# Parts of a Dictionary Entry

- ② homograph number
- ① entry word
- ③ pronunciation
- ⑧ special meaning
- ② homograph number
- ⑯ cross-reference
- ⑤ definition number
- ⑨ parts-of-speech labels
- ⑫ idioms

- ⑮ caption — A blue crab - shell about 15 cm wide
- ⑭ picture
- ⑥ definition
- ⑪ run-on entry
- ⑬ fistnote (etymology)
- ④ restrictive label
- ⑦ example
- ⑩ inflected forms
- ⑪ run-on entry
- ⑥ definition
- ⑦ example
- ⑧ special meaning
- ⑩ inflected forms
- ⑪ run-on entry
- ⑬ fistnote (homonym)

**crab**¹ (krab)  **1** any of a large group of CRUSTACEANS having a short, broad shell, a body composed of 19 segments with a short abdomen, or "tail," that is folded up under the body, four pairs of legs, and one pair of pincers: *Most crabs live in the sea; some are edible.*  **2** any of several other CRUSTACEANS resembling the true crab, such as the hermit crab.  **3** catch crabs for eating.  **4** a machine or apparatus for raising or moving heavy weights.  **5 Crab,** in astrology, the fourth sign of the zodiac; Cancer. See ZODIAC for picture.  1, 2, 4, 5 *n.*, 3 *v.*, **crabbed, crab·bing.** —**crab′ber,** *n.*
☛ *Etym.* OE *crabba* 'crab' related to ON *krabbi* and Old High German *krebiz* 'crab'. See also the note at CRAYFISH.

**crab**² (krab)  **1** CRAB APPLE.  **2** a cross, sour, ill-natured person; one who is always complaining or finding fault.  **3** find fault; complain; criticize: *It doesn't do any good to crab about the weather.*  **4** *Informal.* interfere with; spoil: *His lack of enthusiasm crabbed the deal.*  1, 2 *n.*, 3, 4 *v.*, **crabbed, crab·bing.** —**crab′ber,** *n.*

**blue** (blü)  **1** the colour of the clear sky in daylight or the colour of the part of the spectrum between green and indigo.  **2** of or having this colour or a tone of this colour.  **3** blue dye or pigment.  **4** of the skin, livid; ashen: *blue with cold.*  **5** having or showing low spirits; sad, gloomy, or discouraged: *a blue mood. I was feeling very blue.*  **6** make blue.  **7** use BLUING on.  **8 the blue, a** the sky: *high up in the blue.* **b** the sea.  **9 blues,** *pl.* **a** *Informal.* low spirits: *He's got the blues.* **b** in music, a style of jazz characterized by a tendency to flatten certain notes by a semitone, producing minor sequences and harmonies that give the music a melancholy sound: *The blues developed from black work songs and spirituals.*  1, 3, 8, 9 *n.*, 2, 4, 5 *adj.*, **blu·er, blu·est;**  6, 7 *v.*, **blued, blu·ing** or **blue·ing.** —**blue′ness,** *n.*
**once in a blue moon,** hardly ever; rarely: *Once in a blue moon we get a letter from him.*
**out of the blue,** completely unexpected; from an unknown source or for an unknown reason: *Suddenly, out of the blue, she announced that she was quitting.*
☛ *Hom.* BLEW.

# gage

## Canadian Intermediate DICTIONARY

**gage** EDUCATIONAL PUBLISHING COMPANY
A DIVISION OF CANADA PUBLISHING CORPORATION
Vancouver · Calgary · Toronto · London · Halifax

© 1998, 1991 GAGE EDUCATIONAL PUBLISHING COMPANY
...on of Canada Publishing Corporation

*All rights reserved.* No part of this work covered by the copyrights hereon may be reproduced or used in any form or by any means–graphic, electronic, electrostatic, or mechanical–without the prior written permission of the publisher or, in case of photocopying or other reprographic copying, a licence from the Canadian Reprography Collective.

Any request for photocopying, recording, taping, or information storage and retrieval systems of any part of this book shall be directed in writing to The Canadian Copyright Licensing Agency, 6 Adelaide Street East, Suite 900, Toronto, ON, M5C 1H6.

Gage Educational Publishing Company hereby gives permission to you the purchasing school to reproduce exercise pages, from any of pages vii to xlii, for your own students. This permission does not extend to reproducing pages for any other school.

Illustrations: *Lewis Parker, Lazare and Parker*

Cover design: Campbell Sheffield Design Inc.

Data base design, creation, and imaging: Gandalf Graphics Ltd., Toronto
Printed in the United States by Quebecor Printing Book Group

**Canadian Cataloguing in Publication Data**

Main entry under title:
Gage Canadian dictionary, intermediate

Earlier edition (1979) published under title:
Canadian intermediate dictionary.
ISBN 0-7715-1995-8

1. English language—Dictionaries. English language—Canada—Dictionaries. I. Avis, Walter S., 1919–1979. II. Title: Canadian intermediate dictionary. III. Title: Canadian dictionary, intermediate.

PE3237.G34 1991     423     C90-095675-5

ISBN 0-7715-**1995-8** (School)

ISBN 0-7715-**7553-X** (Trade)

1 2 3 4 5 ARC-QC 01 00 99 98 97

# Gage Canadian Intermediate Dictionary

**Lexicographers**  WALTER S. AVIS
ROBERT J. GREGG
MATTHEW H. SCARGILL
ROSEMARY COURTNEY

**General Editor**  T.K. PRATT
Professor, Department of English
University of Prince Edward Island

**Gage Editorial**  Joe Banel
Caroline Cobham
Chelsea Donaldson
Jean Galt
Darleen Rotozinski
Debbie Sawczak
Paul Shenton
Steven Smith
Lisa St. Louis
Fraser Sutherland
Mary Vasey Fenton
Carol Waldock

**Reviewers**

We would like to thank the following educators for their contribution to the *Gage Canadian Reference Series*.

Robert M. Bilan
English Department Head
Oak Park High School
Winnipeg, Manitoba

Michael Budd
Languages Program Consultant
Essex County Board of Education
Ontario

Carol Chandler
former Curriculum Supervisor
Halifax District School Board
Nova Scotia

Wanda Gibbons
Language Arts Teacher
Magrath Junior/Senior High School
Magrath, Alberta

Stephen Hurley
Language Arts Teacher
Cardinal Newman Catholic School,
Dufferin-Peel RCSSB, Ontario

Glen Kirkland
Assessment Consultant
Edmonton Catholic School Board
Alberta

Mary Ellen Perley-Waugh
Language Arts Teacher
Laurier Heights School
Edmonton, Alberta

Wendy Phillips
Head of English
Palmer Secondary School
Richmond, British Columbia

**Exercises**

Ena Gibson
former English Teacher
McKenzie Middle School
Acton, Ontario

# Gage Canadian Reference Series

Gage Canadian Dictionary
Gage Canadian Thesaurus
Gage Canadian Intermediate Dictionary
Gage Canadian Junior Dictionary
Gage Canadian School Thesaurus

# Contents

| | |
|---|---|
| **Introduction** | vi |
| **Using the Dictionary—Features and Exercises** | vii |
| **Words and Meanings** | vii |
| Looking up a word you can't spell | vii |
| Finding an entry | x |
| Reading an entry | xv |
| What to look up | xx |
| Test A | xxiii |
| **Sounds and Spellings** | xxiv |
| Pronunciation symbols | xxiv |
| Vowel sounds | xxv |
| Consonant sounds | xxvii |
| Pronunciation keys | xxviii |
| Stress | xxix |
| Variant pronunciations | xxxi |
| Variant spellings | xxxiii |
| Test B | xxxiv |
| **Special Features** | xxxv |
| Parts of speech | xxxv |
| Restrictive labels | xxxvi |
| Fistnotes | xxxvii |
| Parts of a dictionary entry | xli |
| Just for fun | xli |
| Test C | xlii |
| **Canadian Intermediate Dictionary** | 1 |
| **Appendix I: General Information** | 1401 |
| Geological time chart | 1401 |
| Periodic table of the elements | 1402 |
| Table of measures | 1403 |
| Money: major currencies of the world | 1404 |
| Prime ministers of Canada | 1405 |
| Examples of wind chill factor | 1405 |
| Beaufort scale of wind speeds | 1405 |
| **Appendix II: Grammar and Usage** | 1406 |

# Introduction

The *Gage Canadian Intermediate Dictionary* is intended as a resource for middle-school students (upper elementary and junior high). With its emphasis throughout on accessibility, this dictionary is also an ideal resource for new Canadians of all ages. This edition has been updated with new entries and definitions. As well, revisions within entries reflect current usage and new developments in technology, geography, science, and the arts; contemporary idioms and cross-curricular terminology are featured.

The *Gage Canadian Intermediate Dictionary*, as part of the Gage Canadian Reference Series, builds on the simpler and smaller *Gage Canadian Junior Dictionary*, preparing students for the more extensive and sophisticated *Gage Canadian Dictionary*, itself recently revised and expanded. The grading of these dictionaries shows not only in the number of entries but also in the treatment of each entry. That is, as the sophistication and background knowledge of the user increases, so each dictionary expands the scope of the linguistic information provided. For example, one feature that has been expanded in the *Intermediate Dictionary* from its introduction in the *Junior Dictionary* is the widespread use of fistnotes to highlight appropriate information on homonyms, usage, pronunciation, synonyms, and etymologies.

**Dictionary Exercises and Tests**
The introductory section, "Using the Dictionary," gives a detailed guide to the use of the dictionary, in the hope that students will learn to take advantage of the full range of benefits that a good dictionary can provide. The introduction incorporates a considerable number of practice exercises and tests. These provide a means of familiarizing students with the dictionary and its features, and of developing the full range of basic dictionary skills.

**Appendix I: General Information**
This edition provides a number of lists and tables of useful information.

**Appendix II: Grammar and Usage**
This edition provides a glossary of terminology associated with grammar, usage, style, and mechanics. It offers students a concise and handy guide to the conventions of written language, with special attention to common errors.

The *Gage Canadian Intermediate Dictionary* is intended for the student who is becoming exposed for the first time to a variety of types and categories of knowledge, as well as to a multiplicity of new ideas. Yet this same student still requires clear and simple definitions that are supported as generously as possible by example sentences, usage notes, pictures, and (in many cases) fuller explanations than are to be found in more advanced dictionaries. It is the consistent attempt to meet these conflicting demands that gives the *Gage Canadian Intermediate Dictionary* its special character and its particular place in the Gage Canadian Reference Series.

# Using the Dictionary—Features and Exercises

Dictionaries give a lot of routine information about how words are spelled and pronounced and what they mean. But you may be surprised to discover some of the questions a dictionary can answer.

## Words and Meanings

Look up the words printed in bold type in the sentences below, and write down the answer to each question.

What is the approximate wingspread of a **swan**?
How is it that **platypus** means "flatfoot"?
When is a word "beside the **point**"?
About how many **decibels** are there in a whisper?
What is the singular of **criteria**?
What does the abbreviation **SPCA** stand for?
What do the letters of **laser** stand for?
What is the largest part of the human **brain**?
What word sounds the same as **faze**?
What is a synonym for **obstinate**?
What is the origin of the word **silhouette**?
How many grains are there in a **scruple**?

## Looking up a word you can't spell

How do you look up a word in the dictionary if you don't know how to spell it? One way is to use the chart of "Common Spellings of English Sounds" on the next two pages. Suppose, for example, that you want to find the spelling and meaning of a word you heard pronounced as follows: (sü′də nim′)?

You are pretty sure that the word does not start with a plain *s*, so you look up the sound "s" in the chart and look at the first column to see how this sound can be spelled at the beginnings of words. You find the following examples of possible spellings: *s*ay, *c*ent, *sc*ience, *ps*alm, *sw*ord. You guess that the correct choice is *ps*, as in *ps*alm, so you look for the word you want under *psoo-* or *psu-*. There is no such word, but you may notice the correct entry word as you are looking.

If you have not yet found the word, go back to the chart, looking at the second column beside the sound "ü" to see what other ways there are of spelling this sound in the middle of words. One spelling you find is *eu*, as in *neutral*, so you look for your word under *pseu-* or *pseud-* (you might even guess that the next letter after the *d* is *o*). Now you can find the right entry word without any trouble; check the pronunciation following the entry word to make sure that you have the right entry, and then you can read the meaning.

What is the correct spelling of (sü′də nim′)?

# Common Spellings of English Sounds

| SOUND | BEGINNINGS OF WORDS | MIDDLES OF WORDS | ENDS OF WORDS |
|---|---|---|---|
| a | *a*nd, *au*nt | h*a*t, pl*ai*d, h*a*lf, l*au*gh | — |
| ā | *a*ge, *ai*d, *eigh*t, *eh* | f*a*ce, f*ai*l, str*aigh*t, p*a*yment, g*ao*l, g*au*ge, br*ea*k, v*ei*n, r*eig*n, n*eigh*bour | s*ay*, w*eigh*, bouqu*et*, th*ey*, matin*ée*, *eh* |
| ä | *ah*, *a*lmond, *a*rt | c*a*lm, b*a*rn, baz*aa*r, serge*a*nt, h*ea*rt | b*aa*, hurr*ah* |
| b | *b*ad | ta*b*le, ra*bb*it | ru*b*, e*bb* |
| ch | *ch*ild, *c*ello | ri*ch*ness, wa*tch*ing, righ*te*ous, ques*ti*on, na*t*ure | mu*ch*, ca*tch* |
| d | *d*o | do*d*o, do*dd*er | re*d* |
| e | *e*nd, *ai*r, *ae*rial, *a*ny | l*e*t, br*ea*d, s*ai*d, s*ay*s, m*a*ny, h*ei*fer, l*eo*pard, fr*ie*nd, b*u*ry | — |
| ē | *e*qual, *ea*t, *ei*ther, *ae*on | n*ee*d, t*ea*m, m*e*tre, bel*ie*ve, rec*ei*ve, k*ey*hole, mach*i*ne, C*ae*sar, ph*oe*be, p*eo*ple | b*ee*, b*e*, k*ey*, pit*y*, fl*ea*, qu*ay*, alg*ae* |
| ėr | *er*mine, *ear*ly, *ir*k, *ur*ge | t*er*m, l*ear*n, f*ir*st, t*ur*n, w*or*d, j*our*ney, m*yr*tle | det*er*, f*ir*, c*ur*, b*urr*, voyag*eur* |
| f | *f*at, *ph*one | hei*f*er, co*ff*ee, lau*gh*ter, go*ph*er | roo*f*, bu*ff*, cou*gh*, lym*ph* |
| g | *g*o, *gh*ost, *g*uess | bo*g*us, bo*gg*le, ro*gu*ish, exa*c*t | ba*g*, e*gg*, ro*gue* |
| h | *h*e, *wh*o (hü), *wh*y (hwī) | block*h*ead | — |
| i | *i*n, *e*namel | p*i*n, s*ie*ve, h*y*mn, b*ui*ld, mess*a*ge, b*u*sy, b*ee*n, w*o*men | — |
| ī | *i*ce, *ei*ther, *ay*e, *ey*e, *ai*sle | l*i*ne, m*igh*t, al*ig*n, skyl*ar*k, h*eigh*t, b*u*ying | l*ie*, h*igh*, *ay*e, *ey*e, b*uy*, sk*y*, r*ye* |
| j | *j*am, *g*em | en*j*oy, tra*g*ic, exa*gg*erate, ba*dg*er, sol*di*er, e*du*cate | ra*ge*, bri*dge* |
| k | *c*oat, *ch*emist, *k*ind, *qu*ick, *qu*ay | re*c*ord, a*cc*ount, c*ch*o, lu*ck*y, a*c*quire, ree*k*ing, li*qu*or, e*x*tra | ba*ck*, see*k* |
| l | *l*and, *ll*ama | on*l*y, fo*ll*ow | coa*l*, fi*ll* |
| m | *m*e | co*m*ing, su*mm*er, cli*m*bing | roo*m*, co*mb*, sole*mn* |
| n | *n*ut, *kn*ife, *gn*aw, *pn*eumonia | mi*n*er, ma*nn*er, jack-*kn*ife | ma*n*, i*nn* |
| ng | — | i*n*k, fi*n*ger, si*ng*er | ri*ng*, to*ngue* |

# Common Spellings of English Sounds (continued)

| SOUND | BEGINNINGS OF WORDS | MIDDLES OF WORDS | ENDS OF WORDS |
|---|---|---|---|
| o | odd, awful, auto, aught, ought, encore, all, almond | hot, bought, cawed, caulk, fall, walk, appal, watch, taut, taught, calm | paw |
| ō | open, oats, oh, own | bogus, soul, flown, boat, folk, brooch, sewn, yeoman | blow, potato, toe, oh, sew, though, beau |
| ô | order, oar | born, board, flooring, mourn, | — |
| oi | oil, oyster | boil, boyhood | boy |
| ou | out, owl | bound, howl, drought | now, thou, bough |
| p | pen | taper, supper | up |
| r | run, rhythm, wrong | parent, hurry | bear, burr |
| s | say, cent, science, psalm, sword | mason, massive, decent, resuscitate, extra | miss, bogus, nice, lax |
| sh | she, sure, chauffeur, schwa | mission, tension, nation, nausea, special, ocean, insurance, conscience, issue, machine | wish, cache |
| t | tell, Thomas, ptomaine | later, latter, debtor | bit, mitt, doubt |
| th | thin | toothpaste | bath |
| ŧH | then | father | smooth, bathe |
| u | up, oven | cup, come, flood, trouble, does | — |
| ů | — | full, good, should, wolf | — |
| ü | ooze | rule, food, fruit, croup, move, neutral, manoeuvre | zoo, blue, threw, caribou, through, shoe |
| yü | use, you, ewe, euchre | duty, feud, beauty | cue, few, ewe, you, queue, adieu |
| v | very | over, Stephen | love, of |
| w | will, wheat | twin, quick, choir | — |
| y | young | canyon, opinion, hallelujah | — |
| z | zero, xylophone | sizing, dazzle, raisin, scissors, exact | buzz, maze, has |
| zh | — | division, measure, azure, garaged | rouge |
| ə | alone, essential, oblige, upon | particular, fountain, moment, pencil, bottle, prism, button, cautious, circus, zephyr | sofa |

> **Exercise**
>
> Use the chart on the previous two pages to help you find the spellings and meanings of the words pronounced as follows:
>
> (ə kwānt′)   (fyü′zhən)   (fə zish′ən)   (ad′ə les′ənt)
>
> (nyü mō′nyə)   (as′folt)   (ō′shē an′ik)   (shō′fər)

# FINDING AN ENTRY

The first need in using a dictionary is to be able to find the right entry for the specific information you want.

## Entry Words

Each word that starts a dictionary entry is called an *entry word*. Entry words are printed in large bold type and usually have a slight space above them. Midline dots between the syllables indicate points at which a word may be hyphenated at the end of a line.

An *entry* consists of an entry word and everything that is said about it—in other words, all the text that comes before another entry word begins.

An entry word may in fact consist of two or more words, or it may consist of only part of a word (a prefix or a suffix), or it may be an abbreviation. If an entry word is a proper name or proper adjective, it begins with a capital letter.

> **Exercise**
>
> Below is part of a column from the dictionary. Look at each entry word, and then answer the following questions.
>
> **dol·o·mite** (dol′ə mīt′)   a rock consisting mainly of calcium and magnesium carbonate.   *n.*
>
> **dol·or·ous** (dol′ə rəs *or* dō′lə rəs)   **1** mournful; sorrowful: *She uttered a heartbroken, dolorous cry.* **2** grievous; painful: *The dolorous day was ending.*   *adj.*
> —**dol′or·ous·ly**, *adv.*
>
> **do·lour** or **do·lor** (dō′lər)   sorrow; grief.   *n.*
>
> **dol·phin** (dol′fən)   **1** any of several related species of small whale having a snout shaped like a beak: *Dolphins are often trained to perform in aquariums.*   **2** either of two species of large, edible, saltwater fish remarkable for their changes of colour when taken from the water.   **3** a BUOY (def. 1) or piling used to mark a channel for ships.   *n.*
>
> **dolphin striker**   on a ship, a small spar under the bowsprit that helps support the JIB BOOM.
>
> **dolt** (dōlt)   a dull, stupid person.   *n.*
>
> **–dom**   a noun-forming suffix meaning:   **1** the position, rank, or realm of a ___: *kingdom = realm of a king.*   **2** the condition of being ___: *martyrdom = condition of being a martyr.*   **3** all those who are ___: *heathendom = all those who are heathen.*
>
> **dom.**   **1** domestic.   **2** dominion.
>
> **do·main** (dō mān′)   **1** the territory under the control of one ruler or government.   **2** the land owned by one person; an estate.   **3** a field of thought, action, etc.: *the domain of science, the domain of politics.*   *n.*   Compare with DEMESNE.

1. How many entry words are there?
2. Which entries are abbreviations?
3. Which word rhymes with *reign*?
4. Which entry word has two spellings?
5. Which entry is a two-word phrase?
6. Which entry is a suffix?
7. What word can you make by adding this suffix to the word *free*?
8. Which entry word is a noun that is not very complimentary?
9. Which entry word is an adjective?
10. Which entry word refers to a kind of rock?

## Alphabetical order

All the entry words in the dictionary are listed in one alphabetical order. A person should be able to go quickly to the right place in this order to find any particular word.

**Exercise**

1. Arrange the words on each line in alphabetical order.
   (a) organ, umpire, film, money
   (b) dynamite, dual, drift, dwarf
   (c) abide, abdicate, abstract, abuse
   (d) malt, malady, malign, male
   (e) dandle, dandy, dandelion, dandruff
   (f) divination, divine, diviner, divinely

2. The following students live in a Canadian city. Write their names in alphabetical order and circle the second letter of each. If correctly done, the circled letter will give you the name of their city.

   Odette _____
   Una _____
   Alanna _____
   Inez _____
   Bob _____
   Polly _____

3. To find out which province the same six students live in, place the following words in alphabetical order, circling the letter indicated by the number at the end of each line.

   deliberative _ _ _ _ _ _ _ _ _ _  4
   delft _ _ _ _ _ _ _ _ _ _ _ _ _  5
   delegation _ _ _ _ _ _ _ _ _ _  9
   delicious _ _ _ _ _ _ _ _ _ _ _  7
   deliberate _ _ _ _ _ _ _ _ _ _  8
   deletion _ _ _ _ _ _ _ _ _ _ _  8
   deliberation _ _ _ _ _ _ _ _ _  7

4. The following words make sense when they are put in alphabetical order. How quickly can you write down the unscrambled sentence?

while George visit a people knowing is
delight to many yachting for

One way to do this last exercise is to draw three columns, like this:

| a to f | g to q | r to z |
|---|---|---|
|  |  |  |

Words starting with *a* to *f* go into the first column, words starting with *g* to *q* go into the middle column, and words starting with *r* to *z* go into the last one. When you have put each word of the scrambled sentence into the proper column, it will be quite easy to alphabetize the words in the first column, then those in the second, and then those in the third.

5. Use the three-column method to put the following words in order, and then write them as a sentence.

Orville loved purple windstorms
here each violent
girl paint utterly through seascapes observing

## Thirding the dictionary

Whenever you want to look up a word in the dictionary, decide if the first letter of the word comes in the beginning (*a* to *f*), the middle (*g* to *q*), or the end (*r* to *z*) of the alphabet. Then try to open the dictionary at approximately the right part.

**Exercise**

At which part (beginning, middle, or end) would you open the dictionary to look up each of the following words?

symposium coquetry theological restitution
hydrolysis momentum endorsement occidental

## Guide words

At the top of the outside column of each page of the dictionary, on either side of the page number, are two words in large bold type. For example:

**Dark Ages**        309        **date**

These words are called *guide words*. They indicate which entries are on that particular page. The guide word on the left is the first entry word to appear on the page. The one on the right is the last entry word to appear on the page. Therefore all the entry words that come alphabetically between the two guide words will appear on the same page.

**Exercise**

1. By looking at the guide words above, decide which of the following will appear as entry words on page 309.

   daylight    dare        darken
   darling     dastardly   dapple
   darn        date        dashing

2. In each question below, the first two words are the guide words of particular pages. Which of the other words would appear as entry words on the same page?

   (a) arena, arithmetician       aria, arise, ark, area
   (b) diabolic, diametric        diadem, diameter, diaper, dialect
   (c) epigrammatic, equalize     equal, epitaph, equate, equity

# Homographs

Sometimes two or more words have the same spellings but different origins and very different meanings. Such words are called *homographs*. In the dictionary they are given as separate entries, but there is a small raised number after each entry word to distinguish one from another. For example:

**fair**[1] (fer)   **1** not favouring one more than the other or others; just; honest: *a fair judge. He is fair even to people he dislikes.*   **2** according to the rules: *fair play.*   **3** pretty good; not bad; average: *She has a fair understanding of the subject. There is only a fair crop of wheat this year.*   **4** favourable; likely; promising: *He is in a fair way to succeed.*   **5** not dark; blond: *fair hair, a fair complexion.*   **6** not cloudy or stormy; clear; sunny: *The weather will be fair today.*   **7** pleasing to the eye or mind; beautiful: *a fair lady. She spoke fair words.*   **8** of good size or amount; ample: *They own a fair piece of property.*   **9** clean or pure; without blemishes: *fair water, a fair copy.*   **10** easily read; plain: *fair handwriting.*   **11** favourable; helpful, especially to a ship's course: *We had fair winds all the way.*   **12** seemingly good at first, but not really so: *His fair promises proved false.*   **13** in an honest, straightforward manner; honestly: *fair-spoken, to play fair.*   **14** directly; straight: *The stone hit him fair on the head.*   1–12 *adj.*, 13, 14 *adv.*   —**fair′ness,** *n.*
**bid fair,**   seem likely; have a good chance.
**fair and square,** *Informal.*   just; honest.

**fair**[2] (fer)   **1** a gathering of people for the purpose of showing goods, products, etc.; exhibition: *the Royal Winter Fair. At the county fair last year, prizes were given for the best farm products and livestock.*   **2** a gathering of people to buy and sell, often held in a certain place at regular times during the year: *a trade fair.*   **3** an entertainment and sale of articles; bazaar: *Our club held a fair to raise money.*   *n.*

In such cases, the small raised number after an entry word is a signal that there is another entry word with the same spelling.

**Exercise**

1. How many homographs are given in the dictionary for each of the following words?
   (a) bore  (c) skate  (e) bowl  (g) duck
   (b) hip   (d) butt   (f) pool  (h) chop

2. Which homograph is used for each of the italicized words?
   Example: She said it was not *fair* to keep her home from the *fair*.
   fair¹, fair²

   (a) The pirate *holds* his captives in the *hold*.
   (b) Only one *school* of fish had eyelids to protect their *pupils*.
   (c) His black *bowler* perched on his head while he *bowled* with his league.
   (d) After a *bit*, the mare took the *bit* between her teeth.
   (e) By using large *bolts*, he made the picnic table *sound*.
   (f) The boat began to *list* near the *levee*.
   (g) She tried to *box* her way out of the cardboard *box*.
   (h) He *ducked* under cover as a *light* rain fell.

## Compound entries and phrases

Many words in English consist of two or more words that have come together to make one. Such words are called *compounds* and they have a meaning different from that of the individual words. Some examples are:

**applesauce**  **go-ahead**  **blue-collar**  **dogtrot**
**half-life**   **blueprint** **flagpole**     **mainstream**

Like most writers, you will often have to look in the dictionary to see if a compound is hyphenated or not. Compounds beginning with *self-* or containing a preposition are hyphenated: *self-evident, mother-in-law*.

**Exercise**

In each of the following, join the two italicized words to make a compound. Look in the dictionary, if necessary, to decide whether or not the compound should have a hyphen.

1. An *ache* in the *head* is a _____ .
2. A *worm* that can *glow* is a _____ .
3. A *snake* that *rattles* is a _____ .
4. In the *day*time, the *light* is called _____ .
5. To *walk* by the *side* of a road, use the _____ .

Some pairs of words are phrases and they are written as two separate words. For example:

**hot seat**   **apple butter**   **heat shield**   **house plant**

Such phrases are entered in the dictionary if their meaning is not obvious from the meanings of the two separate words. For example, a *dead end* is not an end that has died, so it is entered in the dictionary. Do you know what *dead end* means? If not, look it up and then write it in a sentence. Phrases are not labelled as parts of speech but compounds are: *applesauce* is a noun; *blue-collar* is an adjective.

### Exercise

Look up each italicized entry word in the following. Answer each question and give a reason for your answer.
Example: Would you feed hay to a *donkey engine*?
    No, it's a kind of steam engine.

1. Would you be thirsty on a *dry run*?
2. Can you bury a *dead letter*?
3. Does anyone really have a *green thumb*?
4. Does a football player have a *double tackle*?
5. Would a door make a *grand slam*?

Straightforward phrases whose meaning is obvious, such as *racing car* ('a car for racing'), are not entered in the dictionary. Some phrases consist of three words. These are also entered in the dictionary if their meaning is not obvious. Examples are:

**Rocky Mountain juniper    great horned owl    safety deposit box**

# READING AN ENTRY

Having found the entry you want, you may wish only to know how it is spelled (which the entry word tells you) or how it is pronounced (see pages *xxiv–xxxii*). But if you want to know what the word means or how it can be used, you have to look further and study the text of the entry. In fact, the dictionary has three main ways of indicating the meanings of words: definitions, examples, and pictures.

## Definitions

A definition explains the meaning of a word, usually in such a way that all or part of the definition can be substituted in a context for the entry word itself. For example:
**fur·be·low** (fèr′bə lō′)    **1** a bit of elaborate trimming: *a dress with many frills and furbelows.*    **2** trim in an elaborate way.    1 *n.,* 2 *v.*
The definition for the first meaning can be substituted for *furbelow* in the example: *a dress with many frills and bits of elaborate trimming.*

### Exercise

Substitute the appropriate definition for each of the italicized words.

1. Will you *buy* a book for me, please?
2. During the sale, the tent was a great *buy*.
3. He could not *buy* the judge.
4. They watched the *flotilla* sail into the harbour.
5. The spoiled child was *fastidious* when it came to food.
6. The *gyration* of the large pendant was continuous.
7. The thief escaped from the *gendarme*.

## Examples

Many definitions are followed by one or more examples of the word in use. Such examples may be phrases or complete sentences. They are always printed in italics, and the definition before them always ends in a colon. Study the examples in the following entry, and see how they help to distinguish one meaning from another.

**dumb** (dum)   **1** not having the power of speech: *Animals are dumb.*   **2** suffering from an inability to speak as a result of sickness, injury, etc.; mute.   **3** silenced for the moment by fear, surprise, shyness, etc.: *The poor child was dumb with embarrassment.*   **4** not expressed in words: *dumb astonishment, dumb grief.*   **5** unwilling to speak; silent: *They questioned her repeatedly, but she remained dumb.*   **6** *Informal.*   stupid; unintelligent, or foolish: *She's pretty dumb. Dialling the wrong number is a dumb thing to do.*   *adj.*   —**dumb′ly**, *adv.*   —**dumb′ness**, *n.*

Sometimes example sentences give information about meaning over and above that given in the definition, as in the following entry.

**drill²** (dril)   a machine for planting seeds in rows: *The drill makes a small furrow, drops the seed, and then covers the furrow.*   *n.*

### Exercise

1. Look up the following entries and tell what kinds of information the example sentences give.

   | | | | |
   |---|---|---|---|
   | harrow | mustard | paradox | index |
   | radium | hives | knight | inquest |
   | jackal | leap year | lac | quartz |

2. Look up the word *ease*. How many meanings does it have? Tell by the number which definition applies to *ease* as it is used in each of the sentences below.

   (a) Hiring a new assistant should ease his workload.
   (b) The nurse did all she could to ease the patient.
   (c) The expensive glass window was eased into place.
   (d) We admired the ease with which she cleared the jump.
   (e) His tired body found ease in the soft chair.
   (f) As the wind eased, the windmill turned more slowly.
   (g) His ease of manner made him a pleasure to talk to.
   (h) We eased the bandage on his arm as his fingers were turning blue.

3. Choose one of the following words and write your own example sentence for each of its five meanings. Try to make sure that your sentences clearly distinguish each meaning from the others.

   dial     snake

# Pictures

Over 800 entries in the dictionary are accompanied by pictures, and many of these pictures are accompanied by informative captions. Look at the different kinds of information given in the following samples.

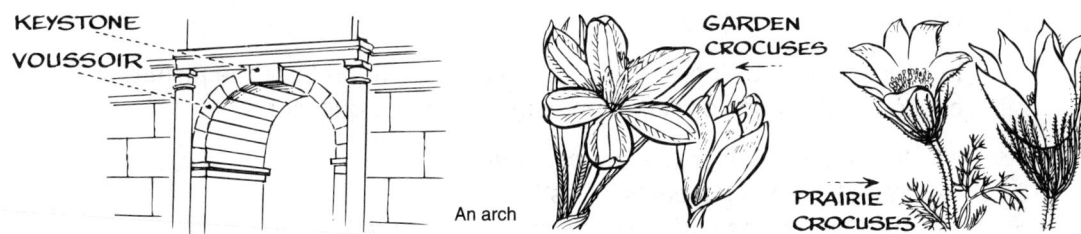

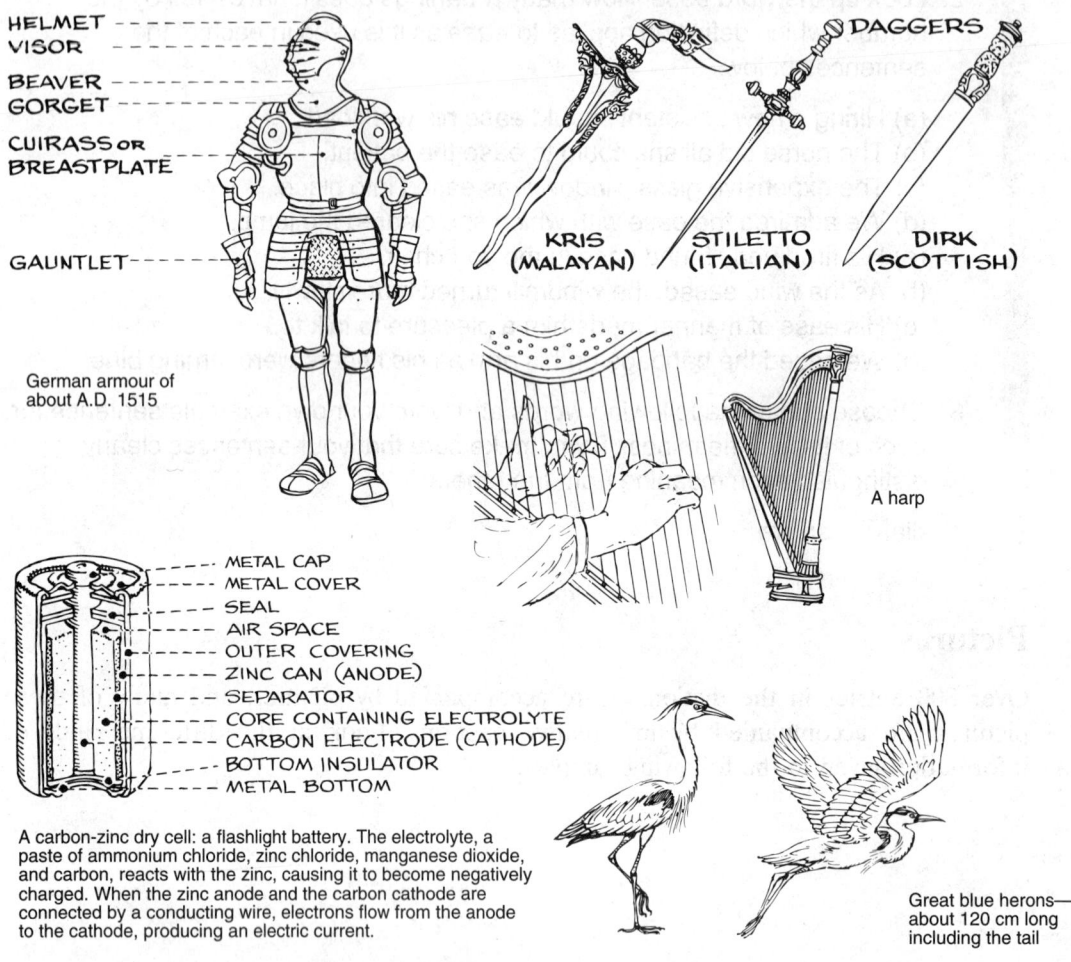

German armour of about A.D. 1515

A harp

A carbon-zinc dry cell: a flashlight battery. The electrolyte, a paste of ammonium chloride, zinc chloride, manganese dioxide, and carbon, reacts with the zinc, causing it to become negatively charged. When the zinc anode and the carbon cathode are connected by a conducting wire, electrons flow from the anode to the cathode, producing an electric current.

Great blue herons— about 120 cm long including the tail

**Exercise**

In each of the following, look up the italicized word and use the picture or caption on this page or at that entry to answer the question.

1. In what part of a ship is the *capstan*?
2. What kind of a *dagger* is a kris?
3. What is the name of the bone of the upper *arm*?
4. About how long is a *walrus*?
5. What three types of *bridge* are shown?
6. What is the name of the square part at the base of a *column*?
7. About how long is a red-tailed *hawk*?
8. What is another name for the breastplate of a suit of *armour*?
9. About how high is a Bactrian *camel*?
10. What four styles of *architecture* are shown?

# Distinguishing meanings

When a word has more than one meaning, each separate definition has a different definition number. Usually the most common meaning is given first, but often that is not the one you are looking for. So you may have to look through several definitions before you find the right one. For example, which definition of *design* fits its use in the following sentence?

He is thought to have designs on the presidency.

**de·sign** (di zīn′) **1** a drawing, plan, or sketch made to serve as a pattern from which to work: *a design for a machine, a dress design.* **2** an arrangement of detail, form, and colour in painting, weaving, building, etc.: *a wallpaper design in tan and brown.* **3** make a first sketch of; plan out; arrange the form and colour of; draw in outline: *to design a dress.* **4** make drawings, sketches, plans, etc.: *He designs for a firm of dressmakers.* **5** the art of making designs, patterns, or sketches: *Architects are skilled in design.* **6** a piece of artistic work. **7** a plan in mind to be carried out: *My sister's design is to be a lawyer.* **8** a scheme of attack; evil plan: *The thief had designs upon the safe.* **9** plan out; form in the mind; contrive: *The author designed an exciting plot.* **10** a purpose; aim, intention: *Whether by accident or design, she overturned the lamp.* **11** have in mind to do; purpose: *Did you design this, or did it just happen?* **12** set apart; intend; plan: *His parents designed him for a musical career.* 1, 2, 5–8, 10 *n.*, 3, 4, 9, 11, 12 *v.*
**by design,** on purpose; by intention.

When looking through a longish entry to find the right meaning, it often saves time to skim through the italic examples until you find one that seems similar to your context for the word.

### Exercise

Rewrite the following sentences substituting the appropriate definition for each of the italicized words. Make any minor changes of wording that are needed to make the definitions fit the sense.

1. Canadians *observe* Thanksgiving in October.
2. I received a hockey ticket through the good *offices* of my friend.
3. You may feel sick if you *gorge* at the table.
4. The teacher gave the tardy student five minutes *grace*.
5. The truck shifted to second gear going up the steep *grade*.
6. Her harsh words *grated* on the rest of us.
7. The politician spoke on many *issues*.
8. Executives are concerned with many matters of *moment*.
9. Can the student earn his *keep*?
10. Daylight begins to *fade* before the sun sets.

# WHAT TO LOOK UP

Sometimes a word that you want to look up is not itself an entry word. Certain forms of words either are not listed or are in small bold type within an entry.

## Inflected forms

Inflected forms—the plural of nouns, tenses of verbs, comparative and superlative of adjectives—are given whenever they are not regularly formed.

> Two stratagems were germinating in his much craftier mind.

If you wanted to know what *stratagems* means in this sentence you would look up its singular form *stratagem*. If you wanted to know what *germinating* means, you would look up the base form *germinate*, and near the end of that entry you would find *germinating* listed as a form of the verb in small bold type.

**ger·mi·nate** (jėr′mə nāt′)   **1** grow or sprout, or cause to grow or sprout: *Seeds germinate in the spring. Warmth and moisture germinate seeds.*   **2** start growing or developing: *An idea was germinating in his head.*   *v.,* **ger·mi·nat·ed, ger·mi·nat·ing.**   —**ger′mi·na′tor,** *n.*

Where would you look in the dictionary to find *craftier*?

> **Exercise**
>
> Write down the entry words that you have to look up to find the meaning of the italicized words in the following passage, which was written by a Grade 8 student. Look up each entry word and then write "yes" or "no" to indicate whether or not the form in the passage is given as an inflected form in small bold type.
>
> > The *shimmering* waters *lapped* against the *freshly* painted sides of the schooner. The captain came out of the cabin clad in *frayed* jeans and a *faded* shift. He *hoisted* the heavy anchor and set sail from the *uninhabited* bay toward the *hushed* and *challenging* ocean.

Inflected forms in *-s*, *-es*, *-ed*, *-ing*, *-er*, and *-est* are not shown in this dictionary if the endings can be added to their root words without any change in spelling. If there is a change in spelling (such as a dropping of *e*, a changing of *y* to *i*, or a doubling of a consonant), the inflected forms are shown in small bold type near the end of the entry for the root word.

Some words do not add *-s* or *-es*, *-ed* or *-ing*, *-er* or *-est* but have quite irregular forms, such as:

| | | |
|---|---|---|
| **goose/geese** | **buy/bought** | **bad/worse/worst** |
| **man/men** | **sing/sang/sung** | **much/more/most** |

In these cases the irregular forms are shown in small bold type, and they are also entered separately as entry words, so that anyone who does not know them can look them up and so be led to their root words.

> **Exercise**
>
> Look up the following, and for each one write down the irregular forms that are given at or near the end of the entry.
>
> 1. many
> 2. datum
> 3. sew
> 4. far
> 5. ply$^1$
> 6. ply$^2$

## Derivatives

Many words in English are formed by adding a suffix, such as *-ly* or *-ness*, to a root word. The resulting words are called *derivatives*. Thus *lopsidedly* ("in a lopsided manner") and *lopsidedness* ("the state of being lopsided") are derivatives of *lopsided*. See how these two words are entered in the dictionary:

**lop·sid·ed** (lop′sī′did)  larger or heavier on one side than the other; unevenly balanced; leaning to one side. *adj.* —**lop′sid′ed·ly**, *adv.* —**lop′sid′ed·ness**, *n.*

A derivative is entered as a *run-on entry* at the end of the root word if there is no major spelling change and if it is formed by using one of the following suffixes: *-able*, *-er*, *-ful*, *-ish*, *-less*, *-like*, *-ly*, *-ment*, *-ness*. However, this is done only if the meaning of the derivative is obvious from the combined meanings of the root word and the suffix. If the meanings of a derivative are not obvious, it is given in the dictionary as a separate entry word. Look up, for example, *clue* and *clueless*.

> **Exercise**
>
> Look up the following words and put a "D" beside each word that is a derivative, or run-on, and an "S" beside each word that is a separate entry.
>
> 1. abiding
> 2. adherent
> 3. adhesiveness
> 4. analysed
> 5. babying
> 6. bachelorhood
> 7. barbecued
> 8. barrenness
> 9. betrayer
> 10. blanket
> 11. censorship
> 12. chunky
> 13. comblike
> 14. converter
> 15. dainties
> 16. defiantly
> 17. dialling
> 18. donation
> 19. faultless
> 20. follower

## Idioms

Idioms are phrases in which one word, called the key word, is used in a way that one does not expect, creating something rather like a metaphor. For example:

*above suspicion*: The key word is *suspicion* since it is not a place that one can be above.
*once in a blue moon*: The key word is *blue* because it is not normally used of the moon.

Idioms are listed after the key words: *cool one's heels* will be found at *heel*.

**Exercise**

In each of the following:

(a) Write down each italicized idiom. Underline the entry word under which the idiom is entered. Check the dictionary if you are not sure which word to underline.

(b) Rewrite the sentence using other words in place of each idiom but without any major change in meaning.

1. He asked his brother to *lend a hand*.
2. They are always *hard up* before payday.
3. Grandmother has a *heart of gold*.
4. We are *in for* a storm.
5. She ran *like mad* for the train.
6. The lake is ten kilometres from here *as the crow flies*.
7. I believe that he *came by* the money honestly.
8. His actions made her *see red*.
9. The pianist *plays by ear*.
10. The spy had to *burn his bridges* behind him.

# Special meanings

In some cases a word has one or more special meanings when it is capitalized, when it is in the plural, when it has *the* before it, or when it is in another special phrase. In these cases the special form is not made a separate entry but is given in small bold type at the beginning or even in the middle of the appropriate definition, usually the last definition. It is then called a *special meaning*. For example:

**mar·i·time** (mar′ə tīm′ *or* mer′ə tīm′)   **1** on or near the sea: *Halifax is a maritime city.*   **2** living near the sea: *Many maritime peoples live from fishing.*   **3** of the sea; having to do with shipping and sailing: *Ships and sailors are governed by maritime law.*   **4 Maritime,** of or having to do with the MARITIME PROVINCES.   *adj.*
☛ *Etym.* See note at MARINE.

**man·ner** (man′ər)   **1** the way something happens or is done: *The trouble arose in a curious manner.*   **2** a way of acting or behaving: *She has a kind manner.*   **3** a style or fashion: *He dresses in a strange manner.*   **4 manners,** *pl.*  **a** ways or customs: *Books and movies show us the manners of other times and places.*   **b** ways of behaving toward others: *bad manners.*   **c** polite behaviour: *It is nice to see a child with manners.*   *n.*

**mer·it** (mer′it)   **1** goodness; worth or value: *The council agreed that our plan for a community playground had merit. Each child will get a mark according to the merit of her work.*   **2** anything that deserves praise or reward.   **3** deserve: *A hardworking girl merits praise.*   **4** Usually, **merits,** *pl.*   actual facts or qualities, whether good or bad: *The judge will consider the case on its merits.*   1, 2, 4 *n.,* 3 *v.*

**mil·i·tar·y** (mil′ə ter′ē)   **1** of soldiers or war: *military training, military history.*   **2** done by soldiers: *military manoeuvres.*   **3** fit for soldiers: *military discipline.*   **4** suitable for war; warlike: *military valour.*   **5** belonging to the armed forces.   **6 the military,** the armed forces; soldiers: *The military did rescue work during the flood.* 1-5 *adj.,* 6 *n.*   —**mil′i·tar′i·ly,** *adv.*

**man·i·tou** or **man·i·tu** (man′ə tü′)   in the traditional religion of the Algonquian peoples:   **1** any of the spirits representing the power that dwells within all things in nature, both weak and strong, and having both good and evil influence.   **2** the impersonal supreme being or supernatural force, author of life and all things; the chief of the manitous, called **gitche** (or **kitshi**) **manitou,** often translated as the Great Spirit.   *n.*

**meas·ure** (mezh′ər)   **1** find out the extent, size, quantity, capacity, etc. of something; estimate by some standard: *to measure a room.*   **2** the act or process of finding the extent, size, quantity, capacity, etc. of something, especially by comparison with a standard. **3** the size, dimensions, quantity, etc. thus ascertained: *Her waist measure is 60 cm.* **Short measure**   means less than it should be; **full measure**   means all it should be.   **4** be of a certain size or amount: *This brick measures 5 × 10 × 20 cm.*   **5** an instrument for measuring: *a litre measure.*

In these examples, *Maritime, manners, merits, the military, gitche manitou, short measure,* and *full measure* are *special meanings.*

### Exercise

Look up the following words and find the special meaning. Tell how it differs in form or meaning from the simple entry word.

| | |
|---|---|
| affair | asset |
| air | attention |
| arctic | attorney-general |
| armada | austerity |
| arrangement | authority |

# TEST A

1. If a new word *bicklet* was added to our language, we would want to know what it meant and we would have to look it up in the dictionary.

   (a) Between which two entry words would we find it?
   (b) What are the guide words for the page it would be on?

2. The word *mark* has eighteen meanings. Which meanings (definitions) are used in the following sentences? Write the number of the definition.

   (a) Which fence marks the end of the property?
   (b) The worn grass marks the path to take.
   (c) A week of celebrations marked the town's centenary.
   (d) She left her mark on every aspect of school activity.
   (e) She received a good mark in English.

3. Compounds often change the original meanings of the words they contain. Use the following in context to show the new meaning.

    air-condition   brushoff   facecloth   browbeat   watershed   canvasback

4. The following paragraphs contain thirteen idioms that include parts of the body. Write down each idiom you find and look it up in your dictionary. Then underline the word under which you found the idiom. For example: <u>twiddle</u> his thumbs

> John couldn't decide if he should twiddle his thumbs and hope for a miracle or rack his brains for the right answers to the science test. He really had his hands full. He had passed the last test by the skin of his teeth, and the teacher had turned a cold shoulder to his excuses. "If you would take to heart my reading assignments, hold your tongue when I explain the lessons, and keep on your toes during class, you wouldn't lose your head every time we have a test," she said.
>
> John realized that he was in trouble. After this he would be all ears in science class. He would really knuckle down. But on this test he was risking his neck making wild guesses, even though he was trying to keep a stiff upper lip.

# Sounds and Spellings

One reason for using a dictionary is to find out how to pronounce a word that you have met for the first time in reading. At other times, you need to look at the pronunciation to make sure the entry word you have found is the word you actually want. So it is important to understand how pronunciations are given in the dictionary and to know the symbols that are used.

## PRONUNCIATION SYMBOLS

The pronunciation of each one-word entry in the dictionary is shown in brackets immediately after the entry word. In the pronunciations, each separate sound is represented by its own symbol, and each symbol always represents the same sound.

Each of the following words shows a different spelling of the same vowel sound, but in the pronunciations following the words, this same vowel sound is always represented by the same symbol:

| plate | (plāt) | steak | (stāk) |
| drain | (drān) | neigh | (nā) |
| clay | (klā) | reins | (rānz) |
| brae | (brā) | obey | (ō bā′) |

On the other hand, each of the following words contains the letters *ough*, but the pronunciation of these letters is different in every case. So the pronunciations use different symbols to show this.

| bough | (bou) | though | (ᴛHō) |
| cough | (kof) | through | (thrü) |
| ought | (ot) | tough | (tuf) |
| hiccough | (hik′up) | | |

# VOWEL SOUNDS

## Vowels

The symbols for vowels are of three types:
1. the simple letters of the alphabet (a, e, i, o, u);
2. those same vowels with special markings
   (ä, ā, ē, ė, ī, ō, ô, ü, u̇);
3. schwa (ə).

## Simple vowel letters

Sometimes a vowel symbol is the same as the letter most commonly used to spell that sound. These are all short vowels. For example:

| | | | |
|---|---|---|---|
| trap | (trap) | flop | (flop) |
| red | (red) | drum | (drum) |
| tip | (tip) | | |

## Specially marked vowel letters

For other vowel sounds, the symbols include special marks over the ordinary vowel letters. For example:

| | | | |
|---|---|---|---|
| brain | (brān) | stone | (stōn) |
| barn | (bärn) | storm | (stôrm) |
| seen | (sēn) | foot | (fu̇t) |
| fern | (fėrn) | hoot | (hüt) |
| type | (tīp) | cute | (kyüt) |

Apart from (u̇) these marked vowels are used either for so-called "long vowel" sounds or for certain vowels as they occur before *r*.

> **Exercise**
>
> 1. Look up each of the following. Then write down the entry word followed by its pronunciation.
>
>    | | | |
>    |---|---|---|
>    | navy | through | soot |
>    | rough | install | boot |
>    | bought | tribute | sky |
>
> 2. Write down the words that are represented by these pronunciations. Check the dictionary to be sure you have the correct word.
>
>    | | | |
>    |---|---|---|
>    | (mās) | (mān′lē) | (kī′ak) |
>    | (maj′ik) | (thėr′ō) | (kēl) |
>    | (mag′nāt) | (thot) | (strān) |

# Schwa

One sound appears only in unstressed syllables, but it can be represented in spelling by any of the five regular vowel letters, by the:

*a* in *tidal* (tī′dəl), *collar* (kol′ər)
*e* in *golden* (gōl′dən), *butter* (but′ər)
*i* in *pencil* (pen′səl), *tapir* (tā′pər)
*o* in *gallon* (gal′ən), *doctor* (dok′tər)
*u* in *circus* (sėr′kəs), *picture* (pik′chər)

The symbol for this sound is (ə). Both the sound and the symbol are called *schwa*.

### Exercise

Write the pronunciations for the following words, copying from the dictionary.

| | | |
|---|---|---|
| abundance | jewel | renewal |
| affect | battle | sailor |
| astronaut | marine | |
| caribou | principle | |

Schwa can also be represented by combinations of vowel letters. For example:

*ai* in *curtain* (kėr′tən), *ou* in *callous* (kal′əs)

### Exercise

Write the pronunciations for the following words, copying from the dictionary. Beside each word write the letters in it that represent the schwa sound.

luncheon    fashion    tortoise    epaulette

# Semivowels

English uses two sounds called semivowels, heard initially in *wet* and *yet*, and represented by (w) and (y):

wet          (wet)               yet          (yet)

They are called *semi-* or *half* vowels, because although they are produced like true vowels, with no interruption of the breath, they cannot form a syllable as true vowels can. There are no English words such as *bwt* or *gyt*.

> **Exercise**
>
> Write the first sound of each of these words. It will be (w) or (y). You may use the dictionary to help you.
>
> yucca    ouananiche    junker    warranty
>
> The letter (y) is often used before (ü) in words like *you*, *yew*, and *ewe* (yü).

## Diphthongs

A diphthong is a combination of two different vowels, the first having primary stress and the second being unstressed. Together they form one syllable. English has the following diphthongs, represented by vowel letters:

(oi) as in boil   (boil)                    (ou) as in foul   (foul)

> **Exercise**
>
> Write the diphthong sound in each of these words. It will be (oi) or (ou).
>
> | toil | plough | joyful | howitzer |
> |---|---|---|---|
> | nowadays | rejoice | ointment | empower |
> | endow | enjoy | ourselves | annoyance |

## CONSONANT SOUNDS

The symbols for most consonant sounds are the same as the letters that regularly represent those sounds. For example:

ride          (rīd)                    ten          (ten)

Remember, however, that a pronunciation symbol represents only one sound and always represents the same sound, even though that sound may be spelled in several different ways.

| access | (ak′ses) | judge | (juj) |
|---|---|---|---|
| debt | (det) | knife | (nīf) |
| laugh | (laf) | rhymes | (rīmz) |

A few consonant sounds are represented by special two-character symbols.

The symbol (ch) represents the first sound in *child*:
child (child)          catcher (kach′ər)          witch (wich)

The symbol (ng) represents the last sound in *long*, even when another (g) sound follows:
long (long)          longer (long′gər)
sing (sing)          singer (sing′ər)                    finger (fing′gər)

The symbol (sh) represents the first sound in *ship*:
ship (ship)　　　session (sesh′ən)　　　mesh (mesh)

The symbol (th) represents the first sound in *thin*:
thin (thin)　　　truthful (trüth′fəl)　　　both (bōth)

The symbol (ᴛʜ) represents the first sound in *then*:
then (ᴛʜen)　　　soothing (sü′ᴛʜing)　　　lithe (līᴛʜ)

The symbol (zh) represents the middle sound in *measure*:
measure (mezh′ər)　　　rouge (rüzh)

*Note*: The sound (ng) never appears in English at the very beginning of words. The sound (zh) begins only a few words, such as *jabot*, which have been borrowed from French.

### Exercise

1. Read the following pronunciations and then write the words in their normal spelling.

   (vul′chər)　　　　　　　　(ang′kəl)

   (bī og′rə fē)　　　　　　　(ling′gər)

   (prok′lə mā′ shən)　　　　(woch′ing)

   (buj′it)　　　　　　　　　(muᴛʜ′ ər)

   (sab′ə täzh′)　　　　　　　(tü′thlis)

2. Write down the pronunciations for the following words. Check your answers in the dictionary. Then rewrite any pronunciations that you did not get right first time.

   rank　　truth　　knack　　seethe　　angle

## PRONUNCIATION KEYS

Each pronunciation symbol used in the dictionary stands for one sound, and each symbol always stands for the same sound. A complete pronunciation key, showing all the symbols used, is given on the endpapers inside the front and back covers of the dictionary. A short pronunciation key, which shows all the special symbols that are used, is given at the top of every right-hand page. The short key looks like this:

hat, āge, fär; let, ēqual, tėrm; it, īce
hot, ōpen, ôrder; oil, out; cup, pùt, rüle
əbove, takən, pencəl, lemən, circəs
ch, child; ng, long; sh, ship
th, thin; ᴛʜ, then; zh, measure

If you are not sure what sound a pronunciation stands for, you can easily find out by looking at this key. For example, the key tells you:

the symbol (a) stands for the sound of *a* as in *hat*;
the symbol (ā) stands for the sound of *a* as in *age*;
the symbol (ä) stands for the sound of *a* as in *far*.

**Exercise**

1. Write down the words represented by the following pronunciations. Use either the complete pronunciation key or the short key as required. Check each one in the dictionary.

   (bā′gəl)              (fā′sof′)
   (bil′yərdz)           (faᴛʜ′əm)
   (dā′vē jōnz′)         (fər get′fəl)
   (di nouns′)           (glüm)
   (dog′kärt′)           (grā′dē ənt)

2. Look up and write down the pronunciations for the following words.

   bacteria      daughter      finagle        binary
   deign         finesse       bon voyage     despicable
   flamenco      brachiopod    displeasure    frugal
   camouflage    fabrication   carcinoma      fatigue

# STRESS

In most words of two or more syllables, one syllable is spoken with more force, or stress, than any of the others. In the dictionary pronunciations, the stressed syllable is shown by a heavy raised mark (′) placed after it. For example, in the following words the stress is always on the first syllable:

bonus (bō′nəs)          fervent (fėr′vənt)        mortal (môr′təl)
patchy (pach′ē)         sudden (sud′ən)           super (sü′pər)

In the following words the stress is always on the second syllable:

below (bi lō′)          chastise (chas tīz′)      deceit (di sēt′)
giraffe (jə raf′)       retire (ri tīr′)          surround (sə round′)

**Exercise**

Say or listen to each of the following and decide which is the stressed syllable in each word. If you are not sure whether a certain syllable is stressed or not, try saying the word with the stress on the other syllable; then decide which pronunciation sounds better. Write the stress mark after the stressed syllable.

| | | |
|---|---|---|
| ca boose | con vey | cui sine |
| cat kin | cous in | cu pid |
| clus ter | cru el | cus tard |
| com pare | crys tal | cy cle |

When you have finished, discuss your answers with your group or with a partner. If you do not agree on where the stress goes in any particular word, look up that word in the dictionary and check your answer against the pronunciation given there.

## Secondary stress

In addition to the main stress, many words have one or two syllables that are spoken with more stress than the others, but with less stress than the main syllable. This lighter stress is shown by means of a lighter mark (′) placed after the syllable. Say or listen to the following examples:

beautify   (byü′tə fī′)           calculation   (kal′kyə lā′shən)

contemplate   (kon′təm plāt′)     hydrophobia   (hī′drəfō′bē ə)

reconcile   (rek′ən sīl′)          saxophone   (sak′sə fōn′)

We call the main stress *primary stress* and the lighter stress *secondary stress*.

Syllables that do not have primary or secondary stress are called *unstressed syllables*. The vowel sound in unstressed syllables is often pronounced as schwa (ə). Reread the six examples above. Say them aloud to yourself, and see how the schwa sound (ə) comes only in unstressed syllables.

> **Exercise**
>
> Say or listen to the following words, and then write their pronunciations in parentheses. Mark the primary and secondary stresses, and remember to use schwa (ə) when it is the sound you hear in unstressed syllables.
>
> | | | |
> |---|---|---|
> | cliff-hanger | emigrate | governmental |
> | combination | emigration | handlebars |
> | commonwealth | even-tempered | haphazard |
> | desperation | flabbergast | hobgoblin |
> | agriculture | fortify | horsewoman |
> | drillmaster | frostbitten | jack-o-lantern |
> | editorial | gate-crasher | kerosene |
>
> When you have finished, check the pronunciations you have written against those in the dictionary.

Compound adjectives have the stress pattern primary followed by secondary when they are used in the attributive position, that is, before a noun. This is the pronunciation given in this dictionary. Example: thick-skinned (thik′skind′). When the compound adjective is in predicative position, that is, after a verb, the stress pattern is reversed: secondary + primary.

# VARIANT PRONUNCIATIONS

For some words the dictionary gives two or more pronunciations. For example:
**fer•tile** (fėr′tīl *or* fėr′təl)
**tu•mult** (tyü′mult *or* tü′mult)
**whim•per** (wim′pər *or* hwim′pər)

In such cases both pronunciations are correct, but the form given first is more common across Canada as a whole. In spite of this, the second form may be more common in a certain area or with certain people.

> **Exercise**
>
> Look up in the dictionary the pronunciations for the following words. Sound out the different pronunciations given, and then for each word write the symbols for the pronunciation that you believe to be more common in your area.
>
> | | | |
> |---|---|---|
> | dew | ocelot | tomato |
> | avenue | arctic | schedule |
> | missile | calm | vase |
> | senile | almond | marry |
> | whine | caramel | vary |

Note that an individual usually pronounces a given word in the same way each time. For *schedule* you may say (skej′ul or shej′ul), but if you chop and change from one pronunciation to the other, you are likely to confuse yourself and your listeners.

Sometimes, however, the pronunciation of a word changes according to its use in a sentence. For example what are the differences in the pronunciations of *permit* in the following pair of sentences?

You need a permit to enter this building.
Will you permit us to leave early?

**Exercise**

1. Look up each italicized word in the following sentences and copy the pronunciation. In each case take care to place the stress mark after the right syllable.

    (a) The foreigner's *accent* is peculiar.
    (b) Please *accent* the right syllable.
    (c) He owns many *transport* trucks.
    (d) Trains *transport* freight across the country.
    (e) The monthly *digest* contained much reading material.
    (f) Eat slowly to *digest* your food.
    (g) There were many *converts* to the new ideas.
    (h) We will *convert* the bedroom to a sewing room.
    (i) Fresh *produce* was bought at the market.
    (j) The factory *produces* plastic toys.
    (k) The hockey player's wrist shot was *perfect*.
    (l) It took many hours of practice to *perfect* it.

2. Another kind of difference is found in the following pairs of sentences.

    (a) There were several hidden *entrances* to the cave.
    The young singer *entrances* her audience.

    (b) The soldier's *wound* looked worse than it was.
    He slowly *wound* up the string of his lost kite.

    Look up *entrance* and *wound* in the dictionary. How many different entry words are there for each form? How many different pronunciations?

3. Write the pronunciation for each italicized word in the following sentences. In each case take care to use the proper vowel symbols and to stress the correct syllable.
    (a) The old house had a *lead* roof.
    (b) A man with red hair played *lead* guitar.
    (c) They tried hard to *console* the orphaned child.
    (d) A young girl sat at the *console* of the organ.
    (e) Behind the wall was a pile of stinking *refuse*.
    (f) She found it hard to *refuse* her friend's request.

Words that have the same spelling but different meanings and sometimes different pronunciations are called *homographs*. See page *xiii* for more information on such words.

# VARIANT SPELLINGS

In certain cases there are two forms of an entry word, showing two alternative spellings. For example:

**la•bour** or **la•bor**
**pro•gram** or **pro•gramme**
**trav•el•ler** or **trav•el•er**

In such cases both spellings are correct, but the form given first is more common across Canada as a whole. In spite of this, the second form may be more common in certain areas or among certain groups of people.

The important thing is to be consistent. You may make it your custom to write *program* or *programme*, but if you mix the two forms—using first one and then the other—your readers are likely to consider you a careless writer.

Some words have a spelling that is much less common than the usual one. Such variations are shown at the end of entries, like this:

**cen•tre** (sen′tər)...Also, **center.**

The less common forms, such as *labor* and *center*, are also entered separately, and are cross-referred to their main entries, unless the two entries come next, or nearly next, to each other in alphabetical order:

**cen•ter** (sen′tər)  See CENTRE.

### Exercise

For each italicized word, write down the other, preferred spelling given in the dictionary.
1. She wrote a *check* for her bicycle.
2. The Christian slaves fought in the *Coliseum*.
3. As the farmer *plowed*, the *colter* hit a stone.
4. The *aboiteau* was opened to let the flood waters through.
5. She flew to Calgary in a large *aeroplane*.
6. She refused to sell any of her family *jewelry*.
7. The horse will *baulk* on the bridge.
8. Be on your best *behavior* today.
9. Mother used *blueing* to whiten her wash.
10. Their visit to the *theater* was a great success.

# TEST B

1. Use your dictionary to answer these questions:
    (a) Does *campanile* rhyme with *crocodile*, *repeal*, or *steely*?
    (b) Does *bury* rhyme with *hurry*, *ferry*, or *fury*?
    (c) Does *faille* rhyme with *mile*, *fail*, or *pal*?
    (d) Does *coup* rhyme with *stoup*, *who*, or *taupe*?
    (e) Does *chamois* rhyme with *tortoise*, *mammy*, or *patois*?
2. The clues for this crossword puzzle are the pronunciations of common words. Copy the puzzle or get a copy from your teacher. Fill in the puzzle with the words that the pronunciations stand for.

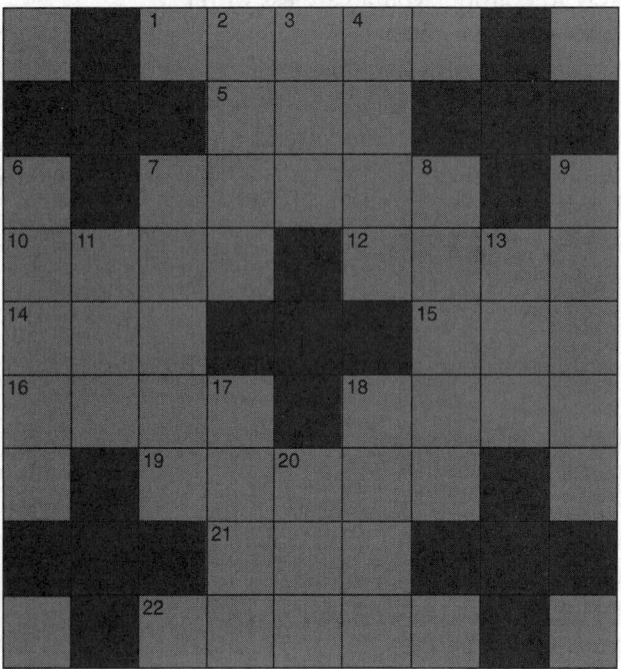

*ACROSS*

1. (brāk)
5. (yüz)
7. (ash′ən)
10. (rōb)
12. (lath)
14. (en′ē)
15. (sē)
16. (nest)
18. (step)
19. (sil′ē)
21. (dī)
22. (nē′dē)

*DOWN*

2. (rüz)
3. (ash)
4. (kēl)
6. (grand)
7. (ə bis′)
8. (nas′tē)
9. (shāp)
11. (wun)
13. (tē)
17. (tīd)
18. (sled)
20. (lī)

# Special Features

## PARTS OF SPEECH

**fish·er·y** (fish′ə rē) **1** the business or industry of catching fish. **2** a place for catching fish: *Salmon is the main catch in the Pacific fisheries.*   *n., pl.* **fish·er·ies.**

**de·ter** (di tėr′)   discourage; keep back; hinder: *The extreme heat deterred us from going downtown.*   *v.,* **de·terred, de·ter·ring.**

Abbreviated labels indicate the parts of speech of all one-word and hyphenated entries in the dictionary. These labels appear at the end of the definitions and example sentences. For example, in the entries above, the label *n.* tells us that *fishery* is a noun and has a typical noun plural, and the label *v.* tells us that *deter* is a verb and has an irregular past tense and past and present participles.

Note that irregular forms such as plurals (*fisheries*) or past tenses and participles (*deterred, deterring*) follow the part-of-speech labels (see page *xx*).

Phrases like **straight face, above reproach, mother superior** are not labelled as parts of speech.

Many words can be used as more than one part of speech. In these cases the appropriate definition numbers are given before the abbreviation for each part of speech. For example:

**gush** (gush)   **1** rush out suddenly; pour out.   **2** a rush of water or other liquid from an enclosed place: *If you get a deep cut, there usually is a gush of blood.*   **3** talk in a silly way about one's affections or enthusiasms.   **4** *Informal.*   silly, emotional talk.   **5** a sudden and violent outbreak; burst: *a gush of anger.*   **6** give forth suddenly or very freely.   1, 3, 6 *v.,* 2, 4, 5 *n.*

The full list of part-of-speech labels is as follows:

| noun | *n.* | pronoun | *pron.* |
| verb | *v.* | preposition | *prep.* |
| adjective | *adj.* | conjunction | *conj.* |
| adverb | *adv.* | interjection | *interj.* |

### Exercise

1. Look up the following words and write beside each one the different parts of speech given for it in the dictionary.

   Example: *major*      major—adj., n., v.

   (a) brown        (d) round       (g) break
   (b) fat          (e) single      (h) hand
   (c) makeshift    (f) square      (i) right

2. Choose one of the following words and write two sentences, using the word as a different part of speech each time. Read your sentences to a partner, asking him or her to tell you the part of speech in which the word is used in each case. (This exercise can also be done as a contest between two teams.)

    date    head    ring    face    light    strike

## RESTRICTIVE LABELS

### Usage labels

Some words are used quite widely but are not appropriate in all kinds of speech or writing. Their use is restricted to certain types of contexts or situations. For example:

**muss** (mus) *Informal.*   **1** put into disorder; rumple: *The child's dress was mussed.*   **2** disorder; untidiness; mess. 1 *v.*, 2 *n.*

**gan·der** (gan′dər)   **1** an adult male goose.   **2** a fool; simpleton.   *n.*
**take a gander,** *Informal.*   take a look: *Take a gander at that outfit.*

*Muss* is marked *Informal*, which means that it is accepted in informal situations but should not be used in formal speech or writing. The idiom of *gander* is marked *Informal*, which means that it is out of place in writing except when one is writing conversation in which such a word would be appropriate.

    *Informal* as used in the above entries is a usage label. If such a label applies to a whole entry (as with *muss*), it appears right after the pronunciation. If a label applies to one meaning only (as with *gander*), it appears immediately after the definition number or idiom.

    The following usage labels are used in the dictionary:

*Informal*
*Humorous*
*Archaic* (old-fashioned, no longer in general use)

### Regional labels

Some words are used in certain parts of the English-speaking world. For example:

**music hall**   *Esp. Brit.*   **1** a theatre for singing, dancing, variety shows, etc.; vaudeville theatre.   **2** vaudeville entertainment.

**mush¹** (mush)   **1** *Esp. U.S.*   corn meal boiled in water. **2** any soft, thick mass: *The heavy rain made mush of the old dirt road.*   **3** *Informal.*   weak sentiment; silly talk.   *n.*

**mush²** (mush) *Cdn.*   **1** a command to advance, given to sled dogs.   **2** urge sled dogs onward by shouting commands: *He mushed his dog team through the blinding storm.*   **3** follow a dogsled on foot: *For six days he mushed across the Barren Lands.*   **4** a journey made by dogsled.

Words or meanings labelled *Cdn.* are ones that came into the English language in Canada. Such words are referred to as Canadianisms. Some of them are used only in speaking or writing that is done in or about Canada.

> **Exercise**
>
> Write down the regional label given in the dictionary for each of the following terms. If the label applies to one meaning only, give a short definition of that meaning.
>
> | | | |
> |---|---|---|
> | corduroy | tram | lorry |
> | wavey | polecat | whisky-jack |

## Language labels

Certain foreign words and phrases are sometimes used in English but are not really accepted as part of the English language. For example: *garçon; auf Wiedersehen*. Such words usually keep their foreign pronunciation. They are underlined in writing and italicized in printing.

> **Exercise**
>
> In the following sentences, look up each of the italicized words in the dictionary and write down its meaning and language of origin.
> 1. The manager gave his secretary *carte blanche* to deal with the problem in his absence.
> 2. "*Eureka!*" cried the detective as she spotted the vital clue.
> 3. There are references to the fur trade in Chapter 2, *passim*.
> 4. They stayed in a small *pension* near Marseilles.

## FISTNOTES

A unique feature of the *Dictionary of Canadian English* series is the use of fistnotes to give special types of information. For example:

**may·be** (mā′bē) possibly or perhaps; it may be so. *adv.*
☞ *Usage.* **Maybe** as an adverb is one word: *Maybe it will rain tomorrow.* **May be** as a verb phrase is two words: *He may be home soon.*

**Ms. or Ms** (miz) a title used in front of the name of a woman or girl: *Ms. Jackson.*
☞ *Usage.* **Ms.** is a form made up in the early 1950's to parallel **Mr.** and **Mrs.** Unlike them, it is not an abbreviation, but it imitates them in being followed by a period. Like **Mr.**, but unlike **Mrs.** or **Miss**, **Ms.** does not identify a person as being married or unmarried.

In this dictionary these fistnotes are used to give information on five different kinds of topic: homonyms, usage, pronunciation, synonyms, and etymology.

# Homonyms

Such notes list words that are pronounced the same as the entry word but are spelled differently. They can often help you to find the entry word you want. For instance, if you look up *alter* and do not find the meaning you want, you should look under *altar*. Alternatively, you may want to know how to spell the word that sounds like *cue* and means a group of people standing in line. If you look up *cue*, the homonym note will lead you to *queue*.

**al·ter** (ol′tər)   1 make different; change; vary: *If this coat is too large, a tailor can alter it to fit you.*   2 become different: *Since her trip to Europe, her whole outlook has altered.*   v.   —**al′ter·a·ble,** *adj.*   —**al′ter·a·bly,** *adv.*
☛ *Hom.*   ALTAR.

**cue**² (kyü)   1 a queue; pigtail.   2 in billiards, pool, etc., a long, tapering stick used for striking the ball.   *n.*
☛ *Hom.*   QUEUE.

### Exercise

1. Write down the homonym(s) given in the dictionary at the fistnote for each of the following words. Then, for each of these entry words and their homonyms, write a sentence to show the word being properly used.

   faint     muscle    gamble
   our       meet      phase

2. (a) What large furry animal sounds as if it is naked?
   (b) This animal sounds expensive.
   (c) What part of a tree makes a noise like a dog?
   (d) She was very pretty at the annual exhibition.
   (e) This tree sounds like a covering of hair.

# Usage

A number of fistnotes give advice about usage. Some refer to choosing between words that are often confused; others deal with specific uses or problems of certain words; still others deal with the appropriate levels of usage for specific words. These are only some of the many kinds of information covered by different usage notes.

**il·lu·sion** (i lü′zhən) ...
☛ *Usage.* Do not confuse **illusion** and ALLUSION. An **illusion** is a misleading appearance: *The large car she drives gives an illusion of wealth.* An **allusion** is an indirect reference or slight mention: *He made allusions to Spain so we gathered he had been there recently.*

**in** (in) ...
☛ *Usage.* **In** generally shows location; INTO generally shows direction: *He was in the house. He came into the house. He was in a stupor. He fell into a deep sleep.* Informally, **in** is often used with certain words instead of **into**: *She fell in the creek.*

### Exercise

Look up the usage notes for the following entries, and then write a sentence for each entry word mentioned, using the word as suggested in the fistnote.

| | | |
|---|---|---|
| each | moral | imply |
| only | maybe | personal |

## Pronunciation

A few fistnotes discuss problems of varieties of pronunciation.

**colo·nel** (kėr′nəl) ...
☛ *Pronunciation.* In the 16c. there were two parallel spellings, *colonel* and *coronel*, each with its own pronunciation. The modern pronunciation (kėr′nəl) comes from the *coronel* form, though the spelling became established as *colonel*.

**creek** (krēk *or* krik) ...
☛ *Pronunciation.* Most Canadians pronounce **creek** the same as **creak,** but in some regions, especially in parts of the West, the pronunciation (krik) is common.

**gen·u·ine** (jen′yü ən *or* jen′yü īn′) ...
☛ *Pronunciation.* The pronunciation (jen′yü īn′) has become established in Canada, though many people still regard it as vulgar or non-standard.

**anti–** (an′tē) ...
☛ *Pronunciation.* The pronunciation given here (an′tē) is still the standard pronunciation in Canada. However, the variant pronunciation (an′tī), which is more typical of usage in the United States, is now making headway in Canada, especially in certain words, such as **antisocial** (an′tī sō′shəl). The same trend can be seen in certain words beginning with **semi-** and **multi-**.

## Synonyms

Some fistnotes bring out differences in meaning or usage between words that have very similar definitions. Such notes can help you to choose the most appropriate synonym for a particular context.

**map** (map) ...
☛ *Syn.* A **map** may refer especially to a plan of road or other routes on land, while CHART is used especially for plans showing air or sea routes. An ATLAS is a book of maps covering a large area or the whole world.

**per·son** (pėr′sən) ...
☛ *Syn.* **Person,** INDIVIDUAL. **Person** is the ordinary word for a human being of either sex: *A well-known person came into the room.* **Individual** emphasizes the person's uniqueness: *A strange individual came into the room.* Unlike **person, individual** can also be applied to animals and objects: *Our cat is a fascinating individual.* The phrase *a person* is often used instead of the impersonal pronoun **one:** *Exercise makes a person hungry.* It is, as a rule, awkward and pretentious to use **individual** in this way.

**Exercise**

Read the synonym note at the entry word that appears in brackets after each of the following sentences. Then use the most appropriate synonym to fill the blank in the sentence.

1. The crazed chemist gave her a _____ dose of poison. (fatal)
2. It is a Ukrainian _____ to decorate Easter eggs. (habit)
3. She was found not guilty as she had been proved to be _____ . (mad)
4. The horse turned _____ and refused to take the jump. (obstinate)

# Etymologies

Many fistnotes provide etymologies, or word histories. A knowledge of the origin and history of a word can help you to use it with more understanding and to recognize the meanings of related words.

To save space, the names of some common languages are abbreviated in the etymologies. The names of other languages are written out in full. The following abbreviations are used:

| | |
|---|---|
| OE | Old English (before A.D. 1100) |
| ME | Middle English (about 1100–1450) |
| AN | Anglo-Norman (1066–about 1350) |
| OF | Old French (before 1400) |
| F | French (modern) |
| Cdn.F | Canadian French |
| ON | Old Norse (before 1300) |
| L | Latin (classical—about 200 B.C. to A.D. 300) |
| Med.L | Medieval Latin (about 700–1500) |
| Gk. | Greek (classical—about 900 B.C. to A.D. 200) |

If the period when a word came into the language is not clear from its being used in, for example, Old English or Middle English, the century in which the word was first used in English is given in the fistnote. For an example, see *penguin*. The abbreviation 16c. means 16th century.

**guil·lo·tine** (gil′ə tēn′ *for noun,* gil′ə tēn′ *for verb*) ...
☞ *Etym.* From F *guillotine,* named after Joseph-Ignace Guillotin, a French doctor and member of the Revolutionary Assembly, who advocated using the machine as a quick and merciful means of execution. 18c.

**in·sect** (in′sekt) ...
☞ *Etym.* From L *insectum,* formed from *insecare* 'to cut into, cut up'; an insect's body is divided into segments that make it look cut up.

**ma·rine** (mə rēn′) ...
☞ *Etym.* MARINA, **marine,** MARINER, and MARITIME all come originally through Italian, French, or Latin forms, from L *mare* (mä′re) 'sea'.

**pen·guin** (pen′gwin *or* peng′gwin) ...
☞ *Etym.* Probably from a Breton word meaning 'white head'. Compare with Welsh *pen* 'head' + *gwyn* 'white', first applied to the great auk, a now extinct bird of the Newfoundland coasts. 16c.

**Exercise**

For each of the following, look up the fistnote giving the etymology of the italicized word, and then answer the question.

1. From what two words was *chortle* made up?
2. What are the meanings of the two Greek elements in *amphibious*?
3. Does the word *cheechako* come from Africa, the Caribbean, or the Pacific Coast of North America?
4. What is the Greek word for *five*?
5. For which god was *Wednesday* named?
6. What two words come originally from the same Latin source as *pawn*?

# PARTS OF A DICTIONARY ENTRY

The following is a list of all the possible parts of an entry in the *Gage Canadian Intermediate Dictionary*. Do you know the name and purpose of each part? To make sure, refer to the chart on the right-hand front endpaper.

1. Entry word
2. Homograph number
3. Pronunciation
4. Restrictive label
5. Definition number
6. Definition
7. Example
8. Special meaning
9. Part-of-speech label
10. Inflected form
11. Run-on entry (derived form)
12. Idiom
13. Fistnote
14. Picture
15. Caption

# JUST FOR FUN

1. **New Words from Old**
   It is possible to create new words by selecting and changing the order of letters in an existing one. For example:
   dreary gives: read, ready, year, red, dry, rear, dear, ear, are, dare, rye, rare, yard

   See how many new words you can make by using some of the letters, and changing the order of letters, in these words:

   | reader | stranger | board | tramp |
   |--------|----------|-------|-------|
   | collar | cellar | starting | nature |

2. **Break the code**
   (a) See if you can decipher this coded message:
   19 E 14 D   20 I 13 E   A 14 D   16 L 1 C 5   15 F   14 E 24 T
   13 E 5 T 9 N 7
   (b) Send a coded message in reply.
   (c) Exchange coded messages with your friends.
   (d) Invent your own code.

# TEST C

Read the following passage. Then look up the italicized words in the dictionary in order to answer the questions below.

## A Study in Contrasts

The stillness at the top of the falls is awesome. Only when one looks near the lip can one see the water starting to surge toward the edge before it *dives* down and becomes a *chute* of angry, turbulent foam. Standing on a ledge, nearly halfway down the cliff and twenty metres or so from the falls, one feels the fall-out from this turbulence as a gentle spray. At certain angles the sunlight catches this spray and is refracted by it into a shimmering rainbow. The colours hang poised in the air, but the water of the falls goes on tumbling like *crazy*, endlessly and irresistibly, until it reaches the bottom in a turmoil of splashing and foaming. It seems impossible to *calculate* the quantity, the force, or the speed of the falling water. Yet, in a hundred metres or so, the gorge widens and the river flows quietly and smoothly, like a gentle *creek* or *snye*, as if its waters had never known the tumultuous fury of the falls. But the spectator cannot forget the tumult, because there is always the noise—the thunderous roaring and pounding of the waters as they smash against each other down the rocky descent and crash into the churning *bedlam* of foam below. So this wonder of untamed nature is a *scene* of many contrasts—sound and silence, turbulence and stillness.

1. What does the usage note say about the two past tenses of *dive*?
2. What homonyms are given for *chute*, *creek*, and *scene*?
3. The idiom *like crazy* seems out of place in this passage. What usage label does the dictionary give for it?
4. Which of the italicized words is a Canadianism? What does it mean?
5. Where is the word *creek* commonly pronounced (krik)?
6. What are the origins of the words *bedlam*, *calculate*, and *snye*?

# Aa Aa

hat, āge, fär; let, ēqual, tėrm; it, īce
hot, ōpen, ôrder; oil, out; cup, pùt, rüle
əbove, takən, pencəl, lemən, circəs
ch, child; ng, long; sh, ship
th, thin; ᴛH, then; zh, measure

**a or A** (ā)   **1** the first letter of the English alphabet.   **2** any speech sound represented by this letter, as in *cat, father, late,* etc.   **3** in music: **a** the sixth tone in the scale of C major.   **b** a symbol representing this tone.   **c** a key, string, etc. of a musical instrument that produces this tone.   **d** the scale or key that has A as its keynote: *a symphony in A.*   **4** any person or thing considered as the first in a series: *Company A in a battalion. A and B are friends.*   **5** a grade rating a person or thing as the best in a group: *grade A eggs. She got an A in the exam.*   **6** a person or thing receiving this rating: *He's an A student.*   *n., pl.* **a's** or **A's.**

**a¹** (ə; *stressed,* ā *or* a)   **1** a word used before singular nouns when the person or thing referred to is not specific: *There's a man at the door. I need a new coat.*   **2** one: *I want a loaf of bread, a watermelon, and a dozen oranges. She took the stairs two at a time.*   **3** any: *A thoughtful person would not have said that.*   *indefinite article.*
☞ *Usage.* **A** is used before words pronounced with an initial consonant sound whether or not that sound is shown by the spelling, as in *a man, a year, a union, a hospital.* Most people also now write *a hotel* or *a historian,* but some use *an* in these cases.
☞ *Usage.* **A** regularly comes before other modifiers but follows *many, such, what,* and any adjective preceded by *as, how, so,* or *too,* as in *many a person, such a bore, so fine a picture, too high a price.*

**a²** (ə; *stressed,* ā *or* a)   **1** in each: *once a year.*   **2** for each: *two dollars a dozen, sixty dollars a day.*   *indefinite article.*
☞ *Usage.* See notes at A¹.

**a–¹**   a prefix meaning:   **1** on or in: *We went aboard. They found a bed.*   **2** in a particular state or condition: *He was fast asleep.*   **3** in a particular manner: *He read the poem aloud.*   **4** in the act or process of: *Luba set the bells a-ringing. They've gone a-fishing. The room was abuzz with conversation.*
☞ *Usage.* Adjectives originally formed with *a–* + noun (such as *alive, asleep*) are not used before a noun. We say *a man who is asleep,* and *a man asleep,* but not *an asleep man.*

**a–²**   a prefix meaning: not or without; a form of AN–¹ occurring before consonants except *h,* as in *atypical, atonal.*

**a–³**   a prefix meaning: from, away, or off; a form of AB–¹ occurring before *m, p,* and *v,* as in *avert.*

**a–⁴**   a prefix meaning: to or toward; a form of AD– occurring before *sc, sp,* and *st,* as in *ascribe, aspire, astringent.*

**a**   **1** anode.   **2** alto.   **3** are².

**a.**   **1** about.   **2** acre; acres.   **3** adjective.   **4** alto.   **5** in the year (for Latin *anno*).   **6** anode.   **7** anonymous.

**A**   **1** ampere.   **2** answer.   **3** one of the four main blood groups.

**A1** or **A–1** *Informal.*   A-one; first-class.

**aard·vark** (ärd′värk′)   a burrowing mammal of Africa, about 1.5 m long, having ears like a donkey, a long, movable snout similar to a pig's, and a very long, flat, sticky tongue with which it catches the ants and termites it eats: *Aardvarks use their strong claws for digging their burrows and for ripping open the nests of ants and termites.*   *n.*

**ab–¹**   a prefix meaning: from, away, away from, or off, as in *abnormal, abduct.*

**ab–²**   a prefix meaning: to or toward; a form of AD– occurring before *b,* as in *abbreviate.*

**AB¹**   Alberta (used in computerized address systems).

**AB²**   one of the four main blood groups.

**a·ba·cá** or **a·ba·ca** (ä′bə kä′ *or* ab′ə kə)   **1** a fibre obtained from the leafstalks of a species of banana plant native to the Philippines; MANILA HEMP.   **2** the plant itself.   *n.*

**a·back** (ə bak′)   now used only in **take aback,** surprise suddenly or startle: *Her answer took me aback. We were taken aback by his strange behaviour.*   *adv.*

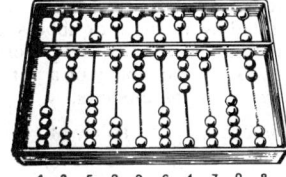

An abacus
The beads above the bar count 5 each when lowered to the bar.
The beads below the bar count 1 each when raised to the bar.
In the picture, the beads are set for 1 352 964 708.

**ab·a·cus** (ab′ə kəs)   a frame with rows of counters or beads that slide back and forth in grooves or on wires, used in calculating.   *n., pl.* **ab·a·cus·es** or **ab·a·ci** (-sī′ or -sē′).

**a·baft** (ə baft′)   **1** back of; behind: *The car was abaft ours.*   **2** of a ship or boat, at the stern; toward the stern: *He went abaft.*   1 *prep.,* 2 *adv.*

**ab·a·lo·ne** (ab′ə lō′nē)   any of several closely related species of edible snail found mainly along the coasts of Japan, Australia, New Zealand, South Africa, and California, having a single, flat, ear-shaped shell with a row of holes along one side and a mother-of-pearl lining that is used to make buttons and ornaments: *The different species of abalone range in size from about 3 to 30 centimetres long.*   *n.*

**a·ban·don** (ə ban′dən)   **1** give up entirely: *She abandoned the idea of becoming an astronaut.*   **2** leave without intending to return to; desert: *A good mother would never willingly abandon her baby.*   **3** a freedom from restraint; yielding completely to impulse: *The students cheered with abandon, waving their arms and shouting.*   1, 2 *v.,* 3 *n.*   —**a·ban′don·er,** *n.*
**abandon oneself to,**   yield oneself completely to a feeling, impulse, etc.: *to abandon oneself to grief.*

**a·ban·doned** (ə ban′dənd)   **1** deserted; forsaken.   **2** completely unrestrained.   *adj.*

**a·ban·don·ment** (ə ban′dən mənt)   **1** abandoning or being abandoned.   **2** a freedom from restraint; ABANDON (def. 3).   *n.*

**a·base** (ə bās′)   make lower in rank, condition, or

character; humiliate; degrade (*used with a pronoun ending in* -**self**): *A man who betrays his country abases himself.* *v.*, **a·based, a·bas·ing.**

**a·base·ment** (ə bās′mənt) a lowering or loss of self-respect; humiliation; degradation. *n.*

**a·bash** (ə bash′) embarrass and confuse; make uneasy or shy and slightly ashamed: *The boy was abashed when the teacher pointed out all his mistakes.* *v.* —**a·bash′ment,** *n.*

**a·bate** (ə bāt′) 1 make less in amount, intensity, etc.; decrease: *The medicine abated her pain.* 2 become less violent, intense, etc.; diminish: *The storm has abated.* 3 in law, do away with; put an end to; annul: *to abate a nuisance, to abate a writ.* *v.*, **a·bat·ed, a·bat·ing.** —**a·bat′er,** *n.*

**a·bate·ment** (ə bāt′mənt) 1 a decrease; lessening. 2 putting an end to. 3 the amount abated; reduction. *n.*

**ab·at·toir** (ab′ə twär′ *or* ab′ə twär′) SLAUGHTERHOUSE. *n.*

**ab·bess** (ab′is *or* ab′es) the woman in charge of an abbey of nuns. *n.*

**ab·bey** (ab′ē) 1 the building or buildings where monks or nuns live a religious life ruled by an abbot or abbess; a monastery or convent. 2 the monks or nuns living there. 3 a church or residence that was once an abbey or a part of an abbey: *Westminster Abbey.* *n., pl.* **ab·beys.**

**ab·bot** (ab′ət) the man in charge of an abbey of monks. *n.*

**abbrev.** or **abbr.** 1 abbreviation. 2 abbreviated.

**ab·bre·vi·ate** (ə brē′vē āt′) 1 make a word or phrase shorter so that a part stands for the whole: *We can abbreviate Saskatchewan to Sask.* 2 make briefer. *v.*, **ab·bre·vi·at·ed, ab·bre·vi·at·ing.** —**ab·bre′vi·a′tor,** *n.*

**ab·bre·vi·a·tion** (ə brē′vē ā′shən) 1 a shortened form of a word or phrase standing for the whole, such as *Ont.* for *Ontario* or *MP* for *Member of Parliament.* 2 making shorter. *n.*

**ABC** (ā′bē′sē′) the elementary principles; the parts to be learned first: *This course is intended to teach you the ABC of flying.* *n.*

**ABC's** (ā′bē′sēz′) the alphabet: *Some children know their ABC's before kindergarten.* *n. pl.*

**ab·di·cate** (ab′də kāt′) 1 give up a position of authority or responsibility; resign: *When the king abdicated his throne, his brother became king.* 2 renounce office or power: *Why did the queen abdicate?* *v.*, **ab·di·cat·ed, ab·di·cat·ing.** —**ab′di·ca′tor,** *n.*

**ab·di·ca·tion** (ab′də kā′shən) an abdicating; giving up a position of authority or responsibility; resigning: *The abdication of King Edward VIII took place in 1936.* *n.*

**ab·do·men** (ab′də mən *or* ab dō′mən) 1 the part of the body containing the stomach, the intestines, and other digestive organs; belly. 2 the last of the three parts of the body of an insect or crustacean. See INSECT for picture. *n.*

**ab·dom·i·nal** (ab dom′ə nəl) of, in, or for the abdomen: *Bending the body exercises the abdominal muscles.* *adj.* —**ab·dom′i·nal·ly,** *adv.*

**ab·duct** (ab dukt′) take a person away by force or by trickery; kidnap. *v.*

**ab·duc·tion** (ab duk′shən) kidnapping. *n.*

**ab·duc·tor** (ab duk′tər) kidnapper. *n.*

**a·beam** (ə bēm′) 1 directly opposite a ship's side: *The pirates started firing when their ship was abeam of ours.* 2 straight across a ship. *adv.*

**Ab·e·na·ki** (ab′ə nak′ē) 1 a member of the First Nations or Native Americans living mainly in southern Québec and the State of Maine. 2 the ALGONQUIAN language spoken by the Abenaki. 3 of or having to do with these people or their language. 1, 2 *n., pl.* **Ab·e·na·ki** or **Ab·e·na·kis;** 3 *adj.*

**Aberdeen Angus** (ab′ər dēn′ ang′gəs) a breed of small, entirely black, hornless beef cattle.

**ab·er·rant** (a ber′ənt) deviating from what is regular, normal, or right: *aberrant behaviour.* *adj.*

**ab·er·ra·tion** (ab′ə rā′shən) 1 a wandering from the right path or usual course of action. 2 a deviation from a standard or ordinary type; abnormal structure or development. 3 a temporary mental disorder. *n.*

**a·bet** (ə bet′) encourage or help, especially in something wrong: *One man did the actual stealing, but two others abetted him by distracting the storekeeper.* *v.*, **a·bet·ted, a·bet·ting.** —**a·bet′ment,** *n.*

**a·bet·tor** or **a·bet·ter** (ə bet′ər) a person who abets. *n.*

**a·bey·ance** (ə bā′əns) a temporary inactivity; state of suspended action: *The judge held the question in abeyance until she had the information necessary to make a decision.* *n.*

**ab·hor** (ab hôr′) shrink from in horror; feel disgust or loathing for; detest: *Some people abhor snakes.* *v.*, **ab·horred, ab·hor·ring.** —**ab·hor′rer,** *n.*

**ab·hor·rence** (ab hô′rəns) a feeling of loathing; horror; great disgust. *n.*

**ab·hor·rent** (ab hô′rənt) causing horror; disgusting; hateful. *adj.* —**ab·hor′rent·ly,** *adv.*

**a·bide** (ə bīd′) 1 put up with; endure; tolerate: *A good housekeeper cannot abide dirt.* 2 stay; remain: *Though much is taken, much abides.* 3 dwell; continue to live in a place. *v.*, **a·bode** or **a·bid·ed, a·bid·ing.** —**a·bid′er,** *n.*

**abide by,** **a** accept and follow out: *I shall abide by your instructions.* **b** remain faithful to; fulfil: *You must abide by your promise.*

**a·bid·ing** (ə bī′ding) unending; lasting: *We hope for an abiding peace.* *adj.*

**a·bil·i·ty** (ə bil′ə tē) 1 the power to perform or accomplish: *A horse has the ability to work.* 2 skill: *He has great ability as a hockey player.* 3 the power to do some special thing; talent: *She showed great musical ability in the way she played that difficult piece on the violin.* 4 the power to do some special things: *This computer has the ability to solve mathematical problems.* *n., pl.* **a·bil·i·ties.**

**ab·ject** (ab′jekt) 1 wretched; miserable: *abject poverty.* 2 deserving contempt; degraded: *abject fear, abject flattery.* 3 slavish: *abject submission.* *adj.* —**ab·ject′ly,** *adv.*

**ab·ju·ra·tion** (ab′jə rā′shən) abjuring. *n.*

**ab·jure** (ab jür′) 1 renounce on oath; repudiate; swear to give up: *He agreed to abjure his evil ways.* 2 abstain

from; avoid: *to abjure alcohol.* *v.,* **ab·jured, ab·jur·ing.**
—**ab·jur′er,** *n.*

**a·blaze** (ə blāz′) **1** on fire: *After the drought the forests were set ablaze by lightning. She set the house ablaze.* **2** shining brightly; brightly lit: *The great hall was ablaze with a hundred lights.* **1** *adv.,* **2** *adj.*

**a·ble** (ā′bəl) **1** having power, skill, means, or talent; competent: *Little children are able to walk, but they are not able to earn a living.* **2** having the necessary qualifications; skilful; competent: *an able seaman.* **3** having more power or skill than most others have; clever: *She is an able teacher.* **4** competently done: *an able speech.* *adj.,* **a·bler, a·blest.**

**-able** an adjective-forming suffix meaning: **1** that can be _____ ed; able to be _____ ed: *Obtainable means that can be obtained.* **2** likely to or suitable for: *Comfortable means suitable for comfort.* **3** inclined toward: *Peaceable means inclined toward peace.* **4** deserving to be _____ ed: *Lovable means deserving to be loved.*

**a·ble–bod·ied** (ā′bəl bod′ēd) strong and healthy. *adj.*

**able–bodied seaman** an experienced sailor who can perform all the ordinary duties of a sailor.

**a·bloom** (ə blüm′) in bloom; blossoming: *The trees are abloom early this year.* *adj.*

**ab·lu·tion** (ə blü′shən) **1** a washing of one's person. **2** washing or cleansing as a religious ceremony of purification. **3** the water or other liquid used in washing. *n.*

**a·bly** (ā′blē) in an able manner; with skill. *adv.*

**Ab·na·ki** (ab′nak′ē) ABENAKI. *n., pl.* **Ab·na·ki** or **Ab·na·kis.**

**ab·ne·gate** (ab′nə gāt) **1** surrender; give up a right or privilege: *They abnegated their claim on the estate.* **2** deny; recant; renounce: *to abnegate one's faith.* *v.,* **ab·ne·gat·ed, ab·ne·gat·ing.** —**ab′ne·ga′tion,** *n.*

**ab·nor·mal** (ab nôr′məl) **1** very different from the normal or ordinary; markedly irregular: *The drug produces an abnormal dilation of the pupil of the eye.* **2** having to do with what is abnormal: *abnormal psychology.* *adj.*
—**ab·nor′mal·ly,** *adv.* —**ab·nor′mal·ness,** *n.*

**ab·nor·mal·i·ty** (ab′nôr mal′ə tē) **1** an abnormal thing or happening. **2** an abnormal condition: *He suffers from an abnormality of the blood.* *n., pl.* **ab·nor·mal·i·ties.**

**a·board** (ə bôrd′) **1** on board; on, in, or into a ship, train, bus, aircraft, etc.: *All passengers should now be aboard.* **2** alongside. **3** on board of: *They went aboard the ship.* **1, 2** *adv.,* **3** *prep.*
**all aboard,** everybody on (conductor's call directing passengers to enter a train, bus, etc. about to start).

**a·bode** (ə bōd′) **1** a place to live in; dwelling; residence. **2** pt. and pp. of ABIDE. **1** *n.,* **2** *v.*

**a·boi·deau** (ab′ə dō′; *French,* äb wä dō′) *Cdn.* in Nova Scotia and New Brunswick: **1** a SLUICE GATE in the DIKES along the Bay of Fundy. **2** the DIKE itself. *n., pl.* **a·boi·deaus** or **a·boi·deaux** (*French,* äb wä dō′).

**a·boi·teau** (ab′ə tō′) ABOIDEAU. *n.*

**a·bol·ish** (ə bol′ish) do away with a law, institution, or custom completely; put an end to: *to abolish slavery.* *v.*
—**a·bol′ish·ment,** *n.*

**ab·o·li·tion** (ab′ə lish′ən) putting an end to; complete

**ablaze**     **3**     **about**

hat, āge, fär; let, ēqual, tėrm; it, īce
hot, ōpen, ôrder; oil, out; cup, pu̇t, rüle
əbove, takən, pencəl, lemən, circəs
ch, child; ng, long; sh, ship
th, thin; ᴛʜ, then; zh, measure

destruction: *In Upper Canada the abolition of slavery took place in 1793.* *n.*

**ab·o·li·tion·ist** (ab′ə lish′ə nist) a person who wishes to have a law or custom ABOLISHed. *n.*

**ab·o·ma·sum** (ab′ə mā′səm) the fourth stomach of cows, sheep, and other animals that chew the CUD: *The abomasum is the stomach that digests the food.* *n.*

**A–bomb** (ā′bom′) ATOMIC BOMB. *n.*

**a·bom·i·na·ble** (ə bom′ə nə bəl) **1** disgusting; hateful; loathsome. **2** *Informal.* very unpleasant; very bad; distasteful. *adj.* —**a·bom′i·na·ble·ness,** *n.*
—**a·bom′i·na·bly,** *adv.*

**abominable snowman** a manlike monster supposed to live in the Himalayan Mountains: *The Tibetan name for the abominable snowman is* YETI.

**a·bom·i·nate** (ə bom′ə nāt′) **1** feel disgust for; hate very much; abhor; detest; loathe. **2** dislike. *v.,*
**a·bom·i·nat·ed, a·bom·i·nat·ing.** —**a·bom′i·na′tor,** *n.*

**a·bom·i·na·tion** (ə bom′ə nā′shən) **1** a disgusting, hateful, or loathsome thing. **2** a feeling of disgust; hate; loathing. *n.*

**ab·o·rig·i·nal** (ab′ə rij′ə nəl) **1** existing from the beginning; first; original; native: *aboriginal inhabitants.* **2** of the earliest-known inhabitants: *The use of horses was not an aboriginal custom in North America.* **3** ABORIGINE. **1, 2** *adj.,* **3** *n.*

**ab·o·rig·i·ne** (ab′ə rij′ə nē) **1** one of the earliest known inhabitants of a country. **2** Usually **Aborigine,** a member of a dark-skinned people who are the first known inhabitants of Australia. *n.*

**a·bort** (ə bôrt′) **1** give birth before the fetus has developed enough to survive outside the womb; have a miscarriage. **2** cause to have an ABORTION (def. 1). **3** bring to an end prematurely; cut short or cancel: *to abort a space flight.* **4** fail to develop. *v.*

**a·bor·tion** (ə bôr′shən) **1** the deliberate ending of a pregnancy by causing the fetus to be expelled, especially before it has developed enough to survive outside the womb. **2** MISCARRIAGE (def. 2). **3** the failure of anything to develop to maturity. **4** anything incompletely developed: *Their revolutionary solar heating system turned out to be a sad abortion.* *n.*

**a·bor·tion·ist** (ə bôr′shə nist) a person who performs ABORTIONS (def. 1). *n.*

**a·bor·tive** (ə bôr′tiv) **1** unsuccessful; fruitless: *Gerard made several abortive attempts to escape.* **2** in biology, not developed properly; rudimentary. *adj.*
—**a·bor′tive·ly,** *adv.* —**a·bor′tive·ness,** *n.*

**a·bound** (ə bound′) be plentiful: *Fish abound in the ocean.* *v.*
**abound in,** be rich in: *Canada abounds in oil.*
**abound with,** be well supplied or filled with: *The ocean abounds with fish.*

**a·bout** (ə bout′) **1** having to do with: *Who Has Seen the Wind? is a novel about a boy on the Prairies.* **2** nearly; almost: *Elizabeth has about finished her work.* **3** all

around: *A collar goes about the neck.* **4** around: *Look about and tell me what you see.* **5** on one's person; with: *Have you a pencil about you?* **6** in the opposite direction: *You are going the wrong way. Face about!* 1, 3, 5 *prep.*, 2, 4, 6 *adv.*
**about to,** on the point of; going, intending, or ready to: *The plane is about to take off.*
**about turn,** a command to face in the opposite direction.

**a·bout–face** (əbout′fās′ *for noun,* ə bout′fās′ *for verb*) **1** turning or going in the opposite direction: *On hearing her name called, she made an about-face and hurried back to the house. At the first hint of opposition, the policy committee did an about-face.* **2** turn or go in the opposite direction. 1 *n.*, 2 *v.*, **a·bout-faced, a·bout-fac·ing.**

**a·bove** (ə buv′) **1** overhead; in a higher place: *The sky is above.* **2** higher than; over: *Henry kept his head above water. A captain is above a sergeant.* **3** more than: *Our club has above thirty members—thirty-five, to be exact.* **4** beyond: *Turn at the first corner above the school.* **5** too high in dignity or character for; superior to: *A great person should be above mean actions.* **6** in heaven. **7** earlier in a book or article: *See the above paragraph. The method discussed above is the best one.* **8** above zero on the Celsius scale of temperature: *It was 10 above that New Year's Day.* **9** something that is above. 1, 6–8 *adv.*, *adj.*, 2–5 *prep.*, 9 *n.*
**above reproach,** beyond reproach: *His conduct has always been above reproach.*

**a·bove·board** (ə buv′bôrd′) **1** in open sight: *Keep your hands aboveboard.* **2** fairly: *to win aboveboard.* 1 *adj.*, 2 *adv.*

**a·bove–men·tioned** (ə buv′men′shənd) previously referred to; mentioned earlier. *adj.*

**ab·ra·ca·dab·ra** (ab′rə kə dab′rə) **1** a word supposed to have magic power, used in incantations or as a charm to ward off disease. **2** meaningless talk; jargon. *n.*

**a·brade** (ə brād′) wear away by rubbing; scrape off: *The rock had been abraded over the years by blowing sand.* *v.*, **a·brad·ed, a·brad·ing.**

**a·bra·sion** (ə brā′zhən) **1** a place scraped or worn by rubbing: *Abrasions of the skin are painful.* **2** a scraping off; a wearing away by rubbing. *n.*

**a·bra·sive** (ə brā′siv) **1** a substance used for grinding, smoothing, or polishing: *Sandpaper, pumice, and emery are abrasives.* **2** wearing away by rubbing; causing abrasion: *the abrasive action of water.* 1 *n.*, 2 *adj.*

**a·breast** (ə brest′) side by side: *The soldiers marched three abreast.* *adv.*
**abreast of** or **abreast with,** keeping up with; not behind; alongside of: *Read the newspapers to keep abreast of what is going on.*

**a·bridge** (ə brij′) **1** make shorter, especially something written or printed: *A long story can be abridged by leaving out unimportant parts.* **2** make less: *The rights of citizens must not be abridged without proper cause.* *v.*, **a·bridged, a·bridg·ing.**

**a·bridged** (ə brijd′) shortened; condensed: *This book is available in an abridged form.* *adj.*

**a·bridg·ment** or **a·bridge·ment** (ə brij′mənt) **1** a shortened form, especially of a book or a long magazine article: *That book is an abridgment of a three-volume history.* **2** making shorter or less; abridging. *n.*

**a·broad** (ə brod′) **1** outside one's country, especially overseas; to a foreign land or lands: *Olga is going abroad this summer to travel in France and Germany.* **2** in a foreign land or lands: *Where's Mario? I hear he's abroad again.* **3** out of doors; in the open air: *They travelled only by night because fewer enemy patrols were abroad then.* **4** going around; in circulation; current: *A rumour is abroad that the principal is leaving.* **5** far and wide; widely: *The news of his arrival spread abroad.* 1, 3, 5 *adv.*, 2 4 *adj.*

**ab·ro·gate** (ab′rə gāt′) do away with; repeal; cancel: *The government once abrogated diplomatic relations with Iran.* *v.* **ab·ro·gat·ed, ab·ro·gat·ing.**
—**ab′ro·ga′tion,** *n.* —**ab′ro·ga′tor,** *n.*

**a·brupt** (ə brupt′) **1** sudden; hasty; unexpected: *He made an abrupt turn to avoid another car.* **2** very steep: *The road made an abrupt rise up the hill.* **3** short or sudden in speech or manner; blunt: *She was very gruff and had an abrupt way of speaking.* *adj.* —**a·brupt′ly,** *adv.* —**a·brupt′ness,** *n.*

**ab·scess** (ab′ses) a collection of pus in the tissues of some part of the body, caused by infection: *Pimples, boils, and carbuncles are abscesses. The dentist treated the abscess at the root of a tooth.* *n.*, *pl.* **ab·scess·es.**

**ab·scessed** (ab′sest) having an ABSCESS. *adj.*

**ab·scond** (ab skond′) go away suddenly and secretly; go off and hide, especially, to escape the law: *The dishonest teller absconded with the bank's money.* *v.*
—**ab·scond′er,** *n.*

**ab·sence** (ab′səns) **1** being away: *His absence was due to illness.* **2** the time of being away: *He returned after an absence of two years.* **3** being without; lack: *Darkness is the absence of light.* *n.*

**absence of mind,** absent-mindedness. Compare with PRESENCE OF MIND.

**ab·sent** (ab′sənt *for adjective,* ab sent′ *for verb*) **1** not present; away: *Three members of the class are absent today.* **2** lacking; not existing: *Trees are almost completely absent in some parts of the Prairies.* **3** ABSENT-MINDED: *She said 'Yes' in an absent way and kept on reading.* *adj.*
**absent oneself,** stay away: *to absent oneself from school.*

**ab·sen·tee** (ab′sən tē′) a person who is away. *n.*

**ab·sen·tee·ism** (ab′sən tē′iz əm) the practice or condition of being away: *Absenteeism was high during the outbreak of flu.* *n.*

**ab·sent·ly** (ab′sən tlē) without paying attention to what is going on around one; inattentively: *He had answered her absently and later on couldn't remember what he had said.* *adv.*

**ab·sent–mind·ed** (ab′sənt mīn′did) not aware of what is going on around one; having one's mind on other things: *She was so absent-minded that day, she threw away my letter and put her shopping list in the mailbox.* *adj.*
—**ab′sent-mind′ed·ly,** *adv.* —**ab′sent-mind′ed·ness,** *n.*

**ab·so·lute** (ab′sə lüt′) **1** complete; whole or entire; perfect: *absolute silence, absolute justice. Try to tell the absolute truth.* **2** not mixed with anything else; pure: *Absolute alcohol has no water in it.* **3** not limited or restricted by a constitution, parliament, etc.: *an absolute monarchy, an absolute ruler.* **4** not qualified or restricted in any way: *absolute freedom.* **5** certain; unquestionable; positive: *absolute proof, absolute certainty.* **6** not compared with or dependent on anything else; not relative: *absolute velocity, an absolute term in logic.*

**7** something that is absolute. 1–6 adj., 7 n.
—**ab′so·lute′ness,** n.

**absolute humidity** the amount of water vapour present in a unit volume of air: *A cubic metre of air containing 10 grams of water vapour has an absolute humidity of 10.* Compare with RELATIVE HUMIDITY.

**ab·so·lute·ly** (ab′sə lü′tlē *for 1, 2,* ab′sə lü′tlē *for 3*) **1** completely: *This can opener is absolutely useless.* **2** positively: *He is absolutely the finest fellow I know.* **3** without question: *"Are you going to the game?" "Absolutely!"* adv.

**absolute monarchy** a monarchy that does not restrict the power of the ruler. Compare with LIMITED MONARCHY.

**absolute zero** the lowest temperature possible according to scientific theory, equal to −273.16°C, or zero kelvins; the lowest theoretical temperature that a gas can reach: *As the temperature of any gas gets lower, its volume gets smaller, and absolute zero is the temperature at which it would theoretically disappear altogether.*

**ab·so·lu·tion** (ab′sə lü′shən) a freeing or freedom from the guilt of sin; forgiveness: *A person who confesses his sins and sincerely repents, intending not to repeat them, is granted absolution by a priest.* n.

**ab·so·lut·ism** (ab′sə lü tiz′əm) a system or form of government in which the power of the ruler is not restricted; DESPOTISM. n.

**ab·so·lut·ist** (ab′sə lü′tist) **1** a person in favour of DESPOTISM or ABSOLUTISM. **2** DESPOTIC. 1 n., 2 adj.

**ab·solve** (ab zolv′ *or* ab solv′) **1** declare free from sin. **2** clear of blame or guilt: *The principal absolved the student of any wrongdoing.* **3** set free from a promise or duty. v., **ab·solved, ab·solv·ing.**

**ab·sorb** (ab zôrb′ *or* ab sôrb′) **1** take in or suck up liquids: *A blotter absorbs ink.* **2** take in and make a part of itself; assimilate: *Canada has absorbed millions of immigrants. Digested food is absorbed into the bloodstream by osmosis.* **3** take up all the attention of; interest very much: *The puzzle has absorbed her for hours.* **4** take in and hold: *Anything black absorbs most of the light rays that fall on it; that is, few of the light rays are reflected from it.* v.

**ab·sorbed** (ab zôrbd′ *or* ab sôrbd′) very much interested; completely occupied: *The girl was so absorbed in watching the chipmunk that she didn't hear her friend call.* adj.

**ab·sorb·ent** (ab zôr′bənt *or* ab sôr′bənt) **1** able to take in moisture, light, or heat: *Absorbent paper is used to dry the hands.* **2** any thing or substance that takes in or sucks up moisture, light, or heat. 1 adj., 2 n.

**ab·sorb·ing** (ab zôr′bing *or* ab sôr′bing) extremely interesting: *The explorer had written an absorbing account of his adventures.* adj. —**ab·sorb′ing·ly,** adv.

**ab·sorp·tion** (ab zôrp′shən *or* ab sôrp′shən) **1** the process of absorbing or of being absorbed: *the absorption of water by a sponge. In the absorption of light rays by black objects, the light rays are changed to heat.* **2** having all one's interest taken up: *They didn't hear the dinner bell because of their absorption in their game.* **3** in biology, the process of taking digested food, oxygen, etc. into the bloodstream by OSMOSIS. n.

**ab·sorp·tive** (ab zôrp′tiv *or* ab sôrp′tiv) able to ABSORB. adj.

**ab·stain** (ab stān′) **1** do without something voluntarily;

**absolute humidity**     **5**     **absurdity**

hat, āge, fär; let, ēqual, tėrm; it, īce
hot, ōpen, ôrder; oil, out; cup, pùt, rüle
əbove, takən, pencəl, lemən, circəs
ch, child; ng, long; sh, ship
th, thin; ŦH, then; zh, measure

refrain (*from*): *Athletes usually abstain from smoking.* **2** decline to vote: *Several delegates abstained from voting because they objected to the wording of the motion.* v.

**ab·stain·er** (ab stā′nər) a person who abstains, especially from the use of alcoholic liquor. n.

**ab·ste·mi·ous** (ab stē′mē əs) sparing in eating and drinking; moderate; temperate. adj.
—**ab·ste′mi·ous·ly,** adv. —**ab·ste′mi·ous·ness,** n.

**ab·sten·tion** (ab sten′shən) **1** ABSTINENCE. **2** the fact of not voting: *There were five votes in favour, four against, and three abstentions.* n.

**ab·sti·nence** (ab′stə nəns) abstaining; giving up or avoiding certain kinds of food, drink, activity, etc. n.

**abs·ti·nent** (ab′stə nənt) ABSTEMIOUS. adj.

**ab·stract** (ab′strakt *for adjective and noun,* ab strakt′ *for verb*) **1** thought of apart from any particular object or real thing: *A lump of sugar is a real thing; the idea of sweetness is abstract.* **2** expressing a quality that is thought of apart from any particular object or real thing: *In "Honesty is the best policy," honesty is an abstract noun.* **3** think of a quality, such as goodness, redness, weight, beauty, or truth, apart from any object or real thing having that quality: *How can we abstract time from the hours, minutes, and seconds by which we measure it?* **4** hard to understand; difficult: *The atomic theory of matter is so abstract that it can be thoroughly understood only by advanced students.* **5** take away; remove: *Can you abstract the watch from my pocket without my knowing it? We can abstract gold from ore.* **6** a short statement of the main ideas or points in an article, book, case in court, etc.; summary. **7** make an abstract of; summarize. **8** in art, representing ideas or feelings by abstracting certain qualities or elements from real things so that the result has little or no direct resemblance to these things: *an abstract painting.* 1, 2, 4, 8 adj., 3, 5, 7 v., 6 n.
—**ab′stract·ly,** adv. —**ab′stract·ness,** n.
**in the abstract,** in theory rather than in practice: *In the abstract, we approve of the Golden Rule; but we do not always follow it.*

**ab·stract·ed** (ab strak′tid) **1** lost in thought; ABSENT-MINDED: *Gemiel could tell from her abstracted look that she hadn't heard a word he said.* **2** pt. and pp. of ABSTRACT. 1 adj., 2 v. —**ab·stract′ed·ly,** adv.

**ab·strac·tion** (ab strak′shən) **1** the idea of a quality thought of apart from any particular object or real thing having that quality; abstract idea or term: *Whiteness, bravery, and length are abstractions. A line that has no width is only an abstraction.* **2** the formation of such an idea. **3** a taking away; removal: *After the abstraction of the juice from an orange, only the pulp and peel are left.* **4** the state of being lost in thought. n.

**ab·struse** (ab strüs′) hard to understand. adj.
—**ab·struse′ly,** adv. —**ab·struse′ness,** n.

**ab·surd** (ab zėrd′ *or* ab sėrd′) plainly not true or sensible; so contrary to reason that it is laughable; foolish; ridiculous. adj. —**ab·surd′ly,** adv. —**ab·surd′ness,** n.

**ab·surd·i·ty** (ab zėr′də tē *or* ab sėr′də tē) **1** something ABSURD; an unreasonable, ridiculous, or silly action, statement, custom, etc.: *Your explanation is an absurdity.* **2** an ABSURD quality or condition; folly: *the absurdity of superstition. n., pl.* **ab·surd·i·ties.**

**a·bun·dance** (ə bun′dəns) a quantity that is more than enough; great plenty; full supply (*of*). *n.*

**a·bun·dant** (ə bun′dənt) more than enough; very plentiful: *There are abundant oil reserves in Alberta. adj.* —**a·bun′dant·ly,** *adv.*

**a·buse** (ə byüz′ *for verb,* ə byüs′ *for noun*) **1** use wrongly; make bad use of: *The policewoman abused her authority by arresting a harmless onlooker.* **2** a wrong or bad use: *the abuse of a privilege.* **3** treat badly: *to abuse a child. Don't abuse your eyes by reading in poor light.* **4** bad treatment: *abuse of a helpless prisoner.* **5** a bad practice or custom: *the abuses of evil dictators.* **6** use harsh and insulting language to: *The angry captain abused the crew at the top of his voice.* **7** harsh and insulting language. 1, 3, 6 *v.,* **a·bused, a·bus·ing;** 2, 4, 5 7 *n.* —**a·bus′er,** *n.*

**a·bu·sive** (ə byü′siv) **1** using harsh and insulting language: *The coach was often abusive to the team.* **2** containing abuse: *an abusive letter.* **3** abusing; treating badly. *adj.* —**a·bu′sive·ly,** *adv.*

**a·but** (ə but′) touch at one end or edge; border (*on*); end (*against*): *The sidewalk abuts on the street. The street abuts against the railway.* *v.,* **a·but·ted, a·but·ting.**

**a·but·ment** (ə but′mənt) a support for an arch or bridge. *n.*

**a·bysm** (ə biz′əm) ABYSS. *n.*

**a·bys·mal** (ə biz′məl) **1** too deep to be measured; bottomless. **2** *Informal.* very bad: *Your work has been abysmal this term. adj.* —**a·bys′mal·ly,** *adv.*

**a·byss** (ə bis′) **1** a very deep crack in the earth; a seemingly bottomless hole. **2** the lowest depth: *the abyss of despair. n.*

**Ab·ys·sin·i·an** (ab′ə sin′ē ən) **1** ETHIOPIAN (defs. 1 and 2). **2** a breed of medium-sized cat having short, fine, silky hair that is light brown in colour. 1 *adj.,* 1, 2 *n.*

**Ac** actinium.

**A/C** or **a/c** account.

**AC, A.C.,** or **a.c.** alternating current.

**a·ca·cia** (ə kā′shə) **1** any of a large, closely related group of flowering trees and shrubs of the pea family found in warm regions, having tiny yellow or white flowers that grow in fluffy round clusters or spikes and having fernlike leaves or wide, flattened stems that look like leaves: *Some species of acacia yield important substances such as tannin and gum arabic.* **2** LOCUST tree. *n.*

**ac·a·dem·ic** (ak′ə dem′ik) **1** of or having to do with schools, colleges, and their studies. **2** concerned with education in the arts, history, philosophy, etc. rather than with commercial, technical, or professional training. **3** scholarly. **4** theoretical; not practical: *"Which came first, the chicken or the egg?" is an academic question.* **5** a scholar or scholarly person. **6 academics,** *pl.* academic courses or studies. 1–4 *adj.,* 5 6 *n.* —**ac′a·dem′i·cal·ly,** *adv.*

**ac·a·dem·i·cal** (ak′ə dem′ə kəl) ACADEMIC (defs. 1–4). *adj.*

**a·cad·e·my** (ə kad′ə mē) **1** a place for instruction. **2** a private high school. **3** a school where some special subject can be studied: *There are academies of medicine and painting, and military or naval academies.* **4** a society of authors, scholars, scientists, artists, etc., for encouraging literature, science, or art. *n., pl.* **a·cad·e·mies.**

**A·ca·di·a** (ə kā′dē ə) *Cdn.* **1** the areas of French settlement and culture in the Maritime Provinces. **2** the Maritime Provinces as a unit. **3** formerly, the French colony comprising the Maritime Provinces and adjacent parts of Quebec and New England. *n.*

**A·ca·di·an** (ə kā′dē ən *or* ə ka′jən) **1** of or relating to Acadia or, sometimes, to Nova Scotia. **2** a native of Acadia or one of his or her descendants. **3** a person of Acadian descent. **4** a variety of CANADIAN FRENCH spoken in the Maritimes. 1 *adj.,* 2–4 *n.*

**a cappella** (ä′kə pel′ə) in music, sung without instrumental accompaniment.

**acc.** **1** accusative. **2** account.

**ac·cede** (ak sēd′) **1** give in (*to*); agree (*to*): *They regretted acceding to the proposal.* **2** come to; attain to an office or dignity: *When the king died, his oldest daughter acceded to the throne.* **3** become a party (*to*): *Our government acceded to the treaty.* *v.,* **ac·ced·ed, ac·ced·ing.**

**accel.** accelerando.

**ac·cel·er·an·do** (ak sel′ə ran′dō *or* a chel′ə ran′dō) in music, gradually increasing in speed. *adv., adj.*

**ac·cel·er·ate** (ak sel′ə rāt′) **1** go or cause to go faster; increase in speed; speed up: *The train accelerated suddenly. By touching the throttle, the pilot accelerated the plane.* **2** cause to happen sooner; hasten: *Rest often accelerates a person's recovery from illness.* **3** in physics, change the velocity of a moving object. *v.,* **ac·cel·er·at·ed, ac·cel·er·at·ing.**

**ac·cel·er·a·tion** (ak sel′ə rā′shən) **1** a speeding up or hastening; increase in speed. **2** a change in velocity: *Positive acceleration is an increase in velocity. Negative acceleration is a decrease in velocity.* **3** the rate of change in the velocity of a moving body. *n.*

**ac·cel·er·a·tor** (ak sel′ə rā′tər) **1** a device for increasing the speed of a machine, especially the pedal that controls the flow of gasoline to an automobile engine. **2** in chemistry, any substance that speeds up a chemical reaction. **3** in physics, any of several kinds of apparatus for accelerating electrically charged atomic particles to high speeds, building up extremely high amounts of energy in them: *Accelerators are used in nuclear research and in medicine and industry. n.*

**ac·cent** (ak′sent *for noun,* ak′sent *or* ak sent′ *for verb*) **1** the degree of force or loudness with which words or syllables in words are uttered; STRESS (def. 6). **2** a mark (′) written or printed to show which syllable or syllables of a word are spoken with the greatest force, as in *yes′ter day, to day′,* and *to mor′row.* Some words have two accents, a primary or main accent (′) and a secondary or lesser accent (′), as in *ac′a dem′ic.* **3** a mark used in writing or printing to indicate a particular sound quality, length of vowel, contraction, etc., or to indicate that a normally silent vowel is to be pronounced: *Accents are used as part of the spelling system of certain languages, such as French or Greek.* **4** a distinctive manner of pronunciation heard in different parts of the same country or in the speech of a person speaking a language other than his native one: *a Scottish accent. Hans still speaks English with a German accent.* **5** mark with an accent.

**6** pronounce with an accent.   **7** the emphasis on certain words or syllables in a line of poetry that gives it a particular rhythm: *In "The stag at eve had drunk his fill," the accents are on* stag, eve, drunk, *and* fill.   **8** in music, emphasis on certain notes or chords.   **9** emphasize; accentuate: *Throughout her speech she accented the gravity of the situation.*   **10 accents,** *pl.* a tone of voice: *The little girl spoke to her doll in tender accents.*   1–4, 7, 8 10 *n.*, 5, 6, 9 *v.*

**ac·cen·tu·al** (ak sen′chü əl)   **1** of ACCENT (def. 1); formed by accent or STRESS (def. 6).   **2** having the same ACCENT (def. 1) or STRESS (def. 6) as ordinary speech: *Much modern poetry is accentual.*   *adj.*

**ac·cen·tu·ate** (ak sen′chü āt′)   **1** emphasize: *Her black hair accentuated the whiteness of her skin.*   **2** pronounce with an ACCENT (def. 1), or STRESS (def. 6): *to accentuate the first syllable of a word.*   **3** mark with an accent.   *v.*, **ac·cen·tu·at·ed, ac·cen·tu·at·ing.**
—**ac·cen·tu·a′tion,** *n.*

**ac·cept** (ak sept′)   **1** take or receive something offered or given; consent to take: *I accept your gift.*   **2** say yes to; agree to: *The government accepted the proposal for a conference on fishing rights.*   **3** take as true or satisfactory; believe in: *She refused to accept our story of what had happened.*   **4** receive with liking and approval; approve: *He was soon accepted by his new classmates.*   **5** regard as normal or inevitable: *to accept one's fate. The right to an education is generally accepted today.*   **6** undertake as a responsibility: *My sister accepted a position as cashier.*   **7** sign and agree to pay: *to accept a note for a loan.*   **8** say yes to an invitation, offer, etc.: *Tiiu asked me to go with her and I accepted.*   *v.*
—**ac·cept′er,** *n.*
☞ *Syn.* See note at RECEIVE.

**ac·cept·a·bil·i·ty** (ak sep′tə bil′ə tē)   the quality of being ACCEPTABLE or satisfactory.   *n.*

**ac·cept·a·ble** (ak sep′tə bəl)   **1** worth ACCEPTing; agreeable; welcome: *Flowers are an acceptable gift for a sick person.*   **2** good enough but not outstanding; satisfactory: *an acceptable performance.*   *adj.*

**ac·cept·a·bly** (ak sep′tə blē)   in a way that pleases.   *adv.*

**ac·cept·ance** (ak sep′təns)   **1** the taking of something offered or given.   **2** a favourable reception; approval.   **3** the taking of something as true and satisfactory.   *n.*

**ac·cept·ed** (ak sep′tid)   **1** generally approved; conventional: *the accepted behaviour at formal dinners.*   **2** pt. and pp. of ACCEPT.   1 *adj.*, 2 *v.*

**ac·cess** (ak′ses)   **1** the right to approach, enter, or use; admission: *All children have access to the library during the afternoon.*   **2** the degree to which a place is reachable; approach: *Access to the mountain town was difficult because of the poor road.*   **3** any way or means of approach: *A ladder was the only access to the attic. He has access to people who help him get work.*   **4** get information out of a computer memory: *You can access information from a computer if you have the codes.*   1–3 *n.*, 4 *v.*

**ac·ces·si·bil·i·ty** (ak ses′ə bil′ə tē)   **1** the condition of being easy to reach or get at.   **2** an openness to influence.   *n.*

**ac·ces·si·ble** (ak ses′ə bəl)   **1** that can be entered or reached.   **2** easy to get at; easy to reach or enter: *A telephone should be put where it will be accessible.*   **3** that can be obtained: *Not many facts about the kidnapping were accessible.*   *adj.*
**accessible to,**   capable of being reached or influenced by;

## accentual     7     acclamation

hat, āge, fär; let, ēqual, tėrm; it, īce
hot, ōpen, ôrder; oil, out; cup, pùt, rüle
əbove, takən, pencəl, lemən, circəs
ch, child; ng, long; sh, ship
th, thin; ᴛʜ, then; zh, measure

susceptible to: *An open-minded person is accessible to reason.*

**ac·ces·si·bly** (ak ses′ə blē)   so as to be ACCESSIBLE.   *adv.*

**ac·ces·sion** (ak sesh′ən)   **1** the act of attaining to a right, office, etc.: *The prince's accession to the throne was welcomed by the people.*   **2** an increase; addition: *the accession of forty pupils.*   **3** the thing added.   *n.*

**ac·ces·so·ry** (ak ses′ə rē)   **1** something added that is useful in some way but not absolutely necessary: *Susanne bought a mirror and some other accessories for her bicycle.*   **2** something worn or carried, such as a hat, shoes, or scarf, that is chosen to set off or complement a dress, suit, etc.: *The appearance of a basic dress can be changed considerably by varying the style and colour of the accessories.*   **3** helping something more important; added; additional; extra: *His tie supplied an accessory touch of colour.*   **4** in law, a person who helps another commit a crime without actually being present: *A person who hides a criminal is an accessory.*   **5** helping to commit or hide a crime.   1, 2, 4 *n., pl.* **ac·ces·so·ries;**   3, 5 *adj.*

**access road**   *Cdn.*   **1** a road that permits entry to an expressway, etc.   **2** a road built to permit entry to a place or an area that is otherwise sealed off, as by dense bush, MUSKEG, etc.

**ac·ci·dent** (ak′sə dənt)   **1** something harmful or unlucky that happens by chance: *an automobile accident.*   **2** something that happens without being planned, intended, wanted, or known in advance: *Their meeting was an accident.*   *n.*
**by accident,**   by chance; not on purpose: *I cut my foot by accident.*

**ac·ci·den·tal** (ak′sə den′təl)   **1** happening by chance: *The finding of the treasure was accidental.*   **2** not planned or intended: *The injury to the player was accidental.*   **3** non-essential; not necessary; incidental: *Songs are essential to musical comedy, but accidental to Shakespeare's plays.*   **4** in music, a sign used to show a change of pitch; a flat (♭), a sharp (♯), or a natural (♮) after the key signature and before the note to be changed.   **5** in music, of or having to do with an accidental.   1–3, 5 *adj.*, 4 *n.*

**ac·ci·den·tal·ly** (ak′sə den′tə lē *or* ak′sə den′tlē)   in an ACCIDENTAL (def. 2) manner; not on purpose.   *adv.*

**ac·claim** (ə klām′)   **1** show satisfaction and approval by words or sounds; shout welcome to; applaud: *The crowd acclaimed the fireman for rescuing two people from the burning house.*   **2** announce with signs of approval; hail: *The newspapers acclaimed the fireman a hero.*   **3** a shout or show of approval; applause; welcome: *The actress was received with great acclaim.*   **4** *Cdn.*   elect to an office without opposition: *The voters acclaimed her mayor.*   1, 2, 4 *v.*, 3 *n.*

**ac·cla·ma·tion** (ak′lə mā′shən)   a shout of welcome or show of approval by a crowd; applause.   *n.*
**by acclamation,**   *Cdn.*   **a** without opposition in an election: *Since no candidate opposed her, Ms. Kress was elected by acclamation.*   **b** with a great majority by an oral vote, rather than by ballot.
☞ *Hom.* ACCLIMATION.

**ac·cli·mate** (ak′lə māt′ *or* ə klī′mit) ACCLIMATIZE. *v.*, ac·cli·mat·ed, ac·cli·mat·ing.

**ac·cli·ma·tion** (ak′lə mā′shən) ACCLIMATIZATION. *n.* ☛ *Hom.* ACCLAMATION.

**ac·cli·ma·ti·za·tion** (ə klī′mə tə zā′shən *or* ə klī′mə tī zā′shən) acclimatizing or being ACCLIMATIZED. *n.*

**ac·cli·ma·tize** (ə klī′mə tīz′) accustom or become accustomed to a new climate or new surroundings or conditions: *It took him a long while to acclimatize himself to the high altitude. They soon became acclimatized to city life.* *v.*, ac·cli·ma·tized, ac·cli·ma·tiz·ing.

**ac·cliv·i·ty** (ə kliv′ə tē) an upward slope of ground. *n., pl.* ac·cliv·i·ties.

**ac·co·lade** (ak′ə lād′ *or* ak′ə läd′) **1** a tap on the shoulder with the flat side of a sword given to mark the bestowal of knighthood on a person. **2** praise; recognition; award. *n.*

**ac·com·mo·date** (ə kom′ə dāt′) **1** have room for; hold comfortably: *This big bedroom will accommodate two beds.* **2** help out; oblige: *Eino wanted change for a dollar, but I could not accommodate him.* **3** furnish with lodging and sometimes with food as well: *Can you accommodate a party of five for two weeks?* **4** provide a person with a loan of money. **5** make fit; make suitable. **6** reconcile; adjust. *v.*, ac·com·mo·dat·ed, ac·com·mo·dat·ing.

**ac·com·mo·dat·ing** (ə kom′ə dā′ting) obliging; willing to help: *The woman was accommodating enough to lend me a dollar.* *adj.* —ac·com′mo·dat′ing·ly, *adv.*

**ac·com·mo·da·tion** (ə kom′ə dā′shən) **1** a help, favour, or convenience: *It will be an accommodation to me if you will meet me tomorrow instead of today.* **2** a loan. **3** a willingness to help out. **4** the fitting of something to a purpose or situation; adjustment: *The accommodation of our desires to a smaller income took some time.* **5** the settlement of differences; reconciliation. **6 accommodations**, *pl.* lodging and sometimes food as well: *The hotel has accommodations for one hundred people.* *n.*

**ac·com·pa·ni·ment** (ə kump′nē mənt *or* ə kum′pə nē mənt) **1** whatever goes along with something else: *Destruction and suffering are accompaniments of war.* **2** in music, a part added to help or enrich the main part: *Yi-Su sang to a piano and violin accompaniment.* *n.*

**ac·com·pa·nist** (ə kum′pə nist) a person who plays a musical ACCOMPANIMENT (def. 2). *n.*

**ac·com·pa·ny** (ə kump′nē *or* ə kum′pə nē) **1** go along with: *May we accompany you on your walk?* **2** be or happen in connection with: *Fire is accompanied by heat.* **3** play or sing a musical accompaniment for or to. *v.*, ac·com·pa·nied, ac·com·pa·ny·ing. —ac·com′pa·ni·er, *n.*

**ac·com·plice** (ə kom′plis) a person who aids another in committing a crime or other unlawful act: *Without an accomplice the thief could not have got into the house so easily.* *n.*

**ac·com·plish** (ə kom′plish) **1** succeed in completing; carry out a promise, plan, etc.: *Did you accomplish your purpose?* **2** finish; complete: *Fred can accomplish more in a day than any other boy in his class.* *v.* —ac·com′plish·er, *n.*

**ac·com·plished** (ə kom′plisht) expert; skilled: *an accomplished surgeon, an accomplished hostess, an accomplished liar.* *adj.*

**ac·com·plish·ment** (ə kom′pli shmənt) **1** doing or carrying out; successful completion: *The accomplishment of his purpose took three months.* **2** something accomplished; achievement; completed undertaking: *The teacher was proud of his pupils' accomplishments.* **3** a skill in some social art or grace: *Anna was a girl of many accomplishments, being skilled in swimming, dancing, and singing.* *n.*

**ac·cord** (ə kôrd′) **1** be in harmony (*with*); agree (*with*): *Her account of the accident accords with yours.* **2** make agree; harmonize; reconcile. **3** agreement; harmony: *Accord was finally reached. The various city groups are now in accord on the parks issue.* **4** a formal agreement between nations or parts of nations. **5** harmony of colour, pitch, or tone. **6** grant a favour, request, etc.: *Accord Tom praise for good work.* 1, 2, 6 *v.*, 3–5 *n.*
**of one's own accord,** without being asked; without suggestion from another: *He usually goes to bed of his own accord now.*
**with one accord,** all agreeing together: *We cheered with one accord when Maria scored the winning basket.*

**ac·cord·ance** (ə kôr′dəns) agreement; harmony: *What he did was in accordance with what he said.* *n.*

**ac·cord·ant** (ə kôr′dənt) agreeing; in harmony. *adj.*

**ac·cord·ing** (ə kôr′ding) **1** agreeing; in harmony. **2** accordingly. **3** ppr. of ACCORD. 1 *adj.*, 2 *adv.*, 3 *v.*
**according as,** in proportion as: *According as you have enriched your own mind, you will have influence upon other minds.*
**according to,** **a** in agreement with: *He came according to his promise.* **b** in proportion to: *Spend according to your income.* **c** on the authority of; as said by: *According to this book a tiger is really a big cat.*

**ac·cord·ing·ly** (ə kôr′ding lē) **1** in agreement with something that has been stated: *These are the rules; you can act accordingly or leave the club.* **2** therefore; for this reason: *She was too sick to stay; accordingly, we sent her home.* *adv.*

A piano accordion

**ac·cor·di·on** (ə kôr′dē ən) **1** a portable musical wind instrument with a bellows, metallic reeds, and keys, played by pressing the keys and the bellows to force air through the reeds: *In a piano accordion, one set of keys is like a piano keyboard and the other keys are buttons.* **2** with folds like the bellows of an accordion: *a skirt with accordion pleats.* *n.*

**ac·cost** (ə kost′) speak to first; come up and speak to; address: *A ragged beggar accosted him, asking for money.* *v.*

**ac·count** (ə kount′) **1** a statement telling in detail about an event or thing; a report or story: *The newspaper published an account of the trial.* **2** an explanation or statement of reasons: *He could give no satisfactory account of his absence.* **3** sake: *Don't wait on my account.* **4** worth or importance: *It was an error of no account. The extra expense is of little account in comparison with the total cost.* **5** profit; advantage: *She turned the incident to her own account.* **6** an arrangement for purchasing goods or services on credit; charge account: *Her firm has an account with that new advertising agency.* **7** an arrangement for depositing one's money in a bank for safekeeping, or the money deposited; BANK ACCOUNT. **8** hold to be; think of as; consider: *The old king was accounted wise. She accounted herself lucky to have escaped with her life.* **9** Usually, **accounts,** *pl.* a statement of money received and spent: *Businesses and factories keep accounts.* 1–7, 9 *n.*, 8 *v.*

**account for,** **a** give a reason or explanation for: *Jennifer couldn't account for the strange message.* **b** be the main or only source or reason for: *Late frosts accounted for the poor fruit crop.* **c** give a reckoning of; tell what has happened to: *The treasurer of the club has to account for all the money received. Have all the passengers been accounted for?* **d** be responsible for the defeat, destruction, or death of: *His squadron accounted for twenty enemy aircraft in the battle.*

**on account,** **a** on the instalment plan: *She bought the coat on account.* **b** as part payment: *If you accept five dollars on account, I can pay the rest next week.*

**on account of,** **a** because of: *The game was put off on account of rain.* **b** for the sake of.

**on no account,** under no circumstances.

**on one's own account,** for one's own sake or benefit: *He helps his father in the garage but also repairs and sells used cars on his own account.*

**take into account** or **take account of,** make allowance for; consider: *When planning a holiday, you have to take travelling time into account.*

**ac·count·a·bil·i·ty** (ə koun′tə bil′ə tē) the state of being ACCOUNTABLE; responsibility. *n.*

**ac·count·a·ble** (ə koun′tə bəl) **1** responsible; liable to be called to account: *Each person is accountable for his own work.* **2** explainable: *His bad temper is easily accountable; he has had a toothache all day.* *adj.*

**ac·count·a·bly** (ə koun′tə blē) in a manner that can be accounted for. *adv.*

**ac·count·ant** (ə koun′tənt) a person trained in ACCOUNTING, especially one who makes it his or her work. *n.*

**ac·count·ing** (ə koun′ting) the system or procedures of recording, sorting, and analysing economic data related to business transactions and preparing statements of the results for individuals or businesses to use in making business decisions. *n.*

**ac·cou·ter** (ə kü′tər) See ACCOUTRE. *v.*

**ac·cou·ter·ments** (ə kü′tər mənts) See ACCOUTREMENTS. *n.*

**ac·cou·tre** (ə kü′tər) equip; array: *Knights were accoutred in armour.* *v.,* **ac·cou·tred** or **ac·cou·tered, ac·cou·tring** or **ac·cou·ter·ing.** Also, **accouter.**

**ac·cou·tre·ments** (ə kü′tər mənts) **1** a soldier's equipment with the exception of his weapons and clothing: *A belt, blanket, and knapsack are parts of a soldier's accoutrements.* **2** personal equipment; outfit. *n. pl.* Also, **accouterments.**

**ac·cred·it** (ə kred′it) **1** give a person credit for; regard a person as having: *to accredit others with kindness.* **2** consider a thing as belonging or due to a person: *We accredit the invention of the telephone to Bell.* **3** accept as true; believe; trust: *Ruth is always truthful, and anything she says will be accredited.* **4** give authority to: *The president has accredited you as her assistant.* **5** send or provide with credentials or a recommendation: *An ambassador is accredited as the representative of his own country in a foreign land.* **6** recognize as coming up to an official standard. *v.*

**ac·cred·it·ed** (ə kred′ə tid) **1** worthy of acceptance, belief, or trust: *Einstein was an accredited authority in physics.* **2** recognized as coming up to an official standard: *This company insists on all its sales representatives taking an accredited business course. Be sure to take your degree at an accredited university.* *adj.*

**ac·cre·tion** (ə krē′shən) **1** growth in size or amount: *the accretion of political power.* **2** a growing together of separate particles or parts. **3** an increase in size by gradual external addition: *the accretion of land by deposits of alluvial soil.* *n.*

**ac·cru·al** (ə krü′əl) **1** an accruing; progressive growth: *Money left in a savings account increases by the accrual of interest.* **2** the amount accrued or accruing. *n.*

**ac·crue** (ə krü′) come as a growth or result: *Ability to think will accrue to you from good habits of study.* *v.,* **ac·crued, ac·cru·ing.** —**ac·crue′ment,** *n.*

**acct.** **1** account. **2** accountant.

**ac·cu·mu·late** (ə kyü′myə lāt′) **1** collect little by little: *Through the years she accumulated sufficient money to buy a farm when she retired.* **2** grow in amount or number; mount up: *Dust had accumulated during the weeks that he was gone.* *v.,* **ac·cu·mu·lat·ed, ac·cu·mu·lat·ing.**

**ac·cu·mu·la·tion** (ə kyü′myə lā′shən) **1** a mass of material collected: *Hannah's accumulation of old papers filled three trunks.* **2** bringing together; collecting: *The accumulation of knowledge is one result of reading.* *n.*

**ac·cu·ra·cy** (ak′yə rə sē) the absence of errors or mistakes; correctness; exactness: *Arithmetic problems must be solved with accuracy.* *n.*

**ac·cu·rate** (ak′yə rit) **1** exactly right; correct: *You must be accurate in arithmetic.* **2** that operates without error: *Our track coach has an accurate stop watch.* *adj.* —**ac′cu·rate·ly,** *adv.* —**ac′cu·rate·ness,** *n.*

**ac·curs·ed** (ə kėr′sid *or* ə kėrst′) **1** damnable; detestable; hateful. **2** under a curse. *adj.* Also, **accurst.**

**ac·curst** (ə kėrst′) ACCURSED. *adj.*

**ac·cu·sa·tion** (ak′yə zā′shən) **1** a charge of having done something wrong, of being something bad, or of having broken the law. **2** the offence charged. *n.*

**ac·cu·sa·tive** (ə kyü′zə tiv) **1** of, having to do with, or being the grammatical case that shows that a noun or pronoun is not part of the subject of the sentence, but is a direct object of a verb or of any of certain prepositions: *The English pronouns* me, her, him, us, *and* them *are accusative cases.* **2** the accusative case. **3** a word in the accusative case. 1 *adj.,* 2, 3 *n.* See OBJECTIVE (defs. 5, 6).

**ac·cu·sa·to·ry** (ə kyü′zə tô′rē) of a statement, manner, etc., containing or expressing an ACCUSATION; accusing: *an accusatory glance, an accusatory tone of voice.* *adj.*

**ac·cuse** (ə kyüz′) charge with having done something wrong, with being something bad, or with having broken the law: *She accused her sister of listening in on the extension.* *v.*, **ac·cused, ac·cus·ing.** —**ac·cus′er,** *n.* —**ac·cus′ing·ly,** *adv.*

**ac·cused** (ə kyüzd′) **the accused,** in law, the person or persons appearing in court on a criminal charge. *n.*

**ac·cus·tom** (ə kus′təm) make familiar with by use or habit; make used to (*used with* **to**): *to accustom a hunting dog to the noise of a gun.* *v.*

**ac·cus·tomed** (ə kus′təmd) **1** usual; customary: *By Monday she was back in her accustomed place.* **2** pt. and pp. of ACCUSTOM. 1 *adj.*, 2 *v.*
**accustomed to,** used to; in the habit of: *He was accustomed to hard work. She is accustomed to getting up early.*

**ace** (ās) **1** a playing card, domino, or side of a die having one spot. **2** a single spot or point. **3** in tennis and certain other games, a point won by a single stroke. **4** a person expert at something: *Peter is an ace at basketball.* **5** of very high quality; expert: *an ace football player.* **6** a combat pilot who has shot down a large number of enemy planes. *n.*

**a·cer·bic** (ə sėr′bik) **1** sour in taste. **2** sharp, bitter or harsh in tone, mood, or temper: *an acerbic remark, an acerbic columnist.* *adj.* —**a·cer′bi·cal·ly,** *adv.*

**a·cer·bi·ty** (ə sėr′bə tē) **1** sharpness of taste; sourness. **2** harshness of manner; severity. *n., pl.* **a·cer·bi·ties.**

**ac·e·tab·u·lum** (as′ə tab′yə ləm) a socket in the hipbone into which the top part of the thighbone fits. See PELVIS for picture. *n., pl.* **ac·e·tab·u·la** (-lə).

**ac·e·tate** (as′ə tāt) **1** a salt or ESTER of ACETIC ACID: *Cellulose acetate is used in making textile fibres, tool handles, industrial parts, cellophane, etc.* **2** an article or material made from this substance, such as photographic film or a kind of silklike cloth. *n.*

**a·ce·tic acid** (ə sē′tik) a very sour, colourless acid, present in vinegar; a compound of hydrogen, carbon, and oxygen.

**ac·e·tone** (as′ə tōn′) a colourless, volatile, flammable liquid, used as a solvent for oils, fats, resins, cellulose, etc. and in making varnishes, etc. *n.*

**a·cet·y·lene** (ə set′ə lēn′) a colourless gas composed of hydrogen and carbon, that burns with a bright light and very hot flame: *Acetylene is used mainly in preparing compounds to make synthetic fibres and vinyl plastics and, combined with oxygen, for welding and cutting metals.* *n.*

**ache** (āk) **1** be in continuous pain: *My back aches.* **2** a dull, steady pain: *a stomach ache, a headache, a toothache.* **3** *Informal.* be eager; wish very much: *During the hot days of August we all ached to go swimming.* 1, 3 *v.*, **ached, ach·ing;** 2 *n.* —**ach′ing·ly,** *adv.*

**a·chene** (ā kēn′) any small, dry, hard fruit consisting of one seed with a thin outer covering that does not burst open when ripe: *Sunflower achenes are commonly called seeds.* *n.*

**a·chieve** (ə chēv′) **1** do; get done; carry out; accomplish: *John soon learned that one cannot achieve much without work.* **2** reach a certain end by one's own efforts; get by effort: *Both sisters achieved distinction in mathematics.* *v.*, **a·chieved, a·chiev·ing.** —**a·chiev′a·ble,** *adj.* —**a·chiev′er,** *n.*

**a·chieve·ment** (ə chēv′mənt) **1** some plan or action carried out with courage or unusual ability: *It was an achievement to sail a submarine under the North Pole.* **2** the carrying out or reaching of an aim or purpose: *the achievement of our goal for the sale of tickets.* *n.*

**Achilles tendon** the strong tendon joining the heel bone to the muscles of the calf: *The Achilles tendon helps to move the ankle joint.*
☛ *Etym.* From the name of *Achilles,* in Greek mythology, a hero of the Greeks at the siege of Troy: *Achilles could not be injured anywhere except in the heel.*

**ach·ro·mat·ic** (ak′rə mat′ik) **1** refracting white light without breaking it up into the colours of the spectrum. **2** having no hue, or colour: *Black, white, and neutral greys are achromatic.* *adj.* —**ach′ro·mat′i·cal·ly,** *adv.*

**ac·id** (as′id) **1** in chemistry, any of various compounds that yield hydrogen ions when dissolved in water and usually react with a BASE to form a SALT: *The water solution of an acid turns blue litmus paper red. Hydrochloric acid and sulphuric acid are two common acids.* **2** of, having to do with, or containing an acid: *an acid solution.* **3** a substance with a sour taste like that of vinegar. **4** sour; sharp or biting to the taste. **5** sour and sharp in manner or temper: *Mother made an acid comment about my untidy room.* 1, 3 *n.*, 2, 4, 5 *adj.* —**ac′id·ly,** *adv.* —**ac′id·ness,** *n.* Compare with ALKALI, ANTACID.

**ac·id·ic** (ə sid′ik) forming ACID. *adj.*

**a·cid·i·fy** (ə sid′ə fī′) **1** make sour. **2** become sour. **3** change into an acid. *v.*, **a·cid·i·fied, a·cid·i·fy·ing.** —**a·cid′i·fi′er,** *n.*

**a·cid·i·ty** (ə sid′ə tē) an acid quality or condition; sourness: *the acidity of vinegar.* *n., pl.* **a·cid·i·ties.**

**ac·i·do·sis** (as′ə dō′sis) a harmful condition in which the blood and tissues are less alkaline than is normal. *n.*

**acid rain** rain or snow that is polluted by acids formed from certain waste chemicals which have been discharged into the air by industrial PLANTs (def. 11).

**acid test** a thorough test to find out the real quality of some person or thing.

**a·cid·u·late** (ə sij′ə lāt′) make slightly acid or sour. *v.*, **a·cid·u·lat·ed, a·cid·u·lat·ing.** —**a·cid′u·la′tion,** *n.*

**a·cid·u·lous** (ə sij′ə ləs) slightly acid or sour. *adj.* —**a·cid′u·lous·ly,** *adv.* —**a·cid′u·lous·ness,** *n.*

**ac·knowl·edge** (ak nol′ij) **1** admit to be true: *Juanita acknowledges her own faults.* **2** recognize the merit, authority, or claims of: *The boys acknowledged him to be the best player on the baseball team.* **3** express thanks for a gift, favour, etc.: *He acknowledged their help by inviting them to dinner.* **4** make known that one has received a service, favour, gift, message, etc.: *I acknowledged her letter today.* *v.*, **ac·knowl·edged, ac·knowl·edg·ing.**

**ac·knowl·edg·ment** or **ac·knowl·edge·ment** (ak nol′ij mənt) **1** a verbal, written, or other recognition of a gift, service, favour, etc.: *She waved in acknowledgment of the crowd's cheers. A receipt is an acknowledgment that a bill has been paid.* **2** the act of admitting the existence or truth of anything: *The accused man made acknowledgment of his guilt.* **3** recognition of authority or claims. **4** an expression of thanks. *n.*

**ac·me** (ak′mē)  the highest point: *To graduate at the top of his class was the acme of his hopes.* *n.*

**ac·ne** (ak′nē)  a skin disease in which the oil glands in the skin become clogged and inflamed, often causing pimples. *n.*

**ac·o·nite** (ak′ə nīt′)  **1** any of a closely related group of plants found in cool northern regions, belonging to the same family as the buttercups and having blue, purple, yellow, or white flowers shaped like hoods: *The roots, seeds, and leaves of some aconites are poisonous.* **2** a poisonous drug obtained from one species of aconite, formerly much used in medicine to deaden pain, slow down the pulse, etc. *n.*

**a·corn** (ā′kôrn)  the nut, or fruit, of an oak tree. See OAK for picture. *n.*

**a·cous·tic** (ə kü′stik)  **1** of or having to do with the sense of hearing: *acoustic nerves, an acoustic stimulus.* **2** having to do with the science of sound: *acoustic phonetics, acoustic energy.* **3** designed to carry sound or to aid in hearing: *An acoustic baffle has been installed in the concert hall.* **4** designed to deaden or absorb sound: *acoustic tile.* *adj.*

**a·cous·ti·cal** (ə kü′sti kəl)  having to do with the science of sound: *an acoustical engineer.* *adj.*

**a·cous·ti·cal·ly** (ə kü′sti klē)  with regard to ACOUSTICS. *adv.*

**a·cous·tics** (ə kü′stiks)  **1** (*used with a plural verb*) the qualities of a room, hall, auditorium, etc. that determine how well sounds can be heard in it; acoustic qualities: *We enjoy singing in the auditorium because the acoustics are so good.* **2** (*used with a singular verb*) the scientific study of sound. *n.*

**ac·quaint** (ə kwānt′)  **1** inform a person about a thing: *They have already acquainted the president with their intention.* **2** make familiar (*with*): *Let me acquaint you with the facts.* *v.*
**be acquainted with,**  have personal knowledge of: *He is acquainted with my mother.*

**ac·quaint·ance** (ə kwān′təns)  **1** a person known to one, but not a close friend. **2** a knowledge of persons or things gained from experience with them; personal knowledge. *n.*

**ac·quaint·ance·ship** (ə kwān′təns ship′)  **1** a personal knowledge; acquaintance. **2** a relation between acquaintances: *Their acquaintanceship dates from before the war.* *n.*

**ac·qui·esce** (ak′wē es′)  accept or agree to by keeping quiet or by not making objections: *We acquiesced in their plan because we could not think of a better one.* *v.*, **ac·qui·esced, ac·qui·esc·ing.**

**ac·qui·es·cence** (ak′wē es′əns)  a consenting without making objections. *n.*

**ac·qui·es·cent** (ak′wē es′ənt)  acquiescing; agreeing; quietly consenting. *adj.*

**ac·quire** (ə kwīr′)  **1** receive or get as one's own; get: *By the time Bela was thirty he had acquired a store of his own.* **2** get by one's own efforts or actions: *He was determined to acquire a university education.* *v.*, **ac·quired, ac·quir·ing.** —**ac·quir′a·ble,** *adj.* —**ac·quir′er,** *n.*

**Acquired Immune Deficiency Syndrome**  a disease of the immune system, caused by a virus transmitted through body fluids, which makes the sufferer susceptible to other diseases from which he or she can die. *Abbrev.*: AIDS.

**ac·quire·ment** (ə kwīr′mənt)  **1** the act of acquiring. **2** something acquired; ATTAINMENT: *Her musical acquirements are unusual for a girl of her age.* *n.*

**ac·qui·si·tion** (ak′wə zish′ən)  **1** an acquiring or getting as one's own: *She spent hundreds of hours in the acquisition of skill with a rifle.* **2** something acquired: *The art gallery is having a special showing of its new acquisitions.* *n.*

**ac·quis·i·tive** (ə kwiz′ə tiv)  fond of acquiring; likely to get and keep: *A miser is acquisitive of money. A great scholar is acquisitive of ideas.* *adj.* —**ac·quis′i·tive·ly,** *adv.*  —**ac·quis′i·tive·ness,** *n.*

**ac·quit** (ə kwit′)  declare a person not guilty of an offence. *v.*, **ac·quit·ted, ac·quit·ting.** —**ac·quit′ter,** *n.*
**acquit oneself,**  do one's part; behave: *The soldiers acquitted themselves well in battle.*

**ac·quit·tal** (ə kwit′əl)  setting free by declaring not guilty; a discharge; release. *n.*

**ac·quit·tance** (ə kwit′əns)  **1** a release from a debt or obligation. **2** the payment of a debt; settlement of a claim. *n.*

**a·cre** (ā′kər)  **1** a unit for measuring land area, equal to about 4047 square metres. **2 acres,** *pl.*  lands; property. *n.*

**a·cre·age** (ā′kə rij)  **1** the number of acres: *What is the acreage of the farm?* **2** area in acres; acres collectively: *We have most of our acreage in barley this year.* **3** a piece of land of several acres: *She bought a small acreage north of town.* *n.*

**ac·rid** (ak′rid)  **1** sharp, bitter, or stinging to the nose, mouth, or skin. **2** having or showing a sharp or irritating temper: *an acrid comment.* *adj.* —**ac′rid·ly,** *adv.* —**ac′rid·ness,** *n.*

**a·crid·i·ty** (ə krid′ə tē)  bitterness; sharpness. *n.*

**ac·ri·mo·ni·ous** (ak′rə mō′nē əs)  sharp and bitter in temper, language, or manner. *adj.* —**ac′ri·mo′ni·ous·ly,** *adv.* —**ac′ri·mo′ni·ous·ness,** *n.*

**ac·ri·mo·ny** (ak′rə mō′nē)  sharpness and bitterness in temper, language, or manner. *n., pl.* **ac·ri·mo·nies.**

**ac·ro·bat** (ak′rə bat′)  a person who can perform tricks on a trapeze, turn handsprings, walk on a tightrope, etc. *n.*

**ac·ro·bat·ic** (ak′rə bat′ik)  **1** of an acrobat: *Dancing on a rope is an acrobatic feat.* **2** like an acrobat's. *adj.* —**ac′ro·bat′i·cal·ly,** *adv.*

**ac·ro·bat·ics** (ak′rə bat′iks)  **1** tricks or performances of an acrobat; gymnastic feats. **2** feats like those of an acrobat: *a monkey's acrobatics.* *n. pl.*

**ac·ro·meg·a·ly** (ak′rō meg′ə lē)  a disease caused by abnormal activity of the pituitary gland: *Acromegaly causes the head, hands, and feet to become permanently enlarged.* *n.*

**ac·ro·nym** (ak′rə nim′)  a word formed from the first letters or syllables of other words, such as UNESCO (United Nations Educational, Scientific, and Cultural Organization). *n.*

**a·crop·o·lis** (ə krop′ə lis)  **1** the fortified hill in the centre of an ancient Greek city, which served as its religious centre as well as its fortress.  **2 the Acropolis**, the fortified hill of Athens, on which the Parthenon was built. *n.*

**a·cross** (ə kros′)  **1** from one side to the other of; to the other side of; over: *a bridge laid across a river. She drew a line across the page.*  **2** from one side to the other: *What is the distance across?*  **3** on the other side of; beyond: *across the sea.*  **4** on or to the other side: *He ran across without looking where he was going.*  **5** on top of and at an angle to: *She laid the board across the sawhorses. She put the coat across the back of a chair.*  **6** into contact with: *We come across unusual words in some books.*  1, 3, 5, 6 *prep.*, 2, 4 *adv.*

**a·cros·tic** (ə′kros′tik)  a composition in verse or an arrangement of words in which the first, last, or certain other letters in each line, taken in order, spell a word or phrase. *n.*

**a·cryl·ic** (ə kril′ik)  **1** a type of colourless, transparent plastic made from an acid. It is used in sheet form for windows, and is also used in making paint, rubber, and glue.  **2** of, or having to do with, or made from ACRYLIC RESIN, ACRYLIC ACID, or ACRYLIC FIBRE.  **3** a kind of paint made with this plastic as a base.  **4** a painting done with such paints: *We bought one of her acrylics.*  **5** a strong, lightweight fibre made from a related acid, and used especially for knitting yarns, pile fabrics, and carpets.  **6** ACRYLIC RESIN.   1, 3–6 *n.*, 2 *adj.*

**acrylic acid**  a colourless liquid that is soluble in water and alcohol, used in making various plastics.

**acrylic fibre**  any of various synthetic textile fibres made from ACRYLIC ACID.

**acrylic resin**  any of various, tough, glasslike plastics used for instrument panels, dental plates, etc.

**act** (akt)  **1** something done; deed: *an act of kindness. Slapping his face was a childish act.*  **2** the process of doing: *He was caught in the act of stealing.*  **3** do something: *The firefighters acted promptly and saved the burning house.*  **4** have effect: *Yeast acts on dough and makes it rise.*  **5** behave: *She has been acting badly in school.*  **6** behave like: *Most people act the fool now and then.*  **7** perform in a theatre, on television, etc.; play a part: *The handsome man acts the part of the hero. She acts very well.*  **8** a legislative decision; decree: *An act of Parliament is a bill that has been passed by Parliament.*  **9** a main division of a play or opera: *Most modern plays have three acts.*  **10** one of several performances on a program: *the juggler's act.*  **11** *Informal.*  a show of pretended behaviour, especially to impress or attract attention: *He seems pleasant, but that's just an act.*  1, 2, 8–11 *n.*, 3–7 *v.*

**act as**,  serve as or do the work of: *Yitzhak acted as class secretary last week. The foam lining acts as insulation.*
**act for**,  take the place of: *While the principal was gone, the assistant principal acted for her.*
**act on**,  follow; obey: *I'll act on your suggestion.*
**act out**,  represent in actions: *Charades is a game in which titles or sayings are acted out.*
**act up**, *Informal.*  **a** behave badly: *He was acting up because he hadn't got his way.*  **b** be troublesome: *The knee I hurt last summer is acting up again.*

**act·ing** (ak′ting)  **1** temporarily taking another's place and doing his or her duties: *While the principal was sick, one of the teachers was acting principal.*  **2** the art of performing: *Her acting was very good.*  **3** ppr. of ACT.  1 *adj.*, 2 *n.*, 3 *v.*

**ac·tin·ic** (ak tin′ik)  **1** of ACTINISM.  **2** producing chemical changes by radiation: *actinic rays.*  *adj.*

**ac·tin·ism** (ak′tə niz′əm)  a property in light that causes chemical changes. *n.*

**ac·tin·i·um** (ak tin′ē əm)  a radio-active chemical element resembling radium, found in pitchblende after uranium has been extracted.  Symbol: Ac  *n.*

**ac·tion** (ak′shən)  **1** the process of doing something; acting: *The quick action of the firefighters saved the building from burning.*  **2** activity: *A soldier is a man of action.*  **3** something done; act: *Giving the dog food was a kind action.*  **4** the effect or influence of something on something else: *the action of wind on a ship's sails.*  **5** the moving parts by which a mechanism operates: *the action of a gun.*  **6** the way a mechanism operates: *a typewriter with a smooth action.*  **7** a battle; part of a battle: *Bella's father was wounded in action in Korea.*  **8** lawsuit.  **9** the series of events in a novel, play, etc.  **10 actions**, *pl.* conduct; behaviour: *Mother punished me for my rude actions.*  *n.*  —**ac′tion·less**, *adj.*
**in action**,  **a** active; taking part.  **b** working.
**take action**,  **a** begin to do something: *The government took action to prevent forest fires.*  **b** start working.  **c** start a lawsuit; SUE.

**ac·ti·vate** (ak′tə vāt′)  **1** make active.  **2** in physics, make radio-active.  **3** in chemistry, speed up a reaction in.  **4** purify sewage by treating it with air and bacteria.  *v.*, **ac·ti·vat·ed, ac·ti·vat·ing.**  —**ac′ti·va′tion**, *n.*

**ac·tive** (ak′tiv)  **1** acting; working: *an active volcano.*  **2** showing much action; moving rather quickly; lively; brisk: *an active stock market. Most children are more active than old people.*  **3** taking an effective part in; participating: *Rupinder took an active part in organizing the stamp club.*  **4** in present use: *an active file.*  **5** showing the subject of a verb as acting: *In "She broke the window," broke is in the active voice.*  **6** the ACTIVE VOICE.  **7** a verb form in the ACTIVE VOICE.  1–5 *adj.*, 6, 7 *n.*  —**ac′tive·ly**, *adv.*  —**ac′tive·ness**, *n.*

**active service** or **duty**  **1** military service with full pay and regular duties.  **2** service in the armed forces in time of war.

**active voice**  in grammar, the form of the verb that shows the subject as acting rather than as being acted on. *In "He broke the window," broke is in the active voice; in "The window was broken," was broken is in the PASSIVE VOICE.*

**ac·tiv·ism** (ak′tə viz′əm)  a doctrine or policy of direct, vigorous action or confrontation in supporting one's own point of view on a controversial social or political issue.  *n.*

**ac·tiv·ist** (ak′tə vist)  **1** a person who practises ACTIVISM.  **2** of or having to do with ACTIVISM or activists.  1 *n.*, 2 *adj.*

**ac·tiv·i·ty** (ak tiv′ə tē)  **1** the state of being active; movement; the use of power: *physical activity, mental activity.*  **2** an action; doing: *the activities of enemy spies.*

3 a vigorous action; liveliness: *the activity of children during recess.* 4 a certain action; something done under certain conditions: *A student who has too many outside activities may find it hard to keep up with her studies.* 5 anything active; active force. *n., pl.* **ac·tiv·i·ties.**

**ac·tor** (ak′tər) 1 a person who acts on a stage, in motion pictures, on television or radio. 2 a person who does something. *n.*

**bad actor,** a person, animal, or thing that is always misbehaving: *That horse is a bad actor; it kicks and bites at anyone who goes near.*

**ac·tress** (ak′tris) a female actor. *n.*

**ac·tu·al** (ak′chü əl) 1 existing as a fact; real: *What she told us was not a dream but an actual happening.* 2 now existing; present; current: *the actual state of affairs. adj.* —**ac′tu·al·ness,** *n.*

**ac·tu·al·i·ty** (ak′chü al′ə tē) 1 actual existence; reality. 2 an actual thing; fact. *n., pl.* **ac·tu·al·i·ties.**

**ac·tu·al·ize** (ak′chü ə līz′) make actual; realize in action or as a fact. *v.,* **ac·tu·al·ized, ac·tu·al·iz·ing.**

**ac·tu·al·ly** (ak′chü ə lē *or* ak′chü lē) really; in fact: *Are you actually going to Europe or just wishing to go? adv.*

**ac·tu·ar·y** (ak′chü er′ē) a person whose work is calculating risks, rates, premiums, etc. for insurance companies. *n., pl.* **ac·tu·ar·ies.**

**ac·tu·ate** (ak′chü āt′) 1 put into action: *This pump is actuated by a belt driven by an electric motor.* 2 influence to act: *She was actuated by love for her mother. v.,* **ac·tu·at·ed, ac·tu·at·ing.** —**ac′tu·a′tion,** *n.* —**ac′tu·a′tor,** *n.*

**a·cu·i·ty** (ə kyü′ə tē) sharpness; acuteness. *n.*

**a·cu·men** (ə kyü′mən *or* ak′yə mən) sharpness and quickness in seeing and understanding; keen insight. *n.*

**ac·u·punc·ture** (ak′yə pungk′chər) a method of relieving pain and treating disease by inserting fine needles into the body at specific points: *Acupuncture has been used in the Far East for thousands of years. n.*

**a·cute** (ə kyüt′) 1 having a sharp point. 2 sharp and severe: *A toothache can cause acute pain.* 3 brief and severe: *An acute disease like pneumonia reaches a crisis within a short time.* 4 threatening; critical: *an acute danger of war.* 5 keen: *Dogs have an acute sense of smell. An acute thinker is clever and shrewd.* 6 high in pitch; shrill: *Some sounds are so acute that we cannot hear them. adj.* —**a·cute′ly,** *adv.* —**a·cute′ness,** *n.*

**acute accent** a mark (´) written or printed to show the spoken quality of a particular letter in a word: *An acute accent placed over an e in French indicates that it is pronounced something like the beginning of the English* (ā) *sound.*

**acute angle** an angle less than a right angle. See ANGLE for picture.

**ad** (ad) *Informal.* ADVERTISEMENT. *n.*

**ad–** a prefix meaning: to; toward, as in *admit, administer, adverb, advert.* Also, (before *b*) **ab–**.

**A.D.** an abbreviation of the Latin words *anno Domini,* meaning in the year of Our Lord, that is, after the birth of Christ: *From 200* B.C. *to* A.D. *500 is 700 years.* Compare with B.C.

**ad·age** (ad′ij) a wise saying that has been much used; well-known proverb: *"Haste makes waste" is an adage. n.*

**a·da·gio** (ə dazh′ē ō′, ə daj′ē ō′, *or* ə dä′jō) 1 in music, slowly. 2 in music, slow. 3 a slow part in a piece of music. 4 in ballet, a slow dance done by a man and a woman. 1 *adv.,* 2 *adj.,* 3 4 *n., pl.* **a·da·gios.**

**ad·a·mant** (ad′ə mənt) 1 a legendary mineral so hard that it could not be cut or broken: *Adamant was identified at different times with the diamond and lodestone.* 2 any extremely hard substance. 3 too hard to be cut or broken. 4 unyielding; firm; immovable: *Columbus was adamant in refusing the requests of his sailors to turn back.* 1, 2 *n.,* 3 4 *adj.*

**ad·a·man·tine** (ad′ə man′tēn *or* ad′ə man′tīn) ADAMANT (defs. 3, 4). *adj.*

**Adam's apple** in men, the lump in the front of the throat, formed by the thyroid cartilage. See WINDPIPE for picture.

**a·dapt** (ə dapt′) 1 make or become fit or suitable: *Good writers adapt their language to the age and interests of their readers.* 2 change one's behaviour so as to fit in with a new situation: *Can you adapt yourself to new situations? She has adapted well to the new school.* 3 modify or alter for a different use: *The farmer can adapt the barn for use as a garage. Her novel has been adapted as a movie. v.* —**a·dapt′er,** *n.*

**a·dapt·a·bil·i·ty** (ə dap′tə bil′ə tē) the power to change easily to fit different conditions. *n.*

**a·dapt·a·ble** (ə dap′tə bəl) easily changed or changing easily to fit different conditions: *an adaptable schedule. Jane is an adaptable person. adj.* —**a·dapt′a·ble·ness,** *n.*

**ad·ap·ta·tion** (ad′ap tā′shən) 1 adapting or being adapted: *Dan made a good adaptation to high school.* 2 something made by adapting: *A film is often an adaptation of a novel.* 3 a change in structure, form, or habits of an animal or plant to fit different conditions: *Wings are adaptations of the upper limbs for flight. n.*

**a·dapt·ed** (ə dap′tid) 1 modified; altered: *a portable radio adapted for installing in a car.* 2 fitted; suitable: *a climate adapted to the growing of oranges. adj.*
☞ **Usage. Adapted** follows the noun it modifies.

**a·dapt·er** (ə dap′tər) 1 a device for fitting together parts that do not match: *We will need an adapter to fit this nozzle onto the larger hose.* 2 a separate plug for attaching to the plug of an electrical appliance, etc. in order to adapt it to a different type of outlet: *North American appliances cannot be used in Europe without adapters.* 3 a device for changing the function of a machine or apparatus. 4 any person or thing that adapts. *n.* Also, **adaptor.**

**a·dap·tive** (ə dap′tiv) 1 able to adapt. 2 showing adaptation. *adj.* —**a·dap′tive·ly,** *adv.* —**a·dap′tive·ness,** *n.*

**a·dap·tor** (ə dap′tər) ADAPTER. *n.*

**ADC, A.D.C.,** or **a.d.c.** aide-de-camp.

**add** (ad) 1 join one thing to another; put together; put with: *Add another stone to the pile. Add 8 and 2 and you have 10.* 2 make or form an addition: *The hotel's new wing has added a number of rooms.* 3 say further; go on

to say or write: *She said goodbye and added that she had had a pleasant visit.* v.
**add to,** increase: *The fine weather added to our pleasure.*
**add up, a** make a total. **b** make sense: *Your story doesn't add up.*

**ad·dax** (ad′aks) a large, heavily built species of antelope found in the deserts of north Africa, standing about 105 cm high at the shoulder and having very long, curving, ringed horns: *The addax has been hunted so much that it is now rare.* n.

**ad·dend** (ad′end *or* ə dend′) a number or quantity to be added to another number or quantity. See ADDITION for picture. n.

**ad·den·da** (ə den′də) pl. of ADDENDUM. n.

**ad·den·dum** (ə den′dəm) **1** a thing to be added. **2** the thing added; appendix: *The addendum to the report shows that Ali disagreed with the committee's findings.* n., pl. **ad·den·da** (-də).

**ad·der**[1] (ad′ər) **1** the common viper, a small poisonous snake of Europe and northern Asia, from 45 to 75 cm long, usually having a black zigzag band along its back: *The adder is the only poisonous snake of Great Britain.* **2** either of two species of viper found in Africa: *The puff adder is a large and dangerous snake; the night adder is small and less dangerous.* **3** Also, **death adder,** a very poisonous snake of Australia, related to the cobras and coral snakes but similar in appearance to a viper. **4** Also, **blowing adder,** any of several species of harmless snake found in the United States. **5** *Informal.* any snake that is thought to be poisonous. n.

**add·er**[2] (ad′ər) a person or thing that adds, especially a machine for adding. n.

**ad·der's–tongue** (ad′ərz tung′) **1** any of a closely related group of fern-like plants belonging to the adder's-tongue family, bearing spores on tall spikes that resemble a snake's tongue. **2** a wildflower of the lily family found in the woods of eastern Canada and the United States; DOGTOOTH VIOLET. n.

**ad·dict** (ad′ikt *for noun,* ə dikt′ *for verb*) **1** a person who is a slave to a habit, especially the use of narcotics: *a heroin addict, a movie addict.* **2** give oneself up to a habit (*used with* **to**): *She has addicted herself to detective novels.* 1 n., 2 v.

**ad·dict·ed** (ə dik′tid) slavishly following a habit or practice; strongly inclined: *He was so addicted to the use of tobacco that he smoked ten cigars a day.* adj.

**ad·dic·tion** (ə dik′shən) the condition of being a slave to a habit; a strong inclination. n.

**ad·dic·tive** (ə dik′tiv) that causes or tends to cause ADDICTION: *It is not known whether the drug is addictive.* adj.

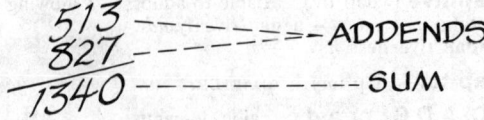

The parts of an addition calculation

**ad·di·tion** (ə dish′ən) **1** the adding of one number or quantity to another: *A simple addition is 2 + 3 = 5.* **2** the adding of one thing to another: *The addition of flour will thicken gravy.* **3** a result of adding; something added: *They made an addition to the building.* n.
**in addition** *or* **in addition to,** besides; also: *In addition to her work as teacher in the school, Ms. Osika gives music lessons after school hours.*

**ad·di·tion·al** (ə dish′ə nəl) added; extra; more. adj.
—**ad·di′tion·al·ly,** adv.

**ad·di·tive** (ad′ə tiv) any substance added in small amounts to a product to add or improve certain desirable qualities or to reduce the effects of undesirable ones: *Additives are put in processed foods to add a desirable colour, act as a preservative, etc. There are additives in gasoline and fuel oil to increase the efficiency of combustion.* n.

**ad·dle** (ad′əl) **1** make or become muddled: *The wine has quite addled her.* **2** muddled; confused (*used only in compounds*): *They called him an addle-pated fool.* **3** of eggs, become rotten; spoil. **4** of eggs, rotten. 1, 3 v., **ad·dled, ad·dling;** 2, 4 adj.

**ad·dled** (ad′əld) muddled; confused: *Her mind always seems so addled, I don't see how she ever accomplishes anything.* adj.

**ad·dress** (ə dres′; *also* ad′res *for 4, 5, and 6*) **1** a speech, especially a formal one: *The prime minister gave a television address.* **2** direct speech or writing to: *He addressed the nation on the subject of the economy.* **3** use titles or other forms in speaking or writing to: *How do you address a mayor?* **4** the place at which a person, business, etc. may be found or reached: *Send the letter to her business address.* **5** the writing on an envelope, package, etc. that shows where it is to be sent: *The letter was returned because the address was incomplete.* **6** write on a letter, package, etc. the information that shows where it is to be sent. **7** manner in conversation: *She was a person of pleasant address.* **8** skill: *The new manager shows much address in getting people to help her.* **9** apply or devote oneself; direct one's energies: *Mauno addressed himself to the task of doing his homework.* **10** a formal request to those in authority to do a particular thing: *an address from the colonists to the king, listing grievances.* **11** direct to the attention: *to address a warning to a friend.* **12** a code label representing the exact location of a piece of data stored in a computer memory. **13 addresses,** pl. attentions paid in courtship. 1, 4, 5, 7, 8, 10, 12, 13 n., 2, 3, 6, 9, 11 v., **ad·dressed** *or* **ad·drest, ad·dress·ing.**
—**ad·dress′er** *or* **ad·dres′sor,** n.

**ad·dress·ee** (ə dres ē′ *or* ad′res ē′) the person to whom a letter, package, etc. is addressed. n.

**ad·duce** (ə dyüs′ *or* ə düs′) give as a reason, proof, or example; cite: *The author has adduced some convincing data in support of her argument.* v., **ad·duced, ad·duc·ing.**

**ad·duc·tion** (ə duk′shən) the bringing forward of arguments. n.

**ad·e·noid** (ad′ə noid′) **1** of the LYMPHATIC glands. **2** like a GLAND; glandular. adj.

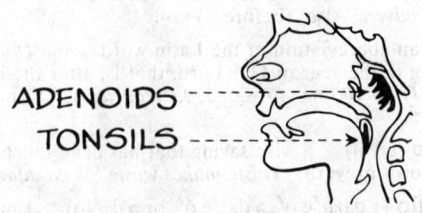

**ad·e·noids** (ad′ə noidz′) **1** normal glandular tissue in the upper part of the throat, just behind the nose, that usually shrinks and disappears in childhood, but sometimes swells and gets in the way of natural breathing and speaking. **2** swollen adenoids: *He had adenoids as a child.* *n. pl.*

**ad·ept** (ad′ept *or* ə dept′ *for noun,* ə dept′ *for adjective*) **1** a thoroughly skilled or expert person: *He is an adept in working crossword puzzles.* **2** thoroughly skilled; expert: *Mette is adept at macramé.* **1** *n.,* **2** *adj.* —**a·dept′ly**, *adv.* —**a·dept′ness**, *n.*

**ad·e·qua·cy** (ad′ə kwə sē) the quality or state of being ADEQUATE; sufficiency. *n.*

**ad·e·quate** (ad′ə kwit) **1** as much as is needed; fully sufficient: *Her wages are adequate to support three people.* **2** suitable; competent: *an adequate person for the job.* *adj.* —**ad′e·quate·ly**, *adv.* —**ad′e·quate·ness**, *n.*

**ad·han** (ə dän′) the Moslem call to prayer, uttered by a MUEZZIN, immediately before each of the five daily prayers. *n.*

**ad·here** (ad hēr′) **1** stick fast; remain attached: *Mud adheres to shoes.* **2** follow closely; carry through (used with *to*): *Paul adhered to his plan in spite of opposition.* **3** be devoted (*to*): *Most people adhere to the religion of their parents.* *v.,* **ad·hered, ad·her·ing.** —**ad·her′er**, *n.*

**ad·her·ence** (ad hē′rəns) **1** attachment or loyalty to a person, group, belief, etc.; faithfulness. **2** holding to and following closely: *rigid adherence to rules.* *n.*

**ad·her·ent** (ad hē′rənt) **1** faithful supporter; follower: *He was an adherent of the Maple Leafs.* **2** sticking fast; attached. **1** *n.,* **2** *adj.*

**ad·he·sion** (ad hē′zhən) **1** the action of sticking fast or joining; the state of being stuck or joined together. **2** a steady or devoted attachment; faithfulness. **3** an agreement; assent. **4** in physics, the attraction between the molecules of different substances: *Capillary attraction, which causes the surface of water to rise against the inside of a glass tube, is the result of adhesion between the liquid and the solid.* Compare with COHESION (def. 2). *n.*

**ad·he·sive** (ad hē′siv) **1** holding fast; adhering easily; sticky. **2** smeared with a sticky substance for holding something fast: *adhesive tape.* **3** any substance, such as paste or gum, used to stick things together: *An adhesive is used to put a patch on an inner tube.* **1, 2** *adj.,* **3** *n.* —**ad·he′sive·ly**, *adv.* —**ad·he′sive·ness**, *n.*

**ad hoc** (ad′ hok′) *Latin.* for a certain purpose, without general application; special: *an ad hoc rule. An ad hoc committee was appointed to discuss the problem.*

**a·dieu** (ə dyü′; *French,* ä dyœ′) goodbye; farewell. *interj., n., pl.* **a·dieus** *or* **a·dieux** (ə dyüz′; *French,* ä dyœ′).

**ad in·fi·ni·tum** (ad′ in′fə nī′təm) *Latin.* without limit.

**a·di·os** (ä′dē ōs′ *or* ad′ē ōs′) *Spanish.* goodbye. *interj., n.*

**ad·i·pose** (ad′ə pōs′) **1** of or having to do with animal fat; fatty: *adipose tissue.* **2** fat: *He has become extremely adipose in the last while.* *adj.*

**ad·i·pos·i·ty** (ad′ə pos′ə tē) a tendency to become fat. *n.*

**adj.** adjective; adjectival.

**ad·ja·cen·cy** (ə jā′sən sē) nearness. *n., pl.* **ad·ja·cen·cies.**

**ad·ja·cent** (ə jā′sənt) lying near or close; adjoining:

---

**adept**     15     **adjudicate**

hat, āge, fär; let, ēqual, tėrm; it, īce
hot, ōpen, ôrder; oil, out; cup, put, rüle
əbove, takən, pencəl, lemən, circəs
ch, child; ng, long; sh, ship
th, thin; ᴛʜ, then; zh, measure

*The house adjacent to ours has been sold.* *adj.* —**ad·ja′cent·ly**, *adv.*

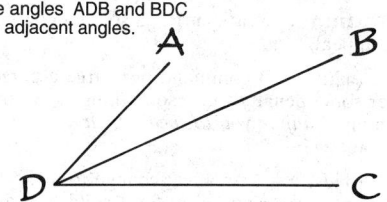

The angles ADB and BDC are adjacent angles.

**adjacent angles** two angles that have the same vertex and the same line as one of their sides. In the diagram, ADB and BDC are adjacent angles.

**ad·jec·ti·val** (aj′ik tī′vəl) **1** of or having to do with an adjective: *The ending* -like *in* childlike *is an adjectival suffix.* **2** used as an adjective: *The form* toy *in* toy poodle *is an adjectival use of the noun* toy. *adj.*

**ad·jec·ti·val·ly** (aj′ik tī′və lē) as an adjective. *adv.*

**ad·jec·tive** (aj′ik tiv) the name given to a class of words that limit or add to the meaning of names of persons, places, ideas, or things: *a green hill, a good reason, an attractive girl.* An adjective that goes in front of the word it describes is called *attributive*: *a warm day.* An adjective that follows a verb is called *predicative*: *The girl is weary.* An adjective that follows the word it describes is called *appositive*: *The child, tired and hungry, started to cry.* *n.*

**ad·join** (ə join′) **1** be next to; be in contact with: *Canada adjoins the United States.* **2** be next or close to each other; be in contact: *These two countries adjoin.* *v.*

**ad·join·ing** (ə joi′ning) **1** being next to or in contact with; bordering: *He and I have adjoining lockers.* **2** ppr. of ADJOIN. **1** *adj.,* **2** *v.*

**ad·journ** (ə jėrn′) **1** suspend or break off for a time: *The meeting was adjourned for lunch. The judge adjourned the court for two hours.* **2** stop business or proceedings for a time: *The court adjourned from Friday until Monday.* **3** go to another place: *After the meeting, we adjourned to the cafeteria.* *v.*

**ad·journ·ment** (ə jėrn′mənt) **1** adjourning or being adjourned. **2** the time during which a court, lawmaking body, etc. is adjourned: *a thirty-day adjournment.* *n.*

**Adjt.** Adjutant.

**ad·judge** (ə juj′) **1** decree or declare by law: *The accused woman was adjudged guilty.* **2** condemn or sentence by law: *The thief was adjudged to prison for two years.* **3** decide or settle by law; judge: *The boy's case was adjudged in the juvenile court.* **4** award or assign by law: *The property was adjudged to the rightful owner.* *v.,* **ad·judged, ad·judg·ing.**

**ad·ju·di·cate** (ə jü′də kāt′) **1** decide or settle; judge. **2** act as judge; pass judgment: *She was asked to adjudicate at the skating competition.* *v.,* **ad·ju·di·cat·ed, ad·ju·di·cat·ing.**

**ad·ju·di·ca·tion** (ə jü′də kā′shən)   1 adjudicating. 2 the decision of a judge, court or adjudicator.   *n.*

**ad·ju·di·ca·tor** (ə jü′də kā′tər)   a person who judges.   *n.*

**ad·junct** (aj′ungkt)   something added that is less important or not necessary, but helpful: *Grammar is not merely an adjunct to composition; it is a study in itself.*   *n.*

**ad·ju·ra·tion** (aj′ə rā′shən)   a solemn command; earnest appeal.   *n.*

**ad·jure** (ə jür′)   1 command or charge a person on oath or under some penalty to do something.   2 ask earnestly or solemnly: *I adjure you to speak the truth.*   *v.*, **ad·jured, ad·jur·ing.**

**ad·just** (ə just′)   1 arrange; change to make fit: *to adjust a seat to the right height for a child.*   2 arrange or set machinery or controls to work as required: *to adjust a radio dial. He adjusted the brakes on his bicycle.*   3 arrange satisfactorily; set right; settle: *to adjust a difference of opinion.*   *v.*   —**ad·just′a·ble,** *adj.*   —**ad·just′er** or **ad·jus′tor,** *n.*

**adjust to,**   fit oneself; adapt to: *She soon adjusted to her job.*

**ad·just·ment** (ə just′mənt)   1 the act or process of adjusting: *The adjustment of the seats took some time.* 2 the orderly arrangement of parts or elements.   3 a means of adjusting: *Most radios have separate adjustments for volume and tone.*   4 a settlement of a dispute, a claim, etc.   *n.*

**ad·ju·tant** (aj′ə tənt)   1 an armed forces officer who assists a commanding officer by sending out orders, writing letters, giving messages, etc.   2 a helper; assistant.   3 helping.   1, 2 *n.*, 3 *adj.*

**ad–lib** (ad′lib′)   *Informal.*   1 make up as one goes along; extemporize freely.   2 freely; on the spur of the moment. 3 not prepared ahead of time; improvised: *an ad-lib speech.*   1 *v.*, **ad·libbed, ad·lib·bing;**   2 *adv.*, 3 *adj.*

**Adm.**   1 Admiral.   2 Admiralty.

**ad·min·is·ter** (ad min′ə stər)   1 manage the affairs of a business, a city, etc.; control on behalf of others; direct: *The Minister of Defence administers a department of the government. A housekeeper administers a household.* 2 give; apply; dispense: *A doctor administers medicine to sick people. Judges administer justice and punishment.* 3 offer or tender an oath.   4 settle or take charge of an estate.   5 act as administrator.   *v.*

**administer to,**   be helpful; add something; contribute to: *to administer to a person's comfort or pleasure.*

**ad·min·is·tra·tion** (ad min′ə strā′shən)   1 the managing of a business, office, etc.; management.   2 a group of persons in charge: *The university administration has improved the enrolment procedure.*   3 the management of public affairs by government officials.   4 the officials as a group; the government in office.   5 the period of office of these officials or of a government.   6 a giving out, applying, or dispensing of medicine, justice, etc.: *The Red Cross handled the administration of aid to the refugees.*   *n.*

**ad·min·is·tra·tive** (ad min′ə strə tiv *or* ad min′ə strā′tiv) having to do with administration; managing; executive. *adj.*   —**ad·min′is·tra·tive·ly,** *adv.*

**ad·min·is·tra·tor** (ad min′ə strā′tər)   1 a person who administers.   2 a person appointed by a court to take charge of or settle the estate of someone who has died. Compare with EXECUTOR (def. 1).   *n.*

**ad·mi·ra·ble** (ad′mə rə bəl)   1 worth admiring. 2 excellent; very good.   *adj.*   —**ad′mi·ra·ble·ness,** *n.* —**ad′mi·ra·bly,** *adv.*

**ad·mi·ral** (ad′mə rəl)   1 the commander-in-chief of a fleet.   2 a naval officer of the second-highest rank. 3 any naval officer above the rank of captain; admiral of the fleet, admiral, vice-admiral, or rear admiral.   4 *Cdn.* formerly in Newfoundland, the leader of a fishing fleet. 5 any of various brightly coloured butterflies.   *n.*

**admiral of the fleet**   a naval officer of the highest rank.

**ad·mi·ral·ty** (ad′mə rəl tē)   1 a law or court dealing with affairs of the sea and ships.   2 **The Admiralty,** in the United Kingdom, until 1963, the government department in charge of naval affairs.   *n., pl.* **ad·mi·ral·ties.**

**ad·mi·ra·tion** (ad′mə rā′shən)   1 a feeling of wonder, pleasure, and approval; delight or satisfaction at something fine, beautiful, or well done.   2 the act of regarding with delight something fine or beautiful: *They paused in admiration of the beautiful view.*   3 a person or thing that is admired: *Helen's talent in painting was the admiration of all her friends.*   *n.*

**ad·mire** (ad mīr′)   1 regard with wonder, approval, and delight: *to admire a brave deed. They stood for a while, admiring the view.*   2 think highly of; esteem: *I admire her very much.*   3 express admiration for: *He was so anxious to please that he enthusiastically admired every piece of furniture in the room.*   *v.*, **ad·mired, ad·mir·ing.**

**ad·mir·er** (ad mī′rər)   1 a person who admires.   2 a person in love with or fond of another; SUITOR (def. 1).   *n.*

**ad·mir·ing** (ad mī′ring)   1 showing or feeling admiration: *an admiring glance. Carole was surrounded by a group of admiring friends.*   2 ppr. of ADMIRE.   1 *adj.*, 2 *v.*   —**ad·mir′ing·ly,** *adv.*

**ad·mis·si·bil·i·ty** (ad mis′ə bil′ə tē)   the quality or state of being ADMISSIBLE.   *n.*

**ad·mis·si·ble** (ad mis′ə bəl)   1 that can be permitted; allowable: *Is it admissible to smoke here?*   2 having the right to enter or use a position, occupation, group, place, etc.: *Only adults are admissible here.*   3 that can be considered as evidence or proof: *Hearsay evidence is not admissible in a court of law.*   *adj.* —**ad·mis′si·ble·ness,** *n.*   —**ad·mis′si·bly,** *adv.*

**ad·mis·sion** (ad mish′ən)   1 allowing a person, animal, etc. to enter; entrance: *admission of aliens into a country.* 2 the power or right to enter or use an office, place, etc.: *Every elementary school graduate has admission to high school.*   3 a price paid for the right to enter. 4 admitting something to be true; confessing: *Puranee's admission that she was to blame kept the others from being punished.*   5 a fact or point acknowledged; something accepted as true or valid.   *n.*

**ad·mit** (ad mit′)   1 say something is real or true; confess: *I admit my mistake.*   2 accept as true or valid. 3 allow to enter or use; let in: *Windows admit light and air to the room.*   4 give the right to enter to: *This ticket admits one person.*   5 allow; permit.   *v.*, **ad·mit·ted, ad·mit·ting.**

**admit of,**   make allowance for; leave room for; be capable of: *His answer admits of no reply.*

**admit to the bar,** give authority to practise law; call to the bar.

**ad·mit·tance** (ad mit′əns) 1 the right to enter; permission to enter: *The reporter had admittance to all theatres free of charge.* 2 the act of admitting. *n.*

**ad·mit·ted·ly** (ad mit′i dlē) without denial; by general consent. *adv.*

**ad·mix** (ad miks′) add in mixing; mix in. *v.*

**ad·mix·ture** (ad miks′chər) 1 mixing or being mixed. 2 the result of mixing; a mixture. 3 anything added in mixing. *n.*

**ad·mon·ish** (ad mon′ish) warn or advise a person about his or her faults in order that he or she may be guided to improve: *The police officer admonished her for driving so fast. The teacher admonished the student for carelessness.* *v.* —**ad·mon′ish·er,** *n.* —**ad·mon′ish·ment,** *n.*

**ad·mo·ni·tion** (ad′mə nish′ən) advice concerning faults a person has shown or may show; a warning. *n.*

**ad·mon·i·to·ry** (ad mon′ə tô′rē) ADMONISHing; warning. *adj.*

**a·do** (ə dü′) activity; stir; fuss; trouble: *The family made much ado about the party.* *n.*

**a·do·be** (ə dō′bē) 1 sun-dried clay or mud. 2 a brick or bricklike piece of such material, used in building. 3 built or made of sun-dried bricks: *Many people in the southwestern United States and in Mexico live in adobe houses.* *n.*

**ad·o·les·cence** (ad′ə les′əns) 1 the period of physical and psychological growth between childhood and maturity. 2 the state of being adolescent. *n.*

**ad·o·les·cent** (ad′ə les′ənt) 1 a person in the state of growth between childhood and maturity. 2 growing up from childhood to manhood or womanhood. 3 of or characteristic of adolescents. 1 *n.*, 2 3 *adj.*

**a·dopt** (ə dopt′) 1 take or use as one's own by choice: *to adopt a new technique. I liked your idea and adopted it.* 2 accept formally: *The club adopted the motion by a vote of 20 to 5.* 3 legally take a child of other parents to bring up as one's own. *v.*

**a·dop·tion** (ə dop′shən) 1 adopting or being adopted: *The English department is considering the adoption of a new text.* 2 the legal taking of a child of other parents to bring up as one's own: *Joe's adoption by his aunt changed his whole life. Adoptions have to be approved by a court of law.* *n.*

**a·dop·tive** (ə dop′tiv) 1 tending to adopt. 2 related by adoption: *She was very happy with her adoptive parents.* *adj.* —**a·dop′tive·ly,** *adv.*

**a·dor·a·ble** (ə dô′rə bəl) 1 worthy of adoration. 2 *Informal.* lovely; delightful. *adj.* —**a·dor′a·bly,** *adv.*

**ad·o·ra·tion** (ad′ə rā′shən) 1 highest respect; devoted love. 2 worship. *n.*

**a·dore** (ə dôr′) 1 respect very highly; love deeply. 2 *Informal.* like very much. 3 worship. *v.*, **a·dored, a·dor·ing.** —**a·dor′ing·ly,** *adv.*

**a·dor·er** (ə dô′rər) 1 a devoted admirer; lover. 2 worshipper. *n.*

**a·dorn** (ə dôrn′) 1 add beauty to; make greater the splendour or honour of; add distinction to. 2 put ornaments on; decorate. *v.* —**a·dorn′er,** *n.*

# admittance 17 adulterer

hat, āge, fär; let, ēqual, tėrm; it, īce
hot, ōpen, ôrder; oil, out; cup, pùt, rüle
əbove, takən, pencəl, lemən, circəs
ch, child; ng, long; sh, ship
th, thin; ᴛʜ, then; zh, measure

**a·dorn·ment** (ə dôrn′mənt) 1 something that adds beauty; an ornament; decoration: *adornments for the hair.* 2 the act of adorning or the state of being adorned: *Lee was busy with the adornment of the bride.* *n.*

**ad·re·nal** (ə drē′nəl) 1 near or on the kidneys. 2 ADRENAL GLAND. 3 of or from the ADRENAL GLANDS. 1, 3 *adj.*, 2 *n.*

**adrenal gland** either of the two ductless glands situated one on top of each kidney. The inner part of the gland, called the MEDULLA, is controlled by the nervous system and produces adrenalin; the outer layer, called the CORTEX, is controlled by the pituitary gland and produces several hormones necessary to life. See KIDNEY for picture.

**ad·ren·al·in** (ə dren′ə lin) 1 a hormone produced by the inner part of the ADRENAL GLANDS in reaction to sudden stress. 2 *Informal.* the state of excitement that is associated with the production of this hormone: *It was pure adrenalin that kept me going.* *n.*

**a·drift** (ə drift′) 1 drifting: *Having lost the paddle, we floated adrift on the lake.* 2 without guidance or security: *adrift in a strange city. The team was adrift for three weeks while the coach was sick.* 1 *adv.*, 2 *adj.*

**a·droit** (ə droit′) 1 expert in the use of the hands; skilful. 2 clever with the mind; resourceful: *A good teacher is adroit in asking questions.* *adj.* —**a·droit′ly,** *adv.* —**a·droit′ness,** *n.*

**ad·sorb** (ad zôrb′ *or* ad sôrb′) gather a gas, liquid, or dissolved substance on a surface in a condensed layer. *v.*

**ad·sorp·tion** (ad zôrp′shən *or* ad sôrp′shən) an ADSORBing or being adsorbed. *n.*

**ad·u·late** (aj′ə lāt′) praise too much; flatter slavishly. *v.*, **ad·u·lat·ed, ad·u·lat·ing.** —**ad′u·la′tor,** *n.*

**ad·u·la·tion** (aj′ə lā′shən) too much praise; slavish flattery. *n.*

**ad·u·la·to·ry** (aj′ə lə tô′rē) praising too much; slavishly flattering. *adj.*

**a·dult** (ə dult′ *or* ad′ult) 1 having full size and strength; grown-up; full-grown; mature. 2 a grown-up person. 3 a person who has reached an age of maturity as defined by law: *In some provinces, one is an adult at 18.* 4 any plant or animal grown to full size and strength. 5 of or for adults. 1, 5 *adj.*, 2–4 *n.* —**a·dult′ness, a·dult′hood,** *n.*

**a·dul·ter·ant** (ə dul′tə rənt) 1 any substance used in adulterating. 2 adulterating. 1 *n.*, 2 *adj.*

**a·dul·ter·ate** (ə dul′tə rāt′) make lower in quality by adding inferior or impure materials: *to adulterate milk with water.* *v.*, **a·dul·ter·at·ed, a·dul·ter·at·ing.**

**a·dul·ter·a·tion** (ə dul′tə rā′shən) 1 the act or process of adulterating. 2 an ADULTERATEd substance; a product that has been adulterated. *n.*

**a·dul·ter·er** (ə dul′tə rər) a person, especially a man, guilty of ADULTERY. *n.*

**a·dul·ter·ess** (ə dul′tris or ə dul′tə ris)   a woman guilty of ADULTERY.   *n.*

**a·dul·ter·ous** (ə dul′tə rəs)   having to do with or characterized by ADULTERY: *an adulterous act.*   *adj.*   —**a·dul′ter·ous·ly,** *adv.*

**a·dul·ter·y** (ə dul′tə rē)   the sexual unfaithfulness of a spouse.   *n., pl.* **a·dul·ter·ies.**

**adv.**   **1** adverb; adverbial.   **2** advertisement.

**ad va·lo·rem** (ad′ və lô′rəm)   *Latin.*   of merchandise, in proportion to the value: *an ad valorem tax.*

**ad·vance** (ad vans′)   **1** move forward; go forward: *The troops advanced.*   **2** bring forward: *The troops were advanced.*   **3** a movement forward: *The caravan's advance was very slow.*   **4** going before: *the advance guard.*   **5** make progress; improve: *We advance in knowledge.*   **6** a step forward; progress: *a great advance in our understanding of the laws of physics.*   **7** help forward; further: *to advance the cause of peace.*   **8** put forward; suggest: *to advance an opinion.*   **9** raise to a higher rank; promote: *to advance her from lieutenant to captain.*   **10** rise in rank; be promoted: *to advance in one's profession.*   **11** raise prices or value: *to advance the price of milk.*   **12** rise in price or value: *The stock advanced three points.*   **13** a rise in price or value: *an advance of one cent a litre.*   **14** make earlier; hasten: *to advance the time of the meeting.*   **15** supply beforehand: *to advance a salesperson funds for expenses.*   **16** ahead of time: *We'll send you advance information on the next meeting.*   **17** the furnishing of money or goods before they are due or as a loan: *The publisher gave her an advance on royalties for her book.*   **18** the money or goods furnished.   **19 advances,** *pl.*   personal approaches toward another or others to settle a difference, to make an acquaintance, etc.   1, 2, 5, 7-12, 14, 15 *v.*, **ad·vanced, ad·vanc·ing;**   3, 4, 6, 13, 16-19 *n.*
**in advance,**   **a** in front; ahead.   **b** ahead of time: *He paid his rent in advance.*

**ad·vanced** (ad vanst′)   **1** in front of others; forward: *an advanced theory of the composition of the atom.*   **2** ahead of most others in progress, ideas, etc.: *The advanced class has studied English for three years.*   **3** far along in life; very old: *He lived to the advanced age of ninety years.*   **4** pt. and pp. of ADVANCE.   1-3 *adj.*, 4 *v.*

**ad·vance·ment** (ad vans′mənt)   **1** a movement forward; advance.   **2** progress; improvement: *the advancement of knowledge through books.*   **3** promotion: *There is good opportunity for advancement in this job.*   *n.*

**ad·van·tage** (ad van′tij)   **1** a favourable condition, circumstance, or opportunity; means helpful in getting something desired: *Good health is always a great advantage.*   **2** any better or superior position: *She has the advantage of Mrs. Allen, who has no money at all.*   **3** the result of a better position: *A person who can think for himself has an advantage when he begins to work.*   **4** give an advantage to; help; benefit.   **5** in a tennis game, the first point scored after deuce.   1-3, 5 *n.*, 4 *v.*, **ad·van·taged, ad·van·tag·ing.**
**take advantage of,**   **a** use to help or benefit oneself: *Take advantage of your illness to catch up on your reading.*   **b** impose upon: *Don't take advantage of me by asking me to run errands on such a hot day.*
**to one's advantage,**   to one's benefit or help: *It will be to your advantage to study hard if you wish to be a scientist.*
**to advantage,**   to a good effect; with a useful effect: *A diamond shows to advantage on a dark background.*

**ad·van·ta·geous** (ad′vən tā′jəs)   giving advantage; favourable; helpful; profitable: *This advantageous position commands three roads.*   *adj.*   —**ad′van·ta′geous·ly,** *adv.*   —**ad′van·ta′geous·ness,** *n.*

**ad·vent** (ad′vent)   the coming; arrival: *The advent of spring was a time for festivals in ancient days.*

**ad·ven·ti·tious** (ad′ven tish′əs)   coming from outside; additional; accidental: *The romantic life of the author gives his book an adventitious interest.*   *adj.*   —**ad′ven·ti′tious·ly,** *adv.*   —**ad′ven·ti′tious·ness,** *n.*

**ad·ven·ture** (ad ven′chər)   **1** a bold and difficult undertaking involving unknown risks and danger: *She has had many adventures in her career as a detective.*   **2** the seeking or encountering of excitement and unknown risks or danger: *the spirit of adventure, yearning after adventure.*   **3** an unusual or exciting experience: *It was an adventure to be entirely on his own in a strange city.*   **4** take part in daring or exciting undertakings: *a summer of adventuring in the wilderness.*   **5** dare to do or go: *to adventure upon an unknown shore.*   1-3 *n.*, 4 5 *v.*, **ad·ven·tured, ad·ven·tur·ing.**

**ad·ven·tur·er** (ad ven′chə rər)   **1** a person who seeks or has adventures.   **2** a soldier ready to serve in any army that will hire him; a MERCENARY.   **3** a person who lives by his or her wits; person who schemes to get money, social position, etc.   **4** SPECULATOR.   *n.*

**ad·ven·ture·some** (ad ven′chər səm)   bold and daring; ADVENTUROUS (def. 1).   *adj.*

**ad·ven·tur·ous** (ad ven′chə rəs)   **1** fond of adventures; ready to take risks; daring: *a bold, adventurous explorer.*   **2** full of risk; dangerous: *An expedition to the North Pole is an adventurous undertaking.*   *adj.*   —**ad·ven′tur·ous·ly,** *adv.*   —**ad·ven′tur·ous·ness,** *n.*

**ad·verb** (ad′vėrb)   a word that extends or limits the meaning of verbs (She sings *well*), especially in place, time, manner, or degree, but is also used to qualify adjectives (She is *very* pretty) or other adverbs (She sings *quite* well). *Soon, here, very, gladly,* and *not* are adverbs. Most adverbs are adjectives or participles plus the ending *-ly:* He rowed *badly*. She was *deservedly* popular. Some adverbs have the same forms as adjectives, such as *cheap, close, deep, loud, much, wrong.*   *n.*
☛ *Usage.*   A few adverbs have two forms: *slow, slowly; cheap, cheaply; second, secondly.* The forms without an adverbial ending are usually found in brief directions: *Drive slow.*

**ad·ver·bi·al** (ad vėr′bē əl)   **1** of an ADVERB.   **2** used as an ADVERB: *The form* home *in* I'm going home *is an adverbial use of the noun* home.   *adj.*

**ad·ver·bi·al·ly** (ad vėr′bē ə lē)   as an ADVERB.   *adv.*

**ad·ver·sar·y** (ad′vər ser′ē)   **1** a person opposing or resisting another person; enemy.   **2** a person or group on the other side in a contest.   *n., pl.* **ad·ver·sar·ies.**

**ad·verse** (ad′vėrs or ad vėrs′)   **1** unfavourable: *adverse criticism.*   **2** harmful: *Dirt and disease have an adverse effect on the health of children.*   **3** acting in a contrary direction; opposing: *Adverse winds hindered the ship.*   *adj.*   —**ad·verse′ly,** *adv.*   —**ad·verse′ness,** *n.*

**ad·ver·si·ty** (ad vėr′sə tē)   **1** a condition of unhappiness, misfortune, or distress.   **2** a stroke of misfortune; an unfavourable or harmful thing or event.   *n., pl.* **ad·ver·si·ties.**

**ad·vert** (ad vėrt′)   direct attention (*to*); refer (*to*) in speaking or writing: *The speaker adverted to the need for more parks.* *v.*

**ad·ver·tise** (ad′vər tīz′) **1** give public notice of in a newspaper, over the radio, etc.: *When people lose something valuable, they advertise it in the newspaper.* **2** ask for by public notice: *to advertise for a job.* **3** make generally known. **4** praise the good qualities of a product, etc. in order to promote sales: *Manufacturers advertise things that they wish to sell.* **5** issue advertising: *It pays to advertise.* **6** call attention to oneself. *v.*, **ad·ver·tised, ad·ver·tis·ing.**

**ad·ver·tise·ment** (ad′vər tī′zmənt *or* ad vėr′ti smənt) a public notice or announcement, especially one that emphasizes the desirable features of a product or service in order to make people want to buy it: *The store has an advertisement in the newspaper.* *n.*

**ad·ver·tis·er** (ad′vər tī′zər) one who ADVERTISES. *n.*

**ad·ver·tis·ing** (ad′vər tī′zing) **1** the business of preparing, publishing, or circulating ADVERTISEMENTS. **2** ADVERTISEMENTS. *n.*

**ad·vice** (ad vīs′) an opinion about what should be done: *Take the doctor's advice.* *n.*

**ad·vis·a·bil·i·ty** (ad vī′zə bil′ə tē) the quality of being ADVISABLE; propriety; expediency: *She questioned the advisability of putting all one's money into stocks.* *n.*

**ad·vis·a·ble** (ad vī′zə bəl) to be recommended; wise; sensible: *It is not advisable for him to go while he is still sick.* *adj.* —**ad·vis′a·bly,** *adv.*

**ad·vise** (ad vīz′) **1** give advice to: *Advise him to be cautious.* **2** give advice: *I shall act as you advise.* **3** give notice; inform (*often with* **of**): *We advised them that we were leaving. We were advised of the dangers before we began our trip.* *v.*, **ad·vised, ad·vis·ing.**

**ad·vised** (ad vīzd′) **1** planned; considered; thought-out. **2** pt. and pp. of ADVISE. 1 *adj.*, 2 *v.*

**ad·vis·ed·ly** (ad vī′zi dlē) after careful consideration; deliberately. *adv.*

**ad·vise·ment** (ad vī′zmənt) careful consideration: *The lawyer took our case under advisement and said he would give us an answer in two weeks.* *n.*

**ad·vis·er** or **ad·vi·sor** (ad vī′zər) **1** a person who gives advice. **2** a person whose job is to give advice, especially a teacher appointed to advise students. *n.*

**ad·vi·so·ry** (ad vī′zə rē) **1** having power to advise: *In her advisory capacity she helps a lot of students.* **2** containing advice. *adj.* —**ad·vi′so·ri·ly,** *adv.*

**ad·vo·ca·cy** (ad′və kə sē) a statement in favour; public recommendation; support: *The Premier's advocacy of the plan got votes for it.* *n.*

**ad·vo·cate** (ad′və kāt′ *for verb,* ad′və kit *or* ad′və kāt′ *for noun*) **1** speak in favour of; recommend publicly: *He advocates building more schools.* **2** any person who pleads or argues for; supporter: *Mrs. Delaney is an advocate of better school buildings.* **3** a lawyer who pleads in a law court; barrister. 1 *v.*, **ad·vo·cat·ed, ad·vo·cat·ing;** 2, 3, *n.* —**ad·vo·ca′tion,** *n.* —**ad′vo·ca′tor,** *n.*

**advt.** advertisement.

Adzes. A man using an adze to shape a log.

**adze** (adz) a tool for shaping wood, resembling an axe, but having a curved blade with its cutting edge set across the end of the handle. *n.* Sometimes, **adz.**

**ae·gis** (ē′jis) **1** a shield or breastplate used by the Greek god Zeus or by his daughter Athena. **2** protection: *He sought the aegis of the ambassador.* *n.* Also, **egis.**
**under the aegis of,** under the protection or patronage of.

**ae·o·li·an harp** (ē ō′lē ən) a box with strings over openings in its top, which gives out musical sounds when currents of air blow across it.
☞ *Etym.* From the name of *Aeolus,* the Greek god of the winds.

**ae·on** (ē′ən *or* ē′on) See EON. *n.*

**aer·ate** (er′āt) **1** expose to air. **2** expose to and mix with air: *Water in some reservoirs is aerated by being tossed high into the air in a fine spray.* **3** fill with a gas: *Soda water is water that has been aerated with carbon dioxide.* **4** expose to chemical action with oxygen: *Blood is aerated in the lungs.* *v.*, **aer·at·ed, aer·at·ing.** —**aer′a′tion,** *n.*

**aer·a·tor** (er′ā tər) a device or apparatus that charges or supplies with air: *Our aquarium is equipped with an aerator.* *n.*

**aer·i·al** (er′ē əl) **1** a radio or television ANTENNA (def. 2). **2** of, having to do with, or existing in the air: *aerial spirits.* **3** done or performed up in the air instead of on the ground: *swallows performing an aerial ballet.* **4** like air; thin, light, and insubstantial as air. **5** of, having to do with, by, or involving aircraft: *aerial navigation, aerial warfare, aerial bombardment.* **6** taken from or designed to be used in an aircraft: *an aerial photograph.* **7** in botany, growing in the air instead of in soil or water: *aerial ferns.* 1 *n.*, 2–7 *adj.* —**aer′i·al·ly,** *adv.*

**aer·ie** (er′ē *or* ēr′ē) See EYRIE. *n., pl.* **aer·ies.**
☞ *Hom.* AIRY (for the first pronunciation of **aerie**).

**aero–** combining form. **1** air, as in *aerospace, aerodynamics.* **2** gas, as in *aerosol.* **3** aircraft or aviation, as in *aeronautics.*

**aer·obe** (er′ōb) a BACTERIUM which uses oxygen to break down food into energy. Compare with ANAEROBE. *n.*

**aer·o·bic** (er ō′bik) **1** living and growing only where there is oxygen: *Some bacteria are aerobic.* **2** having to do with or caused by such bacteria. **3 aerobics,** *pl.* exercises designed to make people breathe more efficiently. 1, 2 *adj.* 3 *n.*

**aer·o·drome** (erʹə drōm′) an airfield or small airport. *n.*

**aer·o·dy·nam·ics** (erʹō dī namʹiks) the branch of physics that deals with the forces exerted by air or other gases in motion, especially with the forces acting on an airplane as it moves through the air. *n.*

**aer·o·lite** (erʹə līt′) METEORITE. *n.*

**aer·o·naut** (erʹə not′) the pilot of an airship or balloon; BALLOONIST. *n.*

**aer·o·nau·tic** (erʹə notʹik) of AERONAUTICS or AERONAUTS. *adj.* —**aerʹo nauʹti·cal·ly**, *adv.*

**aer·o·nau·ti·cal** (erʹə notʹə kəl) AERONAUTIC. *adj.*

**aer·o·nau·tics** (erʹə notʹiks) the science or art having to do with the design, manufacture, and operation of aircraft. *n.*

**aer·o·plane** (erʹə plān′) AIRPLANE. *n.*

**aer·o·sol** (erʹə sol′) 1 a suspension of fine solid or liquid particles in a gas: *Smoke and fog are aerosols.* 2 a substance such as paint or insecticide, packaged in an aerosol bomb. 3 AEROSOL BOMB. *n.*

**aerosol** a small metal can containing a substance such as paint, insecticide, or shaving cream mixed with a liquified gas that is at high pressure and acts as a propellant. When the cap is pushed down to open the inlet, the substance inside shoots out as a mist or foam.

**aer·o·space** (erʹə spās′) 1 the earth's atmosphere and space beyond it, considered as a continuous region or field. 2 the branch of science that deals with the earth's atmosphere and outer space, especially in relation to space travel. 3 the industry of designing, building and operating spacecraft, missiles, etc. 4 of, having to do with, or referring to aerospace, space travel, or the designing, building, and operating of spacecraft, etc.: *aerospace technology. n.*

**aes·thete** (esʹthēt *or* ēsʹthēt) 1 a person who pretends to care a great deal about beauty; person who gives too much attention to beauty. 2 a person who is sensitive to beauty. *n.* Also, **esthete**.

**aes·thet·ic** (es thetʹik *or* ēs thetʹik) 1 having to do with the beautiful, as distinguished from the useful, scientific, etc. 2 sensitive to beauty (*used of persons*). 3 pleasing; artistic (*used of things*). *adj.* Also, **esthetic**.

**aes·thet·i·cal·ly** (es thetʹi klē *or* ēs thetʹi klē) 1 in an AESTHETIC manner. 2 according to AESTHETICS: *an aesthetically pleasing colour combination. adv.* Also, **esthetically**.

**aes·thet·ics** (es thetʹiks *or* ēs thetʹiks) the study of beauty in art and nature; philosophy of beauty; theory of the fine arts. *n.* Also, **esthetics**.

**aes·ti·vate** (esʹtə vāt′) See ESTIVATE. *v.*, **aes·ti·va·ted, aes·ti·vat·ing**.

**aet.** or **aetat.** an abbreviation of a Latin word meaning at the age of.

**ae·ther** (ēʹthər) See ETHER (defs. 2 and 3). *n.*

**ae·the·re·al** (i thēʹrē əl) See ETHEREAL. *adj.*

**AF, A.F.,** or **a.f.** audio frequency

**a·far** (ə färʹ) far; far away; far off: *to see from afar. adv.*

**af·fa·bil·i·ty** (afʹə bilʹə tē) the quality that makes a person easy to talk to; a courteous, pleasant, and friendly manner. *n.*

**af·fa·ble** (afʹə bəl) easy to talk to; courteous, pleasant, and friendly. *adj.* —**afʹfa·ble·ness**, *n.* —**afʹfa·bly**, *adv.*

**af·fair** (ə ferʹ) 1 something done or to be done; matter; concern: *That's my affair.* 2 an action, event, or procedure referred to in vague terms: *The party on Saturday night was a dull affair.* 3 an object or group of objects referred to in vague terms: *This machine is a complicated affair.* 4 a sexual relationship between two people not married to each other, especially one that lasts only a short while. 5 **affairs**, *pl.* matters of interest or concern, especially business, commercial, or public matters: *current affairs, affairs of state. n.*

**affair of honour** or **honor** a duel.

**af·fect**[1] (ə fektʹ) 1 make something happen to; have an effect on; influence: *The small amount of rain last year affected the growth of crops.* 2 act on in a harmful way: *The disease so affected her mind that she lost her memory.* 3 touch the heart of; stir the emotions of: *The stories of starving children so affected him that he spent all his spare money for relief. v.*
☛ *Usage.* See note at EFFECT.

**af·fect**[2] (ə fektʹ) 1 pretend to have or feel: *He affected ignorance of the fight, but we knew that he had seen it.* 2 be fond of; like: *She affects old furniture.* 3 assume, use, or frequent by preference: *She affects carelessness in dress. v.*

**af·fec·ta·tion** (afʹek tāʹshən) 1 an artificial or unnatural way of behaving or talking: *His English accent is an affectation, for he has never lived outside Alberta.* 2 an outward appearance; pretence: *an affectation of ignorance. n.*

**af·fect·ed**[1] (ə fekʹtid) 1 acted on; influenced. 2 influenced injuriously. 3 touched in the heart; moved in feeling: *She was sad and much affected by her sister's illness.* 4 pt. and pp. of AFFECT[1]. 1–3 *adj.*, 4 *v.*

**af·fect·ed**[2] (ə fekʹtid) 1 put on for effect; unnatural; artificial: *His affected manner changed as soon as the guests had gone.* 2 behaving, speaking, writing, etc. unnaturally for effect: *She is very affected.* 3 pt. and pp. of AFFECT[2]. 1, 2 *adj.*, 3 *v.* —**af·fectʹed·ly**, *adv.*

**af·fect·ing** (ə fekʹting) 1 causing emotion; touching the heart, moving the feelings: *The poor woman told an affecting story of hunger and suffering.* 2 ppr. of AFFECT[1]. 1 *adj.*, 2 *v.* —**af·fectʹing·ly**, *adv.*

**af·fec·tion** (ə fekʹshən) 1 a friendly feeling; fondness; tenderness; love. 2 a feeling; inclination. 3 a disease; unhealthy condition. *n.*

**af·fec·tion·ate** (ə fekʹshə nit) loving; fond; having or showing AFFECTION. (def. 1). *adj.* —**af·fecʹtion·ate·ly**, *adv.*

**af·fec·tive** (ə fekʹtiv) of the feelings; emotional. *adj.*

**af·fer·ent** (afʹə rənt) of nerves or blood vessels, carrying inward to a central organ or point. Compare with EFFERENT. *adj.*

**af·fi·ance** (ə fīʹəns) 1 promise in marriage; BETROTH. 2 the pledging of faith; BETROTHAL. 3 trust; confidence. 1 *v.*, **af·fi·anced, af·fi·anc·ing**; 2, 3 *n.*

**af·fi·da·vit** (afʹə dāʹvit) a statement written down and sworn to be true: *An affidavit is usually made before a judge or notary public. n.*

**af·fil·i·ate** (ə fil′ē āt′ *for verb*, ə fil′ē it or ə fil′ē āt′ *for noun*) **1** connect in close association: *The two clubs did not have the same members, but they were affiliated with each other.* **2** associate oneself (*with*): *to affiliate with a political party.* **3** an organization or group associated with other similar bodies. 1, 2 *v.*, **af·fil·i·at·ed, af·fil·i·at·ing;** 3 *n.*

**af·fil·i·a·tion** (ə fil′ē ā′shən) an association; relation. *n.*

**af·fin·i·ty** (ə fin′ə tē) **1** a natural attraction to a person or liking for a thing: *an affinity for dancing. They have a strong affinity for each other.* **2** an attraction or force between certain particles or substances that makes them form chemical compositions. **3** a person to whom one is especially attracted. **4** a relationship by marriage. **5** a similarity or resemblance based on a relationship or connection. *n.*, *pl.* **af·fin·i·ties.**

**af·firm** (ə ferm′) **1** declare to be true; say firmly; assert: *The prisoner affirmed his innocence.* **2** confirm; ratify: *The higher court affirmed the lower court's decision.* **3** declare solemnly, but without taking an oath. *v.*

**af·fir·ma·tion** (af′ər mā′shən) **1** a solemn declaration made without taking an oath: *If a person's religion forbids him or her to take an oath, he or she can make an affirmation.* **2** an assertion; positive statement. *n.*

**af·firm·a·tive** (ə fėr′mə tiv) **1** stating that a fact is so; saying yes: *Marc's answer was affirmative.* **2** a word or statement that gives assent or indicates agreement. **3** the **affirmative,** the side arguing in favour of a question being debated. 1 *adj.*, 2 3 *n.* —**af·firm′a·tive·ly,** *adv.* **in the affirmative,** expressing agreement by saying yes: *The principal replied in the affirmative when we requested that we have a class picnic.*

**af·fix** (ə fiks′ *for verb*, af′iks *for noun*) **1** make firm or fix one thing to or on another: *Ying affixed the stamp to the envelope.* **2** add at the end. **3** something affixed. **4** a syllable or syllables added to the stem or base of a word to modify the meaning; prefix or suffix: *Un-* and *-ly* are *affixes.* **5** make an impression of a seal, etc. **6** connect with; attach: *to affix blame for the accident.* 1, 2, 5 6 *v.*, 3 4 *n.* —**af·fix′er,** *n.*

**af·fla·tus** (ə flā′təs) INSPIRATION. *n.*

**af·flict** (ə flikt′) cause pain to; trouble greatly; distress: *to be afflicted with troubles.* *v.*

**af·flic·tion** (ə flik′shən) **1** a state of pain or distress. **2** a cause of pain, trouble, or distress; misfortune. *n.*

**af·flic·tive** (ə flik′tiv) causing misery or pain; distressing. *adj.*

**af·flu·ence** (af′lü əns) **1** wealth; riches: *Canada is a country of great affluence.* **2** an abundant supply; great abundance: *We have had an affluence of rain this month.* *n.*

**af·flu·ent** (af′lü ənt) **1** very wealthy. **2** abundant; plentiful. **3** a stream flowing into a larger stream, lake, etc. 1, 2 *adj.*, 3 *n.* —**af′flu·ent·ly,** *adv.*

**af·flux** (af′luks) a flow toward a place. *n.*

**af·ford** (ə fôrd′) **1** spare the money for: *We can't afford a new car.* **2** manage to give, spare, have, etc.: *A busy woman cannot afford delay. Can you afford the time?* **3** be able without difficulty; have the means: *I can't afford to take the chance.* **4** furnish from natural resources; yield: *Some trees afford resin.* **5** yield or give as an effect or a result; provide: *Reading affords pleasure.* *v.*

**af·for·est** (ə fôr′ist) plant an area with trees. *v.*

hat, āge, fär; let, ēqual, tèrm; it, īce
hot, ōpen, ôrder; oil, out; cup, pùt, rüle
ə*bove,* tak*ə*n, penc*ə*l, lem*ə*n, circ*ə*s
ch, child; ng, long; sh, ship
th, thin; ᴛʜ, then; zh, measure

**af·fran·chise** (ə fran′chīz) ENFRANCHISE. *v.*, **af·fran·chised, af·fran·chis·ing.**

**af·fray** (ə frā′) a noisy quarrel; fight in public; brawl. *n.*

**af·front** (ə frunt′) **1** insult openly; offend purposely: *The boy affronted the teacher by shouting at her.* **2** a word or act that openly expresses intentional disrespect: *To be called a coward is an affront to a person.* **3** offend the modesty or self-respect of: *The villagers were affronted by the superior airs of the rich newcomer.* **4** a slight or injury to one's dignity. **5** meet face to face; confront. 1, 3, 5 *v.*, 2 4 *n.*

**Af·ghan** (af′gan *or* af′gən) **1** of or having to do with Afghanistan, a country in southwestern Asia, or its people. **2** a native or inhabitant of Afghanistan. **3** AFGHAN HOUND. **4 afghan,** a knitted or crocheted blanket or large shawl, often having a pattern of squares or zigzag stripes. 1 *adj.*, 2–4 *n.*

**Afghan hound** a breed of tall, swift dog having a thick coat of long, silky hair, a long, narrow head, and a thin tail: *Afghan hounds came originally from the Middle East, where they were usually trained as hunting dogs.*

**a·field** (ə fēld′) **1** away from home; away. **2** out of the way; astray. *adv.*

**a·fire** (ə fīr′) **1** on fire: *They set the house afire.* **2** burning: *The building was afire.* 1 *adv.*, 2 *adj.*

**a·flame** (ə flām′) **1** in flames; on fire: *The gas roared aflame.* **2** as if on fire; excited: *Her mind was aflame with curiosity.* 1 *adv.*, 2 *adj.*

**a·float** (ə flōt′) **1** floating on the water or in the air. **2** on a ship: *On the trip around the world, we were afloat 60 days and ashore 30 days.* **3** flooded: *After the rain, our cellar was afloat.* **4** current; in circulation: *Rumours of a revolt were afloat.* 1 *adv.*, 2–4 *adj.*

**a·flut·ter** (ə flut′ər) **1** fluttering: *The excitement set his pigeons aflutter.* **2** in a flutter: *The people were aflutter with expectation.* 1 *adv.*, 2 *adj.*

**a·foot** (ə fùt′) **1** on foot; walking: *Did you come all the way afoot?* **2** going on; in progress: *Preparations for dinner were afoot in the kitchen.* 1 *adv.*, 2 *adj.*

**a·fore·men·tioned** (ə fôr′men′shənd) spoken of before; mentioned above. *adj.*

**a·fore·said** (ə fôr′sed′) spoken of before. *adj.*

**a·fore·thought** (ə fôr′thot′) thought of beforehand; deliberately planned: *Archaic* except in *malice aforethought.* *adj.*

**a for·ti·o·ri** (a′fôr′tē ô′rē *or* ä′fôr′tē ô′rī) *Latin.* for a still stronger reason; all the more.

**a·foul** (ə foul′) **1** in a tangle or collision; entangled: *The propeller ran afoul in the weeds.* **2** in a tangle or collision, entangled: *Our boat remained afoul in the shallows.* 1 *adv.*, 2 *adj.*
**run afoul of,** get into difficulties with.

**a·fraid** (ə frād′) **1** feeling fear, frightened: *Alice is afraid of the dark.* **2** sorry (used to express polite regret or

**a·fresh** (ə fresh′) once more; again: *to start afresh.* *adv.*

**Af·ri·can** (af′rə kən) **1** of or having to do with Africa or its inhabitants. **2** a native or inhabitant of Africa. **3** a person whose recent ancestors came from Africa. **4** of or referring to a race of mankind that includes most of the peoples traditionally inhabiting Africa south of the Sahara: *The Blacks of North and South America and the West Indies belong to the African race.* **5** a member of this race. *1, 4 adj., 2, 3, 5 n.*

**African violet** a small tropical perennial plant having violet, pink, or white flowers, often grown as a house plant in temperate climates.

**Af·ri·kaans** (af′rə käns′ *or* af′rə känz′) **1** one of the official languages of the Republic of South Africa: *Afrikaans developed from 17th-century Dutch.* **2** of or having to do with Afrikaans or Afrikaners. *1 n., 2 adj.*

**Af·ri·ka·ner** (af′rə kä′nər) a native or inhabitant of the Republic of South Africa who is of European, especially Dutch, descent. *n.*

**Af·ro** (af′rō) a hairstyle that takes advantage of the character of very curly hair by leaving it bushy and clipping it into any of various rounded shapes: *an Afro cut.* *n., pl.* **Af·ros.**

Aft and other directions on a boat

**aft** (aft) **1** to the back of a ship, boat, aircraft, or spacecraft; ABAFT: *Take this container aft.* **2** at the back of a ship, boat, aircraft or spacecraft: *the aft cabin.* *1 adv., 2 adj.*

**af·ter** (af′tər) **1** behind in place: *The soldiers marched in line one after another.* **2** behind: *to follow after.* **3** next to; following: *day after day.* **4** in pursuit of; in search of: *The dog ran after the rabbit.* **5** later than the time that: *After he goes, we shall eat.* **6** later in time than: *After dinner we can go.* **7** later: *three hours after.* **8** later: *In after years he regretted the mistakes of his boyhood.* **9** about; concerning: *Your aunt asked after you.* **10** considering; because of: *After the selfish way she acted, who could like her?* **11** in spite of: *After her sufferings, she is still cheerful.* **12** imitating; in imitation of: *He wrote a fable after the manner of Aesop.* **13** lower in rank or importance than: *A captain comes after a general.* **14** for: *named after her cousin.* *1, 3, 4, 6, 9–14 prep., 2 7 adv., 5 conj., 8 adj.*

**after all, a** in spite of everything that has happened, been said, etc.: *We decided to go after all. It didn't make any difference after all.* **b** taking everything into consideration; as a matter of fact: *After all, she's only a child, so you can't expect her to behave like an adult. After all, what does it really matter?*

**af·ter·burn·er** (af′tər bėr′nər) in a TURBOJET aircraft, an extra section between the turbojet engine and the tail pipe, in which additional fuel is sprayed into the burning exhaust gases, greatly increasing the thrust of the exhaust jet: *An afterburner enables a jet aircraft to attain very high speeds.* *n.*

**af·ter·deck** (af′tər dek′) the deck toward or at the STERN of a ship. *n.*

**af·ter–ef·fect** (af′tə ri fekt′) a result or effect that follows something. *n.*

**af·ter·glow** (af′tər glō′) **1** the glow after something bright has gone. **2** the glow in the sky after sunset. *n.*

**af·ter·life** (af′tər līf′) life or existence after death. *n.*

**af·ter·math** (af′tər math′) **1** a result; consequence: *The aftermath of war is hunger and disease.* **2** a crop gathered after the first crop. *n.*

**af·ter·most** (af′tər mōst′) **1** nearest the stern of a ship. **2** hindmost; last. *adj.*

**af·ter·noon** (af′tər nün′ for 1, af′tər nün′ for 2) **1** the part of the day between noon and evening: *They arrived in the afternoon.* **2** of, in, or suitable for the afternoon: *an afternoon visit.* *1 n., 2 adj.*

**af·ter·thought** (af′tər thot′) **1** a thought that comes after the time when it could have been used. **2** a later thought or explanation. *n.*

**af·ter·ward** (af′tər wərd) later. *adv.*

**af·ter·wards** (af′tər wərdz) later. *adv.*

**Ag** silver.

**a·gain** (ə gen′ *or* ə gān′) **1** once more; another time: *to try again.* **2** in return; in reply: *to answer again.* **3** moreover; besides: *Again, he is wrong.* *adv.*
**as much again,** twice as much; twice as many.

**a·gainst** (ə genst′ *or* ə gānst′) **1** upon; toward: *Rain beats against the window. We will sail against the wind.* **2** in opposition to: *He spoke against the suggestion.* **3** directly opposite to; facing: *over against the wall.* **4** in contact with: *to lean against a wall.* **5** in preparation for: *Squirrels store up nuts against the winter.* **6** in defence from: *A fire is a protection against cold.* *prep.*

**a·gape** (ə gāp′) **1** gaping; with the mouth wide open in wonder or surprise: *She stood agape at the sight.* **2** wide open: *The doors were agape.* *1 adv., 2 adj.*

**a·gar–a·gar** (ä′gər ä′gər) a gelatinlike extract obtained from certain seaweeds, used in making cultures for bacteria, fungi, etc. and as a glue. *n.*

**ag·ate** (ag′it) **1** a stone with variously coloured stripes or clouded colours; a kind of QUARTZ. **2** a playing marble resembling an agate. *n.* —**ag′ate·like′**, *adj.*

**a·ga·ve** (ə gā′vē) any of several North American desert plants (the century plant, sisal, etc.): *Soap, alcoholic drinks, and rope are made from some kinds of agave.* *n.*

**age** (āj) **1** time of life: *He died at the age of eighty.* **2** a period in life: *middle age.* **3** the latter part of life: *the wisdom of age.* **4** the full or average term of life: *The age of a horse is from 25 to 30 years.* **5** a period in history: *the golden age, the space age.* **6** a generation: *ages yet unborn.* **7** *Informal.* a long time: *I haven't seen you for an age.* **8** grow old: *He is ageing rapidly.* **9** make old:

*Fear and worry aged her.* **10** improve by keeping for a time; mature: *to age wine.* **1–7** *n.*, **8–10** *v.*, **aged, ag·ing** or **age·ing**.

**of age,** old enough to have full legal rights and responsibilities.

**–age** a noun-forming suffix meaning: **1** the act of: *breakage = act of breaking.* **2** a collection of; group of: *baggage = a group of bags.* **3** the condition of; rank of: *peerage = rank of peer.* **4** the cost of: *postage = cost of posting.* **5** the home of: *orphanage = home of orphans.*

**a·ged** (ā′jid *for 1*, ājd *for 2*) **1** having lived a long time; old: *The aged woman was wrinkled and bent.* **2** of the age of: *The little girl is aged six.* *adj.*

**age·less** (āj′lis) never growing old: *the ageless quality of good literature.* *adj.*

**age·long** (āj′long′) lasting a long time. *adj.*

**a·gen·cy** (ā′jən sē) **1** a means; action: *Snow is drifted by the agency of the wind.* **2** the business of a person or company that has the authority to act for another: *An agency rented my father's house for him.* **3** the place where an agency does business: *We walked down to the agency together.* *n., pl.* **a·gen·cies.**

**a·gen·da** (ə jen′də) **1** things to be done. **2** a list of things to be done or discussed: *The chairman's agenda gave the members of the club an opportunity to acquaint themselves in advance with matters to be discussed.* **1** *n. pl.*, **2** *n. pl.* or *sing.*

**a·gent** (ā′jənt) **1** a person or company that has the authority to act for another: *I made my sister my agent while I was out of the city.* **2** a person who does things. **3** any active power or cause that produces an effect: *Yeast is an important agent in the making of bread.* **4** a means; instrument. *n.*

**agent general** a representative in the United Kingdom of certain Canadian provinces. *n., pl.* **agents general** or **agent generals.**

**age of consent** the age at which a person is legally able to agree to marriage, medical treatment, etc. without the consent of a parent or guardian.

**age–old** (ā′jōld′) having existed for many ages; very old and still continuing: *the age-old question of astrology.* *adj.*

**ag·er·a·tum** (aj′ə rā′təm) a plant having small, dense flower heads, usually blue, sometimes white. *n.*

**ag·glom·er·ate** (ə glom′ə rāt′ *for verb*, ə glom′ə rit *or* ə glom′ə rāt′ *for noun and adjective*) **1** gather together in a mass; cluster together. **2** a mass; collection; cluster. **3** packed together in a mass. **1** *v.*, **ag·glom·er·at·ed, ag·glom·er·at·ing;** **2** *n.*, **3** *adj.*

**ag·glom·er·a·tion** (ə glom′ə rā′shən) a mass of things gathered or clustered together. *n.*

**ag·gran·dize** (ə gran′dīz *or* ag′rən dīz′) increase in power, wealth, rank, etc.; make greater: *The tyrant sought to aggrandize himself at the expense of others.* *v.*, **ag·gran·dized, ag·gran·diz·ing.** —**ag·gran′diz·er,** *n.*

**ag·gran·dize·ment** (ə gran′di zmənt) an increase in power, wealth, rank, etc.; making greater. *n.*

**ag·gra·vate** (ag′rə vāt′) **1** make worse or more severe: *His bad temper was aggravated by his headache.* **2** *Informal.* annoy; irritate; provoke: *The whispering in class aggravated our teacher.* *v.*, **ag·gra·vat·ed, ag·gra·vat·ing.** —**ag′gra·vat′ing·ly,** *adv.*

**ag·gra·va·tion** (ag′rə vā′shən) **1** making worse or more severe: *We were alarmed by the aggravation of the crisis.* **2** being made worse or more severe. **3** something that AGGRAVATES. *n.*

**ag·gre·gate** (ag′rə gāt′ *for verb*, ag′rə git *or* ag′rə gāt′ *for noun and adjective*) **1** formed by the collection of parts or units into one body, mass, or amount; collected, whole, or total: *The aggregate value of all the gifts was $1000.* **2** a mass of separate things joined together or associated; collection: *The report was an aggregate of the viewpoints of the committee members.* **3** the sum total; total amount. **4** in botany: **a** of a flower, composed of many FLORETS forming a head. **b** of a fruit, formed from the development together of several PISTILS of a single flower: *The raspberry and strawberry are aggregate fruits.* **5** in geology, composed of mineral crystals or rock fragments: *Granite is an aggregate rock.* **6** an aggregate rock: *volcanic aggregates.* **7** material such as broken stone, sand, or gravel used to make concrete. **8** collect together or unite. **9** amount to: *The money collected is expected to aggregate over $3000.* **1, 4, 5** *adj.*, **2, 3, 6 7** *n.*, **8 9** *v.*, **ag·gre·gat·ed, ag·gre·gat·ing.** —**ag′gre·gate·ly,** *adv.*

**in the aggregate,** together; as a whole.

**ag·gre·ga·tion** (ag′rə gā′shən) the collection of separate things into one mass or whole. *n.*

**ag·gres·sion** (ə gresh′ən) **1** the making of an unprovoked attack or assault by one nation on the rights or territories of another: *In 1914, Germany was guilty of aggression against Belgium.* **2** any unprovoked attack: *an aggression against a person's rights.* **3** the making of any unprovoked attack or attacks in violation of another's rights: *A libellous speech is a form of aggression.* *n.*

**ag·gres·sive** (ə gres′iv) **1** taking the first step in an attack or quarrel; attacking; quarrelsome: *An aggressive country is always ready to start a war.* **2** active; energetic; forceful: *The police began an aggressive campaign against crime.* *adj.* —**ag·gres′sive·ly,** *adv.* —**ag·gres′sive·ness,** *n.*

**ag·gres·sor** (ə gres′ər) **1** the one that begins an attack or quarrel. **2** a nation that starts a war. *n.*

**ag·grieve** (ə grēv′) injure unjustly; cause grief or trouble to: *Kar-Ling was aggrieved at the insult from her friend.* *v.*, **ag·grieved, ag·griev·ing.**

**ag·grieved** (ə grēvd′) **1** upset or troubled by grief: *We were much aggrieved on learning of our grandfather's death.* **2** wronged; unjustly treated: *The boy felt aggrieved when he was punished for something he didn't do.* **3** *pt.* and *pp.* of AGGRIEVE. **1, 2** *adj.*, **3** *v.*

**a·ghast** (ə gast′) filled with surprise or horror; frightened; terrified. *adj.*

**ag·ile** (aj′il *or* aj′əl) **1** moving quickly and easily; active; lively; nimble: *An acrobat has to be agile.* **2** able to think quickly: *You need an agile mind to solve puzzles.* *adj.* —**ag′ile·ly,** *adv.* —**ag′ile·ness,** *n.*

**a·gil·i·ty** (ə jil′ə tē) **1** the ability to move quickly and easily. **2** activeness; liveliness; nimbleness. *n.*

**ag·i·tate** (aj′ə tāt′) **1** move or shake: *The slightest wind will agitate the leaves of some trees.* **2** disturb; excite the feelings or the thoughts: *She was much agitated by the news*

of her sister's accident.   3 argue about; discuss vigorously.
4 keep arguing about and discussing a matter to arouse public interest: *Anti-slavery leaders agitated the question of slavery for years.*   *v.*, **ag·i·tat·ed, ag·i·tat·ing.**
—**ag′i·tat′ed·ly,** *adv.*

**ag·i·ta·tion** (aj′ə tā′shən)   1 a moving or shaking, usually violent.   2 a disturbed, upset, or troubled condition.   3 the persistent urging of a cause before the public; discussion; debate: *There was much agitation for and against the proposal.*   *n.*

**ag·i·ta·tor** (aj′ə tā′tər)   1 a person who tries to make people discontented with things as they are.   2 a device for shaking or stirring: *The agitator in the washing machine has stuck.*   *n.*

**a·gleam** (ə glēm′)   1 gleaming: *His eyes opened agleam with pleasure.*   2 gleaming: *The hall was agleam with light.*   1 *adv.*, 2 *adj.*

**a·glit·ter** (ə glit′ər)   1 glittering: *The icicles hung aglitter in the frost.*   2 glittering: *The Christmas tree was aglitter with tinsel.*   1 *adv.*, 2 *adj.*

**a·glow** (ə glō′)   1 glowing; in a glow: *The cold turned her pale face aglow.*   2 glowing; in a glow: *The baby's cheeks were aglow with health.*   1 *adv.*, 2 *adj.*

**ag·nos·tic** (ag nos′tik)   a person who believes that nothing is known or can be known about the existence of God or about things outside human experience.   *n.*

**ag·nos·ti·cism** (ag nos′tə siz′əm)   the belief or intellectual attitude of AGNOSTICS.   *n.*

**a·go** (ə gō′)   1 gone by; past: *I met her two years ago.*   2 in the past: *The first Europeans came to Canada long ago.*   1 *adj.*, 2 *adv.*
☞ *Usage.* The adjective **ago** always follows the noun.

**a·gog** (ə gog′)   1 eager; curious; excited: *We were all agog when he arrived.*   2 with eagerness, curiosity, or excitement: *The crowd roared agog at his speech.*   1 *adj.*, 2 *adv.*

**ag·o·nize** (ag′ə nīz′)   1 feel great anguish.   2 cause to suffer extreme pain; torture.   3 struggle.   *v.*, **ag·o·nized, ag·o·niz·ing.**

**ag·o·niz·ing** (ag′ə nī′zing)   causing great pain or suffering.   *adj.*   —**ag′o·niz′ing·ly,** *adv.*

**ag·o·ny** (ag′ə nē)   1 great pain or suffering: *the agony of acute appendicitis.*   2 death throes.   *n., pl.* **ag·o·nies.**

**a·gou·ti** (ə gü′tē)   a rodent animal resembling a guinea pig but having longer legs: *The agouti lives in South America, Central America, and the West Indies.*   *n., pl.* **a·gou·tis** or **a·gou·ties.**

**a·grar·i·an** (ə grer′ē ən)   1 having to do with land, its use, or its ownership: *Most old countries have had agrarian disputes between landlords and tenants.*   2 a person who favours a new division of land.   3 for the support and advancement of the interests of farmers.   4 agricultural.   1, 3, 4 *adj.*, 2 *n.*

**a·gree** (ə grē′)   1 have the same opinion or opinions: *I agree with you. The two partners usually agreed on important issues.*   2 be alike or be similar to; be in harmony; correspond (*with*): *Your story agrees with mine.*   3 get along well together: *Brothers and sisters don't always agree as well as they should.*   4 consent (*to*): *She agreed to accompany us.*   5 come to an understanding, especially in settling a dispute: *Labour and management agreed on the terms for settling the strike.*   6 admit; concede: *Ya-kee agreed that he had been thoughtless.*   7 in grammar, have the same number, case, gender, or person: *That verb agrees with its subject.*   *v.*, **a·greed, a·gree·ing.**
**agree with,** have a good effect on; suit: *This food does not agree with me; it makes me sick.*

**a·gree·a·bil·i·ty** (ə grē′ə bil′ə tē)   the quality of being AGREEABLE.   *n.*

**a·gree·a·ble** (ə grē′ə bəl)   1 pleasant; pleasing: *agreeable manners.*   2 ready to agree; willing: *agreeable to a suggestion.*   3 in agreement; suitable (*to*): *music agreeable to the occasion.*   *adj.*   —**a·gree′a·ble·ness,** *n.*
—**a·gree′a·bly,** *adv.*

**a·greed** (ə grēd′)   1 arranged by common consent.
2 *pt.* and *pp.* of AGREE.   1 *adj.*, 2 *v.*

**a·gree·ment** (ə grē′mənt)   1 an understanding reached by two or more nations, persons, or groups of persons among themselves: *Nations make treaties and individuals make contracts; both are agreements.*   2 sameness of opinion: *There was perfect agreement between the two friends.*   3 harmony; correspondence.   4 coming to an understanding, especially in settling a dispute: *Every obstacle to agreement has been removed.*   5 in grammar, the correspondence of words with respect to number, case, gender, or person: *There must be agreement in number between the subject and verb in an English sentence.*   *n.*

**Ag. Rep.** or **ag. rep.**   agricultural representative; a government official having the function of advising farmers.

**ag·ri·cul·tur·al** (ag′rə kul′chə rəl)   1 of or having to do with farming: *A hoe is an agricultural implement.*
2 promoting the interests or the study of AGRICULTURE: *an agricultural college.*   *adj.*   —**ag′ri·cul′tur·al·ly,** *adv.*

**ag·ri·cul·tur·al·ist** (ag′rə kul′chə rə list)   AGRICULTURIST.   *n.*

**ag·ri·cul·ture** (ag′rə kul′chər)   farming; the raising of crops and livestock; the science or art of cultivating the ground.   *n.*

**ag·ri·cul·tur·ist** (ag′rə kul′chə rist)   a person trained in AGRICULTURE, especially one who makes it his or her work.   *n.*

**a·gron·o·mist** (ə gron′ə mist)   a person trained in AGRONOMY, especially one who makes it his or her work.   *n.*

**a·gron·o·my** (ə gron′ə mē)   the science of managing farm land; branch of AGRICULTURE dealing with crop production; husbandry.   *n.*

**a·ground** (ə ground′)   1 on the shore; on the bottom in shallow water: *The ship ran aground and stuck in the sand.*   2 on the shore; on the bottom in shallow water: *The vessel is still aground.*   1 *adv.*, 2 *adj.*

**agt.**   agent.

**a·gue** (ā′gyü)   1 a malarial fever with chills and sweating that occur at regular intervals.   2 a fit of shivering; chill.   *n.*

**ah** (ä)   an exclamation of pain, sorrow, regret, pity, admiration, surprise, joy, dislike, contempt, etc.: *The meaning of "ah" varies according to the way it is spoken.*   *interj.*

**a·ha** (ä hä′)   an exclamation of triumph, satisfaction, surprise, joy, etc.   *interj.*

**a·head** (ə hed′)   1 in front; before: *He told me to walk ahead.*   2 forward; onward: *Go ahead with this work.*
3 in advance: *Magnus was ahead of his class in reading.*

**4** in front, as in a race or game: *The Maple Leafs shot ahead 3 to 1.* 1, 2, 4 *adv.*, 3 *adj.*
**be ahead,** be to the good: *When recess was over, Fatima was ahead five points.*
**get ahead,** succeed: *One needs a good education to get ahead today.*
**get ahead of,** **a** pass: *The runner tried hard to get ahead of his rival.* **b** do better than: *He studied hard to get ahead of the rest of the class.*

**a·hem** (ə hem′) a sound made by coughing or clearing the throat: *"Ahem" is sometimes used to attract attention, express doubt, or gain time.* *interj.*

**a·hoy** (ə hoi′) a call used by sailors to attract the attention of persons at a distance: *When sailors call to a ship, they shout, "Ship ahoy!"* *interj.*

**A·hu·ra Maz·da** (ə hùr′ə mä′zdə) In Zoroastrianism, the supreme deity; the wise and good lord of creation; the good spirit of the cosmos.

**aid** (ād) **1** give support to; help: *The Red Cross aids flood victims.* **2** help; support: *When my arm was broken, I could not dress without aid.* **3** a helper; assistant: *A dishwasher is an aid to restaurants.* 1 *v.*, 2, 3 *n.*
☛ *Hom.* AIDE.

**aide** (ād) **1** AIDE-DE-CAMP. **2** assistant; helper: *He works as a nurse's aide.* *n.*
☛ *Hom.* AID.

**aide–de–camp** (ād′də kamp′; *French*, ed də käN′) an officer in the armed services who acts as an assistant to a superior officer: *An aide-de-camp takes and sends messages and acts as a secretary.* *n., pl.* **aides-de-camp.**

**AIDS** (ādz) Acquired Immune Deficiency Syndrome. *n.*

**ai·grette** (ā′gret *or* ā gret′) something in the shape of a tuft of feathers worn as an ornament on the head. *n.*

**ail** (āl) **1** be the matter with; trouble: *What ails the man?* **2** be ill; feel sick: *She is ailing.* *v.*
☛ *Hom.* ALE.

**ai·lan·thus** (ā lan′thəs) a tree with many leaflets and clusters of small, greenish flowers: *The flowers of some ailanthus trees have a disagreeable odour.* *n.*

**ai·ler·on** (ā′lə ron′ *or* ā′lə rən) a small, movable section of an airplane wing near the tip for controlling the side-to-side motion of the airplane while flying. See AIRPLANE for picture. *n.*

**ail·ment** (āl′mənt) an illness; sickness. *n.*

**aim** (ām) **1** point or direct a gun, blow, etc. in order to hit a target: *to aim a gun.* **2** the act of pointing or directing at something: *Jimmy's aim was so poor that he missed the target.* **3** direct acts or words so as to influence a particular person or action: *The coach's remarks were aimed at the girls who had not played fair.* **4** the direction aimed in; line of sighting. **5** *Informal.* intend: *I aim to go.* **6** *Informal.* try; direct one's efforts: *He aims to be helpful.* **7** a purpose; intention: *Kim's aim was to do two years' work in one.* 1, 3, 5 6 *v.*, 2, 4, 7 *n.*

**aim·ing piece** (ā′ming) a metal button or other mark at the front of the barrel of a rifle, pistol, etc., by which to take aim.

**aim·less** (ām′lis) without aim or purpose: *He had gone on an aimless walk but happened to meet some friends.* *adj.* —**aim′less·ly,** *adv.* —**aim′less·ness,** *n.*

**ain't** (ānt) **1** am not; are not; is not. **2** have not; has not. *v.*

# ahem 25 air conditioner

hat, āge, fär; let, ēqual, tėrm; it, īce
hot, ōpen, ôrder; oil, out; cup, pùt, rüle
əbove, takən, pencəl, lemən, circəs
ch, child; ng, long; sh, ship
th, thin; ŦH, then; zh, measure

☛ *Usage.* Through a series of different changes, all the forms cited above (**am not, are not, is not; have not, has not**) have come to be represented by the single form **ain't** which has long been used in English. It is, however, unacceptable to most educated speakers in Canada, and should not be used in formal English.

**air** (er) **1** the mixture of gases that surrounds the earth; atmosphere: *Air consists of nitrogen, oxygen, argon, carbon dioxide, hydrogen, small quantities of neon, helium, and other inert gases.* **2** the space overhead; sky: *Birds fly in the air.* **3** put out in the air; let air through: *to air clothes.* **4** make known; mention publicly: *Do not air your troubles.* **5** a light wind; breeze. **6** a melody; tune: *In music, the air is the leading part.* **7** the general character or appearance of anything: *an air of mystery.* **8** bearing; manner: *The famous man had an air of importance.* **9** the medium through which radio waves travel. **10** conducting or supplying air: *an air duct.* **11** compressing or confining air: *an air valve.* **12** using or worked by compressed air: *an air drill.* **13** relating to aviation; done by means of aircraft: *air photography.* **14** be broadcast on radio or television: *The new program will air next week.* **15 airs,** *pl.* unnatural or affected manners: *Your friends will laugh if you put on airs.* 1, 2, 5-13, 15 *n.*, 3, 4, 14 *v.*
**in the air,** **a** going around: *Wild rumours were in the air.* **b** uncertain.
**on the air,** broadcasting; being broadcast.
**take the air,** **a** go outdoors; take a walk or ride. **b** start broadcasting.
**up in the air,** **a** *Informal.* uncertain: *Our plans for the party are still up in the air.* **b** *Informal.* very angry or excited.
**walk on air,** be very happy or pleased.
☛ *Hom.* ERR (er), HEIR.

**air base** a headquarters and airfield for military operations and training involving aircraft.

**air bladder** in some animals and plants, a sac containing air: *Many fish have an air bladder that acts as an aid in breathing or hearing or helps the fish to maintain its buoyancy in the water.*

**air·borne** (er′bôrn′) **1** carried through the air: *airborne seeds, airborne bacteria.* **2** transported by aircraft: *airborne troops.* **3** in the air; in an aircraft, after taking off; flying: *After another delay, we were finally airborne.* *adj.*

**air brake** a brake operated by a piston or pistons worked by compressed air.

**Air Command** *Cdn.* the branch of the Canadian Armed Forces having to do with aircraft, formerly known as the Royal Canadian Air Force.

**air–con·di·tion** (er′kən dish′ən) **1** supply with the equipment for AIR CONDITIONING. **2** treat air by means of AIR CONDITIONING. *v.*

**air–con·di·tioned** (er′kən dish′ənd) having AIR CONDITIONING. *adj.*

**air conditioner** an apparatus used to AIR-CONDITION a room, building, train, etc.

**air conditioning** (er′kən dish′ə ning) a means of treating air in buildings, rooms, trains, etc. to regulate its temperature and amount of moisture and to free it from dust.

**air–cool** (er′kül′) 1 force air onto motor cylinders to remove heat produced by combustion, friction, etc. 2 remove heat in a room by blowing cool air in. *v.*

**air·craft** (er′kraft′) 1 a machine for air navigation that is supported in air by buoyancy (such as a balloon) or by dynamic action (such as an airplane); an airplane, airship, or balloon. 2 such machines collectively or as a class; airplanes, airships or balloons. *n., pl.* **air·craft.**

**aircraft carrier** a warship having a large, flat deck designed as a base for airplanes.

**air cushion** 1 an inflatable rubber or rubberized casing for use as a cushion or pad. 2 the layer of air under pressure that supports a HOVERCRAFT.

**air–cushion vehicle** (er′kush′ən) HOVERCRAFT.

**air drop** a system of dropping food, supplies, etc. from aircraft, especially to allies who are caught behind enemy lines, living in occupied territory, etc.

**Aire·dale** (er′dāl′) a breed of large terrier dog having a wiry tan coat with dark markings on the back and sides. *n.*

**air·field** (er′fēld′) the landing field of an airport. *n.*

**air·foil** (er′foil′) any surface, such as a wing, rudder, etc., designed to help lift or control an aircraft. *n.*

**air force** Often, **Air Force,** the branch of the armed forces that uses aircraft.

**air gun** a gun worked by COMPRESSED AIR.

**air hole** 1 a hole that allows air to pass through. 2 a hole in the ice covering a body of water, often used as a breathing hole by seals, muskrats, etc. 3 AIR POCKET.

**air·i·ly** (er′ə lē) in an AIRY manner; lightly. *adv.*

**air·i·ness** (er′ē nis) an AIRY quality. *n.*

**air·ing** (er′ing) 1 exposure to air for drying, warming, etc.; putting out in the air; letting air through: *I gave my wet coat a thorough airing.* 2 a walk, ride, or drive in the open air. 3 exposure to public discussion, criticism, etc.: *His suggestion is due for an airing at the next meeting. n.*

**air lane** a regular route used by aircraft.

**air·less** (er′lis) 1 without fresh air; stuffy. 2 without a breeze; still. *adj.*

**air·lift** (er′lift′) 1 a system of using aircraft to transport passengers and convey freight to a place when land approaches are closed: *an airlift to the flooded city.* 2 something transported by such a system. 3 transport by such a system. 1, 2 *n.,* 3 *v.*

**air·line** (er′līn′) 1 a company operating a system of transportation by means of aircraft. 2 the system itself. 3 of or having to do with an airline: *airline schedules. n.*

**air·lin·er** (er′līn′ər) a large airplane operated by an airline for carrying passengers. *n.*

**air lock** an airtight compartment in which the air pressure can be adjusted, as between the outside air and the working compartment of a CAISSON. See CAISSON for picture.

**air mail** 1 mail sent by aircraft. 2 a system of sending mail by aircraft.

**air–mail** (er′māl′) send or transport letters or packages by AIR MAIL. *v.*

**air·man** (er′mən) 1 a man connected with flying, especially as a pilot, crew member, or ground technician. 2 formerly, in the ROYAL CANADIAN AIR FORCE, a serviceman below the rank of corporal. *n., pl.* **air·men** (-mən).

**air mattress** an inflatable rubber or rubberized casing designed for use as a mattress: *Air mattresses are often used by campers.*

**air–mind·ed** (er′mīn′did) interested in aviation or aircraft. *adj.* —**air′-mind′ed·ness,** *n.*

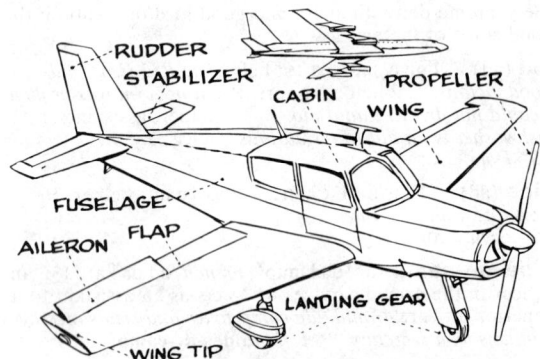

Airplanes: a small, propeller-driven plane and a jet airliner.

**air·plane** (er′plān′) a mechanically driven heavier-than-air aircraft, supported in flight by the action of the air flowing past or thrusting upward on its fixed wings. *n.*

**air pocket** a current or condition in the air that causes a sudden, short drop in the altitude of an aircraft.

**air·port** (er′pôrt′) a place where aircraft regularly come to discharge or take on passengers or freight: *An airport usually has several runways, buildings for passengers and staff, and facilities for sheltering, repairing, and servicing aircraft. n.*

**air pressure** 1 the force exerted by air confined in a restricted space. 2 atmospheric pressure: *Winds are caused by the flow of air from an area of high air pressure to an area of low air pressure.*

**air pump** an apparatus for forcing air in or drawing air out of something.

**air raid** an attack by aircraft carrying bombs.

**air rifle** a rifle that is worked by COMPRESSED AIR and shoots a single pellet or dart.

**air sac** an air-filled space in the body of a bird, connected with the lungs.

**air·ship** (er′ship′) a balloon that can be steered, usually motorized; DIRIGIBLE (def. 1). *n.*

**air·sick** (er′sik′) sick as a result of travelling by air. *adj.* —**air′sick′ness,** *n.*

**air speed** the speed of an aircraft measured in relation to the movement of the air.

**air·strip** (er′strip′) a paved or cleared strip for airplanes to land and take off; temporary airfield. *n.*

**air·tight** (er′tīt′) **1** so tight that no air or gas can get in or out. **2** having no weak points open to an opponent's attack. *adj.*

**air·waves** (er′wāvz′) the medium by which radio and television signals are transmitted. *n. pl.*

**air·way** (er′wā′) **1** a route for aircraft. **2** a passage for air, such as a shaft in a mine. **3** a particular radio frequency for broadcasting. *n.*

**air·ways** (er′wāz′) AIRLINE. *n.*

**air·wo·man** (er′wum′ən) **1** a woman who pilots an aircraft. **2** formerly, in the ROYAL CANADIAN AIR FORCE, a woman holding a rank below that of corporal. *n., pl.* **air·wo·men** (-wim′ən).

**air·wor·thy** (er′wėr′ᴛнē) fit or safe for service in the air. *adj.* —**air′wor′thi·ness,** *n.*

**air·y** (er′ē) **1** like air; not solid or substantial. **2** light as air; graceful; delicate: *an airy melody.* **3** light-hearted; happy: *airy laughter.* **4** open to currents of air; breezy: *a large, airy room.* **5** reaching high into the air; lofty. **6** of air; in the air: *birds and other airy creatures.* **7** unnatural; affected. *adj.,* **air·i·er, air·i·est.**
☛ *Hom.* AERIE, EYRIE (er′ē).

**aisle** (īl) **1** the passage between rows of seats in a hall, theatre, school, etc. **2** the part of a Christian church set off by pillars at the side of the nave, choir, or transept. See BASILICA for picture. **3** any long or narrow passageway, such as the space between shelves of goods in a supermarket. *n.*
☛ *Hom.* I'LL, ISLE.

**a·jar** (ə jär′) **1** slightly open: *Leave the door ajar.* **2** slightly open: *The gate was ajar.* **1** *adv.,* **2** *adj.*

**a·ji·va** (ə jē′və) in Jainism: **1** all that is not JIVA, or living soul. **2** materialism. *n.*

**a.k.a.** also known as.

**A·ke·la** (ə kē′lə *or* ə kā′lə) CUBMASTER. *n.*
☛ *Etym.* From *Akela*, the Lone Wolf, the leader of the wolf pack in Rudyard Kipling's *The Jungle Book.*

**a·kim·bo** (ə kim′bō) **1** with the hands on the hips and the elbows bent outward: *to stand akimbo.* **2** with the hands on the hips and the elbows bent outward: *The boys were akimbo.* **1** *adv.,* **2** *adj.*

**a·kin** (ə kin′) **1** related: *Your aunt is akin to you.* **2** alike; similar: *The friends are akin in their love of sports. adj.*

**–al** a suffix meaning: **1** of; like; having the nature of: *Natural means of or like nature. Ornamental means having the nature of ornament.* **2** the act of _____ ing: *Refusal means the act of refusing.*

**Al** aluminum.

**al·a·bas·ter** (al′ə bas′tər *or* al′ə bäs′tər) **1** a smooth, white, translucent mineral, a variety of GYPSUM: *Alabaster is often carved into ornaments and vases.* *n.*

**à la carte** (a′lə kärt′; *French,* ä lä kärt′) according to the menu, on which each dish is priced separately. Compare with TABLE D'HÔTE.

**a·lac·ri·ty** (ə lak′rə tē) **1** brisk and eager action; liveliness: *Although the woman was very old, she still moved with alacrity.* **2** cheerful willingness. *n.*

**à la mode, a la mode,** or **a·la·mode** (al′ə mōd′ *or* ä′lə mōd′) **1** according to the prevailing fashion; in style. **2** in a certain way: *Desserts à la mode are served with ice cream. Beef à la mode is cooked with vegetables. adv.*

# airtight 27 album

hat, āge, fär; let, ēqual, tėrm; it, īce
hot, ōpen, ôrder; oil, out; cup, put, rüle
əbove, takən, pencəl, lemən, circəs
ch, child; ng, long; sh, ship
th, thin; ᴛн, then; zh, measure

**a·larm** (ə lärm′) **1** sudden fear, fright; excitement caused by fear of danger. **2** fill with sudden fear; frighten: *Francine was alarmed because her friends were so long in returning.* **3** a warning of approaching danger. **4** something that gives such a warning: *a fire alarm.* **5** warn anyone of approaching danger. **6** a call to arms or action: *The sentry sounded the alarm when the attack began.* **7** a device that makes a noise to warn or awaken people. **1, 3, 4, 6, 7** *n.,* **2, 5** *v.*

**alarm clock** a clock that can be set to ring a bell, etc. at any desired time, especially to waken people from sleep.

**a·larm·ing** (ə lär′ming) that alarms; frightening. *adj.* —**a·larm′ing·ly,** *adv.*

**a·larm·ist** (ə lär′mist) a person who is easily alarmed or alarms others needlessly or on very slight grounds. *n.*

**a·las** (ə las′) an exclamation of sorrow, grief, regret, pity, or dread. *interj.*

**A·las·ka cedar** or **cypress** (ə las′kə) YELLOW CYPRESS

**Alaska Highway** a highway that extends from Dawson Creek, in British Columbia, to Fairbanks, Alaska.

**al·ba·core** (al′bə kôr′) a long-finned, edible fish related to the tuna, found in the Atlantic Ocean. *n., pl.* **al·ba·core** or **al·ba·cores.**

**Al·ba·ni·an** (al bā′nē ən) **1** of or having to do with Albania, a country in southeastern Europe, its people, or their language. **2** a native or inhabitant of Albania. **3** the language of Albania: *Albanian is an Indo-European language.* **1** *adj.,* **2, 3** *n.*

**al·ba·tross** (al′bə tros′) any of various large webfooted sea birds, related to the petrel, that can fly long distances. It is 1.2 metres long and has a wingspan of 3.7 metres. *n.*

**al·be·it** (ol bē′it) although; even though. *conj.*

**Al·ber·tan** (al bėr′tən) **1** a native or long-term resident of Alberta, one of the Prairie Provinces. **2** of or having to do with Alberta. **1** *n.,* **2** *adj.*

**al·bi·nism** (al′bə niz′əm) the absence of colour; condition of being an ALBINO. *n.*

**al·bi·no** (al bī′nō *or* al bē′nō) **1** a person who from birth lacks normal pigment and therefore has a pale, milky skin, very light or white hair, and pink eyes. **2** a plant or animal lacking normal colour, especially an animal having white hair or fur and red eyes. *n., pl.* **al·bi·nos.**

**al·bum** (al′bəm) **1** a book with blank pages for holding pictures, stamps, autographs, etc. **2** one or more discs or tape recordings, together with a holder or case in which they are sold and any additional material included in the package, such as lyrics of songs, posters, etc. **3** the disc, recording, or set itself. **4** the holder or case of such a disc, recording, or set. **5** a collection in the form of a book of pictures, musical compositions, souvenirs, etc.: *We made an album of our trip.* *n.*

**al·bu·men** (al byü′mən or al′byə mən) egg white, consisting mostly of ALBUMIN dissolved in water. *n.*
☛ *Hom.* ALBUMIN (for the first pronunciation of **albumen**).

**al·bu·min** (al byü′mən) the protein in egg white and in many other animal and plant tissues and juices: *Albumin is soluble in water and can be coagulated by heat.* *n.*
☛ *Hom.* ALBUMEN (al byü′mən).

**Al·can Highway** (al′kan) ALASKA HIGHWAY.

**al·che·mist** (al′kə mist) in the Middle Ages, a person who practised ALCHEMY (def. 1): *Alchemists tried to turn base metals into gold and to find the elixir of life.* *n.*

**al·che·my** (al′kə mē) **1** a combination of chemistry and magic, studied in the Middle Ages. **2** a seeming magic power or process for changing one thing into another. *n.*

**al·co·hol** (al′kə hol′) **1** a colourless liquid that acts as a drug and is a part of wine, beer, whisky, gin, and other fermented and distilled liquids; grain alcohol; ethyl alcohol: *Alcohol is used in medicines, in manufacturing, and as a fuel.* **2** any strong drink containing this liquid. **3** any of a group of similar organic compounds: *Wood alcohol (methyl alcohol) is very poisonous.* *n.*

**al·co·hol·ic** (al′kə hol′ik) **1** of alcohol. **2** containing alcohol: *alcoholic liquor.* **3** suffering from the excessive use of alcoholic liquors. **4** a person who suffers from ALCOHOLISM. 1–3 *adj.*, 4 *n.*

**al·co·hol·ism** (al′kə hol iz′əm) **1** a disease that has as its chief symptom the inability to moderate the drinking of alcoholic liquors. **2** a diseased condition caused by drinking too much alcoholic liquor. *n.*

An alcove

**al·cove** (al′kōv) a recessed section of a room; nook: *We always have our breakfast in an alcove off the kitchen.* *n.*

**Ald.** Alderman.

**al·der** (ol′dər) any of several trees and shrubs that usually grow in wet land and have clusters of catkins that develop into small, woody cones. *n.*

**al·der·per·son** (ol′dər pėr′sən) a member of the governing body of a city, elected by the people of a particular district or ward of the city: *Our city council consists of the mayor and ten alderpersons.* *n., pl.* **al·der·per·sons.**

**Aldm.** Alderman.

**ale** (āl) a strong beer made from malt and hops. *n.*
☛ *Hom.* AIL.

**a·lee** (ə lē′) **1** toward the side of a ship that is away from the wind: *The small boat came alee.* "Hard alee!" was the captain's order. **2** on the side of a ship that is away from the wind: *Our cabin is alee.* 1 *adv.*, 2 *adj.*

**a·lert** (ə lėrt′) **1** watchful; wide-awake: *A good hunting dog is alert to every sound and movement in the field.* **2** brisk; active; nimble: *A sparrow is very alert in its movements.* **3** a signal warning of an air attack or other approaching danger. **4** the period of time in which this warning is in effect. **5** a signal to troops, etc. to be ready for action. **6** warn of an attack or other danger: *As the storm approached, police tried to alert motorists through radio announcements.* 1, 2 *adj.*, 3–5 *n.*, 6 *v.*
—**a·lert′ly**, *adv.*
**on the alert**, watchful; ready at any instant for what is coming.

**a·lert·ness** (ə lėrt′nis) **1** watchfulness. **2** liveliness; nimbleness. *n.*

**ale·wife** (āl′wīf′) a food fish of the herring family found in sea and fresh waters of eastern North America; GASPEREAU. *n., pl.* **ale·wives.**

**Al·ex·an·dri·an** (al′ig zan′drē ən) **1** of or having to do with Alexander the Great. **2** of or having to do with Alexandria, a seaport in Egypt, or the culture that flourished there in ancient times. *adj.*

**al·fal·fa** (al fal′fə) a plant grown as food for horses and cattle, having deep roots, cloverlike leaves, and bluish-purple flowers: *Alfalfa can be cut several times a season and then dried as hay.* *n.*

**al·ga** (al′gə) sing. of ALGAE. *n.*

**al·gae** (al′jē or al′jī) a group of water plants that can make their own food, and that have chlorophyl but not true stems, roots, or leaves: *Some algae are single-celled and form scum on rocks; others, such as the seaweeds, are very large.* *n. pl.*

**al·ge·bra** (al′jə brə) that part of mathematics in which letters or other symbols are used to represent any one of a set of numbers. The symbols and numbers are combined by adding, subtracting, etc. to form expressions that are used in equations and inequations for representing problem situations. Algebra is also used to illustrate properties of numbers; for example, $x \times 0 = 0$ states that the product of $x$ (any number) and zero is zero. *n.*

**al·ge·bra·ic** (al′jə brā′ik) of ALGEBRA; used in algebra: $(a + b)(a - b) = a^2 - b^2$ is an algebraic statement. *adj.* —**al′ge·bra′i·cal·ly**, *adv.*

**Al·ge·ri·an** (al jē′rē ən) **1** of or having to do with Algeria, a country in North Africa. **2** a native or inhabitant of Algeria or of Algiers, its capital. 1 *adj.*, 2 *n.*

**Al·gon·ki·an** (al gong′kē ən) ALGONQUIAN. *n.*

**Al·gon·kin** (al gong′kin) ALGONQUIN. *n.*

**Al·gon·qui·an** (al gong′kē ən or al gong′kwē ən) **1** a stock or family of languages spoken by a large number of confederacies, tribes, and bands of First Nations and Native American peoples who traditionally occupied much of central and eastern North America, including large areas from Labrador south to Carolina and from the Atlantic west to the Rocky Mountains. Among the languages included in this family are Abenaki, Blackfoot, Cree, Malecite, Micmac, Ojibwa, and Ottawa. **2** a member of any of the First Nations or Native American peoples speaking one of these languages. **3** of, having to do with, or referring to these peoples or their languages. **4** ALGONQUIN (def. 1). 1, 2, 4 *n.*, 3 *adj.*

**Al·gon·quin** (al gong′kwln *or* al gong′kin)   **1** a member of a First Nations living in eastern Ontario and Quebec.   **2** a dialect of Ojibwa, spoken by these people.   **3** of, having to do with, or referring to these people or their language.   *1, 2 n., 3 adj.*

**al·go·rithm** (al′gə riTH′əm)   in mathematics, any special procedure or set of rules for solving a certain type of problem.   *n.*

**a·li·as** (ā′lē əs)   **1** an assumed name; other name: *The spy's real name was Carlos, but he sometimes went by the alias of Pino.*   **2** otherwise called; with the assumed name of: *The thief's name was Wong, alias Chung.*   *1 n., pl.* **a·li·as·es;**   *2 adv.*

**al·i·bi** (al′ə bī′)   **1** the plea or fact that a person accused of an offence was somewhere else when the offence was committed.   **2** *Informal.*   an excuse.   **3** *Informal.*   make an excuse.   *1, 2 n., pl.* **al·i·bis;** *3 v.,* **al·i·bied, al·i·bi·ing.**

**a·li·en** (ā′lē ən *or* ā′ lyən)   **1** a person who is not a citizen of the country in which he lives.   **2** a foreigner; stranger.   **3** a supposed being from some other planet.   **4** of or by another country; foreign: *an alien language, alien domination.*   **5** unfamiliar; strange: *alien ideas.*   *1–3 n., 4, 5 adj.*
**alien to,**   not in agreement with; quite different from: *Unkindness is alien to her nature.*

**a·li·en·ate** (ā′lē ə nāt′ *or* ā′lyə nāt′)   **1** turn away in feeling or affection; make unfriendly: *Her folly alienated her friends.*   **2** transfer the ownership of property to another: *Enemy property was alienated during the war.*   *v.,* **a·li·en·at·ed, a·li·en·at·ing.**

**a·li·en·a·tion** (ā′lē ə nā′shən *or* ā′lyə nā′shən)   a turning away in feeling or affection; making unfriendly.   *n.*

**a·li·en·ist** (ā′lē ə nist *or* ā′lyə nist)   a psychiatrist, especially one who testifies in court.   *n.*

**a·light¹** (ə līt′)   **1** get down; get off: *to alight from a horse.*   **2** come down from the air and settle; come down from flight: *The bird alighted on our window sill.*   *v.,* **a·light·ed, a·light·ing.**
**alight on,**   come upon by chance; happen to find.

**a·light²** (ə līt′)   **1** on fire; lighted up: *The candle continued alight.*   **2** on fire; lighted up: *Her face was alight with happiness.*   *1 adv., 2 adj.*

**a·lign** (ə līn′)   **1** bring into line or ALIGNMENT (def. 1): *to align the sights of a gun with the target, to align the wheels of a car.*   **2** place in a line: *Lombardy poplars were aligned along the drive.*   **3** form an alliance with or against a particular party, group, cause, etc.: *They aligned themselves against the supporters of capital punishment.*   *v.* Also, **aline.**

Alignment

**a·lign·ment** (ə līn′mənt)   **1** arrangement in a straight line: *The troops were in perfect alignment.*   **2** the line or lines formed in this way.   **3** adjustment to a line: *The sights of the rifle were in alignment with the target.*   **4** a joining together of persons, groups, nations, etc. for a particular purpose.   *n.* Also, **alinement.**

**a·like** (ə līk′)   **1** like one another; similar: *These twins are very much alike.*   **2** in the same way: *Robert and his father walk alike.*   **3** similarly; equally: *to share alike.*   *1 adj., 2, 3 adv.*

**al·i·ment** (al′ə mənt)   food; nourishment.   *n.*

**al·i·men·ta·ry** (al′ə men′tə rē)   **1** having to do with food and nutrition.   **2** nourishing; nutritious.   **3** providing support or sustenance.   *adj.*

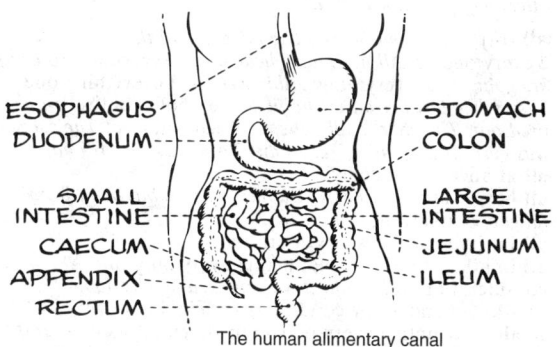
The human alimentary canal

**alimentary canal**   the passage in the body through which food passes while it is being digested: *The alimentary canal extends from the mouth, through the esophagus, stomach, and intestines to the anus.*

**al·i·mo·ny** (al′ə mō′nē)   **1** in law, money paid by a person for the support of his or her spouse under a separation agreement.   Compare with MAINTENANCE (def. 4a).   **2** *Informal.*   money paid for the support of a former spouse after divorce.   *n.*

**a·line** (ə līn′)   See ALIGN.   *v.,* **a·lined, a·lin·ing.**

**a·line·ment** (ə līn′mənt)   See ALIGNMENT.   *n.*

**al·i·quot** (al′ə kwət)   able to divide a number without leaving a remainder: *3 is an aliquot part of 12.*   *adj.*

**a·live** (ə līv′)   **1** living: *Was the snake alive or dead?*   **2** in continued activity or operation: *Keep the principles of liberty alive.*   **3** of all living: *the happiest man alive.*   **4** active; lively; brisk.   *adj.*   —**a·live′ness,** *n.*
**alive to,**   noticing; awake to; sensitive to: *Are you alive to what is going on?*
**alive with,**   full of; swarming with: *The streets were alive with people.*
**look alive!**   hurry up! be quick!
☛ *Usage.*   Not used before a noun.

**a·liz·a·rin** (ə liz′ə rin)   a red dye prepared from COAL TAR, formerly obtained from MADDER.   *n.* Also, **alizarine.**

**a·liz·a·rine** (ə liz′ə rin *or* ə liz′ə rēn′)   See ALIZARIN.   *n.*

**al·ka·li** (al′kə lī′)   **1** in chemistry, any base or

HYDROXIDE that is soluble in water, neutralizes acids and forms salts with them, and turns red litmus blue: *Lye and ammonia are alkalis.* **2** any salt or mixture of salts that neutralizes acids: *Some desert soils contain much alkali.* *n., pl.* **al·ka·lis** *or* **al·ka·lies.** Compare with ACID.

**al·ka·line** (al′kə līn′ *or* al′kə lin) **1** of or like an ALKALI. **2** containing an ALKALI: *The soil around the slough was alkaline.* *adj.* Compare with ACIDIC.

**al·ka·lin·i·ty** (al′kə lin′ə tē) an ALKALINE quality or condition. *n.*

**al·ka·lize** (al′kə līz′) make ALKALINE. *v.,* **al·ka·lized, al·ka·liz·ing.** —**al′ka·li·za′tion,** *n.*

**al·ka·loid** (al′kə loid′) a substance found in or obtained from plants, that resembles an ALKALI and contains nitrogen: *Many alkaloids are drugs, such as cocaine, strychnine, morphine, and quinine. Alkaloids are often very poisonous.* *n.*

**all** (ol) **1** the whole of: *The mice ate all the cheese.* **2** every one of: *All dogs have heads.* **3** everyone: *All of us are going.* **4** everything: *All is well.* **5** everything one has: *Sylvie lost her all in the fire.* **6** wholly; entirely: *all tired out. The cake is all gone.* **7** each; apiece: *The score was even at forty all.* 1, 2 *adj.,* 3 4 *pron.,* 5 *n.,* 6 7 *adv.*
**all at once,** suddenly.
**all but,** almost; nearly: *Damien was all but dead from fatigue, but he struggled on.*
**all in,** *Informal.* weary; worn out.
**all in all,** on the whole; taking everything into consideration: *All in all, it was an exciting election.*
**at all,** **a** under any conditions. **b** in any way.
**in all,** counting every person or thing; altogether: *100 men in all.*
☛ Hom. AWL.

**Al·lah** (a lä′) the Moslem name for the one Supreme Being, or God. *n.*

**all-a·round** (ol′ə round′) ALL-ROUND. *adj.*

**al·lay** (ə lā′) **1** put at rest; quiet: *His fears were allayed by the news of the safety of his family.* **2** relieve; check: *Her fever was allayed by the medicine.* **3** make less; weaken. *v.,* **al·layed, al·lay·ing.**

**all clear** a signal indicating the end of an air raid or some other danger.

**al·le·ga·tion** (al′ə gā′shən) **1** an assertion without proof: *Sheina makes so many wild allegations that no one will believe her.* **2** assertion: *The lawyer's allegation was proved.* *n.*

**al·lege** (ə lej′) **1** assert without proof. **2** state positively; assert; declare: *This man alleges that his watch has been stolen.* **3** give or bring forward as a reason, argument, or excuse: *Vladimir was tardy this morning and alleges that his bus was late.* *v.,* **al·leged, al·leg·ing.** —**al·leg′er,** *n.*

**al·leged** (ə lejd′) **1** asserted without proof: *The alleged theft never really happened.* **2** asserted; declared. **3** brought forward as a reason. *adj.*

**al·leg·ed·ly** (ə lej′id lē) according to what is or has been ALLEGED. *adv.*

**al·le·giance** (ə lē′jəns) **1** the loyalty owed by citizens to their country or by subjects to their ruler. **2** loyalty; faithfulness to a person, cause, etc. that is entitled to obedience or honour: *We owe allegiance to our friends.* *n.*

**al·le·gor·i·cal** (al′ə gô′rə kəl) explaining or teaching something by a story; using ALLEGORY. *adj.* —**al′le·gor′i·cal·ly,** *adv.*

**al·le·go·ry** (al′ə gô′rē) a story that is told to explain or teach something; a long and complicated story with an underlying meaning different from the surface meaning: *Bunyan's The Pilgrim's Progress is an allegory. The incidents of an allegory may stand for political, spiritual, or romantic situations; its characters may be types (such as "Mr. Wiseman") or personifications (such as "Courtesy" or "Jealousy").* *n., pl.* **al·le·go·ries.**

**al·le·gro** (ə lā′grō *or* ə leg′rō) **1** in music, quick; lively. **2** in allegro time. **3** such a part in a piece of music. 1 *adj.,* 2 *adv.,* 3 *n., pl.* **al·le·gros.**

**al·le·lu·ia** (al′ə lü′yə) HALLELUJAH. *n.*

**al·ler·gen** (al′ər jən) a substance that causes an ALLERGIC reaction. *n.*

**al·ler·gic** (ə lèr′jik) **1** having an ALLERGY; extremely sensitive to some substance: *Some people who are allergic to eggs cannot eat them without breaking into a rash.* **2** of or caused by ALLERGY: *Hay fever is an allergic reaction.* **3** *Informal.* having a strong dislike: *I'm allergic to studying.* *adj.*

**al·ler·gy** (al′ər jē) **1** any unusual sensitiveness to a particular substance: *Hay fever and asthma are often caused by allergies to certain pollens and dusts.* **2** *Informal.* strong dislike. *n., pl.* **al·ler·gies.**

**al·le·vi·ate** (ə lē′vē āt′) make easier to endure; relieve; lessen: *Heat often alleviates pain.* *v.,* **al·le·vi·at·ed, al·le·vi·at·ing.** —**al·le′vi·a′tor,** *n.*

**al·le·vi·a·tion** (ə lē′vē ā′shən) **1** the act of alleviating. **2** the condition of being ALLEVIATED. **3** something that ALLEVIATES. *n.*

**al·le·vi·a·tive** (ə lē′vē′ə tiv *or* ə lē′vē ā′tiv) alleviating. *adj.*

**al·ley**[1] (al′ē) **1** a narrow back street in a city or town; alleyway. **2** a path in a park or garden, bordered by trees. **3** a long, narrow, enclosed place for bowling. **4** a building having a number of alleys for bowling. *n., pl.* **al·leys.**

**al·ley**[2] (al′ē) **1** a large, white or coloured, glass marble used to shoot at the other marbles in a game. **2 alleys,** any game played with such marbles. *n., pl.* **al·leys.**

**al·ley·way** (al′ē wā′) **1** an alley in a city or town. **2** a narrow passageway. *n.*

**All Fools' Day** April 1, APRIL FOOLS' DAY.

**all fours** all four legs of an animal.
**on all fours,** on hands and knees: *He went on all fours to amuse the baby.*

**al·li·ance** (ə lī′əns) **1** a formal bond between nations, families, etc. that agree to help each other; joining of interests: *A joining by treaty of the interests of separate nations is an alliance.* **2** the nations, persons, etc. belonging to such a union. *n.*

**al·lied** (ə līd′ *or* al′īd) **1** united by agreement: *allied nations.* **2** associated; connected: *allied banks. Reading and listening are allied activities.* **3** similar in structure or descent; related: *The dog and the wolf are allied animals.* *adj.*

**Al·lied** (ə līd′ *or* al′īd) of or by the ALLIES. *adj.*

**Al·lies** (al′īz *or* ə līz′) **1** the countries that fought against Germany and Austria-Hungary in World War I. **2** the countries that fought against Germany, Italy, and Japan in World War II. *n. pl.*

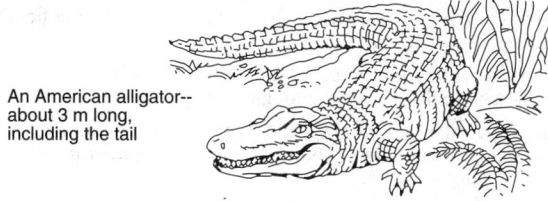
An American alligator—about 3 m long, including the tail

**al·li·ga·tor** (al′ə gā′tər) **1** either of two species of reptile closely related to the crocodile, having a long, thick body and tail, four short legs, powerful jaws with sharp teeth, and eyes and nostrils set on top of the skull. The two species are the American alligator of the southeastern United States and the Chinese alligator of the Yangtze River Valley in China. **2** leather made from the hide of an alligator. **3** made of this leather: *alligator shoes.* *n.*
☛ **Etym.** **Alligator** comes from the Spanish *el lagarto* (the lizard) which in turn goes back to L. *lacertus* (lizard).

**alligator pear** AVOCADO.

**all–im·por·tant** (ol′im pôr′tənt) essential; extremely important. *adj.*

**al·lit·er·ate** (ə lit′ə rāt′) **1** have the same first sound. **2** use ALLITERATION. *v.,* **al·lit·er·at·ed, al·lit·er·at·ing.**

**al·lit·er·a·tion** (ə lit′ə rā′shən) the repetition of the same first sound in a group of words or a line of poetry. *The sun sank slowly* shows alliteration of *s.* *n.*

**al·lit·er·a·tive** (ə lit′ə rə tiv *or* ə lit′ə rā′tiv) having words beginning with the same sound. *adj.* —**al·lit′er·a′tive·ly,** *adv.* —**al·lit′er·a′tive·ness,** *n.*

**al·lo·cate** (al′ə kāt′) **1** ASSIGN OR ALLOT: *The government allocated millions of dollars among many colleges.* **2** locate; fix the place of. *v.,* **al·lo·cat·ed, al·lo·cat·ing.**

**al·lo·ca·tion** (al′ə kā′shən) a distribution; assignment; ALLOTMENT. *n.*

**al·lop·a·thy** (ə lop′ə thē) a method of treating a disease by using remedies to produce effects different from those caused by the disease treated: *Allopathy is the opposite of* HOMEOPATHY. *n.*

**al·lot** (ə lot′) **1** divide and distribute in parts or shares: *The profits have all been allotted among the owners of the company.* **2** give as a share; assign: *The principal allotted each class a part in the end of term program.* *v.,* **al·lot·ted, al·lot·ting.**

**al·lot·ment** (ə lot′mənt) **1** a division and distribution in parts or shares: *The allotment was made on Monday.* **2** a share: *Your allotment is one dollar.* *n.*

**al·lo·trope** (al′ə trōp′) a different form of the same element: *Graphite and diamond are allotropes.* *n.*

**al·lo·trop·ic** (al′ə trōp′ik) occurring in two or more forms that differ in physical and chemical properties but not in the kind of atoms of which they are composed: *Oxygen gas and ozone are allotropic forms of the element oxygen; they are gases composed of the same kind of atoms, but ozone is more active than oxygen, is heavier, and has an irritating odour.* *adj.*

hat, āge, fär; let, ēqual, tėrm; it, īce
hot, ōpen, ôrder; oil, out; cup, put, rüle
əbove, takən, pencəl, lemən, circəs
ch, child; ng, long; sh, ship
th, thin; ᵺ, then; zh, measure

**all out**
**go all out,** use all one's resources; go the whole way, without limiting oneself: *They decided to go all out and hire a band for the dance.*

**all–out** (ol′out′) involving one's entire resources; total; complete: *an all-out effort to win, all-out war.* *adj.*

**all·o·ver** (ol′ō′vər) **1** covering the whole surface. **2** having a pattern that is repeated over the whole surface. *adj.*

**al·low** (ə lou′) **1** let; permit: *The class was not allowed to leave until the bell rang.* **2** let have; give: *His parents allow him $10 a week as spending money.* **3** admit; acknowledge; recognize: *The judge allowed the claim of the man whose property was damaged.* **4** add to make up for something: *The trip will cost you only $50; but you ought to allow $10 more for additional expenses.* *v.*
—**al·low′er,** *n.*
**allow for,** take into consideration; provide for: *She purposely made the dress large to allow for shrinking.*
**allow of,** permit; leave room for; be capable of: *Her answer allows of no reply.*

**al·low·a·ble** (ə lou′ə bəl) ALLOWED by law or by a person in authority; permitted by the rules of the game; not forbidden: *In some parks it is allowable to walk on the grass.* *adj.* —**al·low′a·ble·ness,** *n.*
—**al·low′a·bly,** *adv.*

**al·low·ance** (ə lou′əns) **1** a limited share set apart; a definite portion or amount given out: *My weekly allowance is $10.* **2** the amount added or subtracted to make up for something; discount: *The salesman offered us an allowance of $4 000 on our old car; so we got a $20 000 car for $16 000.* **3** an allowing; conceding: *allowance of a claim.* **4** tolerance: *allowance of slavery.* *n.*
**make allowance for,** take into consideration; allow for: *You must make allowance for the wishes of others.*

**al·loy** (al′oi *for noun,* ə loi′ *for verb*) **1** a metal made by mixing and fusing two or more metals, or a metal and some other substance: *Alloys are often harder, lighter, and stronger than the pure metals. Brass is an alloy of copper and zinc.* **2** make into an alloy. **3** an inferior metal mixed with a more valuable one: *This gold is not pure; there is some alloy in it.* **4** make less valuable by mixing with a cheaper metal. **5** something bad mixed with something better; any injurious addition: *The only alloy in our enjoyment of the vacation was the rainy weather.* **6** make worse by mixing with something bad; debase: *Her happiness was alloyed by the thought of my grief.* 1, 3, 5 *n.,* 2, 4, 6 *v.*

**all–pur·pose** (ol′pėr′pəs) able to be used for any end: *all-purpose flour.* *adj.*

**all right** **1** all correct: *The answers were all right.* **2** satisfactory: *The work was not well done; but it was all right.* **3** yes: *"Will you come with me?" "All right."* **4** in good health; well: *Nicole said she was feeling all right.* **5** in a satisfactory way: *The engine seemed to be working all right.*
☛ *Usage.* See ALRIGHT.

**all-round** (ol′round′) not limited or specialized; able to do many things; useful in many ways. *adj.*

**all·spice** (ol′spīs′) **1** a spice made from the dried unripe berries of the West Indian PIMENTO tree: *Allspice has a flavour similar to cinnamon, nutmeg, and cloves.* **2** the berry of the PIMENTO tree. **3** the tree itself. *n.*

**all–star** (ol′stär′) **1** made up of the best players or performers: *the all-star team.* **2** one of the best players or performers. 1 *adj.*, 2 *n.*

**al·lude** (ə lüd′) *v.*, **al·lud·ed, al·lud·ing.** **allude to,** refer to indirectly; mention in passing: *Do not ask him about his failure; do not even allude to it.*
☛ *Usage.* Do not confuse **allude** with ELUDE.

**al·lure** (ə lür′) **1** tempt or attract very strongly; fascinate; charm: *Circus life allured him with its action and excitement.* **2** fascination; charm: *the allure of the sea.* 1 *v.*, **al·lured, al·lur·ing;** 2 *n.* —**al·lur′er,** *n.*

**al·lure·ment** (ə lür′mənt) **1** charm; fascination. **2** something that allures; temptation; attraction. *n.*

**al·lur·ing** (ə lü′ring) **1** tempting; attracting. **2** charming; fascinating. **3** ppr. of ALLURE. 1, 2 *adj.*, 3 *v.* —**al·lur′ing·ly,** *adv.*

**al·lu·sion** (ə lü′zhən) an indirect or casual reference: *She was hurt by any allusion to her failure.* *n.*
☛ *Usage.* Do not confuse **allusion** and **illusion**. See note at ILLUSION.

**al·lu·vi·al** (ə lü′vē əl) consisting of or formed by sand or mud left by flowing water: *A delta is an alluvial deposit at the mouth of a river.* *adj.*

**all-weath·er** (ol′weᴛH′ər) designed to be usable or practical in all kinds of weather: *an all-weather coat, an all-weather road.* *adj.*

**al·ly** (ə lī′ or al′ī for verb, al′ī or ə lī′ for noun) **1** combine for some special purpose; unite by agreement: *One nation allies itself with another to protect its people and its interests.* **2** a person or nation united with another for some special purpose: *England and France have been allies in some wars.* See also ALLIES. **3** associate; connect: *This newspaper is allied with three others.* **4** be similar in structure, descent, etc.; relate: *Dogs are allied to wolves.* **5** a related animal, plant, form, or thing. **6** a helper; supporter. 1, 3, 4 *v.*, **al·lied, al·ly·ing;** 2, 5, 6 *n.*, *pl.* **al·lies.**

**al·ma ma·ter** or **Al·ma Ma·ter** (al′mə mä′tər, äl′mə mä′tər, *or* al′mə mā′tər) a person's school, college, or university.

**al·ma·nac** (ol′mə nak′) a calendar or table showing the days, weeks, and months: *Many almanacs give information about the weather, sun, moon, stars, tides, and other facts.* *n.*

**al·might·y** (ol mī′tē) **1** having supreme power; all-powerful. **2 the Almighty,** God. 1 *adj.*, 2 *n.* —**al·might′i·ly,** *adv.* —**al·might′i·ness,** *n.*

**al·mond** (o′mənd *or* ä′mənd) **1** the nut, or seed, of a peachlike fruit growing in warm regions. **2** the tree that it grows on. **3** shaped like an almond. **4** made from almonds: *almond paste.* *n.* —**al′mond·like′,** *adj.*

**al·mon·er** (al′mə nər *or* ol′mə nər) a person who distributes ALMS for a king, hospital, etc. *n.*

**al·most** (ol′mōst) nearly. *adv.*

**alms** (omz *or* ämz) money or gifts to help the poor. *n. sing. or pl.*

**alms·giv·er** (omz′giv′ər *or* ämz′giv′ər) a person who helps the poor with money or other gifts. *n.*

**alms·giv·ing** (omz′giv′ing *or* ämz′giv′ing) giving help to the poor. *n., adj.*

**alms·house** (omz′hous′ *or* ämz′hous′) a home for persons who do not have enough money to live on. *n.*

**al·ni·co** (al′ni kō *or* al nē′kō) an ALLOY containing aluminum, nickel, and cobalt: *Alnico is much used in making magnets.* *n.*

**al·oe** (al′ō) **1** any of a large, closely related group of plants of the lily family found mainly in southern Africa, having a long spike of flowers and thick, narrow leaves. **2 aloes,** a bitter drug made from the dried juice of the leaves of certain aloes (*used with a singular verb*). *n., pl.* **al·oes.**

**a·loft** (ə loft′) **1** far above the earth; high up: *Ben climbed aloft.* **2** high above the deck of a ship; up among the sails, rigging, or masts of a ship: *The crow's-nest is aloft.* 1 *adv.*, 2 *adj.*

**a·lone** (ə lōn′) **1** apart from other persons or things: *He was alone.* **2** apart from other persons or things: *One tree stood alone on the hill.* **3** without anyone else: *One girl alone can do this work.* **4** without anything more: *Meat alone is not the best food for children.* **5** only; merely; exclusively. 1, 3, 4 *adj.*, 2, 5 *adv.* —**a·lone′ness,** *n.*
**leave alone,** not bother; not meddle with.
**let alone, a** not bother; not meddle with. **b** not to mention: *It would have been a hot day for summer, let alone early spring.*

**a·long** (ə long′) **1** from one end of something to the other: *Flowers were planted along the path. We walked along the street.* **2** further; onward: *Move along. Pass the word along.* **3** with one; at hand or accompanying one (*often used with* **with**): *He took his dog along. I'll go along with you.* **4** *Informal.* there; present: *I'll be along in a minute.* 1 *prep.*, 2–4 *adv.*
**all along,** from the very beginning: *He was here all along.*
**along with,** together with, in association with: *We had pop along with the food.*
**get along, a** *Informal.* manage with at least some success. **b** agree. **c** go away. **d** advance. **e** succeed; prosper.

**a·long·shore** (ə long′shôr′) near or along the shore. *adv.*

**a·long·side** (ə long′sīd′ *for adverb,* ə long′sīd′ *for preposition*) **1** at the side; close to the side; side by side: *to anchor alongside.* **2** by the side of; beside: *The boat was alongside the wharf.* 1 *adv.*, 2 *prep.*
**alongside of,** beside; next to.

**a·loof** (ə lüf′) **1** at a distance; apart: *One girl stood aloof from all the others.* **2** reserved; withdrawn: *Because of her shyness Chandra seemed to be a very aloof girl.* 1 *adv.*, 2 *adj.* —**a·loof′ly,** *adv.* —**a·loof′ness,** *n.*

**a·loud** (ə loud′) **1** loud enough to be heard; not in a whisper: *He spoke aloud, although he was alone. She read the story aloud to the others.* **2** in a loud voice; loudly: *He groaned aloud with pain.* *adv.*

**alp** (alp) a high mountain See ALPS. *n.*

**al·pac·a** (al pak′ə) **1** a grazing animal found in the mountains of Peru and Bolivia, closely related to the llama and vicuña, having a long neck and small head and a coat of long, soft, silky hair: *Alpacas are raised mainly for their wool, which is straighter and finer than sheep's wool.* **2** the wool of the alpaca. **3** a kind of warm, soft cloth made from this wool. **4** a glossy, wiry cloth made of wool and cotton, usually black. *n.*

**al·pen·stock** (al′pən stok′) a strong staff with an iron point, used as an aid in climbing mountains. *n.*

**al·pha** (al′fə) **1** the first letter of the Greek alphabet (A,α). **2** the beginning of anything; first in a series. *n.*

**alpha and omega** the first and the last letters of the Greek alphabet; the first and the last; the beginning and the end.

**al·pha·bet** (al′fə bet′) **1** a set of letters or characters representing sounds, used in writing a language: *The English alphabet has twenty-six letters.* **2** the letters of a language arranged in their usual order, not as they are in words: *"D" is the fourth letter of the alphabet.* **3** the parts to be learned first; elementary principles. *n.*

**al·pha·bet·ic** (al′fə bet′ik) ALPHABETICAL. *adj.*

**al·pha·bet·i·cal** (al′fə bet′ə kəl) **1** arranged by letters in the order of the ALPHABET (def. 2). **2** of the ALPHABET (def. 2). *adj.* —**al′pha·bet′i·cal·ly,** *adv.*

**al·pha·bet·ize** (al′fə bə tīz′) arrange in ALPHABETICAL (def. 1) order. *v.*, **al·pha·bet·ized, al·pha·bet·iz·ing.**

**alpha particle** a positively charged particle consisting of two protons and two neutrons, released in the disintegration of radium and similar radio-active substances.

**alpha rays** in physics, a stream of ALPHA PARTICLES.

**Al·pine** (al′pīn) **1** of or like the ALPS. **2 alpine, a** of, having to do with, or living or growing on mountains: *alpine meadows, alpine flowers.* **b** having to do with or referring to downhill as opposed to cross-country skiing. *adj.*

**alpine fir** **1** a fir tree found especially in the mountainous regions of western North America, having a narrow, tapering, spire-like crown and greyish-green or bluish-green curved needles. **2** the light, soft, relatively weak wood of this tree.

**Alps** (alps) a range of mountains in southern central Europe, crossing France, Switzerland, Italy, Germany, Austria, Slovenia, and Croatia. *n. pl.*

**al·read·y** (ol red′ē) **1** before this time; by this time; even now: *You are half an hour late already. Krishna has already broken his new toy.* **2** so soon: *Must you go already?* *adv.*

**al·right** (ol rīt′) Informal. ALL RIGHT. *adv.*
☛ Usage. The spelling *alright* is not acceptable by many writers.

**Al·sa·tian** (al sā′shən) **1** of Alsace, a region in northeastern France, or its people. **2** a native or inhabitant of Alsace. **3** *Brit.* GERMAN SHEPHERD. 1 *adj.,* 2, 3 *n.*

**al·so** (ol′sō) in addition; besides; too: *That dress is pretty; it is also cheap.* *adv.*

**al·so-ran** (ol′sō ran′) a loser; unsuccessful contestant; non-entity. *n.*

**alt.** **1** altitude. **2** alternate; alternating. **3** alto.

**Alta.** Alberta.

**al·tar** (ol′tər) **1** a table or stand in the most sacred part of a church, chapel, synagogue, or temple: *In Christian*

**alpenstock** 33 **alternative**

hat, āge, fär; let, ēqual, tėrm; it, īce
hot, ōpen, ôrder; oil, out; cup, put, rüle
əbove, takən, pencəl, lemən, circəs
ch, child; ng, long; sh, ship
th, thin; ᴛʜ, then; zh, measure

*churches the altar is used in the Communion service or in celebrating Mass.* **2** a raised place built of earth or stone on which to make sacrifices or burn offerings to a god. *n.*
**lead to the altar,** marry.
☛ *Hom.* ALTER.

**al·ter** (ol′tər) **1** make different; change; vary: *If this coat is too large, a tailor can alter it to fit you.* **2** become different: *Since her trip to Europe, her whole outlook has altered.* *v.* —**al′ter·a·ble,** *adj.* —**al′ter·a·bly,** *adv.*
☛ *Hom.* ALTAR.

**al·ter·a·tion** (ol′tə rā′shən) a change in the appearance, form, or condition of anything: *to have alterations made in a dress. Intercontinental ballistic missiles have led to great alterations in military planning.* *n.*

**al·ter·cate** (ol′tər kāt′) dispute angrily; quarrel. *v.*, **al·ter·cat·ed, al·ter·cat·ing.**

**al·ter·ca·tion** (ol′tər kā′shən) an angry dispute; quarrel: *The two teams had an altercation over the umpire's decision.* *n.*

**al·ter e·go** (ol′tə rē′gō *or* ol′tə reg′ō) a very intimate friend.

**al·ter·nate** (ol′tər nāt′ *for verb,* ol tėr′nit, ol′tər nit *for adjective,* ol′tər nit *for noun*) **1** occur by turns, first one and then the other; happen or be arranged by turns: *Squares and circles alternate in this row:* ▫●▫●▫●▫●
**2** arrange by turns; do by turns: *We try to alternate work and pleasure.* **3** take turns: *Lucie and her brother alternate in setting the table.* **4** placed or occurring by turns; first one and then the other: *The row has alternate squares and circles.* **5** every other: *We have science on alternate days.* **6** a player who relieves another during a game: *We had ten alternates on our hockey team.* **7** a person appointed to take the place of another if necessary; substitute. **8** interchange regularly: *The sick man alternated two hours of work with one hour of rest.* **9** of an electric current, reverse direction at regular intervals: *Some electric currents alternate 120 times a second.* 1–3, 8, 9 *v.,* **al·ter·nat·ed, al·ter·nat·ing;** 4, 5 *adj.,* 6, 7 *n.*

**al·ter·nate·ly** (ol′tər ni tlē *or* ol tėr′ni tlē) by turns; first one and then the other. *adv.*

**alternating current** an electric current in which the electricity flows regularly in first one direction and then the other, reversing many times per second: *Most electrical circuits now use alternating current, the usual frequency being 60 cycles per second, or 120 reversals in direction per second.* Compare with DIRECT CURRENT.

**al·ter·na·tion** (ol′tər nā′shən) an alternating; occurring by turns, first one and then the other: *There is an alternation of red and white stripes in the flag of the United States.* *n.*

**al·ter·na·tive** (ol tėr′nə tiv) **1** giving or requiring a choice between only two things: *Mother offered the alternative plans of having a picnic or taking a trip on a steamboat.* **2** a choice between two things: *We have the alternative of going to a play or to a movie.* **3** giving a choice from among more than two things: *There are several alternative routes from Ottawa to Toronto.* **4** a choice from among more than two things. 5 one of the things to be chosen: *Ilona chose the first alternative and stayed in school.* 1, 3 *adj.*, 2, 4, 5 *n.* —**al·ter′na·tive·ly**, *adv.*

☛ *Usage.* **Alternative** comes from L *alter*, meaning the second of two persons, things, etc. Because of this origin, some writers use the word only when referring to one of two possibilities (See defs. 1 and 2 above). But it is also commonly used with the meaning as in defs. 3 and 4, that is, to mean one of several possibilities.

**al·ter·na·tor** (ol′tər nā′tər) a DYNAMO or generator for producing an alternating electric current. *n.*

**al·the·a** or **al·thae·a** (al thē′ə) the ROSE OF SHARON, a flowering garden shrub. *n.*

**alt·horn** (alt′hôrn′) a brass musical instrument similar to the FRENCH HORN. *n.*

**al·though** (ol ᴛʜō′) even if; in spite of the fact that; though: *Although it had rained all morning, they went on the hike.* *conj.*

**al·tim·e·ter** (al tim′ə tər *or* al′tə mē′tər) any instrument for measuring altitude: *Altimeters are used in aircraft to indicate height above the earth's surface.* See GAUGE for picture. *n.*

**al·ti·tude** (al′tə tyüd′ *or* al′tə tüd′, ol′tə tyüd′ *or* ol′tə tüd′) 1 height above the earth's surface: *The airplane was flying at an altitude of 3000 metres.* 2 height above sea level: *The altitude of Calgary, Alberta, is 1079 metres.* 3 a high place: *At these altitudes snow never melts.* 4 the angular distance of a star, planet, etc. above the horizon. *n.*

**al·to** (ol′tō *or* al′tō) 1 the lowest female singing voice. 2 the highest adult male singing voice, above tenor; counter tenor: *A male alto is now very rare; the voice has been replaced in music by the female voice that corresponds to it, originally called* contralto *but now usually called* alto. 3 a singer whose range is alto. 4 the part sung by an alto: *Alto is the second highest part in standard four-part harmony for men's and women's voices together.* 5 an instrument having a range lower than that of the soprano, or treble, in a family of instruments. 6 having to do with, having the range of, or designed for an alto. 1–5 *n., pl.* **al·tos;** 6 *adj.*

**al·to·geth·er** (ol′tə geᴛʜ′ər *for adverb,* ol′tə geᴛʜ′ər *for noun*) 1 completely; entirely: *The house was altogether destroyed by fire.* 2 on the whole; considering everything: *Altogether, I'm sorry it happened.* 3 all included: *Altogether there were ten books.* *adv.*
**in the altogether,** *Informal.* nude: *They went swimming in the altogether.*

☛ *Syn.* Do not confuse the adverb **altogether** with the adjective phrase **all together,** which means 'together in a group': *We found the boys all together in the kitchen.*

**alto horn** ALTHORN.

**al·tru·ism** (al′trü iz′əm) unselfishness; unselfish devotion to the interest and welfare of others. *n.*

**al·tru·ist** (al′trü ist) an unselfish person; a person who works for the welfare of others. *n.*

**al·tru·is·tic** (al′trü is′tik) thoughtful of the welfare of others; unselfish. *adj.* —**al′tru·is′ti·cal·ly,** *adv.*

**al·um** (al′əm) 1 a white mineral salt used in medicine and in dyeing: *Alum is sometimes used to stop the bleeding of a small cut.* 2 a colourless, crystalline salt containing ammonia, used in baking powder, etc. *n.*

**al·u·min·i·um** (al′ü min′ē əm) *Esp. Brit.* ALUMINUM. *n.*

**a·lu·mi·num** (ə lü′mə nəm) a silver-white, very light, easily worked metallic element that occurs in nature only in combination: *Aluminum resists tarnish and is used for making utensils, instruments, aircraft parts, etc.* Symbol: Al *n.*

**a·lum·na** (ə lum′nə) a female graduate or former student of a school, college, or university. *n., pl.* **a·lum·nae** (-nē *or* -nī).

**a·lum·nae** (ə lum′nē *or* ə lum′nī) pl. of ALUMNA. *n.*

**a·lum·ni** (ə lum′nī) pl. of ALUMNUS. *n.*

**a·lum·nus** (ə lum′nəs) a graduate or former student, either male or female, of a school, college, or university. *n., pl.* **a·lum·ni.**

**al·ve·o·lus** (al′vē ō′ləs) 1 a small vacuity, pit, or cell: *The air cells of the lungs are alveoli.* 2 the socket of a tooth. *n., pl.* **al·ve·o·li** (-lē *or* lī).

**al·ways** (ol′wiz *or* ol′wāz) 1 every time; at all times: *Night always follows day.* 2 all the time; continually: *Mother is always cheerful.* 3 forever; for all time to come: *I'll love you always.* *adv.*

**a·lys·sum** (ə lis′əm) any of a closely related group of annual or perennial plants of the mustard family, having greyish leaves and fragrant yellow, white, pink, blue, or violet flowers: *Alyssum is a popular garden flower.* *n.*

**Alz·hei·mer's disease** (älts′ hī′mərz) a gradually worsening disease of the brain cells, possibly hereditary, leading eventually to severe mental impairment and death.
☛ *Etym.* Like many diseases, Alzheimer's disease is named after the doctor who described it, in this case the German physician A. *Alzheimer.*

**am** (am; *unstressed,* əm) first person singular, present tense, of BE: *I am a student. I am saving for my holiday.* *v.*

**Am** americium.

**Am.** 1 America. 2 American.

**AM** or **A.M.** amplitude modulation.

**a.m.** or **A.M.** (ā′em′) before noon; ANTE MERIDIEM (*used especially to refer to a particular time after midnight and before noon*): *The store opens at 9:30 a.m.*

**a·mal·gam** (ə mal′gəm) 1 an alloy of mercury with some other metal or metals: *Tin amalgam is used in silvering mirrors. Silver amalgam used to be used as fillings for teeth.* 2 mixture; blend. *n.*

**a·mal·gam·ate** (ə mal′gə māt′) unite; combine; mix; blend: *The two companies amalgamated to form one big company. Many different ethnic groups are being amalgamated in Canada.* *v.,* **a·mal·gam·at·ed, a·mal·gam·at·ing.**

**a·mal·gam·a·tion** (ə mal′gə mā′shən) a union; combination; mixture; blend: *Our nation is an amalgamation of many different peoples.* *n.*

**a·man·u·en·sis** (ə man′yü en′sis) 1 a person who writes down what another says. 2 a person who copies what another has written. *n., pl.* **a·man·u·en·ses** (-sēz).

**am·a·ranth** (am′ə ranth′) 1 *Poetic.* an imaginary flower that never fades. 2 any of a closely related group of annual plants, including some well-known garden plants, such as love-lies-bleeding, and many weeds, including the common pigweed. 3 referring to a family of plants found especially in warm regions, including the cockscomb and the amaranths.   **4** a dark reddish purple.   1–4 *n.*, 4 *adj.*

**am·a·ran·thine** (am′ə ran′thin)   **1** never-fading; undying.   **2** dark reddish purple.   1, 2 *adj.*, 2 *n.*

**am·a·ryl·lis** (am′ə ril′is)   **1** a lily-like plant having clusters of very large, fragrant red, white, or rose flowers on a thick stalk and long narrow leaves that appear after the flowers have withered.   **2** any of various other plants of the same family, having lily-like flowers.   **3** referring to a family of mostly tropical plants that grow from bulbs, corms, or rhizomes, having long narrow leaves and large fragrant flowers with six petals: *The daffodil, jonquil, century plant, and amaryllis belong to the amaryllis family.*   *n., pl.* **am·a·ryl·lis·es** (-ēz).

**a·mass** (ə mas′)   heap together; pile up; accumulate: *The miser amassed a fortune for himself.*   *v.*

**A·mat·er·a·su** (ä′mä te rä′sù)   in Shintoism, the sun goddess; the most highly revered of the many Japanese deities: *The imperial line of Japan have traditionally traced an unbroken ancestry to Amaterasu.*   *n.*

**am·a·teur** (am′ə chər, am′ə chür′, *or* am′ə tyür′)   **1** a person who does something for pleasure, not for money or as a profession.   **2** an athlete who is not a professional: *Only amateurs are permitted to compete in the Olympic games.*   **3** a person who does something without showing the proper skills: *Rachelle plays the piano well but on the violin she is an amateur, completely without training.*   **4** of amateurs; made or done by amateurs: *an amateur orchestra.*   **5** being an amateur: *an amateur pianist.*   1–3 *n.*, 4 5 *adj.*

**am·a·teur·ish** (am′ə chėr′ish, am′ə chü′rish, *or* am′ə tyü′rish)   done as an AMATEUR (defs. 1, 3) might do it; not expert; not very skilful.   *adj.*
—**am′a·teur′ish·ly**, *adv.*

**am·a·teur·ism** (am′ə chə riz′əm, am′ə chü riz′əm, *or* am′ə tyü riz′əm)   **1** an AMATEURISH way of doing things.   **2** the position or rank of an AMATEUR (defs. 1–3).   *n.*

**am·a·to·ry** (am′ə tô′rē)   of love; causing love; having to do with making love or with lovers.   *adj.*

**a·maze** (ə māz′)   surprise greatly; strike with sudden wonder: *The surprise party so amazed her that she could not speak.*   *v.*, **a·mazed, a·maz·ing.**

**a·mazed** (ə māzd′)   greatly surprised.   *adj.*

**a·maz·ed·ly** (ə mā′zi dlē)   lost in wonder or astonishment.   *adv.*

**a·maze·ment** (ə māz′mənt)   great surprise; sudden wonder; astonishment: *The little girl was filled with amazement when she first saw the ocean.*   *n.*

**a·maz·ing** (ə mā′zing)   very surprising; wonderful; astonishing.   *adj.*   —**a·maz′ing·ly**, *adv.*

**Am·a·zon** (am′ə zon′)   **1** in Greek mythology, a member of a race of female warriors supposed to live by the Black Sea.   **2** Also, **amazon**,   a tall, strong, athletic woman.   *n.*

**Am·a·zo·ni·an** (am′ə zō′nē ən)   **1** of the Amazon River or the region it drains.   **2** of the Amazons.   **3** Also, **amazonian**,   of women or girls, aggressive; warlike.   *adj.*

**am·bas·sa·dor** (am bas′ə dər)   **1** a representative of highest rank sent by one government or ruler to another: *An ambassador lives in a foreign country and speaks and acts on behalf of his government or his ruler.*   **2** an unofficial representative of a group: *Boy Scouts who travel abroad can be ambassadors of good will for their country.*   *n.*

**am·bas·sa·do·ri·al** (am bas′ə dô′rē əl)   of an AMBASSADOR (def. 1) or ambassadors.   *adj.*

**am·bas·sa·dor·ship** (am bas′ə dər ship′)   **1** the position or rank of an AMBASSADOR (def. 1).   **2** the term of office of an AMBASSADOR (def. 1).   *n.*

**am·ber** (am′bər)   **1** a hard, translucent yellow or yellowish-brown gum, used for jewellery and in making stems of pipes: *Amber is the fossilized resin of ancient pine trees.*   **2** made of amber.   **3** the colour of amber; yellow; yellowish brown.   **4** yellow; yellowish-brown.   1, 3 *n.*, 2 4 *adj.*

**am·ber·gris** (am′bər grēs′ *or* am′bər gris)   a waxlike, greyish substance that comes from sperm whales: *Ambergris is used in making perfumes.*   *n.*

**am·bi·ance** (am′bē əns)   See AMBIENCE.   *n.*

**am·bi·dex·ter·i·ty** (am′bə dek ster′ə tē)   **1** the ability to use both hands equally well.   **2** an unusual skilfulness.   **3** deceitfulness.   *n.*

**am·bi·dex·trous** (am′bə dek′strəs)   **1** able to use both hands equally well.   **2** very skilful.   **3** deceitful.   *adj.*
—**am′bi·dex′trous·ly**, *adv.*   —**am′bi·dex′trous·ness**, *n.*

**am·bi·ent** (am′bē ənt)   surrounding.   *adj.*

**am·bi·ence** (am′bē əns)   environment or atmosphere: *They felt uncomfortable in the formal ambience of the expensive restaurant.*   *n.*   Also, **ambiance.**

**am·bi·gu·i·ty** (am′bə gyü′ə tē)   **1** the possibility of two or more meanings.   **2** a word or expression that can have more than one meaning.   **3** lack of clarity; vagueness; uncertainty.   *n., pl.* **am·bi·gu·i·ties.**

**am·big·u·ous** (am big′yü əs)   **1** having more than one possible meaning: *After John hit Richard, he ran away is ambiguous because one cannot tell which boy ran away.*   **2** doubtful; not clear; uncertain: *She was left in an ambiguous position by her friend's failure to appear and help her.*   *adj.*   —**am·big′u·ous·ly**, *adv.*
—**am·big′u·ous·ness**, *n.*

**am·bi·tion** (am bish′ən)   **1** a strong desire for fame or honour; a seeking after a high position or great power: *Laurette was filled with ambition and worked afternoons after school and on Saturdays.*   **2** something strongly desired or sought after: *Her ambition was to be a great actress.*   *n.*   —**am·bi′tion·less**, *adj.*

**am·bi·tious** (am bish′əs)   **1** having ambition: *an ambitious person.*   **2** strongly desiring a particular thing; eager: *ambitious to succeed, ambitious of power.*   **3** requiring much skill or effort: *an ambitious undertaking.*   *adj.*   —**am·bi′tious·ly**, *adv.*   —**am·bi′tious·ness**, *n.*

**am·ble** (am′bəl)   **1** the gait of a horse when it lifts first the two legs on one side and then the two on the other.   **2** of a horse, move in that way.   **3** an easy, slow pace in walking.   **4** walk at an easy slow pace.   1, 3 *n.*, 2 4 *v.*, **am·bled, am·bling.**

**am·bler** (am′blər)   **1** a horse or mule that ambles.   **2** a person who ambles.   *n.*

**am·bro·sia** (am brō′zhə *or* am brō′zē ə) **1** the food of the ancient Greek and Roman gods. **2** anything especially delicious. *n.*

**am·bro·sial** (am brō′zhəl *or* am brō′zē əl) like AMBROSIA; especially pleasing to taste or smell. *adj.*

**am·bu·lance** (am′byə ləns) a vehicle, boat, or aircraft equipped to carry sick or wounded persons. *n.*

**am·bu·lant** (am′byə lənt) walking. *adj.*

**am·bu·late** (am′byə lāt′) walk; move about. *v.,* **am·bu·lat·ed, am·bu·lat·ing.** —**am′bu·la′tion**, *n.*

**am·bu·la·to·ry** (am′byə lə tô′rē) **1** having to do with walking; fitted for walking. **2** capable of walking; not bedridden. **3** a covered place for walking; cloister. 1, 2 *adj.*, 3 *n., pl.* **am·bu·la·to·ries.**

**am·bus·cade** (am′bə skād′) **1** an ambush. **2** attack from an ambush. 1 *n.*, 2 *v.,* **am·bus·cad·ed, am·bus·cad·ing.** —**am′bus·cad′er**, *n.*

**am·bush** (am′bùsh) **1** a surprise attack from some hiding place on an approaching enemy. **2** attackers so hidden. **3** the place where they are hidden. **4** attack from an ambush. **5** wait in hiding to make a surprise attack. **6** lying in wait: *They often trapped their enemies by ambush instead of meeting them in open battle.* **7** put soldiers or other persons in hiding for a surprise attack: *The major ambushed his troops in the woods on either side of the road.* 1–3, 6 *n.*, 4, 5, 7 *v.*

**a·me·ba** (ə mē′bə) See AMOEBA. *n., pl.* **a·me·bas** *or* **a·me·bae** (-bē *or* -bī).

**a·me·bic** (ə mē′bik) See AMOEBIC. *adj.*

**a·me·lio·rate** (ə mē′lyə rāt′) **1** make better; improve: *New housing ameliorated living conditions.* **2** become better; improve: *Living conditions ameliorated with the new housing.* *v.,* **a·me·lio·rat·ed, a·me·lio·rat·ing.**

**a·me·lio·ra·tion** (ə mē′lyə rā′shən) improvement. *n.*

**a·me·lio·ra·tive** (ə mē′lyə rə tiv *or* ə mē′lyə rā′tiv) improving. *adj.*

**a·men** (ā′men′ *or* ä′men′) **1** be it so; may it become true. *Amen* is said after a Christian or Jewish prayer. **2** *Informal.* an expression of approval. **3** the saying or writing of 'amen': *Several amens were heard from the crowd.* 1, 2 *interj.*, 3 *n.*

**a·me·na·ble** (ə mē′nə bəl *or* ə men′ə bəl) **1** open to suggestion or advice; responsive; submissive: *A reasonable person is amenable to persuasion.* **2** accountable; answerable: *People living in a country are amenable to its laws.* *adj.* —**a·me′na·ble·ness**, *n.* —**a·me′na·bly**, *adv.*

**a·mend** (ə mend′) **1** change the form of a law, bill, motion, etc. by addition, omission, etc. **2** change for the better; improve: *It is time you amended your poor table manners.* **3** free from faults; make right; correct: *In the new edition of the algebra book, the answers have been amended.* *v.* Compare with EMEND. —**a·mend′a·ble**, *adj.* —**a·mend′er**, *n.*

**a·mend·ment** (ə mend′mənt) **1** a change made in a law, bill, motion, etc. **2** a change for the better; improvement. **3** a change made to remove an error; correction. *n.*

**a·mends** (ə mendz′) payment for loss; satisfaction for an injury; compensation. *n.*
**make amends,** make up (*for*): *He made amends for the insult to her.*

**a·men·i·ty** (ə men′ə tē *or* ə mē′nə tē) **1** pleasant behaviour; a polite act: *Saying "Thank you" and holding the door for a person to pass through are amenities.* **2** a pleasant feature; something which makes life easier and more pleasant: *This house for rent has all amenities.* **3** pleasantness; agreeableness: *the amenity of a warm climate.* *n., pl.* **a·men·i·ties.**

**a·men·sal·ism** (ä men′sə liz′əm) a form of SYMBIOSIS in which one species is harmed, but it is not clear how the other species receives benefit. Compare with COMMENSALISM, MUTUALISM, and PARASITISM. *n.*

**Amer. 1** America. **2** American.

**A·mer·i·can** (ə mer′ə kən) **1** of or having to do with the United States or its people: *an American citizen.* **2** an inhabitant or citizen of the United States, or of the earlier British colonies. **3** of, having to do with, or found in the Western Hemisphere: *the Amazon and other American rivers. The American robin is a different bird from the European robin.* **4** a native or inhabitant of the Western Hemisphere. 1, 3 *adj.*, 2 4 *n.*

**American eagle** the BALD EAGLE: *The coat of arms of the United States has an American eagle on it.*

**American Indian** AMERINDIAN.

**am·er·i·ci·um** (am′ə rish′ē əm) a radio-active metallic element obtained from plutonium. Symbol: Am *n.*

**Am·er·ind** (am′ə rind′) AMERINDIAN. *n.*

**Am·er·in·di·an** (am′ə rin′dē ən) **1** of or referring to a race of mankind, the original inhabitants of the Western Hemisphere south of the Arctic coast. **2** a member of this race: *Amerindians have straight, dark hair and light to dark brown skin.* **3** referring to the aboriginal languages of the Western Hemisphere south of the Arctic coast, forming a number of distinct language families. **4** of or having to do with the Amerindian peoples, their cultures, or their languages. 1, 3, 4 *adj.*, 2 *n.*

**am·e·thyst** (am′ə thist) **1** a purple or violet variety of QUARTZ, used for jewellery. See CRYSTAL for picture. **2** a violet-coloured CORUNDUM, used for jewellery. **3** purple; violet. 1–3 *n.*, 3 *adj.* —**am′e·thyst·like′**, *adj.*

**a·mi·a·bil·i·ty** (ā′mē ə bil′ə tē) friendliness; good nature; pleasantness; agreeableness. *n.*

**a·mi·a·ble** (ā′mē ə bəl) good-natured and friendly; pleasant and agreeable: *She is a sweet, gentle, amiable girl.* *adj.* —**a′mi·a·bly**, *adv.*

**am·i·ca·bil·i·ty** (am′ə kə bil′ə tē) friendliness. *n.*

**am·i·ca·ble** (am′ə kə bəl) peaceable; friendly: *Instead of fighting, the two nations settled their quarrel in an amicable way.* *adj.* —**am′i·ca·bly**, *adv.*

**a·mid** (ə mid′) in the middle of; among. *prep.*

**a·mid·ship** (ə mid′ship) AMIDSHIPS. *adv.*

**a·mid·ships** (ə mid′ships) in or toward the middle of a ship; halfway between bow and stern. *adv.*

**a·midst** (ə midst′) AMID. *prep.*

**a·mi·go** (ə mē′gō) *Spanish.* friend. *n.*

**a·mi·no acids** (ə mē′nō *or* am′ə nō′) certain complex organic compounds of nitrogen that combine in various ways to form proteins.

**a·mir** (ə mēr′) See EMIR. *n.*

**Am·ish** (ä′mish, am′ish, *or* ā′mish)  **1** of, having to do with, or referring to a strict Mennonite sect founded in the 17th century in Switzerland, or its members. **2** the people who belong to this sect: *Today most Amish live in farming communities in southern Ontario and parts of the United States. They form part of the group often called Pennsylvania Dutch.*  1 *adj.*, 2 *n. pl.*

**a·miss** (ə mis′)  **1** not the way it should be; out of order; at fault: *You must be tired; your work seems to be going amiss today.*  **2** improper; wrong: *It would not be amiss to offer an apology, even though you may not have intended harm.*  1 *adv.*, 2 *adj.*
**take amiss,** be offended at because of a misunderstanding: *Mei-Ling had not meant to be rude to her mother but Mother took her answer amiss.*
☞ *Usage.* The adjective always follows a verb and is not used before a noun.

**am·i·ty** (am′ə tē)  peace and friendship; friendly relations: *If there were amity between nations, there would be no wars.*  *n., pl.* **am·i·ties.**

**am·me·ter** (am′mē′tər *or* am′ē′tər)  an instrument for measuring the strength of an electric current in amperes.  *n.*

**am·mo·nia** (ə mō′nyə)  **1** a strong-smelling colourless gas, consisting of nitrogen and hydrogen. **2** this gas dissolved in water: *Ammonia is very useful for cleaning.*  *n.*

**am·mo·ni·ac** (ə mō′nē ak′)  a gum resin used for medicines and as a cement for porcelain.  *n.*

**am·mo·nite** (am′ə nīt′)  one of the coiled fossil shells of an extinct MOLLUSC.  *n.*

**am·mo·ni·um** (ə mō′nē əm)  the radical NH₄, a group of atoms present in ammonia salts.  *n.*

**am·mu·ni·tion** (am′yə nish′ən)  **1** bullets, shells, gunpowder, etc. for guns or other weapons; military supplies that can be used against an enemy. **2** anything that can be shot, hurled, or thrown. **3** a means of attack or defence: *ammunition for his argument.*  *n.*

**am·ne·sia** (am nē′zhə *or* am nē′zē ə)  a loss of memory caused by injury to the brain, by disease, or by shock.  *n.*

**am·nes·ty** (am′ni stē)  **1** a general pardon for past offences against a government: *After order was restored, the king granted amnesty to those who had plotted against him.* **2** give amnesty to; pardon.  1 *n., pl.* **am·nes·ties;**  2 *v.*, **am·nes·tied, am·nes·ty·ing.**

**am·ni·on** (am′nē ən)  a membrane lining the sac that encloses the embryos of reptiles, birds, and mammals.  *n., pl.* **am·ni·ons** *or* **am·ni·a** (-nē ə).

**am·ni·ot·ic** (am′nē ot′ik)  **1** of or contained in the AMNION. **2** having an AMNION.  *adj.*

**a·moe·ba** (ə mē′bə)  a microscopic one-celled animal that moves by forming temporary projections that are constantly changing: *Many amoebas live in water; others live as parasites in other animals.*  *n., pl.* **a·moe·bas** *or* **a·moe·bae** (-bē *or* -bī).  Sometimes, **ameba.**
—**a·moe′ba·like′**, *adj.*

**a·moe·bic** (ə mē′bik)  **1** of or like an AMOEBA or amoebas. **2** caused by AMOEBAS: *amoebic dysentery.* *adj.*  Sometimes, **amebic.**

**a·mok** (ə muk′ *or* ə mok′)  See AMUCK.  *adv.*

**a·mong** (ə mung′)  **1** surrounded by: *a house among the trees.* **2** in with: *She fell among thieves.* **3** a part of; a member of; one of: *Canada is among the largest countries of the world.* **4** in the number or class of: *That book is the best among modern novels.* **5** in comparison with: *one among many.* **6** in equal portions to each of; by or for distribution to: *Divide the money among them.* **7** by the combined action of: *You have among you spoiled the child.* **8** by, with, or through the whole of: *political unrest among the people.*  *prep.*
**among ourselves, yourselves,** *or* **themselves,** **a** some with others: *They fought among themselves.* **b** each with all the others; as a group; mutually: *They agreed among themselves to have a party.*
☞ *Usage.* See note at BETWEEN.

**a·mongst** (ə mungst′)  AMONG.  *prep.*

**am·o·rous** (am′ə rəs)  **1** inclined to love. **2** in love. **3** showing love; loving. **4** having to do with love or courtship.  *adj.* —**am′o·rous·ly,** *adv.*
—**am′o·rous·ness,** *n.*

**a·mor·phous** (ə môr′fəs)  **1** not consisting of crystals: *Glass is amorphous; sugar is crystalline.* **2** of no particular kind or type. **3** having no definite form; shapeless or formless; not organized.  *adj.*
—**a·mor′phous·ly,** *adv.*

**am·or·ti·za·tion** (am′ər tə zā′shən *or* am′ər tī zā′shən)  **1** the act of amortizing or wiping out a debt. **2** the money regularly set aside for this purpose.  *n.*

**am·or·tize** (am′ər tīz′)  set money aside regularly in a special fund for future wiping out of a debt, etc.  *v.,* **am·or·tized, am·or·tiz·ing.**

**a·mount** (ə mount′)  **1** the sum; total: *What is the amount of the day's sales?* **2** the full effect, value, or extent: *The amount of evidence against him is great.* **3** a quantity viewed as a whole: *a great amount of intelligence.*  *n.*
**amount to,** **a** add up to; be equal to: *The loss from the flood amounts to a million dollars.* **b** be the same as in value, force, effect, etc.: *Keeping what belongs to another amounts to stealing.*

**amp.**  **1** ampere. **2** amperage.

**am·per·age** (am′pə rij)  the strength of an electric current measured in AMPERES.  *n.*

**am·pere** (am′pēr *or* am′per)  an SI unit for measuring the rate of flow of an electric current, defined in terms of the magnetic force which a current produces: *About one ampere of current is required to produce 100 watts of electric power. The ampere is one of the seven base units in the SI. Symbol*: A  *n.*

**am·per·sand** (am′pər sand′)  a sign (&) meaning "and."  *n.*

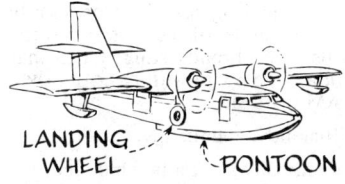

An amphibian (def. 3). The wheels are lowered for coming down on land. For coming down on water, the wheels are drawn up and the pontoon serves as a hull.

**am·phib·i·an** (am fib′ē ən)  **1** any of a class

(**Amphibia**) of cold-blooded vertebrates, most of which have completely scaleless skin, and which produce young that at first breathe by means of gills but usually undergo a complete physical change as they mature, becoming land-living animals with lungs and legs: *Frogs, toads, newts, and salamanders are amphibians.* **2** an animal or plant adapted to life in the water and on land: *Seals, beavers, and water snakes are sometimes called amphibians.* **3** an aircraft that can take off from and come down on either land or water. **4** a vehicle that can travel across land or water. **5** of or having to do with amphibians. **6** AMPHIBIOUS. 1–4 *n.*, 5, 6 *adj.*
☛ *Etym.* **Amphibian,** AMPHIBIOUS. 17c. From modern L from a form of Gr. *amphibios,* literally 'living two lives', made up of *amphi-* 'of both kinds, on both sides' + *bios* 'life'.

**am·phib·i·ous** (am fib′ē əs) **1** able to live both on land and in water: *Frogs are amphibious.* **2** suited for use on land or water: *an amphibious tank.* **3** having two qualities, natures, or parts. **4** by the combined action of land, water, and air forces: *an amphibious attack.* *adj.*
—**am·phib′i·ous·ly,** *adv.* —**am·phib′i·ous·ness,** *n.*
☛ *Etym.* See note at AMPHIBIAN.

**am·phi·the·a·tre** (am′fə thē′ə tər) **1** a circular or oval building with ascending rows of seats around a central open space. **2** a theatre gallery, lecture hall, etc. with ascending rows of seats, especially when forming a semicircle. **3** a place for public contests and games. **4** a level place surrounded by a steeply rising slope. *n.* Sometimes, **amphitheater.**

**am·ple** (am′pəl) **1** large; big; extensive; roomy: *A well-designed house should have ample closets.* **2** more than enough; abundant: *Take an ample supply of food for a day's journey.* **3** enough: *My allowance is ample for my needs.* *adj.,* **am·pler, am·plest.**

**am·pli·fi·ca·tion** (am′plə fə kā′shən) a making greater, stronger, or more extensive; enlargement or expansion. *n.*

**am·pli·fi·er** (am′plə fī′ər) **1** a person or thing that amplifies. **2** a device in or attached to a radio, phonograph, etc. for strengthening electrical impulses. **3** SPEAKER (def. 3). *n.*

**am·pli·fy** (am′plə fī′) **1** make greater or stronger. **2** make fuller and more extensive; expand; enlarge: *to amplify a description, to amplify a point in argument.* **3** write or talk at length. **4** in electronics, increase the strength of an electrical impulse by means of an AMPLIFIER (def. 2). *v.,* **am·pli·fied, am·pli·fy·ing.**

**am·pli·tude** (am′plə tyüd′ or am′plə tüd′) **1** width; breadth; size. **2** abundance; fullness: *A very rich man has an amplitude of money.* **3** one half the range of regular vibrations: *A pendulum swinging through 10 degrees has an amplitude of 5 degrees.* **4** the peak strength of an alternating electric current in a given cycle. *n.*

**amplitude modulation** in radio broadcasting: **1** a method of transmitting the sound signals of a broadcast by changing the strength, or amplitude, of the carrier waves to match the audio signals. **2** a broadcasting system that uses amplitude modulation. Compare with FREQUENCY MODULATION. *Abbrev.:* AM or A.M.

**am·ply** (am′plē) sufficiently; abundantly. *adv.*

**am·pul·la** (am pul′ə *or* am pùl′ə) **1** a two-handled, rounded glass or earthenware flask used in ancient Rome to hold oil, perfume, or wine. **2** a vessel used in Christian churches to hold consecrated oil. **3** in biology, a dilated part of a canal or duct. *n., pl.* **am·pul·lae** (-ē or -ī).

**am·pu·tate** (am′pyə tāt′) cut off, especially in a surgical operation: *The doctor amputated the soldier's wounded leg.* *v.* **am·pu·tat·ed, am·pu·tat·ing.**
—**am′pu·ta′tor,** *n.*

**am·pu·ta·tion** (am′pyə tā′shən) the cutting off of a leg, arm, finger, etc.; cutting off. *n.*

**am·pu·tee** (am′pyə tē′) a person who has had an arm or leg, etc. amputated. *n.*

**am·rit** (äm′rit) a sweetened water used by Sikhs as a sacred drink and as baptismal water. Compare with HOLY WATER. *n.*

**amt.** amount.

**a·muck** (ə muk′) in a murderous frenzy; with a crazy desire to attack. *adv.* Also, **amok.**
**run amuck,** run about in a murderous frenzy.

**am·u·let** (am′yə lit) some object worn as a magic charm against evil. *n.*

**a·muse** (ə myüz′) **1** cause to laugh or smile: *The playful puppy amused the baby.* **2** keep pleasantly interested; entertain: *The new toys amused the children.* *v.,* **a·mused, a·mus·ing.** —**a·mus′er.** *n.*

**a·mused** (ə myüzd′) pleasantly entertained. *adj.*
—**a·mus′ed·ly,** *adv.*

**a·muse·ment** (ə myü′zmənt) **1** the condition of being AMUSED: *The boy's amusement was so great that we all had to laugh with him.* **2** pleasant diversion: *They often window-shop for amusement.* **3** something that amuses or entertains: *His favourite amusement at the Exhibition is the Ferris wheel.* *n.*

**a·mus·ing** (ə myü′zing) **1** entertaining. **2** causing laughter, smiles, etc. **3** ppr. of AMUSE. 1, 2 *adj.,* 3 *v.*
—**a·mus′ing·ly,** *adv.*

**am·y·lase** (am′ə lās) AMYLOPSIN. *n.*

**am·y·lop·sin** (am′ə lop′sin) an enzyme in the pancreatic juice that changes starch into simpler compounds such as GLUCOSE. *n.*

**an** (ən; *stressed,* an) the indefinite article used in place of **a** before a vowel or silent **h**: *an apple, an heir.* **1** any: *Have you an answer to this accusation?* **2** one: *Take an orange.* **3** each; every: *Rajiv earns six dollars an hour.* **4** for each: *He paid fifty cents an apple.* *indefinite article.*

**–an** a suffix meaning: **1** of or having to do with _____: *Mohammedan means of or having to do with Mohammed.* **2** of or having to do with _____ or its people: *Asian means of or having to do with Asia or its people.* **3** a native or inhabitant of _____: *A Venezuelan is a native or inhabitant of Venezuela.* Also, **-ian** in a few words: *Canadian, mammalian.*

**a·nach·ro·nism** (ə nak′rə niz′əm) **1** the putting of a person, thing, or event in some time where it does not belong: *It would be an anachronism to speak of Champlain riding on a bus.* **2** something placed or occurring out of its proper time. *n.*

**a·nach·ro·nis·tic** (ə nak′rə nis′tik) having or involving an ANACHRONISM. *adj.*

**a·nach·ro·nous** (ə nak′rə nəs) placed or occurring out of the proper time. *adj.* —**a·nach′ro·nous·ly,** *adv.*

**an·a·con·da** (an′ə kon′də) **1** a species of snake, a very large tropical American boa, having olive-green skin, often with black rings or spots, and living in trees and in and around water. *The anaconda, averaging about 9 m in length, is not as long as the largest python, but because it has a much thicker body it is considered the largest snake in the world.* **2** any large snake that kills its prey by coiling around it and squeezing until it suffocates. *n.*

**a·nae·mi·a** (ə nē′mē ə)  See ANEMIA. *n.*

**a·nae·mic** (ə nē′mik)  See ANEMIC. *adj.*

**an·aer·obe** (an′er ōb)  a BACTERIUM which does not use oxygen in the air to convert food into energy. Compare with AEROBE. *n.*

**an·aer·o·bic** (an′er ō′bik)  living or growing where there is no free oxygen: *Anaerobic bacteria get oxygen by decomposing compounds containing oxygen.* Compare with AEROBIC. *adj.*

**an·aes·the·sia** (an′əs thē′zhə *or* an′əs thē′zē ə)  See ANESTHESIA. *n.*

**an·aes·thet·ic** (an′əs thet′ik)  See ANESTHETIC. *n., adj.*

**an·aes·the·tist** (ə nēs′thə tist *or* ə nes′thə tist)  See ANESTHETIST. *n.*

**an·aes·the·tize** (ə nēs′thə tīz′ *or* ə nes′thə tīz′)  See ANESTHETIZE. *v.*, **an·aes·the·tized, an·aes·the·tiz·ing.**

**an·a·gram** (an′ə gram′)  **1** a word or phrase formed from another by transposing the letters. *Example: silent—listen.* **2 anagrams,** *pl.*  a game in which the players make words by changing and adding letters. *n.*

**a·nal** (ā′nəl)  **1** of the ANUS.  **2** near the ANUS. *adj.*

**An·a·lects** (an′ə lekts)  in Confucianism, the most revered and influential text containing the sayings and conversations of Confucius. *n.pl.*

**an·a·lem·ma** (an′ə lem′ə)  a graduated scale in the shape of a figure eight, found on many globes, which shows the variation throughout the year between noon according to clock time and noon according to the position of the sun: *The analemma also shows on which two days of the year the sun is directly overhead at midday in the low latitudes.* *n.*

**an·al·ge·si·a** (an′əl jē′zē ə *or* an′əl jē′sē ə)  the state of not being able to feel pain even while completely conscious. *n.*

**an·al·ge·sic** (an′əl jē′zik *or* an′əl jē′sik)  **1** of, having to do with, or causing ANALGESIA: *an analgesic drug.*  **2** a drug or other agent that causes ANALGESIA. 1 *adj.*, 2 *n.*

**an·a·logue** *or* **an·a·log** (an′ə lôg)  **1** something analogous  **2** a kind of measurement in which a constantly changing value, such as a temperature or speed, is understood as a percentage of another value rather than interpreted with separate numbers.  **3** using an analogue computer.  **4** having to do with an electronic system in which the signal is linked to a visible change, as in a phonograph where sound corresponds to a groove.  **5** of a dial, watch, etc. bearing hands rather than digits to indicate an amount.  1-2, *n.*, 3-5, *adj.*

**an·a·log·i·cal** (an′ə loj′ə kəl)  based on ANALOGY; using analogy; having to do with analogy. *adj.*

**a·nal·o·gous** (ə nal′ə gəs)  **1** corresponding in some way; similar in the quality or feature that is being thought of; comparable: *The heart is analogous to a pump.* **2** of animals or plants, corresponding in function but not in structure and origin. *adj.* —**a·nal′o·gous·ly,** *adv.*

## anaemia 39 anathema

hat, āge, fär; let, ēqual, tėrm; it, īce
hot, ōpen, ôrder; oil, out; cup, put, rüle
əbove, takən, penciəl, lemən, circəs
ch, child; ng, long; sh, ship
th, thin; ᴛʜ, then; zh, measure

**a·nal·o·gy** (ə nal′ə jē)  **1** a likeness in some ways between things that are otherwise unlike; similarity: *The analogy between words like* man *and* pan *sometimes causes children to say* mans *for* men.  **2** a comparison of such things: *It is risky to argue by analogy.*  **3** of animals or plants, correspondence in function but not in structure and origin. *n., pl.* **a·nal·o·gies.**

**an·a·lyse** *or* **an·a·lyze** (an′ə līz′)  **1** separate into its parts: *We can analyse water into oxygen and hydrogen.*  **2** examine critically the parts or elements of; find out the essential features of: *After you analyse a sentence, you can explain the form and use of every word in it.*  **3** examine carefully and in detail. *v.*, **an·a·lysed** *or* **an·a·lyzed, an·a·lys·ing** *or* **an·a·lyz·ing.** —**an′a·lys′er** *or* **an′a·lyz′er,** *n.*

**a·nal·y·sis** (ə nal′ə sis)  **1** the separation of a thing into its parts.  **2** examination of a thing's parts to find out their essential features: *An analysis can be made of a book, a person's character, a medicine, soil, etc.*  **3** in chemistry, the intentional separation of a substance into its ingredients or elements to determine their amount or nature. *n., pl.* **a·nal·y·ses** (-sēz′).

**an·a·lyst** (an′ə list)  **1** a person who ANALYSES.  **2** a person who practises PSYCHOANALYSIS. *n.*

**an·a·lyt·ic** (an′ə lit′ik)  ANALYTICAL. *adj.*

**an·a·lyt·i·cal** (an′ə lit′ə kəl)  of ANALYSIS; using analysis: *the analytical methods of science. An analytical balance is an extremely delicate pair of scales for weighing things.* *adj.* —**an′a·lyt′i·cal·ly,** *adv.*

**an·a·lyze** (an′ə līz′)  See ANALYSE. *v.*, **an·a·lyzed, an·a·lyz·ing.**

**an·a·phase** (an′ə fāz′)  the third stage of MITOSIS, in which the chromatids of each chromosome separate and move toward either end of the cell. *n.*

**an·ar·chic** (an är′kik)  lawless; favouring ANARCHY. *adj.*

**an·ar·chism** (an′ər kiz′əm)  **1** the political theory that all systems of government and law are unnecessary and in fact harmful because they prevent individuals from reaching their greatest development: *Anarchism advocates a society based on voluntary co-operation among individuals and groups.*  **2** the support or practice of anarchistic beliefs.  **3** lawlessness or terrorism. *n.*

**an·ar·chist** (an′ər kist)  **1** a person who favours and supports ANARCHISM as a political idea.  **2** a person who uses violent means to overthrow organized government.  **3** a person who promotes disorder or rebels against established laws or customs. *n.*

**an·ar·chis·tic** (an′ər kis′tik)  of or having to do with ANARCHISM or anarchists. *adj.*

**an·ar·chy** (an′ər kē)  **1** the absence of a system of government and law.  **2** a state of political disorder and violence due to the absence of governmental authority.  **3** disorder or confusion. *n.*

**a·nath·e·ma** (ə nath′ə mə)  **1** a solemn curse by Christian authorities excommunicating some person from the church. 2 the denouncing and condemning of some person or thing as evil; a curse. 3 a person or thing accursed. 4 something that is detested and condemned. *n., pl.* **a·nath·e·mas.**

**a·nath·e·ma·tize** (ə nath'ə mə tīz'), pronounce an ANATHEMA against; denounce; curse. *v.* **a·nath·e·ma·tized, a·nath·e·ma·tiz·ing.** —**a·nath'e·ma·ti·za'tion,** *n.* —**a·nath'e·ma·tiz'er.** *n.*

**An·a·to·li·an** (an'ə tō'lē ən) 1 of or having to do with Anatolia (Asia Minor) or its people. 2 a native or inhabitant of Anatolia. 1 *adj.*, 2 *n.*

**an·a·tom·ic** (an'ə tom'ik) ANATOMICAL. *adj.*

**an·a·tom·i·cal** (an'ə tom'ə kəl) of ANATOMY; having to do with anatomy; structural. *adj.* —**an'a·tom'i·cal·ly,** *adv.*

**a·nat·o·mist** (ə nat'ə mist) 1 an expert in ANATOMY. 2 a person who dissects or analyses. *n.*

**a·nat·o·mize** (ə nat'ə mīz') 1 divide into parts to study the structure; dissect. 2 examine the parts of; analyse. *v.*, **a·nat·o·mized, a·nat·o·miz·ing.** —**a·nat'o·mi·za'tion,** *n.*

**a·nat·o·my** (ə nat'ə mē) 1 the structure of an animal or plant: *The anatomy of an earthworm is much simpler than that of a human being.* 2 the science of the structure of animals and plants: *Anatomy is a part of biology.* 3 the dissecting of animals or plants to study their structure. *n., pl.* **a·nat·o·mies.**

**–ance** a noun-forming suffix meaning: 1 the act or fact of _____ing: *Avoidance means the act or fact of avoiding.* 2 the quality or state of being _____ed: *Annoyance means the quality or state of being annoyed.* 3 the quality or state of being _____ant: *Importance means the quality or state of being important.* 4 something that _____s: *Conveyance means something that conveys.* 5 what is _____ed: *Contrivance means what is contrived.*

**an·ces·tor** (an'ses tər) 1 a person from whom one is directly descended, such as one's father, mother, grandfather, or grandmother. 2 an original model or type from which others are developed: *The horseless carriage is the ancestor of the modern automobile.* 3 in biology, an earlier species or type from which a later or existing species is descended: *The mammoth is the ancestor of the elephant. The horse and the donkey have a common ancestor.* *n.* Compare with DESCENDANT.

**an·ces·tral** (an ses'trəl) 1 of or having to do with ANCESTORS: *The ancestral home of the Acadians was France.* 2 inherited from ANCESTORS (def. 1): *Black hair is an ancestral trait in that family.* *adj.* —**an·ces'tral·ly,** *adv.*

**an·ces·tress** (an'ses tris) a woman from whom one is descended. *n.*

**an·ces·try** (an'ses' trē) 1 one's parents, grandparents, and other ancestors: *Many of the early settlers in America had English ancestry.* 2 the line of descent from ancestors; lineage. 3 an honourable descent. *n., pl.* **an·ces·tries.**

Anchors. The traditional ship's anchor on the left is still often used for boats, but ships now commonly use anchors of the type shown in the centre. The grapnel, on the right, is used for dories, etc.

**an·chor** (ang'kər) 1 a heavy piece of iron, usually having hooks, that is fastened to a ship or boat by a chain or rope and dropped into the water: *A ship's anchor grips the bottom of a river, lake, etc. and keeps the ship from drifting.* 2 hold in place with an anchor: *to anchor a ship.* 3 drop anchor; stop or stay in place by using an anchor: *We'll anchor here until morning.* 4 a thing for holding something else in place: *The anchors of the cables of a suspension bridge are at the ends of the cables.* 5 hold in place; fix firmly: *We anchored the tent to the ground.* 6 something that makes a person feel safe and secure. 1, 4, 6 *n.*, 2, 3, 5 *v.*
**at anchor,** held by an anchor.
**cast anchor,** drop the anchor.
**ride at anchor,** be kept at some place by being anchored.
**weigh anchor,** take up the anchor.

**an·chor·age** (ang'kə rij) 1 a place to anchor. 2 the money paid for the right to anchor. 3 anchoring or being anchored. *n*

**an·cho·vy** (an'chō vē) any of a family of very small fish distantly related to the herring, used for food and also for bait: *Most species of anchovy are found in warm seas.* *n., pl.* **an·cho·vies.**

**an·cien régime** (äN syaN Rä zhēm') French. 1 the social and political structure of France before the Revolution of 1789. 2 any former system; the old order of things.

**an·cient** (ān'shənt) 1 of or belonging to times long past, especially the period before the fall of the Roman Empire in A.D. 476: *ancient history, ancient records. We saw the ruins of an ancient temple built four thousand years ago.* 2 of great age; very old: *an ancient city.* 3 a very old person. 4 **the ancients,** *pl.* people who lived long ago, especially the Greeks and Romans. 1, 2 *adj.*, 3 4 *n.* —**an'cient·ness,** *n.*

**ancient history** 1 history from the earliest times to the fall of the western part of the Roman Empire in A.D. 476. 2 *Informal.* a well-known fact or event of the recent past.

**an·cient·ly** (ān'shən tlē) in ancient times. *adv.*

**an·cil·lar·y** (an sil'ə rē) 1 subordinate; dependent: *She owns a factory and several ancillary plants.* 2 additional; supplementary: *Ancillary information can be found in the appendix.* *adj.*

**and** (ənd *or* ən; *stressed,* and) a conjunction used to join grammatically equivalent words, phrases, and clauses: 1 as well as: *windy and cold.* 2 added to; with: *4 and 2 make 6. He likes ham and eggs.* 3 as a result: *The sun came out and the grass dried.* 4 in order to: *Try and do better.* *conj.*

**and.** andante.

**an·dan·te** (an dan'tē *or* än dän'tā) in music: 1 moderately slow; faster than ADAGIO, but slower than ALLEGRETTO: *This section should be performed andante.*

**2** moderately slow; faster than ADAGIO, but slower than ALLEGRETTO: *an andante movement.* **3** a moderately slow movement or piece of music. *1 adv., 2 adj., 3 n.*

**An·de·an** (an dē′ən) of or having to do with the Andes, a mountain system in western South America. *adj.*

**and·i·ron** (an′dī′ərn) one of a pair of metal supports for wood in a fireplace; firedog. See FIREPLACE for picture. *n.*

**an·ec·do·tal** (an′ik dō′təl) of or containing ANECDOTES. *adj.*

**an·ec·dote** (an′ik dōt′) a short account of some interesting or amusing incident or event: *Many anecdotes are told about Sir John A. Macdonald.* *n.*

**a·ne·mi·a** (ə nē′mē ə) an insufficiency of red corpuscles or of HEMOGLOBIN in the blood. *n.* Also, **anaemia**.

**a·ne·mic** (ə nē′mik) of ANEMIA; having anemia. *adj.* Also, **anaemic**.

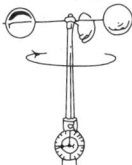
An anemometer. The cups are caught and moved by the wind, causing the vertical shaft to revolve. The speed of these revolutions is shown on the dial.

**an·e·mom·e·ter** (an′ə mom′ə tər) an instrument for measuring the speed of the wind. *n.*

**a·nem·o·ne** (ə nem′ə nē′) **1** any of a closely related group of small flowers of the buttercup family having lobed or divided leaves and large showy flowers: *The crocus of the Prairies is an anemone.* **2** SEA ANEMONE. *n.*

**an·er·oid barometer** (an′ə roid′) a barometer that records the changing pressure of air on the flexible top of an air-tight metal box from which some of the air has been pumped out: *The barometers commonly used in houses and offices are aneroid barometers.* See BAROMETER for picture.

**an·es·the·sia** (an′əs thē′zhə *or* an′əs thē′zē ə) an entire or partial loss of the feeling of pain, touch, cold, etc., produced by drugs, hypnotism, etc. or as the result of hysteria, paralysis, or disease. **General anesthesia** is the loss of feeling in the whole body, causing complete or partial unconsciousness. **Local anesthesia** is the loss of feeling in only part of the body. *n.* Also, **anaesthesia**.

**an·es·thet·ic** (an′əs thet′ik) **1** a substance that causes entire or partial loss of the feeling of pain, touch, etc.: *Halothane, sodium pentothal and procaine are anesthetics used by doctors so that patients will feel no pain during surgery.* **2** causing ANESTHESIA. **3** of or with ANESTHESIA. *1 n., 2 3 adj.* Also, **anaesthetic**.
—**an′es·thet′i·cal·ly** *or* **an′aes·thet′i·cal·ly**, *adv.*

**an·es·the·tist** (ə nēs′thə tist *or* ə nes′thə tist) a person whose work is giving ANESTHETICS (def. 1) during operations, etc. *n.* Also, **anaesthetist**.

**an·es·the·tize** (ə nēs′thə tīz′ *or* ə nes′thə tīz′) make unable to feel pain, touch, cold, etc.; make insensible. *v.*, **an·es·the·tized, an·es·the·tiz·ing.** Also, **anaesthetize.** —**an·es′the·tiz′er** *or* **an·aes′the·tiz′er,** *n.*

**a·new** (ə nyü′ *or* ə nü′) **1** once more; again: *At each meeting the question was raised anew.* **2** in a new form or way: *Rita crossed out the whole paragraph and began anew.* *adv.*

hat, āge, fär; let, ēqual, tėrm; it, īce
hot, ōpen, ôrder; oil, out; cup, pùt, rüle
əbove, takən, pencəl, lemən, circəs
ch, child; ng, long; sh, ship
th, thin; ᴛʜ, then; zh, measure

**an·gel** (ān′jəl) **1** in certain religions, an immortal, spiritual being who is an attendant and messenger of God. **2** in art, a representation of such a being, shown in human form but with wings, white robes, and, often, a halo. **3** a person like an angel in goodness, innocence, or loveliness. **4** any supernatural spirit, either good or bad: *the angel of death.* **5** *Informal.* a person who provides money for a business venture such as the production of a play. **6** an old English gold coin in use between 1465 and 1634. *n.*

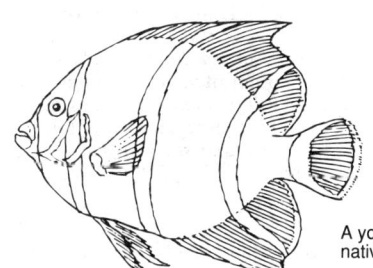
A young French angelfish, native to the Caribbean.

**an·gel·fish** (ān′jəl fish′) **1** any of several quite different species within one family of tropical marine fish, usually brightly coloured and having a deep, narrow body: *Some angelfish are very popular for aquariums.* **2** a species of shark found in warm seas, having large, winglike fins and reaching a length of about 120 cm. *n., pl.* **an·gel·fish** *or* **an·gel·fish·es**.

**an·gel·ic** (an jel′ik) **1** of angels; heavenly. **2** like an angel; pure; innocent; good and lovely. *adj.*
—**an·gel′i·cal·ly,** *adv.*

**an·gel·i·ca** (an jel′ə kə) any of a closely related group of tall perennial herbs of the carrot family found in the Northern Hemisphere and New Zealand, having compound leaves and clusters of white or greenish flowers: *Some species of angelica yield an oil used as a flavouring, in making perfume, etc.* *n.*

**an·gel·i·cal** (an jel′ə kəl) ANGELIC. *adj.*

**an·ger** (ang′gər) **1** the feeling of wanting to retaliate that one has toward some person, animal, or thing that hurts, opposes, offends, or annoys; wrath; strong displeasure. **2** make angry: *The boy's disobedience angered his father.* **3** become angry: *He angers easily.* *1 n., 2 3 v.*

**an·gi·na** (an jī′nə) **1** any inflammatory disease of the mouth or throat, such as quinsy, croup, mumps, or diphtheria, marked by painful attacks of suffocation. **2** ANGINA PECTORIS. *n.*

**angina pectoris** (pek′tə ris) a serious disease of the heart that causes sharp chest pains and a feeling of suffocation.

**an·gi·o·sperm** (an′jē ō spėrm′) any of a class of plants having their seeds enclosed in an ovary or fruit; a flowering plant: *Some angiosperms are the rose, apple, and oak.* *n.*

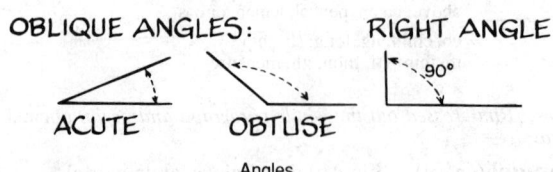
Angles

**an·gle**[1] (ang′gəl) **1** the space between two lines extending in different directions from the same point or two surfaces extending from the same line. See DEGREE for another picture. See also ACUTE ANGLE, ADJACENT ANGLES, OBTUSE ANGLE, RIGHT ANGLE. **2** the figure formed by such lines or surfaces. **3** the difference in direction between two such lines or surfaces: *The roads lie at an angle of about 45 degrees.* **4** move, place, turn, or bend at an angle: *The table will look better if we angle it across the corner. A narrow path angled through the woods.* **5** a corner. **6** *Informal.* a point of view: *From any angle, the job was excellent.* **7** *Informal.* a means or method of obtaining an advantage, especially an unfair one: *She always has an angle for getting the better of you.* **8** one aspect of something; phase. *1–3, 5–8 n., 4 v.*, **an·gled, an·gling.**

**an·gle**[2] (ang′gəl) fish with a hook and line. *v.*, **an·gled, an·gling.**
**angle for,** try to get something by using tricks or schemes: *to angle for an invitation.*

**An·gle** (ang′gəl) a member of a Germanic tribe that migrated from what is now southern Denmark to England in the fifth century A.D. *n.*

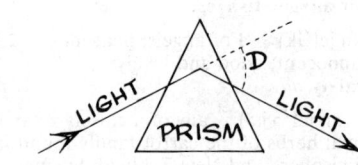
D is the angle of deviation.

**angle of deviation** the angle made between a ray of light as it enters a PRISM (def. 2) or other optical medium and the ray that emerges.

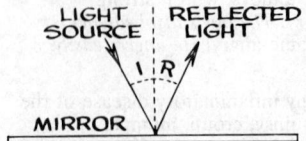
I is the angle of incidence.
R is the angle of reflection.
The angle of incidence is always equal to the angle of reflection.

**angle of incidence** the angle made by a ray of light falling upon a surface with a line perpendicular to that surface.

**angle of reflection** the angle that a ray of light makes on reflection from a surface with a line perpendicular to that surface.

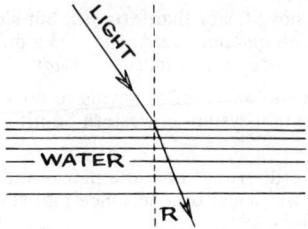
R is the angle of refraction.

**angle of refraction** the angle made between a ray of light that is REFRACTED at a surface separating two media, and a line perpendicular to the surface.

**an·gler** (ang′glər) **1** a person who fishes with a hook and line. **2** a person who tries to get something by using tricks and schemes. **3** any of a family of fishes that live at the bottom of the sea along the coasts of Europe and North America, having a huge mouth and a long, movable filament growing from the head, which serves to attract other fish that the anglers prey on: *The mouth of an angler is so big that it can swallow fish almost as big as itself.* *n.*

**an·gle·worm** (ang′gəl wėrm′) EARTHWORM. *n.*

**An·gli·an** (ang′glē ən) **1** of or having to do with the Angles, their dialect, or customs. **2** an Angle. **3** the dialect of the Angles. *1 adj., 2 3 n.*

**An·gli·cize** (ang′glə sīz′) make or become English in form, pronunciation, habits, customs or character. *v.*, **An·gli·cized, An·gli·ci·zing.** —**An′gli·ci·za′tion,** *n.*

**an·gling** (ang′gling) the act or art of fishing with a rod and line. *n.*

**Anglo–** *combining form.* **1** English or English-speaking: *An Anglo-Canadian is an English-speaking Canadian.* **2** English or British and _____: *Anglo-American means British and American.*

**Ang·lo** or **ang·lo** (ang′glō) *Cdn. Informal.* ANGLO-CANADIAN (defs. 2, 3). *adj., n.*

**An·glo–A·mer–i·can** (ang′glō ə mer′ə kən) **1** British and American. **2** an American, especially a United States citizen of English descent. **3** of or having to do with Anglo-Americans. *1, 3 adj., 2 n.*

**An·glo–Ca·na·di·an** (ang′glō kə nā′dē ən) **1** British and Canadian. **2** of or having to do with English-speaking Canadians. **3** an English-speaking Canadian; a Canadian whose native language is English. *1, 2 adj., 3 n.*

**An·glo–French** (ang′glō french′) **1** the French language as it developed in England after the Norman Conquest, especially after continental French began to have more influence in England than the dialect of the Normans. **2** of or referring to this language. **3** British and French: *an Anglo-French agreement.* *1 n., 2, 3 adj.*

**An·glo–Nor·man** (ang′glō nôr′mən) **1** any of the Normans who settled in England between 1066 and 1154. **2** a descendant of an English Norman. **3** the French dialect of the Normans as used in England after 1066. **4** of or referring to the Anglo-Normans or their dialect. *1–3 n., 4 adj.*

**An·glo·phone** or **an·glo·phone** (ang′glə fōn′) an English-speaking person who lives in a bilingual or multilingual country. *n.*

**An·glo–Sax·on** (ang′glō sak′sən) **1** a member of the nation that dominated England before the Norman

Conquest in 1066, descended from the Germanic tribes who conquered England in the fifth century A.D.  **2** the language of the Anglo-Saxons; Old English.  **3** of or having to do with the Anglo-Saxons or their language.  **4** a person who in any period of history has spoken English as his or her native language.  **5** a person of English descent.   *1, 2, 4 5 n., 3 adj.*

**An·go·ra** (ang gô′rə)  **1** Often, **angora**,  **a** the hair of the ANGORA RABBIT.  **b** yarn made from this hair, used especially for knitting.  **c** mohair.  **2** Often, **angora**, made from this yarn: *an angora sweater.*  **3** ANGORA CAT.  **4** ANGORA GOAT.  **5** ANGORA RABBIT.  *n.*

**Angora cat**  a breed of cat having long, silky hair, a bushy tail, and a ruff of hair around the neck.
☞ *Etym.*  See note at ANGORA GOAT.

**Angora goat**  a breed of goat having spiral horns and long, silky, curly white hair that is used for making cloth: *The hair of the Angora goat or cloth made from it is usually called mohair.*
☞ *Etym.*  From *Angora*, the former name of the Turkish province *Ankara.* The Angora goat and Angora cat came originally from Ankara.

**Angora rabbit**  a breed of rabbit having long, soft, usually white hair that is used for making yarns, especially for knitting: *The Angora rabbit was developed from a species of European wild rabbit.*
☞ *Etym.*  Named after the Angora goat because it has a similar type of hair. See also note at ANGORA GOAT.

**An·gra Main·yu** (äng′rə mī′nyü)  in Zoroastrianism, the evil spirit of the cosmos.

**an·gry** (ang′grē)  **1** feeling or showing anger: *an angry look. She was angry with her brother.*  **2** raging or stormy: *an angry sky.*  **3** moved by anger: *angry words.*  **4** inflamed and sore: *Valerla had an angry cut on her arm.*  *adj.,* **an·gri·er, an·gri·est.**  —**an′gri·ly,** *adv.*  —**an′gri·ness,** *n.*

**ang·strom** or **ång·ström** (ang′strəm)  a unit for measuring length, equal to one ten-millionth of a millimetre: *The angstrom is sometimes used to measure wavelengths of light.*  Symbol: Å   *n.*

**angstrom unit**  ANGSTROM.

**an·guish** (ang′gwish)  very great pain or grief; great suffering or distress: *He was in anguish until the doctor had set his broken leg.*  *n.*

**an·guished** (ang′gwisht)  **1** suffering ANGUISH.  **2** full of ANGUISH; showing anguish: *the anguished face of a mother whose child is lost.*  *adj.*

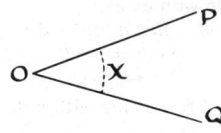
Angular (def. 2). The angular distance of P from Q, when measured from O, is the angle X.

**an·gu·lar** (ang′gyə lər)  **1** having ANGLES; sharp-cornered: *an angular rock.*  **2** measured by an angle: *angular distance.*  **3** somewhat thin and bony; not plump: *He has a tall, angular body.*  *adj.*
—**an′gu·lar·ly,** *adv.*

**an·gu·lar·i·ty** (ang′gyə lar′ə tē *or* ang′gyə ler′ə tē)  the condition of having sharp or prominent corners.  *n.*

**an·hy·dride** (an hī′drīd)  an oxide that unites with water to form an acid or base: *Sulphur trioxide is the anhydride of sulphuric acid.*  *n.*

**an·hy·drous** (an hī′drəs)  **1** without water: *an anhydrous region.*  **2** in chemistry, containing no water of crystallization.  *adj.*

**an·ile** (an′īl *or* ā′nīl)  old-womanish; suitable for a weak or doting old woman.  *adj.*

**an·i·line** (an′ə lin *or* an′ə līn′)  a poisonous, oily liquid, obtained from COAL TAR and, especially from NITRO-BENZENE, used in making dyes, perfumes, plastics, etc.: *Aniline is a compound of carbon, nitrogen, and oxygen.*  *n.*

**aniline dye**  **1** a dye made from ANILINE.  **2** any artificial dye.

**a·nil·i·ty** (ə nil′ə tē)  **1** an ANILE condition.  **2** an ANILE act or notion.  *n., pl.* **a·nil·i·ties.**

**an·i·mad·ver·sion** (an′ə mad vėr′zhən)  criticism; blame; an unfavourable comment.  *n.*

**an·i·mad·vert** (an′ə mad vėrt′)  make criticism; express blame; comment unfavourably (*on*).  *v.*

**an·i·mal** (an′ə məl)  **1** any living thing that is not a plant, fungus, protist or moneran: *Most animals can move about, while most plants cannot; most animals are unable to make their own food from carbon dioxide, water, nitrogen, etc., but most plants can.*  **2** any creature other than a human being; brute; beast.  **3** a person thought of as being like a brute or beast; a person seemingly without human feelings.  **4** of or having to do with the physical nature of human beings, as opposed to the spiritual; carnal: *animal appetites.*  **5** any four-footed creature: *the animals and birds of the forest.*  **6** of, having to do with, or characteristic of animals, especially the higher animals other than humans: *animal intelligence.*  *1–3, 5 n., 4 6 adj.*
☞ *Etym.*  **Animal**, ANIMALISM, ANIMATE, ANIMISM, ANIMOSITY, and ANIMUS can all be traced back to two related Latin words: *anima*, originally meaning 'breath of air' and later 'breath of life' and 'a living being, a soul', and *animus* 'mind, spirit, feeling'. **Animate** comes from L *animare* 'give breath, or life, to', formed from *anima*. **Animal** comes from L *animal* 'living creature', also formed from *anima*. The word **animalism** was formed in English later on and is based on the English meaning of an animal as a living creature other than a human being. **Animism**, on the other hand, was formed in English directly from L *anima* + E suffix *-ism*. **Animosity** comes from F *animosité* or L *animositas* 'spiritedness' which developed from L *animus*; the present-day meaning of 'hostile feeling or spirit' developed later in English. **Animus** was taken into English in the 19c. directly from L *animus*; it now means both 'animating or driving spirit' and 'hostile spirit'.

**an·i·mal·cule** (an′ə mal′kyül)  a minute or microscopic animal.  *n.*

**an·i·mal·ism** (an′ə mə liz′əm)  **1** enjoyment of the natural health and vitality typical of animals.  **2** preoccupation with the satisfying of physical needs and desires.  **3** the belief or doctrine that human beings are no more than animals and that they have no soul or spirit.  *n.*
☞ *Etym.*  See note at ANIMAL.

**an·i·mal·i·ty** (an′ə mal′ə tē) **1** an animal nature or character in man. **2** animal life. *n.*

**animal kingdom** **1** the group of living creatures that can move about and do not use photosynthesis to obtain nourishment. **2** in present-day biology, one of the five basic groups into which all living things are divided: *The animal kingdom includes all living animals, birds, fish, insects, etc.* See also FUNGUS, MONERAN, PLANT and PROTIST.

**animal spirits** natural liveliness; healthy cheerfulness.

**an·i·mate** (an′ə māt′ *for verb,* an′ə mit *for adjective*) **1** give life to; make alive. **2** living; having life: *Animate nature means all living plants and animals.* **3** make lively, cheerful, or vigorous: *Mohammed's funny stories animated the whole party.* **4** inspire; encourage: *A fierce desire to succeed animated her efforts.* **5** put into action; cause to act or work: *Windmills are animated by the wind.* 1, 3–5 *v.,* **an·i·mat·ed, an·i·mat·ing;** 2 *adj.*
☛ *Etym.* See note at ANIMAL.

**an·i·mat·ed** (an′ə mā′tid) **1** lively; vigorous: *The two girls engaged in an animated discussion of yesterday's baseball game.* **2** moving so as to give the appearance of being alive: *animated dolls.* **3** made as an ANIMATED CARTOON: *The movie has some animated sequences and some scenes with live actors.* **4** pt. and pp. of ANIMATE. 1–3 *adj.,* 4 *v.* —**an′i·mat·ed·ly,** *adv.*

**animated cartoon** a series of drawings arranged to be photographed and shown as a motion picture: *Each drawing in an animated cartoon shows a slight change from the one before it.*

**an·i·ma·tion** (an′ə mā′shən) **1** animating or being animated. **2** liveliness; spirit. **3** the process or technique of making ANIMATED CARTOONS. *n.*

**a·ni·ma·to** (ä′ni mä′tō) in music, lively; vigorous. *adj.*

**an·i·mism** (an′ə miz′əm) **1** a belief in the existence of a soul distinct from matter; belief in spiritual beings, such as souls, angels, and devils. **2** a belief that there are living spirits in trees, stones, stars, etc. *n.*
☛ *Etym.* See note at ANIMAL.

**an·i·mos·i·ty** (an′ə mos′ə tē) active or violent dislike; ill will: *Gabriel felt no animosity toward the winner.* *n., pl.* **an·i·mos·i·ties.**
☛ *Etym.* See note at ANIMAL.

**an·i·mus** (an′ə məs) **1** violent hatred; ill will; active dislike or enmity. **2** an animating thought or spirit; intention: *Ambition was his animus.* *n.*
☛ *Etym.* See note at ANIMAL.

**an·i·on** (an′ī ən) **1** an atom or group of atoms having a negative charge. **2** in electrolysis, a negatively charged ION that moves toward the positive pole. See ELECTROLYSIS for picture. *n.*

**an·ise** (an′is) **1** a plant of the same family as the carrot, grown for its fragrant seeds: *Anise grows in the Mediterranean.* **2** the seed of this plant. *n.*

**an·i·seed** (an′ə sēd′) the seed of ANISE (def. 1), used as a flavouring and in medicine. *n.*

**an·i·sette** (an′ə set′ *or* an′ə zet′) a sweet, usually colourless liqueur flavoured with ANISEED. *n.*

**an·kle** (ang′kəl) **1** the part of the human leg between the foot and the calf: *slim ankles.* **2** the protruding part on the outside bottom end of each of the lower leg bones, just above the foot: *I bumped my ankle against the chair. Yaakov has a broken ankle.* **3** the joint formed by the lower leg bones and the TALUS, connecting the foot and the leg: *My ankle is still stiff from when I twisted it.* See LEG for picture. **4** the part of a stocking, sock, or boot that covers the ankle. **5** in a horse, etc., the joint between the CANNON BONE and the PASTERN. *n.*

**an·kle·bone** (ang′kəl bōn′) the protruding part on the outside of the bottom end of each of the lower leg bones, just above the foot. See LEG for picture. *n.*

**an·klet** (ang′klit) **1** a short sock. **2** a chain or band worn around the ankle, especially as an ornament. *n.*

**an·nal·ist** (an′ə list) a writer of ANNALS. *n.*

**an·nals** (an′əlz) **1** a written account of events year by year. **2** historical records; history. *n. pl.*

**an·neal** (ə nēl′) toughen glass, metals, etc. by heating and then cooling; TEMPER (def. 5). *v.*

**an·ne·lid** (an′ə lid) any of the more than 8 000 species of segmented worms making up a PHYLUM of the animal kingdom: *Annelids are grouped into three classes: sea worms, earthworms, and leeches.* *n.*

**an·nex** (ə neks′ *for verb,* an′eks *for noun*) **1** join or add to a larger thing: *Britain annexed Acadia in 1713.* **2** *Informal.* take as one's own; appropriate. **3** something added or attached; an added part: *Our hotel has an annex.* 1, 2, *v.,* 3 *n.*

**an·nex·a·tion** (an′ek sā′shən) **1** ANNEXing or being annexed: *the annexation of Acadia by Britain.* **2** something ANNEXED. *n.*

**Annexation Movement** the name given to groups in Canada that have advocated political union with the United States.

**an·ni·hi·late** (ə nī′ə lāt′) destroy completely; wipe out of existence: *The earthquake annihilated more than thirty towns and villages.* *v.* **an·ni·hi·lated, an·ni·hi·lat·ing.**

**an·ni·hi·la·tion** (ə nī′ə lā′shən) a complete destruction. *n.*

**an·ni·ver·sa·ry** (an′ə vėr′sə rē) **1** the yearly return of a date: *Tomorrow is the anniversary of her birthday.* **2** a celebration of the yearly return of a special date: *a wedding anniversary.* **3** having to do with an anniversary: *an anniversary dinner.* *n., pl.* **an·ni·ver·sa·ries.**

**an·no Dom·i·ni** (an′ō dom′ə nē *or* an′ō dom′ə nī) **1** *Latin.* in the year of Our Lord. **2** any year since the birth of Christ. *Abbrev.:* A.D.

**an·no·tate** (an′ō tāt′) provide with explanatory notes or comments: *Shakespeare's plays are often annotated to make them easier for modern readers to understand.* *v.,* **an·no·tat·ed, an·no·tat·ing.** —**an′no·ta·tor,** *n.*

**an·no·ta·tion** (an′ō tā′shən) **1** furnishing with notes: *That book's annotation required hundreds of hours.* **2** a note added to explain or criticize: *The editor's annotations were printed in small type.* *n.*

**an·nounce** (ə nouns′) **1** make known; give formal or public notice of: *to announce a wedding in the papers. She announced that she was never going to school again.* **2** make known the presence or arrival of: *The butler announced each guest.* *v.,* **an·nounced, an·nounc·ing.**

**an·nounce·ment** (ə nouns′smənt) **1** announcing; making known: *His announcement of his resignation was a surprise.* **2** what is announced or made known by private or public notice: *The announcement appeared in the newspaper.* *n.*

**an·nounc·er** (ə noun′sər)   a person who announces, especially a person in radio and television who introduces programs, reads news, etc.   *n.*

**an·noy** (ə noi′)   **1** make angry; disturb; trouble; irritate: *The baby annoys his sister by pulling her hair.*   **2** hurt; harm; molest: *They began a series of raids designed to annoy the enemy.*   *v.*

**an·noy·ance** (ə noi′əns)   **1** an annoying.   **2** a feeling of being bothered or irritated; vexation: *She replied with annoyance that she had heard that story before.*   **3** anything that annoys: *The heavy traffic on our street is a great annoyance.*   *n.*

**an·noyed** (ə noid′)   **1** disturbed; troubled: *The teacher was annoyed at the interruption.*   **2** molested; hurt.   *adj.*

**an·noy·ing** (ə noi′ing)   disturbing; troublesome.   *adj.* —**an·noy·ing·ly,** *adv.*   —**an·noy·ing·ness,** *n.*

**an·nu·al** (an′yü əl)   **1** coming once a year: *Your birthday is an annual event.*   **2** in a year; for a year: *an annual salary of $45 000.*   **3** accomplished during a year: *the earth's annual course around the sun. You can tell the age of a tree by counting the annual rings.*   **4** of a plant, living just one year or season.   **5** a plant that lives one year or season.   **6** a book or journal published once a year. 1–4 *adj.*, 5, 6 *n.*

**an·nu·al·ly** (an′yü ə lē)   yearly; each year.   *adv.*

**an·nu·i·tant** (ə nyü′ə tənt *or* ə nü′ə tənt)   a person who receives an ANNUITY.   *n.*

**an·nu·i·ty** (ə nyü′ə tē *or* ə nü′ə tē)   **1** a sum of money paid every year.   **2** the right to receive or the duty to pay such a yearly sum: *In her will, she granted a small annuity to her secretary.*   *n., pl.* **an·nu·i·ties.**

**an·nul** (ə nul′)   do away with; destroy the force of; make void; abolish; cancel: *The judge annulled the contract because one of the signers was too young.*   *v.,* **an·nulled, an·nul·ling.**

**an·nu·lar** (an′yə lər)   ringlike; ring-shaped; ringed.   *adj.*

**an·nu·let** (an′yə lit)   **1** a little ring.   **2** a narrow, ringlike moulding of wood, stone, etc.   *n.*

**an·nul·ment** (ə nul′mənt)   an annulling or being annulled; cancellation.   *n.*

**an·num** (an′əm)   *Latin.*   year.   *n.*

**an·nun·ci·a·tion** (ə nun′sē ā′shən)   an announcement.   *n.*

**an·nun·ci·a·tor** (ə nun′sē ā′tər)   **1** an electrical device such as a buzzer or light, that indicates where a signal is coming from: *Annunciators are used in hotel switchboards, in manually operated elevators, etc.*   **2** ANNOUNCER.   *n.*

**A No. 1**   *Informal.*   A-one; first class.

**an·ode** (an′ōd)   **1** the negatively charged electrode of a primary cell or storage battery, through which the electrons leave the cell when the circuit is complete.   See DRY CELL for picture.   **2** in an electrolytic cell, the positive electrode that is connected to the positive terminal of a battery and carries electrons from the cell back to the battery.   See ELECTROLYSIS for picture.   **3** in a vacuum tube, the positively charged electrode that attracts electrons from the cathode, or emitter.   See VACUUM TUBE for picture.   *n.*

**an·o·dyne** (an′ə dīn′)   anything that lessens pain or provides comfort.   *n.*

**a·noint** (ə noint′)   **1** put oil on; rub with ointment; smear: *Anoint sunburned skin with cold cream.*   **2** put oil on in a ceremony as a sign of consecration to office; make sacred with oil: *The archbishop anointed the new king.*   *v.* —**a·noint′ment,** *n.*

**a·nom·a·lous** (ə nom′ə ləs)   departing from the common rule; irregular; abnormal: *A position as head of a department, but with no real authority, is anomalous.*   *adj.*

**a·nom·a·ly** (ə nom′ə lē)   **1** a departure from a general rule; irregularity.   **2** something abnormal: *A dog with six legs would be an anomaly.*   *n., pl.* **a·nom·a·lies.**

**a·non** (ə non′)   **1** in a little while; soon.   **2** at another time; again.   *adv.*
**ever and anon,**   now and then; from time to time.

**anon.**   anonymous.

**an·o·nym·i·ty** (an′ə nim′ə tē)   the quality or state of having one's name unknown: *She wrote under a pen name to preserve her anonymity.*   *n.*

**a·non·y·mous** (ə non′ə məs)   **1** by or from a person whose name is not known or given: *An anonymous book is one published without the name of the author.*   **2** of unknown name; nameless: *The author of this poem is anonymous.*   *adj.* —**a·non′y·mous·ly,** *adv.*

**a·noph·e·les** (ə nof′ə lēz′)   any of several species of mosquito that can transmit malaria.   *n., pl.* **a·noph·e·les.**

**a·no·rak** (an′ə rak′)   **1** a waterproof, hooded outer coat of skins, often worn by Inuit when hunting in a kayak: *The lower edge of an anorak can be fastened tightly around the opening in the kayak.*   **2** a PARKA, especially a waterproof one.   *n.*

**an·o·rex·i·a ner·vo·sa** (an′ə reks′ē ə nər vō′sə)   a fear of becoming fat, marked by a refusal to eat, resulting in excessive weight loss and malnutrition which, if not corrected, can end in death. Also, **anorexia.**

**an·oth·er** (ə nuᴛн′ər)   **1** one more: *Have another glass of milk.*   **2** one more: *He ate a bar of candy and then asked for another.*   **3** different: *That is another matter entirely.*   **4** a different one: *I don't like this book; give me another.*   **5** one of the same kind: *His father is a scholar, and he is another.*   1, 3 *adj.*, 2, 4, 5 *pron.*

**ans.**   **1** answer.   **2** answered.

**an·ser·ine** (an′sə rīn′)   **1** of or belonging to a group of birds that includes geese.   **2** of, like, or having to do with a goose or geese.   **3** stupid; foolish.   *adj.*

**an·swer** (an′sər)   **1** words spoken or written in return to a question: *The girl gave a quick answer.*   **2** make answer; reply: *I asked him a question, but he would not answer.*   **3** reply to: *He answered my question.*   **4** a gesture or act done in return: *A nod was her only answer.*   **5** reply or respond by act: *He knocked on the door, but no one answered.*   **6** act or move in response to: *She answered the doorbell.*   **7** the solution to a problem: *What is the correct answer to this algebra problem?*   **8** serve: *This will answer your purpose. Such a poor excuse will not answer.*   **9** reply to a charge: *to answer a summons.* 1, 4, 7 *n.*, 2, 3, 5, 6, 8, 9 *v.*
**answer back,**   *Informal.*   reply in a rude, saucy way.

**answer for,** bear the consequences of; be responsible for: *to answer for a crime, to answer for his safety.*

**answer to,** correspond to: *This house answers to her description.*

**an·swer·a·ble** (an′sə rə bəl) **1** responsible: *The club treasurer is answerable to the club for the money given to him.* **2** that can be answered. *adj.*

**ant** (ant) any of many kinds of usually wingless insects that live and work in organized groups called colonies, in which each subgroup has specialized functions to perform: *Ants live in tunnels in the ground or in wood.* *n.*
—**ant′like′,** *adj.*
☛ Hom. AUNT.

**-ant** a suffix meaning: **1** _____ ing: *Buoyant means buoying; compliant means complying; triumphant means triumphing.* **2** one that _____ s: *Assistant means one that assists.*

**ant.** antonym.

**ant·ac·id** (an tas′id) **1** a substance that neutralizes acids: *Baking soda and magnesia are antacids.* **2** tending to neutralize acids; counteracting ACIDITY. 1 *n.*, 2 *adj.* Compare with ACID.

**an·tag·o·nism** (an tag′ə niz′əm) active opposition; conflict; hostility. *n.*

**an·tag·o·nist** (an tag′ə nist) one who fights, struggles, or contends with another; an opponent; adversary; rival: *The knight defeated his antagonist.* Compare with PROTAGONIST. *n.*

**an·tag·o·nis·tic** (an tag′ə nis′tik) having or showing conflict or hostility; opposed: *an antagonistic attitude. Cats and dogs are antagonistic.* *adj.*
—**an·tag′o·nis′ti·cal·ly,** *adv.*

**an·tag·o·nize** (an tag′ə nīz′) make an enemy of; arouse dislike in: *Her unkind remarks antagonized people who had been her friends.* *v.,* **an·tag·o·nized, an·tag·o·niz·ing.** —**an·tag′o·niz′er,** *n.*

**ant·arc·tic** (an tärk′tik *or* an tär′tik) **1** Often, **Antarctic,** of, having to do with, referring to, or living or growing in the region south of the Antarctic Circle. **2 the Antarctic,** the south polar region; the region south of the Antarctic Circle. 1 *adj.,* 2 *n.*

**Antarctic Circle** **1** the imaginary circle of the south polar region, parallel to the equator at 23 degrees 30 minutes (23°30′) north of the South Pole. **2** the polar region surrounded by this circle.

**ant bear** the giant ANTEATER of South America.

**ante–** a prefix meaning: **1** before; earlier: *antedate.* **2** in front of: *anteroom.*

**ant·eat·er** (ant′ē′tər) **1** any of a family of toothless mammals found in the tropical forests of South America, having long, tube-shaped head and muzzle with a small mouth opening and a long, slender, sticky, wormlike tongue with which it catches the ants and termites it eats: *The giant, or great, anteater, the largest species, has a long, bushy tail and very strong front claws with which it rips open the nests of ants and termites.* **2** any of several other mammals, such as the AARDVARK and the PANGOLIN, that feed mainly on ants and termites but are not related to the true anteaters. *n.*

**an·te·ced·ence** (an′tə sē′dəns) going before; precedence; priority. *n.*

**an·te·ced·ent** (an′tə sē′dənt) **1** a previous thing or event; something happening before and leading up to another. **2** a word, phrase, or clause that is referred to by a pronoun or relative adverb. In *This is the house that Jack built,* house is the antecedent of *that.* In *I remember the house where I was born,* house is the antecedent of *where.* **3** the first term of a mathematical ratio. **4** coming or happening before; preceding; previous. **5 antecedents,** *pl.* **a** a past life or history: *No one knew the antecedents of the mysterious stranger.* **b** ancestors. 1–3, 5 *n.,* 4 *adj.*

**an·te·cham·ber** (an′tē chām′bər) ANTEROOM. *n.*

**an·te·date** (an′tē dāt′) **1** come before in time; occur earlier than: *Shakespeare's* Hamlet *antedates* Macbeth *by about six years.* **2** give too early a date to. *v.,* **an·te·dat·ed, an·te·dat·ing.**

**an·te·di·lu·vi·an** (an′tē də lü′vē ən) **1** of or having to do with the period before the Flood. **2** a person who lived before the Flood. **3** very old; old-fashioned. **4** an old-fashioned or very old person. 1, 3 *adj.,* 2, 4 *n.*

A Grant's gazelle, a kind of African antelope—about 83 cm high at the shoulder

A pronghorn antelope—about 95 cm high at the shoulder

**an·te·lope** (an′tə lōp′) **1** any of a large group of hoofed, cud-chewing animals found mainly in Africa, having hollow, non-branching horns that grow upward and backward and that are not shed: *Some antelope, such as the gazelles and the impala, resemble deer, but all antelope belong to the same family as cattle and goats.* **2** a very swift, hoofed, cud-chewing animal of the North American plains that belongs to a different family from the African antelope, having horns with a permanent bony core and a black, horny outer layer that is shed every year; PRONGHORN. *n., pl.* **an·te·lope** *or* **an·te·lopes.**

**an·te me·rid·i·em** (an′tē mə rid′ē əm) *Latin.* before noon. *Abbrev.:* a.m. *or* A.M.

**an·ten·na** (an ten′ə) **1** one of two feelers on the head of an insect, lobster, etc. See INSECT for picture. **2** in television and radio, a long wire or set of wires used for sending out or receiving electromagnetic waves; aerial. *n., pl.* **an·ten·nae** *for 1,* **an·ten·nas** *for 2.*

**an·ten·nae** (an ten′ē *or* an ten′ī) *pl.* of ANTENNA (def. 1). *n.*

**an·te·pe·nult** (an′tē pə nult′ *or* an′tē pē′nult) the third syllable from the end of a word: *In the word* anthropology, *the syllable* pol *is the antepenult.* *n.*

**an·te·pe·nul·ti·mate** (an′tē pə nul′tə mit) **1** third from the end; last but two. **2** ANTEPENULT. 1 *adj.,* 2 *n.*

**an·te·ri·or** (an tē′rē ər) **1** toward the front; fore: *The anterior part of a fish contains the head and gills.* **2** going before; earlier; previous. *adj.*

**an·te·room** (an′tē rüm′) a small room leading to a larger one; waiting room. *n.*

**an·them** (an′thəm) **1** a song of praise, devotion, or patriotism: *"O Canada" is sung as the national anthem of Canada.* **2** a piece of Christian sacred music, usually with words from some passage in the Bible: *The choir sang an anthem during the service.* *n.*

**an·ther** (an′thər) the part of the stamen of a flower that bears the pollen. See COMPOSITE and FLOWER for pictures. *n.*

**ant hill** **1** a heap of dirt piled up by ants around the entrance to their underground nest. **2** a TERMITE nest.

**an·thol·o·gist** (an thol′ə jist) a person who makes an ANTHOLOGY. *n.*

**an·thol·o·gy** (an thol′ə jē) a collection of poems or prose selections from various authors. *n., pl.* **an·thol·o·gies.**

**an·tho·zo·an** (an′thə zō′ən) any of a class of flowerlike marine animals having a body that is shaped somewhat like a cylinder, closed above and below by disks of tissue, the upper disk surrounded by a circle of hollow tentacles and having a mouth in the centre: *Sea anemones and corals are anthozoans.* *n.*

**an·thra·cene** (an′thrə sēn′) a colourless crystalline compound used in making ALIZARIN dyes: *Anthracene is a complex compound of hydrogen and carbon, obtained in distilling coal tar.* *n.*

**an·thra·cite** (an′thrə sīt′) a hard, shiny, black type of coal containing a high percentage of carbon and a low percentage of moisture: *Anthracite produces almost no smoke when it burns.* *n.*

**an·thrax** (an′thraks) an infectious, often fatal, disease of cattle, sheep, etc., which may be transmitted to human beings. *n.*

**an·thro·poid** (an′thrə poid′) **1** humanlike; used especially with reference to members of the ape family. **2** APE (def. 1). **1** *adj.,* **2** *n.*

**an·thro·po·log·i·cal** (an′thrə pə loj′ə kəl) of or having to do with ANTHROPOLOGY. *adj.*

**an·thro·pol·o·gist** (an′thrə pol′ə jist) a person trained in ANTHROPOLOGY, especially one who makes it his or her work. *n.*

**an·thro·pol·o·gy** (an′thrə pol′ə jē) the science that deals with the origin, development, races, customs, and beliefs of mankind. *n.*

**an·thro·po·mor·phic** (an′thrə pə môr′fik) attributing human form or qualities to gods or things: *The religion of ancient Greece was anthropomorphic.* *adj.*

**anti–** (an′tē) a prefix meaning: **1** against; opposed to _____: *Anti-aircraft means against aircraft.* **2** not; the opposite of _____: *Antisocial means the opposite of social.* **3** preventing or counteracting _____: *Antiseptic means preventing or counteracting infection.* **4** preventing, curing, or alleviating of _____: *Antiscorbutic means preventing, curing, or alleviating scurvy.*
☛ *Pronunciation.* The pronunciation given here (an′tē) is still the standard pronunciation in Canada. However, the variant pronunciation (an′tī), which is more typical of usage in the United States, is now making headway in Canada, especially in certain words, such as **antisocial**

## anterior 47 antidote

hat, āge, fär; let, ēqual, tėrm; it, īce
hot, ōpen, ôrder; oil, out; cup, pu̇t, rüle
əbove, takən, pencəl, lemən, circəs
ch, child; ng, long; sh, ship
th, thin; ŦH, then; zh, measure

(an′tī sō′shəl). The same trend can be seen in certain words beginning with **semi-** and **multi-**.

**an·ti–air·craft** (an′tē er′kraft′) used in defence against enemy aircraft. *adj.*

**an·ti·bi·ot·ic** (an′tē bī ot′ik) the product of an organism that destroys or weakens harmful micro-organisms: *Penicillin is an antibiotic.* *n.*

**an·ti·bod·y** (an′tē bod′ē) any of various proteins produced in the blood of animals or humans in reaction to foreign substances called ANTIGENS, to provide immunity to diseases: *Different antibodies are produced in reaction to different antigens.* *n., pl.* **an·ti·bod·ies.**

**an·tic** (an′tik) a grotesque action; silly trick. See also ANTICS. *n.*

**an·tic·i·pate** (an tis′ə pāt′) **1** look forward to; expect: *He had anticipated a good vacation in the mountains; but when the time came, he was sick.* **2** do, make, or use in advance: *The Chinese anticipated some modern discoveries.* **3** take care of ahead of time: *The nurse anticipated all the patient's wishes.* **4** be before another in thinking, acting, etc. **5** consider or mention before the proper time: *to anticipate a point in an argument.* **6** cause to happen sooner; hasten: *The lazy office boy anticipated his dismissal by poor work.* *v.,* **an·tic·i·pat·ed, an·tic·i·pat·ing.**

**an·tic·i·pa·tion** (an tis′ə pā′shən) **1** the act of looking forward; expectation: *The settler cut more wood than usual, in anticipation of a long winter.* **2** enjoyment in looking forward to something: *They were waiting for the holidays with great anticipation.* **3** action beforehand that provides for, takes into account, or prevents a later action or occurrence. **4** recognition, realization, or accomplishment beforehand. *n.*

**an·tic·i·pa·to·ry** (an tis′ə pə tô′rē) anticipating. *adj.*

**an·ti·cler·i·cal** (an′tē kler′ə kəl) opposed to the influence of the church and clergy in public affairs. *adj.*

**an·ti·cli·mac·tic** (an′tē klī mak′tik) of or like an ANTICLIMAX. *adj.*

**an·ti·cli·max** (an′tē klī′maks) **1** an abrupt descent from the important to the trivial. *Example:* "*Alas! Alas! what shall I do? I've lost my wife and best hat, too!*" **2** a descent in importance, interest, etc. contrasting with a previous rise. *n.*

**an·ti·cline** (an′ti klīn′) in geology, an arch of stratified rock, in which the layers slope downward in opposite directions from the centre. Compare with SYNCLINE. See SYNCLINE for picture. *n.*

**an·tics** (an′tiks) funny gestures or actions; silly tricks; capers: *the antics of a clown.* *n. pl.*

**an·ti·cy·clone** (an′tē sī′klōn) winds moving around and away from a centre of high pressure, which also moves. Compare with CYCLONE. *n.*

**an·ti·dote** (an′tə dōt′ or an′tē dōt′) **1** any medicine or remedy that counteracts a poison: *Milk is an antidote for some poisons.* **2** anything that counteracts or relieves:

*The plants and paintings served as an antidote to the impersonal atmosphere of the waiting room.* n.

**an·ti·freeze** (an'tē frēz')   a substance added to a liquid to lower its freezing point: *Alcohol is much used as an antifreeze in automobile radiators.* n.

**an·ti·fric·tion** (an'tē frik'shən)   a substance that prevents or reduces friction. n.

**an·ti·gen** (an'tə jən)   any substance that stimulates the production of antibodies or that reacts with antibodies that have already been formed: *Bacteria, viruses, and other micro-organisms are sources of antigens.* n.

**an·ti·his·ta·mine** (an'tē his'tə mēn')   a medicine used in the treatment of colds and allergies. n.

**an·ti·knock** (an'tē nok')   a substance added to the fuel of an INTERNAL-COMBUSTION ENGINE to reduce noise during its operation. n.

**an·ti·ma·cas·sar** (an'tē mə kas'ər)   a small covering used to protect the back and arms of a chair, chesterfield, etc. n.
☛ *Etym.* From *anti-* 'against' + *macassar*, a hair oil originally imported from Macassar, a seaport in Indonesia.

**anti–mis·sile** (an'tē mis'īl *or* an'tē mis'əl)   for use in defence against ballistic missiles, rockets, etc. adj.

**an·ti·mo·ny** (an'tē mō'nē)   a crystalline metal with a bluish-white lustre, used chiefly in ALLOYs to make them harder and in medicinal compounds: *Antimony is a chemical element that occurs chiefly in combination with other elements.* Symbol: Sb   n.

**an·ti·pas·to** (an'tē pas'tō *or* än'tē pä'stō) *Italian.*   an appetizer consisting of fish, meats, etc.; HORS D'OEUVRES. n., pl. **an·ti·pas·tos.**

**an·ti·pa·thet·ic** (an'tē pə thet'ik)   having ANTIPATHY; contrary or opposed in nature or disposition: *Dogs and cats are antipathetic.* adj.

**an·ti·pa·thet·i·cal** (an'tē pə thet'ə kəl) ANTIPATHETIC. adj.

**an·tip·a·thy** (an tip'ə thē)   **1** a strong or fixed dislike; a feeling against.   **2** something or someone that arouses such a feeling. n., pl. **an·tip·a·thies.**

**an·tip·o·dal** (an tip'ə dəl)   **1** on the opposite side of the earth.   **2** directly opposite; exactly contrary. adj.

**an·ti·pode** (an'tē pōd')   anything exactly opposite; direct opposite. n.

**an·tip·o·des** (an tip'ə dēz')   **1** two places on directly opposite sides of the earth: *The North Pole and the South Pole are antipodes.*   **2** a place on the opposite side of the earth.   **3** two opposites or contraries: *Forgiveness and revenge are antipodes.*   1, 3 n. pl., 2 n. pl. or sing.

**an·ti·pro·ton** (an'tē prō'ton)   a tiny particle of the same mass as a PROTON but negatively charged, created when a proton hits a NEUTRON. n.

**an·ti·quar·i·an** (an'tē kwer'ē ən)   **1** having to do with antiques or antiquaries: *The antiquarian section of the museum was full of old furniture and dishes.*   **2** ANTIQUARY.   1 adj., 2 n.

**an·ti·quar·y** (an'tē kwer'ē)   a student or collector of relics from ancient times. n., pl. **an·ti·quar·ies.**

**an·ti·quate** (an'tə kwāt')   make old-fashioned; make out-of-date.   v., **an·ti·quat·ed, an·ti·quat·ing.**
—**an'ti·qua'tion,** n.

**an·ti·quat·ed** (an'tə kwā'tid)   **1** old-fashioned; out-of-date: *antiquated ideas.*   **2** too old for work, service, etc.: *an antiquated truck.* adj.

**an·tique** (an tēk')   **1** of or existing from times long ago: *This antique chair was made in 1750.*   **2** something made at least 50 years ago, especially articles of furniture, decorative objects, etc. sought by collectors: *This carved chest is a real antique.*   **3** exhibiting or selling antiques: *an antique auction, an antique show.*   **4** old-fashioned; out-of-date: *an antique gown, antique manners.*   **5** make furniture, etc. look antique by finishing or refinishing in an antique style.   1, 3, 4 adj., 2 n., 5 v., **an·tiqued, an·tiqu·ing.**

**an·tiq·ui·ty** (an tik'wə tē)   **1** oldness; great age: *We were impressed by the antiquity of the ruins.*   **2** times long ago; early ages of history: *Antiquity usually refers to the period from 5000* B.C. *to* A.D. *476.*   **3** people of long ago.   **4 antiquities,** pl.   **a** things from times long ago.   **b** customs and life of olden times. n., pl. **an·tiq·ui·ties.**

**an·ti·scor·bu·tic** (an'tē skôr byü'tik)   **1** preventing or curing SCURVY.   **2** a remedy for SCURVY.   1 adj., 2 n.

**an·ti–Se·mit·ic** (an'tē sə mit'ik)   having or showing dislike or hatred for Jews; prejudiced against Jews. adj.

**an·ti–Sem·i·tism** (an'tē sem'ə tiz'əm)   a dislike or hatred of Jews; prejudice against Jews. n.

**an·ti·sep·sis** (an'tə sep'sis)   **1** the prevention of infection.   **2** a method of medicine that prevents infection. n.

**an·ti·sep·tic** (an'tə sep'tik)   **1** a substance that kills or prevents the growth of germs and thus prevents infection: *Iodine, peroxide, alcohol, and boric acid are antiseptics.*   **2** preventing infection: *an antiseptic ointment.*   1 n., 2 adj.

**an·ti·sep·ti·cal·ly** (an'tə sep'ti klē)   by the use of ANTISEPTICS (def. 1). adv.

**an·ti·slav·er·y** (an'tē slā'və rē)   opposed to slavery; against slavery. adj.

**an·ti·so·cial** (an'tē sō'shəl)   **1** opposed to the principles upon which society is based: *Murder, stealing, and spreading diseases are antisocial acts.*   **2** not wanting the society or companionship of others; not sociable. adj.

**an·ti·stro·phe** (an tis'trə fē)   **1** the part of an ancient Greek ode sung by the chorus when moving from left to right. Compare with STROPHE.   **2** a group of lines of poetry; stanza. n.

**an·ti·tank** (an'tē tangk')   designed for use against armoured vehicles, especially tanks. adj.

**an·tith·e·sis** (an tith'ə sis)   **1** the direct opposite: *Hate is the antithesis of love.*   **2** a contrast of ideas, expressed by parallel arrangements of words, clauses, etc. Example: "To err is human; to forgive, divine."   **3** an opposition; contrast (*of* or *between*): *antithesis of theory and fact.* n., pl. **an·tith·e·ses** (-sēz').

**an·ti·thet·ic** (an'tə thet'ik)   **1** of or using ANTITHESIS.   **2** contrasted; opposite. adj.

**an·ti·tox·ic** (an'tē tok'sik)   **1** counteracting diseases or poisonings caused by TOXINS.   **2** having to do with or like an ANTITOXIN. adj.

**an·ti·tox·in** (an'tē tok'sin)   **1** a substance formed in the body to counteract a disease or poison.   **2** a serum containing antitoxin. n.

**an·ti·trades** (an′tē trādz′) the winds that blow in a direction opposite to the TRADE WINDS, on a level above them, and descend beyond the trade-wind belt. *n. pl.*

**an·ti·trust** (an′tē trust′) opposed to large corporations that control the trade practices of certain kinds of business. *adj.*

**ant·ler** (ant′lər) **1** the branched horn of a deer or similar animal. **2** a branch of such a horn. *n.*

**ant·lered** (ant′lərd) having ANTLERS. *adj.*

**ant lion** **1** any of several species of insect found in North America and Europe resembling a dragonfly and having short antennae and four narrow wings usually marked with brown or black: *The larva of the ant lion catches small insects for food by lying in wait in a pit it has dug and seizing any insect that falls or slides in.* **2** the larva of the ant lion.

**an·to·nym** (an′tə nim′) a word that means the opposite of another word: *Hot is the antonym of cold.* *n.*

**a·nus** (ā′nəs) the opening at the lower end of the alimentary canal, through which waste material and undigested food pass. *n.*

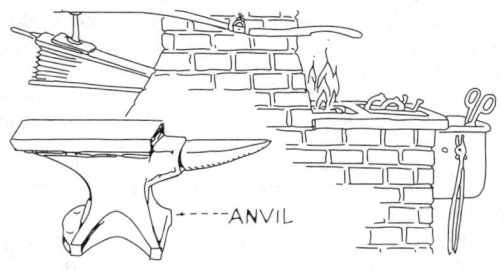

Anvil

**an·vil** (an′vəl) **1** an iron or steel block on which metals are hammered and shaped. **2** INCUS. See EAR¹ for picture. *n.*

**anx·i·e·ty** (ang zī′ə tē) **1** uneasy thoughts or fears about what may happen; a troubled, worried, or uneasy feeling: *We all felt anxiety when Sophie was lost.* **2** an eager desire: *anxiety to succeed. n., pl.* **anx·i·e·ties.**

**anx·ious** (angk′shəs *or* ang′shəs) **1** uneasy because of thoughts or fears of what may happen; troubled; worried: *Her mother was anxious about her. They became anxious at her delay.* **2** causing uneasy feelings or troubled thoughts: *an anxious time.* **3** eagerly desiring; wishing very much; eager: *Indira was anxious for a new bicycle.* *adj.* —**anx′ious·ly**, *adv.* —**anx′ious·ness**, *n.*

**an·y** (en′ē) **1** one (no matter which) out of many: *Any book will do. You can come any day, but you really must come some day.* **2** every: *Any child knows that.* **3** some (used in questions): *Do you have any fresh fruit?* **4** some (used in questions): *I need more paper; do you have any?* **5** no; none (used with words such as **not, seldom, hardly,** etc.): *They seldom have any visitors. She had hardly any money.* **6** no; none (used with negative words): *I asked him for some paper, but he didn't have any.* **7** to some extent or degree; at all (used in questions and with negatives): *Has the sick child improved any? No, she's not any better.* **8** even one (used with negatives and verbs like **forbid** or **prohibit**): *He was forbidden to go to any movie.* **9** even a little (used with negatives and in sentences expressing fear, a threat, etc.): *Do not come any closer. If he comes any closer, I'll run away.* 1, 2, 3, 5, 8 *adj.*, 4, 6 *pron.*, 7, 9 *adv.*

**antitrades** 49 **apartment**

hat, āge, fär; let, ēqual, tėrm; it, īce
hot, ōpen, ôrder; oil, out; cup, pút, rüle
əbove, takən, pencəl, lemən, circəs
ch, child; ng, long; sh, ship
th, thin; ŦH, then; zh, measure

**an·y·bod·y** (en′ē bud′ē *or* en′ē bod′ē) **1** any person; anyone: *Has anybody been here?* **2** an important person: *Is he anybody?* 1 *pron.*, 2 *n., pl.* **an·y·bod·ies.**

**an·y·how** (en′ē hou′) **1** in any way whatever: *It is wrong anyhow you look at it.* **2** in any case; at least: *I can see as well as you, anyhow.* **3** carelessly; in ways that are not right and proper. *adv.*

**any more** *or* **anymore** (en′ē môr′) these days or any longer (used with negatives): *That book is not available any more.* *adv.*
☛ *Usage.* **Any more** is used only in negative constructions in most of Canada. In certain regions, however, it is also quite commonly used in positive constructions with the meaning "these days.": *That's the trouble with the world any more.*

**an·y·one** (en′ē wun′ *or* en′ē wən) any person; anybody. *pron.*

**an·y·place** (en′ē plās′) *Informal.* ANYWHERE. *adv.*

**an·y·thing** (en′ē thing′) **1** any thing. **2** at all; in any way: *This isn't anything like what I expected.* 1 *pron.*, 2 *adv.*

**an·y·way** (en′ē wā′) ANYHOW. *adv.*

**an·y·where** (en′ē wer′ *or* en′ē hwer′) in, at or to any place. *adv.*

**an·y·wise** (en′ē wīz′) in any way; to any degree; at all. *adv.*

**A-one** (ā′wun′) *Informal.* first-rate; first-class; excellent. *adj.*

**a·or·ta** (ā ôr′tə) the main artery that carries the blood from the left side of the heart to all parts of the body except the lungs. See HEART and KIDNEY for pictures. *n., pl.* **a·or·tas** *or* **a·or·tae** (-tē *or* -tī).

**a·or·tic** (ā ôr′tik) having to do with the AORTA. *adj.*

**a·pace** (ə pās′) swiftly; quickly; fast: *Summer flew by, and the time for school was coming on apace.* *adv.*

**A·pach·e** (ə pach′ē) a member of an Athapascan people living in the southwestern United States. *n., pl.* **A·pach·es** *or* **A·pach·e.**

**a·pache** (ə päsh′ *or* ə pach′ē) a gangster of Paris, Brussels, etc. *n.*

**ap·a·nage** (ap′ə nij) See APPANAGE. *n.*

**a·part** (ə pärt′) **1** to pieces; in separate parts: *Take the watch apart.* **2** away from each other: *Keep the dogs apart.* **3** to one side; aside: *Camille stood apart.* **4** away from others; separately; independently: *View each idea apart.* *adv.*
**apart from,** except for; besides.

**a·part·heid** (ə pärt′hīt *or* ə pärt′hāt) South African. racial segregation. *n.*

**a·part·ment** (ə pärt′mənt) a set of rooms, or sometimes a single room, designed as private living quarters and usually located in a building containing other such units: *Apartments in some buildings are rented; in other buildings they are owned by the occupants.* *n.*

**apartment block** a building containing a number of apartments.

**apartment house** APARTMENT BLOCK.

**ap·a·thet·ic** (ap′ə thet′ik) 1 with little interest or desire for action; indifferent. 2 lacking in feeling. *adj.* —**ap′a·thet′i·cal·ly,** *adv.*

**ap·a·thy** (ap′ə thē) 1 a lack of interest or desire for activity; indifference: *The miser heard the old beggar's story with apathy.* 2 a lack of feeling. *n., pl.* **ap·a·thies.**

**ap·a·tite** (ap′ə tīt′) a mineral consisting mainly of calcium phosphate: *Apatite is the main constituent of bones and teeth.* *n.*
☞ *Hom.* APPETITE.

**ape** (āp) 1 any of the family of tail-less primates that most resemble humans, having hairless hands, feet, and faces, long front limbs and short hind limbs, and showing a tendency to stand almost erect: *Chimpanzees, gibbons, gorillas, and orangutans are apes.* 2 any primate other than a human being: *Monkeys are sometimes called apes.* 3 a large, clumsy or boorish person. 4 imitate, mimic, especially in a rather clumsy way. 5 a mimic. 1–3, 5 *n.,* 4 *v.,* **aped, ap·ing.** —**ape′like′,** *adj.*

**ap·er·ture** (ap′ər chər) 1 an opening; gap; hole: *Fernando escaped through an aperture in the wall.* 2 in a camera, telescope, etc.: **a** the opening through which light passes. **b** the diameter of such an opening. *n.*

**a·pex** (ā′peks) 1 the highest point; peak; tip: *the apex of a triangle.* 2 climax. *n., pl.* **a·pex·es** or **ap·i·ces** (ā′pə sēz′ or ap′ə sēz′).

**a·pha·si·a** (ə fā′zhə or ə fā′zē ə) a total or partial loss of the ability to use or understand words: *Aphasia is caused by injury or disease that affects the brain.* *n.*

**a·phe·li·on** (ə fē′lē ən) the point most distant from the sun, in the orbit of a planet or comet. Compare with PERIHELION. *n., pl.* **a·phe·li·ons** or **a·phe·li·a** (-lē ə).

**a·phid** (ā′fid *or* af′id) a tiny, soft-bodied insect that has a tube-shaped mouth and lives by sucking juices from plants; plant louse. *n.*

**a·phis** (ā′fis *or* af′is) APHID. *n., pl.* **aph·i·des** (ā′fə dēz′ *or* af′ə dēz′).

**aph·o·rism** (af′ə riz′əm) 1 a terse sentence expressing a general thought; maxim; proverb. *Example:* "A bird in the hand is worth two in the bush." 2 a concise statement of a principle. *n.*

**aph·o·ris·tic** (af′ə ris′tik) of, containing or like an APHORISM or aphorisms. *adj.*

**a·pi·ar·y** (ā′pē er′ē) a place where bees are kept; group of beehives. *n., pl.* **a·pi·ar·ies.**

**a·pi·cal** (ā′pə kəl *or* ap′ə kəl) of the APEX; at the apex; forming the apex. *adj.*

**a·pi·ces** (ā′pə sēz′ *or* ap′ə sēz′) a pl. of APEX. *n.*

**a·piece** (ə pēs′) for each one; each: *These apples are fifty cents apiece.* *adv.*

**ap·ish** (ā′pish) 1 like an ape. 2 senselessly imitative. 3 foolish; silly. *adj.* —**ap′ish·ly,** *adv.*

**a·plen·ty** (ə plen′tē) *Informal.* in plenty. *adv.*

**a·plomb** (ə plom′) complete self-confidence and assurance; poise. *n.*

**a·poc·a·lypse** (ə pok′ə lips′) revelation. *n.*

**a·poc·a·lyp·tic** (ə pok′ə lip′tik) like or giving a revelation. *adj.*

**a·poc·a·lyp·ti·cal** (ə pok′ə lip′tə kəl) APOCALYPTIC. *adj.*

**a·poc·ry·phal** (ə pok′rə fəl) 1 of doubtful authorship or authority. 2 false; counterfeit. *adj.*

**ap·o·gee** (ap′ə jē′) 1 the point in the orbit of an earth satellite or earth-orbiting vehicle where it is farthest from the earth. Compare with PERIGEE. 2 the furthermost point; highest point. *n.*

**a·pol·o·get·ic** (ə pol′ə jet′ik) 1 making an APOLOGY (def. 1); expressing regret or offering an excuse for a fault or failure: *an apologetic reply.* 2 suggesting uncertainty; unsure: *He answered the principal in an apologetic voice.* 3 defending by speech or writing. *adj.* —**a·pol′o·get′i·cal·ly,** *adv.*

**a·pol·o·gist** (ə pol′ə jist) a person who defends an idea, belief, religion, etc. in speech or writing. *n.*

**a·pol·o·gize** (ə pol′ə jīz′) 1 make an APOLOGY (def. 1); express regret; acknowledge a fault; offer an excuse. 2 make a defence in speech or writing. *v.,* **a·pol·o·gized, a·pol·o·giz·ing.** —**a·pol′o·giz′er,** *n.*

**a·pol·o·gy** (ə pol′ə jē) 1 words of regret for an offence or accident; acknowledgment of a fault or failure; expressing regret and asking pardon: *Make an apology to the lady for hitting her.* 2 a defence in speech or writing; explanation of the truth or justice of something: *an apology for poetry.* 3 a poor substitute; makeshift: *One piece of toast is a skimpy apology for a breakfast.* *n., pl.* **a·pol·o·gies.**

**ap·o·plec·tic** (ap′ə plek′tik) 1 of, having to do with, or causing APOPLEXY. 2 suffering from or showing symptoms of APOPLEXY. 3 of an emotional reaction, likely to bring on APOPLEXY; extreme: *an apoplectic rage.* *adj.*

**ap·o·plex·y** (ap′ə plek′sē) a sudden inability to feel or move, with partial or complete loss of consciousness, caused by injury to the brain when a blood vessel breaks or becomes blocked by a clot; a STROKE (def. 11). *n.*

**a·pos·ta·sy** (ə pos′tə sē) the complete forsaking of one's religion, faith, political party, or principles. *n., pl.* **a·pos·ta·sies.**

**a·pos·tate** (ə pos′tāt) 1 a person who completely forsakes his or her religion, faith, political party, or principles. 2 guilty of APOSTASY. 1 *n.,* 2 *adj.*

**a·pos·ta·tize** (ə pos′tə tīz′) forsake completely one's religion, faith, political party, or principles. *v.,* **a·pos·ta·tized, a·pos·ta·tiz·ing.**

**a pos·te·ri·o·ri** (ā′pos tē′rē ô′rē *or* ā′pos tē′rē ô′rī) *Latin.* from effect to cause; from particular cases to a general rule; based on actual observation or experience.

**a·pos·tro·phe**[1] (ə pos′trə fē) the sign (′) used: 1 to show the omission of one or more letters in contractions, as in *o'er* for *over, can't* for *cannot.* 2 to show the possessive forms of nouns or indefinite pronouns, as in *the lions' den, everybody's business.* 3 to form certain plurals, as in *2 o's, four 9's in 9999.* 4 to show that certain sounds represented in the usual spelling have not been spoken: *'lectric.* *n.*

**a·pos·tro·phe**[2] (ə pos′trə fē) the addressing of words to an absent person as if he or she were present, or to a thing or idea as if it could understand and appreciate the words. *Example:* "Western wind, when wilt thou blow?" *n.*

**a·pos·tro·phize** (ə pos′trə fīz′)   in a speech, poem, etc., address some thing or absent person, usually with emotion: *The poet apostrophizes judgment in these words: "Oh, judgment; thou art fled to brutish beasts."*   *v.*, **a·pos·tro·phized, a·pos·tro·phiz·ing.**

**apothecaries' measure**   a system of units for measuring volume, traditionally used by pharmacists: *One fluid ounce in apothecaries' measure is equal to about 28.4 cubic centimetres.*

60 minims = 1 fluid dram
8 fluid drams = 1 fluid ounce
20 fluid ounces = 1 pint
8 pints = 1 gallon

**apothecaries' weight**   a system of units for measuring mass, traditionally used by pharmacists: *One ounce in apothecaries' weight is equal to about 31.1 grams.* Compare with AVOIRDUPOIS WEIGHT and TROY WEIGHT.

20 grains = 1 scruple
3 scruples = 1 dram
8 drams = 1 ounce
12 ounces = 1 pound

**a·poth·e·car·y** (ə poth′ə ker′ē)   **1** a person who prepares and sells drugs and medicines; druggist. **2** formerly, a person who prescribed medicines and sold them.   *n., pl.* **a·poth·e·car·ies.**

**ap·o·thegm** (ap′ə them′)   a short, forceful saying; maxim. Example: *"Beauty is only skin deep."*   *n.*

**a·poth·e·o·sis** (ə poth′ē ō′sis *or* ap′ə thē′ə sis)   **1** the raising of a human being to the rank of a god; DEIFICATION (def. 1): *The apotheosis of the emperor became a Roman custom.* **2** a glorification; exaltation. **3** a glorified ideal.   *n., pl.* **a·poth·e·o·ses** (-sēz′).

**app.**   appendix.

**ap·pal** *or* **ap·pall** (ə pol′)   fill with horror; dismay; terrify: *We were appalled at the thought of another war. She was appalled when she saw the forest burning.*   *v.*, **ap·palled, ap·pal·ling.**

**ap·pal·ling** (ə pol′ing)   dismaying; terrifying; horrifying.   *adj.*   —**ap·pall′ing·ly,** *adv.*

**ap·pa·nage** *or* **ap·a·nage** (ap′ə nij)   **1** the land, property, or money set aside to support the youngest children of kings, princes, etc.   **2** a person's assigned portion; rightful property.   **3** something that accompanies; an adjunct: *The millionaire had three houses, a yacht, and the other appanages of wealth.*   *n.*

**ap·pa·ra·tus** (ap′ə rā′təs *or* ap′ə rat′əs)   things necessary to carry out a purpose or for a particular use: *apparatus for an experiment in chemistry, gardening apparatus, our digestive apparatus.*   *n., pl.* **ap·pa·ra·tus** *or* **ap·pa·ra·tus·es.**

**ap·par·el** (ə par′əl *or* ə per′əl)   **1** clothing; dress: *Does this store sell women's apparel?*   **2** clothe; dress up: *The horseback riders, colourfully apparelled, formed part of the circus parade.*   **1** *n.*, **2** *v.*, **ap·par·elled** *or* **ap·par·eled, ap·par·el·ling** *or* **ap·par·el·ing.**

**ap·par·ent** (ə par′ənt *or* ə per′ənt)   **1** plain to see; so plain as not to be missed.   **2** easily understood: *It is apparent that the days become shorter in October and November.*   **3** according to appearances; seeming: *The apparent truth was really a lie.*   *adj.*

**ap·par·ent·ly** (ə par′ən tlē *or* ə per′ən tlē)   **1** seemingly; as far as one can judge by appearances: *Apparently the baby had chicken pox.*   **2** clearly; plainly; obviously: *Joselle had quite apparently hurt her leg.*   *adv.*

**ap·pa·ri·tion** (ap′ə rish′ən)   **1** a ghost; phantom.

hat, āge, fär; let, ēqual, tėrm; it, īce
hot, ōpen, ôrder; oil, out; cup, pùt, rüle
əbove, takən, pencəl, lemən, circəs
ch, child; ng, long; sh, ship
th, thin; ᴛʜ, then; zh, measure

**2** something strange, remarkable, or unexpected that comes into view.   **3** the act of appearing; appearance.   *n.*

**ap·peal** (ə pēl′)   **1** make an earnest request (*to* or *for*); apply for help, sympathy, etc.: *The children appealed to their mother to know what to do on a rainy day. We appealed for freedom.*   **2** an earnest request; call for help, sympathy, etc.: *Jane made an appeal to her father to forgive her.*   **3** call on some person to decide some matter in one's favour.   **4** a call on some person for proof, decision, etc.   **5** ask that a case be taken to a higher court or judge to be heard again.   **6** a request to have a case heard again before a higher court or judge.   **7** be attractive, interesting, or enjoyable: *Blue and red appeal to me, but I don't like grey or yellow.*   **8** an attraction; interest: *Movies have a great appeal for most young people.*   1, 3, 5 7 *v.*, 2, 4, 6 8 *n.*   —**ap·peal′ing·ly,** *adv.*

**ap·pear** (ə pēr′)   **1** be seen; come in sight: *One by one the stars appear.*   **2** seem; look: *The apple appeared sound on the outside, but it was rotten inside.*   **3** be published or otherwise presented to the public: *The book appeared in the autumn. The movie will appear soon.*   **4** present oneself publicly or formally: *to appear on the stage.*   **5** become known to the mind: *It appears that we must go.*   **6** stand before an authority: *to appear in court.*   *v.*

**ap·pear·ance** (ə pē′rəns)   **1** appearing; coming in sight: *Anne's appearance in the doorway.*   **2** a coming before the public: *a singer's first appearance in a city.*   **3** the outward look; aspect: *The appearance of the house made us think that it was empty.*   **4** a false show or pretence: *her story's appearance of truth.*   **5** something that appears in sight; object seen.   **6** the coming into court of a party to a lawsuit.   **7 appearances,** *pl.* outward show, especially when thought of in contrast to some underlying fault or misfortune: *After he lost his job, he found it hard to keep up appearances.*   *n.*

**ap·pease** (ə pēz′)   **1** satisfy an appetite or desire: *A good dinner will appease your hunger.*   **2** make calm; quiet: *The mayor appeased the angry crowd by promising to build more houses.*   **3** give in to the demands of, especially those of a potential enemy: *Chamberlain appeased Hitler at Munich.*   *v.*, **ap·peased, ap·peas·ing.**   —**ap·peas′er,** *n.*   —**ap·peas′ing·ly,** *adv.*

**ap·pease·ment** (ə pē′zmənt)   an appeasing or being APPEASED (def. 3); PACIFICATION; satisfaction.   *n.*

**ap·pel·lant** (ə pel′ənt)   **1** a person who APPEALS (def. 5).   **2** APPEALing (def. 5); having to do with appeals.   1 *n.*, 2 *adj.*

**ap·pel·late court** (ə pel′it)   a court having the power to re-examine and reverse the decisions of a lower court.

**ap·pel·la·tion** (ap′ə lā′shən)   **1** a name; title: *In Premier Peterson, the appellation of Peterson is Premier.*   **2** the act of calling by a name.   *n.*

**ap·pend** (ə pend′)   add to a larger thing; attach as a supplement: *The amendments to the British North America Act are appended to it.*   *v.*

**ap·pend·age** (ə pen′dij)   **1** something attached to some larger or more important thing; addition; adjunct.

**2** any of various external or subordinate parts of animals: *Arms, tails, fins, legs, etc. are appendages.* *n.*

**ap·pend·ant** (ə pen′dənt)   **1** added; attached. **2** APPENDAGE.   **1** *adj.*, **2** *n.*

**ap·pen·dec·to·my** (ap′ən dek′tə mē)   the removal of the VERMIFORM APPENDIX by a surgical operation.   *n., pl.* **ap·pen·dec·to·mies.**

**ap·pen·di·ces** (ə pen′də sēz′)   a pl. of APPENDIX.   *n.*

**ap·pen·di·ci·tis** (ə pen′də sī′tis)   an inflammation of the VERMIFORM APPENDIX, the small growth attached to the large intestine.   *n.*

**ap·pen·dix** (ə pen′diks)   **1** an addition at the end of a book or document, containing supplementary material. **2** an outgrowth of some part of the body: *The small growth attached to the large intestine is the vermiform appendix.* See ALIMENTARY CANAL for picture.   *n., pl.* **ap·pen·dix·es** or **ap·pen·di·ces** (-sēz).

**ap·per·tain** (ap′ər tān′)   belong as a part; pertain; relate (*to*): *The control of traffic appertains to the police. Forestry appertains to geography, to botany, and to agriculture.* *v.*

**ap·pe·tite** (ap′ə tīt′)   **1** a desire for food.   **2** a desire: *an appetite for amusement.* *n.*
☛ **Hom.** APATITE.

**ap·pe·tiz·er** (ap′ə tī′zər)   something that arouses the appetite or gives flavour to food: *Pickles and olives are appetizers.* *n.*

**ap·pe·tiz·ing** (ap′ə tī′zing)   arousing or exciting the appetite: *appetizing food.* *adj.*   —**ap′pe·tiz′ing·ly,** *adv.*

**ap·plaud** (ə plod′)   **1** express approval by clapping the hands, shouting, etc.   **2** approve; praise. *v.*

**ap·plause** (ə ploz′)   **1** approval expressed by clapping the hands, shouting, etc.   **2** approval; praise. *n.*

**ap·ple** (ap′əl)   **1** the firm, fleshy, rather round fruit of a tree widely grown in temperate regions: *Apples are usually red, yellow, or green, and are eaten either raw or cooked.* **2** the tree this fruit grows on.   **3** any of various other fruits or fruitlike products, such as the oak apple and love apple. *n.*

**apple of one's eye,**   a person or thing that one cherishes: *Sif is the apple of her father's eye.*

**apple butter**   a smooth, jamlike spread made by boiling tart apples and apple cider together to produce a purée, and then cooking this with sugar and spices such as cinnamon and cloves.

**ap·ple·jack** (ap′əl jak′)   an intoxicating liquor made from apple cider. *n.*

**apple of discord**   **1** in Greek legend, a golden apple inscribed "For the fairest" and claimed by Aphrodite, Athena and Hera: *Paris awarded the apple to Aphrodite.* **2** any cause of jealousy and trouble.

**ap·ple–pol·ish** (ap′əl pol′ish)   try to gain favour by flattering or fawning on a person; TOADY. *v.*
☛ **Etym.** From the traditional custom of children to bring a polished apple as a gift to the teacher.

**ap·ple–pol·ish·er** (ap′əl pol′i shər)   a person who tries to gain favour with another by flattery, etc.   *n.*

**ap·ple·sauce** (ap′əl sos′)   **1** apples cut in pieces and cooked with sugar and water until soft.   **2** *Informal.* nonsense. *n.*

**ap·pli·ance** (ə plī′əns)   **1** a tool, a small machine, or some other device used in doing something: *Can openers, vacuum cleaners, washing machines, refrigerators, etc. are household appliances.*   **2** an applying; the act of putting into use. *n.*

**ap·pli·ca·bil·i·ty** (ap′lə kə bil′ə tē)   the quality of being APPLICABLE. *n.*

**ap·pli·ca·ble** (ap′lə kə bəl)   capable of being put to practical use; appropriate; suitable; fitting: *The rule "Look before you leap" is almost always applicable.* *adj.*

**ap·pli·cant** (ap′lə kənt)   a person who applies for money, position, help, office, etc.: *Are you an applicant for this job?* *n.*

**ap·pli·ca·tion** (ap′lə kā′shən)   **1** the act of using; a use: *The application of what you know will help you solve new problems.*   **2** applying or putting on: *the application of paint to a house.*   **3** ways of using: *Freedom is a word of wide application.*   **4** something applied: *This application is made of cold cream and ointment.*   **5** a request for employment, an award, tickets, etc.: *an application for the position of clerk.*   **6** continued effort; close attention: *By application to the study of law, Rachel became a judge.* *n.*

**ap·plied** (ə plīd′)   put to practical use; used to solve actual problems: *Engineers study applied mathematics.* *adj.*

**applied science**   the science that uses facts, laws, and theories to solve practical problems: *Applied science is used in building a bridge, designing a radio, testing aptitude, etc.*

**ap·pli·qué** (ap′lə kā′ *or* ə plē′kā)   **1** the art or process of sewing or gluing pieces of fabric in various shapes and colours to a larger piece of fabric for decoration: *Appliqué is often used to decorate clothing, table linens, etc.*   **2** a cut-out piece of fabric attached to a larger piece as a decoration: *a skirt with butterfly appliqués.*   **3** trim or ornament with appliqué: *to appliqué a skirt.*   **4** put on as appliqué: *to appliqué flowers on a table cloth.*   **5** make by using appliqué: *an appliquéd wall hanging.*   **1, 2,** *n.*, **3–5** *v.*, **ap·pli·quéd, ap·pli·qué·ing.**

**ap·ply** (ə plī′)   **1** put on or in contact with: *to apply paint to a house. Apply wet towels to the sick boy's face.* **2** put to practical use; put into effect: *Lauren knows the rule but does not know how to apply it.*   **3** be useful or suitable; fit: *When does this rule apply?*   **4** use for a special purpose: *to apply a sum of money to charity.* **5** make a formal request: *to apply for a job.*   **6** use a word or words appropriately with reference to a person or thing: *to apply a nickname. Don't apply that adjective to me.* *v.*, **ap·plied, ap·ply·ing.**

**apply oneself to,**   set to work and stick to it: *She applied herself to learning French.*

**ap·point** (ə point′)   **1** name to an office or position; choose: *This man was appointed postmaster.*   **2** decide on; set: *to appoint a time for the meeting.*   **3** fix; prescribe. **4** furnish; equip: *to appoint an office.* *v.*
—**ap·point′er,** *n.*

**ap·point·ee** (ə poin′tē′)   a person APPOINTED (def. 1). *n.*

**ap·poin·tive** (ə poin′tiv)   filled by APPOINTMENT (def. 1): *Positions in the cabinet are appointive.* *adj.*

**ap·point·ment** (ə point′mənt)   **1** naming to an office or position; choosing: *The appointment of Takako as secretary pleased her friends.*   **2** an office or position. **3** a meeting with someone at a certain time and place; engagement: *I have an appointment to see the doctor at 4 o'clock.*   **4 appointments,** *pl.* furniture; equipment: *The old hotel has rather shabby appointments.* *n.*

**ap·por·tion** (ə pôr′shən)   divide and give out in fair shares; distribute according to some rule: *The father's property was apportioned among his children after his death.*   *v.*

**ap·por·tion·ment** (ə pôr′shən mənt)   the act of dividing and giving out in fair shares.   *n.*

**ap·po·site** (ap′ə zit)   appropriate; suitable; apt.   *adj.* —**ap′po·site·ly**, *adv.*   —**ap′po·site·ness**, *n.*

**ap·po·si·tion** (ap′ə zish′ən)   **1** the act of putting side by side.   **2** a position side by side.   **3** a placing together in the same grammatical relation.   **4** the relation of two members of a sentence when the one is added as an explanation to the other. In "Mr. Brown, our neighbour, has a new car," *Mr. Brown* and *neighbour* are in apposition.   *n.*

**ap·pos·i·tive** (ə poz′ə tiv)   **1** a noun added to another noun as an explanation; a word, phrase, or clause in APPOSITION (def. 4).   **2** placed beside another noun as an explanation.   1 *n.*, 2 *adj.*

**ap·prais·al** (ə prā′zəl)   **1** an estimate of the value, amount, etc.   **2** an appraising; valuation.   **3** the value set on something.   **4** a judgment of the worth or quality of a person or thing: *He let the stranger in after a quick appraisal of his appearance and manner.*   *n.*

**ap·praise** (ə prāz′)   **1** estimate the value, amount, quality: *An employer should be able to appraise ability and character. The ring has been appraised at $600.*   **2** set a price on; fix the value of: *Property is appraised for taxation.*   *v.*, **ap·praised, ap·prais·ing.**   —**ap·prais′ing·ly,** *adv.*

**ap·praise·ment** (ə prāz′mənt)   APPRAISAL.   *n.*

**ap·prais·er** (ə prā′zər)   **1** a person authorized to fix the value of property, imported goods, etc.   **2** a person who APPRAISES.   *n.*

**ap·pre·ci·a·ble** (ə prē′shē ə bəl)   enough to be felt or estimated: *When she was ill, she suffered an appreciable loss of weight.*   *adj.*   —**ap·pre′ci·a·bly,** *adv.*

**ap·pre·ci·ate** (ə prē′shē āt)   **1** think highly of; recognize the worth or quality of; value; enjoy: *Almost everybody appreciates good food.*   **2** have an opinion of the value, worth, or quality of; estimate: *to appreciate knowledge.*   **3** be sensitive to; be aware of: *A musician can appreciate small differences in sounds.*   **4** estimate correctly.   **5** raise in value: *New buildings appreciate the value of land.* Compare with DEPRECIATE (def. 1).   **6** rise in value: *This land will appreciate as soon as good roads are built.* Compare with DEPRECIATE (def. 2).   *v.*, **ap·pre·ci·at·ed, ap·pre·ci·at·ing.**

**ap·pre·ci·a·tion** (ə prē′shē ā′shən)   **1** valuing highly; sympathetic understanding: *She has no appreciation of art and music.*   **2** an appreciating; valuing.   **3** favourable criticism.   **4** a rise in value.   *n.*

**ap·pre·ci·a·tive** (ə prē′shē ə tiv *or* ə prē′shē ā′tiv)   having appreciation; showing appreciation; recognizing the value: *She was appreciative of the smallest kindness.*   *adj.*   —**ap·pre′ci·a·tive·ly,** *adv.*

**ap·pre·hend** (ap′ri hend′)   **1** understand; grasp with the mind: *I apprehended his meaning from his gestures.*   **2** look forward to with fear; fear; dread: *A guilty man apprehends danger in every sound.*   **3** arrest: *The thief was apprehended and put in jail.*   *v.*

**ap·pre·hen·si·bil·i·ty** (ap′ri hen′sə bil′ə tē)   the quality or state of being APPREHENSIBLE.   *n.*

**ap·pre·hen·si·ble** (ap′ri hen′sə bəl)   capable of being

---

apportion    53    appropriate

hat, āge, fär; let, ēqual, tėrm; it, īce
hot, ōpen, ôrder; oil, out; cup, pùt, rüle
əbove, takən, pencəl, lemən, circəs
ch, child; ng, long; sh, ship
th, thin; ᴛʜ, then; zh, measure

---

APPREHENDED (def. 1); understandable.   *adj.* —**ap′pre·hen′si·bly,** *adv.*

**ap·pre·hen·sion** (ap′ri hen′shən)   **1** expectation of evil; fear; dread: *The roar of the hurricane filled us with apprehension.*   **2** understanding; grasping by the mind: *Morag has a clear apprehension of the facts.*   **3** seizing; being seized; arrest: *the apprehension of a thief.*   *n.*

**ap·pre·hen·sive** (ap′ri hen′siv)   **1** fearfully expecting danger or harm; afraid; anxious: *The captain was apprehensive for the safety of his passengers during the storm.*   **2** quick to understand; able to learn.   *adj.* —**ap′pre·hen′sive·ly,** *adv.*   —**ap′pre·hen′sive·ness,** *n.*

**ap·pren·tice** (ə pren′tis)   **1** a person learning a trade or art by working at it under skilled supervision.   **2** set to work as an apprentice: *In earlier times fathers often apprenticed their sons to master craftsmen in any of various trades.*   **3** a beginner; learner.   1, 3 *n.*, 2 *v.*, **ap·pren·ticed, ap·pren·tic·ing.**

**ap·pren·tice·ship** (ə pren′tis ship′)   **1** the condition of being an APPRENTICE (def. 1).   **2** the time during which one is an APPRENTICE (def. 1).   *n.*

**ap·prise** (ə prīz′)   inform; notify; advise: *The dealer was apprised that her goods would be shipped by express. She received a letter apprising her of the change in policy.*   *v.*, **ap·prised, ap·pris·ing.** ☞ *Hom.* APPRIZE.

**ap·prize** (ə prīz′)   APPRAISE.   *v.*, **ap·prized, ap·priz·ing.** ☞ *Hom.* APPRISE.

**ap·proach** (ə prōch′)   **1** come near or nearer in space, time, character, condition, or amount: *Winter is approaching.*   **2** come near or nearer to in character, quality, or amount: *The wind was approaching a gale.*   **3** coming near or nearer: *the approach of night.*   **4** a nearness in quality, likeness, or character: *In mathematics there must be more than an approach to accuracy.*   **5** the way by which a place or person can be reached; ACCESS: *The approach to the house was a narrow path. His best approach to the great man lay through a friend.*   **6** make advances or overtures to: *Will you approach the principal with the idea of arranging an open house?*   **7** an advance; overture: *Our approaches to the principal for an open house were met with a demand for participation.*   **8** a way of dealing with or accomplishing something: *a new approach to mathematics.*   1, 2, 6 *v.*, 3–5, 7 8 *n.*

**ap·proach·a·bil·i·ty** (ə prō′chə bil′ə tē)   an APPROACHABLE quality or condition.   *n.*

**ap·proach·a·ble** (ə prō′chə bəl)   **1** that can be approached: *The fishing camp was approachable from the south only.*   **2** easy to approach: *He looks stern, but is really very friendly and approachable.*   *adj.*

**ap·pro·ba·tion** (ap′rə bā′shən)   **1** APPROVAL (defs. 1, 2); favourable opinion.   **2** SANCTION (def. 1).   *n.*

**ap·pro·pri·ate** (ə prō′prē it *for adjective,* ə prō′prē āt *for verb*)   **1** suitable; proper: *Blue jeans and a sweater are appropriate clothes for the hike.*   **2** set aside for some special use: *The government appropriated money for roads.*   **3** take for oneself: *You should not appropriate* *other people's belongings without their permission.* 1 *adj.*, 2 3 *v.*, **ap·pro·pri·at·ed, ap·pro·pri·at·ing.** —**ap·pro′pri·ate·ly,** *adv.* —**ap·pro′pri·ate·ness,** *n.* —**ap·pro′pri·a′tor,** *n.*

**ap·pro·pri·a·tion** (ə prō′prē ā′shən) 1 a sum of money or other thing set aside for a special use. 2 the act or an instance of appropriating: *Her appropriation of their money was not right. The appropriation of the land made it possible to have a park.* *n.*

**ap·prov·al** (ə prü′vəl) 1 an approving; favourable opinion: *This plan has the teacher's approval.* 2 consent; sanction: *The principal gave her approval to plans for the holiday.* *n.*
**on approval,** so that the customer can decide whether to buy or not; on trial: *We had the car for a day on approval.*

**ap·prov·als** (ə prü′vəlz) items, such as stamps, sent to a customer on APPROVAL. *n. pl.*

**ap·prove** (ə prüv′) 1 think or speak well of; be pleased with: *The teacher looked at Geza's work and approved it.* 2 agree; give approval (*of*): *I'm not sure I approve of what you propose to do.* 3 sanction; consent to: *Parliament approved the bill.* *v.*, **ap·proved, ap·prov·ing.** —**ap·prov′er,** *n.*, —**ap·prov′ing·ly,** *adv.*

**approx.** 1 approximate. 2 approximately.

**ap·prox·i·mate** (ə prok′sə mit *for adjective,* ə prok′sə māt *for verb*) 1 nearly correct: *The approximate area of New Brunswick is* 73 000 km²; *the exact area is* 73 437 km². 2 come near to; approach: *Your account of what happened approximated the truth, but there were several small errors. The crowd approximated a thousand people.* 3 bring near. 4 very near. 5 very like. 1, 4, 5 *adj.*, 2 3 *v.*, **ap·prox·i·mat·ed, ap·prox·i·mat·ing.** —**ap·prox′i·mate·ly,** *adv.*

**ap·prox·i·ma·tion** (ə prok′sə mā′shən) 1 an approximating; approach. 2 a nearly correct amount; close estimate: 40 000 km *is an approximation to the circumference of the earth.* *n.*

**ap·pur·te·nance** (ə pėr′tə nəns) 1 an addition to something more important; added thing; accessory. 2 a minor right or privilege belonging to another one that is more important. *n.*

**Apr.** April.

**ap·ri·cot** (ap′rə kot′ *or* ā′prə kot′) 1 a somewhat small, roundish, orange-coloured fruit that tastes rather like both a peach and a plum. 2 the tree that it grows on. 3 pale orange-yellow. 1–3 *n.*, 3 *adj.*

**A·pril** (ā′prəl) the fourth month of the year: *April has 30 days.* *n.*
☛ *Etym.* From OF *avrill*, from L *Aprilis* 'April.'

**April fool** any person who gets fooled on APRIL FOOLS' DAY.
☛ *Etym.* After the adoption of the Gregorian calendar, New Year's Day was changed from April 1 to January 1. Many people remained unaware of this and were regarded as fools because they continued to observe the New Year on April 1, in accordance with the earlier Julian calendar, introduced by Julius Caesar in 46 B.C.

**April Fools' Day** April 1, a day observed by fooling people with tricks and jokes.

**a pri·o·ri** (ap′rē ô′rē *or* ā′prī ô′rī) 1 from cause to effect; from a general rule to a particular case. 2 based on opinion or theory rather than on actual observation or experience.

**a·pron** (ā′prən) 1 a garment worn over the front part of the body to protect one's clothes: *A carpenter's apron has pockets for nails.* 2 the front part of an area or surface: *The apron of a stage lies in front of the curtain. The apron of an airport is the paved area in front of the hangars or the main building.* *n.* —**a′pron·like′,** *adj.*

**ap·ro·pos** (ap′rə pō′) 1 fittingly; opportunely. 2 fitting; suitable; to the point: *His remarks were quite apropos.* 1 *adv.*, 2 *adj.*
**apropos of,** with regard to.

**apse** (aps) a semicircular or many-sided recess in a Christian church, usually at the east end: *The roof of an apse is arched or vaulted.* See BASILICA for picture. *n.*

**apt** (apt) 1 fitted by nature; likely: *A careless person is apt to make mistakes.* 2 suitable; fitting: *an apt reply.* 3 quick to learn: *an apt pupil.* *adj.* —**apt′ly,** *adv.* —**apt′ness,** *n.*

**apt.** apartment.

**ap·ter·ous** (ap′tə rəs) wingless: *Lice are apterous insects.* *adj.*

**ap·ter·yx** (ap′tə riks) KIWI. *n., pl.* **ap·ter·yx·es** (-ik sēz′).

**ap·ti·tude** (ap′tə tyüd′ *or* ap′tə tüd′) 1 a natural tendency; ability; capacity: *Edison had a great aptitude for inventing new things.* 2 readiness in learning; quickness to understand. 3 some special fitness. *n.*

**aq·ua·lung** (ak′wə lung′) a diving device consisting of cylinders of compressed air strapped to the diver's back and a glass mask placed over the eyes and nose: *The supply of air from an aqualung to the diver is regulated automatically by a valve.* *n.*

**aq·ua·ma·rine** (ak′wə mə rēn′) 1 a transparent, bluish-green precious stone that is a variety of BERYL. 2 light bluish-green. 1, 2 *n.*, 2 *adj.*

**aq·ua·naut** (ak′wə not′) an underwater explorer. *n.*

**aq·ua·plane** (ak′wə plān′) 1 a wide board on which a person rides as he or she is towed by a speeding motorboat. 2 ride on an aquaplane. 3 of a motor vehicle, ride on a film of water that is built up under the tires at high speeds on wet roads, resulting in loss of control over braking and steering. 1 *n.*, 2 3 *v.*, **aq·ua·planed, aq·ua·plan·ing.**

**a·quar·i·um** (ə kwer′ē əm) 1 a pond, tank, or glass bowl in which living fish, water animals, and water plants are kept. 2 a building used for showing collections of living fish, water animals, and water plants. *n., pl.* **a·quar·i·ums** or **a·quar·i·a** (-ē ə).

**A·quar·i·us** (ə kwer′ē əs) 1 in astronomy, a northern constellation thought of as representing a man standing with his left hand extended upward, and with his right pouring a stream of water out of a vase. 2 in astrology, the eleventh sign of the zodiac: *The sun enters Aquarius about January 22.* See ZODIAC for picture. 3 a person born under this sign. *n.*

**a·quat·ic** (ə kwat′ik *or* ə kwot′ik) 1 growing or living in water: *aquatic plants.* 2 taking place in or on water. 3 a plant or animal that lives in water. 4 **aquatics,** *pl.* sports that take place in or on water. 1, 2, *adj.*, 3 4 *n.*

A Roman aqueduct

**aq·ue·duct** (ak′wə dukt′)   **1** an artificial channel or large pipe for bringing water from a distance.   **2** the structure that supports such a channel or pipe.   **3** a canal or passage in the body.   *n.*

**a·que·ous** (ā′kwē əs *or* ak′wē əs)   **1** of water; like water; watery.   **2** containing water; made with water.   **3** produced by the action of water: *Aqueous rocks are formed of sediment carried and deposited by water.*   *adj.*

**aqueous humour** *or* **humor**   the watery liquid that fills the space in the eye between the cornea and the lens. See EYE for picture.

**aq·ui·line** (ak′wə līn′)   **1** of or like an eagle.   **2** curved like an eagle's beak; hooked: *an aquiline nose.*   *adj.*

**a·quiv·er** (ə kwiv′ər)   trembling.   *adj.*

**Ar**   argon.

**Ar·ab** (ar′əb *or* er′əb)   **1** a member of a Semitic people originally from the Arabian Peninsula between the Red Sea and the Persian Gulf, now widely scattered throughout the Middle East and North Africa.   **2** a member of any Arabic-speaking people.   **3** of or having to do with the Arabs.   **4** a swift, graceful horse belonging to a breed of horses that originally came from Arabia.   1, 2, 4 *n.*, 3 *adj.*

**ar·a·besque** (ar′ə besk′ *or* er′ə besk′)   **1** an elaborate and fanciful design of flowers, leaves, geometrical figures, etc.   **2** carved or painted in arabesque.   **3** like arabesque; elaborate and fanciful.   **4** in ballet, a position in which the dancer stands on one leg with the other extended backward, usually, with one arm extended forward and the other backward.   **5** in music, a light, graceful, often elaborate composition or passage.   1, 4, 5 *n.*, 2, 3 *adj.*

**A·ra·bi·an** (ə rā′bē ən)   **1** of or having to do with Arabia or the Arabs.   **2** an ARAB; a native or inhabitant of Arabia.   **3** a swift, graceful horse belonging to a breed of horses that originally came from Arabia.   1 *adj.*, 2, 3 *n.*

**Arabian camel**   a species of camel found mainly in India, the Middle East, and North Africa, used for riding and as a beast of burden, having long legs and one hump, and standing about 2 m high at the shoulder: *When used for riding, an Arabian camel can keep up a speed of 13 to 16 kilometres per hour for 18 hours.* See CAMEL for picture.

**Ar·a·bic** (ar′ə bik *or* er′ə bik)   **1** a Semitic language that is the main language of Saudi Arabia, Yemen, South Yemen, Syria, Lebanon, Jordan, Iraq, Egypt, and parts of North Africa.   **2** of or having to do with the Arabs or their language.   1 *n.*, 2 *adj.*

**Arabic numerals** *or* **figures**   the figures 1, 2, 3, 4, 5, 6, 7, 8, 9, 0. They are called Arabic because they were introduced into western Europe by Arabian scholars, but they probably originated in India. Compare with ROMAN NUMERALS.

## aqueduct   55   arborvitae

hat, āge, fär; let, ēqual, tėrm; it, īce
hot, ōpen, ôrder; oil, out; cup, pùt, rüle
above, takən, pencəl, lemən, circəs
ch, child; ng, long; sh, ship
th, thin; ᴛʜ, then; zh, measure

**ar·a·ble** (ar′ə bəl *or* er′ə bəl)   fit for growing crops: *There is very little arable land in the Canadian Shield.*   *adj.*

**a·rach·nid** (ə rak′nid)   any of a large class of small ARTHROPODS including spiders, scorpions, mites, etc.: *An arachnid breathes air, has four pairs of walking legs, no antennae, and no wings; its body is usually divided into only two segments.*   *n.*

**ar·ba·lest** *or* **ar·ba·list** (är′bə list)   a powerful crossbow with a steel bow.   *n.*

**ar·bi·ter** (är′bə tər)   **1** a person chosen to decide a dispute; judge; umpire.   **2** a person with full power to decide.   *n.*

**ar·bi·tra·ble** (är′bə trə bəl)   capable of being decided by ARBITRATION.   *adj.*

**ar·bit·ra·ment** (är bit′rə mənt)   **1** a decision by an ARBITRATOR or ARBITER.   **2** the power to judge and decide.   *n.*

**ar·bi·trar·y** (är′bə trer′ē)   **1** determined by caprice or whim: *Her sudden arbitrary decision to quit the team cost us the game.*   **2** done or made at random without a reason: *An arbitrary selection of a single ticket decides the winner of a lottery.*   **3** determined by the decision of a judge or tribunal rather than by a specific law.   **4** DESPOTIC; absolute: *arbitrary rule.*   *adj.*   —**ar′bi·trar′i·ly**, *adv.*   —**ar′bi·trar′i·ness**, *n.*

**ar·bi·trate** (är′bə trāt′)   **1** give a decision in a dispute; act as ARBITER: *to arbitrate between two persons in a quarrel.*   **2** settle by ARBITRATION; submit to arbitration: *The two nations finally agreed to arbitrate their dispute.*   *v.*, **ar·bi·trat·ed, ar·bi·trat·ing.**

**ar·bi·tra·tion** (är′bə trā′shən)   the settlement of a dispute by the decision of somebody chosen to be a judge, umpire, or arbiter.   *n.*

**ar·bi·tra·tor** (är′bə trā′tər)   **1** a person chosen to decide a dispute.   **2** a person with full power to judge and decide.   *n.*

**ar·bi·tress** (är′bə tris)   a female ARBITER.   *n.*

**ar·bor**   See ARBOUR.   *n.*

**ar·bo·re·al** (är bô′rē əl)   **1** of trees; like trees.   **2** living in or among trees: *A squirrel is an arboreal animal.*   *adj.*

**ar·bo·re·tum** (är′bə rē′təm)   a botanical garden of trees and shrubs.   *n., pl.* **ar·bo·re·tums** *or* **ar·bo·re·ta** (-tə).

**ar·bor·vi·tae** (är′bər vī′tē *or* är′bər vē′tī)   any of five or six closely related species of medium to very large evergreen tree of the cypress family found in North America and Asia, having small, fragrant, scale-like overlapping leaves, small cones, and very light, soft, fragrant wood that is highly resistant to decay: *The two species of arborvitae native to North America are the eastern white cedar and the western red cedar.*   *n., pl.* **ar·bor·vi·tae.** Also, **arbor-vitae.**

**ar·bour** or **ar·bor** (är′bər) 1 a shady place formed by trees or shrubs, or often by vines growing on latticework. 2 the latticework itself. *n.*

**Arbour Day** or **Arbor Day** a day observed in certain Canadian provinces and in some other countries by planting trees.

**ar·bu·tus** (är byü′təs) 1 a trailing plant, growing in eastern North America, that has clusters of fragrant pink or white flowers very early in the spring: *The arbutus is also called the mayflower or trailing arbutus. It is the provincial flower of Nova Scotia.* 2 a shrub or tree of the same family as the HEATH (def. 2), having clusters of large white flowers and scarlet berries: *The arbutus tree grows in British Columbia. n.*

Arcs of circles

**arc** (ärk) 1 any part of a circle. See COMPLEMENT for picture. 2 a curved line or path: *The football followed a graceful arc as it sailed between the goal posts.* 3 a curved stream of brilliant light or sparks formed as an electric current jumps from one conductor to another. 4 form an arc. 1–3 *n.*, 4 *v.*
☞ Hom. ARK.

**ar·cade** (är kād′) 1 a passageway with an arched roof. 2 any covered passageway: *Some buildings have arcades with small stores along either side.* 3 a row of arches supported by columns. 4 a room with video and other games, which people pay money to play. *n.*

**Ar·ca·di·a** (är kā′dē ə) 1 a mountain district in the southern part of ancient Greece: *Arcadia was famous for the simple, contented life of its people.* 2 any region of simple, quiet contentment. *n.* —**Ar·ca′di·an**, *adj.*, *n.*

An arch

**arch¹** (ärch) 1 a curved structure capable of bearing the weight of the material above it: *Arches often form the tops of doors, windows, and gateways.* 2 a monument forming an arch or arches. 3 bend into an arch; curve: *The wind arched the trees over the road.* 4 furnish with an arch: *The rainbow arches the heavens.* 5 form an arch over; span. 6 ARCHWAY. 7 something like an arch: *the great blue arch of the sky.* 8 the bottom of the foot: *Fallen arches cause flat feet.* See LEG for picture. 1, 2, 6–8 *n.*, 3–5 *v.*

**arch²** (ärch) 1 chief: *When the arch rebel was caught, the revolt died down.* 2 playfully mischievous: *The little girl gave her mother an arch look. adj.* —**arch′ly**, *adv.* —**arch′ness**, *n.*

**arch.** 1 archaic. 2 architect; architecture. 3 archipelago.

**ar·chae·bac·te·ria** (är′kē bak tē′rē ə) tiny organisms much like BACTERIA in appearance, but with different internal structure and chemistry; thought to be ancient life forms, and sometimes classified as a separate kingdom. *n. pl. of* **archaebacterium**.

**ar·chae·o·log·i·cal** (är′kē ə loj′ə kəl) of or having to do with ARCHAEOLOGY. *adj.* Also, **archeological**.

**ar·chae·ol·o·gist** (är′kē ol′ə jist) a person trained in ARCHAEOLOGY, especially one who makes it his or her work. *n.* Also, **archeologist**.

**ar·chae·ol·o·gy** (är′kē ol′ə jē) the study of the people, customs, and life of ancient times: *Students of archaeology excavate, classify, and study the remains of ancient cities, tools, monuments, etc., to reconstruct a picture of life in the past. n.* Also, **archeology**.

**ar·cha·ic** (är kā′ik) 1 no longer in general use: *The phrases* in sooth *and* methinks *are archaic.* 2 old-fashioned; out-of-date. 3 ancient. *adj.*

**ar·cha·ism** (är′kē iz′əm *or* är′kā iz′əm) 1 a word or expression no longer in general use. 2 the use of something out-of-date in language or art. *n.*

**arch·an·gel** (ärk′ān′jel) an angel of high rank. *n.*

**arch·bish·op** (ärch′bish′əp) a bishop of the highest rank: *An archbishop presides over a church district called an archdiocese. n.*

**arch·duch·ess** (ärch′duch′is) 1 the wife or widow of an archduke. 2 a woman with rank equal to that of an archduke. 3 a princess of the former ruling house of Austria. *n.*

**arch·duch·y** (ärch′duch′ē) the territory under the rule of an ARCHDUKE. *n., pl.* **arch·duch·ies**.

**arch·duke** (ärch′dyük′ *or* ärch′dük′) a prince of the former ruling house of Austria. *n.*

**arch·en·e·my** (ärch′en′ə mē) a chief enemy. *n., pl.* **arch·en·e·mies**.

**ar·che·o·log·i·cal** (är′kē ə loj′ə kəl) See ARCHAEOLOGICAL. *adj.*

**ar·che·ol·o·gist** (är′kē ol′ə jist) See ARCHAEOLOGIST. *n.*

**ar·che·ol·o·gy** (är′kē ol′ə jē) See ARCHAEOLOGY. *n.*

**arch·er** (är′chər) a person who shoots with a bow and arrows. *n.*

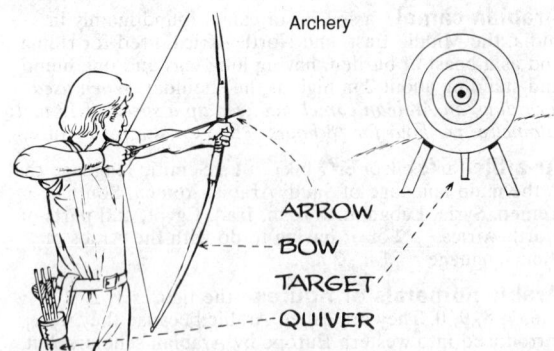
Archery

**arch·er·y** (är′chə rē) 1 the practice or art of shooting

with bows and arrows.   2 a troop of archers.   3 the weapons of an archer; bows, arrows, etc.   *n.*

**ar·che·type** (är′kə tīp′)   an original model or pattern from which copies are made, or out of which later forms develop: *That little engine is the archetype of huge modern locomotives.*   *n.*

**ar·chi·pel·a·go** (är′kə pel′ə gō′)   1 a sea having many islands in it.   2 a group of many islands: *The islands in the Arctic Ocean north of Canada are called the Canadian Archipelago.*   *n., pl.* **ar·chi·pel·a·gos** or **ar·chi·pel·a·goes.**

**ar·chi·tect** (är′kə tekt′)   1 a person trained in ARCHITECTURE (def. 1), especially one whose work is designing buildings and supervising their construction.   2 a maker; creator: *the architects of modern technology.*   *n.*

**ar·chi·tec·ton·ic** (är′kə tek ton′ik)   1 having to do with ARCHITECTURE (def. 1), construction, or design.   2 showing skill in construction or design.   3 directive; controlling: *In this novel, the development of the heroine's character is the architectonic element.*   *adj.*

**ar·chi·tec·tur·al** (är′kə tek′chə rəl)   of ARCHITECTURE (def. 1); having to do with architecture.   *adj.*
—**ar′chi·tec′tur·al·ly,** *adv.*

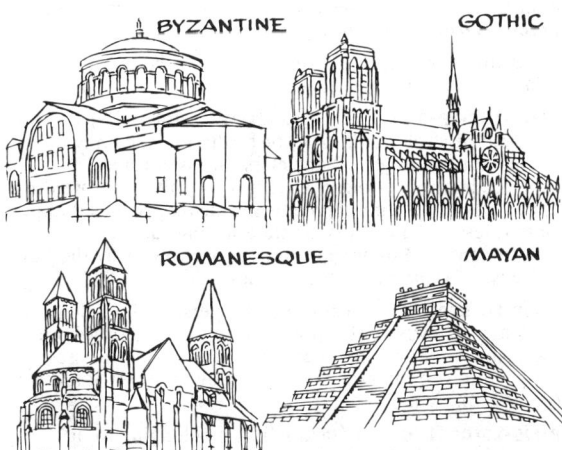
Some styles of architecture

**ar·chi·tec·ture** (är′kə tek′chər)   1 the science and art of building: *Architecture has to do with the design of houses, schools, and public and business buildings.*   2 a style or special manner of building: *Greek architecture made much use of columns.*   3 construction: *The architecture of our school is very substantial.*   4 a building; structure.   *n.*

**ar·chi·trave** (är′kə trāv′)   in architecture:   1 the beam resting directly on the top, or capital, of a column; the lowest part of an ENTABLATURE, below the FRIEZE. See COLUMN for picture.   2 the moulding around a door, window, etc.   *n.*

**ar·chive** (är′kīv)   place material in a reserve file in a computer system: *We have arranged to archive all the data we have collected in the survey.*   *v.,* **ar·chived, ar·chiv·ing.**

**ar·chives** (är′kīvz)   1 a place where public records or historical documents are kept: *The National Archives of Canada are in Ottawa.*   2 the records and documents kept in such a place.   *n. pl.*

**archetype**     57     **area code**

hat, āge, fär; let, ēqual, tėrm; it, īce
hot, ōpen, ôrder; oil, out; cup, pút, rüle
əbove, takən, pencəl, lemən, circəs
ch, child; ng, long; sh, ship
th, thin; ᴛʜ, then; zh, measure

**ar·chiv·ist** (är′ki vist)   a person who looks after ARCHIVES (def. 2).   *n.*

**arch·way** (ärch′wā′)   1 an entrance or passageway with an arch above it.   2 an arch covering a passageway.   *n.*

**arc lamp**   a lamp in which the light comes from an electric ARC.

**arc light**   the brilliant light given by an ARC LAMP.

**arc·tic** (ärk′tik *or* är′tik)   1 extremely cold; frigid.   2 **the Arctic,**   **a** the north polar region; the region north of the Arctic Circle.   **b** the Arctic Ocean.   3 Often, **Arctic,**   of, having to do with, referring to, or living or growing in the region north of the Arctic Circle: *the Arctic fox.*   1, 3 *adj.,* 2 *n.*

**arctic char** or **Arctic char**   a food fish of the salmon and trout family found throughout the Arctic, occurring in two varieties, one of which is landlocked, the other spending most of its life in the sea but moving into fresh water to spawn.

**Arctic Circle**   1 the imaginary circle of the north polar region, running parallel to the equator at 23 degrees 30 minutes (23°30′) south of the North Pole.   2 the polar region surrounded by this circle.

**arctic haze**   a pollution problem in the FAR NORTH, in which particles of pollutants suspended in the arctic air increase in concentration during the winter months.

**ar·dent** (är′dənt)   1 full of zeal; very enthusiastic; eager: *Urho is an ardent student of history.*   2 burning; fiery; hot.   3 glowing.   *adj.*   —**ar′dent·ly,** *adv.*

**ardor** (är′dər)   See ARDOUR.   *n.*

**ar·dour** or **ar·dor** (är′dər)   1 eagerness; warmth of emotion; great enthusiasm: *patriotic ardour.*   2 burning heat.   *n.*

**ar·du·ous** (är′jü əs *or* är′dyü əs)   1 hard to do; requiring much effort; difficult: *an arduous lesson.*   2 using up much energy; strenuous: *an arduous effort to learn the lesson.*   3 hard to climb; steep: *an arduous hill.*   *adj.*   —**ar′du·ous·ly,** *adv.*   —**ar′du·ous·ness,** *n.*

**are**[1] (är; *unstressed,* ər)   the plural and 2nd person singular, present tense of BE: *we are, you are, they are.*   *v.*

**are**[2] (er *or* är)   a measure of area, equal to 100 square metres.   *n.*

**ar·e·a** (er′ē ə)   1 the amount of surface; extent of surface: *The area of this floor is 24 square metres.*   2 range; scope: *The provincial governments often try to limit the area of federal responsibility.*   3 region: *the Rocky Mountain area.*   4 a field of study or activity: *Leo is working in the area of foreign policy.*   5 a level surface or space: *The playing area was marked off with white lines.*   *n.*
☛ *Hom.*  ARIA (er′ē ə).

**area code**   a number consisting of three digits, that identifies the particular area within the whole region served by a telephone system. It is used as part of the telephone number for long-distance calls between areas:

*The area code for all the telephone numbers in Prince Edward Island is 902.*

**a·re·na** (ə rē′nə) **1** a building for indoor sports, having a central space for players or competitors that is surrounded by tiers of seats for spectators: *There is a hockey game at the arena tonight.* **2** a space where contests or shows take place: *Gladiators fought with lions in the arena of the great amphitheatre at Rome.* **3** any sphere of public action, especially one involving conflict: *You have to have stamina to succeed in the political arena.* *n.*

**aren't** (ärnt) **1** are not. **2** am not (*used by some speakers in questions*): *I'm too late, aren't I?* *v.*

**ar·gent** (är′jənt) **1** *Archaic or poetic.* silver. **2** silvery. **1** *n.*, **2** *adj.*

**Ar·gen·tine** (är′jən tēn′ *or* är′jən tīn′) **1** of Argentina, a country in South America, or its people. **2** a native or inhabitant of Argentina. **3 the Argentine,** Argentina. **1** *adj.*, **2 3** *n.*

**ar·gon** (är′gon) a colourless, odourless, inactive gas that forms a very small part of the air: *Argon is used in electric light bulbs and radio tubes. It is a chemical element.* Symbol: Ar *n.*

**Ar·go·naut** (är′gə not′) **1** in Greek mythology, one of the men who sailed with Jason in search of the Golden Fleece. **2** a person who went to California to search for gold in 1849. **3** a person who went from eastern Canada in 1862 to search for gold in the Cariboo in British Columbia. *n.*

**ar·go·sy** (är′gə sē) **1** a large merchant ship. **2** a fleet of such ships. *n., pl.* **ar·go·sies.**

**ar·got** (är′gō *or* är′gət) the specialized language, or jargon, of people who share a particular kind of work or way of life, especially one that is secret, as the language of criminals. *n.*

**ar·gue** (är′gyü) **1** discuss with someone who disagrees: *Luigi argued with his sister about who should wash the dishes.* **2** give reasons for or against something: *to argue a question. He argued against the passage of the bill.* **3** persuade by giving reasons: *Francine argued me into going.* **4** try to prove by reasoning; maintain: *Columbus argued that the world was round.* **5** indicate; show; prove: *Her rich clothes argue her to be wealthy.* **6** raise objections; dispute. *v.,* **ar·gued, ar·gu·ing.** —**ar′gu·er,** *n.*

**argue with,** dispute: *You can't argue with the facts.*

**ar·gu·ment** (är′gyə mənt) **1** a discussion by persons who give reasons for and against different points of view; a debate: *He won the argument by producing figures to prove his point.* **2** an emotional disagreement; a dispute: *Nancy had an argument with her brother about who won the card game.* **3** the reason or reasons given for or against something. **4** a short statement of what is in a book, poem, etc. *n.*

**ar·gu·men·ta·tion** (är′gyə mən tā′shən) **1** the process of arguing; reasoning. **2** a discussion; debate. *n.*

**ar·gu·men·ta·tive** (är′gyə men′tə tiv) **1** fond of arguing. **2** containing argument. *adj.* —**ar′gu·men′ta·tive·ly,** *adv.*

**Ar·gus** (är′gəs) a watchful guardian. *n.*
☞ *Etym.* From **Argus,** the name of a giant in Greek mythology, with a hundred eyes: *Argus was killed by Hermes, and his eyes were put in the peacock's tail.*

**Ar·gus–eyed** (är′gə sīd′) watchful; observant. *adj.*

**ar·hant** (är′hənt) in Buddhism, a title of respect for someone who has attained enlightenment. *n.*

**a·ri·a** (ä′rē ə, ar′ē ə, *or* er′ē ə) an air or melody; melody for a single voice with instrumental or vocal accompaniment. *n.*
☞ *Hom.* AREA (for the third pronunciation of **aria**).

**ar·id** (ar′id *or* er′id) **1** having very little rainfall; very dry; barren: *Desert lands are arid.* **2** dull; uninteresting: *an arid, boring speech.* *adj.* —**ar′id·ly,** *adv.* —**ar′id·ness,** *n.*

**a·rid·i·ty** (ə rid′ə tē) **1** dryness; barrenness. **2** dullness; lack of interest, life, or spirit. *n.*

**Ar·ies** (er′ēz *or* er′ē ēz′) **1** in astronomy, a northern constellation thought of as having the shape of a ram. **2** in astrology, the first sign of the zodiac. The sun enters Aries about March 21. See ZODIAC for picture. **3** a person born under this sign. *n.*

**a·right** (ə rīt′) correctly; rightly. *adv.*

**a·rise** (ə rīz′) **1** rise up; get up: *to arise early.* **2** move upward; ascend; mount: *Smoke arose from the chimney.* **3** come into being or action; come about; appear; begin: *A great wind arose. Accidents arise from carelessness.* *v.,* **a·rose, a·ris·en, a·ris·ing.**

**a·ris·en** (ə riz′ən) pp. of ARISE: *Ramesh has not yet arisen from his bed.* *v.*

**ar·is·toc·ra·cy** (ar′is tok′rə sē *or* er′is tok′rə sē) **1** people of noble rank, title, or birth; a ruling body of nobles; the nobility. **2** any class that is considered superior because of birth, intelligence, culture, or wealth; upper class. **3** a government in which a privileged upper class rules. **4** a country or state having such a government. **5** in ancient times, government by the best citizens. *n., pl.* **ar·is·toc·ra·cies.**

**a·ris·to·crat** (ə ris′tə krat′) **1** a person who belongs to the ARISTOCRACY (def. 1); a noble. **2** a person who has the tastes, opinions, manners, etc. of the upper classes. **3** a person who favours government by an ARISTOCRACY (defs. 1, 2). *n.*

**a·ris·to·crat·ic** (ə ris′tə krat′ik) belonging to or having to do with an ARISTOCRACY. *adj.* —**a·ris′to·crat′i·cal·ly,** *adv.*

**Ar·is·to·te·li·an** (ar′i stə tē′lyən *or* er′i stə tē′lyən) having to do with the Greek philosopher Aristotle (384-322 B.C.) or his philosophy. *adj.*

**arith.** **1** arithmetic. **2** arithmetical.

**a·rith·me·tic** (ə rith′mə tik′) **1** the science of positive, real numbers; the art of computing by figures: *When you study arithmetic, you learn to add, subtract, multiply, and divide.* **2** a textbook or handbook dealing with this science. *n.*

**ar·ith·met·i·cal** (ar′ith met′ə kəl *or* er′ith met′ə kəl) of arithmetic; having to do with arithmetic. *adj.*

**ar·ith·met·i·cal·ly** (ar′ith met′i klē *or* er′ith met′i klē) according to arithmetic; by the use of arithmetic. *adv.*

**arithmetical progression** a series in which there is always the same difference between a number and the one next after it: 2, 4, 6, 8, 10 *are in arithmetical progression; so are* 8, 5, 2, –1.

**a·rith·me·ti·cian** (ə rith′mə tish′ən) a person skilled in arithmetic. *n.*

**arithmetic mean** the average obtained by dividing the sum of several quantities by the number of quantities: *To obtain the arithmetic mean of 3, 9, 18, and 4, add them up and divide the total by 4.*

**ark** (ärk) **1** in the Bible, the large boat in which Noah saved himself, his family, and a pair of each kind of animal from the Flood. **2** *Informal.* any large, clumsy boat. **3** the ARK OF THE COVENANT. *n.*
☞ Hom. ARC.

**Ark of the Covenant** the wooden chest or box in which the ancient Jews kept the two tablets of stone containing the Ten Commandments: *The wooden chest in synagogues symbolizes the Ark of the Covenant.*

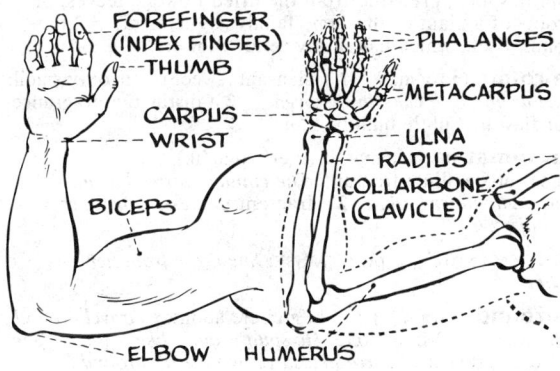

The human arm

**arm¹** (ärm) **1** the part of the human body between the shoulder and the hand. **2** the forelimb of an animal: *The front legs of a bear are sometimes called arms.* **3** anything resembling an arm in shape or use: *the strong arm of the law.* *n.* —**arm′less,** *adj.*
**arm in arm,** with arms linked: *She walked arm in arm with her sister.*
**at arm's length, a** as far as the arm can reach: *He held the picture up at arm's length to look at it.* **b** far enough away to avoid familiarity: *She was never very friendly and kept everyone at arm's length.*
**with open arms,** in a warm, friendly way; cordially.

**arm²** (ärm) **1** any instrument used for fighting; weapon (*usually used in the plural*): *Arms may be used for defence or attack.* **2** supply with weapons: *"Arm yourselves and be ready to fight," said the leader.* **3** take up weapons; prepare for war: *The soldiers armed for battle.* **4** a branch of the armed forces, such as the infantry, the artillery, or the armoured corps. **5** provide with a protective covering. **6** provide with the means to defend or attack something: *Each lawyer entered court armed with the data he planned to use to support his case.* **7 arms,** *pl.* fighting; war: *A soldier is a man of arms.* **8 arms,** *pl.* the symbols and designs used in heraldry or, as emblems of official dignity, by governments, cities, corporations, etc. 1, 4, 7 8 *n.,* 2, 3, 5 6 *v.*
**bear arms, a** serve as a soldier. **b** possess and display a COAT OF ARMS.
**take up arms,** arm for attack or defence: *The settler took up arms against the invaders.*
**to arms!** prepare for battle!
**under arms,** having weapons; equipped for fighting.
**up in arms, a** preparing for battle. **b** very angry; in rebellion.

**ar·ma·da** (är mad′ə *or* är mä′də) **1** a fleet of warships. **2** a fleet of airplanes. **3 the Armada,** the Spanish fleet that was sent to attack England in 1588. *n.*

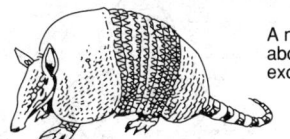

A nine-banded armadillo—about 45 cm long, excluding the tail

**ar·ma·dil·lo** (är′mə dil′ō) any of a family of burrowing mammals found in South America and southern North America, having an armourlike covering of jointed, bony plates, a long, narrow tongue with which it catches insects, and strong claws: *One species of armadillo can roll up into a ball to protect itself when attacked.* *n., pl.* **ar·ma·dil·los.**

**Ar·ma·ged·don** (är′mə ged′ən) a great and final conflict. *n.*

**ar·ma·ment** (är′mə mənt) **1** war equipment and supplies. **2** all the armed forces of a nation. **3** the guns on a ship, tank, airplane, etc. **4** the act or process of preparing for war. *n.*

**ar·ma·ture** (är′mə chər) **1** armour. **2** a part of an animal or plant serving for offence (teeth, suckers) or defence (shells, thorns): *A turtle's shell is an armature.* **3** a piece of soft iron across the poles of a magnet to preserve its magnetic power. **4** a revolving part of an electric motor. **5** the coils of wire that revolve in the magnetic field of a generator to produce an electric current. See GENERATOR for picture. *n.*

**arm·band** (ärm′band′) a circlet of cloth, often black crepe, worn around the sleeve, usually as a sign of mourning. *n.*

**arm·chair** (ärm′cher′) a chair with side pieces to support a person's arms or elbows. *n.*

**armed forces** all the parts of a country's defence organization, including those on land, at sea, in the air, and in space; army, navy, and air force.

**armed services** ARMED FORCES.

**Ar·me·ni·an** (är mē′nē ən) **1** of or having to do with Armenia, a former kingdom of southwestern Asia, its people, or their language. **2** a native or inhabitant of Armenia. **3** the language of the Armenians: *Armenian is an Indo-European language.* 1 *adj.,* 2 3 *n.*

**arm·ful** (ärm′fůl′) as much as one arm or both arms can hold: *Bring in an armful of wood for the fire.* *n., pl.* **arm·fuls.**

**arm·hole** (ärm′hōl′) the hole for the arm in a garment. *n.*

**ar·mi·stice** (är′mə stis) a stop in fighting by agreement on all sides; truce. *n.*

**Armistice Day** November 11, the anniversary of the end of World War I; now called REMEMBRANCE DAY.

**arm·let** (ärm′lit) **1** an ornamental band for the upper arm. **2** a small inlet of the sea. *n.*

**armor** (är′mər) See ARMOUR. *n.*

**ar·mo·ri·al** (är mô′rē əl) having to do with coats of arms or heraldry. *adj.*

**armorial bearings** a COAT OF ARMS.

**ar·mo·ry** (är′mə rē) See ARMOURY. *n.*

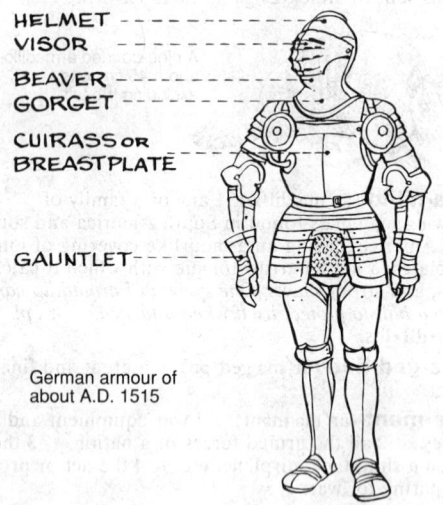

HELMET
VISOR
BEAVER
GORGET
CUIRASS or BREASTPLATE
GAUNTLET

German armour of about A.D. 1515

**ar·mour** or **ar·mor** (är′mər) 1 a covering, often of metal, worn to protect the body in fighting. 2 any kind of protective covering: *A diver's suit and the scales of a fish are armour.* 3 the steel or iron plates or other protective covering of a warship, airplane, or fortification. 4 cover or protect with armour. 5 the tanks and other armoured vehicles of an army. 1–3, 5 *n.*, 4 *v.*

**ar·mour·bear·er** or **ar·mor·bear·er** (är′mər ber′ər) an attendant who carried the armour or weapons of a warrior. *n.*

**ar·moured** or **ar·mored** (är′mərd) 1 covered or protected with armour: *an armoured train, car, etc.* 2 using tanks, armoured cars, etc.: *an armoured regiment.* *adj.*

**ar·mour·er** or **ar·mor·er** (är′mə rər) 1 a maker or repairer of armour. 2 a manufacturer of firearms. 3 a man in charge of firearms: *The armourer of a warship takes care of the revolvers, pistols, and rifles on the ship.* *n.*

**ar·mour·ies** or **ar·mor·ies** (är′mə rēz) *Cdn.* a building where reserve units of the armed forces have their headquarters and training area. *n. pl.*

**armour plate** or **armor plate** a steel or iron plating to protect warships, forts, etc.

**ar·mour·y** or **ar·mor·y** (är′mə rē) 1 a place where weapons are kept; ARSENAL. 2 *U.S.* a place where weapons are made; ARSENAL. 3 ARMOURIES. *n., pl.* **ar·mour·ies** or **ar·mor·ies**.

**arm·pit** (ärm′pit′) the hollow under the arm at the shoulder. *n.*

**ar·my** (är′mē) 1 a large, organized group of soldiers, trained and armed for war. 2 a nation's army. 3 in Canada, the ARMED FORCES on land. 4 part of the name of certain bodies organized on military lines: *The Salvation Army.* 5 a very large number; multitude: *an army of ants.* *n., pl.* **ar·mies**.

**army of occupation** an army sent into a defeated country to enforce a treaty, keep order, etc.

**army worm** 1 a kind of moth caterpillar found in Canada and the United States east of the Rockies, having green and white lengthwise stripes: *Large numbers of these caterpillars often travel together across the fields, like an army, eating any kind of grass or grain and so destroying crops.* 2 any of several kinds of caterpillar that travel to new feeding grounds in large groups, destroying crops on their way.

**ar·ni·ca** (är′nə kə) 1 a healing liquid used on bruises, sprains, etc., prepared from the dried flowers, leaves, or roots of a plant of the same family as the aster. 2 the plant itself, which has showy yellow flowers. *n.*

**a·ro·ma** (ə rō′mə) 1 a pleasant, sweet or savoury smell: *the aroma of a cake in the oven.* 2 a distinctive fragrance or flavour; subtle quality. *n.*

**ar·o·mat·ic** (ar′ə mat′ik *or* er′ə mat′ik) 1 sweet-smelling; fragrant: *The cinnamon tree has an aromatic inner bark.* 2 a fragrant plant or substance. 1 *adj.*, 2 *n.*

**a·rose** (ə rōz′) pt. of ARISE: *She arose from her chair.* *v.*

**a·round** (ə round′) 1 in a circle about: *to travel around the world.* 2 in a circle: *He spun around like a top.* 3 in circumference: *The tree measures two metres around.* 4 closely surrounding: *Ahilia had a coat around her shoulders.* 5 on all sides of: *Woods lay around the house.* 6 on all sides: *A dense fog lay around.* 7 *Informal.* here and there in: *She leaves her books around the house.* 8 here and there: *We walked around to see the town.* 9 *Informal.* somewhere near: *Wait around awhile.* 10 *Informal.* somewhere near: *Please play around the house.* 11 *Informal.* approximately; near in amount, number, etc. to: *That hat cost around twenty-five dollars.* 12 in the opposite direction: *Turn around! You are going the wrong way.* 13 on the far side of: *just around the corner.* 14 along the edge or border of rather than straight through: *On our trip west we drove around Toronto.* 1, 4, 5, 7, 10, 11, 13 14 *prep.*, 2, 3, 6, 8, 9 12 *adv.*

**a·rouse** (ə rouz′) 1 awaken. 2 stir to action; excite: *The attack aroused the whole country.* *v.*, **a·roused**, **a·rous·ing**.

**ar·pent** (är′pənt; *French,* ÄR päN′) *Cdn.* 1 an old French measure of land area, formerly used in Canada, equal to about 3400 square metres: *An arpent contained 100 square PERCHES.* 2 a former measure of length, equal to about 58 metres. *n.*

**ar·que·bus** (är′kwə bəs) HARQUEBUS. *n.*

**ar·raign** (ə rān′) 1 bring before a law court for trial: *The tramp was arraigned on a charge of stealing.* 2 call in question; find fault with; accuse. *v.* —**ar·raign′er**, *n.*

**ar·raign·ment** (ə rān′mənt) 1 the act of bringing before a court to answer a charge; indictment. 2 an unfavourable criticism. *n.*

**ar·range** (ə rānj′) 1 put in the proper order: *The army is arranged for battle.* 2 settle a dispute: *Mother arranged the quarrel between the two girls.* 3 plan; prepare: *Can you arrange to meet me this evening?* 4 adapt a piece of music to voices or instruments for which it was not written: *This music for the violin is also arranged for the piano.* *v.*, **ar·ranged**, **ar·rang·ing**. —**ar·rang′er**, *n.*

**ar·range·ment** (ə rānj′mənt) 1 putting or being put in

proper order.   2 the way or order in which things or persons are put: *You can make six arrangements of the letters A, B, and C.*   3 an adjustment; settlement.   4 something made by arranging separate parts or things in a particular way: *an unusual flower arrangement.*   5 an adaptation of a piece of music to voices or instruments for which it was not written.   6 Usually, **arrangements,** *pl.* a plan; preparation: *to make arrangements for a journey.*   *n.*

**ar·rant** (ar′ənt *or* er′ənt)   extreme; thoroughgoing; downright: *Yussria was such an arrant liar that nobody ever believed her.*   *adj.*

**ar·ras** (ar′əs *or* er′əs)   1 a kind of tapestry.   2 a curtain or hangings of tapestry.   *n.*

**ar·ray** (ə rā′)   1 order: *The troops were formed in battle array.*   2 arrange in order: *The general arrayed his troops for the battle.*   3 a display of persons or things: *an impressive array of wedding gifts. The array of good players on the other team made our side lose confidence.*   4 a military force; soldiers.   5 clothes, especially for some special or festive occasion; dress: *bridal array, gorgeous array.*   6 dress in fine clothes; adorn: *Tuune was arrayed like a queen.*   1, 3–5 *n.*, 2 6 *v.*

**ar·rears** (ə rērz′)   1 money due but not paid; debts.   2 unfinished work; things not done on time.   *n. pl.*
**in arrears,**   behind in payments, work, etc.

**ar·rest** (ə rest′)   1 seize a person or persons by legal authority; take to jail or court: *Police officers arrested the thieves.*   2 the seizing of a person or persons by legal authority; a taking to jail or court.   3 stop; check: *Filling a tooth arrests decay.*   4 a stopping; checking.   5 catch and hold: *Our attention was arrested by the sound of a shot.*   1, 3, 5 *v.*, 2, 4 *n.*   —**ar·rest′er,** *n.*
**under arrest,**   held by the police.

**ar·riv·al** (ə rī′vəl)   1 the act of arriving; coming: *She is waiting for the arrival of the train.*   2 a person or thing that arrives: *The new arrivals were made welcome.*   *n.*

**ar·rive** (ə rīv′)   1 reach the end of a journey; come to a place: *We arrived in Kingston a week ago.*   2 come; occur: *The time has arrived for you to study.*   3 be successful.   *v.*, **ar·rived, ar·riv·ing.**
**arrive at,**   come to; reach: *You must arrive at a decision soon.*

**ar·ro·gance** (ar′ə gəns *or* er′ə gəns)   too great pride; haughtiness.   *n.*

**ar·ro·gant** (ar′ə gənt *or* er′ə gənt)   proud of oneself and disdainful of others; too proud; haughty: *Few people like arrogant boys.*   *adj.*   —**ar′ro·gant·ly,** *adv.*

**ar·ro·gate** (ar′ə gāt′ *or* er′ə gāt′)   1 claim or take without right: *The despotic queen arrogated power to herself.*   2 claim for another without good reason: *The suspicious man arrogated bad motives to other people.*   *v.*, **ar·ro·gat·ed, ar·ro·gat·ing.**

**ar·row** (ar′ō *or* er′ō)   1 a slender shaft or stick having a pointed tip, and feathers at the tail end: *An arrow is made to be shot from a bow.* See ARCHERY for picture.   2 anything resembling an arrow in shape or speed.   3 a sign (→) used to show direction or position in maps, on road signs, and in writing.   *n.*   —**ar′row-like′,** *adj.*

**ar·row·head** (ar′ō hed′ *or* er′ō hed′)   1 the head or tip of an arrow, especially a separately made piece of stone or metal.   2 a marsh or water plant, many varieties of which have leaves shaped like arrowheads.   *n.*

**ar·row·root** (ar′ō rüt′ *or* er′ō rüt′)   1 an easily

# arrant   61   artesian well

hat, āge, fär; let, ēqual, tėrm; it, īce hot, ōpen, ôrder; oil, out; cup, pùt, rüle əbove, takən, pencəl, lemən, circəs ch, child; ng, long; sh, ship th, thin; ᴛʜ, then; zh, measure

digested starch made from the roots of a tropical American plant.   2 the plant itself.   *n.*

**ar·row·y** (ar′ō ē *or* er′ō ē)   1 of arrows.   2 like an arrow in shape or speed.   *adj.*

**ar·roy·o** (ə roi′ō)   1 the dry bed of a stream; gully.   2 a small river.   *n., pl.* **ar·roy·os.**

**ar·se·nal** (är′sə nəl)   a building for storing or manufacturing weapons and ammunition for the armed forces.   *n.*

**ar·se·nate of lead** (är′sə nāt′)   a poison used on vines, trees, etc. to kill insects.

**ar·se·nic** (är′sə nik)   1 a greyish-white chemical element that has a metallic lustre and evaporates when heated.   *Symbol:* As   2 a violent poison that is a compound of this element: *Arsenic is a white, tasteless powder that resembles flour.*   *n.*

**ar·son** (är′sən)   the crime of intentionally setting fire to a building or other property.   *n.*

**ar·son·ist** (är′sə nist)   FIREBUG.   *n.*

**art** (ärt)   1 any form of human activity that is the product of imagination and skill and that appeals mainly to the imagination; especially, drawing, painting, and sculpture, and also architecture, poetry, music, dancing, etc.   2 works produced by such activity: *a museum of art.*   3 a branch or division of learning dealing mainly with human ideas and values and the development of the intellect, such as literature, philosophy, and history; one of the humanities.   4 a craft or trade that requires skill and imagination: *the household arts of cooking and sewing, the weaver's art. Writing compositions is an art.*   5 a particular skill or set of working principles: *the art of making friends, the art of war. There is an art to organizing your work area.*   6 human skill or effort, as opposed to nature: *It was a well-kept, formal garden that owed more to art than to nature.*   7 ARTWORK.   8 cunning; artfulness: *He swore he had used no art to persuade them.*   9 **arts,** *pl.*   in universities, a group of studies that includes literature, languages, history, philosophy, etc. and that excludes the sciences and technical or professional studies.   10 **the arts,** *pl.*   FINE ARTS: *The arts flourished in Elizabethan England.*   *n.*

**ar·te·ri·al** (är tē′rē əl)   1 having to do with or resembling the arteries.   2 having to do with the bright-red blood of the arteries.   3 serving as a major route of transportation, supply, etc.: *an arterial highway.*   4 having a main channel with many branches.   *adj.*

**arterial road**   a main road or highway.

**ar·te·ri·o·scle·ro·sis** (är tē′rē ō sklə rō′sis)   a hardening of the walls of the arteries which makes circulation of the blood difficult.   *n.*

**ar·ter·y** (är′tə rē)   1 any of the blood vessels or tubes that carry blood from the heart to all parts of the body.   2 a main road; important channel: *Yonge Street is one of the main arteries of Toronto.*   *n., pl.* **ar·ter·ies.**

**ar·te·sian well** (är tē′zhən)   a deep-drilled well, especially one from which water gushes up without pumping.

**art·ful** (ärt′fəl) 1 crafty; deceitful: *A swindler uses artful tricks to get people's money away from them.* 2 skilful; clever. 3 artificial. *adj.* —**art′ful·ly**, *adv.* —**art′ful·ness**, *n.*

**ar·thrit·ic** (är thrit′ik) of, having to do with, or affected with ARTHRITIS: *arthritic joints.* *adj.*

**ar·thri·tis** (är thrī′tis) an inflammation of a joint or joints. *n.*

**ar·thro·pod** (är′thrə pod′) any animal belonging to the phylum **Arthropoda**, a large group of invertebrate animals having a segmented body and legs, including insects, spiders, mites, scorpions, and crustaceans: *Arthropods range in size from tiny mites only 0.1 mm long to a giant crab having a leg span of 3.4 m; they make up about three quarters of all the known species of animals on earth.* *n.*

**Arthurian legend** (är thü′rē ən) a body of legends about King Arthur, a supposed king in England in the 6th century. These legends are the source of some of the world's great literature, telling of Arthur's famous knights of the Round Table in Camelot, his sword Excalibur, and the mysterious Isle of Avalon, from which he will one day return to be king again: *Arthurian legend is the basis of some of the world's great literature.*

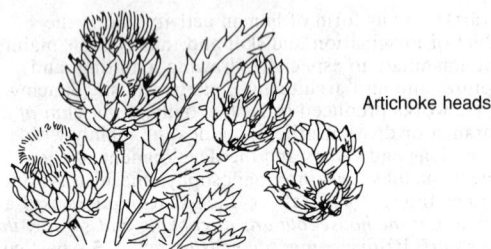
Artichoke heads

**ar·ti·choke** (är′tə chōk′) 1 a thistle-like plant whose flowering head is cooked and eaten. 2 the flowering head. 3 JERUSALEM ARTICHOKE. *n.*

**ar·ti·cle** (är′tə kəl) 1 a literary composition, complete in itself, but forming part of a magazine, newspaper, or book: *an article on gardening in a newspaper.* 2 a clause in a contract, treaty, statute, etc.: *The third article of the club's constitution dealt with the privileges of members.* 3 a particular thing; item: *Bread is a main article of food.* 4 one of the words *a*, *an*, or *the*, which usually accompany nouns. *A* and *an* are indefinite articles; *the* is the definite article. 5 bind by a contract: *The apprentice was articled to serve the master workman for seven years.* 1–4 *n.*, 5 *v.*, **ar·ti·cled, ar·ti·cling.**

**Articles of Confederation** the constitution adopted in 1781 by the thirteen original states of the United States of America. It was replaced by the present Constitution in 1789.

**ar·tic·u·late** (är tik′yə lit *for adjective,* är tik′yə lāt′ *for verb*) 1 uttered in distinct syllables of words: *A baby cries and gurgles, but does not use articulate speech.* 2 speak distinctly: *Be careful to articulate your words so that everyone in the room can understand you.* 3 able to put one's thoughts into words: *Julia is the most articulate of the sisters.* 4 express clearly and logically in words: *She could not articulate her feelings of resentment.* 5 made up of distinct parts; distinct. 6 jointed; segmented.
7 unite by joints. 8 fit together in a joint: *After her knee was injured, she was lame because the bones did not articulate well.* 1, 3, 5 6 *adj.*, 2, 4, 7 8 *v.*, **ar·tic·u·lat·ed, ar·tic·u·lat·ing.** —**ar·tic·u·late·ly**, *adv.*

**ar·tic·u·la·tion** (är tik′yə lā′shən) 1 a way of speaking; enunciation: *If you speak more slowly, your articulation will be improved.* 2 a joint. 3 a connecting or connection by a joint or joints: *the articulation of the bones.* *n.*

**ar·ti·fact** (är′tə fakt′) anything made by human skill or work; an artificial product. *n.*

**ar·ti·fice** (är′tə fis) 1 a clever device; trick: *She will use any artifice to get her own way.* 2 trickery; craft: *His conduct is free from artifice.* 3 skill; cleverness. *n.*

**ar·ti·fi·cer** (är tif′ə sər) 1 a skilled worker; craftsperson. 2 a maker; inventor. *n.*

**ar·ti·fi·cial** (är′tə fish′əl) 1 made by human skill or labour; not natural: *When you read at night, you read by artificial light.* 2 made as a substitute for or in imitation of; not real: *artificial flowers, artificial silk.* 3 put on; assumed; false; affected: *an artificial tone of voice, an artificial manner.* *adj.* —**ar′ti·fi′cial·ly**, *adv.* —**ar′ti·fi′cial·ness**, *n.*

**artificial intelligence** the ability of some computers to recognize and solve problems: *If, given the types of materials to be used, this computer can calculate the weight that each floor of a new building can bear, this is artificial intelligence.*

**ar·ti·fi·ci·al·i·ty** (är′tə fish′ē al′ə tē) 1 an ARTIFICIAL quality or condition. 2 something unnatural or unreal. *n., pl.* **ar·ti·fi·ci·al·i·ties.**

**artificial respiration** the process of restoring the breathing of a person by rhythmically forcing air into and out of his or her lungs, as by breathing directly into the mouth or alternately applying and releasing pressure on the diaphragm.

**ar·til·ler·y** (är til′ə rē) 1 mounted guns; cannon. 2 the part of an army that uses and manages big guns. 3 the science of firing, and of co-ordinating the firing, of guns of larger calibre than machine guns. *n.*

**ar·til·ler·y·man** (är til′ə rē mən) a soldier who belongs to the artillery; GUNNER. *n., pl.* **ar·til·ler·y·men** (-mən).

**artillery piece** a mounted gun or cannon, fixed or movable.

**ar·ti·san** (är′tə zən *or* är′tə zan′) a person skilled in some industry or trade; craftsperson: *Carpenters, masons, plumbers, and electricians are artisans.* *n.*

**art·ist** (är′tist) 1 a person who paints pictures. 2 a person who is skilled in any of the fine arts, such as sculpture, music, or literature. 3 a person who does work with skill and good taste. *n.*

**ar·tiste** (är tēst′) a very skilful performer or worker: *An artiste may be a singer, a dancer, or a cook.* *n.*

**ar·tis·tic** (är tis′tik) 1 of, having to do with, or characteristic of art or artists: *the artistic imagination.* 2 done or made with skill, imagination, and good taste: *an artistic design, an artistic presentation.* 3 having skill in art or an appreciation of art: *She is very artistic.* *adj.*

**ar·tis·ti·cal·ly** (är tis′ti klē) 1 with skill and good taste. 2 from an ARTISTIC point of view. *adv.*

**art·ist·ry** (är′ti strē) artistic work; the workmanship of an artist. *n., pl.* **art·ist·ries.**

**art·less** (är′tlis) 1 not artificial or studied; natural and uncontrived: *She walked with artless grace. Small children ask many artless questions.* 2 without guile or deceit; sincere; innocent: *artless flattery, an artless youth.* 3 lacking knowledge or skill; crude, uncultured, or clumsy. *adj.* —**art′less·ly,** *adv.* —**art′less·ness,** *n.*

**art·work** (ärt′wėrk′) pictures and other decorative or illustrative material in a magazine, book, etc.: *That magazine always has excellent artwork.* *n.*

**art·y** (är′tē) *Informal.* making a pretence or show of being artistic. *adj.,* **art·i·er, art·i·est.** —**art′i·ness,** *n.*

Two species of arum:
a jack-in-the-pulpit (left)
and a calla lily (right)

**ar·um** (er′əm *or* ar′əm) 1 any of various plants belonging to a family of mostly tropical or subtropical plants having small flowers densely clustered on an upright, fleshy part called a SPADIX which is more or less enclosed by a leafy part called a SPATHE: *The* **water arum,** *or* **wild calla,** *is a common Canadian marsh plant having a greenish-white spathe surrounding a yellow spadix.* 2 referring to the family of plants that includes the arums: *The sweet flag, jack-in-the-pulpit, and skunk cabbage belong to the arum family.* *n.*

**Ar·y·an** (ar′ē ən *or* er′ē ən) 1 INDO-EUROPEAN (def. 2). 2 a person belonging to a prehistoric group of people who spoke a language from which the Indo-European languages are descended. 1 *adj.,* 2 *n.*

**as** (əz; *stressed,* az) 1 to the same degree or extent; equally: *as black as coal.* 2 to the same degree or extent that: *She worked just so much as she was told to.* 3 in the same way that: *Run as I do.* 4 during the time that; when; while: *She sang as she worked.* 5 because: *As he was a skilled worker, he received good wages.* 6 though: *Brave as they were, the danger made them afraid.* 7 that the result was: *The child so marked the picture as to spoil it.* 8 in the character of; doing the work of: *Who will act as teacher?* 9 in the manner of: *Will you fight as men, or die as slaves?* 10 a condition or fact that: *She is very careful, as her work shows.* 11 that: *Do the same thing as I do.* 12 for example: *Some animals, as dogs and cats, eat meat.* 1, 12 *adv.,* 2–7 *conj.,* 8 9 *prep.* 10 11 *pron.*
**as for,** about; concerning; referring to: *We're leaving now; as for Sonia, she'll have to come on her own.*
**as if,** as it would be if: *The car looked as if it had been driven on rough roads.*
**as is,** *Informal.* in the present condition: *If you buy the car as is, you will have to put it in running order yourself.*
**as of,** beginning on: *As of April 7, we will be on daylight-saving time.*
**as to,** about; concerning; referring to: *We have no information as to the cause of the riot.*

**such as,** for example.

**As** arsenic.

**as·a·fet·i·da** or **as·a·foet·i·da** (as′ə fet′ə də *or* as′ə fē′tə də) a gum resin with a garliclike odour, used in medicine to prevent spasms. *n.* Also, **assafetida, assafoetida.**

**as·bes·tos** (as bes′təs *or* az bes′təs) 1 a mineral, a silicate of calcium and magnesium that does not burn or conduct heat, usually occurring in fibres. 2 a fireproof fabric made of these fibres: *Asbestos was once used to fireproof buildings.* *n.*

**as·cend** (ə send′) 1 go up; rise; move upward: *Mahmuda watched the airplane ascend.* 2 climb; go to or toward the top of: *to ascend Mt. Everest.* *v.*

**as·cend·ance** (ə sen′dəns) ASCENDANCY. *n.*

**as·cend·an·cy** (ə sen′dən sē) the state of being in the ASCENDANT (def. 3); domination; rule. *n.* Also, **ascendency.**

**as·cend·ant** (ə sen′dənt) 1 ascending; rising. 2 superior; dominant; ruling; controlling. 3 a position of power; controlling influence. 1, 2 *adj.,* 3 *n.* Also, **ascendent.**
**in the ascendant,** **a** supreme; dominant. **b** increasing in influence.

**as·cend·en·cy** (ə sen′dən sē) See ASCENDANCY. *n.*

**as·cend·ent** (ə sen′dənt) See ASCENDANT. *adj., n.*

**as·cen·sion** (ə sen′shən) the act of ascending; ascent. *n.*

**as·cent** (ə sent′) 1 the act of going up; rising: *the sudden ascent of an elevator.* 2 the act of climbing: *the ascent of Mt. Everest.* 3 a place or way that slopes up: *the gradual ascent of the terrace.* *n.*
☛ *Hom.* ASSENT.

**as·cer·tain** (as′ər tān′) find out; determine: *Bulcsu telephoned home to ascertain if his father had arrived.* *v.*

**as·cer·tain·ment** (as′ər tān′mənt) an ASCERTAINing. *n.*

**as·cet·ic** (ə set′ik) 1 a person who practises unusual self-denial and devotion or severe discipline of self for religious reasons. 2 a person who refrains from pleasures and comforts. 3 refraining from pleasures and comforts; self-denying. 1, 2 *n.,* 3 *adj.*
—**as·cet′i·cal·ly,** *adv.*

**as·cet·i·cism** (ə set′ə siz′əm) 1 the life or habits of an ASCETIC (defs. 1, 2). 2 a doctrine that by abstinence and self-denial a person can train himself or herself to be in a high spiritual state. *n.*

**a·scor·bic acid** (ə skôr′bik *or* ā skôr′bik) VITAMIN C.

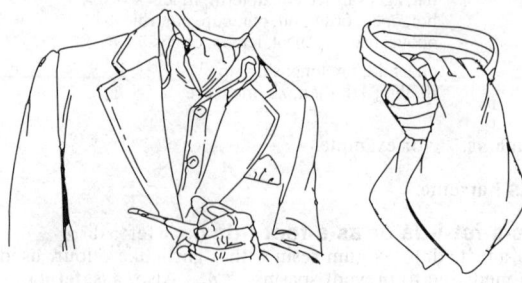
An ascot

**as·cot** (as′kot *or* as′kət) a neck scarf with broad ends, tied so that the ends may be laid flat, one over the other. *n.*

**as·cribe** (ə skrīb′) **1** think of as caused by or coming from; assign; attribute (*to*): *The police ascribed the automobile accident to fast driving.* **2** consider as belonging (*to*): *Men have ascribed their own characteristics to their gods.* *v.*, **as·cribed, as·crib·ing.**

**as·crip·tion** (ə skrip′shən) **1** the act of ascribing: *the ascription of selfishness to a miser.* **2** any statement or words ascribing something. *n.*

**a·sep·sis** (ə sep′sis *or* ā sep′sis) **1** an ASEPTIC condition. **2** ASEPTIC methods or treatment. *n.*

**a·sep·tic** (ə sep′tik *or* ā sep′tik) free from germs causing infection. *adj.*

**a·sex·u·al** (ā sek′shü əl) **1** having no sex. **2** independent of sexual processes: *In liverworts, mosses, and some of the lower animals, sexual and asexual reproduction alternate.* *adj.* —**a·sex′u·al·ly,** *adv.*

**ash¹** (ash) **1** what remains of a thing after it has been thoroughly burned or oxidized by chemical means: *There was cigarette ash on the carpet. We cleaned the ashes out of the fireplace.* **2** the light-grey colour of ashes from wood. **3 ashes,** *pl.* **a** ruins: *a whole city laid in ashes.* **b** the remains of a dead person: *He was buried beside the ashes of his forefathers.* *n.*

**ash²** (ash) **1** a kind of shade tree that is valuable for timber and has greyish bark and twigs and straight-grained wood. **2** its tough, springy wood. *n.*

**a·shamed** (ə shāmd′) **1** feeling shame; disturbed or uncomfortable because one has done something wrong, improper, or silly: *I was ashamed when I cried at the movies. She was ashamed of her dishonesty.* **2** unwilling because of shame: *Gino was ashamed to tell his mother that he had failed.* *adj.*
**ashamed at,** ashamed for another person: *We were surprised and ashamed at his words.*

**ash·en¹** (ash′ən) **1** like ashes; pale as ashes. **2** of ashes. *adj.*

**ash·en²** (ash′ən) **1** of the ash tree. **2** made from the wood of the ash tree. *adj.*

**a·shore** (ə shôr′) **1** to the shore; to land: *The women rowed ashore.* **2** on the shore; on land: *The sailor had been ashore for months.* 1 *adv.*, 2 *adj.*

**ash·tray** (ash′trā′) a container for the ashes of cigarettes, cigars, and pipes. *n.*

**ash·y** (ash′ē) of, like, or covered with ashes. *adj.*, **ash·i·er, ash·i·est.**

**A·sian** (ā′zhən) **1** of, having to do with, or characteristic of Asia or its people. **2** a native or inhabitant of Asia. **3** a person whose recent ancestors came from Asia. 1 *adj.*, 2, 3 *n.*

**a·side** (ə sīd′) **1** on or to one side: *Move the table aside. Yu-wen spoke aside to Winston without our hearing her.* **2** out of one's thoughts, consideration, etc.: *Put your troubles aside.* **3** words meant not to be heard by someone; especially in the theatre, an actor's remark that is meant to be heard by the audience but not by the other characters in the play. 1, 2 *adv.*, 3 *n.*
**aside from,** *Informal.* except for.

**as·i·nine** (as′ə nīn′) stupid; silly: *What an asinine thing to say!* *adj.* —**as′i·nine′ly,** *adv.*

**as·i·nin·i·ty** (as′ə nin′ə tē) stupidity; silliness. *n., pl.* **as·i·nin·i·ties.**

**ask** (ask) **1** try to find out by words; inquire: *Why don't you ask? She asked about our health. Ask the way.* **2** seek the answer to: *Ask any questions you wish.* **3** put a question to; inquire of: *Ask him how old he is.* **4** try to get by words; request: *Ask Kathy to sing. I asked permission to leave the table.* **5** claim; demand: *to ask too high a price for a house.* **6** invite: *She asked ten guests to the party.* **7** need; require: *This job asks hard work.* *v.*
**ask after,** inquire about the health of: *Mother asked after you.*
**asking for,** inviting; causing: *You're asking for trouble.*

**a·skance** (ə skans′) sideways; to one side. *adv.*
**look askance at,** regard with suspicion or disapproval: *The students looked askance at the suggestion of having classes on Saturday.*

**a·skant** (ə skant′) ASKANCE. *adv.*

**a·skew** (ə skyü′) **1** to one side; out of the proper position: *Her hat went askew.* **2** turned or twisted the wrong way: *The bottom line of printing is askew.* 1 *adv.*, 2 *adj.*

**a·slant** (ə slant′) **1** in a slanting direction. **2** slantingly across. **3** slanting. 1 *adv.*, 2 *prep.*, 3 *adj.*

**a·sleep** (ə slēp′) **1** in a condition of sleep; sleeping: *The cat is asleep.* **2** into a condition of sleep: *The tired boy fell asleep.* **3** without feeling; numb: *My foot is asleep.* **4** sluggish; not alert; inactive: *asleep on the job.* **5** dead. 1, 3, 4, 5 *adj.*, 2 *adv.*
☛ *Usage.* **Asleep** as an adjective is never used before a noun.

**a·slope** (ə slōp′) at a slant. *adv., adj.*

**asp** (asp) **1** the Egyptian cobra, a very poisonous snake, about 180 cm long: *The asp was sacred to the Egyptians and became a symbol of royalty.* **2** a small poisonous snake of Europe. *n.*

Leaves and shoots of asparagus

**as·par·a·gus** (ə sparʹə gəs *or* ə sperʹə gəs) **1** a perennial plant of the same family as the lily, but having pulpy fruit and no bulb. The stems have many branches covered with threadlike branchlets, the true leaves being reduced to scales. **2** the stems of one kind of this plant, used as a vegetable. *n.*

**a·spar·kle** (ə spärʹkəl) sparkling. *adj.*

**as·pect** (asʹpekt) **1** one side, part, or view of a subject: *We must consider this plan in its various aspects.* **2** a look; appearance: *I love the ocean in all its aspects, even its stormy, frightening aspect in winter.* **3** countenance; expression: *the solemn aspect of a judge.* **4** the direction in which anything faces; exposure: *This house has a western aspect.* **5** a side fronting in a given direction: *the southern aspect of a house.* *n.*

**as·pen** (asʹpən) **1** any of several poplar trees whose leaves tremble and rustle in the slightest breeze. **2** of this tree. **3** quivering; trembling. **1** *n.*, **2, 3** *adj.*

**as·per·i·ty** (a sperʹə tē) **1** roughness; harshness; severity: *the asperities of a very cold winter.* **2** severity: *We all noticed the asperity in our teacher's voice.* *n., pl.* **as·per·i·ties.**

**as·perse** (ə spėrsʹ) spread damaging or false reports about; slander. *v.*, **as·persed, as·pers·ing.** —**as·persʹer,** *n.*

**as·per·sion** (ə spėrʹzhən) a damaging or false report; slander: *You should not cast aspersions on people.* *n.*

**as·phalt** (asʹfolt) **1** a dark-coloured, almost solid, tarry substance found in natural deposits in many parts of the world and also obtained by evaporating petroleum; bitumen. **2** a smooth, hard mixture of this substance with crushed rock, used for pavements, roofs, etc. *n.*

**as·pho·del** (asʹfə del) **1** a plant of the same family as the lily, having spikes of white or yellow flowers. **2** DAFFODIL. *n.*

**as·phyx·i·a** (as fikʹsē ə) suffocation or an unconscious condition caused by lack of oxygen and excess of carbon dioxide in the blood. *n.*

**as·phyx·i·ate** (as fikʹsē āt) suffocate because of lack of oxygen and excess of carbon dioxide in the blood: *The men trapped in the coal mines were asphyxiated by the gas before help could reach them.* *v.*, **as·phyx·i·at·ed, as·phyx·i·at·ing.**

**as·phyx·i·a·tion** (as fikʹsē āʹshən) ASPHYXIA. *n.*

**as·pic** (asʹpik) a kind of jelly made of meat or fish stock, tomato juice, etc., often set in a mould with seafood, meat, etc. *n.*

**as·pi·dis·tra** (asʹpə disʹtrə) a plant having large, green leaves and very small flowers, much used as a house plant. *n.*

**as·pir·ant** (ə spīʹrənt *or* asʹpə rənt) **1** a person who aspires; person who seeks a position of honour. **2** aspiring. **1** *n.*, **2** *adj.*

**asparagus**    **65**    **assay**

hat, āge, fär; let, ēqual, tėrm; it, īce
hot, ōpen, ôrder; oil, out; cup, put, rüle
əbove, takən, pencəl, lemən, circəs
ch, child; ng, long; sh, ship
th, thin; ᴛʜ, then; zh, measure

**as·pi·rate** (asʹpə rātʹ *for verb*, asʹpə rit *for adjective and noun*) **1** begin a word or syllable with an *h*-sound, as *h* in *hoot* (hüt). **2** pronounced with a breathing or *h*-sound. The *h* in *here* is aspirate. **3** an aspirated sound. **1** *v.*, **as·pi·rat·ed, as·pi·rat·ing;** **2** *adj.*, **3** *n.*

**as·pi·ra·tion** (asʹpə rāʹshən) **1** an earnest desire; longing: *She had aspirations to be an actress.* **2** an object of desire or ambition; goal. **3** the drawing of air into the lungs; breathing. **4** an aspirating of sounds: *There is aspiration of the h in house.* *n.*

**as·pi·ra·tor** (asʹpə rāʹtər) an apparatus or device employing suction: *A vacuum cleaner is an aspirator.* *n.*

**as·pire** (ə spīrʹ) **1** have an ambition for something; desire earnestly; seek: *Scholars aspire after knowledge. Pierre aspired to be captain.* **2** rise high. *v.*, **as·pired, as·pir·ing.** —**as·pirʹing·ly,** *adv.*

**ass** (as) **1** donkey. **2** any of several species of very fast wild animal of Asia and Africa, related to the horse but smaller, and having long ears, a very short mane, and a long tail with a tuft of long hair at the end: *The wild ass of Africa is the ancestor of the common domestic donkey.* **3** *Informal.* a stupid fool; silly or stubborn person. *n.*

**as·sa·fet·i·da** or **as·sa·foet·i·da** (asʹə fetʹə də *or* asʹə fēʹtə də) See ASAFETIDA. *n.*

**as·sa·gai** or **as·se·gai** (asʹə gīʹ) a slender spear or javelin of hard wood, used by some African tribes. *n., pl.* **as·sa·gais** or **as·se·gais.**

**as·sail** (ə sālʹ) **1** set upon with violence; attack: *to assail a fortress.* **2** set upon vigorously with arguments, abuse, etc. *v.* —**as·sailʹa·ble,** *adj.*

**as·sail·ant** (ə sāʹlənt) a person who attacks: *The injured man did not know his assailant.* *n.*

**as·sas·sin** (ə sasʹən) a murderer, especially of a politically important person: *Assassins are often hired to commit murder.* *n.*

**as·sas·si·nate** (ə sasʹə nātʹ) murder someone, especially a politically important person, by a sudden or secret attack. *v.*, **as·sas·si·nat·ed, as·sas·si·nat·ing.** —**as·sasʹsiʹnaʹtor,** *n.*

**as·sas·si·na·tion** (ə sasʹə nāʹshən) murder, usually of an important public figure, by a sudden or secret attack: *The assassination of President Lincoln occurred in 1865.* *n.*

**as·sault** (ə soltʹ) **1** an attack, especially a sudden, vigorous attack. **2** a final phase of a military attack; closing with the enemy in hand-to-hand fighting. **3** make an assault on; attack. **1, 2** *n.*, **3** *v.* —**as·saultʹer,** *n.*

**assault and battery** the crime of striking a person; touching a person to harm him or her.

**as·say** (ə sāʹ) **1** analyse an ore, alloy, etc. to find out the quantity of gold, silver, or other metal in it. **2** an analysis of an ore, alloy, etc. to find out the amount of metal in it. **3** try; test; examine. **4** a trial; test; examination. **1, 3** *v.*, **2 4** *n.* —**as·sayʹer,** *n.*

**as·se·gai** (as′ə gī′) See ASSAGAI. *n.*

**as·sem·blage** (ə sem′blij) **1** a group of persons gathered together; assembly. **2** a collection; group. **3** a bringing together; coming together; meeting. **4** a putting together; fitting together: *the assemblage of the parts of a machine. n.*

**as·sem·ble** (ə sem′bəl) **1** gather or bring together: *All the writer's papers have been assembled into one collection. They were finding it hard to assemble a crew for the yacht.* **2** come together; meet: *After lunch, the delegates assembled in the auditorium.* **3** put together the parts of; fit together: *to assemble a model airplane. The chair should be easy to assemble.* *v.*, **as·sem·bled, as·sem·bling.** —**as·sem′bler,** *n.*

**as·sem·bly** (ə sem′blē) **1** a group of people gathered together for some purpose; meeting: *A reception or a ball may be called an assembly.* **2** a lawmaking group. **3** a putting together; fitting together: *the assembly of the parts of an automobile to make an automobile.* **4** the complete group of parts required to put something together: *the hull assembly of Olaf's model boat.* **5** a signal on a bugle or drum for troops to form in ranks. *n.*, **as·sem·blies.**

**assembly line** a row of workers and machines along which work is passed until the final product is made: *Automobiles are produced on an assembly line.*

**as·sem·bly·man** (ə sem′blē mən) in Prince Edward Island, one of fifteen members of the Legislative Assembly elected by both property and non-property holders; a member of the Legislative Assembly who is not a councillor. *n., pl.* **as·sem·bly·men** (-mən).

**as·sent** (ə sent′) **1** express agreement; agree: *Everyone assented to the plans for the dance.* **2** the acceptance of a proposal, statement, etc.; agreement: *Emoke smiled her assent to the plan. Parliament gave assent to the bill.* **1** *v.*, **2** *n.* —**as·sent′ing·ly,** *adv.*
☛ *Hom.* ASCENT.

**as·sert** (ə sert′) **1** state positively; declare: *Aino asserts that she will go whether we do or not.* **2** insist on a right, a claim, etc.; defend: *to assert one's independence.* *v.* —**as·sert′er** or **as·ser′tor,** *n.*
**assert oneself,** **a** put oneself forward; make oneself noticed. **b** insist on one's rights.

**as·ser·tion** (ə ser′shən) **1** a positive declaration; very strong statement: *Her assertion of innocence was believed by the jury.* **2** an insisting on one's rights, a claim, etc. *n.*

**as·ser·tive** (ə ser′tiv) too confident and certain; positive: *Gunther is an assertive boy, insisting on his own rights.* *adj.* —**as·ser′tive·ly,** *adv.* —**as·ser′tive·ness,** *n.*

**as·sess** (ə ses′) **1** estimate the value of property or income for taxation. **2** fix the amount of a tax, fine, damages, etc. **3** put a tax on or call for a contribution from a person, property, etc.: *Each member was assessed ten dollars for the trip.* *v.* —**as·sess′a·ble,** *adj.*

**as·sess·ment** (ə ses′mənt) **1** the act of assessing. **2** the amount assessed. *n.*

**as·ses·sor** (ə ses′ər) a person who estimates the value of property or income for taxation. *n.*

**as·set** (as′et) **1** something having value: *Ability to get along with people is an asset in business.* **2 assets,** *pl.* **a** things of value; property: *Leslie's assets include a house, car, bonds, and jewellery.* **b** property that can be used to pay debts. *n.*

**as·sev·er·ate** (ə sev′ə rāt′) declare solemnly; state positively. *v.*, **as·sev·er·at·ed, as·sev·er·at·ing.**

**as·sev·er·a·tion** (ə sev′ə rā′shən) a firm, solemn declaration; positive statement. *n.*

**as·si·du·i·ty** (as′ə dyü′ə tē or as′ə dü′ə tē) careful and steady attention; diligence; perseverance. *n., pl.* **as·si·du·i·ties.**

**as·sid·u·ous** (ə sij′ü əs) careful and attentive; diligent. *adj.* —**as·sid′u·ous·ly,** *adv.*

**as·sign** (ə sīn′) **1** give as a share; allot: *The teacher has assigned several problems for homework.* **2** appoint to a post or duty: *The captain assigned two soldiers to guard the gate.* **3** name definitely; fix; set: *The judge assigned a day for the trial.* **4** refer; ascribe; attribute: *Overwork was assigned as the cause of his breakdown.* **5** a person to whom property, a right, etc. is legally transferred. 1–4 *v.*, 5 *n.* —**as·sign′a·ble,** *adj.* —**as·sign′er,** *n.*
**assign to,** **a** transfer or hand over property, a right, etc. legally: *Mr. Jones assigned his home and farm to his creditors.* **b** provide for: *Special funds have been assigned to the needs of poor students.* **c** give someone a task with: *I'll assign an extra man to the case.*

**as·sig·na·tion** (as′ig nā′shən) **1** an appointment for a meeting, especially a secret meeting between lovers; TRYST (def. 1). **2** the meeting or meeting place. **3** the act of assigning: *the assignation of duties. n.*

**as·sign·ment** (ə sīn′mənt) **1** something assigned, especially a piece of work to be done: *Today's assignment in arithmetic is ten problems.* **2** an assigning; appointment: *The soldier was informed of his assignment to a new base.* **3** a legal transfer of some property, right, etc. *n.*

**as·sim·i·la·ble** (ə sim′ə lə bəl) able to be ASSIMILATED. *adj.*

**as·sim·i·late** (ə sim′ə lāt′) **1** absorb; digest: *The girl reads so much that she does not assimilate it all. The human body will not assimilate sawdust.* **2** make or become like the people of a nation, etc. in customs and viewpoint: *We have assimilated immigrants from many lands. All the immigrants have assimilated here readily.* **3** make like: *By living with the Houde family, she was assimilated to them in her thinking.* **4** become like. *v.*, **as·sim·i·lat·ed, as·sim·i·lat·ing.** —**as·sim′i·la′tor,** *n.*

**as·sim·i·la·tion** (ə sim′ə lā′shən) **1** absorbing or being absorbed: *Life depends on the assimilation of food.* **2** making or becoming like. *n.*

**as·sim·i·la·tive** (ə sim′ə lə tiv or ə sim′ə lā′tiv) assimilating: *the assimilative functions of the body. adj.*

**As·sin·i·boine** (ə sin′ə boin′) **1** a member of a First Nations or Native American people living mainly in Alberta, Saskatchewan, and Montana: *The Assiniboines are a Siouan people.* **2** the Siouan language of the Assiniboines. **3** of or having to do with these people or their language. 1, 2 *n.*, 3 *adj.*

**as·sist** (ə sist′) **1** give aid to; help. **2** take part or have a hand (*in*): *Karen assisted in the scoring of the goal.* **3** in hockey, the credit given to a player who helps score a goal. **4** in baseball, the credit given to a player who helps to put an opposing player out. **5** an instance of giving help: *With an assist from me, he soon climbed the fence.* 1, 2 *v.*, 3–5 *n.*

**as·sist·ance** (ə sis′təns) help; aid. *n.*

**as·sist·ant** (ə sis′tənt)  **1** a helper; aid.  **2** helping; assisting: *an assistant teacher.*  1 *n.*, 2 *adj.*

**as·size** (ə sīz′)  **1** an inquest or the verdict of the inquest.  **2 assizes,** *pl.*  **a** periodical sessions of a court of law.  **b** the time or the place of these sessions.  *n.*

**assn.** or **Assn.**  association.

**assoc.** or **Assoc.**  **1** associate.  **2** association.

**as·so·ci·ate** (ə sō′shē āt′ *for verb,* ə sō′shē it *or* ə sō′shē āt′ *for noun and adjective*)  **1** connect in thought: *We associate camping with summer.*  **2** anything that is usually connected with something else.  **3** joined in companionship, interest, action, etc.: *Giuseppe is an associate editor of the school paper.*  **4** join as a companion, partner, or friend: *She associates only with people interested in sports. He has always associated with large enterprises.*  **5** keep company (*with*): *Do not associate with bad companions.*  **6** a companion; partner; ally; friend: *I am one of Ninh-Phung's associates in this scheme.*  **7** join; combine; unite.  **8** combine for a common purpose.  **9** a member without full rights and privileges: *an associate in a law firm.*  1, 4, 5, 7, 8 *v.*, **as·so·ci·at·ed, as·so·ci·at·ing;**  2, 6, 9 *n.*, 3 *adj.*  —**as·so′ci·a′tor,** *n.*

**as·so·ci·a·tion** (ə sō′sē ā′shən *or* ə sō′shē ā′shən)  **1** associating or being associated; alliance: *I look forward to my association with the new students.*  **2** a group of people joined together for some purpose; society: *the Young People's Association.*  **3** companionship; partnership; friendship.  **4** a connection of ideas in thought; relationship.  *n.*

**association area**  the part of the brain that is believed to bring together impulses from the sensory nerves, sort them, and send them to the motor area.

**association football**  SOCCER.

**as·so·ci·a·tive** (ə sō′shē ə tiv *or* ə sō′shē ā′tiv)  **1** of, having to do with, or dependent on association, as of ideas or images.  **2** in mathematics, of or referring to a rule that any change in the grouping of elements in an operation will not affect the result: *Example in addition of real numbers:* $(7 + 3) + 8 = 7 + (3 + 8)$.  *adj.*

**as·so·nance** (as′ə nəns)  a kind of rhyme in which the vowel sounds are alike but the consonants are different. *Examples: brave—vain, lone—show.*  *n.*

**as·sort** (ə sôrt′)  **1** sort out; classify; arrange in sorts.  **2** furnish with an assortment of goods.  **3** group (*with*).  **4** agree in sort or kind; fall into a class.  **5** associate (*with*).  *v.*  —**as·sort′er,** *n.*

**as·sort·ed** (ə sôr′tid)  **1** selected so as to be of different kinds; various: *assorted cakes.*  **2** arranged by kinds; classified: *socks to be assorted by size.*  **3** matched; suited to one another: *They are a poorly assorted couple, always quarrelling.*  *adj.*

**as·sort·ment** (ə sôrt′mənt)  **1** a collection of various kinds: *an assortment of candies.*  **2** arranging by kinds.  **3** a group; class.  *n.*

**asst.** or **Asst.**  assistant.

**as·suage** (ə swāj′)  **1** make easier or milder; quiet; calm: *to assuage pain.*  **2** satisfy; appease; quench: *to assuage thirst.*  *v.*, **as·suaged, as·suag·ing.**  —**as·suag′er,** *n.*

**as·suage·ment** (ə swāj′mənt)  **1** assuaging or being ASSUAGED.  **2** something that ASSUAGES.  *n.*

**as·sume** (ə süm′)  **1** take for granted; suppose: *She assumed that the train would be on time.*  **2** take upon oneself; undertake: *Paavo assumed the leadership in planning the picnic.*  **3** take or put on oneself: *to assume an air of superiority.*  **4** pretend: *He assumed ignorance of the whole matter.*  *v.*, **as·sumed, as·sum·ing.**
☛ *Syn.* See note at PRESUME.

**as·sumed** (ə sümd′ *or* ə syümd′)  **1** pretended; not real.  **2** supposed.  *adj.*

**as·sum·ing** (ə sü′ming *or* ə syü′ming)  taking too much on oneself; presumptuous.  *adj.*

**as·sump·tion** (ə sump′shən *or* ə sum′shən)  **1** taking for granted; assuming: *She bustled about with an assumption of authority.*  **2** something assumed: *Her assumption that she would win the prize proved incorrect.*  **3** presumption; arrogance; unpleasant boldness: *That boy's assumption in always thrusting himself forward made him disliked.*  *n.*

**as·sur·ance** (ə shü′rəns)  **1** making sure or certain.  **2** a positive declaration inspiring confidence: *Mother has given me her assurance that I may go to the circus.*  **3** security; certainty; confidence: *We have the assurance of final victory.*  **4** self-confidence: *Li-Ying's hard studying has given her considerable assurance in school.*  **5** impudence; too much boldness.  **6** insurance: *life assurance.*  *n.*
**self-assurance,**  confidence in oneself.

**as·sure** (ə shur′)  **1** make sure or certain: *The man assured himself that the bridge was safe before crossing it.*  **2** tell positively: *The captain of the ship assured the passengers that there was no danger.*  **3** make safe; secure.  **4** make safe against loss; INSURE: *Is your life assured?*  **5** give or restore confidence to; reassure: *The father assured his frightened son.*  *v.*, **as·sured, as·sur·ing.**  —**as·sur′er,** *n.*

**as·sured** (ə shürd′)  **1** sure; certain: *You may be assured that she is safe.*  **2** confident; bold.  **3** insured against loss.  **4** a person who is the beneficiary of an insurance policy.  **5** a person whose life or property is insured.  1–3 *adj.*, 4 5 *n.*  —**as·sur′ed·ness,** *n.*

**as·sur·ed·ly** (ə shü′ri dlē)  **1** surely; certainly.  **2** confidently; boldly.  *adv.*

**as·ta·tine** (as′tə tēn′)  a radio-active chemical element produced artificially from bismuth: *Astatine is the heaviest of the halogens.*  Symbol: At  *n.*

**as·ter** (as′tər)  any of various mostly perennial plants of the COMPOSITE family, having flower heads consisting of white, purple, blue, or pink ray flowers surrounding a central disk of tiny, tube-shaped flowers: *Asters are popular garden plants.*  *n.*
☛ *Etym.* **Aster,** ASTERISK, and ASTEROID can all be traced back to Gk. *aster* 'star', related to Gk. *astron,* from which ASTRONAUT, ASTRONOMY, etc. are formed.

**as·ter·isk** (as′tə risk)  a star-shaped mark (*) used in printing and writing to call attention to a footnote, indicate an omission, etc.  *n.*
☛ *Etym.* See note at ASTER.

**a·stern** (ə stėrn′)  **1** at or toward the rear of a ship: *The captain went astern.*  **2** backward: *The ship was moving* slowly astern.   **3** behind: *Yachts tow small boats astern.* *adv.*

**as·ter·oid** (as′tə roid′)   any of the many very small planets revolving about the sun, mainly between the orbits of Mars and Jupiter.   *n.*
☛ *Etym.* See note at ASTER.

**as·then·o·sphere** (as then′ə sfēr′)   a region within the mantle of the earth that seems to be partly melted.   *n.*

**asth·ma** (az′mə *or* as′mə)   a chronic disease that causes difficulty in breathing, a feeling of suffocation and coughing.   *n.*

**asth·mat·ic** (az mat′ik *or* as mat′ik)   **1** of or having to do with ASTHMA.   **2** suffering from ASTHMA.   **3** a person suffering from ASTHMA.   1, 2 *adj.*, 3 *n.*

**as·tig·mat·ic** (as′tig mat′ik)   **1** having ASTIGMATISM. **2** having to do with ASTIGMATISM.   **3** correcting ASTIGMATISM.   *adj.*

**a·stig·ma·tism** (ə stig′mə tiz′əm)   a defect of an eye or of a lens that makes objects look indistinct or gives imperfect images: *With perfect focus, all the rays of light from any one point of an object converge at one point on the retina of the eye or other receiving surface; with astigmatism they do not.*   *n.*

**a·stir** (ə stėr′)   **1** in motion; up and about: *The bees came astir in the warmth.*   **2** in motion; up and about: *Even at midnight, the whole town was astir.*   1 *adv.*, 2 *adj.*

**as·ton·ish** (ə ston′ish)   surprise greatly; amaze: *The gift of twenty dollars astonished the little boy.*   *v.*

**as·ton·ish·ing** (ə ston′i shing)   very surprising; amazing: *an astonishing sight.*   *adj.*
—**as·ton′ish·ing·ly,** *adv.*

**as·ton·ish·ment** (ə ston′i shmənt)   **1** great surprise; amazement; sudden wonder.   **2** anything that causes great surprise.   *n.*

**as·tound** (ə stound′)   surprise very greatly; amaze.   *v.*
—**as·tound′ing·ly,** *adv.*

**a·strad·dle** (ə strad′əl)   ASTRIDE (defs. 1, 3).   *adv.*, *adj.*

**as·trag·a·lus** (as trag′ə ləs)   the uppermost bone of the TARSUS; anklebone; TALUS.   *n., pl.* **as·trag·a·li** (-lī′ *or* -lē′)

**as·tra·khan** *or* **as·tra·chan** (as′trə kən)   **1** the curly, furlike wool on the skin of young lambs from Astrakhan.   **2** a woollen cloth that looks like this.   *n.*

**as·tral** (as′trəl)   of, having to do with, or consisting of stars.   *adj.*

**astral body**   a spiritual counterpart, or double, of the human body, believed to be able to leave it at will.

**a·stray** (ə strā′)   **1** out of the right way: *Your reasoning is astray on that subject.*   **2** off the right path: *We seem to have gone astray; we should have turned east by now.*   1 *adj.*, 2 *adv.*

**a·stride** (ə strīd′)   **1** with one leg on each side: *She took an astride position.*   **2** with one leg on each side of something: *Philip sits astride his horse.*   **3** with legs far apart: *He stood with legs astride.*   1, 3 *adj.*, 2 *prep.*

**as·trin·gen·cy** (ə strin′jən sē)   being ASTRINGENT (def. 2).   *n.*

**as·trin·gent** (ə strin′jənt)   **1** a substance that shrinks tissues and checks the flow of blood by contracting blood vessels: *Alum is an astringent.*   **2** having the property of shrinking or contracting.   1 *n.*, 2 *adj.*
—**as·trin′gent·ly,** *adv.*

**as·tro·ge·o·lo·gist** (as′trō jē ol′ə jist)   a person trained in ASTROGEOLOGY, especially one who makes it his or her work.   *n.*

**as·tro·ge·o·lo·gy** (as′trō jē ol′ə jē)   the science that deals with the nature of rocks on other planets and the moon.   *n.*

**as·tro·labe** (as′trə lāb′ *or* as′trə lab′)   an astronomical instrument formerly used for measuring the altitude of the sun or stars, now replaced by the SEXTANT.   *n.*
☛ *Etym.* Through F and L from Gk. *astrolabon*, a noun formed from *astrolabos* 'star-taking'.

**as·trol·o·ger** (ə strol′ə jər)   a person who claims to interpret the influence of the stars and planets on persons, events, etc.   *n.*

**as·tro·log·i·cal** (as′trə loj′ə kəl)   having to do with ASTROLOGY.   *adj.*

**as·trol·o·gy** (ə strol′ə jē)   the study of the stars and planets to reveal their supposed influence on persons, events, etc. and to foretell what will happen.   *n.*
☛ *Etym.* Through F and L from Gk. *astron* 'star' + *-logia* 'treating of'.

**as·tro·naut** (as′trə not′)   a pilot or member of the crew of a spacecraft; a person who travels in outer space.   *n.*
☛ *Etym.* Coined in the 20c. from Gk. *astron* 'star' + *nautēs* 'sailor'. See also note at COSMONAUT.

**as·tro·nau·tics** (as′trə not′iks)   the science that deals with travel in outer space.   *n.*

**as·tron·o·mer** (ə stron′ə mər)   a person trained in ASTRONOMY, especially one who makes it his or her work.   *n.*

**as·tro·nom·ic** (as′trə nom′ik)   ASTRONOMICAL.   *adj.*

**as·tro·nom·i·cal** (as′trə nom′ə kəl)   **1** of ASTRONOMY; having to do with astronomy.   **2** enormous; like the numbers reported in ASTRONOMY: *That trip will cost you an astronomical sum of money.*   *adj.*

**as·tro·nom·i·cal·ly** (as′trə nom′i klē)   according to ASTRONOMY.   *adv.*

**astronomical year**   the period of the earth's revolution around the sun; solar year: *The astronomical year lasts 365 days, 5 hours, 48 minutes, and 45.51 seconds.*

**as·tron·o·my** (ə stron′ə mē)   the science of the sun, moon, planets, stars, and other heavenly bodies. It deals with their composition, motions, positions, distance, sizes, etc.   *n.*
☛ *Etym.* Through OF and L from Gk. *astron* 'star' + *nomos* 'distribution or arrangement'.

**as·tro·phys·ics** (as′trō fiz′iks)   the branch of astronomy that deals with the physical and chemical characteristics of heavenly bodies.   *n.*

**as·tute** (ə styüt′ *or* ə stüt′)   **1** having or showing a keen, discovering mind; clever; sagacious: *an astute remark.* **2** having or showing hard-headed shrewdness; crafty: *an astute business deal.*   *adj.*   —**as·tute′ly,** *adv.*
—**as·tute′ness,** *n.*

**a·sun·der** (ə sun′dər)   **1** in pieces; into separate parts: *The cliff fell asunder.*   **2** apart; separate: *The toy is damaged, its parts are asunder.*   1 *adv.*, 2 *adj.*

**a·sy·lum** (ə sī′ləm)   1 formerly, an institution for the support and care of the mentally ill, the poor, the aged, etc.   2 a refuge; shelter: *The author who had been accused of a political crime was given asylum in another country.*   *n.*

The outline of the tree on the left is asymmetric; the one on the right is symmetric.

**a·sym·met·ric** (ā′sə met′rik *or* as′ə met′rik)   not symmetrical; lacking SYMMETRY.   *adj.*

**a·sym·met·ri·cal** (ā′sə met′rə kəl *or* as′ə met′rə kəl) ASYMMETRIC.   *adj.*

**a·sym·me·try** (ā sim′ə trē *or* a sim′ə trē)   a lack of SYMMETRY.   *n.*

**as·ymp·tote** (as′im tōt′)   in geometry, a straight line that approaches but does not meet a curve.   *n.*

**at** (at; *unstressed*, ət)   1 in; on; by; near: *at school, at the front door.*   2 directly toward; in the direction of: *to aim at the mark. Look at me.*   3 in a place or condition of: *at right angles. England and France were at war.*   4 on or near the time of; at: *at midnight.*   5 through; by way of: *Smoke came out at the chimney.*   6 engaged in; trying to do: *at work.*   7 because of; as a result of: *The shipwrecked sailors were happy at the arrival of the rescue ship.*   8 for: *two books at twenty dollars each.* Symbol: @   9 according to: *at will.*   10 from: *The sick man got good treatment at the hands of his doctor.*   *prep.*

**At**   astatine.

**at.**   atomic.

**at·a·vism** (at′ə viz′əm)   in a plant or animal, the reappearance of a characteristic that has been absent for several generations: *The individual showing atavism is often called a* THROWBACK.   *n.*

**at·a·vis·tic** (at′ə vis′tik)   1 having to do with ATAVISM.   2 having a tendency to ATAVISM.   *adj.*

**a·tax·i·a** (ə tak′sē ə)   the inability to co-ordinate voluntary movements.   *n.*

**ate** (āt)   pt. of EAT. *Wai-Ho ate his dinner.*   *v.*

**–ate¹**   a suffix meaning:   1 of or having to do with: *Collegiate means having to do with college.*   2 having; containing: *Compassionate means having compassion.*   3 having the form of; like: *Palmate means having the form of a palm leaf.*   4 cause to be: *Alienate means cause to be alien.*   5 supply or treat with: *Aerate means treat with air.*   6 combine with: *Oxygenate means combine with oxygen.*

**–ate²**   a suffix meaning: a salt made from _____ic acid: *A sulphate is a salt made from sulphuric acid.*

**–ate³**   a suffix meaning: the office, rule, or condition of: *A caliphate is the office or rule of a caliph.*

**Ath·a·pas·can** (ath′ə pas′kən)   1 a major group of First Nations and Native American languages spoken in northwestern Canada, Alaska, and the southwestern United States, including Chipewyan, Dogrib, Sarcee, Slave, and Navaho.   2 a member of a people speaking any of these languages.   3 of, having to do with, or referring to this group of languages or any of the peoples speaking them.   1, 2 *n.*, 3 *adj.*

**a·the·ism** (ā′thē iz′əm)   a belief that there is no God.   *n.*

**a·the·ist** (ā′thē ist)   a person who believes that there is no God.   *n.*

**a·the·is·tic** (ā′thē is′tik)   of ATHEISM or ATHEISTS.   *adj.*   —a′the·is′ti·cal·ly, *adv.*

**ath·e·nae·um** *or* **ath·e·ne·um** (ath′ə nē′əm)   1 a scientific or literary club.   2 a reading room; library.   *n.*
☛ *Etym.* Through late L from Gk. *Athēnaion*, the temple of Athena at Athens where philosophy was taught.

**A·the·ni·an** (ə thē′nē ən)   1 of Athens, the capital of Greece, or its people.   2 a person having the rights of citizenship in ancient Athens.   3 a native or inhabitant of Athens.   1 *adj.*, 2, 3 *n.*

**Ath·ens** (ath′ənz)   1 the capital city of Greece.   2 any city thought of as being a centre of art and literature like the ancient Greek city of Athens.   *n.*

**ath·er·o·scle·ro·sis** (ath′ə rō sklə rō′sis)   a form of ARTERIOSCLEROSIS characterized by a narrowing and hardening of the arteries due to deposits of cholesterol and fatty acids along the artery walls.   *n.*

**a·thirst** (ə thėrst′)   1 thirsty.   2 eager: *Most young people are athirst for new experiences.*   *adj.*

**ath·lete** (ath′lēt)   a person trained in exercises of physical strength, speed, and skill: *Ballplayers, runners, boxers, and swimmers are athletes.*   *n.*

**athlete's foot**   a contagious skin disease of the feet, caused by a fungus; ringworm of the feet.

**ath·let·ic** (ath let′ik)   1 active and strong; generally enjoying active games and sports and showing natural skill in them: *I'm not very athletic but I do enjoy swimming and horseback riding.*   2 of, like, or suited to an athlete.   3 having to do with active games and sports: *an athletic association.*   *adj.*   —ath·let′i·cal·ly, *adv.*

**ath·let·ics** (ath let′iks)   1 exercises of strength, speed, and skill; active games and sports: *Athletics include baseball and basketball.*   2 the principles of athletic training.   1 *n. pl.*, 2 *n. sing.*

**a·thwart** (ə thwôrt′)   1 crosswise; across from side to side.   2 across.   3 across the line or course of.   4 in opposition to; against.   1 *adv.*, 2–4 *prep.*

**at·i·gi** (at′ə gē *or* ə tē′gē) *Cdn.*   1 a hooded, knee-length inner shirt made of summer skins with the hair inside against the body, used in winter especially by Inuit, often for indoor wear.   2 a hooded outer garment of fur or other material; PARKA.   *n.*

**a·tilt** (ə tilt′)   at a tilt, tilted.   *adj.*, *adv.*

**a·tin·gle** (ə ting′gəl)   tingling; in a tingling or excited condition.   *adj.*

**–ation**   a noun-forming suffix meaning:   1 the act or state of _____ing: *Admiration means the act or state of admiring.*   2 the condition or state of being _____ed: *Cancellation means the condition or state of being cancelled.*

**3** a result of _____ ing: *Civilization means the result of civilizing.*

**–ative** an adjective-forming suffix meaning: **1** tending to _____: *Talkative means tending to talk.* **2** having to do with _____: *Qualitative means having to do with quality.*

**Atlantic Provinces** Newfoundland, Prince Edward Island, Nova Scotia, and New Brunswick.

**Atlantic salmon** a species of salmon found along the Atlantic coasts of North America and Europe, very highly valued as a game and food fish: *The ouananiche, or landlocked salmon, is a variety of Atlantic salmon that spends all its life in fresh water.*

**at·las** (at′ləs) a book of maps. *n., pl.* **at·las·es.**
☞ *Etym.* From the name of **Atlas**, in Greek legend, a giant who supported the heavens.

**atm 1** standard atmosphere; standard atmospheres. **2** atmospheric.

**at·man** (ät′mən) in Hinduism, the soul which is capable of reincarnation. *n.*

**at·mos·phere** (at′mə sfēr′) **1** the air that surrounds the earth. Compare with HYDROSPHERE and LITHOSPHERE. **2** mental and moral surroundings; surrounding influence: *an atmosphere of poverty.* **3** a mass of gases that surrounds any heavenly body. **4** the air in any given place: *The atmosphere in the cave was damp.* **5** STANDARD ATMOSPHERE. **6** the colouring or feeling that pervades a work of art: *music steeped in the atmosphere of old Vienna, the sombre atmosphere of The Scarlet Letter.* *n.*

**at·mos·pher·ic** (at′mə sfer′ik *or* at′mə sfē′rik) **1** of or having to do with the body of gases surrounding the earth and other heavenly bodies. **2** existing or happening in the atmosphere. **3** caused, produced, or worked by the ATMOSPHERE (def. 1): *atmospheric pressure.* *adj.* See ISOBAR for picture.

**at·mos·pher·i·cal·ly** (at′mə sfer′i klē) as regards the ATMOSPHERE; by atmospheric force or influence. *adv.*

**atmospheric pressure** the pressure exerted by the air on the surface of the earth and everything existing on it, caused by the force of gravity: *The standard atmospheric pressure is about 101 kPa; the highest atmospheric pressure ever recorded was about 108 kPa, in Siberia.*

**at. no.** atomic number.

**at·oll** (at′ol *or* ə tol′) a ring of coral that has built up on a sunken land bank or volcano top in the open sea, parts of the ring showing above water as solid coral islands that support vegetation: *The pool in the centre of an atoll is called a* LAGOON. *n.*

**a·tom** (at′əm) **1** the smallest part of an element that has all the properties of the element and can take part in a chemical reaction without being permanently changed: *Atoms are made up of protons, neutrons, and electrons.* **2** a very small particle; tiny bit. *n.*

**atom bomb** ATOMIC BOMB.

**a·tom·ic** (ə tom′ik) **1** of atoms; having to do with atoms: *atomic research.* **2** extremely small; minute. *adj.*

**atomic age** the era marked by the first use of ATOMIC ENERGY.

**atomic bomb** a bomb that uses the energy released by the very rapid splitting of atoms to cause an explosion of tremendous force.

**atomic energy 1** the energy that exists in atoms: *Some atoms can be made to release atomic energy, either slowly in a reactor or very suddenly in a bomb; the energy is generated through alteration of an atomic nucleus.* **2** ATOMIC POWER.

**atomic number** the number used in describing a chemical element and giving its relation to other elements: *The atomic number of an element is the number of positive charges (protons) on the nucleus of one of its atoms.*

**atomic pile** REACTOR.

**atomic power** ATOMIC ENERGY (def. 1) used to generate power for practical uses: *Several generating stations in Canada are now run by atomic power.*

**atomic theory** the theory that all matter is composed of atoms; especially, the modern theory that an atom is made of a positive nucleus around which electrons speed.

**atomic warfare** warfare using atomic bombs.

**atomic weight** the relative weight of an atom of a chemical element, using oxygen or hydrogen as a standard of comparison.

**at·om·ize** (at′ə mīz′) **1** separate into atoms. **2** change a liquid into a fine spray. *v.*, **at·om·ized, at·om·iz·ing.** —**at′om·i·za′tion,** *n.*

**at·om·iz·er** (at′ə mī zər) an apparatus used to blow a liquid in a spray of very small drops: *an atomizer for perfume.* *n.*

**atom smasher** ACCELERATOR (def. 3).

**at·o·my** (at′ə mē) **1** a very small thing; ATOM. **2** a tiny being; PYGMY. *n., pl.* **at·o·mies.**

**a·ton·al** (ā tō′nəl) in music, not having a central or dominant tone, or key; having all tones in equal relation to each other: *Atonal music is often based on the chromatic scale of twelve tones.* *adj.* —**a·ton′al·ly,** *adv.* —**a′to·nal′i·ty,** *n.*

**a·tone** (ə tōn′) make up; make amends (*for*): *George atoned for his unkindness to Petra by taking her to the movies.* *v.*, **a·toned, a·ton·ing.**

**a·tone·ment** (ə tōn′mənt) making up for something; the giving of satisfaction for a wrong, loss, or injury; amends. *n.*
**Day of Atonement,** YOM KIPPUR.

**a·top** (ə top′) **1** on or at the top. **2** on the top of. **1** *adv.*, **2** *prep.*

**at·ra·bil·ious** (at′rə bil′yəs) **1** melancholy; HYPOCHONDRIAC. **2** bad-tempered. *adj.*

**a·tri·um** (ā′trē əm *or* at′rē əm) **1** either of the upper chambers of the heart, that receive the blood from the veins; auricle. See HEART for picture. **2** a high central hall or court in a large building, often having a skylight, or open to the sky. *n., pl.* **a·tri·a** (ā′trē ə *or* at′rē ə) or **atriums.**

**a·tro·cious** (ə trō′shəs) **1** very wicked or cruel; very savage or brutal: *The crime was so atrocious that many details were never made public.* **2** *Informal.* very bad or unpleasant; abominable: *atrocious weather, an atrocious pun.* *adj.* —**a·tro′cious·ly,** *adv.* —**a·tro′cious·ness,** *n.*

**a·troc·i·ty** (ə tros′ə tē) **1** very great wickedness or cruelty. **2** a very cruel or brutal act: *the atrocities of war.* *n., pl.* **a·troc·i·ties.**

**at·ro·phy** (at′rə fē) **1** wasting away; the wasting away of a part or parts of the body: *Some diseases cause atrophy of the muscles in the legs.* **2** waste away or cause to waste away: *After years of not playing a piano, he found his skill had atrophied.* 1 *n.*, 2 *v.*, **at·ro·phied, at·ro·phy·ing.**

**at·ro·pine** (at′rə pēn′) a poisonous drug obtained from BELLADONNA and similar plants: *Atropine is used in medicine in small amounts to relax muscles and dilate the pupil of the eye.* *n.*

**at·tach** (ə tach′) **1** fasten: *She attached the boat to the pier by means of a rope.* **2** connect with for duty, etc.: *He was attached as mate to the ship "Clio."* **3** add at the end; affix: *We attached our names to the petition.* **4** attribute: *The world at first attached little importance to Hitler's acts.* **5** fasten itself; belong (*to*): *The blame for this accident attaches to the man who destroyed the signal.* **6** bind by affection: *Marie is much attached to her cousin.* **7** take a person or property by legal authority: *Her property was attached by the court because she had not paid her debts.* *v.* **—at·tach′a·ble,** *adj.*

**at·ta·ché** (ə tash′ā *or* at′ə shā′) a person on the official staff of an ambassador or minister to a foreign country: *a naval attaché.* *n.*

**attaché case** a briefcase shaped like a small, thin suitcase with a rigid frame and sides.

**at·tach·ment** (ə tach′mənt) **1** attaching or being attached. **2** something that is or can be attached: *A vacuum cleaner has various attachments.* **3** a means of attaching; fastening. **4** affection. **5** the legal taking of a person or property. *n.*

**at·tack** (ə tak′) **1** use force or weapons on to hurt; go against as an enemy; begin fighting against: *The dog attacked the cat.* **2** talk or write against: *to attack a country through propaganda.* **3** begin to work vigorously on: *The hungry boy attacked his dinner.* **4** make an attack: *The enemy attacked at dawn.* **5** attacking; violent opposition: *The attack of the enemy took the town by surprise. The chairman's speech consisted mainly of an attack on wasteful government spending.* **6** act harmfully on: *Fever attacked the man who was bitten by insects.* **7** a sudden occurrence of illness, discomfort, etc.: *an attack of malaria.* 1–4, 6 *v.*, 5 7 *n.* **—at·tack′er,** *n.*

**at·tain** (ə tān′) **1** arrive at; reach: *to attain the age of 80.* **2** gain; accomplish: *to attain a goal.* *v.*
**attain to,** succeed in coming to or getting: *to attain to a position of great influence.*

**at·tain·a·bil·i·ty** (ə tā′nə bil′ə tē) the quality of being ATTAINABLE. *n.*

**at·tain·a·ble** (ə tā′nə bəl) capable of being ATTAINed; that can be reached or achieved: *The office of Governor General is the highest attainable in Canada.* *adj.*

**at·tain·der** (ə tān′dər) the loss of property and civil rights as the result of being sentenced to death or of being outlawed. *n.*

**at·tain·ment** (ə tān′mənt) **1** attaining: *the attainment of our desires.* **2** something attained. **3** an accomplishment; ability: *Leonardo da Vinci was a man of varied attainments; he was an inventor, an artist, and an architect.* *n.*

**at·taint** (ə tānt′) **1** condemn to loss of property and civil rights. **2** stain; disgrace. 1, 2 *v.*, 2 *n.* **—at·taint′ment,** *n.*

**at·tar** (at′ər) a perfume made from the petals of roses or other flowers. *n.*

**at·tempt** (ə tempt′) **1** make an effort at; try: *to attempt to get better marks.* **2** a putting forth of effort to accomplish something, especially something difficult: *to make an attempt to climb Mount Everest.* **3** an attack: *The rebels made an unsuccessful attempt on the king's life.* 1 *v.*, 2 3 *n.*
**attempt the life of,** try to kill.

**at·tend** (ə tend′) **1** be present at: *Children must attend school.* **2** give care and thought; pay attention: *attend to the laboratory instructions. Instead of attending, the child was gazing out of the window.* **3** apply oneself: *Attend to your music if you want to play well.* **4** go with; accompany: *Noble ladies attend the queen.* **5** go with as a result: *Danger attends delay. Success often attends hard work.* **6** wait on; care for; tend: *Nurses attend the sick.* **7** be ready; wait: *They attended her arrival in silence.* *v.*

**at·tend·ance** (ə ten′dəns) **1** being present; attending: *Attendance at all classes is compulsory.* **2** the company present; persons attending: *The attendance at the meeting was over 200 last Wednesday.* *n.*
**dance attendance on,** wait on often and attentively; be excessively polite and obedient to.

**at·tend·ant** (ə ten′dənt) **1** a person who waits on another, such as a servant or a follower. **2** waiting on another to help or serve: *an attendant nurse.* **3** going with as a result; accompanying: *weakness attendant on illness, attendant circumstances.* **4** present: *attendant hearers.* **5** a person who is present. 1, 5 *n.*, 2–4 *adj.*

**at·ten·tion** (ə ten′shən) **1** care and thought; concentration: *Attention to one's lessons is important. The children paid attention to the teacher.* **2** the power of attending; faculty of noticing: *James called my attention to the cat lying in wait for the bird.* **3** consideration: *The boy shows his mother much attention.* **4** a military attitude of readiness: *The soldiers stood at attention during inspection.* **5** a command to come to attention. **6** Usually, **attentions,** *pl.* acts of courtesy or devotion, especially of a suitor: *The girl received many attentions, such as invitations to parties and presents of candy and flowers.* 1–4, 6 *n.*, 5 *interj.*
**come to attention,** take a straight and motionless position.
**stand at attention,** stand straight and still.

**at·ten·tive** (ə ten′tiv) **1** paying attention; observant: *Anita is an attentive pupil.* **2** courteous; showing attention or interest: *an attentive hostess. The nurse was attentive to the patient's needs.* *adj.*
**—at·ten′tive·ly,** *adv.* **—at·ten′tive·ness,** *n.*

**at·ten·u·ate** (ə ten′yü āt′) **1** make or become thin or slender. **2** weaken; reduce. **3** make less dense; dilute. *v.*, **at·ten·u·at·ed, at·ten·u·at·ing.**

**at·ten·u·a·tion** (ə ten′yü ā′shən) an attenuating or being ATTENUATEd. *n.*

**at·test** (ə test′) **1** give proof or evidence of: *The child's good health attests his parents' care.* **2** declare to be true or genuine; certify: *The statement was attested by three witnesses.* **3** put on oath. *v.*
**attest to,** bear witness to; testify to: *The handwriting expert attested to the genuineness of the signature.*

**at·tes·ta·tion** (at′es tā′shən)   1 the act of ATTESTing.   2 proof; evidence.   3 TESTIMONY.   *n.*

**at·tic** (at′ik)   a room or space in a house just below the roof and above the other rooms.   *n.*

**at·tire** (ə tīr′)   1 clothes or dress, especially of a formal kind: *The queen wears rich attire.*   2 dress; array: *He was attired in full military uniform.*   1 *n.*, 2 *v.*, **at·tired, at·tir·ing.**

**at·ti·tude** (at′ə tyüd *or* at′ə tüd′)   1 one's way of thinking, acting, or feeling: *Rosa's attitude toward school changed from dislike to great enthusiasm.*   2 a position of the body suggesting an action, purpose, emotion, etc.: *the attitude of a boxer ready to fight.*   *n.*
**strike an attitude,**   pose for effect.

**attn.**   attention.

**at·tor·ney** (ə tėr′nē)   1 a person who has legal power to act for another.   2 LAWYER.   *n., pl.* **at·tor·neys.**

**attorney at law**   LAWYER.

**at·tor·ney gen·er·al** (ə tėr′nē jen′ə rəl *or* ə tėr′nē jen′rəl)   1 a chief law officer.   2 **Attorney General,**   **a** the chief law officer of Canada: *The Attorney General is the head of the Department of Justice and is a member of the Cabinet.*   **b** the chief law officer of a province.   *pl.* **attorneys general** *or* **attorney generals.**

**at·tract** (ə trakt′)   1 draw to oneself: *A magnet attracts iron.*   2 be pleasing to; win the attention and liking of: *Bright colours attract children.*   *v.*

**at·trac·tion** (ə trak′shən)   1 the act or power of drawing to oneself: *the attraction of a magnet for iron filings.*   2 anything that delights or attracts people: *The elephants were the chief attraction at the circus.*   3 charm; fascination.   4 in physics, the force exerted by molecules on one another, tending to draw or hold them together.   *n.*

**at·trac·tive** (ə trak′tiv)   1 pleasing; winning attention and liking: *an attractive hat.*   2 having or having to do with the power to attract: *the attractive force of a magnet.*   *adj.*   —**at·trac′tive·ly,** *adv.*   —**at·trac′tive·ness,** *n.*

**at·trib·ut·a·ble** (ə trib′yə tə bəl)   that can be ATTRIBUTEd (def. 2): *Some diseases are attributable to lack of cleanliness.*   *adj.*

**at·trib·ute** (ə trib′yüt *for verb,* at′rə byüt′ *for noun*)   1 consider as belonging (*to*) or appropriate (*to*): *They attribute a great deal of intelligence to their dog.*   2 regard as an effect of; think of as caused by: *They attributed his success to intelligence and hard work.*   3 state as having been said or written by: *The newly discovered poem has been attributed to Shakespeare.*   4 a quality considered as belonging to a person or thing; a characteristic: *Kindness is an attribute of a good teacher.*   5 an object considered appropriate to a person, rank, or office; symbol: *A crown is an attribute of a king.*   1–3 *v.,* **at·trib·ut·ed, at·trib·ut·ing;**   4, 5 *n.*

**at·tri·bu·tion** (at′rə byü′shən)   1 the act of attributing.   2 something attributed; an ATTRIBUTE (def. 4).   *n.*

**at·trib·u·tive** (ə trib′yə tiv)   1 of an adjective or other modifier, expressing a quality or ATTRIBUTE (def. 4), especially when coming before the noun it modifies: *An attributive adjective comes before the noun it modifies; a predicate adjective is separated from its noun by a linking verb; an appositive adjective immediately follows its noun.*   2 an attributive noun or adjective: *General is an attributive in* general store.   3 that attributes.   4 of or like an ATTRIBUTE (defs. 4, 5).   1, 3, 4 *adj.*, 2 *n.*
—**at·trib′u·tive·ly,** *adv.*

**at·tri·tion** (ə trish′ən)   1 a wearing away by rubbing: *Pebbles become smooth by attrition.*   2 any gradual process of wearing down: *a war of attrition.*   3 a gradual reduction in the number of employees, due to natural events such as retirement and resignation.   *n.*

**at·tune** (ə tyün′ *or* ə tün′)   1 bring into harmony; adjust (*to*): *He could not attune his ears to the sounds of the big city.*   2 make sensitive (*to*); make responsive (*to*): *Her years in politics had attuned the minister to the shifts in public opinion.*   *v.,* **at·tuned, at·tun·ing.**
—**at·tune′ment,** *n.*

**atty.**   attorney.

**at. wt.**   atomic weight.

**a·typ·i·cal** (ā tip′ə kəl)   not typical; irregular; abnormal: *an atypical specimen.*   *adj.*

**Au**   gold.

**au·ber·gine** (ō′bər zhēn *or* ō′ber jēn)   EGGPLANT.   *n.*

**au·burn** (ob′ərn)   reddish brown.   *n., adj.*

**auc·tion** (ok′shən)   1 a public sale in which each thing is sold to the person who offers the most money for it.   2 sell at an auction.   1 *n.,* 2 *v.*

**auc·tion·eer** (ok′shə nēr′)   1 a person whose business is conducting AUCTIONS.   2 sell at an AUCTION.   1 *n.,* 2 *v.*

**au·da·cious** (o dā′shəs)   1 bold; daring: *It was an audacious plan for rescue, but it succeeded.*   2 too bold; impudent: *The man was vexed by the boys' audacious behaviour.*   *adj.*   —**au·da′cious·ly,** *adv.*
—**au·da′cious·ness,** *n.*

**au·dac·i·ty** (o das′ə tē)   1 boldness; reckless daring.   2 rudeness; impudence: *Rebecca had the audacity to go to the party without being invited.*   *n., pl.* **au·dac·i·ties.**

**au·di·bil·i·ty** (od′ə bil′ə tē)   the condition of being AUDIBLE.   *n.*

**au·di·ble** (od′ə bəl)   capable of being heard; loud enough to be heard: *She spoke in such a low voice that her remarks were barely audible.*   *adj.*   —**au′di·bly,** *adv.*

**au·di·ence** (od′ē əns)   1 the people gathered to hear or see a performance or presentation: *The audience cheered the mayor's speech.*   2 the people reached by radio or television broadcasts, by books, etc.: *The book is intended for a juvenile audience.*   3 a chance to be heard; hearing: *The committee will give you an audience to hear your plan.*   4 a formal interview with a person of high rank: *The queen granted an audience to the famous singer.*   5 the act or fact of hearing.   *n.*

**au·di·o** (od′ē ō)   1 of or having to do with sound.   2 in television, having to do with the broadcasting or receiving of sound: *An audio problem is a sound problem; a video problem involves the image that is supposed to appear on the screen.*   *adj.*

**audio frequency**   a frequency corresponding to audible sound vibrations, from about 20 Hz to about 20 000 Hz for the normal human ear.   *Abbrev.:* AF, A.F., or a.f.

**au·di·om·e·ter** (od′ē om′ə tər)   an instrument for measuring the power of hearing.   *n.*

**au·di·o·vis·u·al** (od′ē ō vizh′ü əl)   of or having to do with both hearing and sight.   *adj.*

**au·dit** (od′it)  1 examine and check business accounts officially.  2 an official examination and check of business accounts.  3 a statement of an account that has been examined and checked authoritatively.  1 v., 2 3 n.

**au·di·tion** (o dish′ən)  1 a trial performance in which an actor, singer, dancer, or other performer demonstrates his or her skills.  2 test or be tested by such a trial performance: *The director is auditioning singers for the musical. Why don't you audition for the chorus?*  3 the power or sense of hearing.  1, 3 n., 2 v.

**au·di·tor** (od′ə tər)  1 a hearer; listener.  2 a person who audits business accounts.  n.

**auditor general** or **Auditor General**  in Canada, an officer, appointed by the Governor General, who is responsible for AUDITing the accounts of the federal government and making an annual report of his or her findings to Parliament.  n., pl. **auditors general** or **auditor generals**.

**au·di·to·ri·um** (od′ə tô′rē əm)  1 a large room for an audience in a theatre, school, etc.; large hall.  2 a building especially designed for lectures, concerts, etc.  n.

**au·di·to·ry** (od′ə tô′rē)  of or having to do with hearing, the sense of hearing, or the organs of hearing: *the auditory nerve.*  adj.

**auf Wie·der·seh·en** (ouf vē′dər zā′ən) German. goodbye; the German equivalent of French *au revoir: Auf Wiedersehen* means "Until we see each other again."

**Aug.** August.

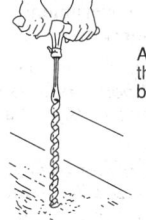
An auger. Each turn makes the spiral cutting edge bite further into the wood.

**au·ger** (og′ər)  1 a tool for boring holes in wood.  2 a tool for boring holes in the earth or ice: *a post-hole auger.* 3 a similar device having a continuous spiral channel inside a tube, used for moving bulk substances such as grain or snow: *An auger is used to move grain from an elevator to a boxcar.*  n.
☞ *Hom.* AUGUR.

**aught** (ot)  cipher; zero; nothing.  n. Sometimes, **ought**.
☞ *Hom.* OUGHT.

**aug·ment** (og ment′)  increase; enlarge: *Michael bought some stamps to augment his collection. He had to augment his income by working in the evenings.*  v.

**aug·men·ta·tion** (og′men tā′shən)  an enlargement; increase; addition: *The power of the nobles declined with the augmentation of the power of the king.*  n.

**au gra·tin** (ō grat′ən; French, ō grä taN′)  sprinkled with grated cheese or grated cheese and bread crumbs and browned in an oven.

**au·gur** (og′ər)  1 in ancient Rome, a priest who made predictions and gave advice.  2 a prophet; fortuneteller. 3 predict; foretell.  4 be a sign or promise of: *The promotion augured a bright future for her.*  1, 2 n., 3 4 v.
**augur ill,**  be a bad sign.

---

**audit** 73 **aurora**

hat, āge, fär; let, ēqual, tėrm; it, īce
hot, ōpen, ôrder; oil, out; cup, put, rüle
əbove, takən, pencəl, lemən, circəs
ch, child; ng, long; sh, ship
th, thin; ᴛʜ, then; zh, measure

**augur well,**  be a good sign.
☞ *Hom.* AUGER.

**au·gu·ry** (og′yə rē)  1 the art or practice of foretelling the future by the flight of birds, the appearance of the internal organs of sacrificed animals, thunder and lightning, etc.  2 a prediction; indication; sign; omen. 3 a rite or ceremony performed by an AUGUR (defs. 1, 2). n., pl. **au·gu·ries.**

**Au·gust** (og′əst)  the 8th month of the year: *August has 31 days.*  n.
☞ *Etym.* OE *August*, from L *Augustus*. The Romans named the month after *Augustus* Caesar, the first Roman emperor.

**au·gust** (o gust′)  inspiring reverence and admiration; majestic; venerable: *The people were silent in the august presence of the queen.*  adj.  —**au·gust′ly,** adv. —**au·gust′ness,** n.

**auk** (ok)  1 any species of a family of swimming and diving sea birds found along northern coasts, all having a short neck, short legs set far back on a heavy body, and short, narrow wings; especially, the **great auk,** a flightless bird about the size of a goose, that has been extinct for over a century, and the **razor-billed auk,** or **razorbill,** similar in appearance, but smaller and able to fly. 2 referring to this family of birds: *Murres, guillemots, auklets, and puffins also belong to the auk family and are sometimes called auks.*  n.

**aunt** (ant *or* änt)  1 the sister of one's father or mother. 2 an uncle's wife.  n.
☞ *Pronunciation.* The pronunciation (ant) is usual in Canada, but (änt) is common in New Brunswick and parts of Nova Scotia.
☞ *Hom.* ANT for the first pronunciation of **aunt.**

**au·ra** (ô′rə)  something supposed to come from a person or thing and surround him, her or it as an atmosphere: *An aura of dignity surrounded the queen.*  n., pl. **au·ras** or **au·rae** (-rē or -rī).

**au·ral** (ô′rəl)  of or having to do with the ear or the sense of hearing.  adj.

**au·re·ole** (ô′rē ōl′)  1 a ring of light; HALO.  2 a ring of light surrounding the sun.  n.

**au re·voir** (ō Rə vwär′) *French.*  goodbye; till we see each other again.

**au·ri·cle** (ô′rə kəl)  1 ATRIUM (def. 1).  See HEART for picture.  2 the outer part of the ear.  n.
☞ *Hom.* ORACLE.

**au·ric·u·lar** (ô rik′yə lər)  1 of, having to do with, or near the ear.  2 heard by or addressed to the ear. 3 shaped like an ear.  4 having to do with an AURICLE (def. 1) of the heart.  adj.

**au·rochs** (ô′roks)  1 the wild ancestor of the modern domestic varieties of cattle found in Europe and America, a huge, black animal, about 185 cm high at the shoulder: *The aurochs became extinct in the 17th century.*  2 WISENT. n., pl. **au·rochs.**

**au·ro·ra** (ô rô′rə)  1 the dawn.  2 streamers or bands of light appearing in the sky at night.  n.

☛ *Etym.* From the name of **Aurora**, in Roman mythology, the goddess of the dawn.

**au·ro·ra aus·tra·lis** (os trā′lis) streamers or bands of light appearing in the southern sky at night.

**au·ro·ra bo·re·al·is** (bô′rē al′is *or* bô′rē ā′lis) streamers or bands of light appearing in the northern sky at night; NORTHERN LIGHTS.

**aus·pic·es** (os′pə siz) **1** omens; signs: *The ancient Romans used to observe the flight of birds for auspices to guide their actions.* **2** favourable circumstances; indications of success. *n. pl.*
**under the auspices of,** under the patronage or favouring influence of: *The school fair was held under the auspices of the Home and School Association.*

**aus·pi·cious** (os pish′əs) **1** with signs of success; favourable: *an auspicious first day in school.* **2** fortunate. *adj.* —**aus·pi′cious·ly,** *adv.*

**aus·tere** (os tēr′) **1** severe; stern; grave: *Frank's father was a silent, austere man, very strict with his children.* **2** strict in moral discipline: *The Puritans were austere.* **3** severely simple: *The tall, plain columns stood against the sky in austere beauty. adj.* —**aus·tere′ly,** *adv.* —**aus·tere′ness,** *n.*

**aus·ter·i·ty** (os ter′ə tē) **1** sternness; strictness; severity. **2** restriction in spending, buying, or using, owing to shortage of money, food, clothing, etc., especially in a time of national emergency. **3** austerities, *pl.* severe practices, such as going without food or sitting up all night to pray. *n., pl.* **aus·ter·i·ties.**

**Aus·tral·a·sian** (os′trə lā′zhən *or* os′trə lā′shən) **1** of or having to do with Australasia, the islands of the southwestern Pacific Ocean, or the people of these islands. **2** a native or inhabitant of Australasia. **1** *adj.,* **2** *n.*

**Aus·tral·ian** (os trā′lyən) **1** of or having to do with the country of Australia or its people. **2** a native or inhabitant of Australia. **3** of, having to do with, or living or growing in the geographical region that includes the continent of Australia and nearby islands. **4** AUSTRALOID. **1, 3, 4** *adj.,* **2, 4** *n.*

**Aus·tra·loid** (os′trə loid′) **1** of or referring to the race of mankind that consists of the original inhabitants of the continent of Australia: *The Australoid race was separated from the rest of mankind for thousands of years before modern times.* **2** a member of the Australoid race: *Australoids have medium brown to very dark skin.* **1** *adj.,* **2** *n.*

**Aus·tri·an** (os′trē ən) **1** of or having to do with Austria, a country in central Europe, or its people. **2** a native or inhabitant of Austria. **3** a person of Austrian descent. **1** *adj.,* **2, 3** *n.*

**au·then·tic** (o then′tik) **1** reliable: *We heard an authentic account of the wreck, given by one of the ship's officers.* **2** genuine: *A comparison of signatures showed that the letter was authentic. adj.*

**au·then·ti·cal·ly** (o then′ti klē) **1** reliably. **2** genuinely. *adv.*

**au·then·ti·cate** (o then′tə kāt′) **1** establish the truth of; show to be valid or genuine. **2** establish the authorship of. *v.,* **au·then·ti·cat·ed, au·then·ti·cat·ing.**

**au·then·ti·ca·tion** (o then′tə kā′shən) authenticating or being AUTHENTICATEd. *n.*

**au·then·tic·i·ty** (oth′en tis′ə tē) **1** reliability. **2** genuineness: *to question the authenticity of a signature. n.*

**au·thor** (oth′ər) **1** a person who writes books, stories, or articles. **2** an author's publications: *Have you read this author?* **3** a person who creates or begins anything: *Are you the author of this scheme? n.*

**au·thor·i·tar·i·an** (ə thô′rə ter′ē ən) **1** favouring obedience to authority instead of individual freedom. **2** a person who favours obedience to authority instead of individual freedom. **1** *adj.,* **2** *n.*

**au·thor·i·tar·i·an·ism** (ə thô′rə ter′ē ə niz′əm) the principle of obeying the authority of one person or a small group of persons. *n.*

**au·thor·i·ta·tive** (ə thô′rə tə tiv *or* ə thô′rə tā′tiv) **1** having authority; officially ordered: *authoritative orders.* **2** commanding: *In authoritative tones, the police officer shouted, "Keep back."* **3** that ought to be believed or obeyed; having the authority of expert knowledge: *A doctor's statement concerning the cause of death is considered authoritative. adj.* —**au·thor′i·ta·tive·ly,** *adv.*

**au·thor·i·ty** (ə thô′rə tē) **1** the power to enforce obedience; right to command or act: *Parents have authority over their children.* **2** a person who has such power or right. **3** an influence that creates respect and confidence: *the authority of his manner.* **4** a government body that runs some activity or business on behalf of the public: *the St. Lawrence Seaway Authority.* **5** a source of correct information or wise advice: *A good dictionary is an authority on the meanings of words.* **6** an expert on some subject: *Sabra is an authority on English history.* **7 the authorities,** *pl.* **a** officials of the government. **b** the persons in control. *n., pl.* **au·thor·i·ties.**

**au·thor·i·za·tion** (oth′ə rə zā′shən *or* oth′ə rī zā′shən) **1** authorizing: *The authorization of police officers to arrest beggars put an end to begging on the streets.* **2** a legal right; sanction; warrant. *n.*

**au·thor·ize** (oth′ə rīz′) **1** give power or right to; sanction: *The Prime Minister authorized her to attend the conference. Parliament authorized the spending of money for day-care.* **2** give authority for; justify: *This dictionary authorizes the two spellings* traveller *and* traveler. *v.,* **au·thor·ized, au·thor·iz·ing.**

**au·thor·ized** (oth′ə rīzd′) **1** having authority; accepted as authoritative. **2** sanctioned by formal or legal authority. **3** pt. and pp. of AUTHORIZE. **1, 2** *adj.,* **3** *v.*

**au·thor·ship** (oth′ər ship′) **1** the occupation of an author; writing. **2** the origin as to author: *What is the authorship of that novel? n.*

**au·tism** (ot′iz əm) a learning and behaviour disorder characterized by difficulty in understanding, or making sense of, what one sees and hears, and in learning to talk and to understand the meanings of words: *Some children suffering from autism have normal or even high intelligence, and many can be helped through special educational programs to cope with their handicap. n.*

**au·tis·tic** (o tis′tik) suffering from AUTISM. *adj.*

**au·to** (ot′ō) AUTOMOBILE. *n., pl.* **au·tos.**

**auto–** combining form. **1** coming from or having to do with the self: *An* autograph *is something written by oneself.* **2** independent: *An* automobile *is a self-propelled vehicle.*
☛ *Etym.* From Gk. *autos* 'self.'

**au·to·bi·og·ra·pher** (ot′ə bī og′rə fər) a person who writes the story of her or his own life. *n.*

**au·to·bi·o·graph·ic** (ot′ə bī′ə graf′ik)  **1** having to do with the story of one's own life.  **2** telling or writing the story of one's own life: *His writings are all autobiographic.* *adj.* —**au′to·bi′o·graph′i·cal·ly**, *adv.*

**au·to·bi·o·graph·i·cal** (ot′ə bī′ə graf′ə kəl) AUTOBIOGRAPHIC. *adj.*

**au·to·bi·og·ra·phy** (ot′ə bī og′rə fē)  the story of a person's life written by that person.  *n., pl.* **au·to·bi·og·ra·phies.**

**auto court**  a group of cabins providing shelter for automobile travellers; MOTEL.

**au·toc·ra·cy** (o tok′rə sē)  **1** a government having absolute power over its citizens.  **2** absolute authority; unlimited power over a group.  *n., pl.* **au·toc·ra·cies.**

**au·to·crat** (ot′ə krat′)  **1** a ruler having absolute power over his or her subjects.  **2** a person who uses power in a harsh way: *My friends think their parents are autocrats.* *n.*

**au·to·crat·ic** (ot′ə krat′ik)  of or like an AUTOCRAT; absolute in power or authority; ruling without checks or limitations.  *adj.* —**au′·to·crat′i·cal·ly**, *adv.*

**au·to·graph** (ot′ə graf′)  **1** a person's signature: *Some people collect the autographs of movie stars.*  **2** write one's signature in or on.  **1** *n.*, **2** *v.*

**au·to·harp** (ot′ō härp′)  a kind of zither having a series of felt dampers that can be pressed down to prevent certain strings from sounding, making it possible to play chords.  *n.*

**au·to–in·tox·i·ca·tion** (ot′ō in tok′sə kā′shən)  poisoning by substances formed within the body.  *n.*

**au·to·mat·ic** (ot′ə mat′ik)  **1** done or made without thought or attention, as from force of habit, etc.; spontaneous or mechanical: *Siu-Wah's automatic reply to questions from reporters was, "No comment."*  **2** mainly or entirely involuntary; reflex: *Breathing is automatic.*  **3** of a mechanism, machine, etc., made or set to move or act by itself; self-regulating or self-acting: *an automatic lock. Her car has an automatic transmission.*  **4** an automobile equipped with an automatic transmission: *Is your car an automatic?*  **5** of a firearm, having a mechanism for repeatedly firing, throwing out the used shell, and reloading until the pressure on the trigger is released or the ammunition is used up.  **6** an automatic firearm.  **7** as a necessary consequence; without exception, or restriction: *automatic promotion after a year of service. Any violation of the rules means automatic disqualification.* 1–3, 5, 7 *adj.*, 4 6 *n.*

**au·to·mat·i·cal·ly** (ot′ə mat′i klē)  in an AUTOMATIC (defs. 1–3, 5, 7) manner.  *adv.*

**automatic transmission**  in a motor vehicle, any of various mechanisms for automatically altering the speed of the driving wheels in relation to engine speed.

**au·to·ma·tion** (ot′ə mā′shən)  the use of automatic controls in the operation of machines: *In automation, electronic or mechanical devices do many of the tasks formerly performed by people.*  *n.*
☛ *Etym.* From *automa*tic and *oper*ation.

**au·tom·a·tism** (o tom′ə tiz′əm)  any action not controlled by the will; involuntary action; automatic action.  *n.*

**au·tom·a·ton** (o tom′ə ton′)  **1** an apparatus that is made to resemble a human being or an animal and operates by a concealed mechanism or by remote control; robot.  **2** a person or animal that acts or appears to act in an automatic or mechanical way.  *n., pl.* **au·tom·a·tons** or **au·tom·a·ta** (-tə).

**au·to·mo·bile** (ot′ə mə bēl′)  **1** a passenger vehicle that carries its own engine and is driven on roads and streets; car.  **2** for use on or in connection with automobiles: *an automobile battery.*  **3** travel by automobile.  1, 2 *n.*,  3 *v.*, **au·to·mo·biled, au·to·mo·bil·ing.**
☛ *Etym.* From 19c. F *automobile* 'self-propelling', a word coined from *auto-* 'independent' + *mobile* 'movable'.

**au·to·mo·bil·ist** (ot′ə mə bē′list)  a person who uses an AUTOMOBILE.  *n.*

**au·to·mo·tive** (ot′ə mō′tiv)  **1** of or having to do with cars, trucks, and other self-propelled vehicles: *automotive engineering.*  **2** self-moving; self-propelling; furnishing its own power.  *adj.*

**au·to·nom·ic** (ot′ə nom′ik)  AUTONOMOUS.  *adj.*

**autonomic nervous system**  the GANGLIA and nerves of the nervous system of vertebrates which control digestive and other involuntary functions of the body.

**au·ton·o·mous** (o ton′ə məs)  self-governing; independent.  *adj.* —**au·ton′o·mous·ly**, *adv.*

**au·ton·o·my** (o ton′ə mē)  **1** self-government; independence.  **2** a self-governing community.  *n., pl.* **au·ton·o·mies.**

**au·top·sy** (ot′op sē)  an examination and dissection of a dead body to find the cause of death or the nature or extent of the damage done to the body by disease, injury, etc.; post-mortem.  Compare with BIOPSY.  *n., pl.* **au·top·sies.**

**au·to·sug·ges·tion** (ot′ō sə jes′chən, or ot′ō səg jes′chən)  in psychology, the suggestion to oneself of ideas that produce subconscious changes in attitudes, behaviour, or physical condition.  *n.*

**au·to·truck** (ot′ō truk′)  TRUCK (def. 1).  *n.*

**au·tumn** (ot′əm)  **1** the season of the year between summer and winter; fall.  **2** of, in, like, or characteristic of autumn: *autumn flowers, autumn rains.*  *n.*

**au·tum·nal** (o tum′nəl)  of, in, or coming in AUTUMN: *autumnal frosts.*  *adj.*

**aux·il·ia·ry** (og zil′yə rē)  **1** helping; assisting: *an auxiliary engine on a sailboat.*  **2** a person or thing that helps; aid: *A microscope is a useful auxiliary to the human eye.*  **3** additional: *The main library has several auxiliary branches.*  **4** an AUXILIARY VERB.  **5 auxiliaries**, *pl.* foreign or allied troops that help the army of a nation at war.  1, 3 *adj.*, 2, 4, 5 *n., pl.* **aux·il·ia·ries.**

**auxiliary verb**  a verb used to form the tenses, moods, or voices of other verbs. *Examples:* be, can, do, have, may, must, shall, and will. I **am** going; he **will** go: they **are** lost; they **were** lost.

**aux·in** (ok′sən)  a plant hormone, natural or synthetic, which controls the growth of various parts of a plant.  *n.*

**av.**  **1** average.  **2** avoirdupois.

**Av.**  Avenue.

**Av or A.V.** audio-visual.

**a·vail** (ə vāl′) **1** be of use or value to: *Money will not avail you after you are dead.* **2** help: *Talk will not avail without work.* **3** use; advantage or help for a purpose (used especially with a negative meaning): *Crying is of little avail now. He tried again and again, but to no avail.* 1, 2 *v.*, 3 *n.*

**avail oneself of,** take advantage of; profit by; make use of: *While he was in Quebec he availed himself of the opportunity to improve his French.*

**a·vail·a·bil·i·ty** (ə vā′lə bil′ə tē) being AVAILABLE; being at hand; being ready: *The availability of water power helped make southern Ontario a manufacturing centre.* *n.*

**a·vail·a·ble** (ə vā′lə bəl) **1** ready or handy to be used; that can be used: *The available water supply had dried up.* **2** that can be obtained: *All available tickets were sold.* **3** willing or free to do something: *Michelle said she was available for the job now.* *adj.* —**a·vail′a·bly,** *adv.*

**av·a·lanche** (av′ə lanch′) **1** a large mass of snow and ice, or of dirt and rocks, sliding or falling down a mountainside. **2** anything like an avalanche: *an avalanche of questions.* **3** move like an avalanche. 1, 2 *n.*, 3 *v.*, **av·a·lanched, av·a·lanch·ing.**

**avalanche lily** any of several species of wild flower of the lily family found in the mountains of western North America, especially the glacier lily.

**a·vant–garde** (*French,* äväɴ gärd′) **1** of or having to do with advanced people or the movements started by them: *an avant-garde artist, avant-garde ideas.* **2 the avant-garde,** the people who develop new and experimental ideas, especially in the arts. 1 *adj.*, 2 *n.*

**av·a·rice** (av′ə ris) an extreme desire for money or property; greed: *It was avarice, not a desire for security, that made them scrimp and save all those years.* *n.*

**av·a·ri·cious** (av′ə rish′əs) greedy for wealth: *A miser is avaricious.* *adj.* —**av′a·ri′cious·ly,** *adv.* —**av′a·ri′cious·ness,** *n.*

**a·va·tar** (av′ə tär) in Hinduism, the descent or appearance of a deity in human or animal form. *n.*

**avdp.** avoirdupois.

**Ave.** or **ave.** Avenue; avenue.

**a·venge** (ə venj′) **1** inflict punishment in return for; take vengeance for: *to avenge an insult.* **2** take vengeance on behalf of: *The clan avenged their slain chief.* **3** get vengeance. *v.*, **a·venged, a·veng·ing.** —**a·veng′er,** *n.*

**avenge oneself on,** get revenge on for a wrong done to oneself: *David swore to avenge himself on those who had betrayed him.*

**av·e·nue** (av′ə nyü′ *or* av′ə nü′) **1** a wide or main street. **2** a road or walk bordered by trees. **3** a way of approach or departure; passage: *There are various avenues to fame.* **4** a city thoroughfare running at right angles to others that are usually called "streets." *n.*

**a·ver** (ə vėr′) state to be true; assert: *Harry avers that he had nothing to do with breaking the windows.* *v.*, **a·verred, a·ver·ring.**

**av·er·age** (av′rij *or* av′ə rij) **1** an arithmetical mean; the quantity found by dividing the sum of several quantities by the number of those quantities: *The average of 3, 5, and 10 is 6.* **2** find the average of. **3** obtained by averaging; being an average: *an average price, the average temperature.* **4** amount on an average to; come close to: *The cost of our lunches at school averaged ten dollars a week.* **5** the usual kind of quality; ordinary amount or rate: *His achievement in school is definitely above the average.* **6** usual; ordinary: *average intelligence.* **7** do, get, etc. on an average: *She averages six hours work a day. We averaged eight litres of gas per 100 kilometres.* **8** divide among several proportionately: *We averaged our gains according to what each had put in.* 1, 5 *n.*, 2, 4, 7 8 *v.*, **av·er·aged, av·er·ag·ing:** 3, 6 *adj.*

**on the average** or **on an average,** considered on the basis of the average: *He works six hours a day on the average.*

**a·ver·ment** (ə vėr′mənt) a statement that something is true; ASSERTION (def. 1). *n.*

**a·verse** (ə vėrs′) opposed (*to*); having an active distaste for; reluctant (*to*): *He was averse to fighting.* *adj.* —**a·verse′ness,** *n.*

**a·ver·sion** (ə vėr′zhən) **1** a strong or fixed dislike; antipathy: *Some people have an aversion to snakes.* **2** a thing or person disliked: *a pet aversion, a secret aversion.* *n.*

**a·vert** (ə vėrt′) **1** prevent; avoid: *Wesley averted an accident by a quick turn of the steering wheel.* **2** turn away; turn aside: *The girl averted her eyes from the wreck.* *v.*

**A·ves** (ā′vēz) a class of vertebrates comprising the birds. *n. pl.*

**A·ves·ta** (ə ves′tə) in Zorastrianism, the sacred scriptures written in the ancient Avesta language. It contains hymns and prayers, and deals with liturgy, ritual, and ethics. *n.*

**a·vi·ar·y** (ā′vē er′ē) a place where many birds are kept. *n., pl.* **a·vi·ar·ies.**

**a·vi·a·tion** (ā′vē ā′shən *or* av′ē ā′shən) the designing, making, and flying of aircraft. *n.*

**a·vi·a·tor** (ā′vē ā′tər *or* av′ē ā′tər) a person who flies an aircraft; pilot of an aircraft. *n.*

**a·vi·a·trix** (ā′vē ā′triks *or* av′ē ā′triks) a female AVIATOR. *n.*

**av·id** (av′id) **1** eager; greedy: *The miser was avid for gold.* **2** enthusiastic: *She is an avid reader.* *adj.* —**av′id·ly,** *adv.*

**a·vid·i·ty** (ə vid′ə tē) eagerness; greediness: *After their long hike the hungry girls looked at the food with avidity.* *n.*

**av·o·ca·do** (av′ə kä′dō) **1** a pear-shaped tropical fruit having a dark green skin and a very large seed; alligator pear. **2** the tree that the avocado grows on. *n., pl.* **av·o·ca·dos.**

**av·o·ca·tion** (av′ə kā′shən) **1** something that a person does besides his or her regular business; minor occupation; hobby: *Maya is a lawyer, but writing stories is her avocation.* **2** *Informal.* regular business; occupation. *n.*

**a·void** (ə void′) **1** keep away from; keep out of the way of: *We avoided driving through large cities on our trip.* **2** in law, make void; annul. *v.* —**a·void′a·ble,** *adj.*

**a·void·ance** (ə voi′dəns) an avoiding; keeping away from: *Lai-Sheung's avoidance of her old friends caused her to be disliked.* *n.*

**av·oir·du·pois** (av′ər də poiz′) **1** AVOIRDUPOIS WEIGHT: *The package weighs three pounds avoirdupois.* **2** *Informal.* a person's mass, or weight. *n.*

**avoirdupois weight** the ordinary system of weighing in Canada before the change to the SI, or metric system: *One pound in avoirdupois weight is equal to about 0.454 kilograms.* Compare with APOTHECARIES' WEIGHT and TROY WEIGHT.

16 drams = 1 ounce
16 ounces = 1 pound
2240 pounds = 1 ton

**a·vouch** (ə vouch′) **1** declare to be true. **2** guarantee. **3** acknowledge; affirm. *v.*

**a·vow** (ə vou′) declare frankly or openly; admit; acknowledge: *Stephen avowed he could not sing.* *v.*

**a·vow·al** (ə vou′əl) a frank or open declaration; admission; acknowledgment. *n.*

**a·vowed** (ə voud′) openly declared; admitted: *Her avowed intention was to try for the party leadership.* *adj.*

**a·vow·ed·ly** (ə vou′i dlē) admittedly; openly. *adv.*

**a·vun·cu·lar** (ə vung′kyə lər) **1** of an uncle. **2** like an uncle. *adj.*

**a·wait** (ə wāt′) **1** wait for; look forward to: *She has awaited your coming for a week.* **2** be ready for; be in store for: *They had no idea what awaited them at the end of the trip.* *v.*

**a·wake** (ə wāk′) **1** wake up; arouse: *We awoke from a sound sleep. The alarm clock awoke me.* **2** roused from sleep; not asleep: *Noboru is always awake early.* **3** on the alert; watchful: *Our government is awake to that peril.* 1 *v.*, **a·woke** or **a·waked**, **a·wak·ing**; 2, 3 *adj.*

**a·wak·en** (ə wā′kən) **1** wake up; rouse from sleep: *The guide awakened the fishermen before dawn.* **2** make alert or watchful. *v.*

**a·wak·en·ing** (ə wā′kə ning) **1** a waking up. **2** arousing: *an awakening to danger.* **3** waking up or reviving: *the sounds of the awakening birds.* 1, 2 *n.*, 3 *adj.*

**a·ward** (ə wôrd′) **1** give after careful consideration; grant: *A medal was awarded to the woman who saved the child.* **2** decide or settle by law; adjudge: *The court awarded damages of $5000 to the injured man.* **3** something given after careful consideration; prize: *Martine's dog won the highest award.* **4** a decision by a judge: *We all thought the award was fair.* 1, 2 *v.*, 3 4 *n.*

**a·ware** (ə wer′) knowing; realizing; conscious: *I was too sleepy to be aware how cold it was. She was not aware of her danger.* *adj.* —**a·ware′ness**, *n.*

**a·wash** (ə wosh′) **1** level with the surface of the water; just covered with water: *The deck of the sinking ship was already awash.* **2** carried about by water; floating: *All kinds of debris were awash and moved by the waves.* 1 *adv.*, 2 *adj.*

**a·way** (ə wā′) **1** at a distance; far: *The barn stands away from the farmhouse.* **2** at a distance; far: *I got very homesick when I was away from home last summer.* **3** from a place; to a distance: *Get away from the fire.* **4** absent; gone: *My mother is away today.* **5** in another direction; aside: *She looked sad and turned away.* **6** out of one's possession, notice, or use: *He gave his boat away.* **7** out of existence: *The sounds died away.* **8** without stopping; continuously: *She worked away at her job.* 1, 3, 5–8 *adv.*, 2 4 *adj.*

**do away with,** **a** put an end to; get rid of. **b** kill.
☞ *Hom.* AWEIGH.

**awe** (o) **1** wonder and reverence inspired by something sacred, mysterious, or magnificent: *They gazed in awe at the mountains towering above them.* **2** great respect and admiration mixed with fear, inspired by power and authority: *They stood in awe of the old woman's disapproval.* **3** cause to feel awe; fill with awe: *The majesty of the mountains awed us.* **4** influence or restrain by awe: *The speaker's words awed the crowd.* 1, 2 *n.*, 3, 4 *v.*, **awed, aw·ing.**

**a·wea·ry** (ə wē′rē) weary; tired. *adj.*

**a·weigh** (ə wā′) raised off the bottom: *The ship sailed off as soon as its anchor was aweigh.* *adj.*
☞ *Hom.* AWAY.

**awe·some** (os′əm) **1** causing AWE: *A great fire is an awesome sight.* **2** showing AWE; awed: *awesome admiration.* *adj.*

**awe–strick·en** (os′trik′ən) AWE-STRUCK. *adj.*

**awe–struck** (os′truk′) filled with AWE: *We watched the northern lights in awe-struck silence.* *adj.*

**aw·ful** (of′əl) **1** dreadful; terrible: *an awful storm.* **2** deserving great respect and reverence: *the awful power of the gods.* **3** filling with AWE; impressive. **4** *Informal.* very bad, ugly, etc.: *His room was in an awful mess.* *adj.* —**aw′ful·ness**, *n.*
☞ *Hom.* OFFAL.

**aw·ful·ly** (of′lē *or* of′ə lē) **1** dreadfully; terribly. **2** *Informal.* very; extremely: *I'm awfully sorry that I hurt your feelings.* *adv.*

**a·while** (ə wīl′ *or* ə hwīl′) for a short time: *Nina stayed awhile.* *adv.*

**awk·ward** (ok′wərd) **1** clumsy; not graceful in movement or shape: *The seal is very awkward on land, but quite at home in the water.* **2** not well-suited to use: *The handle of this pitcher has an awkward shape.* **3** not easily managed: *This is an awkward corner to turn.* **4** embarrassing: *He asked me an awkward question.* *adj.* —**awk′ward·ly**, *adv.* —**awk′ward·ness**, *n.*

**A.W.L.** a military abbreviation for *absent without leave.* Also, **A.W.O.L.**

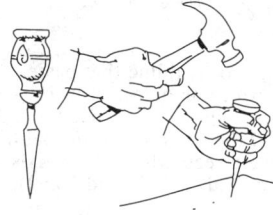

An awl being used to mark places for screws on a piece of wood

**awl** (ol) a pointed tool used for making small holes in leather or wood. *n.*
☞ *Hom.* ALL.

**awn** (on) one of the bristly hairs forming the beard on a head of barley, oats, etc. *n.*
☞ *Hom.* ON.

**awn·ing** (ôn′ing) a rooflike structure consisting of metal, canvas, wood, or plastic spread over a frame and attached over a door, window, etc. as a protection from the sun or rain. *n.*

**a·woke** (ə wōk′) a pt. and pp. of AWAKE: *He awoke at seven.* *v.*

**A.W.O.L.** or **a.w.o.l.** A.W.L.

**a·wry** (ə rī′) **1** with a twist or turn to one side: *Her hat was blown awry by the wind.* **2** wrong: *Our plans remained awry.* 1 *adv.*, 2 *adj.*

An axe

**axe** (aks) **1** a tool with a bladed head on a handle, used for chopping wood. **2** a weapon like this; battle-axe. *n., pl.* **ax·es** (ak′siz). Sometimes, **ax.** —**axe′like′**, *adj.* **have an axe to grind,** have a special purpose or reason for taking action or being interested.

**axe·man** (ak′smən) a man who uses an axe in chopping or fighting. *n., pl.* **axe·men** (-mən).

**ax·es¹** (ak′sēz) pl. of AXIS. *n.*

**ax·es²** (ak′siz) pl. of AXE. *n.*

**ax·i·al** (ak′sē əl) **1** of an AXIS (defs. 1, 2); forming an axis. **2** on or around an AXIS (defs. 1, 2). *adj.*

**ax·il** (ak′sil) the angle between the upper side of a leaf or stem and the supporting stem or branch. *n.*

**ax·i·om** (ak′sē əm) **1** a statement seen to be true without proof; self-evident truth: *Example: Things equal to the same thing are equal to each other.* **2** any established principle. *n.*

**ax·i·o·mat·ic** (ak′sē ə mat′ik) **1** self-evident: *That a whole is greater than any of its parts is axiomatic.* **2** full of AXIOMS or MAXIMS. *adj.*

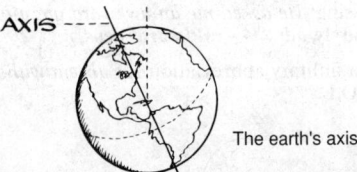
The earth's axis

**ax·is** (ak′sis) **1** an imaginary or real line that passes through an object and about which an object turns or seems to turn: *The earth's axis is an imaginary line through the North and South Poles.* **2** the central or principal line around which parts are arranged regularly. **3 the Axis,** Germany, Italy, Japan, and their allies in World War II. *n., pl.* **ax·es** (ak′sēz).

**ax·le** (ak′səl) **1** a bar or shaft on which or with which a wheel turns. See DIFFERENTIAL and GYROSCOPE for pictures. **2** AXLETREE. *n.*

**ax·le·tree** (ak′səl trē′) a crossbar that connects two opposite wheels: *The wheels turn on or with the ends of their axletree.* *n.*

**ax·o·lotl** (ak′sə lot′əl) any of several closely related species of SALAMANDER found in certain lakes of Mexico and the western United States, that ordinarily never lose their gills and larval form but otherwise live and breed like other salamanders. *n.*

**ax·on** (ak′son) the part of a nerve cell that carries impulses away from the body of the cell. See NEURON for picture. *n.*

**ay·a·tol·lah** (ä′yə tō′lə) among Shiites, a jurist and leader regarded by his followers as the most learned person of the age. *n.*

**aye¹** or **ay¹** (ā) always; ever: *A parent's love lasts forever and aye.* *adv.*

**aye²** or **ay²** (ī) **1** yes: *Aye, aye, sir.* **2** an affirmative answer, vote, or voter: *The ayes were in the majority when the vote was taken.* 1 *adv.*, 2 *n.*
☛ *Hom.* EYE, 1.

**Ayr·shire** (er′shēr *or* er′shər) a breed of red and white or brown and white dairy cattle. *n.*

**a·zal·ea** (ə zā′lyə) any of various species and cultivated varieties of rhododendron, especially those having funnel-shaped flowers and leaves that drop off in the fall. *n.*

**Az·tec** (az′tek) **1** a member of an Amerindian people who ruled Mexico before its conquest by the Spaniards in 1519. **2** their language. **3** of or having to do with the Aztecs or their language: *Aztec architecture.* 1, 2 *n.*, 3 *adj.*

**az·ure** (azh′ər *or* ā′zhər) **1** blue; sky blue: *Azure is not a suitable colour for you.* **2** blue; sky blue: *an azure dress.* 1 *n.*, 2 *adj.*

# B b  *B b*

hat, āge, fär; let, ēqual, tėrm; it, īce
hot, ōpen, ôrder; oil, out; cup, pùt, rüle
ə above, takən, pencəl, lemən, circəs
ch, child; ng, long; sh, ship
th, thin; ᴛʜ, then; zh, measure

**b or B** (bē)  **1** the second letter of the English alphabet. **2** any speech sound represented by this letter. **3** in music, **a** the seventh tone in the scale of C major. **b** a symbol representing this tone. **c** a key, string, etc. of a musical instrument that produces this tone. **d** the scale or key that has B as its keynote. **4** any person or thing considered as second in a series: *Company B in a battalion*. **5** a grade rating a person or thing as good, but not excellent; the second level from the top, or best: *grade B eggs. I hoped for an A but I got only a B on the test*. **6** a person or thing receiving this rating. *n., pl.* **b's** or **B's**.

**B**  **1** boron. **2** one of the four main blood groups. Compare with A, AB and O.

**Ba** barium.

**baa** (bä *or* ba)  BLEAT. *n., v.,* **baaed, baa·ing.**

**bab·bitt** (bab′it)  an ALLOY of tin, antimony, and copper, or a similar alloy, used in bearings, etc. to lessen friction. *n.*

**Babbitt metal**  BABBITT.

**bab·ble** (bab′əl)  **1** make indistinct sounds like a baby. **2** talk that cannot be understood: *A confused babble filled the room*. **3** talk foolishly or too much: *She babbled on and on about her great adventure*. **4** foolish talk. **5** tell secrets; be indiscreet: *Don't tell him anything; he babbles*. **6** make a murmuring sound: *The brook babbles*. **7** murmuring: *the babble of the brook*. **8** reveal foolishly: *to babble a secret*. 1, 3, 5, 6, 8 *v.,* **bab·bled, bab·bling;** 2, 4, 7 *n.* —**bab′bler,** *n.*

**babe** (bāb)  **1** baby. **2** an innocent or inexperienced person; a person who is like a child. *n.*

**Ba·bel** (bā′bəl *or* bab′əl)  **1** BABYLON. **2** Usually, **babel, a** noise; a confusion of many different sounds. **b** a place of noise and confusion. *n.*

**ba·biche** (bä bēsh′ *or* bab′ish)  *Cdn.* rawhide thongs or lacings: *Babiche is often used in making snowshoes*. *n.*

**Ba·bin·sky reflex** (bə bin′skē)  a curling of the toes in response to a stroking of the sole of the foot: *The Babinsky reflex is normal in babies, but otherwise is a sign of nerve damage*.

**ba·boon** (ba bün′)  **1** any of several large African and Arabian species of monkey that live on the ground, having heavy bodies, large heads with large cheek pouches, short tails, and long muzzles: *Baboons live in tightly organized communities dominated by one male leader*. **2** any of a group of African and Arabian monkeys made up of baboons, the drill, and the mandrill. *n.*

**ba·by** (bā′bē)  **1** a very young child. **2** the youngest of a family or group: *the baby of the class*. **3** of or for a baby: *baby shoes*. **4** young: *a baby lamb*. **5** small for its kind; small: *my baby finger*. **6** childish. **7** a person who acts like a baby; childish person: *Don't be a baby*. **8** treat as a baby; pamper: *to baby a sick child*. **9** operate or handle very carefully: *to baby a new car*. 1–7 *n., pl.* **ba·bies;** 8, 9 *v.,* **ba·bied, ba·by·ing.** —**ba′by-like′,** *adj.*

**baby bonus**  *Cdn. Informal.* the FAMILY ALLOWANCE.

**baby buggy**  BABY CARRIAGE.

**baby carriage**  a light four-wheeled carriage used for wheeling a baby about.

**ba·by·hood** (bā′bē hùd′)  **1** the condition or time of being a baby. **2** babies as a group. *n.*

**ba·by·ish** (bā′bē ish)  like a baby; childish; silly. *adj.* —**ba′by·ish·ly,** *adv.* —**ba′by·ish·ness,** *n.*

**Bab·y·lon** (bab′ə lən)  **1** the capital of ancient Babylonia, on the Euphrates River, and, later, of the ancient Chaldean empire: *Babylon was notorious for its wealth, power, magnificence, and wickedness*. **2** any great, rich, or wicked city. *n.*

**Bab·y·lo·ni·an** (bab′ə lō′nē ən)  **1** of or having to do with Babylonia, an ancient empire in southwestern Asia, or Babylon. **2** an inhabitant of Babylonia. **3** the Semitic language of Babylonia. 1 *adj.,* 2, 3 *n.*

**baby's breath**  any of various closely related plants of the pink family native to Europe, Asia, and Africa, having many tiny white or pink flowers on delicate branching stems; gypsophila: *Baby's breath is often used to add a dainty touch to bouquets and to flower arrangements*.

**ba·by–sit** (bā′bē sit′)  take care of a child or children during the temporary absence of the parent or parents. *v.,* **ba·by-sat, ba·by-sit·ting.** —**ba′by-sit′ter,** *n.*

**baby tooth**  one of the first set of teeth; a temporary tooth of a child or young animal.

**bac·ca·lau·re·ate** (bak′ə lô′rē it)  **1** a degree of BACHELOR (def. 3) given by a college or university. **2** a speech delivered to a graduating class at commencement. *n.*

**bac·cha·nal** (bak′ə nəl)  **1** having to do with Bacchus or his worship. **2** a worshipper of Bacchus. **3** a drunken reveller. **4** a wild, noisy party; drunken revelry; orgy. 1 *adj.,* 2–4 *n.*

**bac·cha·na·li·a** (bak′ə nā′lē ə)  a wild, noisy party; drunken revelry; orgy. *n. pl.*
☛ *Etym.* From *Bacchanalia,* the name of an ancient Roman festival in honour of Bacchus, the Roman and Greek god of wine, also called Dionysus by the Greeks.

**bac·cha·na·li·an** (bak′ə nā′lē ən)  **1** having to do with the BACCHANALIA. **2** drunken and riotous. **3** a drunken reveller. 1, 2 *adj.,* 3 *n.*

**bach·e·lor** (bach′ə lər)  **1** a man who has not married. **2** of, for, or referring to a person who is not married or who lives alone: *She lives in a bachelor apartment*. **3** a person who has the first degree offered by a college or university. **4** in the Middle Ages, a young knight serving under the banner of another. *n.*
☛ *Etym.* From OF *bacheler* 'squire', a young gentleman learning the skills and courtesies of knighthood. The English word was first used with this meaning.

**bach·e·lor·hood** (bach′ə lər hùd′)  the condition of being a BACHELOR (def. 1). *n.*

**bach·e·lor's–but·ton** (bach′ə lərz but′ən)  **1** an annual plant of the COMPOSITE family, native to Europe but often grown in North America for its bright blue, mauve, pink, or white flowers; cornflower. **2** Often,

**bachelor's buttons,** a perennial garden plant of the buttercup family native to Europe, having bright yellow double flowers. *n.*

**ba·cil·lar** (bə sil′ər) **1** of or like a BACILLUS. **2** characterized by BACILLI. **3** rod-shaped. *adj.*

**ba·cil·li** (bə sil′ī *or* bə sil′ē) pl. of BACILLUS. See BACTERIA for picture. *n.*

**ba·cil·lus** (bə sil′əs) **1** any of the rod-shaped BACTERIA. **2** any of the bacteria. See BACTERIA for picture. *n., pl.* **ba·cil·li.**

**back** (bak) **1** the part of a person's body opposite to the face and to the front part of the body: *a broad back. She turned her back to the wind.* **2** the upper part of an animal's body, from the neck to the end of the backbone. **3** the side opposite or behind the front: *the back of the head, the back of the room.* **4** the upper, outer, or farther side or part: *the back of the hand, the back of the garden.* **5** opposite or behind the front: *the back seat of a car, the back fence.* **6** the part of a chair, chesterfield, etc. that supports the back of a person sitting down. **7** support or help: *Many of his friends backed his plan.* **8** to or toward the rear; backward; behind: *Please step back.* **9** move or cause to move in reverse or away from the front: *He backed away from the gun. She backed her car slowly out of the driveway.* **10** in or toward the past: *Some years back this land was all in farms.* **11** belonging to the past; not current: *the back numbers of a newspaper.* **12** in return: *Pay back what you borrow.* **13** in or to the place from which something or somebody came: *Put the books back.* **14** in distant or frontier regions: *back country.* **15** due but not yet paid; overdue: *She still has some back debts to clear up.* **16** in football and certain other games, a player whose position is behind the front line. **17** bet on: *to back a baseball team in the World Series.* 1–4, 6, 16 *n.*, 5, 11, 14, 15 *adj.*, 7, 9, 17 *v.*, 8, 10, 12, 13 *adv.*

**back and fill,** **a** trim sails so as to keep a boat in a channel and floating with the current. **b** of cars and trucks, go forward and backward alternately in order to get out of mud or snow or to make a difficult turn. **c** *Informal.* be undecided; keep changing one's mind.
**back away,** **a** move away backwards. **b** withdraw one's opinion.
**back down** or **off,** give up an attempt or claim; withdraw.
**back out (of),** *Informal.* **a** withdraw from an undertaking; pull out: *The village backed out of building a pool when the cost got too high.* **b** break a promise: *I promised to buy everyone ice cream, but I backed out when I realized I had no money with me.*
**back up,** **a** move up backwards. **b** help; support.
**back water,** **a** make a boat go backward. **b** reverse one's course; withdraw from a position, claim, etc.
**behind someone's back,** secretly and with a mean or scheming purpose: *He seemed to be a good friend but then I found out he was talking about me behind my back.*
**get off someone's back,** *Informal.* stop nagging or criticizing someone: *I finally told her if she didn't get off my back I wouldn't do it at all.*
**get one's back up,** *Informal.* make or become angry and stubbornly opposed: *She didn't mean to be critical, so don't get your back up.*
**go back on,** *Informal.* **a** fail to live up to: *go back on one's word.* **b** not be faithful or loyal to: *He went back on his friends.*
**on one's back,** helpless, especially, sick in bed: *He's flat on his back with the flu.*
**put someone's back up,** *Informal.* make angry and stubbornly opposed: *It wasn't what she said, but the way she said it that put my back up.*
**turn one's back on,** **a** reject or ignore in contempt, anger, or indifference: *How can you turn your back on those people when they so obviously need help?* **b** forsake; renounce: *He turned his back on success and returned to his home town.*
**with one's back to the wall,** in a desperate situation; no longer able to run away: *Now, with their backs to the wall, they finally had to admit that they needed help.*

**back·ache** (bak′āk′) a continuous pain in the back. *n.*

**back bacon** bacon cut from the back rather than the sides: *Back bacon has little fat and has a hamlike flavour.*

**back·bench·er** (bak′ben′chər) a member of Parliament or a legislative assembly who is not a member of the cabinet or one of the leading members of an opposition party. *n.*

**back·bit** (bak′bit) pt. and a pp. of BACKBITE. *v.*

**back·bite** (bak′bīt′) say malicious things; slander an absent person. *v.*, **back·bit, back·bit·ten** or (*informal*) **back·bit, back·bit·ing.** —**back′bit·er,** *n.*

**back·bit·ten** (bak′bi tən) a pp. of BACKBITE. *v.*

**back·board** (bak′bôrd′) **1** a board that forms the back of something or acts as a support. **2** a board above and behind the basket on a basketball court. *n.*

**back·bone** (bak′bōn′) **1** in human beings and other vertebrates, the series of small bones along the middle of the back; spinal column. See SPINAL COLUMN for picture. **2** anything like a backbone, such as the keel of a ship or a mountain range. **3** the most important part; the chief strength or support: *She is the backbone of the organization.* **4** strength of character: *A coward lacks the backbone to stand up for his or her beliefs.* *n.*

**back–check** (bak′chek′) in hockey: **1** skate back toward one's own goal in order to interfere with an opponent's rush: *A forward who has lost the puck will often back-check to try to get it back.* **2** the act of back-checking. 1 *v.*, 2 *n.* —**back′-check′er,** *n.*

**back·door** (bak′dôr′) secret; underhand; sly. *adj.*

**back·drop** (bak′drop′) **1** a curtain or scenery at the back of a stage. **2** BACKGROUND (def. 1). *n.*

**back East** *Cdn.* in or to eastern Canada: *People in western Canada speak of Ontario as being back East.*

**back·er** (bak′ər) a person who backs, or supports, another person, some plan, idea, etc. *n.*

**back·field** (bak′fēld′) **1** in football, the players behind the front line; the quarterback, two halfbacks, fullback, and, in Canadian football, the flying wing. **2** in baseball, the outfield. *n.*

**back·fire** (bak′fīr′) **1** in an automobile engine, an explosion, either of fuel igniting too soon in a cylinder or of unburned exhaust gases in the muffler. **2** explode in this way. **3** a fire set to check a forest or prairie fire by burning off the area in front of it. **4** use a backfire in fire-fighting. **5** have an unfavourable result, opposite to an expected favourable one; turn out wrong: *Their scheme to get out of doing the dishes backfired and they ended up cleaning the kitchen as well.* 1, 3 *n.*, 2, 4, 5 *v.*, **back·fired, back·fir·ing.**

**back·gam·mon** (bak′gam′ən) a table game for two

played on a special board with pieces moved according to the throw of dice. *n.*

**back·ground** (bak′ground′) **1** the part of a picture or scene farthest from the viewer: *The cottage stands in the foreground with the mountains in the background.* Compare with FOREGROUND. **2** a surface against which things are seen; surface upon which things are made or placed: *Her dress had pink flowers on a white background.* **3** earlier conditions or events that help to explain some later condition or event: *We studied the background to the news.* **4** past experience, knowledge, and training: *The director is looking for an assistant with a background in musicals.* **5** the accompanying music or sound effects in a play, motion picture, etc. *n.*
**in the background,** out of sight; not in clear view: *The shy boy kept in the background.*

**back·hand** (bak′hand′) **1** a stroke made with the back of the hand turned forward, especially in games like tennis or badminton. **2** handwriting in which the letters slope to the left. **3** BACKHANDED (def. 1). **4** hit or catch backhanded. 1, 2 *n.*, 3 *adj.*, 4 *v.*

**back·hand·ed** (bak′han′did) **1** done or made with the back of the hand turned forward. **2** slanting to the left. **3** awkward or clumsy. **4** indirect or insincere: *A backhanded compliment is really a criticism.* *adj.*

**back·hoe** (bak′hō′) **1** a machine for digging trenches for water mains, etc. **2** use such a machine. 1 *n.*, 2 *v.*, **back·hoed, back·hoe·ing.**

**back·house** (bak′hous′) a small outside toilet; privy. *n.*

**back·ing** (bak′ing) **1** a support or help. **2** supporters or helpers. **3** something placed at the back of anything to support or strengthen it. **4** ppr. of BACK. 1–3 *n.*, 4 *v.*

**back·lash** (bak′lash′) **1** a sudden hostile reaction to an earlier action or series of actions that were not originally seen as a serious threat: *a backlash of anger. The fear of rebellion resulted in a pro-government backlash.* **2** the jarring reaction of a machine or mechanical device. **3** the movement or play between worn or loosely fitting parts. *n.*

**back·log** (bak′log′) **1** a large log at the back of a wood fire. **2** something serving as a basis or support. **3** an accumulation of orders, commitments, etc. that have not yet been filled: *The company hired extra staff to help clear the backlog of orders.* **4** accumulate as a backlog. 1–3 *n.*, 4 *v.*, **back·logged, back·log·ging.**

**back number 1** an old issue of a magazine or newspaper. **2** *Informal.* an old-fashioned person or out-of-date thing.

**back·pack** (bak′pak′) **1** a lightweight bag of nylon, canvas, etc., usually attached to a tubular metal frame that is strapped onto a person's back, used for carrying food, clothing, equipment, etc. **2** travel, especially on foot, while carrying all one's belongings in a backpack: *They backpacked about 200 kilometres last summer.* **3** of or referring to this way of travelling: *a backpack trip.* 1, 3 *n.*, 2 *v.* —**back′pack′er,** *n.*

**back·pack·ing** (bak′pak′ing) **1** the action or sport of travelling, especially on foot, with all one's belongings carried in a BACKPACK (def. 1): *I have had no experience in wilderness backpacking.* **2** ppr. of BACKPACK. 1 *n.*, 2 *v.*

**back seat 1** a seat at or in the back. **2** *Informal.* a place of inferiority or insignificance: *She won't take a back seat to anybody.* —**back-seat,** *adj.*

**background**     **81**     **backward**

hat, āge, fär; let, ēqual, tėrm; it, īce
hot, ōpen, ôrder; oil, out; cup, pùt, rüle
əbove, takən, pencəl, lemən, circəs
ch, child; ng, long; sh, ship
th, thin; ᴛʜ, then; zh, measure

**back-seat driver,** a passenger in a car who tells the driver what to do.

**back·side** (bak′sīd′) **1** the back. **2** *Informal.* the rump or buttocks. *n.*

**back·slid** (bak′slid) pt. and a pp. of BACKSLIDE. *v.*

**back·slide** (bak′slīd′) slide back into wrongdoing; lose one's enthusiasm, especially for religion. *v.*, **back·slid, back·slid·den** or **back·slid, back·slid·ing.** —**back′slid′er,** *n.*

**back·slid·den** (bak′slidən) a pp. of BACKSLIDE. *v.*

**back·stage** (bak′stāj′) **1** in the dressing rooms of a theatre. **2** toward the rear of a stage. **3** not known to the general public; confidential: *backstage negotiations.* 1, 2 *adv.*, 3 *adj.*

**back·stay** (bak′stā′) **1** a rope extending from the top of the mast to the ship's side and helping to support the mast. See SHROUD for picture. **2** a spring, rod, strap, etc. used for support at the back of something. *n.*

**back·stop** (bak′stop′) in various games: **1** a fence or screen used to keep the ball from going too far away. **2** a player who stops balls that get past another player. *n.*

**back·stroke** (bak′strōk′) **1** a swimming stroke made with the swimmer lying on his or her back. **2** a BACKHANDED (def. 1) stroke. *n.*

**back talk** *Informal.* talking back; impudent answers.

**back-to-back** (bak′tə bak′) **1** with the backs against each other or close together and the fronts or faces turned in opposite directions: *We placed the chairs in a back-to-back position.* **2** *Informal.* following one after the other: *The team had back-to-back wins.* *adj.*

**back·track** (bak′trak′) **1** go back over a course or path. **2** withdraw from an undertaking, position, etc.: *Tom backtracked on the claim he had made earlier.* *v.*

**back·up** (bak′up′) **1** a person, group, or thing that serves as a reinforcement: *We need some sort of backup if we're going to convince them.* **2** in computer systems, a copy of important programs or data stored on a disk in case the originals are destroyed or lost. *n.*

**back·ward** (bak′wərd) **1** toward the back: *She glanced backward.* **2** directed toward the back: *a backward look.* **3** with the back foremost: *The little girl was trying to walk backward. He tumbled backward.* **4** toward the starting point: *The rolling ball came to a stop and then began to roll backward.* **5** directed to or toward the starting point; returning: *a backward movement.* **6** opposite to the usual way; in the reverse way: *to read backward.* **7** done in the reverse way or order: *a backward process.* **8** from better to worse: *Educational conditions in the town went backward.* **9** toward the past: *He looked backward forty years and talked about his childhood.* **10** reaching back into the past. **11** slow in development: *Backward children need special help in school.* **12** shy or bashful: *Shake hands; don't be backward.* **13** late, behind time: *This is a backward season; spring is two weeks late.* 1, 3, 4, 6, 8, 9 *adv.*, 2, 5, 7, 10–13 *adj.* —**back′ward·ness,** *n.*

**back·wards** (bak′wərdz) BACKWARD. *adv.*
**fall, lean,** or **bend over backwards,** *Informal.* try extremely hard; be especially accommodating: *He was falling over backwards trying to please the new girl next door.*

**back·wash** (bak′wosh′) **1** a backward-moving current of water such as that thrown back by oars or a motor in a boat. **2** a similar current of air from the propellers of an aircraft. *n.*

**back·wa·ter** (bak′wot′ər) **1** a stretch of still water at the bank of a river or stream: *Because they are not moved by the current, backwaters are often stagnant.* **2** a stretch of water that is held, thrown, or pushed back: *The beaver dam had caused a backwater to form above it at an angle to the main course of the stream.* **3** a condition or place that is thought of as backward, stagnant, etc.: *The town was often referred to as a backwater.* *n.*

**back·woods** (bak′wudz′) **1** uncleared forests or wild regions far away from towns. **2** of the backwoods. **3** crude or rough. 1 *n. pl.*, 2, 3 *adj.*

**back·woods·man** (bak′wudz′mən) a person who lives or works in the BACKWOODS (def. 1). *n., pl.* **back·woods·men** (-zmən).

**back·yard** (bak′yärd′) a yard behind a house: *They have a vegetable garden in their backyard.* *n.*

**ba·con** (bā′kən) the salted and smoked meat from the back and sides of a pig. See PORK for picture. *n.*
**bring home the bacon,** *Informal.* be successful; win the prize.

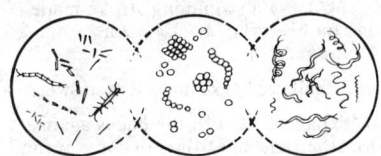
Three main types of bacteria, classified according to shape
BACILLI  COCCI  SPIRILLA

**bac·te·ri·a** (bak tē′rē ə) tiny, one-celled organisms visible only through a microscope, having characteristics of both plants and animals. They are present everywhere: in the air, on land, in the sea, and on and in living things: *Some kinds of bacteria cause disease; other kinds that live in the digestive system act as an aid to digestion.* *n., pl.* of BACTERIUM.

**bac·te·ri·al** (bak tē′rē əl) of or caused by BACTERIA: *bacterial life, bacterial diseases.* *adj.*

**bac·te·ri·o·log·i·cal** (bak tē′rē ə loj′ə kəl) having to do with BACTERIOLOGY. *adj.*

**bac·te·ri·ol·o·gist** (bak tē′rē ol′ə jist) a person trained in BACTERIOLOGY, especially one who makes it his or her work. *n.*

**bac·te·ri·ol·o·gy** (bak tē′rē ol′ə jē) the science that deals with BACTERIA. *n.*

**bac·te·ri·um** (bak tē′rē əm) sing. of BACTERIA. *n.*

**Bac·tri·an camel** (bak′trē ən) a species of camel found in the highlands of central Asia, having two humps and with a heavier build than the Arabian camel: *The Bactrian camel, which is about 2 m high to the top of the humps, cannot travel as fast as the Arabian camel, but it can keep its pace longer in a caravan, averaging about 50 km per day with a load of 180 kg.* See CAMEL for picture.

**bad** (bad) **1** not good; not acceptable; poor or inferior in quality: *bad poetry, a bad shipment. The light was bad. That desk shows bad workmanship.* **2** evil; wicked: *Only a very bad person would deliberately hurt a helpless child.* **3** naughty: *You're a bad boy!* **4** disagreeable; sullen: *a bad mood. She's in a bad temper.* **5** unfavourable; distressing: *bad news. He came at a bad time. I think I made a bad impression on your parents.* **6** harmful: *That kind of food is bad for you.* **7** severe: *a bad cold, a bad storm.* **8** incorrect; faulty: *a bad guess, bad grammar.* **9** rotten; spoiled: *The fish is bad; we'll have to throw it out.* **10** run-down; partly ruined, especially because of neglect: *bad teeth. The car was in bad condition.* **11** sick; suffering: *She's feeling very bad with her cold.* **12** worthless; not valid: *a bad cheque, a bad debt.* **13** sorry; regretful: *I feel bad about losing your baseball.* **14 the bad,** that which is bad; a bad condition, quality, etc.: *She realized she'd have to take the bad with the good.* 1–13 *adj.*, **worse, worst;** 14 *n.* —**bad′ness,** *n.*
**go bad,** become spoiled or rotten: *We forgot about the leftovers and they went bad.*
**not bad,** *Informal.* average; acceptable: *The movie's not bad, but I've seen better.*
**not half bad,** *Informal.* better than average: *I wasn't expecting much of the movie, but it's really not half bad.*
**not so bad,** *Informal.* better than expected: *I was dreading the test, but it wasn't so bad.*
**to the bad,** **a** toward ruin: *It's all gone to the bad in a few short years.* **b** in debt: *That last foolish deal put him several hundred dollars to the bad.*
☛ *Hom.* BADE (bad).

**bad blood** unfriendly feeling; bitterness.

**bade** (bad *or* bād) a pt. of BID: *The king bade her remain.* *v.*
☛ *Hom.* BAD (for the first pronunciation of **bade**).

**badge** (baj) **1** something worn to show that a person belongs to a certain occupation, school, class, club, society, etc.: *The Red Cross badge is a red cross on a white background.* **2** a symbol or sign: *A mayor's badge of office is a chain.* *n.*

**badg·er** (baj′ər) **1** either of two species of large, grey burrowing animal of the weasel family, found in North America, Europe, and Asia, having a long, flat, muscular body, a broad, flattened head on a short neck, and short legs and tail: *The North American badger, found in the western part of the continent, is about 70 cm long.* **2** the fur of a badger. **3** keep after someone; try again and again to convince: *A car salesperson has been badgering my father for weeks.* **4** harass by persistent questioning: *The judge objected to the way the lawyer was badgering the witness.* 1, 2 *n.*, 3, 4 *v.*

**bad·i·nage** (bad′ə näzh′) good-natured joking or banter. *n.*

**bad·lands** (bad′landz′) a barren region marked by ridges, gullies, and weird rock formations caused by erosion, as found in parts of southern Saskatchewan and Alberta. *n.*

**bad·ly** (bad′lē) **1** in a bad manner: *She sings badly.* **2** *Informal.* greatly; very much: *He wants to go badly.* *adv.*

**bad·min·ton** (bad′min tən) a game in which either two or four players use light rackets to volley a shuttlecock over a high net. See RACKET² for picture. *n.*

**bad–tem·pered** (bad′tem′pərd) having a bad temper or disposition. *adj.*

**baf·fle** (baf′əl) **1** be too hard for a person to

understand or solve: *This puzzle baffles me.* **2** a device for hindering or changing the flow of air, water, or sound waves: *a baffle for a jet engine.* 1 *v.*, **baf·fled, baf·fling;** 2 *n.* —**baf′fler,** *n.*

**baf·fle·ment** (baf′əl mənt)  a baffling or being BAFFLED (def. 1). *n.*

**baf·fling** (baf′ling)  **1** puzzling: *a baffling manoeuvre.* **2** hindering; thwarting.  **3** ppr. of BAFFLE. 1, 2 *adj.*, 3 *v.*

**bag** (bag)  **1** a container made of paper, cloth, plastic, leather, etc. that can be pulled together to close at the top.  **2** the amount that a bag can hold: *She liked the candy so much that she finished the whole bag.*  **3** something like a bag in use or shape: *She calls her purse her bag.*  **4** put into a bag or bags.  **5** swell or bulge: *His trousers bag at the knees.*  **6** the game killed or caught at one time by a hunter.  **7** in hunting, kill or catch.  **8** *Informal.* catch, take, or steal.  **9** in baseball, a base. 1–3, 6, 9 *n.*, 4, 5, 7, 8 *v.*, **bagged, bag·ging.** —**bag′like′,** *adj.*
**in the bag,** *Informal.*  sure; certain to succeed or be achieved: *Don't worry; my new job's in the bag.*
**leave someone holding the bag,** *Informal.*  leave someone to take all the responsibility or blame alone instead of sharing it: *We had agreed to do the dishes, but after dinner he suddenly remembered a phone call he had to make and left me holding the bag.*

**bag·a·telle** (bag′ə tel′)  **1** a mere trifle; thing of no importance.  **2** a game resembling billiards.  **3** in music, a short, light composition.  *n.*

**ba·gel** (bā′gəl)  a doughnut-shaped roll of yeast dough that is simmered in water and then baked. *n.*
☞ *Etym.* From Yiddish *beygel,* the word for such a roll, originally from Old High German *boug* 'ring, bracelet'.

**bag·gage** (bag′ij)  **1** the trunks, bags, suitcases, etc. that a person takes when he or she travels.  **2** the equipment that an army takes with it, such as tents, blankets, ammunition, etc.  *n.*

**bag·gy** (bag′ē)  hanging loosely; baglike: *baggy trousers. adj.,* **bag·gi·er, bag·gi·est.**

A bagpipe. The player blows air into the bag and, by pressing with his arm, controls the flow of air into the pipes that produce the sound.

**bag·pipe** (bag′pīp′)  Often, **bag·pipes,** *pl.*  a shrill-toned musical instrument made of a windbag and pipes, associated chiefly with Scotland.  *n.*

**bag·pip·er** (bag′pī′pər)  a person who plays the BAGPIPE. *n.*

**bah** (bä)  an exclamation of scorn or contempt.  *interj.*

**Ba·ha·i** (bə hä′ē)  **1** a person who believes in BAHAISM. **2** BAHAISM.  **3** of or having to do with BAHAISM.  1, 2 *n., pl.* **Ba·ha·is;** 3 *adj.*

**Ba·ha·ism** (bə hä′iz əm)  a religious system founded in 1863 by Mirza Husayn Ali Nuri, a Persian religious leader who taught the basic unity of all religions.  *n.*

**Ba·ha·mi·an** (bə hä′mē ən *or* bä hä′mē ən)  **1** of or having to do with the Bahamas.  **2** a native or inhabitant of the Bahamas.  1 *adj.*, 2 *n.*

**Ba·ha Ul·lah** (bä hä ůl lä′)  the prophet and founder of BAHAISM, who was born Mirza Husayn Ali in Persia, 1817 A.D.  *n.*

**bail**[1] (bāl)  **1** the guarantee necessary to release an arrested person until he or she is to appear for trial.  **2** the amount guaranteed.  **3** the person or persons who stand ready to pay the money guaranteed.  **4** obtain the release of a person under arrest by guaranteeing to pay bail.  1–3 *n.*, 4 *v.*
**bail out,  a** supply bail for.  **b** help out of a difficulty or predicament: *His car was out of gas, but a neighbour bailed him out with some from her lawn mower.*
**go bail for,**  supply bail for.
☞ *Hom.* BALE.

**bail**[2] (bāl)  **1** the arched handle of a kettle or pail.  See PAIL for picture.  **2** a hooplike support: *The bails of a covered wagon hold up the canvas.*  *n.*
☞ *Hom.* BALE.

**bail**[3] (bāl)  **1** a scoop or pail used to throw water out of a boat.  **2** dip and throw water out of a boat with a pail, a dipper, or any other container.  **3** dip water from. 1 *n.*, 2, 3 *v.*
**bail out,  a** drop from an airplane by parachute.  **b** throw water out of with a pail, a dipper, or any other container.  **c** abandon a situation: *We need your help; don't bail out now.*
☞ *Hom.* BALE.

**bail**[4] (bāl)  in cricket, either of two small bars that form the top of a WICKET (def. 4).  *n.*
☞ *Hom.* BALE.

**bail·iff** (bā′lif)  **1** an assistant to a SHERIFF.  **2** an officer of the lower courts of a province, appointed by the Lieutenant-Governor to see that the orders of the court are carried out: *The bailiff's duties include serving summonses and attending all sessions of the court to which she has been appointed.*  **3** the steward of an estate or an agent appointed by a landlord to collect rents or seize property for non-payment of rent.  *n.*

**bail·i·wick** (bā′lə wik′)  **1** the district over which a BAILIFF has authority.  **2** a person's field of knowledge, work, or authority.  *n.*

**bairn** (bern) *Scottish.*  child.  *n.*

**Ba·i·sak·hi Day** (bī′sä′kē)  in Sikhism, the festival commemorating the day upon which Guru Gobind Singh, the tenth and last of the founding Gurus, created the Khalsa, or community of baptized Sikhs.

**bait** (bāt)  **1** anything, especially food, used to attract fish, birds, or animals so that they may be caught.  **2** put bait on a hook or in a trap.  **3** anything used to tempt or attract.  **4** tempt or attract.  **5** set dogs to attack: *Men used to bait bulls and bears for sport.*  **6** attack or torment: *The dogs baited the bear.*  **7** torment or worry by unkind or annoying remarks.  1, 3 *n.*, 2, 4–7 *v.*
☞ *Hom.* BATE.

**baize** (bāz)  a thick woollen or cotton cloth with a nap, used especially for table covers: *Baize is usually dyed green.* *n.*

**bake** (bāk) **1** cook food by dry heat without exposing it directly to the fire: *The cook bakes bread and cakes in the oven.* **2** dry or harden by heat: *to bake bricks or china.* **3** become baked: *Cookies bake quickly.* **4** BAKING (def. 3). 1–3 *v.,* **baked, bak·ing;** 4 *n.*

**bake·ap·ple** (bā′kap′əl) *Cdn.* especially in the Atlantic Provinces: **1** a creeping plant that grows in swampy areas, having single white flowers and amber-coloured, edible berries like small raspberries; cloudberry. **2** the berry of this plant. *n.*

**baked–ap·ple** (bāk′tap′əl) BAKEAPPLE. *n.*

**bak·er** (bā′kər) **1** a person who makes or sells bread, pies, cakes, etc. **2** a small portable oven. *n.*

**baker's dozen** thirteen.

**bak·er·y** (bā′kə rē) a baker's shop; place where bread, pies, cakes, etc. are made or sold. *n., pl.* **bak·er·ies.**

**bake sale** a sale of homemade baked goods, especially one held by a group of people to raise money for charity or some public project.

**bak·ing** (bā′king) **1** cooking in dry heat. **2** drying or hardening by heat. **3** the amount baked at one time; a batch. **4** ppr. of BAKE. 1–3 *n.,* 4 *v.*

**baking powder** a mixture of bicarbonate of soda, starch, and an acid compound such as cream of tartar, used as a LEAVENing agent in making biscuits, cakes, etc.

**baking soda** BICARBONATE OF SODA.

**bal·a·lai·ka** (bal′ə lī′kə) a Russian musical instrument resembling a guitar, but having a triangular body. *n.*

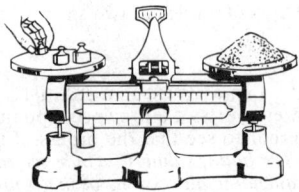

A balance. The thing to be weighed is put on one platform and metal weights of known value are added to the other until the two platforms balance. Fine adjustments are made by moving the weight hung on the bar below the platforms.

**bal·ance** (bal′əns) **1** an instrument for weighing. **2** weigh in a balance or in one's hands to see which of two things is heavier. **3** equality in weight, amount, force, effect, etc.: *He adjusted the balance between the two loudspeakers of his stereo set.* **4** make or be equal to in weight, amount, force, effect, etc.: *The two groups of pictures don't balance; the one on the right looks larger.* **5** a comparison of weight, value, importance, etc.; an estimate. **6** compare the value, importance, etc. of: *Alicia balanced a trip to the Rockies against the chance of a summer job.* **7** harmony; proportion in design. **8** make or be proportionate to. **9** a steady condition or position; steadiness: *He lost his balance and fell off the ladder.* **10** put or keep in a steady condition or position: *Can you balance a coin on its edge?* **11** mental steadiness; poise: *Her balance is never disturbed by the tantrums of others.* **12** anything that counteracts the effect, weight, etc. of something else. **13** counteract the effect, influence, etc. of; make up for. **14** the difference between the credit and debit sides of an account: *I have a balance of $20 in the bank.* **15** make the debit and credit sides of an account equal: *to balance a budget.* **16** be equal in the debit and credit sides of an account. **17** *Informal.* the part that is left over; remainder: *I will be away for the balance of the week.* **18** the wheel that regulates the rate of movement of a clock or watch. **19** the greatest weight, amount, or power. **20** hesitate or waver. 1, 3, 5, 7, 9, 11, 12, 14, 17–19 *n.,* 2, 4, 6, 8, 10, 13, 15, 16, 20 *v.,* **bal·anced, bal·anc·ing. —bal′anc·er,** *n.*

**balance out,** be equal: *The accounts balanced out.*

**in the balance,** undecided: *The outcome of the game was in the balance until the last minute of play.*

**balanced diet** a DIET (def. 1) having the correct amounts of all kinds of foods necessary for health.

**balance of power** an even distribution of military and economic power among nations or groups of nations.

**balance of trade** the difference between the value of all the imports and that of all the exports of a country.

**bal·a·ta** (bal′ə tə) a hard, non-elastic, rubberlike substance made by drying the milky juice of a tropical American tree, used in making golf balls, belting, etc. *n.*

**bal·co·ny** (bal′kə nē) **1** an outside projecting platform with an entrance from an upper floor of a building. **2** in a theatre or hall, a projecting upper floor with seats for an audience. *n., pl.* **bal·co·nies.**

**bald** (bold) **1** completely or partly without hair on the head. **2** without natural covering: *A mountain top with no trees or grass on it is bald.* **3** bare; plain: *The bald truth is that he is a thief.* **4** of birds or mammals, having white on the head. *adj.* **—bald′ly,** *adv.* **—bald′ness,** *n.*

**bald eagle** a species of fish-eating eagle found near the coasts of North America, having dark brown feathers on the body and white feathers on the head and neck and on the tail: *The bald eagle was given its name because the white head contrasts so sharply with the dark body.* See EAGLE for picture.

**bal·der·dash** (bol′dər dash′) nonsense. *n.*

**bald·pate** (bold′pāt′) **1** a person who has a bald head. **2** a species of wild duck found throughout western North America, the male having a noticeable white patch on the forehead and crown; WIDGEON. *n.*

**bald prairie** that part of the western prairie which is almost without trees.

**bale** (bāl) **1** a large bundle of merchandise or material securely wrapped or bound for shipping or storage: *a bale of paper.* **2** make into bales; tie in large bundles. 1 *n.,* 2 *v.,* **baled, bal·ing.**
☞ *Hom.* BAIL.

**ba·leen** (bə lēn′) WHALEBONE (def. 1). *n.*

**bale·ful** (bāl′fəl) evil; harmful. *adj.* **—bale′ful·ly,** *adv.* **—bale′ful·ness,** *n.*

**bal·er** (bā′lər) **1** a person who bales. **2** a machine that compresses and ties up into bundles such things as hay, straw, paper, and scrap metal. *n.*

**Ba·li·nese** (bä′lə nēz′) **1** a native or inhabitant of Bali, an island in Indonesia. **2** the people of Bali. **3** the language of Bali. **4** of Bali, its people, or their language. 1–3 *n., pl.* **Ba·li·nese;** 4 *adj.*

**balk** (bok) **1** stop short and stubbornly refuse to go on: *My horse balked at the bridge. As soon as I suggested a compromise, she balked.* **2** thwart; hinder; check: *The police balked the robber's plans.* **3** a hindrance; check;

defeat: *It was a balk to our plans.* **4** a blunder or mistake. **5** in sports, an incomplete or misleading motion, especially an illegal false move to throw the ball, made by a baseball pitcher when there are runners on base. **6** in sports, make an incomplete or misleading move. 1, 2, 6 *v.*, 3–5 *n.* Also, **baulk.**
**balk at,** refuse to accept: *The management balked at the strikers' latest offer.*

**Bal·kan** (bol′kən) **1** of the Balkan peninsula; having to do with the countries in it. **2** of the people living in these countries. **3** of the Balkan Mountains. **4** the **Balkans,** the Balkan States: *The Balkans have been the scene of much warfare.* 1–3 *adj.*, 4 *n.*

**balk·y** (bok′ē) tending to stop short and stubbornly refuse to go on; likely to BALK (def. 1). *adj.,* **balk·i·er, balk·i·est.**

**ball**¹ (bol) **1** a round or oval object that is thrown, kicked, knocked, bounced, or batted about in various games. **2** a game in which some kind of ball is thrown, hit, or kicked. **3** anything round or roundish; something that resembles a ball: *the ball of the thumb, a ball of string.* **4** make or form into a ball. **5** a ball in motion: *a fast ball.* **6** baseball. **7** in baseball, a ball pitched too high, too low, or not over the plate, which the batter does not strike at. **8** a type of delivery of a ball: *a curved ball.* **9** bullet. **10** a globe; the earth. 1–3, 5–10 *n.*, 4 *v.*
**be on the ball,** *Informal.* be mentally wide awake; be alert: *He's really on the ball today; he sold three cars before noon.*
**play ball,** *Informal.* **a** begin a game or start it again after stopping. **b** get busy. **c** work together; co-operate: *If everyone will play ball, we can get the job done quickly.*
☞ *Hom.* BAWL.
☞ *Etym.* From ME *bal*, ON *bollr*, meaning a globe-shaped object.

**ball**² (bol) **1** a large, formal party with dancing. **2** *Informal.* a very good time; a lot of fun: *We had a ball! n.*
☞ *Hom.* BAWL.
☞ *Etym.* From OF *bal* 'a dance', formed from *baler* 'to dance'.

**bal·lad** (bal′əd) **1** a simple song. **2** a poem that tells a story in a simple verse form, especially one that tells a popular legend. *n.*

**ball–and–socket joint** a flexible joint formed by a ball or knob fitting in a socket, such as the shoulder or hip joint. See SOCKET for picture.

**bal·last** (bal′əst) **1** something heavy carried in a ship to steady it. **2** the weight carried in a balloon or dirigible to control it: *Balloons use bags of sand for ballast.* **3** put ballast in ships, balloons, etc. **4** anything that steadies a person or thing. **5** gravel or crushed rock used in making the bed for a road or railway track. 1, 2, 4, 5 *n.*, 3 *v.*

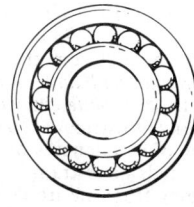

A ball bearing from the hub of a bicycle wheel

**ball bearing** **1** a BEARING (def. 3) in which the shaft turns upon a number of freely moving metal balls contained in a grooved ring around the shaft: *Ball bearings are used to lessen friction.* **2** any of the metal balls so used.

**bal·le·ri·na** (bal′ə rē′nə) a female ballet dancer. *n.,* *pl.* **bal·le·ri·nas.**

**bal·let** (bal′ā *or* ba lā′) **1** an artistic dance that usually tells a story or expresses a mood, performed by either a soloist or a group of dancers in a theatre, concert hall, etc. **2** the art of creating or performing ballets: *He is studying ballet.* **3** a company of dancers that performs ballets. **4** a performance of a ballet: *I went to the ballet last night. n.*

**ball hockey** a hockey-like game played with hockey sticks and a tennis ball.

**bal·lis·tic** (bə lis′tik) **1** having to do with the motion or throwing of PROJECTILES. **2** having to do with the science of BALLISTICS. *adj.*

**ballistic missile** a PROJECTILE powered by a rocket engine or engines but reaching its target as a result of aim at the time of launching.

**bal·lis·tics** (bə lis′tiks) the science that deals with the motion of PROJECTILES such as bullets, shells, or rockets (used with a singular verb). *n.*

**bal·loon** (bə lün′) **1** an airtight bag filled with air or a gas lighter than air, so that it will rise and float. **2** such a bag from which is hung either a car to carry one or more persons or a container to carry instruments. **3** ride in a balloon. **4** swell out like a balloon. **5** puffed out like a balloon: *balloon sleeves.* **6** in a cartoon, a boxed space in which the words of a speaker are written. 1, 2, 5, 6 *n.*, 3, 4 *v.* —**bal·loon′like′,** *adj.*

**bal·loon·ist** (bə lü′nist) **1** a person who goes up in BALLOONS (def. 2). **2** a pilot of a dirigible BALLOON (def. 2). *n.*

**bal·lot** (bal′ət) **1** a piece of paper or other object used in voting. **2** the total number of votes cast. **3** a method of secret voting that uses paper slips, voting machines, etc. **4** vote or decide by using ballots. 1–3 *n.*, 4 *v.,* **bal·lot·ed, bal·lot·ing.**

**ballot box** the box into which voters put their BALLOTs after they have voted.

**ball·play·er** (bol′plā′ər) **1** a baseball player. **2** a person who plays any kind of ball game. *n.*

**ball–point** or **ball·point** (bol′point′) a pen that writes by means of a small metal ball set in its point: *When a ball-point is moved along a surface such as paper, the ball rotates against a cartridge holding ink in semisolid form, transferring the ink to the surface.* *n.*

**ball·room** (bol′rüm′) a large room for dancing. *n.*

**bal·ly·hoo** (bal′ē hü′) *Informal.* **1** noisy advertising; a sensational way of attracting attention. **2** advertise noisily; make exaggerated or false statements about. **3** an uproar or outcry. 1, 3 *n., pl.* **bal·ly·hoos;** 2 *v.*, **bal·ly·hooed, bal·ly·hoo·ing.**

**balm** (bom *or* bäm) **1** a fragrant, oily, sticky resin obtained from certain kinds of trees, used to heal or relieve pain. **2** anything that heals or soothes: *Mother's praise was balm to hurt feelings.* **3** a fragrant plant of the same family as mint. *n.*
☞ *Hom.* BOMB (for the first pronunciation of **balm**).

**balm of Gil·e·ad** (gil′ē əd) **1** a fragrant ointment prepared from the resin of a small evergreen tree of Asia and Africa. **2** the tree itself. **3** a species of poplar tree closely resembling the BALSAM POPLAR but having a broader crown and leaves that are almost heart-shaped. **4** BALSAM FIR.

**bal·mor·al** (bal mô′rəl) a brimless Scottish cap having a round, soft, more or less flat crown that projects all around. See CAP for picture. *n.*

**balm·y** (bom′ē *or* bä′mē) **1** mild; gentle; soothing: *a balmy breeze.* **2** fragrant. *adj.,* **balm·i·er, balm·i·est.** —**balm′i·ly,** *adv.* —**balm′i·ness,** *n.*

**bal·sa** (bol′sə) **1** a tropical American tree with very lightweight, strong wood. **2** the wood of this tree. **3** a raft, especially one consisting of two or more floats fastened to a framework. *n.*

**bal·sam** (bol′səm) **1** a fragrant, oily, sticky substance obtained from certain kinds of trees and shrubs, and used as a base for cough syrups, perfumes, etc. **2** any substance like this, especially a fragrant ointment for healing or soothing. **3** a tree that yields balsam, especially the BALSAM FIR. **4** a garden plant closely related to the common garden IMPATIENS and the wild TOUCH-ME-NOT, having large leaves and double, usually red or pink flowers. *n.*

**balsam fir 1** a fir tree found throughout eastern Canada and parts of the Prairie Provinces, having a narrow, symmetrical crown tapering to a spirelike top and shiny, dark-green needles: *The balsam fir is often used as a Christmas tree and its resin is used in making varnish.* **2** the soft, light, weak wood of this tree, used especially for pulp.

**balsam poplar 1** a North American poplar tree found throughout Canada, having oval leaves that are shiny dark green above and whitish green below; TACAMAHAC (def. 2). **2** the wood of this tree.

**Bal·tic** (bol′tik) **1** having to do with the Baltic Sea. **2** having to do with the Baltic States. **3** a group of Indo-European languages belonging to this region. 1, 2 *adj.,* 3 *n.*

**Bal·ti·more or·i·ole** (bol′tə môr′) a species of North American ORIOLE common throughout central and eastern North America, having a loud, piping whistle: *The male Baltimore oriole has a black head and back and mostly black wings, with a bright orange-yellow underside, rump, and upper tail feathers.*

**bal·us·ter** (bal′ə stər) a support for a railing. See BALUSTRADE for picture. *n.*

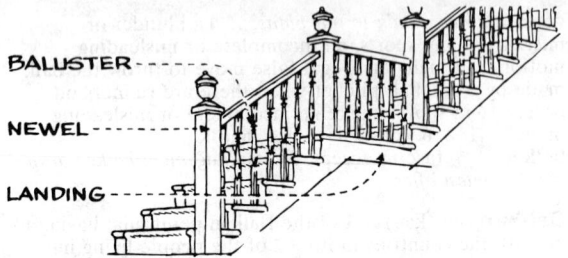

A staircase with a balustrade, or banisters, and a landing

**bal·us·trade** (bal′ə strād′) a row of BALUSTERS and the railing on them. *n.*

**bam·boo** (bam bü′) **1** any of various woody or tree-like tropical or semitropical grasses having stiff, hollow stems with hard, thick joints: *She bought a fishing rod made of bamboo.* **2** of bamboo; made of the stems of this plant. *n., pl.* **bam·boos.**

**Bamboo Curtain** the barrier or dividing line between the People's Republic of China and the western non-communist nations created by the strict censorship of news by the Chinese government.
☞ *Etym.* Coined by analogy with the IRON CURTAIN, a former similar barrier around the Soviet Union and the European nations under its influence.

**bam·boo·zle** (bam bü′zəl) *Informal.* **1** impose upon; cheat or trick. **2** puzzle; perplex. *v.,* **bam·boo·zled, bam·boo·zling.**

**ban** (ban) **1** prohibit; forbid by law or authority: *Swimming is banned in this lake.* **2** the forbidding of an act or speech by authority of the law or public opinion. **3** a solemn curse by the church. **4** a sentence of outlawry or banishment. 1 *v.,* **banned, ban·ning;** 2–4 *n.*

**ba·nal** (bə nal′ *or* bā′nəl) commonplace; trite or trivial: *She made some banal remarks about the weather before coming to the point of her visit. adj.* —**ba′nal·ly,** *adv.*

**ba·nal·i·ty** (bə nal′ə tē) commonplaceness; triteness or triviality. *n., pl.* **ba·nal·i·ties.**

**ba·nan·a** (bə nan′ə) **1** an oblong, slightly curved fruit having a thick yellow or sometimes reddish skin, that is easily peeled off, and firm, creamy flesh. **2** a tree-like tropical plant on which bananas grow. *n.*

**band¹** (band) **1** a group of persons or animals moving or acting together: *a band of robbers, a band of wild dogs.* **2** a group of musicians organized to play together, especially on brass, woodwind, and percussion instruments: *We hired a five-piece band for our dance.* Compare with ORCHESTRA. **3** *Cdn.* a group of Canadian Indian people of a particular region or reserve, recognized by the Federal Government as an administrative unit. *n.*
**band together,** unite or cause to unite in a group: *The children banded together to buy a present for the caretaker.*

**band²** (band) **1** a thin, flat strip of material for binding, trimming, or some other purpose: *a narrow band of lace. The oak box was strengthened with bands of iron.* **2** a loop or ring of material used for holding something together: *I put a rubber band around the bundle of letters.* **3** put a band on a bird. **4** a stripe: *a white cup with a gold band near the rim.* **5** mark with stripes. **6** in radio broadcasting, a particular range of wavelengths or frequencies. **7** anything that binds or restrains. **8 bands,** *pl.* two stripes hanging from the front of a collar in certain academic, clerical, or legal costume. 1, 2, 4, 6–8 *n.,* 3, 5 *v.*

**band·age** (ban′dij)   **1** a strip of some cloth or other material used in binding up and dressing a wound, injured leg, arm, etc.   **2** something like this used to support or protect when there is no injury: *Racehorses often have bandages on their legs.*   **3** bind, tie up, or dress with a bandage.   1, 2 *n.*, 3 *v.*, **band·aged, band·ag·ing.** —**band′ag·er**, *n.*

**band–aid** (ban′dād′)   **1** something quickly brought in or used as a temporary solution; stopgap: *The opposition leader dismissed the proposed tax cuts as nothing but economic band-aids.*   **2** serving as a stopgap; temporary or makeshift: *band-aid solutions.*   *n.*
☞ *Etym.* From the trademark *Band-Aid*, a small bandage for minor wounds, consisting of a thin gauze pad attached to the middle of a strip of adhesive tape.

**ban·dan·a** or **ban·dan·na** (ban dan′ə)   a large, coloured handkerchief worn round the head.   *n.*

**band·box** (band′boks′)   a light cardboard box to put hats, collars, etc. in.   *n.*

**ban·deau** (ban dō′ *or* ban′dō)   **1** a BAND² (def. 1) worn about the head.   **2** a narrow BAND² (def. 1).   *n., pl.* **ban·deaux** (-dōz′ *or* -dōz).

**ban·di·coot** (ban′də küt′)   **1** any of about 20 species of small grey or tan marsupial found in Australia and neighbouring islands, resembling kangaroos but belonging to a different family: *Bandicoots are active at night and sleep during the day.*   **2** BANDICOOT RAT.   *n.*

**bandicoot rat**   a large, burrowing, ratlike rodent found in India and Sri Lanka, having a body about 30 to 38 cm long and a very long tail, and having a short head and a broad muzzle: *The bandicoot rat, which lives in forests, cultivated land, and towns, destroys crops, grains, and poultry.*

**ban·dit** (ban′dit)   a highwayman or robber.   *n., pl.* **ban·dits** or **ban·di·ti** (-ē).

**ban·dit·ry** (ban′di trē)   **1** the work of BANDITS.   **2** BANDITS.   *n.*

**ban·dit·ti** (ban dit′ē)   a pl. of BANDIT.   *n.*

**band·mas·ter** (band′mas′tər)   the leader of a BAND¹ (def. 2) of musicians.   *n.*

**ban·do·lier** or **ban·do·leer** (ban′də lēr′)   **1** a broad belt worn over one shoulder and across the breast: *Some bandoliers have loops for carrying cartridges; others have small cases for bullets, gunpowder, etc.*   **2** one of these cases.   *n.*

**band shell**   a platform for musical concerts that has a shell-shaped rear wall extending up over the platform and serving as a sounding board.

**bands·man** (band′zmən)   a member of a BAND¹ (def. 2) of musicians.   *n., pl.* **bands·men** (-zmən).

**band·stand** (band′stand′)   an outdoor platform, usually roofed, for BAND¹ (def. 2) concerts: *There is a bandstand in the park.*   *n.*

**band·wag·on** (ban′dwag′ən)   a wagon that carries a musical band in a parade.   *n.*
**climb** or **get on the bandwagon,** *Informal.*   join what appears to be the winning side in a political campaign, contest, public issue, etc.

**ban·dy** (ban′dē)   **1** throw back and forth; toss about.   **2** give and take; exchange, especially in a non-serious way: *They spent all their time bandying statistics, without ever getting down to the real issues of the debate.*   **3** having a bend or curve outward: *Some kinds of bulldog have bandy legs.*   1, 2 *v.*, **ban·died, ban·dy·ing;**   3 *adj.*

hat, āge, fär; let, ēqual, tėrm; it, īce
hot, ōpen, ôrder; oil, out; cup, pùt, rüle
əbove, takən, pencəl, lemən, circəs
ch, child; ng, long; sh, ship
th, thin; ᴛʜ, then; zh, measure

**bandy about** or **around,**   talk about.

**ban·dy–leg·ged** (ban′dē leg′id *or* ban′dē legd′)   having legs that curve outward; BOWLEGGED.   *adj.*   Compare with KNOCK-KNEED.

**bane** (bān)   **1** a cause of death, ruin, or harm: *Wild animals were the bane of the mountain village.*   **2** destruction of any kind.   *n.*

**bane·ber·ry** (bān′ber′ē)   **1** any of several species of plant having spikes of small, white flowers and clusters of white or red poisonous berries.   **2** one of these berries.   *n., pl.* **bane·ber·ries.**

**bane·ful** (bān′fəl)   deadly; harmful.   *adj.*
—**bane′ful·ly,** *adv.*

**bang¹** (bang)   **1** a sudden, loud noise: *the bang of a gun.*   **2** make a sudden, loud noise: *The door banged as it blew shut in a sudden gust of wind.*   **3** a violent, noisy blow: *She gave the drum a bang.*   **4** hit with violent and noisy blows; strike noisily: *The baby was banging the pan with a spoon.*   **5** *Informal.*   violently and noisily: *The boy on the bicycle went bang into a telephone pole.*   **6** shut with a noise; slam: *to bang a door.*   **7** handle roughly; damage: *My trunk was banged in the accident.*   **8** an imitation of gunfire: *"Bang! Bang!" shouted the children.*   1, 3 *n.*, 2, 4, 6, 7 *v.*, 5 *adv.*, 8 *interj.*

**bang²** (bang)   **1** Usually, **bangs,** *pl.*   a fringe of hair cut short and worn over the forehead: *She has long hair with bangs.*   **2** cut hair in this way.   1 *n.*, 2 *v.*

**Ban·gla·desh·i** (bang′glə desh′ē *or* bang′glə desh′i)   **1** of or having to do with Bangladesh or its people.   **2** a native or inhabitant of Bangladesh.   1 *adj.*, 2 *n.*

**ban·gle** (bang′gəl)   **1** a bracelet worn around the wrist, arm, or ankle.   **2** a small ornament suspended from a bracelet.   *n.*

**ban·ian** (ban′yən)   See BANYAN.   *n.*

**ban·ish** (ban′ish)   **1** condemn to leave a country; exile: *Napoleon was banished to Elba.*   **2** force to go away; send away; drive away: *Banish the thought of hiking on such a warm day.*   *v.*   —**ban′ish·er,** *n.*

**ban·ish·ment** (ban′i shmənt)   **1** BANISHing.   **2** being BANISHed; exile.   *n.*

**ban·is·ter** (ban′i stər)   **1** BALUSTER.   **2 banisters,** *pl.* the BALUSTRADE of a staircase.   *n.*

A banjo

**ban·jo** (ban′jō)   a stringed musical instrument played with the fingers or a PLECTRUM: *Banjos have either four or five strings.*   *n., pl.* **ban·jos** or **ban·joes.**

**ban·jo·ist** (ban′jō ist)   a person who plays the BANJO, especially a skilled player.   *n.*

**bank**[1] (bangk)   **1** a long pile or heap: *a bank of snow.*   **2** raise a ridge or mound about; border with a bank or ridge.   **3** form into a bank; pile up; heap up: *to bank snow.*   **4** form banks: *Clouds are banking along the horizon.*   **5** the ground bordering a river, lake, etc.   **6** a shallow place in a body of water; shoal: *the fishing banks of Newfoundland.*   **7** slope.   **8** the tilting of an airplane to one side when making a turn.   **9** make an airplane tilt when making a turn: *The pilot banked the plane as she turned toward the landing strip.*   **10** of an airplane, tilt to one side when turning: *The plane banked sharply.*   **11** lessen the draft and cover a fire with ashes or fresh fuel so that it will burn slowly: *to bank a fire for the night.*   1, 5–8 *n.*, 2–4, 7, 9–11 *v.*

**bank**[2] (bangk)   **1** an institution for keeping, lending, exchanging, and paying out money.   **2** operate or manage a bank.   **3** keep money in a bank: *He banks at the branch near his office.*   **4** put money in a bank: *She banked most of the money she earned cutting lawns.*   **5** a small metal, china, or plastic container used to save small sums at home: *a piggy bank.*   **6** in games, a stock of pieces from which players draw.   **7** any place where reserve supplies are kept: *Blood plasma for transfusions is kept in a blood bank.*   **8** in gambling games, the fund out of which the dealer or manager pays his or her losses.   1, 5–8 *n.*, 2–4 *v.* —**bank′a·ble**, *adj.*
**bank on**, *Informal.*   depend on; be sure of.

**bank**[3] (bangk)   **1** a row or close arrangement of things: *a bank of switches, a bank of machines.*   **2** arrange in rows.   **3** a bench for rowers in a galley.   **4** a row or tier of oars.   **5** a row of keys on an organ, typewriter, etc.   1, 3–5 *n.*, 2 *v.*

**bank account**   **1** an arrangement for depositing one's money in a bank for safekeeping until it is needed, involving a record of deposits and withdrawals: *to open a bank account.*   **2** the sum of money kept by a bank for a person or company: *My bank account is very low right now.*

**bank barn**   *Cdn.*   a two-storey barn built into a hill so as to permit entry to the bottom level from one side and to the top level from the other side: *There are many bank barns in Ontario.*

**bank·er**[1] (bang′kər)   **1** a person or company that manages a bank.   **2** the dealer or manager in a gambling game.   *n.*

**bank·er**[2] (bang′kər) *Cdn.*   **1** a fisherman who fishes off the Grand Banks.   **2** a fishing vessel that operates off the Grand Banks.   *n.*

**bank·ing** (bang′king)   **1** the business of operating a BANK[2] (def. 1).   **2** ppr. of BANK.   1 *n.*, 2 *v.*

**bank note**   **1** a piece of paper currency: *In Canada, all bank notes are issued by the Bank of Canada and serve as the currency of this country.*   **2** formerly, a note issued by a bank, that could be redeemed at any time for a specified amount of money, gold, etc.

**Bank of Canada**   the agent of the Government of Canada that issues all Canadian bank notes and carries out monetary policy on behalf of the government.

**bank·rupt** (bang′krupt)   **1** a person declared by a law court to be unable to pay his or her debts: *A bankrupt's property is distributed among his or her creditors.*   **2** unable to pay one's debts; declared legally unable to pay debts.   **3** make bankrupt.   **4** at the end of one's resources; destitute.   1 *n.*, 2, 4 *adj.*, 3 *v.*

**bank·rupt·cy** (bang′krupt sē *or* bang′krəp sē)   a BANKRUPT (def. 2) condition.   *n.*, *pl.* **bank·rupt·cies.**

**ban·ner** (ban′ər)   **1** flag.   **2** a piece of cloth with some design or words on it, attached by its upper edge to a pole or staff.   **3** leading or outstanding; foremost: *Ours is the banner class.*   *n.*

**ban·nock** (ban′ək)   **1** a flat cake, usually unLEAVENed, made of oatmeal or barley flour.   **2** *Cdn.*   a flat, round cake made of flour, salt, water, and, sometimes, baking powder.   *n.*

**banns** (banz)   a public notice, given three times in a Christian church, that a man and a woman are to be married.   *n.pl.*

**ban·quet** (bang′kwit)   **1** feast.   **2** a formal dinner with speeches.   **3** entertain with a banquet: *The visiting celebrity was banqueted by the city.*   **4** take part in a banquet.   1, 2 *n.*, 3, 4 *v.*, **ban·quet·ed, ban·quet·ing.**

**ban·shee** (ban′shē *or* ban shē′)   a spirit whose wails are supposed to mean that there will soon be a death in the family.   *n.*

**ban·tam** (ban′təm)   **1** a very small person, usually one fond of fighting.   **2** small and light.   **3** in sports, a class for players under 15 years: *a bantam hockey league.*   **4** Often, **Bantam**,   any of a number of breeds of dwarf ornamental fowl, raised mainly as a hobby because of the striking colours and arrangement of their feathers: *Bantams usually weigh only about 680 g.*   1, 3, 4 *n.*, 2 *adj.*

**ban·tam·weight** (ban′təm wāt′)   in international and Olympic boxing, a boxer who weighs at least 51 kg and not more than 54 kg.   *n.*

**ban·ter** (ban′tər)   **1** playful teasing; joking: *She didn't mind her friends' banter about her freckles.*   **2** tease or make fun of playfully.   **3** talk in a joking way.   1 *n.*, 2, 3 *v.* —**ban′ter·ing·ly,** *adv.*

**ban·yan** (ban′yən)   a species of tree of India and the East Indies, closely related to the fig tree but having inedible fruit, whose branches have hanging roots that grow down to the ground and start new trunks: *One banyan tree may cover several hectares of ground.*   *n.*   Also, **banian.**

**ba·o·bab** (bā′ō bab′)   a tall, tropical African tree having a very thick trunk, sometimes up to 15 m in diameter: *The fibres of baobab bark are used for making rope, cloth, etc.*   *n.*

**bap·tism** (bap′tiz əm)   **1** the act of baptizing; rite or sacrament of dipping a person into water or sprinkling water on him or her, as a sign of the washing away of sin and of admission into the Christian church.   **2** an experience that cleanses a person or introduces him or her into a new kind of life.   *n.*

**bap·tis·mal** (bap tiz′məl)   having to do with BAPTISM; used in baptism: *a baptismal font, baptismal vows.*   *adj.*

**baptism of fire**   **1** the first time that a soldier is under fire.   **2** a severe trial or test; ordeal.

**bap·tize** (bap tīz′ *or* bap′tīz)   **1** dip into water or sprinkle with water as a sign of the washing away of sin and of admission into the Christian church.   **2** purify or cleanse.   **3** give a first name to a person at BAPTISM; CHRISTEN (def. 1).   **4** give a name to.   *v.*, **bap·tized, bap·tiz·ing.**   —**bap′tiz′er**, *n.*

**bar**[1] (bär)   **1** an evenly shaped piece of some solid, longer than it is wide or thick: *a bar of iron, a bar of soap, a bar of chocolate.*   **2** a pole or rod put across a door, gate, window, etc. to fasten or shut off something.   **3** put bars across; fasten or shut off with a bar: *He bars the door every night.*   **4** anything that blocks the way or prevents progress: *A bar of sand kept boats out of the harbour. A bad temper can be a bar to making friends.*   **5** block or obstruct: *The exits were barred by chairs.*   **6** exclude; forbid: *All talking is barred during a study period.*   **7** except; excluding: *She is the best student, bar none.*   **8** a band of colour; stripe.   **9** mark with stripes or bands of colour: *a chicken with barred feathers.*   **10** in music, a unit of rhythm; measure: *The regular accent falls on the first note of each bar.*   **11** the vertical line between two such units on a musical staff.   **12** a counter where drinks and, sometimes, food are served.   **13** the room or establishment containing such a counter.   **14** a store counter over which certain articles are sold: *a snack bar, a record bar, a hat bar.*   **15** the railing around the place where lawyers sit in a law court.   **16 the bar,   a** the profession of a lawyer: *After passing his law examinations, the young man was called to the bar.*   **b** lawyers as a group: *Judges are chosen from the bar.*   **17** the place where an accused person stands in a law court.   **18** a law court.   **19** anything like a law court: *the bar of public opinion.*   **20** formerly, the mouth of a harbour.   1, 2, 4, 8, 10–20 *n.*, 3, 5, 6, 9 *v.*, **barred, bar·ring;**   7 *prep.*

**bar**[2] (bär)   a unit for measuring pressure, equivalent to 100 KILOPASCALS.   Symbol: bar   *n.*

**barb** (bärb)   **1** a point projecting backward from the main point.   **2** one of the hairlike branches on the shaft of a feather.   **3** a long, thin growth hanging from the mouth: *the barbs of a catfish.*   **4** equip with a barb; furnish with barbs.   1–3 *n.*, 4 *v.*

**Bar·ba·di·an** (bär bā′dē ən)   **1** of or having to do with Barbados, an island in the West Indies, or its people.   **2** a native or inhabitant of Barbados.   1 *adj.*, 2 *n.*

**bar·bar·i·an** (bär ber′ē ən)   **1** a person belonging to a people or to a tribe thought to be uncivilized.   **2** of or like a barbarian; not civilized; cruel and coarse.   **3** a foreigner differing from the speaker or writer in language and customs: *In ancient times a barbarian was successively a person who was not a Greek, a person outside of the Roman Empire, or a person who was not a Christian.*   **4** differing from the speaker or writer in language and customs.   **5** a person without sympathy for literary culture or art; boor.   1, 3, 5 *n.*, 2, 4 *adj.*
☛ *Etym.*   From Gk. *barbaros* through French and Latin. *Barbaros* meant 'foreign' or 'rude', and probably originally referred to the unintelligible sounds of a foreign language. The related words BARBARIC, BARBARISM, and BARBAROUS also come from Gk. through French or Latin. BARBARITY and BARBARIZE were probably formed in English. See also note at BARBARY.

**bar·bar·ic** (bär bar′ik *or* bär ber′ik)   **1** like BARBARIANS; suited to a barbarous people; rough and rude.   **2** crudely rich or splendid: *The explorers were awed by the barbaric splendour of the ancient city.*   *adj.*
☛ *Etym.*   See note at BARBARIAN.

**bar·bar·ism** (bär′bə riz′əm)   **1** the condition of uncivilized people: *People who have no form of writing live in barbarism.*   **2** a BARBAROUS act, custom, or trait.   **3** the use of a word or expression not in accepted use.   **4** a word or expression not in accepted use. *Example:* his'n for his.   *n.*
☛ *Etym.*   See note at BARBARIAN.

**bar·bar·i·ty** (bär bar′ə tē *or* bär ber′ə tē)   **1** brutal cruelty.   **2** an act of cruelty.   **3** a BARBARIC manner, taste, or style.   *n., pl.* **bar·bar·i·ties.**
☛ *Etym.*   See note at BARBARIAN.

**bar·bar·ize** (bär′bə rīz′)   make or become BARBAROUS. *v.*, **bar·ba·rized, bar·ba·riz·ing.**
☛ *Etym.*   See note at BARBARIAN.

**bar·bar·ous** (bär′bə rəs)   **1** not civilized; primitive in culture and customs.   **2** rough and rude; coarse; unrefined.   **3** cruelly harsh; brutal: *They spoke out against the barbarous treatment of prisoners.*   *adj.*
—**bar′ba·rous·ly**, *adv.*   —**bar′ba·rous·ness**, *n.*
☛ *Etym.*   See note at BARBARIAN.

**Bar·ba·ry** (bär′bə rē)   northern Africa west of Egypt.   *n.*
☛ *Etym.*   Named for the **Berbers,** the main non-Arabic inhabitants of the area. **Berber** is the ancient Arabic name for these people, but it is uncertain whether it is a native Arabic word meaning 'foreigner', or whether it is related ultimately to Gk. *barbaros* 'foreign'. See also note at BARBARIAN.

**Barbary ape**   a tail-less monkey of northern Africa and the Rock of Gibraltar.

**bar·be·cue** (bär′bə kyü′)   **1** a grill or open fireplace for cooking meat, usually over charcoal.   **2** an outdoor meal prepared on a barbecue.   **3** meat roasted over an open fire.   **4** roast meat over an open fire.   **5** cook meat or fish in a highly flavoured sauce.   **6** a feast at which animals are roasted whole.   **7** an animal roasted whole.   **8** roast an animal whole.   1–3, 6, 7 *n.*, 4, 5, 8 *v.*, **bar·be·cued, bar·be·cu·ing.**
☛ *Etym.*   In the 17c. from Spanish *barbacoa*, originally from Haitian *barbacoa* 'framework of sticks'.

**barbed** (bärbd)   **1** having a BARB or barbs.   **2** harsh; having a sting: *a barbed remark.*   **3** pt. and pp. of BARB.   1, 2 *adj.*, 3 *v.*

**barbed wire** twisted wire having sharp points on it at short intervals, used for fences, etc.

**bar·bel** (bär′bəl) 1 a long, thin growth hanging from the mouths of some fish. 2 any of several species of large freshwater fish of Europe having such growths. *n.*

**bar·bell** (bär′bel′) a device for performing lifting exercises, similar to a DUMB-BELL but having a longer bar and provision for weights at each end. *n.*

**bar·ber** (bär′bər) 1 a person whose business is cutting hair and shaving or trimming beards. 2 cut the hair of; shave; trim the beard of. 1 *n.*, 2 *v.*

**bar·ber·ry** (bär′ber′ē) 1 any of a closely related group of spiny shrubs having yellow flowers and sour, oblong, red berries. 2 the berry of a barberry. 3 referring to a family of mostly spiny shrubs or herbs found mainly in north temperate regions: *The May apple and the barberries belong to the barberry family.* *n., pl.* **bar·ber·ries.**

**bar·bi·can** (bär′bə kən) a tower for defence, built over a gate or bridge to a city or castle. See CASTLE for picture. *n.*

**bar·bi·tu·rate** (bär bich′ə rāt′, bär′bə tyü′rāt, *or* bär′bə tü′rāt) 1 a salt or ester of BARBITURIC ACID. 2 any of several drugs derived from BARBITURIC ACID, used as sedatives or hypnotics. *n.*

**bar·bi·tu·ric acid** (bär′bə tyü′rik *or* bär′bə tü′rik) an acid much used as the basis of sedatives and hypnotics.

**barb·wire** (bärb′wīr′) BARBED WIRE. *n.*

**bar·ca·role** or **bar·ca·rolle** (bär′kə rōl′) 1 a Venetian boat song. 2 any music imitating the style of a barcarole. *n.*

**bar code** a set of lines printed on a package, so that a computer can read the price. Bar codes can also be used on mail.

**bard** (bärd) 1 a poet and singer of long ago: *Bards sang their own poems to the music of their harps.* 2 poet. *n.*
☞ *Hom.* BARRED.

**Bard of Avon** Shakespeare, so called because he came from Stratford-on-Avon.

**bare** (ber) 1 without covering; not clothed; naked: *bare feet. Trees grew part way up the hill, but the top was bare.* 2 not concealed or disguised; open: *the bare truth.* 3 make bare; uncover; reveal: *to bare one's feelings. The dog bared its teeth.* 4 not furnished; empty: *The room was bare.* 5 plain; unadorned: *He told us just the bare facts.* 6 much worn; THREADBARE (def. 1). 7 just enough and no more; mere: *She earns a bare living by her work.* 1, 2, 4–7 *adj.*, **bar·er, bar·est;** 3 *v.*, **bared, bar·ing.** —**bare′ness,** *n.*
**lay bare,** uncover; expose; reveal: *to lay bare a plot.*
**with one's bare hands,** unaided by tools.
☞ *Hom.* BEAR.

**bare·back** (ber′bak′) 1 without a saddle: *to ride bareback.* 2 on the bare back of a horse, etc.: *a bareback rider.* 1 *adv.*, 2 *adj.*

**bare·faced** (ber′fāst′) 1 with the face bare. 2 not disguised. 3 shameless or impudent: *a barefaced lie.* *adj.*

**bare·foot** (ber′fùt′) 1 without shoes and stockings: *a barefoot child.* 2 with bare feet: *If you go barefoot, watch out for broken glass.* 1 *adj.*, 2 *adv.*

**bare·foot·ed** (ber′fùt′id) BAREFOOT. *adj., adv.*

**bare·hand·ed** (ber′han′did) 1 without any covering on the hands. 2 with empty hands. *adj., adv.*

**bare·head·ed** (ber′hed′id) wearing nothing on the head. *adj., adv.*

**bare·leg·ged** (ber′leg′id *or* ber′legd′) without stockings. *adj., adv.*

**bare·ly** (ber′lē) 1 only just; hardly; scarcely: *He has barely enough money to live on.* 2 poorly or scantily: *The room was furnished barely but neatly.* *adv.*

**bar·gain** (bär′gən) 1 an agreement to trade or exchange: *If you will take $10 for your book, it's a bargain.* 2 something offered for sale cheap, or bought cheap. 3 a good trade or exchange; price below the real value. 4 try to get good terms: *She stood for ten minutes bargaining with the man for the vegetables.* 5 make a bargain; come to terms. 6 trade. 1–3 *n.*, 4–6 *v.* —**bar′gain·er,** *n.*
**bargain for,** be ready for; expect: *The rain wasn't so bad, but the hail was more than we bargained for.*
**bargain on,** depend on; be sure of.
**into the bargain,** besides; also: *It's late and I'm tired into the bargain.*
**strike a bargain,** make a bargain; reach an agreement.

**barge** (bärj) 1 a large, flat-bottomed boat for carrying freight on rivers, canals, etc.: *a grain barge.* 2 carry by barge. 3 a large boat furnished and decorated for use in excursions, pageants, and other special occasions. 4 move heavily or clumsily like a barge. 5 push oneself rudely or abruptly: *Everyone turned as she barged into the room.* 6 a large motorboat or rowboat used by the commanding officer of a flagship. 1, 3, 6 *n.*, 2, 4, 5 *v.*, **barged, barg·ing.**
**barge in,** intrude: *He's forever barging in where he's not wanted.*

**barge·man** (bärj′mən) a man who works on a barge. *n., pl.* **barge·men** (-mən).

**barge·wom·an** (bärj′wùm′ən) a woman who works on a barge: *The bargewoman threw Toad into the river.* *n., pl.* **barge·wom·en** (-wim′ən).

**bar graph** a chart or diagram showing the relationship between different amounts by means of bars of different lengths: *The length of each bar in a bar graph is in proportion to the amount it represents.*

**bar·i·tone** (bar′ə tōn′ *or* ber′ə tōn′) 1 an adult male singing voice having an intermediate range between tenor and bass. 2 a singer who has such a voice. 3 a musical instrument having a low or medium-low range, especially one of a family or group of instruments. 4 having to do with, having the range of, or designed for a baritone. 5 a low-pitched male speaking voice. 1–3, 5 *n.*, 4 *adj.*

**bar·i·um** (bar′ē əm *or* ber′ē əm) a soft, silvery-white metallic element. Symbol: Ba *n.*

**bark¹** (bärk) 1 the tough outer covering of the stems and roots of woody plants, including an outside layer of dead cells, a CORTEX (def. 1), which in twigs and small branches contains chlorophyll, and an inner layer, the PHLOEM, containing the tubes which carry food along the stem or root. 2 a particular kind of bark prepared for use in tanning, as a medicine, etc. 3 strip bark from; especially, cut out a ring of bark around a tree to kill it by interrupting the flow of food. 4 treat or tan with bark. 5 scrape the skin from shins, knuckles, etc.: *I fell down the steps and barked my shins.* 1, 2 *n.*, 3–5 *v.*
☞ *Hom.* BARQUE.

**bark²** (bärk)  **1** the short, sharp sound that a dog makes.  **2** a sound like this: *The bark of a fox, a gun, or a cough.*  **3** make this sound or one like it.  **4** speak sharply or gruffly: *The officer barked out the order.*  **5** *Informal.* cough.  1, 2 *n.*, 3–5 *v.*
**bark up the wrong tree,** have the wrong idea completely.
☛ *Hom.* BARQUE.

**bark³** (bärk)  See BARQUE.  *n.*

**bar·keep** (bär′kēp′)  BARKEEPER.  *n.*

**bar·keep·er** (bär′kē′pər)  a person who tends a BAR¹ (def. 13) where alcoholic drinks are sold.  *n.*

**bar·ken·tine** (bär′kən tēn′)  a three-masted ship with the foremast square-rigged and the other masts fore-and-aft rigged.  *n.* Also, **barquentine.**

**bark·er** (bär′kər)  **1** one that barks.  **2** a person who stands in front of a store, show, etc. urging people to go in.  *n.*

**bar·ley** (bär′lē)  **1** the seed or grain of a cereal grass that has compact spikes of flowers: *Barley is used for food and for making malt.*  **2** the plant yielding this grain.  *n.*

**bar magnet**  a permanent magnet shaped like a bar or rod: *A bar magnet suspended from a string can serve as a compass.*

**bar·maid** (bär′mād′)  a woman who works in a BAR¹ (def. 13), serving alcoholic drinks to customers.  *n.*

**bar·man** (bär′mən)  BARKEEPER.  *n., pl.* **bar·men** (-mən).

**Bar·me·cide feast** (bär′mə sīd′)  **1** a pretended feast with empty dishes.  **2** an empty pretence of hospitality, generosity, etc.
☛ *Etym.* From *Barmecide*, a wealthy man in the *Arabian Nights* who gave a beggar a pretended feast on empty dishes.

**bar mitz·vah** (bär mit′svə)  **1** a ceremony marking the formal admission of a boy into the Jewish religious community, usually held when the boy is thirteen years old.  **2** a boy who has reached the age of thirteen, the age of religious responsibility.  Compare with BAT MITZVAH.  *pl.* **bar mitsvahs** or **mitsvoth** (-vōŦH).
☛ *Etym.* From Hebrew *bar mitsvah* 'son of the divine law'.

**barn** (bärn)  a building for storing hay, grain, and farm machinery and for sheltering farm animals.  *n.*
—**barn′like′,** *adj.*

**bar·na·cle** (bär′nə kəl)  any of a large group of marine crustaceans that spend their entire adult life attached to some underwater object like a rock, ship bottom, or wharf pile, or a sea creature like a turtle or whale: *In the first two of the three stages of a barnacle's life, it has no shell and can swim about freely.*  *n.*

**bar·na·cled** (bär′nə kəld)  covered with BARNACLES.  *adj.*

**barn dance**  **1** a dance held in a barn.  **2** a lively dance resembling a polka.

**barn·storm** (bärn′stôrm′)  *Informal.*  **1** act plays, make speeches, etc. in small towns and country districts.  **2** tour country districts giving short airplane rides, exhibitions of stunt flying, etc.  *v.* —**barn′storm′er,** *n.*

hat, āge, fär; let, ēqual, tėrm; it, īce
hot, ōpen, ôrder; oil, out; cup, pút, rüle
ə*bove, tak*ə*n, penc*ə*l, lem*ə*n, circ*ə*s*
ch, child; ng, long; sh, ship
th, thin; ŦH, then; zh, measure

Barn swallows—about 18 cm long including the tail.

**barn swallow**  a species of swallow found throughout the world, having a dark steel-blue back and reddish-brown throat and breast, and a deeply forked tail: *Barn swallows often nest in crevices of buildings.*

**barn·yard** (bärn′yärd′)  a yard, often fenced, adjoining a barn and used for livestock.  *n.*

**bar·o·graph** (bar′ə graf′ *or* ber′ə graf′)  a barometer that automatically records pressure changes on a revolving drum.  *n.*

An aneroid barometer. A flexible box in this instrument expands or contracts with changes in air pressure and moves one of the pointers. The other pointer is set by hand and remains fixed, acting as a guide to how much the first pointer moves.

**bar·om·e·ter** (bə rom′ə tər)  **1** an instrument for measuring atmospheric pressure: *Barometers are used to indicate probable changes in the weather and for determining the height above sea level.*  **2** something that indicates changes: *Newspapers are often called barometers of public opinion.*  *n.*

**bar·o·met·ric** (bar′ə met′rik *or* ber′ə met′rik)  **1** of a BAROMETER (def. 1).  **2** indicated by a BAROMETER (def. 1).  *adj.*

**bar·on** (bar′ən *or* ber′ən)  **1** a nobleman of the lowest hereditary rank: *In the United Kingdom, a baron has "Lord" before his name, instead of "Baron" as is the case in other European countries.*  **2** during the Middle Ages, an English nobleman who held his lands directly from the king.  **3** a powerful merchant or financier.  *n.*
☛ *Hom.* BARREN.

**bar·on·ess** (bar′ə nis *or* ber′ə nis)  **1** the wife or widow of a BARON: *A baroness has "Lady" before her name.*  **2** a lady whose rank is equal to that of a BARON.  *n.*

**bar·on·et** (bar′ə nit *or* ber′ə nit, bar′ə net′ *or* ber′ə net′) in the United Kingdom, a man below a BARON in rank and next above a knight: *A baronet has "Sir" before his name and "Bart." after it, as in Sir John Brown, Bart.*  *n.*

**ba·ro·ni·al** (bə rō′nē əl)   1 of a BARON; of barons.
2 suitable for a BARON; splendid; stately.   *adj.*

**bar·o·ny** (bar′ə nē *or* ber′ə nē)   1 the lands of a BARON.   2 the rank or title of a BARON.   *n., pl.* **bar·o·nies.**

**ba·roque** (bə rōk′ *or* bə rok′)   1 of or having to do with a style of art, architecture, poetry, or music that flourished in Europe, especially in the 17th century, and was characterized by rich and elaborate ornamentation.
2 ornate or fantastic in style.   3 the baroque style.
4 irregular in shape: *baroque pearls.*   1, 2, 4 *adj.*; 3 *n.*

A barque of the late 19th century

**barque** *or* **bark** (bärk)   1 *Poetic.* any boat or ship.
2 a sailing ship with three masts, square-rigged on the first two masts and fore-and-aft rigged on the other.   *n.*
☞ *Hom.* BARK.

**bar·quen·tine** (bär′kən tēn′)   See BARKENTINE.   *n.*

**bar·rack** (bar′ək *or* ber′ak)   BARRACKS.   *n.*

**bar·racks** (bar′əks *or* ber′əks)   1 a building or group of buildings for members of the armed forces to live in.   2 a building housing local detachments of the Royal Canadian Mounted Police.   3 *Informal.* a training centre of the Royal Canadian Mounted Police: *My brother is training at the RCMP barracks in Regina.*   *n. pl.*
☞ *Usage.* **Barracks** may be used with either a singular or a plural verb: *John wrote that his barracks was a lively place. The barracks were inspected daily.*

**bar·ra·cu·da** (bar′ə kü′də *or* ber′ə kü′də)   any of several closely related species of pikelike fish found in warm seas, having long, pointed jaws with razor-sharp teeth, and ranging in length from about 90 cm to about 120 cm: *Because a barracuda will pursue anything that moves in the water, it is considered by some to be more dangerous than a shark.*   *n., pl.* **bar·ra·cu·da** *or* **bar·ra·cu·das.**

**bar·rage** (bə räzh′ *for* 1–3; bä′rij *for* 4)   1 a barrier of artillery fire to check the enemy or to protect one's own soldiers in advancing or retreating.   2 fire at with artillery; subject to a barrage.   3 a heavy, continuous attack, with words, punches, etc.: *The lawyer met a barrage of questions from reporters as she stepped out of the courtroom.*   4 an artificial barrier in a river; dam.   1, 3, 4 *n.*, 2 *v.*, **bar·raged, bar·rag·ing.**

**bar·ra·try** (bar′ə trē *or* ber′ə trē)   1 fraud or gross negligence of a ship's officer or seaman against owners, insurers, etc.   2 the act of stirring up lawsuits or quarrels.   *n.*

**barred** (bärd)   1 having bars: *a barred window.*
2 marked with stripes: *hens with barred feathers.*   3 pt. and pp. of BAR.   1, 2 *adj.*, 3 *v.*
☞ *Hom.* BARD.

**barred owl**   a fairly large owl with a round head, no ear tufts, and coloured brown and white. Its breast is striped or barred.

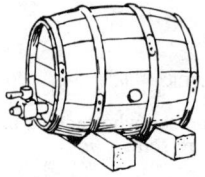

A barrel used for holding liquor

**bar·rel** (bar′əl *or* ber′əl)   1 a large container shaped somewhat like a cylinder, having a flat, round top and bottom and slightly bulging sides, usually made of wide boards held together by hoops.   2 the amount that a barrel can hold.   3 any container, case, or part shaped like a barrel: *the barrel of a drum.*   4 the metal tube of a firearm, through which the bullet travels.   5 any similar tube, such as that in a microscope.   6 put in a barrel.
7 *Informal.* a large quantity or number: *a barrel of fun.*
8 *Informal.* move rapidly: *The children barrelled down the hill. A storm came barrelling in.*   1–5, 7, *n.*, 6, 8 *v.*, **bar·relled** *or* **bar·reled, bar·rel·ling** *or* **bar·rel·ing.**
☞ *Hom.* BERYL (for the second pronunciation of **barrel**).

**barrel organ**   a hand organ.

**bar·ren** (bar′ən *or* ber′ən)   1 not producing anything: *a barren desert.*   2 not able to bear offspring: *Exposure to radio-activity may make animals and plants barren.*
3 **barrens,** *pl. Cdn.* a barren stretch of land; wasteland.
4 **Barrens,** *pl. Cdn.* the BARREN GROUND.   5 without interest; not attractive; dull.   6 fruitless; unprofitable: *a barren attempt to make money.*   1, 2, 5, 6 *adj.*, 3, 4 *n.*
—**bar′ren·ness,** *n.*
☞ *Hom.* BARON.

**Barren Ground**   *Cdn.* the treeless, thinly populated region in northern Canada, lying between Hudson Bay on the east and Great Slave Lake and Great Bear Lake on the west: *Much of the Barren Ground is covered, in season, with short grass, moss, and small flowering plants.*

**Barren Lands**   *Cdn.* the BARREN GROUND.

**bar·rette** (bə ret′)   a small clasp used by women and girls for holding the hair in place.   *n.*

**bar·ri·cade** (bar′ə käd′ *or* ber′ə käd′, bar′ə käd′ *or* ber′ə käd′)   1 a rough, hastily made barrier for defence: *The soldiers cut trees down to make a barricade across the road.*   2 any barrier or obstruction.   3 block or obstruct with a barricade: *The soldiers barricaded the road with fallen trees.*   1, 2 *n.*, 3 *v.*, **bar·ri·cad·ed, bar·ri·cad·ing.**

**bar·ri·er** (bar′ē ər *or* ber′ē ər)   1 something that stands in the way: *A dam is a barrier holding water back.*
2 something stopping progress or preventing approach: *Lack of water was a barrier to the settlement of that region.*
3 something that separates or keeps apart: *The Atlantic Ocean is a barrier between the British Isles and Canada.*   *n.*

**barrier reef**   a long line of rocks or coral reef not far from the mainland.

**bar·ring** (bä′ring)   1 except; not including: *Barring accidents, the train will arrive at twelve.*   2 ppr. of BAR.
1 *prep.*, 2 *v.*

**bar·ris·ter** (bar′i stər *or* ber′i stər)   1 lawyer.   2 in England, a lawyer who can plead in any court.   *n.*

**bar·room** (bär′rüm′) a room with a BAR¹ (def. 12) for the sale of alcoholic drinks. *n.*

**bar·row¹** (bar′ō *or* ber′ō) **1** a frame with two short handles at each end, used for carrying a load. **2** WHEELBARROW. **3** HANDCART. *n.*

**bar·row²** (bar′ō *or* ber′ō) a mound of earth or stones over an ancient grave. *n.*

**bar sinister** a narrow diagonal band on a coat of arms, indicating illegitimacy and going from the top left corner (from the bearer's point of view) to the bottom right. ☞ *Etym.* See note at SINISTER.

**Bart.** Baronet.

**bar·tend·er** (bär′ten′dər) a person who serves or mixes alcoholic drinks for customers at a BAR¹ (def. 12). *n.*

**bar·ter** (bär′tər) **1** trade by exchanging one kind of goods or services for other goods or services without using money. **2** exchange: *She bartered her boat for a car.* **3** the act of bartering. **4** something bartered. 1, 2 *v.*, 3, 4 *n.*
**barter away,** give or trade without an equal return: *In his eagerness to make a fortune, he bartered away his freedom.*

**bar·ti·zan** (bär′tə zən) a small overhanging turret on a wall or tower. *n.*

**bas·al** (bā′səl) **1** of the base; at the base; forming the base. **2** fundamental; basic. *adj.*

**basal metabolism** the amount of energy used by an animal or plant at rest: *The basal metabolism for an average man 30 years old is between 1400 and 1500 calories per day.*

**bas·alt** (bas′olt, bə solt′, *or* bā′solt) a hard, dark-coloured rock of volcanic origin. *n.*

**ba·sal·tic** (bə sol′tik) of or like BASALT. *adj.*

**bas·cule** (bas′kyül) a device that works like a SEESAW. In a **bascule bridge** the rising part pivots on a horizontal shaft at the shore end and is counterbalanced by a weight. See BRIDGE¹ for picture. *n.*

**base¹** (bās) **1** the part of a thing on which it rests; bottom: *The machine rests on a massive base of steel.* **2** make or form a base or foundation for. **3** a basis or foundation; fundamental principle. **4** the most important element of anything; essential part: *This dog food has a meat base.* **5** the part of an animal or plant organ nearest its point of attachment; the point of attachment: *The base of a leaf is the part that joins it to the stem.* **6** in chemistry, a compound that reacts with an acid to form a salt: *Calcium hydroxide is a base.* **7** in certain games, such as baseball, a station or goal: *The player slid into third base.* **8** a starting place; *The base for our hiking trip was a campground beside a brook.* **9** in war, a place from which a military force operates and obtains supplies; headquarters. **10** a permanent camp or other place where units of the armed forces are stationed: *There is a large base at Gagetown, New Brunswick.* **11** the line or surface forming that part of a geometrical figure on which it is supposed to stand: *Any side of a triangle can be its base.* **12** in arithmetic, the number that is the starting point for a numbering system: *The base of the decimal system is ten.* 1, 3–12 *n.*, 2 *v.*, **based, bas·ing.**
**base on,** found on: *Her large business was based on good service.*

---

**barroom** 93 **bashful**

hat, āge, fär; let, ēqual, tėrm; it, īce
hot, ōpen, ôrder; oil, out; cup, pût, rüle
əbove, takən, pencəl, lemən, circəs
ch, child; ng, long; sh, ship
th, thin; ŦH, then; zh, measure

**get to first base,** make the first step successfully: *I worked on the problem for an hour, but couldn't even get to first base.*
**off base,** *Informal.* incorrect; absurdly mistaken: *I think your answer was off base.*
☞ *Hom.* BASS¹.

**base²** (bās) **1** morally low; mean; selfish; cowardly: *To betray a friend for a reward is a base action.* **2** fit for an inferior person or thing; menial; unworthy: *No needful service is to be regarded as base.* **3** having little comparative value; inferior: *Iron and lead are base metals; gold and silver are precious metals.* **4** debased; counterfeit: *base coin. adj.*, **bas·er, bas·est.**
☞ *Hom.* BASS¹.

**base·ball** (bās′bol′) **1** a game played with bat and ball by two teams of nine players each, on a field with four bases. **2** the ball used in this game. *n.*

**base·board** (bās′bôrd′) **1** a line of boards around the walls of a room, next to the floor. **2** a board forming the base of anything. *n.*

**base·born** (bās′bôrn′) **1** born of slaves, peasants, or other humble parents. **2** born of a mother who was not married; illegitimate. *adj.*

**base hit** a successful hitting of the baseball by a batter so that he or she gets at least to first base without the help of an error.

**base·less** (bās′slis) groundless; without foundation: *a baseless rumour. adj.* —**base′less·ness,** *n.*

**base line 1** a line used as a base. **2** a line between bases. **3** Often, **baseline,** a base standard of value against which things are measured or compared: *the artistic baseline of the cinema.*

**base·ly** (bās′slē) as a low, mean, or unworthy person would do. *adv.*

**base·man** (bās′smən) in baseball, a player guarding one of the BASES¹ (def. 7). *n., pl.* **base·men** (-smən).

**base·ment** (bās′smənt) the lowest storey of a building, partly or completely below ground. *n.*

**base metal** any of the non-precious metals, such as lead, zinc, iron, etc.

**base·ness** (bās′snis) low, mean, or unworthy character or conduct. *n.*

**base runner** in baseball, a member of the team at bat who is on a base or trying to reach a BASE¹ (def. 7).

**bas·es¹** (bā′sēz) pl. of BASIS. *n.*

**bas·es²** (bā′siz) pl. of BASE¹. *n.*

**bash** (bash) *Informal.* **1** strike with a smashing blow. **2** a smashing blow. 1 *v.*, 2 *n.*

**bash·ful** (bash′fəl) uneasy and awkward in the presence of strangers; shy. *adj.* —**bash′ful·ly,** *adv.* —**bash′ful·ness,** *n.*

**ba·sic** (bā′sik)   **1** of, at, or forming the BASE¹ (def. 3); fundamental: *Addition, subtraction, multiplication, and division are the basic processes of arithmetic.*   **2** in chemistry, containing a BASE¹ (def. 6); alkaline.   *adj.*

**ba·si·cal·ly** (bā′si klē)   as a BASIC (def. 1) principle; fundamentally.   *adv.*

**bas·il** (baz′əl *or* bā′zəl)   **1** an annual herb of the MINT family having strongly aromatic leaves used as a seasoning in cookery; sweet basil: *Basil is especially good with tomatoes and tomato dishes.*   **2** any of several other closely related herbs of the mint family, not used for cooking.   *n.*

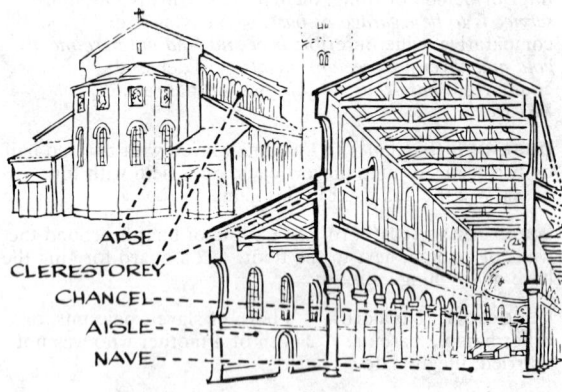

Basilica (def. 2). The 6th-century basilica of Sant'Apollinaire in Classe, Ravenna, Italy

**ba·sil·i·ca** (bə sil′ə kə)   **1** an oblong hall with a row of columns along each side and with a semicircular apse at one end: *The Romans used basilicas for law courts and public meetings.*   **2** an early Christian church built in this form.   *n.*

**bas·i·lisk** (bas′ə lisk′)   **1** in Greek and Roman legend, a fabled reptile whose breath and look were thought to be fatal: *The basilisk was supposed to resemble a lizard and to have a black-and-yellow skin and fiery, red eyes.*   **2** any of a group of tropical American lizards belonging to the iguana family, about 90 cm long, the male having an erect crest on the head, back, and tail.   *n.*

**ba·sin** (bā′sən)   **1** a wide, shallow bowl for holding liquids.   **2** the amount that a basin can hold.   **3** a low place in land, usually containing water.   **4** a shallow area containing water: *Part of the harbour is a basin for sailboats.*   **5** all the land drained by a river and the streams that flow into it: *the St. Lawrence basin.*   *n.*

**ba·sis** (bā′sis)   **1** the BASE¹ (def. 3) or main part; foundation.   **2** a fundamental principle or set of principles; CRITERION.   **3** the principal ingredient: *The basis of this medicine is an oil.*   **4** a starting point; military BASE¹ (defs. 9, 10).   *n., pl.* **ba·ses** (-sēz)·

**bask** (bask)   warm oneself pleasantly: *The cat was basking before the fire.*   *v.*
**bask in**,   take great pleasure in: *She basked in the praise of her friends.*

**bas·ket** (bas′kit)   **1** a container made of twigs, grasses, fibres, strips of wood, etc. woven together.   **2** the amount that a basket holds: *She bought a basket of peaches.*   **3** anything that looks like or is shaped like a basket: *Some baskets for wastepaper are made of metal.*   **4** the structure beneath a balloon for carrying passengers or ballast.   **5** a net shaped like a basket but open at the bottom, used as a goal in basketball.   **6** in basketball, a score made by tossing the ball through the basket.   *n.*
—**bas′ket·like′**, *adj.*

**bas·ket·ball** (bas′kit bol′)   **1** a game played with a large, round leather ball between two teams, usually of five players each.   **2** the ball used in this game.   *n.*

**bas·ket·ry** (bas′ki trē)   **1** basketwork; baskets.   **2** the art of making baskets.   *n.*

**basket weave**   a weave in cloth that looks like the weave in a basket.

**bas·ket·work** (bas′kit wėrk′)   work woven like a basket; WICKERWORK (def. 1).   *n.*

**Basque** (bask)   **1** a member of a people living in the Pyrenees in southern France and northern Spain.   **2** the language of this people.   **3** of or having to do with the Basques or their language.   **4 basque**,   a woman's garment consisting of a close-fitting bodice extending over the hips.   1, 2, 4 *n.*, 3 *adj.*

**bas-re·lief** (bä′ri lēf′ *or* bas′ri lēf′)   low RELIEF (defs. 8, 9) sculpture in which the modelled forms stand out only slightly from the background and no part of the forms is undercut. See RELIEF for picture.   *n.*

**bass¹** (bās)   **1** the lowest adult male singing voice: *He sings bass.*   **2** a singer who has such a voice.   **3** the part sung by a bass: *Bass is the lowest part in standard four-part harmony for men's and women's voices together.*   **4** an instrument having the lowest range in a family of musical instruments, especially a DOUBLE BASS.   **5** having to do with, having the range of, or designed for a bass.   **6** the lower half of the whole musical range for voice or instrument. Compare with TREBLE (def. 5).   **7** having to do with or referring to the lower half of the musical range: *the bass clef.*   **8** a deep, low-pitched male voice or musical sound.   1–4, 6, 8 *n.*, *pl.* **bass·es**;   5, 7 *adj.*
☛ Hom. BASE.

**bass²** (bas)   **1** any of several related species of sea fish found mostly in shallow tropical waters, ranging in length from about 30 cm to about 215 cm: *Bass are considered important game fish.*   **2** any of about six species of large freshwater sunfish native to eastern lakes and streams from southern Canada to northern Mexico: *Largemouth bass, smallmouth bass, and spotted bass are the three most common species.*   *n., pl.* **bass** or **bass·es**.

**bass clef** (bās′ klef′)   a music symbol (𝄢) showing that the pitch of the notes on a staff is below middle C: *In the bass clef, the F below middle C is on the fourth line from the bottom of the staff.* See CLEF for picture.

**bass drum** (bās)   a large drum that makes a deep, low sound when struck.

**bas·set hound** (bas′it)   a breed of heavily built, short-haired hunting dog with a long body, short legs, and very long, drooping ears.

**bass horn** (bās)   TUBA.

**bas·si·net** (bas′ə net′ *or* bas′ə net′)   a baby's basketlike CRADLE (def. 1).   *n.*

**bas·so** (bas′ō; *Italian*, bäs′sō)   a singer with a BASS¹ voice.   *n., pl.* **bas·sos** or **bas·si** (bäs′sē).

A bassoon

hat, āge, fär; let, ēqual, tėrm; it, īce
hot, ōpen, ôrder; oil, out; cup, pùt, rüle
ǝbove, takǝn, pencǝl, lemǝn, circǝs
ch, child; ng, long; sh, ship
th, thin; ᴛʜ, then; zh, measure

**bas·soon** (bǝ sün′)   a deep-toned wind instrument with a double reed, having a long wooden body with a second tube attached at the side, leading to a curved metal mouthpiece.   *n.*

**bass viol** (bās)   DOUBLE BASS.

**bass·wood** (bas′wùd′)   **1** a tall North American shade tree, a kind of LINDEN (def. 1), having heart-shaped leaves.   **2** the light, fine-grained, white wood of this tree.   *n.*

**bast** (bast)   **1** the inner layer of the bark of a tree, which contains cells for carrying sap.   **2** tough fibres in the inner bark of plants such as flax and hemp, used in making rope, matting, etc.   *n.*

**bas·tard** (bas′tǝrd)   **1** a child whose parents are not married to each other; illegitimate child.   **2** born of parents who are not married to each other; illegitimate. **3** anything inferior or not genuine.   **4** inferior; not genuine.   1, 3 *n.*, 2, 4 *adj.*

**baste**[1] (bāst)   drip or pour melted fat, butter, or a sauce on meat, fowl, etc. while roasting: *Meat is basted to keep it from drying out and to improve its flavour.*   *v.*, **bast·ed, bast·ing.**

**baste**[2] (bāst)   sew with long running stitches to hold cloth sections together until the final sewing.   *v.*, **bast·ed, bast·ing.**   —**bast′er**, *n.*

**baste**[3] (bāst)   beat or thrash.   *v.*, **bast·ed, bast·ing.**

**bast·ings** (bā′stingz)   long, loose stitches to hold cloth sections in place until the final sewing: *Bastings are removed after the final sewing.*   *n. pl.*

**bas·tion** (bas′chǝn *or* bas′tē ǝn)   **1** a projecting part of a fortification, made so that the defenders can fire at attackers from as many angles as possible. See FORT for picture.   **2** a defence or fortification.   *n.*

**bas·tioned** (bas′chǝnd *or* bas′tē ǝnd)   provided with or defended by BASTIONS.   *adj.*

**bat**[1] (bat)   **1** in baseball, cricket, etc., a specially shaped wooden stick or club, used to hit the ball.   **2** hit with or as if with a bat.   **3** use a bat: *He's batting well this season.* **4** the act of batting.   **5** a turn at batting: *It's her bat next.* **6** *Informal.*   a stroke or blow.   1, 4, 5, 6 *n.*, 2, 3 *v.*, **bat·ted, bat·ting.**
**at bat**, in position to bat; having a turn at batting.
**go to bat for,** *Informal.*   support the cause of: *I'm sure she'll go to bat for you if you explain exactly what happened.*
**right off the bat,** *Informal.*   immediately; without hesitation: *He accepted the offer right off the bat.*

A little brown bat— about 9 cm long; wingspread about 35 cm

**bat**[2] (bat)   any of several hundred species of flying mammal, resembling other small mammals like mice and shrews in their general body form, but having membranes between the very long bones of the forelimbs, which enable them to fly, hind feet adapted for clinging, and a special radar-like sense organ that enables them to fly in the dark: *Bats sleep during the day by clinging upside down to the ceilings in caves, dark corners of buildings, etc.*   *n.* —**bat′like′**, *adj.*
**blind as a bat,**   completely blind.

**bat**[3] (bat) *Informal.*   blink: *The ball nearly hit her but she didn't bat an eye.*   *v.*, **bat·ted, bat·ting.**

**batch** (bach)   **1** a quantity of bread made at one baking. **2** a quantity of anything made as one lot or set: *a batch of candy.*   **3** a number of persons or things taken together: *I've got a batch of essays to write this month.*   *n.*

**bate** (bāt)   ABATE; lessen; hold back.   *v.*, **bat·ed, bat·ing.**
**with bated breath,**   holding the breath in great fear, awe, interest, etc.: *The boys listened with bated breath to the sailor's story.*
☞ Hom.   BAIT.

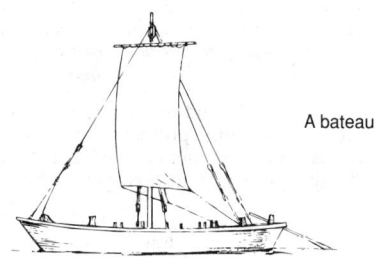
A bateau

**ba·teau** *or* **bat·teau** (ba tō′) *Cdn.*   a light, flat-bottomed river boat: *Bateaux used to carry freight between Montreal and Kingston.*   *n., pl.* **ba·teaux** *or* **bat·teaux** (-tōz′).

**bath** (bath)   **1** a washing of the body.   **2** the water, etc. for a bath: *Your bath is ready.*   **3** a tub, room, or other place for bathing: *In ancient Rome, baths were often elaborate public buildings, which were used also as clubs.* **4** give a bath to: *Mother baths the baby every day.*   **5** take a bath: *He always baths at night.*   **6** a health resort having baths for medical treatment.   **7** a liquid for washing or dipping something, such as a solution for fixing photographic prints or film.   **8** the container holding such liquid.   1–3, 6–8 *n., pl.* **baths** (baᴛʜz)   4, 5 *v.* —**bath′less**, *adj.*

**bathe** (bāᴛʜ)   **1** take a bath: *She bathes regularly.* **2** give a bath to: *Jack is bathing the dog.*   **3** apply water to; wash or moisten with any liquid: *Bathe your feet if they are tired. The doctor told her to bathe her eyes with the lotion.*   **4** go swimming; go into a pool, river, lake, etc. for pleasure.   **5** cover or surround: *The valley was bathed in sunlight.*   *v.*, **bathed, bath·ing.**   —**bath′er**, *n.*

**bath·o·lith** (bath′ǝ lith′)   a great mass of IGNEOUS rock often forming the base of a mountain range and uncovered only by erosion: *There is a batholith in British Columbia that is about 2400 by 160 kilometres.*   *n.*

# bathos — battle-axe

☞ *Etym.* Formed from Greek *bathos* 'depth' + *lithos* 'stone'.

**ba·thos** (bā′thos) **1** dullness or triteness in speech or writing, especially when immediately following more elevated expression. *Example: The exile came back to his home, crippled, unfriended, and hatless.* **2** strained or insincere PATHOS. *n.*

**bath·robe** (bath′rōb′) a loose garment worn when going to and from a bath or when resting or lounging. *n.*

**bath·room** (bath′rüm′) **1** a room fitted up for taking baths or showers and usually equipped with a washbasin and a toilet. **2** a toilet. *n.*
**go to the bathroom,** *Informal.* urinate or defecate.

**bath·tub** (bath′tub′) a tub to bath in. *n.*

**bath·y·scaph** (bath′ə skaf′) a self-contained diving vessel for deep-sea observation, designed to reach great depths in the ocean, consisting of a heavy steel cabin for the observers attached to the underside of a large light hull called a float: *The bathyscaph descends by allowing sea water into the float and ascends again by releasing iron ballast from the float. The record dive for a bathyscaph is 10 916 metres, made in 1960.* *n.*

**bath·y·sphere** (bath′ə sfēr′) a ball-shaped, steel, watertight vessel having portholes, formerly used for observing plant and animal life in the ocean depths: *The bathysphere was suspended from a boat by a cable and was able to descend to a depth of about 900 metres.* *n.*

**ba·tik** (bə tēk′) **1** a method of making designs on cloth by dyeing only part at a time, protecting the remainder with a removable coating of melted wax. **2** cloth dyed in this way. **3** a design formed in this way. **4** of or like batik. *n.*

**ba·tiste** (bə tēst′) **1** a fine, thin cotton cloth in a plain weave. **2** any of various similar fabrics made of polyester, rayon, etc. *n.*

**bat mitz·vah** (bat mit′svə) **1** in some Jewish sects, a ceremony marking the formal admission of a girl into the Jewish religious community, usually held when the girl is twelve years old. **2** a girl who has reached the age of twelve, and has formally accepted her religious responsibilities. Compare with BAR MITZVAH. Also, **bas mitzvah, bath mitzvah.** *pl.* **bat mitzvahs** or **mitzvoth** (-vōth).
☞ *Etym.* From Hebrew *bat mitswāh* 'daughter of the divine law'.

**ba·ton** (ba ton′) **1** a staff or stick used as a symbol of office or authority. **2** a stick used by the leader of an orchestra, chorus, etc., to indicate the beat and direct the performance. **3** a stick passed from runner to runner in a relay race. **4** a light, hollow metal rod twirled by a drum major or majorette as a showy display. *n.*

**bats·man** (bat′smən) in cricket, a player who is batting. *n., pl.* **bats·men** (-smən).

**bat·tal·ion** (bə tal′yən) **1** a formation of four companies within a regiment of infantry, usually commanded by a lieutenant-colonel. **2** any large group organized to act together: *A battalion of volunteers helped to rescue the flood victims.* **3 battalions,** *pl.* armies; military forces. *n.*

**bat·teau** (ba tō′) See BATEAU. *n.*

**bat·ten**[1] (bat′ən) **1** grow fat. **2** fatten. **3** feed greedily. *v.*

**bat·ten**[2] (bat′ən) **1** a large, thick board used for flooring. **2** a strip of wood: *Battens are nailed across parallel boards to strengthen them.* **3** fasten down or strengthen with strips of wood. 1, 2 *n.,* 3 *v.*
**batten down the hatches,** on a ship, fasten tarpaulins over the hatches by means of BATTENS (def. 2).

**bat·ter**[1] (bat′ər) **1** strike with repeated blows; beat so as to bruise, break, or get out of shape; pound: *The police officer battered down the door with a heavy axe.* **2** damage by hard use: *a battered old book.* *v.*

**bat·ter**[2] (bat′ər) a mixture of flour, milk, eggs, etc. that becomes solid when cooked: *Cakes, pancakes, etc. are made from batter.* *n.*

**bat·ter**[3] (bat′ər) in baseball, etc., a player who is batting. *n.*

**battering ram 1** a heavy beam of wood with metal at the striking end, used in ancient and medieval warfare for battering down walls, gates, etc. **2** any heavy object used to break down a door, wall, etc.

**bat·ter·y** (bat′ə rē *or* bat′rē) **1** a container holding materials that produce electricity by chemical action; a single electric cell. See DRY CELL for picture. **2** a set of two or more electric cells that produce electric current: *a car battery.* **3** any set of similar or connected things: *A battery of loudspeakers blared through the hall. If you want this job, you will have to take a battery of tests.* **4** a set of guns or other weapons such as mortars, machine guns, and artillery pieces for combined action in attack or defence. **5** a formation of several troops in an artillery regiment. **6** in baseball, the pitcher and catcher together. **7** in law, assault causing actual bodily harm: *He was charged with assault and battery.* *n., pl.* **bat·ter·ies.**

**bat·ting** (bat′ing) **1** the act or manner of hitting a ball with a bat: *Her batting has improved.* **2** sheets or layers of pressed cotton, wool, or a synthetic fibre, used for lining quilts, stuffing mattresses, packing, etc. **3** ppr. of BAT. 1, 2 *n.,* 3 *v.*

**bat·tle** (bat′əl) **1** a fight between opposing armed forces: *The battle for the island lasted six months.* **2** take part in a battle. **3** fighting or war: *wounds received in battle.* **4** any fight or contest: *a battle of words.* **5** fight; struggle; contend: *The swimmer had to battle a strong current. Our team is battling for first place in hockey.* 1, 3, 4 *n.,* 2, 5 *v.,* **bat·tled, bat·tling.** —**bat′tler,** *n.*

**battle array 1** the order of troops, ships, etc. ready for battle. **2** armour, equipment, etc. for battle.

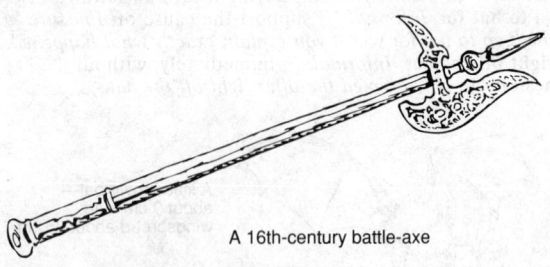

A 16th-century battle-axe

**bat·tle–axe** (bat′ə laks′) formerly, a kind of axe used as a weapon of war. *n.* Sometimes, **battle-ax.**

**battle cruiser** a large, fast warship, not as heavily armoured as a battleship.

**battle cry** 1 formerly, the shout of soldiers in battle. 2 a motto or slogan in any contest or campaign.

**bat·tle·dore** (bat′əl dôr′) a small racket used to hit a SHUTTLECOCK back and forth in the game of battledore and shuttlecock. *n.*

**battle dress** a two-piece uniform consisting of trousers and a short, loose jacket, usually called a BLOUSE (def. 3), that ends in a fitted waistband: *Battle dress is worn by the armed forces for field training and combat.*

**bat·tle·field** (bat′əl fēld′) a place where a battle is fought or has been fought. *n.*

**bat·tle·ground** (bat′əl ground′) BATTLEFIELD. *n.*

**bat·tle·ment** (bat′əl mənt) 1 a low wall for defence at the top of a tower or wall, with indentations through which defending soldiers could shoot. See CASTLE and FORT for pictures. 2 a wall built like this for ornament. *n.*

**bat·tle·ment·ed** (bat′əl men′tid) having BATTLEMENTS. *adj.*

**battle royal** 1 a fight in which several take part. 2 a long, hard fight or dispute.

**bat·tle–scarred** (bat′əl skärd′) 1 injured or damaged during a battle. 2 showing the effects of many battles: *a battle-scarred old soldier. adj.*

**bat·tle·ship** (bat′əl ship′) the largest, most powerful, and most heavily armoured type of warship: *Battleships are seldom used now because they are very vulnerable to attacks from the air. n.*

**bat·tue** (ba tyü′ *or* ba tü′) 1 the driving of game from cover toward the hunters. 2 a hunt where this is done. 3 a general slaughter. *n.*

**bau·ble** (bob′əl) a showy trifle having no real value: *Useless toys and trinkets are baubles. n.*

**baud** (bôd) a unit of speed for transferring data in telecommunications, representing the number of pulses sent per second or especially, between computer systems, the number of bits. *n.pl.*

**baulk** (bok) See BALK. *v., n.*

**baux·ite** (bok′sīt) a clay-like mineral from which aluminum is obtained: *Bauxite is also used in making alum and firebricks. n.*

**Ba·var·i·an** (bə ver′ē ən) 1 of, or having to do with Bavaria, a state in southwestern Germany, its people, or the dialect of German spoken there. 2 a native or inhabitant of Bavaria. 3 a German dialect spoken in Bavaria and in parts of Austria. 1 *adj.*, 2, 3 *n.*

**bawd·y** (bod′ē) 1 lewd or obscene. 2 coarsely humorous: *bawdy songs. adj.,* **bawd·i·er, bawd·i·est.** —**bawd′i·ly,** *adv.* —**bawd′i·ness,** *n.*
☞ *Hom.* BODY.

**bawl** (bol) 1 shout or call out in a noisy way: *The peddler bawled his wares in the street. The sergeant bawled out a command.* 2 weep loudly: *The small boy bawled whenever he hurt himself.* 3 a loud shouting or weeping. 1, 2 *v.*, 3 *n.*

**bawl out,** *Informal.* scold severely or loudly: *We got bawled out for leaving our bicycles in the driveway.*
☞ *Hom.* BALL.

**bay**¹ (bā) a part of a sea or lake extending into the land; a wide indentation that is usually larger than a cove and smaller than a gulf. *n.*
☞ *Hom.* BEY.

hat, āge, fär; let, ēqual, tėrm; it, īce
hot, ōpen, ôrder; oil, out; cup, pút, rüle
əbove, takən, pencəl, lemən, circəs
ch, child; ng, long; sh, ship
th, thin; ᴛʜ, then; zh, measure

**bay**² (bā) 1 a space or division of a wall or building between columns, pillars, buttresses, etc. 2 a space with a window or set of windows in it, projecting out from a wall. 3 a place in a barn for storing hay or grain; MOW². 4 a compartment in an airplane, especially one for carrying bombs. 5 a recess, platform, etc., for a specified purpose: *The truck was backed up to the loading bay of the warehouse. n.*
☞ *Hom.* BEY.

**bay**³ (bā) 1 a long, deep howl or bark, especially as made by hounds, etc. when pursuing or closing in on prey: *The two hunters heard the distant bay of the hounds.* 2 utter a howl or prolonged barks: *The dogs sat and bayed at the moon.* 3 the situation or position of a hunted animal when escape is impossible and it is forced to face its pursuers: *The quarry was brought to bay. The stag stood at bay on the edge of the cliff.* 4 the position or situation of a person forced to face an enemy, a serious difficulty, persecution, etc. 5 the position of the pursuers or enemies kept off: *The deer held the hounds at bay.* 1, 3–5 *n.*, 2 *v.*
☞ *Hom.* BEY.

**bay**⁴ (bā) 1 a large shrub or small tree native to southern Europe and northern Africa, having stiff, glossy evergreen leaves; LAUREL (def. 1): *Bay leaves are used for flavouring food.* 2 **bays,** *pl.* **a** a laurel wreath once given to poets or victors. **b** honour; renown; fame. *n.*
☞ *Hom.* BEY.

**bay**⁵ (bā) 1 reddish brown. 2 a reddish-brown horse. 1, 2 *n.*, 1 *adj.*
☞ *Hom.* BEY.

**bay·ber·ry** (bā′ber′ē) 1 a North American shrub of the wax myrtle family, having clusters of round nuts covered with greyish-white wax: *The leaves of the bayberry are aromatic, and candles made from the wax of the berries burn with a pleasant fragrance.* 2 the fruit of this shrub. 3 a West Indian tree of the myrtle family, closely related to the pimento tree, having leaves that yield an aromatic oil used in making BAY RUM. *n., pl.* **bay·ber·ries.**

**bay laurel** LAUREL (def. 1).

**bay leaf** the dried, aromatic leaf of the LAUREL (def. 1), used as a flavouring in making soups, stews, meat sauces, etc.

**bay·o·net** (bā′ə nit *or* bā′ə net′) 1 a heavy, daggerlike blade for piercing or stabbing, made to be attached to the end of the barrel of a rifle. 2 pierce or stab with a bayonet. 1 *n.*, 2 *v.*
☞ *Etym.* In the 17c. from French *baïonnette,* probably named after the French town *Bayonne* where such daggers or blades were first made.

**bay·ou** (bī′ü) *Esp. U.S.* a marshy inlet or outlet of a lake, river, or gulf. *n., pl.* **bay·ous.**

**bay rum** a fragrant liquid originally made from the leaves of the West Indian BAYBERRY (def. 3), used in medicine and cosmetics.

A bay window

**bay window** a window or set of windows projecting outward from a wall to form an alcove or small space in a room.

**ba·zaar** (bə zär′) 1 especially in Middle Eastern countries, a street or streets full of shops and stalls. 2 a place for the sale of many kinds of goods. 3 a sale of things given by various people, held for some special purpose. *n.* ☞ *Hom.* BIZARRE.

**ba·zoo·ka** (bə zü′kə) a rocket gun used against tanks. *n.*

**BB** (bē′bē) 1 a standard size of shot, about 0.45 cm in diameter. 2 a shot of this size, especially for use in an air rifle. *n., pl.* **BB's**.

**BBC** or **B.B.C.** British Broadcasting Corporation.

**BB gun** AIR RIFLE.

**bbl.** barrels.

**BC** British Columbia.

**B.C.** 1 before Christ; before the birth of Christ: 350 B.C. *is 100 years earlier than 250 B.C.* 2 British Columbia.

**bd. ft.** board foot; board feet.

**bdl.** bundle.

**be** (bē) 1 have reality; live; exist: *The days of the pioneers are no more.* 2 take place; happen: *The circus was last month.* 3 have a particular place or position; remain; continue: *She will be here all year. The food is on the table.* 4 equal; represent: *Let "x" be the unknown quantity.* 5 belong to a particular group or class: *The new baby is a girl. My mother is a doctor. Elephants and mice are mammals.* 6 have or show a particular quality or condition: *I am sad. You are wrong. The book is red.* 7 **Be** is also used as an auxiliary verb with: **a** the present participle of another verb to form the progressive tenses: *I am asking. He was asking. You will be asking.* **b** the past participle of another verb to form the passive voice: *I am asked. You will be asked. He was asked.* 8 **Be** is also used to express future time, duty, intention, and possibility: *She is to be there at nine. No shelter was to be seen.* *v., pres. sing.* **am, are, is,** *pl.* **are;** *pt.* **was, were, was,** *pl.* **were;** *pp.* **been,** *ppr.* **being.** ☞ *Hom.* BEE.

**be-** a prefix meaning: 1 thoroughly; all around: *Bespatter means spatter thoroughly or all around.* 2 at; on; to; for; about; against: *Bewail means wail about.* 3 make; cause to seem: *Belittle means cause to seem little.* 4 provide with: *Bespangle means provide with spangles.*

**Be** beryllium.

**beach** (bēch) 1 the almost flat shore of sand or little stones beside a lake or the sea. 2 run or drive up on shore: *We beached the boat in a little inlet. The newspaper reported that a whale was beached on the island.* 1 *n.,* 2 *v.* —**beach′less,** *adj.* ☞ *Hom.* BEECH.

**beach·comb·er** (bēch′kō′mər) 1 a vagrant or loafer on beaches or in wharf areas, especially in islands of the south Pacific. 2 a long wave rolling in from the ocean. 3 *Cdn.* in British Columbia, a person or vessel that salvages logs broken loose from log booms and returns them to the logging companies for a fee. *n.*

**beach·head** (bēch′hed′) the first position established by an invading army on an enemy shore. *n.*

**bea·con** (bē′kən) 1 a fire or light used as a signal to guide or warn. 2 a marker, signal light, or radio station that guides aircraft through fogs, storms, etc. 3 a tall tower for a signal; lighthouse. 4 give light to; guide; warn. 5 shine brightly. 6 supply with beacons. 1–3 *n.,* 4–6 *v.*

**bead** (bēd) 1 a small ball or bit of glass, metal, etc. with a hole through it, so that it can be strung on a thread with others like it. 2 put beads on; ornament with beads. 3 any small, round object like a drop or bubble: *beads of sweat.* 4 form beads. 5 a small metal knob or ball at the front of a rifle or pistol barrel, used for taking aim. 6 a narrow, semicircular moulding. 7 **beads,** *pl.* **a** a string of beads. **b** a rosary; string of beads used in saying prayers. 1, 3, 5, 6, 7 *n.,* 2, 4 *v.* —**bead′like′,** *adj.* **draw a bead on,** aim at.
**say, tell,** or **count one's beads,** say prayers, using a rosary.

**bead·ed** (bē′did) 1 trimmed with beads; having beads: *a beaded fabric.* 2 formed into beads; like beads. 3 pt. and pp. of BEAD. 1, 2 *adj.,* 3 *v.*

**bead·ing** (bē′ding) 1 a trimming made of beads threaded into patterns. 2 a narrow lace or open-work trimming through which ribbon may be run. 3 on woodwork, silver, etc., a pattern or edge made of small beads. 4 a narrow, rounded moulding. 5 ppr. of BEAD. 1–4 *n.,* 5 *v.*

**bead·work** (bēd′wėrk′) BEADING. *n.*

**bead·y** (bē′dē) 1 small, round, and shiny: *The parakeet has beady eyes.* 2 trimmed with beads. 3 full of bubbles; frothy. *adj.,* **bead·i·er, bead·i·est.**

**bea·gle** (bē′gəl) a breed of small hunting dog having smooth hair, short legs, and drooping ears. *n.*

**beak** (bēk) 1 a bird's bill, especially one that is strong and hooked and useful in striking or tearing: *Eagles, hawks, and parrots have beaks.* 2 a similar part in other animals, such as some turtles or fish. 3 the projecting bow of an ancient warship. *n.*

**beaked** (bēkt) 1 having a beak. 2 shaped like a beak; hooked. *adj.*

**beak·er** (bē′kər) 1 a large cup or drinking glass. 2 the contents of a beaker: *She drank a whole beaker of cold water.* 3 a thin glass or metal cup with a small lip for pouring and no handle, used in laboratories. *n.*

**be-all and end-all** 1 the main purpose or reason for anything. 2 *Informal.* the most important person or thing: *She thinks she is the be-all and end-all.*

**beam** (bēm) 1 a large, long piece of timber, ready for use in building. 2 a similar piece of metal, stone, reinforced concrete, etc. See RIVET for picture. 3 the main horizontal support of a building or ship. 4 the part of a plough by which it is pulled. 5 the crosswise bar of a BALANCE (def. 1), from the ends of which the scales or pans are suspended. 6 the BALANCE (def. 1) itself. 7 a

ray or rays of light or heat: *the beam from a flashlight.* **8** send out rays of light; shine. **9** a bright look or smile. **10** look or smile brightly. **11** a radio signal directed in a straight line, used to guide aircraft, ships, etc. **12** direct a broadcast: *to beam programs at the Yukon.* **13** the widest part of a ship. 1–7, 9, 11, 13 *n.*, 8, 10, 12 *v.*
**on her beam-ends,** of a ship, almost capsizing.
**on one's beam-ends,** *Informal.* short of money.
**on the beam,** **a** of a ship, at right angles with the keel. **b** of an aircraft, in the right path indicated by directing signals. **c** *Informal.* just right.

**beamed** (bēmd) **1** furnished with beams, or as if with beams: *a beamed ceiling.* **2** pt. and pp. of BEAM. 1 *adj.*, 2 *v.*

**beam·ing** (bē′ming) **1** shining or bright. **2** smiling brightly; cheerful: *She came out of the interview just beaming.* **3** ppr. of BEAM. 1, 2 *adj.*, 3 *v.*
—**beam′ing·ly,** *adv.*

**bean** (bēn) **1** any of a number of plants of the pea family, many of them climbing plants, that produce edible, usually kidney-shaped seeds in long pods. **2** the dried mature seed of a bean plant: *Baked beans are often eaten as a meal.* **3** the immature green or yellow pod of a bean plant, used as a vegetable, usually cooked. **4** any of various other seeds or fruits related to or resembling a bean: *Coffee beans are the seeds of the coffee plant.* *n.*
—**bean′like′,** *adj.*
**full of beans,** *Informal.* lively; in high spirits: *She's really full of beans today.*
☛ *Hom.* BEEN (bēn).

**bean·bag** (bēn′bag′) a small cloth bag loosely filled with dry beans, used to toss in play: *Beanbags are often made in the shape of animals.* *n.*

**bean·pole** (bēn′pōl′) a pole stuck in the ground for bean vines to climb on as they grow. *n.*

**bean·stalk** (bēn′stok′) the stem of a bean plant. *n.*

**bear**¹ (ber) **1** carry: *A voice was borne upon the wind.* **2** support: *That board is too thin to bear your weight.* **3** put up with; abide; tolerate: *I can't bear that man.* **4** undergo or experience without giving way; endure: *He cannot bear any more pain.* **5** bring forth; produce; yield: *This tree bears fine apples.* **6** give birth to; have offspring: *to bear a child. That woman has borne four boys. He was born on June 4.* **7** behave; conduct: *She bore herself with great dignity.* **8** bring forward; give: *to bear company, to bear a hand. A person who saw an accident can bear witness to what happened.* **9** hold in mind: *to bear a grudge, affection, etc.* **10** have as an identification or characteristic: *He bears the name of John, the title of earl, and a reputation for learning.* **11** have as a duty, right, privilege, etc.: *The queen bears sway over the empire.* **12** take on oneself as a duty: *to bear the cost. She couldn't bear to tell him.* **13** press; push: *Don't bear down so hard.* **14** move; go: *The ship bore north.* **15** lie; be situated: *The land bore due north of the ship.* **16** allow; permit: *The accident bears two explanations.* *v.*, **bore, borne** or (*for def. 6 when used in the passive voice*) **born, bearing.**
**bear down (on),** **a** put pressure on; press or push: *Don't bear down so hard on him.* **b** move toward; approach: *They watched helplessly as the ship bore down on their rowboat.* **c** try hard; work seriously: *You'll have to bear down if you expect to pass the exam.*
**bear in mind,** remember; consider.
**bear on,** have a connection with; relate to: *Her comment was interesting, but did not bear on the topic.*
**bear out,** support; prove: *The excellent results have borne out his optimism.*
**bear up,** keep one's courage; not lose hope or faith.
**bear with,** put up with; be patient with.
☛ *Hom.* BARE.

**bear**² (ber) **1** any of a family of large, heavily-built mammals found mainly in the temperate regions of the northern hemisphere, having thick, coarse, shaggy hair, a very short tail, short, rounded ears, and large, flat, five-toed paws with powerful claws: *Bears are meat-eating animals but they also feed on berries, young shoots and buds, etc.* **2** a gruff, surly person. **3** a person who tries to lower prices in the stock market, etc. **4** having to do with the lowering of prices in the stock market, etc. **5 Bear,** one of two northern groups of stars; the Little Bear or the Great Bear. *n.*
☛ *Hom.* BARE.

**bear·a·ble** (ber′ə bəl) that can be borne; endurable: *The pain was severe but bearable.* *adj.*
—**bear′a·bly,** *adv.*

TYPES OF BEARD

FULL (EDWARD VII)   GOATEE (DISRAELI)   IMPERIAL (NAPOLEON III)

**beard** (bērd) **1** the hair growing on a man's chin and cheeks. **2** something resembling or suggesting this: *The chin tuft of a goat is a beard; so are the stiff hairs around the beak of certain birds.* **3** the group of hairs on the heads of plants like oats, barley, and wheat; AWNS. **4** face boldly; defy. 1–3 *n.*, 4 *v.* —**beard′like′,** *adj.*

**beard·ed** (bēr′did) **1** having a BEARD. **2** pt. and pp. of BEARD. 1 *adj.*, 2 *v.*

**beard·less** (bērd′lis) **1** without a BEARD. **2** young; immature; youthful. *adj.* —**beard′less·ness,** *n.*

**bear·er** (ber′ər) **1** a person or thing that carries. **2** a person who holds or presents a cheque, draft, or note for payment. **3** a tree or plant that produces fruit or flowers: *This apple tree is a good bearer.* *n.*

**bear·ing** (ber′ing) **1** a way of standing, sitting, walking, etc.; manner: *A queen should have a royal bearing.* **2** connection in thought or meaning; reference or relation: *Her foolish question has no bearing on the problem.* **3** a part of a machine on which another part turns or slides, such as a BALL BEARING. See GYROSCOPE for picture. **4** a supporting part. **5** a single device in a coat of arms: *heraldic bearings.* **6 bearings,** *pl.* **a** a direction; position in relation to other things: *The pilot radioed his bearings.* **b** comprehension of one's position in relation to other things: *Without a guide, she would have soon lost her bearings in the bush.* **7** ppr. of BEAR¹. 1–6 *n.*, 7 *v.*

**bear·ish** (ber′ish) **1** like a bear; rough; surly. **2** aiming at or tending to lower prices in the stock market, etc. *adj.* —**bear′ish·ly,** *adv.* —**bear′ish·ness,** *n.*

**bear·skin** (ber′skin′) **1** the skin of a bear with the fur attached. **2** a tall, black fur cap worn by members of certain regiments. *n.*

**beast** (bēst) **1** any animal except a human being. **2** any four-footed animal. **3** a coarse or brutal person. *n.* —**beast′like′,** *adj.*

**beast·ly** (bē′stlē) **1** like a beast; brutal; coarse; vile. **2** *Informal.* very unpleasant; disagreeable: *a beastly headache.* **3** *Informal.* very; unpleasantly: *It was beastly cold.* 1, 2, *adj.*, **beast·li·er, beast·li·est;** 3 *adv.* —**beast′li·ness,** *n.*

**beast of burden** an animal used for carrying loads.

**beast of prey** any animal that kills other animals for its food.

**beat** (bēt) **1** strike again and again; strike; whip; thrash: *The cruel man beat his horse.* **2** a stroke or blow made again and again: *the beat of a drum, the beat of waves on a beach.* **3** throb: *Her heart beats fast with joy.* **4** pulsation; throb: *the beat of the heart.* **5** drive by blows; force by blows: *He beat the savage dog away from him.* **6** defeat or overcome: *Their team beat ours by a huge score.* **7** *Informal.* baffle: *This problem beats me.* **8** *Informal.* cheat; swindle. **9** make flat; shape with a hammer: *to beat gold into thin strips.* **10** make flat by much walking; tread a path. **11** mix by stirring; mix by striking with a fork, spoon, or other utensil: *to beat eggs.* **12** move up and down; flap: *The bird beat its wings.* **13** make a sound by being struck: *The drums beat loudly.* **14** in music, a unit of time or accent: *three beats to a measure. The good dancer never missed a beat.* **15** mark time with drumsticks or by tapping with hands or feet: *to beat a tattoo.* **16** show a unit of time or accent in music by a stroke of the hand, etc. **17** a stroke of the hand, baton, etc. showing a musical beat. **18** a regular round or route, especially one taken by a police officer or sentry. **19** go through woods or underbrush in a hunt: *The men beat the woods in search of the lost child.* **20** move against the wind by a zigzag course: *The sailboat beat along the coast.* **21** outdo; surpass: *Nothing can beat yachting as a sport.* **22** *Informal.* worn out; exhausted: *He was beat after a hard day at the factory.* 1, 3, 5–13, 15, 16, 19–21 *v.,* **beat, beat·en** or **beat, beat·ing;** 2, 4, 14, 17, 18 *n.,* 22 *adj.*

**beat about,** search around; try to discover: *She beat about in vain for a fitting answer.*

**beat a retreat, a** run away; retreat. **b** sound a retreat on a drum.

**beat around** (or **about**) **the bush,** approach a matter indirectly; avoid coming to the point: *Stop beating around the bush and tell me what you want.*

**beat back,** force to retreat; push back: *The enemy advance was successfully beaten back.*

**beat down,** *Informal.* force to set a lower price.

**beat off, a** drive off or away by blows: *He beat off the two men who attacked him.* **b** drive away; repel: *She beat off her fear by singing to herself.*
☛ *Hom.* BEET.

**beat·en** (bē′tən) **1** whipped; struck: *a beaten dog.* **2** shaped by blows of a hammer: *beaten silver.* **3** much walked on or travelled: *a beaten path.* **4** discouraged by defeat; overcome: *They were a beaten lot.* **5** exhausted. **6** a pp. of BEAT: *We were beaten in football on Saturday.* 1–5 *adj.,* 6 *v.*

**beat·er** (bē′tər) **1** a person who beats, especially someone hired to rouse game during a hunt. **2** a device or utensil for beating eggs, cream, etc.: *an electric beater. n.*

**beat·ing** (bē′ting) **1** whipping; punishment by blows. **2** defeat: *They took a beating in the game.* **3** throbbing; pulsation: *She could hear the beating of her own heart as she waited.* **4** ppr. of BEAT. 1–3 *n.,* 4 *v.*

**be·at·i·tude** (bē at′ə tyüd′ or bē at′ə tüd′) **1** supreme happiness; bliss. **2** a blessing. *n.*

**beat·nik** (bēt′nik) a member of the Beat Generation, a group of young Americans in the 1950s who rebelled against prevailing standards and behaviour. *n.*

**beat–up** (bē′tup) *Informal.* **1** battered. **2** completely exhausted. *adj.*

**beau** (bō) **1** a young man courting a young woman; a suitor or lover. **2** a man who pays much attention to the way he dresses and to the fashion of his clothes. *n., pl.* **beaus** or **beaux** (bōz).
☛ *Hom.* BOW².

**Beau·fort scale** (bō′fərt) an internationally used scale of wind velocities, having code numbers ranging from 0 (calm) to 12 (hurricane).

**beau geste** (bō zhest′) *French.* **1** a graceful or kindly act. **2** a pretence of kindness or unselfishness merely for effect. *pl.* **beaux gestes** (bō zhest′).

**beau i·de·al** (bō′ ī dē′əl; *French,* bō ē dā äl′) a perfect type of excellence or beauty; highest ideal or model.

**beau monde** (bō mond′) *French.* fashionable society.

**beau·te·ous** (byü′tē əs) beautiful. *adj.* —**beau′te·ous·ly,** *adv.* —**beau′te·ous·ness,** *n.*

**beau·ti·fi·er** (byü′tə fī′ər) a person or thing that beautifies. *n.*

**beau·ti·ful** (byü′tə fəl) very pleasing to see or hear; delighting the mind or senses: *a beautiful picture, beautiful music. adj.* —**beau′ti·ful·ly,** *adv.* —**beau′ti·ful·ness,** *n.*

**beau·ti·fy** (byü′tə fī′) **1** make beautiful; make more beautiful: *Flowers beautify a garden.* **2** become beautiful. *v.* **beau·ti·fied, beau·ti·fy·ing.**

**beau·ty** (byü′tē) **1** a quality or combination of qualities that gives great pleasure to the senses or to the mind and spirit: *The richness and beauty of the great hall were almost beyond description. "A thing of beauty is a joy forever." There is great beauty in his poetry.* **2** a person or thing that has beauty, especially a beautiful woman: *She is a renowned beauty.* **3** a feature or trait that gives special pleasure to the mind or senses: *the beauties of the countryside in spring. The beauty of her writing style is its simplicity.* **4** *Informal.* a notable or exceptional example of its kind: *That catch was a beauty! You should see her black eye; it's a beauty! n., pl.* **beau·ties.**

**beauty parlour** or **parlor** BEAUTY SALON.

**beauty salon** a place that provides women with such services as hairdressing, manicuring, and skin treatments. Also, **beauty shop.**

**beaux** (bōz) a pl. of BEAU. *n.*

A beaver—about 75 cm long excluding the tail; tail about 30 cm long and 16 cm wide

hat, āge, fär; let, ēqual, tėrm; it, īce
hot, ōpen, ôrder; oil, out; cup, pu̇t, rüle
above, taken, pencil, lemon, circus
ch, child; ng, long; sh, ship
th, thin; ᴛʜ, then; zh, measure

**bea·ver¹** (bē′vər)   1 any of a family of large rodents that live in and around water, found in North America and Europe, having a thickset body, a broad, flat, scaly tail, which is used as a rudder in swimming, large, webbed hind feet, and long, chisel-like front teeth: *The Canadian beaver has been an emblem of Canada for over two hundred years.* 2 the beaver's thick, soft, glossy fur: *a coat trimmed with beaver.*   3 a man's high silk hat, formerly made of beaver fur.   4 a heavy woollen cloth.   5 *Informal.* an especially hard-working person; an EAGER BEAVER.   *n., pl.* **beavers** or (for def. 1) **beaver.**

**bea·ver²** (bē′vər)   1 a movable piece of armour that protects the chin and mouth. See ARMOUR for picture. 2 the movable front part of a helmet; visor.   *n.*

**be·bop** (bē′bop′)   in music, a style of jazz that evolved in the 1940's, characterized by more complex harmony and more syncopation than in swing; bop.   *n.*

**be·calm** (bi kom′ *or* bi käm′)   1 prevent from moving by lack of wind: *Our boat was becalmed for several hours.* 2 make calm; soothe.   *v.*

**be·came** (bi kām′)   pt. of BECOME: *The seed became a plant.*   *v.*

**be·cause** (bi koz′ *or* bi kuz′)   for the reason that; since: *We play ball because we enjoy the game. Because we were late, we ran.*   *conj.*
**because of,**   by reason of; on account of: *Because of the rain, we did not go.*

**beck** (bek)   1 a motion of the head or hand meant as a call or command.   2 beckon to.   1 *n.,* 2 *v.*
**at one's beck and call,**   a ready whenever wanted. b under one's complete control.

**beck·on** (bek′ən)   signal by a motion of the head or hand: *He beckoned me to follow him.*   *v.*

**be·cloud** (bi kloud′)   1 hide by a cloud or clouds. 2 make obscure: *Too many big words becloud the meaning.*   *v.*

**be·come** (bi kum′)   1 come to be; grow to be: *At his words she became more angry. He became wiser as he grew older.*   2 be suitable for; suit: *The rude comment did not become her position as chairwoman.*   3 look well on: *That dress becomes her.*   *v.,* **be·came, be·come, be·com·ing.**
**become of,**   happen to: *What will become of her? What has become of the box of candy?*

**be·com·ing** (bi kum′ing)   1 fitting; suitable; appropriate: *becoming conduct for a formal occasion.* 2 that looks well on the person wearing it: *a becoming dress.*   3 ppr. of BECOME.   1, 2 *adj.,* 3 *v.*
—**be·com·ing·ly,** *adv.*

**bec·que·rel** (bek′ə rel)   an SI unit for measuring radio-activity, or the rate at which the atoms of radio-active elements disintegrate: *One becquerel is equal to one disintegration per second.*   Symbol: Bq   *n.*

**bed** (bed)   1 anything to sleep or rest on: *A bed usually consists of a mattress raised upon a support and covered with sheets and blankets.*   2 any place where people or animals rest or sleep: *The cat made its bed by the fireplace.* 3 provide with a bed; put to bed: *The man bedded his horse down with straw.*   4 a flat base on which anything rests;

foundation: *They set the pole in a bed of concrete.*   5 fix or set in a permanent position; embed.   6 the ground under a body of water: *The bed of the river is muddy.*   7 a piece of ground in a garden in which plants are grown. 8 plant in a garden bed: *Tulips should be bedded in rich soil.*   9 a layer; STRATUM: *a bed of coal.*   1, 2, 4, 6, 7, 9 *n.,* 3, 5, 8 *v.,* **bed·ded, bed·ding.**
**bed and board,**   sleeping accommodation and meals.
**get up on the wrong side of the bed,** *Informal.*   be irritable or bad-tempered.

**be·daub** (bi dob′)   1 smear with something dirty or sticky.   2 ornament in a gaudy or showy way.   *v.*

**be·daz·zle** (bi daz′əl)   dazzle completely; confuse by dazzling: *He was bedazzled by the brilliant lights.*   *v.,* **be·daz·zled, be·daz·zling.**

**bed·bug** (bed′bug′)   a small, reddish-brown insect about 5 mm long, having a broad, flat body covered with short hairs and bristles, small useless wings, and scent glands that give off a disagreeable odour: *Bedbugs are parasites on human beings; they hide during the day in folds of mattresses, cracks in bedsteads, behind baseboards, etc. and come out at night to suck the blood of people.*   *n.*

**bed·cham·ber** (bed′chām′bər)   BEDROOM.   *n.*

**bed·clothes** (bed′klōz′ *or* bed′klōᴛʜz′)   sheets, blankets, quilts, etc.   *n. pl.*

**bed·ding** (bed′ing)   1 sheets, blankets, quilts, etc.; BEDCLOTHES.   2 material for beds: *Straw is used as bedding for cows and horses.*   3 a foundation; bottom layer.   4 ppr. of BED.   1–3 *n.,* 4 *v.*

**be·deck** (bi dek′)   adorn or decorate: *The street is bedecked with flags for the prince's visit.*   *v.*

**be·dev·il** (bi dev′əl)   1 trouble greatly; torment. 2 confuse completely; muddle.   3 put under a spell; bewitch.   *v.,* **be·dev·illed** or **be·dev·iled, be·dev·il·ling** or **be·dev·il·ing.**

**be·dev·il·ment** (bi dev′əl ment)   1 great trouble; torment.   2 complete confusion or muddle.   3 the state of being under a spell; being bewitched.   *n.*

**bed·fel·low** (bed′fel′ō)   1 the person with whom one shares a bed.   2 a close associate: *The antiwar movement has produced some strange bedfellows.*   *n.*

**be·dim** (bi dim′)   make dim; darken; obscure.   *v.,* **be·dimmed, be·dim·ming.**

**be·di·zen** (bi dī′zən *or* bi diz′ən)   dress in gaudy clothes; ornament with showy finery.   *v.*

**bed·lam** (bed′lam)   1 uproar; confusion: *When the home team won, there was bedlam in the arena. The whole house was bedlam for the first few days.*   2 **Bedlam,** the traditional popular name for a hospital for the mentally ill in England, originally the Hospital of St. Mary of Bethlehem, but now officially named Bethlehem Royal Hospital.   *n.*
☞ *Etym.*   From ME *Bedlem,* a variant form of *Bethlem,* short for the Hospital of St. Mary of Bethlehem in London, England. It became a hospital in 1547.

**bed linen**   sheets and pillowcases for a bed.

**Bed·ou·in** (bed′ü in) **1** a nomad of the deserts and steppes of the Middle East and northern Africa: *Most of the Bedouins of northern Africa are Berbers; those of the Middle East are Arabs.* **2** of or having to do with the Bedouins. **3** any wanderer or nomad. *1, 3 n., 2 adj.*
☛ *Etym.* From OF *beduin*, originally from Arabic *badāwīn* 'desert dwellers'.

**be·drag·gle** (bi drag′əl) make limp and soiled. *v.*, **be·drag·gled, be·drag·gling.**

**be·drag·gled** (bi drag′əld) **1** thoroughly wet and straggly: *bedraggled hair. We didn't let the dog into the house because she was so bedraggled.* **2** soiled by being dragged in the dirt: *a bedraggled skirt.* **3** pt. and pp. of BEDRAGGLE. *1, 2 adj., 3 v.*

**bed·rid** (bed′rid′) BEDRIDDEN. *adj.*

**bed·rid·den** (bed′rid′ən) confined to bed for a long time because of sickness or weakness. *adj.*

**bed·rock** (bed′rok′) **1** the solid rock beneath the soil and looser rocks. **2** a firm foundation. **3** the lowest level; bottom. *n.*

**bed·roll** (bed′rōl′) blankets or a sleeping bag rolled up and tied for carrying. *n.*

**bed·room** (bed′rüm′) a room to sleep in. *n.*

**bed·side** (bed′sīd′) **1** the side of a bed: *The nurse sat by the sick woman's bedside.* **2** with the sick; attending the sick: *Young doctors need bedside practice. She has a good bedside manner.* *n.*

**bed·sore** (bed′sôr′) a sore caused by lying too long in the same position. *n.*

**bed·spread** (bed′spred′) a cover that is spread over other bedclothes to keep them clean and neat. *n.*

**bed·stead** (bed′sted′) the wooden or metal framework of a bed. *n.*

**bed·time** (bed′tīm′) the usual time for going to bed: *His regular bedtime is nine o'clock.* *n.*

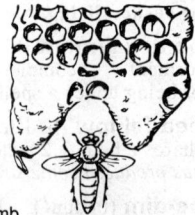

Bee: honeybees with a section of honeycomb

**bee¹** (bē) any of about 20 000 species making up several families of insects that feed their young with a mixture of pollen and honey stored in their nests. Some species of bees are social, living in large, highly organized colonies, but most species are solitary: *The best-known social bees are the honeybee and the bumblebee.* *n.*
**have a bee in one's bonnet** or **one's head,** *Informal.* **a** think of one thing only. **b** be slightly crazy.
☛ *Hom.* BE.

**bee²** (bē) a gathering for work or amusement: *a husking bee, a spelling bee.* *n.*
☛ *Hom.* BE.

**bee·bread** (bē′bred′) a brownish, bitter substance consisting of pollen, or pollen mixed with honey, used by bees as food. *n.*

**beech** (bēch) **1** any of a closely related group of trees found in North America and Europe, having smooth, grey bark, dark green, glossy leaves, and small, sweet, edible nuts. **2** the hard, heavy, strong wood of a beech. **3** a family of trees that includes some species highly valued for their timber: *Beeches, oaks, and chestnuts belong to the beech family.* *n.*
☛ *Hom.* BEACH.

**beech·en** (bē′chən) made of BEECHWOOD. *adj.*

**beech·nut** (bēch′nut′) the small, triangular nut of the BEECH tree. *n.*

**beech·wood** (bēch′wùd′) the wood of a BEECH tree. *n.*

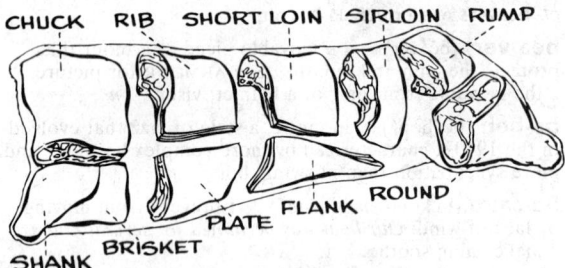

The main cuts of beef

**beef** (bēf) **1** the meat from a steer, cow, or bull. **2** a steer, cow, or bull when full-grown and fattened for food. **3** *Informal.* strength; muscle. **4** *Informal.* weight or heaviness. *n., pl. (def. 2)* **beeves.**
**beef up,** *Informal.* strengthen: *You could beef up your argument by adding more examples.*

**beef cattle** cattle raised for meat.

**beef·eat·er** (bē′fē′tər) the common nickname for a YEOMAN OF THE GUARD who acts as a warder and official guide of the Tower of London. *n.*

**beef·steak** (bēf′stāk′) a slice of beef for broiling or frying. *n.*

**beef tea** a strong beef broth.

**beef·y** (bē′fē) **1** like beef: *The broth has a beefy taste.* **2** strong or muscular. **3** heavy; solid. *adj.*, **beef·i·er, beef·i·est.** —**beef′i·ness,** *n.*

**bee·hive** (bē′hīv′) **1** a hive or house for bees. **2** a busy, swarming place. *n.*

**bee·keep·er** (bē′kē′pər) a person who keeps bees for their honey and wax. *n.*

**bee·keep·ing** (bē′kē′ping) the art of caring for and managing colonies of honeybees so that they will produce more honey than they need for themselves. The extra honey stored by the bees is collected for human use. *n.*

**bee·line** (bē′līn′) the straightest way or line between two places; a straight line, like the flight of a bee to its hive. *n.*
**make a beeline for,** *Informal.* go as quickly and directly as possible to: *The startled calf made a beeline for its mother.*

**been** (bin *or* bēn) pp. of BE: *He has been ill.* *v.*
☛ *Hom.* BIN (for the first pronunciation of **been**); BEAN (for the second pronunciation).

**beer** (bēr) **1** an alcoholic drink made from malt and, usually, hops. **2** a bottle or glass of beer: *She ordered a*

**beer.** 3 a drink made from roots or plants: *root beer, ginger beer.* *n.*
☞ *Hom.* BIER.

**beer and skittles** *Informal.* enjoyment; material comforts: *Life is not all beer and skittles.*

**beer parlour** or **parlor** *Cdn.* a room in a hotel or tavern where beer is sold and drunk; beverage room.

**beest·ings** (bē′stingz) the first milk from a cow after it has given birth to a calf. *n. pl.*

**bees·wax** (bē′zwaks′) 1 a yellowish, pleasant-smelling wax given out by worker bees for constructing the cell walls of their honeycombs: *Beeswax is processed for making candles, furniture polish, modelling wax, etc.* 2 rub, polish, or treat with beeswax. 1 *n.*, 2 *v.*

**beet** (bēt) 1 the thick, fleshy root of a biennial plant: *Red beets are eaten as vegetables. Sugar is made from white beets.* 2 the plant: *The leaves of beets are sometimes eaten as greens.* *n.* —**beet′like′**, *adj.*
☞ *Hom.* BEAT.

LADYBUG    EMERALD-COLOURED BEETLE

Two species of beetle

**bee·tle**¹ (bē′təl) 1 any insect belonging to an order of insects having four wings, the front pair of which are modified into horny coverings that are folded along the back when at rest, hiding the rear pair of wings: *Beetles include some of the largest insects, such as an Asian beetle that is about 18 cm long, and others so small they are almost invisible to the naked eye.* 2 any similar insect. *n.*
**beetle off,** *Informal.* move quickly; scurry: *She grabbed his jacket and beetled off.*
☞ *Hom.* BETEL.

**bee·tle**² (bē′təl) 1 a heavy wooden mallet for ramming, crushing, or smoothing. 2 a wooden household utensil for beating or mashing. 3 pound with a beetle. 1, 2 *n.*, 3 *v.*, **bee·tled, bee·tling.**
☞ *Hom.* BETEL.

**bee·tle**³ (bē′təl) 1 project or overhang: *Great cliffs beetled above the narrow path.* 2 of eyebrows, shaggy and projecting: *His eyes were fierce beneath his beetle brows.* 1 *v.*, **bee·tled, bee·tling;** 2 *adj.*
☞ *Hom.* BETEL.

**bee·tle-browed** (bē′təl broud′) 1 having shaggy, projecting eyebrows. 2 scowling; sullen. *adj.*

**bee·tling** (bē′tling) 1 projecting or overhanging; standing out: *beetling rocks, beetling eyebrows.* 2 ppr. of BEETLE. 1 *adj.*, 2 *v.*

**beet root** the root of a BEET plant.

**beet sugar** the sugar obtained from white BEETS.

**beeves** (bēvz) pl. of BEEF¹ (def. 2). *n.*

**be·fall** (bi fol′) 1 happen to: *An accident must have befallen them.* 2 happen: *Whatever befalls, we'll keep our promise.* *v.*, **be·fell, be·fall·en, be·fall·ing.**

**be·fell** (bi fel′) pt. of BEFALL. *v.*

**be·fit** (bi fit′) be suitable for; be proper for; be suited to: *She always wears clothes that befit the occasion.* *v.*, **be·fit·ted, be·fit·ting.**

**be·fit·ting** (bi fit′ing) 1 suitable; proper. 2 ppr. of BEFIT. 1 *adj.*, 2 *v.* —**be·fit′ting·ly**, *adv.*

**be·fog** (bi fog′) 1 surround with fog; make foggy. 2 obscure or confuse. *v.*, **be·fogged, be·fog·ging.**

**be·fore** (bi fôr′) 1 earlier than: *Come before five o'clock.* 2 rather than: *I'll give up the trip before I'll go with them.* 3 sooner than: *He'd die before giving in.* 4 in the presence of or sight of: *to stand before the king.* 5 in front of; in advance of; ahead of: *Walk before me.* 6 in front; in advance; ahead: *He went before to see if the road was safe.* 7 earlier: *Come at five o'clock, not before.* 8 until now; in the past: *I didn't know that before.* 9 previously to the time when: *Before she goes, I would like to talk to her.* 1, 3–5 *prep.*, 2, 9 *conj.*, 6–8 *adv.*

**be·fore·hand** (bi fôr′hand′) ahead of time; in advance: *I am going to get everything ready beforehand.* *adv.*

**be·foul** (bi foul′) 1 make dirty; cover with filth. 2 entangle: *The rope was befouled by weeds.* *v.*

**be·friend** (bi frend′) act as a friend to; help: *The children were eager to befriend the new girl.* *v.*

**be·fud·dle** (bi fud′əl) 1 stupefy; confuse: *All this arithmetic is befuddling me.* 2 make stupid with alcoholic drink. *v.*, **be·fud·dled, be·fud·dling.**

**beg** (beg) 1 ask help or charity: *He was finally reduced to begging for a living.* 2 ask for food, money, clothes, etc. as a charity: *The tramp begged his meals.* 3 ask as a favour; ask earnestly or humbly: *He begged his mother to forgive him.* 4 ask formally and courteously: *I beg your pardon.* *v.*, **begged, beg·ging.**
**beg off,** ask to be excused or released from an engagement or obligation: *She asked me to go along, but I begged off.*
**beg the question,** take for granted the very thing being argued about.
**go begging,** find no one who will accept.

**be·gan** (bi gan′) pt. of BEGIN: *It began to rain.* *v.*

**be·get** (bi get′) 1 become the father of. 2 cause to be; produce: *Hate always begets hate.* *v.*, **be·got, be·got·ten** or **be·got, be·get·ting.** —**be·get′ter**, *n.*

**beg·gar** (beg′ər) 1 a person who lives by begging. 2 a very poor person. 3 make poor; bring to poverty: *Your reckless spending will beggar your father.* 4 make to seem inadequate or worthless: *The grandeur of Niagara Falls beggars description.* 5 fellow: *a friendly little beggar.* 1, 2, 5 *n.*, 3, 4 *v.*

**beg·gar·ly** (beg′ər lē) fit for a beggar; poor. *adj.* —**beg′gar·li·ness**, *n.*

**beg·gar·y** (beg′ə rē) very great poverty. *n.*

**be·gin** (bi gin′) 1 do the first part; start: *We will begin work soon.* 2 do the first part of: *I began reading the book yesterday.* 3 come into being: *The club began two years ago.* 4 bring into being: *Two sisters began the club.*

**5** be near; come near: *That suit doesn't even begin to fit you.* *v.*, **be·gan, be·gun, be·gin·ning.**

**be·gin·ner** (bi gin′ər) **1** a person who is doing something for the first time; person who lacks skill and experience. **2** a person who begins anything. *n.*

**be·gin·ning** (bi gin′ing) **1** a start: *to make a good beginning.* **2** the time when anything begins. **3** the first part: *The beginning of the book is good, but then it gets boring.* **4** a first cause; source; origin. **5** that begins; first in order: *This is the beginning lesson of the spelling book.* **6** just starting: *a beginning student.* **7** ppr. of BEGIN. 1–4 *n.*, 5, 6 *adj.*, 7 *v.*

**be·go·ni·a** (bi gō′nē ə *or* bi gō′nyə) **1** any of a large, closely related group of flowering plants, including many varieties and hybrids grown for their showy, waxy flowers and often coloured leaves. **2** referring to the family of tropical and subtropical plants that includes the begonias and a few other species: *Most of the plants belonging to the begonia family are herbs native to South America.* *n.*

**be·got** (bi got′) pt. and a pp. of BEGET: *He begot a daughter.* *v.*

**be·got·ten** (bi got′ən) a pp. of BEGET: *He has begotten two sons.* *v.*

**be·grimed** (bi grīmd′) made grimy; soiled and dirty. *adj.*

**be·grudge** (bi gruj′) **1** be reluctant to give something; grudge: *She is so stingy that she begrudges her dog decent food.* **2** envy somebody the possession of: *They begrudge us our new house.* *v.*, **be·grudged, be·grudg·ing.**
—**be·grudg′ing·ly,** *adv.*

**be·guile** (bi gīl′) **1** deceive; cheat: *Her pleasant ways beguiled me into thinking that she was my friend.* **2** take away from deceitfully or cunningly. **3** entertain; amuse; charm: *The old sailor beguiled the boys with stories of his life at sea.* **4** pass or while away pleasantly: *We beguiled the time with reading.* *v.*, **be·guiled, be·guil·ing.**
—**be·guil′er,** *n.*

**be·guil·ing** (bi gī′ling) **1** deceiving. **2** entertaining; amusing. **3** ppr. of BEGUILE. 1, 2 *adj.*, 3 *v.*
—**be·guil′ing·ly,** *adv.*

**be·gum** (bē′gəm) a Moslem title of honour for a woman, used especially in India and Pakistan: *Begum is equivalent to princess.* *n.*

**be·gun** (bi gun′) pp. of BEGIN: *It has begun to rain.* *v.*

**be·half** (bi haf′) interest; favour; support: *His friends will act in his behalf.* *n.*
**in behalf of,** in the interest of; for: *She worked for weeks in behalf of the Community Chest.*
**on behalf of, a** as a representative of: *The lawyer spoke convincingly on behalf of his client.* **b** in behalf of.

**be·have** (bi hāv′) **1** conduct oneself: *The little boy behaves himself badly in school. The ship behaves well.* **2** act well; do what is right: *Did you behave today?* **3** act: *Water behaves in different ways when it is heated and when it is frozen.* *v.*, **be·haved, be·hav·ing.**

**behavior** (bi hā′vyər) See BEHAVIOUR. *n.*

**be·hav·iour** or **be·hav·ior** (bi hā′vyər) **1** a way of acting; actions; acts: *His sullen behaviour showed he was angry.* **2** manners or deportment: *She was on her best behaviour while the visitors were there.* *n.*

**be·hav·iour·ism** or **be·hav·ior·ism** (bi hā′vyə riz′əm) the theory that the objectively observed acts of persons and animals are the chief or only subject matter of scientific psychology. *n.*

**be·hav·iour·ist** or **be·hav·ior·ist** (bi hā′vyə rist) a person who believes in BEHAVIOURISM. *n.*

**be·hav·iour·is·tic** or **be·hav·ior·is·tic** (bi hā′vyə ris′tik) having to do with behaviourists or BEHAVIOURISM. *adj.*

**be·head** (bi hed′) cut off the head of. *v.*

**be·held** (bi held′) pt. and pp. of BEHOLD: *We beheld the approaching storm. You have all beheld beautiful sunsets.* *v.*

**be·he·moth** (bi hē′məth *or* bē′ə məth) **1** in the Bible, a huge and powerful animal: *The behemoth may have been the hippopotamus.* **2** anything of great size or power such as a large truck. *n.*

**be·hest** (bi hest′) a command; order. *n.*

**be·hind** (bi hīnd′) **1** at the back of; in the rear of: *The child hid behind the door.* **2** at or toward the back; in the rear: *The dog's tail hung down behind.* **3** at or on the far side of: *A beautiful valley lies behind the hill.* **4** farther back in place or time: *The rest of the hikers are still far behind.* **5** later than; after: *The letter carrier is behind his usual time today.* **6** not on time; slow; late: *The train is behind today.* **7** concealed by: *Treachery lurked behind the spy's smooth manners.* **8** less advanced than: *She is behind the other children in her class.* **9** remaining after: *The dead man left a family behind him.* **10** in support of; supporting: *Her friends are behind her.* **11** *Informal.* the fleshy part of the body where the legs join the back; buttocks; seat. 1, 3, 5, 7–10 *prep.*, 2, 4, 6 *adv.*, 11 *n.*

**be·hind·hand** (bi hīnd′hand′) **1** behind time; late: *Don't wait for Helen; she is always behindhand.* **2** behind others in progress; backward; slow: *Ali is behindhand in his schoolwork.* **3** in debt; in arrears: *They are behindhand with their rent.* *adj.*
☛ *Usage.* Never used before a noun.

**be·hold** (bi hōld′) see; look at: *They beheld a storm approaching. Behold your new queen.* *v.*, **be·held, be·hold·ing.**

**be·hold·en** (bi hōl′dən) under obligation or in debt to somebody: *I am much beholden to you for your help.* *adj.*
☛ *Usage.* Never used before a noun.

**be·hold·er** (bi hōl′dər) onlooker; spectator. *n.*

**be·hoove** (bi hüv′) be necessary or proper for: *It behooves us to answer the challenge.* *v.*, **be·hooved, be·hoov·ing.**

**be·hove** (bi hōv′) BEHOOVE. *v.*, **be·hoved, be·hov·ing.**

**beige** (bāzh) pale brown; light greyish brown. *n.*, *adj.*

**be·ing** (bē′ing) **1** ppr. of BE: *The dog is being fed.* **2** life; existence: *This world came into being long ago.* **3** nature; constitution: *Her whole being thrilled to the beauty of the music.* **4** a person; living creature: *Men, women, and children are human beings.* 1 *v.*, 2–4 *n.*
**for the time being,** for the present time; for now: *Let's leave that problem for the time being and come back to it later.*

**be·jew·el** (bi jü′əl) adorn with jewels, or as if with jewels: *The sky is bejewelled with stars.* *v.*, **be·jew·elled** or **be·jew·eled, be·jew·el·ling** or **be·jew·el·ing.**

**be·la·bour** or **be·la·bor** (bi lā′bər) **1** beat vigorously:

*The man belaboured his poor donkey.* **2** abuse or ridicule: *The politician was belaboured by the press.* **3** work at or on longer than necessary; harp on: *to belabour a point in an argument.* *v.*

**be·lat·ed** (bi lā′tid) delayed; happening or coming too late: *a belated birthday card. Her belated attempt to make amends was rejected.* *adj.* —**be·lat′ed·ly,** *adv.* —**be·lat′ed·ness,** *n.*

**be·lay** (bi lā′) **1** fasten a rope by winding it around a pin or cleat. **2** *Informal.* stop: *Belay, there!* *v.*, **be·layed, be·lay·ing.**

**belaying pin** a removable pin on the rail of a ship or boat, used for fastening rigging lines. It can quickly be removed to untie a knot.

**belch** (belch) **1** expel gas from the stomach through the mouth. **2** throw out with force: *The volcano belched fire, smoke, and ashes.* **3** the act of belching. **1, 2** *v.*, **3** *n.*

**be·lea·guer** (bi lē′gər) **1** BESIEGE: *The people of the beleaguered city refused to give in.* **2** torment; beset: *Beleaguered by debts, she was finally forced into bankruptcy.* *v.*

**bel·fry** (bel′frē) **1** a tower or steeple containing a bell or bells. **2** a room in a tower, or a cupola or turret in which a bell or bells are hung. *n.*, *pl.* **bel·fries.**

**Bel·gian** (bel′jən) **1** of or having to do with Belgium, a country in western Europe, or its people. **2** a native or inhabitant of Belgium. **3** a person of Belgian descent. **4** a breed of large, strong draft horse. **1** *adj.*, **2–4** *n.*

**Belgian hare** a breed of large European rabbit having reddish-brown hair, raised in many countries for its fur and its meat: *The Belgian hare is the typical domestic rabbit.*

**be·lie** (bi lī′) **1** give a false idea of; misrepresent: *Her frown belied her usual good nature.* **2** show to be false; contradict: *Her actions belie her words.* **3** fail to come up to; disappoint: *He stole again, and so belied our hopes.* *v.*, **be·lied, be·ly·ing.**

**be·lief** (bi lēf′) **1** the state or habit of having confidence in any person or thing; faith; trust: *a belief in God, belief in a person's honesty.* **2** mental acceptance as true or real; acceptance of a statement or fact: *a belief in the existence of ghosts. That statement is unworthy of belief.* **3** the thing believed; a statement or condition accepted as true: *His beliefs are different from mine.* **4** opinion: *It's my belief that we're in for a cold winter.* *n.*

**be·liev·a·ble** (bi lē′və bəl) that can be believed. *adj.* —**be·liev′a·bly,** *adv.*

**be·lieve** (bi lēv′) **1** have faith in a person or thing; trust (used with **in**): *to believe in God. I believe in their sincerity.* **2** think that something is true or real; accept a statement or fact: *We believe that the earth revolves around the sun. I don't believe her story. Do you believe in ghosts?* **3** think that somebody tells the truth: *I don't believe him.* **4** have religious faith: *All who believe are asked to pray for peace.* **5** think or suppose: *I believe we are going to put on a play at graduation.* *v.*, **be·lieved, be·liev·ing.**

**be·liev·er** (bi lē′vər) a person who believes, especially a follower of some religion. *n.*

**be·lit·tle** (bi lit′əl) cause to seem little, unimportant, or less important; speak slightingly of: *Jealous people belittled the explorer's great discoveries.* *v.*, **be·lit·tled, be·lit·tling.** —**be·lit′tler,** *n.*

**belated**     105     **belligerency**

hat, āge, fär; let, ēqual, tėrm; it, īce
hot, ōpen, ôrder; oil, out; cup, pùt, rüle
əbove, takən, pencəl, lemən, circəs
ch, child; ng, long; sh, ship
th, thin; ŦH, then; zh, measure

Bells: a handbell and a bell in a tower

**bell** (bel) **1** a hollow device of metal or sometimes glass, etc., usually shaped like a cup with a flared opening, that makes a musical sound when struck by a clapper or a hammer: *The bells rang to announce the end of the war.* **2** the sound of a bell. **3** on shipboard, the stroke of a bell to indicate a half hour of time. 1 bell = 12:30, 4:30, or 8:30; 2 bells = 1:00, 5:00, or 9:00; and so on up to 8 bells = 4:00, 8:00, or 12:00. **4** put a bell on. **5** a percussion instrument having metal tubes or bars that produce bell-like tones when struck. **6** anything shaped like a bell, such as the COROLLA of a flower. **7** swell out like a bell. **1–3, 5, 6** *n.*, **4, 7** *v.* —**bell′-like′,** *adj.*
**bell the cat,** do something dangerous or daring for the common good.
**ring a bell,** produce a response in one's mind; seem familiar: *I didn't recognize her at first, but the name rang a bell.*
☛ *Hom.* BELLE.

**bel·la·don·na** (bel′ə don′ə) **1** a poisonous plant of Europe having black berries and red, bell-shaped flowers. **2** a drug made from this plant; ATROPINE. *n.*

**bell·boy** (bel′boi′) a man or boy whose work is carrying hand baggage and doing errands for the guests of a hotel or club. *n.*

**bell buoy** a BUOY with a bell that is rung by the movement of the waves.

**belle** (bel) **1** a beautiful woman or girl. **2** the prettiest or most admired woman or girl: *She was the belle of the ball.* *n.*
☛ *Hom.* BELL.

**belles–let·tres** (bel′let′rə) literature, such as poetry, drama, fiction, and personal essays, considered for its artistic appeal rather than for any practical value such as giving information. *n. pl.*

**bell·flow·er** (bel′flou′ər) any of various plants with bell-shaped flowers; CAMPANULA. *n.*

**bell·hop** (bel′hop′) *Informal.* BELLBOY. *n.*

**bel·li·cose** (bel′ə kōs′) warlike; fond of fighting. *adj.*

**bel·li·cos·i·ty** (bel′ə kos′ə tē) a BELLICOSE quality or attitude. *n.*

**bel·lig·er·ence** (bə lij′ə rəns) **1** being warlike; fondness for fighting. **2** fighting or war. *n.*

**bel·lig·er·en·cy** (bə lij′ə rən sē) **1** the state of being a BELLIGERENT (def. 2). **2** BELLIGERENCE. *n.*

**bel·lig·er·ent** (bə lij′ə rənt)   **1** at war; engaged in war; fighting.   **2** a nation or state at war: *The belligerents agreed on a truce.*   **3** having to do with nations or states at war.   **4** having or showing an aggressive or quarrelsome attitude; warlike: *She gets very belligerent if you don't agree with her.*   **5** a person engaged in fighting with another person.   1, 3, 4 *adj.*, 2, 5 *n.*
—**bel·lig′er·ent·ly**, *adv.*

**bell jar**   a bell-shaped container or cover made of glass, used especially in scientific experiments requiring reduced air pressure.

**bell·man** (bel′mən)   a TOWN CRIER.   *n.*, *pl.* **bell·men** (-mən).

**bel·low** (bel′ō)   **1** roar as a bull does.   **2** a roar like a bull's.   **3** shout loudly: *The lifeguard bellowed at the boys to stay near the shore.*   **4** roar with pain or anger: *The pain of the burn made him bellow.*   **5** make a loud, deep noise; roar: *We heard the huge cataract bellowing in the distance.*   **6** any noise made by bellowing; a deep, roaring noise.   1, 3–5 *v.*, 2, 6 *n.*   —**bel·low·er**, *n.*

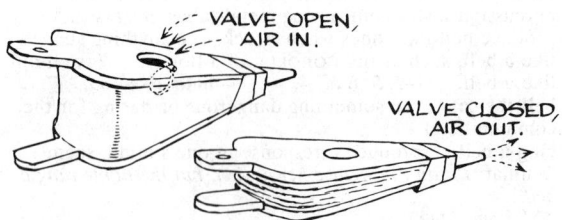

Bellows. Air is sucked into the bellows as the sides are pulled apart. When the sides are pushed together, the valve closes and air is forced out through the nozzle.

**bel·lows** (bel′ōz *or* bel′əs)   **1** an instrument for producing a strong current of air, used for blowing a fire to make it burn or for sounding an organ, accordion, etc.   **2** the folding part of certain cameras, behind the lens.   *n. sing. or pl.*

**bell·weth·er** (bel′weŦH′ər)   **1** a male sheep that wears a bell and leads the flock.   **2** any person, group, or thing thought of as setting a standard or pattern: *The new magazine quickly became the bellwether of fashion.*   *n.*

**bel·ly** (bel′ē)   **1** the lower part of the human body, which contains the stomach and intestines; abdomen.   **2** the under part of an animal's body.   **3** stomach: *a full belly.*   **4** the bulging part of anything; a hollow space in a bulging part: *the belly of a sail.*   **5** swell out or bulge: *The ship's sails bellied in the wind.*   1–4 *n.*, *pl.* **bel·lies**; 5 *v.*, **bel·lied, bel·ly·ing.**

**bel·ly·ache** (bel′ē āk′)   *Informal.*   **1** a pain in the abdomen.   **2** an excuse for complaining; grievance.   **3** complain or grumble, especially over trifles.   1, 2 *n.*, 3 *v.*, **bel·ly·ached, bel·ly·ach·ing.**   —**bel′ly·ach′er**, *n.*

**belly button**   NAVEL.

**bel·ly·ful** (bel′ē fùl′)   *Informal.*   an amount that is more than one wants or can stand: *After listening to complaints for two hours, the store clerk had had a bellyful.*   *n.*

**be·long** (bi long′)   have a proper place: *That book belongs on this shelf.*   *v.*

**belong to,**   **a** be the property of: *Does this cap belong to you?*   **b** be a part of; be connected with: *That top belongs to my bottle.*   **c** be a member of: *Mary belongs to the Girl Guides.*   **d** be the duty or concern of: *This responsibility belongs to the club secretary.*

**be·long·ings** (bi long′ingz)   things that belong to a person; possessions.   *n. pl.*

**be·lov·ed** (bi luv′id *or* bi luvd′)   **1** dearly loved; dear.   **2** a person who is loved; darling.   1 *adj.*, 2 *n.*

**be·low** (bi lō′)   **1** in or to a lower place: *From the airplane we could see the fields below.*   **2** lower than; under: *below the third floor.*   **3** less than; lower in rank or degree than: *It is seven degrees below freezing.*   **4** on or to a lower floor or deck; downstairs: *The sailor went below.*   **5** unworthy of: *below contempt.*   **6** on earth.   **7** in hell.   **8** in a book or article, after: *See the note below.*   **9** below zero on the Celsius or Fahrenheit scale of temperature.   1, 4, 6–9 *adv.*, 2, 3, 5 *prep.*

**belt** (belt)   **1** a strip of leather, cloth, etc. worn around the body to hold in or support clothing, to hold tools or weapons, or as a decoration.   **2** any broad strip or band: *a belt of trees.*   **3** a region having distinctive characteristics: *The wheat belt is the region where wheat is grown.*   **4** put a belt around.   **5** fasten on with a belt.   **6** beat with a belt.   **7** hit suddenly and hard: *The boxer belted his opponent across the ring.*   **8** an endless band that transfers motion from one wheel or pulley to another: *a lathe belt.*   1–3, 8 *n.*, 4–7 *v.*
**below the belt,**   **a** foul; unfair.   **b** foully; unfairly.
**tighten one's belt,**   be more thrifty.

**belt·ed** (bel′tid)   **1** having a belt: *a belted jacket.*   **2** wearing a special belt as a sign of honour: *a belted earl.*   **3** marked by a belt of colour: *A belted kingfisher has a reddish-brown band across its white breast.*   See KINGFISHER for picture.   **4** pt. and pp. of BELT.   1–3 *adj.*, 4 *v.*

**belt·ing** (bel′ting)   **1** material for making belts.   **2** belts.   **3** ppr. of BELT.   1, 2 *n.*, 3 *v.*

**belt line**   a railway, bus line, etc. that takes a more or less circular route around a city or other special area.

**be·lu·ga** (bə lü′gə)   **1** a species of white toothed whale of the same family as the narwhal, found in the Arctic and as far south as the Gulf of St. Lawrence, having no back fin and having broad, rounded flippers; white whale: *The beluga was formerly called the "sea canary" by Arctic whalers because of its musical, trilling voice.*   **2** a species of large white STURGEON, the largest freshwater fish, reaching a length of about seven metres: *The beluga, which is found in the Black and Caspian seas and the Sea of Azov, is the source of most European caviar.*   *n.*
☛ *Etym.*   From the Russian names for both these creatures, formed from *byelo-* 'white' + *-uga* and *-ukha*, suffixes meaning 'large'. 18c.

**be·moan** (bi mōn′)   moan about; bewail.   *v.*

**be·muse** (bi myüz′)   confuse; bewilder; stupefy.   *v.*, **be·mused, be·mus·ing.**

**bench** (bench)   **1** a long seat, usually of wood or stone.   **2** the worktable of a carpenter, or of any worker with tools and materials: *She worked at her bench in the basement.*   **3** the seat where judges sit in a law court.   **4** a judge or group of judges presiding in a law court: *The witness was told by the bench to keep to the point.*   **5** the position or office of a judge: *The lawyer was appointed to the bench.*   **6** a narrow stretch of high, flat land: *Apples are grown on the benches of the Okanagan Valley in British Columbia.*   **7** furnish with benches.   **8** assign a seat on a bench.   **9** take a player out of a game.   1–6 *n.*, 7–9 *v.*
**on the bench,**   **a** sitting in a law court as a judge.   **b** sitting among the substitute players.

**bench·mark** (bench′märk′) **1** a mark made on a rock, post, etc. in surveying: *A benchmark is used as a starting point or guide in a line of levels for the determination of altitudes.* **2** a point of reference; standard. *n.*

**bench warrant** a written order from a court of law or a judge for the arrest of an accused person or a witness who has not appeared in court as required.

**bend** (bend) **1** make, be, or become curved or crooked: *He bent the iron bar as if it had been made of rubber. The branch began to bend as I climbed along it.* **2** a part that is not straight; a curve or turn: *There is a sharp bend in the road here.* **3** move or turn in a certain direction; direct mind or effort; apply: *Her steps were bent toward home. She bent her mind to the new work.* **4** stoop; bow: *She bent to the ground and picked up a stone.* **5** the act of bending: *a bend of the knee.* **6** force to submit: *"I will bend you or break you!" cried the villain.* **7** submit: *But the heroine would not bend.* **8** fasten a sail, rope, etc. **9** a knot for tying two ropes together or tying a rope to something else. **10 the bends,** *Informal.* cramps and paralysis caused by changing too suddenly from high air pressure to ordinary air pressure, as, when coming up from deep water. 1, 3, 4, 6–8 *v.,* **bent, bend·ing;** 2, 5, 9, 10 *n.*
**bend over,** lean toward the ground.
**bend over backwards,** *Informal.* make great effort or take great care.
**bent on,** determined on.

**be·neath** (bi nēth′) **1** below; underneath: *What you drop will fall upon the spot beneath.* **2** below; under; lower than: *The dog sat beneath the tree.* **3** unworthy of; worthy not even of: *A traitor is so low that he is beneath contempt.* 1 *adv.,* 2, 3 *prep.*

**ben·e·dict** (ben′ə dikt′) **1** a recently married man, especially one who was a bachelor for a long time. **2** any married man. *n.*

**ben·e·dic·tion** (ben′ə dik′shən) **1** the asking of a blessing at the end of a religious service. **2** a blessing: *The heavy rainfall was a benediction after the drought.* *n.*

**ben·e·fac·tion** (ben′ə fak′shən) **1** a doing good; a kind act. **2** a benefit conferred; a gift for charity; help given for any good purpose. *n.*

**ben·e·fac·tor** (ben′ə fak′tər *or* ben′ə fak′tər) a person who has helped others, either by gifts of money or some kind act. *n.*

**ben·e·fac·tress** (ben′ə fak′tris *or* ben′ə fak′tris) a woman who has helped others, either by gifts of money or some kind act. *n.*

**be·nef·i·cence** (bə nef′ə səns) **1** the quality of being kind: *Her beneficence is well known.* **2** a kindly act; gift. *n.*

**be·nef·i·cent** (bə nef′ə sənt) **1** kind and good. **2** having good results: *beneficent acts.* *adj.*

**ben·e·fi·cial** (ben′ə fish′əl) favourable; helpful; good for; productive of good: *Sunshine and moisture are beneficial to plants.* *adj.* —**ben′e·fi′cial·ly,** *adv.*

**ben·e·fi·ci·ar·y** (ben′ə fish′ə rē *or* ben′ə fish′ē er′ē) **1** a person who receives benefit: *All the children are beneficiaries of the new playground.* **2** a person who receives or is to receive money or property from an insurance policy, a will, etc. *n., pl.* **ben·e·fi·ci·ar·ies.**

**ben·e·fit** (ben′ə fit) **1** anything for the good of a person or thing; an advantage. **2** do good to; be good for: *Rest will benefit a sick person.* **3** receive good; profit: *He benefited by the medicine. She will benefit from the new way of doing business.* **4** money paid to the sick, disabled, etc. **5** a performance at the theatre, a game, etc. to raise money that goes to a special person or persons or to a worthy cause. 1, 4–5 *n.,* 2, 3 *v.*

**be·nev·o·lence** (bə nev′ə ləns) **1** good will; kindly feeling. **2** an act of kindness; something good that is done; a generous gift. *n.*

**be·nev·o·lent** (bə nev′ə lənt) kindly or charitable. *adj.* —**be·nev′o·lent·ly,** *adv.*

**Ben·ga·lese** (beng′gə lēz′ *or* beng′gə lēz′) **1** a native or inhabitant of Bengal, a former province of northeastern India. **2** of Bengal, its people, or their language. 1 *n., pl.* **Ben·ga·lese;** 2 *adj.*

**Ben·ga·li** (ben gol′ē *or* beng gol′ē) **1** of Bengal, its people, or their language. **2** a native of Bengal. **3** the language of Bengal. 1 *adj.,* 2, 3 *n.*

**be·night·ed** (bi nī′tid) **1** not knowing right from wrong; ignorant. **2** overtaken by night; being in darkness. *adj.*

**be·nign** (bi nīn′) **1** gentle; kindly: *a benign old woman.* **2** favourable; mild: *a benign climate.* **3** doing no harm: *A benign swelling or tumour can usually be cured.* *adj.* —**be·nign′ly,** *adv.*

**be·nig·nan·cy** (bi nig′nən sē) a BENIGNANT quality. *n.*

**be·nig·nant** (bi nig′nənt) **1** kindly; gracious: *a benignant ruler.* **2** favourable; beneficial; benign. *adj.* —**be·nig′nant·ly,** *adv.*

**be·nig·ni·ty** (bi nig′nə tē) **1** kindliness; graciousness. **2** a kind act; favour. *n., pl.* **be·nig·ni·ties.**

**ben·i·son** (ben′ə zən *or* ben′ə sən) BLESSING. *n.*

**Ben·nett buggy** (ben′ət) *Cdn.* in the Depression of the 1930's, an automobile drawn by horses because the owner could not afford gas, oil, or a licence for it: *Bennett buggies usually had the engine removed, and the horses were hitched to poles attached to the front bumper.*
☞ *Etym.* Named after R. B. Bennett, prime minister of Canada from 1930 to 1935, because his government had not succeeded in solving Canada's economic problems as promised.

**bent¹** (bent) **1** pt. and pp. of BEND: *She bent the wire.* **2** not straight; curved or crooked: *His back is bent.* **3** strongly inclined; determined: *She is bent on being a doctor.* **4** an inclination or tendency: *a bent for drawing.* 1 *v.,* 2, 3 *adj.,* 4 *n.*

**bent²** (bent) **1** any of several stiff, wiry grasses that grow on sandy or uncultivated land: *Some species of bent are used in lawn mixtures and for hay.* **2** a heath or moor. *n.*

**be·numb** (bi num′) **1** make numb; deaden. **2** stupefy; make inactive: *A benumbing boredom had set in.* *v.*

**ben·zene** (ben′zēn *or* ben zēn′) a colourless, flammable, liquid hydrocarbon that has a pleasant odour and vaporizes easily: *Benzene is obtained chiefly from coal tar and is used in the manufacture of many chemical*

**benzine** 108 **beside**

products, including detergents, insecticides, and motor fuels. *n.*
☞ *Hom.* BENZINE.

**ben·zine** (ben′zēn *or* ben zēn′) a clear, colourless, flammable liquid consisting of a mixture of hydrocarbons obtained in distilling petroleum, used especially as a solvent and cleaning fluid. *n.*
☞ *Hom.* BENZENE.

**ben·zo·ate** (ben′zō āt′ *or* ben′zō it) a salt or ester of BENZOIC ACID. **Benzoate of soda** is used in foods to preserve them. *n.*

**ben·zo·ic acid** (ben zō′ik) an acid occurring in BENZOIN, cranberries, etc. that is used as an antiseptic or as a food preservative.

**ben·zo·in** (ben′zō in) 1 a fragrant resin obtained from certain species of trees of Java, Sumatra, etc. and used in perfume and medicine. 2 a substance resembling CAMPHOR made from this resin. *n.*

**ben·zol** (ben′zol *or* ben′zōl) 1 BENZENE. 2 a liquid containing about 70 percent of BENZENE and 20 to 30 percent of TOLUENE: *Benzol is obtained from coal tar and is used in making dyes.* *n.*

**be·queath** (bi kwēTH′ *or* bi kwēth′) 1 give or leave property, etc. by a will: *The father bequeathed the farm to his daughter.* 2 hand down to posterity: *One age bequeaths its civilization to the next.* *v.*

**be·quest** (bi kwest′) 1 something bequeathed; LEGACY: *Mr. Hart died and left a bequest of ten thousand dollars to his favourite charity.* 2 the act of bequeathing. *n.*

**be·rate** (bi rāt′) scold sharply: *The teacher berated the girls for being late.* *v.*, **be·rat·ed, be·rat·ing.**

**Ber·ber** (bėr′bər) 1 a member of the original Caucasian peoples of northern Africa: *Most Berbers are now farmers.* 2 the group of languages spoken in this region: *Berber languages are spoken by more than 10 million people scattered through Morocco, Tunisia, Libya, and Egypt.* *n.*
☞ *Etym.* See note at BARBARY.

**be·reave** (bi rēv′) 1 deprive of ruthlessly; rob: *to bereave of hope.* 2 leave desolate: *People are bereaved by the death of relatives and friends.* *v.*, **be·reaved** or **be·reft, be·reav·ing.**

**be·reaved** (bi rēvd′) 1 deprived (*of*) by death: *Bereaved of their mother at an early age, the children learned to take care of themselves.* 2 a pt. and a pp. of BEREAVE. 1 *adj.*, 2 *v.*

**be·reave·ment** (bi rēv′mənt) the state of being bereaved, especially by the loss of a relative or friend by death. *n.*

**be·reft** (bi reft′) a pt. and a pp. of BEREAVE: *The loss bereft him of all hope. He was bereft by the loss of his son.* *v.*

**be·ret** (bə rā′ *or* ber′ā) a soft, round cap of wool, felt, etc. See CAP for picture. *n.*

**berg** (bėrg) ICEBERG. *n.*
☞ *Hom.* BURGH.

**be·rib·boned** (bi rib′ənd) trimmed with many ribbons: *The baby wore a beribboned hat.* *adj.*

**ber·i·ber·i** (ber′ē ber′ē) a disease caused by a lack of THIAMINE, affecting the heart or nervous system and in extreme cases resulting in heart failure or paralysis. *n.*

**ber·ke·li·um** (bər kē′lē əm) a synthetic radio-active element produced by nuclear reaction. Symbol: Bk *n.*

**Ber·mu·da onion** (bər myü′də) a large, mild onion grown in Bermuda, Texas, California, etc.

**Bermuda shorts** short pants that reach to just above the knee.

**ber·ry** (ber′ē) 1 any small, juicy fruit having many seeds instead of a single stone, or pit: *Strawberries and currants are berries.* 2 gather or pick berries. 3 the dry seed or kernel of certain kinds of grain or other plants: *a wheat berry.* 4 the fruit of the coffee tree: *Coffee is made from the beans found inside ripe coffee berries.* 5 a simple fruit with the seeds in the pulp and a skin or rind: *Botanists classify grapes, tomatoes, currants, and bananas as berries.* 1, 3–5 *n.*, *pl.* **ber·ries**; 2 *v.*, **ber·ried, ber·ry·ing.** —**ber′ry-like′** *adj.*
☞ *Hom.* BURY (ber′ē).

**ber·serk** (bər zėrk′ *or* bər sėrk′) in a frenzy. *adj.*, *adv.*

**berth** (bėrth) 1 a place to sleep on a ship, train, or aircraft. 2 enough clear space around a ship for it to manoeuvre safely in the water; sea room. 3 the place where a ship stays when at anchor or at a wharf. 4 a place for a truck or other motor vehicle to load or unload, etc. 5 an appointment or position; job: *My sister has a berth as swimming instructor for the summer.* 6 put in a berth; provide with a berth. 7 have or occupy a berth. 8 *Cdn.* a stand of timber in which an individual or company has the right to fell trees; TIMBER LIMIT (def. 2). 1–5, 8 *n.*, 6, 7 *v.*
**give a wide berth to,** keep well away from; pass well clear of: *Our dog always gives a wide berth to the neighbours' cat.*
☞ *Hom.* BIRTH.

**Ber·til·lon system** (bėr′tə lon′) a system, once widely used, for identifying persons, especially criminals, by their physical measurements, such as length of arms and legs and width and length of the skull: *The Bertillon system has been replaced by fingerprinting.*

**ber·yl** (ber′əl) a very hard mineral, usually green or greenish blue, a silicate of BERYLLIUM and aluminum: *Emeralds and aquamarines are beryls.* *n.*
☞ *Hom.* BARREL (ber′əl).

**be·ryl·li·um** (bə ril′ē əm) a hard, strong, steel-grey metallic element, used mainly in alloys as a hardening agent. Symbol: Be *n.*

**be·seech** (bi sēch′) ask earnestly; beg. *v.*, **be·sought** or **be·seeched, be·seech·ing.**

**be·seech·ing** (bi sē′ching) 1 that BESEECHes: *She gave her mother a beseeching look.* 2 ppr. of BESEECH. 1 *adj.*, 2 *v.* —**be·seech′ing·ly,** *adv.*

**be·seem** (bi sēm′) be proper for; be fitting to; suit: *It does not beseem you to leave your friend without help.* *v.*

**be·set** (bi set′) 1 attack on all sides; attack: *In the swamp we were beset by mosquitoes.* 2 continue to trouble; afflict: *a task beset with many difficulties.* 3 set; stud: *Her bracelet was beset with gems.* *v.*, **be·set, be·set·ting.**

**be·set·ting** (bi set′ing) 1 habitually attacking or troubling: *Laziness is a loafer's besetting sin.* 2 ppr. of BESET. 1 *adj.*, 2 *v.*

**be·side** (bi sīd′) 1 by the side of; near; close to: *Grass grows beside the brook.* 2 in addition to: *Other men* *beside ourselves were helping.* **3** compared with: *Nell seems dull beside her sister.* **4** away from; aside from; not related to: *That question is beside the point.* *prep.*

**beside oneself,** out of one's mind; crazy; upset: *He was beside himself with worry over his lost dog.*

**be·sides** (bi sīdz′) **1** also; moreover; further: *She didn't want to quarrel; besides, she wasn't completely sure she was right.* **2** in addition: *We tried two other ways besides.* **3** in addition to; over and above: *The picnic was attended by others besides our own club members.* **4** otherwise; else: *He is ignorant of politics, whatever he may know besides.* **5** except; other than: *We spoke of no one besides you.* 1, 2, 4 *adv.*, 3, 5 *prep.*

**be·siege** (bi sēj′) **1** make a long-continued attempt to get possession of a place by armed force; surround and try to capture: *For ten years the Greeks besieged the city of Troy.* **2** crowd around: *Hundreds of admirers besieged the famous astronaut.* **3** overwhelm with requests, questions, etc.: *During the flood, the Red Cross was besieged with calls for help.* *v.*, **be·sieged, be·sieg·ing.** —**be·sieg·er,** *n.*

**be·smear** (bi smēr′) smear over. *v.*

**be·smirch** (bi smėrch′) **1** make dirty; soil. **2** sully; dishonour: *to besmirch a good reputation.* *v.*

**be·som** (bē′zəm) a broom made of twigs. *n.*

**be·sot·ted** (bi sot′id) **1** foolish; infatuated. **2** stupefied. **3** intoxicated. *adj.*

**be·sought** (bi sot′) a pt. and a pp. of BESEECH. *v.*

**be·span·gle** (bi spang′gəl) adorn with spangles or anything like them. *v.*, **be·span·gled, be·span·gling.**

**be·spat·ter** (bi spat′ər) **1** spatter all over; soil by spattering. **2** slander. *v.* —**be·spat·ter·er,** *n.*

**be·speak** (bi spēk′) **1** engage in advance; order; reserve: *to bespeak tickets to a play.* **2** show; indicate: *A neat appearance bespeaks care.* **3** point to; foreshadow: *Her early successes bespeak a great future.* *v.*, **be·spoke, be·spo·ken** or **be·spoke, be·speak·ing.**

**be·spec·ta·cled** (bi spek′tə kəld) wearing glasses. *adj.*

**be·spoke** (bi spōk′) pt. and a pp. of BESPEAK. *v.*

**be·spo·ken** (bi spō′kən) a pp. of BESPEAK. *v.*

**be·sprin·kle** (bi spring′kəl) sprinkle all over. *v.*, **be·sprin·kled, be·sprin·kling.**

**Bes·se·mer process** (bes′ə mər) a method of making steel by burning out carbon and impurities in molten iron with a blast of compressed air.
☛ **Etym.** Named after Sir Henry Bessemer (1813–1898), an English engineer, who invented the process.

**best** (best) **1** the most desirable, valuable, superior, etc.: *the best food to eat.* **2** of the greatest advantage, usefulness, etc.: *the best thing to do.* **3** largest; greatest: *We spent the best part of the day just getting organized.* **4** in the most excellent way; most thoroughly: *Who reads best?* **5** in the highest degree: *I like this book best.* **6** the person, thing, part, or state that is best: *We want the best. He is the best in the class.* **7** utmost: *I did my best to finish early.* **8** *Informal.* outdo; defeat: *Our team was bested in the final game.* 1–3 *adj.*, superlative of GOOD; 4, 5 *adv.*, superlative of WELL; 6, 7 *n.*, 8 *v.*

**(all) for the best,** favourable in the end: *At first we were unhappy about the plan, but it turned out to be all for the best.*

**at best,** a even under the most favourable circumstances: *Summer is at best very short.* **b** even when interpreted most favourably: *It was a sad effort at best.*

**get the best of,** defeat.

**had best,** should; ought to; will be wise to: *We had best postpone the party.*

**make the best of,** do as well as possible with: *We'll just have to make the best of a bad job.*

**bes·tial** (bes′chəl *or* bes′tyəl) **1** beastly; brutal; vile. **2** of beasts. *adj.* —**bes′tial·ly,** *adv.*

**bes·ti·al·i·ty** (bes′chē al′ə tē *or* bes′tē al′ə tē) BESTIAL character or conduct. *n.*

**be·stir** (bi stėr′) stir up; rouse; exert: *to bestir oneself to action.* *v.*, **be·stirred, be·stir·ring.**

**best man** the chief attendant of the bridegroom at a wedding.

**be·stow** (bi stō′) **1** give something as a gift; give; confer (*used with* **on** *or* **upon**). **2** make use of; apply (*used with* **on** *or* **upon**): *She bestowed a great deal of thought on the plan.* *v.*

**be·stow·al** (bi stō′əl) the act of BESTOWing. *n.*

**be·strad·dle** (bi strad′əl) bestride; straddle. *v.*, **be·strad·dled, be·strad·dling.**

**be·strew** (bi strü′) **1** strew; scatter; sprinkle (with): *The children bestrewed the path with flowers.* **2** strew around; scatter about. **3** lie scattered over: *Flowers bestrewed the path.* *v.*, **be·strewed, be·strewn** or **be·strewed, be·strew·ing.**

**be·strid** (bi strid′) a pt. and a pp. of BESTRIDE. *v.*

**be·strid·den** (bi strid′ən) a pp. of BESTRIDE. *v.*

**be·stride** (bi strīd′) **1** get on or sit on something with one leg on each side: *One can bestride a horse, a chair, or a fence.* **2** stand over something with one leg on each side. **3** stride across; step over. *v.*, **be·strode** or **be·strid, be·strid·den** or **be·strid, be·strid·ing.**

**be·strode** (bi strōd′) a pt. of BESTRIDE: *He bestrode his horse.* *v.*

**best-seller** (best′sel′ər) **1** anything, especially a book or phonograph record, that has a very large sale. **2** the author of a book with a very large sale. *v.*

**bet** (bet) **1** promise money or something else to a person if that person is proved right about the outcome of an event: *I bet you two dollars I won't pass this test.* **2** *Informal.* be very sure: *I bet you are wrong about that.* **3** an agreement between two persons or groups that the one who is proved wrong about the outcome of an event will give a particular thing or sum of money to the one who is proved right: *I made a two-dollar bet that I wouldn't pass.* **4** the thing or sum of money risked in a bet; the STAKE: *I did pass; so I lost my bet (that is, my two dollars).* **5** a thing to bet on: *That horse is a good bet.* 1, 2 *v.*, **bet** or **bet·ted, bet·ting;** 3–5 *n.*

**bet on,** a risk money on. **b** *Informal.* depend on: *It might work, but don't bet on it.*

**be·ta** (bā′tə *or* bē′tə) **1** the second letter of the Greek alphabet (B, β). **2** the second of a series. *n.*

**be·take** (bi tāk′) (used with a pronoun ending in **-self**) **1** go: *to betake oneself to the mountains.* **2** try doing;

**beta particle**     110     **bevel**

apply oneself: *He betook himself to hard study.*   *v.,* **be·took, be·tak·en, be·tak·ing.**

**beta particle**   an electron or positron given off by an atom in the process of radio-active decay.

**beta ray**   a stream of BETA PARTICLES.

**be·ta·tron** (bā′tə tron′ *or* bē′tə tron′)   an ACCELERATOR (def. 3) that uses rapid changes in a magnetic field to increase the velocity of ELECTRONS.   *n.*

**be·tel** (bē′təl)   a kind of climbing pepper plant of the East Indies: *Betel leaves are chewed together with betel nuts by people in southeastern Asia.*   *n.*
☞ Hom. BEETLE.

**Be·tel·geuse** (bē′təl jüz′ *or* bet′əl jüz′)   a very large, reddish star in the constellation Orion.   *n.*

**betel nut**   the orange-coloured nut of a tropical Asian palm tree (**betel palm**).

**bête noire** (bet nwär′)   French.   a thing or person especially dreaded or detested.

**be·think** (bi thingk′)   think about; call to mind.   *v.,* **be·thought, be·think·ing.**
**bethink oneself,**   **a** consider; reflect.   **b** remember.

**be·thought** (bi thot′)   pt. and pp. of BETHINK: *I bethought myself of my work.*   *v.*

**be·tide** (bi tīd′)   happen to; befall: *Woe betide anyone who touches Lisa's stamp collection.*   *v.,* **be·tid·ed, be·tid·ing.**

**be·times** (bi tīmz′)   **1** early: *He woke up betimes.* **2** soon; before it is too late.   *adv.*

**be·to·ken** (bi tō′kən)   be a sign or token of; indicate; show: *Her smile betokens her satisfaction. Dark clouds betoken a storm.*   *v.*

**be·took** (bi tůk′)   pt. of BETAKE: *He betook himself home as soon as school was out.*   *v.*

**be·tray** (bi trā′)   **1** give away to the enemy: *The traitor betrayed his country.*   **2** be unfaithful to: *She betrayed her friends.*   **3** mislead; deceive.   **4** give away a secret; disclose unintentionally.   **5** reveal; show: *Hari's wet shoes betrayed the fact that he had not worn his rubbers.*   *v.* —**be·tray′er,** *n.*

**be·tray·al** (bi trā′əl)   BETRAYing or being betrayed.   *n.*

**be·troth** (bi trōᴛH′ *or* bi troth′)   promise in marriage; engage: *Azan and Ida are now betrothed. He betrothed his daughter to a rich man.*   *v.*

**be·troth·al** (bi trō′ᴛHəl *or* bi troth′əl)   an engagement to be married.   *n.*

**be·trothed** (bi trōᴛHd′ *or* bi trotht′)   a person engaged to be married: *Azan's betrothed was a young woman named Ida.*   *n.*

**bet·ter**[1] (bet′ər)   **1** more desirable, useful, etc. than another: *a better plan.*   **2** more desirably, usefully, etc.; in a more excellent way: *Do better another time.*   **3** make or become better; improve: *We can better our work by being careful.*   **4** a person, thing, or state that is better: *the better of two roads.*   **5** of superior quality: *better bread.* **6** do better than; surpass: *The other class cannot better our grades.*   **7** less sick: *The child is better today.*   **8** larger: *Four days is the better part of a week.*   **9** in a higher degree; more: *I know her better than anyone else.*   **10 betters,** *pl.*   one's superiors: *Listen to the advice of your betters.*   **1, 5, 7, 8** *adj.,* comparative of GOOD; **2, 9** *adv.,* comparative of WELL; **3, 6** *v.,* **4, 10** *n.*
**better off,**   in a better condition.
**get** or **have the better of,**   be superior to; defeat.
**had better,**   should; ought to; will be wise to: *I had better go before it rains.*
**think better of,**   think over and change one's mind.

**bet·ter**[2] or **bet·tor** (bet′ər)   a person who BETS.   *n.*

**bet·ter·ment** (bet′ər mənt)   improvement: *Doctors work for the betterment of their patients' health.*   *n.*

**be·tween** (bi twēn′)   **1** in or into the space, position, or time separating; in the middle in relation to two persons, things, etc.: *Many cities lie between Halifax and Toronto. There are no more holidays between now and the end of school. A sergeant ranks between a corporal and a warrant officer.*   **2** in or into a position thought of as being in the middle in relation to two or more persons, things, or ideas: *Between dying in captivity and getting killed in escaping, she had little to choose from.*   **3** in or into an intermediate space or time: *We could no longer see the moon, for a cloud had come between. The speeches seemed very long because there was no break between.*   **4** within the range separating two or more quantities, qualities, or times: *a shade between pink and red. The temperature is probably between 20°C and 25°C. She made between $400 and $500 on the deal.*   **5** connecting in space: *There is a paved highway between Flin Flon and The Pas.* **6** connecting in a state or condition; involving: *peace between two nations. There was a strong bond of affection between them.*   **7** in the joint ownership of: *They own the property between them.*   **8** by the combined action or effort of: *The girls caught 12 fish between them. Settle the matter between you.*   **9** in or into portions for: *The estate was divided between the two grandchildren.*   **10** restricted to: *We kept the matter between us.*   **11** in or into a position separating: *They were fast friends and would let no quarrel come between them.*   **12** through the range separating two or more conditions, qualities, or quantities: *all the numbers between 1 and 50.*   **1, 2, 4–12** *prep.,* **3** *adv.*
**between the devil and the deep blue sea,**   in an impossible predicament that leaves no desirable choice; in a DILEMMA.
**between you and me,**   as a secret; confidentially.
**in between,**   **a** in the middle.   **b** in the middle of.
**no love lost between (them),**   strong dislike involving two people; mutual enmity: *It's easy to see that there's no love lost between them.*
☞ Syn. **Between, AMONG. Between** is used when the reference is to two persons or things only: *My sister and I had less than a dollar between us.* **Among** is usually preferred when the reference is to more than two persons or things: *The money was divided among the four of us.* However, **between** is used also when the reference is to a number of persons or things that are thought of in pairs: *Leave a line space between paragraphs.*

**be·twixt** (bi twikst′)   BETWEEN.   *prep., adv.*
**betwixt and between,**   in the middle; neither one nor the other.

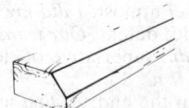 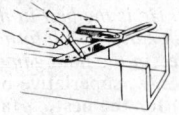
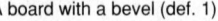

A board with a bevel (def. 1)     A bevel (def. 3) in use

**bev·el** (bev′əl)   **1** a sloping edge: *Plate glass often has a bevel.*   **2** cut at an angle other than a right angle; make slope: *This mirror has bevelled edges.* **3** an instrument for measuring or drawing angles or for adjusting a surface in order to bevel it. **4** slanting; oblique. 1, 3, 4 *n.*, 2 *v.* **bev·elled** or **bev·eled, bev·el·ling** or **bev·el·ing.**

**bev·er·age** (bev′ə rij *or* bev′rij) a liquid used or prepared for drinking: *Milk, tea, coffee, beer, and wine are beverages.* *n.*

**beverage room** *Cdn.* BEER PARLOUR.

**bev·y** (bev′ē) a small group: *a bevy of quail, a bevy of girls.* *n., pl.* **bev·ies.**

**be·wail** (bi wāl′) mourn; weep for, complain of: *to bewail one's fate. The child bewailed her lost tricycle.* *v.*

**be·ware** (bi wer′) be on one's guard against; be careful: *Beware! danger is here.* *v.*
**beware of,** take care about; avoid: *Beware of the dog. Beware of swimming in a strong current.*

**be·wil·der** (bi wil′dər) confuse completely; cause doubt and uncertainty: *Problems in arithmetic bewilder me.* *v.* —**be·wil′der·ment,** *n.*

**be·wil·der·ing** (bi wil′də ring) **1** perplexing; confusing: *a bewildering assortment.* **2** ppr. of BEWILDER. 1 *adj.*, 2 *v.* —**be·wil′der·ing·ly,** *adv.*

**be·witch** (bi wich′) **1** put under a spell; use magic on. **2** charm; delight; fascinate: *a smile that bewitches.* *v.*

**be·witched** (bi wicht′) **1** under the influence of magic. **2** charmed; delighted; fascinated. **3** pt. and pp. of BEWITCH. 1, 2 *adj.*, 3 *v.*

**be·witch·ing** (bi wich′ing) **1** fascinating; delightful; charming. **2** ppr. of BEWITCH. 1 *adj.*, 2 *v.* —**be·witch′ing·ly,** *adv.*

**bey** (bā) **1** in the Ottoman Empire, the governor of a province. **2** a Turkish title of respect for persons of rank. **3** formerly, a native ruler of Tunis or Tunisia. *n., pl.* **beys.**
☛ *Hom.* BAY.

**be·yond** (bi yond′) **1** on or to the farther side of: *He lives beyond the sea.* **2** farther on than: *The school is beyond the last house.* **3** farther away: *Beyond were the hills.* **4** later than; past: *They stayed beyond the time set.* **5** out of the reach, range, or understanding of: *beyond help. The meaning of this story is beyond me.* **6** more than; exceeding: *The price of the suit was beyond what she could pay.* **7** in addition to; besides: *I will do nothing beyond the job given me.* 1, 2, 4, 5, 7 *prep.*, 3 *adv.*, 6 *conj.* **the beyond** or **the great beyond,** life after death.

**bez·el** (bez′əl) **1** a slope, or BEVEL, especially on the edge of a cutting tool. **2** the sloping sides or faces of a cut jewel. **3** a grooved ring or rim that holds a jewel or watch crystal in its place. *n.*

**bg.** bag.

**Bha·ga·vad Gi·ta** (bug′ə vəd gē′tə) in Hinduism, a philosophical and religious dialogue between Krishna and a warrior, Arjuna. It is embodied in the *Mahabharata*, an ancient Sanskrit epic.

**bhak·ti** (buk′tē) in Bhakti Hinduism, the general term for acts of worship and devotion in recognition of a god or gods. *n.*

**bhik·ku** (bik′ü) in Buddhism, a fully ordained monk. *n.*

**bhik·ku·ni** (bi kü′nē) in Buddhism, a fully ordained nun. *n.*

**bi–** a prefix meaning: **1** twice, as in *biannual, bimonthly.* **2** doubly, as in *bipolar, biconcave.* **3** two, as

# beverage 111 biblical

hat, āge, fär; let, ēqual, tėrm; it, īce
hot, ōpen, ôrder; oil, out; cup, pút, rüle
above, tak<ə>n, penc<ə>l, lem<ə>n, circ<ə>s
ch, child; ng, long; sh, ship
th, thin; ŦH, then; zh, measure

in *bicuspid, bilateral.* **4** having two, as in *bicarbonate, bichloride.* **5** appearance or occurrence in intervals of two; every two, as in *bimonthly, biennial.*
☛ *Syn.* See note at BIMONTHLY.

**Bi** bismuth.

**bi·an·nu·al** (bī an′yü əl) occurring twice a year: *Our doctor urges a biannual visit to the dentist.* *adj.*
☛ *Syn.* See note at BIMONTHLY.

**bi·an·nu·al·ly** (bī an′yü ə lē) twice a year. *adv.*

Cloth cut on the bias

**bi·as** (bī′əs) **1** a slanting or oblique line: *Cloth is cut on the bias when it is cut diagonally across the weave.* **2** slanting across the threads of cloth; oblique; diagonal: *a bias cut, cloth with a bias print.* **3** an inclination or preference that makes it difficult or impossible to judge fairly in a particular situation; a general opinion that has an unfair influence on a specific decision: *The newspaper account of the trial showed a bias in favour of the defendant.* **4** cause to have such an inclination or preference: *Several bad experiences biassed her against teenage drivers.* 1–3 *n.*, 4 *v.*, **bi·assed** or **bi·ased, bi·as·sing** or **bi·as·ing.**

**bi·assed** or **bi·ased** (bī′əst) **1** favouring one side too much; warped or prejudiced: *a biassed judge. He was biassed where his children were concerned.* **2** pt. and pp. of BIAS. 1 *adj.*, 2 *v.*

**bi·ath·lon** (bī ath′lən *or* bī ath′lon) an Olympic event or contest in which skiers with rifles race along a twenty-kilometre cross-country course, shooting at four targets spaced along the way. *n.*

**bi·ax·i·al** (bī ak′sē əl) having two AXES[1]. *adj.*

**bib** (bib) **1** a kind of napkin or small apron worn under the chin to protect clothing, especially at meals. **2** the part of an apron or overalls above the waist. *n.*

**bib and tucker** *Informal.* clothes: *Put on your best bib and tucker.*

**bib–cock** (bib′kok′) a tap, or faucet, having a nozzle bent downward. *n.*

**Bi·ble** (bī′bəl) **1** the collection of sacred writings of the Christian religion, comprising the Old and New Testaments. **2** the Holy Scriptures of Judaism, identical with the Old Testament of the Christian Bible. **3** the sacred writings of any religion. **4 bible,** any book accepted as an indisputable authority in a particular field: *The Canada Year Book is the Canadian geographer's bible.* *n.*
☛ *Etym.* From OF *bible*, from church Latin *biblia* 'Bible', which originally came from Greek *biblia* 'books'.

**bib·li·cal** or **Bib·li·cal** (bib′lə kəl) **1** of or having to do with the BIBLE: *biblical literature.* **2** according to the

**bibliographer** 112 **bifurcation**

BIBLE: *biblical history.* **3** in the BIBLE: *a biblical reference to Solomon.* *adj.* —**bib′li·cal·ly** or **Bib′li·cal·ly,** *adv.*

**bib·li·og·ra·pher** (bib′lē og′rə fər) a person who investigates the authorship, editions, dates, etc. of books or other publications or manuscripts. *n.*

**bib·li·o·graph·ic** (bib′lē ə graf′ik) BIBLIOGRAPHICAL. *adj.*

**bib·li·o·graph·i·cal** (bib′lē ə graf′ə kəl) of BIBLIOGRAPHY. *adj.* —**bib′li·o·graph′i·cal·ly,** *adv.*

**bib·li·og·ra·phy** (bib′lē og′rə fē) **1** a list of books, articles, etc. about a subject or person. **2** a list of books, articles, etc. by a certain author. **3** the study of the authorship, editions, dates, etc. of books, articles, etc. *n., pl.* **bib·li·og·ra·phies.**

**bib·li·o·ma·ni·a** (bib′lē ō mā′nē ə) an excessive preoccupation with collecting books. *n.*

**bib·li·o·ma·ni·ac** (bib′lē ō mā′nē ak′) a person who is excessively preoccupied with collecting books. *n.*

**bib·li·o·phile** (bib′lē ə fīl′) a lover of books, especially one who likes to collect books. *n.*

**bib·u·lous** (bib′yə ləs) **1** fond of drinking alcoholic liquor. **2** absorbent. *adj.*

**bi·car·bo·nate** (bī kär′bə nit *or* bī kär′bə nāt′) a salt of CARBONIC ACID that contains a base and hydrogen. *n.*

**bicarbonate of soda** a white, alkaline powder used in cooking and in medicine; sodium bicarbonate; baking soda.

**bi·cen·ten·a·ry** (bī′sen ten′ə rē *or* bī′sen tē′nə rē) **1** having to do with a period of 200 years. **2** a period of 200 years. **3** a 200th anniversary. **4** its celebration. 1 *adj.,* 2–4 *n., pl.* **bi·cen·ten·a·ries.**

**bi·cen·ten·ni·al** (bī′sen ten′ē əl) **1** having to do with a period of 200 years. **2** recurring every 200 years. **3** a 200th anniversary. **4** its celebration. 1, 2 *adj.,* 3, 4 *n.*

**bi·ceps** (bī′seps) any muscle having two heads, or points of origin, especially the large muscle at the front of the upper arm or the large muscle at the back of the upper leg. See ARM[1] for picture. *n. sing. or pl.*

**bi·chlo·ride** (bī klō′rīd) **1** DICHLORIDE. **2** MERCURIC CHLORIDE; bichloride of mercury. *n.*

**bichloride of mercury** MERCURIC CHLORIDE.

**bick·er** (bik′ər) **1** express annoyance to each other over trifles; squabble; engage in a petty quarrel: *The children bickered all afternoon.* **2** a mild quarrel over a trifle or trifles: *After a short bicker they decided on a movie they both wanted to see.* 1 *v.,* 2 *n.*

**bi·con·cave** (bī kon′kāv *or* bī′kon kāv′) concave on both sides. See CONCAVE for picture. *adj.*

**bi·con·vex** (bī kon′veks *or* bī′kon veks′) convex on both sides. See CONVEX for picture. *adj.*

**bi·cul·tur·al** (bī kul′chə rəl) having two distinct cultures existing side by side in the same country, province, etc. *adj.*

**bi·cul·tur·al·ism** (bī kul′chə rə liz′əm) **1** the fact or condition of being BICULTURAL. **2** a policy that favours a country, province, etc. being BICULTURAL. **3** the practice or support of such a policy. *n.*

**bi·cus·pid** (bī kus′pid) **1** a double-pointed tooth: *A human adult has eight bicuspids.* See TEETH for picture. **2** having two points. 1 *n.,* 2 *adj.*

**bi·cy·cle** (bī′sə kəl) **1** a vehicle consisting of a metal frame with two wheels, set one behind the other, handles for steering, and a seat for the rider: *An ordinary bicycle has pedals for pushing; a motor bicycle has an engine.* **2** ride a bicycle. 1 *n.,* 2 *v.,* **bi·cy·cled, bi·cy·cling.** —**bi′cy·cler,** *n.*

**bi·cy·clist** (bī′sə klist) a bicycle rider. *n.*

**bid** (bid) **1** command: *The captain bids his men go forward. Do as I bid you.* **2** a bidding. **3** say or tell: *His friends came to bid him goodbye.* **4** offer: *She bid $22 for the table. He then bid $23.* **5** an offer: *Are you going to make a bid?* **6** the amount offered: *My bid was $24.* **7** offer a price; state a price: *Several companies will bid for the contract.* **8** the price at which one says one can do a certain piece of work: *The lowest bid for building the bridge was two million dollars.* **9** proclaim or declare: *He bade defiance to them all.* **10** in some card games, state what one proposes to make or to win. **11** the amount bid in a card game. **12** an attempt to secure, achieve, etc.: *She made a bid for our sympathy.* **13** *Informal.* an invitation. 1, 3, 4, 7, 9, 10 *v.,* **bade** or **bid, bid·den** or **bid, bid·ding** (for defs. 1, 3, 9); **bid, bid·ding** (for defs. 4, 7, 10); 2, 5, 6, 8, 11–13 *n.*

**bid fair,** seem likely; have a good chance: *The plan bids fair to succeed.*

**bid for,** try to get.

**bid·den** (bid′ən) **1** a pp. of BID. **2** invited. 1 *v.,* 2 *adj.*

**bid·der** (bid′ər) a person who BIDS, especially at an auction or in a card game. *n.*

**bid·ding** (bid′ing) **1** a command. **2** invitation. **3** at an auction, offers; bids: *The bidding was slow at first but soon became lively.* **4** in card games, the bids collectively. **5** ppr. of BID. 1–4 *n.,* 5 *v.*

**do someone's bidding,** obey someone.

**bid·dy**[1] (bid′ē) hen. *n., pl.* **bid·dies.**

**bid·dy**[2] (bid′ē) a talkative old woman. *n., pl.* **bid·dies.**

**bide** (bīd) *Archaic (except in* **bide one's time***).* **1** dwell; abide. **2** continue; wait; stay. **3** wait for. **4** bear; endure; suffer. *v.,* **bode** or **bid·ed, bid·ed, bid·ing.**

**bide one's time,** wait for a good chance: *If you bide your time, you will probably get a good bargain.*

**bi·en·ni·al** (bī en′ē əl) **1** of plants, lasting two years. **2** any plant that lives two years, usually producing flowers and seeds the second year: *Carrots and onions are biennials.* **3** occurring every two years. **4** an event that occurs every two years. 1, 3 *adj.,* 2, 4 *n.*
☛ Syn. See note at BIMONTHLY.

**bi·en·ni·al·ly** (bī en′ē ə lē) once in two years. *adv.*

**bier** (bēr) a movable stand on which a coffin or dead body is placed. *n.*
☛ Hom. BEER.

**bi·fo·cal** (bī fō′kəl) **1** having two focuses: *Bifocal eyeglasses have two parts: the upper part for far vision, the lower for near vision.* **2** a bifocal LENS. **3** **bifocals,** *pl.* eyeglasses having bifocal lenses. 1 *adj.,* 2, 3 *n.*

**bi·fur·cate** (bī′fər kāt′ *or* bī fėr′kāt *for verb,* bī′fər kāt′ *or* bī fėr′kit *for adjective*) **1** divide into two parts or branches. **2** divided into two branches; forked. 1 *v.,* **bi·fur·cat·ed, bi·fur·cat·ing;** 2 *adj.*

**bi·fur·ca·tion** (bī′fər kā′shən) **1** a splitting into two parts. **2** the place where the split occurs. *n.*

**big** (big) **1** great in extent, amount, size, etc.; large: *a big room, a big book, big business.* **2** grown up: *He said he wants to be a firefighter when he's big.* **3** *Informal.* important; great: *This is big news.* **4** full; loud: *a big voice.* **5** generous: *She has a big heart and will always help you out.* **6** boastful: *big talk.* **7** *Informal.* boastfully: *He talks big.* **8** *Informal.* popular: *Compact discs are very big these days.* 1–6, 8 *adj.*, **big·ger, big·gest;** 7 *adv.* —**big′ness,** *n.*

**big·a·mist** (big′ə mist) a person guilty of BIGAMY. *n.*

**big·a·mous** (big′ə məs) **1** guilty of BIGAMY. **2** involving BIGAMY. *adj.* —**big′a·mous·ly,** *adv.*

**big·a·my** (big′ə mē) the criminal offence of marrying someone while still legally married to someone else. *n.*

**Big Dipper** the seven principal stars in the constellation Ursa Major, arranged in a form that suggests a dipper: *The two end stars of the Big Dipper are in a line with the North Star.* Compare with LITTLE DIPPER. See DIPPER for picture.

**big game 1** large animals sought by hunters: *Elephants, tigers, lions, moose, and elk are big game.* **2** a very important thing that is sought.

**big-heart·ed** (big′här′tid) kindly; generous. *adj.*

**big·horn** (big′hôrn′) a large, heavy-bodied wild mountain sheep found mainly in the Rocky Mountains, brown with a white muzzle and rump patch, having long, slender legs and huge brown horns that curl back and down from the forehead. *n., pl.* **big·horn** or **big·horns.**

**bight** (bīt) **1** a long curve in a coastline. **2** a bay; part of a sea or lake extending into the land. **3** a bend, angle, or corner. **4** a loop of rope; the slack of rope between the fastened ends. *n.*
☛ Hom. BITE, BYTE.

**big·ot** (big′ət) a BIGOTED person; an intolerant, prejudiced person. *n.*

**big·ot·ed** (big′ə tid) sticking to an opinion, belief, party, etc. without reason and not tolerating other views; intolerant; prejudiced: *A person may be bigoted in religion or politics. adj.* —**big′ot·ed·ly,** *adv.*

**big·ot·ry** (big′ə trē) BIGOTED conduct or attitude; intolerance; prejudice. *n., pl.* **big·ot·ries.**

**big wheel** *Informal.* an influential or otherwise important person, especially in a particular region, industry, etc.: *a big wheel in hockey, a big wheel in automobile manufacturing, etc.*

**big·wig** (big′wig′) *Informal.* an important person. *n.*

**bike** (bīk) *Informal.* BICYCLE. *n., v.,* **biked, bik·ing.**

**bik·er** (bī′kər) *Informal.* a motorcyclist, especially one who wears leather and belongs to a motorcycle club. *n.*

**bi·ki·ni** (bi kē′nē) **1** a brief two-piece bathing suit for women and girls. **2** brief, close-fitting underpants or men's swimming trunks. *n.*

**bi·la·bi·al** (bī lā′bē əl) **1** having two lips. **2** of or formed by both lips: *bilabial sounds.* **3** a sound formed by both lips: *Bilabials are represented by p, b, m and w.* 1, 2 *adj.*, 3 *n.*

**bi·lat·er·al** (bī lat′ə rəl) **1** having two sides. **2** on two sides. **3** affecting or involving two sides equally: *a bilateral treaty. adj.* —**bi·lat′er·al·ly,** *adv.*

**bil·ber·ry** (bil′ber′ē) **1** any of several shrubs of the HEATH family, closely related to the blueberries, but having flowers that grow singly or in very small clusters.

**2** the sweet, edible bluish or blackish berry of any of these shrubs. *n., pl.* **bil·ber·ries.**

**bile** (bīl) **1** a bitter, yellow or greenish liquid secreted by the liver and stored in the gall bladder: *Bile is discharged into the small intestine, where it aids digestion by neutralizing acids and emulsifying fats.* **2** ill humour; anger. *n.*

**bilge** (bilj) **1** the lowest part of a ship's hold; bottom of a ship's hull. **2** BILGE WATER. **3** break open the bottom of a ship; spring a leak in the bilge. **4** the bulging part of a barrel. **5** bulge; swell out. **6** *Informal.* nonsense: *What a lot of bilge that was.* 1, 2, 4, 6 *n.*, 3, 5 *v.,* **bilged, bilg·ing.**

**bilge water** the dirty water that collects in the bottom of a ship or boat.

**bi·lin·e·ar** (bī lin′ē ər) of, having to do with, or involving two lines. *adj.*

**bi·lin·gual** (bī ling′gwəl *or* bī ling′gyə wəl) **1** able to speak two languages, especially with the fluency of a native speaker. **2** of, containing, or expressed in two languages: *a bilingual dictionary, a bilingual meeting.* **3** *Cdn.* **a** able to speak both English and French. **b** having to do with or catering to speakers of both English and French: *bilingual courts, a bilingual hospital. adj.* —**bi·lin′gual·ly,** *adv.*

**bi·lin·gual·ism** (bī ling′gwə liz′əm *or* bī ling′gyə wə liz′əm) **1** the ability to speak two languages, especially with the fluency of a native speaker. **2** *Cdn.* the ability to speak both English and French. **3** the principle that two languages should enjoy equal status in a country, province, etc. *n.*

**bil·ious** (bil′yəs) **1** suffering from or caused by some trouble with the BILE or the liver: *a bilious attack.* **2** peevish; cross; bad-tempered: *a bilious person. adj.* —**bil′ious·ly,** *adv.* —**bil′ious·ness,** *n.*

**bilk** (bilk) **1** avoid payment of. **2** defraud; cheat; deceive. **3** a fraud; deception. **4** a person who avoids paying his or her bills; petty swindler. 1, 2 *v.,* 3, 4 *n.* —**bilk′er,** *n.*

**bill¹** (bil) **1** a list or statement showing an amount of money owed for work done or things supplied; an account: *We got the bill yesterday.* **2** the amount of money shown on such a statement: *Our phone bill was high last month.* **3** send a statement of charges to: *The store will bill us on the first of the month.* **4** enter in a bill; charge in a bill. **5** a piece of paper money: *a five-dollar bill.* **6** a written or printed public notice; advertisement; poster; handbill. **7** advertise or announce through such notices or posters: *It was billed as the greatest show on earth.* **8** a written or printed statement; list of items: *a bill of fare.* **9** a theatre program. **10** the entertainment in a theatre. **11** list on a theatrical program, poster, etc.: *He was billed as the star.* **12** a proposed law presented to a lawmaking body for its approval: *In Canada, a bill becomes an act if it receives a majority vote in Parliament.* **13** a BILL OF EXCHANGE. 1, 2, 5, 6, 8–10, 12, 13 *n.*, 3, 4, 7, 11 *v.* —**bill′er,** *n.*
**fill the bill,** *Informal.* satisfy requirements.
**foot the bill,** *Informal.* pay or settle the bill.

**bill²** (bil) **1** the horny part of the jaws of a bird; beak. **2** a mouth part shaped like a bird's bill: *the bill of a turtle.* **3** join beaks; touch bills: *Doves often bill in supposed affection.* 1, 2 *n.*, 3 *v.*
**bill and coo,** kiss, caress, and talk as lovers do.

**bill·board** (bil′bôrd′) a large board, usually outdoors, on which advertisements or notices are displayed. *n.*

**billed** (bild) **1** having a BILL² (defs. 1, 2) or beak. **2** pt. and pp. of BILL. 1 *adj.*, 2 *v.*
☛ *Hom.* BUILD.

**bil·let¹** (bil′it) **1** a written order to provide board and lodging, especially for troops in a private home. **2** a place where any person is assigned to be lodged. **3** assign to quarters by billet: *The members of the visiting choir were billeted in people's homes.* **4** a job or position: *A soft billet is an easy, well-paid job.* 1, 2, 4 *n.*, 3 *v.*, **bil·let·ed, bil·let·ing.**

**bil·let²** (bil′it) **1** a thick stick of wood, such as firewood. **2** a bar of iron or steel. *n.*

**bil·let–doux** (bil′ē dü′; *French,* bē ye dü′) a love letter. *n., pl.* **bil·lets-doux** (bil′ē düz′; *French,* bē ye dü′).

**bill·fold** (bil′fōld′) a folding case for carrying money, papers, etc.; wallet. *n.*

**bill·head** (bil′hed′) **1** a sheet of paper with a name and business address printed at the top, used in making out bills. **2** a name and business address printed at the top of a sheet of paper. *n.*

**bill·hook** (bil′hùk′) a tool with a hooked blade, used for pruning or cutting. *n.*

**bil·liard** (bil′yərd) **1** of or for BILLIARDS. **2** in BILLIARDS, a score made by striking one ball so that it hits the other two; CAROM. 1 *adj.*, 2 *n.*

Billiards

**bil·liards** (bil′yərdz) a game played with two white balls and a red one on a special table: *In billiards a long stick called a cue is used to hit the balls.* *n.*

**bill·ing** (bil′ing) **1** on a playbill or similar advertisement, the order in which the names of the performers, acts, etc. are listed. **2** the position in such a listing: *She received star billing.* **3** a listing of the total amount of money owed by a client or customer: *They thought the company's billings were too high.* **4** ppr. of BILL. 1–3 *n.*, 4 *v.*

**bil·lings·gate** (bil′ingz gāt′) vulgar, abusive language. *n.*
☛ *Etym.* From the reputation of *Billingsgate* fish market in London, which was notorious for the abusive language used by the fish-sellers.

**bil·lion** (bil′yən) **1** in Canada, the United States, and France, a thousand million (1 000 000 000). **2** in Britain and Germany, a million million (1 000 000 000 000). *n.*

**bil·lion·aire** (bil′yə ner′) a person whose wealth adds up to at least a BILLION dollars, pounds, marks, francs, etc. *n.*

**bil·lionth** (bil′yənth) **1** last in a series of a BILLION. **2** one of a BILLION equal parts. 1 *adj.*, 2 *n.*

**bill of exchange** a written instruction to pay a certain sum of money to a specified person.

**bill of fare** a list of the articles of food served at a meal or of those that can be ordered; menu.

**bill of health** a certificate stating whether or not there are infectious diseases on a ship or in the port which the ship is leaving: *A ship is not allowed to dock unless it has a clean bill of health from the port it left last.*

**bill of lading** a receipt given by a railway, express agency, etc. showing a list of goods delivered to it for transportation.

**bill of rights 1** a statement of the fundamental rights of the people of a nation. **2 Bill of Rights,** a statement of human rights and basic freedoms in Canada, passed by Parliament in 1960.

**bill of sale** a written statement transferring ownership of something from the seller to the buyer.

**bil·low** (bil′ō) **1** a great wave or surge of the sea. **2** any great wave: *billows of smoke.* **3** rise or roll in big waves: *On a windy day the surf billows.* **4** swell out; bulge: *The sheets on the clothesline billowed in the wind.* 1, 2 *n.*, 3, 4 *v.*

**bil·low·y** (bil′ō ē) **1** rising or rolling in big waves: *a billowy sea.* **2** swelling out; bulging. *adj.*, **bil·low·i·er, bil·low·i·est.**

**bill·post·er** (bil′pō′stər) a person whose work is putting up advertisements or notices in public places. *n.*

**bil·ly¹** (bil′ē) a club or stick: *Police officers sometimes carry billies.* *n., pl.* **bil·lies.**

**bil·ly²** (bil′ē) a can for boiling water or for holding hot liquids. *n., pl.* **bil·lies.**

**billy goat** a male goat.

**bi·month·ly** (bī munth′lē) **1** happening once every two months: *bimonthly meetings.* **2** once every two months: *The magazine is published bimonthly.* **3** happening twice a month. **4** twice a month. **5** a magazine published bimonthly. 1, 3 *adj.*, 2, 4 *adv.*, 5 *n., pl.* **bi·month·lies.**
☛ *Syn.* **Bimonthly,** BIWEEKLY, and BIYEARLY originally meant 'every two months', etc. but are now often used to mean 'twice a month', etc. To avoid confusion, use **semi-monthly** or **twice a month** for one meaning and **every two months** for the other. However, BIANNUAL has only the one meaning: 'twice a year'. The word for 'every two years' is BIENNIAL.

**bin** (bin) a box or enclosed place for holding grain, coal, etc. *n.*
☛ *Hom.* BEEN (bin).

**bi·na·ry** (bī′nə rē) **1** having to do with, consisting of, or involving two; dual. **2** in mathematics and computer technology, having to do with, using, or expressed in

**BINARY DIGITS, or BITS:** *Binary notation is a number system used in computers.* **3** in mathematics and computer technology, a number expressed in BINARY NOTATION. 1, 2 *adj.*, 3 *n.*, *pl.* **bi‧na‧ries.**

**binary digit** in computer technology, either of the digits 0 or 1, that are the basic unit of information in computers. The two digits can be represented as the *off* and *on* states of an electric circuit. Also called **bit.**

**binary notation** a number system used in computers, using the BINARY DIGITS 0 and 1.

**binary star** a pair of stars that revolve around a common centre of gravity, often appearing as a single object.

**bind** (bīnd) **1** tie together; hold together; fasten: *She bound the package with a bright ribbon.* **2** stick together: *Gravel or cinders can be bound by tar or cement.* **3** hold by some force; restrain: *Vines binding that tree will keep it from growing.* **4** hold by a promise, love, duty, etc.; obligate: *She is duty bound to help.* **5** put under legal obligation to serve as an apprentice: *bound out to be a carpenter.* **6** put a bandage on: *to bind up a wound.* **7** put a band or wreath around. **8** put a border or edge on to strengthen or ornament: *They bound the frayed edge of the carpet.* **9** tie up for the sake of appearance or convenience: *She bound her hair with red ribbons.* **10** fasten into a cover; put a cover on: *The pages were bound into a small book.* **11** constipate. **12** anything that binds or ties. 1–11 *v.*, **bound, bind‧ing;** 12 *n.* **bind off,** in knitting, make the last row of stitches to remove the fabric from the needle. **bind over,** put under legal obligation: *bound over to keep the peace.*
☛ *Etym.* All forms of the verb **bind** developed from the OE verb *bindan* 'bind'.

**bind‧er** (bīn′dər) **1** a person who binds, especially a BOOKBINDER. **2** anything that ties or holds together. **3** a cover for holding loose sheets of paper together. **4** a machine that cuts stalks of grain and ties them in bundles. *n.*

**binder twine** *Cdn.* a strong, coarse string used for binding up grain into bales: *On a farm, binder twine has a thousand uses.*

**bind‧er‧y** (bīn′də rē) a place where books are bound. *n.*, *pl.* **bind‧er‧ies.**

**bind‧ing** (bīn′ding) **1** the covering of a book. **2** a strip protecting or ornamenting an edge: *Binding is sometimes used on the seams of dresses.* **3** that binds, fastens, or connects. **4** having force or power to hold to some agreement, pledge, etc.; obligatory: *They signed their names so that the agreement would be binding.* **5** ppr. of BIND. 1, 2 *n.*, 3, 4 *adj.*, 5 *v.*

**binding energy** in physics, the energy necessary to break a particular atomic nucleus into its smaller component particles.

**bind‧weed** (bīnd′wēd′) a plant having long runners that twine around the stems of other plants. *n.*

**bin‧go** (bing′gō) a game of chance in which each player has a card with randomly numbered squares, which he or she covers with markers as the numbers are drawn and called out by a caller. *n.*

**bin‧na‧cle** (bin′ə kəl) a box or stand that contains a ship's compass, placed near the person who is steering. *n.*

**bi‧noc‧u‧lar** (bə nok′yə lər *or* bī nok′yə lər) **1** of, having to do with, using, or for both eyes. **2** Usually, **binoculars,** *pl.* a double telescope joined as a unit for

---

**binary digit**     **115**     **biomass**

hat, āge, fär; let, ēqual, tėrm; it, īce
hot, ōpen, ôrder; oil, out; cup, pút, rüle
əbove, takən, pencəl, lemən, circəs
ch, child; ng, long; sh, ship
th, thin; ₸H, then; zh, measure

---

use with both eyes: *Field glasses and opera glasses are binoculars.* See FIELD GLASSES for picture. 1 *adj.*, 2 *n.*

**bi‧no‧mi‧al** (bī nō′mē əl) **1** consisting of two terms. **2** in mathematics, an expression consisting of two terms connected by a plus or minus sign. **3** in biology, a two-part name by which a plant or animal is identified according to an international system of classification: *The binomial of the North American beaver is* Castor canadensis. 1 *adj.*, 2, 3 *n.*

**bio–** *combining form.* life; living things: *A biography is a written work about a person's life. Biology is the study of living things.*
☛ *Etym.* From Gk. *bios* 'life'.

**bi‧o‧chem‧i‧cal** (bī′ō kem′ə kəl) having to do with BIOCHEMISTRY. *adj.*

**bi‧o‧chem‧ist** (bī′ō kem′ist) a person trained in BIOCHEMISTRY, especially one who makes it his or her work. *n.*

**bi‧o‧chem‧is‧try** (bī′ō kem′i strē) the chemistry of living animals and plants; biological chemistry. *n.*

**bi‧o‧de‧grad‧a‧ble** (bī′ō di grā′də bəl) capable of being broken down, or decomposed, by a natural process such as the action of bacteria: *Plastic containers are not biodegradable.* *adj.*

**biog.** **1** BIOGRAPHICAL. **2** biography.

**bi‧og‧ra‧pher** (bī og′rə fər) a person who writes the life of somebody. *n.*

**bi‧o‧graph‧ic** (bī′ə graf′ik) biographical. *adj.*

**bi‧o‧graph‧i‧cal** (bī′ə graf′ə kəl) **1** of a person's life: *We have little biographical information on Shakespeare.* **2** having to do with BIOGRAPHY. *adj.*
—**bi′o‧graph′i‧cal‧ly,** *adv.*

**bi‧og‧ra‧phy** (bī og′rə fē) **1** the written story of a person's life. **2** the part of literature that consists of biographies. *n.*, *pl.* **bi‧og‧ra‧phies.**

**bi‧o‧log‧ic** (bī′ə loj′ik) BIOLOGICAL. *adj.*

**bi‧o‧log‧i‧cal** (bī′ə loj′ə kəl) **1** of plant and animal life. **2** having to do with BIOLOGY: *a biological laboratory.* *adj.*
—**bi′o‧log′i‧cal‧ly,** *adv.*

**biological warfare** the waging of war by using disease-producing bacteria or other micro-organisms to destroy crops, livestock, or human life.

**bi‧ol‧o‧gist** (bī ol′ə jist) a person trained in BIOLOGY, especially one who makes it his or her work. *n.*

**bi‧ol‧o‧gy** (bī ol′ə jē) the science of life or living matter in all its forms and phenomena; the study of the origin, reproduction, structure, etc. of plant and animal life: *Botany and zoology are the main divisions of biology.* *n.*

**bi‧o‧lu‧mi‧nesc‧ence** (bī′ō lü mi nes′əns) the ability of certain living organisms, such as fireflies, to change chemical energy in the body into light.

**bi‧o‧mass** (bī′ō mas′) the total amount or mass of living organisms in a given area. *n.*

**bi·ome** (bī′ōm) an extensive ecological community, especially one having one dominant type of vegetation. *n.*

**bi·o·nic** (bī on′ik) **1** referring to an artificial body part or a device that strengthens or replaces a natural body function, especially one that operates electronically: *a bionic arm.* **2** in science fiction, referring to a person or animal having superhuman powers due to such a device. **3** of or having to do with the science of BIONICS. *adj.*

**bi·o·nics** (bī on′iks) the study of the functions of the brain, etc. in order to use them as models for the development of computers and other electronic devices or systems (*used with a singular verb*). *n.*

**bi·op·sy** (bī′op sē) the examination of tissue taken from a living person or animal as an aid to medical diagnosis: *A biopsy is often done to find out if cancer cells are present in a particular part of the body.* Compare with AUTOPSY. *n., pl.* **bi·op·sies.**

**bi·o·sphere** (bī′ə sfēr′) the parts of the earth and its atmosphere in which living things are found. *n.*

**bi·o·tech·no·lo·gy** (bī′ō tek nol′ə jē) **1** a combination of biology with technology. **2** the use of living organisms to make industrial products. *n.*

**bi·o·tin** (bī′ə tin) a colourless crystalline vitamin of the B complex that promotes growth and is found especially in yeast, liver, and egg yolk. *n.*

**bi·o·tite** (bī′ə tīt′) black or dark-coloured MICA. *n.*

**bi·par·ti·san** (bī pär′tə zən *or* bī pär′tə zan′) of or representing two political parties: *Bipartisan foreign policy has the support of the two main political parties of a nation.* *adj.*

**bi·par·tite** (bī pär′tīt) having two parts: *An oyster has a bipartite shell.* *adj.*

**bi·par·ty** (bī′pär′tē) combining two different political groups, religious groups, etc. *adj.*

**bi·ped** (bī′ped) **1** an animal having two feet: *Birds are bipeds.* **2** having two feet. **1** *n.*, **2** *adj.*

**bi·plane** (bī′plān′) an airplane having two sets of wings, one above the other. *n.*

**bi·po·lar** (bī pō′lər) **1** having two poles or extremes. **2** of, having to do with, or occurring in both polar regions. **3** characterized by two opposing opinions. *adj.*

**birch** (bėrch) **1** any of a closely related group of trees and shrubs found in the Northern Hemisphere, having light green oval or triangular leaves and usually light-coloured, smooth outer bark that in many species peels off easily in thin layers: *Amerindian peoples of the eastern woodlands traditionally used birchbark for their canoes.* **2** the hard, close-grained wood of a birch. **3** a bundle of birch twigs or a birch stick, used for whipping. **4** whip with a birch; flog. 1–3 *n.*, 4 *v.*

**bird** (bėrd) **1** any of a class of warm-blooded, egg-laying vertebrates having a body covered with feathers, and forelimbs modified into wings by means of which most species can fly: *All birds have keen vision.* **2** a bird hunted for sport. **3** SHUTTLECOCK. *n.*
—**bird′like**′, *adj.*
**bird in the hand,** something certain because one already has it.
**birds of a feather,** people with the same kind of ideas or interests.
**for the birds,** *Informal.* not worth considering; ridiculous, boring, etc.: *The movie was for the birds. I think house cleaning is for the birds.*
**give someone the bird,** *Informal.* jeer or ridicule someone, especially a performer.
**kill two birds with one stone,** get two things done by one action.

**bird·bath** (bėrd′bath′) a shallow basin raised off the ground and filled with water for birds to bathe in or drink from. *n.*

**bird call 1** the sound that a bird makes. **2** an imitation of it. **3** an instrument for imitating the sound that a bird makes.

**bird dog** any of several breeds of dog trained to locate game birds and to bring them back to the hunter after they have been shot: *The various breeds of setter and retriever are usually trained as bird dogs.*

**bird·house** (bėrd′hous′) a small roofed box with one or more openings, built in a tree or on a pole for birds to nest in. *n.*

**bird·ie** (bėr′dē) **1** *Informal.* a little bird. **2** a score of one stroke less than PAR (def. 7) for any hole on a golf course. Compare with BOGEY[1]. *n.*

**bird·lime** (bėrd′līm′) **1** a sticky substance smeared on twigs to catch small birds that light on it. **2** anything that ensnares. *n.*

**bird of paradise** any of about 40 species of songbird of New Guinea and nearby islands, related to the crow, the male of many species having vividly coloured plumes which it displays in elaborate rituals during the mating season: *The largest of these birds is the cinnamon-coloured great bird of paradise, having a yellow and emerald-green head and long, pale yellow plumes rising over the back.*

**bird of peace** DOVE.

**bird of prey** any of many species of bird that kill animals and other birds for food: *Eagles, hawks, and owls are birds of prey.*

**bird·seed** (bėrd′sēd′) a mixture of small seeds used to feed birds. *n.*

**bird's–eye** (bėrd′zī′) **1** an allover woven pattern for cloth, consisting of small diamonds, each having a dot in the centre. **2** cloth of cotton, linen, or synthetic fibres woven with such a pattern. **3** in wood, a small spot resembling a bird's eye. **4** having markings resembling a bird's eyes: *Bird's-eye maple is a wood used in making furniture.*

**bird's–eye view 1** a view from above or from a distance: *You get a bird's-eye view of the town from that hill.* **2** a general or overall view: *The summary will give you a bird's-eye view of the project.*

**bird shot** a small size of shot, used in shooting birds.

**bird–watch** (bėrd′dwoch′) observe and study wild birds in their natural surroundings. *v.*

**bird–watch·er** (bėrd′dwoch′ər) a person for whom BIRD WATCHING is a pastime. *n.*

**bird watching** the observation and study of wild birds in their natural surroundings.

**birth** (bėrth) **1** coming into life; being born: *the birth of a child.* **2** a beginning or origin: *the birth of a nation.* **3** bring forth: *the birth of a plan.* **4** natural inheritance: *a musician by birth.* **5** descent; family: *She is of Spanish birth. He was a man of humble birth.* **6** noble family or descent: *a man of birth and breeding.* *n.*

**give birth to,** a bear; bring forth. **b** be the origin or cause of.
☞ *Hom.* BERTH.

**birth·day** (bėrth′dā′) **1** the day on which a person is born. **2** the day on which something began: *July 1, 1867, was the birthday of Canada.* **3** the anniversary of the day on which a person was born, or on which something began. *n.*

**birth·mark** (bėrth′märk′) a spot or mark on the skin that was there at birth. *n.*

**birth·place** (bėrth′plās′) **1** the place where a person was born. **2** the place of origin. *n.*

**birth rate** the proportion of the number of births per year to the total population or to some other stated number.

**birth·right** (bėrth′rīt′) **1** the rights belonging to a man because he is the oldest son. **2** a right enjoyed by a person because he or she was born in a certain country, or because of any other fact about his or her birth: *"Freedom is our birthright!" she shouted.* *n.*

**birth·stone** (bėrth′stōn′) a jewel associated with a certain month of the year: *A birthstone is supposed to bring good luck when worn by a person born in its month.* *n.*

**bis·cuit** (bis′kit) **1** a kind of bread baked in small, soft cakes, made with baking powder, soda, or yeast. **2** cracker. **3** pale brown. **4** pottery or china that has been fired (baked) once but not yet glazed. 1–4 *n., pl.* **bis·cuits** or **bis·cuit;** 3 *adj.*
☞ *Etym.* From OF *bescuit*, from a Med. L word made up of *bis* 'twice' + *coctus* 'cooked'.

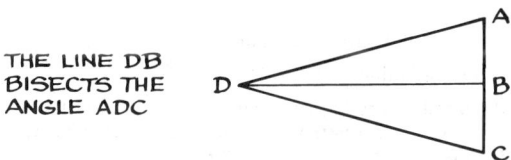

THE LINE DB BISECTS THE ANGLE ADC

**bi·sect** (bī sekt′) **1** divide into two parts; halve. **2** in geometry, divide into two equal parts. *v.*

**bi·sec·tion** (bī sek′shən) **1** the act of BISECTing. **2** the place of BISECTing. **3** one of two equal parts. *n.*

**bi·sec·tor** (bī sek′tər) in geometry, a line that BISECTS something. *n.*

**bi·sex·u·al** (bī sek′shü əl) **1** of, having to do with, or involving both sexes. **2** having male and female reproductive organs in one individual: *Earthworms are bisexual.* **3** sexually attracted to members of both sexes. *adj.*

**bish·op** (bish′əp) **1** a Christian clergyman of high rank who has certain spiritual duties and who administers the affairs of a church district. **2** in chess, one of two pieces held by a player that may be moved diagonally across any number of unoccupied spaces of one colour. *n.*

**bis·muth** (biz′məth) a brittle, reddish-white metallic element: *Some bismuth compounds are used in medicine and in alloys.* Symbol: Bi *n.*

**bi·son** (bī′sən) either of two very closely related species of large animal belonging to the same family as the buffalo of Africa and India, and domestic cattle, found in Europe and North America: *The North American bison is commonly called a buffalo; the European bison is the* WISENT. *n., pl.* **bi·son.**

**bisque** (bisk) **1** a thick soup made from shellfish such as crayfish or lobsters, or from the meat of birds or rabbits. **2** a smooth, creamy soup made of strained tomatoes, asparagus, etc. **3** ice cream containing powdered macaroons or crushed nuts. *n.*

**bis·sex·tile** (bī sek′stīl *or* bi sek′stəl) **1** leap year. **2** containing the extra day of leap year: *February is the bissextile month.* 1 *n.,* 2 *adj.*

**bi·sym·met·ric·al** (bī′si met′rə kəl) having both sides SYMMETRICAL. *adj.*

**bit**¹ (bit) **1** the part of a BRIDLE that goes in a horse's mouth. See HARNESS for picture. **2** put a bit in the mouth of; BRIDLE. **3** anything that curbs or restrains. **4** curb or restrain. **5** the biting or cutting part of a tool. **6** the part of a drill or similar tool that does the actual drilling, or boring: *A drill or brace and bit usually has several interchangeable bits.* See BRACE AND BIT for picture. 1, 3, 5, 6 *n.,* 2, 4 *v.,* **bit·ted, bit·ting.**
☞ *Hom.* BITT.

**bit**² (bit) **1** a small piece; small amount: *I need just a bit of milk. A pebble is a bit of rock.* **2** a small degree or extent: *She wasn't a bit sorry. I'm a bit tired.* **3** *Informal.* a short time: *stay a bit longer.* **4** the basic unit of information in a computer; BINARY DIGIT. *n.*
**do one's bit,** do one's share.
**two bits,** *Informal.* 25 cents: *All I have left is two bits.*
☞ *Hom.* BITT.

**bit**³ (bit) pt. and a pp. of BITE: *The strong trap bit the leg of the fox. A boy was bit by our dog.* *v.*
☞ *Hom.* BITT.

**bitch** (bich) **1** a female dog, wolf, etc. **2** *Informal.* a malicious, treacherous, or bad-tempered woman. **3** *Informal.* anything that is very unpleasant or difficult. **4** *Informal.* complain; grumble: *He's always bitching about something.* **5** *Informal.* botch; bungle (*usually used with* **up**). 1–4 *n.,* 5 *v.*

**bite** (bīt) **1** seize, cut into, or cut off with the teeth: *She bit the apple. The nervous boy bites his fingernails.* **2** a piece bitten off; bit of food; mouthful: *Eat the whole apple, not just a bite.* **3** the act of biting: *The dog gave a bite or two at the bone.* **4** a light meal; snack: *We usually have a bite before going to bed.* **5** cut or pierce: *The sword bit the knight's helmet.* **6** wound or pierce with teeth, fangs, or a sting: *My dog never bites. A mosquito bit me.* **7** the result of a bite, wound, sting, etc.: *The woman soon recovered from the snake's bite.* **8** a sharp, smarting pain: *the bite of a cold wind.* **9** nip; snap: *a dog biting at fleas.* **10** cause a sharp, smarting pain to: *fingers bitten by frost.* **11** take a tight hold on; grip: *The jaws of a vise bite the wood they hold.* **12** a tight hold: *the bite of the wheels on the rails.* **13** take a bait; be caught: *The fish are biting well today.* 1, 5, 6, 9–11, 13 *v.,* **bit, bit·ten** or **bit, bit·ing;** 2–4, 7, 8, 12 *n.* —**bit′er,** *n.*
**bite off more than one can chew,** tackle something too difficult.
**bite one's tongue (off),** regret what one has said: *As soon as I had spoken, I could have bitten my tongue off.*
**bite someone's head off,** be sharply angry with someone.
☞ *Hom.* BIGHT, BYTE.

**bit·ing** (bī′ting) **1** sharp; chilly; cutting: *a biting wind.*

**2** sarcastic; sneering: *a biting remark.* **3** ppr. of BITE. 1, 2 *adj.,* 3 *v.* —**bit′ing·ly,** *adv.*

**bitt** (bit) **1** a strong post on a ship's deck to which ropes, cables, etc. are fastened. **2** put ropes, cables, etc. around the bitts. 1 *n.,* 2 *v.*
☛ *Hom.* BIT.

**bit·ten** (bit′ən) a pp. of BITE. *v.*

**bit·ter** (bit′ər) **1** having a sharp, harsh, unpleasant taste: *bitter medicine. Orange rind is bitter.* **2** unpleasant to the mind or feeling; hard to admit or bear: *a bitter defeat. Failure is bitter.* **3** harsh or cutting: *bitter words.* **4** causing pain; sharp; severe: *a bitter wound, a bitter fight.* **5** of weather, very cold: *a bitter winter.* **6** expressing grief, pain, misery, etc.: *a bitter cry.* **7 the bitter,** that which is bitter; bitterness: *You must take the bitter with the sweet.* 1–6 *adj.,* 7 *n.* —**bit′ter·ly,** *adv.* —**bit′ter·ness,** *n.*
**to the bitter end,** **a** until the very last. **b** to death.

**bit·tern** (bit′ərn) any of several species of mainly brownish wading birds belonging to the same family as the herons, having long legs, short tails, and long necks, which are doubled back against the shoulders in flight: *Bitterns have somewhat shorter legs and necks than herons, and are solitary birds, seldom seen by people.* *n.*

**bit·ter·root** (bit′ər rüt′) a low-growing herb of the PURSLANE family found in the Rocky Mountains, having small, fleshy leaves, large, showy, pink flowers, and starchy, edible roots. *n.*

**bit·ters** (bit′ərz) a liquid, usually alcoholic, flavoured with some bitter plant: *Bitters are sometimes used as medicine.* *n. pl.*

**bit·ter·sweet** (bit′ər swēt′) **1** a woody climbing vine of the nightshade family native to Europe but now common in North America, having clusters of purple flowers and poisonous stems and poisonous scarlet berries: *The bittersweet is so named because its taste is at first bitter and then sweet.* **2** a North American climbing shrub having greenish-white flowers, short, pointed leaves, and orange berry-like fruits that open when ripe, showing red seeds. **3** being bitter and sweet at the same time; especially, being pleasant but including also suffering or regret: *bittersweet memories.* **4** something that is bittersweet. 1, 2, 4 *n.,* 3 *adj.*

**bi·tu·men** (bə tyü′mən, bə tü′mən, *or* bich′ü mən) **1** a heavy, almost solid form of PETROLEUM occurring in natural deposits, as in the Athabasca tar sands: *Bitumen is also often called pitch or asphalt.* **2** any of various tarry substances obtained from the evaporation of PETROLEUM, coal tar, etc. *n.*

**bi·tu·mi·nous** (bə tyü′mə nəs *or* bə tü′mə nəs) **1** containing or made with BITUMEN. **2** like BITUMEN. *adj.*

**bituminous coal** a soft, black type of coal containing less carbon and more moisture than anthracite and burning with a smoky flame: *Bituminous coal is the most important and most plentiful type of coal.*

**bi·va·lence** (bī vā′ləns *or* biv′ə ləns) the quality or condition of being BIVALENT. *n.*

**bi·va·lent** (bī vā′lənt *or* biv′ə lənt) in chemistry: **1** having a VALENCE of two. **2** having two VALENCES. *adj.*

**bi·valve** (bī′valv′) **1** any MOLLUSC whose shell consists of two parts hinged together: *Oysters and clams are bivalves.* **2** having two parts hinged together. 1 *n.,* 2 *adj.*

**biv·ou·ac** (biv′ü ak′) **1** a temporary camp outdoors without tents or with very small tents: *The soldiers made a bivouac for the night in a field.* **2** camp outdoors in this way: *They bivouacked there until morning.* 1 *n.,* 2 *v.,* **biv·ou·acked, biv·ou·ack·ing.**
☛ *Etym.* Early 18c. From F *bivouac,* which probably came from Swiss German *Beiwacht,* a patrol of citizens who assisted the town watch at night. The word in English originally meant a night watch by an army to prevent surprise attack.

**bi·weekly** (bī wē′klē) **1** happening once every two weeks. **2** once every two weeks. **3** happening twice a week. **4** twice a week; semiweekly. **5** a newspaper or magazine published biweekly. 1, 3 *adj.,* 2, 4 *adv.,* 5 *n., pl.* **bi·week·lies.**
☛ *Syn.* See note at BIMONTHLY.

**bi·year·ly** (bī yēr′lē) **1** once every two years: *a biyearly magazine.* **2** appearing every two years: *The magazine comes out biyearly.* **3** *Informal.* BIANNUAL: *You can get a biyearly crop if the weather is right.* **4** *Informal.* twice a year: *You can harvest it biyearly.* 1, 3 *adj.,* 2, 4 *adv.*
☛ *Syn.* See note at BIMONTHLY.

**bi·zarre** (bə zär′) odd; queer; fantastic; grotesque: *The frost made bizarre figures on the windowpanes.* *adj.*
—**bi·zarre′ly,** *adv.* —**bi·zarre′ness,** *n.*
☛ *Hom.* BAZAAR.

**bk.** **1** bank. **2** book.

**Bk** berkelium.

**bkg.** banking.

**bkt.** basket.

**bl.** **1** bale. **2** barrel. **3** blue.

**b.l.** bill of lading.

**blab** (blab) **1** tell secrets; talk too much. **2** blabbing talk; chatter. **3** a person who blabs. 1 *v.,* **blabbed, blab·bing,** 2, 3 *n.* —**blab′ber,** *n.*

**black** (blak) **1** the colour of coal or soot; the opposite of white: *This print is black (adj.). Black is the darkest colour; pure black reflects no light (n.).* **2** black colouring matter. **3** make or become black. **4** without any light; very dark: *With the blinds drawn, the room was black as night.* **5** Often, **Black,** a member of the African race. **6** Often, **Black,** a person having some African ancestors. **7** of or having to do with Blacks. **8** covered with dirt, soot, grease, etc.: *The windows facing the highway were black.* **9** dismal; gloomy: *a black day.* **10** sullen; angry: *She gave him a black look and stomped off.* **11** evil; wicked: *black magic.* **12** black clothes; mourning: *The old gentleman always wore black.* **13** put blacking on shoes, boots, etc. **14** having a dark skin. 1, 4, 7–11, 14 *adj.,* 1, 2, 5, 6, 12 *n.,* 3, 13 *v.*
**black out,** **a** lose consciousness temporarily: *I don't know what happened after that, because I blacked out.* **b** darken completely. **c** hold back; suppress: *The government blacked out all news of the invasion.* **d** prevent television broadcasting of a local game: *The match will be blacked out in Vancouver.*
**in the black,** making a profit; prosperous: *After a year of struggle the company was finally in the black.*

**black-and-blue** (blak′ən blü′) severely bruised. *adj.*

**black and white** writing; print: *I asked her to put her promise down in black and white.*

**black art** black magic.

**black·ball** (blak′bol′) **1** vote against: *Some members of the club blackballed Jack, so he could not become a member.* **2** OSTRACIZE. **3** a vote against a person or thing. 1, 2 *v.*, 3 *n.* —**black′ball′er,** *n.*

**black bass** **1** smallmouth bass. **2** any freshwater bass.

**black bear** a North American species of bear found in forest regions and swamp areas from Mexico north to the edge of the tundra, about 170 cm long, able to swim and climb well, often climbing trees to eat young buds and fruit and to protect itself against attack: *Most black bears are black except for a tan muzzle and a white V on the chest, but much lighter colours occur; cinnamon-coloured black bears are common in western Canada.*

**black·ber·ry** (blak′ber′ē) **1** the small black or dark-purple, edible fruit of various bushes and vines of the rose family, closely related to the raspberry. **2** a bush or vine that produces blackberries. **3** gather blackberries. 1, 2 *n., pl.* **black·ber·ries;** 3 *v.*, **black·ber·ried, black·ber·ry·ing.**

**black·bird** (blak′bėrd′) **1** any of several mainly black species of songbird belonging to the same family as the meadowlarks and North American orioles, ranging in size from about 18 to 33 cm long: *Among the species of blackbird found in Canada are the red-winged blackbird, the rusty blackbird, and the common grackle.* **2** a species of European bird belonging to the thrush family, the male having black feathers and an orange bill, and the female dusky brown feathers and a dark bill: *The blackbird is one of the commonest birds of the British Isles. Its song is beautiful.* *n.*

**black blizzard** *Cdn.* on the Prairies, a storm of wind and dust.

**black·board** (blak′bôrd′) a dark, smooth surface for writing or drawing on with chalk or crayon; chalkboard. *n.*

**black bread** heavy, coarse, dark rye bread.

**black·cap** (blak′kap′) **1** a black raspberry. **2** a bird whose head has a black top, such as the CHICKADEE. *n.*

**Black Death** a violent plague that spread through Asia and Europe in the 14th century: *The Black Death was at its worst in 1348.*

**black·en** (blak′ən) **1** make black. **2** become black or very dark. **3** damage the reputation or good name of; defame. *v.*, **black·ened, black·en·ing.**

**black eye** **1** a bruise around an eye. **2** *Informal.* a cause of disgrace or discredit.

**black–eyed Su·san** (blak′īd′ sü′zən) either of two closely related North American wildflowers of the COMPOSITE family having flower heads consisting of bright golden-yellow ray flowers, surrounding a rounded cluster of tiny dark-brown or purplish FLORETS.

**black·face** (blak′fās′) **1** an actor made up as a caricature of a Black, especially for a minstrel show. **2** the make-up for such a role. **3** in printing, a heavy style of type; BOLDFACE. *n.*

**Black·feet** (blak′fēt′) BLACKFOOT CONFEDERACY. *n. pl.*

**black·fish** (blak′fish′) **1** any of various dark-coloured fish, such as the sea bass, tautog, etc. **2** any of several species of dolphin, mostly black in colour and having a very prominent, rounded forehead. *n.*

**black flag** the pirate's flag: *The black flag usually had a white skull and crossbones on it.*

---

blackball 119 black market

hat, āge, fär; let, ēqual, tėrm; it, īce
hot, ōpen, ôrder; oil, out; cup, pùt, rüle
əbove, takən, pencəl, lemən, circəs
ch, child; ng, long; sh, ship
th, thin; ŦH, then; zh, measure

**black–fly** (blak′flī′) any of many species of small, mostly black or grey flies, found throughout the world and having mouth parts adapted for sucking blood: *The bite of a black-fly can be very painful.* *n., pl.* **black-flies.**

**Black·foot** (blak′fùt′) a member of a First Nations people of the Plains, one of the three Algonquian tribes forming the BLACKFOOT CONFEDERACY. **2** the Algonquian language spoken by the tribes of the BLACKFOOT CONFEDERACY. *n., pl.* **Blackfoot.**

**Blackfoot confederacy** a confederacy of three Algonquian tribes of the Plains, the Blackfoot, Blood, and Piegan.

**black·guard** (blag′ärd′) **1** SCOUNDREL. **2** abuse with vile language. 1 *n.*, 2 *v.* —**black′guard·ly,** *adv.*

**black haw** a shrub of the honeysuckle family, with blue berries.

**black·head** (blak′hed′) **1** a small, black-tipped lump of dead cells and oil plugging a pore of the skin. **2** any of various birds that have a black head. **3** an infectious, often fatal disease that attacks turkeys. *n.*

**black ice** *Cdn.* **1** thin ice on water, appearing black because of its transparency. **2** similar thin ice on the surface of a road.

**black·ing** (blak′ing) **1** a black polish used on shoes, stoves, etc. **2** ppr. of BLACK. 1 *n.*, 2 *v.*

**black·ish** (blak′ish) very dark; almost black. *adj.*

**black·jack** (blak′jak′) **1** a club with a flexible handle, used as a weapon. **2** hit a person with a blackjack. **3** COERCE. **4** a large drinking cup or jug, formerly made of leather. **5** the black flag of a pirate. **6** a small oak tree of the southern United States having a bark which is almost black. **7** a card game. 1, 4–7 *n.*, 2, 3 *v.*

**black lead** GRAPHITE.

**black·leg** (blak′leg′) **1** *Informal.* swindler. **2** *Informal.* a worker who takes a striker's job. **3** an infectious, usually fatal disease of cattle and sheep. *n.*

**black list** a list of persons who are believed to deserve punishment, blame, suspicion, etc.

**black–list** (blak′list′) put on a BLACK LIST. *v.*

**black·ly** (blak′lē) **1** dismally; gloomily. **2** sullenly; angrily. **3** evilly; wickedly. *adv.*

**black magic** evil magic: *Witches were believed to practise black magic.*

**black·mail** (blak′māl′) **1** the money obtained from a person by threatening to reveal something bad about him or her. **2** get or try to get blackmail from. **3** an attempt to get money by threats. 1, 3 *n.*, 2 *v.* —**black′mail′er,** *n.*

**Black Ma·ri·a** (mə rī′ə) **1** a police patrol wagon or prison van. **2** HEARSE.

**black mark** a mark of criticism or punishment.

**black market** **1** the selling of goods at illegal prices or in illegal quantities. **2** a place where such trade is carried on.

**black measles** a severe form of measles.

**black·ness** (blak′nis) **1** the state of being black; black colour; darkness. **2** wickedness. *n.*

**black nightshade** a species of poisonous nightshade native to Europe, but now a common weed throughout eastern North America, having dark green leaves, white flowers, and black berries.

**black·out** (blak′out′) **1** a turning out or concealing of all the lights of a city, district, etc. as a protection against an air raid. **2** a temporary blindness or unconsciousness resulting from lack of circulation of blood in the brain. It may occur after much exertion or be experienced by a pilot during rapid changes in velocity or direction of his or her aircraft. **3** a period of darkness resulting from a failure of electrical power. **4** a turning off of all the lights on the stage of a theatre to suggest the passing of time, or to mark the end of a scene. **5** holding back news or other information by censorship: *News blackouts are common in wartime.* *n.*

**black pepper** a hot-tasting seasoning made from the ground dried berries of the pepper vine. Compare with WHITE PEPPER.

**black sheep** a person who has not lived up to the expectations of his or her family, and is considered a disgrace to it.

**black·smith** (blak′smith′) a person who makes and repairs things of iron, using a forge: *Blacksmiths mend tools and make horseshoes.* *n.*

**black·snake** (blak′snāk′) **1** a harmless, swift-moving snake of southeastern Canada and the eastern United States, belonging to the same family as the garter snake, having a glossy black back and bluish-grey belly, and usually about 120 cm long: *Blacksnakes often climb trees to eat birds' eggs and young birds they find; they also eat insects, frogs, mice, etc., and even other snakes, both poisonous and non-poisonous.* **2** a heavy whip made of braided leather. *n.*

**black spruce** **1** a spruce tree found in moist climates throughout northern Canada up to the edge of the tundra, having small, egg-shaped cones and short, dark bluish-green needles: *The black spruce is the commonest tree of the northern forest.* **2** its soft, moderately light wood.

**black tea** tea made from leaves that have been allowed to wither and ferment in the air for some time, before being dried in ovens.

**black·thorn** (blak′thôrn′) **1** a thorny European shrub, a species of plum having white flowers that appear before the leaves and bearing very small, bluish-black fruits usually called SLOES. **2** a walking stick or club made from the stem of this shrub. *n.*

**black·top** (blak′top′) **1** asphalt mixed with crushed rock, used as a pavement for highways, roads, runways, etc. **2** any surface so paved, such as a highway, driveway, etc. **3** pave or surface a road with blacktop. 1, 2 *n.*, 3 *v.*, **black·topped, black·top·ping.**

**black walnut** **1** a medium-sized North American walnut tree. **2** the heavy, hard, strong brown wood of this tree, highly valued for making furniture, interior panelling, etc. **3** the oily, round, edible nut of this tree.

**black widow** any of a closely related group of poisonous black spiders found in many warm regions of the world, especially any of the three species that occur in the southern United States: *The most common American species, found also in many other countries, has a red hourglass-shaped spot on the underside of its abdomen.*
☛ *Etym.* Named for its colour and the fact that the female often eats the male after mating.

**blad·der** (blad′ər) **1** a soft, thin bag of membrane in the body of an animal, which holds urine received from the kidneys until it is discharged. **2** any similar bag that stores or holds liquid or air in an animal body: *the swim bladder of a fish.* **3** a strong bag, often made of rubber, that will hold liquids or air: *The rubber bag inside a football is a bladder.* **4** a hollow, air-filled bag in plants, as in certain seaweeds. *n.*

**blad·der·wort** (blad′ər wėrt′) **1** any of a closely related group of mainly small, rootless plants found throughout the world, but especially in tropical regions, having many small bladders or bags on their leaves in which they trap insect larvae, small crustaceans, etc.: *Most bladderworts are water or bog plants.* **2** referring to a family of carnivorous plants including the bladderworts and several other groups of plants. *n.*

**blade** (blād) **1** the cutting part of anything like a knife or sword: *My father's hunting knife has a very sharp blade.* See SWORD for picture. **2** sword. **3** swordsman. **4** a smart or dashing fellow. **5** a leaf of grass. **6** the flat, wide part of a leaf as distinguished from the stalk. **7** the flat, wide part of anything: *the blade of an oar or paddle, the shoulder blade.* **8** in the study of speech sounds, the upper part of the tongue, just behind the tip. *n.*
—**blade′like′,** *adj.*

**blad·ed** (blā′did) having a BLADE or blades. *adj.*

**blam·a·ble** (blā′mə bəl) deserving BLAME. *adj.*
—**blam′a·bly,** *adv.*

**blame** (blām) **1** hold responsible for something bad or wrong: *We blamed the fog for our accident.* **2** the responsibility for something bad or wrong: *Lack of care deserves the blame for many mistakes.* **3** find fault with: *The teacher will not blame us if we do our best.* **4** finding fault; reproof. 1, 3 *v.*, **blamed, blam·ing;** 2, 4 *n.*
—**blam′er,** *n.*
**be to blame,** deserve blame: *Each person said somebody else was to blame.*
**blame on,** attribute to: *The accident was blamed on the icy road.*

**blame·less** (blām′lis) not deserving BLAME (def. 2); free from fault. *adj.* —**blame′less·ly,** *adv.*
—**blame′less·ness,** *n.*

**blame·wor·thy** (blām′wėr′ᴛʜē) deserving BLAME (def. 2): *a blameworthy act.* *adj.*

**blanch** (blanch) **1** turn white; become pale: *The boy blanched with fear when he saw the bear coming.* **2** loosen the skins of raw vegetables, nuts, etc. by plunging them first in boiling water and then in cold water. **3** make white; bleach. *v.*

**blanc·mange** (blə mänzh′) a sweet jelly-like dessert made of milk, eggs, sugar, etc. thickened with cornstarch or gelatin. *n.*

**bland** (bland) **1** smooth; mild; gentle; soothing: *a bland spring breeze, a bland diet.* **2** agreeable; polite: *a bland reply, a bland manner.* **3** lacking a distinctive character; uninteresting, dull: *a bland election campaign. Her poems are very bland.* *adj.* —**bland′ly,** *adv.* —**bland′ness,** *n.*

**blan·dish** (blan′dish) coax by flattering. *v.*

**blan·dish·ment** (blan′dish mənt) **1** the act of

BLANDISHing. **2** Usually, **blandishments,** *pl.* flattering remarks, etc. meant to persuade. *n.*

**blank** (blangk) **1** a space left empty or to be filled in: *Leave a blank after each word.* **2** not written or printed on: *blank paper.* **3** a paper with spaces to be filled in: *Fill out this application blank and return it to the manager.* **4** with spaces to be filled in: *a blank cheque. They gave me a blank form to fill in.* **5** an empty or vacant place or space: *When he saw the hard test, his mind became a complete blank.* **6** having or showing no idea or understanding: *His only answer was a blank stare. Her mind suddenly went blank in the middle of the exam.* **7** utter; absolute: *a blank refusal. He looked at her in blank dismay.* **8** become confused or distracted (*used with* **out**): *Just when I wanted to introduce them, I blanked out and couldn't remember their names.* **9** incomplete or lacking some usual feature: *A blank cartridge contains powder but no bullet.* **10** a partly formed piece, ready to be made into a finished object: *a key blank.* **11** in games, keep from scoring. **12** hide; obscure. 1, 3, 5, 10 *n.*, 2, 4, 6, 7, 9 *adj.*, 8, 11, 12 *v.* —**blank′ly,** *adv.* —**blank′ness,** *n.* **draw a blank,** *Informal.* fail; get nowhere; achieve nothing: *They tried to get more information by questioning his friends, but they drew a blank.*

**blan·ket** (blang′kit) **1** a soft, heavy covering woven from wool, cotton, or other material, used to keep people or animals warm. **2** anything like a blanket: *A blanket of snow covered the ground.* **3** cover with a blanket: *Snow blanketed the ground.* **4** cover; hinder; obscure: *Fog blanketed the city.* 1, 2 *n.*, 3, 4 *v.*

**blank verse** unrhymed poetry having a metre based on five IAMBIC feet in each line: *Shakespeare's plays are written mainly in blank verse.*

**blare** (bler) **1** make a loud, harsh sound: *The trumpets blared, announcing the queen's arrival.* **2** utter harshly or loudly. **3** a loud, harsh sound: *The blare of the horn was startling.* **4** brilliance of colour; glare. 1, 2 *v.*, **blared, blar·ing;** 3, 4 *n.*

**blar·ney** (blär′nē) **1** flattering, coaxing talk. **2** flatter; coax. 1 *n.*, 2 *v.*, **blar·neyed, blar·ney·ing.** **kiss the Blarney Stone,** get skill in flattering and coaxing people.
☛ *Etym.* From the *Blarney Stone*, a stone in a wall of Blarney Castle in Ireland, said to give skill in flattery to anyone who kisses it.

**blas·pheme** (blas fēm′) speak about God or sacred things with abuse or contempt; utter BLASPHEMY. *v.*, **blas·phemed, blas·phem·ing.**

**blas·phem·er** (blas fē′mər) a person who BLASPHEMES. *n.*

**blas·phe·mous** (blas′fə məs) showing contempt for God or sacred things; profane: *a blasphemous utterance.* *adj.* —**blas′phe·mous·ly,** *adv.*

**blas·phe·my** (blas′fə mē) abuse of or contempt for God or sacred things. *n., pl.* **blas·phe·mies.**

**blast** (blast) **1** a strong, sudden rush of wind or air: *the icy blasts of winter.* **2** the blowing of a trumpet, horn, etc. **3** the sound so made. **4** a current of air used in smelting, etc. **5** a charge of dynamite or some other explosive that blows up rocks, earth, etc. **6** blow up with dynamite or some other explosive: *The old building was blasted.* **7** a blasting; explosion: *We heard the blast two kilometres away.* **8** a cause of withering, blight, or ruin. **9** wither; blight; ruin; destroy: *The intense heat blasted the vines. His conviction for fraud blasted his reputation.* 1–5, 7, 8 *n.*, 6, 9 *v.* —**blast′er,** *n.*

---

blank 121 bleachers

hat, āge, fär; let, ēqual, tėrm; it, īce
hot, ōpen, ôrder; oil, out; cup, pùt, rüle
ə*bove,* tak*ə*n, penc*ə*l, lem*ə*n, circ*ə*s
ch, child; ng, long; sh, ship
th, thin; ᴛʜ, then; zh, measure

**blast off,** of rockets, missiles, etc., fire; take off: *Make ready to blast off.*
**in full blast,** in full operation.

**blast·ed** (blas′tid) **1** withered; blighted; ruined. **2** *Informal.* detestable; cursed: *This blasted pen won't write.* **3** pt. and pp. of BLAST. 1, 2 *adj.*, 3 *v.*

**blast furnace** a furnace in which ores are smelted by blowing a strong current of air into the furnace from the bottom to make a very great heat.

**blast-off** (blast′of′) of rockets, missiles, etc., the moment or process of taking off; launching. *n.*

**bla·tan·cy** (blā′tən sē) a BLATANT quality. *n.*

**bla·tant** (blā′tənt) **1** offensively obvious; forced on one's attention: *blatant lies, blatant stupidity.* **2** disagreeably noisy; loud-mouthed. *adj.* —**bla′tant·ly,** *adv.*

**blaze**[1] (blāz) **1** a bright flame or fire: *She could see the blaze of the campfire.* **2** burn with a bright flame; be on fire: *A fire was blazing in the fireplace.* **3** a glow of brightness; intense light; glare: *the blaze of the noon sun.* **4** show bright colours or lights: *On the evening of the party, the big house blazed with lights.* **5** a bright display: *The tulips made a blaze of colour.* **6** a violent outburst: *a blaze of temper.* **7** burst out in anger or excitement: *She blazed at the insult.* 1, 3, 5, 6 *n.*, 2, 4, 7 *v.*, **blazed, blaz·ing.**
**blaze away,** fire a gun, etc.
**blaze with,** turn red in the face with: *blazing with anger.*

**blaze**[2] (blāz) **1** a mark made on a tree by chipping off a piece of its bark. **2** mark a tree in this way. **3** mark by blazing trees: *The hunters blazed a trail through the bush.* **4** a white mark on an animal's forehead. 1, 4 *n.*, 2, 3 *v.*, **blazed, blaz·ing.**

**blaze**[3] (blāz) make known; proclaim. *v.*, **blazed, blaz·ing.**

**blaz·er** (blā′zər) **1** a jacket, often dark blue, cut like a suit coat, and usually worn by men as dressy but informal wear. **2** a similar loose or slightly fitted, unbelted jacket worn by women or men, usually having a notched collar and patch pockets. *n.*

**bla·zon** (blā′zən) **1** make known; proclaim: *Big posters blazoned the wonders of the coming circus.* **2** decorate; adorn. **3** a coat of arms; a shield with a coat of arms on it. **4** describe or paint a coat of arms. **5** display or show. 1, 2, 4, 5 *v.*, 3 *n.*

**bla·zon·ry** (blā′zən rē) **1** bright decoration or display. **2** a coat of arms. **3** a description or painting of a coat of arms. *n.*

**bldg.** building.

**bleach** (blēch) **1** whiten by exposing to sunlight: *Bleached bones lay on the desert.* **2** whiten or lighten by using chemicals: *We bleached the stains out of the shirt.* **3** a chemical used in bleaching. **4** turn white or pale; lose colour. **5** the act of bleaching. 1, 2, 4 *v.*, 3, 5 *n.* —**bleach′er,** *n.*

**bleach·ers** (blē′chərz) **1** the roofless rows or tiers of seats at outdoor games such as baseball and football. 2 the similar rows of seats at indoor games such as basketball. *n. pl.*

**bleak** (blēk) 1 swept by winds; bare: *bleak and rocky mountain peaks.* 2 chilly; cold: *a bleak wind.* 3 dreary; dismal: *All their savings were gone, and the future looked bleak.* *adj.* —**bleak′ly,** *adv.* —**bleak′ness,** *n.*

**blear** (blēr) 1 make dim or blurred. 2 BLEARY. 1 *v.*, 2 *adj.*

**blear·y** (blē′rē) of the eyes or vision, dim or blurred, especially from tiredness or tears. *adj.*, **blear·i·er, blear·i·est.** —**blear′i·ness,** *n.*

**bleat** (blēt) 1 the cry made by a sheep, goat, or calf. 2 a sound like it. 3 make the cry of a sheep, goat, or calf, or a sound like it. 1, 2 *n.*, 3 *v.* —**bleat′er,** *n.*

**bled** (bled) *pt.* and *pp.* of BLEED: *The cut bled for ten minutes. Those who have bled for our country shall be remembered.* *v.*

**bleed** (blēd) 1 lose blood: *The cut is bleeding.* 2 shed one's blood; suffer wounds or death: *He bled to death. He fought and bled for his country.* 3 take blood from: *Doctors used to bleed sick people.* 4 lose sap, juice, etc. from a surface that has been cut or scratched: *The injured elm is bleeding.* 5 take sap, juice, etc. from. 6 feel pity, sorrow, or grief: *His heart bled for the poor little orphan.* 7 *Informal.* get money from by extortion. *v.,* **bled, bleed·ing.**

**bleed·er** (blē′dər) a person suffering from a condition in which the blood fails to clot, so that bleeding is hard to stop; HEMOPHILIAC. *n.*

**bleeding heart** 1 a common garden plant that has drooping clusters of red or pink, heart-shaped flowers. 2 *Informal.* a person who is excessively sentimental and allows feelings of pity and sympathy to override judgment.

**blem·ish** (blem′ish) 1 a stain or spot; scar: *A mole is a blemish on a person's skin.* 2 imperfection; flaw: *A quick temper was the only blemish in her character.* 3 make stained or scarred. 4 injure; mar: *One bad deed can blemish a good reputation.* 1, 2 *n.*, 3, 4 *v.* **without blemish,** perfect.

**blench**[1] (blench) draw back; shrink away. *v.*

**blench**[2] (blench) 1 turn pale. 2 make white. *v.*

**blend** (blend) 1 mix together; mix or become mixed so thoroughly that the things mixed cannot be distinguished or separated: *Oil and water will not blend. Blend the first three ingredients in a saucepan.* 2 a thorough mixture made by blending. 3 make by mixing several kinds together: *to blend tea.* 4 a mixture of several kinds: *a blend of coffee.* 5 shade into each other, little by little; merge: *The colours of the rainbow blend into one another.* 6 go well together; harmonize: *The colours in that print do not blend.* 1, 3, 5, 6 *v.,* **blend·ed** or **blent, blend·ing;** 2, 4 *n.*

**blend·er** (blen′dər) a small household appliance for mixing ingredients usually into a liquid. *n.*

**blent** (blent) a *pt.* and *pp.* of BLEND. *v.*

**bless** (bles) 1 make holy or sacred: *to bless a church.* 2 ask God's favour for: *Bless these little children.* 3 wish good to; feel grateful to: *They blessed him for his kindness.* 4 favour with prosperity, success, or happiness: *May this country always be blessed with prosperity.* 5 praise or glorify: *Bless the Lord, O my soul.* 6 guard; protect: *Heaven bless you.* 7 make the sign of the cross over. *v.,* **blessed** or **blest, bless·ing.**

**bless·ed** (bles′id *or* blest) 1 holy; sacred. 2 in heaven; beatified. 3 fortunate; happy: *He had all he wanted now and considered himself blessed.* 4 bringing or accompanied by joy or happiness: *blessed ignorance. The birth of a baby is often called a blessed event.* 5 *Informal.* a word used to express annoyance or anger; darned; confounded: *Now where did I put the blessed thing?* 6 (blest) a *pt.* and a *pp.* of BLESS. 1–5 *adj.*, 6 *v.* —**bless′ed·ness,** *n.*

**Blessed Virgin** the Virgin Mary.

**bless·ing** (bles′ing) 1 a prayer asking God to show His favour; benediction: *At the end of the church service, the bishop gave the blessing.* 2 a giving of God's favour. 3 a wish for happiness or success: *When she left home, she received her parents' blessing.* 4 approval or consent: *The marriage had the blessing of all four parents.* 5 anything that makes one happy or contented: *A good temper is a great blessing.* 6 *ppr.* of BLESS. 1–5 *n.*, 6 *v.*

**blest** (blest) 1 a *pt.* and a *pp.* of BLESS. 2 blessed. 1 *v.*, 2 *adj.*

**blew** (blü) *pt.* of BLOW[2] and BLOW[3]: *All night long the wind blew.* *v.*
☛ *Hom.* BLUE.

**blight** (blīt) 1 any of several plant diseases that cause leaves, stems, or other parts to wither and die: *The apple crop was wiped out by a blight.* 2 a fungus, insect, etc. that causes such a disease: *Rust, smut, and mildew are blights.* 3 anything that causes destruction or ruin: *the blight of high unemployment.* 4 cause to wither and die: *Mildew blighted the June roses.* 5 destroy; ruin. 6 disappoint or frustrate: *All their hopes were blighted.* 7 a person or thing that frustrates or disappoints. 8 the condition of being spoiled, ruined, etc.: *urban blight.* 1–3, 7, 8 *n.*, 4–6 *v.*

**blimp** (blimp) *Informal.* a small, non-rigid dirigible airship. *n.*
☛ *Etym.* Coined in Britain during the first World War, probably from *Type B limp*, a term for the most common type of non-rigid dirigible.

**blind** (blīnd) 1 not able to see; not having the sense of sight: *The man with the white cane is blind.* 2 make unable to see: *The bright lights blinded me for a moment. She was blinded in an accident in childhood.* 3 hard to see; hidden: *a blind seam, blind curve on a highway.* 4 make hard to see; conceal: *Clouds blind the stars from view.* 5 without the help of sight; by means of instruments instead of the eyes: *the blind flying of an aircraft at night* (*adj.*)*, to fly blind* (*adv.*)*.* 6 without thought, judgment, or good sense: *blind fury, a blind guess.* 7 take away the power to understand or judge: *Her prejudices blinded her.* 8 a device on a spring roller that can be rolled down in front of a window in order to screen or shut out light or heat, or to keep heat in: *We have blinds on our bedroom windows.* 9 anything that conceals an action or purpose: *Her cheerful manner was only a blind to conceal her nervousness.* 10 without an opening: *a blind wall.* 11 with only one opening: *a blind canyon.* 12 of or for blind persons. 13 made without previous knowledge: *a blind purchase.* 14 arranged for one by someone else: *a blind date.* 15 a hiding place for a hunter or photographer. 1, 3, 5, 6, 10–14 *adj.*, 2, 4, 7 *v.*, 5 *adv.*, 8, 9, 15 *n.* —**blind′ly,** *adv.* —**blind′ness,** *n.*

**the blind,** people who are unable to see.

**blind to,** make unable to know: *His fine appearance blinded her to his faults.*

**blind alley** 1 a passageway closed at one end. 2 anything that gives no chance for progess or improvement: *His last job proved to be a blind alley.*

**blind date** 1 a social date arranged by a third person for a couple who have not met. 2 either of the two persons thus dated.

**blind·er** (blīn′dər) a leather flap designed to keep a horse from seeing to the side. Also, **blinker**. *n.*

**blind flying** the act of piloting an aircraft by instruments only.

**blind·fold** (blīnd′fōld′) 1 cover the eyes of to prevent seeing: *The robbers blindfolded, gagged, and bound their victim.* 2 something covering the eyes to prevent seeing: *Putting a blindfold on the horse, she led it safely out of the blazing barn.* 3 with the eyes covered: *He said he could walk the line blindfold.* 4 reckless. 1 *v.*, 2 *n.*, 3 *adv.*, 4 *adj.*

**blind·man's buff** (blīnd′manz buf′) a game in which a blindfolded person tries to catch and identify one of the other players. Also, **blindman's bluff**.
☛ *Etym.* The word **buff** in **blindman's buff** is a shortened form of the word **buffet**, meaning 'to knock about' or 'a blow'. See the entry BUFFET[1].

**blind spot** 1 a round spot on the retina of the eye that is not sensitive to light: *The optic nerve enters the eye at the blind spot. The motorist did not see the cyclist as he was riding in her blind spot.* See EYE for picture. 2 a matter on which a person does not know that he or she is prejudiced or poorly informed: *His blind spot is modern music; he refuses to listen to it.* 3 in radio, an area of poor reception.

**blink** (blingk) 1 look with the eyes opening and shutting: *Anna blinked at the sudden light.* 2 close the eyes and open them again quickly; wink: *We blink every few seconds.* 3 shine with an unsteady light: *A lantern blinked through the darkness.* 4 a blinking. 5 look with indifference at; ignore: *You cannot blink the fact that there is war.* 6 a glimpse. 1–3, 5 *v.*, 4, 6 *n.*
**on the blink**, *Informal,* not working properly; out of order: *Our TV set is on the blink again.*

**blink·er** (bling′kər) 1 BLINDER. 2 a warning signal with flashing lights. *n.*

**blip** (blip) an image on a RADAR screen, in the form of a small dot of light, showing that radar waves are being reflected from an object: *The blip shows the location of the object and the direction in which it is moving.* *n.*

**bliss** (blis) 1 great happiness; perfect joy. 2 the joy of heaven; blessedness. *n.*

**bliss·ful** (blis′fəl) very happy; joyful. *adj.* —**bliss′ful·ly**, *adv.* —**bliss′ful·ness**, *n.*

**blis·ter** (blis′tər) 1 a little baglike swelling in the skin filled with watery matter, often caused by a burn or by rubbing. 2 a swelling on the surface of a plant, on metal, on painted wood, etc. 3 raise a blister on. 4 become covered with blisters; have blisters. 5 attack with sharp words. 6 a bubblelike, often transparent, structure on an aircraft, etc. for an observer, navigator, or gunner. 7 a bubblelike shell of transparent plastic used to protect and display merchandise. 1, 2, 6, 7 *n.*, 3–5 *v.*

**blithe** (blīfH *or* blīth) 1 happy; cheerful; light-hearted: *She had a blithe and carefree spirit.* 2 airy; casual; unheeding: *blithe indifference.* *adj.* —**blithe′ly**, *adv.* —**blithe′ness**, *n.*

**blith·er·ing** (blifH′ə ring) talking nonsense; jabbering: *a blithering idiot.* *adj.*

**blithe·some** (blīfH′səm *or* blīth′səm) cheerful; happy; light-hearted. *adj.* —**blithe′some·ly**, *adv.* —**blithe′some·ness**, *n.*

**blitz** (blits) 1 BLITZKRIEG. 2 a sudden, violent attack using many airplanes and tanks. 3 any concerted effort: *The United Way launched a house-to-house blitz in a last attempt to meet their goal.* 4 to subject to a blitz. 1–3 *n.*, 4 *v.*

**blitz·krieg** (blit′skrēg′) warfare in which the offensive is extremely rapid, violent, and hard to resist. *n.*

**bliz·zard** (bliz′ərd) 1 a violent, long-lasting, blinding snowstorm usually accompanied by temperatures of −10°C or colder: *Blizzards sometimes last for more than a day.* 2 any violent winter windstorm with much blowing snow. *n.*

**blk.** 1 black. 2 block. 3 bulky.

**bloat** (blōt) 1 swell up; puff up: *His face was bruised and bloated after the fight.* 2 preserve herring by salting and smoking. 3 a swelling of the abdomen of cattle, sheep, etc. after eating moist feed, caused by gases produced by the fermentation of the feed. 1, 2 *v.*, 3 *n.*

**bloat·er** (blō′tər) a herring preserved by salting and smoking. *n.*

**blob** (blob) 1 a small, soft drop or lump: *Blobs of wax covered the candlestick.* 2 a splash or daub of colour. *n.*

**bloc** (blok) a group of persons, companies, nations, etc. united for some purpose: *Our neighbours formed a bloc to get a new school.* *n.*
☛ *Hom.* BLOCK.

**block** (blok) 1 a solid piece of wood, stone, metal, etc.: *The Pyramids are made of blocks of stone.* 2 fill so as to prevent passage or progress: *The country roads were blocked with snow.* 3 put things in the way of; obstruct; hinder: *Her sickness blocked my plans for the party.* 4 obstruction; hindrance: *We were delayed for half an hour because of a block in traffic.* 5 a space in a city or town bounded by four streets: *one city block.* 6 the length of one side of a block, in a city or town: *Walk one block east.* 7 a number of townships, usually surrounded by land that has not been surveyed: *the Peace River Block.* 8 a group of things of the same kind: *a block of seats in a theatre.* 9 a building containing a number of apartments or offices: *an apartment block, an office block.* 10 a number of buildings close together. 11 a building containing offices, often an annex to another building. 12 a short section of railway track, with signals for spacing trains. 13 a platform where things are put up for sale at an auction. 14 a pulley on a hook: *a block and tackle.* See BLOCK AND TACKLE for picture. 15 in printing, a piece of engraved metal, wood, or other substance. See PRINT for picture. 16 in sports, the hindering of an opponent's play. 17 in sports, hinder an opponent's play. 18 prevent a nerve from transmitting impulses. 19 give shape to something with a mould: *to block a hat.* 20 in computer science, a portion of data already entered, which is identified as a block and can then be moved. 1, 4–16, 20 *n.*, 2, 3, 17–19 *v.*

**block in** or **block out**, plan or sketch roughly without filling in the details; outline.
☛ *Hom.* BLOC.

**block·ade** (blok ād′) **1** in war, the closing off of a harbour, city, etc. by enemy ships or other forces to keep people or supplies from getting through. **2** put under blockade. **3** the forces used to set up a blockade. **4** anything that blocks up or obstructs. **5** block up; obstruct. *1, 3, 4 n., 2, 5 v.,* **block·ad·ed, block·ad·ing.** —**block·ad′er,** *n.*
**run the blockade,** try to get into or out of a port that is being blockaded.

**blockade runner** a ship that tries to get into or out of a port that is being blockaded.

**block·age** (blok′ij) **1** blocking or being blocked. **2** something that blocks: *We cleared the blockage from the pipe.* *n.*

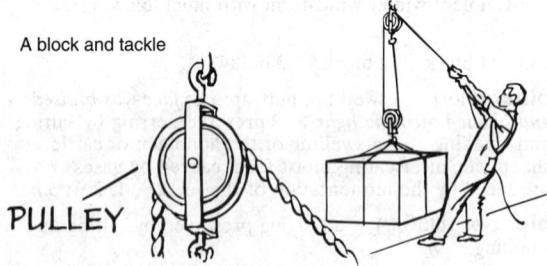

A block and tackle

**block and tackle** an arrangement of pulleys and ropes used in lifting or pulling heavy weights.

**block·bust·er** (blok′bus′tər) *Informal.* **1** an aerial bomb that weighs two or more tonnes, capable of destroying a large area. **2** any person or thing that has a very strong impact or effect: *The new musical is a blockbuster.* *n.*

**block·er** (blok′ər) in football, a player who hinders an opponent's play. *n.*

**block·head** (blok′hed′) a stupid person; fool. *n.*

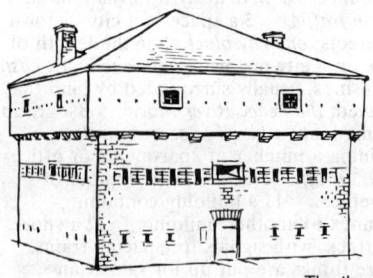

The three-storey concrete blockhouse of Fort Wellington, Prescott, Ontario

**block·house** (blok′hous′) **1** a military fortification built of heavy timbers or concrete, and having loopholes to shoot from. **2** a heavily reinforced building used as a control centre and place of observation for operations involving danger from intense heat, radiation, etc.: *The launching of space vehicles is controlled from a blockhouse.* *n.*

**block signal** a signal to show whether a short section of railway track ahead has a train on it or not.

**block·y** (blok′ē) **1** like a block; chunky. **2** having patches of light and shade. *adj.,* **block·i·er, block·i·est.**

**bloke** (blōk) *Esp. Brit. Informal.* fellow; chap. *n.*

**blond** (blond) **1** light-coloured: *blond hair, blond furniture.* **2** having yellow or light-brown hair, blue or grey eyes, and light skin: *blond people.* **3** a blond man or boy. *1, 2 adj., 3 n.* —**blond′ness,** *n.*
☛ *Syn.* As a noun, **blond** is used for men and boys and BLONDE is used for women and girls. The usual form for the adjective, however, is **blond** in all cases: *a blond young man, a blond actress.* See also note at BRUNET.

**blonde** (blond) a woman or girl having fair hair: *Both sisters are blondes.* *n.*
☛ *Syn.* See note at BLOND.

**blood** (blud) **1** the red liquid in the veins and arteries of vertebrates; the red liquid that flows from a cut: *Blood is circulated by the heart, carrying oxygen and digested food to all parts of the body and taking away waste materials.* **2** the corresponding liquid in other animals: *The blood of most insects looks yellowish.* **3** bloodshed or slaughter. **4** family; birth; relationship; parentage; descent: *Love of the sea runs in her blood.* **5** high lineage, especially royal lineage: *a prince of the blood.* **6** temper; state of mind: *There was bad blood between them.* **7** a man of dash and spirit. **8 Blood,** a member of a First Nations people of the Plains, one of the three Algonquian tribes making up the BLACKFOOT CONFEDERACY. *n., pl.* (def. 8) **Bloods** or **Blood.**
**in cold blood,** on purpose and without emotion: *He lay in wait for the spy and then shot him down in cold blood.*
**make one's blood boil,** make one very angry: *Unfair comments like that make my blood boil.*
**make one's blood run cold,** fill one with terror: *"The Arctic trails have their secret tales/That would make your blood run cold."*

**blood bank** **1** a place for storing blood to be used in transfusions. **2** the blood kept in storage.

**blood count** a count of the number of red and white corpuscles in a sample of a person's blood.

**blood·cur·dling** (blud′kėr′dling) terrifying; horrible: *a bloodcurdling story.* *adj.*

**blood donor** a person who gives his or her blood to a BLOOD BANK.

**blood·ed** (blud′id) **1** coming from good stock; of good breed: *blooded horses.* **2** having blood of a certain kind (*used only in compounds*): *Snakes are called cold-blooded; lions are warm-blooded.* **3** having a temperament of a certain kind (*used only in compounds*): *She is very hot-blooded and gets angry quickly.* *adj.*

**blood group** any of four main groups into which human blood is classified: A, AB, B, and O.

**blood·hound** (blud′hound′) one of a large breed of dog with a very keen sense of smell, long, drooping ears, and a wrinkled face: *A trained bloodhound can follow a trail several hours old.* *n.*

**blood·less** (blud′lis) **1** without blood; pale. **2** without BLOODSHED: *a bloodless revolution.* **3** without energy; spiritless. **4** cold-hearted or cruel. *adj.*

**blood·let·ting** (blud′let′ing) **1** taking blood from a vein as a treatment for disease: *Bloodletting was formerly common, but few diseases are treated in this way today.* **2** BLOODSHED. *n.*

**blood money** **1** the money paid to have somebody

murdered. **2** the money paid as compensation to the next of kin of a person who has been murdered: *In Anglo-Saxon times, blood money was paid to the family of a murdered man by the family of the murderer.* **3** money gained at the cost of another person's life, freedom, welfare, etc.

**blood poisoning** a diseased condition that occurs when the bloodstream is invaded by poisonous substances or disease-causing BACTERIA from a local source of infection.

**blood pressure** the pressure of the blood against the inner walls of the blood vessels, varying with exertion, excitement, health, age, etc.

**blood·root** (blud′rüt′) a common wild plant that has a red root, red sap, and a white flower that blooms in early spring. *n.*

**blood royal** the royal family: *His wife is a princess and belongs to the blood royal.*

**blood·shed** (blud′shed′) the shedding of blood; slaughter. *n.*

**blood·shot** (blud′shot′) of the eyes, red and sore; tinged with blood: *Your eyes become bloodshot if you get dirt in them.* *adj.*

**blood·stain** (blud′stān′) a mark or stain left by blood. *n.*

**blood·stained** (blud′stānd′) **1** stained with blood. **2** guilty of murder or BLOODSHED. *adj.*

**blood·stone** (blud′stōn′) a dark green semiprecious stone having flecks of bright-red jasper or impure quartz through it: *Bloodstone is a kind of translucent quartz.* *n.*

**blood·stream** (blud′strēm′) the blood flowing in the circulatory system of a living body. *n.*

**blood·suck·er** (blud′suk′ər) **1** LEECH¹ (def. 1). **2** a person who gets all he or she can from others. *n.*

**blood test** an examination of a sample of a person's blood to determine the type of blood, diagnose illness, etc.

**blood·thirst·y** (blud′thėr′stē) eager for BLOODSHED; cruel; murderous. *adj.* —**blood′thirst′i·ly,** *adv.* —**blood′thirst′i·ness,** *n.*

**blood type** BLOOD GROUP.

**blood vessel** any tube in the body through which the blood circulates: *Arteries, veins, and capillaries are blood vessels.*

**blood·y** (blud′ē) **1** bleeding: *a bloody nose.* **2** cause to bleed: *His nose was bloodied in the fight.* **3** covered or stained with blood: *a bloody bandage, a bloody sword.* **4** stain with blood. **5** with much BLOODSHED: *a bloody battle.* **6** eager for BLOODSHED; cruel. 1, 3, 5, 6 *adj.,* **blood·i·er, blood·i·est,** 2, 4 *v.,* **blood·ied, blood·y·ing.** —**blood′i·ness,** *n.*

**bloom** (blüm) **1** a flower; BLOSSOM. **2** have flowers; open into flowers; BLOSSOM: *Many plants bloom in the spring.* **3** the condition or time of flowering: *in bloom.* **4** the condition or time of greatest health, vigour, or beauty: *in the bloom of youth.* **5** be in the condition or time of greatest health, vigour, or beauty. **6** a glow of health and beauty. **7** glow with health and beauty. **8** the powdery coating on some fruits and leaves: *There is a bloom on grapes and plums and on the needles of some species of spruce.* 1, 3, 4, 6, 8 *n.,* 2, 5, 7 *v.* —**bloom′er,** *n.*

**bloom·ers** (blü′mərz) **1** loose trousers, gathered at the knee, formerly worn by women and girls for athletics. **2** underwear made like these. *n. pl.*

**bloom·ing** (blü′ming) **1** having flowers; BLOSSOMing. **2** flourishing: *The child is blooming.* **3** ppr. of BLOOM. 1, 2 *adj.,* 3 *v.* —**bloom′ing·ly,** *adv.*

**blos·som** (blos′əm) **1** a flower, especially of a tree or other plant that produces fruit: *apple blossoms.* See PEDICEL for picture. **2** the condition or time of flowering: *a cherry tree in blossom.* **3** have flowers; open into flowers: *The apple trees are beginning to blossom.* **4** open out; develop: *Her talent blossomed under the teacher's expert guidance.* 1, 2 *n.,* 3, 4 *v.*
**blossom into,** develop into: *She's blossoming into a fine athlete.*
**blossom out, a** develop favourably. **b** become more sociable.

**blos·som·y** (blos′ə mē) full of BLOSSOMS. *adj.*

**blot** (blot) **1** a spot or stain: *an ink blot.* **2** make blots on; stain or spot. **3** dry ink, etc. with paper or other material that absorbs: *She blotted her signature before folding the letter.* **4** a blemish; disgrace: *a blot on his reputation.* **5** blemish or disgrace: *His behaviour blotted his record.* 1, 4 *n.,* 2, 3, 5 *v.,* **blot·ted, blot·ting.**
**blot out, a** hide; cover up. **b** wipe out; destroy.

**blotch** (bloch) **1** a large, irregular spot or stain. **2** a place where the skin is red or discoloured. **3** cover or mark with blotches. 1, 2 *n.,* 3 *v.*

**blotch·y** (bloch′ē) having BLOTCHes. *adj.,* **blotch·i·er, blotch·i·est.**

**blot·ter** (blot′ər) **1** a piece of BLOTTING PAPER. **2** a book for writing down happenings or transactions: *A police-station blotter records arrests.* *n.*

**blotting paper** a soft paper used to dry writing by soaking up excess ink.

**blouse** (blouz) **1** a loose or partly fitted, light garment for the upper part of the body, worn by women and girls. **2** any loosely fitting garment for the upper part of the body: *Sailors wear blouses.* **3** the upper part of a battle dress. **4** a kind of smock reaching to the knees, worn by European peasants and workers to protect their clothes. *n.* —**blouse′like′,** *adj.*

**blow¹** (blō) **1** a hard hit; knock; stroke: *a blow with the fist, a hammer, etc.* **2** a sudden happening that causes misfortune or loss; severe shock: *His mother's death was a great blow to him.* **3** a sudden attack or assault: *The army struck a swift blow at the enemy.* *n.*
**come to blows,** start fighting.

**blow²** (blō) **1** send forth a strong current of air: *Blow on the fire or it will go out.* **2** move in a current, especially rapidly or with power: *The wind was blowing from the east.* **3** drive or carry by a current of air: *The wind blew the curtain.* **4** force a current of air into, through, or against: *She blew the embers into flame.* **5** clear or empty by forcing air through: *We blew the eggs before colouring them for Easter.* **6** produce or shape by means of blown or injected air: *to blow bubbles, to blow glass.* **7** the act or fact of forcing air into, through, or against something; blast: *One blow cleared the pipe.*

**8** cause a wind instrument to make a sound: *to blow a trumpet*. **9** make a sound by means of a current of air or steam: *The whistle blew at noon*. **10** break by an explosion; blow up, open, etc.: *The thieves blew the safe*. **11** be out of breath: *The horse was blowing at the end of the race*. **12** make out of breath; cause to pant. **13** make by blasting: *They blew a tunnel through the mountain*. **14** of whales, spout water and air: *"There she blows!"* **15** of insects, lay eggs in: *Some flies blow fruit*. **16** *Informal.* spend recklessly: *She blew her whole allowance in the bookstore*. **17** melt: *A short circuit will blow a fuse*. **18** *Informal.* handle badly; bungle: *The last chance he had to make good, he blew it*. **19** *Informal.* leave; get out of: *He blew town*. **20** blowing: *a blow of the whistle*. **21** a gale of wind: *Last night's big blow brought down several trees*. 1–6, 8–19 *v.*, **blew, blown, blowing;** 7, 20, 21 *n.*
**blow hot and cold,** change from a favourable opinion to an unfavourable one.
**blow in,** appear unexpectedly; drop in.
**blow off,** get rid of noisily.
**blow out, a** extinguish the flame of by blowing: *to blow out a match*. **b** stop blowing: *This wind will soon blow itself out*. **c** burst: *The tire blew out. Windows were blown out by the explosion*.
**blow over, a** pass by or over: *The storm has blown over.* **b** be forgotten.
**blow up, a** explode. **b** fill with air. **c** *Informal.* become very angry. **d** *Informal.* scold; abuse. **e** arise; begin: *A storm suddenly blew up.* **f** enlarge a photograph.

**blow³** (blō) **1** burst into flower; BLOOM (now used mostly as a past participle): *a full-blown rose*. **2** the state of blooming: *The garden was in full blow*. 1 *v.*, **blew, blown, blow·ing;** 2 *n.*

**blow–dry** (blō′drī′) dry and style the hair using a BLOW DRYER: *I don't have to set my hair; I just wash it and blow-dry it.* *v.*, **blow-dried, blow-dry·ing.**

**blow dryer** a hand-held electrical apparatus for drying the hair by means of a strong current of hot air. It has a nozzle for directing the air to a particular part of the hair so that the hair can be styled as it is being dried.

**blow·er** (blō′ər) **1** a person or thing that blows: *a glass blower*. **2** a fan or other machine for forcing air into a building, furnace, mine, etc. **3** WHALE. *n.*

**blow·fly** (blō′flī′) any of several species of large fly, including bluebottles, having metallic blue, green, or bronze bodies and making a loud buzzing sound in flight: *Blowflies are similar to the common housefly, except that they breed mainly in dead flesh, and their larvae will sometimes infest open wounds, causing serious disease*. *n., pl.,* **blow·flies.**

**blow·gun** (blō′gun′) **1** a tube through which a person blows arrows or darts. **2** PEASHOOTER. *n.*

**blow·hole** (blō′hōl′) **1** a hole where air or gas can escape. **2** a hole for breathing, in the top of the head of whales and some other animals. **3** a hole in the ice where whales, seals, etc. come to breathe. **4** a defect or flaw. *n.*

**blown** (blōn) **1** out of breath; exhausted: *He was blown after climbing the steep hill.* **2** tainted by flies; flyblown; tainted. **3** shaped by blowing: *blown glass*. **4** pp. of BLOW² and BLOW³: *The wind has blown itself out*. 1–3 *adj.,* 4 *v.*

**blow·out** (blō′out′) **1** the bursting of a container or casing, such as an automobile tire, by the pressure of the enclosed air, etc. on a weak spot. **2** the sudden, uncontrolled eruption of an oil or gas well. **3** the melting of an electric fuse caused by an overload in a circuit or line. **4** *Informal.* a big party or meal. *n.*

**blow·pipe** (blō′pīp′) **1** a tube for blowing air or gas into a flame to increase the heat. **2** BLOWGUN. *n.*

**blow·torch** (blō′tôrch′) a small torch that shoots out a hot flame: *A blowtorch is used to melt metal and burn off paint.* *n.*

**blow·up** (blō′up′) **1** explosion. **2** *Informal.* an outburst of anger. **3** an enlargement of a photograph. *n.*

**blow·y** (blō′ē) windy. *adj.* **blow·i·er, blow·i·est.**

**blowz·y** (blou′zē) **1** untidy; frowzy. **2** red-faced and coarse-looking. *adj.,* **blowz·i·er, blowz·i·est.**

**blub·ber** (blub′ər) **1** the fat of whales and some other sea animals: *The oil obtained from whale blubber was formerly burned in lamps.* **2** noisy weeping. **3** weep noisily. **4** utter while crying and sobbing: *The child blubbered an apology.* **5** disfigure or swell with crying: *a face all blubbered.* 1, 2 *n.,* 3–5 *v.*

**bludg·eon** (bluj′ən) **1** a short, heavy club, used as a weapon. **2** strike with a club. **3** bully; threaten. 1 *n.,* 2, 3 *v.* —**bludg′eon·er,** *n.*

**blue** (blü) **1** the colour of the clear sky in daylight or the colour of the part of the spectrum between green and indigo. **2** of or having this colour or a tone of this colour. **3** blue dye or pigment. **4** of the skin, livid; ashen: *blue with cold*. **5** having or showing low spirits; sad, gloomy, or discouraged: *a blue mood. I was feeling very blue.* **6** make blue. **7** use BLUING on. **8 the blue, a** the sky: *high up in the blue.* **b** the sea. **9 blues,** *pl.* **a** *Informal.* low spirits: *He's got the blues.* **b** in music, a style of jazz characterized by a tendency to flatten certain notes by a semitone, producing minor sequences and harmonies that give the music a melancholy sound: *The blues developed from black work songs and spirituals.* 1, 3, 8, 9 *n.,* 2, 4, 5 *adj.,* **blu·er, blu·est;** 6, 7 *v.,* **blued, blu·ing** or **blue·ing.** —**blue′ness,** *n.*
**once in a blue moon,** hardly ever; rarely: *Once in a blue moon we get a letter from him.*
**out of the blue,** completely unexpected; from an unknown source or for an unknown reason: *Suddenly, out of the blue, she announced that she was quitting.*
☞ *Hom.* BLEW.

**blue·bell** (blü′bel′) any of various plants having blue flowers shaped like bells, such as the bluebell of Scotland and the wild hyacinth. *n.*

**blue·ber·ry** (blü′ber′ē) **1** a small, sweet, edible blue berry. **2** the shrub that this berry grows on. *n., pl.* **blue·ber·ries.**

**blue·bird** (blü′bird′) any of three closely related species of North American songbird belonging to the thrush family, all about 18 cm long with the tail, the males of all species having mainly bright blue feathers. *n.*

**blue–black** (blü′blak′) bluish black; very dark blue. *n., adj.*

**blue blood 1** aristocratic descent. **2** ARISTOCRAT.

**blue–blood·ed** (blü′blud′id) ARISTOCRATIC. *adj.*

**blue·bon·net** (blü′bon′it) **1** a round, brimless cap made of blue woollen cloth, formerly worn in Scotland. **2** a person wearing such a cap. **3** a Scot. *n.*

**blue·bot·tle** (blü′bot′əl) **1** any of several species of BLOWFLY having a bright, metallic-blue body. **2** any similar fly. **3** CORNFLOWER. *n.*

**blue–col·lar** (blü′kol′ər) of or having to do with industrial or manual workers as a group, or their jobs, attitudes, etc.: *He said he would prefer any blue-collar job to working in an office.* *adj.*
☛ *Etym.* **Blue-collar** refers to a common colour for work shirts and suggests the wearing of coarse or casual clothing for work. The term was coined as a contrast to WHITE-COLLAR.

**blue·fish** (blü′fish′) a species of large blue-and-silver game and food fish of tropical and temperate parts of the Atlantic and Indian oceans, distantly related to the sea basses: *Bluefish move in schools and feed on small fish.* *n., pl.* **blue·fish** or **blue·fish·es.**

**blue flag** an IRIS that has blue flowers.

**blue·grass** (blü′gras′) any of several closely related North American grasses having bluish-green stems, especially **Kentucky bluegrass.** *n.*

**blue·ing** (blü′ing) See BLUING. *n.*

**blue·jack·et** (blü′jak′it) a sailor in the navy. *n.*

Bluejays—about 30 cm long including the tail

**blue·jay** (blü′jā′) a species of jay found in southern Canada and the United States, having a crest on the head, a very long tail, and a blue upper body and head, with a broad black band around the neck: *The bluejay utters a harsh cry.* *n.*

**bluejeans** or **blue jeans** (blü′jēnz′) pants usually made of blue denim, having hip pockets and seams sometimes sewn in thread of a contrasting colour. *n. pl.*

**blue laws** any very strict and puritanical laws.

**blue·line** (blü′līn′) either of the two blue lines drawn midway between the centre of a hockey rink and each goal. *n.*

**Blue·nose** (blü′nōz′) **1** a nickname for a Nova Scotian or, less often, a New Brunswicker: *Many Bluenoses are descended from Loyalists.* **2** of or associated with Nova Scotia. **3** a ship built in Nova Scotia and manned by Nova Scotians. **4** a famous schooner built in Nova Scotia and launched in 1921. The Bluenose was never defeated as the holder of the International Fisherman's Trophy, given to the fastest sailing vessel in the North Atlantic fishing fleets. She was wrecked and lost off Haiti in 1946. The name is generally supposed to come from a nickname given to Nova Scotians. *n.*

**blue–pen·cil** (blü′pen′səl) change or cross out, especially by using a pencil with a blue lead, such as editors usually use. *v.,* **blue-pen·cilled** or **blue-pen·ciled, blue-pen·cil·ling** or **blue-pen·cil·ing.**

**blue·print** (blü′print′) **1** an exact photographic copy of an original drawing of a building plan, map, etc., usually showing white lines on a blue background. **2** a detailed plan for any enterprise. **3** make a blueprint of. **4** make or explain a plan in detail. 1, 2 *n.*, 3, 4 *v.*

**blue ribbon** the first prize; highest honour.

**blue spruce** a spruce tree having bluish-green needles, native to the western United States but commonly used as an ornamental tree throughout North America.

**blue·stock·ing** (blü′stok′ing) *Informal.* a woman who displays great interest in intellectual or literary subjects. *n.*

**blu·et** (blü′it) a small plant of North America having pale bluish flowers. *n.*

**bluff**¹ (bluf) **1** a high, steep bank or cliff. **2** of a cliff, the bow of a ship, etc., rising steeply with a straight, broad front. **3** *Cdn.* a clump of trees standing on the flat prairie; copse: *The farmhouse was screened from the wind and the sun by a poplar bluff.* **4** frank and rough in a good-natured way: *He had a bluff, hearty way about him.* 1, 3 *n.*, 2, 4 *adj.* —**bluff′ly,** *adv.* —**bluff′ness,** *n.*

**bluff**² (bluf) **1** a show of pretended confidence, used to deceive or mislead. **2** deceive by a show of pretended confidence. **3** a threat that cannot be carried out. **4** frighten with a threat that cannot be carried out. **5** a person who bluffs. 1, 3, 5 *n.*, 2, 4 *v.* —**bluff′er,** *n.*
**call someone's bluff,** challenge or expose a bluff: *She backed down when I called her bluff.*
**bluff one's way,** get something one wants by bluffing: *She bluffed her way through this test but she'll never make the final exam.*

**blu·ing** or **blue·ing** (blü′ing) **1** a blue liquid or powder put in water when rinsing white fabrics in order to prevent them from turning yellow. **2** ppr. of BLUE. 1 *n.*, 2 *v.*

**blu·ish** (blü′ish) somewhat blue. *adj.*

**blun·der** (blun′dər) **1** a stupid mistake. **2** make a stupid mistake. **3** do clumsily or wrongly; bungle. **4** move clumsily or blindly; stumble. **5** blurt out; say clumsily or foolishly. 1 *n.*, 2–5 *v.* —**blun′der·er,** *n.*
**blunder on,** discover by chance.

A blunderbuss

**blun·der·buss** (blun′dər bus′) **1** a short gun with a wide muzzle, formerly used to fire a quantity of shot a short distance. **2** a person who blunders. *n.*

**blunt** (blunt) **1** without a sharp edge or point; dull. **2** plainspoken; outspoken; frank: *He thinks that blunt speech proves he is honest.* **3** make less sharp: *You will blunt the scissors if you use them to cut paper.* **4** make less keen: *All the delays have blunted their enthusiasm.* **5** become less sharp. **6** become less keen. **7** slow in perceiving or understanding. 1, 2, 7 *adj.*, 3–6 *v.* —**blunt′ly,** *adv.* —**blunt′ness,** *n.*

**blur** (blėr) **1** make confused in form or outline: *Mist blurred the hills.* **2** make dim: *Tears blurred my eyes.* **3** become dim or indistinct: *Her eyes blurred with tears.* **4** a blurred condition; dimness. **5** something seen dimly or indistinctly: *The countryside was a blur through the rain on the windows.* **6** blot; stain. **7** a blot or stain. **8** smear: *Drops of water had blurred the writing.* 1–3, 6, 8 *v.*, **blurred, blur·ring;** 4, 5, 7 *n.*

**blurb** (blėrb) *Informal.* an advertisement or announcement especially of a book, full of extremely high praise. *n.*

**blur·ry** (blėr′ē) **1** dim; indistinct. **2** smeary; full of blots and stains. *adj.*

**blurt** (blėrt) say suddenly or without thinking (often used with **out**): *In his anger he blurted out the secret.* *v.*

**blush** (blush) **1** a reddening of the skin caused by shame, confusion, or excitement. **2** become red because of shame, confusion, or excitement: *She was so shy that she blushed every time she was spoken to.* **3** be ashamed: *He blushed at his brother's bad table manners.* **4** a rosy colour: *The blush of dawn showed in the east.* **5** be or become rosy. 1, 4 *n.*, 2, 3, 5 *v.*
**at first blush,** at first glance or thought.
**blush for,** be ashamed of.

**blus·ter** (blus′tər) **1** storm or blow noisily and violently: *The wind blustered around the house.* **2** stormy noise and violence. **3** talk noisily and boastfully: *He blusters a lot but he's really a coward.* **4** do or say noisily and violently: *He blustered an oath and slammed the door.* **5** noisy and boastful or threatening talk: *I don't like her bluster.* **6** make or get by blustering. 1, 3, 4, 6 *v.*, 2, 5 *n.* —**blus′ter·er,** *n.*

**blus·ter·y** (blus′tə rē) BLUSTERing. *adj.*

**blvd.** boulevard.

**BNA Act** or **B.N.A. Act** British North America Act.

**bo·a** (bō′ə) **1** any of about 35 species of non-poisonous tropical snakes that give birth to live young, unlike most snakes, and that kill their prey by coiling around it and squeezing until it suffocates: *Boas range in length from about 45 cm to 9 m. One of the smallest boas, called the rubber boa, is found in the valleys in the extreme south of British Columbia.* **2** a long scarf made of fur or feathers, worn around a woman's neck. *n., pl.* **bo·as.**

**boa constrictor 1** a large tropical American BOA, having tan skin with brown markings and averaging about 340 cm in length. **2** any large snake that kills its prey by squeezing it until it suffocates.

**boar** (bôr) **1** the male of the domestic pig. **2** any of several species of wild pig of Europe, northern Africa, and Asia, hunted as a game animal: *Wild boars used to be hunted in the British Isles but have long been extinct there.* *n.*
☛ *Hom.* BOER (bôr), BORE.

**board** (bôrd) **1** a long, flat piece of sawed lumber for use in building, etc. **2** cover with boards: *We board up the windows of our summer cottage in the fall.* **3** a flat piece of wood or other material used for some special purpose: *an ironing board.* **4** pasteboard: *a book with covers of board.* **5** a table to serve food on; table. **6** the food served on a table. **7** meals provided for pay: *Ms. Swinton gives good board.* **8** provide with regular meals, or room and meals, for pay. **9** get meals, or room and meals, for pay: *Mr. Armani boards at our house.* **10** a group of persons managing something; council: *a board of health.* **11** a branch or agency of a government department: *the National Film Board.* **12** get on a ship, train, etc. **13** come alongside or against a ship. **14** *Cdn.* in hockey, body check an opposing player into the boards. **15 the boards, a** the stage of a theatre. **b** *Cdn.* the wooden guard fence surrounding the ice of a hockey rink. 1, 3–7, 10, 11, 15 *n.*, 2, 8, 9, 12–14 *v.*
**across the board,** affecting everybody or everything of a group equally: *Prices have increased across the board again.*
**go by the board,** be given up, neglected, or ignored.
**on board,** on a ship, train, etc.

**board·er** (bôr′dər) **1** a person who pays for regular meals, or for room and meals, at another's house. **2** a person assigned to go on board an enemy ship. *n.*
☛ *Hom.* BORDER.

**board foot** a unit of measure equal to a board one foot square and one inch thick (about 30 cm$^2$ × 2.54 cm), used for measuring logs and lumber; 144 cubic inches (about 2250 cm$^3$).

**board·ing** (bôr′ding) **1** *Cdn.* in hockey, the act of checking an opposing player into the boards of the rink in a rough and illegal manner. **2** wood cut into boards: *We have to order the boarding for our new fence.* **3** a structure made of boards. **4** ppr. of BOARD. 1–3 *n.*, 4 *v.*

**boarding house** a house where regular meals, or room and meals, are provided for pay.

**boarding school** a school that provides lodging and food during the school term for some or all of its students.

**board measure** a system for measuring logs and lumber: *The unit of board measure is the* BOARD FOOT.

**board of education** a name sometimes given to a group of people, usually elected, who manage the schools in a certain area.

**board of health** the department of a local government in charge of public health.

**board·room** (bôr′drüm′) a room that is regularly used to hold meetings of a board of directors, etc. *n.*

**board·sail·ing** (bôrd′sā′ling) a water sport in which one rides a sailboard; windsurfing. *n.*

**board·walk** (bôr′dwok′) a sidewalk or promenade made of boards. *n.*

**boar·hound** (bôr′hound′) any of several breeds of large dog, especially the Great Dane, formerly used in hunting wild boars. *n.*

**boast** (bōst) **1** praise oneself; speak too highly of oneself or one's possessions, etc.; brag: *She is always boasting of her new sports car.* **2** brag about: *He boasts his skill at soccer. She boasted that she was the best player on the team.* **3** a praising of oneself; bragging. **4** something to be proud of. **5** have and be proud of: *Our town boasts many fine parks.* 1, 2, 5 *v.*, 3, 4 *n.*
—**boast′er,** *n.*

**boast·ful** (bōst′fəl) **1** boasting; speaking too highly about oneself: *It is easy to dislike a boastful person.* **2** fond of boasting. *adj.* —**boast′ful·ly,** *adv.*
—**boast′ful·ness,** *n.*

**boat** (bōt) **1** a small, open vessel for travelling on water, such as a motorboat or a rowboat. **2** ship. **3** a boat-shaped dish for gravy, sauce, etc. **4** use a boat; go in a boat. **5** put or carry in a boat. 1–3 *n.*, 4, 5 *v.*
**in the same boat,** in the same position or condition;

taking the same chances: *We're all in the same boat, so stop complaining.*

**miss the boat,** *Informal.* miss an opportunity; lose one's chances.

**boat hook** a metal hook on a pole, used for pulling or pushing a boat, raft, etc.

**boat·house** (bōt′hous′) a house or shed for sheltering a boat or boats. *n.*

**boat·ing** (bō′ting) 1 rowing; sailing. 2 ppr. of BOAT. 1 *n.*, 2 *v.*

**boat·load** (bōt′lōd′) 1 as much or as many as a boat can hold or carry. 2 the load that a boat is carrying. *n.*

**boat·man** (bōt′mən) 1 a person who rents out boats or takes care of them. 2 a person whose work is rowing or sailing small boats or who is skilled in their use. *n.*, *pl.* **boat·men** (-mən).

**boat song** *Cdn.* a song used by the VOYAGEURS to help them maintain a steady rhythm with their paddles.

**boat·swain** (bō′sən; *less often,* bōt′swān′) a ship's officer in charge of the anchors, ropes, rigging, etc.: *The boatswain directs some of the work of the crew.* *n.* Also, **bo's'n, bosun.**

**bob¹** (bob) 1 move up and down, or to and fro, with short, quick motions: *The bird bobbed its head up and down, and its tail bobbed too.* 2 a short, quick motion up and down, or to and fro. 1 *v.*, **bobbed, bob·bing;** 2 *n.*

**bob up,** *Informal.* appear suddenly or unexpectedly.

**bob²** (bob) 1 a short haircut. 2 cut the hair short. 3 a horse's docked tail. 4 a weight on the end of a pendulum or plumb line. 5 a float for a fishing line. 6 fish with a bob. 7 BOBSLED. 1, 3–5, 7 *n.*, 2, 6 *v.*, **bobbed, bob·bing.**

**bob³** (bob) 1 a light rap or tap. 2 rap lightly; tap. 1 *n.*, 2 *v.*, **bobbed, bob·bing.**

**bob·bin** (bob′ən) a reel or spool for holding thread, yarn, etc.: *Bobbins are used in spinning, weaving, machine sewing, and lace-making. Wire is wound on bobbins.* See SHUTTLE for picture. *n.*

**bobby pin** a flat wire clip for the hair, having prongs that press close together.

**bob·by·socks** (bob′ē soks′) *Informal.* ankle-length socks, worn by young girls. *n. pl.*

**bob·by·sox·er** (bob′ē sok′sər) *Informal.* an adolescent girl of the 1940s who followed prevailing fads and fashions. *n.*

**bob·cat** (bob′kat′) a species of lynx found mostly in the United States, closely related to the Canada lynx but generally smaller and having much smaller ear tufts or none at all, and smaller paws: *The bobcat has silky brownish fur with dark spots.* *n.*

**bob·o·link** (bob′ə lingk′) a species of North American songbird of the same family as the meadowlarks and blackbirds, found in fields and meadows, having stiff, pointed tail feathers, the male being mostly black with a white or pale-grey back. *n.*

☛ *Etym.* The name imitates its call.

hat, āge, fär; let, ēqual, tėrm; it, īce
hot, ōpen, ôrder; oil, out; cup, pùt, rüle
əbove, takən, pencəl, lemən, circəs
ch, child; ng, long; sh, ship
th, thin; ŦH, then; zh, measure

Bobskates

**bob·skate** (bob′skāt′) a child's skate that consists of two sections of double runners and is adjustable to the size of the wearer's foot. *n.*

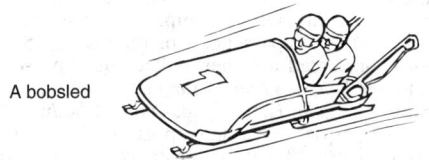

A bobsled

**bob·sled** (bob′sled′) 1 a long sled with two sets of runners, a continuous seat, a steering wheel, and brakes. 2 ride or coast on a bobsled. 1 *n.*, 2 *v.*, **bob·sled·ded, bob·sled·ding.**

**bob·sleigh** (bob′slā′) BOBSLED. *n.*, *v.*, **bob·sleighed, bob·sleigh·ing.**

**bob·stay** (bob′stā′) a rope or chain to hold a bowsprit down. See BOWSPRIT for picture. *n.*

**bob·tail** (bob′tāl′) 1 a short tail; tail cut short. 2 a horse or dog having a bobtail. 3 having a bobtail. *n.*

**bob·white** (bob′wīt′ *or* bob′hwīt′) a species of quail found in southern Ontario and the eastern United States, a small, plump game bird having a reddish-brown back and striped sides. *n.*

☛ *Etym.* The name imitates its call.

**bock** (bok) BOCK BEER. *n.*

**bock beer** a strong, sweet, dark beer brewed in the winter and stored until the spring.

**bode¹** (bōd) be a sign of; indicate beforehand: *Dark clouds boded rain.* *v.*, **bod·ed, bod·ing.**

**bode ill,** be a bad sign.
**bode well,** be a good sign.

**bode²** (bōd) a pt. of BIDE. *v.*

**bod·hi** (bō′dē) in Buddhism: 1 the state of enlightenment attained by one who has achieved salvation. 2 the awakening into NIRVANA. *n.*

**Bod·hi·satt·va** (bō′dē sut′və) in Buddhism, one who has attained enlightenment yet remains in the world to save others. *n.*

**bod·ice** (bod′is) 1 the part of a dress from the shoulders to the waist. 2 an outer garment for women and girls, worn over a blouse and laced up the front: *The bodice is part of the traditional dress of peasant women in some European countries.* *n.*

**–bodied** *combining form.* having a body of a certain kind: *Big-bodied* means having an big body.

**bod·i·less** (bod′ē lis) **1** without a body; lacking the trunk. **2** having no material form: *bodiless spirits.* *adj.*

**bod·i·ly** (bod′ə lē) **1** of or in the body: *bodily pain, assault causing bodily harm.* **2** in person: *The man whom we thought dead walked bodily into the room.* **3** all together; as one unit; entirely: *The audience rose bodily.* 1 *adj.*, 2, 3 *adv.*

**bod·kin** (bod′kin) **1** a large, blunt needle with a large eye, used for pulling tape or ribbon through a casing, etc. **2** a long ornamental hairpin. **3** a small, pointed tool for making holes in fabric or leather. *n.*

**bod·y** (bod′ē) **1** the whole material part of a human being, animal, or plant: *This girl has a strong, healthy body.* **2** the main part, or trunk, of a human being or animal, excluding the head and limbs. **3** the main part of anything, such as the hull of a ship. **4** the part of a vehicle that holds the passengers or the load. **5** a group of persons considered together; collection of persons or things: *A large body of children sang at the concert.* **6** *Informal.* person: *He is a good-natured body.* **7** a dead person; corpse. **8** a mass; portion of matter: *A lake is a body of water.* **9** matter; substance: *Thick soup has more body than thin soup.* **10** provide with a body; give substance to; embody. 1–9 *n.*, *pl.* **bod·ies**; 10 *v.*, **bod·ied, bod·y·ing.**
☞ *Hom.* BAWDY.

**bod·y·check** (bod′ē chek′) *Cdn.* in hockey, lacrosse, etc.: **1** a defensive play by which a player hinders an opponent's progress by body contact. **2** employ a bodycheck. 1 *n.*, 2 *v.* Also (def. 1) **body check.**

**bod·y·guard** (bod′ē gärd′) **1** a person or persons who guard someone. **2** a retinue or escort. *n.*

**body shirt** or **bod·y·shirt** (bod′ē shėrt′) a shirt or blouse for women or girls that ends in a kind of brief pantie with a fastening at the crotch. *n.*

**body stocking** a lightweight, close-fitting, stretchable garment consisting of a top, briefs, and, often, stockings, in one piece: *Body stockings may be worn for exercising, by dancers, or, when made of elastic fabric, as a light support for the body.*

**Boer** (bür *or* bôr) a Dutch colonist or a person of Dutch descent living in South Africa. *n.*
☞ *Hom.* BOOR (for the first pronunciation of **Boer**); BOAR and BORE (for the second pronunciation).

**bog** (bog) **1** soft, wet, spongy ground; a marsh or swamp. **2** sink or get stuck in a bog. 1 *n.*, 2 *v.*, **bogged, bog·ging.**
**bog down,** get stuck, as if in mud.

**bo·gey**[1] (bō′gē) in golf, one stroke over PAR (def. 7): *He shot a bogey on the seventh hole.* *n.* Compare with BIRDIE (def. 2).

**bo·gey**[2] or **bo·gy** (bō′gē) **1** an evil spirit; goblin. **2** a person or thing that causes annoyance or fear; BUGABOO: *His bogey was mathematics.* *n.*, *pl.* **bo·geys** or **bo·gies.** Also, **bogie.**

**bog·gle** (bog′əl) **1** be or become overwhelmed, as by the unexpectedness, difficulty, etc. of something: *His mind boggled at the thought of so much responsibility.* **2** hesitate or shy away. **3** bungle; botch. **4** the act or an instance of boggling. 1–3 *v.*, **bog·gled, bog·gling;** 4 *n.*

**bog·gy** (bog′ē) soft and wet like a bog; marshy; swampy. *adj.*, **bog·gi·er, bog·gi·est.**

**bo·gie** (bō′gē) See BOGEY[2]. *n.*

**bo·gus** (bō′gəs) not genuine; counterfeit; sham: *a bogus twenty-dollar bill.* *adj.*

**bo·gy** (bō′gē) See BOGEY[2]. *n.*, *pl.* **bo·gies.**

**Bo·he·mi·a** (bō hē′mē ə) **1** a former country in central Europe, now a region of Slovakia. **2** a free and easy, unconventional sort of life; a place where artists, writers, etc. live such a life. *n.*

**Bo·he·mi·an** (bō hē′mē ən) **1** of Bohemia, its people, or their language. **2** a native or inhabitant of Bohemia. **3** the language of Bohemia; Czech. **4** free and easy; unconventional. **5** an artist, writer, etc. who lives in a free and easy, unconventional way. **6** Gypsy. 1, 4 *adj.*, 2, 3, 5, 6 *n.*

**Bo·he·mi·an·ism** (bō hē′mē ə niz′əm) a free and easy way of living; unconventional habits. *n.*

**bohemian waxwing** a brownish-grey WAXWING found throughout northern Eurasia and NW North America.

**boil**[1] (boil) **1** of liquids, bubble up and give off steam or vapour: *Water boils when heated to about 100°C.* **2** cause to boil. **3** cook by boiling: *to boil eggs.* **4** of a container, have its contents boil: *The kettle is boiling.* **5** clean or sterilize by boiling. **6** be very excited; be stirred up, especially by anger: *She is still boiling over the incident.* **7** move violently. **8** boiling. **9** a boiling condition. 1–7 *v.*, 8, 9 *n.*
**boil down, a** reduce the bulk of by boiling: *to boil a sauce down.* **b** reduce by getting rid of unimportant parts: *He boiled down his notes to a list of important facts.*
**boil over, a** come to the boiling point and overflow. **b** show excitement or anger.

**boil**[2] (boil) a hard, round abscess in the skin and the tissues just beneath it, consisting of pus around a hard core: *Most boils are caused by bacteria entering an oil or sweat gland, a hair follicle, or a small wound.* *n.*
**blind boil,** a boil that has no visible pus sac.

**boil·er** (boi′lər) **1** a container for heating liquids. **2** a tank for making steam to heat buildings or drive engines. **3** a tank for holding hot water. *n.*

**boiling point** the temperature at which a liquid boils: *The boiling point of water at sea level is 100 degrees Celsius.*

**bois·ter·ous** (boi′stə rəs *or* boi′strəs) **1** noisily cheerful: *a boisterous game.* **2** violent; rough: *a boisterous wind, a boisterous child.* *adj.*
—**bois′ter·ous·ly,** *adv.* —**bois′ter·ous·ness,** *n.*

**bo·la** (bō′lə) a weapon consisting of stone or metal balls tied to cords: *South American cowboys throw a bola so that it winds around the animal at which it is aimed.* *n.*

**bold** (bōld) **1** without fear; daring: *a bold knight, a bold explorer.* **2** showing or requiring courage: *a bold act.* **3** too free in manner; impudent: *The bold little girl made faces at us.* **4** striking; vigorous; free; clear: *The mountains stood in bold outline against the sky. With a few bold strokes, she sketched in the basic design of the painting.* **5** steep or abrupt: *Bold cliffs overlooked the sea.* *adj.*
—**bold′ly,** *adv.* —**bold′ness,** *n.*
**make bold,** take the liberty; dare.

**bold·face** (bōld′fās′) in printing, a heavy type that stands out clearly: **This sentence is in boldface.** *n.*

**bole** (bōl) the trunk of a tree. *n.*
☛ *Hom.* BOLL, BOWL.

**bo·le·ro** (bə ler′ō) **1** a Spanish dance in 3/4 time.
**2** the music for it. **3** a short, loose jacket worn open at the front. *n., pl.* **bo·le·ros**.

**Bo·liv·i·an** (bə liv′ē ən) **1** a native or inhabitant of Bolivia, a country in central South America. **2** of or having to do with Bolivia or its people. **1** *n.*, **2** *adj.*

**boll** (bōl) a rounded seed pod or capsule of a plant, especially that of cotton or flax. See COTTON for picture. *n.*
☛ *Hom.* BOLE, BOWL.

**boll weevil** a small brown or black beetle about 6 mm long, including a long snout about half the length of the body, found in Central America, Mexico, and the southern United States: *Both the larva and adult of the boll weevil feed on the buds and bolls of cotton plants, causing great damage to cotton crops.*

**boll·worm** (bōl′wėrm′) any of several species of moth whose larva feeds on cotton BOLLS and on corn and other crop plants. *n.*

**bo·lo·gna** (bə lō′nē *or* bə lō′nə) a large sausage made of beef, veal, and pork. *n.*

**bolo tie** a tie made of thin cord, kept together with an ornament.

**Bol·she·vik** *or* **bol·she·vik** (bōl′shə vik′ *or* bōl′shə vik′) **1** in Russia, a member of a radical political party that seized power in November, 1917: *The Bolsheviks formed the Communist party in 1918.* **2** of the Bolsheviks or BOLSHEVISM. **3** an extreme radical. **4** extremely radical. **1, 3** *n., pl.* **Bol·she·viks** *or* **bol·she·viks,** **Bol·she·vi·ki** *or* **bol·she·vi·ki** (bōl′shə vē′kē); **2, 4** *adj.*

**Bol·she·vism** *or* **bol·she·vism** (bōl′shə viz′əm *or* bōl′shə viz′əm) **1** the doctrines and methods oı the BOLSHEVIKS (def. 1). **2** extreme radicalism. *n.*

**Bol·she·vist** (bōl′shə vist′ *or* bōl′shə vist′) BOLSHEVIK (def. 1). *n., adj.*

**bol·ster** (bōl′stər) **1** a long pillow for a bed. **2** a pad or cushion. **3** support; keep from falling; prop: *We bolstered the baby up with pillows. His friends have to bolster him, for he gets discouraged easily.* **1, 2** *n.*, **3** *v.*

A bolt with a nut screwed on

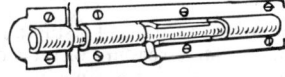
A door bolt

**bolt**[1] (bōlt) **1** a rod made to hold parts together, having a head at one end and a thread on the other: *A bolt is placed through holes that have been drilled for it, and is held in place by a nut screwed onto the threaded end.* **2** a sliding fastener for a door, gate, etc. **3** fasten with a bolt. **4** the part of a lock moved by a key. **5** a short arrow with a thick head: *Bolts were shot from crossbows.* **6** a discharge of lightning: *It came like a bolt from the sky.* **7** a sudden start; running away. **8** dash away; run away: *The horse bolted.* **9** a roll of cloth or wallpaper. **10** swallow food without chewing: *The dog bolted its food.* **1, 2, 4–7, 9** *n.*, **3, 8, 10** *v.*

**bolt upright,** stiff and straight: *Awakened by a noise, he sat bolt upright in bed.*

**bolt**[2] (bōlt) sift through a cloth or sieve: *Flour is bolted to remove the bran.* *v.*

**bolt·er** (bōl′tər) a horse that runs away. *n.*

---

hat, āge, fär; let, ēqual, tėrm; it, īce
hot, ōpen, ôrder; oil, out; cup, put, rüle
əbove, takən, pencəl, lemən, circəs

ch, child; ng, long; sh, ship
th, thin; ᴛʜ, then; zh, measure

**bomb** (bom) **1** a container filled with an explosive charge or a chemical substance, that is exploded by a timing mechanism or by contact when something hits or touches it: *Large bombs are sometimes dropped from aircraft.* **2** a container filled with liquid under pressure, such as paint, insect poison, etc.: *Mother used a bomb to rid the house of moths.* **3** attack, damage, or destroy with a bomb or bombs, especially by dropping bombs from aircraft. **4** a sudden, unexpected happening.
**5** *Informal.* fail completely and miserably: *All the jokes he made in his speech bombed because he was so nervous.*
**6** *Informal.* a miserable failure. **7 the bomb,** nuclear weapons: *Many nations already have the bomb.* **1, 2, 4, 6, 7** *n.*, **3, 5** *v.*
☛ *Hom.* BALM.
☛ *Etym.* In the 17c. from F *bombe,* through Italian and L from Gk. *bombos* 'booming, humming'. Related English words such as BOMBARD and BOMBARDIER have the same origin, but came into English through separate F words.

**bom·bard** (bom bärd′) **1** attack with BOMBS or heavy fire of shot and shell from big guns: *The artillery bombarded the enemy all day.* **2** drop BOMBS on.
**3** keep attacking vigorously: *The lawyer bombarded the witness with one question after another.* **4** in physics, subject atomic nuclei to a stream of fast-moving particles, thus changing the structure of the nuclei. *v.*
☛ *Etym.* See note at BOMB.

**bom·bar·dier** (bom′bə dēr′ *or* bom′ə dēr′) **1** a corporal in the artillery. **2** the person in a bomber who aims and releases the BOMBS. *n.*
☛ *Etym.* See note at BOMB.

A Bombardier

**Bom·bar·dier** (bom′bə dēr′) *Cdn.* a large covered vehicle used for travelling over snow and ice, usually equipped with tracked wheels at the rear and a set of skis at the front. *n.*
☛ *Etym.* Named after Armand *Bombardier* (1908–1964), who invented and manufactured the machine.

**bom·bard·ment** (bom bärd′mənt) **1** an attack with BOMBS or with heavy fire of shot and shell. **2** in physics, the subjection of atomic nuclei to a stream of fast-moving particles. *n.*

**bom·bast** (bom′bast) fine-sounding language that is unsuitable for what is said or written. *n.*

**bom·bas·tic** (bom bas′tik) using many fine words with too little thought. *adj.* —**bom·bas′ti·cal·ly,** *adv.*

**bomb·er** (bom′ər) **1** a combat aircraft used to drop bombs on enemy troops, factories, cities, etc. **2** a person who throws or drops bombs. *n.*

**bomb·proof** (bom′prüf′) strong or deep enough to be safe from bombs and shells: *a bombproof shelter.* *adj.*

**bomb·shell** (bom′shel) **1** bomb. **2** *Informal.* a sudden, unexpected happening; disturbing surprise. *n.*

**bomb·sight** (bom′sīt) an instrument used in aiming the bombs dropped from an aircraft. *n.*

**bo·na fi·de** (bō′nə fīd or bō′nə fī′dē) in good faith; genuine; without make-believe or fraud: *a bona fide signature on the document.*

**bo·nan·za** (bə nan′zə) **1** a rich mass of ore in a mine. **2** *Informal.* any rich source of profit. *n.* ☞ *Etym.* From Spanish *bonanza* 'fair weather, prosperity'. The word was originally used in English to mean a body of rich ore, especially in the gold and silver mines of the southwestern United States in the mid 19c.

**bon·bon** (bon′bon) a piece of candy, usually soft and often having a fancy shape. *n.*

**bond** (bond) **1** anything that ties, binds, or unites: *a bond of affection between sisters.* **2** a certificate of debt issued by a government or company that is borrowing money, promising to pay back, by a certain date, the money borrowed plus interest: *If you buy a $100 government bond, you are lending the government $100.* **3** issue bonds on; mortgage. **4** in law, a written agreement by which a person says he or she will pay a certain sum of money if he or she does not perform certain duties properly: *The judge put her under a bond to keep the peace.* **5** take out an insurance policy to pay for any losses caused by an employee: *The company bonds all its cashiers to protect itself in case any of them proves to be dishonest.* **6** any agreement or binding engagement. **7** BOND PAPER. **8** the condition of goods placed in a warehouse until taxes are paid. **9** put goods under bond. **10** a way of arranging bricks, stones, or boards to bind them together. **11** bind or join firmly together. **12** in chemistry, the electrical forces that hold atoms and molecules together. **13 bonds,** *pl.* chains; shackles. 1, 2, 4, 6–8, 10, 12, 13 *n.,* 3, 5, 9, 11 *v.*

**bond·age** (bon′dij) **1** the lack of freedom; slavery. **2** the condition of being used under some power or influence. *n.*

**bond·ed** (bon′did) **1** guaranteed by a BOND (def. 5) or bonds: *The company's drivers are bonded.* **2** put in a warehouse until taxes are paid. **3** pt. and pp. of BOND. 1, 2 *adj.,* 3 *v.*

**bond·hold·er** (bond′hōl′dər) a person who owns bonds issued by a government or company. *n.*

**bond·man** (bond′mən) **1** slave. **2** in the Middle Ages, a SERF. *n., pl.* **bond·men** (-mən).

**bond paper** a good quality of strong paper, made at least partly from rag pulp: *Bond paper was originally used for documents.*

**bond servant** **1** a servant bound to work without pay, sometimes for a specified time only. **2** a slave.

**bonds·man** (bondz′mən) **1** a person who becomes responsible for another by giving a BOND (def. 4). **2** slave. **3** in the Middle Ages, a SERF. *n., pl.* **bonds·men** (-zmən).

**bond·wom·an** (bond′dwum′ən) a female slave. *n., pl.* **bond·wom·en** (-dwim′ən).

**bone** (bōn) **1** one of the parts of the skeleton of an animal with a backbone: *the bones of the hand, a beef bone for soup.* **2** take bones out of: *to bone fish.* **3** the hard substance of which bones are made. **4** anything like bone: *Ivory is sometimes called bone.* **5** stiffen by putting whalebone or steel strips in. 1, 3, 4 *n.,* 2, 5 *v.,* **boned, bon·ing.** —**bone′less,** *adj.*

**bone up on,** *Informal.* study or get information on, especially at the last minute: *You'd better bone up on your facts before you go for the interview.*

**bone china** a particularly white and translucent type of china made by mixing bone ash or calcium phosphate with clay.

**bon·fire** (bon′fīr) a large fire built on the ground outdoors. *n.*

**bon·go** (bong′gō) one of a pair of small connected drums, one slightly larger than the other, that are played with the hands, usually while being held between the knees. *n., pl.* **bon·gos** or **bon·goes.**

**bo·ni·to** (bə nē′tō) any of several species of food and game fish of the mackerel family, steel blue and silvery in colour, with dark, narrow stripes, found mainly in tropical seas: *Bonitos are similar in form to tuna, but smaller.* *n., pl.* **bo·ni·tos** or **bo·ni·toes.**

**bon·net** (bon′it) **1** a head covering usually tied under the chin with strings or ribbons, worn by babies and little girls. **2** a similar head covering formerly worn by girls and women. **3** a round, brimless cap worn by men and boys in Scotland. **4** WAR BONNET. **5** a metal covering or hood over a machine, chimney, etc. **6** put a bonnet on. 1–5 *n.,* 6 *v.*

**bon·nie** or **bon·ny** (bon′ē) **1** pretty; handsome. **2** fine; excellent. **3** healthy-looking. *adj.,* **bon·ni·er, bon·ni·est,** —**bon′ni·ness,** *n.*

**bon·spiel** (bon′spēl) in curling, a tournament among different clubs or among teams of the same club. *n.*

**bo·nus** (bō′nəs) something extra; something given in addition to what is due: *The company gave all its employees a Christmas bonus.* *n.*

**bon vo·yage** (bôN vwä yäzh′) French. goodbye; a farewell for someone going on a trip.

**bon·y** (bō′nē) **1** of bone. **2** like bone. **3** full of bones. **4** having big bones that stick out. **5** thin. *adj.,* **bon·i·er, bon·i·est.** —**bon′i·ness,** *n.*

**boo** (bü) **1** a sound made to show dislike or contempt or to frighten. **2** make such a sound. **3** cry "boo" at. 1 *n., pl.* **boos;** 1 *interj.,* 2, 3 *v.,* **booed, boo·ing.**

**boo·by** (bü′bē) **1** a stupid person; fool; dunce. **2** a kind of large sea bird of the tropics. **3** a person who does the worst in a game or contest. *n., pl.* **boo·bies.**

**booby trap** **1** a trick arranged to annoy some unsuspecting person. **2** a bomb arranged to explode when an object is grasped, pushed, etc. by an unsuspecting person.

**boog·ie–woog·ie** (bug′ē wug′ē) in music, a style of jazz characterized by a repeating rhythmic pattern of eighth notes in the bass, accompanying a melody that is often improvised: *Boogie-woogie is usually played on the piano.* *n.*

**book** (buk) **1** a set of written or printed sheets of paper stitched or glued together along one edge and usually having attached covers at the front and back: *a book of poetry.* **2** a long work, or composition, that is written or printed: *She writes books about camping.* **3** a set of blank sheets bound together along one edge, used for taking notes, drawing, keeping records, etc. **4** a main division of a literary work: *the books of the Bible.* **5** something fastened together like a book: *a book of tickets, a book of* notes, drawing, keeping records, etc. **4** a main division of a literary work: *the books of the Bible*. **5** something fastened together like a book: *a book of tickets, a book of matches*. **6** the words of an opera, operetta, etc.; libretto. **7** something thought of as providing knowledge if it is studied or "read" like a book: *the book of nature, the book of life*. **8** enter in a book or list. **9** *Informal.* record a charge against a person at a police station: *She was booked on a charge of theft*. **10** engage a place, passage, etc.; make a reservation: *to book a room in a hotel, to book theatre tickets*. **11** hire; make engagements for: *The lecturer is booked for every night this week*. **12** a record of bets. **13** a trick or number of tricks forming a set in a card game. 1–7, 12, 13 *n.*, 8–11 *v.* —**book′er,** *n.* —**book·less,** *adj.*

**by the book,** according to the proper or accepted way; strictly according to the rules: *When she was chairwoman, our meetings were always run by the book.*
**in one's book,** *Informal.* in one's opinion or judgment: *In my book, swearing is always unnecessary.*
**keep books,** keep a record of business accounts.
**know like a book,** understand very well; know everything about: *My mother knows me like a book, and can always tell when I have a problem.*
**read like a book,** guess accurately what a person is thinking, feeling, or planning: *He tried to hide it, but I can always read him like a book and I knew he was afraid.*
**throw the book at,** *Informal.* punish as severely as the law allows: *This is her third offence, so the judge will probably throw the book at her.*

**book·bind·er** (bük′bīn′dər) a person whose work or business is binding books. *n.*

**book·case** (bük′kās′) a piece of furniture with shelves for holding books. *n.*

**book club** a business organization that regularly supplies selected books to subscribers.

**book end** a support placed at the end of a row of books to hold them upright: *Book ends are often made in matching pairs for use at either end of a row of books.*

**book·ish** (bük′ish) **1** fond of reading or studying. **2** knowing books better than real life. **3** having to do with books. *adj.* —**book′ish·ness,** *n.*

**book·keep·er** (bük′kē′pər) a person whose work is BOOKKEEPING. *n.*

**book·keep·ing** (bük′kē′ping) the process or practice of recording, classifying, and summarizing data about the business transactions of a company, according to a particular system. *n.*

**book·let** (bük′lit) a little book; a thin book or pamphlet: *Booklets usually have paper covers*. *n.*

**book·mak·er** (bük′mā′kər) a person who makes a business of accepting bets on horse races. *n.*

**book·mark** (bük′märk′) **1** something put between the pages of a book to mark the place where the reader has finished reading. **2** BOOKPLATE. *n.*

**book·mo·bile** (bük′mə bēl′) a large van or trailer that serves as a travelling branch of a public library. *n.*

**book·plate** (bük′plāt′) a label to paste in books, which has the owner's name or emblem printed on it. *n.*

**book·sell·er** (bük′sel′ər) a person whose business is selling books. *n.*

# bookbinder 133 boorish

hat, āge, fär; let, ēqual, tėrm; it, īce
hot, ōpen, ôrder; oil, out; cup, pút, rüle
əbove, takən, pencəl, lemən, circəs
ch, child; ng, long; sh, ship
th, thin; ᴛʜ, then; zh, measure

**book·shelf** (bük′shelf′) a shelf for holding books. *n.*

**book·shop** (bük′shop′) BOOKSTORE. *n.*

**book·stall** (bük′stol′) a place where books, usually second-hand, are sold, often outdoors. *n.*

**book·store** (bük′stôr′) a store where books are sold. *n.*

**book·worm** (bük′wėrm′) **1** any of various insects whose adult forms or larvae gnaw the bindings or pages of books: *The silverfish is one of the most widely known kinds of bookworm*. **2** a person who is very fond of reading and studying. *n.*

**boom**[1] (büm) **1** a deep, hollow sound like the roar of cannon or of big waves. **2** make a deep, hollow sound: *The big man's voice boomed out above the rest*. **3** utter with such a sound: *The big guns boomed their message*. **4** a sudden activity and increase in business, prices, or values of property; rapid growth: *Our town is having such a boom that it has almost doubled its size in the last six years*. **5** increase suddenly in activity; grow rapidly: *Business is booming*. **6** produced by a boom: *boom prices*. 1, 4, 6 *n.*, 2, 3, 5 *v.*
☛ *Etym.* From ME *bommen* 'to hum', an echoic word originally used to describe a sound such as that made by a bee or beetle.

**boom**[2] (büm) **1** a long pole or beam, used to extend the bottom of a sail. See SLOOP for picture. **2** the lifting or guiding pole of a DERRICK. See CRANE for picture. **3** a chain, cable, or line of timbers used to keep logs from floating away. **4** a large raft of logs being floated over water. *n.*
**lower the boom,** *Informal.* suddenly become more strict or severe; suddenly assert one's authority; crack down: *When she had missed her curfew three times in a row, her parents lowered the boom.*
☛ *Etym.* From Dutch *boom* 'tree, beam, pole'. It was taken into English in the 17c. as a nautical term referring to the long pole used to extend the bottom of a sail.

**boom·er·ang** (bü′mə rang′) **1** a curved flat piece of wood used as a weapon by native peoples of Australia: *One kind of boomerang can be thrown so that it will return to the thrower if it misses its target*. **2** anything that recoils or reacts to harm the doer or user. **3** act as a boomerang. 1, 2 *n.*, 3 *v.*

**boom town** a town that has grown up suddenly.

**boon**[1] (bün) **1** a blessing; a great benefit. **2** something asked or granted as a favour. *n.*

**boon**[2] (bün) jolly; merry. *Archaic* except in **boon companion.** *adj.*

**boor** (bür) **1** a rude, bad-mannered, insensitive person. **2** a person who is clumsy and awkward in unfamiliar social situations. *n.*
☛ *Hom.* BOER (bür).

**boor·ish** (bür′ish) rude; having bad manners; clumsy. *adj.* —**boor′ish·ness,** *n.*

**boost** (büst) *Informal.* **1** a push or shove that helps a person in rising or advancing: *a boost over the fence.* **2** lift or push from below or behind. **3** raise; increase: *to boost prices, to boost sales.* **4** an increase: *a boost in salary.* **5** help by speaking well of or promoting actively: *They're boosting their new product with billboard ads. His speech boosted our campaign.* 1, 4 *n.*, 2, 3, 5 *v.*

**boost·er** (bü′stər) **1** a person or thing that boosts. **2** the first stage of a multistage rocket. **3** the device used to orbit an artificial satellite. *n.*

**booster shot** an injection given to reinforce an earlier INOCULATION.

**booster station** a radio or television installation that amplifies signals from the transmitting station.

**boot¹** (büt) **1** a covering for the foot and lower part of the leg, made of leather, rubber, or a synthetic material such as vinyl. **2** put boots on: *The hunter was booted and spurred.* **3** a kick: *She gave the ball a boot.* **4** give a kick to; drive or move by kicking: *He booted the stone off the sidewalk.* **5** formerly, an instrument of torture used to crush a person's leg. **6** in former times, a place for baggage in a coach. **7** the start-up of a computer program. **8** make a computer start by loading a program into memory. 1, 3, 5, 6, 7 *n.*, 2, 4, 8 *v.*
☞ *Usage.* Often used with **up**: *Once she booted up the computer it ran perfectly.*
☞ *Etym.* See note at BOOT².

**boot²** (büt) *n. Archaic* except in
**to boot,** in addition; besides: *He gave me his knife for my book and fifty cents to boot.*
☞ *Etym.* The word **boot** in the expression **to boot** is an old-fashioned word meaning 'benefit' or 'profit'. This word developed from the OE word *bōt*. It is not related to the other word **boot** (referring to a kind of footwear) which comes from OF *bote*.

**boot·black** (büt′blak′) a person whose work is shining shoes and boots. *n.*

**boot·ee** (bü′tē) **1** a baby's soft shoe. **2** a woman's short boot. *n.*
☞ *Hom.* BOOTY.

**booth** (büth) **1** a place where goods are sold or shown at a fair, market, etc. **2** a small, closed place for a telephone, motion-picture projector, etc. **3** a small, closed place for voting at elections. **4** a partly enclosed space in a restaurant, café, etc., containing a table and seats for a few persons. *n.*, *pl.* **booths** (bü*TH*z *or* büths).
☞ *Etym.* From an early Scandinavian word, probably Old Danish *bōð* 'dwelling'. It came into English in the Middle Ages and originally meant a temporary dwelling or shelter.

**boot·jack** (büt′jak′) a device to help in pulling off boots. *n.*

**boot·leg** (büt′leg′) **1** sell, transport, or make unlawfully. **2** made, transported, or sold unlawfully: *bootleg whisky.* **3** *Informal.* alcoholic liquor made, sold, or transported unlawfully. 1 *v.*, **boot·legged, boot·leg·ging;** 2 *adj.*, 3 *n.*

**boot·leg·ger** (büt′leg′ər) *Informal.* a person who BOOTLEGS (def. 1). *n.*

**boot·less** (büt′lis) useless. *adj.* —**boot′less·ly,** *adv.*
☞ *Etym.* This word is formed from the word **boot**, meaning 'benefit' or 'profit'. See note at BOOT² for more information.

**boot·lick** (büt′lik′) *Informal.* fawn on a person to try to gain favour; TOADY: *She was determined to make it on her own, without bootlicking. They would bootlick anyone with influence.* *v.*

**boot·lick·er** (büt′lik′ər) *Informal.* a person who fawns on another in order to gain favour; flatterer; TOADY. *n.*

**boo·ty** (bü′tē) **1** things taken from the enemy in war. **2** things seized by violence and robbery; plunder: *The pirates fought over the booty from the raided town.* **3** any valuable thing or things obtained; prize. *n.*, *pl.* **boo·ties.**
☞ *Hom.* BOOTEE.

**booze** (büz) *Informal.* **1** any intoxicating liquor. **2** SPREE. **3** drink heavily. 1, 2 *n.*, 3 *v.*, **boozed, booz·ing.**

**bop** (bop) BEBOP. *n.*

**bor.** borough.

**bo·rac·ic** (bə ras′ik) BORIC. *adj.*

**bor·age** (bėr′ij *or* bô′rij) a plant having hairy leaves and blue or purplish flowers, native to southern Europe: *Borage is used in salads, in flavouring beverages, and in medicine.* *n.*

**bo·rate** (bô′rāt) a salt or ester of BORIC ACID. *n.*

**bo·rat·ed** (bô′rā tid) mixed or treated with BORIC ACID or BORAX. *adj.*

**bo·rax** (bô′raks) a white crystalline powder, used as an antiseptic, in washing clothes, in fusing metals, and in preserving foods; sodium borate. *n.*

**bor·der** (bôr′dər) **1** a strip on or near the edge of anything for strength or ornament: *a handkerchief with a lace border. Our lawn has a border of flowers.* **2** the line separating two countries, provinces, etc., or two geographical regions; boundary; frontier: *We reached Detroit by crossing the border at Windsor.* **3** form a boundary to; bound: *Part of the St. Lawrence borders Canada and the United States. A creek borders our property on the west.* **4** put a border on; edge: *We have bordered our lawn with shrubs.* 1, 2 *n.*, 3, 4 *v.*
**border on** *or* **upon,** **a** touch at the border; be next to; adjoin. **b** be close to; approach in character: *The accusations in the newspaper article border on libel.*
☞ *Hom.* BOARDER.

**bor·der·land** (bôr′dər land′) **1** land forming, or next to, a border. **2** an uncertain district or space: *the borderland between sleeping and waking.* *n.*

**bor·der·line** (bôr′dər līn′) **1** a boundary; dividing line. **2** on a border or boundary. **3** uncertain; in between. 1 *n.*, 2, 3 *adj.*

**bore¹** (bôr) **1** make a hole by means of a tool that keeps turning, or as a worm does in fruit: *If you bore through the handle of the brush, you'll be able to hang it up.* **2** make a hole, passage, entrance, etc. by pushing through or digging out: *We bored a tunnel through the snow. A mole has bored its way under our flower bed.* **3** make a round hole in; hollow out evenly. **4** a hole made by a revolving tool. **5** a hollow space inside a pipe, tube, or gun barrel: *He cleaned the bore of his gun.* **6** the distance across the inside of a hole or tube. 1–3 *v.*, **bored, bor·ing;** 4–6 *n.*
☞ *Hom.* BOAR and BOER (bôr).

**bore²** (bôr) **1** make weary by being dull or tiresome: *I was never bored with his stories.* **2** a dull, tiresome person or thing. 1 *v.*, **bored, bor·ing;** 2 *n.*
☞ *Hom.* BOAR and BOER (bôr).

**bore**³ (bôr) pt. of BEAR¹: *She bore her loss bravely.* *v.*
☛ *Hom.* BOAR, BOER (bôr).

**bore**⁴ (bôr) a sudden, high tidal wave that rushes up a channel with great force: *The Bore at Moncton is caused by the powerful tides of the Bay of Fundy.* *n.*
☛ *Hom.* BOAR and BOER (bôr).

**bo·re·al** (bô′rē əl) 1 northern. 2 of or having to do with Boreas, the north wind. *adj.*

**bore·dom** (bôr′dəm) a bored condition; weariness caused by dull, tiresome people or events. *n.*

**bor·er** (bôr′ər) 1 a tool for boring holes. 2 an insect or worm that bores into wood, fruit, etc. *n.*

**bore·some** (bôr′səm) boring; tiresome. *adj.*

**bor·ic** (bô′rik) of or containing BORON. *adj.* Also, **boracic**.

**boric acid** a white crystalline substance used as a mild antiseptic, to preserve food, etc.

**born** (bôrn) 1 brought into life; brought forth. 2 conceived; thought up. 3 by birth; by nature: *a born athlete.* 4 a pp. of BEAR¹: *He was born in 1950.* 1–3 *adj.,* 4 *v.*
☛ *Hom.* BORNE.

**borne** (bôrn) a pp. of BEAR¹: *I have borne it as long as I can.* *v.*
☛ *Hom.* BORN.
☛ *Usage.* **Borne** is the past participle of BEAR¹ for most of its meanings: *The ship was borne along by the breeze. She had borne the pain without complaint. He had borne himself with dignity in the negotiations.* In the meaning "give birth to," however, the past participle of **bear** is **born** in the usual passive usage, as in *He was born in 1962,* but **borne** in other usages, as in *She had borne two children.*

**bo·ron** (bô′ron) a non-metallic chemical element found in BORAX. Symbol: B *n.*

**bor·ough** (ber′ō) a town or township having its own local government: *East York is a borough of Metropolitan Toronto.* *n.*
☛ *Hom.* BURRO, BURROW.

**bor·row** (bô′rō) 1 get something from another person with the understanding that it must be returned. 2 take and use as one's own; adopt; take: *Rome borrowed many ideas from Greece.* 3 take a word or expression from another language to use like a native word: *The word* mukluk *was borrowed from Inuktitut. Many words we think of as English were borrowed from French hundreds of years ago.* 4 in subtraction, decrease the digit in one column of the minuend by 1 in order to increase the value in the column on its right by 10; regroup. *v.* —**bor′row·er,** *n.*
**borrow trouble,** worry about something before there is reason to.

**borsch** (bôrsh) a Russian beet soup. *n.*

**bor·zoi** (bôr′zoi) a breed of tall, slender, swift dog having long, silky hair: *The borzoi was developed in Russia and was originally used to hunt wolves.* *n.*

**bosh** (bosh) *Informal.* nonsense. *n., interj.*

**bo's'n** (bō′sən) See BOATSWAIN. *n.*

**bos·om** (buz′əm) 1 the upper, front part of the human body, especially the female breasts. 2 the part of a garment covering the bosom. 3 the centre or inmost part: *He did not mention it even in the bosom of his family.* 4 the heart, thoughts, affections, desires, etc.: *He kept the secret in his bosom.* 5 the surface of a sea, lake, river, the ground, etc. 6 close; trusted: *a bosom friend.* *n.*

hat, āge, fär; let, ēqual, tėrm; it, īce
hot, ōpen, ôrder; oil, out; cup, pút, rüle
əbove, takən, pencəl, lemən, circəs
ch, child; ng, long; sh, ship
th, thin; ᴛʜ, then; zh, measure

**boss**¹ (bos) *Informal.* 1 a person who hires workers or watches over or directs them; a foreman or manager. 2 give orders to: *She likes to boss people.* 3 direct; control: *Who is bossing this job?* 1 *n.,* 2, 3 *v.*
**boss around** or **about,** give a lot of orders to: *Don't boss me around!*

**boss**² (bos) 1 a raised ornament of silver, ivory, or other material on a flat surface. 2 decorate with bosses. 1 *n.,* 2 *v.*

**boss·y** (bos′ē) *Informal.* fond of telling others what to do and how to do it; domineering. *adj.,* **boss·i·er, boss·i·est.**

**Boston bull** BOSTON TERRIER.

**Boston terrier** a small breed of dog having smooth, short, dark hair with white feet, chest, and face.

**bo·sun** (bō′sən) See BOATSWAIN. *n.*

**bot** (bot) the larva of a BOTFLY. *n.* Also, **bott.**
☛ *Hom.* BOUGHT.

**bo·tan·ic** (bə tan′ik) BOTANICAL. *adj.*

**bo·tan·i·cal** (bə tan′ə kəl) 1 having to do with plants and plant life. 2 having to do with BOTANY. *adj.*

**bo·tan·i·cal·ly** (bə tan′i klē) in a BOTANICAL manner; according to the principles of BOTANY. *adv.*

**bot·a·nist** (bot′ə nist) a person trained in BOTANY, especially one who makes it his or her work. *n.*

**bot·a·nize** (bot′ə nīz′) 1 study plants where they grow. 2 collect plants for study. 3 explore the plant life of. *v.,* **bot·a·nized, bot·a·niz·ing.**

**bot·a·ny** (bot′ə nē) 1 the science of plants; study of plants and plant life: *Botany is concerned with the structure, growth, classifications, diseases, etc. of plants.* 2 a scientific book about plants. *n., pl.* **bot·a·nies.**

**botch** (boch) 1 spoil by poor workmanship; bungle. 2 a poor piece of work. 3 patch or mend clumsily. 4 a clumsy patch. 1, 3 *v.,* 2, 4 *n.* —**botch′er,** *n.*

**botch·y** (boch′ē) botched; poorly made or done. *adj.,* **botch·i·er, botch·i·est.**

**bot·fly** (bot′flī′) any of a number of species of two-winged fly whose larvae are parasites in mammals: *Several species of botfly attack livestock.* *n., pl.* **bot·flies.**

**both** (bōth) 1 two, when only two are considered; the one and the other: *Both houses are white.* 2 the two together: *Both belong to her.* 3 together; alike; equally: *He can sing and dance both* (*adv.*). *She is both strong and healthy* (*conj.*). 1 *adj.,* 2 *pron.,* 3 *adv., conj.*

**both·er** (boᴛʜ′ər) 1 worry; fuss; trouble: *What a lot of bother about nothing.* 2 take trouble; concern oneself: *Don't bother about my breakfast; I'll eat what is here.* 3 a person or thing that causes worry, fuss, or trouble: *A door that will not shut is a bother.* 4 make uneasy, worried, or annoyed; irritate: *Hot weather bothers me.* 1, 3 *n.,* 2, 4 *v.*

**both·er·some** (boᴛʜ′ər səm) causing worry or fuss; troublesome. *adj.*

**bott** (bot) See BOT. *n.*
☞ *Hom.* BOUGHT.

**bot·tle** (bot′əl) 1 a container for holding liquids, made of glass, plastic, etc., usually without handles and with a narrow neck and mouth that can be closed with a cap or stopper. 2 the amount that a bottle can hold: *He could drink a whole bottle of juice.* 3 put into bottles: *to bottle pop.* 4 hold in; keep back; control: *to bottle one's feelings.* 1, 2 *n.*, 3, 4 *v.*, **bot·tled, bot·tling.**
—**bot′tle·like′**, *adj.* —**bot′tler**, *n.*
**bottle up,** hold in; keep back; control: *to bottle up one's anger.*

**bot·tle·neck** (bot′əl nek′) 1 the neck of a bottle. 2 a narrow passageway or street. 3 a person or thing that hinders progress. 4 a situation in which progress is hindered: *They have hit a bottleneck that could delay the decision for weeks.* *n.*

**bot·tle·nose** (bot′əl nōz′) a species of dolphin found in the north Atlantic, dark brown and white in colour and having a short, somewhat upturned snout. *n.*

**bot·tom** (bot′əm) 1 the lowest part: *The berries at the bottom of the basket were crushed.* 2 underside: *The bottom of the shelf was left unpainted. Don't set the glass on the table if the bottom is wet.* 3 the base on which something rests: *There is an inscription around the bottom of the statue.* 4 the ground under a body of water: *the bottom of the sea.* 5 the seat of a chair: *This chair needs a new bottom.* 6 basis; source; origin: *He is at the bottom of this mischief.* 7 *Informal.* the buttocks. 8 the part of a ship's hull below the water line. 9 a ship, especially a cargo ship. 10 touch or rest on the bottom: *The submarine bottomed on the ocean floor.* 11 lowest; last: *bottom prices. I've spent my bottom dollar.* 12 Often, **bottoms,** *pl.* the low land along a river. 13 **bottoms,** *pl.* the trousers of pyjamas. 1–9, 12, 13 *n.*, 10 *v.*, 11 *adj.*
**at bottom,** basically; actually: *At bottom, she's a kind person.*
**bottoms up,** *Informal.* drain your glass! drink up!

**bot·tom·less** (bot′əm lis) 1 without a bottom: *a bottomless chair.* 2 so deep that the bottom cannot be reached; extremely deep: *the bottomless depths of the sea.* *adj.*

**bottom line** the most fundamental point or principle: *What's the bottom line in your negotiations?*

**bot·u·lism** (boch′ə liz′əm) an often fatal kind of food poisoning from poisons produced by certain BACTERIA in improperly canned or smoked food. *n.*

**bou·doir** (bü′dwär *or* bü dwär′) a lady's private sitting room or dressing room. *n.*

**bouf·fant** (bü fänt′) puffed out: *bouffant sleeves, a bouffant hairdo.* *adj.*

**bough** (bou) 1 one of the main branches of a tree. 2 a branch cut from a tree. *n.*
☞ *Hom.* BOW[1], BOW[3].

**bought** (bot) pt. and pp. of BUY: *We bought apples from the farmer.* *v.*
☞ *Hom.* BOT, BOTT.

**bouil·lon** (bùl′yon; *French*, bü yôN′) a clear, thin soup or broth. *n.*

**boul·der** (bōl′dər) a large rock rounded or worn by the action of water or weather. *n.*

**boul·e·vard** (bùl′ə värd′) 1 a broad street. 2 the strip of grass between a sidewalk and a curb. 3 the centre strip dividing any road down the middle. *n.*

**bounce** (bouns) 1 spring, often repeatedly, into the air after striking something, as a rubber ball does: *The baby likes to bounce on the bed. The ball bounced off the porch railing.* 2 cause to bounce: *She bounced the basketball off the backboard.* 3 a bound; spring; bouncing. 4 springiness; ability to bounce: *This ball has lots of bounce.* 5 come or go energetically, noisily, angrily, etc.: *She bounced out of the room.* 6 *Informal.* energy; spirit: *He was in hospital for a week, but now he is as full of bounce as ever.* 1, 2, 5 *v.*, **bounced, bounc·ing;** 3, 4, 6 *n.*

**bounc·er** (boun′sər) 1 something that bounces. 2 *Informal.* a man hired to eject unruly or unwanted people from a BAR[1] (def. 13). *n.*

**bounc·ing** (boun′sing) 1 strong, healthy, and vigorous: *a bouncing baby girl.* 2 ppr. of BOUNCE. 1 *adj.*, 2 *v.*

**boun·cy** (boun′sē) 1 cheerful and spirited; exuberant: *A week after the accident, she was as bouncy as always.* 2 elastic: *a bouncy surface.* *adj.*, **boun·ci·er, boun·ci·est.** —**boun′ci·ly,** *adv.*

**bound**[1] (bound) 1 under some obligation; obliged: *bound by law to keep the peace. He felt himself duty-bound to volunteer.* 2 certain; sure: *It's bound to rain before morning.* 3 confined (*used especially in compounds*): *housebound. We were snowbound for three days.* 4 *Informal.* determined; resolved: *She was bound to go, whether or not we were going.* 5 of a book, having covers; having a binding: *a newly bound book.* 6 pt. and pp. of BIND: *They bound their prisoners with ropes.* 1–5 *adj.*, 6 *v.*
**bound up in** *or* **with,** a closely connected with. b very devoted to.
☞ *Etym.* All forms of the verb **bind** developed from the OE verb *bindan* 'bind'.

**bound**[2] (bound) 1 spring lightly along; move by leaping: *The deer bounded into the woods and was gone.* 2 of a ball, etc., spring back after striking a surface; rebound; bounce: *The ball bounded from the wall and hit the car.* 3 a leap upward or forward: *With one bound, the cat was on the mouse.* 4 the act of rebounding; bounce: *I caught the ball on the bound.* 1, 2 *v.*, 3, 4 *n.*
☞ *Etym.* From the F verb *bondir* 'leap', originally, 'rebound, resound'. 16c.

**bound**[3] (bound) 1 be or form the boundary of: *A poplar bluff bounds the property to the north. The garden is bounded by a flagstone walk.* 2 Usually **bounds,** *pl.* a limit or limiting line: *the farthest bounds of the estate. Keep your hopes within bounds.* 1 *v.*, 2 *n.*
**bound on,** be next to; adjoin: *Canada bounds on the United States.*
**out of bounds,** outside the area allowed by rules, custom, or law: *He kicked the ball out of bounds. The town is out of bounds to the soldiers.*
☞ *Etym.* From AN *bounde* and OF *bunne, bunde* 'landmark'.

**bound**[4] (bound) going; on the way: *I am bound for home. By midnight they were homeward bound.* *adj.*
☞ *Etym.* From ME *boun* 'ready' which came from ON *búinn*, past participle of the verb *búa* 'get ready'. The word was never used as a verb in English and has only the adjective form.

**bound·a·ry** (boun′drē *or* boun′də rē) a limiting line; something that functions as a dividing line, especially between properties, provinces, countries, etc.: *The Ottawa River forms part of the boundary between Ontario and Quebec.* *n.*

**bound·en** (boun′dən)   required; obligatory: *She considered it her bounden duty.*   *adj.*

**bound·less** (boun′dlis)   **1** not limited; infinite: *boundless space.*   **2** seemingly without bounds; vast: *the boundless ocean.*   *adj.*   —**bound′less·ly,** *adv.*   —**bound′less·ness,** *n.*

**bounds** (boundz)   **1** land on or near a boundary.   **2** an area included within boundaries: *The hotels near the camp were declared out of bounds.*   *n. pl.*

**boun·te·ous** (boun′tē əs)   **1** generous; given freely: *bounteous presents.*   **2** plentiful; abundant: *The farmer had a bounteous crop.*   *adj.*   —**boun′te·ous·ly,** *adv.*   —**boun′te·ous·ness,** *n.*

**boun·ti·ful** (boun′tə fəl)   **1** plentiful; abundant: *We have a bountiful supply of tomatoes.*   **2** generous; giving freely: *bountiful friends.*   *adj.*   —**bount′i·ful·ly,** *adv.*   —**boun′ti·ful·ness,** *n*

**boun·ty** (boun′tē)   **1** something given with generosity.   **2** generosity.   **3** a reward or premium, especially one given by a government: *Governments have sometimes offered bounties for animals considered a nuisance.*   *n., pl.* **boun·ties.**

**bou·quet** (bō kā′ *or* bü kā′ *for 1,* bü kā′ *for 2*)   **1** a bunch of flowers.   **2** a fragrance; aroma.   *n.*
☛ *Etym.* From F *bouquet*, earlier *bosquet*, which originally meant a clump of trees. OF *bosquet* came from *bosc*, an earlier form of *bois* 'forest, wood'.

**bour·bon** (bėr′bən)   a kind of whisky distilled from a grain mash that contains at least 51 percent corn.   *n.*

**bour·geois** (bür′zhwä *or* bür zhwä′)   **1** a person of the middle class.   **2** of the middle class.   **3** like the middle class; ordinary: *He has very bourgeois tastes.*   1 *n., pl.* **bour·geois;**   2, 3 *adj.*

**bour·geoi·sie** (bür′zhwä zē′)   the people of the middle class.   *n.*

**bout** (bout)   **1** a trial of strength; contest: *Those are the two boxers who will appear in the main bout.*   **2** a spell; a period, especially one involving illness, effort, or endurance: *I have just had a long bout of the flu. Are you ready for a bout of housecleaning?*   *n.*

**bou·tique** (bü tēk′)   a small shop or a department in a large store that specializes in fashionable clothes and accessories, or in gifts, etc.   *n.*

**bou·ton·niere** *or* **bou·ton·nière** (bü′tə nyer′)   a flower or flowers worn in a buttonhole.   *n.*

**bou·zou·ki** (bü zü′kē)   a Greek stringed musical instrument resembling a mandolin.   *n.*

**bo·vid** (bō′vid)   **1** belonging to or characteristic of the cattle family, a group of domestic and wild cud-chewing, hoofed mammals with permanent, non-branching, hollow horns.   **2** an animal of this group: *Domestic cattle, true antelope, buffalo, bison, the yak, sheep, goats, and the musk-ox are all bovids.*   1 *adj.,* 2 *n.*
☛ *Syn.* **bovid,** BOVINE. **Bovids** are a family of animals. **Bovines** are a group of animals within the bovid family. Sheep and goats are bovids, but not bovines.

**bo·vine** (bō′vīn)   **1** belonging to or characteristic of the subfamily of cud-chewing mammals that includes buffalo, bison, the yak, and domestic cattle.   **2** an animal of this group.   **3** slow; stupid.   **4** without emotions; stolid.   1, 3, 4 *adj.,* 2 *n.*
☛ *Syn.* See note at BOVID.

**bow**[1] (bou)   **1** bend the head or body in greeting, respect, worship, or submission.   **2** a bending of the head or body in this way.   **3** show by bowing: *to bow one's thanks.*   **4** cause to stoop: *The woman was bowed by old age.*   **5** submit; yield: *We must bow to necessity.*   1, 3–5 *v.,* 2 *n.*
**bow down,** **a** weigh down: *bowed down with care.*   **b** to worship.
**bow out,** **a** withdraw (*from*): *He sprained his wrist and had to bow out of the tennis tournament.*   **b** usher out.
**take a bow,** accept praise, applause, etc. for something done.
☛ *Hom.* BOUGH, BOW[3].

**bow**[2] (bō)   **1** a weapon for shooting arrows, usually consisting of a strip of springy wood with a string or cord stretched tight between the two ends.   See ARCHERY for picture.   **2** curve; bend.   **3** something curved; curved part: *A rainbow is a bow.*   **4** a looped knot: *a bow of ribbon.*   **5** a slender rod with horsehairs stretched on it, for playing a violin, etc.   **6** play a violin, etc. with a bow.   1–5 *n.,* 2, 6 *v.*   —**bow′less,** *adj.*   —**bow′-like′,** *adj.*
☛ *Hom.* BEAU.

**bow**[3] (bou)   the forward part of a ship, boat, or aircraft.   See AFT for picture.   *n.*
☛ *Hom.* BOUGH, BOW[1].

**bow·el** (bou′əl)   **1** a part of the bowels; intestine.   **2** Usually, **bowels,** *pl.*   the tube in the body into which food passes from the stomach; intestines.   **3 bowels,** *pl.* the inner part; depths: *Miners dig for coal in the bowels of the earth.*   *n.*

**bowel movement**   **1** discharge of waste matter from the large intestine.   **2** the waste matter discharged; FECES.

**bow·er** (bou′ər)   **1** a shelter of leafy branches.   **2** a summerhouse or arbour.   *n.*

**bow·er·y** (bou′ə rē)   like a bower; leafy; shady.   *adj.*

**bow·head** (bō′hed′)   a species of RIGHT WHALE having a very large head that is almost one third of its total length of about 18 m.   *n.*

**bow·ie knife** (bō′ē *or* bü′ē)   a long, single-edged hunting knife carried in a sheath.

**bow·knot** (bō′not′)   a slipknot such as is made in tying shoelaces: *A bowknot usually has two loops and two ends, and can be untied by pulling the ends.*   See KNOT for picture.   *n.*

**bowl**[1] (bōl)   **1** a hollow, rounded dish, usually without handles.   **2** the amount that a bowl can hold.   **3** a bowl-shaped or concave part: *the bowl of a spoon or a pipe.*   **4** a large drinking cup.   **5** a drink.   **6** a bowl-shaped structure such as an amphitheatre or a stadium.   *n.*   —**bowl′-like′,** *adj.*
☛ *Hom.* BOLE, BOLL.

**bowl**[2] (bōl)   **1** a fairly large, heavy ball used in certain games, especially the weighted or slightly flattened ball used in LAWN BOWLING.   **2** play the game of BOWLS or of LAWN BOWLING.   **3** in the game of BOWLS or in LAWN BOWLING, a throw or casting.   **4** roll or move along rapidly and smoothly: *Our car bowled along on the good road.*   **5** in cricket:   **a** throw the ball to the batsman.   **b** dismiss a batsman, especially by knocking off the BAILS[4] or knocking down a wicket (used with out).  6 bowls, pl. (usually used with a singular verb)  a LAWN BOWLING.  b SKITTLES or TENPINS.  1, 3, 6 n., 2, 4, 5 v.

**bowl over, a** knock over.  **b** *Informal.* make helpless and confused; stun: *I was bowled over by the bad news.*
☛ *Hom.* BOLE, BOLL.

**bow·leg** (bō′leg′)  1 a leg that curves outward at or below the knee.  2 an outward curve of the legs.  *n.*

**bow·leg·ged** (bō′leg′id *or* bō′legd′)  having the legs curved outward at or below the knee; bandy-legged. Compare with KNOCK-KNEED.  *adj.*

**bowl·er**[1] (bō′lər)  1 a person who bowls.  2 in cricket, the player who delivers the ball to the batsman.  *n.*

**bowl·er**[2] (bō′lər)  a man's hat having a small brim and a hard, round crown; a DERBY.  See HAT for picture.  *n.*

**bowl·ful** (bōl′fůl)  as much as a bowl can hold.  *n., pl.* **bowl·fuls**.

**bow·line** (bō′lən *or* bō′līn)  1 a knot used in making a loop.  See KNOT for picture.  2 the rope tied to the edge of a square sail nearest the wind: *The bowline holds the sail steady when sailing into the wind.*  *n.*

**bowline knot**  BOWLINE (def. 1).

**bowl·ing** (bō′ling)  1 a game played indoors, in which balls are rolled down an alley at bottle-shaped wooden pins: *Fivepins, ninepins, and tenpins are forms of bowling.*  2 playing the game of BOWLS (def. 1).  3 ppr. of BOWL.  1, 2 n., 3 v.

**bowling alley**  1 the lane or alley down which balls are rolled in the game of BOWLING.  2 an establishment having a number of lanes for BOWLING: *There is a snack bar at the bowling alley.*

**bowling green**  a smooth, flat stretch of grass for playing BOWLS (def. 1).

**bowls** (bōlz)  1 a game played on grass by rolling a lopsided or weighted ball toward a stationary ball.  2 LAWN BOWLING.  *n.*

**bow·man** (bō′mən)  a soldier armed with bow and arrows; archer.  *n., pl.* **bow·men** (-mən).

**bow·shot** (bō′shot′)  1 a shot from a bow.  2 the distance that a bow will shoot an arrow.  *n.*

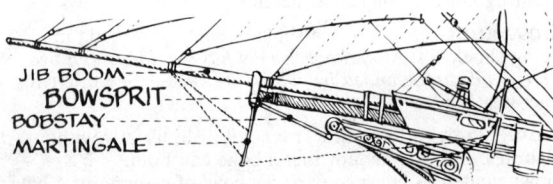

The bow of a French barkentine of the early 20th century

**bow·sprit** (bou′sprit)  a pole or spar projecting forward from the bow of a ship: *Ropes from the bowsprit help to steady sails and masts.*  See SCHOONER for another picture.  *n.*

**bow·string** (bō′string′)  1 a strong cord stretched between the two ends of a bow and pulled back by the archer to send the arrow forward.  2 a cord like this.  *n.*

**box**[1] (boks)  1 a container, usually with a lid, made of wood, metal, cardboard, paper, etc. to pack or put things in.  2 the amount that a box can hold: *We ate a whole box of cereal.*  3 pack in a box; put into a box.  4 in the auditorium of a theatre, etc., a small boxlike space with chairs for a group of people.  5 in a courtroom, an enclosed space for a jury, witnesses, etc.  6 a small shelter: *a box for a sentry.*  7 the driver's seat on a coach, carriage, etc.  8 the place where a baseball pitcher stands to throw the ball.  9 the place where the batter stands to hit the ball.  10 a receptacle in a post office from which a subscriber collects mail.  1, 2, 4–10 n., 3 v.
—**box′like′**, *adj.*

**box in,**  confine, as if in a box; surround; hem in: *We couldn't get out of our parking space because another car had boxed us in.*

**box**[2] (boks)  1 a blow with the open hand or the fist, especially on the side of the head: *She gave him a box on the ear.*  2 strike such a blow.  3 fight as a sport with the fists, which are usually covered with padded gloves: *He had not boxed since he left school.*  1 n., 2, 3 v.

**box**[3] (boks)  1 any of a number of closely related evergreen shrubs and small trees often used for hedges, borders, etc.  2 the hard, durable wood of a box; BOXWOOD.  *n.*

**box·car** (bok′skär′)  a railway freight car enclosed on all sides.  *n.*

**box elder**  MANITOBA MAPLE.

**box·er** (bok′sər)  1 a man who fights with his fists, usually in padded gloves and according to special rules.  2 a breed of medium-sized dog about 55 cm high at the shoulder having a stocky, strong body with a deep chest, short brownish hair, and a short, square muzzle: *The boxer was named for its habit of playfully striking out with its front paws.*  *n.*

**box·ing** (bok′sing)  1 the sport of fighting with the fists.  2 ppr. of BOX.  1 n., 2 v.

**Boxing Day**  December 26, a legal holiday in all provinces except Quebec.

**boxing gloves**  the padded gloves worn when boxing.

**box lacrosse**  *Cdn.*  an indoor version of LACROSSE.

**box office**  1 the place where tickets are sold in a theatre, hall, etc.  2 the money taken in at the box office.  3 the power to attract ticket buyers, or a show or performer having this power: *Adventure movies are good box office.*

**box score**  in baseball, a complete record of the plays of a game arranged in a table by the names of the players.

**box seat**  a chair or seat in a box of a theatre, hall, auditorium, stadium, etc.

**box social**  a social gathering where boxes of sandwiches or other food are auctioned, usually to raise money for some charity.

**box spring**  a base for a bed, consisting of coil springs set in a cloth-covered frame: *A box spring is designed to be used under a mattress.*

**box·wood** (bok′swůd′)  1 the hard, fine-grained wood of the BOX[3].  2 the tree itself.  *n.*

**boy** (boi)  1 a male child from birth to about sixteen.  2 son: *They have two boys.*  3 a male servant.  4 a boy or man employed to run errands, carry things, etc.  5 a familiar term for a man; fellow: *the boys at the office.*  6 *Informal.* used to express surprise, pleasure, etc.: *Boy, was it hot!*  1–5 n., 6 interj.
☛ *Hom.* BUOY (boi).

**boy·cott** (boi′kot)   **1** combine against and have nothing to do with a person, business, nation. etc.: *If people are boycotting someone, they do not associate with him or her, or buy from or sell to him or her, and they try to keep others from doing so.*   **2** refuse to buy or use a product, etc.   **3** the act of boycotting.   **1**, **2** *v.*, **3** *n.*   —**boy′cot·ter**, *n.*
☞ *Etym.*   Named after Captain C.C. *Boycott* (1832–1897), an agent for the owner of an estate in Ireland, who was the victim of such treatment at the hands of the tenants on the estate.

**boy·friend** (boi′frend′)   **1** a male companion of a girl or woman; escort, sweetheart, or lover: *She has a new boyfriend.*   **2** a boy who is one's friend.   *n.*

**boy·hood** (boi′hůd)   **1** the time or condition of being a boy.   **2** boys as a group: *the boyhood of the nation.*   *n.*

**boy·ish** (boi′ish)   **1** of a boy.   **2** like a boy: *The warm spring weather made him feel almost boyish again.*   **3** like a boy's: *a boyish grin.*   **4** fit for a boy: *boyish games.*   *adj.*   —**boy′ish·ly**, *adv.*   —**boy′ish·ness**, *n.*

**Boy Scout**   a member of the BOY SCOUTS.

**Boy Scouts**   an organization for boys and young men to help them to learn to co-operate with people, have confidence in themselves, and be good leaders, also to learn about and appreciate the outdoors, and to develop physically and spiritually. The Boy Scouts of Canada has five programs for different ages: Beavers, Wolf Cubs, Scouts, Venturers, and Rovers.

**boy·sen·ber·ry** (boi′zən ber′ē)   a purple berry like a blackberry in size and shape, and like a raspberry in flavour, probably a cross of loganberry, raspberry, and blackberry.   *n.*, *pl.* **boy·sen·ber·ries**.

**Br**   bromine.

**Br.**   **1** Britain.   **2** British.

**br.**   **1** branch.   **2** brother.

**bra** (brä)   BRASSIERE.   *n.*

**brace** (brās)   **1** something that holds parts together or in place; a support: *An iron rod or a piece of timber used to support a roof or a wall would be called a brace.*   **2** give strength or firmness to; support.   **3** enliven; invigorate: *The walk braced us for the next job.*   **4** a pair or couple: *a brace of ducks.*   **5** a handle for a tool or drill used for boring. See BRACE AND BIT for picture.   **6** either of these signs { } used to enclose words, figures, staves in music, etc.   **7 braces**, *pl.*   a pair of elastic straps for supporting trousers, worn over the shoulders and fastened to the trousers at the back and front; suspenders.   **8** Often, **braces**, *pl.*   an arrangement of wires attached to crooked teeth in order to correct their position.   **1**, **4–8** *n.*, **2**, **3** *v.*, **braced, brac·ing**.
**brace oneself** or **brace up**, *Informal.*   summon one's strength or courage.

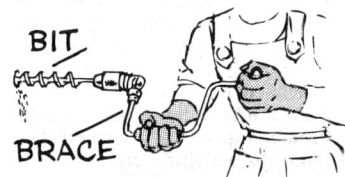

A brace and bit. The user presses with one hand and turns with the other. A bit cuts in much the same way as an auger.

**brace and bit**   a tool for boring, consisting of a bit fitted into a crank-shaped handle.

**brace·let** (brā′slit)   **1** a band or chain worn for ornament around the wrist or arm.   **2** the band of a wristwatch, especially a metal one: *My watch has an expansion bracelet.*   **3** *Informal.*   a handcuff.   *n.*

**brac·er** (brā′sər)   a person or thing that braces; a support.   *n.*

**brach·i·o·pod** (brak′ē ə pod′)   any of the small invertebrate animals of the bottom of the sea that make up a major division of the animal kingdom, all having a shell consisting of an upper and a lower valve and, inside the shell, two coiled arms called brachia on either side of the mouth, used to draw in food-bearing water: *Some brachiopods look very much like clams, but the two groups are not related.*   *n.*

**brac·ing** (brā′sing)   **1** giving strength and energy; refreshing.   **2** a brace or system of braces.   **3** *ppr.* of BRACE.   **1** *adj.*, **2** *n.*, **3** *v.*   —**brac′ing·ly**, *adv.*

**brack·en** (brak′ən)   **1** a large fern.   **2** a clump or field of such ferns.   *n.*

**brack·et** (brak′it)   **1** a piece of stone, wood, metal, etc. projecting from a wall as a support for a shelf, electric fixture, or other weight.   **2** support with a bracket.   **3** a shelf supported by brackets.   **4** either of these signs [ ] used to enclose words, symbols, or figures.   **5** either of these signs ( ), used to enclose words, etc.; parenthesis.   **6** a classification according to age, income, etc.: *a middle-income bracket, the junior age bracket.*   **7** enclose within brackets.   **8** think of together; mention together; group: *She objected to being bracketed with the younger children in the games.*   **1**, **3–6** *n.*, **2**, **7**, **8** *v.*

**brack·ish** (brak′ish)   **1** somewhat salty.   **2** distasteful; unpleasant.   *adj.*   —**brack′ish·ness**, *n.*

**bract** (brakt)   a small leaf at the base of a flower or flower stalk. See COMPOSITE and FLOWER for pictures.   *n.*

**brad** (brad)   a small, thin nail with a small head.   *n.*

**brad·awl** (brad′ol′)   an AWL with a cutting edge for making small holes for BRADS, etc.   *n.*

**brae** (brā) *Scottish.*   a slope; hillside.   *n.*

**brag** (brag)   **1** BOAST.   **2** boasting talk.   **1**, **2** *n.*, **1** *v.*, **bragged, brag·ging**.   —**brag′ger**, *n.*

**brag·ga·do·ci·o** (brag′ə dō′shē ō *or* brag′ə dō′chē ō)   **1** a boasting or bragging.   **2** a boaster or braggart.   *n.*, *pl.* **brag·ga·do·ci·os**.

**brag·gart** (brag′ərt)   **1** BOASTER.   **2** boastful: *a braggart bully.*   *n.*

**Brah·ma** (brä′mə)   **1** a Hindu god, formerly widely worshipped as the highest god, the creator of all things.   **2** Brahman (def. 3); ZEBU.   *n.*

**Brah·man** (brä′mən)   **1** in the classical Hindu religion, the eternal, supreme reality that is the basis of the universe.   **2** a member of the priestly caste, the highest caste in India.   **3** any of several breeds of cattle first developed in India; ZEBU.   *n.*, *pl.* **Brah·mans**. Also, **Brahmin**.

**Brah·man·ism** (brä′mə niz′əm)   **1** the religious beliefs and practices of ancient India, when the priestly caste, the

Brahmans, had great power and prestige: *Sacrificial rituals were very important in Brahmanism.* **2** the principles and practices of the Brahmans themselves. *n.*

**Brah·min** (brä'mən) **1** BRAHMAN (def. 2). **2** a cultured, intellectual person of the upper class. *n., pl.* **Brah·min.**

**braid** (brād) **1** a narrow length of hair, ribbon, straw, etc. formed by weaving together three or more strands or bunches. **2** weave together three or more strands or bunches of: *Her mother always braids her hair.* **3** form or make in this way: *to braid a rug.* **4** ribbon or cord, usually consisting of interwoven strands, used to trim or bind clothing, etc. **5** trim or bind with braid. **6** formed of braiding: *a braid rug.* 1, 4, 6 *n.*, 2, 3, 5 *v.*, —**braid'er**, *n.*

**braid·ed** (brā'did) **1** formed by weaving together three or more strands of hair, ribbon, straw, etc. **2** trimmed or bound with braid. **3** pt. and pp. of BRAID. 1, 2 *adj.*, 3 *v.*

**braille** or **Braille** (brāl) **1** a system of writing and printing for blind people: *The letters in braille are made of groups of raised dots that are read by touch.* **2** the letters themselves. *n.*
☛ *Etym.* Named after Louis *Braille* (1809–1852), the Frenchman who invented this system. Braille was blinded in an accident when he was three years old.

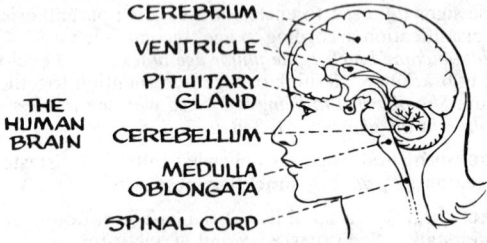
THE HUMAN BRAIN — CEREBRUM, VENTRICLE, PITUITARY GLAND, CEREBELLUM, MEDULLA OBLONGATA, SPINAL CORD

**brain** (brān) **1** the mass of nerve tissue enclosed in the skull or head of vertebrate animals: *The brain interprets impulses received by the senses of sight, touch, hearing, etc., controls and co-ordinates bodily activities, and is the centre of thought and feeling.* **2** a part of the nervous system of invertebrates, corresponding to the brain of vertebrates. **3** *Informal.* an electronic computer. **4** kill by smashing the skull of: *The trapper brained the injured wolf with a large stone.* **5** Often, **brains**, *pl.* **a** intelligence: *She has more brains than anyone else in the family.* **b** the main planner of an organization or project: *She is the brains of the firm.* 1–3, 5 *n.*, 4 *v.*

**brain cell** a nerve cell in the brain; NEURON.

**brain·child** (brān'chīld') an original product of a person's imagination, such as an invention, idea, or plan, especially one that the person is particularly pleased with or proud of. *n.*

**brain·less** (brān'lis) **1** without a brain. **2** stupid; foolish: *That was a brainless thing to do.* *adj.*
—**brain'less·ly**, *adv.*

**brain·storm** (brān'stôrm') **1** *Informal.* a sudden inspired idea. **2** a sudden and violent, but temporary, mental disturbance. **3** try to solve a problem by hearing ideas from all members of a group. 1, 2 *n.*, 3 *v.*

**brain trust** a group of experts acting as advisers to an administrator, a political leader, or an executive.

**brain·wash** (brān'wosh') change the ideas or beliefs of by BRAINWASHING: *The defendant claimed she had taken part in the robbery because she had been brainwashed by her kidnappers.* *v.*

**brain·wash·ing** (brān'wosh'ing) intensive teaching or drilling forced on a person to purge the person's mind of existing political, religious, or social beliefs and to replace them with a completely different set of beliefs. *n.*

**brain wave** **1** a rhythmic increase and decrease of voltage between parts of the brain, that produces an electric current. **2** *Informal.* a sudden inspiration or bright idea.

**brain·y** (brā'nē) *Informal.* intelligent; clever. *adj.*, **brain·i·er, brain·i·est.** —**brain'i·ness**, *n.*

**braise** (brāz) brown meat quickly and then cook it long and slowly in a covered pan with very little water. *v.*, **braised, brais·ing.**

**brake**¹ (brāk) **1** a device used to decrease or stop the motion of a wheel or vehicle by pressing or scraping. **2** slow down or stop by using a brake or brakes: *He had to brake fast to avoid hitting the car ahead. She braked the truck.* 1 *n.*, 2 *v.*, **braked, brak·ing.**
☛ *Hom.* BREAK.

**brake**² (brāk) a thick growth of bushes; thicket. *n.*
☛ *Hom.* BREAK.

**brake**³ (brāk) a large, coarse fern. *n.*
☛ *Hom.* BREAK.

**brake·man** (brāk'mən) a person who helps the conductor or engineer of a railway train: *Brakemen used to work the brakes on steam locomotives.* *n., pl.* **brake·men** (-mən).

**bram·ble** (bram'bəl) **1** one of a large group of plants belonging to the rose family, of which many varieties, such as the blackberry and raspberry, are prickly. **2** any rough, prickly shrub. *n.*

**bram·bly** (bram'blē) **1** full of BRAMBLES. **2** like BRAMBLES; prickly. *adj.*, **bram·bli·er, bram·bli·est.**

**bran** (bran) the broken coat of the grains of wheat, rye, etc. separated from the flour or meal by BOLTing²: *Bran is used as fodder and in cereal, bread, and other foods.* *n.*

**branch** (branch) **1** the part of a tree or other large plant growing out from the main stem; any woody part of a tree above the ground except the trunk: *A bough is a main branch. A twig is a very small branch.* **2** any division that resembles a branch of a tree; an offshoot: *the branches of a deer's antlers, a branch of a river, a branch of a family.* **3** put out branches; spread in branches. **4** divide into branches: *The road branches at the bottom of the hill.* **5** a division or part of a system, subject, etc.: *Botany is a branch of biology.* **6** a local office: *The company's head office is in Moncton, but it has branches in several other cities.* **7** a local branch of a veteran's organization. 1, 2, 5–7 *n.*, 3, 4 *v.* —**branch'less**, *adj.*
—**branch'like**, *adj.*
**branch off,** divide into branches.
**branch out,** **a** put out branches. **b** extend business, interests, activities, etc.

**branch·let** (branch'lit) a small branch. *n.*

**branch plant** a business that is owned and controlled by a company having its headquarters elsewhere: *A corporation may have branch plants in several countries, or in several parts of the same country.*

**branch–plant** (branch′plant′) characterized by or arising from the existence of BRANCH PLANTS and the resulting dependence on decisions made elsewhere: *a branch-plant economy.* *adj.*

**brand** (brand) **1** a certain kind, grade, or make: *a popular brand of shampoo, a good brand of coffee.* **2** brand name or trademark. **3** a mark made by burning the skin with a hot iron: *Cattle and horses on big ranches are marked with brands to show who owns them.* **4** BRANDING IRON. **5** mark by burning the skin with a hot iron: *In former times criminals were often branded.* **6** a mark of disgrace. **7** expose or mark as deserving disgrace: *He has been branded as a traitor.* **8** a piece of wood that is burning or partly burned. 1–4, 6, 8 *n.*, 5, 7 *v.* —**brand′er,** *n.*

**bran·died** (bran′dēd) prepared, mixed, or flavoured with BRANDY. *adj.*

**branding iron** an iron stamp for burning an identification mark on hide, wood, etc.

**bran·dish** (bran′dish) **1** wave or shake threateningly; flourish: *The knight brandished his sword at his enemy.* **2** a threatening shake; flourish. 1 *v.*, 2 *n.*

**brand name** a name given to a product or service by its manufacturer or seller to distinguish from similar ones produced or sold by someone else; trade name: *A brand name is registered and protected as a trademark.* —**brand-name,** *adj.*

**brand–new** (brand′nyü′ *or* brand′nü′) very new; as new as if just made. *adj.*

**bran·dy** (bran′dē) **1** a strong alcoholic liquor distilled from wine. **2** an alcoholic liquor distilled from fermented fruit juice. *n., pl.* **bran·dies.**

**brant** (brant) a small wild goose that breeds in the Arctic tundra and winters in the temperate regions of the Atlantic and Pacific oceans, having a black head, neck, and breast, dark grey upper parts, and a narrow white crescent on either side of the neck: *The brant is closely related to the Canada goose.* *n., pl.* **brants** or (*especially collectively*) **brant.**

**brash** (brash) **1** hasty; rash. **2** impudent; saucy. *adj.*

**brass** (bras) **1** a yellow metal that is an alloy of copper and zinc. **2** something made of brass, such as door fittings or ornaments. **3** made of brass. **4** a musical wind instrument, usually made of brass, such as the trumpet, trombone, tuba, and French horn. **5** *Informal.* money. **6** *Informal.* shamelessness; impudence. **7** *Informal.* high-ranking military officers; any high-ranking person or persons. **8** Often, **brasses,** *pl.* the section of an orchestra or band composed of brass instruments. 1, 2, 4–8 *n.*, 3 *adj.*

**bras·sard** (bras′ärd *or* brə särd′) **1** a band worn above the elbow as a badge. **2** armour for the upper part of the arm. *n.*

**brass hat** *Informal.* a high-ranking military officer, such as a general or staff officer.

**bras·siere** or **bras·sière** (brə zēr′) a breast support worn by women. *n.*

**brass tacks** *Informal.* the actual facts or details: *Let's get down to brass tacks.*

**brass·y** (bras′ē) **1** of brass. **2** like brass. **3** loud and harsh. **4** *Informal.* shameless; impudent. *adj.*, **brass·i·er, brass·i·est.** —**brass′i·ly,** *adv.* —**brass′i·ness,** *n.*

---

**branch-plant**     **141**     **brazen**

hat, āge, fär; let, ēqual, tėrm; it, īce
hot, ōpen, ôrder; oil, out; cup, pút, rüle
əbove, takən, pencəl, lemən, circəs
ch, child; ng, long; sh, ship
th, thin; ᴛʜ, then; zh, measure

**brat** (brat) child, especially one who is irritating, disobedient, rude, etc. *n.*

**bra·va·do** (brə vä′dō) a great show of boldness without much real courage; boastful defiance without much real desire to fight. *n.*

**brave** (brāv) **1** having the strength of mind to control fear and act firmly in the face of danger or difficulties; courageous: *She showed she was brave when she stood up to the bully.* **2** showing bravery: *a brave act.* **3** a courageous person. **4** meet bravely: *Soldiers brave much danger.* **5** dare defy: *She braved the king's anger.* **6** making a fine appearance; showy: *The fair had brave displays.* **7** a North American Indian warrior. **8** fine; excellent. 1, 2, 6, 8 *adj.*, **brav·er, brav·est;** 3, 7 *n.*, 4, 5 *v.*, **braved, brav·ing.** —**brave′ly,** *adv.* —**brave′ness,** *n.*

**brav·er·y** (brā′və rē *or* brā′vrē) **1** strength of mind in the face of danger or difficulties; courage. **2** fine appearance; showy dress; finery. *n., pl.* **brav·er·ies.**

**bra·vo¹** (brä′vo) **1** well done! fine! excellent! **2** the cry of "Bravo!": *The audience applauded the actors loudly and many bravos were heard.* 1 *interj.*, 2 *n., pl.* **bra·vos.**

**bra·vo²** (brä′vō *or* brā′vō) a hired fighter or murderer. *n., pl.* **bra·voes** or **bra·vos.**

**bra·vu·ra** (brə vyü′rə) **1** a piece of music requiring skill and spirit in the performer. **2** a display of daring; an attempt at brilliant performance; dash; spirit. *n.*

**brawl** (brol) **1** a noisy and disorderly quarrel: *The hockey game turned into a brawl.* **2** quarrel in a noisy and disorderly way. **3** BABBLE (def. 6). 1 *n.*, 2, 3 *v.* —**brawl′er,** *n.*

**brawn** (bron) **1** muscle; firm, strong muscles. **2** muscular strength: *Football requires brains as well as brawn.* **3** boiled and pickled meat from a boar or pig. *n.*

**brawn·y** (bron′ē) strong; muscular. *adj.*, **brawn·i·er, brawn·i·est.** —**brawn′i·ness,** *n.*

**bray¹** (brā) **1** the loud, harsh sound made by a donkey. **2** a noise like it. **3** make a loud, harsh sound: *The man brayed with laughter.* **4** utter in a loud, harsh voice. 1, 2 *n.*, 3, 4 *v.*

**bray²** (brā) pound or crush into fine bits; grind into a powder. *v.*

**braze¹** (brāz) **1** cover or decorate with brass. **2** make like brass. *v.*, **brazed, braz·ing.**

**braze²** (brāz) SOLDER with any of various solders having a high melting point. *v.*, **brazed, braz·ing.**

**bra·zen** (brā′zən) **1** shameless; impudent: *brazen behaviour.* **2** make shameless or impudent. **3** made of brass. **4** like brass in colour or strength. **5** loud and harsh: *the brazen bellow of a horn.* 1, 3–5 *adj.*, 2 *v.* —**bra′zen·ly,** *adv.* —**bra′zen·ness,** *n.*
**brazen a thing out** or **through,** act as if one did not feel ashamed of it.

**bra·zier** (brā′zhər *or* brā′zē ər)   a metal container to hold burning charcoal or coal: *Braziers are used in some countries for heating rooms.*   *n.*

**Bra·zil·ian** (brə zil′yən)   **1** of Brazil, a country in South America, or its people.   **2** a native or inhabitant of Brazil.   **1** *adj.*, **2** *n.*

**Brazil nut**   a large, triangular, edible nut of a tropical South American tree.

**breach** (brēch)   **1** an opening made by breaking down something solid; gap: *There is a breach in the hedge where I ran through it with my bicycle.*   **2** break through; make an opening in: *The enemy's fierce attack finally breached the wall.*   **3** the breaking or neglect of a law, promise, duty, etc.: *For her to go away today would be a breach of duty.*   **4** a breaking of friendly relations; quarrel.   **1, 3, 4** *n.*, **2** *v.*
☛ *Hom.* BREECH.

**breach of faith**   a breaking of a promise.

**breach of promise**   a breaking of a promise to marry.

**breach of the peace**   a public disturbance; riot.

**bread** (bred)   **1** a food made of flour or meal mixed with milk or water and, usually, yeast, that is kneaded, shaped into loaves, and baked.   **2** food or livelihood: *How will you earn your daily bread?*   **3** cover with bread crumbs or meal before cooking.   **1, 2** *n.*, **3** *v.*
—**bread′less**, *adj.*

**break bread**,   share a meal.

**cast one's bread upon the waters**,   do good with little or no prospect of reward.

**know which side one's bread is buttered on**,   know what is to one's advantage.
☛ *Hom.* BRED.

**bread and butter**   *Informal.*   necessities; a living.

**bread–and–butter** (bred′ən but′ər)   **1** *Informal.* prosaic; commonplace.   **2** expressing thanks for hospitality: *a bread-and-butter letter.*   *adj.*

**bread·board** (bred′bôrd′)   **1** a board on which dough is kneaded, pastry is rolled, etc.   **2** a board on which bread is cut.   *n.*

**bread·fruit** (bred′früt′)   **1** a large, round, starchy, tropical fruit of the Pacific islands, much used for food: *When baked, breadfruit tastes somewhat like bread.*   **2** the tree that it grows on.   *n.*

**bread line**   a line of people waiting to get food given as charity or relief.

**bread·stuff** (bred′stuf′)   **1** grain, flour, or meal for making bread.   **2** bread.   *n.*

**breadth** (bredth)   **1** how broad a thing is; the distance across; width: *The breadth of his shoulders suggested great strength.*   **2** a piece of certain width: *a breadth of cloth.*   **3** freedom from narrowness in views or taste: *She is known for her breadth of mind.*   **4** great extent or scope: *an unusual breadth of learning.*   *n.*

**breadth·ways** (bred′thwāz′)   in the direction of the BREADTH (def. 1).   *adv.*

**breadth·wise** (bred′thwīz′)   BREADTHWAYS.   *adv.*

**bread·win·ner** (bred′win′ər)   a member of a family who earns the family's living.   *n.*

**break** (brāk)   **1** cause to come to pieces by a blow or pull: *How did my glasses get broken?*   **2** come apart; crack; burst: *The plate broke into pieces when it fell on the floor.*   **3** a broken place; gap; crack: *There's a break in the dam.*   **4** breaking or shattering; fracture; rupture.   **5** destroy evenness, wholeness, etc.: *to break a five-dollar bill. She gave all her china to one daughter because she didn't want to break the set.*   **6** injure; damage; ruin; destroy: *She broke her watch by winding it too tightly.*   **7** fracture the bone of; dislocate: *to break one's arm, one's neck.*   **8** fail to keep; act against: *to break a law, to break a promise.*   **9** force one's way: *to break loose from prison, to break into a house.*   **10** a forcing of one's way out.   **11** come suddenly: *The storm broke within ten minutes.*   **12** become less or stop suddenly: *The spell of rainy weather has broken. Her fever broke after midnight.*   **13** an abrupt or marked change.   **14** a short interruption in work, athletic practice, etc.: *a break for coffee at ten. The coach told us to take a break for five minutes.*   **15** decrease the force of; lessen: *Because the bushes broke his fall, he was not hurt.*   **16** be crushed; give way: *The dog's heart broke when her master died.*   **17** dawn; appear: *The day is breaking.*   **18** stop; put an end to: *to break a habit.*   **19** reduce in rank: *The captain was broken for neglect of duty.*   **20** train to obey; tame: *to break a colt.*   **21** go beyond; exceed: *The speed of the new train has broken all records.*   **22** dig or plough land, especially for the first time: *In the forests of Upper Canada the pioneers had to work hard to break the ground.*   **23** make known; reveal: *to break the bad news gently.*   **24** train away from a habit: *He's trying to break himself of nail biting.*   **25** open an electric circuit.   **26** the act or fact of making an electric circuit incomplete.   **27** *Informal.*   a chance; opportunity: *Finding the money was a lucky break.*   **1, 2, 5–9, 11, 12, 15–25** *v.*, **broke, bro·ken, break·ing;**   **3, 4, 10, 13, 14, 26, 27** *n.*

**break away**,   **a** leave or escape, especially suddenly: *He broke away from his captors. She finally broke away from her parents and got an apartment of her own.*   **b** start before the signal: *The horse was disqualified for breaking away.*

**break down**,   **a** go out of order; cease to work.   **b** collapse; become weak: *Her health broke down.*   **c** begin to cry.   **d** analyse; separate into components: *Water can be broken down into its component elements by passing an electric current through it. We broke our total holiday budget down into expenses for food, hotels, transportation and extras.*

**break even**, *Informal.*   finish with the same amount one started with; not win or lose in: *She had hoped to sell her bicycle at a profit, but she could only break even.*

**break in**,   **a** prepare for work or use; train: *It was his responsibility to break in the new office boy.*   **b** enter illegally or by force: *The thieves broke in through the cellar.*   **c** interrupt: *He broke in with a funny remark.*

**break into**,   **a** enter suddenly, by force, or illegally: *Our house was broken into while we were away. He broke into the room, yelling, "Who took my sweater?"*   **b** begin suddenly: *I almost fell off when my horse broke into a gallop.*   **c** interrupt: *She didn't want to break into the conversation, so she kept quiet.*   **d** enter a profession or activity, especially with some difficulty: *She's been trying for months to break into the advertising business.*

**break of**,   cure of: *How can we break her of biting her nails?*

**break off**,   **a** stop suddenly: *He broke off in the middle of his speech.*   **b** stop being friends.

**break out**,   **a** begin or arise suddenly or unexpectedly: *Fire broke out in the basement.*   **b** have an eruption of pimples, rashes, etc., on the skin: *The child broke out in measles.*   **c** escape from prison: *Ten convicts have broken out in the last year.*

**break short**,   bring to a sudden end.

**break through**,   **a** of the sun, appear from behind clouds.   **b** overcome opposition.   **c** make a new discovery.

**break trail**, *Cdn.* move ahead of a dog team, vehicle, or person, making a way through deep snow: *The leader went ahead on snowshoes, breaking trail for the dogs.*
**break up**, **a** scatter: *The fog is breaking up.* **b** stop; put an end to: *We broke up our meeting early today.* **c** *Informal.* upset; disturb greatly. **d** break into pieces: *to break up lumps of earth.* **e** *Informal.* stop being friends: *They've broken up.* **f** collapse with laughter.
**break with**, stop being friends with: *He broke with me after our fight.*
**get a break** or **the breaks**, *Informal.* have things come easily; have lots of luck.
☛ *Hom.* BRAKE.

**break·a·ble** (brā′kə bəl) that can be cracked or shattered, especially objects of glass, china, etc., or delicate mechanisms: *Is there anything breakable in this box?* *adj.*

**break·age** (brā′kij) **1** a breaking; break. **2** damage or loss caused by breaking. **3** an allowance made for such damage or loss. *n.*

**break dancing** a modern style of dancing in which dancers wriggle and bend the arms and legs and often spin on their backs on the floor. It is performed by individuals or groups to music with a strong beat.

**break·down** (brāk′doun′) **1** a failure to work: *a breakdown in machinery.* **2** a loss of health; weakness; collapse: *a mental breakdown.* **3** a noisy, lively dance. **4** the division of a process into steps or stages; ANALYSIS. *n.*

**break·er** (brā′kər) **1** a wave that breaks into foam on the shore, rocks, etc. **2** a machine for breaking things into smaller pieces. *n.*

**break·fast** (brek′fəst) **1** the first meal of the day. **2** eat breakfast: *We breakfasted at 7:30 a.m.* **1** *n.*, **2** *v.*
☛ *Etym.* From an old phrase *to break one's fast.*

**break–in** (brā′kin′) BURGLARY. *n.*

**breaking and entering** in law, the entry into a house, office, vehicle, etc. with the intention of committing a crime.

**break·neck** (brāk′nek′) likely to cause a broken neck; very dangerous: *breakneck speed.* *adj.*

**break of day** dawn.

**break·out** (brā′kout) **1** the act or condition of escaping from a prison, etc. **2** BREAKTHROUGH (def. 2). *n.*

**break·through** (brāk′thrü′) **1** the solution of a problem, especially in science or technology, that has an important effect on all future research and development: *The development of the transistor was a major breakthrough in electronics.* **2** an offensive military operation that gets all the way through a defensive system into the unorganized area in the rear. *n.*

**break–up** or **break·up** (brā′kup′) **1** *Cdn.* the breaking of the ice on a river or lake in spring: *We stood on the bridge and watched the break-up.* **2** *Cdn.* especially in the North, the time when this happens; spring: *They planned to start work on the new road after break-up.* **3** a scattering; separation. **4** a stopping; end. **5** collapse; decay. *n.*

# breakable 143 breath

hat, āge, fär; let, ēqual, tėrm; it, īce
hot, ōpen, ôrder; oil, out; cup, put, rüle
əbove, takən, pencəl, lemən, circəs
ch, child; ng, long; sh, ship
th, thin; ᴛʜ, then; zh, measure

A concrete breakwater

**break·wa·ter** (brā′kwot′ər) a wall or barrier built near the shore to break the force of waves and make an area of calm water for a harbour or beach. *n.*

**bream**¹ (brēm) **1** a CARP of inland European water. **2** the common freshwater SUNFISH. *n.*, *pl.* **bream** or **breams**.

**bream**² (brēm) clean a ship's bottom. *v.*

**breast** (brest) **1** either of the two milk-producing glands on the chest of the human female. **2** a similar gland in certain other mammals. **3** the upper, front part of the human body; chest. **4** the corresponding part in animals. See LAMB and VEAL for pictures. **5** the upper, front part of a coat, dress, etc. **6** anything suggesting the human breast in shape or position. **7** the heart or feelings. **8** oppose; face; struggle with; advance against: *The experienced swimmer was able to breast the waves. He breasted every trouble as it came.* 1–7 *n.*, 8 *v.*
**make a clean breast of,** confess fully; tell everything.

**breast·bone** (brest′bōn′) the thin, flat bone in the front of the chest to which the ribs are attached; sternum. See COLLARBONE for picture. *n.*

**breast–feed** (brest′fēd′) feed a baby at the mother's breast rather than from a bottle; nurse; suckle. *v.* **breast–fed, breast–feed·ing.**

**breast·pin** (brest′pin′) an ornamental pin worn on the breast; brooch. *n.*

**breast·plate** (brest′plāt′) **1** a piece of armour for the chest. See ARMOUR for picture. **2** formerly, a vestment set with jewels worn by Jewish high priests. *n.*

**breast stroke** a swimming stroke performed while face down in the water, the swimmer bringing both arms forward from the breast and then sweeping them out to the sides and back down, while moving the legs in a frog kick.

**breast·work** (bres′twėrk′) a low, hastily built wall for defence. *n.*

**breath** (breth) **1** air drawn into and forced out of the lungs: *Hold your breath a moment.* **2** a drawing in or forcing out of air: *She took a deep breath.* **3** moisture from breathing: *You can see your breath on a very cold day.* **4** the ability to breathe easily: *Running makes a person lose his breath.* **5** a slight movement of the air. **6** a whisper. **7** a short pause or rest; breather: *Let's take a breath here.* **8** a trace or suggestion: *The slightest breath of scandal would ruin her.* *n.*
**catch one's breath, a** gasp. **b** stop for breath; rest: *They sat down on a rock to catch their breath.*

**in the same breath,** at the same time or almost the same time: *He offered to help and in the same breath said he was very busy.*
**out of breath,** breathing very hard as a result of exertion: *She was so out of breath from the run that she could hardly speak.*
**save one's breath,** *Informal.* avoid useless effort in trying to convince: *I know he won't help, so you might as well save your breath.*
**take one's breath away,** leave one breathless because of awe, surprise, etc.
**under** or **below one's breath,** in a whisper: *She was talking under her breath so we couldn't hear her.*

**breathe** (brēŦH) **1** draw air into the lungs and force it out. **2** stop for breath; rest: *I need a moment to breathe.* **3** say softly; whisper; utter: *"Don't move until I give the signal," she breathed.* **4** be alive; live. **5** draw into the lungs; inhale. **6** send out from the lungs; exhale: *The dragon breathed fire and smoke.* **7** inspire; impart; give: *Her enthusiasm breathed new life into the team.* **8** make apparent; show clearly: *His whole appearance breathes confidence.* **9** blow lightly. **10** allow to rest and breathe: *She stopped several times to breathe her horse.* *v.,* **breathed, breath·ing.**
**breathe again** or **freely,** be relieved; feel easy.
**breathe a word of,** tell a secret.
**breathe down someone's neck,** watch someone closely.
**breathe new life into,** enable to make a fresh start.

**breath·er** (brē'ŦHər) a short stop for breath; rest. *n.*

**breath·ing** (brē'ŦHing) **1** RESPIRATION. **2** a single breath. **3** the time needed for a single breath. **4** ppr. of BREATHE. 1–3 *n.,* 4 *v.*

**breathing space** room or time enough to breathe easily; an opportunity to rest.

**breath·less** (breth'lis) **1** out of breath: *Running very fast makes you breathless.* **2** holding one's breath because of fear, interest, excitement, etc.: *The beauty of the scenery left Anna breathless.* **3** without breath; lifeless. *adj.* —**breath·less·ly,** *adv.* —**breath'less·ness,** *n.*

**breath·tak·ing** (breth'tā'king) thrilling; exciting: *a breathtaking ride on a roller coaster.* *adj.*

**brec·ci·a** (brech'ē ə) a kind of sedimentary rock consisting of angular fragments of older rocks naturally cemented together. *n.*

**bred** (bred) pt. and pp. of BREED: *He bred livestock for market. This child has been very well bred.* *v.*
☞ *Hom.* BREAD.

**breech** (brēch) **1** the lower part; back part. **2** in a firearm, the opening, directly behind the barrel, where the shells are inserted. **3** the rump or buttocks. **4** clothe with BREECHES. 1–3 *n.,* 4 *v.*
☞ *Hom.* BREACH.

**breech·cloth** (brēch'kloth') a covering for the loins consisting of a length of a cloth or leather passed between the legs and fastened around the waist; LOINCLOTH: *Breechcloths were formerly worn by some North American Indian peoples.* *n.*

**breech·es** (brich'iz or brē'chiz) **1** short trousers covering the hips and thighs and fastened snugly at or just below the knees. **2** *Informal.* trousers. *n. pl.*

**breeches buoy** a pair of short canvas trousers fastened to a belt or life preserver: *A breeches buoy slides along a rope on a pulley and is used to move people from one ship to another or from ship to shore, especially in rescue operations.*

**breech·ing** (brich'ing or brē'ching) **1** the part of a harness that passes around a horse's hind quarters. **2** ppr. of BREECH. 1 *n.,* 2 *v.*

**breech-load·ing** (brēch'lō'ding) of guns, loading from behind the barrel instead of at the mouth. *adj.*

**breed** (brēd) **1** produce young: *Rabbits breed rapidly.* **2** mate: *Polar bears breed only every other year.* **3** develop different or superior types of an animal or plant by selective mating of outstanding individuals of one type or of two closely related types: *She breeds horses for harness racing.* **4** bring about; be the cause of: *Despair often breeds violence. Careless driving breeds accidents.* **5** be produced or caused. **6** bring up; train: *He was bred a sailor.* **7** a distinctive type of a particular species of animal having recognizable inherited characteristics that are the result of a long period of selective mating: *By mating only animals showing tendencies toward desired characteristics, people have produced many breeds of dog, horse, pigeon, etc. that suit specific purposes of usefulness or beauty.* **8** kind; sort: *It takes a strong, tough breed of person to survive in the wilderness.* 1–6 *v.,* **bred, breed·ing;** 7, 8 *n.*

**breed·er** (brē'dər) **1** a person who breeds animals: *a dog breeder.* **2** an animal that produces offspring. **3** a source; cause: *Great inequalities are breeders of revolutions.* **4** BREEDER REACTOR. *n.*

**breeder reactor** a nuclear reactor that produces at least as much fissionable material as it uses. One type consumes uranium and produces plutonium.

**breed·ing** (brē'ding) **1** the producing of offspring. **2** the producing of animals or plants, especially to get improved kinds. **3** bringing up or training in social behaviour: *Politeness is a sign of good breeding.* **4** in nuclear physics, the production in a reactor of at least as much fissionable material as is used. **5** ppr. of BREED. 1–4 *n.,* 5 *v.*

**breeze** (brēz) **1** a light wind. **2** *Informal.* a disturbance; quarrel. **3** *Informal.* move or proceed easily or briskly: *She breezed along the corridors.* **4** *Informal.* an easy task: *That math problem was a breeze.* 1, 2, 4 *n.,* 3 *v.,* **breezed, breez·ing.**
**breeze through,** proceed, pass, or perform with ease: *She breezed through her homework. John finally breezed through his driving test.*

**breeze·way** (brē'zwā') a roofed passage open at the sides, between a main building and a lesser building, such as between a house and a garage. *n.*

**breez·y** (brē'zē) **1** that has a breeze; with light winds blowing. **2** brisk; lively; jolly: *We like her breezy, joking manner.* *adj.,* **breez·i·er, breez·i·est.** —**breez'i·ly,** *adv.* —**breez'i·ness,** *n.*

**breth·ren** (breŦH'rən) the male members of a church, society, or religious order. *n. pl.*

**Bret·on** (bret'ən) **1** a native or inhabitant of Brittany, a region in northwestern France. **2** the Celtic language of Brittany. **3** having to do with Brittany, its people, or their language. 1, 2 *n.,* 3 *adj.*

**breve** (brēv) **1** the curved mark (˘) put over a vowel or syllable to show that it is short. **2** in music, a note equal to two whole notes. *n.*

**brev·i·ty** (brev′ə tē) shortness; briefness. *n., pl.* **brev·i·ties.**

**brew** (brü) **1** make beer, ale, etc. from malt, etc. by steeping, boiling, and fermenting. **2** make a drink by steeping, boiling, or mixing: *Tea is brewed in boiling water.* **3** a drink made by brewing. **4** the quantity brewed at one time. **5** bring about; plan; plot: *Those boys are brewing some mischief.* **6** begin to form; gather: *A storm is brewing.* 1, 2, 5, 6, *v.*, 3, 4, *n.*

**brew·er** (brü′ər) a person who brews beer, ale, etc. *n.*

**brew·er·y** (brü′ə rē) a place where beer, ale, etc. are brewed. *n., pl.* **brew·er·ies.**

**brew·ing** (brü′ing) **1** the preparing of a BREW. **2** the amount brewed at one time. **3** ppr. of BREW. 1, 2 *n.*, 3 *v.*

**bri·ar** (brī′ər) See BRIER. *n.*

**bri·ar-root** (brī′ər rüt′) See BRIER-ROOT. *n.*

**bri·ar·wood** (brī′ər wůd′) See BRIERWOOD. *n.*

**bri·ar·y** (brī′ər ē) See BRIERY. *adj.*

**bribe** (brīb) **1** anything given or offered to get someone to do something dishonest or illegal for the benefit of the giver. **2** a reward for doing something that one does not want to do: *She should not need a bribe to do well in school.* **3** influence by giving a bribe; give or offer a bribe to: *A gambler bribed one of the boxers to lose the fight.* 1, 2 *n.*, 3 *v.*, **bribed, brib·ing** —**brib′a·ble,** *adj.* —**brib′er,** *n.*

**brib·er·y** (brī′bə rē) **1** the giving or offering of a BRIBE. **2** the taking of a BRIBE. *n., pl.* **brib·er·ies.**

**bric-a-brac** or **bric-à-brac** (brik′ə brak′) a collection of interesting or curious knick-knacks used as decorations; small ornaments, such as vases, old china, or small statues: *They have a cabinet for all their bric-a-brac.* *n.*

**brick** (brik) **1** a block of clay baked by sun or fire, used in building and paving. **2** such blocks considered together as building material: *Our fireplace is built of brick.* **3** made of bricks. **4** anything shaped like a brick: *Ice cream is often sold in bricks.* **5** build or pave with bricks. **6** cover or line with bricks: *Sheena's father bricked the walk in front of his house.* **7** *Informal.* a good person; one who is generous and dependable. 1–4, 7 *n.*, 5, 6 *v.*
**brick in** or **up,** close or fill up with bricks: *The old doorway was bricked up by the workers.*

**brick·bat** (brik′bat′) **1** a piece of broken brick, especially one used as a missile. **2** *Informal.* an insult. *n.*

**brick·lay·er** (brik′lā′ər) a person whose work is building with bricks. *n.*

**brick·work** (brik′wėrk′) **1** anything made of bricks. See MASONRY for picture. **2** the act or process of building with bricks; laying bricks. *n.*

**brick·yard** (brik′yärd′) a place where bricks are made or sold. *n.*

**bri·dal** (brī′dəl) **1** of a bride or a wedding. **2** wedding. 1 *adj.*, 2 *n.*
☞ *Hom.* BRIDLE.

**bridal wreath** a commonly cultivated species of spiraea having long sprays of small, white flowers that bloom in the spring.

hat, āge, fär; let, ēqual, tėrm; it, īce
hot, ōpen, ôrder; oil, out; cup, půt, rüle
ə*bove, tak*ə*n, penc*ə*l, lem*ə*n, circ*əs
ch, child; ng, long; sh, ship
th, thin; ᴛʜ, then; zh, measure

**bride** (brīd) a woman just married or about to be married. *n.*

**bride·groom** (brīd′grüm′) a man just married or about to be married. *n.*

**brides·maid** (brīdz′mād′) a young, usually unmarried woman who attends the bride at a wedding. *n.*

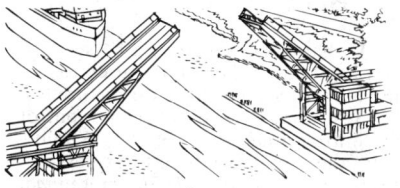

A bascule bridge on the Welland Canal in Ontario

The Quebec Bridge— the longest cantilever span in the world

The suspension bridge at Dunvegan, Alberta

**bridge¹** (brij) **1** a structure built over a river, road, etc. so that people, trains, etc. can get across. **2** build a bridge over: *The engineers bridged the river.* **3** form a bridge over; extend over; span: *A log bridged the brook.* **4** make a way over: *Politeness will bridge many difficulties.* **5** a platform above the deck of a ship for the officer in command. **6** the upper, bony part of the nose. **7** the curved part of a pair of eyeglasses that rests on the nose. **8** a mounting for a false tooth or teeth fastened to the real teeth nearby. **9** a movable piece over which the strings of a violin, etc. are stretched. 1, 5–9 *n.*, 2–4 *v.*, **bridged, bridg·ing.**
**bridge over,** help or deal with for a short time: *This loan will bridge over our difficulties.*
**burn one's bridges,** cut off all chances of retreat.

**bridge²** (brij) a card game for two teams of two players each, played with 52 cards. *n.*

**bridge·head** (brij′hed′) **1** a position obtained and held by advance troops within enemy territory, used as a starting point for further attack. **2** any position taken as a foothold from which to make further advances: *She was able to make her first television job a bridgehead to a spectacular career in broadcasting.* **3** a fortification protecting the end of a bridge nearer to the enemy. *n.*

**bridge·work** (brij′wėrk′) false teeth in a mounting fastened to real teeth nearby. *n.*

**bridg·ing** (brij′ing) **1** the braces placed between two beams to strengthen them and to keep them apart. **2** *ppr.* of BRIDGE. **1** *n.*, **2** *v.*

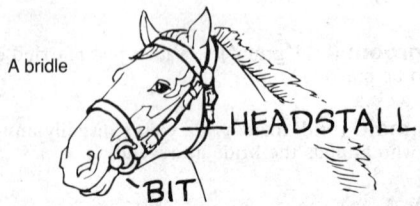
A bridle

**bri·dle** (brī′dəl) **1** a harness fitted about a horse's head, consisting of a headstall, bit, and reins, used to guide or control the horse. See HARNESS for picture. **2** put a bridle on. **3** anything that holds back or controls. **4** hold back; check; control: *Bridle your temper.* **5** hold the head up high with the chin drawn back to express pride, vanity, scorn, or anger: *Geeta bridled when we made fun of her new shoes.* **6** *Cdn.* the loop of a snowshoe in which the toe of the boot or moccasin is placed. **1, 3, 6** *n.*, **2, 4, 5** *v.*, **bri·dled, bri·dling.** —**bri′dler,** *n.* ☛ *Hom.* BRIDAL.

**brief** (brēf) **1** lasting only a short time: *a brief meeting.* **2** using few words: *a brief announcement.* **3** a short statement; summary. **4** a formal statement of opinion for submission to an authority: *She submitted a brief to the Royal Commission on Taxation.* **5** a statement of the facts and the points of law of a case to be pleaded in court. **6** make a brief of; summarize. **7** furnish with a brief. **8** give a BRIEFING to: *She briefed him on how to approach the new client.* **9 briefs,** *pl.* short, close-fitting underpants. **1, 2** *adj.*, **3–5, 9** *n.*, **6–8** *v.* —**brief′ly,** *adv.* —**brief′ness,** *n.*
**hold a brief for,** argue for; support; defend.
**in brief,** in few words.

**brief·case** (brēf′kās′) a flat container for carrying loose papers, books, drawings, etc. *n.*

**brief·ing** (brē′fing) **1** the act or an instance of giving necessary information or exact instructions for a specific job, assignment, etc.: *The briefing for the combat mission was given by the commanding officer.* **2** the information or instruction given. **3** *ppr.* of BRIEF. **1, 2** *n.*, **3** *v.*

**bri·er**[1] (brī′ər) **1** any of various kinds of thorny or prickly bush, especially the wild rose. **2** a thorn or thorny twig. **3** a tangled growth of briers. *n.* Also, **briar.**

**bri·er**[2] (brī′ər) **1** an evergreen shrub of southern Europe having a hard, woody root used for making tobacco pipes. **2** a tobacco pipe made of BRIER-ROOT. *n.* Also (especially def. 2), **briar.**

**bri·er-root** (brī′ər rüt′) **1** the root of the brier, used for tobacco pipes. **2** a pipe made of this root. *n.* Also, **briar-root.**

**bri·er·wood** (brī′ər wùd′) BRIER-ROOT. *n.* Also, **briarwood.**

**bri·er·y** (brī′ə rē) full of thorns or briers: *briery undergrowth.* *adj.* Also, **briary.**

A brig

**brig** (brig) **1** a square-rigged ship with two masts. **2** the prison on a warship. *n.*

**bri·gade** (bri gād′) **1** a part of an army, usually made up of two or more regiments. **2** any group of people organized for some purpose: *Fire brigades fight fires.* **3** *Cdn.* formerly, a fleet of canoes, bateaux, Red River carts, dog sleds, etc. carrying trade goods, supplies, etc. to and from inland posts. *n.*

**brig·and** (brig′ənd) a person who robs travellers on the road; robber; bandit. *n.*

**brig·and·age** (brig′ən dij) robbery; plundering. *n.*

**brig·an·tine** (brig′ən tēn′) a two-masted ship having the foremast square-rigged and the mainmast fore-and-aft rigged. *n.*

**bright** (brīt) **1** giving or reflecting much light; shining: *The sun is too bright to look at directly. Chrome is very bright.* **2** very light or clear: *a bright day.* **3** quick-witted; clever: *She's a bright girl and learns quickly.* **4** vivid; glowing: *bright colours.* **5** lively; cheerful: *a bright smile.* **6** likely to turn out well; favourable: *a bright outlook for the future.* **7** splendid; glorious: *The knight was a bright example of courage in battle.* **8** in a bright manner: *The fire shines bright.* **1–7** *adj.*, **8** *adv.* —**bright′ly,** *adv.* —**bright′ness,** *n.*

**bright·en** (brī′tən) **1** become bright or brighter: *The sky brightened.* **2** make bright or brighter: *She brightened the room with flowers.* **3** make happy or cheerful. **4** become happy or cheerful: *Her face brightened.* *v.*

**Bright's disease** a kidney disease characterized by albumin in the urine.

**brill** (bril) a European flatfish related to the TURBOT. *n.*, *pl.* **brill** or **brills.**

**bril·liance** (bril′yəns) **1** great brightness; radiance; sparkle. **2** splendour; magnificence. **3** great ability: *brilliance as a pianist.* *n.*

**bril·liant** (bril′yənt) **1** shining brightly; sparkling: *brilliant jewels, brilliant sunshine.* **2** splendid; magnificent; distinguished: *They say she has a brilliant future in politics.* **3** having or showing great ability: *a brilliant performance, a brilliant scholar.* **4** a diamond or other gem cut to sparkle brightly. **1–3** *adj.*, **4** *n.* —**bril′liant·ly,** *adv.*

**brim** (brim) **1** the edge of a cup, bowl, etc.; rim: *I filled my glass to the brim.* **2** fill or be full to the brim: *The pond is brimming with water as a result of the hard rains.* **3** the projecting edge of something: *The hat's wide brim shaded her eyes from the sun.* **4** an edge bordering water; water at the edge: *He drank at the fountain's brim.* **1, 3, 4** *n.*, **2** *v.*, **brimmed, brim·ming.** —**brim′less,** *adj.*
**brim over, a** overflow. **b** be full of: *brimming over with joy.*

**brim·ful** (brim′fùl′) full to the brim; full to the very top. *adj.*

**brim·stone** (brim′stōn′) SULPHUR. *n.*

**brin·dle** (brin′dəl) **1** BRINDLED. **2** a BRINDLED colour. **3** a BRINDLED animal. 1 *adj.*, 2, 3 *n.*

**brin·dled** (brin′dəld) grey, tan, or tawny with darker streaks and spots. *adj.*

**brine** (brīn) **1** very salty water: *Pickles are often kept in brine.* **2** a salt lake or sea; ocean. *n.*

**bring** (bring) **1** carry or take with oneself to a place; come to a place with: *I didn't bring enough money. He brought his cousin to the party. Bring me a clean plate, please. The bus brought us home from school.* **2** cause to come: *What brings you into town today?* **3** cause to do something; persuade; induce: *Our arguments finally brought him to agree. I can't bring myself to finish another page tonight.* **4** present before a law court: *She brought a charge against me.* **5** sell for: *Meat is bringing a high price this week.* *v.*, **brought, bring·ing.**
**bring about,** cause; cause to happen: *The flood was brought about by heavy rain.*
**bring around** or **bring round, a** restore to consciousness: *The fresh air soon brought him around.* **b** convince; persuade: *At first her parents refused to let her go to the party, but she brought them around eventually.*
**bring down, a** destroy; kill; defeat. **b** reduce a price. **c** make someone reduce a price. **d** move a digit from one column to another. **e** publish: *bring down a budget.*
**bring forth, a** give birth to; bear. **b** reveal; show.
**bring forward, a** reveal; show. **b** in accounting or bookkeeping, carry over from one page to another. **c** produce for consideration: *In his talk he brought forward several new ideas.*
**bring home to,** make someone understand.
**bring in, a** earn. **b** ask someone to help.
**bring in on,** invite someone to take part in.
**bring off,** carry out successfully: *He brought off the deal.*
**bring on, a** cause; cause to happen: *I think my cold was brought on by lack of sleep.* **b** improve; advance.
**bring out, a** reveal; show: *Her paintings bring out the loneliness of the North.* **b** offer to the public: *She brought out a new book of poems.* **c** make someone more sociable.
**bring over,** convince; persuade.
**bring to, a** restore to consciousness: *We tried to bring him to by loosening his clothing.* **b** stop; check.
**bring up, a** care for in childhood. **b** educate or train, especially in social behaviour: *His good manners showed that he had been well brought up.* **c** suggest for action or discussion: *Please bring your plan up at the meeting.* **d** stop suddenly: *The rider brought her horse up at the high fence.* **e** VOMIT.

**bring·ing–up** (bring′ing up′) **1** care in childhood. **2** education; training. *n.*

**brink** (bringk) **1** the edge at the top of a steep place: *the brink of the cliff.* **2** any edge, such as the shore of a river, etc. *n.*
**on the brink of,** very near: *on the brink of a great discovery. His business is on the brink of ruin.*

**brin·y** (brī′nē) **1** of or like BRINE; salty. **2 the briny,** *Informal.* the sea. 1 *adj.*, **brin·i·er, brin·i·est;** 2 *n.* —**brin′i·ness,** *n.*

**bri·oche** (brē′osh; *French,* bRē osh′) a soft roll or bun rich in butter and eggs. *n.*

**bri·quette** or **bri·quet** (bri ket′) a block of pressed charcoal or coal dust used for fuel. *n.*

**brisk** (brisk) **1** acting, moving, or happening quickly; energetic: *The storekeeper told us that business was brisk.*
*She went for a brisk walk.* **2** keen; sharp: *brisk weather.* *adj.* —**brisk′ly,** *adv.* —**brisk′ness,** *n.*

**bris·ket** (bris′kit) **1** the meat from the breast of an animal. See BEEF for picture. **2** the breast of an animal. *n.*

**bris·tle** (bris′əl) **1** one of the short, stiff hairs of a hog or wild boar, used to make brushes. **2** any short, stiff hair of an animal or plant. **3** a synthetic substitute for a hog's bristles: *My toothbrush has nylon bristles.* **4** provide with bristles. **5** stand up straight: *The angry dog's hair bristled.* **6** cause hair to stand up straight. **7** have one's hair stand up straight: *The dog bristled.* **8** show that one is aroused and ready to fight: *The whole country bristled with indignation.* **9** be thick with; be thickly set: *The harbour bristled with boats and ships. Our path bristled with difficulties.* 1–3 *n.*, 4–9 *v.*, **bris·tled, bris·tling.**

**bris·tle·tail** (bris′əl tāl′) any of about 400 species of mostly very tiny wingless insects found throughout the world, having compound eyes, long, segmented feelers, and three long, movable appendages at the end of the abdomen: *The silverfish is one species of bristletail.* *n.*

**bris·tly** (bris′lē) **1** rough with BRISTLES or hair that is like bristles. **2** resembling BRISTLES; short and stiff; prickly. *adj.*, **bris·tli·er, bris·tli·est.**

**Bristol board** (bris′təl) a heavy, stiff, very smooth cardboard used for printing, drawing, and painting.

**Brit.** **1** Britain; British. **2** Briticism.

**Brit·ain** GREAT BRITAIN. *n.*

**brit·ches** (brich′iz) *Informal.* BREECHES. *n. pl.*

**Brit·i·cism** (brit′ə siz′əm) a word or phrase used especially by the British: *Lorry meaning truck is a Briticism.* *n.*

**Brit·ish** (brit′ish) **1** of or having to do with Great Britain or the United Kingdom, or its people. **2 the British,** *pl.* the people of Great Britain or the United Kingdom. 1 *adj.*, 2 *n.*

**Brit·ish Co·lum·bi·an** (kə lum′bē ən) **1** a native or long-term resident of British Columbia. **2** of or having to do with British Columbia. 1 *n.*, 2 *adj.*

**British Commonwealth of Nations** an association of a large number of countries, many of them now completely independent, that were once under British law and government, and are now united under the British monarchy: *All the independent members of the British Commonwealth of Nations, including Canada and the United Kingdom, have equal status.*

**Brit·ish·er** (brit′ish ər) a native or inhabitant of Great Britain or the United Kingdom. *n.*

**British North America Act** the Act of Parliament that in 1867 created the Dominion of Canada by the union of Ontario, Quebec, Nova Scotia, and New Brunswick. The other six provinces joined the federation as follows: Manitoba, 1870; British Columbia, 1871; Prince Edward Island, 1873; Alberta, 1905; Saskatchewan, 1905; Newfoundland, 1949. Since 1981, it has been called the Constitution Act, 1867.

**British thermal unit** a unit for measuring heat; the amount of heat necessary to raise the temperature of one pound of water one degree Fahrenheit (about 1.06 kJ). *Abbrev.*: BTU, Btu, or B.T.U.

**Brit·on** (brit′ən) 1 a native or inhabitant of Great Britain. 2 a member of a Celtic people who lived in southern Britain at the time of the Roman conquest. *n.*

**brit·tle** (brit′əl) rigid but very easily broken; apt to break with a snap rather than bend: *Thin glass and dead twigs are brittle.* *adj.* —**brit′tle·ness,** *n.*

**bro.** or **Bro.** brother.

**broach** (brōch) 1 a pointed tool for making and shaping holes. 2 open by making a hole: *to broach a barrel of cider.* 3 begin to talk about: *to broach a subject.* 4 a sharp-pointed rod or bar on which meat is roasted; a spit. 1, 4 *n.*, 2, 3 *v.* —**broach′er,** *n.*
☛ *Hom.* BROOCH.

**broad** (brôd) 1 large across; wide: *a broad road.* 2 extensive: *a broad rule. He has broad experience in industry.* 3 not limited; liberal; tolerant: *broad ideas.* 4 not detailed; general: *Give a broad outline of the speech.* 5 clear; full: *broad daylight.* 6 plain; obvious; unmistakable: *a broad hint, a broad accent.* *adj.* —**broad′ly,** *adv.*

**broad·axe** (brôd′aks′) an axe with a broad blade. *n., pl.* **broad·ax·es.** Sometimes, **broadax.**

**broad·brim** (brôd′brim′) a hat with a very wide brim, such as the kind once worn by the Quakers. *n.*

**broad·cast** (brôd′kast′) 1 send out by radio or television: *Her speech will be broadcast tonight.* 2 sent out by radio or television: *a broadcast message.* 3 a radio or television program: *This broadcast is coming from St. John's.* 4 scatter or spread widely: *to broadcast seed.* 5 scattered or spread widely: *broadcast sowing.* 6 over a wide surface: *He scattered the seed broadcast.* 7 the act of broadcasting. 8 make widely known: *He broadcast that story all over town.* 1, 4, 8 *v.*, **broad·cast** or (sometimes for def. 1) **broad·cast·ed, broad·cast·ing;** 2, 5 *adj.*, 3, 7 *n.*, 6 *adv.* —**broad′cast·er,** *n.*

**broad·cloth** (brôd′klôth′) 1 a fine, closely woven cloth with a smooth finish, made of cotton, silk, rayon, synthetics, or blends of these fibres and used for shirts, dresses, pyjamas, etc. 2 a smooth, closely woven woollen cloth having a glossy surface and a short nap, used in making suits, coats, etc. *n.*
☛ *Etym.* Originally, **broadcloth** was good woollen cloth made wider than 29 inches (about 74 cm).

**broad·en** (brôd′ən) make or become broad or broader: *The river broadens at its mouth. Travel had broadened her outlook.* *v.*

**broad–gauge** (brôd′gāj′) of a railway, having a width of track greater than the standard gauge of 56 ½ inches (about 144 cm); especially having a width of track of 66 inches (about 168 cm): *The Grand Trunk and Great Western were originally broad-gauge railways.* *adj.*

**broad jump** 1 LONG JUMP. 2 **standing broad jump,** a LONG JUMP from a standing start.

**broad·loom** (brôd′lüm′) 1 woven on a loom or machine at least 1.8 m wide: *a broadloom carpet.* 2 carpeting made on a broad loom, sold by the square metre or square yard and cut to fit the exact dimensions of a room: *We have broadloom in the living room.* 1 *adj.*, 2 *n.*

**broad–mind·ed** (brôd′mīn′did) respecting opinions, customs, or beliefs, that are different from one's own; liberal; not prejudiced or bigoted. *adj.* —**broad′–mind′ed·ness,** *n.*

**broad·side** (brôd′sīd′) 1 the whole side of a ship above the water line. 2 all the guns that can be fired from one side of a ship. 3 the firing of all these guns at the same time: *The broadside caught the pirates completely by surprise.* 4 a violent attack in words; a storm of abuse: *He was met with a broadside from his sister the minute he got home.* 5 a broad surface or side, as of a house. 6 with the side turned toward an object or point: *The ship drifted broadside to the pier.* 7 a large sheet of paper printed on one or both sides: *Girls were distributing broadsides announcing a big sale.* 1–5, 7 *n.*, 6 *adv.*

**broad·sword** (brôd′sôrd′) a sword with a broad, flat blade. *n.*

**Broad·way** (brôd′wā′) 1 in New York City, a street famous for its bright lights, theatres, night clubs, etc. 2 the New York commercial theatre. *n.*

**bro·cade** (brō kād′) 1 heavy cloth woven with a raised design on it: *silk brocade, velvet brocade.* 2 weave or decorate with raised designs. 1 *n.*, 2 *v.*, **bro·cad·ed, bro·cad·ing.**

**bro·cad·ed** (brō kā′did) 1 woven or wrought into a BROCADE (def. 1). 2 pt. and pp. of BROCADE. 1 *adj.*, 2 *v.*

**broc·co·li** (brok′ə lē) 1 a plant closely related to the cabbage and cauliflower, whose green branching stems and unopened flower heads are eaten as a vegetable. 2 the heads and stems used as a vegetable. *n.*
☛ *Etym.* From the Italian name for this vegetable, *broccoli,* meaning literally 'little cabbage sprouts'.

**bro·chure** (brō shür′) a printed booklet or folder, usually having colourful pictures, that advertises or gives information about a place, a product, etc.: *The provincial government puts out a brochure on its parks.* *n.*

**bro·gan** (brō′gən) a heavy, strong work shoe reaching to the ankle. *n.*

**brogue¹** (brōg) 1 any coarse, strong shoe. 2 an oxford shoe made for comfort and long wear. *n.*

**brogue²** (brōg) 1 an Irish accent in the speaking of English. 2 the accent or pronunciation peculiar to any dialect. *n.*

**broil¹** (broil) 1 cook by placing on a rack directly over a fire or in a pan directly under an electric coil or gas flame; grill. 2 make or be very hot: *You will broil in this hot sun.* 3 broiled meat, etc. 1, 2 *v.*, 3 *n.*

**broil²** (broil) 1 an angry quarrel or struggle; BRAWL. 2 quarrel or fight. 1 *n.*, 2 *v.*

**broil·er** (broi′lər) 1 a pan or rack for broiling food. 2 a young chicken for broiling. *n.*

**broke** (brōk) 1 pt. of BREAK: *She broke her doll.* 2 *Informal.* without money. 1 *v.*, 2 *adj.*

**bro·ken** (brō′kən) 1 pp. of BREAK: *The window was broken by a ball.* 2 crushed; in pieces: *a broken cup.* 3 weakened in strength, spirit, etc.; tamed; crushed: *He looked a broken man after his loss.* 4 rough; uneven: *broken ground, a broken voice.* 5 acted against; not kept: *a broken promise.* 6 imperfectly spoken: *The girl speaks broken French.* 7 interrupted: *broken sleep.* 1 *v.*, 2–7 *adj.* —**bro′ken·ly,** *adv.* —**bro′ken·ness,** *n.*

**bro·ken–down** (brō′kən doun′) **1** shattered; ruined: *broken-down health.* **2** unfit for use: *a broken-down old car.* *adj.*

**bro·ken–heart·ed** (brō′kən här′tid) crushed by sorrow or grief; heartbroken. *adj.*

**bro·ker** (brō′kər) a person who acts as an agent for other people in arranging contracts, purchases, or sales in return for a fee or commission. *n.*

**bro·ker·age** (brō′kə rij) **1** the business of a BROKER. **2** the money charged by a BROKER for his or her services. *n.*

**bro·mid** (brō′mid) BROMIDE (def. 1). *n.*

**bro·mide** (brō′mīd) **1** a compound of BROMINE with another element or radical. **2** POTASSIUM BROMIDE, a drug used to calm nervousness, cause sleep, etc. **3** a commonplace idea; trite remark. *n.*

**bro·min** (brō′min) BROMINE. *n.*

**bro·mine** (brō′mēn *or* brō′mīn) a heavy, non-metallic element that evaporates quickly, resembling chlorine and iodine: *Bromine is a dark-brown liquid that gives off an irritating vapour. Bromine is used in drugs and dyes and in developing photographs.* Symbol: Br *n.*

**bronc** (brongk) BRONCO. *n.*

**bron·chi** (brong′kī *or* brong′kē) **1** the two main branches of the windpipe, one going to each lung. **2** the smaller, branching tubes in the lungs. See LUNG for picture. *n., pl.* of BRONCHUS.

**bron·chi·a** (brong′kē ə) the BRONCHIAL TUBES, especially the smaller tubes. *n. pl.*

**bron·chi·al** (brong′kē əl) of or having to do with the BRONCHIAL TUBES. *adj.*

**bronchial tubes** the BRONCHI and their branching tubes.

**bron·chit·ic** (brong kit′ik) **1** of or having to do with BRONCHITIS. **2** having BRONCHITIS. *adj.*

**bron·chi·tis** (brong kī′tis) an inflammation of the lining of the BRONCHIAL TUBES. *n.*

**bron·cho** (brong′kō) BRONCO. *n., pl.* **bron·chos.**

**bron·chus** (brong′kəs) one of the BRONCHI. *n., pl.* **bron·chi** (-kī *or* -kē).

**bron·co** *or* **bron·cho** (brong′kō) an untamed or partly tamed horse or pony of western North America. *n., pl.* **bron·cos** *or* **bron·chos.**
☛ *Etym.* From Spanish *bronco* 'rough, rude'. It was first used with reference to a half-tamed horse in California and New Mexico in the 19c.

**bron·co·bust·er** *or* **bron·cho·bust·er** (brong′kō bus′tər) *Informal.* in the West, one who breaks wild horses to the saddle. *n.*

**bron·to·sau·rus** (bron′tə sô′rəs) a huge plant-eating dinosaur, having a long neck, small head, a long tail, and walking on all four legs: *A brontosaurus could weigh up to 20 t.* See DINOSAUR for picture. *n.*

**bronze** (bronz) **1** a brown ALLOY of copper and tin. **2** a similar ALLOY of copper with zinc and other metals. **3** a statue, medal, etc. made of bronze: *She won a bronze in the swimming competition.* **4** made of bronze. **5** yellowish brown; reddish brown. **6** make or become reddish brown: *The sailor was bronzed from the sun.* **7** cover with bronze: *She had his baby shoes bronzed.* 1–3, 5 *n.*, 4, 5 *adj.*, 6, 7 *v.*, **bronzed, bronz·ing.**

hat, āge, fär; let, ēqual, tėrm; it, īce
hot, ōpen, ôrder; oil, out; cup, put, rüle
əbove, takən, pencəl, lemən, circəs
ch, child; ng, long; sh, ship
th, thin; ᴛʜ, then; zh, measure

**Bronze Age** the period of history after the Stone Age, when bronze tools, weapons, etc. were used.

**brooch** (brōch) an ornamental pin having the point secured by a clasp or catch: *Brooches are often made of gold or silver.* *n.*
☛ *Hom.* BROACH.

**brood** (brüd) **1** the young birds hatched at one time in the nest or cared for together: *a brood of chicks.* **2** *Informal.* all the children in one family: *They brought their whole brood along to the party.* **3** kept for breeding: *a brood mare.* **4** sit on eggs in order to hatch them. **5** think or worry a long time about some one thing: *She broods a lot these days.* **6** dwell on in thought: *For years he brooded vengeance.* 1–3 *n.,* 4–6 *v.*
**brood on** *or* **over,** **a** keep thinking about. **b** hover over; hang close over.

**brood·er** (brü′dər) **1** a closed place that can be heated, used in raising chicks, etc. **2** somebody or something that BROODS (defs. 4, 6). **3** a hen BROODING (def. 4) or ready to brood eggs. *n.*

**brood·y** (brü′dē) **1** of hens, ready to BROOD (def. 4) eggs: *When hens become broody, they stop laying.* **2** inclined to dwell on in thought. *adj.*

**brook**[1] (brůk) a small, natural freshwater stream; creek. *n.*

**brook**[2] (brůk) put up with; endure; tolerate: *Her pride would not brook such insults.* *v.*

**brook·let** (brůk′lit) a little BROOK[1]. *n.*

**brook trout** a species of freshwater food and game fish of North America, closely related to the lake trout and the Arctic char, having a long, quite narrow, deep body, a large head, and a square tail; speckled char, mud trout: *The colouring of brook trout varies from olive green to dark brown.*

**broom** (brüm) **1** a long-handled brush for sweeping. **2** a shrub of the same family as the pea, with slender branches, small leaves, and yellow flowers. *n.*

**broom·ball** (brüm′bol *or* brüm′bôl) *Cdn.* a game played on a hockey rink in which the players, with or without skates, use corn brooms and volleyballs instead of hockey sticks and pucks. *n.*

**broom·stick** (brüm′stik) the long handle of a BROOM (def. 1). *n.*

**broth** (broth) **1** a thin soup made from water in which meat or fish and, often, vegetables have been boiled. **2** a thick soup, such as Scotch broth. *n.*

**broth·er** (bruᴛʜ′ər) **1** a son of the same parents; sometimes, a son only of the same mother or father (a half brother). **2** a male who is a very close friend or companion; one who fills the role of a brother: *My cousin is a brother to me.* **3** a male who shares a duty, purpose, ideal, or allegiance: *The two soldiers were brothers in arms. All men are brothers.* **4** a male fellow member of a church who is not a priest. **5** a male member of a religious order who is not a priest; monk. **6** being in or of the same profession or calling: *brother officers.* *n., pl.* **broth·ers** or (for def. 4) **breth·ren.**

**broth·er·hood** (bruᴛH′ər hùd′) **1** the biological relationship between brothers: *He claimed brotherhood with the heir.* **2** a spiritual bond between brothers or as if between brothers: *The two inventors had worked closely together for so long that they had a strong feeling of brotherhood.* **3** an association of men with some common aim, characteristic, belief, profession, etc.: *the brotherhood of locomotive engineers.* *n.*

**broth·er–in–law** (bruᴛH′ə rin lo′) **1** the brother of one's husband or wife. **2** the husband of one's sister. **3** the husband of the sister of one's wife or husband. *n., pl.* **broth·ers-in-law.**

**broth·er·ly** (bruᴛH′ər lē) **1** of or having to do with a brother, or brothers: *There was a strong brotherly love between them although they had been separated since childhood.* **2** showing the affection of a brother; friendly; kindly: *He gave her a brotherly hug and wished her luck in the exam.* *adj.* —**broth′er·li·ness,** *n.*

**brougham** (brō′əm *or* brü′əm)   a closed four-wheeled carriage or automobile having an outside seat for the driver. *n.*

**brought** (brot)   pt. and pp. of BRING: *He brought his lunch yesterday. We were brought to school in a bus.* *v.*

**brow** (brou)   **1** the forehead: *a wrinkled brow.* **2** the arch of hair over the eye; eyebrow. **3** the edge of a steep place; the top of a slope: *on the brow of a hill.* *n.*

**brow·beat** (brou′bēt′)   frighten into doing something by overbearing looks or words; bully (*often followed by* into). *v.,* **brow·beat, brow·beat·en, brow·beat·ing.**

**brown** (broun)   **1** a dark colour like that of toast, potato skins, coffee, etc. **2** of or having this colour. **3** something brown. **4** dark-skinned; tanned: *She was very brown from a summer in the sun.* **5** make or become brown: *Brown the onions in butter.* 1, 3 *n.,* 2, 4 *adj.,* 5 *v.* —**brown′ness,** *n.*

**brown bear**   the largest and most widespread species of bear, found throughout the northern parts of the world, having a short neck and large, doglike head and a thick coat of fur varying in colour from cream to blue-black: *The grizzly is a subspecies of the brown bear.*

**brown betty**   a baked pudding made of apples, bread crumbs, sugar, and spices.

**brown bread**   bread made from whole wheat flour.

**brown coal**   LIGNITE.

**brown·ie** (brou′nē)   **1** a good-natured, helpful elf or fairy. **2 Brownie,**   a member of a junior division of the GIRL GUIDES. **3** a small square or bar of a kind of rich chocolate cake usually containing nuts. *n.*

**brown·ish** (brou′nish)   somewhat brown. *adj.*

**brown rice**   rice grains that have not had the outer layer containing the bran removed; unpolished rice.

**brown·stone** (broun′stōn′)   a reddish-brown sandstone, used as a building material. *n.*

**brown study**   the condition of being absorbed in thought; a serious reverie.

**brown sugar**   refined sugar in which the crystals are coated with dark molasses-flavoured syrup.

**browse** (brouz)   **1** feed on growing plants, especially the tender parts of trees and bushes: *The deer moved through the woods, browsing on young shoots and leaves.* **2** tender shoots, leaves, and twigs of trees and shrubs considered as food for animals: *The gorillas in the zoo were fed browse in the morning.* **3** read here and there in a book or in books; especially, pass the time looking at books in a library or bookstore. **4** look casually at articles for sale in a store. 1, 3, 4 *v.,* **browsed, brows·ing.** 2 *n.* —**brows′er,** *n.*

**bru·in** (brü′ən)   a bear, especially a brown bear. *n.*

**bruise** (brüz)   **1** an injury to the body, caused by a fall or a blow, that breaks blood vessels without breaking the skin: *The bruise on my arm turned black and blue.* **2** an injury to the outside of a fruit, vegetable, plant, etc. **3** make or cause a bruise on: *I bruised my leg. Handle the tomatoes carefully so you don't bruise them.* **4** cause to be hurt: *The harsh words bruised her feelings.* **5** become bruised: *I bruise easily.* 1, 2 *n.,* 3–5 *v.,* **bruised, bruis·ing.**

**bruis·er** (brü′zər) *Informal.* **1** a prize fighter. **2** bully. *n.*

**bruit** (brüt)   **1** spread a report or rumour of: *Rumours of the princess's engagement were bruited about.* *v.*
☛ Hom.  BRUTE.

**bru·lé** *or* **bru·le**   (brü lā′) *Cdn.*   **1** a forest area that has been destroyed by fire. **2** rocky land. *n.*

**brunch** (brunch)   a meal taken in the late morning, that combines breakfast and lunch. *n.*
☛ Etym.  From *breakfast* + *lunch.*

**bru·net** (brü net′)   **1** dark-coloured; having an olive colour. **2** having dark-brown or black hair, and usually brown or black eyes and a dark skin. **3** a man or boy having dark hair. 1, 2 *adj.,* 3 *n.*
☛ Syn.  As a noun, **brunet** is used for men and boys and BRUNETTE is used for women and girls. The usual form for the adjective, however, is **brunet** in all cases: *Henry and his sister are both brunet.* See also the note at BLOND.

**bru·nette** (brü net′)   a woman or girl having dark hair: *My mother and my two sisters are all brunettes.* *n.*
☛ Syn.  See note at BRUNET.

**brunt** (brunt)   the main force or violence; the hardest part: *the brunt of the hurricane.* *n.*

**brush¹** (brush)   **1** a tool for cleaning, sweeping, scrubbing, painting, etc.: *A brush is made of bristles, hair, or wires set in a stiff back or fastened to a handle.* **2** clean, sweep, paint, etc. with a brush; use a brush on. **3** brushing; rub with a brush: *Jose gave his puppy a good brush.* **4** remove; wipe away: *The child brushed the tears from his eyes.* **5** touch lightly in passing: *No harm was done; your bumper just brushed ours.* **6** a light touch in passing: *Give the desk a brush with the cloth.* **7** a short, brisk fight or quarrel: *The strikers had a sharp brush with the police, but no one was hurt.* **8** move quickly. **9** the bushy tail of an animal, especially of a fox. **10** a piece of carbon, copper, etc. used to conduct the electricity from the revolving part of a motor or generator to the outside circuit. See GENERATOR for picture. **11** the style of an artist: *She paints with a bold brush.* 1, 3, 6, 7, 9–11 *n.,* 2, 4, 5, 8 *v.*
**brush aside** *or* **away,**   put aside; refuse to consider.
**brush off,** *Informal.*   refuse or dismiss a request, person, etc. in a curt or disdainful way: *He brushed us off when we asked for his autograph.*
**brush up** *or* **brush up on,**   refresh one's memory of by study; review: *I still have to brush up on some theorems for the geometry test tomorrow.*

**brush²** (brush)   **1** branches broken or cut off.

**2** shrubs, brushes, and small trees growing thickly together. **3** a thinly settled country; backwoods. *n.*

**brush·off** (brush′of′) *Informal.* a curt or offhand dismissal or refusal of a request, person, etc.: *When I asked for an appointment, I got a brushoff.* *n.*

**brush wolf** *Cdn.* COYOTE.

**brush·wood** (brush′wůd′) BRUSH² (defs. 1, 2). *n.*

**brush·y¹** (brush′ē) like a brush; rough and shaggy. *adj.*, **brush·i·er, brush·i·est.**

**brush·y²** (brush′ē) covered with bushes, shrubs, etc. *adj.*, **brush·i·er, brush·i·est.**

**brusque** (brusk) abrupt in manner or speech; blunt. *adj.* —**brusque′ly,** *adv.* —**brusque′ness,** *n.*

Brussels sprouts

**Brus·sels sprouts** (brus′əlz) **1** a plant very closely related to broccoli and cabbage, having a thick stem with many small heads growing along it. **2** the heads of this plant, used as a vegetable. Also, **brussels sprouts.**

**bru·tal** (brü′təl) coarse and savage; like a brute; cruel: *The Vikings were brutal in battle.* *adj.* —**bru′tal·ly,** *adv.*

**bru·tal·i·ty** (brü tal′ə tē) **1** BRUTAL conduct; cruelty; savageness. **2** a cruel or savage act. *n., pl.* **bru·tal·i·ties.**

**bru·tal·ize** (brü′tə līz′) **1** make BRUTAL: *War brutalizes many people.* **2** treat brutally: *The judge had harsh criticism for police officers who brutalized people they were questioning.* *v.*, **bru·tal·ized, bru·tal·iz·ing.** —**bru′tal·i·za′tion,** *n.*

**brute** (brüt) **1** an animal without power to reason. **2** not having power to reason: *brute creatures.* **3** a cruel, coarse, or sensual person. **4** cruel; coarse; sensual. **5** without feeling: *the brute forces of nature.* 1, 3 *n.*, 2, 4, 5 *adj.*
☛ *Hom.* BRUIT.

**brut·ish** (brü′tish) coarse; savage. *adj.* —**brut′ish·ness,** *n.*

**bry·o·phyte** (brī′ə fīt′) any of the mosses or liverworts. *n.*

**BTU, Btu,** or **B.T.U.** British thermal unit or units.

**bu.** bushel, bushels.

**bub·ble** (bub′əl) **1** a thin round film of liquid enclosing air or gas: *soap bubbles. The surface of boiling water is covered with bubbles.* **2** a pocket of air or gas in a liquid or solid: *Sometimes there are bubbles in ice or in glass.* **3** have or form bubbles: *Water bubbled up between the stones.* **4** make sounds like water boiling; gurgle: *The baby bubbled and cooed.* **5** the act or process of bubbling; a sound of bubbling: *the bubble of boiling water.* **6** something shaped like a bubble: *A round, domed skylight is often called a bubble.* **7** a plan or idea that looks good, but soon goes to pieces. 1, 2, 5–7 *n.*, 3, 4, *v.*, **bub·bled, bub·bling.** —**bub′bling·ly,** *adv.* —**bub′ble·like′,** *adj.*
**bubble over,** **a** be very full; overflow. **b** be very

---

**brushoff**     **151**     **buckeye**

hat, āge, fär; let, ēqual, tėrm; it, īce
hot, ōpen, ôrder; oil, out; cup, pút, rüle
əbove, takən, pencəl, lemən, circəs
ch, child; ng, long; sh, ship
th, thin; ᴛH, then; zh, measure

enthusiastic: *The girls were bubbling over with ideas for the canoe trip.*

**bubble gum** chewing gum that is very elastic and can be blown up into bubbles from the mouth.

**bubble tower** a device for separating petroleum into various components by distillation.

**bub·bly** (bub′lē) **1** full of BUBBLES. **2** showing enthusiasm or high spirits: *She has a bubbly personality.* *adj.*

**bu·bon·ic** (byü bon′ik) of or having to do with inflamed swelling of the LYMPHATIC glands, especially in the armpit and groin. *adj.*

**bubonic plague** a dangerous contagious disease, accompanied by fever, chills, and swelling of the LYMPHATIC glands: *The bubonic plague is carried to human beings by fleas from rats or squirrels.*

**buc·cal** (buk′əl) **1** of the cheek. **2** of the mouth or of the sides of the mouth. *adj.*
☛ *Hom.* BUCKLE.

**buc·ca·neer** (buk′ə nēr′) a pirate; freebooter. *n.*

**buck¹** (buk) **1** an adult male deer, goat, hare, rabbit, antelope, or sheep. **2** *Informal.* a man, especially a young man who is lively, bold and dashing.

**buck²** (buk) **1** *Informal.* fight against; resist stubbornly: *The swimmer bucked the current with strong strokes. You can't buck progress.* **2** *Informal.* push or hit with the head; butt. **3** in football, charge into the opposing line with the ball. **4** jump into the air with back curved and come down with the front legs stiff: *Her horse began to buck, but she managed to stay on.* **5** throw or attempt to throw a rider in this way: *The cowboy was bucked from the bronco.* **6** a throw or an attempt to throw by bucking. 1–5 *v.*, 6 *n.* —**buck′er,** *n.*
**buck up,** *Informal.* cheer up; be brave or energetic: *Buck up; everything will be all right.*

**buck³** (buk) formerly, a marker placed before a designated player in poker to show that he or she had the responsibility for dealing the cards. *n.*
**pass the buck,** *Informal.* shift the responsibility or blame to someone else: *Whenever his plans don't work out, he passes the buck and someone else gets blamed.*

**buck⁴** (buk) *Informal.* dollar. *n.*

**buck·a·roo** (buk′ə rü′) cowboy. *n., pl.* **buck·a·roos.**

**buck·board** (buk′bôrd′) an open four-wheeled carriage with the seat fastened to a platform of long, springy boards instead of a body and springs. *n.*

**buck·et** (buk′it) **1** a pail, especially a wooden one used for carrying water, milk, etc. **2** the amount that a bucket can hold. **3** the scoop of a dredging machine. *n.*

**buck·et·ful** (buk′it fůl′) the amount that a bucket can hold. *n., pl.* **buck·et·fuls.**

**bucket seat** a small, low, single seat with a rounded back, used in sports cars, small airplanes, etc.

**buck·eye** (buk′ī) *Esp. U.S.* any tree of the horse

**buck·le** (buk′əl) 1 a device used to fasten the loose end or both ends of a belt or strap, usually consisting of a metal or plastic frame through which the end of the belt or strap is pulled. 2 a metal ornament, especially one for a shoe. 3 fasten together with a buckle. 4 bend out of shape; bulge, kink, or wrinkle under heavy strain or pressure: *The heavy snowfall caused the roof of the arena to buckle.* 5 a bend, bulge, kink, or wrinkle. 1, 2, 5 *n.*, 3, 4 *v.*, **buck·led, buck·ling**.
**buckle down (to),** begin to work hard at: *She promised to buckle down to her homework right after supper.*
☞ Hom. BUCCAL.

**buck·ler** (buk′lər) 1 a small, round shield. 2 a protection; defence. *n.*

**buck·ram** (buk′rəm) a coarse cotton or linen cloth made stiff with glue, used in bookbinding and to stiffen hats and other clothing. *n.*

A bucksaw

**buck·saw** (buk′so′) a saw set in a light H-shaped frame and held with both hands: *Bucksaws are used for sawing wood.* *n.*

**buck·shot** (buk′shot′) a coarse lead shot for shotgun shells, used for hunting large game such as deer. *n.*

**buck·skin** (buk′skin′) 1 the skin of a male deer. 2 a soft, strong, yellowish or greyish leather made from this skin, usually having a suede finish: *Buckskin is tougher and coarser than deerskin.* 3 a similar leather made from sheepskin. 4 **buckskins,** *pl.* clothing, especially breeches, made from buckskin (def. 2). *n.*

**buck·thorn** (buk′thôrn′) 1 a small, sometimes thorny, tree or shrub having clusters of black berries, each containing several nutlets. 2 a low, thorny tree with black, cherry-like fruit. *n.*

**buck·wheat** (buk′wēt′ or buk′hwēt′) 1 any of a closely related group of annual plants native to Europe and Asia: *Two species of buckwheat have been extensively grown in North America for their edible seeds, which are used as cereal grains; the plants have escaped from cultivation, becoming common weeds in many parts of Canada.* 2 the seed of a buckwheat, used as food. 3 a twining annual plant of the same family native to Europe, but now growing as a weed throughout Canada. 4 referring to a family of annual or perennial herbs or shrubs found mainly in the northern hemisphere: *Rhubarb, sorrel, dock, and smartweed belong to the buckwheat family.* *n.*
☞ Etym. From 16c. Dutch *boecweite* 'beech wheat' because its fruit is shaped like the nut of the beech.

**buckwheat cake** a pancake made of BUCKWHEAT (def. 2) flour.

**bu·col·ic** (byü kol′ik) 1 of shepherds; pastoral: *Robert Burns and William Wordsworth both wrote some bucolic poems.* 2 rustic; rural. 3 a poem about shepherds. 1, 2 *adj.*, 3 *n.*

**bud** (bud) 1 a small swelling on a plant that will develop into a flower, leaf, or branch. 2 put forth buds: *The rosebush has budded.* 3 graft a bud from one kind of plant into a stem of a different kind. 4 a partly opened flower or leaf. 5 a person or thing not yet developed or mature. 6 begin to grow or develop. 7 a very small, bud-shaped part or organ: *a taste bud.* 1, 4, 5, 7 *n.*, 2, 3, 6 *v.*, **bud·ded, bud·ding**.
**in bud,** budding: *The pear tree is in bud.*
**nip in the bud,** stop at the very beginning.

**Bud·dha** (bud′ə *or* bü′də) the title of Siddhartha Gautama (563?–483? B.C.), the Indian philosopher and religious teacher who founded Buddhism: *Buddha means "Enlightened One."* *n.*

**Bud·dhism** (bud′iz əm *or* bü′diz əm) a religion based on the doctrine of Buddha that pain and suffering cannot be avoided so long as one is subject to wordly desires, but that through meditating and leading a strictly moral life one can eventually reach NIRVANA, a state of liberation and spiritual illumination that is beyond pleasure or pain: *Buddhism is widely practised today in many parts of eastern and central Asia, especially in Burma, Thailand, Sri Lanka, Japan, Cambodia, Laos, and Tibet.* *n.*

**Bud·dhist** (bud′ist *or* bü′dist) 1 of or having to do with BUDDHA or BUDDHISM. 2 a believer in BUDDHISM. 1 *adj.*, 2 *n.*

**bud·ding** (bud′ing) 1 potential: *a budding physicist.* 2 ppr. of BUD. 1 *adj.*, 2 *v.*

**bud·dy** (bud′ē) *Informal.* 1 a good friend; comrade; pal. 2 fellow (used as a form of address): *Say, buddy, can you change a dollar?* *n., pl.* **bud·dies**.

**buddy system** an arrangement in certain types of work or sport that can be dangerous, by which two people stay together to help each other in case of an accident.

**budge** (buj) move or cause to move a little: *He wouldn't budge from his chair, even to pick up the mail.* *v.*, **budged, budg·ing**.

**budg·er·i·gar** (buj′ə ri gär′) a small long-tailed parrot, very popular in many countries as a cage bird but occurring wild only in dry regions of Australia, where it lives in flocks: *Wild budgerigars have green underparts and a yellow back and head with blue and black stripes, but in captivity the birds have been bred to produce individuals of many different colours.* *n.*

**budg·et** (buj′it) 1 an estimate of the amount of money that will be spent for various purposes in a given time by a government, school, business, family, etc.: *We made a budget for our holiday trip so that we wouldn't run out of money before the end.* 2 the amount of money allotted for a particular use or period of time: *My budget won't allow any more movies this month.* 3 make a plan for spending or using: *to budget one's time. She budgets her earnings carefully.* 1, 2 *n.*, 3 *v.*
**budget for,** allot money for a particular purpose: *I forgot to budget for extras so I couldn't buy the record.*

**budg·et·ar·y** (buj′ə ter′ē) of a BUDGET (defs. 1, 2). *adj.*

**budg·ie** (buj′ē) *Informal.* BUDGERIGAR. *n.*

**bud run** *Cdn.* the third run of sugar maple sap,

which makes syrup or sugar of a poor quality. Compare with FROG RUN and ROBIN RUN.

**buff¹** (buf)  **1** a strong, soft, dull yellow leather, made from buffalo skin or ox hide.  **2** a soldier's coat made of this leather.  **3** made of buff.  **4** dull yellow.  **5** a polishing wheel or stick covered with leather.  **6** polish with such a wheel or stick.  *1, 2, 4, 5 n., 3, 4 adj., 6 v.*
**in the buff,** *Informal.* naked.

**buff²** (buf) *Informal.* fan; enthusiast: *a hockey buff, a theatre buff.* *n.*

The buffalo of North America—about 175 cm high at the shoulder

Water buffalo of India—about 155 cm high at the shoulder

**buf·fa·lo** (buf′ə lō′)  **1** a large, powerful animal of the North American plains, a species of bison, having a large hump at the shoulders, coarse dark-brown hair especially long on the head, neck, and shoulders, short curved horns, and a large head that is carried low and cannot be raised to shoulder level: *The buffalo is Canada's largest land mammal; a large bull may weigh up to one tonne.*  **2** any of several species of cattle-like animal found in Africa and India, generally having long horns that curve upward and backward: *Some species of buffalo, such as the water buffalo of India, have been domesticated.*  **3** *Informal.* make unable to answer, proceed, etc.; baffle: *We were all buffaloed by the last question on the exam.*  *1, 2 n.,* **buf·fa·loes, buf·fa·los** or (*esp. collectively*) **buf·fa·lo**; *3 v.,* **buf·fa·loed, buf·fa·lo·ing.**

**buffalo berry**  **1** the edible fruit of a western shrub.  **2** the shrub itself.

**buffalo grass**  a short grass of the plains east of the Rocky Mountains, valued especially for winter pasture.

**buffalo jump**  *Cdn.*  a place where the Plains Indians slaughtered buffalo by stampeding them over a precipice.

**buff·er¹** (buf′ər)  anything that softens the shock of a blow.  *n.*

**buff·er²** (buf′ər)  a person or thing that polishes, especially a leather-covered or cloth-covered device for polishing or buffing.  *n.*

**buffer state**  a small country between two larger countries that are enemies or competitors, thought of as lessening the danger of open conflict between them.

**buf·fet¹** (buf′it)  **1** a blow of the hand or fist.  **2** strike with the hand or fist.  **3** a knock, stroke, or hurt: *She withstood the buffets of the waves.*  **4** knock about; strike; hurt: *The waves buffeted him.*  **5** fight or struggle against: *She reached home exhausted from buffeting the storm.*  *1, 3 n., 2, 4, 5 v.*

**buf·fet²** (bu fā′ *or* bu fā′)  **1** a low cabinet with a flat top, for holding dishes, silver, and table linen.  **2** a counter where food and drinks are served.  **3** a restaurant with such a counter.  **4** a meal at which guests serve themselves from food laid out on a table or counter. *n.*

**buf·fle·head** (buf′əl hed′)  a small, black-and-white,

| buff | 153 | bugle |

hat, āge, fär; let, ēqual, tėrm; it, īce
hot, ōpen, ôrder; oil, out; cup, pùt, rüle
əbove, tāken, pencəl, lemən, circəs
ch, child; ng, long; sh, ship
th, thin; ᴛʜ, then; zh, measure

North American diving duck, the male of which has long, fluffy feathers forming puffs on the sides of the head.  *n.*

**buf·foon** (bu fün′)  a person who amuses people with tricks, pranks, and jokes; clown.  *n.*

**buf·foon·er·y** (bu fü′nə rē)  the tricks, pranks, and jokes of a clown; undignified or rude joking.  *n., pl.* **buf·foon·er·ies.**

**bug** (bug)  **1** any of a large group of sucking insects made up of about 20 000 species, including the bedbug, having generally horizontal wings that overlap on the body when at rest: *Most families of bugs have scent glands that produce a characteristic odour.*  **2** any insect or insectlike animal: *The ladybug and June bug are really beetles. Ants, spiders, and flies are also often called bugs.*  **3** *Informal.* a disease BACTERIUM or VIRUS: *the flu bug.*  **4** *Informal.* a mechanical defect; any structural fault or difficulty: *a bug in the fire alarm system.*  **5** *Informal.* a person who is very enthusiastic about something: *a camera bug.*  **6** *Informal.* annoy, irritate: *Her constant grumbling bugs me.*  **7** *Informal.* a very small hidden microphone, installed for the purpose of listening in on or recording conversation secretly.  **8** *Informal.* hide such a microphone in: *to bug a telephone. The room was bugged.*  **9** *Informal.* listen in on or record secretly by means of a hidden microphone: *to bug a meeting.*  *1–5, 7 n., 6, 8, 9 v.,* **bugged, bug·ging.**

**bug·a·boo** (bug′ə bü′)  a cause of fear; something, usually imaginary, that frightens: *The child was frightened by tales of witches, ghosts, and other bugaboos.*  *n., pl.* **bug·a·boos.**

**bug·bear** (bug′ber′)  **1** a BUGABOO.  **2** something that causes difficulties; a snag.  *n.*

A buggy

**bug·gy¹** (bug′ē)  **1** a light, four-wheeled carriage drawn by one horse and having a single large seat.  **2** a wheeled cart used for shopping in a grocery store, etc.  **3** a baby carriage.  *n., pl.* **bug·gies.**

**bug·gy²** (bug′ē)  swarming with bugs.  *adj.,* **bug·gi·er, bug·gi·est.**

A bugle

**bu·gle** (byü′gəl)  **1** a musical instrument like a small trumpet, made of brass or copper, and sometimes having keys, or valves: *Bugles are sometimes used in the armed*

**bu·gler** (byü′glər) a person who blows a BUGLE. *n.*

**build** (bild) **1** make by putting materials together; construct: *People build houses, dams, bridges, and roads.* **2** form gradually; develop: *to build a business, to build an empire.* **3** establish; base: *to build a case on facts.* **4** make a structure: *We've bought the land, but we won't start to build until next year.* **5** a form, style, or manner of construction; structure: *An elephant has a heavy build.* 1–4 *v.*, **built, build·ing**, 5 *n.*
**build on** or **upon,** depend on.
**build over,** cover with buildings.
**build up,** **a** form gradually; develop: *to build up one's self-confidence. The firm has built up a wide reputation for fair dealing.* **b** gather; come together: *Clouds were building up on the horizon.* **c** fill with houses, etc. **d** promote: *They're using TV ads to build up their new product.*
☛ Hom. BILLED.

**build·er** (bil′dər) **1** a person or animal that builds. **2** a person in the construction business. *n.*

**build·ing** (bil′ding) **1** something built, such as a house, factory, barn, store, etc. **2** the business, art, or process of making houses, bridges, ships, etc. **3** ppr. of BUILD. 1, 2 *n.*, 3 *v.*

**build·up** or **build–up** (bil′dup) **1** the act or process of building up: *a buildup of military strength.* **2** favourable publicity in advance; promotion: *The actor received a tremendous buildup in the local papers before the play opened.* *n.*

**built** (bilt) pt. and pp. of BUILD: *The bird built a nest. It was built of twigs.* *v.*

**built–in** (bilt′in′) built as part of a larger structure, especially a building; not detachable: *a built-in closet. We can't move the bookcase, because it's built-in.* *adj.*

**built–up** (bilt′up′) having many buildings: *a built-up area.* *adj.*

**bulb** (bulb) **1** a round, underground bud from which certain plants grow: *Onions, tulips, and lilies grow from bulbs.* See ONION for picture. **2** the thick part of an underground stem resembling a bulb; TUBER: *a crocus bulb.* **3** an electric light bulb. **4** any object with a rounded end or swelling part: *the bulb of a thermometer.* *n.* —**bulb′less,** *adj.* —**bulb′like′,** *adj.*

**bulb·ar** (bul′bər) of or having to do with a bulb-shaped organ, especially the MEDULLA OBLONGATA, which is the lowest part of the brain. *adj.*

**bulb·ous** (bul′bəs) **1** shaped like a bulb; rounded and swollen: *a bulbous nose.* **2** producing or growing from bulbs: *Daffodils are bulbous plants.* *adj.*

**Bul·gar·i·an** (bul ger′ē ən) **1** of or having to do with Bulgaria, a country in southeastern Europe, its people, or their language. **2** a native or inhabitant of Bulgaria. **3** the Slavic language of Bulgaria. 1 *adj*, 2, 3 *n.*

**bulge** (bulj) **1** swell outward: *His pockets bulged with apples and candy.* **2** cause to swell outward: *The apples bulged her pockets.* **3** an outward swelling. 1, 2 *v.*, **bulged, bulg·ing;** 3 *n.*

**bulg·y** (bul′jē) having a BULGE or bulges. *adj.*

**bu·lim·i·a** (bü lē′mē ə) *n.* a fear of becoming fat, marked by alternate bouts of overeating and self-induced defecation or vomiting. Also, **bulimia nervosa.** —**bul′im·ic,** *adj.*

**bulk** (bulk) **1** size, especially large size: *He had a hard time finding clothes because of his bulk.* **2** the largest part or main mass: *The oceans form the bulk of the earth's surface.* **3** have size; be of importance. **4** grow large; swell. 1, 2 *n.*, 3, 4 *v.*
**bulk large,** seem important.
**in bulk,** **a** loose, not in packages. **b** in large quantities: *We buy rice in bulk, because we use so much.*

**bulk·head** (bulk′hed′) **1** one of the upright partitions dividing a ship into watertight compartments. **2** a similar partition in an aircraft, etc. **3** a wall or partition built to hold back water, earth, rocks, air, etc. **4** a boxlike structure covering the top of a staircase or other opening. *n.*

**bulk·y** (bul′kē) **1** taking up much space; large: *Bulky shipments are often sent by freight.* **2** hard to handle; clumsy: *She dropped the bulky package of curtain rods twice.* *adj.*, **bulk·i·er, bulk·i·est.** —**bulk′i·ly,** *adv.* —**bulk′i·ness,** *n.*

**bull** (bul) **1** the adult male of cattle, buffalo, etc. **2** the adult male of the moose, whale, elephant, seal, and other large animals. **3** like a bull; large and strong. **4** a person who tries to raise prices in the stock market, etc. **5** marked by or having to do with rising prices in the stock market, etc. *n.*

**bull.** bulletin.

A bulldog—about 33 cm high at the shoulder

**bull·dog** (bul′dog′) **1** a breed of heavily built dog with a large head and short hair: *Bulldogs are not large, but they are very muscular and courageous.* **2** like a bulldog's: *bulldog courage.* **3** in the western parts of Canada and the United States, throw a steer, etc. to the ground by grasping its horns and twisting its neck. 1, 2 *n.*, 3 *v.*, **bull·dogged, bull·dog·ging.**

**bull·doze** (bul′dōz′) **1** *Informal.* frighten by violence or threats; bully. **2** move, clear, dig, or level with a BULLDOZER. *v.*, **bull·dozed, bull·doz·ing.**

**bull·doz·er** (bul′dō′zər) **1** a powerful tractor that moves dirt, etc. for grading, road building, etc. by means of a wide steel blade attached to the front. **2** *Informal.* one who BULLDOZES (def. 1). *n.*

**bul·let** (bul′it) a round or pointed piece of lead, steel, or other metal designed to be shot from a rifle, pistol, or other relatively small firearm. See CARTRIDGE for picture. *n.*

**bul·le·tin** (bul′ə tən) **1** a short statement of news: *Newspapers publish bulletins about the latest happenings. Doctors issue bulletins about the condition of a sick person.*

**2** a magazine or newspaper appearing regularly, especially one published by a club or society for its members. **3** make known by a bulletin. 1, 2 *n.*, 3 *v.*

**bulletin board** a board or a sheet of cork, etc. used for posting notices.

**bul·let·proof** (bul'it prüf') made so that a bullet cannot go through: *a bulletproof jacket*. *adj.*

**bull·fight** (bul'fīt') a traditional public performance or ritual in which a man, called a MATADOR, confronts a fierce bull in an arena and performs a series of skilful manoeuvres in avoiding the horns of the charging bull, usually killing the bull with a sword: *Bullfights are common in Spain, Mexico, Colombia, Peru, and Venezuela*. *n.*

**bull·fight·er** (bul'fī'tər) MATADOR. *n.*

**bull·fight·ing** (bul'fī'ting) the act or ritual of fighting a bull in a public arena: *Bullfighting is illegal in Canada and the United States*. *n.*

**bull·finch** (bul'finch') a small, plump-bodied songbird, a species of finch found in the forests of the British Isles, Europe, and Asia, about 16 cm long with the tail, having a short bill and black head, wings, and tail: *The male bullfinch has a pinkish breast and a bluish back, the female a brownish-grey breast and back*. *n.*

**bull·frog** (bul'frog') any of a closely related group of very large frogs found in North America, Africa, and India, the male having a loud call that has been compared to the bellow of a bull: *The North American bullfrog is olive green or reddish brown*. *n.*

**bull·head** (bul'hed') any of several North American fishes having a large, broad head, such as the catfish. *n.*

**bull·head·ed** (bul'hed'id) stupidly stubborn; obstinate. *adj.* —**bull'head'ed·ness**, *n.*

**bull·horn** (bul'hôrn') a megaphone with an electric amplifier. *n.*

**bul·lion** (bul'yən) bricks or bars of gold or silver. *n.*

**bull·ish** (bul'ish) **1** like a bull. **2** trying or tending to raise prices in the stock market, etc. *adj.* —**bull'ish·ly**, *adv.* —**bull'ish·ness**, *n.*

**bull·necked** (bul'nekt') having a thick neck: *a bullnecked wrestler*. *adj.*

**bull·ock** (bul'ək) **1** a young bull. **2** STEER². *n.*

**bull ring** an enclosed arena for bullfights.

**bull session** *Informal.* an informal, rambling discussion, especially a freewheeling discussion among a small group of men.

**bull's-eye** (bulz'ī') **1** the centre of a target. **2** a shot that hits the centre: *She had three bull's-eyes in a row*. **3** a thick disk of glass set in a roof, pavement, the deck or side of a ship, etc. to let in light. **4** a lens shaped like a half sphere to concentrate light. **5** a lantern with such a lens. **6** any small, round opening or window. *n.*
**hit the bull's-eye,** be exactly right or successful.

**bull terrier** a strong, active breed of dog, having a long head and stiff, usually white, hair, originally bred as a cross between a bulldog and a terrier.

**bul·ly** (bul'ē) **1** a person who teases, frightens, or hurts smaller or weaker people. **2** be a bully. **3** frighten into doing something by noisy talk or threats. **4** *Informal.* first-rate; excellent. **5** *Informal.* well done! 1 *n.*, *pl.* **bul·lies;** 2, 3 *v.*, **bul·lied, bul·ly·ing;** 4 *adj.*, 5 *interj.*

**bul·rush** (bul'rush') **1** any of several closely related species of tall marsh plant found in North America,

**bulletin board** 155 **bumptious**

hat, āge, fär; let, ēqual, tėrm; it, īce
hot, ōpen, ôrder; oil, out; cup, put, rüle
əbove, takən, pencəl, lemən, circəs
ch, child; ng, long; sh, ship
th, thin; ᴛʜ, then; zh, measure

Europe, and Asia, having very long, stiff, flat leaves and long, thick, fuzzy, brown flower spikes; CAT-TAIL: *Bulrushes are often used as decoration and also, sometimes, as torches outdoors.* **2** any of a closely related group of grasslike marsh plants of the sedge family found in North America, Europe, and Asia, having long, spongy, usually leafless stems and small flowers growing in a cluster of spikelets: *The stems of the common bulrush of Europe and Asia are used for making mats, baskets, chair seats, thatch, etc.* **3** the PAPYRUS (def. 1) of Egypt, also belonging to the sedge family. *n.*

**bul·wark** (bul'wərk) **1** a support or safeguard; anything, person, or idea that serves as a defence: *They believe that free speech is a bulwark of democracy. Her common sense was our bulwark during the crisis.* **2** defend; protect. **3** an earthwork or other wall for defence against the enemy. **4** a breakwater for protection against the force of the waves. **5** provide with a bulwark or bulwarks. **6** Usually, **bulwarks,** *pl.* the part of the ship's side that extends above the deck level. See SHROUD and CAPSTAN for pictures. 1, 3, 4, 6 *n.*, 2, 5 *v.*

**bum** (bum) *Informal.* **1** an idle or good-for-nothing person; loafer; tramp. **2** loaf around; idle about. **3** drink heavily. **4** a spree. **5** live by taking advantage of the kindness of other people. **6** get something by taking advantage of the kindness of other people: *She tried to bum a ride.* **7** of poor quality. 1, 4 *n.*, 2, 3, 5, 6 *v.*, **bummed, bum·ming;** 7 *adj.*, **bum·mer, bum·mest.**
**bum around,** *Informal.* be lazy; do little.

**bum·ble·bee** (bum'bəl bē') a species of large bee closely related to the honeybees, having a thick, hairy body that is usually banded with yellow: *Bumblebees are social bees, living in large colonies.* *n.*

**bump** (bump) **1** push, throw, or strike against something large or solid: *The children all bumped against one another in their eagerness to be first.* **2** move or proceed with bumps: *Our car bumped along the rough road.* **3** hit or come against with heavy blows: *That truck bumped our car.* **4** a heavy blow or knock. **5** a swelling caused by a bump. **6** any swelling or lump: *She swerved to avoid the bump in the road.* 1–3 *v.*, 4–6 *n.*
**bump into,** *Informal.* meet accidentally.
**bump up,** *Informal.* increase; raise: *bump up your score, bump up the interest rates.*

**bump·er** (bum'pər) **1** the bar or bars of metal or hard rubber across the front and back of a car, bus, or truck that protect it from being damaged if bumped. **2** a fender used to protect a boat or dock. **3** a cup or glass filled to the brim. **4** unusually large: *We had a bumper crop of wheat last year.* **5** *Informal.* something unusually large of its kind. 1, 2, 3, 5 *n.*, 4 *adj.*

**bumper sticker** a piece of gummed paper having a slogan, catchword, or witty saying printed on it, for sticking on the bumper of a motor vehicle.

**bump·kin** (bump'kin) a person from the country who is socially awkward in unfamiliar surroundings, especially in cities. *n.*

**bump·tious** (bump'shəs) unpleasantly assertive or

conceited. *adj.* —**bump′tious·ly,** *adv.* —**bump′tious·ness,** *n.*

**bump·y** (bum′pē) **1** having bumps on the surface; uneven: *a bumpy road.* **2** causing bumps or jolts; rough: *a bumpy ride.* *adj.,* **bump·i·er, bump·i·est.** —**bump′i·ness,** *n.*

**bun** (bun) a small ROLL (def. 26), often sweetened and usually containing raisins. *n.*

**bu·na** (byü′nə *or* bü′nə) an artificial rubber made from BUTADIENE. *n.*

**bunch** (bunch) **1** a group of things of the same kind growing, fastened, placed, or thought of together: *a bunch of grapes, a bunch of flowers.* **2** *Informal.* a group of people, animals, etc.: *They're a friendly bunch.* **3** come together in one place: *The sheep bunched in the shed to keep warm.* **4** bring together and make into a bunch: *We have bunched the flowers for you to carry home.* 1, 2 *n.,* 3, 4 *v.*

**bunch·ber·ry** (bunch′ber′ē) the smallest species of dogwood, a plant growing about 15-20 cm high, having showy blossoms consisting of four petal-like bracts surrounding a cluster of tiny flowers which mature into clusters of bright red berry-like fruits: *The bunchberry is common throughout Canada.* *n., pl.* **bunch·ber·ries.**

**bunch grass** any of various grasses, found in the western parts of Canada and the United States, that grow in bunches or tufts.

**bunch·y** (bun′chē) **1** having bunches. **2** growing in bunches. *adj.,* **bunch·i·er, bunch·i·est.** —**bunch′i·ness,** *n.*

**bun·co** (bung′kō) *Informal.* **1** a scheme in which swindlers join to cheat an unsuspecting person. **2** swindle in this way. 1 *n., pl.* **bun·cos;** 2 *v.,* **bun·coed, bun·co·ing.** Also, **bunko.**

**bun·dle** (bun′dəl) **1** a number of things tied or wrapped together: *a bundle of old newspapers, a bundle of clothing.* **2** a parcel or package: *We made a bundle of all our camp gear and stowed it in the canoe.* **3** wrap or tie together; make into a bundle. **4** *Informal.* a large number or amount; a bunch; a lot: *a bundle of money. The book gave us a bundle of new ideas.* 1, 2, 4 *n.,* 3 *v.,* **bun·dled, bun·dling.** —**bun′dler,** *n.*

**bundle off,** send away in a hurry; hustle: *They bundled her off to the hospital in spite of her protests.*

**bundle up,** dress warmly: *Make sure you bundle up when you go out.*

**bundle of nerves** a person in a state of extreme nervousness and tension: *By the time we got there, he was a bundle of nerves.*

**bung** (bung) **1** a stopper for closing the hole in the side or end of a barrel, keg, or cask. **2** BUNGHOLE. *n.*
**bung up,** **a** close a bunghole with a stopper. **b** stop up; choke up.

**bun·ga·low** (bung′gə lō′) a one-storey house, often small; a house having no living space above the main floor. *n.*
☛ *Etym.* From a language of northwestern India in the 17c. Originally from Hindi *bangla* 'belonging to Bengal'. Part of old Bengal is now Bangladesh, which means 'Bengal nation'.

**bung·hole** (bung′hōl′) a hole in the side or end of a barrel, keg, or cask through which it is filled and emptied. *n.*

**bun·gle** (bung′gəl) **1** spoil by doing or making in a clumsy, unskilful way. **2** a clumsy, unskilful performance or piece of work. 1 *v.,* **bun·gled, bun·gling;** 2 *n.* —**bun′gler,** *n.* —**bun′gling·ly,** *adv.*

**bun·ion** (bun′yən) an enlargement of the first joint of the big toe, causing the toe to be permanently bent inwards. *n.*

**bunk¹** (bungk) **1** a narrow bed attached to a wall like a shelf. **2** a narrow bed, usually one of two built one above the other. **3** *Informal.* any place to sleep. **4** *Informal.* spend the night (*at*): *It was too late to go home so Brigitta bunked at our house.* **5** sleep in or occupy a makeshift bed: *We bunked in an old barn.* **6** provide with a bunk or bed: *This cabin bunks three people.* 1, 2, 3 *n.,* 4–6 *v.*

**bunk²** (bungk) *Informal.* insincere talk; nonsense; humbug. *n.*

**bunk bed** one of two single beds, usually built one above the other.

**bunk·er** (bung′kər) **1** a bin or other place for storing fuel on a ship. **2** a sandy hollow or mound of earth on a golf course, used as an obstacle. **3** a type of shelter, often part of a larger fortification, and built partly or entirely below ground. *n.*

**bunk·house** (bungk′hous′) a building equipped with BUNKS for sleeping: *Men at lumber camps sleep in bunkhouses.* *n.*

**bun·ko** (bung′kō) See BUNCO. *n., v.*

**bun·ny** (bun′ē) a pet name for a rabbit. *n., pl.* **bun·nies.**

**Bun·sen burner** (bun′sən) a gas burner with a very hot, blue flame, used in laboratories: *Air is let in at the base of a Bunsen burner and mixed with gas.*

**bunt** (bunt) **1** strike with the head or horns, as a goat does. **2** push; shove. **3** in baseball, hit a ball lightly so that it goes to the ground and rolls only a short distance. **4** a hit made in this way. **5** a baseball that is bunted. 1–3 *v.,* 2, 4, 5 *n.* —**bunt′er,** *n.*

**bun·ting¹** (bun′ting) **1** a thin cloth used for flags. **2** long pieces of cloth having the colours and designs of a flag, used to decorate buildings and streets on holidays and special occasions; flags. **3** ppr. of BUNT. 1, 2 *n.,* 3 *v.*

**bun·ting²** (bun′ting) a small bird that has a stout bill and resembles a sparrow. *n.*

**bunt·line** (bun′tlin *or* bun′tlīn′) a rope fastened to a sail: *A buntline is used to haul the sail up to the yard for furling.* *n.*

**buoy** (boi *or* bü′ē) **1** a floating object anchored on the water to warn or guide: *Buoys mark hidden rocks or shallows, show the safe part of the channel, etc.* **2** furnish with buoys; mark with a buoy. **3** a cork or plastic belt, ring, or jacket used to keep a person from sinking; a life buoy or life preserver. **4** keep from sinking. **5** hold up; sustain; encourage. 1, 3 *n.,* 2, 4, 5 *v.*
**buoy up,** **a** keep from sinking; hold up: *Her life jacket buoyed her up until rescuers came.* **b** bring to the surface. **c** support or encourage: *Hope buoys him up, even when something goes wrong.*
☛ *Hom.* BOY (for the first pronunciation of **buoy**).

**buoy·an·cy** (boi′ən sē) **1** the power to float: *Wood has more buoyancy than iron.* **2** the power to keep things afloat: *Salt water has greater buoyancy than fresh water.* **3** a tendency to rise: *Hydrogen has approximately 14 times as much buoyancy as air at sea level.* **4** light-heartedness; cheerfulness; hopefulness; the ability to rise above or recover quickly from low spirits: *Her buoyancy kept us from being downhearted.* *n.*

**buoy·ant** (boi′ənt) **1** able to float: *Wood and cork are buoyant in water; iron and lead are not.* **2** able to keep things afloat: *Air is buoyant; balloons float in it.* **3** tending to rise: *A balloon filled with hydrogen is buoyant.* **4** light-hearted; cheerful; hopeful: *Even in the hospital, her spirits were buoyant.* *adj.* —**buoy′ant·ly,** *adv.*

**bu·pres·tid beetle** (byü pres′tid)   a beetle whose larvae poison cattle.

**bur** (bėr)   See BURR¹.   *n., v.*

**bur·ble** (bėr′bəl) **1** make a bubbling noise. **2** speak in a confused, excited manner. *v.,* **bur·bled, bur·bling.**

**bur·bot** (bėr′bət)   a freshwater fish with a slender body, related to the cod.   *n., pl.* **bur·bot** or **bur·bots.**

**bur·den¹** (bėr′dən) **1** something carried; a load of things, duty, work, etc. **2** anything difficult to carry or bear; heavy load: *a burden of debts.* **3** put a burden on; load. **4** load too heavily; oppress. **5** the quantity of freight that a ship can carry; the mass of a ship's cargo. 1, 2, 5 *n.,* 3, 4 *v.*

**bur·den²** (bėr′dən) **1** the main idea or message: *The burden of her speech was the conservation of our natural resources.* **2** chorus; refrain.   *n.*

**burden of proof**   the obligation of proving a statement or accusation that has been made: *In any court case, the burden of proof lies with the accuser.*

**bur·den·some** (bėr′dən səm)   hard to bear; very heavy; oppressive: *burdensome tax, burdensome duties.* *adj.*

**bur·dock** (bėr′dok′)   a coarse weed having prickly burrs and broad leaves.   *n.*

**bu·reau** (byü′rō) **1** dresser. **2** a desk or writing table with drawers. **3** a certain kind of office or business: *a travel bureau.* **4** *Esp. U.S.* a branch of a government department. *n., pl.* **bu·reaus** or **bu·reaux** (-ōz).

**bu·reauc·ra·cy** (byü rok′rə sē) **1** government by groups of officials. **2** the officials administering the government. **3** an excessive concentration of power in administrative offices. **4** an excessive insistence on rigid routine; RED TAPE.   *n., pl.* **bu·reauc·ra·cies.**

**bu·reau·crat** (byü′rə krat′) **1** an official in a BUREAUCRACY. **2** a formal, pretentious government official.   *n.*

**bu·reau·crat·ic** (byü′rə krat′ik) **1** having to do with a BUREAUCRACY or BUREAUCRAT. **2** arbitrary.   *adj.* —**bu′reau·crat′i·cal·ly,** *adv.*

**bur·geon** (bėr′jən) **1** bud; sprout: *burgeoning leaves.* **2** grow; flourish: *the burgeoning talent of the young painter.* **3** a bud; sprout. 1, 2 *v.,* 3 *n.*

**bur·ger** (bėr′gər) *Informal.* HAMBURGER (def. 2).   *n.* ☛ *Hom.* BURGHER.

**–burger** *combining form.* **1** a fried or grilled patty of _____ in a split bun: *fishburger.* **2** a HAMBURGER (def. 2) with _____: *cheeseburger.*

**bur·gess** (bėr′jis) **1** the citizen of a BOROUGH. **2** in Saskatchewan, a property owner who has the right to vote on money by-laws in a municipality.   *n.*

**burgh** (bėrg)   in some countries, a chartered town.   *n.*

☛ *Hom.* BERG.

**burgh·er** (bėr′gər)   a citizen of a BURGH or town; citizen.   *n.*
☛ *Hom.* BURGER.

**bur·glar** (bėr′glər)   a person who breaks into a house or other building, especially at night, to steal or commit some other crime.   *n.*

**bur·glar·ize** (bėr′glə rīz′) *Informal.*   break into a building to steal.   *v.,* **bur·glar·ized, bur·glar·iz·ing.**

**bur·glar·proof** (bėr′glər prüf′)   so strong or safe that burglars cannot break in.   *adj.*

**bur·glar·y** (bėr′glə rē)   breaking into a house or other building, especially at night, to steal or commit some other crime.   *n., pl.* **bur·glar·ies.**

**bur·gle** (bėr′gəl) *Informal.*   BURGLARIZE.   *v.;* **bur·gled, bur·gling.**

**Bur·gun·di·an** (bėr gun′dē ən) **1** of Burgundy, a region in eastern France, its people. **2** a native or inhabitant of Burgundy.   1 *adj.,* 2 *n.*

**bur·i·al** (ber′ē əl *or* bėr′ē əl) **1** putting a dead body in a grave, in a tomb, or in the sea; burying. **2** having to do with burying: *a burial service.*   1 *n.,* 2 *adj.*

**bur·lap** (bėr′lap)   coarse and heavy plain-weave fabric made of jute, hemp, or cotton, used mainly for making sacks, wall coverings, and draperies, and sometimes clothing.   *n.*

**bur·lesque** (bėr lesk′) **1** a literary or dramatic composition in which a serious subject is treated ridiculously, or with mock seriousness: *Mark Twain's story,* A Connecticut Yankee in King Arthur's Court *is a burlesque of some old legends.* **2** imitate so as to ridicule. **3** comical; making people laugh. **4** a cheap, vulgar kind of vaudeville.   1, 3, 4 *n.,* 2 *v.,* **bur·lesqued, bur·les·quing.**

**bur·ly** (bėr′lē)   big, strong, and sturdy; husky.   *adj.,* **bur·li·er, bur·li·est.** —**bur′li·ness,** *n.*

**Bur·man** (bėr′mən)   BURMESE (def. 1).   *n., adj.*

**Bur·mese** (bėr mēz′) **1** a native or inhabitant of Burma, a country in southeast Asia. **2** the language of Burma. **3** of Burma, its people, or their language.   1, 2 *n., pl.* (for def. 1) **Burmese;**   3 *adj.*

**burn¹** (bėrn) **1** be on fire; use up fuel while giving off heat and light and gases; blaze: *The campfire burned all night.* **2** set on fire; cause to burn, especially in order to destroy: *They raked up all the leaves and burned them.* **3** be destroyed or ruined by fire or heat: *Many important documents were burned in the fire. I forgot the roast and it burned to a crisp.* **4** ruin, damage, or injure by fire, heat, acid, electricity, or radiation: *I burned the roast. He burned his finger when he touched the hot pan.* **5** make or produce by burning: *The cigar ashes burned a hole in the tablecloth.* **6** an injury caused by fire, heat, acid, electricity, or radiation: *How do you treat a burn?* **7** a burned place or spot: *Those are cigarette burns on the rug.* **8** become sunburned: *Do you burn easily?* **9** a sunburn. **10** use as fuel: *The stove burns wood or coal. Our car burns*

**burn**

too much gas. **11** fire a rocket engine: *The commander gave the order to burn the engines.* **12** the firing of a rocket engine: *Another burn was needed to correct the spacecraft's orbit.* **13** give light; shine, as if from fire: *Lamps were burning in every room.* **14** feel hot: *the burning sands of the desert. Her forehead burned with fever.* **15** produce or feel pain as if from fire or heat: *My hands were burning from the cold. That ointment burns.* **16** be or become very excited, eager, angry, etc.: *burning with enthusiasm, burning with resentment. It made me burn to see the way she got the better of them.* **17** harden, glaze, etc. by fire or heat: *to burn bricks.* **18** transform into energy by metabolism (*usually used with* **off** *or* **up**): *He's trying to burn off some weight by jogging.* **19** CAUTERIZE. 1–5, 8, 10, 11, 13–19 *v.,* **burned** or **burnt, burn·ing;** 6, 7, 9, 12 *n.*
**burn down, a** burn to the ground: *Their house burned down, but most of their possessions were saved.* **b** burn less strongly as fuel gets low: *We had to get more wood because the fire was beginning to burn down.*
**burn one's boats** or **bridges,** cut off all means of retreat for oneself; commit oneself to a particular course: *She burned her boats when she resigned from her old job before she had found a new one.*
**burn out, a** destroy the inside or contents of by burning: *The store was completely burned out, leaving just a shell.* **b** cease to burn; become extinguished: *The campfire had burned out and we were in darkness.* **c** make or become unserviceable; make or become worn out, especially through long or improper use: *to burn out a motor. One of the light bulbs is burned out.* **d** deprive of a home through fire: *The family was burned out last year and had to live with relatives for two months. The marauders burned the villagers out of their homes.* **e** bring to a state of physical, mental, or emotional exhaustion: *He burned himself out with worry and overwork.*
**burn up, a** burn completely: *By the time the police got there, the papers were burned up.* **b** *Informal.* make angry or annoyed: *Her smug attitude really burns me up.*

**burn**² (bėrn) *Scottish.* a small stream; brook. *n.*

**burn·er** (bėr′nər) **1** the part of a lamp, stove, furnace, etc. where the flame or heat is produced. **2** any thing or part that burns or works by heat. *n.*

**burn·ing** (bėr′ning) **1** glowing; hot. **2** ppr. of BURN. 1 *adj.,* 2 *v.*

**bur·nish** (bėr′nish) polish; shine. *v., n.* —**bur′nish·er,** *n.*

Moroccan burnooses

**bur·noose** or **bur·nous** (bər nüs′) **1** a long cloak with a hood, worn by Moors and Arabs. **2** a similar garment worn by women or men for casual wear. *n.*

**burnt** (bėrnt) a pt. and a pp. of BURN¹. *v.*

**burp** (bėrp) *Informal.* **1** a BELCH. **2** to BELCH. **3** cause to BELCH: *to burp a baby.* 1 *n.,* 2, 3 *v.*

**burr**¹ or **bur** (bėr) **1** the prickly, clinging seed case, fruit husk, or flowers of various plants. **2** a plant bearing burrs. **3** a person or thing that clings like a burr. **4** remove burrs from. **5** a rough ridge or edge left by a tool on metal, wood, etc. after cutting or drilling it. **6** any of several kinds of cutting tool, such as a dentist's drill with a rough head. 1–3, 5, 6 *n.,* 4 *v.*

**burr**² (bėr) **1** a prominent trilling of *r*, as in Scottish pronunciation. **2** pronounce *r* with a trill: *She burrs her r's.* **3** a pronunciation in which *r* sounds are trilled: *a Scottish burr.* **4** speak with a burr. **5** a whirring sound. **6** make a whirring sound. 1, 3, 5 *n.,* 2, 4, 6 *v.*

**bur·ro** (bėr′ō) a kind of small, agile donkey. *n., pl.* **bur·ros.**
☞ *Hom.* BOROUGH, BURROW.
☞ *Etym.* From Spanish *burro,* a shortening of *borrico* 'donkey', which developed from L *burricus* 'small horse'.

**bur·row** (bėr′ō) **1** a hole dug in the ground by an animal for refuge or shelter: *Rabbits live in burrows.* **2** a similar passage for dwelling, shelter, or refuge. **3** dig a hole in the ground: *The mole soon burrowed out of sight.* **4** live in burrows. **5** hide. **6** dig; make burrows in: *Rabbits have burrowed the ground near the river.* **7** search. 1, 2 *n.,* 3–7 *v.*
☞ *Hom.* BOROUGH, BURRO.

**bur·row·er** (bėr′ō ər) one who BURROWS. *n.*

**bur·sa** (bėr′sə) a sac of the body, especially one located between joints and containing a lubricating fluid; a pouch or cavity. *n., pl.* **bur·sae** (-sē *or* -sī) or **bur·sas.**

**bur·sar** (bėr′sər) a treasurer, especially of a college or university. *n.*

**bur·sa·ry** (bėr′sə rē) **1** a grant of money to a student at a college or university. **2** a treasury, especially of a college or university. *n., pl.* **bur·sa·ries.**

**bur·si·tis** (bər sī′tis) inflammation of a BURSA. *n.*

**burst** (bėrst) **1** fly apart suddenly and with force; explode; break open: *The balloon burst when it touched the light bulb.* **2** be full to the breaking point: *The granaries were bursting with grain. She is bursting with enthusiasm.* **3** go, come, do, etc. by force or suddenly: *He burst into the room.* **4** open suddenly or violently: *The trees burst into bloom after the rain. The door burst open. She burst the lock with a screwdriver.* **5** a sudden or violent issuing forth; a sudden opening to sight or view. **6** act or change suddenly in a way suggesting a break or explosion: *She burst into loud laughter.* **7** cause to break open or into pieces; shatter: *to burst a blood vessel.* **8** a bursting, split, or explosion. **9** an outbreak: *a burst of laughter.* **10** a sudden display of activity or energy: *a burst of speed.* **11** a series of shots fired by one pressure of the trigger of an automatic weapon. 1–4, 6, 7 *v.,* **burst, burst·ing;** 5, 8–11 *n.*

**bur·y** (ber′ē *or* bėr′ē) **1** put a dead body in the earth, a tomb, the sea, etc., usually with a ceremony of some kind. **2** cover up with earth or some other material: *The treasure was buried under the old oak tree. We found the essay buried under a lot of papers.* **3** hide from view: *He buried his face in his hands. The story of her exploits was buried in the back pages of the newspaper.* **4** occupy oneself with great concentration: *She buried herself in her work.* **5** put out of mind; put an end to: *They buried their differences and*

*became friends again.* *v.*, **bur·ied, bur·y·ing.** —**bur′i·er,** *n.*
☛ *Hom.* BERRY (for the first pronunciation of **bury**).

**bus** (bus) **1** a large motor vehicle with seats inside and sometimes also upstairs, used to carry passengers along a certain route. **2** transport or travel by bus: *She busses to work. We were bussed to another airport.* **1** *n.*, *pl.* **bus·es** or **bus·ses;** **2** *v.*, **bussed** or **bused, bus·sing** or **bus·ing.**

**bus boy** a waiter's assistant: *A bus boy brings bread and butter, fills glasses, carries off dishes, etc.*

**bus·by** (buz′bē) a tall fur hat with a cloth bag hanging from the top over the right side, worn by hussar regiments. *n.*, *pl.* **bus·bies.**

**bush** (bush) **1** any woody plant having many separate branches starting from or near the ground; shrub: *A bush is usually smaller than a tree.* **2** spread out like a bush; grow thickly. **3** set ground with bushes; cover with bushes. **4** forested wilderness, especially the vast forests beyond settled areas. **5** *Cdn.* a tree-covered area on a farm; a BUSH LOT or woodlot: *The bush was right behind the houses.* **6** *Cdn.* on the Prairies, wooded land on the edge of the plains: *There's more bush west of here.* **1, 4–6** *n.*, **2, 3** *v.*
**beat around the bush,** approach a matter in a roundabout way; not come straight to the point: *Tell me the truth right away and don't beat around the bush.*

**bushed** (busht) *Informal.* **1** *Cdn.* acting strangely as a result of having been isolated from people. **2** exhausted. **3** pt. and pp. of BUSH. **1, 2** *adj.*, **3** *v.*

**bush·el** (bush′əl) **1** a unit for measuring the volume of grain, fruit, vegetables, and other dry things, equal to about 0.036 m³: *One bushel is equal to 4 pecks or 32 quarts.* **2** a container holding a bushel. *n.*

**Bu·shi·do** or **bu·shi·do** (büsh′ē dō′) in Japan, the moral code of the feudal knights and warriors; chivalry: *In its fully developed form, Bushido lasted from the 12th to the 19th centuries.* *n.*

**bush·ing** (bush′ing) **1** a removable metal lining used to protect parts of machinery from wear. **2** ppr. of BUSH. **1** *n.*, **2** *v.*

**bush league** *Informal.* **1** in baseball, a minor league. **2** any second-rate or unimportant group or organization: *Her brilliant performance in court shows that this lawyer is no longer in the bush league.* —**bush-league,** *adj.* —**bush leaguer,** *n.*

**bush line** *Cdn.* an airline that transports freight and passengers over the northern bush country.

**bush lot** *Cdn.* that part of a farm where the trees have been left standing to provide firewood, fence posts, etc.; a WOODLOT.

**bush·man** (bush′mən) **1** *Australian.* a settler in the bush. **2** a person who knows much about living in the woods; woodsman. **3 Bushman, a** a member of a nomadic people of southwestern Africa: *The Bushmen were traditionally hunters.* **b** a language spoken by these people. *n.*, *pl.* **bush·men** (-mən).

**bush pilot** *Cdn.* an aviator who does most of his or her flying in the bush country of the Far North.

**bush·whack** (bush′wak′ or bush′hwak′) **1** live or work in the bush or backwoods. **2** ambush or raid. *v.*

**bush·whack·er** (bush′wak′ər or bush′hwak′ər) **1** a person who lives or works in the bush or backwoods. **2** GUERRILLA. *n.*

**bus**     159     **bustard**

hat, āge, fär; let, ēqual, tėrm; it, īce
hot, ōpen, ôrder; oil, out; cup, pu̇t, rüle
əbove, takən, pencəl, lemən, circəs
ch, child; ng, long; sh, ship
th, thin; ᵺ, then; zh, measure

**bush·work·er** (bush′wėr′kər) *Cdn.* a person who works in the bush, especially a logger. *n.*

**bush·y** (bush′ē) **1** spreading out like a bush; growing thickly: *a bushy beard.* **2** overgrown with bushes: *a bushy hill.* *adj.*, **bush·i·er, bush·i·est.** —**bush′i·ness,** *n.*

**bus·i·ly** (biz′ə lē) in a busy manner; actively. *adv.*

**busi·ness** (biz′nis) **1** whatever one is busy at; work; occupation: *A carpenter's business is building with wood.* **2** a matter; affair: *That adventure was a bad business.* **3** activities of buying and selling; trade; commercial dealings: *This store does a big business.* **4** a commercial enterprise; an industrial establishment: *a bakery business. They sold their business for ten million dollars.* **5** the right to act; responsibility: *It's not your business to decide what she should do.* *n.*
**mean business,** *Informal.* be in earnest; be serious: *Don't argue; he means business.*
**mind your own business,** avoid interfering in the affairs of others.

**business college** an institution that gives training in business-related subjects, especially secretarial skills such as shorthand, keyboarding, and office procedures.

**busi·ness·like** (biz′nis līk′) having system and method; well-managed; practical: *She runs her store in a businesslike manner.* *adj.*

**busi·ness·man** (biz′nis man′ or biz′nis mən) **1** a man in business. **2** a man who is good at business: *He's no businessman.* *n.*, *pl.* **busi·ness·men** (-men′ or -mən).

**busi·ness·wom·an** (biz′nis wu̇m′ən) **1** a woman in business. **2** a woman who is good at business: *The way she handled the project shows that she's a businesswoman.* *n.*, *pl.* **busi·ness·wom·en** (-wim′ən).

**bus·kin** (bus′kin) **1** a boot reaching to the calf or knee, especially an open laced boot worn in ancient times. **2** a similar boot having a very thick sole, worn by actors in Greek and Roman tragedies. **3** tragedy; tragic drama. *n.*

**bus·man's holiday** (bus′mənz) a holiday spent in doing something similar to what one does at one's daily work: *A letter carrier who goes for a walk on her day off is taking a busman's holiday.*

**bus·ses** (bus′iz) a pl. of BUS. *n.*

**bust¹** (bust) **1** a piece of sculpture representing a person's head, shoulders, and chest. **2** the breasts of a woman. **3** the measurement around a woman's body at the level of the bust: *a 92 cm bust.* *n.*

**bust²** (bust) *Informal.* **1** burst. **2** make or become bankrupt. **3** a failure; flop. **4** punch; hit: *He busted me on the nose.* **5** a punch: *I gave him a bust on the head.* **6** arrest: *She was busted for possessing stolen goods.* **7** reduce to a lower rank; demote: *He was busted to private.* **8** break or break down: *Don't bust my watch.* **1, 2, 4, 6–8** *v.*, **bust·ed** or **bust, busting; 3, 5** *n.*

**bus·tard** (bus′tərd) a large game bird having long legs and a heavy body, found on the deserts and plains of Africa, Europe, and Asia. *n.*

**bus·tle¹** (bus′əl) **1** be noisily busy and in a hurry. **2** make others hurry or work hard. **3** noisy or excited activity: *There was a great bustle as the children got ready for the party.* 1, 2 *v.*, **bus·tled, bus·tling;** 3 *n.* —**bus′tler,** *n.*

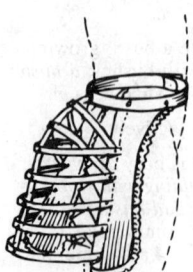 

A dress of the 1870's, with a bustle. The picture at the left shows the steel framework.

**bus·tle²** (bus′əl) a pad formerly used to puff out the upper back part of a woman's skirt. *n.*

**bus·y** (biz′ē) **1** working; active: *a busy person.* **2** make or keep busy: *The stage hands busied themselves in setting up the stage.* **3** in use: *I tried to phone her but her line was busy.* **4** full of work or activity: *a busy day, a busy street.* **5** prying into other people's affairs; meddling: *That inquisitive woman is always busy.* 1, 3–5 *adj.*, **bus·i·er, bus·i·est;** 2 *v.*, **bus·ied, bus·y·ing.**

**bus·y·bod·y** (biz′ē bod′ē) a person who pries into other people's affairs; meddler. *n., pl.* **bus·y·bod·ies.**

**but** (but; *unstressed,* bət) **1** on the other hand; yet: *It rained, but I went anyway.* **2** except; save: *She works every day but Sunday. No one answered but me.* **3** without the result that; unless: *It never rains but it pours.* **4** no more than; only; merely: *He is but a boy.* **5** other than: *We can do nothing but accept their conditions.* **6** objection: *Not so many buts, please.* **7** that: *I don't doubt but she will come.* **8** that not: *He is not so sick but he can eat.* 1, 3, 5, 7, 8 *conj.*, 2 *prep.*, 4 *adv.*, 6 *n.*
**all but,** nearly; almost: *The book was all but finished when the author died.*
☛ *Hom.* BUTT.

**bu·ta·di·ene** (byü′tə dī′ēn) a colourless, flammable gas obtained from petroleum, used in making synthetic rubber. *n.*

**bu·tane** (byü′tān) a colourless, flammable gas obtained from natural gas or petroleum, used as a fuel. *n.*

**butch·er** (buch′ər) **1** a person whose work is killing animals to be sold for food. **2** a person who cuts up and sells meat. **3** kill animals for food. **4** kill cruelly or needlessly: *Many village inhabitants were butchered in the invasion.* **5** a brutal killer or murderer. **6** spoil by poor work; botch: *He butchered the song by singing it much too loudly.* 1, 2, 5 *n.*, 3, 4, 6 *v.* —**butch′er·er,** *n.*

**butch·er·y** (buch′ə rē) **1** brutal or wholesale killing or murder. **2** a slaughterhouse. **3** a butcher's work; the act or business of killing animals for food. *n., pl.* **butch·er·ies.**

**bu·te·o** (byü′tē ō) any of a closely related group of hawks found in many parts of the world, having a thick-set body, broad wings, and a short, broad tail, and feeding mainly on small mammals and beetles: *Buteos will soar high in the air for hours while hunting.* *n.*

**but·ler** (but′lər) the chief male servant of a household, whose duties include supervising other servants, directing the serving of meals and personal services for his employers. *n.*

**but·su·dan** (büt sü dän′) in Japanese tradition: **1** the altar in a temple upon which Buddhist statues are enshrined. **2** the shrine in a Buddhist household, containing statues, pictures, and memorial tablets of family ancestors. *n.*

**butt¹** (but) **1** the thicker end of anything: *The butt of a gun.* **2** the end that is left; a stub or stump: *the butt of a cigarette.* **3** *Informal.* buttocks; rump. *n.*
☛ *Hom.* BUT.

**butt²** (but) **1** target. **2** an object of ridicule or scorn: *She was the butt of their jokes.* **3** join end to end. 1, 2 *n.*, 3 *v.*
☛ *Hom.* BUT.

**butt³** (but) **1** strike or push by knocking hard with the head. **2** a push or blow with the head. 1 *v.*, 2 *n.*
**butt in,** *Informal.* meddle; interfere.
☛ *Hom.* BUT.

**butt⁴** (but) **1** a large barrel for wine or beer. **2** a former unit for measuring liquids, equal to two hogsheads, about 476 L. *n.*
☛ *Hom.* BUT.

A butte

**butte** (byüt) *Cdn.* a steep, often flat-topped hill standing alone: *Buttes are common in southern Alberta.* *n.*

**but·ter** (but′ər) **1** the solid, yellowish fat obtained by churning cream or whole milk. **2** put butter on. **3** something like butter in consistency or use: *peanut butter, apple butter, cocoa butter.* **4** *Informal.* flattery. 1, 3, 4 *n.*, 2 *v.* —**but′ter·less,** *adj.*
**butter up,** *Informal.* flatter in order to get something: *We tried buttering her up, but she still wouldn't give us a ride.*

**but·ter·cup** (but′ər kup′) **1** any of a number of closely related wildflowers found especially in meadows and damp places, having yellow flowers and leaves that are usually deeply lobed. **2** referring to a large family of annual or perennial plants found in temperate and cold regions, especially in the Northern Hemisphere, including many herbs, such as the buttercups, columbines, and anemones, and a few woody vines, such as the clematis: *The buttercup family is also called the crowfoot family.* *n.*

**but·ter·fat** (but′ər fat′) the fatty content of milk from which butter is made: *Whole milk from cows usually contains about 3.8 percent butterfat.* *n.*

**but·ter·fin·gered** (but′ər fing′gərd) *Informal.* always letting things drop or slip through the fingers. *adj.*

**but·ter·fin·gers** (but′ər fing′gərz) *Informal.* a clumsy or awkward person who drops things: *Don't let her handle the china; she's a real butterfingers.* *n.*

**but·ter·fish** (but′ər fish′) a small, silvery fish of the Atlantic coast, used for food. *n., pl.* **but·ter·fish** or **but·ter·fish·es.**

Butterfly: a tiger swallowtail—wingspread about 12 cm

hat, āge, fär; let, ēqual, tėrm; it, īce
hot, ōpen, ôrder; oil, out; cup, pút, rüle
əbove, takən, pencəl, lemən, circəs
ch, child; ng, long; sh, ship
th, thin; ᴛʜ, then; zh, measure

**but·ter·fly** (but′ər flī′)  **1** any of a large group of about six families of insects having a slender body, long, slender antennae with thick, knoblike tips, and four large, often brightly coloured wings: *Butterflies are active in the daytime.*  **2** a person who suggests a butterfly by delicate beauty, bright clothes, fickleness, etc.  **3** a swimming stroke performed face down, in which the outstretched arms move in a circular motion together while the legs are kicking up and down together.  **4 butterflies,** *pl.* an uneasy or queasy feeling caused by nervous anxiety about something that is to happen: *I get butterflies in my stomach just thinking about being in front of all those people.* *n., pl.* **but·ter·flies.**

**butterfly weed**  a milkweed with orange-coloured flowers.

**but·ter·milk** (but′ər milk′)  **1** the sour, fat-free liquid left after butter has been churned from cream.  **2** milk that has been soured by adding certain bacteria. *n.*

**but·ter·nut** (but′ər nut′)  **1** an oily kind of edible walnut grown in North America.  **2** the tree it grows on. *n.*

**but·ter·scotch** (but′ər skoch′)  **1** a candy made from brown sugar and butter.  **2** flavoured with brown sugar and butter: *butterscotch pudding.* *n.*

**butter tart**  *Cdn.*  a rich, sweet tart having a filling made from butter, brown sugar, corn syrup, raisins, spices, etc.: *Recipes for butter tarts vary somewhat and the filling may be runny or firm.*

**but·ter·y**[1] (but′ə rē)  **1** like butter.  **2** containing butter; spread with butter. *adj.*

**but·ter·y**[2] (but′ə rē)  PANTRY (def. 1). *n., pl.* **but·ter·ies.**

**but·tocks** (but′əks)  the fleshy hind part of the body where the legs join the back; rump. *n. pl.*

**but·ton** (but′ən)  **1** a knob or disk of plastic, metal, wood, etc. fixed on clothing or other things, serving to hold parts together when passed through a buttonhole or loop, or used simply to decorate.  **2** close or fasten with buttons.  **3** have buttons for fastening: *The dress buttons down the front.*  **4** a knob or small disk or plate that is pushed or turned to open or close an electric circuit: *an elevator button. You push that button to start the machine.*  **5** a usually round badge of metal or plastic having a catchword, slogan, logo, etc. printed on it, and a pin at the back, for attaching to clothing: *The publisher was giving away buttons to promote the new book.*  1, 4, 5, 6, *n.*, 2, 3 *v.*  —**but′ton·less,** *adj.*  —**but′ton·like′,** *adj.*
**button through,**  of a coat or dress, have buttons from top to bottom.
**button up,**  fasten with buttons.
**on the button,** *Informal.*  exactly; precisely: *She was there at five o'clock on the button.*

**but·ton·ball** (but′ən bol′)  BUTTONWOOD. *n.*

**but·ton·hole** (but′ən hōl′)  **1** the slit through which a button is passed.  **2** make buttonholes in.  **3** sew with the stitch used in making buttonholes.  **4** force someone to listen, as if by holding him or her by the buttonhole of the coat: *He buttonholed me as I tried to sneak out of the room.*  1 *n.*, 2–4 *v.*, **but·ton·holed, but·ton·hol·ing.**  —**but′ton·hol′er,** *n.*

**but·ton·hook** (but′ən huk′)  a hook for pulling the buttons of shoes, gloves, etc. through the buttonholes. *n.*

**but·ton·wood** (but′ən wud′)  the common North American sycamore tree. *n.*

Buttresses. The one on the left is a flying buttress.

**but·tress** (but′ris)  **1** a structure built against a wall or building to strengthen or support it.  **2** something resembling a buttress, such as a projecting rock.  **3** any support; prop: *The experience was a buttress to her faith.*  **4** strengthen with a buttress.  **5** support and strengthen; bolster: *The pilot's report of the flight was buttressed with photographs.*  1–3 *n.*, 4, 5 *v.*

**bux·om** (buk′səm)  vigorously healthy and plump, used especially of a full-bosomed woman. *adj.*

**buy** (bī)  **1** get by paying a price: *You can buy a pencil for 50 cents.*  **2** *Informal.* a bargain: *That book was a real buy.*  **3** *Informal.* something bought; purchase.  **4** bribe: *The prosecution charged that two jury members had been bought.*  1, 4 *v.*, **bought, buy·ing;**  2, 3 *n.*
**buy off,**  get rid of by paying money to.
**buy out,**  buy all the shares, rights, etc. of.
**buy up,**  buy all that one can of; buy.
☞ *Hom.* BY, BYE.

**buy·er** (bī′ər)  **1** a person who buys.  **2** a person whose work is buying goods, especially for a retail store. *n.*

**buyer's market**  an economic situation in which the buyer has the advantage because goods are plentiful and prices tend to be low.  Compare with SELLER'S MARKET.

**buzz** (buz)  **1** a humming sound made by flies, mosquitoes, or bees.  **2** a low, indistinct, murmuring sound of many people talking quietly: *The buzz of conversation stopped when the teacher entered the room.*  **3** make a loud, steady humming sound on one pitch: *The radio needs to be fixed; it buzzes when you turn it on.*  **4** make a low, indistinct murmuring sound: *The whole room buzzed with the news of the class excursion.*  **5** murmur; whisper: *"Here they come," he buzzed in my ear.*  **6** approach quickly and closely with an aircraft or a small boat: *A pilot buzzed our school yesterday.*  **7** *Informal.* a telephone call: *Give me a buzz tonight.*  **8** signal by pressing a buzzer: *She buzzed her secretary.*  **9** *Informal.*

**buzz·ard** (buz′ərd) **1** any of several species of vulture of the Western Hemisphere, especially the turkey vulture, or turkey buzzard. **2** *Esp. Brit.* any of a closely related group of hawks; BUTEO. *n.*

to telephone: *I'll buzz you when I find out.* 1, 2, 7 *n.*, 3–6, 8, 9 *v.*
**buzz about,** move about busily.
**buzz off,** *Informal.* go away.

**buzz bomb** a type of unguided missile heavily loaded with explosives and propelled by a pulsejet, that was invented in Germany and used against England in World War II, especially in the bomb attacks on London.

**buzz·er** (buz′ər) **1** something that buzzes, especially an electrical device that makes a buzzing sound as a signal. **2** the sound of a buzzer: *At the buzzer, they all rushed from the room.* *n.*

**buzz saw** a circular saw.

**by** (bī) **1** near; beside: *The garden is by the house.* **2** along; over; through: *to go by the bridge.* **3** through the action of: *The thief was captured by a police officer. The house was destroyed by fire.* **4** through the means or use of: *They keep in touch by letter. He never travels by plane.* **5** combined with in multiplication or relative dimensions: *a room four by eight metres.* **6** in the measure of: *Eggs are sold by the dozen.* **7** to the extent of: *larger by half.* **8** according to: *They all work by the rules.* **9** in relation to: *She did well by her children.* **10** taken separately as units or groups in a series: *two by two. Algebra must be mastered step by step.* **11** during: *Because of the heat, they travelled by night and rested by day.* **12** not later than: *We'll try to be there by six o'clock.* **13** at hand: *near by.* **14** past: *days gone by. A car dashed by.* **15** aside or away: *She puts by five dollars a week toward a new bicycle.* **16** toward: *The island lies south by east from here.* **17** *Informal.* at, in, or into another's house when passing: *Please come by and see me when you can.* **18** See BYE. 1–12, 16 *prep.*, 13–15, 17 *adv.*, 18 *n.*
**by and by,** after a while; soon: *You will feel stronger by and by.*
**by and large,** on the whole; in general: *It has some faults, but by and large it is a good book.*
**by the by,** incidentally.
**by the way,** **a** incidentally; aside from the main point: *By the way, I still haven't been able to find that book you asked about.* **b** at the roadside: *We stopped by the way to eat.*
☛ *Hom.* BUY, BYE.

**by–** a prefix meaning: **1** secondary; minor; less important: *A by-product is a less important product.* **2** near by: *A bystander is a person standing near by.*

**by–and–by** (bī′ən bī′) the future. *n.*

**bye¹** (bī) **1** in sports, the condition of being the odd player or team not required to play one round of a contest in which players or teams are grouped in pairs: *Our team had a bye to the semifinals.* **2** the player or team not required to play a round. **3** in cricket, a run made on a missed ball. **4** in golf, the holes not played after one player has won. *n.* Also, **by.**
**by the bye,** by the way; incidentally.
☛ *Hom.* BUY, BY.

**bye²** or **'bye** (bī) *Informal.* goodbye. *interj.*
☛ *Hom.* BUY, BY.

**bye–bye** (bī′bī′) *Informal.* goodbye. *interj.*

**by–e·lec·tion** (bī′ə lek′shən) an election held in one riding because of the death or resignation of its Member of Parliament or Legislative Assembly. *n.*

**by·gone** (bī′gon′) **1** gone by; past; former: *The Romans lived in bygone days.* **2** something in the past. **3** the past. 1 *adj.*, 2, 3 *n.*
**let bygones be bygones,** let the past be forgotten.

**by–law** (bī′lo′) **1** a local law; a law made by a city, company, club, etc. for the control of its own affairs: *Our city has by-laws to control parking, traffic, and building practices.* **2** a secondary law or rule; not one of the main rules. *n.*

**by–line** (bī′līn′) a line at the beginning or end of a newspaper or magazine article giving the name of the writer. *n.*

**by·pass** (bī′pas′) **1** a road, channel, pipe, etc. providing a secondary route to be used instead of the main route: *Drivers use the bypass when there is a lot of traffic.* **2** provide a secondary passage for. **3** go around: *to bypass a city.* **4** ignore an intermediate person or level in order to deal directly with a higher authority: *He bypassed the sales manager and took his complaint straight to the president.* **5** set aside or ignore regulations, etc. in order to reach a desired objective. **6** get away from; avoid; escape: *to bypass a question.* 1 *n.*, 2–6 *v.*

**by–path** (bī′path′) a side path or byway. *n.*

**by–play** (bī′plā′) action that is not part of the main action, especially on the stage. *n.*

**by–prod·uct** (bī′prod′əkt) **1** something of value produced in making or doing something else: *Kerosene is a by-product of petroleum refining.* **2** a side effect; a secondary and sometimes unexpected result: *Her new self-confidence is a by-product of her experience as club president.* *n.*

**byre** (bīr) a cowhouse or cow shed. *n.*

**by–road** (bī′rōd′) SIDE ROAD. *n.*

**By·ron·ic** (bī ron′ik) **1** of or having to do with the English poet George Gordon, Lord Byron (1788–1824), or his poetry. **2** having or showing qualities generally associated with Byron or his poetry; arrogant, cynical, unconventional, romantic, etc. *adj.*

**by·stand·er** (bī′stan′dər) a person who stands near or looks on but does not take part. *n.*

**byte** (bīt) a unit of computer memory made up of eight BITS (def. 4). One letter, or character, on the computer keyboard takes one byte of memory. *n.*
☛ *Hom.* BIGHT, BITE.

**by·way** or **by–way** (bī′wā′) a side path or road; a way that is little used. *n.*

**by·word** (bī′wėrd′) **1** a common saying; proverb. **2** a person or thing commonly taken as representing a certain characteristic, especially an unfavourable one: *The courts were a byword for corruption.* **3** an object of contempt; something scorned: *She had become a byword throughout the region.* *n.*

**Byz·an·tine** (biz′ən tēn′ or bi zan′tin) **1** having to do with Byzantium, an ancient city on the Bosporus, or a style of art or architecture developed there: *Byzantine architecture uses round arches, crosses, circles, domes, and mosaics.* See ARCHITECTURE for picture. **2** a native or inhabitant of Byzantium. 1 *adj.*, 2 *n.*

# C c  C c

hat, āge, fär; let, ēqual, tėrm; it, īce
hot, ōpen, ȯrder; oil, out; cup, pu̇t, rüle
әbove, takәn, pencәl, lemәn, circәs
ch, child; ng, long; sh, ship
th, thin; ᴛʜ, then; zh, measure

**c or C** (sē) **1** the third letter of the English alphabet. **2** any speech sound represented by this letter, as in *cell, cat*. **3** in music: **a** the first tone in the scale of C major. **b** a symbol representing this tone. **c** a key, string, etc. of a musical instrument that produces this tone. **d** the scale or key that has C as its keynote. **4** C, the Roman numeral for 100. **5** any person or thing considered as the third in a series: *C works twice as hard as B.* **6** a grade rating a person or thing as fair, or average; the third level from the top, or best: *I got a C on the test.* **7** a person or thing receiving this rating. *n., pl.* **c's** or **C's.**

**c** centi- (an SI prefix).

**c. 1** cent; cents. **2** about; approximately. **3** in sports, catcher. **4** century. **5** centre. **6** copyright. **7** cubic.

**C 1** Celsius. **2** carbon. **3** Central. **4** coulomb.

**C. 1** Cape. **2** Catholic. **3** Conservative.

**C₁₄** carbon 14.

**ca** about; approximately.

**Ca** calcium.

**C.A. 1** chartered accountant. **2** Central America.

**Caa·ba** (kä′bә) See ᴋᴀᴀʙᴀ. *n.*

**cab** (kab) **1** an automobile that can be hired with a driver; taxi. **2** a horse-drawn carriage that can be hired with a driver. **3** the enclosed part of a locomotive, truck, etc. where the operator stands or sits. *n.*

**ca·bal** (kә bal′) **1** a small group of people working or plotting in secret. **2** a secret scheme of such a group; plot. *n.*

**cab·a·lis·tic** (kab′ә lis′tik) having a mystical meaning; secret. *adj.*

**cab·al·le·ro** (kab′ә ler′ō *or* kab′ә lyer′ō; *Spanish,* kä bä lyā′rō) **1** gentleman. **2** knight. *n., pl.* **cab·al·le·ros.**

**ca·ba·na** (kә ban′ә *or* kә bä′nyә) *Spanish.* **1** a small, roughly built house; cabin. **2** a tentlike shelter used for dressing, to provide shade, etc. on the beach. *n.*

**cab·a·ret** (kab′ә rā′) **1** a restaurant offering singing and dancing as an entertainment. **2** the entertainment. *n.*

**cab·bage** (kab′ij) **1** a plant very closely related to the cauliflower and broccoli, having large, round leaves that are closely folded into a compact head growing from a short stem. **2** the head of a cabbage, used as a vegetable. *n.*

**ca·ber** (kā′bәr) a long, heavy pole or beam tossed as a trial of strength in Scottish Highland games. *n.*

**cab·in** (kab′әn) **1** a small, roughly built house; hut. **2** a room for passengers or crew in a ship or boat. **3** a place for passengers in an aircraft. See ᴀɪʀᴘʟᴀɴᴇ for picture. *n.*

**cabin boy** a boy whose work is waiting on the officers and passengers on a ship.

**cabin cruiser** a motorboat having a cabin and equipped with facilities for living on board.

**cab·i·net** (kab′ә nit) **1** an upright piece of furniture having shelves or drawers to store or display things: *a china cabinet, a medicine cabinet.* **2** an upright case holding a radio or television receiver, record turntable, etc. **3** a body of advisers to a head of state, a prime minister, etc. **4** Usually, **Cabinet,** in Canada: **a** an executive committee of the federal government chosen by the prime minister, from members of the majority party in the House of Commons: *Members of the Cabinet have the title of Minister of the Crown.* **b** a similar committee of a provincial government. *n.*

**cab·i·net·mak·er** (kab′ә nit mā′kәr) a person skilled in constructing and finishing fine wooden furniture. *n.*

**cabinet minister** the head of a department of the government of certain countries, including Canada, or of a province; a member of the cabinet.

**cab·i·net·work** (kab′ә nit wėrk′) **1** any beautifully made furniture and woodwork. **2** the making of such furniture and woodwork. *n.*

A cable

**ca·ble** (kā′bәl) **1** a strong, thick rope, usually made of wires twisted together. **2** tie or fasten with a cable. **3** cable's length. **4** a bundle of electric wires protected from each other by insulation: *Telegraph messages are sent under the ocean by cable.* **5** ᴄᴀʙʟᴇɢʀᴀᴍ. **6** send a message by cable. **7** *Informal.* ᴄᴀʙʟᴇ ᴛᴇʟᴇᴠɪsɪᴏɴ: *Do you have cable?* **8** ᴄᴏᴀxɪᴀʟ ᴄᴀʙʟᴇ **1,** 3–5, 7, 8 *n.,* 2, 6 *v.,* **ca·bled, ca·bling.**

**cable car** a car that is pulled along by a moving cable operated by a motor: *Cable cars are used for carrying passengers up and down steep hills.*

**ca·ble·gram** (kā′bәl gram′) a message sent across the ocean by underwater cable. *n.*

**cable television** a system by which signals from various television stations are picked up by a very tall or elevated central antenna and sent by cable to the sets of the individual subscribers: *A television set that is hooked up to cable television does not need any antenna.*

**cable TV** ᴄᴀʙʟᴇ ᴛᴇʟᴇᴠɪsɪᴏɴ.

**ca·ble·vi·sion** (kā′bәl vizh′әn) ᴄᴀʙʟᴇ ᴛᴇʟᴇᴠɪsɪᴏɴ. *n.*

**ca·boose** (kә büs′) **1** a small car on a freight train in which the train crew can work, eat, and sleep: *The caboose is usually the last car on the train.* **2** a kitchen on the deck of a ship. **3** *Cdn.* a mobile bunkhouse used by loggers, threshing crews, etc. **4** *Cdn.* a horse-drawn vehicle consisting of a small cabin mounted on runners and equipped with benches and a stove: *My grandmother remembers driving to school in a caboose in winter.* *n.*

**cab·ri·o·let** (kab′rē ә lā′) **1** an automobile resembling a coupé, but having a folding top.  2 a light carriage with one or two seats and two wheels, pulled by one horse: *A cabriolet often has a folding top.*  *n.*

**ca·ca·o** (kə kā′ō)  1 a tropical American evergreen tree that produces seeds from which chocolate, cocoa, and cocoa butter are obtained.  2 the seed of this tree, also called **cacao bean.**  *n., pl.* **ca·ca·os.**

**cach·a·lot** (kash′ə lot′ or kash′ə lō′)  a large, square-head whale; SPERM WHALE.  *n.*

**cache** (kash)  1 a hiding place.  2 *Cdn.*  a place for storing supplies, furs, equipment, etc. away from foraging animals and the weather: *The explorers dug a hole to serve as a cache for the supplies needed on the return trip.*  3 *Cdn.*  deposit in such a cache.  4 the things hidden or stored in a cache: *We found a cache of acorns in the hollow tree.*  5 hide or conceal.  1, 2, 4 *n.,* 3, 5 *v.,* **cached, cach·ing.**
☛ *Etym.*  From F *cache*, formed from the verb *cacher* 'to hide'. The Canadian meanings come from special French-Canadian uses of the French noun.
☛ *Hom.*  CASH.

**cack·le** (kak′əl)  1 the shrill, broken sound that a hen makes, especially after laying an egg.  2 make this sound.  3 burst of shrill, harsh, or broken laughter.  4 laugh with shrill, harsh, or broken sounds: *After each joke the old woman cackled with enjoyment.*  5 noisy chatter; silly talk.  6 chatter.  1, 3, 5 *n.,* 2, 4, 6 *v.,* **cack·led, cack·ling.**

**ca·coph·o·nous** (kə kof′ə nəs)  harsh and clashing; dissonant; discordant.  *adj.*

**ca·coph·o·ny** (kə kof′ə nē)  a harsh, clashing sound; dissonance; discord.  *n., pl.* **ca·coph·o·nies.**

A species of low-growing cactus, the prickly pear   A giant cactus - up to 20 metres high

**cac·tus** (kak′təs)  a plant with a thick fleshy stem, usually having spines but no leaves: *Cactuses grow in hot, dry regions and often have brightly coloured flowers.*  *n., pl.* **cac·tus·es** or **cac·ti** (-tī or -tē).

**cad** (kad)  a man who does not act like a gentleman; an ill-bred man.  *n.*

**ca·dav·er** (kə dav′ər)  a dead body, especially a human body intended for dissection; corpse.  *n.*

**ca·dav·er·ous** (kə dav′ə rəs)  1 of or like a CADAVER.  2 pale and ghastly.  3 thin and worn.  *adj.*

**cad·die** or **cad·dy** (kad′ē)  1 a person who helps a golf player by carrying the clubs, finding the ball, etc.  2 help a golf player in this way.  1 *n.,* 2 *v.,* **cad·died, cad·dy·ing.**

**cad·dis fly** (kad′is)  an insect resembling a moth, whose larva lives under water and forms itself a case of sand, bits of leaves, or the like.

**cad·dish** (kad′ish)  like a CAD; ungentlemanly.  *adj.*

**caddis worm**  the larva of a CADDIS FLY, used as bait in fishing.

**cad·dy**[1] (kad′ē)  a small box, can, or chest, often used to hold tea.  *n., pl.* **cad·dies.**

**cad·dy**[2] (kad′ē)  See CADDIE.  *n., pl.* **cad·dies;**  *v.,* **cad·died, cad·dy·ing.**

**ca·dence** (kā′dəns)  1 rhythm; measure or beat of any rhythmical movement: *the steady cadence of a march.*  2 a fall of the voice, as at the end of a sentence.  3 a rising and falling sound; modulation: *She speaks with a pleasant cadence.*  4 a series of chords, etc. that brings part of a piece of music to an end.  *n.*

**ca·den·za** (kə den′zə)  in music, an elaborate flourish or showy passage for an unaccompanied voice or solo instrument in an aria, concerto, etc.  *n.*

**ca·det** (kə det′)  1 a young man or woman in training to be an officer in the armed forces: *At the Royal Military College of Canada, the dress uniform for the cadets includes a scarlet tunic and a pillbox.*  2 a young man or woman undergoing training for a police force.  3 an adolescent undergoing basic military training in an organization associated with the armed forces: *There will be sea cadets and air cadets in the parade.*  *n.*

**ca·det·ship** (kə det′ship)  the rank or position of a CADET.  *n.*

**ca·di** (kä′dē or kā′dē)  a Moslem judge responsible for making judgments in religious cases such as those involving inheritance, marriage, or divorce.  *n., pl.* **ca·dis.**

**cad·mi·um** (kad′mē əm)  a soft, bluish-white, ductile metallic element resembling tin, used in plating to prevent rust and in making certain ALLOYS.  *Symbol:* Cd  *n.*

**ca·dre** (kä′dər for 1, usually kad′rē for 2)  1 framework.  2 the staff of trained military personnel necessary to establish and train a new military unit.  *n.*

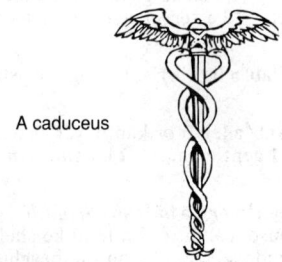

A caduceus

**ca·du·ce·us** (kə dyü′sē əs or kə dü′sē əs)  a staff with two snakes twined around it and a pair of wings on top: *Mercury, or Hermes, the messenger of the gods, is usually shown carrying a caduceus. The caduceus is often used as an emblem of the medical profession.*  *n., pl.* **ca·du·ce·i** (-sē ī′).

**cae·cum** (sē′kəm)  the large pouch, closed at one end, that forms the beginning of the large intestine. See ALIMENTARY CANAL for picture.  *n., pl.* **cae·ca** (-kə). Also, **cecum.**

**Cae·sar** (sē′zer)  1 a title of the Roman emperors from Augustus to Hadrian, and, later, of the heir to the throne.  2 emperor.  3 a dictator or tyrant.  *n.*

**Cae·sar·e·an** (si zer′ē ən or si zar′ē ən)  1 of Julius Caesar or the Caesars.  2 by CAESAREAN SECTION: *a Caesarean birth.*  3 CAESAREAN SECTION.  1, 2 *adj.,* 3 *n.*

Also, **Caesarian** or (sometimes for defs. 2 and 3) **Cesarean** or **Cesarian**.

**Caesarean section**  a method of delivering a child by cutting through the wall of the abdomen and uterus of the mother.
☛ *Etym.*  From the belief that Julius *Caesar* was born in this way.

**cae·sar·ism** (sē′zə riz′əm)  dictatorship; autocracy.  *n.*

**cae·si·um** (sē′zē əm)  See CESIUM.  *n.*

**cae·su·ra** (si zyü′rə *or* si zhü′rə)  a pause in a line of verse, generally agreeing with a pause required by the sense: *A caesura usually comes near the middle of a line, either within or after a metrical foot as indicated by this mark: //.  Example: "to err is human, // to forgive, divine."* *n.*, *pl.* **cae·su·ras**.

**CAF** or **C.A.F.**  Canadian Armed Forces.

**ca·fé** (ka fā′ *or* kə fā′)  **1** a small, informal restaurant.  **2** *French.* coffee.  *n.*
☛ *Syn.*  **Café** usually refers only to a small, informal place to eat. RESTAURANT may refer to any public eating place, from a very formal dining room to a small place with a counter and perhaps two or three tables.

**caf·e·te·ri·a** (kaf′e tēr′ē ə)  a restaurant where customers serve themselves or are served at a counter and carry their meals to tables to eat.  *n.*

**caf·feine** or **caf·fein** (kaf′ēn)  a stimulating drug found in coffee and tea.  *n.*

**caf·tan** (kaf′tan *or* käf tän′)  **1** a loose ankle-length, long-sleeved garment worn with a kind of sash: *Caftans are traditionally worn in eastern Mediterranean countries.*  **2** a similar garment worn in western countries for lounging or recreation.  *n.*

**cage** (kāj)  **1** a frame or box closed in with wires, bars, etc.: *We keep our canary in a cage.*  **2** anything shaped or used like a cage: *The car or closed platform of a mine elevator is a cage.*  **3** a prison.  **4** put or keep in a cage. 1–3 *n.*, 4 *v.*, **caged, cag·ing**.

**cage·ling** (kāj′ling)  a bird kept in a cage.  *n.*

**cage·y** (kā′jē)  **1** *Informal.* shrewd: *a cagey lawyer.*  **2** cautious; wary: *She was too cagey to commit herself completely.*  *adj.*, **cag·i·er, cag·i·est**.  —**cag′i·ly**, *adv.* —**cag′i·ness**, *n.*

**CAHA** or **C.A.H.A.**  Canadian Amateur Hockey Association.

**ca·hoots** (kə hüts′)  *n.*
**in cahoots**, *Informal.*  in partnership, especially for a wrongful purpose; in league: *She was found to be in cahoots with the thief. The two of them are probably in cahoots.*

**ca·hot** (kə hō′)  *Cdn.*  **1** a ridge of snow on a road: *The cahots made the ride a very bumpy one.*  **2** a ridge or bump in an unpaved road.  *n.*

**cai·man** (kā′mən)  a large alligator of tropical America.  *n.*, *pl.* **caimans**.  Also, **cayman**.

**ca·ïque** (kä ēk′)  **1** a long, narrow Turkish rowboat, much used on the Bosporus.  **2** a Mediterranean sailing ship.  *n.*

**cairn** (kern)  a pile of stones heaped up as a memorial, tomb, or landmark.  *n.*

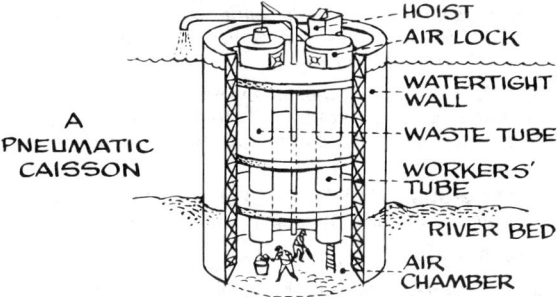

A PNEUMATIC CAISSON

**cais·son** (kā′son *or* kā′sən)  **1** a watertight box or chamber within which work can be carried on under water: *Caissons are used in the construction of bridge piers.*  **2** a watertight float used in raising sunken ships.  **3** a box for ammunition.  **4** a wagon to carry ammunition.  *n.*

**caisson disease**  an illness caused by changing too suddenly from high air pressure to ordinary air pressure.

**ca·jole** (kə jōl′)  persuade by flattery or false promises, especially to overcome reluctance; coax: *His older sister cajoled him into cutting the lawn.*  *v.*, **ca·joled, ca·jol·ing**. —**ca·jol′er**, *n.*

**ca·jol·er·y** (kə jō′lə rē)  persuasion by flattering or deceitful words; flattery; coaxing.  *n.*, *pl.* **ca·jol·er·ies**.

**cake** (kāk)  **1** a baked mixture of flour, sugar, eggs, flavouring, and other things: *a sponge cake, a fruit cake.* **2** batter that has been fried or baked in a small, flat, usually round shape: *buckwheat cakes.*  **3** any small, flat mass of food fried on both sides: *a fish cake.*  **4** a shaped mass: *a cake of soap, a cake of maple sugar.*  **5** form into a solid mass; harden: *Mud cakes as it dries.*  1–4 *n.*, 5 *v.*, **caked, cak·ing**.

**cake·walk** (kāk′wok′)  **1** formerly among Blacks of the United States, an entertainment in which people performed a kind of promenade or walk to music, with a prize of a cake for the best or most original steps.  **2** a popular high-stepping dance based on this walk.  **3** music for this dance.  **4** do a cakewalk.  1–3 *n.*, 4 *v.*

**cal·a·bash** (kal′ə bash′)  **1** a gourd whose dried shell is used to make bottles, bowls, drums, rattles, etc.  **2** the tropical plant or tree that it grows on.  **3** a bottle, bowl, etc. made from such a dried shell.  *n.*

**cal·a·di·um** (kə lā′dē əm)  any of a closely related group of tropical American plants of the ARUM family, having large, showy leaves, often in several colours: *Caladiums are popular house plants.*  *n.*

**cal·a·ma·ry** (kal′ə mer′ē)  a giant edible squid.  *n.*, *pl.* **cal·a·ma·ries**.

**cal·a·mine** (kal′ə mīn′)  a pink, odourless, tasteless powder consisting of ZINC OXIDE and a small amount of ferric oxide, used in skin lotions and ointments.  *n.*

**ca·lam·i·tous** (kə lam′ə təs)  causing CALAMITY; accompanied by calamity; disastrous.  *adj.* —**ca·lam′i·tous·ly**, *adv.*

**ca·lam·i·ty** (kə lam′ə tē)  **1** an event causing great

misery or destruction: *The newspaper reported such calamities as fires and floods.* **2** serious trouble; misery: *Calamity may come to anyone.* *n., pl.* **ca‧lam‧i‧ties.**

**cal‧a‧mus** (kal′ə məs) **1** a marsh plant having long, sword-shaped leaves and a thick, fragrant, underground stem; sweet flag. **2** the dried underground stem of this plant: *Calamus is used as a flavouring agent and also yields an oil that is used in making perfumes and as an insecticide.* *n., pl.* **cal‧a‧mi** (-mī′ or -mē′).

**ca‧lash** (kə lash′) **1** a light, low-wheeled carriage with a folding top. **2** CALÈCHE. **3** a folding carriage top. **4** a woman's folding hood or bonnet, worn in the 18th and 19th centuries. *n.*

**cal‧car‧e‧ous** (kal ker′ē əs) **1** of or containing lime or limestone. **2** of or containing calcium. *adj.*

**cal‧ces** (kal′sēz) a pl. of CALX. *n.*

**cal‧ci‧fi‧ca‧tion** (kal′sə fə kā′shən) **1** the process of CALCIFYing. **2** a calcified part. *n.*

**cal‧ci‧fy** (kal′sə fī′) become hard by the deposit of lime: *An injured cartilage sometimes calcifies.* *v.,* **cal‧ci‧fied, cal‧ci‧fy‧ing.**

**cal‧ci‧mine** (kal′sə mīn′) **1** a white or coloured liquid consisting of a mixture of water, colouring matter, glue, etc., used especially on plastered ceilings and walls. **2** cover with calcimine. **1** *n.,* **2** *v.,* **cal‧ci‧mined, cal‧ci‧min‧ing.** Also, **kalsomine.**

**cal‧ci‧na‧tion** (kal′sə nā′shən) **1** the act or operation of calcining. **2** anything formed by calcining. *n.*

**cal‧cine** (kal′sīn) heat an inorganic substance to a high temperature, but not high enough to melt or fuse it, in order to bring about evaporation of certain matter in it or cause chemical changes such as oxidation: *Limestone is calcined to produce lime.* *v.,* **cal‧cined, cal‧cin‧ing.**

**cal‧ci‧um** (kal′sē əm) a soft, silvery-white metallic element that is a part of limestone, chalk, milk, bone, etc.: *Calcium is used in alloys and its compounds are used in making plaster, in cooking, and as bleaching agents.* *Symbol:* Ca *n.*

**calcium carbide** a heavy, grey crystalline compound that reacts with water to form acetylene gas.

**calcium carbonate** a mineral occurring in rocks as marble and limestone, in animals as bones, shells, teeth, etc., and to some extent in plants.

**calcium chloride** a very absorbent compound of calcium and chlorine, used mainly as a drying agent, preservative, and refrigerant.

**calcium hydroxide** a white compound, $Ca(OH)_2$, produced by the action of water on lime; slaked lime.

**cal‧cu‧la‧ble** (kal′kyə lə bəl) **1** that can be CALCULATED. **2** reliable; dependable. *adj.* —**cal′cu‧la‧bly,** *adv.*

**cal‧cu‧late** (kal′kyə lāt′) **1** find out by adding, subtracting, multiplying, or dividing; figure: *to calculate the cost of furnishing a house.* **2** find out beforehand by any process of reasoning; estimate: *Calculate the day of the week on which your birthday will fall.* **3** *Informal.* plan; intend: *That remark was calculated to hurt my feelings.* **4** *Informal.* think; believe; suppose. **5** rely on; count on: *He calculated an increase in salary to help him.* *v.,* **cal‧cu‧lat‧ed, cal‧cu‧lat‧ing.**

**calculate on,** *Informal.* estimate or anticipate: *We calculated on ten guests, but only two arrived.*
☛ *Etym.* **Calculate** and CALCULUS both come from L *calculus* 'a stone or pebble'. **Calculate** is from the verb *calculare* 'to count', formed from *calculus* because pebbles were used in counting. **Calculus** keeps the additional L meaning of the kind of stone formed in the body.

**cal‧cu‧lat‧ing** (kal′kyə lā′ting) **1** that CALCULATES. **2** shrewd; careful. **3** scheming; selfish. **4** ppr. of CALCULATE. 1–3 *adj.,* 4 *v.*

**cal‧cu‧la‧tion** (kal′kyə lā′shən) **1** the act of calculating: *The calculation of the total cost will take some time.* **2** a result found by calculating: *All my calculations are correct.* **3** careful thinking; deliberate planning. *n.*

**cal‧cu‧la‧tor** (kal′kyə lā′tər) **1** a machine that performs mathematical CALCULATIONS (def. 1) mechanically, especially one that solves difficult mathematical problems. **2** a person who operates such a machine. *n.*

**cal‧cu‧lus** (kal′kyə ləs) **1** in mathematics, a method of reasoning, using a highly specialized system of notation. **2** a stone or hard mass formed in the body. **3** a hard substance that has collected on the teeth, formed by the action of bacteria on saliva and food particles; TARTAR. *n., pl.* **cal‧cu‧lus‧es** or **cal‧cu‧li** (-lī′ or -lē′).
☛ *Etym.* See note at CALCULATE.

**cal‧dron** (kol′drən) See CAULDRON. *n.*

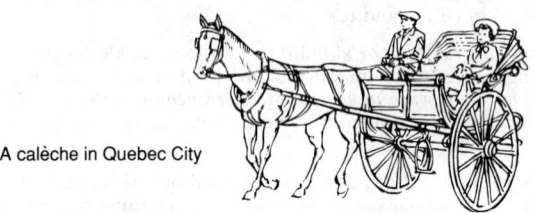

A calèche in Quebec City

**ca‧lèche** (kə lesh′) *Cdn.* a light, two-wheeled, one-horse carriage for two passengers, having a seat in front for the driver and, usually, a folding top. *n.*

**cal‧en‧dar** (kal′ən dər) **1** a table showing the months and weeks of the year and the day of the week on which each day of the month comes. **2** a system by which the beginning, length, and divisions of the year are fixed. **3** a list or schedule; record; register: *We have three winter carnivals on our calendar. The trial had to be delayed because the court calendar was filled.* **4** a volume or booklet issued by a college or university listing rules, courses to be given, etc. **5** enter in a calendar or list; register. 1–4 *n.,* 5 *v.*
☛ *Hom.* CALENDER.

**calendar day** the 24 hours from one midnight to the next midnight.

**calendar month** one of the 12 parts into which a year is divided; month.

**calendar year** a period of 365 days (or in leap year, 366 days) that begins on January 1 and ends on December 31.

**cal‧en‧der** (kal′ən dər) **1** a machine in which cloth, paper, etc. is smoothed and glazed by pressing between rollers. **2** make smooth and glossy by pressing in a calender. 1 *n.,* 2 *v.*
☛ *Hom.* CALENDAR.

**cal·ends** (kal′əndz) in the ancient Roman calendar, the first day of the month. *n. pl.* Also, **kalends**.

**ca·len·du·la** (kə len′jə lə *or* kə len′dyə lə) any of a small, closely related group of herbs of the COMPOSITE family having yellow or orange flowers: *The best-known calendula is the pot marigold.* *n.*

**calf¹** (kaf) **1** the young of the domestic cow or of a related animal such as the buffalo. **2** a young elephant, whale, seal, etc. **3** leather made from the skin of a calf. **4** *Informal.* a clumsy, silly boy or young man. *n., pl.* **calves**.
☛ *Etym.* OE *cælf* 'a young cow or bull'.

**calf²** (kaf) the thick, fleshy part of the back of the leg below the knee. See LEG for picture. *n., pl.* **calves**.
☛ *Etym.* From ON *kálfi*, having the same meaning.

**calf love** PUPPY LOVE.

**calf·skin** (kaf′skin′) **1** the skin of a calf. **2** leather made from it. *n.*

**cal·i·ber** (kal′ə bər) See CALIBRE. *n.*

**cal·i·brate** (kal′ə brāt′) **1** determine, check, or adjust the scale of a thermometer, gauge, or other measuring instrument: *Calibrating is usually done by comparison with a standard instrument.* **2** find the calibre of. *v.,* **cal·i·brat·ed, cal·i·brat·ing.** —**cal′i·bra′tor,** *n.*

**cal·i·bra·tion** (kal′ə brā′shən) calibrating or being CALIBRATED. *n.*

**cal·i·bre** (kal′ə bər) **1** diameter, especially inside diameter: *A .45 calibre revolver has a barrel with an inside diameter of 45/100 of an inch (about 11.4 mm).* **2** degree of quality or worth: *The position of director requires a person of high calibre. How can we improve the calibre of our schools?* *n.* Also, **caliber**.

**cal·i·co** (kal′ə kō) **1** a cotton cloth that usually has coloured patterns printed on one side. **2** made of calico. **3** spotted in colours: *a calico cat.* 1 *n., pl.* **cal·i·coes** or **cal·i·cos;** 2, 3 *adj.*

**cal·i·co·back** (kal′ə kō bak′) a red-and-black bug that feeds on cabbages and other garden plants. *n.*

**calico salmon** *Cdn.* See CHUM³.

**ca·lif** (kā′lif *or* kal′if) See CALIPH. *n.*

**cal·if·ate** (kal′ə fāt′ *or* kā′lə fāt′) See CALIPHATE. *n.*

**Cal·i·for·nia poppy** (kal′ə fôr′nyə) **1** a small poppy having finely divided leaves and orange, yellow, or cream-coloured flowers. **2** its flower.

**cal·i·for·ni·um** (kal′ə fôr′nē əm) a highly radio-active synthetic element, produced by bombarding curium with helium isotopes. Symbol: Cf *n.*
☛ *Etym.* Named after the University of *California*, where it was first produced in 1950.

**cal·i·pers** (kal′ə pərz) See CALLIPERS. *n. pl.*

**ca·liph** (kā′lif *or* kal′if) a traditional title, since the time of Mohammed, of the religious and political leader of the Moslem community: *The office of the caliph was suspended in 1926 until such time as the Moslem peoples can again form one community.* *n.* Also, **calif, khalif**.

**cal·iph·ate** (kal′ə fāt′ *or* kā′lə fāt′) the rank, reign, government, or territory of a CALIPH. *n.* Also, **califate**.

**cal·is·then·ics** (kal′is then′iks) See CALLISTHENICS. *n. pl. or sing.*

hat, āge, fär; let, ēqual, tėrm; it, īce
hot, ōpen, ôrder; oil, out; cup, pùt, rüle
əbove, takən, pencəl, lemən, circəs
ch, child; ng, long; sh, ship
th, thin; ᴛʜ, then; zh, measure

**calk¹** (kok) See CAULK. *v.*
☛ *Hom.* CAULK, COCK.

**calk²** (kok) **1** a projecting piece on a horseshoe that catches in the ground or ice and prevents slipping. **2** a spiked plate attached to the bottom of a shoe to prevent slipping. **3** put calks on. 1, 2 *n.,* 3 *v.*
☛ *Hom.* CAULK, COCK.

**call** (kol) **1** speak loudly; cry; shout: *Morag called from downstairs.* **2** a shout; cry: *a call for help.* **3** of a bird or animal, utter its characteristic sound. **4** the characteristic sound of a bird or other animal. **5** give a signal to: *The bugle called the men to assemble.* **6** a signal given by sound: *Army calls are played on the bugle.* **7** rouse; waken: *Call me at seven o'clock.* **8** summon or command: *Obey when duty calls.* **9** a summon or command: *a call for volunteers.* **10** convene; assemble: *They have called a meeting for Thursday.* **11** bring to action; begin to consider: *Her case will be called in court tomorrow.* **12** a claim or demand: *A busy person has many calls on her time. The store doesn't stock that model any more because there is little call for it.* **13** give a name or label to: *They called the baby John. I hit him because he called me a coward.* **14** consider; think of as being: *Everyone called the party a success. I call that a rude remark.* **15** a need; occasion: *You have no call to meddle in other people's business.* **16** make a short visit or stop: *Please call when you are walking this way.* **17** a short visit or stop. **18** read over aloud: *The teacher called the roll of the class.* **19** end; stop: *The ball game was called on account of rain.* **20** ring up on the telephone; telephone: *Call me tomorrow morning.* **21** a calling by telephone: *I want to make a call to Montreal.* **22** demand payment of: *The bank called my mother's loan.* **23** the act of calling. 1, 3, 5, 7, 8, 10, 11, 13, 14, 16, 18–20, 22 *v.,* 2, 4, 6, 9, 12, 15, 17, 21, 23 *n.*
**call attention to,** bring to people's notice.
**call away,** cause someone to leave: *I'm sorry, she's not here; she's been called away.*
**call back, a** ask a person to return; recall: *Call the letter carrier back.* **b** take back; retract. **c** telephone to someone who has called earlier.
**call down,** *Informal.* scold.
**call for, a** go and get; stop and get: *You can call for the pictures any time after three o'clock.* **b** need; require: *This recipe calls for two eggs. Your remark was uncalled for.* **c** ask for: *to call for the waiter. People are calling for a new law.*
**call forth,** bring into action or being; get: *a play that calls forth strong emotions.*
**call in, a** ask someone to visit: *We had to call in the doctor when Jim got worse.* **b** recall: *The cars were called in because of poor brakes.*
**call off, a** order back; order away: *Call off your dog.* **b** cancel: *We called off our trip.* **c** read aloud from a list: *The names were called off alphabetically.*
**call on** or **upon, a** visit. **b** appeal to: *Emese called upon her friends for help.*
**call out, a** shout loudly. **b** ask someone to help: *Firefighters from three districts were called out.* **c** cause to strike. **d** cause to be used: *The desperate situation called out all his courage.*

**call up, a** bring to mind; bring back. **b** telephone. **c** summon to the service of the country.
**on call, a** subject to payment on demand. **b** available at any time: *There are three doctors on call tonight.* ☛ *Hom.* CAUL.

**cal·la** (kal′ə) any of several plants of the ARUM family having large spear-shaped or heart-shaped leaves and a white, yellow, or pink SPATHE around a yellow SPADIX. *n.*

**calla lily** 1 a showy house or greenhouse plant of the ARUM family having a large white, flaring SPATHE surrounding a yellow SPADIX. See ARUM for picture. 2 CALLA.

**call·boy** (kol′boi′) 1 a bellboy in a hotel, ship, etc. 2 a boy who calls actors from their dressing rooms when they are due to appear on the stage. *n.*

**call·er** (kol′ər) 1 a person who makes a short visit. 2 a person who calls, especially a person who calls out the dance steps at a square dance. *n.* ☛ *Hom.* CHOLER, COLLAR.

**cal·li·graph·ic** (kal′ə graf′ik) having to do with CALLIGRAPHY. *adj.*

**cal·lig·ra·phy** (kə lig′rə fē) 1 handwriting. 2 the art of beautiful handwriting. *n.*

**call·ing** (kol′ing) 1 a business; occupation; profession; trade: *Peter intends to follow the calling of medicine.* 2 a command; summons. 3 ppr. of CALL. 1, 2 *n.*, 3 *v.*

**cal·li·o·pe** (kə lī′ə pē′) a musical instrument having a series of steam whistles played by a keyboard similar to that of an organ. *n.*
☛ *Etym.* From *Calliope*, in Greek mythology, the Muse of eloquence and heroic poetry.

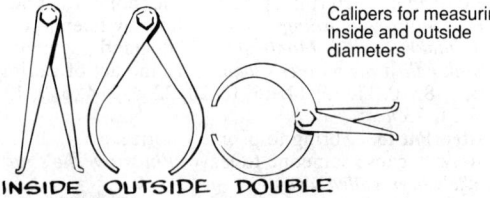
Calipers for measuring inside and outside diameters
INSIDE   OUTSIDE   DOUBLE

**cal·li·pers** or **cal·i·pers** (kal′ə pərz) an instrument used to measure the diameter or thickness of something. *n. pl.*

**cal·lis·then·ics** or **cal·is·then·ics** (kal′is then′iks) 1 exercises without the use of special equipment, designed to develop a strong and graceful body. 2 the practice or art of callisthenics: *Callisthenics is part of our physical education program.* 1 *n. pl.*, 2 *n. sing.*

**call number** a combination of letters and numbers that is part of a system by which a book is classified and assigned to a place on a library shelf.

**cal·los·i·ty** (kə los′ə tē) 1 a hard, thickened place on the skin; callus. 2 lack of feeling; hardness of heart. *n., pl.* **cal·los·i·ties**.

**cal·lous** (kal′əs) 1 hard; hardened: *Going barefoot makes the bottoms of the feet callous.* 2 unfeeling; not sensitive: *Only a callous person can see suffering without trying to relieve it.* *adj.* —**cal′lous·ly,** *adv.* —**cal′lous·ness,** *n.*
☛ *Hom.* CALLUS.

**cal·low** (kal′ō) 1 young and inexperienced. 2 not fully developed. 3 of birds, without feathers sufficiently developed for flight. *adj.* —**cal′low·ness,** *n.*

**call sign** the combination of letters or letters and numbers used to identify a radio station, operator, office, etc.

**cal·lus** (kal′əs) a hard, thickened place on the skin: *He has a callus under his toe.* *n., pl.* **cal·lus·es**.
☛ *Hom.* CALLOUS.

**calm** (kom *or* käm) 1 not stormy or windy; quiet; still; not moving: *a calm sea, a calm day.* 2 the absence of motion or wind; quietness; stillness: *After the storm came the calm.* 3 peaceful; not excited: *Although she was frightened, she answered the summons with a calm voice.* 4 the absence of excitement; peacefulness: *Her arrival shattered the calm of the household.* 5 become calm: *The sea has calmed. The crying baby soon calmed down.* 6 make calm: *She soon calmed the baby.* 1, 3 *adj.*, 2, 4 *n.*, 5, 6 *v.* —**calm′ly,** *adv.* —**calm′ness,** *n.*

**cal·o·mel** (kal′ə mel′) a white, tasteless crystalline powder, a compound of mercury, used in medicine as a CATHARTIC. *n.*

**ca·lor·ic** (kə lô′rik) 1 heat. 2 having to do with heat. 3 having to do with CALORIES. 1 *n.*, 2, 3 *adj.*

**cal·o·rie** or **cal·o·ry** (kal′ə rē) 1 either of two units for measuring heat. A **calorie**, or **small calorie** represents the quantity of heat necessary to raise the temperature of a gram of water one degree Celsius. A **Calorie**, or **large calorie** represents the amount of heat necessary to raise the temperature of one kilogram of water one degree Celsius: *A calorie is equal to about 4.18 joules; a Calorie is equal to about 4.18 kilojoules.* 2 a unit corresponding to a Calorie, used to measure the heat or energy produced by food as it is burned in the body: *Thirty grams of brown sugar produce about 100 calories.* 3 an amount of food capable of producing energy equal to one Calorie. *n., pl.* **cal·o·ries**.

**cal·o·rif·ic** (kal′ə rif′ik) producing heat. *adj.*

**cal·u·met** (kal′yə met′) *Cdn.* a long, ornamented tobacco pipe formerly used by Amerindian peoples of the plains and eastern woodlands, especially in formal peacemaking ceremonies. *n.*

**cal·um·ni·ate** (kə lum′nē āt′) say false and injurious things about; SLANDER. *v.*, **ca·lum·ni·at·ed, ca·lum·ni·at·ing.** —**ca·lum′ni·a′tion,** *n.* —**ca·lum′ni·a′tor,** *n.*

**cal·lum·ni·ous** (kə lum′nē əs) SLANDEROUS. *adj.* —**ca·lum′ni·ous·ly,** *adv.*

**cal·um·ny** (kal′əm nē) a false statement made to injure someone's reputation; SLANDER. *n., pl.* **cal·um·nies**.

**calve** (kav) 1 give birth to a calf. 2 of a glacier, produce or set loose an iceberg or icebergs: *When an advancing arctic glacier reaches the sea, the heavy weight of the ice in the water causes the glacier to calve huge chunks of ice that float away as icebergs.* *v.* **calved, calv·ing**.

**calves** (kavz) pl. of CALF. *n.*

**calx** (kalks) 1 an ashy substance left after a metal or a mineral has been CALCINEd or burned. 2 lime or chalk. *n., pl.* **calx·es** or **cal·ces** (kal′sēz).

**cal·y·ces** (kā′lə sēz′ *or* kal′ə sēz′) a pl. of CALYX. *n.*

**ca·lyp·so** (kə lip′sō) 1 of or referring to a kind of song that originated in Trinidad, characterized by syncopated rhythms and improvisation and usually having satirical or humorous lyrics.   **2** calypso music or a calypso song.   1 *adj.*, 2 *n.*

**ca·lyx** (kā′liks *or* kal′iks)   the outer leaves that surround the unopened bud of a flower: *The calyx is made up of sepals.*   *n.*, *pl.* **ca·lyx·es** *or* **cal·y·ces** (i sēz).

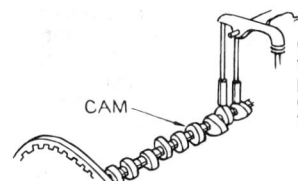
Cams. The cam turns with the shaft. The wheel of the plunger follows the irregular curve of the cam, causing the plunger to move up and down.

**cam** (kam)   a projection on a wheel or shaft that changes a regular circular motion into an irregular circular motion or into a back-and-forth motion.   *n.*

**ca·ma·ra·de·rie** (kä′mə rä′də rē)   comradeship; friendliness and loyalty among comrades.   *n.*

**cam·as** *or* **cam·ass** (kam′əs)   a plant of the same family as the lily: *North American Indians ate the sweet nourishing bulbs of the camas.*   *n.*

**cam·ber** (kam′bər)   **1** arch slightly; bend or curve upward in the middle.   **2** a slight arch; an upward bend or curve in the middle, such as the curve of an airfoil, a ship's deck, a road, or a piece of timber.   1 *v.*, 2 *n.*

**cam·bi·um** (kam′bē əm)   the layer of soft, growing tissue between the bark and the wood of trees and shrubs, from which new bark and new wood grow.   *n.*

**Cam·bri·an** (kam′brē ən)   **1** of, having to do with, or referring to the first period of the Paleozoic era of geological time, or the rock formed during this time: *The Cambrian period began about 575 million years ago.*   **2 the Cambrian,** the Cambrian period.   1 *adj.*, 2 *n.*   See geological time chart in the Appendix.

**cam·bric** (kām′brik)   a fine, thin linen or cotton cloth.   *n.*

**cambric tea**   a drink made of hot water, milk, and sugar, often flavoured with a little tea.

**came** (kām)   pt. of COME: *He came home late.*   *v.*

An Arabian camel - about 2 m high at the shoulder   A Bactrian camel - about 170 cm high at the shoulder

**cam·el** (kam′əl)   either of two species of large, cud-chewing desert mammal of Africa and Asia, having a long neck, broad, padded feet, and one or two humps on the back in which they can store fat for use as food and as a source of water: *Camels are used as beasts of burden and also for their wool, milk, hide, and meat.*   *n.*

**cam·el·lia** (kə mē′lyə)   **1** a shrub or tree having glossy leaves and waxy, white or red flowers shaped like roses.   **2** the flower.   *n.*

**calyx     169     camouflage**

hat, āge, fär; let, ēqual, tėrm; it, īce
hot, ōpen, ôrder; oil, out; cup, pùt, rüle
əbove, takən, pencəl, lemən, circəs
ch, child; ng, long; sh, ship
th, thin; ŦH, then; zh, measure

**Cam·e·lot** (kam′ə lot′)   a legendary place in England where King Arthur had his palace and court.   *n.*

**camel's hair**   **1** the hair of a camel, used in making cloth, paintbrushes, etc.   **2** cloth made of this hair or something like this hair.

**Cam·em·bert** (kam′əm ber′)   a rich, soft cheese.   *n.*

**cam·e·o** (kam′ē ō′)   **1** a precious or semiprecious stone, especially one made up of layers of different colours, carved so that there is a raised part of one colour on a background of another colour: *Agates are commonly used for cameos.*   **2** the technique of carving cameos.   **3** a short literary sketch of a certain character or event.   **4** an appearance by a famous actor or actress in a minor film role, usually in a single brief scene, that presents a distinctive character or is especially suited to the star's talents: *In this movie, he has a cameo as an eccentric landlord.*   **5** a brooch showing a single object in relief.   *n.*, *pl.* **cam·e·os.**

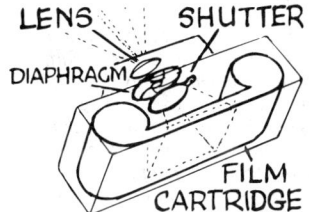
A camera. When the shutter is opened, light rays reflected from the object pass through the lens and are focussed by it onto the film. Because the film is sensitive to light, it records the image.

**cam·er·a** (kam′ə rə)   **1** a lightproof box or chamber for taking photographs or motion pictures, in which film or plates are exposed and the image is formed by means of a lens.   **2** in television, the part of the transmitter that converts images into electronic impulses for transmitting.   **3** a judge's private office.   *n.*, *pl.* **cam·er·as** for 1 and 2, **cam·er·ae** (-ē′ *or* -ī′) for 3.
**in camera,**   **a** in a judge's private office.   **b** privately.

**cam·er·a·man** (kam′ə rə man′)   a person who operates a camera, especially a motion-picture or television camera.   *n.*, *pl.* **cam·er·a·men** (-men′).

**cam·er·a–read·y** (kam′ə rə red′ē)   ready to be photographed for printing: *camera-ready copy.*

**cam·i·on** (kam′ē ən)   **1** a low, heavy cart; dray.   **2** a truck for carrying cannon.   *n.*

**cam·i·sole** (kam′ə sōl′)   a waist-length, sleeveless undergarment worn by women and girls, especially one trimmed with lace or embroidery and worn under a sheer blouse or shirt.   *n.*

**cam·o·mile** (kam′ə mīl′)   a plant of the same family as the aster, having daisy-like flowers: *The flowers and leaves of the camomile are sometimes dried and used in medicine.*   *n.*   Also, **chamomile.**

**cam·ou·flage** (kam′ə fläzh′)   **1** an outward appearance that makes a person, animal, or thing seem to be part of its natural surroundings: *The white fur of a polar bear is a natural camouflage, for it prevents the bear from being easily seen against the snow.*   **2** the practice of giving soldiers, weapons, etc. a false appearance to conceal them from the

**camp** 170 **Canada Medal**

enemy. **3** materials or other means by which something or someone is disguised or concealed: *A camouflage of earth and branches effectively hid the guns.* **4** give a false appearance in order to conceal; disguise: *The hunters were camouflaged with shrubbery so that they blended with the green landscape. The girl camouflaged her embarrassment by laughing.* 1-3 *n.*, 4 *v.*, **cam·ou·flaged, cam·ou·flag·ing.** —**cam'ou·flag'er,** *n.*

**camp** (kamp) **1** a temporary shelter such as a tent, trailer, or cabin, or the ground on which it is set up: *Her camp was right in the bush. It took us three hours to get back to camp.* **2** a temporary community of people living in tents, trailers, cabins, etc. in the country, especially for holidays or outings: *a wilderness camp. They always go to camp for two weeks in summer.* **3** the people in a camp: *The camp was up by seven o'clock.* **4** make a camp; put up tents, huts, etc.: *We decided to camp by the river the first night.* **5** live simply without comforts for a time: *We had to camp in the house until our furniture arrived.* **6** a group of people who promote a particular theory, political doctrine, etc.: *the liberal camp.* **7** military life. 1-3, 6, 7 *n.*, 4, 5 *v.* —**camp'er,** *n.*
**break camp,** pack up tents and equipment and leave.
**camp out,** live in camp.
**make camp,** set up a camp; set up tents, etc.: *We hiked until sunset and then made camp beside a creek.*

**cam·paign** (kam pān') **1** a series of related military operations for some special purpose: *The general's staff planned a campaign to capture the enemy's most important city.* **2** a series of connected activities to do or get something; a planned course of action for some special purpose: *a campaign to raise money for a new hospital, a campaign to advertise some article, a campaign to elect someone to political office.* **3** take part in or serve in a campaign; go on a campaign: *She's campaigning in Saskatchewan this week.* 1, 2 *n.*, 3 *v.* —**cam·paign'er,** *n.*

**cam·pa·ni·le** (kam'pə nē'lē) a bell tower, especially one that is near, but not attached to, a church. *n., pl.* **cam·pa·ni·les** or **cam·pa·ni·li** (-nē'lē).

**cam·pan·u·la** (kam pan'yə lə) a bluebell, Canterbury bell, or other similar plant having bell-shaped flowers. *n.*

**camp·er** (kam'pər) **1** a person who camps. **2** a member of a summer camp for children or adolescents. **3** a vehicle equipped for camping, such as a small covered trailer or a pickup truck: *Campers often have built-in beds, cupboards, etc.* *n.*

**camp·fire** (kamp'fīr') **1** a fire in a camp for warmth or cooking. **2** a social gathering of campers, scouts, guides, etc. *n.*

**camp·ground** (kamp'ground') **1** a place where a camp is. **2** a place where one is permitted to park a camper, trailer, or motor home for the night. *n.*

**cam·phor** (kam'fər) a white, crystalline compound with a strong odour and a bitter taste: *Camphor is used in the manufacture of film, lacquers, etc., in medicine, and in protecting clothes from moths.* *n.*

**cam·phor·at·ed** (kam'fə rā'tid) containing CAMPHOR: *camphorated oil.* *adj.*

**cam·pi·on** (kam'pē ən) any of certain plants of the same family as the pink, with red or white flowers. *n.*

**cam·po·ree** (kam'pə rē') a gathering of scouts or guides for competitions in camp craft, etc. *n.*

**camp robber** *Cdn.* CANADA JAY.

**camp·stool** (kamp'stül') a lightweight folding seat. *n.*

**cam·pus** (kam'pəs) the grounds of a university, college, or school. *n.*

**can**[1] (kan; *unstressed*, kən) a verb used as an auxiliary followed by an infinitive without **to,** to mean: **1** ability: *Can you come tomorrow? I can swim quite well. I can't see because you're standing in my way.* **2** possession of a right or the means to do something: *You can cross the street here. You can go at 4 o'clock.* **3** have power: *This calculator can do much more than the other one.* **4** possibility: *I'm sure you can't mean that.* *v., pres. sing. and pl.* **can,** *pt.* **could.**
☛ *Syn.* **Can** indicates ability but MAY indicates permission: *Although I can skate, Mother says that I may not do so today.*

**can**[2] (kan) **1** a metal container, usually having a separate lid: *a garbage can, an oil can, a milk can.* **2** a small metal container in which foods are sealed to preserve them for later use; tin can. **3** preserve by putting in airtight cans or jars: *to can fruit.* **4** the contents of a can: *We ate a can of peaches.* 1, 2, 4 *n.*, 3 *v.*, **canned, can·ning.**

**Can.** **1** Canada. **2** Canadian.

**Can·a·da Act** (kan'ə də) the Act of 1791 which divided the province of Quebec into Upper and Lower Canada.

**Canada balsam** a sticky, yellow resin obtained from the BALSAM FIR tree.

**Canada Council** a body established by Parliament in 1957 to administer funds for the encouragement of writing, music, painting, and other cultural activities.

**Canada Day** July 1st, Canada's national holiday, formerly called Dominion Day: *The Dominion of Canada was established on July 1st, 1867. The name was officially changed to Canada Day in October, 1982.*

**Canada goose** a large wild goose of North America having a black head and neck, a white throat, and a brownish-grey body. See GOOSE for picture.

Canada jays - about 28 cm long

**Canada jay** a species of jay that is common throughout Canada and the northern United States, having loose, fluffy, grey feathers on the body and a white-and-black head without a crest; grey jay: *The Canada jay has a number of nicknames, including lumberjack, moosebird, and whisky-jack.*

**Canada lynx** a species of lynx found mainly in Canada and Alaska, having very large paws, pointed ears with long tufts, and a thick coat of long, silky, greyish fur mixed with black and dark brown: *The large, well-furred paws of the lynx function like snowshoes in winter, enabling it to run fast over the snow in pursuit of its prey.* See LYNX for picture.

**Canada Medal** an award for conspicuous bravery to

civilians or military personnel, established in 1943. See MEDAL for picture.

**Ca·na·darm** (kə′nə′därm) *n.* an extension, built in Canada, of a spacecraft, which allows astronauts to move and handle objects in space.

**Canada thistle** a kind of thistle that is a very common and troublesome weed throughout Canada: *Canada thistles have small rose-purple, pink, or, sometimes, white flowers.*

**Ca·na·di·an** (kə nā′dē ən) **1** of Canada or its people. **2** a native, inhabitant, or citizen of Canada. 1 *adj.*, 2 *n.*

**Ca·na·di·a·na** (kə nā′dē an′ə *or* kə nā′dē ä′nə) things relating to Canada and its history, especially early Canadian furniture, textiles, books, etc. *n.*

**Canadian Armed Forces** since 1968, the combined land, air, and naval forces of Canada, an integration of the former Royal Canadian Navy, the Royal Canadian Air Force, and the Canadian Army. *Abbrev.*: CAF or CF.

**Canadian Broadcasting Corporation** a Crown corporation in the field of radio and television broadcasting, established by Parliament in 1936. *Abbrev.*: CBC.

**Canadian English** the kind of English spoken by English-speaking Canadians.

**Canadian Forces** CANADIAN ARMED FORCES.

**Canadian French** the kind of French spoken by French-speaking Canadians.

**Ca·na·di·an·ism** (kə nā′dē ə nīz′əm) **1** a word or expression originating in or peculiar to Canada: *"Muskeg" and "caribou" are Canadianisms.* **2** a custom peculiar to Canada. **3** loyalty to Canada as an independent nation and devotion to her customs, traditions, and laws. *n.*

**Ca·na·di·an·ize** (kə nā′dē ə nīz′) **1** make Canadian in character or custom: *Our new neighbours have become so Canadianized they've already taken up curling.* **2** change the content or subject matter of a book, television program, scientific report, etc. to reflect Canadian situations or points of view. **3** bring under Canadian ownership or control: *to Canadianize a foreign-owned industry.* *v.,* **Ca·na·di·an·ized, Ca·na·di·an·iz·ing.** —**Ca·na′di·an·i·za′tion,** *n.*

**Canadian Legion** an organization of Canadian ex-servicemen and women; the ROYAL CANADIAN LEGION.

**Canadian Radio–television and Telecommunications Commission** a Federal Government body established in 1968 to regulate radio and television broadcasting in Canada. It has the power to enforce broadcasting policy and regulate public and private radio and television and cable systems. *Abbrev.*: CRTC

**Canadian Shield** a region of ancient rock, chiefly Precambrian granite, encircling Hudson Bay and covering nearly half the mainland of Canada: *The Canadian Shield is rich in minerals, especially gold, copper, nickel, and iron ore.*

**Ca·na·di·en** (kə nā′dē en′; *French*, kä nä dyeɴ′) a French Canadian. *n.*

**Canadarm** 171 **cancel**

hat, āge, fär; let, ēqual, tèrm; it, īce
hot, ōpen, ôrder; oil, out; cup, pút, rüle
әbove, takәn, pencәl, lemәn, circәs
ch, child; ng, long; sh, ship
th, thin; ᴛн, then; zh, measure

**Ca·na·di·enne** (kə nā′dē en′; *French*, kä nä dyen′) a French-Canadian girl or woman. *n.*

**ca·nal** (kə nal′) **1** a waterway dug across land: *Some canals are for boats and ships; others are for carrying water to places that need it.* **2** a tube in the body or in a plant for carrying food, liquid, or air. **3** a long arm of a large body of water. **4** any of the long, narrow markings sometimes visible on the surface of the planet Mars. *n.*

**canal boat** a long, narrow boat used on canals: *Canal boats are sometimes pulled along by horses.*

**ca·nal·ize** (kə nal′īz *or* kan′ə līz′) **1** make a CANAL or canals through. **2** make into or like a CANAL. *v.,* **ca·nal·ized, ca·nal·iz·ing.**

**ca·nard** (kə närd′) a false rumour; hoax. *n.*

**ca·nar·y** (kə ner′ē) **1** a small yellow or greenish-yellow songbird, a species of finch native to the Canary Islands: *Canaries are often kept as cage birds for their bright plumage and also for their singing.* **2** CANARY YELLOW. **3** a usually sweet wine from the Canary Islands. 1–3 *n., pl.* **ca·nar·ies;** 2 *adj.*
☞ *Etym.* The bird and wine were named for the Canary Islands. The English name of the islands is a 16c. translation of the French name which in turn came through Spanish from the Latin name for one of the islands, *Canaria insula* 'Island of the Dogs', so named because of the large dogs found there. *Canaria* is formed from L *canis* 'dog'.

**canary yellow** light yellow.

**ca·nas·ta** (kə nas′tə) a card game similar to rummy, played by two to six players using two decks of cards: *In canasta the players try to earn as many points as possible by getting sets of seven or more cards.* *n.*

**can·can** (kan′kan′) a kind of dance marked by extravagant kicking, and leaping, performed by women (often in a chorus line) and originating in 19th-century Paris. *n.*

**can·cel** (kan′səl) **1** cross out; mark, stamp, or punch something so that it cannot be used or used again: *to cancel a stamp.* **2** ANNUL; make without value: *The debt was cancelled.* **3** divide the same factor into both the numerator and denominator of a fraction, or into the two sides of an equation. **4** put an end to or withdraw; call off; stop: *She cancelled her order for the books. The meeting has been cancelled.* **5** make up for; balance; compensate; neutralize: *The little boy's sweet smile cancelled his crossness.* **6** a cancelling. **7** a cancelled part. 1–5 *v.,* **can·celled** *or* **can·celed, can·cel·ling** *or* **can·cel·ing;** 6, 7 *n.*

**cancel out,** balance or neutralize one another: *The pros and cons cancelled out and we were back where we started.*
☞ *Etym.* **Cancel,** CHANCEL, and CHANCELLOR came into English through different OF words that had developed from forms of L *cancelli* 'lattice or cross-bars' (as at the gate of a monastery or court). **Cancel** is from a L verb meaning 'to cross out', formed from *cancelli* because crossed lines resembling a lattice were used to cancel documents. The L *cancelli* also came to mean the area behind the lattice, and from this meaning in L and OF comes English **chancel. Chancellor** comes from the L

word for the porter at the gate of a court; it was first used in English to refer to a person of little education but gradually came to refer to persons of greater dignity until today it refers to persons in positions of the highest importance.

**can·cel·la·tion** (kan′sə lā′shən) **1** cancelling or being cancelled: *The cancellation of the game was a great disappointment.* **2** the marks made when something is cancelled or crossed out: *You can hardly see the cancellation on this stamp.* **3** something cancelled. *n.*

**can·cer** (kan′sər) **1** a harmful, uncontrolled growth of new tissue or cells in the body that tends to spread and destroy healthy tissue; a malignant tumour. **2** a condition marked by such harmful growths. **3** any evil or harmful thing that tends to spread: *the cancer of jealousy.* **4 Cancer, a** in astronomy, a northern constellation thought of as having the shape of a crab. **b** in astrology, the fourth sign of the zodiac. The sun enters Cancer about June 21. See ZODIAC for picture. **c** a person born under this sign. **d** Usually, **tropic of Cancer,** an imaginary circle around the world 23 ½° north of the equator. *n.*

**can·cer·ous** (kan′sə rəs) **1** of CANCER (def. 1): *a cancerous growth.* **2** having CANCER (def. 1): *a cancerous rat.* *adj.*

**can·de·la** (kan del′ə) an SI unit for measuring luminous intensity, or candlepower, which is the amount of light shining in one direction from a glowing object: *One candela is the amount of light produced by the inside of a ceramic box that has been heated until it glows; the light is measured as it shines out through a hole in the box. The candela is one of the seven base units in the SI.* Symbol: cd *n.*

**can·de·la·brum** (kan′də lä′brəm) an ornamental candlestick with several branches for candles. *n., pl.* **can·de·la·bra** (-brə) or **can·de·la·brums.**

**can·des·cent** (kan des′ənt) glowing with heat; INCANDESCENT. *adj.*

**can·did** (kan′did) **1** frank; sincere: *a candid reply.* **2** fair; impartial: *a candid decision.* **3** of a photograph, not posed: *The magazine story included several candid shots of the premier's family.* *adj.* —**can′did·ly,** *adv.*

**can·di·da·cy** (kan′də də sē) the state of being a CANDIDATE: *Please support my candidacy for treasurer.* *n.*

**can·di·date** (kan′də dāt′ *or* kan′də dit) **1** a person who seeks or is proposed for an honour, prize, position, office, etc.: *There were three possible candidates for the award. All the job candidates have been interviewed.* **2** a person who seems to have a particular fate in store: *a candidate for fame and fortune, a likely candidate for prison.* *n.*

**can·died** (kan′dēd) **1** glazed, soaked, or cooked with sugar: *candied cherries, a candied apple.* **2** made sweet or agreeable: *His candied words of congratulation hid a great bitterness.* **3** pt. and pp. of CANDY. 1, 2 *adj.*, 3 *v.*

**can·dle** (kan′dəl) **1** a stick of wax or tallow with a wick in it, burned to give light. **2** anything shaped or used like a candle: *Sulphur candles are burned to disinfect rooms.* **3** test eggs for freshness and quality by holding them in front of a light in order to see the size of the air pocket and the position and size of the yolk. **4** a unit for measuring the strength of a light. The **international candle** is the light from 5 square millimetres of platinum at the temperature at which it solidifies. 1, 2, 4 *n.*, 3 *v.*, **can·dled, can·dling.** —**can′dler,** *n.*
**burn the candle at both ends,** try to do more than one's energy or resources allow; make unreasonable demands on one's physical and mental resources: *She's been burning the candle at both ends for so long that she's bound to break down.*
**not hold a candle to,** not compare with: *The cake from the bakery could not hold a candle to the one Eva made.*
☛ *Etym.* **Candle** and CHANDELIER both come originally from L *candella* 'candle', formed from the verb *candere* 'to glisten, burn'. **Candle** has developed from OE *candel*, which was taken directly from L. **Chandelier** came into English much later from F *chandelier* 'candleholder', formed from F *chandelle* 'candle', which had also developed from L *candella*.

**can·dle·fish** (kan′dəl fish′) OOLICHAN. *n.*

**can·dle·hold·er** (kan′dəl hōl′dər) a holder for a candle, having a socket or a spike to make the candle stand upright. *n.*

**can·dle·light** (kan′dəl līt′) **1** the light from a candle or candles. **2** the time when candles are lighted; dusk; twilight; nightfall. *n.*

**can·dle·pow·er** (kan′dəl pou′ər) the intensity of a light source, expressed in CANDLES (def. 4). *n.*

**can·dle·stick** (kan′dəl stik′) a candleholder, especially one having a socket for the candle. *n.*

**can·dle·wick** (kan′dəl wik′) the wick of a candle. *n.*

**can·dor** (kan′dər) See CANDOUR. *n.*

**can·dour** or **can·dor** (kan′dər) **1** saying openly what one really thinks; honesty in giving one's view or opinion. **2** fairness; impartiality. *n.*

**can·dy** (kan′dē) **1** a confection made with sugar or syrup and flavouring: *He doesn't eat much candy.* **2** a piece of this: *She took a candy from the box.* **3** cook or soak in sugar, or glaze with sugar. **4** make sweet or agreeable. 1, 2 *n., pl.* (def. 2) **can·dies;** 3, 4 *v.*, **can·died, can·dy·ing.**

**can·dy-strip·er** (kan′dē strī′pər) a teenage girl who does volunteer work in a hospital. *n.*

**can·dy·tuft** (kan′dē tuft′) a plant of the same family as mustard, having clusters of white, purple, or pink flowers. *n.*

**cane** (kān) **1** a stick to help a person in walking; a walking stick. **2** a stick used to beat with. **3** beat with a cane. **4** a long, jointed stem, such as that of the bamboo. **5** a plant having such stems: *Sugar cane, bamboo, and rattan are canes.* **6** the material made of such stems: *Cane is often used for furniture, chair seats, etc.* **7** make or repair with this material: *to cane a chair seat.* **8** a slender stalk or stem. 1, 2, 4–6, 8 *n.*, 3, 7 *v.*, **caned, can·ing.**

**cane·brake** (kān′brāk′) a thicket of cane plants. *n.*

**cane sugar** sugar from sugar cane.

**ca·nine** (kā′nīn) **1** of or having to do with dogs. **2** like that of a dog: *Her little brother followed her around with canine devotion.* **3** dog. **4** of or having to do with the dog family, a group of meat-eating, four-footed animals that includes the domestic dog, wolf, coyote, Australian dingo, and jackal. **5** a member of the dog family. **6** CANINE TOOTH. 1, 2, 4 *adj.*, 3, 5, 6 *n.*

**canine tooth** one of the four pointed teeth next to the incisors. See TEETH for picture.

**can·is·ter** (kan′i stər)  1 a small covered box or can, especially one used for keeping tea, flour, sugar, coffee, and other dry products.  2 a bullet-filled case that is shot from a CANNON (def. 1).  *n.*

**can·ker** (kang′kər)  1 a spreading sore, especially one in the mouth.  2 a disease of plants that causes slow decay.  3 anything that causes rot or decay or that destroys by a gradual eating away.  4 infect or be infected with canker; decay; rot.  1–3 *n.*, 4 *v.*

**can·ker·ous** (kang′kə rəs)  affected with, caused by, or like CANKER.  *adj.*

**can·ker·worm** (kang′kər wėrm′)  a caterpillar that eats away the leaves of trees and plants.  *n.*

**can·na** (kan′ə)  1 a plant with large, pointed leaves and large red, pink, or yellow flowers.  2 the flower.  *n.*

**can·na·bis** (kan′ə bis)  1 hemp.  2 the dried flowering tops of the female hemp plant: *Hashish is made from cannabis.*  *n.*

**canned** (kand)  1 put in a can; preserved by being put in airtight cans or jars.  2 pt. and pp. of CAN².  1 *adj.*, 2 *v.*

**cannel coal** (kan′əl)  a kind of BITUMINOUS coal in large lumps that burns with a bright flame and a lot of smoke.

**can·ner** (kan′ər)  a person who cans food.  *n.*

**can·ner·y** (kan′ə rē)  a factory where food is canned. *n., pl.* **can·ner·ies.**

**can·ni·bal** (kan′ə bəl)  1 a person who eats human flesh.  2 an animal that eats others of its own kind.  3 of or like cannibals.  *n.*

**can·ni·bal·ism** (kan′ə bə liz′əm)  the practice of eating the flesh of one's own kind.  *n.*

**can·ni·bal·is·tic** (kan′ə bə lis′tik)  of CANNIBALS; characteristic of cannibals.  *adj.*

**can·ni·bal·ize** (kan′ə bə līz′)  1 assemble or repair a vehicle, piece of machinery, etc. by using parts from others which are useless as a whole: *My brother cannibalized a radio set from two old ones that would not work.*  2 take usable parts from a vehicle, piece of machinery, etc. to assemble or repair another: *The soldiers cannibalized the wrecked jeep for tires.*  *v.*, **can·ni·bal·ized, can·ni·bal·iz·ing.**

**can·ni·kin** (kan′ə kin)  a small can; cup.  *n.*

**can·ning** (kan′ing)  1 the process or business of preserving food by putting it in airtight cans or jars.  2 ppr. of CAN².  1 *n.*, 2 *v.*

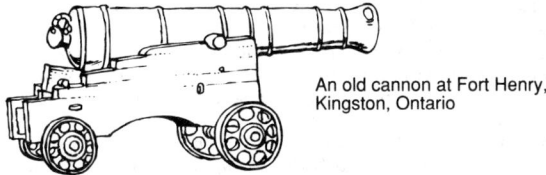

An old cannon at Fort Henry, Kingston, Ontario

**can·non** (kan′ən)  1 a big gun that is fixed to the ground or mounted on a carriage, especially the old-fashioned type of gun that fired cannon balls: *There are a number of fine cannon at Old Fort Henry in Kingston.*  2 CANNON BONE.  3 CAROM.  1–3 *n., pl.* **can·non** or **can·nons;**  3 *v.*

**can·non·ade** (kan′ə nād′)  1 a continued firing of CANNONS.  2 attack with CANNONS.  1 *n.*, 2 *v.*, **can·non·ad·ed, can·non·ad·ing.**

**cannon ball**  a large iron or steel ball, formerly fired from CANNONS (def. 1).

**cannon bone**  in hoofed animals, the long bone between the hock and the fetlock.  See HORSE for picture.

**can·not** (kan′ot *or* kə not′)  can not.  *v.*

**can·ny** (kan′ē)  1 shrewd and cautious.  2 thrifty. *adj.*, **can·ni·er, can·ni·est.**  —**can′ni·ly,** *adv.* —**can′ni·ness,** *n.*

A canoe

**ca·noe** (kə nü′)  1 a light, narrow boat having low, curving sides that come together in a point at each end, and moved by one or more paddles.  2 paddle a canoe; go in a canoe.  1 *n.*, 2 *v.*, **ca·noed, ca·noe·ing.**

**ca·noe·ist** (kə nü′ist)  a person who paddles a canoe, especially one who is skilled at doing this.  *n.*

**ca·noe·man** (kə nü′mən) *Cdn.*  1 VOYAGEUR.  2 a person skilled in handling a canoe.  *n., pl.* **ca·noe·men** (-mən).

**ca·no·la** (kə nō′lə)  RAPE².  *n.*

**ca·ñon** (kan′yən)  See CANYON.  *n.*

**ca·non·i·cal** (kə non′ə kəl)  1 according to or prescribed by the laws of a Christian church. 2 authorized; accepted.  *adj.*  —**ca·non′i·cal·ly,** *adv.*

**can·on·i·za·tion** (kan′ə nə zā′shən *or* kan′ə nī zā′shən)  canonizing or being CANONIZED.  *n.*

**can·on·ize** (kan′ə nīz′)  1 declare a dead person to be a saint; place in the official list of saints: *Joan of Arc was canonized by the Roman Catholic Church in 1920.*  2 treat as a saint; glorify.  3 make or recognize as CANONICAL.  4 authorize.  *v.*, **can·on·ized, can·on·iz·ing.**

**can·o·py** (kan′ə pē)  1 a covering fixed over a bed, throne, entrance, etc. or carried on poles over a person: *There is a striped canopy over the entrance to the hotel.* 2 a rooflike covering; a shelter or shade: *The trees formed a canopy over the old road.*  3 cover with a canopy. 4 the sky.  1, 2, 4 *n., pl.* **can·o·pies;**  3 *v.*, **can·o·pied, can·o·py·ing.**

**cant¹** (kant)  1 insincere talk; moral and religious statements that people make, but few really believe or follow.  2 the peculiar language of a special group, using many words not known to outsiders: *thieves' cant.* 3 peculiar to a special group: *cant words of thieves.*  4 use cant; talk in cant.  1–3 *n.*, 4 *v.*

**cant²** (kant) 1 slant; slope; BEVEL (def. 2). 2 a slant, slope, or BEVEL (def. 1). 3 tip; tilt. 4 throw with a sudden jerk; pitch; toss. 1, 3, 4 v., 2 n.

**can't** (kant) CANNOT. v.

**can·ta·loupe** or **can·ta·loup** (kan'tə lōp') a variety of MUSKMELON with a hard, rough rind and sweet, juicy, orange flesh. n.

**can·tan·ker·ous** (kan tang'kə rəs) showing a disagreeable and ill-natured disposition; hard to get along with because ready to make trouble and oppose anything suggested: *She's very cantankerous these days. The old man had a cantankerous way of speaking.* adj.
—**can·tan'ker·ous·ly,** adv. —**can·tan'ker·ous·ness,** n.

**can·ta·ta** (kən tä'tə or kən tat'ə) a musical composition consisting of a story or play to be sung, but not acted, by a chorus and soloists, usually with orchestral accompaniment. n.

**can·teen** (kan tēn') 1 a small container for carrying water or other drinks. 2 a place in a school, camp, factory, etc. where food and drink and, sometimes, other articles are sold or given out. 3 a store, recreation hall, or club for members of the armed forces. 4 a box of cooking utensils for use in camp. 5 a set of CUTLERY (def. 1) in a box or case. n.

**can·ter** (kan'tər) 1 a horse's gait faster than a trot but slower than a gallop. 2 move with this gait. 1 n., 2 v.

**Can·ter·bur·y bell** (kan'tər ber'ē) a biennial plant with tall stalks of bell-shaped flowers, usually purplish-blue, pink, or white.

**cant–hook** (kant'hùk') *Cdn.* a pole with a movable hook at one end, used to grip and turn over logs; PEAVEY. n.

**can·ti·lev·er** (kan'tə lē'vər or kan'tə lev'ər) 1 a large, projecting bracket or beam that is fastened at one end only. 2 build with cantilevers or a cantilever: *Our balcony is cantilevered; theirs is supported by pillars.* 1 n., 2 v.

**cantilever bridge** a bridge made of two CANTILEVERS whose projecting ends meet but do not support each other. See BRIDGE¹ for picture.

**can·tle** (kan'təl) the part of a saddle that sticks up at the back. n.

**can·to** (kan'tō) one of the main divisions of a long poem: *A canto of a poem corresponds to a chapter of a novel.* n., pl. **can·tos.**

**can·ton** (kan'ton) 1 a small part or political division of a country: *Switzerland is made up of 22 cantons.* 2 township. 3 in Quebec, a municipal unit roughly equal to a township. n.

**Can·ton·ese** (kan'tə nēz') 1 a native or inhabitant of Canton, a city in southern China. 2 the language spoken in or near Canton. 3 of Canton, its people, or their language. 1, 2 n., pl. **Can·ton·ese;** 3 adj.

**can·ton·ment** (kan ton'mənt or kan tōn'mənt) a place where soldiers live; quarters. n.

**can·tor** (kan'tər or kan'tôr) 1 the person who leads the singing of a choir or congregation. 2 a soloist in a synagogue, who leads the congregation in prayer. n.

**Ca·nuck** (kə nuk') *Cdn. Informal.* 1 Canadian. 2 French Canadian. n., adj.

**can·vas** (kan'vəs) 1 a strong cloth made of cotton, flax, or hemp, used to make tents, sails, certain articles of clothing, etc.: *The tops of my sandals are made of canvas.* 2 made of canvas. 3 something made of canvas. 4 a sail or sails. 5 a piece of canvas on which to paint a picture, especially in oils. 6 a picture painted on canvas: *She's got seven canvases ready for the show.* n., pl. **can·vas·es.**
**under canvas, a** in tents. **b** with sails spread: *The boat left the harbour under canvas.*
☛ *Hom.* CANVASS.

**can·vas·back** (kan'vəs bak') a wild duck of North America, having greyish feathers on its back. n.

**can·vass** (kan'vəs) 1 go about asking for subscriptions, votes, orders, etc.: *Each student canvassed his own block for contributions to the Red Cross.* 2 ask for votes, orders, donations, etc.: *The candidate canvassed right up to election day.* 3 the act or process of canvassing, especially a personal visiting of homes or stores in a district to sell something, ask for votes, etc. 4 examine carefully; examine: *Yaakov canvassed the papers, hunting for notices of jobs.* 5 discuss: *The city council canvassed the mayor's plan thoroughly.* 6 examine and count the votes cast in an election. 1, 2, 4–6 v., 3 n.
—**can'vass·er,** n.
☛ *Hom.* CANVAS.

**can·yon** (kan'yən) a narrow valley with high, steep sides, usually with a stream at the bottom. n. Also, **cañon.**
☛ *Etym.* From Spanish *cañón,* originally meaning 'large tube or pipe', which the Spaniards of New Mexico used to describe such deep, narrow valleys.

**caou·tchouc** (kou chùk' or kü'chùk) the gummy, coagulated juice of various tropical plants; rubber. n.

Caps: several different types

**cap** (kap) 1 a close-fitting covering for the head, usually having little or no brim. 2 a special head covering worn to show rank, occupation, etc.: *a nurse's cap.* 3 something that serves as a cover, especially to protect an end, tip, etc. or to close off the end of a pipe, tube, bottleneck, etc.: *a lens cap, a bottle cap.* 4 a top part like a cap: *The top of a mushroom is called a cap.* 5 put a cap on: *to cap a bottle, to cap an oil well.* 6 the highest part; top. 7 put a top on; cover the top of: *Whipped cream capped the dessert.* 8 match one thing with something good or better: *The two clowns kept on capping each other's jokes.* 9 a small quantity of explosive in a wrapper or covering. 1–4, 6, 9 n., 5, 7, 8 v., **capped, cap·ping.** —**cap'less,** adj. —**cap'like',** adj.

**cap.** 1 capital letter. 2 capitalize. 3 capacity. 4 capital.

**ca·pa·bil·i·ty** (kā′pə bil′ə tē) ability to learn or do; power or fitness; capacity. *n., pl.* **ca·pa·bil·i·ties.**

**ca·pa·ble** (kā′pə bəl) having fitness, power, or ability; able; efficient; competent: *a capable teacher. adj.* —**ca′pa·ble·ness,** *n.* —**ca′pa·bly,** *adv.*
**capable of, a** having ability, power, or fitness for: *Some airplanes are capable of going 1500 kilometres per hour.* **b** open to; ready for: *a statement capable of many interpretations.*

**ca·pa·cious** (kə pā′shəs) able to hold much; roomy; large: *a capacious closet. adj.* —**ca·pa′cious·ly,** *adv.* —**ca·pa′cious·ness,** *n.*

**ca·pac·i·ty** (kə pas′ə tē) **1** the amount of room or space inside; the largest amount that can be held by a container: *This can has a capacity of four litres.* **2** the power of receiving and holding: *the capacity of a metal for retaining heat. The theatre has a capacity of 400.* **3** ability to learn or do; power or aptitude: *a great capacity for learning.* **4** a position or relation: *A person may act in the capacity of guardian, trustee, voter, friend, etc.* **5** equal to the maximum capacity: *They had a capacity crowd for the opening night of the play. n., pl.* **ca·pac·i·ties.**

**cap and bells** a cap trimmed with bells, worn by a jester.

**cap and gown** a flat cap, or mortarboard, and loose gown, worn by university professors and students on certain occasions.

**cap-a-pie** or **cap-à-pie** (kap′ə pē′) from head to foot; completely. *adv.*

**ca·par·i·son** (kə par′ə sən *or* kə per′ə sən) **1** an ornamental covering for a horse. See TILT for picture. **2** any rich clothing or equipment. **3** dress richly; fit out. 1, 2 *n.*, 3 *v.*

**cape**[1] (kāp) an outer garment, or part of one, without sleeves, that falls loosely from the shoulders. *n.*

**cape**[2] (kāp) **1** a point of land extending into the water. **2 the Cape,** the Cape of Good Hope. *n.*

**Cape buffalo** a large, savage buffalo of southern Africa.

**cap·e·lin** (kap′lin *or* kā′plin) See CAPLIN. *n.*

**ca·per**[1] (kā′pər) **1** leap or jump about playfully: *The children were capering happily on the lawn.* **2** a playful leap or jump. **3** a playful trick, scheme, or pursuit: *Her newest caper is to tell everyone she's an orphan.* **4** a dishonest scheme or enterprise; racket: *He got five years in jail for that caper.* 1 *v.*, 2–4 *n.*
**cut a caper** or **cut capers,** behave in a frolicsome, playful way: *We really cut a caper at the party last night.*
☛ *Etym.* A shortened form of the English word *capriole,* borrowed from Italian *capriola,* meaning 'leap' which goes back ultimately to L *caper,* meaning 'goat'. **Caper**[2] is an entirely different word, from L *capperis* which was taken from *kapparis,* the Gk. name for the shrub.

**ca·per**[2] (kā′pər) **1** a prickly shrub of the Mediterranean region. **2 capers,** *pl.* the green flower buds of this shrub, pickled and used for seasoning. *n.*
☛ *Etym.* See note at CAPER[1].

**cap gun** a toy gun having a hammer action for setting off a small explosive charge, or CAP (def. 9); cap pistol.

**cap·il·lar·y** (kap′ə ler′ē *or* kə pil′ə rē) **1** one of the very tiny blood vessels connecting the smallest arteries with the smallest veins. **2** any tube having a very slender opening, or bore. **3** of, in, or having to do with capillaries. **4** hairlike; very slender. 1, 2 *n., pl.* **cap·il·lar·ies;** 3, 4 *adj.*

# capability 175 capitalize

hat, āge, fär; let, ēqual, tėrm; it, īce
hot, ōpen, ôrder; oil, out; cup, pùt, rüle
əbove, takən, pencəl, lemən, circəs
ch, child; ng, long; sh, ship
th, thin; ŦH, then; zh, measure

**capillary attraction** in physics, the force that causes a liquid to rise against a vertical surface, resulting when the attraction between the molecules of the liquid is less than the attraction between them and a solid surface: *Capillary attraction causes the surface of water in a glass tube to be slightly higher at the sides where it touches the glass than in the middle.* See MENISCUS for picture.

**capillary repulsion** in physics, the force that causes a liquid to move away from a vertical surface, resulting when the attraction between the molecules of the liquid is greater than the attraction between them and a solid surface: *Capillary repulsion causes the surface of mercury in a glass tube to be slightly higher in the middle than at the sides where it touches the glass.* See MENISCUS for picture.

**cap·i·tal**[1] (kap′ə təl) **1** the city where the government of a country, province, or state is located: *Victoria is the capital of British Columbia.* **2** CAPITAL LETTER: *He printed his name in capitals.* **3** the amount of money or property that a company or a person uses in carrying on a business: *The Smith Company has a capital of $150 000.* **4** of or having to do with capital. **5** a source of power or advantage; resources. **6** capitalists as a group: *Labour and capital have finally reached agreement on the issue.* **7** important; leading: *The invention of the telephone was a capital advance in communications.* **8** main; chief. **9** of the best kind; excellent: *A maple tree gives capital shade.* **10** involving death; punishable by death: *Murder is a capital crime in many countries.* 1–3, 5, 6 *n.*, 4, 7–10 *adj.*
**make capital of,** take advantage of; use to one's own advantage: *He made capital of his mother's fame to get the job.*

**cap·i·tal**[2] (kap′ə təl) the top part of a column or pillar. See COLUMN for picture. *n.*

**capital goods** in economics, goods such as machinery or equipment that can be used to produce other goods. Compare with CONSUMER GOODS.

**cap·i·tal·ism** (kap′ə tə liz′əm) an economic system in which the means of production, such as land or factories, are for the most part privately owned by individuals or corporations which compete with one another to produce goods and services that are offered on a free market for whatever profit may be made. Compare with COMMUNISM and SOCIALISM. *n.*

**cap·i·tal·ist** (kap′ə list) **1** a person whose money and property are used in carrying on business. **2** *Informal.* a wealthy person. **3** a person who favours or supports CAPITALISM. **4** CAPITALISTIC. *n.*

**cap·i·tal·is·tic** (kap′ə tə lis′tik) **1** of or having to do with CAPITALISM. **2** favouring or supporting CAPITALISM. *adj.* —**cap′i·tal·is′ti·cal·ly,** *adv.*

**cap·i·tal·i·za·tion** (kap′ə tə lə zā′shən *or* kap′ə tə lī zā′shən) **1** capitalizing or being CAPITALIZED. **2** the amount at which a company is CAPITALIZED; the capital stock of a business. *n.*

**cap·i·tal·ize** (kap′ə tə līz′) **1** write or print with capital letters. **2** set the capital of a company at a certain amount. **3** turn into CAPITAL (def. 3); use as capital. *v.*, **cap·i·tal·ized, cap·i·tal·iz·ing.**

**capitalize on**, take advantage of; use to one's own advantage: *The children capitalized on the hot weather by setting up lemonade stands at the bus stops.*

**capital letter** the large form of a letter; A, B, C, D, etc., as distinguished from a, b, c, d, etc.: *The first word of a sentence always begins with a capital letter.*

**cap·i·tal·ly** (kap′ə tə lē) very well; excellently. *adv.*

**capital murder** formerly in Canada, murder that carried the death penalty.

**capital punishment** the death penalty for a crime.

**capital ship** a large warship; battleship.

**ca·pit·u·late** (kə pich′ə lāt) **1** surrender under certain terms or conditions: *The men in the fort capitulated on the condition that they be allowed to go free.* **2** give up completely; stop resisting: *She capitulated when she realized that arguing was useless.* *v.*, **ca·pit·u·lat·ed, ca·pit·u·lat·ing.** —**ca·pit·u·la′tor,** *n.*

**ca·pit·u·la·tion** (kə pich′ə lā′shən) **1** the act of capitulating. **2** the terms or conditions of surrender. **3** a statement of the main facts of a subject; summary. *n.*

**cap·lin** or **cape·lin** (kap′lin *or* kā′plin) a small fish of the northern Atlantic, used for food and as bait for cod; a kind of SMELT². *n.*

**ca·pon** (kā′pon *or* kā′pən) a rooster that has been castrated to improve the flesh for eating. *n.*

**ca·pote** (kə pōt′) **1** a long, cloaklike outer garment, usually having a hood. **2** a bonnet formerly worn by women and girls. *n.*

**cap pistol** CAP GUN.

**ca·price** (kə prēs′) **1** a sudden change of mind without reason; unreasonable notion or desire; whim; whimsy: *Her decision to wear only blue clothes was pure caprice.* **2** a tendency to change suddenly and without reason. *n.*

**ca·pri·cious** (kə prish′əs) likely to change suddenly and without reason; changeable; fickle: *a spoiled and capricious child, capricious weather.* *adj.* —**ca·pri′cious·ly,** *adv.* —**ca·pri′cious·ness,** *n.*

**Cap·ri·corn** (kap′rə kôrn) **1** the **tropic of Capricorn**, an imaginary circle around the world 23 ½° south of the equator. See LATITUDE for picture. **2** in astronomy, a southern constellation thought of as having the shape of a goat. **3** in astrology, the tenth sign of the zodiac. The sun enters Capricorn about December 22. See ZODIAC for picture. **4** a person born under this sign. *n.* Compare with CANCER (def. 4).

**caps** or **caps. 1** capital letters. **2** capsule.

**cap·si·cum** (kap′sə kəm) **1** any of a closely related group of small tropical shrubs of the nightshade family, most of which are widely grown for their edible fruit called peppers: *Green peppers, chilies, and pimentos are the fruits of cultivated varieties of capsicum.* **2** such pods prepared for seasoning or medicine. *n.*

**cap·size** (kap sīz′ *or* kap′sīz) turn bottom side up; upset; overturn: *Mark capsized the boat when he stood up in it. The sailboat nearly capsized in the squall.* *v.*, **cap·sized, cap·siz·ing.**

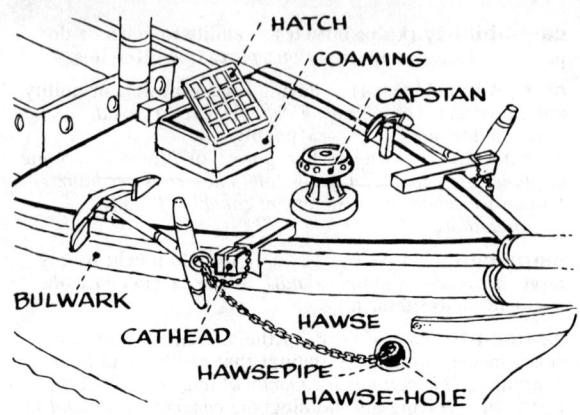

The forward part of a sailing ship

**cap·stan** (kap′stən) a machine for lifting or pulling that revolves on an upright shaft or spindle, now usually operated by an engine: *Sailors on old sailing ships hoisted the anchor by turning the capstan.* *n.*

**capstan bar** a pole used to turn a CAPSTAN.

**cap·stone** (kap′stōn′) the top stone of a wall or other structure. *n.*

**cap·su·lar** (kap′sə lər) **1** of or having to do with a CAPSULE. **2** in a CAPSULE. **3** shaped like a CAPSULE. *adj.*

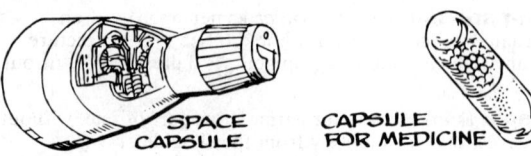

**cap·sule** (kap′səl) **1** a small container of gelatin or other soluble substance for enclosing a dose of medicine. **2** the enclosed front section of a rocket, made to carry instruments, astronauts, etc. into space: *In flight, the capsule can separate from the rest of the rocket and go into orbit or be directed back to earth.* **3** any of various compact containers or coverings. **4** a dry seedcase that opens when ripe. **5** a membrane enclosing an organ of the body; membranous bag or sac. **6** condensed; concise: *She gave a capsule description of the entire plan.* *n.*

**Capt.** Captain.

**cap·tain** (kap′tən) **1** a leader; chief: *Robin Hood was captain of his band.* **2** in the armed forces, a commissioned officer senior to a lieutenant and junior to a major. **3** a commander of a ship. **4** in sports, the leader of a team: *Tom is captain of the football team.* **5** lead or command as captain: *Kalapna will captain the team.* 1–4 *n.*, 5 *v.*

**cap·tain·cy** (kap′tən sē) the rank, commission, or authority of a CAPTAIN. *n., pl.* **cap·tain·cies.**

**cap·tain·ship** (kap′tən ship′) **1** the rank, position, or authority of a CAPTAIN. **2** ability as a CAPTAIN; leadership. *n.*

**cap·tion** (kap′shən) **1** a title or heading at the beginning of a page, article, chapter, etc. **2** an explanation or title accompanying a picture. **3** put a caption on. 1, 2 *n.*, 3 *v.*

**cap·tious** (kap′shəs) hard to please; faultfinding. *adj.* —**cap′tious·ly,** *adv.* —**cap′tious·ness,** *n.*

**cap·ti·vate** (kap′tə vāt′) hold captive by beauty or interest; charm; fascinate: *The children were captivated by the animal story.* *v.,* **cap·ti·vat·ed, cap·ti·vat·ing.** —**cap′ti·vat′ing·ly,** *adv.* —**cap′ti·va′tor,** *n.*

**cap·ti·va·tion** (kap′tə vā′shən) captivating or being CAPTIVATEd. *n.*

**cap·tive** (kap′tiv) **1** a person or animal taken and held by force, skill, or trickery: *The army brought back a thousand captives.* **2** taken and held; captured or kept under control: *a captive balloon. The captive soldiers were kept in a special prison.* **3** obliged to participate; having no choice: *a captive audience, a captive market.* 1 *n.,* 2, 3 *adj.*

**cap·tiv·i·ty** (kap tiv′ə tē) the state of being held CAPTIVE (def. 2): *Some animals cannot bear captivity and die after a few weeks in a cage.* *n., pl.* **cap·tiv·i·ties.**

**cap·tor** (kap′tər) a person who takes or holds a prisoner. *n.*

**cap·ture** (kap′chər) **1** take by force, skill, or trickery; seize: *They were captured during the raid.* **2** anything taken in this way. **3** an act of capturing; the fact of capturing or being captured. **4** get and hold the interest of; attract: *The brightly coloured toy immediately captured the baby's attention.* **5** succeed in preserving: *The artist was able to capture the mood of a rainy fall day.* 1, 4, 5 *v.,* **cap·tured, cap·tur·ing;** 2, 3 *n.*

**cap·u·chin** (kap′yü chin′ *or* kap′yü shin′) **1** a South American monkey having on its head black hair that looks like a hood. See MONKEY for picture. **2** a woman's cloak with a hood. *n.*

**car** (kär) **1** a passenger vehicle that carries its own engine and is used on roads and streets. **2** any vehicle that moves on wheels. **3** a vehicle that runs on rails and is used to carry passengers or freight, such as a railway car or a streetcar. **4** the closed platform of an elevator, balloon, etc. for carrying passengers or cargo. *n.*
☛ *Etym.* From Norman French *carre*, which developed from a form of L *carrus*, meaning 'a wagon for freight or baggage'.

**car·a·cul** (kar′ə kəl *or* ker′ə kəl) a type of flat, loose, curly fur made from the fleece of newborn karakul lambs. *n.* Also, **karakul.**

**ca·rafe** (kə raf′) a glass bottle for holding water, wine, etc. *n.*

**car·a·ga·na** (kar′ə gan′ə *or* ker′ə gan′ə) any of a closely related group of shrubs or small trees of the LEGUME family, having feathery, pale green foliage and yellow flowers that appear in early spring: *Caraganas are widely grown on the Prairies as hedges and windbreaks because they can survive in a dry climate.* *n.*

**car·a·mel** (kar′ə məl, ker′ə məl, *or* kär′məl) **1** sugar browned or burned over heat, used for colouring and flavouring food. **2** a small block of chewy candy flavoured with this sugar. **3** the colour of browned sugar. 1–3 *n.,* 3 *adj.*

**car·a·pace** (kar′ə pās′ *or* ker′ə pās′) the shell on the back of a turtle, lobster, crab, etc. *n.*

**car·at** (kar′ət *or* ker′ət) a unit of mass for precious stones, equal to 200 mg. *n.*
☛ *Hom.* CARET, CARROT, KARAT.

**car·a·van** (kar′ə van′ *or* ker′ə van′) **1** a group of people travelling together, especially for safety through difficult or dangerous country. **2** the vehicles or beasts of burden used by such a group: *a snowmobile caravan.* **3** a covered vehicle that is used as a camper or van. *n.*

## captivate 177 carbonic acid

hat, āge, fär; let, ēqual, tėrm; it, īce
hot, ōpen, ôrder; oil, out; cup, pùt, rüle
əbove, takən, pencəl, lemən, circəs
ch, child; ng, long; sh, ship
th, thin; ᴛʜ, then; zh, measure

**car·a·van·sa·ry** (kar′ə van′sə rē *or* ker′ə van′sə rē) **1** in the Orient, an inn or hotel where caravans rest: *There were many caravansaries on the trade routes from China to Arabia.* **2** any large inn or hotel. *n., pl.* **car·a·van·sa·ries.**

**car·a·vel** (kar′ə vel *or* ker′ə vel′) a small, fast sailing ship of former times. One type was used by Columbus and other navigators of the same period. *n.* Also, **carvel.**

**car·a·way** (kar′ə wā *or* ker′ə wā′) **1** a plant of the same family as the parsley, which yields fragrant, spicy seeds used to flavour bread, rolls, cakes, etc. **2** its seeds. *n.*

**car·bide** (kär′bīd) a compound of carbon with a metal, especially CALCIUM CARBIDE. *n.*

**car·bine** (kär′bīn) a short, light rifle, originally designed for cavalry use. *n.*

**car·bo·hy·drate** (kär′bō hī′drāt′) any of a group of compounds composed of carbon, hydrogen, and oxygen, that take part in the chemical processes in living plants and animals: *Sugar and starch are carbohydrates. In sunlight, green plants make carbohydrates from carbon dioxide and water.* *n.*

**car·bo·lat·ed** (kär′bə lā′tid) containing CARBOLIC ACID. *adj.*

**car·bol·ic acid** (kär bol′ik) a poisonous, corrosive, white crystalline compound present in coal tar and wood tar, used in solution as a disinfectant and antiseptic; phenol.

**car·bon** (kär′bən) **1** a very common non-metallic element found in combination with other elements in all plants and animals. Carbon forms organic compounds in combination with hydrogen, oxygen, etc. Diamonds and graphite are pure carbon; coal and charcoal are impure carbon. *Symbol*: C **2** a piece of carbon used in batteries, arc lamps, etc. **3** a piece of CARBON PAPER. **4** a copy made with CARBON PAPER. *n.*

**carbon 14** a radio-active isotope of CARBON (def. 1), produced by the bombardment of nitrogen atoms: *The extent of the decay of carbon 14 in wood, bone, and other organic matter is evidence of the age of archaeological finds or of geological formations.* *Symbol*: $C_{14}$

**car·bo·na·ceous** (kär′bə nā′shəs) **1** of or containing CARBON (def. 1). **2** like or containing coal. *adj.*

**car·bon·ate** (kär′bə nāt′ *or* kär′bə nit *for noun,* kär′bə nāt′ *for verb*) **1** a salt or ESTER of CARBONIC ACID. **2** change into a carbonate. **3** charge with CARBON DIOXIDE: *Soda water is carbonated to make it bubble and fizz.* 1 *n.,* 2, 3 *v.,* **car·bon·at·ed, car·bon·at·ing.** —**car′bon·a′tion,** *n.*

**carbon dioxide** a heavy, colourless, odourless gas, present in the atmosphere: *The air that comes from the lungs contains carbon dioxide. Plants absorb carbon dioxide from the air and use it to make plant tissue.*

**car·bon·ic** (kär bon′ik) of or containing CARBON. *adj.*

**carbonic acid** the acid made when CARBON DIOXIDE is

dissolved in water: *Carbonic acid gives the sharp taste to soda water.*

**car·bon·i·za·tion** (kär′bə nə zā′shən or kär′bə nī zā′shən)   carbonizing or being CARBONIZEd.   *n.*

**car·bon·ize** (kär′bə nīz′)   **1** change into CARBON (def. 1) by burning.   **2** cover or combine with CARBON (def. 1).   *v.*, **car·bon·ized, car·bon·iz·ing.**

**carbon monoxide**   a colourless, odourless, poisonous gas, formed when carbon burns with an insufficient supply of air: *Carbon monoxide is found in the exhaust gases of automobile engines.*

**carbon paper**   a thin paper having a preparation of carbon or other inky substance on one surface, used for making copies of written or typed material: *Carbon paper is placed between sheets of ordinary paper to make a copy of whatever is written or typed on the top sheet.*

**carbon tet·ra·chlo·ride** (tet′rə klô′rīd)   a colourless, non-flammable liquid, often used in fire extinguishers and in cleaning fluids: *Carbon tetrachloride changes at low temperature to a vapour five times heavier than air. The fumes of carbon tetrachloride are dangerous if taken into the lungs.*

**car·bo·run·dum** (kär′bə run′dəm)   an extremely hard compound of CARBON and SILICON, used for grinding, polishing, etc.   *n.*

**car·boy** (kär′boi)   a large glass bottle, usually enclosed in basketwork or in a wooden box or crate to keep it from being broken.   *n.*

**car·bun·cle** (kär′bung kəl)   a severe abscess of the skin and tissues just beneath the skin, forming a hard, painful, dark red swelling that looks like a group of boils: *A carbuncle discharges pus through several openings.*   *n.*

**car·bu·ret** (kär′bə rāt′)   **1** mix air or gas with CARBON (def. 1) compounds, such as gasoline, benzine, etc.   **2** combine with CARBON (def. 1).   *v.*, **car·bu·ret·ed** or **car·bu·ret·ted, car·bu·ret·ting** or **car·bu·ret·ing.**

**car·bu·re·tion** (kär′bə rā′shən)   CARBURETting or being carburetted.   *n.*

**car·bu·re·tor** (kär′bə rā′tər)   a device for mixing air with a liquid fuel, such as gasoline, to produce an explosive mixture.   *n.*   Also, **carburettor.**

**car·ca·jou** (kär′kə zhü′)   *Cdn.*   WOLVERINE.   *n.*

**car·cass** (kär′kəs)   the body of a dead animal.   *n.*   Also, **carcase.**

**car·cin·o·gen** (kär sin′ə jən)   any substance or agent that causes CANCER (def. 1).   *n.*

**car·cin·o·gen·ic** (kär′sin ə jen′ik)   tending to cause CANCER (def. 1): *The drug was taken off the market because it was found to be carcinogenic.*   *adj.*

**car·ci·no·ma** (kär′sə nō′mə)   a CANCEROUS growth, especially in the skin or the lining of a tube or cavity in the body.   *n., pl.* **car·ci·no·mas** or **car·ci·no·ma·ta** (-mə tə).

**card¹** (kärd)   **1** a piece of stiff paper, thin cardboard, or plastic, usually small and oblong: *a business card, a credit card.*   **2** playing card.   **3** a piece of paper, usually folded, printed with a message or greeting and an illustration and sent in an envelope to mark a special occasion such as a birthday, etc.: *Did you send her a card?*   **4** a round piece of paper, etc. on which the 32 points of the compass are marked.   **5** *Informal.*   an amusing person.   **6** provide with a card.   **7** put on a card.   **8** a flat piece of fibreglass or other material upon which components can be mounted to perform specific functions inside a computer: *graphics card, sound card.*   **9 cards,** *pl.* a any of various games played with a set of playing cards: *She enjoys cards.*   **b** the playing of such a game: *Many of the guests were busy at cards.*   1–5, 8, 9 *n.*, 6, 7 *v.*
**a card up one's sleeve,**   a plan in reserve; extra help kept back until needed: *She doesn't look at all worried; she must have a card up her sleeve.*
**in** or **on the cards,**   sure to happen: *It was in the cards that it would rain; nothing has gone right all day.*
**put one's cards on the table,**   show what one feels or intends to do; be open and frank.

**card²** (kärd)   **1** a toothed tool or wire brush used to separate, clean, and straighten the fibres of raw wool, cotton, etc.   **2** clean or comb with this.   1 *n.*, 2 *v.*

**car·da·mom** or **car·da·mum** (kär′də məm)   **1** a spicy seed used as seasoning and in medicine.   **2** the Asiatic plant that it grows on.   *n.*

**card·board** (kärd′bôrd′)   a fairly thick kind of stiff paper, used to make cards, boxes, cartons, etc.   *n.*

**card catalogue**   a reference catalogue of cards individually listing books and other items in a library or collection; card index.

**card·er** (kärd′ər)   a person or machine that cards wool, cotton, flax, etc.   *n.*

**card game**   a game played with playing cards: *Would you like to learn a new card game?*

**car·di·ac** (kär′dē ak′)   **1** of or having to do with the heart: *cardiac symptoms.*   **2** a medicine that stimulates the heart.   **3** having to do with the upper part of the stomach.   1, 3 *adj.*, 2 *n.*

**car·di·gan** (kär′də gən)   a sweater or knitted jacket that opens down the front and is usually collarless.   *n.*

**car·di·nal** (kär′də nəl)   **1** of first importance; main; chief; principal: *His idea was of cardinal importance to the plan.*   **2** bright red.   **3** one of the high officials of the Roman Catholic Church, appointed by the Pope to the College of Cardinals, and second to him in rank.   **4** a North American songbird, the male having bright red plumage marked with grey and black, and the female being mainly brownish, with reddish wings, tail, and crest.   **5** CARDINAL NUMBER.   1, 2 *adj.*, 2–5 *n.*

**cardinal flower**   **1** the bright red flower of a North American plant.   **2** the plant it grows on.

**cardinal number**   any of the numbers one, two, three, etc. that show quantity, as distinct from first, second, third, etc., which show order.   Compare with ORDINAL NUMBER.

**cardinal points**   the four main directions of the compass; north, south, east, and west.

**cardinal virtues**   prudence, fortitude, temperance, and justice: *The cardinal virtues were considered by the ancient philosophers to be the basic qualities of a good character.*

**card·ing** (kär′ding)   **1** the preparation of the fibres of wool, cotton, flax, etc. for spinning by combing them.   **2** ppr. of CARD².   1 *n.*, 2 *v.*

**car·di·o·gram** (kär′dē ə gram′)   the record made by a CARDIOGRAPH, having the form of a curved line on a graph: *A cardiogram is used in diagnosing heart defects.*   *n.*

**car·di·o·graph** (kär′dē ə graf′)   an instrument that

records the strength and nature of movements of the heart. *n.*

**cardiopulmonary resuscitation** a method of saving life by combining mouth-to-mouth respiration with rhythmical pressure on the heart.

**car·di·o·vas·cu·lar** (kär′dē ō vas′kyə lər) of or having to do with both the heart and the blood vessels: *Hardening of the arteries is a cardiovascular disease.* *adj.*

**care** (ker) **1** a troubled state of mind because of fear of what may happen; worry: *Few people are completely free from care.* **2** serious attention; caution: *A good cook works with care.* **3** an object of worry, concern, or attention: *Keeping records is the care of the secretary of the club.* **4** be concerned; feel an interest: *He cares about conservation. I don't care what they said.* **5** watchful keeping; charge: *The child was left in his sister's care.* **6** food, shelter, and protection: *Your child will have the best of care.* **7** want; wish: *They said they didn't care to come.* **8** to object; mind (*usually used with negatives or in questions*): *Will he care if I borrow his sweater? They don't care if we come home late once in a while.* 1–3, 5, 6 *n.*, 4, 7, 8 *v.*, **cared, car·ing.** **—car′er,** *n.*
**care for, a** have a liking or fondness for: *She doesn't care for him.* **b** want; wish: *I don't care for any dessert tonight.* **c** look after: *The nurse will care for her during the night.*
**care of** or **in care of,** at the address or in the charge of: *Send it care of his father.* Symbol: c/o
**take care,** be careful: *Take care or you'll fall.*
**take care of, a** attend to; take charge of: *The waiter will take care of your order.* **b** look after; provide for: *She has a pension to take care of her basic needs. Her sister took care of her while she was sick.* **c** be careful with; watch over: *Take care of your money.*

**ca·reen** (kə rēn′) **1** lean to one side; tilt; tip: *The ship careened in the strong wind.* **2** cause to lean to one side: *The strong wind careened the ship.* **3** lay a ship over on one side for cleaning, painting, repairing, etc. **4** rush along with a bobbing, leaning movement: *The waitress careened among the tables, balancing a heavy tray on one hand.* *v.*

**ca·reer** (kə rēr′) **1** a general course of action or progress through life: *It is exciting to read about the careers of explorers.* **2** a way of living; an occupation or profession: *Lisa planned to make law her career.* **3** speed; full speed; going with force: *We were in full career when we struck the post.* **4** rush along wildly; dash: *The runaway horse careered through the streets.* 1–3 *n.*, 4 *v.*

**care·free** (ker′frē′) without worry; light-hearted; happy. *adj.*

**care·ful** (ker′fəl) **1** thinking what one says; watching what one does; taking pains; cautious: *He is careful to tell the truth at all times.* **2** done with thought or effort; exact; thorough: *a careful investigation, a careful reading of a text.* **3** full of care or concern; attentive or protective: *She was always careful of the feelings of others.* *adj.*
**—care′ful·ly,** *adv.* **—care′ful·ness,** *n.*

**care·less** (ker′lis) **1** not thinking what one says; not watching what one does; not taking enough pains; not watchful or cautious: *One careless step here may cost a life.* **2** done without enough thought or effort; not exact or thorough: *careless work, a careless worker.* **3** not troubling oneself; indifferent; unconcerned: *Careless of danger, he walked boldly into the enemy camp.* **4** carefree; untroubled. *adj.* **—care′less·ly,** *adv.*
**—care′less·ness,** *n.*

**ca·ress** (kə res′) **1** a gentle, loving touch, stroke, or kiss. **2** any light or gentle touch: *the caress of a summer breeze.* **3** touch or stroke gently, lightly, or lovingly: *He talked to the kitten softly as he caressed it. The wind caressed the treetops.* 1, 2 *n.*, 3 *v.*

**car·et** (kar′ət *or* ker′ət) a mark (^) to show where something should be put in, used in writing and proofreading. *n.*
☛ *Hom.* CARAT, CARROT, KARAT.

**care·tak·er** (ker′tā′kər) a person, especially a JANITOR, who takes care of a building, estate, etc. *n.*

**care·worn** (ker′wôrn′) showing the effects of continuous worry and care. *adj.*

**car·fare** (kär′fer′) the money to pay for riding on a streetcar, bus, etc.: *He had just enough money for carfare home.* *n.*

**car·go** (kär′gō) the load of goods carried on a ship, aircraft, truck, etc.; freight: *a cargo of wheat.* *n., pl.* **car·goes** or **car·gos.**

**car·hop** (kär′hop′) *Informal.* a person who serves customers at a drive-in restaurant. *n.*

**car·i·boo** (kar′ə bü *or* ker′ə bü) CARIBOU. *n.*

Caribou—about 130 cm high at the shoulder

**car·i·bou** (kar′ə bü *or* ker′ə bü) **1** any of several kinds of North American reindeer: *There are great herds of caribou in the Barren Lands.* **2** caribou hide: *caribou parkas, caribou moccasins.* *n., pl.* **car·i·bou** or **car·i·bous.** Sometimes, **caribo.**
☛ *Etym.* From Canadian French *caribou*, from an Algonquian name for this animal meaning 'one that paws or scratches', from the way it paws through snow to reach the grass underneath.

**Caribou** a member of a group of Inuit living on the west side of Hudson Bay.

**car·i·ca·ture** (kar′ə kə chür′ *or* ker′ə kə chür′) **1** a picture, cartoon, description, etc. that deliberately exaggerates the peculiarities or defects of a subject. **2** the art of making such pictures or descriptions. **3** a very poor imitation. **4** make a caricature of. 1–3 *n.*, 4 *v.*, **car·i·ca·tured, car·i·ca·tur·ing.**

**car·i·ca·tur·ist** (kar′ə kə chü′rist *or* ker′ə kə chü′rist, kar′ə kə chə rist *or* ker′ə kə chə rist) a person skilled in drawing CARICATURES (def. 1). *n.*

**car·ies** (ker′ēz *or* ker′ē əz) the decay of teeth, bones, or tissues: *Caries of the teeth is caused by bacteria.* *n.*

**car·il·lon** (kar′ə lon′ *or* ker′ə lon′) **1** a set of bells arranged for playing melodies: *There is a carillon in the*

**carillonneur** Peace Tower in Ottawa. **2** a melody played on such bells. **3** part of an organ imitating the sound of bells. *n.*

**car·il·lon·neur** (kar′ə lə nėr′ *or* ker′ə lə nėr′) a person who plays a CARILLON (def. 1). *n.*

**car·i·ole**[1] *or* **car·ri·ole**[1] (kar′ē ōl′ *or* ker′ē ōl′) **1** a small one-horse carriage. **2** a covered cart. *n.*
☞ *Etym.* From F *carriole*, a light, covered, two-wheeled carriage. 19c. The French word came from Italian *carriuola*, which developed from a variant form of L *carrus*, a freight or baggage wagon. See also notes at CARIOLE[2], CAR.

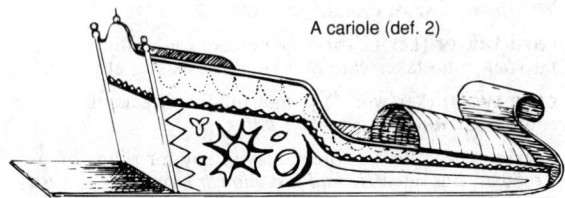

A cariole (def. 2)

**car·i·ole**[2] *or* **car·ri·ole**[2] (kar′ē ōl′ *or* ker′ē ōl′) Cdn. **1** a one-horse sleigh resembling a cutter. **2** a dogsled, often ornately decorated, equipped to carry one person lying down: *The sick trapper was brought to the post in a cariole.* **3** ride in a cariole. 1, 2 *n.*, 3 *v.*, **car·i·oled** *or* **car·ri·oled, car·i·ol·ing** *or* **car·ri·ol·ing.**
☞ *Etym.* From Cdn. F *carriole* 'sled'. 19c. The F *carriole*, from which the Canadian French meanings developed, refers to a light, covered, two-wheeled carriage. See also notes at CARIOLE[1] and CARRYALL.

**car·load** (kär′lōd′) **1** the number or amount that an automobile can carry: *We passed a carload of people bound for the party.* **2** the amount that a freight car can hold or carry: *a carload of grain.* *n.*

**car·mine** (kär′mən *or* kär′mīn) **1** deep red with a tinge of purple. **2** light crimson. **3** a crimson colouring matter found in COCHINEAL, used to stain microscopic slides and, formerly, as a dye. 1–3 *n.*, 1, 2 *adj.*

**car·nage** (kär′nij) the slaughter of a great number of people, as in war. *n.*

**car·nal** (kär′nəl) **1** having to do with the desires and pleasures of the body; sensual: *Gluttony and drunkenness have been called carnal vices.* **2** worldly; not spiritual. *adj.* —**car′nal·ly,** *adv.*

**car·na·tion** (kär nā′shən) **1** any of numerous cultivated varieties of flower derived from the clove pink or gillyflower, widely grown in gardens and greenhouses for their large, many-petalled flowers which usually have a spicy fragrance. **2** the flower of a carnation: *He wore a carnation in his lapel.* *n.*

**car·nel·ian** (kär nē′lyən) a red or reddish-brown stone used in jewellery: *Carnelian is a kind of* QUARTZ. *n.*

**car·ni·val** (kär′nə vəl) **1** a place of amusement, especially a travelling show having merry-go-rounds, side shows, etc. **2** feasting and merrymaking; celebration. **3** an organized program of events involving a particular sport, institution, etc.: *a water carnival.* *n.*
☞ *Etym.* From Italian *carnevale* in the 16c., a development of Med. L *carnelevamen* or *carnelevarium*, the name for the days just before Lent, meaning literally 'the giving up of meat-eating'.

**Car·niv·o·ra** (kär niv′ə rə) an order of mammals that feed chiefly on flesh: *Cats, dogs, lions, tigers, and bears belong to the Carnivora.* *n. pl.*

**car·ni·vore** (kär′nə vôr′) **1** any animal belonging to the order CARNIVORA. **2** any plant that eats insects. *n.*

**car·niv·o·rous** (kär niv′ə rəs) **1** flesh-eating: *Cats, dogs, lions, tigers, and bears are carnivorous animals.* **2** of or having to do with the CARNIVORA. *adj.*

**car·no·tite** (kär′nə tīt′) a yellowish radio-active mineral found in the western and southwestern United States: *Carnotite is a source of radium and uranium.* *n.*

**car·ob** (kar′əb *or* ker′əb) **1** a Mediterranean evergreen tree of the pea family having compound leaves, red flowers, and long, blackish pods. **2** the edible pod of this tree, having a sweet pulp which tastes a little like chocolate. *n.*

**car·ol** (kar′əl *or* ker′əl) **1** a song of joy. **2** a hymn of joy: *Christmas carols.* **3** sing; sing joyously; praise with carols. 1, 2 *n.*, 3 *v.*, **car·olled** *or* **car·oled, car·ol·ling** *or* **car·ol·ing.** —**car′ol·ler** *or* **car′ol·er,** *n.*

**car·om** (kar′əm *or* ker′əm) **1** in billiards, a kind of shot: *In a carom, the ball struck with the cue hits two balls, one after the other.* **2** a similar shot in other games. **3** make a carom. **4** hit and bounce off. **5** a hitting and bouncing off. 1, 2, 5 *n.*, 3, 4 *v.*

**car·oms** (kar′əmz *or* ker′əmz) a game for two or four players, played on a square board, in which the players try to shoot 24 round counters into pockets at the corners. *n. pl.*

**ca·rot·id** (kə rot′id) **1** either of two large arteries, one on each side of the neck, that carry blood to the head. **2** having to do with these arteries. *n.*

**ca·rous·al** (kə rou′zəl) a noisy revel; drinking party. *n.*

**ca·rouse** (kə rouz′) **1** a noisy feast; drinking party. **2** drink heavily; take part in noisy feasts or revels. 1 *n.*, 2 *v.*, **ca·roused, ca·rous·ing.** —**ca·rous′er,** *n.*

**car·ou·sel** *or* **car·rou·sel** (kar′ə sel′ *or* ker′ə sel′) **1** a merry-go-round. **2** at an airport, a revolving platform onto which the baggage of arriving passengers is delivered from a central chute. *n.*

**carp**[1] (kärp) find fault; complain. *v.* —**carp′er,** *n.*

**carp**[2] (kärp) **1** a freshwater fish that has many bones: *Carp feed mostly on plants and sometimes grow quite large.* **2** any of a group of similar fishes, including goldfish, minnows, chub, and dace. *n., pl.* **carp** *or* **carps.**

**car·pal** (kär′pəl) **1** of or having to do with the CARPUS. **2** a carpal bone. 1 *adj.*, 2 *n.*
☞ *Hom.* CARPEL.

**car·pel** (kär′pəl) the central part of a flower containing the OVULES, which develop into seeds: *Some flowers, such as the pea and bean, have a simple pistil composed of only one carpel; other flowers, such as the iris and mock orange, have a compound pistil composed of several carpels fused together.* See FLOWER for picture. *n.*
☞ *Hom.* CARPAL.

**car·pen·ter** (kär′pən tər) **1** a person skilled in CARPENTRY. **2** work at CARPENTRY. 1 *n.*, 2 *v.*

**car·pen·try** (kär′pən trē) the trade or art of building, finishing, and repairing wooden objects or structures. *n.*

**car·pet** (kär′pit) **1** a thick, heavy, woven covering for floors and stairs. **2** the fabric used for such a covering; carpeting. **3** anything like a carpet: *A carpet of grass* stretched down to the lake. **4** cover with a carpet: *In the spring, the ground was carpeted with violets.* 1–3 *n.*, 4 *v.* **on the carpet, a** the condition of being considered or discussed. **b** *Informal.* being scolded or rebuked.

**car·pet·bag** (kär′pit bag′) a travelling bag made of carpeting: *Carpetbags were common in the 19th century.* *n.*

**carpet beetle** any of several species of small beetle whose larvae destroy carpets and other fabrics and furs.

**car·pet·ing** (kär′pi ting) **1** fabric for carpets. **2** carpets. **3** ppr. of CARPET. 1, 2 *n.*, 3 *v.*

**carp·ing** (kär′ping) **1** faultfinding; naggingly critical: *a carping tongue, carping critics.* **2** ppr. of CARP¹. 1 *adj.*, 2 *v.* —**carp′ing·ly,** *adv.*

**car pool** an arrangement by which members of a group take turns at providing transportation in their own cars, especially to and from work.

**car·port** (kär′pôrt′) a roofed space open on two, or sometimes three, sides, used as a garage. *n.*

**car·pus** (kär′pəs) **1** the group of short bones forming the joint between the forearm and the hand; the bones of the wrist. See ARM¹ for picture. **2** the corresponding part in the foreleg of an animal; the knee joint. *n.*, *pl.* **car·pi** (-pī *or* -pē).

**car·riage** (kar′ij *or* ker′ij) **1** a vehicle that moves on wheels: *Carriages are usually pulled by horses and are used to carry people.* **2** a wheeled frame which supports a gun and by which it is moved from place to place. **3** a moving part of a machine that supports some other part: *the carriage of a typewriter.* **4** a manner of holding the head and body; bearing: *She has a queenly carriage.* **5** the taking of persons or goods from one place to another; carrying; transporting: *insurance against loss in carriage, carriage charges.* **6** the cost or price of carrying: *This will be $50 plus $3.50 for carriage.* **7** handling. *n.*

**car·ri·er** (kar′ē ər *or* ker′ē ər) **1** a person or thing that carries something: *A mailman is a mail carrier. Railways, buses, and ships are carriers.* **2** anything designed to carry something in or on. **3** a person or thing that carries or transmits a disease: *Carriers are often healthy persons who are immune to a disease but can pass its germs on to others.* **4** in radio broadcasting, etc., one of the radio-frequency waves that are used to transmit, or carry, the radio-frequency waves representing the sounds being broadcast: *Carriers are also called carrier waves.* **5** an AIRCRAFT CARRIER. *n.*

**Car·rier** (kar′ē ər *or* ker′ē ər) a member of a First Nations people living in the interior of British Columbia. *n.*

**carrier pigeon** a homing pigeon, especially one trained to fly home from great distances carrying written messages.

**car·ri·ole** (kar′ē ōl′ *or* ker′ē ōl′) See CARIOLE. *n.*

**car·ri·on** (kar′ē ən *or* ker′ē ən) **1** dead and decaying flesh: *Buzzards and vultures live on carrion.* **2** dead and decaying. **3** feeding on dead and decaying flesh. **4** rottenness; filth. **5** rotten; filthy. 1, 4 *n.*, 2, 3, 5 *adj.*

**carrion crow** the common European crow.

**car·rot** (kar′ət *or* ker′ət) **1** a plant having feathery, finely divided leaves and a long, thick, tapering orange root. **2** its root, eaten as a vegetable. *n.*
☛ *Hom.* CARAT, CARET, KARAT.

**car·rou·sel** (kar′ə sel′ *or* ker′ə sel′) See CAROUSEL. *n.*

---

**carpetbag** 181 **cart**

hat, āge, fär; let, ēqual, tèrm; it, īce
hot, ōpen, ôrder; oil, out; cup, pùt, rüle
əbove, takən, pencəl, lemən, circəs
ch, child; ng, long; sh, ship
th, thin; ᴛʜ, then; zh, measure

**car·ry** (kar′ē *or* ker′ē) **1** take from one place to another: *Buses carry passengers. He carried the sleepy child up to bed.* **2** bear the weight of; hold up; support; sustain: *Those columns carry the roof.* **3** hold one's body and head in a certain way; have a certain kind of posture: *This girl carries herself well.* **4** capture; win: *Our troops carried the enemy's fort.* **5** get a motion or bill passed or adopted: *The motion to adjourn the meeting was carried.* **6** continue; extend: *to carry a road into the mountains.* **7** cover the distance; have the power of throwing or driving: *His voice carried easily to the back of the room. This gun will carry one kilometre.* **8** the distance covered or the distance that something goes. **9** influence greatly; lead. **10** have as a result; involve: *His judgment carries great weight.* **11** keep in stock: *This store carries men's clothing.* **12** keep on the account books of a business. **13** transfer a number from one place or column in the sum to the next: *A 10 in the 1's column must be carried to the 10's column.* **14** the act of carrying boats and supplies from one river or lake to another. **15** a place where this is done; portage. 1–7, 9–13 *v.*, **car·ried, car·ry·ing;** 8, 14, 15 *n.*, *pl.* **car·ries.**

**carry away,** arouse strong feeling in; influence beyond reason: *The child was carried away by the sad story and began to cry.*
**carry off, a** win a prize, honour, etc. **b** succeed with: *It was her first speech, but she carried it off all right.*
**carry on, a** do; manage or conduct: *She carried on a successful business for many years.* **b** go ahead with; go on with after being stopped. **c** keep going; continue: *We must carry on in our effort to establish world peace.* **d** *Informal.* behave wildly or foolishly: *The small boys really carried on at the party.*
**carry on with,** manage until a later time by using: *The old typewriter will do to carry on with until I can afford a new one.*
**carry out,** do; get done; accomplish; complete: *He carried out his job well.*
**carry over, a** have left over; be left over. **b** keep until later; continue; extend.
**carry through,** fulfil.

**car·ry·all¹** (kar′ē ol′ *or* ker′ē ol′) **1** a covered one-horse carriage. **2** CARIOLE². *n.*
☛ *Etym.* From Cdn. F *carriole* 'sled'. The English word is a kind of translation of the sound of the French word into something that had meaning for English speakers, especially because such vehicles were used for carrying people or things. See also notes at CAR and CARIOLE.

**car·ry·all²** (kar′ē ol′ *or* ker′ē ol′) **1** any of several vehicles so named because of their large capacity. **2** a large bag or basket. *n.*
☛ *Etym.* Carryall² is from the phrase 'carry all'.

**carrying charge** the interest charged on money owing for goods or services bought on credit.

**car·ry·o·ver** (kar′ē ō′vər *or* ker′ē ō′vər) the part left over. *n.*

**car-sick** (kär′sik′) nauseated as a result of motion sickness in a car, etc. *adj.* —**car′-sick′ness,** *n.*

**cart** (kärt) **1** a vehicle with two wheels, used to carry heavy loads: *Horses, donkeys, and oxen are often used to*

**pull carts.** **2** a light wagon, used to deliver goods, etc. **3** a small, wheeled vehicle that is moved by hand: *a grocery cart.* **4** carry in a cart. *1–3 n., 4 v.*
**put the cart before the horse,** reverse the proper or natural order of things.

**cart·age** (kär′tij) **1** the act of carting. **2** the cost of carting. *n.*

**carte blanche** (kär tə blänsh′) *French.* full authority; freedom to use one's own judgment.

**car·tel** (kär tel′) **1** a combination of independent businesses formed to regulate prices, production, and marketing of goods. **2** a written agreement between countries at war, for the exchange of prisoners or some other purpose. *n.*

**car·tel·ize** (kär tel′īz) **1** combine in a CARTEL (def. 1). **2** join with other businesses to form a CARTEL (def. 1). *v.,* **car·tel·ized, car·tel·iz·ing.**

**cart·er** (kär′tər) a person whose work is driving a cart or truck. *n.*

**Car·tha·gin·i·an** (kär′thə jin′ē ən) **1** of or having to do with Carthage, an ancient city and seaport in northern Africa. **2** a native or inhabitant of Carthage. *1 adj., 2 n.*

**cart horse** DRAFT HORSE.

**car·ti·lage** (kär′tə lij) **1** a tough, elastic tissue that forms most of the skeleton of very young vertebrates and, in higher vertebrates, is for the most part changed into bone as the animal matures; gristle: *Cartilage is found in adults at the ends of the long bones, between the bones of the spine, in the nose, etc.* **2** a part formed of cartilage. *n.*

**car·ti·lag·i·nous** (kär′tə laj′ə nəs) **1** of or like CARTILAGE; gristly. **2** having the skeleton formed mostly of CARTILAGE: *Sharks are cartilaginous. adj.*

**cart·load** (kärt′lōd′) as much as a cart can hold or carry. *n.*

**car·tog·ra·pher** (kär tog′rə fər) a person skilled in making maps or charts, especially one who makes it his or her work. *n.*

**car·tog·ra·phy** (kär tog′rə fē) the making of maps or charts. *n.*

**car·ton** (kär′tən) a box or other container made of cardboard: *Pack the books in large cartons. Milk can be bought in cartons. n.*

**car·toon** (kär tün′) **1** a humorous drawing, often having a caption, that shows ridiculous or exaggerated situations; a pictorial joke: *Many magazines and newspapers have cartoons.* **2** an exaggerated drawing or caricature, often accompanied by words, meant to make fun of a political figure or current happenings: *The editorial page of our paper has a cartoon every day.* **3** a full-size drawing of a design or painting, used as a model for a fresco, mosaic, tapestry, etc. **4** a comic strip. **5** a movie made up of a series of drawings; ANIMATED CARTOON: *Cartoons often show animals engaging in human activities.* **6** make a cartoon of. **7** make cartoons. *1–5 n., 6, 7 v.*

**car·toon·ist** (kär tü′nist) a person skilled in drawing CARTOONS (defs. 1, 2, 4). *n.*

**car·touche** (kär tüsh′) **1** an oblong or oval figure found on ancient Egyptian monuments, framing the hieroglyphics representing the name of a ruler. **2** an elaborate frame for a painted or bas-relief inscription on a building. **3** a paper or cardboard container for gun cartridges or the explosive in a firework. *n.*

 A rifle cartridge

**car·tridge** (kär′trij) **1** a tube of metal, cardboard and metal, or plastic containing a charge of explosive and, usually, shot or a bullet, for use in a firearm. **2** a usually long, round case containing a refill of material, such as ink for a fountain pen. **3** a sealed plastic case containing a spool of film together with a take-up spool, designed for use with certain types of camera: *The cartridge is simply dropped into the back of the camera.* See CAMERA for picture. **4** a sealed plastic case containing film or magnetic tape in an endless loop wound on a single reel. **5** of a film projector or tape recorder, designed for use with cartridges. **6** a removable unit in the tone arm of a record player, containing the needle, or stylus, and a crystal or magnet that changes the movements of the needle into electric waves. *n.*

**cart·wheel** (kärt′wēl′ *or* kärt′hwēl′) **1** the wheel of a cart. **2** a sideways handspring or somersault, made with the arms and legs stretched out stiffly like the spokes of a wheel. **3** make such a handspring or somersault. *1, 2 n., 3 v.*

**carve** (kärv) **1** cut into slices or pieces: *to carve meat.* **2** cut; make by cutting: *Statues are often carved from stone or wood.* **3** decorate with figures or designs cut on the surface. *v.,* **carved, carv·ing.**
**carve out,** *Informal.* form or make with difficulty: *She is carving out quite a reputation for herself.*

**car·vel** (kär′vəl) CARAVEL. *n.*

**carv·en** (kär′vən) carved; decorated by carving; sculptured. *adj.*

**carv·er** (kär′vər) **1** a person who carves. **2** CARVING KNIFE. *n.*

**carv·ing** (kär′ving) **1** the act or art of a person who carves. **2** a piece of carved work; a carved decoration: *a wood carving.* **3** ppr. of CARVE. *1, 2 n., 3 v.*

**carving knife** a knife for cutting meat.

**car·y·at·id** (kar′ē at′id *or* ker′ē at′id) in architecture, a supporting column carved in the form of a woman. *n., pl.* **car·y·at·ids** or **car·y·at·i·des** (-ə dēz′).

**ca·sa·ba** or **cas·sa·ba** (kə sä′bə) a variety of winter MUSKMELON with a yellow rind and sweet, light-coloured flesh. *n.*

**cas·cade** (kas kād′) **1** a small waterfall. **2** anything like this: *a cascade of ruffles.* **3** fall in a cascade. *1, 2 n., 3 v.,* **cas·cad·ed, cas·cad·ing.**

**cas·car·a** (kas ker′ə *or* kas kar′ə) **1** a mild LAXATIVE prepared from the bark of a species of buckthorn. **2** the shrub or tree itself, found along the Pacific coast of North America. *n.*

**case¹** (kās) **1** an instance or example: *a case of poor work. He said it was a clear case of reckless driving.* **2** a set of circumstances; situation; state: *You are in a worse case than I.* **3** the actual condition; real situation; true state: *She said she had done the work, but that was not the case.* **4** an instance of a disease or injury: *a case of measles.* **5** a person who has a disease or injury; patient. **6** a matter for a law court to decide. **7** a statement of

facts for a law court to consider.   **8** the set of arguments or supporting facts to justify an action, situation, etc.: *the case for a guaranteed annual income.*   **9** *Informal.* a peculiar or unusual person.   **10** in grammar:   **a** a distinct form of a noun, pronoun, or adjective that shows its relation to other words in a sentence.   **b** the relation shown by such a distinct form. English does not have a case system like German or Latin. English nouns and most pronouns have only two cases indicating grammatical relation: a common, or simple, case (e.g. *boy, woman, somebody*) and a possessive case (*boy's, woman's, somebody's*). Six English pronouns have three cases: the subjective (*I, we, he, she, they, who*), objective (*me, us, him, her, them, whom*), and possessive (*my, our, his, her, their, whose*). English adjectives do not indicate grammatical relation at all.   *n.*
**in any case,**   in or under any circumstances; no matter what happens; in any event; anyhow: *In any case, you should prepare for the worst.*
**in case,**   if; supposing; if it should happen that.
**in case of,**   in the event of; if there should be: *In case of fire, walk quietly to the nearest door.*
**in no case,**   in or under no circumstances.
**case²** (kās)   **1** a strong, heavy box: *a packing case. There is a big case full of books in the hall.*   **2** a covering; sheath: *Put the knife back in the case.*   **3** an outer protective part: *My watch has a steel case.*   **4** the quantity in a box, etc.: *My mother bought a case of ginger ale.*   **5** a frame; casing: *A window fits in a case.*   **6** put in a case; cover with a case.   **7** in printing, a tray for type, with a space for each letter.   1–5, 7 *n.*, 6 *v.*, **cased, cas·ing.**
**lower case,**   small letters.
**upper case,**   CAPITAL LETTERS.
**case history**   all the facts about a person or group that may be useful in deciding what medical or psychiatric treatment, social services, etc. are needed.
**ca·sein** (kā′sēn *or* kā′sē in)   the protein found especially in milk and which is the main ingredient of cheese: *Casein is used in making plastics, paints, and adhesives.*   *n.*
**case·mate** (kās′māt)   **1** a bombproof chamber in a fort or rampart, with openings through which cannon may be fired.   **2** an armoured enclosure protecting guns on a warship.   *n.*
**case·ment** (kās′mənt)   **1** a window opening on vertical hinges.   **2** any window.   **3** a casing; covering; frame.   *n.*
**cash** (kash)   **1** money in the form of coins and bills; ready money.   **2** money, or something that equals money, such as a cheque, paid at the time of buying something: *I don't like charge accounts; I prefer to pay cash.*   **3** get ready money for: *I'll have to cash a cheque to pay for it.*   **4** give ready money for: *That teller will cash your cheque.*   1, 2 *n.*, 3, 4 *v.*
**cash in,** *Informal.*   change into cash.
**cash in on,** *Informal.*   **a** make a profit from.   **b** take advantage of; use to advantage.
☛ Hom.   CACHE.
**cash·book** (kash′bùk)   a book in which a record is kept of money received and paid out.   *n.*
**cash·ew** (kash′ü *or* kə shü′)   **1** a small, edible, kidney-shaped nut.   **2** the tropical American tree that this nut grows on.   **3** referring to the family of trees and shrubs that includes the cashew as well as pistachio, mango, and the sumacs.   *n.*
**cash·ier¹** (ka shēr′)   a person who has charge of money in a business: *Pay the cashier as you leave.*   *n.*

**case** 183 **cassia**

hat, āge, fär; let, ēqual, tėrm; it, īce
hot, ōpen, ôrder; oil, out; cup, pùt, rüle
əbove, takən, pencəl, lemən, circəs
ch, child; ng, long; sh, ship
th, thin; ᴛʜ, then; zh, measure

**cash·ier²** (ka shēr′)   dismiss from the armed forces for some dishonourable act; discharge in disgrace: *The dishonest officer was deprived of his rank and cashiered.*   *v.*
**cash·mere** (kash′mēr)   **1** the soft, downy fibre forming the undercoat of a breed of goats raised especially in Kashmir and Tibet.   **2** a fine, soft cloth made from this fibre.   **3** any fine, soft woollen cloth.   *n.*
**cash on delivery**   payment when goods are delivered. *Abbrev.*: C.O.D.
**cash register**   a machine that records and shows the amount of a sale, and has a drawer where money may be kept.
**cas·ing** (kā′sing)   **1** something to put around something else to cover or contain it; case: *The air in a rubber tire is contained inside a casing made of layers of rubberized cord fabric.*   **2** a lining or liner, especially a metal tube or pipe used to line a water, oil, or gas well.   **3** a frame: *A window fits in a casing.*   **4** a long, narrow space between two layers of fabric, formed by two parallel lines of stitching, used to insert a rod, as for curtains, or a drawstring or elastic, as for clothing.   **5** ppr. of CASE². 1–4 *n.*, 5 *v.*
**ca·si·no** (kə sē′nō)   **1** a building or room for public shows, dancing, gambling, etc.   **2** CASSINO, a card game. *n., pl.* **ca·si·nos.**
**cask** (kask)   **1** barrel: *A cask may be large or small, and is usually made to hold liquids.*   **2** the amount that a cask holds.   *n.*
**cas·ket** (kas′kit)   **1** a small box or chest, used to hold jewels, letters, etc.   **2** coffin.   *n.*
**casque** (kask)   armour for the head; helmet.   *n.*
**cas·sa·ba** (kə sä′bə)   See CASABA.   *n.*
**cas·sa·tion** (ka sā′shən)   an annulment; reversal.   *n.*
**cas·sa·va** (kə sä′və)   **1** a plant of tropical America having a large, starchy root.   **2** a starch from its roots, used as a staple food in the tropics: *Tapioca is made from cassava.*   *n.*
**cas·se·role** (kas′ə rōl′)   **1** a baking dish in which food can be both cooked and served.   **2** the food cooked and served in a casserole: *a chicken-and-rice casserole.*   **3** a small, deep dish with a handle, used in chemical laboratories.   *n.*
**cas·sette** (ka set′ *or* kə set′)   **1** a sealed plastic case containing magnetic tape on a reel together with a take-up reel, designed for use with audio and video recorders. **2** of a tape recorder, designed for use with cassettes: *Cassette recorders are very simple to operate.*   **3** a lightproof plastic case, or magazine, for holding film: *The film for 35 mm cameras is wound on spools in cassettes.* **4** a sealed plastic case containing a spool of film together with a take-up spool; CARTRIDGE (def. 3).   **5** a sealed case containing instructions for a computer.   *n.*
**cas·si·a** (kas′ē ə *or* kash′ə)   **1** a spice similar to cinnamon, but coarser, obtained from the bark of a

tropical Asian tree related to the cinnamon trees. **2** the tree itself. **3** any of several mainly tropical plants whose leaves and pods yield a mild laxative: *The laxative from dried cassia leaves is called senna.* **4** the pods or their pulp. *n.*

**cas·si·no** or **ca·si·no** (kə sē′nō) a card game in which the ten of diamonds and the two of spades have special counting value. *n.*

**cas·so·war·y** (kas′ə wer′ē) any of three closely related species of large, flightless birds found in the forests of New Guinea, northern Australia, and nearby islands, having glossy black, hairlike plumage and a blue, featherless head and neck with a high, bony, helmetlike growth on the head: *The cassowaries are the only members of the cassowary family of birds.* *n.*, *pl.* **cas·so·war·ies.**

**cast** (kast) **1** throw, fling, or hurl. **2** throw one end of a fishing line out into the water. **3** throwing a fishing line: *She made a skilful cast from the river bank.* **4** the distance a thing is thrown; throw: *She made a long cast with her line.* **5** throw off; let fall: *The snake cast its skin.* **6** direct or turn: *He cast a glance of surprise at me.* **7** shape by pouring or squeezing into a mould to harden: *Metal is first melted and then cast.* **8** something made by casting: *A cast in the likeness of Laurier was set up as a monument.* **9** made by casting: *a statue cast in bronze.* **10** a mould used in casting. **11** a plaster support used to keep a broken bone in place while it is mending: *He had his arm in a cast for more than a month.* **12** assign actors and parts in a play: *Our drama teacher has cast Shafeek as the villain.* **13** the actors in a play. **14** the outward form or appearance: *Her face had a gloomy cast.* **15** a kind or sort. **16** a slight amount of colour; tinge: *a white dress with a pink cast.* **17** a slight squint. **18** add; calculate. 1, 2, 5–7, 12, 18 *v.*, **cast, cast·ing;** 3, 4, 8, 10, 11, 13–17 *n.*, 9 *adj.*
**be cast away,** be shipwrecked.
**cast a ballot,** vote.
**cast about,** search; look.
**cast back,** return in memory: *Cast your mind back to our wedding.*
**cast down, a** a turn downward; lower. **b** make sad or discouraged: *He was cast down by the bad news.*
**cast lots,** use LOTS (def. 8) to decide something: *We cast lots for first chance to try out the raft.*
**cast off, a** let loose; set free: *to cast off a boat from its moorings.* **b** in knitting, make the last row of stitches to remove the knitted fabric from the needle. **c** get rid of: *He was able to cast off his illness.*
**cast on,** in knitting, make the first row of stitches.
**cast out,** drive from society.
**cast up, a** turn upward; raise: *He cast up his eyes and groaned in exasperation.* **b** add up; find the sum of.
☞ Hom. CASTE.

 Castanets

**cas·ta·net** (kas′tə net′) a small rhythm instrument made of ivory, hardwood, or plastic, consisting of two parts which are held in the hand and clicked together rhythmically, especially to accompany dancing. *n.*

**cast·a·way** (kas′tə wā′) **1** thrown away; cast adrift. **2** a shipwrecked person. **3** outcast. 1, 3 *adj.*, 2, 3 *n.*

**caste** (kast) **1** one of the four main social classes of India, formerly officially supported by the state and the Hindu religion: *Castes have traditionally been hereditary; a person could never change his or her caste or marry somebody from another caste.* **2** an exclusive social group; distinct class. **3** a social system having distinct classes separated by differences of birth, rank, wealth, or position. *n.*
**lose caste,** lose social rank or position.
☞ Hom. CAST.

**cast·er**[1] (kas′tər) a person or thing that casts. *n.*
☞ Hom. CASTOR.

**cast·er**[2] or **cast·or** (kas′tər) **1** a small wheel on a swivel, set into the base of a piece of furniture or other heavy object to make it easier to move. **2** a bottle containing salt, mustard, vinegar, or other seasoning for table use. **3** the stand or rack for such bottles. *n.*
☞ Hom. CASTOR.

**cas·ti·gate** (kas′tə gāt′) criticize severely; punish. *v.*, **cas·ti·gat·ed, cas·ti·gat·ing.** —**cas′ti·ga′tor,** *n.*

**cas·ti·ga·tion** (kas′tə gā′shən) severe criticism; punishment. *n.*

**Cas·til·ian** (kas til′yən) **1** of Castile, a region and former kingdom of Spain, its people, or their language. **2** Castilian Spanish, originally the dialect of Castile, now the accepted standard form of Spanish as spoken in Spain. **3** a native or inhabitant of Castile. 1 *adj.*, 2, 3 *n.*

**cast·ing** (kas′ting) **1** something shaped by being poured into a mould to harden. **2** the assignment of the parts in a play, film, etc. **3** ppr. of CAST. 1, 2 *n.*, 3 *v.*

**casting vote** a vote by the presiding officer to decide a question when the votes of an assembly or council are evenly divided.

**cast iron** a hard, brittle form of iron containing carbon and silicon, made by re-melting pig iron and pouring it into moulds to harden.

**cast-i·ron** (kas′tī′ərn) **1** made of CAST IRON. **2** hard; not yielding: *He has a cast-iron will.* **3** hardy; strong: *a cast-iron stomach.* *adj.*

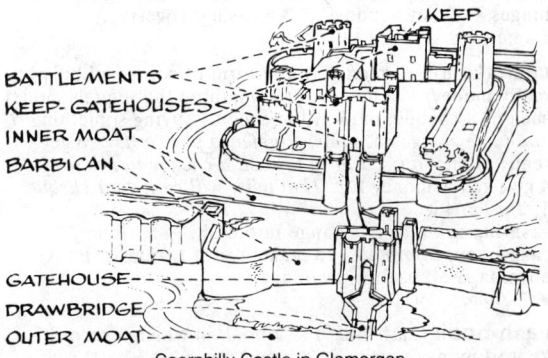

Caerphilly Castle in Glamorgan, Wales, built in the 13th century

**cas·tle** (kas′əl) **1** a building or group of buildings with thick walls, towers, and other defences against attack. **2** a palace that once had defences against attack. **3** a large and imposing residence. **4** in chess, the ROOK[2]. **5** in chess, move the castle, or rook, and the king at the same time. 1–4 *n.*, 5 *v.*, **cas·tled, cas·tling.**

**castle in the air** something imagined but not likely to come true; a daydream.

**cast·off** (kas′tof′) **1** thrown away; abandoned. **2** something that has been thrown away or put aside as no longer useful: *You can use those gloves to work in the garden; they're castoffs.* **3** a person who has been abandoned or cast aside. *1 adj., 2, 3 n.*

**cas·tor**[1] (kas′tər) See CASTER[2]. *n.*

**cas·tor**[2] (kas′tər) **1** a hat made of beaver fur. **2** an oily substance with a strong odour, secreted by beavers: *Castor is used in making perfume and in medicines.* *n.* ☞ *Hom.* CASTER.

**castor bean 1** the CASTOR-OIL PLANT. **2** a seed of this plant.

**castor oil** a yellow oil obtained from CASTOR BEANS, used as a CATHARTIC, a lubricant, etc.

**cas·tor–oil plant** (kas′tə roil′) a tall tropical plant from whose seeds CASTOR OIL is obtained.

**cas·trate** (kas′trāt) **1** remove the testicles of; geld. **2** take away the basic strength or vitality of. *v.*, **cas·trat·ed, cas·trat·ing**.

**cas·tra·tion** (kas trā′shən) the act of castrating. *n.*

**cas·u·al** (kazh′ü əl) **1** happening by chance; not planned or expected; accidental: *a casual meeting.* **2** having or showing lack of concern or interest; careless, nonchalant, or indifferent: *He gave the painting only a casual glance. She takes a very casual approach to her work.* **3** informal; relaxed; easy-going: *casual manners, casual living.* **4** designed for informal use: *casual clothes, casual furniture.* **5** not given or done with any serious purpose or commitment; superficial: *a casual interest in the arts. She's just a casual acquaintance.* **6** happening, active, or employed on an irregular basis; occasional: *casual employment, a casual labourer.* **7** a casual labourer: *The union objected to the hiring of casuals.* **8** a member of the armed forces temporarily attached to a post or station while awaiting transportation to a unit, to a permanent assignment, etc. *1–6 adj., 7, 8 n.* —**cas′u·al·ly**, *adv.* —**cas′u·al·ness**, *n.*

**cas·u·al·ty** (kazh′ü əl tē *or* kazh′əl tē) **1** accident. **2** an unfortunate accident; mishap. **3** a member of the armed forces who has been wounded, killed, or captured as a result of enemy action. **4** a person injured or killed in an accident. *n., pl.* **cas·u·al·ties**.

**cas·u·ist** (kazh′ü ist) **1** a person who is an expert in CASUISTRY (def. 1). **2** a person who reasons cleverly but falsely, especially in regard to right and wrong. *n.*

**cas·u·is·tic** (kazh′ü is′tik) **1** of or like CASUISTRY. **2** too subtle; sophisticated. *adj.* —**cas′u·is′ti·cal·ly**, *adv.*

**cas·u·ist·ry** (kazh′ü i strē) **1** the act or process of deciding questions of right and wrong in regard to conduct, duty, etc. **2** clever but false reasoning. *n., pl.* **cas·u·ist·ries**.

**cat**[1] (kat) **1** a small domestic mammal of the cat family having furry paws with soft pads and retractable claws, a rounded face with a short muzzle, short, pointed ears, and soft fur: *Cats are kept as pets and for catching mice.* **2** any of a family of mostly wild, flesh-eating, tree-climbing mammals characterized by lithe, muscular bodies, spiny tongues, teeth adapted for stabbing, holding, and cutting, but not for chewing, and claws that are retractable in all species but the cheetah: *The cat family is divided into two main groups: the big roaring cats, including the lion, tiger, leopard, snow leopard, and jaguar; and the purring cats,* including the lynxes, wildcats, cougar, and domestic cat. **3** an animal something like a cat. **4** a mean, spiteful woman. **5** catfish. **6** cat-o'-nine-tails. **7** hoist an anchor and fasten it to a beam on the ship's side. **8** tackle for hoisting an anchor. *1–6, 8 n., 7 v.,* **cat·ted, cat·ting**.
**let the cat out of the bag,** tell a secret: *It was supposed to be a surprise party, but she let the cat out of the bag.*
**rain cats and dogs,** rain very hard.

**cat**[2] (kat) CATERPILLAR TRACTOR. *n.*

**cat.** catalogue.

**cat·a·clysm** (kat′ə kliz′əm) **1** a flood or earthquake. **2** any violent change: *World War II was a cataclysm for Europe.* *n.*

**cat·a·clys·mal** (kat′ə kliz′məl) CATACLYSMIC. *adj.*

**cat·a·clys·mic** (kat′ə kliz′mik) of or like a CATACLYSM; extremely sudden and violent. *adj.*

**cat·a·comb** (kat′ə kōm′) an underground gallery forming a burial place. *n.*

**cat·a·falque** (kat′ə falk′) a stand or frame to support the coffin in which a dead person lies. *n.*

**Cat·a·lan** (kat′ə lan′) **1** of Catalonia, a region in northeastern Spain, its people, or their language. **2** a native or inhabitant of Catalonia. **3** the traditional language of Catalonia. *1 adj., 2, 3 n.*

**cat·a·log** (kat′ə log′) *Esp. U.S.* See CATALOGUE. *n., v.,* **cat·a·loged, cat·a·log·ing**.

**cat·a·logue** (kat′ə log′) **1** a list of items in a collection, either identifying each item very briefly or describing it more fully: *A library has a catalogue of its books, arranged in alphabetical order. A company sometimes prints a catalogue with pictures and prices of the things that it sells.* **2** make a catalogue of; put in a catalogue: *She catalogued all the insects in her collection.* *1 n., 2 v.,* **cat·a·logued, cat·a·logu·ing**. —**cat′a·logu′er**, *n.* Also, **catalog**.

**ca·tal·pa** (kə tal′pə) any of several mainly North American trees having large, heart-shaped leaves, clusters of bell-shaped flowers, and long pods. *n.*

**cat·a·lys·er** (kat′ə lī′zər) CATALYST. *n.*

**ca·tal·y·sis** (kə tal′ə sis) in chemistry, the speeding of a chemical reaction by the presence of a substance that is not itself permanently changed. *n., pl.* **ca·tal·y·ses** (-sēz′).

**cat·a·lyst** (kat′ə list) **1** in chemistry, a substance that causes CATALYSIS. **2** an agent that causes or speeds up the occurrence of an event, especially one that is not directly involved or affected by the results. *n.*

**cat·a·lyt·ic** (kat′ə lit′ik) **1** of CATALYSIS. **2** causing CATALYSIS. *adj.*

**catalytic converter** a device in the exhaust system of a vehicle, designed to control the emission of pollution.

A catamaran

**cat·a·ma·ran** (kat′ə mə ran′) 1 a boat having two hulls or floats joined side by side by a frame. 2 Cdn. a type of platform on two runners, used for hauling lumber, etc. 3 a raft made of two or more logs fastened beside each other but some distance apart, used in parts of India, South America, etc. *n.*

**cat·a·mount** (kat′ə mount′) Cdn. any of several large wild members of the cat family, especially the cougar or lynx. *n.*

**cat·a·pult** (kat′ə pult′) 1 an ancient weapon for shooting stones, arrows, etc. 2 slingshot. 3 a device for launching an airplane from the deck of a ship. 4 shoot from a catapult; throw; hurl. 5 move quickly as if shot from a catapult. *1–3 n., 4, 5 v.*

**cat·a·ract** (kat′ə rakt′) 1 a large, steep waterfall. 2 a violent rush or downpour of water; flood. 3 an opaque condition that develops in the lens of the eye, sometimes covering all of the lens and causing total blindness. *n.*

**ca·tarrh** (kə tär′) an inflamed condition of a mucous membrane, usually that of the nose or throat, causing a discharge of mucus or phlegm. *n.*

**ca·tarrh·al** (kə tä′rəl) 1 like CATARRH. 2 caused by CATARRH: *a catarrhal discharge from the nose.* *adj.*

**ca·tas·tro·phe** (kə tas′trə fē) 1 a sudden, widespread, or extraordinary disaster; great calamity or misfortune: *A big earthquake or flood is a catastrophe.* 2 an outcome; conclusion; ending: *The catastrophe of a tragedy usually brings death or ruin to the leading character.* 3 a disastrous end; ruin. *n.*

**cat·a·stroph·ic** (kat′ə strof′ik) of or caused by disaster; calamitous. *adj.*

**cat·bird** (kat′bėrd′) 1 a mainly slate-grey North American songbird belonging to the same family as the mockingbird and the thrashers: *The catbird has a call like the mewing of a cat.* 2 any of several species of Australian bird having a mewing call. *n.*

**catbird seat** a position of advantage or power; an enviable position: *He wasn't at all worried, since he was sitting in the catbird seat.*

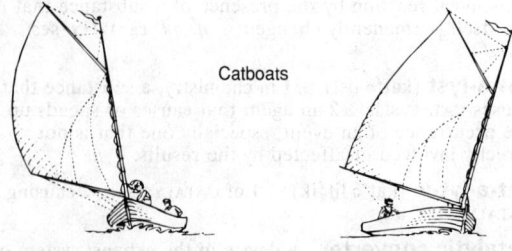

Catboats

**cat·boat** (kat′bōt′) a sailboat having a broad beam and one mast set far forward: *A catboat has no bowsprit or jib.* *n.*

**cat·call** (kat′kol′) 1 a shrill cry or whistle such as to express disapproval: *Poor actors are sometimes greeted by catcalls from the audience.* 2 make catcalls. 3 attack with catcalls: *The audience catcalled the actress.* *1 n., 2, 3 v.*

**catch** (kach) 1 seize and hold, especially after chasing or going after: *She caught the child just as he reached the street. The thief was caught five days after the robbery.* 2 stop the motion of and hold on to: *I caught the ball with one hand. He caught the glass just before it fell.* 3 become affected by; take or get: *to catch the spirit of the celebration. Paper catches fire easily. I think I've caught a cold.* 4 become or cause to become accidentally hooked, pinched, or entangled: *My dress caught in the door.* 5 start burning; take fire: *Tinder catches easily.* 6 come on suddenly; surprise in the act of doing something: *He was caught stealing. My mother caught me hiding her present.* 7 take or get suddenly or for a short while: *to catch a quick nap. They caught a glimpse of her before she disappeared into the crowd.* 8 attract: *Bright colours catch the eye. I tried to catch his attention but he didn't look my way.* 9 reach or get to in time: *If we hurry, we can just catch the next bus.* 10 take notice of; discover: *He thought I wouldn't catch his error.* 11 in baseball, act as catcher: *Who's catching?* 12 the act of catching: *Mario made a fine catch with one hand.* 13 a game of throwing and catching a ball: *They're outside playing catch.* 14 something caught, especially the total quantity caught: *They made a good catch today. Her catch was six trout.* 15 something that holds in place: *We can't fasten the windows because the catch is broken.* 16 Informal. a person worth catching as a spouse, especially because of wealth, position, etc. 17 a hidden or tricky condition or meaning; some difficulty that does not appear on the surface: *There's a catch to that question, so think carefully before you answer.* 18 tricky or deceptive: *a catch question.* 19 a short stopping or blocking of the voice or breath: *There was a catch in his voice as he described the accident.* 20 a ROUND (def. 33). *1–11 v., caught, catch·ing;* *12–20 n.*

**catch alight,** a begin to burn. b become enthusiastic.
**catch at,** try to take hold of; grab at: *She caught at the rope as it swung by her.*
**catch in the act** or **catch red-handed,** find someone in the process of doing something wrong.
**catch it,** Informal. be scolded or punished: *We'll catch it if we're late again.*
**catch on,** Informal. a understand; get the idea: *to catch on to a joke. They were kidding me but I didn't catch on.* b become popular; become widely used or accepted: *The song never caught on.*
**catch out,** discover doing wrong: *to catch him out cheating.*
**catch sight of,** notice; become aware of; see: *The dog suddenly caught sight of the cat.*
**catch up,** a come up even with or overtake a person or thing going the same way: *He ran hard, trying to catch up with his sister.* b pick up suddenly; seize; grab: *He caught the laughing child up in his arms.* c become too much for: *His late nights were beginning to catch up with him.* d bring or become up-to-date; make up for lost time: *to catch up on the news. She's missed a lot of school, but it shouldn't take her too long to catch up.* e involve, especially unwillingly; ensnare (used after the verb BE): *They were both caught up in the scandal.* f absorb completely; engross (used after the verb BE): *He is all caught up in his new boat.*

**catch–all** (kach′ol′) 1 a container for odds and ends:

*The drawer is our kitchen catch-all.* **2** a term, question, etc. used to cover a number of possible examples: *The word* etc. *in the definition is a catch-all.* *n.*

**catch basin** **1** a sievelike receptacle at the entrance of a sewer to retain matter that might block the flow of sewage. **2** a reservoir for catching and holding surface drainage over large areas.

**catch·er** (kach′ər) a person or thing that catches; especially, in baseball, the player who stands behind the batter to catch balls thrown by the pitcher that are not hit by the batter. *n.*

**catch·ing** (kach′ing) **1** liable to spread from one to another; contagious; infectious: *Colds are catching.* **2** attractive; fascinating. **3** ppr. of CATCH. *1, 2 adj., 3 v.*

**catch phrase** a phrase designed to attract attention and be memorable; slogan: *Sheila is trying to think of a good catch phrase to advertise the contest.*

**catch·up** (kach′əp) KETCHUP. *n.*

**catch·word** (kach′wėrd′) **1** a word or phrase used again and again until it becomes accepted as representative of a party, point of view, etc.; slogan: *"Canada first" was a catchword of a late 19th-century movement for cultural independence.* **2** a word placed so as to catch attention, such as a guide word in a dictionary. *n.*

**catch·y** (kach′ē) **1** easy to remember; attractive: *That new song has a very catchy tune.* **2** tricky; misleading; deceptive: *The third question on the test was catchy; nearly everyone in the class gave the wrong answer.* *adj.*, **catch·i·er, catch·i·est.**

**cat·e·chu** (kat′ə chü′ *or* kat′ə kyü′) any of several hard, brittle, ASTRINGENT substances used in dyeing and tanning and in medicine, obtained mainly from certain acacia trees of Asia and Africa. *n.*

**cat·e·gor·i·cal** (kat′ə gôr′ə kəl) **1** without conditions or qualifications; positive. **2** of or in a CATEGORY. *adj.* —**cat′e·gor′i·cal·ly,** *adv.*

**cat·e·go·ry** (kat′ə gôr′ē) a group or division in a general system of classification; class: *Helen groups all people into two categories: those she likes and those she dislikes.* *n., pl.* **cat·e·go·ries.**

**cat·e·nate** (kat′ə nāt′) link together like a chain; connect in a series. *v.,* **cat·e·nat·ed, cat·e·nat·ing.**

**ca·ter** (kā′tər) **1** provide food or supplies: *He runs a restaurant and also caters for weddings and parties.* **2** provide what is needed or wanted (*used with* **to**): *There is a new magazine catering to people interested in crafts.* *v.*

**cat·er-cor·nered** (kat′ər kôr′nərd) KITTY-CORNER. *adv., adj.*

**ca·ter·er** (kā′tə rər) a person who provides food or supplies for entertainments, parties, etc. *n.*

A moth caterpillar - about 7 cm long     A caterpillar tractor

**cat·er·pil·lar** (kat′ər pil′ər) **1** the wormlike larva of

**catch basin**     **187**     **Catholicism**

hat, āge, fär; let, ēqual, tėrm; it, īce
hot, ōpen, ôrder; oil, out; cup, pùt, rüle
ə́bove, takən, pencəl, lemən, circəs
ch, child; ng, long; sh, ship
th, thin; ᴛʜ, then; zh, measure

certain insects, especially butterflies and moths, often brightly coloured and covered with long hairs or spines. **2** CATERPILLAR TRACTOR. *n.*

**caterpillar tractor** a tractor that can travel over rough land on wheels that run inside two endless belts of linked steel plates.

**cat·er·waul** (kat′ər wol′) **1** howl like a cat; screech. **2** such a howl or screech. *1 v., 2 n.*

**cat·fish** (kat′fish′) any of several scale-less fish having around the mouth long, slender feelers that resemble a cat's whiskers. *n., pl.* **cat·fish** *or* **cat·fish·es.**

**cat·gut** (kat′gut′) a very tough cord made from the dried and twisted intestines of sheep or other animals, used for stringing musical instruments and tennis rackets, and for surgical stitches. *n.*

**ca·thar·sis** (kə thär′sis) **1** a purging, especially of the digestive system. **2** an emotional purification or relief. *n.*

**ca·thar·tic** (kə thär′tik) **1** a strong LAXATIVE: *Epsom salts and castor oil are cathartics.* **2** of or bringing about CATHARSIS (def. 2); purifying. *1 n., 2 adj.*

**cat·head** (kat′hed′) a projecting beam on a ship's side near the bow to which the hoisted anchor is fastened. See CAPSTAN for picture. *n.*

**ca·the·dral** (kə thē′drəl) **1** the official church of a bishop: *The bishop of a district or diocese has a throne in the cathedral.* **2** having a bishop's throne. **3** a large or important church. **4** of or like a cathedral. *1, 3 n., 2, 4 adj.*

**cath·ode** (kath′ōd) **1** the positively charged electrode of a primary cell or storage battery: *The cathode of a carbon-zinc dry cell is a mixture of manganese dioxide and carbon powder packed around a central carbon rod.* See DRY CELL for picture. **2** the negative electrode of an electrolytic cell, through which electrons enter the cell. See ELECTROLYSIS for picture. **3** in electronics, the electrode that is the main source of electrons in a vacuum tube; emitter: *The cathode of a vacuum tube gives off electrons when it gets hot.* See VACUUM TUBE for picture. *n.*

**cathode ray** a high-speed, invisible stream of electrons from the heated CATHODE (def. 3) of a vacuum tube.

**cath·ode–ray tube** (kath′ōd drā′) a kind of vacuum tube in which CATHODE RAYS produce a luminous image on a fluorescent screen: *The most common form of cathode-ray tube is the picture tube of a television set.*

**cath·o·lic** (kath′ə lik *or* kath′lik) **1** very broad; general; all-inclusive; universal: *Music has a catholic appeal.* **2** having sympathies with all; broad-minded; liberal. **3** of the whole Christian church. *adj.*

**Cath·o·lic** (kath′ə lik *or* kath′lik) **1** of or having to do with the Christian church governed by the Pope; Roman Catholic. **2** of the ancient undivided Christian church, or of its present representatives. **3** a member of either of these churches. *1, 2 adj., 3 n.*

**Ca·thol·i·cism** (kə thol′ə siz′əm) **1** the faith, doctrine,

**catholicity** 188 **cause**

organization, and practice of the Roman Catholic Church. **2 catholicism,** CATHOLICITY (defs. 1, 2). *n.*

**cath·o·lic·i·ty** (kath′ə lis′ə tē) **1** universality; wide prevalence. **2** broad-mindedness; liberalness. **3 Catholicity,** CATHOLICISM (def. 1). *n.*

**ca·thol·i·cize** (kə thol′ə sīz′) make or become catholic (def. 1) or universal. *v.*, **ca·thol·i·cized, ca·thol·i·ciz·ing.**

**cat·i·on** (kat′ī′ən) an ION having a positive charge: *During electrolysis, cations move toward the cathode.* See ELECTROLYSIS for picture. *n.*

**cat·kin** (kat′kin) the downy or scaly spike of the flowers of willows, poplars, birches, etc. *n.*

**cat·like** (kat′līk′) **1** like a cat: *She stretched in a catlike way.* **2** noiseless; stealthy. **3** active; nimble: *a catlike jump.* *adj.*

**cat nap** a short nap or doze.

**cat·nip** (kat′nip) a plant resembling mint, with scented leaves that cats like. *n.*

**cat-o′-nine-tails** (kat′ə nīn′tālz′) a whip consisting of nine pieces of knotted cord fastened to a handle. *n.*, *pl.* **cat-o′-nine-tails.**

**cat-rigged** (kat′rigd′) rigged like a CATBOAT. *adj.*

**cat's cradle** a game in which a loop of string, stretched over the fingers in an intricate pattern, is passed from one player to another with the object of forming a new pattern each time.

**cat·skin·ner** (kat′skin′ər) *Cdn.* a person who operates a CATERPILLAR TRACTOR: *The catskinners worked long hours on the highway through the bush.* *n.*

**cat's-paw** or **cats·paw** (kat′spo′) **1** a person used by another to do something unpleasant or dangerous. **2** a light breeze that ruffles a small stretch of water. **3** a type of hitch or knot, used for attaching a tackle to a hook. *n.*

**cat·sup** (kat′səp) KETCHUP. *n.*

**cat-swing** (kat′swing′) *Cdn.* CAT-TRAIN. *n.*

**cat-tail** or **cat·tail** (kat′tāl′) any of several closely related species of tall marsh plant having long, flat leaves, and flowers that form thick, brown spikes; BULRUSH (def. 1): *Cat-tails are often used as decoration.* *n.*

**cat·ti·ness** (kat′ē nis) a CATTY (def. 1) quality. *n.*

**cat·tish** (kat′ish) **1** catlike. **2** CATTY (def. 1). *adj.*

**cat·tle** (kat′əl) **1** domesticated BOVINE animals; cows, bulls, steers, or oxen. **2** *Archaic.* any farm animals; livestock. *n.pl.*

**cat·tle·man** (kat′əl mən) a man who raises or takes care of cattle. *n.*, *pl.* **cat·tle·men** (-mən).

**cat-train** (kat′trān′) *Cdn.* a series of large sleds pulled by a CATERPILLAR TRACTOR: *Cat-trains are used in the North for hauling goods over the frozen muskeg in winter time.* *n.*

**cat·ty** (kat′ē) **1** mean; spiteful. **2** of or like cats. *adj.*, **cat·ti·er, cat·ti·est.** —**cat′ti·ly,** *adv.*

**cat·walk** (kat′wok′) a high, narrow place to walk, as on a bridge. *n.*

**Cau·ca·sian** (ko kā′zhən) **1** of or having to do with the Caucasus, a mountainous region in southeastern Europe between the Black and Caspian Seas. **2** a native or inhabitant of the Caucasus. **3** CAUCASOID. 1, 3 *adj.*, 2, 3 *n.*

**Cau·ca·soid** (kok′ə soid′) **1** describing one of the major groups of mankind that includes peoples of Europe, India, the Middle East, Africa: *Caucasoid has nothing to do with skin colour.* **2** a member of this group. 1 *adj.*, 2 *n.*

**cau·cus** (kok′əs) **1** in Canada and the United Kingdom, a meeting of the members of Parliament of one party to discuss policy, plan strategy, etc. **2** in the United States, a meeting of members or leaders of a political party to make plans, choose candidates, decide how to vote, etc. **3** a committee within a political party, whose function is to determine party policy. *n.*
☛ *Hom.* COCCUS.

**cau·dal** (kod′əl) **1** of, at, or near the tail. **2** tail-like. *adj.*

**caught** (kot) pt. and pp. of CATCH: *She caught the ball.* *v.*
☛ *Hom.* COT, CAUGHT.

**caul** (kol) a membrane sometimes covering the head of a child at birth: *A caul was supposed to bring good luck.* *n.*
☛ *Hom.* CALL.

**caul·dron** or **cal·dron** (kol′drən) a large pot, kettle, or boiler. *n.*

A head of cauliflower

**cau·li·flow·er** (kol′ə flou′ər) **1** a plant very closely related to the cabbage and broccoli, having a tightly set flower cluster that forms a solid, white head with a few leaves around it. **2** the head itself, used as a vegetable. *n.*

**cauliflower ear** an ear that has been misshapen as a result of injuries received in boxing, etc.

**caulk** or **calk** (kok) fill up a seam, crack, or joint so that it will not leak; make watertight: *Plumbers caulk joints in pipe with lead.* *v.*
☛ *Hom.* CALK, COCK.

**caus·al** (koz′əl) **1** of a cause; being a cause. **2** involving or having to do with cause and effect. **3** showing a cause or reason: *Because is a causal conjunction.* *adj.* —**caus′al·ly,** *adv.*

**cau·sal·i·ty** (koz al′ə tē) **1** the relation between cause and effect; the principle that nothing can happen or exist without a cause. **2** a CAUSAL quality or agency. *n.*, *pl.* **cau·sal·i·ties.**

**cause** (koz) **1** whatever produces an effect; a person, thing, or event that makes something happen: *The flood was the cause of much damage. Her stubbornness was the cause of the trouble.* **2** produce as an effect; make happen; make do; bring about: *What caused the fire?* **3** an occasion for action; reason; ground; motive: *cause for celebration.* **4** good reason; reason enough: *She was angry without cause.* **5** a subject or movement in which many people are interested and to which they give their support: *World peace is the cause she works for.* **6** in law,

a matter for a court to decide; lawsuit. 1, 3–6 *n.*, 2 *v.*, **caused, caus·ing.**
**make common cause with,** join efforts with; side with; help and support.
☛ *Syn.* See note at REASON.

**cause·less** (koz′lis) **1** without any known cause; happening by chance. **2** without good reason; not having reason enough. *adj.*

**cause·way** (koz′wā′) **1** a raised road or path, usually built across wet ground or shallow water. **2** a paved road; highway. **3** provide with a causeway. **4** pave with cobbles or pebbles. 1, 2 *n.*, 3, 4 *v.*

**caus·tic** (kos′tik) **1** a substance that burns or eats away by chemical action; corrosive substance. **2** able to burn or eat away by chemical action; corrosive: *Lye is caustic soda or caustic potash.* **3** sarcastic; stinging; biting: *The director's caustic remarks made the actors very angry.* 1 *n.*, 2, 3 *adj.*

**caus·ti·cal·ly** (kos′ti klē) sarcastically; stingingly; bitingly. *adv.*

**caustic soda** a brittle, white alkaline compound used in bleaching and in making soap, rayon, paper, etc.; sodium hydroxide.

**cau·ter·i·za·tion** (kot′ə rə zā′shən *or* kot′ə rī zā′shən) cauterizing or being CAUTERIZED. *n.*

**cau·ter·ize** (kot′ə rīz′) destroy defective tissue by burning with heat or chemical agent: *Doctors often remove warts by cauterizing them.* *v.*, **cau·ter·ized, cau·ter·iz·ing.**

**cau·tion** (kosh′ən) **1** the practice of taking care to be safe, or of never taking chances; being very careful: *Use caution in crossing streets.* **2** a warning: *A sign with "Danger" on it is a caution.* **3** warn; urge to be careful. **4** *Informal.* a very unusual person or thing. 1, 2, 4 *n.*, 3 *v.*

**cau·tion·ar·y** (kosh′ə ner′ē) warning; urging to be careful. *adj.*

**cau·tious** (kosh′əs) very careful; taking care to be safe; not taking chances: *a cautious driver.* *adj.*
—**cau′tious·ly,** *adv.* —**cau′tious·ness,** *n.*

**cav·al·cade** (kav′əl kād′) **1** a procession of persons riding on horses, in carriages, or in automobiles. **2** a series of scenes or events: *a cavalcade of sports.* *n.*

**cav·a·lier** (kav′ə lēr′) **1** free and easy; careless in manner; offhand: *a cavalier disregard for danger.* **2** proud and scornful; haughty; arrogant: *People were often irritated by his cavalier attitude.* **3** a horseman, mounted soldier, or knight. **4** a courteous gentleman. **5** a courteous escort for a lady. **6 Cavalier, a** in England, a person who supported Charles I in his struggle with Parliament from 1641 to 1649. **b** of the Cavaliers. 1, 2 *adj.*, 3–6 *n.*
—**cav′a·lier′ly,** *adv.*
☛ *Etym.* From F *cavalier* which comes from Italian *cavaliere*, ultimately from L *caballus*, meaning 'horse'.

**cav·al·ry** (kav′əl rē) **1** army troops trained to fight on horseback or, in recent times, in armoured vehicles. **2** a branch of an army made up of such troops. **3** of, having to do with, or belonging to the cavalry. *n. pl.* **cav·al·ries.**
☛ *Etym.* See note at CAVALIER.

**cav·al·ry·man** (kav′əl rē mən) a CAVALRY (def. 1) soldier. *n., pl.* **cav·al·ry·men** (-mən).

**cave** (kāv) **1** a hollow space underground, often having an opening in the side of a hill or cliff. **2** form a cave in or under; hollow out. 1 *n.*, 2 *v.*, **caved, cav·ing.**
—**cave′like′,** *adj.*

**cave in, a** fall in or down; collapse: *The weight of the snow caused the roof of the arena to cave in.* **b** cause to fall in or down; smash. **c** *Informal.* yield completely; give in to an argument, strain, or hardship.

**cave–in** (kāv′in′) **1** a falling-in, or collapse, of a mine, tunnel, etc. **2** a place where something has caved in: *There's a fence around the cave-in.* *n.*

**cav·ern** (kav′ərn) a large cave. *n.*

**cav·ern·ous** (kav′ər nəs) **1** like a CAVERN; large, dark, or hollow: *cavernous darkness, the cavernous mouth of a whale.* **2** full of CAVERNS: *cavernous mountains.* *adj.*

**cav·i·ar** *or* **cav·i·are** (kav′ē är′) a salty relish made from the eggs of STURGEON. *n.*

**cav·il** (kav′əl) **1** find fault unnecessarily; raise trivial objections. **2** a petty objection; trivial criticism. 1 *v.*, **cav·illed** *or* **cav·iled, cav·il·ling** *or* **cav·il·ing;** 2 *n.*
—**cav′il·ler** *or* **cav′il·er,** *n.*

**cav·i·ty** (kav′ə tē) **1** a hole; a hollow place: *a cavity in a tooth.* **2** an enclosed space inside the body: *the abdominal cavity, the four cavities of the heart.* *n., pl.* **cav·i·ties.**

**ca·vort** (kə vôrt′) *Informal.* prance about; jump around in a frisky way: *The colt cavorted in the pasture.* *v.*

**ca·vy** (kā′vē) any of a small family of mostly rat-sized South American rodents having a very short tail and rough grey or brown hair: *The guinea pig is a cavy.* *n., pl.* **ca·vies.**

**caw** (ko) **1** the harsh cry made by a crow or raven. **2** make this cry. 1 *n.*, 2 *v.*

**cay** (kā *or* kē) a low island; reef; KEY[2]. *n.*
☛ *Hom.* KEY and QUAY (for the second pronunciation of **cay**).

**cay·enne** (kī en′ *or* kā en′) RED PEPPER. *n.*

**cay·man** (kā′mən) See CAIMAN. *n., pl.* **cay·mans.**

**cay·use** (kī yüs′) an Indian pony of the western parts of Canada and the United States. *n.*

**Cb** columbium.

**CB** citizens' band.

**CBC** the Canadian Broadcasting Corporation.

**cc.** or **c.c.** cubic centimetre; cubic centimetres. Now written cm³.

**C.C.** **1** Canada Council. **2** Companion of the Order of Canada.

**CCF** or **C.C.F.** a Canadian political party established in 1932. It joined with the Canadian Labour Congress to form the New Democratic Party in 1961. The name CCF is an abbreviation for Co-operative Commonwealth Federation.

**C clef** in music, a symbol that means that the line on which it is placed represents middle C.

**Cd** cadmium.

**cd.** cord; cords.

**C.D.** or **CD** 1 civil defence. 2 Canadian (Forces) Decoration. 3 compact disc.

**cd. ft.** cord foot.

**Cdn.** Canadian.

**Cdn. Fr.** Canadian French.

**CD-ROM** (sē′dē′rom) compact disc-read-only memory.

**Ce** cerium.

**CE** 1 Canadian English. 2 Civil Engineer.

**cease** (sēs) 1 come to an end; stop: *The music ceased suddenly.* 2 put an end to: *They have ceased their endeavours. Cease your complaining.* *v.,* **ceased, ceas·ing.** **without cease,** without ceasing; continuously: *It rained for hours without cease.*

**cease–fire** (sē′sfīr′) a halt in military operations, especially for the purpose of discussing peace. *n.*

**cease·less** (sē′slis) never stopping; going on all the time; continual: *the ceaseless noise of distant traffic.* *adj.* —**cease′less·ly,** *adv.*

**Ce·cro·pi·a moth** (sə krō′pē ə) a large, colourful silkworm moth of eastern North America: *The Cecropia moth has a wingspan of over 15 cm.*

**ce·cum** (sē′kəm) See CAECUM. *n.*

**ce·dar** (sē′dər) 1 any of several very closely related species of North African and Asian evergreen tree of the pine family, such as the cedar of Lebanon, having long cones and short, sharp needles growing in spirals: *The cedar of Lebanon is the best known of these trees because it often appears in art and literature as a symbol of power and long life.* 2 any of many species of tree, especially several groups of evergreen of the cypress family, such as arborvitae and junipers. 3 the durable, fragrant, usually reddish wood of any of these trees: *Most kinds of cedar are insect repellant and resistant to decay.* 4 made of cedar: *a cedar chest.* *n.*
☞ *Hom.* SEEDER.

**ce·dar·bird** (sē′dər bėrd′) CEDAR WAXWING. *n.*

**cedar waxwing** a small North American bird with a crest and small red markings on its wings; WAXWING.

**cede** (sēd) give up; surrender; hand over to another: *France ceded Louisiana to Spain by the Treaty of Paris in 1763.* *v.,* **ced·ed, ced·ing.**
☞ *Hom.* SEED.

**ce·dil·la** (sə dil′ə) a mark resembling a comma, put under *c* in certain words to show that it has the sound of *s* before *a, o,* or *u.* Example: façade. *n.*

**ceil·ing** (sē′ling) 1 the inside, top covering of a room; the surface opposite to the floor. 2 the greatest height to which an aircraft can go under certain conditions: *That jet has a ceiling of more than 15 000 metres.* 3 the distance between the earth and the lowest clouds. 4 an upper limit: *A ceiling was placed on the amount of rent landlords could charge.* *n.*

**cel·an·dine** (sel′ən dīn′) a plant having yellow flowers, belonging to the same family as the poppy. *n.*

**cel·e·brant** (sel′ə brənt) 1 a person who performs a ceremony or rite. 2 a priest who performs Mass. 3 anyone who CELEBRATES; celebrator. *n.*

**cel·e·brate** (sel′ə brāt′) 1 observe a special time or day with the proper ceremonies or festivities: *To celebrate Canada Day, to celebrate a birthday.* 2 perform publicly with the proper ceremonies and rites: *The priest celebrates Mass in church.* 3 make known publicly; proclaim. 4 praise; honour: *To celebrate the glory of nature.* 5 observe a festival or event with ceremonies or festivities: *On her birthday she was too sick to celebrate.* 6 have a joyful time; make merry: *The people celebrated when the war ended.* *v.,* **cel·e·brat·ed, cel·e·brat·ing.**

**cel·e·brat·ed** (sel′ə brā′tid) 1 famous; well-known; much talked about: *a celebrated author.* 2 pt. and pp. of CELEBRATE. 1 *adj.,* 2 *v.*

**cel·e·bra·tion** (sel′ə brā′shən) 1 an act of celebrating. 2 whatever is done to celebrate something: *A Canada Day celebration often includes a firework display.* *n.*

**cel·e·bra·tor** (sel′ə brā′tər) a person who CELEBRATES. *n.*

**ce·leb·ri·ty** (sə leb′rə tē) 1 a famous person; a person who is well known or much talked about. 2 fame; being well known or much talked about. *n., pl.* **ce·leb·ri·ties.**

**ce·ler·i·ty** (sə ler′ə tē) swiftness; speed. *n.*

**cel·er·y** (sel′ə rē) 1 a plant having long, crisp, pale green stalks with leaves at the top. 2 its stalks, eaten as a vegetable. *n.*

**ce·les·ta** (sə les′tə) a musical instrument with a keyboard: *The tones of a celesta are made by hammers hitting steel plates.* *n.*

**ce·les·tial** (sə les′chəl) 1 of or having to do with the sky or the heavens: *The sun, moon, planets, and stars are celestial bodies.* 2 heavenly; divine; very good or beautiful: *celestial music.* *adj.* —**ce·les′tial·ly,** *adv.*

**celestial equator** the imaginary great circle that represents the intersection of the plane of the earth's equator with the CELESTIAL SPHERE. See ECLIPTIC for picture.

**celestial sphere** the imaginary sphere that apparently encloses the universe, of a size approaching infinity. See ECLIPTIC for picture.

**cel·i·ba·cy** (sel′ə bə sē) an unmarried state, especially because of religious vows. *n.*

**cel·i·bate** (sel′ə bit) 1 an unmarried person, especially one who takes a vow to remain single. 2 unmarried; single, especially because of a vow. 1 *n.,* 2 *adj.*

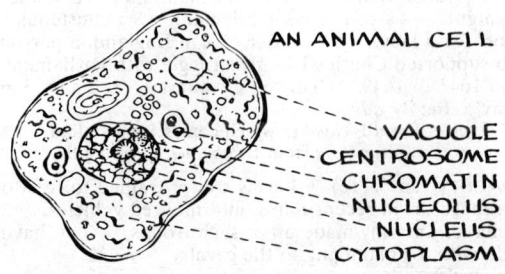

AN ANIMAL CELL — VACUOLE, CENTROSOME, CHROMATIN, NUCLEOLUS, NUCLEUS, CYTOPLASM

**cell** (sel) 1 a small room in a prison, convent, or monastery. 2 any small, hollow place: *Bees store honey in the cells of a honeycomb.* 3 the smallest structural unit of living matter that can function independently: *Most cells consist of protoplasm, have a nucleus near the centre, and are enclosed by a* **cell membrane.** *A plant cell also has a*

**cell wall.** 4 a container holding materials for producing electricity by chemical action; a small battery. 5 a small group that acts as a political, social, or religious unit for a larger, sometimes revolutionary, organization. *n.*
☛ *Hom.* SELL.

**cel·lar** (sel′ər) 1 an underground room or space, usually under a building, used for storing food or fuel, etc. 2 such a room for wines. 3 a supply of wines: *They keep an excellent cellar.* *n.*
☛ *Hom.* SELLER.

**cel·lar·age** (sel′ə rij) 1 space in a cellar. 2 cellars. 3 the charge for storage in a cellar. *n.*

**cell block** an individual building of cells in a prison.

**cell body** the nucleus of a neuron. See NEURON for picture.

**cel·list** or **'cel·list** (chel′ist) a person who plays the CELLO, especially a skilled player. *n.*

**cel·lo** or **'cel·lo** (chel′ō) the second largest instrument of the modern violin family, much larger than the violin and having a lower, mellower tone. When a cello is played it rests upright on the floor and is held between the knees of the player, who is seated. *n., pl.* **cel·los** or **'cel·los.**

**cel·lo·phane** (sel′ə fān′) a transparent substance, somewhat like paper, made from cellulose: *Cellophane is used as a wrapping to keep food, candy, tobacco, etc. fresh and clean.* *n.*

**cel·lu·lar** (sel′yə lər) 1 having to do with cells. 2 consisting of cells: *All animal and plant tissue is cellular.* *adj.*

**cellular radio** a telecommunication system that allows moving vehicles to send and receive messages.

**cellular telephone** a telephone using radio frequencies to send messages in small areas called cells. The frequency needed in moving from one cell to another is obtained with no interruption: *A cellular telephone is a component of many automobiles.*
☛ *Usage.* **cellular telephone** is often shortened to **cell phone.**

**cel·lu·loid** (sel′yə loid′) 1 a hard, transparent, combustible substance made from CELLULOSE and camphor, used now for eyeglass frames, photographic film, etc: *Celluloid was the first plastic to be widely used commercially; it has now been largely replaced by less flammable plastics.* 2 having to do with motion pictures. *n.*

**cel·lu·lose** (sel′yə lōs′) a substance that forms the walls of plant cells; the main substance making up the structure of all plants: *Cellulose is used to make paper, rayon, plastics, explosives, etc.* *n.*

**Cel·si·us** (sel′sē əs) of, based on, or according to the Celsius scale for measuring temperature, in which 0 degrees is the temperature at which water freezes and 100 degrees is the temperature at which water boils at sea level under normal atmospheric pressure. *Symbol:* C *adj.*
☛ *Etym.* Named after Anders *Celsius* (1701–1744), a Swedish astronomer, who invented the Celsius scale.

---

**cellar**     191     **censor**

hat, āge, fär; let, ēqual, tėrm; it, īce
hot, ōpen, ôrder; oil, out; cup, pút, rüle
əbove, takən, pencəl, lemən, circəs
ch, child; ng, long; sh, ship
th, thin; ŦH, then; zh, measure

**Celsius thermometer** a thermometer marked off according to the Celsius scale. See THERMOMETER for picture.

**Celt** (kelt *or* selt) 1 a member of an ancient people of western Europe and the British Isles, including the Britons and Gauls. 2 a descendant of one of these peoples: *The Irish, most Highland Scots, Welsh, and Bretons are Celts.* *n.* Also, **Kelt.**

**Celt·ic** (kel′tik *or* sel′tik) 1 of the Celts or their languages. 2 the group of languages spoken by the Celts, including Irish, Gaelic, Welsh, and Breton. 1 *adj.*, 2 *n.* Also, **Keltic.**

**ce·ment** (sə ment′) 1 a fine, grey powder made by burning clay and limestone. 2 this substance mixed with water and sand, gravel, or crushed stone to form concrete, used to make sidewalks, basement walls and floors, etc.: *Cement becomes hard like stone.* 3 any soft substance that hardens to make things stick together: *rubber cement.* 4 fasten together with cement. 5 pour or spread concrete for: *The workmen were cementing the sidewalk.* 6 anything that joins together or unites. 7 join firmly; unite: *The marriage of her son to their daughter cemented the friendship of the two families.* 1–3, 6 *n.*, 4, 5, 7 *v.*
—**ce·ment′er,** *n.*

**cem·e·ter·y** (sem′ə ter′ē) a place for burying the dead; graveyard. *n., pl.* **cem·e·ter·ies.**

**cen.** central.

**cen·o·taph** (sen′ə taf′) 1 a monument erected in memory of a dead person whose body is elsewhere. 2 a monument in memory of many dead persons, such as all those from one country, city, etc. killed in a war. *n.*

**Ce·no·zo·ic** (sē′nə zō′ik *or* sen′ə zō′ik) in geology: 1 of, having to do with, or referring to the era extending from the end of the Mesozoic, about 70 million years ago, to the present time: *The Cenozoic era is the age of mammals.* 2 of, having to do with, or referring to the system of rocks formed in this era. 3 the Cenozoic era or its rocks. 1, 2 *adj.*, 3 *n.* See geological time chart in the Appendix.

**cen·ser** (sen′sər) a container in which INCENSE is burned. *n.*
☛ *Hom.* CENSOR, SENSOR.

**cen·sor** (sen′sər) 1 a person authorized by a government or other organization to examine and, if necessary, change books, letters, motion pictures, etc. to ensure they contain nothing morally offensive or otherwise objectionable. 2 examine as a censor, often making changes or cutting out parts: *All letters from the battlefront were censored.* 3 take out a part or parts of news reports, letters, books, motion pictures, etc.: *Two scenes in the movie had been censored.* 4 in ancient Rome, a magistrate who took the census and supervised the conduct of citizens. 5 a person who tells others how they ought to behave. 6 a person who likes to find fault. 1, 4–6 *n.*, 2, 3 *v.*
☛ *Hom.* CENSER, SENSOR.

**cen·so·ri·ous** (sen sôr′ē əs)   too ready to find fault; severely critical.   *adj.*   —**cen′so′ri·ous·ly,** *adv.*
—**cen′so′ri·ous·ness,** *n.*

**cen·sor·ship** (sen′sər ship′)   **1** the act, practice, or system of censoring: *Censorship of news is common in time of war.*   **2** the position or work of a censor.   *n.*

**cen·sur·a·ble** (sen′shə rə bəl)   worthy of CENSURE (def. 1).   *adj.*   —**cen′sur·a·bly,** *adv.*

**cen·sure** (sen′shər)   **1** strong disapproval, especially official criticism or condemnation: *a vote of censure.*   **2** an expression of such disapproval: *The minister's speech included a censure of the press for biassed reporting.*   **3** express disapproval of; criticize officially or publicly: *The press in turn censured the government for failure to disclose all the facts.*   **1, 2** *n.,* **3** *v.,* **cen·sured, cen·sur·ing.**
—**cen′sur·er,** *n.*

**cen·sus** (sen′səs)   an official count of the people of a country or district: *A census is taken to find out the number of people living there and the numbers in different age groups, occupations, etc.*   *n.*

**cent** (sent)   **1** a unit of money in Canada equal to one one-hundredth of a dollar.   *Symbol:* ¢   **2** a unit of money equal to one one-hundredth of a dollar in the currencies of the United States, Australia, New Zealand, Trinidad and Tobago, Jamaica, and several other countries.   **3** a unit of money equal to one one-hundredth of the standard unit of currency in certain other countries.   **4** a coin worth one cent.   *n.*
☛ *Etym.* From F *cent*, which came from L *centum*, meaning 'hundred'.
☛ *Hom.* SCENT, SENT.

**cent.**   **1** central.   **2** century.

A centaur

**cen·taur** (sen′tôr)   in Greek mythology, one of a race of monsters that had the head, arms, and chest of a man, and the body and legs of a horse.   *n.*

**cen·te·nar·i·an** (sen′tə ner′ē ən)   **1** a person who is 100 years old or more.   **2** 100 years old or more.   **3** of 100 years.   **1** *n.,* **2, 3** *adj.*
☛ *Etym.* See note at CENT.

**cen·te·na·ry** (sen ten′ə rē or sen tē′nə rē)   **1** a period of 100 years.   **2** a 100th anniversary.   **3** the celebration of the 100th anniversary.   **4** having to do with a period of 100 years.   **1–3** *n., pl.* **cen·ten·a·ries;**   **4** *adj.*
☛ *Etym.* See note at CENT.

**cen·ten·ni·al** (sen ten′ē əl)   **1** of or having to do with 100 years or a 100th anniversary: *a centennial exhibition.*   **2** 100 years old.   **3** a 100th anniversary: *Canada celebrated its centennial in 1967.*   **4** the celebration of the 100th anniversary: *We missed our town's centennial because we were away on holidays.*   **1, 2** *adj.,* **3, 4** *n.*
☛ *Etym.* See note at CENT.

**cen·ten·ni·al·ly** (sen ten′ē ə lē)   once in every hundred years.   *adv.*
☛ *Etym.* See note at CENT.

**cen·ter** (sen′tər)   See CENTRE.   *n., v.*

**cen·tes·i·mal** (sen tes′ə məl)   **1** 100th.   **2** divided into 100ths.   *adj.*
☛ *Etym.* See note at CENT.

**centi–**   *combining form.*   **1** an SI prefix meaning one-hundredth: *A centimetre is one one-hundredth of a metre.*   *Symbol:* c   **2** one hundred, as in *centigrade, centipede.*
☛ *Etym.* See note at CENT.

**cen·ti·grade** (sen′tə grād′)   **1** divided into 100 degrees.   **2** CELSIUS.   *adj.*
☛ *Etym.* See note at CENT.

**cen·ti·me·tre** (sen′tə mē′tər)   an SI unit for measuring length, equal to one one-hundredth of a metre, or ten millimetres: *A nickel has a diameter of just over two centimetres.*   *Symbol:* cm   *n.*   Also, **centimeter.**
☛ *Etym.* See note at CENT.

**cen·ti·pede** (sen′tə pēd′)   a small wormlike ARTHROPOD having a long, flat body and many pairs of legs: *In some centipedes the front pair of legs is connected with a poison gland.*   *n.*
☛ *Etym.* From F *centipède* or L *centipeda*, both meaning 'centipede', formed from L *centum* 'hundred' + *pes, pedis* 'foot'.

**cen·tral** (sen′trəl)   **1** of the centre; being or forming the centre.   **2** at, in, or near the centre: *the central part of the city.*   **3** from the centre.   **4** equally distant from all points; easy to get to or from: *They are looking for a good central location to set up their shop.*   **5** main; chief; principal: *What is the central idea in the story?*   **6** a telephone exchange.   **7** a telephone operator.   **1–5** *adj.,* **6, 7** *n.*
☛ *Etym.* See note at CENTRE.

**cen·tral·i·za·tion** (sen′trə lə zā′shən or sen′trə lī zā′shən)   **1** a coming or bringing to a centre.   **2** concentration at a centre: *Centralization of relief agencies may prevent waste of effort.*   **3** the concentration of administrative power in a central government.   *n.*

**cen·tral·ize** (sen′trə līz′)   **1** collect at a centre; gather together.   **2** bring or come under one control.   *v.,* **cen·tral·ized, cen·tral·iz·ing.**

**cen·tral·ly** (sen′trə lē)   at or near the centre.   *adv.*

**central nervous system**   the brain and spinal cord.

**central processing unit**   that part of a computer in which operations in arithmetic are performed, and which contains a small number of units to hold results of calculations. *Abbrev.:* CPU.

**cen·tre** (sen′tər)   **1** a point within a circle or sphere equally distant from all of the circumference or surface.   **2** the middle part or place: *the centre of a room, the centre of the forehead, the centre of the stage.*   **3** a person or thing that is most important; the chief object of attention, interest, etc.: *She was the centre of attention. The new city hall was the centre of a huge controversy.*   **4** a place of influence or activity; a main area or point: *a shopping centre, a community centre. Toronto is a centre for trade.*   **5** place in or at the centre: *She centred the clock on the mantel.*   **6** gather together; concentrate: *The troops were centred at a temporary camp.*   **7** the player who has the centre position of a forward line in basketball, hockey, football, etc.   **8** a political attitude or policy

characterized by moderate views that are neither right (conservative) nor left (reformist or radical).   **9** all the people and parties having moderate views.   *1–4, 7–9 n.,* *5, 6 v.,*   **cen·tred, cen·tring.**   Also, **center.**
**centre on** or **upon,**   have something as its main theme: *This story centres on two astronauts.*
☛ *Etym.*   From ME *centre*, which came from OF *centre*, from L *centrum*, ultimately from Gk. *kentron*, meaning 'sharp point'.

**centre·board**   (sen′tər bôrd′)   a movable KEEL (def. 1) of a sailboat.   *n.*   Also, **centerboard.**

**centre field**   in baseball, the section of the outfield behind second base.

**centre ice**   in hockey:   **1** the centre of the ice surface from which play begins at the start of each period.   **2** the area of ice surface between the blue lines.

**centre line**   in hockey, a red line passing through centre ice at an equal distance from each of the blue lines.

**centre of gravity**   the point in something around which its mass is evenly balanced.

**cen·trif·u·gal**   (sen trif′ə gəl)   moving away from the centre.   *adj.*   —**cen·trif′u·gal·ly,** *adv.*

**centrifugal force**   an apparent force due to inertia, that tends to move things away from the centre around which they revolve.

**cen·tri·ole**   (sen′trē ōl)   a cylindrical body in an animal cell, located near the nucleus: *The centriole plays a role in cellular division.*   *n.*

**cen·trip·e·tal**   (sen trip′ə təl)   moving toward the centre.   *adj.*   —**cen·trip′e·tal·ly,** *adv.*

**centripetal force**   a force that tends to move things toward the centre around which they are turning: *Gravitation is a centripetal force.*

**cen·tro·mere**   (sen′trə mēr′)   a structure or point by which two sister chromatids are joined to each other and to a spindle during cell division.   *n.*

**cen·tro·some**   (sen′trə sōm′)   a tiny part of many animal cells close to the nucleus that separates into two parts when the cell divides and attracts the divided chromosomes, one group to each part; centrosphere.   See CELL for picture.   *n.*

**cen·tro·sphere**   (sen′trə sfēr′)   **1** CENTROSOME.   **2** in geology, the central part of the earth.   *n.*

**cen·tu·ple**   (sen tü′pəl *or* sen′tü pəl)   **1** 100 times as much or as many; hundredfold.   **2** make 100 times as much or as many; increase a hundredfold.   *1 adj., 2 v.,*   **cen·tu·pled, cen·tu·pling.**
☛ *Etym.*   See note at CENT.

**cen·tu·ri·on**   (sen tyü′rē ən *or* sen tü′rē ən)   in the ancient Roman army, the commander of a group of about 100 soldiers.   *n.*
☛ *Etym.*   See note at CENT.

**cen·tu·ry**   (sen′chə rē)   **1** each 100 years, counting from some special time: *The first century is 1 to 100; the nineteenth century is 1801 to 1900; the twentieth century is 1901 to 2000.*   **2** any period of 100 years: *From 1824 to 1924 is a century.*   **3** a group of 100 people or things. **4** in the ancient Roman army, a body of soldiers: *Originally, a century probably consisted of 100 soldiers.* **5** in ancient Rome, a division of the people for voting: *Each century had one vote.*   **6** in cricket, an individual score of 100 runs.   *n., pl.* **cen·tu·ries.**
☛ *Etym.*   See note at CENT.

# centreboard    193    cerement

hat, āge, fär; let, ēqual, tėrm; it, īce
hot, ōpen, ôrder; oil, out; cup, put, rüle
əbove, takən, pencəl, lemən, circəs
ch, child; ng, long; sh, ship
th, thin; ᴛʜ, then; zh, measure

**ce·phal·ic**   (sə fal′ik)   **1** of or relating to the head. **2** near, on, or in the head.   **3** toward the head.   *adj.*

**ceph·a·lo·pod**   (sef′ə lə pod′)   any animal belonging to the most highly organized class of MOLLUSCS, characterized by long, armlike tentacles around the mouth, a pair of large eyes, and a sharp, birdlike beak: *Cuttlefish and squids are cephalopods.*   *n.*

**ce·phal·o·thor·ax**   (sef′ə lə thô′raks)   the head and body of a CRUSTACEAN.   *n.*

**ce·ram·ic**   (sə ram′ik)   **1** of, having to do with, or referring to pottery, earthenware, porcelain, etc., or the making of them.   **2** an article of pottery, earthenware, porcelain, etc.: *They had some beautiful ceramics at the craft show.*   **3** ceramics,   the art or process of making articles from baked clay (*used with a singular verb*): *Ceramics is taught in art class.*   *1 adj., 2, 3 n.*

**ce·re·al**   (sē′rē əl)   **1** any grass that produces a grain used as food: *Wheat, rice, corn, oats, and barley are cereals.* **2** the grain.   **3** food made from the grain: *Oatmeal and corn meal are cereals. Cereals are often eaten at breakfast.* **4** of or having to do with grain or the grasses producing it: *cereal crops, cereal products.*   *1–3 n., 4 adj.*
☛ *Hom.*   SERIAL.
☛ *Etym.*   Originally an adjective only, formed in the 19c. from L *cerealis* 'having to do with the cultivation of grain', formed from *Ceres*, the name of the Roman goddess of agriculture.

**cer·e·bel·lum**   (ser′ə bel′əm)   the part of the brain that controls the co-ordination of the muscles.   See BRAIN for picture.   *n., pl.* **cer·e·bel·lums** or **cer·e·bel·la** (-bel′ə).

**cer·e·bral**   (sə rē′brəl *or* ser′ə brəl)   **1** of the brain: *A cerebral hemorrhage causes paralysis.*   **2** of the CEREBRUM: *The cerebral cortex is the outer layer of the cerebrum.*   **3** involving or appealing to thought and reason; intellectual: *She enjoys cerebral games like chess. adj.*

**cerebral palsy**   paralysis due to a lesion of the brain: *Children with cerebral palsy have trouble co-ordinating their muscles.*

**cer·e·brate**   (ser′ə brāt′)   use the brain; think.   *v.,* **cer·e·brat·ed, cer·e·brat·ing.**

**cer·e·bra·tion**   (ser′ə brā′shən)   **1** the action of the brain.   **2** thinking.   *n.*

**cer·e·bro·spi·nal**   (sə rē′brō spī′nəl *or* ser′ə brō spī′nəl) of or affecting both the brain and spinal cord.   *adj.*

**cer·e·brum**   (sə rē′brəm *or* ser′ə brəm)   **1** the part of the human brain that is responsible for mental activities such as memory, understanding, and the ability to reason, and also controls fine movements of the smaller muscles of the face, hands, and toes, and the senses of sight, hearing, etc.   See BRAIN for picture.   **2** the part of the brain in all other vertebrates that corresponds structurally to the human cerebrum but has fewer functions.   *n., pl.* **cer·e·brums** or **cer·e·bra** (-brə).

**cere·ment**   (sēr′mənt)   the cloth or garment in which a dead person is wrapped for burial; shroud.   *n.*

**cer·e·mo·ni·al** (serʹə mōʹnē əl)  **1** of or having to do with CEREMONY: *a ceremonial occasion. The ceremonial costumes were beautiful.*  **2** formal actions suitable for an occasion: *Kneeling is a ceremonial of some religions.*  **3** very formal; CEREMONIOUS (def. 2).  1, 3 *adj.*, 2 *n.*
—**cerʹe·moʹni·al·ly**, *adv.*

**cer·e·mo·ni·ous** (serʹə mōʹnē əs)  **1** full of CEREMONY: *The banquet was a ceremonious affair.*  **2** very formal; extremely polite: *He greeted the ambassador with a ceremonious bow.*  *adj.*  —**cerʹe·moʹni·ous·ly**, *adv.*
—**cerʹe·moʹni·ous·ness**, *n.*

**cer·e·mo·ny** (serʹə mōʹnē)  **1** a special form or set of acts to be done on special occasions such as weddings, funerals, graduations, Christmas, Hanukkah.  **2** very polite conduct; a way of conducting oneself that follows all the rules of polite social behaviour: *The old gentleman showed us to the door with a great deal of ceremony.*  **3** an empty form; meaningless formality.  **4** formality; formalities: *The democratic princess disliked the ceremony of the court.*  *n., pl.* **cer·e·mo·nies**.
**stand on ceremony,** be very formal; insist on formal behaviour: *The premier does not stand on ceremony but always makes the people she meets feel comfortable and relaxed.*

**ce·re·us** (sēʹrē əs)  any of several kinds of American cactus. The night-blooming cereus has fragrant flowers that open at night.  *n.*
☛ *Hom.* SERIOUS.

**ce·rise** (sə rēz' *or* sə rēs')  bright pinkish-red.  *n., adj.*

**ce·ri·um** (sēʹrē əm)  a greyish metallic element. Symbol: Ce  *n.*

**cer·tain** (serʹtən)  **1** settled; fixed; definite: *a certain hour. Each investor will receive a certain percentage of the profit.*  **2** that cannot be disputed; established beyond any doubt: *It is certain that 2 and 3 do not make 6.*  **3** sure to happen; inevitable: *Death is certain.*  **4** bound (*to*); sure (*to*): *She is certain to do well in her profession.*  **5** reliable; dependable: *The police have certain evidence of her guilt.*  **6** definite but not named: *A certain person donated $2000 to the project.*  **7** having or showing no doubt; confident; positive: *She was certain of her facts. His reply was quick and certain.*  **8** of a particular but unspecified character, amount, or degree: *There was a certain reluctance in his voice, but he agreed to go. The room had a certain charm that made it very inviting. To a certain extent we are all at fault.*  **9** a definite but unspecified number; some particular ones: *Certain of the students will be asked to give a detailed report.*  1–8 *adj.*, 9 *pron.*  —**cerʹtain·ness**, *n.*
**for certain,** surely, without a doubt: *It will rain for certain.*

**cer·tain·ly** (serʹtən lē)  **1** surely; without doubt.  **2** *Informal.* yes; of course: *May I borrow your music? Certainly, you may.*  *adv.*

**cer·tain·ty** (serʹtən tē)  **1** being certain; freedom from doubt: *The woman's certainty was amusing, for we could all see that she was wrong.*  **2** something certain; a sure fact: *Spring and summer are certainties.*  *n., pl.* **cer·tain·ties**.

**cer·ti·fi·a·ble** (serʹtə fīʹə bəl)  **1** that can be certified.  **2** sick enough in the mind to be legally committed to a mental institution.  *adj.*

**cer·tif·i·cate** (sər tifʹə kit *for noun,* sər tifʹə kāt' *for verb*)  **1** a written or printed statement that declares something to be a fact: *Your birth certificate gives your full name and the date and place of your birth.*  **2** give a certificate to.  **3** authorize by a certificate.  1 *n.*, 2, 3 *v.*,
**cer·tifʹi·cat·ed, cer·tifʹi·cat·ing**.

**cer·ti·fi·ca·tion** (serʹtə fə kāʹshən)  **1** certifying or being CERTIFIED.  **2** a CERTIFIED statement.  *n.*

**cer·ti·fied** (serʹtə fīd')  **1** guaranteed: *The water is certified to be pure.*  **2** having a certificate.  **3** pt. and pp. of CERTIFY.  1, 2 *adj.*, 3 *v.*

**certified cheque**  a cheque that is guaranteed by a bank to be covered by enough money in the account on which it is drawn.

**certified mail**  a postal service that provides proof of delivery of a letter or parcel by means of a card that is signed by the receiver of the mail and is then returned to the sender: *Certified mail is similar to registered mail, but cheaper.*

**cer·ti·fi·er** (serʹtə fīʹər)  one that certifies.  *n.*

**cer·ti·fy** (serʹtə fī')  **1** declare something as true or correct by spoken, written, or printed statement: *The doctor certified the cause of death as a heart attack.*
**2** legally commit a person to a mental institution.
**3** guarantee the quality or value of: *All the meat we buy in the stores has to be certified by the government.*  **4** assure; make certain.  *v.,* **cer·ti·fied, cer·ti·fy·ing**.

**cer·ti·tude** (serʹtə tyüd' *or* serʹtə tüd')  certainty; sureness.  *n.*

**ce·ru·le·an** (sə rüʹlē ən)  sky blue.  *adj., n.*

**cer·vi·cal** (serʹvə kəl)  of or having to do with a CERVIX. See SPINAL COLUMN for picture.  *adj.*

**cer·vi·ces** (sər vīʹsēz)  a pl. of CERVIX.  *n.*

**cer·vine** (serʹvīn)  of or like a deer.  *adj.*

**cer·vix** (serʹviks)  **1** the neck, especially the back of the neck.  **2** a necklike part, especially the narrow opening of the uterus.  *n., pl.* **cer·vix·es** or **cer·vi·ces** (-sēz).

**ce·si·um** or **cae·si·um** (sēʹzē əm)  a silvery metallic element. Symbol: Cs  *n.*

**ces·sa·tion** (se sāʹshən)  ceasing, pause; stop: *There is still hope for a cessation of fighting.*  *n.*

**ces·sion** (seshʹən)  handing over to another; ceding; giving up; surrendering: *the cession of all warships by a conquered nation.*  *n.*
☛ *Hom.* SESSION.

**cess·pool** (sesʹpül')  **1** a pool or pit for house drains to empty into.  **2** any filthy place.  *n.*

**ce·ta·cean** (sə tāʹshən)  **1** any animal belonging to the order Cetacea, a group of fishlike mammals that live in the water, especially in the ocean: *Whales, dolphins, and porpoises are cetaceans.*  **2** of, having to do with, or referring to the cetaceans.  1 *n.*, 2 *adj.*

**ce·ta·ceous** (sə tāʹshəs)  CETACEAN (def. 2).  *adj.*

**Cey·lo·nese** (sēʹlə nēz')  **1** of or having to do with Sri Lanka, an island country in the Indian Ocean, or its people.  **2** a native or inhabitant of Sri Lanka.  1 *adj.*, 2 *n., pl.* **Cey·lo·nese**.

**Cf**  californium.

**cf.**  compare.

**CF**  Canadian Forces.

**CFB**  Canadian Forces Base.

**CFC**  chlorofluorocarbon.  *pl.* **CFC's**.

**CFL** or **C.F.L.**  Canadian Football League.

**C.G.I.T.** or **CGIT** Canadian Girls in Training.
**ch.** or **Ch.** 1 chapter. 2 church.
**C.H.** Companion of Honour.

**chafe** (chāf) 1 rub to make warm: *I chafed my cold hands.* 2 wear or be worn away by rubbing. 3 make sore by rubbing: *The rough collar chafed my neck.* 4 become sore by rubbing: *My neck is chafing.* 5 annoy or make angry: *Their teasing chafed her.* 6 a chafing; irritation. 1–5 *v.*, **chafed, chaf·ing;** 6 *n.*
**chafe at,** become impatient at: *They chafed at the long delay.*
**chafe under,** become annoyed or angry about: *He chafed under their teasing.*

**chaff**[1] (chaf) 1 husks of wheat, oats, rye, etc., especially when separated from grain by threshing. 2 hay or straw cut fine for feeding cattle. 3 worthless stuff. *n.*

**chaff**[2] (chaf) 1 make fun of in a good-natured way: *The girls chaffed the French boy about his mistakes in speaking English.* 2 good-natured joking about a person to his face: *The French boy did not mind their chaff.* 1 *v.*, 2 *n.*

**chaf·fer** (chaf′ər) dispute about a price; bargain. *v.*

**chaf·finch** (chaf′inch) a European songbird with a pleasant, short song, often kept as a cage bird. *n.*

**chaff·y** (chaf′ē) 1 full of CHAFF. 2 like CHAFF; worthless. *adj.*

**chaf·ing dish** (chā′fing) a dish with a heating apparatus under it, used to cook food at the table or to keep it warm.

**cha·grin** (shə grin′) 1 a feeling of embarrassment or vexation caused by disappointment, failure, or humiliation. 2 cause to feel chagrin. 1 *n.*, 2 *v.*

**chain** (chān) 1 a flexible, connected series of links or rings used to bind, connect, or hold, or to decorate: *a gold chain, a steel chain, a paper chain.* 2 a series of things joined or linked together: *a mountain chain, a chain of happenings, a chain of thoughts.* 3 join together or fasten with a chain. 4 anything that binds or restrains. 5 bind; restrain. 6 keep in prison; make a slave of. 7 a measuring instrument consisting of 100 links of iron or steel: *A surveyors' chain is 66 feet long (about 20 m); an engineers' chain is 100 feet long (about 30 m).* 8 a number of similar restaurants, theatres, etc. owned and operated by one person or company. 9 in chemistry, a number of atoms of the same element bonded together like a chain. 10 **chains,** *pl.* **a** bonds; fetters. **b** imprisonment; bondage. 1, 2, 4, 7–10 *n.*, 3, 5, 6 *v.*
**chained to,** be entirely responsible for; be unable to leave: *chained to the house. She is simply chained to her job and never has a vacation.*

**chain gang** in the southern United States, a gang of convicts, etc. chained together while at work outdoors or on their way to work.

**chain letter** a letter that each receiver is asked to copy and send to several others in order to get some supposed benefit.

**chain mail** a kind of flexible armour made of metal rings linked together.

**chain measure** a system of measurement used in surveying: 100 links = 1 chain (about 20 m)
10 chains = 1 furlong
8 furlongs = 1 mile

**chain reaction** 1 in chemistry or nuclear physics, a process that sustains itself when it has once been started because it yields energy and products that cause further reactions of the same kind: *A reactor is designed to produce a controlled chain reaction.* 2 any series of events or happenings, each caused by the one that precedes it.

**chain saw** a portable power saw having teeth linked together in an endless chain.

**chain store** one of a group of retail stores owned and operated by a single company.

**chair** (cher) 1 a seat for one person, that has four legs and a back and, sometimes, arms. 2 a seat of rank, dignity, or authority. 3 the position or authority of a person who has such a seat: *Professor Eagle occupies the chair of Philosophy at this university.* 4 the chairperson of a meeting: *May we have a ruling on this point from the chair?* 5 a covered chair carried on poles by two men; SEDAN CHAIR. 6 ELECTRIC CHAIR. 7 put or carry in a chair. 8 act as a chairperson. 1–6 *n.*, 7, 8 *v.*
**take the chair,** **a** begin a meeting. **b** be in charge of or preside at a meeting.

**chair·man** (cher′mən) 1 a person who presides at or is in charge of a meeting. 2 the head of a committee. 3 in New Brunswick, the elected head of a village council. 4 a man hired to carry or wheel people in a chair: *A sedan chair was carried by two chairmen.* *n., pl.* **chair·men** (-mən).
☞ *Usage.* **Chairman,** CHAIRPERSON, CHAIRWOMAN. The word **chairman** may be used for either a man or a woman in charge of a meeting or committee. The word **chairperson** is now widely used, so that the term **chairwoman** is less frequently needed. Of the three terms, only **chairman** is used as a form of address: *Mr. Chairman, Madam Chairman.*

**chair·man·ship** (cher′mən ship′) 1 the position of CHAIRMAN (defs. 1, 2). 2 the term of office of a CHAIRMAN (defs. 1, 2). *n.*

**chair·per·son** (cher′pėr′sən) 1 a person who presides at or is in charge of a meeting. 2 the head of a committee. *n.*

**chair·wom·an** (cher′wum′ən) 1 a woman who presides at or is in charge of a meeting. 2 a woman at the head of a committee. *n., pl.* **chair·wom·en** (-wim′ən).

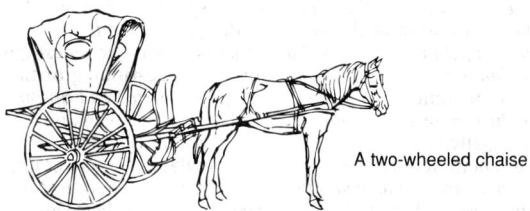

A two-wheeled chaise

**chaise** (shāz) 1 any of several kinds of light carriage, often with a folding top, having two or four wheels and drawn by one or two horses. 2 CHAISE LONGUE. *n.*

**chaise longue** (shāz′long′) a couchlike chair with a long seat, in which a person can sit with outstretched legs. *pl.* **chaise longues** or **chaises longues.**

**chal·ced·o·ny** (kal sed′ə nē *or* kal′sə dō′nē)   **1** a variety of quartz, having a waxy lustre, that occurs in various colours and forms: *Agate, onyx, carnelian, jasper, etc. are chalcedony.*   **2** a gem made from this stone.   *n., pl.* **chal·ced·o·nies.**

**chalcid** (kal′sid)   any of a large family of mostly very small insects whose larvae live as parasites on other insects.   *n.*

**Chal·de·an** (kal dē′ən)   **1** of or having to do with Chaldea, an ancient region in southwestern Asia, its people, or their language.   **2** a native or inhabitant of Chaldea: *The Chaldeans were a Semitic tribe closely related to the Babylonians.*   **3** the language of Chaldea.   **4** of or having to do with astrology or magic.   **5** an astrologer; magician.   1, 4 *adj.,* 2, 3, 5 *n.*

**cha·let** (shal′ā *or* sha lā′)   **1** a herdsman's hut or cabin in the Swiss mountains.   **2** a Swiss house with wide, overhanging eaves.   **3** any house of similar design.   *n.*

**chal·ice** (chal′is)   **1** a cup; goblet, especially one used in the Communion service.   **2** a flower shaped like a cup.   *n.*

**chal·iced** (chal′ist)   **1** having a flower shaped like a cup.   **2** contained in a chalice.   *adj.*

**chalk** (chok)   **1** a soft, white, or grey limestone, made up mostly of tiny fossil sea shells: *Chalk is used for making lime.*   **2** a substance like chalk, used for writing or drawing on a chalkboard.   **3** a piece of this substance.   **4** mark, write, or draw with chalk.   **5** mix or rub with chalk; whiten with chalk.   **6** score; record.   1–3 *n.,* 4–6 *v.*
**chalk up,   a** write down; record.   **b** score: *We chalked up twenty points in that game.*
☛ *Hom.* CHOCK.

**chalk·board** (chok′bôrd′)   a board having a smooth, hard surface for writing or drawing on with chalk.   *n.*

**chalk·y** (chok′ē)   **1** of chalk; containing chalk: *the chalky cliffs of Dover.*   **2** like chalk; white as chalk: *The clown's face was chalky.*   *adj.,* **chalk·i·er, chalk·i·est.** —**chalk′i·ness,** *n.*

**chal·lenge** (chal′ənj)   **1** call to engage in a fight or contest: *to challenge someone to a duel. The new school has challenged us to a basketball tournament.*   **2** a call to a fight or contest: *We have accepted the challenge.*   **3** a call to justify or account for oneself or one's actions: *The sentry called out a challenge as they approached.*   **4** stop a person and question his or her right to do what he or she is doing or to be where he or she is: *When she tried to enter the building, the guard challenged her.*   **5** demand proof; question or dispute something: *My friends challenged my statement that Fredericton was the oldest city in Canada.*   **6** a demand for proof; a questioning of the truth of something: *Their challenge led me to read up on the history of our country.*   **7** in law, object formally, especially to a juror or jury.   **8** such an objection.   **9** demand action or effort from; stimulate: *The possibility of space travel has challenged the human imagination for centuries.*   1, 4, 5, 7, 9 *v.,* **chal·lenged, chal·leng·ing;** 2, 3, 6, 8 *n.*   —**chal′lenge·a·ble,** *adj.*   —**chal′leng·er,** *n.*

**chal·lis** (shal′ē)   a lightweight, usually printed, fabric of wool, wool and cotton, or a synthetic fibre, used for dresses, blouses, etc.   *n.*

**cham·ber** (chām′bər)   **1** a room in a house.   **2** bedroom.   **3** the hall where a legislature or a governing body meets: *the Senate Chamber.*   **4** a group of lawmakers: *The Canadian Parliament has two chambers, the Senate and the House of Commons.*   **5** a group of people organized for some business purpose: *Chamber of Commerce.*   **6** any enclosed space in the body of an animal or plant: *The human heart has four chambers.*   **7** an enclosed space in machinery, especially the part of the bore of a gun that holds the charge, or any of the spaces for cartridges in a revolver: *The part of a gun that holds the charge is called the chamber.*   **8 chambers,** *pl.* **a** a set of rooms in a building to live in or use as offices.   **b** the office of a lawyer or judge.   *n.*

**cham·bered** (chām′bərd)   having a chamber or chambers; divided into compartments.   *adj.*

**cham·ber·lain** (chām′bər lin)   **1** the person who manages the household of a sovereign or a lord; steward.   **2** a high official of a royal court.   *n.*

**cham·ber·maid** (chām′bər mād′)   a maid who makes the beds, cleans the bedrooms, etc., now especially in hotels.   *n.*

**chamber music**   music suited to a room or small hall; music for a trio, quartet, etc.

**Chamber of Commerce**   an organization of business people whose aim is to increase business opportunities by improving the community in which they live.

**cham·bray** (sham′brā)   a fine cloth, especially of cotton, in a plain weave, combining coloured warp threads with white filling threads in various designs.   *n.*

**cha·me·le·on** (kə mē′lē ən)   **1** a lizard that can change the colour of its skin to camouflage itself against different backgrounds.   **2** a changeable or fickle person.   *n.*

**cham·fer** (cham′fər)   **1** a flat slanting surface made by cutting off an edge or corner; BEVEL (def. 1).   **2** cut off at an edge or corner to make a slanting surface.   **3** make a groove or furrow in; FLUTE (def. 5).   **4** a groove or furrow.   1, 4 *n.,* 2, 3 *v.*

**cham·ois** (sham′ē *or for def. 1* sham wä′)   **1** a small, goatlike antelope that lives in the high mountains of Europe and southwestern Asia.   **2** a soft leather made from the skin of sheep, goats, deer, etc.   *n., pl.* **cham·ois.**

**cham·o·mile** (kam′ə mīl′)   See CAMOMILE.   *n.*

**champ**[1] (champ)   **1** bite and chew noisily.   **2** bite on impatiently: *The excited horse champed its bit.*   *v.*
**champ (at) the bit,**   be restless or impatient: *After months with her leg in plaster, the girl was champing at the bit to go skiing again.*

**champ**[2] (champ) *Informal.*   CHAMPION (def. 1).   *n.*

**cham·pagne** (sham pān′)   **1** a sparkling, bubbling wine, first made in northern France.   **2** pale brownish-yellow.   1, 2 *n.,* 2 *adj.*

**cham·pi·on** (cham′pē ən)   **1** a person, animal, or thing that wins first place in a game or contest: *the swimming champion of the world.*   **2** having won first place; ahead of all others: *a champion boxer, a champion rose.*   **3** a person who fights or speaks for another; defender; supporter: *a great champion of peace.*   **4** fight or speak in behalf of; defend; support: *Ingeborg championed her friend.*   1–3 *n.,* 4 *v.*   —**cham′pi·on·less,** *adj.*
☛ *Etym.*   From OF *champion* 'a man who fights on behalf of another', developed from L *campio* 'warrior', formed from *campus* 'field of battle'. The most common meaning today, 'a person who has won the first prize', did not develop until the 19c.

**cham·pi·on·ship** (cham′pē ən ship′)   **1** the position of

CHAMPION (def. 1); first place.   2 defence; support.
3 a competition or series of competitions to decide a
winner.   *n.*

**chance** (chans)   1 opportunity: *a chance to make some
money.*   2 the likelihood of something happening;
probability: *There's a good chance that he'll show up in time
for dinner.*   3 fate; luck.   4 a happening: *Chance led to
the finding of the diamond mine.*   5 happen: *She chanced
to notice a coin in the gutter.*   6 a risk: *She took a chance
when she swam the Channel.*   7 accept the danger of;
risk: *I wouldn't chance going sailing without a life jacket.*
8 not expected or planned; accidental; casual: *a chance
visit.*   1–4, 6, 8 *n.*, 5, 7 *v.*, **chanced, chanc·ing.**
**by chance,**   **a** accidentally: *The meeting came about by
chance.*   **b** by some turn of events: *If by chance the
weather clears, we can go for a swim.*
**chance it,** *Informal.*   take a risk.
**chance upon** or **on,**   happen to find or meet: *He chanced
upon an old friend.*

**chan·cel** (chan′səl)   the space around the altar of a
Christian church, used by the clergy and the choir: *The
chancel is often separated from the rest of the church by a
railing, lattice, or screen.*   See BASILICA for picture.   *n.*
☛ *Etym.* See note at CANCEL.

**chan·cel·ler·y** (chan′sə lə rē)   1 the position of a
CHANCELLOR.   2 the office of a CHANCELLOR.   *n., pl.*
**chan·cel·ler·ies.**

**chan·cel·lor** (chan′sə lər)   1 a high official who is the
secretary of a monarch or noble, or the chief secretary of
an embassy.   2 the prime minister or other very high
official of some European countries.   3 the honorary
head of a university: *The chancellor presides over
convocation and is usually a member of the university senate
and the board of governors.*   *n.*
☛ *Etym.* See note at CANCEL.

**Chancellor of the Exchequer**   in the United
Kingdom, the highest official of the treasury.

**chan·cel·lor·ship** (chan′sə lər ship′)   1 the position of
a CHANCELLOR.   2 the term of office of a
CHANCELLOR.   *n.*

**chan·cer·y** (chan′sə rē)   1 a court that deals with cases
involving fairness and justice outside the scope of common
law or statute law.   2 an office where public records are
kept.   3 the office of a CHANCELLOR.   4 the principle of
equity; the spirit rather than the letter of the law.   *n., pl.*
**chan·cer·ies.**
**in chancery,**   **a** in a court of equity.   **b** in a helpless
position.

**chan·cre** (shang′kər)   a hard, reddish ulcer or sore that
is the first symptom of syphilis.   *n.*

**chan·de·lier** (shan′də lēr′)   a fixture with branches for
lights, usually hanging from the ceiling.   *n.*
☛ *Etym.* See note at CANDLE.

**chan·dler** (chan′dlər)   1 a maker or seller of candles.
2 a dealer in groceries and supplies: *a ship chandler.*   *n.*

**change** (chānj)   1 become different: *He had changed
since she had seen him last. The bus schedule has changed
again.*   2 make different: *She changed the room by
painting the walls green.*   3 put something in place of
another; substitute: *to change dirty clothes for clean ones.
Let's change the subject.*   4 pass from one position or
state to another: *The wind changed from east to west.*
5 give and receive; exchange: *I changed seats with my
brother.*   6 changing; passing from one position or state
to another: *The change from flower to fruit is interesting to
watch. A change from the city to the country in the summer
is good for children.*   7 a changed condition: *Do you see
any changes in her behaviour?*   8 the lack of sameness;
variety: *Let me drive for a change.*   9 a thing to be used
in place of another of the same kind: *a change of clothes.*
10 get or give small units of money that equal a larger
unit: *to change a dollar for ten dimes.*   11 the money
returned to a person when he or she has given an amount
larger than the price of what he or she buys.   12 smaller
units of money given in place of a large unit of money:
*Please give me change for this five-dollar bill.*   13 coins: *I
have a five-dollar bill and some change.*   14 put fresh
clothes or coverings on: *to change the baby, to change the
bed.*   15 put on other clothing: *I want to change first.*
16 transfer from one bus, plane, etc. to another: *It's not a
direct flight; you have to change at Winnipeg.*   1–5, 10,
14–16, *v.*, **changed, chang·ing;**   6–9, 11–13 *n.*
—**chang′er,** *n.*
**change for the better,**   improve.
**change off,**   alternate with another person in doing
something; take turns: *We changed off hoeing and raking to
make the job easier.*
**change over,**   exchange places or tasks.
**change places with,**   have someone else's lifestyle or job.
**change round,**   exchange places or directions.

**change·a·bil·i·ty** (chān′jə bil′ə tē)   a CHANGEABLE
quality or condition.   *n.*

**change·a·ble** (chān′jə bəl)   1 that can change or is
likely to change: *April weather is changeable.*   2 that can
be changed; alterable: *a changeable clause in a contract.*
3 having a colour or appearance that changes: *Silk is called
changeable when it looks different in different lights.*   *adj.*
—**change′a·ble·ness,** *n.*   —**change′a·bly,** *adv.*

**change·ful** (chānj′fəl)   full of changes; likely to
change; changing.   *adj.*   —**change′ful·ly,** *adv.*
—**change′ful·ness,** *n.*

**change·less** (chānj′lis)   not changing; not likely to
change; constant; steadfast.   *adj.*   —**change′less·ly,** *adv.*
—**change′less·ness,** *n.*

**change·ling** (chānj′ling)   1 a child secretly substituted
for another.   2 a strange, stupid, or ugly child, supposed
to have been left by fairies in place of a child carried off
by them.   *n.*

**change of heart**   a change of feeling; conversion.

**change of life**   MENOPAUSE.

**change–o·ver** (chān′jō′vər)   1 a shifting to the
manufacture of a new model.   2 a transfer of ownership
or control.   *n.*

**chan·nel** (chan′əl)   1 the bed of a stream, river, etc.
2 a body of water joining two larger bodies of water: *the
English Channel.*   3 the deeper part of a waterway: *There
is shallow water on both sides of the channel in this river.*
4 a passage for liquids; groove.   5 a means of
communication or expression: *The information came
through secret channels.*   6 a course of action; field of
activity: *He sought to find a suitable channel for his
enthusiasm.*   7 direct into a particular course;
concentrate: *She decided to channel her energies into
politics.*   8 a narrow band of radio or television
frequencies.   9 form a channel in; cut out as a channel:

*The river had channelled its way through the rocks.* 1–6, 8 *n.*, 7, 9 *v.*, **chan·nelled** or **chan·neled, chan·nel·ling** or **chan·nel·ing.**

**chant** (chant) **1** song. **2** sing. **3** a song in which several syllables or words are sung on one tone: *Chants are used in church services.* **4** sing in this way: *A choir chants psalms.* **5** a psalm, prayer, or other song for chanting. **6** a monotonous way of talking. **7** keep talking about; say over and over again: *We chanted, "Go team, go!"* 1, 3, 5, 6 *n.*, 2, 4, 7 *v.* —**chant′er,** *n.*

**chant·ey** (shan′tē *or* chan′tē) See SHANTY². *n., pl.* **chant·eys.**

**chan·ti·cleer** (chan′tə klēr′) ROOSTER. *n.*
☛ *Etym.* From OF *chantecler*, the name of the rooster in the old French story "Reynard the Fox." The French name was formed from *chanter* 'sing, crow' + *cler* 'clear'.

**chant·y** (shan′tē *or* chan′tē) See SHANTY². *n., pl.* **chant·ies.**

**Chanukah** (hä′nu̇ kä′; *Hebrew,* ʜä′nu̇ kä′) See HANUKKAH. *n.*

**cha·os** (kā′os) **1** great confusion; complete disorder: *The whirlwind left chaos behind it.* **2** the infinite space or formless matter thought to have existed before the universe came into being. *n.*

**cha·ot·ic** (kā ot′ik) in great confusion; very confused; completely disordered. *adj.* —**cha·ot′i·cal·ly,** *adv.*

**chap¹** (chap) **1** of skin, crack open; make or become rough: *A person's lips often chap in cold weather. Cold weather chapped her hands.* **2** a place where the skin is chapped. 1 *v.*, **chapped, chap·ping;** 2 *n.*

**chap²** (chap) *Informal. esp. Brit.* a fellow; man; boy. *n.*

**chap.** **1** chapter. **2** chaplain. **3** chapel.

**chap·book** (chap′bu̇k′) a small book or pamphlet of popular tales, ballads, etc., formerly sold on the streets. *n.*

**cha·peau** (sha pō′) *French.* hat. *n., pl.* **cha·peaux** or **cha·peaus** (-pōz′).

**chap·el** (chap′əl) **1** a building for Christian worship, not so large as a church. **2** a small place for worship in a larger building. **3** a room or building for worship in a palace, school, etc. **4** a religious service in a chapel: *She was late for chapel.* *n.*

**chap·er·one** or **chap·er·on** (shap′ə rōn′) **1** a married woman or an older woman who accompanies a young unmarried woman in public for the sake of good form and protection. **2** an older person who attends young people's parties, student dances, etc. for the sake of good form and to ensure proper behaviour. **3** act as a chaperone to. 1, 2 *n.*, 3 *v.*, **chap·er·oned, chap·er·on·ing.**

**chap·lain** (chap′lən) a clergyman officially authorized to perform religious functions for a family, court, society, public institution, or unit in the armed services. *n.*

**chap·lain·cy** (chap′lən sē) the position of a CHAPLAIN. *n.*

**chap·let** (chap′lit) **1** a wreath worn on the head. **2** a string of beads. **3** a string of beads for keeping count in saying prayers, one third as long as a ROSARY. **4** the prayers said with such beads. *n.*

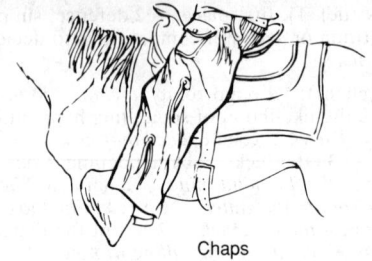
Chaps

**chaps** (shaps *or* chaps) backless leggings of tough leather, worn by cowboys to protect their legs when riding. *n.pl.*

**chap·ter** (chap′tər) **1** a main division of a book or other writing, dealing with a certain part of the story or subject. **2** anything like a chapter; part; section: *The development of radio is an interesting chapter in modern science.* **3** a local division of an organization; branch of a club, society, etc. *n.*

**char¹** (chär) **1** burn to CHARCOAL (def. 1). **2** burn slightly; scorch: *The meat was charred.* *v.*, **charred, char·ring.**

**char²** (chär) any of a closely related group of mostly freshwater fish belonging to the salmon and trout family: *The arctic char, brook trout, and lake trout are species of a char found in Canada.* *n., pl.* **char.**

**char·ac·ter** (kar′ik tər *or* ker′ik tər) **1** the combination of qualities or features that distinguishes one person, group, or thing from another; kind; sort; nature: *The sisters look alike but differ greatly in character. The character of the soil in the southern part of the province is different from that in the central part.* **2** the combined moral, emotional, and mental qualities that a person or group has: *a person of shallow, changeable character.* **3** moral firmness; integrity: *It takes character to endure hardship for very long.* **4** the estimate formed of a person's qualities; reputation: *His meanness was a stain on his character.* **5** position; status; role: *In his character as club secretary, he is responsible for all correspondence.* **6** a person or animal portrayed in a play, novel, or story: *The main character is a miner.* **7** *Informal.* a person who attracts attention for being different or eccentric: *I'd like to meet him; I hear he's really a character.* **8** in biology, a distinctive structure, function, or quality that is determined by heredity: *Marquis wheat is valued for its character of rust resistance.* **9** in writing, computer keyboarding, or printing, a letter, symbol, or other mark: *A, a, %, +, –, 1, 2, and 3 and a space are characters.* **10** a description of a person's qualities. *n.*
**in character,** consistent with a person's known character; as expected: *Her stinging letter to the editor was entirely in character.*
**out of character,** not consistent with a person's known character; not as expected: *It was out of character for her to go off without letting anyone know.*

**char·ac·ter·is·tic** (kar′ik tə ris′tik *or* ker′ik tə ris′tik) **1** marking off or distinguishing a certain person or thing from others; special: *Bananas have their own characteristic smell.* **2** a special quality or feature; whatever distinguishes one person or thing from others: *Cheerfulness is a characteristic that we admire in people. An elephant's trunk is its most noticeable characteristic.* **3** in mathematics, the integral part of a logarithm: *In the logarithm 2.95424, the characteristic is 2 and the mantissa is .95424.* 1 *adj.*, 2, 3 *n.*

**char·ac·ter·is·ti·cal·ly** (kar′ik tə ris′ti klē *or*

ker′ik tə ris′ti klē) in a way that shows CHARACTERISTICS; specially; typically. *adv.*

**char·ac·ter·i·za·tion** (kar′ik tə rə zā′shən *or* kar′ik tə rī zā′shen, ker′ik tə rə zā′shən *or* ker′ik tə rī zā′shən) **1** the act of characterizing; description of CHARACTERISTICS (def. 2). **2** the creation of characters in a play, book, etc. *n.*

**char·ac·ter·ize** (kar′ik tə rīz′ *or* ker′ik tə rīz′) **1** describe the special qualities or features of a person or thing; describe: *I would characterize our teacher as a very friendly person.* **2** be a CHARACTERISTIC (def. 2) of; distinguish: *A camel is characterized by the humps on its back and an ability to go without water for several days.* **3** give CHARACTER (defs. 1, 2) to. *v.*, **char·ac·ter·ized, char·ac·ter·iz·ing.**

**cha·rade** (shə rād′ *or* shə räd′) **1** a word represented by a pantomime, picture, or tableau. **2 charades,** *pl.* a parlour game in which a word, title, proverb, etc. is acted out by a group of people while others try to guess what it is. **3** a very obvious pretence. *n.*

**char·coal** (chär′kōl′) **1** the black substance, a form of CARBON, made by partly burning wood or bones in a place from which the air is shut out: *Charcoal is used as a fuel, filter, and absorbent.* **2** a stick, pencil, or crayon of charcoal for drawing. **3** a drawing made with such a stick, pencil, or crayon. *n.*

**chard** (chärd) a variety of white beet whose leaves and stalks are eaten as a vegetable; Swiss chard. *n.*

**charge** (chärj) **1** ask as a price; put a price on: *This store charges little for hats.* **2** the price asked for or put on something. **3** put down as a debt to be paid: *Some stores will charge things that one buys and let one pay for them later.* **4** a debt to be paid: *Taxes are a charge on property.* **5** load; fill: *A gun is charged.* **6** restore the active materials of a storage battery: *The battery of a car charges automatically when the motor is running.* **7** the quantity needed to load or fill something: *A gun is fired by exploding the charge of powder and shot.* **8** an amount of electricity. **9** give a task, duty, or responsibility to: *The law charges police officers with keeping law and order.* **10** a task; duty; responsibility: *Arresting criminals is the charge of the police.* **11** care; management: *Doctors and nurses have charge of sick people.* **12** a person or thing under the care or management of someone: *Sick people are the charges of doctors and nurses.* **13** give an order or command to; direct: *He charged us to keep the plan secret. The judge charged the jury.* **14** an order; command; direction: *a judge's charge to the jury.* **15** accusation: *He admitted the charge and paid the fine.* **16** attack: *The charge drove the enemy back.* **17** rush with force: *The soldiers charged the enemy.* **18** *Cdn.* in hockey, try to stop an opposing player illegally by taking more than two steps toward him in a direct attack. 1, 3, 5, 6, 9, 13, 17, 18 *v.*, **charged, charg·ing;** 2, 4, 7, 8, 10–12, 14–16 *n.*
**charge off,** a subtract as a loss. b put down as belonging: *A bad mistake must be charged off to experience.*
**charge with,** accuse of, especially in a court of law: *The driver was charged with speeding.*
**in charge,** in command; having control or management: *Who's in charge here?*
**in charge of,** a having control or management of: *Dr. Aziz is in charge of the case.* b under the control or management of: *The class was in the charge of the teacher.* c in command of: *The corporal was in charge of the patrol.*

**charge·a·ble** (chär′jə bəl) **1** that can be charged; likely to be charged: *If you take anything that belongs to someone else, you are chargeable with theft. Taxes are chargeable against the owners of property.* **2** liable to become a public charge. *adj.*

**charge account** an arrangement with a business firm for purchasing goods or services on credit: *We have charge accounts at two department stores.*

**charge card** credit card.

**char·gé d'af·faires** (shär zhā′ də fer′; *French*, shäR zhā dä feR′) an official who takes the place of an ambassador, minister, or other diplomat. *pl.* **char·gés d'af·faires** (shär zhāz′ də fer′; *French*, shäR zhā dä feR′).

**charg·er** (chär′jər) **1** a horse ridden in war. **2** a person or thing that charges. *n.*

**charg·ing** (chär′jing) **1** the act of loading; filling. **2** that charges. **3** ppr. of CHARGE. 1 *n.*, 2 *adj.*, 3 *v.*

**char·i·ly** (cher′ə lē) carefully; warily. *adv.*

**char·i·ness** (cher′ē nis) caution; sparingness. *n.*

**char·i·ot** (char′ē ət *or* cher′ē ət) **1** a two-wheeled vehicle pulled by horses, used in ancient times for fighting, for racing, and in processions. **2** a four-wheeled carriage or coach. *n.*

**char·i·ot·eer** (char′ē ə tēr′ *or* cher′ē ə tēr′) a person who drives a CHARIOT. *n.*

**char·is·ma** (kə riz′mə) **1** a spiritual gift or grace giving a person the gift of prophesying, healing, etc. **2** magnetic and compelling personal power, especially as attributed to leaders who gain the enthusiastic support of large numbers of people. *n., pl.* **cha·ris·ma·ta** (-mə tə).

**char·is·mat·ic** (kar′iz mat′ik *or* ker′iz mat′ik) **1** of or having to do with a CHARISMA (def. 1). **2** having CHARISMA (def. 2); capable of inspiring popular allegiance. *adj.*

**char·i·ta·ble** (char′ə tə bəl *or* cher′ə tə bəl) **1** of or for CHARITY: *Homes for old people are often charitable establishments.* **2** generous in giving help to poor or suffering people. **3** kindly in judging people and their actions. *adj.* —**char′·i·ta·ble·ness,** *n.* —**char′·i·ta·bly,** *adv.*

**char·i·ty** (char′ə tē *or* cher′ə tē) **1** help given to the poor or suffering. **2** an act or work of charity. **3** a fund, institution, or organization for helping the poor or suffering. **4** love for other people. **5** kindness in judging the faults of other people. *n., pl.* **char·i·ties.**

**cha·riv·a·ri** (shiv′ə rē′ *or* shə riv′ə rē′) SHIVAREE. *n., pl.* **cha·riv·a·ris.**

**char·la·tan** (shär′lə tən) a person who pretends to have more knowledge or skill than he or she really has; a QUACK (def. 2). *n.*

**char·la·tan·ism** (shär′lə tə niz′əm) the practices or methods of a CHARLATAN; QUACKERY. *n.*

**char·la·tan·ry** (shär′lə tən rē) CHARLATANISM. *n.*

**char·ley horse** (chär′lē) *Informal.* a very painful cramp or stiffness in a muscle, especially of the leg or arm, caused by strain.

**char·lock** (chär′lək) WILD MUSTARD. *n.*

**char·lotte russe** (shär′lə trüs′) a dessert made of a mould of sponge cake filled with whipped cream or custard.

**charm** (chärm) **1** the power of delighting or fascinating; attractiveness: *We were much impressed by the grace and charm of our hostess.* **2** a very pleasing or fascinating quality or feature: *the charm of old ruins, the charm of novelty.* **3** please greatly; delight; fascinate; attract: *The old sailor's stories of his adventures charmed the boys.* **4** a small ornament or trinket worn in a watch chain, bracelet, etc. **5** a word, verse, act, or thing supposed to have magic power to help or harm people. **6** act on as if by magic: *Laughter charmed away her troubles.* 1, 2, 4, 5, *n.*, 3, 6 *v.* —**charm′less,** *adj.*

**charmed** (chärmd) **1** delighted; fascinated. **2** enchanted. **3** protected as by a charm: *He bears a charmed life.* **4** pt. and pp. of CHARM. 1–3 *adj.*, 4 *v.*

**charm·er** (chär′mər) one who charms, delights, or fascinates. *n.*

**charm·ing** (chär′ming) **1** very pleasing; delightful; fascinating; attractive. **2** ppr. of CHARM. 1 *adj.*, 2 *v.* —**charm′ing·ly,** *adv.*

**Char·o·lais** (shar′ə lā′ *or* sher′ə lā′) a breed of large, white beef cattle. *n.*

**chart** (chärt) **1** a map, especially one for the use of navigators: *A sailor's chart shows the coasts, rocks, and shallow places of a sea. The course of a ship is marked on a chart.* **2** an outline map for showing special conditions or facts other than just geographical information: *a weather chart.* **3** a sheet giving information in lists, pictures, tables, or diagrams. **4** such a list, table, picture, or diagram. **5** make a chart of; show on a chart: *to chart a course.* **6** plan in detail. 1–4 *n.*, 5, 6 *v.* —**chart′less,** *adj.*

**char·ter** (chär′tər) **1** a written grant by a government to a colony, a group of citizens, a commercial company, etc., bestowing the right of organization, with other privileges, and specifying the form of organization: *All Canadian banks must have charters from the federal government.* **2** a written order from the authorities of a society, giving to a group of persons the right to organize a new chapter, branch, or lodge. **3** give a charter to. **4** hire a ship, aircraft, bus, etc. for private use: *to charter a ship.* 1, 2 *n.*, 3, 4 *v.* —**char′ter·less,** *adj.*

**charter member** one of the original members of a club, society, or company.

**char·treuse** (shär trœz′; *also*, shär trüz′ *for 2*) **1** a green, yellow, or white liqueur first made by Carthusian monks. **2** light yellowish-green. 1, 2 *n.*, 2 *adj.*

**char·wom·an** (chär′wum′ən) a woman whose work is cleaning homes, offices, public buildings. *n.*, *pl.* **char·wom·en** (-wim′ən).

**char·y** (cher′ē) **1** careful: *A cat is chary of wetting its paws.* **2** shy: *A bashful person is chary of strangers.* **3** sparing; stingy: *A jealous person is chary of praising others.* *adj.*, **char·i·er, char·i·est.**
☛ *Hom.* CHERRY.

**Cha·ryb·dis** (kə rib′dis) a whirlpool in the strait between Sicily and Italy, opposite the rock Scylla: *Charybdis sucked down ships.* *n.*
**between Scylla and Charybdis,** between two dangers, one of which must be met.

**chase**¹ (chās) **1** run or follow after to catch or kill. **2** going after to catch or kill: *The thieves were caught after a short chase.* **3** drive; drive away: *The English sparrow chases other birds from their nests.* **4** hunt. **5** hunting as a sport: *He was very fond of the chase.* **6** a hunted animal: *The chase escaped the hunter.* **7** follow; pursue: *The catcher chased the ball.* 1, 3, 4, 7 *v.*, **chased, chasing;** 2, 5, 6 *n.*
**chase about,** *Informal.* rush; hurry: *She is always chasing about.*
**chase after,** pursue.
**chase up,** search for.
**give chase,** run after; chase.

**chase**² (chās) **1** a groove; furrow; trench. **2** an iron frame to hold type that is ready to print or make plates from. *n.*

**chas·er** (chā′sər) **1** a person or thing that chases or pursues, such as a hunter or small, speedy aircraft or ship for pursuing the enemy. **2** a gun on the bow or stern of a ship, used when chasing, or being chased by, another ship. **3** *Informal.* a drink of water or something mild after a drink of strong liquor. *n.*

**chasm** (kaz′əm) **1** a deep opening or crack in the earth; a narrow gorge or abyss. **2** a wide difference of feelings or interests between people or groups: *The chasm between England and the American colonies finally resulted in the American Revolution.* *n.*

**chas·sis** (shas′ē *or* chas′ē) **1** the frame that supports the body of an automobile, aircraft, etc. **2** the frame that encloses and supports the working parts of a radio, television set, etc. **3** the frame on which a gun carriage moves backward and forward. *n.*, *pl.* **chas·sis** (shas′ēz *or* chas′ēz).

**chaste** (chāst) **1** pure; virtuous. **2** decent; modest: *chaste behaviour.* **3** simple in taste or style; not too much ornamented. *adj.* —**chaste′ly,** *adv.* —**chaste′ness,** *n.*

**chas·ten** (chā′sən) **1** punish with the intention of improving. **2** make more restrained, humble, etc.; subdue: *The experience chastened them.* *v.* —**chas′ten·er,** *n.*

**chas·tise** (chas tīz′) **1** inflict punishment or suffering on to improve, especially by beating. **2** criticize severely; rebuke: *The coach chastised the players for being late.* *v.*, **chas·tised, chas·tis·ing.** —**chas·tis′er,** *n.*

**chas·tise·ment** (chas′tiz mənt *or* chas tīz′mənt) a punishment; beating. *n.*

**chas·ti·ty** (chas′tə tē) **1** purity; virtue. **2** decency; modesty. **3** simplicity of style or taste; absence of too much decoration. *n.*

**chat** (chat) **1** easy, familiar talk: *a pleasant chat about old times.* **2** talk in an easy, familiar way: *We sat chatting by the fire after supper.* **3** any of several birds with a chattering cry. **4** of or having to do with a branch of a computer network in which participants can have discussions on-line. 1, 3 *n.*, 2 *v.*, **chat·ted, chat·ting;** 4 *adj.*

**châ·teau** *or* **cha·teau** (sha tō′ *or* shə tō′; *French*, shä tō′) **1** a French castle. **2** a large country house in

France. **3** a building resembling such a house. *n., pl.* **châ·teaux** (-tōz′; *French,* -tō′).

**chat·e·laine** (shat′ə lān′) **1** the mistress, or lady, of a castle, CHÂTEAU, or any large, fashionable household. **2** formerly, a chain or clasp worn at a woman's waist for carrying keys, a watch, purse, etc. *n.*

**chat·tel** (chat′əl) a movable possession; a piece of property that is not real estate: *Furniture, automobiles, and domestic animals are chattels. n.*

**chat·ter** (chat′ər) **1** talk constantly, rapidly, and foolishly. **2** rapid, foolish talk. **3** make rapid, indistinct sounds: *Monkeys chatter.* **4** rapid, indistinct sounds: *The chatter of sparrows annoyed her.* **5** rattle together: *Fear or cold sometimes makes a person's teeth chatter.* 1, 3, 5 *v.*, 2, 4 *n.* —**chat′ter·er,** *n.*

**chat·ter·box** (chat′ər boks′) a person who talks all the time. *n.*

**chat·ty** (chat′ē) **1** fond of friendly, familiar talk. **2** having the style and manner of friendly, familiar talk: *He wrote us a nice, chatty letter about his trip.* *adj.*, **chat·ti·er, chat·ti·est.** —**chat′ti·ly,** *adv.* —**chat′ti·ness,** *n.*

**chauf·feur** (shō′fər *or* shō fèr′) **1** a person whose work is driving an automobile, usually as the employee of a private person or a company: *The president of our bank has a chauffeur.* **2** act as a chauffeur to; drive around. 1 *n.*, 2 *v.*

**chau·tau·qua** *or* **Chau·tau·qua** (shə tok′wə) an assembly for education and entertainment of adults by lectures, concerts, etc., held for several days. *n.*

**chau·vin·ism** (shō′və niz′əm) **1** unreasoning enthusiasm for the military glory of one's country; boastful, warlike patriotism. **2** a strong, unreasoning conviction of the natural superiority of one's own group, beliefs, etc. *n.*

**chau·vin·ist** (shō′və nist) a person given to CHAUVINISM. *n.*

**chau·vin·is·tic** (shō′və nis′tik) **1** of or having to do with CHAUVINISM or CHAUVINISTS. **2** showing CHAUVINISM: *a chauvinistic remark.* *adj.* —**chau·vin·is′ti·cal·ly,** *adv.*

**cheap** (chēp) **1** low in price or cost; not expensive: *Eggs are cheap now.* **2** costing less than it is worth. **3** charging low prices: *a cheap market.* **4** easily obtained; costing little effort: *a cheap victory.* **5** of little merit or value; common: *cheap entertainment, cheap jewellery.* **6** stingy; mean: *Don't be so cheap!* **7** cheaply: *After the accident he sold his car cheap.* 1–6 *adj.*, 7 *adv.* —**cheap′ness,** *n.*
**feel cheap,** feel inferior and ashamed.
**hold cheap,** value little: *The lord held the lives of his servants cheap.*
☛ *Hom.* CHEEP.

**cheap·en** (chē′pən) **1** make or become cheap; lower the price of. **2** lower the reputation of; reduce the dignity of: *Rude actions cheapen one.* *v.*

**cheap·ly** (chēp′lē) **1** at a low price; at small cost. **2** with little cost or effort. *adv.*

**cheat** (chēt) **1** deceive or trick; play or do business in a way that is not honest: *The peddler cheated the woman out of two dollars.* **2** act in a dishonest way, by practising fraud or violating rules secretly: *to cheat at cards, to cheat in an exam.* **3** a person who is not honest and does things to deceive and trick. **4** a fraud or trick.

**chatelaine**     **201**     **checker**

hat, āge, fär; let, ēqual, tèrm; it, īce
hot, ōpen, ôrder; oil, out; cup, pụt, rüle
əbove, takən, pencəl, lemən, circəs
ch, child; ng, long; sh, ship
th, thin; ŦH, then; zh, measure

**5** escape; foil: *to cheat death.* 1, 2, 5 *v.*, 3, 4 *n.* —**cheat′er,** *n.*
**cheat (out) of,** deprive of, as by cheating: *She claimed that her father's will cheated her out of her due inheritance.*

**check** (chek) **1** stop suddenly: *The boys checked their steps.* **2** a sudden stop: *The message gave a check to our plans.* **3** hold back; control; restrain: *to check one's anger.* **4** a holding back; control; restrain. **5** any person, thing, or event that controls or holds back action: *a hockey check. A rein used to prevent a horse from lowering its head is a check.* **6** rebuff; repulse; reverse: *to check an enemy attack.* **7** examine or compare to prove true or correct: *We ought to check her statement before we condemn her.* **8** find out; investigate: *When she checked, she found the money was gone.* **9** a test for correctness made by comparing: *My work will be a check on yours.* **10** a mark (✓) to show that something has been examined or compared or that it is true or right: *The teacher put a check beside the correct answers.* **11** mark something examined or compared with a check: *How many answers did the teacher check as right?* **12** used in checking. **13** a ticket or metal piece given in return for a coat, hat, baggage, package, etc., to show ownership. **14** leave or take for safekeeping: *to check one's coat. The hotel checked our baggage.* **15** *Esp. U.S.* See CHEQUE. **16** a written statement of the amount owed in a restaurant: *When we finished eating, Father asked the waitress for the check.* **17** mark in a pattern of squares. **18** a pattern made of squares: *Do you want a check or a stripe for your next suit?* **19** one of these squares: *The checks are small in this pattern.* **20** marked in a pattern of squares. **21** crack; split. **22** in chess, a call warning that an opponent's king is in danger. **23** in chess, the position of an opponent's king when it is in danger and must be moved, or the threatening piece blocked off or removed. **24** have an opponent's king in this position. 1, 3, 6–8, 11, 14, 17, 21, 24 *v.*, 2, 4, 5, 9, 10, 12, 13, 15, 16, 18–20, 23 *n.*, 22 *interj.* —**check′a·ble,** *adj.*
**check in,** arrive and register at a hotel, etc.
**check off,** mark as checked and found true or right.
**check on** *or* **check up on,** find out about; seek more information on: *The police were checking up on her.*
**check out,** **a** leave and pay for a hotel or motel room, or leave a hospital: *We checked out of the hotel at noon.* **b** in a supermarket or other self-service store, check through and pay for one's purchases: *It took a long time to check out.*
**check over,** inspect.
**check up,** examine the health of: *Let your doctor check you up.*
**in check,** held back; controlled.
☛ *Hom.* CHEQUE, CZECH.

**check·book** (chek′bụk′) *Esp. U.S.* See CHEQUEBOOK. *n.*

**checked** (chekt) **1** marked in a pattern of squares. **2** pt. and pp. of CHECK. 1 *adj.*, 2 *v.*

**check·er**[1] (chek′ər) **1** mark in a pattern of squares of alternately different colours, like a chessboard: *The wall was checkered with blue and white tiles.* **2** a pattern made of such squares. **3** one of these squares. **4** mark off with patches different from one another: *The ground under* the trees was checkered with sunlight and shade. **5** change; vary; have ups and downs. **6** one of the flat, round pieces used in a game of CHECKERS. *1, 4, 5 v., 2, 3, 6 n.* Also, **chequer.**

**check·er**[2] (chek′ər) a person or thing that checks, especially a cashier in a self-service store or supermarket. *n.*

**check·er·ber·ry** (chek′ər ber′ē) WINTERGREEN. *n.*

**check·er·board** (chek′ər bôrd′) a square board marked in a pattern of 64 squares of two alternating colours and used in playing checkers or chess. *n.* Also, **chequerboard.**

**check·ered** (chek′ərd) **1** marked in a pattern of squares of different colours. **2** marked in patches. **3** often changing; varied; irregular: *a checkered career.* **4** pt. and pp. of CHECKER. *1–3 adj., 4 v.* Also, **chequered.**

**check·ers** (chek′ərz) a game played by two people, each having 12 round, flat pieces to move on a CHECKERBOARD. *n.* Also, **chequers.**

**check·list** (chek′list′) a complete list of things, such as names, articles on inventory, steps in a procedure, etc., used for checking or comparing. *n.*

**check mark** a mark (✓) to show that something has been checked, etc. or that it is right; CHECK (def. 10).

**check·mate** (chek′māt) **1** in chess, put an opponent's king in CHECK (def. 23) and so win the game. **2** a move that ends the game in this way. **3** defeat completely. **4** a complete defeat. *1, 3 v.,* **check·mat·ed, check·mat·ing;** *2, 4 n.*

**check·off** (chek′of′) a system of collecting union dues through wage deductions made by the employer on behalf of a union. *n.*

**check–out** (chek′out′) **1** in a supermarket or other self-service store, the process by which purchases are checked and paid for: *The check-out took only about a minute.* **2** the counter where this is done: *I went to the express check-out.* **3** in a hotel or motel, the time by which one must leave and pay for a room: *We missed the check-out and had to pay for an extra day.* *n.*

**check·point** (chek′point′) a point or place where a check is made, especially a place on a road or highway where vehicles or persons are inspected by authorities. *n.*

**check·rein** (chek′rān′) **1** a short rein to keep a horse from lowering its head. **2** a short rein connecting the bit of one of a team of horses to the driving rein of the other. *n.*

**check·room** (chek′rüm′) a place where coats, hats, baggage, etc. can be left until called for later. *n.*

**check·up** (chek′up′) **1** a careful examination. **2** a thorough physical examination: *She made an appointment with the doctor for a checkup.* *n.*

**Ched·dar** (ched′ər) a kind of hard, white or yellow cheese. *n.*

**chee·cha·ko** (chē chok′ō) *Cdn.* a newcomer; tenderfoot; greenhorn: *It took the cheechako many months to learn the ways of the Yukon.* *n.*
☛ **Etym.** From Chinook Jargon *cheechako,* formed from *chee* 'new' + *chako* 'come'.

**cheek** (chēk) **1** the side of the face below either eye. **2** anything suggesting the human cheek in form or position. **3** *Informal.* saucy talk or behaviour; impudence: *The girl's cheek annoyed the neighbours.* *n.*

**cheek·bone** (chēk′bōn′) the bone just below either eye. *n.*

**cheek·y** (chē′kē) *Informal.* saucy; impudent. *adj.,* **cheek·i·er, cheek·i·est.** —**cheek′i·ly,** *adv.* —**cheek′i·ness,** *n.*

**cheep** (chēp) **1** make a short, sharp sound like a young bird; chirp; peep. **2** a short, sharp, sound like that of a young bird; chirp; peep. *1 v., 2 n.* —**cheep′er,** *n.*
☛ *Hom.* CHEAP.

**cheer** (chēr) **1** joy; gladness; comfort; encouragement: *The warmth of the fire and a good meal brought cheer to our hearts again.* **2** fill with cheer; give joy to; gladden; comfort; encourage: *It cheered the old woman to have us visit her.* **3** a shout of encouragement, approval, praise, etc.: *Give three cheers for the girls who won the game.* **4** shout encouragement, approval, praise, etc.: *The boys cheered loudly.* **5** urge on with cheers: *Everyone cheered our team.* **6** greet or welcome with cheers. **7** food: *We were invited for Christmas cheer.* **8** a state of mind; condition of feeling: *My friends encouraged me to be of good cheer.* *1, 3, 7, 8 n., 2, 4–6 v.*
**cheer up, a** make happier; make glad. **b** become happier; be glad.

**cheer·ful** (chēr′fəl) **1** full of cheer; joyful; glad: *a smiling, cheerful person.* **2** filling with cheer; pleasant; bright: *a cheerful sunny room.* **3** willing: *A cheerful giver.* *adj.* —**cheer′ful·ly,** *adv.* —**cheer′ful·ness,** *n.*

**cheer·i·o** (chē′rē ō′) *Informal.* **1** goodbye! **2** hello! **3** hurrah! *interj., n., pl.* **cheer·i·os.**

**cheer·lead·er** (chēr′lē′dər) a person who leads the organized cheering, especially at high school or college athletic events: *The cheerleaders spent weeks practising the school yells.* *n.*

**cheer·less** (chēr′lis) without joy or comfort; gloomy; dreary. *adj.* —**cheer′less·ly,** *adv.* —**cheer′less·ness,** *n.*

**cheer·y** (chē′rē) cheerful; pleasant; bright: *The singing of birds is cheery.* *adj.,* **cheer·i·er, cheer·i·est.** —**cheer′i·ly,** *adv.* —**cheer′i·ness,** *n.*

**cheese** (chēz) **1** a solid food made from the curds of milk. **2** a mass of this substance pressed into a shape. *n.* —**cheese′like′,** *adj.*

**cheese·burg·er** (chēz′bėr′gər) a hamburger with a slice of melted cheese on top of the meat. *n.*

**cheese·cake** (chēz′kāk′) a dessert made of cream cheese or cottage cheese, eggs, sugar, etc. baked together. *n.*

**cheese·cloth** (chēz′kloth′) a thin, loosely woven cotton cloth, originally used for wrapping freshly made cheese. *n.*

**chees·y** (chē′zē) of or like cheese. *adj.,* **chees·i·er, chees·i·est.**

**chee·tah** (chē′tə) a tall, rangy, long-legged African and Asian animal of the cat family, thought to be the fastest mammal on earth, having doglike feet with hard pads and claws that cannot be retracted, a small head, and a reddish-yellow coat with black spots: *The cheetah is about 90 cm high at the shoulder and 130 cm long excluding the tail. Cheetahs that have been captured and trained to hunt are often called hunting leopards.* *n.*

**chef** (shef) **1** a head cook, as in a large restaurant. **2** a cook, especially a skilled one. *n.*

**che·la** (kē′lə) a pincer-like claw, such as that of a lobster, crab, or scorpion. *n., pl.* **che·lae** (-lē *or* -lī).

**che·li·ped** (kel′ə ped′) either of the limbs of a CRUSTACEAN bearing a CHELA. *n.*

**chem.** **1** chemistry. **2** chemical. **3** chemist.

**chem·i·cal** (kem′ə kəl) **1** of, having to do with, used in, or produced by CHEMISTRY: *chemical knowledge, a chemical process.* **2** a substance that has been produced by chemical processes in a laboratory, using raw materials such as crude petroleum, rocks, or plant parts, or using basic substances already made in this way to produce more complex substances and finished products: *Phosphates, coal, tar, plastics, drugs, paints, and insecticides are chemicals.* **3** producing or using chemicals: *the chemical industry.* **4** made or produced by chemistry: *a chemical compound. The burning of coal involves chemical change.* 1, 3, 4 *adj.*, 2 *n.*

**chemical element** See ELEMENT (def. 1).

**chemical engineering** the science or profession of using chemistry for industrial purposes.

**chem·i·cal·ly** (kem′i klē) **1** according to CHEMISTRY. **2** by chemical processes. *adv.*

**chem·ist** (kem′ist) **1** a person trained in CHEMISTRY, especially one who makes it his or her work. **2** *Esp. Brit.* DRUGGIST. *n.*

**chem·is·try** (kem′i strē) **1** the science that deals with elements or simple substances, the changes that take place when they combine to form compounds, and the laws of their combination and behaviour under various conditions. **2** the application of this to a certain subject: *the chemistry of foods.* **3** chemical processes, properties, phenomena, etc.: *Some teenagers have acne because of their body chemistry.* *n., pl.* **chem·is·tries.**

**che·mo·syn·thes·is** (kē′mō sin′thə sis *or* kem′ō sin′thə sis) the use by an organism of chemical reaction as an energy source, instead of the sun, to synthesize its organic compounds. Compare with PHOTOSYNTHESIS. —**che′mo·syn·thet′ic,** *adj.*, —**che′mo·syn·thet′ic·al·ly,** *adv.*

**chem·ur·gy** (kem′ər jē) a branch of chemistry that deals with the use of farm products, such as CASEIN and cornstalks, for purposes other than food and clothing. *n.*

**che·nille** (shə nēl′) **1** a fabric, usually cotton, made with a filling of rows of tufted cord arranged in various designs and forming a soft, piled surface: *Chenille is used for bedspreads, robes, rugs, etc.* **2** a tufted cord of silk, cotton, or worsted, used in embroidery, fringe, etc. *n.*

**cheque** (chek) **1** a written order directing a bank to take money from the account of the signer and pay it to the person or company named on it: *Mother pays her bills by cheque.* **2** a blank form on which to write such an order. Sometimes, **check.** ☛ *Hom.* CHECK, CZECH.

**cheque·book** (chek′bùk′) a book of blank cheques. *n.* Sometimes, **checkbook.**

**chequers** (chek′ərz) CHECKERS. *n.*

**cher·ish** (cher′ish) **1** hold dear; treat with affection; care for tenderly: *He cherished his little daughter.* **2** keep in mind; cling to: *For many years the old woman cherished the hope that her wandering son would come home.* *v.*

**che·root** (shə rüt′) a cigar cut square at both ends. *n.*

| chef | 203 | chevron |

hat, āge, fär; let, ēqual, tėrm; it, īce
hot, ōpen, ôrder; oil, out; cup, pùt, rüle
əbove, takən, pencəl, lemən, circəs
ch, child; ng, long; sh, ship
th, thin; ᴛʜ, then; zh, measure

**cher·ry** (cher′ē) **1** a small, round, edible, juicy fruit having a pit in the centre. **2** the tree it grows on. **3** its wood. **4** made of this wood. **5** bright red. 1–3, 5 *n., pl.* **cher·ries;** 4, 5 *adj.* ☛ *Hom.* CHARY.

**cherry picker** a type of crane consisting of a jointed or telescoping arm with a large bucket at the end, in which a person can stand to carry out operations high above the ground, such as repairs to power lines.

**cher·ub** (cher′əb) **1** a picture or statue of a child with wings. **2** a beautiful or good child. **3** a person with a chubby, innocent face. *n., pl.* **cher·u·bim** for 1, **cher·ubs** for 2 and 3.

**cher·u·bic** (chə rü′bik) **1** of or like a CHERUB; angelic. **2** innocent; good. **3** chubby. *adj.* —**che·ru′bi·cal·ly,** *adv.*

**cher·u·bim** (cher′ə bim *or* cher′yə bim) **1** a pl. of CHERUB (def. 1). **2** formerly, CHERUB. 1 *n.pl.,* 2 *n.sing.*

**cher·vil** (chėr′vəl) a plant of the same family as parsley: *The leaves of chervil are used to flavour soups, salads, etc.* *n.*

**Chesh·ire cat** (chesh′ər) **1** the grinning cat in *Alice in Wonderland* by Lewis Carroll. **2** anybody with a fixed grin.

**chess** (ches) a game played on a chessboard by two people, each having 16 pieces. *n.*

**chess·board** (ches′bôrd′) a board marked in a pattern of 64 squares of two alternating colours, used in playing chess. *n.*

**chess·man** (ches′man′) one of the pieces used in playing chess. Each player has 16 chessmen at the start of the game: 1 king, 1 queen, 2 castles (or rooks), 2 knights, 2 bishops, and 8 pawns. *n., pl.* **chess·men** (-men′).

**chest** (chest) **1** the part of a person's or an animal's body enclosed by the ribs. **2** a large box with a lid, used for holding things: *a linen chest, a tool chest, a medicine chest.* **3** a piece of furniture with drawers. **4** a tight container for gas, steam, etc. **5** a place where money is kept; treasury. **6** the money itself. *n.*

**ches·ter·bed** (ches′tər bed′) a CHESTERFIELD (def. 1) that can be opened out to form a bed. *n.*

**ches·ter·field** (ches′tər fēld′) **1** a long, upholstered seat or couch having a back and arms; sofa. **2** a single-breasted overcoat with the buttons hidden by a flap down the front. *n.*

**chest·nut** (ches′nut′ *or* ches′nət) **1** a large tree belonging to the same family as the beech, that bears sweet edible nuts with prickly outer shells. **2** the nut of this tree. **3** the wood of this tree. **4** reddish brown. **5** a reddish-brown horse. **6** *Informal.* a stale joke or story. **7** HORSE CHESTNUT. 1–7 *n.,* 4 *adj.*

**chev·i·ot** (shev′ē ət) **1** a rough, heavy woollen cloth with a nap, used for coats and suits. **2** a heavy, coarse cotton cloth used for shirts. *n.*

**chev·ron** (shev′rən) **1** a V-shaped bar, usually of cloth, often worn on the sleeve of a uniform by members of the armed forces, a police force, etc., to show rank or years of service: *A sergeant wears three chevrons.* **2** any V-shaped design. *n.*

**chew** (chü) **1** crush or grind with or as if with the teeth. **2** chewing: *The puppy gave the rag a good chew.* **3** the thing chewed; a piece for chewing. **4** *Informal.* think over; consider. 1, 4 *v.*, 2, 3 *n.*
**chew out,** *Informal.* scold.

**chew·ing gum** gum, usually sweetened and flavoured, for chewing.

**che·wink** (chi wingk′) a bird of eastern and central North America whose cry sounds somewhat like its name: *The chewink is a species of finch.* *n.*

**chew·y** (chü′ē) requiring chewing; becoming sticky and pliable when chewed. *adj.*

**Chey·enne** (shī en′) **1** a member of a First Nations people now living in Montana and Oklahoma. **2** the Algonquian language of the Cheyenne. *n., pl.* **Chey·enne** or **Chey·ennes.**

**chic** (shēk) **1** style: *a dress with a lot of chic.* **2** stylish. 1 *n.*, 2 *adj.*
☛ *Hom.* SHEIK (shēk).

**chi·cane** (shi kān′) **1** CHICANERY. **2** use CHICANERY. **3** get by CHICANERY. 1 *n.*, 2, 3 *v.*, **chi·caned, chi·can·ing.**

**chi·can·er·y** (shi kā′nə rē) low trickery; unfair practice; quibbling: *Only a dishonest lawyer will use chicanery to win a lawsuit.* *n., pl.* **chi·can·er·ies.**

**chick** (chik) **1** a young chicken. **2** a young bird. **3** child. *n.*

**chick·a·dee** (chik′ə dē′) any of a number of closely related small North American songbirds of the TITMOUSE family having a plump body, long tail, and short bill, and having a large black or brown, caplike patch on the top of the head: *The* **black-capped chickadee** *of Canada and the northern United States is also found in England, where it is called the* **willow tit.** *n.*
☛ *Etym.* The word **chickadee** imitates the bird's call.

**chick·en** (chik′ən) **1** a young hen or rooster. **2** any hen or rooster. **3** the flesh of a chicken used as food. **4** a young bird of certain other kinds. **5** young; small: *a chicken lobster.* **6** *Informal.* cowardly. 1–5 *n.*, 6 *adj.*

**chick·en–heart·ed** (chik′ən här′tid) cowardly; timid: *Don't be chicken-hearted about learning to dive.* *adj.*

**chick·en–liv·ered** (chik′ən liv′ərd) *Informal.* cowardly. *adj.*

**chicken pox** a mild contagious disease accompanied by a fever and a rash on the skin.

**chicken wire** a light wire netting of six-sided mesh, used for fencing, on cages for pets, to protect young trees, etc.

**chick–pea** (chik′pē′) **1** an annual plant of the pea family, native to Asia but now widely grown in the Western Hemisphere for its edible seeds, which grow in short pods. **2** the seed of this plant, resembling the garden pea in shape and flavour. *n.*

**chick·weed** (chik′wēd′) a common weed having small white flowers, whose leaves and seeds are eaten by birds. *n.*

**chic·le** (chik′əl) a tasteless, gumlike substance, the main ingredient of chewing gum, that is prepared from the milky juice of an evergreen tree of tropical America. *n.*

**chic·o·ry** (chik′ə rē) **1** a plant having bright blue flowers, whose leaves are used for salad. **2** its root, roasted and used as a substitute for coffee or to flavour coffee. *n., pl.* **chic·o·ries.**

**chid** (chid) a pt. and a pp. of CHIDE. *v.*

**chid·den** (chid′ən) a pp. of CHIDE. *v.*

**chide** (chīd) reproach; blame; scold: *She chided her son for getting his sweater dirty.* *v.*, **chid·ed** or **chid, chid·ed, chid,** or **chid·den, chid·ing.** —**chid′ing·ly,** *adv.*

**chief** (chēf) **1** the head of a group; leader; the person highest in rank or authority. **2** the head of a tribe or clan. **3** leading; at the head; in authority: *the chief engineer of a building project.* **4** main; most important: *The chief attraction of the midway was the Ferris wheel.* **5** in heraldry, the upper third of a shield. 1, 2, 5 *n.*, 3, 4 *adj.* —**chief′less,** *adj.*
**in chief,** at the head or in the highest position.

**chief justice** in Canada, a judge who is the senior judge in a Supreme Court.

**chief·ly** (chē′flē) **1** mainly; mostly: *This juice is made up chiefly of tomatoes.* **2** first of all; above all. *adv.*

**chief of staff** in the armed forces, an officer at the head of a group of senior officers.

**chief·tain** (chēf′tən) **1** the chief of a tribe or clan. **2** the head of a group; leader. *n.*

**chief·tain·cy** (chēf′tən sē) the position or rank of a CHIEFTAIN. *n.*

**chief·tain·ship** (chēf′tən ship′) CHIEFTAINCY. *n.*

**chif·fon** (shi fon′ *or* shif′on) **1** a delicate, very thin, usually soft fabric, made of silk, rayon, etc. and used for dresses, scarves, veils, etc. **2** soft and light: *chiffon velvet.* 1 *n.*, 2 *adj.*

**chif·fo·nier** (shif′ə nēr′) a high chest of drawers, often having a mirror. *n.*

**chig·ger** (chig′ər) a MITE (def. 1) whose larvae stick to the skin and cause severe itching. *n.*

**chi·hua·hua** (chi wä′wä) a very small dog of an ancient Mexican breed, having large, protruding eyes and large, erect ears. *n.*

**chil·blain** (chil′blān′) an itching sore or redness on the hands or feet caused by cold. *n.*

**child** (chīld) **1** baby. **2** a boy or girl, especially one up to the early or mid teens. **3** a son or daughter: *All their children are already married.* **4** an adult who behaves in a childish way, as if he has not grown up: *My father is such a child when he is sick.* **5** an adult who is more innocent, frank, and trusting than most other adults: *When it comes to politics or business dealings, Aunt Rita is a child.* **6** a result; product: *This is his brain child.* *n., pl.* **chil·dren.**
**with child,** pregnant.

**child·birth** (chīld′bėrth′) the act or process of giving birth to a child. *n.*

**child·hood** (chīld′hud′) **1** the condition of being a child: *the carefree days of childhood.* **2** the time during which one is a child: *His childhood was very happy.* *n.*

**child·ish** (chīl′dish)   1 of a child.   2 like a child: *a childish person.*   3 not suitable for a grown person; weak; silly; foolish: *It was childish of her to make such a fuss.* *adj.* —**child′ish·ly,** *adv.*
☛ **Syn.**   **Childish,** CHILDLIKE differ widely. **Childish** emphasizes the physical helplessness, lack of control over feelings, and undeveloped mind of a child, and therefore expresses an unfavourable opinion when used of an adult: *Such stupid behaviour is childish.* **Childlike** emphasizes the innocence, simplicity, and frankness of children, and suggests a favourable opinion: *She has a childlike belief in her son's innocence.*

**child·ish·ness** (chīl′dish nis)   1 being like a child.   2 weakness; silliness.   *n.*

**child labour** or **labor**   work done by children in factories, business, etc.

**child·less** (chīl′dlis)   having no child.   *adj.* —**child·less·ness,** *n.*

**child·like** (chīl′dlīk′)   1 like a child; innocent; frank; simple: *The charming old woman had an open, childlike manner.*   2 suitable for a child.   *adj.* —**child′like·ness,** *n.*
☛ **Syn.**   See note at CHILDISH.

**chil·dren** (chil′drən)   pl. of CHILD.   *n.*

**child's play**   something very easy to do: *Building a bridge was child's play to him.*

**Chil·e·an** (chil′ē ən)   1 of or having to do with Chile, a country in southwestern South America, or its people.   2 a native or inhabitant of Chile.   1 *adj.*, 2 *n.*

**chil·i** (chil′ē)   1 the small, hot-tasting pod, or fruit, of any of several varieties of pepper (def. 5), used for seasoning: *Chilies are also dried and ground up to make red pepper.*   2 CHILI CON CARNE: *We had chili for supper last night.*   *n., pl.* **chil·ies.** Also, **chilli.**
☛ **Hom.**   CHILLY.

**chil·i con car·ne** (chil′ē kon kär′nē)   ground or cubed beef cooked with chilies or chili powder and, usually, with red or kidney beans and tomatoes.

**chili sauce**   a sauce made of red peppers, tomatoes, and spices, used on meat, fish, etc. Also, **chilli sauce.**

**chill** (chil)   1 a moderate but unpleasant coldness: *a chill in the air.*   2 unpleasantly cold: *a chill wind.*   3 make cold: *We chilled the pop in the refrigerator.*   4 become cold; feel cold.   5 a sudden coldness of the body with shivering: *She was very sick with chills and fever.*   6 feeling cold; shivering.   7 harden a metal surface by sudden cooling.   8 unfriendliness; lack of warmth of feeling: *I felt the chill of his greeting.*   9 cold in manner; unfriendly.   10 a depressing influence; discouraging feeling: *The announcement of renewed fighting cast a chill over the assembled group.*   11 depressing; discouraging.   12 depress; dispirit.   13 a sudden feeling of fear or dread: *A chill went through him at the thought of the coming night.*   1, 5, 8, 10, 13 *n.*, 2, 6, 9, 11 *adj.*, 3, 4, 7, 12 *v.*

**chilled** (child)   1 made cold.   2 pt. and pp. of CHILL.   1 *adj.*, 2 *v.*

**chil·li** (chil′ē)   See CHILI.   *n., pl.* **chil·lies.**

**chill·i·ness** (chil′ē nis)   the quality or state of being CHILLY.   *n.*

**chilli sauce**   CHILI SAUCE.

hat, āge, fär; let, ēqual, tèrm; it, īce
hot, ōpen, ôrder; oil, out; cup, pút, rüle
əbove, takən, pencəl, lemən, circəs

ch, child; ng, long; sh, ship
th, thin; ᴛʜ, then; zh, measure

**chill·y** (chil′ē)   1 unpleasantly cool; rather cold: *a chilly day.*   2 cold in manner; unfriendly: *a chilly greeting.* *adj.*, **chill·i·er, chill·i·est.**
☛ **Hom.**   CHILI.

**chime** (chīm)   1 a set of bells tuned to the musical scale, usually played by hammers or simple machinery.   2 the musical sound made by a set of tuned bells.   3 anything with a pleasantly harmonious sound: *The tinkling chime of the brook.*   4 make musical sounds on a set of tuned bells.   5 ring out musically: *The bells chimed at midnight. The clock chimed three.*   6 agreement; harmony.   7 agree; be in harmony.   8 say or utter in cadence or singsong.   1–3, 6 *n.*, 4, 5, 7, 8 *v.*, **chimed, chim·ing.**
**chime in, a** be in harmony; agree: *Her ideas chimed in beautifully with mine.*   **b** *Informal.*   break into or join in a conversation: *As soon as he arrived, he chimed in with his views.*

**chi·me·ra** or **chi·mae·ra** (kə mē′rə)   1 a horrible creature of the imagination.   2 an absurd or impossible idea; wild fancy: *The hope of changing dirt to gold was a chimera.*   *n., pl.* **chi·me·ras** or **chi·mae·ras.**
☛ **Etym.**   From the name **Chimera,** in Greek mythology, a female monster with a lion's head, a goat's body, and a serpent's tail, supposed to breathe out fire.

**chi·mer·ic** (kə mer′ik)   CHIMERICAL.   *adj.*

**chi·mer·i·cal** (kə mer′ə kəl)   1 unreal; imaginary.   2 absurd; impossible: *chimerical schemes for getting rich.*   3 wildly fanciful; visionary.   *adj.*

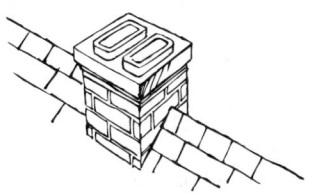   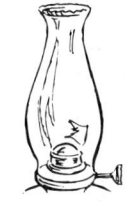

A chimney for a house      A lamp chimney

**chim·ney** (chim′nē)   1 an upright structure used to make a draft for a fire and carry away smoke.   2 the part of this that rises above a roof.   3 a glass tube put around the flame of a lamp.   4 a crack or opening in a rock, mountain, volcano, etc.   *n., pl.* **chim·neys.**

**chimney corner**   the corner or side of a fireplace; place near the fire.

**chimney sweep**   a person whose work is cleaning out chimneys.

**chimney swift**   a short-tailed, very dark grey swift that often nests inside chimneys: *The chimney swift ranges from southern Saskatchewan east to Nova Scotia and south to the upper Amazon region of South America.*

**chi·mo** (chē′mō *or* chī′mō)   *Cdn.*   especially in the North, a call or exclamation of greeting.   *interj.*
☛ **Etym.**   From an Inuit greeting.

**chimp** (chimp) *Informal.*   CHIMPANZEE.   *n.*

A chimpanzee - about 140 cm tall

**chim·pan·zee** (chim′pan zē′ or chim pan′zē) a humanlike ape of Africa, smaller than a gorilla: *The chimpanzee is probably the most intelligent ape.* *n.*

**chin** (chin) **1** the front of the lower jaw below the mouth. **2** *Informal.* chat; gossip. **3** a chat or gossip. 1, 3 *n.*, 2 *v.*, **chinned, chin·ning.** —**chin·less,** *adj.*
**chin oneself,** hang by the hands from a bar and pull up until one's chin is even with or above the bar.

**chi·na** (chī′nə) **1** a fine, white, translucent ceramic ware made of pure clay that has been baked at high temperatures; porcelain: *Coloured designs can be baked into china.* **2** dishes, vases, ornaments, etc. made of china. **3** ceramic dishes of any kind. *n.*
☞ *Etym.* Short for earlier *chinaware*, ware (goods) from China.

**chi·na·ware** (chī′nə wer′) **1** dishes, vases, ornaments, etc. made of CHINA (def. 1). **2** earthen dishes of any kind. *n.*

**chin·chil·la** (chin chil′ə) **1** a South American rodent that resembles a squirrel. **2** its very valuable soft, whitish-grey fur. **3** a thick woollen fabric woven in small, closely set tufts, used for overcoats. *n.*

**chine** (chīn) **1** the backbone; SPINE (def. 1). **2** a piece of an animal's backbone with the meat on it, for cooking. **3** a ridge; crest. *n.*

**Chi·nese** (chī nēz′) **1** a native or inhabitant of China, a large country in eastern Asia. **2** a person of Chinese descent. **3** of China, its people, or their language. **4** any of the languages of China. 1, 2, 4 *n.*, *pl.* (for defs. 1 and 2) **Chi·nese;** 3 *adj.*

**Chinese lantern** a lantern of thin, coloured paper that can be folded up.

**chink**[1] (chingk) **1** a narrow opening; crack; slit: *The chinks between the logs of the cabin let in the wind and snow.* **2** fill up the chinks in: *The cracks in the walls of the cabin were chinked with mud.* 1 *n.*, 2 *v.*

**chink**[2] (chingk) **1** a short, sharp, ringing sound like coins or glasses hitting together. **2** make such a sound. **3** cause to make such a sound: *He chinked the coins in his pocket.* 1 *n.*, 2, 3 *v.*

**chi·nook** (shi nùk′) *Cdn.* **1** a warm winter wind that blows from the southwest across British Columbia and Alberta and into Saskatchewan. **2** blow a chinook. 1 *n.*, 2 *v.*

**Chi·nook** (chə nůk′ *or* shi nůk′) **1** a member of an Amerindian people who lived along the Columbia River in the northwestern United States. **2** the language of the Chinook. **3** CHINOOK JARGON. **4** of or having to do with the Chinook, their language, or CHINOOK JARGON. *n., pl.* **Chi·nook** or **Chi·nooks.**

**chinook arch** *Cdn.* an arch of blue sky above the western horizon, often seen just before or during a CHINOOK.

**Chinook jargon** *Cdn.* a simple trade language of the Pacific coast of North America based on Chinook, with additional words from Nootka, English, and French: *Chinook jargon was formerly used by the Indian peoples and Europeans in their dealings with each other.*

**chinook salmon** SPRING SALMON.

**chintz** (chints) a firm, plain-woven cotton fabric, usually printed with colourful designs and having a glazed surface: *Chintz is used mostly for draperies and slipcovers.* *n.* Compare with CRETONNE.

**chint·zy** (chint′sē) **1** like CHINTZ. **2** *Informal.* showy or gaudy, but cheap or petty.

**chip** (chip) **1** a small, thin piece cut from wood or broken from stone, china, etc. **2** a place in china or stone from which a small piece has been broken: *One of the new plates has a chip.* **3** cut or break small pieces from wood, stones, dishes, etc.: *He chipped off the old paint.* **4** become chipped: *This china chips easily.* **5** shape by cutting at the surface or edge with an axe or chisel. **6** a small, thin piece of food or candy: *chocolate chips.* **7** POTATO CHIP. **8** french fry: *fish and chips.* **9** in electronics, a small wafer of material such as silicon on which many tiny electric circuits have been embedded: *Chips are much used in computers and transistors.* **10** a round, flat piece used for counting in games. **11** a strip of wood, palm leaf, or straw used in making baskets or hats. **12** a piece of dried dung, used for fuel in some regions: *buffalo chips.* 1, 2, 6–12 *n.*, 3–5 *v.*, **chipped, chip·ping.**
**chip in,** *Informal.* **a** join with others in giving money or help: *We all chipped in to buy our teachers a Christmas present.* **b** put in a remark when others are talking.
**chip on one's shoulder,** *Informal.* **a** a readiness to quarrel or fight. **b** a permanent sense of grievance.

**Chip·e·wy·an** (chip′ə wī′ən) **1** a member of a First Nations people living in northern Manitoba and Saskatchewan and the Northwest Territories: *The Chipewyans were traditionally a nomadic people who hunted the caribou.* **2** the language of this tribe. **3** of or having to do with the Chipewyans or their language. *n.*

**chip·munk** (chip′mungk) any of several small North American mammals of the squirrel family that live mainly on the ground, having mostly brown fur with black stripes along the back that are separated by pale grey or creamy stripes: *Chipmunks are smaller than squirrels and have a less bushy tail.* *n.*
☞ *Etym.* From an Algonquian name which was first applied to the red squirrel. The Algonquian word means 'headfirst' and refers to the squirrel's way of going down a tree trunk.

**chip·per** (chip′ər) *Informal.* lively; cheerful: *I was feeling very chipper because everything seemed to be going my way.* *adj.*

**Chip·pe·wa** (chip′ə wä′ *or* chip′ə wä′) OJIBWA. *n., pl.* **Chip·pe·wa** or **Chip·pe·was.**

**chipping sparrow** (chip′ing) a small sparrow of eastern and central North America.

**chips** (chips) **1** POTATO CHIPS. **2** FRENCH FRIES. *n.pl.*

**chi·rog·ra·phy** (kī rog′rə fē) handwriting. *n.*

**chi·rop·o·dist** (kə rop′ə dist) a person trained in CHIROPODY, especially one who makes it his or her work; podiatrist. *n.*

**chi·rop·o·dy** (kə rop′ə dē)   the branch of medicine dealing with the care of human feet and the treatment of foot ailments such as corns and bunions; podiatry.   *n.*

**chi·ro·prac·tic** (kī′rə prak′tik)   **1** the treatment of disorders of the bones, muscles, and nerves by manipulation of the bony segments of the body, especially the spine.   **2** having to do with such treatment.   1 *n.*, 2 *adj.*

**chi·ro·prac·tor** (kī′rə prak′tər)   a person who is qualified to practise CHIROPRACTIC and who makes this his or her work.   *n.*

**Chi·rop·te·ra** (kī rop′tə rə)   an order of mammals (the bats) having forelimbs modified as wings.   *n. pl.*

**chirp** (chėrp)   **1** make a short, sharp sound such as certain birds and insects make: *Sparrows and crickets chirp.* **2** such a sound.   **3** utter with a chirp.   1, 3 *v.*, 2 *n.* —**chirp′er**, *n.*

**chirr** or **churr** (chėr)   **1** make a shrill, trilling sound: *The grasshoppers chirred in the fields.*   **2** a shrill, trilling sound.   1 *v.*, 2 *n.*

**chir·rup** (chėr′əp *or* chir′əp)   **1** chirp again and again: *He chirrupped to his horse to make it go faster.*   **2** utter with chirps or sounds like this.   **3** the sound of chirrupping.   1, 2 *v.*, **chir·rupped** *or* **chir·ruped**, **chir·rup·ping** *or* **chir·rup·ing**;   3 *n.*

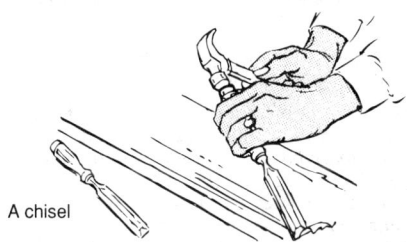

A chisel

**chis·el** (chiz′əl)   **1** a cutting tool with a sharp bevelled edge at the end of a strong blade, used to cut or shape wood, stone, or metal.   **2** cut or shape with a chisel. 1 *n.*, 2 *v.*, **chis·elled** *or* **chis·eled**, **chis·el·ling** *or* **chis·el·ing**.

**chit** (chit)   **1** child.   **2** a saucy, forward girl.   *n.*

**chit–chat** (chit′chat′)   **1** friendly, informal talk; chat. **2** gossip.   *n.*

**chi·tin** (kī′tin)   a semi-transparent, horny substance forming the hard outer covering of beetles, lobsters, crabs, etc.   *n.*

**chi·tin·ous** (kī′tə nəs)   of or like CHITIN.   *adj.*

**chit·ter** (chit′ər)   twitter: *The birds chittered.*   *v.*

**chit·ter·lings** (chit′ər lingz)   parts of the small intestines of pigs, cooked as food.   *n. pl.*

**chiv·al·ric** (shiv′əl rik *or* shə val′rik)   **1** having to do with CHIVALRY (def. 1).   **2** knightly; CHIVALROUS (def. 1). *adj.*

**chiv·al·rous** (shiv′əl rəs)   **1** having the qualities of an ideal knight; brave, courteous, considerate, helpful, and honourable; knightly.   **2** having to do with CHIVALRY (defs. 1, 5).   *adj.*   —**chiv′al·rous·ly**, *adv.* —**chiv′al·rous·ness**, *n.*

☛ *Etym.*   See note at CAVALIER. **Chivalrous** and CHIVALRY are ultimately from the same source as CAVALIER—the L *caballus*, 'horse'. The original *c* changed to *ch* in central F.

**chiropody   207   chock**

hat, āge, fär; let, ēqual, tėrm; it, īce
hot, ōpen, ôrder; oil, out; cup, pùt, rüle
əbove, takən, pencəl, lemən, circəs
ch, child; ng, long; sh, ship
th, thin; ᴛʜ, then; zh, measure

**chiv·al·ry** (shiv′əl rē)   **1** the qualities of an ideal knight in the Middle Ages; bravery, honour, courtesy, respect for women, protection of the weak, generosity, and fairness to enemies.   **2** the rules and customs of knights in the Middle Ages; system of knighthood.   **3** knights as a group.   **4** gallant warriors or gentlemen.   **5** courtesy and honour; chivalrousness.   *n.*

☛ *Etym.*   See note at CHIVALROUS.

**chive** (chīv)   a plant closely related to the onion, having a very small bulb: *The chive's long, slender, hollow leaves are used as seasoning.*   *n.*

**chlo·ral** (klô′rəl)   **1** a colourless, oily, liquid compound that is very irritating to the lungs, used in making DDT and chloral hydrate.   **2** CHLORAL HYDRATE.   *n.*

**chloral hydrate**   a white crystalline drug used to quiet nervousness and induce sleep.

**chlo·rate** (klô′rāt *or* klô′rit)   a salt of chloric acid.   *n.*

**chlo·ric** (klô′rik)   of or containing CHLORINE: *chloric acid.*   *adj.*

**chlo·ride** (klô′rīd)   any of a group of chemical compounds containing CHLORINE and a metal: *Chlorides are chemically classed as salts.*   *n.*

**chlo·rin·ate** (klô′rə nāt′)   **1** combine or treat with CHLORINE: *Paper pulp is chlorinated to bleach it.* **2** disinfect with CHLORINE: *The water in the city reservoirs is chlorinated.*   *v.*, **chlo·rin·at·ed**, **chlo·rin·at·ing**.

**chlo·rin·a·tion** (klô′rə nā′shən)   a chlorinating or being CHLORINATED.   *n.*

**chlo·rine** (klô′rēn *or* klô′rēn′)   a poisonous, greenish-yellow, chemical element that is a gas at normal temperatures, used in making drugs, dyes, explosives, and plastics, and in bleaching and disinfecting: *Chlorine has a sharp, unpleasant smell and is very irritating to the nose, throat, and lungs.*   Symbol: Cl   *n.*

**chlo·ro·fluo·ro·car·bon** (klô′rō flü′ə rō kar′bən)   any of several compounds of carbon used in refrigerators and aerosol cans, etc., and thought to be responsible for damaging the ozone layer of the earth's atmosphere. *Abbrev.*: CFC, *pl.* CFC's.

**chlo·ro·form** (klô′rə fôrm′)   **1** a colourless liquid with a sweetish smell, used as an anesthetic and to dissolve rubber, resin, wax, and many other substances.   **2** make a person or animal unable to feel pain by giving chloroform. **3** kill with chloroform.   1 *n.*, 2, 3 *v.*

**chlo·ro·phyl** or **chlo·ro·phyll** (klô′rə fil′)   the green colouring matter of plants: *In the presence of light, chlorophyl makes carbohydrates, such as starch, from carbon dioxide and water.*   *n.*

**chlo·ro·plast** (klô′rə plast′)   that part of a plant cell that contains CHLOROPHYL.   *n.*   Also, **chloroplastid**.

**chlo·ro·plas·tid** (klô′rə plas′tid)   CHLOROPLAST.   *n.*

**chlor·o·prene** (klô′rə prēn′)   a liquid made from ACETYLENE.   *n.*

**chock** (chok)   **1** a block; wedge: *A chock can be put*

**chock-full** under a barrel or wheel to keep it from rolling. *A boat on a ship's deck is put on chocks.* **2** provide or fasten with chocks. **3** put a boat on chocks. **4** on a ship or boat, a heavy piece of metal or wood with two arms curving inward for a rope to pass through. See ROWBOAT for picture. **5** as close or as tight as can be: *chock up against the wall.* 1, 4 *n.*, 2, 3 *v.*, 5 *adv.*
☞ Hom. CHALK.

**chock–full** (chok′fůl′) as full as can be; completely full. *adj.* Also, **chuck-full.**

**choc·o·late** (chok′lit *or* chok′ə lit) **1** a dark-brown, bitter-tasting substance, the finely ground roasted seeds of the cacao tree, used as a food or flavouring. The basic form of chocolate is a liquid, called **chocolate liquor**, that is produced when the seeds are ground. **2** a hot or cold drink made of chocolate or cocoa, milk or water, and sugar. **3** candy made of chocolate and sugar. **4** made of or flavoured with chocolate: *chocolate cake.* **5** dark brown. 1–3, 5 *n.*, 4, 5 *adj.*

**chocolate bar** a confection consisting of an oblong piece or bar of chocolate or a mixture of things such as nuts, sugar, syrup, marshmallow, flavouring, etc. coated with chocolate.

**choice** (chois) **1** choosing; selection: *Leave the choice of background music to him.* **2** the power or chance to choose: *Her parents have given her a choice between tennis and golf lessons. He had no choice but to accept their statement.* **3** the person or thing chosen: *My choice was cabbage rolls.* **4** a quantity and variety to choose from: *a wide choice of vegetables in the market.* **5** of fine quality; excellent; superior: *The choicest fruit had the highest price.* **6** carefully chosen: *She soon convinced them with a few choice arguments.* 1–4 *n.*, 5, 6 *adj.*, **choic·er, choic·est.**
—**choice′ly,** *adv.* —**choice′ness,** *n.*

**choir** (kwīr) **1** a group of singers, especially a group that sings as part of a church service. **2** the part of a church set apart for such a group. **3** sing all together at the same time. 1, 2 *n.*, 3 *v.*
☞ Hom. QUIRE.

**choke** (chōk) **1** keep from breathing by squeezing or blocking up the windpipe: *The tight collar almost choked her.* **2** be unable to breathe: *The smoke almost choked the firefighters.* **3** the act of choking: *She gave a slight choke, but then got her breath.* **4** the sound of choking: *We heard a choke behind us.* **5** check or extinguish by cutting off the supply of air; smother: *to choke a fire, to choke a motor.* **6** fill up or block; clog: *Sand is choking the river.* **7** something that chokes, such as a valve that cuts off the supply of air to an INTERNAL-COMBUSTION ENGINE. 1, 2, 5, 6 *v.*, **choked, chok·ing;** 3, 4, 7 *n.*
**choke back,** hold back; keep in: *She choked back her angry words.*
**choke down,** control; hold; suppress: *He choked down his anger and said nothing.*
**choke off,** put an end to; stop: *The rock slide choked off our water supply.*
**choke up,** fill with emotion; be or cause to be on the verge of tears: *People in the audience were choked up when the heroine died.*

**choke·ber·ry** (chōk′ber′ē) **1** the berry of a shrub of the rose family, having a bitter taste. **2** the shrub that the berry grows on. *n.*

**choke·bore** (chōk′bôr′) **1** a shotgun bore that narrows toward the muzzle in order to keep the shot from scattering too widely. **2** a gun with such a bore. *n.*

**choke·cher·ry** (chōk′cher′ē) **1** a bitter wild cherry of North America: *Chokecherries are small and grow in clusters.* **2** the tree that it grows on. *n.*, *pl.* **choke·cher·ries.**

**choke·damp** (chōk′damp′) a heavy, suffocating gas, mainly CARBON DIOXIDE and nitrogen, that gathers in mines, old wells, etc. *n.*

**chok·er** (chō′kər) **1** something that causes one to choke. **2** a necklace that fits closely around the neck. **3** *Cdn.* a cable and hook used in logging. *n.*

**chol·er** (kol′ər) an irritable disposition; anger. *n.*
☞ Hom. CALLER, COLLAR.

**chol·er·a** (kol′ə rə) **1** an acute, infectious disease of the stomach and intestines, characterized by vomiting, cramps, and diarrhea: *Asiatic cholera is often fatal.* **2** any of several diseases causing acute diarrhea. *n.*

**chol·er·ic** (kol′ə rik) easily angered; irritable. *adj.*

**cho·les·ter·ol** (kə les′tə rol *or* kə les′tə rōl′) a crystalline fatty alcohol produced by all vertebrate animals and found in the highest concentration in the brain, nerves and spinal cord: *Cholesterol is used by the body to make acids which aid digestion and also to make some hormones. The human body produces most of its own cholesterol, but some enters the body in food and is not always properly absorbed.* *n.*

**chomp** (chomp) **1** chew noisily: *to chomp one's food.* **2** bite down: *He chomped on his cigar.* *v.*

**choose** (chüz) **1** pick out; select from a number: *She chose a book from the library.* **2** prefer and decide on: *I would never choose blue.* **3** think fit; want and decide on: *She did not choose to go. He chose to run for election.* **4** make a choice; decide: *You must choose.* *v.*, **chose, chos·en, choos·ing.** —**choos′er,** *n.*
**cannot choose but,** cannot take an alternative; must: *Since he had received both first prizes, he could not choose but be satisfied.*

**choos·y** (chü′zē) *Informal.* particular; fussy. *adj.*, **choos·i·er, choos·i·est.**

**chop¹** (chop) **1** cut by hitting with something sharp: *to chop wood with an axe.* **2** a cutting stroke. **3** cut into small pieces: *to chop up cabbage.* **4** a slice of lamb, pork, veal, etc. on a piece of rib, loin, or shoulder. See PORK for picture. **5** make quick, sharp movements; jerk. **6** a special short, sharp movement in judo, karate, etc. **7** a short, irregular, broken motion of waves. **8** make by cutting: *She chopped her way through the bushes.* 1, 3, 5, 8 *v.*, **chopped, chop·ping;** 2, 4, 6, 7 *n.*
**chop back,** *Informal.* severely reduce.
**chop down,** make something fall by cutting: *to chop down a tree.*

**chop²** (chop) **1** the jaw. **2 chops,** *pl.* the cheeks or jaws, especially the fleshy covering of an animal's jaws: *The cat is licking the milk off her chops.* *n.*
**lick one's chops,** *Informal.* enjoy the prospect of something good to come: *The children licked their chops over the coming holiday.*

**chop³** (chop) change suddenly; shift quickly: *The wind chopped around from west to north.* *v.*, **chopped, chop·ping.**

**chop·house** (chop′hous′) a restaurant that makes a specialty of serving chops, steaks, etc. *n.*

**chop·per** (chop′ər) **1** a person who chops. **2** a tool or machine for chopping: *A short axe or a heavy knife are kinds of choppers.* **3** *Informal.* helicopter. *n.*

**chop·py**[1] (chop′ē) **1** making quick, sharp movements; jerky: *a choppy ride.* **2** moving in short, irregular, broken waves: *The lake is choppy today.* *adj.*, **chop·pi·er, chop·pi·est.**

**chop·py**[2] (chop′ē) changing suddenly; shifting quickly: *a choppy wind.* *adj.*, **chop·pi·er, chop·pi·est.**

Chopsticks

**chop·stick** (chop′stik′) one of a pair of small, shaped sticks used especially by the Chinese, Japanese, and Koreans to raise food to the mouth. *n.*

**chop su·ey** (chop′sü′ē) a Chinese-American dish consisting of small pieces of meat with vegetables such as bean sprouts, mushrooms, and greens all cooked together in their own juices: *Chop suey is usually served with rice.*

**cho·ral** (kô′rəl) **1** of or having to do with a choir or chorus: *She belongs to a choral group.* **2** sung or designed to be sung by a choir or chorus: *a choral arrangement of a song.* *adj.*
☛ *Hom.* CORAL.

**cho·rale** (kə ral′ *or* kô ral′) a hymn tune, especially a simple one sung in unison. *n.*
☛ *Hom.* CORRAL (for the first pronunciation of **chorale**).

**chord**[1] (kôrd) in music, a combination of two or more notes sounded together in harmony. *n.*
☛ *Hom.* CORD.

**chord**[2] (kôrd) **1** in geometry, a straight line or segment between two points on a curve. **2** a feeling; emotion: *to touch a sympathetic chord.* **3** in architecture, a main, horizontal part of a bridge truss. *n.*
☛ *Hom.* CORD.

**chor·date** (kôr′dāt) any animal belonging to a large PHYLUM of the animal kingdom, including vertebrates, and all other animals that have an internal skeleton and a central nervous system located along the back. *n.*

**chore** (chôr) **1** an odd job; a minor task, especially one that must be done daily: *Feeding the chickens and milking the cows were Ingeborg's chores on the farm.* **2** a task that is disagreeable or irritating: *She found the work quite a chore.* *n.*

**cho·re·a** (kô rē′ə) a nervous disease characterized by involuntary twitching of the muscles; ST. VITUS'S DANCE. *n.*

**chore–boy** (chôr′boi′) a cook's helper or general labourer on a farm or in a mining or logging camp. *n.*

**cho·re·og·ra·pher** (kô′rē og′rə fər) a creator or designer of ballets and other stage dances. *n.*

**cho·re·og·ra·phy** (kô′rē og′rə fē) **1** the art of creating, designing, and arranging dances. **2** the art of stage dancing; ballet dancing. *n.*

**chor·is·ter** (kô′rə stər) **1** a singer in a choir. **2** a boy who sings in a choir. **3** the leader of a choir. *n.*

**cho·roid** (kô′roid) **1** having to do with a delicate coat or membrane between the SCLEROTIC coat and the retina of the eyeball. **2** the choroid coat or membrane. See EYE for picture. **1** *adj.*, **2** *n.*

**choppy**    **209**    **Christian**

hat, āge, fär; let, ēqual, tėrm; it, īce
hot, ōpen, ôrder; oil, out; cup, pút, rüle
əbove, takən, pencəl, lemən, circəs
ch, child; ng, long; sh, ship
th, thin; ŦH, then; zh, measure

**chor·tle** (chôr′təl) **1** chuckle and snort at the same time: *"He chortled in his joy."* **2** a combined chuckle and snort. **1** *v.*, **chor·tled, chor·tling;** **2** *n.* —**chor′tler,** *n.*
☛ *Etym.* Coined by Lewis Carroll for *Through the Looking Glass* by combining parts of the words *ch*uckle and sn*ort*.

**cho·rus** (kô′rəs) **1** a group of singers who sing together, such as a choir. **2** a musical composition to be sung by a large number of singers in several harmonizing voice parts: *The opera ends in a splendid chorus.* **3** the part of a song that is repeated after each stanza; refrain. **4** sing or speak all at the same time. **5** a saying by many at the same time: *My question was answered by a chorus of No's.* **6** a group of singers and dancers: *She was in the chorus of our school musical.* **7** in drama, an actor or group of actors who comment on the action of a play. **8** the part of a play performed by the chorus. 1–3, 5–8 *n., pl.* **cho·rus·es;** 4 *v.*, **cho·rused, chor·us·ing.**
**in chorus,** all together at the same time.

**chose** (chōz) pt. of CHOOSE: *Selma chose a red dress for the Christmas party.* *v.*

**cho·sen** (chō′zən) **1** pp. of CHOOSE: *What have you chosen to play at the recital?* **2** picked out; selected from a group: *the chosen book.* 1 *v.*, 2 *adj.*

**chow** (chou) **1** CHOW CHOW. **2** *Informal.* food. **3** *Informal.* the time when food is served. *n.*

**chow chow** or **Chow Chow** a medium-sized Chinese breed of dog with short, compact body, large head, and thick coat of one colour, usually brown or black.

**chow–chow** (chou′chou′) **1** a Chinese mixed preserve. **2** any mixed pickles chopped up. *n.*

**chow·der** (chou′dər) a thick soup or stew, often made of clams or fish with potatoes, onions, etc. in a milk base. *n.*

**chow mein** (chou′ mān′) a Chinese-American dish consisting of a thickened stew of onions, celery, meat, etc. served over fried noodles.

**Christ** (krīst) **1** Jesus, the founder of the Christian religion. **2** the Messiah; the deliverer foretold by the ancient Jewish prophets. *n.*

**chris·ten** (kris′ən) **1** BAPTIZE a child as a Christian. **2** give a first name to at baptism: *The child was christened Jon.* **3** give a name to: *The new ship was christened before it was launched.* **4** *Informal.* make the first use of: *Let's christen the new radio.* *v.*

**Chris·ten·dom** (kris′ən dəm) **1** Christian countries; the Christian part of the world. **2** all Christians. *n.*

**chris·ten·ing** (kris′ə ning) **1** the act or Christian ceremony of baptizing and naming; BAPTISM. **2** ppr. of CHRISTEN. 1 *n.*, 2 *v.*

**Chris·tian** (kris′chən) **1** of or having to do with Jesus or His teachings. **2** believing in Jesus as Christ; following His example or teachings; belonging to the religion founded by Him: *the Christian church, Christian countries.* **3** a believer in Jesus as Christ; follower of His example or teachings; members of the religion founded by Him. **4** of Christians or Christianity. **5** showing a gentle, humble, helpful spirit: *Christian charity.*

**6** human; not animal. **7** *Informal.* decent; respectable. **8** *Informal.* a decent person. 1, 2, 4–7 *adj.,* 3, 8 *n.* —**Chris′tian·like′,** *adj.* —**Chris′tian·ly,** *adj., adv.*

**Chris·ti·an·i·ty** (kris′chē an′ə tē) **1** the religion taught by Jesus and His followers; the Christian religion that accepts Jesus of Nazareth as the Son of God and the true Messiah foretold by ancient Hebrew prophets. **2** Christian beliefs or faith; Christian spirit or character. **3** all Christians; Christendom. *n.*

**Christian name** one's first name; a given name used by one's friends and family: *Vito is the Christian name of Vito Binetti.*

**Christ·like** (krī′stlīk′) like Christ; like that of Christ; showing the spirit of Christ. *adj.* —**Christ′like′ness,** *n.*

**Christ·ly** (krīs′tlē) of Christ; Christlike. *adj.* —**Christ′li·ness,** *n.*

**Christ·mas** (kris′məs) **1** the yearly celebration of the birth of Christ; December 25. **2** the season of Christmas. **3** for Christmas: *Christmas music.* *n.*

**Christmas Day** December 25.

**Christmas Eve** December 24.

**Christ·mas·tide** (kris′məs tīd′) CHRISTMASTIME. *n.*

**Chris·mas·time** (kris′məs tīm′) the Christmas season, especially from Christmas Eve to New Year's Day, or to Epiphany (January 6). *n.*

**Christmas tree** an evergreen tree hung with decorations at Christmastime.

**chro·mate** (krō′māt) a salt of CHROMIC acid. *n.*

**chro·mat·ic** (krō mat′ik) **1** of or having to do with colour or colours. **2** in music, of, having to do with, or based on the CHROMATIC SCALE. **3 chromatics,** the scientific study of colours with reference to hue and intensity or brightness (*used with a singular verb*). 1, 2 *adj.,* 3 *n.* —**chro·mat′i·cal·ly,** *adv.*

**chromatic scale** in music, a scale in which the octave is divided into 13 half tones.

**chro·ma·tid** (krō′mə tid) either of the two portions of a CHROMOSOME that has doubled in preparation for cell division, held together at the middle by a tiny structure called a **centromere:** *During cell division, the centromere of each doubled chromosome divides and the chromatids separate to become two complete chromosomes that are exactly the same as the parent chromosome.* *n.*

**chro·ma·tin** (krō′mə tin) the substance in the nucleus of a plant or animal cell in a resting stage, made up of a spongy network of CHROMOSOMES. See CELL for picture. *n.*

**chro·ma·tog·raph·y** (krō′mə tog′rə fē) a process by which a solid, liquid, or gas is separated from a solution or mixture by ADSORPTION. *n.*

**chrome** (krōm) **1** CHROMIUM. **2** CHROME STEEL. *n.*

**chrome steel** an extremely hard, strong steel containing CHROMIUM.

**chrome yellow** a yellow colouring matter made from lead CHROMATE.

**chro·mic** (krō′mik) of or containing CHROMIUM. *adj.*

**chro·mite** (krō′mīt) **1** a mineral containing iron and CHROMIUM. **2** a salt of CHROMIUM. *n.*

**chro·mi·um** (krō′mē əm) a shiny, hard, brittle metallic element that does not rust or become dull easily; chrome: *Chromium is used in alloys and in plating.* Symbol: Cr *n.*

**chromium steel** CHROME STEEL.

**chro·mo·some** (krō′mə sōm′) any of the long, thin strands, or fibres, found in the nucleus of every plant and animal cell, composed of protein and DNA, which carries the coded information for heredity in units called GENES: *During cell division, the chromosomes form into pairs of short, fat rods, a characteristic number for each species.* *n.*

**chro·mo·sphere** (krō′mə sfēr′) a scarlet layer of gas around the sun, forming the lower part of the sun's atmosphere, below the CORONA (def. 2): *The chromosphere consists mainly of hydrogen.* *n.*

**chron.** **1** chronological. **2** chronology.

**chron·ic** (kron′ik) **1** of a disease, lasting a long time or recurring often: *Rheumatoid arthritis is chronic.* **2** constant; habitual: *a chronic liar, a chronic smoker.* *adj.*

**chron·i·cal·ly** (kron′i klē) in a chronic manner; always: *The municipality is building a new hospital for chronically ill patients.* *adv.*

**chron·i·cle** (kron′ə kəl) **1** a record of happenings in the order in which they happened; a history or story. **2** record in a chronicle; write the history of; tell the story of. 1 *n.,* 2 *v.,* **chron·i·cled, chron·i·cling.**

**chron·i·cler** (kron′ə klər) the writer of a CHRONICLE (def. 1); a recorder of events; historian. *n.*

**chron·o·graph** (kron′ə graf′) an instrument for measuring intervals of time in terms of seconds or minutes, especially such an instrument used in sports, science and technology, etc.: *A stopwatch is a kind of chronograph.* *n.*

**chron·o·log·er** (krə nol′ə jər) CHRONOLOGIST. *n.*

**chron·o·log·ic** (kron′ə loj′ik) CHRONOLOGICAL. *adj.*

**chron·o·log·i·cal** (kron′ə loj′ə kəl) arranged in the order in which the events happened: *It would be easier to understand your story if you told it in chronological order.* *adj.* —**chron′o·log′i·cal·ly,** *adv.*

**chron·o·lo·gist** (krə nol′ə jist) a person who investigates the exact dates of events and the order in which the events happened. *n.*

**chron·o·lo·gy** (krə nol′ə jē) **1** an arrangement of time in periods; giving the exact dates of events arranged in the order in which they happened. **2** a table or list giving the exact dates of events arranged in the order in which they happened. *n., pl.* **chron·o·lo·gies.**

**chron·om·e·ter** (krə nom′ə tər) a clock or watch that measures time very accurately, especially a **marine chronometer,** used to provide the exact time for observation of celestial bodies to determine the position of a ship at sea. *n.*

**chron·o·scope** (kron′ə skōp′) an instrument for measuring very small intervals of time, especially by visual means such as a pendulum or a falling rod. *n.*

**chrys·a·lid** (kris′ə lid) **1** CHRYSALIS. **2** of a CHRYSALIS. 1 *n.,* 2 *adj.*

**chrys·a·lis** (kris′ə lis) **1** the resting stage, or pupa, of a butterfly, during which it develops into a winged adult. **2** the hard outer covering of the butterfly during this stage: *When the transformation has been completed, the chrysalis splits and the adult butterfly emerges.* **3** a stage of development or change. *n., pl.* **chrys•a•lis•es** or **chry•sal•i•des** (krə sal′ə dēz′).

**chry•san•the•mum** (krə san′thə məm) **1** any of various closely related plants of the COMPOSITE family, some of which are widely cultivated for their large, showy, usually double flowers that bloom in late summer or autumn. **2** the flower of any of these plants: *Chrysanthemums are usually yellow, white, bronze, red, or rose.* *n.*

**chrys•o•lite** (kris′ə līt′) a green or yellow semi-precious stone: *Chrysolite is a silicate of magnesium and iron.* *n.*

**chub** (chub) **1** any of various freshwater game fishes of the cyprinid, or minnow, family: *The lake chub is found throughout Canada and in parts of the N. United States.* **2** any of several North American white fishes. *n., pl.* **chub** or **chubs**.

**chub•by** (chub′ē) round and plump: *chubby cheeks.* *adj.*, **chub•bi•er**, **chub•bi•est**. —**chub′bi•ness**, *n.*

**chuck**[1] (chuk) **1** pat; tap, especially under the chin. **2** throw; toss. **3** *Informal.* give up or finish with: *He's chucked his job.* *v.*

**chuck**[2] (chuk) **1** a device for holding a tool or piece of work in a machine. **2** a cut of beef between the neck and the shoulder. See BEEF for picture. *n.*

**chuck**[3] (chuk) *Cdn.* on the west coast, a large body of water, formerly especially a river, but now usually the ocean. *n.*
☛ *Etym.* From Chinook jargon, from Nootka *ch'a'ak* 'fresh water'.

**chuck–full** (chuk′fůl′) CHOCK-FULL. *adj.*

**chuck•le** (chuk′əl) **1** laugh quietly, as when mildly amused: *Vezna chuckled as she watched the antics of the puppy.* **2** a soft, quiet laugh. **1** *v.*, **chuck•led**, **chuck•ling**; **2** *n.* —**chuck′ler**, *n.*

**chuck race** CHUCKWAGON RACE.

**chuck•wag•on** (chuk′wag′ən) in the West, a wagon that carries food and cooking equipment for cowboys, harvest hands, etc. *n.*

**chuckwagon race** *Cdn.* a race between chuckwagons drawn by horses, a thrilling and highly popular event at rodeos and stampedes in western Canada.

**chug** (chug) **1** a short, loud, explosive sound: *the chug of an engine.* **2** make such sounds. **3** *Informal.* go or move with such sounds: *The engine chugged along.* **1** *n.*, **2**, **3** *v.*, **chugged**, **chug•ging**.

**chuk•ker** or **chuk•kar** (chuk′ər) in polo, one of the periods of play, lasting about eight minutes. *n.*

**chum**[1] (chum) *Informal.* **1** a close friend. **2** be close friends: *Morag and Sabra have chummed for years.* **1** *n.*, **2** *v.*, **chummed**, **chum•ming**.

**chum**[2] (chum) **1** bait for fish. **2** scatter bait to attract fish. **1** *n.*, **2** *v.*

**chum**[3] (chum) *Cdn.* a species of Pacific salmon found especially along the coasts of British Columbia and Alaska, metallic blue and silver in colour and having pale pink flesh. *n.*

**chum•my** (chum′ē) *Informal.* like a CHUM[1] (def. 1); very friendly; intimate. *adj.*, **chum•mi•er**, **chum•mi•est**. —**chum′mi•ly**, *adv.*

**chump** (chump) **1** *Informal.* a foolish or stupid

# chrysanthemum 211 chyle

hat, āge, fär; let, ēqual, tėrm; it, īce
hot, ōpen, ôrder; oil, out; cup, pút, rüle
әbove, takәn, pencәl, lemәn, circәs
ch, child; ng, long; sh, ship
th, thin; ᴛʜ, then; zh, measure

person; blockhead. **2** a short, thick block of wood. **3** a thick, blunt end. *n.*

**chunk** (chungk) a thick piece or lump: *a chunk of earth.* *n.*

**chunk•y** (chung′kē) *Informal.* **1** like a CHUNK; short and thick. **2** stocky. *adj.*, **chunk•i•er**, **chunk•i•est**. —**chunk′i•ly**, *adv.* —**chunk′i•ness**, *n.*

**church** (chėrch) **1** a building for public, especially Christian, worship or religious services: *There is a big church at the end of our street.* **2** public worship or religious service in a church: *They go to church regularly.* **3** a group of people who worship together; congregation: *The whole church spent the weekend at the lake.* **4** the organization of a church; ecclesiastical authority or power: *The church forced Galileo to deny his discoveries.* **5** the profession of the clergy: *He has a brother in the church.* **6** of or having to do with church or a church. **7** the **Church**, all Christians. **8** Usually, **Church**, a body or organization of persons having the same religious beliefs and usually under one authority; denomination: *the Presbyterian Church, the Roman Catholic Church.* *n.* —**church′less**, *adj.* —**church′like**′, *adj.*

**church•yard** (chėrch′yärd′) the ground immediately surrounding and belonging to a church, especially a part used as a burial ground. *n.*

**churl** (chėrl) **1** a rude, surly person. **2** a person of low birth; peasant. *n.*

**churl•ish** (chėr′lish) rude; surly: *a churlish reply.* *adj.* —**churl′ish•ly**, *adv.* —**churl′ishness**, *n.*

**churn** (chėrn) **1** a container or machine in which butter is made from cream or milk by beating and shaking. **2** stir or shake cream or milk in a churn. **3** make butter by using a churn. **4** stir violently; make or become foamy: *The propeller of a steamboat churns the waves.* **5** move as if beaten and shaken: *The excited crowd churned about the speaker's platform.* **6** a violent stirring. **1**, **6** *n.*, **2–5** *v.* —**churn′er**, *n.*

**churn out**, *Informal.* produce as if mechanically.

**churr** (chėr) See CHIRR. *v., n.*

**chute**[1] (shüt) **1** an inclined passage, trough, tube, etc. down which things are dropped or slid to a lower level: *There are chutes for carrying mail, dirty clothes, coal, etc. to a lower level.* **2** a narrow waterfall or rapids in a river. **3** a steep slope. **4** a narrow passageway or stall for controlling an animal while branding or disinfecting it. **5** a similar stall in which a rodeo animal is held before being released into the ring. *n.*
☛ *Hom.* SHOOT.

**chute**[2] (shüt) *Informal.* PARACHUTE. *n., v.*, **chut•ed**, **chut•ing**.
☛ *Hom.* SHOOT.

**chut•ney** (chut′nē) a spicy sauce or relish made of fruits, herbs, pepper, etc.: *tomato chutney.* *n., pl.* **chut•neys**.

**chutz•pah** (hůt′spä) excessive self-confidence; nerve; gall. *n.*

**chyle** (kīl) the milky fluid in the lymphatic vessels of

the body, consisting of lymph and the digested fats that have been absorbed from the intestines: *Chyle is carried by the lymphatic vessels, called lacteals, into the bloodstream.* *n.*

**chyme** (kīm)   the thick, semiliquid mass that is the product of the first stage of digestion in the stomach: *The chyme passes from the stomach into the duodenum and small intestine, where digestion is completed.*   *n.*

**Ci**   curie.

**ci·ca·da** (sə kā′də *or* sə kä′də)   any of a related group of medium to large-sized insects, found mostly in tropical and subtropical regions, having two pairs of transparent wings and noted especially for the loud buzzing sound that the male makes by vibrating membranes on its abdomen: *Several species of cicada have very long cycles of development; one species found in eastern North America lives underground as a larva for 17 years before becoming an adult.*   *n., pl.* **ci·ca·das** *or* **ci·ca·dae** (-dē *or* dī).

**cic·a·trice** (sik′ə tris)    CICATRIX.   *n.*

**cic·a·trix** (sik′ə triks′)   **1** the scar left by a healed wound.   **2** the scar left on a tree or plant by a fallen leaf, branch, etc.   **3** the scar on a seed where it was attached to the pod or seed container.   *n., pl.* **cic·a·tri·ces** (sik′ə trī′sēz).

**cic·e·ro·ne** (sis′ə rō′nē)   a guide for sightseers who explains curiosities, antiquities, etc.   *n., pl.* **cic·e·ro·nes.**

**ci·der** (sī′dər)   **1** the juice pressed out of apples for use as a drink and in making vinegar.   **2** the juice pressed from other fruits.   *n.*

**ci·gar** (sə gär′)   a tight roll of dried tobacco leaves for smoking.   *n.*

**cig·a·rette** (sig′ə ret′ *or* sig′ə ret′)   a small roll of finely cut tobacco enclosed in a thin sheet of paper for smoking.   *n.*   Also, **cigaret.**

**cil·i·a** (sil′ē ə)   **1** EYELASHes.   **2** in biology, tiny hairlike projections found on the surface of many different types of cell, including those lining the human windpipe: *In some one-celled animals, cilia cover the entire surface of the organism and function like oars, allowing the animal to move through its liquid surrounding.*   *n., pl.* of **cil·i·um** (sil′ē əm).

**cil·i·ar·y** (sil′ē er′ē)   **1** of or having do with CILIA. **2** of or having to do with the ciliary body in the eye.   *adj.*

**cil·i·ate** (sil′ē āt′ *or* sil′ē it)   **1** having CILIA (def. 2). **2** any of a large class of microscopic one-celled animals having CILIA (def. 2) on all or part of the body.   **1** *adj.*, **2** *n.*

**cinch** (sinch)   **1** a strong band or belt, usually of leather, for fastening a saddle or pack on a horse. **2** fasten on with a cinch; bind firmly.   **3** *Informal.* a firm hold or grip.   **4** *Informal.* get a firm hold or grip on.   **5** *Informal.* something sure and easy: *We were a cinch to win the game.*   1, 3, 5 *n.*, 2, 4 *v.*

**cin·cho·na** (sing kō′nə)   **1** any of a closely related group of tropical evergreen trees and shrubs of the MADDER family, native to South America: *A few species of cinchona are cultivated in other parts of the world, especially Indonesia, because their bark is a source of quinine, quinidine, and other similar drugs.*   **2** the bitter bark of any species of cinchona tree from which these drugs are obtained.   *n.*

**cinc·ture** (singk′chər)   **1** a belt; girdle.   **2** a border; enclosure.   **3** encircle; surround.   1, 2 *n.*, 3 *v.*, **cinc·tured, cinc·tur·ing.**

**cin·der** (sin′dər)   **1** a piece of burned-up wood or coal. **2 cinders,** *pl.*   **a** wood or coal partly burned but no longer flaming.   **b** ashes.   *n.*

**Cin·der·el·la** (sin′də rel′ə)   **1** in the fairy tale, a girl who was forced by her cruel stepmother to work very hard, but was rescued by her fairy godmother and married to a prince.   **2** a person whose real worth or beauty is not recognized.   *n.*

**cin·e·ma** (sin′ə mə)   **1** a motion picture.   **2** a motion-picture theatre.   **3 the cinema,**   motion pictures as an art form: *She is more interested in the cinema than in live theatre.*   *n.*

**cin·e·rar·i·um** (sin′ə rer′ē əm)   a place for keeping the ashes of cremated bodies.   *n., pl.* **cin·e·rar·i·a** (-ē ə).

**cin·e·rar·y** (sin′ə rer′ē)   **1** used to hold the ashes of a cremated body.   **2** of or for ashes.   *adj.*

**cin·na·bar** (sin′ə bär′)   **1** a reddish or brownish mineral that is the chief source of mercury; native mercuric sulphide.   **2** artificial mercuric sulphide, used as a red pigment in making paints, dyes, etc.   **3** bright red; vermilion.   1–3 *n.,* 3 *adj..*

**cin·na·mon** (sin′ə mən)   **1** a fragrant spice, used especially as a flavouring in baked goods, desserts, and candy, that is the dried inner bark from the branches of a tropical tree of the laurel family: *Most cinnamon comes from Sri Lanka and India.*   **2** the tree itself. **3** flavoured with cinnamon: *cinnamon hearts.*   **4** the colour of cinnamon, a light reddish brown.   1, 2, 4 *n.,* 3, 4 *adj.*

**cin·quain** (sing′kān)   **1** a stanza of five lines.   **2** a five-line poem, usually unrhymed, the lines having 2, 4, 6, 8, 2 syllables or 1, 2, 3, 4, 1 words, respectively.   **3** any group of five.   *n.*

CINQUEFOIL   QUATREFOIL   TREFOIL

**cinque·foil** (singk′foil′)   **1** any of a closely related group of plants of the rose family found mainly in the Northern Hemisphere, having compound leaves with three to seven leaflets and usually yellow or white flowers with five roundish petals: *Several species of cinquefoil are common Canadian weeds.*   **2** in architecture, an ornament made of five connected semicircles or part circles.   *n.*

**ci·pher** (sī′fər)   **1** ZERO; 0.   **2** a person or thing of no importance.   **3** a method of secret writing; code: *She sent me a telegram in cipher.*   **4** something in secret writing or code.   **5** a key to a method of secret writing or code. **6** do arithmetic; use figures.   **7** any Arabic numeral. **8** express in cipher.   1–5, 7 *n.,* 6, 8 *v.*   Also, **cypher.**
▶ **Etym.**   From OF *cifre* 'zero', which came originally from Arabic *ṣifr* 'zero', a noun use which developed from the original meaning 'empty'. From about the 16c. on, the English word was also used to refer to any Arabic numeral. Soon after, it was also used to mean 'secret writing' because early forms of such writing used numerals for letters. See also note at ZERO.

**cir·ca** (sėr′kə) about: *Mohammed was born circa A.D. 570.* Abbrev.: *c.* or *ca. prep., adv.*

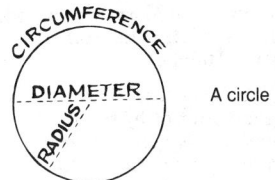
A circle

**cir·cle** (sėr′kəl) **1** a curved line of which every point is equally distant from a point called the centre. **2** a plane figure bounded by such a line. **3** anything shaped like a circle or part of one: *a circle around the moon.* **4** a ring: *The girls danced in a circle.* **5** a set of seats in the balcony of a theatre. **6** go around in a circle; revolve around: *The moon circles the earth. An airplane circles before it lands.* **7** form a circle around; surround; encircle: *A ring of forts circled the city.* **8** identify by drawing a circle around: *Circle the number of the answer you think is correct.* **9** a complete series or course of something that is repeated; cycle: *A year is a circle of 12 months.* **10** the orbit of a heavenly body. **11** the period of revolution of a heavenly body. **12** a group of people held together by the same interests: *the family circle, a circle of friends.* **13** a sphere of influence, action, etc.: *The young executive was at home in the circles of power.* 1–5, 9–13 *n.,* 6–8 *v.,* **cir·cled, cir·cling.** —**cir′cler,** *n.*

**cir·clet** (sėr′klit) **1** a small circle. **2** a round ornament worn on the head, neck, arm, or finger. *n.*

**cir·cuit** (sėr′kit) **1** a complete course, journey, or route, especially one that is more or less circular or that goes around something: *It takes a year for the earth to make its circuit of the sun.* **2** the complete path followed by an electric current. **3** an arrangement and connection of electronic components or elements for the transmission of radio, television, etc.; hookup. **4** the plan of such an arrangement. **5** a route followed repeatedly; a trip made regularly, having several stopovers and returning to the starting point: *Some theatre companies travel over regular circuits.* **6** a periodic journey along such a route: *Some judges make a circuit, stopping at certain places along the way to hold court.* **7** the area or region through which such circuits are made. **8** a district under the jurisdiction of a circuit court. **9** the distance around any space. **10** a group or association of theatres, cinemas, resorts, etc. at which the same plays, films, or other entertainments are presented in turn. **11** a line enclosing any space; boundary line. **12** the space enclosed. **13** make a circuit of; go in a circuit: *The moon circuits the earth.* 1–12 *n.,* 13 *v.*

**circuit breaker** a switch that automatically opens or interrupts an electric circuit when the current gets too strong.

**cir·cu·i·tous** (sər kyü′ə təs) roundabout; not direct: *To avoid unpaved roads, we took a circuitous route home. adj.* —**cir·cu′i·tous·ly,** *adv.* —**cir·cu′i·tous·ness,** *n.*

**cir·cu·lar** (sėr′kyə lər) **1** round: *The full moon is circular.* **2** moving in a circle; going around a circle: *A merry-go-round makes a circular trip.* **3** having to do with a circle: *circular measure.* **4** sent to each of a number of people: *a circular letter.* **5** a letter, notice, or advertisement sent to each of a number of people. **6** roundabout; indirect: *a circular explanation.* 1–4, 6 *adj.,* 5 *n.* —**cir′cu·lar·ly,** *adv.*

hat, āge, fär; let, ēqual, tėrm; it, īce
hot, ōpen, ôrder; oil, out; cup, pùt, rüle
əbove, takən, pencəl, lemən, circəs
ch, child; ng, long; sh, ship
th, thin; ₮H, then; zh, measure

**cir·cu·lar·i·ty** (sėr′kyə lar′ə tē *or* sėr′kyə ler′ə tē) CIRCULAR quality or form. *n., pl.* **cir·cu·lar·i·ties.**

**cir·cu·lar·ize** (sėr′kyə lə rīz′) **1** send CIRCULARS (def. 5) to. **2** make CIRCULAR (def. 1). *v.,* **cir·cu·lar·ized, cir·cu·lar·iz·ing.** —**cir′cu·lar·i·za′tion,** *n.* —**cir′cu·lar·iz′er,** *n.*

**circular measure** **1** a system for measuring angles. There are two main circular measures: **degree measure,** based on the division of a circle into 360 degrees, and **radian measure,** based on a standard angle in which the length of the arc subtending the angle is equal to the radius of the circle. **2** the measurement of the radius, circumference, area, etc. of a circle.

**cir·cu·late** (sėr′kyə lāt′) **1** move around in a circuit; follow a course, especially one that returns to the starting point: *The blood circulates through the body. The house is heated by hot water circulating through a system of pipes.* **2** pass from place to place or person to person freely and continuously: *The gossip circulated rapidly. Money circulates as it goes from person to person.* **3** send around from person to person or place to place: *She circulated the news of the holiday. This book has been widely circulated among the children in the neighbourhood.* **4** move about in a social circle, especially move around at a party, etc., talking to different people. *v.,* **cir·cu·lat·ed, cir·cu·lat·ing.**

**cir·cu·la·tion** (sėr′kyə lā′shən) **1** the movement of anything in a circuit, especially a closed circuit: *Open windows increase the circulation of air in a room. We are learning about the circulation of the blood.* **2** the passage of anything from person to person or place to place: *the circulation of money, the circulation of information or news, the circulation of magazines.* **3** the number of copies of a book, newspaper, magazine, etc. that are sent out during a certain time: *The magazine has a circulation of 50 000. n.*

**cir·cu·la·tor** (sėr′kyə lā′tər) a person or thing that CIRCULATES (def. 2) news, money, gossip, etc. *n.*

**cir·cu·la·to·ry** (sėr′kyə lə tô′rē) having to do with CIRCULATION (def. 1): *Arteries and veins are part of the human body's circulatory system. adj.*

**circum–** a prefix meaning: in a circle; around: *Circumnavigate* means to navigate around; *circumpolar* means around the North or South Pole.

**cir·cum·cise** (sėr′kəm sīz′) cut off the foreskin of. *v.,* **cir·cum·cised, cir·cum·cis·ing.**

**cir·cum·ci·sion** (sėr′kəm sizh′ən) the act or practice of circumcising, either for reasons of hygiene or as a religious rite. *n.*

**cir·cum·fer·ence** (sər kum′fə rəns) **1** the boundary line of a circle: *Every point on the circumference of a circle is at the same distance from the centre.* See CIRCLE for picture. **2** the boundary line of any figure enclosed by a curve. **3** the distance around a circle or an object bounded by a curved surface: *The big tree had a circumference of three metres. n.*

**cir·cum·flex** (sėr′kəm fleks′) **1** a mark ( ˆ or ͡ ) used especially over a vowel in certain languages and phonetic spelling systems to show length, contraction, or quality: *The circumflex was used originally in ancient Greek over long vowels to show a rising-falling tone.* **2** of or having the quality, length, etc. shown by a circumflex. **3** bending or winding around. *1 n., 2, 3 adj.*

**cir·cum·lo·cu·tion** (sėr′kəm lō kyü′shən) a round-about way of speaking: *"The wife of your mother's brother" is a circumlocution for "your aunt."* *n.*

**cir·cum·nav·i·gate** (sėr′kəm nav′ə gāt′) sail completely around: *Magellan's ship circumnavigated the world.* *v.*, **cir·cum·nav·i·gat·ed, cir·cum·nav·i·gat·ing.** —**cir·cum·nav′i·gat′or,** *n.*

**cir·cum·nav·i·ga·tion** (sėr′kəm nav′ə gā′shən) the act of sailing completely around. *n.*

**cir·cum·po·lar** (sėr′kəm pō′lər) **1** around the North or South Pole. **2** around either celestial pole. *adj.*

**cir·cum·scribe** (sėr′kəm skrīb′) **1** draw a line around; mark the boundaries of. **2** surround. **3** limit; restrict: *A prisoner's activities are circumscribed.* **4** draw a figure around another figure so as to touch as many points as possible: *A circle that is circumscribed around a square touches it at four points.* **5** be so drawn around: *A circle can circumscribe a hexagon.* *v.*, **cir·cum·scribed, cir·cum·scribing.**

**cir·cum·scrip·tion** (sėr′kəm skrip′shən) **1** circumscribing or being CIRCUMSCRIBED. **2** the thing that CIRCUMSCRIBES, such as an outline or boundary or a restriction. **3** an inscription around a coin, medal, etc. **4** a space CIRCUMSCRIBED. *n.*

**cir·cum·spect** (sėr′kəm spekt′) careful; cautious; prudent. *adj.* —**cir′cum·spect′ly,** *adv.* —**cir′cumspect′ness,** *n.*

**cir·cum·spec·tion** (sėr′kəm spek′shən) care; caution; prudence. *n.*

**cir·cum·stance** (sėr′kəm stans′) **1** a condition that contributes to or modifies an act or event: *You ought to consider all the circumstances before you judge her action.* **2** a happening; occurrence: *Her arrival on the scene was a fortunate circumstance.* **3** something that is not essential; additional information; detail: *It was her success, not the circumstances of the achievement, that interested her family.* **4** all the unavoidable factors contributing to an event or situation; the sum of the direct and indirect controlling influences (*used only as a singular noun and without the or a*): *a victim of circumstance.* **5** ceremony; display (*used only as a singular noun and without a*): *The royal procession advanced with pomp and circumstance.* **6 circumstances,** *pl.* financial condition: *A rich person is said to be in good or easy circumstances. A poor person is in bad or reduced circumstances.* *n.*
**under no circumstances,** never; no matter what the conditions are.
**under the circumstances,** because of conditions; things being as they are or were.

**cir·cum·stan·tial** (sėr′kəm stan′shəl) **1** depending on circumstances. **2** incidental; not essential; not important: *Minor details are circumstantial compared with the main fact.* **3** giving full and exact details; complete: *a circumstantial report of an accident.* *adj.* —**cir′cum·stan′tial·ly,** *adv.*

**circumstantial evidence** evidence that depends on the accompanying circumstances of a crime: *If stolen jewels are found in a man's possession, it is circumstantial evidence* that he stole them; if somebody saw him steal them, that would be direct evidence.

**cir·cum·stan·ti·ate** (sėr′kəm stan′shē āt′) give all the CIRCUMSTANCES of; support or prove with details. *v.*, **cir·cum·stan·ti·at·ed, cir·cum·stan·ti·at·ing.** —**cir′cum·stan′ti·a′tion,** *n.*

**cir·cum·vent** (sėr′kəm vent′ *or* sėr′kəm vent′) **1** defeat or get the better of by skilful planning; outwit; frustrate: *to circumvent the law. The rebels' plans to take over the radio station were circumvented by the police.* **2** avoid by going around: *We can circumvent the heavy traffic by taking this route.* **3** ENTRAP (def. 2). *v.*

**cir·cum·ven·tion** (sėr′kəm ven′shən) the act of CIRCUMVENTING. *n.*

**cir·cus** (sėr′kəs) **1** a travelling show of acrobats, clowns, horses, riders, and wild animals. **2** the performers who give the show or the performances they give. **3** *Informal.* an amusing person or thing. **4** *Informal.* a lively but disorderly time or place: *Our place was a circus that last night, as we were trying to get organized for the trip.* **5** in ancient Rome, a round or oval space with rows of seats around it, each row higher than the one in front of it. *n.*

**cirque** (sėrk) **1** a circular space. **2** *Poetic.* a circlet; ring. **3** in geology, a large bowl-shaped depression in a mountain, marking the beginning of a valley glacier. *n.*

**cir·rho·sis** (sə rō′sis) a chronic disease of the liver marked by excessive formation of connective tissue. *n.*

**cir·ri·ped** (sir′ə ped′) any of a group of CRUSTACEANS having threadlike appendages instead of legs: *A barnacle is a kind of cirriped.* *n.*

**cir·rus** (sir′əs) a thin, curling, wispy cloud very high in the air. *n., pl.* **cir·ri** (sir′ī *or* sir′ē).

**cis·co** (sis′kō) any of several species of whitefish found throughout the lakes of Canada and the northeastern United States: *Some ciscoes are valuable food fish.* *n., pl.* **cis·coes** *or* **cis·cos.**

**cis·tern** (sis′tərn) **1** a large artificial reservoir, especially a tank, usually underground, for storing rainwater. **2** the tank holding water at the back of, or above, a TOILET (def. 1). *n.*

**cit·a·del** (sit′ə del) **1** a fortress commanding a city: *Halifax has a famous citadel.* **2** a strongly fortified place; stronghold. **3** a strong, safe place; refuge. *n.*

**ci·ta·tion** (sī tā′shən) **1** a quotation or reference given as an authority for facts, opinions, dictionary entries, etc. **2** specific mention in an official dispatch. **3** an honourable mention for bravery in war. **4** the commendation of a person for public service by some official or institution. **5** a summons to appear before a law court. *n.*

**cite** (sīt) **1** quote a passage, book, or author, especially as an authority: *She cited the dictionary and Shakespeare to prove her statement.* **2** refer to; mention as an example: *The lawyer cited another case similar to the one being tried.* **3** mention publicly in recognition of and praise for outstanding service to humanity, one's country, etc. **4** summon to appear before a law court. **5** arouse to action; summon. *v.*, **cit·ed, cit·ing.** —**cite′able,** *adj.*
☛ *Hom.* SIGHT, SITE.

**cit·i·zen** (sit′ə zən) **1** a person who by birth or by choice is a member of a state or nation that gives him or her certain rights and claims his or her loyalty: *Many immigrants have become citizens of Canada.* **2** a person who is not a soldier, police officer, etc.; civilian. **3** an inhabitant of a city or town. *n.*

**cit·i·zen·ry** (sit′ə zən rē) CITIZENS as a group. *n., pl.* **cit·i·zen·ries.**

**citizens' band** a range of radio frequencies reserved for use by the public. *Abbrev.:* CB

**cit·i·zen·ship** (sit′ə zən ship′) **1** the condition of being a CITIZEN (def. 1): *She has Canadian citizenship but her husband doesn't.* **2** the duties, rights, and privileges of a CITIZEN (def. 1). *n.*

**cit·rate** (sit′rāt) a salt or ESTER of CITRIC ACID. *n.*

**cit·ric acid** (sit′rik) a white, odourless, sour-tasting acid that occurs in lemons, limes, etc.: *Citric acid is used as a flavouring, as a medicine, and in making dyes.*

**cit·rine** (sit′rin) pale yellow. *n., adj.*

**cit·ron** (sit′rən) **1** a pale-yellow citrus fruit resembling a lemon but larger, less acid, and with a thicker rind. **2** the tree that this fruit grows on. **3** a small, round variety of watermelon generally considered inedible except for its rind, which is used in preserves. **4** the preserved or candied rind of either of these fruits. *n.*

**cit·ron·el·la** (sit′rə nel′ə) **1** an oil used in making perfume, soap, liniment, etc. and for keeping mosquitoes away. **2** the fragrant tropical grass from which this oil is made. *n.*

**cit·rous** (sit′rəs) having to do with fruits such as lemons, grapefruit, limes, oranges, etc. *adj.*

**cit·rus** (sit′rəs) **1** any of a variety of trees or shrubs growing in warm climates and bearing sweet or tart edible fruit. **2** having to do with one of these trees or its fruit: *Oranges, lemons, limes, grapefruit, and citrons are citrus fruits.* **1** *n.,* **2** *adj.*

**citrus fruit** the fruit of a CITRUS tree.

**cit·y** (sit′ē) **1** a large and important town. **2** in Canada, an incorporated community with fixed boundaries that has been granted status as a city by its provincial government, usually having more financial and social responsibilities and more sources of revenue than a town: *A city is the largest urban municipal unit and in most provinces must have a minimum population of several thousand.* **3** in Britain, a town or district that has a royal charter for the title of city and is usually a cathedral town. **4** in the United States, a municipality, usually with a large population, having a charter granted by the state. **5** the people living in a city. **6** the government of a city: *The city has decided to make more land available for parks.* **7** of, having to do with, or in a city: *city politics. My mother hates city driving. n., pl.* **cit·ies.**

**city editor** the newspaper editor in charge of collecting and editing local news.

**city hall** **1** the headquarters of the local government in a city: *The mayor's office is in the city hall.* **2** the local government itself: *Can you fight city hall?*

**city manager** a person appointed by a city council or commission to manage the government of a city.

**city-state** (sit′ē stāt′) an independent state consisting of a city and the territories depending on it. *n.*

**civ·et** (siv′it) **1** a yellowish secretion of certain glands of the CIVET CAT: *Civet has a musky smell and is used in making perfume.* **2** CIVET CAT. *n.*

# citizenry 215 civilized

hat, āge, fär; let, ēqual, tėrm; it, īce
hot, ōpen, ôrder; oil, out; cup, pùt, rüle
əbove, takən, pencəl, lemən, circəs
ch, child; ng, long; sh, ship
th, thin; ᴛʜ, then; zh, measure

**civet cat** **1** a small, spotted mammal of Africa, Europe, and Asia, having glands that secrete a yellowish substance with a musky odour. **2** any of certain similar animals.

**civ·ic** (siv′ik) **1** of a city. **2** of or having to do with CITIZENSHIP: *Every person has some civic duties, such as obeying the laws, voting, or paying taxes.* **3** of citizens. *adj.*

**civic centre** **1** the headquarters of the government of a city. **2** a building serving as a centre for community activities, concerts, games, etc.

**civ·ics** (siv′iks) the study of the duties, rights, and privileges of CITIZENS (def. 1) (*used with a singular verb*). *n.*

**civ·il** (siv′əl) **1** of a CITIZEN (def. 1) or citizens; having to do with citizens: *Every citizen has civil rights and civil duties.* **2** of or having to do with the government, state, or nation: *civil servants.* **3** not connected with the armed forces or the church: *a civil court, a civil marriage.* **4** polite; courteous: *The girl answered our questions in a very civil way.* **5** having to do with the private rights of individuals and with legal proceedings connected with these rights: *a civil lawsuit. adj.*

**civil defence** or **defense** a program of procedures and planned action for civilian volunteers to cope with a general emergency such as enemy attack or a major natural disaster.

**civil disobedience** the refusal because of one's principles to obey the laws, especially by not paying taxes.

**civil engineer** a person trained in CIVIL ENGINEERING, especially one who makes it his or her work.

**civil engineering** the planning and directing of the construction of bridges, roads, harbours, etc.

**ci·vil·ian** (sə vil′yən) **1** a person who is not in the armed forces. **2** of civilians; not of the armed forces: *Soldiers often wear civilian clothes when on leave.* **1** *n.,* **2** *adj.*

**ci·vil·i·ty** (sə vil′ə tē) **1** politeness; courtesy. **2** an act of politeness or courtesy. *n., pl.* **ci·vil·i·ties.**

**civ·i·li·za·tion** (siv′ə lə zā′shən *or* siv′ə lī zā′shən) **1** a civilized condition; an advanced stage of social and political organization. **2** the nations and peoples thought of as having reached an advanced stage of social and political organization. **3** civilizing or being civilized. **4** the total culture of a nation or people at a given time: *Inuit civilization, 19th-century Canadian civilization. n.*

**civ·i·lize** (siv′ə līz) **1** change a primitive social and political system to a much more complex one that includes knowledge of the arts and sciences: *The Romans civilized a great part of their world.* **2** improve in culture and good manners; refine: *They were given the job of trying to civilize their niece. v.* **civ·i·lized, civ·i·liz·ing.**
—**civ′i·liz′er,** *n.*

**civ·i·lized** (siv′ə līzd′) **1** having a complex social and political system. **2** of civilized nations or persons.

# civilizing     216     clandestine

**3** showing culture and good manners; refined.    **4** pt. and pp. of CIVILIZE.    1–3 *adj.*, 4 *v.*

**civ·i·liz·ing** (siv′ə lī′zing)    **1** that civilizes; promoting CIVILIZATION.    **2** ppr. of CIVILIZE.    1 *adj.*, 2 *v.*

**civil law** the body of law that regulates and protects private rights.

**civil liberty** the right of a person to do and say what he or she pleases as long as he or she does not harm anyone else or break established laws.

**civ·il·ly** (siv′ə lē)    **1** politely; courteously.    **2** according to the civil law.    *adv.*

**civil rights** the rights of a CITIZEN (def. 1).

**civil servant** a member of the CIVIL SERVICE: *A cabinet minister has a staff of civil servants. A deputy minister is a civil servant.*

**civil service** the provincial or federal body of officials, clerks, etc. who do the day-to-day administrative work of government departments: *The civil service looks after such things as the collection of taxes and the issuing of pensions.*

**civil war**    **1** a war between two groups of citizens of one nation.    **2 Civil War, a** in England, the war between the King and Parliament, from 1642 to 1646 and from 1648 to 1652.    **b** in the United States, the war between the northern and southern states from 1861 to 1865; the War between the States.

**Cl** chlorine.

**cl.**    **1** class.    **2** clause.

**clab·ber** (klab′ər)    **1** thick, sour milk.    **2** become thick in souring; curdle.    1 *n.*, 2 *v.*

**clack** (klak)    **1** make or cause to make a short, sharp sound: *Her needles clacked as she knitted.*    **2** a short, sharp sound: *We heard the clack of her heels on the floor.*    **3** chatter.    1, 3 *v.*, 2, 3 *n.*    —**clack′er,** *n.*
☛ *Hom.* CLAQUE.

**clad** (klad)    a pt. and a pp. of CLOTHE: *She was clad all in green.*    *v.*

**claim** (klām)    **1** demand as one's own or one's right; say one has, and demand that others recognize, a right, title, possession, etc.; assert one's right to: *to claim a tract of land. Does anyone claim this pencil?*    **2** a demand for something due; the assertion of a right: *Mary makes a claim to the pencil.*    **3** a right or title to something; a right to demand something: *She has a claim on us because she is my mother's cousin.*    **4** something that is claimed.    **5** a piece of public land that a settler or prospector marks out for himself: *When the government offers the land for sale, the settler must buy his claim or forfeit it.*    **6** require; call for; deserve: *Business claims her attention.*    **7** say strongly; maintain; declare as a fact: *She claimed that her answer was correct.*    **8** the assertion of something as a fact.    1, 6, 7 *v.*, 2–5, 8 *n.*    —**claim′a·ble,** *adj.*
**jump a claim,** illegally seize a piece of land that has been staked for mining by another but not yet formally recorded.
**lay claim to,** declare one's right to; assert one's ownership of; claim: *Since nobody laid claim to the record, we took it home.*
**put in a claim** or **one's claim,** ask for as a right; claim: *I'm putting in my claim right now for my share of the saskatoons we picked.*
**stake (out) a claim,** claim an area of land for mining rights by setting out stakes to mark its boundaries: *After staking out a claim, a person must record his claim at the proper government office within a certain length of time to make it permanent.*

**claim·ant** (klā′mənt)    one who makes a CLAIM (defs. 2, 3, 5).    *n.*

**clair·voy·ance** (kler voi′əns)    **1** the power of knowing about things that are out of sight.    **2** exceptional insight.    *n.*

**clair·voy·ant** (kler voi′ənt)    **1** having the power of seeing things that are out of sight.    **2** a person who has, or claims to have, the power of seeing things that are out of sight: *The clairvoyant claimed to be able to locate lost articles.*    **3** exceptionally keen.    1, 3 *adj.*, 2 *n.*

**clam** (klam)    **1** a MOLLUSC resembling an oyster, having a shell in two halves: *Clams live in sand at the seashore or at the edges of rivers, lakes, etc. Some clams are edible.*    **2** go out after clams; dig for clams.    **3** *Informal.* a person who talks very little.    1, 3 *n.*, 2 *v.*, **clammed, clam·ming.** —**clam′like′,** *adj.*
**clam up,** *Informal.* be silent; say nothing.

**clam·bake** (klam′bāk′)    **1** a picnic where clams are baked or steamed: *A clambake may be an elaborate meal, with much to eat besides clams.*    **2** *Informal.* a large, noisy entertainment or social gathering.    *n.*

**clam·ber** (klam′bər)    **1** climb, using both hands and feet; climb awkwardly or with difficulty; scramble.    **2** an awkward or difficult climb.    1 *v.*, 2 *n.*

**clam·my** (klam′ē)    unpleasantly cold and damp.    *adj.*, **clam·mi·er, clam·mi·est.** —**clam′mi·ness,** *n.*

**clamor** (klam′ər)    See CLAMOUR.    *n., v.*

**clam·or·ous** (klam′ə rəs)    **1** noisy; shouting.    **2** making noisy demands or complaints.    *adj.*
—**clam′or·ous·ly,** *adv.* —**clam′or·ous·ness,** *n.*

**clam·our** or **clam·or** (klam′ər)    **1** a loud, continual noise or uproar; shouting.    **2** make a loud noise or continual uproar; shout.    **3** a noisy demand or complaint.    1, 3 *n.*, 2 *v.* —**clam′our·er** or **clam′or·er,** *n.*
**clamour** or **clamor for,** demand noisily: *The children were clamouring for candy.*

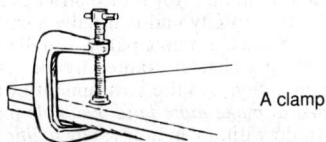
A clamp

**clamp** (klamp)    **1** a brace, band, wedge, or other device for holding things tightly together: *She used a clamp to hold the joint until the glue dried.*    **2** put in a clamp or fasten together or strengthen with a clamp.    **3** impose: *to clamp a tax on imports.*    1 *n.*, 2, 3 *v.*
**clamp down (on),** *Informal.* put pressure (on).

**clan** (klan)    **1** especially in Scotland, a group of related families that claim to be descended from a common ancestor.    **2** a group of people closely joined together by some common interest: *the whole clan of writers.*    *n.*
—**clan′like′,** *adj.*

**clan·des·tine** (klan des′tən *or* klan des′tīn)    secret; concealed; underhand: *a clandestine plan.*    *adj.*
—**clan·des′tine·ly,** *adv.*

**clang** (klang) **1** a loud, harsh sound such as that caused by metal striking metal: *The clang of the fire bell aroused the town.* **2** make or cause to make such a sound. **3** strike together with a clang. **1** *n.*, **2, 3** *v.*

**clangor** (klang′ər *or* klang′gər) See CLANGOUR. *n.*

**clan·gor·ous** (klang′ə rəs *or* klang′gə rəs) clanging. *adj.*

**clan·gour** *or* **clan·gor** (klang′ər *or* klang′gər) a loud clang or continued clanging: *the clangour of many bells.* *n.*

**clank** (klangk) **1** a sharp, harsh sound like the rattle of a heavy chain: *the clank of heavy machinery.* **2** make a sharp, harsh sound: *The swords clashed and clanked as the men fought one another.* **3** cause to clank. **1** *n.*, **2, 3** *v.*

**clan·nish** (klan′ish) **1** having to do with a CLAN. **2** closely united; not liking outsiders. *adj.* —**clan′nish·ly,** *adv.* —**clan′nish·ness,** *n.*

**clans·man** (klanz′mən) a member of a CLAN. *n., pl.* **clans·men** (-mən).

**clap** (klap) **1** a sudden noise, such as a single burst of thunder, the sound of the hands struck together, or the sound of a loud slap. **2** strike together loudly: *to clap one's hands.* **3** applaud by striking the hands together. **4** strike lightly with a quick blow: *She clapped her friend on the back.* **5** put or place quickly and effectively: *The police clapped the thief into jail.* **1** *n.*, **2–5** *v.*, **clapped, clap·ping.**
**clap eyes on,** *Informal.* look at; see: *I liked her from the first time I clapped eyes on her.*

**clap·board** (klap′bôrd *or* klab′ərd) **1** a thin board, thicker along one edge than along the other, used to cover the outer walls of wooden buildings. **2** cover with clapboards. **1** *n.*, **2** *v.*

**clap·per** (klap′ər) **1** a person or thing that claps, especially the movable part inside a bell that strikes the outside part, causing it to ring. **2** a device for making noise: *We had horns and clappers at the party.* *n.*

**clap·trap** (klap′trap′) *Informal.* **1** empty talk or an insincere remark made just to get attention or applause. **2** cheap and showy. **1** *n.*, **2** *adj.*

**claque** (klak) **1** a group of persons hired to applaud in a theatre. **2** a group that applauds or follows another person for selfish reasons. *n.*
☞ *Hom.* CLACK.

**clar·et** (klar′ət *or* kler′ət) **1** a kind of dry red table wine, originally one made in Bordeaux, France. **2** dark purplish-red. **1, 2** *n.*, **2** *adj.*
☞ *Etym.* From OF. Originally used in English as an adjective to describe a light red wine, as in OF *vin claret* which developed from Med. L. *claratum* 'clarified wine', formed from L *clarus* 'clear'. See also note at CLEAR.

**clar·i·fi·ca·tion** (klar′ə fə kā′shən *or* kler′ə fə kā′shən) **1** the act or process of making clear. **2** a freeing from defects or impurities. *n.*

**clar·i·fi·er** (klar′ə fī′ər *or* kler′ə fī′ər) **1** a substance used to CLARIFY (def. 1) liquids. **2** a large metal pan used in CLARIFYing (def. 1) sugar. *n.*

**clar·i·fy** (klar′ə fī′ *or* kler′ə fī′) **1** make or become free of impurities; purify: *We clarified the cloudy liquid by using a filter.* **2** make clear to the understanding; explain: *The news reporter asked her to clarify her statement for the public.* *v.*, **clar·i·fied, clar·i·fy·ing.**
☞ *Etym.* See note at CLEAR.

A clarinet

**clar·i·net** (klar′ə net′ *or* kler′ə net′) a wind instrument consisting of a straight metal or wooden tube ending in a slightly flared bell, having a single reed and played by means of holes and keys. *n.*

**clar·i·net·tist** *or* **clar·i·net·ist** (klar′ə net′ist *or* kler′ə net′ist) a person who plays the CLARINET, especially a skilled player. *n.*

**clar·i·on** (klar′ē ən *or* kler′ē ən) **1** clear and shrill. **2** a trumpet with clear, shrill tones. **3** *Poetic.* the sound made by this trumpet. **4** *Poetic.* a clear, shrill sound like it: *the clarion of a rooster crowing.* **1** *adj.*, **2–4** *n.*
**clarion call,** a clear and emphatic demand.

**clar·i·ty** (klar′ə tē *or* kler′ə tē) clearness. *n.*

**clash** (klash) **1** a loud, harsh, discordant sound like that of two hard things running into each other, or of metal striking metal, or of bells rung together but not in harmony. **2** strike with a clash. **3** throw, shut, etc. with a clash. **4** a strong disagreement; conflict: *a clash of opinion, a clash of colours.* **5** disagree strongly; be in conflict: *Your feelings and your judgment sometimes clash. Orange and pink clash.* **1, 4** *n.*, **2, 3, 5** *v.*

A clasp on a brooch

**clasp** (klasp) **1** a device, usually having a hook of some kind, to fasten two parts or pieces together: *This suede belt has a gold clasp.* **2** fasten together with a clasp. **3** hold closely with the arms or hands: *The mother clasped her baby to her breast.* **4** a close hold with the arms or hands. **5** grip firmly with the hand. **6** a firm grip with the hand: *He gave my hand a warm clasp.* **1, 4, 6** *n.*, **2, 3, 5** *v.*
—**clasp′er,** *n.*

**class** (klas) **1** a group of persons or things alike in some way; kind; sort. **2** a group of students taught together. **3** the meeting time for such a group: *The class was at nine o'clock.* **4** a group of students entering a school together and graduating in the same year: *The class of 1986 graduated in 1986.* **5** a rank or division of society: *the middle class.* **6** a system of ranks or divisions in society. **7** high rank in society. **8** grade; quality: *First class is the best and most costly way to travel.* **9** *Informal.* excellence; style. **10** in biology, a major category in the classification of animals or plants, ranking below a PHYLUM or division and above an ORDER:

Crustaceans and insects are two classes in the phylum of arthropods. Human beings belong to the class of mammals. See biological classification chart in the Appendix. **11** put or be in a class or group. *1–10 n., 11 v.*

**clas·sic** (klas′ik) **1** of the highest rank or quality; serving as an example of excellence for its kind: *a classic example of clear, attractive handwriting, the classic 1937 Ford. The golf champion has a classic swing.* **2** a work of literature or art long considered to be of the highest quality: *The Tin Flute is a classic.* **3** an author or artist of acknowledged excellence whose works serve as a standard, model, or guide: *Shakespeare is a classic.* **4** having to do with the literature and art of ancient Greece and Rome; classical. **5** of or according to established principles of quality in the arts and sciences; simple, regular, and restrained: *the classic style of Bach's music. We admired the classic lines of the new bridge.* **6** famous in literature or history: *the classic smile of the Mona Lisa.* **7 the classics**, the literature of ancient Greece and Rome. *1, 4–6 adj., 2, 3, 7 n.* Compare with CLASSICAL.

**clas·si·cal** (klas′ə kəl) **1** of, having to do with, or referring to ancient Greece and Rome, especially with respect to their art and literature: *classical studies.* **2** knowing much about ancient Greece and Rome, especially their art and literature: *a classical scholar.* **3** modelled on or resembling this literature and art: *Ulysses is a classical poem by Tennyson.* **4** orthodox and sound, but not new or up-to-date: *classical physics.* **5** of or referring to any music composed in the European tradition of written music as developed from early Christian church music, especially works composed during the last 300 years or so: *She prefers classical music to popular or folk music.* **6 Classical,** in music, of, or having to do with, or referring to the music of 18th century European composers such as Mozart and Haydn, as distinct from the Romantic music of composers like Beethoven and Chopin. *adj.* Compare with CLASSIC.

**clas·si·cal·ly** (klas′i klē) **1** in a CLASSICAL style. **2** according to the manner of CLASSIC authors. *adv.*

**clas·si·cism** (klas′ə siz′əm) **1** the principles of the literature and art of ancient Greece and Rome: *Classicism includes simplicity, regularity, and restraint.* **2** the following of these principles. **3** a knowledge of the literature and art of ancient Greece and Rome; classical scholarship. *n.*

**clas·si·cist** (klas′ə sist) **1** a follower of the principles of CLASSICISM in literature and art. **2** an expert in the literature of ancient Greece and Rome. **3** a person who urges the study of Greek and Latin. *n.*

**clas·si·fi·ca·tion** (klas′ə fə kā′shən) **1** an arranging in classes or groups on the basis of similar qualities or features; grouping according to some system. **2** the arrangement or grouping so made: *This library has worked out a simple classification for its books.* **3** in biology, the arranging of plants and animals in groups according to shared characteristics such as body structure. See biological classification chart in the Appendix. *n.*

**clas·si·fied** (klas′ə fīd) **1** of public documents, having a classification such as secret, confidential, or restricted. **2** pt. and pp. of CLASSIFY. *1 adj., 2 v.*

**clas·si·fy** (klas′ə fī′) arrange in classes or groups; group according to some system: *In the post office, mail is classified according to the places where it is to go.* *v.,*  **clas·si·fied, clas·si·fy·ing.** —**clas′si·fi′a·ble**, *adj.* —**clas′si·fi′er**, *n.*

**class·mate** (klas′māt′) a member of the same class in school. *n.*

**class·room** (klas′rüm′) a room where classes meet in school; schoolroom. *n.*

**clat·ter** (klat′ər) **1** a rattling noise: *the clatter of dishes.* **2** move or fall with a rattling noise; make a commotion: *The horses clattered over the stones.* **3** noisy talk. **4** talk fast and noisily. **5** cause to clatter. *1, 3 n., 2, 4, 5 v.*

**clause** (kloz) **1** that part of a sentence having a subject and predicate: *In* He came before we left, He came *is a* main clause, *and* before we left *is a subordinate clause.* A **main clause** can stand alone as a sentence; a **subordinate clause** cannot, since its complete meaning is generally dependent upon the rest of the sentence. A subordinate clause is used as a noun, adjective, or adverb. **2** a single provision of law, treaty, or any other written agreement: *A clause in our lease says we may not keep a dog in this building.* *n.*

**claus·tro·pho·bi·a** (klos′trə fō′bē ə) a morbid fear of enclosed spaces. *n.*

**clave** (klāv) pt. of CLEAVE². *v.*

**clav·i·chord** (klav′ə kôrd′) an early stringed musical instrument with a keyboard: *The piano evolved from the clavichord.* *n.*

**clav·i·cle** (klav′ə kəl) COLLARBONE. See ARM¹ for picture. *n.*

**cla·vier** (klə vēr′) **1** the keyboard of a piano, organ, etc. **2** any musical instrument with a keyboard. **3** a soundless keyboard used for practice. *n.*

**claw** (klo) **1** a sharp, hooked nail on each toe of a bird. **2** a similar nail on each toe of certain animals: *The cat's claws were dangerous.* **3** a foot with such sharp, hooked nails: *The gopher was held tightly in the hawk's claws.* **4** one of the pincers of a lobster, crab, etc. **5** anything like a claw: *The part of a hammer used for pulling nails is the claw.* **6** scratch, tear, seize, or pull with claws or fingernails. *1–5 n., 6 v.* —**claw′-like′**, *adj.*

**claw hammer** **1** a hammer with one end of the head curved like a claw and forked for pulling nails. **2** *Informal.* a dress coat; SWALLOW-TAILED COAT.

**clay** (klā) **1** a stiff, sticky kind of earth with little or no animal or vegetable matter in it, that can be easily shaped when wet and hardens after drying or baking: *Bricks and dishes may be made from clay.* **2** earth. *n.*

**clay·ey** (klā′ē) **1** of, like, or containing clay. **2** covered or smeared with clay. *adj.,* **clay·i·er, clay·i·est.**

**clay·more** (klā′môr′) a heavy, two-edged sword, formerly used by Scottish Highlanders. *n.*

**clay pigeon** a saucerlike clay disk thrown in the air as a flying target for SKEET shooting.

**CLC** Canadian Labour Congress.

**clean** (klēn) **1** free from dirt; not soiled or stained: *clean clothes. Soap and water make us clean.* **2** pure; innocent: *a clean heart.* **3** having the habit of keeping oneself clean: *Cats are clean animals.* **4** of atomic weapons, causing little or no radio-active fall-out. **5** clear; even; regular: *a clean cut.* **6** well-shaped; trim: *She likes the clean lines of her new car.* **7** clever; skilful; free from any clumsiness: *a clean jump.* **8** complete; entire; total: *a clean escape.* **9** honest; fair, as in sports: *a clean player, a clean fighter.* **10** having a few or no corrections or alterations: *I have to make a clean copy to hand in.* **11** blank; new: *I need a clean page.* **12** completely; entirely; totally: *The horse jumped clean over the brook.* **13** in a clean manner. **14** make clean: *to clean a room.* **15** prepare fish, game, chicken, etc. for cooking by removing entrails, scales or feathers, etc. **16** undergo cleaning: *This room cleans easily because it doesn't have much furniture in it.* **17** do cleaning: *I'm going to clean this morning.* **18** not using drugs: *The athlete was found to be clean.* 1–11, 18 *adj.*, 12, 13 *adv.*, 14–17 *v.*

**clean out, a** make clean by emptying: *Clean out your desk.* **b** empty; use up: *The girls cleaned out a whole box of cookies.*

**clean up, a** make clean by removing dirt, rubbish, etc.: *Clean up the yard.* **b** put in order. **c** *Informal.* finish; complete.

**clean–cut** (klēn′kut′) **1** having clear, sharp outlines. **2** well-shaped. **3** clear; definite; distinct. **4** having a neat and wholesome appearance: *a clean-cut young man.* *adj.*

**clean·er** (klē′nər) **1** a person whose work is keeping buildings, windows, etc., clean. **2** a tool or machine for cleaning. **3** anything that removes dirt, grease, or stains; cleanser. *n.*

**clean–limbed** (klēn′limd′) having well-shaped limbs. *adj.*

**clean·li·ness** (klen′lē nis) cleanness; habitual cleanness. *n.*

**clean·ly** (klen′lē *for adverb*, klen′lē *for adjective*) **1** in a clean manner: *The butcher's knife cut cleanly through the meat.* **2** always keeping oneself or one's surroundings clean: *The cat is a cleanly animal.* 1 *adv.*, 2 *adj.*, **clean·li·er, clean·li·est.**

**clean·ness** (klēn′nis) a clean condition or quality: *The cleanness of the rooms pleased the housekeeper.* *n.*

**cleanse** (klenz) **1** make clean. **2** make pure. *v.*, **cleansed, cleans·ing.** —**cleans′a·ble,** *adj.*

**cleans·er** (klenz′ər) a substance that cleans, especially a soap, detergent, disinfectant, or bleaching agent used in household cleaning. *n.*

**clean–up** (klē′nup′) a cleaning up. *n.*

**clear** (klēr) **1** not cloudy, misty, or hazy; bright; light: *a clear day.* **2** easy to see through; transparent: *clear glass.* **3** having a pure, even colour: *a clear blue.* **4** easily seen, heard, or understood; plain; distinct: *a clear idea, a clear voice.* **5** sure; certain: *It is clear that it is going to rain.* **6** not blocked or obstructed; open: *a clear view.* **7** make clear or free of obstruction: *She cleared the land of trees. He cleared his throat before he began to speak. She cleared her desk.* **8** become clear: *It rained all morning, but by noon, the sky was beginning to clear.* **9** remove to leave a space clear: *She cleared the dishes from the table.* **10** without touching; without being caught: *The ship was clear of the iceberg.* **11** get by or over without touching or being caught: *The horse cleared the fence.* **12** free from blame or guilt; innocent: *A careful investigation showed that the suspect was clear.* **13** make free from blame or guilt; prove to be innocent: *The jury's verdict cleared the accused man.* **14** free from debt or charges: *clear profit.* **15** make as profit free from debts or charges. **16** in a clear manner. **17** complete; without limitation: *a clear contradiction.* **18** completely; entirely: *The bullet went clear through the door.* **19** of lumber, free from knots or other imperfections. **20** get a ship or cargo free by meeting requirements on entering or leaving a port. **21** get permission from an authority to proceed

**clean-cut**     **219**     **clearing**

hat, āge, fär; let, ēqual, tėrm; it, īce
hot, ōpen, ôrder; oil, out; cup, pùt, rüle
əbove, takən, pencəl, lemən, circəs
ch, child; ng, long; sh, ship
th, thin; ŦH, then; zh, measure

after inspection of goods, etc.: *It took us half an hour to clear customs.* **22** settle a business account or certify a cheque as valid. 1–6, 10, 12, 14, 17, 19 *adj.*, 7–9, 11, 13, 15, 20–22 *v.*, 16, 18 *adv.* —**clear′ly,** *adv.* —**clear′ness,** *n.*

**clear away** or **off, a** remove to leave a space clear: *to clear away underbrush.* **b** clear dishes and so on from a table: *It's your turn to clear away.*

**clear out,** make clear by throwing out or emptying: *to clear out a cupboard.*

**clear out** or **off,** *Informal.* go away; leave: *You'll have to clear out of the gym by four o'clock because they need it for basketball practice. She cleared off as soon as she heard there was work involved.*

**clear up, a** make or become clear. **b** put in order by clearing. **c** explain or clarify: *Bogdan cleared up the question of why he had not been there by saying that he had been ill.* **d** become clear after a storm.

**in the clear, a** between the outside parts; in interior measurement: *The house was 15 metres wide, in the clear.* **b** *Informal.* free of guilt or blame; innocent: *Her report shows that the suspect is in the clear.* **c** free from limitations or encumbrances: *Having paid all his debts, he was finally in the clear again.*

**make clear,** state definitely: *She made clear her position.*
☞ *Etym.* ME *cler,* from OF *cler,* from L *clarus* 'bright, clear; illustrious, famous'. CLARIFY comes from OF *clarifier* from the late L verb *clarificare,* formed from *clarus.* The original meaning of the verb in English was 'brighten, make illustrious'.

**clear·ance** (klē′rəns) **1** the act of clearing. **2** a clear space, especially the distance between objects or parts that allows free movement: *We had to wait for the other car to move, because there wasn't enough clearance to get our car out. The underpass has a clearance of four metres.* **3** the meeting of requirements to get a ship or cargo free on entering or leaving a port. **4** a certificate showing this. **5** official permission to go ahead; authorization to do a certain thing or have access to a certain place: *The pilot had to wait for clearance from the control tower.* **6** the exchanging of cheques and bills and settling of accounts between different banks. *n.*

**clearance sale** a sale held by a store, etc., to clear out old stock in order to make room for new.

**clear–cut** (klēr′kut′) **1** having clear, sharp outlines. **2** clear; definite; distinct: *Luba had clear-cut ideas about her work.* *adj.*

**clear·cut·ting** (klēr′kut′ing) **1** the clearing from a forest area of all standing timber. **2** the area so cleared. *n.*

**clear–eyed** (klēr′īd′) **1** having bright, clear eyes. **2** having or showing insight and understanding: *a clear-eyed analysis of a complex situation.* *adj.*

**clear–head·ed** (klēr′hed′id) having or showing a clear understanding. *adj.* —**clear′head′ed·ly,** *adv.* —**clear′-head′ed·ness,** *n.*

**clear·ing** (klē′ring) **1** an open space of cleared land in a forest. **2** the exchanging of cheques and bills and settling of accounts between different banks. **3** ppr. of CLEAR. 1–2 *n.*, 3 *v.*

**clearing house** a place where banks exchange cheques and bills and settle their accounts.

**clear-sight·ed** (klēr′sī′tid) 1 able to see clearly. 2 able to understand or think clearly. *adj.* —**clear′-sight′ed·ly**, *adv.* —**clear′-sight′ed·ness**, *n.*

**cleat** (klēt) 1 one of several studs or bars of leather, plastic, etc., attached to the sole of a football boot, soccer boot, etc. to prevent slipping. 2 a strip of wood, metal, leather, etc., fastened across anything for support or for sure footing: *A gangway has cleats to keep people from slipping.* 3 one of the raised bars placed at intervals across the track of a vehicle that travels over snow: *The cleats on a snowmobile track make possible a firmer grip on snow.* 4 a small, wedge-shaped block fastened to a mast, spar, etc., as a support, check, etc. 5 a piece of wood, metal, or plastic having projecting arms or ends, fixed to a boat, wharf, flagpole, etc. and used for securing ropes or lines. See ROWBOAT for picture. 6 fasten to or with a cleat. 1–5 *n.*, 6 *v.*

**cleav·age** (klē′vij) 1 a split or division. 2 the way in which something splits or divides. 3 any of the series of divisions by which a fertilized egg develops into an EMBRYO. *n.*

**cleave**[1] (klēv) 1 cut, divide, or split open: *With one blow of the axe he cleft the log in two.* 2 pass through; pierce; penetrate: *The airplane cleaved the clouds.* 3 make by cutting: *to cleave a path through the wilderness.* *v.*, **cleft, cleaved**, or **clove, cleft, cleaved**, or **clo·ven, cleav·ing**. —**cleav′a·ble**, *adj.*

**cleave**[2] (klēv) hold fast (*to*); cling; be faithful (*to*): *to cleave to an idea.* *v.*, **cleaved, cleaved, cleav·ing**.

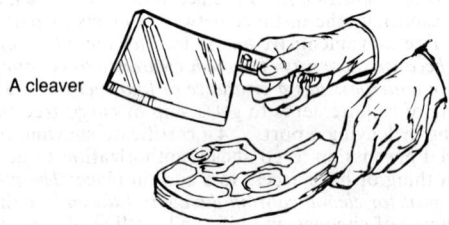
A cleaver

**cleav·er** (klē′vər) a cutting tool with a heavy blade and a short handle: *A butcher uses a cleaver to chop through meat or bone.* *n.*

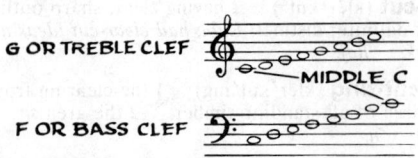
G OR TREBLE CLEF
MIDDLE C
F OR BASS CLEF

**clef** (klef) in music, a symbol indicating the pitch of the notes on a staff. *n.*

**cleft** (kleft) 1 a pt. and a pp. of CLEAVE[1]: *His blow had cleft the log in two.* 2 split; divided: *a cleft stick.* 3 a space or opening made by splitting; crack. 1 *v.*, 2 *adj.*, 3 *n.*

**cleft palate** a narrow opening running lengthways in the roof of the mouth, caused by failure of the two parts of the palate to join.

**clem·a·tis** (klem′ə tis) a vine having clusters of fragrant white, red, or purple flowers. *n.*

**clem·en·cy** (klem′ən sē) 1 mercy; mildness in exercising authority or power: *The Crown recommended clemency for the defendant.* 2 mildness of climate or weather. *n.*, *pl.* **clem·en·cies**.

**clem·ent** (klem′ənt) 1 merciful. 2 mild; gentle. *adj.* —**clem′ent·ly**, *adv.* Compare with INCLEMENT.

**clem·en·tine** (klem′ən tīn′) a small type of orange. *n.*

**clench** (klench) 1 close tightly together: *to clench one's fists, to clench one's teeth.* 2 grasp firmly; grip tightly: *The policeman clenched his prisoner's arm.* 3 a firm grasp; tight grip: *I felt the clench of his hand on my arm.* 4 CLINCH (def. 1) a nail, etc. 1, 2, 4 *v.*, 3 *n.*

**clere·sto·rey** (klēr′stô′rē) 1 in architecture, the upper part of the wall of a church, having windows in it above the roofs of the aisles. See BASILICA for picture. 2 any similar structure. *n.*, *pl.* **clere·sto·reys**.

**cler·gy** (klėr′jē) a body or order of persons specially trained and ordained to perform religious services: *Ministers, pastors, priests, and rabbis are members of the clergy.* Compare with LAITY. *n.*, *pl.* **cler·gies**.

**cler·gy·man** (klėr′jē mən) a man who is a member of the clergy. *n.*, *pl.* **cler·gy·men** (-mən).

**Clergy Reserves** *Cdn.* the lands set aside in Lower and Upper Canada in 1791 for the support of a Protestant clergy.

**cler·ic** (klėr′ik) a member of the clergy. *n.*

**cler·i·cal** (klėr′ə kəl) 1 of or for a clerk or clerks: *Keeping records or accounts and copying letters are clerical jobs in an office.* 2 of, having to do with, or characteristic of the clergy or a member of the clergy: *The priest wore clerical robes in church.* 3 a member of the clergy. 4 in some countries, supporting the power or influence of the clergy in politics. 5 in some countries, a supporter of the power or influence of the clergy in politics. 6 **clericals**, *pl.* the clothes worn by members of the clergy. 1, 2, 4 *adj.*, 3, 5, 6 *n.* —**cler′i·cal·ly**, *adv.*

**clerk** (klėrk; *esp. Brit.*, klärk) 1 a person whose work is waiting on customers and selling goods in a store; a salesman or saleswoman in a store. 2 a person whose work is keeping records or accounts, copying letters, etc. in an office: *a law clerk.* 3 an official who keeps records and takes care of regular business in a law court, legislature, etc.: *a county clerk.* 4 work as a clerk in a store: *He clerks in a drugstore.* 5 a layperson who has minor church duties. 1–3, 5 *n.*, 4 *v.*

**clerk·ship** (klėrk′ship *or* klärk′ship) the position or work of a CLERK. *n.*

**clev·er** (klev′ər) 1 having a quick mind; bright; intelligent: *Kimiko is the cleverest person in our class.* 2 skilful or expert in doing some particular thing: *a clever carpenter.* 3 showing skill or intelligence: *a clever trick, a clever answer.* *adj.* —**clev′er·ly**, *adv.* —**clev′er·ness**, *n.*

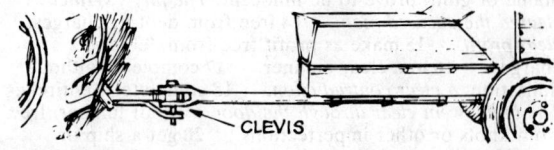
CLEVIS

**clev·is** (klev′is) a U-shaped piece of metal with a bolt

or pin through the ends: *A clevis may be used to fasten a whippletree to a wagon or plough.* *n.*

**clew** (klü) **1** a ball of thread or yarn. **2** a lower corner of a sail. **3** a metal ring fastened there. **4** raise or lower a sail by the clews. 1–3 *n.*, 4 *v.*
☞ *Hom.* CLUE.

**cli·ché** (klē shā′) a timeworn expression or idea. *n.*

**click** (klik) **1** a light, sharp sound: *We heard the click as she turned the key in the lock.* **2** make such a sound: *The clock clicks just before it chimes.* **3** cause to make such a sound: *The soldier clicked his heels together and saluted.* **4** *Informal.* get along well together; be congenial; hit it off: *We clicked from the start.* **5** *Informal.* succeed; go or do well: *This movie should click; it has well-known actors and a popular theme.* 1 *n.*, 2–5 *v.*

**cli·ent** (klī′ənt) **1** a person for whom a lawyer or other professional person acts. **2** customer. **3** in ancient Rome, a poor or humble person depending on a noble or wealthy man for assistance. *n.* —**cli′ent·less**, *adj.*

**cli·en·tele** (klī′ən tel′) **1** CLIENTS (defs. 1, 2); customers. **2** personal followers. **3** a number of CLIENTS (defs. 1, 2). *n.*

**cliff** (klif) a steep, high face of rock or earth; precipice: *Great cliffs overhung the canyon.* *n.* —**cliff′like′**, *adj.*

**cliff–hang·er** (klif′hang′ər) *Informal.* **1** a story, motion picture, etc. that is full of suspense, especially a serial in which each episode ends with the hero or heroine in an extremely dangerous situation. **2** a race, election, or other contest in which the result is in doubt until the very end. *n.*

**cliff swallow** a North American swallow that builds a bottle-shaped nest of mud, straw, and feathers and usually fastens it to a cliff.

**cli·mac·ter·ic** (klī mak′tə rik) **1** the time when some important event occurs, changing the course of things; a crucial period. **2** the period of life around middle age when important physical and emotional changes usually take place: *The climacteric in women is usually called the menopause.* **3** of, having to do with, or referring to a climacteric. 1, 2 *n.*, 3 *adj.*

**cli·mac·tic** (klī mak′tik) of or forming a CLIMAX. *adj.*

**cli·ma·graph** (klī′mə graf′) a graph showing the typical CLIMATE (def. 1) of a selected location in terms of its average monthly temperature and precipitation. *n.* Also, **climograph.**

**cli·mate** (klī′mit) **1** the kind of weather patterns a place has over a period of years: *Climate includes conditions of heat and cold, moisture and dryness, clearness and cloudiness, wind and calm.* **2** a region with certain usual conditions of heat and cold, rainfall, wind, sunlight, etc.: *The doctor ordered Geeta to go to a drier climate.* *n.*

**cli·mat·ic** (klī mat′ik) of or having to do with CLIMATE. *adj.*

**cli·mat·i·cal·ly** (klī mat′i klē) with reference to CLIMATE. *adv.*

**cli·max** (klī′maks) **1** the highest point; the point of greatest interest; the most exciting part: *Shooting the rapids was the climax of our canoe trip.* **2** the arrangement of ideas in a rising scale of force and interest. **3** bring or come to a climax. 1, 2 *n.*, 3 *v.*

**climax community** the last community of plants or animals to develop in a particular area: *The climax*

**clew** 221 **clinical**

hat, āge, fär; let, ēqual, tėrm; it, īce
hot, ōpen, ôrder; oil, out; cup, pu̇t, rüle
ə=above, taken, pencəl, lemən, circəs
ch, child; ng, long; sh, ship
th, thin; ᴛʜ, then; zh, measure

*community will continue provided there is no change in soil conditions or climate in the area.*

**climb** (klīm) **1** go up, especially by using the hands or feet, or both; ascend: *The painter climbed the ladder. We had been climbing for hours but we had not reached the top of the mountain.* **2** rise slowly or with steady effort in rank or fortune: *It took her twelve years to climb to the position of executive director.* **3** grow upward by holding on or twining around: *The ivy is starting to climb up the porch railing.* **4** a climbing; ascent: *Our climb took two hours.* **5** a place to be climbed. **6** slope upward: *The road climbed for more than a kilometre before it began its descent toward the coast.* **7** an increase: *a climb in price.* **8** increase: *The price of coffee has climbed during the past year.* 1–3, 6, 8 *v.*, **climbed, climb·ing;** 4, 5, 7 *n.*
**climb down,** **a** go down by using the hands and feet. **b** *Informal.* give in; back down; withdraw from an impossible position or unreasonable attitude.
☞ *Hom.* CLIME.

**climb·er** (klī′mər) **1** a person or thing that climbs. **2** *Informal.* a person who is always trying to get ahead socially. **3** CLIMBING IRON. **4** climbing plant; vine. *n.*

**climbing iron** one of a pair of frames having metal spikes, attached to boots to help in climbing.

**clime** (klīm) **1** a country or region. **2** CLIMATE. *n.*
☞ *Hom.* CLIMB.

**clinch** (klinch) **1** fasten a driven nail, a bolt, etc. firmly by bending over or flattening the end that has been driven through something and projects from the other side. **2** fasten together in this way. **3** fix firmly; settle decisively: *A deposit of five dollars clinched the bargain.* **4** grasp one another tightly, as in boxing or wrestling; grapple: *When the boxers clinched, the crowd hissed.* **5** a tight grasp in fighting or wrestling; a close grip: *The referee broke the boxers' clinch.* **6** a kind of sailor's knot in which the end of the rope is lashed back. 1–4 *v.*, 5, 6 *n.*

**clinch·er** (klin′chər) **1** a tool for clinching nails, bolts, etc. **2** *Informal.* an argument, statement, etc. that is decisive. *n.*

**cling** (kling) **1** attach oneself firmly; grasp; hold tightly: *The child clung to his mother.* **2** stick; be attached: *A vine clings to its support.* **3** remain attached to a belief, idea, etc.: *They clung to the beliefs of their parents.* **4** keep near: *The clouds cling to the mountains.* *v.* **clung, cling·ing.**

**clin·ic** (klin′ik) **1** a part of a hospital where people are treated for certain kinds of illness without having to stay overnight: *They have the latest equipment in the eye clinic.* **2** a place, separate from a hospital, where a group of doctors work together: *My aunt is a heart specialist in the new clinic.* **3** a session held to treat or prevent certain illnesses or injuries, or to provide a special service: *a blood donor clinic, a rabies clinic for pets.* **4** the practical instruction of medical students by examining or treating patients in the presence of the students. **5** a class of students receiving such instruction. **6** a brief course of practical instruction in some non-medical field: *a football clinic, a writing clinic.* *n.*

**clin·i·cal** (klin′ə kəl) **1** of or having to do with a

CLINIC. **2** having to do with the diagnosis and treatment of disease by observation of the patient, as distinct from dependence on laboratory tests. **3** detached, unemotional, and thorough, suggesting a medical examination or report: *The interviewer looked the applicant over with a clinical eye and then said, "You'll do."* **4** bare, neat, and functional, suggesting a hospital: *The kitchen looked clinical, very different from the large, friendly kitchen in the old house.* *adj.* —**clin′i·cal·ly,** *adv.*

**clinical thermometer** a thermometer for measuring the temperature of the body.

**clink** (klingk) **1** a light, sharp, ringing sound like that of glasses hitting together. **2** make a clink: *The spoons and glasses clinked.* **3** cause to clink: *They clinked glasses in a toast to the mayor.* 1 *n.*, 2, 3 *v.*

**clink·er** (kling′kər) **1** a piece of the rough, hard mass left in a furnace or stove after coal has been burned; large, rough cinder. **2** a very hard brick. **3** a mass of bricks fused together. **4** SLAG (def. 1). *n.*

**clip¹** (klip) **1** cut; cut out or cut short; trim with shears, scissors, or clippers: *to clip the hair. I often clip interesting newspaper articles to send to friends.* **2** cut or trim the hair of a person or animal: *Our dog is clipped every summer.* **3** shear off the fleece of a sheep. **4** the act of clipping. **5** the amount of wool clipped from sheep at one shearing or during one season. **6** anything that has been clipped off, such as a section of filmed material. **7** damage a coin by cutting off the edge. **8** omit sounds in pronouncing. **9** *Informal.* a fast pace: *Our bus passed through the village at quite a clip.* **10** *Informal.* move fast. **11** *Informal.* a sharp blow or punch. **12** *Informal.* hit or punch sharply. **13** *Informal.* one time; a single occasion: *at one clip.* **14** *Informal.* cheat, especially by overcharging: *We got clipped in that restaurant.* 1–3, 7, 8, 10, 12, 14 *v.*, **clipped, clip·ping;** 4–6, 9, 11, 13 *n.*
**a good clip,** a fairly rapid pace: *We were now moving along at a good clip.*

**clip²** (klip) **1** hold tight; fasten: *to clip papers together.* **2** something used for clipping things together: *A clip for papers is often made of a piece of bent wire.* **3** a metal holder for cartridges on some firearms. 1 *v.*, **clipped, clip·ping;** 2, 3 *n.*

**clip·board** (klip′bôrd′) a small board with a heavy spring clip at one end for holding papers while writing. *n.*

**clip joint** *Informal.* a restaurant, nightclub, etc. with a reputation for overcharging.

**clip·per** (klip′ər) **1** a person who clips or cuts. **2** a sailing ship of the mid-19th century, built and rigged for great speed. **3** Often, **clippers,** *pl.* a tool for cutting: *hedge clippers.* *n.*

**clip·ping** (klip′ing) **1** a piece cut from or out of something, especially a piece cut out of a newspaper or magazine. **2** ppr. of CLIP. 1 *n.*, 2 *v.*

**clique** (klēk) a small, exclusive group of people within a larger group: *Members complained that the club was being run by a clique.* *n.*

**cli·quish** (klē′kish) **1** like a CLIQUE. **2** tending to form a CLIQUE. *adj.* —**cli′quish·ness,** *n.*

**clo·a·ca** (klō ā′kə) **1** sewer. **2** privy. **3** a cavity in the body of birds, reptiles, amphibians, etc., into which the intestinal, urinary, and generative canals open. *n., pl.* **clo·a·cae** (-sē *or* -sī).

**cloak** (klōk) **1** an outer garment, usually loose, with or without sleeves, and hanging to the knees. **2** cover with a cloak. **3** anything that hides or conceals: *to do mean deeds under the cloak of friendship.* **4** hide; conceal: *to cloak evil purposes under friendly words.* 1, 3 *n.*, 2, 4 *v.*

**cloak·room** (klōk′rüm′) a room, especially in a school or other public building, where coats, hats, etc. can be left for a time. *n.*

**clob·ber** (klob′ər) *Informal.* **1** attack violently. **2** defeat severely. *v.*

**cloche** (klōsh) a bell-shaped glass cover to protect tender plants. *n.*

**clock** (klok) **1** an instrument for measuring and showing time, especially one that is not carried around like a watch. **2** measure or record the time of; time: *The coach clocked the three girls to see who was the fastest runner.* **3** record time, distance, number, etc. mechanically: *The racing car clocked 240 km/h.* 1 *n.*, 2, 3 *v.* —**clock′er,** *n.* —**clock′like′,** *adj.*
**around the clock,** all day and all night.
**turn** *or* **put the clock back,** go back to an earlier time or to an out-of-date fashion or way of doing things.

**clock·mak·er** (klok′mā′kər) a person whose business is making or repairing clocks. *n.*

**clock radio** a radio with a built-in clock that can be set to turn the radio on or off automatically at any desired time: *Many people use clock radios instead of alarm clocks to wake themselves up in the morning.*

**clock·wise** (klok′wīz′) in the direction in which the hands of a clock move: *Turn the lid clockwise to tighten it.* *adv., adj.*

**clock·work** (klok′wėrk′) **1** the machinery used to run a clock, consisting of gears, wheels, and springs. **2** machinery like this: *Many mechanical toys are run by clockwork.* *n.*
**like clockwork,** with great regularity and smoothness: *The launching of the rocket went off like clockwork.*

**clod** (klod) **1** a lump or chunk, especially of earth or clay. **2** earth; soil. **3** *Informal.* a stupid person; blockhead. *n.*

**clod·hop·per** (klod′hop′ər) **1** a clumsy boor. **2** a large heavy shoe. *n.*

**clog** (klog) **1** block by filling up; stop up: *Greasy water clogged the drain.* **2** become blocked or filled up: *The drain has clogged with leaves.* **3** hinder the operation or movement of; interfere with; hold back: *Heavy clothes clogged the swimmer. Sand clogged the reel of the fishing rod.* **4** something that hinders or interferes. **5** any weight, such as a block of wood, fastened to the leg of an animal to hinder motion. **6** a heavy shoe with a wooden sole. **7** a lighter shoe with a wooden sole, used in clog dancing. **8** dance by beating a heavy rhythm on the floor with such shoes. **9** such a dance. 1–3, 8 *v.*, **clogged, clog·ging;** 4–7, 9 *n.*

**clog dance** a dance in which the dancer wears CLOGS (def. 7) to beat time.

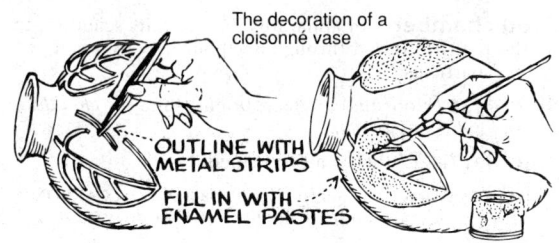
The decoration of a cloisonné vase

**cloi·son·né** (kloi′zə nā′) **1** enamelware in which the different colours of ENAMEL (def. 1) are separated by thin metal strips set on edge on the surface.   **2** enamelled in this way.   1 *n.*, 2 *adj.*

A cloister (def. 1)

**clois·ter** (kloi′stər)   **1** a covered walk along the wall of a building, with a row of pillars on the open side: *A cloister is often built around the courtyard of a monastery, church, or college building.*   **2** a place of religious retirement; convent or monastery.   **3** a quiet place shut away from the world.   **4** shut away in a quiet place.   1–3 *n.*, 4 *v.*

**clone** (klōn)   **1** all the cells or organisms derived from a single individual by means such as cuttings or bulbs, by fission, or by the development of an unfertilized OVUM.   **2** a single organism produced in this way.   **3** produce a new individual in this way.   1, 2 *n.*, 3 *v.*

**clon·ing** (klō′ning)   **1** the technique of producing a duplicate of an organism by replacing the nucleus of an unfertilized OVUM, or egg, with the nucleus of a body cell of the parent organism, causing the ovum to develop into a new organism that is genetically identical to the parent organism.   **2** an individual produced in this way; CLONE (def. 2).   **3** ppr. of CLONE.   1, 2 *n.*, 3 *v.*

**close¹** (klōz)   **1** shut: *Close the door. The sleepy child's eyes are closing.*   **2** stop up; fill; block: *to close a gap.*   **3** bring together; come together: *to close the ranks of troops.*   **4** end; finish: *The meeting closed with a speech by the president.*   **5** an end or finish: *She spoke at the close of the meeting.*   **6** come to terms; agree: *The labour union closed with the company.*   **7** grapple.   1–4, 6, 7 *v.* **closed, clos·ing,**   5 *n.*   —**clos′er,** *n.*
**close down,**   shut completely; stop.
**close in,**   come near; approach from all sides: *The thief gave up when the police closed in. Night closed in swiftly.*
**close in on,**   come near and surround or shut in on all sides: *The wolves closed in on the moose. I felt that the walls were closing in on me.*
**close out,**   **a** sell, usually at a low price to get rid of.   **b** go out of business.
**close up,**   **a** shut completely; stop up; block.   **b** bring or come nearer together.   **c** of a wound, heal.
☛ *Hom.* CLOTHES (klōz).

**close²** (klōs)   **1** with very little in between; near together; near: *close teeth.*   **2** fitting tightly; tight; narrow: *close quarters.*   **3** having its parts near together; compact: *a close texture.*   **4** intimate; dear: *a close friend.*   **5** careful; exact: *a close translation.*   **6** thorough; strict: *close attention.*   **7** stifling; stuffy: *With the windows shut, the room soon became hot and close.*   **8** not fond of talking; keeping quiet about oneself.   **9** secret; hidden.   **10** strictly guarded; confined: *to keep someone close at home.*   **11** restricted; limited.   **12** stingy: *She was close with her money.*   **13** hard to get; scarce.   **14** nearly equal; almost even: *a close contest.*   **15** closed; shut; not open.   **16** in a close manner.   **17** an enclosed place.   **18** the grounds around a cathedral or abbey.   1–15 *adj.,* **clos·er, clos·est;**   16 *adv.,* 17, 18 *n.*   —**close′ness,** *n.*
**close to the wind,**   **a** with the ship pointed as nearly as possible in the direction from which the wind is blowing.   **b** *Informal.*   just barely following rules or laws.

**close call** (klōs) *Informal.*   a narrow escape from disaster: *I had a close call this morning when a car went through a red light and almost hit me.*

**closed shop**   a factory or business that employs only members of labour unions.   Compare with OPEN SHOP.

**closed syllable**   a syllable that ends in a consonant sound. *Example: can-* in *candy.*   Compare with OPEN SYLLABLE.

**close–fist·ed** (klōs′fis′tid)   stingy.   *adj.*

**close–fit·ting** (klōs′fit′ing)   fitting tightly; tight: *a close-fitting jacket.*   *adj.*

**close–grained** (klōs′grānd′)   having a fine, close GRAIN (def. 9): *Mahogany is a close-grained wood.*   *adj.*

**close·ly** (klōs′lē)   in a close manner; to a close degree or extent: *Her coat fits closely. I will examine the matter very closely.*   *adv.*

**close–mouthed** (klōs′mouтнd′ *or* klōs′moutht′)   not fond of talking; reticent.   *adj.*

**close quarters**   a place or position with little space: *They were living in very close quarters.*
**at close quarters,**   very close; at close range: *I had never seen a bear at close quarters before.*

**close shave** (klōs) *Informal.*   a narrow escape; CLOSE CALL.

**clos·et** (kloz′it)   **1** a small room or cupboard used for storing clothes or household supplies: *Most houses and apartments these days have built-in closets.*   **2** a small, private room for prayer or study.   **3** a water closet; toilet.   *n.*
**be closeted with,**   be shut up in a room for a private talk: *The prime minister was closeted with his personal advisers for several hours.*

**close–up** (klōs′up′)   **1** a picture taken at close range.   **2** a close view.   *n.*

**clo·sure** (klō′zhər)   **1** the act of closing or the condition of being closed.   **2** a thing that closes.   **3** the end; finish; conclusion.   **4** a means of ending a debate in a legislative body in order to force an immediate vote: *Closure is used occasionally in the House of Commons.* *n.*

**clot** (klot) **1** a half-solid lump; thickened mass: *A clot of blood formed in the cut and stopped the bleeding.* **2** form into clots: *Milk clots when it turns sour.* **3** CLOD (def. 1). 1, 3 *n.*, 2 *v.*, **clot·ted, clot·ting.**

**cloth** (klôth) **1** material made from wool, cotton, silk, linen, hair, synthetic fibres, etc. by weaving, knitting, or rolling and pressing. **2** a piece of such material used for a special purpose: *a cloth for the table.* **3** the customary clothing worn by the members of the clergy. **4** the profession of a clergyman. **5** made of cloth. **6 the cloth,** the clergy. *n.*, *pl.* **cloths** (klôŦHz *or* klôths).

**clothe** (klōŦH) **1** put clothes on; cover with clothes; dress. **2** provide with clothes: *It costs quite a bit to clothe a family of six.* **3** cover or wrap as if with clothes: *The sun clothes the earth with light.* **4** provide; furnish; equip: *A judge is clothed with the authority of the state.* *v.*, **clothed** or **clad, cloth·ing.**

**clothes** (klōz *or* klōŦHz) **1** coverings for a person's body; garments; apparel; clothing: *summer clothes. Our clothes were very dirty after the hike.* **2** the coverings for a bed. *n. pl.*
☞ Hom. CLOSE¹ (for the first pronunciation of **clothes**).

**clothes·horse** (klōz′hôrs′ *or* klōŦHz′hôrs′) a frame to hang clothes on in order to dry or air them. *n.*

**clothes·line** (klōz′līn′ *or* klōŦH′zlīn′) a rope, wire, etc. to hang clothes on to dry or air them. *n.*

**clothes·peg** (klōz′peg′ *or* klōŦHz′peg′) **1** a peg for hanging clothes on. **2** a CLOTHESPIN. *n.*

**clothes·pin** (klōz′pin′ *or* klōŦHz′pin′) a clip, often wooden, to hold clothes on a clothesline. *n.*

**clothes·press** (klōz′pres′ *or* klōŦHz′pres′) a chest, cupboard, or closet in which to keep clothes. *n.*

**cloth·i·er** (klō′ŦHyər) **1** a seller or maker of clothing. **2** a seller of cloth. *n.*

**cloth·ing** (klō′ŦHing) **1** clothes. **2** covering. **3** ppr. of CLOTHE. 1, 2 *n.*, 3 *v.*

**cloud** (kloud) **1** a white, grey, or almost black mass in the sky, made up of tiny drops of water or ice particles. **2** a mass of smoke or dust. **3** cover with a cloud or clouds. **4** become cloudy: *The sky clouded.* **5** a great number of things moving close together through the air: *a cloud of birds, a cloud of arrows.* **6** a blemish or spot on a polished stone or gem. **7** anything that darkens or dims; a cause of gloom, trouble, suspicion, or disgrace. **8** darken; dim; make or become gloomy or troubled: *Amral's face clouded as he thought of the quarrel.* **9** make or become suspected, or disgraced. 1, 2, 5–7 *n.*, 3, 4, 8, 9 *v.* —**cloud′like′,** *adj.*
**under a cloud,** **a** under suspicion; in disgrace. **b** in gloom or trouble.

**cloud·ber·ry** (kloud′ber′ē) *Cdn.* **1** a berry that grows in northern latitudes and resembles a small raspberry. **2** the bush it grows on. **3** *Cdn.* BAKEAPPLE. *n.*, *pl.* **cloud·ber·ries.**

**cloud·burst** (kloud′bėrst′) a short, sudden, very heavy rainfall. *n.*

**cloud chamber** an apparatus that permits scientists to see the paths followed through a vapour by very small charged particles.

**cloud·less** (kloud′lis) clear; bright; sunny: *a cloudless sky, a cloudless day.* *adj.*

**cloud·let** (kloud′lit) a little cloud. *n.*

**cloud seeding** the scattering of particles of CARBON DIOXIDE or other chemicals in clouds to produce rain.

**cloud·y** (kloud′ē) **1** having clouds; covered with clouds: *a cloudy sky.* **2** characterized by a sky covered with clouds: *The morning was cloudy and cold.* **3** of or like clouds: *A cloudy veil hid the mountaintop.* **4** of a liquid, not clear; murky: *The pond water was cloudy.* **5** streaked; spotted: *cloudy marble.* **6** of ideas, etc., dim or unclear; hazy; clouded by ignorance, etc.: *He had some cloudy, half-formed notions, but no real plan of action.* **7** full of gloom or trouble; made dark or dim by grief, anger, fear, etc.: *a cloudy future.* *adj.*, **cloud·i·er, cloud·i·est.** —**cloud′i·ly,** *adv.* —**cloud′i·ness,** *n.*

**clout** (klout) **1** *Informal.* a hit, especially with the hand; cuff: *a clout on the head.* **2** *Informal.* a long hit in baseball. **3** *Informal.* hit hard: *She finally got exasperated with his teasing and clouted him. He clouted the ball into the stands.* **4** *Informal.* power and influence: *The newspaper doesn't carry any real clout. She has a lot of political clout.* **5** in archery, a white cloth on a frame, used as a target. **6** a shot that hits this. 1, 2, 4–6 *n.*, 3 *v.*

**clove¹** (klōv) **1** the dried flower bud of a tropical tree. **2** the tree it grows on. **3** Often, **cloves,** *pl.* a strong, fragrant spice obtained from dried flower buds. *n.*

**clove²** (klōv) a small, separable section of a bulb: *a clove of garlic.* *n.*

**clove³** (klōv) a pt. of CLEAVE¹. *v.*

**clove hitch** a knot for tying a rope around a pole, spar, etc. See KNOT for picture.

**clo·ven** (klō′vən) **1** a pp. of CLEAVE¹. **2** split; divided. 1 *v.*, 2 *adj.*

**cloven hoof** a split hoof; a hoof divided into two parts: *Cows and sheep have cloven hoofs.*

**clo·ven–hoofed** (klō′vən huft′) having CLOVEN HOOFS. *adj.*

**clove pink** an Old World pink having single flesh-coloured, clove-scented flowers: *The many cultivated varieties of carnation are all derived from the clove pink.*

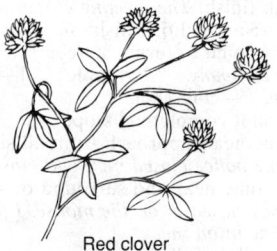
Red clover

**clo·ver** (klō′vər) any of a closely related group of low herbs of the pea family, having leaves consisting of three leaflets and rounded heads of small red, white, or yellow flowers: *Several species of clover are grown as food for horses and cattle.* *n.*
**in clover,** *Informal.* enjoying a life of pleasure and luxury without work or worry.

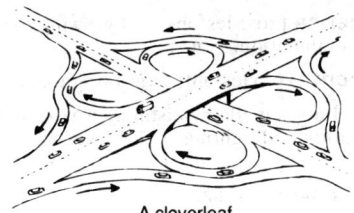
A cloverleaf

**clo·ver·leaf** (klō′vər lēf′) a series of roads at an intersection of two highways, so arranged that traffic may move from one highway to the other without having to cross in front of other traffic. *n.*

**clown** (kloun) 1 a person whose work is to amuse and entertain by tricks, jokes, and antics: *Circuses always have clowns.* 2 act like a clown; play tricks and jokes; act silly: *We were clowning around on the lawn.* 3 a bad-mannered, awkward or uneducated person. 1, 3 *n.*, 2 *v.*

**clown·ish** (klou′nish) like a clown; like a clown's. *adj.* —**clown′ish·ly**, *adv.* —**clown′ish·ness**, *n.*

**cloy** (kloi) 1 overload with something originally pleasurable, such as rich or sweet food, so as to cause dislike: *Claire was cloyed with sweets before the holidays ended.* 2 disgust or make weary with too much of anything originally pleasant: *Her constant helpfulness soon begins to cloy.* *v.*

**club** (klub) 1 a heavy stick of wood, thick at one end, used as a weapon. 2 a stick or bat used in some games to hit a ball: *golf clubs.* 3 beat or hit with a club. 4 a group of people joined together for some special purpose: *a tennis club.* 5 a building or rooms used by a club. 6 a playing card with one or more black designs on it, shaped like this: ♣. 7 **clubs**, *pl.* the suit of such playing cards. 1, 2, 4–7 *n.*, 3 *v.*, **clubbed, club·bing.**
**club together,** unite for some special purpose: *The children clubbed together to buy their mother some flowers for her birthday.*

**club car** a railway passenger coach for day travel, more luxurious than ordinary coaches.

**club·foot** (klub′fut′) 1 a deformity of the foot present at birth, in which the foot is twisted and misshapen, often resembling a club. 2 a foot having this deformity. *n.*, *pl.* **club·feet.**

**club·foot·ed** (klub′fut′id) having a CLUBFOOT. *adj.*

**club·house** (klub′hous′) a building used by a club. *n.*

**club moss** a flowerless plant that grows along the ground and looks much like a vine covered with pine needles.

**club sandwich** a sandwich consisting of toast and at least two layers of meats (especially chicken), lettuce, tomato, etc.

**cluck** (kluk) 1 the sound made by a hen calling her chickens. 2 make such a sound. 3 a sound like this. 4 make a sound like this: *She clucked her disapproval.* 1, 3 *n.*, 2, 4 *v.*

**clue** (klü) 1 a guide to the solving of a mystery or problem: *The police could find no clues to help them in solving the crime. This crossword puzzle has some very hard clues.* 2 *Informal.* tell; give information to: *So what's happening? Clue me! She promised to clue him in on their doings.* 1 *n.*, 2 *v.*
**clue up,** *Informal.* provide with information essential to a position: *The new manager is not clued up yet.*
☛ Hom. CLEW.

**clue·less** (klü′lis) *Informal.* 1 not having any idea; not knowing; in the dark: *I always feel clueless about politics.* 2 generally ignorant or incompetent: *Boy, is he clueless—he just asked me where the cow's nest was!* *adj.*

**clum·ber** (klum′bər) a breed of spaniel with short legs, a long, heavy body, and a silky, mainly white coat. *n.*

**clump** (klump) 1 a cluster: *a clump of trees.* 2 form a clump; plant in clusters. 3 a lump: *a clump of earth.* 4 the sound of heavy, clumsy walking. 5 walk heavily and clumsily. 1, 3, 4 *n.*, 2, 5 *v.*

**clump·y** (klum′pē) 1 full of CLUMPS. 2 like CLUMPS. 3 heavy and clumsy. *adj.*

**clum·si·ness** (klum′zē nis) the state or condition of being CLUMSY; awkwardness. *n.*

**clum·sy** (klum′zē) 1 not graceful or skilful; awkward: *The clumsy boy bumped into all the furniture.* 2 not well-shaped or well-made: *Jack's rowboat was a clumsy affair made out of old boxes.* *adj.*, **clum·si·er, clum·si·est.** —**clum′si·ly**, *adv.*

**clung** (klung) pt. and pp. of CLING: *The child clung to her mother.* *v.*

**clus·ter** (klus′tər) 1 a number of things of the same kind growing or fastened together; bunch: *a cluster of grapes, a cluster of curls.* 2 a group of persons or things: *a cluster of houses in the valley. There was a cluster of people at the theatre doors.* 3 form into a cluster; gather in clusters; group together closely: *The girls clustered around their teacher.* 1, 2 *n.*, 3 *v.*

**clutch**[1] (kluch) 1 a tight grasp; a firm hold by claw, paw, or hand: *The eagle loosened its clutch and the rabbit escaped.* 2 grasp tightly: *The girl clutched her puppy to her breast.* 3 a grasping claw, paw, hand, etc.: *He just managed to stay out of reach of the bear's clutches.* 4 any of several devices for connecting and disconnecting two working parts of a machine: *The clutch in a car connects the engine with the drive shaft, which turns the wheels.* 5 the lever or pedal that operates such a device. 6 Usually, **clutches**, *pl.* control; power: *in the clutches of the police.* 1, 3–6 *n.*, 2 *v.*
**clutch at,** a grasp eagerly for; try to seize or take hold of: *She clutched at the branch, but missed it and fell.* b try to take advantage of: *She'll clutch at the chance to save her children.*

**clutch**[2] (kluch) 1 a nest of eggs. 2 a brood of chickens. *n.*

**clut·ter** (klut′ər) 1 litter; confusion; disorder. 2 litter with things: *Her desk was all cluttered with books and papers.* 3 a confused noise; loud clatter. 4 make a confused noise; clatter loudly. 1, 3 *n.*, 2, 4 *v.*

**Clydes·dale** (klīdz′dāl) a breed of large, strong draft horse. *n.*

**Cm** curium.

**cm** centimetre; centimetres. The symbol for cubic centimetres is $cm^3$.

**C.M.** Canada Medal.

**CMA**  Canadian Medical Association.

**CMHC** or **C.M.H.C.**  Central Mortgage and Housing Corporation.

**CN**  Canadian National Railways. Formerly, **CNR**.

**CNIB**  Canadian National Institute for the Blind.

**co–**  a prefix meaning: **1** with; together: *co-operate = act with or together*. **2** joint; fellow: *co-author = joint or fellow author*. **3** equally: *co-extensive = equally extensive*. See note at COM-.

**c.o.** or **c/o**  in care of.

**Co**  cobalt.

**Co.** or **co.**  **1** Company.  **2** County.

**C.O.**  **1** Commanding Officer.  **2** *Informal.* conscientious objector.

**coach** (kōch)  **1** a large, closed carriage with seats inside and often on top: *Coaches carried passengers along a regular route, stopping for meals and fresh horses.*  **2** carry or ride in a coach.  **3** a passenger car of a railway train, containing adjustable seats but no sleeping accommodation.  **4** a closed automobile like a sedan.  **5** bus.  **6** a person who teaches or trains athletic teams, etc.: *a hockey coach*.  **7** teach; train.  **8** a private teacher who helps a student prepare for a special test.  **9** help to prepare for a special test. 1, 3–6, 8 *n*., 2, 7, 9 *v*.

**coach–and–four** (kōch′ənd fôr′)  a coach pulled by four horses. *n*.

**coach dog**  DALMATIAN.

**coach·man** (kōch′mən)  a person whose work is driving a coach or carriage.  *n*., *pl*. **coach·men** (-mən).

**co·ag·u·late** (kō ag′yə lāt′)  change from liquid form into a thickened mass; thicken; clot: *Cooking coagulates the white of egg. Blood coagulates in air.* *v*.  **co·ag·u·lat·ed, co·ag·u·lat·ing.** —**co·ag′u·la′tor,** *n*.

**co·ag·u·la·tion** (kō ag′yə lā′shən)  **1** the act of coagulating: *If coagulation does not take place after a cut or wound, the injured person may bleed to death.*  **2** a COAGULATED mass. *n*.

**co·ag·u·la·tive** (kō ag′yə lə tiv *or* kō ag′yə lā′tiv)  tending to COAGULATE or cause COAGULATION (def. 1). *adj*.

**coal** (kōl)  **1** a black or brownish-black combustible substance containing varying amounts of carbon, used as a natural fuel and for the manufacture of coal gas, coal tar, etc.: *Coal is a kind of sedimentary rock formed over millions of years from the partial decomposition of vegetable matter away from air and under varying degrees of pressure.*  **2** a piece of coal.  **3** a piece of burning or charred coal, wood, etc.; ember.  **4** charcoal.  **5** supply with or take in coal: *The ship stopped to coal.* 1–4 *n*., 5 *v*.
☞ *Hom.* COLE.

**coal·er** (kōl′ər)  **1** a ship, railway, freight car, etc. used for carrying or supplying coal.  **2** a worker or merchant who supplies coal. *n*.

**co·a·lesce** (kō′ə les′)  **1** grow together.  **2** unite into one body, mass, party, etc.; combine: *Two political groups coalesced to form a new party.* *v*., **co·a·lesced, co·a·lesc·ing.**

**co·a·les·cence** (kō′ə les′əns)  **1** growing together.  **2** a union; combination. *n*.

**co·a·les·cent** (kō′ə les′ənt)  growing together. *adj*.

**coal gas**  **1** a gas made by distilling BITUMINOUS coal, used for heating and lighting.  **2** the gas given off by burning coal.

**coal hod**  COAL SCUTTLE.

**co·a·li·tion** (kō′ə lish′ən)  **1** a union; combination.  **2** a formal arrangement by which statesmen, political parties, etc. agree to work together for a certain period of time or for a special purpose, as, when no one party has a sufficient majority to govern without the aid of another party. *n*.

**coal mine**  a mine or pit where coal is dug from the earth.

**coal oil**  KEROSENE: *Coal-oil lamps are still used in some places where electricity is not available.*

**coal pit**  COAL MINE.

**coal scuttle**  a bucket for holding or carrying coal.

**coal tar**  a dark brown or black, heavy, sticky liquid obtained as a residue after the distillation of BITUMINOUS coal, used especially in making dyes, perfumes, medicines, and explosives.

**coam·ing** (kō′ming)  a raised edge around a hatch or opening in the deck of a ship to prevent water from running down below. See CAPSTAN for picture. *n*.

**coarse** (kôrs)  **1** made up of fairly large parts; not fine: *coarse sand*.  **2** heavy and rough in appearance or texture; not smooth and fine: *Burlap is coarse fabric*.  **3** common; of ordinary or inferior quality: *coarse food. The peasants wore the same coarse clothing, summer and winter.*  **4** rude; rough; vulgar: *coarse manners, a coarse laugh.* *adj.*, **coars·er, coars·est.** —**coarse′ly,** *adv*. —**coarse′ness,** *n*.
☞ *Hom.* COURSE.

**coarse–grained** (kôrs′grānd′)  **1** having a coarse texture; made up of large, coarse fibres.  **2** not delicate or refined; crude. *adj*.

**coars·en** (kôr′sən)  make or become coarse. *v*.

**coast** (kōst)  **1** the land along the sea; seashore.  **2** a region near a coast.  **3** go along or near the coast of.  **4** sail from port to port of a coast.  **5** ride or slide down a hill without using power: *You can coast downhill on a sleigh or bicycle*.  **6** a slope for sliding downhill on a sleigh, etc.  **7** allow a vehicle or vessel to continue to move by its own MOMENTUM.  1, 2, 6 *n*., 3–5, 7 *v*.

**coast·al** (kōs′təl)  of, near, or along a coast: *coastal cities. Those big guns are for coastal defence.* *adj*.

**coastal plain**  a flat stretch of land along a coast.

**coast·er** (kōs′tər)  **1** a person or thing that coasts.  **2** a ship trading along a coast.  **3** a sleigh to coast on.  **4** ROLLER COASTER.  **5** a little tray or decorated mat to hold a glass or bottle. *n*.

**coast guard**  **1** in Canada, a government service responsible mainly for search-and-rescue operations at sea, establishing and maintaining lighthouses, buoys, and other navigation aids, and icebreaking and moving cargo in the North.  **2** a coastal patrol and police whose work is preventing smuggling and protecting lives and property along the coast: *The coast guard is often part of the armed forces of a country*.  **3** a member of such a patrol.

**coasting trade**  **1** the trade carried on by ships between

**coast·land** (kō′stland′) the land along a coast. *n.*

**coast·line** (kō′stlīn′) the outline or contour of a coast: *the rugged coastline of Newfoundland. n.*

**coast·ward** (kō′stwərd) toward the coast. *adv., adj.*

**coast·ways** (kō′stwāz′) COASTWISE. *adv.*

**coast·wise** (kō′stwīz′) along the coast. *adv., adj.*

**coat** (kōt) 1 an outer garment of cloth, fur, etc., with sleeves. 2 an outer covering: *a dog's coat of hair, a coat of bark on a tree.* 3 provide with a coat. 4 a layer covering a surface: *a coat of paint.* 5 cover with a layer: *The old books were coated with dust.* 1, 2, 4 *n.*, 3, 5 *v.* —**coat′less**, *adj.*
☞ Hom. COTE.

**co·a·ti** (kō ä′tē) a small mammal resembling a raccoon, living in Central and South America. *n., pl.* **co·a·tis.**

**coat·ing** (kō′ting) 1 a layer covering a surface: *a coating of paint.* 2 cloth for making coats. 3 ppr. of COAT. 1 *n.*, 2 *v.*

The Canadian coat of arms

**coat of arms** 1 a group of symbols or designs which show the marks of distinction of a noble family, a government, a city, etc.: *In the Middle Ages, each knight or lord had his own coat of arms.* 2 a shield, or drawing of a shield, marked with such symbols or designs. *pl.* **coats of arms.**

A coat of mail

**coat of mail** a garment made of metal rings or plates, worn as armour. *pl.* **coats of mail.**

**co·au·thor** (kō oth′ər) a joint author. *n.*

**coax** (kōks) 1 persuade by soft words; influence by pleasant ways: *She coaxed her father to let her go dancing.* 2 get by coaxing: *The nurse coaxed a smile from the baby.* *v.* —**coax′er**, *n.* —**coax′ing·ly**, *adv.*

**coax·i·al cable** (kō ak′sē əl) a cable containing two or more concentric insulated conductors, used for transmitting computer, telephone, and television signals.

**cob** (kob) 1 the centre part of an ear of corn, on which the kernels grow. 2 a strong horse with short legs, often used for riding. 3 a male swan. *n.*

**co·balt** (kō′bolt) 1 a silver-white metallic element with a pinkish tint that occurs with and is similar to nickel and iron, used especially in alloys and for making pigments. Symbol: Co 2 COBALT BLUE. *n.*
☞ *Etym.* From German *Kobalt*, a variant form of *Kobold*, meaning 'goblin'.

**cobalt blue** 1 a bright-blue pigment made from a mixture of COBALT and aluminum oxides. 2 bright medium blue.

**cobalt 60** a heavy radio-active form of COBALT (def. 1) used as a source of gamma rays for radiotherapy, in industry for detecting flaws in the internal structure of materials, etc.

**cob·ble**[1] (kob′əl) 1 mend shoes, etc.; repair; patch. 2 put together clumsily. *v.*, **cob·bled, cob·bling.** —**cob′bler**, *n.*

**cob·ble**[2] (kob′əl) 1 COBBLESTONE. 2 pave with COBBLESTONES. 1 *n.*, 2 *v.*, **cob·bled, cob·bling.**

**cob·bler** (kob′lər) 1 a fruit pie baked in a deep dish, usually with a crust on top only. 2 an iced drink made of wine, fruit juice, etc. *n.*

**cob·ble·stone** (kob′əl stōn′) a rounded stone that was formerly much used in paving. *n.*

**co·bel·lig·er·ent** (kō′bə lij′ə rənt) a nation that helps another nation carry on a war. *n.*

**CO·BOL** (kō′bol) an abbreviation of *Common Business Oriented Language*, the first computer language designed to handle business transactions. *n.*

**co·bra** (kō′brə) a poisonous snake of Asia and Africa: *A cobra's head and neck can be dilated to assume a hoodlike form. n.*

**cob·web** (kob′web′) 1 a spider's web or the stuff it is made of. 2 anything fine-spun or entangling like a spider's web. *n.*
☞ *Etym.* ME *coppeweb* 'spider web'. A common word for spider in Middle English and early modern English was *spincop* or *coppe*, probably related either to COP 'capture, catch', or OE *cop* 'head'. WEB goes back to OE *webb* 'woven fabric'. See also the note at SPIDER.

**co·ca** (kō′kə) 1 a small tropical shrub growing in South America whose dried leaves are used to make cocaine and other alkaloids. 2 its dried leaves. *n.*

**co·caine** (kō kān′ *or* kō′kān) a drug used to deaden pain and as a stimulant. *n.* Also, **cocain.**

**coc·cus** (kok′əs) 1 a bacterium shaped like a sphere. See BACTERIA for picture. 2 one of the CARPELS making up the compound pistil of such plants as the carrot and celery: *Each coccus contains one seed and breaks away when the fruit is mature. n., pl.* **coc·ci** (kok′sī *or* kok′sē).
☞ Hom. CAUCUS.

**coc·cyx** (kok′siks) a small triangular bone at the lower

end of the spinal column. See SPINAL COLUMN for picture. *n., pl.* **coc·cy·ges** (kok sī′jēz).

**Co·chin** or **co·chin** (kō′chin *or* koch′in) a breed of large domestic fowl developed in Asia, having thickly feathered legs. *n.*

**coch·i·neal** (koch′ə nēl′ *or* koch′ə nēl′) a bright-red dye made from the dried bodies of the females of a scale insect that lives on cactus plants of tropical America. *n.*

**coch·le·a** (kok′lē ə) a spiral-shaped cavity of the inner ear, containing the sensory ends of the auditory nerve. See EAR for picture. *n., pl.* **coch·le·ae** (-lē ē′ *or* -lē ī′).

**cock**[1] (kok) **1** an adult male chicken; rooster. **2** the adult male of other birds. **3** a tap used to turn the flow of a liquid or gas on or off. **4** the hammer of a gun. **5** the position of the hammer of a gun when it is pulled back ready to fire. **6** pull back the hammer of a gun, ready to fire. **7** weathercock. **8** *Informal.* a leader; head; main person: *That big boy thinks he is the cock of the gang.* **1–5, 7, 8** *n.*, **6** *v.*
**cock of the walk,** a person who has power over a group or situation: *It was the first time he had ever been in charge of anything and he really thought he was cock of the walk.*
☛ *Hom.* CALK, CAULK.

**cock**[2] (kok) **1** turn or tilt upward to one side: *The little bird cocked its eye at me. She cocked her ear to listen.* **2** an upward turn or tilt of the nose, eye, or ear. **3** the turn of the brim of a hat. **1** *v.*, **2, 3** *n.*
☛ *Hom.* CALK, CAULK.

**cock**[3] (kok) **1** a small pile of hay, rounded on top. **2** make such piles. **1** *n.*, **2** *v.*
☛ *Hom.* CALK, CAULK.

**cock·ade** (kok ād′) a knot of ribbon or a rosette worn on the hat as a badge. *n.*

**cock·a·too** (kok′ə tü′ *or* kok′ə tü′) any of various large parrots of Australia and the East Indies, having mainly white plumage and a crest on the head. *n., pl.* **cock·a·toos.**

**cock·a·trice** (kok′ə tris) a fabled serpent whose look was supposed to cause death. *n.*

**cock·boat** (kok′bōt′) a small rowboat. *n.*

**cock·chaf·er** (kok′chā′fər) a large European beetle that destroys plants: *The larva of the cockchafer feeds on roots and the adult feeds on the green parts of plants.* *n.*

**cock·er** (kok′ər) COCKER SPANIEL. *n.*

**cock·er·el** (kok′ə rəl) a young rooster not more than one year old. *n.*

**cocker spaniel** a breed of small dog having long, silky hair and drooping ears.

**cock·eyed** (kok′īd) **1** CROSS-EYED. **2** *Informal.* tilting. **3** *Informal.* ridiculous. *adj.*

**cock·fight** (kok′fīt′) a fight between roosters or between gamecocks armed with steel spurs. *n.*

**cock·fight·ing** (kok′fī′ting) fighting by roosters or gamecocks for the sport of spectators. *n.*

**cock·horse** (kok′hôrs′) a child's hobbyhorse; a rocking horse. *n.*

**cock·le**[1] (kok′əl) any of various related saltwater clams having two round convex shells with ridges radiating out from the hinge, especially a common edible European species. *n.*
**cockles of one's heart,** the inmost part of one's heart or feelings: *a welcome that warms the cockles of one's heart.*

**cock·le**[2] (kok′əl) any of several weeds often found in grainfields, especially several plants of the pink family. *n.*

**cock·le·bur** (kok′əl bėr′) any of several closely related plants of the COMPOSITE family found especially along roadsides and in pastures and fields, having spiny burrs. *n.*

**cock·le·shell** (kok′əl shel′) **1** the shell of a COCKLE[1]. **2** a small, light, shallow boat. *n.*

**Cock·ney** or **cock·ney** (kok′nē) **1** a native or inhabitant of the East End of London, England, who speaks a particular dialect. **2** this dialect. **3** of or like this dialect. **4** of or like Cockneys. **1, 2** *n., pl.* **Cock·neys;** **3, 4** *adj.*

**cock·pit** (kok′pit′) **1** a place where the pilot sits in an aircraft. **2** the open place in a boat where the pilot or passengers sit. **3** an enclosed place for cockfights. **4** a scene of many fights or battles: *Belgium is often called the cockpit of Europe.* **5** in former times, rooms below the deck of warships, used as quarters for junior officers, or as a hospital during battle. *n.*

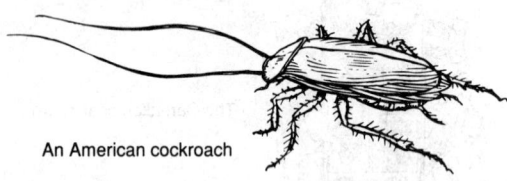

An American cockroach

**cock·roach** (kok′rōch′) any of an order of insects, most of which are active at night, having long feelers and a long, flat, shiny body: *Some species of cockroach are household pests.* *n.*

**cocks·comb** (kok′skōm′) **1** the fleshy, red part on the head of a rooster. See COMB[1] for picture. **2** a pointed cap somewhat like this, worn by a jester or clown. **3** a garden plant of the amaranth family having large, feathery red, orange, or yellow flower heads. *n.*
☛ *Hom.* COXCOMB.

**cock·spur** (kok′spėr′) **1** the spur on the leg of a rooster. **2** a North American hawthorn having side-spreading branches and long, slender thorns. *n.*

**cock·sure** (kok′shur′) **1** too sure; COCKY: *Her cocksure attitude is very irritating.* **2** perfectly sure; absolutely certain: *He hesitated, not being cocksure of his position.* *adj.* —**cock′sure′ness,** *n.*

**cock·swain** (kok′sən *or* kok′swān′) See COXSWAIN. *n.*

**cock·tail** (kok′tāl′) **1** an iced drink, often composed of gin or whisky, mixed with bitters, vermouth, fruit juices, etc. **2** appetizer: *a tomato-juice cocktail.* **3** shellfish served in a small glass with a highly seasoned sauce. **4** mixed fruits, diced and, usually, served in a glass. **5** of, for, or involving the serving and drinking of cocktails: *a cocktail party.* **6** of clothing, semiformal: *a cocktail dress.* *n.*

**cocktail table** COFFEE TABLE.

**cock·y** (kok′ē) *Informal.* conceited; swaggering: *He is a cocky fellow.* *adj.*, **cock·i·er, cock·i·est.**
—**cock′i·ly,** *adv.* —**cock′i·ness,** *n.*

**co·co** (kō′kō)  1 COCONUT PALM.  2 its fruit.  3 made of the fibres of coconut husks: *coco mats.*  *n., pl.* **co·cos.**
☞ *Hom.* COCOA.

**co·coa** (kō′kō)  1 a reddish-brown powder made from chocolate liquor by pressing out most of the fat.  2 a hot drink made from cocoa, milk or water, and sugar.  3 medium reddish brown.  1–3 *n.*, 3 *adj.*
☞ *Hom.* COCO.

**cocoa bean**  the seed of the CACAO.

**cocoa butter**  a yellowish-white fat obtained from chocolate liquor, used in making soap, cosmetics, candy, etc.

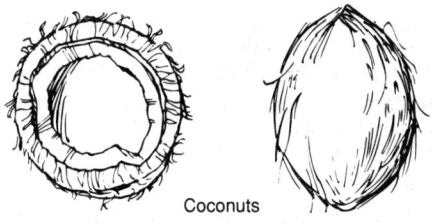
Coconuts

**co·co·nut** (kō′kə nut′)  1 the large, roundish fruit of the COCONUT PALM, having edible white meat in a hard brown shell. The shell of a coconut is enclosed in a thick, fibrous husk which is itself covered by a smooth rind.  2 the meat of the coconut, usually shredded, used as a food or flavouring: *We bought some coconut to sprinkle on top of the cake icing.*  *n.*

**coconut milk**  a sweet liquid found in the hollow centre of an unripe coconut: *Coconut milk is good to drink.*

**coconut oil**  the oil obtained from the dried meat of coconuts, used for making soap, candles, etc.

**coconut palm**  a tall palm tree on which coconuts grow: *The coconut palm has a crown of giant leaves with many leaflets growing along the centre rib.*  See PALM² for picture.

The cocoon of a silkworm

**co·coon** (kə kün′)  1 a covering prepared by the larva of many kinds of insect, including the ant and the moth, to protect itself while it is changing into an adult: *Cocoons are usually of silk fibres produced by the insect, but some kinds include bits of leaves, twigs, etc.*  2 any similar protective covering.  *n.*

**coco palm**  COCONUT PALM.

**cod** (kod)  1 a very important food fish of the colder parts of the northern Atlantic Ocean, having soft fins, a barbel on the chin, and a small, square tail: *The cod is the source of cod-liver oil.*  2 any of several related fishes, especially a closely related Pacific species.  3 referring to a family of fish found in cold and temperate waters, including the cods, haddock, hakes, and pollocks: *Some of the world's most valuable food fishes are in the cod family.*  *n., pl.* **cod** or **cods.**

**C.O.D.** or **c.o.d.**  cash on delivery; collect on delivery.

hat, āge, fär; let, ēqual, tėrm; it, īce
hot, ōpen, ôrder; oil, out; cup, pùt, rüle
əbove, takən, pencəl, lemən, circəs
ch, child; ng, long; sh, ship
th, thin; ᴛʜ, then; zh, measure

**co·da** (kō′də)  in music, a separate and distinct passage at the end of a movement or composition, designed to bring it to a satisfactory close.  *n.*
☞ *Etym.* See note at QUEUE.

**cod·der** (kod′ər) *Cdn.*  in the Maritimes:  1 a boat used for cod fishing.  2 a cod fisherman.  *n.*

**cod·dle** (kod′əl)  1 treat tenderly; pamper: *to coddle sick children.*  2 cook in hot water without boiling: *Eggs are sometimes coddled.*  *v.*, **cod·dled, cod·dling.**

**code** (kōd)  1 a collection of the laws of a country.  2 any set of rules: *A moral code is made up of the notions of right and wrong conduct held by a person, group of persons, or a society.*  3 a system of signals for sending messages by telegraph, flags, etc.: *The Morse code is used in telegraphy.*  4 a system of symbols for representing information in a computer.  5 a system of secret writing; arrangement of words, figures, etc. to keep a message short or secret.  6 change or translate into a code; encode.  1–5 *n.*, 6 *v.* **cod·ed, cod·ing.**
**reveal codes,**  display computer codes on the screen.

**co·deine** (kō′dēn *or* kō′dē in)  a white crystalline drug obtained from opium, used to relieve pain and cause sleep.  *n.*  Also, **codein.**

**co·dex** (kō′deks)  a manuscript; a volume of manuscripts.  *n., pl.* **co·di·ces.**

**cod·fish** (kod′fish′)  COD.  *n., pl.* **cod·fish** or **cod·fish·es.**
**codfish cakes,**  any fried cake made of cod or cod and mashed potato.

**codg·er** (koj′ər) *Informal.*  a peculiar person.  *n.*

**co·di·ces** (kō′də sēz′ *or* kod′ə sēz′)  pl. of CODEX.  *n.*

**cod·i·cil** (kod′ə səl)  1 something added to a will to change it, add to it, or explain it.  2 something added.  *n.*

**cod·i·fi·ca·tion** (kod′ə fə kā′shən *or* kod′ə fə kā′shən)  an arrangement according to a system.  *n.*

**cod·i·fy** (kod′ə fī′ *or* kod′ə fī′)  arrange laws, etc. according to a system: *The laws of France were codified between 1804 and 1810 by order of Napoleon I.*  *v.*, **cod·i·fied, cod·i·fy·ing.**  —**cod′i·fi′er,** *n.*

**cod·lin** (kod′lin)  CODLING.  *n.*

**cod·ling** (kod′ling)  1 a small, unripe apple.  2 a kind of long, tapering apple.  *n.*

**codling moth**  a small moth whose larvae destroy apples, pears, etc.

**cod–liv·er oil** (kod′liv′ər)  the oil extracted from the liver of cod or of related species of fish, used in medicine as a source of vitamins A and D.

**co–ed** or **co·ed** (kō′ed′) *Informal.*  1 a female student at a co-educational school.  2 co-educational.  1 *n.*, 2 *adj.*

**co–ed·u·ca·tion** (kō′ej ù kā′shən)  the education of boys and girls or men and women together in the same school or classes.  *n.*

**co·ed·u·ca·tion·al** (kō′ej u̇ kā′shə nəl) 1 educating boys and girls or men and women together in the same school or classes. 2 having to do with co-education. *adj.* —**co′-ed·u·ca′tion·al·ly**, *adv.*

**co·ef·fi·cient** (kō′ə fish′ənt) a number or symbol put before and multiplying another. In *3x, 3* is the coefficient of *x*; in *axy, a* is the coefficient of *xy*. *n.*

**coe·la·canth** (sē′lə kanth′) any of a group of fishes having rounded scales and lobed fins, considered extinct until 1938 when a live specimen was caught: *A coelacanth is similar to the primitive sea vertebrates that gave rise to all land vertebrates.* *n.*

**coe·len·ter·ate** (si len′tə rāt′) 1 one of a group of saltwater invertebrates with saclike bodies: *Hydras, jellyfish, corals, etc. are coelenterates.* 2 belonging to this group. 1 *n.*, 2 *adj.*

**co·e·qual** (ko ē′kwəl) 1 equal in rank, degree, etc. 2 one that is co-equal. 1 *adj.*, 2 *n.* —**co·e′qual·ly**, *adv.*

**co·erce** (kō ėrs′) 1 compel; force: *The prisoner was coerced into confessing to the crime.* 2 control or restrain by force. *v.*, **co·erced, co·erc·ing.** —**co·erc′er**, *n.*

**co·er·cion** (kō ėr′shən) 1 the use of force; compulsion; constraint. 2 government by force. *n.*

**co·er·cive** (kō ėr′siv) 1 compelling; forcing. 2 restraining. *adj.* —**co·er′cive·ly**, *adv.*

**co·e·val** (kō ē′vəl) 1 of the same age, date, or duration. 2 contemporary. 1, 2 *adj.*, 2 *n.* —**co·e′val·ly**, *adv.*

**co·ex·ist** (kō′eg zist′) exist together or at the same time: *Orange trees have co-existing fruit and flowers.* *v.*

**co·ex·ist·ence** (kō′eg zis′təns) existence together or at the same time. *n.*

**co·ex·ist·ent** (kō′eg zis′tənt) CO-EXISTING. *adj.*

**co·ex·tend** (kō′ek stend′) extend equally or to the same limits. *v.*

**co·ex·ten·sion** (kō′ek sten′shən) 1 extension over an equal amount of space. 2 extension over exactly the same time. *n.*

**co·ex·ten·sive** (kō′ek sten′siv) extending equally; extending over the same space or time. *adj.*

**cof·fee** (kof′ē) 1 a dark-brown drink or flavouring made from the roasted and ground beans of a tall tropical shrub. 2 COFFEE BEANS, especially when roasted and ground: *a kilogram of coffee.* 3 the tall, tropical shrub on which coffee seeds grow. 4 the colour of coffee. 5 a social gathering at which coffee is served. 1–5 *n.*, 4 *adj.*

**coffee bean** the seed of the coffee shrub: *Coffee beans are roasted and ground to make coffee.*

**coffee house** 1 a small, informal restaurant that serves coffee and other refreshments and usually has some live entertainment: *She got her start as a folk singer by singing in coffee houses.* 2 formerly in England, a place where coffee and refreshments were sold, that served as a gathering place for people with similar interests.

**coffee pot** a covered container for making or serving coffee.

**coffee shop** a small, informal restaurant where coffee and other refreshments are served.

**coffee table** a long, low table, usually placed in front of a chesterfield and used for serving refreshments, displaying ornaments or books, etc.

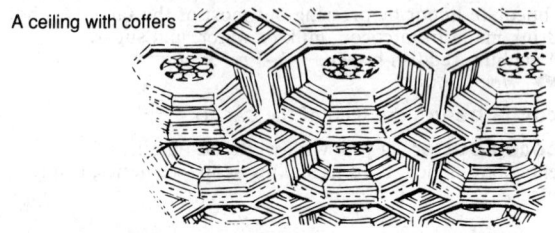
A ceiling with coffers

**cof·fer** (kof′ər) 1 a box, chest, or trunk, especially one used to hold money or other valuable things. 2 an ornamental panel in a ceiling, etc. 3 COFFERDAM. *n.*

**cof·fer·dam** (kof′ər dam′) a watertight enclosure built in a shallow river, lake, etc.: *A cofferdam is pumped dry so that the foundations of a bridge, etc. may be built.* *n.*

**cof·fers** (kof′ərz) treasury; funds. *n. pl.*

**cof·fin** (kof′ən) 1 a box in which a dead person is put to be buried; casket. 2 put into a coffin. 3 shut up tightly. 1 *n.*, 2, 3 *v.*

**cog¹** (kog) 1 one of a series of teeth on the edge of a wheel that transfer motion by locking into the teeth of a similar wheel. 2 a wheel with such a row of teeth on it. 3 a person who plays a small but necessary part in a large and complex organization. *n.*

**cog²** (kog) a projection, or TENON, on a wooden beam, etc. that fits into a hole, or MORTISE, in another beam to form a joint. *n.*

**co·gen·cy** (kō′jən sē) a forcible quality; the power of convincing: *The cogency of his reasoning impressed us all.* *n.*

**co·gent** (kō′jənt) forcible; convincing: *The lawyer's cogent arguments convinced the jury.* *adj.* —**co′gent·ly**, *adv.*

**cogged** (kogd) having COGS. *adj.*

**cog·i·tate** (koj′ə tāt′) think over; consider with care; meditate; ponder. *v.*, **cog·i·tat·ed, cog·i·tat·ing.** —**cog′i·ta′tor**, *n.*

**cog·i·ta·tion** (koj′ə tā′shən) deep thought; careful consideration; pondering; meditation. *n.*

**co·gnac** (kō′nyak; *French,* kô nyȧk′) 1 a brandy produced in Cognac, France. 2 any other kind of brandy. *n.*

**cog·nate** (kog′nāt) 1 related by family or origin: *English, Dutch, and German are cognate languages.* 2 a person, word, or thing related to another by having a common source: *German* Wasser *and English* water *are cognates.* 3 having a similar nature or quality. 1, 3 *adj.*, 2 *n.*

**cog·ni·tion** (kog nish′ən) 1 the mental process by which knowledge is acquired; perception. 2 that which is known, perceived, or recognized. *n.*

**cog·ni·zance** (kog′nə zəns) 1 knowledge; perception; awareness: *The queen had cognizance of plots against her.* 2 in law, an official notice. 3 the right or power to deal with judicially. *n.*

**cog·ni·zant** (kog′nə zənt) aware: *The general was cognizant of the enemy's movements.* *adj.*

**cog·no·men** (kog nō′mən) 1 a surname; family name;

last name. **2** any name, especially a descriptive nickname. *n.*

**cog·wheel** (kog′wēl′ *or* kog′hwēl′) a wheel with teeth cut in the rim that fit with teeth or grooves in another wheel or in a rack or worm so that one can drive the other; gear. See GEAR for picture. *n.*

**co·hab·it** (kō hab′it) **1** live together as husband and wife, especially when not legally married. **2** live in the same place or territory. *v.*

**co·hab·i·ta·tion** (kō hab′ə tā′shən) the act or state of living together as husband and wife, especially when not legally married. *n.*

**co·here** (kō hēr′) **1** stick or hold together as parts of the same mass or substance: *The particles making up a brick cohere.* **2** be connected logically; be consistent. *v.*, **co·hered, co·her·ing.**

**co·her·ence** (kō hēr′əns) **1** a logical connection, consistency. **2** a sticking together; cohesion. *n.*

**co·her·ent** (kō hēr′ənt) **1** logically connected; consistent in structure and thought: *A sentence that is not coherent is hard to understand.* **2** sticking together; holding together. *adj.* —**co·her′ent·ly**, *adv.*

**co·he·sion** (kō hē′zhən) **1** a sticking together; tendency to hold together: *Wet sand has more cohesion than dry sand.* **2** in physics, an attraction between molecules of the same kind, by which the elements of a substance are held together: *The tendency of water to form into drops is a result of cohesion.* Compare with ADHESION (def. 4). *n.*

**co·he·sive** (kō hē′siv) sticking together; tending to hold together. *adj.* —**co·he′sive·ly**, *adv.* —**co·he′sive·ness**, *n.*

**co·ho** (kō′hō) *Cdn.* a species of Pacific salmon found along the coast from southern California to Alaska, metallic blue and silver in colour and having red flesh that fades when cooked: *The coho is very highly valued as a food and game fish.* *n., pl.* **co·hoes** or (*esp. collectively*) **co·ho**. Also, **cohoe**.

**co·hort** (kō′hôrt) **1** in ancient Rome, a part of a legion: *There were from 300 to 600 soldiers in each cohort, and ten cohorts in each legion.* **2** a group or band, especially of soldiers. *n.*

**co·hosh** (kō′hosh) BARBERRY. *n.*

**coif** (koif *for defs. 1 and 2,* kwäf *for defs. 3 and 4*) **1** a cap or hood that fits closely around the head. **2** cover with a coif or something like a coif. **3** COIFFURE. **4** arrange or dress the hair. *1, 3 n., 2, 4 v.*

**coif·fure** (kwä fyür′) a style of arranging the hair. *n.*

**coil** (koil) **1** wind around and around in a series of circles to form a spiral or a tube: *The sailor coiled the rope so it would not take up much space.* **2** form or lie in a series of circles: *The snake coiled around a branch.* **3** one of a series of such circles: *One coil of the rope was smaller than the others.* **4** a series of such circles: *The coil of hose was hung on the wall.* **5** a series of connecting pipes arranged in a coil or row, as in a radiator. **6** a spiral of wire for conducting electricity. **7** move in a winding course. **8** a twist of hair. **9** a small pile of hay rounded on top; cock: *The hay was cut, then piled in coils for drying.* *1, 2, 7 v., 3–6, 8, 9 n.*

**coin** (koin) **1** a piece of metal stamped by a government for use as money: *Nickels, dimes, quarters, and loonies are coins.* **2** metal money: *The Mint makes coin by stamping metal.* **3** make money by stamping metal;

---

**cogwheel**    **231**    **cold**

hat, āge, fär; let, ēqual, tėrm; it, īce
hot, ōpen, ôrder; oil, out; cup, put, rüle
әbove, takәn, pencәl, lemәn, circәs
ch, child; ng, long; sh, ship
th, thin; ᴛʜ, then; zh, measure

mint. **4** make up; invent a word or phrase: *The word* chortle *was coined by Lewis Carroll from* chuckle *and* snort. *1, 2 n., 3, 4 v.*

**coin money,** *Informal.* become rich; have a prospering business: *He is coining money in the oil business.*

**coin·age** (koi′nij) **1** the act or process of coining: *The coinage of money, the coinage of new words.* **2** coins; metal money. **3** a system of coins: *decimal coinage.* **4** a word or phrase that has been made up, or invented. *n.*

**co·in·cide** (kō′in sīd′) **1** occupy the same place in space: *If these triangles △ △ were placed one on top of the other, they would coincide.* **2** occupy the same time; occur at the same time: *The working hours of the two friends coincide.* **3** correspond exactly; agree: *Our opinions coincide.* *v.*, **co·in·cid·ed, co·in·cid·ing.**

**co·in·ci·dence** (kō in′sə dəns) **1** an exact correspondence; agreement; especially, the chance occurrence of two things together in such a way as to seem remarkable, fitting, etc.: *My cousin was born on the very same day that I was. Isn't that a coincidence?* **2** a coinciding; the occupying of the same time or place. *n.*

**co·in·ci·dent** (kō in′sə dənt) **1** coinciding; happening at the same time. **2** occupying the same place or position. **3** in exact agreement (*used with* **with**). *adj.* —**co·in′ci·dent·ly**, *adv.*

**co·in·ci·den·tal** (kō in′sə den′təl) involving or resulting from COINCIDENCE. *adj.* —**co·in′ci·den′tal·ly**, *adv.*

**coin·er** (koi′nər) **1** a person who makes coins. **2** a maker of counterfeit coins. **3** a maker; inventor. *n.*

**coin–op·er·at·ed** (koi′nop′ə rā′təd) worked by inserting a coin or coins: *Coin-operated machines often sell candy, cigarettes, sandwiches, etc.* *adj.*

**co–in·sur·ance** (kō′in shü′rəns) insurance held jointly with another or others. *n.*

**coke** (kōk) **1** a fuel made from soft coal by heating it in a closed oven until the gases have been removed: *Coke burns with much heat and little smoke; it is used in furnaces, for melting metal, etc.* **2** change into coke. *1 n., 2 v.*, **coked, cok·ing.**

**col–** a prefix meaning together or altogether; a form of the prefix **com-** occurring before *l*, as in *collapse.* See note at COM-.

**col.** column.

**co·la** (kō′lə) any of various carbonated soft drinks flavoured with kola nuts, the fruit of a tree related to the cacao tree. *n.*

**col·an·der** (kul′ən dər *or* kol′ən dər) a vessel or dish with many small holes for draining off liquids from foods. *n.*

**col·chi·cum** (kol′chə kəm) **1** a plant with purple or white flowers that resemble crocuses. **2** a medicine for gout, obtained from this plant. *n.*

**cold** (kōld) **1** much less warm than the body: *Snow and ice are cold.* **2** having a relatively low temperature; less warm than desired: *This coffee is cold.* **3** the lack of heat

**cold-blooded** — or warmth; low temperature: *the cold of winter.* **4** not kind and sympathetic; indifferent or unfriendly: *a cold person, a cold greeting.* **5** not influenced by emotion; objective: *cold logic.* **6** faint; weak; not fresh: *a cold trail, a cold scent.* **7** suggesting coolness: *Blue and green are called cold colours.* **8** a common infection that produces a stuffy or running nose and, often, a cough or sore throat. **9** feeling not enough warmth; feeling uncomfortable because of lack of warmth: *She's always complaining that she's cold.* 1, 2, 4–7, 9 *adj.*, 3, 8 *n.*
**catch cold** or **take cold,** become sick with a cold.
**(out) in the cold,** all alone; neglected; ignored: *Most of the neighbourhood children were older than she, so she was often left out in the cold.*
**throw** or **pour cold water on,** actively discourage or belittle: *He was afraid his sister would throw cold water on his bright idea.*

**cold-blood·ed** (kōld′blud′id) **1** having blood whose temperature varies with that of the surroundings: *Snakes and turtles are called cold-blooded creatures, but their blood temperature is actually very close to that of the air or water around them.* **2** feeling the cold because of poor circulation. **3** characterized by a lack of normal feelings of consideration, pity, or kindness; emotionless and cruel: *deliberate, cold-blooded murder. The cold-blooded pirates sold all their captives into slavery.* *adj.*
—**cold′-blood′ed·ly,** *adv.* —**cold′-blood′ed·ness,** *n.*

**cold chisel** a strong, steel chisel for cutting cold metal.

**cold comfort** little or no comfort; something that might be expected to cheer or console but does not, because of particular circumstances or a particular point of view: *She had thirty dollars left for clothes, but that was cold comfort when she wanted the fifty-dollar skirt.*

**cold cream** a creamy, soothing, oil-based salve for softening or cleansing the skin.

**cold cuts** cooked or prepared meats or fowl, such as beef, chicken, salami, or ham, sliced and served cold.

**cold feet** sudden fear or timidity; loss of courage: *He suddenly got cold feet and refused to go on stage.*

**cold frame** a low box with a clear glass or plastic top, built on the ground outdoors and used to protect young or delicate plants from cold while allowing them exposure to sunlight.

**cold front** in meteorology, the front edge of a cold air mass advancing into and replacing a warm one.

**cold-heart·ed** (kōld′här′tid) lacking in feeling; unsympathetic; unkind. *adj.* —**cold′-heart′ed·ly,** *adv.*

**cold light** light without heat: *Phosphorescence and fluorescence are kinds of cold light.*

**cold·ly** (kōld′lē) in a COLD (def. 4) manner; without friendliness, warmth, or sympathy: *She apologized for her rudeness, but she only looked at her coldly and turned away.* *adv.*

**cold·ness** (kōld′nis) **1** the state or quality of being cold. **2** a lack of warmth of feeling or friendliness; indifference. *n.*

**cold shoulder** *Informal.* deliberately unfriendly or indifferent treatment; conscious neglect: *The new friends were plotting something together and gave us the cold shoulder.*

**cold–shoul·der** (kōld′shōl′dər) *Informal.* treat in an unfriendly or indifferent way. *v.*

**cold snap** a sudden spell of cold weather.

**cold sore** a sore on or near the lips, often accompanying a cold or fever, consisting of a group of small blisters that break and form a crust before they begin to heal: *Cold sores are caused by a virus.*

**cold steel** a steel weapon, such as a knife or sword.

**cold storage** storage in a very cold place: *Perishable foods are put in cold storage to keep them from spoiling.*

**cold sweat** perspiration caused by fear or nervousness: *She broke out in a cold sweat just thinking about her narrow escape.*

**cold war** a kind of war in which military weapons are not used, but attempts are made to create fear and suspicion by restrictions on trade and travel, increased movements of troops, and the breaking of diplomatic contacts.

**cold wave¹** a period of very cold weather.

**cold wave²** a process by which hair is pressed into permanent waves or curls by the application of chemicals rather than heat.

**cole** (kōl) any of various plants belonging to the same family as the cabbage, especially rape. *n.*
☛ Hom. COAL.

**co·le·op·ter·ous** (kō′lē op′tə rəs) belonging to a group of insects including beetles and weevils: *In this coleopterous group the front pair of wings is horny, serving to sheathe the second and membranous pair.* *adj.*

**cole·slaw** (kōl′slo′) a salad made of shredded raw cabbage. *n.*

**co·le·us** (kō′lē əs) any of a closely related group of tropical plants of the mint family, grown for their showy, colourful leaves. *n., pl.* **co·le·us.**

**cole·wort** (kōl′wėrt′) **1** COLE. **2** any kind of cabbage having a loosely packed head of curly leaves, such as KALE. *n.*

**col·ic** (kol′ik) severe pains in the abdomen resulting from muscular spasms. *n.*

**col·ick·y** (kol′ik ē) **1** of COLIC. **2** having COLIC. *adj.*

**col·i·se·um** (kol′ə sē′əm) **1** a large building or stadium for games, contests, etc. **2 Coliseum,** See COLOSSEUM. *n.*

**co·li·tis** (kō lī′tis) inflammation of the COLON², often causing severe pain in the abdomen. *n.*

**col·lab·o·rate** (kə lab′ə rāt′) **1** work together: *Two authors collaborated on that book.* **2** aid or co-operate traitorously: *to collaborate with the enemy.* *v.,* **col·lab·o·rat·ed, col·lab·o·rat·ing.**

**col·lab·o·ra·tion** (kə lab′ə rā′shən) the act of collaborating. *n.*

**col·lab·o·ra·tor** (kə lab′ə rā′tər) **1** a person who works with another, usually in literary work. **2** a person who aids or co-operates traitorously. *n.*

**col·lage** (kə läzh′) a picture made by pasting on a background an arrangement of items with different textures, colours, and shapes, such as portions of photographs, newspapers, fabric, string, etc. *n.*
☛ Etym. From F *collage* 'gluing', formed from *colle* 'glue' which originally came from Gk. *kolla* 'glue'.

**col·lapse** (kə laps′) **1** fall down or in suddenly as a result of outside pressure or loss of support; cave in: *They escaped from the burning building just before it collapsed. A football will collapse if the air leaks out.* **2** a falling in or down; a sudden giving away: *A heavy flood caused the collapse of the bridge.* **3** break down; fail suddenly: *Both his health and his business collapsed within a year.* **4** a breakdown; failure: *She is suffering from a mental collapse.* **5** fold or push together: *to collapse a telescope.* 1, 3, 5 *v.*, **col·lapsed, col·laps·ing;** 2, 4 *n.*

**col·laps·i·ble** (kə lap′sə bəl) made so that it can be folded or pushed into a smaller space: *Some umbrellas are collapsible.* *adj.*

**col·lar** (kol′ər) **1** a piece or band of cloth that finishes or is attached to the neckline of a garment, designed to stand up around the neck or lie folded over at the base of the neck, sometimes extending over the shoulders. **2** a piece of jewellery resembling a collar worn around the neck or over the chest and shoulders. **3** a leather or metal band for the neck of a dog or other pet animal. **4** a thick, padded oval ring that forms part of the harness of a draft animal, fitting around the neck and resting against the shoulders and chest: *A horse's collar bears the weight of the load it is pulling.* See HARNESS for picture. **5** a distinctive marking around the neck of an animal or bird, suggesting a collar: *The cliff swallow has a dark blue head and back and a grey collar around the back of the neck.* **6** a ring, disk, or flange on a rod, shaft, etc. that keeps a part from moving to the side. **7** a short pipe connecting two other pipes. **8** put a collar on. **9** *Informal.* capture or seize. 1–7 *n.*, 8, 9 *v.*
—**col′lar·less** *adj.* —**col′lar·like′**, *adj.*
☛ *Hom.* CALLER, CHOLER.

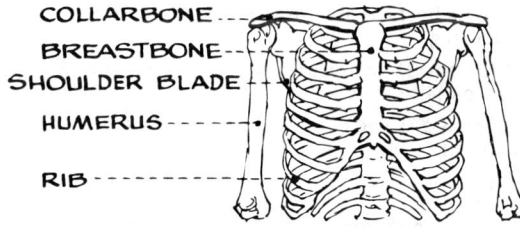

Part of the upper human skeleton, shown from the front

**col·lar·bone** (kol′ər bōn′) the bone connecting the breastbone and the shoulder blade; clavicle. See ARM¹ for another picture. *n.*

**col·late** (kə lāt′ *or* kol′āt) **1** examine and compare carefully in order to note similarities and differences, check for accuracy, etc.: *to collate a copy of a document with the original, to collate the data from several experiments.* **2** arrange in proper order; put together in sequence: *to collate the pages of a report, to collate the sections of a book for binding.* *v.*, **col·lat·ed, col·lat·ing.**
—**col·la′tor,** *n.*

**col·lat·er·al** (kə lat′ə rəl) **1** parallel; side by side. **2** secondary; indirect; related but less important. **3** in a parallel line of descent; descended from the same ancestors, but in a different line: *Cousins are collateral relatives.* **4** a collateral relative. **5** additional. **6** stocks, bonds, etc. pledged as security for a loan. **7** secured by stocks, bonds, etc.: *a collateral loan.* 1–3, 5, 7 *adj.*, 4, 6 *n.* —**col·lat′er·al·ly,** *adv.*

**col·la·tion** (kə lā′shən) **1** a light meal. **2** collating; a careful comparison. *n.*

**collapse** **233** **collectivist**

hat, āge, fär; let, ēqual, tėrm; it, īce
hot, ōpen, ôrder; oil, out; cup, pu̇t, rüle
əbove, takən, pencəl, lemən, circəs
ch, child; ng, long; sh, ship
th, thin; ᴛʜ, then; zh, measure

**col·league** (kol′ēg) an associate or fellow worker: *The doctor asked a colleague to examine the patient.* *n.*

**col·lect** (kə lekt′) **1** gather together; pick up: *The teacher collected the questionnaires.* **2** come together in one place; assemble: *A crowd soon collects at the scene of an accident.* **3** pile up; form into a mass; accumulate: *Drifting snow collects behind snow fences.* **4** gather together as a hobby: *to collect stamps.* **5** ask and receive payment for bills, debts, dues, taxes, etc. **6** to be paid for by the recipient: *a collect telegram* (adj.). *Telephone him collect* (adv.). **7** regain control of: *After a shock a person must collect herself and her thoughts.* 1–5, 7 *v.*, 6 *adj., adv.*

**col·lect·a·ble** *or* **col·lect·i·ble** (kə lek′tə bəl) **1** that may be collected. **2** anything having a current attraction for collectors; an item that might be part of a collection, especially something other than an antique or work of art, or traditionally collected items such as coins or stamps: *a store window full of old picture frames, bottles, and other collectables.* 1 *adj.*, 2 *n.*

**col·lect·ed** (kə lek′tid) **1** brought together; gathered together: *the author's collected works.* **2** not confused or disturbed; calm; in control of one's emotions. **3** pt. and pp. of COLLECT (defs. 1–5, 7). 1, 2 *adj.*, 3 *v.*
—**col·lect′ed·ly,** *adv.* —**col·lect′ed·ness,** *n.*

**col·lect·i·ble** (kə lek′tə bəl) See COLLECTABLE. *adj., n.*

**col·lec·tion** (kə lek′shən) **1** bringing together: *The collection of these stamps took ten years.* **2** a group of things gathered from many places and belonging together: *a large collection of books.* **3** a collecting of money, especially for charity. **4** the money collected: *The collection was larger than expected.* **5** something that has come together in one place; accumulation; heap: *There was a collection of debris on the porch.* *n.*

**col·lec·tive** (kə lek′tiv) **1** of a group; as a group; taken all together: *a collective effort, a collective decision.* **2** COLLECTIVE NOUN. **3** formed by collecting. **4** a farm, factory, or other organization with COLLECTIVISTIC management. 1, 3 *adj.*, 2, 4 *n.* —**col·lec′tive·ly,** *adv.*

**collective bargaining** negotiation about wages, hours, and other working conditions between workers organized as a group and their employer or employers.

**collective noun** in grammar, a noun that is singular in form but refers to a collection of things or persons: *Crowd, team, bunch,* and *orchestra* are collective nouns.
☛ *Usage.* A collective noun is used with a singular verb when it refers to a group as a whole (*The committee was silent*), but with a plural verb when it refers to a group in which the individuals are thought of as acting separately (*The committee were asked to prepare separate reports*).

**col·lec·tiv·ism** (kə lek′ti viz′əm) the control of the production of goods and services and the distribution of wealth by people as a group or by the government. *n.*

**col·lec·tiv·ist** (kə lek′ti vist) **1** a person who favours or supports COLLECTIVISM. **2** COLLECTIVISTIC. 1 *n.*, 2 *adj.*

**col·lec·tiv·is·tic** (kə lek′ti vis′tik) of COLLECTIVISM or COLLECTIVISTS. *adj.*

**col·lec·tor** (kə lek′tər) **1** a person who collects things as a hobby: *a coin collector.* **2** something that collects or appears to collect: *All these ornaments are just dust collectors.* **3** a person hired to collect money owed: *a debt collector.* **4** in a vacuum tube, the positive electrode that attracts electrons from the emitter. See VACUUM TUBE for picture. *n.*

**collector's item** something worth adding to a collection.

**col·leen** (kol′ēn *or* kə lēn′) *Irish.* girl. *n.*

**col·lege** (kol′ij) **1** an institution that offers training or instruction in one or more particular occupations or professions and gives degrees or diplomas: *the Victoria College of Art. My cousin is taking a course in computer programming at a community college.* **2** *Informal.* university: *She's planning to go to college in the fall.* **3** an institution within a university, either offering undergraduate courses in particular subject areas or organized as a social and residential unit with courses in a limited range of subjects: *Students at Erindale College get their degrees from the University of Toronto.* **4** an organized association of persons having certain powers, rights, duties, and purposes: *the College of Cardinals.* **5** a building or buildings used by a college. **6** of or associated with college or university: *college songs, college boys.* *n.*

**col·le·giate** (kə lē′jit) **1** *Cdn.* COLLEGIATE INSTITUTE. **2** *Cdn. Informal.* any high school or secondary school. **3** *Cdn.* of or like a high school or high-school students. **4** of or like a college: *collegiate life.* **5** of or like college students: *collegiate pranks.* 1, 2 *n.,* 3–5 *adj.*

**collegiate institute** *Cdn.* in some provinces, a secondary school providing specified facilities, or having a set minimum number of specialist teachers, over and above those required in a high school.

**col·lide** (kə līd′) **1** come violently into contact; come together with force; crash: *Two large ships collided in the harbour.* **2** clash; conflict. *v.,* **col·lid·ed, col·lid·ing.**

A collie - about 60 cm high at the shoulder

**col·lie** (kol′ē *or* kō′lē) a large, long-haired breed of dog having a long, pointed nose and a bushy tail: *Collies came originally from Scotland where they were trained to tend sheep.* *n.*

**col·lier** (kol′yər) **1** a ship for carrying coal. **2** a coal miner. *n.*

**col·lier·y** (kol′yə rē) a COAL MINE and its buildings and equipment. *n., pl.* **col·lier·ies.**

**col·lin·e·ar** (kə lin′ē ər) **1** lying on the same line. **2** having a common AXIS (def. 2). *adj.*

**col·li·sion** (kə lizh′ən) **1** a violent rushing against; a hitting or striking violently together: *an automobile collision.* **2** a clash; conflict: *a collision of ideas.* *n.*

**col·lo·cate** (kol′ō kāt′) **1** place together. **2** arrange. *v.,* **col·lo·cat·ed, col·lo·cat·ing.**

**col·lo·ca·tion** (kol′ō kā′shən) arrangement: *the collocation of words in a phrase or sentence.* *n.*

**col·lo·di·on** (kə lō′dē ən) a glue-like solution of cellulose nitrate in ether and alcohol that dries very rapidly, leaving a tough, waterproof, transparent film: *Collodion is used for covering burns and wounds.* *n.*

**col·loid** (kol′oid) **1** a solid, liquid, or gaseous substance made up of very small particles, such as single large molecules or groups of smaller molecules, that will remain suspended without dissolving in a different medium: *A colloid may be suspended in a solid, liquid, or gas.* **2** a state of matter consisting of such a substance together with the medium in which it is suspended: *Fog and the protoplasm of plant and animal cells are colloids.* *n.*

**col·loi·dal** (kə loi′dəl) **1** in the form of a COLLOID. **2** of, like, or containing a COLLOID. *adj.*

**colloq. 1** colloquial. **2** colloquialism.

**col·lo·qui·al** (kə lō′kwē əl) used in everyday, informal talk, but not in formal speech or writing. *Beat all hollow* is a colloquial expression. *adj.* —**col·lo′qui·al·ly,** *adv.*

**col·lo·qui·al·ism** (kə lō′kwē ə liz′əm) **1** a COLLOQUIAL word or phrase. **2** a COLLOQUIAL style or usage. *n.*

**col·lo·quy** (kol′ə kwē) a talking together; conversation; conference. *n., pl.* **col·lo·quies.**

**col·lude** (kə lüd′) act together through a secret understanding; conspire in a fraud. *v.,* **col·lud·ed, col·lud·ing.**

**col·lu·sion** (kə lü′zhən) a secret agreement for some wrong purpose. *n.*

**col·lu·sive** (kə lü′siv) involving COLLUSION; fraudulent. *adj.* —**col·lu′sive·ly,** *adv.*

**co·logne** (kə lōn′) a fragrant liquid, not so strong as perfume. *n.*
☞ *Etym.* A shortening of *cologne water,* which is a translation of F *eau de Cologne.* Cologne, a city in West Germany, is where it was first made.

**Co·lom·bi·an** (kə lum′bē ən) **1** a native or inhabitant of Colombia, a country in northwestern South America. **2** of or having to do with Colombia or its people. 1 *n.,* 2 *adj.*

**co·lon**[1] (kō′lən) a mark (:) of punctuation used after an introductory sentence or definition to show that a list, explanation, illustration, long quotation, etc. follows. *n.*

**co·lon**[2] (kō′lən) the main part of the large intestine, from the caecum to the rectum. See ALIMENTARY CANAL for picture. *n., pl.* **co·lons** or **co·la** (kō′lə).

**colo·nel** (kėr′nəl) in the armed forces, a commissioned officer ranking below a brigadier-general and above a lieutenant-colonel: *A colonel usually commands a regiment.* *n.*
☞ *Hom.* KERNEL.
☞ *Pronunciation.* In the 16c. there were two parallel spellings, *colonel* and *coronel,* each with its own pronunciation. The modern pronunciation (kėr′nəl) comes from the *coronel* form, though the spelling became established as *colonel.*

**colo·nel·cy** (kėr′nəl sē) the rank, commission, or authority of a COLONEL. *n., pl.* **colo·nel·cies.**

**co·lo·ni·al** (kə lō′nē əl) **1** of or having to do with a COLONY or colonies. **2** of the time when a nation was a COLONY: *colonial furniture*. **3** a person living in a COLONY. **4** having to do with a group of similar bacteria or of similar plants or animals. **5** one of such a group. 1, 2, 4 *adj.*, 3, 5 *n.* —**co·lo′ni·al·ly,** *adv.*

**col·o·nist** (kol′ə nist) **1** a person who helps to found a COLONY. **2** a person who lives in a COLONY during the period of settlement; settler. *n.*

**colonist car** *Cdn.* formerly, a railway coach having wooden seats and rough berths for sleeping, sometimes also having cooking facilities.

**col·o·ni·za·tion** (kol′ə nə zā′shən *or* kol′ə nī zā′shən) the establishment of a COLONY or colonies: *The English, French, Dutch, and Spanish all took part in the colonization of North America.* *n.*

**col·o·nize** (kol′ə nīz′) establish a COLONY or colonies in: *French fishermen colonized this coast. France colonized parts of Canada before England did.* *v.*, **col·o·nized, col·o·niz·ing.** —**col′o·niz′er,** *n.*

**col·on·nade** (kol′ə nād′) a series of columns set the same distance apart. *n.*

**col·o·ny** (kol′ə nē) **1** a group of people who leave their own country and go to settle in another land, but who still remain citizens of their own country. **2** the settlement made by such a group of people. **3** a territory distant from the country that governs it: *Under Queen Victoria, the United Kingdom added to its colonies in Africa and Asia.* **4** a group of people of one country, faith, or occupation living as a group: *an artists' colony. There is a large Chinese colony in Vancouver. There are several Doukhobor colonies in British Columbia.* **5** a group of animals or plants of the same kind, living or growing together: *a colony of ants. A coral island is a colony.* **6 the Colonies, a** the thirteen British colonies that became the United States of America: New Hampshire, Massachusetts, Rhode Island, Connecticut, New York, New Jersey, Pennsylvania, Delaware, Maryland, Virginia, North Carolina, South Carolina, and Georgia. **b** formerly, the colonies, as opposed to self-governing dominions, within the British Empire. *n., pl.* **col·o·nies.**

**color** See COLOUR. *n., v.*

**col·o·ra·tu·ra** (kul′ə rə tyü′rə *or* kul′ə rə tü′rə) **1** in music, ornamental passages such as trills, runs, etc. **2** characterized by or suitable for such ornamental passages. **3** vocal music having ornamental passages. **4** a soprano who specializes in singing such music. *n.*

**co·los·sal** (kə los′əl) **1** huge; gigantic; vast: *a colossal statue, explosion, etc.* **2** *Informal.* remarkable; outstanding: *a colossal blunder. Her new film is colossal.* *adj.* —**co·los′sal·ly,** *adv.*

**Col·os·se·um** (kol′ə sē′əm) in Rome, a large outdoor theatre, completed in A.D. 80: *The Colosseum was used for games and contests.* *n.* Also, **Coliseum.**

**co·los·sus** (kə los′əs) **1** a huge statue. **2** anything huge; gigantic person or thing. *n., pl.* **co·los·sus** or **co·los·si** (-los′ī *or* -los′ē).

**col·our** or **col·or** (kul′ər) **1** a sensation produced by the effect of waves of light striking the retina of the eye: *Different colours are produced by rays of light having different wave lengths.* **2** any colour other than black, white, or grey; chromatic colour: *Most of the photographs are in colour.* **3** give colour to; put colour on; change the colour of. **4** a paint, dye, or pigment: *oil colours.* **5** the natural healthy colour of a person's face: *The colour drained from his face and we thought he would faint.*
**6** become red in the face; blush. **7** a flush caused by blushing: *The colour rushed to her face when her mistake was pointed out.* **8** the colour of a person's skin due to pigment. **9** an outward appearance; show: *His lies had some colour of truth.* **10** present so as to give a wrong idea: *The general coloured his report of the battle to make his own mistake seem the fault of his officers.* **11** vividness; a distinguishing quality: *Her gift for description adds colour to her stories.* **12** give a distinguishing quality to; affect: *Her report was coloured by her desire to impress the audience. Love of nature coloured all of Sir Charles Roberts' writing.* **13 colours** or **colors,** a badge, ribbon, dress, etc. worn to show allegiance. **14 the colours** or **colors, a** the flag of a nation, regiment, etc.: *She carried the colours in the parade.* **b** the ceremony of raising the flag in the morning and lowering it in the evening. **c** the army, navy, or air force: *Soldiers, sailors, and airmen serve with the colours.* 1, 2, 4, 5, 7–9, 11, 13, 14 *n.*, 3, 6, 10, 12 *v.*

**change colour** or **color,** react by becoming either pale or red in the face: *She took the news calmly and didn't even change colour.*

**lose colour** or **color,** become pale: *He lost a lot of colour during his illness.*

**show one's true colours** or **colors,** show oneself as one really is: *In the fight, the bully showed his true colours and ran away.*

**with flying colours** or **colors,** with great success; triumphantly: *She passed the examination with flying colours.*

**col·our·a·tion** or **col·or·a·tion** (kul′ə rā′shən) a colouring; way in which something is coloured: *The coloration of some animals is like that of their surroundings.* *n.*

**colour bar** or **color bar 1** the denial, especially to Blacks, of rights, privileges, and opportunities enjoyed by white people. **2** the denial of rights, privileges, and opportunities to anyone on the grounds of skin colour.

**colour bearer** or **color bearer** a person who carries the flag or colours; standardbearer.

**col·our-blind** or **col·or-blind** (kul′ər blīnd′) unable to tell certain colours apart; unable to perceive certain colours or, in certain cases, any colours. *adj.* —**col′our-blind′ness** or **col′or-blind′ness,** *n.*

**col·our-code** or **col·or-code** (kul′ər kōd′) use standard colours as a means of identification: *Colour-coded wires are used in electrical systems.* *v.*, **col·our-cod·ed** or **col·or-cod·ed, col·our-cod·ing** or **col·or-cod·ing.**

**col·oured** or **col·ored** (kul′ərd) **1** having colour; not black, white, grey, or clear: *coloured water. He prefers coloured shirts to white ones.* **2** having a certain colour: *red-coloured leaves.* **3** tinged by emotion, prejudice, desire for effect, etc.: *The newspaper published a coloured account of the political convention.* **4** pt. and pp. of COLOUR (defs. 3, 6, 10, 12). 1–3 *adj.*, 4 *v.*

**colour film** or **color film 1** a film for making photographs in colour. **2** a motion picture made with such film.

**col·our·ful** or **col·or·ful** (kul′ər fəl)  1 abounding in colour: *a colourful garden, a colourful design.*  2 picturesque; vivid: *a colourful description.*  *adj.*  —**col′our·ful·ly** or **col′or·ful·ly,** *adv.*  —**col′our·ful·ness** or **col′or·ful·ness,** *n.*

**col·our·ing** or **col·or·ing** (kul′ə ring)  1 the pattern, kind, or degree of colour or colours that a person or thing has: *Her colouring is much better since her health improved.*  2 a substance used to colour something; pigment.  3 a false appearance: *His lies have a colouring of truth.*  4 ppr. of COLOUR.  1–3 *n.*, 4 *v.*

**colouring matter** or **coloring matter**  a substance used to colour something; pigment.

**col·our·less** or **col·or·less** (kul′ər lis)  1 without colour.  2 without excitement or variety; uninteresting: *a colourless personality.*  *adj.*  —**col′our·less·ly** or **col′or·less·ly,** *adv.*  —**col′our·less·ness** or **col′or·less·ness,** *n.*

**colour photography** or **color photography**  photography using colour film.

**colt** (kōlt)  1 a young horse, donkey, etc., especially a male horse under four or five years old.  2 a young or inexperienced person.  *n.*

**col·ter** (kōl′tər)  See COULTER.  *n.*

**colt·ish** (kōl′tish)  like a colt; lively; frisky.  *adj.*

**colts·foot** (kōlt′sfut)  a common European perennial plant of the COMPOSITE family, having heart-shaped leaves and yellow daisy-like flowers.  *n.*

**col·um·bine** (kol′əm bīn′)  any of a closely related group of perennial plants of the buttercup family having showy drooping flowers with five petals each forming a wide-mouthed tube ending in a hooked spur pointing upward: *Several species of columbine grow wild in Canada.*  *n.*

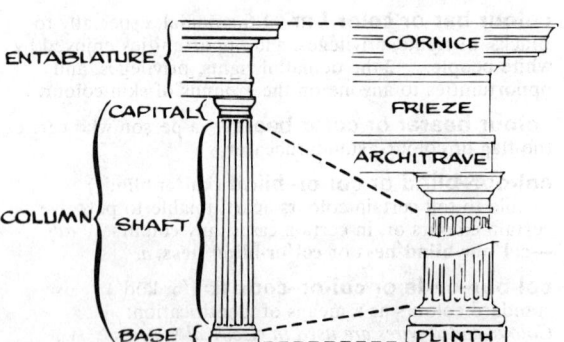

**col·umn** (kol′əm)  1 a slender, upright structure; pillar: *Columns are usually made of stone, wood, or metal, and are used mainly as supports or ornaments to a building. Sometimes a column stands alone as a monument.*  See ORDER for another picture.  2 anything that seems slender and upright like a column: *a column of smoke, a long column of figures.*  3 in the armed forces, an arrangement of persons in rows one behind another.  4 a line of ships or aircraft one behind another.  5 a narrow division of a page reading from top to bottom, kept separate by a line or a blank space: *A newspaper often has eight columns on a page.*  6 a part of a newspaper used for a special subject or written by a special writer: *the children's column.*  *n.*

**co·lum·nar** (kə lum′nər)  1 like a column.  2 made of columns.  3 written or printed in columns.  *adj.*

**col·umned** (kol′əmd)  1 having columns.  2 formed into columns: *columned porches.*  *adj.*

**col·um·nist** (kol′ə mist *or* kol′əm nist)  a person who writes or selects the material for a special column in a newspaper.  *n.*

**com-**  a prefix meaning:  1 with; together: *Commingle* means mingle with one another. *Compress* means press together.  2 altogether; completely: *Comprehend* means to grasp the meaning completely.  The form **com-** (from L *com-,* meaning 'with, together', etc.) is the basic form of this prefix but **com-** occurs only before the consonants *b, m* and *p,* and sometimes also before *f* (as in **comfort**). In other situations we find **co-** before vowels and *h* (**co-operate, cohabit**); **col-** before *l* (**collaborate**); **cor-** before *r* (**correlate**). In all other cases the form **con-** is used (**concoct, conduct, congest, connote, conserve, context, convert,** etc.). Occasionally **con-** also occurs before *f* (**confer, confirm, confluent, conform, confuse**).

**co·ma**¹ (kō′mə)  a prolonged unconsciousness caused by disease, injury, or poison; stupor.  *n., pl.* **co·mas.**

**co·ma**² (kō′mə)  a cloudlike mass around the nucleus of a COMET.  *n., pl.* **co·mae** (-mē *or* mī).

**com·a·tose** (kom′ə tōs′)  in a stupor or COMA¹; unconscious.  *adj.*

The comb of a rooster    A comb for hair

**comb**¹ (kōm)  1 a narrow, short, often somewhat flexible strip of metal, rubber, etc. with teeth, used to arrange or clean the hair or to hold it in place.  2 anything shaped or used like a comb: *One kind of comb cleans and takes out the tangles in wool or flax.*  3 CURRYCOMB.  4 arrange, clean, or take out tangles in, with a comb: *George combs his dog's fur every week.*  5 search through; look everywhere in: *We had to comb the whole city before we found our lost dog.*  6 the thick, red, fleshy piece on the top of the head in some fowls.  7 HONEYCOMB (def. 1).  8 roll over or break at the top: *The big waves combed as they neared the shore.*  9 the top of a wave rolling over or breaking.  1–3, 6, 7, 9 *n.*, 4, 5, 8 *v.*  —**comb′like′,** *adj.*

**comb**² (kum *or* kōm)  See COMBE.  *n.*

**com·bat** (kom′bat; *also* kəm bat′ *for verb*)  1 fight against; struggle with: *Doctors combat disease.*  2 fighting between opposing armed forces; battle: *Bombing planes flew over as we entered the combat. My grandfather was wounded in combat.*  3 designed for or used in combat: *combat training, combat boots.*  4 any fight or struggle.  1 *v.*, **com·bat·ted** or **com·bat·ed, com·bat·ting** or **com·bat·ing;**  2–4 *n.*

**com·ba·tant** (kəm bat′ənt *or* kom′bə tənt)  1 a fighter, especially a member of the armed forces who takes part in the actual combat.  2 battling; fighting.  3 ready to fight; fond of fighting.  1 *n.*, 2, 3 *adj.*

**combat fatigue** a state of mental exhaustion that sometimes occurs among soldiers as a result of warfare in the front lines.

**com·bat·ive** (kəm bat′iv *or* ˌkom′bə tiv) ready to fight or oppose; fond of fighting. *adj.* —**com·bat′ive·ly,** *adv.* —**com·bat′ive·ness,** *n.*

**combe** or **comb** (küm *or* kōm) a narrow valley; a deep hollow surrounded on three sides by hills. *n.*

**comb·er** (kō′mər) **1** a person or thing that combs wool, flax, etc. **2** a wave that rolls over or breaks at the top; BREAKER (def. 1). *n.*

**com·bi·na·tion** (kom′bə nā′shən) **1** combining or being combined; union: *The combination of flour and water makes paste.* **2** one whole made by combining two or more different things. **3** persons or groups joined together for some common purpose. **4** a series of numbers or letters followed in opening or closing a certain kind of lock: *the combination of a safe.* See COMBINATION LOCK. **5** a suit of underwear having the shirt and drawers in one piece. **6** in mathematics, the arrangement of individuals in groups so that each group has a certain number of individuals; the groups thus formed. Possible combinations of *a*, *b*, and *c* are *ab*, *ac*, and *bc*. **7** a union of substances to form a chemical compound. **8** PERMUTATION. *n.*

**combination lock** a lock that is opened either by turning a dial through a pre-selected sequence of numbers or by setting a series of dials at pre-selected numbers. Turning the dial or dials to the correct position aligns the tumblers inside so that the locking mechanism can be released.

**combination square** a carpenter's measuring instrument, usually in the shape of a scalene triangle, which is a combination of an adjustable TRY SQUARE with a SPIRIT LEVEL: *Combination squares are used to check mitre joints and surface levels.* See SQUARE for picture.

**com·bine** (kəm bīn′ *for 1, 5,* kom′bīn *for 2, 3, 4*) **1** join two or more things together; unite: *to combine work and play.* **2** a group of people joined together for business or political purposes: *The companies formed a combine to keep prices up.* **3** a machine that cuts and threshes grain in one operation: *A combine separates the seeds from the stalks as it moves across a field.* **4** use a combine: *We combined the wheat last week.* **5** unite to form a chemical compound: *Two atoms of hydrogen combine with one of oxygen to form water.* 1, 4, 5 *v.*, **com·bined, com·bin·ing;** 2, 3 *n.* —**com·bin′a·ble,** *adj.*

**com·bined** (kəm bīnd′) **1** joined together; united. **2** done by groups, persons, etc. acting together: *a combined effort.* **3** pt. and pp. of COMBINE (defs. 1, 4, 5). 1, 2 *adj.*, 3 *v.*

**combining form** a form of a word used for combining with other words or word elements, suffixes or prefixes. *Examples:* multi-, *as in* multilingual *and* multimillionaire; -phone, *as in* telephone *and* Anglophone.

**com·bus·ti·bil·i·ty** (kəm bus′tə bil′ə tē) a COMBUSTIBLE (def. 1) quality or condition; inflammability. *n.*

**com·bus·ti·ble** (kəm bus′tə bəl) **1** capable of taking fire and burning; easily burned: *Gasoline is highly combustible.* **2** a combustible substance. **3** easily excited; fiery. 1, 3, *adj.*, 2 *n.*

**com·bus·tion** (kəm bus′chən) **1** the act or process of burning: *The explosion in the coal mine was caused by the combustion of gases.* **2** a rapid oxidation accompanied by high temperature and, usually, by light. **3** a slow oxidation not accompanied by high temperature and light: *The cells of the body transform food into energy by combustion.* *n.*

**come** (kum) **1** move toward; approach: *Come this way.* **2** reach a particular place in space or time; arrive: *We come now to a different kind of poem. The time has come for us to decide. The girls come home today.* **3** appear: *Light comes and goes.* **4** reach; extend: *The dress comes to her knees.* **5** progress (Often used with **along**): *She's coming along well now. How is your project coming?* **6** arrive, happen, or belong at a certain position in a series: *She came second in the high jump. V comes after U in the alphabet.* **7** happen; take place; occur: *No harm will come to him.* **8** be caused; result: *You see what comes of meddling.* **9** be derived; originate: *He comes of a poor family. Milk comes from cows.* **10** turn out to be; become: *His dream came true.* **11** enter or be brought into a particular state or condition: *to come into use. My shoelace came undone. When will you come to your senses?* **12** occur to the mind: *The solution of the problem has just come to me.* **13** be available or obtainable: *This sweater comes in white and yellow.* **14** amount or add up (*to*): *The bill comes to $100.* **15** here! look! stop! (*used to express irritation or impatience*). 1–14 *v.*, **came, come, com·ing;** 15 *interj.*
**come about,** take place; happen: *Their meeting came about by accident.*
**come across, a** meet or find by chance: *We came across some of my old toys when we were cleaning out the basement yesterday.* **b** have the desired effect; succeed: *The actor's attempt to portray terror didn't come across.* **c** *Informal.* give an impression of; appear: *He comes across very tough, but he's nice when you get to know him.* **d** *Informal.* give in to a demand, a persistent request, etc.; hand over money, information, etc.: *She came across with a $100 donation.*
**come along,** improve: *She is coming along well now.*
**come back, a** return. **b** be remembered: *The forgotten name came back to her the next day.* **c** *Informal.* return to a former position or condition: *She's making an effort to come back by appearing as guest artist on television shows.*
**come between,** cause separation or unfriendly feeling: *The two friends vowed that they wouldn't let anything come between them.*
**come by,** get; obtain; acquire: *How did you come by that black eye?*
**come down, a** lose position, money, rank, etc: *He has certainly come down in the last year.* **b** be handed down or passed along: *Many fables have come down through the ages.* **c** *Informal.* become ill (*with*): *Camille came down with a bad cold.*
**come forward,** offer oneself for work or duty; volunteer: *Only three people came forward to help with the planning.*
**come from, a** be born in or to; be descended from; descend from: *She comes from a large family.* **b** be a native or former resident of: *They come from Manitoba.*
**come in, a** enter: *Please come in.* **b** begin to be used; be brought into use or fashion: *Steamboats came in soon after the invention of the steam engine.* **c** of trains, planes, etc., arrive: *We got there just as the train came in.* **d** of an oil well, begin producing: *This was the first oil well in the area to come in.*

**come into,** acquire, especially by inheriting: *She has come into a lot of money.*

**come off, a** happen; take place; occur: *When is the final game going to come off?* **b** reach the end; emerge, as from a contest: *She tried out for the team yesterday and came off with flying colours.* **c** become detached: *The label came off when I soaked the jar in water.* **d** *Informal.* turn out to be effective or successful: *His jokes didn't come off at all.*

**come off it!,** *Informal.* stop acting or talking like that.

**come on, a** develop; progress: *Our garden is coming on fine.* **b** meet by chance; find: *When I turned the corner, I came on a strange sight.* **c** in theatre, make an entrance onto the stage: *The murderer comes on in the second act.* **d** *Informal.* make an impression: *Rebecca comes on too strong.*

**come on!,** *Informal.* **a** hurry: *Come on! We're going to be late!* **b** stop behaving that way: *Oh, come on! You know he didn't mean it that way.* **c** an expression of disbelief: *$480,000 for that house? Come on!*

**come out, a** be revealed or made public: *The details of the scandal never came out.* **b** be offered to the public: *A new model came out last year.* **c** result; end: *How did your pictures come out?* **d** put in an appearance; offer to take part: *Quite a few students came out for drama this year.* **e** state publicly: *She came out strongly in favour of the expressway.*

**come out with, a** *Informal.* say openly: *That child comes out with the strangest questions.* **b** offer to the public: *The publisher has come out with a new edition.*

**come over, a** happen to; influence or possess: *A strange feeling came over me. I don't know what's come over her; she's so grumpy lately.* **b** *Informal.* visit: *When are you coming over?*

**come to, a** amount to; total; be equal to: *The bill comes to fifty dollars.* **b** return to consciousness: *The boxer came to in the dressing room.* **c** turn a ship's bow toward the wind. **d** anchor.

**come up,** arise; develop: *The question is sure to come up in class.*

**come upon,** meet or find by chance: *We came upon them at the plaza this morning.*

**come up with,** provide; produce, especially in working on a problem: *He couldn't come up with the right answer.*

**come·back** (kum′bak′) *Informal.* **1** a return to a former condition or position: *The singer made a comeback.* **2** a clever or sharp reply: *She's always ready with a good comeback.* **3** a cause for complaint: *When you buy an appliance "as is," you have no comeback if it doesn't work.* *n.*

**co·me·di·an** (kə mē′dē ən) **1** an actor in comedies; an actor of comic parts. **2** an entertainer who tells jokes or funny stories, sings funny songs, etc.; a comic. **3** a person who amuses others with his or her funny talk and actions. *n.*

**co·me·di·enne** (kə mē′dē en′) **1** an actress in comedies; an actress of comic parts. **2** a female entertainer who tells jokes or funny stories, sings funny songs, etc. *n.*

**come·down** (kum′doun′) *Informal.* a loss of position, rank, money, etc. *n.*

**com·e·dy** (kom′ə dē) **1** an amusing play or show having a happy ending. **2** such plays or shows as a class; the branch of drama concerned with such plays. **3** an amusing happening; a funny incident. *n., pl.* **com·e·dies.**

**come·li·ness** (kum′lē nis) **1** pleasant appearance. **2** fitness; suitableness; propriety. *n.*

**come·ly** (kum′lē) **1** having a pleasant appearance; attractive. **2** fitting; suitable; proper. *adj.,* **come·li·er, come·li·est.**

**come-on** (kum′on′) *Informal.* something offered to attract, especially something extra promised in a sales promotion; gimmick: *The offer of a free sample is just a come-on.* *n.*

**com·er** (kum′ər) **1** a person who comes. **2** a person who has recently come. **3** *Informal.* a person who shows promise or seems likely to succeed: *Our hockey coach says Tom is a comer.* *n.*

**co·mes·ti·ble** (kə mes′tə bəl) **1** something to eat; an article of food. **2** eatable. 1 *n.,* 2 *adj.*

**com·et** (kom′it) a starlike object that travels in an oval orbit around the sun, having a head consisting of an icy nucleus of frozen gases, ice, and dust surrounded by a hazy cloud, and, often, a long, shining tail: *Some comets are visible to the naked eye when they are near the sun. n.*

**come·up·pance** (kə mup′əns) *Informal.* a punishment that is deserved.

**com·fit** (kum′fit) a piece of candy; sweetmeat. *n.*

**com·fort** (kum′fərt) **1** ease the grief or sorrow of; cheer: *She tried to comfort the sobbing child.* **2** anything that makes trouble or sorrow easier to bear: *to bring comfort to a grief-stricken family.* **3** ease; freedom from pain or hardship: *to live in comfort.* **4** give ease to. **5** a person or thing that makes life easier or takes away hardship: *His sister is a great comfort to him.* 1, 4 *v.,* 2, 3, 5 *n.* —**com′fort·ing·ly,** *adv.*

**com·fort·a·ble** (kum′fər tə bəl) **1** giving a feeling of ease: *That's a very comfortable chair. A soft, warm bed is comfortable.* **2** in comfort; at ease; free from pain or hardship: *The warm fire made him feel comfortable after a cold day outdoors.* **3** *Informal.* enough for one's needs; adequate: *Eva has a comfortable income.* *adj.* —**com′fort·a·ble·ness,** *n.* —**com′fort·a·bly,** *adv.*

**com·fort·er** (kum′fər tər) **1** a person or thing that gives comfort. **2** a padded or quilted covering for a bed. **3** a long woollen scarf.

**com·fort·less** (kum′fərt lis) **1** bringing no comfort or ease of mind: *comfortless words.* **2** without the comforts of life: *a bare and comfortless room.* *adj.*

**com·ic** (kom′ik) **1** of comedy or in comedies: *a comic actor.* **2** amusing; funny: *the comic antics of a puppy.* **3** the amusing or funny side of literature, life, etc. **4** *Informal.* a COMIC BOOK. **5** *Informal.* a COMIC STRIP. **6** COMEDIAN (defs. 2, 3) **7 comics,** *pl.* the page or section of a newspaper containing COMIC STRIPS. 1, 2 *adj.,* 3–7 *n.*

**com·i·cal** (kom′ə kəl) amusing; funny: *The clown's actions were comical.* *adj.* —**com′i·cal·ly,** *adv.* —**com′i·cal·ness,** *n.*

**comic book** a book or magazine made up of one or more COMIC STRIPS.

**comic opera** an amusing opera having a happy ending.

**comic strip** a series of drawings that tell a funny story, an adventure, or a series of incidents.

**com·ing** (kum′ing) **1** the approach or arrival. **2** now approaching; next: *this coming spring.* **3** *Informal.* on the way to importance or fame. **4** ppr. of COME. 1 *n.,* 2, 3 *adj.,* 4 *v.*

**com·i·ty** (kom′ə tē) courtesy; civility. *n., pl.* **com·i·ties.**

**com·ma** (kom′ə) a mark (,) of punctuation, used to show a slight separation of elements within a sentence: *Commas are generally used where a slight pause or rise in the voice could be made in speaking, as after an introductory word or phrase, between words in a list, or before and after non-essential phrases or clauses inserted into the middle of a sentence. n.*

**com·mand** (kə mand′) **1** give an order to; direct: *The captain commanded the men to fire.* **2** give orders. **3** an order; direction: *They obeyed the captain's command.* **4** have authority or power over; be in control of: *The captain commands his ship.* **5** be commander. **6** authority; power; control: *The general is in command of the army.* **7** the position of a person who has the right to command. **8** the soldiers, ships, district, etc. under an officer who is appointed to command them: *The captain knew every man in his command.* **9** one of the main tactical formations of the Canadian Armed Forces: *Maritime Command.* **10** have a position of control over; overlook: *A hilltop commands the plain around it.* **11** mastery or control by position; outlook over. **12** have ready for use: *With the political knowledge that she commands, she can answer almost any question on current affairs.* **13** the ability to use; mastery: *An effective speaker or writer must have a good command of the language.* **14** ask for and get; force to be given: *Food commands a higher price when it is scarce.* **15 a** an electronic signal to begin operations in a computer. **b** a specific signal for instructing a computer to perform a special task. 1, 2, 4, 5, 10, 12, 14 *v.*, 3, 6–9, 11, 13, 15 *n.*

**com·man·dant** (kom′ən dant′ *or* kom′ən dänt′) **1** the officer in command of a military base, camp, etc. **2** the officer in charge of a military college or training school. *n.*

**com·man·deer** (kom′ən dēr′) **1** seize private property for military or public use: *All automobiles in the town were commandeered by the army.* **2** force into military service. **3** *Informal.* take by force. *v.*

**com·mand·er** (kə man′dər) **1** a person who commands. **2** an officer in charge of an army or a part of an army. **3** a naval officer ranking next below a captain and next above a lieutenant commander. **4** in Canada, an officer of the navy equivalent in rank to a major. *n.*

**com·mand·er–in–chief** (kə man′də rin chēf′) a person who has complete command of the armed forces of a country in a theatre of war, a garrison, etc. *n., pl.* **com·mand·ers-in-chief.**

**com·mand·ing** (kə man′ding) **1** in command: *a commanding officer.* **2** controlling; powerful: *commanding influences.* **3** authoritative; impressive: *a commanding voice.* **4** having a position of control. **5** ppr. of COMMAND. 1–4 *adj.*, 5 *v.*
—**com·mand′ing·ly,** *adv.*

**com·mand·ment** (kə mand′mənt) an order; law. *n.*

**command module** the main section of a spacecraft, designed to carry the crew and equipment for communication, flight, and re-entry: *A smaller section may be detached from the command module for short independent flights or landing on a planet or the moon.*

**com·man·do** *or* **Com·man·do** (kə man′dō) **1** a soldier who makes brief, daring raids in enemy territory and does close-range fighting. **2** a group of such soldiers. *n., pl.* **com·man·dos** *or* **com·man·does; Com·man·dos** *or* **Com·man·does.**

hat, āge, fär; let, ēqual, tèrm; it, īce
hot, ōpen, ôrder; oil, out; cup, put, rüle
əbove, takən, pencəl, lemən, circəs
ch, child; ng, long; sh, ship
th, thin; ᴛʜ, then; zh, measure

**com·mem·o·rate** (kə mem′ə rāt′) **1** preserve the memory of: *Roman emperors built arches to commemorate their victories.* **2** honour the memory of by some ceremony. *v.*, **com·mem·o·rat·ed, com·mem·o·rat·ing.**
—**com·mem′o·ra′tor,** *n.*

**com·mem·o·ra·tion** (kə mem′ə rā′shən) **1** the act of commemorating. **2** a service, celebration, etc. in memory of some person or event. *n.*
**in commemoration of,** to honour the memory of.

**com·mem·o·ra·tive** (kə mem′ə rə tiv *or* kə mem′ə rā′tiv) **1** calling to remembrance; honouring the memory of. **2** a postage stamp issued to commemorate some person, event, etc. 1 *adj.*, 2 *n.*
—**com·mem′o·ra·tive·ly,** *adv.*

**com·mence** (kə mens′) begin; start: *The opening ceremonies will commence at two o'clock.* *v.*, **com·menced, com·menc·ing.** —**com·menc′er,** *n.*

**com·mence·ment** (kə men′smənt) **1** a beginning; start. **2** the day when a school or college gives diplomas, certificates, etc. to students who have completed the required course of study; graduation day. **3** the ceremonies held on this day. *n.*

**com·mend** (kə mend′) **1** praise: *The volunteers were commended by the city for their help in controlling the flood.* **2** mention favourably; recommend: *A friend commended this book to me.* **3** hand over for safekeeping: *She commended the child to her aunt's care.* *v.*

**com·mend·a·ble** (kə men′də bəl) worthy of praise; deserving approval. *adj.* —**com·mend′a·bly,** *adv.*

**com·men·da·tion** (kom′ən dā′shən) the act of commending, especially recommendation or praise. *n.*

**com·mend·a·to·ry** (kə men′də tô′rē) **1** praising; expressing approval. **2** mentioning favourably; recommending. *adj.*

**com·men·sal·ism** (kə men′sə liz əm) a form of SYMBIOSIS; a relationship between organisms in which one organism benefits while the other is neither helped nor harmed. Compare with AMENSALISM, MUTUALISM, and PARASITISM. *n.*

**com·men·su·ra·ble** (kə men′sə rə bəl *or* kə men′shə rə bəl) measurable by the same set of units: *Greatness and mass are not commensurable.* *adj.*
—**com·men′su·ra·ble·ness,** *n.*
—**com·men′su·ra·bly,** *adv.*

**com·men·su·rate** (kə men′sə rit *or* kə men′shə rit) **1** in the proper proportion; proportionate: *The pay should be commensurate with the work.* **2** of the same size, extent, etc.; equal. **3** measurable by the same set of units: *An ant and an elephant are commensurate, but love and a turnip are not.* *adj.* —**com·men′su·rate·ly,** *adv.*
—**com·men′su·rate·ness,** *n.*

**com·ment** (kom′ent) **1** a short statement, note, or remark that explains, praises, or finds fault with something that has been written, said, or done: *The teacher had written comments in the margin. The reporter asked the mayor for a comment on the proposed bylaw.* **2** a remark. **3** make a comment or comments: *Everyone commented on* her strange behaviour.   4 talk; gossip.   5 talk or gossip. 1, 2, 4 *n.*, 3, 5 *v.*

**com·men·tar·y** (kom′ən ter′ə)   1 a series of notes for explaining the hard parts of a book; explanation or interpretation.   2 anything that explains or illustrates; comment: *The way she dresses is usually a commentary on her mood.*   3 an explanatory essay or treatise.   4 a description of a game or other event while it is in progress.   *n., pl.* **com·men·tar·ies.**

**com·men·ta·tor** (kom′ən tā′tər)   1 a person who describes and discusses news events, etc. while they are in progress, especially for radio or television: *a sports commentator, a fashion-show commentator.*   2 a person who gives a COMMENTARY (def. 4).   *n.*

**com·merce** (kom′ėrs)   1 trade; buying and selling in large amounts between different places; business. 2 communication between people: *After a rude remark like that, there can be no more commerce between us.*   *n.*

**com·mer·cial** (kə mėr′shəl)   1 of or having to do with COMMERCE (def. 1): *commercial law.*   2 made, done, or operating mainly for profit, especially at the expense of quality, artistic merit, etc.: *Her recent plays are very commercial. Their restaurant is very small and not at all commercial.*   3 supported or subsidized by an advertiser or advertisers: *a commercial radio program.*   4 an advertisement on radio or television, broadcast between programs or during a program.   1–3 *adj.*, 4 *n.*
—**com·mer′cial·ly**, *adv.*

**com·mer·cial·ism** (kə mėr′shə liz′əm)   the aims, methods, and spirit of COMMERCE (def. 1), especially as showing too great a concern for profit and success: *Commercialism has almost ruined him as an artist.*   *n.*

**com·mer·cial·ize** (kə mėr′shə līz′)   make a matter of business or trade; apply the methods of business to, often suggesting the loss of some quality or standard: *It's a pity her photography has become so commercialized.*   *v.*, **com·mer·cial·ized, com·mer·cial·iz·ing.**
—**com·mer′cial·i·za′tion**, *n.*

**com·min·gle** (kə ming′gəl)   mingle together; blend. *v.*, **com·min·gled, com·min·gling.**

**com·mis·er·ate** (kə miz′ə rāt′)   feel or express sorrow for; sympathize with; pity.   *v.*, **com·mis·er·at·ed, com·mis·er·at·ing.**

**com·mis·er·a·tion** (kə miz′ə rā′shən)   pity; sympathy.   *n.*

**com·mis·sar** (kom′ə sär′)   formerly in the Soviet Union, the head of a government department.   *n.*

**com·mis·sar·i·at** (kom′ə ser′ē ət)   1 a food supply. 2 formerly in the Soviet Union, any government department.   *n.*

**com·mis·sar·y** (kom′ə ser′ē)   1 a store handling food and supplies in a mining camp, logging camp, etc.   2 a deputy; representative.   *n., pl.* **com·mis·sar·ies.**

**com·mis·sion** (kə mish′ən)   1 a written paper giving certain powers, privileges, and duties.   2 an official certificate giving rank and authority as an officer in the armed forces: *My brother has received his commission as a lieutenant in the infantry.*   3 the rank and authority given. 4 give a commission to.   5 give authority to; give a person the right or power to do something: *Some businessmen commission others to buy or sell property for them.*   6 the authority, power, or right given.   7 a giving of authority.   8 the thing for which authority is given; something trusted to a person to do.   9 a group of people appointed or elected with authority to do certain things: *The prime minister appointed a commission to study the ecological effect of the proposed hydro project.* 10 doing or committing, as a crime: *People are punished for the commission of crimes.*   11 pay based on a percentage of the amount of business done: *She gets a commission of 10 percent on all the sales that she makes.*   12 put in service or use; make ready for service or use: *A new warship is commissioned when it has the officers, sailors, and supplies needed for a voyage.*   1–3, 6–11 *n.*, 4, 5, 12 *v.*
**in commission,**   **a** in service or use.   **b** ready for service or use; in working order.
**out of commission,**   **a** not in service or use.   **b** not ready for use; not in working order.

**com·mis·sion·aire** (kə mish′ə ner′)   1 a person whose job it is to open doors, carry bags, etc. in front of a hotel or a club.   2 a member of the Corps of Commissionaires: *Some Canadian cities employ commissionaires to check parking meters and to issue parking tickets.*   *n.*

**com·mis·sioned** (kə mish′ənd)   1 having a COMMISSION (def. 2): *a commissioned officer.*   2 pt. and pp. of COMMISSION.   1 *adj.*, 2 *v.*

**com·mis·sion·er** (kə mish′ə nər)   1 a member of a COMMISSION (def. 9).   2 an official in charge of some department of a government: *a police commissioner.* 3 one of a group of persons elected or appointed to govern a city or a county.   4 **Commissioner, Cdn.**   **a** the highest ranking officer of the Royal Canadian Mounted Police.   **b** the chief executive officer of the Yukon Territory or the Northwest Territories.   *n.*

**commission merchant**   a person who buys or sells goods for others who pay him or her a commission.

**com·mit** (kə mit′)   1 hand over for safekeeping; deliver: *Hiroko committed her savings bonds to the bank. He committed himself to the doctor's care.*   2 put officially in the care of an institution such as a mental hospital or prison: *The judge committed the accused for psychiatric assessment.*   3 refer to a committee for consideration. 4 do something that is an offence: *to commit a crime.* 5 reveal one's opinion.   6 involve; pledge: *Chandra would not commit herself.*   *v.*, **com·mit·ted, com·mit·ting.**
—**com·mit′ta·ble**, *adj.*
**commit to memory,**   learn by heart.
**commit to paper** or **writing,**   write down.

**com·mit·ment** (kə mit′mənt)   1 committing or being committed.   2 a pledge; promise: *Damien made a commitment to look after his younger sister.*   3 an official order sending a person to prison or to a mental institution.   *n.*

**com·mit·tal** (kə mit′əl)   the act of committing.   *n.*

**com·mit·tee** (kə mit′ē)   a group of persons, appointed or elected by a legislature, club, etc. to consider, investigate, or act on certain matters and report to the main body: *The school board has appointed a committee to study the use of volunteers in the classroom.*   *n.*

**com·mit·tee·man** (kə mit′ē mən)   a member of a committee.   *n., pl.* **com·mit·tee·men** (-mən).

**com·mix·ture** (kə miks′chər)   MIXTURE.   *n.*

**com·mode** (kə mōd′)   1 a chest of drawers.   2 a stand in a bedroom, to hold a washbasin, pitcher of water, etc.; washstand.   *n.*

**com·mo·di·ous** (kə mō′dē əs)   1 roomy. 2 convenient; handy.   *adj.*   —**com·mo′di·ous·ly**, *adv.*
—**com·mo′di·ous·ness**, *n.*

**com·mod·i·ty** (kə mod′ə tē) **1** anything that is bought and sold; an article of trade or commerce: *Groceries are commodities.* **2** a useful thing. *n., pl.* **com·mod·i·ties.**

**com·mo·dore** (kom′ə dôr′) **1** in Canada, an officer of the navy having a rank equivalent to a brigadier general. **2** in the British and other Commonwealth navies, the officer in charge of a convoy of ships. **3** the chief officer of a merchant fleet, yacht club, power squadron, etc. *n.*

**com·mon** (kom′ən) **1** belonging equally to each or all of a group; shared by all; joint: *The two cousins soon discovered that they had a lot of common interests. The house was the common property of the three sisters.* **2** widespread; general: *common knowledge, a common nuisance.* **3** generally accepted; usual; popular as opposed to scientific or technical: *The common name for* Equus caballus *is horse.* **4** often met with; usual; familiar: *Snow is common in cold countries. The dandelion is a common weed.* **5** of the most familiar or abundant kind: *common salt.* **6** of or having to do with the community as a whole; public: *the common good.* **7** without special rank or title: *the common people. A common soldier is a private.* **8** no more or greater than ordinary or average: *common courtesy.* **9** below ordinary; of poor quality; inferior: *a common grade of cloth.* **10** coarse; vulgar: *That was a common thing to say.* **11** land owned or used by all the people of a town, village, etc. **12** in mathematics, belonging equally to two or more quantities: *a common factor, a common multiple.* 1–10, 12 *adj.*, 11 *n.* —**com′mon·ness,** *n.*
**in common,** equally with another or others; owned, used, done, etc. by both or all: *Harriet and her sister have many interests in common.*

**com·mon·al·ty** (kom′ə nəl tē) **1** the common people; persons without rank or title; middle and lower classes of society. **2** people as a group. *n., pl.* **com·mon·al·ties.**

**common carrier** a person or company whose business is conveying goods or people for pay: *A railway company is a common carrier.*

**common denominator** **1** a DENOMINATOR that is a common multiple of the denominators of a group of fractions: *A common denominator of* ½, ⅔, *and* ¾ *is* 12, *because these three fractions can also be expressed as* ⁶⁄₁₂, ⁸⁄₁₂, *and* ⁹⁄₁₂. **2** a quality, opinion, etc. shared by all the persons or things in a group: *A desire to preserve their neighbourhood was the common denominator that brought the residents together.*

**common divisor** a number that will divide two or more other numbers without a remainder: *A common divisor of* 4, 6, 8, *and* 10 *is* 2.

**com·mon·er** (kom′ə nər) **1** one of the common people; a person who is not a nobleman. **2** a member of the House of Commons. *n.*

**common fraction** a FRACTION in which both the numerator and the denominator are whole numbers; SIMPLE FRACTION. *Examples:* ⅝, ²¹³⁄₅₀₀, ⁸⁄₁₅. Compare with COMPLEX FRACTION.

**common gender** in grammar: **1** a classification consisting of nouns that are considered to be either masculine or feminine, so that they may be replaced in different contexts by *he* or *she*. *Examples: friend, person, writer.* **2** a classification consisting of nouns that are considered to be masculine, feminine, or neuter, so that they may be replaced by *he, she* or *it*. *Examples: baby, dog.*

**common law** the law based on common custom and usage dating from ancient times and recognized and confirmed by the judgments of the courts: *The common law is distinguished from law created by legislatures and is based on the ancient unwritten law of England.*

**com·mon-law** (kom′ən lo′) **1** of, having to do with, or based on a COMMON-LAW MARRIAGE: *a common-law husband.* **2** of, having to do with, or based on COMMON LAW. *adj.*

**common-law marriage** a marriage that has not been solemnized in the normal way, but is legally recognized for certain purposes, such as allowance for a widow or dependants, inheritance rights, etc.: *For a relationship to be recognized as a common-law marriage, each of the two partners must agree to the arrangement, and both must be legally able to marry.*

**common logarithm** a LOGARITHM having a base of 10.

**com·mon·ly** (kom′ən lē) usually; as a rule; generally: *Art is commonly taught in elementary schools.* *adv.*

**common multiple** a number that can be divided by two or more other numbers without a remainder: 12 *is a common multiple of* 2, 3, 4, *and* 6.

**common noun** in grammar, any noun that is not a proper noun. A common noun refers to a condition, quality, idea, etc. or to a person, animal, or thing as a member of a class: *In the sentence "The dog's name is Julia,"* dog *and* name *are common nouns;* Julia *is a proper noun.* Compare with PROPER NOUN.
☞ *Usage.* Common nouns are not usually capitalized unless they are used to begin a sentence.

**com·mon·place** (kom′ən plās′) **1** an ordinary or everyday thing: *Sixty years ago broadcasting was a novelty; today it is a commonplace.* **2** an ordinary or obvious remark. **3** not new or interesting; everyday; ordinary: *We thought the speech commonplace.* 1, 2 *n.*, 3 *adj.* —**com′mon·place·ness,** *n.*

**com·mons** (kom′ənz) **1** the common people; people who are not of the nobility. **2** a dining hall or buildings where food is served to a large group at common tables. **3** the food served. **4** food allowance; daily rations. **Short commons** means too little food; not enough rations: *The prisoners were kept on short commons.* **5 the Commons, a** the House of Commons. **b** the members of the House of Commons. *n., pl.*

**common school** in the United States and formerly in Canada, an elementary public school.

**common sense** ordinary good judgment; practical intelligence: *It's just common sense to carry a spare tire in the car.* —**com′mon-sense,** *adj.*

**common stock** ordinary stock in a company, without a definite dividend rate: *A holder of common stock is entitled to dividends only if there is any profit left after all other claims have been paid.* Compare with PREFERRED STOCK.

**com·mon·weal** (kom′ən wēl′) the general welfare; public good. *n.*

**com·mon·wealth** (kom′ən welth′) **1 the Commonwealth,** BRITISH COMMONWEALTH OF NATIONS. **2** the people who make up a nation; citizens of a state.

**3** a democratic state; republic. **4** a group of persons, nations, etc. united by common interest. *n.*

**com·mo·tion** (kə mō′shən) confusion; agitation; violent movement: *We saw a great commotion in the water and then a dolphin surfaced. n.*

**com·mu·nal** (kom′yə nəl *or* kə myü′nəl) **1** of a community; public. **2** owned jointly by all; used or participated in by all members of a group or community. **3** of a COMMUNE². *adj.* —**com′mu·nal·ly,** *adv.*

**com·mune¹** (kə myün′ *for verb,* kom′yün *for noun*) **1** talk intimately. **2** intimate talk. **1** *v.,* **com·muned, com·mun·ing;** **2** *n.*

**com·mune²** (kom′yün) **1** a community of people living together. **2** a unit of local government in China. **3** the smallest division for local government in France, Belgium, and several other European countries. *n.*

**com·mu·ni·ca·ble** (kə myü′nə kə bəl) that can be communicated: *Ideas are communicable by words. Scarlet fever is a communicable disease. adj.*

**com·mu·ni·cant** (kə myü′nə kənt) a person who gives information by talking, writing, etc. *n.*

**com·mu·ni·cate** (kə myü′nə kāt′) **1** exchange information or signals by talk, writing, gestures, etc.; send and receive messages: *The searchers communicated by two-way radio.* **2** pass along; transmit: *A stove communicates heat to a room. She didn't say anything, but she soon communicated her uneasiness to the rest of us.* **3** get in touch with; get through to: *It was impossible to communicate with my family during the storm. The teacher could not communicate with some of the pupils.* **4** be connected: *The dining room communicates with the kitchen.* *v.,* **com·mu·ni·cat·ed, com·mu·ni·cat·ing.** —**com·mu′ni·ca′tor,** *n.*

**com·mu·ni·ca·tion** (kə myü′nə kā′shən) **1** the act or fact of passing along; transmitting. **2** a giving or exchanging of information by talking, writing, etc.: *The government leaders are in close communication on this issue.* **3** information given in this way; message: *Your communication came too late to allow me to change my plans.* **4** a means of going from one place to the other; connection; passage. **5 communications,** *pl.* **a** a system for sending or receiving messages, as by telephone, television, or radio. **b** (*used with a singular verb*) the art and technology of communicating, especially by mechanical or electronic means. *n.*

**communications satellite** an artificial satellite used for radio and television communication: *A communications satellite reflects or relays radio and television signals.*

**com·mu·ni·ca·tive** (kə myü′nə kə tiv *or* kə myü′nə kā′tiv) ready to give information; talkative. *adj.* —**com·mu′ni·ca·tive·ly,** *adv.* —**com·mu′ni·ca·tive·ness,** *n.*

**com·mun·ion** (kə myü′nyən) **1** the act of sharing; a having in common. **2** an exchange of thoughts and feelings; intimate talk; fellowship. **3** a close spiritual relationship. **4** a group of people having the same religious beliefs. **5** HOLY COMMUNION. *n.*

**com·mu·ni·qué** (kə myü′nə kā′ *or* kə myü′nə kā′) an official bulletin, statement, or other communication. *n.*

**com·mu·nism** (kom′yə niz′əm) **1** the political, social, and economic system of certain countries, such as the People's Republic of China, in which the state, governed by a single party without formal opposition, owns all property, controls the production and distribution of goods and services, and, to a great extent, controls the social and cultural life of the people. **2** Often, **Communism,** a philosophy or system derived from MARXISM, advocating state ownership of land and property. **3** any economic system based on ownership of all property and the means of production and distribution by the community or state. Compare with CAPITALISM and SOCIALISM. *n.*

**com·mu·nist** (kom′yə nist) **1** a person who favours or supports COMMUNISM. **2 Communist,** a member of the COMMUNIST PARTY. **3** of, having to do with, or characteristic of COMMUNISM or communists; COMMUNISTIC: *communist doctrine. n.*

**com·mu·nis·tic** (kom′yə nis′tik) **1** of or having to do with communists or COMMUNISM. **2** favouring COMMUNISM. *adj.* —**com′mu·nis′ti·cal·ly,** *adv.*

**Communist Party** a political party that is dedicated to the establishment of COMMUNISM, especially as derived from the principles of Marxism.

**com·mu·ni·ty** (kə myü′nə tē) **1** a group of people having common ties or interests and living in the same locality or district and subject to the same laws: *a farming community. This lake provides water for six communities.* **2** a group of people living together: *a community of nuns.* **3** the public: *the approval of the community.* **4** ownership together; a sharing together: *community of food supplies, community of ideas.* **5** in ecology, a group of animals and plants living in a particular region under similar conditions and interacting with one another, especially in food relationships. **6** likeness; similarity; identity: *Community of interest causes people to work together. n., pl.* **com·mu·ni·ties.**

**community centre** **1** a hall used for recreation, entertainment, public meetings, etc. in a community. **2** *Cdn.* an arena run by the community as a centre for sporting events, skating, dancing, and other forms of entertainment: *The local hockey team plays its home games at the Community Centre.*

**Community Chest** a fund of money contributed voluntarily by people, usually once a year, to support various charitable organizations, in their community: *The United Way is a kind of Community Chest.*

**community college** *Cdn.* an institution for post-secondary and adult education, especially for training in particular occupations and skills: *Community colleges offer diploma courses in many trades and also have courses for the personal interest of people in the community, ranging from philosophy and art appreciation to orienteering.*

**com·mu·tate** (kom′yə tāt′) reverse the direction of an electric current. *v.,* **com·mu·tat·ed, com·mu·tat·ing.**

**com·mu·ta·tion** (kom′yə tā′shən) **1** an exchange; substitution. **2** the reduction of an obligation, penalty, etc. to a less severe one: *The prisoner obtained a commutation of his sentence from death to life imprisonment.* **3** a reversal of the direction of an electric current by a COMMUTATOR. **4** regular, daily travel back and forth to work by train, bus, automobile, etc. *n.*

**com·mu·ta·tive** (kə myü′tə tiv *or* kom′yə tā′tiv) **1** of, having to do with, or involving substitution or exchange. **2** in mathematics, describing an operation in which the ordering of the elements does not affect the result: *Addition and multiplication are commutative because it does not matter which quantity is placed first; subtraction and* division are not commutative because reversing the order of the quantities will produce a different answer. *adj.*

**com·mu·ta·tor** (kom′yə tā′tər) **1** a device for reversing the direction of an electric current. **2** a revolving part in a dynamo or motor that carries the current to or from the brushes. See GENERATOR for picture. *n.*

**com·mute** (kə myüt′) **1** change an obligation, penalty, etc. to an easier one: *The prisoner's sentence of death was commuted to one of life imprisonment.* **2** travel as a COMMUTER: *She commutes from a small town to her job in Montreal.* **3** reverse the direction of an electric current by a COMMUTATOR. **4** exchange; substitute; change: *to commute foreign currency into Canadian dollars.* *v.*, **com·mut·ed, com·mut·ing.**

**com·mut·er** (kə myü′tər) a person who regularly travels a long distance between his or her home in one community and his or her work in another, especially one who travels by train, bus, etc. from a small community or suburb into a city to work. *n.*

**comp. 1** compound. **2** compare. **3** comparative. **4** composition. **5** compositor. **6** composer.

**com·pact**[1] (kom′pakt or kəm pakt′ *for adjective*, kəm pakt′ *for verb*, kom′pakt *for noun*) **1** firmly packed together; closely joined: *The leaves of the cabbage were folded into a compact head.* **2** using few words; brief, well organized, and to the point: *She has developed a compact style of writing.* **3** the second smallest of the four basic sizes of automobile, generally larger than a subcompact and smaller than an intermediate. **4** a small case for carrying face powder or rouge, having a hinged lid with a mirror. **5** pack firmly together; join closely. **6** make by putting together firmly. **7** condense. 1, 2 *adj.*, 3, 4 *n.*, 5–7 *v.* —**com·pact′ly,** *adv.* —**com·pact′ness,** *n.*

**compact**[2] (kom′pakt) agreement: *We made a compact not to tell anyone what we had heard.* *n.*

**compact car** a small car specially designed to be economical.

**compact disc** a thin, flat, round plate on which music, data, games programs, etc. is digitally encoded for a laser beam to play on a computer system or CD-player. *Abbrev.*: CD.

**com·pan·ion**[1] (kəm pan′yən) **1** a person who goes along with or accompanies another; a person who shares in what another is doing; comrade. **2** a person paid to live or travel with another as a friend and helper. **3** anything that matches or goes with another in kind, size, colour, etc. **4** a member of the lowest rank in an order of knighthood. **5** be a companion to; go along with. 1–4 *n.*, 5 *v.* —**com·pan′ion·less,** *adj.*

**com·pan·ion**[2] (kəm pan′yən) **1** a covering over the top of a COMPANIONWAY. **2** COMPANIONWAY. *n.*

**com·pan·ion·a·ble** (kəm pan′yə nə bəl) suited to COMPANIONSHIP; agreeable; pleasant; sociable: *a companionable disposition, a companionable evening.* *adj.* —**com·pan′ion·a·bly,** *adv.*

**com·pan·ion·ate** (kəm pan′yə nit) of or like COMPANIONS. *adj.*

**com·pan·ion·ship** (kəm pan′yən ship′) an association as COMPANIONS; fellowship: *Li-Ying enjoys the companionship of her dog.* *n.*

**com·pan·ion·way** (kəm pan′yən wā′) **1** a stairway leading from the deck of a ship to the rooms below. **2** the space where such a stairway is. *n.*

**commutator**   **243**   **compare**

hat, āge, fär; let, ēqual, tėrm; it, īce
hot, ōpen, ôrder; oil, out; cup, put, rüle
əbove, takən, pencəl, lemən, circəs
ch, child; ng, long; sh, ship
th, thin; ᴛʜ, then; zh, measure

**com·pa·ny** (kum′pə nē *or* kump′nē) **1** a group of people joined together for some purpose: *a business company, a company of actors.* **2** a gathering of persons for social purposes: *He's quite shy in company.* **3** a companion or companions: *You are known by the company you keep.* **4** companionship: *They enjoy each other's company. The dog gives her company.* **5** one or more guests or visitors: *We often have company in the evening.* **6** a group of people: *The chairman led the company in singing.* **7** a part of an army commanded by a captain. **8** a troop of Girl Guides. **9** a ship's crew; the officers and sailors of a ship. **10** partners not named in the title of a firm: *Lasack and Company.* *n., pl.* **com·pa·nies.**
**keep company,** go with; carry on courtship: *They have been keeping company for several months.*
**keep someone company,** stay with for companionship; accompany: *My sister kept me company while I was sick.*
**part company,** **a** go separate ways. **b** end companionship.

**Company of New France** a group formed in 1627 to develop NEW FRANCE.

**company town** a town built by a company for its workers, to whom it rents houses, provides services, etc.

**company union 1** a union of workers in one factory, store, etc. that is not part of a larger union. **2** a union of workers dominated by the employers.

**com·pa·ra·ble** (kom′pə rə bəl *or* kəm per′ə bəl) **1** able to be compared; having qualities in common: *A fire is comparable with the sun; both give light and heat.* **2** fit to be compared: *A cave is not comparable to a house as a comfortable place to live in.* *adj.* —**com′pa·ra·ble·ness,** *n.* —**com′pa·ra·bly,** *adv.*

**com·par·a·tive** (kəm per′ə tiv *or* kəm par′ə tiv) **1** that compares: *the comparative method of studying.* **2** measured by comparison with something else; relative; not absolute: *Screens give us comparative freedom from flies.* **3** in grammar, the second degree of comparison of an adjective or adverb. **4** a form or combination of words that shows this degree. *Fairer, better,* and *more slowly* are the comparatives of *fair, good,* and *slowly.* **5** showing the comparative form. 1, 2, 5 *adj.*, 3, 4 *n.* —**com·par′a·tive·ly,** *adv.*

**com·pare** (kəm per′) **1** find out or point out how persons or things are alike and how they differ: *She compared the two books to see which one had the better pictures.* **2** think, speak, or write of as similar; liken (*to*): *to compare life to a river.* **3** examine two or more things to find similarities and differences: *We compared the fins of a fish with the wings of a bird.* **4** be considered like or as equal to: *Artificial light cannot compare with daylight. One can't compare pearls and diamonds.* **5** in grammar, change the form of an adjective or adverb to show the comparative and superlative degrees; name the positive, comparative, and superlative degrees of. *v.*, **com·pared, com·par·ing.**
**beyond compare,** without an equal; most excellent: *Their cakes are beyond compare.*
**not to be compared with,** **a** very different from. **b** not nearly so good as.

**com·par·i·son** (kəm per′ə sən *or* kəm par′ə sən) **1** the act or process of comparing; finding the likenesses and differences: *The teacher's comparison of the heart to a pump helped the students to understand its action.* **2** likeness; similarity: *There is no comparison between these two cameras; one is much better than the other.* **3** in grammar, a change in an adjective or adverb to show differences of degree: *The three degrees of comparison are positive, comparative, and superlative.* Examples: *good, better, best; cold, colder, coldest; helpful, more helpful, most helpful.* *n.*
**in comparison with,** compared with: *Even a large lake is small in comparison with an ocean.*

**com·part·ment** (kəm pärt′mənt) **1** a separate division or section of anything; part of an enclosed space set off by walls or partitions: *a storage compartment. The human heart has four compartments. A ship's hold is often built in watertight compartments, so that a leak will fill up only one and not the whole ship.* **2** a separate category or aspect: *the compartments of the mind.* *n.*

**com·part·men·tal·iz·a·tion** (kəm pärt′mən·tə lə zā′shən *or* kəm pärt′mən·tə lī zā′shən) division into isolated compartments or categories. *n.*

**com·part·men·tal·ize** (kəm pärt′mən·tə līz′) divide into isolated compartments or categories: *He has a tendency to compartmentalize.* *v.*

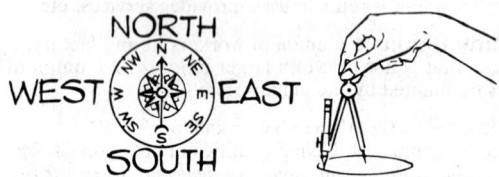

A compass (def. 1). The needle always points to the north, even when the instrument is turned.

A compass (def. 11). The pointed arm remains fixed so that the other arm moves in a circle.

**com·pass** (kum′pəs) **1** an instrument for showing directions, consisting of a magnetized needle suspended by the middle so that it is free to point to the North Magnetic Pole, which is near the North Pole. **2** a boundary or circumference: *The castle had a large dungeon within the compass of its walls.* **3** the extent within limits; scope; range: *The old sailor had had many adventures within the compass of his lifetime.* **4** the range of a voice or musical instrument. **5** a circuit; going around. **6** make a circuit of; go around; move around: *The astronaut compassed the earth many times.* **7** form a circle around; hem in; surround: *a farm house compassed by trees.* **8** do; accomplish; get. **9** plot; scheme. **10** grasp with the mind; understand completely. **11 compasses,** *pl.* an instrument for drawing circles and curved lines and for measuring distances. 1–5, 11 *n.*, 6–10 *v.*

**compass card** a circular card set beneath the needle of a COMPASS (def. 1) showing the 32 points of direction and the degrees of the circle.

**com·pas·sion** (kəm pash′ən) a feeling that leads one to help a person who is suffering; sympathy; pity. *n.*

**com·pas·sion·ate** (kəm pash′ə nit) desiring to relieve another's suffering; sympathetic; merciful. *adj.*
—**com·pas·sion·ate·ly,** *adv.*

**com·pat·i·bil·i·ty** (kəm pat′ə bil′ə tē) the ability to exist together; ability to get on well together; agreement; harmony. *n.*

**com·pat·i·ble** (kəm pat′ə bəl) **1** able to exist together in harmony; that can get on well together: *My two sisters are always arguing; they don't seem to be compatible.* **2** in television, having to do with or referring to the type of colour broadcasting that permits reception in black and white on sets that are not built for colour reception. **3** of a computer, able to use the software of another make: *This computer is not compatible with the central one at the bank.* *adj.* —**com·pat′i·bly,** *adv.*

**com·pa·tri·ot** (kəm pā′trē ət *or* kəm pat′rē ət) **1** a fellow countryman. **2** of the same country. 1 *n.,* 2 *adj.*

**com·peer** (kəm pēr′ *or* kom′pēr) **1** an equal; peer. **2** a comrade or companion. *n.*

**com·pel** (kəm pel′) **1** force or oblige; urge irresistibly: *The cold finally compelled him to surrender. The holdup men compelled the employees to lie face down on the floor.* **2** cause or get: *Her tone of voice compelled obedience. Such brave actions compel our respect.* *v.* **com·pelled, com·pel·ling.** —**com·pel′ling·ly,** *adv.*

**com·pel·ling** (kəm pel′ing) **1** forcing attention or interest: *She has compelling beauty.* **2** strongly persuasive or convincing: *a compelling argument.* **3** ppr. of COMPEL. 1, 2 *adj.,* 3 *v.*

**com·pen·di·ous** (kəm pen′dē əs) brief but comprehensive; CONCISE. *adj.*
—**com·pen·di·ous·ly,** *adv.*

**com·pen·di·um** (kəm pen′dē əm) a summary that gives much information in a little space; CONCISE treatise. *n., pl.* **com·pen·di·ums** or **com·pen·di·a** (-dē ə).

**com·pen·sate** (kom′pən sāt′) **1** make an equivalent or satisfactory return to; reimburse or pay: *The hunter agreed to compensate the farmer for shooting her cow.* **2** balance by equal weight, power, etc.; make up; offset: *A hockey player who is not a very fast skater can sometimes compensate by good positional play.* *v.,* **com·pen·sat·ed, com·pen·sat·ing.** —**com′pen·sa′tor,** *n.*

**com·pen·sa·tion** (kom′pən sā′shən) **1** something given (or received) as an equivalent; a satisfactory return for a loss or injury, or for a service: *Dorothea received compensation from the government for the injury she suffered during the robbery.* **2** offsetting or counterbalancing by an equivalent power, weight, etc.; the act of compensating. **3** a means for offsetting or counterbalancing, especially a particular behaviour or skill developed to offset a defect or lack: *I think his aggressive behaviour is just a compensation for shyness.* *n.*

**com·pen·sa·tive** (kom′pən sā′tiv *or* kom pen′sə tiv) compensating. *adj.*

**com·pen·sa·to·ry** (kəm pen′sə tô′rē) compensating. *adj.*

**com·pete** (kəm pēt′) **1** try hard to obtain something wanted by others; be rivals; contend. **2** take part in a contest: *An injury kept him from competing in the final race.* *v.,* **com·pet·ed, com·pet·ing.**

**com·pe·tence** (kom′pə təns) the quality or state of being COMPETENT: *No one doubted the guide's competence.* *n.*

**com·pe·ten·cy** (kom′pə tən sē) COMPETENCE. *n.*

**com·pe·tent** (kom′pə tənt) **1** able; fit: *a competent*

cook.   2 legally qualified: *The court ruled that the witness was not competent to judge the sanity of the accused.*   *adj.*
—com′pe·tent·ly, *adv.*

**com·pe·ti·tion** (kom′pə tish′ən)   1 an effort to obtain something wanted by others; rivalry: *There is great competition in our class for first place. The two girls enjoyed the spirit of competition that existed between them.*   2 a contest, especially one in which there is a prize for the winner.   *n.*
**in competition with,**   competing against: *She was in competition with five other dancers.*

**com·pet·i·tive** (kəm pet′ə tiv)   1 of, based on, or determined by competition: *a competitive examination for a job.*   2 characterized by a drive to excel; concerned with trying to do better than others: *A first-rate athlete must possess a competitive spirit.*   *adj.*
—com·pet′i·tive·ly, *adv.*   —com·pet′i·tive·ness, *n.*

**com·pet·i·tor** (kəm pet′ə tər)   a person who competes; rival.   *n.*

**com·pi·la·tion** (kom′pə lā′shən)   1 the act of compiling.   2 a book, list, etc. that has been COMPILEd.   *n.*

**com·pile** (kəm pīl′)   1 collect and bring together in one list or account: *He compiled the data for the report.*   2 make a book, report, etc. out of various materials: *to compile an encyclopedia.*   *v.*, **com·piled, com·pil·ing.**

**com·pi·ler** (kəm pī′lər)   1 one who compiles.   2 a program that allows a computer to translate words and numbers into MACHINE LANGUAGE.   *n.*

**com·pla·cence** (kəm plā′səns)   COMPLACENCY.   *n.*

**com·pla·cen·cy** (kəm plā′sən sē)   1 the state or condition of being pleased with oneself; self-satisfaction: *She solved the puzzle easily and smiled with complacency.*   2 contentment.   *n., pl.* **com·pla·cen·cies.**

**com·pla·cent** (kəm plā′sənt)   pleased with oneself; self-satisfied: *The winner's complacent smile annoyed some people.*   *adj.*   —com·pla′cent·ly, *adv.*
☛ *Hom.* COMPLAISANT (kəm plā′sənt).

**com·plain** (kəm plān′)   1 say that something is wrong; find fault: *She complains that the room is cold.*   2 talk about one's pains, troubles, etc.: *Mark is always complaining. She complained of a headache.*   3 make an accusation or charge: *She complained to the police about her neighbour's dog.*   *v.*   —com·plain′er, *n.*
—com·plain′ing, *adj.*   —com·plain′ing·ly, *adv.*

**com·plain·ant** (kəm plā′nənt)   a person who complains, especially one who brings a lawsuit or lays a criminal charge against another: *The complainant accused the defendant of cheating him.*   *n.*

**com·plaint** (kəm plānt′)   1 a voicing of dissatisfaction; complaining; finding fault: *Her letter is filled with complaints about her new job.*   2 a cause for complaining.   3 a formal accusation.   4 a sickness or ailment: *Influenza is a common complaint.*   *n.*

**com·plai·sance** (kəm plā′zəns *or* kəm plā′səns)   1 willingness to please or oblige; agreeableness; courtesy.   2 an obliging or courteous act.   *n.*

**com·plai·sant** (kəm plā′zənt *or* kəm plā′sənt)   inclined to do what is asked; willing to please; obliging; courteous.   *adj.*   —com·plai′sant·ly, *adv.*
☛ *Hom.* COMPLACENT (for the second pronunciation of complaisant).

---

**competition**   245   **complex**

hat, āge, fär; let, ēqual, tėrm; it, īce
hot, ōpen, ôrder; oil, out; cup, pùt, rüle
əbove, takən, pencəl, lemən, circəs
ch, child; ng, long; sh, ship
th, thin; ᴛн, then; zh, measure

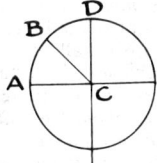

THE ARC BD IS THE COMPLEMENT OF THE ARC AB, AND THE ANGLE BCD IS THE COMPLEMENT OF THE ANGLE ACB

**com·ple·ment** (kom′plə mənt *for noun*, kom′plə ment′ *for verb*)   1 something that completes or makes perfect; something necessary to make a whole: *The complement to the evening was the hour we spent on the shore, listening to the loons.*   2 the full quantity or number; the required amount: *The ship now had its full complement of men.*
3 in grammar, a word or group of words used after a verb to describe or identify the subject or direct object of the sentence. In *The man is feeble*, *feeble* is a complement describing the subject *man*. In *She is chairman*, *chairman* is a complement identifying the subject *she*. In *They made him king*, *king* is a complement identifying the object *him*.
4 in geometry, either one of a pair of angles that together measure 90°: *The complement of a 70° angle is a 20° angle.*
5 either of a pair of COMPLEMENTARY COLOURS: *The complement of red pigment is green.*   6 in music, either of two intervals which together make up an octave.
7 supply a lack of any kind; complete: *My furniture complements my sister's, so that together we have what we need.*   1–6 *n.*, 7 *v.*
☛ *Hom.* COMPLIMENT.

**com·ple·men·ta·ry** (kom′plə men′tə rē *or* kom′plə men′trē)   forming a COMPLEMENT; completing something; supplying what is lacking or needed.   *adj.*
☛ *Hom.* COMPLIMENTARY.

**complementary angles**   two angles which together total 90°.

**complementary colours** *or* **colors**   1 any two colours of the spectrum which, when combined in the right proportions, produce white light.   2 any two colours that absorb the white light reflected by each other: *Red and green are complementary colours in paint.*

**com·plete** (kəm plēt′)   1 with all the parts; lacking nothing; whole; full: *a complete set of Dickens' novels.*
2 make up all the parts of; make whole or entire: *She just needs a platter to complete her set of dishes.*   3 thorough; total; entire: *complete surprise, complete confidence.*
4 make perfect or thorough: *The good news completed my happiness.*   5 ended; finished; done: *My homework is complete.*   6 get done; end; finish: *She completed her homework early in the evening.*   1, 3, 5 *adj.*, 2, 4, 6 *v.*, **com·plet·ed, com·plet·ing.**   —com·plete′ly, *adv.*
—com·plete′ness, *n.*

**com·ple·tion** (kəm plē′shən)   1 the act of completing; finishing.   2 the condition of being completed: *The work is near completion.*   *n.*

**com·plex** (kom′pleks *or* kəm pleks′ *for adjective*, kom′pleks *for noun*)   1 not simple; involved; complicated: *The instructions for building the radio were too complex for us to follow.*   2 made up of a number of connected or interwoven parts; composite: *A complex sentence has one or more subordinate clauses besides the*

**complex fraction** 246 **composite**

main clause. **3** an interconnected or complicated whole: *The whole complex of charges and countercharges had to be sorted out before they could begin to work on a settlement of the dispute.* **4** a group of related or connected units such as buildings or roads: *The new civic complex includes a library, museum, and auditorium.* **5** in psychology, a system of related ideas, feelings, memories, etc. of which a person is usually not aware, which strongly influence his or her behaviour in certain ways. **6** *Informal.* an exaggerated mental tendency; obsession: *Wesley has such a complex about fresh air that he can hardly stay in a room with the windows closed.* 1, 2 *adj.*, 3–6 *n.*
—com′plex′ly, *adv.* —com′plex′ness, *n.*

**complex fraction** a fraction having a fraction in the numerator, in the denominator, or in both; compound fraction. Compare with COMMON FRACTION.
Examples: $\frac{1\frac{3}{4}}{3}, \frac{1}{3\frac{1}{3}}, \frac{\frac{3}{4}}{1\frac{7}{8}}$

**com·plex·ion** (kəm plek′shən) **1** the colour, quality, and general appearance of the skin, particularly of the face. **2** general appearance; nature; character: *The complexion of the war was changed by two great victories.* *n.*

**com·plex·ioned** (kəm plek′shənd) having a certain kind of COMPLEXION: *dark-complexioned.* *adj.*

**com·plex·i·ty** (kem plek′sə tē) **1** the state or quality of being complex: *The complexity of the road map puzzled Tom.* **2** something complex; a difficulty or complication. *n.*, *pl.* **com·plex·i·ties.**

**complex sentence** a sentence having one main clause and one or more subordinate clauses. *Example: When the engineer pulls the cord, the whistle blows.* The whistle blows *is the main clause.* Compare with SIMPLE SENTENCE and COMPOUND SENTENCE.

**com·pli·ance** (kəm plī′əns) **1** the act of COMPLYing or doing as another wishes; the act of yielding to a request or command. **2** a tendency to yield to others. *n.*
**in compliance with,** COMPLYing with; in accordance with.

**com·pli·ant** (kəm plī′ənt) COMPLYing; yielding; obliging: *A compliant person gives in to other people.* *adj.*
—com′pli·ant′ly, *adv.*

**com·pli·cate** (kom′plə kāt′) **1** make hard to understand, settle, cure, etc.; mix up; confuse: *Too many rules complicate a game.* **2** make worse: *a headache complicated by eye trouble.* *v.*, **com·pli·cat·ed, com·pli·cat·ing.**

**com·pli·cat·ed** (kom′plə kā′tid) **1** made up of many parts; involved; intricate; complex. **2** pt. and pp. of COMPLICATE. 1 *adj.*, 2 *v.*

**com·pli·ca·tion** (kom′plə kā′shən) **1** a complex or confused condition that is hard to understand, settle, cure, etc. **2** a difficulty or problem added to one or more already existing: *Pneumonia was the complication they most feared.* **3** the act or process of complicating. *n.*

**com·plic·i·ty** (kəm plis′ə tē) a partnership in wrongdoing; the fact or state of being an ACCOMPLICE: *Knowingly receiving stolen goods is complicity in theft.* *n.*, *pl.* **com·plic·i·ties.**

**com·pli·ment** (kom′plə mənt *for noun,* kom′plə ment′ *for verb*) **1** something good said about a person; something said in praise or congratulation. **2** praise or congratulate; pay a compliment to. **3** give something to a person as a polite attention. **4 compliments,** *pl.* greetings: *In the box of flowers was a card reading "With the compliments of a friend."* 1, 4 *n.*, 2, 3 *v.*
**with compliments,** free of charge.
☛ *Hom.* COMPLEMENT.

**com·pli·men·ta·ry** (kom′plə men′tə rē *or* kom′plə men′trē) **1** giving or containing a COMPLIMENT; expressing courtesy, admiration, or praise. **2** given free: *a complimentary ticket to a concert.* *adj.*
☛ *Hom.* COMPLEMENTARY.

**com·ply** (kəm plī′) act in agreement with a request or a command: *When he asked them to turn down the radio, they immediately complied. You should comply with the doctor's orders.* *v.*, **com·plied, com·ply·ing.**
—com·pli′er, *n.*

**com·po·nent** (kəm pō′nənt) **1** a part; a constituent element: *A chemist can separate a medicine into its components.* **2** forming a part; constituent: *Blade and handle are the component parts of a knife.* **3** one of the main units or parts of an electrical, electronic, or mechanical system: *A printer is one of the components of a computer.* **4** made up of separate units, or components: *In a component stereo system, the amplifier and loudspeakers are separate units.* 1, 3 *n.*, 2, 4 *adj.*

**com·port** (kəm pôrt′) **1** behave (*used with a pronoun ending in* **-self**): *Sheena comported herself with dignity throughout the trial.* **2** agree or suit (*used with* **with**): *His silliness at the meeting did not comport with what we had heard of him.* *v.*

**com·port·ment** (kəm pôrt′mənt) BEHAVIOUR. *n.*

**com·pose** (kəm pōz′) **1** make up; form the substance or the parts of (*usually used in the passive*): *The ocean is composed of salt water. The Commonwealth is composed of a large number of countries.* **2** create, especially in music or in words: *to compose a symphony, to compose a poem.* **3** create works of music, literature, etc.: *She composes only early in the morning.* **4** get oneself ready; put into a proper state: *Nicole composed herself for a long wait.* **5** make oneself or one's mind calm and quiet; put into a state of repose: *Giuseppe tried to compose himself before entering the room.* **6** arrange the parts or elements of; put together in a pleasing or artistic way: *He composes his photographs very carefully.* **7** put into a proper or effective order or arrangement: *The lawyer composed the separate pieces of evidence into a convincing explanation of how the crime must have been committed.* **8** arrange or set up type for printing. *v.*, **com·posed, com·pos·ing.**

**com·posed** (kəm pōzd′) **1** calm; quiet; self-controlled; tranquil. **2** pt. and pp. of COMPOSE. 1 *adj.*, 2 *v.*

**com·pos·ed·ly** (kəm pō′zi dlē) in a composed manner. *adv.*

**com·pos·er** (kəm pō′zər) a person who composes, especially a writer of music. *n.*

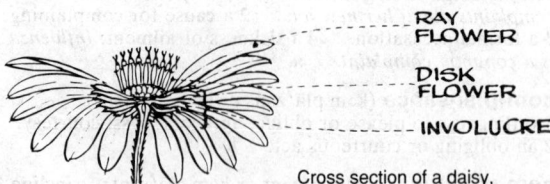

Cross section of a daisy, a composite flower

**com·pos·ite** (kom′pə zit; *sometimes,* kəm poz′it)
**1** made up of various parts; compound: *The photographer*

made a composite picture by putting together parts of several others. **2** referring to a very large family of plants, mostly herbs but including a few shrubs and trees, having flower heads made up of many tiny flowers called FLORETS bunched together so that they appear to be single blooms: *The composite family includes the dandelion, artichoke, sagebrush, thistles, and daisies.* **3** belonging to the composite family: *Goldenrod is a composite plant.* **4** a composite plant: *Many common weeds are composites.* **5** any composite thing; something made up of distinct parts. **6** a column of ancient Roman origin with a capital that combines the Ionic scroll ornamentation with the Corinthian leaf ornamentation. See ORDER for picture. 1-3 *adj.*, 4-6 *n.* —**com′pos·ite·ly,** *adv.*

**composite number** a number that can be exactly divided by some number other than itself or 1; a number that has more than two factors: 8 *is a composite number with four factors: 1, 2, 4 and 8. 5 is not a composite number; its only factors are 1 and 5.*

**composite school** *Cdn.* a secondary school in which a student may receive academic, commercial, or industrial training.

**com·po·si·tion** (kom′pə zish′ən) **1** the make-up of anything or the way it is put together; constitution: *We are studying the composition of light.* **2** a putting together of a whole: *Writing sentences, making pictures, and setting type in printing are all forms of composition.* **3** the thing composed, such as a piece of music, writing, etc. **4** a short essay written as a school exercise. **5** a substance formed by a mixture of different ingredients, used especially in various industries and trades to refer to a particular mixed substance regularly used or manufactured: *The table top is of a composition resembling marble. Shoes can have leather soles or composition soles. Composition picture frames are usually a mixture of wood flakes or chips and a plastic binding agent, shaped and hardened in a mould.* *n.*

**com·pos·i·tor** (kəm poz′ə tər) TYPESETTER. *n.*

**com·post** (kom′pōst) **1** a mixture of decayed vegetable or animal matter, such as leaves or manure, used to fertilize and condition soil. **2** fertilize with compost. **3** convert into compost. 1 *n.*, 2, 3 *v.*

**com·po·sure** (kəm pō′zhər) calmness; quietness; self-control. *n.*

**com·pote** (kom′pōt) **1** a dish with a supporting stem for fruit, candy, etc. **2** stewed fruit. *n.*

**com·pound**[1] (kom′pound *for noun and adjective,* kom pound′ *for verb*) **1** a word made by joining together two or more separate words: *Highway is a compound.* **2** in chemistry, a substance formed by the chemical combination of two or more elements in fixed proportions. The elements lose their individual chemical properties and the compound has new properties: *Water is a compound of hydrogen and oxygen.* Compare with MIXTURE (def. 3). **3** something made by combining or mixing parts; combination or mixture: *Her success in business was due to a compound of common sense and long experience.* **4** having more than one part: *A clover leaf is a compound leaf.* **5** increase or complicate by adding a new element: *The weekend visitors compounded the space problem at our cottage by bringing along their St. Bernard.* **6** calculate interest on a sum of money borrowed plus the accumulated unpaid interest: *The interest is compounded semi-annually.* **7** in law, accept or agree to accept payment not to prosecute: *It is unlawful to compound an indictable offence.* **8** mix or combine: *to compound ingredients.* **9** make by mixing or combining: *to compound a medicine.* 1-3 *n.*, 4 *adj.*, 5-9 *v.*

---

**composite**     **247**     **compressed**
**number**

hat, āge, fär; let, ēqual, tėrm; it, īce
hot, ōpen, ôrder; oil, out; cup, pùt, rüle
əbove, takən, pencəl, lemən, circəs
ch, child; ng, long; sh, ship
th, thin; ₮H, then; zh, measure

**com·pound**[2] (kom′pound) an enclosed yard with buildings in it. *n.*

**compound eye** in biology, an eye made up of many elements, each of which is sensitive to light and forms a part of the total image: *Most insects and some crustaceans have compound eyes.*

**compound flower** in botany, a flower head made up of many small flowers that appear to be a single bloom: *The dandelion, aster, and dahlia are examples of plants that have compound flowers.*

**compound fraction** COMPLEX FRACTION.

**compound fracture** a fracture in which a broken bone cuts through the flesh and sticks out.

**compound interest** the interest paid on both the original sum of money borrowed and on the unpaid interest that has accumulated.

**compound number** a quantity expressed in two or more kinds of related units. Examples: 63° 30′; 12 h 30 min.

**compound sentence** in grammar, a sentence made up of co-ordinate independent clauses. Examples: *He went, but I stayed home. The winds blew, the rains fell, and the water covered the earth.* Compare with COMPLEX SENTENCE and SIMPLE SENTENCE.

**com·pre·hend** (kom′pri hend′) **1** understand the meaning of: *They did not at first comprehend the significance of the new government bill.* **2** include; contain: *His report comprehended all the facts.* *v.* —**com′pre·hend′ing·ly,** *adv.*

**com·pre·hen·si·bil·i·ty** (kom′pri hen′sə bil′ə tē) the quality of being understandable; INTELLIGIBILITY. *n.*

**com·pre·hen·si·ble** (kom′pri hen′sə bəl) understandable. *adj.* —**com′pre·hen′si·bly,** *adv.*

**com·pre·hen·sion** (kom′pri hen′shən) **1** the act or power of understanding; ability to get the meaning: *Arithmetic is not beyond my comprehension.* **2** the act or fact of including. **3** comprehensiveness. *n.*

**com·pre·hen·sive** (kom′pri hen′siv) **1** including much; covering everything or nearly everything: *The term's work ended with a comprehensive review.* **2** able to understand many things: *a comprehensive mind.* *adj.* —**com′pre·hen′sive·ly,** *adv.* —**com′pre·hen′sive·ness,** *n.*

**comprehensive school** *Cdn.* COMPOSITE SCHOOL.

**com·press** (kəm pres′ *for 1, 2;* kom′pres *for 3*) **1** make smaller and more compact by pressure or as if by pressure: *Paper is compressed into bales for recycling. José had to compress his speech because the meeting was running late.* **2** squeeze together: *We could see Nina was angry by the way she compressed her lips.* **3** a pad of cloth applied to some part of the body to stop bleeding or to provide medication, etc. 1, 2 *v.*, 3 *n.*

**com·pressed** (kəm prest′) **1** squeezed together. **2** made smaller by pressure. **3** in biology, not thick or rounded; appearing flattened: *A puffin has a deep, compressed bill. A halibut has a compressed body.* **4** pt. and pp. of COMPRESS (defs. 1, 2) 1-3 *adj.*, 4 *v.*

**compressed air** air put under extra pressure so that it has a great deal of force when released: *Compressed air is used to inflate tires and to operate certain kinds of brakes and guns.*

**com·press·i·bil·i·ty** (kəm pres′ə bil′ə tē) a COMPRESSIBLE quality. *n.*

**com·press·i·ble** (kəm pres′ə bəl) that can be COMPRESSED. *adj.*

**com·pres·sion** (kəm presh′ən) 1 the act or process of COMPRESSING. 2 a COMPRESSED condition. *n.*

**com·pres·sive** (kəm pres′iv) compressing; tending to COMPRESS. *adj.*

**com·pres·sor** (kəm pres′ər) one that COMPRESSES, especially a machine for compressing air, gas, etc. *n.*

**com·prise** (kəm prīz′) consist of; include: *Canada comprises ten provinces and two territories.* *v.*, **com·prised, com·pris·ing.**

**com·pro·mise** (kom′prə mīz) 1 settle a dispute by agreeing that the person or group on each side will give up a part of what they demand. 2 a settlement of a dispute by a partial yielding on both sides. 3 the result of such a settlement. 4 anything halfway between two different things. 5 put in danger or under suspicion, especially one's reputation or character: *You will compromise your good name if you go along with such a cheap trick.* 1, 5 *v.*, **com·pro·mised, com·pro·mis·ing;** 2–4 *n.*

**comp·trol·ler** (kən trō′lər) See CONTROLLER (def. 1). *n.*

**comp·trol·ler·ship** (kən trō′lər ship′) See CONTROLLERSHIP. *n.*

**com·pul·sion** (kəm pul′shən) 1 a compelling or being compelled, or forced: *Azan claimed that he had signed the confession under compulsion.* 2 in psychology, an irresistible impulse to behave or act in a certain way, regardless of whether it is reasonable to do so. 3 an act resulting from such an impulse. *n.*

**com·pul·sive** (kəm pul′siv) 1 of, having to do with, or caused by obsession or COMPULSION (def. 2): *a compulsive liar. He was compulsive about cleanliness.* 2 using COMPULSION (def. 1). *adj.* —**com·pul′sive·ly,** *adv.*

**com·pul·so·ry** (kəm pul′sə rē) 1 required; obligatory: *Attendance at school is compulsory for children.* 2 compelling; using force. *adj.* —**com·pul′so·ri·ly,** *adv.*

**com·punc·tion** (kəm pungk′shən) the pricking of conscience; regret; remorse. *n.*

**com·pu·ta·tion** (kom′pyə tā′shən) 1 reckoning; calculation: *Addition and subtraction are forms of computation.* 2 the conclusion reached as a result of this. *n.*

**com·pute** (kəm pyüt′) find out by arithmetical work; reckon; calculate: *It took some time to compute the cost of our trip.* *v.*, **com·put·ed, com·put·ing.** —**com·put′a·ble,** *adj.*

**com·put·er** (kəm pyü′tər) 1 an electronic machine that can store large amounts of coded data and can be set, or programmed, to perform mathematical and logical operations at high speed. 2 a person skilled or trained in computing. *n.*

**computer–aided learning** a method of learning in which the material to be learned is programmed into a computer in such a way that users can teach themselves, step by step, and test their knowledge after each step.

**computer graphics** the use of a computer, especially one that shows colours, to produce designs, portraits, scenes, etc.

**com·put·er·ize** (kəm pyü′tə rīz) 1 store in a computer: *The bank has computerized all savings accounts.* 2 equip with computers: *Now that the office is computerized, there is no need for filing cabinets.*

**computer literacy** familiarity with computers and the techniques and vocabulary needed to operate them.

**computer terminal** a device with a keyboard, like that of a typewriter, on which information or commands are given to a computer, and a screen similar to a television screen, on which the output from the computer is displayed.

**com·rade** (kom′rad *or* kom′rid) 1 a companion and friend; partner. 2 a person who shares in what another is doing; partner; a fellow worker. 3 a fellow member of a union, political party, etc., especially of the COMMUNIST PARTY. *n.*

**com·rade·ly** (kom′ra dlē *or* kom′ri dlē) of, characteristic of, or like a COMRADE or comrades: *They sat around the fire in comradely silence.* *adj.* —**com′rade·li·ness,** *n.*

**com·rade·ship** (kom′rad ship′ *or* kom′rid ship′) 1 the condition of being a COMRADE. 2 the relation of COMRADES; friendship; fellowship. *n.*

**comte** (kônt) *French.* COUNT. *n.*

**com·tesse** (kôn tes′) *French.* COUNTESS. *n.*

**con**[1] (kon) 1 against: *The two debating teams argued the question pro and con.* 2 a reason against: *The pros and cons of a question are the arguments for and against it.* 1 *adv.*, 2 *n.*

**con**[2] (kon) learn well enough to remember; study. *v.*, **conned, con·ning.**

**con**[3] (kon) *Informal.* 1 trick; swindle: *He was conned into buying a used car that was worthless.* 2 a swindle: *The whole thing was just a con, but I fell for it.* 1 *v.*, **conned, con·ning;** 2 *n.*

**con–** a prefix meaning together or altogether; a form of the prefix **com-** occurring before all consonants except *b, m,* and *p* and, sometimes, *f,* as in *conclusion, confederation.* See note at COM-.

**con.** 1 Cdn. concession road. 2 in music, concerto. 3 continued.

**Con** 1 Conservative. 2 Consul.

**con·cat·e·nate** (kon kat′ə nāt′) 1 link together. 2 linked together. 1 *v.*, **con·cat·e·nat·ed, con·cat·e·nat·ing;** 2 *adj.*

**con·cat·e·na·tion** (kon kat′ə nā′shən) 1 linking or being linked together. 2 a connected series of things or events.

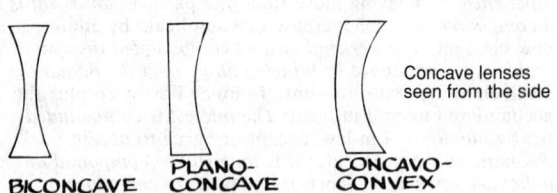

Concave lenses seen from the side

BICONCAVE  PLANO-CONCAVE  CONCAVO-CONVEX

**con·cave** (kon′kāv) 1 hollow and curved like the

inside of a circle or sphere: *The palm of one's hand is slightly concave.* **2** a concave surface or thing. **1** *adj.*, **2** *n.* —**con·cave′ly,** *adv.* Compare with CONVEX.

**con·cav·i·ty** (kon kav′ə tē) **1** a CONCAVE condition or quality. **2** a CONCAVE surface or thing. *n.*, *pl.* **con·cav·i·ties.**

**con·ca·vo–con·vex** (kon kā′vō kon veks′) CONCAVE on one side and CONVEX on the other: *In a concavo-convex lens, the concave side has the greater curvature.* See CONCAVE for picture. *adj.*

**con·ceal** (kən sēl′) **1** hide. **2** keep secret. *v.* —**con·ceal′a·ble,** *adj.* —**con·ceal′er,** *n.*

**con·ceal·ment** (kən sēl′mənt) **1** CONCEALing or being concealed. **2** a means or place for hiding. *n.*

**con·cede** (kən sēd′) **1** admit as true; admit: *Everyone concedes that 2 and 2 make 4.* **2** give what is asked or claimed; grant; yield: *She conceded us the right to hunt on her land.* *v.*, **con·ced·ed, con·ced·ing.**
☛ *Etym.* From L *concedere*, from *com-* 'together' + *cedere* 'yield'.

**con·ceit** (kən sēt′) **1** too high an opinion of oneself or of one's ability, importance, etc.: *In his conceit the track star thought no one could outrun him.* **2** a fanciful notion; witty thought or expression, often a far-fetched one. *n.*

**con·ceit·ed** (kən sē′tid) having too high an opinion of oneself or one's ability, importance, etc.; vain. *adj.* —**con·ceit′ed·ly,** *adv.* —**con·ceit′ed·ness,** *n.*

**con·ceiv·a·ble** (kən sē′və bəl) that can be CONCEIVEd or thought of; imaginable: *We should take every conceivable precaution against fire.* *adj.* —**con·ceiv′a·bly,** *adv.*

**con·ceive** (kən sēv′) **1** form in the mind; think up, plan, or devise: *The plan was poorly conceived. She has conceived a better design for a house that uses solar heating.* **2** develop an idea, feeling, etc.; form in one's mind: *He conceived a strong dislike for his aunt.* **3** have as an idea or opinion; imagine or believe (*often used with* **of**): *It's hard to conceive of such things ever happening. They conceived themselves to be under the protection of the embassy.* **4** become pregnant. **5** become pregnant with: *to conceive a child.* **6** put in words; express: *The warning was conceived in the plainest language.* *v.*, **con·ceived, con·ceiv·ing.**

**con·cen·trate** (kon′sən trāt′) **1** bring or come together to one place: *A convex lens is used to concentrate rays of light.* **2** pay close attention; focus the mind: *He concentrated upon the problem.* **3** make stronger: *We concentrated the solution by boiling off some of the water.* **4** something that has been concentrated: *lemon juice concentrate.* 1–3 *v.*, **con·cen·trat·ed, con·cen·trat·ing;** 4 *n.*

**con·cen·trat·ed** (kon′sən trā′tid) **1** brought together in one place. **2** of liquids and solutions, made stronger. **3** pt. and pp. of CONCENTRATE. 1, 2 *adj.*, 3 *v.*

**con·cen·tra·tion** (kon′sən trā′shən) **1** concentrating or being CONCENTRATEd. **2** close attention: *Josefa gave the problem her full concentration.* **3** the strength of a solution. *n.*

**concentration camp** a camp where political enemies, prisoners of war, and interned foreigners are held.

hat, āge, fär; let, ēqual, tėrm; it, īce
hot, ōpen, ôrder; oil, out; cup, pu̇t, rüle
əbove, takən, pencəl, lemən, circəs
ch, child; ng, long; sh, ship
th, thin; ᴛʜ, then; zh, measure

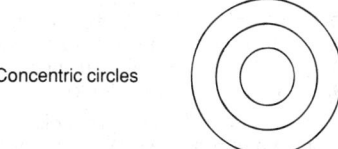
Concentric circles

**con·cen·tric** (kən sen′trik) having the same centre. Compare with ECCENTRIC (def. 3). *adj.* —**con·cen′tri·cal·ly,** *adv.*

**con·cen·tri·cal** (kən sen′trə kəl) CONCENTRIC. *adj.*

**con·cept** (kon′sept) a general notion; an idea of a class of objects; idea: *the concept of equality, basic concepts of chivalry.* *n.*

**con·cep·tion** (kən sep′shən) **1** a thought; idea; impression: *His conception of the problem is different from mine.* **2** the act or power of conceiving. **3** the state of being conceived. **4** becoming pregnant. **5** a design, plan, or concept. *n.*

**con·cep·tu·al** (kən sep′chü əl) having to do with CONCEPTS or general ideas. *adj.* —**con·cep′tu·al·ly,** *adv.*

**con·cern** (kən sėrn′) **1** have to do with; relate to: *The letter concerns the proposal for a new bridge. Nine students from our class are concerned in the play.* **2** involve the interests of; be the proper business or affair of: *The message is private; it concerns nobody but me.* **3** whatever has to do with a person or thing; matter; business; affair: *How I spend my money is my concern, not yours.* **4** troubled state of mind; worry; anxiety; uneasiness: *The mother's concern over her sick child kept her awake all night.* **5** trouble; make anxious: *Krishna didn't want to concern his friends with the details of the accident.* **6** a business company; firm: *She works for a big manufacturing concern in Toronto.* **7** relation; reference: *The special concern of her new book on Saskatchewan history is with the period just after the Depression.* 1, 2, 5 *v.*, 3, 4, 6, 7 *n.*
**as concerns,** about; with reference to.
**concern oneself, a** take an interest; be busy: *She will concern herself in the water sports program.* **b** be troubled or worried; be anxious or uneasy: *Don't concern yourself; I have everything ready.*
**of concern,** of importance; of interest: *a matter of concern.*

**con·cerned** (kən sėrnd′) **1** interested; caring: *Concerned citizens will attend the meeting on pollution.* **2** involved; having a connection: *All the students concerned in the school play were given time off for the dress rehearsal.* **3** troubled; worried; anxious. **4** pt. and pp. of CONCERN. 1–3 *adj.*, 4 *v.*

**con·cern·ing** (kən sėr′ning) **1** having to do with; with regard to; regarding; relating to; about: *The police officer asked many questions concerning the accident.* **2** ppr. of CONCERN. 1 *prep.*, 2 *v.*

**con·cern·ment** (kən sėrn′mənt) **1** importance; interest. **2** worry; anxiety. **3** affair. *n.*

**con·cert** (kon′sərt *for noun,* kən sėrt′ *for verb*) **1** a musical performance. **2** used in concerts; for concerts.

**3** agreement; harmony; union.   **4** arrange by agreement; plan or make together: *The rebels concerted a plan for seizing the town.*   1–3 *n.*, 4 *v.*
**in concert,**   all together; in agreement: *The rebel groups acted in concert to seize the town.*

**con·cert·ed** (kən sėr′tid)   **1** arranged by agreement; planned or made together; combined: *a concerted attack.* **2** arranged in parts for several voices or musical instruments.   **3** pt. and pp. of CONCERT.   1, 2 *adj.*, 3 *v.*

**con·cer·ti·na** (kon′sər tē′nə)   a roundish musical instrument made up of a bellows with a set of button keys at each end: *A concertina is like a small accordion.*   *n.*

**con·cert·mas·ter** (kon′sərt mas′tər)   the leader, usually the first violinist, of an orchestra, ranking next to the conductor.   *n.*

**con·cer·to** (kən cher′tō)   a musical composition, usually in three parts, for one or more solo instruments, such as a violin, piano, etc., accompanied by an orchestra. *n., pl.* **con·cer·tos.**

**con·ces·sion**[1] (kən sesh′ən)   **1** a conceding; granting; yielding: *As a concession, his mother allowed him to stay out an hour longer.*   **2** anything conceded or yielded; admission; acknowledgment.   **3** something conceded or granted by a government or controlling authority; a grant: *Land, privileges, etc. given by a government to a business company are called concessions. A circus leases space for booths as concessions.*   *n.*
☛ *Etym.* From L *concessio, -onis,* from *concedere.* See note at CONCEDE.

**con·ces·sion**[2] (kən sesh′ən) *Cdn.*   **1** mainly in Ontario and Quebec, a subdivision of land in township surveys, formerly one of the rows of thirty-two 200-acre (about 81-hectare) lots into which each new township was divided.   **2** CONCESSION ROAD.   *n.*
☛ *Etym.* From Cdn. F.

**concession road**   *Cdn.*   especially in Ontario, a rural road following the ROAD ALLOWANCE between concessions, running as a rule east and west or sometimes north and south, and connected to other concession roads by north-south or sometimes east-west side roads. Concession roads are usually 1¼ miles (2 km) apart.

**con·ces·sive** (kən ses′iv)   **1** yielding; making or implying concession.   **2** expressing concession. *Though* and *although* are concessive words.   *adj.*

A pink conch of the Caribbean. The animal's body is partly emerged.

**conch** (konch *or* kongk)   **1** any of a group of large sea snails having a spiral shell with the outermost spiral roughly triangular in outline and with a wide lip often curled back, revealing a smooth, pearly lining; especially, any of a number of related plant-eating species found mainly in the Caribbean.   **2** the shell of a conch, used as an ornament or for making cameos.   *n., pl.* **conch·es** (kon′chiz) *or* **conchs** (kongks).

**con·cil·i·ate** (kən sil′ē āt′)   **1** win over; soothe: *Puranee conciliated her angry little sister by promising to take her to the zoo.*   **2** gain good will, regard, favour, etc. by friendly acts.   **3** reconcile; bring into harmony.   *v.,* **con·cil·i·at·ed, con·cil·i·at·ing.**

**con·cil·i·a·tion** (kən sil′ē ā′shən)   conciliating or being CONCILIATEd.   *n.*

**con·cil·i·a·tor** (kən sil′ē ā′tər)   a person who CONCILIATES; arbitrator; peacemaker.   *n.*

**con·cil·i·a·to·ry** (kən sil′ē ə tô′rē)   tending or calculated to win over, soothe, or reconcile: *They hoped the apology would have a conciliatory effect on the angry tenants. He spoke to the crowd in a conciliatory tone of voice.*   *adj.*

**con·cise** (kən sīs′)   expressing much in few words; brief but full of meaning: *He gave a concise report of the meeting.*   *adj.* —**con·cise′ly,** *adv.* —**con·cise′ness,** *n.*

**con·clave** (kon′klāv)   **1** a private meeting.   **2** in the Roman Catholic Church, a meeting of the cardinals for the election of a pope.   **3** the rooms where the cardinals meet in private for this purpose.   *n.*

**con·clude** (kən klüd′)   **1** end; finish: *Sabra concluded her speech with a funny story.*   **2** arrange; settle: *The two countries concluded a trade agreement.*   **3** find out by thinking; reach or arrive at a decision, judgment, or opinion by reasoning; infer: *From the clues we found, we concluded that the thief must have left in a hurry.* **4** decide; resolve: *I concluded not to go.*   *v.,* **con·clud·ed, con·clud·ing.**

**con·clu·sion** (kən klü′zhən)   **1** an end: *the conclusion of the game.*   **2** the last main division of a speech, essay, etc.: *A book or article often has a conclusion summing up all of the important parts.*   **3** a final result; outcome. **4** an arrangement, settlement: *the conclusion of a peace treaty between enemies.*   **5** a decision, judgment, or opinion reached by reasoning: *Fernando came to the conclusion that he must work much harder if he wished to succeed.*   *n.*
**in conclusion,**   finally; lastly; to CONCLUDE (def. 1).

**con·clu·sive** (kən klü′siv)   decisive; convincing; definite: *The evidence against the burglar was conclusive. adj.* —**con·clu·sive·ly,** *adv.* —**con·clu′sive·ness,** *n.*

**con·coct** (kən kokt′ *or* kon kokt′)   **1** prepare by putting together ingredients: *The chef has concocted a delicious new dessert.*   **2** make up, especially something complicated; invent; devise: *What fantastic money-making scheme have you concocted this time? She concocts really clever mystery stories.*   *v.*

**con·coc·tion** (kən kok′shən *or* kon kok′shən)   **1** the act of CONCOCTING.   **2** the thing CONCOCTed.   *n.*

**con·com·i·tance** (kon kom′ə təns)   accompaniment.   *n.*

**con·com·i·tant** (kon kom′ə tənt)   **1** accompanying; attending: *a concomitant result.*   **2** an accompanying thing, quality, or circumstance; accompaniment.   1 *adj.,* 2 *n.* —**con·com′i·tant·ly,** *adv.*

**con·cord** (kon′kôrd *or* kong′kôrd)   **1** agreement; harmony; peace: *concord between friends.*   **2** a harmonious combination of tones sounded together. **3** treaty.   *n.*

**con·cor·dance** (kon kôr′dəns)   **1** an agreement; harmony.   **2** an alphabetical list of the principal words or all the words occurring in a particular body of writing, with identification of the passages in which they occur: *a concordance of Shakespeare.*   *n.*

**con·cord·ant** (kon kôr′dənt) agreeing; harmonious. *adj.* —**con·cord′ant·ly**, *adv.*

**con·cor·dat** (kon kôr′dat) **1** an agreement; compact. **2** a formal agreement between the pope and a government about church affairs. *n.*

**Concord grape** a large, sweet, bluish-black variety of grape used for making jelly, juice, or wine.

**con·course** (kon′kôrs *or* kong′kôrs) **1** a running, flowing, or coming together: *The fort was built at the concourse of two rivers.* **2** a crowd. **3** a place where crowds gather or wait: *the main concourse of a railway station.* *n.*

**con·crete** (kon′krēt *or* kon krēt′) **1** a mixture of crushed stone or gravel, sand, cement, and water that hardens as it dries: *Concrete is used for foundations, whole buildings, sidewalks, roads, dams, and bridges.* **2** the hard substance resulting from the hardening of this mixture: *Ali fell and hurt his head on the concrete.* **3** made of this mixture: *a concrete sidewalk.* **4** real; existing of itself in the material world, not merely as an idea or as a quality: *All actual objects are concrete. A painting is concrete; its beauty is abstract.* **5** specific; particular; not abstract or general: *The lawyer gave concrete examples of the prisoner's cruelty.* **6** naming a thing, especially something perceived by the senses: *Sugar and people are concrete nouns.* 1, 2 *n.*, 3–6 *adj.* —**con·crete′ly**, *adv.* —**con·crete′ness**, *n.*

**con·cre·tion** (kon krē′shən) **1** forming into a mass; solidifying. **2** a solidified mass; hard formation: *Gallstones are concretions.* *n.*

**con·cu·bine** (kong′kyə bīn′ *or* kon′kyə bīn′) **1** a woman who lives with or has a continuing sexual relationship with a man without being legally married to him; mistress: *Concubine was the usual word for a mistress before about the 17th century.* **2** in certain societies where polygamy was accepted, such as that of the ancient Hebrews, a wife having an inferior social and legal status; a second wife. *n.*

**con·cur** (kən kėr′) **1** be of the same opinion; agree: *The judges all concurred in giving John the prize.* **2** work together: *The events of the week concurred to make it a great holiday.* **3** come together; happen at the same time. *v.*, **con·curred, con·cur·ring.**

**con·cur·rence** (kən kėr′əns) **1** the holding of the same opinion; agreement. **2** working together. **3** happening at the same time. **4** coming together; meeting at a point: *the concurrence of many lines of railway track.* *n.*

**con·cur·rent** (kən kėr′ənt) **1** existing side by side; happening at the same time. **2** co-operating. **3** having equal authority or jurisdiction; CO-ORDINATE (def. 1). **4** agreeing; consistent; harmonious. **5** coming together; meeting at a point. *adj.* —**con·cur′rent·ly,** *adv.*

**con·cus·sion** (kən kush′ən) **1** a sudden, violent shaking; shock: *The concussion caused by the explosion broke many windows.* **2** an injury to the brain, spine, etc. caused by a blow, fall, or other shock. *n.*

**con·cus·sive** (kən kus′iv) **1** of or having to do with CONCUSSION. **2** tending to cause CONCUSSION. *adj.*

**con·demn** (kən dem′) **1** express strong disapproval of: *We condemn cruelty and cruel people.* **2** show to be guilty of crime or wrong; convict: *The prisoner is sure to be condemned. Her letters are enough to condemn her.* **3** pass sentence on; doom: *He was condemned to life imprisonment.* **4** declare not sound or suitable for use: *This bridge has been condemned because it is no longer safe.*

**concordant**     **251**     **condition**

hat, āge, fär; let, ēqual, tėrm; it, īce
hot, ōpen, ôrder; oil, out; cup, pu̇t, rüle
əbove, takən, pencəl, lemən, circəs
ch, child; ng, long; sh, ship
th, thin; ᴛʜ, then; zh, measure

**5** assign to an unpleasant fate or condition: *Poverty condemned them to a life of frustration.* *v.*

**con·dem·na·tion** (kon′dem nā′shən) **1** strong disapproval: *Gabriel expressed his condemnation of the new plan.* **2** CONDEMNing or being condemned: *the condemnation of a prisoner by a judge, the condemnation of an unsafe bridge.* **3** a cause or reason for CONDEMNing: *Her refusal to help was her condemnation.* *n.*

**con·dem·na·to·ry** (kən dem′nə tô′rē) condemning; expressing CONDEMNATION. *adj.*

**con·demned** (kən demd′) **1** pronounced guilty of a crime or wrong. **2** declared to be unfit for use: *a condemned house.* **3** pt. and pp. of CONDEMN. 1, 2 *adj.*, 3 *v.*

**con·den·sa·tion** (kon′dən sā′shən) **1** condensing or being CONDENSEd: *the condensation of a story, the condensation of steam into water.* **2** something CONDENSEd; a condensed mass: *A cloud is a condensation of water vapour in the atmosphere. There is a condensation of the book in that magazine.* *n.*

**con·dense** (kən dens′) **1** make or become denser or more compact; reduce the volume of: *Milk is condensed before it is canned.* **2** make stronger; concentrate: *Light is condensed by means of lenses.* **3** change from a gas or vapour to a liquid: *If steam comes into contact with cold surfaces, it condenses or is condensed into water.* **4** put into fewer words; express briefly: *He condensed the paragraph into one line.* *v.*, **con·densed, con·dens·ing.**

**condensed milk** evaporated milk that has been sweetened with sugar before being canned.

**con·dens·er** (kən den′sər) **1** whatever CONDENSES something. **2** a device for receiving and holding a charge of electricity. **3** an apparatus for changing gas or vapour into a liquid. **4** a strong lens or lenses for concentrating light upon a small area. *n.*

**con·de·scend** (kon′di send′) **1** come down willingly or graciously to the level of one's inferiors in rank: *The king condescended to eat with the beggars.* **2** grant a favour in a haughty or patronizing way: *The rich family condescended to visit the poorer people.* **3** stoop or lower oneself: *She would not condescend to taking a bribe.* *v.*

**con·de·scend·ing** (kon′di sen′ding) **1** showing CONDESCENSION; patronizing; acting in a way that shows scorn for others: *The women were annoyed by the condescending manner of the visitor.* **2** ppr. of CONDESCEND. 1 *adj.*, 2 *v.* —**con′de·scend′ing·ly,** *adv.*

**con·de·scen·sion** (kon′di sen′shən) **1** the act or an instance of CONDESCENDing. **2** a patronizing attitude: *I could feel the condescension of the hotel clerk in the way he looked at my old luggage.* *n.*

**con·dign** (kən dīn′) deserved; adequate; fitting: *a condign punishment.* *adj.*

**con·di·ment** (kon′də mənt) something used to give flavour and relish to food, such as pepper and spices. *n.*

**con·di·tion** (kən dish′ən) **1** the state in which a person or thing is: *The accident victim was in critical condition in the hospital. Her car is several years old, but still in very*

good condition. **2** physical fitness; good health: *People who take part in sports must keep in condition.* **3** put in good condition: *Exercise conditions your muscles.* **4** rank; social position: *The premier's parents were people of humble condition.* **5** anything on which something else depends; that without which something else cannot occur or exist: *Available oxygen is a condition of human life. A condition of employment as a sales representative is a willingness to travel.* **6** an ailment or disease: *My aunt has a heart condition.* **7** be a condition of: *Ability and effort usually condition success.* **8** make depend on a condition; subject to a condition: *The increase in his allowance was conditioned on his willingness to help more around the house.* **9** in a legal document, a clause that expresses or contains a condition. **10** shape behaviour of by repeated exposure to particular conditions, with which responses become associated: *This dog has been conditioned to expect food when it obeys a command.* **11** make accustomed to: *Many years of running the store had conditioned her to hard work.* **12 conditions,** circumstances that affect an activity or situation: *poor driving conditions. The working conditions here are excellent.* 1, 2, 4–6, 9, 12 *n.*, 3, 7, 8, 10, 11 *v.* —**con·di′tion·er,** *n.*
**on condition that,** if; provided that: *I'll go on condition that you will too.*
**on no condition,** not at all; never: *On no condition will I do your homework for you.*

**con·di·tion·al** (kən dish′ə nəl) **1** depending on something else; not absolute; limited: *"You may go if the sun shines" is a conditional promise.* **2** expressing or containing a CONDITION (def. 5). "If the sun shines" is a **conditional clause.** *adj.* —**con·di′tion·al·ly,** *adv.*
**conditional clause** in grammar, a clause that expresses a condition: *In* They will leave if permission is given, *the conditional clause is* if permission is given.

**con·di·tioned** (kən dish′ənd) **1** put under a CONDITION; subject to certain conditions. **2** in or having a certain kind of CONDITION. **3** produced by repeated exposure to particular CONDITIONS: *a conditioned reflex.* **4** pt. and pp. of CONDITION. 1–3 *adj.*, 4 *v.*

**con·di·tion·er** (kən dish′ə nər) **1** a lotion or cream used to improve the condition of the hair, skin, etc. **2** any person or thing that conditions. *n.*

**con·do** (kon′dō) *Informal.* CONDOMINIUM (defs. 1, 2). *n., pl.* **con·dos** or **con·does.**

**con·dole** (kən dōl′) express sympathy; sympathize (*used with* **with**): *The widow's friends condoled with her at the funeral.* *v.* **con·doled, con·dol·ing.**

**con·do·lence** (kən dō′ləns) an expression of sympathy: *Her friends sent her many condolences.* *n.*

**con·dom** (kon′dəm *or* kun′dəm) a thin, usually rubber sheath worn over the penis during sexual intercourse to prevent venereal infection and as a contraceptive. *n.*

**con·do·min·i·um** (kon′də min′ē əm) **1** a residential structure in which apartments or townhouses are individually owned as pieces of real estate while the land and common facilities are jointly owned. **2** a unit in such a structure. **3** joint control, especially of two or more countries over the government of another country. *n.*
☛ *Etym.* Formed from the prefix *con-* + L *dominium* 'lordship'. Although the word has been in English for 200 years or so, the meanings given in the first two definitions date only from the 1960's. The original meanings were (a) a territory governed jointly by two countries, (b) that type of joint government. See also note at DOMINION.

**con·do·na·tion** (kon′dō nā′shən) the forgiving of an offence, especially by ignoring or overlooking it. *n.*

**con·done** (kən dōn′) forgive or overlook an offence or fault: *His parents had always condoned his temper tantrums when he was small.* *v.*, **con·doned, con·don·ing.**

**con·dor** (kon′dər) a large vulture having a neck and head bare of feathers: *Condors live on high mountains in South America and California.* *n.*

**con·duce** (kən dyüs′ *or* kən düs′) lead; contribute; be favourable (*to*): *Darkness and quiet conduce to sleep.* *v.*, **con·duced, con·duc·ing.**

**con·du·cive** (kən dyü′siv *or* kən dü′siv) helpful; favourable: *Exercise is conducive to health.* *adj.*

**con·duct** (kon′dukt *for noun,* kən dukt′ *for verb*) **1** behaviour; way of acting: *Her rude conduct was inexcusable. He won a medal for good conduct.* **2** act or behave in a certain way: *The way she conducted herself throughout the crisis showed that she had great courage.* **3** direction; management: *the conduct of an office.* **4** direct; manage: *to conduct the affairs of a business.* **5** direct an orchestra, choir, etc. as leader. **6** go along with and show the way to; guide: *The butler conducted him to the library.* **7** transmit heat, electricity, etc.: *Those pipes conduct steam to the radiators upstairs.* 1, 3 *n.*, 2, 4–7 *v.*

**con·duct·i·bil·i·ty** (kən duk′tə bil′ə tē) the power of CONDUCTING (def. 7) heat, electricity, etc. *n.*

**con·duct·i·ble** (kən duk′tə bəl) **1** capable of CONDUCTING (def. 7) heat, electricity, etc. **2** capable of being CONDUCTED (def. 7). *adj.*

**con·duc·tion** (kən duk′shən) **1** the transmission of heat, electricity, etc. by the transferring of energy from one particle to another: *the conduction of electricity along a wire.* **2** conveying: *the conduction of water through a pipe.* *n.*

**con·duc·tive** (kən duk′tiv) **1** having CONDUCTIVITY. **2** of CONDUCTION (def. 1) *adj.*

**con·duc·tiv·i·ty** (kon′duk tiv′ə tē) the power of CONDUCTING (def. 7) heat, electricity, etc. *n.*

**con·duc·tor** (kən duk′tər) **1** a person who conducts; director; manager; leader; guide. **2** the director of an orchestra, chorus, etc.: *The conductor of an orchestra trains the musicians to work together, selects the music to be used, and directs the players during a performance.* **3** the person in charge of a streetcar, bus, railway train, etc.: *The conductor usually collects the tickets or fares from the passengers.* **4** anything that transmits heat, electricity, light, sound, etc.: *Copper is a good conductor of heat and electricity.* *n.*

**con·duit** (kon′dyü it, kon′dü it, *or* kon′dit) **1** a channel or pipe for carrying liquids long distances. **2** a tube or underground passage for electric wires. *n.*

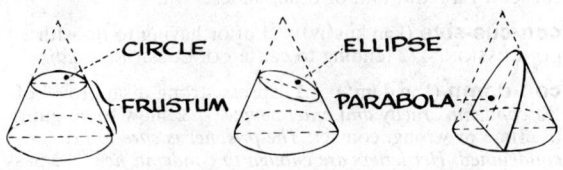

Symmetrical cones, showing conic sections

**cone** (kōn) **1** in geometry, a surface traced by a moving straight line, one point or end of which is fixed, the opposite end passing through all the points of a closed fixed curve. When the fixed curve is a circle and the line from the vertex to the centre of this circle forms a right angle with it, making a symmetrically tapered shape, the surface is called a **right circular cone.** **2** a solid figure bounded by such a surface. See SOLID for another picture. **3** anything shaped somewhat like a cone with evenly tapered sides: *an ice-cream cone, the cone of a volcano.* **4** the part that bears the seeds on pine, cedar, fir, and similar evergreen trees. See FIR, PINE¹, and SPRUCE¹ for pictures. **5** any of the conical cells in the RETINA of the eye that are sensitive to light and colour. *n.*

**co·ney** (kō′nē) **1** rabbit fur: *Coney is used to trim coats.* **2** rabbit. *n., pl.* **co·neys.** Also, **cony.**

**con·fec·tion** (kən fek′shən) a piece of candy, candied fruit, jam, etc. *n.*

**con·fec·tion·er** (kən fek′shə nər) a person whose business is making or selling candies, ice cream, etc. *n.*

**con·fec·tion·er·y** (kən fek′shə nər′ē) **1** candies, sweets, etc.; confections. **2** the business of making or selling confections. **3** a place where confections, ice cream, etc. are made or sold; candy store. *n., pl.* **con·fec·tion·er·ies.**

**con·fed·er·a·cy** (kən fed′ə rə sē) **1** a union of countries or states; a group of people joined together for a special purpose. **2** a league or alliance. **3** conspiracy. **4 Confederacy,** *U.S.* CONFEDERATE STATES OF AMERICA. *n., pl.* **con·fed·er·a·cies.**

**con·fed·er·ate** (kən fed′ə rit *for adjective and noun,* kən fed′ə rāt′ *for verb*) **1** joined together for a special purpose; allied. **2** a country, person, etc. joined with another for a special purpose; ally; companion. **3** an accomplice; partner in crime: *The thief was arrested, but his confederate escaped.* **4** enter a union or alliance: *Newfoundland confederated with Canada in 1949. Four provinces of Canada confederated in 1867.* **5 Confederate,** *U.S.* of or belonging to the CONFEDERATE STATES OF AMERICA: *the Confederate uniform.* **6 Confederate,** *U.S.* a person who lived in and supported the CONFEDERATE STATES OF AMERICA. 1, 5 *adj.*, 2, 3, 6 *n.*, 4 *v.*

**Confederate States of America** *U.S.* the group of eleven southern states that seceded from the United States in 1860 and 1861.

**con·fed·er·a·tion** (kən fed′ə rā′shən) **1** a federation; the act of joining together in a league; the state of being united in a league or alliance: *The conference devised a scheme for the confederation of the foreign colonies.* **2** a group of countries, states, etc. joined together for a special purpose; league. **3 Confederation,** *Cdn.* the name given to the federation of Ontario, Quebec, Nova Scotia, and New Brunswick in 1867. **4 the Confederation, a** *Cdn.* the ten provinces of Canada. **b** the confederation of the American States from 1781 to 1789. *n.*

**con·fer** (kən fėr′) **1** consult together; exchange ideas; talk things over: *The prime minister often confers with his advisers.* **2** give; award; bestow (*on*): *The mayor conferred a medal on the brave firefighter.* *v.,* **con·ferred, con·fer·ring.**

**con·fer·ence** (kon′fə rəns) **1** a meeting of interested persons to discuss a particular subject: *A conference was called to discuss forming a school choir.* **2** the act of taking counsel; the act of talking something over; consultation with a person or a group of persons: *You cannot see Ms. Zamar just now; she is in conference.* **3** an

# coney 253 confidential

hat, āge, fär; let, ēqual, tėrm; it, īce
hot, ōpen, ôrder; oil, out; cup, pút, rüle
əbove, takən, pencəl, lemən, circəs
ch, child; ng, long; sh, ship
th, thin; ᴛʜ, then; zh, measure

association of schools, sports teams, etc. joined together for some special purpose. *n.*

**con·fer·ment** (kən fėr′mənt) giving; bestowal. *n.*

**con·fess** (kən fes′) **1** acknowledge; admit; own up: *I confess you are right on one point.* **2** admit one's guilt: *The prisoner confessed.* **3** tell one's sins to a priest in order to obtain forgiveness. **4** of a priest, hear a person tell his or her sins in order to obtain forgiveness. *v.*

**con·fessed** (kən fest′) **1** acknowledged; admitted. **2** pt. and pp. of CONFESS. 1 *adj.*, 2 *v.* **con·fess′ed·ly,** *adv.*

**con·fes·sion** (kən fesh′ən) **1** acknowledgment; admission; owning up. **2** admission of guilt. **3** the telling of one's sins to a priest in order to obtain forgiveness. **4** the thing confessed. **5** an acknowledgment of belief; profession of faith. **6** the belief acknowledged; creed. *n.*

**con·fes·sion·al** (kən fesh′ə nəl) **1** a small booth where a priest hears CONFESSIONS (def. 3). **2** the practice of CONFESSING sins (def. 3) to a priest. **3** of or having to do with CONFESSION (defs. 1, 2). 1, 2 *n.*, 3 *adj.*

**con·fes·sor** (kən fes′ər) **1** a person who CONFESSES (defs. 1, 2). **2** a priest who has the authority to hear CONFESSIONS (def. 3). **3** a person who acknowledges belief. *n.*

**con·fet·ti** (kən fet′ē) the bits of coloured paper thrown about at carnivals, weddings, etc. *n.*

**con·fi·dant** (kon′fə dant′) a person trusted with one's secrets, private affairs, etc.; a close friend. *n.*

**con·fi·dante** (kon′fə dant′) a woman trusted with one's secrets, etc.; a close woman friend. *n.*

**con·fide** (kən fīd′) **1** tell as a secret: *He confided his troubles to me.* **2** hand over a task, person, etc. in trust; give to another for safekeeping: *The collection of dues is confided to the treasurer.* *v.,* **con·fid·ed, con·fid·ing.** —**con·fid′er,** *n.*
**confide in, a** entrust a secret to: *She always confides in her sister.* **b** put trust in.

**con·fi·dence** (kon′fə dəns) **1** a firm belief; trust: *We have no confidence in a liar.* **2** a firm belief in oneself and one's abilities: *She goes at her work with confidence.* **3** boldness; too much boldness: *Although he could not swim, he dived into the water with confidence.* **4** a feeling of trust; assurance that a person will not tell others what is said: *The story was told to me in strict confidence.* **5** something told as a secret: *I listened to his confidences for half an hour.* *n.*

**con·fi·dent** (kon′fə dənt) **1** firmly believing; certain; sure: *I feel confident that our team will win.* **2** sure of oneself and one's abilities: *a confident person.* **3** too bold; too sure. **4** a close, trusted friend; CONFIDANT(E). 1–3 *adj.*, 4 *n.* —**con′fi·dent·ly,** *adv.*

**con·fi·den·tial** (kon′fə den′shəl) **1** intended for or restricted to secret or private use: *The detective's report* ⸱ *her superior was confidential.* **2** showing trust or intimacy: *He spoke in a confidential tone of voice.* **3** trusted with secrets, private affairs, etc.: *a confi*⸱

secretary. *adj.* —**con′fi·den′tial·ness,** *n.*
—**con′fi·den′tial·ly,** *adv.*

**con·fi·den·ti·al·i·ty** (kən′fə den′shē al′ə tē) the fact or quality of being CONFIDENTIAL. *n.*

**con·fid·ing** (kən fī′ding) **1** trustful; trusting. **2** ppr. of CONFIDE. **1** *adj.,* **2** *v.* —**con·fid′ing·ly,** *adv.*

**con·fig·u·ra·tion** (kən fig′yə rā′shən *or* kən fig′ə rā′shən) the relative position of parts; manner of arrangement; form; shape; outline: *Geographers study the configuration of the surface of the earth.* *n.*

**con·fine** (kən fīn′ *for verb,* kon′fīn *for noun*) **1** keep within limits; restrict: *He was confined in prison for two years.* **2** keep indoors; shut in: *A cold confined her to the house.* **3** imprison. **4** Usually, **confines,** *pl.* a boundary; border; limit: *These people have never been beyond the confines of their own valley.* **1–3** *v.,* **con·fined, con·fin·ing;** **4** *n.* —**con·fin′er,** *n.*
**be confined,** give birth to a child.

**con·fined** (kən fīnd′) **1** restricted. **2** imprisoned. **3** pt. and pp. of CONFINE. **1, 2** *adj.,* **3** *v.*

**con·fine·ment** (kən fīn′mənt) **1** confining or being CONFINED (defs. 1, 2). **2** imprisonment. **3** the period for which a mother is confined to bed during and after childbirth. *n.*

**con·firm** (kən fèrm′) **1** make official by formal statement; approve; consent to: *Parliament confirmed the treaty.* **2** prove to be true or correct; make certain: *to confirm a rumour. The travel agent confirmed her plane reservation.* **3** support; strengthen in an opinion, etc.: *A sudden storm confirmed my decision not to leave.* **4** admit by a special ceremony to full membership in a Christian church after the completion of the required study and preparation. *v.* —**con·firm′a·ble,** *adj.*

**con·fir·ma·tion** (kon′fər mā′shən) **1** making sure; CONFIRMing. **2** something that CONFIRMs; proof: *The lab has sent confirmation of the diagnosis.* **3** an assurance that one's plans have not been changed: *The airline requires confirmation of your reservation.* **4** the ceremony of admitting a person to full membership in a Christian church after completion of the required study and preparation. *n.*

**con·firmed** (kən fèrmd′) **1** firmly established; proved: *confirmed results.* **2** constant; permanent: *a confirmed bachelor.* **3** pt. and pp. of CONFIRM. **1, 2** *adj.,* **3** *v.*

**con·fis·cate** (kon′fi skāt′) **1** seize for the public treasury: *The government confiscated the property of all traitors.* **2** seize by authority; take and keep: *The customs officer confiscated the smuggled cigarettes.* *v.,* **con·fis·cat·ed, con·fis·cat·ing.**

**con·fis·ca·tion** (kon′fi skā′shən) confiscating or being CONFISCATEd: *the confiscation of wealth.* *n.*

**con·fis·ca·to·ry** (kən fis′kə tô′rē) of the nature of confiscation or tending to CONFISCATE. *adj.*

**con·fla·gra·tion** (kon′flə grā′shən) a great, destructive fire: *A conflagration destroyed most of the city.* *n.*

**con·flict** (kon′flikt *for noun,* kən flikt′ *for verb*) **1** a prolonged fight or struggle. **2** direct opposition; a disagreement; clash: *A conflict of opinions divided the members into two groups.* **3** be directly opposed; disagree; clash: *The date conflicts with her vacation plans. Their stories of the accident conflict.* **1, 2** *n.,* **3** *v.*

**con·flict·ing** (kən flik′ting) **1** that conflicts; disagreeing; clashing. **2** ppr. of CONFLICT. **1** *adj.,* **2** *v.*

**conflict of interest** a clash, or opposition, between the private interests and the public responsibilities of a person in a position of trust, such as a government official.

**con·flu·ence** (kon′flü əns) **1** a flowing together: *the confluence of two rivers.* **2** a coming together of people or things; throng. *n.*

**con·flu·ent** (kon′flü ənt) flowing or running together; blending into one: *confluent rivers.* *adj.*

**con·flux** (kon′fluks) a flowing together; CONFLUENCE (def. 1). *n.*

**con·form** (kən fôrm′) **1** act according to law or rule; adapt oneself to or accept the normal standards of business, conduct, worship, etc.: *Members must conform to the rules of the club.* **2** be similar in form or character: *The path conforms to the shoreline of the lake.* **3** make similar in form or character with: *to conform the path to the shoreline. The stranger never conformed his ways to theirs.* *v.* —**con·form′er,** *n.*

**con·form·a·ble** (kən fôr′mə bəl) **1** similar. **2** in agreement; agreeable; harmonious: *The committee felt that the proposal was not conformable to their interests.* **3** obedient; submissive: *The boy was usually conformable to his father's wishes.* *adj.* —**con·form′a·ble·ness,** *n.* —**con·form′a·bly,** *adv.*

**con·form·ance** (kən fôr′məns) the act of conforming; CONFORMITY: *We shall act in conformance with your request.* *n.*

**con·for·ma·tion** (kon′fôr mā′shən) **1** a structure; shape; the form of a thing resulting from the arrangement of its parts. **2** a symmetrical arrangement of the parts of a thing. **3** CONFORMing; adaptation. *n.*

**con·form·ist** (kən fôr′mist) a person who tends to CONFORM (def. 1) to generally accepted usage in behaviour, dress, etc. *n.*

**con·form·i·ty** (kən fôr′mə tē) **1** a similarity; correspondence; agreement. **2** behaviour in agreement with generally accepted standards of business, law, conduct, or worship; fitting oneself and one's actions to the ideas of others; compliance. **3** obedience; submission. *n., pl.* **con·form·i·ties.**

**con·found** (kən found′ *or* kon found′) **1** confuse; mix up; bewilder: *The shock confounded her.* **2** be unable to tell apart: *He confounds "deprecate" and "depreciate."* **3** surprise and puzzle: *The general was confounded by the violence of the enemy attack.* *v.*

**con·found·ed** (kən foun′did) **1** cursed: *"Confounded" is used as a mild curse.* **2** hateful; detestable. **3** pt. and pp. of CONFOUND. **1, 2** *adj.,* **3** *v.*
—**con·found′ed·ly,** *adv.*

**con·frere** (kon′frer) a fellow member; colleague. *n.*

**con·front** (kən frunt′) **1** meet face to face, especially as opponents; stand facing. **2** face boldly; oppose: *She whirled round and confronted the bully.* **3** bring face to face; place before: *The lawyer confronted the prisoner with the forged cheque.* **4** compare. *v.*

**con·fron·ta·tion** (kon′frən tā′shən) **1** a meeting or being met face to face. **2** an open clash between opposing groups, parties, or individuals: *He doesn't believe in confrontation, but would rather try to talk things out* *reasonably.* **3** referring to a tactic or strategy based on open clashes: *confrontation politics.* *n.*

**Con·fu·cian** (kən fyü′shən) **1** of or having to do with CONFUCIUS, his teachings, or his followers. **2** a follower of CONFUCIUS or his teachings. 1 *adj.*, 2 *n.*

**Con·fu·cian·ism** (kən fyü′shə niz′əm) a philosophical and religious system based on the belief in the natural goodness of all human beings, that for more than 2000 years dominated the social and political order in China: *Confucianism teaches that the greatest virtues are love, justice, reverence, wisdom, and sincerity, and emphasizes respect for parents and ancestors.* *n.*

**Con·fu·cian·ist** (kən fyü′shə nist) **1** a supporter or follower of CONFUCIANISM. **2** of or having to do with CONFUCIANISM. 1 *n.*, 2 *adj.*

**Con·fu·cius** (kən fyü′shəs) 551?–479 B.C., a Chinese philosopher and teacher whose teachings form the basis of CONFUCIANISM. *n.*

**con·fuse** (kən fyüz′) **1** mix up; throw into disorder. **2** bewilder: *So many people talking to me at once confused me.* **3** be unable to tell apart; mistake one thing for another: *Even their own mother sometimes confused the twins.* **4** make uneasy and ashamed; embarrass: *Confused by her blunder, she could not say anything for a moment.* *v.*, **con·fused, con·fus·ing.** —**con·fus′ing·ly,** *adv.*

**con·fused** (kən fyüzd′) **1** mixed up; disordered. **2** bewildered. **3** pt. and pp. of CONFUSE. 1, 2 *adj.*, 3 *v.*

**con·fus·ed·ly** (kən fyü′zi dlē) in a CONFUSED manner. *adv.*

**con·fu·sion** (kən fyü′zhen) **1** the act or fact of confusing: *Words like* believe *and* receive *are a source of confusion in spelling.* **2** a confused condition; disorder: *There was confusion in the busy street after the accident.* **3** a failure to distinguish clearly. **4** bewilderment; inability to think clearly: *In his confusion he completely forgot his appointment.* **5** uneasiness and shame: *The child ran from the stage in confusion when she forgot her lines.* *n.*

**con·fu·ta·tion** (kon′fyə tā′shən) **1** the act of confuting; disproving. **2** the thing that CONFUTES. *n.*

**con·fute** (kən fyüt′) **1** prove an argument, testimony, etc. to be false or incorrect: *The lawyer confuted the testimony of the witness by showing actual photographs of the accident.* **2** prove a person to be wrong; overcome by argument: *The speaker confuted her opponents by facts and logic.* *v.*, **con·fut·ed, con·fut·ing.** —**con·fut′er,** *n.* Compare with REFUTE.

**con·ga** (kong′gə) **1** a Cuban dance of African origin, usually performed by a group of people moving one behind the other in a single line. **2** music for this dance, having a strong, syncopated rhythm in 4/4 time. **3** dance the conga. **4** a tall, narrow, low-toned drum that is beaten with the hands. 1, 2, 4 *n.*, 3 *v.*, **con·gaed** or **con·ga'd, con·ga·ing.**

**con·geal** (kən jēl′) **1** harden or make solid by cold; freeze. **2** thicken; clot: *The blood around the wound had congealed.* *v.*

**con·ge·ni·al** (kən jē′nē əl *or* kən jē′nyəl) **1** having similar tastes and interest; getting on well together: *congenial companions.* **2** agreeable; suitable: *congenial work, a congenial atmosphere.* *adj.* —**con·ge′ni·al·ly,** *adv.*

**con·ge·ni·al·i·ty** (kən jē′nē al′ə tē) a CONGENIAL quality: *Congeniality should be considered in choosing a roommate.* *n.*

## Confucian 255 congregation

hat, āge, fär; let, ēqual, tėrm; it, īce
hot, ōpen, ôrder; oil, out; cup, pút, rüle
əbove, takən, pencəl, lemən, circəs
ch, child; ng, long; sh, ship
th, thin; ᴛʜ, then; zh, measure

**con·gen·i·tal** (kən jen′ə təl) existing before or at birth, but not inherited: *A clubfoot is a congenital deformity.* Compare with HEREDITARY. *adj.*

**con·gen·i·tal·ly** (kən jen′ə tə lē) from the time of birth. *adv.*

**con·ger eel** (kong′gər) **1** a large, scaleless ocean eel found along the coasts of Europe, Asia, and Africa, and the Atlantic coast of America: *The conger eel is an important food fish of Europe.* **2** any other eel belonging to the same genus.

**con·ge·ries** (kon jē′rēz *or* kon jē′rē ez) a collection; heap; mass. *n. sing. and pl.*

**con·gest** (kən jest′) **1** fill too full; overcrowd; clog: *The rush-hour traffic congested the streets.* **2** cause too much blood or mucus to gather in one part of the body: *An infection of the mucous membrane in the nose will congest the nasal passages.* *v.*

**con·gest·ed** (kən jes′tid) **1** overcrowded; clogged: *congested hallways.* **2** of a body organ or tissue, containing too much blood or mucus: *congested mucous membranes, congested lungs.* **3** pt. and pp. of CONGEST. 1, 2 *adj.*, 3 *v.*

**con·ges·tion** (kən jes′chən) the quality or state of being CONGESTED: *traffic congestion.* *n.*

**con·glom·er·ate** (kən glom′ə rāt′ *for verb,* kən glom′ə rit *for adjective and noun*) **1** gather in a rounded mass; collect together. **2** gathered into a rounded mass; clustered. **3** made up of miscellaneous materials gathered from various sources. **4** a mass formed of fragments. **5** a kind of sedimentary rock consisting of waterworn boulders, pebbles, etc. held together by a natural cementing material. **6** a large, widely diversified corporation consisting of a number of companies dealing in different products or services. 1 *v.*, **con·glom·er·at·ed, con·glom·er·at·ing;** 2, 3 *adj.*, 4–6 *n.*

**con·glom·er·a·tion** (kən glom′ə rā′shən) a mixed-up mass of various things or persons; mixture. *n.*

**con·grat·u·late** (kən grach′ə lāt′) express one's pleasure at the happiness or good fortune of: *I congratulated my friend on her success.* *v.*, **con·grat·u·lat·ed, con·grat·u·lat·ing.**

**con·grat·u·la·tion** (kən grach′ə lā′shən) **1** congratulating or wishing a person joy: *a letter of congratulation.* **2 congratulations,** *pl.* an expression of pleasure at another's happiness or good fortune: *Congratulations on winning the tournament.* *n.*

**con·grat·u·la·to·ry** (kən grach′ə lə tô′rē) expressing pleasure at another's happiness or good fortune: *a congratulatory note.* *adj.*

**con·gre·gate** (kong′grə gāt′) come together into a crowd or mass; assemble: *Thousands of people congregated in the town square to see the mayor. Bits of steel congregated around the magnet.* *v.*, **con·gre·gat·ed, con·gre·gat·ing.**

**con·gre·ga·tion** (kong′grə gā′shən) **1** a group of people gathered together for religious worship or instruction. **2** a gathering of people or things; assembly.

**3** coming together into a crowd or mass; assembling. **4** a religious community or order having a common rule and with or without solemn vows. *n.*

**con·gre·ga·tion·al** (kong′grə gā′shə nəl) of a CONGREGATION; done by a congregation: *congregational singing. adj.*

**con·gress** (kong′gris) **1** a formal meeting of representatives of interested groups to discuss some subject: *They attended an international congress on conservation.* **2** an organization of people for the purpose of promoting a common interest or concern: *the Canadian Labour Congress.* **3** the lawmaking body of a nation, especially of a republic. **4** meeting; coming together. **5 Congress,** in the United States: **a** the national lawmaking body, consisting of the Senate and the House of Representatives, with members elected from every state. **b** its session. *n.*

**con·gres·sion·al** (kən gresh′ə nəl) **1** of or having to do with a CONGRESS (defs. 1–4) **2 Congressional,** of or having to do with CONGRESS (def. 5). *adj.*

**con·gru·ence** (kong′grü əns) **1** agreement; harmony. **2** the condition of being exactly the same in size and shape, so that all parts match: *Check the congruence of these two triangles. n.*

**con·gru·ent** (kong′grü ənt) **1** agreeing; harmonious. **2** exactly coinciding: *congruent triangles. adj.* —**con′gru·ent·ly,** *adv.*

**con·gru·ous** (kong′grü əs) **1** agreeing; harmonious. **2** fitting; appropriate. **3** exactly coinciding. *adj.* —**con′gru·ous·ly,** *adv.* —**con′gru·ous·ness,** *n.*

**con·ic** (kon′ik) CONICAL. *adj.*

**con·i·cal** (kon′ə kəl) **1** CONE-shaped; like a cone: *The wizard wore a conical hat.* **2** of a CONE. *adj.* —**con′i·cal·ly,** *adv.*

**conic section** in geometry, a curve forming the edge of the flat surface produced when a piece is cut from a cone: *Depending on the angle at which the cut is made, the conic section will be a circle, ellipse, parabola, or hyperbola.* See CONE for picture.

**co·ni·fer** (kō′nə fər *or* kon′ə fər) any tree or shrub belonging to the order **Coniferales,** most species having small, needle-shaped, evergreen leaves and all bearing their seeds in CONES (def. 4): *Pines, spruces, firs, hemlocks, junipers, and cypresses are conifers. n.*

**co·nif·er·ous** (kō nif′ə rəs) **1** bearing CONES (def. 4): *a coniferous tree.* **2** belonging to or having to do with CONIFERS. *adj.*

**conj.** **1** conjunction. **2** conjugation.

**con·jec·tur·al** (kən jek′chə rəl) **1** involving CONJECTURE (defs. 1, 2): *Her opinion was merely conjectural, not proved.* **2** inclined to CONJECTURE (def. 3). *adj.* —**con·jec′tur·al·ly,** *adv.*

**con·jec·ture** (kən jek′chər) **1** the formation of an opinion admittedly without sufficient evidence for proof; guessing. **2** an opinion based on guesswork: *There were many conjectures about how she died, but no one knew for certain.* **3** form an opinion based on guesswork; guess: *She conjectured that they were talking about their uncle.* 1, 2 *n.,* 3 *v.,* **con·jec′tured, con·jec′tur·ing.** —**con·jec′tur·a·ble,** *adj.* —**con·jec′tur·er,** *n.*

**con·join** (kən join′) join together; unite; combine. *v.* —**con·join′er,** *n.*

**con·joint** (kən joint′) **1** joined together; united; combined. **2** formed by two or more in combination; joint. *adj.* —**con·joint′ly,** *adv.*

**con·ju·gal** (kon′jə gəl) **1** of marriage; having to do with marriage. **2** of husband or wife. *adj.* —**con′ju·gal·ly,** *adv.*

**con·ju·gate** (kon′jə gāt′ *for verb,* kon′jə git *or* kon′jə gāt′ *for adjective*) **1** give the forms of a verb according to a systematic arrangement. **2** join together; couple. **3** joined together; coupled. 1, 2 *v.,* **con·ju·gat·ed, con·ju·gat·ing;** 3 *adj.*

**con·ju·ga·tion** (kon′jə gā′shən) **1** a systematic arrangement of the forms of a verb. **2** a group of verbs having similar forms in such an arrangement. **3** the act of giving the forms of a verb according to such an arrangement. **4** a joining together; coupling. *n.*

**con·junc·tion** (kən jungk′shən) **1** a joining or being joined together; union; combination: *A severe illness in conjunction with the hot weather has left the baby very weak.* **2** a word that expresses a particular connection between words, phrases, clauses, or sentences. *And, but,* and *or* are **co-ordinating conjunctions;** *if, as, because,* etc. are **subordinating conjunctions;** *either...or, both...and* are **correlative conjunctions.** **3** the apparent nearness of two or more heavenly bodies. *n.*

**con·junc·ti·va** (kon′jungk tī′və *or* kən jungk′ti və) the mucous membrane that covers the front of the eyeball and the inner surface of the eyelids. *n., pl.* **con·junc·ti·vas** *or* **con·junc·ti·vae** (-vē *or* -vī).

**con·junc·tive** (kən jungk′tiv) **1** joining together; connecting; uniting; combining. **2** joined together; joint; united; combined. **3** like a CONJUNCTION (def. 2); like that of a conjunction. *Then* is a **conjunctive adverb.** **4** a conjunctive word; CONJUNCTION (def. 2). 1–3 *adj.,* 4 *n.* —**con·junc′tive·ly,** *adv.*

☞ *Usage.* **Conjunctive adverbs.** A number of words that are ordinarily adverbs are sometimes used also to connect independent clauses or sentences. They are called **conjunctive adverbs.** Even though they serve as connectives, their adverbial meaning remains important. The most common are: *accordingly, also, anyhow, anyway* (informal), *besides, consequently, furthermore, hence, however, indeed, likewise, moreover, namely, nevertheless, then, therefore.* In a compound sentence, it is normal to use a semicolon before a clause introduced by a conjunctive adverb: *He is extremely conceited; however, he is so charming that people overlook it.*

**con·junc·ti·vi·tis** (kən jungk′tə vī′tis) in medicine, an inflammation of the CONJUNCTIVA. *n.*

**con·ju·ra·tion** (kon′jə rā′shən) **1** the act of invoking by a sacred name. **2** the practice of magic: *The princess had been changed to a toad by conjuration.* **3** a magic form of words used in conjuring; magic spell. *n.*

**con·jure** (kun′jər *or* kon′jər *for 1–3,* kən jür′ *for 4*) **1** compel to appear or disappear by a set form of words: *The witch in the story conjured a dragon.* **2** perform tricks by very quick deceiving movements of the hands. **3** practise magic. **4** make a solemn appeal to: *By all that is holy, I conjure you not to betray your country. v.,* **con·jured, con·jur·ing.**

**conjure up,** *Informal.* **a** cause to appear as if by magic: *Grandma conjured up a bag of toys from the attic.* **b** call to mind: *This book conjures up a world of make-believe.*

**(a person** *or* **thing) to conjure with,** one that has great importance or influence: *Since her last novel, she has become a name to conjure with.*

**con·jur·er** (kun′jə rer *or* kon′jə rər)   **1** magician.   **2** a person who performs tricks with quick, deceiving movements of the hands; juggler.   *n.*   Also, **conjuror.**

**con·nect** (kə nekt′)   **1** join one thing to another; link two things together; fasten together; unite: *The plumber had to connect those pipes before the water could be turned on.*   **2** join in some business or interest; bring into some relation: *This store is connected with a major chain. Ms. Davis is connected with several clubs.*   **3** think of one thing as being associated with or the cause of another: *We usually connect spring with sunshine and flowers.*   **4** be or become connected.   **5** establish a line of communication in a telephone system (*used with* **with**): *Could you please connect me with Mr. LeBlanc's office?*   **6** of an airline flight, bus run, etc., be so arranged that passengers can change to another aircraft, bus, etc. without delay.   *v.*   —**con·nect′er, con·nec′tor,** *n.*

**con·nect·ed** (kə nek′tid)   **1** joined together; fastened together.   **2** joined in order: *connected ideas.*   **3** having ties and associates: *She is well connected socially.*   **4** pt. and pp. of CONNECT.   1–3 *adj.*, 4 *v.*

**con·nec·tion** (kə nek′shən)   **1** the act of connecting or the state of being connected.   **2** something that connects; a connecting part.   **3** any kind of practical relation with another thing or person: *He has no connection with his brother's firm.*   **4** thinking of persons or things together; linking together of words or ideas in a logical order.   **5** the arranged meeting of trains, ships, airplanes, etc. so that passengers can change from one to the other without delay: *You can make a better connection in Montreal if you take the early flight from here.*   **6** a line of communication between two points in a telephone system: *We had a bad connection and couldn't hear her very well.*   **7** a relative: *She is a connection of ours by marriage.*   **8** Usually, **connections,** *pl.*   a group of people with whom one is associated in business dealings, etc.: *She'll probably be able to get tickets through her connections in the city.*   *n.*
**in connection with,** together with; in regard to.

**con·nec·tive** (kə nek′tiv)   **1** that connects.   **2** a thing that connects.   **3** a word used to connect words, phrases, and clauses: *Conjunctions and relative pronouns are connectives.*   1 *adj.*, 2, 3 *n.*

**connective tissue**   tissue that connects, supports, or encloses other tissues and organs in the body.

**con·nie** or **co·ny** (kon′ē) *Cdn.*   the INCONNU, a freshwater food fish of the North.   *n.*

**con·ning tower** (kon′ing)   a small tower on the deck of a submarine, used as an entrance and as a place for observation. See SUBMARINE for picture.

**con·nip·tion** (kə nip′shən) *Informal.*   Often, **conniptions,** *pl.* or **conniption fit,** a fit of rage, hysteria, etc.; tantrum.

**con·niv·ance** (kə nī′vəns)   the act of conniving; a pretended ignorance or secret encouragement of wrongdoing: *He could not have robbed the bank without the connivance of a friend.*   *n.*

**con·nive** (kə nīv′)   **1** shut one's eyes to something wrong; give aid to wrongdoing by not telling of it (*used with* **at**): *The mayor was accused of conniving at the misuse of public funds.*   **2** co-operate secretly; conspire (*with*): *The general connived with the enemies of his country.*   *v.*, **con·nived, con·niv·ing.**   —**con·niv′er,** *n.*

**con·nois·seur** (kon′ə sėr′)   a person having thorough knowledge and able to make fine distinctions and critical judgments, especially in art and matters of taste: *a connoisseur of wine, a connoisseur of antique furniture.*   *n.*

**con·no·ta·tion** (kon′ə tā′shən)   **1** what is suggested by a word or expression in addition to its basic meaning: *The word* slender *has a more favourable connotation than* thin.   **2** the suggesting of a meaning in addition to the basic meaning; connoting: *To say that a man waddles produces a connotation of awkwardness in walking.*   *n.*   Compare with DENOTATION.

**con·note** (kə nōt′)   suggest in addition to the literal meaning; imply: Portly, corpulent, *and* obese *all mean fleshy; but* portly *connotes dignity;* corpulent, bulk; *and* obese, *an unhealthy and unpleasant excess of fat. The smile that accompanied her question connoted that she was not serious.*   *v.*, **con·not·ed, con·not·ing.**

**con·nu·bi·al** (kə nyü′bē əl *or* kə nü′bē əl)   of or having to do with marriage.   *adj.*

**con·quer** (kong′kər)   **1** get by fighting; win in war: *to conquer a country.*   **2** overcome by force; defeat; get the better of: *to conquer an enemy, to conquer a bad habit.*   **3** be victorious; be the conqueror: *The general said he would conquer or die.*   *v.*   —**con′quer·a·ble,** *adj.*

**con·quer·or** (kong′kə rər)   a person who conquers, especially in war.   *n.*

**con·quest** (kon′kwest *or* kong′kwest)   **1** the act of conquering; victory.   **2** the thing conquered; land, people, etc. conquered.   **3** a person whose love or favour has been won.   **4 the Conquest,**   the gaining of the English throne by William, Duke of Normandy, in 1066.   *n.*

**con·quis·ta·dor** (kon kwis′tə dôr′ *or* kon kis′tə dôr′)   **1** one of the Spanish conquerors who came to South America and the southern parts of North America in the 16th century to look for gold: *The conquistadors conquered the Indian civilizations of Mexico and South America in their search for treasure.*   **2** any conqueror.   *n.*, *pl.* **con·quis·ta·dors** or **con·quis·ta·dores.**

**con·san·guin·i·ty** (kon′sang gwin′ə tē)   **1** a relationship by descent from the same parent or ancestor; blood relationship.   **2** any close relationship or connection.   *n.*

**con·science** (kon′shəns)   **1** the sense or awareness of moral right and wrong with respect to one's own conduct or intentions, including the feeling that one ought to do what is right: *Her conscience prompted her to return the book she had stolen.*   **2** obedience to the dictates of conscience: *A person of conscience would not have acted in that way.*   *n.*   —**con′science·less,** *adj.*
**on one's conscience,**   troubling one's conscience; making one feel guilty: *Her theft of the book had been on her conscience for a long time.*

**con·science–strick·en** (kon′shəns strik′ən)   suffering from a feeling of having done wrong.   *adj.*

**con·sci·en·tious** (kon′shē en′shəs)   **1** careful to do what one knows is right; controlled by conscience (def. 1).   **2** done carefully and properly: *Conscientious work is careful and exact.*   *adj.*   —**con′sci·en′tious·ly,** *adv.*   —**con′sci·en′tious·ness,** *n.*

**conscientious objector** a person whose beliefs prevent taking a combatant part in warfare.

**con·scion·a·ble** (kon′shə nə bəl) according to CONSCIENCE (def. 1); just. *adj.* —**con′scion·a·bly,** *adv.*

**con·scious** (kon′shəs) 1 aware; knowing: *She was conscious of a sharp pain.* 2 capable of thought, will, or feeling: *A human being is a conscious animal.* 3 known to oneself; felt: *conscious guilt.* 4 meant; intended; deliberate: *a conscious lie. She's making a conscious effort to improve her writing.* 5 self-conscious; shy; embarrassed. 6 mentally awake: *After about five minutes she became conscious again. adj.* —**con′scious·ly,** *adv.*

**con·scious·ness** (kon′shə snis) 1 the state of being CONSCIOUS (def. 1); awareness: *People and animals have consciousness; plants and stones do not.* 2 all the thoughts and feelings of a person: *Everything of which you are conscious makes up your consciousness.* 3 awareness of what is going on about one: *A severe shock often makes a person lose consciousness for a time. n.*

**con·script** (kən skript′ *for verb,* kon′skript *for adjective and noun*) 1 compel by law to enlist in the armed forces; DRAFT (def. 8). 2 take for government use: *The dictator proposed to conscript both capital and labour.* 3 conscripted; DRAFTED (def. 8). 4 a person who has been conscripted into the armed forces. 1, 2 *v.,* 3 *adj.,* 4 *n.*

**con·scrip·tion** (kən skrip′shən) 1 the compulsory enlistment of people in the armed forces; DRAFT (def. 9). 2 the act or system of forcing contributions of money, labour, or other service to the government or as the government directs. *n.*

**con·se·crate** (kon′sə krāt′) 1 set apart as sacred; make holy: *A church is consecrated to worship.* 2 devote to a purpose; dedicate: *He has consecrated his life to music. v.,* **con·se·crat·ed, con·se·crat·ing.** —**con′se·cra′tor,** *n.*

**con·se·crat·ed** (kon′sə krā′tid) 1 set apart as sacred; made holy. 2 pt. and pp. of CONSECRATE. 1 *adj.,* 2 *v.*

**con·se·cra·tion** (kon′sə krā′shən) 1 consecrating or being consecrated. 2 an ordination to a sacred office, especially that of bishop. *n.*

**con·sec·u·tive** (kən sek′yə tiv) following without interruption; successive: *Monday, Tuesday, and Wednesday are consecutive days. adj.* —**con·sec′u·tive·ly,** *adv.* —**con·sec′u·tive·ness,** *n.*

**con·sen·sus** (kən sen′səs) general agreement: *The consensus of opinion means the opinion of all or most of the people consulted. n.*

**con·sent** (kən sent′) 1 agree; give approval or permission: *His father would not consent to his leaving school. She consented to run for president.* 2 agreement; approval; permission: *We have Mother's consent to go swimming.* 1 *v.,* 2 *n.*

**con·se·quence** (kon′sə kwens′ *or* kon′sə kwəns) 1 a result or effect: *The consequence of his fall was a broken leg.* 2 a logical result; deduction; inference. 3 importance: *The loss of that old coat is a matter of little consequence.* 4 importance in rank or position: *She is a person of consequence in the community. n.*
**in consequence,** as a result; therefore.
**in consequence of,** as a result of; because of.
**take the consequences,** accept any undesirable results of one's actions: *Do it your way if you like, but you'll have to take the consequences if it doesn't work out.*

**con·se·quent** (kon′sə kwent′ *or* kon′sə kwənt) 1 following as a natural result or effect; resulting: *His illness and consequent absence put him behind in his work.* 2 following logical sequence; logically consistent: *the consequent development of an idea.* 3 anything that follows something else; result; effect. 1, 2 *adj.,* 3 *n.*

**con·se·quen·tial** (kon′sə kwen′shəl) 1 following as an effect; resulting. 2 self-important; pompous. *adj.* —**con′se·quen′tial·ly,** *adv.* —**con′se·quen′tial·ness,** *n.*

**con·se·quent·ly** (kon′sə kwen′tlē *or* kon′sə kwən tlē) as a result; therefore. *adv.*

**con·ser·va·tion** (kon′sər vā′shən) 1 a preserving from harm or decay; a protecting from loss or from being used up: *the conservation of forests.* 2 the official protection and care of forests, rivers, wildlife, etc. 3 a forest, etc., or a part of it, under official protection and care. *n.*

**con·ser·va·tion·ist** (kon′sər vā′shə nist) a person who believes in and advocates CONSERVATION (defs. 1, 2) of the forests, rivers, wildlife, etc. of a country. *n.*

**con·serv·a·tism** (kən sėr′və tiz′əm) the inclination to keep things as they are; opposition to change. *n.*

**con·serv·a·tive** (kən sėr′və tiv) 1 inclined to keep things as they are or were in the past; opposed to change. 2 of or belonging to a political party that opposes changes in national institutions. 3 not inclined to take risks; cautious; moderate: *conservative business methods.* 4 free from novelties and fads: *It is economical to choose suits of a conservative style.* 5 having the power to preserve from harm or decay; conserving; preserving. 6 a conservative person; a person who is generally inclined to keep things as they were in the past. 7 a means of preserving. 1–5 *adj.,* 6, 7 *n.* —**con·serv′a·tive·ly,** *adv.* —**con·serv′a·tive·ness,** *n.*

**Con·serv·a·tive** (kən sėr′və tiv) 1 a member of the PROGRESSIVE CONSERVATIVE PARTY, one of the principal Canadian political groups; a person who supports the views and principles of this party. 2 in the United Kingdom, a member of the CONSERVATIVE PARTY. 3 of Conservatives or their party. 1, 2 *n.,* 3 *adj.*

**Conservative Party** 1 in the United Kingdom, a political party that favours existing national institutions or a return to some of those recently existing. 2 in Canada, the PROGRESSIVE CONSERVATIVE PARTY.

**con·serv·a·to·ry** (kən sėr′və tô′rē) 1 a greenhouse or glass-enclosed room for growing and displaying plants. 2 a school for instruction in music. *n., pl.* **con·serv·a·to·ries.**

**con·serve** (kən sėrv′ *for verb,* kon′sėrv *or* kən sėrv′ *for noun*) 1 keep from harm or decay; protect from loss or from being used up: *Try to conserve your strength for the end of the race.* 2 preserve fruit with sugar. 3 fruit preserved in sugar; jam. 1, 2 *v.,* **con·served, con·serv·ing;** 3 *n.*

**con·sid·er** (kən sid′ər) 1 think about in order to decide: *Take time to consider the problem.* 2 think to be; think of as: *We consider Margaret Atwood a great Canadian poet.* 3 allow for; take into account: *This watch runs very well, if you consider how old it is.* 4 be thoughtful of others and their feelings. 5 think carefully; reflect: *He considered for a while before answering. v.*

**con·sid·er·a·ble** (kən sid′ə rə bəl) 1 worth thinking about; important: *a considerable sum of money.* 2 not a little; much: *She has considerable influence in political circles.* **3** *Informal.* a great deal. **1, 2** *adj.*, **3** *n.*

**con·sid·er·a·bly** (kən sid′ər ə blē) a good deal; much: *The boy was considerably older than he looked.* *adv.*

**con·sid·er·ate** (kən sid′ər it) thoughtful of others and their feelings. *adj.* —**con·sid′er·ate·ly,** *adv.* —**con·sid′er·ate·ness,** *n.*

**con·sid·er·a·tion** (kən sid′ə rā′shən) **1** careful thought about something before making a decision: *Please give careful consideration to this question.* **2** something thought of as a reason; something to be considered: *Price and quality are two considerations in buying anything.* **3** money or other payment: *Magnus said he would cut the grass for a small consideration.* **4** thoughtfulness for others and their feelings: *Mary's consideration for her mother was in sharp contrast with her brother's rudeness.* **5** importance. *n.*
**in consideration of, a** because of: *In consideration of his wife's poor health, he moved to a milder climate.* **b** in return for: *She gave him a present in consideration of his helpfulness.*
**on no consideration,** not at all; never.
**take into consideration,** allow for; take into account; consider: *The judge took the boy's age into consideration.*

**con·sid·ered** (kən sid′ərd) **1** carefully thought out: *in my considered opinion.* **2** honoured; respected: *He is highly considered as a poet.* **3** pt. and pp. of CONSIDER. **1, 2** *adj.*, **3** *v.*

**con·sid·er·ing** (kən sid′ər ing) **1** taking into account; making allowance for: *Considering her age, she reads well.* **2** taking everything into account: *He does very well, considering.* **3** ppr. of CONSIDER. **1** *prep.*, **2** *adv.*, **3** *v.*

**con·sign** (kən sīn′) **1** hand over; deliver: *The man was consigned to prison. The father consigned the child to his sister's care.* **2** transmit; send: *The order will be consigned to them by express.* **3** set apart; assign: *These goods are consigned for later delivery.* *v.*

**con·sign·ee** (kon′sī nē′) the person or company to whom goods are CONSIGNed: *The shipment of goods was finally delivered to the consignee.* *n.*

**con·sign·er** (kən sī′nər) See CONSIGNOR. *n.*

**con·sign·ment** (kən sīn′mənt) **1** the act of consigning. **2** a shipment sent to a person or company for safekeeping or sale. *n.*
**on consignment,** of goods, sent to a retailer under an arrangement by which the retailer does not pay the distributor until the goods have been sold.

**con·sign·or** (kən sī′nər *or* kon′sī nôr′) a person or company who consigns goods to another. *n.* Also, **consigner.**

**con·sist** (kən sist′) be made up; be formed (*of*): *A week consists of seven days.* *v.*
**consist in,** have a basis in or be made up of: *Happiness for him consists in being left alone.*

**con·sist·ence** (kən sis′təns) CONSISTENCY. *n.*

**con·sist·en·cy** (kən sis′tən sē) **1** holding together; firmness or density. **2** degree of firmness or density: *Icing for a cake must be of the right consistency to spread easily without dripping.* **3** keeping to a single set of principles, course of action, etc.: *Sophia was much admired for her consistency of purpose.* **4** harmony; agreement; accordance: *It's not always easy to maintain consistency between principles and practice.* *n., pl.* **con·sist·en·cies.**

**con·sist·ent** (kən sis′tənt) **1** keeping or inclined to keep to the same principles, course of action, etc.: *What a* consistent *person says or does today agrees with what he or she said or did yesterday.* **2** in agreement; in accord; compatible: *Driving an automobile very fast is not consistent with safety. Noise and study are not consistent.* *adj.* —**con·sist′ent·ly,** *adv.*

**con·so·la·tion** (kon′sə lā′shən) **1** comfort. **2** a comforting person, thing, or event. *n.*

**con·sole¹** (kən sōl′) comfort. *v.*, **con·soled, con·sol·ing.** —**con·sol′a·ble,** *adj.* —**con·sol′er,** *n.*

**con·sole²** (kon′sōl) **1** the desklike part of an organ, containing the keyboard, stops, and pedals. **2** a cabinet for a television set, record player, or radio made to stand on the floor. **3** a panel of buttons, switches, dials, etc. used to control electrical or other apparatus; control panel. *n.*

**con·sol·i·date** (kən sol′ə dāt) **1** unite; combine; merge: *The two territories were consolidated by the government into one administrative district.* **2** make secure; strengthen: *to consolidate an empire. The army spent a day in consolidating its gains by digging trenches.* **3** make or become solid. *v.*, **con·sol·i·dat·ed, con·sol·i·dat·ing.**

**con·sol·i·dat·ed** (kən sol′ə dā′tid) **1** united; combined. **2** pt. and pp. of CONSOLIDATE. **1** *adj.*, **2** *v.*

**consolidated school** a school for students from several school districts; a school built to replace two or more smaller ones, especially in country districts, so as to provide a greater range of facilities.

**con·sol·i·da·tion** (kən sol′ə dā′shən) consolidating or being CONSOLIDATED. *n.*

**con·sol·ing** (kən sō′ling) **1** that CONSOLES¹. **2** ppr. of CONSOLE¹. **1** *adj.*, **2** *v.* —**con·sol′ing·ly,** *adv.*

**con·som·mé** (kon′sə mā′) a clear soup made by boiling meat and, sometimes, vegetables in water. *n.*

**con·so·nance** (kon′sə nəns) **1** harmony; agreement; accordance. **2** in music, harmony of sounds; a simultaneous combination of tones that is agreeable to the ear. Compare with DISSONANCE. *n.*

**con·so·nant** (kon′sə nənt) **1** a speech sound formed by completely or partially blocking the breath: *Most languages have both consonants and vowels. The first and last sounds in* tab *are consonants.* **2** any letter of the alphabet that is not a vowel: *Examples of consonants are the letters* b, c, d, f, *and* g. **3** harmonious; in agreement; in accord: *Maria's action is consonant with her beliefs.* **4** agreeing in sound. **5** CONSONANTAL. **1, 2** *n.*, **3–5** *adj.* —**con′so·nant·ly,** *adv.*

**con·so·nan·tal** (kon′sə nan′təl) having to do with a CONSONANT (def. 1) or its sound. *adj.*

**con·sort** (kon′sôrt *for noun,* kən sôrt′ *for verb*) **1** a husband or wife, especially of a monarch. **2** an associate. **3** a ship accompanying another; an escort vessel. **4** keep company; associate: *Do not consort with thieves. Rogues and honest men do not consort.* **5** agree; accord: *Our opinions rarely consort.* **1–3** *n.*, **4, 5** *v.*

**con·spec·tus** (kən spek′təs) **1** a general or

---

hat, āge, fär; let, ēqual, tėrm; it, īce
hot, ōpen, ôrder; oil, out; cup, put, rüle
əbove, takən, pencəl, lemən, circəs
ch, child; ng, long; sh, ship
th, thin; ᴛʜ, then; zh, measure

comprehensive view. 2 a short summary or outline of a subject; digest; résumé. *n.*

**con·spic·u·ous** (kən spik′yü əs) 1 easily seen: *A traffic sign should be conspicuous.* 2 attracting notice; striking; remarkable: *Canada has played a conspicuous part in the work of the United Nations.* *adj.*
—**con·spic′u·ous·ly,** *adv.* —**con·spic′u·ous·ness,** *n.*

**con·spir·a·cy** (kən spir′ə sē) 1 a secret scheming or planning together to do something treacherous or evil. 2 the plot or scheme itself: *The conspiracy was revealed as a result of a neighbour's complaint.* 3 in law, an agreement between two or more persons to commit an illegal act: *The four contractors were charged with conspiracy to commit fraud.* 4 a happening or acting together as if by evil design: *It was a conspiracy of the elements to ruin our camping trip.* *n., pl.* **con·spir·a·cies.**

**con·spir·a·tor** (kən spir′ə tər) a person who CONSPIRES; plotter: *Conspirators planned to kill the king.* *n.*

**con·spire** (kən spīr′) 1 plan secretly with others to do something wrong; plot. 2 act together, as if by design: *The rain, the cold, and the mosquitoes conspired to ruin the concert in the park. All things conspired to make her birthday a happy one.* *v.,* **con·spired, con·spir·ing.** —**con·spir′er,** *n.*

**Const.** Constable.

**con·sta·ble** (kon′stə bəl) a member of a police force who is not an officer. *n.*

**con·stab·u·lary** (kən stab′yə ler′ē) 1 the CONSTABLES of a district. 2 having to do with a CONSTABLE: *She performed her constabulary duties very well.* 1 *n. pl.*, **con·stab·u·lar·ies.** 2 *adj.*

**con·stan·cy** (kon′stən sē) 1 the condition of being always the same; the absence of change. 2 firmness in belief or feeling; faithfulness; loyalty: *A country at war depends on the constancy of its allies.* *n.*

**con·stant** (kon′stənt) 1 always the same; not changing: *If you walk due north, your direction is constant.* 2 something that is always the same; a number or quantity that does not change. 3 never stopping: *We had three days of constant rain.* 4 happening often or again and again: *A clock makes a constant ticking sound.* 5 faithful; loyal; steadfast: *A constant friend helps you when you need help.* 1, 3–5 *adj.*, 2 *n.* —**con′stant·ly,** *adv.*

**con·stel·la·tion** (kon′stə lā′shən) 1 a set or group of stars: *Ursa Major is the easiest constellation to locate.* 2 the part of the heavens occupied by such a group. 3 a brilliant gathering. *n.*

**con·ster·na·tion** (kon′stər nā′shən) great dismay; paralysing terror: *To our consternation, the train rushed on toward the burning bridge.* *n.*

**con·sti·pate** (kon′stə pāt′) cause CONSTIPATION in. *v.,* **con·sti·pat·ed, con·sti·pat·ing.**

**con·sti·pat·ed** (kon′stə pā′tid) 1 suffering from CONSTIPATION. 2 pt. and pp. of CONSTIPATE. 1 *adj.*, 2 *v.*

**con·sti·pa·tion** (kon′stə pā′shən) a condition in which the bowels are sluggish or inactive, so that it is difficult or impossible to discharge waste matter from the body. *n.*

**con·stit·u·en·cy** (kən stich′ü ən sē) 1 a district, or RIDING, represented by a Member of Parliament or a Member of the Legislative Assembly. 2 the voters in this district. *n., pl.* **con·stit·u·en·cies.**

**con·stit·u·ent** (kən stich′ü ənt) 1 forming a necessary part; necessary in the composition: *Flour, liquid, salt, and yeast are constituent parts of bread.* 2 a necessary part of a whole; component: *Sugar is the main constituent of candy.* 3 appointing; electing. 4 a person who votes or appoints; a voter in a constituency: *Many of the MP's constituents protested her stand on the issue.* 5 having the power to make or change a political constitution: *a constituent assembly.* 1, 3, 5 *adj.*, 2, 4 *n.*

**con·sti·tute** (kon′stə tyüt′ or kon′stə tüt′) 1 make up; form: *Seven days constitute a week. Hailstorms constitute a serious threat to standing crops.* 2 appoint; elect: *Mr. Chang was constituted president of the Home and School Association.* 3 set up; establish: *Courts are constituted by law to dispense justice.* 4 make by combining parts; frame: *The cabin is well constituted and will withstand the severest weather.* 5 give legal form to: *to constitute a lease.* *v.,* **con·sti·tut·ed, con·sti·tut·ing.**

**con·sti·tu·tion** (kon′stə tyü′shən or kon′stə tü′shən) 1 a person's physical or mental nature or make-up: *A person with a good constitution is strong and healthy.* 2 the way in which anything is organized; structure: *The constitution of the world is the arrangement of all things in it.* 3 the system of fundamental principles according to which a nation, state, or group is governed: *Our club has a written constitution.* 4 a document stating these principles. 5 appointing or making. 6 setting up; establishment. 7 a law; decree. *n.*

**Constitution Act 1867** since 1981, the name of the BRITISH NORTH AMERICA ACT.

**con·sti·tu·tion·al** (kon′stə tyü′shə nəl or kon′stə tü′shə nəl) 1 of or in the CONSTITUTION (def. 1) of a person or thing: *A constitutional weakness makes him subject to colds.* 2 of, in, or according to the CONSTITUTION (def. 3) of a nation, state, or group: *Some lawyers are experts in constitutional law.* 3 for one's health. 4 *Informal.* a walk or other exercise taken for one's health. 1–3 *adj.*, 4 *n.*

**Constitutional Act** the CANADA ACT, 1791.

**con·sti·tu·tion·al·i·ty** (kon′stə tyü′shə nal′ə tē or kon′stə tü′shə nal′ə tē) accordance with the CONSTITUTION (def. 3) of a nation, state, or group: *The constitutionality of the new law was disputed.* *n.*

**con·sti·tu·tion·al·ly** (kon′stə tyü′shə nə lē or kon′stə tü′shə nə lē) 1 in or by CONSTITUTION (def. 1); naturally: *He finds it constitutionally difficult to work on his own.* 2 according to the CONSTITUTION (def. 3). *adv.*

**con·sti·tu·tive** (kon′stə tyü′tiv or kon′stə tü′tiv) having power to establish or enact; constructive; formative; constituent; essential. *adj.*

**con·strain** (kən strān′) 1 force or compel physically or by moral means: *Ruth was constrained to accept her employer's decision or leave her job.* 2 confine; imprison. 3 repress; restrain. *v.* —**con·strain′er,** *n.*

**con·strained** (kən strānd′) 1 forced or compelled by physical means or by pity, love, gratitude, etc.: *He felt constrained to help the wounded man.* 2 restrained; stiff; unnatural: *a constrained smile.* 3 pt. and pp. of CONSTRAIN. 1, 2 *adj.*, 3 *v.*

**con·straint** (kən strānt′) 1 confinement. 2 restraint. 3 a holding back of natural feelings; a forced or unnatural manner; embarrassed awkwardness: *We felt a little constraint with the new neighbour for the first day or so.*

4 force; compulsion: *When he confessed to the crime, he was acting under constraint.* *n.*

**con·strict** (kən strikt′) draw together; contract; compress: *A tourniquet stops the flow of blood by constricting the blood vessels.* *v.*

**con·stric·tion** (kən strik′shən) 1 the act of drawing together; contraction; compression. 2 a feeling of tightness: *She coughed and complained of a constriction in her chest.* 3 a CONSTRICTed part. 4 something that CONSTRICTS. *n.*

**con·stric·tive** (kən strik′tiv) drawing together; contracting; compressing. *adj.*

**con·stric·tor** (kən strik′tər) 1 any snake that kills its prey by squeezing it with its coils. 2 a muscle that constricts a part of the body. *n.*

**con·struct** (kən strukt′) 1 put together; build: *Sentences are constructed of words. The house is constructed of brick.* 2 in mathematics, draw a geometrical figure so as to fulfil given conditions. *v.*

**con·struc·tion** (kən struk′shən) 1 the act of constructing, building, or putting together. 2 the way in which a thing is constructed: *Cracks and leaks are signs of poor construction.* 3 the thing constructed; building: *The doll's house was a construction of wood and cardboard.* 4 a meaning; explanation; interpretation: *He put an unfair construction on what she said.* 5 the arrangement, connection, or relation of words in a sentence, clause, phrase, etc. *n.*

**con·struc·tive** (kən struk′tiv) 1 building up so as to improve; helpful: *People appreciate constructive suggestions, not destructive criticisms.* 2 having to do with construction; structural. 3 not directly expressed; inferred. *adj.* —**con·struc′tive·ly**, *adv.* —**con·struc′tive·ness**, *n.*

**con·struc·tor** (kən struk′tər) a person who constructs; builder. *n.*

**con·strue** (kən strü′) 1 show the meaning of; explain; interpret: *Different lawyers may construe the same law differently.* 2 translate. 3 analyse the arrangement and connection of words in a sentence, clause, phrase, etc. *v.*, **con·strued, con·stru·ing.**

**con·sul** (kon′səl) 1 an official appointed by the government of a country to look after its business interests in a foreign city and also to assist citizens of his or her country living there. 2 either of the two chief magistrates of the ancient Roman republic. 3 one of the three chief magistrates of the first French Republic (1799–1804). *n.*

**con·su·lar** (kon′sə lər) 1 of or belonging to a CONSUL. 2 serving as a CONSUL; having the duties of a consul: *a consular representative.* *adj.*

**con·su·late** (kon′sə lit) 1 the official residence or offices of a CONSUL (def. 1): *He visited the Canadian consulate in New York.* 2 the duties, authority, and position of a CONSUL (def. 1). 3 a CONSUL's (def. 1) term of office. 4 government by CONSULS (def. 3): *France was governed by a consulate from 1799 to 1804.* *n.*

**con·sul·ship** (kon′səl ship′) 1 the duties, authority, and position of a CONSUL. 2 a CONSUL's term of office. *n.*

**con·sult** (kən sult′) 1 seek information or advice from; refer to: *Consult a dictionary for the meaning of a word.* 2 exchange ideas; talk things over: *Helga is consulting with her lawyer.* 3 take into consideration; have regard for: *A good ruler consults the interests and feelings of her people.* *v.*

**con·sult·ant** (kən sul′tənt) 1 a person who consults another. 2 a person who gives professional or technical advice: *a medical consultant.* *n.*

**con·sul·ta·tion** (kon′səl tā′shən) 1 the act of consulting; the act of seeking information or advice. 2 a meeting to exchange ideas or talk things over: *The three doctors held a consultation to decide what was the best way to cure the child.* *n.*

**con·sult·a·tive** (kən sul′tə tiv) having to do with CONSULTATION; advisory. *adj.*

**con·sult·ing** (kən sul′ting) 1 that consults or asks advice. 2 employed in giving professional advice. 3 ppr. of CONSULT. 1, 2 *adj.*, 3 *v.*

**con·sum·a·ble** (kən sü′mə bəl *or* kən syü′mə bəl) 1 intended to be used up: *consumable supplies.* 2 an article that is intended to be used up: *Government offices have been told to cut expenditures on paper, pencils, and other consumables.* 1 *adj.*, 2 *n.*

**con·sume** (kən süm′ *or* kən syüm′) 1 eat or drink up: *We consumed a great deal of food on our hike.* 2 destroy; burn up: *A fire can consume a forest.* 3 use up; spend: *A student consumes much of her time in studying.* 4 waste away; be destroyed. 5 waste time, money, etc. *v.*, **con·sumed, con·sum·ing.**
**consumed with,** absorbed by: *consumed with envy.*

**con·sum·er** (kən sü′mər *or* kən syü′mər) 1 a person who buys and uses food, clothing, or anything grown or made by producers: *A low price for wheat should reduce the price of flour to the consumer.* 2 a person or thing that uses up, makes away with, or destroys. *n.*

**consumer goods** in economics, goods that people use or consume to satisfy their wants: *Food and clothing are two kinds of consumer goods.* Compare with CAPITAL GOODS.

**con·sum·mate** (kon′sə māt′ *for verb,* kon′sə mit *or* kən sum′it *for adjective*) 1 complete; fulfil: *His ambition was consummated when he won the first prize.* 2 complete; perfect; in the highest degree: *The paintings of great artists show consummate skill.* 1 *v.*, **con·sum·mat·ed, con·sum·mat·ing;** 2 *adj.*
—**con·sum′mate·ly**, *adv.*

**con·sum·ma·tion** (kon′sə mā′shən) a completion; fulfilment. *n.*

**con·sump·tion** (kən sump′shən) 1 the act of using or using up: *We took along some food for consumption on our trip. The science of economics deals with the production, distribution, and consumption of wealth.* 2 the amount used up: *Our hydro consumption was up again last month.* 3 a wasting disease of the lungs or of some other part of the body; TUBERCULOSIS of the lungs. *n.*

**con·sump·tive** (kən sump′tiv) 1 having or likely to have TUBERCULOSIS of the lungs. 2 of TUBERCULOSIS of the lungs. 3 a person who has TUBERCULOSIS of the lungs. 4 tending to consume, destructive; wasteful.

1, 2, 4 adj., 3 n. —con·sump′tive·ly, adv.
—con·sump′tive·ness, n.

**con·tact** (kon′takt) **1** the condition of touching; a touching together: *This insecticide should not come in contact with the skin. When two balls are in contact, one can be moved by touching the other.* **2** being in communication; connection; association: *Francine has kept in contact with her school friends. The control tower lost contact with the pilot.* **3** a person with whom one can get in touch, especially for business purposes: *She has a useful contact in an advertising agency.* **4** get in touch with; communicate with: *We could not contact them.* **5** a connection between two conductors of electricity through which a current passes. **6** a device or part for producing such a connection: *The electric light went out when the wire broke off at the contact.* **7 contacts**, pl. *Informal.* CONTACT LENSES. 1–3, 5–7 n., 4 v.

**contact flying** flying an aircraft within sight of the ground: *In contact flying, the pilot directs the aircraft by referring to known points or objects on the ground.* Compare with INSTRUMENT FLYING.

**contact lens** a small, thin plastic lens ground to an optical prescription and worn directly over the pupil of the eye to correct defective vision: *A contact lens fits the curve of the cornea and floats on a thin layer of fluid.*

**con·ta·gion** (kən tā′jən) **1** the spreading of disease by contact. **2** a disease spread in this way; a CONTAGIOUS (def. 1) disease. **3** a means by which disease is spread. **4** the tendency of any influence or emotional or mental state to spread from one person to another: *the contagion of a smile, the contagion of political graft.* **5** a spreading influence or emotional state, especially one that is unpleasant or destructive: *A contagion of fear swept through the crowd and caused a panic.* n.

**con·ta·gious** (kən tā′jəs) **1** spread by contact: *Chicken pox is a contagious disease.* **2** causing contagious diseases. **3** easily spread from one person to another: *Yawning is often contagious.* adj. Compare with INFECTIOUS. —**con·ta′gious·ly,** adv. —**con·ta′gious·ness,** n.

**con·tain** (kən tān′) **1** have within itself; hold as contents; include: *Books contain information. This purse contains much money.* **2** be capable of holding: *That pitcher contains a litre.* **3** be equal to: *A metre contains 100 centimetres.* **4** control; hold back; restrain: *He contained his anger.* **5** of numbers, be exactly divisible by; be divisible by without a remainder: *12 contains 2, 3, 4, and 6.* v. —**con·tain′a·ble,** adj.

**con·tain·er** (kən tā′nər) **1** a box, can, jar, etc. used to hold or contain something. **2 a** a very large, boxlike, standard-sized receptacle for transporting an assortment of cargo. **b** of or having to do with the use of such containers: *a container flatcar, a container service.* n.

**container car** a railway flatcar adapted for carrying CONTAINERS (def. 2a).

**con·tain·er·iz·a·tion** (kən tā′nə rə zā′shən or kən tā′nə rī zā′shən) **1** the sytem of using CONTAINERS (def. 2a) to transport goods. **2** adaptation to such a system. n.

**con·tain·er·ize** (kən tā′nə rīz′) adapt a mode of transport to the use of CONTAINERS (def. 2a). v., con·tain·er·ized, con·tain·er·iz·ing.

**container port** a port with facilities for moving CONTAINERS (def. 2a): *Vancouver is a container port.*

**container ship** a ship adapted to hold CONTAINERS (def. 2a) for moving cargo.

**con·tain·ment** (kən tān′mənt) containing or being contained, especially keeping a hostile political or military force from expanding its territory. n.

**con·tam·i·nate** (kən tam′ə nāt′) make impure by contact; defile; pollute: *Flies can contaminate food.* v., con·tam·i·nat·ed, con·tam·i·nat·ing. —**con·tam′i·na′tor,** n.

**con·tam·i·na·tion** (kən tam′ə nā′shən) **1** contaminating or being CONTAMINATED; pollution: *Food should be kept covered to avoid contamination by flies.* **2** anything that contaminates; impurity. n.

**contd.** continued.

**con·tem·plate** (kon′təm plāt′) **1** look at for a long time; gaze at: *They sat there for some time, contemplating the evening sky.* **2** think about for a long time; consider thoughtfully: *He contemplated his past life, with its successes and failures.* **3** meditate: *I sometimes like to sit and contemplate.* **4** have in mind; consider; intend: *She contemplated going to Europe in July. She is contemplating a change of work.* v., con·tem·plat·ed, con·tem·plat·ing.

**con·tem·pla·tion** (kon′təm plā′shən) **1** the act of looking at or thinking about something for a long time: *contemplation of the sea.* **2** deep thought; meditation: *sunk in contemplation.* **3** expectation; intention: *We are buying tents and other equipment in contemplation of a summer of camping.* n.

**con·tem·pla·tive** (kon′təm plā′tiv) **1** thoughtful; meditative. **2** devoted to religious meditation and prayer. adj.

**con·tem·po·ra·ne·ous** (kən tem′pə rā′nē əs) belonging to the same period of time: *The lives of Macdonald and Laurier were contemporaneous.* adj. —**con·tem′po·ra′ne·ous·ly,** adv.

**con·tem·po·rar·y** (kən tem′pə rer′ē) **1** belonging to or living in the same period of time: *contemporary writers.* **2** a person who belongs to the same period of time as another or others: *Wolfe and Montcalm were contemporaries.* **3** of or having to do with the present time; current: *contemporary theatre, contemporary attitudes.* **4** of the same date: *contemporary issues of the magazine.* **5** a person of the same age: *We all tend to seek the society of our contemporaries.* 1, 3, 4 adj., 2, 5 n., pl. con·tem·po·rar·ies.

**con·tempt** (kən tempt′) **1** the feeling that a person, act, or thing is mean, low, or worthless; scorn; a despising: *We feel contempt for a liar.* **2** the condition of being scorned or despised; disgrace: *A cowardly traitor is held in contempt.* **3** disobedience of or open disrespect for the rules or decisions of a law court, a lawmaking body, etc.: *A person can be put in jail for contempt of court.* n.

**con·tempt·i·ble** (kən temp′tə bəl) deserving CONTEMPT (def. 1) or scorn; mean; low; worthless: *a contemptible act.* adj. —**con·tempt′i·ble·ness,** n. —**con·tempt′i·bly,** adv.

**con·temp·tu·ous** (kən temp′chü əs) showing CONTEMPT (def. 1); scornful: *a contemptuous look.* adj. —**con·temp′tu·ous·ly,** adv. —**con·temp′tu·ous·ness,** n.

**con·tend** (kən tend′) **1** fight; struggle with or against: *The Arctic explorers had to contend with extreme cold, hunger, and loneliness.* **2** take part in a contest; compete: *Five runners were contending in the first race.* **3** argue;

dispute.   **4** declare to be a fact; maintain as true: *Columbus contended that the earth was round.*   *v.*
—**con·tend′er,** *n.*

**con·tent¹** (kon′tent)   **1** the facts or ideas stated; what is written in a book or said in a speech: *The content of her speech was good, but the form was not.*   **2** the power of containing; capacity: *What is the content of the gas tank of this car?*   **3** the proportion of a certain substance contained in something else: *Cream has a higher fat content than milk.*   **4 contents,** *pl.*   what is contained in anything; all things inside: *the table of contents in a book. She drained the contents of the glass in one gulp.*   *n.*

**con·tent²** (kən tent′)   **1** satisfy; please; make easy in mind: *Nothing contents her; she is always complaining.*   **2** not desiring anything more or anything different than what one has; satisfied: *We'll have to be content with whatever accommodations we get.*   **3** contentment; satisfaction; ease of mind.   1 *v.*, 2 *adj.*, 3 *n.*
**content oneself,**   be satisfied.
**to one's heart's content,**   to one's full satisfaction; as much as one pleases: *When exams are over you'll be able to play tennis to your heart's content.*

**con·tent·ed** (kən ten′tid)   **1** satisfied; pleased; easy in mind: *A contented person is happy with what he has.*   **2** pt. and pp. of CONTENT.   1 *adj.*, 2 *v.*   —**con·tent′ed·ly,** *adv.*
—**con·tent′ed·ness,** *n.*

**con·ten·tion** (kən ten′shən)   **1** a statement or point that one has argued for; statement maintained as true: *Columbus's contention that the earth was round proved to be true.*   **2** arguing; disputing; quarrelling: *The main subject of contention was the proposed change in the school curriculum.*   **3** an argument; dispute; quarrel.   **4** a struggle or contest.   *n.*

**con·ten·tious** (kən ten′shəs)   **1** quarrelsome; fond of arguing; given to disputing: *A contentious person argues and disputes about trifles.*   **2** characterized by contention: *a contentious election campaign.*   *adj.*
—**conten′tious·ly,** *adv.*   —**con·ten′tious·ness,** *n.*

**con·tent·ment** (kən tent′mənt)   satisfaction; being pleased; ease of mind: *A cat asleep on the hearth is a picture of contentment.*   *n.*

**con·test** (kon′test *for noun,* kən test′ *for verb*)   **1** a game or competition, especially one in which the entries are rated by judges: *a ploughing contest, a baking contest, a contest to find a name for a new park.*   **2** try to win.   **3** a fight or struggle.   **4** fight for; struggle for: *The soldiers contested every spot of ground.*   **5** an argument or dispute.   **6** argue against; dispute about: *The lawyer contested the claim and tried to prove that it was false.*   **7** take part in a contest.   1, 3, 5 *n.*, 2, 4, 6, 7 *v.*   —**con·test′a·ble,** *adj.*

**con·test·ant** (kən tes′tənt)   a person who contests, especially a person who takes part in a game or competition: *The contestant whose name is selected will win a trip to Paris.*   *n.*

**con·text** (kon′tekst)   the spoken or written text in which a particular word or group of words occurs: *It's unfair to judge her statement without knowing the context in which she made it.*   *n.*

**con·tex·tu·al** (kən teks′chü əl)   having to do with the CONTEXT; depending on the context.   *adj.*

**con·ti·gu·i·ty** (kon′tə gyü′ə tē)   **1** nearness: *The contiguity of the house and garage was a convenience in bad weather.*   **2** a contact.   **3** a continuous mass; unbroken stretch.   *n., pl.* **con·ti·gu·i·ties.**

**con·tig·u·ous** (kən tig′yü əs)   **1** in actual contact; touching: *a fence showed where the two farms were*

**content**   263   **continual**

hat, āge, fär; let, ēqual, tėrm; it, īce
hot, ōpen, ôrder; oil, out; cup, pút, rüle
әbove, takәn, pencәl, lemәn, circәs
ch, child; ng, long; sh, ship
th, thin; ᴛʜ, then; zh, measure

*contiguous.*   **2** adjoining; near.   *adj.*
—**con·tig′u·ous·ly,** *adv.*   —**con·tig′u·ous·ness,** *n.*

**con·ti·nence** (kon′tə nəns)   **1** self-control; self-restraint; moderation.   **2** chastity.   *n.*

**con·ti·nent¹** (kon′tə nənt)   **1** one of the seven great masses of land on the earth: *The continents are North America, South America, Europe, Africa, Asia, Australia, and Antarctica.*   **2** mainland.   **3 the Continent,**   the mainland of Europe: *The Continent does not include the British Isles.*   *n.*

**con·ti·nent²** (kon′tə nənt)   **1** showing restraint with regard to the desires or passions; using self-control; temperate.   **2** CHASTE.   *adj.*   —**con′ti·nent·ly,** *adv.*

**con·ti·nen·tal** (kon′tə nen′təl)   **1** of, having to do with, or characteristic of a CONTINENT¹: *continental rivers.*   **2** Usually, **Continental,**   of, having to do with, or characteristic of the mainland of Europe; of or like that of the Continent: *Continental customs differ from those of England.*   **3** Usually, **Continental,**   a person living on the Continent.   1, 2 *adj.*, 3 *n.*

**continental bed**   a bed that has no headboard or footboard, being made up of a spring mattress set on top of a box-spring base that has short legs.

**Continental Divide**   in North America, the great ridge of the Rocky Mountains: *The Continental Divide separates streams flowing toward the Pacific from those flowing toward the Atlantic or the Arctic.*

**continental drift**   the theory that the earth's land masses move gradually over the surface of the earth on a substratum of magma.   See also PLATE TECTONICS.

**continental shelf**   the submerged shelf of land that borders most continents and ends in a steep slope (the **continental slope**) to deep water.

**con·tin·gen·cy** (kən tin′jən sē)   **1** uncertainty of occurrence; dependence on chance.   **2** an accidental happening; an unexpected event; chance.   **3** a happening or event depending on something that is uncertain; possibility: *The explorer carried supplies for every contingency.*   *n., pl.* **con·tin·gen·cies.**

**con·tin·gent** (kən tin′jənt)   **1** conditional; depending on something not certain: *Our plans for a picnic tomorrow are contingent upon pleasant weather.*   **2** liable to happen or not to happen; possible; uncertain: *Fifteen dollars a day should cover contingent expenses.*   **3** happening by chance; accidental; unexpected.   **4** a share of soldiers, workers, etc. furnished to a force from other sources: *Canada sent a large contingent of troops to France in World War I.*   **5** a group that is part of a larger group: *The Kingston contingent had seats together at the convention.*   **6** an accidental or unexpected event.   1–3 *adj.*, 4–6 *n.*
—**con·tin′gent·ly,** *adv.*

**con·tin·u·al** (kən tin′yü əl)   **1** repeated many times; very frequent: *Dancing requires continual practice.*   **2** never stopping: *the continual flow of the river.*   *adj.*
—**con·tin′u·al·ly,** *adv.*
☛ *Syn.*   Continual, CONTINUOUS. Both these words share the meaning 'without a break', but only **continual** means 'repeated frequently'.

**con·tin·u·ance** (kən tin′yü əns) **1** staying; remaining: *A public official is paid during her continuance in office.* **2** continuing: *his continuance of work in spite of illness.* **3** the time during which anything lasts; duration: *during the continuance of the war.* **4** a continuation; sequel: *the continuance of a story.* **5** in law, an adjournment or postponement. *n.*

**con·tin·u·a·tion** (kən tin′yü ā′shən) **1** the going on with an activity or process: *Shanti was looking forward to university as a continuation of her education.* **2** going on with a thing after stopping; beginning again: *They voted for a continuation of the discussion at the next meeting.* **3** anything by which a thing is continued; an added part: *The continuation of the story will appear in next month's magazine.* **4** the act or fact of not stopping. *n.*

**con·tin·ue** (kən tin′yü) **1** keep up; keep on; go on; go on with: *The road continues for quite a distance. We continued our work at the hospital.* **2** go on or go on with after stopping; begin again: *After lunch she continued her work. The story will be continued next month.* **3** last; endure: *The king's reign continued for 20 years. The cold weather continued for a week.* **4** cause to last. **5** stay: *We continue in school till the end of June.* **6** allow to stay in a position; maintain; retain: *The club continued the president in office for another term.* **7** put off until a later time; postpone; adjourn: *The judge has continued the case until next month.* *v.*, **con·tin·ued, con·tin·u·ing.**
—**con·tin′u·a·ble,** *adj.*

**con·ti·nu·i·ty** (kon′tə nyü′ə tē *or* kon′tə nü′ə tē) **1** being a connected whole or an unbroken series: *The story lacked continuity because there were too many unconnected happenings.* **2** a detailed plan of a motion picture. **3** in radio or television, any connecting comments or announcements between the parts of a program. **4** a script for such comments or announcements. *n., pl.* **con·ti·nu·i·ties.**

**con·tin·u·ous** (kən tin′yü əs) without a stop or break; connected; unbroken: *a continuous line, a continuous sound, continuous work, a continuous procession of cars.* *adj.* —**con·tin′u·ous·ly,** *adv.* —**con·tin′u·ous·ness,** *n.*
☛ *Syn.* See note at CONTINUAL.

**con·tin·u·um** (kən tin′yü əm) a CONTINUOUS quantity, series, etc. *n., pl.* **con·tin·u·a** (-ə).

**con·tort** (kən tôrt′) twist or bend out of shape; distort: *The body of the damaged car was contorted beyond repair.* *v.*

**con·tor·tion** (kən tôr′shən) **1** twisting or bending out of shape; distorting. **2** a CONTORTed condition; distorted form or shape: *The contortion of her face when she tasted the lemon was funny to see.* *n.*

**con·tour** (kon′tür) **1** the outline of a figure; the outline of a country, a lake, a mountain, etc.: *The contour of the Atlantic coast of Canada is very irregular.* **2** showing the outlines of hills, valleys, etc. at regular intervals above sea level: *a contour map.* **3** following the contours of uneven ground in such a way as to minimize erosion: *In contour ploughing, the furrows are made horizontally around the slopes of a hill instead of from top to bottom.* **4** build or shape to fit the outline of something: *The car has bucket seats contoured to fit the body.* 1–3 *n.*, 4 *v.*

**contour line** a line on a map, showing the outline from above of a section of the earth's surface at a particular height above sea level: *A 3000 metre contour line on a map of a mountain shows what its outline would look like from the top if a horizontal cross section were made at that height.*

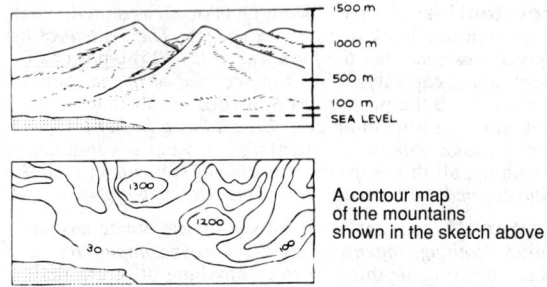

A contour map of the mountains shown in the sketch above

**contour map** a map showing elevations and depressions of the earth's surface by means of a series of CONTOUR LINES made at regular intervals above or below sea level.

**con·tra·band** (kon′trə band′) **1** goods that may not legally be imported or exported: *The plumage of endangered species of birds, such as the ostrich or egret, is contraband in Canada. Some goods, such as firearms, are contraband except under certain circumstances.* **2** trading contrary to law; smuggling. **3** smuggled goods: *The customs official was looking for contraband.* **4** against the law; prohibited: *The sale of stolen goods is contraband.* 1–3 *n.*, 4 *adj.*

**contraband of war** any materials supplied to warring nations by neutral countries: *Ammunition is always contraband of war.*

**con·tra·bass** (kon′trə bās′) **1** the lowest bass instrument of a family of instruments, especially the DOUBLE BASS of the violin family. **2** sounding an octave lower than the normal bass. *n.*

**con·tra·cep·tion** (kon′trə sep′shən) the intentional prevention of CONCEPTION (def. 4). *n.*

**con·tra·cep·tive** (kon′trə sep′tiv) **1** a substance or device for preventing pregnancy, or CONCEPTION (def. 4). **2** of or for CONTRACEPTION. 1 *n.*, 2 *adj.*

**con·tract** (kən trakt′ *for 1–4*; kon′trakt *or* kən trakt′ *for 7*; kon′trakt *for 5, 6*) **1** make or become narrower or shorter; make or become smaller; draw together; shrink: *Wrinkling the forehead contracts the brows. Rubber stretches and contracts.* **2** shorten a word, etc. by omitting some of the letters or sounds: *In talking we contract do not to don't.* **3** form; enter upon; bring on oneself: *to contract a bad habit.* **4** get; catch a disease: *She contracted malaria in the tropics.* **5** an agreement, especially a written agreement that can be enforced by law: *All professional hockey players sign contracts each year, agreeing to play for a certain salary.* **6** a formal agreement of marriage. **7** make a contract; enter into a legal agreement: *The builder contracted to build the new library.* 1–4, 7 *v.*, 5, 6 *n.*

**contract bridge** a card game played by four people divided into two opposing pairs: *In contract bridge, the highest bidder can score toward a game only as many points as he promised to make in his bid.*

**con·trac·tile** (kən trak′tīl *or* kən trak′təl) **1** capable of CONTRACTing (def. 1): *Muscle is contractile tissue.* **2** producing CONTRACTION (def. 1): *Cooling is a contractile force.* *adj.*

**con·trac·tion** (kən trak′shən) **1** CONTRACTING (def. 1) or being contracted: *Cold causes the contraction of liquids,*

gases, and metals, whereas heat causes expansion.
**2** something CONTRACTed (def. 2): a shortened form: *Can't* is *a contraction of* cannot. *n.*

**con·trac·tive** (kən trak′tiv) **1** capable of CONTRACTing (def. 1). **2** producing CONTRACTION (def. 1). **3** of CONTRACTION (def. 1). *adj.*

**con·trac·tor** (kon′trak tər *or* kən trak′tər *for 1*; kən trak′tər *for 2*) **1** a person who agrees to furnish materials or to do a piece of work for a certain price; especially for the construction of buildings. **2** a muscle that draws together some part or parts of the body. Compare with EXTENSOR. *n.*

**con·trac·tu·al** (kən trak′chü əl) **1** of or having to do with a CONTRACT (def. 5). **2** having the nature of a CONTRACT (def. 5). *adj.*

**con·tra·dict** (kon′trə dikt′) **1** express the opposite of a statement; declare to be false or untrue: *She contradicted his version of the accident.* **2** deny the statement of another person: *To contradict a guest is rude.* **3** be contrary to; be inconsistent with: *His quick anger contradicted his previous statement that he never lost his temper.* *v.*

**con·tra·dic·tion** (kon′trə dik′shən) **1** denying what has been said. **2** a statement or act that contradicts another; denial: *Her statement was a clear contradiction of what her father had said.* **3** a contrary condition; disagreement; opposition: *a contradiction in terms.* **4** inconsistency. *n.*

**con·tra·dic·to·ry** (kon′trə dik′tə rē) **1** CONTRADICTing (def. 3); contrary; in disagreement: *First reports of the election were so contradictory that we could not tell who had won.* **2** inclined to CONTRADICT (defs. 1, 2): *Don't be so contradictory!* *adj.*

**con·tra·dis·tinc·tion** (kon′trə dis tingk′shən) a distinction made by opposition or contrast: *The author emphasizes the importance of quality control in contradistinction to speed of production.* *n.*

**con·trail** (kon′trāl) the trail of vapour left by an aircraft flying at a high altitude; vapour trail. *n.*

**con·tral·to** (kən tral′tō *or* kən trol′tō) **1** the lowest female singing voice; alto. **2** a singer who has such a voice. **3** the part sung by a contralto. **4** having to do with, having the range of, or designed for a contralto. 1-3 *n.*, *pl.* **con·tral·tos;** 4 *adj.*

**con·trap·tion** (kən trap′shən) *Informal.* a contrivance; device; gadget: *They invented a crazy contraption for removing the shells from boiled eggs.* *n.*

**con·tra·ri·e·ty** (kon′trə rī′ə tē) **1** the state or quality of being CONTRARY. **2** a CONTRARY fact or statement. *n.*, *pl.* **con·tra·ri·e·ties.**

**con·tra·ri·wise** (kon′trer ē wīz′ *for 1 and 2*, kon′trer ē wīz′ *or* kon trer′ē wīz′ *for 3) Informal.* **1** in the opposite way or direction. **2** on the CONTRARY. **3** perversely. *adv.*

**con·tra·ry** (kon′trer ē; *also* kən trer′ē *for 5*) **1** opposed in purpose, character, etc.; opposite, completely different: *Contrary to all expectations, the party was a great success. The plan is contrary to government policy.* **2** opposite in direction, position, etc. **3** a fact or quality that is the opposite of something else; the opposite: *What she has just told us is the contrary of what we heard yesterday.* **4** unfavourable: *a contrary wind.* **5** opposing others; stubborn; perverse: *A contrary person can be one who argues for the sake of arguing.* **6** in opposition. 1, 2, 4,

**contractive** 265 **contrive**

hat, āge, fär; let, ēqual, tėrm; it, īce
hot, ōpen, ôrder; oil, out; cup, put, rüle
әbove, takәn, pencәl, lemәn, circәs
ch, child; ng, long; sh, ship
th, thin; ŦH, then; zh, measure

5 *adj.*, 3 *n.*, *pl.* **con·tra·ries;** 6 *adv.*
—**con′tra·ri·ly,** *adv.* —**con′tra·ri·ness,** *n.*
**on the contrary,** exactly opposite to what has been said: *He didn't go straight home; on the contrary, he stopped at three different stores and even visited a friend.*
**to the contrary,** with the opposite effect.

**con·trast** (kon′trast *for noun,* kən trast′ *for verb*) **1** a great difference; difference; striking difference: *the contrast between black and white.* **2** anything that shows differences when put side by side with something else: *Black hair is a sharp contrast to light skin.* **3** compare two things so as to show their differences: *My project was to contrast the climate of the Mackenzie Valley and the District of Keewatin.* **4** show differences when compared or put side by side: *Blue and yellow contrast prettily in a design.* **5** form a contrast to; set off (*used with* **with**): *The strained language of his speeches contrasts oddly with the ease and naturalness of his letters.* **6** put close together to heighten an effect by emphasizing differences. 1, 2 *n.*, 3-6 *v.*
—**con·trast′a·ble,** *adj.*

**con·trast·ive** (kən tras′tiv) having to do with or involving CONTRAST (def. 2): *A contrastive study of English and French grammar would show the ways in which the structures of the two languages are different.* *adj.*

**con·trib·ute** (kən trib′yüt) **1** give money, help, etc. along with others; furnish as a share: *to contribute to the Red Cross. Everyone was asked to contribute suggestions for the party.* **2** write articles, stories, etc. for a newspaper or magazine. *v.*, **con·trib·ut·ed, con·trib·ut·ing.**
**contribute to,** help bring about: *Poor food contributed to the child's illness.*

**con·tri·bu·tion** (kon′trə byü′shən) **1** the act of contributing; giving of money, help, etc. along with others. **2** the money, help, etc. given; gift. **3** an article, story, etc. written for a newspaper or magazine. **4** a tax or levy. *n.*

**con·trib·u·tive** (kən trib′yə tiv) contributing; helping to bring about. *adj.* —**con·trib′u·tive·ly,** *adv.*

**con·trib·u·tor** (kən trib′yə tər) **1** a person or thing that contributes. **2** a person who writes articles, stories, etc. for a newspaper or magazine. *n.*

**con·trib·u·to·ry** (kən trib′yə tô′rē) contributing; helping to bring about: *The worker's own carelessness was a contributory cause of the accident.* *adj.*

**con·trite** (kon′trīt *or* kən trīt′) **1** sad and humbled by a sense of having done wrong; penitent. **2** showing deep regret and sorrow: *He wrote an apology in contrite words.* *adj.* —**con·trite′ly,** *adv.* —**con·trite′ness,** *n.*

**con·tri·tion** (kən trish′ən) **1** sorrow for one's wrongdoing; being CONTRITE (def. 1); sincere penitence. **2** deep regret. *n.*

**con·triv·ance** (kən trī′vəns) **1** something invented; a mechanical device. **2** the act or manner of planning or designing: *By careful contrivance she managed to fit all her appointments into one afternoon.* **3** the power or ability of contriving. **4** a plan or scheme. *n.*

**con·trive** (kən trīv′) **1** invent; design: *to contrive a new kind of engine.* **2** scheme; plot: *to contrive a robbery.*

**3** manage; arrange to have something happen: *I will contrive to be there by ten o'clock.* **4** bring about. *v.*, **con·trived, con·triv·ing.**

**con·trol** (kən trōl′) **1** power; authority; direction: *A child is under its parent's control.* **2** have power or authority over; direct: *A captain controls his ship and its crew.* **3** hold back; keep down; restrain: *She controlled her grief.* **4** the power or ability to restrain, check, or keep down: *He lost control of his temper. He spoke in favour of gun control.* **5** a means of restraint; check: *They argued that the new law was not effective as a control against price increases.* **6** regulate: *to control prices and wages.* **7** a device that regulates the working of a machine: *The control for our furnace is in the front hall.* **8** a standard of comparison for testing the results of scientific experiments. **9 controls** *pl.* the instruments and devices by which a car, aircraft, locomotive, etc. is operated: *After the crash, the pilot was found dead at the controls.* 1, 4, 5, 7–9 *n.*, 2, 3, 6 *v.*, **con·trolled, con·trol·ling.**

**con·trol·la·ble** (kən trō′lə bəl) that can be controlled; capable of being checked or restrained. *adj.*

**con·trol·ler** (kən trō′lər) **1** a person employed to supervise expenditures or to manage financial affairs. **2** a person who controls, directs, or regulates: *an air traffic controller.* **3** a device that controls or regulates the speed of a machine. *n.* Also (def. 1), **comptroller.**

**con·trol·ler·ship** (kən trō′lər ship′) the position or office of a CONTROLLER (defs. 1, 2). *n.* Also, **comptrollership.**

**control room** **1** in a radio or television studio, a soundproof room from which the transmission of a broadcast is controlled. **2** a room containing all the instruments necessary to control a complex operation, such as the launching of a rocket.

**control stick** the lever that controls the direction of an aircraft's movement.

**control tower** at an airfield, the building from which the taking off and landing of aircraft is controlled.

**con·tro·ver·sial** (kon′trə vėr′shəl) **1** of, open to, or arousing CONTROVERSY: *a controversial question. She is a controversial politician.* **2** fond of CONTROVERSY. *adj.* —**con′tro·ver′sial·ly,** *adv.*

**con·tro·ver·sial·ist** (kon′trə vėr′shə list) a person who takes part in or is skilled in CONTROVERSY. *n.*

**con·tro·ver·sy** (kon′trə vėr′sē) **1** the act of arguing a question about which differences of opinion exist; a debate or dispute: *The controversy between the company and the union ended in a strike.* **2** a quarrel or wrangle. *n., pl.* **con·tro·ver·sies.**

**con·tro·vert** (kon′trə vėrt′) **1** dispute; deny; oppose: *The statement of the last witness controverts the evidence of the first two.* **2** dispute about; discuss; debate. *v.*

**con·tro·vert·i·ble** (kon′trə vėr′tə bəl) that can be CONTROVERTed; debatable. *adj.*

**con·tu·ma·cious** (kon′tyü mā′shəs *or* kon′tü mā′shəs) stubbornly rebellious; obstinately disobedient. *adj.* —**con′tu·ma′cious·ly,** *adv.*

**con·tu·ma·cy** (kon′tyü mə sē *or* kon′tü mə sē) stubborn resistance to authority; obstinate disobedience. *n., pl.* **con·tu·ma·cies.**

**con·tu·me·ly** (kon′tyü mə lē *or* kon′tü mə lē) **1** insolent contempt; insulting words or actions; humiliating treatment: *The serfs were treated with contumely.* **2** a humiliating insult. *n., pl.* **con·tu·me·lies.**

**con·tuse** (kən tyüz′ *or* kən tüz′) bruise. *v.*, **con·tused, con·tus·ing.**

**con·tu·sion** (kən tyü′zhən *or* kən tü′zhən) a bruise: *He suffered contusions in the accident, but no broken bones.* *n.*

**con·un·drum** (kə nun′drəm) **1** a riddle; a puzzling question whose answer involves a pun or play on words: *"When is a door not a door?" is a conundrum. The answer to this conundrum is "When it's ajar."* **2** any puzzling problem. *n.*

**con·va·lesce** (kon′və les′) regain strength after illness; make progress toward health. *v.*, **con·va·lesced, con·va·lesc·ing.**

**con·va·les·cence** (kon′və les′əns) **1** a gradual recovery of health and strength after illness: *Her convalescence is progressing well.* **2** the time during which a person is convalescing: *She spent a happy convalescence in Acapulco.* *n.*

**con·va·les·cent** (kon′və les′ənt) **1** recovering health and strength after illness: *She is convalescent, but still very weak.* **2** a person recovering after illness: *Such exercise is too strenuous for a convalescent.* **3** of or for persons who are convalescing: *the convalescent ward of a hospital, a convalescent diet.* 1, 3 *adj.*, 2 *n.*

**con·vec·tion** (kən vek′shən) the transfer of heat from one place to another by circulation: *A forced-air furnace system heats a room by convection.* *n.*

**con·vene** (kən vēn′) **1** meet for some purpose; gather together; assemble: *Parliament convenes in Ottawa at least once a year.* **2** call together members of an organization, etc.: *Any member may convene our club in an emergency.* *v.*, **con·vened, con·ven·ing.**

**con·ven·er** (kən vē′nər) See CONVENOR. *n.*

**con·ven·ience** (kən vē′nyəns *or* kən vē′nē əns) **1** the fact or quality of being CONVENIENT: *Many people appreciate the convenience of packaged goods.* **2** comfort; advantage: *Many provincial parks have camping places for the convenience of tourists.* **3** anything handy or easy to use; something that increases comfort and saves trouble or work: *A folding table is a convenience in a small room. Their house is filled with electrical appliances and other modern conveniences.* **4** intended or prepared for people's convenience: *He lives on convenience foods.* **5** Often, **conveniences,** *pl.* toilet or washroom. *n.* **at one's convenience,** so as to suit one as to time, place, or other conditions: *Write at your convenience.*

**convenience store** a small store, often a franchise or one of a chain of stores, that is open every day until late evening and specializes in selling basic food items, such as milk and bread, and a variety of small dry-goods items.

**con·ven·ient** (kən vē′nyənt *or* kən vē′nē ənt) **1** saving trouble; well arranged; easy to use: *to use a convenient tool, to take a convenient bus, to live in a convenient house.* **2** within easy reach; handy: *To meet at a convenient place.* **3** easily done; not troublesome: *Will it be convenient for you to bring your lunch to school?* *adj.* —**con·ven′ient·ly,** *adv.*

**convenient to,** *Informal.* near; easy to reach from: *The library is convenient to our apartment.*

**con·ven·or** (kən vē′nər) a person who is responsible for calling together the members of a committee, club, etc. and who often acts as their chairman. *n.* Also, **convener.**

**con·vent** (kon′vənt *or* kon′vent) **1** a group of nuns who live together and devote their lives to religion. **2** the building or buildings in which they live. *n.*

**con·ven·tion** (kən ven′shən) **1** a meeting for some purpose; gathering; assembly: *A political party holds a convention to choose a new leader.* **2** the delegates to a meeting or assembly. **3** an agreement: *A convention signed by two or more countries is usually about less important matters than those in a treaty.* **4** general agreement; common consent; custom: *Convention decides how people dress in public.* **5** a custom approved by general agreement; a rule based on common consent: *Using the right hand to shake hands is a convention.* **6** in the arts, a procedure or detail not taken literally but accepted by the beholder, reader, etc. as fitting: *It is a convention of the theatre that asides are not heard by persons on the stage with the speaker.* *n.*

**con·ven·tion·al** (kən ven′shə nəl) **1** depending on CONVENTION (def. 4); customary: *"Good morning" is a conventional greeting.* **2** ordinary; not interesting; not original: *conventional furniture.* **3** in art, following custom rather than nature: *Flowers and leaves are often drawn in conventional design without any idea of making them look real.* *adj.* —**con·ven′tion·al·ly,** *adv.*

**con·ven·tion·al·i·ty** (kən ven′shə nal′ə tē) **1** a CONVENTIONAL (def. 2) quality or character: *the conventionality of modern life.* **2** CONVENTIONAL (def. 1) behaviour; adherence to custom: *a slave to conventionality. Conventionality demanded that he at least put in an appearance.* **3** a CONVENTIONAL (def. 1) custom or rule: *The girls at boarding school were required to observe the conventionalities very strictly.* *n., pl.* **con·ven·tion·al·i·ties.**

**con·verge** (kən vėrj′) **1** tend to meet in a point. **2** turn toward each other: *If you look at the end of your nose, your eyes converge.* **3** come together; centre: *The interest of all the students converged upon the celebration.* **4** cause to converge. *v.,* **con·verged, con·verg·ing.**

**con·ver·gence** (kən vėr′jəns) **1** the act, process, or fact of converging; tendency to meet in a point. **2** the point of meeting. *n.*

**con·ver·gent** (kən vėr′jənt) tending to converge; inclining toward each other or toward a common point. *adj.*

**con·ver·sant** (kən vėr′sənt *or* kon′vər sənt) familiar by use or study; acquainted: *Mr. Taylor is thoroughly conversant with modern music.* *adj.*
—**con·ver′sant·ly,** *adv.*

**con·ver·sa·tion** (kon′vər sā′shən) informal or friendly talk; the exchange of thoughts by talking informally together: *There is much pleasure in good conversation.* *n.*

**con·ver·sa·tion·al** (kon′vər sā′shə nəl) **1** of or having to do with CONVERSATION. **2** fond of CONVERSATION; good at conversation. *adj.*

**con·ver·sa·tion·al·ist** (kon′vər sā′shə nə list) a person who is fond of or good at CONVERSATION. *n.*

---

**convenor**    **267**   **convertiplane**

hat, āge, fär; let, ēqual, tėrm; it, īce
hot, ōpen, ôrder; oil, out; cup, pùt, rüle
əbove, takən, pencəl, lemən, circəs
ch, child; ng, long; sh, ship
th, thin; ᵺ, then; zh, measure

**con·ver·sa·tion·al·ly** (kon′vər sā′shə nə lē) in a CONVERSATIONAL, informal manner. *adv.*

**con·verse¹** (kən vėrs′ *for verb,* kon′vėrs *for noun*) **1** talk informally together: *The two old veterans enjoyed conversing about their experiences in the last war.* **2** CONVERSATION. 1 *v.,* **con·versed, con·vers·ing;** 2 *n.*
—**con·vers′er,** *n.*

**con·verse²** (kən vėrs′ *or* kon′vėrs *for adjective,* kon′vėrs *for noun*) **1** opposite, contrary. **2** reversed in order; turned about. **3** something that is opposite or contrary. **4** something that is turned around: *"Honest but poor" is the converse of "Poor but honest."* 1, 2 *adj.,* 3, 4 *n.*

**con·verse·ly** (kən vėr′slē *or* kon′vėr slē) if or when turned the other way around: *Six is more than five; conversely, five is less than six. Grey is lighter than black; conversely, black is darker than grey.* *adv.*

**con·ver·sion** (kən vėr′zhən) **1** the act of CONVERTing (defs. 1, 5, 9, 10) or the process of being converted: *the conversion of inches into centimetres, the conversion of public money to one's own use.* **2** the act or experience of adopting a religion: *She told them about her conversion several years before.* **3** in football, the act or fact of kicking a point after a touchdown. *n.*

**con·vert** (kən vėrt′ *for verb,* kon′vėrt *for noun*) **1** change; turn: *These machines convert pulp into paper. One last effort converted defeat into victory.* **2** change or cause to change from one religion, political party, etc. to another. **3** cause to adopt a religion: *She was converted at a prayer meeting.* **4** a person who has been converted. **5** take and use unlawfully: *The dishonest treasurer converted the club's money to his own use.* **6** in football, a goal kicked after a touchdown. **7** the point made by successfully kicking a convert. **8** kick a goal after a touchdown: *Tom converted all three touchdowns last Saturday.* **9** turn the other way around; invert; transpose. **10** exchange for an equivalent: *He converted his Canadian dollars into French francs before he left.* 1–3, 5, 8–10 *v.,* 4, 6, 7 *n.*

**con·vert·er** (kən vėr′tər) **1** a device for changing alternating electrical current into direct current. **2** a device for adapting a television set to receive more channels than it was designed for. **3** a furnace in which pig iron is changed into steel by the BESSEMER PROCESS. **4** any person or thing that CONVERTs. *n.*

**con·vert·i·bil·i·ty** (kən vėr′tə bil′ə tē) the quality of being CONVERTIBLE. *n.*

**con·vert·i·ble** (kən vėr′tə bəl) **1** capable of being CONVERTED (def. 1): *Wood is convertible into paper. A two-dollar bill is convertible into coins.* **2** an automobile with a roof that can be folded down. 1 *adj.,* 2 *n.*
—**con·vert′i·bly,** *adv.*

**con·vert·i·plane** (kən vėr′tə plān′) an aircraft that operates like a conventional airplane in level flight, but which takes off and lands like a helicopter. *n.*

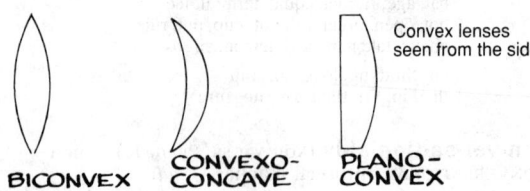
Convex lenses seen from the side

**con·vex** (kon′veks) 1 curved out, like the outside of a circle or sphere: *A watch crystal is slightly convex.* 2 a convex surface or thing. 1 *adj.*, 2 *n.* — **con′vex·ly**, *adv.* Compare with CONCAVE.

**con·vex·i·ty** (kon vek′sə tē) 1 a CONVEX condition or quality. 2 a CONVEX surface or thing. *n., pl.* **con·vex·i·ties**.

**con·vex·o–con·cave** (kon vek′sō kon kāv′) convex on one side and CONCAVE on the other: *In a convexo-concave lens, the convex side has the greater curvature.* See CONVEX for picture. *adj.*

**con·vey** (kən vā′) 1 carry; transport: *A bus conveys passengers.* 2 transmit; conduct: *A wire conveys an electric circuit.* 3 express; make known; communicate: *Her words convey no meaning to me.* 4 transfer the ownership of property from one person to another: *The old farmer conveyed his farm to his daughter.* *v.* —**con·vey′a·ble**, *adj.*

**con·vey·ance** (kən vā′əns) 1 the act of carrying; transportation; transmission. 2 anything that carries people and goods; vehicle: *Trains and buses are public conveyances.* 3 communication: *Books are for the conveyance of ideas.* *n.*

**con·vey·or** or **con·vey·er** (kən vā′ər) 1 a person or thing that CONVEYS. 2 a mechanical device that carries things from one place to another by means of a moving endless belt or a series of rollers: *Grain is carried from one level of an elevator to another by means of a conveyor.* *n.*

**conveyor belt** CONVEYOR (def. 2).

**con·vict** (kən vikt′ *for verb,* kon′vikt *for noun*) 1 prove guilty: *The evidence will surely convict him.* 2 declare guilty: *The jury convicted the prisoner of murder.* 3 a person convicted by a court. 4 a person serving a prison sentence for some crime. 1, 2 *v.*, 3, 4 *n.*

**con·vic·tion** (kən vik′shən) 1 CONVICTing (defs. 1, 2) or being convicted: *a conviction for theft.* 2 the appearance or condition of being CONVINCed: *She spoke with conviction on the benefits of regular exercise.* 3 a firm belief: *It was his conviction that war was inevitable.* *n.*

**con·vince** (kən vins′) make a person feel sure; cause to believe; persuade by argument or proof: *The mistakes Nan made convinced the teacher that she had not studied her lesson.* *v.*, **con·vinced, con·vinc·ing**.

**con·vin·ci·ble** (kən vin′sə bəl) capable of being CONVINCed. *adj.*

**con·vinc·ing** (kən vin′sing) 1 that CONVINCEs: *a convincing argument.* 2 ppr. of CONVINCE. 1 *adj.*, 2 *v.* —**con·vinc′ing·ly**, *adv.* —**con·vinc′ing·ness**, *n.*

**con·viv·i·al** (kən viv′ē əl) 1 fond of eating and drinking with friends; jovial; sociable. 2 of or suitable for a feast or banquet; festive. *adj.* —**con·viv′i·al·ly**, *adv.*

**con·vo·ca·tion** (kon′və kā′shən) 1 calling together; assembling by a summons. 2 an assembly; a number of persons met in answer to a summons: *The convocation of teachers passed a resolution condemning war.* 3 in universities: **a** the officials and graduates as a legislative, advisory, or electoral body. **b** a meeting of this body. **c** an assembly of the members of the university for a specific purpose. **d** a ceremony at which degrees are conferred. *n.*

**con·voke** (kən vōk′) call together; summon to assemble. *v.*, **con·voked, con·vok·ing**. —**con·vok′er**, *n.*

**con·vo·lu·tion** (kon′və lü′shən) 1 a coiling, winding, or twisting together: *the convolutions of a snake.* 2 a coil; winding; twist. 3 an irregular fold or ridge on the surface of the brain. *n.*

**con·vol·vu·lus** (kən vol′vyə ləs) any of a closely related group of plants, usually vines, with flowers shaped like trumpets: *A morning-glory is a convolvulus.* *n., pl.* **con·vol·vu·lus·es** or **con·vol·vu·li** (-lī′ *or* -lē′).

**con·voy** (kon′voi) 1 accompany in order to protect; escort: *Warships convoy merchant ships in time of war.* 2 an escort; protection: *The gold was moved from the truck to the vault under convoy of armed guards.* 3 warships, soldiers, etc. that convoy; a protecting escort. 4 the ship, fleet, supplies, etc. accompanied by a protecting escort. 5 the act of escorting for protection: *The convoy of merchant ships was continued throughout the war.* 1 *v.*, 2–5 *n.*

**con·vulse** (kən vuls′) 1 shake violently: *An earthquake convulsed the island.* 2 cause violent disturbance in; disturb violently: *Rage convulsed his face.* 3 throw into convulsions; affect with muscular spasms: *The sick child was convulsed before the doctor came.* 4 throw into a fit of laughter; cause to shake with laughter: *The clown convulsed us all with his funny acts.* *v.*, **con·vulsed, con·vuls·ing**.

**con·vul·sion** (kən vul′shən) 1 a fit of laughter. 2 a violent disturbance: *The country was undergoing a political convulsion.* 3 Often, **convulsions**, *pl.* a violent, involuntary contracting and relaxing of the muscles; spasm. *n.*

**con·vul·sive** (kən vul′siv) 1 sudden, violent, etc., like a CONVULSION (def. 3). *The dog made convulsive efforts to free itself from the chain.* 2 having CONVULSIONS (def. 3). 3 producing CONVULSIONS (def. 3). *adj.* —**con·vul′sive·ly**, *adv.*

**co·ny** (kō′nē) 1 See CONEY. 2 See CONNIE. *n., pl.* **co·nies**.

**coo** (kü) 1 a soft, murmuring sound made by doves or pigeons. 2 make this sound. 3 murmur softly; speak in a soft, loving manner. 1 *n.*, 2, 3 *v.*, **cooed, coo·ing**. ☛ *Hom.* COUP.

**cook** (kuk) 1 prepare for eating by applying heat, as in boiling, baking, frying, or broiling: *We use coal, wood, gas, oil, and electricity for cooking.* 2 undergo cooking; be cooked: *Let the meat cook slowly.* 3 a person who cooks. 4 acts as cook; work as cook: *He cooked for the whole camp.* 5 *Informal.* tamper with accounts, etc.; doctor; falsify: *She was caught cooking the company's books.* 1, 2, 4, 5 *v.*, 3 *n.* **cook a person's goose**, *Informal.* ruin everything for a person: *If you tell his mother, you'll cook his goose for sure.* **cook up**, *Informal.* **a** make up; prepare. **b** prepare falsely: *The liar had cooked up a story to explain her absence.*

**cook·book** (kuk′buk′) a book of directions for cooking various kinds of food; a book of recipes. *n.*

**cook·er** (kük′ər) an apparatus or container to cook things in. *n.*

**cook·er·y** (kük′ə rē) **1** the art or occupation of cooking. **2** *Cdn.* a COOKHOUSE at a logging camp or mine. *n., pl.* **cook·er·ies.**

**cook·house** (kük′hous′) a room or place for cooking, especially in a large camp. *n.*

**cook·ie** (kük′ē) any of various kinds of small, sweet, more or less flat cake. *n.* Sometimes, **cooky.**
☛ *Etym.* From Dutch *koekje* 'little cake'. 18c.

**cook-out** (kük′out′) cooking and eating a meal out-of-doors; a picnic, etc. where the food is cooked outdoors. *n.*

**cook·y** (kük′ē) See COOKIE. *n., pl.* **cook·ies.**

**cool** (kül) **1** somewhat cold; more cold than hot: *We sat in the shade where it was cool.* **2** allowing or giving a cool feeling: *cool clothes.* **3** not excited; calm and unemotional: *He was always cool in an emergency.* **4** having little enthusiasm or interest; not cordial: *a cool greeting.* **5** a cool part, place, or time: *the cool of the evening.* **6** become cool: *Let the cake cool before you put on the icing.* **7** make cool: *Cool the ginger ale with ice.* **8** bold; impudent: *a cool customer.* **9** *Informal.* without exaggeration or qualification: *a cool million dollars.* **10** of colours, suggesting coolness: *Blue and green are called cool colours. The chesterfield and chair were a cool grey.* **11** *Informal.* control of one's actions, feelings, etc.; self-control: *She managed to keep her cool.* 1–4, 8–10 *adj.*, 5, 11 *n.*, 6, 7 *v.* —**cool′ly,** *adv.* —**cool′ness,** *n.* —**cool′ish,** *adj.*
**cool down** or **off,** *Informal.* lose one's enthusiasm, especially for a person.
**cool it,** *Informal.* calm down; regain one's self-control: *He told his excited little brother to cool it.*

**cool·ant** (kü′lənt) a cooling medium, used for machinery, etc. *n.*

**cool·er** (kü′lər) **1** an apparatus or container that cools foods or drinks, or keeps them cool. **2** anything that cools, such as a cool drink. *n.*

**cool-head·ed** (kül′hed′id) calm; not easily excited. *adj.*

**coo·lie** (kü′lē) **1** an unskilled labourer in parts of Asia. **2** any labourer who does hard work for very little pay. *n.*
☛ *Hom.* COULEE.

**coon** (kün) *Informal.* RACCOON. *n.*

**coop** (küp) **1** a small cage or pen for chickens, rabbits, etc. **2** keep or put in a coop. **3** confine, especially in a very small space: *The children were cooped up indoors by the rain.* 1 *n.,* 2, 3 *v.*
☛ *Hom.* COUPE (küp).

**co-op** (kō′op) *Informal.* CO-OPERATIVE (def. 2). *n.*

**coop·er** (kü′pər) a person who makes or repairs barrels, casks. *n.*

**co-op·er·ate** (kō op′ə rāt′) work together, unite in producing a result: *If we co-operate, we can get the yard cleaned up quickly.* *v.,* **co-op·er·at·ed, co-op·er·at·ing.** Also, **cooperate.** —**co-op′er·a′tor,** *n.*

**co-op·er·a·tion** (kō op′ə rā′shən) the act of working together; united effort or labour: *Co-operation can accomplish many things that no individual could do alone.* *n.* Also, **cooperation.**

**co-op·er·a·tive** (kō op′ə rə tiv *or* kō op′ə rā′tiv) **1** wanting or willing to work together with others: *Dan was helpful and co-operative.* **2** an enterprise owned jointly by a group of people and operated for their mutual benefit: *Co-operatives may take the form of stores, farm marketing agencies, etc.* 1 *adj.,* 2 *n.* Also, **cooperative.** —**co-op′er·a·tive·ly,** *adv.* —**co-op′er·a·tive·ness,** *n.*

**Co-operative Commonwealth Federation** the CCF, a Canadian political party established in 1932. The federal CCF ceased to exist after it joined with the Canadian Labour Congress to form the NEW DEMOCRATIC PARTY in 1961.

**co-opt** (kō opt′) of a committee, etc., add or elect a new member. *v.*

**co-or·di·nate** (kō ôr′də nit *for adjective and noun,* kō ôr′də nāt′ *for verb*) **1** equal in importance; of equal rank. **2** an equal; a co-ordinate person or thing. **3** grammatically equivalent: *A compound sentence contains two or more co-ordinate clauses.* **4** arrange in proper order or relation; harmonize; adjust: *A swimmer should co-ordinate the movements of her arms and legs.* **5 co-ordinates,** *pl.* **a** matching items of clothing or furniture: *This skirt and this sweater are co-ordinates.* **b** in geography, a pair of references, such as latitude or longitude, which fixes a position on a map. **6** usually, **coordinates,** *pl.* in mathematics, an ordered pair of numbers or letters which fixes a position on a grid. 1, 3 *adj.,* 2, 5, 6 *n.,* 4 *v.,* **co-or·di·nat·ed, co-or·di·nat·ing.** —**co-or′di·nate·ly,** *adv.* —**co-or′di·nate·ness,** *n.* Also, **coordinate.**

**co-or·di·na·tion** (kō ôr′də nā′shən) **1** the condition of working together smoothly and easily, often used with reference to muscles: *She became a better swimmer as her co-ordination improved.* **2** arrangement in the proper order or proper relation: *She made an outline for her composition to help in the co-ordination of her ideas.* **3** putting or being put into the same order or rank. *n.* Also, **coordination.**

**coot** (küt) **1** any of a closely related group of dark-grey inland marsh birds of the RAIL[3] family, resembling ducks, but having a smaller bill and toes with scalloplike lobes of skin along the sides; mud hen. **2** a North American SCOTER. **3** *Informal.* a foolish or simple person: *The poor coot couldn't even remember where his hotel was.* *n.*

**cop** (kop) *Informal.* a police officer.

**co·pal** (kō′pəl) a hard, lustrous resin from various tropical trees, used chiefly in making varnish. *n.*

**cope**[1] (kōp) strive or fight with some degree of success; struggled on even terms; deal successfully: *He said he just couldn't cope any more. She was too weak to cope with the extra work.* *v.,* **coped, cop·ing.**

**cope**[2] (kōp) **1** a long cloak. **2** anything like a cope. **3** a COPING. **4** cover with a cope. **5** provide with a COPING. 1–3 *n.,* 4, 5 *v.,* **coped, cop·ing.**

**Co·per·ni·can** (kə pėr′nə kən) of or having to do with Nikolaus Copernicus (1473–1543), a Polish astronomer, or his system of astronomy: *The Copernican system is the theory that the earth revolves on its axis and the planets move in orbits around the sun.* *adj.*

**cope·stone** (kōp′stōn′) **1** the top stone of a wall; a

stone used for or in a COPING.   2 a finishing touch; climax.   *n.*

**cop·i·er** (kop′ē ər)   1 a person who copies; imitator. 2 a person who makes written copies; copyist.   3 a machine that makes copies; duplicator.   *n.*

**co–pi·lot** (kō′pī′lət)   the assistant or second pilot in an aircraft.   *n.*

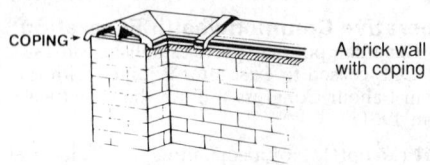
A brick wall with coping

**cop·ing** (kō′ping)   the top layer of a brick or stone wall: *The coping is usually built with a slope to shed water.*   *n.*

**coping saw**   a narrow saw in a U-shaped frame, used to cut curves.

**co·pi·ous** (kō′pē əs)   1 plentiful; abundant: *a copious supply of wheat.*   2 containing much matter. 3 containing many words; wordy: *a copious argument.*   *adj.*   —**co′pi·ous·ly,** *adv.*   —**co′pi·ous·ness,** *n.*

**cop·per** (kop′ər)   1 a tough, reddish-brown metal that is easily shaped into thin sheets or fine wire and resists rust: *Copper is an excellent conductor of heat and electricity.*  Symbol: Cu   2 a large boiler or cauldron.   3 cover with copper.   4 made of copper: *a copper kettle.*   5 reddish brown.   1–3, 5 *n.*, 3 *v.*, 4, 5 *adj.*

**cop·per·as** (kop′ə rəs)   a green sulphate of iron, used in dyeing, photography, making ink, etc.   *n.*

**Copper Eskimo**   a member of a group of Inuit living near the Coppermine River.

**cop·per·head** (kop′ər hed′)   a poisonous North American snake having a copper-coloured head, related to the water moccasin and the rattlesnake.   *n.*

**cop·per·y** (kop′ə rē)   1 of or containing COPPER (def. 1).   2 like COPPER (def. 1).   *adj.*

**cop·ra** (kop′rə)   the dried meat of ripe coconuts, which yields coconut oil, the basic cooking oil of the tropics, and coconut meal, a valuable high-protein food for livestock.   *n.*

**cop·ter** (kop′tər) *Informal.*   HELICOPTER.   *n.*

**cop·u·la** (kop′yə lə)   LINKING VERB.   *n., pl.* **cop·u·las** or **cop·u·lae** (-lē′ *or* -lī′).

**cop·u·late** (kop′yə lāt′)   of human beings or animals, come together in sexual union.   *v.,* **cop·u·lat·ed, cop·u·lat·ing.**

**cop·u·la·tion** (kop′yə lā′shən)   1 sexual union between male and female human beings or animals.   2 in grammar or logic, a joining or being joined together; connection.   *n.*

**cop·y** (kop′ē)   1 anything made to be just like another; anything made on the pattern or model of another; duplicate; reproduction: *One written page, picture, dress, or chair can be an exact copy of another.*   2 make a copy; make a copy of: *Copy this page. She copied her friend's sweater.*   3 be like; follow as a pattern or model; imitate: *The little boy copied his father's way of walking.*   4 one of a number of books, newpapers, magazines, pictures, etc. made at the same printing: *Please get six copies of today's newspaper.*   5 the material to be set up in type for a book, newspaper, or magazine: *She writes advertising copy for a textile company.*   6 in journalism, source material for an article, news report, etc.: *She's always good copy, with her unusual ideas and colourful way of talking.* 1, 4–6 *n., pl.* **copies;**   2, 3 *v.,* **cop·ied, cop·y·ing.**

**cop·y·book** (kop′ē bùk′)   1 a book with models of handwriting to be copied in learning to write. 2 commonplace; conventional; ordinary: *a copybook speech.*   1 *n.*, 2 *adj.*

**co·py·cat** (kop′ē kat′) *Informal.*   a person who slavishly imitates another in dress, behaviour, etc. (*a word used especially by children*).   *n.*

**copy desk**   the desk in a newspaper office where news stories and articles are edited before being set up for printing.

**cop·y·ist** (kop′ē ist)   1 a person who makes written copies.   2 a person who copies; imitator.   *n.*

**cop·y·right** (kop′ē rīt′)   1 a right to copy, granted by law to an author, composer, artist, etc., making him or her for a certain number of years the only person who can sell, print, publish, or copy a particular work, or who can authorize others to do so: *Because Shakespeare's plays are not in copyright, anyone can produce them on stage without paying a fee.*   2 protect by getting a copyright: *Books, pieces of music, plays, etc. are usually copyrighted.*   1 *n.*, 2 *v.*

**cop·y·writ·er** (kop′ē rī′tər)   a person whose work is writing advertisements and other publicity material to be used in newspapers, magazines, radio, or television.   *n.*

**co·quet** (kō ket′)   1 FLIRT.   2 trifle.   *v.,* **co·quet·ted, co·quet·ting.**

**co·quet·ry** (kō′kə trē)   1 FLIRTing.   2 trifling.   *n., pl.* **co·quet·ries.**

**co·quette** (kō ket′)   a woman who tries to attract men merely to please her vanity; FLIRT.   *n.*

**co·quet·tish** (kō ket′ish)   1 of a COQUETTE.   2 like a COQUETTE; like a coquette's: *The pretty girl winked and gave him a coquettish smile.*   *adj.*   —**co·quet′tish·ly,** *adv.*

**cor–**   a form of the prefix **com-** occurring before *r*, as in *correspond.*  See note at COM-.

A modern Welsh coracle

**cor·a·cle** (kôr′ə kəl)   a light, bowl-shaped boat used for many centuries in the British Isles for river fishing, originally made of woven reeds, grasses, or branches with a covering of hides: *The coracles used today in Wales and Ireland have a covering of canvas and tar.*   *n.*

**cor·al** (kôr′əl)   1 a stony or horny substance that forms the skeletal structure built by any of various simple, mostly very tiny sea animals called POLYPS: *The coral forming coral reefs and islands consists of the external skeletons of thousands of polyps. The precious pink or red coral used in jewellery is the internal skeleton of certain other species of polyp.*   2 any of the animals producing coral, especially

any of a group that resemble and are distantly related to sea anemones: *Most corals live in colonies, with their bodies joined together by membranes and their skeletons cemented together.* **3** a colony of such animals with their skeletons, forming a single mass: *The* **fan coral** *often grows to a height of more than two metres.* **4** a piece of coral, especially precious pink or red coral used in jewellery. **5** of, having to do with, or producing coral: *coral polyps, coral reefs.* **6** slightly yellowish deep pink. 1–4, 6 *n.*, 5, 6 *adj.*
☞ *Hom.* CHORAL.

**coral reef** a reef consisting mainly of CORAL (def. 1) produced by many colonies of coral POLYPS over a period of centuries, with new animals building on the skeletons left behind by animals that have died.

**coral snake** any of a genus of poisonous snakes of tropical and subtropical America typically marked with red, black, and yellow or white bands around the body.

**cord** (kôrd) **1** heavy, thick string of several strands or fibres twisted together; thin rope. **2** a thin, flexible, insulated cable having a plug at one end, used to connect an electrical appliance to a source of power. **3** a similar cable for connecting a desk telephone to the main telephone line. **4** a structure in an animal body that resembles a cord: *The spinal cord is in the backbone. The vocal cords are in the* LARYNX. **5** a ridge on cloth. **6** cloth made with such ridges. **7** fasten or tie with heavy string or cord, or provide with cord. **8** a unit for measuring cut firewood, equal to 128 cubic feet (about 3.6 m³): *A standard cord is a stack of 4-foot lengths of wood measuring 8 feet long by 4 feet high (about* 1.2 m × 2.4 m × 1.2 m). *Since fireplaces have become smaller, dealers usually sell wood in* **face cords** *for which the wood is cut in 2-foot (about* 60 cm) *lengths.* **9** pile wood in cords. **10 cords**, *pl.* trousers made of corduroy or other cloth with ridges. 1–6, 8, 10 *n.*, 7, 9 *v.* —**cord′like**, *adj.*
☞ *Hom.* CHORD.

**cord·age** (kôr′dij) **1** CORDS (def. 1); ropes: *The cordage of a ship is its rigging.* **2** a quantity of wood measured in CORDS (def. 8). *n.*

**cor·dial** (kôr′jəl *or* kôr′dē əl) **1** warm; friendly: *His hostess gave him a cordial welcome.* **2** strengthening; stimulating. **3** a food, drink, or medicine that strengthens or stimulates. **4** LIQUEUR. 1, 2 *adj.*, 3, 4 *n.* —**cor′dial·ly**, *adv.* —**cor′dial·ness**, *n.*

**cor·dial·i·ty** (kôr jal′ə tē *or* kôr′dē al′ə tē) a CORDIAL (def. 1) quality or feeling; warmth: *The cordiality of his welcome made Tom feel at home.* *n.*, *pl.* **cor·dial·i·ties**.

**cor·dil·le·ra** (kôr′də lyer′ə *or* kôr dil′ə rə) a long mountain range; a chain of mountains. *n.*

**cor·don** (kôr′dən) **1** a line or circle of soldiers, police, ships, forts, etc. placed at intervals around an area to guard it. **2** a cord, braid, or ribbon worn as an ornament or badge of honour. **3** put a protective line or barrier around (usually used with **off**): *The area around the famous painting was cordoned off.* 1, 2 *n.*, 3 *v.*

**cor·do·van** (kôr′də vən *or* kôr dō′vən) **1** a kind of soft, fine-grained leather first made in Córdoba, Spain: *Cordovan was originally made of goatskin, but now is usually made of split horsehide.* **2** of this leather. *n.*

**cor·du·roy** (kôr′də roi′) **1** cloth, usually of cotton, in a plain or twill weave, having a thick, velvetlike cut pile in wide or narrow ridges called wales. **2** having ridges like corduroy. **3** *Cdn.* a CORDUROY ROAD or bridge. **4 corduroys**, *pl.* corduroy trousers. 1, 3 *n.*, 2 *adj.*

**corduroy bridge** *Cdn.* a temporary bridge made of logs laid crosswise.

**corduroy road** *Cdn.* a temporary road made of logs laid crosswise, often across low, wet land.

**cord·wood** (kôrd′wùd′) **1** wood sold or stacked in CORDS (def. 8). **2** wood or standing timber suitable for use as firewood. *n.*

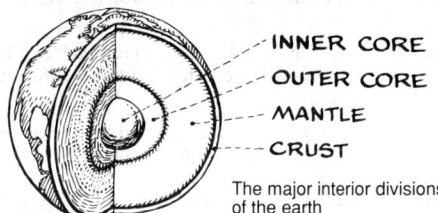

The major interior divisions of the earth

**core** (kôr) **1** the hard central part of some fruits, such as apples and pears, that contains the seeds. **2** take out the core of: *to core apples.* **3** the central part of the earth, beginning at a depth of about 2880 km and having a radius of about 3400 km, believed by most geologists to consist of iron with a small amount of nickel. **4** a base layer of low-grade wood, plywood, etc. to which veneers or plastic laminates are glued: *The wall units are constructed of elm veneers on a plywood core.* **5** a bar of soft iron forming the centre of an electromagnet or of an induction coil. **6** the central or most important part of anything: *the core of a boil, the core of an argument.* 1, 3–6 *n.*, 2 *v.* **cored, cor·ing.**
☞ *Hom.* CORPS.

**co·re·op·sis** (kô′rē op′sis) any of a closely related group of plants of the same family as the aster, having yellow, red-and-yellow, or reddish flowers shaped like daisies. *n.*

**co·ri·an·der** (kô′rē an′dər) **1** an annual herb of the parsley family native to the Mediterranean region, but widely cultivated for its tiny, seedlike, sweet-smelling fruits. **2** its fruit, used as a spice and as a flavouring in liqueurs and medicines. *n.*

**Co·rin·thi·an** (kə rin′thē ən) **1** of or having to do with Corinth, a seaport in southern Greece, or its people. **2** a native or inhabitant of Corinth. **3** of or having to do with the most elaborate of the three types of Greek architecture: *The capital of a Corinthian column is adorned with acanthus leaves.* See ORDER for picture. 1, 3 *adj.*, 2 *n.*

**Coriolis force** (kô′rē ō′lis) the force resulting from the rotation of the earth that causes a moving body on or above the earth's surface to drift from its course to the right in the Northern Hemisphere and to the left in the Southern Hemisphere: *The Coriolis force must be taken into account in plotting ocean currents, cyclones, and artificial satellites.*

**cork** (kôrk) **1** the light, thick, outer bark of the CORK OAK, used for bottle stoppers, floats for fishing lines, inner soles of shoes, floor and wall coverings, etc. **2** anything made of cork, especially a stopper for a bottle: *Bottles of wine are usually closed with a cork.* **3** any stopper made of glass, rubber, etc. **4** stop up with a cork. **5** made of

**cork or with cork.** 6 confine; restrain; check. 7 blacken with burnt cork. 8 an outer bark of woody plants, serving as a protective covering. 1–3, 5, 8 *n.*, 4, 6, 7 *v.*

**cork oak** an oak tree from which cork is obtained.

**cork·screw** (kôrk′skrü′) 1 a tool for pulling corks out of bottles. 2 shaped like a corkscrew; spiral: *The plane did a corkscrew dive.* 3 move or advance in a spiral or zigzag course. 1, 2 *n.*, 3 *v.*

**corm** (kôrm) a fleshy, bulblike underground stem that has leaves and buds on the upper surface and roots usually on the lower. *n.*

**cor·mo·rant** (kôr′mə rənt) 1 a large, black sea bird that has a pouch under its beak for holding captured fish. 2 a greedy person. *n.*

**corn**[1] (kôrn) 1 a species of tall cereal plant having seeds, or kernels, that grow in rows along a thick, woody axis called a cob; maize; Indian corn. 2 the kernels, used for food or fodder. 3 any small, hard seed or grain, especially of cereal plants. 4 in England, grain in general, especially wheat. 5 in Scotland and Ireland, oats. 6 *Informal.* anything trite, too sentimental, or unsophisticated. 7 preserve meat with strong salt water or with dry salt. 1–6 *n.*, 7 *v.*

**corn**[2] (kôrn) a hardening and thickening of the skin, usually on a toe: *Corns are caused by pressure or rubbing and are often very painful.* *n.*

**corn boil** a CORN ROAST.

**corn borer** the larva of a small moth that destroys corn and other plants.

**corn bread** bread made of CORNMEAL instead of flour.

**corn·cob** (kôrn′kob′) 1 the central, woody part of an ear of corn, on which the kernels grow. 2 a tobacco pipe with a bowl hollowed out of a piece of dried corncob. *n.*

**corn crake** a species of short-billed RAIL[3] native to Europe and Asia, commonly found in European grainfields.

**corn·crib** (kôrn′krib′) a bin or small, ventilated building for storing unshelled corn. *n.*

**cor·ne·a** (kôr′nē ə) the transparent part of the outer coat of the eyeball: *The cornea covers the iris and the pupil.* See EYE for picture. *n.*

**cor·ne·al** (kôr′nē əl) of or having to do with the CORNEA. *adj.*

**corned** (kôrnd) 1 preserved with strong salt water or dry salt: *corned beef.* 2 pt. and pp. of CORN. 1 *adj.*, 2 *v.*

**cor·nel·ian** (kôr nē′lyən) CARNELIAN. *n.*

**cor·ne·ous** (kôr′nē əs) horny; of or like horn. *adj.*

**cor·ner** (kôr′nər) 1 the point or place where lines or surfaces meet: *A diagonal joins two opposite corners of a rectangle.* 2 the space between two lines or surfaces near where they meet; ANGLE: *There was a bookcase in the far corner of the room.* 3 the place where two streets meet. 4 at a corner: *the corner drugstore.* 5 for a corner: *a corner shelf.* 6 put in a corner; drive into a corner: *I finally cornered our dog and got the leash on her.* 7 something that forms, protects, or decorates a corner: *The leather wallet has gold corners.* 8 a secret or secluded place: *The money was hidden in odd corners all over the house.* 9 a region or part; a place that is far away: *People have searched in all corners of the earth for gold.* 10 an awkward or difficult position; a place from which escape is impossible: *His enemies had driven him into a corner.* 11 force into an awkward or difficult position; drive into a place from which escape is impossible. 12 a buying up of the available supply of some stock or article to raise its price: *a corner in copper.* 13 buy up all or nearly all that can be had of something to raise its price: *Some speculators have tried to corner wheat.* 1–5, 7–10, 12 *n.*, 6, 11, 13 *v.*

**cut corners,** a shorten the way by going across corners. b save money, effort, time, etc.

**turn the corner,** pass the worst or most dangerous point.

**cor·ner·stone** (kôr′nər stōn′) 1 a stone at the corner of two walls that holds them together. 2 such a stone built into the corner of a building as its formal beginning: *The laying of a cornerstone is often accompanied with ceremonies.* 3 a main part on which something else rests; foundation; basis: *Clear thinking is the cornerstone of good writing.* *n.*

**cor·ner·ways** (kôr′nər wāz′) CORNERWISE. *adj.*

**cor·ner·wise** (kôr′nər wīz′) 1 with the corner in front; so as to form a corner. 2 from corner to corner; diagonally. *adv.*

**cor·net** (kôr′nit *or* kôr net′) 1 a valved brass wind instrument resembling a trumpet, now used mostly in brass bands: *The cornet was very popular for all orchestral music in the late 19th century, before the valve trumpet was adopted.* 2 a piece of paper rolled into a cone and twisted at one end, used to hold candy, nuts, etc. *n.*

**cor·net·tist** *or* **cor·net·ist** (kôr net′ist) a person who plays the CORNET (def. 1), especially a skilled player. *n.*

**corn·field** (kôrn′fēld′) a field of growing corn. *n.*

**corn·flow·er** (kôrn′flou′ər) a plant having blue, pink, white, or purple flowers; BACHELOR'S-BUTTON. *n.*

**corn·husk** (kôrn′husk′) the husk of an ear of corn. *n.*

**cor·nice** (kôr′nis) 1 in architecture, the moulded, projecting, topmost part of the upper section of a wall or storey supported on columns or pilasters; the top part of an entablature. See COLUMN for picture. 2 an ornamental moulding around the top of a wall. 3 furnish or finish with a cornice. 1, 2 *n.*, 3 *v.*, **cor·niced, cor·nic·ing.**

**Cor·nish** (kôr′nish) 1 of or having to do with Cornwall, a county in southwestern England, its people, or the language formerly spoken by them. 2 the ancient Celtic language of Cornwall. 1 *adj.*, 2 *n.*

**Cor·nish·man** (kôr′nish mən) a male native or inhabitant of Cornwall. *n., pl.* **Cor·nish·men** (-mən).

**Cor·nish·wo·man** (kôr′nish wù′mən) a female native or inhabitant of Cornwall. *n., pl.* **Cor·nish·wo·men** (-wi′mən).

**corn·meal** (kôrn′mēl′) meal made from ground-up corn. *n.*

**corn roast** a picnic held usually in the fall, at which corn is roasted or boiled for eating off the COB (def. 1).

**corn silk** the long, glossy STYLES that emerge in a silky tuft from the tip of an ear of corn.

**corn snow** snow consisting of granular particles suggesting cornmeal, formed by alternate periods of thawing and freezing.

**corn·stalk** (kôrn′stok′) a stalk of a corn plant. *n.*

**corn·starch** (kôrn′stärch′) a starchy flour made from corn, used to thicken sauces, etc. *n.*

**corn sugar** sugar made from cornstarch.

**corn syrup** syrup made from corn.

A cornucopia, or horn of plenty

**cor·nu·co·pi·a** (kôr′nyə kō′pē ə) 1 a horn-shaped container or ornament: *Cornucopias are hung on Christmas trees.* 2 a decorated curved horn overflowing with fruits and flowers, used as a symbol of a good harvest or any time of prosperity. *n.*

**corn·y** (kôr′nē) *Informal.* too trite, sentimental, or unsophisticated: *corny jokes. That movie has some corny scenes.* *adj.*, **corn·i·er, corn·i·est.**

**co·rol·la** (kə rol′ə) the internal envelope or floral leaves of a flower, usually of some colour other than green; the petals: *The corolla can consist of separate petals, as in the rose, or fused petals, as in the morning-glory.* *n.*

**cor·ol·lar·y** (kə rol′ə rē *or* kô′rə ler′ē) 1 something proved incidentally in proving something else. 2 an inference; deduction. 3 a natural consequence or result: *She believes her good health is a corollary of her simple way of life.* 4 like a corollary; resulting. *n., pl.* **cor·ol·lar·ies.**

**co·ro·na** (kə rō′nə) 1 in meteorology, a ring of usually coloured light visible around a shining body such as the sun or moon when it is seen through a thin cloud of water droplets or, sometimes, dust particles in the atmosphere. Compare with HALO (def. 1). 2 in astronomy, a layer of gases forming the outer part of the sun's atmosphere: *The corona is visible to the naked eye only when the direct rays of the sun are blocked during a total eclipse.* 3 an upper or crownlike part. 4 a cigar with blunt ends. *n., pl.* **co·ro·nas** *or* **co·ro·nae** (-nē *or* -nī).

**cor·o·nar·y** (kô′rə ner′ē) 1 of or referring to either or both of the two arteries branching from the aorta that supply blood to the muscular tissue of the heart. See HEART for picture. 2 a CORONARY THROMBOSIS. 3 having to do with or resembling a crown. 1, 3 *adj.*, 2 *n.*

**coronary thrombosis** the stopping up of a branch of a coronary artery by a blood clot.

**cor·o·na·tion** (kô′rə nā′shən) 1 the ceremony of crowning a monarch. 2 of or having to do with a coronation: *coronation robes.* *n.*

**cor·o·ner** (kô′rə nər) a person, usually a medical doctor, appointed by a provincial government for a particular community or area to investigate the cause of any sudden or unexpected death that may be the result of a crime or of a situation that could be dangerous to other people. *n.*

**cor·o·net** (kô′rə net′) 1 a small crown worn as a mark of noble rank below that of a monarch: *A monarch wears a crown; princes and nobles wear coronets.* 2 a circle of gold, jewels, or flowers worn around the head as an ornament. *n.*

**Corp.** Corporation.

**cor·po·ral**[1] (kôr′pə rəl) of or having to do with the body; physical: *corporal punishment.* *adj.* —**cor′po·ral·ly,** *adv.*

**cor·po·ral**[2] (kôr′pə rəl) 1 the lowest-ranking non-commissioned officer in the armed forces: *A corporal is one rank below a master corporal.* 2 in the RCMP, a rank next above constable. *n.*

**corporal punishment** physical punishment; punishment given by striking the body, as in spanking, strapping, beating, or whipping.

**cor·po·rate** (kôr′pə rit) 1 forming a corporation; incorporated. 2 belonging to a corporation; having to do with a corporation. 3 united; combined. *adj.*

**cor·po·ra·tion** (kôr′pə rā′shən) 1 a group of persons who obtain a charter giving them as a group certain legal rights and privileges distinct from those of the individual members of the group: *A corporation can buy and sell, own property, manufacture goods, etc. as if its members were a single person.* 2 a group of persons with authority to act as a single person: *The mayor and aldermen of a city are a corporation.* *n.*

**cor·po·re·al** (kôr pô′rē əl) 1 of or for the body; bodily: *Food and water are corporeal nourishment.* 2 of a material nature; tangible: *Land, trees, and buildings are corporeal things.* *adj.* —**cor·po′re·al·ly,** *adv.*

**corps** (kôr) 1 in the armed forces, a formation made up of more than one division. 2 a branch of the armed forces that provides special services: *the Signal Corps.* 3 a group of people organized for working together: *a corps of volunteers.* *n., pl.* **corps** (kôrz).
☛ *Hom.* CORE.

**corps de bal·let** (kôr′ də ba′lā; *French,* kôR də bä lā′) all the dancers in a ballet company not classed as soloists: *The members of the corps de ballet usually dance as a group.*

**corpse** (kôrps) a dead body, especially of a human being. *n.*

**Corps of Commissionaires** an organization of former members of the armed forces who can be hired as gatekeepers, guards, night watchmen, etc.: *Members of the Corps of Commissionaires, who wear dark-blue uniforms, are often employed to protect property.*

**cor·pu·lence** (kôr′pyə ləns) fatness. *n.*

**cor·pu·lent** (kôr′pyə lənt) fat; stout. *adj.*

**cor·pus** (kôr′pəs) 1 a complete collection of writings on some subject or of some period, or of laws, etc. 2 a body, especially the dead body of a person or animal. *n., pl.* **cor·po·ra** (-pə rə).

**cor·pus·cle** (kôr′pə səl *or* kôr′pus əl) 1 any of the cells that float in the blood, lymph, etc.: *Red corpuscles carry oxygen and carbon dioxide; some white corpuscles destroy disease germs.* 2 a very small particle. *n.*

**cor·pus de·lic·ti** (kôr′pəs di lik′tī *or* di lik′tē) *Latin* for "the body of the crime." **1** the actual facts which prove that a crime or offence against the law has been committed. **2** the body of a murdered person.

**corr. 1** correspondent. **2** corresponding. **3** correspondence. **4** correct. **5** corrected.

**cor·ral** (kə ral′) **1** an enclosed space for keeping horses, cattle, etc. **2** a circular camp formed by wagons for defence against attack. **3** drive into and keep in a corral. **4** hem in; surround; capture. 1, 2 *n.*, 3, 4 *v.*, **cor·ralled, cor·ral·ling.**

**cor·rect** (kə rekt′) **1** agreeing with fact or reason; free from mistakes or faults; right: *the correct answer.* **2** agreeing with a general standard of good taste; proper: *correct manners.* **3** change to what is right; remove mistakes or faults from: *Correct any wrong spellings that you find.* **4** alter or adjust to agree with some standard: *to correct the reading of a barometer.* **5** point out or mark the errors of: *The teacher corrects the test papers and returns them to the students.* **6** set right by punishing; find fault with in order to improve; punish: *The mother corrected the child.* **7** counteract something hurtful; cure; overcome: *to correct a bad habit. He was given medicine to correct his stomach trouble.* 1, 2 *adj.*, 3–7 *v.*
—**cor·rect′ly,** *adv.* —**cor·rect′ness,** *n.* —**cor·rec′tor,** *n.*

**cor·rect·ed** (kə rek′tid) **1** made free from mistakes or faults. **2** pt. and pp. of CORRECT. 1 *adj.*, 2 *v.*

**cor·rec·tion** (kə rek′shən) **1** the act or process of correcting: *The correction of all my mistakes took nearly an hour.* **2** something put in place of an error or mistake: *Write in your corrections neatly.* **3** a punishment; rebuke; scolding: *A prison is sometimes called a house of correction.* **4** an amount added or subtracted to correct a result. *n.*

**cor·rec·tion·al** (kə rek′shə nəl) of or having to do with correction; CORRECTIVE. *adj.*

**correction line** *Cdn.* on the Prairies, a surveyor's line that runs north and south every six miles (about 10 km) on the surveyor's original base line that runs east and west to mark townships and municipalities, both lines often used as trails or roads.

**cor·rec·tive** (kə rek′tiv) **1** tending to correct; setting right; making better: *Corrective exercises will make weak muscles strong.* **2** something that tends to correct or set right anything that is wrong or hurtful. 1 *adj.*, 2 *n.*
—**cor·rec′tive·ly,** *adv.*

**cor·re·late** (kô′rə lāt′) **1** be related one to the other; have a mutual relation: *The results of the study on television advertising correlate closely with earlier findings.* **2** place in or bring into proper relation with one another; show the connection or relation between: *Try to correlate your ideas with the facts.* *v.*, **cor·re·lat·ed, cor·re·lat·ing.**

**cor·re·la·tion** (kô′rə lā′shən) **1** the mutual relation of two or more things: *There is a close correlation between climate and crops.* **2** correlating or being CORRELATEd. *n.*

**cor·rel·a·tive** (kə rel′ə tiv) **1** mutually dependent; so related that each implies the other. **2** either of two closely related things. **3** having a mutual relation and commonly used together: *Conjunctions used in pairs, such as either...or and both...and, are correlative words.* **4** a correlative word. 1, 3 *adj.*, 2, 4 *n.*

**cor·re·spond** (kô′rə spond′) **1** be in harmony; agree: *Her friendly manner corresponded with what they had been told of her.* **2** be similar; have the same function, value, effect, etc. in its own context: *The arms of a person correspond to the wings of a bird.* **3** agree in amount or position. **4** exchange letters; write letters to each other: *Let's correspond while I'm away.* *v.*

**cor·re·spond·ence** (kô′rə spon′dəns) **1** an agreement; harmony: *There was no correspondence between the two accounts of the events.* **2** a similarity; resemblance: *Historians have noted a correspondence between the careers of the two women.* **3** an exchange of letters; letter writing. **4** letters: *She found a pile of correspondence on her desk when she returned from her holidays.* **5** in mathematics, a matching of the members of one set of objects with the members of a second set of objects. *n.*

**cor·re·spond·ent** (kô′rə spon′dənt) **1** a person who exchanges letters with another: *They have been regular correspondents for over two years.* **2** a person employed by a newspaper, a radio or television network, etc. to send news from a distant place: *A foreign correspondent is a reporter who gathers news in another country.* **3** a person or company that has regular business with another in a distant place: *This big bank has correspondents in all the large cities of the world.* **4** corresponding; in agreement. **5** anything that corresponds to something else. 1–3, 5 *n.*, 4 *adj.*

**cor·re·spond·ing** (kô′rə spon′ding) **1** agreeing; in harmony. **2** similar; matching. **3** handling or carrying on correspondence. **4** ppr. of CORRESPOND. 1–3 *adj.*, 4 *v.* —**cor′re·spond′ing·ly,** *adv.*

**cor·ri·dor** (kô′rə dər) **1** a long hallway; a passage in a large building from which doors lead into rooms: *My mother's office is at the end of the corridor.* **2** a narrow strip of land connecting two parts of a country or an inland country with a seaport. *n.*

**cor·ri·gen·dum** (kô′rə jen′dəm) **1** an error in a book, manuscript, etc. to be corrected. **2 corrigenda,** *pl.* a list of errors with their corrections, in a book. *n., pl.* **cor·ri·gen·da** (-də).

**cor·rob·o·rate** (kə rob′ə rāt′) make more certain; confirm: *Witnesses corroborated the police officer's statement.* *v.*, **cor·rob·o·rat·ed, cor·rob·o·rat·ing.** —**cor·rob′o·ra′tor,** *n.*

**cor·rob·o·ra·tion** (kə rob′ə rā′shən) **1** confirmation by additional proof. **2** something that CORROBORATES; additional proof: *His aunt's letter was corroboration of his claim to the inheritance.* *n.*

**cor·rob·o·ra·tive** (kə rob′ə rə tiv *or* kə rob′ə rā′tiv) corroborating; confirming. *adj.*

**cor·rob·o·ra·to·ry** (kə rob′ə rə tô′rē) CORROBORATIVE. *adj.*

**cor·rob·o·ree** (kə rob′ə rē) **1** a tribal dance of Australian aborigines, held at night. **2** *Esp. Australian.* a noisy gathering or celebration. *n.*

**cor·rode** (kə rōd′) **1** eat or wear away gradually, especially by chemical action: *Rust had corroded the steel rails.* **2** become corroded: *Iron corrodes quickly.* *v.*, **cor·rod·ed, cor·rod·ing.**

**cor·ro·sion** (kə rō′zhən) **1** the act or process of corroding. **2** a CORRODEd condition. **3** a product of corroding, such as rust. *n.*

**cor·ro·sive** (kə rō′siv) **1** producing CORROSION; corroding; eating away. **2** a substance that CORRODES: *Most acids are corrosives.* 1 *adj.*, 2 *n.*
—**cor·ro′sive·ly,** *adv.*

**corrosive sublimate** MERCURIC CHLORIDE.

**cor·ru·gate** (kô′rə gāt′) bend or shape a surface or a thin sheet of material into wavelike folds; make wrinkles in; furrow. *v.*, **cor·ru·gat·ed, cor·ru·gat·ing.** —**cor′ru·ga′tion,** *n.*

**cor·ru·gat·ed** (kô′rə gā′tid) **1** bent or shaped into a row of wavelike ridges: *corrugated iron.* **2** pr. and pp. of CORRUGATE. 1 *adj.*, 2 *v.*

**corrugated paper** paper or cardboard that is bent into a row of wavelike ridges, used in wrapping packages, etc.

**cor·rupt** (kə rupt′) **1** evil; wicked: *a corrupt man, corrupt desires.* **2** make evil or wicked: *Her intense desire for wealth finally corrupted her.* **3** influenced by bribes; dishonest: *a corrupt judge.* **4** bribe; influence by bribes: *He failed in his attempt to corrupt the police officer.* **5** damaged by inaccurate copying, insertions, alterations, or the like: *The manuscript is so corrupt that parts of it make no sense at all.* **6** make worse by changing; make impure or incorrect: *The original text had been corrupted by scribes who copied it.* **7** rotten; decayed. **8** rot; decay. **9** become corrupt. 1, 3, 5, 7 *adj.*, 2, 4, 6, 8, 9 *v.* —**cor·rupt′er,** *n.* —**cor·rupt′ly,** *adv.* —**cor·rupt′ness,** *n.*

**cor·rupt·i·bil·i·ty** (kə rup′tə bil′ə tē) the quality of being CORRUPTIBLE. *n.*

**cor·rupt·i·ble** (kə rup′tə bəl) **1** that can be CORRUPTED (defs. 2, 4). **2** liable to be CORRUPTED (defs. 2, 4). *adj.* —**cor·rupt′i·ble·ness,** *n.* —**cor·rupt′i·bly,** *adv.*

**cor·rup·tion** (kə rup′shən) **1** making or being made evil or wicked. **2** evil conduct; wickedness. **3** bribery; dishonesty: *The police force must be kept free of corruption.* **4** a changing for the worse; making impure or incorrect: *the corruption of a text through careless copying.* **5** rot; decay. **6** corrupting influence; thing that causes corruption. *n.*

**cor·rup·tive** (kə rup′tive) tending to CORRUPT; causing CORRUPTION. *adj.*

**cor·sage** (kôr säzh′) a single flower or a small bouquet to be worn on a woman's dress. *n.*

**cor·sair** (kôr′ser) **1** PIRATE. **2** a pirate ship. **3** PRIVATEER. *n.*

**corse·let** (kôr′slit *for 1*, kôr′sə let′ *for 2*) **1** a piece of armour for the body. **2** a light corset, with few or no stays. See FARTHINGALE for picture. *n.* Also, (def. 1) **corslet.**

**cor·set** (kôr′sit) a firm, close-fitting undergarment stiffened and reinforced by stays, worn, especially by women, to support or shape the torso. *n.*

**cors·let** (kôr′slit) See CORSELET (def. 1). *n.*

**cor·tege** or **cor·tège** (kôr tāzh′ or kôr tezh′) **1** a procession: *Many cars were in the writer's funeral cortege.* **2** a group of followers, attendants, etc.; retinue. *n.*

**cor·tex** (kôr′teks) **1** in botany, a complex layer of tissue between the epidermis or corky layer and the vascular tissue of a stem or root, made up mainly of PARENCHYMA cells. **2** the bark or rind of a plant used as medicine. **3** the outer part of an internal organ such as the kidneys or the adrenal glands. **4** the thin layer of grey matter that covers the CEREBRUM of the brain. *n.*, *pl.* **cor·ti·ces** (-tə sēz′).

**cor·ti·cal** (kôr′tə kəl) **1** of or having to do with a CORTEX (defs. 3, 4). **2** consisting of CORTEX (defs. 1, 2). *adj.* —**cor′ti·cal·ly,** *adv.*

**cor·ti·sone** (kôr′tə zōn′) one of the hormones produced by the CORTEX (def. 3) of the adrenal glands, necessary for the regulation of many functions of the body: *Cortisone is used in the treatment of various diseases, including arthritis and leukemia.* *n.*

**co·run·dum** (kə run′dəm) an extremely hard mineral, aluminum oxide, sometimes containing iron, magnesia, or silica: *Dark-coloured corundum is used for polishing and grinding. Sapphires and rubies are transparent varieties of corundum.* *n.*

**cor·us·cate** (kô′rə skāt′) give off flashes of light; sparkle; glitter. *v.*, **cor·us·cat·ed, cor·us·cat·ing.**

**cor·vette** or **cor·vet** (kôr vet′) **1** formerly, a warship with sails and only one tier of guns: *A corvette was smaller than a frigate.* **2** a small, fast warship for use in antisubmarine and convoy work. *n.*

**cor·vine** (kôr′vīn or kôr′vin) of or like a CROW. *adj.*

**cor·y·phée** (kô′rə fā′) in ballet, a leading member of the CORPS DE BALLET: *A coryphée dances in the front row of the corps de ballet or in a small group.* *n.*

**cos.** **1** companies. **2** countries.

**co·se·cant** (kō sē′kənt or kō sē′kant) in trigonometry, the ratio of the length of the hypotenuse to the length of the opposite side; the SECANT of the complement of a given angle or arc. See SINE for picture. *n.*

**co·si·ly** (kō′zə lē) in a snug and comfortable manner. *adv.* Also, **cozily.**

**co·sine** (kō′sīn′) in trigonometry, the ratio of the length of the adjacent side to the length of the hypotenuse; the SINE of the complement of a given angle or arc. See SINE for picture. *n.*

**co·si·ness** (kō′zē nis) being cosy. *n.* Also, **coziness.**

**cos·met·ic** (koz met′ik) **1** a preparation for beautifying the skin, hair, nails, etc.: *Powder, lipstick, and face creams are cosmetics.* **2** beautifying to the skin, hair, nails, etc. 1 *n.*, 2 *adj.*

**cosmetic surgery** surgery performed to improve a person's appearance, especially of the face.

**cos·mic** (koz′mik) **1** of or belonging to the COSMOS (def. 1); having to do with the whole universe: *Cosmic forces produce stars and meteors.* **2** vast. *adj.*

**cos·mi·cal·ly** (koz′mi klē) according to COSMIC (def. 1) laws; on a vast or cosmic scale. *adv.*

**cosmic dust** fine particles of matter falling upon the earth from outer space.

**cosmic rays** streams of mostly electrically charged protons and alpha particles that travel through space at speeds nearly equal to that of light; some of these enter the earth's atmosphere, where they collide with atoms in the air, producing secondary cosmic rays of enormous energy which are eventually converted into heat: *The*

hat, āge, fär; let, ēqual, tėrm; it, īce
hot, ōpen, ôrder; oil, out; cup, pùt, rüle
əbove, takən, pencəl, lemən, circəs
ch, child; ng, long; sh, ship
th, thin; ᴛʜ, then; zh, measure

radiation from cosmic rays in outer space is a hazard for space travellers.

**cos·mog·o·ny** (koz mog′ə nē) **1** the creation or origin of the universe. **2** any theory of its creation or origin. *n., pl.* **cos·mog·o·nies.**

**cos·mog·ra·phy** (koz mog′rə fē) **1** the science that describes and maps the general appearance and structure of the universe: *Cosmography includes astronomy, geography, and geology.* **2** a general description of the universe or the earth. *n., pl.* **cos·mog·ra·phies.**

**cos·mol·o·gy** (koz mol′ə jē) **1** the branch of learning that deals with the description of the universe as an ordered whole made up of parts and subject to laws by which it functions: *Cosmology may be considered as a branch of philosophy or of natural science.* **2** a particular theory or account of the structure and workings of the universe. *n.*

**cos·mo·naut** (koz′mə not′) ASTRONAUT. *n.*
☞ *Etym.* From Gk. *cosmos* 'universe' + *nautes* 'sailor'. It was coined in Russian and is used in English to refer to Soviet space travellers or explorers. See also note at ASTRONAUT.

**cos·mo·pol·i·tan** (koz′mə pol′ə tən) **1** belonging to all parts of the world; not limited to any one country or its inhabitants: *Music is one of the most cosmopolitan of the arts.* **2** free from national or local prejudices; feeling at home in any part of the world. **3** a cosmopolitan person or thing; a person who feels at home in all parts of the world. **4** in biology, found in many or all parts of the world: *Ants are cosmopolitan insects.* **5** showing the influence of many different cultures: *Toronto is a cosmopolitan city.* 1, 2, 4, 5 *adj.*, 3 *n.*

**cos·mop·o·lite** (koz mop′ə līt′) **1** a COSMOPOLITAN (def. 2) person. **2** an animal or plant found in all or many parts of the world. *n.*

**cos·mos** (koz′məs) **1** the universe thought of as an orderly, harmonious system. **2** any complete system that is orderly and harmonious. **3** order; harmony: *Cosmos is the opposite of chaos.* **4** a tall garden plant of the same family as the aster, with much-divided leaves and white, pink, purple, or orange flowers that bloom in the fall. *n.*

**Cos·sack** (kos′ak) a member of a people living in Ukraine, noted as horsemen. *n.*

**cos·set** (kos′it) **1** a pet, especially a pet lamb. **2** make a pet of; treat as a pet; pamper. 1 *n.*, 2 *v.*

**cost** (kost) **1** the price paid: *The cost of this hat was $38.* **2** a loss or sacrifice: *The fox escaped from the trap at the cost of a leg.* **3** have a price of: *This hat costs $38.* **4** require spending of money, effort, suffering, etc.: *The other hat costs a lot more. The school play cost much time and effort.* **5** cause someone the loss or sacrifice of: *The accident almost cost him his life. Her many absences finally cost her her job.* **6 costs,** *pl.* the expenses of a lawsuit or case in court: *Mr. Brown had to pay a $1000 fine and $50 costs.* 1, 2, 6 *n.*, 3–5 *v.*, **cost, cost·ing.**
**at all costs** or **at any cost,** regardless of expense; by all means; no matter what must be done: *They had to catch the next boat at all costs, or lose their chance to escape.*

**cos·ta** (kos′tə) a rib or riblike structure or marking of a plant or animal. *n.*

**cos·tal** (kos′təl) near, on, or having to do with a rib or the ribs. *adj.*

**co-star** (kō′stär′ *for noun,* kō′stär′ *for verb*) **1** an actor or actress of equal prominence with another or others playing a leading role in a motion picture, play, etc. **2** be or cause to be a co-star. 1 *n.*, 2 *v.*, **co-starred, co-star·ring.**

**Costa Ri·can** (kos′tə rē′kən) **1** of Costa Rica, a country in Central America, or its people. **2** a native or inhabitant of Costa Rica.

**cos·ter·mon·ger** (kos′tər mung′gər) *Brit.* a person who sells fruit, vegetables, fish, etc. from a handcart or a stand in the street. *n.*

**cos·tive** (kos′tiv) CONSTIPATED. *adj.*

**cost·li·ness** (kos′tlē nis) great cost; expensiveness. *n.*

**cost·ly** (kos′tlē) **1** of great value: *costly jewels.* **2** costing much: *costly mistakes.* **3** costing too much. *adj.*, **cost·li·er, cost·li·est.**

**cos·tume** (kos′tyüm *or* kos′chüm *for noun,* kos tyüm′ *or* kos chüm′ *for verb*) **1** a style of dress of a particular time, place, or social class, including garments, hairstyles, jewellery or other ornaments, etc. **2** dress belonging to another time, or place, worn on stage, at masquerades, etc.: *The actors wore Spanish costumes.* **3** a complete set of outer garments: *a street costume, a hunting costume.* **4** provide a costume or costumes for; dress. 1–3 *n.*, 4 *v.*, **cos·tumed, cos·tum·ing.**

**cos·tum·er** (kos tyü′mər *or* kos′chü mər) a person who makes, sells, or rents costumes or dresses. *n.*

**co·sy** (kō′zē) **1** warm and comfortable; snug: *She liked to read in a cosy corner by the fire.* **2** a cover, usually of padded or knitted cloth, used to keep a teapot warm. 1 *adj.*, **co·si·er, co·si·est;** 2 *n., pl.* **co·sies.** Also, **cozy.**

**cot¹** (kot) a narrow bed: *A cot is sometimes made of canvas stretched on a frame that folds together.* *n.*
☞ *Hom.* CAUGHT.

**cot²** (kot) **1** cottage. **2** something small built for shelter or protection; COTE. *n.*
☞ *Hom.* CAUGHT.

**co·tan·gent** (kō tan′jənt) in trigonometry, the ratio of the length of the adjacent side (not the hypotenuse) to the length of the opposite side; the TANGENT of the complement of a given angle or arc. See SINE for picture. *n.*

**COTC** or **C.O.T.C.** Canadian Officers Training Corps.

**cote** (kōt) a shelter or shed for small animals, birds, etc.: *a dovecote.* *n.*
☞ *Hom.* COAT.

**co·te·rie** (kō′tə rē) a set or circle of acquaintances; group of people who often meet socially. *n.*

**co·til·lion** (kə til′yən) a dance with complicated steps and much changing of partners, led by one couple. *n.*

**cot·tage** (kot′ij) **1** a house at a summer resort. **2** a small house. *n.*

**cottage cheese** a soft, white cheese made from the curds of sour skim milk.

**cot·tag·er** (kot′i jər) **1** a person who lives in a cottage. **2** a summer resident in a rural or resort area: *The first cottagers of the season usually arrived on the Victoria Day weekend.* *n.*

**cot·ter¹** (kot′ər) **1** a wedge or other tapered piece used to hold parts of a structure together. **2** COTTER PIN. *n.*

**cot·ter²** or **cot·tar** (kot′ər) in Scotland, a man who

works for a farmer and is allowed to use a small cottage and a plot of land. *n.*

A cotter pin

**cotter pin** a long metal strip, round on one side and flat on the other, that is bent double and used for inserting into a slot or hole to hold small parts of machinery together: *The two ends of the cotter pin are flared out after it is inserted, to keep it in place.*

A cotton plant

**cot·ton** (kot′ən) **1** soft, downy white or yellowish fibres obtained from the seed pods of any of several closely related plants and used in making fabrics, thread, etc.: *The cotton is attached to the seeds in a fluffy mass.* **2** any of the plants that produce these fibres: *Cotton grows in warm climates.* **3** the crop of such plants. **4** thread or cloth made from cotton fibres. **5** made of cotton. **6** any downy substance resembling cotton fibres, growing on other plants. **7** *Informal.* agree, get along. **8** *Informal.* take a liking (*to*): *I cottoned to her at once.* 1–6 *n.,* 7, 8 *v.*
**cotton on,** *Informal.* understand: *He still hasn't cottoned on that it was only a joke.*
**cotton up,** *Informal.* flatter (*used with* **to**): *Did you see the way he was cottoning up to the coach?*

**cotton batting** soft, fluffy cotton pressed into thin layers, used as padding in quilting, for dressing wounds, etc.

**cotton gin** a machine for separating the fibres of cotton from the seeds.

**cot·ton·seed** (kot′ən sēd′) the seed of cotton, used for making COTTONSEED OIL, fertilizer, cattle food, etc. *n., pl.* **cot·ton·seed** or **cot·ton·seeds.**

**cottonseed oil** oil pressed from COTTONSEED, used for cooking, making soap, etc.

**cot·ton·tail** (kot′ən tāl′) any of several species of rabbit, the common wild rabbit of North America, having brownish or greyish fur and a fluffy tail with a white or light grey underside. See RABBIT for picture. *n.*

**cot·ton·wood** (kot′ən wùd′) **1** a North American poplar tree having cottonlike tufts on the seeds. **2** the soft wood of this tree. *n.*

**cotton wool** **1** COTTON BATTING. **2** raw cotton.

hat, āge, fär; let, ēqual, tėrm; it, īce
hot, ōpen, ôrder; oil, out; cup, pùt, rüle
əbove, takən, pencəl, lemən, circəs
ch, child; ng, long; sh, ship
th, thin; ᴛʜ, then; zh, measure

**cot·ton·y** (kot′ə nē) **1** of cotton. **2** like cotton; soft; fluffy; downy. *adj.*

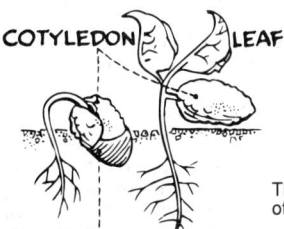

The cotyledons of a bean seedling

**cot·y·le·don** (kot′ə lē′dən) an embryo leaf in the seed of a plant; the first leaf, or either of the first pair of leaves, growing from a seed. *n.*

**couch** (kouch) **1** chesterfield; sofa. **2** any long piece of furniture for reclining or sitting on, especially one that is upholstered. **3** any place to sleep or rest: *The deer sprang up from its grassy couch.* **4** put on a couch. **5** lie down on a couch. **6** put in words; express: *Poets couch their ideas in beautiful language.* **7** lower; bring down; put in a level position ready to attack: *The knights couched their lances and prepared to charge.* **8** lie hidden ready to attack. 1–3 *n.,* 4–8 *v.* —**couch′like′,** *adj.*

**couch grass** (kouch *or* küch) a coarse, perennial grass that is native to Europe but has become a common weed in North America, having long, wiry, white or yellowish underground stems by which it spreads; quack grass.

**couch potato** *Informal.* someone who is sedentary, watches television a lot, etc.

A cougar – about 183 cm long excluding the tail

**cou·gar** (kü′gər) a large, usually sandy-coloured wild animal of the cat family found in many parts of North and South America, having short, black ears and a very long black-tipped tail; mountain lion; puma. *n.*

**cough** (kof) **1** force air from the lungs suddenly with a short, harsh noise or series of noises. **2** the act of coughing. **3** the sound of coughing. **4** repeated acts of coughing. **5** a condition marked by frequent coughing: *She has a bad cough.* 1 *v.,* 2–5 *n.*
**cough up, a** expel from the throat or lungs by coughing. **b** *Informal.* give; bring out; produce; pay what is due: *The crook tried to keep more than his share, but the rest of the gang made him cough up.* **c** *Informal.* confess.

**cough drop** a small tablet containing medicine to relieve coughs, hoarseness, etc.

**cough·ing** (kof′ing) **1** the forcing of air from the lungs with a harsh sound. **2** ppr. of COUGH. 1 *n.*, 2 *v.*

**could** (kůd) pt. of CAN. **1** used to express past time: *Once she could sing beautifully.* **2** used to indicate a possibility: *Perhaps I could write a poem, but I doubt it.* **3** used to make a request more polite: *Could you lend me some money?* *v.*

**could·n't** (kůd′ənt) could not.

**cou·lee** (kü′lē) **1** *Cdn.* especially on the Prairies, a deep ravine or gulch that is usually dry in summer. **2** a stream of lava. *n.*
☛ *Hom.* COOLIE.

**cou·lomb** (kü′lŏm *or* kü′lom) an SI unit for measuring the quantity, or charge, of electricity flowing past a given section of an electric current within a given time: *One coulomb is the electric charge furnished by a current of one ampere in one second.* Symbol: C *n.*

**coul·ter** or **col·ter** (kōl′tər) a sharp blade or disk on a plough to cut the earth ahead of the ploughshare. *n.*

**coun·cil** (koun′səl) **1** a group of people called together to give advice, talk things over, or settle questions: *a council of war.* **2** a small group of people elected by citizens to make laws for and govern a township, city, municipal district, etc. *n.*
☛ *Hom.* COUNSEL.

**coun·cil·lor** or **coun·ci·lor** (koun′sə lər) **1** an elected member of council of a town, village, etc. **2** *Cdn.* in Prince Edward Island, a member of the Legislative Assembly elected by the property owners. *n.*
☛ *Hom.* COUNSELLOR.

**Council of the Northwest Territories** the legislative body responsible for local government in the Northwest Territories, consisting of 15 elected members. It has powers similar to those of a provincial legislature, but all natural resources except game are under federal control.

**coun·sel** (koun′səl) **1** talking things over; consultation or deliberation: *There was little time for counsel.* **2** advice: *A wise person gives good counsel.* **3** a lawyer or group of lawyers: *She is acting as counsel for the defence.* **4** give advice to; advise: *She counsels high school students.* **5** recommend: *He counselled immediate action.* **6** wisdom; prudence. **7** exchange ideas; consult together; deliberate. 1–3, 6 *n., pl.* (def. 3) **counsel;** 4, 5, 7 *v.*, **coun·selled** or **coun·seled, coun·sel·ling** or **coun·sel·ing.**
**hold** or **take counsel,** talk things over; consult or deliberate: *The stranded travellers held counsel to decide what they should do next. He took counsel with his friends.*
☛ *Hom.* COUNCIL.

**coun·sel·lor** or **coun·se·lor** (koun′sə lər) **1** a person who gives advice; adviser. **2** lawyer. **3** a person who supervises, especially at a summer camp. *n.*
☛ *Hom.* COUNCILLOR.

**count**[1] (kount) **1** name numbers in order: *The child can count to ten.* **2** add up; find out how many: *She counted the books and found there were fifty.* **3** adding up; finding out how many: *The count showed that 5000 votes had been cast.* **4** the total number; amount: *The exact count was 5170.* **5** include in counting; take into account: *Let's not count that game.* **6** be included in counting; be taken into account: *Your first race is only for practice; it won't count.* **7** have an influence; be of value: *All our tests and projects count toward our final grade.* **8** consider; think of

as: *He counts himself fortunate in having good health.* **9** in law, each charge in a formal accusation. **10** the ten seconds counted to give a fallen boxer time to get up before he is declared the loser. 1, 2, 5–8 *v.*, 3, 4, 9, 10 *n.*
**count for,** be worth: *Her argument counted for little against theirs.*
**count in,** *Informal.* include: *Count me in for the party!*
**count off,** divide into equal groups by counting: *Count off in fours from the left.*
**count on, a** depend on; rely on; trust: *Can I count on you to help?* **b** reckon on; plan on; expect: *Count on spending at least thirty dollars for dinner.*
**count out, a** *Informal.* not include in a plan: *If you go skiing, count me out.* **b** declare a fallen boxer the loser when he cannot get up after ten seconds have been counted: *He was counted out in the third round of the fight.*

**count**[2] (kount) a European nobleman having a rank about the same as that of a British earl. *n.*

**count·down** or **count-down** (kount′doun′) **1** the period of time immediately preceding the firing of a missile, rocket, etc. **2** the calling out of the minutes and seconds, in the last stage of this period, as they pass. *n.*

**coun·te·nance** (koun′tə nəns) **1** an expression of the face: *an angry countenance.* **2** a face or features: *The king had a noble countenance.* **3** approval; encouragement: *He gave countenance to our plan, but no active help.* **4** approve; encourage: *The parents countenanced the girls' friendship.* **5** calmness; composure. 1–3, 5 *n.*, 4 *v.*, **coun·te·nanced, coun·te·nanc·ing.**
**keep one's countenance, a** be calm; not show feeling. **b** keep from smiling or laughing.

**count·er**[1] (koun′tər) **1** something used for counting. **2** an imitation coin. **3** a fixture in a store, restaurant, etc. having a long, flat, relatively narrow top surface for displaying goods, serving food, etc., and closed sides, usually with shelves or drawers: *a lunch counter.* **4** a similar fixture built in against one wall in a kitchen or bathroom and usually including a sink or washbasin: *I left the groceries on the kitchen counter.* *n.*

**count·er**[2] (koun′tər) a person or thing that counts. *n.*

**count·er**[3] (koun′tər) **1** in the opposite direction; opposed; contrary: *His wild idea runs counter to common sense.* **2** opposite; contrary: *Your plans are counter to ours.* **3** go or act counter to; oppose: *She did not like our plan, so she countered it with one of her own.* **4** that which is opposite or contrary to something else. **5** meet or answer a blow or move with another in return. **6** a blow or move to answer or meet another. **7** a stiff piece inside the back of a shoe around the heel. **8** the part of a ship's stern from the water line up to the end of the curved part. 1 *adv.*, 2 *adj.*, 3, 5 *v.*, 4, 6–8 *n.*

**counter–** combining form. **1** against; in opposition to: *Counteract means act against.* **2** in return: *Counterattack means attack in return.* **3** so as to correspond: *Counterpart means the part that corresponds.*

**coun·ter·act** (koun′tə rakt′) act against; neutralize the action or effect of; hinder. *v.*

**coun·ter·ac·tion** (koun′tə rak′shən) an action opposed to another action; hindrance. *n.*

**coun·ter·at·tack** (koun′tə rə tak′) **1** an attack made to counteract an attack. **2** attack in return. 1 *n.*, 2 *v.*

**coun·ter·bal·ance** (koun′tər bal′əns *for noun*, koun′tər bal′əns *for verb*) **1** a mass balancing another mass. **2** influence, power, etc. balancing or offsetting another.   **3** act as a counterbalance to; offset; neutralize: *The two friends' different personalities seem to counterbalance each other.*   **1, 2** *n.*, **3** *v.*, **coun·ter·bal·anced, coun·ter·bal·anc·ing.**

**coun·ter·charge** (koun′tər chärj′ *for noun*, koun′tər chärj′ *for verb*)   **1** a charge or accusation made to oppose one made by an accuser.   **2** make a charge or accusation after being oneself charged or accused.   **1** *n.*, **2** *v.*

**coun·ter·check** (koun′tər chek′)   **1** something that restrains or opposes; obstacle.   **2** restrain or oppose by some obstacle.   **3** a check made upon a check; a double check for verification.   **4** make a second check of; check again.   **1, 3** *n.*, **2, 4** *v.*

**counter cheque**   a blank cheque obtainable for use in a bank or at a store.

**coun·ter·claim** (koun′tər klām′)   an opposing claim; claim made by a person to offset a claim made against him or her.   *n.*

**coun·ter–clock·wise** (koun′tər klok′wīz′)   in the direction opposite to that in which the hands of a clock move.   *adv., adj.*

**coun·ter–es·pi·o·nage** (koun′tə res′pē ə näzh′ *or* koun′tə res′pē ə nij)   the taking of measures to prevent or confuse enemy ESPIONAGE.   *n.*

**coun·ter·feit** (koun′tər fit)   **1** copy money, pictures, etc., in order to deceive or defraud.   **2** a copy made to deceive or defraud and passed as genuine: *The store manager refused to accept the fifty-dollar bill because she suspected it was a counterfeit.*   **3** resemble closely.   **4** not genuine; sham: *a counterfeit stamp.*   **5** pretend; dissemble: *The old miser's widow counterfeited a grief she did not feel.*   **6** pretended; dissembled.   **1, 3, 5** *v.*, **2** *n.*, **4, 6** *adj.*   —**coun′ter·feit′er,** *n.*

**coun·ter·mand** (kount′tər mand′)   **1** withdraw or cancel an order, command, etc.: *The order was countermanded and they were sent back to the base.*   **2** an order that cancels or is contrary to a previous order.   **1** *v.*, **2** *n.*

**coun·ter·march** (koun′tər märch′)   march in the opposite direction; march back.   *v., n.*

**coun·ter·mis·sile** (koun′tər mis′īl *or* koun′tər mis′əl)   a missile designed to intercept and destroy another missile.   *n.*

**coun·ter·of·fen·sive** (koun′tə rə fen′siv)   an attack on a large scale undertaken by a defending force to take the initiative back from an attacking force.   *n.*

**coun·ter·pane** (koun′tər pān′)   an outer covering for a bed; bedspread.   *n.*

☞ *Etym.* Before the 15c. the word was *counterpoint*, from OF *contrepointe* 'bed covering', which developed from Med. L *culcita puncta* 'quilt, or stitched mattress'. The English word *counterpoint* became **counterpane** from association with the original meaning of **pane** 'piece of cloth'. See also note at PANE.

**coun·ter·part** (koun′tər pärt′)   **1** a person or thing closely resembling another: *The twin is her sister's counterpart.*   **2** a person or thing that corresponds to another; equivalent: *The federal energy minister is holding talks with her provincial counterparts.*   **3** a person or thing that complements another: *Night is the counterpart of day.*   *n.*

**coun·ter·plot** (koun′tər plot′)   plot to defeat another plot.   *n., v.*, **coun·ter·plot·ted, coun·ter·plot·ting.**

**coun·ter·point** (koun′tər point′)   in music:   **1** a melody added to another as an accompaniment.   **2** the art of combining two or more melodies so that they form a harmonious unit but the individual melodies can still be distinguished.   *n.*

**coun·ter·poise** (koun′tər poiz′)   **1** a mass balancing another mass.   **2** an influence, power, etc. balancing or offsetting another.   **3** balance; equilibrium.   **4** act as a counterpoise to; offset.   **1–3** *n.*, **4** *v.*, **coun·ter·poised, coun·ter·pois·ing.**

**coun·ter·rev·o·lu·tion** (koun′tər rev′ə lü′shən)   a revolution against a government established by a previous revolution.   *n.*

**coun·ter·rev·o·lu·tion·ar·y** (koun′tər rev′ə lü′shə ner ē)   **1** of or having to do with a COUNTER-REVOLUTION.   **2** one who supports a COUNTER-REVOLUTION.   **1** *adj.*, **2** *n.*

**coun·ter·shaft** (koun′tər shaft′)   a shaft that transmits motion from the main shaft to the working part of a machine.   *n.*

**coun·ter·sign** (koun′tər sīn′)   **1** a password given in answer to the challenge of a sentinel: *The soldier had to give the countersign before he could pass the sentry.*   **2** a secret sign or signal given in answer to another.   **3** a signature added to another signature to confirm it.   **4** sign something already signed by another to confirm it.   **1–3** *n.*, **4** *v.*

**coun·ter·sink** (koun′tər singk′)   **1** enlarge the upper part of a hole to make room for the head of a screw, bolt, etc.   **2** sink the head of a screw, bolt, etc. into such a hole so that it is even with or below the surface.   **3** a countersunk hole.   **4** a tool for countersinking holes.   **1, 2** *v.*, **coun·ter·sunk, coun·ter·sink·ing;**   **3, 4** *n.*

**coun·ter·ten·or** (koun′tər ten′ər)   **1** a very high adult male singing voice: *Countertenor usually involves falsetto in its upper range.*   **2** a singer who has such a voice.   **3** having to do with, having the range of, or designed for a countertenor.   **1, 2** *n.*, **3** *adj.*

**coun·ter·weight** (koun′tər wāt′)   a mass that balances another mass.   *n.*

**count·ess** (koun′tis)   **1** the wife or widow of an earl or count.   **2** a woman whose rank is equal to that of an earl or count.   *n.*

**counting house**   a building or office used for keeping accounts and doing business.

**count·less** (koun′tlis)   too many to count; very many; innumerable: *the countless grains of sand on the seashore, the countless stars.*   *adj.*

**coun·tri·fied** (kun′tri fīd′)   **1** looking or acting like a person from the country; rustic.   **2** like the country; rural.   *adj.*

**coun·try** (kun′trē)   **1** the land; a region or district: *The hill country to the north was rough and mountainous.*   **2** a nation; state: *She came from France, a country across the sea.*   **3** the people of a nation: *All the country hated the dictator.*   **4** the land where a person was born or is a citizen: *In my own country the customs are very different.*   **5** land without many houses such as wild, open land or

**country and western** 280 **course**

farmland: *Bob likes the country better than the city.* **6** of, in, or like the country as opposed to the city; rural: *She likes country food and country air.* **7** COUNTRY MUSIC. *n., pl.* **coun·tries.**

**country and western** COUNTRY MUSIC.

**country club** a club in the country near a city, or in the suburbs, having a clubhouse and facilities for outdoor sports.

**country cousin** *Informal.* a rural relative who finds the city confusing or frightening.

**coun·try·folk** (kun′trē fōk′) people who live in the country. *n.*

**coun·try·man** (kun′trē mən) **1** a man of one's own country; compatriot: *They met many of their countrymen in their travels through Europe.* **2** a man who lives in the country; a rustic. *n., pl.* **coun·try·men** (-mən).

**country music** a style of music that developed from the traditional folk music of the southern United States: *Modern country music has spread throughout North America and other countries and contains many elements of blues, popular music, and rock.*

**coun·try·side** (kun′trē sīd′) **1** land outside cities and towns, especially with reference to its features such as trees, flowers, hills and valleys, and its general appearance: *The countryside looked beautiful in the fall sun.* **2** a certain section of the country. **3** its people. *n.*

**coun·try·wide** (kun′trē wīd′) NATION-WIDE. *adj.*

**coun·try·wom·an** (kun′trē wùm′ən) **1** a woman of one's own country; compatriot. **2** a woman living in the country; a rustic. *n., pl.* **coun·try·wom·en** (-wim′ən).

**coun·ty** (koun′tē) **1** one of the geographical districts into which certain countries, states, and provinces are divided for purposes of government. The county is the largest administrative district for local government in New Brunswick, Nova Scotia, Prince Edward Island, Quebec, and Alberta; Ontario also has counties, but some have been combined into larger districts called *regions*. In Great Britain and Ireland, a county is a major division for administrative, judicial, and political purposes. **2** the people of a county. **3** of or in a county: *a county road.* *n., pl.* **coun·ties.**

**county court** a court with limited jurisdiction in the county or district where it is held.

**county seat** a town or city where the county government is located.

**coup** (kü) a sudden, brilliant action; unexpected, clever move; master stroke. *n., pl.* **coups** (küz).
☛ *Hom.* COO.

**coup d'é·tat** (kü dā tä′) *French.* a sudden and decisive use of force by a small group of people, especially in the violent overthrow of a government.

**coupe** (küp) a closed, two-door automobile, usually seating two to five people and smaller than a sedan. Compare with CONVERTIBLE (def. 2). *n.*
☛ *Hom.* COOP.

**cou·pé** (kü pā′ *for 1,* kü pā′ *or* küp *for 2*) **1** a closed carriage with a seat for two people inside and a seat for the driver outside. **2** COUPE. *n.*

**cou·ple** (kup′əl) **1** two things of the same kind that go together; a pair. **2** a man and woman who are married or engaged. **3** the partners in a dance. **4** join together; join together in pairs: *to couple two freight cars.* **5** COPULATE. **6** *Informal.* a few; several (*used with* **of**): *It shouldn't take longer than a couple of days.* 1–3, 6 *n.*, 4, 5 *v.*, **cou·pled, cou·pling.**

**cou·pler** (kup′lər) **1** a person or thing that couples. **2** a device used to join together two railway cars. **3** a device used to connect electric circuits in order to transfer energy from one to the other. *n.*

**cou·plet** (kup′lit) **1** two successive lines of poetry that rhyme and have the same rhythm.
*Example:* Be not the first by whom the new are tried,
   Nor yet the last to lay the old aside.
**2** couple; pair. *n.*

**cou·pling** (kup′ling) **1** the act or process of joining. **2** a device for joining parts of machinery. **3** a device used to join two railway cars. **4** a device or arrangement for transferring electrical energy from one circuit to another. **5** ppr. of COUPLE. 1–4 *n.*, 5 *v.*

**cou·pon** (kü′pon *or* kyü′pon) **1** a part of a ticket, advertisement, package, etc. that entitles the person who holds it to get something in exchange: *She saved the coupons that came with each box of soap to get free cups and saucers.* **2** a printed statement of interest due on a bond, which can be cut from the bond and presented for payment. *n.*

**cour·age** (ker′ij) bravery; the strength of mind to control fear and act firmly in the face of danger or difficulties. *n.*
**have the courage of one's convictions,** act as one believes one should.

**cou·ra·geous** (kə rā′jəs) full of courage; brave. *adj.*
—**cou·ra′geous·ly,** *adv.* —**cou·ra′geous·ness,** *n.*

**cou·reur de bois** (kü rėr′ də bwo′; *French,* kü ROER də bwä′) *Cdn.* in former times in the North and Northwest, a French or Métis fur trader or woodsman: *Radisson and Groseilliers were coureurs de bois.* *pl.* **cou·reurs de bois** (kü rėr′də bwo′).

**cour·i·er** (ker′ē ər *or* kü′rē ər) **1** a person whose work is carrying messages, especially official government messages. **2** a person who goes with a group of travellers and takes care of hotel reservations, tickets, etc. **3** an agency that undertakes to deliver letters and parcels very rapidly. *n.*

**course** (kôrs) **1** an onward movement: *the course of events. She gets little rest in the course of her daily work.* **2** a direction taken: *The ship's course was east.* **3** a line of action or conduct: *The only sensible course was to go home.* **4** a way; path or track; channel: *the course of a stream.* **5** a series of similar things arranged in some regular order: *a course of medical treatment, a course of lectures in history.* **6** the regular order; the ordinary way of proceeding: *the course of nature.* **7** a body of prescribed studies that make up a curriculum leading to a degree or diploma in a university, college, or school: *a hairdressing course. She has almost completed the course work for an M.A. degree.* **8** a unit within such a body of studies; subject: *How many courses are you taking next year?* **9** a part of a meal served at one time: *Soup was the first course.* **10** an area marked out for a game or sport: *a race course, a golf course.* **11** race; run: *The blood courses through the arteries.* **12** hunt with hounds. **13** cause hounds to hunt for game. **14** a layer of bricks, stones, shingles, etc.; row. **15** the lowest square sail on any mast of a square-rigged ship. 1–10, 14, 15 *n.*, 11–13 *v.*, **coursed, cours·ing.**

**in due course,** at the proper or usual time; after a while: *I know he will be here in due course.*
**of course,** **a** as might be expected; needless to say; naturally: *Of course it will rain on the weekend.* **b** certainly; without question: *Of course I'll do it.*
☛ *Hom.* COARSE.

**cours·er** (kôr′sər) a swift horse. *n.*

**course·ware** (kôr′swer) computer SOFTWARE that presents instruction in a variety of subjects: *Our school uses courseware to help with the teaching of chemistry.* *n.*

**court** (kôrt) **1** a space partly or wholly enclosed by walls or buildings: *The apartment house is built around a court.* **2** a short street, especially a wide lane opening off a street and having buildings on three sides. **3** a place marked or walled off for any of various games: *a tennis court, a squash court.* **4** the residence of a king, queen, or other sovereign; a royal palace. **5** the family, household, or followers of a sovereign: *The court of King Louis XVI was noted for its splendour.* **6** a sovereign and his or her advisers as a ruling power: *By order of the Court of St. James means by order of the British government.* **7** a formal assembly held by a sovereign. **8** a place where justice is administered: *The unruly spectator was removed from the court.* **9** the persons who are chosen to administer justice; a judge or judges: *The court found him guilty.* **10** an assembly of such persons to administer justice: *The prisoner was brought to court for trial.* **11** attention paid to get favour; an effort to please. **12** pay attention to a person to get his or her favour; try to please. **13** try to gain the love of, especially with the intention of marrying; woo. **14** the act of wooing; seeking to marry. **15** try to get; act so as to get; seek: *It is foolish to court danger.* **16** lay oneself open to, especially unthinkingly or foolishly: *Taking a shortcut through that yard when the dog is around is courting disaster.* 1–11, 14 *n.*, 12, 13, 15, 16 *v.*
**pay court to,** **a** pay attention to a person to get his or her favour; try to please. **b** WOO.

**cour·te·ous** (kėr′tē əs) polite; thoughtful of others: *It is a courteous act to help an old lady to cross the street safely.* *adj.* —**cour′te·ous·ly,** *adv.* —**cour′te·ous·ness,** *n.*

**cour·te·san** (kôr′tə zən *or* kôr′tə zan′) a prostitute. *n.*

**cour·te·sy** (kėr′tə sē) **1** polite or gracious behaviour; thoughtfulness for others. **2** Usually, **courtesies,** *pl.* a polite or thoughtful act or expression: *They exchanged courtesies and each went his own way.* *n., pl.* **cour·te·sies.**
**by courtesy,** as a favour, rather than as something rightfully owing.
**by courtesy of** *or* **through the courtesy of,** with the consent of; with the permission or approval of: *The poem is included in the book by courtesy of the author.*

**court·house** (kôrt′hous′) a building where law courts are held. *n.*

**cour·ti·er** (kôr′tē ər) **1** a person often present at the court of a king, queen, prince, etc.; a court attendant. **2** a person who tries to win the favour of another by flattering and pleasing him or her. *n.*

**court·li·ness** (kôrt′lē nis) politeness; elegance; polish. *n.*

**court·ly** (kôrt′lē) **1** suitable for a royal court; polite; elegant: *courtly manners, courtly hospitality.* **2** of or having to do with a royal court. *adj.*, **court·li·er, court·li·est.**

**courser** **281** **cover**

hat, āge, fär; let, ēqual, tėrm; it, īce
hot, ōpen, ôrder; oil, out; cup, pút, rüle
əbove, takən, pencəl, lemən, circəs
ch, child; ng, long; sh, ship
th, thin; ᴛʜ, then; zh, measure

**court–mar·tial** (kôrt′mär′shəl) **1** a court made up of commissioned officers in the armed forces for the purpose of trying personnel accused of breaking military law. **2** a trial by such a court: *The captain's court-martial will be held next week.* **3** try by such a court. 1, 2 *n.*, *pl.* **courts-mar·tial;** 3 *v.*, **court-mar·tialled** *or* **court-mar·tialed, court-mar·tial·ling** *or* **court-mar·tial·ing.**

**court·room** (kôr′trüm′) a room where a law court is held. *n.*

**court·ship** (kôrt′ship) the condition or time of courting with the intention of marrying; wooing. *n.*

**court·yard** (kôr′tyärd′) a space enclosed by walls, in or near a large building. *n.*

**cous·cous** (küs′küs) a North African food made from steamed grain and usually served with cooked chicken: *Couscous is cooked and used in much the same way that rice is.* *n.*

**cous·in** (kuz′ən) **1** the son or daughter of one's uncle or aunt: *First cousins have the same grandparents; second cousins have the same great-grandparents; and so on for third and fourth cousins. Your father's or mother's first cousin is your first cousin once removed.* **2** a distant relative. **3** a citizen of a related nation: *The British, Canadians, and Americans might be called cousins.* **4** formerly, a term used by one sovereign in speaking to another sovereign or to a great nobleman. *n.*
☛ *Hom.* COZEN.

**cous·in–ger·man** (kuz′ən jėr′mən) a son or daughter of one's uncle or aunt; first cousin. *n., pl.* **cous·ins-ger·man.**

**cous·in·ly** (kuz′ən lē) **1** of, like, or characteristic of a COUSIN. **2** in a cousinly manner. 1 *adj.*, 2 *adv.*

**cove** (kōv) **1** a small, sheltered bay; an inlet on the shore; the mouth of a creek. **2** a sheltered NOOK. *n.*

**cov·en** (kuv′ən) **1** a gathering of witches. **2** a company, community, or congregation of witches; especially, traditionally, a group of thirteen. *n.*

**cov·e·nant** (kuv′ə nənt) **1** a solemn agreement between two or more persons or groups to do or not to do a certain thing; a compact. **2** a legal contract or agreement. **3** solemnly agree to do certain things. 1, 2 *n.*, 3 *v.* —**cov′e·nant·er,** *n.*

**cov·er** (kuv′ər) **1** put something over or around so as to protect, keep warm, hide, etc.: *He covered the sleeping child with his coat. Pull the blind to cover the window.* **2** lie thickly on the surface of, be spread or scattered over: *Dust covered her shoes. Snow covered the ground.* **3** clothe; wrap up: *People in the Arctic cover themselves with furs.* **4** extend over; occupy: *Their farm covers 300 acres (about 120 hectares).* **5** hide; conceal: *to cover a mistake.* **6** protect, screen, or shelter: *to cover someone's retreat.* **7** go over; travel: *We covered more than 500 kilometres on the first day of our trip.* **8** include; take in: *The review covered everything we learned last term.* **9** be enough for; provide for: *I had just enough money to cover the cost of the meal plus a tip.* **10** aim a gun straight at: *One robber covered the cashier while the other emptied the cash drawer.*

**11** have within range: *The guns of the fort on the hill covered the territory down to the sea.* **12** protect by insurance; insure against a particular risk: *The house is covered but not the contents. The insurance does not cover flood damage.* **13** in journalism, act as a reporter or photographer of an event or subject: *She covers the city police court.* **14** anything that covers: *He always puts covers on his new schoolbooks. Put the cover on the box. Good ground cover will prevent erosion.* **15** protection; shelter: *We took cover in an old barn during the storm. The soldiers attacked under cover of dark.* **16** something that hides or disguises: *Her job as a newspaper reporter was just a cover for her activities as a spy.* **17** a place for one person at a table, set with a plate, fork, spoon, napkin, etc. **18** stand behind; support: *The shortstop covered the second baseman in case the ball got by him.* **19** Informal. act as a substitute while someone is absent: *He's covering for the manager while she's away.* **20** deposit the equivalent of money deposited in betting; accept the conditions of a bet. **21** buy commodities, securities, etc. for future delivery as a protection against loss. 1–13, 18–21 *v.*, 14–17 *n.* —**cov′er•er,** *n.* —**cov′er•less,** *adj.*
**break cover,** come out of hiding, especially suddenly: *She broke cover and ran for the house.*
**cover up, a** cover completely; hide; conceal: *She did her best to cover up her error.* **b** hide knowledge or an act in order to protect oneself or someone else: *He's obviously trying to cover up. She will always cover up for a colleague.* **c** seek to protect oneself: *The boxer covered up under the onslaught of blows.*
**under cover, a** hidden; secret; disguised: *The company tried to keep its new manufacturing process under cover.* **b** secretly: *Spies work under cover.*

**cov•er•alls** (kuv′ə rolz′) a strong outer garment that includes shirt and pants in a single unit, usually worn to protect other clothing: *Mechanics wear coveralls.* *n. pl.*

**cover charge** a charge made in some nightclubs, restaurants, etc. for service, entertainment, etc. in addition to the charge for food and drink.

**cover crop** a crop sown in a field or orchard to protect the soil, especially in winter.

**cov•ered** (kuv′ərd) **1** having a cover or covering. **2** wearing one's hat or cap. **3** pt. and pp. of COVER. 1, 2 *adj.*, 3 *v.*

A covered wagon

**covered wagon** a large wagon having a removable, arched canvas cover.

**cov•er•ing** (kuv′ə ring) **1** anything that covers: *bed coverings.* **2** ppr. of COVER. 1 *n.*, 2 *v.*

**cov•er•let** (kuv′ər lit) **1** an outer covering for a bed; bedspread. **2** any covering. *n.*

**cov•ert** (kuv′ərt *or* kō′vərt *for 1*) **1** secret; hidden; disguised: *covert glances.* **2** a shelter; a hiding place. **3** a thicket in which animals hide. 1 *adj.*, 2, 3 *n.* —**cov′ert•ly,** *adv.* —**cov′ert•ness,** *n.*

**cov•et** (kuv′it) desire eagerly something that belongs to another: *The boy coveted his cousin's new bat.* *v.*

**cov•et•ous** (kuv′ə təs) desiring things that belong to others. *adj.* —**cov′et•ous•ly,** *adv.* —**cov′et•ous•ness,** *n.*

**cov•ey** (kuv′ē) **1** a BROOD (def. 1) of partridges, quail, etc. **2** a small flock, especially of partridges, quail, etc.; group. *n., pl.* **cov•eys.**

**cow¹** (kou) **1** the full-grown female of any BOVINE animal, especially of domestic cattle. **2** the female of various other large mammals: *an elephant cow, a buffalo cow, a cow moose.* *n., pl.* **cows** *or* **kine.**

**cow²** (kou) make afraid; frighten: *Don't let his threats cow you.* *v.*

**cow•ard** (kou′ərd) **1** a person who lacks courage or gives in to fear; a person who runs from danger, trouble, etc. **2** lacking courage; cowardly. 1 *n.*, 2 *adj.*

**cow•ard•ice** (kou′ər dis) lack of courage; the quality of being easily overcome by fear in the face of danger, pain, etc. *n.*

**cow•ard•ly** (kou′ər dlē) **1** lacking courage. **2** of a coward; suitable for a coward. **3** in a cowardly manner. 1, 2 *adj.*, 3 *adv.* —**cow′ard•li•ness,** *n.*

**cow•bell** (kou′bel′) a bell hung around a cow's neck so that its sounds will indicate where she is. *n.*

**cow•bird** (kou′bėrd′) a small North American blackbird that is often found with cattle: *Most cowbirds lay their eggs in the nests of other birds.* *n.*

**cow•boy** (kou′boi′) especially in western Canada and the United States, a man who looks after cattle on a ranch and on the range: *A cowboy performs many of his duties on horseback.* *n.*

**cow•catch•er** (kou′kach′ər) a metal apron at the bottom of the front of a locomotive, designed to roll to one side any obstruction on the tracks. *n.*

**cow•er** (kou′ər) **1** crouch in fear or shame: *The whipped dog cowered under the table.* **2** draw back tremblingly from another's threats, blows, etc. *v.*

**cow•girl** (kou′gėrl′) a woman or girl who looks after cattle. *n.*

**cow hand** a COWBOY or COWGIRL.

**cow•herd** (kou′hėrd′) a person whose work is looking after cattle while they are at pasture. *n.*

**cow•hide** (kou′hīd′) **1** the hide of a cow. **2** leather made from it. *n.*

**Cow•i•chan sweater** *or* **Cow•i•chan** (kou′i chən) *Cdn.* a heavy sweater of unbleached wool having a knitted design on the front and back; especially such a sweater knitted by the Cowichans, an Indian people of Vancouver Island: *Cowichan sweaters were originally always black and white, but now they are sometimes made in other colours.*

**cowl** (koul) **1** a monk's cloak with a hood. **2** the hood itself. **3** put on a monk's cowl. **4** anything shaped like a hood, such as a covering for the top of a chimney, designed to increase the draft. **5** the part of an automobile body that includes the windshield and the dashboard. **6** a COWLING. **7** cover with a cowl or something resembling a cowl. 1, 2, 4–6 *n.*, 3, 7 *v.*

**cow•lick** (kou′lik′) *Informal.* a small tuft of hair that will not lie flat, usually just above the forehead. *n.*

**cowl·ing** (kou′ling)   1 a removable metal covering over the engine of an aircraft.   2 ppr. of COWL.   1 n., 2 v.

**cow·man** (kou′mən)   an owner of cattle; ranchman.   n., pl. **cow′men** (-mən).

**co–work·er** (kō′wėr′kər)   one who works with a person; fellow worker: *She's one of his co-workers.*   n.

**cow·poke** (kou′pōk′) *Informal.*   COWBOY.   n.

**cow·pox** (kou′poks′)   a disease of cows causing small PUSTULES on cows' udders: *Vaccine for smallpox was obtained from cows that had cowpox.*   n.

**cow·punch·er** (kou′pun′chər) *Informal.*   COWBOY.   n.

**cow·skin** (kou′skin′)   COWHIDE.   n.

**cow·slip** (kou′slip)   1 a European primrose having crinkled leaves and clusters of bright yellow flowers that bloom in spring.   2 MARSH MARIGOLD   n.

**cox** (koks) *Informal.*   COXSWAIN.   n.

**cox·comb** (koks′kōm′)   a vain, empty-headed man; a conceited dandy.   n.
☛ *Hom.* COCKSCOMB.

**cox·comb·ry** (koks′kōm′rē)   1 silly vanity; empty-headed conceit.   2 an example of this.   n., pl. **cox·comb·ries.**

**cox·swain** (kok′sən *or* kok′swān′)   a person who steers a boat, racing shell, etc. and is in charge of the crew.   Also, **cockswain.**

**coy** (koi)   1 shy; modest; bashful.   2 pretending to be shy: *The actress wore a coy smile.*   adj.   —**coy′ly,** adv.   —**coy′ness,** n.

A pair of coyotes - about 45 cm high at the shoulder

**coy·ote** (kī′ōt *or* kī′ōt′; *also, esp. U.S.* kī ō′tē)   a North American wild animal of the dog family found throughout the continent, but especially on the plains, resembling a small wolf, having a buff coat and bushy, black-tipped tail, and noted for its nighttime calls that range from long mournful howls to short barks: *Coyotes feed mainly on small wild animals such as gophers, rats, mice, and hares.*   n., pl. **coy·otes** or (*esp. collectively*) **coy·ote.**

**coy·pu** (koi′pü)   a large beaverlike water rodent native to South America, having an undercoat of soft reddish-brown fur called NUTRIA that is commercially valuable.   n., pl. **coy·pus** or (*esp. collectively*) **coy·pu.**

**coz** (kuz) *Informal.*   cousin.   n.

**coz·en** (kuz′ən)   1 cheat; defraud (*usually used with* **out of** *or* **of**): *The child was cozened out of his inheritance.*   2 deceive; beguile: *They cozened her into signing the papers.*   v.   —**coz′en·er,** n.
☛ *Hom.* COUSIN.

**coz·en·age** (kuz′ə nij)   a cozening; fraud; deception.   n.

**co·zi·ly** (kō′zə lē)   See COSILY.   adv.

**co·zi·ness** (kō′zē nis)   See COSINESS.   n.

hat, āge, fär; let, ēqual, tėrm; it, īce
hot, ōpen, ôrder; oil, out; cup, pút, rüle
əbove, takən, pencəl, lemən, circəs
ch, child; ng, long; sh, ship
th, thin; ᴛʜ, then; zh, measure

**co·zy** (kō′zē)   See COSY.   adj., n.

**cp.**   compare.

**c.p.**   1 candle power.   2 chemically pure.

**CP**   Canadian Pacific.

**C.P.**   1 Chemically Pure.   2 Communist Party.

**C.P.A.**   Certified Public Accountant.

**cpd.**   compound.

**Cpl.**   Corporal.

**CPR**   1 Canadian Pacific Railway.   2 cardiopulmonary resuscitation.

**CPU**   Central Processing Unit.

**cr.**   1 creditor.   2 credit.

**Cr**   chromium.

**Cr.**   1 Crescent.   2 Creek.

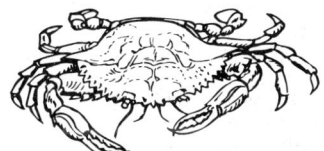
A blue crab - shell about 15 cm wide

**crab¹** (krab)   1 any of a large group of CRUSTACEANS having a short, broad shell, a body composed of 19 segments with a short abdomen, or "tail," that is folded up under the body, four pairs of legs, and one pair of pincers: *Most crabs live in the sea; some are edible.*   2 any of several other CRUSTACEANS resembling the true crab, such as the hermit crab.   3 catch crabs for eating.   4 a machine or apparatus for raising or moving heavy weights.   5 **Crab,** in astrology, the fourth sign of the zodiac; Cancer.   See ZODIAC for picture.   1, 2, 4, 5 n., 3 v., **crabbed, crab·bing.**   —**crab′ber,** n.
☛ *Etym.* OE *crabba* 'crab' related to ON *krabbi* and Old High German *krebiz* 'crab'. See also the note at CRAYFISH.

**crab²** (krab)   1 CRAB APPLE.   2 a cross, sour, ill-natured person; one who is always complaining or finding fault.   3 find fault; complain; criticize: *It doesn't do any good to crab about the weather.*   4 *Informal.* interfere with; spoil: *His lack of enthusiasm crabbed the deal.*   1, 2 n., 3, 4 v., **crabbed, crab·bing.**   —**crab′ber,** n.

**crab apple**   1 any of various small, sour apples, used for making jelly.   2 a small, sour, wild apple.   3 a tree that bears crab apples.

**crabbed** (krab′id *or* krabd)   1 CRABBY.   2 hard to understand; perplexing.   3 hard to read or decipher because irregular: *The teacher objected to crabbed handwriting.*   4 (krabd) pt. and pp. of CRAB.   1–3 adj., 4 v.   —**crab′bed·ly,** adv.   —**crab′bed·ness,** n.

**crab·by** (krab′ē) *Informal.*   cross, peevish, or ill-natured: *She's so crabby today, you can't even talk to her.*   adj., **crab·bi·er, crab·bi·est.**

**crab grass** any of various coarse grasses that spread rapidly: *Crab grass is considered a lawn pest.*

**crab·wise** (krab′wīz′) moving sideways like a crab: *The car went out of control and slid crabwise into the fence.* *adv.*

**crack** (krak) **1** a place, line, surface, or opening made by breaking without separating into two parts: *There is a crack in this cup.* **2** break without separating into parts: *You have cracked the window.* **3** break with a sudden, sharp noise: *The tree cracked and fell. He cracked the egg with the edge of the knife.* **4** a sudden, sharp noise: *The crack of a whip.* **5** make or cause to make a sudden, sharp noise: *The whip cracked. He cracked the whip.* **6** *Informal.* a blow that makes a sudden sharp noise. **7** *Informal.* hit with a sudden, sharp noise. **8** a narrow opening: *There were cracks between the boards of the old floor.* **9** of the voice, change or cause to change sharply in pitch or quality because of hoarseness or emotion. **10** of the voice, change in pitch in male adolescents. **11** *Informal.* an instant or moment. **12** *Informal.* a try; effort; attempt: *Let me take a crack at opening the jar.* **13** *Informal.* a joke. **14** *Informal.* a nasty or sharp remark: *What do you mean by that crack?* **15** *Informal.* give way; break down. **16** *Informal.* break into: *to crack a safe.* **17** separate petroleum, coal tar, etc. into various substances. **18** *Informal.* very good; excellent; first-rate: *a crack shot, a crack regiment.* 1, 4, 6, 8, 11–14 *n.*, 2, 3, 5, 7, 9, 10, 15–17 *v.*, 18 *adj.*
**crack a bottle,** *Informal.* open a bottle and drink what is in it.
**crack a joke,** tell a joke; say something funny.
**crack down,** *Informal.* take stern measures.
**crack up, a** crash or smash. **b** *Informal.* suffer a breakdown in mental or physical health. **c** *Informal.* respond or cause to respond with a fit of laughter: *I almost cracked up when he said that. This TV program always cracks her up.* **d** *Informal.* praise; tout: *That book is not what it's cracked up to be.*

**crack–brained** (krak′brānd′) *Informal.* crazy; insane. *adj.*

**cracked** (krakt) **1** broken without separating into parts. **2** lacking evenness; broken; having harsh notes: *to speak in a cracked voice.* **3** *Informal.* crazy; insane. **4** pt. and pp. of CRACK. 1–3 *adj.*, 4 *v.*

**crack·er** (krak′ər) **1** a thin, crisp biscuit or wafer: *a soda cracker, a graham cracker.* **2** a small paper roll used as a party favour, containing a motto, a paper cap, etc.: *A cracker explodes when it is pulled at both ends.* **3** a person or instrument that cracks. *n.*

**crack·er·jack** (krak′ər jak′) **1** a person or thing especially fine of its kind. **2** of superior ability or quality. **3** candied popcorn. 1, 3 *n.*, 2 *adj.*

**crack·ing** (krak′ing) **1** the process of changing certain hydrocarbons in petroleum and other oils into lighter hydrocarbons by heat and pressure: *Gasoline may be produced by cracking.* **2** ppr. of CRACK. 1 *n.*, 2 *v.*

**crack·le** (krak′əl) **1** make slight, sharp sounds: *A fire crackled on the hearth.* **2** a slight, sharp sound, such as paper makes when it is crushed. **3** very small cracks on the surface of some kinds of china, glass, etc. 1 *v.*, **crack·led, crack·ling;** 2, 3 *n.*

**crack·ling** (krak′ling) **1** the crisp rind of roasted pork. **2** Usually, **cracklings,** *pl.* the crisp remains of rendered animal fat, especially from pork. **3** ppr. of CRACKLE. 1, 2 *n.*, 3 *v.*

**crack·pot** (krak′pot′) *Informal.* **1** a very eccentric or crack-brained person. **2** eccentric; crack-brained; impractical. 1 *n.*, 2 *adj.*

**cracks·man** (kraks′mən) a burglar, especially a safe-cracker. *n., pl.* **cracks·men** (-smən).

**crack–up** (krak′up′) **1** a smash-up; crash: *That pilot has been in more than one crack-up.* **2** *Informal.* a mental or physical collapse. *n.*

A cradle on a scythe

**cra·dle** (krā′dəl) **1** a baby's little bed, usually on rockers or swinging on a frame. **2** hold as in a cradle: *She cradled the child in her arms.* **3** put or rock in a cradle. **4** the place where a thing begins its growth: *Authorities seem to disagree on where we should look for the cradle of civilization.* **5** shelter or train in early life. **6** a frame to support a ship, aircraft, or other large object while it is being built, repaired, lifted, etc. **7** support in a cradle. **8** the part of a telephone that supports the receiver. **9** a box on rockers designed to wash gold from earth. **10** wash in a cradle. **11** a frame attached to a scythe for laying grain evenly as it is cut. **12** CRADLE SCYTHE. **13** cut with a CRADLE SCYTHE. 1, 4, 6, 8, 9, 11, 12 *n.*, 2, 3, 5, 7, 10, 13 *v.*, **cra·dled, cra·dling.** —**cra′dle·like′,** *adj.*

A cradle-board

**cra·dle–board** (krā′dəl bôrd′) *Cdn.* a North American Indian device for carrying a baby, consisting of a thin, rectangular board to which a kind of bag is fastened, formerly widely used throughout North America except in the Arctic; tikinagan. *n.*

**cradle scythe** a SCYTHE with a frame attached to it for laying grain evenly as it is cut.

**cradle song** or **cra·dle·song** (krā′dəl song′) LULLABY. *n.*

**craft** (kraft) **1** skill or art, especially in handwork; CRAFTSMANSHIP: *The craft of the artist is evident in the fine detail of the carving.* **2** a trade or a kind of work requiring special skill: *Carpentry and weaving are crafts.* **3** an article made by hand: *The store sells books and crafts.* **4** skill in deceiving others; slyness; trickiness: *He used craft* *to get all their money from them.* **5** a boat, ship, or aircraft. **6** of or for a craft or crafts: *craft supplies, a craft sale.* **7** construct or form: *The store is featuring oak furniture crafted in England. This quilt was crafted by hand.* 1–6 *n., pl. (defs. 2, 3)* **crafts,** *(def. 5)* **craft**; 7 *v.*

**craft·i·ness** (kraf′tē nis) skill in deceiving others; the art or fact of being CRAFTY; cunning. *n.*

**crafts·man** (kraft′smən) **1** a person who practises a trade or handicraft: *a journal for leather craftsmen.* **2** a person who is highly skilled in the techniques of a craft or art: *a craftsman in wood. Her latest work shows she is a craftsman.* *n., pl.* **crafts·men** (-smən).

**crafts·man·like** (kraft′smən līk′) showing craftsmanship: *a craftsmanlike piece of work.* *adj.*

**crafts·man·ship** (kraft′smən ship′) skill in artistic or exacting work; skilled workmanship. *n.*

**crafts·peo·ple** (kraft′spē′pəl) people who are craftsmen; craftspersons. *n. pl.*

**crafts·per·son** (kraft′spėr′sən) CRAFTSMAN. *n.*

**crafts·wom·an** (kraft′swum′ən) **1** a woman who practises a trade or handicraft. **2** a woman who is highly skilled in the techniques of a craft or art. *n., pl.* **crafts·wom·en** (-swim′ən).

**craft union** a labour union made up of persons in the same craft: *Unions of carpenters, plumbers, or bricklayers are craft unions.*

**craft·y** (kraf′tē) skilful in deceiving others; sly; tricky: *The crafty thief escaped by disguising himself as a waiter.* *adj.,* **craft·i·er, craft·i·est.** —**craft′i·ly,** *adv.*

**crag** (krag) a steep, rugged rock or cliff; a projecting rock. *n.*

**crag·gy** (krag′ē) **1** having many CRAGs; rocky: *a craggy hillside.* **2** suggesting the hardness and unevenness of a CRAG; rugged; rough: *a craggy face.* *adj.,* **crag·gi·er, crag·gi·est.** —**crag′gi·ness,** *n.*

**cram** (kram) **1** force; stuff: *He crammed all his clothes quickly into the bag.* **2** fill too full: *The hall was crammed, with many people standing.* **3** eat too fast or too much. **4** *Informal.* stuff with knowledge or information. **5** *Informal.* learn hurriedly: *She is cramming facts and dates for her history examination.* *v.,* **crammed, cram·ming.** —**cram′mer,** *n.*

**cramp**¹ (kramp) **1** a painful, involuntary contracting of muscles from a sudden chill, strain, etc.: *The swimmer was seized with a cramp.* **2** a temporary paralysis of particular muscles as a result of overexercising them: *Writer's cramp can be brought on by excessive writing.* **3** cause a painful numbness or stiffness: *I was cramped from sitting in one position so long.* **4 cramps,** *pl.* sharp, continuous pains in the abdomen. 1, 2, 4 *n.;* 3 *v.*

**cramp**² (kramp) **1** a small metal bar with both ends bent, used in building to hold timbers, stone or concrete blocks, etc. permanently in place. **2** a CLAMP. **3** fasten together with a cramp. **4** confine in small space; limit; restrict: *If the flowerpot is too small, it will cramp the roots of the plant. The three girls were cramped in one little tent. Cramped handwriting is small and hard to read.* **5** turn the wheels of an automobile, etc. sharply. 1, 2 *n.,* 3–5 *v.* **cramp one's style,** *Informal.* restrict or interfere with one's natural or usual behaviour: *She didn't let the setback cramp her style for long.*

A crampon harnessed to a boot

**cram·pon** (kram′pən) **1** a strong iron bar with hooks at one end, used to lift heavy things; a GRAPPLING IRON. **2** an iron plate set with spikes that is fastened to the bottom of a shoe to prevent slipping. *n.*

**cran·ber·ry** (kran′ber′ē) **1** a firm, sour, dark-red berry produced by any of several closely related climbing or trailing plants of the HEATH family: *Cranberries are used for jelly, sauces, etc.* **2** a plant that produces these berries. **3** any of several species of VIBURNUM often grown for ornament. The **highbush cranberry** has edible fruit. *n., pl.* **cran·ber·ries.**
☞ *Etym.* From Low German *kraanbere,* from *kraan* 'crane' + *bere* 'berry'.

Crane (def. 1): a derrick

A sandhill crane - about 95 cm long including the tail

**crane** (krān) **1** a large machine with a long, swinging arm, for lifting and moving heavy weights. **2** move by, or as if by, such a machine. **3** any of several devices usually consisting of a horizontal arm swinging on a vertical axis, such as a metal arm in a fireplace used to hold a kettle over the fire, or a BOOM for holding a motion-picture or television camera. **4** any of a family of tall, grey, brown, or white wading birds having long legs, a long neck and bill, and a partly naked head: *Cranes resemble herons, but they fly with the neck stretched out while herons fly with the neck curved back.* **5** any of various herons, especially the GREAT BLUE HERON. **6** stretch the neck as a crane does: *He craned his neck, trying to see over the crowd.* 1, 3–5 *n.,* 2, 6 *v.,* **craned, cran·ing.**

**cra·ni·al** (krā′nē əl) of, from, or having to do with the SKULL. *adj.*

**cranial nerve** any of the nerves beginning in the lower part of the brain, which control certain bodily senses and movements: *Mammals, birds, and reptiles have 12 pairs of cranial nerves.*

**cra·ni·um** (krā′nē əm)  **1** the skull of a VERTEBRATE. **2** the part of the skull enclosing the brain.  *n., pl.* **cra·ni·ums, cra·ni·a** (-nē ə).

**crank** (krangk)  **1** a part or handle of a machine connected at right angles to a shaft to transmit motion: *to turn the crank of a pencil sharpener.*  **2** work or start by means of a crank: *to crank a window open.*  **3** bend into the shape of a crank.  **4** *Informal.*  a person with queer notions or habits, especially one possessed by some idea: *The police got a few calls from cranks when they asked for information about the missing boy.*  **5** *Informal.*  a cross or ill-tempered person; grouch: *I wouldn't ask any favours of that old crank.*  **6** a fanciful turn of speech: *quips and cranks.*  **7** a fantastic or queer idea or action.  **8** of machinery, loose and unsteady.  1, 4–7 *n.*, 2, 3 *v.*, 8 *adj.*

**crank·case** (krangk′kās′)  a heavy metal case forming the bottom part of an INTERNAL-COMBUSTION ENGINE: *The crankcase of a gasoline engine encloses the crankshaft, connecting rods, etc.*  *n.*

**crank·shaft** (krangk′shaft′)  the shaft turning or turned by a CRANK (def. 1).  *n.*

**crank·y** (krang′kē)  **1** cross; irritable; ill-natured. **2** odd; queer.  **3** liable to capsize; loose; shaky.  *adj.*, **crank·i·er, crank·i·est.**  —**crank′i·ly,** *adv.*  —**crank′i·ness,** *n.*

**cran·ny** (kran′ē)  a small, narrow opening; a crack or crevice: *There were many nooks and crannies in the wall.* *n., pl.* **cran·nies.**

**crape** (krāp)  **1** a piece of black crepe used as a sign of mourning.  **2** See CREPE (def. 1).  *n.*
☛ *Hom.* CREPE.

**crap·pie** (krap′ē)  either of two closely related species of small North American freshwater fish belonging to the SUNFISH family: *Crappies are good to eat.*  *n.*

**craps** (kraps)  a gambling game played with dice.  *n.*

**crash¹** (krash)  **1** a sudden, very loud noise like many dishes falling and breaking, or like sudden, loud band music: *a crash of thunder. There was a crash as the platform collapsed. The huge tree fell with a crash.*  **2** make a sudden, loud noise: *The thunder crashed.*  **3** fall, hit, or break with force and a loud noise: *The dishes crashed to the floor.*  **4** a hitting, colliding, or breaking with force and a loud noise; a violent impact or fall: *the crash of an airplane.*  **5** an instance of this: *There was a serious car crash at this intersection last night.*  **6** go or move into or through with force and a loud noise: *A bullet crashed through the window. He crashed into the room.*  **7** collide: *The two cars crashed right in front of our house.*  **8** of a pilot or aircraft, make a crash landing: *She crashed the plane but wasn't badly hurt. The plane crashed in a field.* **9** a sudden and severe decline or failure, as in business: *a stock market crash.*  **10** fail or decline suddenly: *The stock market crashed.*  **11** *Informal.*  enter or attend without an invitation, ticket, etc.: *to crash a party.*  **12** *Informal.* characterized by great hurry or speed and by concentrated effort: *a crash course in Italian, a crash campaign to raise money.*  **13** the failure of a computer system or of one of its components: *Yesterday's computer crash caused the bank's automatic teller machines to fail.*  **14** of a computer system, cease to function due to some hardware or software error.  1, 4, 5, 9, 12, 13 *n.*, 2, 3, 6–8, 10, 11, 14 *v.*  —**crash′er,** *n.*

**crash²** (krash)  a coarse linen cloth, used for towels, curtains, upholstering, etc.  *n.*

**crash–dive** (krash′dīv′)  **1** of a submarine, make a fast descent in an emergency.  **2** of an aircraft, make a downward plunge that ends in a CRASH (def. 4).  *v.*, **crash·dived, crash·div·ing.**

**crash dive**  **1** a fast descent made by a submarine in an emergency.  **2** of an aircraft, a downward plunge ending in a CRASH (def. 4).

**crash–land** (krash′land′)  of an aircraft or its pilot, make a forced landing in an emergency, usually with damage to the aircraft: *The plane crash-landed on the beach.*  *v.*

**crash landing**  a forced landing made by an aircraft in an emergency, usually with damage to the aircraft.

**crass** (kras)  **1** gross; stupid: *crass ignorance.*  **2** thick; coarse.  *adj.*  —**crass′ly,** *adv.*  —**crass′ness,** *n.*

**crate** (krāt)  **1** a large frame, box, basket, etc., used to pack furniture, glass, fruit, etc. for shipping or storage. **2** pack in a crate.  1 *n.*, 2 *v.*, **crat·ed, crat·ing.**

**cra·ter** (krā′tər)  **1** the depression around the opening at the top of a volcano.  **2** a bowl-shaped hole: *The battlefield was full of craters made by exploding shells.*  *n.*

**cra·vat** (krə vat′)  **1** a scarf or cloth formerly worn around the neck: *A cravat was wound around the neck several times outside the standing collar of the shirt.* **2** ASCOT.  *n.*

**crave** (krāv)  **1** long for; yearn for; desire strongly: *The thirsty man craved water.*  **2** ask earnestly; beg: *to crave a favour.*  *v.*, **craved, crav·ing.**

**cra·ven** (krā′vən)  **1** cowardly: *a craven act.*  **2** a coward.  1 *adj.*, 2 *n.*  —**cra′ven·ly,** *adv.* —**cra′ven·ness,** *n.*
**cry craven,**  surrender; admit defeat.

**crav·ing** (krā′ving)  **1** a longing or yearning; strong desire: *The hungry man had a craving for food.*  **2** ppr. of CRAVE.  1 *n.*, 2 *v.*

**craw** (kro)  **1** the crop of a bird or insect.  **2** the stomach of any animal.  *n.*

**craw·fish** (krof′ish)  **1** CRAYFISH.  **2** *Informal.* move backwards.  1 *n.*, *pl.* **craw·fish** or **craw·fish·es;** 2 *v.*
☛ *Etym.* See note at CRAYFISH.

**crawl** (krol)  **1** move slowly, with the body close to or dragging on the ground: *Worms, snakes, and insects crawl.* **2** move slowly on hands and knees; creep: *to crawl through a hole in a fence. Babies usually crawl before they learn to walk.*  **3** move slowly: *The traffic crawled on the icy roads.*  **4** a slow movement; crawling: *The traffic was moving at a crawl.*  **5** swarm with crawling things: *The ground was crawling with ants.*  **6** feel creepy: *My flesh crawled at the thought of the huge snakes.*  **7** behave or move slavishly or abjectly; fawn: *She came crawling to me, begging to be taken back on the team.*  **8** a fast way of swimming, using alternative overarm strokes and a continuous kicking motion.  **9** swim in this way.  1–3, 5–7, 9 *v.*, 4, 8 *n.* —**crawl′er,** *n.*

**crawl·y** (krol′ē)  feeling as if things were crawling over one's skin; creepy.  *adj.*, **crawl·i·er, crawl·i·est.**

**cray·fish** (krā′fish′)  any of a large group of freshwater CRUSTACEANS resembling small lobsters, found almost throughout the world, having a segmented body with a long abdomen ending in a fanlike part, four pairs of legs

and one pair of pincers, and two pairs of feelers: *Crayfish often move backwards.* *n., pl.* **cray·fish** *or* **cray·fish·es.**
☛ *Etym.* From OF *crevice* 'crab' which came from an older Germanic word related to Old High German *krebiz* 'crab'. The word was formerly a general term for any of the larger edible crustaceans, including lobsters, crabs, etc. It came into Middle English as *crevisse*, pronounced (krā vis′), but it became **crayfish** because the second syllable of *crevisse* was mistakenly associated with **fish**. See also the note at CRAB.¹ The alternative form CRAWFISH developed in a divergent dialect of English.

**cray·on** (krā′on *or* krā′ən) **1** a stick or pencil of chalk, charcoal, or a waxlike, coloured substance, for drawing or writing. **2** draw with a crayon or crayons. **3** a drawing made with crayons. *1, 3 n., 2 v.,* **cray·oned, cray·on·ing.**

**craze** (krāz) **1** something everybody is very much interested in for a short time; a fad: *Rings and bracelets were last year's craze; this year everyone is wearing scarves.* **2** make crazy: *She was nearly crazed with the pain.* **3** make tiny cracks all over the surface of earthenware, pottery, etc. **4** become minutely cracked. *1 n., 2–4 v.,* **crazed, craz·ing.**

**cra·zy** (krā′zē) **1** affected with madness; insane. **2** distracted or temporarily out of control as a result of some violent emotion: *crazy with fear, a thrill-crazy mob.* **3** *Informal.* very foolish or wild; not sensible: *a crazy driver. He has some crazy idea about walking from Dawson to Whitehorse.* **4** *Informal.* very enthusiastic; excessively preoccupied (*used with* **about**): *She's crazy about cars.* **5** *Informal.* extremely fond; infatuated (*used with* **about**): *He's crazy about her.* **6** *Informal.* unusual and conspicuous; odd: *She likes crazy jewellery.* **7** not strong or sound; shaky and frail: *a crazy old bridge.* *adj.,* **cra·zi·er, cra·zi·est;** —**cra′zi·ly,** *adv.* —**cra′zi·ness,** *n.*
**like crazy,** *Informal.* to an extreme degree; extremely hard, fast, etc.: *laughing like crazy. He took off on his bike, pedalling like crazy.*
☛ *Syn.* See note at MAD.

**crazy paving** PAVING (def. 2) arranged in an irregular pattern to achieve a decorative effect.

**creak** (krēk) **1** squeak loudly: *Hinges creak when they need oiling.* **2** a creaking noise. *1 v., 2 n.*
☛ *Hom.* CREEK (krēk).

**creak·y** (krē′kē) likely to CREAK; creaking: *creaky floors, hinges, etc.* *adj.,* **creak·i·er, creak·i·est.** —**creak′i·ly,** *adv.* —**creak′i·ness,** *n.*

**cream** (krēm) **1** the yellowish part of milk that contains fat: *Cream rises to the top when milk that is not homogenized is allowed to stand. Butter is made from cream.* **2** put cream in. **3** take cream from. **4** form like cream on the top; foam; froth. **5** food made of cream; food like cream: *ice cream, chocolate creams.* **6** containing cream or milk; resembling cream: *cream sauce, cream soup.* **7** cook with cream, milk, or a sauce made of cream or milk with butter and flour. **8** make into a smooth mixture like cream: *The cook creamed the butter and sugar together for a cake.* **9** an oily preparation put on the skin to make it smooth and soft. **10** yellowish white. **11** *Informal.* **a** in sports, defeat soundly. **b** damage severely. **12 the cream,** the best part of anything: *the cream of the crop. The cream of a class is made up of the best students.* *1, 5, 9, 10, 12 n., 2–4, 7, 8, 11 v., 6, 10 adj.*
**cream off,** *Informal.* select the best.

**cream·er** (krē′mər) a small pitcher for holding CREAM (def. 1). *n.*

hat, āge, fär; let, ēqual, tėrm; it, īce
hot, ōpen, ôrder; oil, out; cup, pùt, rüle
əbove, takən, pencəl, lemən, circəs
ch, child; ng, long; sh, ship
th, thin; ᴛʜ, then; zh, measure

**cream·er·y** (krē′mə rē) **1** a place where butter and cheese are made. **2** a place where cream, milk, and butter are sold or bought. **3** a place where milk is set for cream to rise. *n., pl.* **cream·er·ies.**

**cream·y** (krē′mē) **1** like cream; smooth and soft. **2** having much cream in it. **3** having the colour of cream; yellowish-white. *adj.,* **cream·i·er, cream·i·est.** —**cream′i·ly,** *adv.* —**cream′i·ness,** *n.*

**crease** (krēs) **1** a line or mark made by folding cloth, paper, etc.; fold; wrinkle. **2** make a crease or creases in. **3** become creased or wrinkled. **4** *Cdn.* in hockey and lacrosse, a small area marked off in front of each goal: *The crease is reserved for the goal tender and prohibited to attacking players except when the puck or ball is inside it.* **5** in cricket, **a** either of two lines at each end of the pitch that define the positions of the bowler and the batsman. **b** the space enclosed by these two lines. *1, 4 n., 2, 3 v.,* **creased, creas·ing.** —**creas′er,** *n.*

**cre·ate** (krē āt′) **1** make a thing that has not existed before. **2** make something original by intelligence and skill: *She created this garden in the desert.* **3** make by giving a new character, function, or status to: *to create a man a knight.* **4** give rise to; cause: *Do not create a disturbance.* *v.,* **cre·at·ed, cre·at·ing.**

**cre·a·tion** (krē ā′shən) **1** creating or being created. **2** all things created; the world and everything in it; the universe. **3** a thing produced by intelligence and skill, usually something important or original: *That painting is a magnificent creation.* **4 the Creation,** the creating of the universe by God. *n.*

**Cre·a·tion·ism** (krē ā′shə niz əm) the belief that God created the universe. *n.*

**cre·a·tive** (krē ā′tiv) having the power to create; inventive; productive: *Sculptors are creative artists.* *adj.* —**cre·a′tive·ly,** *adv.* —**cre·a′tive·ness,** *n.*

**cre·a·tor** (krē ā′tər) **1** a person who creates. **2 the Creator,** God. *n.*

**crea·ture** (krē′chər) **1** anything created. **2** a living being; an animal or person. **3** a person who is completely under the influence of another; a person who is ready to do anything that another asks. *n.*

**crèche** (kresh *or* krāsh) **1** a DAY-CARE centre. **2** a model showing the Christ child in the manger, with Mary and Joseph and, often, other figures: *Crèches are displayed in many homes, churches, etc. at Christmas.* *n.*

**cre·dence** (krē′dəns) belief: *The kind-hearted old lady never gave credence to gossip.* *n.*

**cre·den·tials** (kri den′shəlz) letters of introduction; references: *After showing his credentials, the new inspector was allowed to see the bank's records.* *n. pl.*

**cre·di·bil·i·ty** (kred′ə bil′ə tē) the fact or quality of being CREDIBLE. *n.*

**cred·i·ble** (kred′ə bəl) believable or reliable; trustworthy: *It seems hardly credible that Bill has grown so tall in one year.* *adj.* —**cred′i·ble·ness,** *n.* —**cred′i·bly,** *adv.*

**cred·it** (kred′it) **1** belief in the truth of something; faith; trust: *One cannot be blamed for placing little credit in the words of a liar.* **2** believe in the truth of something; have faith in; trust: *It was difficult to credit the girl's strange explanation for her absence.* **3** confidence or trust in a person's ability and intention to pay later for something he or she wishes to buy now: *She had no trouble getting credit for her purchase.* **4** the time allowed for delayed payment: *They give only short-term credit.* **5** the amount of money a person has in an account: *He had a credit of $5000 in his savings account.* **6** add to an account as a deposit: *The bank credited his account with $100.* **7** reputation with respect to payment of debts: *If you pay your bills on time, your credit will be good.* **8** good reputation: *a man of credit.* **9** recognition; honour: *The person who does the work should get the credit.* **10** a source of honour or praise: *The author's latest novel is a credit to her.* **11** official recognition that a student has passed a course of study: *He needs two more credits to complete his year.* **12** Usually, **credits**, *pl.* a listing of the producers, directors, actors, technicians, and others who have contributed their skills to a motion picture, radio or television program, or a play. 1, 3–5, 7–9, 10–12 *n.*, 2, 6 *v.*
**credit a person with,** attribute to a person: *You will have to credit her with some sense for not panicking during the fire.*
**do credit to,** bring honour or recognition to: *Her quick action did credit to her courage.*
**give credit to,** believe; have faith in; trust.
**give a person credit for,** believe or acknowledge that a person has: *Give him credit for some intelligence and let him try the job himself.*
**on credit,** on a promise to pay later: *She bought her car on credit.*

**cred·it·a·ble** (kred′ə tə bəl) bringing CREDIT (def. 9) or honour: *a creditable record of perfect attendance.* *adj.* —**cred′it·a·ble·ness,** *n.* —**cred′it·a·bly,** *adv.*

**credit card** an identification card entitling its holder to charge the cost of goods or services.

**Cred·i·tiste** (kred′i tēst′) *Cdn.* **1** of or having to do with the SOCIAL CREDIT RALLY. **2** a member of this party. 1 *adj.*, 2 *n.*

**Creditiste Party** SOCIAL CREDIT RALLY.

**cred·i·tor** (kred′ə tər) a person to whom money or goods are due; one to whom a debt is owed. *n.*

**credit union** a co-operative association that makes loans to its members at low rates.

**cre·du·li·ty** (krə dyü′lə tē *or* krə dü′lə tē) too great a readiness to believe. *n.*

**cred·u·lous** (krej′ə ləs) too ready to believe; easily deceived: *She was so credulous that the other children could fool her easily.* *adj.* —**cred′u·lous·ly,** *adv.* —**cred′u·lous·ness,** *n.*

**Cree** (krē) **1** a member of a First Nations people living mainly in the Prairie Provinces. **2** the language of these people: *Cree is an Algonquian language.* **3** of or having to do with the Cree or their language. 1, 2 *n.*, *pl.* **Cree** or **Crees;** 3 *adj.*

**creed** (krēd) **1** a formal statement of the essential points of religious belief as authorized by a church. **2** a set of beliefs, principles, or opinions: *It was his creed that work should come before play.* *n.*

**creek** (krēk *or* krik) **1** a small freshwater stream. **2** a narrow bay, running inland for some distance. *n.*
☞ *Hom.* CREAK (for the first pronunciation of **creek**); CRICK (for the second pronunciation).
☞ *Pronunciation.* Most Canadians pronounce **creek** the same as **creak**, but in some regions, especially in parts of the West, the pronunciation (krik) is common.

**creel** (krēl) **1** a basket for holding fish that have been caught. **2** a basketlike trap for fish, lobsters, etc. *n.*

**creep** (krēp) **1** move with the body close to the ground or floor; crawl: *The cat crept toward the mouse. A baby creeps on its hands and knees.* **2** move slowly: *The traffic is creeping over the narrow bridge.* **3** creeping; a slow movement. **4** grow along the ground or over a wall by means of clinging stems: *a creeping plant. Ivy had crept up the wall of the old house.* **5** feel as if things were creeping over the skin: *It made my flesh creep to hear her moan.* **6** move in a timid, stealthy, or servile manner: *The dog crept into the living room. The robbers crept toward their victims.* **7** slip slightly out of place: *The hall rug creeps until we pull it back.* **8** *Informal.* a person who gives one the creeps. **9 the creeps,** *Informal.* a feeling as if things were creeping over one's skin. 1, 2, 4–7 *v.*, crept, creep·ing; 3, 8, 9 *n.*
**creep up on,** approach slowly: *Darkness was creeping up on the forest. The soldiers crept up on the enemy sentry.*

**creep·er** (krē′pər) **1** a person or thing that creeps. **2** any plant that grows along a surface, sending out rootlets from the stem, such as the Virginia creeper and ivy. **3** any of a family of small, mostly brownish birds that climb along the trunk and branches of trees looking for insects. The one North American species is the **brown creeper. 4** a piece of canvas or other material that is attached to the bottom of a ski for better gripping in climbing uphill. **5** CLIMBING IRON. **6 creepers,** *pl.* a one-piece garment combining top and pants, worn by babies. *n.*

**creep·y** (krē′pē) **1** having a feeling of horror, as if things were creeping over one's skin: *The ghost story made us feel creepy.* **2** causing such a feeling: *a creepy howl.* **3** creeping; moving slowly. *adj.*, **creep·i·er, creep·i·est.** —**creep′i·ness,** *n.*

**creep·y-crawl·y** (krē′pē krol′ē) *Informal.* **1** making one feel shivery or afraid, as some people think small insects do: *I had a nightmare in which there were creepy-crawly things all over me.* **2** a small insect or other creature, especially when thought of as frightening. **3 the creepy-crawlies,** *pl.* the feeling of fear such insects may give: *He looked dazed, as if he had the creepy-crawlies again.* 1 *adj.*, 2, 3 *n.*, *pl.* **creep·y-crawl·ies.**

**creese** (krēs) See KRIS.

**cre·mate** (kri māt′ *or* krē′māt) burn to ashes; especially, burn a dead body to ashes. *v.*, **cre·mat·ed, cre·mat·ing.** —**cre′ma·tor,** *n.*

**cre·ma·tion** (kri mā′shən) the burning of a dead body to ashes. *n.*

**cre·ma·to·ri·um** (krē′mə tô′rē əm *or* krem′ə tô′rē əm) **1** a furnace for cremation. **2** an establishment that has a furnace for cremation. *n.*, *pl.* **cre·ma·to·ri·ums** or **cre·ma·to·ria** (-rē ə).

**cre·ma·to·ry** (krē′mə tô′rē *or* krem′ə tô′rē) **1** of or having to do with CREMATION. **2** CREMATORIUM. 1 *adj.*, 2 *n.*, *pl.* **cre·ma·to·ries.**

**Cre·ole** (krē′ōl) **1** a person who is a descendant of the original French settlers of Louisiana. **2** a person of French or Spanish ancestry, or of mixed black and European ancestry, born in Spanish America or the West

Indies.  **3** the variety of French spoken by some Blacks in Louisiana.  **4** the language spoken by Blacks in Haiti, based on French but with West African influences.  **5** of or having to do with the Creoles.  *1–4 n., 5 adj.*

**cre·ole** (krē′ōl)  **1** a language that is based on two or more languages and is the native tongue of a community of speakers.  **2** of or typical of a creole.  **3** cooked in a sauce of stewed tomatoes, peppers, etc.  *1 n., 2–3 adj.*

**cre·o·sol** (krē′ə sōl′ *or* krē′ə sol′)  a colourless oily liquid obtained from wood tar and the resin of lignum vitae, used as an antiseptic.  *n.*

**cre·o·sote** (krē′ə sōt′)  **1** any oily liquid with a penetrating odour, obtained by distilling wood tar, used to preserve wood and to make cough medicine.  **2** a similar substance obtained from COAL TAR.  **3** treat with creosote.  *1, 2 n., 3 v.,* **cre·o·sot·ed, cre·o·sot·ing.**

**creosote bush**  an evergreen shrub with a smell like that of CREOSOTE, found in New Mexico and other parts of southwestern U.S.A.

**crepe** *or* **crêpe** (krāp)  **1** a kind of cloth woven with a crinkled surface.  **2** CREPE PAPER.  **3** a raw or synthetic rubber made with a crinkled surface, often used for the soles of shoes.  **4** a piece of black crepe used as a sign of mourning: *The officers all wore crepe armbands to the funeral.*  **5** Usually, **crêpe,**  a large, very thin pancake usually served folded or rolled up with a filling.  *n.*  Also, **crape** for **crepe** (def. 1).
☛ *Hom.* CRAPE.

**crepe paper**  thin, crinkled, stretchy paper used for making party decorations, etc.

**crept** (krept)  pt. and pp. of CREEP: *We had crept up on the enemy without their seeing us.*  *v.*

**cres.** *or* **cresc.**  crescendo.

**cre·scen·do** (krə shen′dō)  in music:  **1** a gradual increase in force or loudness. The sign for a crescendo is <  **2** gradually increasing in force or loudness.  **3** a passage to be played or sung with a crescendo.  *1, 3 n., pl.* **cre·scen·dos;**  *2 adj., adv.*  Compare with DIMINUENDO.

**cres·cent** (kres′ənt)  **1** the shape of the moon as seen from the earth in its first or last quarter. See MOON for picture.  **2** anything having this or a similar shape: *A curved street or a curved row of houses is sometimes called a crescent.*  **3** shaped like the moon in its first or last quarter.  **4** growing; increasing.  *1, 2 n., 3, 4 adj.*
—**cres′cent·like′,** *adj.*
☛ *Etym.*  Through Anglo-French from OF *creissant*, which developed from the Latin verb *crescere* 'to grow, increase'. The word was first used in English to describe the visible shape of the moon during the first quarter.

**cre·sol** (krē′sol *or* krē′sol)  an oily liquid obtained from tar, used as a disinfectant.  *n.*

**cress** (kres)  any of several plants whose leaves have a peppery taste, used as a garnish or in salads.  *n.*

**crest** (krest)  **1** a tuft of hair or feathers, or a growth of skin on the head of a bird or animal.  **2** a decoration, plumes, etc. on the top of a helmet.  **3** a decoration at the top of a coat of arms: *A family crest is sometimes put on silverware, dishes, stationery, etc.*  **4** an emblem, usually of felt cloth, worn by members of various organizations, athletic teams, etc.: *a hockey crest. The soldier wore his regimental crest on the breast pocket of his blue blazer.*  **5** a similar emblem awarded as a sign of merit in studies, athletics, etc.  **6** the top part; the top of a hill, wave, ridge, etc.; peak; summit.  *n.*  —**crest′like′,** *adj.*

**crest·ed** (kres′tid)  having a crest: *a crested bird, a crested shield.*  *adj.*

**crest·fall·en** (krest′fol′ən)  dejected; discouraged: *Nell came home crestfallen because she had failed the examination.*  *adj.*  —**crest′fall′en·ly,** *adv.*

**Cre·tan** (krē′tən)  **1** of or having to do with Crete or its people.  **2** a native or inhabitant of Crete.  *1 adj., 2 n.*
☛ *Hom.*  CRETIN (krē′tən).

**cre·tin** (kret′ən *or* krē′tən)  a person who is severely mentally retarded, especially one afflicted with CRETINISM.  *n.*
☛ *Hom.*  CRETAN (for the second pronunciation of **cretin**).

**cre·tin·ism** (kret′ə niz′əm *or* krē′tə niz′əm)  an abnormal condition, usually present from birth, in which physical and mental growth is stunted because the THYROID GLAND cannot produce enough thyroid hormone.  *n.*

**cre·tonne** (kri ton′)  a strong cotton cloth with designs printed in colours on one or both sides, used for curtains, furniture covers, etc.  *n.*  Compare with CHINTZ.

**cre·vasse** (krə vas′)  a deep crack or crevice in the ice of a GLACIER.  *n.*

**crev·ice** (krev′is)  a narrow split or crack: *Tiny ferns grew in crevices in the stone wall.*  *n.*

**crew¹** (krü)  **1** a group of people who work together; gang: *A camera crew looks after the filming of a television program. A repair crew is working on the hydro lines.*  **2** the people who operate a ship, sometimes including the officers and captain.  **3** the people who operate an aircraft.  **4** a team of people who operate a boat.  **5** *Informal.*  a group or crowd: *The whole crew came to our place for dinner.*  *n.*

**crew²** (krü)  a pt. of CROW¹: *The cock crew at dawn.*  *v.*

**crew cut**  a kind of very short haircut for men.

**crew neck**  a plain, round neckline on a pullover, sweatshirt, etc., fitting closely around the base of the neck.

**crib** (krib)  **1** a small bed with high, barred sides: *The sides on a crib are intended to keep a baby from falling out.*  **2** a rack or manger for horses and cows to eat from.  **3** a building or box for storing grain, salt, etc.: *a corn crib.*  **4** a framework of logs or timbers used in building: *The wooden lining inside a mine shaft is a crib.*  **5** provide with a crib.  **6** *Informal.*  the use of another's words or ideas as one's own.  **7** *Informal.*  use another's words or ideas as one's own.  **8** *Informal.*  notes or helps that are unfair to use in doing schoolwork or in examinations.  **9** *Informal.*  use notes or helps unfairly in doing schoolwork or in examinations. **10** a small room or house. 1–4, 6, 8, 10 *n.*, 5, 7, 9 *v.*, **cribbed, crib·bing.**

**crib·bage** (krib′ij)   a card game for two, three, or four people: *In cribbage, the players keep score with a narrow board into which movable pegs fit.* *n.*

**crick** (krik)   a sudden muscular cramp; painful stiffness of muscles.   *n.*
☞ *Hom.* CREEK (krik).

**crick·et**[1] (krik′it)   any of a very large family of insects resembling grasshoppers, having long, threadlike antennae, long hind legs for jumping, and two pairs of wings: *Male crickets produce their characteristic chirping noise by rubbing a kind of scraper on one of the leathery forewings against a row of teeth on the other.* *n.*

**crick·et**[2] (krik′it)   **1** an outdoor game played by two teams of eleven players each, with ball, bats, and wickets: *Cricket is very popular in Victoria.* See WICKET for picture.   **2** play this game.   **3** *Informal.*   fair play; good sportsmanship (*usually negative*): *That's not cricket.* 1, 3 *n.*, 2 *v.*

**crick·et·er** (krik′ə tər)   one who plays CRICKET[2] (def. 1).   *n.*

**cried** (krīd)   pt. and pp. of CRY: *The baby cried for its mother.* *v.*

**cri·er** (krī′ər)   **1** an official who shouts out public announcements.   **2** a person who cries or shouts.   *n.*

**cries** (krīz)   pl. of CRY.   *n.*

**crime** (krīm)   **1** an act that is against the law: *Murder and swindling are crimes.*   **2** the activity of criminals; violation of law.   **3** a wrong act; sin: *War is a crime against humanity.*   *n.*

**crim·i·nal** (krim′ə nəl)   **1** a person guilty of a crime. **2** guilty of crime.   **3** having to do with crime: *criminal law.*   **4** like crime; illegal; wrong; immoral: *criminal behaviour.*   1 *n.*, 2–4 *adj.*

**crim·i·nal·i·ty** (krim′ə nal′ə tē)   **1** the state of being a CRIMINAL (def. 1); guilt.   **2** a CRIMINAL (def. 4) act.   *n.*, *pl.* **crim·i·nal·i·ties.**

**crim·i·nal·ly** (krim′ə nə lē)   **1** in a CRIMINAL (def. 4) manner.   **2** according to CRIMINAL (def. 3) law.   *adv.*

**crim·i·nol·o·gist** (krim′ə nol′ə jist)   an expert in CRIMINOLOGY.   *n.*

**crim·i·nol·o·gy** (krim′ə nol′ə jē)   the scientific study of crime and CRIMINALS (def. 1), and of the treatment of criminals.   *n.*

**crimp** (krimp)   **1** press into small, narrow folds; make wavy: *The girl crimped her hair before going to the party.* **2** a crimping.   **3** something crimped; fold; wave.   **4** a waved or curled lock of hair.   1 *v.*, 2–4 *n.*
**put a crimp in,** *Informal.*   interfere with; hinder: *That will put a crimp in his foolish plans.*

**crim·son** (krim′zən)   **1** deep red.   **2** turn deep red: *His face crimsoned with shame.*   1 *n.*, *adj.*, 2 *v.*

**cringe** (krinj)   **1** shrink from danger or pain; crouch in fear.   **2** bow down timidly; try to get favour or attention by servile behaviour: *The beggar cringed as he put out his hand for money.*   **3** a cringing.   1, 2 *v.*, **cringed, cring·ing;**   3 *n.*   —**cring′er,** *n.*

**crin·kle** (kring′kəl)   **1** become or cause to be wrinkled: *Her suit was crinkled from lying on the floor.*   **2** a wrinkle; ripple.   **3** rustle: *Paper crinkles when it is crushed.*   **4** a rustle.   1, 3 *v.*, **crin·kled, crin·kling;**   2, 4 *n.*

**crin·kly** (kring′klē)   full of CRINKLES (def. 2).   *adj.*, **crin·kli·er, crin·kli·est.**

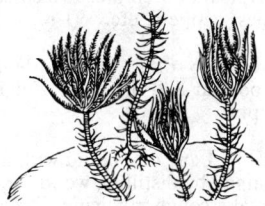
Crinoid: sea lilies

**cri·noid** (krī′noid *or* krin′oid)   **1** any of a class of flowerlike sea animals having a more or less cup-shaped body and long feathery arms. Some crinoids have long stalks by which they are attached to the sea bottom; others swim about freely: *Sea lilies are crinoids.*   **2** of or referring to the class of crinoids.   1 *n.*, 2 *adj.*

**crin·o·line** (krin′ə lin *or* krin′ə lēn′)   **1** a stiff cloth used as a lining to hold a skirt out, make a coat collar stand up, etc.   **2** a petticoat of crinoline formerly used to hold a skirt out.   **3** a HOOP SKIRT.   *n.*

**crip·ple** (krip′əl)   **1** a person or animal that cannot use the legs, arms, or body properly because of injury, deformity, or lack; lame person or animal.   **2** make a cripple of.   **3** damage; disable; weaken: *The ship was crippled by the storm.*   1 *n.*, 2, 3 *v.*, **crip·pled, crip·pling.**   —**crip′pler,** *n.*

**cri·sis** (krī′sis)   **1** the turning point in a serious illness, after which it is known whether the patient is expected to live or die.   **2** an important or deciding event.   **3** a time or state of danger or anxious waiting: *The British people faced a crisis during the Battle of Britain.*   *n.*, *pl.* **cri·ses** (-sēz).

**crisp** (krisp)   **1** firm and stiff, but breaking or snapping easily and sharply: *Dry toast and fresh celery are crisp.* **2** fresh; sharp and clear; bracing: *The air was cool and crisp.*   **3** clear-cut; decisive: *"Don't talk; fight" is a crisp sentence.*   **4** curly and wiry: *crisp hair.*   **5** make or become crisp.   1–4 *adj.*, 5 *v.*   —**crisp′ness,** *n.*

**crisp·ly** (kris′plē)   in a CRISP manner.   *adv.*

**crisp·y** (kris′pē)   CRISP.   *adj.*, **crisp·i·er, crisp·i·est.**

**criss·cross** (kris′kros′)   **1** marked or made with crossed lines; crossed; crossing: *Plaids have a crisscross pattern.*   **2** crosswise.   **3** mark or cover with crossed lines.   **4** come and go across: *Buses and cars crisscross the city.*   **5** a mark or pattern made of crossed lines.   1 *adj.*, 2 *adv.*, 3, 4 *v.*, 5 *n.*

**cri·te·ri·a** (krī tē′rē ə)   a pl. of CRITERION.   *n.*

**cri·te·ri·on** (krī tē′rē ən)   a rule or standard for making a judgment; test: *Money is only one criterion of success.*   *n.*, *pl.* **cri·te·ri·a** or **cri·te·ri·ons.**

**crit·ic** (krit′ik)   **1** a person who makes judgments of the merits and faults of books, music, pictures, plays, acting, etc.   **2** a person whose profession is writing such judgments for a newspaper, magazine, etc.   **3** a person who disapproves or finds fault; faultfinder.   *n.*

**crit·i·cal** (krit′ə kəl)   **1** inclined to find fault or disapprove: *a critical disposition.*   **2** skilled as a CRITIC (defs. 1, 2).   **3** coming from one who is skilled as a

CRITIC (defs. 1, 2): *She knows enough to make a critical judgment.* **4** belonging to the work of a CRITIC (def. 2): *critical essays.* **5** of a CRISIS; being important at a time of danger and difficulty: *the critical moment.* **6** full of danger or difficulty: *His delay was critical. She is in critical condition in the hospital.* **7** of supplies, labour, or resources, necessary for some work or project but existing in inadequate supply. *adj.* —**crit′i·cal·ly,** *adv.* —**crit′i·cal·ness,** *n.*

**crit·i·cism** (krit′ə siz′əm) **1** disapproval; fault-finding. **2** the making of judgments; approving or disapproving; analysis of merits and faults. **3** the rules and principles used in making careful judgments of the merits and faults of books, music, pictures, plays, acting, etc. **4** a critical comment, essay, review, etc. *n.*

**crit·i·cize** (krit′ə sīz′) **1** disapprove; find fault with: *Do not criticize him until you know all the facts.* **2** judge or speak as a CRITIC (defs. 1, 2). *v.*, **crit·i·cized, crit·i·ciz·ing.**

**cri·tique** (kri tēk′) **1** a CRITICAL (def. 3) essay or review: *Some newspapers have critiques of new books.* **2** the art of CRITICISM (defs. 2, 3); CRITICISM (def. 4). *n.*

**croak** (krōk) **1** a deep, hoarse sound, made by a frog, crow, or raven. **2** make a deep, hoarse sound. **3** utter in a deep, hoarse voice. **4** be always prophesying misfortune; be dissatisfied; grumble. **1** *n.*, **2–4** *v.* —**croak′er,** *n.*

**croak·ing** (krō′king) **1** the act of making a deep, hoarse sound. **2** ppr. of CROAK. **1** *n.*, **2** *v.*

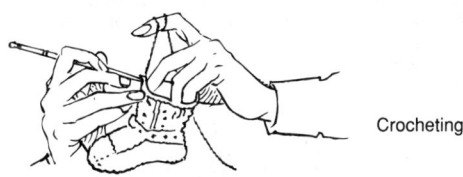
Crocheting

**cro·chet** (krō shā′) **1** a kind of lacy needlework made by interlocking loops of a single thread, using a hook: *Crochet may be fine or heavy, and is used for making sweaters, shawls, doilies, tablecloths, etc.* **2** make of crochet: *to crochet a shawl.* **3** do crochet: *I like to crochet.* **1** *n.*, **2, 3** *v.*, **cro·cheted,** (-shād′), **cro·chet·ing** (-shā′ing). —**cro·chet′er** (-shā′ər), *n.*

**crock** (krok) **1** a pot or jar made of baked clay. **2** such a pot or jar filled with something: *a crock of jam.* **3** *Informal.* a person or car that is very old and considered useless. *n.*

**crock·er·y** (krok′ər ē) dishes, jars, etc. made of baked clay; EARTHENWARE. *n.*

**croc·o·dile** (krok′ə dīl′) any of a family of large water reptiles found mainly in the warm parts of Africa, America, and Asia, having a thick, scaly skin, a long, round body, four short legs, and a powerful tail: *Crocodiles closely resemble alligators, to which they are related, but they are faster moving and have a narrower snout.* *n.*
☞ *Etym.* From OF, from L *crocodilus,* from Gk. *krokodilos,* meaning 'lizard', ultimately from Gk. *kroke* 'pebble' + *drilos* 'worm', with reference to its habit of basking on shingle.

**crocodile tears** pretended or insincere grief.

hat, āge, fär; let, ēqual, tėrm; it, īce
hot, ōpen, ôrder; oil, out; cup, pút, rüle
əbove, takən, pencəl, lemən, circəs
ch, child; ng, long; sh, ship
th, thin; ᴛʜ, then; zh, measure

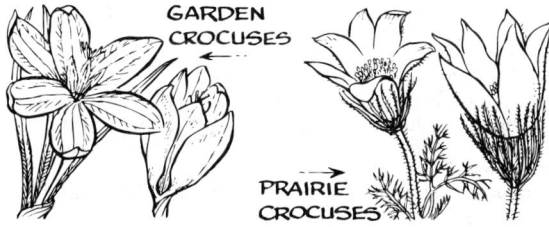
GARDEN CROCUSES
PRAIRIE CROCUSES

**cro·cus** (krō′kəs) **1** any of a large, closely related group of small plants of the IRIS family, growing from a fleshy underground stem and having long, slender leaves and a single large, cup-shaped flower that may be white, yellow or purple: *Crocuses bloom early in spring and are popular garden plants.* **2** *Cdn.* a small wildflower of central North America, a species of ANEMONE having fine silky hairs on the stem and leaves and a single large, mauve, cup-shaped flower that blooms very early in spring; pasqueflower: *The crocus is the floral emblem of Manitoba.* **3** the flower of a crocus. *n., pl.* **cro·cus·es** or **cro·ci** (-sī or -sē).

**Croe·sus** (krē′səs) **1** a very rich king of Lydia from 560 to 546 B.C. **2** a very rich person. *n.*

**croft** (kroft) **1** a small enclosed field. **2** a very small rented farm. *n.*

**croft·er** (krof′tər) a person who cultivates a small farm. *n.*

**Cro–Mag·non** (krō mag′non) **1** belonging to a group of prehistoric people who lived in southwestern Europe. **2** a person of this group: *Cro-Magnons used stone and bone implements; some of them were skilled artists.* **1** *adj.*, **2** *n.*

**crone** (krōn) a shrivelled, wrinkled old woman. *n.*

**cro·ny** (krō′nē) a very close friend; chum. *n., pl.* **cro·nies.**

**crook** (krúk) **1** something having a hooked or bent form or part, such as a CROSIER or a shepherd's staff. **2** a hooked or bent part of something: *the crook of a hockey stick, the crook of an umbrella handle.* **3** bend or curve: *She beckoned to the children by crooking her finger at them.* **4** *Informal.* a thief or swindler. **5** a bend or curve: *a crook in a stream.* **1, 2, 4, 5** *n.*, **3** *v.*, **crooked** (krúkt), **crook·ing.**

**crook·ed** (krúk′id) **1** not straight; bent, curved, or twisted: *narrow, crooked streets, a crooked piece of lumber. Your skirt is crooked.* **2** not perpendicular or parallel; slanted: *The picture on the wall is crooked.* **3** dishonest: *a crooked person, a crooked deal.* *adj.* —**crook′ed·ly,** *adv.* —**crook′ed·ness,** *n.*

**crook·neck** (krúk′nek′) a kind of squash with a long, curved neck. *n.*

**croon** (krün) **1** murmur or hum; sing in a low tone: *The mother was crooning to her baby.* **2** a low singing; a humming or murmuring. **3** sing popular ballads in a low voice. **1, 3** *v.*, **2** *n.* —**croon′er,** *n.*

**crop** (krop) **1** a product grown or gathered for use, especially for use as food or fibre: *Wheat is the main crop* of the Prairie Provinces.   **2** the total amount of grain, vegetable, or fruit produced in one season: *The potato crop was very small this year.*   **3** plant and cultivate a crop.   **4** anything like a crop; group; collection: *a crop of new paperbacks in the bookstore.*   **5** cut or bite off the top of: *Sheep crop grass very short.*   **6** clip; cut short; *The horse's tail was cropped.*   **7** the act or result of cropping: *A short haircut is a crop.*   **8** a mark produced by clipping the ears.   **9** the baglike swelling in a bird's food passage, where food is prepared for digestion.   **10** a short whip having a loop instead of a lash: *a riding crop.*   **11** the handle of a whip. *1, 2, 4, 7–11 n., 3, 5, 6 v.,* **cropped, crop·ping.**

**crop out,**   appear or come to the surface: *Great ridges of rock cropped out all over the hillside.*

**crop up,**   appear or occur unexpectedly: *All sorts of difficulties cropped up.*

**crop·per** (krop′ər)   **1** a person or thing that CROPS.   **2** *Informal.*   a heavy fall.   **3** *Informal.*   a failure; collapse.   *n.*

**come a cropper,** *Informal.*   **a** fall heavily.   **b** fail; collapse.

**cro·quet** (krō kā′)   an outdoor game played by knocking wooden balls through small wire arches by means of mallets. See MALLET and WICKET for pictures.   *n.*

**cro·quette** (krō ket′)   a small ball or cake of chopped or ground cooked meat, fish, vegetables, etc., coated with crumbs and fried.   *n.*

Crosses (def. 3)

**cross** (kros)   **1** an upright post with another across it near the top, upon which condemned persons were executed by the ancient Romans.   **2** any object, design, or mark shaped somewhat like a cross, consisting of at least two lines which cross: *A person who cannot write his name represents his signature with a cross.*   **3** draw a line across: *In writing you cross the letter* t.   **4** cancel by drawing a line or lines through (*used with* **off** *or* **out**): *Cross my name off your list. He crossed out the wrong word.*   **5** set or lay crosswise one over the other; put one thing across another: *She crossed her arms.*   **6** go across; go to the other side of: *to cross a bridge.*   **7** lie or extend across; form a cross: *Lansdowne Avenue crosses Main Street. The two streets cross.*   **8** pass: *Our letters crossed in the mail, and I got hers the same day she got mine.*   **9** trace the form of a cross with the right hand as an act of Christian devotion (*used with a pronoun ending in* **-self**): *He knelt and crossed himself.*   **10** oppose or hinder; thwart: *crossed in love. If anyone crosses him, he gets very angry.*   **11** in a bad temper; grumpy: *Just leave her alone; she's feeling very cross this morning.*   **12** a burden of duty; suffering or trouble that must be endured: *She considers her sickness a cross that she must bear.*   **13** cause two different breeds, varieties, or species of animals or plants to mate in order to produce a new kind: *Canadian breeders have crossed domestic cattle with buffalo to produce the cattalo.*   **14** the act of crossing breeds, varieties, or species of animals or plants.   **15** the result of such crossing: *Our dog is a cross between chihuahua and fox terrier.*   **16** something that is like a combination of two different things or is intermediate between them: *Documentary drama is a cross between theatre and journalism.*   **17 the Cross,**   in the Christian religion, **a** the cross on which Jesus died.   **b** the sufferings and death of Jesus; the Atonement.   *1, 2, 12, 14–17 n., 3–10, 13 v., 11 adj.*   —**cross′ly,** *adv.*   —**cross′ness,** *n.*

**cross (one's) fingers,**   put one finger over another in a superstitious gesture intended to keep trouble away, or when saying something but keeping back part of one's thoughts.

**cross (one's) heart,**   make the sign of the cross over one's heart when swearing that something is true.

**cross one's mind,**   occur to one; be thought of: *It never crossed my mind that he might forget.*

**cross (someone's) path,**   meet a person.

**cross swords,**   **a** fight with swords in single combat.   **b** engage in controversy.

**cross the floor,**   of a member of a legislature, leave one's party by moving from one's assigned seat with that party to a seat in another section of the chamber.

**cross·bar** (kros′bär′)   a bar, line, or stripe going crosswise.   *n.*

**cross·beam** (kros′bēm′)   a large beam that crosses another or extends from wall to wall.   *n.*

**cross·bill** (kros′bil′)   any of a small genus of finches having a strong bill with points that cross each other, with which the birds pry open conifer cones in order to feed on the seeds.   *n.*

**cross·bones** (kros′bōnz′)   two large bones placed crosswise: *A pirate flag has crossbones below a skull as a symbol of death. Poisonous products are marked with a skull and crossbones.*   *n. pl.*

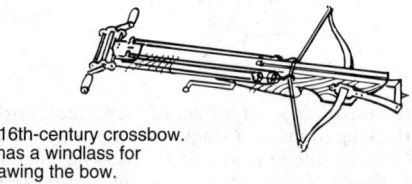

A 16th-century crossbow. It has a windlass for drawing the bow.

**cross·bow** (kros′bō′)   a medieval weapon consisting of a bow fixed across a wooden stock with a groove along the middle to direct the arrows, stones, etc.   *n.*

**cross·bow·man** (kros′bō′mən)   a soldier who uses a CROSSBOW.   *n., pl.* **cross·bow·men** (-mən).

**cross·brace** (kros′brās′)   CROSSBEAM.   *n.*

**cross·bred** (kros′bred′)   produced by CROSSBREEDing.   *adj.*

**cross·breed** (kros′brēd′)   **1** breed by mixing kinds or breeds.   **2** an individual or breed produced by crossbreeding: *A mule is a crossbreed developed by crossing a horse and a donkey.*   *1 v.,* **cross·bred, cross·breed·ing;** *2 n.*

**cross–check** (kros′chek′)   **1** check again or check against another source: *He checked his lists and then cross-checked them to make sure that they were correct.*   **2** in hockey or lacrosse, check an opponent illegally by holding one's stick in both hands and pushing it in front of the opponent's face or body.   **3** the act of cross-checking. *1, 2 v., 3 n.*

**cross-coun·try** (kros′kun′trē) **1** across fields or open country instead of by road or over a track: *a cross-country race.* **2** going or reaching across a country: *Fly cross-country from Vancouver to Halifax.* **3** of or referring to the sport of skiing over relatively flat country, using long, narrow skis. **4** for use in cross-country skiing: *cross-country skis.* 1, 3, 4 *adj.*, 2 *adv.*

**cross·cut** (kros′kut′) **1** a cut, course, or path going across: *a crosscut through the fields.* **2** used or made for cutting across: *a crosscut saw.* **3** cut across. **4** shortcut. 1, 4 *n.*, 2 *adj.*, 3 *v.*, **cross·cut, cross·cut·ting.**

**crosscut saw** a saw used or made for cutting across the grain of wood. See SAW¹ for picture.

**cross–ex·am·i·na·tion** (kros′eg zam′ə nā′shən) **1** an examination to check a previous examination; especially, the questioning of a witness by the lawyer for the opposing side to test the truth of the witness's evidence. **2** a close or severe questioning. *n.*

**cross–ex·am·ine** (kros′eg zam′ən) **1** in law, question closely to test the truth of evidence given: *The defence counsel spent two hours cross-examining the first Crown witness.* **2** question closely or severely. *v.* **cross–ex·am·ined, cross–ex·am·in·ing.** —**cross′–ex·am′in·er,** *n.*

**cross–eyed** (kros′īd′) having one eye or both eyes turned in toward the nose. *adj.*

**cross–fer·ti·li·za·tion** (kros′fėr′tə lə zā′shən *or* kros′fėr′tə lī zā′shən) the fertilization of one flower by pollen from another. *n.*

**cross–fer·ti·lize** (kros′fėr′tə līz′) **1** cause the CROSS-FERTILIZATION of. **2** be subjected to CROSS-FERTILIZATION. *v.*, **cross–fer·ti·lized, cross–fer·ti·liz·ing.**

**cross–grained** (kros′grānd′) **1** having the grain running across the regular grain; having an irregular or gnarled grain. **2** *Informal.* hard to get along with; contrary. *adj.*

**cross·hatch** (kros′hach′) mark or shade with two sets of parallel lines crossing each other. *v.*

**cross·ing** (kros′ing) **1** a place where things cross each other: *The place where a railway crosses a road is called a railway crossing.* **2** a place at which a street, etc. may be crossed: *White lines mark the crossing.* **3** the act of crossing, especially a voyage across water. **4** ppr. of CROSS. 1–3 *n.*, 4 *v.*

**crossing guard** a member of a school patrol, or other individual, who escorts children across busy streets.

**cross–leg·ged** (kros′leg′id *or* kros′legd′) **1** with the ankles crossed and the knees bent and spread wide apart: *We all sat cross-legged on the floor.* **2** with one leg crossed in front of the other: *A cross-legged position is hard to maintain for very long.* 1 *adv.*, 2 *adj.*

**cross·piece** (kros′pēs′) a piece that is placed across something. *n.*

**cross–pol·li·na·tion** (kros′pol′ə nā′shən) the transfer of pollen from the ANTHER of one flower to the STIGMA of another: *Bees are agents of cross-pollination.* *n.*

**cross–pur·pose** (kros′pėr′pəs) an opposing or contrary purpose. *n.*
**at cross-purposes, a** misunderstanding each other's purpose. **b** acting under such a misunderstanding.

**cross–ques·tion** (kros′kwes′chən) **1** question closely or severely; CROSS-EXAMINE. **2** a question asked in cross-examining. 1 *v.*, 2 *n.*

**cross–re·fer** (kros′ri fėr′) **1** refer from one part to another. **2** make a CROSS-REFERENCE. *v.*, **cross–re·ferred, cross–re·fer·ring.**

**cross–ref·er·ence** (kros′ref′ə rəns) **1** a reference or instruction in one part of a book, index, etc. to another part for more information. Under CRUPPER, the instruction "See HARNESS for picture" is a cross-reference: *Cross-references in this dictionary are printed in* SMALL CAPITALS. **2** CROSS-REFER. 1 *n.*, 2 *v.*

**cross·road** (kros′rōd′) **1** a road that crosses another. **2** a road connecting main roads. **3 crossroads, a** a place where roads cross (*used with a plural verb*): *The crossroads are to be our meeting place.* **b** a critical point, especially where a decision has to be made (*used with a singular verb*): *An economic crossroads looms ahead.* *n.*

**cross section 1** a cutting across; a cutting made at right angles to an AXIS: *Tomatoes are usually sliced by making a series of cross sections.* **2** a part cut off by making a cross section: *They have a coffee table made from a cross section of a tree trunk.* **3** a drawing, etc. of the surface exposed by such a cutting: *The chart shows cross sections of different kinds of plant stems.* **4** a small selection of people, things, etc. thought to be typical of all the members of a larger, whole group to which they belong, and chosen to stand for the whole group; a representative sample: *The newspaper wanted to get the views of a cross section of the community.*

**cross–stitch** (kros′stich′) **1** one stitch crossed over another, forming an X. **2** embroidery made with this stitch. See EMBROIDERY for picture. **3** embroider or sew with one stitch crossed over another. 1, 2 *n.*, 3 *v.*

**cross·trees** (kros′trēz′) two horizontal bars of wood near the top of a mast. See MAST for picture. *n. pl.*

**cross·walk** (kros′wok′) a street crossing marked with white lines: *In some cities all vehicles must stop when pedestrians are using a crosswalk.* *n.*

**cross·way** (kros′wā′) CROSSROAD. *n.*

**cross·ways** (kros′wāz′) CROSSWISE. *adv.*

**cross·wise** (kros′wīz′) **1** so as to cross; across. **2** in the form of a cross. **3** opposite to what is required; wrongly. *adv.*

**cross·word puzzle** (kros′wėrd′) a puzzle with numbered clues to certain words and with sets of blank squares to be filled in, one letter to a square, with the answers. Some of the words read across and some down so that some letters belong to two words that cross each other.

**cross·yard** (kros′yärd′) a pole or spar fastened CROSSWISE. *n.*

**crotch** (kroch) **1** a forked piece or part; a place where a tree, bough, etc. divides into two limbs or branches. **2** the place where the human body divides into its two legs. *n.*

**crotched** (krocht) having a CROTCH; forked. *adj.*

**crotch·et** (kroch′it) **1** an odd notion; unreasonable whim. **2** a small hook or hooklike part. **3** in music, a QUARTER NOTE. *n.*

**crotch·et·y** (kroch′ə tē) full of odd notions or unreasonable whims. *adj.* —**crotch′et·i·ness**, *n.*

**cro·ton** (krō′tən) **1** any of a closely related group of shrubs of the SPURGE family, especially a tropical shrub native to Malaysia, widely cultivated for its showy, many-coloured leaves that may be flat or crinkled and may have smooth or deeply lobed edges. **2** any of a closely related group of mostly tropical shrubs, trees, and herbs also of the SPURGE family, several of which yield substances formerly used in medicine. *n.*

**croton bug** a species of small, winged cockroach.

**crouch** (krouch) **1** stoop low with legs bent like an animal ready to spring, or in hiding, or shrinking in fear. **2** bow down in a timid or slavish manner; cower. **3** bend low. **4** the act or state of crouching. **5** a crouching position: *A baseball catcher's squatting stance is called a crouch.* 1–3 *v.*, 4, 5 *n.*

**croup**[1] (krüp) an inflammation or diseased condition of the throat and windpipe characterized by a hoarse cough and difficult breathing. *n.*

**croup**[2] (krüp) the rump of a horse, etc. See HORSE for picture. *n.*

**croup·y** (krü′pē) **1** sick with CROUP[1]. **2** hoarse and having difficulty in breathing. **3** of CROUP[1]; resembling croup[1]. *adj.*

**crow**[1] (krō) **1** a loud cry made by a rooster. **2** make the cry of a rooster. **3** a happy sound made by a baby. **4** make the happy sound of a baby. **5** show happiness and pride; boast: *The winning team crowed over its victory.* 1, 3 *n.*, 2, 4, 5 *v.*, **crowed** (or **crew** for 2), **crowed, crow·ing**.

**crow**[2] (krō) **1** a large, glossy, black bird that has a harsh cry or caw. **2** any similar bird, such as a raven, magpie, jay, etc. **3** CROWBAR. *n.*
**as the crow flies,** in a straight line; in or by the straightest way: *The nearest town is about 10 kilometres away as the crow flies, but about 15 kilometres by road.*

**crow·bar** (krō′bär′) a strong iron or steel bar, used as a lever. *n.*

**crowd** (kroud) **1** a large number of people together: *A crowd gathered to hear the speaker.* **2** the common people; people in general; the masses: *Many newspapers appeal to the crowd.* **3** *Informal.* a group; set: *Joanne and her crowd went to the dance.* **4** a large number of things together. **5** collect in large numbers: *to crowd around the swimming pool.* **6** fill; fill too full: *Shoppers crowded the store.* **7** push; shove. **8** press forward; force one's way: *to crowd into a building.* 1–4 *n.*, 5–8 *v.*
**crowd out,** exclude because of lack of space.

**crowd·ed** (krou′did) **1** filled with a crowd. **2** filled; filled too full; packed. **3** close together; too close together. **4** *pt.* and *pp.* of CROWD. 1–3 *adj.*, 4 *v.*

**crow·foot** (krō′fut′) **1** any of a number of closely related wildflowers having yellow or white flowers and deeply lobed leaves that look somewhat like birds' feet: *The crowfoots are closely related to the buttercup.* **2** referring to a family of plants found in temperate and cold regions, including the buttercups, columbines, anemones, and clematis: *The crowfoot family is also called the buttercup family.* **3** an arrangement of small ropes used to suspend awnings, etc., on a ship. **4** a piece of zinc used as one of the poles or electrodes in some kinds of batteries. *n., pl.* **crow·foots** for *1*, **crow·feet** for *3, 4*.

**crown** (kroun) **1** a head covering of precious metal and jewels, worn by a monarch. **2** a monarch; a king, queen, etc. **3** make king, queen, etc. **4** of a crown; having to do with a crown: *the crown jewels.* **5** a design or thing shaped like a crown. **6** a wreath for the head: *The winner of the race received a crown.* **7** honour; reward: *Her work was crowned with success.* **8** the head. **9** the top; highest part: *the crown of the head, the crown of a hat.* **10** be on top of; cover the highest part of: *A fort crowns the hill.* **11** the highest state or quality of anything. **12** make perfect or complete; add the finishing touch to: *Success crowned his efforts.* **13** the part of a tooth above the gum. **14** an artificial substitute for this part. **15** put a crown on. **16** the leaves and branches of a tree: *The balsam fir has a symmetrical pyramid-shaped crown.* **17 the Crown, a** the power and authority of a monarch, or of the officials who exercise that authority: *The Crown granted lands to the Hudson's Bay Company.* **b** a monarch acting in his or her official capacity. 1, 2, 4–6, 8, 9, 11, 13, 14, 16, 17 *n.*, 3, 7, 10, 12, 15 *v.*
—**crown′like′**, *adj.*

**crown colony** a colony under the power and authority of the British government.

**Crown corporation** an agency or company through which the Government of Canada or one of the provincial governments carries on certain activities: *The CBC and the St. Lawrence Seaway Authority are Crown corporations.*

**crown fire** a forest fire that spreads from treetop to treetop.

**crown land** **1** public land; land belonging to a government. **2** land that is the personal property of a monarch.

**crown prince** the oldest living son of a king, queen, etc.; the HEIR APPARENT to a kingdom.

**crown princess** **1** the wife of a CROWN PRINCE. **2** a girl or woman who is HEIR APPARENT to a kingdom.

**crow's–foot** (krōz′fut′) a wrinkle at the outer corner of the eye. *n., pl.* **crow's-feet**.

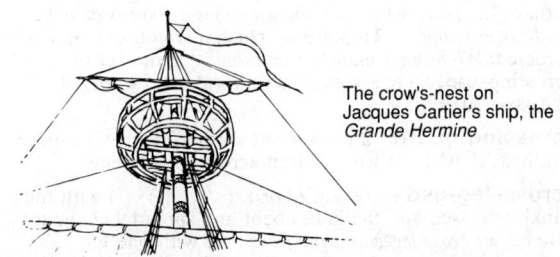

The crow's-nest on Jacques Cartier's ship, the *Grande Hermine*

**crow's–nest** or **crows–nest** (krō′znest′) **1** a small, enclosed platform near the top of a ship's mast, used by the lookout. **2** any similar platform ashore. *n.*

**CRT** cathode-ray tube.

**CRTC** Canadian Radio-television and Telecommunications Commission.

**cru·cial** (krü′shəl) **1** very important; critical; decisive. **2** very trying; severe. *adj.* —**cru′cial·ly,** *adv.*

**cru·ci·ble** (krü′sə bəl) **1** a container in which metals, ores, etc. can be melted. **2** a severe test or trial. *n.*

**cru·ci·fix** (krü′sə fiks′) **1** a cross with a figure of the crucified Christ on it. **2** a cross. *n.*

**cru·ci·fix·ion** (krü′sə fik′shən) **1** the act of crucifying. **2 the Crucifixion, a** the crucifying of Christ. **b** a picture, statue, etc. of Christ's death on the cross. *n.*

**cru·ci·form** (krü′sə fôrm′) shaped like a cross. *adj.*

**cru·ci·fy** (krü′sə fī′) **1** put to death by nailing or binding the hands and feet to a cross. **2** treat severely; persecute; torture. **3** blame and punish for the errors and crimes of someone else: *The newspapers crucified the mayor for a mistake made by her secretary.* *v.*, **cru·ci·fied, cru·ci·fy·ing.** —**cru′ci·fi′er,** *n.*

**crude** (krüd) **1** in a natural or raw state; not yet prepared for use; unprocessed: *crude rubber.* **2** not skilfully or carefully made or done; rough, careless, or unfinished: *a crude shack, a crude attempt.* **3** lacking taste, grace, or tact; rude or vulgar: *a crude remark.* **4** bare and undisguised or unadorned: *the crude truth.* **5** *Informal.* CRUDE OIL; petroleum. **1-4** *adj.*, **crud·er, crud·est;** **5** *n.* —**crude′ly,** *adv.* —**crude′ness,** *n.*

**crude oil** petroleum as it comes from the well, before it is refined.

**cru·di·tés** (krü′di tā′; *French,* kRY dē tā′) small pieces of raw vegetable, eaten as an appetizer or snack. *n. pl.*

**cru·di·ty** (krü′də tē) **1** a crude quality or condition; roughness; lack of finish. **2** a crude action, thing, etc. *n., pl.* **cru·di·ties.**

**cru·el** (krü′əl) **1** fond of causing pain to others and delighting in their suffering; not caring about the pain and suffering of others; hardhearted: *a cruel master.* **2** showing a cruel nature: *cruel acts.* **3** causing pain and suffering: *a cruel war, a cruel winter.* *adj.* —**cru′el·ly,** *adv.* —**cru′el·ness,** *n.*

**cru·el·ty** (krü′əl tē) **1** the state or condition of being CRUEL; readiness to give pain to others or to delight in their suffering. **2** a CRUEL act. *n., pl.* **cru·el·ties.**

**cru·et** (krü′it) **1** a glass bottle to hold vinegar, oil, etc. for the table. **2** a set of such bottles on a stand. *n.*

**cruise** (krüz) **1** sail about from place to place on pleasure or business; sail over or about: *He bought a yacht so that he could cruise along the coast.* **2** the act of sailing about from place to place on pleasure or business. **3** journey or travel from place to place, with or without a special destination: *The taxi cruised about in search of passengers. Many police cars are cruising the streets.* **4** travel in an airplane or car at the speed of maximum efficiency. **5** *Cdn.* in the forest industry, examine a tract of forest to estimate the value of the timber on it, especially for a logging company. **1, 3, 4, 5** *v.*, **cruised, cruis·ing;** **2** *n.*

**cruise control** in a car, a device to maintain engine speed at a constant rate.

**cruis·er** (krü′zər) **1** a warship having less armour and more speed than a battleship. **2** an airplane, taxi, power boat, etc. that cruises. **3** a police car connected with headquarters by radio; a patrol car or squad car used for patrolling streets and highways. **4** *Cdn.* a person who goes out in the woods to estimate the volume of timber standing on a particular acreage: *A cruiser works for a logging company.* **5** a CABIN CRUISER. *n.*

**crul·ler** (krul′ər) a kind of doughnut made by twisting together pieces of rich, sweet dough and frying them in hot fat. *n.* Also, **kruller.**

**crumb** (krum) **1** a very small piece of bread, cake, etc. broken from a larger piece. **2** break into crumbs. **3** cover with crumbs for frying or baking. **4** *Informal.* brush or wipe the crumbs from a tablecloth, etc. **5** the soft, inside part of bread. **6** a little bit: *a crumb of comfort.* **7** *Informal.* a worthless person; a person of no importance. **1, 5-7** *n.*, **2-4** *v.*

**crum·ble** (krum′bəl) **1** break into very small pieces or crumbs: *to crumble dirt between your hands.* **2** fall to pieces; decay: *The old wall was crumbling away at the edges.* *v.*, **crum·bled, crum·bling.**

**crum·bly** (krum′blē) tending to crumble; easily crumbled. *adj.*, **crum·bli·er, crum·bli·est.**

**crum·pet** (krum′pit) a round, flat cake, thicker than a pancake, baked on a griddle: *Crumpets are usually toasted and eaten while hot.* *n.*

**crum·ple** (krum′pəl) **1** crush together; wrinkle: *She crumpled the letter into a ball.* **2** fall down: *He crumpled to the floor.* **3** a wrinkle made by crushing something together. **1, 2** *v.*, **crum·pled, crum·pling;** **3** *n.*

**crunch** (krunch) **1** crush noisily with the teeth. **2** produce a crunching noise: *The hard snow crunched under our feet.* **3** proceed with a crunching noise: *The children crunched through the snow.* **4** the act or sound of crunching. **5** *Informal.* a crucial stage or turning point; CRISIS: *They talked bravely beforehand, but when the crunch came they fell apart.* **1-3** *v.*, **4, 5** *n.*

**crup·per** (krup′ər) **1** a strap attached to the back of a harness and passing under a horse's tail. See HARNESS for picture. **2** the rump of a horse. *n.*

**cru·sade** (krü sād′) **1** a war having a religious purpose and approved by the church. **2** a vigorous campaign against a public evil or in favour of some new idea: *Everyone was asked to join the crusade against tuberculosis.* **3** take part in a crusade. **4** Often, **Crusade,** any one of the Christian military expeditions between the years 1096 and 1272 to recover the Holy Land from the Moslems. **1, 2, 4** *n.*, **3** *v.*, **cru·sad·ed, cru·sad·ing.**

**cru·sad·er** (krü sā′dər) a person who takes part in a CRUSADE. *n.*

**crush** (krush) **1** squeeze together so violently as to break or bruise. **2** wrinkle or crease by wear or rough handling: *His hat was crushed when the girl sat on it.* **3** break into fine pieces by grinding, pounding, or pressing. **4** flatten by heavy pressure. **5** a violent pressure like grinding or pounding. **6** a mass of people crowded close together. **7** subdue; conquer: *to crush a revolt.* **8** oppress or burden; overwhelm: *He was crushed by her refusal to marry him.* **9** *Informal.* a sudden, strong liking for a person. **10** *Informal.* the object of a sudden, strong liking. **1-4, 7, 8** *v.*, **5, 6, 8, 9** *n.* —**crush′a·ble,** *adj.* —**crush′er,** *n.*

**crust** (krust) **1** the hard, outside part of bread. **2** a piece of this; any hard, dry piece of bread. **3** the baked outside covering of a pie. **4** any hard outside covering: *The snow had a crust that was thick enough to walk on.* **5** the outer layer of the earth, about 30 to 50 kilometres thick, composed of rock. See CORE for picture. **6** cover or become covered with a crust. **7** form or collect into a crust: *By the next day the snow had crusted over.* 1–5 *n.*, 6, 7 *v.* —**crust′like′**, *adj.*

**crus·ta·cean** (krus tā′shən) **1** any of a large class (Crustacea) of ARTHROPODs, most of them water animals having hard shells, jointed bodies with appendages, and two pairs of antennae: *Barnacles, crabs, lobsters, shrimps, and wood lice are crustaceans.* **2** of or having to do with crustaceans. 1 *n.*, 2 *adj.*

**crust·y** (krus′tē) **1** having a crust; hard; crustlike: *crusty bread.* **2** harsh in manner, speech, etc. *adj.*, **crust·i·er, crust·i·est.** —**crust′i·ly**, *adv.* —**crust′i·ness**, *n.*

**crutch** (kruch) **1** a support to help a lame or disabled person walk, usually consisting of a long, rubber-tipped staff with a padded crosspiece at the top that fits under the armpit and with a handgrip lower down. **2** a support or brace with a forked top. **3** anything that serves as a prop or support: *She is such a poor manager that she has to use her assistant as a crutch.* *n.*

**crux** (kruks) **1** the essential part; the most important point. **2** a puzzling or perplexing question; a difficult point to explain. *n., pl.* **crux·es** or **cru·ces** (krü′sēz).

**cry** (krī) **1** a sound made by a person or animal to show some strong feeling, such as pain, fear, anger, or sorrow; a noise that shows grief, pain, etc. **2** make such a sound. **3** shed tears; weep. **4** a spell of shedding tears; a fit of weeping. **5** the noise or call of an animal: *a gull's cry, the cry of a wolf.* **6** make such a noise. **7** a loud call or shout: *We heard the drowning man's cry for help.* **8** call loudly; shout. **9** announce in public: *Peddlers cry their wares in the street to sell them. The queen ordered the news cried in the streets.* **10** a call to action; slogan: *The cheerleaders of our football team use "Varsity" as their cry.* **11** a call for help; appeal; entreaty. 1, 4, 5, 7, 10, 11 *n., pl.* **cries;** 2, 3, 6, 8, 9 *v.*, **cried, cry·ing.**
**a far cry, a** a long way. **b** a great difference.
**cry down,** make little of; speak of as unimportant or less valuable; deprecate.
**cry up,** praise; speak of as important or valuable.
**in full cry,** in close pursuit.

**cry·ba·by** (krī′bā′bē) a person who cries easily or pretends to be hurt. *n., pl.* **cry·ba·bies** (-bēz).

**cry·ing** (krī′ing) **1** that cries. **2** demanding attention; very bad: *a crying evil.* **3** ppr. of CRY. 1, 2 *adj.*, 3 *v.*

**cry·o·gen** (krī′ə jən) a substance for producing low temperatures. *n.*

**cry·o·gen·ic** (krī′ə jen′ik) **1** of or having to do with cryogenics. **2 cryogenics,** the branch of physics dealing with the production of extremely low temperature, approaching absolute zero, and the effect of such temperatures on matter (*used with a singular verb*). 1 *adj.*, 2 *n.*

**crypt** (kript) an underground room or vault: *The crypt beneath the main floor of a church was formerly often used as a burial place.* *n.*

**cryp·tic** (krip′tik) having a hidden meaning; secret;

mysterious: *a cryptic message, a cryptic reply.* *adj.* —**cryp′ti·cal·ly**, *adv.*

**cryp·to·gram** (krip′tə gram′) something written in secret code or CIPHER (def. 3). *n.*

Crystal (def. 7): mineral crystals

**crys·tal** (kris′təl) **1** a clear, transparent mineral, a kind of QUARTZ, that looks like ice. **2** a piece of crystal cut to a form for use or ornament: *Crystals are used as beads or hung around lights.* **3** made of crystal: *crystal ornaments.* **4** clear and transparent like crystal. **5** transparent glass of good quality: *The wine glasses were made of fine crystal.* **6** the glass over the face of a watch. **7** a regular-shaped piece with angles and flat surfaces, into which a substance solidifies: *Crystals of sugar can be distinguished from crystals of snow by their difference in form.* **8** a piece of QUARTZ used in radio: *The first radios used crystals instead of tubes.* 1, 2, 5–8 *n.*, 3, 4 *adj.*

**crys·tal·line** (kris′tə līn′ or kris′tə lin) **1** consisting of CRYSTALS (def. 7); solidified in the form of crystals: *Sugar and salt are crystalline.* **2** made of CRYSTAL (defs. 1, 5). **3** clear and transparent like CRYSTAL (defs. 1, 5). *adj.*

**crystalline lens** the LENS of the eye.

**crys·tal·li·za·tion** (kris′tə lə zā′shən or kris′tə lī zā′shən) **1** a crystallizing or being CRYSTALLIZED. **2** a CRYSTALLIZED substance or formation. *n.*

**crys·tal·lize** (kris′tə līz′) **1** form into CRYSTALS (def. 7); solidify into crystals: *Water crystallizes to form snow.* **2** form into definite shape: *His vague ideas crystallized into a clear plan.* **3** coat with sugar. *v.*, **crys·tal·lized, crys·tal·liz·ing.**

**crys·tal·lized** (kris′tə līzd′) **1** formed into CRYSTALS (def. 7). **2** coated with sugar. **3** pt. and pp. of CRYSTALLIZE. 1, 2 *adj.*, 3 *v.*

**Cs** cesium.

**CSC 1** Civil Service Commission. **2** Canadian Services College.

**ct.** cent.

**ctn.** carton.

**cu.** cubic.

**Cu** copper.

**cub** (kub) **1** a young bear, fox, lion, etc. **2** a boy who belongs to the WOLF CUBS. **3** an inexperienced or awkward boy. **4** a boy who behaves badly. *n.*

**Cu·ban** (kyü′bən) **1** of or having to do with Cuba, an island country in the West Indies, or its people. **2** a native or inhabitant of Cuba. 1 *adj.*, 2 *n.*

**cub·by·hole** (kub′ē hōl′) a small, enclosed space. *n.*

**cube** (kyüb) **1** a solid with six equal, square sides. See SOLID for picture. **2** make or form into the shape of a cube: *The beets we had for supper were cubed instead of sliced.* **3** an ice cube. **4** use a number three times as a factor: *5 cubed is 125, for $5 \times 5 \times 5 = 125$.* **5** the product obtained when a number is cubed: *The cube of 4 is 64.* 1, 3, 5 *n.*, 2, 4 *v.*, **cubed, cub·ing.**

**cu·beb** (kyü′beb) a dried, unripe berry of an East Indian vine of the pepper family, used as a spice and in medicine. *n.*

**cube root** a number used as the FACTOR (def. 2) of a cube: *The cube root of 125 is 5.*

**cu·bic** (kyü′bik) **1** shaped like a CUBE (def. 1). **2** having length, breadth, and thickness: *A cubic centimetre is the volume of a cube whose edges are one centimetre long. The cubic content of a room is the number of cubic metres it contains.* **3** having to do with or involving the CUBES (def. 5) of numbers. *adj.*

**cu·bi·cal** (kyü′bə kəl) shaped like a CUBE (def. 1). *adj.*
☞ *Hom.* CUBICLE.

**cu·bi·cle** (kyü′bə kəl) a small room or compartment, especially one of the divisions of a large dormitory. *n.*
☞ *Hom.* CUBICAL.

**cubic measure** a unit or series of units for measuring volume or capacity:
   1000 cubic millimetres = 1 cubic centimetre
   1000 cubic centimetres = 1 cubic decimetre
   1000 cubic decimetres = 1 cubic metre

**cu·bit** (kyü′bit) an ancient unit for measuring length, varying from about 45 to 50 cm: *The cubit was based on the length of the arm from the elbow to the tip of the middle finger.* *n.*

**cub·mas·ter** (kub′mas′tər) a man in charge of a pack of WOLF CUBS. *n.*

**cu·boid** (kyü′boid) **1** shaped like a cube. **2** a solid having six flat sides, each one a rectangle: *A cube is a special kind of cuboid.* **3** a bone between the HEEL and the INSTEP. **1** *adj.*, **2**, **3** *n.*

**cub pack** a group made up of several dens or sixes of WOLF CUBS.

**cub reporter** a young, inexperienced newspaper reporter.

**cuck·oo** (kü′kü *or, sometimes for noun,* kùk′ü) **1** a bird whose name imitates its call: *The European cuckoo lays its eggs in the nests of other birds instead of hatching them itself. The North American cuckoo builds its own nest.* **2** the call of the cuckoo. **3** *Informal.* crazy; silly. **1**, **2** *n., pl.* **cuck·oos**; **3** *adj.*

**cuckoo clock** a clock with a toy bird that pops out of a little door at regular intervals and makes a sound like that of a European cuckoo to mark the hour, half-hour, etc.

**cu·cum·ber** (kyü′kum bər) **1** the long, fleshy fruit of a vine of the GOURD family, having a green skin and white flesh, commonly used as a vegetable: *Cucumbers are eaten raw, often in salads, and are also pickled.* **2** the vine it grows on. *n.*

**cud** (kud) food that has been brought up into the mouth from the first and second stomachs of cattle, deer, camels, and similar animals to be chewed before being swallowed again: *Animals that chew the cud are called ruminants.* *n.*

**cud·dle** (kud′əl) **1** hold closely and lovingly in one's arms or lap: *The father cuddled his baby.* **2** lie close and snug; curl up: *The two puppies cuddled together in front of the fire.* **3** a hug. **1**, **2** *v.*, **cud·dled**, **cud·dling**; **3** *n.*

**cudg·el** (kuj′əl) **1** a short, thick stick used as a weapon; club. **2** beat with a cudgel. **1** *n.*, **2** *v.*, **cudg·elled** or **cudg·eled**, **cudg·el·ling** or **cudg·el·ing**. **cudgel one's brains,** try very hard to think.

**cue¹** (kyü) **1** a hint or suggestion as to what to do or when to act: *Being a stranger, she took her cue from the actions of the natives.* **2** an action or speech on or behind the stage, which gives the signal for an actor, singer, musician, etc. to enter or to begin: *In a play the last word or words of one actor's speech is the cue for another to come on the stage, begin speaking, etc.* **3** give a cue to; give a suggestion, hint or signal to: *Don't forget to cue her when to start the song.* **4** the part one is to play; course of action. **1**, **2**, **4** *n.*, **3** *v.*, **cued**, **cu·ing** or **cue·ing**.
**cue in,** give a cue to.
**on cue,** at the right moment: *They started on cue.*
☞ *Hom.* QUEUE.

**cue²** (kyü) **1** a QUEUE (def. 3); pigtail. **2** in billiards, pool, etc., a long tapering stick used for striking the ball. *n.*
☞ *Hom.* QUEUE.

**cuff¹** (kuf) **1** the part of a sleeve or glove that goes around the wrist. **2** a turned-up fold around the bottom of a trouser leg. **3** a HANDCUFF. *n.*
**off the cuff,** without preparation; impromptu: *He had no notes but spoke off the cuff.*

**cuff²** (kuf) hit with the hand; slap. *v., n.*

**cuff link** an ornamental link for joining together the open ends of a shirt CUFF (def. 1).

**cu. ft.** cubic foot; cubic feet.

**cu. in.** cubic inch; cubic inches.

**cui·rass** (kwi ras′) **1** a piece of armour for the body, made of a breastplate and a plate for the back fastened together. **2** the breastplate alone. See ARMOUR for picture. *n.*

**cui·ras·sier** (kwē′rə sēr′) a cavalry soldier wearing a CUIRASS. *n.*

**cui·sine** (kwi zēn′) **1** a style of cooking or preparing food. **2** food. **3** kitchen. *n.*

**cuke** (kyük) *Informal.* CUCUMBER. *n.*

**cul–de–sac** (kul′də sak′ *or* kùl′də sak′; *French,* kY də säk′) a street or passage open at only one end; blind alley. *n.*

**cu·lex** (kyü′leks) any of a genus of mosquitoes found throughout the world, and including the common mosquito of North America and Europe. *n., pl.* **cu·li·ces** (-lə sēz′).

**cul·i·nar·y** (kyü′lə ner′ē *or* kul′ə ner′ē) **1** having to do with cooking or the kitchen: *Mother is often praised for her culinary skill.* **2** used in cooking: *culinary herbs.* *adj.*

**cull** (kul) **1** pick out; select: *The lawyer culled important facts from the mass of evidence.* **2** pick over; make selections from. **3** something picked out as inferior or worthless: *Poor fruit, stale vegetables, lumber, and animals not up to standard are called culls.* **4** select for slaughter: *The herd is culled to keep the numbers down to a point where the remainder have a good chance of survival through the winter.* **1**, **2**, **4** *v.*, **3** *n.*

**cul·mi·nate** (kul′mə nāt′) **1** rise to or form a highest point: *The church tower had a long winding staircase that culminated in a lookout platform.* **2** reach the decisive point or climax: *The dramatic action of the play culminates in a murder.* *v.,* **cul·mi·nat·ed, cul·mi·nat·ing.**

**cul·mi·na·tion** (kul′mə nā′shən) **1** the highest point; climax. **2** a reaching of the highest point. *n.*

**cu·lottes** (kyü lots′ *or* kü lots′) women's and girls' trousers cut with very wide legs to resemble a flared skirt: *Culottes may reach to the knees or ankles.* *n. pl.*

**cul·pa·bil·i·ty** (kul′pə bil′ə tē) the fact or condition of deserving blame. *n.*

**cul·pa·ble** (kul′pə bəl) deserving blame: *The police officer was dismissed for culpable neglect of duty.* *adj.* —**cul′pa·ble·ness,** *n.* —**cul′pa·bly,** *adv.*

**cul·prit** (kul′prit) **1** a person guilty of a fault or a crime; offender. **2** a prisoner in court who has been accused of a crime. *n.*

**cult** (kult) **1** a system of religious worship. **2** great admiration for a person, thing, idea, etc.: *a cult for sunbathing.* **3** a group showing such admiration; worshippers. *n.*

**cul·ti·va·ble** (kul′tə və bəl) that can be CULTIVATED. *adj.*

**cul·ti·vat·a·ble** (kul′tə vāt′ə bəl) CULTIVABLE. *adj.*

**cul·ti·vate** (kul′tə vāt′) **1** prepare and use land to raise crops by ploughing it, planting seeds, and taking care of the growing plants. **2** help plants grow by labour and care. **3** loosen the ground around growing plants to kill weeds, etc. **4** improve; develop by study or training: *It takes time, thought, and effort to cultivate your mind.* **5** give time, thought, and effort to mastering; practise: *An artist cultivates her craft.* **6** seek better acquaintance with; try to win the friendship of: *She cultivated people who could help her.* *v.,* **cul·ti·vat·ed, cul·ti·vat·ing.**

**cul·ti·vat·ed** (kul′tə vā′tid) **1** prepared and used to raise crops: *A field of wheat is cultivated land; a pasture is not.* **2** produced by cultivation; not wild: *The American Beauty rose is a cultivated flower.* **3** improved; developed. **4** cultured; refined. **5** pt. and pp. of CULTIVATE. 1–4 *adj.,* 5 *v.*

**cul·ti·va·tion** (kul′tə vā′shən) **1** the act or practice of cultivating. **2** the result of improvement or growth through education or experience; culture: *a man of cultivation.* *n.*
**under cultivation,** of land, planted with crops or prepared for planting: *Most of their land is now under cultivation.*

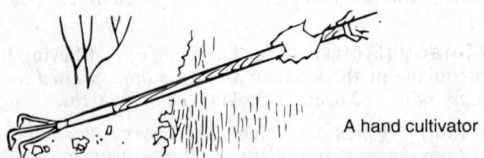
A hand cultivator

**cul·ti·va·tor** (kul′tə vā′tər) **1** a tool or machine used to loosen the ground and destroy weeds: *A cultivator is pulled or pushed between rows of growing plants.* **2** any person or thing that CULTIVATES. *n.*

**cul·tur·al** (kul′chə rəl) of or having to do with CULTURE (def. 2): *Music and art are cultural studies.* *adj.* —**cul′tur·al·ly,** *adv.*

**cul·ture** (kul′chər) **1** fineness of feelings, thoughts, tastes, manners, etc. **2** the arts, beliefs, habits, institutions, and other human endeavours considered together as being characteristic of a particular community, people, or nation: *Modern Canadian culture is strongly influenced by television and the other mass media.* **3** the development of the mind or body by education, training, etc. **4** the preparation of land to raise crops by ploughing, planting, and necessary care; CULTIVATION. **5** proper care given to the raising of bees, fish, silkworms, viruses, etc. **6** a growth of living material such as bacteria in a special medium for scientific study or medicinal use. **7** cultivate. 1–6 *n.,* 7 *v.,* **cul·tur·ing.**

**cul·tured** (kul′chərd) **1** having or showing CULTURE (def. 1); refined. **2** produced or raised under artificial conditions, as in a laboratory, etc.: *cultured pearls.* **3** pt. and pp. of CULTURE. 1, 2 *adj.,* 3 *v.*

**cul·vert** (kul′vərt) a small channel or drain that allows water to run under a road, railway, canal, etc. *n.*

**cum·ber** (kum′bər) **1** burden; trouble: *Household cares cumber a busy mother.* **2** hinder; hamper: *The logger's heavy boots cumbered him in walking.* **3** hindrance. 1, 2 *v.,* 3 *n.*

**cum·ber·some** (kum′bər səm) hard to manage; clumsy; unwieldy; burdensome: *The armour worn by medieval knights seems cumbersome to us today. Long, awkward sentences are cumbersome.* *adj.* —**cum′ber·some·ly,** *adv.* —**cum′ber·some·ness,** *n.*

**cum·brous** (kum′brəs) CUMBERSOME. *adj.* —**cum′brous·ly,** *adv.* —**cum′brous·ness,** *n.*

**cum·in** *or* **cum·min** (kum′ən) a small plant whose seedlike fruits are used in cookery and medicine. *n.*

**cum lau·de** (kùm lou′dā) *Latin.* with praise or honour: *To graduate "cum laude" is to graduate with high standing.*

**cum·quat** (kum′kwot) KUMQUAT. *n.*

**cu·mu·late** (kyü′myə lāt′) **1** heap up; accumulate. **2** heaped up. 1 *v.,* **cu·mu·lat·ed, cu·mu·lat·ing;** 2 *adj.*

**cu·mu·la·tion** (kyü′myə lā′shən) **1** a heaping up; accumulating. **2** a heap; ACCUMULATION (def. 1). *n.*

**cu·mu·la·tive** (kyü′myə lə tiv *or* kyü′myə lā′tiv) heaped up; accumulated; increasing or growing in amount, force, etc. by additions: *A cumulative dividend is one that must be added to future dividends if not paid when due.* *adj.* —**cu′mu·la′tive·ly,** *adv.* —**cu′mu·la′tive·ness,** *n.*

**cu·mu·lus** (kyü′myə ləs) **1** a cloud formation of rounded heaps having a flat base. **2** heap. *n., pl.* **cu·mu·li** (-lī′ *or* -lē′).

**cu·ne·ate** (kyü′nē it *or* kyü′nē āt′) tapering to a point at the base; wedge-shaped. *adj.*

Cuneiform characters

**cu·ne·i·form** (kyü′nē ə fôrm′ *or* kyü nē′ə fôrm′) **1** wedge-shaped. **2** the wedge-shaped characters used in the writing of ancient Babylonia, Assyria, Persia, etc. 1 *adj.,* 2 *n.*

**cun·ning** (kun′ing) **1** clever in getting what one wants or in deceiving one's enemies; crafty; wily: *a cunning rogue.* **2** craftiness; wiliness: *A fox has a great deal of* *cunning.* **3** showing craftiness or wiliness: *a cunning plot.* **4** *Informal.* attractively small, delicate, quaint, etc.; cute: *a cunning baby.* 1, 3, 4 *adj.*, 2 *n.* —**cun′ning·ly,** *adv.* —**cun′ning·ness,** *n.*

**cup** (kup) **1** a small container in the shape of a bowl to drink from: *Most cups have handles.* **2** as much as a cup holds; a cupful: *He ordered a cup of tea.* **3** anything shaped like a cup: *The petals of some flowers form a cup.* **4** shape like a cup: *She cupped her hands to catch the ball. The old man cupped a hand behind one ear.* **5** an ornamental TROPHY (def. 2) often in the shape of a vase, given to the winner of a contest: *the Stanley Cup, in hockey.* **6** take or put in a cup. **7** a drink or mixture: *a claret cup.* **8** a cup used in Communion. **9** the wine, etc. used in Communion. **10** something to be endured or experienced; fate: *Hers was a bitter cup.* 1–3, 5, 7–10 *n.*, 4, 6 *v.*, **cupped, cup·ping.** —**cup′like′,** *adj.* **in one's cups,** *Informal.* drunk.

**cup·bear·er** (kup′ber′ər) a person who fills and passes around the cups in which drinks are served. *n.*

**cup·board** (kub′ərd) **1** a closet or cabinet with shelves for dishes, food, etc. **2** a closet for storing clothing and other things. *n.*

**cup·cake** (kup′kāk′) a small cake baked in a cup-shaped container. *n.*

**cup·ful** (kup′fùl′) as much as a cup can hold. *n., pl.* **cup·fuls.**

**cu·pid·i·ty** (kyü pid′ə tē) eager desire; greed. *n.*

**cu·po·la** (kyü′pə lə) **1** a round dome forming the roof of a building or part of a building. **2** a small structure on top of a roof. *n.*

**cur** (kėr) **1** a worthless dog; MONGREL. **2** an ill-bred, worthless person. *n.*

**cur·a·bil·i·ty** (kyü′rə bil′ə tē) being CURABLE. *n.*

**cur·a·ble** (kyü′rə bəl) that can be cured. *adj.* —**cur′a·ble·ness,** *n.* —**cur′a·bly,** *adv.*

**cu·ra·re** (kyü rä′rē) a poisonous, blackish, resinlike extract of certain tropical American plants, which causes paralysis of the muscles. It is used medicinally as a muscle relaxant and has long been used by South American Indian peoples as an arrow poison in hunting game. Also, **curari.**

**cur·a·tive** (kyü′rə tiv) **1** having the power to cure; curing; tending to cure. **2** a means of curing. 1 *adj.*, 2 *n.*

**cu·ra·tor** (kyü rā′tər) the person in charge of all or part of a museum, library, etc.: *The curator of an art museum knows a great deal about pictures.* *n.*

**curb** (kėrb) **1** a raised border of concrete or stone along the edge of a street, driveway, etc. **2** a chain or strap fastened to a horse's bit and passing under its lower jaw: *When the reins are pulled tight, the curb checks the horse.* **3** anything that checks or restrains. **4** hold in check; restrain. **5** provide with a curb. **6** a market that deals in stocks and bonds not listed on the regular stock exchange. 1–3, 6 *n.*, 4, 5 *v.*

**curb bit** a horse's bit having a CURB (def. 2).

**curb·stone** (kėrb′stōn′) a stone or stones forming a CURB (def. 1); a raised border of concrete, etc. along the sides of a street, driveway, etc. *n.*

**curd** (kėrd) **1** the thick part of milk that separates from the watery part when milk sours. **2** form into curds; CURDLE. 1 *n.*, 2 *v.*

**cup** 299 **curl**

hat, āge, fär; let, ēqual, tėrm; it, īce
hot, ōpen, ôrder; oil, out; cup, pùt, rüle
əbove, takən, pencəl, lemən, circəs
ch, child; ng, long; sh, ship
th, thin; ᴛʜ, then; zh, measure

**cur·dle** (kėr′dəl) **1** form into CURDS: *Milk curdles when it is kept too long.* **2** thicken. *v.*, **cur·dled, cur·dling.** **curdle the blood,** horrify; terrify.

**cur·dled** (kėr′dəld) **1** formed into curds. **2** pt. and pp. of CURDLE. 1 *adj.*, 2 *v.*

**cure** (kyùr) **1** bring back to health or to a normal, sound, or proper condition: *The sick child was soon cured. The punishment was meant to cure her of lying.* **2** get rid of: *to cure a cold, to cure a bad habit.* **3** recovery from a disease; bringing or being brought back to health: *Her cure took a long time.* **4** a period or course of treatment for a disease: *a rest cure.* **5** something that restores to health; a successful medical treatment, drug, etc.: *Researchers have not yet found a cure for cancer.* **6** anything that permanently relieves or corrects a problem or a harmful situation: *a cure for laziness. The proposals are not a cure for inflation, but merely a stopgap.* **7** prepare for keeping; preserve: *They cured the meat by drying and salting it.* **8** prepare for use: *Tobacco is cured by drying it.* 1, 2, 7, 8 *v.*, **cured, cur·ing;** 3–6 *n.* —**cure′less,** *adj.* —**cur′er,** *n.*

**cure-all** (kyùr′rol′) a remedy supposed to cure all diseases or evils. *n.*

**cur·few** (kėr′fyü) **1** the giving of a signal, such as a bell ringing, at a fixed time every evening: *In the Middle Ages, the curfew was a signal to put out lights and cover fires. More recently the curfew has been used as a signal for persons, usually children, to leave streets and public places.* **2** the signal given: *"The curfew tolls the knell of parting day."* **3** the time when it is given: *Everyone was indoors before curfew.* **4** a formal regulation forbidding persons to be on the streets after a certain hour. *n.*
☛ *Etym.* From OF *coevrefeu,* from *coevre* 'cover' + *feu* 'fire'.

**Cu·ri·a** (kyùr′ē ə) the administrative arm of the Roman Catholic Church, with the Pope as its supreme head. *n.*

**cu·rie** (kyùr′ē *or* kyü rē′) a unit for measuring radio-activity, equal to 37 gigabecquerels. *Symbol:* Ci *n.*

**cu·ri·o** (kyùr′ē ō′) an object valued as a curiosity: *The traveller brought back many curios from foreign lands.* *n., pl.* **cu·ri·os.**

**cu·ri·os·i·ty** (kyùr′ē os′ə tē) **1** an eager desire to know: *Her curiosity made her open the forbidden door.* **2** a strange, rare, or novel object. *n., pl.* **cu·ri·os·i·ties.**

**cu·ri·ous** (kyùr′ē əs) **1** eager to know: *a curious student.* **2** too eager to know; prying: *The old woman is too curious about other people's business.* **3** strange; odd; unusual: *a curious old book.* **4** very careful; exact: *a curious inquiry into the customs of the Blackfoot.* **5** *Informal.* very odd; eccentric: *curious notions.* *adj.* —**cu′ri·ous·ly,** *adv.* —**cu′ri·ous·ness,** *n.*

**cu·ri·um** (kyùr′ē əm) an element produced by the bombardment of plutonium and uranium by helium ions. *Symbol:* Cm *n.*

**curl** (kėrl) **1** twist or roll into coils: *Mother has to curl her hair, but mine curls naturally.* **2** take the form of coils or twists: *Paper curls when it burns.* **3** grow or rise in coils or spirals: *The smoke curled slowly from the chimney.* **4** a curled lock of hair. **5** anything like it: *A carpenter's shavings are curls.* **6** form into a curve; twist: *Her lip curled in a sneer.* **7** move in curves or twists; wind: *A stream curled through the woods.* **8** curling or being curled. **9** in the game of CURLING, slide a CURLING STONE down the ice. **10** engage in the game of CURLING. 1–3, 6, 7, 9, 10 *v.*, 4, 5, 8 *n.*

**curl up,** take a comfortable position sitting or lying down with one's legs drawn up: *The child curled up in the big chair and went to sleep.*

**curl·er** (kėr′lər) **1** a person who takes part in the game of CURLING. **2** a device on which hair is twisted to make it curl. *n.*

**cur·lew** (kėr′lü) a wading bird having a long, thin bill. *n., pl.* **cur·lews** or (*esp. collectively*) **cur·lew**.

**curl·i·cue** (kėr′lə kyü′) a fancy twist, curl, flourish, etc.: *Curlicues in handwriting make it hard to read.* *n.*

**curl·ing** (kėr′ling) **1** a game played on ice, in which large, heavy, round stones are slid toward a target at the end of the rink. **2** ppr. of CURL. 1 *n.*, 2 *v.*

A curling stone    A woman curling

**curling stone** or **rock** the object, usually made of granite, that is slid down the ice in the game of CURLING.

**curl·y** (kėr′lē) **1** curling; having a tendency to curl; wavy: *curly hair.* **2** having curls: *a curly head.* *adj.,* **curl·i·er, curl·i·est.** —**curl′i·ness,** *n.*

**cur·mudg·eon** (kər muj′ən) a rude, stingy, bad-tempered person. *n.*

**cur·rant** (kėr′ənt) **1** a small, seedless raisin used in cakes, etc. **2** a small, sour, edible berry that grows in bunches: *Currants are red, white, or black and are used for jelly, wine, preserves, etc.* **3** a bush that bears currants. *n.*
☛ Hom. CURRENT.

**cur·ren·cy** (kėr′ən sē) **1** the money in actual use in a country: *Canadian currency cannot be used in Mexico.* **2** a passing from person to person; circulation: *The people who spread a rumour give it currency.* **3** general use or acceptance; common occurrence: *Informal words often obtain currency.* *n., pl.* **cur·ren·cies.**

**cur·rent** (kėr′ənt) **1** a flow or stream of water or air in one direction, especially within a larger body of water or air: *Stay near the shore so you don't get caught in the current.* **2** the flow of electricity along a wire, etc. **3** the rate or amount of such a flow, usually expressed in amperes: *Electrical heating requires much more current than lighting does.* **4** a course or tendency of events, ideas, etc.; a general direction or drift: *the current of public opinion.* **5** of or at the present time: *current fashions, the current month. Her current job involves a lot of travelling.* **6** most recent: *The current issue of a magazine is the one most recently published.* **7** generally used or accepted; common or prevalent: *Many slang expressions of the mid eighties are no longer current.* **8** going around; passing from person to person: *A rumour is current that prices will go up.* 1–4 *n.*, 5–8 *adj.*
☛ Hom. CURRANT.

**cur·rent·ly** (kėr′ən tlē) at the present time or in the present period: *The prime minister is currently vacationing in the Maritimes. Her songs are currently very popular.* *adv.*

**cur·ric·u·lar** (kə rik′yə lər) having to do with a CURRICULUM. *adj.*

**cur·ric·u·lum** (kə rik′yə ləm) **1** the whole range of studies offered in a school, college, etc., or in a type of school: *the university curriculum. Our high-school curriculum includes English, mathematics, science, history, and foreign languages.* **2** a program of studies leading to a particular degree, certificate, etc.: *the curriculum of the Law School.* *n., pl.* **cur·ric·u·lums** or **cur·ric·u·la** (-lə).

**cur·rish** (kėr′ish) of or like a CUR; snarling; ill-bred; worthless. *adj.* —**cur′rish·ly,** *adv.*

**cur·ry**¹ (kėr′ē) **1** rub and clean a horse, etc. with a brush or CURRYCOMB. **2** prepare tanned leather for use by soaking, scraping, beating, colouring, etc. *v.,* **cur·ried, cur·ry·ing.**
**curry favour,** seek favour by flattery, attention, etc.

**cur·ry**² (kėr′ē) **1** a peppery sauce or powder containing a mixture of spices, seeds, vegetables, etc. **2** food flavoured with curry. **3** prepare or flavour with curry: *curried rice, curried lamb.* 1, 2 *n., pl.* **cur·ries;** 3 *v.,* **cur·ried, cur·ry·ing.**

**cur·ry·comb** (kėr′ē kōm′) **1** a brush with metal teeth for rubbing and cleaning a horse. **2** use a currycomb on; brush with a currycomb. 1 *n.,* 2 *v.*

**curse** (kėrs) **1** call on a supernatural or divine being to bring evil or harm to: *to curse one's enemies.* **2** the words that a person says when he curses someone or something: *The last line of the epitaph on Shakespeare's tomb is a curse: "And curst be he that moves my bones."* **3** a person or thing that is or ought to be cursed; a source of evil or harm: *The stolen money proved to be a curse to them. Malaria was the curse of the expedition.* **4** harm or evil that comes as if in answer to a curse or as a retribution: *They claimed that there was a curse on the diamond.* **5** bring evil or harm to; torment or afflict: *cursed with poverty, cursed by the gods.* **6** rail at by using blasphemous words; revile: *to curse one's fate, to curse the gods.* **7** use blasphemous or obscene words to express anger, hatred, frustration, etc.; swear or swear at: *He cursed when he hit his thumb with the hammer. She cursed her servant for his clumsiness.* **8** blasphemous or obscene words used to express anger, hatred, frustration, etc.: *Their talk was full of curses.* 1, 5, 6, 7 *v.,* **cursed** or **curst, curs·ing;** 2–4, 8 *n.* —**curs′er,** *n.*

**curs·ed** (kėr′sid *or* kėrst) **1** under a CURSE (defs. 2, 4). **2** deserving a CURSE (defs. 2, 4); evil; hateful. **3** (kėrst) a pt. and a pp. of CURSE. 1, 2 *adj.,* 3 *v.*
—**curs′ed·ly,** *adv.*

**cur·sive** (kėr′siv) **1** written with the letters joined together: *Ordinary handwriting is cursive.* **2** a letter made to join other letters. 1 *adj.,* 2 *n.* —**cur′sive·ly,** *adv.*

**cur·sor** (kėr′sər) a mark on the video display of a computer that indicates where the next character will be placed. *n.*

**cur·so·ri·al** (kėr sô′rē əl) **1** for running. **2** having legs fitted for running: *The ostrich is a cursorial bird.* *adj.*

**cur·so·ry** (kėr′sə rē)   hasty; superficial; without attention to details: *Even a cursory reading of the letter showed many errors.*   *adj.*   —**cur′so·ri·ly,** *adv.*

**curst** (kėrst)   **1** CURSED.   **2** a pt. and a pp. of CURSE.   1 *adj.*, 2 *v.*

**curt** (kėrt)   short; rudely brief; abrupt: *Her curt answer made him angry.*   *adj.*   —**curt′ly,** *adv.*   —**curt′ness,** *n.*

**cur·tail** (kėr tāl′)   cut short; cut off part of; reduce; lessen: *He curtailed his son's allowance.*   *v.*

**cur·tail·ment** (kėr tāl′mənt)   a CURTAILing.   *n.*

**cur·tain** (kėr′tən)   **1** a piece of cloth or other similar material hung at windows or in doorways to protect from sun, wind, or rain, to separate, conceal, or darken, or to decorate.   **2** in the theatre:   **a** a movable hanging screen that separates the stage from the part where the audience sits.   **b** the opening or raising of the curtain at the beginning of an act or scene, or the fall or closing of the curtain at the end of an act or scene.   **3** provide with or as if with a curtain: *We haven't curtained the living room windows yet.*   **4** anything that hides or acts as a barrier: *a curtain of fog. They had placed a curtain of secrecy over all their movements.*   **5** hide or cover with or as if with a curtain.   **6** the part of a wall between two bastions, towers, or the like.   1, 2, 4, 6 *n.*, 3, 5 *v.*

**curtain call**   a call for an actor, musician, etc. to return to the stage and acknowledge the applause of the audience.

**curtain raiser**   **1** a short play given before the main play in a theatre.   **2** any preliminary event before something more important: *The first film was just a curtain raiser before the main feature.*

**curt·sey** (kėrt′sē)   See CURTSY.   *n.*, *pl.* **curt·seys;**   *v.*, **curt·seyed, curt·sey·ing.**

**curt·sy** (kėrt′sē)   **1** a bow of respect or greeting by women, made by bending the knees and lowering the body slightly.   **2** make a curtsy.   1 *n.*, *pl.* **curt·sies;**   2 *v.*, **curt·sied, curt·sy·ing.**

**cur·va·ture** (kėr′və chər *or* kėr′və chür′)   **1** a curving or bending: *We watched the gradual curvature of the plane's vapour trail.*   **2** a curved condition, especially one that is not normal: *curvature of the spine.*   **3** a curved piece or part; curve.   *n.*

**curve** (kėrv)   **1** a line that has no straight part.   **2** something having the shape of a curve; bend: *The automobile had to slow down for the curves in the road.*   **3** bend so as to form a curve.   **4** move in the course of a curve.   **5** curved.   **6** in baseball, a ball pitched with a spin that causes it to swerve just before it reaches the batter: *A good curve is difficult to hit.*   1, 2, 6 *n.*, 3, 4 *v.*, 5 *adj.*   **curved, curv·ing;**

**curved** (kėrvd)   **1** bent so as to form a curve.   **2** pt. and pp. of CURVE.   1 *adj.*, 2 *v.*

**cur·vet** (kėr′vit *for noun,* kėr vet′ *or* kėr′vit *for verb*)   **1** a leap in the air made by a horse: *In a curvet the forelegs are first raised and then the hind legs, so that all legs are off the ground for a second.*   **2** leap in this way.   **3** make a horse do this.   1 *n.*, 2, 3 *v.*, **cur·vet·ted** *or* **cur·vet·ed, cur·vet·ting** *or* **cur·vet·ing.**

**cur·vi·lin·e·ar** (kėr′və lin′ē ər)   consisting of a curved line or lines; enclosed by curved lines.   *adj.*

**cush·ion** (kùsh′ən)   **1** a soft pillow or pad used to sit, lie, or kneel on.   **2** anything used or shaped like a cushion: *Air or steam forms a cushion in some machines to protect from sudden shocks or jars.*   **3** put or rest on a cushion; support with cushions.   **4** supply with a cushion.   **5** *Cdn.* the enclosed ice surface, especially an outdoor one, on which hockey is played.   **6** protect from sudden shocks or jars with a cushion of air or steam.   **7** the elastic lining of the sides of a billiard table.   1, 2, 5, 7 *n.*, 3, 4, 6 *v.*   —**cush′ion·like′,** *adj.*

**cush·y** (kùsh′ē) *Informal.*   easy: *a cushy summer job.*   *adj.*, **cush·i·er, cush·i·est.**

**cusk** (kusk)   a species of CODFISH.   *n.*

**cusp** (kusp)   **1** a pointed end; point: *A crescent has two cusps.*   **2** a blunt or pointed protuberance of the crown of a tooth.   *n.*

**cus·pid** (kus′pid)   a tooth having one cusp; a CANINE TOOTH.   *n.*

**cus·pi·dal** (kus′pə dəl)   **1** of or having to do with a CUSP.   **2** having a pointed end.   *adj.*

**cus·pi·date** (kus′pə dāt′)   having a sharp, pointed end.   *adj.*

**cus·pi·dor** (kus′pə dôr′)   a container to spit into; spittoon.   *n.*

**cuss** (kus) *Informal.*   **1** curse: *He cussed me out for a whole half minute.*   **2** an odd or troublesome person or animal: *Tell that cuss to get over here now.*   **3** a curse.   1 *v.*, 2, 3 *n.*

**cus·tard** (kus′tərd)   a baked, boiled, or frozen food made of eggs and milk, usually sweetened.   *n.*

**custard apple**   **1** a heart-shaped tropical fruit with sweet, yellowish flesh.   **2** the tree that it grows on.   **3** any tree or shrub of the same family, such as the North American pawpaw: *In Canada, the custard apple grows in the Niagara Peninsula.*

**cus·to·di·al** (kus tō′dē əl)   having to do with CUSTODY or CUSTODIANS.   *adj.*

**cus·to·di·an** (kus tō′dē ən)   **1** the person in charge; guardian or keeper: *the custodian of a museum, the legal custodian of a child.*   **2** a caretaker; janitor.   *n.*

**cus·to·di·an·ship** (kus tō′dē ən ship′)   the position or duties of a CUSTODIAN.   *n.*

**cus·to·dy** (kus′tə dē)   **1** the keeping; charge; care: *Parents have the custody of their young children.*   **2** being confined or detained; imprisonment.   *n.*, *pl.* **cus·to·dies. in custody,**   in the care of the police; in prison.   **take into custody,**   arrest.

**cus·tom** (kus′təm)   **1** a usual action; habit: *It was her custom to rise early.*   **2** a habit maintained for so long that it has almost the force of law: *The social customs of many countries differ from ours.*   **3** the regular business given by a customer: *That store would like to have your custom.*   **4** made specially for individuals; made to order; not ready-made: *custom clothes.*   **5** making things to order; not selling ready-made goods: *a custom tailor.*   **6** in feudal times, a tax or service regularly due from tenants to their lord.   **7 customs,** *pl.*   **a** duty paid to the government on things brought in from a foreign country.   **b** the office at a seaport, international airport, or border-crossing point where imported goods are checked.

**c** the department of the government that collects duty. 1–3, 6, 7 *n.*, 4, 5 *adj.*
☞ *Syn.* See note at HABIT.

**cus·tom·ar·i·ly** (kus′tə mer′ə lē *or* kus′tə mer′ə lē) in a CUSTOMARY manner; usually. *adv.*

**cus·tom·ar·y** (kus′tə mer′ē) according to custom; as a habit; usual. *adj.*

**cus·tom–built** (kus′təm bilt′) built to order for individuals; not ready-made: *a custom-built bedroom suite. adj.*

**cus·tom·er** (kus′tə mər) **1** a person who buys. **2** *Informal.* a person; fellow: *Don't get mixed up with him; he's a rough customer. n.*

**custom house** *or* **customs house** a government building or office where taxes on things brought into a country are collected.

**cus·tom·ize** (kus′tə mīz) make or alter according to individual requirements; make or alter to order: *to customize a van. v.*, **cus·tom·ized, cus·tom·iz·ing.**

**cus·tom–made** (kus′təm mād′) made to order; made specially for individuals; not ready-made. *adj.*

**cut** (kut) **1** open, remove, or separate with something sharp: *to cut meat, timber, grass, one's nails, etc.* **2** make by cutting: *He cut a hole through the wall with the axe.* **3** be cut; admit of being cut: *Stale bread cuts better than fresh bread.* **4** of a cutting tool, function or be effective: *This knife cuts well.* **5** that has been cut: *a cut pie.* **6** shaped or formed by cutting. **7** pierce or wound with something sharp: *She cut her finger on the broken glass.* **8** a wound or opening made by cutting. **9** a passage, channel, etc. made by cutting or digging. **10** a piece cut off or cut out: *a cut of meat.* **11** the way in which a thing is cut; a style or fashion: *the cut of a coat.* **12** haircut. **13** reduce; decrease: *to cut expenses.* **14** reduced: *at cut prices.* **15** a reduction; decrease. **16** go by a direct way; go: *He cut across the field to save time.* **17** change direction suddenly: *She had to cut to the right to avoid the oncoming car.* **18** a way straight across or through; short cut. **19** cross; divide by crossing: *A brook cuts that field.* **20** hit or strike sharply: *The cold wind cut me to the bone.* **21** a sharp blow or stroke. **22** the act of cutting: *He made a quick cut in the cardboard.* **23** hit with a slicing stroke: *He cut the ball so that it bounded almost backward.* **24** a slicing stroke. **25** hurt the feelings of: *His mean remark cut me.* **26** an action or speech that hurts the feelings. **27** *Informal.* refuse to recognize socially: *No one in the class cut the new girl, although she was shy.* **28** *Informal.* a refusal to recognize socially. **29** *Informal.* be absent from a class, lecture, etc.: *She wanted to cut history when she heard there was going to be a test.* **30** *Informal.* an absence from a class, lecture, etc. **31** in printing, a block or plate with a picture engraved on it. **32** a picture made from such a block or plate. **33** make less sticky or stiff; dissolve: *Gasoline cuts grease and tar.* **34** divide a pack of cards at random. **35** *Informal.* do; perform; make: *to cut a caper.* **36** shorten by omitting some part or parts: *Your speech will be more effective if you cut it in several places.* **37** *Informal.* share: *Each partner has a cut of the profits.* 1–4, 7, 13, 16, 17, 19, 20, 23, 25, 27, 29, 33–36 *v.*, **cut, cut·ting;** 5, 6, 14 *adj.*, 8–12, 15, 18, 21, 22, 24, 26, 28, 30–32, 37 *n.*
**a cut above,** *Informal.* somewhat superior to.
**cut across,** go straight across or through: *We had to go around the field because it was too muddy to cut across.*
**cut and dried,** arranged in advance.
**cut back, a** go back suddenly. **b** shorten (a plant) by cutting off the end. **c** reduce output, etc.
**cut both ways,** have disadvantages as well as advantages.
**cut down, a** cause to fall by cutting: *to cut down a tree.* **b** reduce; decrease: *to cut down expenses.*
**cut in, a** go in suddenly. **b** break in; interrupt: *to cut in with a remark.* **c** interrupt a dancing couple to take the place of one of them. **d** move a vehicle suddenly into a line of moving traffic. **e** connect, join, etc., especially to a machine or working part.
**cut it out,** *Informal.* stop doing it.
**cut off, a** remove from the outside of something by cutting: *to cut off the bark of a tree.* **b** shut off: *Our power was cut off for an hour.* **c** stop suddenly. **d** break; interrupt. **e** disinherit.
**cut out, a** remove from inside of by cutting: *He cut the core out of the apple.* **b** take out; leave out. **c** take the place of; get the better of. **d** make by cutting; make; form: *Her cousin showed her how to cut out paper dolls.* **e** stop doing, using, making, etc.: *cut out candy. He was told to cut out the teasing.* **f** move out of an assigned or expected position: *The reckless driver suddenly cut out from his own lane.*
**cut short,** interrupt.
**cut teeth,** have teeth grow through the gums.
**cut up, a** cut into small pieces. **b** *Informal.* hurt by causing lacerations. **c** *Informal.* show off; play tricks: *The father was annoyed because his daughter was cutting up.*
**cut up rough, a** become physically violent. **b** make difficulties. **c** misbehave badly.

**cu·ta·ne·ous** (kyü tā′nē əs) of, on, or having to do with the skin. *adj.*

**cut·a·way** (kut′ə wā′) **1** a coat having the lower part cut back in a curve or slope from the waist in front to the tails in back: *Cutaways are used by men for formal wear in the daytime.* **2** of or referring to a drawing or model of a building, machine, etc. having part of the outside wall or surface cut away to show its internal structure or workings. 1 *n.*, 2 *adj.*

**cut·back** (kut′bak′) a reduction in output, etc.: *The company has had to make cutbacks in expenditures because of a slump in sales. n.*

**cut·bank** (kut′bangk′) the outer side of a stream or river where the force of the current has cut away the earth, leaving an overhanging bank. *n.*

**cute** (kyüt) *Informal.* **1** pleasing or attractive because pretty, lovable, dainty, etc.: *a cute puppy, a cute dress, a cute girl.* **2** clever; shrewd; cunning: *a cute trick. adj.*, **cut·er, cut·est.** —**cute′ly,** *adv.* —**cute′ness,** *n.*

**cut glass** glass shaped or decorated by grinding and polishing.

**cu·ti·cle** (kyü′tə kəl) **1** the outer layer of skin of vertebrates; EPIDERMIS. **2** the strip of hardened or dead skin at the base of a fingernail or toenail. *n.*

**cut·lass** (kut′ləs) a short, heavy, slightly curved sword with a single-edged blade. *n.*

**cut·ler** (kut′lər) a person who makes, sells, or repairs knives, scissors, and other cutting instruments. *n.*

**cut·ler·y** (kut′lə rē) **1** knives, forks, and spoons for table use. **2** knives, scissors, and other cutting instruments. **3** the business of a CUTLER. *n.*

**cut·let** (kut′lit) **1** a slice of meat for broiling or frying:

a veal cutlet.   2 a flat, fried cake of chopped meat or fish.

**cut·off** (kut′ôf′)   1 the act of cutting off, especially the limit set for an activity, process, etc.   2 a short way across or through; shorter road or passage.   3 a stopping of the passage of steam or working fluid to the cylinder of an engine.   4 the mechanism or device that does this.   *n.*

**cut·out** (kut′out′)   1 a shape or design that has been cut out or is to be cut out: *Some books for children have cutouts.*   2 a device that allows the exhaust gases of an INTERNAL-COMBUSTION ENGINE to pass straight into the air instead of going through a muffler.   3 a device for breaking an electric current.   *n.*

A cutter

**cut·ter** (kut′ər)   1 a person who cuts, especially one whose work is cutting cloth to be made up into clothes.   2 a tool or machine for cutting: *a meat cutter.*   3 a small, light sleigh, usually pulled by one horse.   4 a kind of sleigh pulled as a trailer by a snowmobile.   5 a small sailboat with one mast.   6 a boat belonging to a warship, used to carry people and supplies to and from the ship.   7 a small armed ship used for patrolling coastal waters.   *n.*

**cut·throat** (kut′thrōt′)   1 murderer.   2 murderous.   3 relentless; merciless; severe: *cutthroat competition.*   1 *n.*, 2, 3 *adj.*

**cut·ting** (kut′ing)   1 something cut off or cut out.   2 a small shoot cut from a plant to grow a new plant.   3 a newspaper or magazine clipping.   4 a place or way cut through high ground for a road, track, etc.   5 the act of one that cuts.   6 that cuts; sharp: *A cutlass has a blade with one cutting edge.*   7 that hurts the feelings; sarcastic: *a cutting remark.*   8 ppr. of CUT.   1–5 *n.*, 6, 7 *adj.*, 8 *v.*
—**cut·ting·ly**, *adv.*

**cut·tle** (kut′əl)   CUTTLEFISH.   *n.*

**cut·tle·bone** (kut′əl bōn′)   the hard internal shell of CUTTLEFISH, used as a food supplement for caged birds and, in powder form, as a polishing agent.   *n.*

**cut·tle·fish** (kut′əl fish′)   a saltwater MOLLUSC having ten sucker-bearing arms and a hard internal shell: *One kind of cuttlefish squirts out an inky fluid when frightened.*   *n., pl.* **cut·tle·fish** or **cut·tle·fish·es.**

**cut·wa·ter** (kut′wot′ər)   1 the front part of a ship's prow.   2 the wedge-shaped edge of a bridge pier, designed to break the force of the current.   *n.*

**cut·worm** (kut′wėrm′)   a moth caterpillar that feeds on the stalks of young plants, cutting them off near or below the surface of the ground.   *n.*

**cwt.**   hundredweight.

**–cy**   a noun-forming suffix meaning:   1 the office, position, or rank of, as in *captaincy.*   2 the quality, state, condition, or fact of being, as in *bankruptcy.*

**cy·an·a·mide** (sī an′ə mīd′)   a white crystalline compound prepared by the action of ammonia on cyanogen chloride and in other ways.   *n.*

---

**cutoff**  303  **cyclopedia**

hat, āge, fär; let, ēqual, tėrm; it, īce
hot, ōpen, ôrder; oil, out; cup, pùt, rüle
әbove, takәn, pencәl, lemәn, circәs
ch, child; ng, long; sh, ship
th, thin; ᴛʜ, then; zh, measure

**cy·an·ic acid** (sī an′ik)   a colourless, poisonous liquid.

**cy·a·nide** (sī′ə nīd′)   a salt of hydrocyanic acid, especially potassium cyanide, a powerful poison.   *n.*

**cy·an·o·gen** (sī an′ə jən)   a colourless, poisonous, inflammable gas having the odour of bitter almonds.   *n.*

**cy·a·no·sis** (sī′ə nō′sis)   blueness of the skin, caused by lack of oxygen in the blood.   *n.*

**cy·ber·na·tion** (sī′bər nā′shən)   automation in manufacturing, etc. by means of computers.   *n.*

**cy·ber·net·ics** (sī′bər net′iks)   the comparative study of complex calculating machines and the human nervous system in order to understand better the functioning of the human brain.   *n.*

**cy·cad** (sī′kad)   a large, tropical, palmlike plant with a cluster of long fernlike leaves either rising from an underground stem or borne at the top of a thick trunk that resembles a column.   *n.*

**cyc·la·men** (sī′klə mən *or* sik′lə mən)   any of a group of closely related plants of the primrose family, having heart-shaped leaves and showy white, purple, pink, or crimson flowers, whose five petals bend backwards.   *n.*

**cy·cle** (sī′kəl)   1 a period of time or complete process of growth or action that repeats itself in the same order: *The seasons of the year—spring, summer, autumn, and winter—make a cycle.*   2 a complete set or series.   3 pass through a cycle; occur over and over again in the same order.   4 all the stories, poems, legends, etc. about a great hero or event: *There is a cycle of stories about the adventures of King Arthur and his knights.*   5 a very long period of time; age.   6 a bicycle, tricycle, or motorcycle.   7 ride a cycle, especially a bicycle.   8 a complete or double alternation or reversal of an alternating electric current.   9 the series of strokes of a piston in the cylinder of an engine.   1, 2, 4–6, 8, 9 *n.*, 3, 7 *v.*, **cy·cled, cy·cling.**

**cy·clic** (sī′klik *or* sik′lik)   1 of a CYCLE (defs. 1, 2).   2 moving or occurring in CYCLES (defs. 1, 2).   *adj.*

**cy·cli·cal** (sī′klə kəl *or* sik′lə kəl)   CYCLIC.   *adj.*

**cy·clist** (sī′klist)   the rider of a CYCLE (def. 6), such as a bicycle or motorcycle.   *n.*

**cy·clom·e·ter** (sī klom′ə tər)   an instrument that records the number of revolutions that a wheel makes, used to measure the distance that a vehicle travels.   *n.*

**cy·clone** (sī′klōn)   1 a severe windstorm resulting from a condition of low pressure, with winds moving in a spiral toward the centre, where the air pressure is lowest: *Hurricanes and typhoons are cyclones.*   2 a low-pressure condition or weather system that can produce such storms: *Cyclones are sometimes thousands of kilometres across.* Compare with ANTI-CYCLONE.   3 any violent windstorm with spiralling winds, such as a tornado.   *n.*

**cy·clon·ic** (sī klon′ik)   of or like a CYCLONE.   *adj.*

**cy·clo·pe·di·a** *or* **cy·clo·pae·di·a** (sī′klə pē′dē ə)   a book giving information on all branches of one subject: *A cyclopedia is different from an encyclopedia in that it does*

**cy·clo·pe·dic** or **cy·clo·pae·dic** (sī′klə pē′dik)
1 wide and varied. 2 having to do with a CYCLOPEDIA. *adj.*

**cy·clo·ram·a** (sī′klə ram′ə) 1 a large picture of a landscape, battle, etc. on the wall of a circular room. 2 a curved screen crossing the width of a stage and used as a background for the scenery. *n.*

**cy·clo·tron** (sī′klə tron′) an apparatus for giving very high speeds to electrically charged particles. The accelerated particles may be used to bombard, and to effect changes in, atomic nuclei. *n.*

**cyg·net** (sig′nit) a young swan. *n.*
☛ *Hom.* SIGNET.

**cyl.** 1 cylinder. 2 cylindrical.

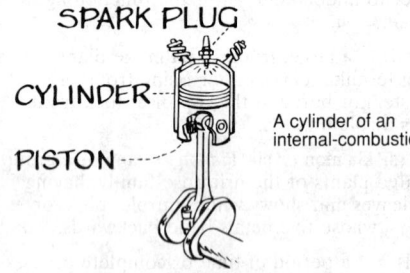
A cylinder of an internal-combustion engine

**cyl·in·der** (sil′ən dər) 1 a solid bounded by two equal, parallel circles and a curved surface formed by moving a straight line of fixed length so that its ends always lie on the two parallel circles. See SOLID for picture. 2 the volume of such a solid. 3 any long, round object, solid or hollow, with flat ends: *Rollers and tin cans are cylinders.* 4 the part of a revolver that contains chambers for cartridges. 5 the piston chamber of an engine. See STEAM ENGINE for another picture. *n.*

**cy·lin·dric** (sə lin′drik) CYLINDRICAL. *adj.*

**cy·lin·dri·cal** (sə lin′drə kəl) shaped like a CYLINDER (def. 1); having the form of a cylinder: *Silos, candles, and water pipes are usually cylindrical.* *adj.*
—**cy·lin′dri·cal·ly,** *adv.*

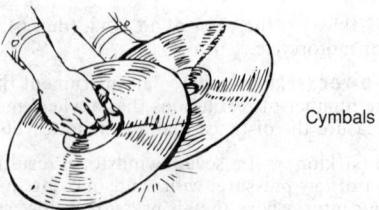
Cymbals

**cym·bal** (sim′bəl) one of a pair of metal plates, used as a musical instrument: *Cymbals are struck together to make a ringing sound. A cymbal can also be struck with a drumstick, hammer, or wire brush.* *n.*
☛ *Hom.* SYMBOL.

**cyme** (sīm) a flower cluster in which there is a flower at the top of the main stem and of each branch of the cluster: *The sweet william has cymes.* See INFLORESCENCE for picture. *n.*

**cyn·ic** (sin′ik) 1 a person inclined to believe that the motives for people's actions are insincere and selfish. 2 a sneering, sarcastic person. 3 CYNICAL. 1, 2 *n.*, 3 *adj.*
☛ *Etym.* From the name of a group of ancient Greek philosophers who taught that self-control is the essential part of virtue.

**cyn·i·cal** (sin′ə kəl) 1 doubting the sincerity and goodness of others. 2 sneering; sarcastic. *adj.*
—**cyn′i·cal·ly,** *adv.* —**cyn′i·cal·ness,** *n.*

**cyn·i·cism** (sin′ə siz′əm) 1 a CYNICAL quality or disposition. 2 a CYNICAL remark. *n.*

**cy·no·sure** (sī′nə shùr′ *or* sin′ə shùr′) 1 something that is the centre of attraction or interest: *She was the cynosure of all eyes.* 2 **Cynosure,** a the constellation containing the North Star, now usually called Ursa Minor, or Little Bear. b the North Star. *n.*

**cy·pher** (sī′fər) See CIPHER. *n.*, *v.*

**cy·press** (sī′prəs) 1 any of a group of closely related evergreen trees found in North America, southern Europe, and Asia, having small, scale-like, overlapping leaves and round, upright cones: *There are no cypresses native to Canada.* 2 any of several other species of evergreen tree, such as the yellow cypress, which belongs to the same family as the true cypress, and the bald cypress, which belongs to the same family as the redwoods. 3 referring to a family of coniferous trees: *The cypress family includes the true cypresses, junipers, and arborvitae.* *n.*

**cyp·ri·nid** (sip′rə nid) 1 any of a family of mainly soft-finned, freshwater fishes found in North America, Africa, Europe, and Asia, having toothless jaws, sometimes with BARBELS: *Carps, minnows, and goldfish are cyprinids.* 2 of, having to do with, or referring to this family of fishes: *The cyprinid family is also called the minnow family.* 1 *n.*, 2 *adj.*

**cyp·ri·noid** (sip′rə noid′) CYPRINID. *n.*, *adj.*

**Cyp·ri·ot** (sip′rē ət) 1 of or having to do with Cyprus, an island country in the eastern Mediterranean Sea, south of Turkey. 2 a native or inhabitant of Cyprus. 1 *adj.*, 2 *n.*

**cyp·ri·pe·di·um** (sip′rə pē′dē əm) any of a closely related group of orchids that have drooping flowers with a protruding saclike lip, including lady's-slippers. *n.*, *pl.* **cyp·ri·pe·di·a** (-dē ə).

**Cy·ril·lic** (si ril′ik) of, having to do with, or referring to an ancient Slavic alphabet from which the Russian, Ukrainian, Bulgarian, and Serbian alphabets have developed. *adj.*
☛ *Etym.* From St. *Cyril,* an apostle to the Slavs in the 9c., who is traditionally supposed to have invented it.

**cyst** (sist) 1 an abnormal, saclike growth in animals or plants that usually contains fluid and has no outside opening. 2 a saclike structure in animals or plants. *n.*

**cys·tic** (sis′tik) 1 of or like a CYST. 2 having a CYST or cysts. *adj.*

**cys·tic fib·ro·sis** (fī brō′sis) a congenital disease of some children, causing frequent respiratory infections and malfunction of the pancreas.

**cy·tol·o·gist** (sī tol′ə jist) a person who knows much about CYTOLOGY, especially one who makes it his or her work. *n.*

**cy·tol·o·gy** (sī tol′ə jē) the branch of biology that deals with the formation, structure, and function of the cells of animals and plants. *n.*

**cy·to·plasm** (sī′tə plaz′əm) the living substance or protoplasm of a cell, exclusive of the nucleus. See CELL for picture. *n.*

**cy·to·plas·mic** (sī′tə plaz′mik) having to do with CYTOPLASM. *adj.*

**czar** or **tsar** (zär) **1** emperor: *Czar was the title of the former emperors of Russia.* **2** an autocrat; person with absolute power: *Al Capone was a czar of crime.* *n.* Also, **tzar**.

**cza·ri·na** or **tsa·ri·na** (zä rē′nə) the wife of a czar; a Russian empress. *n.* Also, **tzarina**.

**Czech** (chek) **1** a native or inhabitant of the Czech Republic, a country in central Europe. **2** the Slavic language of the Czechs. **3** of or having to do with the Czech Republic, its people, or their language. 1–2 *n.*, 3 *adj.*
☛ *Hom.* CHECK, CHEQUE.

**Czech·o·slo·vak** (chek′ə slō′vak) **1** of or having to do with Czechoslovakia, formerly a country in central Europe. **2** a native or inhabitant of the former Czechoslovakia. 1 *adj.*, 2 *n.*

**Czech·o·slo·va·ki·an** (chek′ə slō vak′ē ən) CZECHOSLOVAK. *adj.*, *n.*

hat, āge, fär; let, ēqual, tėrm; it, īce
hot, ōpen, ôrder; oil, out; cup, pùt, rüle
əbove, takən, pencəl, lemən, circəs

ch, child; ng, long; sh, ship
th, thin; ᴛʜ, then; zh, measure

# D d *D d*

Daffodils

**d or D** (dē) **1** the fourth letter of the English alphabet. **2** any speech sound represented by this letter. **3** in music: **a** the second tone in the scale of C major. **b** a symbol representing this tone. **c** a key, string, etc. of a musical instrument that produces this tone. **d** the scale or key that has D as its keynote. **4** any person or thing considered as the fourth in a series. **5** a grade rating a person's work or performance as being below average and barely acceptable. **6** a person receiving such a grade. **7 D,** the Roman letter used as the numeral for 500. *n., pl.* **d's** or **D's.**

**d** **1** day. **2** deci- (an SI prefix).

*d* diameter.

**D** deuterium.

**da** deca- (an SI prefix).

**dab** (dab) **1** touch lightly; pat with something soft or moist; tap: *He dabbed at the spot with his napkin.* **2** a quick, light touch or blow; pat; tap: *The cat made a dab at the butterfly.* **3** put on with light strokes: *She dabbed some powder on her nose.* **4** a small, soft or moist mass: *a dab of butter.* **5** a little bit. 1, 3 *v.,* **dabbed, dab·bing;** 2, 4, 5 *n.* —**dab′ber,** *n.*

**dab·ble** (dab′əl) **1** dip the hands, feet, etc. in and out of water; splash. **2** work at a little; do in a half-hearted or superficial way: *to dabble at painting, to dabble in stocks.* *v.,* **dab·bled, dab·bling.** —**dab′bler,** *n.*

**dace** (dās) any of several species of small, quick freshwater fish belonging to the minnow and carp family: *The pearl dace is found from Nova Scotia west to the Peace River district.* *n., pl.* **dace** or **daces.**

**dachs·hund** (dash′hùnd′ or daks′hùnd′; *German,* däks′hùnt′) a breed of small dog having a long body, long, drooping ears, a slender muzzle, and very short legs: *The dachshund was originally developed in Germany for hunting badgers. The word means 'badger dog'.* *n.*

**dad** (dad) *Informal.* father. *n.*

**dad·dy** (dad′ē) *Informal.* father. *n., pl.* **dad·dies.**

**dad·dy–long–legs** (dad′ē long′legz′) any of several species of small animal related to the spider, having a rounded, segmented body and six very long, thin, bent legs: *Daddy-longlegs are arachnids.* *n., pl.* **dad·dy–long·legs.**

**da·do** (dā′dō) **1** the part of a pedestal between the base and the cap. **2** the lower part of an inside wall, when covered with a special finish of wood, wallpaper, etc. *n., pl.* **da·does** or **da·dos.**

**dae·mon** (dē′mən) **1** an attendant or guardian spirit. **2** in Greek mythology, a supernatural being ranking less than a god but more than a human being. *n.*
☞ *Hom.* DEMON.

**daf·fo·dil** (daf′ə dil′) **1** a narcissus having yellow, white, or partly white flowers and long, slender leaves: *The flower of a daffodil has a long, trumpet-shaped corona growing out from the centre of its petals.* **2** the flower. **3** bright yellow. 1–3 *n.,* 3 *adj.*

**daft** (daft) **1** silly; foolish. **2** crazy; insane. *adj.* —**daft′ly,** *adv.* —**daft′ness,** *n.*

**dag·ger** (dag′ər) **1** a small weapon with a short, pointed blade, used for stabbing. **2** in printing, a sign (†) used to refer the reader to a footnote, a note at the back of the book, etc. *n.*
**look daggers at,** look at with hatred or anger.

**da·guerre·o·type** (də ger′ə tīp′) **1** an early photographic process: *In daguerreotype, the pictures were made on light-sensitive silver-coated metal plates.* **2** a picture made in this way. *n.*

**dahl·ia** (dā′lyə *or* dal′yə) **1** a tall plant of the same family as the aster, which has large, showy flowers in the fall. **2** the flower of this plant. *n.*

**dai·ly** (dā′lē) **1** done, happening, or appearing every day, or every day but Sunday: *a daily paper, a daily visit.* **2** a newspaper appearing every day, or every day but Sunday. **3** every day; day by day: *He visited her daily while she was in hospital.* 1 *adj.,* 2 *n., pl.* **dai·lies;** 3 *adv.*

**dain·ti·ness** (dān′tē nis) the quality of being DAINTY. *n.*

**dain·ty** (dān′tē) **1** having delicate beauty; pretty and graceful: *a dainty flower.* **2** having or showing delicate and refined tastes and feeling; particular: *She is dainty about her eating.* **3** overly refined and delicate; too particular. **4** good to eat; delicious: *a dainty morsel.* **5** something very good to eat; a delicious bit of food. 1–4 *adj.,* **dain·ti·er, dain·ti·est;** 5 *n., pl.* **dain·ties.** —**dain′ti·ly,** *adv.*

**dair·y** (der′ē) **1** a room or building where milk and cream are kept and made into butter and cheese. **2** a business that processes and sells or distributes milk and milk products. **3** DAIRY FARM. *n., pl.* **dair·ies.**

**dairy cattle** cows kept for the milk they give.

**dairy farm** a farm where milk and milk products are produced.

**dair·y·maid** (der′ē mād′) a girl or woman who works in a dairy. *n.*

**dair·y·man** (der′ē mən) **1** a person who owns or manages a dairy farm. **2** a person who works in a dairy. *n., pl.* **dair·y·men** (-mən).

**da·is** (dā′is) a raised platform at one end of a hall or large room: *A throne, seats of honour, a lecture desk, etc. are set on a dais.* *n.*
☞ *Etym.* See note at DISH.

**dai·sy** (dā′zē) **1** any of a number of closely related plants of the COMPOSITE family, especially the **ox-eye daisy,** a common wildflower and weed introduced to North

America from its native Europe, or the **Shasta daisy,** a popular garden flower: *Daisies have tall, leafy stems and showy flower heads consisting of a yellow central disk surrounded by usually white, petal-like ray flowers.* **2** any of various other plants of the COMPOSITE family, such as the **English daisy** or **Michaelmas daisy,** which are grown as garden flowers. **3** the flower of any of these plants. *n., pl.* **dai·sies.** —**dai′sy-like,** *adj.*
☞ *Etym.* OE *dæges ēage* 'eye of day'. The flower was given this name for its bright-yellow central disk surrounded by radiating petals which close at night.

**daisy wheel** a wheel that produces the printing in an electronic typewriter or computer printer.

**Da·ko·ta** (də kō′tə) **1** a member of a First Nations or Native American people living on the plains of southern Canada and the northern United States. **2** the language of these people. **3** of or having to do with the Dakotas or their language. *1, 2 n., pl.* **Da·ko·tas** or **Da·ko·ta;** *3 adj.*

**Da·lai La·ma** (dä lī′ lä′mə) the chief priest of the religion of Lamaism in Tibet and Mongolia.

**dale** (dāl) valley. *n.*

**dalles** (dal′əs *or* dalz) *Cdn.* **1** a natural slide or chute in a river; rapids. **2** a narrow stretch of river between high rock walls, with whirlpools, rapids, and treacherous currents. *n. pl.*

**dal·li·ance** (dal′ē əns) **1** flirtation. **2** a playing; trifling. *n.*

**dal·ly** (dal′ē) **1** loiter; linger idly; waste time: *He was late because he dallied along the way. She dallied away the whole afternoon.* **2** play or toy (*with*): *She dallied with her necklace as she spoke.* **3** behave in a playful manner, especially flirt (with a person). *v.,* **dal·lied, dal·ly·ing.**

**Dal·ma·tian** (dal mā′shən) **1** a breed of medium-sized, short-haired dog, usually white with black spots; coach dog. **2** a native or inhabitant of Dalmatia, a region in Yugoslavia. **3** of or having to do with Dalmatia or its people. *1, 2 n., 3 adj.*

**dam¹** (dam) **1** a wall built to hold back flowing water. **2** the water held back by a dam. **3** anything resembling a dam. **4** provide with a dam; hold back by means of a dam: *Beavers had dammed the stream.* **5** hold back; block: *He tried to dam back his tears.* *1–3 n., 4, 5 v.,* **dammed, dam·ming.** —**dam′like′,** *adj.*
☞ *Hom.* DAMN.

**dam²** (dam) the female parent of four-footed animals. *n.*
☞ *Hom.* DAMN.

**dam·age** (dam′ij) **1** injury or harm that lessens value or usefulness: *The accident did very little damage to the car.* **2** injure or harm so as to lessen value or usefulness; harm; hurt: *I damaged my sweater in football practice.* **3 damages,** *pl.* the money claimed by law or paid to make up for some harm done to a person or property: *The man who was hit by the car asked for $5000 damages.* *1, 3 n., 2 v.,* **dam·aged, dam·ag·ing.** —**dam′age·a·ble,** *adj.* —**dam′ag·ing·ly,** *adv.*

**Da·mas·cus steel** (də mas′kəs) a kind of ornamented steel, used in making swords, etc.

**dam·ask** (dam′əsk) **1** reversible linen, silk, or cotton fabric with woven designs: *hangings of damask.* **2** a linen material of this type, used especially for tablecloths and serviettes. **3** made of damask. **4** pink; rose-coloured: *damask cheeks.* **5** a rose colour; pink. *1, 2, 5 n., 3, 4 adj.*

# daisy wheel 307 damsel

hat, āge, fär; let, ēqual, tėrm; it, īce
hot, ōpen, ôrder; oil, out; cup, pùt, rüle
əbove, takən, pencəl, lemən, circəs
ch, child; ng, long; sh, ship
th, thin; ᴛʜ, then; zh, measure

**dame** (dām) **1** in former times, a lady. **2** an elderly woman. **3 Dame, a** in the United Kingdom, the title of a woman who belongs to an order of knighthood. It is used before the given name. **b** the legal title of the wife or widow of a knight or baronet. **c** in former times, a title given to a woman in authority in a household. *n.*

**damn** (dam) **1** declare to be bad or inferior; condemn: *The critics damned the new book.* **2** cause to fail; ruin. **3** doom to eternal punishment; condemn to hell. **4** swear or swear at by saying "damn"; curse. **5** a saying of "damn"; a curse. *1–4 v., 5 n., interj.*
**damn with faint praise,** praise with so little enthusiasm as to condemn.
☞ *Hom.* DAM.

**dam·na·ble** (dam′nə bəl) **1** abominable; outrageous; detestable. **2** deserving damnation. *adj.* —**dam′na·bly,** *adv.*

**dam·na·tion** (dam nā′shən) **1** a damning or being damned; condemnation. **2** a condemnation to eternal punishment. **3** a curse. *n.*

**damned** (damd) **1** condemned as bad or inferior. **2** doomed to eternal punishment. **3** cursed; abominable. **4 the damned,** the souls in hell. **5** pt. and pp. of DAMN. *1–3 adj., 4 n., 5 v.*

**Dam·o·cles** (dam′ə klēz′) a flatterer and courtier of Dionysius, king of Syracuse. Damocles thought Dionysius must be the happiest of men, but Dionysius asked him to share the happiness of a king. He gave a banquet for Damocles, seating his guest beneath a naked sword that hung above his head by a single hair. Thus Damocles was made aware of the dangers surrounding kings. *n.*
**sword of Damocles,** any imminent danger.

**Da·mon** (dā′mən) in Roman legend, a man who pledged his life for his friend Pythias, who had been sentenced to death. *n.*
**Damon and Pythias,** any loyal and devoted friends.

**damp** (damp) **1** slightly wet; moist: *My house is damp in rainy weather.* **2** moisture: *One could feel the damp in the morning air.* **3** moisten; DAMPEN (def. 1). **4** anything that checks or deadens: *His ill-humoured objections put a damp on our spirits.* **5** slow down the combustion of a fire by cutting off most of the air supply: *She damped down the fire for the night.* **6** discourage; check: *Weariness damped the traveller's enthusiasm.* **7** any foul or explosive gas that collects in mines, such as CHOKEDAMP or FIREDAMP: *The mine disaster was caused by exploding damp.* *1 adj., 2, 4, 7 n., 3, 5, 6 v.* —**damp′ly,** *adv.* —**damp′ness,** *n.*

**damp·en** (dam′pən) **1** make moist or slightly wet: *We dampen clothes before ironing them.* **2** deaden; depress; discourage: *The bad news dampened our spirits.* *v.* —**damp′en·er,** *n.*

**damp·er** (dam′pər) **1** a person or thing that discourages or depresses. **2** a movable plate to control the draft in a stove or furnace. **3** a device for checking vibration, especially of piano strings. *n.*

**dam·sel** (dam′zəl) a maiden or young girl. *n.*

**dam·son** (dam′zən)  1 a small, dark-purple plum.  2 the tree that it grows on.  *n.*

**dance** (dans)  1 move in rhythm, usually in time with music: *Helen can dance very well.*  2 a movement in rhythm, usually in time with music.  3 some special group of steps, etc.: *The waltz and fox trot are well-known dances.*  4 do or take part in a dance.  5 one round of dancing.  6 a piece of music for dancing.  7 a party where people dance.  8 jump up and down; move in a lively way: *See that boat dancing on the water.*  9 bob up and down.  10 cause to dance; lead or conduct by dancing: *He danced his partner across the ballroom floor.*  11 a movement up and down; lively movement.  12 of or for dancing.   1, 4, 8–10 *v.*, **danced, danc·ing;**   2, 3, 5–7, 11, 12 *n.* —**danc′ing·ly,** *adv.*

**dance attendance on,**  wait on often and attentively; be excessively polite and obedient to.

**dance hall**  a public hall or room in which dances are held.

**danc·er** (dan′sər)  1 a person who dances.  2 a person whose occupation is dancing.  *n.*

**dan·de·li·on** (dan′də lī′ən)  any of a closely related group of plants of the COMPOSITE family, native to Europe and Asia but now found throughout the temperate regions of North America, having long, often toothed leaves radiating from the base of the plant and a single, bright-yellow flower head made up of many ray flowers: *The common dandelion occurs as a weed throughout Canada and is also grown for its edible leaves and flowers.*  *n.*

**dan·dle** (dan′dəl)  1 move a child up and down on one's knees or in one's arms.  2 pet; pamper.  *v.*, **dan·dled, dan·dling.** —**dan′dler,** *n.*

**dan·druff** (dan′drəf)  small, whitish scales that flake off the scalp.  *n.*

**dan·dy** (dan′dē)  1 a man who is too careful of his dress and appearance.  2 of a dandy; too carefully dressed.  3 *Informal.*  anything that is excellent or pleasing.  4 *Informal.*  excellent; first-rate: *Everything is just dandy.*   1, 3 *n.*, *pl.* **dan·dies;**   2, 4 *adj.*, **dan·di·er, dan·di·est.**

**Dane** (dān)  1 a native or inhabitant of Denmark, a country in northern Europe.  2 a person of Danish descent.  3 formerly, a person from any part of what is now Scandinavia: *King Alfred fought many battles against the Danes.*  *n.*
☛ *Hom.* DEIGN.

**dan·ger** (dān′jər)  1 a chance of harm; nearness to harm; risk or peril: *A mountain climber's life is full of danger.*  2 anything that may cause harm: *Hidden rocks are a danger to ships.*  *n.*

**in danger of,**  liable to (with the accompanying threat of injury, harm, or death): *The old bridge is in danger of collapsing. The sick man is in danger of dying.*

**dan·ger·ous** (dān′jə rəs)  likely to cause harm; not safe; risky: *The mountain road is dangerous.*  *adj.* —**dan′ger·ous·ly,** *adv.*  —**dan′ger·ous·ness,** *n.*

**dan·gle** (dang′gəl)  1 hang and swing loosely: *The curtain cord dangles.*  2 hold or carry something so that it swings loosely: *The nurse dangled the toys in front of the baby.*  3 be a hanger-on or follower: *He was always dangling after the older boys.*  4 hold before a person as a temptation: *to dangle false hopes before a person.*  *v.*, **dan·gled, dan·gling.** —**dan′gler,** *n.*

**Dan·iel** (dan′yəl)  an upright judge or other person of great wisdom.  *n.*
☛ *Etym.* From the name of a Hebrew prophet whose great faith in God kept him unharmed in the lions' den.

**Dan·ish** (dā′nish)  1 of or having to do with Denmark, its people, or their language.  2 the language of Denmark.  3 *Informal.*  DANISH PASTRY: *Let's have a Danish for dessert.*   1 *adj.*, 2, 3 *n.*

**Danish pastry**  a rich, flaky pastry made with yeast.

**dank** (dangk)  unpleasantly damp; moist; wet: *The cave was dark, dank, and chilly.*  *adj.* —**dank′ly,** *adv.* —**dank′ness,** *n.*

**daph·ni·a** (daf′nē ə)  a freshwater crustacean used as food for aquarium fish.  *n.*, *pl.* **daph·ni·a.**

**dap·per** (dap′ər)  1 neat; trim; spruce.  2 small and active.  *adj.* —**dap′per·ly,** *adv.*  —**dap′per·ness,** *n.*

**dap·ple** (dap′əl)  1 spotted: *a dapple horse.*  2 a spotted appearance or condition.  3 an animal having a spotted or mottled skin.  4 mark or become marked with spots: *The lawn under the trees was dappled with spots of sunlight.*   1 *adj.*, 2, 3 *n.*, 4 *v.*, **dap·pled, dap·pling.**

**dap·pled** (dap′əld)  1 spotted.  2 pt. and pp. of DAPPLE.   1 *adj.*, 2 *v.*

**dap·ple–grey** (dap′əl grā′)  grey with spots of darker grey.  *adj.*

**dare** (der)  1 have courage; be bold; be bold enough to: *He doesn't dare dive from the bridge.*  2 have courage; not be afraid of; face or meet boldly: *The explorer dared the dangers of the Arctic.*  3 meet and resist; face and defy.  4 challenge: *I dare you to jump.*  5 a challenge: *Will you take the dare?*   1–4 *v.*, **dared** or **durst, dared, dar·ing;**   5 *n.* —**dar′er,** *n.*

**I dare say,**  probably; maybe; perhaps: *I dare say her success was due to hard work.*

**dare·dev·il** (der′dev′əl)  1 a recklessly adventurous person; one who does bold and dangerous things that are unnecessary.  2 reckless: *a daredevil stunt.*   1 *n.*, 2 *adj.*

**dar·ing** (der′ing)  1 the courage to take risks; boldness.  2 courageous; bold.  3 ppr. of DARE.   1 *n.*, 2 *adj.*, 3 *v.* —**dar′ing·ly,** *adv.*  —**dar′ing·ness,** *n.*

**dark** (därk)  1 without light or with very little light: *the dark side of the moon. It was a dark, moonless night. I thought he must be in bed, because his window was dark.*  2 the time when the dark of night begins; nightfall: *The children are not allowed out after dark. They waited until dark to continue their journey.*  3 allowing only some light to pass through: *She was wearing her dark glasses.*  4 not light-complexioned: *a dark skin, dark good looks.*  5 deep in shade; closer in colour to black than white: *dark green, white lettering on a dark background, dark hair.*  6 a dark colour: *There was a striking contrast between the darks and lights in the painting.*  7 secret; hidden: *He kept his past dark.*  8 evil; wicked: *a dark deed.*  9 gloomy and sad; dismal: *Those were dark days. Don't always look on the dark side of things.*  10 sullen or angry: *She gave him a dark look.*  11 hard to understand; obscure: *dark sayings.*  12 ignorant; unenlightened: *a culturally dark age.*  13 **the dark,**  the absence of light; darkness: *He's afraid of the dark. It was a shock to step from the dark of the cave into the sunlight.*   1, 3–5, 7–12 *adj.*, 2, 6, 13 *n.* —**dark′ly,** *adv.*  —**dark′ness,** *n.*

**in the dark,**  not knowing or understanding; in ignorance: *I'm still in the dark about what I'm supposed to do on the project.*

**Dark Ages** **1** the early part of the Middle Ages in Europe, from the 5th to the 11th century. **2** the period between ancient and modern times, from about A.D. 500 to about A.D.1450; the MIDDLE AGES.

**dark·en** (där′kən) **1** make dark or darker. **2** become dark or darker. *v.*

**dark horse** **1** an unexpected winner that little is known about. **2** a person who is unexpectedly nominated for a political or other office.

**dark·ish** (där′kish) somewhat dark. *adj.*

**dark lantern** a lantern whose light can be hidden by a cover or a dark glass.

**dark·room** (där′krüm′) a room arranged for developing photographs: *A darkroom usually has a very dim, coloured light.* *n.*

**dar·ling** (där′ling) **1** a person very dear to another; a person much loved. **2** very dear. **3** a favourite: *He's the darling of the jet set.* **4** *Informal.* very attractive; pleasing; charming: *a darling little hat.* **1, 3** *n.,* **2, 4** *adj.*

**darn**[1] (därn) **1** mend by weaving rows of thread or yarn across a hole or torn place. **2** the act of darning. **3** a place mended by darning. **1** *v.,* **2, 3** *n.*

**darn**[2] (därn) *Informal.* a EUPHEMISM for the word **damn** used to express annoyance, irritation, or anger. *n., v., adj., adv., interj.*

**dar·nel** (där′nəl) a weed that resembles rye: *Darnel often grows in grain fields.* *n.*

**darn·ing** (där′ning) **1** the act of mending with stitches. **2** articles darned or to be darned. **3** ppr. of DARN. **1, 2** *n.,* **3** *v.*

**darning needle** **1** a long needle with a large eye for heavy thread, used for darning. **2** DRAGONFLY.

**dart** (därt) **1** a small, slender, pointed missile usually having feathers at the back, for throwing by hand or shooting from a tube or gun. **2** throw or shoot suddenly and quickly: *The hunter darted the spear at the seal.* **3** move suddenly and quickly: *The deer darted away. She darted across the street.* **4** a sudden quick movement: *He made a dart for the window.* **5** direct or send suddenly: *She darted an angry glance at her sister.* **6** a sharp look, word, etc. **7** a tapered fold, or tuck, in a garment to shape it to a part of the body or to make it hang better: *Long, narrow sleeves usually have darts at the elbow.* **8 darts,** an indoor game in which players throw darts at a round board marked off in concentric circles and numbered radiating sections (*used with a singular verb*). **1, 4, 6–8** *n.,* **2, 3, 5** *v.*

**dash** (dash) **1** throw: *We dashed water over him.* **2** splash: *She dashed some paint on the paper and called it a tree.* **3** rush: *They dashed by in a car.* **4** strike violently against something: *She dashed her head against the wall when she fell.* **5** smash: *He dashed the bowl to bits on a rock.* **6** ruin: *Our hopes were dashed.* **7** depress; discourage. **8** anything that depresses or discourages a check: *The accident was a dash to our hopes.* **9** mix with a small amount of something else. **10** a small amount: *Put in just a dash of pepper.* **11** a short race: *the hundred-metre dash.* **12** in writing or printing, a mark (—) used especially to show a break in sense or in the structure of a sentence. **13** in telegraphy, a long sound or signal that represents a letter or part of a letter: *Morse code uses dots and dashes.* **14** DASHBOARD (def. 1). **15** energy; spirit; liveliness. **16** showy appearance or behaviour. **1–7, 9** *v.,* **8, 10–16** *n.*

hat, āge, fär; let, ēqual, tėrm; it, īce
hot, ōpen, ôrder; oil, out; cup, pùt, rüle
əbove, takən, pencəl, lemən, circəs
ch, child; ng, long; sh, ship
th, thin; ᴛн, then; zh, measure

**dash off,** do, make, write, etc. quickly: *He dashed off a short letter to his friend.*

**dash·board** (dash′bôrd′) **1** a panel with controls and gauges below the windshield in front of the operator in an automobile, aircraft, etc. **2** a screen on the front of a wagon, boat, etc. to provide protection from splashing mud or water. *n.*

**dash·er** (dash′ər) **1** one that dashes. **2** a device with blades for stirring the cream in a churn or ice-cream freezer. **3** *Cdn.* the fence surrounding the ice of a hockey rink; the boards. *n.*

**dash·ing** (dash′ing) **1** full of energy and spirit; lively. **2** showy. **3** ppr. of DASH. **1, 2** *adj.,* **3** *v.* —**dash′ing·ly,** *adv.*

**das·tard** (das′tərd) **1** a mean coward; a sneak. **2** mean and cowardly; sneaking. *n.*

**das·tard·ly** (das′tər dlē) like a dastard; mean and cowardly; sneaking. *adj.* —**das′tard·li·ness,** *n.*

**da·ta** (dā′tə *or* dat′ə) facts; things known or accepted; information from which conclusions can be drawn: *Names, ages, and other data about the class are written in the teacher's record book.* *n., pl.* of **datum.**
☛ *Usage.* In informal English **data** is often used with a singular verb when it refers to a group of facts considered together: *The data you have collected is not enough to convince me.* In formal English, however, **data** is always treated as a plural: *The data are now being analysed.*

**data bank** DATA BASE.

**data base** or **da·ta·base** (dā′tə bās′ *or* dat′ə bās′) information stored in a computer for easy access and retrieval. *n.*

**data processing** the use of a DATA BASE to produce such things as financial statements, lists of books divided into categories, etc.

**date**[1] (dāt) **1** the time when something happens or happened: *1492 is the date of the discovery of America by Columbus.* **2** a statement of time: *There is a date stamped on every piece of Canadian money.* **3** mark with a date; put a date on: *Please date your letter.* **4** find out the date of; give a date to: *The scientist was unable to date the fossil.* **5** a period of time: *At that date there were no airplanes.* **6** belong to a certain period of time; have its origin (*usually used with* **from**): *That house dates from the late 18th century.* **7** an appointment for a certain time, especially for a social engagement with a person of the opposite sex: *She's made a date with him for Saturday.* **8** the social engagement itself: *She said it was a boring date. He's out on a date.* **9** *Informal.* the person with whom one has such an engagement: *Who's your date for the dance?* **10** make a social appointment with a person of the opposite sex: *He's been trying for months to date her.* **11** go out regularly with a particular person of the opposite sex; go on dates: *They've been dating for a long time. She dates a fellow from another school.* **1, 2, 5, 7–9** *n.,* **3, 4, 6, 10, 11** *v.,* **dat·ed, dat·ing.**

**out-of-date,** old-fashioned; not in present use: *That dress looks out-of-date.*

**to date,** till now; up to the present moment; yet: *There have been no replies to date.*

**up-to-date, a** to the present time. **b** modern; according to the latest style or idea; in fashion: *His clothes are always up-to-date.*

**date²** (dāt) **1** the oblong, fleshy, sweet fruit of a kind of palm tree. **2** a DATE PALM. *n.*

**dat·ed** (dā′tid) **1** marked with a date; showing a date on it. **2** out-of-date. **3** pt. and pp. of DATE. 1, 2 *adj.*, 3 *v.*

**date·less** (dā′tlis) **1** without a date; not dated. **2** endless; unlimited. **3** so old that it cannot be given a date. **4** old but still admirable, in good style, etc. *adj.*

**date line 1** an imaginary line agreed upon as the place where each calendar day first begins. It runs north and south through the Pacific, mostly along the 180th meridian. When it is Sunday just east of the date line, it is Monday just west of it. **2** a line in a letter, newspaper, etc. giving the date and place of writing.

**date palm** a palm tree on which dates grow.

**da·tive** (dā′tiv) **1** of, having to do with, or being the grammatical case that in many languages shows that a noun, pronoun, or adjective is an indirect object of a verb or an object of any of certain prepositions: *German and Latin have a dative case. English has no dative case, but expresses such a grammatical relationship by prepositions such as* to *or* for *and through word order.* **2** the dative case. **3** a word in this case. 1 *adj.*, 2, 3 *n.*

**da·tum** (dā′təm *or* dat′əm) a fact from which conclusions can be drawn. *n., pl.* **da·ta.**

**daub** (dob) **1** coat or cover with plaster, clay, mud, etc. **2** apply greasy or sticky stuff. **3** anything daubed on. **4** make dirty; soil; stain. **5** paint unskilfully. **6** a badly painted picture. 1, 2, 4, 5 *v.*, 3, 6 *n.* —**daub′er,** *n.*

**daugh·ter** (dot′ər) **1** a female child (immediate descendant of parents). **2** a female descendant. **3** a girl or woman thought of as related to something in the same way that a child is related to its parents: *a daughter of France.* **4** anything thought of as a daughter in relation to its origin: *Skill is the daughter of hard work.* *n.*

**daughter element** an element produced by the decay of a radio-active element.

**daugh·ter-in-law** (dot′ə rin lo′) the wife of one's son. *n., pl.* **daugh·ters-in-law.**

**daugh·ter·ly** (dot′ər lē) **1** of a daughter. **2** like that of a daughter. **3** proper for a daughter. *adj.*

**daunt** (dont) frighten; discourage: *Danger did not daunt the explorer.* *v.*

**daunt·less** (don′tlis) not to be frightened or discouraged; brave: *She is a dauntless pilot.* *adj.* —**daunt′less·ly,** *adv.*

**dau·phin** (dof′ən; *French,* dō faN′) from 1349 to 1830, the title of the oldest son of the king of France. *n.*

**dav·en·port** (dav′ən pôrt′) **1** a long couch having a back and arms; a chesterfield or sofa: *Some davenports can be opened up to make a bed.* **2** a writing desk with drawers and a hinged shelf to write on. *n.*

**dav·it** (dav′it *or* dā′vit) **1** one of a pair of curved arms at the side of a ship, used to hold or lower a small boat. **2** a crane for raising or lowering the anchor of a ship. *n.*

**Da·vy Jones** (dā′vē jōnz′) the evil spirit of the sea; the sailor's devil.

**Davy Jones's locker** the sea, especially as the grave of those who have drowned or been buried at sea.

**daw** (do) JACKDAW. *n.*

**daw·dle** (dod′əl) waste time; idle; loiter: *Don't dawdle over your work.* *v.*, **daw·dled, daw·dling.** —**daw′dler,** *n.*

**dawn** (don) **1** the break of day; the first light in the east. **2** the beginning: *before the dawn of history.* **3** grow light: *The day dawned bright and clear.* **4** grow clear to the eye or mind: *It dawned on me that she was expecting a present.* **5** begin; appear: *A new era is dawning.* 1, 2 *n.*, 3–5 *v.*
☛ Hom. DON.

**day** (dā) **1** the time between sunrise and sunset: *Days are longer in summer than in winter.* **2** the light of day; daylight: *When he awoke, it was already day.* **3** the 24 hours of day and night; the time it takes the earth to turn once on its axis: *There are 31 days in January.* **4** in astronomy, the time needed by any celestial body to turn once on its axis. **5** a certain day on which something happened, set aside for a particular purpose or for celebration: *Christmas Day.* **6** the hours for work: *She works a seven-hour day.* **7** a certain period of time: *the present day, in days of old.* **8** a period of life, activity, power, or influence: *He has had his day.* **9** the conflict or contest of a particular day: *Our team won the day. The day is ours.* *n.*

**call it a day,** *Informal.* stop work: *I'm tired; let's call it a day.*

**day·break** (dā′brāk′) DAWN (def. 1); the time when it first begins to get light in the morning. *n.*

**day camp** a summer camp for children in which they have daytime activities as at a regular camp but return home for the night.

**day-care** (dā′ker′) **1** of, having to do with, or providing care and training for babies and preschool children outside the home during the day: *She takes her baby to the neighbourhood day-care centre every morning on her way to work.* **2** the care and training of babies and preschool children outside the home during the day: *The taxpayers were asking for more funds for day-care.* 1 *adj.*, 2 *n.*

**day coach** an ordinary railway passenger car.

**day·dream** (dā′drēm′) **1** a dreamy thinking about pleasant things. **2** a pleasant plan or fancy, unlikely to come true. **3** think dreamily about pleasant things. 1, 2 *n.*, 3 *v.*, **day·dreamed** *or* **day·dreamt, day·dream·ing.**

**day·light** (dā′līt′) **1** the light of day: *Artificial light is not as good for the eyes as daylight.* **2** the daytime. **3** the DAWN (def. 1); daybreak: *He was up at daylight.* **4** publicity; openness. **5** open space; a gap. *n.*

**daylight-saving time** time that is one hour in advance of standard time and so gives more daylight after working hours: *Clocks are set ahead one hour in the spring and back one hour in the fall to allow for daylight-saving time.*

**day·lin·er** (dā′lī′nər) a railway train which runs express between two cities, or between suburbs and a city, during the day. *n.*

**day·long** (dā′long′) through the whole day. *adj., adv.*

**day nursery** a nursery for the care of small children during the day.

**day school** 1 a school held in the daytime. 2 a private school for students who live at home.

**days of grace** the three extra days allowed for payment after a bill or note falls due.

**day·time** (dā′tīm′) the time when it is day. *n.*

**daze** (dāz) 1 confuse; bewilder; cause to feel stupid; stun: *She was so dazed by her fall that she didn't know where she was.* 2 dazzle. 3 a confused state of mind; bewilderment: *He was in a daze from the accident and he could not understand what was happening.* 1, 2 *v.*, **dazed, daz·ing;** 3 *n.*

**daz·zle** (daz′əl) 1 confuse, dim, or overpower the eyes with too bright or with quick-moving lights: *To look straight at the sun dazzles the eyes.* 2 overcome the sight or the mind by brightness, display, etc.: *The young pianist's performance dazzled the critics.* 3 the act or fact of dazzling; bewildering brightness: *the dazzle of powerful electric lights.* 1, 2 *v.*, **daz·zled, daz·zling;** 3 *n.*
—**daz′zling·ly,** *adv.* —**daz′zler,** *n.*

**dB** decibel.

**dbl.** double.

**D.C.** or **d.c.** direct current.

**D–day** (dē′dā′) 1 in World War II, the day when the Allies landed in France; June 6, 1944. 2 the day on which a previously planned military attack is to be made or on which an operation is to be started. *n.*

**DDT** a chemical compound that is a very powerful and long-lasting poison, formerly much used as an insecticide.
☛ *Etym.* From *d*ichloro-*d*iphenyl-*t*richloro-ethane.

**de–** a prefix meaning: 1 do the opposite of, as in *decamp, decentralize, demobilize.* 2 down, as in *depress, descend.* 3 away; off, as in *deport, detract.* 4 cause to leave something, as in *derail.* 5 entirely; completely, as in *despoil.* 6 remove, as in *defrost.*

**dead** (ded) 1 no longer living; that has died: *dead flowers.* 2 without life. 3 like death: *in a dead faint.* 4 not active; dull; quiet. 5 without force, power, spirit, or feeling. 6 no longer in use: *dead languages.* 7 out of play; not in the game: *a dead ball.* 8 *Informal.* very tired; worn-out. 9 sure; certain: *a dead shot, a dead certainty.* 10 complete; absolute: *a dead loss, dead silence.* 11 completely; absolutely: *You are dead right.* 12 directly; straight: *Walk dead ahead two kilometres.* 13 the time of greatest darkness, quiet, cold, etc.: *the dead of night.* 14 **the dead,** those who are dead; all who no longer have life: *We remember the dead of our wars on Remembrance Day.* 1–10 *adj.*, 11, 12 *adv.*, 13, 14 *n.*
—**dead′ness,** *n.*

**dead·en** (ded′ən) 1 make dull or weak; lessen the intenseness or force of: *Some medicines are given to deaden pain. The force of the blow was deadened by his heavy clothing.* 2 reduce the sound of: *Thick walls deaden the noises from the street.* *v.*

**dead end** 1 a street, passage, etc. closed at one end. 2 a point in a discussion, plan, etc. beyond which progress is impossible: *When the committee reached a dead end, they decided to drop the plan.*

**dead·eye** (ded′ī′) a round, flat, wooden block that is used to fasten the shrouds of a ship. See SHROUD for picture. *n.*

**dead·fall** (ded′fol′) 1 a trap for animals made so that

**day nursery**     311     **deal**

hat, āge, fär; let, ēqual, tėrm; it, īce
hot, ōpen, ôrder; oil, out; cup, put, rüle
əbove, takən, pencəl, lemən, circəs
ch, child; ng, long; sh, ship
th, thin; ᴛʜ, then; zh, measure

a heavy weight falls upon and holds or kills the animal. 2 a mass of fallen trees and underbrush. *n.*

**dead·head** (ded′hed′) 1 *Informal.* a person who rides on a bus, train, etc. or sees a game or show without paying. 2 a train, railway car, truck, etc. travelling without passengers or freight. 3 *Cdn.* a log or fallen tree partly or entirely submerged in water, usually with one end embedded in the bottom. *n.*

**dead heat** a race that ends in a tie.

**dead letter** 1 an unclaimed letter; a letter that cannot be delivered or returned to the sender because the address is wrong, impossible to read, or incomplete. 2 a law, rule, etc. that is not enforced.

**dead·line** (ded′līn′) 1 a time limit; the latest possible time to do something. 2 a line or boundary that must not be crossed. *n.*

**dead·lock** (ded′lok′) 1 a position in which it is impossible to act or continue because of disagreement: *Employers and strikers were at a deadlock.* 2 bring or come to such a position: *The talks were deadlocked for weeks.* 1 *n.*, 2 *v.*

**dead·ly** (ded′lē) 1 causing death; liable to cause death; fatal: *a deadly wound, the deadly berries of a poisonous bush.* 2 like death: *deadly paleness* (*adj.*), *deadly pale* (*adv.*). 3 filled with hatred that lasts till death: *deadly enemies.* 4 causing death of the spirit: *deadly sin.* 5 *Informal.* extreme; intense. 6 *Informal.* extremely. 7 dull: *The party was a deadly affair.* 1–5, 7 *adj.*, **dead·li·er, dead·li·est;** 2, 6 *adv.*
☛ *Syn.* See note at FATAL.

**deadly nightshade** 1 BLACK NIGHTSHADE. 2 BELLADONNA.

**dead·pan** (ded′pan′) *Informal.* 1 an expressionless face. 2 without expression: *a deadpan face.* 3 in a deadpan manner. 4 act, tell, or behave in a deadpan manner: *deadpan a joke. The clown deadpanned all through the scene.* 1 *n.*, 2 *adj.*, 3 *adv.*, 4 *v.*, **dead·panned, dead·pan·ning.**

**dead reckoning** the calculation of the location of a ship or aircraft without observations of the sun, stars, etc., by using a compass and studying the record of the voyage.

**dead weight** 1 the heavy weight of anything inert. 2 a very great or oppressive burden.

**deaf** (def) 1 not able to hear. 2 not able to hear well. 3 not willing to hear; heedless: *A miser is deaf to all requests for money.* *adj.* —**deaf′ly,** *adv.* —**deaf′ness,** *n.*

**deaf·en** (def′ən) 1 make deaf. 2 stun with noise. 3 drown out by a louder sound. *v.* —**deaf′en·ing,** *adj.*
—**deaf′en·ing·ly,** *adv.*

**deaf–mute** (def′myüt′) a person who is deaf and cannot speak. *n.*

**deal¹** (dēl) 1 have to do (*with*): *Arithmetic deals with numbers.* 2 occupy oneself; take action: *The courts deal with those who break the laws.* 3 act or behave: *Deal fairly with everyone.* 4 do business; buy and sell: *A butcher deals in meat.* 5 *Informal.* a bargain; a

**deal** business arrangement: *If you buy this television set now, I can give you a good deal.* **6** give: *One fighter dealt the other a blow.* **7** give a share of to each; distribute. **8** *Informal.* a distribution; arrangement; plan: *a new deal.* **9** distribute playing cards. **10** in card games, the distribution of cards. **11** a player's turn to deal. **12** the time during which one deal of cards is being played. **13** a quantity; amount: *I took a deal of trouble.* 1–4, 6, 7, 9 *v.*, **dealt, deal·ing;** 5, 8, 10–13 *n.*
**deal out,** give out or distribute.
**a good deal** or **a great deal, a** a large part, portion, or amount: *She spends a great deal of her money on holiday trips.* **b** to a great extent or degree; much: *He smokes a good deal.*
**square deal,** an honest business transaction; a fair arrangement.

**deal²** (dēl) **1** a board of pine or fir, usually more than 7 inches wide and 6 feet long and less than 3 inches thick (about $18 \times 180 \times 7.6$ cm). **2** pine or fir wood in the form of deals. **3** made of deal: *a deal table. n.*

**deal·er** (dē′lər) **1** a person who trades; any person engaged in buying and selling. **2** in a card game, a person who distributes the cards to the players. *n.*

**deal·er·ship** (dē′lər ship′) the business, franchise, or territory of a dealer. *n.*

**deal·ing** (dē′ling) **1** a way of doing business: *The storekeeper is respected for his honest dealing.* **2** a way of acting; behaviour toward others: *Mr. Just is honoured for his fair dealing.* **3** the act or process of distributing. **4 dealings,** *pl.* **a** business relations: *The fur trader was honest in his dealings with the trappers.* **b** actions; behaviour: *The teacher tried to be fair in all his dealings with students.* **5** ppr. of DEAL. 1–4 *n.*, 5 *v.*

**dealt** (delt) pt. and pp. of DEAL¹: *The knight dealt his enemy a blow. The cards are dealt. v.*

**dean** (dēn) **1** the head of a division or school in a college or university. **2** a member of the faculty of a college or university who has charge of the behaviour or studies of the students. **3** a high official of a church: *A dean is often in charge of a cathedral.* **4** the member who has belonged to a group longest. *n.*

**dean·er·y** (dē′nə rē) **1** the position or authority of a DEAN (def. 3). **2** the residence of a DEAN (def. 3). *n., pl.* **dean·er·ies.**

**dean·ship** (dēn′ship) the position, office, or rank of a DEAN (defs. 1–3). *n.*

**dear** (dēr) **1** much loved; precious: *His sister was very dear to him.* **2** a dear one: *"Come, my dear," said Mother.* **3** with affection; fondly: *He held his wife dear.* **4** much valued; highly esteemed. *Dear* is used as a polite form of address at the beginning of letters: *Dear Sir, Dear Isabel.* **5** high-priced; costly; expensive: *Fruit is still too dear to can.* **6** at a high price; at a great cost. **7** an exclamation of surprise, trouble, etc.: *Oh, dear! My head aches.* 1, 4, 5 *adj.*, 2 *n.*, 3, 6 *adv.*, 7 *interj.*
—**dear′ly,** *adv.* —**dear′ness,** *n.*
**hold dear,** value highly.
☛ Hom. DEER.

**dearth** (dėrth) **1** a scarcity; lack; too small a supply. **2** a scarcity of food; famine. *n.*

**death** (deth) **1** the act or fact of dying; the ending of life in human beings, animals, or plants: *She faced death with courage.* **2** the state or condition of being dead. **3** any ending that is like dying; total destruction: *the death of an empire, the death of all our hopes.* **4** any condition like being dead. **5** a cause of death: *Alcoholism was the death of her.* **6** bloodshed; murder. **7** Often, **Death,** the power that destroys life, often represented as a skeleton dressed in black and carrying a scythe. *n.*
**at death's door,** dying; about to die; almost dead.
**be death on,** be very strongly opposed to: *He's death on all drugs.*
**put to death,** kill or execute.
**to death,** almost beyond endurance; extremely: *She said she was bored to death.*
**to the death,** to the last resource; to the last extreme: *a fight to the death.*

**death·bed** (deth′bed′) **1** the bed on which a person dies. **2** the last hours of life. **3** during the last hours of life: *The murderer made a deathbed confession. n.*

**death·blow** (deth′blō′) **1** a blow that kills. **2** anything that puts an end to something else. *n.*

**death cup** a very poisonous mushroom that has a cuplike enlargement at the base of the stem.

**death house** a place where condemned prisoners are kept until put to death.

**death·less** (deth′lis) never dying; living forever; immortal; eternal. *adj.* —**death′less·ness,** *n.*

**death·like** (deth′līk′) like that of death: *a deathlike silence. adj.*

**death·ly** (deth′lē) **1** like that of death: *Her face was deathly white.* **2** causing death; deadly: *a deathly famine.* **3** of death: *a deathly hush.* **4** as if dead. **5** extremely: *deathly ill.* 1–3 *adj.*, 4, 5 *adv.*

**death mask** a clay, wax, or plaster likeness of a person's face made from a cast taken after his or her death.

**death rate** the proportion of the number of deaths per year to the total population or to some other stated number.

**death's–head** (deths′hed′) a human skull, used as a symbol of death. *n.*

**death·trap** (deth′trap′) **1** an unsafe building or structure where the risk of fire or other hazard is great. **2** a very dangerous situation. *n.*

**de·ba·cle** (dā bä′kəl *or* di bak′əl) **1** a disaster; overthrow; downfall. **2** the breaking up of ice in a river. **3** a violent rush of waters carrying debris. *n.*

**de·bar** (di bär′) bar out; shut out; prevent; prohibit (*from*): *John was debarred from playing on the school team because his work had been so poor. v.,* **de·barred, de·bar·ring.** —**de·bar′ment,** *n.*

**de·bark** (di bärk′) land or cause to land from a ship or aircraft; DISEMBARK. *v.*

**de·bar·ka·tion** (dē′bär kā′shən) debarking or being debarked; a landing from a ship or aircraft. *n.*

**de·base** (di bās′) **1** make low in quality or character; dishonour or cheapen: *to debase oneself by a mean act.* **2** lower the exchange value of currency: *Poor management by a country of its financial affairs will generally debase its currency on world markets.* **3** lower the content value of a coin or coinage by increasing the proportion of base metal in it. *v.,* **de·based, de·bas·ing.** —**de·bas′er,** *n.*

**de·base·ment** (di bās′mənt) the action of debasing or the fact or state of being debased: *the debasement of coinage. n.*

**de·bat·a·ble** (di bā′tə bəl)   **1** capable of being debated; open to debate: *To be debatable, a topic must have at least two sides.*   **2** not decided; in dispute.   *adj.*

**de·bate** (di bāt′)   **1** discuss reasons for and against something; consider: *I am debating buying a car.*   **2** a discussion of reasons for and against: *There has been much debate about whom to choose for captain.*   **3** argue about a question, topic, etc. in a public meeting.   **4** a public argument for and against a question in a meeting: *A formal debate is a contest between two sides to see which one has more skill in speaking and reasoning.*   **5** a discussion that takes place in Parliament: *The debate on defence costs lasted for two weeks.*   1, 3 *v.*, **de·bat·ed, de·bat·ing;**   2, 4, 5 *n.*   —**de·bat′er,** *n.*

**de·bauch** (di bôch′)   **1** lead away from virtue or morality; corrupt morally or seduce: *debauched by bad companions.*   **2** corrupt or spoil the senses, taste, judgment, etc.: *a mind debauched by prejudice.*   **3** a bout or period of debauchery.   **4** DEBAUCHERY.   1, 2 *v.*, 3, 4 *n.* —**de·bauch′er,** *n.* —**de·bauch′ment,** *n.*

**de·bauch·er·y** (di bôch′ə rē)   **1** too much indulgence in sensual pleasures; DISSIPATION.   **2** a leading away from virtue or morality.   *n., pl.* **de·bauch·er·ies.**

**de·ben·ture** (di ben′chər)   a bond, especially one issued by a corporation rather than a government and backed by the general assets of the corporation.   *n.*

**de·bil·i·tate** (di bil′ə tāt′)   weaken: *A hot, wet climate is debilitating.*   *v.* **de·bil·i·tat·ed, de·bil·i·tat·ing.** —**de·bil′i·ta′tion,** *n.*

**de·bil·i·ty** (di bil′ə tē)   weakness: *Long illness may cause general debility.*   *n., pl.* **de·bil·i·ties.**

**deb·it** (deb′it)   **1** the entry of something owed in an account.   **2** the left-hand side of an account where such entries are made.   **3** enter on the debit side of an account.   Compare with CREDIT (def. 6).   **4** charge with or as a debt: *Debit his account $500.*   1, 2 *n.*, 3, 4 *v.*

**deb·o·nair** or **deb·o·naire** (deb′ə ner′)   **1** happy; cheerful.   **2** pleasant; courteous.   *adj.* —**deb′o·nair′ly,** *adv.*

**de·bouch** (di büsh′)   come out from a narrow or confined place into open country: *The soldiers debouched from the valley into the plain.*   *v.*

**de·brief** (dē brēf′)   question a combat pilot, intelligence agent, etc. immediately on return from a mission to find out the results of the mission and anything else the person learned while on the mission.   *v.*

**de·brief·ing** (dē brē′fing)   **1** the action or process of questioning a combat pilot, etc. on return from a mission. **2** ppr. of DEBRIEF.   1 *n.*, 2 *v.*

**de·bris** or **dé·bris** (də brē′ or dā′brē; French, dā brē′)   **1** scattered fragments; ruins; rubbish: *The street was covered with debris from the explosion.*   **2** a mass of fragments of rock, etc.: *the debris left by a glacier.*   *n.*

**debt** (det)   **1** something owed to another: *He paid off all his debts in a year.*   **2** a liability or obligation to pay or render something: *to be in debt to the grocer, to get out of debt.*   *n.*

**debt of honour** or **honor**   a gambling debt.

**debt·or** (det′ər)   a person who owes something to another: *If I borrow a dollar from you, I am your debtor.*   *n.*

**de·bug** (dē bug′)   **1** locate and remove errors or malfunctions in: *to debug a computer program.*   **2** locate and remove hidden microphones in a room, etc.   **3** remove insects from.   *v.*, **de·bugged, de·bug·ging.**

**de·bunk** (di bungk′)   **1** expose as false, exaggerated, empty, etc.: *to debunk a theory. She wrote an article debunking the manufacturer's claims.*   **2** expose the false reputation of: *to debunk a hero.*   *v.* —**de·bunk′er,** *n.*

**de·but** or **dé·but** (dā′byü; French, dā bY′)   **1** a first public appearance: *an actor's debut on the stage.*   **2** a first formal appearance in society.   *n.*

**deb·u·tante** or **dé·bu·tante** (deb′yə tänt′; French, dā bY tänt′)   **1** a girl during her first season in society.   **2** a woman making a DEBUT.   *n.*

**Dec.**   December.

**deca–** (dek′ə)   an SI prefix meaning ten: *A decagram is ten grams.*   Symbol: da

**dec·ade** (dek′ād)   **1** ten years: *From 1980 to 1990 was a decade.*   **2** a group of ten.   *n.*

**de·ca·dence** (dek′ə dəns or di kā′dəns)   a falling off; decline; decay: *The decadence of morals was one of the causes of the fall of Rome.*   *n.*

**dec·a·dent** (dek′ə dənt or di kā′dənt)   **1** falling off; declining; growing worse.   **2** a decadent person.   1 *adj.*, 2 *n.*

**de·caf·fein·ate** (dē kaf′ə nāt′)   remove the CAFFEINE from: *They drink only decaffeinated coffee.*   *v.*, **de·caf·fein·at·ed, de·caf·fein·at·ing.**

**dec·a·gon** (dek′ə gon′)   a plane figure having ten interior angles and ten sides.   See POLYGON for picture.   *n.*

**dec·a·he·dron** (dek′ə hē′drən)   a solid figure having ten plane surfaces, or faces.   *n., pl.* **dec·a·he·drons** or **dec·a·he·dra** (-drə).

**de·cal** (dē′kal, dē′kəl or di kal′)   DECALCOMANIA.   *n.*

**de·cal·co·ma·ni·a** (di kal′kə mā′nē ə)   **1** a design or picture treated so that it will stick to glass, wood, etc. **2** a process of decorating glass, wood, etc. by applying these designs or pictures.   *n.*

**de·camp** (di kamp′)   **1** depart quickly, secretly, or without ceremony.   **2** leave a camp.   *v.* —**de·camp′ment,** *n.*

**de·cant** (di kant′)   **1** pour off liquor or a solution gently without disturbing the sediment.   **2** pour from one container to another.   *v.*

**de·cant·er** (di kan′tər)   a glass bottle with a stopper, used for serving wine or liquor.   *n.*

**de·cap·i·tate** (di kap′ə tāt′)   cut off the head of; behead.   *v.*, **de·cap·i·tat·ed, de·cap·i·tat·ing.** —**de·cap′i·ta′tion,** *n.*

**dec·a·pod** (dek′ə pod′)   **1** any of an order of CRUSTACEANS having five pairs of appendages with one or more pair modified into pincers: *Lobsters, shrimps, and crabs are decapods.*   **2** any of an order of MOLLUSCS having ten arms, including squid and cuttlefish.   **3** of, having to do with, or referring to a decapod.   *n.*

**de·cath·lete** (di kath′lēt) an athlete who competes in the DECATHLON. *n.*

**de·cath·lon** (di kath′lon) an athletic contest consisting of 10 separate events for the competitor, in which the winner is the person who has the highest total of points from all the events: *The decathlon consists of the 100-metre, 400-metre, and 1500-metre runs, and the long jump, high jump, pole vault, shot put, javelin and discus throws, and the 110-metre hurdles.* *n.*

**de·cay** (di kā′) **1** become rotten: *Fruits and vegetables decay. Teeth decay if they are not taken care of.* **2** a rotting condition. **3** grow less in power, strength, wealth, beauty, etc.: *The power of the Roman Empire was decaying under Nero.* **4** a loss of power, strength, wealth, beauty, etc. **5** a loss in quantity of a radio-active substance through disintegration of its component nuclei. 1, 3 *v.*, 2, 4, 5 *n.*

**de·cease** (di sēs′) **1** death: *His decease was unexpected.* **2** die. 1 *n.*, 2 *v.*, **de·ceased, de·ceas·ing.**

**de·ceased** (di sēst′) **1** dead (*used of persons*). **2 the deceased,** a particular person or persons who have died recently: *a memorial service for the deceased.* **3** pt. and pp. of DECEASE. 1 *adj.*, 2 *n.*, 3 *v.*

**de·ce·dent** (di sē′dənt) in law, a deceased person: *The decedent's will was read in court.* *n.*

**de·ceit** (di sēt′) **1** the act or practice of making a person believe as true something that is false: *Her friendliness toward the newcomers was outright deceit.* **2** a dishonest trick; a lie spoken or acted: *That excuse was one deceit too many.* **3** the quality of being deceitful; deceitfulness: *Boris was so full of deceit that he believed his own lies.* *n.*

**de·ceit·ful** (di sēt′fəl) **1** ready or willing to deceive or lie: *a deceitful person.* **2** meant to deceive: *a deceitful friendliness.* **3** tending to deceive; deceptive: *a deceitful mildness in the air.* *adj.* —**de·ceit′ful·ly,** *adv.* —**de·ceit′ful·ness,** *n.*

**de·ceive** (di sēv′) **1** cause to accept as true something that is not true; mislead: *Ahmed's attempt to hide his unhappiness did not deceive them. It is illegal to try to deceive the public through false advertising.* **2** use deceit: *"Ah, what a tangled web we weave, When first we practise to deceive."* *v.*, **de·ceived, de·ceiv·ing.** —**de·ceiv′a·ble,** *adj.* —**de·ceiv′ing·ly,** *adv.*

**de·ceiv·er** (di sē′vər) a person who deceives. *n.*

**de·cel·er·ate** (dē sel′ə rāt′) decrease the VELOCITY of; slow down. Compare with ACCELERATE. *v.*, **de·cel·er·at·ed, de·cel·er·at·ing.** —**de·cel·er·a′tion,** *n.* —**de·cel′er·a′tor,** *n.*

**De·cem·ber** (di sem′bər) the twelfth and last month of the year: *December has 31 days.* *n.*
☛ *Etym.* From OF *decembre*, from L *December*, the Roman name for this month, formed from *decem* 'ten'. December was the tenth month of the ancient Roman calendar.

**de·cen·cy** (dē′sən sē) **1** the quality or state of being DECENT; conforming to accepted standards of behaviour, good taste, courtesy, etc.: *Common decency requires that you pay for the window you broke.* **2 the decencies,** *pl.* **a** the generally accepted standards of behaviour; proper and suitable actions: *She tried hard to observe the decencies although the situation was unfamiliar to her.* **b** the things needed for a proper standard of living. *n., pl.* **de·cen·cies.**

**de·cen·ni·al** (di sen′ē əl) **1** of or for ten years. **2** happening every ten years. **3** a tenth anniversary. 1, 2 *adj.*, 3 *n.*

**de·cent** (dē′sənt) **1** proper and right: *a decent burial. The decent thing to do is to apologize.* **2** not vulgar, immodest, or obscene: *decent language. His stories are usually decent.* **3** conforming to generally accepted standards of honesty, goodness, sincerity, etc.: *decent people.* **4** meeting at least the minimum standards of quality, etc.; reasonably good; adequate: *a decent wage. You can't even get a decent meal in this town.* **5** not severe; rather kind: *His boss was very decent about his being late for work.* *adj.* —**de′cent·ly,** *adv.* —**de′cent·ness,** *n.*

**de·cen·tral·ize** (dē sen′trə līz′) spread or distribute authority, power, etc. among more groups or local governments. *v.*, **de·cen·tral·ized, de·cen·tral·iz·ing.** —**de·cen′tral·i·za′tion,** *n.*

**de·cep·tion** (di sep′shən) **1** the act of deceiving. **2** the state of being deceived. **3** something that deceives; an ILLUSION. **4** a trick meant to deceive; fraud; SHAM. *n.*

**de·cep·tive** (di sep′tiv) **1** tending to deceive; misleading: *a deceptive calm before the storm.* **2** meant to deceive; deceiving: *The deceptive mildness of his manner did not fool them for long.* *adj.* —**de·cep′tive·ly,** *adv.* —**de·cep′tive·ness,** *n.*

**deci–** (des′ə) an SI prefix meaning tenth: *A decimetre is one tenth of a metre.* Symbol: d

| DECIBELS | SOUNDS |
|---|---|
| 1 | faintest sound heard |
| 10 | whisper; rustling of leaves |
| 30 | quiet conversation |
| 50 | quiet radio; average home |
| 70 | typewriter; average factory |
| 90 | police whistle; heavy traffic |
| 110 | deafening factory noise |
| 130 | sound vibrations *felt*, as with thunder or a jet plane close by |

**dec·i·bel** (des′ə bel′) a unit for measuring the loudness of sounds. Symbol: dB *n.*

**de·cide** (di sīd′) **1** settle a question, dispute, etc. by giving victory to one side; give a judgment or decision: *Let us decide the question by tossing a coin. Mother decided in favour of a small car.* **2** make up one's mind; resolve: *Sven decided to be a sailor.* **3** cause a person to reach a decision. *v.*, **de·cid·ed, de·cid·ing.**

**de·cid·ed** (di sī′did) **1** clear; definite; unquestionable: *The home team had a decided advantage.* **2** firm; determined: *Tom was a very decided person.* **3** pt. and pp. of DECIDE. 1, 2 *adj.*, 3 *v.* —**de·cid′ed·ness,** *n.*
☛ *Syn.* Do not confuse **decided** with DECISIVE. **Decided** means 'definite': *Bela's height gave him a decided advantage in the game.* **Decisive** means 'having or giving a definite or clear result': *The battle ended in a decisive victory.*

**de·cid·ed·ly** (di sī′did lē) **1** clearly; definitely; unquestionably: *Alicia's work is decidedly better than Frank's.* **2** firmly; in a determined manner. *adv.*

**de·cid·u·ous** (di sij′ü əs) **1** falling off at a particular season or stage of growth: *deciduous leaves, deciduous horns.* **2** shedding leaves annually: *Maples, elms, and most oaks are deciduous trees.* *adj.*

**de·cil·lion** (di sil′yən)  **1** in Canada, the United States, and France, 1 with 33 zeros following it.  **2** in the United Kingdom and Germany, 1 with 60 zeros following it.  *n.*

**dec·i·mal** (des′ə məl)  **1** based on or having to do with the number 10: *The metric system is a decimal system of measurement.*  **2** a numeral having a decimal point; DECIMAL NUMBER: *The numerals 23.6, 3.09, and 0.728 are decimals.*  **3** DECIMAL POINT: *Put the decimal between the units and the tenths.*  1 *adj.*, 2, 3 *n.*

**decimal fraction**  **1** a DECIMAL NUMBER.  **2** a DECIMAL NUMBER less than one.

**dec·i·mal·ly** (des′ə mə lē)  **1** by means of decimals.  **2** by tens.  *adv.*

**decimal number**  a number including a fraction whose denominator is 10, 100, 1000, etc., usually written in decimal form. *Examples*: 0.2, 9.93, 4.1.

**decimal point**  the period between the units and the tenths of a decimal number: *The decimal point separates the whole number from the fractional part of a decimal number.*

**dec·i·mate** (des′ə māt′)  **1** destroy much of; kill a large part of: *War had decimated the tribe.*  **2** select by lot and execute every tenth man of.  **3** take or destroy one tenth of.  *v.*, **dec·i·mat·ed, dec·i·mat·ing.** —**dec′i·ma′tion,** *n.* —**dec′i·ma′tor,** *n.*

**dec·i·me·tre** (des′ə mē′tər)  an SI unit for measuring length, equal to one tenth of a metre or ten centimetres: *One cubic decimetre is equal to one litre.*  Symbol: dm  *n.*  Also, **decimeter.**

**de·ci·pher** (di sī′fər)  **1** make out the meaning of something that is not clear: *I can't decipher this poor handwriting. We will try to decipher the mystery.*  **2** interpret secret writing by using a key; change something in cipher or code to ordinary language.  *v.* —**de·ci′pher·a·ble,** *adj.*

**de·ci·sion** (di sizh′ən)  **1** the act of making up one's mind; resolution.  **2** the deciding or settling of a question, dispute, etc. by giving judgment to one side.  **3** a judgment reached or given: *The judge gives a decision in a lawsuit.*  **4** firmness; determination: *A man of decision makes up his mind what to do and then does it.*  *n.*

**de·ci·sive** (di sī′siv)  **1** having or giving a clear result; settling something beyond question: *a decisive victory.*  **2** having or showing decision: *a decisive answer.*  *adj.* —**de·ci′sive·ly,** *adv.*  —**de·ci′sive·ness,** *n.*
☛ *Syn.* See note at DECIDED.

**deck** (dek)  **1** a floor or platform extending from side to side and often from end to end of a ship: *Often the upper deck has no roof over it.*  **2** a raised floor or platform against an outside wall of a house or cottage, usually having no roof, used for sunbathing, etc.  **3** any floor, platform, or shelf resembling the deck of a ship.  **4** a pack of playing cards.  **5** decorate or trim: *The hall was decked with flags.*  **6** dress splendidly or elegantly (*used with* **out**): *She was all decked out in blue satin.*  1–4 *n.*, 5, 6 *v.*
**on deck,** *Informal.* **a** ready for work, etc.; on hand: *We were all on deck for the cleanup.* **b** next in line, especially for batting in baseball.

**deck·er** (dek′ər) *Cdn.*  in baseball, a catcher's mitt.  *n.*

**deck hand**  a sailor who works on deck; an ordinary sailor.

**de·claim** (di klām′)  **1** recite in public; make a formal speech.  **2** speak in a loud and emotional manner; speak or write for effect.  *v.* —**de·claim′er,** *n.*

**dec·la·ma·tion** (dek′lə mā′shən)  **1** the act or art of reciting in public; making a formal speech or speeches.  **2** a selection of poetry, prose, etc. for reciting; formal speech.  **3** the act of talking loudly and emotionally.  **4** loud and emotional talk.  *n.*

**de·clam·a·to·ry** (di klam′ə tô′rē)  **1** having to do with DECLAMATION.  **2** loud and emotional.  *adj.*

**dec·la·ra·tion** (dek′lə rā′shən)  **1** the act of declaring: *a declaration of love.*  **2** a public statement or formal announcement: *a declaration of war.*  **3** a document containing a declaration.  **4** a statement acknowledging possession of income, goods, etc. for purposes of taxation.  **5** a strong statement.  *n.*

**Declaration of Independence**  in the United States, the public statement adopted by the Continental Congress on July 4, 1776, in which the American colonies were declared free and independent of the United Kingdom.

**de·clar·a·tive** (di klar′ə tiv *or* di kler′ə tiv)  making a statement: *I'm hungry and Dogs have four legs are declarative sentences.*  *adj.*

**de·clar·a·to·ry** (di klar′ə tô′rē *or* di kler′ə tô′rē)  DECLARATIVE.  *adj.*

**de·clare** (di kler′)  **1** announce publicly and formally; make known; proclaim: *Parliament has the power to declare war. The company has just declared a dividend on its stock.*  **2** say strongly; assert: *She declared that she would solve the problem if it took her all night.*  **3** state one's opinion or decision; proclaim oneself for or against something (*used with a pronoun ending in* **-self**): *They declared themselves against the use of violence.*  **4** acknowledge being in possession of income, goods, etc.: *Travellers returning to Canada must declare to the customs officers what they have bought abroad.*  *v.*, **de·clared, de·clar·ing.** —**de·clar′er,** *n.*

**de·clen·sion** (di klen′shən)  **1** in the grammar of certain languages, a variation in the form of nouns, pronouns, and adjectives according to their case.  **2** a class of nouns, etc. having similar forms for the different cases: *Latin nouns are usually grouped in five declensions.*  **3** a downward movement, bend, or slope.  **4** a sinking or falling into a lower or inferior condition; deterioration or decline.  *n.*

**de·clin·a·ble** (di klī′nə bəl)  that can be declined; especially in grammar, having different forms to show different cases: *English personal pronouns are declinable.*  *adj.*

**dec·li·na·tion** (dek′lə nā′shən)  **1** a downward bend or slope.  **2** a polite refusal.  **3** the deviation of a compass needle from true north or south.  *n.*

**de·cline** (di klīn′)  **1** refuse, especially politely, to accept or do something: *The man declined my offer of help. She declined the invitation.*  **2** bend or slope down: *The hill declines to a fertile valley.*  **3** decay; grow less in strength, power, value, etc.; grow worse: *Great nations have risen and declined.*  **4** a falling or sinking to a lower level: *the decline of the sun to the horizon, a decline in*

**declivity** 316 **dedication**

prices. **5** a growing worse; a losing of strength, power, value, etc.: *the decline of a person's strength, the decline of the Roman Empire.* **6** the last part of anything: *the decline of the day or of a person's life.* **7** in grammar, give the different cases or case endings of a noun, pronoun, or adjective. 1–3, 7 *v.*, **de·clined, de·clin·ing;** 4–6 *n.* —**de·clin′er,** *n.*

**de·cliv·i·ty** (di kliv′ə tē) a downward slope. *n., pl.* **de·cliv·i·ties.**

**de·coct** (di kokt′) extract desired substances from herbs, etc. by boiling. *v.*

**de·coc·tion** (di kok′shən) **1** the act of boiling to extract some desired substance. **2** a preparation made by boiling a substance in water or other liquid; an extract obtained by boiling. *n.*

**de·code** (dē kōd′) translate secret writing from code into ordinary language. *v.*, **de·cod·ed, de·cod·ing.** —**de·cod′er,** *n.*

**dé·colle·té** (dā′kol ə tā′; *French,* dā kol tā′) **1** of a dress, blouse, etc., low-necked. **2** wearing a low-necked dress, blouse, etc. *adj.*

**de·com·pose** (dē′kəm pōz′) **1** decay; rot or become rotten. **2** separate a substance into what it is made of: *A prism decomposes sunlight into its many colours.* **3** of a substance, become separated into its parts. *v.*, **de·com·posed, de·com·pos·ing.**

**de·com·po·si·tion** (dē′kom pə zish′ən) **1** the act or process of decomposing. **2** decay; rot. *n.*

**de·con·ges·tant** (dē kən jes′tənt) a medication used to relieve congestion of the lungs and nasal cavities. *n.*

**de·con·tam·i·nate** (dē′kən tam′ə nāt′) **1** make free from poison gas or harmful radio-active agents. **2** free from any sort of contamination. *v.*, **de·con·tam·i·nat·ed, de·con·tam·i·nat·ing.** —**de′con·tam·i·na′tion,** *n.*

**de·con·trol** (dē′kən trōl′) **1** remove controls from: *to decontrol the price of meat.* **2** a removing of controls. 1 *v.*, **de·con·trolled, de·con·trol·ling;** 2 *n.*

**dé·cor** or **de·cor** (dā kôr′) **1** decoration. **2** the overall style and arrangement of the furnishings of a room, etc. **3** a stage setting. *n.*

**dec·o·rate** (dek′ə rāt′) **1** furnish with ornamental things, especially for a particular occasion: *to decorate a Christmas tree. The room was decorated with flowers for the reception.* **2** plan the style, colour, and arrangement of interior furnishings, wallpaper, etc. **3** paint or paper a room, house, etc. **4** give a medal, ribbon, etc. to a person as a mark of honour: *The firefighter was decorated for bravery.* *v.*, **dec·o·rat·ed, dec·o·rat·ing.**

**dec·o·ra·tion** (dek′ə rā′shən) **1** the act or process of decorating. **2** anything used to add beauty; ornament. **3** a medal, ribbon, etc. awarded as a mark of honour: *The general wore many decorations.* *n.*

**dec·o·ra·tive** (dek′ə rə tiv *or* dek′ə rā′tiv) decorating; helping to adorn; ornamental: *The flowered curtains were highly decorative.* *adj.* —**dec′o·ra·tive·ly,** *adv.* —**dec′o·ra·tive·ness,** *n.*

**dec·o·ra·tor** (dek′ə rā′tər) **1** a person who decorates, especially one who specializes in designing colour schemes and the style and arrangement of furnishings for rooms, etc.: *They hired an interior decorator to do their living and dining rooms.* **2** designed for use in the decoration of rooms, etc.: *decorator fabrics, decorator colours.* *n.*

**dec·o·rous** (dek′ə rəs *or* di kô′rəs) well-behaved; acting properly; in good taste; dignified. *adj.* —**dec′o·rous·ly,** *adv.* —**dec′o·rous·ness,** *n.*

**de·co·rum** (di kô′rəm) **1** propriety of action, speech, dress, etc.: *You behave with decorum when you do what is proper.* **2** an observance or requirement of polite society: *Mary's mother had taught her to observe all the little decorums that mark a lady.* *n.*

**de·cou·page** or **dé·cou·page** (dā′kü pazh′) **1** the art of decorating surfaces by pasting on cutout pictures or designs of paper, foil, etc. and then applying several coats of varnish or lacquer to finish the surface: *Decoupage is often used to decorate small boxes.* **2** work done by decoupage. *n.*

**de·coy** (di koi′ *for verb,* dē′koi *for noun*) **1** lure wild birds, animals, etc. into a trap or within gunshot. **2** an artificial bird used to lure real birds into a trap or within range of a hunter's gun. **3** a bird or other animal trained to lure others of its kind into a trap. **4** a place into which wild birds or animals are lured. **5** lead or tempt into danger. **6** *Cdn.* DEKE. **7** any person or thing used to lead or tempt into danger. 1, 5, 6 *v.*, 2–4, 6, 7 *n.*

**de·crease** (di krēs′ *for verb,* dē′krēs *or* di krēs′ *for noun*) **1** become less: *Hunger decreases as one eats.* **2** make less: *to decrease prices.* **3** the process of becoming less: *A decrease in humidity made the hot weather more bearable.* **4** the amount by which a thing becomes or is made less: *The decrease in the value of the shares was eight percent.* 1, 2 *v.*, **decreased, de·creas·ing;** 3, 4 *n.* —**de·creas′ing·ly,** *adv.*
**on the decrease,** decreasing.

**de·cree** (di krē′) **1** something ordered or settled by authority; an official decision: *A government decree sets the date of Thanksgiving Day.* **2** order or settle by authority: *The government decreed that the election would take place July 8.* **3** decide; determine. 1 *n.*, 2, 3 *v.*, **de·creed, de·cree·ing.**

**de·crep·it** (di krep′it) broken down or weakened by old age; old and feeble. *adj.* —**de·crep′it·ly,** *adv.*

**de·crep·i·tude** (di krep′ə tyüd′ *or* di krep′ə tüd′) feebleness, usually from old age; a DECREPIT condition; weakness. *n.*

**decresc.** decrescendo.

**de·cre·scen·do** (dē′krə shen′dō) in music: **1** a gradual decrease in force or loudness; diminuendo. The sign of a decrescendo is >. **2** with a gradual decrease in force or loudness. **3** a passage to be played or sung with decrescendo. 1, 3 *n., pl.* **de·cre·scen·dos;** 2 *adj., adv.* Compare with CRESCENDO.

**de·cry** (di krī′) **1** CONDEMN: *The minister decried gambling in all its forms.* **2** make little of; try to lower the value of: *The lumber dealer decried the use of concrete for houses.* *v.*, **de·cried, de·cry·ing.**

**ded·i·cate** (ded′ə kāt′) **1** set apart for a sacred or solemn purpose: *The land on which the battle was fought was dedicated to the memory of the soldiers who had died there.* **2** give up wholly or earnestly to some person or purpose: *The doctor dedicated her life to healing the sick.* **3** address a book, poem, etc. to a friend or patron as a mark of affection, respect, gratitude, etc. *v.*, **ded·i·cat·ed, ded·i·cat·ing.** —**ded′i·ca′tor,** *n.*

**ded·i·ca·tion** (ded′ə kā′shən) **1** a setting apart or being set apart for a sacred or solemn purpose: *the* dedication of a church. **2** very great and constant interest; close attachment; complete loyalty (to some person or purpose): *a dedication to music. Because of his dedication to his queen, the baron refused to join the revolt.* **3** the words dedicating a book, poem, etc. to a friend or patron. *n.*

**ded·i·ca·to·ry** (ded′ə kə tô′rē) of DEDICATION. *adj.*

**de·duce** (di dyüs′ *or* di düs′) infer from a general rule or principle; reach a conclusion by reasoning: *After looking at the evidence, the detective deduced the cause of the fire.* *v.*, **de·duced, de·duc·ing.**

**de·duc·i·ble** (di dyü′sə bəl *or* di dü′sə bəl) capable of being DEDUCED or inferred. *adj.*

**de·duct** (di dukt′) take away; subtract. *v.*

**de·duct·i·ble** (di duk′tə bəl) that can be DEDUCTED. *adj.*

**de·duc·tion** (di duk′shən) **1** the act of taking away; subtraction: *No deduction in salary is made for absence due to illness.* **2** the amount deducted. **3** the act of reaching a conclusion by reasoning; inference. A person using deduction reasons from general laws to particular cases. Example: *All animals die; a cat is an animal; therefore, a cat will die.* Compare with INDUCTION (def. 2). **4** a conclusion reached by this method of reasoning: *Sherlock Holmes made brilliant deductions.* *n.*

**de·duc·tive** (di duk′tiv) of or using DEDUCTION; reasoning by deduction. *adj.* —**de·duc′tive·ly,** *adv.*

**deed** (dēd) **1** something done; an act: *To feed the hungry is a good deed.* **2** a brave, skilful, or unusual act: *the deeds of Joan of Arc.* **3** an action; doing; performance: *Deeds, not words, are needed.* **4** a written or printed document, sealed and signed, containing some contract: *The buyer of real estate receives a deed legally transferring the ownership.* **5** transfer by deed. 1–4 *n.*, 5 *v.*

**deem** (dēm) think; believe; consider: *The lawyer deemed it unwise to take the case to court.* *v.*

**deep** (dēp) **1** going far down or back: *a deep well.* **2** from far down or back: *Take a deep breath.* **3** far down or back: *The men dug deep before they found water.* **4** far on: *He studied deep into the night.* **5** in depth: *a tank 3 metres deep.* **6** from front to back: *The lot on which the house stands is 40 metres deep.* **7** low in pitch: *a deep voice.* **8** strong and dark in colour: *a deep red.* **9** strong; great; intense; extreme: *deep sorrow, a deep sleep.* **10** requiring or showing much thought and study: *a deep book.* **11** with the mind fully taken up: *deep in thought.* **12** wise; shrewd. **13** sly; crafty. **14** a deep place. **15** the most intense part: *the deep of winter.* **16 the deep,** the sea. 1, 2, 5–13 *adj.,* 3, 4 *adv.,* 14–16 *n.* —**deep′ly,** *adv.* —**deep′ness,** *n.*

**deep·en** (dē′pən) make or become deeper: *It was necessary to deepen the ditch. His frown deepened as he became more worried.* *v.*

**deep–root·ed** (dē′prü′tid) **1** deeply rooted. **2** firmly fixed: *deep-rooted traditions, a deep-rooted dislike.* *adj.*

**deep–sea** (dēp′sē′) of or in the deeper parts of the sea: *a deep-sea diver.* *adj.*

**deep–seat·ed** (dēp′sē′tid) **1** far below the surface. **2** firmly fixed: *The disease was so deep-seated that it could not be cured.* *adj.*

**deep–set** (dēp′set′) **1** set deeply. **2** firmly fixed. *adj.*

---

**dedicatory**     317     **defaulter**

hat, āge, fär; let, ēqual, tėrm; it, īce
hot, ōpen, ôrder; oil, out; cup, pùt, rüle
əbove, takən, pencəl, lemən, circəs
ch, child; ng, long; sh, ship
th, thin; ᴛʜ, then; zh, measure

**deer** (dēr) **1** any of a number of related cud-chewing animals having long, slender legs with small, split hoofs, the males (and in some species, some females) having solid, bony antlers that are shed each year. **2** any animal belonging to the same family as the true deer: *Moose, elk, and caribou are deer.* **3** *Cdn. North.* CARIBOU. *n., pl.* **deer** or (*rarely*) **deers.**
☛ *Hom.* DEAR.

**deer·fly** (dēr′flī′) a small blood-sucking fly, related to the horsefly. *n., pl.* **deer·flies.**

**deer·hound** (dēr′hound′) a breed of large dog resembling a greyhound, but larger and having shaggy hair: *The deerhound comes from Scotland, where it was originally bred for hunting deer.* *n.*

**deer mouse** a small North American mouse having white feet and large ears.

**deer·skin** (dēr′skin′) **1** the hide of a deer. **2** leather made from it: *deerskin moccasins.* **3 deerskins,** *pl.* clothing made from this leather. *n.*

**def. 1** definition. **2** defined. **3** defendant. **4** deferred. **5** defective.

**de·face** (di fās′) spoil the appearance of; mar: *Scribbled pictures and notes defaced the pages of the book.* *v.*, **de·faced, de·fac·ing.** —**de·fac′er,** *n.*

**de·face·ment** (di fās′mənt) **1** the act of defacing. **2** the state of being defaced. **3** anything that defaces. *n.*

**de fac·to** (dē′fak′tō) *Latin.* **1** in fact; in reality. **2** actually existing, whether legal or not: *a de facto government.*

**de·fal·cate** (di fal′kāt) steal or misuse money trusted to one's care. *v.*, **de·fal·cat·ed, de·fal·cat·ing.** —**de·fal′ca·tor,** *n.*

**de·fal·ca·tion** (dē′fal kā′shən) **1** the theft or misuse of money entrusted to one's care: *The cashier's defalcation was discovered.* **2** the amount stolen or misused: *a defalcation of $5000.* *n.*

**def·a·ma·tion** (def′ə mā′shən) defaming or being DEFAMED; slander; libel. *n.*

**de·fam·a·to·ry** (di fam′ə tô′rē) defaming; slanderous. *adj.*

**de·fame** (di fām′) attack the good name of; harm the reputation of; speak evil of; slander: *People in public life are sometimes defamed by opponents.* *v.*, **de·famed, de·fam·ing.** —**de·fam′er,** *n.*

**de·fault** (di folt′) **1** a failure to do something or to appear somewhere when due; neglect: *If in any contest, one side does not appear, it loses by default.* **2** fail to do something or appear somewhere when due: *They defaulted in the tennis tournament.* **3** a failure to pay when due. **4** fail to pay when due. **5** lack; absence: *In default of tools, she used a hairpin and a nail file.* 1, 3, 5 *n.,* 2, 4 *v.*

**de·fault·er** (di fol′tər) **1** a person who DEFAULTs. **2** a person who steals or misuses money trusted to his or her care. *n.*

**de·feat** (di fēt′) **1** win a victory over; overcome: *to defeat another school in basketball.* **2** make useless: *to defeat someone's plans.* **3** defeating or being defeated: *Sandra's defeat in the chess competition was a big surprise. It was the defeat of all our hopes for the championship.* 1, 2 *v.*, 3 *n.*

**de·feat·ism** (di fē′tiz əm) the attitude or behaviour of a DEFEATIST. *n.*

**de·feat·ist** (di fē′tist) a person who expects, wishes for, or admits the defeat of his or her country, cause, etc. *n.*

**def·e·cate** (def′ə kāt′) have a movement of the bowels. *v.*, **def·e·cat·ed, def·e·cat·ing.** —**def′e·ca′tion,** *n.*

**de·fect** (dē′fekt *or* di fekt′ *for noun*, di fekt′ *for verb*) **1** a fault; blemish; imperfection: *A hearing aid helps to overcome defects in hearing.* **2** the lack of something essential to completeness; a falling short: *A bad temper was the one defect in his kind and generous nature.* **3** forsake one's own country, group, etc. for another, especially for one opposed to it. 1, 2 *n.*, 3 *v.* —**de·fec′tor,** *n.*

**de·fec·tion** (di fek′shən) **1** a falling away from loyalty, duty, religion, etc.; desertion: *The candidate denied any defection from the principles of his party.* **2** failure. *n.*

**de·fec·tive** (di fek′tiv) **1** having a serious flaw or blemish; faulty: *His hearing is defective. We returned the toaster because it was defective.* **2** in grammar, lacking one or more of the usual forms of inflection: *Ought is a defective verb.* **3** of a person, below normal in intelligence. **4** a defective person or thing. 1–3 *adj.*, 4 *n.* —**de·fec′tive·ly,** *adv.* —**de·fec′tive·ness,** *n.*

**de·fence** *or* **de·fense** (di fens′) **1** the act of defending or protecting; guarding against attack or harm: *The armed forces are responsible for the defence of the country.* **2** anything that defends or protects; something used to guard against attack or harm: *A wall around a city was a defence against enemies. A well-built house or a warm coat is a defence against cold weather.* **3** in boxing or fencing, the act of defending oneself. **4** in games, a team or player defending a goal. **5** an action, speech, or writing in favour of something. **6** the answer of a defendant to an accusation or lawsuit against him or her. **7** a defendant and his or her lawyers. *n.*

**de·fence·less** *or* **de·fense·less** (di fens′lis) having no defence; unprotected; helpless against attack or harm: *A baby is defenceless.* *adj.*

**de·fence·man** *or* **de·fense·man** (di fens′mən) in hockey, football, etc., a player whose job is to prevent the opposing players from approaching the goal. *n.*, *pl.* **de·fence·men** *or* **de·fense·men** (-smən).

**de·fend** (di fend′) **1** guard from attack or harm; protect: *Soldiers are trained to defend their country.* **2** in sports: **a** try to keep an opponent away from: *to defend a goal.* **b** maintain one's position as champion by playing or fighting against a challenger: *He will forfeit his title unless he defends it within a year.* **3** justify or maintain against opposition, criticism, etc.: *to defend one's argument. She defended their conduct in a letter to the editor.* **4** act as counsel for in a court of law: *He has hired a well-known lawyer to defend him.* **5** resist or deny the claim of a plaintiff; contest a charge or lawsuit: *Is she going to defend the speeding charge?* *v.*

**de·fen·da·ble** (di fen′də bəl) DEFENSIBLE. *adj.*

**de·fend·ant** (di fen′dənt) a person accused or sued in a law court: *This defendant is accused of theft.* *n.*

**de·fend·er** (di fen′dər) **1** a protector or guardian. **2** in sports, the holder of a championship who is defending it by playing or fighting against a challenger. *n.*

**de·fense** (di fens′) See DEFENCE. *n.*

**de·fense·less** (di fens′lis) See DEFENCELESS. *adj.*

**de·fense·man** (di fens′mən) See DEFENCEMAN. *n.*

**de·fen·si·ble** (di fen′si bəl) **1** capable of being defended. **2** justifiable; proper. *adj.* —**de·fen′si·bly,** *adv.*

**de·fen·sive** (di fen′siv) **1** ready to defend; defending. **2** for defence: *Their team had a good defensive strategy.* **3** of DEFENCE: *a defensive attitude.* **4** a position or attitude of DEFENCE. **5** anything that defends. 1–3 *adj.*, 4, 5 *n.* —**de·fen′sive·ly,** *adv.* —**de·fen′sive·ness,** *n.*
**on the defensive,** ready to defend, apologize, or explain: *Mei-Ling has been criticized so much that she is always on the defensive.*

**de·fer**[1] (di fėr′) put off; delay: *The examinations were deferred because so many children were sick.* *v.*, **de·ferred, de·fer·ring.**

**de·fer**[2] (di fėr′) yield; submit to another's judgment, opinion, or wishes: *Carl deferred to his sister's wishes.* *v.*, **de·ferred, de·fer·ring.**

**def·er·ence** (def′ə rəns) **1** a yielding to the judgment or opinion of another; courteous submission. **2** respect; regard: *The insolent children should have shown more deference to their principal.* *n.*
**in deference to,** out of respect or regard for: *In deference to his father's wishes, Urho worked hard at his studies.*

**def·er·en·tial** (def′ə ren′shəl) showing DEFERENCE; respectful. *adj.* —**def′er·en′tial·ly,** *adv.*

**de·fer·ment** (di fėr′mənt) a putting off; delay. *n.*

**de·ferred** (di fėrd′) **1** postponed; delayed. **2** pt. and pp. of DEFER. 1 *adj.*, 2 *v.*

**de·fi·ance** (di fī′əns) **1** the act or an instance of openly resisting or opposing: *Rebellion always involves defiance against authority.* **2** intent or willingness to openly resist or oppose: *Her defiance showed clearly on her face. He shouted his defiance.* *n.*
**in defiance of,** in open opposition to; showing contempt or disregard for: *She took the car in defiance of her father's wishes.*

**de·fi·ant** (di fī′ənt) showing DEFIANCE; openly resisting or offering a challenge; hostile. *adj.* —**de·fi′ant·ly,** *adv.* —**de·fi′ant·ness,** *n.*

**de·fi·cien·cy** (di fish′ən sē) **1** a lack or absence of something needed or required; incompleteness: *Mother's illness was caused by a deficiency of certain vitamins.* **2** the amount by which something falls short or is too small: *If a bill to be paid is $10 and you have only $6, the deficiency is $4.* *n.*, *pl.* **de·fi·cien·cies.**

**de·fi·cient** (di fish′ənt) **1** incomplete; defective: *His knowledge of geography is deficient.* **2** not sufficient in quantity, force, etc.; lacking: *Her diet is deficient in protein.* *adj.* —**de·fi′cient·ly,** *adv.*

**def·i·cit** (def′ə sit) the amount by which a sum of money falls short; shortage: *Since the club owed $15 and had $10 in the treasury, there was a deficit of $5.* *n.*

**de·fi·er** (di fī′ər)  a person who defies. *n.*

**de·file**[1] (di fīl′)  **1** make filthy or dirty; make disgusting in any way.  **2** destroy the purity or cleanness of; corrupt.  **3** violate the sanctity of: *During the war many shrines and churches were defiled by marauding raiders.*  **4** stain; dishonour: *Charges of corruption defiled the reputation of the government.*  *v.*, **de·filed, de·fil·ing.** —**de·fil′er,** *n.*

**de·file**[2] (di fīl′ *or* dē′fīl)  **1** march in a line.  **2** a narrow way or passage through which troops can march only in narrow columns.  **3** a steep and narrow valley. **1** *v.*, **de·filed, de·fil·ing; 2, 3** *n.*

**de·file·ment** (di fīl′mənt)  **1** the act of defiling.  **2** the state of being defiled.  **3** something that defiles. *n.*

**de·fine** (di fīn′)  **1** make clear the meaning of; explain: *A dictionary defines words.*  **2** make clear; make distinct.  **3** fix; settle: *The powers of the courts are defined by law.*  **4** settle the limits of: *to define the boundaries of a piece of property.*  *v.*, **de·fined, de·fin·ing.** —**de·fin′a·ble,** *adj.* —**de·fin′er,** *n.*

**def·i·nite** (def′ə nit)  **1** clear and exact in meaning or expression; free of ambiguity or doubt: *He wouldn't give a definite answer. She was very definite about the time of the shot. Is it definite that we're going?*  **2** precisely defined; having exact limits; fixed: *a definite area, a definite number of players.*  **3** in grammar, limiting or specifying: *The definite article is used to show that a noun is specific.* *adj.* —**def′i·nite·ness,** *n.*

**definite article**  in English, the word *the.*

**def·i·nite·ly** (def′ə ni tlē)  **1** in a definite manner. **2** certainly: *Are you going? Definitely. They're definitely taking the dog along.*  *adv.*

**def·i·ni·tion** (def′ə nish′ən)  **1** the act of explaining; the act of making clear the meaning of a word or group of words.  **2** a statement that makes clear the meaning of a word or group of words; explanation.  **3** the power of making clear and distinct: *The capacity of a lens to give a clear, distinct image of an object is called its definition.*  **4** clearness; distinctness.  **5** the accuracy with which sound or images are reproduced by a radio or television receiver. *n.*

**de·fin·i·tive** (di fin′ə tiv)  **1** conclusive; final. **2** limiting; defining.  **3** a word that limits or defines a noun. *The, this, all, none,* etc. are definitives. Compare with DETERMINER.  **1, 2** *adj.*, **3** *n.* —**de·fin′i·tive·ly,** *adv.* —**de·fin′i·tive·ness,** *n.*

**def·la·grate** (def′lə grāt′)  burn with great heat.  *v.*, **def·la·grat·ed, def·la·grat·ing.** —**de′fla·gra′tion,** *n.*

**de·flate** (di flāt′)  **1** let air or gas out of a balloon, tire, football, etc.  **2** reduce the amount or importance of; reduce: *to deflate prices, to deflate currency.*  *v.*, **de·flat·ed, de·flat·ing.** Compare with INFLATE.

**de·fla·tion** (di flā′shən)  **1** the act of letting the air or gas out: *the deflation of a tire.*  **2** a reduction.  **3** the reduction of the amount of available money in circulation so that prices go down.  *n.* Compare with INFLATION.

**de·fla·tion·ar·y** (di flā′shə ner′ē)  of or having to do with DEFLATION (def. 3). Compare with INFLATIONARY. *adj.*

**de·flect** (di flekt′)  bend or turn aside; change the direction of.  *v.* —**de·flec′tor,** *n.*

**de·flec·tion** (di flek′shən)  **1** a bending or turning aside.  **2** the amount of bending or turning. *n.*

---

**defier**    **319**   **degeneration**

hat, āge, fär; let, ēqual, tėrm; it, īce
hot, ōpen, ôrder; oil, out; cup, pu̇t, rüle
əbove, takən, pencəl, lemən, circəs
ch, child; ng, long; sh, ship
th, thin; ᴛʜ, then; zh, measure

**de·flec·tive** (di flek′tiv)  **1** causing DEFLECTION. **2** tending to DEFLECT. *adj.*

**de·for·est** (dē fô′rist)  clear of trees: *The land had to be deforested before the settlers could farm it.*  *v.* —**de·for′est·a′tion,** *n.* —**de·for′est·er,** *n.*

**de·form** (di fôrm′)  **1** spoil the form or shape of: *Shoes that are too tight deform the feet.*  **2** make ugly; disfigure: *a face deformed by rage.*  *v.* —**de·form′er,** *n.*

**de·for·ma·tion** (dē′fôr mā′shən *or* def′ər mā′shən) DEFORMing or being deformed. *n.*

**de·formed** (di fôrmd′)  **1** especially of the body or a part of it, not properly formed; distorted or misshapen: *a deformed foot.*  **2** pt. and pp. of DEFORM.  **1** *adj.*, **2** *v.*

**de·form·i·ty** (di fôr′mə tē)  **1** a part that is not properly formed.  **2** the condition of being improperly formed.  **3** an improperly formed person or thing. **4** ugliness.  *n.*, *pl.* **de·form·i·ties.**

**de·fraud** (di frod′)  take money, rights, etc. away from by fraud; cheat: *They defrauded the widow of her savings.*  *v.* —**de·fraud′er,** *n.*

**de·fray** (di frā′)  pay costs or expenses: *The expenses of national parks are defrayed by the taxpayers.*  *v.*

**de·fray·al** (di frā′əl)  a payment of expenses, etc.  *n.*

**de·fray·ment** (di frā′mənt)  DEFRAYAL.  *n.*

**de·frost** (dē frost′)  **1** remove frost or ice from: *to defrost a refrigerator.*  **2** thaw out frozen foods.  *v.*

**de·frost·er** (dē fros′tər)  a device that removes ice or prevents its formation, either through heat or chemically: *Defrosters are used on automobile windshields and the wings of planes.* *n.*

**deft** (deft)  skilful; nimble: *the deft fingers of a violinist or a surgeon.*  *adj.* —**deft′ly,** *adv.* —**deft′ness,** *n.*

**de·funct** (di fungkt′)  dead; extinct.  *adj.*

**de·fy** (di fī′)  **1** set oneself openly against authority; resist boldly: *Now that the young man was earning his own living, he could defy his father's strict rules.*  **2** withstand; resist: *This strong fort defies capture.*  **3** challenge a person to do something: *We defy you to show that our playing is not fair.*  *v.*, **de·fied, de·fy·ing.**

**deg.**  degree; degrees.

**de·gen·er·a·cy** (di jen′ə rə sē)  a DEGENERATE condition.  *n.*

**de·gen·er·ate** (di jen′ə rāt′ *for verb,* di jen′ə rit *for adjective and noun*)  **1** decline in physical, mental, or moral qualities; grow worse.  **2** sink to a lower type; lose the normal or more highly developed characteristics of its race or kind.  **3** that has degenerated; showing a decline in physical, mental, or moral qualities: *The thief was a degenerate member of a fine family.*  **4** a person who shows degraded and debased physical, mental, or moral qualities: *Only a degenerate could have committed such a horrible crime.*  **1, 2** *v.*, **de·gen·er·at·ed, de·gen·er·at·ing; 3** *adj.*, **4** *n.* —**de·gen′er·ate·ly,** *adv.*

**de·gen·er·a·tion** (di jen′ə rā′shən)  **1** the process of

**degenerating.** 2 a DEGENERATE (def. 3) condition. 3 a deterioration in tissues or organs caused by disease, injury, etc. *n.*

**de·gen·er·a·tive** (di jen′ə rə tiv *or* di jen′ə rā′tiv) 1 tending to DEGENERATE (defs. 1, 2). 2 characterized by DEGENERATION; showing degeneration. *adj.*

**deg·ra·da·tion** (deg′rə dā′shən) 1 degrading. 2 being DEGRADED (def.1): *Failure to obey orders caused the captain's degradation to the rank of a private.* 3 a DEGRADED (def. 2) condition: *The drunkard, filthy and half-starved, lived in degradation.* *n.*

**de·grade** (di grād′) 1 reduce to a lower rank; take away a position, an honour, etc. from: *The captain was degraded for disobeying orders.* 2 make bad; lower in value; debase: *You degrade yourself when you tell a lie.* 3 wear down by erosion. *v.*, **de·grad·ed, de·grad·ing.** —**de·grad′er,** *n.*

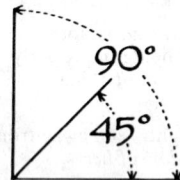
Two angles with the degrees marked

**de·gree** (di grē′) 1 a stage or step in a scale or process. 2 a step in direct line of descent: *a cousin two degrees removed.* 3 the amount, intensity, or extent of an action or condition: *To what degree is he interested in reading?* 4 a unit for measuring temperature: *The boiling point of water is 100 degrees Celsius.* Symbol: ° 5 a unit used with the SI for measuring plane angles, especially in navigation, surveying, etc.: *There are 360 degrees in a circle and 90 degrees in a right angle. One degree is equal to (π ÷ 180) radians.* Symbol: ° 6 rank: *A princess is a lady of high degree.* 7 a rank or title given by a college or university to a student whose work fulfils certain requirements, or to a person as an honour: *an M.A. degree, a D.Mus. degree.* 8 in grammar, one of the three stages in the comparison of adjectives or adverbs: *Fast is the positive degree; faster, the comparative degree; fastest, the superlative degree.* 9 in law, the relative measure of guilt: *murder in the first degree.* 10 a measure of damage to body tissue: *She suffered a second-degree burn when the pot of water overturned.* *n.*
**by degrees,** gradually: *By degrees the lake became warm enough to swim in.*
**to a degree, a** to a large amount; to a great extent. **b** somewhat; rather.

**degree Celsius** a unit used with the SI for measuring temperature: *On a thermometer, zero degrees Celsius (0°C)is the temperature at which water freezes, and one hundred degrees Celsius (100°C)is the temperature at which water boils. A temperature interval of one degree Celsius is equal to one kelvin (1°C = 1K).* Symbol: °C

**de·his·cent** (dē his′ənt) bursting open to scatter seeds. *adj.*

**de·horn** (dē hôrn′) remove the horns from. *v.*

**de·hu·man·ize** (dē hyü′mə nīz′) deprive of human qualities, interest, sympathy, etc. *v.*, **de·hu·man·ized, de·hu·man·iz·ing.**

**de·hy·drate** (dē hī′drāt) 1 deprive a chemical compound of water or the elements of water. 2 take water or moisture from; dry. 3 lose water or moisture. *v.*, **de·hy·drat·ed, de·hy·drat·ing.**

**de·hy·dra·tion** (dē′hī drā′shən) 1 the removal of water from a chemical compound or from vegetables, fruits, etc. 2 an excessive loss of body fluids. *n.*

**de–ice** (dē īs′) prevent the formation of ice on; remove ice from an aircraft, etc. *v.*, **de-iced, de-ic·ing.** —**de-ic′er,** *n.*

**de·i·fi·ca·tion** (dē′ə fə kā′shən) 1 a DEIFYing: *The deification of the emperor was customary in ancient Rome.* 2 being deified: *After his deification, altars were erected to him.* *n.*

**de·i·fy** (dē′ə fī′) 1 make a god of. 2 worship or regard as a god: *Some people deify wealth.* *v.*, **de·i·fied, de·i·fy·ing.** —**de′i·fi′er,** *n.*

**deign** (dān) 1 CONDESCEND; think fit: *So conceited a man would never deign to notice us.* 2 CONDESCEND to give an answer, a reply, etc. *v.*
☛ Hom. DANE.

**de·ism** (dē′iz əm) 1 the belief that God exists entirely apart from our world and does not influence the lives of human beings. 2 a belief in God without accepting any particular religion. *n.*

**de·ist** (dē′ist) a person who believes in DEISM. *n.*

**de·i·ty** (dē′ə tē) 1 a god or goddess: *Neptune was a deity of the sea.* 2 a divine nature; the state of being a god. 3 **the Deity,** God. *n., pl.* **de·i·ties.**

**de·ject·ed** (di jek′tid) in low spirits; sad; discouraged: *The defeated boxer wore a dejected frown.* *adj.* —**de·ject′ed·ly,** *adv.* —**de·ject′ed·ness,** *n.*

**de·jec·tion** (di jek′shən) lowness of spirits; sadness; discouragement: *Her face showed her dejection at missing the party.* *n.*

**deka–** (dek′ə) *U.S.* DECA-.

**deke** (dēk) *Cdn.* in hockey: 1 a fake shot or movement intended to draw a defending player out of position. 2 draw a defending player out of position by faking a shot or movement. 3 manoeuvre (oneself or the puck) by feinting so as to outsmart a defending player. 1 *n.*, 2, 3 *v.*, **deked, dek·ing.**

**del.** 1 delete. 2 delegate. 3 delivery.

**de·lay** (di lā′) 1 put off till a later time: *We will delay the party for a week.* 2 make late; keep waiting; hinder the progress of: *The accident delayed the train for two hours. Ignorance delays progress.* 3 be late; wait; go slowly; stop along the way: *She asked him not to delay on his errand.* 4 delaying: *We were so late that we could afford no further delay.* 5 the fact of being delayed: *The delay upset our plans.* 1–3 *v.*, 4, 5 *n.* —**de·lay′er,** *n.*

**de·lec·ta·ble** (di lek′tə bəl) very pleasing; delightful. *adj.* —**de·lec′ta·ble·ness,** *n.* —**de·lec′ta·bly,** *adv.*

**de·lec·ta·tion** (dē′lek tā′shən) delight; pleasure; entertainment: *The magician did many tricks for our delectation.* *n.*

**del·e·gate** (del′ə git *or* del′ə gāt′ *for noun,* del′ə gāt′ *for verb*) 1 a person given power or authority to act for others; representative: *Our club sent two delegates to the national meeting.* 2 appoint or send a person as a delegate: *Each club delegated one member to attend the first meeting.* 3 give over one's power or authority to another as agent or deputy: *The provinces have delegated some of their rights to the Federal Government.* 1 *n.*, 2, 3 *v.*, **del·e·gat·ed, del·e·gat·ing.**

**del·e·ga·tion** (del′ə gā′shən) 1 delegating or being DELEGATED (def. 3): *the delegation of authority.* 2 a group of DELEGATES (def. 1): *Each province sent a delegation to the national convention.* *n.*

**de·lete** (di lēt′) strike out or take out anything written or printed; remove; cross out. *v.,* **de·let·ed, de·let·ing.**

**del·e·te·ri·ous** (del′ə tē′rē əs) harmful; injurious. *adj.* —**del′e·te′ri·ous·ly,** *adv.*

**de·le·tion** (di lē′shən) 1 the act of deleting. 2 the fact of being deleted. 3 a deleted part. *n.*

**delft** (delft) a kind of glazed earthenware made in Holland: *Delft is usually decorated in blue.* *n.*

**de·lib·er·ate** (di lib′ə rit *for adjective,* di lib′ə rāt′ *for verb*) 1 carefully thought out; made or done on purpose: *Her excuse was a deliberate lie.* 2 slow and careful in deciding what to do: *A deliberate person takes a long time to make up his or her mind.* 3 slow but with firmness and purpose: *The old man walked with deliberate steps.* 4 think over carefully; consider. 5 discuss reasons for and against something; DEBATE: *Parliament was deliberating the question of raising taxes.* 1–3 *adj.,* 4, 5 *v.,* **de·lib·er·at·ed, de·lib·er·at·ing.** —**de·lib′er·ate·ly,** *adv.* —**de·lib′er·ate·ness,** *n.* —**de·lib′er·a′tor,** *n.*

**de·lib·er·a·tion** (di lib′ə rā′shən) 1 careful thought. 2 a discussion of reasons for and against something; DEBATE: *the deliberations of the Legislative Assembly.* 3 slowness and care: *The hunter aimed his gun with great deliberation.* *n.*

**de·lib·er·a·tive** (di lib′ə rə tiv *or* di lib′ə rā′tiv) 1 for DELIBERATION (def. 2); having to do with deliberation; discussing reasons for and against something: *Parliament is a deliberative body.* 2 characterized by DELIBERATION; coming as a result of deliberation. *adj.* —**de·lib′er·a·tive·ly,** *adv.*

**del·i·ca·cy** (del′ə kə sē) 1 a delicate quality or nature; slightness and grace: *the delicacy of lace, the delicacy of a flower, the delicacy of a baby's skin.* 2 fineness of feeling for small differences; sensitiveness: *delicacy of hearing or touch.* 3 need of care, skill, or tact: *A matter of great delicacy is one that requires careful handling.* 4 thought or regard for the feelings of others. 5 a shrinking from what one considers offensive or not modest. 6 weakness; the condition of being easily hurt or made ill: *The child's delicacy was a worry to her parents.* 7 a choice kind of food; DAINTY (def. 5). *n., pl.* **del·i·ca·cies.**

**del·i·cate** (del′ə kit) 1 light and pleasant to taste or smell: *delicate foods, a delicate fragrance.* 2 soft or fine in structure or make: *delicate features, delicate silks for blouses.* 3 easily crushed, broken, or torn; fragile: *a delicate flower, a delicate china cup.* 4 requiring skill and care in handling: *a delicate situation, a delicate heart operation.* 5 of a colour, pale; not intense: *a delicate shade of green.* 6 capable of responding to very slight changes of condition; very sensitive: *delicate instruments, a delicate sense of touch.* 7 easily hurt or made ill: *a delicate child. She has a delicate constitution.* 8 very subtle; marked by fine distinctions: *delicate shades of meaning, delicate irony.* *adj.* —**del′i·cate·ly,** *adv.* —**del′i·cate·ness,** *n.*

**del·i·ca·tes·sen** (del′ə kə tes′ən) 1 a store that sells prepared foods, such as cooked meats, smoked fish, cheese, salads, pickles, etc. 2 the foods sold at such a store. *n.*

**de·li·cious** (di lish′əs) 1 very pleasing to taste or smell. 2 very pleasing; delightful: *a delicious colour combination.* *adj.* —**de·li′cious·ly,** *adv.* —**de·li′cious·ness,** *n.*

**de·light** (di līt′) 1 great pleasure; joy. 2 something that gives great pleasure: *Dancing is his delight.* 3 please greatly: *The circus delighted the audience.* 4 have great pleasure (*in*): *Children delight in surprises.* 1, 2 *n.,* 3, 4 *v.* —**de·light′er,** *n.*

**de·light·ed** (di lī′tid) 1 greatly pleased; joyful; glad. 2 pt. and pp. of DELIGHT. 1 *adj.,* 2 *v.* —**de·light′ed·ly,** *adv.*

**de·light·ful** (di līt′fəl) very pleasing; giving joy: *a delightful ride, a delightful person.* *adj.* —**de·light′ful·ly,** *adv.* —**de·light′ful·ness,** *n.*

**De·li·lah** (di lī′lə) any false, treacherous woman; temptress. *n.*
▶ *Etym.* From the name of the woman who betrayed Samson, her lover, to the Philistines.

**de·lim·it** (di lim′it) fix the limits of; mark the boundaries of. *v.* —**de·lim′i·ta′tion,** *n.*

**de·lin·e·ate** (di lin′ē āt′) 1 trace the outline of. 2 draw or sketch. 3 describe in words. *v.* **de·lin·e·at·ed, de·lin·e·at·ing.** —**de·lin′e·a′tor,** *n.*

**de·lin·e·a·tion** (di lin′ē ā′shən) 1 a drawing or sketch. 2 description. *n.*

**de·lin·quen·cy** (di ling′kwən sē) 1 the failure to do what is required by law or duty; guilt. 2 a fault; offence. 3 the condition or habit of behaving unlawfully: *Juvenile delinquency is greatly increased by wartime conditions.* *n., pl.* **de·lin·quen·cies.**

**de·lin·quent** (di ling′kwənt) 1 failing to do what is required by law or duty; guilty of a fault or an offence. 2 a delinquent person; offender; criminal. 3 due and unpaid; overdue: *The owner lost her house when it was sold for delinquent taxes.* 4 having to do with delinquents. 1, 3, 4 *adj.,* 2 *n.* —**de·lin′quent·ly,** *adv.*

**de·lir·i·ous** (di lir′ē əs) 1 temporarily out of one's senses; wandering in mind; raving. 2 wildly excited: *delirious with joy.* 3 caused by DELIRIUM. *adj.* —**de·lir′i·ous·ly,** *adv.*

**de·lir·i·um** (di lir′ē əm) 1 a temporary disorder of the mind that occurs during fevers, insanity, drunkenness, etc.: *Delirium is characterized by excitement, irrational talk, and hallucinations.* 2 any wild excitement that cannot be controlled. *n., pl.* **de·lir·i·ums** *or* **de·lir·i·a** (-ē ə).

**delirium tre·mens** (trē′mənz) violent tremblings and terrifying hallucinations, caused by excessive drinking of alcoholic liquor.

**de·liv·er** (di liv′ər) 1 carry and give out; distribute. 2 hand over; give up: *to deliver a fort to the enemy.* 3 give forth in words: *The traveller delivered an interesting talk about her journey. The jury delivered its verdict.* 4 strike; throw: *The fighter delivered a blow.* 5 set free; rescue; save from evil or trouble: *"Deliver us from evil."* 6 help in the birth of: *The doctor delivered the baby at noon.* *v.* —**de·liv′er·a·ble,** *adj.* —**de·liv′er·er,** *n.*
**be delivered of,** give birth to.

**de·liv·er·ance** (di liv′ə rəns *or* di liv′rəns) 1 the act of setting free or the state of being set free; a rescue or release: *The men rejoiced in their deliverance from prison.* 2 a formal opinion or judgment. *n.*

**de·liv·er·y** (di liv′ə rē) 1 the act of carrying and handing over letters, goods, etc.; the act of distributing: *The mail delivery was late today.* 2 a giving up; handing over: *The captive was released upon the delivery of her ransom.* 3 a manner of speaking; way of giving a speech, lecture, etc.: *Our MP has an excellent delivery.* 4 an act or way of striking, throwing, etc. 5 a rescue or release. 6 the act of giving birth: *a difficult delivery.* 7 the act of assisting at a birth. 8 anything that is delivered; goods to be delivered. *n., pl.* **de·liv·er·ies.**

**dell** (del) a small, sheltered glen or valley, usually having trees in it. *n.*

**de·louse** (dē lous′ *or* dē louz′) remove lice from. *v.*

**del·phin·i·um** (del fin′ē əm) LARKSPUR. *n.*

**del·ta** (del′tə) 1 the deposit of earth and sand, usually three-sided, that collects at the mouth of some rivers. 2 the fourth letter of the Greek alphabet (Δ or δ). *n.*

**Del·ta–wing** or **del·ta–wing** (del′tə wing′) of a jet plane, having a triangular structure. *adj.*

**de·lude** (di lüd′) mislead; deceive: *He deluded himself into believing he would pass his examinations without studying.* *v.,* **de·lud·ed, de·lud·ing.** —**de·lud′er,** *n.*

**del·uge** (del′yüj) 1 a great flood. 2 a heavy fall of rain. 3 flood. 4 overwhelm as if by a flood: *The movie star was deluged with requests for her autograph.* 5 any overwhelming rush: *Most stores have a deluge of orders just before Christmas.* 1, 2, 5 *n.,* 3, 4 *v.,* **del·uged, del·ug·ing.**

**de·lu·sion** (di lü′zhən) 1 the act of deluding or the state of being DELUDED: *In his delusion, he had expected his friends to come to his rescue.* 2 a false notion or belief: *The voyages of Columbus destroyed the common delusion that the earth was flat.* 3 in psychiatry, a fixed belief maintained in spite of all evidence from one's own senses and the objective world that it is false: *The old man suffered from the delusion that his food was being poisoned.* *n.*

**de·lu·sive** (di lü′siv) misleading; deceptive; false. *adj.*

**de luxe** or **de·luxe** (də lúks′ *or* də luks′) of exceptionally good quality; elegant; costly. *adj.*

**delve** (delv) 1 search carefully for information: *The scholar delved in many libraries for facts.* 2 dig. *v.,* **delved, delv·ing.**

**de·mag·net·ize** (dē mag′nə tīz′) deprive of MAGNETISM (def. 1). *v.,* **de·mag·net·ized, de·mag·net·iz·ing.** —**de·mag′net·i·za′tion,** *n.*

**dem·a·gog** (dem′ə gog′) See DEMAGOGUE. *n.*

**dem·a·gog·ic** (dem′ə goj′ik) 1 of a DEMAGOGUE. 2 like a DEMAGOGUE or demagogues. *adj.*

**dem·a·gogue** (dem′ə gog′) a popular leader who stirs up the people by appealing to their emotions and prejudices: *The chief aim of most demagogues is to get power for themselves.* *n.* Also, **demagog.**

**dem·a·gogu·er·y** (dem′ə gog′ə rē) the methods or principles of a DEMAGOGUE. *n.*

**dem·a·go·gy** (dem′ə gō′jē, dem′ə goj′ē *or* dem′ə gog′ē) DEMAGOGUERY. *n.*

**de·mand** (di mand′) 1 ask for with authority: *to demand a trial. The police officer demanded her driver's licence.* 2 claim as a right: *to demand payment of a debt.* 3 ask urgently or insistently: *"What have you done with my hockey stick?" she demanded.* 4 an urgent or insistent request: *a demand for an answer.* 5 call for; require or need: *Training a puppy demands patience.* 6 the thing demanded: *His demand was the immediate release of all the prisoners.* 7 a claim; call: *With two jobs to look after, she has many demands on her time.* 8 a seeking or being sought after; request or need: *Because of the large crop, the supply of apples was greater than the demand. Taxis are in great demand on rainy days.* 1–3, 5 *v.,* 4, 6–8 *n.* —**de·mand′er,** *n.*
**on demand,** as and when requested: *a loan payable on demand.*

**de·mand·ing** (di man′ding) 1 EXACTING: *a demanding person, a demanding job.* 2 ppr. of DEMAND. 1 *adj.,* 2 *v.*

**de·mar·cate** (dē′mär kāt′) 1 set and mark the limits of. 2 separate; distinguish. *v.,* **de·mar·cat·ed, de·mar·cat·ing.**

**de·mar·ca·tion** (dē′mär kā′shən) 1 the act of setting and marking the limits: *the demarcation of infancy from childhood.* 2 a separation; distinction: *the demarcation of a country's authority.* *n.*

**de·mean**[1] (di mēn′) lower in dignity or standing; humble: *The dictator's actions demeaned all his subjects.* *v.*
☞ *Hom.* DEMESNE (di mēn′).

**de·mean**[2] (di mēn′) behave or conduct (oneself): *The duke's son demeans himself well.* *v.*

**de·mean·our** or **de·mean·or** (di mē′nər) the way a person looks and acts; behaviour; conduct; manner: *Amy has a quiet, modest demeanour.* *n.*

**de·ment·ed** (di men′tid) insane; crazy. *adj.*

**de·mer·it** (dē mer′it) 1 a fault; defect. 2 a mark against a person's record given for unsatisfactory performance or behaviour or for violation of a rule or law: *Many provinces have a system of demerits for certain driving offences.* *n.*

**de·mesne** (di mān′ *or* di mēn′) 1 the possession and actual use of land. 2 on an estate, the house and land reserved for the owner's use. 3 a domain; district; region. *n.* Compare with DOMAIN.
☞ *Hom.* DEMEAN (for the second pronunciation of **demesne**).

**dem·i·god** (dem′ē god′) 1 in mythology: **a** a god that is partly human; the offspring of a god or goddess and a human being: *Hercules was a demigod.* **b** a minor or lesser god. 2 a person who is so outstanding in some way that he or she seems to be godlike: *The famous hockey player was a demigod to his young fans.* *n.*

**dem·i·john** (dem′ē jon′) a large bottle of glass or earthenware enclosed in wicker. *n.*

**de·mil·i·tar·ize** (dē mil′ə tə rīz′) free from military control. *v.,* **de·mil·i·tar·ized, de·mil·i·tar·iz·ing.** —**de·mil′i·ta·ri·za′tion,** *n.*

**de·mise** (di mīz′) 1 death. 2 the transfer of an estate by a will or lease. 3 the transfer of royal power by death or abdication. *n.*

**dem·i·tasse** (dem′ē tas′) 1 a very small cup for

serving black coffee.   **2** a very small cup of black coffee.   *n.*

**de·mo·bi·lize** (dē mō′bə līz′)   **1** disband: *When a war is over, the armies are demobilized.*   **2** release from military service: *I'm still waiting to be demobilized.*   *v.,* **de·mo·bi·lized, de·mo·bi·liz·ing.** —**de·mo·bi·li·za′tion,** *n.*

**de·moc·ra·cy** (di mok′rə sē)   **1** a system of government by means of elected representatives: *Under a democracy, the people rule either by direct vote at public meetings or indirectly through the election of certain representatives to govern them.*   **2** the ideals and principles of such a government, such as equality of rights and opportunities and the rule of the majority.   **3** a country, state, or community having such a government: *Canada is a democracy.*   **4** the treatment of others as one's equals.   *n., pl.* **de·moc·ra·cies.**

**dem·o·crat** (dem′ə krat′)   **1** a person who believes that a government should be run by the people who live under it.   **2** a person who treats other people as equals.   **3** a light, four-wheeled, horse-drawn vehicle having two double seats, one behind the other.   **4** *U.S.* a member of the DEMOCRATIC PARTY.   *n.*

**dem·o·crat·ic** (dem′ə krat′ik)   **1** of or like a DEMOCRACY.   **2** treating other people as one's equals: *She was very democratic in her treatment of the employees.*   **3** *U.S.* of or having to do with the DEMOCRATIC PARTY.   *adj.* —**dem′o·crat′i·cal·ly,** *adv.*

**Democratic Party**   one of the two main political parties in the United States.

**de·moc·ra·tize** (di mok′rə tīz′)   make or become DEMOCRATIC.   *v.,* **de·moc·ra·tized, de·moc·ra·tiz·ing.** —**de·moc·ra·ti·za′tion,** *n.*

**de·mol·ish** (di mol′ish)   **1** pull or tear down; wreck; raze: *The old train station will be demolished this summer.*   **2** break into pieces; smash or crush: *The whole pile of books fell on the doll and demolished it.*   **3** show to be false or weak; ruin or discredit: *The government's arguments for the new bill were demolished by the opposition.*   *v.* —**de·mol′ish·er,** *n.* —**de·mol′ish·ment,** *n.*

**dem·o·li·tion** (dem′ə lish′ən)   destruction; ruin.   *n.*

**de·mon** (dē′mən)   **1** an evil spirit; devil; fiend.   **2** a very wicked or cruel person.   **3** an evil or undesirable influence or condition: *The demon of greed ruined the miser's happiness.*   **4** a person who has great energy, vigour, or skill: *She's a demon for work.*   **5** Usually spelled **daemon:** **a** an attendant or guardian spirit. **b** in Greek mythology, a supernatural being ranking less than a god and more than a human being.   *n.* —**de′mon·like′,** *adj.*
☛ *Hom.* DAEMON.

**de·mo·ni·ac** (dē mō′nē ak′)   **1** of demons.   **2** devilish; fiendish: *Burning people alive was a demoniac custom.*   **3** raging; frantic.   **4** possessed by an evil spirit.   **5** a person supposed to be possessed by an evil spirit.   1–4 *adj.,* 5 *n.*

**de·mo·ni·a·cal** (dē′mə nī′ə kəl)   DEMONIAC.   *adj.*

**de·mon·ic** (di mon′ik)   of or caused by evil spirits.   *adj.*

**de·mon·stra·bil·i·ty** (di mon′strə bil′ə tē)   the quality or condition of being DEMONSTRABLE.   *n.*

**de·mon·stra·ble** (di mon′strə bəl)   capable of being proved.   *adj.*

---

**demobilize**   323   **demote**

hat, āge, fär; let, ēqual, tėrm; it, īce
hot, ōpen, ôrder; oil, out; cup, pùt, rüle
əbove, takən, pencəl, lemən, circəs
ch, child; ng, long; sh, ship
th, thin; ᴛʜ, then; zh, measure

**de·mon·stra·bly** (di mon′strə blē)   **1** in a manner that can be proved; clearly.   **2** by DEMONSTRATION (defs. 1, 2).   *adv.*

**dem·on·strate** (dem′ən strāt′)   **1** establish the truth of; prove.   **2** explain and illustrate with the aid of examples, experiments, etc.: *We watched the lab instructor demonstrate the process of electrolysis.*   **3** try to prove the quality, usefulness, etc. of a product to a prospective buyer or buyers by showing it in use: *The salesman demonstrated the electric drill for her by drilling holes in thick steel.*   **4** show clearly and openly: *She demonstrated her love for her niece by giving her a big hug.*   **5** publicly show feelings or views about a particular person, issue, etc.: *An angry crowd demanding better police protection demonstrated in front of the city hall.*   *v.,* **dem·on·strat·ed, dem·on·strat·ing.**

**dem·on·stra·tion** (dem′ən strā′shən)   **1** a clear proof: *a demonstration of the defendant's guilt, a demonstration that the earth is round.*   **2** an explanation with the use of examples, experiments, etc.: *a demonstration of weaving techniques.*   **3** a showing of a product in use to illustrate its merits to a prospective buyer or buyers: *the demonstration of a new overhead projector.*   **4** an open show or expression of feeling: *a demonstration of joy.*   **5** a public show of feelings or views about a person, cause, etc. by many people in a parade or meeting.   **6** a display of military strength.   *n.*

**de·mon·stra·tive** (di mon′strə tiv)   **1** expressing one's affections freely and openly: *The girl's demonstrative greetings embarrassed her shy brother.*   **2** showing clearly; explanatory.   **3** giving proof; conclusive.   **4** in grammar, pointing out the one or ones referred to as distinct from others of the same group or class: *The adjective* this *in this book is a demonstrative adjective which serves to distinguish one particular book from all others.*   **5** a pronoun, adjective or adverb that points out: *That* and *there are demonstratives.*   1–4 *adj.,* 5 *n.* —**de·mon′stra·tive·ly,** *adv.* —**de·mon′stra·tive·ness,** *n.*

**dem·on·stra·tor** (dem′ən strā′tər)   **1** a person who demonstrates a process, procedure, or product for an audience, such as one who shows a medical or dental procedure or conducts a laboratory experiment for students, or one who shows how a machine or apparatus is used.   **2** a person who takes part in a demonstration of protest or demand: *Several demonstrators were hurt in a scuffle with guards.*   **3** a sample product used by a seller to demonstrate the merits of the product: *She got a very good deal on her new car because it was a demonstrator.*   *n.*

**de·mor·al·i·za·tion** (di môr′ə lə zā′shən *or* di môr′ə lī zā′shən)   a demoralizing or being DEMORALIZED.   *n.*

**de·mor·al·ize** (di môr′ə līz′)   **1** corrupt the morals of: *The drug habit demoralizes people.*   **2** weaken the spirit, courage, or discipline of; dishearten: *Lack of food and ammunition demoralized the besieged soldiers.*   **3** throw into confusion or disorder: *Threats of war demoralized the stock market.*   *v.,* **de·mor·al·ized, de·mor·al·iz·ing.**

**de·mote** (di mōt′)   put back to a lower grade; reduce

in rank: *She was demoted from corporal to private.* *v.*, **de·mot·ed, de·mot·ing.**

**de·mo·tion** (di mō′shən) **1** the act of demoting. **2** the fact of being DEMOTEd. *n.*

**de·mount·a·ble** (dē moun′tə bəl) that can be removed: *a demountable wheel rim.* *adj.*

**de·mul·cent** (di mul′sənt) **1** soothing. **2** a soothing ointment or medicine. 1 *adj.*, 2 *n.*

**de·mur** (di mėr′) **1** object: *The clerk demurred at working overtime without extra pay.* **2** objection. 1 *v.*, **de·murred, de·mur·ring;** 2 *n.*

**de·mure** (di myùr′) **1** quiet and modest in behaviour: *a demure young lady.* **2** artificially proper; assuming an air of modesty; coy: *the demure smile of a flirt.* *adj.*, **de·mur·er, de·mur·est.** —**de·mure′ly**, *adv.* —**de·mure′ness**, *n.*

**den** (den) **1** a wild animal's home; lair: *The bear's den was in a cave.* **2** a room in a home where a person can read, work, or think in privacy: *There is a small, cosy den off the living room.* **3** a small, dirty, unattractive room, house, etc.: *The beggars lived in dens along the waterfront.* **4** a place used as a hideout or for secret activities: *a den of thieves.* **5** a group of eight to ten WOLF CUBS. **6** live in or retire to a den. **7** escape into or hide in a den. 1–5 *n.*, 6, 7 *v.*, **denned, den·ning.** —**den′like**, *adj.*

**de·na·tion·al·ize** (dē nash′ə nə līz′ or dē nash′nə līz′) **1** deprive of national rights, scope, or character. **2** of industries, return from national to private control or ownership. *v.*, **de·na·tion·al·ized, de·na·tion·al·iz·ing.** —**de·na′tion·al·i·za′tion**, *n.*

**de·nat·u·ral·ize** (dē nach′ə rə līz′ or dē nach′rə līz′) **1** make unnatural. **2** withdraw citizenship from a naturalized citizen. *v.*, **de·nat·u·ral·ized, de·nat·u·ral·iz·ing.** —**de·nat′u·ral·i·za′tion**, *n.*

**de·na·ture** (dē nā′chər) **1** change the nature of. **2** make alcohol, food, etc. unfit for drinking or eating without destroying its usefulness for other purposes. *v.*, **de·na·tured, de·na·tur·ing.** —**de·na′tur·a′tion**, *n.*

**den·drite** (den′drīt) **1** a stone or mineral with branching, tree-like markings. **2** a tree-like marking. **3** the branching part at the receiving end of a nerve cell. See NEURON for picture. *n.*

**Den·e Nation** (den′ā or den′ē) *Cdn.* the official organization representing the Athapascan peoples of the Northwest Territories: *The Dene Nation was formerly called the Northwest Territories Indian Brotherhood.*

**den·gue** (deng′gā) an infectious fever with skin rash and severe pain in the joints and muscles. *n.*

**de·ni·al** (di nī′əl) **1** a statement that something is not true: *a denial of the existence of ghosts.* **2** a statement that one does not hold to or accept something: *a public denial of a belief.* **3** refusing: *His denial of our request was impolite.* **4** a disowning; refusing to acknowledge. **5** doing without things one wants; SELF-DENIAL. *n.*

**de·ni·er** (di nī′ər) a person who denies. *n.*

**den·im** (den′əm) **1** a heavy, coarse cotton cloth with a diagonal weave, usually woven with a coloured warp and white filling threads: *Denim is used mainly for work and casual clothes, upholstery, etc.* **2 denims,** *pl.* pants or overalls made of denim, usually blue. *n.*
☛ *Etym.* A shortening of F *serge de Nîmes* 'serge from Nîmes'. *Serge* is a common name for fabric with a diagonal weave, and this kind of serge was first made in Nîmes, a manufacturing town in southern France. 17c.

**den·i·zen** (den′ə zən) **1** an inhabitant; occupant: *Fish are denizens of the sea.* **2** a foreigner who is given certain rights. **3** a foreign word, plant, animal, etc. that has been naturalized: *The common English sparrow is a denizen of North America.* *n.*

**de·nom·i·nate** (di nom′ə nāt′ *for verb,* di nom′ə nit *or* di nom′ə nāt′ *for adjective*) **1** give a name to; name. **2** representing a unit of measure. *The 6 and 4 in 6 cm and 4 kg are* **denominate numbers.** 1 *v.*, **de·nom·i·nat·ed, de·nom·i·nat·ing;** 2 *adj.*

**de·nom·i·na·tion** (di nom′ə nā′shən) **1** a name for a group or class of things; name. **2** a religious group, usually represented by a number of local churches: *Presbyterian and Baptist are two large Protestant denominations.* **3** a class or kind of unit: *The Canadian coin of lowest denomination is a cent.* **4** the act of naming. *n.*

**de·nom·i·na·tion·al** (di nom′ə nā′shə nəl) having to do with some religious DENOMINATION (def. 2) or denominations; SECTARIAN (def. 1). *adj.* —**de·nom′i·na′tion·al·ly**, *adv.*

**de·nom·i·na·tion·al·ism** (di nom′ə nā′shə nə liz′əm) **1** DENOMINATIONAL principles. **2** a division into DENOMINATIONS (def. 2). *n.*

**de·nom·i·na·tive** (di nom′ə nə tiv *or* di nom′ə nā′tiv) **1** giving a distinctive name; naming. **2** in grammar, formed from a noun or an adjective: *To centre and to whiten are* **denominative verbs. 3** a word formed from a noun or an adjective. 1, 2 *adj.*, 3 *n.* —**de·nom′i·na·tive·ly**, *adv.*

**de·nom·i·na·tor** (di nom′ə nā′tər) **1** the number below the line in a fraction, stating the size of the parts in their relation to the whole: *In* $3/4$, *4 is the denominator, and 3 is the numerator.* **2** a person or thing that names. *n.*

**de·no·ta·tion** (dē′nō tā′shən) **1** the meaning, especially the exact, literal meaning: *The denotation of* home *is "the place where one lives," but the word has many* connotations *as well.* Compare with CONNOTATION. **2** denoting or marking out. **3** a mark or sign. *n.*

**de·note** (di nōt′) **1** be the sign of; indicate: *A fever usually denotes sickness. If a teacher writes "Excellent" on a pupil's exercise, it denotes very good work.* **2** be a name for; mean: *The word "stool" denotes a small chair without a back.* *v.*, **de·not·ed, de·not·ing.**

**dé·noue·ment** (dā nü′män; *French,* dā nü män′) the solution of a plot in a play, a story, etc.; outcome; end. *n.*

**de·nounce** (di nouns′) **1** condemn publicly; express strong disapproval of: *The judge denounced drinking drivers.* **2** inform against; accuse: *He denounced his own brother to the military police as a spy.* **3** give formal notice of the termination of a treaty, etc. *v.*, **de·nounced, de·nounc·ing.** —**de·nounc′er**, *n.*

**de·nounce·ment** (di nouns′mənt) the act of denouncing; DENUNCIATION. *n.*

**dense** (dens) **1** closely packed together; thick: *a dense fog, a dense growth of weeds.* **2** stupid; dull; slow-thinking: *Mette's dense look showed she did not understand the problem.* *adj.*, **dens·er, dens·est.** —**dense′ly**, *adv.* —**dense′ness**, *n.*

**den·si·ty** (den′sə tē) **1** a dense condition or quality; having parts very close together; compactness; thickness:

*The density of the forest prevented us from seeing more than a little way ahead.* **2** the quantity of matter in a particular unit of volume; the ratio of the mass of a given volume of a substance to that of an equal volume of a standard substance: *A cubic metre of lead has more mass than a cubic metre of wood, so we say lead has a greater density than wood. Water is the standard of density for solids and liquids, and air for gases.* **3** stupidity. *n., pl.* **den·si·ties.**

**dent** (dent) **1** a hollow made by a blow or pressure; a DINT: *Bullets had made dents in the soldier's steel helmet.* **2** make a dent in; DINT: *The blow from the hammer dented the table.* **3** become dented. *1 n., 2, 3 v.*
☞ *Etym.* **Dent** and DINT both developed from OE *dynt* 'stroke or blow'. Because they were so similar in sound to the verb INDENT, originally meaning 'make a toothlike cut', they came to mean the hollow or mark made by a blow. The modern phrase **by dint of** comes from the old expression *by dint of sword,* in which *dint* had its original meaning of 'a blow'. See also the note at INDENT.

**den·tal** (den′təl) **1** of or for the teeth. **2** of, by, or for dentistry. *adj.*

**dental floss** a thin, strong, smooth thread used to remove PLAQUE and food particles from between the teeth.

**den·ti·frice** (den′tə fris) a paste, powder, or liquid for cleaning the teeth. *n.*

**den·tin** (den′tin) DENTINE. *n.*

**den·tine** (den′tēn) the hard, bony material beneath the enamel of a tooth, forming the main part of a tooth. *n.* Also, **dentin.**

**den·tist** (den′tist) a person who is qualified to practise the prevention and treatment of tooth decay and other problems and diseases of the teeth and gums, and to fit patients with false teeth. *n.*

**den·tist·ry** (den′ti strē) the art or occupation of a DENTIST. *n.*

**den·ti·tion** (den tish′ən) **1** the growth of teeth; teething. **2** the kind, number, and arrangement of the teeth: *Dogs and wolves have the same dentition.* *n.*

**den·ture** (den′chər) **1** a set of artificial teeth. **2** an artificial tooth or group of teeth. *n.*

**den·tur·ist** (den′chə rist) a person trained to make and fit DENTURES. *n.*

**de·nu·da·tion** (dē′nyü dā′shən *or* dē′nü dā′shən) **1** denuding. **2** a DENUDED condition. *n.*

**de·nude** (di nyüd′ *or* di nüd′) make bare; strip of clothing, covering, etc.: *Deciduous trees are denuded of their leaves in winter.* *v.*, **de·nud·ed, de·nud·ing.**

**de·nun·ci·a·tion** (di nun′sē ā′shən) **1** public condemnation; an expression of strong disapproval: *the teacher's denunciation of cheating.* **2** the act of informing against; accusation. **3** a formal notice of the intention to end a treaty, etc. **4** a declaration of a curse, revenge, etc.; warning; threat. *n.*

**de·nun·ci·a·to·ry** (di nun′sē ə tô′rē) condemning; accusing; threatening. *adj.*

**de·ny** (di nī′) **1** declare something is not true: *The prisoner denied the charges.* **2** say that one does not hold to or accept: *She denied the principles of communism.* **3** refuse: *to deny a favour.* **4** refuse to acknowledge; disown: *Indira denied her signature.* *v.*, **de·nied, de·ny·ing.**

**deny oneself,** do without the things one wants.

**dent**     **325**     **depend**

hat, āge, fär; let, ēqual, tėrm; it, īce
hot, ōpen, ôrder; oil, out; cup, pùt, rüle
əbove, takən, pencəl, lemən, circəs
ch, child; ng, long; sh, ship
th, thin; ᴛʜ, then; zh, measure

**deny oneself to,** refuse to see: *Illness forced Mrs. Smith to deny herself to all callers.*

**de·o·dor·ant** (dē ō′də rənt) **1** a preparation that destroys, prevents, or masks an undesirable odour, especially a powder, liquid, or salve used on the body. **2** capable of destroying, preventing, or masking undesirable odours. *1 n., 2 adj.*

**de·o·dor·ize** (dē ō′də rīz′) remove undesirable odours from: *to deodorize a bathroom.* *v.*, **de·o·dor·ized, de·o·dor·iz·ing.** —**de·o′dor·i·za′tion,** *n.*

**de·o·dor·iz·er** (dē ō′də rī′zər) a substance used to destroy or mask odours, especially in a room, on articles of furniture, etc.: *He bought some deodorizer for the dog's bed.* *n.*

**de·ox·i·dize** (dē ok′sə dīz′) remove oxygen from. *v.*, **de·ox·i·dized, de·ox·i·diz·ing.** —**de·ox′i·diz′er,** *n.*

**de·ox·y·gen·ate** (dē ok′sə jə nāt′) remove oxygen from; deoxidize. *v.*, **de·ox·y·gen·at·ed, de·ox·y·gen·at·ing.**

**de·ox·y·ri·bo·nu·cle·ic acid** (dē ok′si rī′bō nyü klē′ik *or* dē ok′si rī′bō nü klē′ik) DNA, an essential component of all living matter, that in higher organisms contains the genetic codes determining heredity.

**dep. 1** deputy. **2** deposit. **3** depot. **4** department. **5** deponent.

**de·part** (di pärt′) **1** go away; leave: *The train departs at 6:15.* **2** turn away; change (*from*): *Petra departed from her usual way of working.* **3** go away from (chiefly used of life): *He departed this life at the age of seventy.* **4** die. *v.*

**de·part·ed** (di pär′tid) **1** a dead person or persons. **2** dead. **3** gone; past. **4** pt. and pp. of DEPART. *1 n. sing. and pl., 2, 3 adj., 4 v.*

**de·part·ment** (di pärt′mənt) **1** a separate part or division of a larger unit, such as a government, business, school, etc.: *the city fire department, the furniture department of a store, the department of external affairs of the federal government, the English department of a school.* **2** a field or range of activity or influence: *He said that handling complaints from customers was not his department.* **3** in France and some Latin American countries, an administrative district similar to a province. *n.*

**de·part·men·tal** (dē′pärt men′təl) **1** having to do with a DEPARTMENT. **2** divided into DEPARTMENTS. *adj.*

**department store** a store that sells many different kinds of articles arranged in separate departments.

**de·par·ture** (di pär′chər) **1** the act of going away; the act of leaving: *His departure was very sudden.* **2** a turning away; change: *a departure from our old custom.* **3** a starting on a new course of action or thought: *Learning to ski will be a new departure for me, for I have never done anything like it.* *n.*

**de·pend** (di pend′) **1** rely; trust: *You can depend on this timetable from the depot.* **2** get support; rely for help: *Children depend on their parents.* **3** be a result of; be controlled or influenced by: *The success of our picnic depends partly on the weather.* **4** hang down. *v.* **that depends** or **it depends,** the answer will be determined by certain conditions or actions that are not yet definitely known or understood: *"That depends,"* answered mother.

**de·pend·a·bil·i·ty** (di pen′də bil′ə tē) reliability; trustworthiness. *n.*

**de·pend·a·ble** (di pen′də bəl) reliable; trustworthy: *Newspapers ought to be dependable. adj.* —**de·pend′a·ble·ness,** *n.* —**de·pend′a·bly,** *adv.*

**de·pend·ant** (di pen′dənt) **1** a person who depends on someone else for support: *A man's wife and children are usually his dependants.* **2** See DEPENDENT (def. 1). 1 *n.,* 2 *adj.*
☛ *Hom.* DEPENDENT.

**de·pend·ence** (di pen′dəns) **1** reliance on another for support or help: *The girl wished to go to work so that she could end her dependence on her aunt.* **2** reliance; trust: *Do not put your dependence in him, for he sometimes fails us.* **3** the condition of being a result of another thing; the fact of being controlled or influenced by something else: *the dependence of crops on the weather.* **4** a person or thing relied on. *n.*

**de·pend·en·cy** (di pen′dən sē) **1** a country or territory controlled by another country: *Gibraltar is a dependency of the United Kingdom.* **2** DEPENDENCE. **3** a thing that depends on another for existence, support, or help. *n., pl.* **de·pend·en·cies.**

**de·pend·ent** (di pen′dənt) **1** relying on another for support or help: *A child is dependent on its parents.* **2** See DEPENDANT (def. 1). **3** resulting from another thing; controlled or influenced by something else: *Good crops are dependent on the weather. Being promoted is dependent on doing good enough work in school.* **4** hanging down. 1, 3, 4 *adj.,* 2 *n.*
☛ *Hom.* DEPENDANT.

**de·pict** (di pikt′) **1** represent by drawing, painting, or carving; picture: *A famous painting by Leonardo depicts the Mona Lisa.* **2** describe in words: *Who Has Seen the Wind depicts life on the Prairies during the Depression. v.*

**de·pic·tion** (di pik′shən) a description in words, music, painting, and sculpture. *n.*

**de·pil·a·to·ry** (di pil′ə tô′rē) **1** capable of removing hair. **2** a paste, liquid, or other preparation for removing hair. 1 *adj.,* 2 *n., pl.* **de·pil·a·to·ries.**

**de·plete** (di plēt′) empty; exhaust: *The traveller went home because her funds were depleted. v.,* **de·plet·ed, de·plet·ing.**

**de·ple·tion** (di plē′shən) **1** depleting. **2** being DEPLETEd. *n.*

**de·plor·a·ble** (di plô′rə bəl) **1** to be DEPLOREd; regrettable; lamentable: *a deplorable accident.* **2** wretched; miserable. *adj.* —**de·plor′a·bly,** *adv.*

**de·plore** (di plôr′) be very sorry about; regret deeply; lament: *We deplore the accident. v.,* **de·plored, de·plor·ing.**

**de·ploy** (di ploi′) spread out troops, military units, etc. from a column into a long battle line. *v.*
—**de·ploy′ment,** *n.*

**de·po·nent** (di pō′nənt) a person who testifies, especially in writing, under oath. *n.*

**de·pop·u·late** (dē pop′yə lāt′) deprive of inhabitants: *The conquerors depopulated the enemy's country, driving the inhabitants away or killing them. v.,* **de·pop·u·lat·ed, de·pop·u·lat·ing.** —**de·pop′u·la′tor,** *n.*

**de·pop·u·la·tion** (dē pop′yə lā′shən) **1** a depopulating. **2** being DEPOPULATEd. *n.*

**de·port** (di pôrt′) **1** banish; expel; remove: *When an alien is deported, he or she is sent out of the country, usually back to his or her native land.* **2** behave or conduct oneself in a particular manner: *The boys were trained to deport themselves like gentlemen. v.*

**de·por·ta·tion** (dē′pôr tā′shən) banishment; expulsion; removal: *Deportation of criminals from England to Australia was once common. n.*

**de·port·ment** (di pôrt′mənt) **1** the way a person acts; behaviour; conduct: *A gentleman is known by his deportment.* **2** good bearing; graceful movement: *Young ladies once took lessons in deportment. n.*

**de·pose** (di pōz′) **1** put out of office or a position of authority; remove from a throne: *The queen was deposed by the revolution.* **2** declare under oath; testify: *He deposed that he had seen the prisoner on the day of the murder. v.,* **de·posed, de·pos·ing.**

**de·pos·it** (di poz′it) **1** put down; lay down; leave lying: *Lee deposited her bundles on the table. The flood deposited a layer of mud in the streets.* **2** the material laid down or left lying by natural means: *a deposit of mud and sand at the mouth of a river.* **3** put in a place for safekeeping: *People deposit money in banks.* **4** something put in a place of safekeeping: *Money put in a bank is a deposit.* **5** pay as a pledge to do something or to pay more later: *If you deposit part of the price, a store will keep an article for you until you pay the rest.* **6** the money paid as a pledge to do something or to pay more later. **7** a mass of some mineral in rock or in the ground: *deposits of tin.* 1, 3, 5 *v.,* 2, 4, 6, 7 *n.*
**on deposit, a** in a place for safekeeping. **b** in a bank.

**dep·o·si·tion** (dep′ə zish′ən *or* dē′pə zish′ən) **1** the act of putting out of office or a position of authority; removal from a throne. **2** in law: **a** the act of testifying under oath. **b** TESTIMONY given under oath; especially, such testimony taken down in writing to be used as evidence later in court: *The witness made a deposition because she was not able to testify in court.* **3** the act or process of depositing: *the deposition of sediment at the mouth of a river.* **4** something deposited; DEPOSIT. *n.*

**de·pos·i·tor** (di poz′ə tər) a person who deposits, especially one who deposits money in a bank. *n.*

**de·pos·i·to·ry** (di poz′ə tô′rē) a place where a thing is put for safekeeping or storage; storehouse. *n., pl.* **de·pos·i·to·ries.**

**dep·ot** (dē′pō *or* dep′ō) **1** a bus or railway station. **2** a storehouse, especially for military supplies. **3** a military recruiting and distribution centre: *After his release from hospital, the soldier was sent to a depot before being returned to his regiment. n.*

**de·prave** (di prāv′) make morally bad; corrupt: *Drinking too much liquor often depraves a person's character. v.,* **de·praved, de·prav·ing.**

**de·praved** (di prāvd′) **1** corrupt; perverted: *He was completely depraved, having no regard for human life.* **2** pt. and pp. of DEPRAVE. 1 *adj.,* 2 *v.*

**de·prav·i·ty** (di prav′ə tē) **1** wickedness; corruption. **2** a corrupt act; bad practice. *n.*, *pl.* **de·prav·i·ties.**

**dep·re·cate** (dep′rə kāt′) express strong disapproval of; plead against; protest against: *Lovers of peace deprecate war.* *v.*, **dep·re·cat·ed, dep·re·cat·ing.** —**dep′re·cat′ing·ly,** *adv.* —**dep′re·ca′tor,** *n.*

**dep·re·ca·tion** (dep′rə kā′shən) a strong expression of disapproval; a pleading or protesting against something. *n.*

**dep·re·ca·to·ry** (dep′rə kə tô′rē) **1** deprecating. **2** *Informal.* apologetic. *adj.*

**de·pre·ci·ate** (di prē′shē āt′) **1** lessen the value or price of. **2** lessen in value: *Certain goods depreciate if they are kept very long.* **3** speak slightingly of; belittle: *She depreciates the value of exercise.* *v.*, **de·pre·ci·at·ed, de·pre·ci·at·ing.** —**de·pre′ci·at′ing·ly,** *adv.* —**de·pre′ci·a′tor,** *n.*

**de·pre·ci·a·tion** (di prē′shē ā′shən) **1** a lessening or lowering in value. **2** speaking slightingly of; belittling. *n.*

**de·pre·ci·a·to·ry** (di prē′shē ə tô′rē) tending to DEPRECIATE, disparage, or undervalue. *adj.*

**dep·re·da·tion** (dep′rə dā′shən) the act of plundering; robbery; ravaging. *n.*

**de·press** (di press′) **1** make sad or gloomy; cause to have low spirits: *She was depressed by the bad news from home.* **2** press down; push down; lower: *When you play the piano, you depress the keys.* **3** lower in amount or value: *The price of potatoes has been depressed by the tremendous size of the harvest this year.* **4** reduce the activity of; weaken: *Some medicines depress the action of the heart.* *v.* —**de·press′ing·ly,** *adv.*

**de·pres·sant** (di pres′ənt) **1** decreasing the rate of vital activities; quieting. **2** a medicine that lessens pain or excitement; SEDATIVE (def. 1). **1** *adj.*, **2** *n.*

**de·pressed** (di prest′) **1** sad or gloomy; low-spirited: *He was depressed by his mother's illness.* **2** pressed down or lowered. **3** pt. and pp. of DEPRESS. **1, 2** *adj.*, **3** *v.*

**de·pres·sion** (di presh′ən) **1** the state of feeling sad or gloomy; low spirits. **2** in psychiatry, a condition in which a person has continual feelings of extreme sadness or hopelessness not directly caused by real events. **3** the action of pressing down: *Depression of the gas pedal causes an automobile to accelerate.* **4** a lowering of amount, force, activity, or quality: *A rapid depression of the mercury in a barometer usually indicates a storm.* **5** a low place or part; hollow: *Depressions in the lawn were filled with water after the rain.* **6** a period of low economic activity, accompanied by high levels of unemployment. **7 the Depression,** the severe economic depression of the 1930's. *n.*

**dep·ri·va·tion** (dep′rə vā′shən) **1** the act of depriving. **2** the state of being DEPRIVED; loss; privation. *n.*

**de·prive** (di prīv′) **1** take away from by force: *The people deprived the cruel king of his power.* **2** keep from having or doing: *Worrying deprived her of sleep.* *v.*, **de·prived, de·priv·ing.**

**de pro·fun·dis** (dē′ prō fun′dis *or* dā′ prō fun′dēs) *Latin.* from the depths (of sorrow, misery, despair, etc.).

**dept.** **1** department. **2** deputy.

**depth** (depth) **1** the quality of being deep; deepness. **2** the distance from top to bottom: *the depth of a hole.* **3** the distance from front to back: *The depth of our house lot is 30 metres.* **4** a deep place. **5** the deepest part: *in the depths of the earth.* **6** the most central part; middle: *in the depth of the forest, in the depth of winter.* **7** profoundness: *A philosopher should have depth of mind.* **8** lowness of pitch. **9** intensity of colour, etc. *n.* **out of one's depth, a** in water so deep that one cannot touch bottom. **b** in a situation too difficult to understand or cope with: *He was out of his depth in the mathematics class.*

**depth bomb** DEPTH CHARGE.

**depth charge** an explosive charge dropped from a ship or airplane and arranged to explode at a certain depth under water.

**dep·u·ta·tion** (dep′yə tā′shən) **1** the act of deputing. **2** a group of persons appointed to act for others: *The ratepayers' association sent a deputation to call on the mayor to present their petition.* *n.*

**de·pute** (di pyüt′) **1** appoint to do one's work or to act in one's place: *The teacher deputed a pupil to take charge of the room while she was gone.* **2** give work, authority, etc. to another. *v.*, **de·put·ed, de·put·ing.**

**dep·u·tize** (dep′yə tīz′) **1** appoint as DEPUTY. **2** act as DEPUTY. *v.*, **dep·u·tized, dep·u·tiz·ing.**

**dep·u·ty** (dep′yə tē) **1** a person appointed to do the work of or to act in the place of another: *A deputy minister is an assistant to a minister of the cabinet.* **2** a representative to or in certain assemblies: *In Quebec the members of the National Assembly are often called deputies.* **3** acting as a deputy. *n.*, *pl.* **dep·u·ties.**

**deputy minister** in Canada, a senior civil servant who acts as assistant to a cabinet minister.

**deputy returning officer** in Canada, an official appointed by the returning officer of a constituency to look after the procedure of voting at a particular polling station: *The deputy returning officer is in charge of counting the ballots.* *Abbrev.:* DRO

**de·rail** (dē rāl′) **1** cause a train, etc. to run off the rails. **2** run off the rails. *v.* —**de·rail′ment,** *n.*

**de·range** (di rānj′) **1** disturb the order or arrangement of; throw into confusion: *Sudden illness in the family deranged our plans for the trip.* **2** make insane: *The mother of the kidnapped baby was temporarily deranged by grief.* *v.*, **de·ranged, de·rang·ing.**

**de·range·ment** (di rānj′mənt) **1** a disturbance of order or arrangement. **2** a mental disorder; insanity. *n.*

**der·by** (dėr′bē; *esp. Brit.*, där′bē) **1** any contest or race: *a fishing derby, a dog derby, a bicycle derby.* **2** a man's stiff hat having a rounded crown and narrow brim; BOWLER². See HAT for picture. **3 Derby, a** a famous horse race in England, founded by the Earl of Derby in 1780 and run every year at Epsom Downs, near London. **b** any of several annual horse races of similar importance: *the Kentucky Derby.* *n.*, *pl.* **der·bies.**

**der·e·lict** (der′ə likt′) **1** abandoned; deserted; forsaken: *a derelict ship.* **2** a ship abandoned at sea. **3** any worthless, deserted person or thing: *The ragged old* *derelict begged for money to buy a meal.* **4** failing in one's duty; negligent. 1, 4 *adj.*, 2, 3 *n.*

**der·e·lic·tion** (der'ə lik'shən) **1** a failure in one's duty; negligence. **2** an abandonment; desertion; forsaking. *n.*

**de·ride** (di rīd') make fun of; laugh at in scorn; ridicule with contempt. *v.*, **de·rid·ed, de·rid·ing.** —**de·rid'er,** *n.* —**de·rid'ing·ly,** *adv.*

**de ri·gueur** (də rē gœR') *French.* required by etiquette; according to custom; proper.

**de·ri·sion** (di rizh'ən) **1** scornful laughter; ridicule; contempt: *Children dread the derision of their playmates.* **2** an object of ridicule. *n.*

**de·ri·sive** (di rī'siv) mocking; ridiculing: *a derisive smile. adj.* —**de·ri'sive·ly,** *adv.* —**de·ri'sive·ness,** *n.*

**de·ri·so·ry** (di rī'sə rē) DERISIVE. *adj.*

**der·i·va·tion** (der'ə vā'shən) **1** the act or process of deriving. **2** the state of being derived. **3** the source; origin: *Many English words are of French derivation.* **4** the formation of new words from old, through use of prefixes and suffixes and other methods. *Example: Quickness = quick +* suffix *-ness.* **5** a statement of how a word was formed. *n.* —**der'iva'tion·al,** *adj.*

**de·riv·a·tive** (di riv'ə tiv) **1** DERIVED (def. 1); not original. **2** something DERIVED (def. 3): *Words formed by adding prefixes and suffixes to other words are called derivatives.* 1 *adj.*, 2 *n.* —**de·riv'a·tive·ly,** *adv.*

**de·rive** (di rīv') **1** receive or obtain from a particular source: *She derives great pleasure from music. Gasoline is derived from petroleum.* **2** come from a source or origin; originate or develop: *Our word table derives from Latin* tabula. **3** make or create new words by adding suffixes or prefixes: *The words* kindness, kinder, *and* unkind *are derived from* kind. **4** trace the development or origin of a custom, condition, word, etc.: *Scholars derive many modern English words from Old French. He derives all his present troubles from the loss of his job years ago.* **5** obtain by reasoning; deduce: *Hannah derived her conclusion from the large amount of data she had collected. v.*, **de·rived, de·riv·ing.** —**de·riv'a·ble,** *adj.* —**de·riv'er,** *n.*

**derived word** a word formed by adding one or more prefixes or suffixes to an existing word or root.

**der·ma** (dėr'mə) **1** the sensitive layer of skin beneath the epidermis. **2** the skin. *n.*

**der·mal** (dėr'məl) of the skin. *adj.*

**der·ma·ti·tis** (dėr'mə tī'tis) inflammation of the skin. *n.*

**der·ma·tol·o·gist** (dėr'mə tol'ə jist) a doctor who is an expert in DERMATOLOGY. *n.*

**der·ma·tol·o·gy** (dėr'mə tol'ə jē) the science that deals with the skin and its diseases. *n.*

**der·mis** (dėr'mis) DERMA. See EPIDERMIS for picture. *n.*

**der·o·gate** (der'ə gāt') **1** take away; detract (*from*): *The king felt that summoning a parliament would derogate from his authority.* **2** become worse; degenerate. *v.*, **der·o·gat·ed, der·o·gat·ing.**

**der·o·ga·tion** (der'ə gā'shən) **1** a lessening or impairment of power, law, position, etc.; detraction. **2** the state of becoming worse; deterioration; debasement. *n.*

**de·rog·a·to·ry** (di rog'ə tô'rē) **1** disparaging; belittling; showing an unfavourable opinion of some person or thing. **2** lessening the value; detracting. *adj.* —**de·rog'a·to'ri·ly,** *adv.*

**der·rick** (der'ik) **1** a machine for lifting and moving heavy objects: *A derrick has a long arm that swings at an angle from the base of an upright post or frame.* **2** a towerlike framework over an oil well, gas well, etc., which holds the drilling and hoisting machinery. *n.*
☛ *Etym.* From the name of a London hangman of the early 17c. The word originally meant 'hangman' or 'gallows'.

**der·ring·er** (der'ən jər) a short pistol that has a large CALIBRE (def. 1). *n.*

**der·vish** (dėr'vish) a member of any of several Moslem religious orders dedicated to a life of poverty and chastity: *The dervishes of some orders practise religious rites that include whirling, dancing, etc. n.*

**des·cant** (des kant' *for verb,* des'kant *for noun*) **1** in music: **a** a separate melody or counterpoint sung above the basic melody. **b** the highest part or melody in harmonic music; soprano or treble. **2** talk at great length; discourse freely: *to descant upon the wonders of nature.* 1 *n.*, 2 *v.*

**de·scend** (di send') **1** go or come down from a higher place to a lower place: *We descend stairs and mountains. The river descends to the sea.* **2** pass from an earlier to a later time: *We still have many superstitions descended from the Middle Ages.* **3** go in sequence from greater to smaller, or higher to lower: *The numerals 100, 75, 50, 25 form a series arranged in descending order.* **4** extend or slope downward: *The road descended in a winding path to the sea.* **5** make a sudden appearance or attack (*used with* on *or* upon): *The wolves descended on the sheep and killed them. Many tourists descended upon the town during the exhibition.* **6** be handed down from parent to child; pass by inheritance: *The land has descended in the family for 150 years.* **7** come down from a source, especially an ancestor (*usually used after the verb* be): *George is descended from a pioneer family.* **8** lower oneself; stoop: *He descended to cheating in an effort to win the scholarship. v.*

**de·scend·ant** (di sen'dənt) **1** a person born of a certain family or group: *a descendant of the United Empire Loyalists.* **2** an offspring; child; great-grandchild, etc.: *You are a direct descendant of your parents, grandparents, great-grandparents, etc. n.*

**de·scent** (di sent') **1** the act or process of coming down or going down from a higher to a lower place: *The balloon made a rapid descent.* **2** a downward slope: *the sharp descent of the ground to the sea.* **3** a way or passage down; a means of descending: *We took the steep descent carefully.* **4** a family line; ancestry: *Our family is of Turkish descent. They can trace their descent back to the 18th century.* **5** a transmitting or handing down of property, qualities, etc. from parent to child; transmission through inheritance: *The estate was acquired by descent. We can trace the descent of red hair in our family through five generations.* **6** a sinking to a lower condition or quality; a decline: *Nina was disturbed by her friend's descent to bigotry and racism.* **7** a sudden attack or unexpected appearance: *The descent of the invaders on the town led to the slaughter of many people. n.*
☛ *Hom.* DISSENT.

**de·scribe** (di skrīb') **1** tell in words how a person looks, feels, or acts, or how a place, a thing, or an event

looks; tell or write about: *The reporter described the accident in detail.* **2** draw the outline of; trace: *The skater described a figure 8.* *v.*, **de•scribed, de•scrib•ing.**
—**de•scrib′a•ble,** *adj.* —**de•scrib′er,** *n.*

**de•scrip•tion** (di skrip′shən) **1** the act of describing; the act of giving a picture or account in words. **2** a composition or account that describes or gives a picture in words. **3** a kind or sort: *In the crowd there were people of every description.* **4** the act of tracing; the act of drawing in outline. *n.*

**de•scrip•tive** (di skrip′tiv) describing; that tells about by using DESCRIPTION (def. 1): *Write a descriptive paragraph about a flower garden.* *adj.*
—**de•scrip′tive•ly,** *adv.* —**de•scrip′tive•ness,** *n.*

**de•scry** (di skrī′) catch sight of; be able to see; make out: *The shipwrecked sailor at last descried an island far away on the horizon.* *v.*, **de•scried, de•scry•ing.**

**des•e•crate** (des′ə krāt′) treat or use without respect; disregard the sacredness of: *The enemy desecrated the temple by using it as a stable.* *v.*, **des•e•crated, des•e•crat•ing.** —**des′e•crat′er, des′e•cra′tor,** *n.*

**des•e•cra•tion** (des′ə krā′shən) **1** the act of desecrating: *The Puritans thought that work or amusement was a desecration of the Sabbath.* **2** the fact or state of being desecrated. *n.*

**de•seg•re•gate** (dē seg′rə gāt′) abolish any law or practice that requires the members of a particular race or particular races to be isolated for any purpose from the rest of the population: *to desegregate the schools.* *v.*, **de•seg•re•gat•ed, de•seg•re•gat•ing.**

**de•seg•re•ga•tion** (dē seg′rə gā′shən) **1** the act or process of desegregating. **2** the state of being DESEGREGATED. *n.*

**de•sen•si•tize** (dē sen′sə tīz′) **1** make less sensitive. **2** in photography, make less sensitive to light. *v.*, **de•sen•si•tized, de•sen•si•tiz•ing.**
—**de•sen′si•ti•za′tion,** *n.* —**de•sen′si•tiz′er,** *n.*

**des•ert**[1] (dez′ərt) **1** a dry, barren region, usually sandy and without trees: *the Sahara Desert.* **2** dry; barren. **3** a region that is not inhabited or cultivated; wilderness. **4** not inhabited or cultivated; wild: *Robinson Crusoe was shipwrecked on a desert island.* *n.*

**de•sert**[2] (di zėrt′) **1** go away and leave; abandon; forsake: *The woman was guilty of deserting her family.* **2** run away from duty. **3** leave military service without permission and with no intention of returning: *The soldier who had deserted was caught and brought back for trial.* **4** fail; leave: *The girl's courage deserted her when she met the angry dog.* *v.* —**de•sert′er,** *n.*
☛ *Hom.* DESERT[3], DESSERT.

**de•sert**[3] (di zėrt′) Usually, **deserts,** *pl.* what is deserved; a suitable reward or punishment: *The robber got his just deserts when he was sentenced to five years in prison.* *n.*
☛ *Hom.* DESERT[2], DESSERT.

**de•ser•tion** (di zėr′shən) **1** deserting. **2** being deserted. **3** running away from duty. **4** leaving military service without permission. *n.*

**de•serve** (di zėrv′) **1** have a claim or right to; be worthy of: *Good work deserves good pay.* **2** be worthy: *She deserves well.* *v.*, **de•served, de•serv•ing.**

**de•serv•ed•ly** (di zėr′vi dlē) according to what is deserved; justly; rightly: *The criminal was deservedly punished.* *adv.*

**de•serv•ing** (di zėr′ving) **1** that deserves; worthy of something. **2** worth helping: *Scholarships are usually awarded to deserving students.* **3** ppr. of DESERVE. 1, 2 *adj.*, 3 *v.* —**de•serv′ing•ly,** *adv.*

**des•ic•cate** (des′ə kāt′) **1** dry thoroughly: *The soil in a desert is desiccated.* **2** preserve by drying thoroughly: *desiccated fruit.* *v.*, **des•ic•cat•ed, des•ic•cat•ing.**
—**des′ic•ca′tion,** *n.*

**de•sid•er•a•ta** (di sid′ə rā′tə *or* di sid′ə rat′ə) pl. of DESIDERATUM.

**de•sid•er•a•tum** (di sid′ə rā′təm *or* di sid′ə rat′əm) something desired or needed: *His consent was a desideratum.* *n., pl.* **de•sid•er•a•ta.**

**de•sign** (di zīn′) **1** a drawing, plan, or sketch made to serve as a pattern from which to work: *a design for a machine, a dress design.* **2** an arrangement of detail, form, and colour in painting, weaving, building, etc.: *a wallpaper design in tan and brown.* **3** make a first sketch of; plan out; arrange the form and colour of; draw in outline: *to design a dress.* **4** make drawings, sketches, plans, etc.: *He designs for a firm of dressmakers.* **5** the art of making designs, patterns, or sketches: *Architects are skilled in design.* **6** a piece of artistic work. **7** a plan in mind to be carried out: *My sister's design is to be a lawyer.* **8** a scheme of attack; evil plan: *The thief had designs upon the safe.* **9** plan out; form in the mind; contrive: *The author designed an exciting plot.* **10** a purpose; aim, intention: *Whether by accident or design, she overturned the lamp.* **11** have in mind to do; purpose: *Did you design this, or did it just happen?* **12** set apart; intend; plan: *His parents designed him for a musical career.* 1, 2, 5–8, 10 *n.*, 3, 4, 9, 11, 12 *v.*
**by design,** on purpose; by intention.

**des•ig•nate** (dez′ig nāt′) **1** mark out; point out; indicate definitely: *Red lines designate main roads on this map. Her uniform designates her rank.* **2** name; entitle: *The ruler of the country was designated queen.* **3** select for duty, office, etc.; appoint: *That is the woman designated as the new Governor General.* *v.*, **des•ig•nat•ed, des•ig•nat•ing.**

**des•ig•na•tion** (dez′ig nā′shən) **1** the act of marking out or of pointing out; definite indication: *The designation of places on a map should be clear.* **2** a descriptive title; name: *"Her Majesty" is a designation given to the Queen.* **3** the appointment or selection for a duty, office, position, etc.: *The designation of cabinet officers is one of the powers of the prime minister.* *n.*

**de•sign•ed•ly** (di zī′ni dlē) purposely; intentionally. *adv.*

**de•sign•er** (di zī′nər) **1** a person who DESIGNS: *A dress designer makes patterns and sketches for women's clothes.* **2** a plotter; schemer. *n.*

**de•sign•ing** (di zī′ning) **1** scheming; plotting: *a designing rogue.* **2** the art of making designs, patterns, sketches, etc.: *She studies dress designing at school.* **3** ppr. of DESIGN. 1 *adj.*, 2 *n.*, 3 *v.*

**de•sir•a•bil•i•ty** (di zī′rə bil′ə tē) the state or quality of being desirable: *Nobody doubts the desirability of good health.* *n.*

**de·sir·a·ble** (di zīr′ə bəl)   worth wishing for; worth having; pleasing; good; excellent.   *adj.*
—**de·sir′a·ble·ness,** *n.*   —**de·sir′a·bly,** *adv.*

**de·sire** (di zīr′)   **1** long for; wish strongly for.   **2** a strong wish; a longing: *His desire is to travel.*   **3** express a wish for; ask for or request, especially in a formal manner: *The Governor General desires your presence in her office.*   **4** an expressed wish; request: *The queen graciously granted the knight's desire.*   **5** something desired.   1, 3 *v.*, **de·sired, de·sir·ing;**   2, 4, 5 *n.*

**de·sir·ous** (di zī′rəs)   having or showing desire or longing; strongly wishing: *desirous of fame. Desirous to learn all she could, she questioned the old man closely. He was desirous that his true identity should not be revealed.* *adj.*

**de·sist** (di sist′ *or* di zist′)   stop; cease: *The judge ordered him to desist from fighting.*   *n.*

**desk** (desk)   a piece of furniture with one or more drawers and a flat or sloping top on which to write or to rest books, papers, etc.   *n.*
☞ *Etym.*   See note at DISH.

**desktop publishing**   the preparation of camera-ready copy for printing, using a computer.

**des·o·late** (des′ə lit *for adjective,* des′ə lāt′ *for verb*)   **1** barren; laid waste; devastated: *desolate land.*   **2** make unfit to live in; lay waste: *The Vikings desolated the lands they attacked.*   **3** not lived in; deserted: *a desolate house.*   **4** deprive of inhabitants.   **5** left alone; solitary; lonely.   **6** unhappy; wretched; forlorn: *The ragged, hungry child looked desolate.*   **7** make lonely, unhappy, or forlorn: *He was desolated to hear that his old friend was going away.*   **8** dreary; dismal: *She has led a desolate life.*   1, 3, 5, 6, 8 *adj.*, 2, 4, 7 *v.*, **des·o·lat·ed, des·o·lat·ing.**
—**des′o·late·ly,** *adv.*   —**des′o·late·ness,** *n.*

**des·o·la·tion** (des′ə lā′shən)   **1** the action of making desolate: *the desolation of a vast area by fire.*   **2** the condition of being desolated; devastation: *the desolation left by the forest fire.*   **3** the condition of being solitary, deserted, or uninhabited: *the desolation of the Barren Ground.*   **4** a lonely or isolated place.   **5** lonely sorrow or misery; grief: *There was desolation in the eyes of the condemned woman.*   *n.*

**de·spair** (di sper′)   **1** a complete loss of hope; the state of being without hope; a feeling that nothing good can happen: *Despair seized us as we felt the boat sinking. In despair, she took her own life.*   **2** a person or thing that causes despair: *The girl was the despair of her parents.*   **3** lose hope; be without hope: *The doctors despaired of saving the sick man's life.*   1, 2 *n.*, 3 *v.*

**de·spair·ing** (di sper′ing)   **1** feeling, showing, or expressing DESPAIR (def. 1); hopeless.   **2** ppr. of DESPAIR.   1 *adj.*, 2 *v.*   —**de·spair′ing·ly,** *adv.*
—**de·spair′ing·ness,** *n.*

**des·patch** (di spach′)   See DISPATCH.   *v.*, *n.*

**des·patch·er** (di spach′ər)   See DISPATCHER.   *n.*

**des·per·a·do** (des′pə rä′dō *or* des′pə rā′dō)   a bold or reckless criminal; a dangerous outlaw.   *n.*, *pl.* **des·per·a·does** or **des·per·a·dos.**

**des·per·ate** (des′pə rit)   **1** having lost all hope: *She would have to be desperate before she asked for help.*   **2** make reckless or violent through loss of hope: *a desperate criminal.*   **3** resulting from loss of hope; showing recklessness caused by despair: *a last, desperate bid for freedom.*   **4** giving little or no hope of improvement; very dangerous or serious: *a desperate illness. The situation is desperate.*   **5** having an extreme need or desire: *desperate for affection. After a week of being cooped up in the cabin, he was desperate for something to do.*   **6** extreme: *in desperate need of assistance.*   *adj.*
—**des′per·ate·ly,** *adv.*   —**des′per·ate·ness,** *n.*

**des·per·a·tion** (des′pə rā′shən)   recklessness caused by DESPAIR (def. 1); willingness to do anything, regardless of risks or consequences: *Desperation finally made her give herself up. He saw that the stairs were on fire and in desperation he jumped out of the window.*   *n.*

**des·pic·a·ble** (des pik′ə bəl *or* des′pi kə bəl)   to be DESPISED; contemptible: *Cowards and liars are despicable.* *adj.*   —**des·pic′a·ble·ness,** *n.*   —**des·pic′a·bly,** *adv.*

**de·spise** (di spīz′)   look down on; feel contempt for; scorn: *Most people despise a traitor.*   *v.*, **de·spised, de·spis·ing.**   —**de·spis′er,** *n.*

**de·spite** (di spīt′)   **1** in spite of: *The girls went for a walk despite the rain.*   **2** insult; injury.   1 *prep.*, 2 *n.* **in despite of,**   in spite of.

**de·spoil** (di spoil′)   rob; plunder.   *v.*

**de·spond** (di spond′)   lose heart, courage, or hope.   *v.*   —**de·spond′ing·ly,** *adv.*

**de·spond·ence** (di spon′dəns)   DESPONDENCY.   *n.*

**de·spond·en·cy** (di spon′dən sē)   loss of courage or hope; discouragement; dejection.   *n.*

**de·spond·ent** (di spon′dənt)   without courage or hope; discouraged; dejected.   *adj.*
—**de·spond′ent·ly,** *adv.*

**des·pot** (des′pot *or* des′pət)   **1** a tyrant; oppressor.   **2** a monarch, etc. having unlimited power; absolute ruler.   **3** any person who uses his or her power to get his or her own way: *Some fathers are despots in the eyes of their children.*   *n.*

**des·pot·ic** (des pot′ik)   of a DESPOT; tyrannical; having unlimited power.   *adj.*

**des·pot·i·cal·ly** (des pot′i klē)   in a DESPOTIC manner; with absolute power.   *adv.*

**des·pot·ism** (des′pə tiz′əm)   **1** tyranny; oppression.   **2** government by a monarch, etc. having unlimited power.   *n.*

**des·sert** (di zėrt′)   a course served at the end of a meal: *Pie, cake, fruit, cheese, etc. are desserts.*   *n.*
☞ *Hom.*   DESERT², DESERT³.

**des·ti·na·tion** (des′tə nā′shən)   **1** the place to which a person or thing is going or is being sent.   **2** a setting apart for a particular purpose or use; intention.   *n.*

**des·tine** (des′tən)   **1** set apart for a particular purpose or use; intend: *The prince was destined from birth to be a king.*   **2** cause by fate: *My letter was destined never to reach her.*   *v.*, **des·tined, des·tin·ing.**
**destined for,**   **a** intended to go to; bound for: *ships destined for England.*   **b** intended for: *Her brother was destined for a musical career.*

**des·tiny** (des′tə nē)   **1** one's lot or fortune; what becomes of a person or thing in the end: *It was his destiny to die in battle.*   **2** what is predetermined to happen in spite of all efforts to change or prevent it: *She struggled in vain against her destiny.*   **3** the power that foreordains; overruling necessity; fate: *Do you believe in destiny?*   *n.*, *pl.* **des·ti·nies.**

**des·ti·tute** (des′tə tyüt′ or des′tə tüt′)   **1** lacking necessities such as food, clothing, and shelter: *The family is destitute and needs help.*   **2** not having; being without, especially something desirable or needed (*used with* **of**): *a region destitute of trees. The tyrant was destitute of pity.* *adj.*

**des·ti·tu·tion** (des′tə tyü′shən or des′tə tü′shən)   **1** a DESTITUTE (def. 1) condition; extreme poverty.   **2** the state of being without; lack.   *n.*

**de·stroy** (di stroi′)   **1** ruin or wreck by tearing down, breaking, etc. or as if by tearing down, breaking, etc.; demolish: *Hail destroyed their crop. Many paintings were destroyed in the flood. His reputation has been destroyed by his involvement in the scandal.*   **2** defeat completely: *The enemy was destroyed.*   **3** put an end to; bring to nothing: *A heavy rain destroyed all hope of a picnic. Repeated failures have destroyed her confidence.*   **4** kill: *The injured dog had to be destroyed.*   *v.*

**de·stroy·er** (di stroi′ər)   **1** a person or thing that destroys.   **2** a small, fast warship equipped with guns, torpedoes, and other weapons: *In wartime, the Royal Canadian Navy used destroyers for hunting submarines.*   *n.*

**de·struct·i·bil·i·ty** (di struk′tə bil′ə tē)   the quality of being DESTRUCTIBLE.   *n.*

**de·struct·i·ble** (di struk′tə bəl)   capable of being destroyed.   *adj.*

**de·struc·tion** (di struk′shən)   **1** the act or process of destroying: *A crowd watched the destruction of the old building.*   **2** the condition or fact of being destroyed; ruin: *The storm left destruction behind it.*   **3** anything that destroys; the cause or means of destruction: *That letter was the destruction of all her hopes.*   *n.*

**de·struc·tive** (di struk′tiv)   **1** tending to destroy; liable to cause destruction: *Termites are destructive insects.*   **2** destroying; causing destruction: *Fires and earthquakes are destructive forces.*   **3** guilty of destroying; in the habit of causing destruction: *Destructive children should be corrected.*   **4** not helpful; not constructive: *His criticism was destructive because it showed what was wrong, but did not show how to correct it.*   *adj.*   —**de·struc′tive·ly,** *adv.*   —**de·struc′tive·ness,** *n.*

**des·ue·tude** (des′wə tyüd′ or des′wə tüd′)   disuse: *Many words once commonly used have fallen into desuetude.*   *n.*

**des·ul·to·ry** (des′əl tô′rē)   jumping from one thing to another; unconnected; without aim or method: *The careful study of a few books is better than the desultory reading of many.*   *adj.*   —**des′ul·to′ri·ly,** *adv.*   —**des′ul·to′ri·ness,** *n.*

**de·tach** (di tach′)   **1** loosen and remove; unfasten; separate: *She detached a charm from her bracelet.*   **2** separate a number of soldiers, ships, tanks, etc. from the main body for some special duty: *One squad of soldiers was detached to guard the camp.*   *v.*   —**de·tach′a·ble,** *adj.*

**de·tached** (di tacht′)   **1** separate from others; isolated: *A detached house is not in a solid row with others.*   **2** not influenced by one's interests and prejudices, or those of others; impartial; aloof.   **3** pt. and pp. of DETACH.   1, 2 *adj.*, 3 *v.*

**de·tach·ment** (di tach′mənt)   **1** separation.   **2** a standing apart; aloofness.   **3** a freedom from prejudice or bias; impartial attitude: *Students were surprised at the professor's air of detachment in talking about her own books.*   **4** a group of troops, ships, tanks, etc. sent on or assigned to some special duty: *He belonged to the machine gun detachment.*   **5** the state of being on special duty: *a squad of soldiers on detachment.*   **6** the smallest unit in the organization of the ROYAL CANADIAN MOUNTED POLICE or other police force: *Some rural detachments of the RCMP have only one or two officers.*   *n.*

**de·tail** (dē′tāl or di tāl′)   **1** a small part of something; a particular item that is not of great importance in itself: *She worked out the general program but left the details to her assistants. The two drawings were alike in every detail.*   **2** dealing with or showing things individually or one by one: *He doesn't care for the detail involved in accounting. This new map has more detail than the old one.*   **3** give the particulars of; report or tell in full: *She detailed all the things she had seen and done on her trip. The particulars are detailed in the enclosed brochure.*   **4** any of the small parts that go to make up a painting, etc.: *The details are beautifully painted, but the general effect is dull.*   **5** a reproduction of a part of a painting or other work of art: *The picture on the card is a detail of a painting by Leonardo da Vinci.*   **6** a small group selected for or sent on some special duty: *The captain sent a detail of six soldiers to guard the road.*   **7** the task or duty itself.   **8** select for or send on special duty: *Police officers were detailed to hold back the crowd.*   1, 2, 4–7 *n.*, 3, 8 *v.*
**go into detail,**   give all the parts or particulars separately: *There was no time to go into detail, so she just gave them a general outline of the situation.*
**in detail,**   part by part; giving all the particulars: *She described the inside of the airplane in detail.*

**de·tailed** (dē′tāld or di tāld′)   **1** having much detail: *a detailed description, a detailed map.*   **2** pt. and pp. of DETAIL.   1 *adj.*, 2 *v.*

**de·tain** (di tān′)   **1** hold back; keep from going; delay.   **2** keep in custody; confine: *The police detained the suspected thief for questioning.*   **3** withhold.   *v.*

**de·tain·ment** (di tān′mənt)   DETENTION.   *n.*

**de·tect** (di tekt′)   **1** find out; discover: *to detect a crime.*   **2** discover the existence of: *Can you detect an odour in the room?*   **3** change the alternating currents in a radio set by a DETECTOR (def. 2).   *v.*

**de·tect·a·ble** (di tek′tə bəl)   capable of being DETECTed.   *adj.*

**de·tec·tion** (di tek′shən)   **1** finding out; discovery.   **2** being found out or discovered.   **3** the change of alternating currents in a radio set.   *n.*

**de·tec·tive** (di tek′tiv)   **1** a police officer whose work is investigating crimes.   **2** a person who works for a company or organization as an investigator.   **3** having to do with detectives and their work: *detective stories.*   **4** designed for or used in detecting something: *detective devices.*   *n.*

**de·tec·tor** (di tek′tər)   **1** a device or apparatus for detecting the presence of something, such as electric waves, radio-activity, or smoke.   **2** in radio, a device for changing radio waves into sound waves at the receiver.   **3** any person or thing that detects.   *n.*

**de·ten·tion** (di ten′shən)   **1** the act of detaining or holding back; especially, keeping in custody: *A jail is used for the detention of persons who have been arrested.*   **2** a

**de·ter** (di tėr′) discourage; keep back; hinder: *The extreme heat deterred us from going downtown.* *v.*, **de·terred, de·ter·ring.**

**de·ter·gent** (di tėr′jənt) **1** a chemical compound that acts like a soap, used for cleansing: *Detergents are responsible for some pollution in our lakes.* **2** cleansing: *the detergent action of suds.* **1** *n.*, **2** *adj.*

**de·te·ri·o·rate** (di tē′rē ə rāt′) **1** become worse; lessen in value; depreciate: *Machinery deteriorates if it is not given good care.* **2** make worse: *A hot, damp climate deteriorates leather.* *v.*, **de·te·ri·o·rat·ed, de·te·ri·o·rat·ing.**

**de·te·ri·o·ra·tion** (di tē′rē ə rā′shən) **1** a deteriorating. **2** the condition of having DETERIORATED (def. 1): *The Umbertis moved away because of the deterioration of the neighbourhood.* *n.*

**de·ter·ment** (di tėr′mənt) **1** a DETERring. **2** something that DETERS. *n.*

**de·ter·mi·na·ble** (di tėr′mə nə bəl) **1** capable of being settled or decided. **2** capable of being found out exactly. *adj.*

**de·ter·mi·nant** (di tėr′mə nənt) **1** something that determines. **2** determining: *The longer vacation offered was the determinant factor in Mr. Injit's change of position.* **1** *n.*, **2** *adj.*

**de·ter·mi·nate** (di tėr′mə nit) **1** with exact limits; fixed; definite. **2** settled; positive. **3** determined; resolute. *adj.* —**de·ter′mi·nate·ly,** *adv.* —**de·ter′mi·nate·ness,** *n.*

**de·ter·mi·na·tion** (di tėr′mə nā′shən) **1** the act of formally settling or deciding a question, problem, controversy, etc.: *the determination of the boundary lines of the provinces. The determination of the best name for our club took a long time.* **2** the result of settling or deciding; settlement or decision: *They were unable to come to any determination on the question of inheritance.* **3** the act of finding out the exact amount, position, or kind by calculating, measuring, etc.: *the determination of the amount of gold in a sample of ore.* **4** the result of finding out by calculating, etc.; conclusion or solution: *Their research was based on earlier scientific determinations.* **5** the result of coming to a decision; a fixed purpose: *She left with the determination to find out who her real parents were.* **6** great firmness in carrying out a purpose; the quality of being DETERMINED: *The boy's determination was not weakened by the difficulties he met.* *n.*

**de·ter·mine** (di tėr′mən) **1** make up one's mind firmly; resolve: *He determined to become the best Scout in his troop.* **2** settle; decide. **3** find out exactly; fix: *The captain determined the latitude and longitude of his ship's position.* **4** fix the geometrical position of. **5** be the deciding fact in reaching a certain result; bring about a certain result: *Tomorrow's events will determine whether we are to go or stay.* **6** fix or settle beforehand: *Can we now determine the date for our party?* **7** give an aim to; direct; impel: *Let hope determine your thinking.* **8** limit; define: *The meaning of a word is partly determined by its use in a particular sentence.* **9** put an end to; conclude. **10** come to an end. *v.*, **de·ter·mined, de·ter·min·ing.**

**de·ter·mined** (di tėr′mənd) **1** with one's mind firmly made up; resolved: *The determined explorer kept on her way in spite of the storm.* **2** firm; resolute: *She made a determined effort to win the race.* **3** pt. and pp. of DETERMINE. **1, 2** *adj.*, **3** *v.*

**de·ter·mined·ly** (di tėr′mən dlē) in a DETERMINED manner. *adv.*

**de·ter·min·er** (di tėr′mə nər) in grammar, a specifying word such as *the, a, her,* or *this,* that comes before a noun or before an adjective followed by a noun. Compare with DEFINITIVE (def. 3). *n.*

**de·ter·rent** (di tėr′ənt) **1** DETERring, restraining. **2** something that DETERS: *Fear of consequences is a common deterrent from wrongdoing.* **1** *adj.*, **2** *n.*

**de·test** (di test′) dislike very much; hate. *v.*

**de·test·a·ble** (di tes′tə bəl) deserving to be DETESTED; hateful. *adj.* —**de·test′a·ble·ness,** *n.*

**de·tes·ta·tion** (dē′tes tā′shən) **1** a very strong dislike; hatred. **2** a DETESTED person or thing: *Snakes are her detestation.* *n.*

**de·throne** (di thrōn′) deprive of the power to rule; remove from a throne; depose. *v.*, **de·throned, de·thron·ing.**

**de·throne·ment** (di thrōn′mənt) dethroning or being DETHRONED. *n.*

**det·o·nate** (det′ə nāt′) **1** cause to explode with a loud noise: *The workmen detonated the dynamite.* **2** explode with a loud noise: *The bomb detonated.* *v.*, **det·o·nat·ed, det·o·nat·ing.**

**det·o·na·tion** (det′ə nā′shən) **1** an explosion with a loud noise. **2** a loud noise. *n.*

**det·o·na·tor** (det′ə nā′tər) a device, such as a fuse, percussion cap, etc., used to set off an explosive. *n.*

**de·tour** (dē′tůr) **1** a road that is used when the main or direct road cannot be travelled. **2** a roundabout way. **3** use a roundabout way; make a detour: *We detoured around the flooded part of the highway.* **4** cause to use a detour. **1, 2** *n.*, **3, 4** *v.*

**de·tract** (di trakt′) take away from the quality, value, etc. of something: *The ugly frame detracts from the beauty of the picture.* *v.*

**de·trac·tion** (di trak′shən) **1** the act of speaking evil; belittling. **2** taking away; detracting. *n.*

**de·trac·tive** (di trak′tiv) **1** tending to DETRACT. **2** speaking evil; belittling. *adj.* —**de·trac′tive·ly,** *adv.*

**de·trac·tor** (di trak′tər) a person who speaks evil of or belittles another. *n.*

**det·ri·ment** (det′rə mənt) **1** damage; injury; harm: *Teresa continued working long hours, apparently without detriment to her health.* **2** something that causes damage or harm. *n.*

**det·ri·men·tal** (det′rə men′təl) damaging; injurious; harmful: *Lack of sleep is detrimental to one's health.* *adj.* —**det′ri·men·tal·ly,** *adv.*

**de·tri·tus** (di trī′təs) particles of rock or other material worn away from a mass. *n.*

**deuce¹** (dyüs *or* düs) **1** the number two in a game of cards or dice. **2** a playing card marked with a 2. **3** the side of a die having two spots. **4** in tennis, a tie score at 40 each in a game. *n.*

**deuce²** (dyüs *or* düs) *Informal.* a mild oath used to express annoyance or surprise: *What the deuce does she want now?* *interj.*

**deu·te·ri·um** (dyü tē′rē əm *or* dü tē′rē əm)   an isotope of hydrogen having a mass double that of ordinary hydrogen; heavy hydrogen.   *Symbol:* D or ²H   *n.*

**de·val·u·ate** (dē val′yü āt′)   DEVALUE.   *v.*, **de·val·u·at·ed, de·val·u·at·ing.**

**de·val·u·a·tion** (dē val′yü ā′shən)   devaluing or being DEVALUEd (def. 1): *the devaluation of the dollar.*   *n.*

**de·val·ue** (dē val′yü)   **1** officially reduce the value of currency in relation to other currencies or to gold. **2** lessen or take away the importance or value of.   *v.*, **de·val·ued, de·val·u·ing.**

**dev·as·tate** (dev′ə stāt′)   make desolate; destroy; ravage: *A long war devastated the border towns.*   *v.*, **dev·as·tat·ed, dev·as·tat·ing.**  —**dev′as·ta′tor,** *n.*

**dev·as·ta·tion** (dev′ə stā′shən)   **1** the act of laying waste or of destroying; destruction.   **2** the condition or state of being laid waste; desolation: *The people were shocked at the devastation caused by the forest fire.*   *n.*

**de·vel·op** (di vel′əp)   **1** come into being gradually through successive stages of growth and change: *Many plants develop from seeds. Land animals are believed to have developed from sea animals.*   **2** bring into being through successive stages: *The modern power loom was developed from a simple hand loom.*   **3** go from earlier to later stages, especially by a natural process of growth and change; become gradually bigger, fuller, more mature, etc.: *She is developing into a fine, healthy child. The idea had been developing in his mind for some time.*   **4** cause to grow and mature: *Exercise and wholesome food develop healthy bodies.*   **5** come to have; acquire bit by bit: *to develop an aversion for seafood. She has developed an interest in stamp collecting.*   **6** work out in more and more detail; make bigger, better, fuller, etc.: *to develop an argument. Gradually they developed their plans for the Boys' Club.*   **7** make or become known; reveal: *No new facts developed from the detective's inquiry.*   **8** change, especially by means of construction work, from a natural or near natural state to one that serves another purpose: *The plan to develop the park area was strongly opposed by the public. The government is developing the water power of the northern rivers for industry.*   **9** make more urban, more up-to-date, or more industrialized: *They have developed the old downtown area.*   **10** treat with chemicals to bring out the image recorded on a photographic plate or film: *The film was developed commercially but she made the prints herself.*   **11** of a photographic image, be brought out; become visible: *We watched the picture develop.*   *v.*

**de·vel·op·er** (di vel′ə pər)   **1** a person whose business is developing real estate on a large scale: *A developer buys a tract of land and builds an office complex, an apartment building, houses, etc. on it for the purpose of selling them.* **2** a chemical used to bring out the picture on an exposed photographic film, plates, etc.   **3** any person or thing that develops.   *n.*

**de·vel·op·ment** (di vel′əp mənt)   **1** the act of working out in greater detail: *The development of a feasible plan took many hours of work.*   **2** the process of developing; growth: *The parents followed their child's development with pride.*   **3** a happening; an outcome or result; news: *Newspapers give information about the latest developments in world affairs.*   **4** bringing into being through successive stages: *the development of a new kind of motor.* **5** progression through successive stages by a natural process of growth and change: *the development of a caterpillar into a butterfly.*   **6** changing something from a natural or older state for a particular purpose: *the development of the waterfront for industry.*   **7** the product or result of developing in this way: *The old farm is now a large housing development.*   **8** a group of buildings constructed by the same person or company: *The new development will have business offices and stores.*   **9** the developing of a film.   *n.*

**de·vel·op·men·tal** (di vel′əp men′təl)   having to do with DEVELOPMENT.   *adj.*

**de·vi·ate** (dē′ vē āt′)   turn aside from a way, course, rule, truth, etc.; DIVERGE (def. 3): *His statements sometimes deviated slightly from the truth.*   *v.*, **de·vi·at·ed, de·vi·at·ing.**  —**de′vi·a′tor,** *n.*

**de·vi·a·tion** (dē′vē ā′shən)   a turning aside from a way, course, rule, truth, etc.; DIVERGENCE: *No deviation from the rules was allowed. The deviation of the compass needle was caused by the iron on the ship.*   *n.*

**de·vice** (di vīs′)   **1** a mechanical invention used for a special purpose; machine; apparatus: *a device for lighting a gas stove.*   **2** a plan; scheme; trick: *By some device or other he got the girl to let him into the house.*   **3** a drawing or figure used in a pattern or as an ornament.   **4** a picture or design on a coat of arms, often accompanied by a motto.   **5** motto.   *n.*
**leave to one's own devices,**   leave to do as one thinks best: *The teacher left us to our own devices in choosing a book for our report.*

**de·vil** (dev′əl)   **1** an evil spirit; fiend; demon.   **2** a wicked or cruel person.   **3** a very dashing, energetic, or reckless person.   **4** an unfortunate or wretched person: *The poor devil didn't even hear the warning.*   **5** anything that is hard to handle, solve, understand, etc.: *That last problem was a real devil.*   **6** something very bad; an evil influence or power: *the devil of greed.*   **7** an errand boy or apprentice in a printing office.   **8** tease; bother; harass. **9** prepare food with hot seasoning: *to devil ham, devilled eggs.*   **10** any of various machines for tearing or shredding paper, rags, etc.   **11 the Devil,** the supreme spirit of evil; the enemy of goodness; Satan.   1–7, 10, 11 *n.*, 8, 9 *v.*, **dev·illed** or **dev·iled, dev·il·ling** or **dev·il·ing.**
**between the devil and the deep blue sea,** between two equally dangerous and unpleasant alternatives; in a dilemma.
**give the devil his due,**   be fair even to a bad or disliked person.

**dev·il·fish** (dev′əl fish′)   **1** any of several species of very large ray found in warm seas.   **2** any large sea animal with tentacles, especially an octopus.   *n., pl.* **dev·il·fish** or **dev·il·fish·es.**

**dev·il·ish** (dev′ə lish)   **1** of, having to do with, like, or worthy of a devil or devils; cruel, wicked, mischievous, etc.: *a devilish scheme for getting the inheritance.* **2** *Informal.*   very great; extreme: *She's always in such a devilish hurry.*   **3** *Informal.*   very ; extremely: *They worked devilish hard.*   1, 2 *adj.,* 3 *adv.*
—**dev′il·ish·ly,** *adv.*  —**dev′il·ish·ness,** *n.*

**dev·il–may–care** (dev′əl mā ker′)   happy-go-lucky or reckless: *She showed a devil-may-care attitude toward authority.*   *adj.*

**dev·il·ment** (dev′əl mənt)   **1** an evil action; wicked behaviour.   **2** mischief; daring behaviour.   *n.*

**dev·il·ry** (dev′əl rē)   DEVILTRY.   *n., pl.* **dev·il·ries.**

**dev·il·try** (dev′əl trē)   **1** an evil action; wicked behaviour.   **2** daring behaviour.   **3** mischief.   **4** great cruelty or wickedness.   *n., pl.* **dev·il·tries.**

**de·vi·ous** (dē′vē əs)   **1** winding; twisting; roundabout: *We took a devious route through side streets and alleys to avoid the crowded main streets.*   **2** straying from the right course; not straightforward; going astray: *His devious nature was shown in lies and small dishonesties.*   *adj.*   —**de′vi·ous·ly,** *adv.*   —**de′vi·ous·ness,** *n.*

**de·vise** (di vīz′)   **1** think out; plan; contrive; invent: *The girls devised a scheme for earning money during the summer vacation.*   **2** give or leave land, buildings, etc. by a will.   **3** a giving or leaving of land, buildings, etc. by a will.   **4** a will or part of a will doing this.   **5** land, buildings, etc. given or left in this way.   1, 2 *v.,* **de·vised, de·vis·ing;** 3–5 *n.*   —**de·vis′a·ble,** *adj.*

**de·vi·tal·i·za·tion** (dē vī′tə lə zā′shən *or* dē vī′tə lī zā′shən)   **1** devitalizing.   **2** being DEVITALIZEd.   *n.*

**de·vi·tal·ize** (dē vī′tə līz′)   **1** kill; take the life of.   **2** weaken; exhaust; make less vital.   *v.,* **de·vi·tal·ized, de·vi·tal·iz·ing.**

**de·void** (di void′)   not having; lacking (*used with* **of**): *a speech completely devoid of humour.*   *adj.*

**de·voir** (də vwär′)   **1** an act of courtesy or respect.   **2** duty.   *n.*

**de·volve** (di volv′)   **1** transfer duty, work, etc. to someone else.   **2** be handed down to someone else; be transferred: *If the president is unable to handle her duties, they devolve upon the vice-president.*   *v.,* **de·volved, de·volv·ing.**

**de·vote** (di vōt′)   **1** give up oneself, one's money, time, or efforts to some person, purpose, or service: *The mother devoted herself to her children.*   **2** set apart and consecrate to God or to a sacred purpose.   **3** set apart for any particular purpose: *That museum is devoted to modern art.*   *v.,* **de·vot·ed, de·vot·ing.**

**de·vot·ed** (di vō′tid)   **1** loyal; faithful: *a devoted friend.*   **2** set apart for some purpose; dedicated; consecrated.   **3** pt. and pp. of DEVOTE.   1, 2 *adj.,* 3 *v.*   —**de·vot′ed·ly,** *adv.*   —**de·vot′ed·ness,** *n.*

**dev·o·tee** (dev′ə tē′)   **1** a person deeply devoted to something.   **2** a person earnestly devoted to religion.   *n.*

**de·vo·tion** (di vō′shən)   **1** a deep, steady affection; a feeling of loyalty; faithfulness: *the devotion of a lifelong friend.*   **2** the act of devoting.   **3** the state of being devoted: *the devotion of much time to study.*   **4** earnestness in religion.   **5** **devotions,** *pl.* religious worship; prayers.   *n.*

**de·vo·tion·al** (di vō′shə nəl)   having to do with DEVOTION (defs. 4, 5); used in worship.   *adj.*   —**de·vo′tion·al·ly,** *adv.*

**de·vour** (di vour′)   **1** of animals, eat: *The wolves devoured the caribou.*   **2** eat hungrily or greedily: *They devoured their meal in about 10 minutes.*   **3** consume; destroy: *The fire quickly devoured the whole building.*   **4** take in with eyes or ears in a hungry, greedy way: *to devour a book.*   **5** completely absorb the attention or emotions of: *devoured by curiosity, devoured by envy.*   *v.*   —**de·vour′er,** *n.*   —**de·vour′ing·ly,** *adv.*

**de·vout** (di vout′)   **1** active in worship and prayer; religious.   **2** devoted; earnest; sincere; hearty: *devout thanks, a devout follower.*   *adj.*   —**de·vout′ly,** *adv.*   —**de·vout′ness,** *n.*

**dew** (dyü *or* dü)   **1** the moisture from the air that condenses and collects in small drops on cool surfaces during the night.   **2** moisture in small drops.   **3** make wet with dew; moisten.   **4** anything fresh or refreshing like dew: *the dew of youth.*   1, 2, 4 *n.,* 3 *v.*   —**dew′less,** *adj.*
☛ *Hom.* DO¹ (for the second pronunciation of **dew**); DUE.

**dew·ber·ry** (dyü′ber′e *or* dü′ber′ē)   **1** any of several species of trailing blackberry.   **2** the fruit of any of these plants.   *n., pl.* **dew·ber·ries.**

**dew·drop** (dyü′drop′ *or* dü′drop′)   a drop of dew.   *n.*

**dew·lap** (dyü′lap′ *or* dü′lap′)   a loose fold of skin under the throat of cattle and some other animals. See ZEBU for picture.   *n.*

**dew point**   the temperature at which the water vapour in air that is cooling begins to condense as dew.

**dew–worm** (dyü′wėrm′ *or* dü′wėrm′) *Cdn.*   a large earthworm that comes to the surface at night when there is dew on the grass: *Dew-worms make excellent fish bait.*   *n.*

**dew·y** (dyü′ē *or* dü′ē)   **1** wet with dew.   **2** of dew.   **3** like dew; refreshing; sparkling; coming gently; vanishing quickly.   *adj.* **dew·i·er, dew·i·est.**   —**dew′i·ness,** *n.*

**dex·ter·i·ty** (dek ster′ə tē)   **1** skill in using the body, especially the hands: *A good surgeon works with dexterity.*   **2** skill in using the mind; cleverness: *Dexterity in questioning witnesses helped the lawyer win many cases.*
☛ *Etym.* **Dexterity** and DEXTEROUS can be traced back to L *dexter* 'on or to the right'. The right hand was early associated with skilfulness or cleverness. Compare the note at SINISTER.

**dex·ter·ous** (dek′stə rəs *or* dek′strəs)   **1** having or showing skill in using the hands and body: *A typist, a dressmaker, and a pianist need to be dexterous.*   **2** having or showing skill in using the mind; clever: *A leader is dexterous in handling people.*   *adj.* Also, **dextrous.**   —**dex′ter·ous·ly,** *adv.*   —**dex′ter·ous·ness,** *n.*
☛ *Etym.* See note at DEXTERITY.

**dex·tral** (dek′strəl)   **1** of the right hand; right-hand.   **2** right-handed.   *adj.*

**dex·trin** (dek′strin)   a gummy substance obtained from starch, used as an adhesive, for sizing paper, etc.   *n.*

**dex·trine** (dek′strin *or* dek′strēn)   DEXTRIN.   *n.*

**dex·trose** (dek′strōs)   a sugar that is less sweet than cane sugar; a form of GLUCOSE.   *n.*

**dex·trous** (dek′strəs)   DEXTEROUS.   *adj.*

**dhar·ma** (där′mə)   **1** in Buddhism, law.   **2** in Hinduism, virtue; righteousness; correct behaviour.   *n.*

**Dhar·ma·pa·da** (där′mə pä′də)   in Buddhism, a sacred book covering almost every aspect of Buddhist teaching about truth, duty, and enlightenment.   *n.*

**di·a·be·tes** (dī′ə bē′tis)   a disease in which the digestive system is unable to absorb normal amounts of sugar and starch.   *n.*

**di·a·bet·ic** (dī′ə bet′ik *or* dī′ə bē′tik)   **1** of or having to do with DIABETES. **2** having DIABETES. **3** a person having DIABETES. 1, 2 *adj.*, 3 *n.*

**di·a·bol·ic** (dī′ə bol′ik) **1** devilish; like the Devil; very cruel or wicked; fiendish. **2** having to do with the Devil or devils. *adj.* —**di′a·bol′i·cal·ly,** *adv.*

**di·a·bol·i·cal** (dī′ə bol′ə kəl) DIABOLIC. *adj.*

**di·a·crit·ic** (dī′ə krit′ik) **1** DIACRITICAL. **2** a DIACRITICAL MARK. 1 *adj.*, 2 *n.*

**di·a·crit·i·cal** (dī′ə krit′ə kəl) **1** used to distinguish. **2** capable of seeing distinctions. *adj.* —**di′a·crit′i·cal·ly.** *adv.*

**diacritical mark** a mark like ¨ ^ ´ ` or ˛ placed over or under a letter to indicate pronunciation, stress, etc.

**di·a·dem** (dī′ə dem′) **1** a crown. **2** an ornamental band of cloth formerly worn as a crown. **3** royal power, authority, or dignity. *n.*

**di·aer·e·sis** (dī er′ə sis) DIERESIS. *n., pl.* **di·aer·e·ses** (-sēz′).

**di·ag·nose** (dī′əg nōs′) make a DIAGNOSIS of; find out the nature of by an examination: *Doctors diagnose disease.* *v.*, **di·ag·nosed, di·ag·nos·ing.** —**di′ag·nos′a·ble,** *adj.*

**di·ag·no·sis** (dī′əg nō′sis) **1** the act or process of finding out what disease a person or animal has by examination and careful study of the symptoms: *The doctor used X rays and blood tests in her diagnosis.* **2** a careful study of the facts about something to find out its essential features, faults, etc.: *a diagnosis of a plane crash.* **3** a decision reached after a careful study of symptoms or facts. *n., pl.* **di·ag·no·ses** (-sēz).

**di·ag·nos·tic** (dī′əg nos′tik) of or helping in DIAGNOSIS: *diagnostic tests.* *adj.*

**di·ag·nos·ti·cian** (dī′əg nos tish′ən) a person who is expert in making diagnoses. *n.*

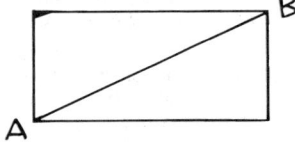
Line AB is a diagonal.

**di·ag·o·nal** (dī ag′ə nəl) **1** a straight line joining any two corners that are not next to each other, of a figure having four or more sides. **2** taking the direction of a diagonal; slanting; oblique: *a ship sailing on a diagonal course, a diagonal stripe in cloth.* **3** having slanting lines, ridges, etc. **4** any slanting line, row, course, etc. **5** connecting two corners that are not next to each other. 1, 4 *n.*, 2, 3, 5 *adj.* —**di·ag′o·nal·ly,** *adv.*

**di·a·gram** (dī′ə gram′) **1** a drawing or sketch showing important parts of a thing: *A diagram may be an outline, a plan, a drawing, a figure, a chart, or a combination of any of these, made to show clearly what a thing is or how it works. He drew a diagram to show us how to get to his house. The engineer drew a diagram of the bridge.* **2** put on paper, a chalkboard, etc. in the form of a drawing or sketch; make a diagram of. 1 *n.*, 2 *v.*, **di·a·grammed** or **di·a·gramed, di·a·gram·ming** or **di·a·gram·ing.**

**di·a·gram·mat·ic** (dī′ə grə mat′ik) **1** in the form of a DIAGRAM (def. 1). **2** in outline only; sketchy. *adj.*

**di·a·gram·mat·i·cal** (dī′ə grə mat′ə kəl) DIAGRAMMATIC. *adj.*

**di·a·gram·mat·i·cal·ly** (dī′ə grə mat′i klē) in the form of a DIAGRAM. *adv.*

**diabolic** 335 **diametric**

hat, āge, fär; let, ēqual, tėrm; it, īce
hot, ōpen, ôrder; oil, out; cup, put, rüle
əbove, takən, pencəl, lemən, circəs
ch, child; ng, long; sh, ship
th, thin; ᴛʜ, then; zh, measure

**di·al** (dī′əl *or* dīl) **1** a marked surface on which a moving pointer indicates a measurement of some kind: *The face of a clock or of a compass is a dial. A dial may show the amount of water in a tank or the amount of steam pressure in a boiler.* **2** the plate or disk on a radio or television set marked with numbers to identify the station frequencies, and having a movable indicator connected to a tuning knob for tuning in different stations. **3** a disk on a telephone that is rotated in order to make connection with another telephone line. **4** the control knob in the centre of the face of a combination lock, that must be rotated through a particular sequence of numbers in order to open the lock. **5** use a dial in order to operate, select, etc.: *to dial a combination on a lock, to dial a favourite program. Dial carefully when you use the phone. He dialled a wrong number.* 1–4 *n.*, 5 *v.*, **di·alled** or **di·aled, di·al·ling** or **di·al·ing.**

**dial direct,** make a telephone call without using an operator: *I dialled direct but got a wrong number.*

**di·a·lect** (dī′ə lekt′) **1** a form of speech characteristic of a fairly definite region or class: *the Cockney dialect, the dialect spoken in Lunenburg, Nova Scotia.* **2** one of a group of closely related languages: *Some of the dialects descended from the Latin language are French, Italian, Spanish, Portuguese, and Romanian.* **3** the words and pronunciations used by certain professions, classes of people, etc. **4** of or having to do with a dialect: *a dialect dictionary.* *n.*
☛ *Usage.* Dialects exist because of the separation of groups of speakers, either regionally or socially. Where several regional dialects exist, one may attain the highest status because it may be spoken in the area which contains the centre of government, education, or trade. A dialect is a valid form of a language; it is not to be confused with a misuse of standard form.

**di·a·lec·tal** (dī′ə lek′təl) of a DIALECT; like that of a dialect. *adj.* —**di′a·lec′tal·ly,** *adv.*

**di·a·logue** (dī′ə log′) **1** conversation. **2** a literary work in the form of a conversation. **3** the conversation written for a story, play, motion picture, etc.: *That novel has a good plot and clever dialogue.* *n.*

**dial tone** the humming sound that is heard on a dial or push-button telephone when the receiver is lifted: *The dial tone indicates the line is in service and open.*

**di·al·y·sis** (dī al′ə sis) **1** the separation of crystalloids from colloids in solution by the application of the principle that crystalloids diffuse readily through a membrane, and colloids not at all or very slightly. **2** the separation of waste matter from the blood in an artificial kidney, using this process. *n., pl.* **di·al·y·ses** (-sēz′).

**diam.** diameter.

**di·am·e·ter** (dī am′ə tər) **1** a straight line passing from one side to the other through the centre of a circle, sphere, etc. **2** the length of such a line; the measurement from one side to the other through the centre; width; thickness: *The tree trunk was almost 60 cm in diameter.* *n.*

**di·a·met·ric** (dī′ə met′rik) **1** of or along a DIAMETER. **2** direct; absolute; exactly opposite. *adj.*

**di·a·met·ri·cal** (dī′ə met′rə kəl) DIAMETRIC. *adj.*

**di·a·met·ri·cal·ly** (dī′ə met′ri klē) **1** as a DIAMETER. **2** directly; exactly; entirely. *adv.*
**diametrically opposed,** directly opposite; exactly contrary.

**dia·mond** (dī′ə mənd *or* dī′ mənd) **1** a colourless or tinted precious stone formed of pure carbon in crystals: *Diamond is the hardest substance known. Inferior diamonds are used to cut glass.* **2** a tool having a diamond tip for cutting glass. **3** a plane figure shaped like this ♦. **4** in baseball, the space inside the lines that connect the bases. **5** a playing card having one or more red diamond-shaped designs on it. **6 diamonds,** *pl.* the suit of playing cards marked with this design. *n.*
**rough diamond,** a person who has poor manners but good qualities such as kindness, generosity, etc.

**di·a·pa·son** (dī′ə pā′zən) **1** harmony. **2** a melody; strain. **3** a swelling musical sound. **4** the whole range of a voice or instrument. **5** a fixed standard of pitch. **6** either of two principal stops in an organ. *n.*

**di·a·per** (dī′ə pər) **1** a piece of cloth folded up, or a pad of other absorbent material, used as underpants for a baby; NAPKIN (def. 2). **2** put a diaper on: *to diaper a baby.* **3** a pattern of small, constantly repeated geometric figures. **4** a white cotton or linen cloth woven with such a pattern. 1, 3, 4 *n.*, 2 *v.*

**di·aph·a·nous** (dī af′ə nəs) TRANSPARENT: *Gauze is a diaphanous fabric. adj.* —**di·aph′a·nous·ly,** *adv.*

**di·a·phragm** (dī′ə fram′) **1** in the body, a partition of muscles and tendons separating the cavity of the chest from the cavity of the abdomen. See LIVER for picture. **2** a thin partition in some shellfish, etc. **3** a thin disk or cone that moves rapidly to and fro when sounds or electrical signals are directed at it, used in telephone receivers, microphones, earphones, and in similar instruments. **4** a device for controlling the amount of light entering a camera, microscope, etc. **5** a contraceptive device, consisting of a flexible, moulded cap, usually made of thin rubber, that is fitted over the entrance to the uterus to prevent the entry of sperm. *n.*

**di·a·rist** (dī′ə rist) a person who keeps a DIARY. *n.*

**di·ar·rhe·a** or **di·ar·rhoe·a** (dī′ə rē′ə) the condition of having too many and too loose movements of the bowels. *n.*

**di·a·ry** (dī′ə rē) **1** an account, written down each day, of what one has done, thought, etc. during the day. **2** a book for keeping such an account, with a blank space for each day of the year. *n., pl.* **di·a·ries.**
☛ Etym. Diary and JOURNAL are related words. Diary comes from L *diarium* 'diary', formed from *diarius* 'daily'. Journal comes from F *journal* 'journal', and JOURNALISM and JOURNALIST come from French words which developed from *journal*. F *journal* in turn developed from L *diurnalis* 'a daily portion'. *Diurnalis* and *diarius* were both formed from L *dies* 'day'. See also the note at JOURNEY.

**di·as·to·le** (dī as′tə lē) the normal, rhythmical dilation of the heart, especially that of the ventricles. Compare with SYSTOLE. *n.*

**di·as·tol·ic** (dī′ə stol′ik) having to do with the DIASTOLE. Compare with SYSTOLIC. *adj.*

**di·a·tom** (dī′ə tom′) any of numerous microscopic, one-celled algae that have hard shells composed mostly of silica. *n.*

**di·a·ton·ic** (dī′ə ton′ik) in music, of or using the tones of a standard major or minor scale. *adj.*

**diatonic scale** in music, a standard major or minor scale of eight tones in the octave.

**di·a·tribe** (dī′ə trīb′) a bitter and violent denunciation of some person or thing. *n.*

**dib** (dib) **1** a small marble, usually made of clay: *He bought some dibs at the store.* **2 dibs,** *pl.* the game played with such marbles. *n.*

**dib·ble** (dib′əl) a pointed tool for making holes in the ground for seeds, young plants, etc. *n.*

**dice** (dīs) **1** small cubes with a different number of spots (one to six) on each side, used in playing games and gambling. **2** *Informal.* a single one of these cubes; DIE³. **3** a game of chance played with such cubes (*used with a singular verb*). **4** play dice, tossing them to see how many spots there will be on the sides turned up. **5** lose by gambling with dice (*used with* **away**): *She diced away her inheritance.* **6** take serious risks: *dicing with death.* **7** cut vegetables, etc. into small cubes: *to dice carrots.* **8** small cubes of food. 1–3, 8 *n., pl.* of **die**³; 4–7 *v.*, **diced, dic·ing.** —**dic′er,** *n.*

**di·chlo·ride** (dī klô′rīd) a compound composed of CHLORINE and one other element or a radical, with two atoms of chlorine for every atom of the other element or radical. *n.*

**di·chot·o·mous clas·si·fi·ca·tion** a system of classifying objects by repeatedly categorizing into one of two possible sets.

**di·chot·o·my** (dī kot′ə mē) a division into two parts. *n., pl.* **di·chot·o·mies.**

**dick·er** (dik′ər) **1** trade by barter or by petty bargaining. **2** a petty bargain: *I made a dicker with him to trade my coins for his stamps.* 1 *v.*, 2 *n.*

**dick·ey** (dik′ē) **1** a shirt front that can be detached. **2** a high collar on a shirt. **3** a sleeveless, sideless woman's waist, for wearing under a dress or suit. **4** a child's bib or pinafore. *n., pl.* **dick·eys.**

**di·cot·y·le·don** (dī kot′ə lē′dən) a flowering plant that has two COTYLEDONS or seed leaves; any of a group of plants that have two seed leaves: *Many trees and most of the cultivated plants are dicotyledons.* Compare with MONOCOTYLEDON. *n.*

**dic·ta** (dik′tə) a pl. of DICTUM. *n.*

**dic·tate** (dik′tāt *or* dik tāt′ *for verb*, dik′tāt *for noun*) **1** say or read something aloud for another person or other persons to write or type: *The teacher dictated a spelling list. The businessman dictated to his secretary.* **2** command with authority; give orders that must be obeyed: *The country that won the war dictated the terms of peace to the country that lost. No one is going to dictate to me.* **3** a direction or order that is to be carried out or obeyed: *Follow the dictates of your conscience.* 1, 2 *v.*, **dic·tat·ed, dic·tat·ing;** 3 *n.*

**dic·ta·tion** (dik tā′shən) **1** the act of saying or reading something aloud for another person or persons to write or type: *The students wrote to the teacher's dictation.* **2** the words said or read aloud to be written down: *We have dictation during our spelling class.* **3** the act of commanding with authority; the act of giving orders that must be obeyed: *The group members acted at the dictation of their leader.* *n.*

**dic·ta·tor** (dik′tā tər *or* dik tā′tər)   **1** a person exercising absolute authority; especially, a person who, without having any claim through inheritance or free popular election, seizes control of a government.   **2** a person whose authority is widely accepted in some special field: *a dictator of men's fashions.*   **3** a person who dictates words or sentences for someone else to record.   *n.*

**dic·ta·to·ri·al** (dik′tə tô′rē əl)   **1** of or like that of a DICTATOR: *dictatorial government.*   **2** imperious; domineering; overbearing: *The soldiers disliked the dictatorial manner of that officer.*   *adj.*
—**dic′ta·to′ri·al·ly,** *adv.*

**dic·ta·tor·ship** (dik′tā tər ship′ *or* dik tā′tər ship′)   **1** the position or rank of a DICTATOR (def. 1).   **2** the term of a DICTATOR (def. 1); period of time a dictator rules.   **3** absolute authority; power to give orders that must be obeyed.   **4** a country under the rule of a DICTATOR (def. 1).   *n.*

**dic·tion** (dik′shən)   **1** the manner of expressing ideas in words; style of speaking or writing: *Good diction implies grammatical correctness, a wide vocabulary, and skill in the choice and arrangement of words.*   **2** pronunciation and enunciation in speaking or singing: *clear diction.*   *n.*

**dic·tion·ar·y** (dik′shə ner′ē)   **1** a book of words arranged alphabetically, with information about their meanings, forms, and, usually, pronunciations and history: *Some dictionaries also give information on how words are used in sentences and idiomatic expressions.*   **2** a book of names or words of some special subject or activity, arranged alphabetically, with information on meanings, uses, etc.: *a law dictionary, a dictionary of trade names.*   **3** a book of alphabetically arranged words of one language with equivalent words or meanings in another language: *an English-Czech dictionary, a French-English dictionary.*   *n., pl.* **dic·tion·ar·ies.**

**dic·tum** (dik′təm)   **1** a formal comment; authoritative opinion: *The dictum of the critics was that the play was excellent.*   **2** a maxim; saying.   *n., pl.* **dic·tums** *or* **dic·ta** (-tə).

**did** (did)   pt. of DO¹: *I did my work.*   *v.*

**di·dac·tic** (dī dak′tik)   **1** intended to instruct: *The fables of Aesop are didactic stories; each one has an instructive moral.*   **2** inclined to instruct others; teacherlike: *The older sister was called "Professor" because of her didactic manner.*   *adj.*

**di·dac·ti·cal** (dī dak′tə kəl)   DIDACTIC.   *adj.*
—**di·dac′ti·cal·ly,** *adv.*

**di·dac·ti·cism** (dī dak′tə siz′əm)   a DIDACTIC quality, character, or manner.   *n.*

**did·n't** (did′ənt)   did not.   *v.*

**di·do** (dī′dō)   *Informal.*   a prank; trick; mischievous or disorderly action.   *n., pl.* **di·dos** *or* **di·does.**

**die¹** (dī)   **1** cease to live; stop living; become dead.   **2** come to an end; lose force or strength; stop: *The motor sputtered and died.*   **3** *Informal.*   want very much; be very desirous (usually a participle with a form of *be*, followed by an infinitive or by *for*): *I'm dying to go to Alaska. We are dying for a home in the country.*   *v.,* **died, dy·ing.**

**die away** *or* **down,**   stop or end little by little; lose force or strength gradually: *The music died away. The noisy conversation of the class died down suddenly when the teacher came into the room.*

**die hard,**   struggle with death; resist to the very end; refuse to give in.

**die off,**   die one after another until all are dead: *The whole herd of cattle died off in the epidemic.*

**die out,**   **a** stop or end little by little.   **b** cease or end completely.

☛ *Hom.*   DYE.

☛ *Usage.*   **Die** is generally followed by *of* when illness is the cause of death: *He died of cancer.* However, *from* is sometimes used when injury is the cause: *He died from a wound.*

A die for cutting the threads of bolts. As the die is turned, it screws onto the bolt, cutting a thread on it.

**die²** (dī)   **1** any tool or apparatus for shaping, cutting, or stamping things, usually under pressure: *A die is usually a metal block or plate cut in a certain way.*   **2** a tool for cutting threads on pipes, bolts, etc.   *n., pl.* **dies.**
☛ *Hom.*   DYE.

**die³** (dī)   a small cube marked with a different number of spots (from one to six) on each face, used for gambling and playing certain games: *Dice are often used in pairs.* See also DICE.   *n., pl.* **dice.**

**the die is cast,**   the decision is made and cannot be changed.
☛ *Hom.*   DYE.

**die·back** (dī′bak′)   a disease of trees and other woody plants in which the twigs and tips of branches die first: *Dieback is caused especially by parasites.*   *n.*

**die–hard** (dī′härd′)   **1** resisting to the very end; refusing to give in.   **2** a person who refuses to give in.   1 *adj.,* 2 *n.*

**di·er·e·sis** *or* **di·aer·e·sis** (dī er′ə sis)   two dots (¨) placed over the second of two consecutive vowels to indicate that the second vowel is to be pronounced in a separate syllable. *Example: naïve.*   *n., pl.* **di·er·e·ses** *or* **di·aer·e·ses** (-sēz′).

**die·sel** (dē′zel)   **1** DIESEL ENGINE.   **2** a vehicle powered by a diesel engine.   **3** powered by a diesel engine: *a diesel train.*   **4** of or for diesel engines: *diesel fuel.*   *n.*

**diesel engine**   an internal-combustion engine that burns fuel oil which is ignited by heat from compressed air instead of by an electric spark, as in a gasoline engine.
☛ *Etym.*   Named for Rudolf *Diesel* (1858–1913), the German engineer who invented it.

**die·sink·er** (dī′sing′kər)   a person who makes dies for shaping or stamping.   *n.*

**di·et¹** (dī′ət)   **1** the usual food and drink for a person or animal: *The diet of the giraffe consists of young leaves and shoots. A rich diet is not wholesome.*   **2** a special selection of food and drink eaten during illness, in an attempt to lose or gain weight, etc.   **3** eat or cause to eat special food and drink as a part of a doctor's treatment, in order to gain or lose weight, etc.   1, 2 *n.*, 3 *v.*, **di·et·ed, di·et·ing.** —**di′et·er,** *n.*

**di·et²** (dī′ət)   **1** a formal assembly.   **2** in certain countries, the national lawmaking body.   *n.*

**di·e·tar·y** (dī′ə ter′ē)   **1** of or having to do with DIET: *Dietary rules tell what food to eat for healthy living and how to prepare it.*   **2** a system of rules for eating and drinking.   **3** a daily allowance of food in a prison, hospital, etc.   1 *adj.*, 2, 3 *n.*, *pl.* **di·e·tar·ies.**

**di·e·tet·ic** (dī′ə tet′ik)   having to do with DIET.   *adj.*

**di·e·tet·ics** (dī′ə tet′iks)   the science that deals with the amount and kinds of food needed by the body (*used with a singular verb*).   *n.*

**di·e·ti·tian** or **di·e·ti·cian** (dī′ə tish′ən)   a person trained to plan meals that have the proper proportion of various kinds of food: *Many hospitals and schools employ dietitians.*   *n.*

**diff.**   **1** difference.   **2** different.

**dif·fer** (dif′ər)   **1** be unlike; be different (*from*): *My answers to the arithmetic problems differed from Mary's.*   **2** have or express a different opinion; disagree (*with*): *Peter is a stubborn boy, determined to differ with his sister at every turn.*   *v.*

**dif·fer·ence** (dif′ə rəns *or* dif′rəns)   **1** the condition of being different: *the difference of night and day.*   **2** the way of being different; the point in which people or things are different.   **3** what is left after subtracting one number from another: *The difference between 6 and 15 is 9.*   See SUBTRACTION for picture.   **4** the amount or extent by which one thing differs from another: *The difference in size between Nova Scotia and Ontario is great.*   **5** the condition of having a different opinion; disagreement.   **6** dispute.   *n.*
**make a difference,**   **a** give or show different treatment.   **b** matter; be important; having an effect or influence.
**split the difference,**   **a** divide what is left in half.   **b** meet halfway; compromise.

**dif·fer·ent** (dif′ə rənt *or* dif′rənt)   **1** not alike; not like: *People have different names. An automobile is different from a cart.*   **2** not the same; separate; distinct: *I saw her three different times today.*   **3** not like others or most others; unusual: *Rajiv insists on being different in the way he dresses.*   *adj.*   —**dif′fer·ent·ly,** *adv.*

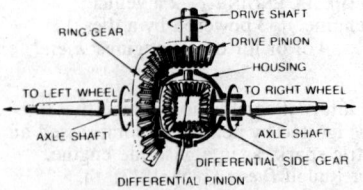

The differential of an automobile. The pinions mesh with the two side gears connected to the axle shafts, allowing the wheels to rotate at different speeds.

**dif·fer·en·tial** (dif′ə ren′shəl)   **1** of a difference; showing a difference; depending on a difference: *Differential duties, rates, charges, etc. are those that differ according to circumstances.*   **2** a differential duty or rate; the difference involved.   **3** distinguishing; distinctive.   **4** having to do with distinguishing characteristics or specific differences: *Differential diagnosis is distinguishing between two similar diseases or objects of natural history.*   **5** an arrangement of gears in an automobile that allows one of the rear wheels to turn faster than the other in going round a corner or curve.   1, 3, 4 *adj.*, 2, 5 *n.*

**dif·fer·en·tial·ly** (dif′ə ren′shə lē)   in a DIFFERENTIAL (def. 1) manner; with reference to a difference between quantities or forces.   *adv.*

**dif·fer·en·ti·ate** (dif′ə ren′shē āt′)   **1** show or mark a difference between or in: *an act of kindness that differentiates real consideration for others from mere politeness.*   **2** recognize or see a distinction; discriminate: *The twins were so much alike that it was almost impossible to differentiate between them.*   **3** become different in character: *The words* metal *and* mettle *have the same origin but have differentiated over the centuries to become two separate words.*   *v.*, **dif·fer·en·ti·at·ed, dif·fer·en·ti·at·ing.**

**dif·fer·en·ti·a·tion** (dif′ə ren′shē ā′shən)   the act or process of differentiating; alteration; modification; distinction.   *n.*

**dif·fi·cult** (dif′ə kult *or* dif′ə kəlt)   **1** hard to do or understand: *Cutting down the tree was difficult. Physics is difficult for some people.*   **2** hard to deal with, get along with, or please: *The secretary found her new employer difficult.*   *adj.*

**dif·fi·cul·ty** (dif′ə kul′tē)   **1** the fact or condition of being difficult: *the difficulty of a job.*   **2** hard work; much effort: *Some children have a great deal of difficulty learning how to spell.*   **3** trouble: *What is your difficulty?*   **4** financial trouble.   **5** something that is difficult; something in the way; an obstacle, such as lack of money, lack of people to help, lack of understanding, or objections to plans.   **6** a disagreement or quarrel.   *n.*, *pl.* **dif·fi·cul·ties.**
**in difficulties,**   in trouble, especially money trouble: *Our spendthrift friend is in difficulties again.*
**make difficulties,**   cause trouble; hinder by raising objections: *We will get the meeting finished quickly if no one makes difficulties.*

**dif·fi·dence** (dif′ə dəns)   lack of self-confidence; shyness.   *n.*

**dif·fi·dent** (dif′ə dənt)   lacking in self-confidence; shy.   *adj.*   —**dif′fi·dent·ly,** *adv.*

**dif·fract** (di frakt′)   break up by DIFFRACTION.   *v.*

**dif·frac·tion** (di frak′shən)   **1** a breaking up of a ray of light into a series of light and dark bands or into coloured bands of the spectrum.   **2** a similar breaking up of sound waves, electricity, etc.   *n.*

**dif·fuse** (di fyüz′ *for verb*, di fyüs′ *for adjective*)   **1** spread out so as to cover a larger space or surface; scatter widely: *Light, heat, kindness, good humour, and knowledge can be diffused.*   **2** not concentrated together at a single point; spread out: *diffuse light.*   **3** mix together by spreading into one another, as one gas with another or one liquid with another.   **4** using many words where a few would do: *a diffuse writer.*   1, 3 *v.*, **dif·fused, dif·fus·ing;**   2, 4 *adj.*   —**dif·fuse′ness,** *n.*

**dif·fus·i·ble** (di fyü′zə bəl)   capable of being DIFFUSEd (defs. 1, 3).   *adj.*

**dif·fu·sion** (di fyü′zhən)   **1** the act or fact of diffusing; spreading widely; scattering: *The invention of printing greatly increased the diffusion of knowledge.*   **2** being widely spread or scattered; a diffused condition.   **3** a mixing together of the molecules of gases or of liquids by spreading into one another.   **4** wordiness.   *n.*

**dif·fu·sive** (di fyü′siv)   **1** tending to DIFFUSE (defs. 1, 3).   **2** showing DIFFUSION.   **3** using too many words;

wordy. *adj.* —**dif·fu′sive·ly,** *adv.* —**dif·fu′sive·ness,** *n.*

**dig** (dig) **1** use a shovel, spade, hands, claws, or snout to make a hole or to turn over ground: *After digging for three hours, they were still only one metre down. She's out in the garden digging for earthworms.* **2** make or form by removing earth or other material: *to dig a hole, to dig a basement.* **3** prepare by turning over ground: *to dig a garden.* **4** make a way by digging: *to dig through a snowbank, to dig under a fence.* **5** get by digging: *to dig potatoes, to dig clams.* **6** an archaeological excavation. **7** make a careful search or inquiry for information, or into a book, etc.: *We will really have to dig for that information.* **8** make a thrust or stab into; prod: *The rider dug her spurs into the horse.* 1–5, 7, 8, *v.,* **dug, dig·ging;** 6 *n.* **dig in, a** work hard. **b** make a protective trench. **c** secure one's position: *He has really dug in at the factory.* **d** *Informal.* eat heartily.

**di·gest** (dī jest′ *or* di jest′ *for verb,* dī′jest *for noun*) **1** change food in the stomach so that it can be taken into the blood and used as nourishment: *We digest our food.* **2** undergo this process; be digested: *Some foods digest more quickly than others.* **3** understand and absorb mentally; arrange in the mind: *It often takes a long time to digest new ideas.* **4** condense and arrange according to some system; summarize. **5** information condensed and arranged according to some system; summary: *a digest of law.* 1–4 *v.,* 5 *n.*

**di·gest·i·bil·i·ty** (dī jes′tə bil′ə tē *or* di jes′tə bil′ə tē) the quality of being DIGESTIBLE. *n.*

**di·gest·i·ble** (dī jes′tə bəl *or* di jes′tə bəl) capable of being digested; easily digested. *adj.*

**di·ges·tion** (dī jes′chən *or* di jes′chən) **1** the digesting of food. **2** the ability to digest food. **3** the act of digesting books, etc. *n.*

**di·ges·tive** (dī jes′tiv *or* di jes′tiv) **1** of or for DIGESTION (def. 1): *Saliva is one of the digestive juices.* **2** helping DIGESTION (def. 2): *digestive tablets.* **3** something that aids DIGESTION (defs. 1, 2). 1, 2 *adj.,* 3 *n.*

**dig·ger** (dig′ər) **1** a person who digs. **2** the part of a machine that turns up the ground. **3** any tool for digging. *n.*

**dig·gings** (dig′ingz) **1** a mine or place where digging is being done. **2** the stuff that is dug out. *n.pl.*

**dig·it** (dij′it) **1** a finger or toe. **2** any one of the figures 0, 1, 2, 3, 4, 5, 6, 7, 8, 9: *Sometimes 0 is not called a digit but is known as a cipher.* *n.*

**dig·it·al** (dij′ə təl) **1** of or having to do with the fingers or toes. **2** of or having to do with numerals (digits) or calculation by numerals. **3** of, having to do with, or providing information in the form of numerals: *A digital clock shows the time in the form of changing numerals rather than by hands moving over a dial.* **4** of or by means of a DIGITAL COMPUTER. *adj.*

**digital computer** a computer that uses a BINARY system of numbers to solve mathematical problems.

**dig·i·tal·is** (dij′ə tal′is) **1** a medicine used for stimulating the heart, obtained from the dried leaves of the purple foxglove. **2** FOXGLOVE. *n.*

**dig·ni·fied** (dig′nə fīd′) having or showing DIGNITY (defs. 1, 4); noble or stately. *adj.* —**dig′ni·fied′ly,** *adv.*

**dig·ni·fy** (dig′nə fī′) **1** give DIGNITY (defs. 1, 4) to; make noble or worthy: *The little farmhouse was dignified by the great elms around it.* **2** give a high-sounding name to. *v.,* **dig·ni·fied, dig·ni·fy·ing.**

# dig   339   dilemma

hat, āge, fär; let, ēqual, tėrm; it, īce hot, ōpen, ôrder; oil, out; cup, put, rüle ə*bove, ta*ken, penc*i*l, lem*o*n, circ*u*s ch, child; ng, long; sh, ship th, thin; ᴛʜ, then; zh, measure

**dig·ni·tar·y** (dig′nə ter′ē) a person who has a position of honour: *A bishop is a dignitary of the Christian church.* *n., pl.* **dig·ni·tar·ies.**

**dig·ni·ty** (dig′nə tē) **1** a proud and self-respecting manner; stateliness and formality: *He replied with dignity that he was not interested in their scheme. She had great dignity of bearing.* **2** self-respect; self-esteem: *She maintained that lying about the matter would be beneath her dignity.* **3** high rank, office, or position, or the honour or esteem attached to it: *He felt that casual dress was not in keeping with the dignity of his position as director.* **4** the quality of being worthy of honour or esteem; true worth, nobility, or excellence: *The dignity of labour.* **5** a stately appearance: *the dignity of a castle.* *n., pl.* **dig·ni·ties.**

**di·graph** (dī′graf) two letters used together to spell a single sound: *Examples: ea in each, th in with.* *n.*

**di·gress** (dī gres′ *or* di gres′) turn aside; get off the main subject in talking or writing. *v.*

**di·gres·sion** (dī gresh′ən *or* di gresh′ən) a turning aside; a getting off the main subject in talking or writing. *n.*

**di·gres·sive** (dī gres′iv *or* di gres′iv) tending to DIGRESS; digressing. *adj.* —**di·gres′sive·ness,** *n.*

**dike** (dīk) **1** a bank of earth or a dam built as a defence against flooding. **2** provide with a dike or dikes. **3** a ditch or channel for water. **4** drain with a ditch or channel for water. **5** a bank of earth thrown up in digging; low wall of earth or stone; causeway. **6** a barrier; obstacle. **7** in geology, a long, usually narrow mass of igneous rock that was thrust, while molten, into a fissure of older rock and that cuts across the existing rock at an angle. 1, 3, 5, 6, 7 *n.,* 2, 4 *v.,* **diked, dik·ing.** Also, **dyke.**

**di·lap·i·dat·ed** (di lap′ə dā′tid) falling to pieces; partly ruined or decayed through neglect: *a dilapidated house.* *adj.*

**di·lap·i·da·tion** (di lap′ə dā′shən) a falling to pieces; decay; ruin; tumble-down condition: *The house was in the last stage of dilapidation.* *n.*

**di·late** (dī lāt′ *or* di lāt′) **1** make or become larger or wider: *The pupil of the eye dilates when the light gets dim. The doctor used a drug to dilate the pupils of her eyes.* **2** speak or write in a very complete or detailed manner: *The mayor did not have time to dilate on the subject.* *v.,* **di·lat·ed, di·lat·ing.**

**di·lat·ed** (dī lā′tid *or* di lā′tid) **1** widened; expanded. **2** pt. and pp. of DILATE. 1 *adj.,* 2 *v.*

**di·la·tion** (dī lā′shən *or* di lā′shən) **1** the act of dilating; enlargement; widening. **2** a DILATED condition. **3** a DILATED part. *n.*

**dil·a·to·ry** (dil′ə tô′rē) **1** tending to delay; not prompt. **2** causing delay. *adj.* —**dil′a·to′ri·ly,** *adv.* —**dil′a·to′ri·ness,** *n.*

**di·lem·ma** (di lem′ə) a situation requiring a choice between two things when either one is unpleasant or undesirable; a difficult choice: *Her dilemma was either the loss of her job or a reduction in salary.* *n.*

**dil·et·tan·te** (dil′ə tan′tē or dil′ə tänt′) 1 a lover of the fine arts. 2 a person who is interested in some art or other subject only as an amusement; a dabbler or trifler. *n., pl.* **dil·et·tan·tes** or **dil·et·tan·ti** (-tē).

**dil·et·tan·ti** (dil′ə tan′tē or dil′ə tän′tē) a pl. of DILETTANTE. *n.*

**dil·et·tant·ism** (dil′ə tan′tiz əm or dil′ə tän′tiz əm) the quality or practice of a DILETTANTE. *n.*

**dil·i·gence** (dil′ə jəns) 1 the quality of being DILIGENT; careful effort; the ability to work hard and steadily; industry: *The student's diligence was rewarded with high marks.* *n.*

**dil·i·gent** (dil′ə jənt) 1 hard-working; industrious. 2 careful and steady. *adj.* —**dil′i·gent·ly**, *adv.*

**dill** (dil) 1 a tall plant of the parsley family native to Europe, but widely grown in North America: *Dill is grown for its spicy seeds or leaves, which are used as flavouring for cucumber pickles, soups, stews, etc.* 2 the seeds or leaves of this plant. 3 DILL PICKLE: *Dills are my favourite pickles.* *n.*

**dill pickle** a cucumber pickle flavoured with dill.

**dil·ly–dal·ly** (dil′ē dal′ē) waste time; loiter; trifle. *v.*, **dil·ly-dal·lied, dil·ly-dal·ly·ing.**

**di·lute** (di lüt′ or dī lüt′) 1 make weaker or thinner by adding water or some other liquid. 2 weaken; lessen. 3 become diluted. 4 weakened or thinned by the addition of water or other liquid: *a dilute acid.* 1–3 *v.*, **dil·ut·ed, di·lut·ing;** 4 *adj.*

**di·lut·ed** (di lü′tid or dī lü′tid) 1 weakened; thinned. 2 pt. and pp. of DILUTE. 1 *adj.*, 2 *v.*

**di·lu·tion** (di lü′shən or dī lü′shən) 1 the act of diluting. 2 the fact or state of being diluted. 3 something diluted. *n.*

**dim** (dim) 1 not bright, clear, or distinct: *a dim light, a dim outline.* 2 not clearly or completely perceived or distinguished; vague: *He had a dim memory of the event.* 3 not able to see or perceive clearly and distinctly: *Her eyesight was getting dim.* 4 not likely to have a good result or outcome: *Her future looks dim.* 5 make or become dim: *The theatre lights were dimmed.* 6 change the headlights of a motor vehicle to the low beam: *We dim our lights for oncoming cars.* 1–4 *adj.*, **dim·mer, dim·mest;** 5, 6 *v.*, **dimmed, dim·ming.** —**dim′ly**, *adv.* —**dim′ness**, *n.*

**dim out,** make nearly but not absolutely dark, by allowing light to appear only through slits, by use of blue lights, etc.: *to dim out the lights on stage.*

**take a dim view of,** disapprove of; look on with disfavour: *He takes a dim view of practical jokes.*

**dim.** 1 diminuendo. 2 diminutive.

**dime** (dīm) a coin of Canada and the United States, equal to one tenth of a dollar; a ten-cent coin. *n.*

**a dime a dozen,** *Informal.* cheap and commonplace: *Those comic T-shirts are a dime a dozen.*

**dime novel** a sensational or melodramatic novel, usually published as a cheap paperback: *Dime novels are all he ever reads.*

**di·men·sion** (di men′shən or dī men′shən) 1 the measurement of length, breadth, or thickness: *The dimensions of my room are 4.2 metres by 3.1 metres.* 2 Usually, **dimensions,** *pl.* the size; extent: *It was a project of large dimensions.* *n.*

**di·men·sion·al** (di men′shə nəl or dī men′shə nəl) having to do with DIMENSION or dimensions. *adj.*

**dime store** a store selling a large variety of low-priced articles.

**dimin.** 1 diminuendo. 2 diminutive.

**di·min·ish** (di min′ish) make or become smaller in size, amount, or importance; lessen; reduce: *The heat diminished as the sun went down.* *v.*

**di·min·u·en·do** (di min′yü en′dō) in music: 1 a gradual lessening in force or loudness. The sign for a diminuendo is >. 2 gradually lessening in force or loudness. 3 a passage to be played or sung with a diminuendo. 1, 3 *n., pl.* **di·min·u·en·dos;** 2 *adj., adv.* Compare with CRESCENDO.

**dim·i·nu·tion** (dim′ə nyü′shən or dim′ə nü′shən) a DIMINISHing; lessening; reduction; decrease. *n.*

**di·min·u·tive** (di min′yə tiv) 1 small; little; tiny. 2 a small person or thing. 3 expressing smallness. 4 a word or part of a word expressing smallness, such as the suffixes *-let* and *-kin.* 1, 3 *adj.*, 2, 4 *n.* —**di·min′u·tive·ly**, *adv.* —**di·min′u·tive·ness**, *n.*

**dim·i·ty** (dim′ə tē) a thin cloth, usually of cotton, woven with heavy threads at intervals in a striped or cross-barred arrangement, used for dresses, curtains, etc. *n., pl.* **dim·i·ties.**

**dim·mer** (dim′ər) 1 a device for dimming an electric light: *We have a dimmer for the light in our dining room.* 2 a switch for changing the headlights of a motor vehicle to the low beam. 3 any person or thing that dims. *n.*

**dim·ple** (dim′pəl) 1 a small natural hollow on the surface of a plump part of the body, such as on the cheek, the chin, or the back of the hand. 2 any small, hollow place: *A golf ball has dimples.* 3 make dimples in: *The rain dimpled the smooth surface of the pond.* 4 have or form dimples: *Her cheeks dimple when she smiles.* 1, 2 *n.*, 3, 4 *v.* **dim·pled, dim·pling.**

**din** (din) 1 a loud, confused noise that lasts for some time. 2 make a din. 3 strike with a din. 4 say over and over: *He was always dinning into our ears the importance of hard work.* 1 *n.*, 2–4 *v.*, **dinned, din·ning.**

**dine** (dīn) 1 eat dinner. 2 give a dinner to or for: *The Chamber of Commerce dined the famous traveller.* *v.*, **dined, din·ing.**

**dine out,** eat dinner away from home.

**din·er** (dī′nər) 1 a person who is eating dinner. 2 a railway car in which meals are served. 3 a restaurant shaped like such a car. 4 a small eating place, usually near a main highway. *n.*

**di·nette** (dī net′) a small dining room. *n.*

**ding** (ding) 1 make a sound like a bell; ring continuously. 2 the sound made by a bell. 3 *Informal.* say over and over. 1, 3 *v.*, 2 *n.*

**ding–dong** (ding′dong′) the sound made by a bell or anything like a bell; continuous ringing. *n.*

**din·gey** (ding′gē or ding′ē) DINGHY. *n., pl.* **din·geys.**

**din·ghy** (ding′gē or ding′ē) 1 a small rowboat. 2 a small boat used as a tender or lifeboat by a large boat. 3 a small sailboat. *n., pl.* **din·ghies.**

**din·gle** (ding′gəl) a small, deep, shady valley. *n.*

**din·go** (ding′gō)   a wolflike wild dog of Australia.   *n.*, *pl.* **din·goes.**

**din·gy** (din′jē)   dirty-looking; not bright and fresh; dull: *The old curtains were torn and dingy.*   *adj.*, **din·gi·er, din·gi·est.**   —**din′gi·ly,** *adv.*   —**din′gi·ness,** *n.*

**dink·ey** (ding′kē)   a small locomotive, used for pulling freight cars around in a railway yard, for hauling logs, etc.   *n.*, *pl.* **dink·eys.**

**dining room**   a room in which dinner and other meals are served.

**din·ner** (din′ər)   **1** one of the three main meals of the day, especially the largest meal: *Some people have dinner at noon; others have a lunch at noon and dinner in the evening.*   **2** a formal social event including dinner: *They're having a dinner to celebrate their parents' wedding anniversary.*   **3** the food served at dinner.   **4** a packaged, prepared meal, designed for quick and convenient preparation: *a TV dinner.*   *n.*

**dinner jacket**   TUXEDO (def. 1).

**din·ner·time** (din′ər tīm′)   the time at which dinner is eaten.   *n.*

**di·no·flag·el·late** (dē′nə flaj′ə lāt)   a member of an order of marine organisms, some of which are very toxic.   *n.*

**di·no·saur** (dī′nə sôr′ or din′ə sôr′)   any of a group of extinct four-limbed reptiles, often of huge size.   *n.*

**dint** (dint)   **1** a hollow made by the force of a blow or by pressure; a dent.   **2** make a dent in.   **3** become dented.   **1** *n.*, **2, 3** *v.*
**by dint of,**   by the force of or by means of: *By dint of hard work the job was completed on schedule.*
☛ *Etym.*   See note at DENT.

**di·o·ram·a** (dī′ə ram′ə)   **1** a picture that is usually looked at through a small opening: *A diorama is lighted in such a way as to be very realistic.*   **2** a scene to be viewed through a window-like opening, showing a painted background and a foreground occupied by sculptured figures (life-size or smaller) of animals, people, etc. and appropriate accessory objects.   *n.*

**di·ox·ide** (dī ok′sīd)   an OXIDE having two atoms of oxygen per molecule and one atom of a metal or other element.   *n.*

**dip** (dip)   **1** put under water or any liquid and lift quickly out again: *Mary dipped her hand into the pool.*   **2** go under water and come quickly out again.   **3** a dipping of any kind, especially a plunge into and out of a tub of water, the ocean, etc.   **4** dye by dipping in a liquid.   **5** wash or clean by dipping in a liquid.   **6** a liquid in which to dip something: *sheep dip.*   **7** make a candle by putting a wick into hot tallow or wax.   **8** a candle made by dipping.   **9** take up in the hollow of the hand or with a pail, pan, or other container: *to dip up water from a well, to dip up a sample of wheat.*   **10** put one's hand, a spoon, etc. into to take out something.   **11** that which is taken out or up by dipping.   **12** a creamy mixture of foods eaten by dipping into it with a cracker, piece of bread, etc.: *a cheese dip.*   **13** lower and raise again quickly: *The flag is dipped as a kind of salute.*   **14** sink or drop down: *A bird dips in its flight.*   **15** a sudden drop: *a dip in prices, a dip in the road.*   **16** slope downward: *The road dips.*   **17** the amount of slope down.   1, 2, 4, 5, 7, 9, 10, 13, 14, 16 *v.*, **dipped** or **dipt, dip·ping**; 3, 6, 8, 11, 12, 15, 17 *n.*
**dip into,**   read or look at for a short time; glance at.

**diph·the·ri·a** (dif thē′rē ə or dip thē′rē ə)   a

# dingo 341 diplomatist

hat, āge, fär; let, ēqual, tėrm; it, īce
hot, ōpen, ôrder; oil, out; cup, pùt, rüle
əbove, takən, pencəl, lemən, circəs
ch, child; ng, long; sh, ship
th, thin; ᴛʜ, then; zh, measure

dangerous, infectious disease of the throat, usually accompanied by a high fever and by the formation of membranes that hinder breathing.   *n.*

**diph·thong** (dif′thong or dip′thong)   **1** a vowel sound made up of two identifiable vowel sounds in immediate sequence and pronounced in one syllable, as *ou* in *house*, *oi* in *noise*.   **2** two vowel letters representing a single vowel sound, properly called a DIGRAPH, as *ea* in *eat*.   **3** several letters joined together in printing, such as æ and œ, properly called a LIGATURE.   *n.*   Compare with MONOPHTHONG.

**diph·thon·gal** (dif thong′gəl or dip thong′gəl)   of or like a DIPHTHONG.   *adj.*

**di·plod·o·cus** (di plod′ə kəs)   a dinosaur of North America that lived by eating plants.   *n.*

**di·ploid** (dip′loid)   **1** double or twofold.   **2** of or referring to a nucleus, cell, or organism having paired homologous chromosomes (twice the haploid number of chromosomes).   **3** a diploid nucleus, cell, or organism.   1, 2 *adj.*, 3 *n.*   Compare with HAPLOID.

**di·plo·ma** (di plō′mə)   **1** a certificate given by a school, college, or university to its graduating students.   **2** any certificate that bestows certain rights, privileges, honours, etc.   *n.*

**di·plo·ma·cy** (di plō′mə sē)   **1** the management of relations between nations: *The making of treaties, international agreements, etc. is an important part of diplomacy.*   **2** skill in managing such relations.   **3** skill in dealing with others; tact: *Our son showed diplomacy in being very helpful at home the day he wanted to use the car.*   *n.*, *pl.* **di·plo·ma·cies.**

**dip·lo·mat** (dip′lə mat′)   **1** a person employed in DIPLOMACY (def. 1), especially a representative of a nation who is located in a foreign country with the duty of looking after the interests of his or her own nation in the foreign country.   **2** a person who is skilful in dealing with others; a tactful person.   *n.*

**dip·lo·mat·ic** (dip′lə mat′ik)   **1** of or having to do with the management of relations between nations or with the people conducting such relations: *diplomatic immunity. Ambassadors and high commissioners are the highest-ranking members of the diplomatic service.*   **2** having or showing skill in dealing with others; tactful: *a diplomatic police officer. She gave a diplomatic answer to avoid hurting her friend's feelings.*   *adj.*

**dip·lo·mat·i·cal·ly** (dip′lə mat′i klē)   in a DIPLOMATIC (def. 2) manner; with diplomacy.   *adv.*

**diplomatic corps**   all of the ambassadors, ministers, etc. of foreign nations in the capital of a country.

**di·plo·ma·tist** (di plō′mə tist)   DIPLOMAT.   *n.*

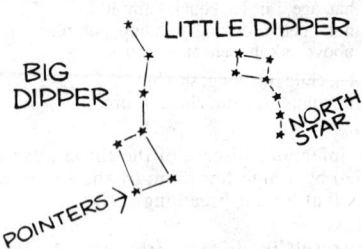

**dip·per** (dip′ər) 1 a person or thing that dips. 2 a long-handled cup or larger vessel for dipping water or other liquids. 3 **Dipper,** either of two groups of stars in the northern sky resembling dippers in shape; the BIG DIPPER or the LITTLE DIPPER. *n.*

**dip·so·ma·ni·a** (dip′sə mā′nē ə) an abnormal, uncontrollable craving for alcoholic liquor. *n.*

**dip·so·ma·ni·ac** (dip′sə mā′nē ak′) a person who has DIPSOMANIA. *n.*

**dipt** (dipt) a pt. and a pp. of DIP. *v.*

**dire** (dīr) 1 causing great fear or suffering; terrible: *a dire flood, a dire enemy.* 2 desperate; urgent; extreme: *dire poverty. They were in dire distress.* *adj.,* **dir·er, dir·est.** —**dire′ly,** *adv.* —**dire′ness,** *n.*

**di·rect** (di rekt′ *or* dī rekt′) 1 manage; control; guide: *The teacher directs the work of the pupils.* 2 order; command: *The captain directed his men to advance.* 3 tell or show the way; give information about where to go, what to do, etc.: *Can you direct me to the railway station? Signposts direct travellers.* 4 point; aim: *The fireman directed his hose at the flames. We should direct our efforts to a useful end.* 5 put the address on a letter, package, etc. 6 address words, etc. to a person: *to direct a request to the queen.* 7 turn a thing straight to. 8 proceeding in a straight line; without a stop or turn; straight: *a direct route.* 9 in an unbroken line of descent: *a direct descendant of Queen Victoria.* 10 immediate: *He took direct charge of the library.* 11 without anyone or anything in between; by oneself or itself; not through others: *a direct tax.* 12 straightforward; frank; plain; truthful: *a direct answer. She made a direct denial of the charge of cheating.* 13 exact; absolute: *the direct opposite.* 14 directly: *The flight goes to Winnipeg direct, without changing planes.* 1–7 *v.,* 8–13 *adj.,* 14 *adv.* —**di·rect′ness,** *n.*

**direct current** a steady electric current that flows in one direction. Compare with ALTERNATING CURRENT.

**direct discourse** a quoting of what a person says in his or her exact words. *Example:* She said, "Let's go now." Compare with INDIRECT DISCOURSE.

**di·rec·tion** (di rek′shən *or* dī rek′shən) 1 guidance; management; control: *The school is under the direction of a good principal.* 2 an order or command. 3 knowing or telling what to do, how to do, where to go, etc.; instruction: *Can you give me directions how to reach Montreal?* 4 the address on a letter or package. 5 the course taken by a moving body, such as a ball or a bullet. 6 any way in which one may face or point: *North, south, east, and west are directions.* 7 a line of action; tendency, etc.: *The town shows improvement in many directions. The crime investigation has taken a new direction.* *n.*

**di·rec·tion·al** (di rek′shə nəl *or* dī rek′shə nəl) 1 of or having to do with direction in space. 2 fitted for determining the direction from which radio signals come, or for sending radio signals in one direction only. *adj.*

**di·rec·tive** (di rek′tiv *or* dī rek′tiv) 1 an order or instruction as to procedure. 2 directing. 1 *n.,* 2 *adj.*

**di·rect·ly** (di rek′tlē *or* dī rek′tlē) 1 in a direct line or manner; straight: *This road runs directly north.* 2 exactly; absolutely: *directly opposite.* 3 immediately; at once: *Come home directly.* *adv.*

**direct object** a grammatical term for a word showing by its position or form the person or thing undergoing the action expressed by the verb. In "The car struck me," *me* is the direct object. Compare with INDIRECT OBJECT.

**di·rec·tor** (di rek′tər *or* dī rek′tər) 1 a person who leads or controls; manager: *the director of a private school, the director of a building restoration project.* 2 one of a group of persons chosen to direct the overall affairs of a company or institution: *She is on the board of directors of a large corporation.* 3 a person who plans, guides, and rehearses the staging of a play, opera, motion picture, etc. 4 a person who leads a choir, orchestra, etc.; conductor. *n.*

**di·rec·tor·ate** (di rek′tə rit *or* dī rek′tə rit) 1 the position of director. 2 a group of directors. *n.*

**di·rec·tor·ship** (di rek′tər ship′ *or* dī rek′tər ship′) the position or term of office of a director. *n.*

**di·rec·to·ry** (di rek′tə rē *or* dī rek′tə rē) 1 a list of names and addresses: *A telephone book is a directory.* 2 a book of rules or instructions. 3 a group of directors; DIRECTORATE (def. 2). 4 directing; advisory. 5 a list of files on one disk, available in a computer. 1–3, 5 *n., pl.* **di·rec·to·ries;** 4 *adj.*

**direct question** a question quoted in a person's exact words. *Example:* He asked, "Shall we go now?" Compare with INDIRECT QUESTION.

**di·rec·tress** (di rek′tris *or* dī rek′tris) a woman director. *n.*

**direct tax** a tax demanded of the persons who must pay it: *Poll taxes, income taxes, property taxes, and inheritance taxes are direct taxes.*

**dire·ful** (dīr′fəl) dire; dreadful; terrible. *adj.* —**dire′ful·ly,** *adv.* —**dire′ful·ness,** *n.*

**dirge** (dėrj) a song or tune of grief for a person's death. *n.*

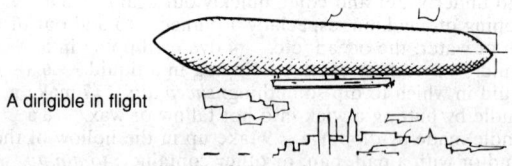

A dirigible in flight

**dir·i·gi·ble** (dir′ə jə bəl *or* di rij′ə bəl) 1 a kind of aircraft having a long, gas-filled hull that keeps it up in the air and a steering and propelling mechanism underneath the hull; airship: *Some dirigibles have a rigid hull; in others the hull is non-rigid.* 2 capable of being steered. 1 *n.,* 2 *adj.*
☛ *Etym.* Short for *dirigible balloon;* that is, a balloon capable of being directed, or steered.

**dirk** (dėrk) 1 a short, straight dagger. See DAGGER for picture. 2 stab with a dirk. 1 *n.,* 2 *v.*

**dirn·dl** (dėrn′dəl) 1 an Alpine peasant girl's costume consisting of a blouse, a tight bodice, and a full, bright-coloured skirt, gathered at the waist. **2** a dress imitating this. **3** a skirt of this type. *n.*

**dirt** (dėrt) **1** mud, dust, earth, or anything like them: *Dirt soils whatever it gets on.* **2** loose earth; soil: *He dropped his glove in the dirt.* **3** lewdness of speech or thought. **4** anything worthless or contemptible: *She had treated them like dirt.* **5** malicious gossip: *He delighted in spreading all the latest dirt.* *n.* —**dirt′less**, *adj.*
**eat dirt**, *Informal.* submit to a humiliating experience, such as making an apology or taking back something one has said.

**dirt bike** a motorcycle designed for riding over rough ground. It cannot be licensed for use on roads.

**dirt·y** (dėr′tē) **1** soiled by dirt; unclean: *Children playing in the mud get dirty.* **2** not clear or pure in colour; clouded: *a dirty red.* **3** low; mean; vile: *a dirty trick.* **4** not decent; lewd or obscene: *a dirty joke.* **5** make dirty; soil. **6** stormy; windy: *dirty weather.* 1–4, 6 *adj.*, **dirt·i·er, dirt·i·est;** 5 *v.*, **dirt·ied, dirt·y·ing.** —**dirt′i·ly**, *adv.* —**dirt′i·ness**, *n.*

**dis-** a prefix meaning: **1** the opposite of, as in *discontent.* **2** do the reverse of, as in *disentangle.*

**dis·a·bil·i·ty** (dis′ə bil′ə tē) **1** the condition of being DISABLEd: *an accident resulting in permanent disability.* **2** something that DISABLES (def. 1): *Paralysis is a physical disability.* **3** in law, something that disqualifies: *Her relationship to the accused was a disability that disqualified her from serving on the jury at his trial.* *n., pl.* **dis·a·bil·i·ties.**

**dis·a·ble** (di sā′bəl) **1** deprive of ability or power; make useless; cripple: *My father was disabled in the accident.* **2** disqualify legally. *v.*, **dis·a·bled, dis·a·bling.** —**dis·a′ble·ment**, *n.*

**dis·a·bled** (di sā′bəld) **1** deprived of ability or power; crippled. **2** pt. and pp. of DISABLE. 1 *adj.*, 2 *v.*

**dis·a·buse** (dis′ə byüz′) free from deception or error: *Education should disabuse people of prejudice.* *v.*, **dis·a·bused, dis·a·bus·ing.**

**dis·ad·van·tage** (dis′əd van′tij) **1** a lack of advantage; unfavourable condition: *The deaf child was at a disadvantage in school.* **2** harm; loss: *The candidate's enemies spread rumours to his disadvantage.* *n.*

**dis·ad·van·taged** (dis′əd van′tijd) **1** suffering from severe economic or social disadvantage. **2 the disadvantaged,** *pl.* all those who are disadvantaged. 1 *adj.*, 2 *n.*

**dis·ad·van·ta·geous** (di sad′vən tā′jəs) causing disadvantage; unfavourable. *adj.* —**dis·ad′van·ta′geous·ly**, *adv.* —**dis·ad′van·ta′geous·ness**, *n.*

**dis·af·fect·ed** (dis′ə fek′tid) **1** unfriendly; discontented. **2** no longer loyal; disloyal: *a disaffected Communist.* *adj.*

**dis·af·fec·tion** (dis′ə fek′shən) **1** unfriendliness; discontent: *The new tax caused general disaffection.* **2** disloyalty; desertion: *The party was weakened by the disaffection of many of its members.* *n.*

**dis·a·gree** (dis′ə grē′) **1** fail to agree; differ: *The witness disagreed with the lawyer about the time of the crime. Doctors sometimes disagree.* **2** quarrel; dispute. **3** have a bad effect; be harmful: *Strawberries disagree with him.* *v.*, **dis·a·greed, dis·a·gree·ing.**

**dis·a·gree·a·ble** (dis′ə grē′ə bəl) **1** not to one's liking; unpleasant: *A headache is disagreeable.*

**dirt**     **343**     **disarray**

hat, āge, fär; let, ēqual, tėrm; it, īce
hot, ōpen, ôrder; oil, out; cup, pùt, rüle
above, takən, pencəl, lemən, circəs
ch, child; ng, long; sh, ship
th, thin; ᴛH, then; zh, measure

**2** bad-tempered; cross: *Maria is sometimes disagreeable until she has had her breakfast.* *adj.* —**dis′a·gree′a·bly**, *adv.*

**dis·a·gree·ment** (dis′ə grē′mənt) **1** a failure to agree; difference of opinion. **2** a quarrel or dispute. **3** a difference; unlikeness: *There is a striking disagreement between the two species.* *n.*

**dis·al·low** (dis′ə lou′) refuse to allow; deny the truth or value of; reject: *The request for a new trial was disallowed.* *v.*

**dis·ap·pear** (dis′ə pēr′) **1** pass from sight: *The little dog disappeared down the road.* **2** pass from existence; stop being; be lost: *When spring comes, the snow disappears.* *v.*

**dis·ap·pear·ance** (dis′ə pē′rəns) the act of disappearing: *The disappearance of the little boy brought about a search of the area.* *n.*

**dis·ap·point** (dis′ə point′) **1** fail to satisfy or please; leave one wanting or expecting something: *The circus disappointed him, for there was no elephant.* **2** fail to keep a promise to: *You promised to come; do not disappoint me.* **3** keep from happening; oppose and defeat. *v.*

**dis·ap·point·ment** (dis′ə point′mənt) **1** the state of being or feeling disappointed: *When she did not get the new bicycle, the disappointment seemed too great to bear.* **2** a person or thing that causes disappointment: *Her lazy son was a disappointment to her.* **3** the act or fact of disappointing. *n.*

**dis·ap·pro·ba·tion** (dis′ap rə bā′shən) DISAPPROVAL: *He showed his disapprobation of my laziness.* *n.*

**dis·ap·prov·al** (dis′ə prü′vəl) **1** an opinion or feeling against; expression of an opinion against; dislike. **2** a refusal to consent; rejection. *n.*

**dis·ap·prove** (dis′ə prüv′) **1** have or express an opinion against. **2** show dislike (*of*): *The boy disapproved of going to school in the summer.* **3** refuse consent to; reject: *The judge disapproved the verdict.* *v.*, **dis·ap·proved, dis·ap·prov·ing.** —**dis′ap·prov′ing·ly**, *adv.*

**dis·arm** (di särm′) **1** take weapons away from: *The police captured the bandits and disarmed them.* **2** stop having armed forces; reduce or limit the size of the armed forces. **3** remove suspicion from; make friendly; calm the anger of: *The speaker's frankness disarmed the angry men, and they began to cheer him.* **4** make harmless: *The expert disarmed the bomb.* *v.*

**dis·ar·ma·ment** (di sär′mə mənt) **1** the act of disarming. **2** the reduction or limitation of military forces and equipment. *n.*

**dis·ar·range** (dis′ə rānj′) disturb the arrangement of; put out of order: *The wind disarranged her hair.* *v.*, **dis·ar·ranged, dis·ar·rang·ing.** —**dis′ar·range′ment**, *n.*

**dis·ar·ray** (dis′ə rā′) **1** a disorder; confusion. **2** put into disorder or confusion. **3** a disorder of clothing. 1, 3 *n.*, 2 *v.*

**dis·as·sem·ble** (dis′ə sem′bəl)   take apart.   *v.*
**dis·as·sem·bled, dis·as·sem·bling.**

**dis·as·ter** (də zas′tər)   an event that causes much suffering or loss; great misfortune: *A destructive fire, flood, earthquake, or shipwreck is a disaster.*   *n.*

**disaster area**   an area officially designated as having suffered some kind of DISASTER: *Disaster areas are usually given government aid.*

**dis·as·trous** (də zas′trəs)   bringing DISASTER; causing great danger, suffering, loss, pain, or sorrow: *The train wreck was disastrous.*   *adj.*   —**dis·as′trous·ly,** *adv.*

**dis·a·vow** (dis′ə vou′)   deny that one knows about, approves of, or is responsible for; DISCLAIM (def. 1): *The prisoner disavowed the confession bearing his signature.*   *v.*

**dis·a·vow·al** (dis′ə vou′əl)   a DISAVOWing; denial of knowledge, approval, or responsibility.   *n.*

**dis·band** (dis band′)   **1** dismiss from service: *Most of the army was disbanded after the war.*   **2** break ranks; become scattered.   *v.*   —**dis·band′ment,** *n.*

**dis·bar** (dis bär′)   deprive a lawyer of the right to practise his or her profession.   *v.,* **dis·barred, dis·bar·ring.**   —**dis·bar′ment,** *n.*

**dis·be·lief** (dis′bi lēf′)   a lack of belief; refusal to believe.   *n.*

**dis·be·lieve** (dis′bi lēv′)   have no belief in: *His mother disbelieved his story.*   *v.,* **dis·be·lieved, dis·be·liev·ing.**   —**dis′be·liev′er,** *n.*

**dis·bur·den** (dis bėr′dən)   relieve of a burden: *The boy disburdened his mind to his sister by confessing what he had done.*   *v.*

**dis·burse** (dis bėrs′)   pay out; expend: *Our city treasurer disburses thousands of dollars each week.*   *v.,* **dis·bursed, dis·burs·ing.**   —**dis·burs′er,** *n.*

**dis·burse·ment** (dis bėr′smənt)   **1** the act of paying out: *Our treasurer attends to the disbursement of funds.*   **2** the money paid out; expenditure.   *n.*

**disc** (disk)   See DISK.   *n.*

**dis·card** (di skärd′ *for verb,* dis′kärd *for noun*)   **1** give up as useless or worn out; throw aside: *You can discard clothes, ways of doing things, or beliefs.*   **2** the act of throwing aside as useless.   **3** something thrown aside as useless or not wanted: *That old book is a discard from the school library.*   **4** get rid of useless or unwanted playing cards by throwing them aside or playing them.   **5** throw out an unwanted card.   **6** the unwanted card thrown aside; a card played as useless.   1, 4, 5 *v.,* 2, 3, 6 *n.*

**dis·cern** (di sėrn′ *or* di zėrn′)   perceive; see clearly; distinguish; recognize: *When I looked closely I could discern a faint outline through the fog. It is often hard to discern the truth.*   *v.*   —**dis·cern′er,** *n.*

**dis·cern·i·ble** (di sėr′nə bəl *or* di zėr′nə bəl)   capable of being DISCERNed.   *adj.*   —**dis·cern′i·bly,** *adv.*

**dis·cern·ing** (di sėr′ning *or* di zėr′ning)   **1** shrewd; acute; discriminating.   **2** ppr. of DISCERN.   1 *adj.,* 2 *v.*
—**dis·cern′ing·ly,** *adv.*

**dis·cern·ment** (di sėrn′mənt *or* di zėrn′mənt)   **1** keenness in perceiving and understanding; good judgment; shrewdness.   **2** the act of DISCERNing.   *n.*

**dis·charge** (dis chärj′ *for verb,* dis chärj′ *or* dis′chärj *for noun*)   **1** unload a ship, train, bus, etc.; unload from a ship; unload.   **2** unloading: *The discharge of this cargo will not take long.*   **3** fire; shoot: *to discharge a gun.*   **4** a firing off of a gun, a blast, etc.: *The discharge of the dynamite could be heard for blocks.*   **5** release; let go; dismiss: *to discharge a patient from a hospital, to discharge a committee.*   **6** dismiss from a job; fire: *He was discharged for incompetence.*   **7** a release; the act of letting go; dismissing: *the discharge of a convict from prison.*   **8** a piece of writing that shows a person's release or dismissal; certificate of release: *A soldier or sailor gets a discharge when his service is ended.*   **9** give off; let out: *The wound was still discharging pus.*   **10** giving off; letting out: *In a thunderstorm there is a discharge of electricity from the clouds.*   **11** something given off or let out: *the watery discharge from a sore.*   **12** come or pour forth: *The river discharged into a bay.*   **13** the rate of flow: *The discharge from the pipe is 45 cubic decimetres per second.*   **14** rid of an electric charge; withdraw electricity from.   **15** the transference of electricity between two charged bodies when placed in contact or near each other.   **16** pay; settle: *to discharge a debt.*   **17** payment.   **18** perform; carry out: *to discharge one's duty.*   **19** carrying out; performance: *A public official should be honest in the discharge of her duties.*   **20** in law, cancel or set aside a court order.   1, 3, 5, 6, 9, 12, 14, 16, 18, 20 *v.,*
**dis·charged, dis·charg·ing;**   2, 4, 7, 8, 10, 11, 13, 15, 17, 19 *n.*   —**dis·charg′er,** *n.*

**disc harrow**   a harrow that turns and loosens soil by means of one or more rows of revolving saucer-shaped blades set at an angle.   See HARROW for picture.

**dis·ci·ple** (də sī′pəl)   a person who believes in and helps to spread the ideas and teachings of another; follower.   *n.*

**dis·ci·pli·nar·i·an** (dis′ə plə ner′ē ən)   **1** a person who enforces discipline or who believes in strict discipline.
**2** DISCIPLINARY.   1 *n.,* 2 *adj.*

**dis·ci·pli·nar·y** (dis′ə plə ner′ē)   **1** of or having to do with discipline.   **2** for discipline.   *adj.*

**dis·ci·pline** (dis′ə plin)   **1** training, especially of the mind or character.   **2** the training effect of experience, adversity, etc.   **3** a trained condition of order and obedience.   **4** order among school pupils, members of the armed services, or members of any group: *When the fire broke out, the students showed good discipline.*   **5** train; bring to a condition of order and obedience; bring under control: *A good officer must know how to discipline people.*
**6** a particular system of rules for conduct.   **7** the methods or rules for regulating the conduct of members of a church.   **8** the control exercised over members of a church.   **9** punishment; chastisement: *A little discipline would do him a world of good.*   **10** punish: *The rebellious convicts were severely disciplined.*   **11** a branch of instruction or education: *the discipline of science.*   1–4, 6–9, 11 *n.,* 5, 10 *v.,* **dis·ci·plined, dis·ci·plin·ing.**
—**dis′ci·plin·er,** *n.*

**disc jockey**   *Informal.*   a person who chooses, plays, and introduces recorded music for a radio program, party, or dance. Also called *deejay. Abbrev.:* DJ.

**dis·claim** (di sklām′)   **1** refuse to recognize as one's own; deny connection with: *The motorist disclaimed responsibility for the accident.*   **2** give up all claim to: *She disclaimed any share in the invention.*   *v.*

**dis·claim·er** (di sklā′mər)   **1** DISCLAIMing (def. 1); denial; rejection.   **2** a person who DISCLAIMS.   *n.*

**dis·close** (di sklōz′)   **1** open to view; uncover: *The lifting of the curtain disclosed a beautiful interior scene.*

2 make known; reveal: *This letter discloses a secret.* *v.*, **dis·closed, dis·clos·ing.** —**dis·clos′er,** *n.*

**dis·clo·sure** (di sklō′zhər) 1 the act of disclosing. 2 the thing DISCLOSED. *n.*

**disco** *Informal.* DISCOTHÈQUE. *n.*

**dis·col·our** or **dis·col·or** (di skul′ər) 1 change or spoil the colour of; stain: *Smoke had discoloured the building.* 2 become changed in colour: *Many materials discolour if exposed to sunshine.* *v.*

**dis·col·our·a·tion** or **dis·col·or·a·tion** (di skul′ə rā′shən) 1 discolouring or being discoloured. 2 a discoloured spot: *There was a slight discolouration at the bottom of the curtain.* *n.*

**dis·com·fit** (di skum′fit) 1 overthrow completely; defeat; rout. 2 defeat the plans or hopes of; frustrate. 3 embarrass greatly; confuse; disconcert. *v.*

**dis·com·fi·ture** (di skum′fi chər) 1 a complete overthrow; defeat; rout. 2 the defeat of plans or hopes; frustration. 3 confusion. *n.*

**dis·com·fort** (di skum′fərt) 1 a lack of comfort: *He felt considerable discomfort after the operation.* 2 a feeling of embarrassment, confusion, etc.: *Her discomfort increased as her guilt became more and more evident.* 3 something that causes discomfort. 4 make uncomfortable or uneasy. 1–3 *n.*, 4 *v.*

**dis·com·pose** (dis′kəm pōz′) disturb the self-possession of; make uneasy; bring into disorder: *His friend's grin discomposed Vito when he tried to make his speech.* *v.*, **dis·com·posed, dis·com·pos·ing.**

**dis·com·po·sure** (dis′kəm pō′zhər) the state of being disturbed; uneasiness; EMBARRASSMENT (def. 2). *n.*

**dis·con·cert** (dis′kən sėrt′) 1 disturb the self-possession of; embarrass greatly; confuse: *Her arrest of the wrong man disconcerted the police officer.* 2 upset; disorder. *v.* —**dis′con·cert′ing·ly,** *adv.*

**dis·con·cert·ed** (dis′kən sėr′tid) 1 disturbed; confused. 2 pt. and pp. of DISCONCERT. 1 *adj.*, 2 *v.* —**dis′con·cert′ed·ly,** *adv.*

**dis·con·nect** (dis′kə nekt′) undo or break the connection of; unfasten; separate: *She disconnected the electric fan by pulling out the plug.* *v.*

**dis·con·nect·ed** (dis′kə nek′tid) 1 not connected; separate. 2 without order or connection; incoherent; broken: *The injured man could give only a disconnected account of the accident.* 3 pt. and pp. of DISCONNECT. 1, 2 *adj.*, 3 *v.* —**dis′con·nect′ed·ly,** *adv.*

**dis·con·nec·tion** (dis′kə nek′shən) 1 the act of disconnecting. 2 the state of being disconnected; separation. *n.*

**dis·con·so·late** (di skon′sə lit) without hope; forlorn; unhappy; cheerless: *Gina was disconsolate because her kitten died.* *adj.* —**dis·con′so·late·ly,** *adv.* —**dis·con′so·late·ness,** *n.*

**dis·con·tent** (dis′kən tent′) 1 a dislike of what one has and a desire for something different; an uneasy feeling of dissatisfaction. 2 dissatisfy; displease. 1 *n.*, 2 *v.*

**dis·con·tent·ed** (dis′kən ten′tid) 1 not contented; not satisfied; displeased and restless; disliking what one has and wanting something different. 2 pt. and pp. of DISCONTENT. 1 *adj.*, 2 *v.* —**dis′con·tent′ed·ly,** *adv.* —**dis′con·tent′ed·ness,** *n.*

**dis·con·tent·ment** (dis′kən tent′mənt) DISCONTENT (def. 1). *n.*

hat, āge, fär; let, ēqual, tėrm; it, īce
hot, ōpen, ôrder; oil, out; cup, pút, rüle
ə*bove*, *tak*ə*n*, *penc*ə*l*, *lem*ə*n*, *circ*ə*s*
ch, child; ng, long; sh, ship
th, thin; ᴛʜ, then; zh, measure

**dis·con·tin·u·ance** (dis′kən tin′yü əns) stopping or being stopped. *n.*

**dis·con·tin·u·a·tion** (dis′kən tin′yü ā′shən) 1 a breaking off; stopping; ceasing. 2 a break; interruption. *n.*

**dis·con·tin·ue** (dis′kən tin′yü) 1 cause to cease; put an end or stop to: *The morning train has been discontinued. After the patient got well, the doctor discontinued her visits.* 2 cease from; cease to take, use, etc.: *You may discontinue the medicine after three days.* 3 terminate a law suit by request of the plaintiff or by his or her failing to continue it. *v.*, **dis·con·tin·ued, dis·con·tin·u·ing.**

**dis·con·ti·nu·i·ty** (dis′kon tə nyü′ə tē or dis′kon tə nü′ə tē) lack of connection and unity: *The discontinuity of the plot made the novel clumsy and hard to understand.* *n.*

**dis·con·tin·u·ous** (dis′kən tin′yü əs) not continuous; broken; interrupted. *adj.* —**dis′con·tin′u·ous·ly,** *adv.*

**dis·cord** (dis′kôrd) 1 a difference of opinion; unfriendly relations; disagreement: *Angry discord spoiled the meeting.* 2 in music, a lack of harmony in notes sounded at the same time. 3 harsh, clashing sounds. *n.*

**dis·cord·ance** (di skôr′dəns) 1 a DISCORD (defs. 2, 3) of sounds. 2 disagreement. *n.*

**dis·cord·ant** (di skôr′dənt) 1 not in harmony: *a discordant note in music.* 2 not in agreement; not fitting together: *Many discordant views were expressed.* 3 harsh; clashing: *The sound of some automobile horns is discordant.* *adj.* —**dis·cord′ant·ly,** *adv.*

**disc·o·thèque** (dis′kə tek′) a type of night club where one may listen and dance to music on records. *n.*

**dis·count** (dis′kount *or* di skount′ *for verb*, dis′kount *for noun*) 1 deduct a certain percentage of the amount or cost: *The store discounts 3 percent on all bills paid when due.* 2 a deduction from the amount or cost: *During the sale the dealer allowed a 10 percent discount on all cash purchases.* 3 having or referring to a price less than the current average retail price: *discount merchandise, discount prices.* 4 allow for exaggeration, prejudice, or inaccuracy in; believe only part of: *You must discount what Rita tells you, for she is too fond of a good story.* 5 make less effective by anticipating: *The price of stock fell before its dividend was reduced, for the reduction had already been discounted.* 6 lend money, deducting the interest in advance. 7 the interest deducted in advance. 1, 4–6 *v.*, 2, 3, 7 *n.* —**dis′count·a·ble,** *adj.*
**at a discount, a** at less than the regular price; below par. **b** easy to get because not in demand.

**dis·coun·te·nance** (di skoun′tə nəns) 1 refuse to approve; discourage: *This school discountenances secret societies.* 2 abash; disconcert. *v.*, **dis·coun′te·nanced, dis·coun′te·nanc·ing.**

**discount rate** the percentage charged for discounting notes.

**discount store** a retail store that sells merchandise for

**dis·cour·age** (di skėr′ij) **1** take away the courage of; lessen the hope or confidence of: *Repeated failures discouraged her.* **2** prevent or hinder through fear, loss of incentive, etc.: *Lack of recognition discouraged him from writing more novels. Fear that war might break out discouraged us from going to the Middle East.* **3** try to prevent by disapproving; frown upon: *All Nell's friends discouraged her from such a dangerous swim.* **4** make unattractive; make to seem not worthwhile: *The chill of winter soon discouraged our picnics.* *v.*, **dis·cour·aged, dis·cour·ag·ing.** —**dis·cour′ag·ing·ly**, *adv.*

**dis·cour·age·ment** (di skėr′ij mənt) **1** the state of being or feeling discouraged. **2** the thing that discourages: *The defeat was a great discouragement to the troops.* **3** the act of discouraging. *n.*

**dis·course** (dis′kôrs *for noun*, di skôrs′ *for verb*) **1** a formal speech or writing: *Lectures and sermons are discourses.* **2** speak or write formally. **3** a conversation; talk. **4** converse; talk. 1, 3 *n.*, 2, 4 *v.*, **dis·coursed, dis·cours·ing.** —**dis·cours′er**, *n.*

**dis·cour·te·ous** (dis kėr′tē əs) not courteous; rude; impolite. *adj.* —**dis·cour′te·ous·ly**, *adv.* —**dis·cour′te·ous·ness**, *n.*

**dis·cour·te·sy** (dis kėr′tə sē) **1** a lack of courtesy; rudeness; impoliteness. **2** a rude or impolite act. *n.*, *pl.* **dis·cour·te·sies.**

**dis·cov·er** (dis kuv′ər) see or learn of for the first time; find out: *No one has discovered a way to turn copper into gold.* *v.* —**dis·cov′er·a·ble**, *adj.* —**dis·cov′er·er**, *n.*

**dis·cov·er·y** (dis kuv′ə rē) **1** the act of discovering. **2** the thing discovered: *One of Benjamin Franklin's discoveries was that lightning is caused by electricity.* *n.*, *pl.* **dis·cov·er·ies.**

**dis·cred·it** (dis skred′it) **1** destroy trust in; show to be unworthy of belief or trust: *to discredit a witness. Science has discredited the theory that the earth is flat.* **2** reason for disbelief; doubt; distrust: *The new evidence throws discredit on her testimony.* **3** refuse to believe; give no credit to: *I see no reason to discredit her statement.* **4** do harm to the reputation of; give a bad reputation to: *Losing five battles discredited the general among his troops.* **5** the loss of good name or standing: *His conduct brought discredit on his firm.* **6** a person or thing that causes loss of good name or standing; disgrace: *Her behaviour was a discredit to the school.* 1, 3, 4 *v.*, 2, 5, 6 *n.*

**dis·cred·it·a·ble** (dis skred′ə tə bəl) bringing DISCREDIT (def. 5). *adj.* —**dis·cred′it·a·bly**, *adv.*

**dis·creet** (di skrēt′) **1** prudent and tactful in speech or behaviour; restrained: *A lawyer must be discreet and not violate the confidence of a client. The discreet servant never let on that he had heard the argument.* **2** showing prudence and tact; polite: *The salesman maintained a discreet distance while they discussed their finances. Her criticism was so discreet that he was not offended.* **3** not lavish or ostentatious; modest: *the discreet elegance of their home.* *adj.* —**dis·creet′ly**, *adv.* —**dis·creet′ness**, *n.*
☛ *Hom.* DISCRETE.

**dis·crep·an·cy** (di skrep′ən sē) **1** a lack of CONSISTENCY (def. 4); difference; disagreement: *The lawsuit was lost because of discrepancies in the statements of the witnesses.* **2** an example of INCONSISTENCY (def. 1). *n.*, *pl.* **dis·crep·an·cies.**

**dis·crete** (di skrēt′) **1** separate; distinct. **2** consisting of distinct parts. *adj.* —**dis·crete′ly**, *adv.* —**dis·crete′ness**, *n.*
☛ *Hom.* DISCREET.

**dis·cre·tion** (di skresh′ən) **1** the freedom to judge or choose: *Making final plans was left to the president's discretion.* **2** the quality of being discreet; good judgment; carefulness in speech or action; wise caution: *You will need discretion to criticize her without hurting her feelings.* *n.*

**dis·cre·tion·ar·y** (di skresh′ə ner′ē) with freedom to decide or choose; left to one's own judgment: *The law gave the mayor certain discretionary powers.* *adj.*

**dis·crim·i·nate** (di skrim′ə nāt′) **1** note or see the difference; make a distinction (*between*): *It is often difficult to discriminate between a mere exaggeration and a deliberate falsehood.* **2** make a biased distinction; act according to or be motivated by PREJUDICE (def. 2) (*used with* **against**): *That company discriminates against older people.* **3** see the difference in or between; distinguish with the mind: *The study of literature helps a person discriminate good writing from poor writing.* *v.*, **dis·crim·i·nat·ed, dis·crim·i·nat·ing.** —**dis·crim′i·nate·ly**, *adv.*

**dis·crim·i·nat·ing** (di skrim′ə nā′ting) **1** having or showing the ability to DISCRIMINATE (defs. 1, 3) well: *a discriminating judgment. A discriminating buyer will be able to see that this fabric is inferior.* **2** that DISCRIMINATES (def. 1): *The discriminating mark of measles is a rash on the skin.* **3** ppr. of DISCRIMINATE. 1, 2 *adj.*, 3 *v.*
—**dis·crim′i·nat′ing·ly**, *adv.*

**dis·crim·i·na·tion** (di skrim′ə nā′shən) **1** the act of making or recognizing differences and distinctions: *Do not buy clothes without discrimination.* **2** the ability to make fine distinctions: *Her discrimination in such matters is well-known.* **3** the act or practice of making or showing a difference based on PREJUDICE (def. 2): *He was happy to work for a firm in which there was no discrimination.* *n.*

**dis·crim·i·na·tive** (di skrim′ə nə tiv *or* dis krim′ə nā′tiv) **1** that distinguishes; discriminating. **2** DISCRIMINATORY; biassed: *a discriminative tax.* *adj.*

**dis·crim·i·na·to·ry** (di skrim′ə nə tô′rē) marked by or showing partiality or PREJUDICE (def. 2); BIASSED: *discriminatory laws.* *adj.*

**dis·cur·sive** (di skėr′siv) wandering or shifting from one subject to another; rambling: *Zilla's carefully planned speech was not discursive, for she developed one topic only.* *adj.* —**dis·cur′sive·ly**, *adv.* —**dis·cur′sive·ness**, *n.*

**dis·cus** (dis′kəs) a heavy, circular plate of stone or metal, used in athletic games as a test of skill and strength in throwing. *n.*
☛ *Etym.* See note at DISH.

**dis·cuss** (di skus′) **1** talk about together, bringing in various points of view; talk over informally: *The class discussed several problems this morning.* **2** explain in detail; expound in speech or writing: *Her new book discusses the future of the publishing industry in Canada.* *v.*

**dis·cus·sion** (di skush′ən) **1** talking about together, going over the reasons for and against; the act of discussing things informally: *After two hours' discussion, we seemed no nearer a decision.* **2** a formal, detailed presentation of a topic in speech or writing; DISCOURSE (def. 1): *He concluded his talk with a discussion of the social implications of a guaranteed annual wage.* *n.*

**dis·dain** (dis dān′) **1** look down on; consider beneath oneself; scorn: *The honest official disdained the offer of a bribe.* **2** the act of disdaining; scorn: *That selfish boy treated his younger brothers and sisters with disdain.* 1 *v.*, 2 *n.*

**dis·dain·ful** (dis dān′fəl) feeling or showing DISDAIN (def. 2); contemptuous; scornful. *adj.* —**dis·dain′ful·ly**, *adv.* —**dis·dain′ful·ness**, *n.*

**dis·ease** (də zēz′) **1** a condition in which an organ, system, or part does not function properly; sickness; illness: *People, animals, and plants are all liable to suffer from disease.* **2** any particular illness: *Chicken pox is an infectious disease.* **3** a disordered or bad condition of mind, morals, public affairs, etc. *n.*

**dis·eased** (də zēzd′) **1** having a disease; showing signs of sickness or illness; being diseased: *a diseased hand.* **2** disordered: *a diseased mind.* *adj.*

**dis·em·bark** (dis′em bärk′) **1** go ashore from a ship or leave an aircraft: *We disembarked at Montreal.* **2** unload from a ship or aircraft: *to disembark passengers.* *v.*

**dis·em·bar·ka·tion** (dis′em bär kā′shən) **1** the act of DISEMBARKing. **2** being DISEMBARKed. *n.*

**dis·em·bod·y** (dis′em bod′ē) separate a soul, spirit, etc. from the body: *Ghosts are usually thought of as disembodied spirits.* *v.*, **dis·em·bod·ied, dis·em·bod·y·ing.** —**dis·em·bod′i·ment**, *n.*

**dis·em·bow·el** (dis′em bou′əl) take or rip out the bowels of. *v.*, **dis·em·bow·elled** or **dis·em·bow·eled, dis·em·bow·el·ling** or **dis·em·bow·el·ing.** —**dis·em′bow′el·ment**, *n.*

**dis·en·chant** (dis′en chant′) **1** free from a magic spell or illusion. **2** free from wrong ideas about something; disillusion: *The bad weather disenchanted us with the Rockies.* *v.* —**dis·en·chant′ment**, *n.*

**dis·en·chant·ed** (dis′en chan′tid) **1** disappointed; disillusioned: *After a few weeks, Tim felt disenchanted with his new job.* **2** pt. and pp. of DISENCHANT. 1 *adj.*, 2 *v.*

**dis·en·cum·ber** (dis′en kum′bər) free from a burden, annoyance, or trouble. *v.*

**dis·en·fran·chise** (dis′en fran′chīz) DISFRANCHISE. *v.*, **dis·en·fran·chised, dis·en·fran·chis·ing.**

**dis·en·fran·chise·ment** (dis′en fran′chīz mənt) DISFRANCHISEMENT. *n.*

**dis·en·gage** (dis′en gāj′) **1** free from an engagement, pledge, obligation, etc. **2** detach; loosen: *The mother disengaged her hand from that of the sleeping child.* *v.*, **dis·en·gaged, dis·en·gag·ing.** —**dis·en′gage′ment**, *n.*

**dis·en·gaged** (dis′en gājd′) **1** not busy; free from appointments. **2** released; detached. **3** pt. and pp. of DISENGAGE. 1, 2 *adj.*, 3 *v.*

**dis·en·tan·gle** (dis′en tang′gəl) free from tangles or complications; untangle. Compare with ENTANGLE. *v.*, **dis·en·tan·gled, dis·en·tan·gling.** —**dis·en·tan′gle·ment**, *n.*

**dis·en·twine** (dis′en twīn′) DISENTANGLE. *v.*, **dis·en·twined, dis·en·twin·ing.**

**dis·es·tab·lish** (dis′es tab′lish) deprive of the character of being established; especially, withdraw state recognition or support from a church. *v.* —**dis·es·tab′lish·ment**, *n.*

**dis·es·teem** (dis′es tēm′) scorn; dislike. *v.*, *n.*

**disdain** 347 **disgust**

hat, āge, fär; let, ēqual, tėrm; it, īce
hot, ōpen, ôrder; oil, out; cup, pùt, rüle
əbove, takən, pencəl, lemən, circəs
ch, child; ng, long; sh, ship
th, thin; ᴛʜ, then; zh, measure

**dis·fa·vour** or **dis·fa·vor** (di sfā′vər) **1** unfavourable opinion; disapproval: *The employees looked with disfavour on any attempt to change their cafeteria.* **2** the state or condition of having lost favour or trust; being regarded with disapproval: *The ambassador was in disfavour with the government at home.* **3** view with disapproval; withhold favour from: *They disfavour controversy.* 1, 2 *n.*, 3 *v.*

**dis·fig·ure** (di sfig′ər *or* di sfig′yər) spoil the appearance of; mar the beauty of: *Large billboards disfigured the countryside.* *v.*, **dis·fig·ured, dis·fig·ur·ing.** —**dis·fig′ur·er**, *n.*

**dis·fig·ure·ment** (di sfig′ər mənt *or* di sfig′yər mənt) **1** the act of disfiguring. **2** a DISFIGUREd condition. **3** something that DISFIGURES; defect. *n.*

**dis·fran·chise** (di sfran′chīz) **1** take the rights of citizenship away from: *A disfranchised person cannot vote or hold office.* **2** take a right or privilege from. *v.*, **dis·fran·chised, dis·fran·chis·ing.** Also, **disenfranchise.**

**dis·fran·chise·ment** (di sfran′chīz mənt) **1** a disfranchising. **2** being DISFRANCHISEd. *n.* Also, **disenfranchisement.**

**dis·gorge** (dis gôrj′) **1** throw up what has been swallowed; VOMIT forth. **2** pour forth; discharge: *Swollen streams disgorged their waters into the river.* **3** give up unwillingly: *The robbers were forced to disgorge their plunder.* *v.*, **dis·gorged, dis·gorg·ing.**

**dis·grace** (dis grās′) **1** a loss of respect or honour: *The boy's disgrace was deeply felt by his family.* **2** cause to lose honour or respect; bring shame upon: *She disgraced her family by her behaviour.* **3** a person or thing that causes dishonour or shame: *To be put in prison is usually considered a disgrace.* **4** the state or condition of having fallen from honour and good repute: *The girl was in disgrace with her teachers and friends for having cheated on an exam.* 1, 3, 4 *n.*, 2 *v.*, **dis·graced, dis·grac·ing.** —**dis·grac′er**, *n.*

**dis·grace·ful** (dis grā′sfəl) causing loss of honour or respect; shameful. *adj.* —**dis·grace′ful·ly**, *adv.* —**dis·grace′ful·ness**, *n.*

**dis·grun·tled** (dis grun′təld) in bad humour; discontented; disgusted; displeased. *adj.*

**dis·guise** (dis gīz′) **1** make changes in clothes or appearance to hide who one really is or to look like someone else: *The spy disguised himself as an old man.* **2** the use of a changed or unusual dress and appearance in order not to be recognized: *The criminal resorted to disguise to escape from jail.* **3** clothes, actions, etc. used to hide who one really is or to make a person look like someone else: *Woman's clothes and a wig formed his disguise.* **4** hide what something really is; make something seem like something else: *The pirates had disguised their ship. Martine disguised her handwriting. He disguised his hate by a show of friendliness.* **5** a false or misleading appearance; deception; concealment: *Her seeming friendliness was a disguise.* 1, 4 *v.*, **dis·guised, dis·guis·ing**; 2, 3, 5 *n.* —**dis·guis′er**, *n.*

**dis·gust** (dis gust′) **1** a strong, sickening dislike; loathing: *Bad odours or tastes can arouse disgust. Many* people wrote to express their disgust at the newspaper's sensational account of the murder trial. **2** arouse loathing in; be very offensive to: *The strong smell of garbage in the kitchen disgusted her.* **3** weary indignation or dissatisfaction: *His excuses for not helping out were so silly that she finally hung up in disgust.* **4** cause weary indignation or dissatisfaction in: *Their unwillingness to recognize the weaknesses in the plan disgusted him to the point where he resigned.* 1, 3 *n.*, 2, 4 *v.*

**dis·gust·ed** (dis gus'tid) **1** filled with DISGUST (defs. 1, 3). **2** *Informal.* fed up; tired: *She said she was disgusted with their constant quarrelling.* **3** pt. and pp. of DISGUST. 1, 2 *adj.*, 3 *v.* —**dis·gust'ed·ly**, *adv.* —**dis·gust'ed·ness**, *n.*

**dis·gust·ing** (dis gus'ting) **1** that disgusts; unpleasant; distasteful. **2** ppr. of DISGUST. 1 *adj.*, 2 *v.* —**dis·gus'ting·ly**, *adv.*

**dish** (dish) **1** any vessel or container, usually shallow and flat-bottomed, used for holding or serving food: *The vegetables were served in a covered dish.* **2** the amount of food served in a dish: *I ate two dishes of ice cream.* **3** a particular kind of food: *My favourite dish is sliced peaches and cream.* **4** put food into a dish ready for serving: *You may dish the dinner now.* **5** something shallow and hollow like a dish. **6** shape like a dish; make concave. **7 dishes**, *pl.* cups, saucers, glasses, plates, bowls, etc. together: *It's your turn to wash the dishes.* 1–3, 5, 7 *n.*, 4, 6 *v.*

**dish out**, *Informal.* hand out; give out: *to dish out punishment.*

**dish up**, **a** serve food: *Are you ready to dish up? They dished up a hot meal for us.* **b** present facts, etc. neatly: *to dish up a good argument.*

☛ *Etym.* OE *disc* from L *discus* 'a quoit', which came from Gk. *diskos.* DISCUS and, probably, DISK came in the 17c. from L *discus*, though *disk* may have come through F *disque.* DAIS, which meant first a head table in a hall and then the platform on which such a table stood, came into Middle English through OF *deis* from Med. L *discus*, which had the additional meaning 'table'. DESK came into Middle English from Med. L *desca* 'table', which had also developed from L *discus.*

**dish·cloth** (dish'kloth') a small cloth to wash dishes with. *n.*

**dis·heart·en** (dis här'tən) discourage; depress: *A long drought disheartens a farmer.* *v.* —**dis·heart'en·ing**, *adj.* —**dis·heart'en·ing·ly**, *adv.*

**di·shev·elled** or **di·shev·eled** (də shev'əld) **1** rumpled; mussed; disordered; untidy: *a dishevelled appearance.* **2** hanging loosely or in disorder: *dishevelled hair.* *adj.*

**dish·ful** (dish'fùl) as much as a dish can hold. *n.*, *pl.* **dish·fuls**.

**dis·hon·est** (di son'ist) **1** lacking honesty or integrity; inclined to cheat, steal, deceive, etc.: *You cannot expect a fair deal from a dishonest merchant.* **2** showing falseness or deceit: *a dishonest advertisement, a dishonest account of the accident.* **3** arranged to work in an unfair way: *a dishonest card game, dishonest scales.* *adj.* —**dis·hon'est·ly**, *adv.*

**dis·hon·es·ty** (di son'i stē) **1** lying, cheating, or stealing; a lack of honesty. **2** a dishonest act. *n.*, *pl.* **dis·hon·es·ties**.

**dishonor** (di son'ər) See DISHONOUR. *n.*, *v.*

**dis·hon·or·a·ble** (di son'ə rə bəl) See DISHONOURABLE. *adj.*

**dis·hon·our** or **dis·hon·or** (di son'ər) **1** a loss of honour or reputation; shame; disgrace. **2** the cause of dishonour: *A man who steals is a dishonour to his family.* **3** cause or bring dishonour to. **4** a refusal or failure to pay a cheque, bill, etc. **5** refuse or fail to pay a cheque, bill, etc.: *A bank will dishonour your cheques if you do not have money in the bank to pay them.* 1, 2, 4 *n.*, 3, 5 *v.*

**dis·hon·our·a·ble** or **dis·hon·or·a·ble** (di son'ə rə bəl) **1** causing loss of honour; shameful; disgraceful. **2** without honour. *adj.* —**dis·hon'our·a·ble·ness** or **dis·hon'or·a·ble·ness**, *n.* —**dis·hon'our·a·bly** or **dis·hon'or·a·bly**, *adv.*

**dish·pan** (dish'pan') a large pan or basin in which to wash dishes. *n.*

**dish·rag** (dish'rag') DISHCLOTH. *n.*

**dish towel** a cloth for drying dishes; tea towel.

**dish·wash·er** (dish'wosh'ər) **1** a machine for washing, rinsing, and drying dishes in one continuous operation. **2** a person who washes dishes, especially one employed by a restaurant, hospital, etc. *n.*

**dish·wa·ter** (dish'wot'ər) water in which dishes are being or have been washed. *n.*

**dis·il·lu·sion** (dis'i lü'zhən) **1** free from illusion: *People are apt to become disillusioned as they grow old.* **2** freeing or being freed from illusion. 1 *v.*, 2 *n.*

**dis·il·lu·sion·ment** (dis'i lü'zhən mənt) DISILLUSIONing or being disillusioned. *n.*

**dis·in·cli·na·tion** (di sin'klə nā'shən) unwillingness. *n.*

**dis·in·cline** (dis'in klīn') make or be unwilling. *v.*, **dis·in·clined, dis·in·clin·ing**.

**dis·in·clined** (dis'in klīnd') **1** unwilling. **2** pt. and pp. of DISINCLINE. 1 *adj.*, 2 *v.*

**dis·in·fect** (dis'in fekt') destroy the disease germs in or on: *A doctor's instruments are disinfected before they are used.* *v.* —**dis'in·fect'or**, *n.*

**dis·in·fect·ant** (dis'in fek'tənt) **1** a means for destroying disease germs: *Alcohol, chlorine, and carbolic acid are disinfectants.* **2** destroying disease germs. 1 *n.*, 2 *adj.*

**dis·in·fec·tion** (dis'in fek'shən) the destruction of disease germs. *n.*

**dis·in·gen·u·ous** (dis'in jen'yü əs) not frank; insincere. *adj.* —**dis'in·gen'u·ous·ly**, *adv.*

**dis·in·her·it** (dis'in her'it) prevent from inheriting; deprive of an inheritance: *A father disinherits his daughter if he leaves none of his property to his daughter.* *v.*

**dis·in·her·it·ance** (dis'in her'ə təns) **1** the act of DISINHERITing. **2** the state of being DISINHERITed. *n.*

**dis·in·te·grate** (di sin'tə grāt') **1** break up; separate into small parts or bits: *Time had caused the old books to disintegrate into a pile of fragments and dust.* **2** change in nuclear structure through bombardment by charged particles. *v.*, **dis·in·te·grat·ed, dis·in·te·grat·ing**.

**dis·in·te·gra·tion** (di sin'tə grā'shən) a breaking up; separation into small parts or bits: *Rain and frost had caused the gradual disintegration of the rock.* *n.*

**dis·in·te·gra·tor** (di sin'tə grā'tər) **1** a person or thing that causes DISINTEGRATION. **2** a machine for disintegrating a substance. *n.*

**dis·in·ter** (dis′in tėr′) **1** take out of a grave or tomb; dig up. **2** bring to light; discover and reveal. *v.*, **dis·in·terred, dis·in·ter·ring.** —**dis′in·ter′ment,** *n.*

**dis·in·ter·est** (di sin′trist *or* di sin′tə rist) lack of interest; indifference. *n.*

**dis·in·ter·est·ed** (di sin′tri stid *or* di sin′tə res′tid) not having or showing selfish motives; not concerned with one's own interests; impartial; fair: *The mayor's support of the building program was completely disinterested.* *adj.* —**dis′in′ter·est′ed·ly,** *adv.* —**dis′in′ter·est′ed·ness,** *n.*
☞ *Usage.* See note at INTERESTED.

**dis·join** (dis join′) separate; keep from joining; prevent from being joined. *v.*

**dis·joint** (dis joint′) **1** take apart at the joints: *to disjoint a chicken.* **2** break up; disconnect; put out of order: *The girl's speech was stumbling and disjointed.* **3** put out of joint; dislocate: *a disjointed wrist.* **4** come apart; be put out of joint. *v.*

**dis·joint·ed** (dis join′tid) **1** taken apart at the joints. **2** broken up; disconnected; incoherent. **3** out of joint. **4** pt. and pp. of DISJOINT. 1–3 *adj.*, 4 *v.* —**dis·joint′ed·ly,** *adv.* —**dis·joint′ed·ness,** *n.*

**disk** or **disc** (disk) **1** a round, thin, flat object. **2** a round, flat or apparently flat surface: *the sun's disk.* **3** the round central part of the flower head of most COMPOSITE plants: *The daisy has a yellow disk.* **4** in anatomy and zoology, any round, flat structure, especially any of the masses of cartilage between the bones of the spinal column. **5** a round, thin, flat plate coated with a magnetic substance, used for storing data for a computer. **6** Usually, **disc,** a phonograph record. **7** Usually, **disc,** **a** any of the round, concave blades of a DISC HARROW. **b** DISC HARROW. *n.* —**disk′like′** or **disc′like,** *adj.*
☞ *Etym.* See note at DISH.

**disk drive** an electronic device in a computer that reads data on magnetized disks.

**disk·ette** (dis′ket′) a small flexible plastic disk on which data for a computer can be stored. *n.*

**disk flower** any of the tiny flowers that make up the central disk of the flower head of a COMPOSITE plant. See COMPOSITE for picture.

**disk harrow** See DISC HARROW.

**disk jockey** See DISC JOCKEY.

**disk operating system** a program that runs a personal computer's internal functions and enables the user to manage the computer's operations. *Abbrev.*: DOS

**dis·like** (dis līk′) **1** a feeling of not liking; a feeling against: *I have a dislike of rain and fog.* **2** not like; object to; have a feeling against: *Marc dislikes studying and would rather play football.* 1 *n.*, 2 *v.*, **dis·liked, dis·lik·ing.**

**dis·lo·cate** (dis′lō kāt′) **1** cause one or more of the bones of a joint to be shifted out of place: *The football player dislocated his shoulder when he fell.* **2** put out of order; disturb; upset: *Our plans for the picnic were dislocated by the bad weather.* *v.*, **dis·lo·cat·ed, dis·lo·cat·ing.**

**dis·lo·ca·tion** (dis′lō kā′shən) **1** the act of dislocating. **2** the state of being DISLOCATED. *n.*

**dis·lodge** (dis sloj′) drive or force out of a place, position, etc.: *Heavy gunfire dislodged the enemy from the fort.* *v.*, **dis·lodged, dis·lodg·ing.**

**dis·lodg·ment** (dis sloj′mənt) **1** the act of dislodging. **2** the state of being DISLODGED. *n.*

| hat, āge, fär; let, ēqual, tėrm; it, īce |
| hot, ōpen, ôrder; oil, out; cup, pùt, rüle |
| əbove, takən, pencəl, lemən, circəs |
| ch, child; ng, long; sh, ship |
| th, thin; ŦH, then; zh, measure |

**dis·loy·al** (di sloi′əl) not loyal; unfaithful. *adj.* —**dis·loy′al·ly,** *adv.*

**dis·loy·al·ty** (di sloi′əl tē) **1** a lack of LOYALTY; unfaithfulness: *Refusing to defend parents, school, or country is disloyalty.* **2** a DISLOYAL act. *n., pl.* **dis·loy·al·ties.**

**dis·mal** (diz′məl) **1** dark; gloomy: *Damp caves and rainy days are dismal.* **2** dreary; miserable: *Sickness often makes a person feel dismal.* *adj.* —**dis′mal·ly,** *adv.*

**dis·man·tle** (di sman′təl) **1** strip of covering, equipment, furniture, guns, rigging, etc.: *The warship was dismantled before the hull was sold for scrap metal.* **2** pull down; take down; take apart: *We had to dismantle the bookcases in order to move them.* *v.*, **dis·man·tled, dis·man·tling.**

**dis·may** (di smā′) **1** a loss of courage because of fear of what is about to happen: *The mother was filled with dismay when her son confessed that he had robbed a store.* **2** trouble greatly; make afraid: *The thought that she might fail the history test dismayed her.* 1 *n.,* 2 *v.*

**dis·mem·ber** (di smem′bər) **1** pull apart; cut to pieces; separate or divide into parts: *The Austro-Hungarian Empire was dismembered after the First World War.* **2** cut or tear the limbs from: *to dismember a body.* *v.* —**dis·mem′ber·ment,** *n.*

**dis·miss** (di smis′) **1** send away; allow to go: *At noon the teacher dismissed the class.* **2** remove from a position or office; discharge; fire: *The clerk was dismissed because she was always late for work.* **3** put out of mind; stop thinking about: *Dismiss your troubles and be happy.* **4** refuse to consider a complaint, plea, etc. in a law court. *v.*

**dis·miss·al** (di smis′əl) **1** the act of dismissing: *The dismissal of the teacher was the cause of a demonstration by the students.* **2** the state or fact of being dismissed. **3** a written or spoken order dismissing someone. *n.*

**dis·mis·sion** (di smish′ən) DISMISSAL. *n.*

**dis·mount** (di smount′) **1** get off a horse, bicycle, etc. **2** knock, throw, or otherwise remove from a horse; unhorse: *The first knight dismounted the second.* **3** take something from its setting or support: *The cannon was dismounted for shipping to another fort.* **4** take apart; take to pieces. *v.*

**dis·o·be·di·ence** (dis′ə bē′dē əns) a refusal to obey; failure to obey: *Disobedience cannot be allowed in the army.* *n.*

**dis·o·be·di·ent** (dis′ə bē′dē ənt) refusing to obey; failing to obey. *adj.* —**dis′o·be′di·ent·ly,** *adv.*

**dis·o·bey** (dis′ə bā′) fail to follow orders or rules; refuse to obey. *v.* —**dis′o·bey′er,** *n.*

**dis·o·blige** (dis′ə blīj′) **1** neglect to oblige; refuse to oblige; refuse to do a favour for. **2** give offence to. *v.*, **dis·o·bliged, dis·o·blig·ing.** —**dis′o·blig′ing·ly,** *adv.*

**dis·or·der** (di sôr′dər) **1** a lack of order; confusion: *The room was in such disorder that it was impossible to find anything.* **2** destroy the order of; throw into confusion: *A* series of accidents disordered the shop. **3** a public disturbance; riot. **4** a sickness or disease: *a disorder of the stomach.* **5** upset the functions of; cause sickness in: *Such food is likely to disorder the stomach.* 1, 3, 4 *n.*, 2, 5 *v.*

**dis·or·dered** (di sôr′dərd) **1** not in order; disturbed. **2** sick. **3** pt. and pp. of DISORDER. 1, 2 *adj.*, 3 *v.*

**dis·or·der·ly** (di sôr′dər lē) **1** not orderly; in confusion: *The books and papers lay in a disorderly pile on the floor.* **2** causing disorder; making a disturbance; breaking rules; unruly: *a disorderly mob.* **3** in law, acting against public peace and order. *adj.* —**dis·or′der·li·ness,** *n.*

**dis·or·gan·ize** (di sôr′gə nīz′) throw into confusion and disorder; upset the order and arrangement of: *Heavy snowstorms disorganized the train schedule.* *v.*, **dis·or·gan·ized, dis·or·gan·iz·ing.** —**dis·or′gan·i·za′tion,** *n.*

**dis·own** (di sōn′) refuse to recognize as one's own; cast off: *He disowned his disobedient daughter. The politician disowned her former views on the subject.* *v.*

**dis·par·age** (di spar′ij *or* di sper′ij) **1** speak slightingly of; try to lessen the importance or value of; belittle: *The coward disparaged the hero's brave rescue.* **2** lower the reputation of; discredit. *v.*, **dis·par·aged, dis·par·ag·ing.** —**dis·par′ag·ing·ly,** *adv.*

**dis·par·age·ment** (di spar′ij mənt *or* di sper′ij mənt) **1** the act of disparaging. **2** something that lowers a thing or person in worth or importance. **3** lessening in esteem or standing: *Say nothing that will be to Jo's disparagement with her new employer.* *n.*

**dis·pa·rate** (dis′pə rit) distinct in kind; essentially different; unlike. *adj.* —**dis′pa·rate·ness,** *n.*

**dis·par·i·ty** (di spar′ə tē *or* di sper′ə tē) inequality; difference: *There will be a disparity in the accounts of the same event given by several people.* *n.*, *pl.* **dis·par·i·ties.**

**dis·part** (di spärt′) separate; divide into parts. *v.*

**dis·pas·sion·ate** (di spash′ə nit) free from emotion or prejudice; calm; impartial: *To a dispassionate observer, the drivers of both cars seemed equally at fault.* *adj.* —**dis·pas′sion·ate·ly,** *adv.*

**dis·patch** or **des·patch** (di spach′) **1** send off to some place or for some purpose: *He dispatched a messenger to tell the king what had happened.* **2** a sending of a letter, a messenger, etc.: *Please hurry up the dispatch of this telegram.* **3** a written message such as a news report or a report to a government by an ambassador or other official: *This dispatch has been two days on the way.* **4** get something done promptly or speedily. **5** promptness; speed: *Ruth works with neatness and dispatch.* **6** give the death blow to; kill: *He dispatched the deer at his first shot.* **7** putting to death; killing. **8** *Informal.* eat up: *The hungry girl quickly dispatched the meal.* **9** an agency for conveying goods, etc. 1, 4, 6, 8 *v.*, 2, 3, 5, 7, 9 *n.*

**dis·patch·er** or **des·patch·er** (di spach′ər) a person who DISPATCHES (def. 1): *She is a dispatcher for a taxi company.* *n.*

**dis·pel** (di spel′) drive away and scatter; disperse: *The captain's cheerful laugh dispelled our fears.* *v.*, **dis·pelled, dis·pel·ling.** —**dis·pel′ler,** *n.*

**dis·pen·sa·ble** (di spen′sə bəl) **1** that may be done without; unimportant. **2** capable of being DISPENSEd (defs. 1, 2) or administered. *adj.* —**dis·pen′sa·ble·ness,** *n.*

**dis·pen·sa·ry** (di spen′sə rē) **1** a place where medicines and medical advice are given free or for a small charge. **2** that part of a hospital where medicines are prepared and stored. *n.*, *pl.* **dis·pen·sa·ries.**

**dis·pen·sa·tion** (dis′pən sā′shən) **1** the act of giving out; the act of distributing: *the dispensation of charity to the poor.* **2** the thing given out or distributed: *They gave thanks for the dispensations of the king.* **3** rule; management: *England under the dispensation of Elizabeth I.* *n.*

**dis·pense** (di spens′) **1** give out; distribute: *The Red Cross dispensed food and clothing to the refugees.* **2** carry out; put in force; apply: *In our country, judges and law courts dispense justice.* **3** prepare and give out: *Druggists dispense medicines.* **4** grant a dispensation for. *v.*, **dis·pensed, dis·pens·ing.**

**dispense with, a** get rid of; make unnecessary: *The new evaluation system dispenses with the need for oral examinations.* **b** get along without; do without: *He found he could dispense with rich food when he began to eat properly.*

**dis·pens·er** (di spen′sər) **1** a device, often automatic and often coin-operated, which is made to release its contents one at a time or in measured amounts: *There are dispensers for gum, chocolate bars, coffee, sandwiches, cigarettes, paper cups, etc.* **2** a container, such as a spray bottle, that sprays or feeds out its contents in a handy form or amount. *n.*

**dis·per·sal** (di spėr′səl) a dispersion; the act of scattering or state of being scattered: *the dispersal of a crowd.* *n.*

**dis·perse** (di spėrs′) **1** send in different directions; scatter: *The police dispersed the rioters.* **2** go in different directions: *The crowd dispersed when the game was over.* **3** divide white light into its coloured rays. *v.*, **dis·persed, dis·pers·ing.**

**dis·per·sion** (di spėr′zhən *or* di spėr′shən) **1** dispersing. **2** being DISPERSEd (defs. 1, 2). **3** the separation of light into its different colours. *n.*

**dis·pir·it** (di spir′it) depress; discourage; dishearten: *A week of rain dispirited us all.* *v.*, —**dis·pir′it·ed·ly,** *adv.*

**dis·place** (di splās′) **1** put something else in the place of; take the place of: *The automobile has almost displaced the horse and buggy.* **2** remove from a position of authority: *The chief of police was displaced by a younger man.* **3** put out of place; move from the usual position. *v.*, **dis·placed, dis·plac·ing.**

**displaced person** a person forced out of his or her own country by war, famine, political disturbance, etc.

**dis·place·ment** (di splā′smənt) **1** displacing or being DISPLACED. **2** the volume or mass of a fluid DISPLACED (def. 1) by something floating in it; especially, the volume or mass of water displaced by a ship. *n.*

**dis·play** (di splā′) **1** expose to view, especially in such a way so as to show to advantage: *Many ancient weapons are displayed in the museum. The new spring clothes are already being displayed in store windows.* **2** a planned showing of something for some special purpose; exhibit: *Our class had a display of drawings at the Exhibition.* **3** make plain or clear; show: *She displayed great tact in her handling of a delicate situation.* **4** an obvious showing or revealing; making plain or clear: *a shocking display of bad* temper, a display of courage. **5** showing off; ostentation: *Her fondness for display led her to buy showy clothes.* **6** spread out; unfold or unfurl: *to display a flag, to display a newspaper.* **7** in printing, the choice and arrangement of type so as to make certain words or parts prominent. **8** present (electronic signals) in visual form, as on the screen of a computer or electronic typewriter. **9 a** a device for presenting computerized information or electronic signals visually, such as a computer screen. **b** the information so presented. *1, 3, 6, 8 v., 2, 4, 5, 7, 9 n.*

**dis·please** (di splēz′) offend, annoy, or be disagreeable to: *She was displeased by their apparent lack of respect. The new furnishings displeased him.* *v.*, **dis·pleased, dis·pleas·ing.**

**dis·pleasure** (di splezh′ər) the feeling of being DISPLEASEd; slight anger; annoyance; disapproval. *n.*

**dis·port** (di spôrt′) amuse oneself; sport; play: *People laughed at the clumsy bears disporting themselves in the water.* *v.*

**dis·pos·a·ble** (di spō′zə bəl) **1** capable of being DISPOSED of. **2** at one's DISPOSAL; available. *adj.*

**dis·pos·al** (di spō′zəl) **1** the act or process of getting rid of something: *The city looks after the disposal of garbage.* **2** the act or process of selling or giving away to another: *She arranged for the disposal of her property in her will.* **3** a final arranging of matters; a settling of affairs: *The chairman's disposal of the difficulty satisfied everybody.* **4** the act or process of putting in a certain order or position: *The disposal of the chairs around the sides of the room left plenty of space in the middle.* *n.* **at one's disposal,** ready for one's use or service at any time; under one's control or management: *She put all her books at her guests' disposal. Does he have a car at his disposal?*

**dis·pose** (di spōz′) **1** put in a certain order or position; arrange: *The battleships were disposed in a straight line.* **2** arrange matters; settle affairs; determine. **3** make ready or willing; incline: *More pay and shorter hours of work disposed her to take the new job.* **4** make liable or subject: *Getting your feet wet disposes you to catching cold.* *v.*, **dis·posed, dis·pos·ing.** —**dis·pos′er**, *n.* **dispose of, a** get rid of: *to dispose of a lot of old papers.* **b** sell or give away: *to dispose of one's property.* **c** eat or drink up: *We disposed of the whole watermelon with no trouble.* **d** arrange; settle: *The club disposed of its business in an hour.*

**dis·posed** (di spōzd′) **1** having a particular DISPOSITION or attitude: *How were they disposed toward the plan? He was a well-disposed young man—friendly and sympathetic.* **2** pt. and pp. of DISPOSE. *1 adj., 2 v.* **disposed to,** inclined to; tending to: *She is always disposed to get mad at the least little thing.*

**dis·po·si·tion** (dis′pə zish′ən) **1** one's habitual way of acting toward others or of thinking about things; nature: *a cheerful disposition, a selfish disposition.* **2** a tendency or inclination: *a disposition to argue.* **3** the act or process of putting in order or position; orderly arrangement: *the disposition of troops in battle.* **4** final arrangement; settlement: *the satisfactory disposition of a difficult problem.* *n.*

**dis·pos·sess** (dis′pə zes′) **1** force to give up the possession of a house, land, etc.; OUST: *The farmer was dispossessed for not paying her rent.* **2** deprive: *Fear dispossessed him of his senses.* *v.* —**dis′pos·ses′sion,** *n.*

**dis·praise** (di sprāz′) **1** express DISAPPROVAL of; speak against; blame. **2** expression of DISAPPROVAL; blame. *1 v.*, **dis·praised, dis·prais·ing;** *2 n.*

**dis·proof** (di sprüf′) **1** disproving; REFUTATION. **2** a fact, reason, etc. that disproves something. *n.*

**dis·pro·por·tion** (dis′prə pôr′shən) **1** a lack of PROPORTION (def. 2); lack of proper proportion; lack of symmetry. **2** make DISPROPORTIONATE. *1 n., 2 v.*

**dis·pro·por·tion·ate** (dis′prə pôr′shə nit) out of PROPORTION (def. 2); lacking in proper proportion: *They missed the deadline because they spent a disproportionate amount of time on details.* *adj.*

**dis·pro·por·tion·ate·ly** (dis′prə pôr′shə ni tlē) in a DISPROPORTIONATE degree; inadequately or excessively. *adv.*

**dis·prove** (di sprüv′) prove false or incorrect; REFUTE: *Carlos disproved Sandra's statement that he had less candy by weighing both boxes.* *v.*, **dis·proved, dis·prov·ing.** —**dis·prov′a·ble,** *adj.*

**dis·put·a·ble** (di spyü′tə bəl *or* dis′pyə tə bəl) liable to be DISPUTEd (def. 4); uncertain; questionable. *adj.*

**dis·pu·tant** (dis′pyə tənt *or* di spyü′tənt) a person who takes part in a DISPUTE (def. 2) or debate. *n.*

**dis·pu·ta·tion** (dis′pyə tā′shən) **1** a debate; CONTROVERSY. **2** a DISPUTE (defs. 2, 3). *n.*

**dis·pu·ta·tious** (dis′pyə tā′shəs) fond of disputing; inclined to argue. *adj.* —**dis′pu·ta′tious·ly,** *adv.*

**dis·pute** (di spyüt′) **1** argue; debate. **2** an argument; debate. **3** quarrel. **4** disagree with a statement; declare not true; call in question: *The insurance company disputed her claim for damages to her car.* **5** fight against; oppose; resist. **6** fight for; fight over: *The soldiers disputed every metre of ground when the enemy attacked.* **7** contend for; try to win: *The losing team disputed the victory until the very end of the game.* *1, 3–7 v.*, **dis·put·ed, dis·put·ing;** *2, 3 n.* —**dis·put′er,** *n.*

**dis·qual·i·fi·ca·tion** (di skwol′ə fə kā′shən) **1** DISQUALIFYing. **2** being disqualified. **3** something that disqualifies. *n.*

**dis·qual·i·fy** (di skwol′ə fī′) **1** make unfit; make unable to do something: *His injury disqualified him from playing football.* **2** declare unfit or unable to do something; deprive of a right or privilege: *He was disqualified from voting because he was in jail.* **3** in sports, etc., withhold the right to play or the right to win a competition: *The hockey team was disqualified by the referee for refusing to come out on the ice.* *v.*, **dis·qual·i·fied, dis·qual·i·fy·ing.**

**dis·qui·et** (di skwī′ət) **1** make uneasy or anxious; disturb: *Rumours of a revolution disquieted the queen.* **2** uneasiness; anxiety: *Her disquiet made the rest of us uneasy too.* *1 v., 2 n.*

**dis·qui·et·ing** (di skwī′ə ting) **1** disturbing: *a disquieting rumour.* **2** ppr. of DISQUIET. *1 adj., 2 v.*

**dis·qui·e·tude** (di skwī′ə tyüd′ *or* di skwī′ə tüd′) uneasiness; anxiety. *n.*

---

displease 351 disquietude

hat, āge, fär; let, ēqual, tėrm; it, īce
hot, ōpen, ôrder; oil, out; cup, pùt, rüle
əbove, takən, pencəl, lemən, circəs
ch, child; ng, long; sh, ship
th, thin; ᴛʜ, then; zh, measure

**dis·qui·si·tion** (dis′kwə zish′ən)   a long or formal speech or writing about a subject.   *n.*

**dis·re·gard** (dis′ri gärd′)   **1** pay no attention to; take no notice of: *Disregarding her clothing, she jumped into the lake to save the child.*   **2** lack of attention; neglect: *a disregard for fame and fortune, disregard of traffic laws.*   **3** treat without proper regard or respect; slight.   **4** a lack of proper regard or respect: *Her action showed a shocking disregard for the feelings of others.*   1, 3 *v.*, 2, 4 *n.*

**dis·rel·ish** (dis rel′ish)   DISLIKE.   *v., n.*

**dis·re·pair** (dis′ri per′)   a bad condition; need of repairs.   *n.*

**dis·rep·u·ta·ble** (dis rep′yə tə bəl)   **1** having a bad reputation; shady: *a disreputable dance hall.*   **2** not respectable; dishonourable: *disreputable conduct, a disreputable politician.*   **3** shabby; much worn: *a disreputable old jacket.*   *adj.*   —**dis·rep′u·ta·bly,** *adv.*

**dis·re·pute** (dis′ri pyüt′)   disgrace; discredit; disfavour: *Many old remedies are now in disrepute.*   *n.*

**dis·re·spect** (dis′ri spekt′)   a lack of RESPECT (def. 1); rudeness; impoliteness: *Older people disliked the boy because of his disrespect to his parents.*   *n.*

**dis·re·spect·ful** (dis′ri spekt′fəl)   rude; showing no RESPECT (def. 1); lacking in courtesy to elders or superiors: *The disrespectful boy laughed at his mother.*   *adj.*   —**dis′re·spect′ful·ly,** *adv.*   —**dis′re·spect′ful·ness,** *n.*

**dis·robe** (dis rōb′)   UNDRESS (def. 1).   *v.*, **dis·robed, dis·rob·ing.**

**dis·rupt** (dis rupt′)   break up; split: *A violent quarrel disrupted the meeting.*   *v.*

**dis·rup·tion** (dis rup′shən)   **1** breaking up; splitting.   **2** being broken up; being split.   *n.*

**dis·rup·tive** (dis rup′tiv)   tending to break up; causing DISRUPTION: *a disruptive influence.*   *adj.*

**dis·sat·is·fac·tion** (dis′sat i sfak′shən)   discontent; displeasure.   *n.*

**dis·sat·is·fied** (dis sat′i sfīd′)   **1** discontented; displeased.   **2** showing discontent or displeasure.   *adj.*

**dis·sat·is·fy** (dis sat′i sfī′)   fail to satisfy; make discontented; displease: *Envy may dissatisfy us with our lot.*   *v.*, **dis·sat·is·fied, dis·sat·is·fy·ing.**

**dis·sect** (di sekt′ *or* dī sekt′)   **1** cut in pieces; divide into parts.   **2** cut up or separate the parts of an animal, plant, etc. in order to examine or study its structure.   **3** examine carefully part by part; analyse: *The lawyer dissected the testimony to show where the witnesses had contradicted themselves.*   *v.*

**dis·sect·ed** (di sek′tid *or* dī sek′tid)   **1** cut or divided into many parts: *These plants have dissected leaves.*   **2** pt. and pp. of DISSECT.   1 *adj.*, 2 *v.*

**dis·sec·tion** (di sek′shən *or* dī sek′shən)   **1** the act of separating or dividing an animal or plant into parts in order to examine or study the structure.   **2** an animal, plant, etc. that has been dissected.   **3** an analysis; consideration of something in detail or point by point.   *n.*

**dis·sec·tor** (di sek′tər *or* dī sek′tər)   **1** a person who DISSECTS.   **2** an instrument used in DISSECTing (defs. 1, 2).   *n.*

**dis·sem·ble** (di sem′bəl)   **1** disguise or hide one's real feelings, thoughts, plans, etc.: *She dissembled her anger with a smile.*   **2** conceal one's motives, etc.; be a HYPOCRITE.   **3** pretend; feign: *The bored listener dissembled an interest she didn't feel.*   **4** pretend not to see or notice; disregard; ignore.   *v.*, **dis·sem·bled, dis·sem·bling.**   —**dis·sem′bler,** *n.*

**dis·sem·i·nate** (di sem′ə nāt)   scatter widely; spread abroad.   *v.*, **dis·sem·i·nat·ed, dis·sem·i·nat·ing.**   —**dis·sem′i·na′tion,** *n.*   —**dis·sem′i·na′tor,** *n.*

**dis·sen·sion** (di sen′shən)   disputing; quarrelling; hard feelings caused by a difference in opinion: *Their political disagreement caused dissension.*   *n.*

**dis·sent** (di sent′)   **1** differ in opinion; disagree: *Two of the judges dissented from the decision of the other three.*   **2** a difference of opinion; disagreement: *Dissent among the members broke up the club meeting.*   **3** refuse to conform to the rules and beliefs of an established church.   **4** a refusal to conform to the rules and beliefs of an established church: *The dissent of some Puritans caused their separation from the Church of England.*   1, 3 *v.*, 2, 4 *n.*   —**dis·sent′er,** *n.*   Compare with ASSENT.
☛ *Hom.* DESCENT.

**dis·sen·tient** (di sen′shənt)   **1** DISSENTing, especially from the opinion of the majority.   **2** a person who DISSENTS.   1 *adj.*, 2 *n.*

**dis·ser·ta·tion** (dis′ər tā′shən)   a formal discussion of a subject; TREATISE.   *n.*

**dis·serv·ice** (dis sėr′vis)   bad treatment; harm; injury.   *n.*

**dis·sev·er** (di sev′ər)   sever; separate.   *v.*

**dis·si·dence** (dis′ə dəns)   disagreement; DISSENT (def. 2).   *n.*

**dis·si·dent** (dis′ə dənt)   **1** disagreeing; dissenting.   **2** a person who disagrees or dissents.   1 *adj.*, 2 *n.*

**dis·sim·i·lar** (di sim′ə lər)   not similar; unlike; different: *dissimilar opinions.*   *adj.*   —**dis·sim′i·lar·ly,** *adv.*

**dis·sim·i·lar·i·ty** (di sim′ə lar′ə tē *or* di sim′ə ler′ə tē)   lack of similarity; unlikeness; difference.   *n., pl.* **dis·sim·i·lar·i·ties.**

**dis·si·mil·i·tude** (dis′sə mil′ə tyüd′ *or* dis′sə mil′ə tüd′)   unlikeness; difference.   *n.*

**dis·sim·u·late** (di sim′yə lāt′)   disguise or hide under a pretence; DISSEMBLE (defs. 1–3).   *v.*, **dis·sim·u·lat·ed, dis·sim·u·lat·ing.**   —**dis·sim′u·la′tor,** *n.*

**dis·sim·u·la·tion** (di sim′yə lā′shən)   the act of dissembling; HYPOCRISY; pretence; deceit.   *n.*

**dis·si·pate** (dis′ə pāt′)   **1** spread in different directions; scatter: *The crowd soon dissipated.*   **2** disappear: *The fog had dissipated by mid morning.*   **3** cause to disappear; dispel: *The sun dissipated the mists.*   **4** spend foolishly; waste on things of little value: *The extravagant son soon dissipated his mother's fortune.*   **5** indulge too much in foolish or harmful pleasures.   *v.*, **dis·si·pat·ed, dis·si·pat·ing.**

**dis·si·pat·ed** (dis′ə pā′tid)   **1** indulging too much in foolish or harmful pleasures; DISSOLUTE: *a dissipated youth.*   **2** scattered.   **3** wasted.   **4** pt. and pp. of DISSIPATE.   1–3 *adj.*, 4 *v.*

**dis·si·pa·tion** (dis′ə pā′shən)   **1** dissipating or being

DISSIPATED. **2** an amusement; diversion, especially harmful amusements. **3** too much indulgence in foolish or harmful pleasures; intemperance. *n.*

**dis·so·ci·ate** (di sō′shē āt′ *or* di sō′sē āt′) **1** break the connection or association with; separate: *When the honest man discovered that his companions were thieves, he dissociated himself from them.* **2** separate or decompose by DISSOCIATION (def. 2). *v.*, **dis·so·ci·at·ed, dis·so·ci·at·ing.**

**dis·so·ci·a·tion** (di sō′shē ā′shən *or* di sō′sē ā′shən) **1** the act of dissociating or state of being DISSOCIATEd (def. 1). **2** the separation of molecules of an electrolyte into constituent ions; ionization: *Sodium and chlorine ions are formed by the dissociation of sodium chloride molecules in water.* *n.*

**dis·sol·u·bil·i·ty** (di sol′yə bil′ə tē) the fact or quality of being DISSOLUBLE. *n.*

**dis·sol·u·ble** (di sol′yə bəl) capable of being DISSOLVED (defs. 1, 2). *adj.* —**dis·sol′u·ble·ness,** *n.*

**dis·so·lute** (dis′ə lüt′) living an evil life; wicked; lewd; immoral. *adj.* —**dis′so·lute·ly,** *adv.* —**dis′so·lute·ness,** *n.*

**dis·so·lu·tion** (dis′ə lü′shən) **1** breaking up; an ending: *The partners arranged for the dissolution of their partnership.* **2** the ending of an assembly, especially of a parliament prior to an election. **3** ruin; destruction. **4** death. *n.*

**dis·solve** (di zolv′) **1** make or become liquid, especially by putting or being put into a liquid; form into a solution in a liquid: *Salt or sugar will dissolve in water.* **2** break up; end: *to dissolve a partnership.* **3** dismiss or end an assembly, especially a parliament before an election. **4** fade away: *The dream dissolved when she woke up.* **5** solve; explain; clear up. **6** separate into parts; decompose. **7** the gradual disappearing of the figures of a motion picture or television scene while those of a succeeding scene slowly take their place. **8** of a motion picture or television scene, give way gradually to a following sequence. 1–6, 8 *v.*, **dis·solved, dis·solv·ing;** 7 *n.* —**dis·solv′a·ble,** *adj.*
**dissolve in tears,** shed many tears.

**dis·so·nance** (dis′ə nəns) **1** a combination of sounds that is not harmonious; harshness and unpleasantness of sound; DISCORD (def. 2). Compare with CONSONANCE. **2** a disagreement of views, opinions, etc.; lack of harmony. *n.*

**dis·so·nant** (dis′ə nənt) **1** harsh in sound; clashing; not harmonious. **2** out of harmony with other views or persons; disagreeing: *Her dissonant views always made the meetings unpleasant.* *adj.*

**dis·suade** (di swād′) persuade not to do something (used with **from**): *The father dissuaded his son from leaving school.* *v.*, **dis·suad·ed, dis·suad·ing.**

**dis·sua·sion** (di swā′zhən) the act of dissuading. *n.*

**dis·syl·lab·ic** (dis′sə lab′ik) DISYLLABIC. *adj.*

**dis·syl·la·ble** (dis′sil′ə bəl) DISYLLABLE. *n.*

**dist.** **1** district. **2** distance.

**dis·taff** (dis′taf) **1** a stick, cleft at the tip, to hold wool, flax, etc. for spinning into thread. **2** the part of a spinning wheel that holds the wool or flax. **3** woman's work or affairs. **4** the female sex; woman or women. *n.*

**distaff side** the mother's side of a family. Compare with SPEAR SIDE.

hat, āge, fär; let, ēqual, tėrm; it, īce
hot, ōpen, ôrder; oil, out; cup, pùt, rüle
əbove, takən, pencəl, lemən, circəs
ch, child; ng, long; sh, ship
th, thin; ⟨TH⟩, then; zh, measure

**dis·tance** (dis′təns) **1** the space in between; the extent of separation in space: *Is the theatre within walking distance? The distance from here to town is five kilometres.* **2** a long way; far away: *The farm is situated quite a distance from the highway.* **3** a place far away: *a light in the distance.* **4** the time in between; interval. **5** in music, the interval or difference between two tones. **6** a lack of friendliness or familiarity; coolness of manner; reserve. **7** leave far behind; do much better than: *The big black horse distanced the others.* **8** keep (oneself) at an emotional distance (from); choose to have no connection with: *The British government has tried to distance itself from the controversial author and his novel.* 1–6 *n.*, 7, 8 *v.*, **dis·tanced, dis·tanc·ing.**
**keep at a distance,** refuse to be friendly or familiar with; treat with reserve: *We tried to be friendly but she kept us at a distance.*
**keep one's distance,** **a** remain some distance away: *The dog might be dangerous, so keep your distance.* **b** be not too friendly or familiar; be or stay aloof: *She prefers to keep her distance with her employees.*

**dis·tant** (dis′tənt) **1** far away in space: *Vancouver is distant from Quebec City. The moon is distant from the earth.* **2** away: *The town is three kilometres distant.* **3** far apart in time, relationship, likeness, etc.; not close: *A third cousin is a distant relative.* **4** not friendly: *a distant nod.* *adj.* —**dis′tant·ly,** *adv.*

**dis·taste** (di stāst′) dislike: *She has always had a distaste for carrots.* *n.*

**dis·taste·ful** (di stāst′fəl) unpleasant; disagreeable; offensive: *a distasteful medicine, a distasteful task.* *adj.* —**dis·taste′ful·ly,** *adv.* —**dis·taste′ful·ness,** *n.*

**dis·tem·per**[1] (di stem′pər) **1** an infectious virus disease of dogs and other animals, accompanied by a short, dry cough and a loss of strength. **2** any sickness of the mind or body; disorder; disease. **3** make unbalanced; disturb; disorder. **4** disturbance. 1, 2, 4 *n.*, 3 *v.*

**dis·tem·per**[2] (di stem′pər) **1** a method or process of painting in which powdered colours are mixed with glue or other sizing, used especially for painting interior walls, scenes for theatre sets, etc.: *Distemper is a kind of tempera.* **2** the paint used in distemper painting. **3** paint with distemper. 1, 2 *n.*, 3 *v.*

**dis·tend** (di stend′) stretch out; swell out; expand: *His cheeks distended when he blew his bugle. The balloon was distended almost to the bursting point.* *v.*

**dis·ten·sion** or **dis·ten·tion** (di sten′shən) DISTENDing or being distended. *n.*

**dis·til** or **dis·till** (di stil′) **1** heat a liquid or other substance and condense the vapour given off: *Distilled water is pure because the impurities in the original water do not vaporize when the water does.* See STILL[2] for picture. **2** obtain by distilling: *Gasoline is distilled from crude oil.* **3** extract; refine: *A jury must distil the truth from the testimony of witnesses.* **4** give off in drops: *Flowers distil nectar.* **5** fall or let fall in drops; drip. *v.*, **dis·tilled, dis·til·ling.**

**dis·til·late** (dis′tə lit *or* dis′tə lāt′) a distilled liquid; something obtained by distilling. *n.*

**dis·til·la·tion** (dis′tə lā′shən) **1** a distilling: *the distillation of water to purify it.* **2** something distilled; extract; essence: *Kerosene is a distillation of petroleum. n.*

**dis·tilled** (di stild′) **1** obtained by distilling. **2** pt. and pp. of DISTIL. 1 *adj.*, 2 *v.*

**dis·till·er** (di stil′ər) a person or thing that distils, especially a person or company that makes whisky, rum, brandy, etc. *n.*

**dis·till·er·y** (di stil′ə rē) a place where distilling is done, especially of whisky, rum, brandy, etc. *n., pl.* **dis·till·er·ies.**

**dis·tinct** (di stingkt′) **1** not the same; separate: *There are two distinct questions to be considered.* **2** different in quality or kind: *Mice are distinct from rats.* **3** clear; plain: *distinct writing.* **4** unmistakable; definite; decided: *a distinct lisp, a distinct advantage. adj.*
—**dis·tinct′ness,** *n.*

**dis·tinc·tion** (di stingk′shən) **1** the act of making a difference; distinguishing from others: *He treated all alike, without distinction.* **2** the quality or state of being distinguishable; difference: *What is the distinction between ducks and geese?* **3** a point of difference; a distinguishing quality or feature: *There are only minor distinctions between our house and the others on the block.* **4** honour or esteem: *The title is given as a mark of distinction.* **5** a mark or sign of honour: *He won many distinctions for bravery.* **6** excellence that distinguishes one from others; superiority: *a man of distinction. The novel has true distinction. The nurse had served with distinction. n.*

**dis·tinc·tive** (di stingk′tiv) clearly distinguishing from others; special; characteristic: *Police officers wear a distinctive uniform. adj.* —**dis·tinc′tive·ly,** *adv.*
—**dis·tinc′tive·ness,** *n.*

**dis·tinct·ly** (di stingkt′lē) **1** clearly; plainly: *to speak distinctly.* **2** unmistakably; decidedly: *The prisoner was distinctly unhappy. adv.*

**dis·tin·guish** (di sting′gwish) **1** tell apart; see or show the difference between: *Can you distinguish cotton cloth from linen?* **2** see or show the difference (*often used with* **between** *or* **among**): *I find it hard to distinguish between Maria's handwriting and her sister's.* **3** see or hear clearly; make out plainly: *It was much too dark for me to distinguish the outline of the house.* **4** make different; be a special quality or feature of: *The ability to talk distinguishes human beings from animals.* **5** make famous or well-known: *She distinguished herself by winning all three prizes.* **6** separate into different groups; classify. *v.*

**dis·tin·guish·a·ble** (di sting′gwi shə bəl) capable of being separated or differentiated. *adj.*
—**dis·tin′guish·a·bly,** *adv.*

**dis·tin·guished** (di sting′gwisht) **1** having or showing excellence, honour, or greatness: *She is a distinguished artist. He received a medal for distinguished conduct.* **2** suited for or having the appearance of a great or honoured person: *a distinguished profile. He was tall and distinguished.* **3** pt. and pp. of DISTINGUISH. 1, 2 *adj.*, 3 *v.*

**dis·tort** (di stôrt′) **1** pull or twist out of shape; change the normal appearance of: *Rage distorted his face.* **2** change from the truth; twist the meaning of: *The man distorted the facts of the accident to escape blame. v.*

**dis·tor·tion** (di stôr′shən) **1** the act of DISTORTing (def. 2): *The statement was not a direct lie but it was certainly a distortion of the truth.* **2** the result of DISTORTing; anything distorted: *The article contains many distortions. They laughed at the distortions produced by the curved mirrors. n.*

**dis·tract** (di strakt′) **1** draw away the mind, attention, etc.: *The nurse distracted the baby while the doctor gave the injection. The music distracted him from his studies.* **2** confuse the attention of; disturb; bewilder: *Several people talking at once can distract a listener.* **3** put out of one's mind; make frantic or crazed (*used only after the verb* **be**): *Karen was nearly distracted by the thought of her brother trapped in the mine. v.* —**dis·tract′i·ble,** *adj.*
—**dis·tract′ing·ly,** *adv.*

**dis·tract·ed** (di strak′tid) **1** confused; bewildered: *She looked about her in a distracted way, trying to remember what she had come into the room for.* **2** in a frenzy; frantic; crazed: *He stood on the roof of the burning building, distracted with terror.* **3** pt. and pp. of DISTRACT. 1, 2 *adj.*, 3 *v.* —**dis·tract′ed·ly,** *adv.*

**dis·trac·tion** (di strak′shən) **1** DISTRACTing or being distracted; confusion of mind: *In their distraction, the parents of the missing child hardly knew what they were doing.* **2** anything that draws away the attention, mind, etc.: *Noise can be a distraction when you are studying.* **3** something that relieves the mind or spirit; a relief from continued thought, effort, grief, etc.: *Movies are a convenient and popular distraction. n.*

**dis·train** (di strān′) seize goods for unpaid rent or other debts. *v.*

**dis·traught** (di strot′) **1** in a state of mental conflict and confusion: *The lost child wandered about distraught with fear.* **2** crazed. *adj.*

**dis·tress** (di stres′) **1** great mental or physical pain; trouble. **2** cause pain, grief, or suffering to; make miserable or troubled. **3** misfortune: *economic distress.* **4** a dangerous or desperate situation: *A ship sinking or burning at sea is in distress.* 1, 3, 4 *n.*, 2 *v.*
—**dis·tress′ing·ly,** *adv.*

**dis·tressed** (di strest′) **1** troubled; anxious; agitated. **2** damaged: *distressed furniture, distressed produce.* **3** pt. and pp. of DISTRESS. 1, 2 *adj.*, 3 *v.*

**distressed area** a region characterized by an abnormally low standard of living because of unemployment, poverty, etc.

**dis·tress·ful** (di stres′fəl) **1** causing DISTRESS; painful. **2** feeling or showing DISTRESS; suffering. *adj.*
—**dis·tress′ful·ly,** *adv.*

**dis·trib·ute** (di strib′yüt) **1** give some of to each; divide and give out in shares: *The teacher distributed paper to the class.* **2** spread; scatter: *Distribute the paint evenly over the wall.* **3** divide into parts: *The children were distributed into three groups for the tour.* **4** arrange; classify. *v.*, **dis·trib·ut·ed, dis·trib·ut·ing.**

**dis·tri·bu·tion** (dis′trə byü′shən) **1** the act of distributing: *Everyone was waiting for the distribution of the prizes.* **2** the position, arrangement, or spread of anything over an area or space or a period of time: *an even distribution of paint. Caribou have a wide distribution in the North.* **3** the marketing of products; the process by which goods get to the consumers: *She is in charge of distribution for the company. n.*

**dis·trib·u·tive** (di strib′yə tiv)   **1** of or having to do with DISTRIBUTION; distributing.   **2** in mathematics, referring to a property of an operation by which the operation has the same result when applied to a set of quantities as it has when applied to individual members of the set. *Multiplication is distributive over addition since $a(b + c)$ is the same as $ab + ac$.*   *adj.*

**dis·trib·u·tive·ly** (di strib′yə ti vlē)   by DISTRIBUTION; not collectively.   *adv.*

**dis·trib·u·tor** (di strib′yə tər)   a person or thing that DISTRIBUTES.   *n.*

**dis·trict** (dis′trikt)   **1** a part of a larger area; region: *Northern Ontario is the leading gold-mining district in Canada. They lived in a fashionable district of the city.*   **2** a part of a country, a province, or a city marked off for a special purpose, such as providing schools, electing officials, etc.: *a school district, a local improvement district. The Northwest Territories are divided into three districts: Mackenzie, Keewatin, and Franklin.*   **3** divide into districts.   *1, 2 n., 3 v.*

**dis·trust** (dis trust′)   **1** not trust; have no confidence in; be suspicious of.   **2** a lack of trust or confidence; suspicion: *She could not overcome her distrust of the stranger.*   *1 v., 2 n.*

**dis·trust·ful** (dis trust′fəl)   not trusting; suspicious. *adj.*   —**dis·trust′ful·ly**, *adv.* **distrustful of**,   lacking confidence in.

**dis·turb** (dis tėrb′)   **1** destroy the peace, quiet, or rest of: *The noise of the road construction disturbed us so much that we couldn't sleep.*   **2** break in upon with noise or change; interrupt: *Don't disturb him now; he's studying.*   **3** make uneasy; trouble: *The party officials were disturbed by the results of the survey.*   **4** put out of order: *Someone has disturbed all my papers.*   *v.*   —**dis·turb′er**, *n.* —**dis·turb′ing·ly**, *adv.*

**dis·turb·ance** (dis tėr′bəns)   **1** DISTURBing or being disturbed.   **2** anything that DISTURBs: *The roar of the traffic was a disturbance.*   **3** confusion; disorder: *The police were called to quell the disturbance.*   **4** uneasiness; trouble; worry: *mental disturbance.*   *n.*

**di·sul·phide** or **di·sul·fide** (dī sul′fīd)   a compound consisting of two atoms of SULPHUR combined with another element or radical.   *n.*

**dis·un·ion** (dis yü′nyən)   **1** separation; division.   **2** a lack of unity; disagreement.   *n.*

**dis·u·nite** (dis′yə nīt′)   **1** separate; divide.   **2** destroy the unity of; cause to disagree.   *v.*, **dis·u·nit·ed**, **dis·u·nit·ing**.

**dis·u·ni·ty** (dis yü′nə tē)   lack of unity; disunion.   *n.*

**dis·use** (dis yüs′)   lack of use; not being used: *The old tools were rusted from disuse. Many words common in Shakespeare's time have fallen into disuse.*   *n.*

**di·syl·lab·ic** (dī′si lab′ik *or* dis′ i lab′ik)   having two SYLLABLES: *Ditto is a disyllabic word.*   *adj.*   Also, **dissyllabic**.

**di·syl·la·ble** (dī′sil ə bəl *or* dī sil′ə bəl, dis′il ə bəl *or* di sil′ə bəl)   a word having two SYLLABLES.   *n.*   Also, **dissyllable**.

**ditch** (dich)   **1** a long, narrow trench dug in the earth, usually used to carry off water.   **2** dig a ditch in.   **3** drive a vehicle into a ditch: *He ditched his car.*   **4** abandon, especially an aircraft in flight: *The pilot ditched the airplane because two engines were on fire.*   **5** *Informal*. get rid of.   *1 n., 2–5 v.*

**dith·y·ramb** (dith′ə ram′ *or* dith′ə ramb′)   **1** a Greek choral song in honour of Dionysus.   **2** a poem that is full of wild emotion, enthusiasm, etc.   **3** any speech or writing like this.   *n.*

**dit·to** (dit′ō)   **1** the same; exactly the same as appeared before.   **2** inverted commas or apostrophes (″) that stand for ditto; DITTO MARK.   **3** as said or done before; likewise.   **4** copy or repeat: *She simply dittoed what I had said.*   **5** make a copy or copies of on a duplicating machine: *to ditto a memo.*   **6** a copy made in this way. *1, 2, 6 n., pl.* **dit·tos**;   *3 adv.*, *4, 5 v.*, **dit·toed**, **dit·to·ing**.

**ditto mark**   a small mark (″) used in lists, tables, etc. directly under something written to show that it is repeated. *Example:*
10 copies at 10¢ each = $1.00
40 ″ ″ 5¢ ″ = $2.00

**dit·ty** (dit′ē)   a short, simple song or poem.   *n., pl.* **dit·ties**.

**di·ur·nal** (dī ėr′nəl)   **1** occurring every day; daily: *the diurnal course of the sun.*   **2** of or belonging to the daytime.   **3** of animals, active during the day and not at night: *Most birds are diurnal.*   **4** of flowers, opening during the day and closing at night.   **5** lasting a day. *adj.*

**di·ur·nal·ly** (dī ėr′nə lē)   **1** daily; every day.   **2** by day; during the daytime.   *adv.*

**di·va** (dē′və)   a PRIMA DONNA; a famous female opera singer.   *n., pl.* **di·vas**.

**Di·va·li** (də vä′lē)   a Hindu festival celebrated in the fall. It is dedicated to Lakshmi and is also known as the Festival of Lights.   *n.*

**di·van** (dī′van *or* də van′)   a long, low, soft couch or sofa.   *n.*

**dive** (dīv)   **1** plunge headfirst into the water.   **2** the act of diving.   **3** go down or out of sight suddenly: *He dived into an alley.*   **4** of an aircraft, missile, etc., plunge downward at a steep angle.   **5** of a submarine, submerge.   **6** the downward plunge of an aircraft, missile, submarine, etc.   **7** plunge the hand suddenly into anything: *He dived into his pocket and fished out a dollar.*   **8** penetrate with the mind: *Eva has been diving into the history of the Incas.* *1, 3–5, 7, 8 v.*, **dived** or **dove**, **dived**, **div·ing**;   *2, 6 n.*
☛ *Usage.* **Dived** and **dove** are both used for the past tense, though **dived** seems to be more widely preferred in writing and in formal English.

**dive bomber**   a bomber that releases its bomb load just before it pulls out of a dive toward the target.

**div·er** (dī′vər)   **1** a person or thing that dives. See SKINDIVER for another picture.   **2** a person whose occupation is to work under water.   **3** a diving bird: *The loon is a well-known Canadian diver.*   *n.*

**di·verge** (di vėrj′ *or* dī vėrj′)   **1** move or extend in different directions from one point; branch off: *Their paths diverged at the fork in the road.*   **2** differ or vary: *They usually agreed, but their opinions diverged on this matter.*   **3** turn away from a set course; DEVIATE.   *v.*, **di·verged**, **di·verg·ing**.

**di·ver·gence** (di vėr′jəns *or* dī vėr′jəns)   the act or state of diverging; difference: *The committee couldn't come to an agreement because of the wide divergence of opinion among its members.*   *n.*

**di·ver·gent** (di vėr′jənt *or* dī vėr′jənt)   diverging; different.   *adj.*

**di·verse** (di vėrs′, dī′vėrs′, *or* dī′vėrs)   **1** different; completely unlike: *Many diverse opinions were expressed at the meeting.*   **2** varied: *A person of diverse interests can talk on many subjects.*   *adj.*   —**di·verse′ness,** *n.*

**di·verse·ly** (di vėr′slē *or* dī vėr′slē)   in different ways or directions; differently; variously.   *adv.*

**di·ver·si·fi·ca·tion** (di vėr′sə fə kā′shən *or* dī vėr′sə fə kā′shən)   **1** the act or process of DIVERSIFYing.   **2** the state of being diversified.   *n.*

**di·ver·si·fy** (di vėr′sə fī *or* dī vėr′sə fī)   **1** give variety to; vary: *He joined a travel club to diversify his interests.*   **2** expand or extend business activities into different fields: *The company has recently diversified and now produces a whole range of cleaning products.*   *v.*, **di·ver·si·fied, di·ver·si·fy·ing.**   —**di·ver′si·fi′er,** *n.*

**di·ver·sion** (di vėr′zhən *or* dī vėr′zhən)   **1** a manoeuvre intended to draw attention away from a planned activity or attack; FEINT.   **2** an amusement; entertainment; pastime: *Golf is my mother's favourite diversion.*   **3** turning aside: *High tariffs often cause a diversion of trade from one country to another.*   *n.*

**di·ver·sion·ar·y** (di vėr′zhə ner′ē *or* dī vėr′zhə ner′ē)   of or like a DIVERSION (def. 1) or feint, especially in military tactics.   *adj.*

**di·ver·si·ty** (di vėr′sə tē *or* dī vėr′sə tē)   **1** a complete difference; unlikeness: *Diversity in opinions need not prevent friendship.*   **2** variety: *The diversity of food on the table made it hard for him to choose. Diversity of opinion is encouraged in a democracy.*   *n., pl.* **di·ver·si·ties.**

**di·vert** (di vėrt′ *or* dī vėrt′)   **1** turn aside: *A ditch diverted water from the stream into the fields.*   **2** amuse; entertain: *She browsed through the bookstore, looking for something to divert her during the flight.*   *v.*

**di·ver·tisse·ment** (dē veR tē smän′)   French.   **1** entertainment; amusement.   **2** a short ballet.   *n.*

**di·vest** (di vest′ *or* dī vest′)   **1** strip; rid; free: *The police divested the pretended officer of his stolen uniform and fake decorations.*   **2** force to give up; deprive: *Citizens were divested of their right to vote.*   *v.*

**di·vide** (di vīd′)   **1** separate into parts: *A brook divides the field. The river divides and forms two streams.*   **2** in mathematics, separate into equal parts: *Divide 8 by 2, and you get 4.*   Symbol: ÷   **3** give some of to each; share: *The children divided the candy among them.*   **4** disagree or cause to disagree; differ or cause to differ in feeling, opinion, etc.: *The school divided on the choice of a motto. Jealousy divided us.*   **5** separate into two groups in voting.   **6** a ridge of land separating the regions drained by two different river systems.   1–5 *v.*, **di·vid·ed, di·vid·ing;** 6 *n.*

**di·vid·ed** (di vī′did)   **1** separated.   **2** of a leaf, cut to the base so as to form distinct portions.   **3** pt. and pp. of DIVIDE.   1, 2 *adj.*, 3 *v.*

**divided highway**   a road, such as an expressway, having a median strip or boulevard between lanes of traffic going in opposite directions.

**divided skirt**   a woman's garment that looks like a flared skirt but is divided and sewn in the manner of trousers.

**div·i·dend** (div′ə dend′)   **1** a number or quantity to be divided by another: *In 8 ÷ 2, 8 is the dividend.*   See DIVISION for picture.   **2** money to be shared by those to whom it belongs: *If a company makes a profit, it declares a dividend to its shareholders.*   **3** a share of such money.   *n.*

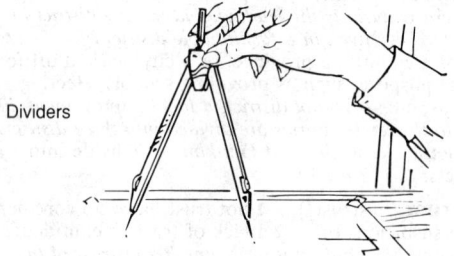

Dividers

**di·vid·er** (di vī′der)   **1** a person or thing that divides.   **2** **dividers,** *pl.*   an instrument for dividing lines, measuring distances, etc.; COMPASS (def. 2).   *n.*

**div·i·na·tion** (div′ə nā′shən)   **1** the art or act of foreseeing the future or revealing the unknown by supernatural means.   **2** a skilful guess or prediction.   *n.*

**di·vine** (di vīn′)   **1** of God or a god: *divine wisdom.*   **2** by or from God.   **3** to or for God; sacred; holy.   **4** like God or a god; heavenly.   **5** *Informal.* delightful; excellent; unusually good: *"What a divine hat!" cried Sue.*   **6** a person who knows much about theology, especially a minister or priest.   **7** find out, or foretell by supernatural means.   **8** find out by intuition or by guessing: *She divined their plan and immediately set out to stop them.*   **9** locate water, minerals, etc. underground by using a DIVINING ROD.   1–5 *adj.*, 6 *n.*, 7–9 *v.*, **di·vined, di·vin·ing.**   —**di·vine′ness,** *n.*

**di·vine·ly** (di vīn′lē)   **1** in a DIVINE or godlike manner.   **2** by the agency or influence of God.   **3** supremely.   *adv.*

**di·vin·er** (di vī′nər)   **1** a person who DIVINEs (defs. 7, 8), especially one who foresees the future or perceives the unknown, or professes to do these things.   **2** a person who locates water, minerals, etc. underground by using a DIVINING ROD: *a water diviner.*   *n.*

**diving bell**   a large, hollow, bell-shaped container open at the bottom, used as a chamber for people to work in under water: *A diving bell is supplied with air through a hose; the pressure of the air keeps the water out.*

**diving suit**   a waterproof suit with a helmet into which air can be pumped through a tube: *Diving suits are worn by persons working under water.*   See DIVER for picture.

**divining rod**   a forked stick, usually of willow or hazel, used to indicate the location of water or metal underground by bending downward.

**di·vin·i·ty** (di vin′ə tē)   **1** a divine being; a god or goddess.   **2** divine nature or quality.   **3** theology: *a student of divinity.*   **4** a creamy fudge.   *n., pl.* **di·vin·i·ties.**

**di·vis·i·bil·i·ty** (di viz′ə bil′ə tē)   the quality of being DIVISIBLE.   *n.*

**di·vis·i·ble** (di viz′ə bəl) **1** capable of being divided: *People have learned that the atom is divisible.* **2** capable of being divided without leaving a remainder: *Any even number is divisible by 2.* *adj.*

The parts of a division problem:

$$15 \overline{)78}$$ — DIVISOR 15, DIVIDEND 78, QUOTIENT 5, 75, REMAINDER 3

**di·vi·sion** (di vizh′ən) **1** dividing or being divided. **2** the act or process of giving some to each; distribution: *a division of labour.* **3** the process of dividing one number by another: *26 ÷ 2 = 13 is a simple division.* **4** something that divides, such as a boundary or partition. **5** a part; group; section. **6** in Canada, an army formation usually consisting of three infantry brigades supported by artillery, armoured, and other supporting units: *A division is usually commanded by a major-general.* **7** a difference of opinion, thought, or feeling; disagreement. **8** in a legislative body, the process of separating into two groups for voting. **9** a major category in the classification of plants, corresponding to the phylum in the classification of animals. This category is more specific than the kingdom and more general than the class. See classification chart in the Appendix. *n.*

**di·vi·sion·al** (di vizh′ə nəl) of, having to do with, or belonging to a DIVISION: *a divisional commander.* *adj.*

**di·vi·sor** (di vī′zər) **1** a number or quantity by which another is divided: *In 8 ÷ 2, 2 is the divisor.* See DIVISION for picture. **2** a number or quantity that divides another without a remainder. *n.*

**di·vorce** (di vôrs′) **1** the legal ending of a marriage. **2** end a marriage legally: *The judge divorced Mr. and Mrs. Antonietti.* **3** end marriage with one's spouse by getting a divorce: *Mrs. Volo divorced her husband.* **4** complete separation: *The pamphlet advocated the divorce of church and state.* **5** separate or detach something (*from*): *She led a lonely life, divorced from all her childhood friends and pleasures.* 1, 4 *n.*, 2, 3, 5 *v.*, **di·vorced, di·vorc·ing.**

**di·vor·cée** (dē vôr sā′) French. a divorced woman. *n.*

**di·vor·cee** (dē vôr′sē′) a divorced person. *n.*

**di·vorce·ment** (di vôr′smənt) DIVORCE. *n.*

**div·ot** (div′ət) a small piece of turf or earth dug up by a golf club in making a stroke. *n.*

**di·vulge** (di vulj′) reveal something secret; make known; make public: *The traitor divulged secret plans to the enemy.* *v.*, **di·vulged, di·vulg·ing.** —**di·vulg′er,** *n.*

**Dix·ie** (dik′sē) the southern states of the United States. *n.*

**dizziness** a DIZZY (def. 1) condition. *n.*

**diz·zy** (diz′ē) **1** having a sensation that things about one are whirling or spinning around and that one is about to fall: *Most of the midway rides make me dizzy.* **2** confused; bewildered: *He felt quite dizzy from all the advice they were giving him.* **3** make dizzy: *The ride on the merry-go-round had dizzied her.* **4** causing or likely to cause dizziness: *The mountaineer climbed to a dizzy height.* **5** *Informal.* foolish; silly: *What a dizzy thing to do!* 1, 2, 4, 5 *adj.*, **diz·zi·er, diz·zi·est;** 3 *v.*, **diz·zied, diz·zy·ing.** —**diz′zi·ly,** *adv.*

**djinn** (jin) JINN. *n.*

**dm** decimetre or decimetres.

hat, āge, fär; let, ēqual, tėrm; it, īce hot, ōpen, ôrder; oil, out; cup, pùt, rüle əbove, takən, pencəl, lemən, circəs ch, child; ng, long; sh, ship th, thin; ᴛʜ, then; zh, measure

**DNA** any of various acids that are an essential component of all living matter and that in higher organisms contain the genetic codes determining heredity. ☞ *Etym.* An abbreviation of *deoxyribonucleic acid.*

**DND** or **D.N.D.** Department of National Defence.

**do**[1] (dü) **1** carry out; perform: *That's easier said than done. She did her work.* **2** act; work: *Do or die.* **3** complete; finish; end: *That's done!* **4** make; produce: *Walt Disney did a movie about Snow White and the seven dwarfs.* **5** be the cause of; bring about: *Do good. Your work does you credit.* **6** act; behave: *Do wisely.* **7** render: *to do homage, to do justice.* **8** deal with as the case may require; take care of: *to do the dishes, to do one's hair, to have one's hair done.* **9** get along; manage; fare: *How do you do?* **10** be satisfactory; be enough; serve: *He said any kind of paper would do. These boots will have to do for another year.* **11** work out; solve: *to do a puzzle, to do a sum.* **12** cook: *The roast will be done in an hour.* **13** cover; traverse: *We did 100 kilometres in an hour.* **14** *Informal.* cheat; trick. **15** *Informal.* celebration: *They had a big do for us when we got back.* **16 Do** is also used in certain constructions as an auxiliary verb: **a** in asking questions: *Do you like milk?* **b** to emphasize a verb: *I do want to go.* **c** to stand for a verb already used: *My dog goes where I do.* **d** in negative statements that contain **not**: *I do not think they will come. He enjoyed the movie but she did not.* **e** in inverted constructions after the adverbs *rarely, hardly, little,* etc.: *Rarely did she laugh.* 1–14, 16 *v.*, *pres. sing.* 1 **do,** 2 **do,** 3 **does,** *pl.* **do;** *pt.* **did;** *pp.* **done;** *ppr.* **do·ing;** 15 *n.*
**do away with, a** abolish: *to do away with a rule.* **b** kill.
**do for, a** look after the needs of, as housekeeper, etc.: *Who did for her while she was sick?* **b** *Informal.* ruin; destroy, or kill: *That job almost did for me.*
**do in,** *Informal.* **a** ruin or kill: *That exercise is enough to do anybody in.* **b** tire out: *I'm all done in.*
**do up, a** close or fasten a zipper, buttons, laces, etc.: *Do up your shoe laces. He had trouble doing up the top button.* **b** close the fastenings of: *to do up a coat.* **c** wrap up: *to do up a package.* **d** clean and get ready for use: *to do up a room.*
**how do you do?** how are you? (used as a greeting).
**it isn't done,** it is not considered good manners, good taste, etc.
☞ *Hom.* DEW (dü), DUE (dü).

**do**[2] (dō) in music: **1** the first and last tones of an eight-tone major scale: *do, re, mi, fa, sol, la, ti, do.* **2** the tone C. *n.*
☞ *Hom.* DOE, DOUGH.

**do.** ditto.

**do·a·ble** (dü′ə bəl) that can be done. *adj.*

**dob·bin** (dob′ən) a farm horse, especially a quiet, plodding one. *n.*

**Do·ber·man pin·scher** (dō′bər mən pin′shər) a breed of medium-sized, slender, alert dog having short, dark hair: *Doberman pinschers are often trained as watchdogs.*

**dob·son fly** (dob′sən) a large insect whose larva is often used as bait by anglers.

**do·cile** (dō′sīl, dos′īl, *or* dos′əl)   1 easily managed; obedient: *a docile dog.*   2 easily taught; willing to learn: *a docile pupil.*   *adj.*   —**do′cile·ly,** *adv.*

**do·cil·i·ty** (dō sil′ə tē)   a DOCILE quality.   *n.*

Docks (defs. 1 and 2) with a ship loading

**dock¹** (dok)   1 a platform built on the shore or out from the shore; a WHARF or pier.   2 the water between two piers, permitting the entrance of ships.   3 bring a ship alongside a dock: *The sailors docked the ship and began to unload it.*   4 come into a dock: *The ship will dock at ten o'clock.*   5 join spacecraft together in space.   6 a DRY DOCK.   1, 2, 6 *n.*, 3, 4, 5 *v.*

**dock²** (dok)   1 the solid, fleshy part of an animal's tail.   2 cut short; cut the end off: *Horses' and dogs' tails are sometimes docked.*   3 cut down; take away part of: *The company docked the employees' wages if they came to work late.*   1 *n.*, 2, 3 *v.*

**dock³** (dok)   the place where an accused person stands in criminal court.   *n.*
**in the dock,**   on trial.

**dock⁴** (dok)   any of several closely related plants of the buckwheat family, some of which are troublesome weeds.   *n.*

**dock·et** (dok′it)   1 a list of cases to be tried by a court: *There are 12 cases on this morning's docket.*   2 any list of matters to be considered by some group of people; AGENDA.   3 enter on a docket.   4 a summary or list of law-court decisions.   5 make such a summary or list of.   6 a label or ticket giving the contents of a package, document, etc.   7 mark with such a label or ticket.   1, 2, 4, 6 *n.*, 3, 5, 7 *v.*

**dock·yard** (dok′yärd′)   a place where ships are built, equipped, and repaired: *A dockyard contains docks, workshops, and warehouses for supplies.*   *n.*

**doc·tor** (dok′tər)   1 a person who is qualified to treat diseases and physical or mental disorders and who makes this his or her work; a physician, surgeon, psychiatrist, or veterinarian.   2 dentist.   3 any person who treats diseases: *a witch doctor.*   4 give medical treatment to; try to heal: *She doctors her children when they have colds or stomach aches.*   5 *Informal.*   practise medicine.   6 a person who has received the highest degree possible in a university: *A Doctor of Laws, a Doctor of Philosophy.*   7 alter or weaken, especially for a bad purpose: *The whisky had been doctored with water. The dishonest teller doctored the accounts.*   8 mend; repair, especially machinery, etc.   1–3, 6 *n.*, 4, 5, 7, 8 *v.*

**doc·tor·al** (dok′tə rəl)   of or having to do with a DOCTOR (def. 6) or DOCTORATE.   *adj.*

**doc·tor·ate** (dok′tə rit)   the degree of DOCTOR (def. 6) given by a university.   *n.*

**doc·tri·naire** (dok′trə ner′)   1 an impractical theorist; a person who tries to apply a theory without considering the actual circumstances.   2 characteristic of a doctrinaire; theoretical and impractical: *a doctrinaire approach.*   1 *n.*, 2 *adj.*

**doc·tri·nal** (dok′trī′nəl *or* dok′trə nəl)   of, characterized by, or having to do with DOCTRINE: *a doctrinal sermon.*   *adj.*

**doc·trine** (dok′trən)   1 what is taught as the belief of a church, nation, or group of persons.   2 what is taught; teachings.   3 a belief, especially a religious one.   *n.*

**doc·u·ment** (dok′yə mənt *for noun,* dok′yə ment′ *for verb*)   1 something written, printed, etc. that gives information or proof of some fact; any original or official paper that can be used as evidence: *Letters, maps, and pictures are documents.*   2 provide with original or official papers.   3 prove or support by means of such papers.   4 provide with references to authoritative material and original sources that support a claim, argument, or theory: *Her article on the effects of artificial lighting is well documented.*   5 demonstrate or illustrate in a book, motion picture, etc.: *The film documents the changing face of the North.*   1 *n.*, 2–5 *v.*   —**doc′u·men·ta′tion,** *n.*

**doc·u·men·ta·ry** (dok′yə men′tə rē *or* dok′yə men′trē)   1 consisting of DOCUMENTS (def. 1); in writing, print, etc.: *The man's own letters were documentary evidence of his guilt.*   2 presenting or recording factual information in an artistic fashion: *a documentary film.*   3 a documentary book, motion picture, or radio or television program.   1, 2 *adj.*, 3 *n., pl.* **doc·u·men·ta·ries.**

**doc·u·men·ta·tion** (dok′yə mən tā′shən)   material that explains the use of some equipment: *There was no documentation to help us understand our new microwave.*   *n.*

**dod·der¹** (dod′ər)   1 shake; tremble.   2 move unsteadily; totter: *The man dodders about as if he were ninety years old.*   *v.*

**dod·der²** (dod′ər)   any of a closely related group of annual plants of the morning-glory family, having no leaves, chlorophyl, or roots when mature, and living as parasites by twining around other plants and drawing food from them through suckers.   *n.*

**do·dec·a·he·dron** (dō′dek ə hē′drən)   a solid figure having 12 faces: *The faces of a dodecahedron are regular pentagons.*   *n.*

**dodge** (doj)   1 move quickly to one side: *She dodged into the shadow of the house.*   2 move quickly in order to get away from a person, a blow, or something thrown: *He dodged the bat as it came flying toward him.*   3 a sudden movement to one side.   4 get away from or avoid an obligation, problem, etc. by trickery, cunning, or evasion; evade: *She is trying to dodge her responsibilities as leader by not taking a stand on the issue.*   5 *Informal.*   a trick or scheme: *a clever dodge.*   1, 2, 4 *v.*, **dodged, dodg·ing;** 3, 5 *n.*

**dodge·ball** (doj′bol′)   a game in which players forming a circle or two opposite lines try to hit opponents in the centre with a large ball.   *n.*

**dodg·er** (doj′ər)   1 a person who DODGES (def. 4), especially one who uses tricky or cunning devices.   2 a small handbill.   *n.*

**do·do** (dō′dō)   either of two extinct species of large, heavy bird having a large hooked bill, short legs, and small wings that were useless for flying: *The dodos, believed to be most closely related to the pigeon family, were found on islands in the Indian Ocean.*   *n., pl.* **do·dos** *or* **do·does.**

**dead as a dodo,** defunct or obsolete, with no chance of revival: *That issue is dead as a dodo.*

**doe** (dō) the female of a deer, antelope, rabbit, hare, and of most other animals whose male is called a BUCK (def. 1). *n.*
☛ *Hom.* DO², DOUGH.

**Doe** (dō) See JOHN DOE. *n.*

**do·er** (dü′ər) a person who does something, especially with energy and enthusiasm: *Anna is a dreamer, but her elder brother Gerard is a doer.* *n.*

**does** (duz) third person singular, present tense, of DO¹: *He does all his work. Does she sing well?* *v.*

**doe·skin** (dō′skin′) **1** the skin of a female deer. **2** a very soft leather made from this skin. **3** a smooth, soft woollen cloth with a short nap, used for suits, sportswear, etc. *n.*

**does·n't** (duz′ənt) does not.

**doff** (dof) **1** take off; remove: *to doff one's clothes.* **2** take off or lift one's hat in greeting: *He doffed his hat to her.* **3** get rid of; throw aside: *When he became mayor, he doffed his casual manner.* *v.*
☛ *Etym.* Originally a 14c. contraction of *do off,* meaning 'take or put off, remove'. Compare with DON².

**dog** (dog) **1** a domesticated, meat-eating mammal, kept as a pet or used for such purposes as guarding people or property, hunting, or leading the blind: *Two breeds of dog are the cocker spaniel and the greyhound.* **2** referring to the family of meat-eating animals that includes the dog as well as wolves, coyotes, jackals, and foxes. **3** a male dog, fox, wolf, etc. **4** any of various animals resembling a dog, such as the PRAIRIE DOG. **5** hunt or follow like a dog: *The police dogged the thief's footsteps until they caught him.* **6** a mean, contemptible man. **7** *Informal.* a man; fellow: *You're a lucky dog.* **8** a device to hold or grip something. 1–4, 6–8 *n.,* 5 *v.,* **dogged, dog·ging.**
—**dog′like′,** *adj.*
**go to the dogs,** be ruined.
**put on the dog,** *Informal.* behave or dress in a showy and affected manner: *Everyone really put on the dog for the civic reception.*

**dog·bane** (dog′bān′) **1** any of a closely related group of mainly tropical plants having clusters of small, white or pink, bell-shaped flowers: *Some dogbanes are poisonous.* **2** referring to the family of herbs, shrubs, and trees that includes dogbanes and periwinkles. *n.*

**dog·cart** (dog′kärt′) **1** a small cart pulled by dogs. **2** a small, open, usually two-wheeled carriage with two seats that are back to back. *n.*

**dog·catch·er** (dog′kach′ər) a person whose job is to pick up stray dogs and take them to the POUND³ (def. 1). *n.*

**dog days** a period of very hot, humid, and uncomfortable weather during July and August.

**doge** (dōj) the chief magistrate of Venice or Genoa when they were republics. *n.*

**dog-ear** (dog′ēr′) **1** a folded-down corner of a page in a book: *I made a dog-ear to mark the page where I stopped reading.* **2** fold down the corner of. 1 *n.,* 2 *v.* Also, **dog's-ear.**

**dog-eared** (dog′ērd′) **1** having a dog-ear: *Find the dog-eared page.* **2** having many pages with dog-ears: *a dog-eared old schoolbook.* **3** looking much used; shabby: *Almost everything in the room is dog-eared.* **4** pt. and pp. of DOG-EAR. 1–3 *adj.,* 4 *v.*

hat, āge, fär; let, ēqual, tėrm; it, īce
hot, ōpen, ôrder; oil, out; cup, pút, rüle
əbove, takən, pencəl, lemən, circəs
ch, child; ng, long; sh, ship
th, thin; ᴛʜ, then; zh, measure

**dog-eat-dog** (dog′ēt′dog′) marked by ruthless or vicious competition: *a dog-eat-dog society.* *adj.*

**dog·fight** (dog′fīt′) **1** a fight between dogs. **2** any rough fight or uproar. **3** a combat between individual fighter planes. *n.*

**dog·fish** (dog′fish′) any of several species of small shark found in temperate and warm seas, especially the **spiny dogfish,** having a spine in front of each back fin. *n., pl.* **dog·fish** or **dog·fishes.**

**dog·ged** (dog′id) stubborn; persistent; not giving up: *In spite of failures, she kept on with dogged determination.* *adj.* —**dog′ged·ly,** *adv.* —**dog′ged·ness,** *n.*

**dog·ger·el** (dog′ə rəl) **1** poor poetry; poetry that is trivial and not well written: *Doggerel is often written for a comic effect.* **2** of or referring to doggerel; not artistic; poor. 1 *n.,* 2 *adj.*

**dog·gie** (dog′ē) a child's word or a pet name for a dog. *n.*

**doggie bag** a bag given to a patron by a restaurant for the purpose of carrying home food left over from the patron's meal.

**dog·gy** (dog′ē) **1** of or like a dog: *There's a doggy smell in the car.* **2** *Informal.* outwardly showy. *adj.,* **dog·gi·er, dog·gi·est.**

**dog·house** (dog′hous′) a small house or shelter for a dog. *n.*
**be in the doghouse,** *Informal.* be in disfavour with somebody: *She's in the doghouse with her brother because she borrowed his sweater and got it dirty.*

**do·gie** (dō′gē) in the western parts of Canada and the United States, a motherless calf on the range or in a range herd. *n.*

**dog·ma** (dog′mə) **1** in theology, a belief or body of beliefs authorized by a church. **2** a doctrine or belief. **3** an opinion asserted in a positive manner as if it were authoritative. *n.*

**dog·mat·ic** (dog mat′ik) **1** having to do with DOGMA (defs. 1, 2); doctrinal. **2** asserting opinions as if one were the highest authority; positive; overbearing: *She is extremely dogmatic and uncompromising.* **3** asserted without proof: *a dogmatic statement.* *adj.*
—**dog·mat′i·cal·ly,** *adv.*

**dog·ma·tism** (dog′mə tiz′əm) a positive or authoritative assertion of opinion. *n.*

**dog·ma·tist** (dog′mə tist) **1** a person who asserts opinions as if they were authoritative. **2** a person who states DOGMAs (defs. 1, 2). *n.*

**dog·ma·tize** (dog′mə tīz′) **1** assert opinions in a positive or authoritative manner. **2** express as a DOGMA (defs. 1, 2). *v.,* **dog·ma·tized, dog·ma·tiz·ing.**

**Dog·rib** (dog′rib) **1** a member of a First Nations people who live in the Northwest Territories: *The Dogrib traditionally occupied the region between Great Bear Lake and Great Slave Lake.* **2** the Athapascan language of these people. **3** of or having to do with the Dogrib or their language. 1, 2 *n., pl.* **Dog·rib** or **Dog·ribs;** 3 *adj.*

**dog salmon** chum, a species of Pacific salmon.

**dog's–ear** (dog′zēr′) DOG-EAR. *n., v.*

**dog·sled** (dog′sled′) *Cdn.* a sled pulled by dogs. See SLED for picture. *n.*

**dog's life** a miserable life: *He lived a dog's life when he was young, because nobody wanted him.*

**Dog Star** Sirius.

**dog's–tooth violet** (dogz′tüth′) DOGTOOTH VIOLET.

**dog–tired** (dog′tīrd′) very tired. *adj.*

**dog·tooth violet** (dog′tüth′) any of a closely-related group of plants of the lily family, having yellow, white, or purple lily-like flowers and long, pointed, oval-shaped leaves; especially a species with yellow flowers found in the woods of eastern North America, also called **adder's-tongue.**

**dog·trot** (dog′trot′) a gentle, easy trot. *n.*

**dog·wood** (dog′wùd′) **1** any of a closely related group of trees, shrubs, and herbs having clusters of small flowers, often surrounded by showy, petal-like bracts, and red, dark blue, or white fruit: *The Pacific or western flowering dogwood is the provincial flower of British Columbia.* **2** the heavy, hard wood of any of these trees or shrubs. **3** referring to a family of shrubs, trees, or herbs found throughout the world: *The dogwood family consists of about 100 species, including the flowering dogwoods and the bunchberry.* *n.*

**doi·ly** (doi′lē) a small piece of linen, lace, or paper used on or under plates, vases, etc. *n. pl.* **doi·lies.**

**do·ings** (dü′ingz) **1** things done; actions. **2** social activities or behaviour. *n. pl.*

**dol·drums** (dol′drəmz *or* dōl′drəmz) **1** certain regions of the ocean near the equator where the wind is very light or constantly shifting: *Sailing ships caught in the doldrums were often unable to move for days.* **2** dullness; a gloomy feeling; low spirits: *The whole family was in the doldrums because of the rainy weather.* *n. pl.*

**dole** (dōl) **1** a portion of money, food, etc. given in charity. **2** deal out in portions to the poor. **3** a small portion. **4** give in small portions: *Mother doles out one piece of candy a day to each child.* **5** the relief money given by a government to unemployed people. 1, 3, 5 *n.*, 2, 4 *v.*, **doled, dol·ing.**

**dole·ful** (dōl′fəl) sad; mournful; dreary; dismal: *She wore a doleful expression.* *adj.* —**dole′ful·ly,** *adv.* —**dole′ful·ness,** *n.*

**doll** (dol) **1** a child's plaything made to look like a baby, child, or grown person. **2** a pretty child, girl or woman. *n.*

**dol·lar** (dol′ər) **1** a unit of money in Canada, the United States, and some other countries: *There are one hundred cents in a dollar.* Symbol: $ **2** a coin worth one dollar: *He gave me four quarters for a dollar.* *n.*
☛ *Etym.* Through Low German *daler* from German *taler or thaler,* short for *Joachimsthaler,* a kind of silver coin. *Joachimsthal* was a valley in Bohemia (formerly a province in the Austrian Empire, but now part of Czechoslovakia), where the silver for this coin was mined.

**dol·lop** (dol′əp) *Informal.* **1** a portion or serving, large or small: *a dollop of ice cream.* **2** apply or spread on heavily. 1 *n.*, 2 *v.*

**doll's house** a miniature house, often less than 50 cm high, used as a toy: *Our mother made all the wooden furniture for our doll's house.*

**doll·y** (dol′ē) **1** a child's name for a doll. **2** a small, low frame on wheels, used to move heavy things: *The fridge was moved on a dolly.* *n., pl.* **doll·ies.**

A dolmen on the downs in Wiltshire, England

**dol·men** (dol′mən) a prehistoric monument, generally regarded as a tomb, made by laying a large, flat stone across several upright stones. *n.*

**dol·o·mite** (dol′ə mīt′) a rock consisting mainly of calcium and magnesium carbonate. *n.*

**dol·or·ous** (dol′ə rəs *or* dō′lə rəs) **1** mournful; sorrowful: *She uttered a heartbroken, dolorous cry.* **2** grievous; painful: *The dolorous day was ending.* *adj.* —**dol′or·ous·ly,** *adv.*

**do·lour** *or* **do·lor** (dō′lər) sorrow; grief. *n.*

**dol·phin** (dol′fən) **1** any of several related species of small whale having a snout shaped like a beak: *Dolphins are often trained to perform in aquariums.* **2** either of two species of large, edible, saltwater fish remarkable for their changes of colour when taken from the water. **3** a BUOY (def. 1) or piling used to mark a channel for ships. *n.*

**dolphin striker** on a ship, a small spar under the bowsprit that helps support the JIB BOOM.

**dolt** (dōlt) a dull, stupid person. *n.*

**–dom** a noun-forming suffix meaning: **1** the position, rank, or realm of a _____: *kingdom = realm of a king.* **2** the condition of being _____: *martyrdom = condition of being a martyr.* **3** all those who are _____: *heathendom = all those who are heathen.*

**dom.** **1** domestic. **2** dominion.

**do·main** (dō mān′) **1** the territory under the control of one ruler or government. **2** the land owned by one person; an estate. **3** a field of thought, action, etc.: *the domain of science, the domain of politics.* *n.* Compare with DEMESNE.
☛ *Etym.* See note at DOMINION.

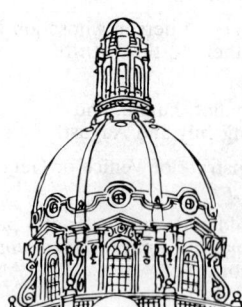

The dome of the Alberta legislature

**dome** (dōm) **1** a large, rounded roof on a circular or many-sided base. **2** anything that is or appears high and rounded: *the dome of the sky, the dome of a hill.* **3** cover with a dome. **4** form into the shape of a dome. **5** rise

or swell like a dome.   1, 2 *n.*, 3–5 *v.*, **domed, dom·ing.**
—**dome′like′,** *adj.*
☛ *Etym.* See note at DOMINION.

**dome fastener**   *Cdn.*   a metal or plastic fastener consisting of two parts, one with a small, round projection in the centre that snaps into a socket in the centre of the other.

**Domesday Book** (dümz′dā′)   a record of the value and ownership of the lands in England, made in 1086 at the order of William the Conqueror.   Also, **Doomsday Book.**

**do·mes·tic** (də mes′tik)   **1** of the home, household, or family affairs: *domestic cares, a domestic scene.*   **2** fond of home and family life: *Since his marriage he has become quite domestic.*   **3** a servant in a household: *Cooks, butlers, and maids are domestics.*   **4** of animals, not wild; tame: *Cats, dogs, cows, horses, sheep, and pigs are domestic animals.*   **5** of one's own country; not foreign: *domestic news, domestic affairs.*   **6** made in one's own country; native: *domestic cheese.*   1, 2, 4–6 *adj.*, 3 *n.*
☛ *Etym.* See note at DOMINION.

**do·mes·ti·cal·ly** (də mes′ti klē)   in a DOMESTIC (def. 1) manner; so far as concerns domestic affairs.   *adv.*

**do·mes·ti·cate** (də mes′tə kāt′)   **1** change animals or plants from a wild to a tame or cultivated state; tame. **2** make fond of home and family life.   **3** bring a foreign word, custom, etc. into accepted use in a region or country; adopt.   *v.*, **do·mes·ti·cat·ed, do·mes·ti·cat·ing.**

**do·mes·ti·ca·tion** (də mes′tə kā′shən)   domesticating or being DOMESTICATEd.   *n.*

**do·mes·tic·i·ty** (dō′mes tis′ə tē)   **1** home and family life.   **2** fondness for home and family life.
**3 domesticities,** *pl.*   domestic affairs.   *n., pl.* **do·mes·tic·i·ties.**

**dom·i·cile** (dom′ə sīl′ *or* dom′ə səl)   **1** a dwelling place; home; residence.   **2** a place of permanent residence: *One may have several residences, but only one legal domicile at a time.*   **3** settle in a domicile.   1, 2 *n.*, 3 *v.*, **dom·i·ciled, dom·i·cil·ing.**
☛ *Etym.* See note at DOMINION.

**dom·i·cil·i·ar·y** (dom′ə sil′ē er′ē)   of or having to do with a dwelling place.   *adj.*

**dom·i·nance** (dom′ə nəns)   dominating or being DOMINANT (def. 1); rule; control.   *n.*

**dom·i·nant** (dom′ə nənt)   **1** controlling, ruling, or governing; strongest and most influential: *The dominant influence in her life has been her grandmother.*   **2** rising high above its surroundings; towering: *The window looked out on the dominant hills to the west.*   **3** in music, the fifth tone in an eight-tone scale: *G is the dominant in the key of C.*   **4** of or referring to a gene in one of a pair of chromosomes that dominates over the corresponding gene in the other chromosome and is therefore expressed as a trait in the organism: *If one of such a pair of genes inherited by a person is for brown eyes and the other is for blue, the person will have brown eyes because that gene is dominant.*   Compare with RECESSIVE.   1, 2, 4 *adj.*, 3 *n.*
—**dom′i·nant·ly,** *adv.*
☛ *Etym.* See note at DOMINION.

**dom·i·nate** (dom′ə nāt′)   **1** control or rule by strength or power: *A person of strong will will often dominates others. Dandelions will dominate over lawn grass if they are not kept out.*   **2** rise high above; tower over: *The mountain dominates the harbour.*   **3** have the foremost place or the greatest influence in: *The new hockey team already*

# dome fastener   361   donate

hat, āge, fär; let, ēqual, tėrm; it, īce
hot, ōpen, ôrder; oil, out; cup, put, rüle
əbove, takən, pencəl, lemən, circəs
ch, child; ng, long; sh, ship
th, thin; ᴛʜ, then; zh, measure

*dominates the league. Their products dominate the market.*
*v.,* **dom·i·nat·ed, dom·i·nat·ing.**   —**dom′i·na′tor,** *n.*

**dom·i·na·tion** (dom′ə nā′shən)   dominating or being DOMINATEd (def. 1); control; rule: *The country was under the domination of a tyrant for many years.*   *n.*

**dom·i·neer** (dom′ə nēr′)   rule over at one's own will; tyrannize; be overbearing in asserting one's authority: *He tried to domineer over the other members of the committee.*   *v.*

**dom·i·neer·ing** (dom′ə nē′ring)   **1** inclined to DOMINEER; overbearing: *a domineering attitude, a domineering person.*   **2** ppr. of DOMINEER.   1 *adj.*, 2 *v.*
—**dom′i·neer′ing·ly,** *adv.*

**do·min·ion** (də min′yən)   **1** supreme authority; rule; control: *The British had dominion over a large part of the world.*   **2** a territory or country under the control of one ruler or government: *The old king divided his dominion between his sons.*   **3 Dominion,   a** a name used for certain self-governing countries in the Commonwealth of Nations: *the Dominion of New Zealand.*   **b** in Canada, under the control or authority of the federal government: *the Dominion Fire Commissioner.*   **c** in Canada, relating to the country as a whole; national in scope.   *n.*
☛ *Etym.* From OF *dominion* from L *dominium* 'property, lordship', derived from *dominus* 'master, lord'. *Dominus* was in turn derived from L *domus* 'house', which has also given us several other English words. DOMAIN, DOME, DOMESTIC, DOMICILE, DOMINANT, etc. all came into English through French from separate Latin words derived from *domus*. See also notes at CONDOMINIUM and DOMINO.

**Dominion Day**   the former name for a national holiday commemorating the establishment of the Dominion of Canada on July 1, 1867. The name was officially changed to Canada Day in October, 1982.

**dom·i·no** (dom′ə nō′)   **1** one of the pieces used in playing the game of dominoes.   **2** a long, loose, hooded cloak and a mask for the upper part of the face, worn as a disguise, especially at masquerades.   **3** a mask, usually black, for the upper part of the face.   **4** a person wearing a domino.   **5 dominoes,** *pl.*   a game played with flat, oblong pieces of wood, bone, etc. that are either blank or marked with dots on one side (*used with a singular verb*).   *n., pl.* **dom·i·noes** or **dom·i·nos.**
☛ *Etym.* From F *domino*, originally meaning a priest's winter cloak with a hood, later developing the meanings that were taken into English. The French word probably developed from L *dominus* 'master', as of a house, derived from *domus* 'house'. 18c. See also note at DOMINION.

**don**[1] (don)   in some Canadian universities and colleges, an official in charge of a student residence.   *n.*
☛ *Hom.* DAWN.

**don**[2] (don)   put on: *Sir Richard donned his armour.*   *v.,* **donned, don·ning.**
☛ *Hom.* DAWN.
☛ *Etym.* Originally a 14c. contraction of *do on*, meaning 'put on'. Compare with DOFF.

**do·nate** (dō′nāt *or* dō nāt′)   give; contribute, especially to an institution or public service: *My mother donates* *blood regularly. He donated fifty dollars to the charity.* v., **do·nat·ed, do·nat·ing.**

**do·na·tion** (dō nā′shən) **1** the act of giving or contributing. **2** a gift or contribution: *Our class made a donation to the United Way.* n.

**done** (dun) **1** completed; finished; ended; through. **2** *Informal.* worn-out; exhausted. **3** cooked; cooked enough: *Are the potatoes done?* **4** proper; fitting; conforming to custom or convention: *This is the done thing. Eating peas with a knife is not done.* **5** pp. of DO¹: *Have you done your homework?* 1–4 *adj.*, 5 *v.*
☛ Hom. DUN.

**don·jon** (dun′jən) the large, strongly fortified inner tower of a castle; KEEP (def. 18). n.
☛ Hom. DUNGEON.

**don·key** (dong′kē) **1** any of several species of tame or wild four-footed animal related to the horse but smaller, and having larger ears, a shorter neck and mane, and smaller hooves than a horse. See PANNIER for another picture. **2** a stubborn person. **3** a silly or stupid person. *n., pl.* **don·keys.**

**donkey engine** a small steam engine: *Donkey engines are used on a ship for hoisting anchor, etc.*

**Don·ny·brook** (don′ē brùk′) *Informal.* a riot; a brawl: *The players engaged in a terrific Donnybrook after the hockey game.* n.
☛ *Etym.* From *Donnybrook Fair*, an annual event held in Donnybrook, a suburb of Dublin, Ireland. The fair used to be known for its brawls. 19c.

**do·nor** (dō′nər) a person who contributes; giver: *The Red Cross is calling for blood donors.* n.

**Don Qui·xo·te** (don′ kē hō′tē *or* kwik′sət; *Spanish,* dông′ kē Hō′tä) **1** the chivalrous and idealistic, but very impractical, hero of a story by Cervantes. **2** any person of high but impractical ideals.

**don't** (dōnt) do not.

**doo·dle** (dü′dəl) **1** make drawings or marks of any kind while thinking of something else; draw absent-mindedly: *He doodled while he was talking on the telephone.* **2** a drawing or mark made absent-mindedly. 1 *v.*, **doo·dled, doo·dling;** 2 *n.*

**doo·dle·bug** (dü′dəl bug′) *Informal.* **1** a small car or other vehicle. **2** any of various devices with which it is claimed mineral and oil deposits can be located. n.

**doo·hick·ey** (dü′hik ē) *Informal.* **1** any small mechanical device; gadget. **2** any small device, whose name has been temporarily forgotten: *Pass that doohickey for opening windows.* n.

**doom** (düm) **1** fate. **2** make a bad or undesirable outcome certain: *The weather doomed our hopes for a picnic.* **3** an unhappy or terrible fate; ruin; death: *The soldiers marched to their doom.* **4** destine to an unhappy or terrible fate: *the doomed men.* **5** judgment; sentence: *The judge pronounced the guilty man's doom.* **6** condemn to punishment: *The prisoner was doomed to life imprisonment.* **7** the end of the world; God's final judgment of mankind. 1, 3, 5, 7 *n.*, 2, 4, 6 *v.*

**dooms·day** (dümz′dā′) the end of the world; the day of God's final judgment of mankind. n.

**Doomsday Book** See DOMESDAY BOOK.

**door** (dôr) **1** a movable structure of wood, metal, glass, etc. intended for closing up an entrance to a building or room: *Doors usually swing or slide open and shut.* **2** a similar structure designed to close off an opening giving access to a cupboard, closet, etc.: *a bookcase with sliding glass doors.* **3** an opening where a door is; doorway: *I saw him just as he came through the door.* **4** the room or building to which a particular door belongs: *Her house is three doors down the street.* **5** any means by which to go in or out; a way to get something; access: *an open door to the Yukon.*

**lay at the door of,** blame for: *Don't lay this offence at my door.*

**next door,** in the adjacent dwelling: *They live just next door from us.*

**out of doors,** not in a house or building; outside.

**show a person the door,** ask or order a person to leave.

**door·bell** (dôr′bel′) a bell to be rung by pressing a button or pulling a handle on the outside of a door as a signal that someone wishes to have the door opened. n.

**door·jamb** (dôr′jam′) the upright piece forming the side of a doorway. n.

**door·keep·er** (dôr′kē′pər) **1** a person who guards a door or entrance. **2** DOORMAN. n.

**door·knob** (dôr′nob′) a knob on a door that releases the latch of the door when turned. n.

**door·man** (dôr′mən *or* dôr′man′) **1** a person whose work is opening the door of a hotel, store, apartment house, etc. for people going in or out. **2** a person who guards a door. *n., pl.* **door·men** (-mən *or* -men′).

**door·nail** (dôr′nāl′) a nail with a large head. n.
**dead as a doornail,** entirely dead.

**door·plate** (dôr′plāt′) a metal plate on a door with a name, number, etc. on it. n.

**door·post** (dôr′post′) DOORJAMB. n.

**door·sill** (dôr′sil′) THRESHOLD. n.

**door·step** (dôr′step′) a step leading from an outside door to the ground. n.

**door–to–door** (dôr′ tə dôr′) **1** making a call, often uninvited, at each residential or business address in turn in a particular area or district: *a door-to-door salesperson, a door-to-door canvasser.* **2** made or done by going from one address to the next: *door-to-door selling.* **3** at or to each address in turn: *She went door-to-door, campaigning for the election.* **4** going from the original starting point to the final destination: *The courier service offers door-to-door delivery.* **5** from starting point to destination: *The taxi cost us twenty dollars door-to-door.* 1, 2, 4 *adj.*, 3, 5 *adv.*

**door·way** (dôr′wā′) an entrance to be closed by a door. n.

**door·yard** (dôr′yärd′) the yard near the door of a house; yard around a house. n.

**dope** (dōp) **1** *Informal.* a harmful narcotic drug, such as heroin or opium. **2** oil, grease, etc. used to make machinery run smoothly. **3** a thick varnish or similar liquid applied to a fabric to strengthen or waterproof it. n. —**dop′er,** n.

**do·ra·do** (də rä′dō) either one of two DOLPHINS (def. 2) valued as game fish. n.

**do·ré** (dô′rā) *Cdn.* YELLOW WALLEYE. n.

**Dor·ic** (dô′rik) **1** of, having to do with, or referring to the oldest and simplest of the classical Greek styles of architecture. See ORDER for picture. **2** the Greek dialect spoken in Doris, a small region in the central part of ancient Greece.  **3** of Doris, its people, or their language.  *1, 3 adj., 2 n.*

**dorm** (dôrm) *Informal.* DORMITORY.  *n.*

**dor·man·cy** (dôr′mən sē)  a DORMANT condition.  *n.*

**dor·mant** (dôr′mənt)  **1** sleeping or apparently sleeping: *Bears are dormant during the winter.*  **2** in a state of rest or inactivity: *a dormant volcano.*  *adj.*

A dormer

**dor·mer** (dôr′mər)  **1** an upright window that projects from a sloping roof.  **2** the projecting part of a roof that contains such a window.  *n.*

**dormer window**  DORMER (def. 1).

**dor·mice** (dôr′mīs′)  pl. of DORMOUSE.  *n.*

**dor·mi·to·ry** (dôr′mə tô′rē)  **1** a sleeping room containing a number of beds.  **2** a building with many rooms providing sleeping and living accommodation for many people as at a college.  *n., pl.* **dor·mi·to·ries.**

**dor·mouse** (dôr′mous′)  a small rodent found in Africa, Asia, and Europe, related to the rat and mouse, having fine, soft fur, large black eyes, and a tail as long as its body.  *n., pl.* **dor·mice.**

**dor·sal** (dôr′səl)  of, on, or near the back: *a dorsal fin, a dorsal nerve.*  *adj.*

**dor·sal·ly** (dôr′sə lē)  on, by, or toward the back.  *adv.*

**do·ry** (dô′rē)  a rowboat with a flat bottom and high sides, often used by ocean fishermen.  *n., pl.* **do·ries.**

**DOS**  DISK OPERATING SYSTEM.

**dos·age** (dō′sij)  **1** the amount of a medicine to be taken at one time.  **2** the giving of medicine in DOSES.  *n.*

**dose** (dōs)  **1** the amount of a medicine to be given or taken at one time.  **2** give medicine in doses; treat with medicine: *The doctor dosed the boy with quinine.*  **3** a portion; the amount of anything given at one time as a punishment, remedy, treatment, etc.: *a dose of flattery.*  **4** blend or adulterate: *to dose wine with sugar.*  *1, 3 n., 2, 4 v.,* **dosed, dos·ing.**  —**dos′er,** *n.*

**dot** (dot)  **1** a tiny, round mark; a very small spot; a point: *A dot after a note or rest in music makes it half as long again.*  **2** a small round spot: *a blue necktie with white dots.*  **3** mark with a dot or dots: *He never dots his i's when he writes.*  **4** be here and there in; give variety to: *Trees and bushes dotted the broad lawn.*  **5** a short sound used in sending messages by telegraph or radio.  *1, 2, 5 n., 3, 4 v.,* **dot·ted, dot·ting.**  —**dot′er,** *n.*
**on the dot,** *Informal.*  at exactly the right time; at the specified time: *Be there on the dot.*

**dot·age** (dō′tij)  a weak-minded and childish condition that sometimes accompanies old age.  *n.*

**do·tard** (dō′tərd)  a person who is weak-minded and childish because of old age.  *n.*

**dote** (dōt)  **1** be weak-minded and childish because of old age.  **2** (*used with* **on** *or* **upon**) be foolishly fond; be too fond: *He dotes on his daughter.*  *v.,* **dot·ed, dot·ing.**  —**dot′er,** *n.*

**dot·ing** (dō′ting)  **1** foolishly fond; too fond.  **2** ppr. of DOTE.  *1 adj., 2 v.*  —**dot′ing·ly,** *adv.*

**dot·ted** (dot′id)  **1** marked with or as with a dot or dots: *She wore a dress of pale yellow cotton dotted with tiny white flowers.*  **2** pt. and pp. of DOT.  *1 adj., 2 v.*

**dot·ty** (dot′ē)  **1** *Informal.*  feeble-minded or mentally unbalanced.  **2** *Informal.*  unsteady; shaky; feeble.  **3** full of dots.  *adj.,* **dot·ti·er, dot·ti·est.**

**dou·ble** (dub′əl)  **1** twice as much, as many, as large, as strong, etc.: *double pay, a double letter.*  **2** twice.  **3** the number or amount that is twice as much: *Four is the double of two.*  **4** make twice as much or twice as many: *Rocco doubled his money in six years by making a shrewd investment.*  **5** become twice as much or as many: *Money left in a savings account will double in about 10 years.*  **6** for two: *a double bed.*  **7** two together: *The blow made him see double.*  **8** made of two like parts; in a pair: *double doors.*  **9** made of two unlike parts; combining two in one: *He leads a double life as a lawyer and as a dentist.*  **10** a person or thing just like another: *In a movie an actor often has a double to do the dangerous parts. I saw your double in the bus yesterday.*  **11** be used for another; be the double of.  **12** take another's place: *Tom doubled for me when I couldn't get to the meeting.*  **13** serve two purposes; play two parts: *The maid doubled as cook.*  **14** fold; bend: *He doubled his fists in anger. Sonia doubled her slice of bread to make a sandwich.*  **15** turn suddenly and sharply; turn back on one's own trail: *The fox doubled on its track to get away from the dogs.*  **16** a sharp backward bend or turn; shift.  **17** go around: *The ship doubled the cape.*  **18** insincere; deceitful; false: *a double tongue.*  **19** having more than one set of petals: *Some roses are double; others are single.*  **20** in baseball, a hit by which a batter gets to second base.  **21** in baseball, make a two-base hit.  **22** in bridge, increase the points or penalties of an opponent's bid.  **23** the act of doubling a bid in bridge.  **24 doubles,** *pl.*  any game with two players on each side.  *1, 6, 8, 9, 18, 19 adj., 2, 7 adv., 3, 10, 16, 20, 23, 24 n., 4, 5, 11–15, 17, 21, 22 v.,* **dou·bled, dou·bling.**  —**dou′bler,** *n.*
**double back,**  **a** fold over: *She doubled back the cloth to make a hem.*  **b** go back the same way that one came: *He decided he must have passed the house, so he doubled back.*
**double up,**  **a** fold back; fold up: *He doubled up the five-dollar bill and put it in his pocket.*  **b** draw the knees up toward the chest; bend the upper part of the body toward the lower part: *She doubled up in pain.*  **c** share a room, a bed, etc. with another: *When guests came, the two sisters had to double up.*
**on the double,**  quickly; at a run.

**double bar**  in music, a double line on a STAFF (def. 6) that marks the end of a movement or of an entire piece of music.

**dou·ble–bar·relled** *or* **dou·ble–bar·reled** (dub′əl bar′əld *or* dub′əl ber′əld)  **1** having two barrels: *a double-barrelled shotgun.*  **2** having a two-fold purpose.  *adj.*

A double bass

**double bass** a stringed instrument with a deep bass tone, the largest member of the modern violin family, played standing upright on the floor with the player standing behind it. The double bass, which has four strings, is derived directly from one of the seventeenth-century viols, not from the violins.

**double bassoon** a large BASSOON, an octave lower in pitch than the ordinary bassoon.

**dou·ble–breast·ed** (dub′əl bres′tid) of clothing, overlapping enough to make two thicknesses across the breast and having two rows of buttons. *adj.*

**double chin** a soft fold of flesh under the chin.

**dou·ble–cross** (dub′əl krôs′) *Informal.* promise to do one thing and then do another; be treacherous to. *v.* —**dou′ble–cross′er,** *n.*

**dou·ble–deal·er** (dub′əl dē′lər) a person guilty of DOUBLE-DEALING. *n.*

**dou·ble–deal·ing** (dub′əl dē′ling) pretending to do one thing and then doing another; deceiving. *n., adj.*

**double eagle** a former gold coin of the United States, worth 20 dollars.

**dou·ble–edged** (dub′əl ejd′) 1 two-edged. 2 as much against as for. *adj.*

**dou·ble–faced** (dub′əl fāst′) 1 having two faces or aspects. 2 of cloth, having a nap or finish on both sides. 3 TWO-FACED. *adj.*

**double feature** a motion-picture program with two full-length films.

**dou·ble–glazed** (dub′əl glāzd′) having two layers of glass. *adj.*

**double glazing** windows having two layers of glass for insulation.

**dou·ble–head·er** (dub′əl hed′ər) 1 two baseball games between the same teams on the same day, one right after the other. 2 a railway train pulled by two engines. *n.*

**dou·ble–joint·ed** (dub′əl join′tid) having very flexible joints that allow fingers, arms, legs, etc. to bend in unusual ways. *adj.*

**double knit** a knitted fabric made on a machine with a double set of needles to produce a double thickness of cloth: *Double knits are often reversible.*

**double–knit** (dub′əl nit′) knitted on a machine with a double set of needles: *double-knit jersey.* *adj.*

**dou·ble–park** (dub′əl pärk′) park a car, etc. beside another car that is occupying the area where parking is allowed: *It is usually illegal to double-park.* *v.*

**dou·ble–quick** (dub′əl kwik′) 1 in marching, the next quickest step to a run. 2 very quick. 3 in double-quick time; very quickly. 4 march in double-quick step. 1 *n.*, 2 *adj.*, 3 *adv.*, 4 *v.*

**double star** two stars so close together that they look like one to the naked eye.

A doublet

**dou·blet** (dub′lit) 1 a man's close-fitting jacket: *Men in Europe wore doublets in the 15th, 16th, and 17th centuries.* 2 a pair of two similar or equal things. 3 one of a pair. *n.*

**double tackle** a pulley with two grooved wheels.

**double talk** talk that is purposely made confusing so as to cloak ignorance or deceit.

**double time** 1 payment at twice the normal rate: *They get double time for working on Sundays or holidays.* 2 a rate of marching in which 180 paces, each of about a metre, are taken in a minute. 3 DOUBLE-QUICK.

**double window** a window together with a storm window, made either in one piece or as separate structures.

**dou·bly** (dub′lē) 1 twice; twice as: *doubly kind.* 2 two at a time. *adv.*

**doubt** (dout) 1 not believe; not be sure of; feel uncertain about. 2 be uncertain. 3 a lack of belief or sureness; uncertainty: *Faith casts out doubt.* 4 a state of uncertainty: *The outcome of the game was in doubt till the end.* 5 be afraid; fear; suspect: *They doubted a sinister motive in the king's friendliness.* 1, 2, 5 *v.*, 3, 4 *n.* —**doubt′er,** *n.* —**doubt′ing·ly,** *adv.*
**no doubt, a** surely; certainly: *No doubt we will win in the end.* **b** probably: *Even if he had money, he'd no doubt expect me to pay the bill.*
**without doubt,** without question; certainly: *She will pass the test without doubt.*
☛ *Usage.* In negative statements the verb **doubt** is followed by **that:** *I don't doubt that she is clever.* In positive statements use **whether** (in formal use) or **if** (informal) to show uncertainty: *I doubt whether she can pass the exam.* To show real lack of belief, use **that:** *I doubt that she can answer this question.*

**doubt·ful** (dout′fəl) 1 unclear; not distinct; not certain: *a doubtful advantage. It is doubtful whether he ever saw his friend again.* 2 full of doubt; feeling uncertain: *He looked doubtful.* 3 open to question or suspicion: *Her sly answers made her sincerity doubtful.* *adj.* —**doubt′ful·ly,** *adv.* —**doubt′ful·ness,** *n.*

**doubt·ing Thom·as** (tom′əs) a person who doubts everything.

**doubt·less** (dou′tlis) 1 surely; certainly. 2 probably. *adv.*

**dough** (dō) **1** a soft, thick mixture of flour, liquid, and other ingredients for baking: *Bread, pie crust, etc. are made from dough.* **2** any soft, thick mass like this. **3** *Slang.* money. *n.* —**dough′-like′**, *adj.*
☛ *Hom.* DO², DOE.

**dough·nut** (dō′nut′) a small cake, often ring-shaped, fried in deep fat. *n.*

**dough·ty** (dou′tē) brave; valiant; strong: *King Arthur's doughty knights fought valiantly.* *adj.*, **dough·ti·er**, **dough·ti·est.** —**dough′ti·ness**, *n.*

**dough·y** (dō′ē) of or like dough; soft and thick; pale and flabby. *adj.* **dough·i·er**, **dough·i·est.**

**Doug·las fir** (dug′ləs) **1** a very tall evergreen tree of the pine family found in western North America, having long, narrow, hanging cones and flat needles growing singly along the stem: *The Douglas fir occurs in two forms: an inland form having bluish-green needles, that is usually less than 45 metres high; and a coastal form, a huge tree, usually more than 50 metres high and occasionally reaching a height of 90 metres, having bright yellowish-green needles.* **2** the hard, strong wood of this tree. *n.*

**Douk·ho·bor** or **Douk·ho·bour** (dü′kə bôr′) a member of a 200-year-old Christian sect originally from Russia, that traditionally believes that every person knows what is right and must be guided by this knowledge rather than by any outside authority: *Several thousand Doukhobors left Russia in 1898 and settled in western Canada.* *n.*
☛ *Etym.* From a Russian word meaning 'spirit wrestlers'.

**dour** (dür *or* dour) **1** gloomy; sullen: *dour silence.* **2** stern; severe: *a dour look.* **3** stubborn. *adj.* —**dour′ly**, *adv.* —**dour′ness**, *n.*

**douse** (dous) **1** plunge into water or any other liquid. **2** throw water over; drench. **3** put out a light; extinguish: *We doused the candles.* **4** lower or slacken a sail in haste. **5** close a porthole. *v.*, **doused, dous·ing.**

**dove**¹ (duv) **1** any of various species of pigeon, especially any of several of the smaller, wild species. **2** an innocent, gentle, or loving person. *n.*

**dove**² (dōv) a pt. of DIVE. *v.*
☛ *Usage.* See note at DIVE.

**dove·cot** (duv′kot′) DOVECOTE. *n.*

**dove·cote** (duv′kōt′) a small house or shelter for doves or pigeons. *n.*

**dove·tail** (duv′tāl′) **1** a wedge-shaped projection at the end of a piece of wood, metal, etc. that can be fitted into a corresponding opening at the end of another piece to form a joint. **2** the joint formed in this way. See JOINT for picture. **3** fasten, join, or fit together with projections that fit into openings. **4** fit together exactly: *The various bits of evidence dovetailed so completely that the mystery was solved at once.* **1, 2** *n.*, **3, 4** *v.*

**dow·a·ger** (dou′ə jər) **1** a woman who holds some title or property from her dead husband: *The queen and her mother-in-law, the queen dowager, were both present.* **2** *Informal.* a dignified elderly woman. *n.*

**dow·dy** (dou′dē) **1** dressed in a dull or unimaginative way: *a dowdy person.* **2** not stylish; shabby: *The old lady wore a dowdy coat and a shapeless hat.* **3** a woman whose clothes are dowdy. **1, 2** *adj.*, **dow·di·er, dow·di·est; 3** *n.*, *pl.* **dow·dies.** —**dow′di·ly**, *adv.* —**dow′di·ness**, *n.*

**dow·el** (dou′əl) **1** a peg on a piece of wood, metal, etc., made to fit into a corresponding hole on another piece and so form a joint fastening the two pieces together. See JOINT for picture. **2** fasten with dowels.

hat, āge, fär; let, ēqual, tėrm; it, īce
hot, ōpen, ôrder; oil, out; cup, pút, rüle
əbove, takən, pencəl, lemən, circəs
ch, child; ng, long; sh, ship
th, thin; ᴛʜ, then; zh, measure

**1** *n.*, **2** *v.*, **dow·elled** or **dow·eled, dow·el·ling** or **dow·el·ing.**

**dow·er** (dou′ər) **1** a widow's share of her dead husband's property. **2** *Archaic or poetic.* DOWRY (def. 1). **3** a natural gift, talent, or quality; endowment. **4** provide with a dower; endow. **1–3** *n.*, **4** *v.* —**dow′er·less**, *adj.*

**down**¹ (doun) **1** from a higher to a lower place or condition: *The soldiers laid down their arms. They ran down from the top of the hill.* **2** in a lower place or condition: *Down in the valley the fog still lingered.* **3** to or in a place or condition thought of as lower: *He lives in Newfoundland, but goes down to Florida in the winter. He has gone down East.* **4** to a position or condition that is difficult, dangerous, etc.: *The dogs ran the fox down.* **5** from an earlier to a later time or person: *The house was handed down from father to son.* **6** from a larger to a smaller amount, degree, etc.: *everyone from the hotel manager down to the shoeshine boy. The temperature has gone down.* **7** down along, through, or into: *One can ride down a hill, sail down a river, walk down a street.* **8** going or pointed down: *the down escalator.* **9** put down; get down: *She downed the medicine at one swallow. Adolph downed Percy and sat on top of him.* **10** lie down: *Down, Fido!* **11** a downward movement. **12** a period of bad luck or unhappiness: *the ups and downs of life.* **13** actually; really: *Stop talking, and get down to work.* **14** on paper; in writing: *Take down what I say.* **15** when bought: *You can pay part of the price down and the rest later.* **16** sick; ill: *She is down with a cold.* **17** sad; discouraged: *He felt down about his failure.* **18** of a football, no longer in play. **19** in football, a chance to move the ball forward: *In Canadian football a team is allowed three downs in which to move the ball forward ten yards.* **20** behind an opponent by a certain number. **21** of a computer, not working. **1–6, 13–15** *adv.*, **7** *prep.*, **8, 16–18, 20, 21** *adj.*, **9, 10** *v.*, **11, 12, 19** *n.*

**down**² (doun) **1** the short, soft, fluffy feathers beneath the outer feathers of adult birds and forming the plumage of young birds: *Down is used in pillows and as a lightweight insulation for winter clothing, etc.* **2** soft hair or fluff; fuzz: *The down on a boy's chin develops into a beard.* *n.*

**down**³ (doun) Usually, **downs**, *pl.* a stretch of high, rolling, grassy land. *n.*

**down–beat** (doun′bēt′) in music: **1** the first beat in a measure. **2** the downward gesture of the conductor's hand to indicate this beat. *n.*

**down·cast** (doun′kast′) **1** directed downward: *Ashamed of his mistake, he stood with downcast eyes.* **2** dejected; sad; discouraged: *She was downcast by her failure to make the team.* *adj.*

**down·fall** (doun′fol′) **1** a coming to ruin; sudden overthrow of a great person, institution, or nation through a change in fortune: *the downfall of a hero, the downfall of an empire.* **2** a heavy fall of rain or snow. *n.*

**down·fall·en** (doun′fol′ən) fallen; overthrown. *adj.*

**down–filled** (doun′fild′) filled or insulated with down

from birds: *Down-filled pillows are very soft. Down-filled clothing is very light and warm.* *adj.*

**down·grade** (doun′grād′) **1** a downward slope. **2** a going down toward an inferior state or condition: *He's been on the downgrade since he missed that promotion.* **3** lower the status and rate of pay of a job or person: *The position has been downgraded.* **4** think of or refer to in a slighting way; belittle: *Don't downgrade the novel; it was a first attempt.* 1, 2 *n.,* 3, 4 *v.,* **down·grad·ed, down·grad·ing.**

**down·heart·ed** (doun′här′tid) discouraged; dejected; depressed. *adj.* —**down′heart′ed·ly,** *adv.* —**down′heart′ed·ness,** *n.*

**down·hill** (doun′hil′) **1** down the slope of a hill; toward the bottom of a hill: *For the last part of our hike we were going downhill.* **2** sloping or going downward: *a downhill run.* **3** having to do with or referring to skiing down hillsides or mountainsides, as opposed to cross-country. **4** toward a worse condition or state (*used especially in the expression* **go downhill**): *Her business has been going downhill for some time.* **5** *Informal.* proceeding smoothly and without effort; easy: *After we got the members signed up, the rest of the planning was all downhill.* 1, 4 *adv.,* 2, 3, 5 *adj.*

**Down·ing Street** (dou′ning) **1** in London, England, a street where several important offices of the British government are located. **2** the British government.

**down·load** (doun′lōd) deliver (files, programs, etc.) from one computer to another computer via a telecommunications link. *v.*

**down·pour** (doun′pôr′) a heavy rainfall. *n.*

**down·right** (doun′rīt′) **1** thorough; complete: *a downright thief, a downright lie.* **2** thoroughly; completely: *She was downright rude to me.* **3** plain; positive: *Her downright answer left no doubt as to what she thought.* 1, 3 *adj.,* 2 *adv.*

**Down Syndrome** (dounz) a condition of mental retardation accompanied by certain abnormal physical characteristics, such as a broad, short skull, skin folds on the upper eyelids, a thick tongue, and broad hands with short fingers: *Down Syndrome is not inherited, but exists from birth because it is caused by an abnormal development of one of the 46 chromosomes in some or all cells.*

**down·stage** (doun′stāj′) in a theatre, toward or at the front of the stage. *adj., adv.*

**down·stairs** (doun′sterz′) **1** down the stairs: *Juanita slipped and fell downstairs.* **2** on a lower floor: *Look downstairs for my glasses* (*adv.*). *The downstairs rooms are dark* (*adj.*). **3** to a lower floor: *I went downstairs for breakfast.* **4** the lower floor or floors: *The downstairs is usually much warmer.* 1–3 *adv.,* 2 *adj.,* 4 *n.*

**down·stream** (doun′strēm′) **1** in the direction of the current of a stream or river. **2** farther along in the direction of a stream or river: *The sawmill was downstream from the town.* 1 *adv.,* 2 *adj.*

**down time** or **down·time** (doun′tīm′) a time during which the computer is not working. *n.*

**down·town** (doun′toun′) **1** to, toward, or in the lower part of a town. **2** to the main part or business part of a town: *I'm going downtown.* **3** in the main part or business part of a town: *Her office is in downtown Toronto.* **4** the business section or main part of a town. 1, 2 *adv.,* 3 *adj.,* 4 *n.*

**down·trod** (doun′trod′) DOWNTRODDEN. *adj.*

**down·trod·den** (doun′trod′en) **1** tyrannized over; oppressed. **2** trodden down. *adj.*

**down under** the region of Australia, New Zealand, etc.

**down·ward** (doun′wərd) **1** toward a lower place. **2** from an earlier to a later time: *downward through history.* **3** toward a lower or worse condition or state: *There is a downward trend in the economy.* 1, 2 *adv.,* 3 *adj.*

**down·wards** (doun′wərdz) DOWNWARD. *adv.*

**down·y** (dou′nē) **1** of soft feathers or hair: *a downy pillow.* **2** covered with soft feathers or hair: *a downy duckling.* **3** like down; soft; fluffy. *adj.,* **down·i·er, down·i·est.** —**down′i·ness,** *n.*

**downy woodpecker** a small black and white woodpecker with a broad white stripe down the middle of its back.

**dow·ry** (dou′rē) **1** the money, property, etc. that a bride brings to her husband. **2** a natural gift, talent, or quality; endowment from nature: *a dowry of good health and intelligence.* *n., pl.* **dow·ries.** Also, **dower.**

**dowse** (douz) use a DIVINING ROD to locate water, etc. *v.,* **dowsed, dows·ing.** —**dows′er,** *n.*

**doz.** dozen; dozens.

**doze** (dōz) **1** sleep lightly; be half asleep: *I was dozing on the chesterfield when I heard a light knock on the door.* **2** fall into a light sleep (*used with* **off**): *He dozed off during the news broadcast.* **3** a light sleep; a nap. 1, 2 *v.,* **dozed, doz·ing;** 3 *n.* —**doz′er,** *n.*

**do·zen** (duz′ən) a group of 12: *Eggs are sold by the dozen.* *n., pl.* **doz·ens** or **doz·en.**
☛ *Usage.* After a number, the plural **dozen** is used: *Five dozen eggs are too many.*

**doz·enth** (duz′ənth) the twelfth. *adj.*

**do·zer** (dō′zər) *Informal.* BULLDOZER. *n.*

**D.P.** or **DP** displaced person.

**dr.** **1** dram; drams. **2** debtor. **3** drawer. **4** debit.

**Dr.** or **Dr** **1** Doctor. **2** Drive.

**drab** (drab) **1** dull, monotonous; unattractive: *the drab houses of the mining town.* **2** dull brownish-grey. **3** a khaki drill uniform: *The soldiers wore drab on manoeuvres.* 1, 2 *adj.,* **drab·ber, drab·best;** 2, 3 *n.* —**drab′ly,** *adv.* —**drab′ness,** *n.*

**drachm** (dram) See DRAM. *n.*

**drae·ger·man** (drāg′ər mən *or* drā′gər mən) *Cdn.* especially in the Maritimes, a coal miner trained in underground rescue work and the use of special oxygen equipment effective in gas-filled mines. *n., pl.* **drae·ger·men** (-mən).
☛ *Etym.* Named for Alexander B. *Dräger* (1870–1928), a German physicist who invented the equipment used by these rescue workers.

**draft** (draft) **1** a current of air inside a building or other enclosed space. **2** a device for regulating a current of air: *Opening the draft of a furnace makes the fire burn faster.* **3** a plan; sketch. **4** a rough, unpolished version of a piece of writing: *The first draft of an essay is often quite different from the finished work.* **5** make up or prepare a plan, sketch, or rough version of: *to draft new legislation. She drafted the letter to the editor in the bus on* *her way home.* **6** a selection of persons or things from a group for some special purpose. **7** the person or things selected. **8** select from a group for some special purpose, such as for military service or for special duty within the armed forces: *Ten men from the battalion were drafted for guard duty.* **9** *Esp. U.S.* **a** a system for selecting persons for compulsory military service. **b** a group of persons selected in this way. **10** the act of pulling loads. **11** the quantity or thing pulled. **12** used for pulling loads: *Draft horses are bigger and stronger than horses used for riding.* **13** the pulling in of a net to catch fish. **14** the quantity of fish caught in a net at one time. **15** a written order requiring the payment of a stated amount of money, especially a cheque drawn by one branch of a bank on another. **16** a heavy demand or drain on anything: *A long illness is a draft on one's resources.* **17** the depth of water that a ship draws or needs for floating, especially when loaded. **18** the act or an instance of drinking or inhaling: *He emptied the glass at one draft.* **19** the amount drunk or inhaled: *She took in a large draft of fresh air.* **20** the act of drawing beer, ale, etc. from a keg or other container. **21** the amount drawn at one time: *a draft of ale.* **22** drawn from a keg, etc. when ordered: *Some people prefer draft beer to bottled beer.* **23** beer, ale, etc. drawn from a keg, etc. when ordered: *Do they sell draft there?* 1–4, 6, 7, 9–23 *n.*, 5, 8 *v.* Also, **draught.**

**on draft,** of beer, ale, etc., available for drawing directly from a keg, etc. when ordered: *Most taverns have beer on draft.*

☛ *Usage.* **Draft** has become the preferred spelling for all senses, though **draught** is still widely used for such meanings as in *a draught of fish, a ship's draught,* or *beer on draught.*

**draft horse** a large, strong, heavily built horse used for hauling heavy loads, pulling a plough, etc.: *Draft horses are now bred mainly for show.* See HORSE for picture.

**draft·i·ness** (draf′tē nis) a DRAFTY condition. *n.*

**drafts·man** (draft′smən) **1** a person who makes plans or sketches: *A draftsman draws designs or diagrams from which buildings and machines are made.* **2** a person who draws up legal or official documents. **3** an artist who is especially skilled in drawing. *n., pl.* **drafts·men** (-smən) Also, **draughtsman.**

**drafts·man·ship** (draft′smən ship′) the work of a DRAFTSMAN. *n.* Also, **draughtsmanship.**

**draft·y** (draf′tē) having, letting in, or exposed to currents of air: *a drafty room, a drafty window. adj.,* **draft·i·er, draft·i·est.** Also, **draughty.** —**draft′i·ly,** *adv.*

**drag** (drag) **1** pull or move along heavily or slowly; pull or draw along the ground: *A team of horses dragged the big log out of the forest.* **2** go too slowly: *Time drags when you have nothing to do. A piece of music drags if played too slowly.* **3** trail along the ground: *Your scarf is dragging.* **4** pull a net, hook, harrow, etc. over or along for some purpose: *to drag a lake for fish or for a drowned person's body.* **5** a net, hook, etc. used in dragging. **6** the act of dragging. **7** the thing dragged. **8** any person or thing that holds back; an obstruction or hindrance: *outworn ideas that are a drag on progress. A lazy player is a drag on a hockey team.* **9** a low, strong sled for carrying heavy loads; STONEBOAT. **10** a big coach with seats inside and on top. **11** a heavy harrow or other implement drawn over land to level it and break up clods. **12** take part in a DRAG RACE. 1–4, 12 *v.*, **dragged, dragg·ing;** 5–11 *n.*
**drag in,** bring something irrelevant into a discussion: *Whatever we talk about, you drag in hockey.*
**in drag,** of a man, dressed and made up as a woman.

# draft horse 367 drainage

hat, āge, fär; let, ēqual, tėrm; it, īce
hot, ōpen, ôrder; oil, out; cup, pút, rüle
əbove, takən, pencəl, lemən, circəs
ch, child; ng, long; sh, ship
th, thin; ᴛʜ, then; zh, measure

**drag·gle** (drag′əl) **1** make wet or dirty by dragging through mud, water, dust, etc. **2** trail along the ground. **3** follow slowly; lag behind; STRAGGLE. *v.,* **drag·gled, drag·gling.**

**drag·net** (drag′net′) **1** a net pulled over the bottom of a river, pond, etc. or along the ground: *Fish and small birds could be caught in the dragnet.* **2** an extensive search or hunt to catch or round up criminals, etc.: *Twenty of the criminals were arrested in the police dragnet. n.*

**drag·on** (drag′ən) **1** in legend, a huge, fierce animal supposed to look like a snake or lizard with wings and claws: *Some dragons were said to breathe fire.* **2** a fierce, violent person. **3** a very strict and watchful woman; a stern CHAPERONE. **4** any of a number of species of small, brilliantly coloured tree lizard of southern Asia and the East Indies, having winglike membranes. *n.* —**drag′on·like′,** *adj.*

A dragonfly— wingspread about 7 cm

**drag·on·fly** (drag′ən flī′) any of a large group of large, harmless insects having a long, slender body and two pairs of gauzy wings: *Dragonflies dart rapidly about catching flies, mosquitoes, and other insects. n., pl.* **drag·on·flies.**

**dra·goon** (drə gün′) **1** in former times, a soldier who was mounted on a horse and was armed with a heavy musket. **2** a soldier in any of several cavalry regiments: *Most dragoon regiments are now equipped with tanks or other armoured vehicles.* **3** force by violence; bully or oppress: *He was dragooned into signing a false statement.* 1, 2 *n.,* 3 *v.*

**drag race** a contest with motor vehicles to see which can accelerate fastest.

**drain** (drān) **1** draw a liquid off slowly: *A ditch drains water from a swamp.* **2** flow off gradually: *The water drains into a river.* **3** draw water or other liquid from; empty or dry by draining: *They drained the swamp to get more land for crops.* **4** a means, such as a channel or pipe, for carrying off water or other liquid. **5** dry by the flowing off of water: *Set the dishes here to drain.* **6** take away from slowly; use up little by little; deprive: *The long war had drained the country of its young people and its resources.* **7** a slow taking away or withdrawing; a gradual outflow or lessening: *Lack of opportunity at home caused a serious drain of talent to other regions.* **8** anything that causes such an outflow or lessening: *The big car soon became a drain on her budget.* 1–3, 5, 6 *v.,* 4, 7, 8 *n.*

**drain·age** (drā′nij) **1** the act or process of draining; a gradual flowing off: *The drainage of the swamp cleared the area of mosquitoes.* **2** a system of channels or pipes for carrying off water or waste of any kind. **3** what is drained off: *The drainage flows into the river.* **4** the area that is drained. *n.*

**drain·pipe** (drān′pīp′) a pipe for carrying off water or other liquid. *n.*

**drake** (drāk) the adult male duck. *n.*

**dram** (dram) **1** in APOTHECARIES' WEIGHT, a unit equal to 60 grains or ⅛ ounce (about 3.89 g). **2** in AVOIRDUPOIS WEIGHT, a unit equal to 27.34 grains or 1/16 ounce (about 1.77 g). **3** a small drink of alcoholic liquor. *n.* Also, **drachm.**

**dra·ma** (dram′ə *or* drä′mə) **1** a story written to be acted out by actors on a stage; a play such as one sees in a theatre. **2** a series of happenings that seem like those of a play: *The history of Arctic exploration is a great and thrilling drama.* **3** the art of writing, acting, or producing plays; the branch of literature having to do with plays: *She is studying drama.* **4** acting; playing in role: *creative drama.* *n.*

**dra·mat·ic** (drə mat′ik) **1** of or having to do with plays or drama: *dramatic arts.* **2** seeming like a drama or play; full of action or feeling; exciting: *There was a dramatic pause and then she leaped onto the stage.* *adj.*
—**dra·mat′i·cal·ly,** *adv.*

**dra·mat·ics** (drə mat′iks) **1** the art or practice of acting or producing plays (*usually used with a singular verb*): *She is studying dramatics.* **2** exaggerated emotional behaviour or expression: *Don't pay any attention to his dramatics.* *n. pl.*

**dram·a·tist** (dram′ə tist) a writer of plays. *n.*

**dram·a·ti·za·tion** (dram′ə tə zā′shən *or* dram′ə tī za′shən) **1** the act of dramatizing. **2** what is DRAMATIZEd. *n.*

**dram·a·tize** (dram′ə tīz′) **1** make a drama of; arrange in the form of a play: *to dramatize a novel.* **2** show or express in a dramatic way; make exciting and thrilling: *to dramatize a small problem.* *v.*, **dram·a·tized, dram·a·tiz·ing.** —**dram′a·tiz′er,** *n.*

**drank** (drangk) pt. of DRINK: *She drank her milk.* *v.*

**drape** (drāp) **1** cover or hang with cloth falling loosely in graceful folds, especially as a decoration: *The buildings were draped with red, white, and blue bunting.* **2** arrange clothes, hangings, etc. in graceful folds: *The designer draped the robe around the model's shoulders.* **3** fall in graceful folds: *Soft fabrics drape well.* **4** arrangement of cloth in folds: *The bodice of the dress has a soft drape.* **5** the way a garment hangs on the body: *I don't like the drape of the skirt.* **6** stretch out loosely or lazily: *He draped his legs over the arm of the chesterfield.* **7 drapes,** *pl.* large curtains that are made to hang in folds; draperies: *There are drapes on the large windows in the living room.* 1–3, 6 *v.*, **draped, drap·ing;** 4, 5, 7 *n.*

**dra·per·y** (drā′pə rē) **1** clothing or hangings arranged in graceful folds, especially on figures in paintings or sculpture. **2** the graceful arrangement of hangings or clothing. **3** cloth or fabric. **4 draperies,** *pl.* DRAPES: *draperies for a large window.* *n., pl.* **dra·per·ies.**

**dras·tic** (dras′tik) **1** acting with force or violence; forceful and violent: *The general was a drastic man who showed no mercy.* **2** extreme; severe; harsh: *The police took drastic measures to put a stop to the crime wave.* *adj.*
—**dras′ti·cal·ly,** *adv.*

**draught** (draft) See DRAFT. *n., v.* —**draught′er,** *n.*

**draughts** (drafts) *Brit.* the game of CHECKERS. *n. pl.*

**draughts·man** (draft′smən) See DRAFTSMAN. *n., pl.* **draughts·men** (-smən).

**draughts·man·ship** (draft′smən ship′) See DRAFTSMANSHIP. *n.*

**draught·y** (draf′tē) See DRAFTY. *adj.*, **draught·i·er, draught·i·est.**

**draw** (dro) **1** pull; drag: *A horse draws a wagon.* **2** pull out; pull up; pull back: *He drew his hand from his pocket.* **3** bring out; take out; get out: *Draw a pail of water from the well.* **4** take out a pistol, sword, etc. for action. **5** the act of doing this: *quick on the draw.* **6** take; get; receive: *I drew another idea from the story. Vezna draws her pay each Friday.* **7** make; cause; bring: *Your actions draw blame or praise on yourself.* **8** move; come; go: *We drew near the fire to get warm.* **9** attract; cause to come: *A parade draws a crowd.* **10** anything that attracts. **11** make a picture or likeness of with pencil, pen, chalk, crayon, etc.; represent by lines. **12** make pictures or likenesses with pen, pencil, chalk, crayon, etc.; make drawings: *She draws very well for a six-year old.* **13** write out in proper form; frame; draft: *to draw up a deed.* **14** write an order to pay money: *to draw a cheque.* **15** obtain resources or assistance, etc. from: *You can always draw on your savings if you have to. He had a vast store of knowledge to draw on.* **16** make a current of air to carry off smoke: *A chimney draws.* **17** breathe in; inhale; take in: *to draw a breath.* **18** of time, etc., come or go gradually but steadily: *The day drew to a close. Night draws on. Death was drawing nigh her.* **19** in certain games, a tie: *If neither side wins, it is a draw.* **20** make the same score in a game; finish with neither side winning. **21** pull out to make tense; extend completely; stretch: *The men drew the rope taut.* **22** make or become small or smaller; shrink. **23** of a ship or boat, sink to a depth of; need for floating: *A ship draws more water when it is loaded than when it is empty. The big ship draws 8.5 metres of water.* **24** remove the insides of poultry; EVISCERATE. **25** find out by reasoning; infer: *draw a conclusion.* **26** a small land basin into or through which water drains; valley: *The rancher found his strayed cattle grazing in a draw.* **27** lottery: *Olga won a bicycle in a draw run by the club.* 1–4, 6–9, 11–18, 20–25 *v.*, **drew, drawn, draw·ing;** 5, 10, 19, 26, 27 *n.*

**draw a blank,** fail completely to get what one wants: *She tried to get information from their neighbours but drew a blank.*

**draw in,** of evening or night, approach slowly.

**draw out, a** extend too much; prolong: *Don't draw out the story so much. The movie was long and drawn out.* **b** persuade to talk; get to respond freely: *We tried to draw him out because we knew he was just shy.*

**draw the line,** set a limit, especially for behaviour: *She doesn't know where to draw the line in playing pranks.*

**draw up, a** arrange in order: *to draw up a squad on the parade square.* **b** write out in proper form: *The will was drawn up by a lawyer.* **c** come or bring to a stop: *A taxi drew up at the entrance.*

**draw·back** (dro′bak′) something unfavourable or unpleasant; something that lessens satisfaction or success; a disadvantage or hindrance: *Our trip was interesting but the rainy weather was a drawback. The plan has some serious drawbacks and will have to be revised.* *n.*

**draw·bridge** (dro′brij′) a bridge that can be wholly or partly lifted, lowered, or moved to one side: *In old castles drawbridges were lifted to prevent enemies from entering. A drawbridge over a river is lifted to let boats pass.* See CASTLE for picture. *n.*

**draw·er** (dro′ər) **1** a person who draws liquor, as at a bar. **2** DRAFTSMAN (def. 3). **3** a person who writes an order to pay money.  **4** any person or thing that draws.  **5** a box built to slide in and out of a table, dresser, desk, etc.: *He kept his shirts in a drawer in the dresser.*  **6 drawers,** *pl.* an undergarment for the lower part of the body, fitting around the waist and having long or short legs; underpants.  *n.*

**draw·ing** (drō′ing)  **1** the art or act of making a picture or design with lines drawn on a surface: *Drawing is usually done with a pencil, pen, chalk, or crayon.*  **2** a picture or design made in this way: *I like her drawings better than her paintings.*  **3** ppr. of DRAW. 1, 2 *n.*, 3 *v.*

**drawing board**  **1** a board used as a support for drawing or drafting on paper.  **2** the planning stage: *The new fighter plane is still on the drawing board. The scheme failed completely and they were forced to go back to the drawing board.*

**drawing room**  **1** a room for receiving or entertaining guests; parlour.  **2** a private compartment in a passenger car of a train, including beds for one or more persons, toilet, etc., and often specially made up to order for a person or group.

**drawl** (drol)  **1** talk in a slow way, making the vowels of words very long: *He drawled a lazy answer.*  **2** a way of speaking in which the vowels of words are made long: *English speakers in some regions speak with a drawl.*  1 *v.*, 2 *n.*  —**drawl′er,** *n.*

**drawn** (dron)  pp. of DRAW: *That old horse has drawn many loads.*  *v.*

**dray** (drā)  **1** a low, strong cart for hauling heavy loads.  **2** transport or carry on a cart.  1 *n.*, 2 *v.*

**dread** (dred)  **1** look forward to with fear or extreme uneasiness or reluctance: *He dreaded the long walk back home in the dark. She dreaded the interview.*  **2** fear, especially of something that will or may happen: *The old woman lived in dread of winter.*  **3** a person or thing inspiring fear.  **4** dreaded; dreadful: *The dread tyrant ruled without mercy.*  **5** held in awe; awe-inspiring.  1 *v.*, 2, 3 *n.*, 4, 5 *adj.*

**dread·ful** (dred′fəl)  **1** causing DREAD (def. 2); terrible or awe-inspiring: *The dragon was a dreadful creature.*  **2** *Informal.* very bad; very unpleasant: *I have a dreadful cold.*  *adj.*  —**dread′ful·ness,** *n.*

**dread·ful·ly** (dred′fə lē)  **1** in a DREADFUL (def. 1) manner.  **2** *Informal.* very; exceedingly: *He was dreadfully upset.*  *adv.*

**dread·nought** or **dread·naught** (dred′nôt′)  a big, powerful battleship with heavy armour and large guns: *Dreadnoughts are no longer in use.*  *n.*

**dream** (drēm)  **1** something thought, felt, seen, or heard during sleep.  **2** something unreal, like a dream: *The girl had dreams of being a heroine.*  **3** the state in which a person has dreams.  **4** have a dream or dreams: *He dreamed he was a Mountie.*  **5** have daydreams: *The girl dreamed of being a famous scientist.*  **6** think of something as possible; suppose in a vague way; imagine: *We never dreamed there would be rain today.*  **7** spend in dreaming (usually used with **away**): *He dreamed the afternoon away.*  **8** something having great beauty or charm.  1–3, 8 *n.*, 4–7 *v.*, **dreamed** or **dreamt, dream·ing.**  —**dream′less,** *adj.*  —**dream′like′,** *adj.*

**dream of,**  (usually negative) consider: *I wouldn't dream of hurting an animal.*

**dream up,** *Informal.* devise; conceive an idea, invention, etc. in the mind; think up: *She was always dreaming up fanciful machines.*

**dream·er** (drē′mər)  **1** a person who has dreams.

**drawing** 369 **dress**

hat, āge, fär; let, ēqual, tėrm; it, īce  
hot, ōpen, ôrder; oil, out; cup, pu̇t, rüle  
əbove, takən, pencəl, lemən, circəs  
ch, child; ng, long; sh, ship  
th, thin; ᴛʜ, then; zh, measure

**2** a person whose ideas do not fit real conditions; impractical person.  *n.*

**dream·land** (drēm′land′)  **1** a place where a person seems to be when he or she is dreaming.  **2** a beautiful and desirable place.  **3** an ideal place existing only in the imagination.  **4** sleep.  *n.*

**in dreamland,**  asleep.

**dreamt** (dremt)  a pt. and a pp. of DREAM.  *v.*

**dream·y** (drē′mē)  **1** like something in a dream; vague; dim: *a dreamy recollection.*  **2** full of dreams: *a dreamy sleep.*  **3** fond of thinking about pleasant things that are unreal; impractical: *a dreamy person.*  **4** soft and soothing: *dreamy songs.*  **5** *Informal.* wonderful; exciting; attractive.  *adj.*, **dream·i·er, dream·i·est.**  —**dream′i·ly,** *adv.*  —**dream′i·ness,** *n.*

**drear·y** (drē′rē)  **1** dull; gloomy; cheerless; depressing.  **2** sad; sorrowful.  **3** uninteresting; boring: *We heard a dreary speech last Tuesday.*  *adj.*, **drear·i·er, drear·i·est.**  —**drear′i·ly,** *adv.*  —**drear′i·ness,** *n.*

**dredge¹** (drej)  **1** a machine with a scoop or series of buckets for removing mud, sand, or other materials from the bottom of a river, harbour, etc.  **2** clean out or deepen a channel, harbour, etc. with a dredge.  **3** an apparatus with a net, used for gathering oysters, etc.: *A dredge is dragged along the bottom of the sea.*  **4** bring up or gather with a dredge.  1, 3 *n.*, 2, 4 *v.*, **dredged, dredg·ing.**  —**dredg′er,** *n.*

**dredge²** (drej)  sprinkle: *to dredge meat with flour.*  *v.*, **dredged, dredg·ing.**  —**dredg′er,** *n.*

**dregs** (dregz)  **1** the solid bits of matter that settle to the bottom of a liquid: *After pouring the tea, she rinsed the dregs out of the teapot.*  **2** the most worthless part: *the dregs of society.*  *n. pl.*

**drench** (drench)  **1** wet thoroughly; soak: *We were drenched in the cloudburst.*  **2** a thorough wetting; soaking.  1 *v.*, 2 *n.*

**dress** (dres)  **1** an outer garment consisting of a bodice and skirt, usually in one piece, worn by women and girls.  **2** of or for a dress: *dress fabric.*  **3** an outer covering or appearance: *The trees were in their summer dress.*  **4** clothes: *They care very little about dress.*  **5** put clothes on.  **6** wear clothes properly and attractively: *Her sister really knows how to dress.*  **7** formal clothes.  **8** put formal clothes on: *They always dress for dinner.*  **9** of or characterized by formal dress: *It was a dress occasion.*  **10** worn on formal occasions: *a dress suit.*  **11** clothes suitable for a characteristic of a certain time or occasion: *formal dress, casual dress. The play was performed in modern dress.*  **12** decorate; trim; adorn: *The store windows were dressed for Christmas.*  **13** make ready for use; prepare: *A butcher dresses a chicken by pulling out the feathers, cutting off the head and feet, and taking out the insides.*  **14** arrange the hair by curling, combing, etc.: *She just had her hair dressed.*  **15** put a medicine, bandage, etc. on a wound or sore: *The nurse dressed the wound every day.*  **16** form in a straight line: *The captain ordered the soldiers to dress their ranks.*  **17** smooth;

finish: *to dress leather.* 1–4, 7, 9–11 *n.*, 5, 6, 8, 12–17 *v.*, **dressed** or **drest, dress·ing.**

**dress·er**[1] (dres′ər) 1 a person who dresses another person, especially one whose work is helping actors or entertainers dress for their performances. 2 a person whose work is decorating and arranging displays in store windows. 3 a person who dresses attractively or in a particular way: *He's a smart dresser.* 4 a tool or machine to prepare things for use. *n.*

**dress·er**[2] (dres′ər) 1 a piece of furniture with drawers for clothes and, usually, a mirror. 2 a piece of furniture with shelves for dishes. *n.*

**dress·ing** (dres′ing) 1 what is put on or in something to get it ready for use. 2 a sauce for salads, fish, meat, etc. 3 a stuffing of bread crumbs, seasoning, etc. for chicken, turkey, etc. 4 the medicine, bandage, etc. put on a wound or sore. 5 fertilizer. 6 formation: *The soldiers are noted for their dressing on parade.* 7 preparations before and during getting dressed: *She took care with her dressing for the dance.* 8 preparation for display: *the dressing of a store window.* 9 ppr. of DRESS. 1–8 *n.*, 9 *v.*

**dress·ing–down** (dres′ing doun′) *Informal.* a severe scolding. *n.*

**dressing gown** a loose robe worn while dressing or resting.

**dressing room** a room for getting dressed in, especially a room behind the stage in a theatre, in which actors dress.

**dressing table** a table with a mirror, at which one can sit to put on cosmetics, brush or arrange the hair, etc.

**dress·mak·er** (dres′mā′kər) 1 a person whose work is making dresses, etc. 2 of women's clothing, having soft or flowing lines and fine decoration: *a dressmaker suit.* Compare with TAILORED. 1 *n.*, 2 *adj.*

**dress·mak·ing** (dres′mā′king) the act or occupation of making dresses, etc. *n.*

**dress parade** a formal military parade in dress uniform.

**dress rehearsal** a rehearsal of a play with costumes, scenery and lighting just as for a regular performance.

**dress·y** (dres′ē) 1 stylish and formal; not casual: *That outfit is too dressy for a wiener roast.* 2 fond of wearing showy clothes. *adj.*, **dress·i·er, dress·i·est.** —**dress′i·ness,** *n.*

**drest** (drest) a pt. and pp. of DRESS. *v.*

**drew** (drü) pt. of DRAW: *He drew a picture.* *v.*

**drib·ble** (drib′əl) 1 flow or let flow in drops, small amounts, etc.; trickle: *Gasoline dribbled from the leak in the tank.* 2 a dropping; dripping; trickle: *All we could get out of the hose was a dribble.* 3 let saliva run from the mouth: *The baby dribbles on his bib.* 4 a very light rain. 5 move a ball along by bouncing it or giving it short kicks. 6 the act of moving a ball in this way. 1, 3, 5 *v.*, **drib·bled, drib·bling;** 2, 4, 6 *n.* —**drib′bler,** *n.* Compare with DRIVEL (defs. 1–3), DROOL.

**drib·let** (drib′lit) a small amount: *He paid off the debt in driblets, a dollar or two a week.* *n.*

**dried** (drīd) pt. and pp. of DRY: *I dried my hands. This bread has been dried in the oven.* *v.*

**dri·er** (drī′ər) 1 the comparative of DRY. 2 See DRYER. 1 *adj.*, 2 *n.*

**drift** (drift) 1 carry or be carried along by currents of water or air: *The wind drifted the boat onto the rocks. A raft drifts if it is not steered.* 2 go along without knowing or caring where one is going: *Some people have a purpose in life; others just drift.* 3 a drifting: *the drift of an iceberg.* 4 the direction of drifting: *The drift of the current is to the south.* 5 a tendency; trend: *The drift of opinion was against war.* 6 the meaning; direction of thought; *I caught the drift of her speech, but I couldn't understand all the details.* 7 snow, sand, etc. heaped up by the wind. 8 heap or be heaped up by the wind: *The wind is so strong it's drifting the snow. The snow is drifting badly.* 9 a slow current of water, especially a slow ocean current. 10 the distance that a ship or aircraft is off its course because of currents. 11 the sand, gravel, rocks, etc. moved from one place and left in another by a river, glacier, etc. 12 an almost horizontal passageway in a mine along a vein of ore, coal, etc. 1, 2, 8 *v.*, 3–7, 9–12 *n.* —**drift′er,** *n.*

**drift–ice** (drift′īs′) *Cdn.* small masses of ice drifting in the sea. *n.*

**drift·wood** (drift′twud′) wood drifting in water or washed ashore. *n.*

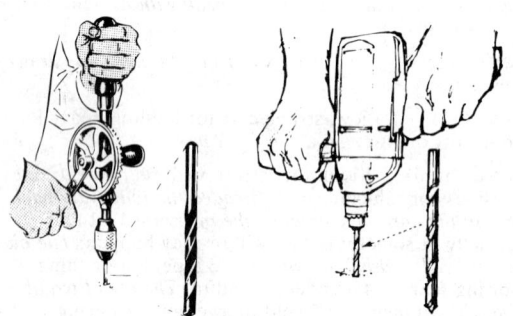

A hand drill and an electric drill. The cutting part, called the bit, works like an auger.

**drill**[1] (dril) 1 a tool or machine for boring holes. 2 bore a hole in; pierce with a drill. 3 a snail that bores into and destroys oysters. 4 the process of teaching or training by having the learners do a thing over and over again: *The teacher gave the class plenty of drill in arithmetic.* 5 teach or train in this way. 6 be taught or trained in this way. 7 group instruction and training in physical exercises or in marching, handling a gun, and other duties of soldiers. 8 do or cause to do physical or military exercises. 1, 3, 4, 7 *n.*, 2, 5, 6, 8 *v.* —**drill′er,** *n.*

**drill**[2] (dril) a machine for planting seeds in rows: *The drill makes a small furrow, drops the seeds, and then covers the furrow.* *n.*

**drill**[3] (dril) a strong, twilled cotton cloth similar to denim, used for overalls, uniforms, ticking, etc. *n.*

**drill**[4] (dril) a BABOON of Western Africa, closely related to the MANDRILL but smaller. *n.*

**drill·mas·ter** (dril′mas′tər) an instructor who teaches by drilling, especially one who drills soldiers in marching, handling guns, etc. *n.*

**dri·ly** (drī′lē) See DRYLY. *adv.*

**drink** (dringk) 1 swallow liquid. 2 any liquid swallowed or to be swallowed. 3 swallow the liquid contents of: *She drank the whole glass.* 4 take and hold;

absorb: *The dry ground drank up the rain.*   **5** alcoholic liquor.   **6** drink liquor: *Does he drink?*   **7** excessive drinking of liquor.   **8** drink liquor to excess.   **9** drink in honour of: *They drank his health.*   1, 3, 4, 6, 8, 9 *v.*, **drank, drunk, drink•ing;**   2, 5, 7 *n.*   —**drink′less,** *adj.*

**drink in,**   take in eagerly with the senses: *Our ears had drunk in the music.*

**drink to,**   drink in honour of; drink with good wishes for.

**drink•a•ble** (dring′kə bəl)   fit to drink.   *adj.*

**drink•er** (dring′kər)   a person who drinks, especially one who drinks liquor as a habit or to excess.   *n.*

**drip** (drip)   **1** fall or let fall in drops: *Rain drips from an umbrella.*   **2** a falling in drops.   **3** the liquid that falls in drops.   **4** be so wet that drops fall: *Her forehead was dripping with perspiration.*   **5** a part that projects to keep water off the parts below.   1, 4 *v.*, **dripped** or **dript, drip•ping;**   2, 3, 5 *n.*

**drip–dry** (drip′drī′)   **1** made to be dried by being let drip after washing, then needing little or no ironing: *drip-dry curtains.*   **2** let drip until dry.   1 *adj.*, 2 *v.*, **drip-dried, drip-dry•ing.**

**drip•ping** (drip′ing)   **1** the melted fat and juices that drip down from meat while roasting: *Some people like beef dripping spread on bread.*   **2** ppr. of DRIP.   1 *n.*, 2 *v.*

**dript** (dript)   a pt. and a pp. of DRIP.   *v.*

**drive** (drīv)   **1** make go; cause to move: *Drive the dog away.*   **2** make go by hitting; propel: *to drive a spike.*   **3** force into or out of some place, condition, act, etc.: *That dog's barking drives me crazy. Hunger drove him to steal.*   **4** manage; operate; guide by steering: *drive a car, drive a motorboat, drive a supertanker.*   **5** go or travel in a car or other vehicle: *We drove out into the country for the afternoon.*   **6** travel over or across in a car, etc.; cover: *We drove 300 kilometres without stopping.*   **7** a trip, usually short, taken in a car or other vehicle: *a Sunday drive.*   **8** carry or transport in a car or other vehicle: *The truck driver drove the girls all the way to Toronto.*   **9** a road (*used mainly in street names*): *Winona Drive.*   **10** a DRIVEWAY (def. 1): *He left his car in the drive all night.*   **11** capacity for hard work; forceful action; energy: *Her success was largely due to her great drive.*   **12** bring about or obtain by being clever, shrewd, forceful, etc.: *He drove a good bargain when he bought his bicycle.*   **13** an impelling force; pressure: *The craving for approval is a strong drive in people.*   **14** a special effort of a group for some purpose: *The town had a drive to get money for charity.*   **15** work hard or compel to work hard: *The men said their boss drove them too harshly.*   **16** dash or rush with force: *The ship drove on the rocks.*   **17** hit very hard and fast: *to drive a golf ball.*   **18** a very hard, fast hit.   **19** aim; strike.   **20** a military attack, often a large-scale, forceful attack.   **21** the moving overland of a herd of cattle by cowboys.   **22** *Cdn.*   the floating of a great many logs down a river: *Drives are held when the ice melts in spring.*   **23** *Cdn.*   a great many logs floating down a river.   **24** *Cdn.*   move logs in large numbers down a river.   **25** DISC DRIVE.   1–6, 8, 12, 15–17, 19, 24 *v.*, **drove, driv•en, driv•ing;**   7, 9–11, 13, 14, 18, 20–23, 25 *n.*

**drive at,**   mean; intend: *I didn't understand what she was driving at.*

**let drive,**   aim; strike: *The boxer let drive a left to the jaw.*

**drive–in** (drīv′in′)   a place where customers may make purchases, eat, attend movies, etc. while seated in their cars.   *n.*

**driv•el** (driv′əl)   **1** let saliva run from the mouth.   **2** saliva running from the mouth.   **3** flow like saliva

---

**drinkable**   371   **drone**

hat, āge, fär; let, ēqual, tėrm; it, īce
hot, ōpen, ôrder; oil, out; cup, pùt, rüle
əbove, takən, pencəl, lemən, circəs
ch, child; ng, long; sh, ship
th, thin; ᴛʜ, then; zh, measure

running from the mouth.   **4** talk or say in a stupid, foolish manner; talk silly nonsense.   **5** stupid, foolish talk; silly nonsense.   **6** waste time, energy, etc. in a stupid, foolish way.   1, 3 4, 6 *v.*, **driv•elled** or **driv•eled, driv•el•ling** or **driv•el•ing;**   2, 5 *n.*   Compare with DRIBBLE (def. 3), DROOL.

**driv•el•ler** or **driv•el•er** (driv′ə lər)   a person who DRIVELS (defs. 4, 6).   *n.*

**driv•en** (driv′ən)   **1** pp. of DRIVE: *Mrs. Yousif has just driven past.*   **2** carried along and gathered into heaps by the wind; drifted.   1 *v.*, 2 *adj.*

**driv•er** (drī′vər)   **1** a person or thing that drives.   **2** a person who directs the movement of an engine, automobile, horses, etc.   **3** a person who makes the people under him or her work very hard.   **4** a golf club with a large wooden head, used in hitting the ball from the tee.   *n.*

**drive shaft**   a shaft that transmits power or motion, such as the shaft in a motor vehicle that connects the transmission to the axle of the driving wheels.   See DIFFERENTIAL and UNIVERSAL JOINT for pictures.

**drive•way** (drīv′wā′)   **1** a private road: *A driveway usually leads from a house to the public street or road.*   **2** *Cdn.*   a road, usually one that is lined with trees and lawns.   *n.*

**driz•zle** (driz′əl)   **1** rain in very small drops resembling mist.   **2** very small drops of rain resembling mist.   1 *v.*, **driz•zled, driz•zling;**   2 *n.*

**driz•zly** (driz′lē)   drizzling.   *adj.*

**DRO**   deputy returning officer.

**drogue** (drōg)   **1** a device shaped like a large funnel at the end of a hose, used to refuel planes in flight: *The pilot of the plane being refuelled guides the nose of her plane into the drogue.*   **2** a small parachute that springs open when a parachute pack is opened and helps to draw out the main parachute.   **3** a similar device attached to a space capsule, etc. to stabilize it or slow it down.   *n.*

**droll** (drōl)   amusingly odd; humorously quaint; laughable: *We smiled at the monkey's droll tricks.*   *adj.*

**droll•er•y** (drō′lə rē)   **1** something odd and amusing; a laughable trick.   **2** quaint humour.   **3** jesting.   *n., pl.* **droll•er•ies.**

**drom•e•dar•y** (drom′ə der′ē).   a swift camel raised for racing and riding, especially the one-humped Arabian camel.   See CAMEL for picture.   *n., pl.* **drom•e•dar•ies.**

**drone**[1] (drōn)   **1** the male of a bee, especially the honeybee, that has no sting and does not gather honey.   **2** a person not willing to work; idler; loafer.   **3** a pilotless aircraft, missile, or vessel directed by remote control.   **4** spend time idly; loaf.   1–3 *n.*, 4 *v.*, **dron•ed, dron•ing.**

**drone**[2] (drōn)   **1** make a deep, continuous, humming sound: *Bees droned among the flowers.*   **2** such a sound: *the drone of airplane motors.*   **3** talk or say in a monotonous voice: *to drone a poem.*   **4** any of the pipes on a bagpipe that sound a continuous tone.   1, 3 *v.*, **droned, dron•ing;**   2, 4 *n.*

**drool** (drül) **1** let saliva run from the mouth as a teething baby does. **2** saliva running from the mouth. **3** *Informal.* make an excessive show of pleasure or enthusiasm (*over*): *drooling over the rock group's latest recording.* 1, 3 *v.*, 2 *n.* Compare with DRIBBLE (def. 3), DRIVEL (defs. 1–3).

**droop** (drüp) **1** hang down; bend down: *These flowers will soon droop if they are not put in water.* **2** a bending position; the act or condition of hanging down: *The droop of the branches brought them within our grasp.* **3** become weak; lose strength and energy: *The boy's spirit drooped when he failed to make the team. The patient drooped as her illness got worse.* **4** become discouraged or depressed; be sad and gloomy: *She's been drooping around the house all day.* 1, 3, 4 *v.*, 2 *n.* —**droop′ing·ly**, *adv.*

**drop** (drop) **1** a small, roundish mass of liquid, usually formed in falling: *a drop of rain, a drop of blood.* **2** something small and roundish, resembling such a mass: *a cough drop, a lemon drop. Some earrings are called drops.* **3** fall or let fall in small masses of liquid: *Rain drops from the sky. Penina had to drop some medicine into her sore eye.* **4** a very small amount of liquid: *Drink a drop of this.* **5** a very small amount of anything: *a drop of kindness.* **6** a sudden fall or decrease: *a drop in temperature, a drop in prices.* **7** the distance down; the length of fall: *a drop of ten metres.* **8** take a sudden fall or decrease: *The price of tomatoes always drops in August.* **9** let fall: *He dropped the package.* **10** cause to fall: *The boxer dropped his opponent with one hard punch.* **11** fall dead or wounded: *The soldier dropped when the bullet hit him.* **12** fall from exhaustion: *I'm so tired, I could drop.* **13** cause to fall dead or wounded; kill: *The hunter dropped the deer with one shot.* **14** something arranged to fall or let fall: *A letter drop is a slot, usually with a hinged cover.* **15** go lower; sink: *The sun dropped below the horizon.* **16** make lower; cause to become lower: *Drop your voice.* **17** pass into a less active or worse condition: *She finally dropped into a coma.* **18** let go; dismiss: *Members who do not pay will be dropped from the club.* **19** leave out; omit: *Drop the 'e' in 'drive' before adding 'ing'. Don't drop your h's.* **20** stop; end; close: *They agreed to let the quarrel drop.* **21** give or express casually: *In saying good-bye, she dropped the hint that she wanted to go, too.* **22** go along gently with the current or tide: *The raft dropped down the river.* **23** set down from a ship, automobile, carriage, etc.: *The taxi driver dropped her passengers at the corner.* **24 drops**, *pl.* liquid medicine given in drops. 1, 2, 4–7, 14, 24 *n.*, 3, 8–13, 15–23 *v.*, **dropped** or **dropt, drop·ping**.
**drop behind** or **back**, lag behind; fall behind: *He started out strongly in the race but soon dropped back to fourth place.*
**drop by, in,** or **over,** come (to visit): *Drop over to our house tonight.*
**drop in the bucket** or **ocean,** a very small amount compared with the rest.
**drop off, a** go to sleep. **b** become less; decrease: *Sales of chewing gum have dropped off.* **c** stop: *I think I'll drop off at the grocery store.*
**drop out,** leave school, a training program, etc. without completing the course.

**drop–forge** (drop′fôrj′) beat hot metal into shape with a very heavy hammer or weight. *v.*, **drop-forged, drop-forg·ing.**

**drop–in centre** (drop′in) an informal place for people to come to for help, recreation, or companionship: *Drop-in centres are often run by a church or social service organization.*

**drop kick** a kick given to a football as it touches the ground after being dropped from the hands.

**drop leaf** a hinged section of the surface of a table. Such a leaf can be folded down when not in use.

**drop–leaf** (drop′lēf′) having a drop leaf: *a drop-leaf dining table.* *adj.*

**drop·let** (drop′lit) a tiny drop. *n.*

**drop–off** (drop′of′) **1** a lessening or decline: *a drop-off in sales.* **2** a sudden, sharp slope. *n.*

**drop·out** (drop′out′) **1** a person who leaves school, a training program, etc. without completing the course. **2** the act or fact of dropping out. *n.*

**drop pass** in hockey, a type of passing play in which the player in possession of the puck draws opposing players out of position and drops the puck back for a team-mate.

**drop·per** (drop′ər) a small glass tube with a hollow rubber cap at one end and a small opening at the other end from which a liquid can be made to fall in drops. *n.*

**drop·pings** (drop′ingz) **1** what is dropped. **2** the dung of animals and birds. *n. pl.*

**drop·si·cal** (drop′sə kəl) **1** of or like DROPSY. **2** having DROPSY. *adj.*

**drop·sy** (drop′sē) an abnormal accumulation of watery fluid in certain tissues or cavities of the body; EDEMA. *n.*

**dropt** (dropt) a pt. and a pp. of DROP. *v.*

**drosh·ky** or **dros·ky** (drosh′kē) a low, open, four-wheeled Russian carriage. *n., pl.* **drosh·kies** or **dros·kies.**

**dro·soph·i·la** (drō sof′ə lə) any of a closely related group of flies whose larvae feed on fruit and decaying plants; the fruit fly. *n., pl.* **dro·soph·i·lae** (-lē′ or -lī).

**dross** (dros) **1** the water or scum that comes to the surface of melting metals; slag. **2** waste material; rubbish. *n.*

**drought** (drout) **1** a long period of dry weather; continued lack of rain. **2** a prolonged shortage of anything. *n.*

**drought·y** (drou′tē) showing or suffering from DROUGHT. *adj.*

**drove**[1] (drōv) pt. of DRIVE. *v.*

**drove**[2] (drōv) **1** a group of cattle, sheep, pigs, etc. moving or driven along together; a herd or flock: *The rancher sent a drove of cattle to market.* **2** many people moving along together; a crowd. *n.*

**dro·ver** (drō′vər) **1** a person who drives cattle, sheep, pigs, etc. to market. **2** a dealer in cattle. *n.*

**drown** (droun) **1** die under water or some other liquid because of lack of air to breathe. **2** kill by keeping under water or some other liquid. **3** cover with water; flood. **4** be stronger or louder than; keep from being heard (*usually used with* **out**): *The boat's whistle drowned out what she was trying to tell us.* **5** get rid of: *He tried to drown his sorrow in excitement.* *v.*

**drowse** (drouz) **1** be sleepy; be half asleep; doze: *He's drowsing in the hammock.* **2** make sleepy. **3** pass time in drowsing (*used with* **away**): *She drowsed the day away.*

**4** the state of being half asleep; sleepiness. *1–3 v.*, **drowsed, drows·ing;** *4 n.*

**drow·sy** (drou′zē) **1** half asleep; sleepy. **2** causing sleepiness or half sleep; lulling: *It was a warm, quiet, drowsy afternoon.* **3** caused by sleepiness. *adj.*, **drow·si·er, drow·si·est.** —**drow′si·ly,** *adv.* —**drow′si·ness,** *n.*

**drub** (drub) **1** beat with a stick; thrash; whip soundly. **2** defeat by a large margin in a fight, game, contest, etc. *v.*, **drubbed, drub·bing.** —**drub′ber,** *n.*

**drub·bing** (drub′ing) **1** a beating. **2** a thorough defeat. **3** ppr. of DRUB. *1, 2 n., 3 v.*

**drudge** (druj) **1** a person who does hard, tiresome, or disagreeable work. **2** do hard, tiresome, or disagreeable work. *1 n., 2 v.*, **drudged, drudg·ing.**

**drudg·er·y** (druj′ə rē) hard, uninteresting, or disagreeable work. *n., pl.* **drudg·er·ies.**

**drug** (drug) **1** a substance (other than food) that, when taken into the body, produces a change in functions of the body; a substance used as a medicine: *Acetaminophen and antibiotics are drugs.* **2** a substance that brings drowsiness or sleep, or lessens pain by dulling the nerves; narcotic: *Opium is a habit-forming drug.* **3** give drugs to, particularly drugs that are harmful or cause sleep: *The witch drugged the princess.* **4** put a harmful or poisonous drug in food or drink: *The spy drugged the soldier's drink.* **5** affect or overcome the body or senses in a way not natural: *The wine drugged her.* *1, 2 n., 3–5 v.*, **drugged, drug·ging.** —**drug′less,** *adj.*
**drug on the market,** an article that is too abundant, is no longer in demand, or has too slow a sale.

**drug·gist** (drug′ist) **1** a person who sells drugs, medicines, etc. **2** a person licensed to fill prescriptions; a PHARMACIST. *n.*

**drug·store** (drug′stôr′) a store where drugs and other medicines are sold: *A drugstore often sells soft drinks, cosmetics, magazines, etc. as well as drugs.* *n.*

**drum** (drum) **1** a musical instrument that makes a sound when it is beaten, tapped, or brushed: *A drum is usually a hollow cylinder with a covering stretched tightly over each end.* **2** the sound made when a drum is struck; any sound like this. **3** beat or play a drum; make a sound like this. **4** beat, tap, or strike again and again: *Stop drumming on the table with your fingers.* **5** force into one's mind by repeating over and over: *Algebra had to be drummed into me because I didn't understand it.* **6** anything shaped somewhat like a drum. **7** the part around which something is wound in a machine. **8** a drum-shaped container to hold oil, food, etc. **9** eardrum. **10** the hollow part of the middle ear. *1, 2, 6–10 n., 3–5 v.*, **drummed, drum·ming.** —**drum′like′,** *adj.*
**drum out of,** send away from in disgrace.
**drum up, a** call together: *We could not drum up enough players for our game.* **b** get by asking again and again: *to drum up support for a project.*

**drum·head** (drum′hed′) the parchment or membrane stretched tightly over the end of a drum. *n.*

**drumhead court–martial** a court-martial on the battlefield or while troops are moving, held in order to try offenders without delay.

**drum·lin** (drum′lən) a ridge or oval hill formed by deposit from a glacier. *n.*

**drum major** the leader or director of a marching band.

**drowsy**     373     **dry battery**

hat, āge, fär; let, ēqual, tėrm; it, īce
hot, ōpen, ôrder; oil, out; cup, pút, rüle
əbove, takən, pencəl, lemən, circəs
ch, child; ng, long; sh, ship
th, thin; ᴛʜ, then; zh, measure

**drum majorette** a girl who accompanies a marching band, twirling a BATON (def. 4).

**drum·mer** (drum′ər) **1** a person who plays a drum, especially a skilled player. **2** *Informal.* a travelling salesman. *n.*

**drum·stick** (drum′stik′) **1** a stick for beating a drum. **2** the lower, meaty part of the leg of a cooked chicken, turkey, or other edible bird. *n.*

**drunk** (drungk) **1** overcome by alcoholic liquor; intoxicated. **2** *Informal.* a person who is often drunk; drunkard. **3** *Informal.* a spell of drinking liquor; drinking spree: *a three-day drunk.* **4** very much excited or affected: *drunk with success.* **5** pp. of DRINK: *He had drunk all the milk.* *1, 4 adj., 2, 3 n., 5 v.*
☛ *Usage.* **drunk,** DRUNKEN. When used as an adjective, the form is usually **drunk** after a verb and **drunken** before a noun: *The man was drunk. The drunken man lurched against the wall.*

**drunk·ard** (drung′kərd) a person who is often drunk; a person who frequently drinks too much liquor. *n.*

**drunk·en** (drung′kən) **1** DRUNK (def. 1). **2** caused by or resulting from being drunk: *a drunken quarrel, drunken words.* **3** often drinking too much liquor. *adj.* —**drunk′en·ly,** *adv.* —**drunk′en·ness,** *n.*
☛ *Usage.* See note at DRUNK.

**drupe** (drüp) a soft, fleshy fruit having a thin, skinlike covering and, in the centre, a hard pit or stone containing the seed: *Cherries and peaches are drupes.* *n.*

**drupe·let** (drü′plit) a small DRUPE: *A raspberry or blackberry is a mass of drupelets.* *n.*

**dry** (drī) **1** not wet; not moist: *Dust is dry. This bread is dry.* **2** make or become dry: *He was drying dishes. The towels soon dried in the breeze.* **3** having little or no rain: *a dry climate.* **4** not giving milk: *That cow has been dry for a month.* **5** containing no water or other liquid: *The kettle is dry.* **6** not shedding tears or accompanied by tears: *a dry sob. Her eyes were dry.* **7** wanting a drink; thirsty. **8** not liquid; solid: *dry measure, on dry land.* **9** apparently matter-of-fact but actually ironic: *His dry humour does not seem intentional.* **10** not interesting; dull: *a dry speech.* **11** without butter: *dry toast.* **12** free from sweetness or fruity flavour: *dry wine.* **13** *Informal.* having or favouring laws against making and selling alcoholic drinks: *a dry township.* **14** *Informal.* a person who favours laws against making and selling alcoholic drinks. *1, 3–13 adj.*, **dri·er, dri·est;** *2 v.*, **dried, dry·ing;** *14 n., pl.* **drys.**
**dry up, a** make or become completely dry: *The creek dried up last summer.* **b** *Informal.* stop talking: *Why don't you dry up?*

**dry battery** **1** a set of DRY CELLS connected to produce electric current. **2** a DRY CELL.

# dry cell

A carbon-zinc dry cell: a flashlight battery. The electrolyte, a paste of ammonium chloride, zinc chloride, manganese dioxide, and carbon, reacts with the zinc, causing it to become negatively charged. When the zinc anode and the carbon cathode are connected by a conducting wire, electrons flow from the anode to the cathode, producing an electric current.

**dry cell** an electrochemical cell in which the electrolyte is in the form of a paste so that it cannot spill.

**dry-clean** (drī′klēn′) clean clothes, drapes, etc. by DRY CLEANING. *v.*

**dry-clean·a·ble** (drī′klē′nə bəl) that can be dry-cleaned: *Most fabrics are dry-cleanable.* *adj.*

**dry cleaner** a person or company that does DRY CLEANING (def. 1).

**dry cleaning** 1 the cleaning of fabrics without water, using a solvent: *Most commercial dry cleaning today is done with synthetic or petroleum-base solvents.* 2 something that is to be or has been dry-cleaned: *I have to pick up the dry cleaning on my way home today.*

**dry dock** an area set between two piers, built watertight so that water may be pumped out or kept high: *Dry docks are used for building or repairing ships.*

**dry-dock** (drī′dok′) 1 place in a DRY DOCK. 2 go into DRY DOCK. *v.*

**dry·er** or **dri·er** (drī′ər) 1 an appliance or machine for drying things quickly, especially by heat or blowing air: *A clothes dryer dries clothes by blowing air over them as they are tumbled in a revolving drum.* 2 a stand or rack for hanging clothes up to dry. 3 Usually, **drier**, a substance added to oil paint, varnish, etc. to make it dry faster. 4 any person or thing that dries. *n.*

**dry-eyed** (drī′īd′) not weeping; not shedding tears: *She remained dry-eyed at the funeral.* *adj.*

**dry-farm** (drī′färm′) farm land where there is no irrigation and little rain. *v.*

**dry farming** a way of farming land in dry regions where there is no irrigation, using methods that save soil moisture and raising crops that survive drought.

**dry goods** cloth, ribbon, lace, etc.

**dry law** a law prohibiting the making and selling of liquor.

**dry·ly** or **dri·ly** (drī′lē) in a DRY (def. 9) manner: *He spoke dryly of his experiences at election time.* *adv.*

**dry measure** a system for measuring such things as grain, flour, or fruit:
```
2 pints = 1 quart
8 quarts = 1 peck
4 pecks = 1 bushel
```

**dry·ness** (drī′nis) the state of being dry; dry quality. *n.*

**dry rot** the decay of seasoned wood, causing it to crumble to a dry powder, due to various fungi.

**dry run** a practice test or session.

**dry-shod** (drī′shod′) having dry shoes; without getting the feet wet. *adj.*

**dry·wall** (drī′wol or drī′wəl) 1 a construction method of interior walls, using plasterboard instead of wet plaster. 2 PLASTERBOARD. 3 made of plasterboard: *drywall panelling.* 4 construct a wall with plasterboard instead of wet plaster. 1–3 *n.*, 4 *v.*

**d.s.** daylight saving.

**D.S.T., DST,** or **d.s.t.** daylight-saving time.

**du·al** (dyü′əl or dü′əl) 1 of two; showing two. 2 consisting of two parts; double; twofold: *The airplane had dual controls, one set for each pilot.* *adj.*
☞ *Hom.* DUEL.

**dub¹** (dub) 1 make a person a member of an order of knighthood by striking his shoulder lightly with a sword: *He was dubbed a knight.* 2 give a title to; call; name: *Because of his very blond hair, the boys dubbed him 'Whitey'.* *v.*, **dubbed, dub·bing.**

**dub²** (dub) *Informal.* an awkward, clumsy person. *n.*

**dub³** (dub) 1 add or alter sounds, especially on a motion-picture film: *It was a Spanish film, but English dialogue had been dubbed in.* 2 the sounds thus added or altered. 1 *v.*, **dubbed, dub·bing;** 2 *n.*

**du·bi·e·ty** (dyü bī′ə tē or dü bī′ə tē) 1 doubtfulness; uncertainty. 2 something which is doubtful. *n., pl.* **du·bi·e·ties.**

**du·bi·ous** (dyü′bē əs or dü′bē əs) 1 doubtful; uncertain: *a dubious compliment, dubious authorship, a dubious friend.* 2 of a questionable character; probably bad: *She called it a dubious scheme for making money.* *adj.* —**du′bi·ous·ly,** *adv.* —**du′bi·ous·ness,** *n.*

**du·cal** (dyü′kəl or dü′kəl) of a duke or dukedom. *adj.*

**duc·at** (duk′ət) a gold or silver coin formerly used in some European countries. *n.*

**duch·ess** (duch′is) 1 the wife or widow of a duke. 2 a woman with a rank equal to that of a duke. *n.*

**duch·y** (duch′ē) the territory under the rule of a duke or duchess; dukedom. *n., pl.* **duch·ies.**

A mallard duck and drake - about 60 cm long including the tail

**duck¹** (duk) 1 any of many species of small or medium-sized swimming bird having a thick body, short neck and legs, flat bill, and webbed feet. 2 a female duck. Compare with DRAKE. 3 the flesh of a duck used for food. 4 *Informal.* a darling; pet. 5 *Informal.* a person, especially one considered strange but harmless: *He's a strange old duck.* *n.*

**duck²** (duk) **1** dip or plunge suddenly under water and out again. **2** a sudden dip or plunge under water and out again. **3** lower the head or bend the body suddenly to keep from being hit, seen, etc. **4** lower the head or bend the body suddenly. **5** a sudden lowering of the head or bending of the body to keep from being hit, seen, etc. **6** *Informal.* get or keep away from; avoid: *He is always ducking his responsibilities.* 1, 3, 4, 6 *v.*, 2, 5 *n.*

**duck³** (duk) **1** a strong cotton or linen cloth with a lighter and finer weave than canvas: *Duck is used to make small sails and clothes for sailors or people living in hot climates.* **2 ducks,** *pl. Informal.* trousers made of duck. *n.*

**duck⁴** (duk) a military vehicle that looks something like a truck, but has a watertight body so that it may move through the water like a boat. *n.*

**duck·bill** (duk′bil′) PLATYPUS. *n.*

**duckbilled platypus** PLATYPUS. *n.*

**ducking stool** a stool on which a person was tied and ducked into water as a punishment.

**duck·ling** (duk′ling) a young duck. *n.*

**duck·pins** (duk′pinz′) a game resembling bowling, but played with smaller balls and pins. *n.*

**duck·weed** (duk′wēd′) any of various tiny plants that grow in water, often forming a coating on the surface. *n.*

**duct** (dukt) **1** a tube, pipe, or channel for carrying liquid, air, wires, etc. **2** a tube in the body for carrying a bodily fluid: *tear ducts.* *n.* —**duct′less,** *adj.*

**duc·tile** (duk′tīl *or* duk′təl) **1** capable of being hammered out thin or drawn out into a wire: *Gold and copper are ductile metals.* **2** easily moulded or shaped: *Wax is ductile.* **3** easily managed or influenced; docile. *adj.*

**duc·til·i·ty** (duk til′ə tē) a DUCTILE quality. *n., pl.* **duc·til·i·ties.**

**ductless gland** a gland without a duct whose secretion passes directly into the blood or lymph circulating through it; ENDOCRINE GLAND: *The thyroid, the spleen, and the thymus are ductless glands.*

**dud** (dud) *Informal.* **1** a shell or bomb that fails to explode. **2** a failure. *n.*

**dude** (düd *or* dyüd) **1** a man who pays too much attention to his clothes; dandy. **2** in the western parts of Canada and the United States, a city-bred person who spends a holiday on a ranch. *n.*

**dude ranch** a ranch that is run as a tourist resort.

**dudg·eon** (duj′ən) anger; resentment. *n. Archaic* except in **in high dudgeon,** very angry; resentful.

**dud·ish** (dü′dish *or* dyü′dish) like that of a DUDE. *adj.*

**due** (dyü *or* dü) **1** owed as a debt; to be paid as a right: *Money is due her for her work. Respect is due to older people.* **2** something owed as a debt or to be paid as a right: *Courtesy is a person's due as long as he is your guest.* **3** proper; suitable; rightful: *Good deeds deserve due reward; bad deeds deserve due punishment.* **4** as much as needed; enough: *Use due care to be safe in crossing streets.* **5** promised to come or be ready; looked for; expected: *The train is due at noon. Your report is due tomorrow.* **6** straight; directly; exactly: *The wind is due east.* **7 dues,** *pl.* **a** the amount of money owed or to be paid; a fee; tax. **b** the amount of money owed or to be paid to a club, etc. by a member: *Members are expected to pay their dues promptly.* 1, 3–5 *adj.*, 2, 7 *n.*, 6 *adv.*

**due to,** caused by: *The accident was due to his careless use of the gun.*

**give a person his or her due,** be fair to a person.

☛ *Hom.* DEW; DO¹ (for the second pronunciation of **due**).

☛ *Usage.* **Due to** is often used in the sense of 'because of': *Due to an avalanche, the road was impassable.* In formal English, however, many insist that **due to** should be used only at the beginning of an adjective clause immediately following some form of the verb **to be**: *The road blockage was due to an avalanche.* Nevertheless, the use of **due to** (meaning 'because of')—and the similar expression **owing to**—is becoming increasingly frequent in all styles except the most formal.

**du·el** (dyü′əl *or* dü′əl) **1** a formal fight between two men armed with swords or firearms: *Duels were arranged to settle quarrels, avenge insults, etc., and were fought in the presence of witnesses, called seconds.* **2** any fight or contest between two opponents: *a duel of wits.* **3** fight in a duel. 1, 2 *n.*, 3 *v.*, **du·elled** *or* **du·eled, du·el·ling** *or* **du·el·ing.**

☛ *Hom.* DUAL.

**du·el·list** *or* **du·el·ist** (dyü′ə list *or* dü′ə list) a person who fights a DUEL or duels. *n.*

**du·et** (dyü et′ *or* dü et′) **1** a piece of music to be sung or played by two people. **2** two singers or players performing together. *n.*

**duff** (duf) a flour pudding boiled in a cloth bag. *n.*

**duf·fel bag** *or* **duf·fle bag** (duf′əl) **1** a large bag of heavy cloth or canvas, used by campers, hunters, soldiers, etc. for carrying personal belongings. **2** any bag of stout material.

**duf·fel coat** *or* **duf·fle coat** a knee-length, usually hooded coat made of coarse woollen cloth with a thick nap.

**duf·fer** (duf′ər) *Informal.* a useless, clumsy, or stupid person. *n.*

**dug¹** (dug) pt. and pp. of DIG: *The dog dug a hole under the garden fence. The potatoes have all been dug.* *v.*

**dug²** (dug) a nipple; teat. *n.*

**dug·out** (dug′out′) **1** a rough shelter made by digging into the side of a hill, trench, etc.: *During war, soldiers use dugouts for protection against bullets and bombs.* **2** in baseball, a small shelter near the diamond, used by players who are not at bat or not in the game. **3** a boat made by hollowing out a large log. **4** *Cdn.* a large excavation used to hold water: *Some dugouts are used for watering livestock; others are used for irrigating land.* *n.*

**duke** (dyük *or* dük) **1** a nobleman ranking next below a prince and above a marquis. **2** a prince who rules a small state or country called a duchy. *n.*

**duke·dom** (dyük′dəm *or* dük′dəm) **1** the territory under the rule of a duke or duchess; duchy. **2** the title or rank of a duke. *n.*

**Duk·ho·bor** (dü′kə bôr′) See DOUKHOBOR. *n.*

**dul·cet** (dul′sit) soothing, especially to the ear; sweet; pleasing. *adj.*

**dul·ci·mer** (dul′sə mər) a musical instrument with metal strings, played by striking the strings with two hammers. *n.*

**dull** (dul) **1** not sharp or pointed: *a dull knife.* **2** not bright or clear: *dull eyes, a dull day, a dull sound, a dull colour.* **3** slow in understanding; stupid: *a dull mind, a dull girl.* **4** showing a lack of liveliness in the senses or feelings. **5** not interesting; tiresome; boring: *a dull book.* **6** having little life, energy, or spirit; not active: *Business is dull these days.* **7** not felt sharply: *a dull pain.* **8** make or become dull. *1–7 adj., 8 v.* —**dull′ness** or **dul′ness,** *n.*

**dull·ard** (dul′ərd) a stupid person who learns very slowly. *n.*

**dul·ly** (dul′ē) in a dull manner. *adv.*

**dulse** (duls) any of several coarse, edible seaweeds that have red fronds. *n.*

**du·ly** (dyü′lē *or* dü′lē) **1** according to what is due; properly; rightfully: *The debt was duly paid.* **2** as much as is needed; enough. **3** when due; at the proper time. *adv.*

**dumb** (dum) **1** not having the power of speech: *Animals are dumb.* **2** suffering from an inability to speak as a result of sickness, injury, etc.; mute. **3** silenced for the moment by fear, surprise, shyness, etc.: *The poor child was dumb with embarrassment.* **4** not expressed in words: *dumb astonishment, dumb grief.* **5** unwilling to speak; silent: *They questioned her repeatedly, but she remained dumb.* **6** *Informal.* stupid; unintelligent, or foolish: *She's pretty dumb. Dialling the wrong number is a dumb thing to do.* *adj.* —**dumb′ly,** *adv.* —**dumb′ness,** *n.*

**dumb–bell** (dum′bel′) a short bar of wood or iron with large, heavy, round ends: *Dumb-bells are generally used in pairs and are lifted or swung around to exercise the muscles of the arms, back, etc.* *n.*

**dumb·found** (dum′found′) See DUMFOUND. *v.*

**dumb show** gestures without words; pantomime.

**dumb·wait·er** (dum′wā′tər) **1** a small box with shelves, pulled up and down a shaft like an elevator to send dishes, food, rubbish, etc. from one floor to another. **2** a small stand placed near a dining table, for holding dishes, etc. *n.*

**dum·dum** (dum′dum) a soft-nosed bullet that spreads out when it strikes, causing a large, jagged wound. *n.*

**dumdum bullet** DUMDUM.

**dum·found** (dum′found′) amaze to the point of making unable to speak; bewilder; confuse. *v.*

**dum·my** (dum′ē) **1** a figure of a person, used to display clothing in store windows, to shoot at in rifle practice, to tackle in football, etc. **2** *Informal.* a stupid person; blockhead. **3** made to resemble the real thing; make-believe; imitation; counterfeit: *The children played soldier with dummy swords made of wood.* **4** a person supposedly acting for himself or herself, but really acting for another. **5** acting for another while supposedly acting for oneself. **6** a cardplayer whose cards are laid face up on the table and played by his or her partner. **7** a hand of cards played in this way. **8** played with a hand of cards exposed. *1–4, 6, 7 n., pl.* **dum·mies;** *3, 5, 8 adj.*

**dump** (dump) **1** empty out; throw down; unload in a mass: *The truck backed up to the curb and dumped the topsoil on the driveway.* **2** unload rubbish. **3** a place for unloading rubbish. **4** a heap of rubbish. **5** a place for storing military supplies: *an ammunition dump.* **6** put goods on the market in large quantities and at a low price; especially, do so in a foreign country at a price below that in the home country. *1, 2, 6 v., 3–5 n.*

**dump·ling** (dum′pling) **1** a rounded piece of dough, boiled or steamed and served with meat. **2** a small pudding made by enclosing fruit in a piece of dough and baking or steaming it. *n.*

**dumps** (dumps) *Informal.* low spirits; gloomy feelings. *n. pl.*
**(down) in the dumps,** *Informal.* feeling gloomy or sad: *Kim's in the dumps because her best friend is moving away.*

**dump·y** (dum′pē) short and fat. *adj.,* **dump·i·er, dump·i·est.** —**dump′i·ly,** *adv.* —**dump′i·ness,** *n.*

**dun**¹ (dun) **1** demand payment of a debt from, again and again. **2** a demand for payment, especially of a debt. **3** a person constantly demanding payment of a debt. *1 v.,* **dunned, dun·ning;** *2, 3 n.*
☞ *Hom.* DONE.

**dun**² (dun) dull greyish-brown. *n., adj.*
☞ *Hom.* DONE.

**dunce** (duns) **1** a child slow at learning his or her lessons in school. **2** a stupid person. *n.*

**dunce cap** *or* **dunce's cap** a tall, cone-shaped cap formerly worn as a punishment by a child who was slow in learning his or her lessons in school.

**dun·der·head** (dun′dər hed′) a stupid, foolish person; dunce; blockhead. *n.*

**dune** (dün *or* dyün) a mound or ridge of loose sand heaped up by the wind. *n.*

**dung** (dung) waste matter from the bowels of animals; manure: *Dung is a good fertilizer.* *n.*

**dun·ga·ree** (dung′gə rē′) **1** a coarse cotton cloth used for work clothes, sails, etc., especially blue denim. **2 dungarees,** *pl.* trousers or clothing made of this cloth. *n.*
☞ *Etym.* From Hindi *dungrī,* a coarse Indian calico cloth. 17c.

**dun·geon** (dun′jən) a dark underground room to keep prisoners in. *n.*
☞ *Hom.* DONJON.

**dung·hill** (dung′hil′) **1** a heap of dung. **2** a vile place or person. *n.*

**dunk** (dungk) **1** dip something to eat into a liquid: *to dunk doughnuts in coffee.* **2** *Informal.* push somebody into water. *v.* —**dunk′er,** *n.*

**dun·lin** (dun′lən) a small wading bird. *n., pl.* **dun·lins** or (*esp. collectively*) **dun·lin.**

**du·o** (dyü′ō *or* dü′ō) **1** DUET. **2** *Informal.* pair. *n., pl.* **du·os.**

**du·o·dec·i·mal** (dyü′ō des′ə məl *or* dü′ō des′ə məl) **1** having to do with twelfths or twelve; proceeding by twelves. **2** one twelfth. **3 duodecimals,** *pl.* in mathematics, a system of numbering or computing, using twelve as a base instead of ten as in the decimal system. *1 adj., 2, 3 n.*

**du·o·de·nal** (dyü′ō dē′nəl *or* dü′ō dē′nəl) of or in the DUODENUM: *a duodenal ulcer.* *adj.*

**du·o·de·num** (dyü′ō dē′nəm *or* dü′ō dē′nəm) the first part of the small intestine, just below the stomach. See ALIMENTARY CANAL for picture. *n., pl.* **du·o·de·na** (-nə).

**dupe** (dyüp *or* düp) **1** a person easily deceived or tricked. **2** one who is being deluded or tricked: *The young politician's inexperience is making her the dupe of some unscrupulous schemers.* **3** deceive; trick. 1, 2 *n.*, 3 *v.*, **duped, dup·ing.** —**dup′er,** *n.*

**du·ple** (dyü′pəl *or* dü′pəl) DOUBLE. *adj.*

**du·plex** (dyü′pleks *or* dü′pleks) **1** double; twofold. **2** *Cdn.* a building consisting of two dwellings under one roof, either side by side or one above the other: *Most of the houses on this street are duplexes.* **3** *Cdn.* one of the dwellings of such a building. 1 *adj.*, 2, 3 *n.*

**du·pli·cate** (dyü′plə kit *or* dü′plə kit *for adjective and noun,* dyü′plə kāt′ *or* dü′plə kāt′ *for verb*) **1** exactly alike; corresponding exactly: *We have duplicate keys for the front door.* **2** an exact copy; reproduction; replica: *Cassandra made a duplicate of her letter to the editor of the newspaper.* **3** a counterpart; double: *This chair is a duplicate of one we have at home.* **4** make an exact copy of; reproduce: *to duplicate a document.* **5** repeat exactly; equal: *She was never able to duplicate the record she had set during training.* **6** having or consisting of two similar or corresponding parts: *A person's lungs are duplicate.* **7** in card games, having the same hands played by a second set of players in order to compare scores: *duplicate bridge.* 1, 6, 7 *adj.*, 2, 3 *n.*, 4, 5 *v.*, **du·pli·cat·ed, du·pli·cat·ing.** **in duplicate,** in two copies exactly alike: *This application must be made out in duplicate.*

**du·pli·ca·tion** (dyü′plə kā′shə n *or* dü′plə kā′shən) **1** duplicating or being DUPLICATEd (defs. 4, 5). **2** a DUPLICATE (def. 1) copy. *n.*

**du·pli·ca·tor** (dyü′plə kā′tər *or* dü′plə kā′tər) a machine for making exact copies of anything written, drawn, typed, etc. *n.*

**du·plic·i·ty** (dyü plis′ə tē *or* dü plis′ə tē) deceitfulness; treachery; secretly acting one way and publicly acting another in order to deceive. *n., pl.* **du·plic·i·ties.**

**du·ra·bil·i·ty** (dyü′rə bil′ə tē *or* dü′rə bil′ə tē) the quality of being DURABLE; ability to stand wear. *n., pl.* **du·ra·bil·i·ties.**

**du·ra·ble** (dyü′rə bəl *or* dü′rə bəl) able to last a long time; not soon injured or worn out. *adj.* —**du′ra·ble·ness,** *n.* —**du′ra·bly,** *adv.*

**du·rance** (dyü′rəns *or* dü′rəns) imprisonment. *n.*

**du·ra·tion** (dyü rā′shən *or* dü rā′shən) length of time; the time during which something lasts: *The strike was expected to be of short duration.* *n.* **for the duration,** until the end, especially of a war.

**dur·bar** (dėr′bär) in India: **1** an official court or audience chamber. **2** any formal reception or assembly held by a governmental authority. **3** formerly in British India, a formal assembly held to mark special occasions such as the proclamation of Queen Victoria as Empress of India. *n.*

**du·ress** (dyü res′ *or* dü res′) **1** compulsion: *A person cannot be legally forced to fulfil a contract signed under duress.* **2** imprisonment. *n.*

**Dur·ham boat** (dėr′əm) a large boat much used in the early 19th century on the St. Lawrence and its tributaries for carrying freight and passengers. It could be propelled by sails or poles.
☞ *Etym.* Named after a Pennsylvania boatbuilder called Robert *Durham,* who designed a similar boat about 1750.

**dur·ing** (dyü′ring *or* dü′ring) **1** throughout; through the entire time of: *The old woman stays in the house during the day, but usually goes for a walk in the evening. The children played tag during recess.* **2** at some time in; in the course of: *They're going to drop in and see us sometime during the day.* *prep.*

**dur·ra** (du̇′rə) a kind of SORGHUM that produces grain, widely grown in dry regions of Asia and northern Africa. *n.*

**du·rum** (dyu̇′rəm *or* du̇′rəm) a hard wheat from which the flour used in macaroni, spaghetti, etc. is made. *n.*

**dusk** (dusk) **1** the time just before dark; twilight. **2** shade; gloom. **3** make or become dusky or shadowy. 1, 2 *n.*, 3 *v.*

**dusk·y** (dus′kē) **1** somewhat dark; dark-coloured: *a dusky complexion.* **2** dim; obscure. *adj.,* **dusk·i·er, dusk·i·est.** —**dusk′i·ly,** *adv.* —**dusk′i·ness,** *n.*

**dust** (dust) **1** fine, dry earth; any fine powder: *Dust lay thick in the street. The old papers had turned to dust.* **2** get dust off; brush or wipe the dust from: *My job is dusting the furniture.* **3** sprinkle with dust, powder, etc.: *to dust crops with an insecticide. The nurse dusted powder over the baby.* **4** the earth, especially as a place of burial. **5** what is left of a dead body after decay: *The tomb contains the dust of kings.* **6** a low or humble condition. **7** a worthless thing. 1, 4–7 *n.*, 2, 3 *v.*
**dust off,** brush or wipe the dust from.
**lick the dust,** humble oneself slavishly.
**shake the dust off one's feet,** go away feeling angry or scornful.
**throw dust in someone's eyes,** deceive or mislead a person: *The escape plan depended on her success in throwing dust in the eyes of the police.*

**dust bowl** especially in the western parts of Canada and the United States, a region that suffers from severe DUST STORMS due to long periods of drought.

**dust·er** (dus′tər) **1** a person or thing that dusts, especially a cloth, brush, etc. used to get dust off things. **2** a light dress or robe that opens down the front, usually without a belt and worn especially when doing light household chores. **3** a long, lightweight coat worn over the clothes to protect them from dust. **4** *Informal.* a DUST STORM. *n.*

**dust jacket** a removable paper cover for a book, folded over the cover to protect it and to display the book effectively for selling purposes.

**dust·less** (dus′tlis) **1** without dust. **2** not causing dust. *adj.*

**dust·pan** (dust′pan′) a flat pan, shaped like a short, broad shovel with a straight edge, for sweeping dust or debris into from the floor. *n.*

**dust storm** a strong wind carrying clouds of dust across or from a dry region.

**dust-up** (dus′tup′) *Informal.* a quarrel; argument. *n.*

**dust·y** (dus′tē) **1** covered with or full of dust. **2** like dust; dry and powdery. **3** having the colour of dust; greyish: *a dusty pink. adj.*, **dust·i·er, dust·i·est.** —**dust′i·ly,** *adv.* —**dust′i·ness,** *n.*

**Dutch** (duch) **1** of or having to do with the Netherlands, a small country in western Europe, its people, or their language. **2 the Dutch,** the people of the Netherlands. **3** their language. 1 *adj.*, 2, 3 *n.*

**Dutch elm disease** a killing disease of elm trees, caused by a fungus and carried by insects.

**Dutch·man's–breech·es** (duch′mənz brich′iz) **1** a spring wild flower shaped somewhat like breeches. **2** the plant that bears it. *n. sing.* or *pl.*

**Dutch oven 1** a large, heavy metal pot with a high, rounded lid, used for cooking roasts, etc. in the oven. **2** a metal box with an open side, used for roasting meat, etc. before an open fire: *The open side of the Dutch oven faces toward the fire.* **3** a brick oven of which the walls are heated, and into which food is put to cook after the fire goes out or is removed.

**du·te·ous** (dyü′tē əs *or* dü′tē əs) DUTIFUL; obedient. *adj.* —**du′te·ous·ly,** *adv.* —**du′te·ous·ness,** *n.*

**du·ti·a·ble** (dyü′tē ə bəl *or* dü′tē ə bəl) on which a duty or tax must be paid: *Perfumes imported into Canada are dutiable goods. adj.*

**du·ti·ful** (dyü′tə fəl *or* dü′tə fəl) **1** doing the duties required of one; obedient: *a dutiful daughter.* **2** required by duty; proceeding from or expressing a sense of duty: *dutiful words. adj.* —**du′ti·ful·ly,** *adv.* —**du′ti·ful·ness,** *n.*

**du·ty** (dyü′tē *or* dü′tē) **1** the thing that a person ought to do; something that is right to do: *It is your duty to obey the laws.* **2** the feeling of having to do what is right: *Joselle acted from a sense of duty although she was afraid.* **3** the thing that a person has to do in his or her work; action required by one's occupation or position: *One of her duties as a reporter is to cover the meetings of the city council.* **4** the proper behaviour owed to an older or superior person; obedience; respect. **5** a tax due to the government, especially on goods brought into or taken out of a country. *n., pl.* **du·ties.**
**do duty for,** serve in place of.
**in duty bound,** compelled to do something as a duty.
**off duty,** away from one's work or occupation: *He's off duty till six o'clock.*
**on duty,** at or to one's work or occupation: *She goes on duty at midnight.*

**duty–free** (dyü′tē frē′ *or* dü′tē frē′) exempt from customs duty. *adj.*

**du·um·vir** (dyü um′vər *or* dü um′vər) in ancient Rome, either of two men who shared one governmental position. *n., pl.* **du·um·virs** *or* **du·um·vi·ri** (və rī′ or -və rē′).

**du·um·vir·ate** (dyü um′və rit *or* dü um′və rit) **1** a governmental position shared by two people simultaneously: *The consulship in ancient Rome was a duumvirate.* **2** two people jointly holding such a position. *n.*

**du·ve·tyn** (dü′və tēn′) a soft, closely woven cloth having a velvety finish. *n.*

**DVD** digital versatile disc or digital video disc, similar to a compact disc but with greater data capacity. It has video, audio, and computer applications.

**dwarf** (dwôrf) **1** a person, animal, or plant much smaller than the usual size for its kind. **2** in fairy tales, a tiny, often ugly, person who has magic powers. **3** much smaller than the usual size of its kind; checked in growth. **4** keep from growing large; check in growth. **5** cause to seem small by contrast or by distance: *That tall building dwarfs the other.* 1–3 *n., pl.* **dwarfs** or **dwarves** (dwôrvz); 4, 5 *v.*
☛ *Syn.* **Dwarf,** MIDGET, PYGMY. **Dwarf** applies particularly to a very small person whose growth has been stunted, usually by glandular deficiency, and who often has a head large enough for a normal person of his or her age, or larger, or a body deformed in some way. **Dwarf** may also be applied to a stunted animal or plant. With plants, however, **dwarf** usually refers not to the individual but to a *kind* or *variety* smaller than related varieties, either because of natural differentiation or because of breeding: *dwarf marigolds, the dwarf birch.* **Midget** applies to a tiny person who is perfectly shaped and normal in every way except size. A **pygmy** is one of a diminutive race found in Africa; but the word may be used as a synonym for both **dwarf** and **midget.**

**dwarf·ish** (dwôr′fish) like a dwarf; smaller than usual. *adj.* —**dwarf′ish·ly,** *adv.* —**dwarf′ish·ness,** *n.*

**dwarf star** a star of relatively low mass and brightness.

**dwell** (dwel) make one's home; live: *The princess dwelt in a beautiful castle. v.*, **dwelt** or **dwelled, dwell·ing.**
**dwell on, a** think, write, or speak about for a long time. **b** put stress on.

**dwell·er** (dwel′ər) a person who lives in a place: *a city dweller, a cliff dweller. n.*

**dwell·ing** (dwel′ing) **1** a house; a place in which people live: *a two-family dwelling.* **2** ppr. of DWELL. 1 *n.*, 2 *v.*

**dwelling place** DWELLING.

**dwelt** (dwelt) a pt. and a pp. of DWELL: *They dwelt in the country for years. v.*

**dwin·dle** (dwin′dəl) become smaller and smaller; shrink; diminish: *During the war the supply of food dwindled rapidly. v.*, **dwin·dled, dwin·dling.**

**dwt.** pennyweight; pennyweights.

**DX** or **D.X.** in radio, distance; distant.

**Dy** dysprosium.

**dye** (dī) **1** a colouring matter used to colour cloth, hair, etc., or a liquid containing it: *Some dyes are vegetable, others chemical. We bought some blue dye.* **2** a colour produced by treatment with such colouring matter; tint; hue: *A good dye will not fade.* **3** colour cloth, hair, etc. by dipping into or treating with a liquid containing colouring matter: *to have a dress dyed.* **4** colour; stain: *The spilled grape juice dyed the tablecloth purple.* **5** become coloured when treated with a dye: *This material dyes easily and quickly.* 1, 2 *n.*, 3–5 *v.*, **dyed, dye·ing.**
**of deepest** or **blackest dye,** of the lowest or vilest kind.
☛ *Hom.* DIE.

**dyed–in–the–wool** (dī′din ᴛʜə wúl′) **1** of people, thorough-going, especially in a political sense; unchanging: *a dyed-in-the-wool conservative.* **2** of materials, dyed before being woven into cloth. *adj.*

**dye·ing** (dī′ing) **1** the colouring of fabrics with DYE. **2** ppr. of DYE. 1 *n.*, 2 *v.*
☛ Hom. DYING.

**dy·er** (dī′ər) a person whose business is dyeing fabrics. *n.*

**dye·stuff** (dī′stuf′) any substance yielding a dye or used as a dye: *Indigo and cochineal are dyestuffs.* *n.*

**dy·ing** (dī′ing) **1** about to die: *a dying man.* **2** coming to an end: *the dying year.* **3** death. **4** of death; at death. **5** ppr. of DIE¹: *The storm is dying down.* 1, 2, 4 *adj.*, 3 *n.*, 5 *v.*
**dying for,** *Informal.* wanting very much: *I'm dying for a cup of coffee.*
**dying to,** *Informal.* wanting to very much: *I'm dying to see Jane again.*
☛ Hom. DYEING.

**dyke** (dīk) See DIKE. *n.*, *v.*, **dyked, dyk·ing.**

**dy·nam·ic** (dī nam′ik) **1** having to do with energy or force in motion. **2** having to do with DYNAMICS. **3** active; energetic; forceful: *The teacher has a dynamic way of talking.* *adj.*

**dy·nam·i·cal·ly** (dī nam′i klē) in a DYNAMIC (def. 3) manner. *adv.*

**dy·nam·ics** (dī nam′iks) **1** the branch of physics that deals with the study of the motion of bodies (KINEMATICS) and the relation between motion and the forces producing it (KINETICS). **2** KINETICS. **3** MECHANICS (def. 1), including KINETICS, KINEMATICS, and STATICS. **4** any set of forces that produce change, growth, or interaction: *the dynamics of glacier motion, the dynamics of family life.* **5** a branch of study dealing with such forces: *She is an expert on population dynamics.* **6** in music, the effect of variation and contrast in force or loudness. *n. sing. or pl.*

**dy·na·mite** (dī′nə mīt′) **1** a powerful explosive often used in blasting rock, tree stumps, etc., made of nitroglycerin mixed with an absorbent material and pressed into round sticks. **2** blow up or destroy with dynamite: *They planned to dynamite the bridge.* 1 *n.*, 2 *v.*, **dy·na·mit·ed, dy·na·mit·ing.** —**dy′na·mit′er,** *n.*

**dy·na·mo** (dī′nə mō′) **1** GENERATOR (def. 1). See GENERATOR for picture. **2** a very energetic and forceful person. *n.*, *pl.* **dy·na·mos.**

**dy·na·mo–e·lec·tric** (dī′nə mō i lek′trik) having to do with the transformation of mechanical energy into electric energy, or electric energy into mechanical energy. *adj.*

**dy·na·mom·e·ter** (dī′nə mom′ə tər) an apparatus for measuring force or power, especially one for measuring the power of an engine. *n.*

**dy·na·mom·e·try** (dī′nə mom′ə trē) the art or process of measuring forces. *n.*

**dy·na·mo·tor** (dī′nə mō′tər) a combined electric motor and dynamo for changing the voltage of an electric current. *n.*

**dy·nast** (dī′nast *or* din′ast) **1** a member of a DYNASTY; hereditary ruler. **2** any ruler. *n.*

**dy·nas·tic** (dī nas′tik *or* di nas′tik) of or having to do with a DYNASTY. *adj.*

**dy·nas·ty** (dī′nə stē *or* din′ə stē) **1** a succession of rulers who belong to the same family: *The Bourbon dynasty, the Hapsburg dynasty.* **2** the period of time during which a dynasty rules. *n.*, *pl.* **dy·nas·ties.**

**dyne** (dīn) a former unit for measuring force: *One dyne is the force required to give an acceleration of one centimetre per second squared to a mass of one gram. It is equal to one one-hundred-thousandth of a* NEWTON. *n.*

**dys·en·ter·y** (dis′ən ter′ē *or* dis′ən trē) a painful disease of the intestines, producing diarrhea with blood and mucus. *n.*

**dys·func·tion** (di sfungk′shən) a functional abnormality or impairment, as of a body organ. *n.*

**dys·func·tion·al** (di sfungk′shə nəl) **1** having to do with DYSFUNCTION. **2** performing badly or improperly; malfunctioning. *adj.*

**dys·gen·ic** (dis jen′ik) having to do with or causing degeneration in the type of offspring produced. *adj.*

**dys·pep·si·a** (di spep′sē ə) poor digestion; indigestion: *Bad eating habits may cause dyspepsia.* Compare with EUPEPSIA. *n.*

**dys·pep·tic** (di spep′tik) **1** having to do with or causing DYSPEPIA. **2** suffering from DYSPEPSIA. **3** a person who has DYSPEPSIA. **4** gloomy; pessimistic. 1, 2, 4 *adj.*, 3 *n.* Compare with EUPEPTIC.
—**dys·pep′ti·cal·ly,** *adv.*

**dys·pro·si·um** (di sprō′sē əm) a rare chemical element, the most magnetic substance known. Symbol: Dy *n.*

**dz.** dozen; dozens.

# E e  *E e*

**e or E** (ē) **1** the fifth letter of the alphabet. **2** any speech sound represented by this letter. **3** in music: **a** the third tone in the scale of C major. **b** a symbol representing this tone. **c** a key, string, etc. of a musical instrument that produces this tone. **d** the scale or key that has E as its keynote. **4** any person or thing considered as the fifth in a series. *n., pl.* **e's** or **E's**.

**e 1** in physics, erg. **2** in baseball, error.

**e.** in theatre, entrance.

**E 1** east; eastern. **2** English. **3** excellent.

**E. 1** East; Eastern. **2** Earl. **3** Engineering. **4** English. **5** Earth.

**ea.** each.

**each** (ēch) **1** every one of two or more persons or things considered separately or one by one: *Each dog has a name.* **2** every single one: *He gave a pencil to each.* **3** all of a group, thought of as individuals: *We each have our work to do.* **4** for each; to each; apiece: *These pencils cost fifty cents each.* 1 *adj.*, 2, 3 *pron.*, 4 *adv.*
☛ *Usage.* As a pronoun, **each** is singular: *Each of the four players has seven cards.* When **each** is used as an adjective modifying a noun, however, it is the noun that decides whether a following verb or pronoun is singular or plural: *Each player looks at his seven cards.* (sing.) *The four players each look at their seven cards.* (pl.)

**each other 1** each of two in an action or relation that is common to both: *They struck each other* (that is, they struck, each *striking the other*). **2** one another: *They struck at each other.*

**ea·ger** (ē′gər) **1** wanting very much; desiring strongly; impatient to do or get something: *The child is eager to have the candy.* **2** characterized by or showing keenness of desire or feeling: *eager looks.* *adj.* —**ea′ger·ly**, *adv.* —**ea′ger·ness**, *n.*

**eager beaver** *Informal.* an especially hard-working person.

A bald eagle— about 88 cm long including the tail

**ea·gle** (ē′gəl) **1** any of a number of large, strong birds of prey belonging to the same family as hawks, having very keen eyes and powerful wings: *Eagles eat small animals, fish, or other birds.* **2** a standard bearing the figure of an eagle as an emblem. **3** in golf, two strokes less than par for any hole on a course. *n.*

**eagle eye** the ability to see far and clearly; sharp eye.

**ea·gle–eyed** (ē′gə līd′) **1** able to see far and clearly. **2** observant. *adj.*

**ea·glet** (ē′glit) a young EAGLE (def. 1). *n.*

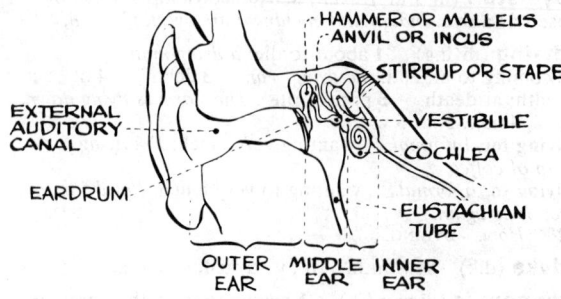
The human ear

**ear¹** (ēr) **1** the part of the body by which human beings and animals hear, usually consisting of three parts (**external ear, middle ear,** and **inner ear**); the organ of hearing. **2** the external ear; visible part of the ear. **3** the sense of hearing. **4** the ability to distinguish small differences in sounds: *That musician has a good ear.* **5** favourable attention; listening; attention: *to give ear to something.* **6** anything shaped like the external part of an ear. *n.* —**ear′like**, *adj.*
**be all ears,** *Informal.* listen eagerly; pay careful attention.
**give ear,** listen or attend.
**go in one ear and out the other,** make no impression.
**lend an ear,** listen; pay attention.
**play by ear,** play an instrument or a composition without using written music.
**wet behind the ears,** *Informal.* inexperienced; not yet able to cope; quite immature.

**ear²** (ēr) **1** the mature spike of cereal plants, containing the seeds, or kernels: *An ear of corn consists of rows of kernels surrounding the outside of a long, thick, woody cob.* **2** of such plants, develop ears; mature: *Soon the corn will ear.* 1 *n.*, 2 *v.*

**ear·ache** (ēr′āk′) a pain in the ear. *n.*

**ear·drop** (ēr′drop′) EARRING, especially one with a hanging ornament. *n.*

**ear·drum** (ēr′drum′) **1** the thin membrane that stretches across the middle ear and vibrates when sound waves strike it; tympanic membrane. See EAR¹ for picture. **2** the middle ear. *n.*

**ear·flap** (ēr′flap′) a part of a cap that can be turned down over the ear to keep it warm. *n.*

**earl** (ėrl) a British nobleman ranking below a marquis and above a viscount: *The wife or widow of an earl is called a countess.* *n.*

**earl·dom** (ėrl′dəm) **1** the territory under the rule of an earl. **2** the rank or title of an earl. *n.*

**ear·ly** (ėr′lē) **1** near the beginning: *The sun is not hot early in the day.* **2** that happens or arrives before the usual, normal, or expected time: *an early dinner, an early spring.* **3** before the usual or expected time: *Call me early.* **4** long ago; far back in time; in ancient times: *The plough was an early invention.* **5** before very long; in the near future; soon: *Let us have an early reply.* 1, 3 *adv.*, 2, 4, 5 *adj.*, **ear·li·er, ear·li·est. —ear′li·ness,** *n.*

**early bird** *Informal.* a person who gets up or arrives early.

**ear·mark** (ēr′märk′) 1 a mark made on the ear of an animal to show who owns it. 2 a special mark, quality, or feature that identifies or gives information about a person or thing; sign. 3 make an earmark on. 4 identify or give information about: *Careful work earmarks a good student.* 5 set aside for some special purpose: *Five thousand dollars is earmarked to buy books for the library.* 1, 2 *n.*, 3–5 *v.*

**ear·muffs** (ēr′mufs′) a pair of coverings to put over the ears to keep them warm. *n.pl.*

**earn** (ėrn) 1 receive for work or service; be paid: *She earns one hundred dollars a day.* 2 do enough work for; deserve; be worth: *He is paid more than he really earns.* 3 bring or get as deserved: *Her unselfish acts earned her the respect of all who knew her.* *v.* —**earn′er,** *n.*
☞ Hom. URN.

**ear·nest**[1] (ėr′nist) 1 sincerely zealous; strong and firm in purpose; serious: *He is very earnest in his desire to help people. An earnest pupil has her mind on her work.* 2 important: *"Life is real, life is earnest."* *adj.* —**ear′nest·ly,** *adv.* —**ear′nest·ness,** *n.*
**in earnest, a** seriously: *I speak in earnest.* **b** sincerely zealous; serious: *We could see she was in earnest about the project.*

**ear·nest**[2] (ėr′nist) 1 the part given or done in advance as a pledge for the rest: *Take this as an earnest of what is to come.* 2 anything that shows what is to come; pledge; token. *n.*

**earnest money** money paid as a pledge.

**earn·ings** (ėr′ningz) money earned; wages; profits. *n.pl.*

**ear·phone** (ēr′fōn′) a receiver for a radio, telephone, hearing aid, etc. that fits over or is inserted into the ear: *Many portable radios have earphones for private listening.* *n.*

**ear·plug** (ēr′plug′) a round piece of pliable rubber, plastic, etc. inserted into the ear to keep out water or noise. *n.*

**ear·ring** (ēr′ring′) an ornament for the lobe of the ear, held in place either by a wire or post passed through a hole pierced in the lobe, or by a screw or clip. *n.*

**ear·shot** (ēr′shot′) the distance a sound can be heard; range of hearing: *He was out of earshot and could not hear our shouts.* *n.*

**earth** (ėrth) 1 the planet on which we live; the third planet from the sun, and the fifth in size. 2 all the people who live on this planet. 3 this world, in contrast with heaven and hell. 4 dry land. 5 ground; soil; dirt: *The earth in the garden is soft.* 6 the ground: *The arrow fell to earth 100 metres away.* 7 the hole of a fox or other burrowing animal. 8 worldly matters. *n.*
**down to earth,** seeing things as they really are; practical.

**earth·bound** (ėrth′bound′) bound or limited to this earth. *adj.*

**earth·en** (ėrth′ən) 1 made of earth. 2 made of baked clay. *adj.*

**earth·en·ware** (ėrth′ən wer′) 1 any of the coarser kinds of dishes, containers, etc. made of baked clay:

**early bird**     **381**     **ease**

hat, āge, fär; let, ēqual, tėrm; it, īce
hot, ōpen, ôrder; oil, out; cup, put, rüle
əbove, taken, pencəl, lemən, circəs
ch, child; ng, long; sh, ship
th, thin; ᴛʜ, then; zh, measure

*Pottery or crockery is earthenware.* 2 baked clay.
3 made of earthenware. 1, 2 *n.*, 3 *adj.*

**earth·ly** (ėrth′lē) 1 having to do with the earth, the human world, and not with heaven: *He thinks only of earthly things.* 2 possible; conceivable: *That rubbish is of no earthly use.* *adj.*, **earth·li·er, earth·li·est.** —**earth′li·ness,** *n.*

**earth·nut** (ėrth′nut′) an underground part of certain plants, such as a root, tuber, or underground pod: *Peanuts are earthnuts.* *n.*

**earth·quake** (ėrth′kwāk′) a shaking of the earth's surface, caused by the sudden movement of masses of rock or by changes beneath the earth's surface. *n.*

**earth station** a receiving station, usually a concave dish, for electronic signals transmitted from an artificial satellite, especially one transmitting television programs.

**earth·ward** (ėrth′wərd) toward the earth. *adv., adj.*

**earth·wards** (ėrth′wərdz) toward the earth. *adv.*

**earth·work** (ėrth′wėrk′) 1 a bank of earth piled up for a fortification. 2 a moving of earth in engineering operations. *n.*

**earth·worm** (ėrth′wėrm′) a reddish-brown or greyish worm that lives in the soil; angleworm. See WORM for picture. *n.*

**earth·y** (ėr′thē) 1 of earth or soil. 2 like earth or soil. 3 not spiritual; worldly. 4 not refined; coarse: *earthy humour.* *adj.*, **earth·i·er, earth·i·est.** —**earth′i·ness,** *n.*

**ear trumpet** a trumpet-shaped instrument held to the ear by a hearing-impaired person as an aid in hearing.

**ear·wax** (ēr′waks′) the sticky, yellowish substance in the canal of the outer ear. *n.*

**ear·wig** (ēr′wig′) any of numerous insects having long, jointed antennae and a long, slender body, with a pair of appendages at the tail end that are like forceps: *Some earwigs can be garden pests because they eat the leaves and flowers of plants.* *n.*

**ease** (ēz) 1 freedom from pain or trouble; comfort: *When school is out, I am going to live a life of ease for a whole week.* 2 make free from pain or trouble; give relief or comfort to. 3 freedom from trying hard; lack of effort: *He enjoyed the ease of his part-time job.* 4 freedom from constraint; a natural or easy manner. 5 lessen; lighten: *This medicine eased my pain.* 6 make easy; loosen: *The belt is too tight; ease it a little.* 7 move slowly and carefully: *She eased the big box through the narrow door.* 8 become less rapid, less tense, etc. 1, 3, 4 *n.*, 2, 5–8 *v.*, **eased, eas·ing.**
**at ease, a** free from pain or trouble; comfortable.
**b** with the hands behind the back, the feet apart, and the body somewhat relaxed: *The soldiers stood at ease.*
**ease off** or **up, a** lessen; lighten. **b** loosen.
**with ease,** without having to try hard; with little effort: *She learned to spell with ease.*

**ea·sel** (ē′zəl)   a support or frame for holding an artist's canvas, a chalkboard, etc. upright.   *n.*

**ease·ment** (ē′zmənt)   a right held by one person in land owned by another.   *n.*

**eas·i·ly** (ē′zə lē)   **1** in an easy manner; without difficulty or great effort: *She solved the puzzle easily.*   **2** without pain or trouble; comfortably: *The patient was resting easily.*   **3** smoothly; freely: *The cowboy rode his horse easily.*   **4** by far; beyond question: *She is easily the best singer in the choir.*   **5** very likely: *A war may easily begin.*   *adv.*

**eas·i·ness** (ē′zē nis)   **1** the quality, condition, or state of being easy.   **2** carelessness, indifference.   *n.*

**east** (ēst)   **1** the direction of sunrise; point of the compass to the right as one faces north. See COMPASS for picture.   **2** toward the east: *They travelled east for two more days.*   **3** from the east: *an east wind.*   **4** in the east.   **5** Also, **East,**   the part of any country toward the east: *Nova Scotia is in the East.*   **6 the East, a** the eastern part of Canada and the United States.   **b** the countries in Asia; the Orient: *China is in the East.*   **c** the Eastern Roman Empire.   1, 5, 6 *n.*, 2 *adv.*, 3, 4 *adj.*
**back East** or **down East,**   in Canada: **a** any point to the east of Winnipeg, especially that part east of Quebec.   **b** in or toward any place east of Winnipeg, especially that part east of Quebec.
**east of,**   farther east than.

**east·bound** (ēst′bound′)   going toward the east.   *adj.*

**East·er** (ē′stər)   **1** the yearly Christian celebration commemorating Christ's rising from the dead: *In most churches, Easter comes between March 21 and April 26, on the first Sunday after the first full moon after March 21.*   **2** of Easter; for Easter: *Easter music.*   1 *n.*, 2 *adj.*

**Easter egg**   a coloured egg, either real or made of chocolate, glass, etc. used as a gift or ornament at Easter.

**Easter lily**   **1** a wildflower of the lily family found in the open woods and fields of southern British Columbia and the northwestern United States, closely related to the glacier lily: *The Easter lily has white flowers that bloom in April and May.*   **2** any of several cultivated varieties of lily having large, waxy, white flowers shaped like trumpets, grown especially for Easter.

**east·er·ly** (ē′stər lē)   **1** toward the east.   **2** from the east: *an easterly wind.*   1 *adv.*, 2 *adj.*

**east·ern** (ē′stərn)   **1** toward the east: *an eastern trip.*   **2** from the east: *eastern tourists.*   **3** of or in the east; of or in the eastern part of the country: *Halifax is an eastern port.*   **4** of or in the Orient, or Asia: *eastern countries, eastern customs.*   **5** of or having to do with the Soviet Union and its East European satellites.   *adj.*

**East·ern·er** (ēs′tər nər)   a person born in or living in the eastern part of the country: *In the West, Ontario people are referred to as Easterners; in Ontario, Maritimers are referred to as Easterners.*   *n.*

**east·ern·most** (ēs′tərn mōst′)   farthest east.   *adj.*

**eastern red cedar**   RED JUNIPER.

**eastern white cedar**   a medium-sized evergreen tree, a species of ARBORVITAE, found especially in eastern Canada and the United States, having a tapered trunk and a dense, narrow, conical crown: *Because the wood of the eastern white cedar is extremely light in mass and resistant to decay, it is valuable for poles, shingles, canoes, etc.*

**Eastern Townships**   most of that part of Quebec lying south of the St. Lawrence River Valley and west of a line drawn southeast from Quebec City to the United States border: *The Eastern Townships were first settled by United Empire Loyalists.*

**East Indian**   **1** of or having to do with India or the East Indies or their inhabitants.   **2** a native or inhabitant of India or the East Indies.   **3** a person of East Indian descent.   1 *adj.*, 2, 3 *n.*

**east–north·east** (ēst′nôr thēst′)   **1** a direction or compass point midway between east and northeast.   **2** in, toward, or from this direction.   1 *n.*, 2 *adj.*, *adv.*

**east–south·east** (ēst′sou thēst′)   **1** a direction or compass point midway between east and southeast.   **2** in, toward, or from this direction.   1 *n.*, 2 *adj.*, *adv.*

**east·ward** (ēs′twərd)   **1** toward the east; east: *an eastward slope.*   **2** in an easterly direction: *to ride eastward.*   **3** an eastward part, direction, or point.   1 *adj.*, 2 *adv.*, 3 *n.*

**east·ward·ly** (ēs′twər dlē)   **1** toward the east.   **2** in an easterly direction.   **3** of winds, from the east.   1, 3 *adj.*, 2 *adv.*

**east·wards** (ēs′twərdz)   EASTWARD (def. 2).   *adv.*

**eas·y** (ē′zē)   **1** requiring little effort; not hard: *easy work.*   **2** free from pain, discomfort, trouble, or worry: *an easy life.*   **3** giving comfort or rest: *an easy chair.*   **4** fond of comfort or rest; lazy.   **5** not harsh; not severe; not strict: *easy terms. That teacher is an easy marker.*   **6** not hard to influence; ready to agree with, believe in, or help anyone.   **7** smooth and pleasant; not awkward: *easy manners.*   **8** not tight; loose: *an easy fit.*   **9** not fast; slow: *an easy pace.*   **10** not much in demand; not hard to get.   **11** *Informal.*   in an easy manner; with ease.   1–10 *adj.*, **eas·i·er, eas·i·est;**   11 *adv.*
**on easy street,**   in comfortable circumstances.
**take it easy,**   relax.

**easy chair**   a comfortable chair, usually having arms and cushions.

**eas·y·go·ing** (ē′zē gō′ing)   usually taking matters easily; tending not to worry: *an easygoing person.*   *adj.*

**easy mark**   *Informal.*   a person who is easily imposed on.

**eat** (ēt)   **1** chew and swallow.   **2** have a meal: *Where shall we eat?*   **3** gnaw; devour: *Termites have eaten the posts and ruined them.*   **4** destroy as if by eating; corrode; wear away: *The sea has eaten into the north shore. The acid has eaten through the metal.*   **5** make by eating: *Moths ate holes in my wool coat.*   *v.*, **ate, eat·en, eat·ing.**
—**eat′er,** *n.*
**eat one's words,** *Informal.*   take back what one has said; retract.
**eat up, a** eat all of.   **b** use up; waste away: *Extravagance ate up his inheritance.*

**eat·a·ble** (ē′tə bəl)   **1** fit to eat; edible.   **2** Usually, **eatables,** *pl.*   food.   1 *adj.*, 2 *n.*

**eat·en** (ē′tən)   pp. of EAT: *Have you eaten your dinner?*   *v.*

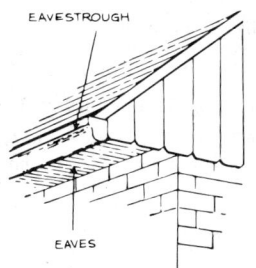

hat, āge, fär; let, ēqual, tėrm; it, īce
hot, ōpen, ôrder; oil, out; cup, pùt, rüle
əbove, takən, pencəl, lemən, circəs
ch, child; ng, long; sh, ship
th, thin; ᴛʜ, then; zh, measure

**eaves** (ēvz) the lower edges of a roof projecting beyond the wall of a building. *n. pl.*

**eaves·drop** (ēvz′drop′) listen to what one is not supposed to hear; listen secretly to private conversation. *v.*, **eaves·dropped, eaves·drop·ping.** —**eaves′drop′per,** *n.*

**eaves·trough** (ēvz′trof′) a gutter placed under the eaves of a roof to catch rainwater and carry it away. See EAVES for picture. *n.*

**ebb** (eb) 1 a flowing of the tide away from the shore; the fall of the tide. 2 flow out; fall: *We waded farther out as the tide ebbed.* 3 a growing less or weaker; decline. 4 a point of decline: *Her fortunes were at their lowest ebb.* 5 grow less or weaker; decline: *His courage began to ebb.* 1, 3, 4 *n.*, 2, 5 *v.*

**ebb and flow** 1 the falling and rising of the tide. 2 constantly changing circumstances; a period of growth followed by a period of decline: *the ebb and flow of business.*

**ebb tide** the flowing of the tide away from the shore: *Ebb tide occurs once in about thirteen hours.*

**eb·on·ite** (eb′ə nīt′) a hard, black substance made by heating rubber together with a large quantity of sulphur; vulcanite: *Ebonite is used for combs and buttons and for electric insulation. n.*

**eb·on·y** (eb′ə nē) 1 a hard, usually black wood, used especially for such ornamental objects as statues and inlays on wooden furniture. 2 a tropical tree that yields this wood. 3 made of ebony. 4 like ebony; black; dark. 1, 2 *n., pl.* **eb·on·ies;** 3, 4 *adj.*

**e·bul·li·ence** (i bul′yəns *or* i bul′ē əns) an overflow of excitement, liveliness, etc.; great enthusiasm. *n.*

**e·bul·li·ent** (i bul′yənt *or* i bul′ē ənt) 1 overflowing with excitement, liveliness, etc.; very enthusiastic. 2 boiling; bubbling. *adj.* —**e·bul′lient·ly,** *adv.*

**eb·ul·li·tion** (eb′ə lish′ən) 1 a boiling; bubbling up. 2 an outburst of feeling, etc. *n.*

**ec·cen·tric** (ek sen′trik) 1 out of the ordinary; odd; peculiar: *eccentric clothes, eccentric habits. It would be eccentric for you to turn around after every ten steps.* 2 a person who behaves in an unusual manner. 3 not having the same centre: *These circles ⊙ are eccentric.* Compare with CONCENTRIC. 4 not moving in a circle but in a related line: *The orbit of an eccentric planet is not circular.* 5 off centre; having its axis set off centre: *an eccentric wheel.* 6 a disk or wheel set off centre so that it can change circular motion into back-and-forth motion. 1, 3–5 *adj.*, 2, 6 *n.* —**ec·cen′tri·cal·ly,** *adv.*

**ec·cen·tric·i·ty** (ek′sen tris′ə tē) 1 something queer or out of the ordinary; oddity; peculiarity: *One of Dr. Johnson's eccentricities was the habit of touching every lamppost he passed.* 2 an eccentric condition; the state of being unusual or out of the ordinary. *n., pl.* **ec·cen·tric·i·ties.**

**ec·cle·si·as·tic** (i klē′zē as′tik) 1 clergyman. 2 ECCLESIASTICAL. 1 *n.*, 2 *adj.*

**ec·cle·si·as·ti·cal** (i klē′zē as′tə kəl) of or having to do with the church or the clergy. *adj.* —**ec·cle′si·as′ti·cal·ly,** *adv.*

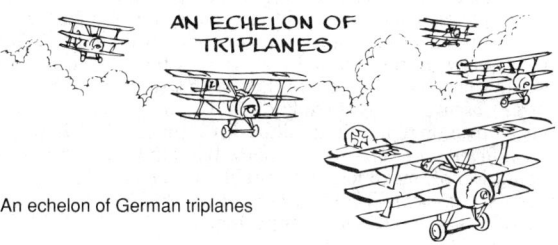

An echelon of German triplanes

**ech·e·lon** (esh′ə lon′) 1 an arrangement of troops, ships, etc. in a steplike formation. 2 form into a steplike arrangement. 3 the level of command. 1, 3 *n.*, 2 *v.*

**e·chid·na** (i kid′nə) a small, egg-laying, ant-eating mammal of Australia having a covering of spines and a long, slender snout. It is classified as a MONOTREME. *n., pl.* **e·chid·nas** or **e·chid·nae** (-nē *or* -nī).

**e·chi·no·derm** (i kī′nə dėrm′) a starfish, sea urchin, or other similar small sea animal having a spiny, stony shell and a body whose parts are arranged radially. *n.*

**ech·o** (ek′ō) 1 sounding again; a repeating of a sound: *An echo is heard when sound waves are bounced back from a cliff or hill.* 2 send back or repeat sound: *The hills echoed the sound of the explosion.* 3 be repeated in sound; resound: *The boom echoed through the valley.* 4 repeat the words or imitate the feelings, acts, etc. of another: *That girl is always echoing her mother.* 5 a person who repeats the words or imitates the feelings, acts, etc. of another. 6 the act of repeating the words or imitating the feelings, acts, etc. of another. 1, 5, 6 *n., pl.* **ech·oes;** 2–4 *v.*, **ech·oed, ech·o·ing.** —**ech′o·er,** *n.* —**ech′o·ic,** *adj.*

**é·clair** (ē kler′ *or* ā kler′) an oblong piece of pastry filled with whipped cream or custard and covered with icing. *n.*

**é·clat** (ā klä′) 1 a brilliant success. 2 fame; glory. *n.*

**ec·lec·tic** (ek lek′tik) 1 selecting and using what seems best from various sources. 2 a follower of an eclectic method. 3 made up of selections from various sources. 1, 3 *adj.*, 2 *n.*

**ec·lec·ti·cism** (ek lek′tə siz′əm) 1 the use or advocacy of an ECLECTIC method. 2 an ECLECTIC system of philosophy, medicine, etc. *n.*

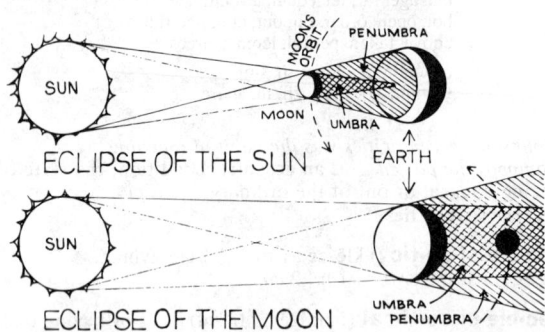

**e·clipse** (ē klips′) **1** a darkening of the sun, moon, etc. when some other heavenly body is in a position that partly or completely cuts off its light as seen from some part of the earth's surface. A **solar eclipse** occurs when the moon passes between the sun and the earth. A **lunar eclipse** occurs when the moon enters the earth's shadow. **2** cut off or obscure the light from; darken. **3** a loss of importance or reputation; failure for a time: *This boxer has suffered an eclipse.* **4** obscure the importance or reputation of; make less outstanding by comparison; surpass: *Napoleon eclipsed other generals of his time.* 1, 3 *n.*, 2, 4 *v.*, **e·clipsed, e·clips·ing.**

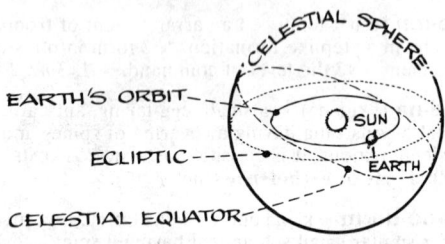

**e·clip·tic** (ē klip′tik) **1** the great circle on the celestial sphere that is the apparent annual path of the sun around the earth. It is the plane that contains the orbit of the earth. **2** of or having to do with the ecliptic or an ECLIPSE (def. 1). 1 *n.*, 2 *adj.*

**e·clip·ti·cal** (ē klip′tə kəl) ECLIPTIC (def. 2). *adj.*

**ec·logue** (ek′log) a short poem about country life, often written as a dialogue between shepherds. *n.*

**eco–** *combining form.* of or having to do with the environment or habitat; ecological: *ecosystem.*
☞ *Etym.* See note at ECOLOGY.

**é·cole** (ā kol′) *French.* school. *n.*

**ec·o·log·i·cal** (ek′ə loj′ə kəl *or* ē′kə loj′ə kəl) of or having to do with ECOLOGY. *adj.*
—**ec′o·log′i·cal·ly,** *adv.*

**ec·ol·o·gist** (ē kol′ə jist) a person trained in ECOLOGY, especially one who makes it his or her work. *n.*

**ec·ol·o·gy** (ē kol′ə jē) the branch of biology that deals with the relation of living things to their environment and to each other. *n.*
☞ *Etym.* From German *Ökologie*, coined by a German scientist in the 19c. from Gk. *oikos* 'house, dwelling' + *-logos* 'study'. See note at -LOGY. The form *eco-* is now used in English as a combining form meaning 'of the habitat or environment', as in ECOSPHERE, ECOSYSTEM, etc. See also the note at ECONOMY.

**econ.** **1** economic. **2** economics. **3** economy.

**e·co·nom·ic** (ē′kə nom′ik *or* ek′ə nom′ik) **1** having to do with economics: *Economic problems have to do with the production, distribution, and consumption of wealth.* **2** having to do with the management of the income, supplies, and expenses of a household, community, government, etc. *adj.*

**e·co·nom·i·cal** (ē′kə nom′ə kəl *or* ek′ə nom′ə kəl) **1** avoiding waste; saving; thrifty: *An efficient engine is economical in its use of fuel.* **2** having to do with ECONOMICS. *adj.*

**e·co·nom·i·cal·ly** (ē′kə nom′i klē *or* ek′ə nom′i klē) **1** in an ECONOMICAL (def. 1) manner. **2** from the point of view of ECONOMICS. *adv.*

**e·co·nom·ics** (ē′kə nom′iks *or* ek′ə nom′iks) the science of the production, distribution, and consumption of wealth: *Economics deals with the material welfare of people and the problems of capital, labour, wages, prices, tariffs, taxes, etc.* *n.*
☞ *Etym.* See note at ECONOMY.

**e·con·o·mist** (i kon′ə mist) a person trained in ECONOMICS, especially one who makes it his or her work. *n.*

**e·con·o·mize** (i kon′ə mīz′) **1** manage so as to avoid waste; use to the best advantage. **2** cut down expenses. *v.*, **e·con·o·mized, e·con·o·miz·ing.**
—**e·con′o·miz′er,** *n.*

**e·con·o·my** (i kon′ə mē) **1** making the most of what one has; freedom from waste in the use of anything; thrift. **2** an instance of this; saving: *Many little economies were necessary.* **3** the managing of affairs and resources to the best advantage; management. **4** an efficient arrangement of parts; organization; system. **5** a system of managing the production, distribution, and consumption of goods: *feudal economy.* *n., pl.* **e·con·o·mies.**
☞ *Etym.* **Economy**, ECONOMICS, and other words derived from them came through L *oeconomia* from Gk. *oikonomia*, which was made up from *oikos* 'house, dwelling' + *nemein* 'manage'. See also the note at ECOLOGY.

**e·co·sphere** (ē′kō sfēr *or* ek′ō sfēr) BIOSPHERE. *n.*

**e·co·sys·tem** (ē′kō sis′təm *or* ek′ō sis′təm) the system formed by the interaction of all the living things of a particular environment with one another and with their habitat. *n.*

**ec·ru** or **é·cru** (ek′rü) pale brown; light tan. *n., adj.*

**ec·sta·sy** (ek′stə sē) **1** a state of great joy; thrilling or overwhelming delight; rapture: *Speechless with ecstasy, the little girl gazed at the toys.* **2** any strong feeling that completely absorbs the mind; uncontrollable emotion. **3** TRANCE. *n., pl.* **ec·sta·sies.**

**ec·stat·ic** (ek stat′ik) **1** full of ecstasy; showing ecstasy. **2** caused by ecstasy. **3** likely to show ecstasy. **4** a person subject to fits of ecstasy. **5 ecstatics,** *pl.* fits of ecstasy; raptures. 1–3 *adj.*, 4, 5 *n.*
—**ec·stat′i·cal·ly,** *adv.*

**ECT** or **E.C.T.** electro-convulsive therapy.

**ec·to·derm** (ek′tə dėrm′) the outer layer of cells formed during the development of the embryos of animals: *Skin, hair, nails, the enamel of teeth, and essential parts of the nervous system grow from the ectoderm.* *n.*

**ec·to·plasm** (ek′tə plaz′əm) the outer portion of the CYTOPLASM of a cell. *n.*

**Ec·ua·do·re·an** or **Ec·ua·do·ri·an** (ek′wə dô′rē ən) **1** of or having to do with Ecuador, a country in South America, or its people. **2** a native or inhabitant of Ecuador. **1** *adj.*, **2** *n.*

**ec·u·men·i·cal** (ek′yə men′ə kəl) **1** general; universal. **2** of or representing the whole Christian Church. **3** promoting unity among all Christians or Christian denominations. *adj.*

**ec·ze·ma** (ek′sə mə *or* eg zē′mə) an inflammation of the skin, characterized by redness, itching, and the formation of patches of scales. *n.*

**–ed**[1] a suffix forming the past tense of most English verbs, as in *wanted* from *want*, *edged* from *edge*, *tried* from *try*.

**–ed**[2] **1** a suffix forming the past participle, as in *echoed*. **2** a suffix meaning: having or supplied with, as in *bearded*, *long-legged*, *pale-faced*, *tender-hearted*. **3** a suffix meaning: having the characteristics of, as in *honeyed*.

**ed.** **1** editor. **2** edition. **3** edited.

**E·dam** (ē′dam *or* ē′dəm) EDAM CHEESE. *n.*

**Edam cheese** **1** a round, yellow cheese made in Holland, usually coloured red on the outside. **2** any cheese resembling this.

**ed·dy** (ed′ē) **1** water, air, etc. moving against the main current, especially when having a whirling motion; a small whirlpool or whirlwind. **2** move against the main current in a whirling motion; whirl: *The water eddied down the drain*. **3** move in circles. **1** *n.*, *pl.* **ed·dies**; **2, 3** *v.*, **ed·died**, **ed·dy·ing**.

**e·del·weiss** (ā′dəl vīs′) a small Alpine plant of the COMPOSITE family, having heads of very small, yellow flowers in the centre of star-shaped clusters of fuzzy leaves. *n.*

**e·de·ma** (i dē′mə) a swelling caused by an abnormal accumulation of watery fluid in the tissues of the body: *Edema is usually a symptom of a disease and has many causes*. *n.*, *pl.* **e·de·ma·ta** (-mə tə).

**e·den·tate** (ē den′tāt) **1** toothless. **2** one of a group of mammals that are toothless or lack incisors: *Armadillos and sloths are edentates*. **1** *adj.*, **2** *n.*

**edge** (ej) **1** the line or place where something ends; part farthest from the middle; side: *the edge of the paper*. **2** the brink; verge: *We walked to the edge of the water*. **3** a thin, sharp side that cuts: *The blade of a knife, axe, or razor has an edge*. **4** sharpness; keenness. **5** put an edge on; form an edge on: *Anne edged the path with white stones*. **6** move in a sideways manner: *She edged through the crowd*. **7** move little by little: *He edged his chair nearer to the fire*. **8** *Informal.* an advantage: *We have a slight edge on the second team in the league*. **9** *Informal.* win a narrow victory over: *Our hockey team edged the visitors 3–2*. **1–4, 8** *n.*, **5–7, 9** *v.*, **edged**, **edg·ing**.
**edge in,** manage to get in.
**on edge,** **a** disturbed; nervous; tense: *Everyone was on edge during the air raid. When he quit smoking, his nerves were on edge for days*. **b** tense with eagerness; anxious; impatient: *We were all on edge until we arrived at the station*.
**set on edge,** **a** disturb; cause to feel excited or irritable. **b** make eager, anxious, or impatient.
**take the edge off,** deprive of force, strength, or enjoyment.

---

**ectoplasm  385  editorially**

hat, āge, fär; let, ēqual, tèrm; it, īce
hot, ōpen, ôrder, oil, out; cup, pùt, rüle
əbove, takən, pencəl, lemən, circəs
ch, child; ng, long; sh, ship
th, thin; ᴛʜ, then; zh, measure

**edge·ways** (ej′wāz′) with the edge forward; in the direction of the edge. *adv.*
**get a word in edgeways,** manage to say a few words during a conversation or conference.

**edge·wise** (ej′wīz′) EDGEWAYS; sideways. *adv.*

**edg·ing** (ej′ing) **1** anything forming an edge or put on along an edge. **2** a border or trimming for an edge. **3** ppr. of EDGE. **1, 2** *n.*, **3** *v.*

**edg·y** (ej′ē) **1** sharply defined: *edgy outlines*. **2** impatient; irritable. *adj.*, **edg·i·er**, **edg·i·est**.

**ed·i·bil·i·ty** (ed′ə bil′ə tē) fitness for eating. *n.*

**ed·i·ble** (ed′ə bəl) **1** fit to eat; eatable: *Not all mushrooms are edible*. **2** **edibles**, *pl.* things fit to eat. **1** *adj.*, **2** *n.*

**e·dict** (ē′dikt) a public order or command by some authority; decree. *n.*

**ed·i·fi·ca·tion** (ed′ə fə kā′shən) moral improvement; spiritual benefit; instruction: *Good books provide edification*. *n.*

**ed·i·fice** (ed′ə fis) a building, especially a large or imposing one. *n.*

**ed·i·fy** (ed′ə fī′) improve morally; benefit spiritually; instruct. *v.*, **ed·i·fied**, **ed·i·fy·ing**.

**ed·it** (ed′it) **1** prepare for publication, correcting errors, checking facts, etc.: *The teacher is editing famous speeches for use in schoolbooks*. **2** have charge of a newspaper, magazine, dictionary, etc. and decide what shall be printed in it. **3** revise or give final form to (motion-picture film, tape recordings, etc.) by such means as cutting and splicing. **4** compile or modify a computer file or program. *v.*

**e·di·tion** (i dish′ən) **1** all the copies of a book, newspaper, etc. printed alike and issued at or near the same time: *In the second edition of the book many of the errors in the first edition had been corrected*. **2** the form in which a book is printed or published: *The reading matter in the cheaper one-volume edition was exactly the same as in the three-volume edition. Some books appear in pocket editions*. *n.*

**ed·i·tor** (ed′ə tər) **1** a person who EDITs, especially one whose occupation is preparing material for publication or broadcasting. **2** a person who is responsible for the content of a periodical or newspaper, or for a particular section or department of one: *a sports editor*. *n.*

**ed·i·to·ri·al** (ed′ə tô′rē əl) **1** an article in a newspaper or magazine, or a comment in a radio or television broadcast, giving the opinion or attitude of the publisher, editor, speaker, etc. regarding some subject. **2** of or having to do with an EDITOR; by an editor or editors. **1** *n.*, **2** *adj.*

**ed·i·to·ri·al·ize** (ed′ə tô′rē ə līz′) **1** write news articles as if they were editorials, including comment and criticisms in the articles. **2** write an editorial. *v.*, **ed·i·to·ri·al·ized**, **ed·i·to·ri·al·iz·ing**.

**ed·i·to·ri·al·ly** (ed′ə tô′rē ə lē) **1** in an editorial manner. **2** in an editorial. *adv.*

**ed·i·tor·ship** (ed′ə tər ship′) the position, duties, or authority of an EDITOR. *n.*

**E.D.P.** or **EDP** electronic data processing.

**ed·u·ca·ble** (ej′ü kə bəl) capable of being educated, taught, or trained. *adj.*

**ed·u·cate** (ej′ü kāt′) 1 develop in knowledge, skill, ability, or character by training, study, or experience; teach; train. 2 send to school. *v.*, **ed·u·cat·ed, ed·u·cat·ing.**

**ed·u·ca·tion** (ej′ü kā′shən) 1 a development in knowledge, skill, ability, or character by teaching, training, study, or experience; teaching; training: *In Canada, public schools offer an education to all children.* 2 the knowledge, skill, ability, or character developed by teaching, training, study, or experience: *A person with education knows how to speak, write, and read well.* 3 the science and art that deals with the principles, problems, etc. of teaching and learning. *n.*

**ed·u·ca·tion·al** (ej′ü kā′shə nəl *or* ej′ə kā′shnəl) 1 of or having to do with education: *an educational association.* 2 giving education; tending to educate: *an educational motion picture.* *adj.* —**ed′u·ca′tion·al·ly,** *adv.*

**ed·u·ca·tive** (ej′ü kā′tiv) that educates; instructive. *adj.*

**ed·u·ca·tor** (ej′ü kā′tər) 1 a person whose profession is education; teacher. 2 a leader in education; authority on methods and principles of education. *n.*

**e·duce** (i dyüs′ *or* i düs′) bring out; draw forth; elicit; develop: *The teacher's questions educed many facts about home gardens.* *v.*, **e·duced, e·duc·ing.**

**–ee** a suffix often added to verbs to form nouns: 1 a person who is _____: *An absentee is a person who is absent.* 2 a person who is _____ed: *An appointee is a person who is appointed.* 3 a person to whom something is _____ed: *A mortgagee is a person to whom something is mortgaged.* 4 a person who _____s: *A standee is a person who stands.*

**EEC** European Economic Community.

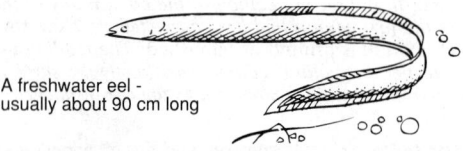

A freshwater eel - usually about 90 cm long

**eel** (ēl) 1 any fish belonging to the order *Apodes*, a group of fishes having a long, usually scaleless, snakelike body and no pelvic fins: *A film of mucus that covers the body of eels makes them very slippery.* 2 any of various other fishes that are similar in shape, such as the ELECTRIC EEL or the LAMPREY. *n.*

**ee·rie** (ē′rē) 1 causing fear; strange; weird: *an eerie scream.* 2 timid because of superstition. *adj.*, **ee·ri·er, ee·ri·est.** —**ee′ri·ness,** *n.*
☛ *Hom.* EYRIE (ē′rē).

**ee·ri·ly** (ē′rə lē) in an eerie way; in a way that causes fear: *The shutters in the old, deserted house creaked eerily.* *adv.*

**ee·ry** (ē′rē) EERIE. *adj.*, **ee·ri·er, ee·ri·est.**

**ef·face** (ə fās′) 1 rub out; blot out; do away with; destroy; wipe out: *The inscriptions on many ancient monuments have been effaced by time. It takes many years to efface the unpleasant memories of a war.* 2 keep oneself from being noticed; make inconspicuous: *The shy boy effaced himself by staying in the background.* *v.*, **ef·faced, ef·fac·ing.** —**ef·fac′a·ble,** *adj.*

**ef·face·ment** (ə fās′mənt) an effacing or being effaced. *n.*

**ef·fect** (i fekt′) 1 whatever is produced by a cause; something made to happen by a person or thing; result: *The overturned boats were the effect of the gale.* 2 produce as an effect; make happen; get done; bring about: *The war effected changes all over the world.* 3 force; power; influence: *The medicine had an immediate effect.* 4 the impression produced. 5 the combination of colour or form in a picture, etc.: *Sunshine coming through leaves makes a lovely effect.* 6 purport; intent; meaning: *She spoke to the effect that we would all fail our test.* 7 **effects,** *pl.* personal property; belongings; goods: *He lost all his personal effects in the fire.* 1, 3–7 *n.*, 2 *v.*
**for effect,** for show; to impress or influence others.
**give effect to,** put in operation; make active.
**in effect, a** in result; in fact; really. **b** in operation: *The new rules are now in effect.*
**into effect,** in operation; in action; in force.
**take effect,** begin to operate; become active: *The new prices will take effect on January 1st.*
☛ *Usage.* Because effect and AFFECT sound similar, they are often confused in writing. Most commonly, **effect** is a noun, meaning 'result', and **affect** is a verb, meaning 'to influence': *We don't know what effect the new rule will have. The new rule will affect everybody.* However, in formal English **effect** is also used as a verb meaning 'get done, bring about': *He effected an improvement in the working conditions.* Thus *to affect a proposal* means to influence it or make a change in it, while *to effect a proposal* means to get it done or bring it to completion.

**ef·fec·tive** (i fek′tiv) 1 producing an effect: *Several new drugs are effective in treating serious diseases.* 2 producing the desired effect. 3 in operation; active: *These laws will become effective on New Year's Day.* 4 striking; impressive. 5 equipped and ready for fighting in the armed forces. *adj.* —**ef·fec′tive·ly,** *adv.* —**ef·fec′tive·ness,** *n.*

**ef·fec·tu·al** (i fek′chü əl) 1 producing the effect desired; capable of producing the effect desired: *Quinine is an effectual preventive of malaria.* 2 VALID (def. 3). *adj.* —**ef·fec′tu·al·ly,** *adv.*

**ef·fec·tu·ate** (i fek′chü āt′) cause; make happen; bring about; accomplish. *v.*, **ef·fec·tu·at·ed, ef·fec·tu·at·ing.**

**ef·fem·i·na·cy** (ə fem′ə nə sē) lack of manly qualities; unmanly weakness or delicacy. *n.*

**ef·fem·i·nate** (ə fem′ə nit) lacking in manly qualities; showing a weakness or delicacy that is not manly. *adj.* —**ef·fem′i·nate·ly,** *adv.*

**ef·fer·ent** (ef′ə rənt) conveying outward from a central organ or point: *Efferent nerves carry impulses from the brain to the muscles.* Compare with AFFERENT. *adj.*

**ef·fer·vesce** (ef′ər ves′) 1 give off bubbles of gas; bubble: *Ginger ale effervesces.* 2 be lively and merry; be excited. *v.*, **ef·fer·vesced, ef·fer·vesc·ing.**

**ef·fer·ves·cence** (ef′ər ves′əns) 1 the act or process of bubbling. 2 liveliness; gaiety. *n.*

**ef·fer·ves·cent** (ef′ər ves′ənt) 1 giving off bubbles of gas; bubbling. 2 lively; merry. *adj.*

**ef·fete** (i fēt′) no longer able to produce; worn out; exhausted. *adj.* —**ef·fete′ness,** *n.*

**ef·fi·ca·cious** (ef′ə kā′shəs) producing the desired results; effective: *Vaccination for flu is usually efficacious.* *adj.* —**ef′fi·ca′cious·ly,** *adv.* —**ef′fi·ca′cious·ness,** *n.*

**ef·fi·ca·cy** (ef′ə kə sē) the power to produce a desired effect or result; effectiveness. *n., pl.* **ef·fi·ca·cies.**

**ef·fi·cien·cy** (ə fish′ən sē) **1** the ability to produce the effect wanted without waste of time, energy, etc. **2** efficient operation: *Friction lowers the efficiency of a machine.* *n., pl.* **ef·fi·cien·cies.**

**ef·fi·cient** (ə fish′ənt) **1** able to produce the effect wanted without waste of time, energy, etc.; capable; competent: *An efficient cook receives good pay.* **2** actually producing an effect: *Heat is the efficient cause in changing water to steam.* *adj.* —**ef·fi′cient·ly,** *adv.*

**ef·fi·gy** (ef′ə jē) a statue, etc. of a person; image: *The dead man's monument bore his effigy.* *n., pl.* **ef·fi·gies.** **burn** or **hang in effigy,** burn or hang a stuffed image of a person to show hatred or contempt.

**ef·flo·resce** (ef′lə res′) burst into bloom; blossom out. *v.,* **ef·flo·resced, ef·flo·resc·ing.**

**ef·flo·res·cence** (ef′lə res′əns) **1** a blooming; flowering. **2** a mass of flowers. **3** anything resembling a mass of flowers. *n.*

**ef·flo·res·cent** (ef′lə res′ənt) blooming; flowering. *adj.*

**ef·flu·ence** (ef′lü əns) **1** an outward flow. **2** the thing that flows out; emanation. *n.*

**ef·flu·ent** (ef′lü ənt) **1** flowing out or forth. **2** that which flows out or forth; an outflow, especially of SEWAGE. **3** a stream flowing out of another stream, lake, etc. **1** *adj.,* **2, 3** *n.*

**ef·flu·vi·a** (i flü′vē ə) a pl. of EFFLUVIUM. *n.*

**ef·flu·vi·um** (i flü′vē əm) **1** an unpleasant vapour or odour. **2** a vapour; odour. *n., pl.* **ef·flu·vi·a** (-ə) or **ef·flu·vi·ums.**

**ef·fort** (ef′ərt) **1** the use of energy and strength to do something; trying hard: *Climbing a steep hill takes effort.* **2** a hard try; strong attempt. **3** the result of effort; anything done with effort; achievement: *Handel's 'Messiah' was his greatest effort.* **4** the amount of energy required to perform a physical task: *To lift a mass of one kilogram requires effort equivalent to ten newtons.* *n.*

**ef·fort·less** (ef′ər tlis) requiring or involving no effort; easy. *adj.* —**ef′fort·less·ly,** *adv.* —**ef′fort·less·ness,** *n.*

**ef·fron·ter·y** (ə frun′tə rē) shameless boldness; impudence: *The candidate had the effrontery to ask the people she had insulted to vote for her.* *n., pl.* **ef·fron·ter·ies.**

**ef·ful·gence** (i ful′jəns) brightness; radiance: *the effulgence of the stars.* *n.*

**ef·ful·gent** (i ful′jənt) shining brightly; radiant. *adj.*

**ef·fuse** (i fyüz′) pour out; spill; shed. *v.,* **ef·fused, ef·fus·ing.**

**ef·fu·sion** (i fyü′zhən) **1** pouring out: *the effusion of blood.* **2** an unrestrained expression of feeling, etc. in talking or writing. *n.*

**ef·fu·sive** (i fyü′siv) showing too much feeling; too emotional in expression. *adj.* —**ef·fu′sive·ly,** *adv.* —**ef·fu′sive·ness,** *n.*

---

**effete** 387 **egoism**

hat, āge, fär; let, ēqual, tėrm; it, īce
hot, ōpen, ôrder; oil, out; cup, pùt, rüle
əbove, takən, pencəl, lemən, circəs
ch, child; ng, long; sh, ship
th, thin; ᴛʜ, then; zh, measure

**eft** (eft) **1** a newt in the land stage. **2** formerly, a small newt or lizard. *n.*

**e.g.** for example.

**egg¹** (eg) **1** the roundish body, covered with a shell or membrane, that is laid by the female of birds, many reptiles, amphibians, fish, and other types of animals: *Young animals come from these eggs.* **2** a female GERM CELL. **3** anything shaped like a hen's egg. *n.* —**egg′less,** *adj.* —**egg′like′,** *adj.*

**egg²** (eg) urge; encourage (*used with* **on**): *The other boys egged him on to fight.* *v.*

**egg·beat·er** (eg′bē′tər) a kitchen utensil for beating or whipping eggs, cream, etc., especially a hand-operated one with rotary blades. *n.*

**egg cell** the mature female reproductive cell produced by the ovary of a plant or animal; a female GAMETE; ovum: *A new plant or animal develops from a fertilized egg cell.*

**egg cup** a small cup in which a boiled egg is placed to be eaten.

**egg·head** (eg′hed′) *Informal.* an intellectual; highbrow. *n.*

**egg·nog** (eg′nog′) a drink made of eggs beaten up with milk, spices, and sugar, often containing whisky, brandy, or wine. *n.*

**egg·plant** (eg′plant′) **1** a large, egg-shaped fruit, used as a vegetable and having a glossy purple skin when ripe; aubergine. **2** the plant bearing such fruit. *n.*

**egg roll** a small, filled pastry containing chopped vegetables and, often, pieces of chicken, shrimp, etc.: *Egg rolls are deep-fried in fat.*

**egg·shell** (eg′shel′) **1** the shell covering an egg. **2** like an eggshell; very thin and delicate. **3** a semi-mat finish on paint when dry: *eggshell paint, eggshell finish.* **1** *n.,* **2, 3** *adj.*

**egg timer** a measuring device, shaped like a miniature hour-glass, for timing the boiling of an egg to the desired firmness.

**e·gis** (ē′jis) See AEGIS. *n.*

**eg·lan·tine** (eg′lən tīn′) a wild rose with a tall, prickly stem and single, pink flowers; SWEETBRIER. *n.*

**e·go** (ē′gō) **1** the individual as a whole in his or her capacity to think, feel, and act; self. **2** *Informal.* conceit: *The boy's ego annoyed many people.* *n., pl.* **e·gos.**

**e·go·cen·tric** (ē′gō sen′trik *or* eg′ō sen′trik) **1** looking upon oneself as the focus and object of all experience and events; seeing everything in relation to oneself; self-centred; EGOISTIC. **2** an egocentric person. **1** *adj.,* **2** *n.*

**e·go·ism** (ē′gō iz′əm *or* eg′ō iz′əm) **1** the quality of seeking the welfare of oneself only; selfishness. **2** the act or practice of talking too much about oneself; conceit. *n.*

**e·go·ist** (ē′gō ist *or* eg′ō ist)   1 a person who seeks the welfare of himself or herself only; selfish person.   2 a person who talks too much about himself or herself; conceited person.   *n.*

**e·go·is·tic** (ē′gō is′tik *or* eg′ō is′tik)   1 seeking the welfare of oneself only; selfish.   2 talking too much about oneself; conceited.   *adj.*   —**e′go·is′ti·cal**, *adj.* —**e′go·is′ti·cal·ly**, *adv.*

**e·go·tism** (ē′gə tiz′əm *or* eg′ə tiz′əm)   EGOISM.   *n.*

**e·go·tist** (ē′gə tist *or* eg′ə tist)   EGOIST.   *n.*

**e·go·tis·tic** (ē′gə tis′tik *or* eg′ə tis′tik)   EGOISTIC. *adj.*   —**eg′o·tis′ti·cal·ly**, *adv.*

**e·go·tis·ti·cal** (ē′gə tis′tə kəl *or* eg′ə tis′ti kəl) EGOISTIC.   *adj.*

**e·gre·gious** (i grē′jəs)   1 remarkably or extraordinarily bad; outrageous; flagrant: *an egregious lie.*   2 remarkable; extraordinary.   *adj.*   —**e·gre′gious·ly**, *adv.*

**e·gress** (ē′gres)   1 going out: *The enemy blocked the narrow pass so that no egress was possible for our exhausted soldiers.*   2 a way out; exit.   3 the right to go out.   *n.* Compare with INGRESS.

**e·gret** (ē′gret)   any of various herons that in mating season grow tufts of beautiful, long plumes, which were formerly much used as ornaments for the head.   *n.*

**E·gyp·tian** (i jip′shən)   1 of or having to do with Egypt, a country in northeastern Africa, or its people. 2 a native or inhabitant of Egypt.   3 the language of the ancient Egyptians.   1 *adj.*, 2, 3 *n.*

**eh** (ā)   1 an exclamation expressing doubt, surprise, or failure to hear exactly.   2 an exclamation suggesting "Yes" for an answer: *Wasn't it lucky, eh?*   3 in Canadian English, a word used to convert a statement into a question: *So that's what you think, eh?*   *interj.*

**ei·der** (ī′dər)   a large northern sea duck, usually black and white, with very soft feathers on its breast.   *n.*

**ei·der–down** (ī′dər doun′)   1 the soft feathers from the breasts of EIDERS, used to stuff pillows, bed quilts, etc. 2 a quilt stuffed with these feathers.   *n.*

**eider duck**   EIDER.

**eight** (āt)   1 one more than seven; 8: *We've used up two of the rolls, so there are eight left. She sneezed eight times.* 2 the numeral 8: *He makes his eights with two circles.* 3 the eighth in a set or series; especially, a playing card having eight spots: *the eight of diamonds.*   4 being eighth in a set or series (*used mainly after the noun*): *Section Eight is missing.*   5 in rowing:   **a** a crew of eight rowers.   **b** the boat they use.   6 any set or series of eight persons or things: *The computer was programmed to count in eights.* 1–3, 5, 6 *n.*, 1, 4 *adj.*

**behind the eight ball**,   in a most unfavourable situation: *Your letter of refusal puts you behind the eight ball because you can't accept the job now.*

☛ *Etym.*   From OE *ehta, eahta*, related to German *acht* and having the same INDO-EUROPEAN source as L *octo* and Gk. *oktō*. See also the note at OCTAGON.

**eight·een** (ā′tēn′)   1 eight more than ten; 18: *It was just fifteen degrees an hour ago, but it's already gone up to eighteen. I sent eighteen postcards.*   2 the numeral 18: *The 18 is not in line with the other figures in the column.*   3 the eighteenth in a set or series.   4 being eighteenth in a set or series (*used after the noun*): *Chapter Eighteen.*   5 a set or series of eighteen persons or things.   1–3, 5 *n.*, 1, 4 *adj.*

**eight·eenth** (ā′tēnth′)   1 next after the 17th; last in a series of eighteen; 18th.   2 one of 18 equal parts. *adj.*, *n.*

**eighth** (ātth)   1 next after the seventh; last in a series of eight; 8th.   2 one of 8 equal parts.   3 in music, one octave.   1, 2 *adj.*, 1–3 *n.*

**eighth note**   in music, a short note; one eighth of a whole note; QUAVER (def. 5).   See NOTE for picture.

**eighth rest**   in music, a rest, or sign for silence, lasting as long as an EIGHTH NOTE.   See REST¹ for picture.

**eight·i·eth** (ā′tē ith)   1 next after the 79th; last in a series of 80; 80th.   2 one, or being one, of 80 equal parts.   *adj.*, *n.*

**eight·y** (ā′tē)   1 eight times ten; 80.   2 **eighties**, *pl.* the years from eighty through eighty-nine, especially of a century or of a person's life: *My great-grandmother is in her eighties.*   1, 2 *n.*, *pl.* **eight·ies;**   1 *adj.*

**Ein·stein equation** (īn′stīn)   an equation expressing the relation of mass and energy: $E = MC^2$. E = the energy in joules; M = the mass in grams; C = the velocity of light in centimetres per second.

**ein·stein·i·um** (īn stī′nē əm)   a rare, radio-active artificial element, produced as a by-product of nuclear fission.   *Symbol*: Es   *n.*

**ei·ther** (ē′ᴛʜər *or* ī′ᴛʜər)   1 one or the other of two: *Either hat is becoming.*   2 one or the other of two things or people: *Either of the hats is becoming.*   3 one or the other of two actions: *Either come in or go out.*   4 each of two: *On either side of the river lie cornfields.*   5 any more than another; also: *If you do not go, I shall not go either.* 6 *Informal.*   a word used to strengthen a negative in contradiction or retraction: *I've finished all my homework; no, I haven't either.*   1, 4 *adj.*, 2 *pron.*, 3 *conj.*, 5, 6 *adv.*

**e·jac·u·late** (i jak′yə lāt′)   say suddenly and briefly; exclaim.   *v.*, **e·jac·u·lat·ed, e·jac·u·lat·ing.**

**e·jac·u·la·tion** (i jak′yə lā′shən)   something said suddenly and briefly; exclamation.   *n.*

**e·jac·u·la·to·ry** (i jak′yə lə tô′rē)   said suddenly and briefly; containing exclamations.   *adj.*

**e·ject** (i jekt′)   1 throw out: *The volcano ejected lava and ashes.*   2 force out; expel: *The landlady ejected the tenant who did not pay his rent.*   *v.*   —**e·jec′tor**, *n.*

**e·jec·tion** (i jek′shən)   1 an ejecting.   2 being ejected. 3 something ejected: *Lava is a volcanic ejection.*   *n.*

**e·ject·ment** (i jekt′mənt)   an ejecting; dispossessing; ousting.   *n.*

**eke** (ēk) *Archaic*,   except in

**eke out**,   **a** supply what is lacking to; supplement: *The clerk eked out his wages by working evenings.*   **b** barely make a living by various schemes or makeshifts.

**e·lab·o·rate** (i lab′ə rit *for adjective,* i lab′ə rāt′ *for verb*) 1 worked out with great care; having many details; complicated: *The scientists made elaborate preparations for studying the eclipse.*   2 work out with great care; add details to: *The inventor spent months elaborating his plans for a new engine.*   3 talk, write, etc. in great detail; give added details: *The witness was asked to elaborate upon one of her statements.*   4 make with labour; produce.   1 *adj.*, 2–4 *v.*, **e·lab·o·rat·ed, e·lab·o·rat·ing.** —**e·lab′o·rate·ly**, *adv.*   —**e·lab′o·rate·ness**, *n.*

**e·lab·o·ra·tion** (i lab′ə rā′shən)   **1** elaborating.   **2** being elaborated.   **3** something elaborated.   *n.*

**é·lan** (ā lon′; *French*, ā läN′)   enthusiasm; liveliness.   *n.*

**e·land** (ē′lənd)   a large, heavily built African antelope with twisted horns.   *n.*

**e·lapse** (i laps′)   slip away; glide by; pass: *Hours elapsed while she slept.*   *v.,* **e·lapsed, e·laps·ing.**

**e·las·mo·branch** (i las′mə brangk′)   any of a group of fish whose skeletons are formed of CARTILAGE (def. 1) and whose gills are thin and platelike: *Sharks and rays are elasmobranchs.*   *n.*

**e·las·tic** (i las′tik)   **1** having the quality of springing back to its original size, shape, or position after being stretched, squeezed, bent, etc.: *Toy balloons, sponges, and steel springs are elastic.*   **2** springing back; springy: *an elastic step.*   **3** being able to recover quickly from weariness, low spirits, or misfortune; buoyant: *Her elastic spirits never let her be discouraged for long.*   **4** easily altered to suit changed conditions; flexible; adaptable.   **5** tape or fabric woven partly of rubber threads.   **6** a RUBBER BAND.   1–4 *adj.,* 5, 6 *n.*   —**e·las′ti·cal·ly,** *adv.*

**e·las·tic·i·ty** (i las′tis′ə tē *or* ē′las tis′ə tē)   **1** an elastic quality: *Rubber has great elasticity.*   **2** flexibility: *Good and evil are words having great elasticity of meaning.*   *n.*

**e·late** (i lāt′)   put in high spirits; make joyful or proud.   *v.,* **e·lat·ed, e·lat·ing.**

**e·lat·ed** (i lā′tid)   **1** in high spirits; joyful; proud.   **2** pt. and pp. of ELATE.   1 *adj.,* 2 *v.*   —**e·lat′ed·ly,** *adv.*

**e·la·tion** (i lā′shən)   high spirits; joyous pride; exultant gladness: *Ruth was filled with elation at having won the prize.*   *n.*

**el·bow** (el′bō)   **1** the joint between the upper arm and forearm. See ARM¹ for picture.   **2** the outer part of this joint, especially the point formed when the arm is bent.   **3** anything resembling a bent elbow in shape or position: *A sharp turn in a road or river may be called an elbow.*   **4** push with the elbow: *Don't elbow me off the sidewalk.*   **5** make one's way by pushing: *He elbowed his way through the crowd.*   1–3 *n.,* 4, 5 *v.*
**at one's elbow,**   near at hand; close by: *When Juan did his homework, his dictionary was always at his elbow.*

**elbow grease**   effort or enthusiasm.

**el·bow·ing** (el′bō ing)   **1** in hockey, an offence, resulting in a penalty, of jabbing one's elbows into an opponent's body.   **2** ppr. of ELBOW.   1 *n.,* 2 *v.*

**elbow room** or **el·bow·room** (el′bō rüm′)   plenty of room; enough space to move or work in.   *n.*

**el·der**¹ (el′dər)   **1** born, produced, or formed before something else; older; senior: *my elder sister, an elder statesman.*   **2** prior in rank, validity, etc.: *an elder title to an estate.*   **3** earlier; former.   **4** an older person: *The children showed respect for their elders.*   **5** an aged person.   **6** an ancestor.   **7** one of the older and more influential people of a tribe or community; a chief, ruler, member of council, etc.   **8** any of various important officers of certain churches.   1–3 *adj.,* 4–8 *n.*

**el·der**² (el′dər)   ELDERBERRY.   *n.*

**el·der·ber·ry** (el′dər ber′ē)   **1** a shrub or tree having flat clusters of white flowers and black or red berries that are sometimes used in making wine.   **2** the berry of such a plant.   *n., pl.* **el·der·ber·ries.**

hat, āge, fär; let, ēqual, tėrm; it, īce
hot, ōpen, ôrder; oil, out; cup, put, rüle
əbove, takən, pencəl, lemən, circəs
ch, child; ng, long; sh, ship
th, thin; ŦH, then; zh, measure

**eld·er·ly** (el′dər lē)   rather old; beyond middle age; near old age.   *adj.*

**eld·est** (el′dist)   OLDEST.   *adj.*

**El·do·ra·do** or **El Do·ra·do** (el′də rä′dō)   any fabulously wealthy place.   *n., pl.* **El·do·ra·dos** or **El Do·ra·dos.**
☞ *Etym.* From *El Dorado,* a legendary place of very great wealth sought by early explorers in South America.

**elec.**   **1** electricity.   **2** electrical.   **3** electrician.

**e·lect** (i lekt′)   **1** choose or select for an office by voting: *The club members elect a new president each year.*   **2** elected but not yet in office (*used after the noun*): *president elect.*   **3** choose; select: *We elected to play baseball.*   **4** specially chosen; selected.   **5 the elect,** people who belong to a group with special rights and privileges.   1, 3 *v.,* 2, 4 *adj.,* 5 *n.*

**e·lec·tion** (i lek′shən)   **1** choice.   **2** a choosing by vote.   **3** a GENERAL ELECTION.   *n.*

**e·lec·tion·eer** (i lek′shə nēr′)   work for the success of a candidate or party in an ELECTION (def. 2).   *v.*

**e·lec·tive** (i lek′tiv)   **1** chosen by an ELECTION (def. 2): *Aldermen are elective officials.*   **2** filled by an ELECTION (def. 3): *The office of President of the United States is elective.*   **3** having the right to vote in an ELECTION (def. 2).   **4** open to choice; not required: *elective surgery. German is an elective subject in many high schools.*   **5** a subject or course of study that may be taken but is not required.   1–4 *adj.,* 5 *n.*

**e·lec·tor** (i lek′tər)   **1** a person who has the right to vote in an ELECTION (def. 2).   **2** one of the princes who had the right to elect the emperor of the Holy Roman Empire.   *n.*

**e·lec·tor·al** (i lek′tə rəl)   **1** of ELECTORS (def. 1).   **2** of an ELECTION (def. 2).   *adj.*

**electoral college**   *U.S.*   a group of people chosen by the voters to elect the President and Vice-President of the United States.

**e·lec·tor·ate** (i lek′tə rit)   the persons having the right to vote in an ELECTION (defs. 2, 3).   *n.*

**electr.**   **1** electricity.   **2** electrical.   **3** electrician.

**e·lec·tric** (i lek′trik)   **1** of electricity; having to do with electricity.   **2** charged with electricity: *an electric battery.*   **3** capable of giving an electric shock: *an electric eel.*   **4** run by electricity: *an electric train.*   **5** making use of electricity: *an electric guitar.*   **6** exciting; thrilling.   *adj.*
☞ *Etym.* **Electric,** ELECTRON, and ELECTRO- can all be traced back to Gk. *ēlektron* 'amber'. Amber is a resin that has the power of attracting other substances when it is rubbed. Our word **electron** was made up in the late 19c. from the stem of *electric* + a scientific suffix *-on.* **Electric** goes back to the 17c.

**e·lec·tri·cal** (i lek′trə kəl)   ELECTRIC.   *adj.*

**electrical engineering**   the branch of engineering which deals with electricity, especially in its practical application to communications, power supplies, etc.

**e·lec·tri·cal·ly** (i lek′tri klē)   by electricity.   *adv.*

**electrical transcription** 1 a system of radio broadcasting from a special phonograph record. 2 a special phonograph record used for such broadcasting.

**electric chair** the chair used in electrocuting criminals.

**electric eel** a large, eel-like fish of South America, capable of giving strong electric shocks.

**electric eye** a PHOTO-ELECTRIC CELL: *An electric eye can operate a mechanism that will make a door open when the light reaching the cell is interrupted or changed by a person, car, etc. that passes in front of it.*

**electric field** the space surrounding an electrically charged body within which it produces electric force.

**e·lec·tri·cian** (i lek′trish′ən) a person whose work is installing or repairing electric wires, lights, motors, etc. *n.*

**e·lec·tric·i·ty** (i lek′tris′ə tē) 1 a form of energy that can produce light, heat, magnetism, and chemical changes, and that can be generated by friction, induction, or chemical changes. 2 an electric current; a flow of electrons: *Most refrigerators are run by electricity.* 3 the branch of physics that deals with electricity. *n.*

**electric light bulb** the glass bulb and the enclosed filament by which electricity is converted to light for illumination.

**electric storm** or **electrical storm** a storm accompanied by much thunder and lightning.

**e·lec·tri·fi·ca·tion** (i lek′trə fə kā′shən) 1 an ELECTRIFYing (defs. 2, 5). 2 being electrified. *n.*

**e·lec·tri·fy** (i lek′trə fī) 1 charge with electricity. 2 equip to use electricity: *Some railways once run by steam are now electrified.* 3 give an electric shock to. 4 excite; thrill: *The speaker electrified her audience.* 5 provide with electric power service: *Many rural areas will soon be electrified.* *v.*, **e·lec·tri·fied, e·lec·tri·fy·ing.**

**electro–** combining form: 1 electric, as in *electromagnet.* 2 electrically, as in *electropositive.* 3 electricity, as in *electrochemistry.* ☛ Etym. See note at ELECTRIC.

**e·lec·tro·chem·i·cal** (i lek′trō kem′ə kəl) of, having to do with, or involving the principles or processes of ELECTROCHEMISTRY. *adj.* —**e·lec′tro·chem′i·cal·ly,** *adv.*

**electrochemical cell** a device capable of producing an electric current by means of chemical action, consisting of a container with two electrodes of different metals in a paste or liquid that will conduct electricity: *An electrochemical cell generates a current when the electrodes are connected by a conducting wire. A flashlight battery is an electrochemical cell.* See DRY CELL for picture.

**e·lec·tro·chem·is·try** (i lek′trō kem′i strē) the branch of chemistry that deals with chemical changes produced by electricity and the production of electricity by chemical changes. *n.*

**electro-convulsive therapy** the treatment of mental disorder, especially depression, through shock induced by electrical means.

**e·lec·tro·cute** (i lek′trə kyüt′) kill by means of an electric current. *v.*, **e·lec·tro·cut·ed, e·lec·tro·cut·ing.**

**e·lec·tro·cu·tion** (i lek′trə kyü′shən) killing by electricity. *n.*

**e·lec·trode** (i lek′trōd) a conductor through which an electric current enters or leaves a conducting medium such as an electrolyte, gas, or vacuum in a battery, electron tube, etc. See VACUUM TUBE for picture. *n.*

**e·lec·tro·dy·nam·ics** (i lek′trō dī nam′iks) the branch of physics that deals with the action of electricity or with electric currents. *n.*

**e·lec·tro·lyse** (i lek′trə līz′) decompose by ELECTROLYSIS (def. 1). *v.*, **e·lec·tro·lysed, e·lec·tro·lys·ing.** —**e·lec′tro·ly·sa′tion,** *n.* —**e·lec′tro·lys′er,** *n.*

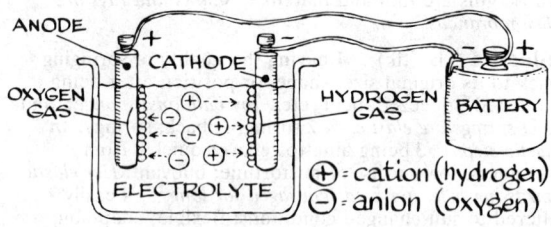

The electrolysis (def. 1) of water. The electrolyte is water with salt (or sulphuric acid, etc.) added to ionize it.

**e·lec·trol·y·sis** (i lek′trol′ə sis) 1 the decomposition of a chemical compound into ions by the passage of an electric current through a solution of it. 2 the removal of excess hair, moles, etc. by destruction with an electrified needle. *n.*

**e·lec·tro·lyte** (i lek′trə līt′) 1 a solution that will conduct an electric current. 2 a chemical compound whose water solution will conduct an electric current: *Acids, bases, and salts are electrolytes.* *n.*

**e·lec·tro·lyt·ic** (i lek′trə lit′ik) having to do with ELECTROLYSIS or with an ELECTROLYTE. *adj.* —**e·lec′tro·lyt′i·cal·ly,** *adv.*

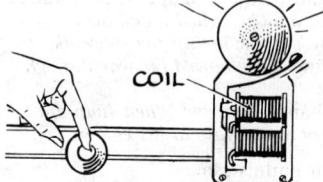

An electromagnet used in an electric doorbell. When the button is pushed to complete the circuit, the electromagnet is activated and attracts the metal bar to which the clapper is attached. This causes the clapper to strike the bell.

**e·lec·tro·mag·net** (i lek′trō mag′nit) a strong MAGNET (def. 1) made by coiling wire around an iron core and applying an electrical current to the coil. *n.*

**e·lec·tro·mag·net·ic** (i lek′trō mag net′ik) of, having to do with, or caused by ELECTROMAGNETISM. *adj.*

**electromagnetic spectrum** the whole range of wavelengths (or frequencies) of electromagnetic waves, from the longest radio waves (wavelength $10^5$ metres) to the shortest cosmic rays (wavelength $10^{-17}$ metres).

**electromagnetic wave** a wave of energy, such as a radio wave, light wave, or X ray that can travel through space or matter.

**e·lec·tro·mag·net·ism** (i lek′trō mag′nə tiz′əm) 1 MAGNETISM (def. 1) produced by a current of electricity. 2 the branch of physics that deals with this. *n.*

**e·lec·trom·e·ter** (i lek′trom′ə tər) an instrument for measuring differences in electrical charge or potential. *n.*

**e·lec·tro·mo·tive** (i lek′trə mō′tiv) **1** producing a flow of electricity. **2** of or having to do with ELECTROMOTIVE FORCE. *adj.*

**electromotive force** the amount of energy derived from an electric source in one second when one unit of current is passing through the source: *Electromotive force is produced by differences in electrical charge or potential.*

**e·lec·tron** (i lek′tron) in chemistry and physics, an elementary particle carrying one unit of negative electric charge, found outside the nucleus of every kind of ATOM (def. 1). *n.*
☛ *Etym.* See note at ELECTRIC.

**electron beam** a stream of ELECTRONS moving in the same direction at the same speed. The electron beam inside the picture tube of a television set inscribes the picture on the screen.

**e·lec·tro·neg·a·tive** (i lek′trō neg′ə tiv) **1** charged with negative electricity. **2** tending to pass to the positive pole in ELECTROLYSIS (def. 1). **3** non-metallic; acid. *adj.*

**electron gun** a device that guides the flow and greatly increases the speed of atomic particles: *Electron guns are being developed for use in oil refining and various other industries.*

**e·lec·tron·ic** (i lek′tron′ik) of or having to do with an ELECTRON or electrons, especially with the action of electrons in motion. *adj.* —**e·lec·tron′ic·al·ly,** *adv.*

**electronic brain** COMPUTER (def. 1).

**electronic mail** messages sent from one terminal to another or others by users of a computer network; e-mail.

**electronic music** music created, usually on magnetic tape, from sound made by electronic generators and filters.

**e·lec·tron·ics** (i lek′tron′iks) the branch of physics that deals with the production, activity, and effects of ELECTRONS in motion (*used with a singular verb*): *Radar, radio, television, etc. are based on the principles of electronics.* *n.*

**electron microscope** a microscope that uses beams of ELECTRONS instead of beams of light, and has much higher power than any ordinary microscope: *The enlarged images of the electron microscope are not observable directly by the eye, but are projected upon a fluorescent surface or photographic plate.*

**electron tube** a device for producing a controlled flow of ELECTRONS, consisting of a sealed glass or metal tube, etc., either having a vacuum inside or containing a gas at low pressure through which the electrons can move readily to carry current between the electrodes inside the tube: *Microwave tubes and cathode-ray tubes are two kinds of electron tube.*

**e·lec·tron·volt** (i lek′tron vōlt′) a unit used with the SI for measuring the kinetic energy of electrons. One electronvolt is equal to the energy acquired by an electron when it is accelerated through a potential difference of one volt. Symbol: eV *n.*

**e·lec·tro·plate** (i lek′trə plāt′) **1** cover with a coating of metal by means of ELECTROLYSIS (def. 1). **2** silverware, etc. covered in this way. **1** *v.*, **e·lec·tro·plat·ed, e·lec·tro·plat·ing;** **2** *n.* —**e·lec′tro·plat′er,** *n.*

**e·lec·tro·pos·i·tive** (i lek′trō poz′ə tiv) **1** charged with positive electricity. **2** tending to pass to the negative pole in ELECTROLYSIS. **3** metallic; basic. *adj.*

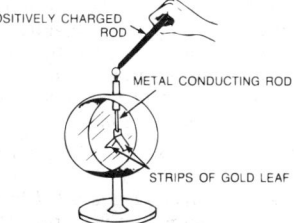

hat, āge, fär; let, ēqual, tėrm; it, īce
hot, ōpen, ôrder; oil, out; cup, pùt, rüle
əbove, takən, pencəl, lemən, circəs
ch, child; ng, long; sh, ship
th, thin; ᴛʜ, then; zh, measure

**e·lec·tro·scope** (i lek′trə skōp′) any of various devices or instruments for detecting the presence of a minute electric charge on a body and showing whether the charge is positive or negative. *n.*

**e·lec·tro·stat·ic** (i lek′trə stat′ik) having to do with electricity at rest or with stationary electric charges. *adj.*

**e·lec·tro·stat·ics** (i lek′trə stat′iks) the branch of physics that deals with objects charged with electricity. *n.*

**e·lec·tro·ther·a·py** (i lek′trō ther′ə pē) the treatment of disease by electricity. *n.*

**e·lec·tro·type** (i lek′trə tīp′) **1** a metal or composition plate used in printing. An electrotype is a copy of a page of type, an engraving, etc., consisting of a thin shell of metal deposited by electrolytic action in a wax mould of the original and backed with type metal. **2** a print made from such a plate. **3** make such a plate or plates of. **1, 2** *n.*, **3** *v.*, **e·lec·tro·typed, e·lec·tro·typ·ing.** —**e·lec′tro·typ′er,** *n.*

**el·ee·mos·y·nar·y** (el′ə mos′ə ner′ē) **1** of or for charity; charitable. **2** provided by charity; free. **3** dependent on charity; supported by charity. *adj.*

**el·e·gance** (el′ə gəns) **1** refined grace and richness; luxury free from coarseness: *We admired the elegance of her clothes.* **2** something elegant. *n.*

**el·e·gant** (el′ə gənt) **1** having or showing good taste; gracefully and richly refined: *The palace had elegant furnishings.* **2** expressed with taste; correct and polished in expression or arrangement: *an elegant speech.* **3** *Informal.* fine; excellent; superior. *adj.* —**el′e·gant·ly,** *adv.*

**el·e·gize** (el′ə jīz′) **1** write an ELEGY about. **2** write an ELEGY; lament. *v.*, **el·e·gized, el·e·giz·ing.**

**el·e·gy** (el′ə jē) a mournful or melancholy poem; poem that is a lament for the dead: *Milton's "Lycidas" and Shelley's "Adonais" are elegies.* *n., pl.* **el·e·gies.**

**elem.** **1** element; elements. **2** elementary.

**el·e·ment** (el′ə mənt) **1** one of the simple substances, such as gold, iron, carbon, sulphur, oxygen, and hydrogen, that have not yet been separated into simpler parts by chemical means; a substance composed of atoms that are chemically alike. See the chemical elements chart in the

# elemental — eliminate

Appendix. 2 one of the parts of which anything is made up: *Honesty, industry, and kindness are elements of a good life.* 3 one of the four substances—earth, water, air, and fire—that were once thought to make up all other things. 4 the place, condition, activities, etc. best suited to or preferred by a person or thing: *She was in her element tinkering with old clocks.* 5 **the elements,** *pl.* **a** the simple, necessary parts to be learned first; the first principles: *We learned the elements of arithmetic before the seventh grade.* **b** the atmospheric forces: *The storm seemed a war of the elements.* *n.*

**el·e·men·tal** (el′ə men′təl) 1 of the four elements —earth, water, air, and fire. 2 of the forces of nature: *Explorers in unknown lands often faced elemental dangers.* 3 as found in nature; simple but powerful: *Hunger is an elemental feeling.* 4 being a necessary or essential part. 5 ELEMENTARY (defs. 2, 3). *adj.*

**el·e·men·ta·ry** (el′ə men′tə rē *or* el′ə men′trē) 1 of or dealing with the simple, necessary parts to be learned first; having to do with first principles; introductory: *elementary arithmetic.* 2 made up of only one chemical element; not a compound: *Silver is an elementary substance.* 3 having to do with a chemical element or elements. 4 ELEMENTAL (defs. 3, 4). *adj.*

**elementary school** a school of six, seven, or eight grades for children aged six and over, which is followed by high school or junior high school. Some elementary schools also include kindergarten.

An African elephant - about 3.5 m high at the shoulder

**el·e·phant** (el′ə fənt) any of several species of huge, strong animal of Africa and Asia, having thick, almost hairless, grey skin, large ears, thick legs, and a long, muscular snout called a trunk. Elephants, which form a separate class of mammals, are the largest four-footed animals now living. *n.*

**el·e·phan·ti·a·sis** (el′ə fan tī′ə sis) a disease in which parts of the body, usually the legs, become greatly enlarged, and the skin thickened and broken: *Elephantiasis is caused by parasitic worms that block the flow of lymph.* *n.*

**el·e·phan·tine** (el′ə fan′tīn *or* el′ə fan′tēn) 1 like an elephant; huge; heavy; clumsy; slow. 2 of elephants. *adj.*

**el·e·vate** (el′ə vāt′) 1 lift up; raise: *She spoke from an elevated platform.* 2 raise in rank or station: *The actor was elevated to knighthood.* 3 raise in quality: *Reading good books elevates your mind.* 4 put in high spirits; make joyful or proud; elate. *v.,* **el·e·vat·ed, el·e·vat·ing.**

**el·e·vat·ed** (el′ə vā′tid) 1 lifted up; raised; high. 2 dignified; lofty; noble. 3 in high spirits; joyful; proud. 4 *Informal.* ELEVATED RAILWAY. 5 pt. and pp. of ELEVATE. 1–3 *adj.,* 4 *n.,* 5 *v.*

**elevated railway** a railway raised above the ground on a supporting frame high enough for streetcars, automobiles, etc. to pass underneath.

**el·e·va·tion** (el′ə vā′shən) 1 a raised place; high place: *A hill is an elevation.* 2 the height above the earth's surface: *The airplane fell from an elevation of 1000 metres.* 3 the height above sea level: *The elevation of Calgary is 1045 metres.* 4 dignity; loftiness; nobility. 5 a raising; lifting up: *the elevation of Caesar to be the ruler of Rome.* 6 being raised or lifted up. 7 a flat drawing of the front, rear, or side of a building. *n.*

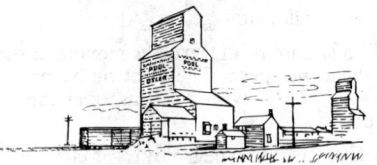

A Prairie elevator

**el·e·va·tor** (el′ə vā′tər) 1 anything that raises or lifts up. 2 a moving platform or cage to carry people and freight up and down in a building, mine, etc. 3 a building for storing grain. 4 a hinged piece, usually on the tail of an aircraft, that is raised or lowered to make the aircraft go upward or downward. *n.*

**elevator shaft** a vertical passageway for an elevator.

**e·lev·en** (i lev′ən) 1 one more than ten; 11: *Margit just borrowed another dollar, so now she owes me eleven. There were eleven empty seats.* 2 the numeral 11: *That looks like an 11.* 3 the eleventh in a set or series. 4 being eleventh in a set or series (*used after the noun*): *Chapter Eleven.* 5 in cricket, soccer, etc., a team of eleven players: *This year our school has the best eleven ever.* 6 any set or series of eleven persons or things. 1–3, 5, 6 *n.,* 1, 4 *adj.*

**e·lev·enth** (i lev′ənth) 1 next after the 10th; last in a series of 11; 11th. 2 one, or being one, of 11 equal parts. 1 *adj.,* 2 *n.*

**eleventh hour** the last possible moment; the time just before it is too late to do something.

**elf** (elf) 1 a tiny, mischievous fairy. 2 a small, mischievous person. *n., pl.* **elves.** —**elf′like′,** *adj.*

**elf·in** (el′fən) 1 of or suitable for elves; like an elf's: *an elfin smile.* 2 elf. 1 *adj.,* 2 *n.*

**elf·ish** (el′fish) elflike; ELFIN (def. 1); mischievous. *adj.* —**elf′ish·ly,** *adv.* —**elf′ish·ness,** *n.*

**e·lic·it** (i lis′it) draw forth: *to elicit a reply, to elicit applause, to elicit the truth. I succeeded in eliciting from her friend the information I needed.* *v.*
☛ Hom. ILLICIT.

**e·lic·i·ta·tion** (i lis′ə tā′shən) drawing forth or being drawn forth. *n.*

**e·lide** (i līd′) omit or slur over in pronunciation: *The e in the is elided in "th' inevitable hour."* *v.,* **e·lid·ed, e·lid·ing.** See ELISION.

**el·i·gi·bil·i·ty** (el′ə jə bil′ə tē) fitness; qualification; desirability. *n., pl.* **el·i·gi·bil·i·ties.**

**el·i·gi·ble** (el′ə jə bəl) 1 fit or proper to be chosen; desirable: *an eligible bachelor.* 2 properly qualified; meeting all requirements set by law or rule: *Players had to pass in all subjects to be eligible for the school team.* 3 an eligible person. 1, 2 *adj.,* 3 *n.* —**el′i·gi·bly,** *adv.*

**e·lim·i·nate** (i lim′ə nāt′) 1 get rid of; remove: *The new bridge over the railway tracks eliminated the danger in crossing.* 2 pay no attention to; leave out of consideration; omit: *The architect eliminated furniture, rugs, etc. in figuring the cost of the house.*  **3** in algebra, get rid of an unknown quantity by combining equations.  **4** put out of a championship competition by reason of defeat: *Our school was eliminated in the first round of the hockey playoffs.*  **5** expel waste from the body; EXCRETE.  *v.*, **e·lim·i·nat·ed, e·lim·i·nat·ing.**

**e·lim·i·na·tion** (i lim′ə nā′shən)  **1** an eliminating.  **2** being eliminated.  *n.*
**elimination round,** that part of a competition which eliminates a competitor from the championship round.

**e·li·sion** (i lizh′ən)  the suppression of a vowel or a syllable in pronunciation: *Elision is often used in poetry, and generally consists in cutting off a vowel at the end of a word when the next begins with a vowel.*  *n.*  See ELIDE.

**e·lite** or **é·lite** (i lēt′ or ā lēt′)  the choice or distinguished part; those thought of as the best people: *The elite of society attended the reception.*  *n.*

**e·lix·ir** (i lik′sər)  **1** a substance supposed to have the power of changing lead, iron, etc. into gold or of lengthening life indefinitely, sought by the alchemists of the Middle Ages.  **2** a universal remedy; cure-all.  **3** a medicine made of drugs or herbs mixed with alcohol and syrup.  *n.*

**E·liz·a·be·than** (i liz′ə bē′thən *or* i liz′ə beth′ən)  **1** of or having to do with the time of Queen Elizabeth I (1533–1603).  **2** a person, especially a writer, of the time of Queen Elizabeth I: *Shakespeare is a famous Elizabethan.*  **1** *adj.*, **2** *n.*

**elk** (elk)  **1** a large North American mammal, the second largest member of the deer family, having a light or dark brown coat with a light-coloured rump patch, long, shaggy, dark-brown hair covering the neck and shoulders, and, in the adult male, large antlers, usually with five tines; wapiti: *Some authorities consider the elk to be of the same species as the European red deer.*  **2** a large deer of Europe and Asia, considered by many authorities to be of the same species as the North American moose: *The elk closely resembles the moose, but is considerably smaller.*  **3** any of several other large deer of Asia.  *n.*, *pl.* **elks** or (*esp. collectively*) **elk.**

**ell**[1] (el)  an old measure of length, chiefly used in measuring cloth: *In the British Isles, the ell was equal to 45 inches (about 115 cm). Give him an inch (a little) and he'll take an ell (much).*  *n.*

**ell**[2] (el)  **1** the letter L, l.  **2** something shaped like a capital L.  **3** an extension of a building at right angles to it.  *n.*

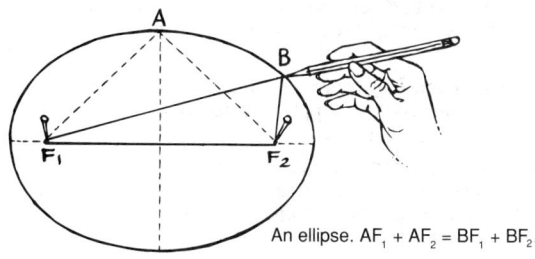

An ellipse. $AF_1 + AF_2 = BF_1 + BF_2.$

**el·lipse** (i lips′)  an oval having both ends alike. An ellipse is the path of a point that moves so that the sum of its distances from two fixed points remains the same. Any CONIC SECTION formed by a cutting plane inclined to the base but not passing through the base is an ellipse.  See CONE and OVAL for more pictures.  *n.*, *pl.* **el·lip·ses** (-siz).

**el·lip·ses** (i lip′siz *for 1,* i lip′sēz *for 2*)  **1** pl. of ELLIPSE.  **2** pl. of ELLIPSIS.  *n.*

**el·lip·sis** (i lip′sis)  **1** the omission of a word or words that could complete the grammatical construction of a sentence. Example: *In She is almost as tall as her brother there is a permissible ellipsis of is tall after brother.*  **2** marks (…or * * *) used to show an omission in writing or printing.  *n.*, *pl.* **el·lip·ses** (-sēz).

**el·lip·tic** (i lip′tik)  ELLIPTICAL.  *adj.*

**el·lip·ti·cal** (i lip′tə kəl)  **1** shaped like an ELLIPSE; of an ellipse.  **2** having a word or words omitted.  *adj.*

**el·lip·ti·cal·ly** (i lip′ti klē)  **1** shaped like an ELLIPSE.  **2** with an ELLIPSIS.  *adv.*

**elm** (elm)  **1** a tall, graceful shade tree.  **2** its hard, heavy wood.  *n.*

**el·o·cu·tion** (el′ə kyü′shən)  **1** the art of speaking or reading clearly and effectively in public; art of public speaking, including the appropriate and effective use of the voice, gestures, etc.  **2** a manner of speaking or reading in public.  *n.*

**el·o·cu·tion·ar·y** (el′ə kyü′shə ner′ē)  of or having to do with ELOCUTION (def. 1).  *adj.*

**el·o·cu·tion·ist** (el′ə kyü′shə nist)  **1** a person skilled in ELOCUTION (def. 1).  **2** a teacher of ELOCUTION (def. 1).  *n.*

**e·lon·gate** (i long′gāt)  **1** lengthen; extend; stretch: *A rubber band can be elongated to several times its normal length.*  **2** lengthened.  **3** long and thin: *the elongate leaf of a willow.*  **1** *v.*, **e·lon·gat·ed, e·lon·gat·ing;** **2, 3** *adj.*

**e·lon·ga·tion** (ē′long gā′shən)  **1** a lengthening; extension.  **2** a lengthened part; continuation.  *n.*

**e·lope** (i lōp′)  run away with a lover: *Juliet planned to elope with Romeo.*  *v.*, **e·loped, e·lop·ing.**
—**e·lope′ment,** *n.*  —**e·lop′er,** *n.*

**el·o·quence** (el′ə kwəns)  **1** a flow of speech that has grace and force: *The eloquence of the speaker moved all hearts.*  **2** the power to win by speaking; the art of speaking so as to stir the feelings.  *n.*

**el·o·quent** (el′ə kwənt)  **1** having ELOQUENCE.  **2** very expressive: *Indira's frown was eloquent of her displeasure.*  *adj.*  —**el′o·quent·ly,** *adv.*

**else** (els)  **1** other; different; instead: *What else could I say?*  **2** in addition: *The Browns are here; do you expect anyone else?*  **3** differently: *How else can it be done?*  **4** otherwise; if not: *Hurry, else you will be late.*  **1, 2** *adj.*, **3, 4** *adv.*
**or else,** *Informal.*  or suffer for it; or pay a penalty: *You'd better return my bike, or else.*

**else·where** (els′wer′ *or* els′hwer′)  somewhere else; in or to some other place.  *adv.*

**e·lu·ci·date** (i lü′sə dāt′)  make clear; explain: *The*

**elucidation** *scientist elucidated her theory by a few simple experiments.* *v.*, **e·lu·ci·dat·ed, e·lu·ci·dat·ing.**

**e·lu·ci·da·tion** (i lü′sə dā′shən) making clear; explanation. *n.*

**e·lude** (i lüd′) 1 slip away from; avoid or escape by cleverness, quickness, etc.: *The sly fox eluded the dogs.* 2 escape discovery by; baffle: *The cause of cancer will not long elude research.* *v.*, **e·lud·ed, e·lud·ing.**
—**e·lud′er,** *n.*
☞ *Usage.* Do not confuse **elude** with ALLUDE. **Elude** means 'avoid or escape from': *The thief eluded his pursuers.* **Allude** means 'mention or refer to': *She alluded briefly to the minister's speech.*

**e·lu·sion** (i lü′zhən) an eluding; clever avoidance. *n.*
☞ *Hom.* ILLUSION.

**e·lu·sive** (i lü′siv) 1 hard to describe or understand; baffling: *an elusive idea.* 2 tending to elude: *The elusive fox got away from the hunters.* *adj.* —**e·lu′sive·ly,** *adv.*
—**e·lu′sive·ness,** *n.*
☞ *Hom.* ILLUSIVE.

**e·lu·so·ry** (i lü′sə rē) ELUSIVE. *adj.*
☞ *Hom.* ILLUSORY.

**el·ver** (el′vər) a young eel. *n.*

**elves** (elvz) pl. of ELF. *n.*

**elv·ish** (el′vish) ELFISH; elflike. *adj.*

**el·y·tron** (el′ə tron′) one of the hardened front wings of beetles and some other insects, that form a protective covering for the hind pair. *n., pl.* **el·y·tra** (el′ə trə)

**em** (em) the letter M, m. *n., pl.* **ems.**

**e·ma·ci·ate** (i mā′shē āt′ *or* i mā′sē āt′) make unnaturally thin; cause to lose flesh or waste away. *v.*, **e·ma·ci·at·ed, e·ma·ci·at·ing.**

**e·ma·ci·at·ed** (i mā′shē ā′tid *or* i mā′sē ā′tid) 1 thin from losing flesh: *The invalid was pale and emaciated.* 2 pt. and pp. of EMACIATE. 1 *adj.,* 2 *v.*

**e·ma·ci·a·tion** (i mā′shē ā′shən *or* i mā′sē ā′shən) an unnatural thinness caused by loss of flesh; wasting away. *n.*

**e-mail** ELECTRONIC MAIL.

**em·a·nate** (em′ə nāt′) come forth: *Light and heat emanate from the sun. Fragrance emanated from the flowers. The rumour emanated from Ottawa.* *v.*, **em·a·nat·ed, em·a·nat·ing.**

**em·a·na·tion** (em′ə nā′shən) 1 coming forth. 2 anything that comes forth from a source: *Light and heat are emanations from the sun.* 3 a gas given off by a disintegrating radio-active substance. *n.*

**e·man·ci·pate** (i man′sə pāt′) release from slavery or restraint; set free. *v.*, **e·man·ci·pat·ed, e·man·ci·pat·ing.**

**e·man·ci·pa·tion** (i man′sə pā′shən) a release from slavery or restraint; setting free: *the emancipation of slaves, emancipation from the authority of parents.* *n.*

**e·man·ci·pa·tor** (i man′sə pā′tər) a person who EMANCIPATES. *n.*

**e·mas·cu·late** (i mas′kyə lāt′ *for verb,* i mas′kyə lit *or* i mas′kyə lāt′ *for adjective*) 1 remove the male glands of; castrate. 2 destroy the force of; weaken: *The editor emasculated the speech by cutting out its strongest passages.* 3 deprived of vigour; weakened; effeminate. 1, 2 *v.*, **e·mas·cu·lat·ed, e·mas·cu·lat·ing;** 3 *adj.*
—**e·mas′cu·la′tion,** *n.*

**em·balm** (em bom′ *or* em bäm′) 1 treat a dead body with drugs, chemicals, etc. to keep it from decaying. 2 keep in memory; preserve: *Many fine sentiments are embalmed in poetry.* 3 fill with sweet scent; perfume: *Roses embalmed the June air.* *v.* Also, **imbalm.**
—**em·balm′er,** *n.*

**em·bank** (em bangk′) protect, enclose, or confine with a raised bank of earth, stones, etc. *v.*

EMBANKMENT

**em·bank·ment** (em bangk′mənt) 1 a raised bank of earth, stones, etc. used to hold back water, support a roadway, etc. 2 a protecting, enclosing, or confining with a bank of this kind. *n.*

**em·bar·go** (em bär′gō) 1 an order of a government forbidding ships to enter or leave its ports: *During the war, an embargo was placed on certain vessels.* 2 any restriction put on commerce by law. 3 a restriction; restraint; hindrance. 4 lay an embargo on; forbid to enter or leave port. 1–3 *n., pl.* **em·bar·goes;** 4 *v.*, **em·bar·goed, em·bar·go·ing.**

**em·bark** (em bärk′) 1 go on board ship: *to embark for Europe.* 2 enter an airplane, train, etc. as a passenger. 3 put on board ship: *The general embarked his troops.* 4 involve a person in an enterprise; invest money in an enterprise: *She foolishly embarked much money in the swindler's scheme.* *v.*
**embark on,** begin or enter upon: *After leaving university the young woman embarked on a business career.*

**em·bar·ka·tion** (em′bär kā′shən) an embarking. *n.*

**em·bar·rass** (em bar′əs *or* em ber′əs) 1 disturb; make self-conscious: *Meeting strangers embarrassed the shy boy so that he blushed and stammered.* 2 complicate; mix up; make difficult: *She embarrasses discussion of the simplest subject by the use of a difficult technical vocabulary.* 3 involve in difficulties; hinder: *Heavy equipment embarrassed the army's movements.* 4 burden with debt; involve in financial difficulties. *v.*

**em·bar·rassed** (em bar′əst *or* em ber′əst) 1 in a state of embarrassment. 2 pt. and pp. of EMBARRASS. 1 *adj.,* 2 *v.*

**em·bar·rass·ing** (em bar′ə sing *or* em ber′ə sing) 1 that embarrasses. 2 ppr. of EMBARRASS. 1 *adj.,* 2 *v.*
—**em·bar′rass·ing·ly,** *adv.*

**em·bar·rass·ment** (em bar′əs mənt *or* em ber′əs mənt) 1 an embarrassing. 2 being embarrassed. 3 something that embarrasses: *The bad-mannered boy was an embarrassment to his parents.* *n.*

**em·bas·sy** (em′bə sē) 1 an ambassador and his or her staff of assistants: *An embassy ranks next above a legation.* 2 the official residence, offices, etc. of an ambassador in a foreign country. 3 the position or duties of an ambassador. 4 a person or group officially sent to a foreign government with a special errand. 5 a special errand; important mission; official message. *n., pl.* **em·bas·sies.**

**em·bat·tle**[1] (em bat′əl) prepare for battle; form into battle order. *v.,* **em·bat·tled, em·bat·tling.**

**em·bat·tle**[2] (em bat′əl) provide with battlements; fortify. *v.,* **em·bat·tled, em·bat·tling.**

**em·bay** (em bā′) **1** put or bring into a bay for shelter; force into a bay. **2** shut in; surround. *v.*

**em·bed** (em bed′) **1** plant in a bed: *He embedded the bulbs in a box of sand.* **2** fix or enclose in a surrounding mass: *Precious stones are found embedded in rock.* **3** fix firmly in the mind: *Every detail is embedded in my memory.* *v.,* **em·bed·ded, em·bed·ding.** Also, **imbed.**

**em·bel·lish** (em bel′ish) **1** decorate; adorn; ornament: *We embellished our room with new rugs, lamps, and pictures.* **2** make more interesting by adding real or imaginary details; elaborate: *She embellished the old stories so that they sounded new.* *v.*

**em·bel·lish·ment** (em bel′ish mənt) **1** a decoration; adornment; ornament. **2** a detail, often imaginary, added to make a story, account, etc. more interesting. *n.*

**em·ber**[1] (em′bər) **1** a piece of wood or coal still glowing in the ashes of a fire. **2 embers,** *pl.* ashes in which there is still some fire. *n.*

**em·bez·zle** (em bez′əl) steal by putting to one's own use money held in trust for some other person or group of persons: *The treasurer embezzled $2000 from the club's funds.* *v.,* **em·bez·zled, em·bez·zling.** —**em·bez′zler,** *n.*

**em·bez·zle·ment** (em bez′əl mənt) the theft of money, securities, etc. held in trust for some other person or group of persons. *n.*

**em·bit·ter** (em bit′ər) make bitter; make more bitter: *The old man was embittered by his loss.* *v.*

**em·bla·zon** (em blā′zən) **1** display conspicuously; picture in bright colours. **2** decorate; adorn: *The knight's shield was emblazoned with his coat of arms.* **3** praise highly; honour publicly; make known the fame of: *King Arthur's exploits were emblazoned in song and story.* *v.* —**em·bla′zon·er,** *n.* —**em·bla′zon·ment,** *n.*

**em·bla·zon·ry** (em blā′zən rē) **1** brilliant decoration; adornment; conspicuous display. **2** the display of coats of arms, etc.; heraldic decoration. *n., pl.* **em·bla·zon·ries.**

**em·blem** (em′bləm) **1** an object or representation that stands for an invisible quality, idea, etc. by some connection of thought; the sign of an idea; symbol: *The beaver and the maple leaf are both emblems of Canada. The dove is an emblem of peace.* See OLIVE BRANCH for picture. **2** a heraldic device. *n.*

**em·blem·at·ic** (em′blə mat′ik) used as an emblem; symbolical: *A white flag is emblematic of surrender.* *adj.*

**em·blem·at·i·cal** (em′blə mat′ə kəl) EMBLEMATIC. *adj.*

**em·bod·i·ment** (em bod′ē mənt) **1** embodying. **2** being embodied. **3** that in which something is embodied; a person or thing symbolizing some idea, quality, etc.: *King Arthur was the embodiment of knighthood.* **4** something embodied. *n.*

**em·bod·y** (em bod′ē) **1** put into visible form; express in definite form: *The building embodied the idea of the architect.* **2** bring together and include in a single book, law, system, etc.; organize: *The British North America Act embodies the conditions of Confederation.* **3** make part of

**embattle** **395** **embroidery**

hat, āge, fär; let, ēqual, tėrm; it, īce
hot, ōpen, ôrder; oil, out; cup, pùt, rüle
əbove, takən, pencəl, lemən, circəs
ch, child; ng, long; sh, ship
th, thin; ᵺ, then; zh, measure

an organized book, law, system, etc.; incorporate: *The new engineer's suggestions were embodied in the revised plan of the bridge.* *v.,* **em·bod·ied, em·bod·y·ing.**

**em·bold·en** (em bōl′dən) make bold; encourage. *v.*

**em·bo·lism** (em′bə liz′əm) the obstruction of a blood vessel by a clot, a bit of fat, or other obstacle carried there by the blood. *n.*

**em·bon·point** (äṅ bôṅ pwaN′) *French.* plumpness. *n.*

**em·boss** (em bos′) **1** decorate with a design, pattern, etc. that stands out from the surface, made by pressing or moulding: *Canadian coins are embossed with letters and figures.* **2** cause to stand out from the surface: *Helga ran her finger over the letters to see if they had been embossed.* *v.*

**em·boss·ment** (em bos′mənt) **1** embossing. **2** a figure carved or moulded in relief. **3** a part that sticks out; bulge. *n.*

**em·bou·chure** (om′bü shür′; *French,* äṅ bü shYR′) **1** the mouth of a river. **2** the widening of a river valley into a plain. **3** the mouthpiece of a wind instrument. *n.*

**em·brace** (em brās′) **1** clasp or hold in the arms to show love or friendship; hug. **2** hug one another: *The two lovers embraced.* **3** take up; take for oneself; accept: *to embrace an opportunity.* **4** include; contain: *The cat family embraces cats, lions, tigers, and similar animals.* **5** surround; enclose: *Vines embraced the hut.* **6** embracing; a hug. **1–5** *v.,* **em·braced, em·brac·ing; 6** *n.* —**em·brace′a·ble,** *adj.*

**em·bra·sure** (em brā′zhər) **1** an opening in a wall for a gun, with sides that spread outward to permit the gun to swing through a wide arc. **2** a slanting of the wall at an oblique angle on the inner sides of a window or door. *n.*

**em·broi·der** (em broi′dər) **1** ornament cloth, leather, etc. with a design, pattern, etc. of stitches. **2** make a design, pattern, etc. on cloth, leather, etc. with stitches: *She embroidered stars on her blue dress.* **3** do embroidery. **4** add imaginary details to: *He didn't tell lies, but he did embroider his stories.* *v.*

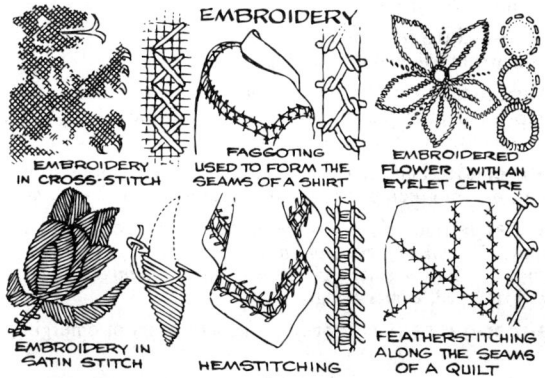

EMBROIDERY

EMBROIDERY IN CROSS-STITCH

FAGGOTING USED TO FORM THE SEAMS OF A SHIRT

EMBROIDERED FLOWER WITH AN EYELET CENTRE

EMBROIDERY IN SATIN STITCH

HEMSTITCHING

FEATHERSTITCHING ALONG THE SEAMS OF A QUILT

**em·broi·der·y** (em broi′dər ē) **1** the act or art of

**EMBROIDERing** (defs. 1, 2).   **2** raised and ornamental designs in cloth, leather, etc. sewn with a needle; **EMBROIDERED** (def. 1) work or material.   *n., pl.* **em·broi·der·ies.**

**em·broil** (em broil′)   **1** involve a person, country, etc. in a quarrel: *She did not wish to become embroiled in the dispute.*   **2** throw affairs, etc. into a state of confusion.   *v.*   —**em·broil′ment,** *n.*

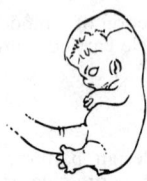 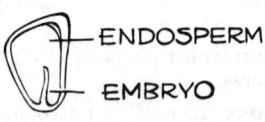

A human embryo, about 6 weeks old

The embryo of a corn plant inside a seed

**em·bry·o** (em′brē ō′)   **1** an animal during the period of its growth from the fertilized egg until its organs have developed so that it can live independently: *A chicken within an egg is an embryo. A human embryo more than three months old is usually called a fetus.*   **2** an undeveloped plant within a seed.   **3** embryonic; undeveloped; not mature: *an embryo idea.*   1, 2 *n., pl.* **em·bry·os;**   3 *adj.*
**in embryo,** in an undeveloped stage.

**em·bry·o·log·ic** (em′brē ə loj′ik)   EMBRYOLOGICAL. *adj.*

**em·bry·o·log·i·cal** (em′brē ə loj′ə kəl)   of or having to do with EMBRYOLOGY.   *adj.*

**em·bry·ol·o·gist** (em′brē ol′ə jist)   a person trained in EMBRYOLOGY, especially one who makes it his or her work.   *n.*

**em·bry·ol·o·gy** (em′brē ol′ə jē)   the branch of biology that deals with the formation and development of EMBRYOS (def. 1).   *n.*

**em·bry·on·ic** (em′brē on′ik)   **1** of the EMBRYO (defs. 1, 2).   **2** undeveloped; not mature.   *adj.*

**em·cee** (em′sē′) *Informal.*   **1** a master of ceremonies. **2** act as master of ceremonies.   1 *n.,* 2 *v.,* **em·ceed, em·cee·ing.**   Also, **M.C.**

**e·mend** (i mend′)   free a faulty text, document, etc. from errors; correct.  Compare with AMEND.   *v.*

**e·men·date** (ē′men dāt′)   EMEND.   *v.,* **e·men·dat·ed, e·men·dat·ing.**

**e·men·da·tion** (ē′men dā′shən)   **1** a correction; improvement.   **2** a suggested change to free a faulty text, document, etc. from errors.   *n.*

**em·er·ald** (em′ə rəld)   **1** a bright-green precious stone; transparent green beryl.   **2** bright green.   1, 2 *n.,* 2 *adj.*

**e·merge** (i mėrj′)   **1** come out; come up; come into view: *The sun emerged from behind a cloud.*   **2** become known: *Many facts emerged as a result of the investigation.*   *v.,* **e·merged, e·merg·ing.**

**e·mer·gence** (i mėr′jəns)   the act or fact of emerging; coming into view.   *n.*

**e·mer·gen·cy** (i mėr′jən sē)   **1** a sudden need for immediate action: *I keep a fire extinguisher in my car for use in an emergency.*   **2** for a time of a sudden need: *an emergency brake.*   **3** carried out or performed in a situation requiring immediate action: *an emergency operation.*   1, 2 *n., pl.* **e·mer·gen·cies;**   3 *adj.*

**e·mer·gent** (i mėr′jənt)   emerging.   *adj.*

**e·mer·i·tus** (i mer′ə təs)   retired from active service, but still holding one's rank and title: *At the age of seventy, Professor Timshi became a professor emeritus.*   *adj.*

**e·mer·sion** (i mėr′zhən *or* i mėr′shən)   emerging: *On emersion from the cocoon a moth slowly unfolds its wings.*   *n.*
☛ *Hom.* IMMERSION.

**em·er·y** (em′ə rē *or* em′rē)   a hard, dark mineral used for grinding, smoothing, and polishing.   *n.*

**emery paper**   a fine grade of sandpaper, used for final smoothing.

**e·met·ic** (i met′ik)   **1** causing vomiting.   **2** a medicine that causes vomiting.   1 *adj.,* 2 *n.*

**EMF, emf,** or **E.M.F.**   electromotive force.

**em·i·grant** (em′ə grənt)   **1** a person who leaves his or her own country or region to settle in another. **2** emigrating.   1 *n.,* 2 *adj.*
☛ *Usage.*  See note at EMIGRATE.

**em·i·grate** (em′ə grāt′)   leave one's own country or region to settle in another: *Many people emigrated from Russia during the revolution.*  Compare with IMMIGRATE. *v.,* **em·i·grat·ed, em·i·grat·ing.**
☛ *Usage.*  **Emigrate** means 'move out of a country or region'; IMMIGRATE means 'move into a country or region'. So a man might *emigrate* from Norway and *immigrate* to Canada; he would be an *emigrant* from Norway and an *immigrant* to Canada.

**em·i·gra·tion** (em′ə grā′shən)   **1** the act of leaving one's own country or region to settle in another: *In recent years there has been much emigration from Asia to Canada.* **2** a movement of emigrants.   *n.*

**é·mi·gré** (em′ə grā′; *French,* ā mē grā′)   **1** an emigrant.   **2** a royalist refugee from France during the French Revolution.   **3** a refugee from Russia during and after the Russian revolution.   *n., pl.* **é·mi·grés** (-grāz′; *French,* -grā′).

**em·i·nence** (em′ə nəns)   **1** a rank or position above all or most others; high standing; greatness; fame: *Bell won eminence as an inventor.*   **2** a high place; lofty hill.   *n.*

**Em·i·nence** (em′ə nəns)   in the Roman Catholic Church, the title of honour given to a cardinal.   *n.*

**em·i·nent** (em′ə nənt)   **1** distinguished; exalted: *The Governor General is an eminent man.*   **2** conspicuous; noteworthy: *The judge was a woman of eminent fairness.* **3** high; lofty.   **4** prominent; projecting.   *adj.*
☛ *Usage.*  Do not confuse **eminent** with IMMINENT, which means 'likely to happen soon'.

**em·i·nent·ly** (em′ə nən tlē)   in an EMINENT (def. 2) degree; so as to be conspicuous and distinguished from others.   *adv.*

**e·mir** (ə mēr′)   **1** a Moslem title given to rulers, governors, and military and naval commanders.   **2** a title of dignity given to the descendants of Mohammed.   *n.*  Also, **amir.**

**e·mir·ate** (ə mē′rit)   **1** the rank or authority of an EMIR (def. 1).   **2** the territory governed by an EMIR (def. 1).   *n.*

**em·is·sar·y** (em′ə ser′ē)   a person sent on a mission

or errand, especially one sent secretly. *n., pl.* **em·is·sar·ies.**

**e·mis·sion** (i mish′ən) **1** the act or fact of emitting: *the emission of light from the sun.* **2** the thing emitted. *n.*

**emission control** a device attached to a vehicle to reduce pollution from the exhaust system.

**e·mis·sive** (i mis′iv) emitting. *adj.*

**e·mit** (i mit′) **1** give off; send out; discharge: *Volcanoes emit lava. The trapped lion emitted roars of rage.* **2** put into circulation; issue. *v.*, **e·mit·ted, e·mit·ting.**

**e·mit·ter** (i mit′ər) in electronics, the electrode in a vacuum tube that emits, or gives off, electrons. See VACUUM TUBE for picture. *n.*

**e·mol·lient** (i mol′yənt *or* i mol′ē ənt) **1** softening; soothing. **2** something that softens and soothes: *Cold cream is an emollient for the skin.* 1 *adj.*, 2 *n.*

**e·mol·u·ment** (i mol′yə mənt) the profit from a job, office, or position; salary; fee. *n.*

**e·mote** (i mōt′) *Informal.* display emotion in an exaggerated, theatrical manner. *v.*, **e·mot·ed, e·mot·ing.**

**e·mo·tion** (i mō′shən) **1** a strong feeling: *Fear, anger, love, joy, and grief are emotions.* **2** feeling as opposed to reason. *n.*

**e·mo·tion·al** (i mō′shə nəl) **1** of the emotions. **2** showing emotion. **3** appealing to the emotions: *The next speaker made an emotional plea for money to help disabled children.* **4** easily affected by emotion: *Emotional people are likely to cry if they hear sad music or read sad stories.* *adj.* —**e·mo′tion·al·ly,** *adv.*

**e·mo·tion·al·ism** (i mō′shə nə liz′əm) **1** an emotional quality or character. **2** an appeal to the emotions. **3** a tendency to display emotion too easily. *n.*

**e·mo·tive** (i mō′tiv) **1** showing or causing emotion. **2** having to do with the emotions. *adj.*

**em·pan·el** (em pan′əl) IMPANEL. *v.*, **em·pan·elled** or **em·pan·eled, em·pan·el·ling** or **em·pan·el·ing.**

**em·per·or** (em′pə rər) a man who is the ruler of an empire. *n.*

**em·pha·sis** (em′fə sis) **1** special force; stress; importance: *My high school puts much emphasis on studies that prepare its students for college.* **2** the special force given to particular syllables, words, or phrases: *A speaker puts emphasis on important words.* *n., pl.* **em·pha·ses** (-sēz′).

**em·pha·size** (em′fə sīz′) **1** give special force to; stress; make important: *She emphasized the word by saying it very loudly.* **2** call attention to: *The great number of automobile accidents emphasizes the need for careful driving.* *v.*, **em·pha·sized, em·pha·siz·ing.**

**em·phat·ic** (em fat′ik) **1** spoken or done with force or stress; strongly expressed: *Her answer was an emphatic "No!"* **2** speaking with force or stress; expressing oneself strongly: *The emphatic speaker often pounded the table and shouted.* **3** attracting attention; very noticeable; striking: *The club made an emphatic success of their party.* *adj.*

**em·phat·i·cal·ly** (em fat′i kle) in an EMPHATIC manner; to an emphatic degree. *adv.*

**em·pire** (em′pīr) **1** a group of countries or states under the same ruler or government, one country having some measure of control over the rest: *Napoleon I governed the French Empire from 1804 to 1815.* **2** a

# emission 397 empty

hat, āge, fär; let, ēqual, tėrm; it, īce
hot, ōpen, ôrder; oil, out; cup, pút, rüle
əbove, takən, pencəl, lemən, circəs
ch, child; ng, long; sh, ship
th, thin; ᴛʜ, then; zh, measure

country ruled by an emperor or empress: *the Japanese Empire.* **3** absolute power; supreme authority. **4** a very large business controlled by one person or group. *n.*

**em·pir·ic** (em pir′ik) **1** a person who lacks theoretical or scientific knowledge and relies entirely on practical experience. **2** a person without regular or proper training; quack. **3** EMPIRICAL. 1, 2 *n.*, 3 *adj.*

**em·pir·i·cal** (em pir′ə kəl) **1** based on experiment and observation: *Chemistry is largely an empirical science.* **2** based entirely on practical experience, without regard to science or theory: *The witch doctor had only an empirical knowledge of medicine.* *adj.* —**em·pir′i·cal·ly,** *adv.*

**em·pir·i·cism** (em pir′ə siz′əm) **1** the use of methods based on experiment and observation, especially as practised in the natural sciences. **2** a theory that the only basis of knowledge is experience. **3** reliance on experience without the aid of science; unscientific practice. *n.*

**em·pir·i·cist** (em pir′ə sist) a person who practises or advocates EMPIRICISM. *n.*

**em·place·ment** (em plā′smənt) **1** a space or platform for a heavy gun or guns. **2** an assigning to a place; locating. *n.*

**em·ploy** (em ploi′) **1** use the services of; give work and pay to: *The big factory employs many workers.* **2** being employed; service for pay; employment: *There are many workers in the employ of the government.* **3** use: *One employs a knife, fork, and spoon in eating.* **4** engage the attention of; keep busy; occupy: *Instead of wasting time, she employed herself in reading.* 1, 3, 4 *v.*, 2 *n.* —**em·ploy′a·ble,** *adj.*

**em·ploy·ee** (em ploi′ē) a person who works for some person or firm for pay. *n.* Also, **employé** or **employe.**

**em·ploy·er** (em ploi′ər) **1** a person or firm that employs one or more persons. **2** user. *n.*

**em·ploy·ment** (em ploi′mənt) **1** an employing or being employed. **2** what a person does for a living; work. **3** use: *There is a clever employment of colour in that painting.* *n.*

**em·po·ri·um** (em pô′rē əm) **1** a centre of trade; market place. **2** a large store selling many different things. *n., pl.* **em·po·ri·ums** or **em·po·ri·a** (-rē ə).

**em·pow·er** (em pou′ər) **1** give power or authority to: *The secretary was empowered to sign certain contracts.* **2** enable; permit: *A human being's erect position empowers him or her to use the hands freely.* *v.* Also, **impower.**

**em·press** (em′pris) **1** the wife of an emperor. **2** a woman who is the ruler of an empire. *n.*

**emp·ty** (emp′tē) **1** with nothing or no one in it: *The birds had gone, and their nest was empty.* **2** pour out or take out the contents of; make empty: *Empty the box of rubbish into the fire.* **3** become empty: *The hall emptied as soon as the concert was over.* **4** flow out; discharge: *The St. Lawrence River empties into the Gulf of St. Lawrence.* **5** not real; meaningless: *An empty promise is insincere.* **6** *Informal.* hungry. **7** *Informal.* something that is empty; an empty container, freight car,

bottle, etc. 1, 5, 6 *adj.*, **emp·ti·er, emp·ti·est;** 2–4 *v.*, **emp·tied, emp·ty·ing;** 7 *n., pl.* **emp·ties.**
—**emp′ti·ly,** *adv.* —**emp′ti·ness,** *n.*
**empty of,** without; lacking.

**emp·ty-hand·ed** (emp′tē han′did) having nothing in the hands; bringing or taking nothing. *adj.*

**emp·ty-head·ed** (emp′tē hed′id) silly; stupid. *adj.*

**empty set** in mathematics, a set that has no members. *Example: the set of human beings who have landed on Pluto.*

**em·pur·pled** (em pėr′pəld) made purple; coloured with purple. *adj.*

**em·pyr·e·al** (em pir′ē əl, em pī′rē əl, or em′pə rē′əl) of the EMPYREAN (defs. 1, 2); celestial; heavenly. *adj.*

**em·py·re·an** (em′pī rē′ən *or* em′pə rē′ən) 1 the highest heaven; region of pure light. 2 the sky; firmament; vault of the heavens. 3 EMPYREAL. 1, 2 *n.*, 3 *adj.*

**e·mu** (ē′myü) a large Australian bird resembling an ostrich but smaller: *Emus cannot fly, but they can run very fast.* *n.*

**em·u·late** (em′yə lāt′) try to equal or excel: *The fable tells us to emulate the industry of the ant.* *v.*, **em·u·lat·ed, em·u·lat·ing.**

**em·u·la·tion** (em′yə lā′shən) an imitation in order to equal or excel; the ambition or desire to equal or excel. *n.*

**em·u·la·tive** (em′yə lə tiv *or* em′yə lā′tiv) 1 tending to emulate. 2 of or caused by emulation. *adj.*

**em·u·la·tor** (em′yə lā′tər) one who EMULATES. *n.*

**em·u·lous** (em′yə ləs) wishing to equal or excel. *adj.* —**em′u·lous·ly,** *adv.* —**em′u·lous·ness,** *n.*

**e·mul·si·fi·ca·tion** (i mul′sə fə kā′shən) 1 EMULSIFYING. 2 being emulsified. *n.*

**e·mul·si·fy** (i mul′sə fī′) make into an EMULSION. *v.*, **e·mul·si·fied, e·mul·si·fy·ing.** —**e·mul′si·fi·er,** *n.*

**e·mul·sion** (i mul′shən) 1 a mixture of liquids that do not dissolve in each other: *In an emulsion very fine drops of one of the liquids are evenly distributed throughout.* 2 a milky liquid containing very tiny drops of fat, oil, etc.: *Cod-liver oil is made into an emulsion to improve its taste.* 3 a coating on a camera film, plate, etc. that is sensitive to light. *n.*

**en·a·ble** (en ā′bəl) give ability, power, or means to; make able: *Airplanes enable people to travel through the air.* *v.*, **en·a·bled, en·a·bling.**

**en·act** (en akt′) 1 pass a bill giving it validity as law; make into a law. 2 decree; order. 3 play the part of; act out; play: *to enact Hamlet.* *v.*

**en·act·ment** (en akt′mənt) 1 enacting. 2 being enacted. 3 law. *n.*

**e·nam·el** (i nam′əl) 1 a glasslike substance melted and then cooled to make a smooth, hard surface: *Different colours of enamel are used to cover or decorate metal, pottery, etc.* 2 a paint or varnish used to make a smooth, hard, glossy surface. 3 the smooth, hard, glossy outer layer of the teeth. 4 cover or decorate with enamel. 5 anything covered or decorated with enamel. 6 any smooth, hard, shiny coating or surface. 7 form an enamel-like surface upon. 8 adorn with various colours; decorate as if with enamel. 1–3, 5, 6 *n.*, 4, 7, 8 *v.*, **e·nam·elled** *or* **e·nam·eled, e·nam·el·ling** *or* **e·nam·el·ing.** —**e·nam′el·ler** *or* **e·nam′el·er,** *n.*

**e·nam·el·ware** (i nam′əl wer′) pots, pans, etc. that are made of metal coated with enamel. *n.*

**en·am·our** *or* **en·am·or** (en am′ər) arouse to love; charm: *Her beauty enamoured the prince.* *v.*

**en·am·oured** *or* **en·am·ored** (en am′ərd) 1 very much in love; very fond; charmed: *The enamoured prince married the beautiful peasant girl.* 2 pt. and pp. of ENAMOUR. 1 *adj.*, 2 *v.*

**enamoured of** *or* **enamored of,** in love with; very fond of; charmed by.

**en bloc** (en′blok′; *French,* äN blôk′) all together; in one lump.

**en·camp** (en kamp′) 1 make a camp: *It took the soldiers only an hour to encamp.* 2 stay in a camp: *They encamped there for three weeks.* 3 put in a camp: *They were encamped in tents.* *v.* —**en·camp′ment,** *n.*

**en·camp·ment** (en kamp′mənt) 1 the act of forming a camp. 2 camp. *n.*

**en·case** (en kās′) INCASE. *v.*, **en·cased, en·cas·ing.**

**–ence** a suffix meaning: 1 the act, fact, quality, or state of _____ing, as in *abhorrence, dependence, indulgence.* The suffix -ence is often added to verbs to form nouns. 2 the quality or state of being _____ent, as in *absence, confidence, competence, independence, prudence.* The suffix -ence is the noun suffix often corresponding to the adjective suffix -ent. See also -ENCY.

**en·ce·phal·ic** (en′sə fal′ik) of or having to do with the brain. *adj.*

**en·ceph·a·li·tis** (en sef′ə lī′tis) an inflammation of the brain caused by injury, infection, poison, etc.: *Sleeping sickness is one kind of encephalitis.*

**en·ceph·a·lon** (en sef′ə lon′) the brain. *n.*

**en·chain** (en chān′) 1 put in chains; fetter. 2 attract and fix firmly; hold fast: *The speaker's earnestness enchained the attention of her audience.* *v.*

**en·chant** (en chant′) 1 use magic on; put under a spell: *The witch enchanted the princess.* 2 delight greatly; charm: *The music enchanted us all.* *v.* —**en·chant′er,** *n.*

**en·chant·ing** (en chan′ting) 1 very delightful; charming. 2 bewitching. 3 ppr. of ENCHANT. 1, 2 *adj.*, 3 *v.*

**en·chant·ment** (en chant′mənt) 1 the use of magic; the act of putting under a spell. 2 the condition of being put under a magic spell. 3 a magic spell: *An enchantment froze the river.* 4 delight; rapture. 5 something that delights or charms; great delight; charm. *n.*

**en·chan·tress** (en chan′tris) 1 a woman who makes magic spells; witch. 2 a delightful, charming woman. *n.*

**en·chase** (en chās′) 1 engrave: *Her initials were enchased on the back of the watch.* 2 ornament with engraved designs; decorate with gems, inlay, etc.: *The shield was enchased with gold and silver.* 3 place in a setting; mount; frame. *v.*, **en·chased, en·chas·ing.**

**en·cir·cle** (en sėr′kəl) 1 form a circle around; surround: *Trees encircled the pond.* 2 go in a circle around: *The moon encircles the earth.* *v.*, **en·cir·cled, en·cir·cling.**

**en·cir·cle·ment** (en sėr′kəl mənt) an encircling. *n.*

**en·clave** (en′klāv) **1** a country or district surrounded by the territory of another country. **2** a separate or distinct unit enclosed within a larger one. *n.*

**en·close** (en klōz′) **1** shut in on all sides; surround. **2** put a wall or fence around: *The farmer enclosed her pasture.* **3** include in an envelope or package along with something else: *A cheque was enclosed with the letter.* *v.*, **en·closed, en·clos·ing.** Also, **inclose.**

**en·clo·sure** (en klō′zhər) **1** an enclosing or being enclosed. **2** an enclosed place: *Those cages are enclosures for the monkeys.* **3** something that encloses: *A wall or fence is an enclosure.* **4** something enclosed, especially additional material enclosed in an envelope with a letter. *n.* Also, **inclosure.**

**en·code** (en kōd′) **1** put into code: *The spy encoded his message before mailing it.* **2** express in writing. *v.*, **en·cod·ed, en·cod·ing.**

**en·co·mi·ast** (en kō′mē ast′) a writer or speaker of ENCOMIUMS; eulogist. *n.*

**en·co·mi·um** (en kō′mē əm) an elaborate expression of praise; high praise; eulogy. *n.*, *pl.* **en·co·mi·ums** or **en·co·mi·a** (-mē ə).

**en·com·pass** (en kum′pəs) **1** surround completely; shut in on all sides; encircle: *The atmosphere encompasses the earth.* **2** enclose; contain. *v.* —**en·com′pass·ment,** *n.*

**en·core** (ong′kôr *or* on′kôr) **1** once more; again. **2** a demand by the audience for the repetition of a song, a piece of music, etc., or for another appearance of the performer or performers. **3** the repetition of a song, etc. in response to such a demand. **4** an additional song, etc. given in response to such a demand. **5** call for a repetition of a song, etc., or the reappearance of a performer, etc.: *The audience encored the singer by applauding.* **1** *interj.*, 2–4 *n.*, 5 *v.*, **en·cored, en·cor·ing.**

**en·coun·ter** (en koun′tər) **1** meet unexpectedly: *I encountered an old friend on the train.* **2** a meeting; an unexpected meeting. **3** meet with difficulties, opposition, etc.; be faced with. **4** meet as an enemy; meet in a fight or battle. **5** a meeting of two opposed forces, teams, etc.; a fight or battle. 1, 3, 4 *v.*, 2, 5 *n.*

**en·cour·age** (en kėr′ij) **1** give courage to; increase the hope or confidence of; urge on: *Success encourages you to go ahead and do better.* **2** be favourable to; help; support: *High prices for farm products encourage farming.* *v.*, **en·cour·aged, en·cour·ag·ing.** —**en·cour′ag·er,** *n.* —**en·cour′ag·ing·ly,** *adv.*

**en·cour·age·ment** (en kėr′ij mənt) **1** an encouraging. **2** the state of being or feeling encouraged. **3** something that encourages. *n.*

**en·croach** (en krōch′) **1** go beyond proper or usual limits: *The sea encroached upon the shore and submerged the beach.* **2** trespass upon the property or rights of another; intrude: *He is a good salesman and will not encroach upon his customer's time.* *v.*

**en·croach·ment** (en krōch′mənt) **1** an encroaching: *The cliff is being worn back by the encroachments of the sea.* **2** something taken by encroaching. *n.*

**en·crust** (en krust′) INCRUST. *v.*

**en·cum·ber** (en kum′bər) **1** hold back from running, doing, etc.; hinder; hamper: *Heavy shoes encumber anybody*

## encirclement 399 end

hat, āge, fär; let, ēqual, tėrm; it, īce
hot, ōpen, ôrder; oil, out; cup, pùt, rüle
əbove, takən, pencəl, lemən, circəs
ch, child; ng, long; sh, ship
th, thin; ᵺ, then; zh, measure

*in the water.* **2** make difficult to use; fill; obstruct: *Rubbish and old boxes encumbered the fire escape.* **3** weigh down; burden: *The doctor is encumbered with the care of too many patients.* **4** of property, put under a mortgage or a legal claim. See ENCUMBRANCE (def. 4): *The farm was encumbered with a heavy mortgage.* *v.* Also, **incumber.**

**en·cum·brance** (en kum′brəns) **1** anything that encumbers; hindrance; obstruction: *Shoes would be a serious encumbrance to a swimmer.* **2** an annoyance; trouble; burden. **3** a dependent person; child. **4** a claim, mortgage, etc. on property. *n.* Also, **incumbrance.**

**–ency** a noun-forming suffix meaning: **1** the act, fact, quality, or state of _____ing, as in *dependency*. **2** the quality or state of being _____ent, as in *clemency, frequency.* **3** other meanings, as in *agency, currency.* See also -ENCE.

**encyc.** *or* **ency.** encyclopedia.

**en·cy·clo·pe·di·a** *or* **en·cy·clo·pae·di·a** (en sī′klə pē′dē ə) **1** a book or series of books giving information, usually arranged alphabetically, on all branches of knowledge. **2** a book treating one subject very thoroughly, with its articles arranged alphabetically: *a medical encyclopedia.* *n.*

**en·cy·clo·pe·dic** *or* **en·cy·clo·pae·dic** (en sī′klə pē′dik) **1** covering a wide range of subjects; possessing wide and varied information. **2** having to do with an encyclopedia. *adj.*

**en·cy·clo·pe·dist** *or* **en·cy·clo·pae·dist** (en sī′klə pē′dist) a person who makes or compiles an encyclopedia. *n.*

**en·cyst** (en sist′) enclose or become enclosed in a cyst or sac. *v.* —**en·cyst′ment,** *n.*

**end** (end) **1** the last part; conclusion: *He read through to the end of the book.* **2** the edge or outside limit of an object or area; boundary: *Those trees mark the end of their property.* **3** the point where something that has length stops or ceases to be: *Every stick has two ends.* **4** have a boundary: *Their property ends here.* **5** bring or come to an end; stop; finish: *Let us end this fight.* **6** form the end of; be the end of: *This chapter ends the book.* **7** a purpose; object: *The end of work is to get something done.* **8** a result; outcome: *It is hard to tell what the end will be.* **9** death; destruction: *Luba met her end in the accident.* **10** destroy; kill. **11** a part left over; remnant; fragment. **12** in rugby football, the player at either end of the line. **13** in curling, one of the divisions of a game: *We were beaten in the last end.* **14** the farthest or most distant part; extreme point: *The police will hunt the murderer to the ends of the earth.* **15** surpass: *It was a holiday to end all holidays.* 1–3, 7–9, 11–14 *n.*, 4–6, 10, 15 *v.*

**at loose ends, a** not settled or established. **b** in confusion or disorder.

**end to end,** with the end of one object set next to the end of another; endways: *The dominoes were arranged end to end on the table.*

**end up,** finish: *She ended up a judge. He'll end up at the top of his class.*

**hold** or **keep one's end up,** do one's part or carry one's share fully in an undertaking or performance: *He was less experienced than the others, but he kept his end up very well.*
**in the end,** finally; at last: *Everything will turn out all right in the end.*
**make both ends meet, a** spend no more than one has. **b** just manage to live on what one has.
**no end,** *Informal.* very much; very many: *We had no end of trouble with that car.*
**on end, a** upright in position: *She stood the dominoes on end.* **b** one after another: *It snowed for days on end.*
**put an end to,** stop; do away with; destroy; kill.

**en·dan·ger** (en dān′jər) cause danger to; expose to loss or injury: *Fire endangered the hotel's guests, but no lives were lost.* *v.*

**endangered species** any species of life that is threatened with extinction.

**en·dear** (en dēr′) make dear: *Her kindness endeared her to all of us.* *v.*

**en·dear·ment** (en dēr′mənt) 1 endearing. 2 the thing that endears. 3 an act or word showing love or affection; caress. *n.*

**en·deav·our** or **en·deav·or** (en dev′ər) 1 try hard; attempt earnestly; make an effort; strive: *A runner endeavours to win a race.* 2 an earnest attempt; effort. 1 *v.*, 2 *n.*

**en·dem·ic** (en dem′ik) 1 regularly found in a particular people or locality: *Cholera is endemic in India.* 2 an endemic disease. 1 *adj.*, 2 *n.* Compare with EPIDEMIC.

**en dés·ha·bil·lé** (än dā zä bē yā′) *French.* partly or carelessly dressed.

**end·ing** (en′ding) 1 the last part; an end: *The story had a sad ending.* 2 death. 3 an INFLECTION (def. 2) added to a word or stem to change its meaning or to show how it is used in relation to other words. The common plural ending in English is -*s* or -*es*, as in *kings, dresses.* 4 ppr. of END. 1-3 *n.*, 4 *v.*

**en·dive** (en′dīv) 1 a kind of chicory with finely divided, curly leaves, used for salads. 2 a kind of chicory that looks like very smooth, white celery, used for salads. *n.*

**end·less** (en′dlis) 1 having no end; never stopping; lasting or going on forever: *the endless motion of the stars.* 2 appearing to have no end; seeming never to stop: *an endless task.* 3 with the ends joined; continuous: *A bicycle chain is an endless chain.* *adj.*
—**end′less·ly,** *adv.* —**end′less·ness,** *n.*

**end·most** (end′mōst) nearest to the end; last; farthest. *adj.*

**en·do·carp** (en′dō kärp′) the inner layer of a fruit or ripened OVARY (def. 2): *A peach stone is an endocarp.* Compare with EPICARP. *n.*

**en·do·crine** (en′dō krīn′ *or* en′dō krin) 1 producing secretions that pass directly into the blood or lymph instead of into a duct: *The thyroid is an endocrine gland.* 2 of or having to do with the ENDOCRINE GLANDS. 3 an ENDOCRINE GLAND. 4 its secretion. 1, 2 *adj.*, 3, 4 *n.* Also, **endocrin.**

**endocrine gland** any of various glands which produce secretions that pass directly into the blood stream or lymph, and which secrete hormones that influence other organs in the body.

**en·do·derm** (en′dō dėrm′) the inner layer of cells formed during development of animal embryos: *The lining of the organs of the digestive system develops from endoderm.* *n.*

**end of steel** *Cdn.* 1 the limit to which tracks have been laid for a railway. 2 a town at the end of a railway line; the terminus of a northern railway: *A road will soon connect us with the end of steel.*

**en·dog·e·nous** (en doj′ə nəs) growing from the inside; originating within. *adj.*

**en·do·plasm** (en′dō plaz′əm) the inner portion of the cytoplasm of a cell. *n.*

**en·dor·sa·tion** (en′dôr sā′shən) approval; support: *His proposals received wide endorsation.* *n.*

**en·dorse** (en dôrs′) 1 write one's name or instructions on the back of a cheque, money order, or other document: *She had to endorse the cheque before cashing it.* 2 approve; support: *Parents endorsed the plan for a playground.* *v.*, **en·dorsed, en·dors·ing.**
—**en·dors′er,** *n.* Also, **indorse.**

**en·dor·see** (en dôr′sē′) a person to whom a cheque, note, or other document is assigned by ENDORSEMENT (def. 1). *n.* Also, **indorsee.**

**en·dorse·ment** (en dôr′smənt) 1 the act of writing on the back of a cheque or other document. 2 a name, comment, instruction, etc. written on the back of a cheque or other document. 3 approval; support: *The proposal for a new stadium has our endorsement.* *n.* Also, **indorsement.**

**en·do·skel·e·ton** (en′dō skel′ə tən) the internal supporting structure of all vertebrates and some other groups of animals such as starfish, sea urchins, and some varieties of coral. Compare with EXOSKELETON. *n.*

**en·do·sperm** (en′dō spėrm′) the nourishment for the embryo enclosed with it in the seed of a plant. See EMBRYO for picture. *n.*

**en·dow** (en dou′) 1 give money or property to provide an income for: *The rich man endowed the college he had attended.* 2 furnish at birth; provide with some ability, quality, or talent: *Nature endowed her with both a good mind and good looks.* *v.*

**en·dow·ment** (en dou′mənt) 1 the money or property given to provide an income: *This college has a large endowment.* 2 a gift from birth; ability; talent: *A good sense of rhythm is a natural endowment.* 3 the act of endowing. *n.*

**end product** 1 the last stable member of a series of isotopes, each produced by the radio-active decay of the preceding isotope. 2 the final result of any series of changes, activities, etc.

**en·due** (en dyü′ *or* en dü′) 1 provide with a quality or power; furnish; supply: *The wisest man cannot be endued with perfect wisdom.* 2 put on. 3 clothe. *v.*, **en·dued, en·du·ing.** Also, **indue.**

**en·dur·ance** (en dyür′əns *or* en dü′rəns) 1 the power to last or keep on: *A person must have great endurance to run in a marathon.* 2 the power to put up with, bear, or stand: *Her endurance of the pain was remarkable.* 3 an act or instance of enduring pain, hardship, etc. 4 duration. *n.*

**en·dure** (en dyür′ *or* en dür′) 1 keep on; last: *These statues have endured for a thousand years.* 2 undergo;

bear; tolerate: *Those brave people endured much pain.* *v.*, **en·dured, en·dur·ing.** —**en·dur′a·ble,** *adj.*

**en·dur·ing** (en dyü′ring *or* en dü′ring) **1** lasting; permanent. **2** ppr. of ENDURE. **1** *adj.,* **2** *v.*

**end·ways** (en′dwāz′) **1** on end; upright. **2** with the end forward; in the direction of the end; lengthways. **3** end to end. *adv.*

**end·wise** (en′dwīz′) ENDWAYS. *adv.*

**end zone** **1** in rugby football, the part of the field between each goal line and the corresponding end of the field. **2** in hockey, the ice between each blue line and the corresponding end of the rink.

**ENE** or **E.N.E.** east-northeast.

**en·e·ma** (en′ə mə) an injection of liquid into the rectum to flush the bowels. *n., pl.* **en·e·mas.**

**en·e·my** (en′ə mē) **1** a person or group that hates and tries to harm another. **2** a hostile force, nation, army, fleet, or air force; person, ship, etc. of a hostile nation. **3** of an enemy. **4** anything harmful: *Frost is an enemy of plants.* **1, 2, 4** *n., pl.* **en·e·mies;** **3** *adj.*

**en·er·get·ic** (en′ər jet′ik) **1** full of energy; eager to work: *Cool autumn days make some people feel energetic.* **2** full of force; active. *adj.*

**en·er·get·i·cal·ly** (en′ər jet′i klē) with energy. *adv.*

**en·er·gize** (en′ər jīz′) give energy to; make active: *Ambition energizes people.* *v.*, **en·er·gized, en·er·giz·ing.** —**en′er·giz′er,** *n.*

**en·er·gy** (en′ər jē) **1** active strength or force; the will to work or act; vigour: *Young people have more energy than old people.* **2** strength; force; power: *All our energies were used in fighting the fire.* **3** the capacity for doing work, such as lifting or moving an object, or causing change: *Energy is measured in joules.* **4** natural resources such as oil, coal, hydro-electric power needed to make things work, especially industrial machinery, heating and lighting systems: *We must conserve oil to help our energy policy.* *n., pl.* **en·er·gies.**

**en·er·vate** (en′ər vāt′) lessen the vigour or strength of; weaken: *A hot, damp climate enervates people who are not used to it.* *v.*, **en·er·vat·ed, en·er·vat·ing.** —**en′er·va′tion,** *n.*

**en·fee·ble** (en fē′bəl) make feeble; weaken. *v.*, **en·fee·bled, en·fee·bling.** —**en·fee′ble·ment,** *n.*

**en·fi·lade** (en′fə lād′) fire guns from the side at a line of troops or at the position held by them. *v.*, **en·fi·lad·ed, en·fi·lad·ing.**

**en·fold** (en fōld′) **1** fold in; wrap up: *The old lady was enfolded in a shawl.* **2** embrace; clasp: *The mother enfolded her baby in her arms.* *v.* —**en·fold′er,** *n.* Also, **infold.**

**en·force** (en fôrs′) **1** force obedience to; put into force: *Police officers and judges enforce the laws.* **2** force; compel: *The robbers enforced obedience to their demand by threats of violence. Illness enforced me to remain idle.* **3** urge with force; emphasize: *The teacher enforced the principle by examples.* *v.*, **en·forced, en·forc·ing.** —**en·force′a·ble,** *adj.* —**en·forc′er,** *n.*

**en·force·ment** (en fôr′smənt) an enforcing; putting into force: *Strict enforcement of the laws against speeding will reduce automobile accidents.* *n.*

**en·fran·chise** (en fran′chīz) **1** give the right to vote: *All adult Canadian citizens are enfranchised.* **2** set free; release from slavery or restraint. *v.*, **en·fran·chised,**

**enduring** 401 **engineer**

hat, āge, fär; let, ēqual, tėrm; it, īce
hot, ōpen, ôrder; oil, out; cup, pút, rüle
əbove, takən, pencəl, lemən, circəs
ch, child; ng, long; sh, ship
th, thin; ᴛʜ, then; zh, measure

**en·fran·chis·ing.** —**en·fran′chis·er,** *n.* Also, **af·fran·chise.**

**en·fran·chise·ment** (en fran′chiz mənt) **1** an enfranchising. **2** being enfranchised. *n.*

**Eng.** **1** England. **2** English. **3** Engineer.

**eng.** **1** engineer. **2** engineering. **3** engraving. **4** engraved. **5** engraver.

**en·gage** (en gāj′) **1** keep busy; occupy: *Work engages much of his time.* **2** hire; employ: *She engaged a cook for the summer.* **3** arrange to secure for occupation or use; reserve: *We engaged a room in the hotel.* **4** bind by a promise or contract; pledge: *I will engage to be there on time.* **5** promise or pledge to marry: *Nikos and Olga are engaged. Nikos is engaged to Olga.* **6** catch and hold; attract: *Bright colours engaged the baby's attention.* **7** fit into; lock together; interlock: *The teeth of one gear engage with the teeth of another. The teeth engage each other.* See COGWHEEL for picture. **8** come into contact with in battle; attack: *Our soldiers engaged the enemy.* *v.*, **en·gaged, en·gag·ing.** —**en·gag′er,** *n.*

**engage in,** **a** keep busy with; take part in; be active in: *He engages in many sports.* **b** take up the attention of: *They were engaged in repairing the car.*

**en·gaged** (en gājd′) **1** promised or pledged to marry: *The engaged girl had a diamond ring.* **2** busy; occupied: *Engaged in conversation, they did not see us.* **3** taken for use or work; hired. **4** fitted together. **5** involved in a fight or battle. **6** pt. and pp. of ENGAGE. **1–5** *adj.,* **6** *v.*

**en·gage·ment** (en gāj′mənt) **1** the act of engaging. **2** the fact or condition of being engaged. **3** a promise or pledge: *An honest person fulfils all his or her engagements.* **4** the time between becoming pledged to marry and the actual wedding: *They got married after an engagement of six months.* **5** a meeting with someone at a certain time; appointment: *A previous engagement prevented her from coming to our party.* **6** the period of being hired; time of use or work. **7** a fight; battle. *n.*

**en·gag·ing** (en gā′jing) **1** very attractive; pleasing; charming: *an engaging smile.* **2** ppr. of ENGAGE. **1** *adj.,* **2** *v.* —**en·gag′ing·ly,** *adv.* —**en·gag′ing·ness,** *n.*

**En·gel·mann spruce** (eng′gəl mən) **1** a tall spruce tree found throughout the interior mountain regions of British Columbia and Alberta, having oval cones and curved, bluish-green needles often covered with a whitish, powdery coating called a bloom. **2** the light, soft wood of this tree.

**en·gen·der** (en jen′dər) bring into existence; produce; cause: *Filth engenders disease.* *v.*

**en·gine** (en′jən) **1** a machine that applies power to some work, especially one that can start others moving. **2** the machine that pulls a railway train; locomotive. **3** a machine; device; instrument: *Those big guns are engines of war.* *n.*

**en·gi·neer** (en′jə nēr′) **1** a person who takes care of or runs engines: *The driver of a locomotive is an engineer.* **2** a person skilled in a branch of engineering. **3** a member of a group of people who do engineering work in the armed forces. **4** plan, build, direct, or work as an engineer.   5 manage; guide: *Although many opposed his plan, he engineered it through to final approval.*   1–3 *n.*, 4, 5 *v.*

**en·gi·neer·ing** (en′jə nē′ring)   the application of science to such practical uses as the design and building of structures and machines, and the making of many products of modern technology: *Knowledge of engineering is needed in building railways, bridges, and dams.*   *n.*

**Eng·lish** (ing′glish)   1 of or having to do with England, its people, or their language.   2 **the English,** *pl.*   the people of England collectively.   3 the English language, including Old English or Anglo-Saxon (before 1100), Middle English (about 1100–1500), and Modern English (from about 1500): *English is spoken in the British Isles, Canada, the United States, South Africa, Australia, New Zealand, and many other places. The English spoken in Canada is called Canadian English.*   1 *adj.*, 2 *n. pl.*, 3 *n. sing.*

**English horn**   a wooden musical instrument resembling an oboe, but larger and having a lower tone.

**Eng·lish·man** (ing′glish mən)   1 a man who is a native or inhabitant of England.   2 a man of English descent.   *n., pl.* **Eng·lish·men** (-mən).

**English setter**   a long-haired, black-and-white hunting dog, sometimes having tan spots: *The English setter is trained to hunt with its nose pointed toward game.*

**English sparrow**   a small, brownish-grey bird, a European finch now very common in North America.

**English walnut**   1 a walnut tree from Asia, cultivated in Europe and North America.   2 its edible nut, used in candy, cakes, etc.

**Eng·lish·wom·an** (ing′glish wùm′ən)   1 a woman who is a native or inhabitant of England.   2 a woman of English descent.   *n., pl.* **Eng·lish·wom·en** (-wim′ən).

**en·gorge** (en gôrj′)   1 swallow greedily.   2 glut; gorge.   3 feed greedily.   4 congest with blood.   *v.*, **en·gorged, en·gorg·ing.**

**engr.**   1 engineer.   2 engraved.   3 engraver.

**en·graft** (en graft′)   1 insert or graft a shoot from one tree or plant into or on another: *Peach trees can be engrafted upon plum trees.*   2 add permanently; implant: *Honesty and thrift are engrafted in his character.*   *v.*   Also, **ingraft.**

**en·grave** (en grāv′)   1 cut in; carve artistically; decorate by engraving: *The jeweller engraved the boy's initials on the back of his watch.*   2 cut in lines on a metal plate, block of wood, etc. for printing.   3 print from such a plate, block, etc.   4 impress deeply; fix firmly: *His mother's face was engraved on his memory.*   *v.*, **en·graved, en·grav·ing.**

**en·grav·er** (en grā′vər)   a person who ENGRAVES (def. 2) metal plates, blocks of wood, etc. for printing.   *n.*

**engraver beetle**   a beetle that lives in the trunks of trees and engraves channels that weaken the tree.

**en·grav·ing** (en grā′ving)   1 the art of an ENGRAVER; cutting lines in metal plates, blocks of wood, etc. for printing.   2 a picture printed from an engraved plate, block, etc.   3 an engraved plate, block, etc.   4 ppr. of ENGRAVE.   1–3 *n.*, 4 *v.*

**en·gross** (en grōs′)   1 occupy wholly; take up all the attention of: *She was engrossed in a story.*   2 copy or write in large letters of the kind once used for legal documents.   *v.*   —**en·gross′ment,** *n.*

**en·gulf** (en gulf′)   swallow up; overwhelm; submerge: *A wave engulfed the small boat.*   *v.*   Also, **ingulf.**

**en·hance** (en hans′)   make greater; add to; heighten: *Gardens enhanced the beauty of the stately old house.*   *v.*, **en·hanced, en·hanc·ing.**   —**en·hance′ment,** *n.*

**e·nig·ma** (i nig′mə)   1 a puzzling statement; riddle: *To most of the audience the philosopher seemed to speak in enigmas.*   2 a baffling or puzzling problem, situation, person, etc.: *The strange behaviour of the child was an enigma even to his parents.*   *n.*

**en·ig·mat·ic** (en′ig mat′ik)   ENIGMATICAL.   *adj.*

**en·ig·mat·i·cal** (en′ig mat′ə kəl)   like a riddle; baffling; puzzling; mysterious.   *adj.*   —**en′ig·mat′i·cal·ly,** *adv.*

**en·join** (en join′)   1 order; direct; urge: *Parents enjoin good behaviour on their children.*   2 issue an authoritative command to: *Through an injunction a judge may enjoin a person to do (or not do) some act.*   *v.*

**en·joy** (en joi′)   1 have or use with joy; be happy with; take pleasure in.   2 have as an advantage or benefit: *He enjoyed good health.*   *v.*

**enjoy oneself,**   be happy; have pleasure; have a good time: *Enjoy yourself at the party.*

**en·joy·a·ble** (en joi′ə bəl)   capable of being enjoyed; giving enjoyment; pleasant.   *adj.*   —**en·joy′a·bly,** *adv.*

**en·joy·ment** (en joi′mənt)   1 an enjoying.   2 something enjoyed.   3 joy; happiness; pleasure.   4 the condition of having as an advantage or benefit; possession; use: *Laws protect the enjoyment of our rights.*   *n.*

**en·kin·dle** (en kin′dəl)   1 arouse; excite; stir up.   2 light up; brighten.   *v.*, **en·kin·dled, en·kin·dling.**

**en·lace** (en lās′)   1 wind about; encircle; enfold.   2 twine together; interlace.   *v.*, **en·laced, en·lac·ing.**

**en·large** (en lärj′)   make or become larger; increase in size.   *v.*, **en·larged, en·larg·ing.**   —**en·larg′er,** *n.*

**enlarge on,**   talk or write more about: *The chairman of the school board enlarged on her earlier statement about the plan for a new school.*

**en·large·ment** (en lärj′mənt)   1 an enlarging or being enlarged.   2 anything that is an enlarged form of something else.   3 in photography, a print that is made larger than the negative.   4 anything that enlarges something else; addition.   *n.*

**en·light·en** (en lī′tən)   give the light of truth and knowledge to; free from prejudice, ignorance, etc.   *v.*

**en·light·en·ment** (en lī′tən mənt)   an ENLIGHTENing or being ENLIGHTENed.   *n.*

**en·list** (en list′)   1 get someone to join a branch of the armed forces.   2 enrol in a branch of the armed forces.   3 induce to join in some cause or undertaking; secure the help or support of: *The mayor enlisted the volunteers of our city to work for more parks.*   4 join in some cause or undertaking; give help or support.   *v.*   —**en·list′er,** *n.*

**en·list·ment** (en list′mənt)   1 an ENLISTing (defs. 1, 2).   2 being ENLISTed (def. 1).   3 the time for which a person ENLISTs (def. 2).   *n.*

**en·liv·en** (en lī′vən)   make lively, active, or cheerful: *The speaker enlivened his speech with humour. Bright curtains enliven a room.*   *v.*

**en masse** (on′mas′; *French,* äN mäs′) in a group; all together.

**en·mesh** (en mesh′) catch in a net; enclose in meshes; entangle. *v.*

**en·mi·ty** (en′mə tē) the feeling that enemies have for each other; hatred. *n., pl.* **en·mi·ties.**

**en·no·ble** (en nō′bəl) **1** give a title or rank of nobility to; raise to the rank of nobleman. **2** raise in the respect of others; dignify; exalt: *A good deed ennobles the person who does it.* **3** make finer or more noble in nature: *Her character had been ennobled through suffering.* *v.,* **en·no·bled, en·no·bling.** —**en·no′ble·ment,** *n.*

**en·nui** (on′wē; *French,* äN nYē′) a feeling of weariness and discontent from lack of occupation or interest; BOREDOM. *n.*

**e·nor·mi·ty** (i nôr′mə tē) **1** extreme wickedness; outrageousness: *The cruel murderer was put to death for the enormity of his crime.* **2** an extremely wicked crime; outrageous offence. *n., pl.* **e·nor·mi·ties.**

**e·nor·mous** (i nôr′məs) **1** extremely large; huge: *Long ago enormous animals lived on the earth.* **2** extremely wicked; outrageous. *adj.* —**e·nor′mous·ness,** *n.*

**e·nor·mous·ly** (i nôr′məs lē) in or to an enormous degree; extremely; vastly; beyond measure. *adv.*

**e·nough** (i nuf′) **1** as much or as many as needed or wanted: *Buy enough food for the picnic* (*adj.*). *I have had enough to eat* (*n.*). *Have you played enough?* (*adv.*). **2** quite; fully: *He is willing enough to take a hint.* **3** rather; fairly: *She talks well enough for a baby.* 1 *adj., n.,* 1–3 *adv.*

**e·nounce** (i nouns′) **1** proclaim; make a public or formal statement. **2** speak; pronounce; enunciate. *v.,* **e·nounced, e·nounc·ing.**

**en·quire** (en kwīr′) See INQUIRE. *v.,* **en·quired, en·quir·ing.**

**en·quir·y** (en kwīr′ē *or* en′kwə rē) See INQUIRY. *n., pl.* **en·quir·ies.**

**en·rage** (en rāj′) put into a rage; make very angry; make furious. *v.,* **en·raged, en·rag·ing.**

**en rap·port** (äN rä pôr′) *French.* in sympathy; in agreement.

**en·rapt** (en rapt′) rapt; filled with great delight. *adj.*

**en·rap·ture** (en rap′chər) fill with great delight; ENTRANCE[2] (def. 2): *The audience was enraptured by the singer's beautiful voice.* *v.,* **en·rap·tured, en·rap·tur·ing.**

**en·rich** (en rich′) **1** make rich or richer: *An education enriches one's mind. Fertilizer enriches soil.* **2** raise the nutritive value of a food by adding vitamins and minerals in processing. *v.*

**en·rich·ment** (en rich′mənt) **1** an ENRICHing. **2** being ENRICHed. **3** anything that ENRICHes. *n.*

**en·rol** *or* **en·roll** (en rōl′) **1** write in a list: *The secretary enrolled our names.* **2** have one's name written in a list. **3** make a member. **4** become a member. **5** enlist: *Vito enrolled in the armed forces.* *v.,* **en·rolled, en·rol·ling.**

**en·rol·ment** *or* **en·roll·ment** (en rōl′mənt) **1** an enrolling. **2** the number enrolled: *The school has an enrolment of 200 students.* *n.*

**en route** (on rüt′; *French,* äN Rüt′) on the way: *We shall stop at Toronto en route from Montreal to Winnipeg.*

hat, āge, fär; let, ēqual, tėrm; it, īce
hot, ōpen, ôrder; oil, out; cup, pu̇t, rüle
əbove, takən, pencəl, lemən, circəs
ch, child; ng, long; sh, ship
th, thin; ᴛH, then; zh, measure

**en·sconce** (en skons′) **1** shelter safely; hide: *The soldiers were ensconced in strongly fortified trenches.* **2** settle comfortably and firmly: *The cat ensconced itself in the armchair.* *v.,* **en·sconced, en·sconc·ing.**

**en·sem·ble** (on som′bəl) **1** all the parts of a thing considered together; the general effect. **2** a united performance of the full number of singers, musicians, etc.: *After the solo, all the singers joined in the ensemble.* **3** a group of musicians, or the musical instruments used, in taking part in such a performance: *Two violins, a cello, and a harp made up the string ensemble.* **4** a complete, harmonious costume. *n.*

**en·shrine** (en shrīn′) **1** enclose in a shrine: *A holy relic is enshrined in the cathedral.* **2** keep sacred; cherish: *Memories of happier days were enshrined in the old beggar's heart.* *v.,* **en·shrined, en·shrin·ing.**

**en·shrine·ment** (en shrīn′mənt) **1** an enshrining. **2** anything that enshrines or surrounds. *n.*

**en·shroud** (en shroud′) cover; hide; veil: *Fog enshrouded the ship, but we could hear its siren.* *v.*

**en·sign** (en′sīn *or* en′sən) **1** a flag or banner: *the Red Ensign.* **2** in former times, a British army officer whose duty was carrying the flag. **3** the sign of one's rank, position, or power; symbol of authority. *n.*

**en·si·lage** (en′sə lij) **1** the preservation of green fodder by packing it in a silo or pit. **2** green fodder preserved in this way: *Ensilage is used to feed cattle in winter.* *n.*

**en·slave** (en slāv′) make a slave or slaves of; take away freedom from. *v.,* **en·slaved, en·slav·ing.**

**en·slave·ment** (en slāv′mənt) **1** an enslaving. **2** being ENSLAVed. *n.*

**en·snare** (en sner′) catch in a snare; trap. *v.,* **en·snared, en·snar·ing.** Also, **insnare.**

**en·sue** (en sü′ *or* en syü′) **1** come after; follow: *The ensuing year means the next year.* **2** happen as a result: *In his anger he hit the man, and a fight ensued.* *v.,* **en·sued, en·su·ing.**

**en·sure** (en shu̇r′) **1** make sure or certain: *Careful planning and hard work ensured the success of the party.* **2** make sure of getting; secure: *A letter of introduction will ensure you an interview.* **3** make safe; protect: *Proper clothing ensured us against the cold.* *v.,* **en·sured, en·sur·ing.**

☞ *Syn.* Do not confuse **ensure** with INSURE. **Ensure** means 'make sure or certain'; INSURE means 'arrange for money payment in case of loss, accident, or death': *Check your work to ensure its accuracy. They insured their house against fire.*

**–ent** a suffix often added to a verb to form an adjective or a noun: **1** _____ing, as in *absorbent, indulgent, coincident.* **2** one that _____s, as in *correspondent, president, superintendent.* **3** other meanings, as in *competent, confident.*

**en·tab·la·ture** (en tab′lə chər) in architecture, a horizontal band forming the top of a wall or storey, supported by columns or pilasters: *In classical architecture,*

**en·tail** (en tāl′) **1** impose; require: *Owning an automobile entailed greater expense than he had expected.* **2** limit the inheritance of property, etc. to a specified line of heirs so that it cannot be left to anyone else: *An entailed estate usually passes to the eldest son.* **3** an entailing. **4** an entailed inheritance. **5** the order of descent specified for an entailed estate. 1, 2 *v.*, 3–5 *n.*

**en·tail·ment** (en tāl′mənt) **1** an ENTAILing (def. 2). **2** being ENTAILed (def. 2). *n.*

**en·tan·gle** (en tang′gəl) **1** get twisted up and caught; tangle: *Loose string is easily entangled.* **2** get into difficulty; involve: *The villain tried to entangle the heroine in an evil scheme.* **3** perplex; confuse. *v.*, **en·tan·gled, en·tan·gling.**

**en·tan·gle·ment** (en tang′gəl mənt) **1** an entangling or being ENTANGLED. **2** anything that ENTANGLES: *a barbed wire entanglement.* *n.*

**en·tente** (on tont′; *French* äN tänt′) **1** an understanding; agreement between two or more governments. **2** the parties to an understanding; governments that have made an agreement. *n.*

**en·tente cor·diale** (äN tänt kôr dyäl′) *French.* a friendly understanding or agreement.

**en·ter** (en′tər) **1** go into; come into: *She entered the house.* **2** go in; come in: *Let them all enter.* **3** become a part or member of; join: *The singer entered the choir.* **4** cause to join; enrol; obtain admission for: *Parents enter their children in school.* **5** begin; start: *After years of training, the doctor entered the practice of medicine.* **6** write or print in a book, list, etc.: *A dictionary enters words in alphabetical order.* **7** put in regular form; record: *The injured woman entered a complaint in court.* **8** in the theatre, come on stage. **9** take part in: *He will enter the piano competition.* **10** input data or instructions into a computer. *v.*

**enter into, a** begin to take part in: *He entered into conversation with the woman.* **b** form a part of: *That question doesn't enter into the problem.* **c** consider; discuss: *enter into a question of law.*

**enter on** or **upon, a** begin; start: *Nina entered on her professional duties as soon as she finished law school.* **b** take possession of.

**en·ter·prise** (en′tər prīz′) **1** an important, difficult, or dangerous undertaking. **2** an undertaking; project: *a business enterprise.* **3** a readiness to start projects; courage and energy in starting projects: *The successful businessman showed great enterprise.* **4** the carrying on of enterprises; taking part in enterprises. *n.*

**en·ter·pris·ing** (en′tər prī′zing) ready to try new, important, difficult, or dangerous plans; courageous and energetic in starting projects. *adj.*

**en·ter·tain** (en′tər tān′) **1** amuse; please; interest: *The circus entertained the children.* **2** have as a guest or guests: *She entertained ten people at dinner.* **3** have guests; invite people to one's home or a restaurant: *They entertain a great deal.* **4** take into the mind; consider: *They refuse to entertain such a foolish idea.* **5** hold in the mind; maintain: *Even after failing twice, we still entertained a hope of success.* *v.*

**en·ter·tain·er** (en′tər tā′nər) a singer, musician, reciter, etc. who takes part in public ENTERTAINMENTS (def. 2). *n.*

**en·ter·tain·ing** (en′tər tā′ning) **1** very interesting; pleasing; amusing. **2** ppr. of ENTERTAIN. 1 *adj.*, 2 *v.* —**en′ter·tain′ing·ly,** *adv.*

**en·ter·tain·ment** (en′tər tān′mənt) **1** an ENTERTAINing or being entertained. **2** something that interests, pleases, or amuses: *A show or play is an entertainment.* **3** hospitality; the act or practice of paying attention to the comfort and desires of guests: *I devoted myself to the entertainment of my guests.* *n.*

**en·thral** or **en·thrall** (en throl′) **1** captivate; fascinate; charm: *The explorer enthralled the audience with the story of her exciting adventures.* **2** make a slave of; enslave. *v.*, **en·thralled, en·thral·ling.** Also, **inthral** or **inthrall.** —**en·thral′ment** or **en·thrall′ment,** *n.*

**en·throne** (en thrōn′) **1** set on a throne. **2** place highest of all; exalt: *Sir Wilfrid Laurier is enthroned in the hearts of his countrymen.* **3** invest with authority, especially as a sovereign or as a bishop. *v.*, **en·throned, en·thron·ing.** Also, **inthrone.** —**en·throne′ment,** *n.*

**en·thuse** (en thüz′ *or* en thyüz′) *Informal.* **1** show ENTHUSIASM. **2** fill with ENTHUSIASM. *v.*, **en·thused, en·thus·ing.**

**en·thu·si·asm** (en thü′zē az′əm *or* en thyü′zē az′əm) eager interest; zeal: *The great leader filled his followers with enthusiasm.* *n.*

**en·thu·si·ast** (en thü′zē ast′ *or* en thyü′zē ast′) **1** a person who is filled with eager interest or zeal: *a baseball enthusiast.* **2** a person who is carried away by his or her feelings for a cause. *n.*

**en·thu·si·as·tic** (en thü′zē as′tik *or* en thyü′zē as′tik) full of ENTHUSIASM; eagerly interested. *adj.* —**en·thu′si·as′ti·cal·ly,** *adv.*

**en·tice** (en tīs′) tempt by arousing hopes or desires; attract by offering some pleasure or reward: *The robber enticed his victims into a cave by promising to show them a gold mine.* *v.*, **en·ticed, en·tic·ing.** —**en·tic′er,** *n.* —**en·tic′ing·ly,** *adv.*

**en·tice·ment** (en tīs′mənt) **1** an enticing. **2** being ENTICEd. **3** the thing that ENTICES: *Enticements of milk and meat induced the frightened cat to come down from the tree.* *n.*

**en·tire** (en tīr′) having all the parts or elements; whole; complete: *Our new radio is not entire: two parts are missing. The entire class has passed the examination.* *adj.*

**en·tire·ly** (en tīr′lē) **1** wholly; completely; fully. **2** solely: *It was entirely my fault.* *adv.*

**en·tire·ty** (en tīr′tē *or* en tī′rə tē) **1** wholeness; completeness. **2** a complete thing; the whole. *n., pl.* **en·tire·ties.**

**in its entirety,** wholly, completely: *He enjoyed the concert in its entirety.*

**en·ti·tle** (en tī′təl) **1** give the title of; call by the name of: *She read a poem entitled "Trees."* **2** give a claim or right to; provide with a reason to ask or get something: *Their age and experience entitle old people to respect.* *v.*, **en·ti·tled, en·ti·tling.** Also, **intitle.**

**en·ti·ty** (en′ti tē) **1** something that has a real and separate existence either actually or in the mind; anything real in itself: *Persons, mountains, languages, and beliefs are distinct entities.* **2** a state of being; existence. *n., pl.* **en·ti·ties.**

**en·tomb** (en tüm′) **1** place in a tomb; bury. **2** shut

**en·to·mo·log·i·cal** (en′tə mə loj′ə kəl) of or having to do with ENTOMOLOGY. *adj.*

**en·to·mol·o·gist** (en′tə mol′ə jist) a person trained in ENTOMOLOGY. *n.*

**en·to·mol·o·gy** (en′tə mol′ə jē) the branch of zoology that deals with insects. *n.*

**en·tou·rage** (on′tü räzh′) a group of attendants or people usually accompanying a person. *n.*

**en·trails** (en′trālz *or* en′trəlz) **1** the inner parts of a human being or animal. **2** the intestines; bowels. **3** any inner parts. *n. pl.*

**en·train** (en trān′) **1** get on a train. **2** put on a train: *The students were entrained at night.* *v.*

**en·trance**¹ (en′trəns) **1** the act of entering: *The actor's entrance was greeted with applause.* **2** a place by which to enter; door, passageway, etc. **3** the freedom or right to enter; permission to enter: *The princess had entrance to the best society.* *n.*

**en·trance**² (en trans′) **1** put into a trance. **2** fill with joy; delight; charm: *The girl was entranced by her new book.* *v.*, **en·tranced, en·tranc·ing.** —**en·tranc′ing·ly**, *adv.*

**en·trance·ment** (en tran′smənt) **1** an entrancing. **2** being ENTRANCED². **3** something that ENTRANCES². *n.*

**en·trance·way** (en′trən swā′) a place by which to enter. *n.*

**en·trant** (en′trənt) **1** a person who enters. **2** a new member in a profession, club, association, etc. **3** a person who takes part in a contest. *n.*

**en·trap** (en trap′) **1** catch in a trap. **2** bring into difficulty or danger; deceive; trick: *By clever questioning, the lawyer entrapped the witness into contradicting himself.* *v.*, **en·trapped, en·trap·ping.** —**en·trap′ment**, *n.*

**en·treat** (en trēt′) ask earnestly; beg and pray; implore: *The captives entreated the enemy not to kill them.* *v.* Also, **intreat.**

**en·treat·y** (en trē′tē) an earnest request; prayer: *The enemy paid no attention to their captives' entreaties for mercy.* *n.*, *pl.* **en·treat·ies.**

**en·tree** *or* **en·trée** (on′trā) **1** the freedom or right to enter; access. **2** the main dish of food at dinner or lunch. *n.*

**en·trench** (en trench′) **1** surround with a trench; fortify with trenches: *Our soldiers were entrenched opposite the enemy.* **2** establish firmly: *Your rights as a citizen are entrenched in the Charter of Rights.* **3** trespass; encroach; infringe (*on* or *upon*): *Do not entrench upon the rights of others.* *v.* Also, **intrench.**

**en·trench·ment** (en trench′mənt) **1** an ENTRENCHing. **2** an ENTRENCHed position. **3** a defence consisting of a trench and a rampart of earth or stone. *n.* Also, **intrenchment.**

**en·tre·pre·neur** (on′trə prə nėr′) a person who organizes and manages a business or industrial enterprise, taking the risk of not making a profit but getting the profit when there is one. *n.*

**en·trust** (en trust′) **1** charge with a trust; trust: *The club entrusted the treasurer with all of its money.* **2** give the care of; hand over for safekeeping: *While travelling, they entrusted their daughter to her grandparents.* *v.* Also, **intrust.**

## entomological 405 enviable

hat, āge, fär; let, ēqual, tėrm; it, īce
hot, ōpen, ôrder; oil, out; cup, pút, rüle
əbove, takən, pencəl, lemən, circəs
ch, child; ng, long; sh, ship
th, thin; ŦH, then; zh, measure

**en·try** (en′trē) **1** the act of entering. **2** a place by which to enter; way to enter: *A vestibule is an entry.* **3** something written or printed in a book, list, etc.: *Each word explained in a dictionary is an entry.* **4** a person or thing that takes part in a contest. **5** in law, the act of taking possession of lands or buildings by entering or setting foot on them. *n.*, *pl.* **en·tries.**

**entry word** in a dictionary, one of the words listed in alphabetical order and followed by information concerning its pronunciation, meaning, etc.: *Entry words are usually printed in heavy black type.*

**en·twine** (en twīn′) **1** twine together. **2** twine around: *Roses entwined the little cottage.* *v.*, **en·twined, en·twin·ing.**

**e·nu·mer·ate** (i nyü′mə rāt′ *or* i nü′mə rāt′) **1** name one by one; give a list of: *She enumerated the days of the week.* **2** count. **3** *Cdn.* make up or enter in a list of voters in an area. *v.*, **e·nu·mer·at·ed, e·nu·mer·at·ing.**

**e·nu·mer·a·tion** (i nyü′mə rā′shən *or* i nü′mə rā′shən) **1** an enumerating; listing; counting. **2** a list. *n.*

**e·nu·mer·a·tive** (i nyü′mə rə tiv *or* i nü′mə rə tiv, i nyü′mə rā′tiv *or* i nü′mə rā′tiv) that ENUMERATES; having to do with ENUMERATION. *adj.*

**e·nu·mer·a·tor** (i nyü′mə rā′tər *or* i nü′mə rā′tər) **1** *Cdn.* a person appointed to list, prior to an election, the eligible voters in a polling area. **2** any person or thing that lists or counts. *n.*

**e·nun·ci·ate** (i nun′sē āt′) **1** pronounce words: *He is a well-trained actor and enunciates very distinctly.* **2** state definitely; announce: *After performing many experiments, the scientist enunciated a new theory.* *v.*, **e·nun·ci·at·ed, e·nun·ci·at·ing.** —**e·nun′ci·a′tor**, *n.*

**e·nun·ci·a·tion** (i nun′sē ā′shən) **1** one's manner of pronouncing words. **2** a definite statement; announcement: *the enunciation of a set of rules.* *n.*

**en·ure** (i nyür′) See INURE. *v.*

**en·vel·op** (en vel′əp) **1** wrap; cover: *The baby was so enveloped in blankets that we could hardly see her face.* **2** surround: *Our soldiers enveloped the enemy and captured them.* **3** hide; conceal: *Fog enveloped the village.* *v.*, **en·vel·oped, en·vel·op·ing.**

**en·ve·lope** (en′və lōp′ *or* on′və lōp′) **1** a paper cover in which a letter or anything flat and fairly thin can be mailed, filed, etc.: *An envelope can usually be folded over and sealed by wetting a gummed edge.* **2** a covering; wrapper. **3** the bag that holds the gas in a balloon or airship. *n.*

**en·vel·op·ment** (en vel′əp mənt) **1** an ENVELOPing. **2** being ENVELOPed. **3** something that ENVELOPS (def. 1); wrapping; covering. *n.*

**en·ven·om** (en ven′əm) **1** make poisonous. **2** fill with bitterness, hate, etc.: *The wicked boy envenomed his father's mind against his half brother.* *v.*

**en·vi·a·ble** (en′vē ə bəl) to be envied; desirable; worth

**having:** *She has an enviable school record.* *adj.* —**en′vi·a·ble·ness,** *n.* —**en′vi·a·bly,** *adv.*

**en·vi·ous** (en′vē əs) full of envy; feeling or showing envy: *She was envious of her friend's new bicycle. The weak are often envious of the strong.* *adj.* —**en′vi·ous·ly,** *adv.* —**en′vi·ous·ness,** *n.*

**en·vi·ron** (en vī′rən) surround; enclose. *v.*

**en·vi·ron·ment** (en vī′rən mənt) **1** all the surrounding conditions and influences that affect the development of a living thing: *A person's character is influenced by his or her environment. Differences in environment often account for differences in the same kind of plant found in different places.* **2** surroundings: *an environment of poverty. Banff has a beautiful environment.* **3** the act or fact of surrounding. *n.*

**en·vi·ron·men·tal** (en vī′rən men′təl) having to do with ENVIRONMENT (def. 1). *adj.*

**en·vi·rons** (en vī′rənz) surrounding districts; suburbs: *We visited Toronto and its environs.* *n. pl.*

**en·vis·age** (en viz′ij) foresee; visualize: *I envisage no difficulty with our plans.* *v.*, **en·vis·aged, en·vis·ag·ing.**

**en·vi·sion** (en vizh′ən) have a mental picture of; imagine, especially something that does not yet exist; picture to oneself; look forward to: *It is difficult to envision a state of world peace.* *v.*

**en·voy** (en′voi) **1** messenger. **2** a diplomat ranking next below an ambassador and next above a minister. *n.*

**en·vy** (en′vē) **1** discontent or ill will at another's good fortune because one wishes it were one's own; dislike for a person who has what one wants: *The boys were filled with envy when they saw her new bicycle.* **2** the object of such feeling: *She was the envy of the younger girls in the school.* **3** feel envy toward: *Some people envy the rich.* **4** feel envy because of: *Carlos envied his friend's success.* 1, 2 *n., pl.* **en·vies;** 3, 4 *v.*, **en·vied, en·vy·ing.**
☛ *Etym.* From OF *envie* which came from L *invidia*, ultimately from the L verb *invidere*, meaning 'to look with enmity at'.

**en·womb** (en wüm′) enclose in, or as if in, a womb. *v.*

**en·wrap** (en rap′) enclose; envelop; wrap. *v.*, **en·wrapped, en·wrap·ping.** Also, **inwrap.**

**en·wreathe** (en rēth′) wreathe around; encircle. *v.*, **en·wreathed, en·wreath·ing.** Also, **inwreathe.**

**en·zyme** (en′zīm) a chemical substance, produced in living cells, that can cause changes in other substances within the body without being changed itself: *Pepsin is an enzyme.* *n.*

**e·o·lith·ic** or **E·o·lith·ic** (ē′ə lith′ik) of or having to do with a very early stage of human culture, characterized by the use of the most primitive stone instruments. *adj.*

**e·on** (ē′ən *or* ē′on) a very long period of time; many thousands of years: *Eons passed before life existed on earth.* *n.* Also, **aeon.**

**ep·au·lette** or **ep·au·let** (ep′ə let′) an ornament on the shoulder of a uniform: *Epaulettes are usually worn only by officers in the armed forces.* *n.*

**e·phem·er·al** (i fem′ə rəl) lasting for only a day; lasting for only a very short time; very short-lived. *adj.*

**e·phem·er·id** (i fem′ə rid) the May fly, a type of insect living a day or two in the adult form, but from one to three years in the immature stage. *n.*

**eph·od** (ef′od) a vestment worn by Jewish priests in performing sacred duties. *n.*

**ep·ic** (ep′ik) **1** a long poem that tells of the adventures of one or more great heroes: *An epic is written in a dignified, majestic style and often gives expression to the ideals of a nation or people. The "Iliad," the "Aeneid," and "Paradise Lost" are epics.* **2** any writing having the qualities of an epic. **3** any story or series of events worthy of being the subject of an epic. **4** *Informal.* a spectacular motion picture or other entertainment. **5** of or having to do with an epic. **6** like an epic; grand in style; heroic: *epic deeds.* 1–4 *n.*, 5, 6 *adj.* —**ep′i·cal·ly,** *adv.*

**ep·i·cal** (ep′ə kəl) EPIC (defs. 5, 6). *adj.*

**ep·i·carp** (ep′ə kärp′) the outer layer of a fruit or ripened OVARY (def. 2) of a plant: *The skin of a pear is its epicarp.* Compare with ENDOCARP. *n.*

**ep·i·cen·tre** or **ep·i·cen·ter** (ep′ə sen′tər) the point from which earthquake waves seem to go out: *The epicentre is situated directly above the true centre of the earthquake.* *n.*

**ep·i·cure** (ep′ə kyür′) a person who has a refined taste in eating and drinking and cares much about food and drink. *n.*

**ep·i·cu·re·an** (ep′ə kyə rē′ən) **1** like an epicure; fond of pleasure and luxury. **2** fit for an epicure: *an epicurean banquet.* **3** a person fond of pleasure and luxury; epicure. **4** of Epicurus or his philosophy. 1, 2, 4 *adj.*, 3 *n.*
☛ *Etym.* From *Epicurus*, a Greek philosopher (341–270 B.C.) who taught a belief in pleasure as the greatest good.

**ep·i·dem·ic** (ep′ə dem′ik) **1** a rapid spreading of a disease so that many people have it at the same time: *All the schools in the city were closed because of an epidemic of scarlet fever.* **2** the rapid spread of an idea, fashion, etc. **3** affecting many people at the same time; widespread: *an epidemic disease. The wild rumours had reached epidemic proportions.* 1, 2 *n.*, 3 *adj.* Compare with ENDEMIC.

**ep·i·der·mal** (ep′ə der′məl) of or having to do with the EPIDERMIS. *adj.*

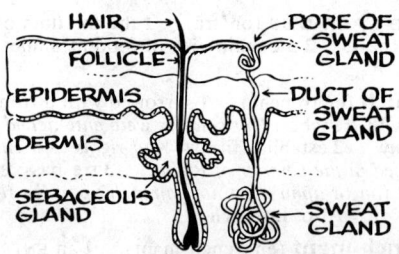

The layers of human skin as seen through a microscope

**ep·i·der·mis** (ep′ə der′mis) **1** the outer layer of the skin of vertebrates. **2** the outer covering on the shells of many MOLLUSCS. **3** any of various other outer layers of invertebrates. **4** a skinlike layer of cells in seed plants and ferns. *n.*

**ep·i·glot·tis** (ep′ə glot′is) a thin, triangular plate of cartilage that covers the entrance to the windpipe during swallowing, so that food, etc. does not enter the lungs. See WINDPIPE for picture. *n.*

**ep·i·gram** (ep′ə gram′) **1** a short, pointed or witty

saying: *Example:* "The only way to get rid of temptation is to yield to it." **2** a short poem ending in a witty or clever turn of thought. *Example:*

> Here lies our Sovereign Lord the King,
> Whose word no man relies on,
> Who never said a foolish thing,
> Nor ever did a wise one.  *n.*

**ep·i·gram·mat·ic** (ep′ə grə mat′ik)  **1** of EPIGRAMS; full of epigrams.  **2** like an EPIGRAM; terse and witty.  *adj.*  —**ep′i·gram·mat′i·cal·ly,** *adv.*

**e·pig·ra·phy** (i pig′rə fē)  **1** inscriptions.  **2** the branch of knowledge that deals with the deciphering and interpretation of inscriptions.  *n.*

**ep·i·lep·sy** (ep′ə lep′sē)  a disorder of the nervous system whose attacks cause convulsions and total or partial loss of consciousness.  *n.*

**ep·i·lep·tic** (ep′ə lep′tik)  **1** of or having to do with EPILEPSY: *Most epileptic seizures can be controlled with drugs.*  **2** having EPILEPSY.  **3** a person having EPILEPSY. 1, 2 *adj.*, 3 *n.*

**ep·i·logue** (ep′ə log′)  **1** a concluding section added to a novel, poem, etc. and serving to round out or interpret the work.  **2** a speech or poem after the end of a play, addressed to the audience and spoken by one of the actors.  *n.* Also, **epilog.**

**ep·i·phyte** (ep′ə fīt′)  any of various plants that grow on other plants for support, but not for nourishment: *Many mosses, lichens, and orchids are epiphytes.*  *n.*

**e·pis·co·pal** (i pis′kə pəl)  **1** of or having to do with bishops.  **2** governed by bishops.  *adj.*

**ep·i·sode** (ep′ə sōd′)  **1** an incident or experience that stands out from others: *The year in France was an important episode in her life.*  **2** a set of events or actions separate from the main plot of a novel, story, etc.  **3** a similar digression in a musical composition.  **4** a portion of a serial play, film, etc.: *The concluding episode will be shown next week.*  *n.*

**ep·i·sod·ic** (ep′ə sod′ik)  **1** like an EPISODE (def. 2); incidental; occasional.  **2** consisting of a series of EPISODES (def. 4): *Her new novel is loosely episodic.*  *adj.*

**e·pis·tle** (i pis′əl)  a letter, especially an instructive or a formal one.  *n.*

**e·pis·to·lar·y** (i pis′tə ler′ē)  **1** carried on by letters; contained in letters.  **2** of letters; suitable for writing letters.  *adj.*

**ep·i·taph** (ep′ə taf′)  a short statement in memory of a dead person, usually put on a tombstone.  *n.*

**ep·i·the·li·al** (ep′ə thē′lē əl)  of the EPITHELIUM.  *adj.*

**ep·i·the·li·um** (ep′ə thē′lē əm)  a thin layer of cells forming a tissue that covers surfaces, and lines hollow organs.  *n., pl.* **ep·i·the·li·ums** or **ep·i·the·li·a** (-lē ə).

**ep·i·thet** (ep′ə thet′)  a descriptive expression; adjective or noun, or even a clause, expressing some quality or attribute: *In "crafty Ulysses" and "Richard the Lion-Hearted," the epithets are "crafty" and "the Lion-Hearted."*  *n.*

**e·pit·o·me** (i pit′ə mē)  **1** a condensed account; summary: *An epitome contains only the most important points of a literary work, subject, etc.*  **2** a person or thing that is typical or representative of a quality; an ideal or typical example: *Solomon is spoken of as the epitome of wisdom.*  *n.*

## epigrammatic 407 equalize

hat, āge, fär; let, ēqual, tėrm; it, īce
hot, ōpen, ôrder; oil, out; cup, pùt, rüle
əbove, takən, pencəl, lemən, circəs
ch, child; ng, long; sh, ship
th, thin; ŦH, then; zh, measure

**e·pit·o·mize** (i pit′ə mīz′)  make an EPITOME (def. 1) of; summarize.  *v.*, **e·pit·o·mized, e·pit·o·miz·ing.**

**ep·i·zo·ot·ic** (ep′ə zō ot′ik)  **1** temporarily prevalent among animals.  **2** an epizootic disease.  1 *adj.*, 2 *n.*

**ep·och** (ē′pok *or* ep′ək)  **1** a period of time; ERA.  **2** a period of time in which striking things happened: *The years leading to Confederation were an epoch in Canada's history.*  **3** the starting point of such a period: *The invention of the steam engine marked an epoch in the evolution of industry.*  *n.*

**ep·och·al** (ep′ə kəl *or* ē′pok əl)  **1** having to do with an EPOCH.  **2** EPOCH-MAKING.  *adj.*

**ep·och–mak·ing** (ē′pok mā′king *or* ep′ək mā′king)  beginning an epoch; causing important changes.  *adj.*

**ep·o·nym** (ep′ə nim′)  a person from whom a nation, tribe, place, etc. gets or is reputed to get its name: *Romulus is the eponym of Rome.*  *n.*

**e·pon·y·mous** (ep on′ə məs)  giving one's name to a nation, tribe, place, book, etc.: *David Copperfield is the eponymous hero of the novel* David Copperfield.  *adj.*

**ep·ox·y** (ep ok′sē)  **1** containing oxygen as a bond between two different atoms already united in another way: *Epoxy resins are extremely durable plastics used for adhesives, varnishes, etc.*  **2** an epoxy resin.  1 *adj.*, 2 *n., pl.* **ep·ox·ies.**

**Epsom salts**  a bitter, white, crystalline powder used in medicine, especially as a laxative.

**eq.**  **1** equal.  **2** equivalent.  **3** equator.  **4** equation.

**eq·ua·bil·i·ty** (ek′wə bil′ə tē)  an EQUABLE condition or quality.  *n.*

**eq·ua·ble** (ek′wə bəl)  changing little; uniform; even; tranquil: *an equable temperature, an equable disposition.*  *adj.*  —**eq′ua·bly,** *adv.*

**e·qual** (ē′kwəl)  **1** the same in amount, size, number, value, degree, rank, etc.; as much; neither more nor less: *These two roasts are equal in weight.*  **2** person or thing similar in rank or excellence: *In spelling she had no equal.*  **3** something that is equal: *Add equals to equals.* *7 + 3 is the equal of 5 × 2.*  **4** be the same as: *Four times five equals twenty.*  Symbol: =  **5** make or do something equivalent to; match: *She tried hard to equal the scoring record.*  **6** the same throughout; even; uniform.  1, 6 *adj.*, 2, 3 *n.*, 4, 5 *v.*, **e·qualled** or **e·qualed, e·qual·ling** or **e·qual·ing.**  —**e′qual·ly** *adv.*

**equal to,**  **a** the same as: *Ten dimes are equal to one dollar.*  **b** capable of; strong enough or brave enough for: *One horse is not equal to pulling a load of five tonnes.*

**e·qual·i·ty** (i kwol′ə tē)  being EQUAL; sameness in amount, size, number, value, degree, rank, etc.  *n., pl.* **e·qual·i·ties.**

**e·qual·i·za·tion** (ē′kwə lə zā′shən *or* ē′kwə lī zā′shən)  **1** an equalizing.  **2** being EQUALIZED.  *n.*

**e·qual·ize** (ē′kwə līz′)  **1** make the same.  **2** make even or uniform.  *v.*, **e·qual·ized, e·qual·iz·ing.**  —**e′qual·iz·er,** *n.*

**e·qual sign** (ē′kwəl sīn′)   the sign =, used in equations.

**e·qua·nim·i·ty** (ē′kwə nim′ə tē *or* ek′wə nim′ə tē)   evenness of mind or temper; calmness: *A wise person bears misfortune with equanimity.*   *n.*

**e·quate** (i kwāt′)   **1** state to be EQUAL; put in the form of an EQUATION.   **2** consider, treat, or represent as EQUAL.   **3** make EQUAL.   *v.*, **e·quat·ed, e·quat·ing.**

**e·qua·tion** (i kwā′zhən)   **1** a statement of equality between two quantities. *Examples:* (4 × 8) + 12 = 44. C = 2πr.   **2** an expression that uses chemical formulas and symbols to show the substances used and produced in a chemical change. *Example:* HCl + NaOH = NaCl + H₂O.   **3** an equating or being equated.   *n.*

**e·qua·tor** (i kwā′tər)   **1** an imaginary circle around the middle of the earth, halfway between the North Pole and the South Pole. See LATITUDE for picture.   **2** a similarly situated circle on any heavenly body.   **3** a great circle (**celestial equator**) of the **celestial sphere**, the plane of which is perpendicular to the axis of the earth. See ECLIPTIC for picture.   *n.*

**e·qua·to·ri·al** (ek′wə tô′rē əl *or* ē′kwə tô′rē əl)   **1** of, at, or near the EQUATOR (def. 1): *equatorial countries.*   **2** like conditions at or near the EQUATOR (def. 1): *This heat is almost equatorial.*   *adj.*

**eq·uer·ry** (ek′wə rē)   **1** formerly, an officer of a royal or noble household who had charge of the horses or who accompanied his master's carriage.   **2** an attendant on a royal or noble person.   *n., pl.* **eq·uer·ries.**

**e·ques·tri·an** (i kwes′trē ən)   **1** of horsemen or horsemanship; having to do with horseback riding: *Riders should have equestrian skill.*   **2** on horseback; mounted on horseback: *An equestrian statue shows a person riding a horse.*   **3** a rider or performer on horseback.   1, 2 *adj.*, 3 *n.*

**e·ques·tri·enne** (i kwes′trē en′)   a woman rider or performer on horseback.   *n.*

**e·qui·an·gu·lar** (ē′kwē ang′gyə lər)   having all angles equal: *A square is equiangular.*   *adj.*

**e·qui·dis·tant** (ē′kwə dis′tənt)   equally distant: *All points on the circumference of a circle are equidistant from the centre.*   *adj.*   —**e′qui·dis′tant·ly**, *adv.*

**e·qui·lat·er·al** (ē′kwə lat′ə rəl)   **1** having all sides equal.   **2** a figure having all sides equal. See TRIANGLE for picture.   1 *adj.*, 2 *n.*   —**e′qui·lat′er·al·ly**, *adv.*

**e·qui·li·brate** (ē′kwə lī′brāt)   balance.   *v.*, **e·qui·li·brat·ed, e·qui·li·brat·ing.**

**e·qui·li·bra·tion** (ē′kwə lī brā′shən)   a balancing evenly; a being balanced evenly.   *n.*

**e·qui·lib·ri·um** (ē′kwə lib′rē əm *or* ek′wə lib′rē əm)   **1** a state of balance; condition in which opposing forces exactly balance or equal each other: *The acrobat in the circus maintained her equilibrium on a tightrope. Scales are in equilibrium when the weights on each side are equal.*   **2** mental poise: *She is a sensible person and will not let little annoyances upset her equilibrium.*   *n.*

**e·quine** (ē′kwīn *or* ek′wīn)   **1** of horses; like a horse; like that of a horse.   **2** horse.   1 *adj.*, 2 *n.*

**e·qui·noc·tial** (ē′kwə nok′shəl *or* ek′wə nok′shəl)   **1** having to do with either EQUINOX: *Equinoctial points are two points on the celestial equator where the sun crosses that equator.*   **2** occurring at or near the EQUINOX: *equinoctial gales.*   **3** a storm occurring at or near the EQUINOX.   **4** at or near the earth's EQUATOR (def. 1): *Borneo is an equinoctial island.*   1, 2, 4 *adj.*, 3 *n.*

**equinoctial line**   the celestial equator. See EQUATOR (def. 3).

**e·qui·nox** (ē′kwə noks′ *or* ek′wə noks′)   either of the two times in the year when the centre of the sun crosses the celestial equator and day and night are of equal length all over the earth: *The vernal (spring) equinox occurs about March 21, the autumnal equinox about September 22.*   *n.*
☞ Etym. From L *aequinoctium*, formed from *aequus* 'equal' + *nox, noctis* 'night'. 14c.

**e·quip** (i kwip′)   furnish with all that is needed; fit out; provide: *The school equips each player with a complete hockey outfit.*   *v.*, **e·quipped, e·quip·ping.**

**eq·ui·page** (ek′wə pij)   **1** carriage.   **2** a carriage with its horses, driver, and servants.   **3** equipment; outfit.   *n.*

**e·quip·ment** (i kwip′mənt)   **1** the act of equipping.   **2** the state of being equipped.   **3** what a person or thing is equipped with; an outfit.   **4** knowledge or skill; ability.   *n.*

**e·qui·poise** (ē′kwə poiz′ *or* ek′wə poiz′)   **1** a state of balance.   **2** a balancing force; counterbalance.   *n.*

**eq·ui·ta·ble** (ek′wə tə bəl)   **1** fair; just: *Paying a person what he or she has earned is equitable.*   **2** having to do with or dependent upon EQUITY (def. 3); valid in equity, as distinguished from common law and statute law.   *adj.*   —**eq′ui·ta·ble·ness**, *n.*   —**eq′ui·ta·bly**, *adv.*

**eq·ui·ta·tion** (ek′wə tā′shən)   horseback riding.   *n.*

**eq·ui·ty** (ek′wə tē)   **1** fairness; justice.   **2** what is fair and just.   **3** a system of rules and principles based on fairness and justice: *Equity supplements common law and statute law by covering cases in which fairness and justice require a settlement not covered by law.*   **4** a claim or right according to equity.   **5** the amount that a property is worth beyond what is owed on it.   *n. pl.* **eq·ui·ties.**

**e·quiv·a·lence** (i kwiv′ə ləns)   being equivalent; equality in value, force, significance, etc.   *n.*

**e·quiv·a·lent** (i kwiv′ə lənt)   **1** equal in value, measure, force, effect, meaning, etc.: *Nodding one's head is equivalent to saying yes.*   **2** having the same extent: *A triangle and a square of equal area are equivalent.*   **3** something equivalent: *He accepted the equivalent of his wages in groceries.*   1, 2 *adj.*, 3 *n.*
—**e·quiv′a·lent·ly**, *adv.*

**e·quiv·o·cal** (i kwiv′ə kəl)   **1** having two or more meanings; intentionally vague or ambiguous: *His equivocal answer left us uncertain as to his real opinion.*   **2** undecided; uncertain: *The result of the experiment was equivocal and proved nothing.*   **3** questionable; rousing suspicion: *The stranger's equivocal behaviour made it unlikely that anyone would trust her.*   *adj.*
—**e·quiv′o·cal·ly**, *adv.*

**e·quiv·o·cate** (i kwiv′ə kāt′)   use expressions of double meaning in order to mislead: *When asked if he had finished his arithmetic, Gunther equivocated by saying, "I was working on that an hour ago."*   *v.*, **e·quiv·o·cat·ed, e·quiv·o·cat·ing.**   —**e·quiv′o·ca′tor**, *n.*

**e·quiv·o·ca·tion** (i kwiv′ə kā′shən)   **1** the use of EQUIVOCAL (def. 1) expressions in order to mislead.   **2** an EQUIVOCAL (def. 1) expression.   *n.*

**–er**[1]   a noun-forming suffix meaning:   **1** a person or thing that _____s: *An admirer is a person who admires;*

*a burner is something that burns.* **2** a native or inhabitant of _____: *A Newfoundlander is a person living in Newfoundland; a villager is a person living in a village.* **3** a person who makes or works with _____: *A hatter is a person who makes hats.* **4** a person or thing that is or has _____: *A six-footer is a person who is six feet tall.*

**—er²** a suffix meaning the person or thing connected with, as in *officer.*

**—er³** a suffix forming the comparative degree: **1** of adjectives as in *softer, smoother.* **2** of adverbs, as in *slower.*
☛ **Usage.** Normally, **-er** ('more') and **-est** ('most') are used with all adjectives and adverbs of one syllable and with some of two syllables: *sweet—sweeter, soon—sooner, narrow—narrowest.* **More** and **most** are used with most adjectives and adverbs of two syllables and with all of more than two syllables: *most famous, more quickly, most beautiful.*

**Er** erbium.

**E.R.** an abbreviation of L *Elizabeth Regina*, 'Elizabeth the Queen'; Queen Elizabeth.

**e·ra** (ē′rə) **1** a historical period distinguished by certain important or significant happenings; an age in history: *The decade from 1929 to 1939 is often called the Depression Era.* **2** a system of reckoning time: *the Common Era.* **3** a system of reckoning time from some important or significant happenings, given date, etc.: *The era of travel in outer space dates from October, 1957, when the first artificial satellite was launched.* **4** one of five very extensive periods of time in geological history. See Appendix for geological time chart. *n.*

**e·rad·i·ca·ble** (i rad′ə kə bəl) that can be ERADICATEd. *adj.*

**e·rad·i·cate** (i rad′ə kāt′) **1** get rid of entirely; destroy completely: *Yellow fever has been eradicated in some countries.* **2** pull out by the roots: *to eradicate weeds from a garden.* *v.* **e·rad·i·cat·ed, e·rad·i·cat·ing.** —**e·rad′i·ca′tor,** *n.*

**e·rad·i·ca·tion** (i rad′ə kā′shən) an eradicating; complete destruction. *n.*

**e·rase** (i rās′) **1** rub out; scrape out: *She erased the wrong answer and wrote in the right one.* **2** remove all trace of; blot out: *The blow on his head erased from his memory the details of the accident.* **3** remove marks or recorded information from: *Please erase the chalkboard. She accidentally erased the whole tape while recording.* *v.* **e·rased, e·ras·ing.** —**e·ras′a·ble,** *adj.*

**e·ras·er** (i rā′sər) a piece of rubber or any other substance for erasing marks made with pencil, ink, chalk, etc. *n.*

**e·ra·sure** (i rā′shər *or* i rā′zhər) **1** an erasing. **2** an erased word, letter, etc. **3** a place where a word, letter, etc. has been erased. *n.*

**er·bi·um** (ėr′bē əm) a rare metallic element of the yttrium group. Symbol: Er *n.*

**e·rect** (i rekt′) **1** straight up; upright: *A chimney stands erect.* **2** put straight up; set upright: *They erected the flagpole in ten minutes. The pole was erected on a firm base.* **3** build; put up: *That house was erected forty years ago.* **4** put together; set up: *When the missing parts arrived, we erected the machine.* **5** raised; bristling: *The cat faced the dog with fur erect.* 1, 5 *adj.,* 2–4 *v.* —**e·rect′ly,** *adv.* —**e·rect′ness,** *n.* —**e·rec′tor,** *n.*

**e·rec·tion** (i rek′shən) **1** an erecting: *The erection of the tent took only a few minutes.* **2** being erected. **3** anything erected; a building or other structure. *n.*

**erg** (ėrg) a former unit for measuring work or energy: *An erg is the amount of work done by one* DYNE *acting through a distance of one centimetre. n.*

**er·got** (ėr′gət *or* ėr′got) **1** a disease of rye and other cereals in which the grains are replaced by blackish fungous growths. **2** a medicine made from these growths, used to stop bleeding and to contract muscles. *n.*

**er·mine** (ėr′mən) **1** any of several kinds of weasel of northern climates, which are brown in summer but white with a black-tipped tail in winter. **2** a soft, white fur of the winter phase, used for women's coats, trimming, etc.: *The official robes of English judges are trimmed with ermine as a symbol of purity and fairness.* **3** the position, rank, or duties of a judge. *n., pl.* **er·mines** or (*esp. collectively*) **er·mine.**

**e·rode** (i rōd′) **1** eat into; eat or wear away gradually: *Running water erodes soil and rocks.* **2** form by a gradual eating or wearing away: *The stream eroded a channel in the solid rock.* *v.* **e·rod·ed, e·rod·ing.**

**e·ro·sion** (i rō′zhən) **1** a gradual eating or wearing away by glaciers, running water, waves, or wind: *Trees help prevent the erosion of soil by running water.* **2** the condition of being eaten or worn away. *n.*

**e·ro·sive** (i rō′siv) eroding; causing EROSION: *Running water has an erosive action.* *adj.*

**e·rot·ic** (i rot′ik) of or arousing sexual desire. *adj.* —**e·rot′i·cal·ly,** *adv.*

**err** (ėr *or* er) **1** go wrong; make mistakes: *Everyone errs at some time or other.* **2** be wrong; be mistaken or incorrect. **3** do wrong: *"To err is human; to forgive divine."* *v.*
☛ Hom. AIR, HEIR (for the second pronunciation of **err**).

**er·rand** (er′ənd) **1** a trip to do something: *The little boy goes to the stores and runs other errands for his parents.* **2** what one is sent to do: *She did ten errands in one trip.* **3** the purpose or object of a trip. *n.*

**er·rant** (er′ənt) **1** travelling in search of adventure; wandering; roving. **2** wrong; mistaken; incorrect. *adj.*

**er·ra·ta** (ə rat′ə *or* ə rä′tə) pl. of ERRATUM. *n.*

**er·rat·ic** (ə rat′ik) **1** not steady; uncertain; irregular: *An erratic mind jumps from one idea to another.* **2** odd; unusual: *erratic behaviour.* *adj.* —**er·rat′i·cal·ly,** *adv.*

**er·ra·tum** (ə rat′əm *or* ə rä′təm) an error or mistake in writing or printing. *n., pl.* **er·ra·ta** (-tə).

**er·ro·ne·ous** (ə rō′nē əs) wrong; mistaken; incorrect: *Many people once held the erroneous belief that the earth was flat.* *adj.* —**er·ro′ne·ous·ly,** *adv.*

**er·ror** (er′ər) **1** something wrong; what is incorrect; a mistake: *A false belief is an error. I failed my test because of errors in spelling.* **2** wrongdoing. **3** in baseball, a faulty play in fielding a ball that permits the batter to remain at bat or allows a runner to advance. *n.*

**in error, a** wrong or mistaken: *The teacher was in error.* **b** by mistake: *He got on the westbound bus in error.*

**er·u·dite** (er′yə dīt′ *or* er′ə dīt′) scholarly; learned. *adj.* —**er′u·dite′ly,** *adv.*

**er·u·di·tion** (er′yə dish′ən *or* er′ə dish′ən) acquired knowledge; scholarship; learning. *n.*

**e·rupt** (i rupt′) **1** burst forth: *Hot water erupted from the geyser.* **2** throw forth: *The volcano erupted lava and ashes.* **3** break out in a rash: *Her skin erupted when she had measles.* **4** break through the gums: *When the baby was seven months old, its teeth started to erupt.* *v.*

**e·rup·tion** (i rup′shən) **1** a bursting forth. **2** a throwing forth of lava, etc. from a volcano or of hot water from a geyser. **3** a breaking out in a rash: *When a person has measles, his skin is in a state of eruption.* **4** red spots on the skin; a rash: *Scarlet fever causes an eruption on the body.* **5** a breaking through the gums: *The eruption of teeth made the baby fretful.* **6** an outbreak; outburst: *eruptions of racial or national hatred.* *n.*

**e·rup·tive** (i rup′tiv) **1** bursting forth; tending to burst forth. **2** causing the skin to break out: *Measles is an eruptive disease.* **3** of or formed by volcanic eruptions. *adj.*

**–ery** a noun-forming suffix meaning: **1** a place for _____ing, as in *cannery, hatchery.* **2** a place for _____s, as in *rookery.* **3** the occupation or business of a _____, as in *cookery.* **4** the state or condition of a _____, as in *slavery.* **5** the qualities, actions, etc. of a _____, as in *knavery.* **6** _____s as a group, as in *machinery.*

**er·y·sip·e·las** (er′ə sip′ə ləs) an acute infectious disease caused by streptococcus bacteria and characterized by a fever and a deep red inflammation of the skin. *n.*

**Es** einsteinium.

**–es¹** a suffix used to form plurals; the form -es is used after the sounds (s, z, sh, zh, ch and j) at the end of nouns such as *mass, buzz, dish, mirage, church, bridge*; also, -es is used to form the plurals of nouns ending in -y which changes to -i before adding -es, as in *family,* plural *families;* nouns ending in -f which changes to -v before adding -es, as in *scarf,* plural *scarves;* some nouns ending in a vowel, such as *tomato,* plural *tomatoes.*

**–es²** a suffix used to form the third person singular, present tense, of verbs ending in the letters *s, z, sh,* and *ch: kisses, buzzes, rushes, matches.*

**es·ca·drille** (es′kə dril′) a small fleet of airplanes or warships, together with the equipment and men needed to keep them in use. *n.*

**es·ca·late** (es′kə lāt′) **1** increase or decrease in accordance with some standard: *As prices go up, costs escalate.* **2** increase or expand by stages: *Small battles can easily escalate into major wars.* *v.,* **es·ca·lat·ed, es·ca·lat·ing.** —**es′ca·la′tion,** *n.*

**es·ca·la·tor** (es′kə lā′tər) a continuous moving stairway: *Many department stores have escalators to carry the customers from one floor to another.* *n.*

**es·cal·lop** (es kol′əp) **1** bake in a cream sauce or with bread crumbs. **2** food cooked in this way: *escallop of veal.* **3** SCALLOP. **1** *v.,* **2, 3** *n.*

**es·ca·pade** (es′kə pād′) a breaking loose from rules or restraint; wild adventure or prank: *Shooting the rapids on a raft was a crazy escapade.* *n.*

**es·cape** (es kāp′) **1** get free; get out and away: *The convict escaped from the prison.* **2** get free from: *She thinks she will never escape hard work.* **3** keep free or safe from; avoid: *We all escaped the measles. He escaped being killed in the blast because he had not gone to work.* **4** avoid capture, trouble, etc.: *The thief has escaped.* **5** an escaping. **6** a way of escaping: *There was no escape from the trap.* **7** providing a way of escape or avoidance. **8** come out of without being intended: *A cry escaped her lips.* **9** fail to be noticed or remembered by: *The pin escaped my eye. I knew his face, but his name escaped me.* **10** a relief from boredom, trouble, etc.: *to find escape in mystery stories.* **11** an outflow or leakage of gas, water, etc. **1–4, 8, 9** *v.,* **es·caped, es·cap·ing;** **5, 6, 10, 11** *n.,* **7** *adj.*

**escape clause** a clause that frees a signer of a contract from certain responsibilities under specified circumstances.

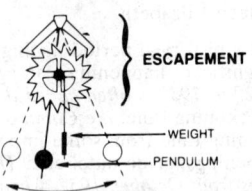

A simplified diagram of an escapement in a pendulum clock. The falling weight turns the barrel on which its line is coiled, and this in turn moves the notched wheel. The hooked arms above the wheel, connected to the pendulum, allow only one tooth of the wheel to escape for each swing of the pendulum.

**es·cape·ment** (es kāp′mənt) **1** a device in a timepiece by which the motion of the wheels and the motion of the pendulum or balance wheel are accommodated to each other, so that one tooth of the wheel escapes at each swing of the pendulum. **2** a mechanism that controls the movement of a typewriter carriage. *n.*

**escape velocity** the velocity that must be given to a body such as a man-made satellite to escape the gravitational pull of the earth, sun, or moon; about eleven kilometres per second.

**es·cap·ism** (es kā′piz əm) a habitual avoidance of unpleasant realities by recourse to imagination or to entertainment. *n.*

**es·ca·role** (es′kə rōl′) a kind of ENDIVE that has broad leaves, used for salads. *n.*

**es·carp·ment** (es kärp′mənt) **1** a steep slope; cliff. **2** ground made into a steep slope as part of a fortification. *n.*

**es·chew** (es chü′) avoid; shun; keep away from: *A wise person eschews bad company.* *v.*

**es·cort** (es′kôrt *for noun,* es kôrt′ *for verb*) **1** a person or a group of persons going with another to give protection, show honour, etc.: *an escort of ten Mounties.* **2** a man or boy who accompanies a woman or girl on a walk, to a dance, etc.: *Her escort to the party was a tall young man.* **3** one or more ships, aircraft, etc. serving as a guard: *During World War II Canada's destroyers served as escorts to many convoys.* **4** the act of going with another as an escort. **5** accompany as an escort: *Warships escorted the royal yacht. Four policemen escorted the dangerous criminal to prison. Vladimir escorted Kim to the movies.* **1–4** *n.,* **5** *v.*

**es·crow** (es′krō *or* es krō′)   a deed, bond, or other written agreement put in the charge of a third person until certain conditions are fulfilled by two other parties.   *n.*
**in escrow**,   held by a third party in accordance with an agreement.

**es·cu·lent** (es′kyə lənt)   suitable for food; edible.   *adj.*

**es·cutch·eon** (es kuch′ən)   a shield or shield-shaped surface on which a coat of arms is put.   *n.*

**–ese**   a suffix often added to a noun to form an adjective or another noun:   **1** of or having to do with: *She admires Japanese art.*   **2** a native or inhabitant of a country: *The Portuguese colonized Brazil.*   **3** the language of: *Do you speak Chinese?*   **4** the typical style or vocabulary of: *Journalese means newspaper style.*

**ESE** or **E.S.E.**   east-southeast.

**es·ker** (es′kər)   a winding ridge of sand, gravel, etc., believed to have been deposited by meltwater streams flowing inside the retreating glaciers of the Ice Age.   *n.* Also, **eskar**.

**Es·ki·mo** (es′kə mō′)   **1** See INUIT.   **2** See INUKTITUT. (Origin uncertain)   *n., pl.* **-mos** or **mo**.
☛ *Etym.*   From an Algonquian word meaning 'eaters of raw flesh'. 18c. It probably came through F *Esquimaux* with the spelling influenced by Danish *Eskimo*. The word is not used by the people it names, who have always called themselves *Inuit*. See note at INUIT.

An Eskimo dog - about 60 cm high at the shoulder

**Eskimo dog**   *Cdn.*   a breed of large, very strong dog native to the North, long used by the Inuit for pulling sleds and for hunting: *An Eskimo dog can go for several days without food and still pull a load of 50 kg.*

**Eskimo pie**   a chocolate-coated ice-cream bar.

**e·soph·a·gus** (ē sof′ə gəs *or* i sof′ə gəs)   the passage for food from the mouth to the stomach; gullet.   See ALIMENTARY CANAL and WINDPIPE for pictures.   *n., pl.* **e·soph·a·gi** (-jī *or* -gē).   Also, **oesophagus**.

**es·o·ter·ic** (es′ə ter′ik)   **1** understood only by the select few; intended for an inner circle of disciples, scholars, etc.   **2** private; secret; confidential.   *adj.* —**es′o·ter′i·cal·ly**, *adv.*

**E.S.P.** or **ESP**   extrasensory perception.

**esp.** or **espec.**   especially.

**es·pe·cial** (es pesh′əl)   special; particular; exceptional: *my especial friend, of no especial value.*   *adj.*

**es·pe·cial·ly** (es pesh′ə lē)   particularly; chiefly; unusually: *This book is difficult, especially for young students.*   *adv.*

**Es·pe·ran·to** (es′pə ran′tō *or* es′pə rän′tō)   an artificial language for international use, whose vocabulary

hat, āge, fär; let, ēqual, tėrm; it, īce
hot, ōpen, ôrder; oil, out; cup, pùt, rüle
әbove, takәn, pencәl, lemәn, circәs
ch, child; ng, long; sh, ship
th, thin; ŦH, then; zh, measure

and grammar are based on forms common to the principal European languages.   *n.*

**es·pi·al** (es pī′əl)   **1** spying.   **2** watching. **3** discovery.   *n.*

**es·pi·o·nage** (es′pē ə nij *or* es′pē ə näzh′)   the use of spies; especially, the use of spies by one country to find out the military or political secrets of another; spying.   *n.*

**es·pla·nade** (es′plə näd′ *or* es′plə näd′)   **1** any open, level space used for public walks or drives.   **2** an open space separating a fortress from the houses of a town.   *n.*

**es·pous·al** (es pou′zəl)   **1** an espousing; adoption of a cause, etc.   **2** the ceremony of becoming engaged or married.   *n.*

**es·pouse** (es pouz′)   **1** marry.   **2** take up or make one's own: *Late in life he espoused a new religion.*   *v.,* **es·poused, es·pous·ing**.

**es·prit** (es prē′)   lively wit; spirit.   *n.*

**es·prit de corps** (es prē də kôr′) *French.*   a sense of union and of common interests and responsibilities in some group: *The team had a strong esprit de corps.*

**es·py** (es pī′)   see or catch sight of something, especially something far away, small, or partly hidden. *v.,* **es·pied, es·py·ing**.

**Es·qui·mau** (es′kə mō′)   ESKIMO.   *n., pl.* **Es·qui·maux** (-mō′ *or* -mōz′).

**es·quire** (es kwīr′ *or* es′kwīr)   **1** in the Middle Ages, a young man of noble family who attended a knight until he himself was made a knight.   **2** an Englishman ranking next below a knight.   *n.*

**ess** (es)   **1** the 19th letter of the alphabet (S, s). **2** anything in the shape of this letter: *an ess-bend in the road.*   *n.*

**–ess**   a suffix meaning female, as in *heiress, hostess, lioness.*

**es·say** (es′ā *for noun, defs. 1 and 2,*   es′ā *or* e sā′ *for noun, def. 4;* e sā′ *for verb*)   **1** a literary composition on a certain subject: *An essay is usually shorter and less methodical than a treatise.*   **2** a written composition assigned as an exercise in school.   **3** try; attempt: *She essayed a very difficult jump.*   **4** a try or attempt.   *1, 2, 4 n., 3 v.*

**es·say·ist** (es′ā ist)   a writer of essays.   *n.*

**es·sence** (es′əns)   **1** that which makes a thing what it is; the necessary part or parts; important feature or features: *Kindness is the essence of politeness.*   **2** a concentrated substance that has the characteristic flavour, fragrance, or effect of the plant, fruit, etc. from which it is obtained: *Atropine is the essence of the belladonna plant.*   **3** a solution of such a substance in alcohol: *Essence of peppermint is oil of peppermint dissolved in alcohol.*   **4** a perfume.   *n.*

**es·sen·tial** (ə sen′shəl)   **1** needed to make a thing what it is; basic; necessary; very important: *Good food and*

## essential oil

*enough rest are essential to good health.* **2** an absolutely necessary element or quality; a basic part; fundamental feature: *Learn the essentials first; then learn the details.* **3** of, like, or constituting the essence of a substance. 1, 3 *adj.*, 2 *n.* —**es·sen′tial·ly,** *adv.*

**essential oil** a volatile oil that gives a plant, fruit, etc. its characteristic flavour, fragrance, or effect: *Essential oils are used to make perfume and flavouring.*

**-est** a suffix forming the superlative degree: **1** of adjectives, as in *warmest.* **2** of adverbs, as in *slowest.*
☞ *Usage.* See note at -ER³.

**est.** **1** established. **2** estate. **3** estuary.

**es·tab·lish** (es tab′lish) **1** set up permanently: *to establish a government or a business. The English established colonies in America.* **2** settle in a position; set up in a business: *A new doctor has established herself on our street.* **3** bring about permanently; cause to be accepted: *to establish a custom.* **4** show beyond dispute; prove: *to establish a fact.* **5** make a church a national institution recognized and supported by the government. *v.*

**established church** a church that is a national institution recognized and supported by the government.

**es·tab·lish·ment** (es tab′lish mənt) **1** setting up; establishing. **2** being established. **3** something established: *A household, business, church, or army may be called an establishment.* **4** the recognition of a church by the state as the official church. **5** the number of men in a regiment, a ship's company, etc., as set by regulations: *The regiment needed three officers to complete its establishment.* **6 the Establishment, a** the Church of England or the Presbyterian Church of Scotland. **b** the people having the greatest social and political influence in a country and generally being opposed to change and the influence of other groups. *n.*

**es·tate** (es tāt′) **1** a large piece of land belonging to a person; landed property: *He has a beautiful country estate with a house and a swimming pool.* **2** that which a person owns; property; possessions: *Land and buildings are real estate. When a person dies, his or her estate is divided up among those to whom he or she has left it.* **3** a condition or stage in life: *He will receive his inheritance when he reaches man's estate.* **4** a class or group of people in a nation: *The press is often called the fourth estate.* *n.*
**the three estates,** the noblemen, clergymen, and people without special rank or title.

**es·teem** (es tēm′) **1** have a very favourable opinion of; regard highly: *We esteem people of good character.* **2** a very favourable opinion; high regard: *Courage is held in esteem.* **3** think; consider: *People have often esteemed happiness the greatest good.* 1, 3 *v.*, 2 *n.*

**es·ter** (es′tər) a compound resulting from the reaction of an acid with an alcohol, so that the hydrogen ion of the acid is replaced by the hydrocarbon radical of the alcohol: *Animal and vegetable fats and natural waxes are esters.* *n.*

**es·thete** (es′thēt *or* ēs′thēt) See AESTHETE. *n.*

**es·thet·ic** (es thet′ik *or* ēs thet′ik) See AESTHETIC. *adj.*

**es·thet·i·cal·ly** (es thet′i klē *or* ēs thet′i klē) See AESTHETICALLY. *adv.*

**es·thet·ics** (es thet′iks *or* ēs thet′iks) See AESTHETICS. *n.*

**es·ti·ma·ble** (es′tə mə bəl) **1** worthy of ESTEEM (def. 2); deserving high regard. **2** capable of being ESTIMATED (def. 2) or calculated. *adj.*
—**es′ti·ma·bly,** *adv.*

**es·ti·mate** (es′tə mit *or* es′tə māt′ *for noun*, es′tə māt′ *for verb*) **1** a judgment or opinion about how much, how many, how good, etc.: *My estimate of the length of the room was 7 metres; it actually measured 6 metres 91 centimetres.* **2** form a judgment or opinion about how much, how many, how good, etc.: *Mother estimated that it would take four hours to weed the garden.* **3** a statement of what certain work will cost, made by one willing to do the work: *The contractor's estimate for painting the house was $4 000.* **4** fix the worth, size, amount, etc., especially in a rough way; calculate approximately. 1, 3 *n.*, 2, 4 *v.*,
**es·ti·mat·ed, es·ti·mat·ing.** —**es′ti·ma′tor,** *n.*

**es·ti·ma·tion** (es′tə mā′shən) **1** judgment; opinion: *In my estimation, your plan will not work.* **2** esteem; respect; regard: *hold in high estimation.* **3** the act or process of estimating. *n.*

**es·ti·vate** (es′tə vāt′) of animals, spend the summer in a dormant or torpid condition: *Some snakes estivate.* Compare with HIBERNATE. *v.*, **es·ti·vat·ed, es·ti·vat·ing.** Also, **aestivate.**

**Es·to·ni·an** (es tō′nē ən) **1** of or having to do with Estonia, a republic in the western Soviet Union, its people, or their language. **2** a native or inhabitant of Estonia. **3** a person of Estonian descent. **4** the Finno-Ugric language of Estonia. 1 *adj.*, 2–4 *n.*

**es·trange·ment** (es tranj′mənt) **1** an estranging. **2** being estranged: *A misunderstanding between the two friends had caused their estrangement.* *n.*

**es·tu·ar·y** (es′chü er′ē) **1** a broad mouth of a river flowing into the sea, where its current meets the tide and is influenced by it. **2** an inlet of the sea. *n., pl.*
**es·tu·ar·ies.**

**ETA** estimated time of arrival.

**et al.** and others (an abbreviation of Latin *et alii*).

**etc.** et cetera.
☞ *Usage.* Etc. is usually read 'and so forth'. For example, the definition of **equality** reads 'exact likeness in size, number, value, rank, etc.' Etc. in such definitions shows that the meaning applies to many items similar to the ones mentioned.

**et cet·er·a** (et set′ə rə) *Latin.* and so forth; and others; and the rest; and so on; and the like.
☞ *Usage.* Et cetera is a Latin phrase meaning 'and so forth'. Since the *et* itself means 'and', there is no need to put *and* before it. It is wrong to write *and et cetera* or *and etc.*

**et·cet·er·as** (et set′ə rəz) extra things; usual additions. *n. pl.*

**etch** (ech) **1** engrave by using acid to eat a drawing or design into a metal plate, glass, etc. **2** engrave a drawing or design on by means of acid: *The artist etched only a few copper plates.* **3** make drawings or designs by this method. **4** make an impression on the mind: *The event remains etched in my memory.* *v.* —**etch′er,** *n.*

**etch·ing** (ech′ing) **1** a picture or design printed from an ETCHed plate. **2** an ETCHed plate; etched drawing or design. **3** the art of an ETCHer; process of engraving a drawing or design on a metal plate, glass, etc. by means of acid. **4** *ppr.* of ETCH. 1–3 *n.*, 4 *v.*

**e·ter·nal** (i tėr′nəl) **1** without beginning or ending; lasting throughout all time. **2** always and forever the same. **3** seeming to go on forever; occurring very frequently. *adj.*

**e·ter·nal·ly** (i tėr′nə lē) **1** without beginning or ending; throughout all time. **2** always and forever. **3** constantly; incessantly. *adv.*

**e·ter·ni·ty** (i tėr′nə tē) **1** time without beginning or ending; all time. **2** an eternal quality; endlessness. **3** the endless period after death. **4** a seemingly endless period of time. *n., pl.* **e·ter·ni·ties.**

**e·ter·nize** (i tėr′nīz) make ETERNAL; perpetuate; immortalize. *v.,* **e·ter·nized, e·ter·niz·ing.**

**eth·ane** (eth′ān) a colourless, odourless, flammable gas present in natural gas and coal gas. *n.*

**e·ther** (ē′thər) **1** a colourless, strong-smelling liquid that burns and evaporates readily: *Ether fumes cause unconsciousness when deeply inhaled. Ether is used as a solvent for fats and resins.* **2** the upper regions of space beyond the earth's atmosphere; clear sky; aether. **3** the invisible, elastic substance formerly supposed to be distributed evenly through all space and to conduct light waves, electric waves, etc.; aether. *n.*

**e·the·re·al** (i thē′rē əl) **1** light; airy; delicate: *Her ethereal beauty made her seem more like a spirit than a human being.* **2** not of the earth; heavenly. **3** of or having to do with the aether (or ETHER, defs. 2 and 3). *adj.* Also, **aethereal.** —**e·the′re·al·ly,** *adv.*

**e·the·re·al·ize** (i thē′rē ə līz′) make ETHEREAL. *v.,* **e·the·re·al·ized, e·the·re·al·iz·ing.**

**eth·i·cal** (eth′ə kəl) **1** having to do with standards of right and wrong; of ETHICS or morality. **2** in accordance with formal or professional rules of right and wrong: *It is not considered ethical for a doctor to repeat a patient's confidences.* *adj.* —**eth′i·cal·ly,** *adv.*

**eth·ics** (eth′iks) **1** the study of standards of right and wrong; that part of science and philosophy dealing with moral conduct, duty, and judgment (*used with a singular verb*). **2** a book about ethics (*used with a singular verb*). **3** formal or professional rules of right and wrong; system of conduct or behaviour (*used with a plural verb*): *Medical ethics do not permit doctors and surgeons to advertise.* 1, 2 *n. sing.,* 3 *n. pl.*

**E·thi·o·pi·an** (ē′thē ō′pē ən) **1** of or having to do with Ethiopia or its people. **2** a native or inhabitant of Ethiopia. 1 *adj.,* 2 *n.*

**eth·nic** (eth′nik) **1** of or having to do with various groups of people and their characteristics, customs, and languages. **2** *Cdn. Informal.* an immigrant who is not a native speaker of English or French; a person of foreign birth or descent: *There are ethnics in Toronto from many parts of Europe.* **3** *Cdn.* of or having to do with such persons: *ethnic dances, the ethnic vote.* 1, 3 *adj.,* 2 *n.*

☛ **Usage.** The use of **ethnic** in definitions 2 and 3 has become established in Canada and is spreading to the United States, though many people consider it unacceptable. While the word is useful in that it recognizes that different nationalities have individual qualities and customs, it becomes insulting if it is used to refer scornfully to people not of English or French descent.

**eth·nog·ra·phy** (eth nog′rə fē) the science that deals with the description and classification of the various groups of people. *n.*

**eth·no·log·ic** (eth′nə loj′ik) ETHNOLOGICAL. *adj.*

**eth·no·log·i·cal** (eth′nə loj′ə kəl) having to do with ETHNOLOGY. *adj.* —**eth′no·log′i·cal·ly,** *adv.*

## eternally 413 Eucharist

hat, āge, fär; let, ēqual, tėrm; it, īce
hot, ōpen, ôrder; oil, out; cup, pùt, rüle
əbove, takən, pencəl, lemən, circəs
ch, child; ng, long; sh, ship
th, thin; ᴛʜ, then; zh, measure

**eth·nol·o·gist** (eth nol′ə jist) a person trained in ETHNOLOGY. *n.*

**eth·nol·o·gy** (eth nol′ə jē) the science that deals with the various groups of people, their origin, distribution, characteristics, language, customs, institutions, and culture. *n.*

**ethyl alcohol** ordinary alcohol, made by the fermentation of grain, sugar, etc.

**eth·yl·ene** (eth′ə lēn′) a colourless, flammable gas with an unpleasant odour, used as an anesthetic, in making organic compounds, and for colouring and ripening citrus fruits. *n.*

**e·ti·ol·o·gy** (ē′tē ol′ə jē) **1** an assigning of a cause. **2** the science that deals with origins or causes. **3** the theory of the causes of disease. *n.*

**et·i·quette** (et′ə ket′) **1** the conventional rules for conduct or behaviour in polite society: *Etiquette requires a man to rise when a woman enters the room.* **2** the formal rules or conventions governing conduct in a profession, official ceremony, etc.: *medical etiquette.* *n.*

**E·trus·can** (i trus′kən) **1** of or having to do with Etruria, an ancient country in western Italy, its people, their language, art, or customs. **2** a native or inhabitant of Etruria. **3** the language of Etruria. 1 *adj.,* 2, 3 *n.*

**et seq.** and the following (an abbreviation of Latin *et sequens*).

**–ette** a suffix often added to a noun to form a new noun: **1** little, as in *kitchenette, statuette.* **2** female, as in *suffragette.* **3** a substitute for; imitation, as in *leatherette.*

**étude** (ā tyüd′ *or* ā tüd′) **1** a study. **2** a piece of music intended to develop or display skill in technique. *n.*

**et·y·mo·log·i·cal** (et′ə mə loj′ə kəl) having to do with the origin and history of words. *adj.* —**et′y·mo·log′i·cal·ly,** *adv.*

**et·y·mol·o·gist** (et′ə mol′ə jist) a person trained in ETYMOLOGY. *n.*

**et·y·mol·o·gy** (et′ə mol′ə jē) **1** an explanation of the origin of a word and a description of the changes it has gone through in its history. **2** a study dealing with linguistic changes, especially with individual word origins. *n., pl.* **et·y·mol·o·gies.**

**Eu** europium.

**eu·ca·lyp·tus** (yü′kə lip′təs) a very tall tree that grows in Australia and elsewhere, valued for its timber and for the oil from its leaves, used as medicine. *n., pl.* **eu·ca·lyp·tus·es** or **eu·ca·lyp·ti** (-tī *or* -tē).

**eu·ca·ry·ote** (yü kar′ē ət *or* yü ker′ē ət) an organism with a membrane-bound nucleus, and all higher organisms, having two kinds of cell, diploid and somatic: *A eucaryote has a nuclear membrane, but a procaryote has not.* *n.* Also, **eukaryote.**

**Eu·cha·rist** (yü′kə rist) **1** the sacrament of the Lord's

Supper; HOLY COMMUNION. 2 the consecrated bread and wine used in this sacrament. *n.*

**Eu·cha·ris·tic** (yü′kə ris′tik) having to do with the EUCHARIST. *adj.*

**eu·chre** (yü′kər) 1 a simple card game for two, three, or four players, using the 32 (or 28, or 24) highest cards in the pack. 2 defeat the side that declared the trump at euchre. 3 a social gathering during which people play euchre. 1, 3 *n.*, 2 *v.*, **eu·chred, eu·chring.**

**eu·gen·ic** (yü jen′ik) 1 having to do with improvement of the race; improving the offspring produced; improving the race. 2 coming of good stock. *adj.*

**eu·gen·i·cal·ly** (yü jen′i klē) in a EUGENIC manner; with respect to racial improvement. *adv.*

**eu·gen·ics** (yü jen′iks) 1 the science of improving the human race by a careful selection of parents in order to develop healthier and more intelligent children. 2 the science of improving offspring. *n. sing.* or *pl.*

**eu·ka·ry·ote** (yü kar′ē ət *or* yü ker′ē ət) See EUCARYOTE. *n.*

**eu·la·chon** (yü′lə kən) OOLICHAN. *n.*

**eu·lo·gist** (yü′lə jist) a person who EULOGIZES. *n.*

**eu·lo·gis·tic** (yü′lə jis′tik) praising highly. *adj.* —**eu′lo·gis′ti·cal·ly,** *adv.*

**eu·lo·gis·ti·cal** (yü′lə jis′tə kəl) EULOGISTIC. *adj.*

**eu·lo·gize** (yü′lə jīz′) praise very highly. *v.*, **eu·lo·gized, eu·lo·giz·ing.** —**eu′lo·giz′er,** *n.*

**eu·lo·gy** (yü′lə jē) 1 a speech or writing in praise of a person, action, etc.: *She pronounced a eulogy upon the hero.* 2 high praise. *n., pl.* **eu·lo·gies.**

**eu·nuch** (yü′nək) 1 a castrated man. 2 a castrated man in charge of a harem or the household of an Oriental ruler. *n.*

**eu·pep·si·a** (yü pep′sē ə) good digestion. Compare with DYSPEPSIA. *n.*

**eu·pep·tic** (yü pep′tik) 1 having good digestion. 2 aiding digestion. *adj.* Compare with DYSPEPTIC.

**eu·phe·mism** (yü′fə miz′əm) 1 the use of a mild or indirect expression instead of one that is harsh or unpleasantly direct. 2 a mild or indirect expression used in this way: *Pass away is a common euphemism for die.* *n.*

**eu·phe·mist** (yü′fə mist) a person who uses EUPHEMISMS. *n.*

**eu·phe·mis·tic** (yü′fə mis′tik) of or showing EUPHEMISM; containing a euphemism. *adj.*

**eu·phe·mis·ti·cal·ly** (yü′fə mis′ti klē) by way of EUPHEMISM; using euphemism. *adv.*

**eu·phon·ic** (yü fon′ik) 1 having to do with EUPHONY. 2 EUPHONIOUS. *adj.*

**eu·pho·ni·ous** (yü fō′nē əs) sounding well; pleasing to the ear; harmonious. *adj.* —**eu·pho′ni·ous·ly,** *adv.* —**eu·pho′ni·ous·ness,** *n.*

**eu·pho·ni·um** (yü fō′nē əm) a brass musical instrument, like a tuba, having a loud, deep tone. *n.*

**eu·pho·ny** (yü′fə nē) 1 agreeableness of sound; a pleasing effect to the ear; harmony of speech sounds as uttered or combined in utterance. 2 the tendency to change speech sounds so as to favour ease of utterance. *n., pl.* **eu·pho·nies.**

**eu·phor·bi·a** (yü fôr′bē ə) any of a variety of plants having acrid, milky juice and small, inconspicuous flowers; spurge: *Some euphorbia resemble cactuses.* *n.*

**eu·pho·ri·a** (yü fô′rē ə) a feeling of well-being. *n.*

**eu·phu·ism** (yü′fyü iz′əm) any affected, elegant style of writing; flowery, artificial language. *n.*

**eu·phu·ist** (yü′fyü ist) one who uses EUPHUISM. *n.*

**eu·phu·is·tic** (yü′fyü is′tik) using or containing EUPHUISM; like euphuism. *adj.* —**eu′phu·is′ti·cal·ly,** *adv.*

**Eur.** 1 Europe. 2 European.

**Eur·a·sian** (yü rā′zhən) 1 of or having to do with Europe and Asia or the people. 2 a person of mixed European and Asian parentage. 3 of mixed European and Asian parentage. 1, 3 *adj.*, 2 *n.*

**eu·re·ka** (yü rē′kə) *Greek.* I have found it! an exclamation of triumph about some discovery. *interj.*

**eu·rhyth·mics** (yü riŦH′miks *or* yü rith′miks) a system for the development of rhythm and grace by the performing of bodily movements in response to music. *n.* Also, **eurythmics.**

**Eu·ro·pe·an** (yü′rə pē′ən) 1 of or having to do with Europe or its inhabitants. 2 a native or inhabitant of Europe. 3 a person whose recent ancestors came from Europe. 1, *adj.*, 2, 3, *n.*

**European Common Market** EUROPEAN ECONOMIC COMMUNITY.

**European Community** the expanded European Economic Community, now consisting of fifteen countries: France, Germany, Italy, the Netherlands, Belgium, Luxembourg, Denmark, Irish Republic, The United Kingdom, Sweden, Finland, Austria, Greece, Spain, and Portugal.

**European Economic Community** a European common market to eliminate tariffs and work toward complete economic union, established in 1958 and including France, West Germany, Italy, the Netherlands, Belgium, and Luxembourg; European Common Market.

**Eu·ro·pe·an·ize** (yür′ə pē′ə nīz′) 1 make European in appearance, habit, way of life, etc. 2 integrate (a country) into the EEC. *v.*, **Eu·ro·pe·an·ized, Eu·ro·pe·an·iz·ing.**

**eu·ro·pi·um** (yü rō′pē əm) a rare metallic element of the same group as cerium. *Symbol:* Eu *n.*

**eu·ryth·mics** (yü riŦH′miks *or* yü rith′miks) See EURHYTHMICS. *n.*

**Eu·sta·chi·an tube** (yü stā′kē ən *or* yü stā′shən) a slender canal between the pharynx and the middle ear, which equalizes the air pressure on the two sides of the eardrum. See EAR[1] for picture.

**eu·tha·na·sia** (yü′thə nā′zhə) 1 any easy, painless death. 2 a painless killing, especially to end a painful and incurable disease. *n.*

**eu·then·ics** (yü then′iks) the science or art of improving the environment or living conditions. *n.*

**eV** electronvolt(s).

**e·vac·u·ate** (i vak′yü āt′) 1 leave empty; withdraw

from: *After surrendering, the soldiers evacuated the fort.* **2** withdraw; remove: *Efforts were made to evacuate all foreign residents from the war zone.* **3** make empty: *to evacuate the bowels.* *v.*, **e·vac·u·at·ed, e·vac·u·at·ing.** —**e·vac′u·a′tor,** *n.*

**e·vac·u·a·tion** (i vak′yü ā′shən) **1** leaving empty; withdrawal from occupation or possession; the act or process of evacuating. **2** removal. **3** making empty. **4** a discharge. *n.*

**e·vac·u·ee** (i vak′yü ē′) one who is evacuated from a dangerous place. *n.*

**e·vade** (i vād′) **1** get away from by trickery; avoid by cleverness: *The thief evaded his pursuers and escaped. The witness tried to evade an embarrassing question.* **2** avoid the truth by indefinite or misleading statements: *When Mother asked who broke the window, Ruth evaded the question by changing the subject.* *v.*, **e·vad·ed, e·vad·ing.**

**e·vad·er** (i vā′dər) one who EVADES. *n.*

**e·val·u·ate** (i val′yü āt′) **1** judge the worth, quality, or importance of: *Our essays are being evaluated by the new teacher.* **2** find or decide the value of: *An expert evaluated the old clock at $900.* *v.*, **e·val·u·at·ed, e·val·u·at·ing.**

**e·val·u·a·tion** (i val′yü ā′shən) **1** an evaluating. **2** an estimate of worth or quality: *The coach made too high an evaluation of the centre's ability to score.* *n.*

**ev·a·nesce** (ev′ə nes′) disappear gradually; fade away; vanish. *v.*, **ev·a·nesced, ev·a·nes·cing.**

**ev·a·nes·cence** (ev′ə nes′əns) **1** a gradual disappearance; fading away; vanishing. **2** a tendency to disappear or fade away; inability to last long. *n.*

**ev·a·nes·cent** (ev′ə nes′ənt) tending to disappear or fade away; able to last only a short time: *The colours of the rainbow are evanescent.* *adj.*

**e·van·gel·ism** (i van′jə liz′əm) **1** a preaching of the Gospel; earnest effort for the spread of the Gospel. **2** the work of an EVANGELIST. **3** belief in the doctrines of an evangelical church or party. *n.*

**e·van·gel·ist** (i van′jə list) a preacher of the Gospel. *n.*

**e·van·gel·is·tic** (i van′jə lis′tik) of or by EVANGELISTS. *adj.*

**e·van·gel·ize** (i van′jə līz′) **1** preach the Gospel to. **2** convert to Christianity by preaching. *v.*, **e·van·gel·ized, e·van·gel·iz·ing.** —**e·van′gel·i·za′tion,** *n.*

**e·vap·o·rate** (i vap′ə rāt′) **1** change into a vapour: *Boiling water evaporates rapidly. Some solids, such as moth balls, evaporate without melting.* **2** remove moisture, especially water, from: *Heat is used to evaporate milk.* **3** give off moisture. **4** vanish; disappear; fade away: *Her good resolutions evaporated soon after New Year's Day.* *v.*, **e·vap·o·rat·ed, e·vap·o·rat·ing.**

**evaporated milk** a thick, unsweetened canned milk, prepared by evaporating some of the water from ordinary milk.

**e·vap·o·ra·tion** (i vap′ə rā′shən) **1** a changing of a liquid or solid into vapour: *Wet clothes on a line become dry by evaporation.* **2** being changed into vapour. **3** the removal of water or other liquid. *n.*

**e·vap·o·ra·tor** (i vap′ə rā′tər) an apparatus for evaporating water or other liquid: *an evaporator for drying paints.* *n.*

# evacuation 415 event

hat, āge, fär; let, ēqual, tėrm; it, īce
hot, ōpen, ôrder; oil, out; cup, pút, rüle
əbove, takən, pencəl, lemən, circəs

ch, child; ng, long; sh, ship
th, thin; ᴛʜ, then; zh, measure

**e·va·sion** (i vā′zhən) **1** getting away from something by trickery; avoiding by cleverness: *Evasion of one's duty is contemptible.* **2** an attempt to escape an argument, a charge, a question, etc.: *The prisoner's evasions of the lawyer's questions convinced the jury he was guilty.* **3** a means of evading; trick or excuse used to avoid something. *n.*

**e·va·sive** (i vā′siv *or* i vā′ziv) tending or trying to EVADE: *Perhaps is an evasive answer.* *adj.* —**e·va′sive·ly,** *adv.* —**e·va′sive·ness,** *n.*

**eve** (ēv) **1** the evening or day before a holiday or some other special day: *New Year's Eve.* **2** the time just before: *Everything was quiet on the eve of the battle.* *n.*

**e·ven** (ē′vən) **1** level; flat; smooth: *Even country has no hills.* **2** at the same level; in the same plane or line: *The snow was even with the windowsill.* **3** always the same; regular; uniform: *An even motion does not change.* **4** equal: *They divided the money in even shares.* **5** make equal; tie: *even the score.* **6** make level or of similar length: *She evened the edges by trimming them.* **7** of a number, having no remainder when divided by 2. **8** neither more nor less; exact: *Twelve apples make an even dozen.* **9** owing nothing: *When he paid all of his debts, he was even.* **10** not easily disturbed or angered; calm: *an even temper.* **11** not favouring one more than another; fair: *Justice is even treatment.* **12** in an even manner. **13** just; exactly: *She left even as you came.* **14** indeed: *He is ready, even eager to go.* **15** fully; quite: *He was faithful even unto death.* **16** though one would not expect it; as one would not expect: *Even the least noise disturbs her. Even young children can understand it.* **17** still; yet: *You can do even better if you try.* 1–4, 7–11 *adj.*, 5, 6 *v.*, 12–17 *adv.* —**e′ven·er,** *n.* —**e′ven·ly,** *adv.* —**e′ven·ness,** *n.*
**be even,** **a** owe nothing. **b** have revenge.
**break even,** *Informal.* have equal gains and losses.
**even if,** in spite of the fact that; although: *I will come, even if it rains.*
**even though,** *Informal.* although.
**get even,** **a** owe nothing. **b** have revenge.

**e·ven–hand·ed** (ē′vən han′did) impartial; fair; just. *adj.*

**eve·ning** (ēv′ning) **1** the last part of day and early part of night; the time between day and night. **2** the time between sunset and bedtime. **3** the last part: *Old age is the evening of life.* **4** in the evening; of the evening. 1–3 *n.*, 4 *adj.*

**evening dress** **1** men's formal clothes worn in the evening. **2** a woman's gown for formal wear in the evening.

**evening star** a bright planet seen in the western sky after sunset: *Venus is often the evening star.* See MORNING STAR.

**even number** a number that has no remainder when divided by 2: *The even numbers are 4, 6, 8, etc.*

**e·ven·song** (ē′vən song′) a church service said or sung in the late afternoon or early evening; vespers. *n.*

**e·vent** (i vent′) **1** a happening: *current events.* **2** an important happening: *The discovery of oil in Alberta was*

*certainly an event.* **3** the result or outcome: *We made careful plans and awaited the event.* **4** an item or contest in a program of sports: *The broad jump was the last event.* *n.*
**at all events** or **in any event,** in any case; whatever happens.
**in the event of,** in the case of; if there is; if there should be: *In the event of rain the party will be held indoors.*
**in the event that,** if it should happen that; supposing: *In the event that the roads are icy, we will not come.*

**e·ven·tem·pered** (ē'vən tem'pərd) not easily disturbed or angered; calm. *adj.*

**e·vent·ful** (i vent'fəl) **1** full of events; having many unusual events: *Our day at the fall fair was highly eventful.* **2** having important results; important: *July 1, 1867, Dominion Day, was an eventful day for Canada.* *adj.* —**e·vent'ful·ly,** *adv.*

**e·ven·tu·al** (i ven'chü əl) coming in the end; final: *Her eventual success after several failures surprised us.* *adj.* —**e·ven'tu·al·ly,** *adv.*

**e·ven·tu·al·i·ty** (i ven'chü al'ə tē) a possible occurrence or condition; possibility: *We hope for rain but are ready for the eventuality of drought.* *n., pl.* **e·ven·tu·al·i·ties.**

**e·ven·tu·ate** (i ven'chü āt') come out in the end; happen finally; result. *v.,* **e·ven·tu·at·ed, e·ven·tu·at·ing.**

**ev·er** (ev'ər) **1** at any time: *Is she ever at home?* **2** at all times; always: *ever at your service.* **3** at all; by any chance; in any case: *What did you ever do to make him so angry?* *adv.*
**ever so,** *Informal.* very: *The ocean is ever so deep.*
**for ever and a day,** always.

**ev·er·glade** (ev'ər glād') *U.S.* a large tract of low, wet ground partly covered with tall grass; a large swamp or marsh. *n.*

**ev·er·green** (ev'ər grēn') **1** remaining green all year: *evergreen leaves.* **2** having leaves or needles all year: *evergreen tree.* **3** a tree, shrub, or plant that keeps its leaves or needles all year: *Pine, spruce, cedar, ivy, box, rhododendrons, etc. are evergreens.* **4 evergreens,** *pl.* evergreen twigs or branches used for decoration, especially at Christmas. 1, 2 *adj.*, 3, 4 *n.*

**ev·er·last·ing** (ev'ər las'ting) **1** lasting forever; never ending or stopping. **2** lasting a long time. **3** lasting too long; repeated too often; tiresome: *his everlasting quibbles.* **4** eternity. **5** a flower that keeps its shape and colour when dried. 1–3 *adj.*, 4, 5 *n.* —**ev'er·last'ing·ly,** *adv.*

**ev·er·more** (ev'ər môr') always; forever. *adv., n.*

**eve·ry** (ev'rē) **1** all, regarded singly or separately; each and all: *Every written word is made of letters.* **2** all possible; complete: *We showed her every consideration.* **3** at a regular interval of: *A bus leaves every two hours.* *adj.*
**every now and then,** from time to time: *Every now and then, we have a frost that ruins the crop.*
**every other,** each first, third, fifth, etc., or second, fourth, sixth, etc.: *The magazine is published every other month.*
**every which way,** *Informal.* in all directions; helter-skelter: *He had packed his suitcase every which way.*

**eve·ry·bod·y** (ev'rē bud'ē *or* ev'rē bod'ē) every person; everyone: *Everybody likes the new teacher.* *pron.*
☛ *Usage.* The pronoun **everybody** is always written as one word.

**eve·ry·day** (ev'rē dā') **1** of every day; daily: *Accidents are everyday occurrences.* **2** for every ordinary day; not for Sundays or holidays: *She wears everyday clothes to work.* **3** not exciting or unusual; ordinary: *He's just an everyday writer.* *adj.*
☛ *Usage.* **Everyday** is written as one word when it is an adjective, but it is written as two words when **day** is a noun modified by **every**: *Being late is an everyday occurrence. Every day seemed like a year.*

**eve·ry·one** or **every one** (ev'rē wun' *or* ev'rē wən) every person; everybody: *Everyone took the purchases home.* *pron.*
☛ *Usage.* **Everyone** is usually written as one word, but it is written as two words when **one** is stressed or emphasized: *Everyone wants to attend the concert. Our winning this game depends on every one of you.*

**eve·ry·thing** (ev'rē thing') **1** every thing; all things: *Nan does everything she can to help her mother.* **2** something extremely important; very important thing: *This news means everything to us.* 1 *pron.,* 2 *n.*
☛ *Usage.* **Everything** is written as one word when it is a noun or pronoun, but it is written as two words when **thing** is a noun modified by **every**: *Everything has its proper place. There is a noun for every thing or idea you can name.*

**eve·ry·where** (ev'rē wer' *or* ev'rē hwer') in every place; in all places: *We looked everywhere for our lost dog.* *adv.*

**e·vict** (i vikt') **1** expel by a legal process from land, a building, etc.; eject a tenant: *The tenant was evicted for not paying his rent.* **2** expel or put out by force: *The police evicted the gunman from the occupied building.* *v.*

**e·vic·tion** (i vik'shən) an EVICTING or being EVICTED; expulsion. *n.*

**ev·i·dence** (ev'ə dəns) **1** whatever makes clear the truth or falsehood of something: *The evidence showed that she had not been near the place.* **2** facts established and accepted in a court of law: *Before deciding a case, the judge or jury hears all the evidence given by both sides.* **3** an indication or sign: *A smile gives evidence of pleasure.* **4** make easy to see or understand; show clearly; prove: *His smiles evidenced his pleasure.* 1–3 *n.,* 4 *v.,* **ev·i·denced, ev·i·denc·ing.**
**in evidence,** easily seen or noticed.

**ev·i·dent** (ev'ə dənt) easy to see or understand; clear; plain: *He has brought Betty a kitten, to her evident joy.* *adj.*

**ev·i·dent·ly** (ev'ə dən tlē) plainly; clearly. *adv.*

**e·vil** (ē'vəl) **1** morally bad; wrong; sinful; wicked: *an evil life, an evil character.* **2** something bad; wickedness. **3** causing harm or injury: *an evil plan.* **4** something that causes harm or injury; something that takes away happiness and prosperity: *War is a great evil.* **5** unfortunate. **6** due to bad character or conduct: *an evil reputation.* 1, 3, 5, 6 *adj.,* 2, 4 *n.* —**e'vil·ly,** *adv.* —**e'vil·ness,** *n.*

**e·vil·do·er** (ē'vəl dü'ər) one who does evil. *n.*

**e·vil·do·ing** (ē'vəl dü'ing) the doing of evil. *n.*

**evil eye** the power that some people are supposed to have of causing harm or bringing bad luck to others by looking at them.

**e·vil-mind·ed** (ē′vəl mīn′did) having an evil mind; wicked; malicious. *adj.*

**e·vince** (i vins′) **1** show clearly: *The dog evinced its dislike of strangers by growling.* **2** show that one has a certain quality, trait, etc. *v.*, **e·vinced, e·vinc·ing.**

**e·vis·cer·ate** (i vis′ə rāt′) **1** remove the bowels from; disembowel. **2** deprive of something essential. *v.*, **e·vis·cer·at·ed, e·vis·cer·at·ing.** —**e·vis′cer·a′tion,** *n.*

**ev·o·ca·tion** (ev′ō kā′shən) an evoking. *n.*

**e·voke** (i vōk′) call forth; bring out: *A good joke evokes a laugh.* *v.*, **e·voked, e·vok·ing.**

**ev·o·lu·tion** (ev′ə lü′shən *or* ē′və lü′shən) **1** any process of formation or growth; gradual development: *the evolution of a flower from a bud.* **2** something evolved; a product of development; not a sudden discovery or creation. **3** the theory that all living things developed from a few simple forms of life, or from a single form. **4** a movement of ships or soldiers, planned beforehand. **5** a movement that is a part of a definite plan, design, or series: *the graceful evolutions of a ballet dancer.* **6** a releasing; giving off; setting free: *the evolution of heat from burning coal.* *n.*

**ev·o·lu·tion·ar·y** (ev′ə lü′shə ner′ē *or* ē′və lü′shə ner′ē) **1** having to do with EVOLUTION or development. **2** in accordance with the theory of EVOLUTION (def. 3). **3** performing EVOLUTIONS (def. 5); having to do with evolutions. *adj.*

**ev·o·lu·tion·ist** (ev′ə lü′shə nist *or* ē′və lü′shə nist) a student of, or believer in, the theory of EVOLUTION (def. 3). *n.*

**e·volve** (i volv′) **1** develop gradually; work out: *The girls evolved a plan for earning money during their summer vacation.* **2** develop by a process of growth and change to a more highly organized condition. **3** release; give off; set free. *v.*, **e·volved, e·volv·ing.**

**e·volve·ment** (i volv′mənt) **1** an evolving. **2** being EVOLVED. *n.*

**ewe** (yü) a female sheep. *n.*
☛ *Hom.* YEW, YOU.

**ew·er** (yü′ər) a wide-mouthed water pitcher: *The ewer and basin are on the washstand.* *n.*

**ex** (eks) **1** the 24th letter of the alphabet (X, x). **2** anything shaped like an X. *n.*

**ex–** a prefix meaning: **1** out of; from; out, as in *express, exit, export.* **2** utterly; thoroughly, as in *exterminate, exasperate.* **3** former; formerly, as in *ex-president, ex-member.*

**ex.** **1** example. **2** examined. **3** exchange. **4** exercise.

**ex·ac·er·bate** (eg zas′ər bāt′ *or* ek sas′ər bāt′) **1** make worse; aggravate pain, disease, or anger. **2** irritate a person's feelings. *v.*, **ex·ac·er·bat·ed, ex·ac·er·bat·ing.**

**ex·ac·er·ba·tion** (eg zas′ər bā′shən *or* ek sas′ər bā′shən) **1** AGGRAVATION (def. 1). **2** irritation. *n.*

**ex·act** (eg zakt′) **1** without any error or mistake; strictly correct; accurate; precise: *an exact measurement, the exact amount.* **2** strict; severe; rigorous. **3** characterized by or using strict accuracy: *A scientist should be an exact thinker.* **4** demand and get; force to be paid: *If he does the work, he can exact payment for it.* **5** call for; need; require: *A hard piece of work exacts effort and patience.* 1–3 *adj.*, 4, 5 *v.* —**ex·act′ness,** *n.*

## evil-minded 417 example

hat, āge, fär; let, ēqual, tèrm; it, īce
hot, ōpen, ôrder; oil, out; cup, pùt, rüle
əbove, takən, pencəl, lemən, circəs
ch, child; ng, long; sh, ship
th, thin; ᴛʜ, then; zh, measure

**ex·act·ing** (eg zak′ting) **1** requiring much; making severe demands; hard to please: *an exacting employer.* **2** requiring effort, care, or attention: *Flying an airplane is exacting work.* **3** ppr. of EXACT. 1, 2 *adj.*, 3 *v.*

**ex·ac·tion** (eg zak′shən) **1** an exacting; demanding and getting; forcing to be paid: *The ruler's exactions of money left the people very poor.* **2** the thing exacted: *Taxes, fees, etc., forced to be paid, are exactions.* *n.*

**ex·ac·ti·tude** (eg zak′tə tyüd′ *or* eg zak′tə tüd′) exactness. *n.*

**ex·act·ly** (eg zak′tlē) **1** in an exact manner; accurately; precisely. **2** just so; quite right. *adv.*

**exact science** a science in which facts can be accurately observed and results can be accurately predicted: *Mathematics and physics are exact sciences.*

**ex·ag·ger·ate** (eg zaj′ə rāt′) **1** make something greater than it is; overstate: *She exaggerated the dangers of the trip in order to frighten them.* **2** increase or enlarge abnormally. **3** say or think something is greater than it is; go beyond the truth: *He always exaggerates when he tells about things he has done.* *v.*, **ex·ag·ger·at·ed, ex·ag·ger·at·ing.** —**ex·ag′ger·a′tor,** *n.*

**ex·ag·ger·a·tion** (eg zaj′ə rā′shən) **1** a statement that goes beyond the truth: *It is an exaggeration to say that you would rather die than touch a snake.* **2** the act of going beyond the truth: *His constant exaggeration made people distrust him.* **3** being exaggerated. *n.*

**ex·alt** (eg zolt′) **1** place high or raise in rank, honour, power, character, quality, etc.: *We exalt a man when we elect him to high office.* **2** fill with pride, joy, or noble feeling. **3** praise; honour; glorify. *v.*

**ex·al·ta·tion** (eg′zol tā′shən) **1** an EXALTing. **2** being EXALTed. **3** lofty emotion; rapture. *n.*

**ex·am** (eg zam′) *Informal.* EXAMINATION (def. 2). *n.*

**ex·am·i·na·tion** (eg zam′ə nā′shən) **1** a careful test; inspection: *The doctor made a careful examination of my eyes.* **2** a set of questions to test knowledge or skill; a formal test: *an examination in arithmetic.* **3** the answers given in a test. *n.*

**ex·am·ine** (eg zam′ən) **1** look at closely and carefully: *The doctor examined the wound.* **2** test the knowledge or qualifications of; ask questions of; test. *v.*, **ex·am·ined, ex·am·in·ing.** —**ex·am′in·er,** *n.*

**ex·am·ple** (eg zam′pəl) **1** one thing taken to show what others are like; a case that shows something; sample: *Vancouver is an example of a busy city.* **2** a model; pattern of something to be imitated or avoided: *That mother is a good example to her daughters.* **3** an instance or sample that serves to illustrate a way of doing or making something: *The problems in the arithmetic textbook were accompanied by examples.* **4** an instance or case, especially of punishment intended as a warning to others: *As an example, the captain made the shirkers clean up the camp.* *n.*

**for example,** as an illustration or illustrations; for instance: *Children play many games: baseball, for example.*

**make an example of,** treat sternly, or punish, as a

sample of the result of misbehaviour: *The judge made an example of the careless driver by a heavy fine.*
**set an example,** behave so that others may imitate; be a model or pattern of conduct.
**without example,** with nothing like it before.

**ex·as·per·ate** (eg zas′pə rāt′) irritate very much; annoy extremely; make angry: *The child's endless questions exasperated her father.* *v.,* **ex·as·per·at·ed, ex·as·per·at·ing.**

**ex·as·per·a·tion** (eg zas′pə rā′shən) extreme annoyance, irritation, or anger. *n.*

**exc.** except.

**Exc.** Excellency.

**Ex·cal·i·bur** (eks kal′ə bər) in the legends about King Arthur, Arthur's magic sword. *n.*

**ex ca·the·dra** (ek′skə thē′drə) *Latin,* meaning 'from the throne of a bishop'. **1** with authority; from the seat of authority. **2** spoken with authority.

**ex·ca·vate** (ek′skə vāt′) **1** make a hole by removing dirt, sand, rock, etc.: *The construction company will begin to excavate tomorrow.* **2** make by digging; dig: *The tunnel was excavated through solid rock.* **3** dig out; scoop out: *Earth movers excavated the dirt.* **4** get or uncover by digging: *They excavated the ancient buried city.* *v.,* **ex·ca·vat·ed, ex·ca·va·ting.**

**ex·ca·va·tion** (ek′skə vā′shən) **1** a digging; digging out or up. **2** a hole or hollow made by digging. *n.*

**ex·ca·va·tor** (ek′skə vā′tər) a person or thing that EXCAVATES: *An earth mover is an excavator.* *n.*

**ex·ceed** (ek sēd′) **1** go beyond; be more or greater than; do more than; surpass: *The sum of 5 and 7 exceeds 10. The motorist was fined for exceeding the speed limit.* **2** be more or greater than others. *v.*

**ex·ceed·ing** (ek sē′ding) **1** surpassing; very great; unusual; extreme: *Helen is a girl of exceeding beauty.* **2** ppr. of EXCEED. 1 *adj.,* 2 *v.*

**ex·ceed·ing·ly** (ek sē′ding lē) extremely; unusually; very: *Today is an exceedingly hot day.* *adv.*

**ex·cel** (ek sel′) **1** be better than; do better than: *Sonia excelled her classmates in history.* **2** be better than others; do better than others: *The old king excelled in wisdom.* *v.,* **ex·celled, ex·cel·ling.**

**ex·cel·lence** (ek′sə ləns) an unusually good quality; being better than others; superiority: *The hotel was famous for the excellence of its food.* *n.*

**ex·cel·len·cy** (ek′sə lən sē) **1** EXCELLENCE. **2 Excellency,** a title of honour used in speaking to or of the Governor General, an ambassador, etc. *n., pl.* **ex·cel·len·cies.**

**ex·cel·lent** (ek′sə lənt) unusually good; better than others; first-class: *She is an excellent golfer. Excellent work deserves high praise.* *adj.* —**ex′cel·lent·ly,** *adv.*

**ex·cel·si·or** (ek sel′sē ər) short, fine, curled shavings of soft wood used as a packing material or as stuffing. *n.*

**ex·cept** (ek sept′) **1** leaving out; but; other than: *every day except Sunday.* **2** *Informal.* only (*often used with* **that**): *I'd like to go with you except that I can't swim.* **3** with any purpose other than; otherwise than: *He hardly ever goes out except to visit his brother.* **4** take out or leave out; EXCLUDE: *All the children, the baby excepted, were helping to clean up the backyard.* 1 *prep.,* 2, 3 *conj.,* 4 *v.*

**except for,** leaving out; other than: *It's a good movie, except for a few boring scenes near the beginning.*

**ex·cept·ing** (ek sep′ting) **1** except; leaving out; other than: *The whole group went to the beach, excepting the two girls who were sick.* **2** ppr. of EXCEPT. 1 *prep.,* 2 *v.*

**ex·cep·tion** (ek sep′shən) **1** the act of leaving out or excluding: *I like all the paintings, with the exception of this one. They said they could make no exception, and that everyone would have to pay the full fee.* **2** an unusual instance; a case that does not follow the rule: *She usually comes on time; today was an exception.* *n.*

**take exception,** object or protest: *He took exception to the editorial, and wrote a letter to the newspaper about it.*

**ex·cep·tion·a·ble** (ek sep′shə nə bəl) liable to objection; objectionable. *adj.*

**ex·cep·tion·al** (ek sep′shə nəl) out of the ordinary; unusual: *This warm weather is exceptional for January. Sheila is an exceptional student.* *adj.* —**ex·cep′tion·al·ly,** *adv.*

**ex·cerpt** (ek′sėrpt *for noun,* ek sėrpt′ *for verb*) **1** a selected passage; quotation; extract: *The article included excerpts from several medical books.* **2** take out; select passages from; quote; make extracts from. 1 *n.,* 2 *v.*

**ex·cess** (ek ses′ *or, esp. for 4,* ek′ses) **1** the action or an instance of going beyond what is usual, enough, or right: *The excesses of the last city council were exposed in the report. He was opposed to all excess in eating and drinking.* **2** an amount or degree beyond what is usual, enough, or right: *an excess of grief. She said he never drank to excess.* **3** the amount by which one quantity or thing is more than another: *She had to pay for an excess of five kilograms on her luggage.* **4** more than the usual permitted, or proper amount: *Airlines charge for excess baggage.* *n.*

**in excess of,** more than; over: *They expect the contributions to be in excess of $5000.*

**to excess,** too much: *He eats candy to excess.*

**ex·ces·sive** (ek ses′iv) too much; too great; going beyond what is necessary or right: *She didn't buy the couch because she felt the price was excessive. Marc spends an excessive amount of time telephoning.* *adj.* —**ex·ces′sive·ly,** *adv.* —**ex·cess′ive·ness,** *n.*

**ex·change** (eks chānj′) **1** give for something else: *She would not exchange her house for a palace.* **2** give in trade for something regarded as equivalent: *I will exchange ten dimes for a dollar.* **3** give and receive things of the same kind: *to exchange letters.* **4** replace a purchase or have it replaced: *We cannot exchange swimsuits.* **5** an exchanging; giving and receiving: *Ten dimes for a dollar is a fair exchange.* **6** what is traded. **7** a place where things are traded: *Stocks are bought, sold, and traded in a stock exchange.* **8** a central telephone office. **9** a system of settling accounts in different places by exchanging BILLS OF EXCHANGE that represent money instead of exchanging money itself. **10** the changing of the money of one country into the money of another. **11** a fee charged for settling accounts or changing money. **12** the rate of exchange; a varying rate or sum in one currency given for a fixed sum in another currency: *What is the exchange now on the American dollar?* 1–4 *v.,* **ex·changed, ex·chang·ing;** 5–12 *n.*

**ex·change·a·bil·i·ty** (eks chān′jə bil′ə tē) the quality or condition of being EXCHANGEABLE. *n.*

**ex·change·a·ble** (eks chān′jə bəl) capable of being EXCHANGED. *adj.*

**ex·cheq·uer** (eks chek′ər) **1** a treasury, especially the treasury of a state or nation. **2** *Informal.* finances; funds. **3 Exchequer, a** the department of the British government in charge of its finances and the public revenues. **b** the offices of this department of the British government. **c** the funds of the British government. *n.*

**ex·cise**[1] (ek′sīz *or* ek sīz′) a tax on the manufacture, sale, or use of certain articles made, sold, or used within a country: *There is an excise on tobacco.* *n.*

**ex·cise**[2] (ek sīz′) cut out; remove: *The editor excised passages from the book.* *v.*, **ex·cised, ex·cis·ing.**

**ex·cis·ion** (ek sizh′ən) cutting out; removal: *the excision of a tumour.* *n.*

**ex·cit·a·bil·i·ty** (ek sī′tə bil′ə tē) the quality of being easily excited. *n.*

**ex·cit·a·ble** (ek sī′tə bəl) easily stirred up and aroused: *Our dog is excitable and will bark at anything.* *adj.* —**ex·cit′a·ble·ness,** *n.* —**ex·cit′a·bly,** *adv.*

**ex·cit·a·tion** (ek′sī tā′shən) **1** an exciting or being EXCITED (def. 1). **2** the production of a magnetic field by means of electricity or the raising of an atom or nucleus to a higher level of energy. *n.*

**ex·cite** (ek sīt′) **1** stir up the feelings of; move to strong emotion: *It excited her just to think of what she would do with the money.* **2** arouse: *His new jacket excited envy in some of the other boys.* **3** stir to action or activity: *Don't excite the dogs.* **4** in physics, produce magnetism in: *to excite an electromagnet.* **5** in physiology, produce or increase a response in an organ, tissue, organism, etc.; stimulate: *to excite a nerve.* **6** in physics, raise an atom, nucleus, or molecule to a higher level of energy. *v.* **ex·cit·ed, ex·cit·ing.** —**ex·cit′er,** *n.*

**ex·cit·ed** (ek sī′tid) **1** stirred up; aroused: *He was so excited he couldn't sleep.* **2** in physics, raised to a higher level of energy: *an excited atom.* **3** pt. and pp. of EXCITE. **1, 2** *adj.*, **3** *v.* —**ex·cit′ed·ly,** *adv.*

**ex·cite·ment** (ek sīt′mənt) **1** an exciting; arousing: *the excitement of nations to war.* **2** the state of being EXCITED (def. 1): *The baby's first steps caused great excitement in the family.* **3** something that EXCITES (def. 1): *The hockey game provided first-rate excitement.* **4** noisy activity; commotion; ado: *What's all the excitement?* *n.*

**ex·cit·ing** (ek sī′ting) **1** arousing; stirring: *an exciting piece of news, an exciting game.* **2** ppr. of EXCITE. **1** *adj.*, **2** *v.*

**ex·claim** (ek sklām′) say or speak suddenly in surprise or strong feeling; cry out: *"Here you are at last!" exclaimed Jack's mother.* *v.*

**ex·cla·ma·tion** (ek′sklə mā′shən) an expression of strong feeling either in one word or in a complete sentence. *n.*

**exclamation mark** or **point** a mark (!) of punctuation used after a word or sentence to show that it is an exclamation. This mark is also used, within parentheses, to suggest that some statement or situation is remarkable, absurd, or the like: *"The poet John Milton was born in Vancouver"(!).*
☞ *Usage.* Take care not to overuse exclamation marks. If too many are used in a piece of writing, they quickly lose their effectiveness. Except in very familiar writing, don't use more than one exclamation mark after any one word, phrase, or sentence.

**ex·clam·a·to·ry** (ek sklam′ə tô′rē) using, containing,

hat, āge, fär; let, ēqual, tėrm; it, īce
hot, ōpen, ôrder; oil, out; cup, pút, rüle
əbove, takən, pencəl, lemən, circəs
ch, child; ng, long; sh, ship
th, thin; ᴛʜ, then; zh, measure

or expressing EXCLAMATION: *an exclamatory sentence.* *adj.*

**ex·clude** (ek sklüd′) **1** shut out; keep out: *Blinds exclude light. Faith excludes doubt.* **2** keep from a place, privilege, activity, etc.; keep from including or considering: *Professional players are excluded from the competition. The invitation excludes children.* *v.*, **ex·clud·ed, ex·clud·ing.** —**ex·clud′er,** *n.*

**ex·clud·ing** (ek sklü′ding) **1** except for; with the exception of; not counting: *All the neighbours, excluding those away on holidays, will be at the picnic.* **2** ppr. of EXCLUDE. **1** *prep.*, **2** *v.*

**ex·clu·sion** (ek sklü′zhən) shutting out or being shut out: *Amy's exclusion from the club hurt her feelings.* *n.* **to the exclusion of,** so as to exclude: *She worked away at her science project, to the exclusion of everything else.*

**ex·clu·sive** (ek sklü′siv) **1** each shutting out the other: *Baby and adult are exclusive terms since a person cannot be both.* **2** shutting out all or most other things, considerations, etc.: *He demanded our exclusive attention. She has an exclusive interest in sports.* **3** not divided or shared with others; single; sole: *An inventor has an exclusive right for a certain number of years to make what he or she has invented and patented.* **4** excluding certain people or groups for social, financial, or other reasons: *an exclusive club, an exclusive school.* **5** selling only expensive items: *an exclusive boutique.* **6** not available elsewhere or to anyone else: *an exclusive design, an exclusive interview.* **7** something exclusive, especially an article, news story, etc. published by only one periodical. **1–6** *adj.*, **7** *n.* —**ex·clu′sive·ly,** *adv.* —**ex·clu′sive·ness,** *n.*
**exclusive of,** excluding; leaving out, not counting or considering: *There are 26 days in that month, exclusive of Sundays. The label says the dress is all cotton, exclusive of trimming.*

**ex·clu·sive·ly** (ek sklü′si vlē) with the exclusion of all others: *That selfish girl looks out for herself exclusively.* *adv.*

**ex·com·mun·i·cate** (ek′skə myü′nə kāt′) cut off from membership in a church; expel formally from the fellowship of a church; prohibit from participating in any of the rites of a church. *v.*, **ex·com·mu·ni·cat·ed, ex·com·mu·ni·cat·ing.**

**ex·com·mu·ni·ca·tion** (ek′skə myü′nə kā′shən) **1** a formal expulsion from the fellowship of a church; prohibition from participating in any of the rites of a church. **2** the formal, official statement announcing excommunication. *n.*

**ex·co·ri·ate** (ek skô′rē āt′) **1** strip or rub off the skin of; make raw and sore. **2** denounce violently. *v.*, **ex·co·ri·at·ed, ex·co·ri·at·ing.** —**ex·co′ri·a′tion,** *n.*

**ex·cre·ment** (ek′skrə mənt) waste matter discharged from the bowels; feces. *n.*

**ex·cres·cence** (ek skres′əns) **1** an unnatural or disfiguring growth or addition, such as a wart or bunion. **2** any unnatural outgrowth. *n.*

**ex·cres·cent** (ek skres′ənt) forming an unnatural growth or a disfiguring addition. *adj.*

**ex·crete** (ek skrēt′) discharge waste matter from the body; separate waste matter from the blood or tissues: *The pores of the skin excrete sweat.* *v.*, **ex·cret·ed, ex·cret·ing.**

**ex·cre·tion** (ek skrē′shən) **1** the discharge of waste matter from the body; separation of waste matter from the blood or tissues. **2** the waste matter discharged from the body; waste matter separated from the blood or tissues: *Sweat is an excretion.* *n.*

**ex·cre·to·ry** (ek′skrə tô′rē *or* ek skrē′tə rē) of EXCRETION; that EXCRETES: *The kidneys are excretory organs.* *adj.*

**ex·cru·ci·at·ing** (ek skrü′shē ā′ting) very painful; torturing; causing great suffering: *an excruciating toothache.* *adj.*

**ex·cul·pate** (ek′skul pāt′) free from blame; prove innocent: *The evidence of the witness exculpated him.* *v.*, **ex·cul·pat·ed, ex·cul·pat·ing.**

**ex·cul·pa·tion** (ek′skul pā′shən) **1** a freeing from blame; proving innocent. **2** a vindication; proof of innocence; excuse. *n.*

**ex·cur·sion** (ek skėr′zhən) **1** a short journey made with the intention of returning; pleasure trip: *Our club went on an excursion to the mountains.* **2** a round trip at a reduced fare, usually involving a restriction on the length of time spent on the trip, dates of travel, etc. *n.*

**ex·cur·sion·ist** (ek skėr′zhə nist) a person who goes on an EXCURSION. *n.*

**ex·cur·sive** (ek skėr′siv) off the subject; wandering; rambling. *adj.* —**ex·cur′sive·ly,** *adv.*

**ex·cus·a·ble** (ek skyü′zə bəl) that can or ought to be EXCUSED (def. 1): *Her anger was excusable since they had been so rude.* *adj.* —**ex·cus′a·bly,** *adv.*

**ex·cuse** (ek skyüz′ *for verb*, ek skyüs′ *for noun*) **1** overlook a fault, etc.; pardon; forgive: *He excused her carelessness in upsetting his paint.* **2** give a reason or apology for; try to clear of blame: *She excused her own faults by blaming others.* **3** be a reason or explanation for; clear of blame: *Sickness excused his absence from school.* **4** not demand or require; dispense with: *We will excuse your presence.* **5** a real or pretended reason or explanation: *She had many excuses for coming late.* **6** an apology given: *If you must leave early, be sure to make your excuses to your hostess.* **7** the act of excusing. 1–4 *v.*, **ex·cused, ex·cus·ing;** 5–7 *n.*
**be excused from,** be given permission to avoid; be let off: *Those who passed the first test are excused from the second one.*
**excuse me,** **a** I apologize. **b** please may I leave?
**excuse oneself,** **a** ask to be pardoned. **b** ask permission to leave: *I excused myself from the table.*

**exec.** **1** executive. **2** executor.

**ex·e·cra·ble** (ek′sə krə bəl) **1** abominable; detestable: *an execrable crime.* **2** *Informal.* very bad: *execrable taste in art.* *adj.* —**ex′e·cra·bly,** *adv.*

**ex·e·crate** (ek′sə krāt′) **1** express or feel extreme loathing for; abhor: *The former leader's cruelty was execrated by his disillusioned followers.* **2** curse. *v.*, **ex·e·crat·ed, ex·e·crat·ing.**

**ex·e·cra·tion** (ek′sə krā′shən) **1** the action of execrating; denouncing or cursing. **2** a curse: *The mob shouted angry execrations.* **3** a person or thing execrated. *n.*

**ex·e·cute** (ek′sə kyüt′) **1** carry out; do: *The nurse executed the doctor's orders.* **2** put into effect; enforce: *to execute a law.* **3** put to death according to law: *The convicted murderer was executed.* **4** make according to a plan or design: *The tapestry was executed with great skill.* **5** perform or play a piece of music. **6** in law, make a deed, lease, contract, will, etc. complete or valid by signing, sealing, or doing whatever is necessary. **7** in computers, follow (an instruction); cause (a program) to be in action. *v.*, **ex·e·cut·ed, ex·e·cut·ing.**

**ex·e·cu·tion** (ek′sə kyü′shən) **1** carrying out; doing, performing, or producing: *the execution of one's duties, the execution of a statue in marble.* **2** putting into effect; enforcing: *the execution of a law.* **3** the manner of carrying out or doing something: *the skilful execution of a difficult piece of music.* **4** putting to death according to law. **5** making according to a plan or design. **6** in law, making complete or valid by signing, sealing, or doing what is necessary. **7** a written order from a court directing a judgment to be carried out. *n.*

**ex·e·cu·tion·er** (ek′sə kyü′shə nər) **1** a person who carried out the death penalty according to law. **2** any person who puts another to death. *n.*

**ex·ec·u·tive** (eg zek′yə tiv) **1** having to do with carrying out or managing affairs: *an executive committee. The principal of a school has an executive position.* **2** a person who carries out or manages affairs: *The president of a company is an executive.* **3** suitable or designed for executives: *an executive suite, executive toys, executive socks.* **4** having the duty and power of putting the laws into effect: *The Cabinet is the executive branch of our federal government.* **5** a person, group, or branch of government that has the duty and power of putting the laws into effect. **6** a group of people responsible for running the affairs of a society, association, or club: *She's on the executive of our ski club.* **7** involving or having to do with this group of people: *There's an executive meeting this afternoon.* 1, 3, 4, 7 *adj.*, 2, 5, 6 *n.* —**ex·ec′u·tive·ly,** *adv.*

**Executive Council** the cabinet of a provincial government, consisting of the Premier and his or her ministers.

**ex·ec·u·tor** (eg zek′yə tər *for 1*, ek′sə kyü′tər *for 2*) **1** a person named in a will to carry out the provisions of the will. Compare with ADMINISTRATOR (def. 2). **2** a person who performs or carries out things. *n.*

**ex·ec·u·trix** (eg zek′yə triks′) a female EXECUTOR. *n.*

**ex·em·plar** (eg zem′plər) **1** a person or thing worth imitating; an ideal model or pattern: *They looked on her as the exemplar of courage.* **2** a typical case; example: *She was belligerent and defensive, the exemplar of the insecure child.* *n.*

**ex·em·pla·ry** (eg zem′plə rē) **1** worth imitating; being a good model or pattern: *exemplary conduct. She showed exemplary courage.* **2** of a penalty or punishment, serving as a warning or deterrent: *a sentence of exemplary severity.* **3** serving as an example; typical: *exemplary passages from a book.* *adj.*

**ex·em·pli·fi·ca·tion** (eg zem′plə fə kā′shən) **1** showing by example; the act or fact of being an example. **2** something that serves to illustrate; example: *The sudden price increases were an exemplification of the law of supply and demand.* *n.*

**ex·em·pli·fy** (eg zem′plə fī′) show by example; be an example of: *The knights exemplified courage and courtesy.* *v.*, **ex·em·pli·fied, ex·em·pli·fy·ing.**

**ex·empt** (eg zempt′) **1** make free from a duty, obligation, rule, etc.; release: *She was exempted from the test because she had been away from school.* **2** freed from a duty, obligation, rule, etc.; released: *Food is exempt from sales tax.* **3** a person who has been exempted. 1 *v.*, 2 *adj.*, 3 *n.*

**ex·emp·tion** (eg zemp′shən) **1** exempting or being exempted; freedom from a duty, obligation, rule, etc.; immunity: *Poor people have exemption from taxes.* **2** something that is exempted, especially a part of a person's income that does not have to be taxed: *There is a basic tax exemption that can be claimed by everyone.* *n.*

**ex·er·cise** (ek′sər sīz′) **1** activity to train or develop the body or keep it healthy: *Running and playing volleyball are forms of exercise.* **2** take part or cause to take part in such activity: *A person should exercise daily. The man on the sidewalk was exercising his dog.* **3** a particular activity or series of activities designed to develop or train the body or develop some skill or faculty: *He does exercises every morning. There is an exercise at the end of each lesson.* **4** active use or practice, employment: *the exercise of one's right to vote, the exercise of care to promote safety.* **5** use actively; employ: *to exercise one's mind or imagination, to exercise care in crossing the street.* **6** carry out in action; perform or fulfil: *to exercise the duties of one's office.* **7** the performance of duties, functions, etc. **8** have as an effect: *What others think exercises a great influence on most of us.* **9 exercises,** *pl.* a formal activity; ceremony: *the opening exercises in a new school.* 1, 3, 4, 7, 9 *n.*, 2, 5, 6, 8 *v.*, **ex·er·cised, ex·er·cis·ing.** —**ex′er·cis′er,** *n.*

**ex·ert** (eg zėrt′) use; use actively; put into action: *A clever fighter exerts both strength and skill. A ruler exerts authority.* *v.*

**exert oneself,** make an effort; try hard; strive: *We will have to exert ourselves if we want to get there on time.*

**ex·er·tion** (eg zėr′shən) **1** effort: *The exertion of moving the piano was too much for him and he collapsed. It was through the exertions of many volunteers that the fair succeeded.* **2** putting into action; active use; use: *an exertion of authority.* *n.*

**ex·ha·la·tion** (eks′hə lā′shən) **1** an exhaling: *Breathing out is an exhalation of air.* **2** something exhaled; air, vapour, smoke, odour, etc. *n.*

**ex·hale** (eks hāl′) **1** breathe out: *to exhale air from the lungs. The doctor told him to exhale completely.* **2** give off air, vapour, smoke, odour, etc. **3** pass off as vapour; rise like vapour: *Sweet odours exhale from the flowers.* *v.*, **ex·haled, ex·hal·ing.**

**ex·haust** (eg zost′) **1** empty completely: *to exhaust a well.* **2** use up: *to exhaust one's money.* **3** tire very much: *The climb up the hill exhausted us.* **4** drain of strength, resources, etc.: *The long war exhausted the country.* **5** draw off: *to exhaust the air in a jar.* **6** leave nothing important to be found out or said about; study or treat thoroughly: *Her book about tulips exhausted the subject.* **7** the escape of used steam, gasoline fumes, etc. from a machine. **8** a means or way for used steam, gasoline fumes, etc. to escape from an engine. **9** the used steam, gasoline fumes, etc. that escape. **10** be discharged; go forth: *Gases from an automobile exhaust through a pipe.* 1–6, 10 *v.*, 7–9 *n.*

**ex·haust·ed** (eg zos′tid) **1** used up. **2** worn out; very tired: *The exhausted child had fallen asleep on the floor.* **3** pt. and pp. of EXHAUST. 1, 2 *adj.*, 3 *v.*

hat, āge, fär; let, ēqual, tėrm; it, īce
hot, ōpen, ôrder; oil, out; cup, pùt, rüle
əbove, takən, pencəl, lemən, circəs
ch, child; ng, long; sh, ship
th, thin; ᴛн, then; zh, measure

**ex·haust·i·bil·i·ty** (eg zos′tə bil′ə tē) the quality of being EXHAUSTIBLE; capability of being exhausted. *n.*

**ex·haust·i·ble** (eg zos′tə bəl) capable of being EXHAUSTED (defs. 1–6). *adj.*

**ex·haus·tion** (eg zos′chən) **1** EXHAUSTing or being exhausted. **2** extreme fatigue. *n.*

**ex·haus·tive** (eg zos′tiv) leaving out nothing important; thorough; comprehensive: *Her conclusions are based on an exhaustive study of the subject.* *adj.* —**ex·haus′tive·ly,** *adv.*

**ex·haust·less** (eg zos′tlis) that cannot be EXHAUSTed. *adj.*

**ex·hib·it** (eg zib′it) **1** show; display: *He exhibits interest whenever I mention dogs.* **2** show publicly: *You should exhibit your roses in the flower show.* **3** the thing or things shown publicly: *His exhibit of coins won the prize.* **4** a public show; small exhibition; part of an exhibition: *Have you seen the art exhibit?* **5** show in court as evidence; submit for consideration or inspection. **6** something shown in court as evidence. 1, 2, 5 *v.*, 3, 4, 6 *n.*

**ex·hi·bi·tion** (ek′sə bish′ən) **1** the act of showing; display: *He said he had never seen such an exhibition of bad manners.* **2** a public show: *The art school holds an exhibition every year.* **3** a thing or things shown publicly. **4** a public showing of livestock, produce, manufactured goods, etc., often accompanied by side shows, rides, games, and other forms of entertainment; big fair: *The Canadian National Exhibition.* *n.*

**ex·hi·bi·tion·ism** (ek′sə bish′ə niz′əm) **1** an excessive tendency to seek attention or to show off one's abilities. **2** a compulsive tendency to expose the genitals in public. **3** an instance of such exposure. *n.*

**ex·hi·bi·tion·ist** (ek′sə bish′ə nist) **1** a person who tends to seek attention or show off his or her abilities excessively. **2** a person given to compulsive exposure of the genitals in public. *n.*

**ex·hib·i·tor** (eg zib′ə tər) a person, company or group that EXHIBITS (def. 2). *n.*

**ex·hil·a·rate** (eg zil′ə rāt′) **1** refresh; invigorate: *The girls were exhilarated by their early-morning swim.* **2** make merry or lively; put into high spirits: *He was exhilarated by the prospect of getting home a day early.* *v.*, **ex·hil·a·rat·ed, ex·hil·a·rat·ing.**

**ex·hil·a·ra·tion** (eg zil′ə rā′shən) **1** an EXHILARATEd feeling or condition; high spirits; stimulation. **2** the act of exhilarating. *n.*

**ex·hort** (eg zôrt′) urge strongly; advise or warn earnestly: *The teacher exhorted his class to work harder.* *v.* —**ex·hort′er,** *n.*

**ex·hor·ta·tion** (eg′zôr tā′shən *or* ek′sôr tā′shən) **1** a strong urging; earnest advice or warning. **2** a speech, sermon, etc. that exhorts. *n.*

**ex·hu·ma·tion** (eks′hyə mā′shən) an exhuming. *n.*

**ex·hume** (eg zyüm′ *or* eks hyüm′) **1** take out of a grave or out of the ground; dig up. **2** reveal. *v.*, **ex·humed, ex·hum·ing.**

**ex·i·gen·cy** (eg zij′ən sē *or* ek′sə jən sē) **1** the state or quality of being urgent: *The exigency of the case justified his rudeness.* **2** a situation demanding immediate action or attention; urgent case: *The tablecloth had caught fire, but she proved equal to the exigency and put out the flames with a heavy rug.* **3 exigencies,** *pl.* urgent needs; requirements of a particular situation: *The exigencies of business kept her from attending the conference. n., pl.* **ex·i·gen·cies.**

**ex·i·gent** (eg′zə jənt *or* ek′sə jənt) **1** demanding immediate action or attention; urgent: *The exigent pangs of hunger sent him on a search for food.* **2** demanding a great deal; exacting: *an exigent occupation. adj.*

**ex·ile** (eg′zīl *or* ek′sīl) **1** force a person to leave his or her country or home; banish: *After the revolution, many people were exiled from the country.* **2** being exiled; banishment: *Napoleon's exile to Elba was brief.* **3** an exiled person: *He has been an exile for ten years.* **4** any prolonged absence from one's own country: *After a few years of exile, many artists and actors have returned to work in Canada.* 1 *v.,* **ex·iled, ex·il·ing;** 2–4 *n.*

**ex·ist** (eg zist′) **1** have actual existence; be; be real: *The world has existed a long time. Do elves exist or not?* **2** continue to be: *The problem still exists.* **3** live; have life: *A person cannot exist without air.* **4** be present; occur; be recorded; be known as a matter of record: *Cases exist of persons who cannot smell anything. v.*

**ex·ist·ence** (eg zis′təns) **1** real or actual being; being: *to come into existence. Most people do not now believe in the existence of ghosts.* **2** way of life; life: *Many bush pilots lead a dangerous existence.* **3** an occurrence; presence: *They admitted the existence of isolated cases of the disease but claimed that there was no public danger.* **4** all that exists. **5** something that exists. *n.*

**ex·ist·ent** (eg zis′tənt) **1** existing. **2** existing now; of the present time. *adj.*

**ex·is·ten·tial·ism** (eg′siz ten′shə liz′əm) a philosophy stressing that people are totally free to make their own decisions in a world lacking purpose. *n.*

**ex·it** (eg′zit *or* ek′sit) **1** a way out: *The theatre had six exits.* **2** going out; departure: *When the cat came in, the mouse made a hasty exit.* **3** the departure of an actor from the stage: *The actor made a graceful exit.* **4** go out; depart. **5** in stage directions, the signal for an actor to go into the wings. 1–3, 5 *n.,* 4 *v.*

**ex li·bris** (eks′ lī′bris *or* lē′brēs) *Latin,* meaning 'from the books'. **1** from the library (*of*); an inscription used on a bookplate, followed by the name of the book's owner. **2** bookplate.

**ex·o·dus** (ek′sə dəs) **1** going out; departure, especially of a large number of people: *Every summer there is an exodus from the city.* **2** Often, **Exodus,** the departure of the Israelites from Egypt under Moses. *n.*

**ex of·fi·ci·o** (ek′sə fish′ē ō′) *Latin.* because of one's office: *The secretary is, ex officio, a member of all committees.*

**ex·og·en·ous** (ek soj′ə nəs) **1** having stems that grow by the addition of layers of wood on the outside under the bark. **2** originating from the outside; caused by external conditions. *adj.*

**ex·on·er·ate** (eg zon′ə rāt′) **1** free from blame; prove or declare innocent: *Witnesses of the accident completely exonerated the driver of the truck.* **2** relieve from a duty, task, obligation, etc. *v.,* **ex·on·er·at·ed, ex·on·er·at·ing.**

**ex·on·er·a·tion** (eg zon′ə rā′shən) exonerating or being EXONERATED. *n.*

**ex·or·bi·tance** (eg zôr′bə təns) being EXORBITANT. *n.*

**ex·or·bi·tant** (eg zôr′bə tənt) going beyond what is customary, right, or reasonable; very excessive: *Five dollars is an exorbitant price for a dozen eggs. adj.* —**ex·or′bi·tant·ly,** *adv.*

**ex·or·cise** (ek′sôr sīz′) **1** drive out an evil spirit by prayers, ceremonies, etc. **2** free a person or place from an evil spirit. *v.,* **ex·or·cised, ex·or·cis·ing.** —**ex′or·cis′er,** *n.* Also, **exorcize.**

**ex·or·cism** (ek′sôr siz′əm) **1** the act of exorcising. **2** the prayers, ceremonies, etc. used in exorcising. *n.*

**ex·or·cist** (ek′sôr sist) a person who EXORCISES. *n.*

**ex·or·cize** (ek′sôr sīz′) See EXORCISE. *v.,* **ex·or·cized, ex·or·ciz·ing.**

**ex·o·skel·e·ton** (ek′sō skel′ə tən) the hard, external structure that protects or supports the bodies of many invertebrates, such as oysters, lobsters, or insects. Compare with ENDOSKELETON. *n.*

**ex·ot·ic** (eg zot′ik) **1** foreign; not native: *Many exotic plants are grown in Canada as house plants.* **2** strange or unusual in a way that is fascinating or beautiful; strikingly unusual: *She had an exotic glamour.* **3** something exotic. 1, 2 *adj.,* 3 *n.* —**ex·ot′i·cal·ly,** *adv.*

**exp.** **1** export. **2** express. **3** expenses.

**ex·pand** (ek spand′) **1** increase in size; enlarge; swell: *The balloon expanded as it was filled with air. Heat expands metal.* **2** spread out; open out; unfold; extend: *As the plant grew, its leaves and flowers gradually expanded. A bird expands its wings before flying.* **3** express in greater detail; enlarge (*upon*): *She expanded on the theme in the second chapter.* **4** in mathematics, express a quantity as a sum of terms, product of terms, etc. *v.*

**ex·pan·da·ble** (ek span′də bəl) EXPANSIBLE. *adj.*

**ex·panse** (ek spans′) a large, unbroken space or stretch; a widespread area or surface: *The Pacific Ocean is a vast expanse of water. n.*

**ex·pan·si·bil·i·ty** (ek span′sə bil′ə tē) a capacity for EXPANDing. *n.*

**ex·pan·si·ble** (ek span′sə bəl) capable of being EXPANDed. *adj.*

**ex·pan·sile** (ek span′sīl *or* ek span′səl) **1** capable of EXPANSION. **2** of or having to do with EXPANSION. *adj.*

**ex·pan·sion** (ek span′shən) **1** spreading out so as to occupy more space: *Heat caused the expansion of the gas in the balloon.* **2** growing larger; swelling: *The expanding gas caused the expansion of the balloon.* **3** being expanded; increase in size, volume, etc.: *The expansion of the factory doubled the amount of goods it produced.* **4** the amount or degree of expansion. **5** in mathematics, the expression of a quantity as a sum of terms, product of terms, etc. **6** a part or thing that is the result of expanding: *The thesis is an expansion of a paper she wrote last year. n.*

**ex·pan·sive** (ek span′siv) **1** capable of expanding or tending to EXPAND. **2** wide; spreading. **3** taking in much or many things; broad; extensive. **4** showing one's feelings freely and openly; demonstrative: *He is a very*

*expansive and hospitable person.* *adj.*
—**ex·pan′sive·ly,** *adv.* —**ex·pan′sive·ness,** *n.*

**ex·pa·ti·ate** (ek spā′shē āt′) write or talk much (*on*): *She expatiated on the thrills of her trip.* *v.*, **ex·pa·ti·at·ed, ex·pa·ti·at·ing.** —**ex·pa′ti·a′tor,** *n.*

**ex·pa·ti·a·tion** (ek spā′shē ā′shən) **1** the act of writing or talking much. **2** an extended talk, description, etc. *n.*

**ex·pa·tri·ate** (ek spā′trē āt′ *for verb,* ek spā′trē it *or* ek spā′trē āt′ *for adjective and noun*) **1** banish; exile. **2** withdraw oneself from one's country; renounce one's citizenship: *Some Canadians expatriate themselves and live in Europe.* **3** expatriated: *There are many expatriate Canadians in New York.* **4** an expatriated person; exile. 1, 2 *v.*, **ex·pa·tri·at·ed, ex·pa·tri·at·ing;** 3 *adj.*, 4 *n.* —**ex′pa·tri·a′tion,** *n.*

**ex·pect** (ek spekt′) **1** look forward to; think likely to come or happen: *We expect hot days in summer.* **2** look forward to with reason or confidence; desire and feel sure of getting: *They expect to be married in April. He's expecting a bonus from his company.* **3** count on as reasonable, necessary, or right: *A soldier is expected to be properly dressed. She expected a reward for finding and returning the dog.* **4** think; suppose; guess: *I expect they'll be coming by car.* **5** look forward to the arrival of: *We'll expect you for dinner on Thursday. I expected her last night.* **6** await the birth of: *My sister is expecting her first baby.* *v.*

**ex·pect·an·cy** (ek spek′tən sē) **1** expecting or being EXPECTed. **2** what is EXPECTed, especially the expected amount based on statistical information: *a life expectancy of 67 years.* *n., pl.* **ex·pect·an·cies.**

**ex·pect·ant** (ek spek′tənt) **1** having or showing expectation: *He opened his birthday present with an expectant smile.* **2** a person who expects something. 1 *adj.*, 2 *n.* —**ex·pect′ant·ly,** *adv.*
**expectant mother,** a woman who is expecting a baby.

**ex·pec·ta·tion** (ek′spek tā′shən) **1** expecting something to come or happen; anticipation: *Contrary to expectation, he turned out to be an excellent student.* **2** something expected; the thing looked forward to. **3** Usually, **expectations,** *pl.* a reason for expecting something; a prospect, especially of advancement or prosperity: *They say she has great expectations.* *n.*

**ex·pect·ing** (ek spek′ting) **1** *Informal.* pregnant. **2** ppr. of EXPECT. 1 *adj.*, 2 *v.*

**ex·pec·to·rate** (ek spek′tə rāt′) cough up and spit out phlegm, etc.; spit. *v.*, **ex·pec·to·rat·ed, ex·pec·to·rat·ing.**

**ex·pec·to·ra·tion** (ek spek′tə rā′shən) **1** the act of expectorating. **2** the EXPECTORATEd matter. *n.*

**ex·pe·di·ence** (ek spē′dē əns) EXPEDIENCY. *n.*

**ex·pe·di·en·cy** (ek spē′dē ən sē) **1** usefulness; suitability for bringing about a desired result; desirability or fitness under the circumstances: *Consider expediency in what you say.* **2** personal advantage; self-interest: *Her offer to help was prompted by expediency, not kindness.* *n., pl.* **ex·pe·di·en·cies.**

**ex·pe·di·ent** (ek spē′dē ənt) **1** fit for bringing about a desired result; desirable or suitable under the circumstances; useful: *She decided it would be expedient to take an umbrella. It is expedient to be friendly and pleasant if you want to have friends.* **2** a means of bringing about a desired result: *Having no ladder or rope, the prisoner tied sheets together and escaped by this expedient.* **3** prompted by a concern for personal advantage; based on

---

**expatiate**     **423**     **experience**

hat, āge, fär; let, ēqual, tėrm; it, īce
hot, ōpen, ôrder; oil, out; cup, pùt, rüle
әbove, takәn, pencәl, lemәn, circәs
ch, child; ng, long; sh, ship
th, thin; ᴛH, then; zh, measure

self-interest; politic. 1, 3 *adj.*, 2 *n.* —**ex·pe′di·ent·ly,** *adv.*

**ex·pe·dite** (ek′spə dīt′) **1** make easy and quick; speed up: *If everyone will help, it will expedite matters.* **2** do quickly. *v.*, **ex·pe·dit·ed, ex·pe·dit·ing.**

**ex·pe·dit·er** (ek′spə dī′tər) a person who EXPEDITES, especially one employed to look after supplying raw materials or delivering finished products on schedule. *n.*

**ex·pe·di·tion** (ek′spə dish′ən) **1** a journey for some special purpose: *A voyage of discovery or a march against the enemy is an expedition.* **2** the group of people, ships, etc. that make such a journey: *a well-equipped expedition.* **3** efficient and prompt action; speed: *He completed his work with expedition.* *n.*

**ex·pe·di·tion·ar·y** (ek′spə dish′ə ner′ē) of, concerning, or making up an EXPEDITION (defs. 1, 2). *adj.*

**ex·pe·di·tious** (ek′spə dish′əs) quick; speedy; efficient and prompt. *adj.* —**ex′pe·di′tious·ly,** *adv.*

**ex·pel** (ek spel′) **1** force out; force to leave: *When the gunpowder exploded, the bullet was expelled from the gun.* **2** put out; dismiss permanently: *A troublesome pupil may be expelled from school.* *v.*, **ex·pelled, ex·pel·ling.**

**ex·pend** (ek spend′) spend; use up. *v.* —**ex·pend′er,** *n.*

**ex·pend·a·ble** (ek spen′də bəl) **1** normally consumed or used up in service: *Pencils, paper, stamps, etc. are expendable items.* **2** that may be sacrificed if necessary; more convenient, economical, etc. to sacrifice in certain situations than to rescue or protect: *People don't usually like to think of themselves as expendable in their jobs.* **3** Usually, **expendables,** *pl.* expendable persons or things. 1, 2 *adj.*, 3 *n.*

**ex·pend·i·ture** (ek spen′də chər *or* ek spen′də chür′) **1** spending; using up: *Such a large piece of work requires the expenditure of much money, time, and effort.* **2** the amount of money, time, energy, etc. spent or used up: *Limit your expenditures to what is necessary.* *n.*

**ex·pense** (ek spens′) **1** the cost; charge: *The expense of the trip was slight. He travelled at his uncle's expense. They had many a laugh at his expense.* **2** a cause of spending: *Running a car is an expense.* **3** an expending; the paying out of money; outlay: *Her time at university put her parents to considerable expense.* **4** loss; sacrifice. **5 expenses,** *pl.* **a** the charges incurred in running one's business or doing one's job. **b** the money to repay such charges: *Because she has to travel a lot as a consultant, she gets expenses besides her salary.* *n.*
**at the expense of,** with the loss or sacrifice of: *He achieved the prosperity he had desired, but it was at the expense of his health.*

**ex·pen·sive** (ek spen′siv) costly; high-priced: *He had a very expensive knife that cost $60.* *adj.*
—**ex·pen′sive·ly,** *adv.* —**ex·pen′sive·ness,** *n.*

**ex·pe·ri·ence** (ek spē′rē əns) **1** what has happened to one; what is or has been met with or felt; anything or everything observed, done, or lived through: *The expedition*

through the jungle was an exciting experience for her. **2** the act of living through something; observing or taking part in events: *He has learned a lot by experience.*
**3** everything gone through that makes up the life of a person, community, race, etc.: *No parallel for such wickedness can be found in human experience.* **4** skill, practical knowledge, or wisdom gained by observing, doing, or living through things: *a person of wide experience. Have you had any experience in this kind of work?* **5** have happen to one; meet with; feel; live through: *Visiting the Calgary Stampede was the greatest thrill I ever experienced.* 1–4 *n.*, 5 *v.*, **ex·pe·ri·enced, ex·pe·ri·enc·ing.**

**ex·pe·ri·enced** (ek spē′rē ənst) **1** skilful or wise because of much experience in a particular field or activity; expert; practised: *an experienced nurse, an experienced driver.* **2** pt. and pp. of EXPERIENCE. 1 *adj.*, 2 *v.*

**ex·pe·ri·en·tial** (ek spē′rē en′shəl) having to do with EXPERIENCE; based on or coming from experience. *adj.*

**ex·per·i·ment** (ek sper′ə ment *or* ek sper′ə mənt *for verb,* ek sper′ə mənt *for noun*) **1** try in order to find out; make trials or tests: *He has been experimenting with dyes to get the colour he wants.* **2** a test or trial to find out something new or to demonstrate something that is known: *a cooking experiment to test a new kind of flour. We did an experiment in school today to show how electricity produces magnetism.* **3** a conducting of such tests or trials; experimentation: *Scientists test out theories by experiment.* 1 *v.*, 2, 3 *n.* —**ex·per′i·ment′er,** *n.*

**ex·per·i·men·tal** (ek sper′ə men′təl) **1** based on EXPERIMENTS (def. 2): *Chemistry is an experimental science.* **2** used for EXPERIMENTS (def. 2): *an experimental farm.* **3** based on EXPERIENCE (def. 2), not on theory or authority. **4** for testing or trying out: *They are growing an experimental variety of wheat at the university farm.* **5** tentative: *The new drug is still in the experimental stage.* *adj.* —**ex·per′i·men′tal·ly,** *adv.*

**ex·per·i·men·ta·tion** (ek sper′ə men tā′shən) the act or process of EXPERIMENTing or making experiments: *More experimentation is needed to confirm the results.* *n.*

**ex·pert** (ek′spėrt *for noun,* ek′spėrt *or* ek spėrt′ *for adjective*) **1** a very skilful person; one who knows a great deal about some special thing. **2** very skilful; knowing a great deal about some special thing: *He is an expert chemist.* **3** from an expert; requiring or showing knowledge about some special thing: *an expert opinion.* 1 *n.*, 2, 3 *adj.* —**ex′pert·ly,** *adv.* —**ex′pert·ness,** *n.*

**ex·pi·ate** (ek′spē āt′) make amends for a wrong, etc.; atone for: *The young king tried to expiate injustices of his uncle's rule.* *v.*, **ex·pi·at·ed, ex·pi·at·ing.**

**ex·pi·a·tion** (ek′spē ā′shən) **1** making amends for a wrong, etc.; atonement: *He made a public apology in expiation of his error.* **2** amends; a means of atonement. *n.*

**ex·pi·ra·tion** (ek′spə rā′shən) **1** coming to an end: *the expiration of a lease.* **2** breathing out: *the expiration of used air from the lungs.* *n.*

**ex·pir·a·to·ry** (ek spī′rə tô′rē) having to do with breathing out air from the lungs. *adj.*

**ex·pire** (ek spīr′) **1** come to an end: *You must obtain a new automobile licence when your old one expires.* **2** die. **3** breathe out: *to expire used air from the lungs.* *v.*, **ex·pired, ex·pir·ing.**

**ex·pi·ry** (ek spī′rē) EXPIRATION (def. 1). *n., pl.* **ex·pi·ries.**

**ex·plain** (ek splān′) **1** make clear or understandable; tell what something means or how something is done, organized, formed, used, etc.: *The teacher explained how a generator works. Can you explain what refraction is? I explained the paragraph to her.* **2** tell the significance of; interpret: *to explain a dream. Nobody could explain his strange behaviour.* **3** give an acceptable reason for; excuse or justify: *She couldn't explain her absence.* **4** give an explanation: *Wait! Let me explain!* *v.* —**ex·plain′a·ble,** *adj.*

**explain away,** get rid of or make insignificant by giving reasons or as if by giving reasons: *to explain away someone's fears. There is a lot of evidence against her that cannot be explained away.*

**explain oneself, a** make one's meaning clear: *I guess I didn't explain myself very well because nobody understood.* **b** justify or give reasons for one's conduct: *Why did you go off and leave your little sister alone? Explain yourself.*

**ex·pla·na·tion** (ek′splə nā′shən) **1** the act or process of explaining: *Her explanation of electricity was easy to follow. Their attitude toward the new members requires explanation.* **2** something that explains: *That book was a good explanation of the principle of atomic fission. What's your explanation for your absence?* *n.*

**ex·plan·a·to·ry** (ek splan′ə tô′rē) explaining; serving or helping to explain or make clear: *Read the explanatory part of the lesson before you try to do the problems.* *adj.*

**ex·ple·tive** (ek′splə tiv *or* ek splē′tiv) **1** an oath or exclamation as an expression of surprise, anger, annoyance, etc.: *The expressions* Damn! *and* My goodness! *are expletives.* **2** a syllable, word, or phrase added to fill out a line of verse, etc. without adding anything to the sense. **3** in grammar, a word used in a sentence to take the normal place of the subject or object, which is identified later. *There* and *it* in the following sentences are expletives: *There is a book on the table. It is too bad that the book has no pictures. They thought it terrible that the book should cost so much.* *n.*

**ex·pli·ca·ble** (ek splik′ə bəl *or* ek′splə kə bəl) capable of being EXPLAINed. *adj.*

**ex·pli·cate** (ek′splə kāt′) **1** develop the meaning or implication of a principle, doctrine, etc.; analyse logically. **2** EXPLAIN. *v.*, **ex·pli·cat·ed, ex·pli·cat·ing.**

**ex·pli·ca·tion** (ek′splə kā′shən) EXPLANATION. *n.*

**ex·plic·it** (ek splis′it) **1** clearly expressed; distinctly stated; definite and unambiguous: *an explicit statement of intentions. He gave such explicit directions that everyone understood them.* Compare with IMPLICIT. **2** clear and unreserved in expression; frank; outspoken: *The description of the accident victim's injuries was so explicit that it shocked some people.* *adj.* —**ex·plic′it·ly,** *adv.* —**ex·plic′it·ness,** *n.*

**ex·plode** (ek splōd′) **1** burst violently and noisily because of pressure from within; blow up: *The building was destroyed when the defective boiler exploded.* **2** undergo an uncontrolled chemical or nuclear reaction that produces a violent expansion of gases, along with noise, heat, light, etc.: *The bomb exploded.* **3** cause to explode; set off: *to explode dynamite.* **4** react suddenly with noise or violence: *The speaker's mistake was so funny the audience exploded with laughter.* **5** cause to be rejected; destroy belief in: *to explode a rumour. Columbus helped to explode the theory that the earth is flat.* **6** increase rapidly in an uncontrolled way: *an exploding population.* *v.*, **ex·plod·ed, ex·plod·ing.** —**ex·plod′er,** *n.*

**ex·ploit** (ek′sploit *for noun*, ek sploit′ *for verb*)   **1** a bold, unusual act; daring deed: *Old stories tell about the exploits of famous heroes.*   **2** make use of; turn to practical account: *A mine is exploited for its minerals.*   **3** make unfair or selfish use of: *Nations sometimes exploit their colonies, taking as much wealth out of them as they can.*   **1** *n.*, **2, 3** *v.*   —**ex·ploit′a·ble,** *adj.*   —**ex·ploit′er,** *n.*

**ex·ploi·ta·tion** (ek′sploi tā′shən)   **1** use.   **2** selfish or unfair use.   *n.*

**ex·plo·ra·tion** (ek′splə rā′shən)   the act or circumstance of exploring: *exploration for oil, the exploration of new territory.*   *n.*

**ex·plor·a·tive** (ek splô′rə tiv)   **1** EXPLORATORY.   **2** inclined to make EXPLORATIONS.   *adj.*

**ex·plor·a·to·ry** (ek splô′rə tô′rē)   of, having to do with, or related to EXPLORATION: *exploratory surgery, exploratory travels.*   *adj.*

**ex·plore** (ek splôr′)   **1** go or travel over land or water for the purpose of finding out about geographical features, natural resources, etc.: *Champlain explored the Ottawa River and Georgian Bay. We spent all afternoon exploring the bush behind the house. Let's go exploring.*   **2** go or search through a place, etc., in order to find out about it: *to explore one's surroundings. They explored the abandoned house.*   **3** look into closely and carefully; investigate: *We will have to explore all the possibilities before deciding on a course of action.*   **4** examine carefully, especially by touch: *She explored the wall with her fingers, searching for the light switch. The doctor explored the wound.*   *v.*, **ex·plored, ex·plor·ing.**

**ex·plor·er** (ek splô′rər)   a person who explores, especially in unknown regions.   *n.*

**ex·plo·sion** (ek splō′zhən)   **1** blowing up; bursting with a loud noise: *the explosion of a bomb.*   **2** a loud noise caused by something blowing up: *People 15 kilometres away heard the explosion.*   **3** a noisy bursting forth; outbreak: *an explosion of laughter.*   *n.*

**ex·plo·sive** (ek splō′siv)   **1** capable of exploding; likely to EXPLODE (defs. 1, 2): *Gunpowder is explosive.*   **2** a substance that is capable of exploding: *Explosives are used in making fireworks.*   **3** tending to burst forth noisily: *The irritable old woman had an explosive temper.*   **1, 3** *adj.*, **2** *n.*   —**ex·plo′sive·ly,** *adv.*   —**ex·plo′sive·ness,** *n.*

**ex·po·nent** (ek spō′nənt)   **1** a person or thing that explains, interprets, etc.   **2** a person or thing that favours or speaks for (*used with* **of**): *She is an exponent of the guaranteed annual wage.*   **3** a person or thing that stands as an example, type, or symbol of something: *This man is a famous exponent of self-education.*   **4** in mathematics, an index or small number written above and to the right of an algebraic symbol or quantity to show how many times the symbol or quantity is to be used as a factor. Examples: $2^2 = 2 \times 2$; $a^3 = a \times a \times a$.   *n.*

**ex·po·nen·tial** (ek′spō nen′shəl)   having to do with algebraic EXPONENTS (def. 4); involving unknown or variable quantities as exponents.   *adj.*   —**ex′po·nen′tial·ly,** *adv.*

**ex·port** (ek spôrt′ *or* ek′spôrt *for verb*, ek′spôrt *for noun*)   **1** send articles or goods out of one country for sale and use in another: *Canada exports millions of tonnes of wheat each year.*   **2** the act of selling or shipping articles or goods to another country.   **3** the goods or articles so sold and shipped: *Clothing is an important export of Quebec.*   **4** of a kind or quality suitable for export: *export liquors. Export quality is usually higher than the regular domestic quality.*   **5** of or having to do with exports or exporting: *export duty.*   **1** *v.*, **2–5** *n.*

hat, āge, fär; let, ēqual, tėrm; it, īce
hot, ōpen, ôrder; oil, out; cup, půt, rüle
əbove, takən, pencəl, lemən, circəs
ch, child; ng, long; sh, ship
th, thin; ᴛH, then; zh, measure

**ex·por·ta·tion** (ek′spôr tā′shən)   the act or process of EXPORTing.   *n.*

**ex·port·er** (ek spôr′tər *or* ek′spôr tər)   a person or company whose business is EXPORTING goods.   *n.*

**ex·pose** (ek spōz′)   **1** lay open; leave unprotected; uncover: *The deer in the open field were exposed to the hunters' gunfire. His foolish actions exposed him to ridicule.*   **2** lay open to view, especially something that was hidden; display or make visible: *to expose a card in a card game. They stripped off the paint around the fireplace, exposing the original tile surface.*   **3** make known; show up; reveal: *to expose a murderer. The investigators exposed the takeover plot.*   **4** in photography, allow light to reach and act on a sensitive film, plate, or paper.   **5** put out without shelter; abandon: *The ancient Spartans used to expose babies that they did not want.*   *v.*, **ex·posed, ex·pos·ing.**   —**ex·pos′er,** *n.*

**ex·po·sé** (ek′spō zā′)   a showing up of crime, dishonesty, fraud, etc.   *n.*

**ex·posed** (ek spōzd′)   **1** uncovered or unprotected: *These flowers should not be planted in an exposed location.*   **2** open to view; not concealed: *an exposed card.*   **3** pt. and pp. of EXPOSE.   **1, 2** *adj.*, **3** *v.*

**ex·po·si·tion** (ek′spə zish′ən)   **1** a public show or exhibition: *The Canadian National Exhibition is an exposition.*   **2** a detailed explanation: *the exposition of a scientific theory.*   **3** a speech or writing explaining a process or idea.   *n.*

**ex·pos·i·tor** (ek spoz′ə tər)   a person who explains or EXPOUNDS; interpreter or commentator.   *n.*

**ex·pos·i·to·ry** (ek spoz′ə tô′rē)   of, having to do with, or including EXPOSITION (def. 3): *expository writing.*   *adj.*

**ex post fac·to** (ek′ pōst′ fak′tō)   made or done after something, but applying to it. An **ex post facto** law applies to actions done before the law was passed.

**ex·pos·tu·late** (ek spos′chə lāt′)   reason earnestly with a person, protesting against something he or she means to do or has done; remonstrate (*with*): *They expostulated with their daughter about the foolishness of leaving school.*   *v.*, **ex·pos·tu·lat·ed, ex·pos·tu·lat·ing.**   —**ex·pos′tu·la′tor,** *n.*

**ex·pos·tu·la·tion** (ek spos′chə lā′shən)   an earnest protest; remonstrance: *The manager's expostulations failed, and he resorted to threats.*   *n.*

**ex·pos·tu·la·to·ry** (ek spos′chə lə tô′rē)   of or characteristic of EXPOSTULATION.   *adj.*

**ex·po·sure** (ek spō′zhər)   **1** the act or instance of exposing: *The exposure of the real criminal cleared the innocent man. Anyone would dread public exposure of all his or her faults.*   **2** the condition or an instance of being EXPOSED (def. 1): *Years of exposure to the rain had ruined the machinery.*   **3** appearance in public, as on television, etc.: *His campaign manager thought he needed more television exposure.*   **4** a position in relation to the sun and the wind: *A house with a southern exposure is open to*

sun and wind from the south. **5** the time during which light reaches and acts on a photographic film or plate: *A longer exposure is needed to take a photograph in shade than in sunlight.* **6** the part of a photographic film for one picture. *n.*
**die of exposure,** die from HYPOTHERMIA due to lack of shelter or adequate clothing.

**exposure meter** a device for measuring the intensity of light, used to indicate the correct EXPOSURE (def. 5) needed for taking a photograph under particular light conditions: *Some cameras have a built-in exposure meter.*

**ex·pound** (ek spound′) **1** make clear; explain or interpret: *The teacher expounds each new principle in arithmetic to the class.* **2** set forth or state in detail. *v.*

**ex·press** (ek spres′) **1** put into words: *Express your ideas clearly.* **2** show by look, voice, or action; reveal: *A smile expresses joy.* **3** show by a sign, figure, etc.; indicate: *The sign × expresses multiplication.* **4** clear; plain; definite: *It was his express wish that we should go without him.* **5** special; for a particular purpose: *She came for the express purpose of seeing you.* **6** exact: *Sheina is the express image of her mother.* **7** a special messenger or message sent for a particular purpose. **8** a quick or direct means of sending things: *Packages and money can be sent by express in trains or airplanes.* **9** a system or company for sending parcels, money, etc.: *Canadian National Express.* **10** having to do with express: *An express agency or company is in the express business.* **11** things sent by express. **12** send by express. **13** by express; directly. **14** travelling fast and making few stops: *an express train.* **15** a train, bus, elevator, etc. making few stops. **16** for fast travelling: *an express highway.* **17** press out; squeeze out: *The juice is expressed from grapes to make wine.* 1–3, 12, 17 *v.*, 4–6 *adj.*, 7–11, 14–16 *n.*, 13 *adv.*
**express oneself,** **a** say what one thinks: *A good speaker expresses herself clearly.* **b** show one's feelings: *The children are only expressing themselves.*

**ex·press·i·ble** (ek spres′ə bəl) capable of being EXPRESSED (def. 1). *adj.*

**ex·pres·sion** (ek spresh′ən) **1** putting into words: *Her clear expression of the plan made it easier for us to understand.* **2** a word or group of words used as a unit: *"Wise guy" is a slang expression.* **3** showing by look, voice, or action: *Her sigh was an expression of sadness.* **4** an indication of feeling, spirit, character, etc.; look that shows feeling: *A grin is a happy expression.* **5** the bringing out of the meaning or beauty of something read, spoken, played, sung, etc.: *Try to read with more expression.* **6** showing by sign, figure, etc.: *In mathematics, the sign = is the expression of equality.* **7** pressing out: *the expression of oil from plants.* *n.*

**ex·pres·sion·ism** (ek spresh′ə niz′əm) **1** a movement in art and literature in the late 19th and early 20th centuries, marked by the attempt to express the artist's subjective feelings without regard to accepted forms or tradition. It began as a revolt against naturalism and impressionism. **2** a similar movement in music. *n.*

**ex·pres·sion·less** (ek spresh′ən lis) without EXPRESSION (def. 4): *an expressionless face, an expressionless voice.* *adj.*

**ex·pres·sive** (ek spres′iv) **1** serving as a sign or indication; representing (*used with* **of**): *Alas is a word expressive of sadness.* **2** full of EXPRESSION (def. 5); having or showing much feeling, meaning, etc.: *an expressive pause. He has a very expressive face.* **3** of or having to do with EXPRESSION (def. 1): *She is a writer of great expressive power.* *adj.* —**ex·pres′sive·ly,** *adv.* —**ex·pres′sive·ness,** *n.*

**ex·press·ly** (ek spres′lē) **1** clearly; plainly; definitely: *You were expressly forbidden to touch it.* **2** specially; for the particular purpose: *She came expressly to see you.* *adv.*

**ex·press·way** (ek spres′wā) a divided highway for fast driving; a highway that stretches for long distances with few intersections: *Most interchanges on expressways are built on two levels so that vehicles do not have to cross in front of each other on the highway.* *n.*

**ex·pro·pri·ate** (ek sprō′prē āt′) **1** take property away from an owner, especially for public use: *The provincial government expropriated 50 000 square metres of land for a public housing development.* **2** put a person out of possession; dispossess. *v.*, **ex·pro·pri·at·ed,** **ex·pro·pri·at·ing.** —**ex·pro′pri·a′tion,** *n.*

**ex·pul·sion** (ek spul′shən) an expelling or being expelled: *expulsion of air from the lungs. The threat of expulsion from school did not help.* *n.*

**ex·pul·sive** (ek spul′siv) expelling or having the power to expel: *the expulsive power of steam under pressure.* *adj.*

**ex·punge** (ek spunj′) remove completely; blot out; erase: *The secretary was directed to expunge certain items from the record.* *v.*, **ex·punged, ex·pung·ing.**

**ex·pur·gate** (ek′spər gāt′) remove objectionable passages or words from a book, letter, etc. *v.*, **ex·pur·gat·ed, ex·pur·gat·ing.** —**ex′pur·ga′tor,** *n.*

**ex·pur·ga·tion** (ek′spər gā′shən) the removing or removal from a book, etc. of something that seems objectionable. *n.*

**ex·qui·site** (ek′skwi zit *or* ek skwiz′it) **1** very lovely in a delicate way: *exquisite lace. Violets are exquisite flowers.* **2** of highest excellence; most admirable: *an exquisite painting technique, exquisite taste.* **3** keenly sensitive: *an exquisite ear for music.* **4** sharp; intense: *exquisite pain, exquisite joy.* *adj.* —**ex′qui·site·ly,** *adv.* —**ex′qui·site·ness,** *n.*

**ex·tant** (ek′stənt *or* ek stant′) still in existence; currently existing: *Some of Sir John A. Macdonald's letters are extant.* *adj.*

**ex·tem·po·ra·ne·ous** (ek stem′pə rā′nē əs) **1** spoken or done without preparation; impromptu: *an extemporaneous speech.* **2** made for the occasion; makeshift: *an extemporaneous shelter against a storm.* *adj.* —**ex·tem′po·ra′ne·ous·ly,** *adv.* —**ex·tem′po·ra′ne·ous·ness,** *n.*

**ex·tem·po·re** (ek stem′pə rē) **1** on the spur of the moment; without preparation; offhand or impromptu: *an extempore speech.* **2** in an impromptu manner: *Each pupil will be called on to speak extempore.* 1 *adj.*, 2 *adv.*

**ex·tem·po·rize** (ek stem′pə rīz′) **1** speak, play, sing, or dance, composing as one proceeds: *The pianist was extemporizing.* **2** compose offhand; make for the occasion: *The campers extemporized a shelter for the night.* *v.*, **ex·tem·po·rized, ex·tem·po·riz·ing.** —**ex·tem′po·ri·za′tion,** *n.*

**ex·tend** (ek stend′) **1** stretch out: *Extend your hand.* **2** be continued in time, space, or direction: *The beach extended for more than a kilometre in each direction.* **3** straighten out: *Extend your arms in front of you.* **4** lengthen: *to extend a deadline. They have extended the ski* trail another three kilometres. **5** enlarge or broaden: *to extend a gym, to extend one's knowledge.* **6** give; grant: *to extend help to someone in need, to extend credit.* *v.*

**ex·tend·ed** (ek sten′did) **1** extensive; widespread: *the extended family.* **2** stretched out; prolonged. **3** widened. **4** spread out; outstretched. **5** pt. and pp. of EXTEND. 1–4 *adj.*, 5 *v.*

**ex·tend·i·ble** (ek sten′də bəl) EXTENSIBLE. *adj.* —**ex·tend′i·bil′i·ty**, *n.*

**ex·ten·si·bil·i·ty** (ek sten′sə bil′ə tē) the quality of being EXTENSIBLE. *n.*

**ex·ten·si·ble** (ek sten′sə bəl) capable of being protruded, stretched, or opened out: *an extensible tongue.* *adj.*

**ex·ten·sile** (ek sten′sīl *or* ek sten′səl) capable of being EXTENDED (defs. 1, 2). *adj.*

**ex·ten·sion** (ek sten′shən) **1** EXTENDING (def. 1) or being extended: *The extension of one's right hand is a sign of friendship.* **2** an EXTENDED (def. 2) part; addition: *The new extension to the school will have several classrooms and a gym.* **3** an extra telephone connected to a line: *He heard it all because he was listening in on the extension.* **4** an increase in time, especially in the time allowed for something: *I got an extension on my essay deadline because I had been sick.* **5** an education program provided by a university for people who cannot take regular courses: *People who have full-time jobs can upgrade their education by taking evening classes through extension.* **6** of, in, or referring to such a program: *She's taking an extension course.* *n.*

**extension cord** an electrical cord having a plug at one end and a socket at the other, used to lengthen the cord attached to an electrical appliance: *With an extension cord, an appliance may be moved a greater distance from an outlet.*

**ex·ten·sive** (ek sten′siv) **1** of great extent; wide; broad; large: *an extensive park. She has extensive knowledge in several branches of science.* **2** far-reaching; affecting many things; comprehensive: *extensive changes.* **3** depending on the use of large areas: *extensive agriculture.* *adj.* —**ex·ten′sive·ly**, *adv.* —**ex·ten′sive·ness**, *n.*

**ex·ten·sor** (ek sten′sər) a muscle that extends or straightens out a limb or other part of the body. Compare with CONTRACTOR (def. 2). *n.*

**ex·tent** (ek stent′) **1** the size, space, length, amount, or degree to which a thing extends: *Railways carry people and goods through the whole extent of the country. The extent of a judge's power is limited by law.* **2** something extended; an extended space: *a vast extent of prairie.* *n.*

**ex·ten·u·ate** (ek sten′yü āt′) make guilt, a fault, an offence, etc. seem less; excuse in part: *Ignorance does not extenuate your offence.* *v.*, **ex·ten·u·at·ed, ex·ten·u·at·ing.**

**ex·ten·u·a·tion** (ek sten′yü ā′shən) **1** extenuating: *The lawyer pleaded her client's youth in extenuation of the crime.* **2** something that lessens the seriousness of guilt, a fault, an offence, etc.; partial excuse. *n.*

**ex·te·ri·or** (ek stē′rē ər) **1** an outer surface or part; the outward appearance; outside: *The exterior of the house was of brick. The gruff old man has a harsh exterior but a kind heart.* **2** on the outside; outer: *The skin of an apple is its exterior covering.* **3** coming from without; happening outside: *exterior influences.* 1 *n.*, 2, 3 *adj.*

**exterior angle** **1** any of the four angles formed on the outer sides of two parallel lines by a straight line cutting through the parallel lines. **2** the angle formed on the outside of a polygon between one of its sides and an extension of a side next to it. Compare with INTERIOR ANGLE.

**ex·ter·mi·nate** (ek stėr′mə nāt′) destroy completely: *This poison will exterminate rats.* *v.*, **ex·ter·mi·nat·ed, ex·ter·mi·nat·ing.**

**ex·ter·mi·na·tion** (ek stėr′mə nā′shən) complete destruction: *This poison is useful for the extermination of rats.* *n.*

**ex·ter·mi·na·tor** (ek stėr′mə nā′tər) a person or thing that EXTERMINATES, especially a person whose business is exterminating cockroaches, bedbugs, rats, etc. *n.*

**ex·ter·nal** (ek stėr′nəl) **1** on the outside; outer: *the external wall of a house.* **2** an outer surface or part; outside. **3** to be used on the outside of the body: *Liniment and rubbing alcohol are external remedies.* **4** entirely outside; coming from without: *external air. External influences affect our lives.* **5** having existence outside one's mind: *external reality.* **6** for outward appearance; superficial: *His politeness is only external.* **7** not essential or basic: *His decision was influenced too much by external factors.* **8** having to do with international affairs; foreign: *a nation's external trade.* **9 externals,** *pl.* clothing, manners, outward acts, or appearances: *He judges people by such externals as clothing and length of hair.* 1, 3–8 *adj.*, 2, 9 *n.* —**ex·ter′nal·ly**, *adv.*

**ex·tinct** (ek stingkt′) **1** no longer in existence: *The dinosaur is an extinct animal.* **2** no longer active; extinguished: *an extinct volcano.* *adj.*

**ex·tinc·tion** (ek stingk′shən) **1** extinguishing or being extinguished: *The sudden extinction of the lights left the room in darkness.* **2** being or becoming EXTINCT: *The caribou was once threatened with extinction.* **3** a suppression; a doing away with completely; wiping out; destruction: *The RCMP brought about the extinction of the spy ring.* *n.*

**ex·tin·guish** (ek sting′gwish) **1** put out; quench: *Water extinguished the fire.* **2** put an end to; do away with; wipe out; destroy: *One failure after another extinguished her hope.* **3** eclipse or obscure by superior brilliance: *Her dress extinguished all others at the ball.* *v.* —**ex·tin′guish·a·ble,** *adj.* —**ex·tin′guish·ment,** *n.*

**ex·tin·guish·er** (eks ting′gwi shər) **1** a person or thing that extinguishes. **2** a device for quenching fires. *n.*

**ex·tir·pate** (ek′stər pāt′ *or* ek stėr′pāt) **1** remove or destroy completely; abolish or exterminate: *to extirpate a prejudice.* **2** tear up by the roots. *v.*, **ex·tir·pat·ed, ex·tir·pat·ing.**

**ex·tir·pa·tion** (ek′stər pā′shən) **1** complete removal or destruction. **2** a tearing up by the roots. *n.*

**ex·tol** *or* **ex·toll** (ek stōl′) praise highly; commend: *The article extolled the virtues of the simple life.* *v.*, **ex·tolled, ex·tol·ling.** —**ex·tol′ler,** *n.*

**ex·tort** (ek stôrt′) obtain money, a promise, etc. by

---

hat, āge, fär; let, ēqual, tėrm; it, īce
hot, ōpen, ôrder; oil, out; cup, pùt, rüle
əbove, takən, pencəl, lemən, circəs

ch, child; ng, long; sh, ship
th, thin; ᴛʜ, then; zh, measure

threats, force, fraud, or illegal use of authority: *Blackmailers try to extort money from their victims.* *v.* —**ex·tort′er**, *n.*

**ex·tor·tion** (ek stôr′shən) **1** the act or practice of obtaining money, a promise, etc. by threats, force, fraud, or illegal use of authority: *Very high interest on loans is considered extortion and is forbidden by law.* **2** the money, promise, etc. obtained in this way. *n.*

**ex·tor·tion·ate** (ek stôr′shə nit) **1** characterized by EXTORTION (def. 1): *extortionate demands.* **2** much too great; exorbitant: *an extortionate price.* *adj.* —**ex·tor′tion·ate·ly**, *adv.*

**ex·tor·tion·er** (ek stôr′shə nər) a person who is guilty of EXTORTION (def. 1). *n.*

**ex·tor·tion·ist** (ek stôr′shə nist) EXTORTIONER. *n.*

**ex·tra** (ek′strə) **1** more, greater, or better than what is usual, expected, or needed: *extra pay, an extra workload. Do you have an extra pencil?* **2** something for which an additional charge is made: *The rear window defroster is an extra. Her bill for extras was $30.* **3** something in addition to what is usual, expected, or needed: *As an added extra, we'll give you a free film with this camera.* **4** a special edition of a newspaper: *Every paper in town came out with extras when the news of the budget came through.* **5** an extra worker, especially a person hired by the day to act in crowd scenes, etc. in a motion picture. **6** more than usually: *The quality is extra fine. They like their coffee extra strong.* 1 *adj.*, 2–5 *n.*, 6 *adv.*

**extra–** a prefix meaning: beyond; outside: *Extraordinary* means beyond the ordinary.

**ex·tract** (ek strakt′ *for verb*, ek′strakt *for noun*) **1** pull out or draw out, usually with some effort: *to extract a tooth.* **2** obtain by pressing, distilling, etc., or by a chemical process: *to extract oil from olives.* **3** draw out or obtain against a person's will: *to extract payment, to extract a confession.* **4** deduce: *to extract a principle from a collection of facts.* **5** derive: *to extract pleasure from a situation.* **6** take out; select a passage from a book, speech, etc. **7** something drawn out or taken out; passage taken from a book, speech, etc.: *Magazines often publish extracts from new novels.* **8** a concentrated preparation of a substance: *Vanilla extract, made from vanilla beans, is used as flavouring.* **9** in mathematics, calculate or find the root of a number. 1–6, 9 *v.*, 7, 8 *n.* —**ex·trac′tor**, *n.*

**ex·trac·tion** (ek strak′shən) **1** EXTRACTing (def. 1) or being extracted: *the extraction of a tooth.* **2** descent; origin: *Ms. Del Rio is of Spanish extraction.* *n.*

**ex·trac·tive** (ek strak′tiv) EXTRACTing. *adj.*

**ex·tra–cur·ric·u·lar** (ek′strə kə rik′yə lər) outside the regular course of study: *His extra-curricular activities are football and debating.* *adj.*

**ex·tra·dite** (ek′strə dīt′) **1** give up or deliver a fugitive or prisoner to another nation or legal authority for trial or punishment: *If an escaped prisoner from Canada is caught in the United States, he or she can be extradited from the United States to Canada.* **2** obtain the EXTRADITION of such a person. *v.*, **ex·tra·dit·ed, ex·tra·dit·ing**.

**ex·tra·di·tion** (ek′strə dish′ən) the surrender of a fugitive or prisoner by one state, nation, or legal authority to another for trial or punishment. *n.*

**ex·tra–le·gal** (ek′strə lē′gəl) beyond the control or influence of law. *adj.*

**ex·tra·mu·ral** (eks′trə myü′rəl) **1** occurring or done outside the boundaries of a school or college: *extramural activities.* **2** between schools or colleges: *extramural hockey.* *adj.*

**ex·tra·ne·ous** (ek strā′nē əs) **1** coming from outside; foreign: *Sand or some other extraneous matter had got into the butter.* **2** not essential to what is under consideration; irrelevant: *In her talk on conservation, she made several interesting but extraneous remarks about wildlife photography.* *adj.*

**ex·traor·di·nar·i·ly** (ek strôr′də ner′ə lē) in an EXTRAORDINARY manner or to an extraordinary degree; most unusually. *adv.*

**ex·traor·di·nar·y** (ek strôr′də ner′ē *or* ek strə ôr′də ner′ē) **1** far beyond what is ordinary; most unusual; very remarkable: *Two and a half metres is an extraordinary height for a person. He is an extraordinary child.* **2** outside of or additional to the regular class of officials; special. An **envoy extraordinary** is an envoy sent on a special mission; he or she ranks below an ambassador. *adj.*

**ex·tra·sen·so·ry** (ek′strə sen′sə rē) beyond the normal scope or range of the senses: *Mental telepathy is one kind of extrasensory perception.* *adj.*

**extrasensory perception** the perceiving of thoughts, actions, etc. in other than a normal fashion; mental telepathy.

**ex·tra·ter·res·tri·al** (ek′strə tə res′trē əl) **1** coming from or existing beyond the limits of the earth's atmosphere: *extra-terrestrial life.* **2** a supposed creature from another planet. 1 *adj.*, 2 *n.*

**ex·tra·ter·ri·to·ri·al** (ek′strə ter′ə tô′rē əl) outside the laws of the country that a person is living in: *Any ambassador to a foreign country has certain extra-territorial privileges.* *adj.*

**ex·trav·a·gance** (ek strav′ə gəns) **1** careless and lavish spending; wastefulness: *His extravagance kept him always in debt.* **2** going beyond the bounds of reason; excess: *The extravagance of the sales representative's claims caused us to doubt the worth of the product.* **3** an EXTRAVAGANT action, idea, purchase, etc. *n.*

**ex·trav·a·gant** (ek strav′ə gənt) **1** spending carelessly and lavishly; wasteful: *An extravagant person usually has extravagant tastes and habits.* **2** beyond the bounds of reason; excessive: *People laughed at the inventor's extravagant praise of her invention. He refused to buy the ring because of the extravagant price.* **3** costing more than is fit and proper: *They spent a whole day's pay on an extravagant dinner.* *adj.* —**ex·trav′a·gant·ly**, *adv.*

**ex·trav·a·gan·za** (ek strav′ə gan′zə) a lavish or spectacular play, piece of music, literary composition, etc.: *Musical comedies having elaborate scenery, gorgeous costumes, etc. are extravaganzas.* *n.*

**ex·treme** (ek strēm′) **1** much more than usual; very great; very strong: *extreme love for one's country, extreme poverty.* **2** very severe or harsh: *The government took extreme measures to crush the revolt.* **3** farthest from the centre; outermost: *the extreme outlying districts of the city.* **4** farthest from the centre in political opinion, etc.; in favour of strong measures; not moderate: *She's a member of the extreme right.* **5** far from the usual or ordinary: *an extreme mode of dress.* **6** something extreme; one of two things as far or as different as possible from each other: *Love and hate are two extremes of feeling.* **7** an extreme

degree: *Joy is happiness in the extreme.* **8** in mathematics, the first or last term in a proportion or series: *In the proportion, 2 is to 4 as 8 is to 16, 2 and 16 are the extremes; 4 and 8 are the means.* **1–5** *adj.*, **ex·trem·er, ex·trem·est;** **6–8** *n.* —**ex·treme′ness,** *n.*
**go to extremes,** do or say too much; resort to extreme measures.

**ex·treme·ly** (ek strēm′lē) much more than usual; very. *adv.*

**extremely high frequency** the highest range of frequencies in the radio spectrum, between 30 and 300 gigahertz: *Extremely high frequency is the range next above superhigh frequency.*

**extremely low frequency** the lowest range of frequencies in the radio spectrum, between 30 and 300 hertz.

**ex·trem·ist** (ek strē′mist) **1** a person who goes to extremes, especially one who takes an EXTREME (def. 4) view or position in politics; a radical. **2** having or showing EXTREME (def. 4) views or ideas; radical: *an extremist position. He is too extremist ever to get elected in this riding.* **1** *n.*, **2** *adj.*

**ex·trem·i·ty** (ek strem′ə tē) **1** the very end; farthest possible place; last part or point. **2** an EXTREME (def. 1) need, danger, suffering, etc.: *In their extremity, the people on the sinking ship bore themselves bravely.* **3** the highest degree; the ultimate: *Joy is the extremity of happiness.* **4** an EXTREME (def. 2) action: *The soldiers were forced to the extremity of firing their rifles to scatter the angry mob.* **5 the extremities,** *pl.* the hands and feet. *n., pl.* **ex·trem·i·ties.**

**ex·tri·ca·ble** (ek′strə kə bəl) capable of being extricated. *adj.*

**ex·tri·cate** (ek′strə kāt′) set free from entanglements, difficulties, embarrassing situations, etc.; release: *Tom extricated his younger brother from the barbed-wire fence.* *v.*, **ex·tri·cat·ed, ex·tri·cat·ing.** —**ex′tri·ca′tion,** *n.*

**ex·trin·sic** (ek strin′sik) **1** not essential or inherent; caused by external circumstances. **2** being, coming, or acting from outside of a thing: *extrinsic aid, an extrinsic stimulus.* *adj.* Compare with INTRINSIC.

**ex·trin·si·cal·ly** (ek strin′si klē) in an EXTRINSIC manner; from without; externally. *adv.* Compare with INTRINSICALLY.

**ex·tro·ver·sion** (ek′strə vėr′zhən) the tendency to be more interested in other persons and in what is going on around one than in one's own thoughts and feelings. Compare with INTROVERSION. *n.*

**ex·tro·vert** (ek′strə vėrt′) a person more interested in other persons and in what is going on around him or her than in his or her own thoughts and feelings; a person who is active and expressive rather than thoughtful. Compare with INTROVERT. *n.*

**ex·trude** (ek strüd′) **1** thrust out; push out. **2** stick out; protrude. *v.*, **ex·trud·ed, ex·trud·ing.**

**ex·tru·sion** (ek strü′zhən) extruding or being extruded. *n.*

**ex·tru·sive** (ek strü′siv) **1** tending to EXTRUDE. **2** of a rock, formed on the surface of the earth. *adj.*

**ex·u·ber·ance** (eg zü′bə rəns) **1** the quality or state of being EXUBERANT: *an exuberance of shrubbery.* **2** an EXUBERANT (defs. 1, 2) action or expression. *n.*

**ex·u·ber·ant** (eg zü′bə rənt) **1** having or showing high spirits and unrestrained joy: *She gave us an exuberant*

---

# extremely 429 eye

hat, āge, fär; let, ēqual, tėrm; it, īce
hot, ōpen, ôrder; oil, out; cup, pu̇t, rüle
əbove, tākən, pencəl, lemən, circəs
ch, child; ng, long; sh, ship
th, thin; ᵺ, then; zh, measure

*welcome.* **2** too elaborate or lavish: *an exuberant use of metaphors.* **3** very abundant; overflowing: *exuberant good health.* **4** profuse in growth; luxuriant: *the exuberant vegetation of the jungle.* *adj.* —**ex·u′ber·ant·ly,** *adv.*

**ex·u·da·tion** (ek′syə dā′shən) **1** an exuding. **2** something exuded, such as sweat. *n.*

**ex·ude** (ek syüd′ *or* eg züd′) **1** come or send out in drops; ooze: *Sweat exudes from the pores in the skin.* **2** show conspicuously or abundantly: *She exudes self-confidence.* *v.*, **ex·ud·ed, ex·ud·ing.**

**ex·ult** (eg zult′) be very glad; rejoice greatly: *The winners exulted in their victory.* *v.* —**ex·ult′ing·ly,** *adv.*

**ex·ult·ant** (eg zul′tənt) rejoicing greatly; exulting; triumphant: *He gave an exultant shout.* *adj.* —**ex·ult′ant·ly,** *adv.*

**ex·ul·ta·tion** (eg′zul tā′shən *or* ek′sul tā′shən) the act of exulting; great rejoicing; triumph: *There was exultation over the team's victory.* *n.*

**–ey** an adjective-forming suffix meaning: full of, containing, or like: *A clayey substance would be something that contains clay or is sticky like clay.*

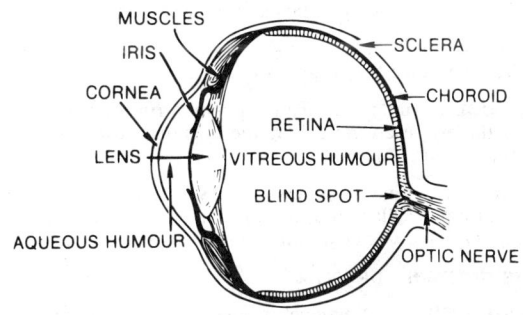

A diagram of the human eye, shown from the side

**eye** (ī) **1** either of the two organs of the body by which people and animals see; organ of sight. **2** the coloured part of this organ; iris: *He has brown eyes.* **3** this organ and all the visible structures on and around it, including the eyelids, eyelashes, etc.: *The blow gave him a black eye.* **4** any organ that is sensitive to light. **5** the ability to see small difference in things: *A good artist must have an eye for colour.* **6** a look or glance: *He cast an eye in her direction.* **7** a watchful look. **8** fix the gaze on; look at: *He sat there, curiously eyeing everything in the room.* **9** look at watchfully or sharply: *The dog eyed the stranger.* **10** something like or suggesting an eye: *the eye of a needle, the eye of a potato.* **11** the calm, clear area at the centre of a hurricane, cyclone, etc. **12** Often, **eyes,** *pl.* the sense of seeing; vision; sight: *She has very good eyes.* **13** Often, **eyes,** *pl.* a way of thinking or considering; view; opinion; judgment: *She can do no wrong in his eyes. Beauty is in the eye of the beholder.* **1–7, 10–13** *n.*, **8, 9** *v.*, **eyed, ey·ing** *or* **eye·ing.**
**an eye for an eye,** punishment or revenge as severe as the offence or injury.

**be all eyes,** watch eagerly and attentively: *The children were all eyes as he began to open the box.*
**catch one's eye,** attract one's attention: *A notice in the newspaper caught his eye.*
**have an eye for,** be a sound and appreciative judge of: *She has an eye for a good painting.*
**have an eye to,** look out for; pay attention to.
**in the eye(s) of,** in the judgment, opinion, or view of: *In the eyes of most doctors, smoking is dangerous to health.*
**in the public eye,** often seen in public or often mentioned in newspaper or magazine articles, etc.: *She is very much in the public eye since her record-breaking swim.*
**keep an eye on,** watch; take care of: *Keep an eye on the baby.*
**make eyes at,** look at in a flirtatious or loving way.
**my eye,** *Informal.* an exclamation used to express disagreement or contradiction: *Tired, my eye! She's just lazy.*
**open a person's eyes,** make a person see what is really happening: *That experience opened our eyes to what he was really like.*
**see eye to eye,** agree entirely; have exactly the same opinion: *They often don't see eye to eye, but they never actually fight.*
**set eyes on,** see; look at: *I knew who he was the minute I set eyes on him.*
**shut one's eyes to,** refuse to see or consider: *You can't shut your eyes to the problem forever.*
☛ *Hom.* AYE, I.

**eye·ball** (ī′bol′) the ball-shaped part of the eye without the surrounding lids and bony socket. *n.*

**eye·brow** (ī′brou′) 1 the arch of hair above the eye. 2 the bony ridge that it grows on. *n.*

**eye·cup** (ī′kup′) a small cup with a rim shaped to fit over the eye, used in washing the eyes or putting medicine in them. *n.*

**eyed** (īd) 1 having an eye or eyes. 2 having an eye or eyes of a particular kind, colour, number, etc. (used only in compounds): *a one-eyed pirate, a dark-eyed girl.* *adj.*

**eye dropper** DROPPER.

**eye·ful** (ī′fùl) 1 as much as the eye can see at one time. 2 *Informal.* a good look. *n.*

**eye·glass** (ī′glas′) 1 a glass lens to aid poor vision. 2 EYECUP. 3 EYEPIECE. 4 **eyeglasses,** *pl.* a pair of glass or plastic lenses in a frame, worn in front of the eyes to help vision; glasses: *The doctor prescribed eyeglasses to help my poor sight.* *n.*

**eye·hole** (ī′hōl′) 1 the bony socket for the eyeball. 2 a hole to look through. 3 a round opening for a pin, hook, rope, etc. to go through. *n.*

**eye·lash** (ī′lash′) 1 one of the hairs on the edge of the eyelid. 2 one row or fringe of such hairs. *n.*

**eye·less** (ī′lis) blind or without eyes. *adj.*

**eye·let** (ī′lit) 1 a small, round hole for a lace or cord to go through. 2 a metal ring that is set around such a hole to strengthen it; GROMMET. 3 a hole to look through. 4 a small, round hole edged with fine stitches, used as a decorative pattern in embroidery. See EMBROIDERY for picture. 5 cloth having an allover pattern of such eyelets. *n.*
☛ *Hom.* ISLET.

**eye·lid** (ī′lid′) the movable fold of skin over the eye. *n.*

**eye·lin·er** (ī′lī′nər) a coloured cosmetic applied as a fine line along the base of the lashes to emphasize the contour of the eyes. *n.*

**eye-o·pen·er** (ī′ō′pə nər *or* ī′ōp′nər) a happening or discovery that comes as a revelation: *Her behaviour during the trial was an eye-opener; I had no idea she could be so cool-headed.* *n.*

**eye-o·pen·ing** (ī′ō′pə ning *or* ī′ōp′ning) enlightening or revealing: *an eye-opening experience.* *adj.*

**eye·piece** (ī′pēs′) the lens or set of lenses nearest the eye of the user in a telescope, microscope, etc. See MICROSCOPE and TELESCOPE for pictures. *n.*

**eye shadow** a cosmetic in any of various colours applied to the eyelids to accent the eye.

**eye·shot** (ī′shot′) the range of vision. *n.*

**eye·sight** (ī′sīt′) 1 the power of seeing; sight: *He has good eyesight.* 2 the range of vision; view. *n.*

**eye socket** the bony cavity in which the eyeball is set.

**eye·sore** (ī′sôr′) something unpleasant to look at: *A garbage heap is an eyesore.* *n.*

**eye·spot** (ī′spot′) the simplest kind of organ for seeing, found in many invertebrates, consisting of a spot of pigment that is sensitive to light. *n.*

**eye·strain** (ī′strān′) a tired or weak condition of the muscles of the eye caused by overuse or by an uncorrected defect, such as shortsightedness. *n.*

**eye·tooth** (ī′tüth′) either of the two pointed, upper teeth between the incisors and the bicuspids; upper CANINE TOOTH. *n., pl.* **eye·teeth.**

**eye·wit·ness** (ī′wit′nis) a person who actually sees or has seen some act or happening, and thus can give testimony concerning it. *n.*

**ey·rie** (ī′rē *or* ē′rē) 1 the nest of an eagle or other bird of prey high on a mountain or cliff. 2 a house, castle, etc. built in a high place. *n.* Also, **aerie.**
☛ *Hom.* EERIE (for the second pronunciation of **eyrie**).

# F f  *F f*

hat, āge, fär; let, ēqual, tėrm; it, īce
hot, ōpen, ôrder; oil, out; cup, pùt, rüle
ə above, ə taken, ə pencil, ə lemon, ə circus
ch, child; ng, long; sh, ship
th, thin; ᴛʜ, then; zh, measure

**f** or **F**  **1** the sixth letter of the English alphabet.  **2** any speech sound represented by this letter.  **3** in music: **a** the fourth tone in the scale of C major.  **b** a symbol representing this tone.  **c** a key, string, etc. of a musical instrument that produces this tone.  **d** the scale or key that has F as its keynote.  **4** any person or thing considered as the sixth in a series.  **5** a grade rating a person's work or performance as failing.  **6** a person receiving such a grade.  *n., pl.* **f's** or **F's**.

**F**  fluorine.

**F.** or **F**  **1** Fahrenheit.  **2** French.  **3** Friday.  **4** February.

**f.**  **1** female.  **2** feminine.  **3** forte.  **4** franc.  **5** in mathematics, function.  **6** frequency.  **7** the following page, line, etc.: *p. 83f.* means page 83 and the following page.  **8** frame.

**fa**  (fä)  in music:  **1** the fourth tone of an eight-tone major scale.  **2** the tone F. See ᴅᴏ² for picture.  *n.*

**fa·ble**  (fā′bəl)  **1** a story made up to teach a lesson: *Fables are often about animals who can talk, such as "The Hare and the Tortoise" and "The Fox and the Crow."*  **2** an untrue story; falsehood.  **3** a legend; myth.  *n.*

**fa·bled**  (fā′bəld)  **1** told about in fables, legends, or myths.  **2** having no real existence; made up; fictitious.  *adj.*

**fab·ric**  (fab′rik)  **1** any woven, knitted, or pressed material; cloth: *Velvet, canvas, linen, felt, and flannel are fabrics.*  **2** the texture or quality of such material: *Cloth may have a smooth or rough fabric.*  **3** a structure; something constructed of combined parts; framework: *the fabric of society.*  *n.*

**fab·ri·cate**  (fab′rə kāt′)  **1** build; construct; manufacture.  **2** make by fitting together standardized parts: *Some automobiles may be fabricated from parts made in different factories.*  **3** make up; invent stories, lies, excuses, etc.  *v.,* **fab·ri·cat·ed, fab·ri·cat·ing.**

**fab·ri·ca·tion**  (fab′rə kā′shən)  **1** manufacture; fabricating.  **2** something fabricated, especially a story, lie, excuse, etc.  *n.*

**fab·u·lous**  (fab′yə ləs)  **1** not believable; amazing; exaggerated: *That antique shop charges fabulous prices.*  **2** of or belonging to a fable; imaginary: *The phoenix is a fabulous bird.*  **3** like a fable.  **4** wonderful; exciting: *We had a fabulous time at the party.*  *adj.* —**fab′u·lous·ly,** *adv.* —**fab′u·lous·ness,** *n.*

**fa·çade**  (fə säd′)  **1** the front part of a building.  **2** any side of a building that faces a street or other open space.  **3** a front or outward part or appearance of anything, especially when thought of as concealing something: *a façade of honesty.*  *n.* Also, **facade**.

**face**  (fās)  **1** the front part of the head, from forehead to chin: *a beautiful face, a wide face.*  **2** an expression or look: *His face was sad.*  **3** a distortion of the face, usually expressing annoyance, disgust, etc. or meant to amuse: *He made a face and said he didn't like the coat. A little girl on the bus was making faces at people.*  **4** outward appearance or aspect: *On the face of it, he seems to have a good chance to win. We have new information that puts a different face on the matter.*  **5** the upper or outer surface of something: *the face of the earth.*  **6** the front or main side of something: *the face of a clock, the face of a playing card.*  **7** in mathematics, any of the plane surfaces of a solid: *A cube has six faces.*  **8** have the face toward: *The dancers stood facing each other. Our house faces east.*  **9** turn the face toward: *He was told to face the wall.*  **10** be opposite to: *Look at the picture facing page 60.*  **11** dignity, self-respect, or prestige: *To some people, loss of face is a disaster. She tried to save face by changing the subject.*  **12** gall; nerve; impudence: *I didn't think she would have the face to come back after being asked to leave.*  **13** meet bravely or boldly; confront: *The mayor went out to face the angry demonstrators. She has the courage to face her problems.*  **14** present itself to: *Another problem now faced us. They were faced with a difficult decision.*  **15** cover the surface of with a layer of different material: *a wooden house faced with brick.*  **16** apply a facing to a garment, etc.  **17** smooth the surface of stone, etc.  1–7, 11, 12 *n.,* 8–10, 13–17 *v.,* **faced, fac·ing.**

**face off,** *Cdn.*  in hockey, lacrosse, etc., put a puck, ball, etc. into play by dropping it between the sticks of two players facing each other: *The referee starts a hockey game by facing off the puck at centre ice.*
**face to face, a** with faces toward each other: *The skaters were lined up face to face.*  **b** in person; personally: *I never expected to meet him face to face.*
**face to face with,**  in the actual presence of: *The wounded soldier knew he was face to face with death.*
**face up to,**  meet bravely and boldly: *to face up to a difficult situation, to face up to an enemy.*
**face with,**  present with a problem: *They faced him with an impossible request.*
**in the face of, a** in the presence of: *She showed no fear in the face of danger.*  **b** in spite of: *He has succeeded in the face of tremendous difficulties.*
**lose face,**  lose dignity or prestige.
**pull a long face,**  look unhappy or disapproving.
**put a good** (or **brave,** etc.) **face on,**  make the best of; face cheerfully, bravely, etc.
**set one's face against,**  oppose and resist: *He has set his face against any kind of change.*
**to a person's face,**  boldly or impudently, in the presence of: *He repeated the gossip to the teacher's face.*

**face card**  the king, queen, or jack of a suit of playing cards.

**face·cloth**  (fās′klôth′)  a small cloth, usually made of towelling, for washing the face or body.  *n.*

**faced**  (fāst)  **1** having a face of a certain kind or with a certain appearance (*used mainly in compounds*): *sad-faced, round-faced.*  **2** *pt.* and *pp.* of ꜰᴀᴄᴇ.  1 *adj.,* 2 *v.*

**face-off**  (fās′ôf′) *Cdn.*  in hockey, lacrosse, etc., the act of putting the puck, ball, etc. into play; the act of facing off: *The last goal was scored from the face-off.*  *n.*

**face-sav·ing**  (fās′sā′ving)  that preserves or is intended to preserve one's dignity, self-respect, etc.: *That was just a face-saving gesture.*  *adj.*

The facets of a diamond

**fac·et** (fas′it) **1** any one of the small, polished surfaces of a cut gem. **2** anything like the facet of a gem. **3** any one of several sides or views, as of a character or personality: *Selfishness was a facet of his character that we seldom saw.* **4** cut facets on. 1–3 *n.*, 4 *v.*, **fac·et·ed, fac·et·ing.**

**fa·ce·tious** (fə sē′shəs) **1** having the habit of joking. **2** said in fun; not to be taken seriously: *facetious remarks.* *adj.* —**fa·ce′tious·ly,** *adv.* —**fa·ce′tious·ness,** *n.*

**face value 1** the value stated on a bond, cheque, coin, bill, etc.: *He paid much more than the face value for the silver quarters in his collection.* **2** the apparent worth or meaning: *He took the compliment at face value and did not worry about any possible sarcasm.*

**fa·cial** (fā′shəl) **1** of the face: *facial features, facial expression.* **2** for the face: *a facial treatment, facial tissue.* **3** a massage or cosmetic treatment of the face. 1, 2 *adj.*, 3 *n.*

**fa·cile** (fas′īl, fas′əl, *or* fas′əl) **1** easily done, used, etc.: *a facile task, facile methods.* **2** moving, acting, working, etc. with ease; fluent or ready: *a facile hand, a facile tongue, a facile pen.* **3** showing little thought, effort, depth, etc.; superficial or insincere: *facile answers to complex questions, facile repentance.* *adj.* —**fac′ile·ly,** *adv.*

**fa·cil·i·tate** (fə sil′ə tāt′) make easy; lessen the labour of; help forward; assist: *A vacuum cleaner facilitates housework.* *v.*, **fa·cil·i·tat·ed, fa·cil·i·tat·ing.**

**fa·cil·i·ty** (fə sil′ə tē) **1** the absence of difficulty; ease: *The boy ran and dodged with such facility that no one could catch him. The facility of communication is far greater now than it was a hundred years ago.* **2** the ability to do anything easily, quickly, or smoothly; fluency or skill. **3** Usually, **facilities,** *pl.* something, such as equipment, furnishings, etc., that makes an action or activity possible or easier: *The library provides facilities for studying. The school has excellent sports facilities.* *n., pl.* **fa·cil·i·ties.**

**fac·ing** (fā′sing) **1** a layer of material covering a surface, used for protection or ornament: *The front of the courthouse has a marble facing.* **2** a lining along the inside edges of the front opening, neckline, etc. of a garment in the same or a contrasting fabric: *A facing is often meant to be turned back, as a collar or cuff.* **3** **facings,** *pl.* the cuffs, collar, and trimmings of a military or military-style coat, usually in a contrasting colour. **4** *ppr.* of FACE. 1–3 *n.*, 4 *v.*

**fac·sim·i·le** (fak sim′ə lē) **1** an exact copy or likeness; a perfect reproduction. **2** a process for transmitting printed matter, photographs, etc. by electronic means such as telephone or radio. **3** make a facsimile of. 1, 2 *n.*, 3 *v.*, **fac·sim·i·led** (-lēd′), **fac·sim·i·le·ing** (-lē′ing). **in facsimile,** exactly.

**fact** (fakt) **1** anything known to be true or have really happened; something that has or had actual existence: *historical facts, the fact of the existence of gravity. It is a fact that he was there, because several people identified him. Space travel is a fact.* **2** the quality of being real; the state of things as they are or have happened; reality; truth: *The fact of the matter is, she never wanted to go. I want fact, not fantasy.* **3** something said or believed to be true or to have really happened: *Check your facts before you present your argument.* **4** an actual deed or act, especially a criminal act: *She was charged with being an accessory after the fact.* *n.*

**as a matter of fact, in fact,** *or* **in point of fact,** in truth; actually: *He hasn't had much education; in fact, he never got past grade five.*

**facts and figures,** factual information: *You need facts and figures to prove your theory.*

**fac·tion** (fak′shən) **1** a group of people in a political party, club, etc. acting together, usually in opposition to another such group or the main body: *A faction often seeks to promote only its own interests at the expense of the group as a whole.* **2** strife or quarrelling among the members of a political party, club, etc.: *They allowed faction to destroy their club.* *n.*

**fac·tion·al** (fak′shə nəl) **1** of or having to do with factions; partisan. **2** causing faction. *adj.*

**fac·tious** (fak′shəs) **1** fond of causing strife or faction. **2** of or caused by strife or faction: *a factious issue.* *adj.* —**fac′tious·ly,** *adv.* —**fac′tious·ness,** *n.*

**fac·ti·tious** (fak tish′əs) developed by effort; not natural; artificial: *Extensive advertising can cause a factitious demand for an article.* *adj.* —**fac·ti′tious·ly,** *adv.*

**fact of life 1** a part of life or existence that cannot be changed or ignored, especially an unpleasant or harsh part. **2 facts of life,** *pl. Informal.* **a** the realities of life: *He wouldn't face the facts of life, but lived in a dream world.* **b** information about human sexual functions.

**fac·tor** (fak′tər) **1** any element, condition, quality, etc. that helps to bring about a result: *Endurance is an important factor of success in sports.* **2** any of the numbers, algebraic expressions, etc. that produce a given number or quantity when multiplied together: *5, 3, and 4 are factors of 60.* See MULTIPLICATION for picture. **3** separate into factors. **4** *Cdn.* a person who acts as a representative of a company; agent: *The Hudson's Bay Company employed many factors in its fur-trading posts throughout the Northland.* 1, 2, 4 *n.*, 3 *v.*

**fac·to·ry** (fak′tə rē *or* fak′trē) **1** a building or group of buildings where things are manufactured. **2** *Cdn.* in former times, a trading post: *Moose Factory, Ontario.* *n., pl.* **fac·to·ries.**

**fac·to·tum** (fak tō′təm) a person employed to do all kinds of work. *n.*

**fac·tu·al** (fak′chü əl) of, containing, or consisting of fact or facts: *The newspaper simply gave a factual report of the fire, without speculating on possible causes.* *adj.* —**fac′tu·al·ly,** *adv.*

**fac·ul·ty** (fak′əl tē) **1** a power of the mind or body: *the faculty of hearing, the faculty of memory. She is over ninety years old, but she still has all her faculties.* **2** the power to do some special thing, especially a power of the mind: *a faculty for arithmetic.* **3** the teachers of a college or university. **4** a department of learning in a university: *the faculty of theology, the faculty of law.* **5** the members of a profession: *The medical faculty is made up of doctors, surgeons, etc.* *n., pl.* **fac·ul·ties.**

**fad** (fad) something many people are very much interested in for a short time; a craze or rage: *Crossword puzzles became a fad several years ago.* *n.*

**fad·dist** (fad′ist) a person devoted to a fad or a person who takes up fads. *n.*

**fade** (fād) **1** lose colour or brightness: *The bedroom* *curtains have faded a lot.* **2** lose freshness or strength; wither: *Most of the garden flowers had faded by September.* **3** die away; disappear: *The sound of the train faded in the distance.* **4** cause to fade: *Sunlight will fade the colours in some fabrics.* *v.*, **fad·ed, fad·ing.**

**fade in,** of a motion-picture image or electronic signal, slowly become more distinct or louder.

**fade out,** of a motion-picture image or electronic signal, slowly become less distinct or quieter.

**fade–in** (fād′in′) in motion pictures, radio, or television, a gradual increase in brightness, distinctness, or sound. *n.*

**fade–out** (fād′dout′) **1** in motion pictures, radio, or television, a gradual decrease in brightness, distinctness, or sound. **2** a gradual disappearance. *n.*

**fae·cal** (fē′kəl) See FECAL. *adj.*

**fae·ces** (fē′sēz) See FECES. *n.*

**fag** (fag) **1** work hard or until wearied: *Tom fagged away at his arithmetic.* **2** tire by work: *The horse was fagged.* **3** a person who does hard work; drudge. 1, 2 *v.*, **fagged, fag·ging;** 3 *n.*

**fag end 1** the last and poorest part of anything; remnant. **2** the coarse, unfinished end of a piece of cloth. **3** an untwisted end of rope.

**fag·got** or **fag·ot** (fag′ət) **1** a bundle of sticks or twigs tied together: *She built the fire with faggots.* **2** a bundle of iron rods or pieces of iron or steel to be welded. **3** tie or fasten together into bundles; make into a faggot. 1, 2 *n.*, 3 *v.*

**fag·got·ing** or **fag·ot·ing** (fag′ə ting) **1** a style of embroidery in which a group of crosswise threads is pulled out of a fabric and the lengthwise threads thus exposed are tied together in groups resembling faggots. **2** a decorative openwork method of joining two finished edges. See EMBROIDERY for picture. *n.*

**Fahr.** Fahrenheit.

**Fahr·en·heit** (far′ən hīt′ *or* fer′ən hīt′) of, based on, or according to the Fahrenheit scale for measuring temperature, on which 32 degrees marks the freezing point of water and 212 degrees the boiling point. *adj.*

**Fahrenheit thermometer** a thermometer marked according to the Fahrenheit scale. See THERMOMETER for picture.

**fai·ence** (fī ons′; *French*, fä yäns′) a glazed earthenware or porcelain, usually of fine quality. *n.*

**fail** (fāl) **1** not succeed; fall short of success: *He tried hard, but failed to achieve his goal.* **2** be unsuccessful in an examination, course of study, etc.; receive a mark of failure: *She failed her first year.* **3** give a mark of failure to: *The teacher failed a third of the class.* **4** fall far short of what is wanted or expected; come to nothing: *The project failed. The crops failed again this year.* **5** decrease to the point of not being enough; run out: *A rescue party found them just before their supplies failed.* **6** not remember or choose to do; neglect: *He failed to follow our advice.* **7** not be able (*to*): *I fail to understand why she didn't even show up.* **8** be of no use to, when needed: *Words failed her and she could think of nothing to say. His friends failed him when he was in trouble.* **9** stop performing or operating: *We were still far from home when the engine failed.* **10** lose strength; become weak or weaker: *The sick man's heart was failing.* **11** not make enough profit to stay in business; go bankrupt: *That company will fail.* *v.*

---

**fade-in**      **433**      **fair**

hat, āge, fär; let, ēqual, tėrm; it, īce
hot, ōpen, ôrder; oil, out; cup, pút, rüle
əbove, takən, pencəl, lemən, circəs
ch, child; ng, long; sh, ship
th, thin; ᴛʜ, then; zh, measure

**without fail,** without failing to do, happen, etc.; for certain; surely: *She promised to write regularly without fail.*
☛ *Hom.* FAILLE (fāl).

**fail·ing** (fā′ling) **1** failure. **2** a fault or weakness; defect: *He is a charming person in spite of his failings.* **3** in the absence of; in default of; lacking: *Failing good weather, the party will be held indoors.* **4** ppr. of FAIL. 1, 2 *n.*, 3 *prep.*, 4 *v.*

**faille** (fīl *or* fāl) a kind of cloth, usually soft and somewhat glossy, having flat crosswise ribs or cords on the surface: *Faille is often of silk, cotton, or synthetics and is used for coats, dresses, handbags, etc.* *n.*
☛ *Hom.* FAIL (for the second pronunciation of **faille**).

**fail·ure** (fā′lyər) **1** a falling short of success; lack of success. **2** the fact of not being successful in an examination, course, etc. **3** not doing; neglecting. **4** a falling short of what is wanted or expected: *the failure of crops.* **5** a loss of strength; becoming weak; dying away: *failure of eyesight.* **6** not making enough profit to stay in business; becoming bankrupt: *the failure of a company.* **7** a person or thing that has failed: *The picnic was a failure because it rained.* *n.*

**faint** (fānt) **1** not clear or plain; dim: *faint idea, faint colours. We could see a faint outline of trees through the fog.* **2** weak; exhausted; feeble: *a faint voice.* **3** done feebly or without zest: *a faint attempt.* **4** a condition in which a person is unconscious for a short time, caused by an insufficient flow of blood to the brain: *He fell to the floor in a faint.* **5** lose consciousness temporarily: *He fainted at the sight of his bleeding finger.* **6** ready to faint; about to faint: *I feel faint.* 1–3, 6 *adj.*, 4 *n.*, 5 *v.*
—**faint′ly,** *adv.* —**faint′ness,** *n.*
**feel faint,** feel ready to faint.
☛ *Hom.* FEINT.

**faint–heart·ed** (fānt′här′tid) lacking courage; cowardly; timid. *adj.* —**faint′-heart′ed·ly,** *adv.*
—**faint′-heart′ed·ness,** *n.*

**fair**¹ (fer) **1** not favouring one more than the other or others; just; honest: *a fair judge. He is fair even to people he dislikes.* **2** according to the rules: *fair play.* **3** pretty good; not bad; average: *She has a fair understanding of the subject. There is only a fair crop of wheat this year.* **4** favourable; likely; promising: *He is in a fair way to succeed.* **5** not dark; blond: *fair hair, a fair complexion.* **6** not cloudy or stormy; clear; sunny: *The weather will be fair today.* **7** pleasing to the eye or mind; beautiful: *a fair lady. She spoke fair words.* **8** of good size or amount; ample: *They own a fair piece of property.* **9** clean or pure; without blemishes: *fair water, a fair copy.* **10** easily read; plain: *fair handwriting.* **11** favourable; helpful, especially to a ship's course: *We had fair winds all the way.* **12** seemingly good at first, but not really so: *His fair promises proved false.* **13** in an honest, straightforward manner; honestly: *fair-spoken, to play fair.* **14** directly; straight: *The stone hit her fair on the head.* 1–12 *adj.*, 13, 14 *adv.* —**fair′ness,** *n.*
**bid fair,** seem likely; have a good chance.
**fair and square,** *Informal.* just; honest.
☛ *Hom.* FARE.

**fair**² (fer) **1** a gathering of people for the purpose of

showing goods, products, etc.; exhibition: *the Royal Winter Fair. At the county fair last year, prizes were given for the best farm products and livestock.* **2** a gathering of people to buy and sell, often held in a certain place at regular times during the year: *a trade fair.* **3** an entertainment and sale of articles; bazaar: *Our club held a fair to raise money.* *n.*
☞ *Hom.* FARE.

**fair ball** in baseball, a hit that is not a foul.

**fair game** **1** animals or birds that it is lawful to hunt. **2** a person or thing that is considered a suitable or legitimate object of pursuit or attack: *She was fair game for political cartoonists because of her odd way of dressing.*

**fair·ground** (fer′ground′) an outdoor space, usually having equipment for exhibitions and entertainment, where fairs are held. *n.*

**fair–haired** (fer′herd′) having light-coloured hair. *adj.*

**fair·ish** (fer′ish) fairly good, well, or large. *adj.*

**fair·ly** (fer′lē) **1** in a fair manner. **2** to a fair degree. **3** justly; honestly. **4** rather; somewhat: *The pay was fairly good.* **5** actually or really: *He fairly beamed when he saw his picture in the paper.* **6** clearly. *adv.*

**fair–mind·ed** (fer′mīn′did) not prejudiced; just; impartial. *adj.* —**fair′-mind′ed·ness,** *n.*
—**fair′-mind′ed·ly,** *adv.*

**fair–spo·ken** (fer′spō′kən) speaking smoothly and pleasantly; civil; courteous. *adj.*

**fair·way** (fer′wā′) **1** an unobstructed passage or way: *The fairway in a harbour is the channel for ships.* **2** the part in a golf course where the grass is kept short, between the TEE (def. 2) and the putting green. *n.*

**fair–weath·er** (fer′weᴛH′ər) **1** of or fitted for fair weather. **2** weakening or failing in time of need: *a fair-weather friend.* *adj.*

**fair·y** (fer′ē) **1** a supernatural being of folklore and myth having magical powers and able to help or harm human beings: *In recent legend, fairies have been pictured as very small, and sometimes very lovely and delicate. In medieval story, however, fairies were often of full human size.* **2** of fairies. **3** like a fairy; lovely; delicate: *wings of fairy gossamer.* **1** *n., pl.* **fair·ies;** **2, 3** *adj.*
☞ *Hom.* FERRY.

**fair·y·land** (fer′ē land′) **1** the imaginary place where the fairies live. **2** any charming and pleasant place. *n.*

**fairy ring** a ring of mushrooms and darker grass, etc. growing around the edge of a body of underground fungi: *It used to be thought that fairy rings were made by fairies when dancing.*

**fairy tale** **1** a story involving fairies or other beings with magical powers and containing strange adventures, enchantments, marvellous deeds, etc. **2** an untrue story, especially one intended to deceive; lie.

**fait ac·com·pli** (fet′ə kom′plē; *French,* fe tä kôn plē′) something done and no longer worth opposing.

**faith** (fāth) **1** believing without proof; trust; confidence; reliance: *We have faith in our friends.* **2** belief in God, religion, or spiritual things. **3** what is believed. **4** religion: *the Islamic faith, the Catholic faith.* **5** being faithful; loyalty: *Good faith is honesty of intention; bad faith is intent to deceive.* **6** a promise to remain loyal: *The captured soldiers refused to break faith even under torture.* **1–6** *n.*
**in bad faith,** dishonestly or insincerely.
**in faith,** truly; indeed.
**in good faith,** honestly; sincerely: *Although the boys had done the wrong thing, they had acted in good faith.*
**keep faith,** keep one's promise.

**faith·ful** (fāth′fəl) **1** worthy of trust; doing one's duty; keeping one's promise; loyal: *a faithful friend, a faithful servant.* **2** true; accurate: *The witness gave a faithful account of what happened.* **3** full of faith. **4 the faithful,** **a** true believers. **b** loyal followers or supporters. **1–3** *adj.,* **4** *n.* —**faith′ful·ly,** *adv.*
—**faith′ful·ness,** *n.*

**faith·less** (fāth′lis) **1** unworthy of trust; failing in one's duty; breaking one's promise; not loyal: *A traitor is faithless.* **2** not reliable. **3** without faith; unbelieving: *He was a faithless, godless man.* *adj.*
—**faith′less·ly,** *adv.* —**faith′less·ness,** *n.*

**fake** (fāk) **1** make to seem satisfactory; falsify; counterfeit: *The picture was faked by pasting together two photographs.* **2** a fraud; deception: *The beggar's limp was a fake.* **3** intended to deceive; false: *a fake testimonial.* **4** intentionally give a false appearance of; simulate: *to fake an illness.* **1, 4** *v.,* **faked, fak·ing;** **2** *n.,* **3** *adj.*
—**fak′er,** *n.*

**fa·kir** (fā′kər *or* fə kēr′) **1** a Moslem holy man who lives by begging. **2** a Hindu ascetic. *n.*

**fal·chion** (fol′chən) **1** a medieval sword having a broad, short blade with an edge that curves to a point. See SWORD for picture. **2** *Poetic.* any sword. *n.*

**fal·con** (fol′kən *or* fal′kən) **1** a bird of prey related to the hawk and eagle, having a hooked bill and long, strong, pointed wings for swift flight. **2** a falcon or hawk trained to hunt and kill birds and small game: *In the Middle Ages, hunting with falcons was a popular sport.* *n.*

**fal·con·er** (fol′kə nər *or* fal′kə nər) **1** a man who hunts with falcons. **2** a breeder and trainer of falcons. *n.*

**fal·con·ry** (fol′kən rē *or* fal′kən rē) **1** the sport of hunting with falcons. **2** the training of falcons to hunt. *n.*

**fal·de·ral** (fol′də rol′) **1** a flimsy thing; trifle. **2** nonsense; rubbish. **3** a meaningless refrain in songs. *n.*

**fall** (fol) **1** drop or come down from a higher place: *The snow falls fast. Leaves fall from the trees.* **2** a falling; dropping from a higher place: *The fall from his horse hurt him.* **3** the amount that falls: *We had a heavy fall of snow last winter.* **4** the distance that anything falls: *The fall of the river between here and the bridge is one metre.* **5** waterfall. **6** come down suddenly from an erect position: *He fell on his knees.* **7** a coming down suddenly from an erect position: *The child had a bad fall when she tripped on the step.* **8** hang down: *Her curls fell upon her shoulders.* **9** a hanging down; dropping. **10** droop: *His spirits fell when he heard they weren't going.* **11** give in to temptation: *She was tempted and fell.* **12** giving in to temptation. **13** lose position, power, dignity, etc.: *The dictator fell from the people's favour.* **14** a loss of position, power, dignity, etc.: *a politician's fall from public favour.* **15** be captured, overthrown, or destroyed: *The fort fell to the enemy.* **16** a capture; overthrow; destruction. **17** drop wounded or dead; especially, be killed in battle: *The plaque carried the names of those who fell in the last war.* **18** pass into a certain condition: *She fell asleep. The rent falls due on Monday.* **19** come;

arrive: *When night falls, the stars appear.*  **20** come by chance or lot: *Our choice fell on her.*  **21** come to pass; happen; occur: *My birthday falls on a Sunday this year.*  **22** come by right; be put properly: *The money fell to the only daughter. The principal stress of* farmer *falls on the first syllable.*  **23** the proper place: *the fall of a stress.*  **24** become lower or less: *Prices fell sharply. The water in the river has fallen 80 centimetres. Her voice fell.*  **25** a lowering; becoming less: *a fall in prices, the fall of the tide.*  **26** be divided: *The story falls into five parts.*  **27** look sad or disappointed: *His face fell at the news.*  **28** slope downward: *The land falls gradually to the beach.*  **29** a downward slope.  **30** be directed: *The light falls on my books.*  **31** the season of the year between summer and winter; autumn.  **32** of, having to do with, or for autumn: *fall weather, a fall coat.*  **33** in wrestling, being thrown on one's back.  **34** a contest in wrestling.  **35 falls,** *pl.* **a** a waterfall; cataract; cascade: *Niagara Falls.*  **b** an apparatus used in lowering and raising a ship's boat. 1, 6, 8, 10, 11, 13, 15, 17–22, 24, 26–28, 30 *v.,* **fell, fall·en, fall·ing;**  2–5, 7, 9, 12, 14, 16, 23, 25, 29, 31–35 *n.*
**fall away,** become less.
**fall back,**   retreat; go toward the rear: *The soldiers fell back to a stronger position.*
**fall back on, a** go back to for safety.   **b** turn to for help or support: *He knew he could fall back on his father.*
**fall behind, a** fail to keep up; drop back: *Before the race was half over, the slow runners had fallen a lap behind.* **b** be late: *Don't let your rent fall behind.*
**fall down,**   fail: *Our plans could fall down if we're not careful.*
**fall in, a** collapse; cave in: *The roof fell in from the weight of the snow.*  **b** in the armed forces, take one's place in line; line up in the correct formation.
**fall in with, a** meet by chance: *On our trip, we fell in with some interesting people.*  **b** agree to: *They fell in with our plans.*
**fall off,**   drop; become less: *Attendance at baseball games falls off late in the season.*
**fall on, a** attack: *Thieves fell on the man and stole his money.*  **b** be the responsibility of: *It falls on me to give the vote of thanks.*
**fall out, a** in the armed forces, leave one's place in line. **b** quarrel; stop being friends.  **c** happen; turn out.
**fall over backwards,** *Informal.*   try very hard to do something.
**fall short of,**   be less than required: *The supply of goods fell short of the estimated demand.*
**fall through,**   fail: *Her plans fell through.*
**fall to, a** begin to fight or attack: *The swordsman fell to with great enthusiasm.*  **b** begin to eat: *The girls fell to as soon as they sat down.*  **c** go into place; close by itself.
**fall under,**   belong under; be classified as.
**fall upon,**   attack: *The pirates fell upon the city.*

**fal·la·cious** (fə lā′shəs)   **1** deceptive; misleading: *fallacious hopes for a lasting peace.*  **2** containing or being a FALLACY; logically unsound: *fallacious reasoning.*  *adj.* —**fal·la′cious·ly,** *adv.*  —**fal·la′cious·ness,** *n.*

**fal·la·cy** (fal′ə sē)   **1** a false idea; a mistaken belief; error: *It is a fallacy to suppose that riches always bring happiness.*  **2** a mistake in reasoning; a misleading or unsound argument.   *n., pl.* **fal·la·cies.**

**fall·en** (fol′ən)   **1** *pp.* of FALL: *Much rain has fallen.*  **2** dropped: *They picked up some fallen apples.*  **3** on the ground; down flat: *a fallen tree.*  **4** degraded.  **5** overthrown; destroyed.  **6 the fallen,** *pl.*   all those killed in battle: *The memorial commemorates the fallen of the First World War.*   1 *v.,* 2–5 *adj.,* 6 *n.*

**fall fair**   *Cdn.*   a fair held in the fall in a community for the exhibiting and judging of livestock, produce, and crafts, often with horse races, dances, and other forms of entertainment.

**fal·li·bil·i·ty** (fal′ə bil′ə tē)   a FALLIBLE quality or nature: *It is wise to remember the fallibility of human nature.*  *n.*

**fal·li·ble** (fal′ə bəl)   **1** liable to be deceived or mistaken; liable to err.  **2** liable to be erroneous, inaccurate, or false.  *adj.*

**falling star**   METEOR.

**Fal·lo·pi·an tubes** (fə lō′pē ən)   in female mammals, a pair of slender tubes through which ova from the ovaries pass to the uterus.

**fall–out** (fol′out′)   **1** the radio-active particles or dust that fall to the earth after a nuclear explosion.  **2** any incidental result.   *n.*

**fal·low** (fal′ō *or, esp. in the Prairie Provinces,* fol′ō)  **1** ploughed and left unseeded for a season or more; uncultivated; inactive: *fallow land.*  **2** of land, the state of being ploughed and left unseeded for a season, in order to destroy weeds, improve the soil, etc.  **3** land ploughed and left unseeded in this way: *The ground was wet, so they walked around the fallow.*   1 *adj.,* 2, 3 *n.*
☛ *Hom.* FOLLOW (for the second pronunciation of **fallow**).

**fallow deer**   a small European deer having a yellowish coat that is spotted with white in the summer.

**false** (fols)   **1** not true; not correct; wrong: *false statements, false testimony.*  **2** not truthful; lying: *a false witness.*  **3** not loyal; not faithful: *a false friend.*  **4** made or done so as to deceive: *The fugitive left a false trail for his pursuers. The dishonest butcher used false scales.*  **5** in music, not true in pitch: *a false note.*  **6** not real; artificial: *false diamonds.*  **7** based on wrong notions; ill-founded: *false pride, a false sense of security.*  **8** improperly called or named: *The false acacia is really a locust tree.*  **9** in a false manner.  **10** not structurally essential; fitted over or in front of another part to strengthen it, disguise it, etc.: *They put in a false ceiling to hide the pipes. The store had a false front.*  1–8, 10 *adj.,* **fals·er, fals·est;**  9 *adv.*  —**false′ly,** *adv.*  —**false′ness,** *n.*
**false step, a** a wrong step; stumble: *One false step and the climber would fall to her death.*  **b** a mistake or blunder: *The police were waiting for the suspect to make a false step.*
**play false,**   deceive; cheat; trick; betray.

**false bottom**   the bottom of a trunk, suitcase, etc. that forms a secret or a supplementary compartment.

**false colours** or **colors**   **1** a flag of another country.  **2** false pretences.

**false face**   a funny or ugly mask; mask.

**false·hood** (fols′hud)   **1** lack of truth or accuracy; falsity.  **2** a false idea, theory, etc.  **3** the practice of making false statements; lying.  **4** a false statement; lie.  *n.*

**false pride**   pride based on mistaken ideas.

**false ribs** the ribs not attached to the breastbone: *Human beings have five pairs of false ribs.*

**fal·set·to** (fol set′ō) **1** an adult male voice pitched artificially high, especially a singing voice that goes above the normal full tenor range. **2** a singer who uses falsetto. **3** in falsetto: *He sang the part falsetto.* 1, 2 *n., pl.* **fal·set·tos;** 3 *adv.*

**fal·si·fi·ca·tion** (fol′sə fə kā′shən) falsifying or being falsified. *n.*

**fal·si·fy** (fol′sə fī′) **1** make false; change in order to deceive; misrepresent. **2** make false statements; lie. **3** prove to be false; disprove. *v.*, **fal·si·fied, fal·si·fy·ing.** —**fal′si·fi′er,** *n.*

**fal·si·ty** (fol′sə tē) **1** being false; incorrectness: *the falsity of her smile. Education showed him the falsity of his superstitions.* **2** something false; lie. **3** untruthfulness; deceitfulness. *n., pl.* **fal·si·ties.**

**fal·ter** (fol′tər) **1** lose courage; draw back; hesitate; waver: *The soldiers faltered for a moment as their captain fell.* **2** move unsteadily; stumble; totter. **3** speak in hesitating, broken words; stammer: *Greatly embarrassed, he faltered out his thanks.* **4** come forth in hesitating, broken sounds: *Her voice faltered.* **5** the act of faltering. **6** a faltering sound. 1–4 *v.,* 5, 6 *n.* —**fal′ter·er,** *n.*

**fame** (fām) **1** being very well-known; having much said or written about one. **2** what is said about one; reputation. *n.*

**famed** (fāmd) famous; celebrated; well-known. *adj.*

**fa·mil·iar** (fə mil′yər) **1** often seen or experienced; well-known; common: *a familiar tune, a familiar face. A knife is a familiar tool.* **2** well acquainted: *She is familiar with French.* **3** close; personal; intimate: *familiar friends. They are on familiar terms.* **4** a close friend. **5** not formal; friendly. **6** too friendly; presuming; forward: *They didn't like his familiar manner.* **7** a spirit or demon supposed to serve a particular person: *A black cat was thought to be a witch's familiar.* 1–3, 5, 6 *adj.,* 4, 7 *n.* —**fa·mil′iar·ly,** *adv.*

**fa·mil·iar·i·ty** (fə mil′yar′ə tē *or* fə mil′yer′ə tē) **1** close acquaintance. **2** a freedom of behaviour suitable only to friends; lack of formality or ceremony: *Our friendly host treated us with easy familiarity.* **3** an instance of such behaviour: *She dislikes such familiarities as the use of her first name by people she has just met.* *n., pl.* **fa·mil·iar·i·ties.**

**fa·mil·iar·ize** (fə mil′yə rīz′) **1** make well acquainted: *Before playing the new game, familiarize yourself with the rules.* **2** make well-known: *Radio has familiarized the word broadcast.* *v.,* **fa·mil·iar·ized, fa·mil·iar·iz·ing.** —**fa·mil′iar·i·za′tion,** *n.*

**fam·i·ly** (fam′ə lē *or* fam′lē) **1** a father, mother, and their children; a parent and his or her child or children. **2** the children of a father and mother: *Do they have a family?* **3** one's spouse and children: *She says her family doesn't want to move.* **4** a group of people living in the same house. **5** all of a person's relatives. **6** a group of related people; tribe. **7** in biology, a major category in the classification of plants and animals, ranking between an order and a genus: *Lions, tigers, and leopards belong to the cat family. The prairie lily, dogtooth violet, and trillium belong to the lily family. See Appendix for classification chart.* **8** in linguistics, a group of related languages descending from a single language: *English, French,* German, Hindi, Italian, and Russian are some of the languages belonging to the Indo-European family. **9** any group of related or similar things. *n., pl.* **fam·i·lies.**

**Family Allowance** formerly, in Canada, an allowance paid by the Federal Government for children under the age of 18 who are maintained by parents or guardians. Provincial governments can vary the rates within certain limits, and a few provinces have their own program to supplement the federal one.

**Family Compact** in Canada, the name applied to the governing class of Upper Canada before 1837 and, in particular, to the executive and legislative councils of Upper Canada.

**family name** the last name of all the members of a certain family; surname.

**family skeleton** a cause of shame that a family tries to keep secret.

**family tree** **1** a diagram showing the relationships and descent of all the members and ancestors of a family; a genealogical chart. **2** all the members of a family line.

**fam·ine** (fam′ən) **1** starvation. **2** an extreme lack of food in a place; a time of starving: *Many people died during the famine in India.* **3** a very great shortage of anything: *a coal famine.* *n.*

**fam·ish** (fam′ish) be or make extremely hungry; make or become weak from hunger. *v.*
**be famished** or **famishing,** *Informal.* be very hungry: *Let's eat; I'm famished.*

**fa·mous** (fā′məs) **1** very well-known; noted: *a famous writer.* **2** *Informal.* first-rate; excellent. *adj.* —**fa′mous·ly,** *adv.*

Three kinds of fan

**fan¹** (fan) **1** an instrument or device with which to stir the air in order to cool, ventilate, etc. **2** make a current of air with a fan, etc. **3** direct a current of air toward with a fan, etc.: *Fan the fire to make it burn faster.* **4** drive away with a fan, etc.: *She fanned the flies from the sleeping child.* **5** stir up; arouse: *Bad treatment fanned their dislike into hate.* **6** anything spread out like an open fan. **7** spread out like an open fan. **8** winnow. **9** a winnowing machine. **10** in baseball, strike out: *He fanned three times in one game. The pitcher fanned five batters.* 1, 6, 9 *n.,* 2–5, 7, 8, 10 *v.,* **fanned, fan·ning.** —**fan′like′,** *adj.* —**fan′ner,** *n.*
**fan out,** spread out like an open fan.

**fan²** (fan) *Informal.* **1** a person extremely interested in a sport, one of the performing arts, etc., especially as a spectator: *a hockey fan, a movie fan.* **2** an admirer of an actor, writer, etc. *n.*

**fa·nat·ic** (fə nat′ik) **1** a person who is carried away beyond reason by his or her feelings or beliefs: *My friend was such a fanatic about fresh air that she would not stay in any room with the windows closed.* **2** enthusiastic or zealous beyond reason. 1 *n.,* 2 *adj.*

**fa·nat·i·cal** (fə nat′ə kəl)   unreasonably enthusiastic; extremely zealous.   *adj.*   —**fa·nat′i·cal·ly,** *adv.*

**fa·nat·i·cism** (fə nat′ə siz′əm)   an unreasonable enthusiasm; extreme zeal.   *n.*

**fan belt**   the belt that drives the fan to cool an automobile engine and other machines.

**fan·cied** (fan′sēd)   **1** imagined; imaginary: *She took offence at a fancied slight.*   **2** pt. and pp. of FANCY.   1 *adj.*, 2 *v.*

**fan·ci·er** (fan′sē ər)   a person who is especially interested in and knowledgeable about something, especially the growing or breeding of particular kinds of plants or animals: *She's a dog fancier.*   *n.*

**fan·ci·ful** (fan′sē fəl)   **1** marked by fancy or caprice; quaint; whimsical: *fanciful designs or decorations.*   **2** influenced by fancy; indulging in fancies: *He was in a fanciful mood when he wrote this delightful story.*   **3** suggested by fancy; imaginary; unreal: *She gave a fanciful account of the events.*   *adj.*   —**fan′ci·ful·ly,** *adv.*   —**fan′ci·ful·ness,** *n.*

**fan·cy** (fan′sē)   **1** one's power to imagine; imagination, especially of a decorative, whimsical, or playful kind: *Poetic fancy has produced some great works of literature.*   **2** something imagined or supposed; something unreal: *Is it just fancy, or do I hear a sound?*   **3** form an idea of; imagine: *Can you fancy yourself living in that house?*   **4** an idea or notion: *She had a sudden fancy to go for a swim.*   **5** have an idea; suppose; guess: *I fancy she is about sixty.*   **6** a liking or fondness based mainly on whim: *They took a fancy to each other right away.*   **7** like or be fond of: *He fancied the idea of having a reunion.*   **8** having or showing great technical skill and grace: *He showed us some fancy dancing.*   **9** not plain or simple; decorated, ornamental, or elaborate; showy: *a fancy table setting, a fancy costume.*   **10** of high quality: *These canned peaches are labelled fancy.*   **11** extravagant, especially of prices: *It's a nice place, but they also have fancy prices.*   **12** of an animal or plant, bred for special ornamental or odd qualities that have no practical function.   1, 2, 4, 6 *n.*, *pl.* **fan·cies;**   3, 5, 7 *v.*, **fan·cied, fan·cy·ing;**   8–12 *adj.*, **fan·ci·er, fan·ci·est.**
**fancy oneself,**   think highly of oneself: *That girl really fancies herself.*

**fancy dress**   a costume for a masquerade, especially one representing an animal, a person from history or fiction, etc.

**fan·cy·work** (fan′sē wėrk′)   ornamental needlework; embroidery, crocheting, etc.   *n.*

**fan·fare** (fan′fer)   **1** a short tune or call sounded by trumpets, bugles, hunting horns, etc.   **2** a loud show of activity, talk, etc.; showy flourish.   *n.*

The fangs of a rattlesnake

**fang** (fang)   **1** a long, sharp tooth by which certain animals, such as dogs, wolves, etc. seize and hold prey; CANINE TOOTH: *The hungry wolf buried its fangs in the caribou's neck.*   **2** a hollow or grooved tooth by which a poisonous snake injects poison into its prey.   **3** a long, slender, tapering part of anything, such as the root of a tooth or the prong of a fork.   *n.*

**fan·light** (fan′līt′)   **1** a semicircular window with bars spread out like an open fan.   **2** any semicircular or other window over a door.   *n.*

**fan mail**   the mail received by a celebrity from fans.

**fan·tail** (fan′tāl′)   **1** a tail, end, or part spread out like an open fan.   **2** a variety of domestic pigeon whose tail spreads out like an open fan.   *n.*

**fan–tan** (fan′tan′)   **1** a Chinese gambling game in which the players bet on the number of coins or beans that will be left in a hidden pile when it has been counted off in fours.   **2** a card game in which the player who gets rid of his or her cards first wins the game.   *n.*

**fan·ta·si·a** (fan tā′zhē ə *or* fan tā′zē ə)   in music, a composition following no fixed form or style.   *n.*

**fan·ta·size** (fan′tə sīz′)   indulge in vivid and often extravagant daydreams or fantasies: *He often fantasized about living the life of a rock star.*   *v.*, **fan·ta·sized, fan·ta·siz·ing.**

**fan·tas·tic** (fan tas′tik)   **1** very fanciful; capricious; eccentric; irrational: *The idea of space travel seemed fantastic a hundred years ago.*   **2** existing only in the imagination; unreal: *There are many fantastic creatures in The Wizard of Oz.*   **3** very odd or queer; wild and strange in shape; showing unrestrained fancy: *The firelight cast weird, fantastic shadows on the walls.*   **4** *Informal.* unbelievably good, quick, high, etc.: *That store charges fantastic prices.*   *adj.*   —**fan·tas′ti·cal·ly,** *adv.*

**fan·tas·ti·cal** (fan tas′tə kəl)   FANTASTIC.   *adj.*

**fan·ta·sy** (fan′tə sē *or* fan′tə zē)   **1** the play of the mind; imagination or fancy: *The idea of space travel was once pure fantasy.*   **2** a fanciful or fantastic idea or notion; a caprice or whim: *It was a mere fantasy, not to be taken seriously.*   **3** wild imagining or day-dreaming; the creation of unrealistic or far-fetched mental images to satisfy desires not fulfilled in real life: *living in a world of fantasy.*   **4** such an idea or mental image: *fantasies about sudden wealth and fame.*   **5** fiction featuring strange and grotesque characters and fantastic acts or events in a coherent setting: *The Lord of the Rings is a fantasy.*   **6** FANTASIA.   *n.*, *pl.* **fan·ta·sies.**   Also, **phantasy.**

**fan·wise** (fan′wīz′)   spread out like an open fan.   *adv.*

**FAO**   in the United Nations, the Food and Agricultural Organization.

**far** (fär)   **1** distant; not near: *a far country.*   **2** more distant: *the far side of the hill.*   **3** a long way off in time or space: *far distant.*   **4** very much: *It is far better to be overcautious than to be careless in driving.*   1, 2 *adj.*, **far·ther** or **fur·ther, far·thest** or **fur·thest;**   3, 4 *adv.*
**by far,**   very much: *She was by far the better swimmer.*
**far and away,**   very much: *He was far and away the best student.*
**far and near,**   everywhere.
**far and wide,**   everywhere; even in distant parts.
**go far,**   **a** last long: *That new shampoo doesn't go very far.*   **b** tend very much.   **c** get ahead: *She shows great promise; she should go far.*
**how far,**   to what distance, point, or degree.
**in so far as,**   to the extent that.
**so far,**   **a** to this or that point: *He accepts teasing just so*

**farad** 438 **farthingale**

far and then he gets angry. **b** until now or then: *Our team has won every game so far this season.*

**far·ad** (far′əd *or* fer′əd) an SI unit of electrical capacity: *A farad is the capacity of a condenser having a charge of one coulomb when the potential across the plate is one volt.* Symbol: F *n.*

**far·a·way** (fä′rə wā′) **1** distant, far away: *faraway countries.* **2** dreamy: *A faraway look in her eyes showed that she was thinking of something else.* *adj.*

**farce** (färs) **1** a play intended merely to make people laugh, full of ridiculous happenings, absurd actions, and improbable situations. **2** the kind of humour found in such plays; broad humour. **3** ridiculous mockery; absurd pretence: *The trial was a mere farce.* *n.*

**far·ci·cal** (fär′sə kəl) of or like a farce; ridiculous; absurd; improbable. *adj.* —**far′ci·cal·ly,** *adv.*

**far cry** **1** a long way. **2** completely different.

**fare** (fer) **1** the sum of money paid to ride in a train, airplane, bus, etc. **2** a passenger on a train, airplane, bus, etc. **3** food provided or eaten: *party fare.* **4** eat food; be fed: *We fared very well at Grandmother's.* **5** get along; do: *If you fare well, you have good luck or success.* **6** turn out; happen: *It will fare hard with the thief if he is caught.* **7** go; travel: *to fare on a journey.* 1–3 *n.*, 4–6, 7 *v.*, **fared, far·ing.** —**far′er,** *n.*
☛ *Hom.* FAIR.

**Far East** China, Japan, and other parts of eastern Asia.

**fare·well** (fer′wel′ *for 1–3*, fer′wel′ *for 4*) **1** an expression of good wishes at parting. **2** good-bye; good luck. **3** a departure; leave-taking. **4** of farewell; parting; last: *The singer gave a farewell performance.* 1, 2 *interj.*, 1–3 *n.*, 4 *adj.*

**far–fetched** (fär′fecht′) not likely; hard to believe; forced; strained: *a far-fetched excuse.* *adj.*

**far–flung** (fär′flung′) covering a large area: *a far-flung empire.* *adj.*

**fa·ri·na** (fə rē′nə) **1** flour or meal made from grain, potatoes, beans, nuts, etc. **2** starch. **3** a coarse, white corn meal. *n.*

**far·i·na·ceous** (far′ə nā′shəs *or* fer′ə nā′shəs) consisting of flour or meal; starchy; mealy: *Cereals, bread, and potatoes are farinaceous foods.* *adj.*

**farm** (färm) **1** the buildings and land used in raising crops or animals. **2** raise crops or animals on a farm: *Angela and her brother farm for a living.* **3** cultivate land: *They farm 100 hectares.* **4** anything like a farm: *A sheet of water for cultivating oysters is an oyster farm.* **5** let the labour or services of a person for hire. 1, 4 *n.*, 2, 3, 5 *v.*
**farm out, a** send a professional athlete to a less advanced league so that he can gain experience. **b** turn over to a person, company, etc. for a special purpose: *She farms out the right to pick berries on her land.*

**farm club** *or* **team** in sports, a minor-league team that trains players for the major leagues.

**farm·er** (fär′mər) a person who raises crops or animals on a farm. *n.*

**farm hand** a person employed to work on a farm.

**farm·house** (färm′hous′) the dwelling on a farm. *n.*

**farm·ing** (fär′ming) **1** the business of raising crops or animals on a farm; agriculture. **2** ppr. of FARM. 1 *n.*, 2 *v.*

**farm·land** (färm′land′ *or* färm′lənd) land suitable for or used for raising crops or grazing. *n.*

**farm·stead** (färm′sted′) a farm with its buildings. *n.*

**farm·yard** (färm′yärd′) the yard connected with the buildings of a farm or enclosed by them. *n.*

**Far North** in Canada, the Arctic and sub-Arctic regions; the territories lying north of the provinces.

**far·o** (fer′ō) a gambling game played by betting on the order in which certain cards will appear. *n.*
☛ *Hom.* FARROW (fer′ō), PHAROAH.

**far–off** (fä′rof′) distant; far away: *far-off lands.* *adj.*

**far–reach·ing** (fär′rē′ching) having a wide influence or effect; extending far. *adj.*

**far·ri·er** (far′ē ər *or* fer′ē ər) a blacksmith who shoes horses. *n.*

**far·row** (far′ō *or* fer′ō) **1** a litter of pigs. **2** give birth to a litter of pigs: *The sow farrowed yesterday. She farrowed a litter of six.* 1 *n.*, 2 *v.*
☛ *Hom.* FARO, PHAROAH (for the second pronunciation of **farrow**.)

**far–see·ing** (fär′sē′ing) **1** able to see far. **2** looking ahead; planning wisely for the future. *adj.*

**far–sight·ed** (fär′sī′tid) **1** having a condition of the eyes in which the visual images of nearby objects come to a focus behind the retina, so that they are not clear: *A far-sighted person has better vision for distant objects than for near objects.* Compare with NEAR-SIGHTED. **2** looking ahead; planning wisely for the future. *adj.*
—**far′-sight·ed·ly,** *adv.* —**far′-sight·ed·ness,** *n.*

**far·ther** (fär′ᴛʜər) **1** more distant: *Three kilometres is farther than two.* **2** at or to a greater distance: *Go no farther.* **3** at or to a more advanced point: *He has investigated the subject farther than most people.* **4** in addition; also. 1 *adj.*, a comparative of **far;** 2–4 *adv.*
☛ *Syn.* In formal English **farther** is used for physical distance and FURTHER for abstract and metaphysical senses: *We have moved our campsite farther from the road. His criticisms of the school went further than mine.* Informally, **further** is often used in all senses.

**far·ther·most** (fär′ᴛʜər mōst′) most distant; farthest. *adj.*

**far·thest** (fär′ᴛʜist) **1** most distant. **2** to or at the greatest distance. **3** most. **4** longest: *His last trip was the farthest he had ever taken.* 1, 4 *adj.*, a superlative of **far;** 2, 3 *adv.*

 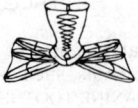

A farthingale of the mid 18th century. The framework of cane and whalebone, attached to a corselet, is shown on the right.

**far·thin·gale** (fär′ᴛʜing gāl′) a hoop skirt or framework for expanding a woman's skirt, worn in England from about 1550 to about 1650. *n.*

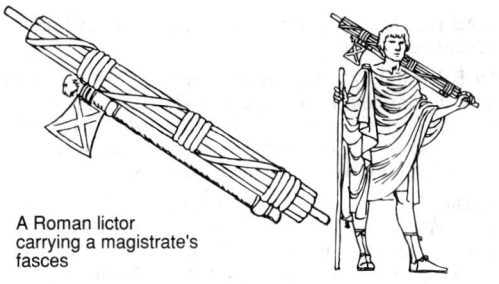

A Roman lictor carrying a magistrate's fasces

**fas·ces** (fas′ēz)   in ancient Rome, a bundle of rods or sticks containing an axe with the blade projecting, carried before a magistrate as a symbol of authority.   *n., pl.* of **fas·cis** (fas′is).

**fas·ci·a** (fash′ē ə *or* fā′shə)   a long, flat band or surface, such as a horizontal band forming part of a cornice or architrave, or a flat surface above a shop window, often carrying the name of the shop.   See FRAME for picture.   *n.*

**fas·ci·cle** (fas′ə kəl)   **1** a small bundle, especially, in botany, a small cluster of flowers, leaves, roots, etc. **2** one of the parts of a book published in instalments.   *n.*

**fas·ci·nate** (fas′ə nāt′)   **1** attract very strongly; enchant by charming qualities: *The actress's great beauty and cleverness fascinated everyone.*   **2** hold motionless by strange power, terror, etc.: *Snakes are said to fascinate small birds.*   *v.*, **fas·ci·nat·ed, fas·ci·nat·ing.**

**fas·ci·nat·ing** (fas′ə nā′ting)   **1** captivating; enchanting; charming.   **2** ppr. of FASCINATE.   **1** *adj.,* **2** *v.* —**fas′ci·nat′ing·ly,** *adv.*

**fas·ci·na·tion** (fas′ə nā′shən)   **1** fascinating or being FASCINATED.   **2** a very strong attraction; charm; enchantment.   *n.*

**fas·ci·na·tor** (fas′ə nā′tər)   **1** formerly, a long, lightweight scarf, usually knitted or crocheted, worn by women over the head or around the neck.   **2** a person who FASCINATES (def. 1).   *n.*

**fas·cine** (fa sēn′)   a bundle of sticks tied together, formerly used to fill ditches, strengthen earthworks, etc.   *n.*

**fas·cism** (fash′iz əm)   **1** any system of government in which property is privately owned, but in which all industry and business is regulated by a strong national government.   **2** Usually, **Fascism,   a** a strongly nationalistic movement in favour of government control of industry and labour and opposed to radical socialism and communism: *Fascism seized control of the Italian government in 1922 under the leadership of Mussolini.* **b** the doctrines, principles, or methods of the Fascists.   *n.*

**Fas·cist** or **fas·cist** (fash′ist)   **1** a person who favours and supports FASCISM.   **2** of or having to do with FASCISM or the Fascists.   **1** *n.,* **2** *adj.*

**fash·ion** (fash′ən)   **1** a manner or way: *to walk in a peculiar fashion.*   **2** the prevailing style; current custom in dress, manners, speech, etc.: *She follows the fashion very closely.*   **3** a garment in the current style: *That shop carries all the latest fashions.*   **4** of or concerned with fashion or fashions: *a fashion magazine, a fashion designer.* **5** make; shape; form: *She fashioned a whistle out of the stick.*   **1–4** *n.,* **5** *v.* **after** or **in a fashion,**   in some way or other; not very well.

**fashion after** or **on,**   model after: *Pierre always fashioned himself on his father. My dress is fashioned after the bride's.* **set the fashion,**   fix the fashion, method, etc. for others to follow.

**fash·ion·a·ble** (fash′ə nə bəl)   **1** following the fashion; in fashion; stylish: *Her clothes are fashionable, but they do not always suit her.*   **2** of, like, or used by people of fashion: *They are members of a fashionable club.*   *adj.* —**fash′ion·a·ble·ness,** *n.*

**fash·ion·a·bly** (fash′ə nə blē)   in a fashionable manner.   *adv.*

**fast¹** (fast)   **1** quick; rapid; swift: *a fast runner.* **2** quickly; rapidly; swiftly: *Airplanes go fast.*   **3** indicating a time ahead of the correct time: *My watch is fast.*   **4** too free; wild; not restrained in pleasures: *He led a fast life, drinking and gambling.*   **5** firm; secure; tight: *a fast hold on a rope.*   **6** firmly; securely; tightly: *She held fast to the bar as the roller-coaster car started to hurtle downhill. The fox was caught fast in the trap.*   **7** loyal; faithful: *They have been fast friends for years.*   **8** that will not fade easily: *Good cloth is dyed with fast colour.*   **9** thoroughly; completely; soundly: *He was fast asleep.*   **10** adapted for speed; helping to produce or increase speed: *a fast track.* **11** with greater than average speed, force, etc.: *a fast pitcher.*   **12** in photography, making a short exposure possible: *Fast film can be used in dim light.*   **1, 3–5, 7, 8, 10–12** *adj.,* **2, 6, 9** *adv.* **play fast and loose,**   be tricky, insincere, or unreliable: *to play fast and loose with the truth.*

**fast²** (fast)   **1** go without food; eat little or nothing; go without certain kinds of food: *Members of some religions fast on certain days.*   **2** a fasting.   **3** a day or period of fasting.   **1** *v.,* **2, 3** *n.*

**fast·back** (fast′bak′)   **1** an automobile roof that slopes downward in a long curve to the back.   **2** an automobile with such a roof.   *n.*

**fast·ball** (fast′bol′)   a variety of softball having a number of features to add speed and action, making the game more like baseball.   *n.*

**fast day**   a day observed by fasting, especially a day regularly set apart for this purpose by a religion.

**fas·ten** (fas′ən)   **1** fix firmly in place; tie, lock, or shut: *to fasten a dress, to fasten a door.*   **2** fix; impose: *He tried to fasten the blame on his companions.*   **3** direct; fix: *The dog fastened its eyes on the boy.*   **4** become fixed in place: *The door wouldn't fasten properly.*   *v.* **fasten down,**   fix to a decision: *We have been unable to fasten the supplier down to a definite date.* **fasten on** or **upon,**   **a** take hold of; seize.   **b** choose.

**fas·ten·er** (fas′ə nər)   **1** a person who fastens.   **2** an attachment, device, etc. used to fasten a door, garment, etc.   *n.*

**fas·ten·ing** (fas′ə ning)   **1** a device used to fasten things together: *Locks, bolts, clasps, hooks, and buttons are all fastenings.*   **2** ppr. of FASTEN.   **1** *n.,* **2** *v.*

**fas·tid·i·ous** (fas tid′ē əs *or* fas tid′yəs)   hard to please; extremely refined or critical; easily disgusted: *a* *fastidious eater. He's fastidious about clothes.* adj. —**fas‧tid′i‧ous‧ly,** adv. —**fas‧tid′i‧ous‧ness,** n.

**fast‧ness** (fast′nis) **1** a strong, safe place; stronghold: *The bandits hid in their mountain fastness.* **2** being fast. n.

**fast time** *Informal.* daylight-saving time.

**fat** (fat) **1** any of various kinds of white or yellow oily substance formed in the bodies of animals and also in some seeds. **2** any animal tissue mainly composed of such a substance. **3** any of a class of organic chemical compounds of which the natural fats are mixtures. **4** consisting of or containing fat; oily: *fat meat.* **5** abounding in some element; fertile: *fat land.* **6** yielding much money; profitable: *a fat job.* **7** affording good opportunities. **8** full of good things; plentifully supplied; plentiful. **9** fleshy; plump; round and well-fed: *He has got quite fat.* **10** thick; broad. **11** dull; stupid. **12** make fat; become fat. **13** too fat; corpulent; obese. 1–3 *n.,* 4–11, 13 *adj.,* **fat‧ter, fat‧test;** 12 *v.,* **fat‧ted, fat‧ting.** —**fat′like′,** *adj.* —**fat′ly,** *adv.* —**fat′ness,** *n.* **live off the fat of the land,** have the best of everything.

**fa‧tal** (fā′təl) **1** causing death: *fatal accidents.* **2** causing destruction or ruin: *The loss of all that money was fatal to their plans.* **3** decisive; fateful: *At last the fatal day for the contest arrived.* **4** influencing fate. *adj.*
☛ *Syn.* **Fatal,** DEADLY, MORTAL, and LETHAL can all mean 'causing death'. **Fatal** and **mortal** are used of something that has caused death or is sure to cause it: *a fatal disease, a mortal wound.* **Deadly** and **lethal** describe something that could cause death but will not inevitably cause it: *a deadly weapon, a lethal poison.* **Mortal** is used to refer to a state, event, etc. but not to a weapon: *a mortal wound.* **Lethal** is used of something sure to kill and designed or intended to do so: *a lethal dose.*

**fa‧tal‧ism** (fā′tə liz′əm) **1** the belief that fate controls everything that happens. **2** submission to everything that happens as inevitable. *n.*

**fa‧tal‧ist** (fā′tə list) a believer in FATALISM. *n.*

**fa‧tal‧is‧tic** (fā′tə lis′tik) **1** of or having to do with FATALISM. **2** believing that fate controls everything; accepting things and events as inevitable. *adj.* —**fa‧tal‧is′ti‧cal‧ly,** *adv.*

**fa‧tal‧i‧ty** (fə tal′ə tē *or* fā tal′ə tē) **1** a fatal accident or happening; death: *There were several fatalities on the highways last weekend.* **2** a fatal influence or effect; deadliness: *Doctors are trying to reduce the fatality of diseases.* **3** liability to disaster. **4** the condition of being controlled by fate; inevitable necessity: *We struggle against fatality in vain.* *n., pl.* **fa‧tal‧i‧ties.**

**fa‧tal‧ly** (fā′tə lē) **1** in a manner leading to death or disaster: *He was fatally wounded.* **2** according to fate. *adv.*

**fat‧back** (fat′bak′) salted and dried strips of fat from the back of a hog. *n.*

**fate** (fāt) **1** a power believed to fix beforehand and control everything that happens: *Fate is beyond human control. She does not believe in fate.* **2** what is caused by fate. **3** one's lot or fortune: *He deserved a better fate. History shows the fate of nations.* **4** what becomes of a person or thing: *The jury settled the fate of the accused.* **5** death; ruin. *n.*
☛ *Hom.* FETE.

**fat‧ed** (fāt′id) **1** controlled by fate. **2** destined; predestined. *adj.*

**fate‧ful** (fāt′fəl) **1** controlled by fate. **2** determining what is to happen; decisive: *a fateful battle.* **3** showing what fate decrees; prophetic: *fateful words.* **4** causing death, destruction, or ruin; disastrous: *a fateful flood.* *adj.* —**fate′ful‧ly,** *adv.* —**fate′ful‧ness,** *n.*

**fa‧ther** (foᴛн′ər) **1** a male parent. **2** produce or bring forth, as a father; beget: *He has fathered three children.* **3** take care of as a father does; act as a father to. **4** a person who is like a father. **5** a male ancestor; forefather: *the customs of our fathers.* **6** a person who helped to make something; founder, leader, inventor, author, oldest member, etc.: *Fathers of Confederation. Alexander Graham Bell was the father of the telephone.* **7** make; originate: *The inventor of the light bulb fathered many other inventions.* **8** acknowledge oneself as the father of. **9** a title of respect used in addressing priests or some other clergymen. **10** a clergyman having this title. **11** a title of respect to an old man. **12** the **Father,** God. 1, 4–6, 9–12 *n.,* 2, 3, 7, 8 *v.*

**father confessor** **1** a priest who hears confessions. **2** a person to whom one confides everything.

**fa‧ther‧hood** (foᴛн′ər hud′) the condition of being a father. *n.*

**fa‧ther‑in‑law** (foᴛн′ə rin lo′) the father of one's husband or wife. *n., pl.* **fa‧thers‑in‑law.**

**fa‧ther‧land** (foᴛн′ər land′) one's native country; the land of one's ancestors. *n.*

**fa‧ther‧less** (foᴛн′ər lis) **1** without a father. **2** without a known father. *adj.*

**fa‧ther‧ly** (foᴛн′ər lē) **1** of or belonging to a father: *fatherly responsibilities.* **2** like a father; kindly. *adj.* —**fa′ther‧li‧ness,** *n.*

**Fathers of Confederation** the men, led by Sir John A. Macdonald, who brought about the confederation of the original provinces of Canada in 1867.

**fath‧om** (faᴛн′əm) **1** a unit of measure equal to six feet (about 1.83 m), used mostly in measuring the depth of water and the length of ships' ropes, cables, etc. **2** measure the depth of; sound. **3** get to the bottom of; understand fully: *I can't fathom what you're driving at.* 1 *n., pl.* **fath‧oms** or (*esp. collectively*) **fath‧om;** 2, 3 *v.*

**fath‧om‧a‧ble** (faᴛн′ə mə bəl) **1** that can be measured. **2** understandable. *adj.*

**fath‧om‧less** (faᴛн′əm lis) **1** too deep to be measured. **2** impossible to be fully understood: *the fathomless riddle of the universe.* *adj.*

**fa‧tigue** (fə tēg′) **1** physical or mental weariness. **2** cause fatigue in; weary. **3** any task or exertion producing weariness: *The doctor has not yet recovered from the fatigues of the epidemic.* **4** a weakening of metal caused by long-continued use or strain. **5** weaken by much use or strain. **6** FATIGUE DUTY. **7** having to do with fatigue. **8** **fatigues,** *pl.* clothes worn during FATIGUE DUTY. 1, 3, 4, 6, 8 *n.,* 2, 5 *v.,* **fa‧tigued, fa‧ti‧guing;** 7 *adj.*

**fatigue duty** non-military work done by members of the armed forces.

**fat‧ten** (fat′ən) **1** make fat: *Pigs are fattened for market.* **2** become fat. *v.*
**fatten on** or **upon,** taken advantage of in order to live well: *She has been fattening on her sons for years.*

**fat‧tish** (fat′ish) somewhat fat. *adj.*

**fat·ty** (fat′ē)  1 of fat; containing fat: *fatty tissue.*  2 like fat; oily or greasy.  *adj.,* **fat·ti·er, fat·ti·est.**  —**fat′ti·ness,** *n.*

**fa·tu·i·ty** (fə tyü′ə tē *or* fə tü′ə tē)  self-satisfied stupidity; folly; silliness.  *n., pl.* **fa·tu·i·ties.**

**fat·u·ous** (fach′ü əs)  stupid but self-satisfied; silly.  *adj.*  —**fat′u·ous·ly,** *adv.*  —**fat′u·ous·ness,** *n.*

**fau·cet** (fos′it)  a device containing a valve for controlling the flow of water or other liquid from a pipe, tank, barrel, etc., by opening or closing; a tap.  *n.*

**faugh** (fo)  an exclamation of disgust.  *interj.*

**fault** (folt)  1 something that is not as it should be; a flaw or defect: *Sloppiness is her greatest fault. Her dog has two faults: it eats too much and it howls at night.*  2 a mistake.  3 a cause for blame; responsibility: *Whose fault was it?*  4 in geology, a break in a mass of rock with the segment on one side of the break pushed up or down.  5 in tennis and similar games, a failure to serve the ball into the right place.  6 in tennis and similar games, fail to serve the ball into the right place: *She faulted twice and lost the match.*  7 find fault with: *Her work could not be faulted.*  1–5 *n.,* 6, 7 *v.*
**find fault,**  pick out faults; complain: *The boy said that his father was always finding fault.*
**find fault with,**  object to; criticize: *The teacher was always finding fault with badly done homework.*

**fault·find·er** (folt′fīn′dər)  a person who finds fault; complainer.  *n.*

**fault·find·ing** (folt′fīn′ding)  finding fault; complaining; pointing out faults.  *n., adj.*

**fault·less** (folt′lis)  without a single fault; free from blemish or error; perfect: *a faultless performance of a difficult dance step.*  *adj.*  —**fault′less·ly,** *adv.*  —**fault′less·ness,** *n.*

**fault·y** (fol′tē)  having faults; containing blemishes or errors; wrong; imperfect.  *adj.,* **fault·i·er, fault·i·est.**  —**fault′i·ness,** *n.*

**fau·na** (fon′ə)  all the animals of a particular region or time: *the fauna of Australia.*  *n.*

**faux pas** (fō′ pä′ *or* fō′ pä′; French, fō pä′)  a slip in speech, conduct, manners, etc.; a breach of etiquette; a blunder.  *pl.* **faux pas** (fō′ pä′ *or* fō′ päz′; French, fō pä′)

**fa·vor** (fā′vər)  See FAVOUR.  *n., v.*

**fa·vor·a·ble** (fā′və rə bəl *or* fā′vrə bəl)  See FAVOURABLE.  *adj.*

**fa·vored** (fā′vərd)  See FAVOURED.  *adj., v.*

**fa·vor·ite** (fā′və rit *or* fā′vrit)  See FAVOURITE.  *adj.*

**fa·vor·it·ism** (fā′və rə tiz′əm *or* fā′vrə tiz′əm)  See FAVOURITISM.  *n.*

**fa·vour** *or* **fa·vor** (fā′vər)  1 an act of kindness: *Will you do me a favour?*  2 show kindness to; oblige: *Favour us with a song.*  3 liking; approval: *They will look with favour on your plan.*  4 the condition of being liked or approved: *A fashion in favour this year may be out of favour next year.*  5 like; approve: *They favour Heinz's plan.*  6 more than fair treatment; favouring one or some more than others; favouritism.  7 give more than fair treatment to: *The teacher favours you.*  8 be on the side of; support: *to favour legal reform.*  9 be to the advantage of; help.  10 a gift or token: *The knight wore his lady's favour on his arm.*  11 a small gift, especially one given as a souvenir at a party.  12 treat gently: *The dog favours his sore foot when she walks.*  13 look like: *She favours her mother.*  1, 3, 4, 6, 10, 11 *n.,* 2, 5, 7–9, 12, 13 *v.*
**in favour of,**  a on the side of; supporting.  b to the advantage of; helping.  c to be paid to: *Make the cheque out in favour of the company, not the sales representative.*
**in one's favour,**  for one; to one's benefit.

**fa·vour·a·ble** *or* **fa·vor·a·ble** (fā′və rə bəl *or* fā′vrə bəl)  1 favouring; approving: *a favourable answer.*  2 being to one's advantage; helping: *a favourable wind.*  3 boding well; promising: *It was a favourable time for our trip, since business was light.*  *adj.*  —**fa′vour·a·ble·ness** *or* **fa′vor·a·ble·ness,** *n.*  —**fa′vour·a·bly** *or* **fa′vor·a·bly,** *adv.*

**fa·voured** *or* **fa·vored** (fā′vərd)  1 treated with favour.  2 having special advantages; talented.  3 having a certain appearance.  4 pt. and pp. of FAVOUR.  1–3 *adj.,* 4 *v.*

**fa·vour·ite** *or* **fa·vor·ite** (fā′və rit *or* fā′vrit)  1 liked better than others; liked very much: *What is your favourite flower?*  2 a person or thing liked better than others; one liked very much: *Hank is a favourite with everybody.*  3 a person treated with special favour.  4 a person, horse, etc. expected to win a contest.  1 *adj.,* 2–4 *n.*

**fa·vour·it·ism** *or* **fa·vor·it·ism** (fā′və rə tiz′əm *or* fā′vrə tiz′əm)  1 a favouring of one or some more than others; having favourites.  2 the state of being a favourite.  *n.*

**fawn**[1] (fon)  1 a deer less than a year old.  2 light yellowish brown.  1, 2 *n.,* 2 *adj.*  —**fawn′like′,** *adj.*

**fawn**[2] (fon)  1 cringe and bow to get favour or attention; act slavishly: *Flattering relatives fawned on the rich old woman.*  2 of dogs, etc., show fondness by crouching, wagging the tail, licking the hand, etc.  *v.*  —**fawn′er,** *n.*

**fawn lily**  DOG-TOOTH VIOLET.

**fax** (faks)  1 a system for transmitting printed and other material by electronic means such as telephone or cable.  2 the equipment used: *Does your office have a fax?*  3 the material sent: *Here is the fax you expected.*  4 use the system: *Your letter will be faxed today.*  1–3 *n., pl.* **fax·es;** 4 *v.,* **faxed, fax·ing.**
☛ Etym. A shortening/abbreviation and respelling of *facsimile.*

**fay** (fā)  FAIRY.  *n.*

**faze** (fāz)  *Informal.*  disturb; worry; bother: *A scolding doesn't faze her at all.*  *v.,* **fazed, faz·ing.**
☛ Hom.  PHASE.

**F clef**  in music, the bass clef.  See CLEF for picture.

**F.D.**  Fire Department.

**Fe**  iron.

**fe·al·ty** (fē′əl tē)  1 the loyalty and duty owed by a vassal to his feudal lord: *The nobles swore fealty to the king.*  2 loyalty; faithfulness; allegiance.  *n., pl.* **fe·al·ties.**

**fear** (fēr)  1 being afraid; wanting to escape from a danger, pain, or evil that one feels is near; dread: *In spite*

*of his fear, he opened the door and stepped out into the dark.* **2** feel fear. **3** feel fear of: *Our cat fears big dogs. Our baby sister fears loud noises.* **4** a cause for fear; danger; chance: *There is no fear of our losing.* **5** an uneasy feeling or anxious thought; concern: *She had no fear of opposition.* **6** have an uneasy feeling or anxious thought; feel concern: *He fears that the children will be sick.* **7** a feeling of awe and reverence. **8** have awe and reverence for. 1, 4, 5, 7 *n.*, 2, 3, 6, 8 *v.*
**fear for,** worry about.

**fear·ful** (fēr′fəl) **1** causing fear; terrible; dreadful: *The great fire was a fearful sight.* **2** full of fear; afraid: *fearful of the dark.* **3** showing or caused by fear: *She cast a fearful glance about her.* **4** *Informal.* very bad, unpleasant, etc.: *a fearful cold. adj.* —**fear′ful·ly,** *adv.* —**fear′ful·ness,** *n.*

**fear·less** (fēr′lis) without fear; afraid of nothing; brave; daring. *adj.* —**fear′less·ly,** *adv.* —**fear′less·ness,** *n.*

**fear·some** (fēr′səm) **1** causing fear; frightful: *a fearsome sight.* **2** timid; afraid: *fearsome of danger. adj.* —**fear′some·ly,** *adv.* —**fear′some·ness,** *n.*

**fea·si·bil·i·ty** (fē′zə bil′ə tē) the quality of being easily done or carried out. *n.*

**fea·si·ble** (fē′zə bəl) **1** capable of being done or carried out easily; practicable: *The committee selected the plan that seemed most feasible.* **2** likely; probable: *The witness's explanation of the accident sounded feasible.* **3** suitable; convenient: *The road was too rough to be feasible for travel by automobile. adj.* —**fea′si·bly,** *adv.* —**fea′si·ble·ness,** *n.*

**feast** (fēst) **1** an elaborate meal prepared for some special occasion and for a number of guests: *We went to the wedding feast.* **2** an unusually delicious or abundant meal. **3** have a feast. **4** provide with a feast: *The queen feasted the ambassadors.* **5** something that gives pleasure or joy; a special treat. **6** give pleasure or joy to: *We feasted our eyes on the magnificent view.* **7** a religious festival or celebration: *Every religion has its special feasts.* 1, 2, 5, 7 *n.*, 3, 4, 6 *v.* —**feast′er,** *n.*

**feat** (fēt) a great or unusual deed; an act showing great skill, daring, strength, etc. *n.*
☛ *Hom.* FEET.

**feath·er** (feŦH′ər) **1** one of the light, thin growths that cover a bird's skin: *Because they are soft and light, feathers are often used to fill pillows.* **2** something like a feather in shape or lightness. **3** supply or cover with feathers. **4** grow like feathers. **5** move like feathers. **6** turn an oar after a stroke so that the blade is flat and keep it that way until the next stroke begins. **7** the act of feathering an oar. **8** turn the blade of an aircraft propeller to decrease wind resistance. 1, 2, 7 *n.*, 3–6, 8 *v.* —**feath′er·like′,** *adj.*
**feather in one's cap,** something to be proud of.
**feather one's nest,** take advantage of chances to get rich.
**in feather,** covered with feathers.
**in fine** (or **high** or **good**) **feather,** in very good humour; exuberantly happy: *We were all in fine feather the first day on the trail.*

**feather bed 1** a soft, warm mattress filled with feathers. **2** *Informal.* an easy way of living.

**feath·er–bed·ding** (feŦH′ər bed′ing) requiring an employer to pay more employees than he or she considers are needed, or to pay full wages for unnecessary work or for restricted output. *n.*

**feath·er·brain** (feŦH′ər brān′) a silly, frivolous or foolish person: *Only a featherbrain would take the lid off a blender while it's operating.* *n.*

**feath·er·brained** (feŦH′ər brānd′) silly; foolish; scatterbrained: *That was a featherbrained thing to do! adj.*

**feath·ered** (feŦH′ərd) **1** having feathers; covered with feathers. **2** equipped and supplied with feathers: *a feathered dart.* **3** swift; rapid: *birds in their feathered flight.* **4** pt. and pp. of FEATHER. 1–3 *adj.*, 4 *v.*

**feath·er·edged** (feŦH′ə rejd′) having a very thin edge. *adj.*

**feath·er·stitch** (feŦH′ər stich′) **1** a zigzag embroidery stitch. See EMBROIDERY for picture. **2** make such stitches. **3** decorate with such stitches. 1 *n.*, 2, 3 *v.*

**feath·er·weight** (feŦH′ər wāt′) **1** a very light thing or person. **2** a boxer who weighs between 55 and 57 kilograms. **3** very light. **4** of or having to do with featherweights. **5** an unimportant person or thing: *He is a featherweight on the political scene.* **6** unimportant. 1, 2, 5 *n.*, 3, 4, 6 *adj.*

**feath·er·y** (feŦH′ə rē) **1** having feathers; covered with feathers. **2** like feathers; soft, light, etc. *adj.*

**fea·ture** (fē′chər) **1** a part of the face: *The eyes, nose, mouth, chin, and forehead are features.* **2** a distinct part or quality; something that stands out and attracts attention: *Your plan for the picnic has many good features. An outstanding feature of Alberta and British Columbia is the Rocky Mountains.* **3** a main attraction, especially a full-length motion picture. **4** a special article, comic strip, etc. in a newspaper or magazine. **5** make a feature of; give special prominence to: *The movie featured an outstanding actress. The store was featuring radios in its sale.* **6** be featured; have a prominent part (*in*): *She features in several recent films.* **7** features, *pl.* the face. 1–4, 7 *n.*, 5, 6 *v.*, **fea·tured, fea·tur·ing.**
☛ *Usage.* The term **feature article** or **feature story** is often used for a newspaper or magazine article that gives the writer's feelings and opinions about an event or situation, as opposed to a **news story,** which gives the facts without personal comment.

**fea·tured** (fē′chərd) **1** having a certain kind of facial feature (*used mainly in compounds*): *a hard-featured woman.* **2** shown or advertised as a special feature: *The featured entertainers this week are a group from Halifax.* **3** pt. and pp. of FEATURE. 1, 2 *adj.*, 3 *v.*

**fea·ture·less** (fē′chər lis) without striking features; not distinctive or impressive: *a featureless landscape. adj.*

**Feb.** February.

**fe·brile** (fē′brīl *or* fē′brəl, feb′rīl *or* feb′rəl) **1** of fever; feverish. **2** caused by fever. *adj.*

**Feb·ru·ary** (feb′rü er′ē *or* feb′yü er′ē) the second month of the year: *February has 28 days except in leap years, when it has 29.* *n., pl.* **Feb·ru·ar·ies.**
☛ *Etym.* Through OF from the Latin name for this month. The Romans named the month after the *februarius mensis,* a festival of purification held at this time of year.

**fe·cal** (fē′kəl) having to do with FECES. *adj.* Also, **faecal.**

**fe·ces** (fē′sēz) the waste matter discharged from the intestines. *n. pl.* Also, **faeces.**

**feck·less** (fek′lis) **1** futile; ineffective. **2** careless: *feckless behaviour.* *adj.*

**fe·cund** (fek′ənd *or* fē′kənd) fruitful; productive; fertile: *Edison had a fecund mind.* *adj.*

**fe·cun·di·ty** (fi kun′də tē) fruitfulness; productiveness; fertility. *n.*

**fed** (fed) pt. and pp. of FEED: *We fed the birds. Have they been fed today?* *v.*

**fed·er·al** (fed′ə rəl) **1** formed by an agreement between groups establishing a central organization to handle their common affairs while the parties to the agreement keep control of local affairs: *The Canadian Federation of Agriculture is a federal organization of farm representatives.* **2** of or having to do with the central government formed in this way: *Parliament is the federal lawmaking body of Canada.* **3** Also, **Federal**, of or having to do with the central government of Canada. *adj.*

**Federal Government 1** the government of Canada, located in Ottawa. Its responsibilities are specified by the Constitution Act, 1867. **2** the prime minister and his or her Cabinet.

**fed·er·al·ism** (fed′ə rə liz′əm) the federal principle of government. *n.*

**fed·er·al·ist** (fed′ə rə list) a person who favours the federal principle of government. *n.*

**fed·er·al·ize** (fed′ə rə līz′) **1** put under the control of the federal government. **2** unite into a federal union. *v.*, **fed·er·al·ized, fed·er·al·iz·ing.**

**fed·er·ate** (fed′ə rāt′ *for verb*, fed′ə rit *for adjective*) **1** form into a federation. **2** formed into a federation; federation. **1** *v.*, **fed·er·at·ed, fed·er·at·ing;** **2** *adj.*

**fed·er·a·tion** (fed′ə rā′shən) **1** the act or process of federating, especially the formation of a federal union. **2** a nation formed by federation; a union of a number of separate provinces, states, etc.: *Canada and the United States are both federations.* **3** a union formed by agreement of organizations, states, or nations; league: *a federation of student groups.* *n.*

**fed·er·a·tive** (fed′ə rə tiv *or* fed′ə rā′tiv) of, like, or forming a federation. *adj.*

**fe·do·ra** (fi dô′rə) a man's soft felt hat with a curved brim and a crown creased lengthwise. *n.*

**fee** (fē) **1** a sum of money asked or paid for a service or privilege; a charge: *Doctors and lawyers get fees for their services. What is the annual fee for the tennis club?* **2** in a feudal society, the right to keep and use land; FIEF. **3** land held in this way. **4** an inherited estate in land. **5** ownership. **6 fees,** *pl.* the money paid for instruction at a school or university. *n.*
**hold in fee,** have legal possession of; own.
☛ *Etym.* Fee, with the basic meanings of 'property, payment', comes from Anglo-Norman *fee* which developed from Med. L. *feodum, feudum.* The Latin word probably came from an early Germanic word related to OE *fēoh* 'cattle, property'. FEUDAL and words related to it are believed to have come from the same source. See also the note at FELLOW.

**fee·ble** (fē′bəl) **1** lacking strength; weak: *a feeble old woman.* **2** weak intellectually or morally: *a feeble mind.* **3** lacking in force; ineffective: *a feeble attempt.* **4** lacking in volume, brightness, etc.: *a feeble cry.* *adj.*, **fee·bler, fee·blest.** —**fee′ble·ness,** *n.* —**fee′bly,** *adv.*

**fee·ble–mind·ed** (fē′bəl mīn′did) weak in mind; lacking normal intelligence. *adj.* —**fee′ble·mind′ed·ly,** *adv.* —**fee′ble·mind′ed·ness,** *n.*

**feed** (fēd) **1** give food to: *We feed a baby because she cannot feed herself.* **2** give as food to: *Feed this grain to the chickens.* **3** food for animals; an allowance of food for an animal: *Give the chickens their feed.* **4** of animals, eat: *Don't disturb the cows while they're feeding.* **5** *Informal.* a meal for a person. **6** supply with material: *to feed a machine, to feed a furnace.* **7** supplying a machine with material. **8** the material supplied. **9** the part of a machine that supplies material. **10** satisfy; gratify: *Praise fed his vanity.* **11** nourish: *He fed his anger with thoughts of revenge.* 1, 2, 4, 6, 10, 11 *v.*, **fed, feed·ing;** 3, 5, 7–9 *n.*
**feed in** or **into,** supply to a machine: *You feed the paper in here. Feed the pages into the copier.*
**feed on** or **upon,** **a** live at the expense of. **b** derive satisfaction from: *The artist feeds on admiration from the public.*
**feed to,** supply to: *The agency feeds news stories to all the radio stations.*
**fed up,** tired, bored, or frustrated.

**feed·back** (fēd′bak′) **1** the return to a system, machine, etc. of part of its output in order to change or control future output. **2** *Informal.* information on the results of one's actions that will influence one's future decisions or actions. *n.*

**feed·er** (fē′dər) **1** a person or thing that feeds. **2** a device that supplies food to a person or animal: *a bird feeder.* **3** anything that supplies something else with material: *a brook is a feeder for a river.* *n.*

**feeder line** a branch airline, railway, pipeline, etc.

**feel** (fēl) **1** touch: *Feel this cloth.* **2** try to find or make one's way by touch: *She felt her way across the room when the lights went out.* **3** test or examine by touching: *to feel someone's pulse.* **4** search by touch; grope: *He felt in his pockets for a dime.* **5** find out by touching: *Feel how cold my hands are.* **6** be aware of: *to feel the cool breeze.* **7** have the feeling of being; be: *She feels well.* **8** give the feeling of being; seem: *The air feels cold.* **9** have in one's mind; experience: *She feels joy.* **10** have pity or sympathy: *She feels for all who suffer.* **11** be influenced or affected by: *The ship feels its helm.* **12** think; believe; consider: *I feel that we will win.* **13** the way in which something feels to the touch: *Wet soap has a greasy feel.* **14** the sense of touch. 1–12 *v.*, **felt, feel·ing;** 13, 14 *n.*
**feel for** or **with,** sympathize with.
**feel like,** *Informal.* **a** have a desire for; want: *I feel like an ice-cream cone.* **b** seem as if it is going to: *It feels like rain.* **c** seem like to the sense of touch: *The cat's fur felt like silk.*
**feel out,** find out about in a cautious way.
**feel up to,** feel able to do something.

**feel·er** (fē′lər) **1** a special part of an animal's body for touching: *An insect's antennae are its feelers.* See INSECT for picture. **2** a suggestion, remark, hint, question, etc. made to find out what others are thinking or planning: *She has put out some feelers to try to find out how people like the idea.* *n.*

**feel·ing** (fē′ling) 1 the sense of touch: *By feeling we can distinguish between something hard and something soft.* 2 a sensation experienced through this sense: *a feeling of pain.* 3 the ability or power to experience physical sensation: *She had no feeling in her left hand.* 4 emotion: *Joy, sorrow, fear, and anger are feelings.* 5 full of feeling; sensitive; emotional: *a feeling heart.* 6 pity; sympathy. 7 an opinion; sentiment: *Her feeling was that right would win.* 8 **feelings**, *pl.* **a** susceptibilities: *The remark hurt her feelings.* **b** sympathies: *His feelings were touched by the child's cry of pain.* 9 ppr. of FEEL. 1–4, 6–8 *n.*, 5 *adj.*, 9 *v.* —**feel′ing·ly**, *adv.*

**fee simple** the ownership of land with the right to sell or give it to anyone.

**feet** (fēt) pl. of FOOT. *n.*
**carry off one's feet,** **a** make very enthusiastic. **b** impress.
**sit at someone's feet,** be a pupil or admirer of.
**stand on one's own feet,** be independent.
☞ *Hom.* FEAT.

**feign** (fān) 1 put on a false appearance of; make believe; pretend: *Some animals feign death when in danger.* 2 make up with intent to deceive; invent falsely: *to feign an excuse.* *v.*

**feigned** (fānd) 1 imagined; not real. 2 pretended: *a feigned attack.* 3 invented to deceive: *a feigned headache.* 4 pt. and pp. of FEIGN. 1–3 *adj.*, 4 *v.*

**feint** (fānt) 1 a movement intended to deceive; pretended blow; sham attack. 2 make a pretended blow or sham attack: *The fighter feinted with his right hand and struck with his left.* 3 a false appearance; pretence: *She made a feint of studying while actually listening to the radio.* 1, 3 *n.*, 2 *v.*
☞ *Hom.* FAINT.

**feist·y** (fī′stē) 1 aggressively energetic and exuberant. 2 touchy or quarrelsome. *adj.*, **feist·i·er, feist·i·est.**

**feld·spar** (feld′spär) any of several crystalline minerals composed mostly of aluminum silicates: *Feldspar is used for making glass and pottery.* *n.*

**fe·lic·i·tate** (fə lis′ə tāt′) formally express good wishes to; congratulate: *Giovanni's friends felicitated him on his good fortune.* *v.*, **fe·lic·i·tat·ed, fe·lic·i·tat·ing.**

**fe·lic·i·ta·tion** (fə lis′ə tā′shən) a formal expression of good wishes; congratulation. *n.*

**fe·lic·i·tous** (fə lis′ə təs) 1 well chosen for the occasion; unusually appropriate: *The poem was full of striking and felicitous similes.* 2 having a gift for apt speech. *adj.* —**fe·lic′i·tous·ly**, *adv.* —**fe·lic′i·tous·ness**, *n.*

**fe·lic·i·ty** (fə lis′ə tē) 1 happiness; bliss. 2 good fortune; blessing. 3 a pleasing aptness in expression; appropriateness; grace: *The famous writer phrased her ideas with felicity.* 4 a happy turn of thought; a well-chosen phrase. *n.*, *pl.* **fe·lic·i·ties.**

**fe·line** (fē′līn) 1 of or having to do with the cat family. 2 any animal belonging to the cat family: *Lions, tigers, leopards, and panthers are felines.* 3 catlike; stealthy; sly: *The hunter stalked the deer with noiseless feline movements.* 1, 3 *adj.*, 2 *n.*

**fell¹** (fel) pt. of FALL: *Snow fell last night.* *v.*

**fell²** (fel) 1 cause to fall; knock down: *One blow felled him to the ground.* 2 cut down a tree. 3 all the trees cut down in one season. 4 turn down and stitch one edge of a seam over the other. 5 a seam made by felling. 1, 2, 4 *v.*, 3, 5 *n.*

**fell³** (fel) 1 cruel; fierce; terrible: *a fell blow.* 2 deadly; destructive: *a fell disease.* *adj.*

**fell⁴** (fel) the skin or hide of an animal. *n.*

**fel·lah** (fel′ə) in Egypt and other Arabic-speaking countries, a peasant or farm labourer. *n.*, *pl.* **fel·la·hin** (fel′ə hēn′).

**fell·er** (fel′ər) a person or thing that fells. *n.*

**fel·loe** (fel′ō) the circular rim of a wheel into which the outer ends of the spokes are inserted. See WHEEL for picture. *n.* Also, **felly.**
☞ *Hom.* FELLOW (fel′ō).

**fel·low** (fel′ō; often fel′ə for defs. 1, 2, and 3) 1 a man or boy: *Never mind, old fellow. Poor fellow!* 2 *Informal.* boyfriend: *She's got a new fellow.* 3 a friendly term of address for a dog, horse, etc. 4 a companion; comrade; associate: *She was cut off from her fellows.* 5 one of the same class or rank; equal: *The world has not his fellow.* 6 the other one of a pair; mate: *I have the fellow of your glove.* 7 belonging to the same class; united by the same work, interests, aims, etc.; being in the same or a like condition: *fellow citizens, fellow sufferers.* 8 a graduate student who has a fellowship in a university or college. 9 a member of a learned society. *n.*
**hail fellow well met,** very friendly.
☞ *Etym.* From OE *fēolaga* 'partner, associate', which came from ON *félagi*, literally a 'fee-layer', one who lays down a fee for a joint venture or partnership. See also the note at FEE.
☞ *Hom.* FELLOE.

**fellow feeling** sympathy.

**fel·low·ship** (fel′ō ship′) 1 companionship; friendliness. 2 taking part with others; sharing: *I have enjoyed my fellowship with you in this club.* 3 a group of people having similar tastes, interests, etc.; brotherhood; corporation. 4 a position or sum of money given to a person, such as a graduate student, to enable him or her to go on with his or her studies. *n.*

**fellow traveller** or **traveler** a person sympathizing with, though not a member of, a political movement or party, especially the COMMUNIST PARTY.

**fel·ly** (fel′ē) FELLOE. *n.*, *pl.* **fel·lies.**

**fel·on¹** (fel′ən) a person who has committed a FELONY. *n.*

**fel·on²** (fel′ən) a painful, usually pus-filled infection on a finger or toe, especially near the nail. *n.*

**fe·lo·ni·ous** (fə lō′nē əs) of, having to do with, or being a FELONY. *adj.* —**fe·lo′ni·ous·ly**, *adv.* —**fe·lo′ni·ous·ness**, *n.*

**fel·o·ny** (fel′ə nē) INDICTABLE OFFENCE. *n.*, *pl.* **fel·o·nies.**

**felt¹** (felt) pt. and pp. of FEEL: *She felt the soft fur of the cat. Things are felt with the hands.* *v.*

**felt²** (felt) 1 a kind of cloth that is not woven but is made by rolling and pressing together wool, hair, or fur, used to make hats, slippers, and pads. 2 something made of felt. 3 made of felt: *a felt hat.* *n.*

**fem.** 1 female. 2 feminine.

**fe·male** (fē′māl) 1 a woman or girl. 2 of or having to do with women or girls. 3 belonging to the sex that gives birth to young or produces eggs.  4 an animal belonging to this sex.  5 in botany, indicating or having to do with any reproductive structure that produces or contains elements that need fertilization from the male element; having pistils.  6 a flower having a pistil or pistils and no stamens.  7 a plant bearing only flowers with pistils.  8 of pipe fittings, etc., referring to or having a hollow part into which a corresponding part fits.  1, 4, 6, 7 n., 2, 3, 5, 8 adj.

**fem·i·nine** (fem′ə nin)  1 of women or girls: *Jewellery and lace are usually feminine belongings.*  2 like a woman; womanly; gentle.  3 like that of a woman; not suited to a man.  4 of or belonging to the female sex: *feminine graces.*  5 of the gender to which names of females belong: *Actress, queen,* and *vixen* are feminine nouns.  6 the feminine gender.  7 a word or form in the feminine gender: *Lioness* is the feminine of *lion*.  1–5 *adj.*, 6, 7 *n.*

**fem·i·nin·i·ty** (fem′ə nin′ə tē)  1 a FEMININE quality or condition.  2 women.  *n.*

**fem·i·nism** (fem′ə niz′əm)  a social movement promoting the advancement of increased rights and activities for women.  *n.*

**fem·i·nist** (fem′ə nist)  a person who believes in or favours FEMINISM.  *n.*

**fe·mur** (fē′mər)  the thighbone.  See LEG and PELVIS for pictures.  *n.*, *pl.* **fe·murs** or **fem·o·ra** (fem′ə rə).

**fen** (fen) *Brit.*  a marsh or swamp; bog.  *n.*

**fence** (fens)  1 a railing, wall, or other means of enclosing a yard, garden, field, farm, etc. to show where it ends or to keep people or animals out or in.  See PALE² for picture.  2 put a fence around; enclose with a fence; keep out or in with a fence.  3 fight, now only in sport or in theatre or film, with long, slender swords called foils; compete in FENCING (def. 1).  4 parry; evade.  5 a person who buys and sells stolen goods.  6 buy and sell stolen goods.  7 a place where stolen goods are bought and sold.  1, 5, 7 *n.*, 2–4, 6 *v.*, **fenced, fenc·ing**.
**fence in,**  keep in with a fence: *to fence in the chickens.*
**fence with,**  avoid giving a direct answer to.
**on the fence,** *Informal.*  not having made up one's mind which side to take; doubtful; hesitating.

**fenc·er** (fen′sər)  1 a person who fences with a sword or foil.  2 a person who makes or mends fences.  *n.*

Fencing with foils

**fenc·ing** (fen′sing)  1 the art of fighting, now only as a sport or in theatre or film, with swords or foils.  2 material for making fences.  3 fences.  4 ppr. of FENCE.  1–3 *n.*, 4 *v.*

**fend** (fend) *Archaic* or *poetic* except in
**fend for oneself,**  provide for oneself; get along by one's own efforts: *A young child cannot fend for itself.*
**fend off,**  ward off; keep off: *to fend off blows with one's arm.*

**fend·er** (fen′dər)  1 a curved protective covering over the wheels of an automobile, truck, etc.; mudguard.  2 a guard, made of rubber, rope, plastic, etc., hung over the sides of a boat or attached to a dock to protect the boat in docking; bumper.  3 a metal guard, frame, or screen in front of a fireplace to keep hot coals and sparks from the room.  4 anything that keeps or wards something off.  *n.*

**fen·nel** (fen′əl)  a tall perennial plant having yellow flowers: *The aromatic seeds of the fennel are used in medicine and cooking.*  *n.*

**fe·ral** (fē′rəl *or* fer′əl)  1 wild; untamed.  2 brutal; savage.  3 of a human being, living in the wild and not brought up by other humans: *Feral children never learn language.*  *adj.*
☛ Hom.  FERRULE, FERULE (for the second pronunciation of **feral**).

**fer·ment** (fər ment′ *for verb*, fėr′ment *for noun*)  1 undergo a gradual chemical change that involves the production of heat and the giving off of bubbles of gas, caused by yeast, bacteria, etc.: *Vinegar is formed when cider ferments.*  2 cause this chemical change in.  3 a substance or organism that causes fermentation: *Yeast is used as a ferment in brewing beer.*  4 cause unrest in; excite; agitate.  5 be excited; seethe with agitation or unrest.  6 excitement; agitation; unrest: *Rumours of war created a ferment.*  1, 2, 4, 5 *v.*, 3, 6 *n.*

**fer·men·ta·tion** (fėr′men tā′shən)  1 the act or process of FERMENTing (def. 1): *Fermentation causes milk to sour and bread to rise.*  2 excitement; agitation; unrest: *There was a long period of fermentation before the outbreak of revolution.*  3 a chemical change caused by a FERMENT (def. 3).  *n.*

**fer·mi·um** (fėr′mē əm)  a rare, radio-active metallic element, produced artificially.  *Symbol:* Fm  *n.*

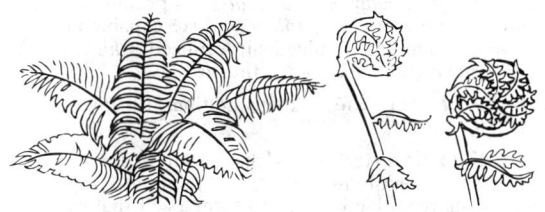
Fern: an ostrich fern, common in the Maritimes   Fiddleheads of this fern

**fern** (fėrn)  any of a group of plants that have roots, stems, and leaves, but no flowers, and reproduce by spores instead of seeds: *Maidenhair, bracken, club mosses, etc. are ferns.*  *n.*

**fern·y** (fėr′nē)  1 of or like FERNS.  2 covered with ferns: *the forest's ferny floor.*  *adj.*

**fe·ro·cious** (fə rō′shəs)  savage; fierce.  *adj.*
—**fe·ro′cious·ly,** *adv.*

**fe·roc·i·ty** (fə ros′ə tē)  savage behaviour; fierceness.  *n.*, *pl.* **fe·roc·i·ties**.

**fer·ret** (fer′it)  1 a white or yellowish-white weasel used for killing rats, hunting rabbits, etc.  2 hunt with ferrets.  3 hunt; search (*usually used with* **out**): *The detectives* *ferreted out the criminal.* **4** find or find out by persistent searching (*usually used with* **out**): *to ferret out the truth of the matter.* 1 *n.*, 2–4 *v.*

**fer·ric** (fer′ik) of or containing iron, especially iron with a valence of three. Compare with FERROUS. *adj.*

**Fer·ris wheel** (fer′is) a large, revolving framework of steel like an upright wheel, equipped with swinging seats that hang from its rim: *Ferris wheels are found in the amusement areas of fairs, exhibitions, and carnivals.*

**fer·rous** (fer′əs) of or containing iron, especially iron with a valence of two. Compare with FERRIC. *adj.*

**fer·rule** (fer′ül *or* fer′əl) a metal ring or cap put around the end of a cane, wooden handle, umbrella, etc. for strength and protection. *n.* Also, **ferule**.
☞ *Hom.* FERULE, FERAL (for the second pronunciation of **ferrule**).

**fer·ry** (fer′ē) **1** a boat that carries people and goods back and forth across a river or narrow stretch of water. **2** carry back and forth on a ferry, etc., especially as a regular service: *Hundreds of cars are ferried across Northumberland Strait every day.* **3** a place where a ferry operates. **4** go across in a ferryboat: *They ferried to Wolfe Island last Sunday.* **5** carry back and forth across a wide stretch of water in an aircraft. **6** fly an aircraft to a destination for delivery. **7** delivering aircraft to a destination by flying them. 1, 3, 7 *n.*, *pl.* **fer·ries**; 2, 4–6 *v.*, **fer·ried, fer·ry·ing.**
☞ *Hom.* FAIRY.

**fer·ry·boat** (fer′ē bōt′) FERRY (def. 1). *n.*

**fer·ry·man** (fer′ē mən) **1** a person who owns or has charge of a FERRY. **2** a person who works on a FERRY. *n.*, *pl.* **fer·ry·men** (-mən).

**fer·tile** (fer′tīl *or* fer′təl) **1** capable of reproduction; able to produce seeds, fruit, young, etc. **2** of soil, capable of producing plants, crops, etc.: *Sand is not very fertile.* **3** capable of producing many young; prolific: *Rabbits are fertile creatures, for they have litters of young more often than most other animals.* **4** productive of many ideas; inventive: *a fertile mind.* **5** capable of developing into a new individual; fertilized: *Chicks hatch from fertile eggs.* *adj.* —**fer′tile·ness**, *n.*

**fer·til·i·ty** (fer til′ə tē) the condition of being FERTILE. *n.*

**fer·ti·li·za·tion** (fer′tə lə zā′shən *or* fer′tə lī zā′shən) **1** the application of FERTILIZER. **2** the union of male and female reproductive cells to form a cell that will develop into a new individual. *n.*

**fer·ti·lize** (fer′tə līz′) **1** make FERTILE or productive: *A crop of alfalfa fertilized the soil by adding nitrates to it.* **2** put FERTILIZER on. **3** of a male reproductive cell, or sperm, unite with an egg cell in fertilization. *v.*, **fer·ti·lized, fer·ti·liz·ing.**

**fer·ti·liz·er** (fer′tə lī′zər) a person or thing that FERTILIZES, especially a substance put on land to make it able to produce more: *Manure is a fertilizer.* *n.*

**fer·ule**[1] (fer′ül *or* fer′əl) **1** a stick or ruler used for punishing children by striking them, especially on the hand. **2** punish with a stick or ruler. 1 *n.*, 2 *v.*, **fer·uled, fer·ul·ing.**
☞ *Hom.* FERRULE, FERAL (for the second pronunciation of **ferule**).

**fer·ule**[2] (fer′ül *or* fer′əl) See FERRULE. *n.*

**fer·ven·cy** (fer′vən sē) a great warmth of feeling; intensity; ardour. *n.*

**fer·vent** (fer′vənt) **1** showing warmth of feeling; ardent; intense: *a fervent plea.* **2** hot; glowing. *adj.* —**fer′vent·ly**, *adv.*

**fer·vid** (fer′vid) **1** showing great warmth of feeling; intensely emotional: *a fervid orator.* **2** intensely hot. *adj.* —**fer′vid·ly**, *adv.*

**fer·vour** *or* **fer·vor** (fer′vər) **1** great warmth of feeling; intense emotion: *The patriot's voice trembled from the fervour of his emotion.* **2** intense heat. *n.*

**fes·cue** (fes′kyü) **1** a tough grass used for pasture. **2** a small stick, straw, etc. for pointing out the letters in teaching a child to read. *n.*

**fes·tal** (fes′təl) of a feast, festival, or holiday; joyous; festive: *A wedding or a birthday is a festal occasion.* *adj.*

**fes·ter** (fes′tər) **1** form pus: *The neglected wound festered and became very painful.* **2** a sore that forms pus; small ulcer. **3** cause pus to form. **4** cause pain or bitterness; rankle: *Resentment festered in his heart.* **5** decay; rot. 1, 3–5 *v.*, 2 *n.*

**fes·ti·val** (fes′tə vəl) **1** a day or special time of rejoicing or feasting, often in memory of some great happening or person: *A Mozart Festival is held in Salzburg.* **2** a celebration; entertainment: *Every year the city has a music festival during the first week in May.* **3** a competition among drama groups, orchestras, etc., for recognition as the best in a region: *a high-school drama festival.* **4** merry-making; revelry. **5** having to do with a festival. *n.*

**fes·tive** (fes′tiv) of or for a feast, festival, or holiday; joyous; merry: *A birthday or wedding is a festive occasion.* *adj.* —**fes′tive·ly**, *adv.*

**fes·tiv·i·ty** (fes tiv′ə tē) **1** a festive activity; something done to celebrate: *the festivities of Canada Day.* **2** gaiety; merriment. **3** festival. *n.*, *pl.* **fes·tiv·i·ties.**

**fes·toon** (fes tün′) **1** a hanging curve of flowers, leaves, ribbons, etc.: *The flags were hung on the wall in colourful festoons.* **2** decorate with festoons: *The Christmas tree was festooned with tinsel.* **3** form into festoons; hang in curves: *Draperies were festooned over the window.* 1 *n.*, 2, 3 *v.*

**fe·tal** *or* **foe·tal** (fē′təl) of, having to do with, or like a FETUS. *adj.*

**fetch** (fech) **1** go and get; bring: *Please fetch me my glasses.* **2** cause to come; succeed in bringing. **3** be sold for: *Eggs were fetching a good price that year.* **4** *Informal.* attract; charm. **5** *Informal.* hit; strike. *v.*

**fetch·ing** (fech′ing) **1** *Informal.* attractive; charming: *She wore a fetching hat.* **2** ppr. of FETCH. 1 *adj.*, 2 *v.*

**fete** *or* **fête** (fāt; *French*, fet) **1** a festival; a gala entertainment or celebration, usually held outdoors: *A large fete was given for the benefit of the town hospital.* **2** honour with a fete; entertain: *The engaged couple were feted by their friends.* 1 *n.*, 2 *v.*, **fet·ed** *or* **fêt·ed, fet·ing** *or* **fêt·ing.**
☞ *Hom.* FATE.

**fet·id** (fet′id *or* fē′tid) smelling very bad; stinking. *adj.* —**fet′id·ly**, *adv.* —**fet′id·ness**, *n.*

**fet·ish** (fet′ish *or* fē′tish) **1** any material object supposed to have magic power. **2** anything regarded with unreasoning reverence or devotion: *Some people make a fetish of fashionable clothes.* *n.*

**fet·ish·ism** (fet′i shiz′əm *or* fē′ti shiz′əm) belief in or worship of FETISHes. *n.*

**fet·lock** (fet′lok) **1** the tuft of hair above a horse's hoof on the back part of the leg. **2** the part of a horse's leg where this tuft grows. See HORSE for picture. *n.*

**fet·ter** (fet′ər) **1** a chain or shackle for the feet to prevent escape. **2** bind with fetters; chain the feet of. **3** anything that shackles or binds; restraint. **4** bind; restrain: *The boy had to learn to fetter his temper.* 1, 3 *n.*, 2, 4 *v.*

**fet·tle** (fet′əl) condition; trim: *The horse is in fine fettle and should win the race.* *n.*

**fe·tus** or **foe·tus** (fē′təs) an embryo of human beings, animals, or birds, especially during the later stages of its development in the womb or in the egg. *n.*

**feud**[1] (fyüd) **1** a long and deadly quarrel between families, tribes, etc., often passed down from generation to generation. **2** continued strife between two persons, groups, etc. **3** a quarrel. **4** engage in a deadly quarrel, especially one involving families: *They have been feuding with their neighbours for years.* 1–3 *n.*, 4 *v.*

**feud**[2] (fyüd) a feudal estate; FIEF. *n.*

**feu·dal** (fyü′dəl) **1** of or having to do with FEUDALISM. **2** of or having to do with FIEFs. *adj.*
☛ *Etym.* See note at FEE.

**feu·dal·ism** (fyü′də liz′əm) **1** the social, economic, and political system of western Europe in the Middle Ages. Under this system vassals gave military and other services to a lord in return for protection and the use of land owned by the lord. **2** any social, economic, or political system that suggests or resembles this. *n.*

**feu·dal·is·tic** (fyü′də lis′tik) **1** of or having to do with FEUDALISM. **2** tending toward or favouring FEUDALISM. *adj.*

**feudal system** FEUDALISM.

**feu·da·to·ry** (fyü′də tô′rē) **1** owing feudal services (*to*). **2** a feudal vassal: *The duke summoned his feudatories to aid him in war.* **3** holding or held as a feudal estate or FIEF. **4** a feudal estate; FIEF. 1, 3 *adj.*, 2, 4 *n.*, *pl.* **feu·da·to·ries**.

**feud·ist** (fyü′dist) a person engaging in a FEUD (defs. 1–3). *n.*

**fe·ver** (fē′vər) **1** an unhealthy condition of the body in which the temperature is higher than normal. **2** any of various diseases that cause fever and make the heart beat rapidly, such as scarlet fever and typhoid fever. **3** an excited, restless condition: *When gold was discovered, the miners were in a fever of excitement.* **4** affect with fever or excite as if with fever. **5** a current fad or enthusiasm for something or for some person. 1–3, 5 *n.*, 4 *v.*
—**fe′ver·less**, *adj.*

**fe·vered** (fē′vərd) **1** having fever; hot with fever: *a fevered brow.* **2** excited; restless. **3** pt. and pp. of FEVER. 1, 2 *adj.*, 3 *v.*

**fe·ver·few** (fē′vər fyü′) a perennial plant of the same family as the aster, having small, white, daisy-like flowers. *n.*

**fe·ver·ish** (fē′və rish) **1** having fever, especially a slight fever. **2** caused by fever: *feverish thirst, feverish dreams.* **3** causing fever: *a feverish climate.* **4** infested with fever: *a feverish swamp.* **5** excited; restless: *a feverish anxiety.* *adj.* —**fe′ver·ish·ly**, *adv.* —**fe′ver·ish·ness**, *n.*

# fetishism 447 fibreglass

hat, āge, fär; let, ēqual, tėrm; it, īce
hot, ōpen, ôrder; oil, out; cup, pu̇t, rüle
əbove, takən, pencəl, lemən, circəs
ch, child; ng, long; sh, ship
th, thin; ᴛʜ, then; zh, measure

**fe·ver·ous** (fē′və rəs) FEVERISH. *adj.*

**fever pitch** a state of intense excitement or frenzied activity.

**fe·ver–root** (fē′vər rüt′) a coarse plant whose roots are sometimes used for medicine. *n.*

**fever sore** a COLD SORE.

**few** (fyü) **1** not many: *There are few women more than 185 centimetres tall.* **2** a small number: *Only a few of the boys had bicycles.* **3 the few,** the minority, especially a small, privileged group. 1 *adj.*, 2, 3 *n.* —**few′ness**, *n.*
**few and far between,** very few or infrequent.
**quite a few,** *Informal.* a good many: *We caught ten fish, but quite a few got away.*
☛ *Syn.* Few, LESS. Few refers to number and to things that are countable: *Few cars were on the road. There were fewer than sixty present.* In formal usage **less** refers only to amount or quantity and to things that are measured: *There was a good deal less lateness in the second term. There was even less hay than the summer before.*

**fez** (fez) a felt cap, usually red, having a high crown with a flat top and ornamented with a long, black tassel: *The fez was formerly the national headdress of Turkish men.* See CAP for picture. *n.*, *pl.* **fez·zes**.

**ff** fortissimo.

**ff.** **1** the following pages, sections, etc.: *p. 26 ff.* means page 26 and the following few pages. **2** folios.

**fi·an·cé** (fē′än sā′ *or* fē än′sā) a man to whom a woman is engaged to be married. *n.*

**fi·an·cée** (fē′än sā′ *or* fē än′sā) a woman to whom a man is engaged to be married. *n.*

**fi·as·co** (fē as′kō) a failure; breakdown: *The picnic was a fiasco because of a cloudburst.* *n.*, *pl.* **fi·as·cos** or **fi·as·coes**.

**fi·at** (fī′ət *or* fī′at) **1** an authoritative order or command; decree: *The emperor's fiat must be obeyed.* **2** sanction: *He acted under the fiat of the king.* *n.*

**fib** (fib) *Informal.* **1** a lie about some small matter. **2** tell such a lie: *He fibbed when he said he had not eaten the last cookie in the box.* 1 *n.*, 2 *v.*, **fibbed, fib·bing.**
—**fib′ber**, *n.*

**fi·bre** (fī′bər) **1** one of the threadlike parts or strands that form certain plant and animal substances: *muscle fibres.* **2** a substance made up of such threadlike parts: *Hemp fibre can be spun into rope or woven into a coarse cloth.* **3** texture: *cloth of coarse fibre.* **4** character; nature: *A person of strong moral fibre can resist temptation.* **5** a slender, threadlike root of a plant. **6** ROUGHAGE (def. 2). *n.* Also, **fiber.**

**fi·bre·board** (fī′bər bôrd′) a building material made by compressing fibres, especially of wood, into flat sheets: *Fibreboard is often used in constructing partitions between rooms.* *n.* Also, **fiberboard.**

**fi·bre·glass** (fī′bər glas′) a strong, fireproof material made from fine threads of glass. It is used in thick mats for insulation, or mixed with plastic for making boats, etc. *n.* Also, **fiberglass.**

**fibre optics** 1 the technology of using a very long, fine, flexible glass or acrylic fibre or a bundle of such fibres for transmitting light or optical images by total internal reflection or refraction. 2 designating such a fibre or a bundle of such fibres forming part of a telecommunications system, optical instruments, etc.

**fi·bril** (fī′brəl) 1 a small or very slender fibre. 2 one of the hairs on the roots of small plants. *n.*

**fi·brin** (fī′brən) a tough, elastic, insoluble protein forming the fibrous network of a blood clot: *Fibrin is formed from fibrinogen by the action of an enzyme in the blood. n.*

**fi·brin·o·gen** (fī brin′ə jen′) a soluble protein found especially in blood plasma, that is converted into FIBRIN by the action of an enzyme when blood clots. *n.*

**fi·brous** (fī′brəs) made up of fibres; having fibres; like fibre. *adj.*

**fib·u·la** (fib′yə lə) 1 the outer, thinner of the two bones in the human lower leg: *The fibula extends from knee to ankle.* See LEG for picture. 2 a similar bone in the hind leg of animals. 3 a clasp or brooch, often highly ornamented, used by the ancient Greeks and Romans: *A fibula resembles a safety pin. n., pl.* **fib·u·lae** (-lē′ or -lī′) or **fib·u·las.**

**fib·u·lar** (fib′yə lər) of or having to do with the FIBULA. *adj.*

A muslin fichu of the mid 19c. in Europe

**fich·u** (fish′ü) a three-cornered piece of muslin, lace, or other soft material worn by women about the neck, with the ends drawn together or crossed on the breast. *n.*

**fick·le** (fik′əl) likely to change without reason; changing; not constant: *fickle fortune, a fickle friend. adj.* —**fick′le·ness,** *n.*

**fic·tion** (fik′shən) 1 novels, short stories, and other prose writings that tell about imaginary, and sometimes real, people and happenings. Both characters and events in fiction may sometimes be partly real. 2 what is imagined or made up; imaginary happenings; make-believe: *The explorer exaggerated so much in telling about his remarkable adventures that it was impossible to separate fact from fiction.* 3 an imaginary account or statement; a made-up story: *His account of the accident is a fiction from beginning to end. n.*

**fic·tion·al** (fik′shə nəl) of or having to do with FICTION: *Historical novels give a fictional treatment to actual events. adj.* —**fic′tion·al·ly,** *adv.*

**fic·ti·tious** (fik tish′əs) 1 not real; imaginary; made-up: *Characters in novels are usually entirely fictitious.* 2 assumed in order to deceive; false: *The criminal used a fictitious name. adj.* —**fic·ti′tious·ly,** *adv.* —**fic·ti′tious·ness,** *n.*

**fid·dle** (fid′əl) 1 *Informal.* VIOLIN. 2 *Informal.* play on a violin. 3 make aimless movements; play nervously or restlessly; toy: *The embarrassed boy fiddled with his hat.* 4 trifle: *She fiddled away the whole day doing nothing.* 1 *n.,* 2–4 *v.,* **fid·dled, fid·dling.** —**fid′dler,** *n.*
**fit as a fiddle,** in excellent physical condition.
**play second fiddle,** take a secondary part.

**fid·dle·head** (fid′əl hed′) the young leaves, or fronds, of certain ferns, eaten as a delicacy: *Fiddleheads are eaten especially in Nova Scotia and New Brunswick.* See FERN for picture. *n.*

**fid·dle·neck** (fid′əl nek′) FIDDLEHEAD. *n.*

**fiddler crab** a small burrowing crab.

**fid·dle·stick** (fid′əl stik′) 1 a violin bow. 2 a mere nothing; trifle. *n.*

**fid·dle·sticks** (fid′əl stiks′) nonsense! rubbish! *interj.*

**fi·del·i·ty** (fə del′ə tē *or* fī del′ə tē) 1 faithfulness to a trust or vow; steadfast faithfulness; loyalty. 2 accuracy; exactness, as in a copy or in the reproduction of sound by a radio transmitter or receiver, a record player, etc. *n., pl.* **fi·del·i·ties.**

**fidg·et** (fij′it) 1 move about restlessly; be uneasy: *A child fidgets if he or she has to sit still a long time.* 2 make uneasy. 3 the condition of being restless or uneasy. 4 a person who moves about restlessly. 5 **the fidgets,** a fit of restlessness or uneasiness. 1, 2 *v.,* 3–5 *n.*

**fidg·et·y** (fij′ə tē) restless; uneasy. *adj.*

**fi·du·ci·ar·y** (fə dyü′shē er′ē *or* fə dü′shē er′ē) 1 held in trust: *fiduciary estates.* 2 holding in trust: *A fiduciary possessor is legally responsible for what belongs to another.* 3 trustee. 4 of a trustee; of trust and confidence: *A guardian acts in a fiduciary capacity.* 1, 2, 4 *adj.,* 3 *n., pl.* **fi·du·ci·ar·ies.**

**fief** (fēf) in feudal times, a piece of land held from a lord in return for military and other services as required; feudal estate. *n.*

**field** (fēld) 1 a piece of land used for crops or pasture: *a wheat field.* 2 land with few or no trees: *They rode through forest and field.* 3 a piece of land used for some special purpose: *a playing field.* 4 land yielding some product: *the coal fields of Alberta, the gold fields of South Africa.* 5 the place where a battle is or has been fought. 6 a battle: *The English won the field.* 7 a region where certain military operations, scientific activities, etc. are conducted. 8 a large, flat space; broad surface: *A field of ice surrounds the North Pole.* 9 the surface on which some emblem is pictured or painted: *the field of a coat of arms.* 10 a range of opportunity or interest; sphere of activity or operation: *Many great discoveries have been made in the field of science.* 11 in physics, the space throughout which a force operates: *A magnet has a magnetic field around it.* 12 the space or area in which things can be seen through a telescope, microscope, etc. without moving it: *the field of vision.* 13 the entire screen area occupied by a television image. 14 all those participating in a game, contest, or outdoor sport: *At the halfway mark in the marathon, a Canadian was leading the field.* 15 all those participating in a game or contest except one or more specified: *to bet on one horse against the field.* 16 in baseball, cricket, etc., stop or catch and return a ball. 17 act as a fielder in baseball, cricket, etc. 18 have as players: *We field a strong team.* 1–15 *n.,* 16–18 *v.*
**field a question,** answer a question asked unexpectedly.
**take the field,** begin a battle, campaign, game, etc.

**field artillery** artillery mounted on carriages for easy movement by armies in the field.

**field day** 1 a day set aside for athletic contests and outdoor sports. 2 a day when soldiers perform drills, mock fights, etc. 3 a day of unusual activity, display, or success.

**field·er** (fēl′dər) 1 in baseball, a player who is stationed around or outside the diamond to stop the ball and throw it in. 2 in cricket, a person playing in a similar position. *n.*

Field glasses

**field glasses** or **field glass** a small binocular telescope.

**field goal** in football, a goal counting three points, scored by kicking the ball between the uprights and above the crossbar of the goal post.

**field hockey** a game played on a grass field by two teams whose players, except the goalie, use curved sticks and try to drive a ball into the opposing team's goal.

**field hospital** a temporary hospital near a battlefield.

**field house** a building near an athletic field, used for storing equipment, for dressing rooms, etc.

**field magnet** an electromagnet used in a generator or motor to make a strong electric field.

**field mouse** a medium-sized VOLE found throughout most of Canada and the northern United States.

**field officer** an army officer ranking above a captain and below a brigadier: *Colonels, lieutenant-colonels, and majors are field officers.*

**field of fire** the area that a gun or battery covers effectively.

**field trip** a trip to give students special opportunities for observing facts relating to a particular field of study.

**field work** scientific or technical work done in the field by surveyors, geologists, linguists, etc.

**field·work** (fēl′dwėrk′) a temporary fortification for defence made by soldiers in the field. *n.*

**fiend** (fēnd) 1 an evil spirit; devil. 2 a very wicked or cruel person. 3 *Informal.* a person who indulges excessively in some habit, practice, game, etc.: *He is a fiend for work.* *n.* —**fiend′like′**, *adj.*
☛ *Etym.* From OE *fēond* 'enemy'. related to *fēogan* 'to hate'. See also the note at FRIEND.

**fiend·ish** (fēn′dish) very cruel or wicked; devilish: *fiendish tortures, a fiendish yell.* *adj.* —**fiend′ish·ly**, *adv.* —**fiend′ish·ness**, *n.*

**fierce** (fērs) 1 savage; wild: *a fierce lion.* 2 raging; violent: *a fierce wind.* 3 very eager or active; ardent: *a fierce determination to win.* 4 *Informal.* intense; extreme: *The heat was fierce.* *adj.*, **fierc·er, fierc·est.** —**fierce′ly**, *adv.* —**fierce′ness**, *n.*

**fier·y** (fī′rē) 1 consisting of fire; containing fire;

---

**field artillery** 449 **fight**

hat, āge, fär; let, ēqual, tėrm; it, īce
hot, ōpen, ôrder; oil, out; cup, pút, rüle
әbove, takәn, pencәl, lemәn, circәs
ch, child; ng, long; sh, ship
th, thin; ᴛн, then; zh, measure

burning; flaming. 2 like fire; very hot; brilliant; glowing: *a fiery red.* 3 full of feeling or spirit; ardent: *a fiery speech.* 4 easily aroused or excited: *a fiery temper.* 5 inflamed: *a fiery sore.* *adj.*, **fier·i·er, fier·i·est.** —**fier′i·ly**, *adv.* —**fier′i·ness**, *n.*

**fi·es·ta** (fē es′tә) 1 a religious festival; saint's day. 2 a holiday; festivity. *n.*

**fife** (fīf) 1 a small, shrill musical instrument like a flute: *Fifes and drums are used in playing marches.* 2 play on a fife. 1 *n.*, 2 *v.*, **fifed, fif·ing.** —**fif′er**, *n.*

**fif·teen** (fif′tēn′) 1 five more than ten; 15: *Fifteen isn't enough. Fifteen people answered the ad.* 2 the numeral 15: *The 15 refers to the song number, not the page.* 3 the fifteenth in a set or series. 4 being fifteenth in a set or series (*used after the noun*): *Chapter Fifteen.* 5 a set or series of fifteen persons or things. 1–3, 5 *n.*, 1, 4 *adj.*

**fif·teenth** (fif′tēnth′) 1 next after the 14th; last in a series of fifteen; 15th. 2 one, or being one, of 15 equal parts. *adj.*, *n.*

**fifth** (fifth) 1 next after the fourth; last in a series of five; 5th. 2 one, or being one, of 5 equal parts. 3 in music, the fifth tone from the keynote of a scale; the dominant. 4 the interval between such tones. 5 a combination of such tones. 1, 2 *adj.*, 1–5 *n.*

**fifth column** any persons within a country who secretly aid its enemies.

**fifth columnist** a member of the FIFTH COLUMN.

**fifth·ly** (fifth′lē) in the fifth place. *adv.*

**fifth wheel** *Informal.* a person or thing that is not needed.

**fif·ti·eth** (fif′tē ith) 1 next after the 49th; last in a series of fifty; 50th. 2 one, or being one, of 50 equal parts. *adj.*, *n.*

**fif·ty** (fif′tē) 1 five times ten; 50. 2 the numeral 50. 3 the fiftieth in a set or series. 4 a 50-dollar bill: *She asked the teller for two fifties.* 5 being fiftieth in a set or series (*used after the noun*): *Chapter Fifty.* 6 a set or series of fifty persons or things. 7 **fifties**, *pl.* the years from fifty through fifty-nine, especially of a century or of a person's life: *Her grandfather is in his fifties.* 1–4, 6, 7 *n.*, *pl.* **fif·ties;** 1, 5 *adj.*

**fif·ty-fif·ty** (fif′tē fif′tē) *Informal.* half-and-half; in or with equal shares. *adv.*, *adj.*

**fig** (fig) 1 a small, soft, sweet fruit that grows in warm regions: *Figs are usually dried like dates and raisins.* 2 the tree that figs grow on. 3 a very small amount: *I don't care a fig for your opinion.* *n.*

**fig.** figure.

**fight** (fīt) 1 a struggle; battle; conflict; combat; contest. 2 an angry dispute. 3 take part in a fight. 4 take part in a fight against; war against: *to fight disease.* 5 carry on a fight, conflict, etc. 6 get or make by fighting. 7 cause to fight. 8 disagree angrily; quarrel: *The boys were always fighting about one thing or another.* 9 the power or will to fight: *There is fight in the old dog yet.* 1, 2, 9 *n.*, 3–8 *v.*, **fought, fight·ing.**

**fight back,** a offer resistance: *They had no heart to fight back.* b struggle to control: *She fought back her tears.*
**fight down,** control: *to fight down a feeling of fear.*
**fight it out,** fight until one side wins.
**fight off,** a turn back; repel: *Fight off an enemy attack.* b overcome; stop the progress of: *to fight off a cold.*
**fight on,** continue struggling.
**fight shy of,** keep away from; avoid.
**show fight,** resist; be ready to fight: *The hunted animal was too weary to show fight.*

**fight·er** (fī′tər) 1 one that fights. 2 a professional boxer. 3 a FIGHTER PLANE. *n.*

**fighter plane** a highly manoeuvrable and heavily armed airplane used mainly for attacking enemy aircraft or strafing ground forces.

**fighting chance** *Informal.* the possibility of success, but only after a long, hard struggle.

**fig·ment** (fig′mənt) something imagined; a made-up story. *n.*

**fig·ur·a·tion** (fig′ə rā′shən *or* fig′yə rā′shən) 1 a form; shape. 2 a forming; shaping. 3 a representation by a likeness or symbol. *n.*

**fig·ur·a·tive** (fig′ə rə tiv *or* fig′yə rə tiv) 1 using words out of their literal meaning to add beauty or force. 2 having many figures of speech: *Much poetry is figurative.* 3 representing by a likeness or symbol: *A globe is a figurative model of the world.* *adj.*
—**fig′ur·a·tive·ly,** *adv.* —**fig′ur·a·tive·ness,** *n.*

**fig·ure** (fig′ər *or* fig′yər) 1 a symbol for a number: *The symbols 1, 2, 3, etc. are called figures.* 2 use figures to find the answer to a problem; reckon; compute; show by figures. 3 an amount or value given in figures: *The price is too high; ask a lower figure.* 4 a form or shape: *In the darkness she saw dim figures moving.* 5 a form enclosing a surface or space: *Circles, triangles, squares, cubes, and spheres are all geometrical figures.* 6 a person; character: *Samuel de Champlain is a great figure in Canadian history.* 7 a human form; a person considered from the point of view of appearance, manner, etc.: *The poor old woman was a figure of distress.* 8 be conspicuous; appear: *The names of great leaders figure in the story of human progress.* 9 an image or likeness. 10 a picture or drawing; a diagram or illustration: *This dictionary makes use of many figures to help explain the meaning of words.* 11 show by a figure; represent in a diagram. 12 a design or pattern: *Cloth or wallpaper often has figures on it.* 13 decorate with a figure or pattern. 14 an outline traced by movements: *figures made by an airplane.* 15 a set of movements in dancing or skating. 16 FIGURE OF SPEECH. 17 think; consider. 18 *Informal.* make sense: *That figures.* 19 picture mentally; imagine: *Figure to yourself a happy family, secure in their own home.* 20 **figures,** *pl.* calculations using figures; arithmetic: *She was never very good at figures.* 1, 3–5, 9, 10, 12, 14–16, 20 *n.*, 2, 8, 11, 13, 17–19 *v.*, **fig·ured, fig·ur·ing.** —**fig′ur·er,** *n.*
**figure on,** *Informal.* a depend on; rely on: *We are figuring on your help in painting the house.* b consider as part of a plan or undertaking.
**figure out,** a find out by using figures: *She soon figured out how much it would cost.* b think out; understand: *She couldn't figure out what was meant.*

**fig·ured** (fig′ərd *or* fig′yərd) 1 decorated with a design or pattern; not plain. 2 shown by a figure, diagram, or picture. 3 formed; shaped: *figured in bronze.* 4 pt. and pp. of FIGURE. 1–3 *adj.*, 4 *v.*

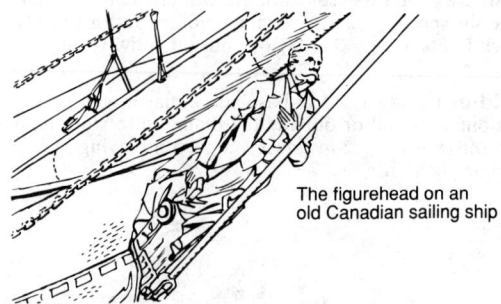

The figurehead on an old Canadian sailing ship

**fig·ure·head** (fig′ər hed *or* fig′yər hed′) 1 a person who is the head in name only, and has no real authority or responsibility. 2 a statue or carving decorating the bow of a ship. *n.*

**figure of speech** an expression in which words are used with a figurative meaning or in exceptional combinations to add beauty or force: *Similes and metaphors are figures of speech.*

**fig·ure–skate** (fig′ər skāt′ *or* fig′yər skāt′) engage in FIGURE SKATING. *v.*, **fig·ure-skat·ed, fig·ure-skat·ing.**

**fig·ure–skat·er** (fig′ər skā′tər *or* fig′yər skā′tər) a person who FIGURE-SKATES. *n.*

**figure skating** the art or practice of performing figures and ballet programs on ice skates, often to music.

**fig·ur·ine** (fig′ə rēn′ *or* fig′yə rēn′) a small ornamental figure made of stone, pottery, etc.; statuette. *n.*

**fig·wort** (fig′wėrt′) 1 a tall, coarse plant with small, greenish-purple or yellow flowers that have a disagreeable odour. 2 any similar plant. *n.*

**Fi·ji·an** (fē′jē ən *or* fē jē′ən) 1 of or having to do with the Fiji Islands, a group of islands in the south Pacific, their people, or their language. 2 a native or inhabitant of the Fiji Islands. 3 the language of the Fijians. 1 *adj.*, 2, 3 *n.*

**fil·a·ment** (fil′ə mənt) 1 a very fine thread. 2 a very slender, threadlike part: *The wire that gives off light in an electric light bulb is a filament.* 3 the stalklike part of the stamen of a flower. It supports the ANTHER. See FLOWER for picture. *n.*

**fil·bert** (fil′bərt) 1 hazelnut, the thick-shelled, sweet nut of the cultivated European hazel tree: *Filberts are good to eat.* 2 the tree or shrub it grows on. *n.*

**filch** (filch) steal in small quantities; pilfer: *He filched apples from the basket.* *v.* —**filch′er,** *n.*

**file**[1] (fīl) 1 a place for keeping papers in order: *You will find the letter in the file.* 2 a set of papers kept in order. 3 put away papers, etc. in order: *Please file this letter.* 4 a collection of information stored in a computer. 5 a line of people or things one behind another: *a file of soldiers.* 6 march or move in such a line: *The class filed out quietly.* 7 a small detachment of soldiers. 8 make application. 1, 2, 4, 5, 7 *n.*, 3, 6, 8 *v.*, **filed, fil·ing.** —**fil′er,** *n.*
**in file,** one after another; in succession: *We walked in file.*
**on file,** in a file; put away and kept in order: *The principal keeps all our school reports on file.*

Files

**file²** (fīl) **1** a steel tool with many small ridges or teeth on it: *The rough surface of a file is used to wear away hard materials or to make rough materials smooth.* **2** smooth or wear away with a file. 1 *n.*, 2 *v.*, **filed, fil·ing.**
—**fil′er**, *n.*

**file clerk** a person whose work is taking care of the files in an office.

**fi·let** (fi lā′, fil′ā *or* fē′lā) **1** a net or lace having a square mesh. **2** fillet; a slice of fish, meat, etc. without bones or fat. *n.*

**filet mignon** a small, round, thick piece of choice beef, cut from the tenderloin.

**fil·i·al** (fil′ē əl) of a son or daughter; due from a son or daughter: *The children treated their parents with filial respect.* *adj.* —**fil′i·al·ly,** *adv.*

**fil·i·bus·ter** (fil′ə bus′tər) **1** a member of a legislature who deliberately hinders the passage of a bill by long speeches or other means of delay. **2** deliberately hinder the passage of a bill by long speeches or other means of delay. **3** the deliberate hindering of the passage of a bill by such means. **4** a person who fights against another country without the authorization of his or her government; FREEBOOTER. **5** fight against another country without the authorization of one's government; act as a FREEBOOTER. 1, 3, 4 *n.*, 2, 5 *v.*
—**fil′i·bus′ter·er,** *n.*

**fil·i·gree** (fil′ə grē′) **1** very delicate, lacelike ornamental work of gold or silver wire. **2** a lacy, delicate, or fanciful pattern in any material: *The frost made a beautiful filigree on the window pane.* *n.*

**filing cabinet** a set of steel or wooden drawers for storing files of letters or other papers.

**fil·ings** (fī′lingz) the small pieces of iron, wood, etc. that have been removed by a file. *n. pl.*

**Fil·i·pine** (fil′ə pēn′) See PHILIPPINE.

**Fil·i·pi·no** (fil′ə pē′nō) **1** a native or inhabitant of the Philippines, a country consisting of about 7000 islands in the western Pacific Ocean. **2** of or having to do with the Philippines or its inhabitants; Philippine. 1 *n., pl.* **Filipinos;** *feminine* **Filipina, Filipinas;** 2 *adj.*

**fill** (fil) **1** make full; put into until there is room for no more: *to fill a cup, to be filled with joy.* **2** become full: *The hall filled rapidly.* **3** take up all the space in: *The crowd filled the hall.* **4** enough to fill something. **5** satisfy the hunger or appetite of. **6** supply what is needed for: *A store fills orders, prescriptions, etc.* **7** all that is needed or wanted: *Eat and drink your fill; there is plenty.* **8** stop up or close by putting something in: *A dentist fills decayed teeth.* **9** something that fills: *Earth or rock used to make uneven land level is called fill.* **10** hold and do the duties of a position, office, etc. **11** supply a person for or appoint a person to a position, office, etc. 1–3, 5, 6, 8, 10, 11 *v.*, 4, 7, 9 *n.*
**fill in, a** fill with something put in. **b** complete by filling. **c** put in to complete something. **d** acquaint with; bring up to date: *Would you be good enough to fill me in as to what happened during my absence?*

**fill in for,** substitute for: *Can you fill in for me tonight?*
**fill out, a** make larger; grow larger; swell. **b** make rounder; grow rounder. **c** complete by filling. **d** complete a questionnaire, etc.; enter requested information on a form.
**fill the bill,** come up to requirements.
**fill up,** fill; fill completely.

**fill·er** (fil′ər) **1** a person or thing that fills. **2** anything put in to fill something: *A pad of paper for a notebook, a preparation put on wood before painting it, and the tobacco inside cigars are all fillers.* *n.*

**fil·let** (fil′ət, *usually* fi lā′ *for 4, 5*) **1** a narrow band, ribbon, etc. put around the head to keep the hair in place or as an ornament. **2** a narrow band or strip of any material. **3** bind or decorate with a narrow band, ribbon, strip, etc. **4** a slice of fish, meat, etc. without bones or fat; filet. **5** cut fish, meat, etc. into fillets. 1, 2, 4 *n.*, 3, 5 *v.*

**fill·ing** (fil′ing) **1** anything put in to fill something: *A dentist puts a filling in a decayed tooth. Get me a can of cherry filling for the pie.* **2** the threads running from side to side across a woven fabric. **3** making full; becoming full. **4** ppr. of FILL. 1–3 *n.*, 4 *v.*

**filling station** a place where gasoline and oil for automobiles are sold.

**fil·lip** (fil′əp) **1** strike with the fingernail as it is snapped quickly from the end of the thumb. **2** toss or cause to move by striking in this way: *He filliped a coin into the beggar's cup.* **3** a quick, light blow given by striking with the fingernail as it is snapped quickly from the end of the thumb. **4** anything that rouses, revives, or stimulates: *Relishes serve as fillips to the appetite.* **5** rouse; revive; stimulate. 1, 2, 5 *v.*, 3, 4 *n.*

**fil·ly** (fil′ē) **1** a young female horse; a mare that is less than four or five years old. **2** *Informal.* a lively girl. *n., pl.* **fil·lies.**

**film** (film) **1** a very thin layer, sheet, surface or coating: *a film of dew. Oil poured on water will spread and make a film.* **2** cover or become covered with a film: *Her eyes filmed with tears.* **3** a roll or sheet of thin, flexible material covered with a special coating and used in making photographs: *This film is coated with an emulsion that is sensitive to light. He bought two rolls of film for the camera.* **4** such a roll for making motion pictures. **5** motion picture. **6** make a motion picture of: *They filmed the story of Moby Dick.* **7** photograph for motion pictures: *They filmed the scene three times.* **8** be photographed for motion pictures: *Action scenes usually film well. Some singers film better than others.* 1, 3–5 *n.*, 2, 6–8 *v.* —**film′like′,** *adj.*
**film over,** become covered with or as with a film: *The lens of my microscope is filmed over with moisture.*

**film·y** (fil′mē) **1** of or like a film; very thin. **2** covered with a film. *adj.*, **film·i·er, film·i·est.**
—**film′i·ness,** *n.*

**fil·ter** (fil′tər) **1** a device for straining out substance from a liquid or gas by putting it slowly through felt, paper, sand, charcoal, etc.: *A filter is used to remove*

impurities from drinking water.   2 the felt, paper, sand, charcoal, or other porous material used in such a device.   3 any of various devices for removing dust, smoke, germs, etc. from the air.   4 a device for controlling certain light rays, electric currents, etc.: *Putting a yellow filter in front of a camera lens causes less blue light to reach the film.*   5 pass through a filter; strain: *to filter water for drinking.*   6 act as a filter for: *The charcoal filtered the water.*   7 pass or flow very slowly: *Water filters through the sandy soil into the well.*   1–4 *n.*, 5–7 *v.*   —**fil′ter·er,** *n.*
**filter out,**   a remove or control by a filter: *Filter out the dirt before using the water.*   b of news, leak out.

**fil·ter·a·ble** (fil′tə rə bəl)   1 that can be filtered.   2 capable of passing through a filter that arrests bacteria: *a filterable virus.   adj.*

**filter tip**   1 a cigarette with an attached filter, for filtering impurities from the smoke before it is inhaled.   2 the filter itself.

**filth** (filth)   1 foul, disgusting dirt: *The alley was littered with garbage and other filth.*   2 obscene words or thoughts; vileness: *moral corruption.   n.*
☛ *Etym.*   From OE *fylth* 'the condition of being foul, or decomposed'. FOUL developed from the related OE *fūl*.

**filth·i·ness** (fil′thē nis)   a filthy state or condition.   *n.*

**filth·y** (fil′thē)   1 disgustingly dirty; foul.   2 vile.   *adj.*, **filth·i·er, filth·i·est.**   —**filth′i·ly,** *adv.*

**fil·tra·ble** (fil′trə bəl)   FILTERABLE.   *adj.*

**fil·trate** (fil′trāt)   1 liquid that has been passed through a filter.   2 pass through a filter.   1 *n.*, 2 *v.*, **fil·trat·ed, fil·trat·ing.**

**fil·tra·tion** (fil trā′shən)   1 filtering.   2 being filtered.   *n.*

**fin** (fin)   1 a movable, winglike part of a fish's body: *Moving the fins enables the fish to swim, guide, and balance itself in the water.* See FISH for picture.   2 anything shaped or used like a fin: *Some airships have fins to help balance them in flight.*   3 FLIPPER (def. 2).   *n.*
—**fin′less,** *adj.*   —**fin′like′,** *adj.*
☛ *Hom.* FINN.

**fi·na·gle** (fə nā′gəl)   *Informal.*   1 manage craftily or cleverly.   2 cheat.   *v.*, **fi·na·gled, fi·na·gling.**
—**fi·na′gler,** *n.*

**fi·nal** (fī′nəl)   1 at the end; last; with no more after it: *The last day of school each year is the final one for students who are graduating from high school.*   2 deciding; settling the question; not to be changed: *Decisions of the judges will be final.*   3 something final: *The last examination of a school term is a final.*   4 having to do with purpose: *a final clause.*   5 **finals,** *pl.*   the last or deciding set in a series of contests, examinations, etc.   1, 2, 4 *adj.*, 3, 5 *n.*

**fi·na·le** (fə nal′ē *or* fə näl′ē)   1 the last part of a piece of music or a play.   2 the last part; end.   *n.*

**fi·nal·ist** (fī′nə list)   a person who takes part in the last or deciding set in a series of contests, etc.   *n.*

**fi·nal·i·ty** (fī nal′ə tē)   1 being final, finished, or settled: *John recognized the finality of his father's decision.*   2 something final; a final act, speech, etc.   *n., pl.*   **fi·nal·i·ties.**

**fi·nal·ize** (fī′nə līz′)   bring to a conclusion; complete or finish in such a manner as to be final: *The committee hopes to finalize its report next week.   v.*

**fi·nal·ly** (fī′nə lē)   1 at the end; at last.   2 in such a way as to decide or settle the question.   *adv.*

**fi·nance** (fī′nans *or* fə nans′)   1 money matters: *The millionaire boasted of his skill in finance.*   2 the management of large sums of public or private money: *Management of government revenue and expenditure is called public finance.*   3 provide money for: *His friends helped him finance a new business.*   4 manage the finances of.   5 **finances,** *pl.*   money matters; money; funds; revenues.   1, 2, 5 *n.*, 3, 4 *v.*, **fi·nanced, fi·nanc·ing.**

**fi·nan·cial** (fī nan′shəl *or* fə nan′shəl)   1 having to do with money matters: *Her financial affairs are in bad condition.*   2 having to do with the management of large sums of public or private money.   *adj.*

**fi·nan·cial·ly** (fī nan′shə lē *or* fə nan′shə lē)   in relation to finances; in respect to money matters.   *adv.*

**fin·an·cier** (fī′nən sēr′ *or* fin′ən sēr′)   1 a person skilled in finance: *Bankers are financiers.*   2 a person active in matters involving large sums of money.   *n.*

**fin·back** (fin′bak′)   a kind of whale having a fin on its back; rorqual.   *n.*

**finch** (finch)   any of a group of small songbirds that have cone-shaped bills: *Sparrows, buntings, grosbeaks, canaries, and cardinals are finches.   n.*

**find** (fīnd)   1 come upon; happen on; meet with: *She found a dime in the road.*   2 look for and get: *Please find my hat for me.*   3 discover; learn: *We found that he could not swim.*   4 see; know; feel; perceive: *He found that he was growing sleepy.*   5 get; get the use of: *Can you find time to do this?*   6 arrive at; reach: *Water finds its level.*   7 decide and declare: *The jury found the accused man guilty.*   8 provide; supply: *She tried to find food and lodging for her friend.*   9 FINDING (def. 1).   10 something found.   1–8 *v.*, **found, find·ing;**   9, 10 *n.*
**find oneself,**   learn one's abilities and make good use of them.
**find out,**   learn about; come to know; discover.

**find·er** (fīn′dər)   1 a person or thing that finds.   2 a small extra lens on the outside of a camera that shows what is being photographed.   *n.*

**find·ing** (fīn′ding)   1 discovery.   2 the thing found.   3 Often, **findings,** *pl.*   the decision or conclusion reached after an examination of facts, data, etc. by a commission, judge, scholar, etc.: *The Commission will publish its findings next spring.*   4 **findings,** *pl.*   the tools and supplies, other than the main materials, used by a shoemaker, dressmaker, or other artisan: *A jeweller's findings include swivels, clasps, and wire.*   5 ppr. of FIND.   1–4 *n.*, 5 *v.*

**fine**[1] (fīn)   1 of very high quality; very good; excellent: *a fine sermon, a fine view, a fine scholar.*   2 very small or thin: *fine wire.*   3 sharp: *a tool with a fine edge.*   4 not coarse or heavy; delicate: *fine linen.*   5 refined; elegant: *fine manners.*   6 subtle: *The law makes fine distinctions.*   7 too highly decorated; showy: *fine language or writing.*   8 good-looking: *a fine young man.*   9 clear; pleasant; bright: *fine weather.*   10 without impurities: *Fine gold is gold not mixed with any other metal.*   11 having a stated proportion of gold or silver in it: *A gold alloy that is $^{925}/_{1000}$ fine is 92.5% gold.*   12 well; in good health: *I feel fine.*   13 *Informal.*   very well; excellently.   1–12 *adj.*, **fin·er, fin·est;**   13 *adv.*   —**fine′ly,** *adv.*

**fine**[2] (fīn)   1 a sum of money paid as a punishment.

**2** cause to pay a fine: *The judge fined Mr. Vick forty dollars for speeding.* **1** *n.*, **2** *v.*, **fined, fin·ing.**
**in fine, a** finally. **b** in a few words; briefly.

**fi·ne³** (fē′nā) the end; in music, a direction marking the end of a passage that has to be repeated. *n.*

**fine arts** the arts that depend upon taste and appeal to the sense of beauty; painting, drawing, sculpture, and architecture: *Literature, music, dancing, and acting are often included in the fine arts.*

**fine-drawn** (fīn′drôn′) **1** drawn out until very small or thin. **2** very subtle: *Fine-drawn distinctions are difficult to understand.* *adj.*

**fine-grained** (fīn′grānd′) having a fine, close grain: *Mahogany is a fine-grained wood.* *adj.*

**fine·ness** (fīn′nis) **1** thinness: *the fineness of a line, thread, needle, or wire.* **2** sharpness: *the fineness of an edge or point.* **3** degree of purity: *the fineness of a metal.* **4** clearness: *the fineness of the weather.* **5** fine quality; perfection: *the fineness of materials.* *n.*

**fin·er·y** (fī′nə rē) showy clothes, ornaments, etc. *n., pl.* **fin·er·ies.**

**fine-spun** (fīn′spun′) **1** spun or drawn out until very small or thin. **2** very subtle. *adj.*

**fi·nesse** (fə nes′) **1** delicacy of execution; skill: *That artist shows wonderful finesse.* **2** the skilful handling of a delicate situation to one's advantage; craft; strategem: *A shrewd diplomat must be a master of finesse.* **3** use finesse. **4** bring or change by finesse. **5** in bridge, whist, etc., attempt to take a trick with a lower card while holding a higher card, in the hope that the card or cards between may not be played. **6** make a finesse with a card. **1, 2** *n.*, **3–6** *v.*, **fi·nessed, fi·ness·ing.**

**fin·ger** (fing′gər) **1** one of the five end parts of the hand, especially the four other than the thumb. **2** the part of a glove that covers a finger. **3** anything shaped or used like a finger. **4** touch or handle with the fingers; use the fingers on. **5** perform or mark a passage of music with a certain fingering. **6** the breadth of a finger; 2 cm. **7** the length of a finger. **8** pilfer; filch; steal. **1–3, 6, 7** *n.*, **4, 5, 8** *v.*
**put one's finger on,** point out exactly.
**twist around one's little finger,** manage easily; control completely: *He can twist his teacher around his little finger.*

**finger bowl** a small bowl to hold water for rinsing the fingers after or during a meal.

**fin·ger·ing** (fing′gə ring) **1** a touching or handling with the fingers; a way of using the fingers: *In playing certain musical instruments, the fingering is important.* **2** the signs marked on a piece of music to show which fingers are to be used in playing particular notes. **3** a fine type of yarn, usually woollen, used in knitting. **4** ppr. of FINGER. **1–3** *n.*, **4** *v.*

**fin·ger·ling** (fing′gər ling) **1** a small fish no longer than a finger. **2** something very small. *n.*

**fin·ger·nail** (fing′gər nāl′) the hard layer of hornlike substance at the end of a finger. *n.*

**fin·ger·paint** (fing′gər pānt′) paint with the fingers, palms, etc. instead of with brushes. *v.*

**finger painting** **1** a technique of applying paint using fingers, palms, etc. instead of with brushes. **2** a design or picture so painted.

**fin·ger·print** (fing′gər print′) **1** an imprint of the markings on the inner surface of the last joint of a finger or thumb: *He was identified by his fingerprints on the gun.*

---

**fine**         **453**        **fiord**

hat, āge, fär; let, ēqual, tėrm; it, īce
hot, ōpen, ôrder; oil, out; cup, pu̇t, rüle
əbove, takən, pencəl, lemən, circəs
ch, child; ng, long; sh, ship
th, thin; ᴛʜ, then; zh, measure

See WHORL for picture. **2** take the fingerprints of. **1** *n.*, **2** *v.*

**fin·i·cal** (fin′ə kəl) FINICKY. *adj.* —**fin′i·cal·ly,** *adv.*

**fin·ick·y** (fin′ə kē) too dainty or particular; too precise or fussy: *She's terribly finicky about her food.* *adj.*

**fin·is** (fin′is) end. *n.*

**fin·ish** (fin′ish) **1** bring action, speech, etc. to an end; end. **2** an end: *to fight to a finish.* **3** bring work, affairs, etc. to completion; complete: *She started the race but did not finish it.* **4** come to an end: *There was so little wind that the sailing race didn't finish until after dark.* **5** use up completely: *to finish a spool of thread.* **6** *Informal.* overcome completely: *My answer finished him.* **7** *Informal.* destroy; kill: *to finish a wounded animal.* **8** perfect; polish. **9** a polished condition or quality; perfection: *There is an expert finish to this photographer's work.* **10** prepare the surface of in some way: *to finish cloth with nap.* **11** the way in which the surface is prepared: *a smooth finish.* **12** something used to finish something else. **1, 3–8, 10** *v.*, **2, 9, 11, 12** *n.*
—**fin′ish·er,** *n.*
**finish off, a** complete. **b** overcome completely; destroy; kill.
**finish up, a** complete. **b** use up completely.
**finish with, a** complete. **b** stop being friends with.
☞ *Hom.* FINNISH.

**fin·ished** (fin′isht) **1** ended. **2** completed. **3** perfected; polished; most excellent. **4** pt. and pp. of FINISH. **1–3** *adj.*, **4** *v.*

**finishing school** a private school that prepares young women for social life rather than for business or a profession.

**fi·nite** (fī′nīt) **1** having limits or bounds; not infinite: *Death ends a person's finite existence.* **2** what is finite; something finite. **3** having definite grammatical person, number, and tense; not an infinitive or participle. In *To write the letter seemed a tiresome task* the finite verb is *seemed.* **1, 3** *adj.*, **2** *n.*

**Finn** (fin) **1** a native or inhabitant of Finland, a country in northern Europe. **2** a member of those peoples that speak a language similar to Finnish. *n.*
☞ *Hom.* FIN.

**fin·nan had·die** (fin′ən had′ē) smoked haddock.

**Finn·ish** (fin′ish) **1** of or having to do with Finland, its people, or their language. **2** the Finno-Ugric language of Finland. **1** *adj.*, **2** *n.*
☞ *Hom.* FINISH.

**fin·ny** (fin′ē) **1** abounding with fish: *The sea is sometimes called the finny deep.* **2** having fins. **3** like a fin. *adj.*

**fiord** or **fjord** (fyôrd) a long, narrow bay of the sea between high banks or cliffs: *Norway has many fiords.* *n.*

A branch of fir with cones

**fir** (fėr) **1** any of a group of about 40 closely related species of evergreen tree of the pine family found throughout the north temperate regions of the world, having leaves shaped like flattened needles and upright cones: *The four species of fir native to Canada are balsam fir, alpine fir, amabilis fir, and grand fir.* **2** the wood of any of these trees. *n.*
☛ *Hom.* FUR.

**fire** (fīr) **1** the flame, heat, and light caused by something burning. **2** a burning mass of fuel: *Put more wood on the fire.* **3** fuel arranged for burning: *A fire was laid in the fireplace.* **4** a destructive burning: *A great fire destroyed the furniture factory.* **5** a preparation that will burn: *Red fire is used in signalling.* **6** cause to burn: *The gardener fired the pile of dead leaves.* **7** begin to burn; burst into flame. **8** supply fuel to; tend: *The men fired the steamship's huge furnaces.* **9** dry with heat; bake: *Bricks are fired to make them hard.* **10** something that suggests a fire because it is hot, glowing, brilliant, or light: *the fire of lightning, an insane fire in her eye, the fire in a diamond.* **11** grow or make hot, red, glowing, etc. **12** any feeling that suggests fire; passion, fervour, enthusiasm, excitement, etc.: *Their hearts were filled with patriotic fire.* **13** arouse; excite; inflame: *Stories of adventure fire the imagination.* **14** a fever; inflammation; burning pain: *the fire of a wound.* **15** a severe trial or trouble. **16** the shooting or discharge of guns, etc.: *the enemy's fire.* **17** discharge a gun, bomb, gas mine, etc.: *He fired his gun four times.* **18** discharge or propel a missile, etc. from or as if from a gun; shoot: *to fire a rocket. The soldiers fired from the fort. The hunter fired small shot.* **19** *Informal.* dismiss from a job, etc. 1–5, 10, 12, 14–16 *n.*, 6–9, 11, 13, 17–19 *v.*, **fired, fir·ing.** —**fir′er**, *n.*
**between two fires,** attacked from both sides.
**catch fire,** begin to burn: *Be careful that the curtains don't catch fire from the lamp.*
**fire away,** *Informal.* begin; start; go ahead.
**fire up,** start a fire in a furnace, boiler, etc.: *The men did not have time to fire up.*
**hang fire, a** be slow in going off. **b** be slow in acting. **c** be delayed.
**lay a fire,** build a fire ready to be lit.
**on fire, a** burning. **b** full of feeling or spirit; excited: *The team were on fire with the desire for victory.*
**play with fire,** meddle with something dangerous.
**set fire to,** cause to burn.
**set on fire, a** cause to burn. **b** fill with feeling or spirit.
**under fire, a** exposed to shooting from the enemy's guns. **b** attacked; blamed.

**fire alarm 1** the signal that a fire has broken out. **2** a device that gives such a signal.

**fire·arm** (fī′rärm′) rifle, pistol, or other weapon to shoot with, usually such as a person can carry. *n.*

**fire·ball** (fīr′bol′) **1** the great billowing mass of fire produced by an atomic explosion. **2** in baseball, a very fast pitch to the batter. *n.*

**fire·boat** (fīr′bōt′) a boat equipped with apparatus for putting out fires on a dock, ship, etc. *n.*

**fire·box** (fīr′boks′) the place for the fire in a furnace, boiler, etc. *n.*

**fire·brand** (fīr′brand′) **1** a piece of burning wood. **2** a person who stirs up angry feelings in others. *n.*

**fire·break** (fīr′brāk′) a strip of land that has been cleared of trees or on which the sod has been turned over so as to prevent the spreading of a forest fire or a prairie fire. *n.*

**fire·brick** (fīr′brik′) a brick that can stand great heat, used to line furnaces and fireplaces. *n.*

**fire·bug** (fīr′bug′) *Informal.* a person who purposely sets houses or property on fire; pyromaniac. *n.*

**fire clay** clay capable of resisting high temperatures, used for making crucibles, firebricks, etc.

**fire·crack·er** (fīr′krak′ər) a paper roll containing gunpowder and a fuse: *A firecracker explodes with a loud noise.* *n.*

**fire·damp** (fīr′damp′) methane, a gas formed in coal mines. It is dangerously explosive when mixed with certain proportions of air. *n.*

**fire department** a municipal department in charge of the fighting and preventing of fires.

**fire·dog** (fīr′dog′) ANDIRON. See FIREPLACE for picture. *n.*

**fire drill** drill for firefighters, a ship's crew, pupils in a school, etc. to train them for duties or for orderly exit in case of fire.

**fire–eat·er** (fī′rē·tər) **1** an entertainer who pretends to eat fire. **2** a person who is too ready to fight or quarrel. *n.*

**fire engine** a truck with a machine for throwing water, chemicals, etc. and with ladders and other equipment to put out fires.

**fire escape** a stairway, ladder, etc. in or on a building, to use in case of fire.

**fire extinguisher** a container filled with chemicals that can be sprayed upon fire to extinguish it.

**fire·fight·er** (fīr′fī′tər) **1** a member of a fire department. **2** a person who fights forest fires. *n.*

**fire·fight·ing** (fīr′fī′ting) the act or process of fighting fires. *n.*

**fire·fly** (fīr′flī′) a small beetle that gives off flashes of light that can be seen in the dark; lightning bug. *n., pl.* **fire·flies.**

**fire hall** *Cdn.* **1** a building in which firefighting equipment is kept. **2** the headquarters of a fire department: *Permits for burning rubbish may be obtained at the fire hall.*

**fire·less** (fīr′lis) without a fire. *adj.*

**fireless cooker** an insulated container that stays hot a long time without heat from outside, used to cook food or keep it hot.

**fire·light** (fīr′līt′) the light from a fire. *n.*

**fire line 1** a FIREBREAK. **2** the front edge of a forest fire or a prairie fire.

**fire·lock** (fīr′lok′) an old type of gun, fired by a spark falling on the gunpowder; FLINTLOCK. *n.*

**fire·man** (fīr′mən) **1** a man whose work is putting out fires. **2** a man whose work is taking care of the fire in a furnace, boiler, locomotive, etc. *n., pl.* **fire·men** (-mən).

A fireplace

**fire·place** (fīr′plās′)   a place built in the wall of a room or out-of-doors to hold a fire. *n.*

**fire plug**   HYDRANT.

**fire·pow·er** (fīr′pou′ər)   the ability to deliver FIRE (def. 16); the amount of fire delivered by a military unit or by a particular weapon. *n.*

**fire·proof** (fīr′prüf′)   **1** that will not burn; almost impossible to burn: *A building made entirely of steel and concrete is fireproof.* **2** make fireproof. 1 *adj.*, 2 *v.*

**fire–rang·er** (fīr′rān′jər)   a government employee engaged in preventing and putting out forest fires on Crown lands. *n.*

**fire screen**   a screen to be placed in front of a fire as protection against heat or flying sparks.

**fire·side** (fīr′sīd′)   **1** the space around a fireplace or hearth.   **2** the home.   **3** home life.   **4** beside the fire: *fireside comfort.* 1–3 *n.*, 4 *adj.*

**fire station**   FIRE HALL.

**Fire Temple**   in Zoroastrianism, a temple or shrine in which a sacred fire is always burning.

**fire·trap** (fīr′trap′)   **1** a building hard to get out of when it is on fire.   **2** a building that will burn very easily. *n.*

**fire·truck** (fīr′truk′)   FIRE ENGINE. *n.*

**fire·ward·en** (fīr′wôr′dən)   an official whose duty is preventing and putting out fires in forests, camps, etc. *n.*

**fire·wa·ter** (fīr′wot′ər)   any strong alcoholic drink. *n.*

**fire·weed** (fīr′wēd′)   **1** a tall plant that flourishes especially in newly burned areas, having long, showy spikes of purplish-pink flowers, found throughout much of Canada and the northern United States: *The fireweed is the floral emblem of the Yukon.*   **2** any of several other plants that commonly grow in burned areas. *n.*

**fire·wood** (fīr′wud′)   wood for burning in a stove, fireplace, etc. *n.*

**fire·work** (fīr′wėrk′)   **1** a firecracker, bomb, rocket, etc. that makes a loud noise or a beautiful fiery display, especially at night.   **2 fireworks**, a firework display. *n.*

**firing line**   **1** any line where soldiers are stationed to shoot at the enemy.   **2** the soldiers on such a line.   **3** the foremost position in a controversy, campaign for a cause, etc.

**firing squad**   **1** a group of soldiers formed to carry out a death penalty.   **2** a group of soldiers who fire shots as a tribute at a military funeral.

**fir·kin** (fėr′kən)   **1** a quarter of a barrel, used as a measure of capacity.   **2** a small wooden cask for butter, etc. *n.*

**firm¹** (fėrm)   **1** not yielding easily to pressure or force; solid; hard: *firm flesh, firm ground.*   **2** not easily moved or shaken; tightly fastened or fixed: *a tree firm in the earth.*   **3** not easily changed; determined; resolute; positive: *a firm purpose, voice, character, or belief.*   **4** not changing; staying the same; steady: *a firm price.*   **5** make or become firm: *to firm the earth around transplanted seedlings.*   1–4 *adj.*, 5 *v.* —**firm′ly,** *adv.* —**firm′ness,** *n.*
**firm up,** *Informal.*   arrange definitely: *When can we firm up the date for our meeting?*

**firm²** (fėrm)   a company or partnership of two or more persons in business together: *an old and trusted firm.*   *n.*

**fir·ma·ment** (fėr′mə mənt)   the arch of the heavens; sky.   *n.*

**first** (fėrst)   **1** coming before all others; 1st: *Gino is first in his class.*   **2** before all others; before anything else: *Women and children go first.*   **3** before some other thing or event: *First bring me the chalk.*   **4** for the first time: *when I first visited Italy.*   **5** a person, thing, place, etc. that is first.   **6** the winning position in a race, etc.   **7** beginning.   **8** in an automobile or similar machine, the first, or lowest, gear; low.   **9** rather; sooner: *I'll go to jail first.*   **10** in music, highest in pitch.   **11** in music, playing or singing the part highest in pitch: *first violin, first soprano.*   **12 firsts,** *pl.* articles of the best quality.   1, 10, 11 *adj.*, 2–4, 9 *adv.*, 5–8, 12 *n.*
**at first,**   in the beginning: *At first Bela did not like school.*
**first and foremost,**   chiefly; above all.
**first and last,**   taking all together.
**from the first,**   since the beginning.

**first aid**   the emergency treatment given to an injured person before a doctor comes. —**first′-aid′,** *adj.*

**first–born** (fėrst′bôrn′)   **1** born first; oldest.   **2** the first-born child.   1 *adj.*, 2 *n.*

**first–class** (fėrst′klas′)   **1** of the highest class or best quality; excellent.   **2** on a first-class ship, train, aircraft, etc.; in or on the first-class section: *to travel first-class.*   **3** of or having to do with the class of mail that includes letters, postcards, etc.   **4** by first-class mail.   1, 3 *adj.*, 2, 4 *adv.*

**first finger**   the finger next to the thumb.

**first fruits**   **1** the earliest fruits of the season.   **2** the first products or results.

**first–hand** (fėrst′hand′)   from the original source; direct: *first-hand information.* *adj., adv.*

**first·ling** (fėr′stling)   **1** the first of its kind.   **2** the first product or result.   **3** the first offspring of an animal.   *n.*

**first·ly** (fėr′stlē)   in the first place; first.   *adv.*

**first name**   a person's first given name or, sometimes, the second (or third) given name if that is what that person is usually known by: *Her first name is Alicia.*

**First Nations**   **1** the original peoples of Canada.   **2** of or designating these peoples.

**first person** the form of a pronoun or verb used to refer to the speaker or speakers. *I, me, my,* and *we, us, our* are pronouns of the first person.

**first quarter** the period between a new moon and the first half moon after the new moon. See MOON for picture.

**first–rate** (fėr′strāt′) **1** of the highest class. **2** *Informal.* excellent; very good. *adj.*

**firth** (fėrth) especially in Scotland, a narrow arm of the sea; the estuary of a river. *n.*

**fis·cal** (fis′kəl) **1** financial. **2** having to do with a treasury or exchequer: *Important changes were made in the government's fiscal policy.* **3** in some countries, a public prosecutor. **1, 2** *adj.,* **3** *n.*

**fiscal year** the time between one yearly settlement of financial accounts and another.

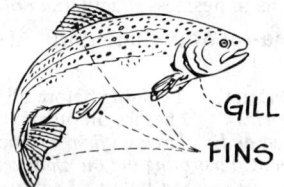
Fish: a rainbow trout – about 30 cm long including the tail

**fish** (fish) **1** a cold-blooded vertebrate that lives in water and has gills instead of lungs for breathing: *Fish are usually covered with scales and have fins for swimming.* **2** the flesh of fish used for food. **3** catch fish; try to catch fish: *to fish for salmon.* **4** try to catch fish in: *to fish a pool.* **5** try to get back or pick up as if with a hook: *Maria fished for the dime with a stick.* **6** search by groping inside something: *She fished in her purse for a coin.* **7** find and take out: *He fished the map from the back of the drawer.* **8** *Informal.* a person or fellow. **9** a long strip of iron, wood, etc. used to strengthen a joint, etc. **1, 2, 8, 9** *n., pl.* **fish** or **fish·es; 3–7** *v.*
—**fish′less,** *adj.* —**fish′like,** *adj.*

**a fish out of water,** a person who is uncomfortable or ill at ease as a result of being out of his or her usual environment.

**fish for, a** look for; try to find: *She was fishing for some papers in the file.* **b** try to get, often by indirect or underhand means: *He is always fishing for information.*
☞ Usage. The plural is usually **fish,** but **fishes** is used when referring to different kinds of fish: *She caught eight fish. He has written a book on the fishes of Canada.*

**fish and chips** pieces of fish fried in a batter and served with French fries.

**fish·er** (fish′ər) **1** one who catches fish for a living or as a hobby. **2** an animal or bird that catches fish for food. **3** a slender mammal like a weasel but larger; the marten of North America. **4** its dark-brown fur. *n.*
☞ *Hom.* FISSURE.

**fish·er·man** (fish′ər mən) **1** a person who fishes for a living or for pleasure. **2** a ship used in fishing. *n., pl.* **fish·er·men** (-mən).

**fish·er·y** (fish′ə rē) **1** the business or industry of catching fish. **2** a place for catching fish: *Salmon is the main catch in the Pacific fisheries.* *n., pl.* **fish·er·ies.**

**fish flake** a slatted platform used for drying fish.

**fish–hawk** (fish′hok′) a large bird that feeds on fish; osprey. *n.*

**fish–hook** (fish′hůk′) a hook used for catching fish. *n.* See BARB for picture.

**fish·ing** (fish′ing) **1** the catching of fish for a living or for pleasure. **2** ppr. of FISH. **1** *n.,* **2** *v.*

**fishing ground** a place where fish are plentiful.

**fishing line** a line used in fishing.

**fishing pole** FISHING ROD.

**fishing rod** a slender rod, made of bamboo, plastic, etc. used for fishing.

**fishing tackle** rods, lines, hooks, etc. used in catching fish.

**fish line** FISHING LINE.

**fish·pond** (fish′pond′) a pond in which there are fish, especially an ornamental pool where fish, such as goldfish, are kept in captivity. *n.*

**fish stick 1** a frozen fish fillet packaged in the form of a short, oblong stick for ease in shipping and handling: *The Maritimes ship fish sticks to central Canada.* **2** a portion of fish, often breaded and pre-cooked, frozen and packaged for retail sale.

**fish story** *Informal.* an exaggerated, unbelievable story.

**fish·tail** (fish′tāl′) like a fish's tail in shape or action. *adj.*

**fish·way** (fish′wā′) a special waterway built to enable fish, such as salmon, to swim more easily past waterfalls on their way to their spawning grounds up river. *n.*

**fish·wife** (fish′wīf′) a woman who uses coarse and abusive language. *n., pl.* **fish·wives.**

**fish·y** (fish′ē) **1** like a fish in smell, taste, or shape. **2** of fish. **3** full of fish. **4** *Informal.* doubtful; unlikely; suspicious. **5** without expression or lustre; dull: *fishy eyes.* *adj.,* **fish·i·er, fish·i·est.** —**fish′i·ly,** *adv.* —**fish′i·ness,** *n.*

**fis·sile** (fis′īl *or* fis′əl) **1** easily split. **2** capable of nuclear FISSION (def. 2). *adj.*

**fis·sion** (fish′ən) **1** splitting apart; division into parts. **2** the splitting that occurs when the nucleus of an atom under bombardment absorbs a neutron: *Nuclear fission releases tremendous amounts of energy when heavy elements, especially plutonium and uranium, are involved.* *n.*

**fis·sion·a·ble** (fish′ə nə bəl) capable of nuclear FISSION (def. 2). *adj.*

**fission bomb** ATOMIC BOMB.

**fis·sure** (fish′ər) **1** a split or crack; a long, narrow opening: *a fissure in a rock.* **2** splitting apart; division into parts. **3** split apart; divide into parts; become split. **1, 2** *n.,* **3** *v.,* **fis·sured, fis·sur·ing.**
☞ *Hom.* FISHER.

**fist** (fist) **1** the hand closed tightly. **2** *Informal.* the hand. **3** *Informal.* handwriting. **4** a symbol (☞) used in printing; fistnote. *n.* —**fist′like′,** *adj.*

**fist·fight** (fist′fīt′) a fight using the closed bare hands. *n.*

**fist·ic** (fis′tik) *Informal.* having to do with fighting with the fists; done with the fists. *adj.*

**fist·i·cuffs** (fis′ti kufs′) **1** a fight with the fists. **2** blows with the fists. *n. pl.*

**fist·note** (fist′nōt′) in printed texts, a special note preceded by a FIST (def. 4). *n.*

**fis·tu·la** (fis′chə lə) a tubelike sore. *n., pl.* **fis·tu·las** or **fis·tu·lae** (-lē′ or -lī′).

**fis·tu·lar** (fis′chə lər) **1** tubelike; tubular. **2** made up of tubelike parts. **3** having to do with a FISTULA. *adj.*

**fit**[1] (fit) **1** having the necessary qualities; suitable: *Grass is a fit food for cows; it is not fit for human beings.* **2** right; proper: *It is fit that we give thanks.* **3** be suited or suitable to; be fit for: *Let the punishment fit the crime.* **4** make right, proper, or suitable: *to fit the action to the word.* **5** have the right size or shape; have the right size or shape for: *The last piece of the puzzle didn't fit. The dress fitted Olga.* **6** try to make fit; adjust: *Father was fitting new seat covers on our car.* **7** install; attach: *It took two hours to fit the new radio in the car.* **8** the manner in which one thing fits another: *the fit of a coat, a tight fit.* **9** something that fits: *This coat is a good fit.* **10** ready; prepared: *He is fit for high school.* **11** make ready; prepare. **12** in good health; in good physical condition: *She is now well and fit for work.* **13** supply with what is needed; equip: *fit a store with counters.* 1, 2, 10, 12 *adj.*, **fit·ter, fit·test;** 3–7, 11, 13 *v.*, **fit·ted, fit·ting;** 8, 9 *n.* **fit out** or **up,** supply with what is needed; equip. **see** or **think fit,** consider suitable or appropriate.

**fit**[2] (fit) **1** a sudden, sharp attack of sickness: *a fit of colic.* **2** a sudden attack of illness characterized by loss of consciousness or by convulsions: *a fainting fit, a fit of epilepsy.* **3** any sudden, sharp attack: *In a fit of anger he hit his friend.* **4** a short period of doing one thing: *a fit of laughter.* *n.* **by fits and starts,** irregularly; starting, stopping, beginning again, and so on.

**fit·ful** (fit′fəl) going on and then stopping awhile; irregular: *a fitful sleep, a fitful conversation.* *adj.* —**fit′ful·ly,** *adv.* —**fit′ful·ness,** *n.*

**fit·ly** (fit′lē) **1** in a suitable manner. **2** at a proper time. *adv.*

**fit·ness** (fit′nəs) **1** suitability. **2** physical and muscular health. **3** for physical health: *a fitness club.* *n.*

**fit·ter** (fit′ər) **1** a person who fits. **2** a person who fits dresses, suits, etc. on people. **3** a person who adjusts parts of machinery. **4** a person who supplies and fixes anything necessary for some purpose: *A gas fitter sells and installs gas fixtures, stoves, etc.* *n.*

**fit·ting** (fit′ing) **1** right; proper; suitable. **2** a trying on of unfinished clothes to see if they will fit. **3 fittings,** *pl.* furnishings; fixtures: *Desks, chairs, and files are office fittings.* **4** ppr. of FIT. 1 *adj.*, 2, 3 *n.*, 4 *v.* —**fit′ting·ly,** *adv.*

**five** (fīv) **1** one more than four; 5: *I counted only five. We ordered five tickets.* **2** the numeral 5: *I think it's a five, but I'm not sure.* **3** the fifth in a set or series; especially, a playing card or side of a die having five spots: *a pair of fives.* **4** a five-dollar bill: *She gave me two fives.* **5** being fifth in a set or series (*used mainly after the noun*): *Lesson Five is easier than Lesson Four.* **6** a set or series of five persons or things: *The Romans counted in fives.* 1–4, 6 *n.*, 1, 5 *adj.* ☞ *Etym.* From OE *fíf,* related to German *fünf* and having the same Indo-European source as L *quinque* (giving F *cinq*) and Gk. *pente.* See also the note at PENTA-.

**five·fold** (fīv′fōld′) **1** five times as much or as many. **2** having five parts. 1, 2 *adj.*, 1 *adv.*

**Five Nations** a former confederacy of Iroquois tribes, consisting of the Mohawks, Oneidas, Onondagas, Cayugas, and Senecas: *Members of the Five Nations (now the Six Nations) lived in Ontario and Quebec.*

**five pins** a bowling game in which a large ball is rolled down a long, indoor alley with the aim of knocking down all of the five pins arranged upright at the other end: *Five pins is a popular Canadian game.*

**fix** (fiks) **1** make firm; become firm; fasten tightly; be fastened tightly: *We fixed the post in the ground.* **2** commit to memory: *The boy fixed the spelling lesson in his mind.* **3** settle; set: *He fixed the price at one dollar.* **4** direct or hold steady the eyes, attention, etc.; be directed or held steadily. **5** make or become rigid: *eyes fixed in death.* **6** put definitely: *She fixed the blame on the leader.* **7** treat to keep from changing or fading: *A dye or photograph is fixed with chemicals.* **8** mend or repair: *to fix a watch.* **9** *Informal.* put in order; arrange: *to fix one's hair.* **10** prearrange or influence the outcome of a game, race, trial, etc. by payment or other inducement: *The jury had been fixed.* **11** *Informal.* a position hard to get out of; awkward state of affairs: *The boy who cried "Wolf" got himself into a bad fix.* 1–10 *v.*, **fixed, fix·ing;** 11 *n.* —**fix′a·ble,** *adj.* **fix on** or **upon,** decide on; choose; select. **fix up,** *Informal.* **a** mend; repair. **b** put in order; arrange.

**fix·a·tion** (fik sā′shən) **1** the act of fixing or condition of being fixed. **2** a treatment to keep something from changing or fading: *the fixation of a photographic film.* **3** a morbid attachment or prejudice. **4** the process of converting atmospheric nitrogen into molecules containing nitrogen that plants can use. *n.*

**fix·a·tive** (fik′sə tiv) **1** a substance used to keep something from fading or changing. **2** that prevents fading or change. 1 *n.*, 2 *adj.*

**fixed** (fikst) **1** not movable; firm. **2** settled; set; definite: *fixed charges for taxicabs.* **3** steady; not moving. **4** made stiff or rigid. **5** *Informal.* prearranged privately or dishonestly: *The horse race was fixed.* **6** pt. and pp. of FIX. 1–5 *adj.*, 6 *v.*

**fix·ed·ly** (fik′si dlē) in a fixed manner; without change; intently. *adv.*

**fix·ed·ness** (fik′sid nis) being fixed; intentness. *n.*

**fixed star** a star whose position in relation to other stars appears not to change.

**fix·ings** (fik′singz) *Informal.* **1** furnishings; trimmings. **2** ingredients. *n. pl.*

**fix·i·ty** (fik′sə tē) **1** a fixed condition or quality; permanence; steadiness; firmness. **2** something fixed. *n., pl.* **fix·i·ties.**

**fix·ture** (fiks′chər) **1** something put in place to stay: *bathroom fixtures, electric-light fixtures.* **2** a person or thing that stays in one place, job, etc.: *After twenty-five years' service, she is considered a fixture in the factory.* **3** a game or some other sports event for which a date has been fixed. *n.*

**fiz** (fiz) See FIZZ. *v.*, **fizzed, fiz·zing;** *n.*

**fizz** (fiz) **1** make a hissing sound. **2** a hissing sound. **3** a bubbling drink, such as champagne, soda water, etc. 1 *v.*, 2, 3 *n.*

**fiz·zle** (fiz′əl) **1** hiss or sputter weakly: *The firecracker fizzled instead of exploding with a bang.* **2** a hissing; sputtering. **3** *Informal.* fail. **4** *Informal.* failure. 1, 3 *v.*, fiz·zled, fiz·zling; 2, 4 *n.*
**fizzle out,** *Informal.* end in failure.

**fizz·y** (fiz′ē) that fizzes. *adj.* fizz′i·er, fizz′i·est.

**fjord** (fyôrd) See FIORD. *n.*

**fl. 1** fluid. **2** flourished.

**flab·ber·gast** (flab′ər gast′) *Informal.* amaze. *v.*

**flab·by** (flab′ē) lacking firmness or force; soft; weak: *flabby cheeks.* *adj.,* flab·bi·er, flab·bi·est.
—flab′bi·ly, *adv.* —flab′bi·ness, *n.*

**flac·cid** (flak′sid) limp; weak: *flaccid muscles, a flaccid will.* *adj.*

**flac·cid·i·ty** (flak sid′ə tē) a FLACCID quality or condition. *n.*

**fla·con** (flä kon′) a small bottle with a stopper, used for perfume, smelling salts, etc. *n.*

The Canadian flag

**flag**[1] (flag) **1** a piece of cloth, often rectangular, that shows the emblem of a country, of a unit of the armed forces, or of some other organization: *Canadian flag, the regimental flag.* **2** a piece of cloth, often rectangular and of bright colour, used as a decoration: *The hall was decorated with many flags.* **3** a piece of cloth of a certain shape, colour, or design that has a special meaning: *A red flag is often a sign of danger, a white flag of surrender, a black flag of disaster.* **4** something that suggests a flag: *The tail of a deer or of a setter dog is a flag.* **5** something like a flag. **6** a large cloth used to keep lights from interfering with a television camera. **7** put a flag or flags over or on; decorate with flags. **8** stop or signal, especially by waving a flag: *to flag a train, to flag down a cab.* **9** communicate by a flag: *to flag a message.* 1–6 *n.,* 7–9 *v.,* flagged, flag·ging.

**flag**[2] (flag) **1** an iris having blue, purple, yellow, or white flowers and sword-shaped leaves. See IRIS for picture. **2** the sweet flag, a plant having a sweet-smelling rootstock. **3** the flower of either of these plants. **4** the leaf of either of these plants. *n.*

**flag**[3] (flag) get tired; grow weak; droop: *After you do the same thing for a long time, your interest flags.* *v.,* flagged, flag·ging.

**flag**[4] (flag) FLAGSTONE. *n.*

**flag·el·lant** (flaj′ə lənt) **1** a person who whips or is whipped. **2** a religious fanatic who whips himself or herself for religious discipline or for penance. *n.*

**flag·el·late** (flaj′ə lāt′) whip; flog. *v.,* flag·el·lat·ed, flag·el·lat·ing.

**flag·el·la·tion** (flaj′ə lā′shən) a whipping; flogging. *n.*

**fla·gel·lum** (flə jel′əm) **1** a long, whiplike tail or part, which is an organ of locomotion in certain cells, bacteria, protozoa, etc. **2** a whip. **3** a runner of a plant. *n.,* *pl.* fla·gel·la (flə jel′ə) or fla·gel·lums.

**flag·eo·let** (flaj′ə let′) a small wind instrument resembling a flute, with a mouthpiece at one end, six main finger holes, and sometimes keys. *n.*

**flag football** a game following the rules of Canadian football but in which tackling is outlawed, the ball carrier being stopped in his advance when a handkerchief is snatched from his back pocket.

**flag·ging** (flag′ing) **1** drooping; tired; weak. **2** ppr. of FLAG. **1** *adj.,* 2 *v.*

**flag·man** (flag′mən) **1** a person who has charge of or carries a flag. **2** a person who signals with a flag or lantern at a railway crossing, road construction zone, etc. *n., pl.* flag·men (-mən).

**flag officer** a naval officer entitled to display a flag on his or her ship indicating his or her rank or command: *An admiral, vice-admiral, rear admiral, or officer in command of a fleet or squadron is a flag officer.*

**flag of truce** a white flag used as a signal of surrender or of a desire to confer with the enemy.

**flag·on** (flag′ən) **1** a container for liquids, usually having a handle and a spout, and often a cover. **2** a large bottle, holding about two litres. *n.*

**flag·pole** (flag′pōl′) a pole from which a flag is flown. *n.*

**fla·gran·cy** (flā′grən sē) a FLAGRANT nature or quality. *n.*

**fla·grant** (flā′grənt) notorious; outrageous; scandalous. *adj.* —fla′grant·ly, *adv.*

**flag·ship** (flag′ship′) **1** the ship that carries the officer in command of a fleet or squadron and displays his or her flag. **2** the most outstanding member of any group. **3** main; leading: *The chain's flagship store is in Toronto.* 1, 2 *n.,* 3 *adj.*

**flag·staff** (flag′staf′) a pole from which a flag is flown. *n.*

**flag·stone** (flag′stōn′) a large, flat stone, used for paving walks, patios, etc. *n.*

**flail** (flāl) **1** an instrument for threshing grain by hand: *A flail consists of a wooden handle with a short, heavy stick fastened at one end by a thong.* **2** strike with a flail. **3** beat; thrash. 1 *n.,* 2, 3 *v.*

**flair** (fler) **1** a keen perception: *That trader had a flair for bargains.* **2** a natural talent: *The poet had a flair for making clever rhymes.* *n.*
☛ Hom. FLARE.

**flak** (flak) gunfire from the ground against airplanes. *n.*

**flake** (flāk) **1** a small, light mass; a soft, loose bit: *a flake of snow.* **2** a thin, flat piece or layer: *flakes of rust, flakes of ice floating on the pond, corn flakes.* **3** come off in flakes; take off, chip, or peel in flakes: *Dirty, grey spots showed where the paint had flaked off.* **4** break or separate into flakes. **5** cover or mark with flakes; make spotted. **6** form into flakes. **7** a slatted platform used for drying fish; FISH FLAKE. **8** *Informal.* a strange, eccentric person. 1, 2, 7, 8 *n.*, 3-6 *v.*, **flaked, flak·ing.**

**flak·y** (flā′kē) **1** consisting of flakes: *Mica is a flaky substance.* **2** easily broken or separated into flakes. **3** *Informal.* weird; eccentric. *adj.* **flak·i·er, flak·i·est.** —**flak′i·ness,** *n.*

**flam·beau** (flam′bō) **1** a flaming torch. **2** a large, decorated candlestick. *n., pl.* **flam·beaux** (-bōz) or **flam·beaus.**

**flam·boy·ance** (flam boi′əns) a flamboyant nature or quality. *n.*

**flam·boy·ant** (flam boi′ənt) **1** gorgeously brilliant; flaming: *flamboyant colours.* **2** very ornate; excessively decorated: *flamboyant architecture.* **3** given to display; ostentatious; showy: *a flamboyant person.* **4** having wavy lines or flamelike curves: *flamboyant designs.* *adj.* —**flam·boy′ant·ly,** *adv.*

**flame** (flām) **1** one of the glowing red or yellow tongues of light that shoot out from a blazing fire: *The house burst into flames.* **2** a burning gas or vapour. **3** burn with flames; blaze: *The dying fire suddenly flamed brightly.* **4** burning with flames; a blaze: *The dying fire suddenly burst into flame.* **5** a thing or condition that suggests flame. **6** grow hot, red, etc.: *Her cheeks flamed.* **7** a bright light. **8** shine brightly; give out a bright light. **9** a burning feeling; zeal. **10** have or show a burning feeling. **11** burst out quickly and hotly; be or act like a flame. **12** *Informal.* sweetheart. **13** bright reddish yellow or reddish orange. 1, 2, 4, 5, 7, 9, 12, 13 *n.*, 3, 6, 8, 10, 11 *v.*, **flamed, flam·ing;** 13 *adj.* —**flame′like′,** *adj.*

**fla·men·co** (flə meng′kō) **1** a style of Spanish Gypsy dance performed with castanets to fast, fiery, vigorous rhythms. **2** a song or piece of music in this style, or for such a dance. *n.*

**flame·out** (flām′out′) the sudden failure of a jet engine to function, especially while the aircraft containing it is in flight. *n.*

**flame thrower** a weapon or device that directs a jet of burning gasoline mixture, napalm, etc. through the air.

**flam·ing** (flā′ming) **1** burning with flames. **2** like a flame; very bright; brilliant. **3** showing or arousing strong feeling; violent; vehement. **4** ppr. of FLAME. 1-3 *adj.,* 4 *v.*

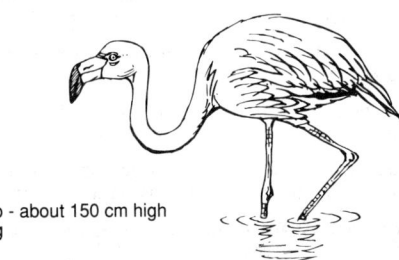
A red flamingo - about 150 cm high when standing

**fla·min·go** (flə ming′gō) any of several related species of tropical wading bird having very long legs and neck, and feathers that vary from pink to scarlet. *n., pl.* **fla·min·gos** or **fla·min·goes.**

hat, āge, fär; let, ēqual, tėrm; it, īce
hot, ōpen, ôrder; oil, out; cup, pút, rüle
above, takən, pencəl, lemən, circəs
ch, child; ng, long; sh, ship
th, thin; ᴛʜ, then; zh, measure

**flam·ma·bil·i·ty** (flam′ə bil′ə tē) the quality of being FLAMMABLE. *n.*

**flam·ma·ble** (flam′ə bəl) easily set on fire; inflammable. *adj.*
☛ *Usage.* **Flammable** and INFLAMMABLE mean the same, but **inflammable** is sometimes misunderstood because it looks like a negative, such as *inactive.* **Inflammable** comes from Latin; the *in-* meant 'extremely'. It is more usual in Canada–except in science and industry, where care is taken to use **flammable.** Whichever form is used, the opposite is NONFLAMMABLE.

A flange for attaching a pipe to a surface

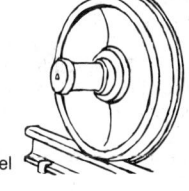
A flange on a wheel of a railway car

**flange** (flanj) a projecting edge, rim, collar, etc. on an object for keeping it in place, attaching it to another object, strengthening it, etc.: *Railway cars and locomotives have wheels with flanges to keep them on the track.* *n.*

**flank** (flangk) **1** of animals or people, the part of the body between the hips and the ribs. **2** a piece of meat cut from this part of an animal. See BEEF, LAMB and VEAL for pictures. **3** the side of a mountain, building, etc. **4** be at the side of: *High buildings flanked the dark, narrow alley.* **5** the far right or far left side of an army, fleet, etc. **6** get around the far right or the far left side of. **7** attack from or on the side. 1-3, 5 *n.*, 4, 6, 7 *v.* —**flank′er,** *n.*

**flan·nel** (flan′əl) **1** a soft, warm, woollen cloth. **2** made of flannel. **3** FLANNELETTE. **4** FACECLOTH. **5 flannels,** *pl.* **a** a clothes, especially trousers, made of flannel. **b** woollen underwear. 1, 3-5 *n.*, 2 *adj.*

**flan·nel·ette** (flan′ə let′) a soft, warm, cotton cloth with a nap, that looks like flannel. *n.*

**flap** (flap) **1** swing or sway about loosely: *Curtains flapped in the wind.* **2** move wings, arms, etc. up and down: *The crow flapped its wings.* **3** fly by moving wings up and down: *The bird flapped away.* **4** a flapping motion. **5** a noise caused by flapping. **6** strike noisily with something broad and flat. **7** a blow from something broad and flat: *a flap from a beaver's tail.* **8** a broad, flat piece fastened at one edge only: *Her coat had flaps on the pockets.* **9** a small, movable section of an airplane wing near the fuselage that is lowered to increase lift at low air speeds. See AIRPLANE for picture. 1-3, 6 *v.,* **flapped, flap·ping;** 4, 5, 7-9 *n.*

**flap·jack** (flap′jak′) a pancake; griddlecake. *n.*

**flap·per** (flap′ər) **1** something broad and flat to strike with. **2** a broad, flat, hanging piece; flap. **3** a young bird just able to fly. *n.*

A flared skirt

**flare** (fler) **1** flame up briefly or unsteadily, sometimes with smoke: *A gust of wind made the torches flare.* **2** a bright, unsteady light or blaze that lasts only a short time: *The flare of a match showed us his face. Carry flares in your car to put round an accident.* **3** a dazzling light that burns for a short time, used for signalling, lighting up a battlefield, etc. **4** signal by lights: *The rockets flared a warning.* **5** a sudden outburst. **6** spread out in the shape of a bell: *The skirt flared out from the waist to the hem.* **7** a spreading out into a bell shape. **8** a part that spreads out: *the flare of a skirt.* **9** burst out: *Suddenly her temper flared.* 1, 4, 6, 9 *v.*, **flared, flar‧ing;** 2, 3, 5, 7, 8 *n.*
**flare up** or **out,** **a** burst into sudden flame: *The dying fire flared up briefly.* **b** break out in a sudden burst of emotion, such as anger or hatred: *His temper flared up and he struck out with his fist.*
☞ Hom. FLAIR.

**flare‧pot** (fler′pot′) a metal sphere, usually containing kerosene, that may be lit as a warning signal. *n.*

**flare–up** (fler′up′) **1** an outburst of flame. **2** *Informal.* a sudden outburst of anger, violence, etc. *n.*

**flar‧ing** (fler′ing) **1** flaming. **2** gaudy. **3** spreading gradually outward in form. **4** ppr. of FLARE. 1–3 *adj.*, 4 *v.*

**flash** (flash) **1** a sudden, brief light or flame: *a flash of lightning.* **2** give out such a light or flame: *The lighthouse flashes signals twice a minute.* **3** come suddenly; pass quickly: *A bird flashed across the field.* **4** cause to flash. **5** a sudden, brief feeling, outburst, or display: *a flash of hope, a flash of temper, a flash of wit.* **6** a very brief time; instant: *It all happened in a flash.* **7** give out or send out like a flash. **8** communicate by flashes; send by telegraph, radio, etc. **9** a brief news report, usually received by teletype, or given over the radio or television: *a news flash.* **10** flashy. **11** a bright, showy display. **12** *Informal.* show off. 1, 5, 6, 9, 11 *n.*, 2–4, 7, 8, 12 *v.*, 10 *adj.* —**flash′er,** *n.*
**flash back,** of a film, return to an earlier time.
**flash in the pan,** a sudden, showy attempt or effort that often fails or is not followed by further efforts.
**in a flash,** in a very short time: *It all happened in a flash.*

**flash–back** (flash′bak′) in film, a return to an earlier time. *n.*

**flash bulb** **1** a bulb, often containing magnesium, used to give a bright light for taking photographs indoors, in shadow, or at night. **2** a portable electric device to hold and set off such a bulb.

**flash burn** a severe burn caused by instantaneous thermal radiation, such as from an atomic bomb.

**flash card** one of a set of cards displaying letters, words, figures, pictures, etc., intended to be shown briefly for drills in reading, arithmetic, and other school subjects, or to be used for various other purposes.

**flash cube** a cube-shaped device containing four flash bulbs, that can be attached to certain kinds of cameras so that four flash pictures can be taken without having to change bulbs.

**flash flood** a very sudden, violent flooding of a river, stream, etc.

**flash gun** in photography, an apparatus for holding and setting off a flash bulb.

**flash‧ing** (flash′ing) **1** the pieces of sheet metal used to cover and protect the joints and angles of a building to make them watertight. **2** ppr. of FLASH. 1 *n.*, 2 *v.*

**flash‧light** (flash′līt′) **1** a light that flashes, used in a lighthouse or for signalling. **2** a portable electric light, usually operated by batteries. **3** a preparation that makes a very bright flash of light, used for taking photographs indoors, in shadow, or at night. *n.*

**flash‧y** (flash′ē) **1** very bright for a short time; flashing. **2** showy; gaudy: *He tries to impress people by wearing flashy clothes.* *adj.*, **flash‧i‧er, flash‧i‧est.** —**flash′i‧ly,** *adv.* —**flash′i‧ness,** *n.*

**flask** (flask) **1** any bottle-shaped container, especially one having a narrow neck: *Flasks of thin glass are used in chemical laboratories for heating liquids.* **2** a small glass, plastic, or metal bottle with flat sides, made to be carried in the pocket. *n.*

**flat¹** (flat) **1** smooth and level; even: *flat land. This floor is flat.* **2** spread out; at full length; *The storm left the trees flat.* **3** not very deep or thick: *A plate is flat.* **4** with little air in it: *A nail or sharp stone can cause a flat tire.* **5** something flat. **6** a FLATBOAT. **7** a shallow box or basket. **8** a FLATCAR. **9** a piece of theatrical scenery. **10** *Informal.* a tire with little air in it. **11** a flat part: *The front of an open hand is the flat.* **12** flat land. **13** land covered with shallow water; marsh; swamp. **14** positive; not to be changed: *A flat refusal is complete. A flat rate has no extra charges.* **15** without much life, interest, flavour, etc.; dull: *flat food, a flat voice.* **16** not shiny or glossy: *a flat yellow.* **17** not clear or sharp in sound. **18** in music, below the true pitch: *to sing flat.* **19** in music, one half step or half note below natural pitch. **20** such a tone or note: *music written in B flat.* **21** the sign ♭ that shows such a tone or note in music. **22** in a flat manner; flatly: *Eva lay flat on the floor.* **23** make or become flat. 1–4, 14–19 *adj.*, **flat‧ter, flat‧test;** 5–13, 20, 21 *n.*, 18, 22 *adv.*, 23 *v.*, **flat‧ted, flat‧ting.** —**flat′ly,** *adv.* —**flat′ness,** *n.*
**fall flat,** fail completely; have no effect or interest: *One actor forgot her lines, and the scene fell flat.*

**flat²** (flat) an apartment or set of rooms on one floor. *n.*

**flatbed** (flat′bed′) a truck or trailer without sides, used for carrying heavy machinery.

**flat‧boat** (flat′bōt′) a large boat with a flat bottom, often used for carrying goods on a river or canal. *n.*

**flat‧bot‧tomed** (flat′bot′əmd) having a flat bottom. *adj.*

**flat‧bread** (flat′bred′) a thin, dry cracker usually made from rye flour. *n.*

**flat‧car** (flat′kär′) a railway freight car without a roof or sides. *n.*

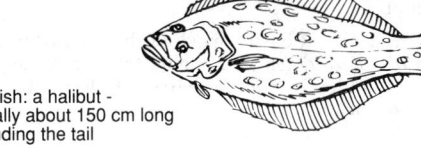

Flatfish: a halibut - usually about 150 cm long including the tail

**flat·fish** (flat′fish′) any of an order of saltwater fishes with flat bodies, and with both eyes on the side that is kept uppermost when lying flat: *Halibut, flounder, and sole are flatfish.* *n., pl.* **flat·fish** or **flat·fish·es.**

**flat·foot** (flat′fút′) 1 a foot with a flattened arch. 2 condition in which the feet have flattened arches. *n., pl.* **flat·feet.**

**flat–foot·ed** (flat′fút′id) 1 having feet with flattened arches. 2 *Informal.* not to be changed or influenced; firm; uncompromising. 3 *Informal.* unprepared. *adj.* —**flat′foot′ed·ness,** *n.*

**Flat·head** (flat′hed′) a member of several North American Indian tribes, including the Chinook, who, formerly, used to flatten artificially the heads of their children. *n.*

**flat·i·ron** (flat′ī′ərn) an iron with a flat surface that, when heated, is used for smoothing wrinkles out of cloth: *A flatiron is heated by placing it on a hot surface.* *n.*

**flat·ten** (flat′ən) make or become flat: *One can flatten the surface of a grass tennis court by using a roller.* *v.* **flatten out,** spread out flat.

**flat·ter** (flat′ər) 1 praise too much or beyond what is true; praise insincerely. 2 show to be better looking than is really the case: *The picture flatters her.* 3 try to please or win over by flattering. 4 cause to be pleased or feel honoured. *v.* —**flat′ter·er,** *n.* —**flat′ter·ing·ly,** *adv.* **flatter oneself,** **a** be pleased to know or think: *She flattered herself that she would be the best-dressed girl at the formal.* **b** overestimate oneself.

**flat·ter·y** (flat′ə rē) 1 the act or fact of FLATTERing. 2 words of praise, usually untrue or overstated. *n., pl.* **flat·ter·ies.**

**flat·tish** (flat′ish) somewhat flat. *adj.*

**flat·u·lence** (flach′ə ləns) 1 gas in the stomach or intestines. 2 pompous speech or behaviour; vanity; emptiness. *n.*

**flat·u·lent** (flach′ə lənt) 1 having gas in the stomach or intestines. 2 causing gas in the stomach or intestines. 3 pompous in speech or behaviour; vain; empty. *adj.*

**flat·ways** (flat′wāz′) with the flat side forward, upward, or touching. *adv.*

**flat·worm** (flat′wėrm′) a worm having a flat body, which lives in water or as a parasite on some animal: *Tapeworms are flatworms.* *n.*

**flaunt** (flont) 1 show off: *She flaunts her riches before her friends.* 2 wave proudly: *banners flaunting in the breeze.* 3 a flaunting. 1, 2 *v.,* 3 *n.* —**flaunt′ing·ly,** *adv.*

**flau·tist** (flot′ist) FLUTIST. *n.*

**fla·vor** (flā′vər) See FLAVOUR. *n., v.*

**fla·vor·ing** (flā′və ring) See FLAVOURING. *n.*

**fla·vour** or **fla·vor** (flā′vər) 1 a taste, especially a characteristic taste: *Chocolate and vanilla have different flavours.* 2 give an added taste to; season: *We use salt, pepper, and spices to flavour food.* 3 anything used to give a certain taste to food or drink; flavouring. 4 a characteristic quality: *Stories about ships and sailors have a flavour of the sea.* 5 give a characteristic quality to: *Many exciting adventures flavour an explorer's life.* 6 an aroma; odour. 1, 3, 4, 6 *n.,* 2, 5 *v.* —**fla′vour·less,** *adj.*

**fla·vour·ing** or **fla·vor·ing** (flā′və ring) 1 something used to give a certain taste to food or drink: *vanilla flavouring, chocolate flavouring.* 2 ppr. of FLAVOUR. 1 *n.,* 2 *v.*

**flaw** (flo′) 1 a defective place; crack: *A flaw in the dish caused it to break.* 2 a fault; defect: *a flaw in a man's character.* 3 make or become defective; crack. 1, 2 *n.,* 3 *v.*

**flaw·less** (flol′is) perfect; without a flaw: *The actor gave a flawless performance.* *adj.* —**flaw′less·ly,** *adv.* —**flaw′less·ness,** *n.*

**flax** (flaks) 1 a plant having small, narrow leaves, blue or yellow flowers, and slender stems about 30–60 cm tall: *Linseed oil is made from flax seeds.* 2 the fibres from the stems of this plant prepared for spinning: *Flax is spun into linen thread for making linen cloth.* *n.*

**flax·en** (flak′sən) 1 made of flax. 2 like the colour of flax; pale yellow: *flaxen hair.* *adj.*

**flax·seed** (flaks′sēd′) the seed of flax; linseed: *Flaxseed is used for linseed oil and some medicines.* *n.*

**flay** (flā) 1 strip the skin or outer covering from by whipping or lashing: *The tyrant had his enemies flayed alive.* 2 scold severely; criticize without pity or mercy: *The angry man flayed his servant with his tongue.* 3 rob; cheat. *v.* —**flay′er,** *n.*

**fld.** field.

A flea. The line beside it shows its actual length.

**flea** (flē) any of an order of small, wingless, jumping insects that live as parasites on animals, sucking their blood. *n.*
☞ *Hom.* FLEE.

**fleck** (flek) 1 a spot or patch of colour, light, etc.: *Freckles are brown flecks on the skin.* 2 a small particle; flake. 3 sprinkle with spots or patches of colour, light, etc.; speckle: *Sunlight coming through the branches flecked the shadow cast by the tree.* 1, 2 *n.,* 3 *v.*

**flecked** (flekt) 1 sprinkled with spots or patches of colour, light, etc.; speckled: *The bird's breast is flecked with brown.* 2 pt. and pp. of FLECK. 1 *adj.,* 2 *v.*

**flec·tion** (flek′shən) 1 a bending: *Every flection of her arm caused the muscles to bulge.* 2 a bent part; bend. *n.*

**fled** (fled) pt. and pp. of FLEE: *The clouds fled before the wind. The thieves had already fled.* *v.*

**fledge** (flej) 1 grow the feathers needed for flying.

**fledg·ling** or **fledge·ling** (flej′ling) 1 a young bird just able to fly. 2 a young, inexperienced person. *n.*

**flee** (flē) 1 run away; try to get away by running. 2 run away from; try to get away from by running. 3 go quickly; move swiftly: *The clouds are fleeing before the wind.* 4 pass away; cease; vanish: *The shadows flee at dawn.* *v.*, **fled, flee·ing.** —**fle′er,** *n.*
☛ Hom. FLEA.

**fleece** (flēs) 1 the wool that covers a sheep or similar animal. 2 the quantity of wool cut from a sheep at one time. 3 cut the fleece from. 4 strip of money or belongings; rob; cheat: *The gamblers fleeced him of a large sum.* 5 something like a fleece: *a fleece of hair, the fleece of new fallen snow.* 1, 2, 5 *n.*, 3, 4 *v.*, **fleeced, fleec·ing.** —**fleec′er,** *n.*

**fleec·y** (flē′sē) 1 like a fleece; soft and white: *fleecy clouds.* 2 covered with fleece. 3 made of fleece. *adj.*, **fleec·i·er, fleec·i·est.** —**fleec′i·ness,** *n.*

**fleet**¹ (flēt) 1 a group of warships under one command; navy: *the Canadian fleet.* 2 a group of boats, aircraft, automobiles, etc. moving or working together: *a fleet of trucks.* *n.*

**fleet**² (flēt) 1 swift; rapid: *a fleet horse.* 2 pass swiftly; move rapidly. 1 *adj.*, 2 *v.* —**fleet′ly,** *adv.* —**fleet′ness,** *n.*

**fleet·ing** (flē′ting) 1 passing swiftly; moving rapidly; soon gone. 2 ppr. of FLEET. 1 *adj.*, 2 *v.* —**fleet′ing·ly,** *adv.*

**Flem·ing** (flem′ing) 1 a native of Flanders, a region on the North Sea extending from northeastern France to the southwestern Netherlands. 2 a Belgian whose native language is Flemish. *n.*

**Flem·ish** (flem′ish) 1 of or having to do with Flanders, its people, or their language. 2 **the Flemish,** *pl.* the people of Flanders. 3 their language. 1 *adj.*, 2, 3 *n.*

**flesh** (flesh) 1 the soft substance of a human or animal body that covers the bones and is covered by skin: *Flesh consists mostly of muscles and fat.* 2 the tissue or muscles of animals. 3 fatness. 4 meat, especially of a sort not usually eaten by human beings: *horseflesh.* 5 the body, not the soul or spirit. 6 the physical side of human nature, as distinguished from the spiritual or moral side. 7 the human race; people as a group. 8 all living creatures: *All flesh must die.* 9 one's family or relatives by birth. 10 the soft or edible part of fruits or vegetables: *The McIntosh apple has crisp, juicy, white flesh.* 11 the colour of a white person's skin; pinkish white with a little yellow. *n.* —**flesh′less,** *adj.*
**flesh and blood,** a one's family or relatives by birth; a child or relative by birth. b a human body.
**in the flesh,** a alive. b in person: *There stood Rita in the flesh.*

**flesh–col·oured** or **flesh–col·ored** (flesh′kul′ərd) pinkish-white with a tinge of yellow. *adj.*

**flesh fly** a fly whose larvae feed on decaying flesh.

**flesh·ly** (flesh′lē) 1 of the flesh; bodily. 2 sensual. *adj.*, **flesh·li·er, flesh·li·est.** —**flesh′li·ness,** *n.*

**flesh·pots** (flesh′pots′) good food and living; luxuries. *n. pl.*

**flesh wound** a wound that merely injures the flesh; slight wound.

**flesh·y** (flesh′ē) 1 having much flesh: *The calf is the fleshy part of the lower leg.* 2 plump; fat. 3 of flesh; like flesh. 4 pulpy. *adj.*, **flesh·i·er, flesh·i·est.** —**flesh′i·ness,** *n.*

Two styles of fleur-de-lis. The one on the left is from the Canadian coat of arms.

**fleur–de–lis** (flėr′də lē′ *or* flėr′də lēs′) 1 a design or device used in heraldry, representing a lily. 2 the former royal coat of arms of France. 3 the unofficial floral emblem of the province of Quebec. 4 the iris flower or plant. *n.*, *pl.* **fleurs-de-lis** (flėr′də lē′ *or* flėr′də lēz′).

**flew** (flü) pt. of FLY: *The bird flew slowly away.* *v.*
☛ Hom. FLU, FLUE.

**flex** (fleks) 1 bend: *He slowly flexed his stiff arm.* 2 of muscles, tighten and relax alternately. *v.*

**flex·i·bil·i·ty** (flek′sə bil′ə tē) a FLEXIBLE quality. *n.*

**flex·i·ble** (flek′sə bəl) 1 easily bent; not stiff; bending without breaking: *Leather, rubber, and wire are flexible materials.* 2 easily adapted to fit various uses, purposes, etc.: *flexible plans. The actor's flexible voice accommodated itself to every emotion.* 3 easily managed; willing to yield to influence or persuasion. *adj.* —**flex′i·bly,** *adv.*

**flex·ure** (flek′shər) 1 a bending; curving. 2 a bend; curve. *n.*

**flick** (flik) 1 quick, light blow; a sudden, snapping stroke: *By a flick of her whip, she drove the fly from the horse's head.* 2 the light, snapping sound of such a blow or stroke. 3 strike lightly with a quick, snapping blow: *He flicked the dust from his shoes with a handkerchief.* 4 make a sudden, snapping stroke with: *The boys flicked wet towels at each other.* 5 flutter; move quickly and lightly. 6 a sudden jerk; a short, quick movement: *The fisherman made a short cast with a flick of his wrist.* 7 a streak; splash; fleck. 1, 2, 6, 7 *n.*, 3–5 *v.*

**flick·er**¹ (flik′ər) 1 shine with a wavering light; burn with an unsteady flame: *A dying fire flickered on the hearth.* 2 a wavering, unsteady light or flame. 3 a brief flame; spark. 4 move quickly and lightly in and out or back and forth: *The tongue of a snake flickers.* 5 a quick, light movement: *the flicker of an eyelash.* 1, 4 *v.*, 2, 3, 5 *n.*

**flick·er**² (flik′ər) any of various types of North American woodpecker: *The yellowhammer is one kind of flicker.* *n.*

**fli·er** (flī′ər) See FLYER. *n.*

**flight**¹ (flīt) 1 the act or manner of flying: *the flight of a bird through the air.* 2 the distance a bird, bullet, aircraft, etc. can fly. 3 a group of things flying through the air together: *a flight of six birds.* 4 an air-force unit of either planes or personnel. 5 a trip in an aircraft. 6 a swift movement. 7 a soaring above or beyond what is ordinary: *a flight of fancy.* 8 a set of stairs or steps between landings or storeys of a building. *n.*

**flight**² (flīt) 1 the act of fleeing or running away: *The defeated army was in flight.* 2 escape: *The flight of the prisoners was soon discovered.* *n.*
**put to flight,** force to flee.
**take to flight,** flee.

**flight·less** (flīt′lis) unable to fly. *adj.*

**flight·y** (flī′tē) **1** likely to have sudden fancies; full of whims; frivolous: *She was too flighty to be reliable.* **2** slightly crazy; light-headed. *adj.*, **flight·i·er, flight·i·est.** —**flight′i·ly,** *adv.* —**flight′i·ness,** *n.*

**flim·flam** (flim′flam′) *Informal.* **1** nonsense; rubbish. **2** deception; a low trick. **3** cheat a person out of money; trick. 1, 2 *n.*, 3 *v.*, **flim·flammed, flim·flam·ming.**

**flim·sy** (flim′zē) **1** light and thin; frail: *Muslin is too flimsy to be used for sails.* **2** not serious or convincing; inadequate: *a flimsy excuse.* **3** a thin paper used by reporters. **4** a newspaper report on this paper. **5** a sheet of very thin paper for typing or writing. 1, 2 *adj.*, **flim·si·er, flim·si·est;** 3–5 *n.*, *pl.* **flim·sies.** —**flim′si·ly,** *adv.* —**flim′si·ness,** *n.*

**flinch** (flinch) **1** draw back from difficulty, danger, or pain; shrink: *The baby flinched when she touched the hot radiator.* **2** drawing back: *He took his punishment without a flinch.* **3** a game played with cards bearing numbers from 1 to 14. 1 *v.*, 2, 3 *n.*

**fling** (fling) **1** throw forcefully; hurl violently: *The angry man flung his hat on the floor.* **2** a violent throw. **3** move rapidly; rush; flounce: *She flung angrily out of the room.* **4** plunge; kick. **5** put suddenly or violently: *Fling him into jail.* **6** move a part of the body in an impulsive, unrestrained way: *The girl happily flung her arms around her mother's neck.* **7** a time of doing as one pleases: *He had his fling when he was young; now he must work.* **8** a lively Scottish dance: *the Highland fling.* 1, 3–6 *v.*, **flung, fling·ing;** 2, 4, 7, 8 *n.* **have** or **take a fling at,** *Informal.* **a** try; attempt. **b** make scornful remarks about.

**flint** (flint) **1** a very hard grey or brown stone that makes a spark when struck against steel: *Flint is a kind of quartz.* **2** a piece of this stone used with steel to light fires, explode gunpowder, etc.: *Flints are used in cigarette lighters.* **3** anything very hard or unyielding: *He had a heart of flint.* *n.*

**flint·lock** (flint′lok′) **1** a gunlock in which a flint striking against steel makes sparks that explode the gunpowder: *Flintlocks were used on guns from the 1600's to the 1800's.* **2** an old-fashioned gun with such a gunlock. *n.*

**flint·y** (flin′tē) **1** containing flint: *a flinty rock formation.* **2** hard like flint: *The girls were tired after walking over the flinty asphalt.* **3** hard; unyielding: *The sergeant had flinty eyes.* *adj.*, **flint·i·er, flint·i·est.** —**flint′i·ness,** *n.*

**flip¹** (flip) **1** toss or move with a snap of a finger and thumb: *She flipped a coin on the counter.* **2** jerk; turn or move with a jerk; flick: *She flipped her fan shut. The branch flipped back. The driver flipped his whip at a fly.* **3** a smart tap; snap; a sudden jerk: *The cat gave the kitten a flip on the ear.* **4** turn over quickly: *He flipped the pages of the magazine. She flipped the eggs before serving them.* **5** a quick overturning: *The airplane took a flip just before it crashed.* **6** *Informal.* FLIPPANT. 1, 2, 4 *v.*, **flipped, flip·ping;** 3, 5 *n.*, 6 *adj.*, **flip·per, flip·pest.**

**flip²** (flip) a hot drink containing beer, ale, cider, etc., with sugar and spice. *n.*

**flip·pan·cy** (flip′ən sē) being FLIPPANT: *Avoid flippancy in addressing a judge.* *n.*, *pl.* **flip·pan·cies.**

**flip·pant** (flip′ənt) smart or pert in speech; not respectful: *a flippant answer.* *adj.* —**flip′pant·ly,** *adv.*

hat, āge, fär; let, ēqual, tèrm; it, īce
hot, ōpen, ôrder; oil, out; cup, pùt, rüle
ə*bove,* tak*ə*n, penc*ə*l, lem*ə*n, circ*ə*s
ch, child; ng, long; sh, ship
th, thin; ᴛн, then; zh, measure

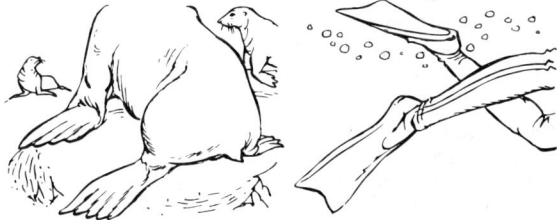

The flippers of a seal    Rubber flippers for the feet

**flip·per** (flip′ər) **1** a broad, flat fin especially adapted for swimming: *Seal flippers are a popular food in Newfoundland.* **2** a piece of rubber or plastic that fits onto the foot and has a broad, flat blade extending from the toe, used by swimmers to give extra power, especially when swimming under water: *A pair of flippers is part of every skindiver's equipment.* **3** comparative of FLIP. 1, 2 *n.*, 3 *adj.*

**flirt** (flėrt) **1** play at being in love with someone; try frivolously or playfully to win a person's attention and affection: *The girl's parents advised her not to flirt with boys.* **2** a person who flirts. **3** trifle; toy: *She flirted with the idea of going to Europe, though she couldn't afford it.* **4** move quickly to and fro; flutter: *She flirted her program impatiently.* **5** a quick movement or flutter: *With a flirt of its tail, the bird flew away.* **6** toss; jerk. 1, 3, 4, 6 *v.*, 2, 5, 6 *n.*

**flir·ta·tion** (flėr tā′shən) **1** pretending to be in love with someone. **2** a love affair that is not serious. *n.*

**flir·ta·tious** (flėr tā′shəs) **1** inclined to flirt. **2** having to do with FLIRTATION. *adj.* —**flir·ta′tious·ly,** *adv.* —**flir·ta′tious·ness,** *n.*

**flit** (flit) **1** fly lightly and quickly; flutter: *Birds flitted from tree to tree.* **2** pass lightly and quickly: *Many idle thoughts flitted through her mind as she lay in the sun.* **3** a light, quick movement. 1, 2 *v.*, **flit·ted, flit·ting;** 3 *n.*

**flitch** (flich) a side of a pig salted and cured; side of bacon. *n.*

**float** (flōt) **1** stay on top or be held up by a fluid, such as air or water: *A cork floats, but a stone sinks.* **2** move with a moving liquid; drift: *The boat floated out to sea.* **3** rest or move in a liquid, the air, etc. **4** cause to float. **5** cover with liquid; flood. **6** set going as a company. **7** sell securities: *to float an issue of stock.* **8** anything that stays up or holds up something else in water, such as a raft. **9** a cork on a fish line. **10** an air-filled organ that supports a fish. **11** a hollow, metal ball that regulates the level, supply, or outlet of a liquid. **12** a flat board of a water wheel or paddle wheel. **13** a low, flat car that carries an exhibit to be shown in a parade. **14** the car and exhibit together. **15** a drink consisting of ginger ale or a similar beverage with ice cream in it. 1–7 *v.*, 8–15 *n.* —**float′a·ble,** *adj.*

**float·er** (flō′tər) **1** a person or thing that floats. **2** *Informal.* a person who often changes his or her place of living, working, etc. **3** a person who can fill in for anyone absent from work. *n.*

**float·ing** (flō'ting) **1** that floats. **2** not fixed; not staying in one place; moving around. **3** in use or circulation; not permanently invested. **4** ppr. of FLOAT. 1–3 *adj.*, 4 *v.*

**floating ribs** the ribs not attached to the breastbone; the last two pairs of ribs.

**floc·cu·lent** (flok'yə lənt) **1** like bits of wool. **2** made up of soft, woolly masses. **3** covered with a soft, woolly substance. *adj.*

**flock** (flok) **1** animals of one kind that feed and move about in a group, especially sheep, goats, or birds. **2** a large group; crowd. **3** go or gather in a flock; come crowding: *Sheep usually flock together. The children flocked around the storyteller.* **4** people of the same church group; a band or company: *The minister served her flock well until her retirement.* 1, 2, 4 *n.*, 3 *v.*

**floe** (flō) **1** a field or sheet of floating ice: *Seals are hunted on ice floes.* **2** a floating piece broken off from such a field or sheet. *n.*
☞ *Hom.* FLOW.

**flog** (flog) whip very hard; beat with a whip, stick, etc. *v.*, **flogged, flog·ging.** —**flog'ger,** *n.*

**flood** (flud) **1** a flow of water over what is usually dry land. **2** flow over or into: *When the heavy snow melted last spring, the river rose and flooded our fields.* **3** fill much fuller than usual; fill to overflowing: *A wave flooded the holes I had dug in the sand.* **4** become covered or filled with water: *During the thunderstorm, our cellar flooded.* **5** cover the surface of something with water: *The attendants flooded the ice before every hockey game.* **6** a large amount of water; ocean; sea; lake; river. **7** a great outpouring of anything: *a flood of light, a flood of words.* **8** pour out or stream like a flood: *Sunlight flooded into the room.* **9** fill, cover, or overcome like a flood: *The rich woman was flooded with requests for money. The room was flooded with moonlight.* **10** flow like a flood: *The tide flooded in.* **11** a flowing of the tide toward the shore; rise of the tide. **12 the Flood,** in the Bible, the water that covered the earth in the time of Noah. 1, 6, 7, 11, 12 *n.*, 2–5, 8–10 *v.*
**in flood,** filled to overflowing with an unusual amount of water: *The river was in flood.*

**flood control** the control of floods and the prevention of damage caused by them by the use of dams, dikes, extra outlets, reforestation, etc.

**flood·gate** (flud'gāt') **1** the gate in a canal, river, stream, etc. to control the flow of water. **2** something that controls any flow or passage. *n.*

**flood·light** (flud'līt') **1** a lamp that gives a broad beam of light: *Several floodlights were used to illuminate the stage.* **2** the broad beam of light from such a lamp. **3** illuminate with floodlights. 1, 2 *n.*, 3 *v.* **flood·light·ed** or **flood·lit, flood·light·ing.**

**flood plain** a plain bordering a river and made of soil deposited by floods.

**flood tide** the flowing of the tide toward the shore; rise of the tide.

**floor** (flôr) **1** the inside bottom covering of a room. **2** put a floor in or over: *We shall floor this room with oak.* **3** a storey of a building: *Five families live on the fourth floor.* **4** a flat surface at the bottom of anything: *They dropped their net to the floor of the ocean.* **5** the part of a room or hall where members of a lawmaking body, etc. sit and from which they speak: *the floor of the House of Commons.* **6** the right or privilege to speak in a lawmaking body, etc.: *The chairperson decides who has the floor.* **7** knock down. **8** *Informal.* defeat. **9** *Informal.* confuse or puzzle completely: *The last question on the examination floored us all.* 1, 3–6 *n.*, 2, 7–9 *v.*

**floor hockey** an indoor game derived from hockey, in which the players use a long stick to carry and pass a plastic puck or a ring resembling a quoit of rope or felt.

**floor·ing** (flôr'ing) **1** a floor. **2** floors collectively. **3** material for making floors: *Tile is often used as flooring for bathrooms.* **3** ppr. of FLOOR. 1, 2 *n.*, 3 *v.*

**floor show** an entertainment consisting of music, singing, dancing, etc., presented at a night club, hotel, etc.

**floor·walk·er** (flôr'wok'ər) a person employed in a large store to oversee sales, direct customers, etc. *n.*

**flop** (flop) **1** move loosely or heavily; flap around clumsily: *The fish flopped helplessly on the deck.* **2** fall, drop, throw, or move heavily or clumsily: *She flopped down into a chair.* **3** flopping. **4** the sound made by flopping. **5** change or turn suddenly. **6** *Informal.* failure: *The new play was a flop.* **7** *Informal.* fail. 1, 2, 5, 7 *v.*, flopped, flop·ping; 3, 4, 6 *n.* —**flop'per,** *n.*

**flop·py** (flop'ē) *Informal.* flopping; tending to flop: *She bought a sunhat with a floppy brim.* *adj.*, **flop·pi·er, flop·pi·est.** —**flop'pi·ness,** *n.*

**floppy disk** a thin, round, and magnetized flexible plate used for storing data for a computer.

**flo·ra** (flô'rə) the plants of a particular region or time: *The Sahara Desert has scanty flora.* *n.*

**flo·ral** (flô'rəl) **1** of or having to do with flowers: *floral decorations.* **2** resembling flowers: *a floral design.* *adj.*

**Flor·en·tine** (flô'rən tēn') **1** of or having to do with Florence, a city in Italy. **2** a native or inhabitant of Florence. 1 *adj.*, 2 *n.*

**flo·res·cence** (flô res'əns) **1** the act of blossoming. **2** the condition of blossoming. **3** the period of blossoming. *n.*
☞ *Hom.* FLUORESCENCE (flô res'əns).

**flo·res·cent** (flô res'ənt) blossoming. *adj.*
☞ *Hom.* FLUORESCENT (flô res'ənt).

**flo·ret** (flô'rit) a small flower. *n.*

**flo·ri·cul·ture** (flô'rə kul'chər) the cultivation of flowers. *n.*

**flor·id** (flô'rid) **1** highly coloured; ruddy: *a florid complexion.* **2** elaborately ornamented; flowery; showy; ornate: *florid language, florid architecture.* *adj.*
—**flor'id·ly,** *adv.* —**flor'id·ness,** *n.*

**flo·rist** (flô'rist) one who raises or sells flowers. *n.*

**floss** (flos) **1** short, loose silk fibres. **2** a shiny, untwisted silk thread made from such fibres: *Floss is used for embroidery. Floss is used for cleaning between the teeth.* **3** soft, silky fluff or fibres: *Milkweed pods contain white floss.* *n.*

**floss·y** (flos'ē) **1** of floss. **2** like floss. **3** *Informal.* fancy; glamorous; highly decorated. *adj.*, **floss·i·er, floss·i·est.**

**flo·ta·tion** (flō tā'shən) **1** floating or launching. **2** getting started or established. **3** selling or putting on sale. *n.*

**flo·til·la** (flō til′ə) 1 a small fleet. 2 a fleet of small ships. *n.*

**flot·sam** (flot′səm) the wreckage of a ship or its cargo found floating on the sea. *n.*
**flotsam and jetsam,** a wreckage or cargo found floating on the sea or washed ashore. b odds and ends; useless things. c people without steady work or permanent homes.

**flounce**[1] (flouns) 1 go with an angry or impatient movement of the body: *She flounced out of the room in a huff.* 2 an angry or impatient fling or turn of the body. 3 twist; turn; jerk. 1, 3 *v.*, **flounced, flounc·ing;** 2, 3 *n.*

**flounce**[2] (flouns) 1 a wide strip of cloth, gathered along the top edge and sewn to a dress, skirt, etc. as trimming; a wide ruffle. 2 trim with a flounce or flounces. 1 *n.*, 2 *v.*, **flounced, flounc·ing.**

**floun·der**[1] (floun′dər) 1 struggle awkwardly without making much progress; plunge about: *Men and horses were floundering in the deep snowdrifts.* 2 be clumsy or confused and make mistakes: *The frightened girl could only flounder through her song.* 3 a floundering movement or action. 1, 2 *v.*, 3 *n.*

**floun·der**[2] (floun′dər) a flatfish that has a large mouth. *n., pl.* **floun·der** or **floun·ders.**

**flour** (flour *or* flou′ər) 1 a fine, powdery substance made by grinding and sifting wheat or other grain. 2 any fine, soft powder. 3 cover with flour. 1, 2 *n.*, 3 *v.*
☛ *Hom.* FLOWER (for the second pronunciation of **flour**).

**flour·ish** (flėr′ish) 1 grow or develop with vigour; thrive; do well: *Her newspaper business grew and flourished.* 2 be in the best time of life or activity. 3 wave a sword, stick, arm, etc. in the air: *Pablo flourished the letter when he saw us.* 4 a waving in the air: *He removed his hat with a flourish.* 5 a showy decoration in handwriting. 6 in music, a showy trill or passage: *a flourish of trumpets.* 7 a showy display of enthusiasm, heartiness, etc.: *The agent showed us about the house with much flourish.* 8 make a showy display. 1–3, 8 *v.*, 4–7 *n.* —**flour′ish·ing·ly,** *adv.*

**flour mill** 1 a machine for grinding wheat or other grain into flour. 2 a place or establishment where there is such a machine or machines.

**flour·y** (flou′rē *or* flou′ə rē) 1 of or like flour. 2 covered or white with flour. *adj.*
☛ *Hom.* FLOWERY (for the second pronunciation of **floury**).

**flout** (flout) 1 treat with contempt or scorn; mock; scoff at: *The disobedient boy flouted his mother's advice.* 2 show contempt or scorn; scoff. 3 a contemptuous speech or act; insult; mockery; scoffing. 1, 2 *v.*, 3 *n.* —**flout′er,** *n.* —**flout′ing·ly,** *adv.*

**flow** (flō) 1 run like water; move in a current or stream. 2 pour out; pour along. 3 move easily or smoothly; glide: *a flowing movement in a dance, flowing verse.* 4 hang loosely and waving: *flowing robes, a flowing tie.* 5 be plentiful; be full and overflowing: *a land flowing with milk and honey.* 6 the act or way of flowing: *a flow of blood.* 7 any continuous movement like that of water in a river: *a rapid flow of speech.* 8 the rate of flowing. 9 something that flows; a current; stream: *There is a constant flow of water from the spring.* 10 the flowing of the tide toward the shore; rise of the tide. 11 flow in; rise. 1–5, 11 *v.*, 6–10 *n.*
☛ *Hom.* FLOE.

**flow chart** a diagram showing the sequence of operations and the relationship between different elements of a complex system or process, as in manufacturing or data processing.

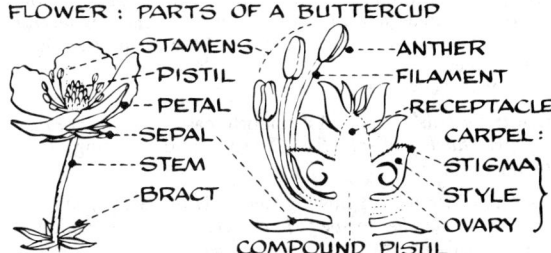

Flower: the parts of a buttercup

**flow·er** (flou′ər) 1 the part of a plant that produces the seed; blossom: *A flower is a shortened branch with modified leaves called petals.* 2 a plant grown for its blossoms. 3 any of several kinds of reproductive structures in lower plants, such as the mosses. 4 have flowers; produce flowers. 5 cover or decorate with flowers. 6 the finest part: *The flower of the country's youth was killed in the war.* 7 the time of being at one's best: *a man in the flower of life.* 8 be at one's best. 1–3, 6, 7 *n.*, 4, 5, 8 *v.* —**flow′er·less,** *adj.* —**flow′er·like**′, *adj.*
**in flower,** flowering.
☛ *Hom.* FLOUR (flou′ər).

**flower bed** a border or area of earth in a garden in which flowers are grown.

**flow·ered** (flou′ərd) 1 having flowers. 2 covered or decorated with flowers. 3 pt. and pp. of FLOWER. 1, 2 *adj.*, 3 *v.*

**flow·er·et** (flou′ə rit) a small flower. *n.*

**flower head** a bloom, or blossom, composed of many tiny flowers grouped together so that they appear to be a single flower; compound flower: *Composite plants, such as the daisy and dandelion, have flower heads.* See COMPOSITE for picture.

**flow·er·ing** (flou′ə ring) 1 having flowers. 2 ppr. of FLOWER. 1 *adj.*, 2 *v.*

**flow·er·pot** (flou′ər pot′) a pot to hold soil for a plant to grow in. *n.*

**flow·er·y** (flou′ə rē) 1 having many flowers. 2 containing many fine words and fanciful expressions: *a flowery speech.* *adj.*, **flow·er·i·er, flow·er·i·est.** —**flow′er·i·ness,** *n.*
☛ *Hom.* FLOURY (flou′ə rē).

**flown** (flōn) pp. of FLY[2]: *The bird has flown. The flag is flown on all government buildings.* *v.*

**FLQ** or **F.L.Q.** Front de Libération du Québec.

**flu** (flü) *Informal.* INFLUENZA. *n.*
☛ *Hom.* FLEW, FLUE.

**flub** (flub) *Informal.* do something very clumsily; make a mess of. *v.* **flubbed, flub·bing.**

**fluc·tu·ate** (fluk′chü āt′) **1** rise and fall; change continually; vary irregularly: *The temperature fluctuates from day to day.* **2** move in waves. *v.*, **fluc·tu·at·ed, fluc·tu·at·ing.**

**fluc·tu·a·tion** (fluk′chü ā′shən) **1** rising and falling; continual change; irregular variation. **2** a wavelike motion. *n.*

**flue** (flü) **1** a tube, pipe, or other enclosed passage for conveying smoke, hot air, etc.: *A chimney often has several flues.* **2** a flue pipe in an organ. **3** the air passage in such a pipe. *n.*
☞ Hom. FLEW, FLU.

**flu·en·cy** (flü′ən sē) **1** a smooth, easy flow: *The orator had great fluency of speech.* **2** easy, rapid speaking or writing. *n.*

**flu·ent** (flü′ənt) **1** flowing smoothly or easily: *Long practice enabled her to speak fluent French.* **2** speaking or writing easily and rapidly: *He is a fluent lecturer.* *adj.* —**flu′ent·ly,** *adv.*

**flue pipe** an organ pipe in which the sound is made by a current of air striking the mouth or opening in the pipe.

**fluff** (fluf) **1** soft, light, downy particles: *Woollen blankets often have fluff on them.* **2** a soft, light, downy mass: *The little kitten looked like a fluff of fur.* **3** shake up into a soft, light, downy mass: *I fluffed the pillows when I made the bed.* **4** become fluffy. 1, 2 *n.*, 3, 4 *v.*

**fluff·y** (fluf′ē) **1** soft and light like fluff: *Whipped cream is fluffy.* **2** covered with fluff; downy: *fluffy chicks.* *adj.*, **fluff·i·er, fluff·i·est.** —**fluff′i·ness,** *n.*

**flu·id** (flü′id) **1** any liquid or gas; any substance that flows: *Water, mercury, air, and oxygen are fluids.* **2** in the state of a fluid; like a fluid; flowing: *He poured the fluid mass of hot candy into a dish to harden.* **3** of or having to do with fluids. **4** changing easily; not fixed. 1 *n.*, 2–4 *adj.* —**flu′id·ly,** *adv.*

**fluid dram** one eighth of a FLUID OUNCE (about 3.6 cm³).

**flu·id·i·ty** (flü id′ə tē) a FLUID condition or quality. *n.*

**fluid ounce** a unit for measuring liquids, equal to one-twentieth of a pint, or about 28.4 cm³.

**fluke¹** (flük) **1** the pointed part of an anchor that catches in the ground. See ANCHOR for picture. **2** the barbed head or any barb of an arrow, harpoon, etc. **3** either half of a whale's tail.

**fluke²** (flük) *Informal.* **1** in billiards or pool, a lucky shot. **2** in billiards or pool, make or hit by a lucky shot. **3** a lucky chance; fortunate accident. **4** get by chance or accident. 1, 3 *n.*, 2, 4 *v.*, **fluked, fluk·ing.**

**fluke³** (flük) **1** a flatfish. **2** a parasitic flatworm shaped like a flatfish; trematode. *n.*

**flume** (flüm) **1** a deep, narrow valley with a stream running through it. **2** a large, inclined trough or chute for carrying water: *Flumes are used to transport logs or to furnish water for power or irrigation.* *n.*

**flung** (flung) pt. and pp. of FLING: *The girl flung the ball. The paper was flung away.* *v.*

**flunk** (flungk) *Informal.* **1** fail in school work: *He flunked his chemistry examination but passed all the others.* **2** cause to fail. **3** mark or grade as having failed. **4** failure. **5** give up; back out. 1–3, 5 *v.*, 4 *n.*
**flunk out,** *Informal.* dismiss or be dismissed from school, college, etc. for inferior work.

**flunk·ey** (flung′kē) **1** manservant who wears livery; footman. **2** flattering, fawning person. **3** a farm hand; a cook's assistant. *n., pl.* **flunkeys.** Also, **flunky.**

**flunk·y** (flung′kē) See FLUNKEY. *n., pl.* **flunkies.**

**flu·o·resce** (flü′ə res′ or flô res′) give off light by FLUORESCENCE. *v.*, **flu·o·resced, flu·o·resc·ing.**

**flu·o·res·cence** (flü′ə res′əns or flô res′əns) **1** a giving off of light from a substance while exposed to certain rays (X rays and ultraviolet rays). **2** the property of a substance that causes this: *Fluorescence is an ability to transform light so as to emit rays of a different wave length or colour.* **3** the light given off in this way. *n.*
☞ Hom. FLORESCENCE (for the second pronunciation of **fluorescence**).

**flu·o·res·cent** (flü′ə res′ənt or flô res′ənt) that gives off light by FLUORESCENCE: *Fluorescent substances glow in the dark when exposed to X rays.* *adj.*
☞ Hom. FLORESCENT (for the second pronunciation of **fluorescent**).

**fluorescent lamp** a type of electric lamp, usually a cathode-ray tube containing a gas or vapour that produces light (**fluorescent light**) when acted on by an electric current.

**flu·or·ic** (flü ô′rik) of, having to do with, or obtained from FLUORITE or FLUORINE. *adj.*

**fluor·i·date** (flü′ə rə dāt′ or flô′rə dāt′) add small amounts of a FLUORIDE to drinking water, especially to decrease tooth decay in children. *v.*, **fluor·i·dat·ed, fluor·i·dat·ing.**

**fluor·i·da·tion** (flü′ə rə dā′shən or flô′rə dā′shən) the act or process of fluoridating. *n.*

**flu·o·ride** (flü′ə rīd′ or flô′rīd) a compound of FLUORINE and another element or radical. *n.*

**flu·o·rine** (flü′ə rēn′ or flô′rēn; flü′ə rin or flô′rin) a poisonous, greenish-yellow gaseous chemical element, similar to chlorine. Symbol: F *n.*

**flu·o·rite** (flü′ə rīt′ or flô′rīt) a transparent crystalline mineral that occurs in many colours; calcium fluoride: *Fluorite is used for fusing metals, making glass, etc.* *n.*

**fluor·o·scope** (flü′ə rə skōp′ or flô′rə skōp′) a device containing a FLUORESCENT screen for examining objects exposed to X rays or other radiations: *The parts of the object not penetrated by the rays of the fluoroscope cast shadows on the screen.* *n.*

**flur·ry** (flėr′ē) **1** a sudden gust of wind: *A flurry upset the small sailboat.* **2** a light fall of snow or, less usually, rain: *snow flurries.* **3** a sudden excitement, confusion, or disturbance. **4** excite; confuse; disturb: *Noise in the audience flurried the actor so that he forgot his lines.* 1–3 *n., pl.* **flur·ries;** 4 *v.*, **flur·ried, flur·ry·ing.**

**flush¹** (flush) **1** blush; glow: *The girl flushed when they laughed at her* (*v.*). *The flush of sunrise was on the clouds* (*n.*). **2** cause to blush or glow: *Exercise flushed his face.* **3** rush suddenly; flow rapidly: *Embarrassment caused the blood to flush to her cheeks.* **4** a sudden rush; rapid flow. **5** wash or cleanse with a rapid flow of water: *The city streets were flushed every night.* **6** excite; make joyful and proud: *The team was flushed with its first victory.* **7** an excited condition or feeling; sudden rush of joyous pride, etc. **8** a sudden, fresh growth: *April brought the first flush of grass.* **9** glowing vigour; freshness: *the first flush of* youth.   **10** a fit of feeling very hot.   1–3, 5, 6 *v.*, 1, 4, 7–10 *n.*

**flush²** (flush)   **1** even; level: *The edge of the new shelf must be flush with the old one.*   **2** evenly; so as to be level.   **3** well supplied; having plenty: *The rich woman was always flush with money.*   **4** abundant; plentiful: *Money is flush when times are good.*   **5** liberal; lavish.   **6** prosperous.   **7** glowing; ruddy.   **8** direct; square.   **9** directly; squarely: *The fighter hit him flush on the nose.*   1 *v.*, 1, 3–8 *adj.*, 2, 9 *adv.*

**flush³** (flush)   **1** fly or start up suddenly.   **2** cause to fly or start up suddenly: *The hunter's dog flushed a partridge in the woods.*   *v.*   —**flush′er**, *n.*

**flush⁴** (flush)   in cards, a hand all of one suit.   *n.*

**flu·sol** (flü′sol)   artificial blood for emergency use.   *n.*

**flus·ter** (flus′tər)   **1** make nervous and excited; confuse.   **2** nervous excitement; confusion.   1 *v.*, 2 *n.*

A flute

**flute** (flüt)   **1** a long, slender musical instrument, played by blowing across a hole near one end: *Different notes are made on a flute by opening and closing holes along the tube with the fingers or with keys.*   **2** play on a flute.   **3** sing or whistle so as to sound like a flute.   **4** a long, round groove: *Some pillars have flutes.*   **5** make long, round grooves in.   1, 4 *n.*, 2, 3, 5 *v.*, **flut·ed, flut·ing.**

**flut·ed** (flü′tid)   **1** having long, round grooves: *fluted columns.*   **2** pt. and pp. of FLUTE.   1 *adj.*, 2 *v.*

Fluting used to decorate a fireplace

**flut·ing** (flü′ting)   **1** a decoration made with long, round grooves.   **2** ppr. of FLUTE.   1 *n.*, 2 *v.*

**flut·ist** (flü′tist)   a person who plays the flute, especially a skilled player.   *n.* Also, **flautist.**

**flut·ter** (flut′ər)   **1** wave back and forth quickly and lightly: *The flag fluttered in the breeze.*   **2** flap the wings; flap: *The chickens fluttered excitedly when they saw the dog.*   **3** come or go with a fluttering motion: *The young birds fluttered to the ground.*   **4** move restlessly.   **5** tremble; move quickly and unevenly: *Her heart fluttered.*   **6** beat feebly and irregularly: *Her pulse fluttered.*   **7** a fluttering.   **8** confuse; excite.   **9** a confused or excited condition: *The appearance of the Queen caused a great flutter in the crowd.*   1–6, 8 *v.*, 7, 9 *n.*   Also, **flitter.**   —**flut′ter·er,** *n.*
—**flut′ter·ing·ly,** *adv.*

**flu·vi·al** (flü′vē əl)   of, found in, or produced by a river: *A delta is a fluvial deposit.*   *adj.*

**flux** (fluks)   **1** a flow; flowing.   **2** a flowing in of the tide.   **3** continuous change: *Atomic science is in a state of flux.*   **4** an unnatural discharge of blood or liquid matter from the body.   **5** cause such a discharge in; purge.   **6** a substance used to help metals or minerals melt together: *Rosin is used as a flux in soldering.*   **7** melt together; heat with a substance of this kind.   **8** the rate of flow of a fluid, heat, etc. across a certain surface or area.   1–4, 6, 8 *n.*, 5, 7 *v.*

**flux·ion** (fluk′shən)   **1** a flowing; flow.   **2** discharge.   *n.*

**fly¹** (flī)   **1** housefly. See MAGGOT for picture.   **2** any of a large group of insects that have two wings, including houseflies, mosquitoes, gnats, etc.   **3** any insect with transparent wings, such as a May fly.   **4** a fish-hook with feathers, silk, tinsel, etc. on it to make it look like an insect: *Some fishermen make their own flies.*   *n., pl.* **flies.**
**fly in the ointment,**   a small thing that spoils something else or lessens its value.

**fly²** (flī)   **1** move through the air with wings: *Birds fly.*   **2** float or wave in the air: *Our flag flies every day.*   **3** cause to fly: *Children fly kites.*   **4** travel through the air in an aircraft.   **5** travel over in an airplane or airship.   **6** manage an airplane or airship.   **7** carry in an airplane or airship.   **8** move swiftly; go rapidly: *Clouds fly before the wind.*   **9** run away; flee; flee from; shun.   **10** in baseball, a ball hits high into the air with a bat: *She enjoys catching flies.*   **11** hit a baseball high into the air with a bat: *The batter flied into left field.*   **12** a piece of canvas that serves as an extra outer flap or roof for a tent.   **13** an opening in a garment, especially in the front of trousers.   1–9, 11 *v.*, **flew, flown, fly·ing** (defs. 1–9), **flied, fly·ing** (def. 11).   10, 12, 13 *n., pl.* **flies.**
**fly at,**   attack violently.
**fly in the face of,**   disobey openly; defy.
**fly off,**   leave suddenly; break away.
**fly up,**   be promoted from Brownie to Girl Guide.
**let fly, a** aim; shoot; throw: *The hunter let fly an arrow.*   **b** say violently.
**on the fly,**   while still in the air.

**fly·a·way** (flī′ə wā′)   **1** fluttering; streaming.   **2** frivolous; flighty.   *adj.*

**fly-blown** (flī′blōn′)   **1** tainted by the eggs or larvae of flies.   **2** spoiled.   **3** covered with FLY SPECKS.   *adj.*

**fly-by-night** (flī′bī nīt′)   **1** not reliable; not to be trusted.   **2** *Informal.*   a person who avoids paying his or her debts by leaving secretly at night.   **3** an unreliable or irresponsible person.   1 *adj.*, 2, 3 *n.*

**fly·catch·er** (flī′kach′ər)   any of a family of songless perching birds having small, weak feet, short necks, and large heads with broad, flattened bills hooked at the tip: *The kingbird, phoebe, and crested flycatcher are common types of flycatcher.*   *n.*

**fly·er** or **fli·er** (flī′ər)   **1** a person or thing that flies.   **2** a pilot.   **3** a very fast train, ship, bus, etc.   **4** a handbill, used for advertising.   *n.*

**fly·ing** (flī′ing) **1** that flies; moving through the air. **2** floating or waving in the air. **3** swift. **4** short and quick; hasty: *Aunt Michelle paid us a flying visit last week.* **5** of cattle brands, wavy. **6** ppr. of FLY. *1–5 adj., 6 v.*
**with flying colours** or **colors,** successfully; triumphantly: *She passed the examination with flying colours.*

**flying boat** a type of seaplane having a boatlike hull.

**flying buttress** an arched support or brace built between the wall of a building and a supporting column to bear some of the weight of the roof. See BUTTRESS for picture.

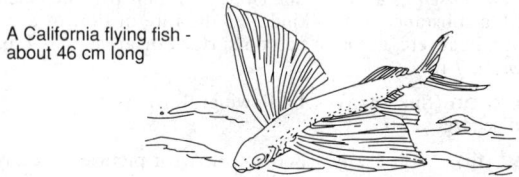
A California flying fish - about 46 cm long

**flying fish** any of numerous related fishes mainly of tropical seas that have winglike pectoral fins which help them glide for some distance through the air after leaping from the water.

**flying fox** any of several fruit-eating bats with a head like a fox.

**flying jib** a small triangular sail set in front of the regular jib.

**flying saucer** a disklike object that some people claim to have seen flying at great speed over various parts of the world; UFO.

**flying squirrel** a squirrel that can make long, gliding leaps through the air.

**flying wing** in Canadian rugby football, a player whose position is variable behind the line of scrimmage: *There is no flying wing on American football teams.*

**fly·leaf** (flī′lēf′) a blank sheet of paper at the beginning or end of a book, pamphlet, etc. *n., pl.* **fly·leaves.**

**fly·pa·per** (flī′pā′pər) a sticky paper to catch flies. *n.*

**fly·past** (flī′past′) a display in which aircraft in formation fly over a reviewing stand located on the ground: *We were thrilled by the flypast at the air show.* *n.*

**fly specks** the tiny dark spots left by flies on windows, light bulbs, etc.; fly dung.

**fly swatter** a device for killing flies, usually consisting of a long wooden or wire handle to which is attached a broad, flat piece of perforated rubber, plastic, etc.

**fly·trap** (flī′trap′) **1** a plant that traps insects. **2** a trap to catch flies. *n.*

**fly–up** (flī′up′) a ceremony at which BROWNIES (def. 2) are promoted to GIRL GUIDES. *n.*

**fly·way** (flī′wā′) an established route followed by migrating birds. *n.*

**fly·weight** (flī′wāt′) a boxer who weighs between 49 and 51 kilograms. *n.*

**fly·wheel** (flī′wēl′ *or* flī′hwēl′) a heavy wheel attached to machinery to keep the speed even. See STEAM ENGINE for picture. *n.*

**Fm** fermium.

**FM, F.M.,** or **f.m.** frequency modulation.

**fm.** fathom.

**foal** (fōl) **1** a young horse, donkey, etc.; a colt or filly. **2** give birth to a foal. *1 n., 2 v.*

**foam** (fōm) **1** a mass of very small bubbles. **2** form or gather foam. **3** cause to foam. **4** break into foam: *The stream foams over the rocks.* **5** a spongy, flexible material made from plastics, rubber, etc. *1, 5 n., 2–4 v.* —**foam′less,** *adj.* —**foam′like′,** *adj.*

**foam rubber** a firm, spongy foam of natural or synthetic rubber, used especially for mattresses and upholstery.

**foam·y** (fō′mē) **1** covered with foam; foaming. **2** made of foam. **3** like foam. *adj.,* **foam·i·er, foam·i·est.** —**foam′i·ly,** *adv.* —**foam′i·ness,** *n.*

**fob¹** (fob) **1** a small pocket in trousers or vest to hold a watch, etc. **2** a short watch chain, ribbon, etc. that hangs out of a watch pocket. **3** an ornament worn at the end of such a chain, ribbon, etc. *n.*

**fob²** (fob) trick; deceive; cheat. *v.,* **fobbed, fob·bing.**
**fob off, a** put off or deceive by a trick. **b** palm off or get rid of by a trick.

**f.o.b.** or **F.O.B.** of prices, free on board: *$850, f.o.b. Halifax,* means *a price of $850 at Halifax; further costs for shipping from Halifax to another point are extra.*

**fo·cal** (fō′kəl) of a FOCUS; having to do with a focus: *The focal length of a lens is the distance of its focus from the optical centre of the lens.* *adj.*
☞ *Etym.* See note at FOCUS.

**fo·cal·ize** (fō′kə līz′) **1** FOCUS (defs. 2, 5, 6). **2** bring into FOCUS (def. 1). *v.,* **fo·cal·ized, fo·cal·iz·ing.** —**fo′cal·i·za′tion,** *n.*

**fo·ci** (fō′sī *or* fō′sē) a plural of FOCUS. *n.*

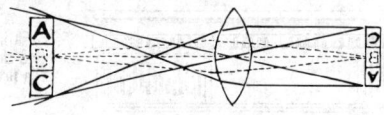
Rays of light brought to a focus by a lens

**fo·cus** (fō′kəs) **1** a point where rays of light, heat, etc. meet, appear to meet, or should meet after being bent by a lens, curved mirror, etc. **2** bring rays of light, heat, etc. to such a point: *The lens focussed the sun's rays on a piece of paper so that they burned a hole in it.* **3** the distance of this point from the lens, curved mirror, etc.: *A near-sighted eye has a shorter focus than a normal eye.* **4** the correct adjustment of a lens, the eye, etc. to make a clear image: *If the camera is not brought into focus, the photograph will be blurred.* **5** adjust a lens, the eye, etc. to make a clear image: *A near-sighted person cannot focus accurately on distant objects.* **6** make an image, etc. clear by adjusting a lens, the eye, etc. **7** the central point of attention, activity, disturbance, etc.: *The focus of a disease is the part of the body where it is most active.* **8** concentrate: *When studying, he focussed his mind on his lessons.* *1, 3, 4, 7 n., pl.* **fo·cus·es** *or* **fo·ci;** *2, 5, 6, 8 v.,* **fo·cus·ses** or **fo·cus·es, fo·cussed** or **fo·cused, fo·cus·sing** or **fo·cus·ing.**

☛ *Etym.* From L. *focus* 'hearth, fireplace'—the centre of the home.

**fod·der** (fod′ər) coarse food for horses, cattle, etc.: *Hay and cornstalks are fodder.* *n.*

**foe** (fō) enemy. *n.*

**foe·tal** (fē′təl) See FETAL. *adj.*

**foe·tus** (fē′təs) See FETUS. *n.*

**fog** (fog) **1** a cloud of fine drops of water that forms just above the earth's surface; thick mist. **2** cover with fog. **3** a darkened condition; dim, blurred state. **4** darken; dim; blur: *Something fogged six of our photographs.* **5** a confused or puzzled condition: *His mind was in a fog during most of the examination.* **6** confuse; puzzle. 1, 3, 5 *n.*, 2, 4, 6 *v.*, **fogged, fog·ging.**

**fog bank** a dense mass of fog.

**fog-bound** (fog′bound′) **1** of airplanes or ships, prevented by fog from travelling. **2** of an airport or port, unable to operate because of fog. *adj.*

**fo·gey** (fō′gē) one who is behind the times or lacks enterprise. *n.*, *pl.* **fo·geys.** Also, **fogy.**

**fog·gy** (fog′ē) **1** having much fog; misty. **2** not clear; dim; blurred: *Her understanding of geography was rather foggy.* **3** confused; puzzled. *adj.*, **fog·gi·er, fog·gi·est.** —**fog′gi·ly,** *adv.* —**fog′gi·ness,** *n.*

**fog·horn** (fog′hôrn′) **1** a horn or siren used in foggy weather to warn ships of danger from rocks, collision, etc. **2** a loud, harsh voice. *n.*

**fo·gy** (fō′gē) See FOGEY. *n.*, *pl.* **fo·gies.**

**foi·ble** (foi′bəl) a weak point; a weakness in character: *Talking too much is one of her foibles.* *n.*

**foil¹** (foil) prevent from carrying out plans, attempts, etc.; get the better of; turn aside or hinder: *The heroine foiled the villain.* *v.*

**foil²** (foil) **1** metal beaten, hammered, or rolled into a very thin sheet: *tin foil, aluminum foil.* **2** anything that makes something else look or seem better by contrast: *The green dress was a foil for Juanita's red hair.* *n.*

**foil³** (foil) **1** a long, narrow sword with a knob or button on the point to prevent injury, used in fencing. See FENCING for picture. **2 foils,** *pl.* FENCING (def. 1). *n.*

**foist** (foist) **1** palm off as genuine; impose slyly: *The dishonest shopkeeper foisted inferior goods on his customers.* **2** put in secretly or slyly: *The author discovered that the translator had foisted several passages into his book.* *v.*

**fold¹** (fōld) **1** bend or double over on itself: *She folded the letter and put it in an envelope.* **2** a layer of something folded. **3** a hollow place made by folding. **4** bring together with the parts in or around one another. **5** bring close to the body: *He folded his arms across his chest.* **6** put the arms around and hold tenderly: *A mother folds her child to her breast.* **7** wrap; enclose: *He folded the pills in a piece of blue paper.* **8** in geology, a bend in a layer of rock. **9** bring or come to a halt; cease doing business: *The restaurant folded after only three months.* 1, 4–7, 9 *v.*, 2, 3, 8 *n.*
**fold up, a** make or become smaller by folding. **b** fail.

**fold²** (fōld) **1** a pen to keep sheep in. **2** sheep kept in a pen. **3** put or keep sheep in a pen. **4** a church group; congregation; church. 1, 2, 4 *n.*, 3 *v.*
**return to the fold, a** return to active membership of one's church. **b** return to the place or the group of people to which one naturally belongs.

hat, āge, fär; let, ēqual, tėrm; it, īce
hot, ōpen, ôrder; oil, out; cup, pút, rüle
əbove, takən, pencəl, lemən, circəs
ch, child; ng, long; sh, ship
th, thin; ŦH, then; zh, measure

**–fold** a suffix meaning: **1** times as many; times as great, as in *tenfold*. **2** formed or divided into _____ parts, as in *manifold*.

**fold·er** (fōl′dər) **1** a person or thing that folds. **2** a holder for papers, made by folding a piece of cardboard. **3** a small book made of one or more folded sheets. *n.*

**fo·li·a·ceous** (fō′lē ā′shəs) **1** leaflike; leafy. **2** made of leaflike plates or thin layers. *adj.*

**fo·li·age** (fō′lē ij) **1** the leaves of a plant, especially of a tree. **2** a decoration made of carved or painted leaves, flowers, etc. *n.*

**fo·li·ate** (fō′lē it *or* fō′lē āt′ *for adjective*, fō′lē āt′ *for verb*) **1** having leaves; covered with leaves. **2** put forth leaves. **3** decorate with leaflike ornaments. 1 *adj.*, 2, 3 *v.*, **fo·li·at·ed, fo·li·at·ing.**

**fo·li·a·tion** (fō′lē ā′shən) **1** a growing of leaves; a putting forth of leaves: *foliation of trees in the spring.* **2** being in leaf. **3** a decoration with leaflike ornaments or foils. *n.*

**folic acid** (fō′lik) a crystalline compound of the vitamin complex, found in green leaves, mushrooms, and some animal tissue, and used in the treatment of anemia.

**fo·li·o** (fō′lē ō′) **1** a large sheet of paper folded once to make two leaves, or four pages, of a book, etc. **2** a book of the largest size, having pages made by folding large sheets of paper once (that is, with four pages to each sheet); a volume having pages of the largest size: *A folio is usually any book more than 11 inches (about 28 cm) in height.* **3** of the largest size; made of large sheets of paper folded once: *The encyclopedia was in twenty volumes folio.* **4** in printing, a page number of a book, etc. **5** a leaf of a book, manuscript, etc., numbered on the front side only. *n.*, *pl.* **fo·li·os.**
**in folio,** of folio size or form.

**fo·li·ose** (fō′lē ōs) FOLIATE (def. 1). *adj.*

**folk** (fōk) **1** people as a group: *Most city folk know very little about farming.* **2** a tribe; nation. **3** of or having to do with the people of a region or country, their beliefs, legends, customs, etc.: *folk tales, folk tunes.* **4** of or having to do with folk songs or folk music: *a folk festival.* **5 folks,** *pl.* **a** people. **b** *Informal.* the members of one's own family; one's relatives: *How are all your folks?* 1, 2, 5 *n.*, *pl.* **folk** or **folks;** 3, 4 *adj.*

**folk dance 1** a dance originating and handed down among the people of a region or country. **2** the music for such a dance.

**folk etymology** a popular misconception of the origin of a word that often results in a change to its sound or spelling. Thus, ME *crevice* became E *crayfish*, influenced by *fish*.

**folk·lore** (fōk′lôr′) the beliefs, legends, customs, etc. of a people, tribe, etc. *n.*

**folk·lor·ist** (fōk′lôr′ist) a person who studies or knows much about folklore. *n.*

**folk music 1** music originating and handed down among the people of a region or country. **2** any of many kinds of modern popular music, usually similar in style to traditional folk music.

**folk song** 1 a song originating, as a rule, among the people of a region or country and handed down from generation to generation: *"Alouette" is a well-known French-Canadian folk song.* 2 a modern song imitating or similar to a traditional folk song: *Many folk songs are being written today.*

**folk·sy** (fōk′sē) *Informal.* 1 friendly; social: *It was just a nice, folksy evening.* 2 plain and unpretentious: *folksy furniture.* *adj.*, **folk·si·er, folk·si·est.**

**folk tale** a story or legend originating, as a rule, among the people of a region or country and handed down from generation to generation.

**folk·way** (fōk′wā′) a custom or habit that has grown up within a social group and is very common among the members of this group. *n.*

**fol·li·cle** (fol′ə kəl) a small cavity, sac, or gland: *Hair grows from follicles.* See EPIDERMIS for picture. *n.*

**fol·low** (fol′ō) 1 go or come after: *Night follows day. She leads; we follow.* 2 result from; result: *Misery follows war. If you eat too much candy, a stomach ache may follow.* 3 go along: *Follow this road to the corner.* 4 go along with; accompany: *My dog followed me to school.* 5 pursue: *The dogs followed the fox.* 6 act according to; take as a guide; use; obey: *Follow her advice.* 7 keep the eyes or attention on: *I could not follow that bird's flight.* 8 keep the mind on; keep up with and understand: *He found it hard to follow the conversation.* 9 take as one's work or profession; be concerned with: *She expects to follow the law.* 10 the act of following. 1-9 *v.*, 10 *n.*
**follow out,** carry out to the end.
**follow suit,** a play a card of the same suit as that first played. b follow the example of another.
**follow through,** a continue a stroke or motion through to the end: *Most golfers follow through after hitting the ball.* b carry out fully; complete: *When one begins a job, one should try to follow it through.*
**follow up,** a follow closely and steadily. b carry out to the end. c increase the effect of by further action: *He followed up his first request by asking again a week later.*
☞ Hom. FALLOW (fol′ō).

**fol·low·er** (fol′ō ər) 1 a person or thing that follows. 2 a person who follows the ideas or beliefs of another: *Buddhists are followers of Buddha.* 3 an attendant; servant. 4 a part of a machine that takes its motion from another part. See CAM for picture. *n.*

**fol·low·ing** (fol′ō ing) 1 followers; attendants. 2 that follows; next after: *That was Sunday, then the following day must have been Monday.* 3 **the following,** the persons, things, items, etc. now to be named, related, described, etc. 4 ppr. of FOLLOW. 1, 3 *n.*, 2 *adj.*, 4 *v.*

**fol·ly** (fol′ē) 1 being foolish; lack of sense; unwise conduct. 2 a foolish act, practice, or idea; something silly. 3 a costly but foolish undertaking, especially a tower or other architectural structure built for show rather than for use. *n., pl.* **fol·lies.**

**fo·ment** (fō ment′) 1 promote; foster trouble, rebellion, etc. 2 apply warm water, hot cloths, etc. to a hurt or pain. *v.* —**fo·ment′er,** *n.*

**fo·men·ta·tion** (fō′men tā′shən) 1 stirring up; instigation; encouragement. 2 the application of moist heat. 3 a hot, moist application. *n.*

**fond** (fond) 1 loving; liking: *a fond look.* 2 loving foolishly or too much. 3 cherished: *fond hopes.* *adj.* —**fond′ly,** *adv.* —**fond′ness,** *n.*
**be fond of,** a having a liking for: *My uncle is fond of children.* b like to eat: *Most cats are fond of fish.*

**fon·dant** (fon′dənt) a creamy sugar candy, usually used as a filling or coating for other candies. *n.*

**fon·dle** (fon′dəl) pet; caress lovingly: *Parents like to fondle their babies.* *v.*, **fon·dled, fon·dling.** —**fon′dler,** *n.*

**fon·due** (fon′dü *or* fon dü′) a dish made of melted cheese and, usually, other ingredients into which small pieces of bread, toast, etc. are dipped and eaten. *n.*

**font¹** (font) 1 a basin holding water for baptism. 2 a basin for holy water. *n.*

**font²** (font) in printing, a complete set of type of one size and style. *n.*

**fon·ta·nel** (fon′tə nel′) a membrane-covered spot on the growing skull of an infant or fetus. *n.*

**food** (füd) 1 what an animal or plant takes in to enable it to live and grow. 2 what is eaten: *Give him food and drink.* 3 a particular kind or article of food. 4 what helps anything to live and grow. 5 what sustains or serves for consumption in any way: *food for thought.* *n.*

**food chain** edible things regarded as links in a chain: *Grass, rabbits, and foxes form a food chain.*

**food·stuff** (füd′stuf′) any material for food: *Grain and meat are foodstuffs.* *n.*

**fool** (fül) 1 a person without sense; an unwise or silly person. 2 a clown formerly kept by a king or lord to amuse people; jester. 3 act like a fool for fun; play; joke: *The teacher told him not to fool during class.* 4 make a fool of; deceive; trick: *He tried to fool me by disguising his voice.* 5 a person who has been deceived or tricked; dupe. 1, 2, 5 *n.*, 3, 4 *v.*
**fool around,** *Informal.* waste time foolishly.
**fool away,** *Informal.* waste foolishly.
**fool with,** *Informal.* meddle foolishly with.

**fool·er·y** (fü′lə rē) a foolish action. *n., pl.* **fool·er·ies.**

**fool·har·dy** (fül′här′dē) foolishly bold; rash. *adj.*, **fool·har·di·er, fool·har·di·est.** —**fool′har′di·ness,** *n.*

**fool hen** any of various grouse or quail: *The fool hen is so called because of its foolish curiosity.*

**fool·ish** (fü′lish) 1 like a fool; without sense; unwise; silly. 2 ridiculous. *adj.* —**fool′ish·ly,** *adv.* —**fool′ish·ness,** *n.*

**fool·proof** (fül′prüf′) so safe or simple that even a fool can use or do it: *a foolproof device, a foolproof plan.* *adj.*

**fool's cap** 1 a cap or hood worn by the fool or jester of a king or lord. 2 a dunce cap.

**fools·cap** (fülz′skap′) writing paper in sheets usually about 21 cm wide by 35 cm long. *n.*

**fool's gold** a mineral that looks like gold; iron pyrites or copper pyrites.

**foot** (fut) 1 the end part of a leg; part that a person, animal, or thing stands on. 2 the part near the feet; end toward which the feet are put. 3 the lowest part; bottom; base: *the foot of a column, the foot of a hill, the foot of a page.* 4 the part that covers the foot. 5 make or renew the foot of a stocking, etc. 6 soldiers that go on foot; infantry. 7 walk: *The boys footed the whole ten*

*kilometres.* **8** dance. **9** a measure of length (30.48 centimetres) equalling 12 inches: *Three feet equal one yard.* Symbol: ′ **10** one of the parts into which a line of poetry is divided: *The following line has four feet:* "The boy I stood on I the burn I ing deck." **11** add: *Foot this column of numbers.* **12** *Informal.* pay: *Mother foots the bill.* 1–4, 6, 9, 10 *n., pl.* **feet;** 5, 7, 8, 11, 12 *v.*
**on foot,** **a** standing or walking. **b** going on.
**put one's foot down,** *Informal.* make up one's mind and act firmly.
**put one's foot in it,** *Informal.* get into trouble by meddling; blunder.
**under foot,** **a** in the way. **b** in one's power; in subjection.

**foot·age** (fŭt′ij) length in feet. *n.*

**foot–and–mouth disease** a dangerous contagious disease of cattle and some other animals, causing blisters in the mouth and around the hoofs.

**foot·ball** (fŭt′bôl) **1** an air-filled, leather-covered ball used in games that involve kicking: *Footballs of different shapes are used in soccer and Canadian or American football.* **2** a game in which a football is kicked, passed, or carried toward the opposing goal: *Canadian football (or rugby football) is somewhat different from American football with regard to rules, size of field, number of players, number of downs, etc.* **3** a game in which the ball must be driven toward the opposing goal without the use of the hands: *This kind of football is usually called soccer in Canada.* *n.*

**foot·board** (fŭt′bôrd′) **1** a board or small platform to be used as a support for the feet. **2** an upright piece across the foot of a bed. *n.*

**foot·bridge** (fŭt′brij′) a bridge for pedestrians only. *n.*

**foot–can·dle** (fŭt′kan′dəl) a non-metric unit for measuring illumination: *A foot-candle is the amount of light produced by a standard candle at a distance of one foot (about 10.8 lux).* *n.*

**foot·ed** (fŭt′id) **1** having a certain kind or number of feet: *a four-footed animal.* **2** pt. and pp. of FOOT. 1 *adj.,* 2 *v.*

**foot·fall** (fŭt′fol′) the sound of steps coming or going. *n.*

**foot·gear** (fŭt′gēr′) shoes, boots, etc. *n.*

**foot·hill** (fŭt′hil′) a low hill at the base of a mountain or mountain range: *We visited a cattle ranch in the foothills of the Rockies.* *n.*

**foot·hold** (fŭt′hōld′) **1** a place to put a foot; support for the feet; surface to stand on: *She climbed the steep cliff by getting footholds in cracks in the rock.* **2** a firm footing or position: *It is hard to break a habit that has gained a foothold.* *n.*

**foot·ing** (fŭt′ing) **1** a firm placing or position of the feet: *He lost his footing and fell down on the ice.* **2** the position of the feet: *When he changed his footing, he lost his balance.* **3** a place to put a foot; a support for the feet; surface to stand on: *The steep cliff gave us no footing.* **4** a firm place or position: *The newly rich family struggled for a footing in society.* **5** a basis of understanding; relationship: *Canada and the United States are on a friendly footing.* **6** an adding. **7** the amount found by adding; sum; total. **8** the act of moving on the feet; walking, dancing, etc. **9 footings,** *pl.* the concrete foundations of a building, wall, etc. **10** ppr. of FOOT. 1–9 *n.,* 10 *v.*

**footage** 471 **foppery**

hat, āge, fär; let, ēqual, tėrm; it, īce
hot, ōpen, ôrder; oil, out; cup, pút, rüle
əbove, takən, pencəl, lemən, circəs
ch, child; ng, long; sh, ship
th, thin; ᴛʜ, then; zh, measure

**foot·less** (fŭt′lis) **1** without a foot or feet. **2** without support; not substantial. *adj.*

**foot·lets** (fŭt′lits) very short socks sometimes worn by women. *n.pl.*

**foot·lights** (fŭt′līts′) **1** a row of lights at the front of a stage. **2** the profession of acting; stage; theatre. *n.pl.*

**foot·loose** (fŭt′lüs′) *Informal.* free to go anywhere or do anything. *adj.*

**foot·man** (fŭt′mən). **1** a male servant who answers the bell, waits on table, goes with an automobile or carriage to open the door, etc.: *Footmen, who usually wear special uniforms, are now found mainly in royal palaces.* **2** a FOOT SOLDIER. *n., pl.* **foot·men** (-mən).

**foot·note** (fŭt′nōt′) a note at the bottom of a page about something on the page. *n.*

**foot·pad** (fŭt′pad′) a highway robber who goes on foot only. *n.*

**foot·path** (fŭt′path′) a path for pedestrians. *n.*

**foot–pound** (fŭt′pound′) in a system that is not metric, a unit for measuring energy, equal to the energy needed to raise a weight of one pound to a height of one foot, about 1.36 joules. *n.*

**foot·print** (fŭt′print′) a mark made by a foot: *The robber was traced by his footprints in the snow.* *n.*

**foot·rest** (fŭt′rest′) a support on which to rest the feet. *n.*

**foot rule** a wooden or metal ruler one foot long (30.48 cm.).

**foot soldier** a soldier who fights on foot; infantryman.

**foot·sore** (fŭt′sôr′) having sore feet from much walking: *The farmer was footsore after ploughing all day.* *adj.*

**foot·step** (fŭt′step′) **1** a person's step. **2** the distance covered in one step. **3** the sound of steps coming or going. **4** the mark made by a foot; footprint. **5** a step on which to go up or down. *n.*
**follow in someone's footsteps,** do as another has done.

**foot·stool** (fŭt′stül′) a low stool on which to rest the feet when one is sitting in a chair. *n.*

**foot·way** (fŭt′wā′) a path for pedestrians only; sidewalk. *n.*

**foot·wear** (fŭt′wer′) shoes, slippers, stockings, etc. *n.*

**foot·work** (fŭt′werk′) the way of using the feet: *Footwork is important in boxing and dancing.* *n.*

**foot·worn** (fŭt′wôrn′) **1** worn by feet: *a footworn path.* **2** having tired feet. *adj.*

**fop** (fop) a vain man who is very fond of fine clothes and has affected manners; an empty-headed dandy. *n.*

**fop·per·y** (fop′ə rē) foppish behaviour; fine clothes, affected manners, etc. suitable for a fop. *n., pl.* **fop·per·ies.**

**fop·pish** (fop′ish) 1 of a fop; suitable for a fop. 2 vain; empty-headed; affected. *adj.*

**for** (fôr; *unstressed,* fər) 1 in place of: *We used boxes for chairs.* 2 in support of; in favour of: *She voted for Laurier.* 3 representing; in the interest of: *A lawyer acts for his or her client.* 4 in return for; in consideration of: *These apples are two for a dollar. We thanked him for his kindness.* 5 with the object or purpose of taking, achieving, or obtaining: *She went for a walk. He is looking for a job.* 6 in order to become, have, keep, etc.: *The navy trains men for sailors. He ran for his life.* 7 in search of: *She is hunting for her cat.* 8 in order to get to: *She has just left for Toronto.* 9 meant to belong to or with, or to be used by or with; suited to: *a box for gloves, books for children.* 10 because of; by reason of: *shout for joy. He was punished for stealing.* 11 because: *We can't go, for it is raining.* 12 in honour of: *A party was given for her.* 13 with a feeling toward: *She has an eye for beauty. We longed for home.* 14 with respect or regard to: *It is warm for April. Eating too much is bad for one's health.* 15 as far or as long as; throughout; during: *We walked for a kilometre. He worked for an hour.* 16 as being: *They know it for a fact.* 17 in spite of: *For all his faults, we like him still.* 18 in proportion to: *For one poisonous snake there are many harmless ones.* 19 to the amount of: *His sister gave him a cheque for $20.* 1–10, 12–19 *prep.,* 11 *conj.* ☞ Hom. FORE, FOUR.

**for.** 1 foreign. 2 forestry.

**for·age** (fôr′ij) 1 food for horses, cattle, etc. 2 supply with food; feed. 3 hunt or search for anything, especially food: *The girls foraged in the kitchen till they found some cookies. The man made a living foraging for metal.* 4 a hunt or search for something such as food: *We went on a forage for supplies.* 5 get by hunting or searching about: *The campers foraged some dry wood for the fire.* 6 get or take food from; plunder: *The soldiers foraged the villages near the camp.* 1, 4 *n.,* 2, 3, 5, 6 *v.,* **for·aged, for·ag·ing.** —**for′ag·er,** *n.*

**for·as·much as** (fô′rəz much′) in view of the fact that; because; since.

**for·ay** (fô′rā) 1 a raid for plunder. 2 plunder; lay waste; pillage. 1 *n.,* 2 *v.*

**for·bad** (fər bad′) See FORBADE. *v.*

**for·bade** (fər bad′ *or* fər bād′) pt. of FORBID: *The doctor forbade the sick girl to leave her bed.* *v.* Also, **forbad.**

**for·bear**[1] (fôr ber′) 1 hold back; keep from doing, saying, using, etc.: *The boy forbore to hit back because the other boy was smaller.* 2 be patient; control oneself. *v.,* **for·bore, for·borne, for·bear·ing.** —**for·bear′ing·ly,** *adv.*

**for·bear**[2] (fôr′ber) forebear; ancestor. *n.*

**for·bear·ance** (fôr ber′əns) 1 the act of forbearing. 2 patience; self-control. *n.*

**for·bid** (fər bid′) 1 order one not to do something; make a rule against; prohibit. 2 keep from happening; prevent: *God forbid!* 3 command to keep away from; exclude from: *I forbid you the house.* *v.,* **for·bade** or **for·bad, for·bid·den** or **for·bid, for·bid·ding.**

**for·bid·den** (fər bid′ən) 1 not allowed; against the law or rules: *He was fined for parking in a forbidden area.* 2 pp. of FORBID: *My father has forbidden me to go swimming in that river.* 1 *adj.,* 2 *v.*

**for·bid·ding** (fər bid′ing) 1 causing fear or dislike; hostile; grim: *The enemy soldier's look was forbidding.* 2 looking dangerous or unpleasant; threatening: *The coast was rocky and forbidding.* 3 ppr. of FORBID. 1, 2 *adj.,* 3 *v.* —**for·bid′ding·ly,** *adv.*

**for·bore** (fôr bôr′) pt. of FORBEAR[1]: *He forbore from showing his anger.* *v.*

**for·borne** (fôr bôrn′) pp. of FORBEAR[1]: *We have forborne from vengeance.* *v.*

**force** (fôrs) 1 strength; power. 2 strength used against a person or thing; violence: *The rebels captured the village by force.* 3 the power to control, influence, persuade, convince, etc.; effectiveness; vividness: *She writes with force.* 4 use force on. 5 make or drive by force: *Give it to me at once, or I will force you to.* 6 get or take by force: *He forced the key out of her hand.* 7 put by force. 8 break open or through by force: *to force the door.* 9 urge to violent effort. 10 make by an unusual or unnatural effort; strain. 11 hurry the growth or development of: *The rhubarb was forced by growing it in a dark, warm place.* 12 in baseball, compel a player to leave one base and try in vain to reach the next. 13 a group of people working or acting together: *our office force.* 14 a group of sailors, soldiers, police, etc. 15 any cause that produces, changes, or stops the motion of a body: *the force of gravitation, electric force.* 16 meaning. 17 **the forces,** *pl.* the armed forces; armed services. 1–3, 13–17 *n.,* 4–12 *v.,* **forced, forc·ing.** —**forc′er,** *n.*
**in force, a** in effect or operation; binding; valid: *The old rules are still in force.* **b** with full strength: *The enemy attacked us in force.*

**forced** (fôrst) 1 made, compelled, or driven by force: *The work of slaves is forced labour.* 2 made by an unusual or unnatural effort; strained; not natural: *She hid her dislike with a forced smile.* 3 pt. and pp. of FORCE. 1, 2 *adj.,* 3 *v.*

**forced march** an unusually long, fast march.

**force·ful** (fôr′sfəl) full of force; strong; powerful; vigorous; effective: *a forceful manner.* *adj.* —**force′ful·ly,** *adv.* —**force′ful·ness,** *n.*

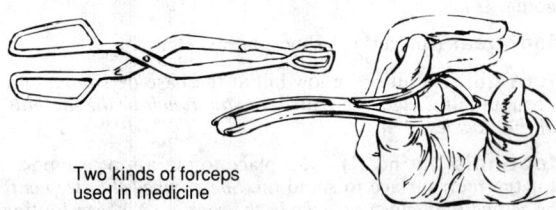

Two kinds of forceps used in medicine

**for·ceps** (fôr′seps *or* fôr′səps) a pair of small pincers or tongs used by surgeons, dentists, etc. for seizing, holding, and pulling. *n., pl.* **for·ceps.**

**for·ci·ble** (fôr′sə bəl) 1 made or done by force; using force: *The thieves were charged with forcible entry into the house.* 2 having or showing force; strong; powerful; effective; convincing: *a forcible speech.* *adj.* —**for′ci·bly,** *adv.*

**ford** (fôrd) 1 a place where a river or stream is shallow enough to cross by walking, riding, or driving through the water. 2 cross a river, etc. by walking, riding, or driving through the water: *They were looking for a place to ford the river.* 1 *n.,* 2 *v.* —**ford′a·ble,** *adj.*

**fore** (fôr) **1** at the front; toward the beginning or front; forward. **2** the forward part; front, especially of a ship or boat. See AFT for picture. **3** in golf, a shout of warning to persons ahead who are liable to be struck by the ball. **1** *adj., adv.,* **2** *n.,* **3** *interj.*
**to the fore, a** into full view; into a conspicuous place or position. **b** at hand; ready; alive.
☛ Hom. FOR, FOUR.

**fore–** a prefix meaning: **1** front, as in *foremost*. **2** before; beforehand, as in *foreknow, foresee.*

**fore and aft 1** at or toward both bow and stern of a ship. **2** lengthwise on a ship; from bow to stern; placed lengthwise.

**fore–and–aft** (fô′rən daft′) lengthwise on a ship; from bow to stern; placed lengthwise: *A fore-and-aft-rigged ship has the sails set lengthwise. adj.*

**fore·arm¹** (fô′rärm′) that part of the arm between the elbow and wrist. *n.*

**fore·arm²** (fô rärm′) prepare for trouble ahead of time; arm beforehand. *v.*

**fore·bear** (fôr′ber) an ancestor; forefather: *He is proud of his pioneer forebears. n.* Also, **forbear.**

**fore·bode** (fôr bōd′) **1** give warning of; predict: *Black clouds forebode a storm.* **2** have a feeling that something bad is going to happen. *v.,* **fore·bod·ed, fore·bod·ing.** —**fore·bod′er,** *n.*

**fore·bod·ing** (fôr bō′ding) **1** a prediction or warning. **2** a feeling that something bad is going to happen: *As the storm grew worse, the travellers were filled with foreboding.* **3** ppr. of FOREBODE. **1, 2** *n.,* **3** *v.*

**fore·brain** (fôr′brān′) the front section of the brain: *The forebrain consists of the cerebrum, the pituitary gland, and the pineal body. n.*

**fore·cast** (fôr′kast′) **1** prophesy; predict: *Cooler weather is forecast for tomorrow.* **2** a prophecy or prediction. **3** be a prophecy or prediction of. **4** foresee; plan ahead. **5** a planning ahead; foresight. **1, 3, 4** *v.,* **fore·cast** or **fore·cast·ed, fore·cast·ing;** **2, 5** *n.* —**fore′cast·er,** *n.*

**fore·cas·tle** (fōk′səl *or* fôr′kas′əl) **1** the upper deck in front of the foremast of a ship or boat. **2** the sailors' quarters in a merchant ship, formerly in the forward part of the ship. *n.*

**fore·close** (fôr klōz′) **1** shut out; prevent; exclude. **2** take away the right to redeem a mortgage: *When the conditions of a mortgage are not met, the holder can foreclose and have the property sold to satisfy his or her claim. v.,* **fore·closed, fore·clos·ing.**

**fore·clo·sure** (fôr klō′zhər) the foreclosing of a mortgage. *n.*

**fore·doom** (fôr düm′) doom beforehand. *v.*

**fore·fa·ther** (fôr′fo₮H′ər) ancestor. *n.*

**fore·fin·ger** (fôr′fing′gər) the finger next to the thumb; first finger; index finger. See ARM¹ for picture. *n.*

**fore·foot** (fôr′fút′) **1** one of the front feet of an animal. **2** the forward end of a ship's keel. *n., pl.* **fore·feet.**

**fore·front** (fôr′frunt′) **1** the place of greatest importance, activity, etc. **2** foremost part. *n.*

**fore·gath·er** (fôr ga₮H′ər) See FORGATHER. *v.*

**fore·go¹** (fôr gō′) do without; give up: *He chose to forego the movies and do his work. v.,* **fore·went, fore·gone, fore·go·ing.** —**fore·go′er,** *n.* Also, **forgo.**

**fore·go²** (fôr gō′) precede; go before. *v.,* **fore·went, fore·gone, fore·go·ing.** —**fore·go′er,** *n.*

**fore·go·ing** (fôr′gō′ing) **1** preceding; previous: *There are many pictures in the foregoing pages.* **2** ppr. of FOREGO. **1** *adj.,* **2** *v.*

**fore·gone** (fôr′gon) **1** that has gone before; previous. **2** pp. of FOREGO. **1** *adj.,* **2** *v.*

**foregone conclusion** a fact or result that was almost surely known beforehand: *It was a foregone conclusion that there would be traffic jams while the road was being repaired.*

**fore·ground** (fôr′ground′) the part of a picture or scene nearest the observer; the part toward the front. *n.*

**fore·hand** (fôr′hand′) **1** made with the palm of the hand turned forward. **2** a stroke made with the palm of the hand turned forward. **3** a position in front or above; an advantage. **1** *adj.,* **2, 3** *n.*

**fore·hand·ed** (fôr′han′did) **1** providing for the future; prudent; thrifty. **2** done beforehand; early; timely. *adj.* —**fore′hand′ed·ness,** *n.*

**fore·head** (fôr′hed′ *or* fô′rid) **1** the part of the face above the eyes. **2** a front part. *n.*

**for·eign** (fô′rən) **1** outside one's own country: *She has travelled much in foreign countries.* **2** of, characteristic of, or coming from outside one's own country: *a foreign ship, a foreign language, foreign money.* **3** having to do with other countries; carried on or dealing with other countries: *foreign trade.* **4** not belonging; not related: *Sitting still all day is foreign to a healthy child's nature.* **5** coming from an outside source: *English has many foreign words. adj.*

**foreign affairs** a country's relations with other countries.

**for·eign–born** (fô′rən bôrn′) born in another country. *adj.*

**for·eign·er** (fô′rə nər) a person from another country; an alien. *n.*

**foreign legion** part of an army made up largely of soldiers who are volunteers from other countries: *the French Foreign Legion.*

**Foreign Office** *Brit.* the government department in charge of foreign affairs.

**fore·judge** (fôr juj′) judge beforehand. *v.,* **fore·judged, fore·judg·ing.**

**fore·knew** (fôr nyü′ *or* fôr nü′) pt. of FOREKNOW. *v.*

**fore·know** (fôr nō′) know beforehand. *v.,* **fore·knew, fore·known, fore·know·ing.**

**fore·knowl·edge** (fôr′nol′ij) knowledge of a thing before it happens. *n.*

**fore·known** (fôr nōn′) pp. of FOREKNOW. *v.*

---

hat, āge, fär; let, ēqual, tėrm; it, īce
hot, ōpen, ôrder; oil, out; cup, pút, rüle
əbove, takən, pencəl, lemən, circəs
ch, child; ng, long; sh, ship
th, thin; ₮H, then; zh, measure

**fore·land** (fôr′land′) a cape; headland; promontory. *n.*

**fore·leg** (fôr′leg′) one of the front legs of an animal. *n.*

**fore·lock** (fôr′lok′) a lock of hair that grows just above the forehead. *n.*
**take time by the forelock,** act promptly.

**fore·man** (fôr′mən) 1 the man in charge of a group of workers or of some part of a factory. 2 the chairman of a jury. *n., pl.* **fore·men** (-mən).

**fore·mast** (fôr′mast′ *or* fôr′məst) the mast nearest the bow of a ship. See BRIG, MAST and SCHOONER for pictures. *n.*

**fore·most** (fôr′mōst′) 1 first: *I am foremost in line* (*adj.*). *She fell head foremost* (*adv.*). 2 chief; leading; most notable. 1, 2 *adj.*, 1 *adv.*

**fore·name** (fôr′nām′) first name. *n.*

**fore·noon** (fôr′nün′) 1 the time between early morning and noon. 2 between early morning and noon. 1 *n.*, 2 *adj.*

**fo·ren·sic** (fə ren′sik) 1 of or suitable for a law court or public debate. 2 a spoken or written exercise in argumentation, as in a college or high-school class in speech or rhetoric. 1 *adj.*, 2 *n.*

**fore·or·dain** (fôr′ôr dān′) ordain beforehand; predestine. *v.*

**fore·or·di·na·tion** (fôr′ôr də nā′shən) an ordaining beforehand; predestination. *n.*

**fore·part** (fôr′pärt′) the front part. *n.*

**fore·paw** (fôr′po′) a front paw. *n.*

**fore·quar·ter** (fôr′kwôr′tər) 1 a front leg, shoulder, and nearby ribs of beef, lamb, pork, etc.; a front quarter. 2 FORECASTLE (def. 1). 3 FORECASTLE (def. 2). *n.*

**fore·run·ner** (fôr′run′ər) 1 a person going before or sent before to show that another or something more is coming; herald. 2 a sign or warning of something to come: *Black clouds are forerunners of a storm.* 3 a predecessor; ancestor. *n.*

**fore·sail** (fôr′sāl′ *or* fôr′səl) 1 the principal sail on the foremast of a schooner. 2 the lowest sail on the foremast of a square-rigged ship. *n.*

**fore·saw** (fôr′so′) pt. of FORESEE: *Mother put up a big picnic lunch, because she foresaw how hungry we would be.* *v.*

**fore·see** (fôr′sē′) see or know beforehand: *Fortunetellers claim to foresee the future.* **fore·saw, fore·seen, fore·see·ing.** —**fore·see′a·ble,** *adj.*

**fore·seen** (fôr′sēn′) pp. of FORESEE: *Nobody could have foreseen how cold it would be on the beach.* *v.*

**fore·shad·ow** (fôr shad′ō) indicate beforehand; be a warning of: *Black clouds foreshadow a storm.* *v.*

**fore·shank** (fôr′shangk′) 1 the upper part of the foreleg of an animal. 2 a cut of meat from this part. *n.*

**fore·sheet** (fôr′shēt′) one of the ropes used to hold a foresail in place. *n.*

**fore·sheets** (fôr′shēts′) the space in the forward part of an open boat. *n.pl.*

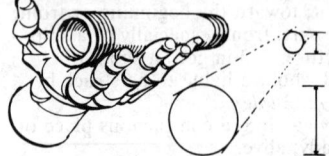
Foreshortening. The hand and the cylinder are both foreshortened to suggest depth in the drawing.

**fore·short·en** (fôr shôr′tən) represent lines, etc. in a drawing or painting as of less than true length in order to give the illusion of correct size and distance. *v.*

**fore·sight** (fôr′sīt′) 1 the power to see or realize beforehand what is likely to happen. 2 careful thought for the future; prudence. 3 looking ahead; view into the future. *n.*

**fore·sight·ed** (fôr′sī′tid *or* fôr′sī′tid) having or showing foresight. *adj.* —**fore′sight′ed·ness,** *n.*

**fore·skin** (fôr′skin′) the fold of skin that covers the end of the penis. *n.*

**for·est** (fô′rist) 1 a large area of land covered with trees; thick woods; woodland. 2 the trees themselves. 3 of or in a forest: *forest fires.* 4 plant with trees; cover with trees. 1–3 *n.,* 4 *v.* —**for′est·less,** *adj.*

**fore·stall** (fôr stol′) 1 prevent by acting first: *The mayor forestalled a riot by having the police ready.* 2 deal with in advance; anticipate; be ahead of. 3 buy up in advance in order to increase the price. *v.* —**fore·stall′er,** *n.*

**for·est·a·tion** (fô′ri stā′shən) the planting or taking care of forests. *n.*

**fore·stay** (fôr′stā′) the rope or cable reaching from the top of a ship's foremast to the bowsprit: *The forestay helps to support the foremast.* *n.*

**for·est·er** (fô′ri stər) 1 a government official whose job it is to guard against fires and to protect timber in a forest. 2 a person trained in FORESTRY. *n.*

**forest preserve** a forest protected by the government from wasteful cutting, fires, etc.

**for·est·ry** (fô′ri strē) 1 the science of planting and taking care of forests. 2 the art of making and managing forests. *n.*

**fore·taste** (fôr′tāst′ *for noun,* fôr tāst′ *for verb*) 1 a preliminary taste; anticipation: *The boy got a foretaste of business life by working during his vacation.* 2 taste beforehand; anticipate. 1 *n.,* 2 *v.,* **fore·tast·ed, fore·tast·ing.**

**fore·tell** (fôr tel′) tell or show beforehand; predict; prophesy: *Who can foretell what a baby will do next?* *v.,* **fore·told, fore·tell·ing.**

**fore·thought** (fôr′thot′) 1 previous thought or consideration; planning. 2 careful thought for the future; prudence; foresight: *A little forethought will often prevent mistakes.* *n.*

**fore·to·ken** (fôr tō′kən *for verb,* fôr′tō′kən *for noun*) 1 indicate beforehand; be an omen of. 2 an indication of something to come; omen. 1 *v.,* 2 *n.*

**fore·told** (fôr tōld′) pt. and pp. of FORETELL: *She foretold the war. The Weather Office had foretold the cold wave.* *v.*

**fore·top** (fôr′top′ *or* fôr′təp) a platform at the top of the FOREMAST. *n.*

**fore–top·mast** (fôr′top′mast′ *or* fôr′top′məst) the mast next above the FOREMAST. *n.*

**fore-top·sail** (fôr′top′sāl′ *or* fôr′top′səl)   the sail set on the FORE-TOPMAST and next above the FORESAIL.   *n.*

**for·ev·er** (fə rev′ər)   **1** for always; without ever coming to an end.   **2** all the time; always: *That woman is forever talking.*   *adv.*

**for·ev·er·more** (fə rev′ər môr′)   forever.   *adv.*

**fore·warn** (fôr wôrn′)   warn beforehand: *The dark clouds forewarned us of a thunderstorm.*   *v.*

**fore·went** (fôr went′)   pt. of FOREGO.   *v.*

**fore·word** (fôr′wėrd′)   an introduction; preface.   *n.*

**for·feit** (fôr′fit)   **1** lose or have to give up as a penalty for some act, neglect, fault, etc.: *He forfeited his life by his careless driving.*   **2** something lost or given up because of some act, neglect, or fault; penalty; fine: *A headache was the forfeit she paid for staying up late.*   **3** lost or given up as a penalty; forfeited.   **4** the loss or giving up of something as a penalty.   1 *v.*, 2, 4 *n.*, 3 *adj.*   —**for′feit·er**, *n.*

**for·fei·ture** (fôr′fi chər)   **1** the loss or giving up of something as a penalty; forfeiting.   **2** the thing forfeited; penalty; fine.   *n.*

**for·gath·er** (fôr gaŦH′ər)   **1** gather together; assemble; meet.   **2** meet by accident.   **3** be friendly; associate.   *v.* Also, **foregather.**

**for·gave** (fər gāv′)   pt. of FORGIVE: *She forgave my mistake.*   *v.*

**forge**[1] (fôrj)   **1** a furnace or open fireplace where metal is heated to a high temperature before being hammered into shape: *The blacksmith took the white-hot horseshoes out of the forge.*   **2** a blacksmith's shop; smithy.   **3** heat metal to a high temperature and then hammer it into shape: *The blacksmith forged a bar of iron into a big, strong hook.*   **4** a place where iron or some other metal is melted and refined.   **5** make; shape or form: *They forged a strong and lasting friendship.*   **6** make or write something false or counterfeit: *The supposed will of the dead woman had been forged.*   **7** sign another's name falsely to deceive: *She was sent to jail for forging cheques.*   1, 2, 4 *n.*, 3, 5–7 *v.*, **forged, forg·ing.**   —**forg′er**, *n.*

**forge**[2] (fôrj)   move forward slowly but steadily: *One runner forged ahead of the others and won the race.*   *v.*, **forged, forg·ing.**

**for·ger·y** (fôr′jə rē)   **1** the act of forging a signature, etc.   **2** something made or written falsely to deceive: *The painting was a forgery. The signature on the cheque was not mine but a forgery.*   *n.*, *pl.* **for·ger·ies.**

**for·get** (fər get′)   **1** let go out of the mind; fail to remember; be unable to remember: *I couldn't introduce her because I had forgotten her name.*   **2** omit or neglect without meaning to: *She said she would not forget to send him a postcard.*   **3** leave behind unintentionally: *She had to return home because she had forgotten her purse.*   *v.*, **for·got, for·got·ten** *or* **for·got, for·get·ting. forget oneself,  a** not think of oneself and one's interests; be unselfish.   **b** fail to consider what one should do or be; say or do something improper.

**for·get·ful** (fər get′fəl)   **1** apt to forget; having a poor memory.   **2** heedless: *forgetful of danger.*   **3** *Poetic.* causing to forget.   *adj.*   —**for·get′ful·ly**, *adv.*   —**for·get′ful·ness**, *n.*

**for·get–me–not** (fər get′mē not′)   any of several small plants of the same family as the BORAGE, having hairy leaves and clusters of small blue or white flowers.   *n.*

---

**fore-topsail**   **475**   **form**

hat, āge, fär; let, ēqual, tėrm; it, īce
hot, ōpen, ôrder; oil, out; cup, put, rüle
əbove, takən, pencəl, lemən, circəs
ch, child; ng, long; sh, ship
th, thin; ŦH, then; zh, measure

**for·give** (fər giv′)   **1** give up the wish to punish or get even with; pardon; excuse; not have hard feelings about or toward: *She forgave her mother for breaking her doll. Please forgive my mistake.*   **2** give up all claim to; not demand payment for: *to forgive a debt.*   *v.*, **for·gave, for·giv·en, for·giv·ing.**   —**for·giv′a·ble**, *adj.*

**for·giv·en** (fər giv′ən)   pp. of FORGIVE: *Your mistakes are forgiven.*   *v.*

**for·give·ness** (fər giv′nis)   **1** the act of forgiving; pardon.   **2** willingness to forgive.   *n.*

**for·giv·ing** (fər giv′ing)   **1** that forgives; willing to forgive.   **2** ppr. of FORGIVE.   1 *adj.*, 2 *v.*   —**for·giv′ing·ly**, *adv.*   —**for·giv′ing·ness**, *n.*

**for·go** (fôr gō′)   See FOREGO[1].   *v.*

**for·gone** (fôr gon′)   pp. of FORGO[1].   *v.*

**for·got** (fər got′)   pt. and a pp. of FORGET: *Ahmed forgot to do his homework.*   *v.*

**for·got·ten** (fər got′ən)   a pp. of FORGET: *He has forgotten much of what he learned.*   *v.*

**fork** (fôrk)   **1** an instrument having a handle and two or more long, pointed prongs at one end: *A small fork is used to lift food. A much larger fork, called a pitchfork, is used to lift and throw hay.*  See PITCHFORK for picture. *Another kind of fork is used for digging.*   **2** lift, throw, or dig with a fork.   **3** make in the shape or form of a fork.   **4** anything shaped like a fork: *The place where a tree, road, or stream divides into branches is a fork.*   **5** one of the branches into which anything is divided.   **6** have a fork or forks; divide into branches: *There is a garage where the road forks.*   1, 4, 5 *n.*, 2, 3, 6 *v.*   —**fork′like**, *adj.*

**forked** (fôrkt)   **1** having a fork or forks; divided into branches.   **2** zigzag: *forked lightning.*   **3** pt. and pp. of FORK.   1, 2 *adj.*, 3 *v.*
**speak with a forked tongue,**   speak untruths; tell lies.

**for·lorn** (fôr lôrn′)   **1** left alone; neglected; deserted: *The lost kitten, a forlorn little animal, was wet and dirty.*   **2** wretched in feeling or looks; unhappy: *The weeping child looked very forlorn.*   **3** hopeless; desperate.   **4** bereft (*of*): *forlorn of hope.*   *adv.*,   —**for·lorn′ly**, *adv.*   —**for·lorn′ness**, *n.*

**forlorn hope**   **1** a desperate enterprise.   **2** an undertaking almost sure to fail.   **3** a party of soldiers engaged in a very dangerous job.

**form** (fôrm)   **1** a shape; appearance apart from colour or materials: *Circles and triangles are simple forms.*   **2** a shape of body; the body of a person or animal.   **3** something that gives shape to something else: *A mould is a form.*   **4** give shape to; make: *The cook formed the dough into loaves.*   **5** be formed; take shape: *Clouds form in the sky.*   **6** become: *Water forms ice when it freezes.*   **7** make up; compose: *People who are related form a family.*   **8** organize; establish: *We formed a club.*   **9** develop: *Form good habits while you are young.*   **10** arrange in some order: *The soldiers formed themselves into lines.*   **11** an orderly arrangement of parts: *The effect of a work of literature, art, or music comes from its form as well as its content.*   **12** a way of doing something; manner; method:

**formal**     476     **forswear**

*He is a fast runner, but his form in running is bad.* **13** a set way of doing something; set way of behaving according to custom or rule; formality; ceremony: *Shaking hands is a form. Many forms have little or no real meaning.* **14** a set order of words: *A written agreement to buy, sell, or do something follows a certain form.* **15** a document with printing or writing on it and blank spaces to be filled in: *To get a licence, you must fill out a form.* **16** the way in which a thing exists, takes shape, or shows itself; condition; character; manifestation: *Water appears also in the forms of ice, snow, and steam.* **17** a kind; sort; variety: *Heat, light, and electricity are forms of energy.* **18** a good condition of body or mind: *Athletes exercise to keep in form.* **19** any of the ways in which a word is spelled or pronounced to express different ideas and relations. *Boys* is the plural form of *boy. Saw* is the past form of *see. My* and *mine* are the possessive forms of *I*. **20** a grade in school, especially in high school: *Freda is now in the fifth form.* **21** a long seat; bench. **22** type fastened in a frame ready for printing or making plates. 1–3, 11–22 *n.*, 4–10 *v*.
    **bad form,** behaviour contrary to accepted customs.
    **good form,** behaviour in accord with accepted customs.

**for·mal** (fôr′məl) **1** with strict attention to outward forms and ceremonies; not familiar and homelike; stiff: *A judge has a formal manner in a law court.* **2** according to set customs or rules. **3** done with the proper forms; clear and definite: *A written contract is a formal agreement to do something.* **4** very regular; symmetrical; orderly. **5** having to do with the form, not the content. **6** of language, conforming to established convention in grammar, syntax, and pronunciation. **7** a social gathering at which formal dress is worn. **8** a gown worn to formal social gatherings: *She was dressed in her first formal.* 1–6 *adj.*, 7, 8 *n.* —**for′mal·ly,** *adv*.
☞ *Usage.* Do not confuse **formally** with FORMERLY.
☞ *Usage.* See note at INFORMAL.

**form·al·de·hyde** (fôr mal′də hīd′) a colourless gas with a sharp, irritating odour, used in solution as a disinfectant and preservative. *n*.

**for·ma·lin** (fôr′mə lin) a solution of FORMALDEHYDE in water. *n*.

**for·mal·ism** (fôr′mə liz′əm) strict attention to outward forms and ceremonies. *n*.

**for·mal·is·tic** (fôr′mə lis′tik) of FORMALISM. *adj*.

**for·mal·i·ty** (fôr mal′ə tē) **1** a procedure required by custom or rule; outward form; ceremony: *the formalities of a wedding or a funeral.* **2** attention to forms and customs: *Visitors at the court of a queen are received with formality.* **3** stiffness of manner, behaviour, or arrangement: *The formality of the party made Amy shy.* *n., pl.* **for·mal·i·ties.**

**for·mal·ize** (fôr′mə līz′) **1** make formal. **2** give a definite form to. *v.*, **for·mal·ized, for·mal·iz·ing.**

**for·mat** (fôr′mat) **1** the shape, size, and general arrangement of a book, magazine, etc. **2** the design, plan, or arrangement of anything: *the format of a television show.* **3** to prepare a computer disk for use by having the operating system write certain essential data on it; initialize: *He had to format the diskette before he could save his spreadsheet on it.* 1, 2 *n.*, 3 *v*.

**for·ma·tion** (fôr mā′shən) **1** forming or being formed: *Heat causes the formation of steam from water. The formation of words is a fascinating study.* **2** the way in which a thing is arranged; arrangement; order: *troops in battle formation. Geese fly in formation. There was an interesting formation of ice crystals on the windows.* **3** the thing formed: *Clouds are formations of tiny drops of water in the sky.* **4** a series of layers or deposits of the same kind of rock or mineral. *n*.

**form·a·tive** (fôr′mə tiv) **1** having to do with formation or development; forming; moulding: *Home and school are the chief formative influences in a child's life.* **2** used to form words: *Words may be made from other words by adding formative endings, such as -ly and -ness.* *adj*.

**for·mer** (fôr′mər) **1** first of two: *Canada and the United States are in North America; the former country lies north of the latter.* Compare with LATTER. **2** earlier; past; long past: *In former times cooking was done in fireplaces instead of on stoves.* **3 the former,** the first of two: *When Sue is offered ice cream or pie, she always chooses the former.* 1, 2 *adj.*, 3 *n*.

**for·mer·ly** (fôr′mər lē) in the past; some time ago: *Mrs. Tumanov was formerly known as Miss Snell.* *adv*.
☞ *Usage.* Do not confuse **formerly** with FORMALLY.

**for·mic acid** (fôr′mik) a colourless liquid that is irritating to the skin: *Formic acid occurs in ants, spiders, nettles, etc.*

**for·mi·da·ble** (fôr′mə də bəl) hard to overcome; hard to deal with; to be dreaded: *a formidable opponent.* *adj*. —**for′mi·da·bly,** *adv*.

**form·less** (fôrm′lis) without definite or regular form; shapeless. *adj.* —**form′less·ly,** *adv*. —**form′less·ness,** *n*.

**for·mu·la** (fôr′myə lə) **1** a set form of words, especially one that by much use has partly lost its meaning: *"How do you do?" is a polite formula.* **2** a statement of religious belief or doctrine. **3** a rule for doing something, especially as used by those who do not know the reason on which it is based. **4** a recipe; prescription: *a formula for making soap.* **5** an expression showing by chemical symbols the composition of a compound: *The formula for water is $H_2O$.* **6** an expression showing by algebraic symbols a rule, principle, etc. $(a + b)^2 = a^2 + 2ab + b^2$ is an algebraic formula. *n., pl.* **for·mu·las** or **for·mu·lae** (-lē *or* lī)

**for·mu·lae** (fôr′myə lē *or* fôr′myə lī) a pl. of FORMULA. *n*.

**for·mu·lar·y** (fôr′myə ler′ē) **1** a collection of formulas. **2** a set form of words; formula. **3** having to do with formulas. 1, 2 *n., pl.* **for·mu·lar·ies;** 3 *adj*.

**for·mu·late** (fôr′myə lāt′) **1** state definitely; express in systematic form: *Our ideas of fair treatment for all Canadians are formulated in a Bill of Rights.* **2** express in a formula; reduce to a formula. *v.*, **for·mu·lat·ed, for·mu·lat·ing.** —**for′mu·la′tor,** *n*.

**for·mu·la·tion** (fôr′myə lā′shən) **1** a definite statement; expression in systematic form. **2** expression in a formula. *n*.

**for·sake** (fôr sāk′) give up; leave alone; leave; abandon: *Robert ran away from home, forsaking his family.* *v.*, **for·sook, for·sak·en, for·sak·ing.**

**for·sak·en** (fôr sā′kən) **1** pp. of FORSAKE: *That girl has forsaken her old friends.* **2** deserted; abandoned; forlorn: *a forsaken house.* 1 *v.*, 2 *adj*.

**for·sook** (fôr sůk′) pt. of FORSAKE: *He forsook his family.* *v*.

**for·swear** (fôr swer′) **1** renounce on oath; swear or promise solemnly to give up: *The coach asked the team to* *forswear smoking.* **2** deny solemnly or on oath. **3** be untrue to one's sworn word or promise; perjure oneself. *v.*, **for·swore, for·sworn, for·swear·ing.**

**for·swore** (fôr swôr′) pt. of FORSWEAR. *v.*

**for·sworn** (fôr swôrn′) **1** untrue to one's sworn word or promise; perjured. **2** pp. of FORSWEAR: *Harry has forsworn his bad habits.* 1 *adj.*, 2 *v.*

**for·syth·i·a** (fôr sith′ē ə *or* fôr sī′thē ə) a shrub having many bell-shaped, yellow flowers in early spring before its leaves come out. *n.*

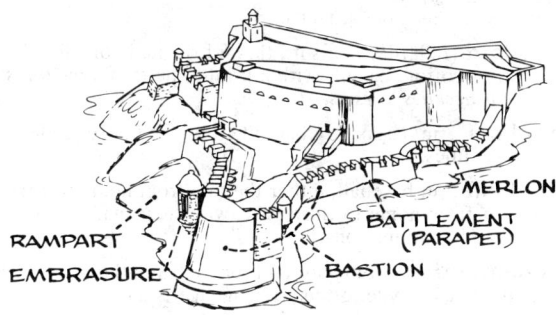

**fort** (fôrt) **1** a strong building or place that can be defended against an enemy: *Forts were often protected by earthworks or stockades.* **2** a trading post usually fortified in the early days of the fur trade: *Winnipeg is built on the site of Fort Garry, an old Hudson's Bay Company post.* *n.* **hold the fort, a** make a defence. **b** be in charge.

**forte**[1] (fôrt) something a person does very well; strong point: *Cooking is her forte.* *n.*

**for·te**[2] (fôr′tā) in music: **1** loud. **2** loudly. 1 *adj.*, 2 *adv.*

**forth** (fôrth) **1** forward; onward: *From that day forth she lived alone.* **2** into view or consideration; out: *The sun came forth from behind the clouds.* **3** away. *adv.* **and so forth,** and so on; and the like: *We ate cake, candy, nuts, and so forth.*
☛ Hom. FOURTH.

**forth·com·ing** (fôrth′kum′ing *or* fôrth kum′ing) **1** about to appear; approaching: *The forthcoming week will be busy.* **2** an appearance; approach. **3** ready when wanted: *She needed help, but none was forthcoming.* 1, 3 *adj.*, 2 *n.*

**forth·right** (fôrth′rīt′ for adjective, also fôrth rīt′ for adverb) **1** frank and outspoken; straightforward; direct: *Mr. Tumiak made forthright objections to the proposal.* **2** straight ahead; directly forward: *The soldiers marched forthright to battle.* **3** at once; immediately. 1 *adj.*, 2, 3 *adv.* —**forth′right′ness,** *n.*

**forth·with** (fôrth′with′ *or* fôrth′wiTH′) at once; immediately: *She said she would be there forthwith.* *adv.*

**for·ti·eth** (fôr′tē ith) **1** next after the 39th; last in a series of forty; 40th. **2** one, or being one, of 40 equal parts. *adj.*, *n.*

**for·ti·fi·ca·tion** (fôr′tə fə kā′shən) **1** fortifying: *Soldiers were busy with the fortification of the village.* **2** anything used in fortifying; a fort, wall, ditch, etc. **3** a fortified place. **4** the enriching of foods with vitamins and minerals. *n.*

**for·ti·fy** (fôr′tə fī′) **1** build forts, walls, etc.; strengthen against attack; provide with forts, walls, etc. **2** give support to; strengthen. **3** add something that strengthens or enriches: *Brandy is used to fortify port wine. Refined foods are often fortified with vitamins and minerals.* *v.*, **for·ti·fied, for·ti·fy·ing.**

**for·tis·si·mo** (fôr tis′ə mō′) in music: **1** very loud. **2** very loudly. 1 *adj.*, 2 *adv.*

**for·ti·tude** (fôr′tə tyüd′ *or* fôr′tə tüd′) courage in facing pain, danger, or trouble; firmness of spirit. *n.*

**fort·night** (fôrt′nīt′) two weeks. *n.*

**fort·night·ly** (fôrt′nī′tlē) **1** once in every two weeks. **2** appearing or happening once in every two weeks. 1 *adv.*, 2 *adj.*

**FOR·TRAN** (fôr′tran) a computer language using algebraic symbols for the solution of scientific problems. *n.*
☛ *Etym.* From the first letters of *for*mula and *tran*slation.

**for·tress** (fôr′tris) a fortified place; a large and well-protected fort. *n.*

**for·tu·i·tous** (fôr tyü′ə təs *or* fôr tü′ə təs) happening by chance; accidental: *a fortuitous meeting, a fortuitous acquaintance.* *adj.* —**for·tu′i·tous·ly,** *adv.*

**for·tu·i·ty** (fôr tyü′ə tē *or* fôr tü′ə tē) chance; accident. *n.*, *pl.* **for·tu·i·ties.**

**for·tu·nate** (fôr′chə nit) **1** having good luck; lucky. **2** bringing good luck; having favourable results: *a fortunate event.* *adj.* —**for′tu·nate·ly,** *adv.*

**for·tune** (fôr′chən) **1** a great deal of money or property; riches; wealth: *One of the gold seekers made a fortune.* **2** what is going to happen to a person; fate: *Gypsies often claim that they can tell people's fortunes.* **3** good luck; prosperity; success. **4** what happens; luck; chance: *Fortune was against us; we lost.* *n.*

**fortune hunter** **1** a person who tries to get a fortune by marrying someone rich. **2** anybody who seeks wealth.

**for·tune·tell·er** (fôr′chən tel′ər) a person who claims to be able to tell what will happen to people. *n.*

**for·ty** (fôr′tē) **1** four times ten; 40. **2 forties,** *pl.* the years from forty through forty-nine, especially of a century or of a person's life: *She achieved success as a playwright in her forties.* 1, 2 *n.*, *pl.* **for·ties;** 1 *adj.*

**forty winks** a short nap.

**fo·rum** (fô′rəm) **1** in ancient Rome, the public square or market place of a town: *The forum in Rome was used for public assemblies and business.* **2** an assembly for discussing questions of public interest. **3** a law court; tribunal. *n.*

**for·ward** (fôr′wərd *or* (*nautical*) fô′rəd) **1** ahead; onward: *They marched forward.* **2** toward the front: *Come forward* (*adv.*), *the forward part of a ship* (*adj.*). **3** advanced; far ahead: *A child four years old that can read is forward for her age.* **4** out; into view or consideration: *In his talk he brought forward several new ideas.* **5** send on further: *Please forward my mail to my new address.* **6** help along: *He did all he could to forward his friend's plan.* **7** ready; eager: *He knew his lesson and was forward with his answers.* **8** pert; bold: *Don't be so forward.*

**9** in certain games, a player whose position is in the front line.   1, 2, 4 *adv.*, 2, 3, 7, 8 *adj.*, 5, 6 *v.*, 9 *n.*
—**for′ward·er,** *n.*

**for·ward·ness** (fôr′wərd nis)   **1** readiness; eagerness. **2** pertness; boldness.   *n.*

**forward pass**   the throwing of a football to a player on the same team in the direction of the opponents' goal.

**for·wards** (fôr′wərdz)   FORWARD (def. 1).   *adv.*

**for·went** (fôr went′)   pt. of FORGO.   *v.*

**fosse** (fos)   a ditch; trench; canal; moat.   *n.*

**fos·sil** (fos′əl)   **1** the remains of prehistoric animals or plants preserved in rocks where they have become petrified: *Bone fossils of dinosaurs have been discovered in Alberta. Fossils of ferns are sometimes found in coal.* **2** traces of animal life preserved in ancient rocks: *fossil footprints.*   **3** forming a fossil; of the nature of a fossil. **4** a very old-fashioned person, set in his ways. **5** belonging to the outworn past: *fossil ideas.*   1, 2, 4 *n.*, 3, 5 *adj.*   —**fos′sil-like′**, *adj.*

**fossil fuels**   fuels obtained from the earth, such as coal, petroleum, and natural gas.

**fos·sil·if·er·ous** (fos′ə lif′ə rəs)   containing FOSSILS (defs. 1, 2).   *adj.*

**fos·sil·ize** (fos′ə līz′)   **1** change into a FOSSIL; turn into stone. **2** make or become antiquated, set, stiff, or rigid. *v.*, **fos·sil·ized, fos·sil·iz·ing.**

**fos·ter** (fos′tər)   **1** help the growth or development of; encourage: *Ignorance fosters superstition.*   **2** care for fondly; cherish.   **3** bring up; rear.   **4** in the same family, but not related by birth: *a foster brother.*   1–3 *v.*, 4 *adj.*

**foster brother**   a boy brought up with another child or children of different parents.

**foster child**   a child brought up by a person who is not his or her parent.

**foster father**   a man who brings up a child or children of other parents.

**foster mother**   a woman who brings up a child or children of other parents.

**foster parent**   a person who brings up a child or children of other parents: a foster father or foster mother.

**foster sister**   a girl brought up with another child or children of different parents.

**fought** (fot)   pt. and pp. of FIGHT: *He fought bravely yesterday. A battle was fought.*   *v.*

**foul** (foul)   **1** very dirty; impure; nasty; smelly; containing or covered with filth: *Open the windows and let out the foul air.*   **2** make dirty or impure; pollute; soil; defile: *Exhaust fumes fouled the air.*   **3** become dirty or impure: *Spark plugs foul if not cared for properly.* **4** dishonour; disgrace: *a name fouled by misdeeds.* **5** very wicked; vile: *Murder is a foul crime.*   **6** unfair; against the rules.   **7** in football, basketball, etc., unfair play; something done contrary to the rules.   **8** make a foul; make a foul against.   **9** a foul ball.   **10** hit a baseball in this way.   **11** hit against: *One boat fouled the other.* **12** hitting against: *One boat was foul of the other.*   **13** get tangled up with; catch: *The rope fouled the anchor chain.* **14** tangled up; caught: *The sailor cut the foul rope.*   **15** clog up: *Grease fouled the drain.*   **16** clogged up: *The fire will not burn because the chimney is foul.*   **17** cover a ship's bottom with seaweed, barnacles, etc.   **18** of a ship, having the bottom covered with seaweed, barnacles, etc. **19** unfavourable; stormy: *Foul weather delayed the ship.* **20** contrary: *a foul wind.*   1, 5, 6, 12, 14, 16, 18–20 *adj.*, 2–4, 8, 10, 11, 13, 15, 17 *v.*, 7, 9 *n.*   —**foul′ly,** *adv.* —**foul′ness,** *n.*

**foul up,**   **a** make a mess of; bungle:   **b** put out of order: *A piece of loose rope fouled up the boat's propeller.* **c** make dirty or impure.   **d** become dirty or impure.
☞ *Hom.*   FOWL.
☞ *Etym.*   See note at FILTH.

**fou·lard** (fü lärd′)   a soft, thin fabric made of silk, rayon, or cotton, usually with a printed pattern: *Foulard is used for neckties, dresses, etc.*   *n.*

**foul ball**   in baseball, a ball hit so that it falls outside the base lines.

**foul line**   in baseball, either the line from home to first base, or from home to third base, with their marked or unmarked continuations.

**foul-mouthed** (foul′mouTHd or foul′moutht′) habitually using vile, offensive language.   *adj.*

**foul play**   **1** unfair play; a thing or things done against the rules.   **2** treachery; violence: *The man seemed to have died in his sleep, but the police suspected foul play.*

**found¹** (found)   pt. and pp. of FIND: *We found the treasure. The lost child was found.*   *v.*

**found²** (found)   **1** establish; set up: *Champlain founded Quebec City in 1608.*   **2** rest for support; base: *He founded his claim on facts.*   *v.*

**found³** (found)   melt and mould metal; make of molten metal; cast.   *v.*

**foun·da·tion** (foun dā′shən)   **1** the part on which the other parts rest for support; base: *the foundation of a house.*   **2** the basis of a belief, idea, argument, etc.: *The report has no foundation in fact.*   **3** a founding or establishing: *The foundation of Quebec City took place in 1608.*   **4** a being founded or established.   **5** an institution founded and endowed: *a charitable foundation.* **6** a fund given to support an institution.   *n.*

**foun·der¹** (foun′dər)   **1** fill with water and sink: *The ship foundered in the storm.*   **2** break down; go lame; stumble: *Her horse foundered.*   **3** become worn out; fail. **4** cause a horse to break down, fall lame, etc.   *v.*

**foun·der²** (foun′dər)   a person who founds or establishes something.   *n.*

**Founder's Day**   the festival celebrated in October, commemorating the introduction of Buddhism to Canada in 1905, and the assembly of Buddhists in Toronto in 1930 which led to the formation of the Buddhist Council of Canada.

**found·ling** (foun′dling)   a baby or child found deserted.   *n.*

**found·ry** (foun′drē)   **1** a place where metal is melted and moulded; place where things are made of molten metal.   **2** the melting and moulding of metal; the process of making things of molten metal.   *n.*, *pl.* **found·ries.**

**fount** (fount)   **1** fountain.   **2** source: *She is a fount of knowledge.*   *n.*

**foun·tain** (foun′tən)   **1** a stream or spray of water rising into the air.   **2** a decorative structure through which water is forced into the air in a stream of spray.

**foun·tain·head** (foun′tən hed′) 1 the source of a stream. 2 an original source. *n.*

**fountain pen** a pen for writing that automatically supplies liquid ink to the nib from a rubber or plastic tube inside.

**four** (fôr) 1 one more than three; 4: *There are four left in the box. She saw the movie four times.* 2 the numeral 4: *She crossed the 3 out and put a 4 in its place.* 3 the fourth in a set or series; especially a playing card or side of a die having four spots: *He threw a four.* 4 being fourth in a set or series (*used mainly after the noun*): *I don't understand Section Four of the manual.* 5 in rowing: **a** a crew of four rowers. **b** the boat they use. 6 any set or series of four persons or things: *They set up a four to play tennis.* 1–3, 5, 6 *n.*, 1, 4 *adj.*
**on all fours, a** on all four feet. **b** on hands and knees.
☞ *Hom.* FOR, FORE.
☞ *Etym.* For OE *fēower*, related to German *vier* and having the same Indo-European source as L *quattuor* (giving F *quatre*).

**four·fold** (fôr′fōld′) 1 four times as much or as many. 2 having four parts. 1, 2 *adj.*, 1 *adv.*

**four–foot·ed** (fôr′fùt′id) having four feet. *adj.*

**four–hand·ed** (fôr′han′did) 1 having four hands. 2 for four players. *adj.*

**Four-H clubs** or **4-H clubs** a national system of clubs to teach rural children agriculture and home economics: *The purpose of Four-H clubs is the improvement of head, heart, hands, and health.*

**four–in–hand** (fô′rin hand′) 1 a necktie tied in a slip knot with the ends left hanging. 2 a carriage pulled by four horses driven by one person. 3 a team of four horses. *n.*

**four–o'clock** (fô′rə klok′) a small plant having red, white, or yellow trumpet-shaped flowers that open late in the afternoon and close in the morning. *n.*

**four·score** (fôr′skôr′) four times twenty; 80. *adj., n.*

**four·some** (fôr′səm) 1 a group of four people. 2 a game played by four people, two on each side. 3 the players. *n.*

**four·square** (fôr′skwer′) 1 square. 2 frank; outspoken. 3 not yielding; firm. 4 a square. 1–3 *adj.*, 4 *n.*

**four·teen** (fôr′tēn′) 1 four more than ten; 14: *That's only fourteen; we need two more* (*n.*). *They stayed for fourteen days* (*adj.*). 2 the numeral 14: *That should be a 14, not a 15.* 3 the fourteenth in a set or series. 4 being fourteenth in a set or series (*used after the noun*): *Lesson Fourteen.* 5 a set or series of fourteen persons or things. 1–3, 5 *n.*, 1, 4 *adj.*

**four·teenth** (fôr′tēnth′) 1 next after the 13th; last in a series of fourteen; 14th. 2 one, or being one, of 14 equal parts. *adj., n.*

**fourth** (fôrth) 1 next after the third; last in a series of four; 4th. 2 one of 4 equal parts. 3 in automobiles and similar machines, the forward gear next above third; high gear in a four-gear system. 4 in music, the fourth tone from the keynote of a scale. 5 the interval between such tones. 6 a combination of such tones. 1, 2 *adj.*, 1–6 *n.*
☞ *Hom.* FORTH.

**fourth dimension** a dimension in addition to length, width, and thickness: *Time has been thought of as a fourth dimension.*

**fourth estate** the press; newspapers and those who work for them.

**fourth·ly** (fôr′thlē) in the fourth place. *adv.*

**Fourth of July** U.S. the holiday in honour of the adoption of the Declaration of Independence on July 4, 1776.

**four–wheeled** (fôr′wēld′ *or* fôr′hwēld′) having four wheels; running on four wheels. *adj.*

**fowl** (foul) 1 any bird: *a water fowl.* 2 any of several kinds of large birds such as chickens, geese, and turkeys, raised for meat and eggs. 3 the flesh of such a bird used for food. *n., pl.* **fowls** or (*esp. collectively*) **fowl**.
☞ *Hom.* FOUL.

**fowl·er** (fou′lər) a person who hunts, shoots, catches, or traps wild birds. *n.*

**fowling piece** a light gun for shooting wild birds.

A red fox - about 65 cm long excluding the tail

**fox** (foks) 1 a wild animal related to the dog, having a pointed muzzle and a bushy tail: *Foxes are sly and crafty.* 2 the fur of this animal. 3 a sly, crafty person; a person noted for his or her ability to get the better of other people. 4 *Informal.* trick by being sly and crafty. 1–3 *n.*, 4 *v.* —**fox′like′**, *adj.*

**fox·glove** (foks′gluv′) a plant with tall stalks having many bell-shaped flowers: *Digitalis is obtained from the leaves and seeds of the foxglove. n.*

**fox·hole** (foks′hōl′) a hole in the ground for protection against enemy fire. *n.*

**fox·hound** (foks′hound′) a hound having a keen sense of smell, bred and trained to hunt foxes. *n.*

**fox·tail** (fok′stāl′) 1 the tail of a fox. 2 a kind of grass with soft, brushlike spikes of flowers. *n.*

**fox terrier** a small, active dog of a breed once trained to drive foxes from their holes: *Fox terriers are white with brown or black spots and may have smooth or rough hair.* See TERRIER for picture.

**fox trot** 1 a dance with short, quick steps. 2 the music for such a dance.

**fox–trot** (fok′strot′) dance the FOX TROT. *v.*,
**fox-trot·ted, fox-trot·ting.**

**fox·y** (fok′sē) like a fox; sly; crafty. *adj.*, **fox·i·er, fox·i·est.** —**fox′i·ly,** *adv.* —**fox′i·ness,** *n.*

**foy·er** (foi′ər *or* foi′ā) **1** an entrance hall used as a lounging room in a theatre or hotel; lobby. **2** an entrance hall. *n.*

**fr. 1** franc. **2** from. **3** fragment.

**Fr** francium.

**Fr. 1** France. **2** French. **3** Father. **4** Friday.

**fra·cas** (frā′kəs *or* frak′əs) a noisy quarrel or fight; disturbance; uproar; brawl. *n.*

**frac·tion** (frak′shən) **1** one or more of the equal parts of a whole: $\frac{1}{2}$ *and* $\frac{7}{8}$ *are fractions.* **2** a very small part, amount, etc.; fragment. **3** breaking. *n.*

**frac·tion·al** (frak′shə nəl) **1** having to do with fractions. **2** forming a fraction: *440 metres is a fractional part of a kilometre.* **3** small by comparison; insignificant. *adj.*

**frac·tious** (frak′shəs) **1** cross; fretful; peevish. **2** hard to manage; unruly. *adj.* —**frac′tious·ly,** *adv.* —**frac′tious·ness,** *n.*

**frac·ture** (frak′chər) **1** break; crack: *The boy fell from a tree and fractured his arm.* **2** a break; crack. **3** breaking or being broken. **4** a breaking of a bone or cartilage. **5** the surface of a freshly broken mineral. **1** *v.*, **frac·tured, frac·tur·ing;** **2**–**5** *n.*

**frag·ile** (fraj′īl *or* fraj′əl) easily broken, damaged, or destroyed; delicate; frail. *adj.* —**frag′ile·ly,** *adv.*

**fra·gil·i·ty** (frə jil′ə tē) a fragile quality. *n.*

**frag·ment** (frag′mənt *for noun,* frag ment′ *for verb*) **1** a broken piece; a part broken off. **2** an incomplete or disconnected part: *She could hear only fragments of the conversation.* **3** a part of an incomplete or unfinished work. **4** break or divide into fragments. **1**–**3** *n.*, **4** *v.*

**frag·men·tar·y** (frag′mən ter′ē) made up of fragments; incomplete; disconnected: *fragmentary remains of a temple, fragmentary evidence, a fragmentary account.* *adj.*

**frag·men·ta·tion** (frag′mən tā′shən) the actual process of breaking into many pieces. *n.*

**fragmentation bomb** a bomb, grenade, etc. that throws bits of metal in all directions as it bursts.

**fra·grance** (frā′grəns) a sweet smell; pleasing odour. *n.*

**fra·grant** (frā′grənt) having or giving off a pleasing odour; sweet-smelling. *adj.* —**fra′grant·ly,** *adv.*

**frail** (frāl) **1** not very strong; weak; physically delicate: *a frail child.* **2** easily broken, damaged, or destroyed; fragile: *Be careful, those branches are a very frail support.* **3** morally weak; liable to yield to temptation. *adj.* —**frail′ness,** *n.*

**frail·ty** (frāl′tē) **1** being frail. **2** moral weakness; liability to yield to temptation. **3** a fault or sin caused by moral weakness. *n., pl.* **frail·ties.**

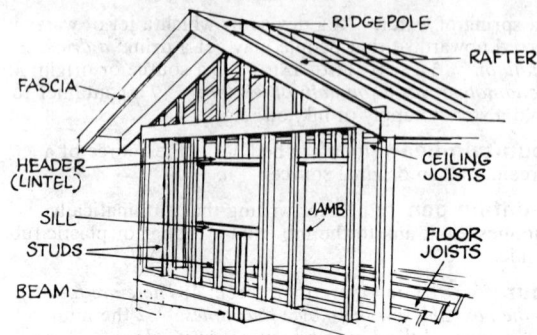
Part of the frame of a house

**frame** (frām) **1** a supporting structure over which something is stretched or built: *the frame of a house.* **2** the body; bodily structure: *a man of heavy frame.* **3** skeleton. **4** the way in which a thing is put together. **5** an established order; plan; system. **6** shape; form. **7** put together; plan; make: *Laws are framed in Parliament.* **8** the border in which a thing is set: *a window frame, a picture frame.* **9** one of the individual pictures on a strip of motion-picture film. **10** one image transmitted by television. **11** put a border around; enclose with a frame: *to frame a picture.* **12** *Informal.* make seem guilty. **13** any of the divisions of a bowling game when the pins are set up again. **1–6, 8–10, 13** *n.*, **6, 7, 11, 12** *v.*, **framed, fram·ing.** —**fram′er,** *n.*

**frame house** a house made of a wooden framework covered with boards.

**frame of mind** a way of thinking or feeling; disposition; mood.

**frame·work** (frām′wèrk′) **1** a support over which a thing is stretched or built; the stiff part that gives shape to a thing: *A bridge often has a steel framework.* **2** the way in which a thing is put together; structure; system. *n.*

**fran·chise** (fran′chīz) **1** a privilege or right granted by a government: *The city granted the company a franchise to operate buses on the city streets.* **2** the right to vote: *In 1920 Canada established a universal franchise for persons of 21 years and over.* **3** the privilege, often exclusive, of selling the products of a manufacturer or providing a company's service in a given area. *n.*

**fran·ci·um** (fran′sē əm) a rare radio-active element. Symbol: Fr *n.*

**Fran·co–** combining form. **1** French or French-speaking, as in *Francophone.* **2** French and _____: *the Franco-Prussian war.* **3** French-Canadian: *Franco-Albertan.*

**Fran·co·phone** or **fran·co·phone** (frang′kə fōn) *Cdn.* in a bilingual country, a person whose native language is French. *n.*

**fran·gi·ble** (fran′jə bəl) breakable. *adj.*

**frank** (frangk) **1** free in expressing one's real thoughts, opinions, and feelings; not hiding what is in one's mind; not afraid to say what one thinks: *a frank way of talking.* **2** clearly manifest; undisguised; plain: *frank mutiny.* **3** send a letter, package, etc. without charge. **4** a mark to show that a letter, package, etc. is to be sent without charge. **5** the right to send letters, packages, etc. without charge. **6** a letter, package, etc. sent without charge. **7** put a postmark on: *Have all the letters been franked?* **1, 2** *adj.*, **3, 7** *v.*, **4–6** *n.* —**frank′ly,** *adv.* —**frank′ness,** *n.*

**Frank·en·stein** (frang′kən stīn′) **1** the hero of a

novel, who creates a monster that he cannot control. **2** anything that causes the ruin of its creator. *n.*

**frank·furt** (frangk′fərt) FRANKFURTER; wiener. *n.*

**frank·furt·er** (frangk′fér tər) WIENER. *n.*

**frank·in·cense** (frang′kin sens′) a fragrant resin from certain Asiatic or African trees that gives off a sweet, spicy odour when burned. *n.*

**fran·tic** (fran′tik) **1** very much excited: *She made frantic motions to stop the approaching car.* **2** wild with rage or pain: *The couple was frantic when their baby was stolen.* *adj.*

**fran·ti·cal·ly** (fran′ti klē) in a frantic manner; with excitement: *He signalled frantically for the train to stop.* *adv.*

**frap·pé** (fra pā′) **1** iced; cooled. **2** fruit juice sweetened and frozen. **3** any frozen or iced food or drink. 1 *adj.*, 2, 3 *n.*

**fra·ter·nal** (frə tér′nəl) **1** brotherly. **2** having to do with a FRATERNAL ORDER. **3** of twins, coming from two separately fertilized egg cells, as distinguished from IDENTICAL (def. 3) twins. *adj.* —**fra·ter′nal·ly,** *adv.*

**fraternal order** a group of people joined for some common aim; society; fraternity: *Many fraternal orders were established to provide insurance and health benefits for their members.*

**fra·ter·ni·ty** (frə tér′nə tē) **1** a group of men or women joined together for fellowship or for some other purpose; society: *There are student fraternities in some Canadian universities.* **2** a group having the same interests, kind of work, etc. **3** fraternal feeling; brotherhood. *n., pl.* **fra·ter·ni·ties.**

**frat·er·nize** (frat′ər nīz′) **1** associate in a brotherly way; be friendly. **2** of soldiers, etc., associate in a friendly way with the citizens of a hostile nation during occupation of their territory. *v.* **frat·er·nized, frat·er·niz·ing.** —**frat′er·ni·za′tion,** *n.*

**frat·ri·cid·al** (frat′rə sī′dəl) **1** having to do with FRATRICIDE (def. 1). **2** having to do with the killing of relatives or fellow citizens: *A civil war is a fratricidal struggle.* *adj.*

**frat·ri·cide** (frat′rə sīd′) **1** the act of killing one's own brother or sister. **2** a person who kills his or her own brother or sister. *n.*

**fraud** (frod) **1** deceit; cheating; dishonesty: *Any intent to deceive is considered a fraud.* **2** a dishonest act, statement, etc.; something done to deceive or cheat; trick. **3** *Informal.* a person who is not what he or she pretends to be. *n.*

**fraud·u·lence** (froj′ə ləns) being FRAUDULENT. *n.*

**fraud·u·lent** (froj′ə lənt) **1** deceitful; cheating; dishonest. **2** intended to deceive. **3** done by fraud; obtained by trickery. *adj.* —**fraud′u·lent·ly,** *adv.*

**fraught** (frot) loaded; filled: *A battlefield is fraught with horror.* *adj.*

**fray¹** (frā) a noisy quarrel; fight. *n.*

**fray²** (frā) **1** separate into threads; make or become ragged or worn along the edge. **2** wear away; rub: *Long wear had frayed the collar and cuffs of his old shirts.* *v.*

**fraz·zle** (fraz′əl) *Informal.* **1** tear to shreds; fray; wear out. **2** tire out, weary. **3** a frazzled condition. 1, 2 *v.*, **fraz·zled, fraz·zling;** 3 *n.*

**freak** (frēk) **1** something very queer or unusual: *A green* 

---

**frankfurt**     481     **freeborn**

hat, āge, fär; let, ēqual, tėrm; it, īce
hot, ōpen, ôrder; oil, out; cup, pút, rüle
əbove, takən, pencəl, lemən, circəs
ch, child; ng, long; sh, ship
th, thin; ŦH, then; zh, measure

*leaf growing in the middle of a rose would be called a freak of nature.* **2** very queer or unusual. **3** a sudden change of mind without reason; an odd notion or fancy. 1, 3 *n.*, 2 *adj.*

**freak·ish** (frē′kish) full of freaks; very queer or unusual. *adj.*

**freck·le** (frek′əl) **1** a small, light-brown spot on the skin. **2** make freckles on; cover with freckles: *The sun freckles the skin of some people.* **3** become marked or spotted with freckles. 1 *n.*, 2, 3 *v.*, **freck·led, freck·ling.**

**freck·le–faced** having many FRECKLEs on the face. *adj.*

**freck·ly** (frek′lē) covered with FRECKLES. *adj.*

**free** (frē) **1** not under another's control; having liberty; able to do, act, or think as one pleases: *a free life, free speech, free nations.* **2** showing liberty; caused by liberty. **3** not held back, fastened, or shut up; released; loose. **4** not hindered; easy: *a free step.* **5** clear; open. **6** open to all: *a free port.* **7** without cost or payment: *These tickets are free.* (adj.) *Children under 12 attend free.* (adv.) **8** without paying a tax or duty. **9** generous: *I appreciated his free offer to carry my suitcase.* **10** giving or using much. **11** abundant. **12** not following rules, forms, or words exactly; not strict. **13** saying what one thinks; frank. **14** not restrained enough by manners or morals. **15** not combined with something else: *Oxygen exists free in air.* **16** relieve from any kind of burden, bondage, or slavery; make free: *The prisoner was freed early for good behaviour.* **17** let loose; release: *to free a boat from weeds.* **18** clear: *She will have to free herself of this charge of stealing.* **19** in a free manner. 1–15 *adj.*, **fre·er, fre·est;** 7, 19 *adv.*, 16–18 *v.*, **freed, free·ing.** —**free′ness,** *n.*

**free and easy,** paying little attention to rules and customs: *His free and easy manner was not typical of the diplomatic service.*

**free from** or **of,** without; lacking: *free from fear, air free of dust.*

**free with,** giving or using much.

**make free with,** use as if one had complete rights.

**set free,** make free; let loose; release.

☛ *Etym.* From OE *frēo*, which can be traced back to much earlier Germanic and Indo-European forms meaning 'dear, loved'. The people who were dear to each other in a household were the members of the family, the free people, as opposed to the slaves. The word is related to OE *frīgu* 'love' and *Frīg,* the Germanic goddess of love (see note at FRIDAY). It is also related to the OE verb *frēogan* 'to love' (see note at FRIEND).

**free·bee** (frē′bē) FREEBIE. *n.*

**free·bie** (frē′bē) a little free gift. *n., pl..* **freebies.** Also, **freebee, freeby.**

**free·board** (frē′bôrd′) that part of a ship's side between the water line and the deck or gunwale. *n.*

**free·boot·er** (frē′bü′tər) a pirate; buccaneer. *n.*

**free·boot·ing** (frē′bü′ting) piracy; buccaneering. *n.*

**free·born** (frē′bôrn′) **1** born free; not in slavery. **2** of or suitable for people born free. *adj.*

**free·by** (frē′bē) FREEBIE. *n.*

**free city** a city forming an independent state.

**freed·man** (frēd′mən) a man freed from slavery. *n.*, *pl.* **freed·men** (-mən).

**free·dom** (frē′dəm) **1** the state or condition of being free. **2** the condition of not being under another's control; the power to do, say, or think as one pleases; liberty. **3** free use: *We give a guest the freedom of our home.* **4** lack of restraint; frankness: *We did not like the freedom of his manner.* **5** ease of movement or action. *n.*

**freed·wom·an** (frē′dwum′ən) a woman freed from slavery. *n.*, *pl.* **freed·wom·en** (-dwim′ən).

**free–for–all** (frē′fə rol′) **1** open to all. **2** a fight, race, etc. open to all. *1 adj., 2 n.*

**free·hand** (frē′hand′) done by hand without using instruments, measurements, etc.: *freehand drawing.* *adj.*

**free·hand·ed** (frē′han′did) generous; liberal. *adj.*

**free·hold** (frē′hōld′) **1** a piece of land held for life or with the right to transfer it to one's heirs. **2** the holding of land in this way. *n.*

**free·hold·er** (frē′hōl′dər) a person who has a FREEHOLD. *n.*

**free lance** **1** a writer, artist, etc. who works independently and sells his or her work to anyone who will buy it. **2** in the Middle Ages, a soldier who fought for any person, group, or state that would pay him. **3** a person who fights or works for any cause that he or she chooses.

**free–lance** (frē′lans′) of writers, artists, etc., work as a FREE LANCE (def. 1). *v.*, **free-lanced, free-lanc·ing.**

**free·ly** (frē′lē) **1** in a free manner. **2** generously; willingly: *He gave freely of his time.* *adv.*

**free·man** (frē′mən) **1** a person who is not a slave or a serf. **2** a person who has civil or political freedom; citizen. *n.*, *pl.* **free·men** (-mən).

**free on board** delivered free of charge on a train, ship, etc. *Abbrev.*: f.o.b. or F.O.B.

**free port** **1** a port open to traders of all countries on the same conditions. **2** a port where no taxes or duties must be paid.

**free press** a press not censored or controlled by the government.

**free·sia** (frē′zhə) a plant of the same family as the iris, which has clusters of fragrant white, yellow, purple, or pink flowers: *Freesias are grown from bulbs.* *n.*

**free–spo·ken** (frē′spō′kən) speaking freely; saying what one thinks; frank. *adj.*

**free·stone** (frē′stōn′) **1** any stone, such as limestone or sandstone, that can easily be cut without splitting. **2** a fruit stone, or pit, that can be easily separated from the pulp. **3** a fruit having such a stone. **4** having such a stone: *freestone peaches.* *n.*

**free·think·er** (frē′thing′kər) a person who forms his or her religious opinions independently of authority or tradition. *n.*

**free thought** religious opinions formed independently of authority or tradition.

**free trade** trade unrestricted by taxes, imposts, or differences of treatment; especially, international trade free from protective duties and subject only to tariff for revenue: *The United Kingdom had free trade for many years.*

**free·trad·er** (frē′trā′dər) a person who favours the system of FREE TRADE. *n.*

**free trader** *Cdn.* formerly, a man who traded in furs independently of such companies as the Hudson's Bay Company. *n.*

**free verse** poetry not restricted by rules of metre, rhyme, etc.

**free·way** (frē′wā′) *Esp. U.S.* a high-speed highway on which no tolls are charged. *n.*

**free·wheel·ing** (frē′wē′ling *or* frē′hwē′ling) independent or unhampered: *a freewheeling operation.* *adj.*

**free·will** (frē′wil′) of one's own accord; voluntary: *a freewill offering to the Red Cross.* *adj.*

**free will** a voluntary choice; freedom of decision.

**freeze** (frēz) **1** turn into ice; harden by cold: *to freeze ice cream. The water in the pond has frozen.* **2** cause something to become hard and stiff by lowering the temperature to below the FREEZING POINT (0°C): *By freezing meat we can keep it from spoiling.* **3** become very cold. **4** kill or damage by frost. **5** be killed or damaged by frost. **6** freeze over. **7** become clogged by pieces of ice: *The car stalled because the gas line froze.* **8** fix or become fixed to something by freezing. **9** a state of extreme coldness; frost; freezing: *The freeze last night damaged the apple trees.* **10** a period during which there is freezing weather. **11** make or become stiff and unfriendly. **12** chill or be chilled with fear, etc. **13** become motionless, usually because of fear: *The mouse froze as the snake moved toward it.* **14** fix a price at a definite amount, usually by governmental decree. **15** make funds, bank balances, etc. unusable and inaccessible by governmental decree. **16** make a part of the body numb by injecting or applying some kind of drug: *The dentist froze the patient's gums before taking out the tooth.* *1–8, 11–16 v.*, **froze, fro·zen, freez·ing;** *9, 10 n.* **freeze out,** *Informal.* force out; keep out: *The clique's unfriendliness froze out all newcomers.*
☛ *Hom.* FRIEZE.

**freeze–dry** (frēz′drī′) preserve (food, vaccine, etc.) by quick-freezing it and then evaporating the frozen moisture content in a high vacuum. Freeze-dried substances keep for a long period without refrigeration. *v.*, **freeze-dried, freeze-drying.**

**freez·er** (frē′zər) **1** a refrigerator cabinet within which a temperature below FREEZING POINT is maintained. **2** a machine to freeze ice cream. *n.*

**freeze–frame** (frēz′frām′) a picture held still in a movie or television program. *n.*

**freeze–up** (frēz′up′) *Cdn.* the time of year when the rivers and lakes freeze over; the onset of winter. *n.*

**freez·ing** (frē′zing) **1** ppr. of FREEZE: *The water in the puddles is freezing.* **2** FREEZING POINT, especially that of water: *It's below freezing outside.* **3** *Informal.* very cold: *It's freezing in here!* *1 v., 2 n., 3 adj.*

**freezing point** the temperature at which a liquid freezes: *The freezing point of water at sea level is zero degrees Celsius.* See THERMOMETER for picture.

**freight** (frāt) **1** the load of goods carried on a train, ship, etc.: *It took a whole day to unload the freight.* **2** the carrying of goods on a train, ship, etc.: *She sent the box by freight.* **3** the charge for this. **4** a train for carrying goods: *The freight was early last night.* **5** load with freight. **6** carry as freight. **7** send as freight. **8** load; burden. 1–4, 8 *n.*, 5–8 *v.*

**freight car** a railway car for carrying freight.

**freight·er** (frā′tər) a ship or aircraft for carrying freight. *n.*

**French** (french) **1** of or having to do with France, its people, or their language. **2 the French,** *pl.* the people of France. **3** the French language: *The kind of French spoken in Canada is called Canadian French.* **4** French Canadian; of or having to do with French Canada, French Canadians, or their language. 1, 4 *adj.*, 2, 3 *n.*

**French and Indian War** the name given to the part of the Seven Years' War fought in North America between Great Britain and France, with their Indian allies (1754–1763).

**French Canada 1** French Canadians as a group; all French Canadians. **2** that part of Canada inhabited mainly or entirely by French Canadians, especially the province of Quebec.

**French Canadian 1** a Canadian whose ancestors came from France. **2** of or having to do with French Canada or French Canadians: *French-Canadian customs.* **3** the language of the French Canadians; Canadian French.

**French Community** an association formed in 1958 of France, its dependent territories, and many of its former colonies.

**French cuff** a sleeve cuff that is folded back at the wrist and fastened with a cuff link instead of a button.

**French fries** potatoes that have been **French fried,** that is, cut into long, square-sided strips and cooked in boiling fat until crisp on the outside.

A french horn

**French horn** a brass wind instrument that has a mellow tone.

**French·man** (french′mən) **1** a male native or inhabitant of France. **2** a male citizen of France. **3** a French-Canadian male. *n., pl.* **French·men** (-mən).

**French Shore** *Cdn.* **1** the west coast of Newfoundland, where the French held fishing and other rights from 1713 till 1904. **2** an area originally settled by the Acadian French, located on the southwest coast of Nova Scotia.

**French toast** slices of bread dipped in a mixture of egg and milk and then fried in very little fat.

**French·wom·an** (french′wum′ən) **1** a female native or inhabitant of France. **2** a female citizen of France. **3** a French-Canadian woman. *n., pl.* **French·wom·en** (-wim′ən).

**fre·net·ic** (frə net′ik) FRENZIED; frantic. *adj.*

hat, āge, fär; let, ēqual, tėrm; it, īce hot, ōpen, ôrder; oil, out; cup, pùt, rüle әbove, takәn, pencәl, lemәn, circәs
ch, child; ng, long; sh, ship th, thin; ᴛʜ, then; zh, measure

**fren·zied** (fren′zēd) greatly excited; frantic. *adj.*

**fren·zy** (fren′zē) **1** a state of near madness: *She was in a frenzy of grief when she heard of her son's death.* **2** a state of very great excitement: *The spectators were in a frenzy after the home team scored the winning goal.* *n., pl.* **fren·zies.**

**fre·on** (frē′on) any of a group of nonflammable, inert gaseous or liquid fluorocarbons used especially as refrigerants. *n.*

**fre·quen·cy** (frē′kwən sē) **1** the rate of occurrence: *The flashes of light came with a frequency of three per minute.* **2** a frequent occurrence. **3** the number of complete cycles per second of an alternating current or any type of wave motion: *Different radio stations broadcast at different frequencies so that their signals can be heard distinctly.* *n., pl.* **fre·quen·cies.**

**frequency modulation** (moj′ə lā′shən) in radio broadcasting: **1** a method of transmitting the sound signals of a broadcast by changing the frequency of the carrier waves to match the sound signals. **2** a broadcasting system that uses frequency modulation. Compare with AMPLITUDE MODULATION. *Abbrev.:* FM, F.M., or f.m.

**fre·quent** (frē′kwənt *for adjective,* fri kwent′ *for verb*) **1** occurring often, near together, or every little while: *In my part of the country, storms are frequent in March.* **2** regular; habitual: *She is a frequent caller at our house.* **3** go often to; be often in: *Frogs frequent ponds, streams, and marshes.* 1, 2 *adj.*, 3 *v.*

**fre·quent·er** (fri kwen′tər) a habitual visitor: *He is not a frequenter of dance halls.* *n.*

**fre·quent·ly** (frē′kwən tlē) often; repeatedly; every little while. *adv.*

**fres·co** (fres′kō) **1** the act or art of painting with water colours on damp, fresh plaster. **2** a picture or design so painted: *Beautiful frescoes covered the walls and ceiling of the cathedral.* **3** paint in fresco. 1, 2 *n., pl.* **fres·coes** or **fres·cos;** 3 *v.*, **fres·coed, fres·co·ing.**

**fresh** (fresh) **1** newly made, arrived, or obtained: *fresh footprints.* **2** not known, seen, or used before; new; recent: *Is there any fresh news from home?* **3** additional; further; another: *After her failure she made a fresh start.* **4** not salty: *There is fresh water in the Great Lakes.* **5** not spoiled; newly grown, produced, or gathered; not stale: *fresh vegetables, fresh milk.* **6** not artificially preserved: *Fresh foods usually have more flavour than canned ones.* **7** not wearied; vigorous; lively: *Use fresh horses.* **8** not faded or worn; bright. **9** looking healthy or young. **10** clean; newly washed: *a fresh shirt.* **11** pure; cool; refreshing: *a fresh breeze.* **12** fairly strong; brisk: *A fresh wind is more than a breeze.* **13** not experienced. *adj.* —**fresh′ly,** *adv.* —**fresh′ness,** *n.*

**fresh·en** (fresh′ən) **1** make new, pure, or bright: *She thought it would be a good idea to freshen the paint on the house.* **2** become stronger: *The wind freshened at sunset.* *v.*

**freshen up,** do something to make, or feel, fresh: *He freshened up by taking a bath and changing his clothes.*

**fresh·et** (fresh′it) 1 a flood caused by heavy rains or melted snow. 2 a rush of fresh water flowing into the sea. *n.*

**fresh·man** (fresh′mən) 1 a student in the first year of a university course. 2 beginner. *n., pl.* **fresh·men** (-mən).

**fresh·wa·ter** (fresh′wot′ər) 1 of, having to do with, or living in water that is not salty: *The catfish is a freshwater fish.* 2 not used to sailing on the sea: *a freshwater sailor.* *adj.*

**fret¹** (fret) 1 be peevish, unhappy, discontented, or worried: *A baby sometimes frets in hot weather. Don't fret about your mistake.* 2 make peevish, unhappy, discontented, or worried: *Lola's failures fretted her.* 3 a peevish complaining; worry; discontented condition. 4 eat away; wear; rub. 5 roughen; disturb. 1, 2, 4, 5 *v.*, **fret·ted, fret·ting;** 3 *n.* —**fret′ter,** *n.*

**fret²** (fret) 1 an ornamental pattern made of straight lines bent or combined at angles. 2 decorate with FRETWORK. 1 *n.,* 2 *v.,* **fret·ted, fret·ting.**

**fret³** (fret) one of a series of ridges of wood, ivory, or metal on a guitar, banjo, etc. to show where to put the fingers to produce particular tones. *n.*

**fret·ful** (fret′fəl) inclined to fret; peevish; unhappy; discontented: *My baby brother is fretful because he is cutting his teeth.* *adj.* —**fret′ful·ly,** *adv.* —**fret′ful·ness,** *n.*

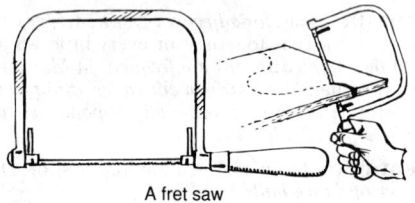
A fret saw

**fret saw** a saw with a long, slender blade and fine teeth, used to cut thin wood into patterns.

Traditional fretwork on the gable of a house in rural Ontario

**fret·work** (fret′wėrk′) ornamental openwork or carving: *Some houses are decorated with fretwork.* *n.*

**Fri.** Friday.

**fri·a·bil·i·ty** (frī′ə bil′ə tē) the state of being FRIABLE. *n.*

**fri·a·ble** (frī′ə bəl) easily crumbled: *Dry soil is friable.* *adj.*

**fric·as·see** (frik′ə sē′) 1 meat cut up, stewed, and served in a sauce made with its own gravy. 2 prepare meat in this way. 1 *n.,* 2 *v.,* **fric·as·seed, fric·as·see·ing.**

**fric·tion** (frik′shən) 1 a rubbing of one object against another; rubbing: *Matches are lighted by friction.* 2 the resistance to motion of surfaces that touch: *A sleigh moves more easily on smooth ice than on rough ground because there is less friction.* 3 conflict of differing ideas, opinions, etc.; disagreement: *Political differences caused friction between the two countries.* *n.*

**fric·tion·al** (frik′shə nəl) having to do with FRICTION; caused by friction. *adj.*

**Fri·day** (frī′dā′ *or* frī′dē) 1 the sixth day of the week, following Thursday. 2 the servant of Robinson Crusoe. 3 any faithful servant or devoted follower. *n.*
☛ *Etym.* From OE *Frīgedæg* 'day of Frig'. *Frīg* (ON *Frigg*) was the Germanic goddess of love. See also the note at FREE.

**fridge** (frij) *Informal.* a refrigerator: *Get the milk out of the fridge.* *n.*

**fried** (frīd) 1 cooked in hot fat. 2 pt. and pp. of FRY¹: *I fried the ham. Are the potatoes fried?* 1 *adj.,* 2 *v.*

**friend** (frend) 1 a person who knows and likes another. 2 a person who favours and supports: *She was a friend to the poor.* 3 a person who belongs to the same side or group: *Are you friend or foe?* *n.* —**friend′less,** *adj.*
☛ *Etym.* From OE *frēond,* originally the present participle of the verb *frēogan* 'to love' (see note at FREE). The word **fiend** developed from OE *fēond,* related to *fēogan,* which means the exact opposite, 'to hate'. See also the note at FIEND.

**friend·ly** (frend′lē) 1 of a friend; having the attitude of a friend; kind: *a friendly greeting.* 2 like a friend; like a friend's. 3 on good terms; not hostile: *friendly relations between countries.* 4 wanting to be a friend: *a friendly dog.* 5 favouring and supporting; favourable: *a friendly breeze.* 6 in a friendly manner; as a friend. 1–5 *adj.,* **friend·li·er, friend·li·est;** 6 *adv.* —**friend′li·ness,** *n.*

**friend·ship** (frend′ship) 1 the state of being friends. 2 a liking between friends. 3 a friendly feeling; friendly behaviour: *Her smile radiated friendship.* *n.*

**fries** (frīz) FRENCH FRIES. *n. pl.*

**frieze¹** (frēz) 1 a horizontal band of decoration around a room, building, mantel, etc. 2 in architecture, a horizontal band forming part of the upper section of a wall, often ornamental with sculpture: *The frieze is the part of an entablature between the cornice and the architrave.* See COLUMN for picture. *n.*
☛ *Hom.* FREEZE.

**frieze²** (frēz) a thick woollen cloth with a shaggy nap on one side. *n.*
☛ *Hom.* FREEZE.

**frig·ate** (frig′it) 1 a modern warship smaller than a destroyer: *The Canadian Forces use frigates as escort vessels.* 2 formerly, a three-masted sailing warship of medium size. *n.*

**frigate bird** a strong-flying, tropical sea bird that steals other birds' food.

**fright** (frīt) 1 sudden fear; sudden terror. 2 *Informal.* a person or thing that is ugly, shocking, or ridiculous: *She looked a fright in that hat.* 3 *Poetic.* frighten. 1, 2 *n.,* 3 *v.*

**fright·en** (frī′tən) 1 fill with fright; make afraid; scare. 2 become afraid. *v.*

**fright·ened** (frī′tənd) 1 filled with fright; afraid. 2 pt. and pp. of FRIGHTEN. 1 *adj.,* 2 *v.*

**fright·en·ing** (frīt′ning *or* frī′tə ning) 1 capable of causing fright or fear: *a frightening experience.* 2 ppr. of FRIGHTEN. 1 *adj.,* 2 *v.*

**fright·ful** (frīt′fəl) **1** causing fright or horror; dreadful; terrible: *a frightful thunderstorm.* **2** ugly; shocking. **3** *Informal.* disagreeable; unpleasant: *a frightful person, a frightful trip.* **4** *Informal.* very great. *adj.*
—**fright′ful·ly**, *adv.* —**fright′ful·ness**, *n.*

**frig·id** (frij′id) **1** very cold: *a frigid climate.* **2** cold in feeling or manner; stiff; chilling: *frigid conversation.* *adj.*
—**frig′id·ly**, *adv.* —**frig′id·ness**, *n.*

**fri·gid·i·ty** (fri jid′ə tē) being FRIGID. *n.*

**Frigid Zone** a region within the Arctic or the Antarctic Circle.

**frill** (fril) **1** a ruffle. **2** decorate with a ruffle; adorn with ruffles. **3** *Informal.* anything added merely for show; useless ornament; affectation of dress, manner, speech, etc.: *It was a plain house with few frills.* **4** a fringe of feathers, hair, etc. around the neck of a bird or animal. 1, 3, 4 *n.*, 2 *v.* —**frill′y**, *adj.*

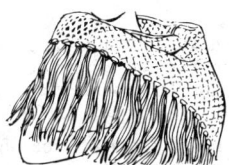

A shawl with a fringe

**fringe** (frinj) **1** a border or trimming made of threads, cords, etc., either loose or tied together in small bunches: *My scarf has a fringe at both ends.* **2** anything like this; border: *A fringe of hair hung over her forehead.* **3** anything thought of as marginal rather than central: *She belongs to the radical fringe of the labour movement.* **4** make a border for. **5** be a border for; border: *Bushes fringed the road.* **6** of the border or outside. **7** apart from the main purpose; secondary: *They didn't want to spend too much time on fringe issues.* 1–3, 6, 7 *n.*, 4, 5 *v.*, **fringed, fring·ing.**

**fringe tree** any member of the OLIVE family with white flowers.

**frip·per·y** (frip′ə rē) **1** cheap, showy clothes; gaudy ornaments. **2** a showing off; foolish display; pretended refinement: *Affectations of manner and speech are mere frippery.* *n.*, *pl.* **frip·per·ies.**

**frisk** (frisk) **1** run and jump about playfully; skip and dance joyously; frolic. **2** search a person for concealed weapons, stolen goods, etc. by running a hand quickly over the person's clothes. *v.*

**frisk·y** (fris′kē) playful; lively. *adj.*, **frisk·i·er, frisk·i·est.** —**frisk′i·ly**, *adv.* —**frisk′i·ness**, *n.*

**frith** (frith) FIRTH. *n.*

**frit·ter¹** (frit′ər) **1** waste little by little: *She frittered away the afternoon trying to decide what to do.* **2** cut or tear into small pieces; break into fragments. *v.*
—**frit′ter·er**, *n.*

**frit·ter²** (frit′ər) a small cake of batter, sometimes containing fruit or other food, fried in fat: *corn fritters, apple fritters.* *n.*

**fri·vol·i·ty** (fri vol′ə tē) **1** being FRIVOLOUS. **2** a FRIVOLOUS act or thing. *n.*, *pl.* **fri·vol·i·ties.**

**friv·o·lous** (friv′ə ləs) **1** lacking in seriousness or sense; silly: *Frivolous behaviour is out of place in Parliament.* **2** of little worth or importance; trivial: *He wasted his time on frivolous matters.* *adj.*
—**friv′o·lous·ly**, *adv.* —**friv′o·lous·ness**, *n.*

hat, āge, fär; let, ēqual, tėrm; it, īce
hot, ōpen, ôrder; oil, out; cup, put, rüle
above, takən, pencəl, lemən, circəs
ch, child; ng, long; sh, ship
th, thin; ŦH, then; zh, measure

**frizz** or **friz** (friz) **1** form into small, crisp curls; curl. **2** hair curled in small, crisp curls or a very close crimp. 1 *v.*, **frizzed, friz·zing;** 2 *n.*, *pl.* **friz·zes.**

**friz·zle¹** (friz′əl) **1** form into small, crisp curls; curl. **2** a small, crisp curl. 1 *v.*, **friz·zled, friz·zling;** 2 *n.*

**friz·zle²** (friz′əl) **1** make a hissing, sputtering noise when cooking; sizzle. **2** a hissing, sputtering noise; sizzle. **3** fry or broil until crisp. 1, 3 *v.*, **friz·zled, friz·zling;** 2 *n.*

**friz·zly** (friz′lē) full of small, crisp curls; curly. *adj.*, **friz·zli·er, friz·zli·est.**

**friz·zy** (friz′ē) FRIZZLY. *adj.*, **friz·zi·er, friz·zi·est.**

**fro** (frō) from; back. *adv.*
**to and fro,** first one way and then back again; back and forth: *A rocking chair goes to and fro.*

**frock** (frok) **1** a gown or dress. **2** a loose outer garment. **3** a robe worn by a clergyman. **4** clothe in a frock. 1–3 *n.*, 4 *v.*

A leopard frog - head and body about 7 cm long

**frog¹** (frog) **1** any of various small, smooth-skinned, tail-less, leaping animals, most of which live in or near water: *Frogs are amphibians.* **2** the arrangement of a rail where a railway track crosses or branches from another. **3** a pad of horny substance in the middle of the bottom of a foot of a horse, donkey, etc. *n.*
**frog in the throat,** *Informal.* a slight hoarseness caused by soreness or swelling in the throat.

**frog²** (frog) an ornamental fastening for a coat or dress. *n.*

**frog kick** in swimming, a movement of the legs in which the swimmer draws the knees forward and then kicks out to the sides and brings both legs together again: *The frog kick is done in the breast stroke.*

**frog·man** (frog′man′ *or* frog′mən) a skindiver, especially one in or working for the armed forces: *Most of the world's navies now have frogmen.* See SKINDIVER for picture. *n.*, *pl.* **frog·men** (-men′ *or* -mən).

**frog run** *Cdn.* in sugaring-off operations, the second run of sap in the maple trees, inferior to the first, or ROBIN RUN, for making syrup or sugar. Compare with BUD RUN and ROBIN RUN.

**frol·ic** (frol′ik) **1** a merry prank; fun. **2** a merry game or party. **3** play; have fun; make merry. **4** full of fun; merry. **5** a bee or gathering for work. 1, 2, 5 *n.*, 3 *v.*, **frol·icked, frol·ick·ing;** 4 *adj.* —**frol′ick·er**, *n.*

**frol·ic·some** (frol′ik səm) full of fun; merry. *adj.*

**from** (frum *or* from; *unstressed,* frəm) **1** out of; of: *Bricks are made from clay.* **2** starting out from; beginning with: *the train from Montreal. Study the lesson from page 10 to page 15.* **3** originating in; having as a source: *The river flows from the mountain. Much of our clothing is from Quebec.* **4** caused by; because of; by reason of: *to act from a sense of duty. The woman was weak from hunger.* **5** as being unlike: *Anyone can tell peas from beans.* **6** off: *a book from the table.* **7** out of the control or possession of: *She took the knife from the baby.* *prep.*

**frond** (frond) a divided leaf of a fern, palm, etc. *n.*

**front** (frunt) **1** the first part; foremost part: *the front of a car.* **2** the part that faces frontward: *the front of a dress.* **3** something fastened or worn on the front. **4** in war, the place where fighting is going on; line of battle: *He spent many weeks at the front.* **5** a sphere of activity combining different groups in a political or economic battle: *the labour front.* **6** the forces fighting for some political or social aim. **7** the land facing a street, river, lake, etc. **8** of, on, in, or at the front: *the front page.* **9** have the front toward; face: *Helen's house fronts the park.* **10** be in front of. **11** meet face to face; defy; oppose. **12** a manner of looking or behaving. **13** *Informal.* an outward appearance of wealth, importance, etc. **14** *Informal.* a person appointed to add respectability or prestige to an enterprise. **15** *Informal.* a person or thing that serves as a cover for illegal activities. **16** the forehead. **17** the face. **18** the dividing surface between two dissimilar air masses: *The weather report says there is a cold front approaching from the northwest.* 1–7, 12–18 *n.*, 8 *adj.*, 9–11 *v.*

**eyes front!** look forward! direct the eyes ahead!
**in front of,** in a place or position before a person or thing: *He stood in front of me.*
☛ *Etym.* From OF *front*, which developed from L *frons, frontis* 'forehead'. This was the original meaning in Old French and Middle English.

**front·age** (frun′tij) **1** the front of a building or of a lot. **2** the length of this front. **3** the direction that the front of a building or lot faces. **4** the land facing a street, river, etc. **5** the land between a building and a street, river, etc. *n.*

**fron·tal** (frun′təl) **1** of, on, in, or at the front: *a frontal attack.* **2** of the forehead: *frontal bones.* **3** a bone of the forehead. 1, 2 *adj.*, 3 *n.*

**front bench** **1** in a legislative chamber, the front seats on either side, reserved for the party leaders. **2** the party leaders.

**fron·tier** (fron tēr′, frun tēr′, or fron′tēr) **1** the farthest part of a settled country, where the wilds begin: *The Yukon is part of Canada's present-day frontier. Frontier life is often harsh.* **2** a part of one country that touches on the border of another; a boundary line or border between two countries. **3** an uncertain or undeveloped region: *the frontiers of science.* *n.*

**fron·tiers·man** (fron tērz′mən *or* frun tērz′mən) a man who lives on the FRONTIER. *n., pl.* **fron·tiers·men** (-zmən).

**fron·tis·piece** (frun′ti spēs′) **1** a picture facing the title page of a book or of a division of a book. **2** a pediment over a door, gate, etc. *n.*

**front·let** (frunt′lit) **1** a band or ornament worn on the forehead. **2** the forehead of an animal. *n.*

**front-page** (frunt′pāj′) suitable for the front page of a newspaper; important. *adj.*

**frost** (frost) **1** a freezing condition; very cold weather; temperature below the point at which water freezes: *There was frost in the air last night.* **2** moisture frozen on or in a solid surface; feathery crystals of ice formed when water vapour in the air condenses at a temperature below freezing: *frost on the grass, frost on windows.* **3** cover with frost. **4** cover with anything that suggests frost; cover with frosting: *The cook frosted the cake.* **5** kill or injure by frost. **6** a coldness of manner or feeling. 1, 2, 6 *n.*, 3–5 *v.* —**frost′less,** *adj.* —**frost′like′** *adj.*

**frost·bite** (frost′bīt′) an injury to a part of the body caused by severe cold: *Experienced skiers take precautions against frostbite.* *n.*

**frost·bit·ten** (frost′bit′ən) injured by severe cold: *My ears were frostbitten.* *adj.*

**frost·ed** (fros′tid) **1** covered with frost: *a frosted window.* **2** finished or decorated with a surface suggesting frost: *frosted glass.* **3** covered with icing: *a frosted cake.* **4** frozen. **5** pt. and pp. of FROST. 1–4 *adj.*, 5 *v.*

**frost·ing** (fros′ting) **1** a mixture of sugar and some liquid, with flavouring, etc., used to cover and decorate a cake; icing. **2** a dull finish on glass, metal, etc. **3** ppr. of FROST. 1, 2 *n.*, 3 *v.*

**frost·y** (fros′tē) **1** cold enough for frost; freezing: *a frosty morning.* **2** covered with frost: *The glass is frosty.* **3** covered with anything like frost. **4** cold in manner or feeling; unfriendly: *a frosty greeting.* **5** hoary or grey, as if covered with frost. *adj.*, **frost·i·er, frost·i·est.** —**frost′i·ly,** *adv.* —**frost′i·ness,** *n.*

**froth** (froth) **1** a mass of very small bubbles; foam: *The bottle of pop had been shaken so much that it was half froth.* **2** give out froth; foam. **3** cover with foam. **4** cause to foam by beating, pouring, etc. **5** something light and trifling; trivial notions, unimportant talk, etc. 1, 5 *n.*, 2–4 *v.*

**froth·y** (froth′ē) **1** of or like froth; foamy: *frothy soapsuds.* **2** light; trifling; shallow; unimportant: *frothy conversation.* *adj.*, **froth·i·er, froth·i·est.** —**froth′i·ness,** *n.*

**frou–frou** (frü′frü′) **1** a swishing sound; rustling, especially of a woman's clothes. **2** *Informal.* fancy or fussy trimmings; frills. *n.*

**fro·ward** (frō′wərd) not easily managed; willful; contrary. *adj.* —**fro′ward·ness,** *n.*

**frown** (froun) **1** a drawing together of the brows, usually in deep thought or disapproval. **2** any expression or show of disapproval. **3** draw the brows together, in deep thought or disapproval: *She frowned, trying to remember the name.* **4** show displeasure or anger. **5** express by frowning: *He frowned his annoyance.* 1, 2 *n.*, 3–5 *v.* —**frown′ing·ly,** *adv.*
**frown on,** disapprove of: *They frown on gambling.*
☛ *Syn.* **Frown** and SCOWL both mean draw the brows together or downward, usually to express a feeling of displeasure. **Frown** is used especially for expressing displeasure at something specific: *The teacher frowned when we came in late.* **Scowl** is used more for looking sullen or sour out of a general feeling of discontent: *He is so disagreeable that he scowls all day.*

**frowz·y** (frou′zē) slovenly; dirty; untidy. *adj.*, **frowz·i·er, frowz·i·est.** —**frowz′i·ly,** *adv.* —**frowz′i·ness,** *n.* Also, **frowsy.**

**froze** (frōz) pt. of FREEZE: *The water in the pond froze.* *v.*

**fro·zen** (frō′zən) **1** turned into ice; hardened by cold: *a* frozen dessert. *The water in the pail was frozen.* **2** very cold: *the frozen north.* **3** kept at a temperature below freezing to prevent spoiling: *frozen foods.* **4** killed or injured by frost: *frozen flowers.* **5** covered or clogged with ice: *a frozen lake, a frozen water main.* **6** too frightened or stiff to move; made motionless as if turned to ice: *frozen to the spot in horror.* **7** without affection or feeling: *a frozen heart.* **8** temporarily forbidden to be sold or exchanged: *frozen assets.* **9** of prices, wages, etc., fixed at a particular amount or level. **10** pp. of FREEZE. 1–9 *adj.*, 10 *v.*

**frt.** freight.

**fruc·ti·fi·ca·tion** (fruk′tə fə kā′shən) **1** a forming or bearing of fruit. **2** the fruit. *n.*

**fruc·ti·fy** (fruk′tə fī′) **1** bear fruit. **2** make fruitful; FERTILIZE. *v.*, **fruc·ti·fied, fruc·ti·fy·ing.**

**fruc·tose** (fruk′tōs) a sugar occurring in three different forms, the best known being fruit sugar. *n.*

**fru·gal** (frü′gəl) **1** avoiding waste; saving; tending to avoid unnecessary spending: *A frugal housekeeper buys and uses food carefully.* **2** costing little; barely sufficient: *She ate a frugal supper of bread and milk.* *adj.* —**fru′gal·ly,** *adv.*

**fru·gal·i·ty** (frü gal′ə tē) thrift; avoidance of waste; a tendency to avoid unnecessary spending. *n., pl.* **fru·gal·i·ties.**

**fruit** (früt) **1** the sweet or tart, fleshy, edible, usually seed-bearing product of a flowering tree, shrub, or vine, usually eaten raw and as a dessert: *Apples, oranges, raspberries, and saskatoons are fruits.* **2** in botany, the part of a plant that contains the seeds: *A fruit is the ripened ovary of a flower and the tissues connected with it. Pea pods, acorns, grains of wheat, cucumbers, tomatoes, etc. are fruits.* **3** the useful product of plants: *the fruits of the earth.* **4** a product; result: *Her invention was the fruit of much effort.* **5** produce or cause to produce fruit. 1–4 *n.*, 5 *v.* —**fruit′like′,** *adj.*

**fruit·age** (frü′tij) **1** the bearing of fruit. **2** fruit; crop of fruit. **3** a product; result. *n.*

**fruit·cake** (früt′kāk′) a rich cake containing preserved fruit, nuts, raisins, spices, etc. *n.*

**fruit cup** mixed fruits served in a cup or glass as an appetizer or a dessert.

**fruit fly** any of various small, two-winged flies whose larvae feed on decaying fruits and vegetables.

**fruit·ful** (früt′fəl) **1** producing or bearing much fruit; productive or fertile: *a fruitful tree, a fruitful garden, fruitful soil.* **2** producing much of anything; especially producing good results: *a fruitful discussion. The trade mission proved to be fruitful.* *adj.* —**fruit′ful·ly,** *adv.* —**fruit′ful·ness,** *n.*

**fru·i·tion** (frü ish′ən) **1** the state of having results; fulfilment; realization: *Her plans have at last come to fruition.* **2** the bearing of fruit. *n.*

**fruit·less** (früt′lis) **1** having no results; useless; unsuccessful: *fruitless efforts.* **2** producing no fruit; barren. *adj.* —**fruit′less·ly,** *adv.*

**fruit nappie** or **nappy** a small bowl or dish in which dessert such as fruit may be served.

**fruit sugar** a crystalline sugar found in sweet fruits and honey; levulose.

**fruit tree** a tree bearing edible fruit.

# frt. 487 frying pan

hat, āge, fär; let, ēqual, tėrm; it, īce
hot, ōpen, ôrder; oil, out; cup, pùt, rüle
əbove, takən, pencəl, lemən, circəs
ch, child; ng, long; sh, ship
th, thin; ᴛʜ, then; zh, measure

**fruit·y** (frü′tē) tasting or smelling like fruit. *adj.*, **fruit·i·er, fruit·i·est.**

**fru·men·ty** (frü′mən tē) hulled wheat boiled in milk and flavoured with sugar, cinnamon, etc. *n.*

**frump** (frump) a dowdy, unattractive woman or girl. *n.*

**frump·ish** (frum′pish) FRUMPY. *adj.*

**frump·y** (frum′pē) dowdy and out of style in general appearance: *a frumpy woman, a frumpy old coat.* *adj.*

**frus·trate** (frus′trāt) **1** bring to nothing; make useless or worthless: *Heavy rain frustrated our plan for a picnic.* **2** prevent from succeeding; oppose successfully; defeat: *to frustrate an opponent.* **3** make discouraged or discontented by preventing the realization of a purpose or desire: *It's very frustrating to stand in line for an hour to get into a movie and then not get seats.* *v.*, **frus·trat·ed, frus·trat·ing.**

**frus·trat·ed** (frus′trā tid) **1** foiled or defeated in one's chosen or desired goal: *He makes a good living as an accountant, but he's actually a frustrated painter.* **2** filled with FRUSTRATION (def. 3); feeling discontented or discouraged because of not being able to fulfil one's desires or purposes: *Everything had gone wrong that day, and by evening she was so frustrated, she couldn't enjoy the show. He's just a frustrated old busybody.* **3** pt. and pp. of FRUSTRATE. 1, 2 *adj.*, 3 *v.*

**frus·tra·tion** (frus trā′shən) **1** the act of frustrating. **2** the state or condition of being frustrated: *After spending two hours trying to find the place, she gave up in frustration.* **3** a feeling of discontent or discouragement, because of not being able to achieve one's desires: *He takes out his frustrations on unsuspecting customers.* **4** something that frustrates: *the frustrations of city driving.* *n.*

**frus·tum** (frus′təm) **1** the part of a cone-shaped solid left after the top has been cut off by a plane parallel to the base. See CONE for picture. **2** the part of a solid between two cutting planes, especially two parallel planes. *n., pl.* **frus·tums** or **frus·ta** (-tə).

**fry¹** (frī) **1** cook in a pan or on a griddle over direct heat, usually in hot fat or oil. **2** undergo frying: *While the hamburgers were frying, he set the table.* **3** fried food; a dish of fried meat, fish, etc. **4** a social gathering at which food is fried and eaten: *a fish fry.* 1, 2 *v.*, **fried, fry·ing;** 3, 4 *n., pl.* **fries.**

**fry²** (frī) **1** the young of fish. **2** small adult fish that live together in large groups, or schools: *Sardines are classed as fry.* **3** young creatures; offspring; children. *n., pl.* **fry.**

**small fry, a** children: *This movie is not for small fry.* **b** people or things having little importance: *The police raid netted only small fry.*

**fry·er** (frī′ər) a chicken young and tender enough for frying: *A fryer usually weighs less than 1.5 kg.* *n.*

**frying pan** a shallow pan with a long handle, used for frying food.

**out of the frying pan into the fire,** straight from one danger or difficulty into a worse one.

**ft.** 1 foot; feet. 2 fort.

**fuch·sia** (fyü′shə) 1 any of a closely related group of mainly tropical shrubs and small trees having showy, funnel-shaped, usually hanging flowers that are rose, purple, or red: *Fuchsias are popular garden flowers, often grown in hanging baskets.* 2 vivid purplish red. *1, 2 n., 2 adj.*

**fud·dle** (fud′əl) 1 make stupid with alcohol; intoxicate. 2 confuse; muddle. *v.,* **fud·dled, fud·dling.**

**fudge** (fuj) 1 a soft candy made of sugar, milk, butter, and a flavouring such as chocolate or caramel. 2 nonsense; empty talk. 3 a word used to express annoyance or disbelief. 4 avoid committing oneself on an issue or coming to grips with a problem; hedge; waffle: *Don't let him fudge on the issue.* 5 put together in a makeshift or dishonest way; fake. *1, 2 n., 3 interj., 4, 5 v.,* **fudged, fudg·ing.**

**fu·el** (fyü′əl) 1 something burned to provide heat or power: *Coal, wood, gas, and oil are fuels.* 2 a material from which atomic energy can be obtained, as in a reactor. 3 material that supplies nutrients for a living organism: *Your body needs fuel to live and grow.* 4 anything that keeps up or increases a feeling: *Her insults were fuel to his hatred.* 5 supply with fuel. 6 get fuel. *1–4 n., 5, 6 v.,* **fu·elled** or **fu·eled, fu·el·ling** or **fu·el·ing.**

**fu·gi·tive** (fyü′jə tiv) 1 a person who is fleeing or who has fled: *a fugitive from justice.* 2 fleeing; having fled; runaway: *a fugitive slave.* 3 lasting only a very short time; passing swiftly: *fugitive thoughts, the fugitive hours.* *1 n., 2, 3 adj.* —**fu′gi·tive·ness,** *n.*

**fugue** (fyüg) in music, a composition based on one or more short themes in which different voices or instruments repeat the same melody at different times with slight variations. *n.*

**–ful** a suffix meaning: 1 full of, as in *cheerful.* 2 characterized by or having the qualities of, as in *careful, masterful.* 3 having a tendency or the ability to, as in *forgetful, harmful, mournful.* 4 enough to fill, as in *cupful, handful.*

**ful·crum** (ful′krəm *or* ful′krəm) the support on which a lever turns or is supported in moving or lifting something. See LEVER for picture. *n., pl.* **ful·crums** or **ful·cra** (-krə).

**ful·fil** or **ful·fill** (ful fil′) 1 carry out a promise, prophecy, etc.; cause to happen or take place. 2 do or perform a duty; obey a command, law, etc. 3 satisfy a requirement, condition, etc.; serve a purpose: *fulfil a need.* 4 finish; complete: *fulfil a contract.* *v.,* **ful·filled, ful·fil·ing.**

**ful·fil·ment** or **ful·fill·ment** (ful fil′mənt) a fulfilling; completion; accomplishment: *Winning the race brought him a feeling of fulfilment.* *n.*

**full** (ful) 1 able to hold no more; with no empty space; filled: *a full cup. The box is full of firewood.* 2 complete; entire: *a full supply, a full treatment. I waited a full hour.* 3 completely; entirely: *Fill the pail full.* 4 of the greatest size, amount, extent, development, etc.: *She was running at full speed. The rose is in full bloom.* 5 more than enough to satisfy: *She ate a full meal.* 6 having had enough food: *a full stomach. He was full after the first course.* 7 very: *He knew full well that he would have to go back.* 8 plump; round; well filled out: *a full face.* 9 having a large amount or number (used with **of**): *Her room was full of toys. The lake is full of fish.* 10 made with a large amount of material, in gathers, folds, pleats, etc.: *a full skirt, full sleeves.* 11 of the highest grade or rank: *a full professor.* 12 of sound, strong and deep; sonorous: *a full alto voice.* 13 squarely; directly: *The blow hit him full in the face.* 14 completely taken up with; absorbed (used with **of**): *He's full of his latest project.* 15 **the full,** the greatest size, amount, etc.: *The moon is past the full.* *1, 2, 4–6, 8–12, 14 adj., 3, 7, 13 adv., 15 n.*

**in full,** a to or for the complete amount: *The account has been paid in full.* b written or said with all the words; not shortened: *Write your name in full.*

**to the full,** completely; entirely: *He satisfied his ambition to the full.*

**full·back** (ful′bak′) in football and other games, a player whose position is farthest behind the front line. *n.*

**full blast** *Informal.* in full operation; at highest speed or largest capacity: *The copy machine has been going full blast all day.*

**full–blood·ed** (ful′blud′id) 1 of pure race, breed, or strain; thoroughbred. 2 vigorous; hearty. *adj.*

**full–blown** (ful′blōn′) 1 in full bloom. 2 completely developed or matured. *adj.*

**full–bod·ied** (ful′bod′ēd) having considerable strength, flavour, etc.: *a full-bodied wine.* *adj.*

**full dress** the formal clothes worn in the evening or on important occasions.

**full–dress** (ful′dres′) 1 having to do with or requiring full dress; formal: *a full-dress reception.* 2 utilizing all resources; all-out; exhaustive: *a full-dress report, a full-dress debate.* *adj.*

**full·er** (ful′ər) a person whose work is cleaning and thickening cloth. *n.*

**fuller's earth** a soft, clay-like mixture used for removing grease from cloth and for purifying oil.

**full–fledged** (ful′flejd′) 1 fully developed. 2 of full rank or standing: *Wai-Ho is now a full-fledged Boy Scout.* *adj.*

**full–grown** (ful′grōn′) fully grown; mature: *a full-grown dog.* *adj.*

**full house** 1 in theatre, the fact or state of every seat being occupied. 2 in poker, a hand made up of three cards of one kind and two of another, such as three sixes and two kings.

**full–length** (ful′length′) 1 showing or for the full length of the human figure: *a full-length portrait, a full-length mirror.* 2 reaching almost to the floor: *full-length windows, a full-length dress.* 3 of traditional or standard size, lengths, duration, etc.: *a full-length novel, a full-length chesterfield.* *adj.*

**full moon** 1 the moon seen as a whole circle. See MOON for picture. 2 the period when this occurs.

**full·ness** (ful′nis) the state or condition of being full: *The bag bulged because of its fullness.* *n.* Also, **fulness.**

**full–rigged** (ful′rigd′) 1 completely equipped with masts and sails. 2 completely equipped. *adj.*

**full sail** 1 with all sails set. 2 with all possible power and energy.

**full–scale** (ful′skāl′) 1 made in the original or actual size: *a full-scale drawing, a full-scale working model.* 2 using or involving all available resources; total or all-out: *a full-scale investigation, full-scale fighting.* *adj.*

**full stop** in punctuation, a period.
**come to a full stop,** end abruptly.

**full swing** 1 full operation; vigorous activity or movement: *The party was in full swing.* 2 with vigour: *She ran full swing.*

**full–time** (fül′tīm′) for the usual or normal length of time. *adj., adv.*

**ful·ly** (fül′ē) 1 in a full manner or degree; completely: *She was now fully awake. He could not fully describe what he had seen.* 2 abundantly; plentifully: *fully covered by insurance.* 3 at least: *It was fully three hours before they could reach her.* *adv.*

**ful·mi·nant** (ful′mə nant) exploding suddenly. *adj.*

**ful·mi·nate** (ful′mə nāt) 1 thunder forth censure, threats, decrees, etc.: *The newspapers fulminated against the crime wave.* 2 denounce violently; censure strongly. 3 explode violently. 4 a violent explosive. 1–3 *v.*, **ful·mi·nat·ed, ful·mi·nat·ing;** 4 *n.*

**ful·mi·na·tion** (ful′mə nā′shən) 1 a violent denunciation; strong censure. 2 a violent explosion. *n.*

**ful·ness** (fül′nis) See FULLNESS. *n.*

**ful·some** (fül′səm) so much as to be disgusting; offensive. *adj.* —**ful′some·ly,** *adv.* —**ful′some·ness,** *n.*

**fum·ble** (fum′bəl) 1 feel or grope about clumsily; search awkwardly: *He fumbled about in his pockets for the ticket. Jane fumbled for words to express her thanks.* 2 handle awkwardly: *He fumbled the introduction.* 3 an awkward groping or handling. 4 fail to catch and hold a ball. 5 a failure to catch and hold a ball. 1, 2, 4 *v.*, **fum·bled, fum·bling;** 3, 5 *n.* —**fum′bler,** *n.* —**fum′bling·ly,** *adv.*

**fume** (fyüm) 1 a vapour, gas, or smoke, especially if harmful, strong, or odorous: *The strong fumes of the acid nearly choked him.* 2 give off fumes: *The candle fumed and sputtered.* 3 pass off in fumes. 4 an angry or irritable mood: *She was obviously in a fume.* 5 be in a state of anger or great irritation: *By the time we got there, he was fuming.* 6 treat with fumes: *to fume oak.* 1, 4 *n.*, 2, 3, 5, 6 *v.*, **fumed, fum·ing.**

**fumed oak** oak darkened and coloured by exposure to ammonia fumes.

**fu·mi·gate** (fyü′mə gāt′) expose to fumes in order to kill vermin or to disinfect: *The whole apartment building needs to be fumigated.* *v.,* **fu·mi·gat·ed, fu·mi·gat·ing.** —**fu′mi·ga′tion,** *n.*

**fu·mi·ga·tor** (fyü′mə gā′tər) 1 a person who fumigates. 2 an apparatus for fumigating. *n.*

**fun** (fun) 1 lively play or playfulness; amusement: *an evening full of fun.* 2 a source of amusement: *That game is a lot of fun.* 3 *Informal.* amusing or entertaining: *It was a fun evening.* 4 ridicule: *He became a figure of fun.* *n.*
**for fun** or **in fun,** not seriously; as a joke; playfully: *The trick was meant in fun.*
**make fun of** or **poke fun at,** laugh at; ridicule.

**func·tion** (fungk′shən) 1 proper work; normal action or use; purpose: *The function of the stomach is to digest food. The program committee has an important function in the club.* 2 work; be used; act: *My new pen does not function very well.* 3 have a function; serve (*as*): *That heavy old china ornament functions as a doorstop then.* 4 a formal public or social gathering for some purpose: *All the dignitaries attended the great function to welcome the Queen.* 5 in mathematics, a quantity whose value depends on, or varies with, the value given to one or more related quantities: *The volume of a sphere is a function of the radius.* 1, 4, 5 *n.*, 2, 3 *v.*

**func·tion·al** (fungk′shə nəl) 1 of or having to do with a function or functions. 2 having a function; working; acting. 3 stressing usefulness instead of beauty: *a functional approach to furniture design.* 4 designed or developed mainly from the point of view of usefulness: *functional clothing.* 5 in medicine, affecting the function of an organ or part of the body, but not its structure: *functional heart disease.* *adj.* —**func′tion·al·ly,** *adv.*

**func·tion·ar·y** (fungk′shə ner′ē) 1 an official. 2 official. 1 *n., pl.* **func·tion·ar·ies;** 2 *adj.*

**fund** (fund) 1 a sum of money set aside for a special purpose: *The school has a fund of $10 000 to buy books with.* 2 a stock or store ready for use; supply: *There is a fund of information in a dictionary.* 3 provide funds for: *A summer recreation program is being funded by the community association.* 4 set aside a sum of money to pay the interest on a debt. 5 change a debt from a short term to a long term. 6 **funds,** *pl.* money available for use: *He had to cancel his trip because he ran out of funds.* 1, 2, 6 *n.,* 3–5 *v.*

**fun·da·men·tal** (fun′də men′təl) 1 of or forming a foundation or basis; essential; basic: *the fundamental principles of design.* 2 a principle, rule, law, etc. that forms a foundation or basis; an essential part: *the fundamentals of grammar.* 3 involving or affecting a basic structure, function, etc.; radical: *a fundamental change of attitude.* 4 principal; main: *The fundamental purpose of her campaign is to block the legislation.* 5 in music, having to do with the lowest note of a chord. 6 in music, the lowest note of a chord. 1, 3–5 *adj.*, 2, 6 *n.* —**fun′da·men′tal·ly,** *adv.*

**fu·ner·al** (fyü′nə rəl *or* fyün′rəl) 1 the ceremonies that accompany the burial or burning of the dead, which usually include holding a religious service and taking the body to the place of burial or burning. 2 the procession taking a dead person's body to the place where it is to be buried or burned. 3 of or suitable for a funeral: *A funeral march is very slow.* *n.*

**funeral director** a person who manages a FUNERAL HOME; undertaker.

**funeral home** a business establishment that makes arrangements for or conducts funeral services and has facilities for preparing the bodies of the dead for burial or cremation.

**funeral parlour** or **parlor** FUNERAL HOME.

**fu·ner·ar·y** (fyü′nə rer′ē) of a FUNERAL or burial: *A funerary urn holds the ashes of a dead person's body.* *adj.*

**fu·ne·re·al** (fyü nē′rē əl) 1 of or suitable for a FUNERAL. 2 sad; gloomy; dismal. *adj.* —**fu·ne′re·al·ly,** *adv.*

**fun fair** 1 a local fund-raising bazaar offering many attractions for children. 2 *Brit.* an amusement park.

---

hat, āge, fär; let, ēqual, tėrm; it, īce
hot, ōpen, ôrder; oil, out; cup, pút, rüle
əbove, takən, pencəl, lemən, circəs
ch, child; ng, long; sh, ship
th, thin; ᴛʜ, then; zh, measure

**fun·gi** (fung′gī *or* fung′gē, fun′jī *or* fun′jē) pl. of FUNGUS. *n.* See FUNGUS for picture.

**fun·gi·cid·al** (fung′gə sī′dəl *or* fun′jə sī′dəl) that destroys FUNGI. *adj.*

**fun·gi·cide** (fung′gə sīd′ *or* fun′jə sīd′) any substance that destroys FUNGI. *n.*

**fun·goid** (fung′goid) resembling a FUNGUS; having spongy, unhealthful growths. *adj.*

**fun·gous** (fung′gəs) **1** of a FUNGUS or fungi; like a fungus; spongy. **2** growing or springing up suddenly, but not lasting. **3** caused by a FUNGUS. *adj.*
☛ Hom. FUNGUS.

Fungi growing on a tree

**fun·gus** (fung′gəs) **1** any of a group of plants without flowers, leaves, or chlorophyll: *Mushrooms, moulds, smuts, and mildews are fungi.* **2** something that grows or springs up rapidly like a mushroom. **3** a diseased, spongy growth on the skin. **4** FUNGOUS. *n., pl.* **fun·gi** *or* **fun·gus·es**.
☛ Hom. FUNGOUS.

**fu·nic·u·lar** (fyü nik′yə lər) of, hanging from, or operated by a rope or cable. A **funicular railway** is a railway system in which the cars are moved by cables. *adj.*

**funk** (fungk) *Informal.* **1** a state of extreme fear; panic. **2** a depressed mood: *He's been in a funk since he and his girlfriend broke up.* **3** be afraid of. **4** frighten. **5** shrink from; shirk. 1, 2 *n.*, 3–5 *v.*

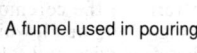
A funnel used in pouring

**fun·nel** (fun′əl) **1** a tapering tube with a wide, cone-shaped mouth, used for pouring a liquid or powder into a container with a small opening: *She used a funnel to pour the gas into the tank.* **2** anything shaped like a funnel. **3** a round metal chimney; smokestack: *The steamship had two funnels.* **4** a flue. **5** pass or feed through a funnel. 1–4 *n.*, 5 *v.*, **fun·nelled** *or* **fun·neled**, **funnel·ling** *or* **fun·nel·ing**.

**fun·ny** (fun′ē) **1** causing laughter; amusing or comical: *a funny story, a funny accident. My little brother was very funny the first time he tried to skate.* **2** trying or intended to amuse: *She was just being funny.* **3** *Informal.* strange; peculiar; odd: *That's funny; I thought I left my wallet right here.* **4** deceptive or tricky: *Don't try anything funny or you might get hurt.* **5 funnies,** *pl.* **a** COMIC STRIPS. **b** a section of a newspaper devoted to comic strips: *Who's got the funnies?* 1–4 *adj.*, **fun·ni·er**, **fun·ni·est;** 5 *n.* —**fun′ni·ly,** *adv.* —**fun′ni·ness,** *n.*

**funny bone** the part of the elbow over which a nerve passes: *When the funny bone is struck, a sharp tingling sensation is felt in the arm and hand.*

**funny paper** *or* **papers** the section of a newspaper containing the COMIC STRIPS.

**fur** (fėr) **1** the thick covering of hair on the skin of certain animals. **2** skin with such hair on it: *Fur is used to make, cover, trim, or line clothing.* **3** make, cover, trim, or line with fur. **4** a furlike coating, such as the whitish matter on the tongue during illness. **5** coat or become coated with such matter. **6** fasten thin strips of wood to beams, walls, etc. to make a support for laths, etc. or to provide air spaces. **7** Usually, **furs,** *pl.* a garment made of fur. 1, 2, 4, 7 *n.*, 3, 5, 6 *v.* **furred, fur·ring.** —**fur′less,** *adj.*
☛ Hom. FIR.

**fur.** **1** furlong. **2** furnished.

**fur·be·low** (fėr′bə lō′) **1** a bit of elaborate trimming: *a dress with many frills and furbelows.* **2** trim in an elaborate way. 1 *n.*, 2 *v.*

**fur·bish** (fėr′bish) **1** brighten by rubbing or scouring; polish. **2** restore to good condition; make usable again (usually used with **up**): *Before going to France, he furbished up his half-forgotten French.* *v.*

**fur brigade** *Cdn.* formerly, a convoy of freight canoes, dog sleds, York boats, etc. that carried furs and other goods from remote trading posts.

**fu·ri·ous** (fyü′rē əs) **1** intensely violent; raging: *a furious storm.* **2** full of wild, fierce anger. **3** of unrestrained energy, speed, etc.: *furious activity.* *adj.* —**fu′ri·ous·ly,** *adv.* —**fu′ri·ous·ness,** *n.*

**furl** (fėrl) **1** roll up; fold up: *to furl a sail, to furl a flag.* **2** the act of furling. 1 *v.*, 2 *n.* —**furl′er,** *n.*

**fur·long** (fėr′long) a unit for measuring distance, equal to one-eighth of a mile (about 0.2 km). *n.*

**fur·lough** (fėr′lō) **1** leave of absence, especially for a soldier. **2** give leave of absence to. 1 *n.*, 2 *v.*

**fur·nace** (fėr′nis) **1** an enclosed structure for providing heat for buildings by warming water or air that circulates through pipes and radiators, hot-air registers, etc. **2** an enclosed structure for providing intense heat for use in separating metal from ore, in treating metal, in producing coke, etc. **3** a very hot place: *The room was a furnace when the windows were closed.* *n.*

**fur·nish** (fėr′nish) **1** supply a room, house, etc. with furniture, equipment, etc.: *We furnished the living room.* **2** supply; provide: *The sun furnishes heat.* *v.* —**fur′nish·er,** *n.*

**fur·nish·ings** (fėr′ni shingz) **1** the furniture or equipment for a room, house, etc. **2** accessories of dress; articles of clothing: *The store sells men's furnishings.* *n. pl.*

**fur·ni·ture** (fėr′nə chər) **1** the movable articles needed in a room, house, etc.: *Beds, chairs, tables, and desks are furniture.* **2** articles needed; equipment: *The harness and ornamental coverings for a horse were called furniture in the Middle Ages.* *n.*

**fu·ror** (fyü′rôr) **1** an outburst of wild enthusiasm or excitement among a group; uproar: *There was a great furor in the crowd when the announcement was made.* **2** an inspired or excited mood: *She wrote the poem in a furor.* **3** fury; rage. *n.*

**furred** (fėrd) **1** having fur. **2** made, covered, trimmed, or lined with fur. **3** wearing fur. **4** coated with matter suggesting fur: *A furred tongue is a sign of illness.* **5** provided with furring strips: *a furred wall.* **6** pt. and pp. of FUR. *1–5 adj., 6 v.*

**fur·ri·er** (fėr′ē ər) **1** a dealer in furs. **2** a person whose work is preparing furs or making and repairing fur garments. *n.*

**fur·ring** (fėr′ing) **1** fur used to make, cover, trim, or line clothing. **2** a coating of matter suggesting fur. **3** the application of thin strips of wood to beams, walls, etc. to make a level support for laths, etc. or to provide air spaces. **4** the strips used for this, also called **furring strips.** **5** ppr. of FUR. *1–4 n., 5 v.*

Furrows cut by ploughshares

**fur·row** (fėr′ō) **1** a long, narrow groove or track cut in the ground by a plough. **2** any long, narrow groove or track: *Heavy trucks made deep furrows in the muddy road.* **3** make furrows in. **4** a wrinkle: *a furrow in one's brow.* **5** wrinkle: *His face was furrowed with age.* *1, 2, 4 n., 3, 5 v.*

**fur·ry** (fėr′ē) **1** consisting of fur. **2** covered with or wearing fur: *a little furry animal.* **3** looking or feeling like fur. *adj.,* **fur·ri·er, fur·ri·est.** —**fur′ri·ness,** *n.*

**fur seal** any of various eared seals highly valued as a source of sealskin because of their thick coats with fine underfur.

**fur·ther** (fėr′ŦHər) **1** farther; more distant: *Our house is on the further side.* **2** at or to a greater distance: *Seek no further for happiness.* **3** to a greater extent: *Inquire further into the matter.* **4** more: *I have no further need of it.* **5** moreover; furthermore; besides: *He said further that he would support us in any way he could.* **6** help forward; promote: *Let us further the cause of peace.* *1, 4 adj., a comparative of* FAR; *2, 3, 5 adv., 6 v.*
☞ *Syn.* See note at FARTHER.

**fur·ther·ance** (fėr′ŦHə rəns) an act of furthering; helping forward; advancement; promotion. *n.*

**fur·ther·more** (fėr′ŦHər môr′) moreover; also; besides. *adv.*

**fur·ther·most** (fėr′ŦHər mōst′) FURTHEST. *adj.*

**fur·thest** (fėr′ŦHist) **1** farthest in space or time. **2** to the greatest degree or extent. *1 adv., 1, 2 adj., a superlative of* FAR.

**fur·tive** (fėr′tiv) **1** done stealthily; secret: *She made a furtive attempt to read her sister's letter.* **2** sly; stealthy; shifty: *The thief had a furtive manner.* *adj.* —**fur′tive·ly,** *adv.* —**fur′tive·ness,** *n.*

**fu·ry** (fyü′rē) **1** wild, fierce anger; a rage. **2** violence; fierceness: *the fury of a hurricane.* **3** a raging or violent person. *n., pl.* **fu·ries.**
**like fury,** *Informal.* violently; very rapidly.

**furze** (fėrz) **1** a low, prickly, European evergreen shrub of the pea family having yellow flowers, common on wastelands; gorse. **2** any of several related plants. *n.*

---

hat, āge, fär; let, ēqual, tėrm; it, īce
hot, ōpen, ôrder; oil, out; cup, pùt, rüle
əbove, takən, pencəl, lemən, circəs
ch, child; ng, long; sh, ship
th, thin; ŦH, then; zh, measure

**fuse¹** (fyüz) **1** a safety device in an electric circuit, consisting of a metal strip or wire that melts and breaks the connection when the current becomes dangerously strong. **2** a slow-burning wick or other device to detonate dynamite, a shell, a bomb, etc.: *Firecrackers have fuses.* *n.*

**fuse²** (fyüz) **1** melt; melt together: *The wax from the two candles fused as they burned.* **2** blend; unite. *v.,* **fused, fus·ing.**

**fu·see** (fyü zē′) a coloured flare used as a warning signal. *n.*

**fu·se·lage** (fyü′zə läzh′ *or* fyü′zə lij) the body of an aircraft that holds passengers, cargo, etc.: *The wings and tail are attached to the fuselage.* See AIRPLANE for picture. *n.*

**fu·sel oil** (fyü′zəl) a sharp or bitter, poisonous, oily liquid that occurs in alcoholic liquors when they are not distilled enough.

**fu·si·bil·i·ty** (fyü′zə bil′ə tē) being FUSIBLE. *n.*

**fu·si·ble** (fyü′zə bəl) that can be fused or melted. *adj.*

**fu·si·form** (fyü′zə fôrm′) rounded and tapering from the middle toward each end; spindle-shaped: *A milkweed pod is somewhat fusiform.* *adj.*

**fu·sil** (fyü′zəl) a light flintlock musket. *n.*

**fu·sil·ier** (fyü′zə lēr′) **1** formerly, a soldier armed with a light flintlock musket called a fusil. **2** a private soldier in a regiment that used to be armed with fusils. *n.*

**fu·sil·lade** (fyü′zə lād′) **1** a discharge of many firearms at the same time or in rapid succession. **2** attack or shoot down by a fusillade. **3** something that resembles a fusillade: *The reporters greeted the mayor with a fusillade of questions.* *1, 3 n., 2 v.,* **fu·sil·lad·ed, fu·sil·lad·ing.**

**fu·sion** (fyü′zhən) **1** a melting; melting together; fusing: *Bronze is made by the fusion of copper and tin.* **2** a blending or union: *A new party was formed by the fusion of two political groups.* **3** a fused mass. **4** in nuclear physics, the combining of nuclei of light elements to create nuclei of greater mass: *The fusion of the nuclei of certain light elements releases tremendous amounts of energy, which can be used in nuclear bombs.* *n.*

**fusion bomb** HYDROGEN BOMB.

**fu·sion·ist** (fyü′zhə nist) a person taking part in a union of political parties or factions. *n.*

**fuss** (fus) **1** much bother about small matters; useless talk and worry: *Why make a fuss over the loss of a dime?* **2** make a fuss: *Nervously she fussed about her work.* **3** make nervous or worried; bother. *1 n., 2, 3 v.* —**fuss′er,** *n.*

**fuss·y** (fus′ē) **1** inclined to fuss; hard to please; very particular: *A sick person is sometimes fussy about food.* **2** much trimmed; elaborately made: *fussy clothes.* **3** full of details; requiring much care. *adj.,* **fuss·i·er, fuss·i·est.** —**fuss′i·ly,** *adv.* —**fuss′i·ness,** *n.*

**fus·tian** (fus′chən) **1** a coarse, heavy cloth made of

cotton and flax: *Fustian was used for clothing in Europe throughout the Middle Ages.* **2** a thick cotton cloth like corduroy. **3** pompous, high-sounding language. *n.*

**fus·tic** (fus′tik) **1** a tropical American tree of the mulberry family. **2** the wood of this tree, which yields a yellow dye. **3** this dye. *n.*

**fust·y** (fus′tē) **1** having a stale smell; musty; mouldy; stuffy. **2** old-fashioned; out-of-date: *fusty opinions.* *adj.*, **fust·i·er, fust·i·est.** —**fust′i·ly**, *adv.* —**fust′i·ness**, *n.*

**fut.** future.

**fu·tile** (fyü′tīl *or* fyü′təl) not successful; useless: *Hannah made a futile attempt to solve the puzzle.* *adj.* —**fu′tile·ly**, *adv.*

**fu·til·i·ty** (fyü til′ə tē) **1** uselessness. **2** a useless action, event, etc. *n., pl.* **fu·til·i·ties.**

**fu·ton** (fü′ton *or* fyü′ton) a Japanese padded quilt that can be placed on the floor to sleep on: *Futons have become popular in Canada.* *n.*

**fut·tock** (fut′ək) one of the curved timbers that form the middle of a rib in a ship. *n.*

**fu·ture** (fyü′chər) **1** the time to come; the days, years, etc. ahead: *She has not done very well so far but hopes to do better in the future.* **2** what is to come; what will be: *She claims she can foretell the future.* **3** coming; that is to come; that will be: *They wished him happiness in his future years.* **4** a chance or expectation of success and prosperity: *a young woman with a future.* **5** in grammar, of, having to do with, or being a verb tense that indicates time to come. *Will go* is the future tense of *go.* **6** a FUTURE TENSE or future verb form. **7 futures**, *pl.* commodities or stocks bought or sold to be received or delivered at a future date. 1, 2, 4, 6, 7 *n.*, 3, 5 *adj.*

**future perfect** the form of a verb which shows that an action will be completed in the future: *Example: They will have finished their work next week.*

**future tense** a verb form that expresses occurrence in time to come.

**fu·tur·ism** (fyü′chə riz′əm) **1** a movement in art, literature, and music that began in Italy in the early 20th century, and that rejected traditional forms and methods in an attempt to express the violence, speed, and noise of contemporary civilization. **2** the practice or policy of concentrating on predictions of what will happen in the future as the basis for present-day decisions and actions. *n.*

**fu·tur·ist** (fyü′chə rist) **1** a person who practises or studies FUTURISM. **2** of or having to do with FUTURISM or the future. 1 *n.*, 2 *adj.*

**fu·tur·is·tic** (fyü′chə ris′tik) **1** of or having to do with the future or what is thought of as characteristic of the future: *a futuristic movie, set in the year 2050. The display featured futuristic designs in furnishings.* **2** of or having to do with FUTURISM. *adj.*

**fu·tu·ri·ty** (fyü chü′rə tē *or* fyü tyü′rə tē) **1** the time to come; future. **2** a future state or event. **3** the quality of being future. *n., pl.* **fu·tu·ri·ties.**

**fuzz** (fuz) **1** loose, fine, light fibres or hairs; fluff or down: *Peaches and some caterpillars are covered with fuzz.* **2** become fuzzy: *This blanket is fuzzing.* **3** make fuzzy. 1 *n.*, 2, 3 *v.*

**fuzz·y** (fuz′ē) **1** of fuzz: *The baby's hair was just a fuzzy halo.* **2** like fuzz: *My hair gets fuzzy when it's humid outside.* **3** covered with fuzz: *a fuzzy caterpillar.* **4** not clear or distinct; blurred or imprecise: *Everything looks fuzzy when I don't have my glasses on. That argument is an example of fuzzy thinking.* *adj.*, **fuzz·i·er, fuzz·i·est.** —**fuzz′i·ly**, *adv.* —**fuzz′i·ness**, *n.*

**fwd.** forward.

**–fy** a verb-forming suffix meaning: **1** make or make into; cause to be, as in *simplify, intensify, pacify, horrify.* **2** become, as in *solidify, putrify.*

# G g  G g

hat, āge, fär; let, ēqual, tėrm; it, īce
hot, āge, ôrder; oil, out; cup, pút, rüle
above, taken, pencəl, lemən, circəs
ch, child; ng, long; sh, ship
th, thin; ŦH, then; zh, measure

**g or G** (jē)  **1** the seventh letter of the English alphabet. **2** any speech sound represented by this letter.  **3** in music: **a** the fifth tone in the scale of C major.  **b** a symbol representing this tone.  **c** a key, string, etc. of a musical instrument that produces this tone.  **d** the scale or key that has G as its keynote.  **4** any person or thing classed as the seventh in a series.  *n., pl.* **g's** or **G's**.

**g.** or **g**  **1** gravity.  **2** guinea.  **3** gauge.  **4** genitive. **5** gender.

**G**  **1** German.  **2** giga- (an SI prefix).

**G.**  **1** gravity.  **2** German.  **3** Gulf.

**Ga**  gallium.

**gab** (gab) *Informal.*  **1** chatter; gabble; idle talk.  **2** talk too much; chatter; gabble.  1 *n.,* 2 *v.,* **gabbed, gab·bing. gift of the gab,**  fluency of speech; glibness.

**gab·ar·dine** (gab′ər dēn′)  **1** a closely woven woollen, cotton, or rayon cloth having small, diagonal ribs on its surface, used for raincoats, suits, etc.  **2** a garment of gabardine.  *n.*  Also, **gaberdine.**

**gab·ble** (gab′əl)  **1** make unintelligible or animal sounds: *They heard the geese gabbling in the yard.*  **2** talk rapidly, without making much sense: *She was gabbling on excitedly about a fire she had seen.*  **3** rapid, nonsensical talk or unintelligible sounds: *the gabble of geese.*  1, 2 *v.,* **gab·bled, gab·bling;**  3 *n.*  —**gab′bler,** *n.*

**gab·by** (gab′ē) *Informal.*  very talkative.  *adj.,* **gab·bier, gab·bi·est.**

**gab·er·dine** (gab′ər dēn′)  **1** a man's long, loose coat or cloak worn in the Middle Ages, especially by Jews. **2** See GABARDINE.  *n.*

Green Gables, the farm house near Cavendish, P.E.I. that is featured in *Anne of Green Gables,* by L.M. Montgomery

**ga·ble** (gā′bəl)  **1** the end of a ridged roof, with the triangular upper part of the wall that it covers.  **2** an end wall topped by a gable.  **3** a triangular ornament or canopy over a door, window, etc. See FRETWORK for picture.  *n.*

**ga·bled** (gā′bəld)  built with a gable or gables; having or forming gables.  *adj.*

**gable roof**  a ridged roof that forms a gable at each end. See ROOF for picture.

**gable window**  **1** a window in a GABLE (def. 1).  **2** a window with an ornamental GABLE (def. 3) over it.

**gad**[1] (gad)  **1** go about looking for pleasure or excitement: *She was always gadding about town.*  **2** move about restlessly.  *v.,* **gad·ded, gad·ding.**  —**gad′der,** *n.*

**gad**[2] (gad)  GOAD.  *n., v.*

**gad·a·bout** (gad′ə bout′) *Informal.*  **1** a person who goes about looking for pleasure or excitement.  **2** a person fond of going from place to place.  *n.*

**gad·fly** (gad′flī′)  **1** any of several large flies that sting cattle, horses, etc.: *The horsefly and botfly are gadflies.* **2** a person who irritates others or rouses them from a state of self-satisfaction by calling attention to their faults, etc. *n., pl.* **gad·flies.**

**gadg·et** (gaj′it) *Informal.*  a small mechanical, electrical, or electronic device or contrivance; any ingenious device: *She's always buying gadgets for her car; the latest one is a coffee maker that plugs into the lighter.*  *n.*

**gad·o·lin·i·um** (gad′ə lin′ē əm)  a rare magnetic metallic element.  Symbol: Gd  *n.*

**Gael** (gāl)  **1** a Scottish Highlander.  **2** a Celt who is a native or inhabitant of Scotland, Ireland, or the Isle of Man.  *n.*
☞ *Hom.* GALE.

**Gael·ic** (gā′lik; *also, esp. Scottish,* gä′lik)  **1** of or having to do with the Gaels, especially the Scottish Highlanders, or their language.  **2** the language of the Gaels: *Gaelic is a Celtic language, related to Welsh.*  1 *adj.,* 2 *n.*

**gaff** (gaf)  **1** a strong hook or barbed spear for pulling large fish out of the water.  **2** hook or pull a fish out of the water with a gaff.  **3** a sharp metal spur fastened to the leg of a gamecock.  **4** a spar or pole extending along the upper edge of a fore-and-aft sail. See SLOOP for picture.  1, 3, 4 *n.,* 2 *v.*

**gaf·fer** (gaf′ər) *Informal.*  **1** an old man.  **2** the chief electrician on a television program or motion picture. *n.*

**gaff·top·sail** (gaf′top′sāl′ *or* gaf′top′səl)  a topsail set above a GAFF (def. 4).  *n.*

**gag** (gag)  **1** something thrust into a person's mouth to keep him or her from talking, crying out, etc.  **2** keep from talking, crying out, etc. by means of a gag: *The bandits tied the watchman's arms and gagged him.* **3** anything used to silence a person; restraint or hindrance to free speech.  **4** force to keep silent; restrain or hinder from free speech.  **5** choke or strain in an effort to vomit.  **6** cause to choke or strain in an effort to vomit. **7** *Informal.*  a joke; something said to cause a laugh; an amusing trick: *The comedian's gags made the audience laugh.*  1, 3, 7 *n.,* 2, 4–6 *v.,* **gagged, gag·ging.**  —**gag′ger,** *n.*

**gage** (gāj)  See GAUGE.  *n., v.,* **gaged, gag·ing.** —**gage′a·ble,** *adj.*  —**gag′er,** *n.*
☞ *Hom.* GAUGE.

**gag·gle** (gag′əl)  **1** a flock of geese.  **2** of geese, cackle.  **3** *Informal.*  a group or cluster of people: *A gaggle of autograph hunters waited outside the door.*  1, 3 *n.,* 2 *v.,* **gag·gled, gag·gling.**

**gai·e·ty** (gā′ə tē)  **1** cheerful liveliness; merriment: *Her gaiety helped the party.*  **2** lively entertainment.  **3** bright appearance; showiness; finery: *gaiety of dress.*  *n., pl.* **gai·e·ties.**  Also, **gayety.**

**gai·ly** (gā′lē)  **1** in a gay manner; happily; merrily: *She* ran gaily to meet them. *The children chattered gaily.* **2** brightly; showily: *The room was gaily decorated.* *adv.* Also, **gayly**.

**gain** (gān) **1** get; obtain; secure: *The king gained possession of more lands.* **2** an increase in profit or advantage: *He has made a substantial gain over his opponent in this competition.* **3** get as an increase, addition, advantage, or profit: *How much did I gain by that?* **4** getting wealth: *Greed is love of gain.* **5** an increase in amount or degree: *a gain in speed, a gain of ten percent.* **6** make progress; advance; improve: *The sick child is gaining and will soon be well.* **7** win; be the victor in: *gain the prize; gain the battle.* **8** get to; arrive at; reach: *The swimmer gained the shore.* **9** of a timepiece, run too fast: *My watch gains about six minutes a week.* **10 gains,** *pl.* profits; earnings; winnings. 1, 3, 6–9 *v.*, 2, 4, 5, 10 *n.*

**gain on, a** come closer to; get nearer to: *The pirate ship was slowly gaining on them.* **b** advance in competition with: *We are beginning to gain on our competitors in business.*

**gain·er** (gā′nər) **1** one that gains. **2** a fancy dive in which the diver turns a back somersault in the air. *n.*

**gain·ful** (gān′fəl) bringing in money or advantage; profitable. *adj.* —**gain′ful·ly,** *adv.*

**gait** (gāt) **1** the kind of step used in walking or running: *A gallop is one of the gaits of a horse.* **2** a way of walking or running: *He has a lame gait because of an injured foot.* *n.*
☛ Hom. GATE.

**gait·ed** (gā′tid) having a certain gait: *heavy-gaited oxen.* *adj.*

**gai·ter** (gā′tər) **1** a cloth or leather covering for the lower leg and ankle, held on by buckles or buttons on the side and, often, a strap under the foot; leggings: *Gaiters were worn by men especially in the 19th and early 20th centuries.* **2** an ankle-high shoe with an elastic insert in each side and no laces. See SHOE for picture. *n.*

**gal** (gal) a unit in geodesy and geophysics for measuring acceleration due to gravity. It is equal to one centimetre per second per second (1 cm/s²).
☛ *Etym.* After *Galileo* (1564–1642), Italian mathematician, astronomer, and physicist.

**gal.** gallon; gallons.

**ga·la** (gā′lə *or* gal′ə) **1** a festive occasion; festival. **2** of, for, or involving festivity: *a gala occasion.* *n.*

**ga·lac·tic** (gə lak′tik) in astronomy, of or having to do with a GALAXY of stars, especially the Milky Way. *adj.*

**galactic cluster** any diffuse group of stars, usually numbering over a hundred, such as the Pleiades.

**Gal·a·had** (gal′ə had′) **1** in the legends about King Arthur, the noblest and purest knight of the Round Table: *Sir Galahad was the only knight who was allowed to look into the Holy Grail.* **2** any man considered to be very noble and pure. *n.*

**gal·an·tine** (gal′ən tēn′) veal, chicken, or other white meat boned, boiled, and seasoned, and then served cold in its own jelly. *n.*

**gal·ax·y** (gal′ək sē) **1** in astronomy, any of the many systems or groupings of stars making up the universe: *A galaxy may contain millions or billions of stars.* **2** a brilliant or splendid group: *The queen was followed by a galaxy of brave knights and fair ladies.* **3 Galaxy,** the Milky Way, the faintly luminous band of countless stars that stretches across the sky. *n., pl.* **gal·ax·ies**.

**gale¹** (gāl) **1** a very strong wind. **2** a wind with a velocity of 55–88 km/h (28–47 knots): *Winds of gale force are represented by numbers 7 to 9 on the Beaufort scale.* **3** a noisy outburst: *gales of laughter.* *n.*
☛ Hom. GAEL.

**gale²** (gāl) SWEET GALE, a shrub that grows in marshy places. *n.*
☛ Hom. GAEL.

**ga·le·na** (gə lē′nə) a grey metallic ore consisting of lead sulphide: *Galena is the most important lead ore.* *n.*

**gall¹** (gol) **1** a bitter yellow, brown, or greenish liquid secreted by the liver and stored in the gall bladder; bile. **2** anything very bitter or harsh. **3** bitterness; hate: *Her heart was filled with gall.* **4** *Informal.* too great boldness; impudence: *He had a lot of gall talking to his employer in such a nasty way.* *n.*

**gall²** (gol) **1** make or become sore by rubbing: *The rough strap galled the horse's skin.* **2** a sore spot on the skin caused by rubbing. **3** annoy; irritate: *The boy's continual interruptions galled his teacher.* **4** a cause of annoyance or irritation. 1, 3 *v.*, 2, 4 *n.*

**gall³** (gol) a growth, or tumour, on the leaves, stems, or roots of plants, caused by insects, fungi, bacteria, etc.: *The galls of oak trees contain tannic acid, used in making ink, medicine, etc.* *n.*

**gal·lant** (gal′ənt *for 1–3*; gə lant′, gə lont′ *or* gal′ənt *for 4–7*) **1** noble; brave; daring: *King Arthur was a gallant knight. They made a gallant effort to save the building.* **2** grand; fine; stately: *a gallant ship.* **3** showy in dress or appearance. **4** very polite and attentive to women. **5** a man who is very polite and attentive to women. **6** amorous. **7** lover. 1–4, 6 *adj.*, 5, 7 *n.*
—**gal′lant·ly,** *adv.* —**gal′lant·ness,** *n.*

**gal·lant·ry** (gal′ən trē) **1** noble spirit or conduct; bravery; dashing courage. **2** great politeness and attention to women. **3** a gallant act or speech. *n., pl.* **gal·lant·ries**.

**gall bladder** a sac attached to the liver, in which excess bile is stored until needed.

A galleon

**gal·le·on** (gal′yən *or* gal′ē ən) a large, heavy sailing ship, usually having three or four decks, used in Europe as a warship and armed trading ship, especially from the 15th to the end of the 16th century: *The Spaniards used many galleons in the fleet of the Armada.* *n.*

**gal·ler·y** (gal′ə rē) **1** a long, narrow platform or passage projecting from the wall of a building. **2** a projecting upper floor in a church, theatre, or hall with seats or room for part of the audience; balcony. **3** the highest floor of this kind in a theatre. **4** the people who sit in the highest balcony of a theatre. **5** a group of people watching or listening. **6** a long, narrow room or passage; hall. **7** a covered walk or porch. **8** an underground passage. **9** a room or building where works of art are shown: *an art gallery.* **10** a collection of works of art. **11** a room or building where photographs are taken, shooting is practised, etc. *n., pl.* **gal·ler·ies.**

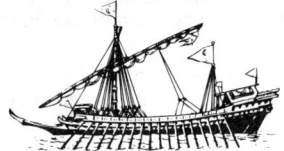
A medieval galley

**gal·ley** (gal′ē) **1** a long, low ship propelled mainly by one or more banks of oars, used in ancient and medieval times as a warship and a trading ship. Ancient galleys sometimes carried a square sail. The medieval Mediterranean galleys had a large LATEEN sail. **2** the kitchen of a ship or aircraft. **3** in printing, a shallow oblong tray for holding type that has been set. **4** a proof taken from the type in a galley, used to make corrections before the type is made up into pages. *n., pl.* **gal·leys.**

**galley proof** GALLEY (def. 4).

**galley slave** **1** a person compelled or condemned to row a GALLEY (def. 1). **2** a drudge.

**gall·fly** (gol′flī′) any of various small insects that deposit their eggs on plants and cause GALLS[3] that the larvae feed on. *n., pl.* **gall·flies.**

**Gal·lic** (gal′ik) **1** of or having to do with Gaul or its people. **2** French. *adj.*

**gal·lic acid** (gal′ik) an acid obtained especially from GALLS[3] on plants, used in making ink, dyes, etc.

**Gal·li·cism** or **gal·li·cism** (gal′ə siz′əm) **1** a French idiom or expression. **2** a French trait or characteristic. *n.*

**gal·li·na·ceous** (gal′ə nā′shəs) of or having to do with an order of heavy-bodied birds that nest on the ground and fly only short distances, including chickens, turkeys, pheasants, and grouse. *adj.*

**gall·ing** (gol′ing) bitterly disappointing; very annoying or irritating: *a galling defeat at the hands of an inferior opponent. adj.*

**gal·li·nule** (gal′ə nyül′ *or* gal′ə nül′) any of several species of marsh bird of the rail family found throughout the world, having long thin toes and a fleshy shield on the forehead. *n.*

**gal·li·pot** (gal′ə pot′) a small pot or jar of glazed earthenware: *Gallipots were used by druggists to hold medicine, salve, etc. n.*

**gal·li·um** (gal′ē əm) a shiny, soft, bluish-white metallic element similar to mercury, with a low melting point: *Gallium is used as a substitute for mercury in thermometers.* Symbol: Ga  *n.*

**gal·li·vant** (gal′ə vant′) travel or roam for pleasure: *They're gallivanting around Europe this summer. v.*

**gall·nut** (gol′nut′) a nutlike GALL[3] on plants. *n.*

**gal·lon** (gal′ən) a unit for measuring liquids, equal to 4 quarts: *The traditional Canadian gallon was equal to about 4.55 dm$^3$; the United States gallon is equal to about 3.79 dm$^3$. n.*

**gal·lop** (gal′əp) **1** a fast gait of a horse or other four-footed animal: *In a gallop all four feet are off the ground together once in each stride.* **2** ride at a gallop: *The cowboy galloped across the field.* **3** a ride taken at

# galley 495 gamble

hat, āge, fär; let, ēqual, tėrm; it, īce
hot, ōpen, ôrder; oil, out; cup, pùt, rüle
əbove, takən, pencəl, lemən, circəs
ch, child; ng, long; sh, ship
th, thin; ₮H, then; zh, measure

this gait. **4** go at a gallop: *The pony galloped up to the fence.* **5** cause to gallop: *Dino galloped his horse down the road.* **6** go very fast; hurry: *She came galloping downstairs to tell us the news.* 1, 3 *n.*, 2, 4–6 *v.*  —**gal′lop·er,** *n.*

**gal·lows** (gal′ōz) **1** a wooden frame made of a crossbar on two upright posts, used for hanging criminals. **2 the gallows,** punishment by hanging: *Many people are against the gallows. n., pl.* **gal·lows** or **gal·lows·es.**

**gall·stone** (gol′stōn′) a pebble-like mass that forms in the GALL BLADDER or its duct: *When one or more gallstones stop the flow of bile, a painful illness results. n.*

**Gal·lup poll** (gal′əp) a poll or opinion on social and political issues, etc., taken from a selected group of people and intended to reflect the opinion of the general public.

**ga·lore** (gə lôr′) in abundance: *There were flowers galore all over the house from friends and family. adv.*
☞ *Etym.* From Irish *go leór* or Scots Gaelic *gu leóir* 'enough; plenty'.
☞ *Usage.* Galore must follow the noun it is attached to.

**ga·losh** (gə losh′) a high overshoe having a rubber or plastic sole and a rubber, plastic, or fabric top, worn in wet or snowy weather (*usually used in the plural*): *I hate wearing galoshes. n.*

**gal·van·ic** (gal van′ik) **1** producing a direct current of electricity, especially by chemical action. **2** of or caused by an electric current. **3** affecting as if by GALVANISM; startling or stimulating: *a galvanic personality.* **4** produced as if by an electric shock: *a galvanic reaction. adj.*

**gal·va·nism** (gal′və niz′əm) **1** a direct electrical current, especially one produced by chemical action. **2** in medicine, the use of such electricity to stimulate muscles and nerves. *n.*

**gal·va·nize** (gal′və nīz′) **1** apply an electric current to. **2** arouse suddenly; startle: *The whole country was galvanized by the threat of war.* **3** cover iron or steel with a thin coating of zinc to prevent rust. *v.,* **gal·va·nized, gal·va·niz·ing.** —**gal′va·ni·za′tion,** *n.*

**galvanized iron** iron covered with a thin coating of zinc, which resists rust.

**gal·va·nom·e·ter** (gal′və nom′ə tər) an instrument for detecting and measuring a small electric current. *n.*

**gal·va·no·scope** (gal′və nə skōp′ *or* gal van′ə skōp′) an instrument for detecting very small electric currents and showing their direction. *n.*

**gam·bit** (gam′bit) **1** a way of opening a game of chess by purposely sacrificing a pawn or a piece to gain some advantage. **2** any rather risky move or strategem intended to gain an advantage: *His opening gambit was to call for an investigation.* **3** any opening move, such as in a conversation. *n.*

**gam·ble** (gam′bəl) **1** play games of chance for money or some other prize or stake. **2** take a risk in order to gain some advantage: *She decided to gamble by refusing the job offer and hoping for a better one.* **3** a risky venture or undertaking: *Investing money in newly discovered mines is a*

**gambler**     **496**     **gander**

*gamble.*   **4** bet; wager.   **5** lose or squander by gambling (*used with* **away**): *He gambled away his inheritance.*   1, 2, 4, 5 *v.,* **gam·bled, gam·bling;**   3, 4 *n.*
**gamble on,**   be sure of (*used only in negatives or questions*): *You can't gamble on getting that job.*
☛ *Hom.*   GAMBOL.

**gam·bler** (gam′blər)   a person who GAMBLES a great deal, especially one who lives on money won in games of chance.   *n.*

**gam·bling** (gam′bling)   **1** the playing of games of chance for money or some other prize or stake.   **2** the taking of risks in order to gain some advantage.   **3** ppr. of GAMBLE.   1, 2 *n.,* 3 *v.*

**gam·bol** (gam′bəl)   **1** a running and jumping about in play; caper; frolic.   **2** frisk about; run and jump about in play: *Lambs gambolled in the meadow.*   1 *n.,* 2 *v.,* **gam·bolled** or **gam·boled, gam·bol·ling** or **gam·bol·ing.**
☛ *Hom.*   GAMBLE.

**gambrel roof** (gam′brəl)   a two-sided roof having two slopes on each side, with the lower slope steeper than the upper one. See ROOF for picture.

**game**¹ (gām)   **1** an activity done for entertainment or amusement; a way of playing: *Football, solitaire, and chess are games.*   **2** the equipment, etc. necessary to play a particular game, especially any of various table games: *We got several games for Christmas.*   **3** a physical or mental exercise with certain rules, played either alone or with another person or group, and often involving competition: *a game of tag. Are you going to the game tonight?*   **4** any one of a number of contests making up a set or series: *The tennis champion won four games out of six.*   **5** the condition of the score in a game: *At the end of the first period the game was 6 to 3 in our favour.*   **6** the number of points required to win.   **7** a particular manner of playing: *She plays a good game.*   **8** any activity or undertaking that is carried on as if under set rules and that tests one's skill or endurance: *the game of life, the game of diplomacy.*   **9** *Informal.*   any business venture, profession, etc.: *the acting game.*   **10** a plan or scheme: *He tried to trick us, but we saw through his game.*   **11** what is hunted or pursued.   **12** wild animals, birds, or fish hunted or caught for sport or for food.   **13** the flesh of wild animals or birds used for food.   **14** having to do with game hunting, or fishing: *Game laws protect wildlife.* **15** brave; plucky: *The losing team put up a game fight.* **16** having spirit or will enough: *The explorer was game for any adventure.*   **17** gamble.   1–13 *n.,* 14–16 *adj.,* **gam·er, gam·est;**   17 *v.,* **gamed, gam·ing.**  —**game′ly,** *adv.* —**game′ness,** *n.*
**die game,**   die fighting; die bravely.
**make game of,**   make fun of; laugh at; ridicule.
**play the game,** *Informal.*   follow the rules; be a good sport.
**the game is up,** *Informal.*   the plan or scheme has failed.

**game**² (gām)   lame; crippled; injured: *The veteran had a game leg.*   *adj.*

**game bag**   **1** a bag for carrying game that has been killed.   **2** the amount of game killed.

**game bird**   a bird hunted for sport or food.

**game·cock** (gām′kok′)   a rooster bred and trained for fighting: *Fighting with gamecocks is against the law in Canada.*   *n.*

**game fish**   a fish that fights to get away when hooked: *Trout are considered game fish; suckers are not.*

**game fowl**   a fowl of a breed trained for fighting.

**game·keep·er** (gām′kē′pər)   a person employed to breed and look after game animals and birds on an estate and to prevent anyone from stealing them or killing them without permission.   *n.*

**game law**   a law made to restrict and regulate hunting and fishing in order to preserve or protect game animals, birds, and fish.

**game of chance**   any game depending on luck, not skill.

**game·some** (gām′səm)   full of play; sportive; ready to play.   *adj.* —**game′some·ly,** *adv.*

**game·ster** (gām′stər)   GAMBLER.   *n.*

**gam·ete** (gam′ēt *or* gə mēt′)   a mature reproductive cell capable of uniting with another to form a fertilized cell that can develop into a new plant or animal: *Gametes are produced by a special type of cell division called meiosis; each gamete has only half the number of chromosomes of other body cells.*   *n.*

**game warden**   an official whose duty is to enforce the game laws in a certain district.

**gam·in** (gam′ən)   **1** a neglected boy left to roam about the streets; urchin.   **2** any small, lively person.   **3** like an urchin; impudent.   *n.*
☛ *Hom.*   GAMMON.

**gam·ine** (gam ēn′)   a slender young woman who looks and behaves a little like a boy.   *n.*

**gam·ing** (gā′ming)   **1** the playing of games of chance for money; GAMBLING (def. 1).   **2** ppr. of GAME.   1 *n.,* 2 *v.*

**gam·ma** (gam′ə)   **1** the third letter of the Greek alphabet (Γ, γ = English G, g).   **2** the third in any series or group.   *n.*

**gamma glob·u·lin** (glob′yə lin)   in chemistry, the constituent of blood plasma that contains the most antibodies and is often used for temporary immunization against infectious diseases such as measles and hepatitis.

**gamma rays**   in physics, electromagnetic radiation of very high frequency and great penetrating power, given off by radio-active substances: *Gamma rays are similar to X rays, but shorter in wave length.*

**gam·mon** (gam′ən)   **1** the lower end of a side of bacon.   **2** a smoked or cured ham.   *n.*
☛ *Hom.*   GAMIN.

**gam·ut** (gam′ət)   **1** in music, the whole series of recognized notes.   **2** the complete scale of any key, especially the major scale.   **3** the entire range of anything: *This book covers the whole gamut of poetry from children's rhymes to 'Paradise Lost'.*
**run the gamut,**   go through the whole range of something.

**gam·y** (gā′mē)   **1** having a taste or smell characteristic of the meat of wild animals or birds when it is too strong, as when the meat is tainted or improperly cooked. **2** especially of animals, brave or plucky.   **3** scandalous or racy.   *adj.,* **gam·i·er, gam·i·est.**  —**gam′i·ly,** *adv.* —**gam′i·ness,** *n.*

**gan·der** (gan′dər)   **1** an adult male goose.   **2** a fool; simpleton.   *n.*
**take a gander,** *Informal.*   take a look: *Take a gander at that outfit.*   *n.*

**Ga·nesh·a** (gə nā′shə)   in Hinduism, the god of success.   *n.*

**gang** (gang)   **1** a group of people acting or going around together, especially for criminal or other purposes generally considered antisocial.   **2** a group of people working together under one supervisor: *Two gangs of workers were repairing the road.*   **3** a group of people closely associated for social purposes: *Let's have the gang over for coffee after the show.*   **4** a set of tools, machines, or components arranged to work together: *a gang plough.*   **5** *Informal.*   form a gang.   **6** *Informal.*   attack in a gang.   1–4 *n.*, 5, 6 *v.*
**gang up,**   come together into a group for some purpose: *We ganged up to give a party for our coach.*
**gang up on,**   oppose as a group: *Let's gang up on that bully.*

**gan·gli·a** (gang′glē ə)   a pl. of GANGLION.   *n.*

**gan·gling** (gang′gling)   awkwardly tall and slender; lank and loosely built.   *adj.*

**gan·gli·on** (gang′glē ən)   **1** a mass of nerve cells forming a nerve centre outside of the brain or spinal cord.   **2** a centre of force, activity, etc.   *n., pl.* **gan·gli·a** (-glē ə) or **gan·gli·ons.**

**gan·gly** (gang′glē)   GANGLING.   *adj.*

A gangplank

**gang·plank** (gang′plangk′)   a movable bridge used in getting on and off a ship, etc.   *n.*

**gang plough** or **plow**   a plough consisting of several shares for turning several furrows at a time.

**gan·grene** (gang′grēn)   **1** the decay of tissue in a part of a living person or animal when the blood supply is interfered with by injury, infection, freezing, etc.   **2** affect or become affected with gangrene: *The wounded leg gangrened and had to be amputated.*   1 *n.*, 2 *v.*, **gan·grened, gan·gren·ing.**

**gan·gre·nous** (gang′grə nəs)   of or having GANGRENE; decaying.   *adj.*

**gang·ster** (gang′stər)   a member of a gang of criminals.   *n.*

**gang·way** (gang′wā′)   **1** passageway.   **2** a passageway on a ship.   **3** GANGPLANK.   **4** *Informal.*   get out of the way! stand aside and make room!   1–3 *n.*, 4 *interj.*

**gan·net** (gan′it)   any of several related species of large, white, fish-eating sea bird having long, black-tipped wings, a pointed bill and tail, and webbed feet: *Gannets nest in colonies on cliffs.*   *n.*

**gan·oid** (gan′oid)   **1** of or having to do with a group of living and extinct fish having hard, shiny, enamelled scales, including the sturgeons, garfish, and paddlefish.   **2** a ganoid fish.   1 *adj.*, 2 *n.*

**gant·let** (gont′lit)   See GAUNTLET².   *n.*

**gan·try** (gan′trē)   **1** a movable, bridgelike structure for carrying a travelling crane, consisting of side towers on parallel tracks that support a horizontal framework along which the crane moves.   **2** a similar structure spanning several railway tracks, used to carry block signals.   **3** a towerlike, movable framework with platforms at different levels, used for servicing a rocket on its launching pad.   **4** a frame for supporting a barrel or cask on its side.   *n., pl.* **gan·tries.**

**gap** (gap)   **1** a broken place; hole or opening, as in a fence, hedge, or wall.   **2** an empty part; unfilled space; blank: *My diary is not complete; there are several gaps in it.*   **3** a wide difference of opinion, character, etc.; disparity: *the generation gap.*   **4** a pass through mountains.   *n.*

**gape** (gāp)   **1** open wide: *A deep crevasse gaped before us.*   **2** a wide opening.   **3** open the mouth wide, as when hungry or yawning.   **4** the act of opening the mouth wide.   **5** stare with the mouth open: *The children gaped when they saw the huge birthday cake.*   **6** an open-mouthed stare.   **7 the gapes, a** a fit of yawning.   **b** a disease of poultry.   1, 3, 5 *v.*, **gaped, gap·ing;**   2, 4, 6, 7 *n.*   —**gap′er,** *n.*

**gar** (gär)   **1** any of a small family of freshwater fishes having a long, slender, round body covered with an armour of very hard scales and a long, narrow, alligatorlike snout with many needle-like teeth: *The gars, found only in North and Central America, make up a separate order of fishes.*   **2** NEEDLEFISH.   *n., pl.* **gar** or **gars.**

**ga·rage** (gə räzh′, gə raj′ *or* gə razh′)   **1** a shelter for automobiles.   **2** a shop for repairing automobiles.   **3** put or keep in a garage.   1, 2 *n.*, 3 *v.*, **ga·raged, ga·rag·ing.**

**garage sale**   an informal sale of household items usually held in a private garage or driveway.

**garb** (gärb)   **1** the way one is dressed; a characteristic style of clothing: *a doctor's garb, a painter's garb.*   **2** clothe: *The doctor was garbed in white.*   **3** the outward covering, form, or appearance.   1, 3 *n.*, 2 *v.*

**gar·bage** (gär′bij)   **1** waste animal or vegetable matter from a kitchen, store, etc. to be thrown away.   **2** any worthless material: *We threw out several boxes of garbage when we cleaned out the attic.*   **3** *Informal.*   inferior, worthless, or offensive speech, writings, etc.: *That argument is a lot of garbage and shouldn't be taken seriously.*   *n.*

**gar·ban·zo** (gär ban′zō)   CHICK-PEA.   *n.*

**gar·ble** (gär′bəl)   **1** make unfair or misleading selections from facts, statements, writings, etc.; omit parts of, often in order to misrepresent: *The newspapers gave a garbled account of his speech.*   **2** confuse or mix up statements, words, etc. unintentionally.   *v.*, **gar·bled, gar·bling.**   —**gar′bler,** *n.*

**gar·çon** (gár sôN′) *French.*   **1** a young man or boy.   **2** a male servant.   **3** waiter.   *n., pl.* **gar·çons** (-sôN′).

**gar·den** (gär′dən)   **1** a piece of ground used for growing vegetables, herbs, flowers, or fruits.   **2** make, take care of, or work in a garden: *He loves to garden.*   **3** growing or grown in a garden; for a garden.   **4** a park or other place where plants or animals may be viewed by the public: *The city has a fine botanical garden.*   **5** a fertile and delightful spot; a well-cultivated region.   1, 3–5 *n.*, 2 *v.*   —**gar′den·like′,** *adj.*

**lead up** or **down the garden path,** *Informal.* lead on; lure; deceive.

**garden cress** an annual plant of the mustard family, native to Asia, but widely cultivated as a salad plant.

**gar·den·er** (gär′də nər *or* gärd′nər) 1 a person whose occupation is taking care of a garden, lawn, etc. 2 a person who makes a garden or works in a garden: *She's an enthusiastic gardener.* *n.*

**garden heliotrope** 1 the common heliotrope, a garden plant having wrinkled leaves and clusters of lilac or blue flowers with a fragrance like vanilla. 2 the common valerian, a garden plant having clusters of tiny, very fragrant, white or reddish flowers.

**gar·de·nia** (gär dē′nyə *or* gär dē′nē ə) 1 any of a large, closely related group of tropical and subtropical trees and shrubs of the madder family, having fragrant, roselike, white or yellow flowers with waxy petals. 2 a flower of any of these trees or shrubs: *Gardenias are often worn as corsages.* *n.*

**gar·den·ing** (gär′də ning *or* gärd′ning) 1 the preparation and care of gardens: *Some people find great pleasure in gardening.* 2 ppr. of GARDEN. 1 *n.*, 2 *v.*

**gar·fish** (gär′fish′) GAR. *n.*

**Gar·gan·tu·an** (gär gan′chü ən) gigantic; huge. *adj.*

**gar·gle** (gär′gəl) 1 wash or rinse the inside of the throat with liquid kept in motion in the throat by the air that is slowly expelled from the lungs. 2 a liquid used for gargling. 3 utter with a sound like gargling. 1, 3 *v.*, **gar′gled, gar′gling;** 2 *n.*

A gargoyle

**gar·goyle** (gär′goil) 1 a spout for carrying off rain water, projecting from the gutter of a building and usually having the form of a grotesquely shaped animal or imaginary creature: *Gargoyles are found mostly on Gothic buildings.* 2 on a building, a projection or ornament resembling a gargoyle. *n.*

**gar·ish** (ger′ish *or* gar′ish) 1 unpleasantly bright; glaring: *a garish yellow.* 2 showy; gaudy: *a garish suit.* *adj.* —**gar′ish·ly,** *adv.* —**gar′ish·ness,** *n.*

**gar·land** (gär′lənd) 1 a wreath of flowers, leaves, etc. worn on the head or hung as a decoration: *Garlands are often used as symbols of peace, victory, etc.* 2 decorate with garlands. 1 *n.*, 2 *v.*

**gar·lic** (gär′lik) 1 a perennial plant of the lily family, closely related to the onion, widely grown for its strong-smelling and strong-tasting bulb: *The bulb of garlic is made up of small sections called cloves.* 2 a bulb or clove of this plant, used to season meats, sauces, salads, etc.: *a garlic dressing on the fish.* *n.*

**gar·ment** (gär′mənt) 1 any article of clothing. 2 an outer covering. 3 clothe. 1, 2 *n.*, 3 *v.* —**gar′ment·less,** *adj.*

**gar·ner** (gär′nər) 1 gather and store away: *Wheat is cut and garnered at harvest time. Squirrels garner nuts in the fall.* 2 a storehouse for grain; granary. 3 a store of anything. 4 earn. 1, 4 *v.*, 2, 3 *n.*

**gar·net** (gär′nit) 1 a brittle silicate mineral occurring mainly in red crystals: *The transparent, deep-red variety of garnet is used as a semiprecious gemstone; other varieties are used as abrasives.* 2 deep red. 1, 2 *n.*, 2 *adj.* —**gar′net·like′,** *adj.*

**gar·nish** (gär′nish) 1 something laid on or around food as a decoration: *a garnish of parsley.* 2 decorate food. 3 decoration; trimming. 4 decorate; trim. 1, 3 *n.*, 2, 4 *v.* —**gar′nish·er,** *n.*
**garnish with,** embellish with: *His writing is garnished with images.*

**gar·nish·ee** (gär′ni shē′) in law, take money or property from a person by the authority of a court to pay a debt: *If a creditor garnishees a debtor's salary, a certain portion of the salary is withheld and paid to the creditor.* *v.*, **gar·nish·eed, gar·nish·ee·ing.**

**gar·ni·ture** (gär′nə chər) decoration; trimming; garnish, especially of food. *n.*

**ga·rotte** (gə rot′ *or* gə rōt′) See GARROTE. *n.*, *v.*

**gar pike** a species of GAR found in eastern North America from southern Ontario and Quebec to the Gulf of Mexico.

**gar·ret** (gar′it *or* ger′it) a space in a house just below a sloping roof; attic. *n.*

**gar·ri·son** (gar′ə sən *or* ger′ə sən) 1 the soldiers stationed in a fort, town, etc., usually for purposes of defending it. 2 a place where such troops are stationed. 3 station troops in a fort, town, etc. to defend it. 4 take over or occupy as a garrison. 5 of, associated with, or having a garrison: *Kingston is a garrison town.* 1, 2, 5 *n.*, 3, 4 *v.*

**gar·rote** (gə rot′ *or* gə rōt′) 1 a cord, wire, etc. used for strangling in a robbery, a surprise attack on an enemy, etc. 2 strangling, especially in order to rob. 3 attack or kill with a garrote. 1, 2 *n.*, 3 *v.*, **gar·rot·ed, gar·rot·ing.** Also, **garotte, garrotte.** —**gar·rot′er,** *n.*

**gar·rotte** (gə rot′ *or* gə rōt′) See GARROTE. *n.*, *v.*

**gar·ru·li·ty** (gə rü′lə tē) being GARRULOUS. *n.*

**gar·ru·lous** (gar′yə ləs *or* ger′yə ləs, gar′ə ləs *or* ger′ə ləs) 1 talking too much about trifles. 2 using too many words. *adj.* —**gar′ru·lous·ly,** *adv.* —**gar′ru·lous·ness,** *n.*

**gar·ter** (gär′tər) 1 a band or strap, usually of elastic, used to hold up a stocking or sock. 2 fasten with a garter. 3 **Garter, a Order of the,** the oldest and most important British order of knighthood, established about 1344. **b** the badge of this order. **c** membership in this order. 1, 3 *n.*, 2 *v.*

**garter snake** a small, harmless, brownish or greenish snake having long, yellow stripes.

**gas**[1] (gas) 1 any fluid substance that can expand without limit; not a solid or liquid: *Oxygen and nitrogen are gases.* 2 any gas or mixture of gases except air. 3 any mixture of gases that can be burned, obtained from coal and other substances: *Gas was once much used for lighting, but is now used for cooking and heating.* 4 any gas used as an anesthetic, such as nitrous oxide (laughing gas) or ether. 5 supply with gas. 6 treat with gas; use gas on: *Some kinds of seeds are gassed to hasten sprouting.* 7 give off gas. 8 in mining, an explosive mixture of FIREDAMP with air. 9 a substance that vaporizes and then poisons, suffocates, or stupefies, such as mustard gas, tear gas, etc. **10** attack with gas; use gas on: *The police were forced to gas the violent criminals who refused to leave the building.* **11** gas accumulated in or released from the stomach, usually as a result of indigestion or some other stomach disorder: *She suffers from gas pains.* 1–4, 8, 9, 11 *n., pl.* **gas·es;** 5–7, 10 *v.,* **gassed, gas·sing.** —**gas′less,** *adj.*

**gas²** (gas) *Informal.* **1** GASOLINE. **2** fill the tank of a motor vehicle with gasoline (usually used with **up**): *We gassed up before we left the city.* 1 *n.,* 2 *v.,* **gassed, gas·sing.**

**step on the gas, a** push down the accelerator of a motor vehicle. **b** go or act faster; hurry: *We'd better step on the gas and get these dishes done.*

**gas·e·ous** (gas′ē əs *or* gā′sē əs) in the form of gas; of or like a gas: *Steam is water in a gaseous condition.* *adj.*

**gas giant** a planet that is a huge ball of gas and that appears to have no solid surface.

**gash** (gash) **1** a long, deep cut or wound. **2** make a long, deep cut or wound in. 1 *n.,* 2 *v.*

**gas jet** **1** a small nozzle or burner at the end of a gas fixture where the gas comes out. **2** a flame of gas.

**gas·ket** (gas′kit) **1** a ring or strip of rubber, metal, plaited hemp, etc., packed around a piston, pipe joint, etc. to make it leakproof. **2** a cord or small rope used to secure a furled sail on a yard. *n.*

**gas mask** a helmet or mask that covers the mouth and nose and is supplied with a filter containing chemicals to neutralize poisons: *The wearer of a gas mask breathes only filtered air.*

**gas·o·hol** (gas′ə hol) a mixture of gasoline and alcohol used as a fuel for motor vehicles. *n.*

**gas·o·lene** (gas′ə lēn′ *or* gas′ə lēn′) GASOLINE. *n.*

**gas·o·line** (gas′ə lēn′ *or* gas′ə lēn′) a colourless liquid consisting of a mixture of hydrocarbons, which evaporates and burns very easily and is made by distilling petroleum: *Gasoline is used mainly as a fuel in internal-combustion engines.* *n.* Also, **gasolene.**

**gasp** (gasp) **1** a sudden, short intaking of breath through the mouth: *A gasp often indicates suspense, shock, or fear.* **2** one of a series of short breaths caused by having difficulty in breathing: *After her hard run, her breath came in gasps.* **3** breathe with gasps. **4** utter with gasps: *"Help! Help!" gasped the drowning woman.* 1, 2 *n.,* 3, 4 *v.*

**at the last gasp, a** about to die. **b** at the final moment.

**gasping for,** *Informal.* wanting very much: *Pat had been gasping for a chance to play with the team.*

**gas·pe·reau** (gas′pə rō′) a species of herring; an ALEWIFE. *n., pl.* **gas·pe·reaux** (-rōz′; *French,* -rō′).

**Gas·pe·sian** (gas pā′zhən *or* gas pē′zhen) *Cdn.* **1** a native or inhabitant of the Gaspé Peninsula. **2** of or having to do with the Gaspé or its inhabitants. 1 *n.,* 2 *adj.*

**gas station** a place for supplying automobiles with gasoline, motor oil, water, etc.

**gas·sy** (gas′ē) **1** full of gas; containing gas. **2** like gas: *a gassy smell.* *adj.,* **gas·si·er, gas·si·est.**

**gas·tric** (gas′trik) of, in, or near the stomach. *adj.*

hat, āge, fär; let, ēqual, tėrm; it, īce
hot, ōpen, ôrder; oil, out; cup, pu̇t, rüle
əbove, takən, pencəl, lemən, circəs
ch, child; ng, long; sh, ship
th, thin; ᴛʜ, then; zh, measure

**gastric juice** the digestive fluid secreted by glands in the mucous membrane that lines the stomach: *The gastric juice contains pepsin and other enzymes and hydrochloric acid.*

**gas·tri·tis** (gas trī′tis) inflammation of the stomach, especially of its mucous membrane. *n.*

**gas·tro·nom·ic** (gas′trə nom′ik) of or having to do with GASTRONOMY. *adj.*

**gas·tron·o·my** (gas tron′ə mē) the art or science of good eating. *n.*

**gas·tro·pod** (gas′trə pod′) **1** any of a large class of MOLLUSCS having one-piece shells or no shells, most of which move by means of a single, broad, disklike foot attached to the undersurface of their bodies: *Snails, limpets, and slugs are gastropods.* **2** of such MOLLUSCS. 1 *n.,* 2 *adj.*

**gate** (gāt) **1** a movable part or frame for closing an opening in a wall, fence, etc.: *A gate turns on hinges or slides open and shut.* **2** an opening in a fence, etc., usually fitted with a door, turnstile, or some other barrier; gateway. **3** a way to go in or out; a way to get to something. **4** a barrier intended to prevent entrance, stop traffic, etc.: *Level crossings are often equipped with gates to stop cars when a train is passing.* **5** a door, valve, etc. for stopping or controlling the flow of water in a pipe, dam, lock, etc. **6** the number of people who pay to see a contest, exhibition, performance, etc.: *The rink manager was expecting a good gate at the play-off game.* **7** the total amount of money received from these people: *The teams divided a gate of $3,250.* **8** *Informal.* require a young person to stay home: *I've been gated for staying out too late.* 1–7 *n.,* 8 *v.* —**gate′less,** *adj.* —**gate′like′,** *adj.*

**give the gate to,** *Informal.* **a** dismiss or turn away. **b** in hockey, give a player a penalty, thus putting him or her off the ice.

☞ *Hom.* GAIT.

**gate–crash·er** (gāt′krash′ər) *Informal.* a person who attends parties, gatherings, etc. without an invitation; an uninvited guest. *n.*

**gate·house** (gāt′hous′) a house at or over a gate, used as the keeper's quarters. See CASTLE for picture. *n.*

**gate·keep·er** (gāt′kē′pər) a person employed to guard a gate and control passage through it. *n.*

**gate·post** (gāt′pōst′) one of the posts on either side of a gate: *A swinging gate is fastened to one gatepost and closes against the other.* *n.*

**gate·way** (gāt′wā′) **1** an opening in a wall, fence, etc. fitted with a gate or some other barrier. **2** a way to go in or out; way to get to or attain something: *A college education is one of the gateways to success. Winnipeg is known as the "Gateway to the West."* *n.*

**Gath·as** (gä′təz) in Zoroastrianism, that portion of the Avesta containing the hymns written by Zoroaster. *n. pl.*

**gath·er** (gaᴛʜ′ər) **1** bring into one place or group: *Rudi gathered his books and papers and started off to school.* **2** come together; assemble: *A crowd gathered at*

the scene of the accident. **3** get together gradually or from various places or sources: *to gather sticks for a fire.* **4** form a mass; collect: *Tears gathered in her eyes.* **5** pick and collect; take: *Farmers gather their crops.* **6** get or gain little by little: *The train gathered speed as it left the station.* **7** collect oneself, one's strength, energies, thoughts, etc. for an effort: *He gathered his thoughts for a final decision.* **8** put together in the mind; conclude; infer: *I gathered from his words that he was really upset.* **9** pull together in folds; wrinkle: *She gathered her brows in a frown.* **10** pull together in little folds and stitch: *The skirt is gathered at the waist.* **11** one of the little folds between the stitches when cloth is pulled together in this way. **12** come to a head and form pus: *A boil is a painful swelling that gathers under the skin.* 1–10, 12 *v.*, 11 *n.*
**be gathered to one's fathers,** die and be buried.
**gather oneself together,** prepare oneself mentally.
**gather up, a** pick up and put together. **b** pull together; bring into a smaller space. **c** prepare by collecting: *Gather up your courage for the competition.*
**gather up the threads,** begin something again after an interruption.

**gath·er·ing** (gaŦH′ə ring) **1** the act of one that gathers. **2** that which is gathered. **3** a meeting; assembly; party; crowd. **4** a swelling that comes to a head and forms pus. **5** ppr. of GATHER. 1–4 *n.*, 5 *v.*

**Gat·ling gun** (gat′ling) an early type of machine gun consisting of a revolving cluster of barrels around a central axis.
☞ **Etym.** Named after Richard J. *Gatling* (1818–1903), an American inventor.

**GATT** (gat) General Agreement on Tariffs and Trade.

**gauche** (gōsh) awkward or clumsy in social situations; tactless. *adj.* —**gauche′ly,** *adv.* —**gauche′ness,** *n.*

**gau·che·rie** (gō′shə rē *or* gō′shə rē′) **1** awkwardness in social situations; tactlessness. **2** an awkward or tactless movement, act, etc. *n.*

**gau·cho** (gou′chō) a cowboy or herdsman in the southern plains of South America. *n., pl.* **gau·chos.**

**gaud·y** (gôd′ē) bright or ornate in a cheap and tasteless way: *gaudy jewellery. adj.,* **gaud·i·er, gaud·i·est.** —**gaud′i·ly,** *adv.* —**gaud′i·ness,** *n.*

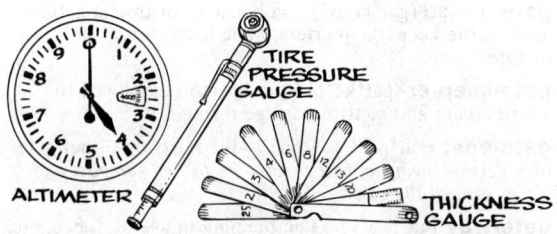

**gauge** (gāj) **1** a standard measure; scale of standard measurements; measure: *There are gauges of the capacity of a barrel, the thickness of sheet iron, the diameter of a shotgun bore, the diameter of wire, etc.* **2** an instrument for measuring. A **steam gauge** measures the pressure of steam. **3** measure accurately with a measuring device: *She had a special instrument to gauge the width of the metal strip.* **4** estimate; judge: *It is difficult to gauge the character of a stranger.* **5** a means of estimating or judging. **6** size, capacity, or extent. **7** the distance between the rails of a railway track or between the right and left wheels of a wagon, automobile, etc.: *Standard gauge between rails is 56½ inches (about 144 cm).* **8** the position of one sailing ship with reference to another and to the wind: *A ship having the weather gauge of another is to the windward of it.* 1, 2, 5–8 *n.*, 3, 4 *v.*, **gauged, gaug·ing.** Also, **gage.** —**gauge′a·ble,** *adj.* —**gaug′er,** *n.*
☞ **Hom.** GAGE.

**gaunt** (gont) **1** very thin and bony; having hollow eyes and a starved look: *Hunger and suffering make people gaunt.* **2** looking bare and gloomy; desolate, forbidding, or grim: *The ancient castle stood gaunt on the hilltop. adj.* —**gaunt′ly,** *adv.* —**gaunt′ness,** *n.*

**gaunt·let¹** (gont′lit) **1** a stout, heavy glove, usually of leather covered with plates of iron or steel, that was part of a knight's armour. See ARMOUR for picture. **2** a stout, heavy glove with a wide, flaring cuff, used for protection in industry, etc. **3** the wide, flaring cuff. *n.*
**take up the gauntlet, a** accept a challenge. **b** take up the defence of a person, opinion, etc.
**throw down the gauntlet,** challenge.

**gaunt·let²** (gont′lit) a former military punishment in which the offender had to run between two rows of men who struck him with clubs or other weapons as he passed. *n.* Also, **gantlet.**
**run the gauntlet, a** carry out an action in spite of danger threatening on all sides: *During the war, convoys ran the gauntlet of enemy submarines.* **b** pass between two rows of men each of whom strikes the runner as he passes. **c** be exposed to unfriendly attacks, criticism, etc.

**Gau·ta·ma** (got′ə mə *or* gou′tə mə) BUDDHA. *n.* Also, **Gotama.**

**gauze** (goz) **1** a very thin, light cloth of cotton, silk, etc., easily seen through: *Cotton gauze is often used for bandages.* **2** a thin haze. **3** a semi-transparent theatre curtain. *n.* —**gauze′like′,** *adj.*

**gauz·y** (goz′ē) like gauze; thin and light as gauze. *adj.,* **gauz·i·er, gauz·i·est.** —**gauz′i·ness,** *n.*

**gave** (gāv) pt. of GIVE: *He gave me some candy. v.*

**gav·el** (gav′əl) a small mallet used by a presiding officer to signal for attention or order or by an auctioneer to announce that the bidding is over. *n.*

**ga·vi·al** (gā′vē əl) a large crocodile of India that has a long, slender snout. *n.*

**gawk** (gok) **1** an awkward person; clumsy fool. **2** *Informal.* stare rudely or stupidly. 1 *n.,* 2 *v.*

**gawk·y** (gok′ē) awkward; clumsy. *adj.,* **gawk·i·er, gawk·i·est.** —**gawk′i·ly,** *adv.* —**gawk′i·ness,** *n.*

**gay** (gā) **1** happy and full of fun: *gay laughter.* **2** bright-coloured; showy: *gay decorations.* **3** fond of pleasures: *They had led a gay and wild life.* **4** homosexual. 1–4 *adj.,* **gay·er, gay·est;** 4 *n.* —**gay′ness,** *n.*

**gay·e·ty** (gā′ə tē) See GAIETY. *n.*

**gay·ly** (gā′lē) See GAILY. *adv.*

**gaze** (gāz) **1** look long and steadily: *For hours she sat gazing at the stars.* **2** a long, steady look: *She was embarrassed by the child's gaze.* 1 *v.,* **gazed, gaz·ing;** 2 *n.* —**gaz′er,** *n.*

**ga·ze·bo** (gə zē′bō) a summerhouse, balcony, etc. that commands a wide view. *n.*

**ga·zelle** (gə zel′) any of a number of species of small, graceful antelope of Africa and Asia, having soft, lustrous eyes. See ANTELOPE for picture. *n.*

**ga·zette** (gə zet′) **1** newspaper: *the "Weekly Gazette."* **2** an official government journal containing lists of appointments, promotions, etc. **3** publish, list, or announce in a gazette. 1, 2 *n.*, 3 *v.*, **ga·zet·ted, ga·zet·ting.**

**gaz·et·teer** (gaz′ə tēr′) **1** a dictionary of geographical names. **2** a writer for a gazette. **3** an official appointed to publish a gazette. *n.*

**gaz·pa·cho** (gä spä′chō) a vegetable soup served cold, made with tomatoes, cucumbers, onions, peppers, olive oil, etc. *n.*

**G.B.** Great Britain.

**GCD, G.C.D.,** or **g.c.d.** greatest common divisor.

**GCF, G.C.F.,** or **g.c.f.** greatest common factor.

**G clef** in music, the treble clef. See CLEF for picture.

**Gd** gadolinium.

**Ge** germanium.

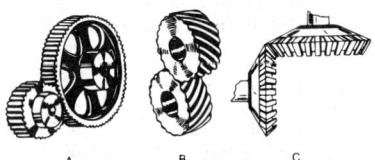

Gears:
A, to change the speed of axle rotation
B, with angled teeth to run more quietly
C, to change the direction of rotation

**gear** (gēr) **1** a wheel having teeth that fit into the teeth of another wheel of the same kind: *If the wheels of two gears are of different sizes, they will turn at different speeds.* See DIFFERENTIAL and RACK for more pictures. **2** connect by gears: *An automobile moves when the motor is geared to the driving wheels.* **3** fit or work together; mesh: *The cogs gear smoothly.* **4** any arrangement of gears or moving parts for transmitting or changing motion; mechanism; machinery: *The car ran off the road when the steering gear broke.* **5** a working order; adjustment: *Her watch got out of gear and would not run.* **6** the equipment needed for some purpose: *Harness, clothes, household goods, tools, tackle, and rigging are various kinds of gear.* **7** provide with gear; equip; harness. **8** make fit; adjust; adapt: *The steel industry was geared to the needs of war.* 1, 4–6 *n.*, 2, 3, 7, 8 *v.*
**in gear, a** connected to the motor, etc. **b** in working order.
**out of gear, a** disconnected from the motor, etc. **b** not working well; disorganized.
**shift gears,** change from one set of gears to another.

**gear·ing** (gēr′ing) **1** a set of gears, chains, etc. for transmitting motion or power; gears. **2** ppr. of GEAR. 1 *n.*, 2 *v.*

**gear·shift** (gēr′shift′) a device for connecting a motor, etc. to any of several sets of gears. *n.*

**geck·o** (gek′ō) any of several small, soft-skinned, insect-eating lizards found in the tropics, having suction pads on its toes for climbing. *n., pl.* **geck·os** or **geck·oes.**

hat, āge, fär; let, ēqual, tėrm; it, īce
hot, ōpen, ôrder; oil, out; cup, pùt, rüle
əbove, takən, pencəl, lemən, circəs
ch, child; ng, long; sh, ship
th, thin; ᴛʜ, then; zh, measure

**gee¹** (jē) **1** a command to horses, oxen, etc. directing them to turn to the right. **2** turn to the right. 1 *interj.*, 2 *v.*, **geed, gee·ing.**

**gee²** (jē) an exclamation or mild oath. *interj.*

**geese** (gēs) pl. of GOOSE. *n.*

**Gei·ger counter** (gī′gər) a device that detects and counts ionizing particles: *A Geiger counter is used to measure radio-activity, test cosmic-ray particles, etc.*
☞ *Etym.* Named after Hans *Geiger* (1882–1945), a German physicist and co-inventor of the device.

**gei·sha** (gā′shə *or* gē′shə) a Japanese girl specially trained in singing, dancing, the art of conversation, etc., in order to act as a hostess or companion for men. *n., pl.* **gei·sha** or **gei·shas.**

**gel·a·tin** or **gel·a·tine** (jel′ə tən) **1** an odourless, tasteless substance obtained by boiling animal tissues, bones, hoofs, etc.: *Gelatin dissolves easily in hot water and becomes jelly-like when cool; it is used in making jellied desserts, camera film, glue, etc.* **2** any of various vegetable substances having similar properties. **3** a preparation or product in which gelatin is the basic constituent. *n.*

**ge·lat·i·nous** (jə lat′ə nəs) **1** jelly-like; of the consistency of jelly. **2** of or containing gelatin. *adj.*

**geld** (geld) remove the testicles of an animal, especially a horse; castrate. *v.*, **geld·ed** or **gelt, geld·ing.**

**geld·ing** (gel′ding) **1** a gelded horse or other animal. **2** ppr. of GELD. 1 *n.*, 2 *v.*

**gel·id** (jel′id) cold as ice; frosty. *adj.*

**gelt** (gelt) a pt. and a pp. of GELD. *v.*

**gem** (jem) **1** a precious stone; jewel: *Diamonds and rubies are gems.* **2** a person or thing that is very precious, beautiful, etc.: *The gem of his collection was a rare Persian stamp.* **3** set or adorn with gems, or set as if with gems: *Stars gem the sky.* **4** a kind of muffin made of coarse flour. 1, 2, 4 *n.*, 3 *v.*, **gemmed, gem·ming.**
—**gem′like**, *adj.*

**gem·i·nate** (jem′ə nāt′ *for verb,* jem′ə nit *or* jem′ə nāt′ *for adjective*) **1** make or become double; combine in pairs. **2** combined in a pair or pairs; coupled. 1 *v.*, **gem·i·nat·ed, gem·i·nat·ing;** 2 *adj.*
—**gem′i·na′tion**, *n.*

**Gem·i·ni** (jem′ə nī′ *or* jem′ə nē′) (used with a singular verb) **1** in astronomy, a northern constellation containing the two bright stars Castor and Pollux. **2** in astrology, the third sign of the zodiac. The sun enters Gemini about May 21. See ZODIAC for picture. **3** a person born under this sign. *n.pl.*

**gems·bok** (gemz′bok′) a large antelope of southern Africa, having long, straight horns and a long, tufted tail. *n.*

**–gen** a suffix meaning: producing or produced, as in *antigen, nitrogen.*

**gen.** **1** gender. **2** general. **3** genitive. **4** genus. **5** generator.

**gen·darme** (zhon′därm; *French*, zhäN däRM′)
**1** especially in France, one of a body of soldiers employed as armed police officers. **2** any police officer. *n., pl.* **gen·darmes** (-därmz; *French*, -däRM′).

**gen·der** (jen′dər) **1** in many languages, a system of grouping words such as nouns, pronouns, and adjectives into two or more classes, either arbitrarily or according to certain features of structure or meaning. In English, except in pronouns (*him—her*) and a few nouns with endings such as *-ess* (*actress*), *-trix* (*aviatrix*), gender is now indicated only by the meaning of the word: *man—woman, nephew—niece, rooster—hen.* **2** one of such classes. **3** *Informal.* sex. *n.*

**gene** (jēn) in a plant or animal cell, a minute part of a chromosome that determines the nature and development of an inherited characteristic: *The genes inherited from its parents determine what kind of plant or animal will develop from a fertilized egg cell.* *n.*
☛ *Hom.* JEAN.

**ge·ne·a·log·i·cal** (jē′nē ə loj′ə kəl *or* jen′ē ə loj′ə kəl) having to do with GENEALOGY: *A genealogical table or chart shows the descent of a person or family from an ancestor.* *adj.* —**ge′ne·a·log′i·cal·ly,** *adv.*

**ge·ne·al·o·gist** (jē′nē al′ə jist *or* jen′ē al′ə jist) a person who traces genealogies; a person who makes a study of genealogies. *n.*

**ge·ne·al·o·gy** (jē′nē al′ə jē *or* jen′ē al′ə jē) **1** an account or record of the descent of a person or family from an ancestor or ancestors. **2** the descent of a person or family from an ancestor; pedigree; lineage. **3** the study or investigation of lines of descent; study of pedigrees. *n., pl.* **ge·ne·al·o·gies.**

**gen·er·a** (jen′ə rə) a pl. of GENUS. *n.*

**gen·er·al** (jen′ə rəl *or* jen′rəl) **1** of all; for all; from all: *A government takes care of the general welfare.* **2** common to many or most; not limited to a few; widespread: *There is a general interest in sports.* **3** not specialized; not limited to one kind, class, department, or use: *A general reader reads different kinds of books.* **4** not detailed; sufficient for practical purposes: *general instructions.* **5** indefinite; vague: *She referred to her trip in a general way.* **6** a general fact, idea, principle, or statement. **7** of or for all those forming a group: *"Cat" is a general term for cats, lions, and tigers.* **8** in chief; of highest rank: *The Postmaster General is the head of the Post Office.* **9** the head of a religious order. 1–5, 7, 8 *adj.*, 6, 9 *n.*
**in general, a** referring to all those mentioned. **b** usually; for the most part: *In general, people get along fairly well together.*

**General Assembly** the legislative body of the United Nations.

**general delivery** a department of a post office that handles mail which is not addressed to a street number or box number.

**general election** **1** an election involving all the voters of a country. **2** in Canada, an election in which either a new federal Parliament or a new provincial legislative assembly is elected.

**gen·er·al·is·si·mo** (jen′ə rə lis′ə mō′) in certain countries: **1** the commander-in-chief of all the military forces of a country. **2** the commander-in-chief of several armies in the field. *n., pl.* **gen·er·al·is·si·mos.**

**gen·er·al·i·ty** (jen′ə ral′ə tē) **1** a general statement; word or phrase not definite enough to have much meaning or value: *The candidate spoke only in generalities; not once did he mention definite laws that he and his party would try to pass.* **2** a general principle or rule: *"Nothing happens without a cause" is a generality.* **3** the greater part; main body; mass: *The generality of people must work for a living.* **4** general quality or condition: *A rule of great generality has very few exceptions.* *n., pl.* **gen·er·al·i·ties.**

**gen·er·al·i·za·tion** (jen′ə rə lə zā′shən, jen′ə rə lī zā′shən, jen′rə lə zā′shən *or* jen′rə lī zā′shən) **1** the act or process of generalizing. **2** a general idea, statement, principle, or rule: *Her argument was weakened by too many generalizations.* *n.*

**gen·er·al·ize** (jen′ə rə līz′ *or* jen′rə līz′) **1** make into one general statement; bring under a common heading, class, or law: *All men, women, and children can be generalized under the term "human being."* **2** infer a general rule from particular facts: *If you have seen cats, lions, leopards, and tigers eat meat, you can generalize that the cat family eats meat.* **3** state in a more general form; extend in application: *The statement that $5 + 3 = 8$ and $50 + 30 = 80$ can be generalized to the form $5a + 3a = 8a$.* **4** talk indefinitely or vaguely; use generalities: *The commentator generalized because he knew no details.* **5** make general; bring into general use or knowledge. **6** make general inferences. *v.*, **gen·er·al·ized, gen·er·al·iz·ing.**

**gen·er·al·ly** (jen′ə rə lē *or* jen′rə lē) **1** as a rule; in most cases; usually: *She is generally on time.* **2** by or to most people; commonly; widely: *It was once generally believed that the earth is flat.* **3** in a general way; without giving details; not specially: *Generally speaking, our coldest weather comes in January.* *adv.*

**gen·er·al–pur·pose** (jen′ə rəl pėr′pəs) suitable for use for a number of different purposes; having a number of different uses. *adj.*

**gen·er·al·ship** (jen′ə rəl ship′) **1** ability as a general; skill in commanding an army. **2** skilful management; leadership. **3** the rank, commission, authority, or term of office of a general. *n.*

**general staff** a group of high army officers who make plans for war or national defence.

**general store** a small store that carries a wide variety of goods for sale but is not divided into departments: *General stores are usually located in small communities and rural areas.*

**gen·er·ate** (jen′ə rāt′) **1** produce; cause to be: *Rubbing generates heat. Steam can be used to generate power or electricity.* **2** produce offspring. **3** in mathematics, form a line, surface, figure, or solid by moving a point, line, or plane. *v.*, **gen·er·at·ed, gen·er·at·ing.**

**gen·er·a·tion** (jen′ə rā′shən) **1** all the people born about the same time: *Your parents belong to one generation; you belong to the following generation.* **2** the average time from the birth of one generation to the birth of the next generation; about 30 years. **3** one step, or stage, in the history of a family: *The picture showed four generations—great-grandmother, grandmother, mother, and baby.* **4** the production of offspring. **5** production; a causing to be; a generating: *Steam and water power are used for the generation of electricity.* *n.*

**gen·er·a·tive** (jen′ə rə tiv *or* jen′ə rā′tiv) **1** having to do with the production of offspring. **2** having the power of producing. *adj.*

A DC generator as used in older automobiles. An electric current is generated in the copper wires of the armature as it rotates through the lines of magnetic force of the field coils. The current is transferred to an outside circuit by the brushes and commutator.

hat, āge, fär; let, ēqual, tėrm; it, īce
hot, ōpen, ôrder; oil, out; cup, pu̇t, rüle
ǝbove, takǝn, pencǝl, lemǝn, circǝs
ch, child; ng, long; sh, ship
th, thin; ᴛʜ, then; zh, measure

**gen·i·tal** (jen′ǝ tǝl) of or having to do with sexual reproduction or the sex organs. *adj.*

**gen·i·tals** (jen′ǝ tǝlz) the external sex organs. *n. pl.*

**gen·i·tive** (jen′ǝ tiv) 1 of, having to do with, or being the grammatical case that in many languages shows that a noun, pronoun, or adjective refers to the possessor or source of something or to a part of a larger whole. In *his books* and *the girl's books*, *his* and *girl's* are both in the genitive case. 2 the genitive case. 3 a word or construction in the genitive case. 1 *adj.*, 2, 3 *n.*

**gen·ius** (jē′nē ǝs *or* jē′nyǝs) 1 a very great natural power of mind: *Genius is shown by extraordinary ability to think, invent, or create.* 2 a person having such power: *Shakespeare was a genius.* 3 a great natural ability of some special kind: *Mozart played the piano well, but he had a genius for composing.* 4 the special character or spirit of a person, nation, age, language, etc. 5 a guardian spirit of a person, place, institution, etc. 6 either of two spirits, one good and one evil, supposed to influence a person's fate. 7 a spirit or genie; JINN. *n., pl.* **ge·ni·us·es** for 1-4, 7, **ge·ni·i** (jē′nē ī′) for 5, 6.

**gen·o·cid·al** (jen′ǝ sī′dǝl) of or having to do with GENOCIDE. *adj.*

**gen·o·cide** (jen′ǝ sīd′) the deliberate, systematic killing of a whole cultural or racial group. *n.*

**Gen·o·ese** (jen′ō ēz′) 1 of or having to do with Genoa, a city in Italy, or its people. 2 a native or inhabitant of Genoa. 1 *adj.*, 2 *n., pl.* **Gen·o·ese**.

**gen·o·type** (jen′ǝ tīp′) 1 the arrangement or combination of genes in an organism. 2 a group of organisms each having the same combinations of hereditary characteristics. *n.*

**gen·re** (zhon′rǝ; *French,* zhänʀ) kind; sort; style, especially of works of literature, art, etc.: *The novel and the drama are two literary genres.* *n.*

**Gent.** or **gent.** gentleman; gentlemen.

**gen·teel** (jen tēl′) 1 belonging or suited to polite society. 2 polite; well-bred; fashionable; elegant. 3 trying to be aristocratic, but not really being so. *adj.* —**gen·teel′ly**, *adv.* —**gen·teel′ness**, *n.*

**gen·tian** (jen′shǝn *or* jen′shē ǝn) any of a large family of plants having funnel-shaped flowers, stemless leaves, and bitter juice. *n.*

**gentian violet** a crystalline derivative of aniline that forms a violet solution in water, used as a dye, chemical indicator, and antiseptic.

**gen·tile** or **Gen·tile** (jen′tīl) 1 a person who is not a Jew. 2 not Jewish. 3 heathen; pagan. 1, 3 *n.*, 2, 3 *adj.*

**gen·til·i·ty** (jen til′ǝ tē) 1 noble birth; membership in the aristocracy or upper class. 2 good manners; refinement: *The lady had an air of gentility.* 3 pretended refinement. *n., pl.* **gen·til·i·ties**.

**gen·tle** (jen′tǝl) 1 not severe, rough, or violent; mild: *a gentle tap.* 2 soft; low: *a gentle sound.* 3 moderate: *gentle heat, a gentle slope.* 4 kindly; friendly: *a gentle*

---

**gen·er·a·tor** (jen′ǝ rā′tǝr) 1 a machine that changes mechanical energy into electrical energy. 2 an apparatus for producing gas or steam. 3 any person or thing that generates; originator. *n.*

**ge·ner·ic** (jǝ ner′ik) 1 in biology, having to do with or characteristic of a GENUS of plants or animals: *Cats and lions show generic differences.* 2 of, having to do with, or applied to a whole class or group of things; general; not specific: *Liquid is a generic term that includes water, gasoline, and milk.* 3 of or having to do with a group or class as distinct from a brand name: *Most drugs have a generic name as well as one or more brand names.* *adj.* —**ge·ner′i·cal·ly**, *adv.*

**gen·er·os·i·ty** (jen′ǝ ros′ǝ tē) 1 being generous; willingness to share with others; unselfishness. 2 nobleness of mind; absence of meanness: *He accepted the apology with great generosity.* 3 a generous act. *n., pl.* **gen·er·os·i·ties**.

**gen·er·ous** (jen′ǝ rǝs *or* jen′rǝs) 1 willing to share with others; unselfish. 2 having or showing a noble mind; willing to forgive; not mean: *a generous mind.* 3 large; plentiful: *A quarter of a pie is a generous serving.* 4 fertile: *generous fields.* 5 rich and strong: *a generous wine.* *adj.* —**gen′er·ous·ly**, *adv.* —**gen′er·ous·ness**, *n.*

**gen·e·sis** (jen′ǝ sis) origin; creation; coming into being. *n., pl.* **gen·e·ses** (-sēz′).

**ge·net·ic** (jǝ net′ik) 1 having to do with origin and natural growth. 2 of or having to do with GENETICS. *adj.*

**ge·net·i·cal·ly** (jǝ net′i klē) 1 with respect to genesis or origin. 2 according to the laws of genetics. *adv.*

**ge·net·i·cist** (jǝ net′ǝ sist) a person trained in GENETICS, especially one who makes it his or her work. *n.*

**ge·net·ics** (jǝ net′iks) 1 the branch of biology dealing with the principles of heredity and variation in animals and plants of the same or related kinds. 2 the genetic make-up of an individual organism or a type or group. *n.*

**Ge·ne·va Convention** (jǝ nē′vǝ) an agreement between nations providing for the neutrality of members and building of medical departments on battlefields and for the proper treatment of prisoners.

**ge·ni·al** (jē′nē ǝl *or* jē′nyǝl) 1 smiling and pleasant; cheerful and friendly; kindly: *a GENIAL welcome.* 2 helping growth; pleasantly warming; comforting: *genial sunshine.* *adj.* —**gen′ial·ly**, *adv.* —**gen′ial·ness**, *n.*

**ge·ni·al·i·ty** (jē′nē al′ǝ tē) a GENIAL quality. *n.*

**ge·nie** (jē′nē) a spirit; JINN: *When Aladdin rubbed his lamp, the genie came to do whatever Aladdin asked.* *n.*

**ge·ni·i** (jē′nē ī) a pl. of GENIUS. *n.*

disposition. **5** easily handled or managed: *a gentle dog.* **6** of good family and social position; well-born: *The princess was of a gentle origin.* **7** honourable; good; superior. **8** refined; polite. **9** treat in a soothing way: *The rider gentled his excited horse.* 1–8 *adj.*, **gen·tler, gen·tlest;** 9 *v.*, **gen·tled, gent·ling.** —**gen′tle·ness,** *n.*

**gen·tle·folk** (jen′təl fōk′) people of good family and social position. *n. pl.*

**gen·tle·man** (jen′təl mən) **1** a man of good family and social position. **2** a man who is honourable, polite, and considerate of others. **3** a polite term for any man. *n., pl.* **gen·tle·men** (-mən). —**gen′tle·man·like′,** *adj.*

**gen·tle·man–in–wait·ing** (jən′təl mən in wā′ting) a man of good family who attends a king or prince. *n., pl.* **gen·tle·men-in-wait·ing.**

**gen·tle·man·ly** (jen′təl mən lē) of, characteristic of, or suitable for a gentleman: *a gentlemanly bow, a gentlemanly sport.* *adj.* —**gen′tle·man·li·ness,** *n.*

**gentleman's agreement** or **gentlemen's agreement** an unwritten agreement that is not legally binding but depends only on the honour of the people or countries that participate in it.

**gen·tle·wom·an** (jen′təl wům′ən) **1** a woman of good family and social position. **2** a well-bred woman; lady. **3** a woman attendant of a lady of rank. *n., pl.* **gen·tle·wom·en** (-wim′ən). —**gen′tle·wom′an·ly,** *adj.*

**gen·tly** (jen′tlē) **1** in a gentle way; tenderly; softly. **2** gradually: *a gently sloping hillside.* *adv.*

**gen·tri·fi·ca·tion** (jen′trə fə kā′shən) upgrading, such as of a city area. *n.*

**gen·tri·fy** (jen′trə fī′) upgrade something such as a city area. *v.,* **gen·tri·fied, gen·tri·fy·ing.**

**gen·try** (jen′trē) **1** people of good family and social position; formerly, in the British Isles, members of the class of wealthy landowners ranking just below the nobility. **2** people of a particular class: *the academic gentry.* *n.*

**gen·u·flect** (jen′yə flekt′) bend the knee as an act of reverence or worship. *v.*

**gen·u·flec·tion** (jen′yə flek′shən) the bending of the knee as an act of reverence or worship. *n.*

**gen·u·ine** (jen′yü ən *or* jen′yü īn′) **1** actually being what it seems or is claimed to be; real; true: *The table is genuine mahogany, not wood stained to look like it.* **2** without pretence; sincere; frank: *genuine sorrow.* *adj.* —**gen′u·ine·ly,** *adv.* —**gen′u·ine·ness,** *n.*
☛ Pron. The pronunciation (jen′yü īn′) has become established in Canada, though many people still regard it as vulgar or non-standard.

**ge·nus** (jē′nəs *or* jen′əs) **1** in biology, a major category in the classification of plants and animals, ranking between a family and a species: *The prairie crocus and Canada anemone belong to one genus of flowers. The whooping crane and sandhill crane belong to one genus of birds. The scientific name of every animal or plant is made up of the name of the genus followed by the name of the species.* See Appendix for chart. **2** any kind or sort. *n., pl.* **gen·er·a** or **ge·nus·es.**

**geo–** a word element meaning: earth; land, as in *geocentric.*

**ge·o·cen·tric** (jē′ō sen′trik) **1** as viewed or measured from the earth's centre. **2** having or representing the earth as a centre: *The people of medieval times had a geocentric view of the universe.* Compare with HELIOCENTRIC. *adj.* —**ge′o·cen′tri·cal·ly,** *adv.*

**ge·o·chem·ist** (jē′ō kem′ist) a person trained in GEOCHEMISTRY, especially one who makes it his or her work. *n.*

**ge·o·chem·is·try** (jē′ō kem′i strē) the science dealing with the chemistry of the earth. *n.*

**ge·o·des·ic** (jē′ə des′ik *or* jē′ə dē′zik) **1** the shortest possible distance between two points along a surface, especially a curved surface. **2** of or having to do with the geometry of curved lines. **3** in architecture, built with short, straight, lightweight struts forming a spherical grid of triangles: *A geodesic dome uses the minimum amount of material to produce a given volume.* 1 *n.,* 2, 3 *adj.*

**ge·od·e·sy** (jē od′ə sē) the branch of applied mathematics dealing with the shape and dimensions of the earth or large areas on its surface, determining the exact position of points on the surface, and variations in the earth's gravity and magnetism: *Geodesy is based on the notion of measuring a sphere by dividing its surface area into triangles.* *n.*

**ge·o·det·ic** (jē′ə det′ik) of, having to do with, or involving GEODESY: *geodetic measurements, a geodetic project.* *adj.* —**ge′o·det′i·cal·ly,** *adv.*

**ge·og·ra·pher** (jē og′rə fər) a person trained in GEOGRAPHY, especially one who makes it his or her work. *n.*

**ge·o·graph·ic** (jē′ə graf′ik) GEOGRAPHICAL. *adj.*

**ge·o·graph·i·cal** (jē′ə graf′ə kəl) of or having to do with GEOGRAPHY. *adj.* —**ge′o·graph′i·cal·ly,** *adv.*

**geographical mile** the distance of a mile (1.6 km) over land. Compare with NAUTICAL MILE.

**ge·og·ra·phy** (jē og′rə fē) **1** the science that deals with the earth's surface and its division into continents and countries, and the climate, animal and plant life, peoples, resources, industries, and products of these divisions. **2** the surface features of a place or region: *the geography of Ungava.* **3** a book about geography. *n., pl.* **ge·og·ra·phies.**

**geol.** **1** geology. **2** geologic.

**ge·o·log·ic** (jē′ə loj′ik) GEOLOGICAL. *adj.*

**ge·o·log·i·cal** (jē′ə loj′ə kəl) of or having to do with GEOLOGY. *adj.* —**ge′o·log′i·cal·ly,** *adv.*

**ge·ol·o·gist** (jē ol′ə jist) a person trained in GEOLOGY (def. 1), especially one who makes it his or her work. *n.*

**ge·ol·o·gy** (jē ol′ə jē) **1** the science that deals with the earth's crust, the layers of which it is composed, and their history. **2** the features of the earth's crust in a place or region; rocks, rock formation, etc. of a particular area. **3** a book about geology. *n., pl.* **ge·ol·o·gies.**

**geom.** **1** geometry. **2** geometric.

**ge·o·met·ric** (jē ə met′rik) **1** of GEOMETRY or according to its principles: *geometric proof.* **2** consisting of or characterized by straight lines, circles, triangles, etc.; regular and symmetrical: *a geometric design.* *adj.*

**ge·o·met·ri·cal** (jē′ə met′rə kəl) GEOMETRIC. *adj.* —**ge′o·met′ri·cal·ly,** *adv.*

**ge·om·e·tri·cian** (jē om′ə trish′ən *or* jē′ə met′rish′ən) a person trained in GEOMETRY, especially one who makes it his or her work. *n.*

**geometric progression** in mathematics, a series in which each following number is obtained by multiplying the preceding number by the same factor. 2, 4, 8, 16, and 32 form a geometric progression. So also do 3125, 625, 125, 25, 5, 1, 1/5, and 1/25.

**ge·om·e·trid** (jē om′ə trid) any of a group of grey or greenish moths having slender bodies, whose larvae are called measuring worms or inchworms: *Geometrids move by bringing the rear end of the body forward, thus forming a loop, and then advancing the front end.* *n.*

**ge·om·e·try** (jē om′ə trē) **1** the branch of mathematics that deals with lines, angles, surfaces, and solids: *Geometry includes the definition, comparison, and measurement of squares, triangles, circles, cubes, cones, spheres, etc.* **2** a book about geometry. *n., pl.* **ge·om·e·tries.**

**ge·o·mor·phic** (jē′ō môr′fik) of or having to do with the shape or the surface features of the earth or a heavenly body such as the moon. *adj.*

**ge·o·mor·pho·log·i·cal** (jē′ō môr′fə loj′ə kəl) of or having to do with GEOMORPHOLOGY. *adj.*

**ge·o·mor·phol·o·gist** (jē′ō môr fol′ə jist) a person trained in GEOMORPHOLOGY, especially one who makes it his or her work. *n.*

**ge·o·mor·phol·o·gy** (jē′ō môr fol′ə jē) the science that deals with the surface features of the earth or a heavenly body such as the moon, and with the origin and development of these features and their relationship with geological structures. *n.*

**ge·o·phys·i·cal** (jē′ō fiz′ə kəl) of or having to do with GEOPHYSICS. *adj.*

**ge·o·phys·i·cist** (jē′ō fiz′ə sist) a person trained in GEOPHYSICS, especially one who makes it his or her work. *n.*

**ge·o·phys·ics** (jē′ō fiz′iks) the science that deals with the relations between the features of the earth and the forces that produce them; the physics of the earth (*used with a singular verb*): *Geophysics includes magnetism, meteorology, oceanography, seismology, etc.* *n.*

**ge·o·po·lit·i·cal** (jē′ō pə lit′ə kəl) of, having to do with, or involved in GEOPOLITICS. *adj.* —**ge′o·po·lit′i·cal·ly,** *adv.*

**ge·o·pol·i·ti·cian** (jē′ō pol′ə tish′ən) a person who has special skill in, or knowledge of, GEOPOLITICS. *n.*

**ge·o·pol·i·tics** (jē′ō pol′ə tiks) the study of government and its policies as affected by physical geography. *n.*

**George Cross** in the British Commonwealth of Nations, the highest award for civilian courage, established by King George VI. See MEDAL for picture.

**geor·gette** (jôr jet′) a thin, fine, transparent cloth, of silk, etc., having a slightly wavy surface and used for dresses, etc. *n.*

**Geor·gian** (jôr′jən) **1** of or having to do with the four Georges, kings of Great Britain and Ireland from 1714 to 1830. **2** of or having to do with, especially, George V, king from 1910 to 1936, or with George VI, king from 1936 to 1952. **3** a person, especially a writer, of either of the Georgian periods in England. 1, 2 *adj.*, 3 *n.*

**ge·o·syn·cline** (jē′ō sin′klīn) a sediment-filled trough that surrounds continents. *n.*

**ge·o·ther·mal** (jē′ō thėr′məl) of or having to do with heat energy produced deep inside the earth. *adj.*

| **geometric progression** | **505** | **German measles** |

hat, āge, fär; let, ēqual, tėrm; it, īce
hot, ōpen, ôrder; oil, out; cup, pút, rüle
əbove, takən, pencəl, lemən, circəs
ch, child; ng, long; sh, ship
th, thin; ᴛʜ, then; zh, measure

**ge·o·trop·ic** (jē′ə trop′ik) in biology, affected by GEOTROPISM; responding to gravity. *adj.*

**ge·ot·ro·pism** (jē ot′rə piz′əm) in biology, a response to gravity: *Geotropism can be positive or negative.* *n.*

**ge·ra·ni·um** (jə rā′nē əm *or* jə rā′nyəm) **1** a cultivated plant having large clusters of showy flowers and fragrant leaves: *The geranium is often grown as a window plant.* **2** a wild plant having pink or purple flowers, deeply notched leaves, and long, pointed pods. *n.*

**ger·bil** (jėr′bəl) any of a group of rodents having long hind legs, native to Asia and Africa: *Gerbils are often kept as pets.* *n.*

**ger·fal·con** (jėr′fol′kən) See GYRFALCON. *n.*

**ger·i·at·rics** (jer′ē at′riks) the branch of medicine that deals with the study of old age and its diseases. Compare with GERONTOLOGY. *n.*

**germ** (jėrm) **1** a microscopic animal or plant, especially one that causes disease: *the germ of scarlet fever.* **2** the earliest form of a living thing; seed; bud. **3** the beginning of anything; origin: *Counting was the germ of arithmetic.* *n.* —**germ′less,** *adj.* —**germ′like′,** *adj.*

**Ger·man** (jėr′mən) **1** a native or inhabitant of Germany, a country in western and central Europe. **2** a person of German descent. **3** the Germanic language of Germany and Austria and parts of Switzerland; especially, the standard form used in literature, on radio, television, and the stage, etc. **4** of or having to do with Germany, Germans, or German. 1–3 *n.*, 4 *adj.*

**ger·man** (jėr′mən) **1** having the same parents. Children of the same father and mother are **brothers-german** or **sisters-german.** **2** being a child of one's uncle or aunt. A **cousin-german** is a first cousin. *adj.*

**ger·mane** (jėr mān′) closely connected; to the point; pertinent: *Your statement is not germane to the discussion.* *adj.*

**Ger·man·ic** (jėr man′ik) **1** a main branch of the Indo-European family of languages, including English, German, Dutch, Frisian, Flemish, Danish, Norwegian, Swedish, Icelandic, and Gothic, that have developed from a common language spoken in Europe up to about 2500 years ago. **2** of, having to do with, or referring to this group of languages or the language they descended from. **3** of, having to do with, or referring to the peoples speaking any of these languages. **4** German. 1 *n.*, 2–4 *adj.*

**ger·ma·ni·um** (jėr mā′nē əm) a rare, greyish-white, brittle, metallic element: *Germanium is used in making transistors.* Symbol: Ge *n.*

**German measles** a contagious virus disease resembling measles, but much less serious.

A German shepherd—about 60 cm high at the shoulder

**German shepherd** a breed of large, intelligent dog developed in Germany, often trained to work with soldiers and police, to guide the blind, etc.; Alsatian.
**German silver** NICKEL SILVER.
**germ cell** a cell that can produce a new individual usually after union with another cell of the opposite sex; egg or sperm cell; gamete.
**ger·mi·cid·al** (jėr′mə sī′dəl) capable of killing germs. *adj.*
**ger·mi·cide** (jėr′mə sīd′) any substance that kills germs, especially disease germs. *n.*
**ger·mi·nal** (jėr′mə nəl) 1 of, like, or characteristic of germs or germ cells. 2 in the earliest stage of development; embryonic. *adj.*
**ger·mi·nate** (jėr′mə nāt′) 1 grow or sprout, or cause to grow or sprout: *Seeds germinate in the spring. Warmth and moisture germinate seeds.* 2 start growing or developing: *An idea was germinating in his head.* *v.*, ger·mi·nat·ed, ger·mi·nat·ing. —ger′mi·na′tor, *n.*
**ger·mi·na·tion** (jėr′mə nā′shən) the process of starting to sprout or develop: *the germination of a plan. Germination takes place when seeds are warm and moist.* *n.*
**germ plasm** a substance in germ cells that transmits hereditary characteristics to the offspring.
**germ warfare** the spreading of germs to produce disease among the enemy in time of war.
**ger·on·tol·o·gy** (jer′ən tol′ə jē) the branch of science that studies the aging process and the problems of old people. Compare with GERIATRICS. *n.*
**ger·ry·man·der** (jer′ē man′dər *or* ger′ē man′dər) 1 arrange the political boundaries of a riding, constituency, etc. so as to give the party in power an unfair advantage in an election. 2 such an arrangement. 1 *v.*, 2 *n.*
**ger·und** (jer′ənd) a verb form used as a noun. In English, gerunds end in *-ing*, having the same form as present participles but differing in use. Gerund (able to take an object): *Running a hotel appealed to her.* Participle (modifying a noun or pronoun): *Running around the corner, he bumped into a police officer.* *n.*
**ge·run·di·al** (jə run′dē əl) 1 of a GERUND. 2 used as a GERUND. *adj.*
**ges·so** (jes′ō) a plastic or liquid coating used to give surfaces the correct finish for painting: *Gesso usually contains plaster of Paris.* *n.*
**Ge·sta·po** (gə stap′ō *or* gə stä′pō; *German,* gə shtä′pō) in Nazi Germany, the secret state police. *n.*
**ges·ta·tion** (jes tā′shən) 1 the act or period of carrying young in the uterus from conception to birth; pregnancy. 2 the formation and development of a project, etc. in the mind. *n.*

**ges·tic·u·late** (jes tik′yə lāt′) 1 make or use gestures. 2 make or use many vehement gestures: *The speaker gesticulated by raising his arms, pounding the desk, and stamping his foot.* *v.*, ges·tic·u·lat·ed, ges·tic·u·lat·ing. —ges·tic′u·la′tor, *n.*
**ges·tic·u·la·tion** (jes tik′yə lā′shən) 1 the act of gesticulating. 2 gesture. *n.*
**ges·tic·u·la·tive** (jes tik′yə lə tiv *or* jes tik′yə lā′tiv) making or using gestures. *adj.*
**ges·ture** (jes′chər) 1 a movement of the hands, arms, or any part of the body, used instead of words or with words to help express an idea or feeling: *A speaker often makes gestures with the hands or arms to stress something that he or she is saying.* 2 any action for effect or to impress others: *Her refusal was merely a gesture; she really wanted to go.* 3 make or use gestures. 1, 2 *n.*, 3 *v.*, ges·tured, ges·tur·ing.

**get** (get) 1 come to have; obtain; receive; gain: *I got a new coat yesterday. She got first prize in the spelling contest.* 2 reach: *I got home early last night. Your letter got here yesterday.* 3 catch; get hold of: *I have got a bad cold.* 4 cause to be or do: *He got his hair cut yesterday. They got the fire under control.* 5 *Informal.* be obliged (used with some form of **have**): *We have got to win.* 6 become: *to get sick.* 7 be: *Don't get nervous when you have to take the test.* 8 go; come: *His boat got in yesterday.* 9 persuade; influence: *Try to get Anna to come too.* 10 prepare: *Sabra helped her mother get dinner.* 11 begin; start: *We soon got talking about our days at camp.* 12 possess; have (used with some form of **have**): *She has got black hair.* 13 usually of animals, beget. 14 *Informal.* hit; strike: *The bullet got the soldier in the arm.* 15 *Informal.* kill. 16 *Informal.* puzzle; annoy. 17 *Informal.* understand: *I don't get the point.* *v.*, **got, got** *or* **got·ten, get·ting.**
**get about,** a go from place to place. b spread; become widely known.
**get across,** *Informal.* a make clear or understood: *The teacher used slides to get the idea across.* b succeed. c annoy.
**get after,** a scold. b urge.
**get along,** a go away. b advance. c manage. d succeed; prosper. e be on good terms: *He doesn't get along with his neighbours.*
**get around,** a go from place to place. b become widely known; spread. c overcome opposition by charm, flattery, etc.; win over: *Her winning smile often helped her to get around her father.* d deceive; trick.
**get at,** a reach. b find out: *Try to get at the truth.* c *Informal.* tamper with; influence with money or threats.
**get away,** a go away. b escape. c start.
**get away with,** *Informal.* succeed in taking or doing something and escaping safely: *Ahmed thought he could get away with being late but he was caught.*
**get back,** a return. b recover. c *Informal.* get revenge.
**get behind,** a support; endorse. b fail to keep up to a schedule.
**get by,** a pass. b not be noticed or caught. c do well enough; manage all right: *They got by on her small salary.*
**get down,** make downhearted; discourage; depress: *The hot weather was getting her down.*
**get down to,** a begin: *It took him a long time to get down to work.* b reach by removing what stands in the way: *After much questioning of the witness, the lawyer got down to the truth.*
**get even,** a pay back for a wrong done; obtain revenge: *He threatened to get even with his sister for twisting his arm.*

**b** win back what was lost: *After Sven had lost 25 marbles, he played all afternoon trying to get even.*
**get in,** **a** go in. **b** put in. **c** arrive. **d** become friendly or familiar.
**get into,** **a** find out about. **b** get control of.
**get off,** **a** come down from or out of. **b** take off. **c** escape the full punishment deserved: *The naughty boy got off with a scolding.* **d** help to escape. **e** start. **f** put out; issue. **g** say or express a joke. **h** deliver a speech.
**get on,** **a** go up on or into. **b** put on. **c** advance. **d** manage. **e** succeed. **f** agree; be friendly.
**get out,** **a** go out. **b** take out. **c** go away. **d** escape. **e** help to escape. **f** become known. **g** publish. **h** find out.
**get over,** **a** recover from: *Gerard was a long time getting over his illness.* **b** overcome.
**get there,** succeed.
**get through,** **a** get to the end of; finish: *She always gets through her homework quickly.* **b** complete or cause to complete successfully: *She got through the test. His friend's help got him through.* **c** make or get a telephone connection: *I tried to phone you but I couldn't get through.* **d** make oneself understood; succeed in communicating: *No one can get through to her when she's angry.*
**get together,** **a** bring or come together; meet; assemble. **b** come to an agreement: *The workers and their employer couldn't get together about wages.*
**get up,** **a** get out of bed, etc. **b** stand up. **c** prepare; arrange: *She spent all evening getting up the next day's lesson.* **d** dress up. **e** go ahead.

**get·a·way** (get′ə wā′) *Informal.* **1** the act of getting away; escape. **2** the start of a race. *n.*

**get–to·geth·er** (get′tə geTH′ər) *Informal.* an informal social gathering or party. *n.*

**get–up** (get′up′) *Informal.* **1** the way a thing is put together; arrangement; style. **2** a dress; costume. *n.*

**gew·gaw** (gyü′gô) a showy trifle; gaudy, useless ornament or toy; bauble. *n.*

**gey·ser** (gī′zər *or* gā′zər) a spring that sends a column of hot water and steam into the air at intervals. *n.*

**ghast·ly** (gast′lē) **1** horrible: *Murder is a ghastly crime.* **2** like a dead person or ghost; deathly pale: *The sick man's face was ghastly.* **3** *Informal.* shocking: *a ghastly failure.* **4** in a ghastly manner. 1–3 *adj.*, **ghast·li·er, ghast·li·est;** 4 *adv.* —**ghast′li·ness,** *n.*

**ghee** (gē) in India, a liquid butter, clarified by boiling, from the milk of buffaloes and cows. *n.*

**gher·kin** (gėr′kən) **1** a variety of cucumber having small prickly fruit often used for pickles. **2** the pickled fruit of this plant. **3** the immature fruit of any variety of cucumber when pickled. *n.*

**ghet·to** (get′ō) **1** a part of a city inhabited mainly or entirely by a minority group that is obliged to live there for reasons of poverty, prejudice, or government policy. **2** formerly, a part of a city where Jews were obliged to live. *n., pl.* **ghet·tos.**

**ghost** (gōst) **1** the spirit of a dead person: *A ghost is supposed to live in another world and appear to living people as a pale, dim, shadowy form.* **2** anything pale, dim, or shadowy like a ghost; a faint image; slightest suggestion: *a ghost of a smile, not a ghost of a chance.* **3** *Informal.* a ghost writer. **4** write as a ghost writer: *Her autobiography was ghosted by a journalist.* **5** a secondary or multiple image resulting from the reflection of a transmitted television signal. 1–3, 5 *n.,* 4 *v.* —**ghost′like′,** *adj.*
**give up the ghost,** die.

# getaway 507 giddy

hat, āge, fär; let, ēqual, tėrm; it, īce
hot, ōpen, ôrder; oil, out; cup, pút, rüle
ǝbove, takǝn, pencǝl, lemǝn, circǝs
ch, child; ng, long; sh, ship
th, thin; ᴛʜ, then; zh, measure

**ghost·ly** (gōst′lē) like a ghost; pale, dim, and shadowy: *In the darkness he seemed to see ghostly forms.* *adj.,* **ghost·li·er, ghost·li·est.** —**ghost′li·ness,** *n.*

**ghost town** a town that has become empty and lifeless: *When the gold rush was over, the once-flourishing community became a ghost town.*

**ghost writer** a person who writes something for another who pretends to be the author.
—**ghost′-write′,** *v.*

**ghoul** (gül) **1** in Arabic stories, a horrible demon, believed to feed on corpses. **2** a person who robs graves or corpses. **3** a person who enjoys what is revolting, brutal, and horrible. *n.*
☛ *Etym.* From Arabic *ghūl* meaning an ogre or monster.

**ghoul·ish** (gü′lish) like a ghoul; revolting, brutal, and horrible. *adj.* —**ghoul′ish·ly,** *adv.*

**gi·ant** (jī′ənt) **1** a legendary being having human form, but superhuman size and strength. **2** a person or thing of unusual size, strength, importance, etc. **3** like a giant; unusually big and strong; huge. **4** an unusually large star. 1, 2, 4 *n.,* 3 *adj.*

**giant arborvitae** WESTERN RED CEDAR.

**gi·ant·ess** (jī′ən tis) a female giant. *n.*

**giant panda** PANDA (def. 1).

**gib·ber** (jib′ər *or* gib′ər) **1** chatter senselessly; talk rapidly and indistinctly: *The monkeys gibbered angrily at each other.* **2** senseless chattering; rapid indistinct talking. 1 *v.,* 2 *n.*

**gib·ber·ish** (jib′ə rish *or* gib′ə rish) meaningless chatter or unintelligible language: *the gibberish of monkeys.* *n.*

**gib·bet** (jib′it) **1** an upright post with a projecting arm at the top, from which the bodies of criminals were hung after execution. **2** hang on a gibbet. **3** hold up to public scorn or ridicule. **4** GALLOWS (def. 1). **5** put to death by hanging. 1, 4 *n.,* 2, 3, 5 *v.,* **gib·bet·ed, gib·bet·ing.**

**gib·bon** (gib′ən) a small, long-armed ape of southeastern Asia and the East Indies: *Gibbons live in trees.* *n.*

**gib·bous** (gib′əs) **1** curved out; bulging. **2** referring to the moon or a planet in the phase when more than half the disk is illuminated, but less than the whole disk. See MOON for picture. **3** hump-backed. *adj.*

**gibe** *or* **jibe** (jīb) jeer; scoff; sneer. *v.,* **gibed, gib·ing;** *n.* —**gib′er,** *n.* —**gib′ing·ly,** *adv.*

**gib·lets** (jib′lits) the heart, liver, and gizzard of a fowl, usually cooked separately or used in making gravy. *n. pl.*

**gid·dy** (gid′ē) **1** having a confused, whirling feeling in one's head; dizzy: *It makes me giddy to go on a merry-go-round.* **2** likely to make dizzy; causing dizziness: *a giddy height. The couples whirled and whirled in their giddy dance.* **3** rarely or never serious; living for the pleasure of the moment; flighty; heedless: *Nobody can tell* *what that giddy girl will do next.* *adj.,* **gid·di·er,** **gid·di·est.** —**gid′di·ly,** *adv.* —**gid′di·ness,** *n.*

**gift** (gift) **1** something given; a present: *a birthday gift.* **2** the act of giving: *The house came to her by gift from an uncle.* **3** the power or right of giving: *The job is within his gift.* **4** a natural ability; special talent: *a gift for painting.* *n.*

**gift·ed** (gif′tid) having natural ability or special talent: *a gifted musician.* *adj.*

**gift–wrap** (gif′trap′) **1** wrap for presentation as a gift, using decorative paper, ribbon, etc. **2** decorative paper, etc. suitable for wrapping gifts. 1 *v.*, **gift-wrapped, gift-wrap·ping;** 2 *n.*

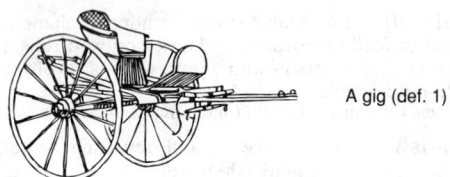
A gig (def. 1)

**gig¹** (gig) **1** a light, open two-wheeled carriage drawn by one horse. **2** a small boat used by a ship's captain for going to and from shore. *n.*

**gig²** (gig) **1** a fish spear; harpoon. **2** spear fish with a gig. 1 *n.,* 2 *v.,* **gigged, gig·ging.**

**gig³** (gig) *Informal.* an engagement for a band, singer, etc. to perform, especially for one night only. *n.*

**giga–** (jī′gə *or* gī′gə, jig′ə *or* gig′ə) an SI prefix meaning billion: *A gigametre is one billion metres.* Symbol: G

**gi·gan·tic** (jī gan′tik) **1** like a giant: *Paul Bunyan was a gigantic logger.* **2** huge; enormous: *a gigantic building project.* *adj.* —**gi·gan′ti·cal·ly,** *adv.*

**gig·gle** (gig′əl) **1** laugh in a silly or nervous way. **2** a silly or nervous laugh. 1 *v.,* **gig·gled, gig·gling;** 2 *n.* —**gig′gler,** *n.* —**gig′gling·ly,** *adv.*

**gig·gly** (gig′lē) having a tendency to giggle. *adj.*

**gig·o·lo** (jig′ə lō′) a man who is paid for being a dancing partner or escort for a woman. *n., pl.* **gig·o·los.**

**gild¹** (gild) **1** cover with a thin layer of gold or gold-coloured material; make golden. **2** make a thing look bright and pleasing: *The light from the setting sun gilded the windows.* **3** make a thing seem better than it is. *v.*
**gild the lily,** **a** adorn something that is beautiful enough not to need adornment; adorn unnecessarily. **b** praise something fine or beautiful excessively or unnecessarily.
☞ *Hom.* GUILD.

**gild²** (gild) See GUILD. *n.*

**gild·ing** (gil′ding) **1** a thin layer of gold or gold-coloured material with which a thing is gilded. **2** an attractive outer appearance hiding an unattractive or unpleasant reality or fact. **3** ppr. of GILD. 1, 2 *n.,* 3 *v.*

**gill¹** (gil) **1** one of the breathing organs of certain animals that live under water: *Fish, tadpoles, and crabs have gills.* See FISH for picture. **2** any of the thin, leaflike radiating structures on the underside of the cap of a mushroom. **3 gills,** *pl.* **a** flesh under a person's jaws. **b** the red, hanging flesh under the throat of a fowl; WATTLE. *n.*

**gill²** (jil) a unit for measuring liquids, equal to one fourth of a pint (about 142 mL). *n.*

**gil·lie** (gil′ē) **1** in the Scottish Highlands, a man who acts as an attendant or guide for a hunter or fisherman. **2** formerly, a male servant or attendant to a Highland chief. *n.* Also, **gilly.**

**gill net** a net suspended upright in the water, for catching fish by entangling their gills in its meshes.

**gil·ly** (gil′ē) See GILLIE. *n., pl.* **gil·lies.**

**gil·ly·flow·er** (jil′ē flou′ər) any of various flowers that have a spicy fragrance, such as the wallflower, stock, and clove pink. *n.*

**gilt** (gilt) **1** gilded. **2** a thin layer of gold or gold-coloured material with which a thing is gilded; gilding. 1 *adj.,* 2 *n.*
**gilt on the gingerbread,** an additional adornment to something that is already sufficiently attractive.
☞ *Hom.* GUILT.

**gilt–edged** (gil′tejd′) **1** having gilded edges. **2** of the very best quality: *gilt-edged stocks and securities.* *adj.*

**gim·crack** (jim′krak′) **1** a showy, useless trifle. **2** showy but useless. 1 *n.,* 2 *adj.*

**gim·let** (gim′lit) a small tool with a screw point, for boring holes. *n.*

**gim·let–eyed** (gim′li tīd′) having eyes that are sharp and piercing. *adj.*

**gim·mick** (gim′ik) **1** *Informal.* any small device, especially one used secretly or in a tricky manner. **2** a deceptive thing or quality; trick. **3** something to attract attention; stunt. *n.*

**gin¹** (jin) a strong, colourless, alcoholic drink, usually made from grain and usually flavoured with juniper berries. *n.*

**gin²** (jin) **1** a machine for separating cotton from its seeds. **2** separate cotton from its seeds. **3** a trap; snare. **4** trap. 1, 3 *n.,* 2, 4 *v.,* **ginned, gin·ning.** —**gin′ner,** *n.*

**gin·ger** (jin′jər) **1** a spice made from the root of a tropical plant, used for flavouring and in medicine. **2** the root: *Ginger is sometimes preserved in syrup and sometimes candied.* **3** the plant. **4** *Informal.* liveliness; energy: *That horse has plenty of ginger.* **5** light reddish or brownish yellow: *a girl with ginger hair.* 1–5 *n.,* 5 *adj.*
**ginger up,** *Informal.* make more lively: *Your story needs gingering up with some action.*

**ginger ale** a non-alcoholic, sweetened, carbonated drink flavoured with ginger.

**ginger beer** a drink similar to ginger ale, but made with fermenting ginger.

**gin·ger·bread** (jin′jər bred′) **1** a cake flavoured with ginger and sweetened with molasses. **2** intricate wooden decoration, such as fretwork or carving on the gables of houses, etc.: *Many old houses, especially in central and eastern Canada, are trimmed with gingerbread.* **3** of or referring to such decoration. **4** showy or gaudy. *n.*

**gin·ger·ly** (jin′jər lē) with extreme care or caution. *adv., adj.* —**gin′ger·li·ness,** *n.*

**gin·ger·snap** (jin′jər snap′) a thin, crisp cookie flavoured with ginger and molasses. *n.*

**gin·ger·y** (jin′jə rē) **1** like ginger; hot and sharp; spicy. **2** light reddish or brownish yellow. **3** alert; full of vigour. *1–3 adj., 2 n.*

**ging·ham** (ging′əm) **1** a kind of cloth, usually cotton or part cotton: *The patterns of gingham are usually in stripes, plaids, or checks.* **2** made of gingham: *a gingham dress. n.*

**gink·go** (ging′kō *or* jing′kō) a large deciduous tree native to China but widely cultivated in temperate regions as an ornamental tree, having fan-shaped leaves and yellow fruit. *n., pl.* **gink·goes.**

**gin·seng** (jin′seng) **1** either of two closely related species of plant found in North America and eastern Asia, having compound leaves composed of five leaflets and a thick, aromatic branched root. **2** the root of either of these plants, used as a medicine. *n.*

**Gip·sy** *or* **gipsy** (jip′sē) See GYPSY. *n., pl.* **Gip·sies.**

**gipsy moth** See GYPSY MOTH.

**gi·raffe** (jə raf′) a large African mammal having a very long neck and legs and a spotted skin: *Giraffes are the tallest of living animals. n.*

**gird** (gėrd) **1** put a belt or band around. **2** fasten with a belt or band. **3** surround; enclose. **4** get ready for action: *They girded themselves for battle.* **5** clothe, furnish, equip, etc. *v.,* **girt** *or* **gird·ed, gird·ing.**

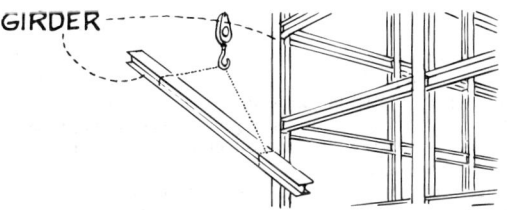

**gird·er** (gėr′dər) a main supporting beam, usually horizontal: *Steel girders are often used to make the framework of bridges and tall buildings. n.*

**gir·dle** (gėr′dəl) **1** a belt, sash, cord, etc. worn around the waist. **2** anything that surrounds or encloses: *a girdle of trees around the pond.* **3** a support like a corset worn about the hips or waist. **4** form a girdle around; encircle: *Wide roads girdle the city.* **5** cut away the bark so as to make a ring around a tree, branch, etc.: *If you girdle a tree, it will die.* **6** put a girdle on or around. *1–3 n., 4–6 v.,* **gir·dled, gir·dling.**

**girl** (gėrl) **1** a female child. **2** a young, unmarried woman. **3** a female servant. **4** *Informal.* sweetheart: *He took his girl to the movies. n.*

**girl·friend** (gėrl′frend′) **1** a female companion of a boy or man; sweetheart or lover: *Does he have a girlfriend?* **2** a girl who is one's friend. *n.*

**Girl Guide** a member, aged nine to twelve, of the GIRL GUIDES.

**Girl Guides** a nonpolitical, nondenominational organization for girls and young women whose aim is to help them to learn co-operation, leadership, self-reliance, and consideration for others, and to develop physical fitness and spiritual values, in order to become responsible, resourceful, and happy members of society. The Girl Guides of Canada have five programs for different ages: Sparks, Brownies, Guides, Pathfinders, and Cadets and Rangers.

**girl·hood** (gėrl′hùd) the time or condition of being a girl: *The old woman recalled her girlhood with pleasure. n.*

**girl·ie** (gėr′lē) *Informal.* a girl or woman. *n.*

**girl·ish** (gėr′lish) **1** of a girl. **2** like that of a girl. **3** proper or suitable for girls: *She thought she was too old now for such girlish games. adj.* —**girl′ish·ly,** *adv.* —**girl′ish·ness,** *n.*

**girt** (gėrt) **1** a pt. and a pp. of GIRD: *The knight girt himself for battle.* **2** put a belt, girdle, or girth around; gird. **3** fasten with a belt, girdle, or girth. *v.*

**girth** (gėrth) **1** the measure around anything: *a man of large girth, the girth of a tree.* **2** measure in girth. **3** a strap or band that keeps a saddle, pack, etc. in place on a horse's back. See HARNESS and SADDLE for pictures. **4** fasten with a strap and band. *1, 3 n., 2, 4 v.*

**gist** (jist) the essential part; real point or main idea; the substance of an argument: *The gist of his long speech was that we should build a new school. n.*

**give** (giv) **1** hand over as a present; make a present of: *My brother gave me his watch.* **2** hand over; deliver: *to give a person into custody, to give one's word.* **3** hand over in return for something; pay: *I gave it to her for $5.* **4** let have; cause to have: *Give me permission to leave.* **5** deal; administer: *He gives hard blows even in play. She gave the ball a kick.* **6** offer or present: *This newspaper gives a full story of the game.* **7** put forth; make; do; utter: *He gave a cry of pain.* **8** furnish; supply: *to give aid to the enemy.* **9** produce; yield; deliver: *to give a lecture.* **10** cause; create: *Don't give the teacher any trouble.* **11** yield to pressure or force: *The lock gave when she pushed hard against the door.* **12** a yielding to force or pressure; elasticity: *You need a fabric with give for this pattern. 1–11 v.,* **gave, giv·en, giv·ing;** *12 n.* —**giv′er,** *n.*

**give and take,** exchange evenly or fairly.
**give away,** *Informal.* **a** give as a present. **b** give as a bride: *The bride's father gave her away.* **c** cause to become known; reveal; betray: *The spy gave away secrets to the enemy.*
**give back,** return: *Give back the book you borrowed.*
**give in, a** stop fighting and admit defeat; yield. **b** hand in: *Mario gave in his history project when it was due.*
**give off,** send out; put forth.
**give out, a** send out; put forth: *The roses gave out a sweet smell.* **b** distribute: *The girls gave out the handbills.* **c** make known: *The news was given out at midnight.* **d** become used up: *The food gave out during the famine.* **e** become worn out or exhausted: *The old man's strength gave out during the long walk.* **f** fail to operate: *The engine gave out.*
**give over, a** hand over; deliver. **b** stop.
**give up, a** hand over; deliver; surrender. **b** stop having or doing. **c** stop trying: *Don't give up now; we're almost there.* **d** have no more hope for: *They've given him up as dead.* **e** devote entirely: *Hans gave himself up to his studies.*

**give–and–take** (giv′ən tāk′) **1** an even or fair exchange. **2** good-natured banter. *n.*

**give·a·way** (giv′ə wā′) *Informal.* **1** an unintentional revelation; exposure; betrayal. **2** a radio or television

**given** (giv′ən) **1** stated; fixed; specified: *You must finish the test in a given time.* **2** assigned as a basis of calculating, reasoning, etc.: *Given that the radius is 19 cm, find the circumference.* **3** pp. of GIVE: *That book was given to me.* 1, 2 *adj.*, 3 *v.*
**given to,** inclined or disposed toward: *The old soldier was given to boasting.*

**given name** a name given to a person in addition to the family name: *Gordon and Charles are the given names of Gordon Charles McRae.*

**giz·zard** (giz′ərd) **1** a bird's second stomach, where the food from the first stomach is ground up fine. **2** a muscular organ in insects and earthworms that is behind the crop and serves to grind the food. *n.*

**gla·cé** (gla sā′) **1** coated with a glaze of sugar. **2** frozen. **3** finished with a glossy surface: *glacé silk.* *adj.*

**gla·cial** (glā′shəl) **1** of ice or glaciers; having much ice or many glaciers: *During the glacial period, much of the northern hemisphere was covered with great ice sheets.* **2** relating to a glacial epoch or period. **3** made by the pressure and movement of ice or glaciers: *a glacial plain.* **4** like ice; very cold; icy: *She gave him a glacial stare.* *adj.* —**gla′cial·ly,** *adv.*

**glacial epoch** **1** any of the times when much of the earth was covered with glaciers. **2** the most recent time when much of the northern hemisphere was covered with glaciers.

**glacial period** a period that includes the GLACIAL EPOCHS; ice age.

**gla·ci·ate** (glā′shē āt′) **1** cover with ice or glaciers. **2** expose to or change by the action of glaciers. *v.*, **gla·ci·at·ed, gla·ci·at·ing.** —**gla′ci·a′tion,** *n.*

**gla·cier** (glā′shər *or* glā′syər) a large mass of ice formed from snow on high ground wherever winter snowfall exceeds summer melting: *A glacier moves very slowly down a mountain or along a valley.* *n.*

**glacier lily** *Cdn.* a plant of the lily family, closely related to the adder's-tongue of eastern North America, found in the mountains of western North America; snow lily; dogtooth violet: *The yellow flowers of the glacier lily appear in May and June, often before the snow has disappeared.*

**glad** (glad) **1** happy; experiencing joy: *I'm glad you could come. I'll be glad when exams are over.* **2** bringing joy; very pleasant: *glad news.* **3** caused by or expressing happiness: *We heard her glad shout when she saw us.* **4** very willing: *I'd be glad to help out.* **5** bright and cheerful. *adj.*, **glad·der, glad·dest.** —**glad′ly,** *adv.* —**glad′ness,** *n.*

**glad·den** (glad′ən) make or become glad: *Her heart was gladdened by the good news.* *v.*

**glade** (glād) an open space in a wood or forest. *n.*

**glad·i·a·tor** (glad′ē ā′tər) **1** in ancient Rome, a slave, captive, or paid fighter who fought at the public shows. **2** a person who argues, fights, wrestles, etc. with great skill. *n.*

**glad·i·a·to·ri·al** (glad′ē ə tô′rē əl) of or having to do with GLADIATORS. *adj.*

**glad·i·o·lus** (glad′ē ō′ləs) any of a large, closely related group of plants of the iris family that grow from bulblike underground stems, having stiff, sword-shaped leaves and spikes of large showy flowers all growing on one side of the stem: *Gladioli are widely grown for their flowers.* *n., pl.* **glad·i·o·li** (-lī *or* -lē) *or* **glad·i·o·lus·es.**

**glad·some** (glad′səm) **1** glad; joyful; cheerful. **2** causing gladness; pleasant; delightful. *adj.*

**glam·or** (glam′ər) See GLAMOUR. *n.*

**glam·or·ize** (glam′ə rīz′) See GLAMOURIZE. *v.*

**glam·or·ous** (glam′ə rəs) full of GLAMOUR; fascinating; charming. *adj.* —**glam′or·ous·ly,** *adv.*

**glam·our** (glam′ər) **1** a romantic or exciting fascination; alluring charm: *the glamour of show business. The mysterious stranger had a glamour about him.* **2** a magic spell or influence. *n.* Sometimes, **glamor.**
☞ *Etym.* From an altered form of *grammar* with the general meaning of 'learning' and the specific meaning of 'occult learning, magic'. **Glamour** was used in Scotland in the 18c. to mean 'magic, magic spell' and later to mean 'magical beauty or fascination'.

**glam·our·ize** (glam′ə rīz′) make someone or something glamorous. *v.*, **glam·our·ized, glam·our·iz·ing.** Also, **glamorize.**

**glance** (glans) **1** a quick look: *I gave her only a glance.* **2** look quickly. **3** a flash of light; gleam. **4** flash with light; gleam: *eyes glancing.* **5** hit and go off at a slant: *The spear glanced off the wall and missed him.* **6** a glancing off; deflected motion; swift, oblique movement. **7** make a short reference and go on to something else. **8** a passing reference; brief allusion. 1, 3, 6, 8 *n.*, 2, 4, 5, 7 *v.*, **glanced, glanc·ing.**
**glance off,** fail to affect: *Criticism just seems to glance off him.*

**gland** (gland) an organ in the body by which certain substances are separated from the blood and changed into some secretion for use in the body, such as bile, or into a product to be discharged from the body, such as sweat: *The liver, the kidneys, the pancreas, and the thyroid are glands.* *n.*

**glan·du·lar** (glan′jə lər *or* glan′dyə lər) of or like a gland; having glands; made up of glands. *adj.*

**glare**[1] (gler) **1** a strong, bright light; light that shines so brightly that it hurts the eyes: *The glare from the ice made her eyes sore.* **2** give off a strong, bright light; shine so brightly as to hurt the eyes. **3** a fierce, angry stare. **4** stare fiercely and angrily: *The angry man glared at his disobedient daughter.* **5** express by a fierce, angry stare. **6** too great brightness and showiness. **7** be too bright and showy. 1, 3, 6 *n.*, 2, 4, 5, 7 *v.*, **glared, glar·ing.**

**glare**[2] (gler) **1** a bright, smooth surface. **2** bright and smooth. 1 *n.*, 2 *adj.*

**glare ice** *Cdn.* ice that has a smooth, glassy surface.

**glar·ing** (gler′ing) **1** shining very brightly: *She was dazzled by the glaring headlights.* **2** too bright and showy. **3** very easily seen; conspicuous: *The student made a glaring error in spelling.* **4** ppr. of GLARE. 1–3 *adj.*, 4 *v.*

**glass** (glas) **1** a hard, brittle substance that is usually transparent, made by fusing sand with soda, potash, lime, or other substances: *Windows are made of glass.* **2** a tumbler or similar drinking vessel made of glass, plastic, etc.: *She knocked a glass off the table.* **3** the amount that a glass can hold: *to drink a glass of water.* **4** something made of glass: *A piece of glass for a picture frame, a windowpane, a mirror, a watch crystal, a lens to correct defective eyesight, a telescope, a thermometer, a barometer, or an hourglass is a glass.* **5** made of glass: *a glass dish.* **6** things made of glass; glassware. **7** with glass put in it; covered with glass. **8** put glass in; cover or protect with glass. **9** reflect. **10** mirror: *Look at yourself in the glass.* **11 glasses,** *pl.* **a** a pair of lenses to correct defective eyesight; eyeglasses; spectacles. **b** field glasses; binoculars. *1–7, 10, 11 n., 8, 9 v.*

**glass blowing** the art or process of shaping glass by blowing while it is still hot and soft.

**glass·ful** (glas′fúl) as much as a drinking glass holds. *n., pl.* **glass·fuls.**

**glass·ware** (glas′wer′) articles made of glass. *n.*

**glass·wort** (glas′wèrt′) a plant having juicy, leafless stems that grows in saltwater marshes: *The ashes of glasswort were formerly used as a source of soda in making glass.* *n.*

**glass·y** (glas′ē) **1** like glass; smooth or easily seen through: *glassy water.* **2** having a fixed, stupid stare: *The dazed man's eyes were glassy.* *adj.,* **glass·i·er, glass·i·est.** —**glass′i·ly,** *adv.* —**glass′i·ness,** *n.*

**glau·co·ma** (glo kō′mə *or* glou kō′mə) a disease of the eye, characterized by increasing pressure within and hardening of the eyeball and gradual loss of sight. *n.*

**glau·cous** (glok′əs) **1** light bluish-green. **2** covered with whitish powder as plums and grapes are. *adj.*

**glaze** (glāz) **1** put glass in; cover with glass: *Pieces of glass cut to the right size are used to glaze windows and picture frames.* **2** a smooth, glassy surface or glossy coating: *the glaze on a china cup, a glaze of ice.* **3** a substance used to make such a surface or coating on things. **4** make a smooth, glassy surface or glossy coating on china, food, etc. **5** become smooth, glassy, or glossy. *1, 4, 5 v., glazed, glaz·ing; 2, 3 n.*

**gla·zier** (glā′zhər, glā′zhē ər *or* glā′zē ər) a person whose work is putting glass in windows, picture frames, etc. *n.*

**gleam** (glēm) **1** a flash or beam of light: *We saw the gleam of headlights through the rain.* **2** to flash or beam with light. **3** a short or faint light. **4** shine with a short or faint light. **5** a short appearance; faint show: *After one gleam of hope, all was discouraging and dark.* **6** appear suddenly; be shown briefly. *1, 3, 5 n., 2, 4, 6 v.*

**glean** (glēn) **1** gather grain left on a field by reapers. **2** gather little by little or slowly: *The spy gleaned information from the soldier's talk.* *v.* —**glean′er,** *n.*

**glee** (glē) **1** joy; delight; mirth. **2** a song for three or more usually male voices each singing a different part: *A glee is usually sung without accompaniment.* *n.*

**glee club** a society or group organized for singing glees or other part songs.

**glee·ful** (glē′fəl) filled with glee; merry; joyous: *a gleeful laugh.* *adj.* —**glee′ful·ly,** *adv.* —**glee′ful·ness,** *n.*

**glee·some** (glē′səm) GLEEFUL. *adj.*

**glen** (glen) a small, narrow valley. *n.*

**glen·gar·ry** (glen gar′ē *or* glen ger′ē) a Scottish cap with straight sides and a lengthwise crease in the top, often having short ribbons at the back. See CAP for picture. *n., pl.* **glen·gar·ries.**

**glib** (glib) **1** speaking or spoken too smoothly and easily to be sincere: *a glib sales talk. No one believed her glib excuses.* **2** without depth; not thought out; superficial: *a glib solution.* *adj.,* **glib·ber, glib·best.** —**glib′ly,** *adv.* —**glib′ness,** *n.*

**glide** (glīd) **1** move along smoothly, evenly, and easily: *Birds, ships, dancers, and skaters glide.* **2** a smooth, even, easy movement. **3** pass gradually, quietly, or imperceptibly: *The years glided past.* **4** come down slowly at a slant without using a motor: *Under favourable circumstances, an airplane can glide about 1.6 kilometres for every 300 metres that it is above the ground.* **5** of an airplane, coming down slowly at a slant without using a motor. **6** in music, a SLUR. *1, 3, 4 v.,* **glid·ed, glid·ing;** *2, 5, 6 n.*

A glider

**glid·er** (glī′dər) **1** a person or thing that glides, especially an aircraft resembling an airplane but without a motor: *A glider has very long wings in proportion to the body, and is kept up in the air by rising air currents.* **2** a type of chair with a sliding base. *n.*

**glim·mer** (glim′ər) **1** a faint or unsteady light. **2** shine with a faint or unsteady light: *The candle glimmered and went out.* **3** a vague idea or feeling; a faint glimpse: *The doctor's report gave us only a glimmer of hope.* **4** appear faintly or dimly. *1, 3 n., 2, 4 v.*

**glim·mer·ing** (glim′ə ring) **1** GLIMMER (defs. 1, 3). **2** ppr. of GLIMMER. *1 n., 2 v.*

**glimpse** (glimps) **1** a short, quick view: *I caught a glimpse of the falls as our train went by.* **2** catch a short, quick view of. **3** look quickly; glance. **4** a short, faint appearance. *1, 4 n., 2, 3 v.* **glimpsed, glimps·ing.**

**glint** (glint) gleam; flash: *There was a glint of steel as the man swung his axe. Her eyes glinted fiercely in the light.* *n., v.*

**glis·san·do** (gli sän′dō) in music: **1** performed with a gliding effect: *A pianist plays a glissando passage by running one finger rapidly over the white keys on a piano.* **2** a gliding effect. **3** a glissando passage. *1 adj., 2, 3 n., pl.* **glis·san·di** (-dē).

**glis·ten** (glis′ən) sparkle; glitter; shine: *The leaves glistened after the rain.* *v., n.*

**glit·ter** (glit′ər) **1** glisten; sparkle; shine with a bright, sparkling light: *Jewels and new coins glitter.* **2** a bright sparkling light. **3** be bright and showy. **4** brightness; showiness; a bright display. **5** the bright, sparkling ice that forms on everything outdoors after a rain that freezes. **6** become covered with such ice. *1, 3, 6 v., 2, 4, 5 n.*

**glit·ter·y** (glit′ə rē) glittering. *adj.*

**glitz** (glits) *Informal.* glitter. *n.*

**glitzy** (glit′sē) *Informal.* glittering. *adj.*

**gloam·ing** (glō′ming) evening twilight; dusk. *n.*

**gloat** (glōt) gaze intently; ponder with pleasure; stare: *The miser gloated over his gold.* *v.* —**gloat′er**, *n.* —**gloat′ing·ly**, *adv.*

**glob·al** (glō′bəl) 1 of the earth as a whole; worldwide: *the threat of global war.* 2 shaped like a globe. *adj.* —**glob′al·ly**, *adv.*

**globe** (glōb) 1 anything round like a ball; sphere. 2 the earth; world. 3 a sphere with a map of the earth or sky on it. 4 anything rounded like a globe: *An electric light bulb is a globe.* *n.*

**globe·fish** (glōb′fish′) a fish that can make itself nearly globe-shaped by drawing in air. *n., pl.* **globe·fish** or **globe·fish·es**.

**globe·flow·er** (glōb′flou′ər) a plant of the same family as the buttercup, having globe-shaped, yellow flowers. *n.*

**globe·trot·ter** (glōb′trot′ər) a person who travels widely over the world, especially for pleasure. *n.*

**globe·trot·ting** (glōb′trot′ing) travelling widely throughout the world, especially as a tourist. *n.*

**glob·u·lar** (glob′yə lər) 1 shaped like a globe or GLOBULE; round; spherical. 2 consisting of GLOBULES. *adj.*

**glob·ule** (glob′yül *or* glob′yəl) a very small ball; tiny drop: *globules of sweat.* *n.*

**glob·u·lin** (glob′yə lin) any of a group of proteins, found in plant and animal tissues, that are soluble in weak salt solutions but insoluble in pure water. *n.*

**glock·en·spiel** (glok′ən spēl′) a musical instrument consisting of a graduated series of small, tuned bells, metal bars, or tubes mounted in a frame and struck by two little hammers. *n.*

**gloom** (glüm) 1 darkness; deep shadow; dimness. 2 be or become dark, dim, or dismal. 3 low spirits; sadness. 4 be in low spirits; feel miserable. 5 a dejected or sad look. 6 look sad or dismal. 1, 3, 5 *n.*, 2, 4, 6 *v.*

**gloom·y** (glü′mē) 1 dark; dim: *a gloomy winter day.* 2 in low spirits; sad; melancholy: *a gloomy mood.* 3 causing low spirits; discouraging; dismal: *a gloomy book.* *adj.*, **gloom·i·er**, **gloom·i·est**. —**gloom′i·ly**, *adv.* —**gloom′i·ness**, *n.*

**glo·ri·fi·ca·tion** (glô′rə fə kā′shən) glorifying or being glorified. *n.*

**glo·ri·fy** (glô′rə fī′) 1 give glory to; make glorious. 2 praise; honour; worship. 3 make more beautiful or splendid: *Sunset glorified the valley.* 4 exalt to the glory of heaven. *v.*, **glo·ri·fied**, **glo·ri·fy·ing**. —**glo′ri·fi′er**, *n.*

**glo·ri·ous** (glô′rē əs) 1 having or deserving glory; illustrious. 2 giving glory; worthy of high praise: *a glorious victory.* 3 magnificent; splendid: *a glorious pageant.* 4 *Informal.* admirable; delightful; fine: *have a glorious time. Isn't it a glorious day?* *adj.* —**glo′ri·ous·ly**, *adv.*

**glo·ry** (glô′rē) 1 great praise and honour; fame; renown. 2 that which brings praise and honour; a source of pride and joy: *Her real glory was not her beauty but her success as a doctor.* 3 adoring praise and thanksgiving. 4 be proud; rejoice. 5 radiant beauty; brightness; magnificence; splendour: *Her hair was her crowning glory.* 6 a condition of magnificence, splendour, or greatest prosperity. 7 the splendour and bliss of heaven; heaven. 8 a halo. 1–3, 5–8 *n., pl.* **glo·ries**; 4 *v.*, **glo·ried**, **glo·ry·ing**.
**glory in**, take great pride or delight in: *Her father gloried in her success as a pianist.*

**gloss**[1] (glos) 1 a smooth, shiny surface; lustre: *Varnished furniture has a gloss.* 2 put a smooth, shiny surface on. 3 an outward appearance or surface that covers faults underneath. 1, 3 *n.*, 2 *v.*
**gloss over**, smooth over something or try to make something appear right even though it is wrong: *Daniel wished to gloss over the errors in his essay.*

**gloss**[2] (glos) 1 an explanation; comment. 2 comment on; explain. 3 a GLOSSARY. 1, 3 *n.*, 2 *v.* —**gloss′er**, *n.*

**glos·sa·ry** (glos′ə rē) a list of special, technical, or difficult words with explanations or comments: *a glossary to Shakespeare's plays, a glossary of terms used in chemistry. Textbooks sometimes have glossaries at the end.* *n., pl.* **glos·sa·ries**.

**gloss·y** (glos′ē) 1 smooth and shiny: *glossy paint.* 2 a photograph printed on glossy paper. 1 *adj.*, **gloss·i·er**, **gloss·i·est**. 2 *n.* —**gloss′i·ly**, *adv.* —**gloss′i·ness**, *n.*

**glot·tis** (glot′is) the opening at the upper part of the windpipe, between the vocal cords. See WINDPIPE for picture. *n.*

**glove** (gluv) 1 a covering for the hand, having separate sections for each of the four fingers and the thumb. 2 a padded covering to protect the hand: *a hockey glove, a baseball glove.* 3 cover or provide with a glove or gloves. 4 in baseball, catch a ball. 1, 2 *n.*, 3, 4 *v.*, **gloved**, **glov·ing**. —**glove′less**, *adj.*
**handle with (kid) gloves**, treat gently or carefully.

**glov·er** (gluv′ər) a person who makes or sells gloves. *n.*

**glow** (glō) 1 the shine from something that is red-hot or white-hot. 2 any similar shine: *The firefly's glow was fascinating.* 3 shine as if red-hot or white-hot. 4 brightness: *the glow of sunset.* 5 a warm feeling or colour in the body: *the glow of health on his cheeks.* 6 show a warm colour; look warm; be red or bright: *Her cheeks glowed as she danced.* 7 be hot; burn. 8 an eager look on the face: *a glow of interest or excitement.* 9 be eager or animated. 1, 2, 4, 5, 8 *n.*, 3, 6, 7, 9 *v.*

**glow·er** (glou′ər) 1 stare angrily; scowl: *The fighters glowered at each other.* 2 an angry or sullen look. 1 *v.*, 2 *n.* —**glow′er·ing·ly**, *adv.*

**glow·ing** (glō′ing) 1 shining from something that is red-hot or white-hot. 2 bright: *glowing colours.* 3 showing a warm colour: *glowing cheeks.* 4 eager; animated: *a glowing description.* 5 ppr. of GLOW. 1–4 *adj.*, 5 *v.* —**glow′ing·ly**, *adv.*

**glow–worm** (glō′wėrm′) any insect larva or wormlike insect that glows in the dark: *Fireflies develop from some glow-worms.* *n.*

**glox·in·i·a** (glok sin′ē ə) a cultivated plant having large, white, red, or purple, bell-shaped flowers. *n.*

**gloze** (glōz) smooth or gloss (*over*): *Michelle's friends glozed over her faults.* *v.*, **glozed**, **gloz·ing**.

**glu·cose** (glü′kōs) 1 a kind of sugar occurring

naturally in fruits: *Glucose is about half as sweet as cane sugar.* **2** a syrup made from starch. *n.*

**glue** (glü) **1** a substance used to stick things together, often made by boiling the hoofs, skins, and bones of animals in water. **2** any similar sticky substance made of casein, rubber, etc.; adhesive: *Glues are stronger than pastes.* **3** stick together with glue. **4** fasten tightly; attach firmly: *During the ride down the mountain, her hands were glued to the steering wheel.* **5** regard or look at fixedly: *He walked on, his eyes glued to the road.* 1, 2 *n.*, 3, 4, 5 *v.*, **glued, glu·ing.**

**glue·y** (glü′ē) **1** like glue; sticky. **2** full of glue; smeared with glue. *adj.*, **glu·i·er, glu·i·est.**

**glum** (glum) gloomy; dismal; sullen: *a glum look.* *adj.*, **glum·mer, glum·mest.** —**glum′ly,** *adv.*

**glut** (glut) **1** fill full; feed or satisfy fully: *A year of war glutted her appetite for adventure.* **2** a full supply; great quantity. **3** fill too full; supply too much for: *The price of wheat dropped when the market was glutted with it.* **4** too great a supply. 1, 3 *v.*, **glut·ted, glut·ting;** 2, 4 *n.*

**glu·ten** (glü′tən) a tough, sticky substance that remains in flour when the starch is taken out. *n.*

**glu·te·nous** (glü′tə nəs) **1** like GLUTEN. **2** containing much GLUTEN. *adj.*
☛ *Hom.* GLUTINOUS.

**glu·ti·nous** (glü′tə nəs) sticky. *adj.*
☛ *Hom.* GLUTENOUS.

**glut·ton¹** (glut′ən) **1** a greedy eater; person who eats too much. **2** a person who never seems to have enough of something. *n.*

**glut·ton²** (glut′ən) a clumsy, heavily built mammal of northern regions; wolverine. See WOLVERINE for picture. *n.*

**glut·ton·ous** (glut′ə nəs) greedy about food; having the habit of eating too much. *adj.*
—**glut′ton·ous·ly,** *adv.*

**glut·ton·y** (glut′ə nē) greediness about food; the habit of eating too much. *n., pl.* **glut·ton·ies.**

**glyc·er·in** (glis′ə rin) a colourless, syrupy, sweet liquid obtained from fats and oils, used in ointments, lotions, antifreeze solutions, and explosives. *n.* Also, **glycerine** (glis′ər ēn′).

**glyc·er·ol** (glis′ə rōl) GLYCERIN. *n.*

**gly·co·gen** (glī′kə jən) a starchlike substance in the liver and other animal tissues that is changed into sugar when needed. *n.*

**G.M.T.** Greenwich mean time.

**gnarl** (närl) a knot in wood; hard, rough lump: *Wood with gnarls is hard to cut.* *n.*

**gnarled** (närld) **1** having many knots or hard, rough lumps; knotty and twisted: *a gnarled old cypress.* **2** rough and hard; rugged and sinewy, as the hands of a person who has done much hard, rough manual work. *adj.*

**gnash** (nash) strike or grind the teeth together; grind together. *v.*

**gnat** (nat) any of various small two-winged insects or flies: *Most gnats are bloodsucking and make bites that itch.* *n.*
**strain at a gnat,** object to some small or very trifling thing.

**gnaw** (no) **1** wear away by biting: *to gnaw a bone. The mouse has gnawed right through the oatmeal box.* **2** make by biting: *to gnaw a hole.* **3** wear away; consume or corrode: *The river has been gnawing the bank.* **4** torment: *A feeling of guilt gnawed my conscience.* *v.*, **gnawed, gnawed** or **gnawn, gnaw·ing.** —**gnaw′er,** *n.*
—**gnaw′ing·ly,** *adv.*

**gnawn** (non) a pp. of GNAW. *v.*

**gneiss** (nīs) a metamorphic rock composed of quartz, feldspar, and mica or hornblende. It is distinguished from granite by its layered structure. *n.*
☛ *Hom.* NICE.

**gnome** (nōm) in folklore, a dwarf that lives in the earth and guards treasures of precious metals and stones. *n.*

**gno·mic** (nō′mik *or* nom′ik) full of maxims or instructive sayings; aphoristic. *adj.*

**GNP** or **G.N.P.** gross national product.

**gnu** (nyü *or* nü) any of several species of large African antelope having an oxlike head, curved horns, and a long tail; wildebeest. *n., pl.* **gnus** or (*esp. collectively*) **gnu.**
☛ *Hom.* KNEW, NEW.

**go** (gō) **1** move along: *Go straight home.* **2** move away; leave: *It is time for us to go.* **3** be in motion; act; work; run: *Does your watch go well?* **4** get to be; become: *to go mad.* **5** be habitually; be: *to go hungry.* **6** proceed; advance: *to go to Edmonton.* **7** attend on a regular basis: *She goes to the vocational school.* **8** be current: *A rumour went through the town.* **9** be known: *She went under a false name.* **10** put oneself: *Don't go to any trouble for me.* **11** extend; reach: *His memory does not go back that far.* **12** pass: *The summer holidays go quickly.* **13** be given: *First prize goes to the winner.* **14** be sold: *The painting goes to the highest bidder.* **15** tend; lead: *This goes to show that you must work harder.* **16** turn out; have a certain result: *How did the game go?* **17** have its place; belong: *This book goes on the top shelf.* **18** make a certain sound: *The cow went "moo".* **19** have certain words; be said: *How does that song go?* **20** refer; appeal: *to go to court.* **21** stop being; be given up, used up, or lost: *Her eyesight is going.* **22** die: *His wife went first.* **23** break down; give way: *The engine in the old car finally went.* **24** *Informal.* put up with; stand: *I can't go tea.* **25** the act of going. **26** *Informal.* spirit; energy. **27** *Informal.* the state of affairs; way that things are. **28** *Informal.* a fashion; style; rage. **29** *Informal.* a try; attempt; chance: *Let's have another go at this problem.* **30** something successful; a success: *She seems to be making a go of her new store.* 1–24 *v.*, **went, gone, go·ing;** 25–30 *n., pl.* **goes.** —**go′er,** *n.*
**as people** or **things go,** considering how others are.
**go about, a** be busy at; work on. **b** move from place to place. **c** turn around; change direction.
**go ahead,** proceed without hesitating; carry on: *He went ahead with his plan, in spite of their objections.*
**go along,** agree; co-operate.
**go around, a** move from place to place. **b** be enough to give some to all.
**go at, a** attack: *With a snarl, the dog went at the intruder.* **b** *Informal.* make a start on: *The girls went at the dinner as if they were starving.*

**go back on, a** be not faithful or loyal to: *He went back on his friends.* **b** fail to live up to: *She went back on her word.*
**go by, a** pass. **b** be guided by; follow: *He promised to go by the rules.* **c** be controlled by. **d** be known by: *She goes by the nickname of "Slim."*
**go down, a** descend; decline; sink. **b** be defeated; lose.
**go for,** *Informal.* **a** try to get. **b** favour, support. **c** be attracted to. **d** attack.
**go in for,** try to do; take part in; spend time and energy at: *She used to go in for basketball.*
**go into, a** in arithmetic, be contained in: *3 goes into 9 three times.* **b** investigate.
**go in with,** join; share with.
**go it,** *Informal.* go fast.
**go it alone,** *Informal.* manage without help.
**go off, a** leave; depart. **b** be fired; explode: *The gun went off accidentally.* **c** stop functioning; cease working: *The hydro went off during the storm.* **d** take place; happen.
**go on, a** go ahead; go forward. **b** start functioning: *The radio goes on when you turn this switch.* **c** manage. **d** behave: *If you go on that way, you'll get into trouble.* **e** happen: *What's going on here?*
**go out, a** leave a room, one's home, etc.: *She went out at eight o'clock.* **b** stop burning: *Don't let the candle go out.* **c** go dark: *The lights went out during the storm.* **d** go to parties, movies, about town, etc.: *They don't go out much.* **e** date; keep company: *Are she and Rocco still going out?* **f** of the heart, feelings, etc., feel sympathy for a person or persons: *Her heart went out to them.* **g** go on strike.
**go over, a** look at carefully. **b** do again. **c** read again. **d** succeed.
**go through, a** go to the end of; do all of; finish: *I went through two books over the weekend.* **b** undergo; experience: *She went through some hard times.* **c** search: *He went through his pockets to find a nickel.* **d** use up; spend; exhaust: *She went through all her money.* **e** be accepted or approved: *The new schedule did not go through.*
**go through with,** complete; carry out to the end: *Vito disliked the job so much that he refused to go through with it.*
**go together,** keep steady company.
**go under, a** be overwhelmed or sunk. **b** be ruined; fail.
**go up, a** ascend; rise. **b** increase: *The price went up.*
**go with, a** accompany. **b** keep company with: *He's been going with Peg for a long time.* **c** be in harmony with: *That tie goes with your suit.*
**go without,** do without the thing stated or implied.
**let go, a** allow to escape. **b** give up one's hold. **c** give up. **d** fail to keep in good condition.
**let oneself go, a** give way to one's feelings or desires. **b** fail to keep oneself in good condition.
**no go,** *Informal.* not to be done or had; useless; worthless.
**on the go,** *Informal.* always moving or acting: *He is so busy that he's on the go from morning till night.*
**to go,** of prepared food, for taking away from the place where it was bought, to be eaten elsewhere: *She ordered two hamburgers to go.*

☛ *Usage.* The phrase **go and** is used informally to introduce or emphasize a verb: *Go and try it yourself* (no actual movement meant). *She went and shot the bear herself.* Sometimes the phrase suggests criticism of the action referred to: *He went and bought that rusty old car.* Though **go and** is appropriate in writing dialogue and in some narration, it should be omitted in exposition and in all formal writing.

**goad** (gōd) **1** a sharp-pointed stick for driving cattle, etc. **2** anything that drives or urges one on. **3** drive or urge on; act as a goad to: *Hunger goaded her to steal a loaf of bread.* 1, 2 *n.,* 3 *v.*

**go-a·head** (gō′ə hed′) *Informal.* **1** the action of going forward; ambition; spirit. **2** the authority to proceed. **3** disposed to push ahead. 1, 2 *n.,* 3 *adj.*

**goal** (gōl) **1** in certain games, the space between two posts into which a player tries to shoot a puck, kick a ball, etc. in order to score. **2** the act of scoring in such a manner. **3** the point or points counted for scoring a goal; a score: *Our team won, four goals to three.* **4** the finish line of a race. **5** something for which an effort is made; something wanted; one's aim or an object in doing something: *Her goal was to be a great doctor.* *n.* —**goal′·less,** *adj.*
**play goal,** *Informal.* be the goalie.

**goal·er** (gōl′ər) GOALIE. *n.*

**goal·ie** (gōl′ē) the player who guards the goal to prevent scoring in such games as football, hockey, lacrosse, etc.; goalkeeper. *n.*

**goal·keep·er** (gōl′kē′pər) GOALIE. *n.*

**goal line** the line marking the goal in a game.

**goal post** one of a pair of posts with a bar across them, forming a goal in football, hockey, lacrosse, etc.

**goal tender** GOALIE.

Domestic goats— about 90 cm high at the shoulder

**goat** (gōt) **1** a cud-chewing mammal with hollow horns and, usually, long hair: *Goats are closely related to sheep but are stronger, less timid, and more active.* **2** *Informal.* a person made to take the blame or suffer for the mistakes of others; scapegoat. *n., pl.* **goats** or (*esp. collectively*) **goat.** —**goat′like′,** *adj.*
**get one's goat,** *Informal.* make a person angry or annoyed; get any reaction from a person by teasing.

**goat·ee** (gō tē′) a small pointed beard on a man's chin. See BEARD for picture. *n.*

**goat·herd** (gōt′hėrd′) a person who tends goats. *n.*

**goat·skin** (gōt′skin′) **1** the hide of a goat. **2** leather made from the hide of goats. **3** something made of goatskin, such as a container for wine or water. *n.*

**goat·suck·er** (gōt′suk′ər) a bird having a flat head, wide mouth, and long wings. It flies at night and feeds on flying insects: *A whip-poor-will is a goatsucker.* *n.*

**gob** (gob) *Informal.* a lump; mass: *She put a big gob of honey on her bread.* *n.*

**gob·ble**[1] (gob′əl) **1** eat fast and greedily; swallow quickly in big pieces. **2** *Informal.* seize upon eagerly (*used with* **up**): *He gobbled up every piece of information he could find on the rock group.* *v.,* **gob·bled, gob·bling.**

**gob·ble**[2] (gob′əl) **1** make the throaty sound that a turkey does. **2** the throaty sound that a turkey makes. 1 *v.,* **gob·bled, gob·bling;** 2 *n.*

**gob·ble·dy·gook** or **gob·ble·de·gook** (gob′əl dē gŭk′) *Informal.* speech or writing that is unnecessarily complicated or involved: *Official documents are often full of gobbledygook.* *n.*

**gob·bler** (gob′lər) a male turkey. *n.*

**go–be·tween** (gō′bi twēn′) a person who goes back and forth between others with messages, proposals, suggestions, etc.; intermediary: *She acted as a go-between in the settlement of the strike.* *n.*

**gob·let** (gob′lit) a drinking glass with a base and stem. *n.*

**gob·lin** (gob′lən) in folklore, an ugly sprite that is mischievous or evil. *n.*

**go·by** (gō′bē) a bony fish living near seacoasts: *The ventral fins of gobies are united to form a cup-shaped suction pad with which they cling to rocks.* *n., pl.* **go·by** or **go·bies**.

**go–by** (gō′bī′) *Informal.* a going by; casting off; intentional neglect: *to give one the go-by.* *n.*

**go·cart** (gō′kärt′) **1** a low seat on wheels to take a small child around on. **2** a small framework with casters in which children sometimes learn to walk. **3** a light carriage. **4** See GO-KART. *n.*

**god** (god) **1** a being thought of as superior to nature and to human beings and considered worthy of worship. **2** a male god. **3** an image of a god; idol. **4** a person or thing intensely admired and respected: *His father was a god to him.* **5 God**, in the Christian, Jewish, Moslem and certain other religions, the maker and ruler of the universe; the Supreme Being, perfect in goodness, knowledge and power. *n.*

**god·child** (god′chīld′) a child for whom a grownup person takes vows at its baptism. *n., pl.* **god·chil·dren**.

**god·daugh·ter** (god′dot′ər) a female GODCHILD. *n.*

**god·dess** (god′is) **1** a female god. **2** a very beautiful or charming woman. *n.*

**god·fa·ther** (god′foтH′ər) a man who takes vows for a child when it is baptized. *n.*

**god·less** (god′lis) **1** not believing in God; not religious. **2** wicked; evil. *adj.* —**god′less·ness,** *n.*

**god·like** (god′līk′) **1** like God or a god; divine. **2** suitable for God or a god. *adj.*

**god·ly** (god′lē) obeying God's laws; religious; pious; devout. *adj.* **god·li·er, god·li·est.** —**god′li·ness,** *n.*

**god·moth·er** (god′muтH′ər) woman who takes vows for a child when it is baptized. *n.*

**god·par·ent** (god′per′ənt) a godfather or godmother. *n.*

**god·send** (god′send′) something unexpected and very welcome, as if sent from God: *The chance to go to a warm climate was a godsend to the sick man.* *n.*

**god·son** (god′sun′) a male GODCHILD. *n.*

**goes** (gōz) third person singular, present tense, of GO: *She goes to school.* *v.*

**go–get·ter** (gō′get′ər) *Informal.* an energetic or aggressive person. *n.*

**gog·gle** (gog′əl) **1** stare with wide-open or bulging eyes: *We all goggled at the huge dog.* **2** of the eyes, bulge or open very wide: *The children's eyes goggled as the magician pulled a rabbit out of the empty hat.* **3 goggles,**

hat, āge, fär; let, ēqual, tėrm; it, īce
hot, ōpen, ôrder; oil, out; cup, pút, rüle
əbove, takən, pencəl, lemən, circəs
ch, child; ng, long; sh, ship
th, thin; ᴛʜ, then; zh, measure

*pl.* a pair of large, close-fitting spectacles to protect the eyes from light, dust, etc.: *She wore goggles while she was welding the broken steel rod.* **4** bulging: *A frog has goggle eyes.* 1, 2 *v.,* **gog·gled, gog·gling;** 3 *n.,* 4 *adj.*

**gog·gle–eyed** (gog′ə līd′) having rolling, bulging, or staring eyes. *adj.*

**go·ing** (gō′ing) **1** a going away; leaving: *His going was sudden.* **2** moving; acting; working; running. **3** the condition of the ground or road for walking, riding, etc.: *The going is bad on a muddy road.* **4** that goes; that can or will go. **5** in existence; existing; current: *the going price for gold.* **6** ppr. of GO. 1, 3 *n.,* 2, 4, 5 *adj.,* 6 *v.* **be going to,** will; be about to: *It is going to rain soon.* **going on,** almost; nearly: *It is going on four o'clock.*

**going concern** a company, store, etc. that is doing good business.

**go·ings–on** (gō′ing zon′) actions; behaviour; conduct: *Her parents were unhappy about the goings-on at the party.* *n. pl.*

**goi·tre** (goi′tər) **1** a disease of the thyroid gland, which often produces a large swelling in the neck, usually caused by a diet with too little iodine. **2** the swelling itself. *n.* Also, **goiter.**

**go–kart** (gō′kärt′) **1** a small, four-wheeled racing vehicle that consists of a bare chassis and a low-powered engine. *n.* Also, **gocart.**

**gold** (gōld) **1** a shiny, yellow, non-rusting, precious metal that is soft and malleable, used especially for making jewellery and coins: *Gold is a chemical element. Symbol:* Au. **2** coins made of gold. **3** money in large sums; wealth; riches. **4** a bright, beautiful or precious thing or material: *Wheat is sometimes called prairie gold.* **5** made of gold. **6** of or like gold. **7** bright yellow. 1–4, 7 *n.,* 5–7 *adj.*

**gold brick** *Informal.* anything that looks good at first but turns out to be worthless.

**gold·en** (gōl′dən) **1** made or consisting of gold: *a golden goblet.* **2** containing or yielding gold. **3** shining or coloured like gold; bright yellow: *golden hair.* **4** very good; most excellent; extremely favourable, valuable, or important: *a golden opportunity.* **5** very happy and prosperous; flourishing: *the golden days of youth, a golden age.* **6** having to do with the fiftieth year or event in a series: *a golden wedding anniversary.* *adj.*

**Golden Age** **1** in Greek and Roman mythology, the first age of the human race, an era of perfect prosperity, happiness, and innocence. **2 golden age,** a period of great progress, cultural achievement, etc.

**golden eagle** a large eagle with dark brown feathers on the back of its neck.

**golden mean** the avoidance of extremes; the safe, sensible way of doing things; moderation.

**golden retriever** a breed of medium-sized retriever dog, having a golden, water-resistant coat, and often trained to retrieve game, especially waterfowl.

**gold·en·rod** (gōl′dən rod′) a plant of the same family

as the aster, that blooms in the autumn and has many small yellow flowers on tall, branching stalks. *n.*

**golden rule** a rule of conduct, common to most great religions, that people should behave toward others as they would want others to behave toward them.

**gol·den·seal** (gōl'dən sēl') a North American plant of the buttercup family once used as a medicine. *n.*

**golden wedding** the 50th anniversary of a wedding.

**gold·eye** (gōl'dī') *Cdn.* an edible freshwater fish that is native to rivers and lakes from Ontario to the Northwest Territories: *Goldeye is smoked and dyed for marketing as a table delicacy. n., pl.* **gold·eye** or **gold·eyes.**

**gold–filled** (gōld'fild') made of cheap metal covered with a layer of gold. *adj.*

**gold·finch** (gōld'finch') **1** a small American songbird: *The male goldfinch is yellow marked with black.* **2** a European songbird having yellow on its wings. *n.*

**gold·fish** (gōld'fish') a small, reddish-golden fish: *Goldfish are often kept in garden pools or glass bowls. n., pl.* **gold·fish** or **gold·fish·es.**

**gold·i·locks** (gōl'dē loks') **1** a person with yellow hair. **2** a plant having many small, yellow flowers. *n.*

**gold leaf** gold beaten into very thin sheets.

**gold mine 1** a mine where ore yielding gold is obtained. **2** the source of something of great value.

**gold–plate** (gōld'plāt') coat (another metal or a metal object) with gold, especially by electroplating: *Gold-plated silver is called vermeil. v.,* **gold–plat·ed, gold–plat·ing.**

**gold rush** a sudden movement of people to a place where gold has just been found: *The Klondike Gold Rush began after gold was discovered there in 1896.*

**gold·smith** (gōld'smith') an artisan whose work is making articles of gold. *n.*

**gold standard** the use of gold as the standard of value for the money of a country: *Using the gold standard means that a nation's unit of money value is declared by the government to be equal to and exchangeable for a certain amount of gold.*

**gold·thread** (gōld'thred') any one of a number of North American plants of the buttercup family, especially one with white flowers. *n.*

**golf** (golf) **1** an outdoor game played with a small, hard ball and a set of long-handled clubs having wooden or iron heads: *A golfer tries to drive the ball into each of 9 or 18 successive holes with as few strokes as possible.* **2** play the game of golf: *She golfs every Saturday.* **1** *n.,* **2** *v.*

**golf club 1** one of the set of long-handled clubs having wooden or iron heads that is used in playing golf. **2** a group of people joined together for the purpose of playing golf. **3** the buildings, land, etc. used by such a group.

**golf course** a place where golf is played, having tees, greens, and fairways.

**gol·fer** (gol'fər) one who plays golf. *n.*

**golf links** GOLF COURSE.

**gol·ly** (gol'ē) a word used to express surprise, etc. *interj.*

**gon·ad** (gō'nad *or* gon'ad) an organ in which reproductive cells develop: *Ovaries and testes are gonads.* *n.*

A gondola

**gon·do·la** (gon'də lə) **1** a long, narrow, flat-bottomed boat with a high peak at each end, used on the canals of Venice. **2** a large, flat-bottomed river boat with pointed ends. **3** a freight car that has low sides and no top. **4** a car that hangs under a dirigible and holds the motors, passengers, etc. **5** the passenger basket of a hot-air balloon. **6** *Cdn.* a broadcasting booth built up near the roof of a hockey arena. **7** a car that hangs from and moves along a cable: *We went up the mountain on the gondola.* *n.*

**gon·do·lier** (gon'də lēr') a man in charge of a GONDOLA (def. 1). *n.*

**gone** (gon) **1** moved away; left. **2** lost: *a gone case.* **3** dead. **4** used up. **5** failed; ruined. **6** weak, faint: *a gone feeling.* **7** pp. of GO: *He has gone far away.* 1–6 *adj.,* 7 *v.*
**far gone,** much advanced; deeply involved.
**gone on,** *Informal.* in love with.

**gon·er** (gon'ər) *Informal.* a person or thing that is dead, ruined, past help, etc. *n.*

**gong** (gong) a piece of metal shaped like a bowl or saucer and making a loud noise when struck: *A gong is a kind of bell.* *n.*

**gon·or·rhe·a** or **gon·or·rhoe·a** (gon'ə rē'ə) a contagious venereal disease that causes inflammation of the genital and urinary organs. *n.*

**good** (gu̇d) **1** having the right qualities; admirable; desirable: *a good book, a good game.* **2** as it ought to be; right; proper: *Do what seems good to you.* **3** well-behaved: *a good girl.* **4** kind; friendly: *Say a good word for me.* **5** doing right: *a good king.* **6** honourable; worthy: *my good friend.* **7** reliable; dependable: *good judgment.* **8** real; genuine: *It is hard to tell counterfeit money from good money.* **9** agreeable; pleasant: *Have a good time.* **10** beneficial; advantageous; useful: *drugs good for a fever.* **11** benefit; advantage; use: *to work for the common good.* **12** well-suited to its purpose: *A carpenter insists on good tools.* **13** satisfying; sufficient in size and quality: *a good meal.* **14** not spoiled; sound: *a good apple.* **15** thorough; complete: *do a good job.* **16** skilful; clever: *a good manager, to be good at arithmetic.* **17** fairly great; more than a little: *a good while.* **18** that which is good: *She always looked for the good in people.* **19** a good thing. **20** good people. **21** That is good! 1–10, 12–17 *adj.,* **bet·ter, best;** 11, 18–20 *n.,* 21 *interj.*
**as good as,** almost the same as; almost; practically: *The day is as good as over.*
**feel good,** *Informal.* feel well or elated.
**for good** or **for good and all,** forever; finally; permanently: *She has left Canada for good.*
**good and,** *Informal.* very; extremely: *She was good and angry.*
**good for, a** able to do, live, or last. **b** able to pay. **c** worth.
**make good, a** make up for; give or do in place of; pay for: *He made good the damage done by his car.* **b** fulfil;

**carry out:** *to make good a promise.* **c** succeed in doing. **d** succeed; prosper: *His parents expected him to make good.* **e** prove.
**to the good,** on the side of profit or advantage; in one's favour.

**good afternoon** a form of greeting or farewell said in the afternoon.

**good·bye** or **good–bye** (gud′bī′) an expression of good wishes on parting or ending a telephone conversation; farewell. *interj., n., pl.* **good·byes** or **good-byes.** Sometimes, **good-by.**

**good cheer** 1 feasting and merrymaking; *A wedding is a time of good cheer.* 2 good food and drink. 3 a spirit of optimism and courage: *Be of good cheer.*

**good day** a form of greeting or farewell said in the daytime.

**good deal** 1 much; many: *It cost a good deal more than I expected.* 2 *Informal.* a favourable business transaction; bargain: *It was a good deal all around.*

**good evening** a form of greeting or farewell said in the evening.

**good–for–noth·ing** (gud′fər nuth′ing) 1 worthless; useless. 2 a person who is worthless or useless. 1 *adj.,* 2 *n.*

**Good Friday** the Friday before Easter, observed by Christians in commemoration of Christ's crucifixion.

**good–heart·ed** (gud′här′tid) kind and generous. *adj.* —**good′-heart′ed·ly,** *adv.* —**good′-heart′ed·ness,** *n.*

**good humour** or **humor** a cheerful, pleasant disposition or mood.

**good–hu·moured** or **good–hu·mored** (gud′hyü′mərd *or* gud′yü′mərd) cheerful; pleasant. *adj.* —**good′-hu′moured·ly** or **good′-hum′ored·ly,** *adv.*

**good·ish** (gud′ish) *Informal.* 1 pretty good. 2 fairly great; considerable: *There was a goodish amount of work involved.* *adj.*

**good–look·ing** (gud′luk′ing) having a pleasing appearance; handsome; attractive: *a good-looking woman.* *adj.*

**good looks** a handsome or pleasing appearance.

**good·ly** (gud′lē) considerable: *a goodly quantity.* *adj.,* **good·li·er, good·li·est.** —**good′li·ness,** *n.*

**good morning** a form of greeting or farewell said in the morning.

**good nature** a pleasant or kindly disposition; cheerfulness; agreeableness.

**good–na·tured** (gud′nā′chərd) pleasant; kindly; cheerful; agreeable. *adj.* —**good′-na′tured·ly,** *adv.* —**good′-na′tured·ness,** *n.*

**good·ness** (gud′nis) 1 the quality or state of being good. 2 excellence; virtue. 3 kindness: friendliness. 4 the valuable quality; best part. 5 an exclamation of surprise. 1–4 *n.,* 5 *interj.*

**good night** a form of farewell said at night.

**goods** (gudz) 1 personal property; belongings: *She gave half of her goods to the poor.* 2 things for sale; wares. 3 material for clothing; cloth.

**good–sized** (gud′sīzd′) large or somewhat large; ample: *a good-sized helping.* *adj.*

**good speed** a farewell expressing a wish for success or good luck.

hat, āge, fär; let, ēqual, tėrm; it, īce
hot, ōpen, ôrder; oil, out; cup, pùt, rüle
əbove, takən, pencəl, lemən, circəs
ch, child; ng, long; sh, ship
th, thin; ᴛʜ, then; zh, measure

**good–tem·pered** (gud′tem′pərd) easy to get along with; cheerful; agreeable. *adj.* —**good′-tem′pered·ly,** *adv.*

**good turn** a kind or friendly act; favour.

**good will** 1 a kindly or friendly feeling. 2 cheerful consent; willingness. 3 the reputation and steady trade that a business has with its customers.

**good·y** (gud′ē) *Informal.* 1 something very good to eat; a piece of candy or cake: *There were lots of goodies at the party.* 2 an exclamation of pleasure: *Are we going? Oh, goody!* 3 making too much of being good; GOODY-GOODY. 1 *n., pl.* **good·ies;** 2 *interj.,* 3 *adj.*

**good·y–good·y** (gud′ē gud′ē) 1 making too much of being good; good in an affected, prim, or weak way. 2 a person who makes too much of being good. 1 *adj.,* 2 *n., pl.* **good·y-good·ies.**

Canada geese—about 85 cm long including the tail

**goose** (güs) 1 a wild or tame web-footed swimming bird resembling a duck, but larger and having a longer neck. 2 the female of this bird. A male goose is called a gander. 3 the flesh of this bird used as food. 4 a silly person: *"What a goose you are!"* 5 a tailor's smoothing iron that has a long, curved handle like a goose's neck. *n., pl.* **geese** for 1–4, **gooses** for 5. —**goose′like′,** *adj.*
**cook one's goose,** ruin one's reputation, plan, chances, etc.
**the goose hangs high,** all is well; prospects are good.

**goose·ber·ry** (güs′ber′ē *or* güz′ber′ē) 1 a small, sour berry, used to make pies, tarts, jam, etc.: *Some kinds of gooseberry have prickly skins.* 2 the thorny bush that this berry grows on. *n., pl.* **goose·ber·ries.**

**goose bumps** a rough condition of the skin caused by cold or fear.

**goose flesh** GOOSE BUMPS.

**goose·foot** (güs′fut′) a plant having coarse leaves, clusters of very small flowers, and dry, seedlike fruits: *Beets and spinach are goosefoots.* *n., pl.* **goose·foots.**

**gooseneck lamp** an electric light supported by a movable tube like a goose's neck.

**goose pimples** GOOSE BUMPS.

**goose step** a marching step in which the leg is swung high with straight, stiff knees.

A gopher (def. 1)— about 20 cm long excluding the tail

**go·pher** (gō′fər) 1 a species of buff-coloured, burrowing ground squirrel found in the central plains of North America, having short legs, short, rounded ears, small pouches inside the cheeks, and a slightly bushy tail about one third as long as the body: *The gopher is one of the commonest mammals of the Canadian Prairies.* 2 any of the several other ground squirrels. 3 POCKET GOPHER. *n.*
☛ *Etym.* Probably from F *gaufre* 'honeycomb', from the effect of the animal's burrowing and tunnelling the ground; possibly also influenced by the name of a burrowing land tortoise of the southern United States, also called a *gopher* or, earlier *magofer*. 19c.

**Gor·di·an knot** (gôr′dē ən) 1 a knot tied by Gordius, an ancient king of Phrygia, to be undone only by the person who should rule Asia. Alexander the Great cut it with his sword. 2 an intricate or baffling problem. **cut the Gordian knot,** solve an intricate or vexing problem by some quick and drastic means.

**gore**[1] (gôr) blood that is shed; thick blood; clotted blood: *The battlefield was covered with gore.* *n.*

**gore**[2] (gôr) wound with a horn or tusk: *The bull gored the old bullfighter to death.* *v.*, **gored, gor·ing.**

**gore**[3] (gôr) 1 a long, tapering piece of cloth put or made in a skirt, sail, etc. to give greater width or change the shape. 2 put or make a gore in. 1 *n.*, 2 *v.*, **gored, gor·ing.**

**gorge** (gôrj) 1 a deep, narrow valley, usually steep and rocky. 2 eat greedily until full; stuff with food. 3 fill full; stuff. 4 a gorging; gluttonous meal. 5 the contents of a stomach. 6 a feeling of disgust, indignation, resentment, or the like. 7 a narrow rear entrance from a fort into an outwork or outer part. 8 a mass stopping up a narrow passage: *An ice gorge blocked the river.* 1, 4–8 *n.*, 2, 3 *v.*, **gorged, gorg·ing.**
—**gorg′er**, *n.*
**stick in one's gorge,** be hard to accept.

**gor·geous** (gôr′jəs) richly coloured; splendid: *a gorgeous sunset.* *adj.* —**gor′geous·ly**, *adv.* —**gor′geous·ness**, *n.*

**gor·get** (gôr′jit) 1 a piece of armour for the throat. See ARMOUR for picture. 2 a covering for the neck and breast, formerly worn by women. *n.*

**Gor·gon** (gôr′gən) 1 in Greek legend, any of three horrible sisters who had snakes for hair and whose look turned the beholder to stone. Medusa is the best-known of the three Gorgons. 2 **gorgon,** any very ugly or terrible woman. *n.*

**go·ril·la** (gə ril′ə) the largest and most powerful species of ape, found in the forests of central Africa. *n.*
☛ *Hom.* GUERRILLA.

**gorse** (gôrs) FURZE; whin. *n.*

**gor·y** (gô′rē) very bloody. *adj.*, **gor·i·er, gor·i·est.**
—**gor′i·ly**, *adv.* —**gor′i·ness**, *n.*

**gosh** (gosh) an exclamation or mild oath. *interj.*

**gos·hawk** (gos′hok′) a powerful, short-winged hawk, formerly used in falconry. *n.*

**gos·ling** (goz′ling) a young goose. *n.*

**gos·pel** (gos′pəl) 1 the teachings of Jesus and the Apostles. 2 *Informal.* anything earnestly believed or taken as a guide for action: *Drink plenty of water; that is my gospel.* 3 the absolute truth: *They take her words for gospel.* 4 a type of music associated with prayer meetings. 5 **Gospel, a** any one of the first four books of the New Testament of the Bible, by Matthew, Mark, Luke, or John. **b** a part of one of these books read during a religious service. *n.*
☛ *Etym.* From OE *gōdspel* 'good news'.

**gos·sa·mer** (gos′ə mər) 1 a film or thread of cobweb. 2 a very thin, light cloth: *a dress of gossamer.* 3 a thin, light, waterproof cloth or coat. 4 like gossamer; very light and thin; filmy: *gossamer wings.* 5 anything very light and thin. 1–3, 5 *n.*, 4 *adj.*

**gos·sip** (gos′ip) 1 idle talk, not always true, about other people and their affairs. 2 repeat what one knows, or the idle talk that one hears, about other people and their affairs. 3 a person who gossips a good deal. 1, 3 *n.*, 2 *v.*, **gos·siped, gos·sip·ing.** —**gos′sip·er**, *n.*

**gos·sip·y** (gos′i pē) 1 fond of gossip. 2 full of gossip. *adj.*

**got** (got) pt. and a pp. of GET: *We got the letter yesterday. We had got tired of waiting for it.* *v.*
☛ *Usage.* **Gotten,** the older past participle of the verb *get*, has largely been replaced by **got.** Nevertheless, depending on the meaning of the sentence, the form **gotten** (instead of **got**) is still considered acceptable by some people. However, only **got** should be used as a way of intensifying "have" in the sense of "possess" (*Have you got a pencil?*) or "be obligated" (*I've got to study now.*).

**Go·ta·ma** (gō′tə mə) GAUTAMA. *n.*

**Goth** (goth) 1 a member of a Germanic tribe that overran the Roman Empire in the 3rd, 4th, and 5th centuries A.D.: *The Goths settled in southern and eastern Europe.* 2 an uncivilized person; barbarian. *n.*

**Goth·ic** (goth′ik) 1 a style of architecture using pointed arches and high, steep roofs, developed in Western Europe during the Middle Ages, from about 1150 to 1550. See ARCHITECTURE for picture. 2 of this kind of architecture: *Gothic cathedrals often have windows of stained glass.* 3 of the Goths or their language. 4 the language of the Goths. 5 uncivilized; crude; barbarous. 6 medieval. 7 a kind of type used in printing. *This sentence is in Gothic.* 1, 4, 7 *n.*, 2, 3, 5, 6 *adj.*

**got·ten** (got′ən) a pp. of GET: *He has gotten himself into trouble twice this week.* *v.*
☛ *Usage.* See note at GOT.

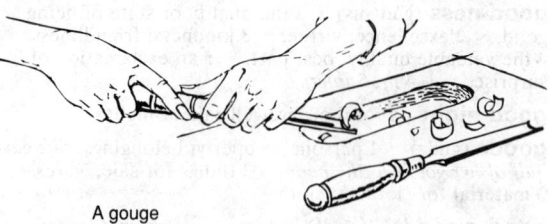

A gouge

**gouge** (gouj) 1 a chisel with a concave blade: *Gouges are used for cutting round grooves or holes in wood, stone, etc.* 2 cut with a gouge or something like it: *to gouge a* piece of wood. **3** make by gouging: *to gouge a channel.* **4** a groove, trench, or hole made by gouging: *There was a long gouge in the desk top.* **5** dig or tear (*out*): *to gouge out dirt.* **6** *Informal.* overcharge or swindle. **7** *Informal.* a swindle. 1, 4, 7 *n.*, 2, 3, 5, 6 *v.*, **gouged, goug·ing.**

**gou·lash** (gü′lash) a highly seasoned stew made of beef or veal and vegetables: *Goulash is usually seasoned with paprika.* *n.*

Gourds

**gourd** (gôrd *or* gürd) **1** the hard-shelled fruit of certain vines: *Gourds are dried and hollowed out to be used as cups, bowls, etc.* **2** the vine that gourds grow on. **3** a bowl, bottle, etc. made from the dried shell of a gourd. **4** referring to a family of climbing or trailing plants that includes some common vegetables and fruits: *Gourds, cucumbers, pumpkins, muskmelons, and squashes belong to the gourd family.* *n.*

**gour·mand** (gür′mənd) a person who is fond of good eating. *n.*

**gour·met** (gür′mā) a person expert in judging and choosing fine foods, wines, etc.; epicure. *n.*

**gout** (gout) **1** a painful disease of the joints, often characterized by a painful swelling of the big toe. **2** a drop; splash; clot: *gouts of blood.* *n.*

**gout·y** (gou′tē) **1** swollen with GOUT (def. 1): *a gouty toe.* **2** of or like gout. **3** causing or caused by gout. **4** having or tending to have gout. *adj.*, **gout·i·er, gout·i·est.** —**gout′i·ness,** *n.*

**Gov.** or **gov.** **1** governor. **2** government.

**gov·ern** (guv′ərn) **1** control and direct the affairs of a state, nation, etc.; rule: *To govern a country.* **2** control and direct oneself or one's passions, etc.; curb; bridle: *to govern one's temper.* **3** exercise a directing or restraining influence over; determine: *the motives governing a person's decision.* **4** hold back; restrain; check. **5** be a rule or law for: *the principles governing a case.* **6** in grammar, require a word to be in a certain case or mood; require a certain case or mood. *v.* —**gov′ern·a·ble,** *adj.*

☛ *Etym.* **Govern** and the related words GOVERNMENT, GOVERNOR, etc. can all be traced back through Old French to a Latin verb *gubernare* 'to steer, direct, rule', which itself came from Gk. *kubernân* 'to steer'.

**gov·ern·ance** (guv′ər nəns) government; rule; control. *n.*

**gov·ern·ess** (guv′ər nis) a woman who teaches children in a private house. *n.*

**gov·ern·ment** (guv′ərn mənt *or* guv′ər mənt) **1** the rule or authority over a country, a province, district, etc.; direction of the affairs of state. **2** a person or persons ruling a country, province, district, etc.; administration: *The government was defeated in the general election.* **3** a system of ruling: *Canada has democratic government.* **4** the country, district, etc. ruled. **5** rule; control: *self-government.* **6** in grammar, the influence of one word in determining the case, number, or mood of another. *n.*
☛ *Etym.* See note at GOVERN.

**gov·ern·men·tal** (guv′ərn men′təl *or* guv′ər men′təl) of or having to do with government: *National defence is under governmental supervision.* *adj.*
—**gov′ern·men′tal·ly,** *adv.*

**Government House** **1** the official residence of the Governor General in Ottawa, also known as Rideau Hall. **2** in some provinces, the official residence of the Lieutenant-Governor.

**gov·er·nor** (guv′ər nər) **1** the appointed ruler of a colony; the representative of a monarch in a colony. **2** in the United States, an official elected as the executive head of a state. **3** a person who manages or directs a club, society, institution, etc.: *A club often has a board of governors.* **4** an automatic device that controls the supply of steam, gas, etc. and keeps a machine going at a certain speed. *n.*
☛ *Etym.* Through OF *governeor* from L *gubernator* 'steersman, helmsman, ruler'. See also the note at GOVERN.

**governor general** **1** a governor who has subordinate or deputy governors under him or her. **2** **Governor General, a** in Canada, the representative of the Crown, appointed on the advice of the prime minister for a term of five years. **b** the representative of the Crown in certain other independent countries of the British Commonwealth of Nations. *pl.* **governors general.** Also, **governor-general.**

**gov·er·nor·ship** (guv′ər nər ship′) the position or term of office of GOVERNOR (defs. 1–3). *n.*

**Govt.** or **govt.** government.

**gown** (goun) **1** a woman's dress, especially a formal or evening dress. **2** a loose outer garment: *Judges, clergymen, members of a university, and students graduating from university wear gowns to show their position, profession, etc.* **3** a nightgown or dressing gown. **4** put a gown on; dress in a gown. **5** the members of a university. 1–3, 5 *n.*, 4 *v.*

**gp.** group.

**G.P.** in medicine, general practitioner.

**gr.** **1** grain; grains. **2** gross. **3** grade. **4** grammar. **5** group. **6** great.

**grab** (grab) **1** seize suddenly; snatch: *The dog grabbed the meat and ran.* **2** snatching; a sudden seizing: *She made a grab for the apple.* **3** that which is grabbed. **4** a mechanical device for firmly holding something that is to be lifted or raised. **5** of a vehicle's brakes, take hold suddenly or jerkily. 1, 5 *v.*, **grabbed, grab·bing;** 2–4 *n.* —**grab′ber,** *n.*
**up for grabs,** *Informal.* available.

**grace** (grās) **1** beauty of form, movement, or manner; a pleasing or agreeable quality. **2** give or add grace to; set off with grace: *She was asked to grace the party with her presence.* **3** favour; good will: *I wonder if I am in the teacher's good graces.* **4** mercy; pardon. **5** God's free

**graceful** 520 **graft**

and undeserved favour to and love for people; the influence of God operating in a person to improve or strengthen him or her. **6** a short prayer of thanks before or after a meal. **7** the favour shown by granting a delay. **8** an allowance of time: *The bank gave him three days' grace.* **9** do a favour or honour to: *The Queen graced the ball with her presence.* **10** virtue; merit; excellence. **11** behaviour put on to seem attractive: *Do you like that girl's little airs and graces?* **12** in music, a note or group of notes added for ornament and not essential to the harmony or melody. **13** add such notes to. **14 Grace**, a title used in speaking to or of a duke, duchess, or archbishop: *May I assist Your Grace? He spoke to His Grace the Duke of Bedford.* 1, 3–8, 10–12, 14 *n.*, 2, 9, 13 *v.*, **graced, grac·ing.**
**have the grace,** have the goodness or courtesy: *He had the grace to say he was sorry.*
**in one's bad graces,** out of favour or disliked by.
**in one's good graces,** favoured or liked by: *I wonder if I am in the teacher's good graces or bad graces.*
**with bad grace,** unpleasantly; unwillingly.
**with good grace,** pleasantly; willingly.

**grace·ful** (grā'sfəl) having or showing grace; beautiful in form, movement, or manner; pleasing; agreeable: *a graceful speech. A good dancer must be graceful.* *adj.*
—**grace'ful·ly,** *adv.* —**grace'ful·ness,** *n.*

**grace·less** (grā'slis) **1** without grace. **2** not caring for what is right or proper: *The boy is a graceless rascal.* *adj.* —**grace'less·ly,** *adv.* —**grace'less·ness,** *n.*

**grace note** in music, a note or group of notes added for ornament and not essential to the harmony or melody.

**gra·cious** (grā'shəs) **1** pleasant; kindly; courteous: *She welcomed her guests in a gracious manner that made them feel at ease.* **2** pleasant, kindly, and courteous to people of lower social position: *The Queen greeted the crowd with a gracious smile.* **3** of God, merciful; kindly. **4** an exclamation of surprise. 1–3 *adj.*, 4 *n.*
—**gra'cious·ly,** *adv.* —**gra'cious·ness,** *n.*

**grack·le** (grak'əl) a kind of blackbird whose black feathers have a bronze lustre: *Grackles are often mistaken for starlings.* *n.*

**gra·da·tion** (grā dā'shən *or* grə dā'shən) **1** a change by steps or stages; gradual change: *Her career showed a gradation from poverty to wealth.* **2** a step, stage, or degree in a series: *There are many gradations between poverty and wealth. The rainbow shows gradations of colour.* **3** the act or process of grading. *n.*

**grade** (grād) **1** any one division of a school arranged according to the pupils' progress: *grade seven.* **2** a step or stage in course or process. **3** a degree in a scale of rank, quality, value, etc.: *Grade A butter is the best in quality.* **4** a group of people or things having the same rank, quality, value, etc. **5** arrange in classes; arrange according to size, value, etc.; sort: *These apples are graded by size.* **6** be of a particular grade or quality. **7** a number or letter that shows how well one has done: *Her grade in English is B.* **8** give a grade to: *The teacher graded the papers.* **9** the slope of a road, railway track, etc.: *a steep grade.* **10** the amount of slope. **11** make more nearly level: *The workers graded the land around the new house.* **12** change gradually; go through a series of steps, stages, or degrees: *Red and yellow grade into orange.* 1–4, 7, 9, 10 *n.*, 5, 6, 8, 11, 12 *v.*, **grad·ed, grad·ing.**
**at grade,** on the same level.
**down grade,** **a** going down. **b** getting worse.
**make the grade,** **a** ascend a steep slope. **b** overcome difficulties.
**up grade,** **a** going up. **b** getting better.

**grade crossing** LEVEL CROSSING.

**grad·er** (grā'dər) **1** a person or thing that grades, especially a machine for levelling earth. **2** a person who is in a certain grade in elementary or secondary school (*used only in compounds*): *a sixth-grader.* *n.*

**grade school** U.S. ELEMENTARY SCHOOL.

**gra·di·ent** (grā'dē ənt) **1** the rate at which a road, railway track, etc. rises. **2** the sloping part of a road, etc. **3** the rate at which temperature or pressure changes. **4** going up or down gradually. **5** moving by taking steps; walking. 1–3 *n.*, 4, 5 *adj.*

**grad·u·al** (graj'ü əl) by degrees too small to be separately noticed; little by little: *a gradual increase in sound. The hill had a gradual slope.* *adj.*
—**grad'u·al·ly,** *adv.*

**grad·u·and** (graj'ü and') a student who is about to graduate. *n.*

**grad·u·ate** (graj'ü āt' *for verb*, graj'ü it *or* graj'ü āt' *for noun*, graj'ü it *for adjective*) **1** finish a course of study at a school, college, or university and receive a diploma or paper saying one has done so: *Mary's brother graduated from university last year.* **2** give a diploma to for finishing a course of study. **3** a person who has graduated. **4** that is a graduate: *a graduate student.* **5** of or for graduates: *a graduate school.* **6** mark with degrees for measuring: *A thermometer is graduated.* **7** a container marked with degrees for measuring. **8** arrange in regular steps, stages, or degrees: *An income tax is graduated so that the people who make the most money pay the highest rate of taxes.* **9** change gradually. 1, 2, 6, 8, 9 *v.*, **grad·u·at·ed, grad·u·at·ing;** 3, 7, *n.*, 4, 5 *adj.*
—**grad'u·a'tor,** *n.*

**grad·u·a·tion** (graj'ü ā'shən) **1** a graduating from a school, college, or university. **2** the ceremony of graduating; graduating exercises. **3** a marking with degrees for measuring. **4** a mark or set of marks to show degrees for measuring. **5** an arrangement in regular steps, stages, or degrees. *n.*

**graf·fi·ti** (grə fē'tē) verses, sayings, or pictures drawn, scribbled, or scratched on a public surface such as a wall or fence: *Graffiti are usually anonymous and are often cleverly done.* *n., pl.* of **graffito.**
☛ *Etym.* From Italian *graffiti* 'a scribbling' from Italian and L *graffio* 'a scratch, scribble', from Gk. *graphein* 'write, draw'. See also note at -GRAPH.

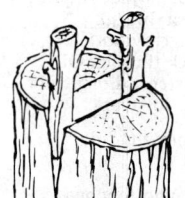

Three kinds of plant graft. The pieces are tied or taped together and kept moist until the graft begins to grow.

**graft**[1] (graft) **1** insert a shoot, bud, etc. from one tree or plant into a slit in another so that it will grow there permanently. **2** the shoot, bud, etc. used. **3** the place on a tree or plant where the shoot, bud, etc. is inserted. **4** a tree or plant that has had a shoot, bud, etc. grafted on it. **5** the act of grafting. **6** produce or improve fruit, flower, etc. by grafting. **7** do grafting on. **8** transfer a piece of skin, bone, etc. from one part of the body to another so that it will grow there permanently. **9** a piece of skin, bone, etc. so transferred. 1, 6–8 *v.*, 2–5, 9 *n.* —**graft′er,** *n.*

**graft²** (graft) **1** the taking of money dishonestly, especially in connection with city or government business; political dishonesty, corruption, etc. **2** a method of getting money dishonestly. **3** money dishonestly taken or obtained. **4** *Informal.* make money dishonestly through one's job, especially in political positions. 1–3 *n.*, 4 *v.* —**graft′er,** *n.*

**gra·ham** (grā′əm) referring to or made from a finely ground, unsifted, whole-wheat flour: *graham crackers.* *n.*
☞ *Etym.* Named after an American, Sylvester Graham (1794–1851), who supported reforms in nutrition.

**Grail** (grāl) the cup or dish supposed to have been used by Christ at the Last Supper, in which one of His followers received the last drops of blood from Christ's body on the cross; Holy Grail. *n.*

**grain** (grān) **1** a single seed or seedlike fruit of wheat, oats, and similar cereal grasses. **2** the seeds or seedlike fruits of such plants in the mass. **3** the plants that these seeds or seedlike fruits grow on. **4** a tiny, hard particle of sand, salt, sugar, etc. **5** form into grains. **6** a unit for measuring mass, equal to 0.065 grams: *The grain is the smallest unit in avoirdupois, troy, and apothecaries' weight.* **7** the smallest possible amount; tiniest bit: *a grain of truth.* **8** the arrangement or direction of fibres in wood, layers in stone, etc.: *Wood and stone split along the grain.* **9** the little lines and other markings in wood, marble, etc.: *That mahogany table has a fine grain.* **10** paint in imitation of the grain in wood, marble, etc. **11** the rough surface of leather: *The grain in leather is on the side of the skin from which the hair has been removed.* **12** remove the hair from a skin or skins. **13** soften and raise the grain of leather. **14** natural character; disposition: *Laziness was against the grain for her.* 1–4, 6–9, 11, 14 *n.*, 5, 10, 12, 13 *v.* —**grain′less,** *adj.*

**grain alcohol** ETHYL ALCOHOL, often made from grain.

**grained** (grānd) **1** having little lines and markings. **2** painted in imitation of the grain in wood, marble, etc. **3** roughened on the surface. **4** pt. and pp. of GRAIN. 1–3 *adj.*, 4 *v.*

**grain elevator** a building for storing grain. See ELEVATOR for picture.

**grain·field** (grān′fēld′) a field in which grain grows. *n.*

**gram** (gram) an SI unit for measuring mass, equal to one one-thousandth of a kilogram: *A nickel has a mass of about five grams.* Symbol: g *n.* Also, **gramme.**

**gram·mar** (gram′ər) **1** the scientific study and classification of a language with reference to the sounds and forms of words and the structure of sentences. **2** a systematic study comparing the forms and constructions of two or more languages. **3** a systematic study comparing present with past forms and usage of a language. **4** a treatise or book on one of these subjects. **5** the system of the forms and uses of words in a particular language: *Grammar is often thought of as a set of rules.* **6** the use of words according to this system: *Good grammar is important in formal writing.* **7** the elements of any subject: *the grammar of painting.* *n.*

**gram·mar·i·an** (grə mer′ē ən) an expert in GRAMMAR. *n.*

## graft 521 grandeur

hat, āge, fär; let, ēqual, tėrm; it, īce
hot, ōpen, ôrder; oil, out; cup, put, rüle
above, takən, pencəl, lemən, circəs
ch, child; ng, long; sh, ship
th, thin; ᴛʜ, then; zh, measure

**grammar school** **1** a public school having the grades between primary school and high school. **2** in the United Kingdom, a secondary school that prepares students for university.

**gram·mat·i·cal** (grə mat′ə kəl) **1** according to the GRAMMAR (def. 5) of a particular language: *My new friend speaks grammatical English but has a French accent.* **2** of GRAMMAR (def. 6): *"They am" is a grammatical mistake.* *adj.* —**gram·mat′i·cal·ly** *adv.*

**gramme** (gram) See GRAM. *n.*

**Gram-neg·a·tive** (gram′neg′ə tiv) designating bacteria that do not retain the violet colour when stained by GRAM'S METHOD. *adj.*

**gram·o·phone** (gram′ə fōn′) PHONOGRAPH. *n.*

**Gram-pos·i·tive** (gram′poz′ə tiv) designating bacteria that retain the violet colour when stained by GRAM'S METHOD. *adj.*

**gram·pus** (gram′pəs) **1** a type of large dolphin. **2** a blackfish or killer whale. *n.*

**Gram's method** (gramz) in bacteriology, a technique for classifying bacteria, by which they are stained with gentian violet and then treated with an agent that removes colour. Certain species (called Gram-positive bacteria) retain the violet stain after this treatment, while others (Gram-negative bacteria) lose it.

**gran·a·ry** (gran′ə rē, grā′nə rē *or* grān′rē) **1** a place or building where grain is stored. **2** a region having much grain. *n., pl.* **gran·a·ries.**

**grand** (grand) **1** large and of fine appearance: *grand mountains.* **2** fine; noble; dignified; stately; splendid: *grand music, a grand old man.* **3** highest or very high in rank; chief: *a grand duchess, a grand master in chess.* **4** great; important; main: *the grand staircase.* **5** complete; comprehensive: *grand total.* **6** *Informal.* very pleasing: *a grand time.* **7** in names of relationship, in the second degree of ascent or descent: *grandmother, grandson.* *adj.* —**grand′ly,** *adv.* —**grand′ness,** *n.*

**gran·dad** *or* **grand·dad** (gran′dad′ *or* grand′dad′) *Informal.* grandfather (def. 1). *n.*

**grand-aunt** (gran′dant′) great-aunt. *n.*

**Grand Banks** *or* **Grand Bank** a shallow region, or shoal, of the ocean lying southeast of Newfoundland: *The Grand Banks are famous as a fishing ground for cod.*

**grand·child** (gran′chīld′ *or* grand′chīld′) a child of one's son or daughter. *n., pl.* **grand·chil·dren.**

**grand·daugh·ter** (gran′dot′ər) a daughter of one's son or daughter. *n.*

**gran·dee** (gran dē′) **1** a Spanish or Portuguese nobleman of the highest rank. **2** a person of high rank or great importance. *n.*

**gran·deur** (gran′jər *or* gran′jùr) greatness; majesty; nobility; dignity; splendour: *the grandeur of the mountains.* *n.*

**grand·fa·ther** (gran′foTH′ər or grand′foTH′ər) 1 the father of one's father or mother. 2 any forefather. *n.*

**grandfather clock** or **grandfather's clock** a clock in a tall wooden case.

**grand·fa·ther·ly** (gran′foTH′ər lē or grand′foTH′ər lē) 1 of a grandfather. 2 like or characteristic of a grandfather. *adj.*

**gran·dil·o·quence** (gran dil′ə kwəns) the use of lofty or pompous words. *n.*

**gran·dil·o·quent** (gran dil′ə kwənt) using lofty or pompous words. *adj.* —**gran·dil′o·quent·ly**, *adv.*

**gran·di·ose** (gran′dē ōs′) 1 grand in an imposing or impressive way; magnificent. 2 grand in an affected or pompous way; trying to seem magnificent. *adj.* —**gran′di·ose·ly**, *adv.*

**Grand Lama** DALAI LAMA.

**grand·ma** (gran′mä′, gram′mä′, or grand′mä′) *Informal.* grandmother. *n.*

**grand march** a ceremony at a ball in which the guests march around the ballroom together.

**grand master** 1 the head of a military order of knighthood, of a lodge, etc. 2 an expert chess player who has consistently done well in international championships.

**grand·moth·er** (gran′muTH′ər or grand′muTH′ər) 1 the mother of one's father or mother. 2 a female ancestor. *n.*

**grand·moth·er·ly** (gran′muTH′ər lē or grand′muTH′ər lē) 1 of a grandmother. 2 like or characteristic of a grandmother. *adj.*

**grand·neph·ew** (gran′nef′yü or grand′nef′yü) the son of one's nephew or niece. *n.*

**grand·niece** (gran′nēs′ or grand′nēs′) the daughter of one's nephew or niece. *n.*

**grand opera** a musical drama in which all the speeches are sung, usually to the accompaniment of an orchestra.

**grand·pa** (gran′pä′, gram′pä′, or grand′pä′) *Informal.* grandfather. *n.*

**grand·par·ent** (gran′per′ənt or grand′per′ənt) grandfather or grandmother. *n.*

**grand piano** a large, harp-shaped piano with horizontal frame and strings. Compare with UPRIGHT PIANO. See PIANO for picture.

**grand slam** 1 the winning of all the tricks in a hand of bridge. 2 the winning of several major tournaments in sports like tennis and golf. 3 a victory in any series: *She had a grand slam in all her final examinations.*

**grand·son** (gran′sun′ or grand′sun′) a son of one's son or daughter. *n.*

**grand·stand** (gran′stand′ or grand′stand′) 1 the main seating place for people at an athletic field, race track, parade, etc.: *Grandstands are usually covered.* 2 act or speak ostentatiously to impress an audience. 1 *n.*, 2 *v.*

**grand·un·cle** (gran′dung′kəl) great-uncle. *n.*

**grange** (grānj) a farm with its buildings; farmstead. *n.*

**gran·ite** (gran′it) a hard igneous rock consisting chiefly of quartz and feldspar: *Granite is much used for buildings and monuments.* *n.*

**gran·ite·ware** (gran′i twer′) ironware covered with grey enamel. *n.*

**gran·nie** or **gran·ny** (gran′ē) *Informal.* 1 grandmother. 2 an old woman. 3 a fussy person. *n., pl.* **gran·nies.**

**grannie knot** or **granny knot** a knot differing from a square knot in having the ends crossed in the opposite way: *A grannie knot is not as secure as a square knot.*

**grant** (grant) 1 give what is asked; allow: *to grant a request.* 2 admit to be true; accept without proof; concede: *I grant that you are right.* 3 bestow or confer a right, etc. by formal act; transfer or convey the ownership of property, especially by deed or writing. 4 something granted, such as a privilege, right, sum of money, or tract of land: *The companies that built the railways received large grants of land from the government.* 5 the act of granting. 1–3 *v.*, 4, 5 *n.* —**grant′a·ble**, *adj.* —**grant′er**, *n.*
**take for granted**, assume to be true, accept as proved or as agreed to: *It is taken for granted that one must eat to live. We took it for granted that Dennis would do well.*

**gran·u·lar** (gran′yə lər) 1 consisting of or containing grains or granules: *Granular sugar is coarser than icing sugar.* 2 resembling grains or granules. *adj.* —**gran′u·lar·ly**, *adv.*

**gran·u·late** (gran′yə lāt′) 1 form into grains or granules. 2 roughen on the surface. 3 become granular; develop granulations: *Wounds granulate in healing.* *v.*, **gran·u·lat·ed, gran·u·lat·ing.**

**gran·u·lat·ed** (gran′yə lā′tid) 1 formed into grains or granules: *granulated sugar.* 2 roughened on the surface. 3 having granulations. 4 pt. and pp. of GRANULATE. 1–3 *adj.*, 4 *v.*

**gran·u·la·tion** (gran′yə lā′shən) 1 a formation into grains or granules. 2 a roughening on the surface. 3 a granule on a roughened surface. *n.*

**gran·ule** (gran′yül) 1 a small grain. 2 a small bit or spot like a grain, especially one of the small brilliant spots that appear on the sun's photosphere and last only a few minutes. *n.*

**gran·u·lose** (gran′yə lōs′) that part of a starch granule on which diastase and saliva act. *n.*

**grape** (grāp) a small round fruit of various colours that grows in bunches on a vine: *Grapes are eaten raw or made into raisins and wine.* *n.* —**grape′like′**, *adj.*

**grape·fruit** (grāp′früt′) 1 a pale-yellow, roundish citrus fruit like an orange, but larger and not as sweet: *Grapefruit grow in clusters, like grapes.* 2 the subtropical evergreen tree that produces this fruit. *n., pl.* **grape·fruit** or **grape·fruits.**

**grape·shot** (grāp′shot′) a cluster of small iron balls formerly used as a charge for cannon. *n.*

**grape sugar** sugar formed in all green plants, but especially in grapes; dextrose.

**grape·vine** (grāp′vīn′) 1 the vine that bears grapes. 2 *Informal.* a way by which reports are mysteriously spread: *She learned through the grapevine that she had passed the examination.* *n.*

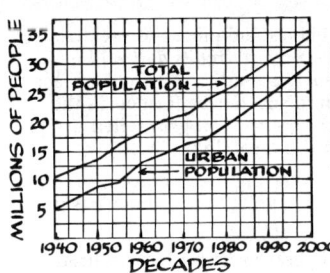

A graph of Canadian population trends projected to the year 2000. It shows that the total population is increasing, and also that the urban population is increasing relative to the rural.

**graph** (graf) **1** a line or diagram showing how one quantity depends on or changes with another. **2** in mathematics, any line or lines representing the relations of equations or functions. **3** draw such a line or diagram; draw a line representing some change, equation, or function. 1, 2 *n.*, 3 *v.*
☞ *Etym.* See note at -GRAPH.

**-graph** *combining form.* **1** make a picture, draw, or write, as in *photograph*. **2** a machine that makes a picture, draws, or writes, as in *seismograph, barograph*. **3** drawn or written, as in *autograph*. **4** something drawn or written, as in *lithograph*.
☞ *Etym.* **-graph**, GRAPH, and GRAPHIC can all be traced back to Gk. *graphein* 'to write'. While **-graph** comes directly from the Greek combining form *-graphos*, **graph** is a shortened form of the phrase *graphic formula*. **Graphic** comes through Latin from the Greek adjective *graphikos*. See also the note at GRAFFITI.

**graph·ic** (graf′ik) **1** lifelike, clear, and vivid: *a graphic account of the battle*. **2** of or about diagrams and their use. **3** shown by a graph: *a graphic record of school attendance for a month*. **4** of or about drawing, painting, engraving, or etching: *the graphic arts*. **5** a piece of graphic work. **6** of or used in handwriting: *graphic symbols*. **7** written; inscribed. **8 graphics**, the art or technique of producing graphic work: *Computers are often used in graphics*. 1–4, 6, 7 *adj.*, 5, 8 *n.*
☞ *Etym.* See note at -GRAPH.

**graph·i·cal·ly** (graf′i klē) **1** by a diagram or pictures. **2** vividly. *adv.*

**graphic arts** drawing, painting, engraving, etching, etc.: *Some artists make use of computers to produce graphic arts.*

**graph·ite** (graf′īt) a soft, black form of carbon found in nature, having a metallic lustre, used for lead in pencils, for lubricating machinery, etc. *n.*

**graph·ol·o·gy** (gra fol′ə jē) the study of handwriting, especially as a means of analysing a person's character. *n.*

**graph paper** paper with small ruled squares for the drawing of diagrams, graphs, etc.: *Graph paper has squares measured in centimetres to allow accuracy in producing diagrams.*

**grap·nel** (grap′nəl) **1** an instrument with one or more hooks for seizing and holding something. **2** a small anchor having three or more hooks. See ANCHOR for picture. *n.*

**grap·ple** (grap′əl) **1** seize and hold fast; grip or hold firmly. **2** seizing and holding fast; firm grip or hold. **3** struggle; fight: *The wrestlers grappled in the centre of the ring.* **4** an iron bar with hooks at one end for seizing and holding fast an object; grappling iron; grapnel. **5** use a grappling iron; search with a grappling iron. **6** try to deal with: *She grappled with the problem for an hour before she solved it.* 1, 3, 5 *v.*, **grap·pled**, **grap·pling**; 2, 4 *n.* —**grap′pler**, *n.*

# graph 523 grate

hat, āge, fär; let, ēqual, tėrm; it, īce
hot, ōpen, ôrder; oil, out; cup, pu̇t, rüle
əbove, takən, pencəl, lemən, circəs
ch, child; ng, long; sh, ship
th, thin; ᴛʜ, then; zh, measure

**grappling iron** GRAPNEL (def. 1).

**grasp** (grasp) **1** seize and hold fast by closing the fingers around. **2** a seizing and holding tightly; clasp of the hand. **3** the power of seizing and holding; reach: *She has a strong grasp. Success is within his grasp.* **4** control; possession. **5** understand. **6** understanding: *He has a good grasp of mathematics.* 1, 5 *v.*, 2–4, 6 *n.*
—**grasp′a·ble**, *adj.* —**grasp′er**, *n.*
**grasp at**, **a** try to take hold of. **b** accept eagerly: *Joan grasped at the opportunity.*

**grasp·ing** (gras′ping) **1** eager to get all that one can; greedy. **2** ppr. of GRASP. 1 *adj.*, 2 *v.*
—**grasp′ing·ly**, *adv.*

**grass** (gras) **1** non-woody green plants that grow in pastures and meadows and are suitable as food for grazing animals: *Horses, cows, and sheep eat grass.* **2** any of a large family of plants having jointed, non-woody stems, long, narrow leaves, and flowers in spikelets: *Wheat, corn, sugar cane, and bamboo are grasses.* **3** land covered with grass: *There was a sign saying "Keep off the grass".* **4** pasture: *The horses were put out to grass.* **5** seed to grass; grow grass over or on. **6** feed on grass: *to grass livestock.* 1–4 *n.*, 5, 6 *v.* —**grass′less**, *adj.*
—**grass′like′**, *adj.*
**go to grass**, **a** graze; go to pasture. **b** take a rest.
**let the grass grow under one's feet**, waste time; lose chances.

**grass hockey** *Cdn.* FIELD HOCKEY.

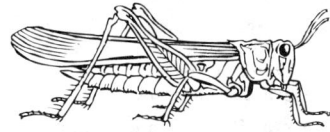

A common North American grasshopper— about 3 cm long

**grass·hop·per** (gras′hop′ər) any of a number of insects having biting mouth parts, two pairs of wings, and long, strong hind legs, adapted for jumping: *Grasshoppers eat plants and are often serious pests in grainfields.* *n.*

**grass·land** (gras′land′) land with grass on it, used for pasture. *n.*

**grass roots** **1** in politics, people and party organizations at the local level, especially in rural communities. **2** soil near or at the surface. **3** the beginning or source. —**grass′-roots′**, *adj.*

**grass snake** a harmless, greyish-green snake living in marshy places.

**grass widow** a woman whose husband is temporarily away.

**grass widower** a man whose wife is temporarily away.

**grass·y** (gras′ē) **1** covered with grass: *a grassy meadow.* **2** of or like grass. *adj.* **grass·i·er, grass·i·est.**
—**grass′i·ness**, *n.*

**grate**[1] (grāt) **1** a framework of iron bars to hold a fire: *A coal furnace has a grate.* See FIREPLACE for picture. **2** fireplace. **3** a framework of bars over a window or

opening; grating. 4 furnish with a grate or grating. 1–3 n., 4 v., **grat·ed, grat·ing.** —**grate′like′**, adj.
☛ Hom. GREAT.

**grate²** (grāt) 1 have an annoying or unpleasant effect: *His rude manners grate on people.* 2 make a grinding sound; sound harshly. 3 move with a harsh sound: *The door grated on its old, rusty hinges.* 4 wear down or grind off in small pieces: *to grate cheese.* v., **grat·ed, grat·ing.**
☛ Hom. GREAT.

**grate·ful** (grāt′fəl) 1 feeling gratitude; thankful: *We were grateful for their help.* 2 pleasing; welcome: *a grateful breeze.* adj. —**grate′ful·ly**, adv. —**grate′ful·ness**, n.

**grat·er** (grā′tər) a device with a rough surface for wearing down into shreds or particles: *a cheese grater.* n.

**grat·i·fi·ca·tion** (grat′ə fə kā′shən) 1 gratifying or being gratified: *The gratification of every wish of every person is not possible.* 2 something that satisfies or pleases: *Nina's success was a great gratification to her parents.* n.

**grat·i·fy** (grat′ə fī) 1 give pleasure or satisfaction to; please: *Flattery gratifies a vain person.* 2 satisfy; indulge: *A drunkard gratifies his craving for liquor.* v., **grat·i·fied, grat·i·fying.** —**grat′i·fi′er**, n. —**grat′i·fy′ing·ly**, adv.

**grat·ing¹** (grā′ting) 1 a framework of bars over a window or opening. 2 ppr. of GRATE¹. 1 n., 2 v.

**grat·ing²** (grā′ting) 1 unpleasant; annoying; irritating. 2 harsh or jarring in sound: *a grating voice.* 3 ppr. of GRATE². 1, 2 adj., 3 v.

**grat·is** (grat′is or grā′tis) for nothing; free of charge. adv., adj.

**grat·i·tude** (grat′ə tyüd′ or grat′ə tüd′) a thankful feeling because of a favour received; thankfulness. n.

**gra·tu·i·tous** (grə tyü′ə təs or grə tü′ə təs) 1 freely given or obtained; free. 2 without reason or cause; unnecessary; uncalled for: *a gratuitous insult.* adj. —**gra·tu′i·tous·ly**, adv. —**gra·tu′i·tous·ness**, n.

**gra·tu·i·ty** (grə tyü′ə tē or grə tü′ə tē) a present of money in return for service; tip: *Gratuities are given to waiters, porters, etc.* n., pl. **gra·tu·i·ties.**

**grave¹** (grāv) 1 a hole dug in the ground where a dead body is to be buried. 2 a mound or monument over it. 3 any place that becomes the receptacle of what is dead: *a watery grave.* 4 death: *an early grave.* n.

**grave²** (grāv for 1–4, gräv or grāv for 5–7) 1 important; weighty; momentous: *It was a grave decision to make.* 2 serious; threatening: *grave questions, doubts, symptoms, news.* 3 dignified; sober; solemn: *a grave face, a grave ceremony.* 4 sombre: *grave colours.* 5 in phonetics, low in pitch; not acute. 6 having a grave accent. 7 grave accent. 1–6 adj., **grav·er, grav·est;** 7 n. —**grave′ly**, adv. —**grave′ness**, n.

**grave³** (grāv) 1 engrave; carve; sculpture. 2 impress deeply; fix firmly. v., **graved, graved** or **graven, grav·ing.** —**grav′er**, n.

**grave accent** (gräv or grāv) a mark ( ` ) placed over a vowel to indicate stress, pitch, or quality of sound (as in French *père*), or syllabic value (as in *belovèd*). Compare with ACUTE ACCENT.

**grave·dig·ger** (grāv′dig′ər) a person whose work is digging graves. n.

**grav·el** (grav′əl) 1 pebbles and pieces of rock coarser than sand: *Gravel is much used for roads and walks.* 2 cover with gravel: *to gravel a road.* 3 a road surfaced with gravel. 4 small, hard substances formed in the bladder and kidneys. 1, 3, 4 n., 2 v., **grav·elled** or **grav·eled, grav·el·ling** or **grav·el·ing.**

**grav·el·ly** (grav′ə lē) 1 having much gravel: *gravelly soil.* 2 consisting of or like gravel. 3 rough; rasping; grating: *a gravelly voice.* adj.

**grav·en** (grā′vən) 1 engraved; carved; sculptured. 2 deeply impressed; firmly fixed. 3 a pp. of GRAVE³: *Figures were graven in the rock.* 1, 2 adj., 3 v.

**graven image** 1 a statue. 2 idol.

**grave·stone** (grāv′stōn′) a stone that marks a grave. n.

**grave·yard** (grāv′yärd′) a place for burying the dead; cemetery; burial ground. n.

**graveyard shift** *Informal.* night work.

**grav·id** (grav′id) pregnant. adj.

**graving dock** (grā′ving) a DRY DOCK where ships are repaired or have their hulls cleaned.

**grav·i·tate** (grav′ə tāt′) 1 move or tend to move by gravitation. 2 settle down; sink; fall: *The sand and dirt in the water gravitated to the bottom of the bottle.* 3 tend to go; be strongly attracted: *The attention of the crowd gravitated to the new jet.* v., **grav·i·tat·ed, grav·i·tat·ing.**

**grav·i·ta·tion** (grav′ə tā′shən) 1 the fact that the earth pulls any object toward it and that the sun, moon, stars, and other such bodies in the universe do the same; the force or pull that makes bodies in the universe tend to move toward one another. 2 a moving or tendency to move caused by this force. 3 a settling down; sinking; falling. 4 a natural tendency toward some point or object of influence: *the gravitation of population to the cities.* n.

**grav·i·ta·tion·al** (grav′ə tā′shə nəl) of gravitation; having to do with gravitation. adj.

**grav·i·ty** (grav′ə tē) 1 the natural force that causes objects to move or tend to move toward the centre of the earth or moon, or a planet: *The gravity is slightly less at the top of a high mountain than at sea level.* 2 the natural force that makes objects move or tend to move toward each other; gravitation. 3 heaviness; weight (used especially in **centre of gravity**): *The centre of gravity of an object is where most of its weight appears to be. The toy was hard to tip over because it had a low centre of gravity.* 4 a serious manner; serious behaviour; solemnity; earnestness: *a look of gravity.* 5 a serious or critical character: *When she had explained the gravity of the situation, they were all willing to help.* n., pl. **grav·i·ties.**

**gra·vy** (grā′vē) 1 a sauce for meat, potatoes, etc. made from the juice that comes out of meat in cooking. 2 the juice itself. n., pl. **gra·vies.**

**gray** (grā) See GREY. n., adj., v.

**gray·beard** (grā′bērd′) See GREYBEARD. n.

**gray–head·ed** (grā′hed′id) See GREY-HEADED. adj.

**gray·ish** (grā′ish) See GREYISH. adj.

**gray jay** GREY JAY.

**gray·ling** (grā′ling) any of a very small family of freshwater fishes found in the cold, clear streams of northern North America, Europe, and Asia, famous as a food and game fish and also for their beautiful colouring and the smell of wild thyme that freshly caught specimens have: *Some zoologists place the graylings in the salmon and trout family.* *n.*

**gray matter** GREY MATTER.

**graze**[1] (grāz) **1** feed on growing grass: *Cattle and sheep graze.* **2** put cattle, sheep, etc. to feed on growing grass or a pasture. **3** tend or look after cattle, sheep, etc. while they are grazing. *v.*, **grazed, graz·ing.**
—**graz′er,** *n.*

**graze**[2] (grāz) **1** touch lightly in passing; rub lightly against: *The car grazed the garage door.* **2** scrape the skin from: *The bullet grazed his shoulder.* **3** a slight wound made by grazing. **4** the act of grazing. 1, 2 *v.*, **grazed, graz·ing;** 3, 4 *n.*

**graz·ing** (grā′zing) **1** the growing grass that cattle, sheep, etc. feed on; pasture: *There is good grazing in the east pasture in June.* **2** ppr. of GRAZE. 1 *n.*, 2 *v.*

**Gr. Brit.** or **Gr. Br.** Great Britain.

**grease** (grēs) **1** animal fat that has been melted and then allowed to cool to a soft solid. **2** any thick, oily substance, especially one used as a lubricant. **3** smear with grease; put grease on or in: *Grease the casserole dish well. Long-distance swimmers grease their bodies for protection against the cold water.* **4** lubricate with grease: *He took his car in to have it greased.* 1, 2 *n.*, 3, 4 *v.*, **greased, greas·ing.**

**grease·wood** (grē′swu̇d) a stiff, prickly shrub having narrow leaves, growing in alkaline regions in the western parts of Canada and the United States. *n.*

**greas·y** (grē′sē) **1** smeared with grease; having grease on it. **2** containing much grease: *greasy food.* **3** like grease; smooth; slippery: *The roads were greasy after the snowfall.* *adj.*, **greas·i·er, greas·i·est.**
—**greas′i·ly,** *adv.* —**greas′i·ness,** *n.*

**great** (grāt) **1** big; large: *a great house, a great crowd.* **2** more than usual; much: *great ignorance.* **3** important; remarkable; famous: *a great composer.* **4** most important; main; chief: *the great seal.* **5** noble; generous: *a great heart.* **6** much in use; favourite: *That is a great habit of hers.* **7** very much of a: *a great talker.* **8** *Informal.* very good; fine: *We had a great time at the party.* **9** in names of relationship, of the next generation before or after: *great-grandmother, great-grandson.* *adj.*
—**great′ly,** *adv.* —**great′ness,** *n.*
☞ *Hom.* GRATE.

**great·aunt** (grāt′ant′) an aunt of one's father or mother; grandaunt. *n.*

**Great Bear** the constellation Ursa Major; its seven bright stars form the Big Dipper. See DIPPER for picture.

**great blue heron** the largest heron common in southern Canada, having a bill about 12.7 cm long, and greyish blue plumage. See HERON for picture.

**Great Britain** the principal island of the United Kingdom, including England, Scotland, and Wales.

**great circle** any circle on the surface of a sphere having its plane passing through the centre of the sphere: *The equator is one of the great circles of the earth.*

**great·coat** (grāt′kōt′) a heavy overcoat, especially one worn by members of the armed forces. *n.*

**Great Dane** a breed of large, powerful, short-haired dog.

**Great Divide** in Canada, the height or crest of land extending northwest along the Rocky mountain range, from which rivers flow west to the Pacific Ocean or east and north to Hudson Bay and the Arctic Ocean; the Continental Divide.

**great–grand·child** (grāt′gran′chīld′ or grāt′grand′chīld′) a grandchild of one's son or daughter. *n.*, *pl.* **great-grand·chil·dren.**

**great–grand·daugh·ter** (grāt′gran′dot′ər) a granddaughter of one's son or daughter. *n.*

**great–grand·fa·ther** (grāt′gran′foᴛн′ər *or* grāt′grand′foᴛн′ər) a grandfather of one's father or mother. *n.*

**great–grand·moth·er** (grāt′gran′muᴛн′ər *or* grāt′grand′muᴛн′ər) a grandmother of one's father or mother. *n.*

**great–grand·son** (grāt′gran′sun′ *or* grāt′grand′sun′) a grandson of one's son or daughter. *n.*

**great grey owl** a very large owl of coniferous forests of the northern hemisphere, having a round head with a very large face, yellow eyes, a long tail, and grey plumage. It is the largest North American owl.

**great–heart·ed** (grāt′här′tid) **1** noble; generous. **2** brave; fearless. *adj.* —**great′-heart′ed·ness,** *n.*

**great horned owl** a powerful bird of prey, the largest Canadian owl, mostly brown and white and having large ear tufts.

**Great Lakes** the five large bodies of fresh water that are included in the St. Lawrence Seaway; Lakes Superior, Michigan, Huron, Erie, and Ontario.

**great·ly** (grāt′lē) to a great degree; very much. *adv.*

**great seal** the most important seal of a country, province, etc. stamped on official documents as proof of their approval by the government.

**great–uncle** (grāt′tung′kəl) an uncle of one's father or mother; granduncle. *n.*

**Great Wall of China** a huge stone wall on the boundary between northern and northwestern China and Mongolia, about 2400 kilometres long.

**Great War** the First World War, from 1914 to 1918.

**grebe** (grēb) **1** a diving bird resembling a loon and having partly webbed feet and a pointed bill: *Most grebes have crests or ruffs during the nesting season.* **2** its breast feathers, used to trim hats, etc. *n.*

**Gre·cian** (grē′shən) Greek. *adj.*

**Gre·co–Ro·man** (grē′kō rō′mən) Greek and Roman. *adj.*

**greed** (grēd) the quality of wanting more than one's share; extreme or excessive desire: *a miser's greed for money.* *n.*

**greed·y** (grē′dē) **1** wanting to get more than one's share; having a very great desire to possess something. **2** wanting to eat or drink a great deal in a hurry; piggish. **3** eager; keen: *greedy for new experiences.* *adj.*, **greed·i·er, greed·i·est.** —**greed′i·ly,** *adv.*
—**greed′i·ness,** *n.*

**Greek** (grēk) **1** of or having to do with Greece, its people, or their language. **2** a native or inhabitant of Greece. **3** the language of Greece. **Ancient** or **classical Greek** was the language until about A.D. 200; **modern Greek** is the language from about A.D. 1500 on. **1** *adj.*, **2, 3** *n.*
**it's Greek to me,** I can't understand it.

**Greek cross** a cross whose four arms are of the same length and form right angles.

**Greek fire** a flammable substance whose flames could not be put out by water, used in warfare in ancient and medieval times.

**Greek Orthodox** of or having to do with a group of Christian churches, especially the main Christian churches in eastern Europe and western Asia, which are united by common beliefs and traditions.

**green** (grēn) **1** the colour of most growing plants, grass, and leaves; the colour in the spectrum between yellow and blue. **2** having this colour. **3** make or become green. **4** green colouring matter, dye, paint, etc. **5** green cloth or clothing. **6** covered with growing plants, grass, leaves, etc.: *green fields*. **7** characterized by growing grass, etc.: *a green Christmas*. **8** grassy land or a plot of grassy ground. **9** a putting green on a golf course. **10** full of life and strength: *green old age*. **11** not dried, cured, seasoned, or otherwise prepared for use: *green tobacco*. **12** not ripe; not fully grown: *green peaches*. **13** not trained or experienced; not mature in age, judgment, etc.: *He is certainly green in business*. **14** easily fooled; easy to trick or cheat. **15** recent; fresh; new: *a green wound*. **16** having a pale, sickly colour because of fear, jealousy, or sickness. **17 greens,** *pl.* **a** green leaves and branches used for decoration, wreaths, garlands, etc. **b** leaves and stems of plants used as food: *salad greens*. 1, 4, 5, 8, 9, 17 *n.*, 2, 6, 7, 10–16 *adj.*, 3 *v.*
—**green′ness,** *n.*

**green corn** sweet corn in the young, tender, milky stage, suitable for eating roasted or boiled.

**green·er·y** (grē′nə rē) **1** green plants, grass, or leaves; verdure. **2** a place where green plants are grown or kept. *n., pl.* **green·er·ies.**

**green–eyed** (grē′nīd′) **1** having green eyes. **2** jealous. *adj.*

**green·horn** (grēn′hôrn′) *Informal.* **1** a person without experience. **2** a person easy to trick or cheat. *n.*

**green·house** (grēn′hous′) a building with a glass roof and glass sides, kept warm for growing plants; hothouse. *n.*

**greenhouse effect** the result of the emission of carbon dioxide ($CO_2$) into the atmosphere, leading to the trapping of heat on the planet by the layer of $CO_2$: *The greenhouse effect is raising the world's temperature.*

**green·ish** (grē′nish) somewhat green. *adj.*

**green light** *Informal.* permission to proceed on a particular task or undertaking.

**greenstick fracture** a breaking of part of a bone, leaving the rest intact.

**green·sward** (grēn′swôrd′) green grass; turf. *n.*

**green tea** tea made from leaves that have been steamed and then crushed and dried in ovens: *Green tea has not been fermented like black tea.*

**green thumb** a remarkable ability to grow flowers, vegetables, etc., especially as a hobby: *When Aunt Mary saw our garden, she said Mother must certainly have a green thumb.*

**Green·wich mean time** (grin′ij, grin′ich, *or* gren′ich) the basis for setting standard time in England and elsewhere, reckoned from the meridian passing through Greenwich: *Greenwich mean time is the basic time used in sea navigation.* Also, **Greenwich time.** *Abbrev.*: G.M.T.

**green·wood** (grēn′wùd′) the forest in spring and summer when the trees are green with leaves. *n.*

**greet** (grēt) **1** speak or write to in a friendly, polite way; address in welcome. **2** address; salute: *She greeted him sternly.* **3** receive: *His speech was greeted with cheers.* **4** present itself to; meet: *A strange sight greeted her eyes.* *v.* —**greet′er,** *n.*

**greet·ing** (grē′ting) **1** the act or words of a person who greets another; welcome. **2 greetings,** *pl.* friendly wishes on a special occasion: *birthday greetings*. **3** ppr. of GREET. 1, 2 *n.*, 3 *v.*

**gre·gar·i·ous** (grə ger′ē əs *or* grə gar′ē əs) **1** living in flocks, herds, or other groups: *Sheep and cattle are gregarious*. **2** fond of being with others: *A human being is a gregarious animal.* **3** of or having to do with a flock or crowd. *adj.* —**gre·gar′i·ous·ly,** *adv.* —**gre·gar′i·ous·ness,** *n.*

**Gregorian calendar** (grə gô′rē ən) the calendar now in use in most countries, introduced by Pope Gregory XIII in 1582. According to this calendar, the ordinary year has 365 days, and leap year has 366 days: *The Gregorian calendar is a correction of the calendar of Julius Caesar.*

**grem·lin** (grem′lən) an imaginary, mischievous spirit or goblin, especially one supposed to trouble airplane pilots. *n.*

**gre·nade** (grə nād′) **1** a small bomb, usually thrown by hand: *The soldiers threw grenades into the enemy's trenches.* **2** a round, glass bottle filled with chemicals that scatter as the glass breaks: *Fire grenades are thrown on fires to put them out.* *n.*

**gren·a·dier** (gren′ə dēr′) **1** originally, a soldier who threw grenades. **2** today, a soldier in any one of several infantry regiments: *The Grenadier Guards of Canada are the ceremonial guards of Parliament in Ottawa.* *n.*

**gren·a·dine**[1] (gren′ə dēn′ *or* gren′ə dēn′) a thin, openwork fabric used for women's dresses. *n.*

**gren·a·dine**[2] (gren′ə dēn′ *or* gren′ə dēn′) a syrup made from pomegranate or currant juice. *n.*

**grew** (grü) pt. of GROW: *It grew cold. Farmers grew crops.* *v.*

**grey** (grā) **1** the colour made by mixing black and white. **2** having this colour: *Ashes are grey.* **3** make or become grey. **4** grey cloth or clothing. **5** a grey horse. **6** something grey. **7** having grey hair. **8** old; ancient. **9** dark; gloomy; dismal. 1, 4–6 *n.*, 2, 7–9 *adj.*, 3 *v.* Also, **gray.** —**grey′ly,** *adv.* —**grey′ness,** *n.*

**grey·beard** (grā′bērd′) an old man. *n.* Also, **graybeard.**

**Grey Cup 1** a trophy awarded to the champion professional football team each year in Canada, first presented in 1909 by Earl Grey. **2** the game played to decide the winner of this trophy.

**grey–head·ed** (grā′hed′id) having grey hair. *adj.* Also, **gray-headed.**

A greyhound—about 70 cm high at the shoulder

**grey·hound** (grā′hound′) a breed of tall, slender, swift dog. *n.*

**grey·ish** (grā′ish) somewhat grey. *adj.* Also, **grayish**.

**grey jay** CANADA JAY. Also, **gray jay**.

**grey matter** 1 the greyish tissue in the brain and spinal cord that contains nerve cells and some nerve fibres. 2 *Informal.* intelligence; brains. Also, **gray matter**.

**grid** (grid) 1 a framework of parallel iron bars; grating; gridiron. 2 the numbered squares drawn on military maps and used for map references. 3 the system of survey lines running parallel to lines of latitude and longitude, used in the division of an area into counties, sections, lots, etc. 4 one of these lines. 5 the lead plate in a storage battery. 6 the electrode in a vacuum tube that controls the flow of current between the filament and the plate. See VACUUM TUBE for picture. *n.*

**grid·dle** (grid′əl) a heavy, flat plate of metal or soapstone, used for cooking bacon, pancakes, etc. *n.*

**grid·dle·cake** (grid′əl kāk′) a thin, flat cake of batter cooked on a griddle; pancake; flapjack: *Griddlecakes are often served with maple syrup.* *n.*

**grid·i·ron** (grid′ī′ərn) 1 metal framework, often with a handle, used for broiling meat, fish, etc.; grill. 2 any framework or network that looks like a gridiron. 3 a football field. 4 a structure above the stage of a theatre, from which scenery that is hung, etc. is manipulated. *n.*

**grid road** *Cdn.* a municipal road that follows a grid line established by survey. In Saskatchewan, these roads are built two miles (about 3.2 km) apart from north to south and one mile (about 1.6 km) from east to west.

**grief** (grēf) 1 deep sadness caused by trouble or loss; heavy sorrow. 2 a cause of sadness or sorrow: *Her son's incurable illness was a great grief to her.* *n.*
**come to grief,** have trouble; fail: *Although he worked hard, his plan came to grief.*

**griev·ance** (grē′vəns) a real or imagined wrong; reason for being angry or annoyed; cause for complaint. *n.*

**grieve** (grēv) 1 feel grief; be very sad: *She grieved over her kitten's death.* 2 cause to feel grief; make very sad; afflict: *His lawless deeds grieved his parents.* *v.*, **grieved**, **griev·ing**. —**griev′er**, *n.* —**griev′ing·ly**, *adv.*

**griev·ous** (grē′vəs) 1 hard to bear; causing great pain or suffering: *grievous cruelty.* 2 flagrant; atrocious: *Wasting food when people are starving is a grievous wrong.* 3 causing grief: *a grievous loss.* 4 full of grief; showing grief: *a grievous cry.* *adj.* —**griev′ous·ly**, *adv.* —**griev′ous·ness**, *n.*

**grif·fin** (grif′ən) a mythical creature with the head, wings, and forelegs of an eagle, and the body, hind legs, and tail of a lion. *n.* Also, **gryphon** or **griffon**.

**grill** (gril) 1 a cooking utensil consisting of a framework of parallel iron bars for broiling meat, fish, etc.; gridiron. 2 broil. 3 a dish of broiled meat, fish, etc. 4 a restaurant or dining room that specializes in serving broiled meat, fish, etc. 5 torture with heat. 6 question severely and persistently: *The detective grilled the prisoner until he finally confessed.* 1, 3, 4 *n.*, 2, 5, 6 *v.* —**grill′er**, *n.*
☞ *Hom.* GRILLE.

**grille** (gril) an openwork metal structure or screen, used as a gate, door, or window; grating. *n.*
☞ *Hom.* GRILL.

**grill·work** (gril′wərk) GRILLE. *n.*

**grilse** (grils) a salmon that is returning from the sea to fresh water. *n.*, *pl.* **grilse** or **grils·es**.

**grim** (grim) 1 without mercy; stern; harsh; fierce: *grim, stormy weather.* 2 not yielding; not relenting: *The losing team fought on with grim resolve.* 3 looking stern, fierce, or harsh: *Mother was grim when she was told about the broken windows.* 4 horrible; ghastly: *He made grim jokes about death and ghosts.* *adj.*, **grim·mer**, **grim·mest**. —**grim′ly**, *adv.* —**grim′ness**, *n.*

**gri·mace** (grim′is *or* grə mās′) 1 a twisting of the face; ugly or funny smile: *a grimace caused by pain.* 2 make grimaces. 1 *n.*, 2 *v.*, **gri·maced**, **gri·mac·ing**. —**gri·mac′er**, *n.*

**gri·mal·kin** (grə mal′kən) 1 a cat. 2 an old female cat. 3 a spiteful old woman. *n.*

**grime** (grīm) 1 dirt rubbed deeply and firmly into a surface: *the grime on a coal miner's hands.* 2 cover with grime; make dirty. 1 *n.*, 2 *v.*, **grimed**, **grim·ing**.

**grim·y** (grī′mē) covered with grime; very dirty. *adj.*, **grim·i·er**, **grim·i·est**. —**grim′i·ly**, *adv.* —**grim′i·ness**, *n.*

**grin** (grin) 1 smile broadly. 2 a broad smile. 3 show, make, or express by smiling broadly: *He grinned approval.* 4 draw back the lips and show the teeth in anger, pain, scorn, etc.: *A snarling dog grins.* 5 the act of showing the teeth in anger, pain, scorn, etc. 1, 3, 4 *v.*, **grinned**, **grin·ning**; 2, 5 *n.* —**grin′ner**, *n.*

**grind** (grīnd) 1 crush into bits or into powder: *Your back teeth grind food. The mill grinds corn into meal and wheat into flour.* 2 produce or make by grinding: *to grind flour.* 3 crush by harshness or cruelty: *The slaves were ground down by their masters.* 4 sharpen, smooth, or wear by rubbing on something rough: *to grind an axe.* 5 rub harshly on, into, against, or together: *to grind one's heel into the earth, to grind one's teeth in anger.* 6 work by turning a crank; produce by turning a crank: *A man grinds a hand organ to grind out music.* 7 the act of grinding. 8 *Informal.* long hard work or study. 9 *Informal.* work or study long and hard. 10 *Informal.* a person who works long and hard at his or her studies. 1–6, 9 *v.*, **ground**, **grind·ing**; 7, 8, 10 *n.*

**grind·er** (grīn′dər) 1 a person or thing that grinds: *a coffee grinder.* 2 a person or machine that sharpens tools. 3 a back tooth for grinding food; molar. *n.*

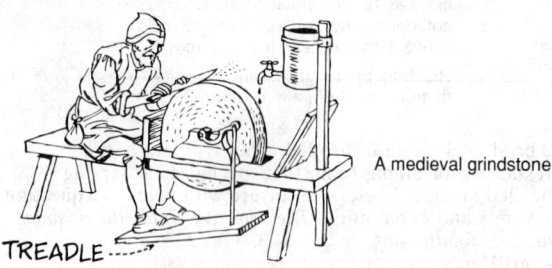

A medieval grindstone

TREADLE

**grind·stone** (grīn′stōn′ or grīnd′stōn′) a flat, round stone set in a frame and turned by a crank, treadle, etc.: *A grindstone is used to sharpen tools, such as axes and knives, or to smooth and polish things.* *n.*

**have, keep** or **put one's nose to the grindstone,** work long and hard.

**grip** (grip) **1** a firm hold; seizing and holding tight; tight grasp. **2** take a firm hold on; seize and hold tight: *The dog gripped the stick.* **3** the power of gripping. **4** something for gripping something else. **5** a part to take hold of; handle: *the grip of a suitcase.* **6** a special way of shaking hands. **7** a small suitcase; handbag. **8** firm control: *The country is in the grip of winter.* **9** mental grasp. **10** get and keep the interest and attention of: *An exciting story grips the reader.* **11** a sudden, sharp pain. **12** GRIPPE; influenza. 1, 3–9, 11, 12 *n.*, 2, 10 *v.*, **gripped, grip·ping.** —**grip′less,** *adj.* —**grip′per,** *n.*

**come to grips,** fight hand to hand; struggle close together.

**come to grips with,** begin to work at: *It's time you came to grips with that problem.*

☛ *Hom.* GRIPPE.

**gripe** (grīp) **1** clutch; pinch. **2** oppress; distress. **3** cause pain in the bowels. **4** *Informal.* complain: *She was always griping about something.* **5** a fast hold; gripping; clutch. **6** grasp; control: *The empire held small nations in its gripe.* **7** *Informal.* complaint. 1–4 *v.*, **griped, grip·ing;** 5–7 *n.*

**grippe** (grip) a contagious disease like a very severe cold with fever; influenza. *n.*

☛ *Hom.* GRIP.

**grip·ping** (grip′ing) **1** that grips; especially, that catches and holds the attention or interest. **2** ppr. of GRIP. 1 *adj.*, 2 *v.*

**gris·ly** (griz′lē) frightful; horrible; ghastly: *a grisly sight.* *adj.*, **gris·li·er, gris·li·est.** —**gris′li·ness,** *n.*

☛ *Hom.* GRIZZLY.

**grist** (grist) **1** grain to be ground. **2** grain that has been ground; meal or flour. *n.*

**grist to one's mill,** a source of profit to one.

**gris·tle** (gris′əl) cartilage; firm, tough, elastic tissue: *Babies have gristle instead of bone in some parts of the skull.* *n.*

**gris·tly** (gris′lē) of, containing, or like gristle. *adj.*, **gris·tli·er, gris·tli·est.**

**grist mill** a mill for grinding grain.

**grit** (grit) **1** very fine bits of gravel or sand: *There was grit in the spinach.* **2** a coarse sandstone. **3** *Informal.* courage; pluck: *The fighter showed lots of grit.* **4** grate; grind: *She gritted her teeth and plunged into the cold water.* **5 Grit,** *Cdn. Informal.* **a** a member of the Liberal party in Canada. **b** of or associated with the Liberals. 1–3, 5 *n.*, 4 *v.*, **grit·ted, grit·ting.**

**grits** (grits) **1** coarsely ground corn, oats, etc. with the husks removed. **2** *U.S.* coarse hominy. *n.pl.*

**grit·ty** (grit′ē) **1** of or containing grit; like grit; sandy: *This spinach tastes gritty.* **2** *Informal.* courageous; plucky. *adj.*, **grit·ti·er, grit·ti·est.** —**grit′ti·ness,** *n.*

**griz·zled** (griz′əld) **1** grey; greyish. **2** grey-haired. *adj.*

**griz·zly** (griz′lē) **1** greyish; grey. **2** grey-haired. **3** a GRIZZLY BEAR. 1, 2 *adj.*, **griz·zli·er, griz·zli·est;** 3 *n.*, *pl.* **griz·zlies.**

☛ *Hom.* GRISLY.

**grizzly bear** a large, fierce, grey or brownish grey bear of western North America.

**groan** (grōn) **1** a deep-throated sound expressing grief, pain, or disapproval; deep, short moan: *We heard the groans of the wounded men.* **2** give a groan or groans. **3** be loaded or overburdened: *The table groaned with food.* **4** express by groaning. **5** suffer greatly. 1 *n.*, 2–5 *v.*, —**groan′er,** *n.*

☛ *Hom.* GROWN.

**groats** (grōts) hulled grain; hulled and crushed grain. *n.pl.*

**gro·cer** (grō′sər) a merchant who sells food and household supplies. *n.*

**gro·cer·y** (grō′sə rē) **1** a store that sells food and household supplies. **2** the business of a grocer. **3 groceries,** *pl.* food and household supplies sold by a grocer. *n.*

**gro·ce·te·ri·a** (grō′sə tē′rē ə) a grocery store in which the customers wait on themselves, paying for their purchase at a cashier's counter. *n.*

**grog** (grog) *Esp. Brit.* **1** a drink made of rum or any other strong alcoholic liquor diluted with water. **2** any strong alcoholic liquor. *n.*

**grog·gy** (grog′ē) *Informal.* **1** shaky; unsteady. **2** drunk; intoxicated. *adj.*, **grog·gi·er, grog·gi·est.** —**grog′gi·ly,** *adv.* —**grog′gi·ness,** *n.*

**groin** (groin) **1** the hollow on either side of the body where the thigh joins the abdomen. **2** a curved line where two vaults of a roof cross. **3** form or build with groins. 1, 2 *n.*, 3 *v.*

**grom·met** (grom′it) **1** a metal eyelet. **2** a ring of rope, used as an oarlock, to hold a sail on its stays, etc. *n.*

**groom** (grüm) **1** a person who has charge of horses. **2** feed and take care of horses; rub down and brush. **3** take care of the appearance of; make neat and tidy: *She was brought up to groom herself carefully.* **4** prepare a person for a job, political office, etc. **5** a man just married or about to be married; bridegroom. **6** any of several officers of the British royal household. 1, 5, 6 *n.*, 2–4 *v.* —**groom′er,** *n.*

**grooms·man** (grümz′mən) the man who attends the bridegroom at a wedding. *n.*, *pl.* **grooms·men** (-zmən).

**groove** (grüv) **1** a long, narrow channel or furrow, especially one cut by a tool: *The plate rests in a groove on the rack.* **2** any similar channel; rut: *Wheels leave grooves in a dirt road.* **3** make a groove in. **4** a fixed way of doing things: *It is hard to get out of a groove.* 1, 2, 4 *n.*, 3 *v.*, **grooved, groov·ing.**

**grope** (grōp) **1** feel about with the hands: *She groped* for a flashlight when the lights went out.   2 search blindly and uncertainly: *The detectives groped for some clue to the murder.*   3 find by feeling about with the hands; feel one's way slowly: *The blind man groped his way to the door.* *v.*, **groped, grop·ing.**   **—grop'ing·ly,** *adv.*

**gros·beak** (grōs'bēk')   a finch having a large, stout, cone-shaped bill.   *n.*

**gros·grain** (grō'grān')   a closely woven silk or rayon cloth with heavy cross threads and a dull finish.   *n.*

**gross** (grōs)   1 with nothing taken out; whole; entire: *The gross receipts are all the money taken in before costs are deducted.*   2 the whole sum; total amount.   3 a unit consisting of twelve dozen; 144.   4 obviously bad; glaring: *gross misconduct. She makes gross errors in pronunciation.*   5 coarse; vulgar: *Her manners are too gross for a lady.*   6 too big and fat; overfed.   7 thick; heavy; dense: *the gross growth of a jungle.*   1, 4–7 *adj.*, 2, 3 *n., pl.* **gross·es** for 2, **gross** for 3.   **—gross'ly,** *adv.*   **—gross'ness,** *n.*   **in the gross,**   **a** as a whole; in bulk.   **b** wholesale.

**gross national product**   the total market value of a nation's goods and services, before allowances or deductions.   *Abbrev.:* GNP or G.N.P.

**gro·tesque** (grō tesk')   1 odd or unnatural in shape, appearance, manner, etc.; fantastic; queer: *The book had pictures of hideous dragons and other grotesque monsters.*   2 ridiculous; absurd: *The monkey's grotesque antics made the children laugh.*   3 a painting, sculpture, etc. combining designs, ornaments, figures of persons or animals, etc. in a fantastic or unnatural way.   4 a fantastic character in a play or film.   1, 2 *adj.*, 3, 4 *n.*   **—gro·tesque'ly,** *adv.*   **—gro·tesque'ness,** *n.*

**grot·to**[1] (grot'ō)   1 a cave.   2 an artificial cave made for coolness or pleasure.   3 a shrine in or like a cave. *n., pl.* **grot·toes** or **grot·tos.**

**grot·to**[2] (grot'ō)   a local group of Satanists who hold regular meetings.   *n., pl.* **grot·toes** or **grot·tos.**

**grouch** (grouch) *Informal.*   1 be sulky or ill-tempered; complain.   2 a sulky person.   3 a sulky, discontented feeling.   1 *v.*, 2, 3 *n.*

**grouch·y** (grou'chē) *Informal.*   sulky; sullen; grumbling; discontented.   *adj.*, **grouch·i·er, grouch·i·est.**   **—grouch'i·ly,** *adv.*   **—grouch'i·ness,** *n.*

**ground**[1] (ground)   1 the solid part of the earth's surface: *Snow covered the ground.*   2 earth; soil; dirt: *The ground was hard.*   3 of, on, at, or near the ground; living or growing in, on, or close to the ground: *the ground floor of a building.*   4 put on the ground; cause to touch the ground.   5 run aground; hit the bottom or shore: *The boat grounded in shallow water.*   6 a particular piece of land; land for some special purpose: *The Cariboo was her favourite hunting ground.*   7 the foundation for what is said, thought, claimed, or done; basis; reason: *There is no ground for complaining of her conduct.*   8 put on a firm foundation or basis; establish firmly.   9 instruct in the first principles or elements: *The class is well grounded in arithmetic.*   10 underlying surface; background: *The cloth has a blue pattern on a white ground.*   11 furnish with a background.   12 the connection of an electrical conductor with the earth.   13 connect an electric wire or other conductor with the earth.   14 the connection in a radio, television set, etc. for the conductor that leads to the ground.   15 **grounds,** *pl.*   **a** land or area for some purpose or special use.   **b** the land, lawns, and gardens around a house, college, etc.   **c** the small bits that sink to the bottom of a drink such as coffee or tea; dregs; sediment.   **d** foundation; basis: *What grounds do you have for your accusation?*   1, 2, 6, 7, 10, 12, 14, 15 *n.*, 3 *adj.*, 4, 5, 8, 9, 11, 13 *v.*

**above ground,**   alive.
**break ground,**   **a** dig; plough.   **b** begin building.
**break new ground,**   **a** do something for the first time.   **b** do something in a new and original manner.
**cover ground,**   **a** go over a certain distance or area.   **b** travel.   **c** do a certain amount of work, etc.
**cut the ground from under one's feet,**   spoil a person's defence or argument by meeting it in advance.
**fall to the ground,**   fail; be given up.
**from the ground up,**   completely; entirely; thoroughly: *She learned her father's business from the ground up.*
**gain ground,**   **a** go forward; advance; progress: *During the second day of fighting, the army began to gain ground.*   **b** become more common or widespread.
**give ground,**   retreat; yield: *Under our attack the enemy was forced to give ground.*
**hold one's ground,**   keep one's position; not retreat or yield.
**lose ground,**   **a** retreat; yield.   **b** fall back; give up what has been gained: *As soon as the runner became tired, she began to lose ground.*   **c** become less common or widespread.
**on the grounds of,**   because of; by reason of.
**run into the ground,** *Informal.*   overdo.
**shift one's ground,**   change one's position; use a different defence or argument.
**stand one's ground,**   keep one's position; refuse to retreat or yield: *Even though the boxer was hurt, he stood his ground.*

**ground**[2] (ground)   *pt.* and *pp.* of GRIND: *The wheat was ground to make flour.*   *v.*

**ground crew**   the non-flying personnel responsible for the conditioning and maintenance of airplanes.

**ground·er** (groun'dər)   a baseball hit or thrown so as to bound or roll along the ground.   *n.*

**ground floor**   1 the first floor of a building. 2 *Informal.*   the best position in relation to a business deal, etc.

**ground hemlock**   a common low-growing shrub, a species of yew found in forests from Newfoundland to Manitoba and the northeastern United States.

A groundhog—about 50 cm long excluding the tail

**ground·hog** (ground'hog')   a North American burrowing animal of the marmot family; woodchuck: *Groundhogs grow fat in summer and sleep in their burrows all winter.*   *n.*

**Groundhog Day**   February 2, when the groundhog is supposed to come out of its hole to see whether the sun is shining; if the sun is shining and it sees its shadow, it returns to its hole for six more weeks of winter.

**ground·less** (groun′dlis) without foundation, basis, or reason. *adj.* —**ground′less·ly**, *adv.* —**ground′less·ness**, *n.*

**ground·ling** (groun′dling) **1** a plant or animal that lives close to the ground. **2** a fish that lives at the bottom of the water. **3** a spectator or reader who has poor taste. *n.*

**ground·nut** (groun′nut′) **1** any of various plants having edible underground parts, such as the peanut. **2** the edible tuber, pod, etc. of such a plant. *n.*

**ground plan 1** the plan of a floor of a building. **2** the first or fundamental plan.

**ground·sel** (groun′səl) a plant having small heads of yellow flowers: *The seeds of some kinds of groundsel are used for bird food.* *n.*

**ground squirrel** any one of various burrowing rodents belonging to the same family as the squirrel, especially the chipmunk.

**ground swell** broad, deep waves caused by a distant storm, earthquake, etc.

**ground wire** a wire connecting electric wiring, a radio, etc. with the ground.

**ground·work** (groun′dwėrk′) foundations; basis. *n.*

**ground zero** the exact point where a bomb strikes the ground or, in an atomic explosion, the area directly beneath the core of radiation.

**group** (grüp) **1** a number of persons or things together: *A group of children were playing tag.* **2** a number of persons or things belonging or classed together: *Wheat, rye, and oats belong to the grain group.* **3** form into a group: *The children grouped themselves at the monkey's cage.* **4** bring together; put in a group. **5** arrange in groups. 1, 2 *n.*, 3–5 *v.*

**group·er** (grü′pər) a large food fish of warm seas. *n., pl.* **group·er** or **group·ers**.

**group·ing** (grü′ping) **1** a placing or manner of being placed in a group or groups. **2** ppr. of GROUP. 1 *n.*, 2 *v.*

A ruffed grouse—about 45 cm long including the tail

**grouse**[1] (grous) a game bird having feathered legs: *The prairie chicken and ruffed grouse are different kinds of grouse.* *n., pl.* **grouse**.

**grouse**[2] (grous) *Informal.* **1** grumble; complain. **2** a complaining; complaint. **3** a person who complains; grumbler. 1 *v.*, **groused, grous·ing**; 2, 3 *n.* —**grous′er**, *n.*

**grove** (grōv) a group of trees standing together. *n.*

**grov·el** (grov′əl *or* gruv′əl) **1** lie face downward, crawl at someone's feet; humble oneself: *The slaves grovelled before their master.* **2** enjoy low, mean, or contemptible things. *v.*, **grov·elled** or **grov·eled, grov·el·ling** or **grov·el·ing**. —**grov′el·ler** or **grov′el·er**, *n.*

**grow** (grō) **1** become bigger by taking in food, as plants and animals do. **2** exist; sprout; spring; arise: *a tree growing only in the tropics.* **3** become greater; increase: *Her fame grew.* **4** become gradually attached or united by growth: *The vine has grown fast to the wall.* **5** become: *to grow old.* **6** cause to grow; produce; raise: *to grow corn.* **7** allow to grow: *to grow a beard.* **8** develop. *v.*, **grew, grown, grow·ing**.
**grow on** or **upon**, have an increasing effect or influence on: *The habit grew on me.*
**grow out of**, **a** grow too big for. **b** grow too old for.
**grow up**, **a** advance to or arrive at full growth and maturity: *What will you be when you grow up?* **b** come into being; be produced; develop. **c** behave maturely.

**grow·er** (grō′ər) **1** a person who grows something: *a fruit grower.* **2** a plant that grows in a certain way: *a quick grower.* *n.*

**growl** (groul) **1** make a deep, low, angry sound: *The dog growled at the tramp.* **2** a deep, low, angry sound; deep, warning snarl. **3** express by growling. **4** complain angrily: *The soldiers growled about the poor food.* **5** an angry complaint. **6** rumble. **7** a rumble. 1, 3, 4, 6 *v.*, 2, 5, 7 *n.*

**growl·er** (grou′lər) a person or animal that growls. *n.*

**grown** (grōn) **1** arrived at full growth: *A grown woman is an adult.* **2** covered with a growth. **3** pp. of GROW: *This flower has grown very tall.* 1, 2 *adj.*, 3 *v.*
☛ Hom. GROAN.

**grown–up** (grō′nup′) **1** adult: *The girl went to the theatre with the grown-ups.* **2** characteristic of or suitable for adults: *grown-up clothes.* 1, 2 *adj.*, 1 *n.*

**growth** (grōth) **1** the process of growing; development. **2** the amount of growing or developing; increase: *one year's growth.* **3** what has grown or is growing: *A thick growth of bushes covered the ground.* **4** an unhealthy mass of tissue formed in or on the body: *Cancer causes a growth.* *n.*

**grub** (grub) **1** a wormlike form or larva of an insect: *A grub is usually the smooth, thick larva of a beetle.* **2** dig: *Pigs grub for roots.* **3** root out of the ground; dig up: *It took the farmer weeks to grub the stumps on her land.* **4** rid ground of roots, etc. **5** a drudge. **6** drudge; toil. **7** *Informal.* food. 1, 5, 7 *n.*, 2–4, 6 *v.*, **grubbed, grub·bing**. —**grub′ber**, *n.*

**grub·by** (grub′ē) **1** dirty; grimy: *grubby hands.* **2** infested with grubs: *grubby apples.* *adj.*, **grub·bi·er, grub·bi·est**. —**grub′bi·ness**, *n.*

**grub·stake** (grub′stāk′) *Informal.* **1** the food, outfit, money, etc. supplied to a prospector on the condition of sharing in whatever he or she finds. **2** the money or the means to buy food and other provisions for a certain period: *He was afraid his grubstake would run out before he could work again.* **3** supply with a grubstake. 1, 2 *n.*, 3 *v.*, **grub·staked, grub·stak·ing**. —**grub′stak′er**, *n.*

**grudge** (gruj) **1** ill will; a sullen feeling against; dislike of long standing. **2** feel anger or dislike toward a person because of something; envy the possession of: *She grudged me my little prize even though she had won a bigger one.* **3** give or let have unwillingly: *The mean man grudged his*

horse the food that it ate.   1 n., 2, 3 v., **grudged, grudg·ing.**
**bear a grudge,** have and keep a grudge.

**grudg·ing·ly** (gruj′ing lē)   unwillingly.   adv.

**gru·el** (grü′əl)   **1** a thin, almost liquid food made by boiling oatmeal, etc. in water or milk: *Gruel is often given to those who are sick or old.*   **2** *Informal.* tire out completely; exhaust.   1 n., 2 v., **gru·elled** or **gru·eled, gru·el·ling** or **gru·el·ing.**

**gru·el·ling** or **gru·el·ing** (grü′ə ling) *Informal.*
**1** exhausting; very tiring: *a gruelling contest.*   **2** an exhausting or very tiring experience.   **3** ppr. of GRUEL.   1 adj., 2 n., 3 v.

**grue·some** (grü′səm)   horrible; frightful; revolting: *a gruesome sight.*   adj.   —**grue′some·ly,** adv.   —**grue′some·ness,** n.

**gruff** (gruf)   **1** deep and harsh; hoarse: *a gruff voice.*   **2** rough; rude; unfriendly; bad-tempered: *a gruff manner.*   adj.   —**gruff′ly,** adv.   —**gruff′ness,** n.

**grum·ble** (grum′bəl)   **1** mutter in discontent; complain in a bad-tempered way.   **2** a mutter of discontent; a bad-tempered complaint.   **3** express by grumbling.   **4** rumble: *Her stomach was grumbling from hunger.*   1, 3, 4 v., **grum·bled, grum·bling;**   2 n.   —**grum′bler,** n.

**grump·y** (grum′pē)   surly; ill-humoured; gruff: *The grumpy old woman used to find fault with everything.*   adj., **grump·i·er, grump·i·est.**   —**grump′i·ly,** adv.   —**grump′i·ness,** n.

**Grun·dy, Mrs.** (grun′dē)   a character who personifies prudish or narrow-minded disapproval of manners, actions, etc.: *What would Mrs. Grundy say to such brief bathing suits?*   n.
☞ *Etym.* From a person often referred to by the characters in the play *Speed the Plough,* by Thomas Morton (1764–1838).

**grunt** (grunt)   **1** the deep, hoarse sound that a pig makes.   **2** a sound like this: *The old man got out of his chair with a grunt.*   **3** make the deep, hoarse sound of a pig.   **4** say with this sound: *The sullen girl grunted her apology.*   **5** an edible sea fish that grunts when taken out of the water.   1, 2, 5 n., 3, 4 v.   —**grunt′er,** n.

**gt.**   great.

**Gt. Br.** or **Gt. Brit.**   Great Britain.

**gtd.**   guaranteed.

**gua·na·co** (gwä nä′kō)   a wild South American mammal like a small camel without a hump: *Llamas and alpacas are thought to have been domesticated from guanacos.*   n., pl. **gua·na·cos.**

**gua·no** (gwä′nō)   **1** the manure of sea birds, found especially on islands near Peru: *Guano is an excellent fertilizer.*   **2** an artificial fertilizer made from fish.   n., pl. **gua·nos.**

**guar·an·tee** (gar′ən tē′, ger′ən tē′ or gä′rən tē′)   **1** a promise to pay or do something if another fails; pledge to replace or repair goods if they are not as represented; backing.   **2** a person who so promises.   **3** one to whom such a pledge is made.   **4** stand behind; give a guarantee for; assure genuineness or permanence of; answer for fulfilment of a contract, etc.: *This company guarantees its clocks for a year. The mother guaranteed her son's future behaviour.*   **5** undertake to secure for another: *She will guarantee us possession of the house by May.*   **6** secure

# grudgingly 531 guardian

hat, āge, fär; let, ēqual, tėrm; it, īce
hot, ōpen, ôrder; oil, out; cup, pu̇t, rüle
əbove, taken, pencəl, lemən, circəs
ch, child; ng, long; sh, ship
th, thin; ᴛʜ, then; zh, measure

against or from: *His insurance guaranteed him against money loss in case of fire.*   **7** promise to do something: *I will guarantee to prove every statement I made.*   **8** pledge that something has been or will be: *The advance payment of money guarantees the good faith of the purchaser.*   **9** make sure or certain: *Wealth does not guarantee happiness.*   **10** an assurance, promise: *Wealth is not a guarantee of happiness.*   1–3, 10 n., 4–9 v., **guar·an·teed, guar·an·tee·ing.**

**guar·an·tor** (gar′ən tôr′ or ger′ən tôr′)   one who makes or gives a guarantee.   n.

**guar·an·ty** (gar′ən tē or ger′ən tē)   **1** the act or fact of giving security.   **2** a pledge or promise given as security; security.   **3** GUARANTEE (def. 4).   1, 2 n., pl. **guar·an·ties;**   3 v., **guar·an·tied, guar·an·ty·ing.**

**guard** (gärd)   **1** keep safe; watch over carefully; take care of: *The dog guards the house.*   **2** defend; protect: *The goalie guards the goal.*   **3** keep from escaping: *The soldiers guarded the prisoners day and night.*   **4** keep in check; hold back; keep under control: *Guard your tongue.*   **5** a person or group that guards: *A soldier or group of soldiers guarding a person or place is a guard.*   **6** take precautions against.   **7** anything that gives protection; a contrivance or appliance to protect against injury, loss, etc.: *A guard was placed in front of the fire.*   **8** a careful watch: *A soldier kept guard over the prisoners.*   **9** a picked body of soldiers: *a guard of honour.*   **10** defence; protection.   **11** in boxing, fencing, or cricket, a position of defence.   **12** arms or weapons held in a position of defence.   **13** in rugby football, a player on either side of the centre.   **14** in basketball, either of the two players serving as defencemen.   **15** *Brit.* a person in charge of a railway train; brakeman.   **16** in former times, the man in charge of a stagecoach.   **17 the Guards, a** certain British regiments whose duties include guarding the Sovereign.   **b** certain Canadian regiments: *the Governor General's Horse Guards.*   1–4, 6 v., 5, 7–17 n.   —**guard′er,** n.
**guard against,**   avoid or prevent by being careful: *Paula's mother told her to guard against getting her feet wet.*
**off guard,**   unready; unprepared: *The pitcher was off guard when the ball was hit to him.*
**on guard,**   ready to defend or protect; watchful: *A dog stood on guard near the door.*
**stand guard,**   do sentry duty: *The soldier stood guard at the gate of the fort.*
☞ *Etym.* See note at WARD.

**guard·ed** (gär′did)   **1** kept safe; carefully watched over; protected.   **2** careful; cautious: *"Maybe" is a guarded answer to a question.*   **3** pt. and pp. of GUARD.   1, 2 adj., 3 v.   —**guard′ed·ness,** n.

**guard·ed·ly** (gär′did lē)   in a GUARDED (def. 2) manner.   adv.

**guard·house** (gärd′hous′)   **1** a building used as a jail for soldiers.   **2** a building used by soldiers on guard.   n.

**guard·i·an** (gär′dē ən or gär′dyən)   **1** a person who takes care of another or of some special thing.   **2** a person appointed by law to take care of the affairs of

someone who is young or cannot take care of them himself or herself.  **3** protecting: *a guardian angel.*  *1, 2 n., 3 adj.*
☞ *Etym.* See note at WARD

**guard·i·an·ship** (gär′dē ən ship′ *or* gär′dyən ship′) the position or care of a GUARDIAN.  *n.*

**guard·rail** (gär′drāl′) a rail or railing for protection.  *n.*

**guard·room** (gär′drüm′)  **1** a room used by soldiers on guard.  **2** a room used as a jail for soldiers.  *n.*

**guards·man** (gärd′zmən)  **1** a guard.  **2** a private in any one of several infantry regiments called Guards.  **3** any man serving in such a regiment.  *n., pl.* **guards·men** (-zmən).

**gua·va** (gwä′və)  **1** a tropical American tree or shrub having a yellowish, pear-shaped fruit.  **2** the fruit, used for jelly, jam, etc.  *n.*

**gu·ber·na·to·ri·al** (gyü′bər nə tô′rē əl *or* gü′bər nə tô′rē əl) of, or having to do with a GOVERNOR (defs. 1–3).  *adj.*

**gudg·eon** (guj′ən)  **1** a small European freshwater fish that is easy to catch and is often used for bait.  **2** minnow.  **3** a person easily fooled or cheated.  *n.*

**guer·ril·la** (gə ril′ə)  **1** a member of a small independent band of fighters who harass the enemy by sudden raids, ambushes, etc.  **2** warfare carried on by such fighters.  **3** of or by guerrillas.  *1, 2 n., 3 adj.*
☞ *Hom.* GORILLA.

**guess** (ges)  **1** form an opinion of without really knowing: *to guess the height of a tree.*  **2** an opinion formed without really knowing: *My guess is that it will rain tomorrow.*  **3** get right or find out by guessing: *to guess a riddle.*  **4** think; believe; suppose: *I guess she is really sick after all.*  *1, 3, 4 v., 2 n.*  —**guess′er,** *n.*

**guess·tim·ate** (ges′tə mət) *Informal.*  **1** an estimate based on guesswork.  **2** make a guesstimate of.  *1 n., 2 v.,* **guess·tim·at·ed, guess·tim·at·ing.**

**guess·work** (ges′wėrk′) work, action, or results based on guessing; guessing: *There is a lot of guesswork involved in buying a used car.*  *n.*

**guest** (gest)  **1** a person who is received and entertained at another's home, club, etc.  **2** a person who is not a regular member; visitor.  **3** a person staying at a hotel, motel, boarding house, etc.  **4** on television or radio, be or appear as a guest: *She guested on the new talk show last night.*  *1–3 n., 4 v.*

**guff** (guf) *Informal.* foolish talk, especially when used in an attempt to hide the real facts.  *n.*

**guf·faw** (gu fo′)  **1** a loud, coarse burst of laughter.  **2** laugh loudly and coarsely.  *1 n., 2 v.*

**guid·ance** (gī′dəns)  **1** a guiding; leadership; direction: *Under her mother's guidance, Nan learned how to cook.*  **2** something that guides.  **3** in education, studies and counselling intended to help students understand their school environment, make the most of their opportunities, and plan for the future.  *n.*

**guide** (gīd)  **1** show the way; lead; conduct; direct: *The Indian guided the hunters.*  **2** manage; control; regulate.

**3** a person or thing that shows the way, leads, conducts, or directs: *Tourists and hunters sometimes hire guides.*  **4** a part of a machine for directing or regulating motion or action.  **5** guidebook.  **6 Guide,** GIRL GUIDE.  *1, 2 v.,* **guid·ed, guid·ing;** *3–6 n.* —**guid′er,** *n.*
—**guide′less,** *adj.*

**guide·board** (gīd′bôrd′) a board or sign with directions for travellers, often attached to a guidepost.  *n.*

**guide·book** (gīd′bůk′) a book of directions and information, especially one for travellers, tourists, etc.  *n.*

**guided missile** a projectile that can be guided accurately, often for great distances and usually by means of transmitted electronic impulses.

**guide·line** (gīd′līn′) a principle or instruction set forth as a guide.  *n.*

**guide·post** (gīd′pōst′) A post with signs and directions on it for travellers: *A guidepost where roads meet tells travellers what places each road goes to and how far it is to each place.*  *n.*

**Guid·er** (gī′dər) an adult who is associated in some way with the GIRL GUIDES or BROWNIES.  *n.*

**guide word** in dictionaries and similar reference works, either of two words appearing at the top of a page: *The guide word at the left is the same as the first entry word on the page; the one at the right is the same as the last entry word on the page.*

**gui·don** (gī′dən *or* gī′don)  **1** a small flag or streamer carried as a guide by soldiers, or used for signalling.  **2** a soldier who carries the guidon.  *n.*

**guild** (gild)  **1** a society for mutual aid or for some common purpose: *the Canadian Guild of Potters.*  **2** in the Middle Ages, a union of the men in one trade, formed to keep standards high and to protect their common interests: *the guild of silversmiths.*  *n.* Also, **gild.**
☞ *Hom.* GILD.

**guild·hall** (gild′hol′)  **1** the hall in which a guild meets.  **2** a town hall; city hall.  *n.*

**guilds·man** (gild′zmən) a member of a guild.  *n., pl.* **guilds·men** (-zmən).

**guile** (gīl) crafty deceit; craftiness; sly tricks: *A swindler uses guile; a robber uses force.*  *n.*

**guile·ful** (gīl′fəl) crafty and deceitful; sly and tricky.  *adj.*  —**guile′ful·ly,** *adv.*  —**guile′ful·ness,** *n.*

**guile·less** (gīl′lis) without guile; honest; frank; sincere.  *adj.*  —**guile′less·ly,** *adv.*  —**guile′less·ness,** *n.*

**guil·le·mot** (gil′ə mot′) any of several narrow-billed arctic diving birds of the same family as the auk.  *n.*

**guil·lo·tine** (gil′ə tēn′ *for noun,* gil′ə tēn′ *for verb*)  **1** a machine for beheading persons by means of a heavy blade that slides down between two grooved posts: *The guillotine was much used during the French Revolution.*  **2** behead with this machine.  **3** a machine for cutting paper.  **4** cut with this machine.  *1, 3 n., 2, 4 v.,* **guil·lo·tined, guil·lo·tin·ing.**  —**guil′lo·tin′er,** *n.*
☞ *Etym.* From F *guillotine,* named after Joseph-Ignace *Guillotin,* a French doctor and member of the Revolutionary Assembly, who advocated using the machine as a quick and merciful means of execution. 18c.

**guilt** (gilt)   1 the fact or state of having done wrong; being guilty; being to blame: *The evidence proved Ray's guilt.*   2 guilty action or conduct; crime; offence; wrongdoing.   *n.*
☛ *Hom.* GILT.

**guilt·less** (gil′tlis)   not guilty; free from guilt; innocent.   *adj.*

**guilt·y** (gil′tē)   1 having done wrong; deserving to be blamed and punished: *The jury pronounced the prisoner guilty of murder.*   2 knowing or showing that one has done wrong: *The one who did the crime had a guilty conscience and a guilty look.*   *adj.*, **guilt·i·er, guilt·i·est.** —**guilt′i·ly,** *adv.*  —**guilt′i·ness,** *n.*

**guimpe** (gimp *or* gamp)   a blouse worn under a jumper and showing at the neck or at the neck and arms.   *n.*

**guin·ea** (gin′ē)   1 an amount equal to 21 shillings, formerly used in the British Isles in stating prices, fees, etc.   2 a former British gold coin worth 21 shillings. 3 GUINEA FOWL.   *n.*
☛ *Etym.* A **guinea** was first (17c.) a coin made of gold from *Guinea,* a part of the west coast of Africa originally named *Guiné* by the Portuguese. A GUINEA FOWL came from the same area, but the term **guinea** was applied also to things or animals from other distant countries, as in GUINEA PIG, which actually came from South America.

A guinea fowl—about 60 cm long including the tail

**guinea fowl**   a domestic fowl resembling a pheasant, having dark-grey feathers with small, white spots.
☛ *Etym.* See note at GUINEA.

**guinea hen**   1 GUINEA FOWL.   2 a female GUINEA FOWL.

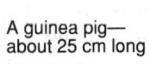

A guinea pig—about 25 cm long

**guinea pig**   1 a short-eared, short-tailed rodent kept as a pet and for experiments: *A guinea pig is like a big, fat, harmless rat.*   2 any person or thing serving as a subject for experiment or testing: *The school used our class as guinea pigs to test the new timetable.*
☛ *Etym.* See note at GUINEA.

**Guin·e·vere** (gwin′ə vēr′)   in the legends about King Arthur, Arthur's wife, who became the mistress of Lancelot.   *n.*

**guise** (gīz)   1 a style of dress; garb: *The soldier went in the guise of a monk so that he would not be recognized.* 2 external appearance; aspect; semblance: *Her theory is nothing but an old idea in a new guise.*   3 an assumed appearance, pretence: *Under the guise of friendship he plotted treachery.*   *n.*

hat, āge, fär; let, ēqual, tėrm; it, īce
hot, ōpen, ôrder; oil, out; cup, put, rüle
 ǝbove, takǝn, pencǝl, lemǝn, circǝs
ch, child; ng, long; sh, ship
th, thin; ᴛʜ, then; zh, measure

Guitars: a Spanish guitar and an electric guitar

**gui·tar** (gǝ tär′)   1 a musical instrument which, as a rule, has six strings played with the fingers or with a pick. 2 an electric guitar.   *n.*
☛ *Etym.* **Guitar** came into English in the 17c. from Spanish *guitarra,* while ZITHER came in the 19c. from German. Both the Spanish and German words can be traced back to Gk. *kitharā,* the name of a stringed instrument similar to a lyre.

**gulch** (gulch)   a deep, narrow ravine with steep sides, especially one marking the course of a stream or torrent.   *n.*

**gulf** (gulf)   1 a large bay; an arm of an ocean or sea extending into the land: *The Gulf of St. Lawrence lies at the mouth of the St. Lawrence River, on the east coast of Canada.*   2 a very deep break or cut in the earth.   3 any wide separation: *The quarrel left a gulf between the old friends.*   4 something that swallows up; whirlpool.   *n.* —**gulf′like′,** *adj.*

**Gulf Stream**   a current of warm water in the Atlantic Ocean, flowing north from the Gulf of Mexico along the United States coast to Newfoundland and then northeast toward the British Isles.

**gulf·weed** (gul′fwēd′)   an olive-brown seaweed having many berry-like sacs that keep it afloat.   *n.*

Herring gulls—about 60 cm long including the tail

**gull**¹ (gul)   a graceful grey-and-white bird having long wings, webbed feet, and a thick, strong beak, living on or near large bodies of water.   *n.*

**gull**² (gul)   1 deceive; cheat.   2 a person who is easily deceived or cheated.   1 *v.,* 2 *n.*

**gul·let** (gul′it)   1 a passage for food from the mouth to the stomach; esophagus.   2 throat.   *n.*

**gul·li·bil·i·ty** (gul′ǝ bil′ǝ tē)   being GULLIBLE; tendency to be easily deceived or cheated.   *n.*

**gul·li·ble** (gul′ǝ bǝl)   easily deceived or cheated: *The*

**gul·ly** (gul′ē) **1** a narrow gorge; small ravine. **2** a ditch made by heavy rains or running water: *After the storm, the newly seeded lawn was covered with gullies.* **3** make gullies in. *1, 2 n., pl.* **gul·lies;** *3 v.,* **gul·lied, gul·ly·ing.**

...gullible woman believed everything the glib salesman said. *adj.* —**gul′li·bly,** *adv.*

**gulp** (gulp) **1** swallow eagerly or greedily. **2** the act of swallowing. **3** the amount swallowed at one time; mouthful. **4** keep in; choke back; repress: *The disappointed boy gulped down a sob.* **5** gasp; choke. *1, 4, 5 v., 2, 3 n.*

**gum¹** (gum) **1** a sticky juice, obtained from or given off by certain trees and plants, that hardens in the air and dissolves in water: *Gum is used to make glue, drugs, candy, etc.* **2** any similar secretion, such as resin, gum resin, etc. **3** a preparation of such a substance for use in industry or the arts. **4** CHEWING GUM. **5** the substance on the back of a stamp, the flap of an envelope, etc.; mucilage; glue. **6** rubber. **7** a gum tree; eucalyptus. **8** smear, stick, stick together, or stiffen with gum: *The stamp was gummed onto the letter.* **9** give off gum; form gum. **10** make or become sticky; clog with something sticky: *Jeanne's pocket was all gummed with candy.* *1–7 n., 8–10 v.,* **gummed, gum·ming.**

**gum²** (gum) Often, **gums,** *pl.* the flesh around the teeth. *n.*

**gum ammoniac** a natural mixture of gum and resin used in medicine.

**gum arabic** the gum obtained from acacia trees, used in making candy, medicine, mucilage, etc.

**gum·bo** (gum′bō) **1** the OKRA plant. **2** its sticky pods. **3** soup thickened with OKRA pods: *chicken-gumbo soup.* **4** soil that contains much silt and becomes very sticky when wet, especially that found on the western prairies: *It took her an hour to clean the gumbo off her boots.* *n., pl.* **gum·bos.**
☞ *Etym.* From Louisiana French *gombo*, ultimately from a Bantu word *kingombo*, a name for the okra plant, which is native to Africa. 19c.

**gum·boil** (gum′boil′) a small abscess on the gums. *n.*

**gum·drop** (gum′drop′) a stiff, jelly-like piece of candy made of gum arabic, gelatin, etc., sweetened and flavoured. *n.*

**gum·my** (gum′ē) **1** sticky like gum. **2** covered with gum. **3** giving off gum. *adj.,* **gum·mi·er, gum·mi·est.** —**gum′mi·ness,** *n.*

**gump·tion** (gump′shən) *Informal.* **1** initiative; energy. **2** common sense; good judgment. *n.*

**gum resin** a natural mixture of gum and resin, obtained from certain plants.

**gum·shoe** (gum′shü) a rubber overshoe. *n.*

**gum tree** a tree that yields gum: *The sweet gum, sour gum, and eucalyptus are gum trees.*

**gum·wood** (gum′wùd) the wood of a GUM TREE. *n.*

**gun** (gun) **1** a weapon with a long, metal tube for shooting bullets, shot, etc.: *An artillery piece or a cannon is properly a gun; rifles, pistols, and revolvers are commonly called guns.* **2** anything resembling a gun in use or shape: *a spray gun.* **3** the shooting of a gun as a signal or salute. **4** shoot with a gun; hunt with a gun. *1–3 n., 4 v.,* **gunned, gun·ning.**
**spike someone's guns,** make a person powerless; defeat him or her.
**stick to one's guns,** keep one's position; refuse to retreat or yield.

**gun·boat** (gun′bōt′) a small warship, often one that can be used in shallow water. *n.*

**gun carriage** a structure on which a gun is mounted or moved and on which it is fired.

**gun·cot·ton** (gun′kot′ən) an explosive made by treating cotton with nitric and sulphuric acids. *n.*

**gun·fire** (gun′fīr′) **1** the shooting of a gun or guns. **2** the sound of shooting. *n.*

**gun·lock** (gun′lok′) the part of a gun by which the charge is fired. *n.*

**gun·man** (gun′mən) a person who uses a gun to threaten, rob, kill, etc. *n., pl.* **gun·men** (-mən).

**gun metal 1** a dark-grey alloy used for chains, buckles, handles, etc. **2** a dark grey. **3** a kind of bronze formerly used for making guns. *n.*

**gun·nel** (gun′əl) See GUNWALE. *n.*

**gun·ner** (gun′ər) **1** a man trained to fire artillery pieces; soldier who handles and fires big guns. **2** a naval officer in charge of a ship's guns. **3** a person, especially a private serving in the artillery. **4** in the air force, a man who fires the guns of an aircraft. **5** a person who hunts with a shotgun, rifle, etc. *n.*

**gun·ner·y** (gun′ə rē) **1** the art and science of constructing and managing big guns. **2** the use of guns; shooting of guns. **3** guns collectively. *n.*

**gun·ning** (gun′ing) **1** the act of shooting with a gun; hunting with a gun. **2** ppr. of GUN. *1 n., 2 v.*

**gun·ny** (gun′ē) **1** a strong, coarse fabric used for sacks, bags, etc. **2** a sack, bag, etc. made of this fabric. *n., pl.* **gun·nies.**

**gun·pow·der** (gun′pou′dər) a powder that explodes with force when brought into contact with fire: *Gunpowder is used in guns, fireworks, and blasting. One kind of gunpowder is made of saltpetre, sulphur, and charcoal.* *n.*

**gun·shot** (gun′shot′) **1** a shot fired from a gun. **2** the shooting of a gun: *We heard gunshots.* **3** the distance that a gun will shoot: *within gunshot.* *n.*

**gun·smith** (gun′smith′) a person whose work is making or repairing small guns. *n.*

**gun·stock** (gun′stok′) the wooden support or handle to which the barrel of a gun is fastened. *n.*

**gun·wale** (gun′əl) the upper edge of a ship's or boat's side. See ROWBOAT for picture. *n.* Also, **gunnel.**

**gup·py** (gup′ē) a very small, brightly coloured fish of tropical fresh water: *The female guppy bears live young instead of producing eggs.* *n., pl.* **gup·pies.**

**gur·dwa·ra** (gėr dwä′rə) a Sikh temple in which services of worship are held on Sundays. It also serves as a Sikh community centre. *n.*

**gur·gle** (gėr′gəl) **1** flow or run with a bubbling sound: *Water gurgles when it is poured out of a bottle or flows over stones.* **2** a bubbling sound. **3** make a bubbling sound: *The baby gurgled happily.* **4** express with a gurgle. *1, 3, 4 v.,* **gur·gled, gur·gling;** *2 n.*

**gu·ru** (gü′rü) **1** in Hinduism, a revered religious

teacher, often accompanied by a group of devoted students. **2** an honorary title for any popular leader: *The young activist was hailed as a guru of pop culture.* *n.*

**Gu·ru** (gü′rü) in Sikhism: **1** any of the ten founding teachers of Sikhism. **2** the honorific title given to the Granth, the Sikh holy book. *n.*

**Gu·ru Granth Sa·hib** in Sikhism: **1** the sacred scriptures containing the teachings of the ten founding Gurus. **2** the one visible holy object of the Sikh religion.

**gush** (gush) **1** rush out suddenly; pour out. **2** a rush of water or other liquid from an enclosed place: *If you get a deep cut, there usually is a gush of blood.* **3** talk in a silly way about one's affections or enthusiasms. **4** *Informal.* silly, emotional talk. **5** a sudden and violent outbreak; burst: *a gush of anger.* **6** give forth suddenly or very freely. 1, 3, 6 *v.*, 2, 4, 5 *n.*

**gush·er** (gush′ər) **1** an oil well that gives oil in large quantities without pumping. **2** a gushy person. *n.*

**gush·ing** (gush′ing) **1** that gushes. **2** effusive. **3** ppr. of GUSH. 1, 2 *adj.*, 3 *v.*

**gush·y** (gush′ē) showing silly feeling; effusive; sentimental. *adj.*, **gush·i·er, gush·i·est.** —**gush′i·ness,** *n.*

**gus·set** (gus′it) **1** a triangular piece of material inserted in a dress, the upper part of a shoe, etc. to give greater strength or more freedom of movement. **2** a bracket or plate used to reinforce the joints of a structure. *n.*

**gust** (gust) **1** a sudden, violent rush of wind: *A gust upset the small sailboat.* **2** a sudden burst of rain, smoke, sound, etc. **3** an outburst of anger, enthusiasm, etc.: *Gusts of laughter greeted the clown.* *n.*

**gus·ta·to·ry** (gus′tə tô′rē) of the sense of taste; having to do with tasting. *adj.*

**gus·to** (gus′tō) **1** keen relish; hearty enjoyment: *The hungry girl ate her dinner with gusto.* **2** a liking or taste. *n., pl.* **gus·tos.**

**gust·y** (gus′tē) **1** coming in gusts; windy; stormy. **2** marked by outbursts: *gusty laughter.* *adj.*, **gust·i·er, gust·i·est.** —**gust′i·ly,** *adv.* —**gust′i·ness,** *n.*

**gut** (gut) **1** intestine. **2** a tough string made from the dried and twisted intestines of sheep or other animals; catgut: *Gut is used for violin strings and for the strings in tennis rackets.* **3** remove the entrails of; disembowel. **4** plunder or destroy the inside of: *Fire gutted the building and left only the brick walls standing.* **5** a narrow channel or gully. **6 guts,** *pl.* **a** entrails; bowels. **b** pluck; courage; endurance. 1, 2, 5, 6 *n.*, 3, 4 *v.*, **gut·ted, gut·ting.**

**gut·ta-per·cha** (gut′ə pėr′chə) a substance resembling rubber, obtained from the thick, milky juice of certain tropical trees, used in dentistry, in insulating electrical wires, etc. *n.*

**gut·ter** (gut′ər) **1** a channel or ditch along the side of a street or road to carry off water; low part of a street beside the sidewalk. **2** a channel or trough along the lower edge of a roof to carry off rain water; eavestrough. **3** any channel or groove. **4** form gutters in. **5** flow or melt in streams: *A candle gutters when the melted wax runs down its sides.* **6** become channelled. **7** a low, poor, or wretched place: *a child of the gutter.* 1–3, 7 *n.*, 4–6 *v.*

**gut·ter·snipe** (gut′ər snīp′) *Informal.* **1** an urchin who lives in the streets. **2** any ill-bred person. *n.*

**gut·tur·al** (gut′ə rəl) **1** of the throat. **2** formed in the throat; harsh: *The woman spoke in a guttural voice.* *adj.* —**gut′tur·al·ly,** *adv.*

**guy**[1] (gī) **1** a rope, chain, wire, etc. attached to something to steady or secure it. **2** steady or secure with a guy or guys: *The mast was guyed by four ropes.* 1 *n.*, 2 *v.*, **guyed, guy·ing.**
☛ *Etym.* Probably through French or Dutch from an old Low German word meaning a small rope for trussing up sails. 14c.

**guy**[2] (gī) **1** *Informal.* any person, young or old. **2** a queer-looking person. **3** *Informal.* make fun of; tease. 1, 2 *n.*, 3 *v.*, **guyed, guy·ing.**
☛ *Etym.* From the name of Guy Fawkes, who was hanged for his part in an unsuccessful plot to blow up the British king (James I) and parliament in 1605. A custom developed of burning a dummy 'guy' at celebrations on November 5 each year. **Guy** came to refer to any strange-looking person, and later became an informal term meaning simply 'person'.

**guy rope** one of several ropes attached to a tent, marquee, etc. for pegging it to the ground as a means of support.

**guz·zle** (guz′əl) drink greedily; drink too much. *v.*, **guz·zled, guz·zling.** —**guz′zler,** *n.*

**gym** (jim) GYMNASIUM. *n.*

**gym·na·si·a** (jim nā′zē ə) a pl. of GYMNASIUM. *n.*

**gym·na·si·um** (jim nā′zē əm) a room, building, etc. fitted up for physical exercise or training and for indoor athletic sports. *n., pl.* **gym·na·si·ums** or **gym·na·si·a.**

**gym·nast** (jim′nast) an expert in GYMNASTICS. *n.*

**gym·nas·tic** (jim nas′tik) of or having to do with bodily exercise or activities. *adj.* —**gym·nas′ti·cal·ly,** *adv.*

**gym·nas·tics** (jim nas′tiks) physical exercises for developing the muscles, such as are performed in a gymnasium. *n. pl.*

**gym·no·sperm** (jim′nə spėrm′) any of a large group of plants having the seeds exposed: *The pine, fir, and spruce, which bears seeds on the surface of cone scales instead of in pods, are gymnosperms.* *n.*

**gyp** (jip) *Informal.* **1** cheat; swindle: *She gypped me out of three dollars.* **2** a swindle; fraud: *That show was a big gyp; it wasn't anything like the ad.* **3** a cheat; swindler. 1 *v.*, **gypped, gyp·ping;** 2, 3 *n.* —**gyp′per,** *n.*

**gyp·soph·i·la** (jip sof′ə lə) a plant having many small, fragrant, white or pink flowers on delicate, branching stalks with few leaves. *n.*

**gyp·sum** (jip′səm) a mineral used for making plaster of Paris, fertilizer, etc.; hydrated calcium sulphate: *Alabaster is one form of gypsum.* *n.*

**gypsum board** PLASTERBOARD.

**Gyp·sy** (jip′sē) **1** Also, **gypsy, a** a wandering person having dark skin and black hair, who probably came from northern India originally. **b** a member of this group. **2** the language of these people. **3 gypsy,** a person who looks or lives like a Gypsy. **4 gypsy,** of,

having to do with, or like a Gypsy or Gypsies. 1–3 *n.*, *pl.* **Gyp·sies**, 4 *adj.*
☛ *Etym.* Formed in the 16c. from *Egyptian* because, when the gypsies first came to Britain, they were thought to have come from Egypt.

**gypsy moth** a brownish or white moth whose larvae eat the leaves of trees. Also, **gipsy moth.**

**gy·rate** (jī′rāt) move in a circle or spiral; whirl; rotate: *A top gyrates.* *v.*, **gy·rat·ed, gy·rat·ing.** —**gy·ra′tor,** *n.*

**gy·ra·tion** (jī rā′shən) a circular or spiral motion; whirling; rotation. *n.*

**gy·ra·to·ry** (jī′rə tô′rē) gyrating. *adj.*

**gyr·fal·con** (jėr′fol′kən) the largest species of falcon, found mainly in arctic and subarctic regions, varying in colour from almost pure white with black streaks and speckles to dark greyish-brown. *n.*

**gy·ro·com·pass** (jī′rō kum′pəs) a compass using a motor-driven GYROSCOPE instead of a magnetic needle to point to the north: *The gyrocompass points to the geographic north instead of to the magnetic pole.* *n.*

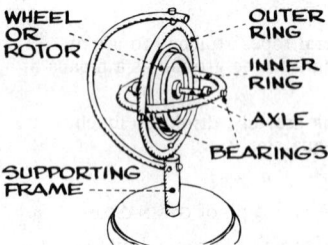
A gyroscope. Once it is set spinning rapidly, it will continue to rotate in the same plane regardless of magnetic forces and no matter which way the supporting frame is turned.

**gy·ro·scope** (jī′rə skōp′) a heavy wheel or disk mounted so that its axis can turn freely in one or more directions. *n.*

**gy·ro·scop·ic** (jī′rə skop′ik) having to do with a GYROSCOPE. *adj.*

**gy·ro·sta·bil·iz·er** (jī′rō stā′bə lī′zər) a device for stabilizing a sea-going vessel by counteracting its rolling motion. *n.*

**gyve** (jīv) fetter; shackle. *n.*, *v.*, **gyved, gyv·ing.**

# H h  *H h*

hat, āge, fär; let, ēqual, tėrm; it, īce
hot, ōpen, ôrder; oil, out; cup, pu̇t, rüle
ə above, takən, pencəl, lemən, circəs
ch, child; ng, long; sh, ship
th, thin; ᴛʜ, then; zh, measure

**h or H**   1 the eighth letter of the English alphabet. 2 any speech sound represented by this letter.   3 any person or thing classed as the eighth in a series. 4 something shaped like the letter H.   *n.*, *pl.* **h's** or **H's**.

**h**   1 hour.   2 hecto- (an SI prefix).

**h.**   1 harbour.   2 hard.   3 high.   4 height.   5 in baseball, hit or hits.

**H**   hydrogen.

**ha¹** (hō, hä, *or* ha)   1 an exclamation of surprise, joy, triumph, etc.: "Ha! I've caught you!" cried the giant to Jack. 2 in writing, a way of indicating laughter: "Ha! ha! ha!" laughed the girls.   *interj.*

**ha²**   hectare.

**Ha**   hahnium.

**ha·be·as cor·pus** (hā′bē əs kôr′pəs)   a writ or order requiring that a prisoner be brought before a judge or into a court to decide whether he or she is being held lawfully: *The right of habeas corpus is a protection against unjust imprisonment.*

**hab·er·dash·er** (hab′ər dash′ər)   1 a dealer in men's furnishings, such as hats, ties, shirts, socks, etc.   2 a dealer in small articles, such as buttons, needles, trimmings, etc.   *n.*

**hab·er·dash·er·y** (hab′ər dash′ə rē)   1 the articles sold by a HABERDASHER.   2 the shop of a HABERDASHER. *n.*, *pl.* **hab·er·dash·er·ies**.

**ha·bil·i·ment** (hə bil′ə mənt)   1 articles of clothing. 2 dress; attire.   *n.*

**hab·it** (hab′it)   1 a tendency to act in a certain way or to do a certain thing; usual way of acting: *Everyone should form the habit of brushing the teeth after every meal.*   2 the distinctive dress or costume worn by members of a religious order: *Monks and nuns wear habits.*   3 a woman's riding dress.   4 put a habit on; dress.   5 the characteristic form, mode of growth, etc. of an animal or plant: *The woodbine is of a twining habit.*   1–3, 5 *n.*, 4 *v.*
☞ *Syn.* **Habit** and CUSTOM both refer to an established practice. **Habit** refers more to a personal practice, something one does without thinking about it: *Biting one's fingernails is a bad habit.* **Custom** refers especially to a practice adopted by a group of people or an individual and continued over a long period of time: *It was a custom in her family to play euchre every Friday evening.*

**hab·it·a·ble** (hab′ə tə bəl)   fit to live in.   *adj.*

**hab·it·ant** (hab′ə tənt *for 1*, hab′ə tont′ *for 2 and 3*; *French*, ä bē tän′)   1 inhabitant.   2 *Cdn.*   a French-Canadian farmer.   3 *Cdn.*   having to do with French Canadians or French Canada, especially with regard to country life.   1, 2 *n.*, 3 *adj.*

**hab·i·tat** (hab′ə tat′)   1 the place where an animal or plant naturally lives or grows: *The jungle is the habitat of tigers.*   2 a place of living; dwelling place.   *n.*

**hab·i·ta·tion** (hab′ə tā′shən)   1 a place to live in; home; dwelling.   2 inhabiting: *Is this house fit for habitation?*   *n.*

**ha·bit·u·al** (hə bich′ü əl)   1 done by habit; caused by habit: *a habitual smile, habitual courtesy.*   2 being or doing something by habit: *A habitual reader reads a great deal.*   3 often done, seen, or used; usual; customary: *Ice and snow are habitual sights in arctic regions.*   *adj.* —**ha·bit′u·al·ly**, *adv.*

**ha·bit·u·ate** (hə bich′ü āt′)   make used (*to*); accustom (*to*): *Loggers are habituated to hard work.*   *v.*, **ha·bit·u·at·ed, ha·bit·u·at·ing**. —**ha·bit′u·a′tion**, *n.*

**hab·i·tude** (hab′ə tyüd′ *or* hab′ə tüd′)   1 a characteristic condition of body or mind.   2 CUSTOM (def. 1).   *n.*

**ha·bit·u·é** (hə bich′ü ā′ *or* hə bich′ü ā′)   a person who has the habit of going to any place frequently: *a habitué of the theatre.*   *n.*

**ha·ci·en·da** (hä′sē en′də; *American Spanish* ä syen′dä) a large ranch; landed estate; country house.   *n.*

**hack¹** (hak)   1 cut roughly or unevenly; deal cutting blows: *She hacked the box apart with a dull axe.*   2 a rough cut.   3 a tool or instrument for hacking or cutting, such as an axe, pick, hoe, etc.   4 a notch cut in the ice at one end of a curling rink, used as a foothold when a player throws his or her rock.   5 give short, dry coughs. 6 a short, dry cough.   1, 5 *v.*, 2–4, 6 *n.* —**hack′er**, *n.*

**hack²** (hak)   1 a carriage for hire: *Hacks were waiting at the railway station.*   2 *Informal.*   taxi.   3 an old or worn-out horse.   4 a horse for ordinary riding: *They rented hacks at the riding stable.*   5 ride on horseback over roads.   6 *Informal.*   drive a taxi.   7 a person hired to do routine literary work; drudge.   8 working or done merely for money; hired; drudging: *a hack writer.* 9 a plodding, faithful, but undistinguished worker in an organization such as a political party: *an old party hack.* 1–4, 7, 9 *n.*, 5, 6 *v.*, 8 *adj.*

**hack·ber·ry** (hak′ber′ē)   1 a tree related to the elm, that has small, cherry-like fruit.   2 the fruit.   *n.*, *pl.* **hack·ber·ries**.

**hack·er** (hak′ər)   a person skilled in the use of computers, especially one who uses this skill to gain access illegally to government or business data.   *n.*

**hack·le¹** (hak′əl)   1 a comb used in dressing flax, hemp, etc.   2 comb flax, hemp, etc. with a hackle.   3 one of the long, slender feathers on the neck of certain birds. 4 the neck plumage of certain birds.   5 a wingless artificial fly used by fishermen.   1, 3–5 *n.*, 2 *v.*, **hack·led, hack·ling**.
**raise the hackles**, *Informal.*   arouse suspicion or anger.

**hack·le²** (hak′əl)   cut roughly; hack; mangle.   *v.*, **hack·led, hack·ling**.

**hack·man** (hak′mən)   the driver of a hack or carriage for hire.   *n.*, *pl.* **hack·men** (-mən).

**hack·ma·tack** (hak′mə tak′)   any of several evergreen trees, including the larch and the juniper.   *n.*

**hack·ney** (hak′nē)   1 a horse for ordinary riding.   2 a carriage for hire.   3 hired; let out, employed, or done for hire: *a hackney coach.*   1, 2 *n.*, *pl.* **hack·neys;**   3 *adj.*

**hack·neyed** (hak′nēd) used too often; commonplace: *"White as snow" is a hackneyed comparison.* *adj.*

A hacksaw

**hack·saw** (hak′sò′) a saw for cutting metal, consisting of a narrow, fine-toothed blade fixed in a frame. *n.*

**had** (had; *unstressed* həd *or* əd) pt. and pp. of HAVE: *She had a party. A fine time was had by all who came.* *v.*

**had·dock** (had′ək) a food fish of the northern Atlantic Ocean, resembling a cod but smaller. *n., pl.* **had·dock** or **had·docks**.

**Ha·des** (hā′dēz) 1 in Greek mythology, the home of the dead, below the earth. 2 **hades**, *Informal.* hell. *n.*

**had·ith** (ha dēth′) in Islam, a compilation of the teachings, sayings, and actions of the prophet Mohammed, collected by his followers. *n.*

**had·n't** (had′ənt) had not.

**hae·mo·glo·bin** (hē′mə glō′bən *or* hem′ə glō′bən) See HEMOGLOBIN. *n.*

**hae·mo·phil·i·a** (hē′mə fil′ē ə *or* hem′ə fil′ē ə) See HEMOPHILIA. *n.*

**hae·mo·phil·i·ac** See HEMOPHILIAC. *n.*

**haem·or·rhage** (hem′ə rij) See HEMORRHAGE. *n.*

**haem·or·rhoid** (hem′ə roid′) See HEMORRHOID. *n.*

**ha·fiz** (hä′fiz) a title of respect for one who can recite the entire Koran from memory. *n.*

**haf·ni·um** (haf′nē əm) a rare metallic element resembling zirconium. *Symbol*: Hf *n.*

**haft** (haft) 1 the handle of a knife, sword, dagger, etc. 2 furnish with a handle or hilt; set in a haft. 1 *n.*, 2 *v.*

**hag** (hag) 1 a very ugly old woman, especially one who is vicious or malicious. 2 WITCH¹. *n.*

**hag·fish** (hag′fish′) a small saltwater fish shaped like an eel: *Hagfish attach themselves to other fish by their round mouths and bore into them with their horny teeth.* *n., pl.* **hag·fish** or **hag·fish·es**.

**Hag·ga·dah** or **Hag·ga·da** (hə gä′də) 1 a story or legend in the Talmud that explains or illustrates the Jewish law. 2 the section of the Talmud containing such stories and legends. 3 the religious rites for the first two nights of the Jewish Passover. *n., pl.* **Hag·ga·doth** (-dōth′).

**hag·gard** (hag′ərd) wild-looking from pain, fatigue, worry, hunger, etc.; gaunt; careworn. *adj.*
—**hag′gard·ly**, *adv.* —**hag′gard·ness**, *n.*

**hag·gis** (hag′is) *Scottish.* the heart, lungs, and liver of a sheep mixed with suet and oatmeal and boiled in the stomach of the animal. *n.*

**hag·gle** (hag′əl) 1 dispute about a price or the terms of a bargain; wrangle. 2 mangle in cutting; hack. *v.*, **hag·gled, hag·gling.** —**hag′gler**, *n.*

**hag·rid·den** (hag′rid′ən) worried or tormented, as if by witches; harassed. *adj.*

**hah** (hä) HA¹. *interj.*

**hahn·i·um** (hä′nē əm) an artificially produced radio-active element. *Symbol*: Ha *n.*

**Hai·da** (hī′də) 1 a member of a First Nations people of western British Columbia. 2 the language of these people. 3 of or having to do with the Haida or their language. 1, 2 *n., pl.* **Hai·da** *or* **Hai·das;** 3 *adj.*

**hai·den** (hī den′) the small outer shrine of a Shinto temple which worshippers may enter for their devotions. *n.*

**hai·ku** (hī′kü) a Japanese verse form consisting of three lines of five, seven, and five syllables respectively. *n.*

**hail¹** (hāl) 1 greet; cheer; shout in welcome to: *The crowd hailed the winner.* 2 a greeting; cheer; shout of welcome. 3 greet as; call: *They hailed him leader.* 4 call loudly to; shout to: *The captain hailed the passing ship.* 5 a loud call; shout: *The ship sailed on, paying no attention to our hails.* 1, 3, 4 *v.*, 2, 5 *n.* —**hail′er**, *n.*
**hail fellow well met,** very friendly.
**hail from,** come from: *Both these ships hail from Montreal.*
**within hail,** near enough to hear a call or shout.
☞ *Hom.* HALE.

**hail²** (hāl) 1 small, roundish pieces of ice coming down from the clouds in a shower; frozen rain: *Hail fell with such violence that it broke windows.* 2 come down in hail: *Sometimes it hails during a summer thunderstorm.* 3 a shower resembling hail: *A hail of bullets met the soldiers.* 4 pour down in a shower like hail: *The angry mob hailed blows on the thief.* 1, 3 *n.*, 2, 4 *v.*
☞ *Hom.* HALE.

**hail·stone** (hāl′stōn′) a small, roundish piece of ice coming down from the clouds. *n.*

**hail·storm** (hāl′stôrm′) a storm with hail. *n.*

**hair** (her) 1 a fine, threadlike outgrowth from the skin of human beings and animals. See EPIDERMIS for picture. 2 a mass of such growths. 3 a fine threadlike growth from the outer layer of plants. 4 made of or with hair. 5 a very small space or thing; least degree. 1–3, 5 *n.*, 4 *adj.* —**hair′like**′, *adj.*
**get in one's hair,** annoy; be a nuisance to.
**not turn a hair,** not show any sign of being disturbed or embarrassed.
**split hairs,** make too fine distinctions.
☞ *Hom.* HARE.

**hair·breadth** (her′bredth′) 1 very narrow; extremely close: *a hairbreadth escape.* 2 a very narrow space; a very small distance. 1 *adj.*, 2 *n.*

**hair·brush** (her′brush′) a brush for taking care of the hair. *n.*

**hair·cloth** (her′klòth′) a cloth made of horsehair or camel's hair, used to cover furniture, stiffen garments, etc.: *The hermit wore haircloth shirts as a penance.* *n.*

**hair·cut** (her′kut′) 1 the act or manner of cutting the hair of the head. 2 the trimming of head hair: *He needs a haircut.* 3 a style of haircut. *n.*

**hair·do** (her′dü′) the way in which the hair, especially of a woman, is arranged. *n., pl.* **hair·dos**.

**hair·dress·er** (her′dres′ər)   a person who takes care of or cuts people's hair.  *n.*

**haired** (herd)   having hair, especially of a specified kind (*used in compounds*): *dark-haired, curly-haired.*  *adj.*

**hair·less** (her′lis)   without hair.  *adj.*

**hair·line** (her′līn′)   **1** a very thin line.   **2** the irregular outline where hair growth ends on the head or forehead.  *n.*

**hair·pin** (her′pin′)   **1** a pin, usually a U-shaped piece of wire, shell, etc., used by women to keep the hair in place.   **2** shaped like a hairpin; U-shaped: *a hairpin bend.*  **1** *n.,* **2** *adj.*

**hair–rais·ing** (her′rā′zing) *Informal.*   making the hair seem to stand on end; terrifying: *hair-raising stories.*  *adj.*

**hair's–breadth** or **hairs·breadth** (herz′bredth′) HAIRBREADTH.  *adj., n.*

**hair shirt**   a rough shirt or girdle made of horsehair, worn as a penance.

**hair·split·ting** (her′split′ing)   making too fine distinctions.  *n., adj.*

**hair·spring** (her′spring′)   a fine, hairlike spring that regulates the motion of the balance wheel in a watch or clock.  *n.*

**hair·style** (her′stīl′)   a way of arranging or wearing the hair: *Her new hairstyle is very attractive. Men's hairstyles have changed a lot in the last 30 years.*  *n.*

**hair·styl·ist** (her′stī′list)   a person whose work is choosing and arranging individual hairstyles.  *n.*

**hair trigger**   a trigger that operates by very slight pressure.

**hair·y** (her′ē)   **1** covered with hair; having much hair: *hairy hands, a hairy ape.*   **2** of or like hair: *hairy cloth, a hairy texture.*  *adj.,* **hair·i·er, hair·i·est.**
—**hair′i·ness,** *n.*

**Hai·tian** (hā′tē ən *or* hā′shən)   **1** of or having to do with Haiti, a republic in the West Indies, or its people.  **2** a native or inhabitant of Haiti.   **3** the native language of Haiti, a dialect of French.   **1** *adj.,* **2, 3** *n.*

**haj** (haj)   in Islam, a pilgrimage to the sacred shrine at Mecca, to be undertaken at least once in the lifetime of all devout Moslems.  *n.*

**ha·ji** (haj′ē)   one who has performed the HAJ.  *n., pl.* **ha·jis.**

**hake** (hāk)   a sea fish related to the cod but slenderer and inferior as food.  *n., pl.* **hake** or **hakes.**

**ha·kim**[1] (hə kēm′)   among Moslems:   **1** a wise or learned man.   **2** doctor.  *n.*

**ha·kim**[2] (hä′kim)   a Moslem ruler, judge, or governor.  *n.*

**hal·berd** (hal′bərd)   a weapon that is both a spear and a battle-axe, used in warfare in the 15th and 16th centuries.  *n.*

**hal·berd·ier** (hal′bər dēr′)   formerly, a soldier armed with a halberd: *There were many Swiss halberdiers in the 15th century.*  *n.*

**hal·bert** (hal′bərt)   HALBERD.  *n.*

**hal·cy·on** (hal′sē ən)   calm; peaceful; happy.  *adj.*

**hale**[1] (hāl)   strong and well; healthy.  *adj.,* **hal·er, hal·est.**
☛ **Hom.** HAIL.

# hairdresser   539   half-mast

hat, āge, fär; let, ēqual, tėrm; it, īce
hot, ōpen, ôrder, oil, out; cup, pùt, rüle
əbove, takən, pencəl, lemən, circəs
ch, child; ng, long; sh, ship
th, thin; ᴛн, then; zh, measure

**hale**[2] (hāl)   **1** drag by force.   **2** compel to go: *The woman was haled into court.*  *v.,* **haled, hal·ing.**
☛ **Hom.** HAIL.

**half** (haf)   **1** one of two equal parts: *A half of 4 is 2.*   **2** forming a half; being or making half of.   **3** to half of the full amount or degree: *a glass half full of milk.*   **4** one of two equal periods in certain games.   **5** one of two nearly equal parts: *Which is the bigger half?*   **6** not complete; being only part of: *A half truth is often no better than a lie.*   **7** partly: *half cooked. She spoke half aloud.*  **8** almost: *half dead from hunger.*   **1, 4, 5** *n., pl.* **halves; 2, 6** *adj.,* **3, 7, 8** *adv.*
**by half,**   by far.
**not half,**   **a** to a very slight extent.   **b** *Informal.*   not at all; the reverse of: *not half bad.*

**half–and–half** (haf′ənd haf′)   **1** half one thing and half another.   **2** not clearly one thing or the other.   **3** in two equal parts.   **4** a mixture of milk and cream.   **1, 2** *adj.,* **3** *adv.,* **4** *n.*

**half–back** (haf′bak′)   in football, soccer, etc., a player whose position is behind the forward line.  *n.*

**half–baked** (haf′bākt′)   **1** not cooked enough.   **2** *Informal.*   not fully worked out; incomplete.   **3** *Informal.*   not experienced; showing poor judgment.  *adj.*

**half–blood** (haf′blud′)   a person related to another person through one parent only.  *n.*

**half blood**   the relationship between persons who are related through one parent only.

**half–blood·ed** (haf′blud′id)   related through one parent only.  *adj.*

**half boot**   a boot reaching about halfway to the knee.

**half brother**   a brother related through one parent only.

**half–caste** (haf′kast′)   a person whose parents belong to different races, especially an offspring of a European father and an Asiatic mother.  *n.*

**half dollar**   a coin of Canada and the United States, worth 50 cents.

**half–heart·ed** (haf′här′tid)   lacking interest or enthusiasm; not earnest: *a half-hearted attempt.*  *adj.*
—**half′–heart′ed·ly,** *adv.*   —**half′–heart′ed·ness,** *n.*

**half hitch**   a knot formed by passing the end of a rope under and over its standing part and then inside the loop. See KNOT for picture.

**half–hour** (haf′our′ *for noun;* haf′our′ *for adjective*)   **1** thirty minutes.   **2** the halfway point in an hour.   **3** of or lasting one half-hour.   **1, 2** *n.,* **3** *adj.*
—**half′–hour′ly,** *adv.*

**half–life** (haf′līf′)   the time needed for a radio-active substance to lose half its radio-activity.  *n.*

**half–mast** (haf′mast′)   a position halfway or part way down from the top of a mast, staff, etc.: *When the Governor General died, flags were lowered to half-mast as a mark of respect.*  *n.*

**half moon** 1 the moon when only half of its surface appears bright. See MOON for picture. 2 something shaped like a half moon or crescent.

**half nelson** in wrestling, a hold applied by hooking one arm under an opponent's armpit and putting a hand on the back of his or her neck.

**half note** in music, a note held half as long as a whole note. See NOTE for picture.

**half rest** in music, a rest lasting as long as a half note. See REST¹ for picture.

**half-section** (haf′sek′shən) *Cdn.* an area of land covering 130 hectares. *n.*

**half sister** a sister related through one parent only.

**half step** the difference in pitch between two adjacent keys on a piano; half tone.

An English half-timbered house of Tudor times

**half-tim·bered** (haf′tim′bərd) built with a timber frame with the spaces filled by plaster, stone, or brick. *adj.*

**half-time** (haf′tīm′) 1 the interval between two halves of a game. 2 having to do with this period: *the half-time score.* *n.*

**half-tone** (haf′tōn′) 1 a process in photo-engraving for making pictures for books and magazines. 2 a picture made by this process. 3 in paintings, a tone between the high light and the deep shades. *n.*

**half tone** in music, an interval equal to half a tone on the scale; a half step.

**half-track** or **half·track** (haf′trak′) an army motor vehicle that has wheels in front and short tracks in the rear for driving, used to carry personnel and weapons. *n.*

**half-volley** (haf′vol′ē) in tennis, the striking of the ball on its first bounce after hitting the court. *n.*

**half·way** (haf′wā′) 1 half the way; half the required distance: *The rope reached only halfway to the boat.* 2 midway: *The inn served as a halfway house between the two towns.* 3 not going far enough; incomplete; inadequate: *Halfway measures are never satisfactory.* 4 not completely; partially: *The concert is halfway finished.* 1, 4 *adv.,* 2, 3 *adj.*
**go** or **meet halfway,** do one's share toward reaching an agreement or toward patching up a quarrel.

**half-wit** (haf′wit′) 1 a feeble-minded person. 2 a stupid, foolish person: *Only a half-wit would try to ski on that icy slope.* *n.*

**half-wit·ted** (haf′wit′id) 1 feeble-minded. 2 very stupid; foolish. *adj.*

**hal·i·but** (hal′ə bət) a large flatfish much used for food, sometimes weighing several hundred kilos. *n., pl.* **hal·i·but** or **hal·i·buts.**

**hal·ide** (hal′īd *or* hā′līd) any compound of a HALOGEN with another element or radical: *Sodium chloride is a halide.* *n.*

**Hal·i·go·ni·an** (hal′i gō′nē ən) 1 a native or inhabitant of Halifax. 2 of or having to do with Halifax. 1 *n.,* 2 *adj.*

**hal·i·to·sis** (hal′ə tō′sis) bad or offensive breath. *n.*

**hall** (hol) 1 a way to go through a building; passageway: *A hall ran the length of the upper floor of the house.* 2 a passageway or room at the entrance of a building: *Leave your umbrella in the hall.* 3 a large room for holding meetings, parties, banquets, etc.: *No hall in town was large enough for the graduation dance.* 4 a building for public business: *The mayor's office is in the town hall.* 5 a building of a school, college, or university. 6 the residence of an English landowner. *n.*
☞ *Hom.* HAUL.

**Halley's comet** (hal′ēz) the comet that Halley predicted could be seen about every 75 years, last seen in 1986.
☞ *Etym.* Named after Edmund *Halley* (1656–1742), an English astronomer.

**hal·liard** (hal′yərd) See HALYARD.

**hall·mark** (hol′märk′) 1 an official mark indicating standard of purity, put on gold and silver articles. 2 a mark or sign of genuineness or good quality: *Courtesy and self-control are hallmarks of a gentleman.* 3 put a hallmark on. 1, 2 *n.,* 3 *v.*

**hal·loo** (hə lü′) 1 a shout to make hounds run faster. 2 a call or shout to attract attention. 3 shout; call. 1, 2 *interj.,* 1–3 *n., pl.* **hal·loos;** 3 *v.,* **hal·looed, hal·loo·ing.**

**hal·low¹** (hal′ō) 1 make holy; make sacred. 2 honour as holy or sacred. *v.*
☞ *Etym.* **Hallow** and HOLY both come from OE *hālig* 'holy'. The verb **hallow** had the OE form *hālgian.* There was also a noun *hallow* meaning 'saint'. So All Saints' Day was *All Hallows* (later *Allhallows*) and the previous day was *All Hallow Eve* or *Even,* which was shortened to *Hallowe'en* and, without the apostrophe, HALLOWEEN.

**hal·low²** (hə lō′) HALLOO. *interj., n., v.*

**hal·lowed** (hal′ōd; *in worship, often* hal′ō id) 1 made holy; sacred; consecrated: *A churchyard is hallowed ground.* 2 honoured or observed as holy. 3 pt. and pp. of HALLOW. 1, 2 *adj.,* 3 *v.*
☞ *Etym.* See note at HALLOW¹.

**Hal·low·een** or **Hal·low·e'en** (hal′ō ēn′, hal′ə wēn′, *or* hol′ə wēn′) the evening of October 31: *Halloween is the eve of Allhallows or All Saints' Day.* *n.*
☞ *Etym.* See note at HALLOW¹.

**hal·lu·ci·na·tion** (hə lü′sə nā′shən) 1 seeing or hearing things that have no basis outside a person's brain: *A person alone in a perfectly quiet room suffers from hallucination if he or she sees people there or hears voices.* 2 a thing seen or heard when there is no external cause for it. *n.*

**hal·lu·cin·o·gen** (ha lü′sə nə jən) a drug or substance that produces HALLUCINATIONS. *n.*

**hal·lu·cin·o·gen·ic** (hə lü′sə nə jen′ik) of, producing, or tending to produce, HALLUCINATIONS. *adj.*

**hall·way** (hol′wā) **1** a way to go through a building; passageway; corridor. **2** a passageway or room at the entrance of a building. *n.*

**ha·lo** (hā′lō) **1** a series of coloured rings appearing around the sun or moon when it is seen through a cloud of ice crystals suspended in the atmosphere: *The colours of the halo range from a red inner ring to a blue outer ring.* Compare with CORONA (def. 1). **2** a ring or circle of light shown around the head of a saint or divine being in a painting to symbolize saintliness; nimbus. **3** a kind of splendour, glory, or glamour that surrounds an idealized person or thing: *A halo of romance surrounds King Arthur and his knights.* **4** surround with a halo. 1–3 *n., pl.* **ha·los** or **ha·loes**; 4 *v.*, **ha·loed, ha·lo·ing.**

**hal·o·gen** (hal′ə jən) any of the five chemical elements, iodine, bromine, chlorine, fluorine, and astatine, that combine directly with metals to form salts: *The halogens are the most active elements.* *n.*

**halt**[1] (holt) **1** stop for a time; stop: *The soldiers halted and rested from their march.* **2** cause to stop for a time: *The police officer halted the traffic.* **3** a stop for a time; stopping. **4** a command to stop or come to a halt. 1, 2 *v.*, 3 *n.*, 4 *interj.*
**call a halt,** order a stop.

**halt**[2] (holt) **1** be in doubt; hesitate; waver: *Shyness made her halt as she talked.* **2** be faulty or imperfect: *A poor argument halts.* **3 the halt,** persons who halt, limp, or hesitate. 1, 2 *v.*, 3 *n.* —**halt′ing·ly,** *adv.*

**hal·ter** (hol′tər) **1** a rope, strap, etc. for leading or tying an animal. **2** put a halter on; tie with a halter. **3** a rope for hanging a person; noose. **4** death by hanging. **5** a backless and sleeveless blouse that usually fastens behind the neck and across the back. 1, 3–5 *n.*, 2 *v.*

**halve** (hav) **1** divide into two equal parts; share equally: *The two girls agreed to halve expenses on their trip.* **2** reduce to half: *The new machine halves the time of doing the work by hand.* *v.*, **halved, halv·ing.**
☞ *Hom.* HAVE.

**halves** (havz) *pl.* of HALF. *n.*
**by halves,** **a** not completely; partly. **b** in a half-hearted way.
**go halves,** share equally.

**hal·yard** (hal′yərd) a rope or tackle used on a ship to raise or lower a sail, yard, flag, etc. *n.* Also, **halliard.**

**ham** (ham) **1** salted and smoked meat from the upper part of a pig's hind leg. **2** the upper part of an animal's hind leg, used for food. See PORK for picture. **3** the back of the thigh; thigh and buttock. **4** the part of the leg behind the knee. **5** *Informal.* any person who overacts or exaggerates his or her part in a play or show: *a ham actor.* **6** *Informal.* insincere, exaggerated acting. **7** *Informal.* act in such a way; overact. **8** *Informal.* an amateur radio operator. 1–6, 8 *n.*, 7 *v.*, **hammed, ham·ming.**

**ham·burg** (ham′bėrg) HAMBURGER. *n.*

**ham·burg·er** (ham′bėr′gər) **1** ground beef. **2** this meat shaped into flat cakes and fried or broiled, especially when served in a split bun or roll. *n.*

**hame** (hām) either of two curved pieces on either side of the collar in a horse's harness: *The traces are fastened to the hames.* See HARNESS for picture. *n.*

**ham·let** (ham′lit) a small group of houses together with a few businesses and services such as stores and a post office, situated in the country and having no fixed boundaries: *A hamlet is usually smaller than a village and has no local government of its own.* *n.*

A hammer

**ham·mer** (ham′ər) **1** a tool with a metal head and a handle, used to drive nails and beat metal into shape. **2** something shaped or used like a hammer: *The hammer of a gun explodes the charge.* **3** drive, hit, or work with a hammer: *to hammer nails.* **4** beat into shape with a hammer: *The metal was all hammered into ornaments.* **5** fasten by using a hammer. **6** hit again and again: *The angry man hammered at the door with his fist.* **7** force by many efforts: *She hammered the formulas into her head until she had memorized them.* **8** MALLEUS. See EAR[1] for picture. 1, 2, 8 *n.*, 3–7 *v.* —**ham′mer·er,** *n.* —**ham′mer·like′,** *adj.*
**hammer and tongs,** with all one's force and strength: *The two boys fought hammer and tongs.*
**hammer at,** work hard at; keep working hard at: *She hammered at her homework until it was finished.*
**hammer away,** **a** work hard at; keep working at: *She hammered away at her homework. He hammered away till the job was done.* **b** keep nagging; badger: *He hammered away at his father till he got what he wanted.*
**hammer out,** **a** beat into shape with a hammer. **b** flatten or spread with a hammer. **c** remove with a hammer. **d** work out with much effort. **e** make clear by much thinking or talking: *The girls finally hammered out the plans for their clubhouse.*

**hammer and sickle** the symbol of a sickle and hammer crossed, used on the flag of the former Soviet Union since 1923. The two elements represent the farmer and the labourer.

**ham·mer·head** (ham′ər hed′) a fierce shark whose wide head resembles a double-headed hammer. *n.*

**ham·mer·less** (ham′ər lis) having no hammer or no visible hammer: *A hammerless pistol has its hammer covered.* *adj.*

**hammer lock** in wrestling, a hold in which an opponent's arm is twisted and held behind his or her back.

**ham·mock** (ham′ək) a swinging bed or couch made of canvas, netted cord, etc. that is suspended at both ends. *n.*

**ham·per**[1] (ham′pər) hold back; hinder: *The heavy bundle hampered Joe.* *v.*

**ham·per**[2] (ham′pər) a large container, often a wicker basket, usually having a cover: *a picnic hamper, a clothes hamper.* *n.*

**ham·ster** (ham′stər) a small, short-tailed rodent having large cheek pouches, often kept as a pet. *n.*

**ham·string** (ham′string′) **1** in human beings, one of the tendons at the back of the knee. **2** in four-footed animals, the great tendon at the back of the hock. **3** cripple by cutting the hamstring. **4** cripple; disable; destroy the activity, efficiency, etc. of. *1, 2 n., 3, 4 v.*
**ham·strung** or *(rare)* **ham·stringed, ham·string·ing.**

**ham·strung** (ham′strung′) a pt. and a pp. of HAMSTRING (def. 4): *Our building plans have been hamstrung by the bad weather. v.*

**hand** (hand) **1** the end part of an arm; part that a person grasps and holds things with. **2** the end of any limb that grasps, holds, or clings: *We call a monkey's feet hands.* **3** something resembling a hand in shape, appearance, or use: *The hands of a clock or watch show the time.* **4** a hired worker who uses his or her hands: *a factory hand, a farm hand.* **5** give with the hand; pass; pass along: *Please hand me the butter.* **6** help with the hand: *The hotel doorman handed the lady into her car.* **7** a part or share in doing something: *She had no hand in the matter.* **8** side: *At her left hand stood two men.* **9** source: *She heard his story at first hand.* **10** one's style of handwriting: *She writes in a clear hand.* **11** a person's signature. **12** skill; ability: *The artist's work showed a master's hand.* **13** a person, with reference to action, skill, or ability: *She is a great hand at thinking up new games.* **14** a round of applause or clapping: *The crowd gave the winner a big hand.* **15** a promise of marriage. **16** a measure used in giving the height of horses, etc.; the breadth of a hand, about 10 centimetres: *This horse is 18 hands high.* **17** the cards held by a player in one round of a card game. **18** one round of a card game. **19** a player in a card game. **20** of, for, by, or in the hand. *1–4, 7–19 n., 5, 6 v., 20 adj.* **—hand′like′,** *adj.*
**all hands, a** all sailors of a ship's crew. **b** *Informal.* all members of a group.
**at hand, a** within reach; near; close. **b** ready.
**at second hand,** from a source other than the original source: *The story she had heard at second hand proved to be an exaggeration.*
**bear** or **give a hand,** help.
**by hand,** by using the hands, not machinery.
**change hands,** pass from one person to another: *During the sale, a lot of money changed hands.*
**eat out of one's hand,** follow one's ideas, leadership, etc.; submit to one's authority.
**force one's hand, a** make a person do something. **b** make a person show what he or she is going to do.
**from hand to mouth,** without being able to put something aside for the future: *During the long strike, many families lived from hand to mouth.*
**hand and glove,** intimate; in close relations.
**hand down, a** pass along: *Her old clothes were handed down to her younger sister.* **b** deliver: *The judge will hand down her decision tomorrow.*
**hand in,** give or pass to a person in authority: *The tests were handed in to the teacher.*
**hand in glove,** intimate; in close relations.
**hand in hand, a** holding hands. **b** together.
**hand it to,** *Informal.* express admiration of: *I have to hand it to you for completing the job on time.*
**hand on, a** pass along: *He read the note and handed it on to the person next to him.* **b** pass to a later generation: *It is our task to hand on our knowledge to our children.*
**hand out,** give out; distribute: *The storekeeper handed out free suckers.*
**hand over, a** give to another; deliver: *When Jake asked for his book, I handed it over.* **b** pass control of: *The colonel handed over command of the unit to the major.*
**hand to hand,** close together; at close quarters: *to fight hand to hand.*
**have one's hands full,** be very busy; be able to do no more; have as much to do as one can manage.
**in hand, a** under control. **b** in possession. **c** going along; being done.
**in one's hands, a** in one's possession or control: *The property is no longer in my hands.* **b** in one's care or charge: *George left his bicycle in Helga's hands.*
**join hands, a** become partners. **b** marry.
**keep one's hand in,** keep up one's skill; keep in practice.
**lay hands on, a** seize; take; get. **b** arrest. **c** attack; harm. **d** bless by touching with the hands.
**lend a hand,** help or assist: *He asked his brother to lend a hand with the chores.*
**off one's hands,** out of one's care or charge: *The babysitter was glad when the sick child was taken off his hands.*
**on hand, a** within reach; near; close. **b** ready; in stock: *The supermarket has lots of oranges on hand.* **c** present: *I will be on hand again tomorrow.*
**on one's hands,** in one's care or charge.
**on the other hand,** considering the other side of the question or argument; from the opposite point of view: *I want the bicycle very much; on the other hand, I can't afford to buy it.*
**out of hand, a** out of control: *The angry crowd soon got out of hand.* **b** at once; without hesitation: *The girl was expelled out of hand.* **c** finished; done with.
**out of one's hands,** off one's hands: *When Luigi got sick, the job was taken out of his hands.*
**take in hand, a** bring under control. **b** consider; deal with: *The principal promised to take the matter in hand.* **c** attempt.
**tie one's hands,** make one unable to do something.
**to hand, a** within reach; near; close. **b** in one's possession.
**try one's hand,** try to do; test one's ability: *After trying her hand at politics, she soon went back into business.*
**turn one's hand to,** work at.
**wash one's hands of,** have no more to do with; refuse to be responsible for.

**hand·bag** (han′bag′ or hand′bag′) **1** a woman's small bag for money, keys, cosmetics, etc.; purse. **2** a small travelling bag to hold clothes, etc. *n.*

**hand·ball** (han′bol′ or hand′bol′) **1** a game played by hitting a small ball against a wall with the hand. **2** the ball used in this game. *n.*

**hand·bell** (han′bel′ or hand′bel′) a bell with a handle, to be rung by hand, used especially as one of a set for a musical performance. *n.*

**hand·bill** (han′bil′ or hand′bil′) a printed announcement, advertisement, etc. to be handed out to people. *n.*

**hand·book** (han′bùk′ or hand′bùk′) **1** a small book of directions or reference, especially in some field of study; manual: *a handbook of engineering.* **2** a guidebook for tourists. *n.*

**hand·breadth** (han′bredth′ or hand′bredth′) the breadth of a hand, used as a measure. It varies from about 6 to 10 cm. *n.*

**hand·cart** (han′kärt′, hang′kärt′, or hand′kärt′) a small cart pulled or pushed by hand. *n.*

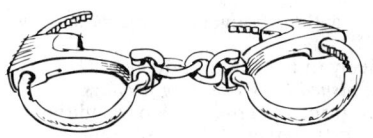
A pair of handcuffs

**hand·cuff** (han′kuf′, hang′kuf′, or hand′kuf′) **1** a device to keep a person from using the hands, usually consisting of a pair of metal clasps joined by a short chain and fastened around the wrists. **2** put handcuffs on; fasten by handcuffs: *He was handcuffed to the post.* **1** *n.*, **2** *v.*

**hand·ful** (han′fůl or hand′fůl) **1** as much or as many as the hand can hold: *a handful of candy.* **2** a small number or quantity: *A handful of men could defend this pass against hundreds.* **3** *Informal.* a person or thing that is hard to handle or control: *That girl is quite a handful.* *n., pl.* **hand·fuls.**

**hand·grip** (han′grip′ or hand′grip′) **1** a grip or grasping of the hand, used in greeting. **2** a handle. *n.* **come to handgrips,** get into a hand-to-hand fight.

**hand·gun** (han′gun′, hang′gun′, or hand′gun′) a firearm that is held and fired with one hand: *A revolver is a handgun.* *n.*

**hand–held** (hand′held′) of an appliance, machine, etc., designed to be operated while being held in the hand: *a hand-held electric mixer.* *adj.*

**hand·i·cap** (han′di kap′ or han′dē kap′) **1** something that puts a person at a disadvantage; hindrance; mental or physical defect: *A sore throat is a handicap to a singer.* **2** put at a disadvantage as by a mental or physical defect; hinder: *The pitcher was handicapped by a lame arm.* **3** a contest in which rules are applied to ensure that nobody has an unfair advantage or is at an unfair disadvantage. **4** the disadvantage or advantage given in such a contest or game: *If a runner has a handicap of 5 metres in a 100-metre dash, it means that she has to run either 95 metres or 105 metres.* **5** give a handicap to: *The Sports Committee handicapped me 5 metres.* 1, 3, 4 *n.*, 2, 5 *v.*, **hand·i·capped, hand·i·cap·ping.** —**hand′i·cap′per,** *n.*

**hand·i·capped** (han′di kapt′) having a handicap. —*v.* pt. and pp. of HANDICAP.

**hand·i·craft** (han′di kraft′ or han′dē kraft′) **1** skilful use of the hands: *The design on the leather purse showed fine handicraft.* **2** a trade or art requiring skill with the hands: *Basket weaving is a handicraft.* **3** an article made by hand, especially one requiring skill or imagination to make: *The display of handicrafts included wooden ware, pottery, and children's clothes.* *n.*

**hand·i·work** (han′di werk′ or han′dē werk′) **1** work done with the hands. **2** work that a person has done. **3** result of a person's action. *n.*

**hand·ker·chief** (hang′kər chif′ or hang′kər chēf′) **1** a piece of fine cotton, linen, silk, etc., usually square, used for wiping the nose, face, eyes, etc. **2** a piece of cloth worn over the head or around the neck; kerchief. *n.*

**han·dle** (han′dəl) **1** a part of a thing made to be held or grasped by the hand: *Spoons, pitchers, hammers, and pails have handles.* See PAIL for picture. **2** touch, feel, hold, or move with the hands; use the hands on: *Handle that book carefully.* **3** manage; direct; control: *The captain handles his soldiers well.* **4** behave or perform in a certain way when driven, managed, directed, etc.: *This car handles easily.* **5** deal with; treat: *The boy handled his kitten roughly.* **6** deal in; trade in: *That store handles groceries.* **7** a chance; opportunity; occasion: *Don't let your conduct give any handle for gossip.* 1, 7 *n.*, 2–6 *v.*, **han·dled, han·dling.**
**handle to one's name,** *Informal.* a title.

**han·dle·bars** (han′dəl bärz′) the bars, usually curved, in front of the rider, by which a bicycle, etc. is guided. *n.*

**han·dler** (han′dlər) **1** a person or thing that handles. **2** a person who helps to train a boxer, or who acts as his second during a boxing match. **3** a person who shows dogs or cats or other animals in a contest. *n.*

**hand·made** (han′mād′ or hand′mād′) made by hand, not by machinery; not machine-made. *adj.*
☞ *Hom.* HANDMAID.

**hand·maid** (han′mād′ or hand′mād′) **1** a female servant. **2** a female attendant. *n.*
☞ *Hom.* HANDMADE.

**hand·maid·en** (han′mā′dən or hand′mā′dən) HANDMAID. *n.*

**hand organ** a large music box that is made to play tunes by turning a crank.

**hand·out** (han′dout′) *Informal.* **1** a portion of food handed out: *The tramp was given a handout.* **2** a news story or piece of publicity issued to the press by a business organization, government agency, etc. *n.*

**hand–picked** (han′pikt′) **1** picked by hand. **2** carefully selected. *adj.*

**hand·rail** (han′drāl′) a railing used as a guard or support on a stairway, platform, etc. *n.*

**hand·saw** (han′so′ or hand′so′) a saw used with one hand. *n.*

**hand·shake** (han′shāk′ or hand′shāk′) a clasping and shaking of hands by two people as a sign of friendship when meeting or parting, or to seal a bargain. *n.*

**hand·some** (han′səm) **1** good-looking; pleasing in appearance: *We usually say that a man is handsome, but that a woman is pretty or beautiful.* **2** fairly large; considerable: *Ten thousand dollars is a handsome sum of money.* **3** generous: *a handsome gift.* *adj.*, **hand·som·er, hand·som·est.** —**hand′some·ly,** *adv.* —**hand′some·ness,** *n.*
☞ *Hom.* HANSOM.

**hands–on** (han′zon′) making use of personal, especially physical, involvement: *A hands-on learning process is better than theory.* *adj.*

**hand·spike** (han′spīk′ or hand′spīk′) a bar used as a lever, especially on a ship. *n.*

**hand·spring** (han′spring′ or hand′spring′) a somersault made from a standing position, in which the person comes down first on the hands, turning the body forward or backward in a full circle and landing again on the feet. *n.*

**hand·stand** (han′stand′ or hand′stand′) an act or feat of supporting the body on the hands alone, while the trunk and legs are stretched in the air. *n.*

**hand-to-hand** (han′tə hand′ *or* hand′tə hand′)   close together; at close quarters: *a hand-to-hand fight.* *adj.*

**hand-to-mouth** (han′tə mouth′ *or* hand′tə mouth′)   having nothing to spare; being unable to save or provide for the future.   *adj.*

**hand-tooled** (han′tüld′)   ornamented by handwork, not by machinery.   *adj.*

**hand·work** (han′dwėrk′)   work done by hand, not by machinery.   *n.*

**hand·wov·en** (han′dwō′vən)   **1** woven on a loom operated by hand.   **2** of basketwork, etc., woven by hand.   *adj.*

**hand·writ·ing** (han′drī′ting)   **1** writing done by hand; writing done with pen, pencil, etc.   **2** manner or style of writing: *He recognized his mother's handwriting on the envelope.* *n.*

**hand·y** (han′dē)   **1** easy to reach or use; saving work; useful; convenient: *handy shelves, a handy tool.*   **2** skilful with the hands: *Rose is handy with tools.*   **3** easy to handle or manage.   *adj.*, **hand·i·er, hand·i·est.**   —**hand′i·ly,** *adv.*   —**hand′i·ness,** *n.*

**han·dy·man** (han′di man′ *or* han′dē man′)   a person who does odd jobs.   *n., pl.* **han·dy·men** (-men′).

**hang** (hang)   **1** fasten or be fastened to something above: *Hang your cap on the hook. The swing hangs from a tree.*   **2** fasten or be fastened so as to swing or turn freely: *to hang a door on its hinges.*   **3** put or be put to death by hanging with a rope around the neck: *He was hanged several weeks after being sentenced to death.*   **4** die by hanging.   **5** cover or decorate with things that hang: *to hang a window with curtains. The walls were hung with pictures.*   **6** bend down; droop: *Enver hung his head in shame.*   **7** fasten in position.   **8** attach paper, etc. to walls.   **9** depend.   **10** hold fast; cling.   **11** be doubtful or undecided; hesitate; waver.   **12** keep a jury from making a decision or reaching a verdict: *One member can hang a jury by refusing to agree with the others.*   **13** the way that a thing hangs: *She didn't like the hang of her skirt.*   **14** loiter; linger.   **15** hover.   1–12, 14, 15 *v.*, **hung** or (*esp. for execution or suicide*) **hanged, hang·ing;** 13 *n.*
**get the hang of,** *Informal.*   get the knack of; discover how to operate, do, etc.: *She had never used a calculator before, but it didn't take her long to get the hang of it.*
**give** or **care a hang,** *Informal.*   care or be concerned about something (*usually used with a negative*): *He doesn't give a hang about anybody.*
**hang about** or **around,**   **a** loiter in a particular place, or in the company of a particular person, but with no definite purpose in mind.   **b** wait near: *There's a small crowd hanging about the door.*
**hang back,**   be unwilling to go forward; be backward.
**hang in,** *Informal.*   be persistent; not give up.
**hang in the balance,**   be undecided.
**hang it!**   an expression of annoyance.
**hang on,**   **a** hold tight.   **b** be unwilling to let go, stop, or leave: *The dying man hung on to life for several days.*   **c** depend on: *My decision hangs on your answer.*   **d** consider or listen to very carefully: *She hung on the teacher's every word.*   **e** wait on the telephone.
**hang one's head,**   be ashamed.
**hang onto,**   **a** try to keep control or possession of.   **b** depend for comfort or support on: *Hang onto this thought, it may help you.*
**hang out,** *Informal.*   gather; frequent: *Where do the boys hang out?*
**hang over,**   **a** be likely to happen to; threaten: *The possibility of being punished hung over him for days.*   **b** *Informal.*   remain from an earlier time or condition.
**hang together,**   **a** stick together.   **b** be coherent or consistent: *The story does not hang together.*
**hang up,**   **a** put on a hook, peg, etc.   **b** put a telephone receiver back in place.   **c** hold back; delay; detain.
☛ *Usage.*   In formal English, the preferred form of the past tense and past participle for def. 3 only is **hanged**: *The murderer was hanged.* In informal English, however, **hung** is often used: *He was hung for his crimes.*

**hang·ar** (hang′ər)   **1** a shed for aircraft.   **2** a shed.   *n.*
☛ *Hom.* HANGER.

**hang·bird** (hang′bėrd′)   any bird that builds a hanging nest, especially the Baltimore oriole.   *n.*

**hang·dog** (hang′dog′)   ashamed; sneaking.   *adj.*

**hang·er** (hang′ər)   **1** a person who hangs things: *A paperhanger puts on wallpaper.*   **2** a tool or machine that hangs things.   **3** anything on which something else is hung: *a coat hanger.*   **4** a loop, ring, etc. attached to something to hang it up by.   **5** a kind of short, light sword formerly worn by sailors on their belts.   *n.*
☛ *Hom.* HANGAR.

**hang·er-on** (hang′ə ron′)   **1** a follower; dependent.   **2** an undesirable follower.   **3** a person who often goes to a place.   *n., pl.* **hang·ers-on.**

**hang-glider** (hang′glī′dər)   a large, flat, usually delta-shaped kite with an attached harness or seat, designed to carry a person through the air for a short while. The flyer runs into the wind toward the edge of a cliff and soars down to earth, suspended from the kite.   *n.*

**hang-gliding** (hang′glī′ding)   the sport of gliding through the air while suspended from a HANG-GLIDER.   *n.*

**hang·ing** (hang′ing)   **1** death by hanging with a rope around the neck.   **2** deserving to be punished by hanging: *a hanging crime.*   **3** something that hangs from a wall, bed, etc.: *Curtains and draperies are hangings.*   **4** fastened to something above.   **5** leaning over or down.   **6** located on a height or steep slope.   **7** ppr. of HANG.   1, 3 *n.*, 2, 4–6 *adj.*, 7 *v.*

**hang·man** (hang′mən)   a man who hangs criminals who have been sentenced to death by hanging.   *n., pl.* **hang·men** (-mən).

**hang·nail** (hang′nāl′)   a bit of skin that hangs partly loose near a fingernail.   *n.*

**hang·o·ver** (hang′ō′vər) *Informal.*   **1** something that remains from an earlier time or condition.   **2** a sick state resulting from drinking too much liquor.   *n.*

**hank** (hangk)   **1** a coil or loop.   **2** a loop or coil of yarn, especially one containing a definite length.   *n.*

**han·ker** (hang′kər)   wish; crave.   *v.*

**han·ker·ing** (hang′kə ring)   **1** a longing; craving: *As soon as summer comes, I have a hankering for strawberries.*   **2** ppr. of HANKER.   1 *n.*, 2 *v.*

**hank·y** (hang′kē) *Informal.*   HANDKERCHIEF.   *n., pl.* **hank·ies.**

**hank·y-pank·y** (hang′kē pang′kē) *Informal.*   underhand or questionable dealing or behaviour; dishonest or illicit goings-on: *Hans denied that there was any hanky-panky involved in his getting the contract.* *n.*

**Han·sard** (han′sərd) the printed record of the proceedings of the Canadian or British House of Commons. *n.*

**Hansen's disease** an infectious disease which causes sores on the skin and injury to the nerves, and which may result in paralysis and deformity; leprosy.

An English hansom cab, widely used for public transport in the second half of the 19th century.

**han·som** (han′səm) a two-wheeled cab for two passengers, drawn by one horse. *n.*
☛ *Hom.* HANDSOME.

**Ha·nu·ka, Ha·nuk·kah,** or **Ha·nuk·ka** (hä′nu̇ kä′; Hebrew, Hä′nu̇ kä′) the Feast of Dedication or the Feast of Lights, an eight-day Jewish festival, falling in December. *n.* Also, **Chanukah.**

**hap·haz·ard** (hap′haz′ərd) 1 random, casual; not planned: *Haphazard answers are usually wrong.* 2 by chance; at random; casually: *She took a card haphazard from the deck.* 1 *adj.,* 2 *adv.* —**hap′haz′ard·ly,** *adv.*

**hap·less** (hap′lis) unlucky; unfortunate: *The hapless ship struck an iceberg on its maiden voyage.* *adj.*

**hap·loid** (hap′loid) in biology, 1 having the complete number of chromosomes that occur in a mature germ cell; for human beings, the number is 46. 2 such a cell. 1 *adj.,* 2 *n.* Compare with DIPLOID.

**hap·pen** (hap′ən) 1 take place; occur: *Nothing interesting happens here.* 2 be or take place by chance: *Accidents will happen.* 3 have the fortune to; chance to: *I happened to sit next to a famous hockey player.* 4 be done to; go wrong with: *Something has happened to this lock; the key won't turn.* *v.*
**as it happens,** by chance; as it turns out: *As it happens, I have no money with me.*
**happen on** or **upon,** a meet by chance. b find by chance: *She happened on a dime while looking for her ball.*
**happen to,** be the fate of; become of: *Nobody knew what happened to the last explorer.*

**hap·pen·ing** (hap′ə ning) 1 anything that happens; event; occurrence. 2 ppr. of HAPPEN. 1 *n.,* 2 *v.*

**hap·pen·stance** (hap′ən stans′) *Informal.* a situation or circumstance that is the result of chance: *The success of the deal was more happenstance than shrewd bargaining.* *n.*

**hap·pi·ly** (hap′ə lē) 1 in a happy manner; with pleasure, joy, and gladness: *She lives happily.* 2 luckily; fortunately: *Happily, he saved her from falling.* 3 aptly; appropriately. *adv.*

**hap·pi·ness** (hap′ē nis) 1 being happy; gladness. 2 good luck; good fortune. 3 aptness. *n.*

**hap·py** (hap′ē) 1 feeling or showing pleasure and joy; glad; pleased; contented: *a happy smile.* 2 lucky; fortunate: *By a happy chance, I found the lost money.* 3 clever and fitting; apt; successful and suitable: *a happy way of expressing an idea.* *adj.,* **hap·pi·er, hap·pi·est.**

**hap·py-go-luck·y** (hap′ē gō luk′ē) taking things easily; trusting to luck: *Those people are certainly happy-go-lucky.* *adj.*

hat, āge, fär; let, ēqual, tėrm; it, īce
hot, ōpen, ôrder; oil, out; cup, pu̇t, rüle
ə*bove,* tak*ə*n, penc*ə*l, lem*ə*n, circ*ə*s
ch, child; ng, long; sh, ship
th, thin; ŦH, then; zh, measure

**ha·rangue** (hə rang′) 1 a noisy speech. 2 a long, pompous speech. 3 address in a harangue. 4 deliver a harangue. 1, 2 *n.,* 3, 4 *v.,* **ha·rangued, ha·rangu·ing.**

**har·ass** (har′əs, her′əs, *or* hə ras′) 1 trouble by repeated attacks; harry: *Pirates harassed the villages along the coast.* 2 disturb; worry; torment: *After his long illness Arend was harassed by debt.* *v.*

**har·ass·ment** (har′ə smənt, her′ə smənt, *or* hə ras′mənt) 1 harassing. 2 being harassed; worry. 3 something that harasses. *n.*

**har·bin·ger** (här′bin jər) 1 one that goes ahead to announce another's coming; forerunner: *The robin is a harbinger of spring.* 2 announce beforehand; announce. 1 *n.,* 2 *v.*
☛ *Etym.* See note at HARBOUR.

**har·bor** (här′bər) See HARBOUR. *n., v.*

**har·bor·age** (här′bə rij) See HARBOURAGE. *n.*

**harbor master** See HARBOUR MASTER.

**har·bour** or **har·bor** (här′bər) 1 a naturally or artificially sheltered area of deep water where ships may dock or anchor: *Many yachts are in the harbour.* 2 any place of shelter. 3 give shelter to; give a place to hide: *The dog's shaggy hair harbours fleas.* 4 take shelter or refuge. 5 keep or nourish in the mind: *Don't harbour unkind thoughts.* 1, 2 *n.,* 3–5 *v.* —**har′bour·less,** *adj.*
☛ *Etym.* From OE *herebeorg* 'lodgings', originally meaning 'shelter for soldiers' and made up of *here* 'army' + *beorg* 'shelter'. The earlier Germanic form from which the Old English word developed also led to OF *herbergere* 'a person who finds or provides lodgings', from which, in Middle English, came HARBINGER.

**har·bour·age** or **har·bor·age** (här′bə rij) 1 a shelter for ships and boats. 2 any shelter. *n.*

**harbour master** or **harbor master** an officer who has charge of a harbour or port and enforces the rules respecting it.

**hard** (härd) 1 solid and firm to the touch; not soft: *Rocks are hard.* 2 so as to be hard, solid, or firm: *frozen hard.* 3 firmly formed; tight: *Her muscles were hard.* 4 firmly; tightly: *Don't hold hard.* 5 difficult; needing much ability, effort, or time: *a hard problem, a hard job, a hard lesson, a hard man to get on with.* 6 with difficulty: *to breathe hard.* 7 severe; causing much pain, trouble, care, etc.: *a hard illness.* 8 stern; unfeeling: *He was a hard father.* 9 not pleasant; harsh: *a hard face, a hard laugh.* 10 acting or done with energy, persistence, etc.: *a hard worker.* 11 with steady effort or much energy: *Try hard.* 12 vigorous; violent: *a hard storm, a hard run.* 13 with vigour or violence: *He hit hard.* 14 fully; to the extreme limit. 15 containing mineral salts that interfere with the action of soap: *hard water.* 16 containing much alcohol: *hard liquor.* 17 of wheat, having a hard kernel and high gluten content. 18 *Informal.* real and significant: *hard facts, hard news.* 19 the pronunciation of *c* and *g* as (k) (*corn*) and (g) (*get*), and not as in *city* and *gem.* 1–3, 5, 7, 8–10, 12, 15–19 *adj.,* 4, 6, 11, 13, 14 *adv.* —**hard′ness,** *n.*

**hard-bitten**     **546**     **Harlequin**

**go hard with,** cause severe trouble or pain; deal harshly with: *It will go hard with the murderer if he is caught.*
**hard and fast,** that cannot be changed or broken; strict.
**hard by,** near; close: *The house stands hard by the bridge.*
**hard of hearing,** somewhat deaf.
**hard put to it,** in much difficulty or trouble.
**hard up,** *Informal.* needing money or anything very badly: *He is always hard up the day before he is paid. It rained throughout our holiday, and we were hard up for things to do.*

**hard–bit·ten** (härd'bit'ən) stubborn; unyielding. *adj.*

**hard–boiled** (härd'boild') 1 boiled until hard: *hard-boiled eggs.* 2 *Informal.* not easily influenced by the feelings; tough; rough. *adj.*

**hard cider** fermented cider, containing alcohol.

**hard coal** ANTHRACITE.

**hard copy** information that can be read without special equipment, such as a computer printout.

**hard·cov·er** (härd'kuv'ər) 1 of a book or edition, having relatively rigid covers of board, cloth, leather, etc. 2 a book or edition bound in such a way. 1 *adj.*, 2 *n.*

**hard drive** or **hard disk** a large capacity storage device used to retain computer programs and data.

**hard edge** a style of painting in which the edges of the objects painted are sharply defined.

**hard·en** (här'dən) 1 make or become hard. 2 make or become capable of endurance. 3 make or become unfeeling or pitiless. *v.*

**hard–head·ed** (härd'hed'id) 1 not easily excited or deceived; practical; shrewd. 2 stubborn; obstinate. *adj.* —**hard'-head'ed·ly**, *adv.* —**hard'-head'ed·ness**, *n.*

**hard–heart·ed** (härd'här'tid) without pity; cruel; unfeeling. *adj.* —**hard'-heart'ed·ly**, *adv.* —**hard'-heart'ed·ness**, *n.*

**har·di·hood** (här'dē hud) boldness; daring. *n.*

**har·di·ness** (här'dē nis) 1 endurance; strength. 2 hardihood. *n.*

**hard·ly** (härd'lē) 1 only just; barely: *We hardly had time for breakfast.* 2 not quite; not altogether: *hardly strong enough.* 3 most probably not: *She will hardly come now.* 4 with trouble or effort: *money hardly earned.* 5 in a hard manner; harshly; severely: *to deal hardly with a person.* *adv.*
☞ *Usage.* **Hardly** (defs. 1-3) and SCARCELY are treated as negatives and so should not have another negative with them: *The film showed hardly anything that was new to them* (not *hardly nothing*). *I scarcely had enough money* (not *I didn't scarcely have*).

**hard·pan** (härd'pan') hard, firm earth underneath the topsoil. *n.*

**hard·rock** (härd'drok') in mining, rock, such as quartz, that can be removed only by drilling or blasting. *n.*

**hard sell** *Informal.* a forceful and direct method of advertising a product; high-pressure salesmanship: *More and more companies are using the hard sell.*

**hard·ship** (härd'ship) something hard to bear; hard condition of living: *Hunger, cold, and sickness are hardships.* *n.*

**hard·tack** (härd'tak') a very hard, dry biscuit. *n.*

**hard·top** (härd'top') *Informal.* an automobile having a body design similar to that of a convertible except that the top is rigid. *n.*

**hard·ware** (härd'wer') 1 articles made from metal: *Locks, nails, hinges, utensils, and tools are hardware.* 2 in military use, manufactured equipment such as guns, tanks, aircraft, or missiles. 3 the mechanical or electronic parts of a computer or a teaching machine: *The hardware of large computers is very sophisticated.* Compare with SOFTWARE. *n.*

**hard water** water containing minerals that hinder the action of soap.

**hard·wood** (härd'wud') 1 any hard, heavy wood. 2 in forestry, any tree that has broad leaves, or does not have needles. 3 the wood of such a tree: *Oak, cherry, maple, etc. are hardwoods; pine and fir are softwoods.* *n.*

**hard·work·ing** (härd'wer'king) usually working hard; diligent: *She is a hardworking student.* *adj.*

**har·dy** (här'dē) 1 able to bear hard treatment, fatigue, etc.; strong; robust. 2 able to withstand the cold of winter in the open air: *hardy plants.* 3 bold; daring. 4 too bold; rash. *adj.*, **har·di·er, har·di·est.** —**har'di·ly**, *adv.*

**hare** (her) a gnawing animal resembling a rabbit but larger: *A hare has long ears, long hind legs, a short tail, and a divided upper lip.* *n., pl.* **hares** or (*esp. collectively*) **hare.** —**hare'like'**, *adj.*
☞ *Hom.* HAIR.

**hare·bell** (her'bel') a slender plant having blue, bell-shaped flowers; bluebell. *n.*

**hare·brained** (her'brānd') giddy; heedless; reckless: *Only a harebrained driver would attempt to pass another car on that curve.* *adj.*

**hare·lip** (her'lip') a deformity caused when parts of the lip fail to grow together before birth. *n.* —**hare'lipped'**, *adj.*

**har·em** (her'əm) 1 the part of a Moslem house where the women live. 2 its occupants; the wives, female relatives, female servants, etc. of a Moslem household. *n.*

**har·i·cot** (har'ə kō' *or* her'ə kō') STRING BEAN. *n.*

**hark** (härk) listen. *v.*
**hark back,** **a** go back; turn back: *His ideas hark back twenty years.* **b** return to a previous point or subject: *He is always harking back to his time at camp.*

**hark·en** (här'kən) See HEARKEN. *v.*

Harlequin, brandishing his wooden sword

**Har·le·quin** (här'lə kwin' *or* här'lə kin') 1 a character in comedy and pantomime who is usually masked, has a

costume of varied colours, and carries a wooden sword.
**2 harlequin,** a mischievous person; buffoon.   **3** varied in colour; many-coloured.   *n.*

**har·lot** (här′lət)   prostitute.   *n.*

**harm** (härm)   **1** hurt; damage: *The accident did a lot of harm to the car.*   **2** evil; wrong: *What harm is there in borrowing a friend's bicycle?*   **3** damage; injure; hurt: *An unkind and untrue story harmed her reputation.*   1, 2 *n.*, 3 *v.*

**harm·ful** (härm′fəl)   causing harm; injurious; hurtful.   *adj.*   —**harm′ful·ly,** *adv.*   —**harm′ful·ness,** *n.*

**harm·less** (härm′lis)   causing no harm; that would not harm anyone or anything.   *adj.*   —**harm′less·ly,** *adv.*   —**harm′less·ness,** *n.*

**har·mon·ic** (här mon′ik)   **1** in music, having to do with HARMONY (defs. 3, 4).   **2** having to do with fainter and higher tones heard along with the main tones.   **3** musical.   **4** a fainter and higher tone heard along with the main tone; overtone.   1–3 *adj.*, 4 *n.*

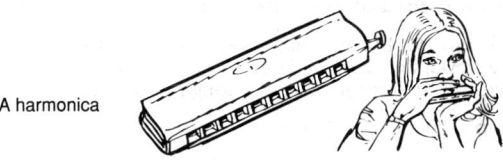

A harmonica

**har·mon·i·ca** (här mon′ə kə)   a small, oblong musical instrument having several metal reeds, which are caused to vibrate by air from the mouth controlled by the tongue and lips; mouth organ.   *n.*

**har·mon·ics** (här mon′iks)   the science of musical sounds.   *n.*

**har·mo·ni·ous** (här mō′nē əs)   **1** agreeing in feelings, ideas, or actions; getting along well together: *The children played together in a harmonious group.*   **2** arranged so that the parts are orderly or pleasing; going well together: *A beautiful picture has harmonious colours.*   **3** sweet-sounding; musical.   *adj.*   —**har·mo′ni·ous·ly,** *adv.*

**har·mo·ni·um** (här mō′nē əm)   a small organ with metal reeds.   *n.*

**har·mo·nize** (här′mə nīz′)   **1** bring into harmony or agreement: *The chairperson had to harmonize several different points of view.*   **2** go or put together in a pleasing way: *The colours in the room harmonized.*   **3** in music, add tones to a melody to make successive chords.   *v.,* **har·mo·nized, har·mo·niz·ing.**   —**har′mo·niz′er,** *n.*

**har·mo·ny** (här′mə nē)   **1** an agreement of feeling, ideas, or actions; getting along well together: *The two brothers lived and worked in perfect harmony.*   **2** an orderly or pleasing arrangement of parts; going well together: *a harmony of design and colour.*   **3** in music, a sounding together of notes in a chord.   **4** in music, the study of chords and of relating them to successive chords.   **5** a sweet or musical sound; music.   **6** the act of harmonizing, especially of singing voices: *The quartet achieved excellent harmony.*   **7** a grouping of passages on the same subject from different stories or accounts, showing their points of agreement.   *n., pl.* **har·mo·nies.**

**harlot**   547   **harpsichord**

hat, āge, fär; let, ēqual, tėrm; it, īce
hot, ōpen, ôrder; oil, out; cup, pùt, rüle
əbove, takən, pencəl, lemən, circəs
ch, child; ng, long; sh, ship
th, thin; ᴛʜ, then; zh, measure

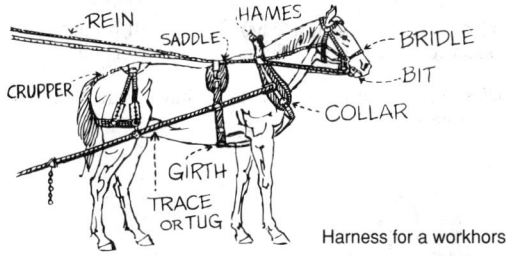

Harness for a workhorse

**har·ness** (här′nis)   **1** a combination of leather straps, bands, and other pieces used to hitch a horse or other animal to a carriage, wagon, plough, etc.   **2** an arrangement of straps to fasten or hold: *a parachute harness, a shoulder harness. We need a harness for the baby's crib.*   **3** put harness on: *Harness the horse.*   **4** cause to produce power: *Water in a stream is harnessed by building a dam and putting in machinery for the water to turn.*   1, 2 *n.,* 3, 4 *v.*
**harness to,**   make use of for: *If only we could find a way of harnessing children's energy to their school work.*
**in harness,**   at one's regular work: *She was content to be back in harness after a good holiday.*

A harp

**harp** (härp)   **1** a musical instrument with strings set in a triangular frame, played by plucking the strings with the fingers.   **2** play on a harp.   1 *n.,* 2 *v.*   —**harp′er,** *n.*
**harp on,**   keep on tiresomely talking or writing about; refer continually to.

**harp·ist** (här′pist)   a person who plays the harp, especially a skilled player.   *n.*

**har·poon** (här pün′)   **1** a barbed spear with a rope tied to it, used for catching large fish and other sea animals: *Harpoons are thrown by hand or shot from a gun.*   **2** strike, catch, or kill with a harpoon: *The sailor skilfully harpooned the seal.*   1 *n.,* 2 *v.*   —**har·poon′er,** *n.*

**harp seal**   a species of seal found in the arctic and subarctic waters of the Atlantic Ocean, mainly pale grey in colour, with a dark-brown or black head and a large, irregular horseshoe-shaped marking on its back.

**harp·si·chord** (härp′sə kôrd′)   a stringed musical instrument like a piano, used especially from about 1550 to 1750: *The harpsichord has a soft and tinkling sound because the strings are plucked by leather or quill points instead of being struck by hammers.*   *n.*

**har·que·bus** (här′kwə bəs)    a kind of gun used before muskets were invented.   *n.*   Also, **arquebus.**

**har·ri·dan** (har′ə dən *or* her′ə dən)    a bad-tempered, disreputable old woman.   *n.*

**har·ri·er**[1] (har′ē ər *or* her′ē ər)    **1** a small hound of the kind used to hunt hares.   **2** a cross-country runner.   *n.*

**har·ri·er**[2] (har′ē ər *or* her′ē ər)    a hawk that preys on small animals.   *n.*

A disc harrow

**har·row** (har′ō *or* her′ō)    **1** a heavy frame with iron teeth or upright disks: *Harrows are drawn over ploughed land to break up clods, cover seeds, etc.*   **2** draw a harrow over land, etc.   **3** hurt; wound.   **4** arouse uncomfortable feelings in; distress; torment: *He harrowed us with a tale of ghosts.*   1 *n.*, 2–4 *v.*   —**har′row·er,** *n.*

**har·ry** (har′ē *or* her′ē)    **1** raid and rob with violence: *The pirates harried the towns along the coast.*   **2** keep troubling; worry; torment: *Fear of losing his job harried the clerk.*   *v.*, **har·ried, har·ry·ing.**   —**har′ri·er,** *n.*

**harsh** (härsh)    **1** rough to the touch, taste, eye, or ear; sharp and unpleasant: *a harsh voice, a harsh climate.*   **2** without pity; cruel; severe: *a harsh woman.*   *adj.*   —**harsh′ly,** *adv.*   —**harsh′ness,** *n.*

**hart** (härt)    a male deer; stag, usually a male red deer after its fifth year.   *n., pl.* **harts** or (*esp. collectively*) **hart.**   ☞ *Hom.* HEART.

**har·te·beest** (här′tə bēst′ *or* härt′bēst′)    a large, swift African antelope having ringed, curved horns bent backwards at the tips.   *n., pl.* **har·te·beests** or (*esp. collectively*) **har·te·beest.**

**harts·horn** (härts′hôrn′)    **1** ammonia dissolved in water.   **2** smelling salts; sal volatile.   *n.*

**har·um–scar·um** (her′əm sker′əm)    **1** reckless; rash; thoughtless: *What a harum-scarum child you are!*   **2** recklessly; wildly: *He rushed harum-scarum down the main street.*   **3** a reckless person.   1 *adj.*, 2 *adv.*, 3 *n.*

**har·vest** (här′vist)    **1** a reaping and gathering in of grain and other food crops, usually in the late summer or early autumn.   **2** the time or season when grain, fruit, etc. are gathered in.   **3** gather in for use: *to harvest wheat.*   **4** one season's yield of any natural product; crop: *The oyster harvest was small this year.*   **5** the result or consequences: *He is reaping the harvest of his lies.*   1, 2, 4, 5 *n.*, 3 *v.*

**har·vest·er** (här′vi stər)    **1** a person who works in a harvest field; reaper.   **2** a machine for harvesting crops, especially grain.   *n.*

**harvest home**   **1** the end of harvesting.   **2** a festival to celebrate the end of harvesting.

**harvest moon**   the full moon at harvest time, or about September 23.

**harvest special**   *Cdn.*   a train taking part in a low-fare railway trip for field-workers travelling to the West to harvest grain.

**has** (haz; *unstressed*, həz *or* əz)    third person singular, present indicative of HAVE: *Who has my book?*   *v.*

**has–been** (haz′bin′)   *Informal.*   a person or thing whose best days are past.   *n.*

**hash** (hash)    **1** a mixture of cooked meat, potatoes, etc. chopped into small pieces and fried or baked.   **2** chop into small pieces.   **3** a mixture; jumble.   **4** mess or muddle.   **5** *Informal.*   talk about in detail; discuss or review thoroughly: *The two leaders hashed over their dispute for hours.*   1, 3, 4 *n.*, 2, 4, 5 *v.*
**make a hash of,**   make a mess of: *She made a hash of mounting stamps in her album.*
**settle one's hash,** *Informal.*   subdue or silence someone completely; put an end to someone.

**hash·eesh** (hash′ēsh)    HASHISH.   *n.*

**hash·ish** (hash′ēsh *or* hash′ish)    an extract from the dried flowers of the female hemp plant, that is smoked, chewed, or drunk for its intoxicating effect.   *n.*

**has·n't** (haz′ənt)    has not.

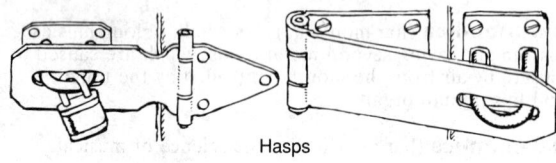
Hasps

**hasp** (hasp)    a clasp or fastening for a door, window, trunk, box, etc., especially a hinged metal clasp that fits over a staple or into a hole and is fastened by a peg, padlock, etc. See PADLOCK for another picture.   *n.*

**has·sle** (has′əl)   *Informal.*   **1** a struggle; argument: *There was a hassle about who was going to ride in the front seat of the car.*   **2** trouble; annoyance; bother: *Driving in city traffic is too much of a hassle. Traffic jams create a lot of hassle.*   **3** struggle; argue.   **4** worry; annoy; bother: *The film star was being hassled by newspaper reporters.*   1, 2 *n.*, 3, 4 *v.*, **has·sled, has·sling.**

**has·sock** (has′ək)    **1** a thick cushion to rest the feet on, sit on, or kneel on.   **2** a tuft or bunch of coarse grass.   *n.*

**haste** (hāst)    **1** a trying to be quick; hurrying: *The queen's business required haste.*   **2** quickness without thought or care: *Haste makes waste.*   *n.*
**in haste,**   **a** in a hurry; quickly: *Bring the doctor in haste.*   **b** without careful thought; rashly.
**make haste,**   hurry; be quick.

**has·ten** (hā′sən)    **1** cause to be quick; speed; hurry: *Do not hasten everyone off to bed.*   **2** be quick; go fast: *Let me hasten to explain.*   *v.*

**hast·y** (hā′stē)    **1** hurried; quick: *a hasty visit.*   **2** not well thought out; rash: *Her hasty decisions caused many mistakes.*   **3** easily angered; quick-tempered.   *adj.*, **hast·i·er, hast·i·est.**   —**hast′i·ly,** *adv.*   —**hast′i·ness,** *n.*

HATS: SHAKO, TOP HAT, PILL BOX, SOMBRERO, DERBY

**hat** (hat) **1** a covering for the head, usually with a crown and brim and usually worn outdoors. **2** a red head covering worn by a cardinal of the Roman Catholic Church. **3** the dignity or office of a cardinal. **4** cover or furnish with a hat. *1–3 n., 4 v.,* **hat·ted, hat·ting.** —**hat′less,** *adj.* —**hat′like′,** *adj.*
**old hat,** out-of-date or fashion; commonplace.
**pass the hat,** take up a collection.
**take off one's hat to, a** remove the hat, as a salute or sign of respect. **b** honour; hail.
**hat·band** (hat′band′) a band around the crown of a hat, just above the brim. *n.*
**hatch**[1] (hach) **1** bring forth young from an egg or eggs: *A hen hatches chickens.* **2** keep an egg or eggs warm until the young come out: *The heat of the sun hatches turtles' eggs.* **3** come out from the egg: *Three chickens hatched today.* **4** produce living young: *Not all eggs hatch properly.* **5** the act of hatching. **6** the brood hatched: *There are twelve chicks in this hatch.* **7** arrange; plan, especially in secret; plot: *The robbers were hatching an evil scheme.* *1–4, 7 v., 5, 6 n.* —**hatch′er,** *n.*
**hatch**[2] (hach) **1** an opening in a ship's deck, especially one that leads to the hold and is used for loading cargo. See CAPSTAN for picture. **2** the trapdoor covering such an opening. **3** an opening in the floor or roof of a building, etc.: *an escape hatch.* **4** the lower half of a divided door. *n.*
**hatch**[3] (hach) **1** draw, cut, or engrave fine parallel lines on: *With a sharp pencil the artist hatched certain parts of the picture to darken and shade them.* **2** one of such a set of lines. *1 v., 2 n.*
**hatch·back** (hach′bak′) **1** a sloping back on a two-door or four-door automobile, the whole of which swings up like a hatch, giving access to the interior of the car. **2** an automobile having a hatchback. *n.*
**hatch·er·y** (hach′ə rē) a place for hatching eggs of fish, hens, etc. *n., pl.* **hatch·er·ies.**
**hatch·et** (hach′it) **1** a small axe with a short handle, for use with one hand. **2** a tomahawk. *n.*
**bury the hatchet,** make peace.
**dig up the hatchet,** make war.
**hatch·ing** (hach′ing) **1** fine, parallel lines drawn, cut, or engraved close together. See CROSSHATCH for picture. **2** ppr. of HATCH. *1 n., 2 v.*
**hatch·way** (hach′wā′) **1** an opening in the deck of a ship to the lower part. **2** a similar opening in a floor, roof, etc. *n.*
**hate** (hāt) **1** dislike very strongly. **2** a strong dislike: *She felt a hate of snakes. Hate is the opposite of love.* **3** dislike: *I hate to study.* **4** an object of hatred. *1, 3 v.,* **hat·ed, hat·ing;** *2, 4 n.* —**hat′er,** *n.*
**hate·ful** (hāt′fəl) **1** causing to; to be hated: *hateful behaviour.* **2** feeling hate; showing hate: *She was always making hateful remarks. adj.* —**hate′ful·ly,** *adv.* —**hate′ful·ness,** *n.*
**hat·pin** (hat′pin′) a long pin used by women to fasten a hat to the hair. *n.*
**hat·rack** (hat′rak′) a rack, shelf, or arrangement of hooks or pegs to put hats on. *n.*
**ha·tred** (hā′trid) very strong dislike; hate. *n.*
**hat·ter** (hat′ər) a maker or seller of hats. *n.*
**hat trick 1** in hockey and soccer, three goals scored in a single game by the same player. **2** in cricket, the taking of three wickets with three successive balls. **3** *Informal.* any feat consisting of three or more victories in a row.
☞ *Etym.* From the fact of a *hat* formerly being the prize for this feat in cricket.
**haugh·ti·ness** (hot′ē nis) being haughty; arrogance; looking down on other people. *n.*
**haugh·ty** (hot′ē) **1** too proud of oneself and too scornful of others: *A haughty girl is always unpopular.* **2** showing too great pride of oneself and scorn for others: *a haughty smile. adj.,* **haugh·ti·er, haugh·ti·est.** —**haugh′ti·ly,** *adv.*
**haul** (hol) **1** pull or drag with force: *The logs were hauled by horses.* **2** the act of hauling; hard pull. **3** transport by truck or railway: *Those trains haul coal to Vancouver.* **4** the load hauled: *Powerful trucks are used for heavy hauls.* **5** the distance that a load is hauled. **6** the amount won, taken, etc. at one time; catch: *The fishing boats made a good haul today.* **7** change the course of a ship. **8** change; shift: *The wind hauled around to the east.* *1, 3, 7, 8 v., 2, 4–6 n.* —**haul′er,** *n.*
**haul off, a** turn a ship away from an object. **b** draw away; withdraw. **c** *Informal.* draw back one's arm to give a blow.
**haul on** or **to the wind,** sail closer to the direction of the wind.
**haul up, a** turn a ship nearer to the direction of the wind. **b** change the course of a ship.
☞ *Hom.* HALL.
**haunch** (honch) **1** the part of the body around the hip; the hip. **2** a hind quarter of an animal: *A dog sits on its haunches.* **3** a cut of meat consisting of the leg and loin of a deer, sheep, etc. *n.*
**haunt** (hont) **1** of a ghost, appear frequently to a person or in a place; be continually present at a place: *People say ghosts haunt that old house.* **2** go often to; visit frequently: *They haunt the new bowling alley.* **3** a place frequently gone to or often visited: *The swimming pool was the favourite haunt of the girls in the summer.* **4** be often with; come often to: *Memories of his youth haunted the old man.* *1, 2, 4 v., 3 n.* —**haunt′ing·ly,** *adv.*
**haunt·ed** (hon′tid) **1** visited by ghosts. **2** pt. and pp. of HAUNT. *1 adj., 2 v.*
**haut·boy** (hō′boi) oboe. *n.*
**hau·teur** (hō tėr′) haughtiness; a haughty manner or spirit. *n.*

A red-tailed hawk—about 55 cm long including the tail

**have** (hav; *unstressed,* həv *or* əv)   **1** hold: *I have a book in my hand.*   **2** possess; own: *She has a big house and farm.*   **3** cause somebody to do something or cause something to be done: *Please have the boy bring my mail. She will have the car washed for me.*   **4** obtain; receive; take; get: *Have a seat.*   **5** show by action: *to have the courage to.*   **6** experience: *to have a pain, to have fear. They had trouble with this engine.*   **7** engage in; carry on; perform: *Have a talk with her.*   **8** allow; permit: *Ann won't have any noise while she is reading.*   **9** maintain; assert: *They will have it so.*   **10** keep; retain: *He has the directions in mind.*   **11** know; understand: *He has no Latin.*   **12** hold in the mind: *to have an idea.*   **13** be in a certain relation to: *She has three brothers.*   **14** *Informal.* hold an advantage over: *You have him there.*   **15** *Informal.* outwit or cheat.   **16** become the father or mother of: *My sister plans to have children.*   **17** *Have* is used with past participles to express completed action: *They have come. She had gone before. I have called her. They will have seen her by Sunday.*   **18** a person or country that has property or wealth: *the haves and have-nots.*   1–17 *v., pres.* **1 have,** 2 **have,** 3 **has,** *pl.* **have;** *pt. and pp.* **had;** *ppr.* **hav·ing;** 18 *n.*
**have at,**   attack; hit.
**have done,**   stop; be through.
**have it in for,** *Informal.*   have a grudge against; try to get revenge on.
**have it out,**   argue or fight until a question is settled.
**have to,**   must: *All animals have to sleep. We will have to go now.*
**have to do with,**   **a** be connected with; be related to.   **b** be a companion, partner, or friend of; associate with.
**to have and to hold,**   to keep and possess.
☛ *Hom.* HALVE.

**have·lock** (hav′lok)   a white cloth covering for a cap: *The havelock falls over the back of the neck and gives protection against the sun.* *n.*

**ha·ven** (hā′vən)   **1** a harbour, especially one providing shelter from a storm.   **2** a place of shelter and safety: *The hunters found the cabin a welcome haven from the storm.*   **3** shelter in a haven.   1, 2 *n.,* 3 *v.*

**have–not** (hav′not′) *Informal.*   a person or country that has little or no property or wealth. *n.*

**have·n't** (hav′ənt)   have not.

**hav·er·sack** (hav′ər sak′)   a bag used by soldiers and hikers to carry food, utensils, etc. *n.*

**hav·oc** (hav′ək)   very great destruction or injury: *Tornadoes, severe earthquakes, and plagues create widespread havoc.* *n.*
**play havoc with,**   injure severely; ruin; destroy.

**haw¹** (ho)   **1** the red berry of the HAWTHORN.   **2** the HAWTHORN. *n.*

**haw²** (ho)   **1** a stammering sound between words.   **2** make this sound; stammer.   1 *interj., n.,* 2 *v.*

**haw³** (ho)   **1** a word of command to horses, oxen, etc., directing them to turn to the left.   **2** turn to the left.   1 *interj., n.,* 2 *v.*

**Ha·wai·ian** (hə wī′yən)   **1** of or having to do with Hawaii, a group of islands in the Pacific Ocean, its people, or their language.   **2** a native or inhabitant of Hawaii, especially one of Polynesian descent.   **3** the language of the Hawaiians.   1 *adj.,* 2, 3 *n.*

**hawk¹** (hok)   **1** a bird of prey having a strong hooked beak, large curved claws, short rounded wings, and a long tail.   **2** a bird of prey like a hawk; a buzzard or kite.   **3** hunt with trained hawks.   **4** a person who preys on others.   1, 2, 4 *n.,* 3 *v.*   —**hawk′like**′, *adj.*
☛ *Hom.* HOCK.

**hawk²** (hok)   **1** carry goods about for sale as a street peddler does.   **2** advertise by shouting that goods are for sale.   **3** spread a report. *v.*
☛ *Hom.* HOCK.

**hawk³** (hok)   **1** clear the throat noisily.   **2** a noisy effort to clear the throat.   1 *v.,* 2 *n.*
☛ *Hom.* HOCK.

**hawk·er¹** (hok′ər)   a person who carries his or her wares around and offers them for sale by shouting; peddler. *n.*

**hawk·er²** (hok′ər)   a person who hunts with a hawk. *n.*

**hawk–eyed** (hok′īd′)   having sharp eyes like a hawk. *adj.*

**hawk·ing** (hok′ing)   **1** the act of hunting with hawks; falconry.   **2** *ppr.* of HAWK.   1 *n.,* 2 *v.*

**hawks·bill turtle** (hoks′bil′)   a sea turtle whose mouth is shaped like a hawk's beak.

**hawse** (hoz *or* hos)   **1** the part of a ship's bow where the hawseholes are located.   **2** HAWSEPIPE.   **3** the distance between the bow of a moored ship and the anchor or anchors. *n.*

**hawse·hole** (hoz′hōl′)   a hole in the bow of a ship for a hawser or anchor chain to pass through. *n.*

**hawse·pipe** (hoz′pīp′)   a heavy iron or steel pipe lining a HAWSEHOLE: *A hawsepipe has a curled rim that fits tightly against the edge of the hawsehole.*   See CAPSTAN for picture. *n.*

**haw·ser** (hoz′ər)   a large, stout rope or a thin, steel cable, used for mooring or towing ships. *n.*

**haw·thorn** (hoth′ôrn′)   a thorny shrub or tree having clusters of white, red, or pink blossoms and small, red berries called haws. *n.*

**hay** (hā)   **1** grass, alfalfa, clover, etc. that has been cut and dried for use as food for cattle, horses, etc.   **2** cut and dry grass, alfalfa, clover, etc. for hay: *The men are haying in the east field.*   **3** supply with hay.   1 *n.,* 2, 3 *v.*
**make hay,**   **a** cut and dry grass, alfalfa, clover, etc. for hay.   **b** *Informal.*   take advantage of some opportunity.
☛ *Hom.* HEY.

**hay·cock** (hā′kok′)   a small, cone-shaped pile of hay in a field. *n.*

**hay·coil** (hā′koil′)   HAYCOCK. *n.*

**hay fever**   an allergy with effects like those of a cold, caused by the pollen of ragweed and other plants.

**hay·field** (hā′fēld′) a field where grass, alfalfa, clover, etc. is grown or cut for hay. *n.*

**hay·loft** (hā′loft′) the upper storey of a stable or barn, where hay is stored. *n.*

**hay·mak·er** (hā′mā′kər) a person who tosses and spreads cut hay to dry. *n.*

**hay·mow** (hā′mou′ *or* hā′mō′) **1** the place in a barn where hay is stored; HAYLOFT. **2** a heap of hay stored in a barn. *n.*

**hay·rack** (hā′rak′) **1** a rack or frame used for holding hay to be eaten by cattle, horses, etc. **2** a framework on a wagon used in hauling hay, straw, etc. **3** the wagon and framework together. *n.*

**hay·rick** (hā′rik′) HAYSTACK. *n.*

**hay·seed** (hā′sēd′) **1** grass seed, especially that shaken out of hay. **2** small bits of chaff, etc. of hay. *n.*

**hay·stack** (hā′stak′) a large pile of hay outdoors. *n.*

**hay·wire** (hā′wīr′) **1** wire used to tie up bales of hay. **2** *Informal.* out of order; wrong. *n.*

**haz·ard** (haz′ərd) **1** a risk; danger; peril: *The life of an explorer is full of hazards.* **2** a chance. **3** take a chance with; risk; venture: *I would hazard my life on her honesty.* **4** any obstruction on a golf course. **5** an early dice game, the origin of CRAPS. **6** expose to risk. 1, 2, 4, 5 *n.*, 3, 6 *v.*
**at all hazards,** whatever the risk; in spite of great danger or peril.

**haz·ard·ous** (haz′ər dəs) dangerous; risky; perilous. *adj.* —**haz′ard·ous·ly,** *adv.* —**haz′ard·ous·ness,** *n.*

**haze**[1] (hāz) **1** a small amount of mist, smoke, dust, etc. in the air: *A thin haze veiled the mountains.* **2** vagueness of the mind during which one sees things indistinctly: *After he was hit on the head, everything was in a haze for him.* **3** general vagueness; a slight confusion of the mind. *n.*

**haze**[2] (hāz) **1** force to do unnecessary or ridiculous tasks; bully: *The freshmen resented being hazed by the older students.* **2** in western Canada and the United States, drive (cattle, horses, etc.) from horseback. *v.*, **hazed, haz·ing.** —**haz′er,** *n.*

**ha·zel** (hā′zəl) **1** a shrub or small tree of the same family as the birch, having light-brown, edible nuts. **2** greenish-brown: *hazel eyes.* 1, 2 *n.*, 2 *adj.*

**ha·zel·nut** (hā′zəl nut′) the nut of a HAZEL (def. 1). *n.*

**ha·zy** (hā′zē) **1** full of haze; misty; smoky: *hazy air.* **2** confused; vague; obscure: *hazy ideas.* *adj.*, **ha·zi·er, ha·zi·est.** —**ha′zi·ly,** *adv.* —**ha′zi·ness,** *n.*

**H.B.C.** Hudson's Bay Company.

**H–bomb** (āch′bom′) hydrogen bomb. *n.*

**H.C.** House of Commons.

**he** (hē; *unstressed,* ē *or* i) **1** a boy, man, or male animal already referred to and identified: *Carlos has to work hard, but he likes his job, and it pays him well.* **2** anyone; a person: *He who hesitates is lost.* *pron.*, *nom.*, **he;** *poss.*, **his;** *obj.*, **him;** *pl. nom.*, **they;** *poss.*, **theirs, their;** *obj.*, **them.**

**He** helium.

**HE** *or* **H.E.** high explosive.

---

# hayfield 551 head

hat, āge, fär; let, ēqual, tėrm; it, īce
hot, ōpen, ôrder; oil, out; cup, put, rüle
əbove, takən, pencəl, lemən, circəs
ch, child; ng, long; sh, ship
th, thin; ᴛʜ, then; zh, measure

**H.E.** **1** His Eminence. **2** His Excellency; Her Excellency.

**head** (hed) **1** the top part of the human body where the eyes, ears, nose, and mouth are. **2** the corresponding part of an animal's body. **3** the top part of anything: *the head of a pin, the head of a page.* See RIVET for picture. **4** the foremost part or end of anything; the front: *the head of a procession.* **5** a likeness of a head, especially as a work of art: *A marble head of the emperor was in the museum.* **6** at the head, top, or front: *the head division of a parade.* **7** be or go at the head, top, or front of: *to head a parade.* **8** coming from in front: *a head wind.* **9** cause to move or face in a certain direction: *to head a boat toward shore.* **10** move or go in a certain direction: *It's getting late; we'd better head for home.* **11** the chief person; leader; commander; director. **12** the position of head; chief authority; leadership; command; direction. **13** chief; leading; commanding; directing. **14** be the head or chief of; lead; command; direct: *to head a business.* **15** a person; an individual: *Kings and queens are crowned heads.* **16** a unit used in counting animals: *She sold fifty head of cattle and ten head of horses.* **17** anything rounded like a head: *a head of cabbage or lettuce.* **18** in botany, a cluster of small flowers growing closely together, as in composite plants or clover. **19** the part of a boil or pimple where pus is about to break through the skin. **20** the striking part of a tool or implement: *the head of a hammer.* **21** a piece of skin stretched tightly over the end of a drum, etc. **22** either end of a barrel or cask. **23** put a head on; furnish with a head. **24** form a head; come to a head. **25** cut off the head of. **26** mind; understanding; intelligence; intellect: *The old woman has a wise head.* **27** topic; point: *He arranged his speech under four main heads.* **28** a crisis; conclusion; decisive point: *Her sudden refusal brought matters to a head.* **29** strength or force gained little by little: *As more people joined, the movement gathered head.* **30** pressure of water, steam, etc. **31** the source of a river or stream. **32** foam; froth. **33** in soccer, direct the movement of the ball with one's head: *He headed the ball away from his opponent.* **34** the device in a tape-recorder or a computer that records or deletes information on a magnetic tape or disk. **35** the component of a computer peripheral (disk drive, tape drive, etc.) that contacts or is situated very close to the recording surface for purposes of reading or writing data. **36** Usually, **heads,** the side of a coin bearing the likeness of a head, especially that of a king, queen, president, etc.: *The tossed coin came up heads. The head of a Canadian coin carries a portrait of Queen Elizabeth II.* 1–5, 11, 12, 15–22, 26–32, 34, 35, 36 *n.*, 7, 9, 10, 14, 23–25, 33 *v.*, 6, 8, 13 *adj.* —**head′like**′, *adj.*
**come to a head,** **a** of boils, pimples, etc., reach the stage where they are about to break through the skin. **b** reach a decisive stage: *The international crisis came to a head and war was declared.*
**eat one's head off,** **a** eat very much. **b** cost more to feed than one is worth.
**give someone his or her head,** let someone go as he or she pleases.
**go to one's head,** **a** affect one's mind. **b** make one dizzy. **c** make one conceited.
**hang one's head,** be ashamed and show that one is so.

**head off,** get in front of and turn back or aside: *The cowboys tried to head off the stampeding herd.*
**head on,** with the head or front first: *The car crashed head on into the wall.*
**head over heels, a** in a somersault. **b** hastily; rashly. **c** completely; thoroughly.
**heads up,** be careful; watch out: *Heads up! The principal's coming.*
**hide one's head,** be ashamed and show that one is so.
**keep one's head,** not get excited; stay calm.
**keep one's head above water,** keep out of trouble or difficulty, especially financial difficulty: *He's finding it hard to keep his head above water these days.*
**lay heads together, a** confer; consult. **b** plot; conspire.
**lose one's head,** get excited; lose one's self-control.
**make head,** move forward; make progress; advance.
**make head or tail of,** understand.
**off** or **out of one's head,** *Informal.* crazy; insane.
**on** or **upon one's head,** on one's responsibility.
**over one's head, a** beyond one's power to understand. **b** to a person higher in authority: *She threatened that she would go over the foreman's head.*
**put heads together, a** confer; consult. **b** plot; conspire.
**take it into one's head, a** get the idea. **b** plan; intend.
**turn one's head, a** affect the mind. **b** make one dizzy. **c** make one conceited.

**head·ache** (hed′āk′) **1** a pain in the head. **2** *Informal.* a thing, situation, etc. that is the cause of great bother, annoyance, etc. *n.*

**head·band** (hed′band′) **1** a band of cloth, ribbon, leather, etc. worn around the head: *Headbands are often worn to hold the hair in place.* **2** a flexible metal or plastic band that holds an earphone or earphones in place over the ear. *n.*

**head·board** (hed′bôrd′) a board or frame that forms the head of a bed. *n.*

**head·cheese** (hed′chēz′) a jellied loaf formed of parts of the head and feet of pigs cut up, cooked, and seasoned. *n.*

**head·dress** (hed′dres′) **1** a covering or decoration for the head. **2** a way of wearing or arranging the hair. *n.*

**head·er** (hed′ər) **1** a person, tool, or machine that puts on or takes off heads of grain, barrels, pins, nails, etc. **2** *Informal.* a plunge or dive headfirst: *She took a header into the water.* **3** a brick or stone laid with its length across the thickness of a wall. **4** a beam forming part of the framework around an opening in a floor or roof, placed so as to fit between two long beams and support the ends of short ones. *n.*

**head·first** (hed′fèrst′) **1** with the head first: *She slid headfirst down the hill.* **2** hastily; rashly. *adv.*

**head·fore·most** (hed′fôr′mōst′) HEADFIRST. *adv.*

**head·gate 1** an upstream gate of a lock in a canal or river. **2** the floodgate of a sluice, race, etc. *n.*

**head·gear** (hed′gēr′) **1** a covering for the head; hat, cap, etc. **2** the harness for an animal's head. *n.*

**head·ing** (hed′ing) **1** the part forming the head, top, or front. **2** something written or printed at the top of a page. **3** the title of a page, chapter, etc.; topic. **4** the direction of a ship or aircraft as indicated by a compass. **5** ppr. of HEAD. **1–4** *n.,* **5** *v.*

**head·lamp** (hed′lamp′) **1** a small lamp worn on the cap or the forehead. **2** a headlight on a train, automobile, etc. *n.*

**head·land** (hed′lənd *or* hed′land′) a point of land jutting out into water; cape. *n.*

**head·less** (hed′lis) **1** having no head. **2** without a leader. **3** *Informal.* without brains; stupid. *adj.*

**head·light** (hed′līt′) **1** of vehicles such as an automobile, one of two large lights at the front. **2** a large single light at the front of a locomotive or streetcar. **3** on a ship, a light at a masthead. *n.*

**head·line** (hed′līn′) **1** the words printed at the top of an article in a newspaper or magazine to indicate the topic. **2** a line printed at the top of a page giving the running title, page number, etc. **3** furnish with a headline. **1, 2** *n.,* **3** *v.,* **head·lined, head·lin·ing.**

**head·long** (hed′long′) **1** headfirst: *to plunge headlong into the sea.* **2** with great speed and force: *to rush headlong into the crowd.* **3** in too great a rush; without stopping to think: *The girl was always rushing headlong into trouble.* **4** rash. **5** rashly. **1–3, 5** *adv.,* **4** *adj.*

**head·man** (hed′man′ *or* hed′mən) a chief or leader. *n., pl.* **head·men** (-men′ *or* -mən).

**head·mas·ter** (hed′mas′tər) a person in charge of a school, especially of a private school; principal. *n.*

**head·most** (hed′mōst′) first; most advanced. *adj.*

**head of steel** *Cdn.* END OF STEEL.

**head–on** (hed′on′) with the head or front first: *a head-on collision.* *adj.*

**head·phone** (hed′fōn′) a telephone or radio receiver held on the head, against the ears. *n.*

**head·piece** (hed′pēs′) **1** a piece of armour for the head; helmet. **2** a hat, cap, or other covering for the head. **3** headphone. **4** the head; mind; intellect. **5** a decoration at the head of a page, chapter, etc. *n.*

**head·quar·ters** (hed′kwôr′tərz) **1** the place from which the chief or commanding officer of an army, police force, etc. sends out orders. **2** the centre from which any organization is controlled and directed; main office: *The headquarters of the Canadian Red Cross Society are in Toronto.* *n.pl.* or *sing.*

**head·rest** (hed′rest′) a support for the head: *The dentist's chair has a headrest.* *n.*

**head·room** (hed′rüm *or* hed′rùm) HEADWAY (def. 3).

**head·set** (hed′set′) a pair of earphones. *n.*

**head·ship** (hed′ship′) the position of head; chief authority. *n.*

**heads·man** (hedz′mən) a man who puts criminals to death by cutting off their heads. *n., pl.* **heads·men** (-zmən).

**head·stall** (hed′stol′) **1** the part of a bridle or halter that fits over a horse's head. See BRIDLE for picture. **2** halter. *n.*

**head start 1** an advantage or lead allowed someone at the beginning of a race: *The smaller girl was given a head start.* **2** an advantage gained by beginning something before somebody else: *That team is playing better hockey than we are because they had a head start in practising.*

**head·stone** (hed′stōn′) **1** a stone set at the head of a grave; tombstone. **2** the principal stone in a foundation; cornerstone. *n.*

**head·stream** (hed′strēm′) a stream that is the source of a larger stream. *n.*

**head·strong** (hed′strong′) **1** rashly or foolishly determined to have one's own way; hard to control or manage; obstinate. **2** showing rash or foolish determination to have one's own way: *a headstrong action*. *adj.*

**head·wait·er** (hed′wā′tər) a man in charge of the waiters in a restaurant, hotel, etc. *n.*

**head·wa·ters** (hed′wot′ərz) the sources or upper parts of a river. *n. pl.*

**head·way** (hed′wā′) **1** forward motion: *The ship could make no headway against the strong wind and tide*. **2** progress with work, etc. **3** a clear space overhead in a doorway or under an arch, bridge, etc.; clearance. **4** the interval of time between two trains, streetcars, ships, etc. going in the same direction over the same route. *n.*

**head wind** a wind blowing straight against the front of a ship, aircraft, etc.

**head·word** (hed′wėrd′) a word that is modified by another word or words; the main word of a phrase. *n.*

**head·y** (hed′ē) **1** hasty; rash. **2** apt to affect the head and make one dizzy; intoxicating. *adj.*, **head·i·er, head·i·est.** —**head′i·ness,** *n.*

**heal** (hēl) **1** make whole, sound, or well; bring back to health; cure a disease or wound. **2** become whole or sound; get well; return to health; be cured: *Her cut finger soon healed*. **3** free from anything bad. **4** get rid of anything bad. *v.* —**heal′er,** *n.*
☞ *Hom.* HEEL, HE'LL (hēl).

**health** (helth) **1** being well; freedom from sickness. **2** a condition of body or mind: *She is in poor health*. **3** a toast drunk in honour of a person with a wish for health and happiness: *We all drank a health to the bride*. *n.*

**health·ful** (helth′fəl) giving health; good for the health: *healthful exercise, a healthful diet*. *adj.* —**health′ful·ly,** *adv.* —**health′ful·ness,** *n.*
☞ *Syn.* In formal English, a distinction is usually made between **healthful,** meaning 'giving health', and HEALTHY, meaning 'having good health'. Places, food, etc. are **healthful;** people and animals are **healthy.**

**health·y** (hel′thē) **1** having good health: *a healthy baby*. **2** showing good health: *a healthy appearance*. **3** HEALTHFUL. *adj.*, **health·i·er, health·i·est.** —**health′i·ly,** *adv.* —**health′i·ness,** *n.*
☞ *Syn.* See note at HEALTHFUL.

**heap** (hēp) **1** a pile of many things thrown or lying together: *a heap of stones, a sand heap*. **2** form into a heap; gather in heaps: *She heaped the dirty clothes beside the washing machine*. **3** a large amount. **4** give generously or in large amounts. **5** fill to the point of overflowing; load: *His mother heaped potatoes on his plate. His friends heaped praise on him.* 1, 3 *n.*, 2, 4, 5 *v.*

**hear** (hēr) **1** perceive by the ear: *to hear sounds, to hear voices*. **2** be able to perceive by the ear: *A deaf child cannot hear well*. **3** listen to: *to hear a person's explanation*. **4** listen. **5** give a chance to be heard; give a formal hearing to, as a king, a judge, a teacher, or an assembly does. **6** find out by hearing: *to hear news*. **7** be told; receive news or information. **8** listen to with favour: *The magistrate refused to hear the prisoner's plea*. *v.*, **heard, hear·ing.** —**hear′er,** *n.*
 **hear from,** **a** receive news or information from: *Have you heard from your friend?* **b** receive a reprimand from.
 **hear! hear!** shouts of approval; cheering.
 **hear of,** have some knowledge of: *I've never heard of her.*
 **hear out,** listen to till the end.
 **will not hear of it,** will not listen to, think of, agree to, or allow it.
☞ *Hom.* HERE.

**heard** (hėrd) pt. and pp. of HEAR: *I heard the noise. The gun was heard two kilometres away.* *v.*
☞ *Hom.* HERD.

**hear·ing** (hē′ring) **1** the sense by which sound is perceived: *The old man's hearing is poor*. **2** the act or process of perceiving sound: *Hearing the good news made her happy*. **3** a formal or official listening: *The Royal Commission has set a date for its next hearing*. **4** the trial of an action: *The judge gave both sides a hearing in court*. **5** a chance to be heard: *Give us a hearing*. **6** the distance that a sound can be heard: *to be within hearing of the baby, to talk freely in the hearing of others*. **7** ppr. of HEAR. 1–6 *n.*, 7 *v.*

**hearing aid** a device used to improve hearing: *Most modern hearing aids are operated by batteries, which provide power for making sounds louder.*

**heark·en** (här′kən) listen; listen attentively. *v.* Also, **harken.**

**hear·say** (hēr′sā′) common talk; gossip. *n.*

**hearse** (hėrs) an automobile, carriage, etc. used in funerals to carry a dead person to the grave or crematorium. *n.*

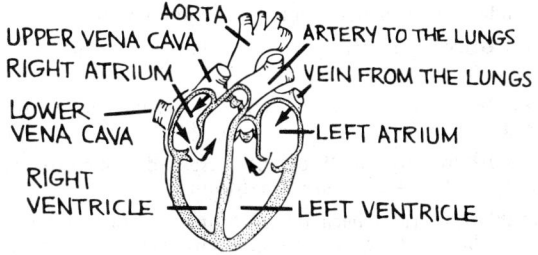

The human heart

**heart** (härt) **1** a hollow, muscular organ that pumps the blood throughout the body by contracting and dilating. See LUNG for another picture. **2** the feelings; mind or soul: *She has a kind heart*. **3** the source of the emotions, especially of love: *to give one's heart*. **4** a person loved or praised: *a group of stout hearts*. **5** kindness; sympathy: *to have no heart*. **6** spirit; courage; enthusiasm: *The losing team showed plenty of heart*. **7** the innermost part; middle; centre: *in the heart of the forest*. **8** the main part; vital or most important part: *the very heart of the matter*. **9** a figure shaped like a heart: *There was a big red heart on the front of the valentine card*. **10** a playing card with one or more red, heart-shaped figures. **11 hearts,** *pl.* **a** a suit of playing cards with red designs like hearts on them. **b** a game in which the players try to get rid of cards of this suit. *n.*
 **after one's own heart,** just as one likes it; pleasing one perfectly.

**at heart,** in one's deepest thoughts or feelings; really: *He is kind at heart, though he appears to be gruff.*
**break the heart of,** crush with sorrow or grief.
**by heart, a** by memory. **b** from memory.
**eat one's heart out,** feel great sorrow, grief, or worry.
**from one's heart,** with deepest feeling; sincerely.
**get to the heart of,** find out the secret or hidden meaning of.
**have a heart,** *Informal.* be kind, merciful, or sympathetic.
**have one's heart in one's boots** or **mouth,** be very frightened.
**have one's heart in the right place,** mean well; have good intentions.
**heart and soul,** with all one's affections and energies.
**heart of gold,** extremely kind, generous, and sympathetic feelings.
**in one's heart of hearts,** in one's deepest thoughts or feelings; really.
**lay to heart, a** keep in mind; remember. **b** think seriously about.
**near one's heart,** of great value or interest to one.
**take heart,** be encouraged.
**take to heart,** think seriously about; be deeply affected by; grieve over.
**wear one's heart on one's sleeve,** show one's feelings too plainly.
**with all one's heart, a** sincerely. **b** gladly.
☛ *Hom.* HART.

**heart·ache** (härt′āk′) sorrow; grief. *n.*
**heart attack** a sudden destruction of muscle tissue in the heart, especially when caused by an interruption of the blood supply to the tissue due to a clot in a coronary artery.
**heart·beat** (härt′bēt′) a pulsation of the heart, including one complete contraction and dilation. *n.*
**heart·break** (härt′brāk′) a crushing sorrow or grief. *n.*
**heart·break·ing** (härt′brā′king) crushing with sorrow or grief. *adj.*
**heart·bro·ken** (härt′brō′kən) crushed with sorrow or grief. *adj.* —**heart′bro′ken·ly,** *adv.*
**heart·burn** (härt′bėrn′) a burning sensation in the lower chest and the stomach, generally caused by digestive juices escaping from the stomach up into the esophagus. *n.*
**heart·burn·ing** (härt′bėr′ning) a feeling of envy or jealousy. *n.*
**heart·ed** (här′tid) having a heart of a certain kind (used only in compounds): *good-hearted, light-hearted. adj.*
**heart·en** (här′tən) encourage; cheer up: *Good news heartens you. v.*
**heart·felt** (härt′felt′) sincere; genuine: *The shipwrecked sailor gave heartfelt thanks to his rescuer. adj.*
**hearth** (härth) **1** the floor of a fireplace. **2** the home; fireside: *The traveller longed for his own hearth. n.*
**hearth·side** (härth′sīd′) **1** the side of a hearth. **2** home. *n.*
**hearth·stone** (härth′stōn′) **1** a stone forming a hearth. **2** the home; fireside. *n.*

**heart·i·ly** (här′tə lē) **1** sincerely; genuinely; in a warm, friendly way: *to express good wishes very heartily.* **2** with enthusiasm; with a good will; vigorously: *to set to work heartily.* **3** with a good appetite: *Most active girls eat heartily.* **4** very; completely; thoroughly: *I'm heartily sick of his complaining. adv.*
**heart·i·ness** (här′tē nis) **1** sincerity. **2** warmth: *The heartiness of his laugh was pleasant. n.*
**heart·less** (härt′lis) without kindness or sympathy; unfeeling; cruel. *adj.* —**heart′less·ly,** *adv.* —**heart′less·ness,** *n.*
**heart–rend·ing** (härt′ren′ding) causing mental anguish; very distressing. *adj.* —**heart′-rend′ing·ly,** *adv.*
**hearts ease** or **heart's–ease** (härt′sēz′) **1** peace of mind. **2** WILD PANSY. *n.*
**heart·sick** (härt′sik′) sick at heart; very much depressed; very unhappy. *adj.*
**heart·sore** (härt′sôr′) feeling or showing grief; grieved. *adj.*
**heart–strick·en** (härt′strik′ən) struck to the heart with grief; shocked with fear; dismayed. *adj.*
**heart·strings** (härt′stringz′) deepest feelings; strongest affections. *n.pl.*
**heart–to–heart** (härt′tə härt′) without reserve; frank; sincere: *a heart-to-heart talk. adj.*
**heart·wood** (härt′wůd′) the hard, central wood of a tree. *n.*
**heart·y** (här′tē) **1** warm and friendly; genuine; sincere: *a hearty welcome.* **2** strong and well; vigorous: *The old woman was still hale and hearty.* **3** full of energy and enthusiasm; not restrained: *He burst out in a loud, hearty laugh.* **4** with plenty to eat; nourishing: *A hearty meal satisfied her hunger.* **5** requiring or using much food: *a hearty eater.* **6** a fellow sailor; a brave and good comrade. 1–5 *adj.,* **heart·i·er, heart·i·est;** 6 *n., pl.* **heart·ies.** —**heart′i·ness,** *n.*
**heat** (hēt) **1** hotness; high temperature. **2** the degree of hotness; temperature. **3** the sensation or perception of hotness or warmth. **4** in physics, a form of energy that consists of the motion of the molecules of a substance. The rate at which the molecules move determines the temperature. **5** make hot or warm; become hot or warm. **6** the hot weather: *the heat of summer.* **7** warmth or intensity of feeling; anger; violence; excitement; eagerness; ardour: *He replied with great heat that he had never been so insulted.* **8** fill with strong feeling; inflame; excite; become excited. **9** the hottest point; most violent or active state: *In the heat of the fight he lost his temper.* **10** one trial in a race: *She won the first heat, but lost the final race.* **11** one operation of heating in a furnace or a forge. 1–4, 6, 7, 9–11 *n.,* 5, 8 *v.*
**heat barrier** THERMAL BARRIER.
**heat·ed** (hē′tid) **1** angry or excited: *a heated debate, a heated reply.* **2** pt. and pp. of HEAT. 1 *adj.,* 2 *v.* —**heat·ed·ly,** *adv.*
**heat·er** (hē′tər) a device that gives heat or warmth, especially one that is not part of a central heating system: *an electric baseboard heater. They have a block heater for their car. n.*
**heath** (hēth) **1** open wasteland with heather or low bushes growing on it; moor: *A heath has few or no trees.* **2** any of a family of shrubs and plants, especially any of

several evergreen shrubs of this family that grow on such land: *Common heather is a species of heath.*  3 referring to a family of woody plants: *The heath family includes the blueberry, cranberry, heather, and rhododendrons.*  *n.*
**one's native heath,**  the place where one was born or brought up.

**hea·then** (hē′ᴛʜən)  1 a person who does not believe in the God of the Bible; person who is not a Christian, Jew, or Moslem.  2 of or having to do with heathens or their religion or customs: *heathen temples.*  3 a person who is thought to have no religion or culture.  4 not religious or cultured; unenlightened.  *n., pl.* **hea·thens** or **hea·then.**
☞ *Etym.*  From OE *hǽthen* 'heath dwellers', with the suggestion of their being savage or uncivilized. See also note at PAGAN.
☞ *Usage.*  Both **heathen** and PAGAN have a basic connotation of 'unenlightened' or 'unbelieving'. People belonging to established religions other than Christian, Jewish, and Moslem object to being called pagan. **Heathen,** in particular, is sometimes used as a term of insult. The words, therefore, are best used in historical contexts: *Julius Caesar was a pagan. The Goths were heathen.*

**hea·then·dom** (hē′ᴛʜən dəm)  1 heathen worship or ways.  2 heathen lands or people.  *n.*

**hea·then·ish** (hē′ᴛʜə nish)  resembling or characteristic of the heathen; barbarous.  *adj.*

**hea·then·ism** (hē′ᴛʜə niz′əm)  1 heathen worship or ways.  2 the lack of religion or culture; barbarism.  *n.*

**heath·er** (heᴛʜ′ər)  any of several species of evergreen shrub characteristic of a heath, especially the common heather of the north, having clusters of tiny, bell-shaped, usually purplish-pink flowers: *Heather is common in the British Isles.*  *n.*

**heath·er·y** (heᴛʜ′ə rē)  1 of or like heather. 2 covered with heather.  *adj.*

**heating element**  the part of an electrical heating device that gets hot.

**heat lightning**  flashes of light without any thunder, seen near the horizon, especially on hot summer evenings.

**heat pump**  a device using mechanical energy to transfer heat from one place or space to another one that is at a higher temperature: *A heat pump can be used to heat a house in winter when the air is warmer inside, and to cool it in summer when the air is warmer outside.*

**heat shield**  a coating or covering of special material on the nose cone of a missile or spacecraft to protect it from the heat produced when it re-enters the earth's atmosphere.

**heat·stroke** (hēt′strōk′)  a serious illness produced by long exposure to extreme heat and humidity, in which the body temperature rises dangerously high because the sweating system can no longer function to cool the body.  *n.*

**heat wave**  a long period of very hot weather.

**heave** (hēv)  1 lift with force or effort: *She heaved the heavy box into the wagon.*  2 lift and throw: *The sailors heaved the anchor overboard.*  3 pull with force or effort; haul: *They heaved on the rope.*  4 utter with effort: *She heaved a sigh of relief.*  5 rise and fall rhythmically: *The sea was heaving.*  6 rise; swell or bulge: *The ground heaved during the earthquake.*  7 pant: *His chest was heaving from the exertion.*  8 try to vomit; retch.  9 of a ship, move in a certain direction: *A ship hove in sight.* 10 the act or fact of heaving: *With a great heave, they got*

**heathen**  555  **heavy**

hat, āge, fär; let, ēqual, tėrm; it, īce
hot, ōpen, ôrder; oil, out; cup, pùt, rüle
əbove, takən, pencəl, lemən, circəs
ch, child; ng, long; sh, ship
th, thin; ᴛʜ, then; zh, measure

*the dresser into the truck.*  11 **heaves,**  a disease of horses characterized by difficult breathing, coughing, and heaving of the flanks (used with a singular verb).  1–9 *v.,* **heaved** or (*esp. in nautical use*) **hove, heav·ing;**  10, 11 *n.* —**heav′er,** *n.*

**heave ho!**  a sailor's cry when pulling up the anchor, or pulling on any rope or cable.
**heave in sight,**  come into view.
**heave to,**  stop a ship; stop.

**heav·en** (hev′ən)  1 in Christian religious use, the place where God and His angels live and where the blessed go after death: *Heaven is usually thought of as beyond the sky.*  Compare with HELL.  2 a place or condition of greatest happiness: *It was heaven just to be able to relax after the uproar.*  3 **Heaven,**  God; Providence: *They felt it was the will of Heaven.*  4 Usually, **heavens,** *pl.*  the space that appears to be a dome over the earth, in which the sun, moon, and stars are seen; sky: *Millions of stars were shining in the heavens.*  *n.*
**for heaven's sake!** or **good heavens!**  an exclamation of surprise or protest.
**move heaven and earth,**  do everything possible.

**heav·en·ly** (hev′ən lē)  1 of or in heaven; divine; holy: *heavenly choirs.*  2 like or suitable for heaven; of more than human excellence: *heavenly peace.*  3 *Informal.* delightful; excellent: *a heavenly spot for a picnic, heavenly weather.*  4 of or in the heavens; in the sky: *The sun, moon, stars, planets, and comets are heavenly bodies.*  *adj.* —**heav′en·li·ness,** *n.*

**heav·en·ward** (hev′ən wərd)  toward heaven.  *adv., adj.*

**heav·en·wards** (hev′ən wərdz)  HEAVENWARD.  *adv.*

**heav·i·ly** (hev′ə lē)  in a heavy way or manner: *He fell heavily to the floor.*  *adv.*

**heav·i·ness** (hev′ē nis)  1 the state or condition of being heavy; great mass.  2 sadness: *The loss filled them with heaviness.*  *n.*

**Heav·i·side layer** (hev′ē sīd′)  1 the second, or middle, layer of the ionosphere, which reflects radio waves of frequencies produced in short-wave broadcasting. 2 the ionosphere.
☞ *Etym.*  Named after British physicist Oliver *Heaviside* (1850–1925), who predicted its existence as an explanation for the fact that radio waves follow the earth's curvature instead of travelling in a straight line.

**heav·y** (hev′ē)  1 hard to lift or carry; of great weight: *a heavy load.*  2 having much mass for its size; of great density: *heavy metal.*  3 of more than usual mass for its kind: *heavy silk.*  4 of great amount, force, or intensity; greater than usual; large: *a heavy vote, heavy strain, heavy sea, heavy sleep, heavy rain, heavy meal, heavy crop.* 5 being such in an unusual degree: *a heavy buyer, heavy smoker.*  6 hard to bear or endure: *heavy taxes, a heavy responsibility.*  7 hard to deal with; trying or difficult in any way: *A heavy road is hard to travel over because it is muddy, sandy, etc. A heavy slope is a steep one. Heavy food is hard to digest. Heavy soil is hard to work.*  8 weighted down; laden: *air heavy with moisture. Her eyes were heavy with sleep.*  9 sorrowful; gloomy: *heavy news.*  10 grave;

serious; sober; sombre: *a heavy part in a play.* **11** cloudy: *a heavy sky.* **12** broad; thick; coarse: *a heavy line, heavy features.* **13** clumsy; sluggish; slow: *a heavy walk.* **14** ponderous; dull: *heavy reading.* **15** loud and deep: *the heavy roar of cannon.* **16** in military use, heavily armed or equipped: *heavy tanks.* **17** in military use, of large size: *heavy artillery.* **18** not risen enough: *heavy bread.* **19** in physics, referring to an isotope possessing a greater atomic weight than the most abundant isotope of the same element: *heavy water.* **20** a heavy person or thing. **21** in a heavy manner; heavily. **22** *Informal.* the villain in a play. **23** *Informal.* emotionally involving. 1–19, 23 *adj.*, **heav·i·er, heav·i·est;** 20, 22 *n.*, *pl.* **heav·ies;** 21 *adv.*

**hang heavy,** of time, pass slowly and boringly: *She had nothing to do, and time was hanging heavy on her hands.*

**heavy with child,** pregnant, especially in the last months of pregnancy.

**heav·y-du·ty** (hev′ē dyü′tē *or* hev′ē dü′tē) durably built to withstand unusual strain or very hard use: *a heavy-duty vacuum cleaner.* *adj.*

**heav·y-hand·ed** (hev′ē han′did) **1** clumsy; awkward: *Her heavy-handed attempts at humour were embarrassing.* **2** harsh; cruel. *adj.*

**heav·y-heart·ed** (hev′ē här′tid) sad; gloomy; in low spirits. *adj.*

**heavy hydrogen** an isotope of hydrogen having a mass number of 2; deuterium: *Heavy hydrogen has one proton and one neutron in its nucleus, while ordinary hydrogen has no neutrons.* Symbol: D or $^2$H

**heav·y·set** (hev′ē set′) of a sturdy, compact, and often stout build: *a heavyset man.* *adj.*

**heavy water** water composed of oxygen and heavy hydrogen, represented by the formula $D_2O$, present in very small quantities in ordinary water: *If ordinary water is electrolysed, the percentage of heavy water in it is increased. Heavy water is used in nuclear power plants to moderate and control nuclear reactions.*

**heav·y·weight** (hev′ē wāt′) **1** a person or thing of much more than average mass. **2** a boxer weighing more than 81 kilograms. **3** *Informal.* a person of great importance or influence: *a heavyweight in the political field.* *n.*

**He·bra·ic** (hi brā′ik) of or having to do with the Hebrews or their language or culture; Hebrew. *adj.*

**He·brew** (hē′brü) **1** a member of any of a group of Semitic peoples of ancient Palestine, especially an Israelite. **2** a descendant of any of these peoples, especially the Israelites. **3** the Semitic language of the ancient Hebrews. **4** the modern form of this language, one of the official languages of present-day Israel. **5** of or having to do with the Hebrews or their language. 1–4 *n.*, 5 *adj.*

**hec·a·tomb** (hek′ə tōm′) **1** in ancient Greece and Rome, the sacrifice of 100 oxen or cattle at one time. **2** any great slaughter. *n.*

**heck·le** (hek′əl) harass and annoy a speaker, etc. by asking bothersome questions, etc. *v.*, **heck·led, heck·ling.** —**heck′ler,** *n.*

**hect–** (hekt) an SI prefix, a form of HECTO– used before a vowel.

**hec·tare** (hek′ter *or* hek′tär) a unit used with the SI for measuring land area, equal to 10 000 square metres. Symbol: ha *n.*

**hec·tic** (hek′tik) **1** filled with or characterized by great excitement or confusion: *a hectic life. We spent three hectic days packing for the move.* **2** showing signs of a fever: *a hectic flush, hectic cheeks.* **3** of or referring to the fever characteristic of such diseases as tuberculosis: *hectic fever, a hectic cough.* **4** CONSUMPTIVE (def. 1). *adj.*

**hecto–** (hek′tə) an SI prefix meaning hundred: *A hectometre is one hundred metres.* Symbol: h

**hec·to·met·re** (hek′tom′ē tər) a measure of length equal to one hundred metres. *n.*

**hec·tor** (hek′tər) **1** a bragging, bullying fellow. **2** bluster; bully. 1 *n.*, 2 *v.*

**he'd** (hēd; *unstressed*, ēd, id, *or* hid) **1** he had. **2** he would.
☛ *Hom.* HEED (for the stressed pronunciation of **he'd**); HID (for the third unstressed pronunciation).

**hedge** (hej) **1** a thick row of bushes or small trees, planted as a fence or boundary. **2** any barrier or boundary. **3** enclose or separate with a hedge; put a hedge around or along: *to hedge a garden.* **4** avoid giving a direct answer; evade questions; avoid taking a definite stand: *Stop hedging and tell us what you want to do.* **5** the act of hedging. **6** protect oneself from losing money on a bet, investment, etc. by making other bets, investments, etc. as a counterbalance. 1, 2, 5 *n.*, 3, 4, 6 *v.*, **hedged, hedg·ing.**

**hedge in,** **a** hem in; surround on all sides: *The town was hedged in by mountains and a forest.* **b** keep from getting away or moving freely.

A hedgehog— about 23 cm long

**hedge·hog** (hej′hog′) **1** any of a closely related group of small mammals of Europe, Asia, and Africa, having a short tail, long nose, and short, thick, sharp spines on the back: *When attacked or frightened, hedgehogs roll up into a bristling ball.* **2** the porcupine of North America. *n.*

**hedge-hop** (hej′hop′) fly an aircraft very low. *v.*, **hedge-hopped, hedge-hop·ping.** —**hedge′-hop′per,** *n.*

**hedge-hop·ping** (hej′hop′ing) **1** flying an aircraft very low. **2** ppr. of HEDGE-HOP. 1 *n.*, 2 *v.*

**hedge·row** (hej′rō′) a thick row of bushes or small trees forming a hedge. *n.*

**he·don·ism** (hē′də niz′əm) the doctrine that pleasure or happiness is the highest good. *n.*

**he·don·ist** (hē′də nist) a person who believes in or practises HEDONISM. *n.*

**heed** (hēd) **1** give careful attention to; take notice of: *Now heed what I say.* **2** careful attention; notice: *She went on as before, paying no heed to the warning signal.* 1 *v.*, 2 *n.* —**heed′er,** *n.*
☛ *Hom.* HE'D (hēd).

**heed·ful** (hēd′fəl) careful; mindful; attentive. *adj.* —**heed′ful·ly,** *adv.* —**heed′ful·ness,** *n.*

**heed·less** (hē′dlis) careless; thoughtless: *Heedless of traffic, the girl ran across the busy highway.* *adj.* —**heed′less·ly,** *adv.* —**heed′less·ness,** *n.*

**hee·haw** (hē′hô′) **1** the braying sound made by a donkey. **2** make the braying sound of a donkey. **3** a loud, coarse laugh. **4** laugh loudly and coarsely. *1, 3 n., 2, 4 v.*

**heel**¹ (hēl) **1** the back part of a person's foot, below the ankle. **2** the part of a stocking or shoe that covers the heel. **3** the part of a shoe or boot that is under the heel or raises the heel. **4** the part of the hind leg of an animal that corresponds to a person's heel. **5** follow closely behind someone: *I'm teaching my dog to heel.* **6** put a heel or heels on. **7** touch or drive forward with the heel or as if with the heel: *She heeled the horse.* **8** *Informal.* an untrustworthy or contemptible person. **9** anything shaped, used, or placed at an end like a heel: *The end crust of a loaf of bread is sometimes called a heel.* *1–4, 8, 9 n., 5–7 v.* —**heel′·less,** *adj.*
**at heel,** near the heels; close behind.
**cool one's heels,** *Informal.* be kept waiting a long time: *She was left cooling her heels for an hour in the waiting room.*
**down at the heel** or **heels, a** of a shoe or shoes, with the heels worn down. **b** in a shabby or run-down condition: *The whole place looked very down at the heel.*
**kick up one's heels,** behave in a merry and exuberant way; have fun: *She really kicked up her heels at the party.*
**lay by the heels,** put in prison or in stocks.
**out at the heels, a** with the heel of the stocking or shoe worn through. **b** shabby and run-down.
**show a clean pair of heels,** run away.
**take to one's heels,** run away.
**to heel, a** near the heels; close behind: *The dog walked to heel.* **b** under control: *He soon brought the mutineers to heel.*
☛ *Hom.* HEAL, HE'LL (hĕl).

**heel**² (hēl) **1** lean over to one side; tilt; tip: *The ship heeled as it turned.* **2** the act of heeling. *1 v., 2 n.*
☛ *Hom.* HEAL, HE'LL (hĕl).

**heft** (heft) *Informal.* **1** mass or heaviness. **2** judge the mass or heaviness of by lifting: *She hefted the baseball bat to get the feel of it.* **3** lift; heave. *1 n., 2, 3 v.*

**heft·y** (hef′tē) *Informal.* **1** weighty; heavy: *That's a hefty load.* **2** large; considerable: *They got a hefty bill for repairs.* **3** big and strong. *adj.*, **heft·i·er, heft·i·est.**

**he·gem·o·ny** (hi jem′ə nē *or* hej′ə mō′nē) political domination; especially, leadership or domination by one state over others in a group. *n., pl.* **he·gem·o·nies.**

**He·gi·ra** (hi jī′rə) **1** the flight of Mohammed from Mecca to Medina in A.D. 622. The Moslems use a calendar reckoned from this date. **2** the Moslem era. **3** *hegira,* a journey, especially to escape; flight. *n.* Also, **Hejira.**

**heif·er** (hef′ər) a young cow that has not had a calf. *n.*

**heigh** (hī *or* hā) a sound used to attract attention, give encouragement, express surprise, etc. *interj.*

**heigh–ho** (hī′hō′ *or* hā′hō′) a sound made to express surprise, boredom, weariness, etc. *interj.*

**height** (hīt) **1** the measurement from top to bottom; the tallness of anyone or anything; the point to which anything rises above ground: *My father's height is 187 centimetres.* **2** the distance above sea level. **3** a fairly great distance up: *rising at a height above the valley.* **4** a high point or place; hill: *the height overlooking the river, on the mountain heights.* **5** the highest part; top: *She reached the height of her career by the age of forty.* **6** the highest point; greatest degree: *the height of folly.* **7** high rank; high degree. *n.*

hat, āge, fär; let, ēqual, tėrm; it, īce
hot, ōpen, ôrder; oil, out; cup, put, rüle
above, takən, pencəl, lemən, circəs
ch, child; ng, long; sh, ship
th, thin; ŦH, then; zh, measure

**height·en** (hīt′ən) **1** make or become higher. **2** make or become stronger, greater, more intense, etc.: *The background music heightened the feeling of suspense.* *v.*

**height of land** **1** a region higher than its surroundings. **2** *Cdn.* a watershed; DIVIDE (def. 6): *A height of land marks the boundary between Labrador and Quebec.* *n.*

**Heimlich manoeuvre** an emergency procedure used to dislodge food from a person's airway by pressing one's fist into the victim's abdomen, and giving upward thrusts.
☛ *Etym.* From its inventor, H. J. *Heimlich,* an American doctor.

**hei·nous** (hā′nəs *or* hē′nəs) very wicked; atrocious; abominable: *a heinous murder.* *adj.* —**hei′nous·ly,** *adv.* —**hei′nous·ness,** *n.*

**heir** (er) **1** a person who receives, or has the right to receive, someone's property or title after the death of its owner; a person who inherits property. **2** a person who inherits anything; a person who receives or has something from someone before him or her. *n.*
☛ *Hom.* AIR, ERR (er).

**heir apparent** a person who will be the first to succeed to a property or title: *The Queen's oldest son is heir apparent to the throne.* *pl.* **heirs apparent.**

**heir·ess** (er′is) **1** a female heir. **2** a female heir to great wealth. *n.*

**heir·loom** (er′lüm′) a special possession handed down from generation to generation: *This clock is a family heirloom.* *n.*

**heir presumptive** a person who will be heir unless someone with a stronger claim is born. *pl.* **heirs presumptive.**

**heir·ship** (er′ship) the position or rights of an heir; right of inheritance; inheritance. *n.*

**He·ji·ra** (hi jī′rə) See HEGIRA. *n.*

**held** (held) pt. and pp. of HOLD¹: *David held the baby. The swing is held by strong ropes.* *v.*

**hel·i·cal** (hel′ə kəl) having to do with, or having the form of, a HELIX (def. 1); spiral. *adj.*

**hel·i·ces** (hel′ə sēz′) a pl. of HELIX. *n.*

**hel·i·con** (hel′ə kon′) a large bass tuba having a circular spiral shape designed for placing around the body of the player. *n.*

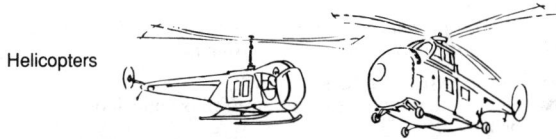

Helicopters

**hel·i·cop·ter** (hel′ə kop′tər) **1** an aircraft having one or more horizontal propellers, or rotors, by means of which it can hover, take off and land vertically, and move forward, backward, or sideways in the air. **2** travel or carry by helicopter. *1 n., 2 v.*

■ *Etym.* From F *hélicoptère* which was formed from Gk. *heliko* 'spiral' + *ptéron* 'wing'. 19c.

**he·li·o·cen·tric** (hē′lē ō sen′trik) **1** viewed or measured from the centre of the sun. **2** having or representing the sun as a centre: *The Copernican system of astronomy is heliocentric.* Compare with GEOCENTRIC. *adj.*

**he·li·o·graph** (hē′lē ə graf′) **1** a device for signalling by means of a movable mirror that flashes beams of light to a distance: *The flashes of the mirror of a heliograph represent the dots and dashes of the Morse code.* **2** communicate or signal by heliograph. **3** an apparatus for taking photographs of the sun. 1, 3 *n.*, 2 *v.*

**he·li·o·trope** (hē′lē ə trōp′) **1** any of a closely related group of herbs or shrubs of the borage family having spikes or clusters of small white, lilac, or blue flowers that always turn to face the sun: *The common heliotrope is a popular garden plant having oval, wrinkled leaves and clusters of lilac or blue flowers with a fragrance like vanilla.* **2** the common valerian, also called GARDEN HELIOTROPE (def. 2). **3** reddish purple. **4** bloodstone, a semiprecious stone. 1–4 *n.*, 3 *adj.*

**he·li·ot·ro·pism** (hē′lē ot′rə piz′əm) of certain plants and other organisms, a tendency to respond to sunlight by turning or bending toward it or away from it: *Sunflowers exhibit positive heliotropism; that is, the flowers turn toward the sunlight.* *n.*

**hel·i·pad** (hel′ə pad′) a small piece of level surface for helicopters to land or take off. *n.*

**hel·i·port** (hel′ə pôrt′) a place for helicopters to land or take off: *Heliports are sometimes built on rooftops.* *n.*

**he·li·um** (hē′lē əm) a very light, colourless, inert gas that will not burn, much used in balloons and dirigibles: *Helium is a rare element, first discovered in the sun's atmosphere.* Symbol: He *n.*

**he·lix** (hē′liks) **1** a spiral: *A screw thread and a watch spring are helices.* **2** in architecture, an ornamental spiral as on the capital of a Corinthian or Ionic column. **3** the rim of the outer ear. *n.*, *pl.* **hel·i·ces** or **he·lix·es.**

**hell** (hel) **1** in religious use, the home of the devil, where wicked persons suffer eternal punishment after death: *Hell is usually thought of as below or within the earth.* Compare with HEAVEN (def. 1). **2** the abode of the dead. **3** a place or state of wickedness, torment, or misery: *War is hell.* **4** *Informal.* a severe scolding, punishment, etc.: *His mother gave him hell for being so rude.* **5** *Informal.* wild, mischievous spirits: *The kids were full of hell that day.* *n.*

**come hell or high water,** whatever difficulties or problems arise: *I'm going, come hell or high water.*

**hell and high water,** extreme difficulties or problems, whatever they may be: *She will keep her word through hell and high water.*

**raise hell,** *Informal.* cause trouble; make a disturbance: *The disgruntled prisoners started raising hell.*

**he'll** (hēl; *unstressed*, hil) he will.
■ *Hom.* HEAL, HEEL (for the stressed pronunciation of he'll).

**hell·cat** (hel′kat′) **1** a mean, spiteful woman. **2** a WITCH¹.

**hel·le·bore** (hel′ə bôr′) **1** any of a genus of poisonous plants of the buttercup family, especially the **black hellebore,** an evergreen plant having showy white or pinkish flowers. **2** the dried underground stem of the black hellebore, or an extract from it, formerly used in medicine. **3** any of various poisonous, north temperate plants of the lily family. **4** the dried underground stem of this plant, or an extract made from it. *n.*

**Hel·lene** (hel′ēn) a Greek. *n.*

**Hel·len·ic** (he len′ik) **1** a Greek. **2** of Greek history, language, or culture from about 776 B.C. to the death of Alexander the Great in 323 B.C. *adj.*

**hell·fire** (hel′fīr′) the fire of hell; punishment in hell. *n.*

**hell·gram·mite** (hel′grə mīt′) the larva of a DOBSON FLY, often used for fish bait. *n.*

**hell·hole** (hel′hōl′) *Informal.* a dreadful place; a place of great discomfort, filth, squalor, etc. *n.*

**hell·ion** (hel′yən) *Informal.* a very mischievous or troublesome person. *n.*

**hell·ish** (hel′ish) **1** fit to have come from hell; devilish; fiendish. **2** of hell. *adj.* —**hell′ish·ly,** *adv.* —**hell′ish·ness,** *n.*

**hel·lo** (he lō′ or hə lō′) **1** an exclamation to attract attention or to express a greeting or surprise. **2** a call of greeting or surprise, or to attract attention: *The girl gave a loud hello to tell us where she was.* **3** shout; call. 1 *interj.*, 2 *n.*, *pl.* **hel·los;** 3 *v.*, **he·lloed, hel·lo·ing.**

**helm** (helm) **1** the handle or wheel by which a ship is steered. **2** a position of control or guidance: *The situation began to improve soon after the new director took over the helm.* *n.* —**helm′less,** *adj.*

Helmets worn by a knight, a football player, and an astronaut

**hel·met** (hel′mit) a covering to protect the head: *Knights wore helmets as part of their armour. Soldiers wear steel helmets; firefighters wear fireproof plastic helmets. Motorcyclists must wear crash helmets.* See ARMOUR for another picture. *n.* —**hel′met·like′,** *adj.*

**hel·minth** (hel′minth) an intestinal worm, such as the tapeworm, roundworm, etc. *n.*

**helms·man** (helm′zmən) the person at the helm of a ship. *n.*, *pl.* **helms·men** (-zmən).

**help** (help) **1** provide with what is needed or useful: *to help a person with one's money.* **2** anything done or given in helping: *Your advice is a great help.* **3** aid; assist: *to help someone with his or her work.* **4** give aid or assistance: *We could finish the job faster if she would help.* **5** aid; assistance: *I need some help with my work.* **6** a person or thing that helps; helper. **7** a hired helper or group of hired helpers: *The storekeeper treats his help well.* **8** wait on or serve in a store, etc.: *"May I help you?"* asked the clerk. **9** make better; relieve: *This medicine might help your cough.* **10** a means of making better; remedy. **11** prevent; stop: *It can't be helped.* **12** a means of preventing or stopping. **13** avoid; keep from: *She can't help yawning.* 1, 3, 4, 8, 9, 11, 13 *v.*, 2, 5–7, 10, 12 *n.*

**cannot help but,** cannot avoid, cannot fail to: *I cannot help but admire her endurance.*

**help oneself,** **a** take what one wishes, etc.: *Help yourself*

to a drink while you wait. **b** control oneself: *She couldn't help herself.*
**help out,** give temporary help.
**so help me** or **so help me God,** as I solemnly promise; as I speak the truth.

**help·er** (hel′pər) a person or thing that helps, especially a person who assists or supports another. *n.*

**help·ful** (help′fəl) giving help; useful. *adj.* —**help′ful·ly,** *adv.* —**help′ful·ness,** *n.*

**help·ing** (hel′ping) **1** the portion of food served to a person at one time: *He had two helpings of dessert.* **2** ppr. of HELP. 1 *n.*, 2 *v.*

**help·less** (hel′plis) **1** not able to help oneself; weak. **2** without help, protection, etc. *adj.* —**help′less·ly,** *adv.* —**help′less·ness,** *n.*

**help·mate** (help′māt′) a companion and helper, especially a wife or husband. *n.*

**help·meet** (help′mēt′) HELPMATE. *n.*

**hel·ter–skel·ter** (hel′tər skel′tər) **1** with headlong, disorderly haste: *The children ran helter-skelter when the dog rushed at them.* **2** noisy and disorderly haste, confusion, etc. **3** carelessly hurried; disorderly; confused. **4** a ride at an amusement park; a spiral slide around a building. 1 *adv.*, 2, 4 *n.*, 3 *adj.*

Hems on a serviette and a skirt

**hem¹** (hem) **1** a finished border or edge on an article made of cloth; especially, an edge made by folding the cloth over and sewing it down: *The skirt has a narrow hem.* **2** fold over and sew down the edge of: *I hemmed the serviettes by hand.* **3** any rim or margin. 1, 3 *n.*, 2 *v.*, **hemmed, hem·ming.**
**hem in, around,** or **about,** **a** surround on all sides. **b** keep from getting away or moving freely.

**hem²** (hem) **1** a word used to attract attention or to show doubt or hesitation. **2** make a sound like that of clearing the throat: *"Uh...," she hemmed, and then kept quiet.* 1 *n.*, 2 *v.*, **hemmed, hem·ming.**
**hem and haw,** hesitate in order to avoid committing oneself; stall: *The committee hemmed and hawed for several weeks and then turned the problem over to a subcommittee.*

**hem·a·tite** (hem′ə tīt′ or hē′mə tīt′) an important iron ore that is reddish-brown when powdered. *n.*

**hemi–** a prefix meaning half, as in *hemisphere.*

**he·mip·ter·an** (hi mip′tə rən) **1** a HEMIPTEROUS insect. **2** of or referring to an order comprising these insects. 1 *n.*, 2 *adj.*
☞ Usage. See note at HETEROPTEROUS.

**he·mip·ter·ous** (hi mip′tə rəs) **1** of or having to do with a large order (**Hemiptera**) of sucking insects that includes the heteropterans (the "true bugs", such as the bedbug) and the homopterans (scale insects, aphids, etc.). **2** of or having to do with heteropterans; heteropterous. *adj.*
☞ Usage. See note at HETEROPTEROUS.

**hem·i·sphere** (hem′ə sfēr′) **1** half of a sphere or globe. **2** half of the earth's surface: *North America and South America are in the Western Hemisphere. Europe, Asia, Africa, and Australia are in the Eastern Hemisphere. All countries north of the equator are in the Northern Hemisphere.* See MERCATOR PROJECTION for picture. *n.*

**hem·i·spher·i·cal** (hem′ə sfer′ə kəl) **1** shaped like a hemisphere. **2** of a hemisphere. *adj.*

**hem·i·stich** (hem′ə stik′) half a line of verse, especially one separated from the rest of the line by a CAESURA. *n.*

**hem·lock** (hem′lok) **1** any of a group of about 10 closely related species of evergreen tree of the pine family found in North America and eastern Asia, having hanging cones, needle-like leaves growing spirally along the stem, and bark that is rich in tannin: *The three species of hemlock native to Canada are the western hemlock, mountain hemlock, and eastern hemlock.* **2** the relatively hard wood of any of these trees. **3** a poisonous European plant of the same family as the carrot and parsley, having spotted stems, finely divided leaves, and small, white flowers. **4** a poison made from this plant. *n.*

**hemo–** combining form. blood.

**he·mo·glo·bin** (hē′mə glō′bən or hem′ə glō′bən) the protein matter in the red corpuscles of the blood of vertebrates, which carries oxygen from the lungs to the tissues and carbon dioxide from the tissues to the lungs. *n.* Also, **haemoglobin.**

**he·mo·phil·i·a** (hē′mə fil′ē ə or hem′ə fil′ē ə) an inherited condition in which the blood does not clot normally, resulting in excessive bleeding after the slightest cut. *n.* Also, **haemophilia.**

**he·mo·phil·i·ac** (hē′mə fil′ē ak′ or hem′ə fil′ē ak′) a person suffering from HEMOPHILIA. *n.* Also, **haemophiliac.**

**hem·or·rhage** (hem′ə rij) **1** a discharge of blood from the blood vessels, especially a heavy discharge. **2** suffer from a heavy or uncontrollable bleeding. 1 *n.*, 2 *v.*, **hem·or·rhaged, hem·or·rhag·ing.** Also, **haemorrhage.**

**hem·or·rhoid** (hem′ə roid′) Usually, **hemorrhoids,** *pl.* swollen tissue near the anus caused by the dilation of blood vessels: *Hemorrhoids are painful.* *n.* Also, **haemorrhoid.**

**hemp** (hemp) **1** a tall Asiatic plant whose tough fibres are made into heavy string, rope, coarse cloth, etc. **2** the tough fibres of this plant. **3** hashish, marijuana, or some other drug obtained from the female hemp plant. *n.*

**hemp·en** (hem′pən) of, made of, or resembling HEMP (defs. 1, 2). *adj.*

**hem·stitch** (hem′stich′) **1** an ornamental stitch made by pulling out several parallel threads at or near a hem and gathering the remaining cross threads into small bunches. See EMBROIDERY for picture. **2** ornamental needlework made in this way. **3** hem or decorate with hemstitch. 1, 2 *n.*, 3 *v.*

**hen** (hen) **1** the adult female of the domestic fowl. **2** the adult female of certain other birds and a few animals

such as the lobster: *a hen sparrow, a hen lobster.* n.
—**hen′like′,** adj.
**like a hen with one chicken,** Informal.   very fussy.
**scarce as hens' teeth,** Informal.   very scarce.

**hen·bane** (hen′bān′)   a poisonous plant of the nightshade family native to Europe and Asia but now growing in North America, having large, sticky, hairy leaves and funnel-shaped yellowish flowers and having a strong, unpleasant smell: *Henbane yields several powerful drugs used in medicine.* n.

**hence** (hens)   **1** as a result of this; therefore: *The attempts to raise money have failed; hence the project will have to be abandoned.*   **2** from now; from this time onward: *A year hence, the incident will have been forgotten.*   **3** from here; away: *She went hence many years ago.*   **4** from this world or life.   **5** from this source or origin: *Hence came several problems.* adv.

**hence·forth** (hens′fôrth′)   from this time on; from now on.   adv.

**hence·for·ward** (hens′fôr′wərd)   HENCEFORTH. adv.

**hench·man** (hench′mən)   **1** a follower or aide who obeys orders without scruple: *He had one of his henchmen collect the blackmail money.*   **2** a trusted attendant or follower.   n., pl. **hench·men** (-mən).
☛ Etym. From OE *hengest, hengst* 'male horse' + *man.* The original meaning may have been 'horse attendant'; a later meaning was 'page, squire'. The unfavourable sense of definition 1 seems to have developed in the 19c.

**hen·coop** (hen′küp′)   a coop for poultry.   n.

**hen·house** (hen′hous′)   a house for poultry.   n.

**hen·na** (hen′ə)   **1** a small shrub of the LOOSESTRIFE family found in Africa, the Mediterranean region, Australia, and Asia, having small, fragrant white flowers and lance-shaped leaves which yield a dark orange-red dye: *Henna is often grown as an ornamental and has become naturalized in the warmer regions of the Western Hemisphere.*   **2** the dye made from the leaves of this shrub: *Henna has been used in different periods since ancient times to colour fingernails, hair, beards, parts of the hands and feet, the manes and hoofs of horses, and also leather, wool, and silk.*   **3** reddish brown.   **4** colour with henna: *hennaed hair.*   1–3 n., 3 adj., 4 v., **hen·naed, hen·na·ing.**

**hen·ner·y** (hen′ə rē)   a place where fowls are kept. n., pl. **hen·ner·ies.**

**hen·pecked** (hen′pekt′)   Informal.   domineered over by one's wife: *He's a tyrant at work, but henpecked at home.* adj.

**hen·ry** (hen′rē)   an SI unit for measuring inductance: *When a current varying at the rate of one ampere per second induces an electromotive force of one volt, the circuit has inductance of one henry.* Symbol: H   n., pl. **hen·rys.**

**he·pat·ic** (hi pat′ik)   **1** of, having to do with, or affecting the liver.   **2** resembling the liver, especially in colour.   adj.

**he·pat·i·ca** (hi pat′ə kə)   any of a closely related group of small, stemless plants of the buttercup family found in wooded areas of the temperate regions of North America, Europe, and Asia, having lobed leaves and purple, blue, pink, or white flowers that bloom in early spring.   n.

**hep·a·ti·tis** (hep′ə tī′tis)   an inflammation of the liver.   n.

**hep·ta·gon** (hep′tə gon′)   a plane figure having seven angles and seven sides.   n.

**hep·tag·o·nal** (hep tag′ə nəl)   in the form of a HEPTAGON.   adj.

**her** (hėr; *unstressed,* hər *or* ər)   **1** the objective form of SHE: *I like her.*   **2** a possessive form of SHE: of, belonging to, or made or done by her or herself: *She raised her hand. Her graduation is next week. That's one of her paintings.*   1 *pron.,* 2 *adj.*
☛ Usage.   **Her** and HERS are possessive forms of **she. Her** is always followed by a noun: *This is her bicycle.* **Hers** stands alone: *This bicycle is hers.*

**her·ald** (her′əld)   **1** in the Middle Ages, in western Europe, an officer who carried messages, made announcements, arranged and supervised tournaments and other public ceremonies, and regulated the use of armorial bearings.   **2** a person who carries official messages, or makes important announcements: *The herald brought the good news.*   **3** bring news of; announce: *The robins heralded the arrival of spring.*   **4** a forerunner; harbinger: *Dawn is the herald of day.*   **5** in Britain, an officer in charge of granting arms and recording arms and pedigrees, who also has important duties in various royal ceremonies. 1, 2, 4, 5 *n.,* 3 *v.*

**he·ral·dic** (he ral′dik)   of or having to do with HERALDRY (def. 1) or heralds.   adj.

**her·ald·ry** (her′əld rē)   **1** the science or art dealing with coats of arms: *Heraldry deals with a person's right to use a coat of arms, the tracing of family descent, the creating of a coat of arms for a new country, etc.*   **2** a heraldic device; collection of such devices.   **3** a coat of arms. **4** the ceremony or pomp connected with the life of noble families; pageantry.   n., pl. **her·ald·ries.**

**herb** (ėrb *or* hėrb)   **1** any flowering plant whose stalk or stem lives only one season: *Herbs do not form woody tissue as shrubs and trees do, though their roots may live many years. Peonies, buttercups, corn, wheat, cabbage, lettuce, etc. are herbs.*   **2** any of many sweet-scented herbs used in medicine, for flavouring food, or for perfumes: *Sage, mint, and lavender are herbs.*   n.

**her·ba·ceous** (hėr bā′shəs)   **1** of or like an herb; having stems that are soft and not woody.   **2** in botany, having the colour, texture, etc. of a leaf: *a flower with herbaceous sepals.*   adj.

**herb·age** (ėr′bij *or* hėr′bij)   **1** herbs collectively, especially grass used for grazing.   **2** the green leaves and soft stems of plants.   n.

**herb·al** (hėr′bəl *or* ėr′bəl)   **1** of, having to do with, or made of herbs: *herbal tea.*   **2** a book about herbs, especially one that describes their uses as medicine. 1 *adj.,* 2 *n.*

**her·bar·i·um** (hėr ber′ē əm)   **1** a collection of dried plants systematically arranged.   **2** a room or building where such a collection is kept.   n., pl. **her·bar·i·ums** or **her·bar·i·a** (-ber′ē ə).

**her·bi·cide** (hėr′bə sīd′)   any chemical substance used to destroy plants or stop their growth.   n.

**her·bi·vore** (hėr′bə vôr′)   any animal that feeds on plants, especially hoofed animals such as cows, horses, or deer.   n.

**her·biv·o·rous** (hėr biv′ə rəs) feeding on grass or other plants: *Cattle are herbivorous animals.* *adj.*

**her·cu·le·an** (hėr′kyə lē′ən *or* hėr kyü′lē ən) **1** requiring or showing great strength or courage; very hard to do: *a herculean task, a herculean effort.* **2** having great strength or courage. **3 Herculean,** of or having to do with Hercules or his labour. *adj.*

**Her·cu·les** (hėr′kyü lēz) **1** in Greek and Roman mythology, a hero famous for his great strength, which allowed him to perform twelve difficult tasks or labours. **2** a northern constellation. **3** any man of great strength. *n.*

**herd** (hėrd) **1** a number of animals of one kind together: *a herd of cows, a herd of horses, a herd of elephants.* **2** people as a mass, group or mob; rabble: *the common herd.* **3** bring or come together in a herd or as if in a herd: *The cattle were herded into the corral. Many animals herd for protection.* **4** drive or take care of cattle, sheep, etc.: *His job is herding sheep.* **5** the keeper of a herd (*usually used in compounds*): *cowherd, goatherd.* 1, 2, 5 *n.*, 3, 4 *v.*
☛ *Hom.* HEARD.

**herd·er** (hėr′dər) HERDSMAN. *n.*

**herds·man** (hėrd′zmən) a manager or keeper of a herd or herds of animals. *n., pl.* **herds·men** (-zmən).

**here** (hėr) **1** in or at this place: *Put it down here. We have lived here for two years.* **2** to this place: *Come here.* **3** this place: *Here is a good place to stop. Fill the bottle up to here.* **4** at this point in argument, conversation, etc.: *Here the speaker paused.* **5** an answer showing that one is present when roll is called. **6** an exclamation expressing indignation, rebuke, etc.: *Here! Give me that! Here, that's not the way to talk!* **7** a word used to call attention to the presence of a person or thing mentioned: *Here is your scarf. Al here could probably tell you where they are.* **8** on earth; in this life. **9** this life. 1, 2, 4, 7, 8 *adv.*, 3, 5, 9 *n.*, 6 *interj.*
**here and there,** in various places; at scattered intervals: *Here and there we saw an early crocus blooming.*
**here, there, and everywhere,** in many different places: *There were toys here, there, and everywhere throughout the house.*
**neither here nor there,** not to the point; off the subject; unimportant: *Why he took it is neither here nor there; what we want to know is what he did with it.*
☛ *Hom.* HEAR.

**here·a·bout** (hēr′ə bout′) around here; about this place; near here: *There are several points of historic interest hereabout.* *adv.*

**here·a·bouts** (hēr′ə bouts′) HEREABOUT. *adv.*

**here·af·ter** (hē raf′tər) **1** after this; in the future. **2** in life after death. **3 the hereafter, a** the future. **b** life after death. 1, 2 *adv.*, 3 *n.*

**here·by** (hėr bī′) by this means; in this way: *The licence read, "You are hereby given the right to hunt in Ontario."* *adv.*

**he·red·i·ta·ble** (hə red′ə tə bəl) that can be inherited. *adj.*

**he·red·i·tar·y** (hə red′ə ter′ē) **1** coming by inheritance: *Prince is a hereditary title.* **2** holding a position by inheritance: *The Queen is a hereditary ruler.* **3** in biology, transmitted or caused by heredity: *Colour blindness is hereditary.* Compare with CONGENITAL. **4** derived from one's parents or ancestors; established by tradition: *hereditary beliefs, a hereditary enemy.* **5** of or having to do with inheritance or heredity. *adj.*

## herbivorous 561 hermaphrodite

hat, āge, fär; let, ēqual, tėrm; it, īce
hot, ōpen, ôrder; oil, out; cup, pút, rüle
əbove, takən, pencəl, lemən, circəs

ch, child; ng, long; sh, ship
th, thin; ŦH, then; zh, measure

**he·red·i·ty** (hə red′ə tē) **1** in biology, the transmission of physical or mental characteristics or qualities from parent to offspring through elements called genes in the chromosomes of the germ cells that produce the offspring. **2** the qualities that have come to offspring from parents. **3** the tendency of offspring to be like the parents. *n., pl.* **he·red·i·ties.**

**Here·ford** (her′ə fərd *or* hėr′fərd) any of a breed of beef cattle having a red body, white face, and white markings on the underside of the body. *n.*

**here·in** (hē rin′) **1** in this place. **2** in this matter or way: *It is herein that the difference lies.* *adv.*

**here·in·af·ter** (hē′rin af′tər) afterward in this document, statement, etc. *adv.*

**here·in·be·fore** (hē rin′bi fôr′) before in this document, statement, etc. *adv.*

**here·in·to** (hē rin′tü) **1** into this place. **2** into this matter. *adv.*

**here·of** (hē rov′ *or* hē ruv′) of or about this. *adv.*

**here·on** (hē ron′) **1** on this. **2** immediately after this. *adv.*

**here's** (hērz) here is.

**her·e·sy** (her′ə sē) **1** a belief different from the accepted belief of a church, school, profession, etc. **2** the holding of such a belief. *n., pl.* **her·e·sies.**

**her·e·tic** (her′ə tik) **1** a person who holds a belief that is different from the accepted belief of his or her religion, school, profession, etc. **2** holding such a belief. 1 *n.*, 2 *adj.*

**he·ret·i·cal** (hə ret′ə kəl) **1** of or having to do with HERESY or heretics. **2** containing HERESY; characterized by heresy. *adj.* —**he·ret′i·cal·ly,** *adv.*

**here·to** (hėr tü′) to this place, thing, etc. *adv.*

**here·to·fore** (hėr′tə fôr′) before this time; until now. *adv.*

**here·un·to** (hē′run tü′) to this. *adv.*

**here·up·on** (hē′rə pon′) **1** upon this. **2** immediately after this. *adv.*

**here·with** (hėr with′ *or* hėr wiŦH′) **1** with this. **2** by this means; in this way. *adv.*

**her·it·a·ble** (her′ə tə bəl) capable of being inherited. *adj.*

**her·it·age** (her′ə tij) **1** what is or may be handed on to a person from his or her ancestors; inheritance. **2** something that a person has as a result of having been born in a certain time, place, condition, etc.: *a heritage of violence. Their heritage was freedom.* *n.*

**her·maph·ro·dite** (hėr maf′rə dīt′) **1** an animal or plant having the reproductive organs of both sexes. **2** a person or thing that combines opposite qualities. *n.*

**hermaphrodite brig** a sailing ship with two masts, square-rigged forward and schooner-rigged aft.

**her·maph·ro·dit·ic** (hėr maf′rə dit′ik) of or like a HERMAPHRODITE. *adj.*

**her·met·ic** (hėr met′ik) closed tightly so that air cannot get in; airtight. *adj.* —**her·met′i·cal·ly,** *adv.*

**her·mit** (hėr′mit) **1** a person who goes away from other people and lives alone in some lonely or out-of-the-way place, often for religious reasons. **2** a kind of spiced cookie made with molasses or brown sugar and usually containing raisins and nuts. *n.* —**her′mit·like′,** *adj.*

**her·mit·age** (hėr′mə tij) **1** the home of a hermit. **2** a place to live away from other people; a retreat. *n.*

**hermit crab** any of numerous species of small, soft-bodied crab found throughout the world, mainly in the ocean, having the eyes on the end of long stalks and living in the empty shells of snails or similar animals: *Most hermit crabs are only about two or three centimetres long.*

**hermit thrush** a North American songbird of the same family as the robin, nightingale, and blue birds, having a brown back, reddish-brown tail, and spotted breast and noted for its beautiful, varied evening song.

**her·ni·a** (hėr′nē ə) the protrusion of a part of the intestine or some other organ through a break in its surrounding walls; a rupture. *n., pl.* **her·ni·as** or **her·ni·ae** (-nē ē *or* -nē ī).

**he·ro** (hē′rō) **1** a person who does great and brave deeds and is admired for them: *the heroes of old.* **2** a person admired for contributing to a particular field: *a football hero, heroes of science.* **3** the most important male person in a story, play, motion picture, etc. **4** in mythology and legend, a man of more than human qualities: *Hercules was a hero. n., pl.* **he·roes.**

**he·ro·ic** (hi rō′ik) **1** like a hero or heroine in deeds or in qualities; brave; noble: *the heroic deeds of our firefighters.* **2** of or about heroes and their deeds: *The Iliad and the Odyssey are heroic poems.* **3** unusually daring or bold: *Only heroic measures could save the town from the flood.* **4** unusually large; larger than life size. **5** a heroic poem. **6 heroics,** *pl.* **a** heroic behaviour. **b** extravagant or pretentious talk or action: *We are all getting a little tired of his heroics.* 1–4 *adj.*, 5, 6 *n.* —**he·ro′i·cal·ly,** *adv.*

**he·ro·i·cal** (hi rō′ə kəl) HEROIC (defs. 1–4). *adj.*

**her·o·in** (her′ō in) a very powerful, habit-forming sedative drug made from morphine. *n.*
☞ *Hom.* HEROINE.

**her·o·ine** (her′ō in) **1** a woman or girl admired for her bravery or great deeds: *Laura Secord and Madeleine de Verchères are Canadian heroines.* **2** the most important female person in a story, play, motion picture, etc. **3** in mythology and legend, a woman or girl having more than human qualities. *n.*
☞ *Hom.* HEROIN.

**her·o·ism** (her′ō iz′əm) **1** the actions and qualities of a hero or heroine; great bravery; daring courage. **2** a very brave act or quality. *n.*

Great blue herons— about 120 cm long including the tail

**her·on** (her′ən) any of a number of species of wading bird belonging to the same family as the bitterns and egrets, having a long neck, long bill, long legs, and a short tail. *n.*

**he·ro–wor·ship** (hē′rō wėr′ship) **1** idolize; worship as a hero. **2** in ancient Greece and Rome, the worship of ancient heroes as gods. **3** the idolizing of great people, or of persons thought of as heroes. 1 *v.*, 2, 3 *n.* Also (for defs. 2 and 3), **hero worship.**

**her·pes** (her′pēz) any of several virus diseases of the skin or mucous membranes, characterized by clusters of blisters. **Herpes simplex** is a type of herpes marked by watery blisters especially on the mouth and lips. *n.*

**her·pe·tol·o·gist** (her′pə tol′ə jist) a person trained in HERPETOLOGY, especially one who makes it his or her work. *n.*

**her·pe·tol·o·gy** (her′pə tol′ə jē) the branch of zoology dealing with the study of reptiles and amphibians. *n.*

**her·ring** (her′ing) **1** a small, silvery sea fish found in the Atlantic and Pacific oceans that is one of the most important food fishes in the world: *Herring are caught in huge quantities and sold fresh, salted, smoked, dried, or pickled, and are also canned, when they are called sardines.* **2** any of a number of related fishes. **3** referring to the family of sea and freshwater fishes that includes the herrings: *The alewife, pilchard, and shad also belong to the herring family.* **4** any of various other fishes of different families, such as the lake herring, or cisco, and the yellow herring, or goldeye. *n., pl.* **her·ring** or **her·rings.**

A band of decorative brickwork in a herringbone pattern on a house in Edam in the Netherlands

**her·ring·bone** (her′ing bōn′) **1** a zigzag pattern. **2** cloth in a twill weave with a small, woven zigzag pattern: *He chose a herringbone for his suit.* **3** a zigzag arrangement of bricks, tiles, etc. **4** of or referring to a herringbone: *a herringbone tweed, a herringbone pattern.* **5** produce such a pattern on. **6** in skiing, a method of going up a slope by pointing the front of the skis outward and putting the weight on the inner side. **7** go up a slope in this way. 1–4, 6 *n.*, 5, 7 *v.*, **her·ring·boned, her·ring·bon·ing.**

**herring gull** a large gull widely distributed throughout the Northern Hemisphere, the adults having white plumage with pearl-grey back and black wing tips: *The herring gull is common in most of Canada, including the interior regions.* See GULL[1] for picture.

**hers** (herz) a possessive form of SHE: *that which*

belongs to her: *This money is hers. My answers were wrong, but hers were right.* *pron.*
☞ *Usage.* See note at HER.

**her·self** (hėr self′) **1** a reflexive pronoun, the object of a reflexive verb with **she** as subject: *She asked herself if it was really worth all the trouble.* **2** an intensive pronoun, used to emphasize the noun or pronoun it follows: *She herself brought the book. She herself did it.* **3** her usual self: *In those fits she is not herself.* *pron.*

**hertz** (hėrts) an SI unit for measuring the frequency, or rate of occurrence, of waves and vibrations, equal to one cycle per second: *The musical tone A above middle C on the piano has a frequency of 440 vibrations per second, or 440 hertz.* Symbol: Hz *n., pl.* **hertz.**

**he's** (hēz; *unstressed*, ēz, iz, *or* hiz) **1** he is. **2** he has: *He's broken his hockey stick.*

**hes·i·tance** (hez′ə təns) HESITANCY. *n.*

**hes·i·tan·cy** (hez′ə tən sē) hesitation; doubt; indecision. *n., pl.* **hes·i·tan·cies.**

**hes·i·tant** (hez′ə tənt) hesitating; doubtful; undecided. *adj.* —**hes′i·tant·ly**, *adv.*

**hes·i·tate** (hez′ə tāt′) **1** hold back because one feels doubtful; be undecided; show that one has not yet made up one's mind: *I hesitated about taking his side until I knew the whole story.* **2** feel that perhaps one should not; be unwilling; not want: *I hesitated to ask you because you were so busy.* **3** stop for an instant; pause: *She hesitated before asking the question.* **4** speak with stops or pauses; stammer. *v.,* **hes·i·tat·ed, hes·i·tat·ing.**

**hes·i·tat·ing·ly** (hez′ə tā′ting lē) with hesitation. *adv.*

**hes·i·ta·tion** (hez′ə tā′shən) **1** the act of hesitating; doubt or indecision: *After some hesitation she decided to come with us.* **2** speaking with short stops or pauses. *n.*

**Hessian fly** (hesh′ən) a small, two-winged fly whose larvae are very destructive to wheat.

**hetero–** *combining form.* other; different, as in *heterogeneous.*

**het·er·o·dox** (het′ər ə doks′) **1** contrary to or differing from an acknowledged standard; not ORTHODOX: *a heterodox belief.* Compare with ORTHODOX (def. 1). **2** rejecting the regularly accepted beliefs or doctrines: *a heterodox priest.* *adj.*

**het·er·o·dox·y** (het′ə rə dok′sē) **1** the rejection of regularly accepted beliefs or doctrines; departure from an acknowledged standard; opposite of ORTHODOXY. **2** a belief, doctrine, or opinion not in agreement with what is regularly accepted. *n., pl.* **het·er·o·dox·ies.**

**het·er·o·dyne** (het′ə rō dīn′) **1** having to do with or referring to a strong, stable radio frequency called a beat, produced by combining the high unstable incoming frequency with another slightly different one given out by an oscillator in the receiver itself: *The heterodyne frequency is the difference between the original two frequencies.* **2** combine two similar frequencies to produce a beat. **1** *adj.,* **2** *v.*

**het·er·o·ge·ne·i·ty** (het′ə rō jə nē′ə tē) the quality or state of being HETEROGENEOUS; dissimilarity. *n., pl.* **het·er·o·ge·ne·i·ties.**

**het·er·o·ge·ne·ous** (het′ə rō jē′nē əs) **1** different in kind; unlike; not at all similar; varied. **2** made up of unlike elements or parts; miscellaneous. *adj.*
—**het′er·o·ge′ne·ous·ly,** *adv.*

**herself** 563 **hexameter**

hat, āge, fär; let, ēqual, tėrm; it, īce
hot, ōpen, ôrder; oil, out; cup, pùt, rüle
əbove, takən, pencəl, lemən, circəs
ch, child; ng, long; sh, ship
th, thin; ᴛʜ, then; zh, measure

**het·er·o·nym** (het′ə rə nim′) a word spelled the same as another but having a different sound and meaning: Example: lead, *to conduct,* and lead, *a metal.* *n.*

**het·er·op·ter·an** (het′ə rop′tə rən) **1** a HETEROPTEROUS insect. **2** of or referring to the order comprising these insects. **1** *n.,* **2** *adj.*
☞ *Usage.* See note at HETEROPTEROUS.

**het·er·op·ter·ous** (het′ə rop′tə rəs) of or having to do with an order (**Heteroptera**) of sucking insects that includes the bedbug: *Heteropterous insects usually have two pairs of wings, with the front pair thickened at the base; the wings are folded flat on the back when at rest.* *adj.*
☞ *Usage.* Some authorities classify all sucking insects as belonging to a single order (Hemiptera) with two suborders: Heteroptera (bedbugs, etc.) and Homoptera (aphids, scale insects, etc.). However, most authorities today consider that the distinctions between the two groups of insects are great enough to warrant classifying them as two separate orders.

**het·er·o·sex·u·al** (het′ə rə sek′shü əl *or* het′rə sek′shü əl) **1** in biology, of or having to do with the different sexes. **2** of, having to do with, or characterized by sexual feeling for a person of the opposite sex. Compare with HOMOSEXUAL. **3** a heterosexual person. **1, 2** *adj.,* **3** *n.*

**heu·ris·tic** (hyü ris′tik) **1** guiding or helping one to discover: *heuristic reasoning.* **2** having to do with an educational method that encourages students to use personal investigation, observation, etc. so that they may find things out for themselves. **3** in computer science, a technique or procedure used to solve a particular problem with apparent intelligence. **1, 2** *adj.,* **3** *n.*

**hew** (hyü) **1** cut with an axe, sword, etc.: *He hewed down the tree.* **2** cut into shape; form by cutting with an axe, adze, etc.: *to hew stone for building, to hew logs into beams.* **3** make or produce with cutting blows: *The knight hewed his way through the enemy.* **4** conform (*to*): *The newspaper hews strictly to the party line.* *v.,* **hewed, hewed** *or* **hewn, hew·ing.**
☞ *Hom.* HUE.

**hew·er** (hyü′ər) a person or thing that hews. *n.*

**hewn** (hyün) a pp. of HEW. *v.*

**hex** (heks) *Informal.* **1** practise witchcraft on; bewitch. **2** witch. **3** a magical spell. **1** *v.,* **2, 3** *n.*

**hex·a·gon** (hek′sə gon′) a plane figure having six interior angles and six sides. See POLYGON for picture. *n.*

**hex·ag·o·nal** (hek sag′ə nəl) **1** of or having the form of a HEXAGON. **2** having a HEXAGON as base or cross section. *adj.*

**hex·a·he·dral** (hek′sə hē′drəl) having six faces, or surfaces. *adj.*

**hex·a·he·dron** (hek′sə hē′drən) a solid figure having six faces. *n., pl.* **hex·a·he·drons** *or* **hex·a·he·dra** (-drə).

**hex·am·e·ter** (hek sam′ə tər) **1** a line of poetry consisting of six metrical feet. Example: This is the /

**fórest pri / méval.** The / múrmuring / pínes and the / hémlocks. **2** poetry consisting of hexameters. **3** of, having to do with, or consisting of hexameters. *n.*

**hex·an·gu·lar** (hek sang′gyə lər) having six angles. *adj.*

**hex·a·pod** (hek′sə pod′) a true insect; any of a class of ARTHROPODS having six legs. *n.*

**hey** (hā) a sound made to attract attention, to express surprise, etc. or to ask a question: *"Hey, stop!" interj.*
☞ *Hom.* HAY.

**hey·day** (hā′dā′) the period of greatest strength, vigour, spirits, prosperity, etc.: *In her heyday, she was the darling of the jet set.* *n.*

**Hf** Hafnium.

**HF, H.F.,** or **h.f.** high frequency.

**Hg** mercury.

**H.G.** His Grace; Her Grace.

**H.H.** **1** His Highness; Her Highness. **2** His Holiness.

**hi·a·tus** (hī ā′təs) **1** an empty space; gap; space that needs to be filled. **2** a slight pause between two vowels that come together in successive syllables or words: *There is a hiatus between the e's in* pre-eminent. *n., pl.* **hi·a·tus·es** or **hi·a·tus.**

**hi·ba·chi** (hē bä′chē) a cast iron or similar container in which charcoal is burned for cooking, heating, etc. *n.*

**hi·ber·na·cu·lum** (hī′bər nak′yə ləm) a structure in which dormant animals hibernate. *n., pl.* **hi·ber·na·cu·la** (-lə).

**hi·ber·nate** (hī′bər nāt′) **1** spend the winter in sleep or in an inactive condition, as bears, groundhogs, and some other wild animals do. **2** be or become inactive: *I think I'll just hibernate for the first week of my holidays.* *v.*, **hi·ber·nat·ed, hi·ber·nat·ing.**

**hi·ber·na·tion** (hī′bər nā′shən) hibernating. *n.*

**hi·bis·cus** (hə bis′kəs) any of a closely related group of herbs, shrubs, and small trees of the MALLOW family found in temperate and tropical regions around the world, often cultivated for their large, usually bell-shaped, white, pink, red, blue, or yellow flowers: *The rose of Sharon is a hibiscus.* *n.*

**hic·cough** (hik′up) See HICCUP. *n., v.*

**hic·cup** (hik′up) **1** a sudden, involuntary contraction of the diaphragm that causes the glottis to close just when one is inhaling, producing a characteristic short clicking sound. **2** make a hiccup: *He hiccupped.* **3** **hiccups,** *pl.* the state of having one hiccup after another: *I've got the hiccups.* 1, 3 *n.,* 2 *v.,* **hic·cupped, hic·cup·ping.** Also, **hiccough.**

**hick·o·ry** (hik′ə rē) **1** a North American tree having hard, edible nuts, of the same family as the walnut. **2** the tough, hard wood of this tree. **3** made of hickory. 1, 2 *n., pl.* **hick·o·ries;** 3 *adj.*

**hid** (hid) pt. and a pp. of HIDE¹: *The dog hid his bone.* *v.*
☞ *Hom.* HE'D (hid).

**hid·den** (hid′ən) **1** concealed or secret: *a hidden staircase.* **2** mysterious or obscure: *a statement full of hidden meanings.* **3** a pp. of HIDE¹: *They had hidden the treasure in a cave.* 1, 2 *adj.,* 3 *v.*

**hide¹** (hīd) **1** put out of sight; conceal: *She hid the presents in the attic. He hid his face in the pillow.* **2** shut off from sight; screen or obscure: *Clouds hid the moon.* **3** keep secret: *She hid her anxiety.* **4** conceal oneself: *I'll hide, and you find me. The shy little boy hid behind his mother's skirt.* **5** a shelter for hiding from birds or animals; BLIND (def. 15). 1–4 *v.,* **hid, hid·den** or **hid, hid·ing;** 5 *n.* —**hid′er,** *n.*
**hide out** or **up,** remain concealed: *The bandits hid out for several weeks in a mountain shack.*

**hide²** (hīd) **1** the skin of an animal, either raw or tanned. **2** a person's skin. **3** *Informal.* beat; thrash. 1, 2 *n.,* 3 *v.,* **hid·ed, hid·ing.**
**neither hide nor hair,** nothing at all.

**hide–and–seek** (hī′dən sēk′) a children's game in which one player has to find all the others, who are hidden in different places. The player who has to find the others is called "it." *n.* Also, **hide-and-go-seek.**

**hide·a·way** (hī′də wā′) **1** a place of hiding. **2** a quiet, restful place, especially one in an isolated area, for a person or small group of people to be alone: *He had a little hideaway by a lake where he went to escape from the noise and confusion of the city.* *n.*

**hide·bound** (hīd′bound′) **1** with the skin sticking close to the bones. **2** narrow-minded and stubborn: *He was too hidebound to accept new ideas.* *adj.*

**hid·e·ous** (hid′ē əs) very ugly; frightful; horrible: *a hideous monster.* *adj.* —**hid′e·ous·ly,** *adv.* —**hid′e·ous·ness,** *n.*

**hide–out** or **hide·out** (hī′dout′) a place for hiding or being alone. *n.*

**hid·ing¹** (hī′ding) **1** the condition of being hidden; concealment: *The bandits are still in hiding in the mountains. They went into hiding right after the robbery.* **2** ppr. of HIDE¹. 1 *n.,* 2 *v.*

**hid·ing²** (hī′ding) *Informal.* **1** a beating; thrashing. **2** ppr. of HIDE². 1 *n.,* 2 *v.*

**hi·er·ar·chi·cal** (hī′ə rär′kə kəl) of, having to do with, or belonging to a HIERARCHY. *adj.*

**hi·er·ar·chy** (hī′ə rär′kē) **1** an organization of persons or things in higher and lower ranks: *A hierarchy is a graded series.* **2** church government by a hierarchy of priests or other clergy. **3** a body of clergy organized in orders or ranks, especially members of the highest orders. *n., pl.* **hi·er·ar·chies.**

Egyptian hieroglyphics

A KINGLY
GIFT OF AN
OFFERING TABLE
TO
RA-HORUS
THE GREAT
GOD
LORD OF
HEAVEN

**hi·er·o·glyph·ic** (hī′ə rə glif′ik) **1** a picture or symbol standing for a word, idea, or sound: *The ancient Egyptians used hieroglyphics instead of an alphabet like ours.* **2** of or written in hieroglyphics. **3** a symbol, word, etc. that is hard to understand. **4** hard to read. **5 hieroglyphics,** *pl.* **a** a system of writing that uses hieroglyphics (*used with a singular or plural verb*). **b** *Informal.* writing that

is hard to read: *I can't read her hieroglyphics.* 1, 3, 5 *n.*, 2, 4 *adj.* —**hi′er·o·glyph′i·cal·ly,** *adv.*
☞ *Etym.* Through French or late Latin from Gk. *hierogluphikos* 'sacred writing', which was formed from *hieros* 'sacred' + *gluphē* 'carving'. 16c.

**hi-fi** (hī′fī′ *for adjective,* hī′fī′ *for noun*) *Informal.*
**1** HIGH-FIDELITY. **2** HIGH-FIDELITY reproduction of music, etc. or the equipment for such reproduction. 1 *adj.*, 2 *n.*

**hig·gle·dy-pig·gle·dy** (hig′əl dē pig′əl dē) **1** in jumbled confusion: *They ran higgledy-piggledy out the door.* **2** jumbled; confused: *a higgledy-piggledy arrangement of odds and ends.* **3** jumble; confusion. 1 *adv.*, 2 *adj.*, 3 *n.*

**high** (hī) **1** of more than usual height; tall: *a high building.* **2** rising to a specified extent: *The mountain is 6100 metres high.* **3** far above the ground or some base: *an airplane high in the air.* **4** extending to or done from a height: *a high leap, a high dive.* **5** senior to others in rank or position: *a high official.* **6** superior; above others in personal qualities: *a person of high character.* **7** greater, stronger, or better than average; great: *high temperature.* **8** most important; chief; main: *the high altar.* **9** extreme of its kind: *high crimes.* **10** costly: *Strawberries are high in winter.* **11** above the normal pitch; shrill; sharp: *a high voice.* **12** advanced to its peak: *high summer.* **13** smelling bad as a result of decay; tainted: *Some people prefer to eat game after it has become high.* **14** haughty: *a high manner.* **15** at or to a high point, place, rank, amount, degree, price, pitch, etc.: *The eagle flies high.* **16** something that is high: *The high for today will be 19°C.* **17** in automobiles and similar machines, an arrangement of gears to give the greatest speed. 1–14 *adj.*, 15 *adv.*, 16, 17 *n.*
**fly high,** have big ideas, plans, hopes, ambitions, etc.
**high and dry, a** up out of the water: *The fish was high and dry on the beach.* **b** all alone; without help: *He has left me high and dry with all this work to do.*
**high and low,** everywhere: *We looked high and low but couldn't find the letter.*
**on high, a** high above; up in the air. **b** in heaven.
☞ *Hom.* HIE.

**high·born** (hī′bôrn′) of noble birth. *adj.*

**high·boy** (hī′boi′) a tall chest of drawers on legs. *n.*

**high·bred** (hī′bred′) **1** of superior breeding or stock. **2** well-mannered; very refined. *adj.*

**high·brow** (hī′brou′) *Informal.* **1** a person who has intellectual and cultural interests and, sometimes, a feeling of superiority because of this. **2** of or suitable for a highbrow: *highbrow music, a highbrow discussion.* 1 *n.*, 2 *adj.*

**high–class** (hī′klas′) of high quality; superior: *a high-class restaurant.* *adj.*

**high–col·oured** or **high–col·ored** (hī′kul′ərd) **1** having a deep or vivid colour. **2** florid; red. *adj.*

**High Commission** the embassy of one Commonwealth country in another.

**High Commissioner** the chief representative of one Commonwealth country in another: *A High Commissioner has the status of an ambassador.*

**high·er–up** (hī′ə rup′) *Informal.* a person occupying a superior position: *The higher-ups have vetoed the change.* *n.*

**high–fi·del·i·ty** (hī′fī del′ə tē *or* hī′fə del′ə tē) **1** indicating reproduction of the full range of sound, or something approaching it, with a minimum of distortion.
**2** of or having to do with high-fidelity reproduction, equipment, recordings, etc. *adj.*

**high–flown** (hī′flōn′) **1** aspiring; extravagant. **2** attempting to be elegant or eloquent: *high-flown compliments.* *adj.*

**high frequency** the range of radio frequencies between 3 and 30 megahertz: *High frequency is the range next above medium frequency.* —**high′-fre′quen·cy,** *adj.*

**high–grade** (hī′grād′) **1** of fine quality; superior: *high-grade ore, a high-grade performance.* **2** gold nuggets or rich ore. **3** gold nuggets or rich ore stolen in small quantities from a mine. **4** steal small quantities of gold or ore from a mine. **5** in logging, take only the best timber from a stand. 1 *adj.*, 2, 3 *n.*, 4, 5 *v.*, **high-grad·ed, high-grad·ing.**

**high–hand·ed** (hī′han′did) arbitrary or overbearing; disregarding the feelings of others: *The club members began to resent his high-handed way of running things.* *adj.* —**high′-hand′ed·ly,** *adv.* —**high′-hand′ed·ness,** *n.*

**high hat** a tall, black silk hat; a top hat.

**high·jack** (hī′jak′) See HIJACK. *v.*

**high·jack·er** (hī′jak′ər) See HIJACKER. *n.*

**high jump 1** an athletic contest or event in which the contestants try to jump as high as possible. **2** a jump of this kind.

**high·land** (hī′lənd) **1** a country or region that is higher and hillier than the neighbouring country. **2** of, having to do with, or in such country: *a highland meadow.* **3 the Highlands,** a hilly region in northern and western Scotland. **4 Highland,** of, having to do with, or in the Highlands. *n.*

**High·land·er** (hī′lən dər) **1** a native or inhabitant of the Highlands of Scotland. **2** a soldier of a regiment from the Highlands of Scotland. *n.*

**Highland fling** a lively dance of the Highlands of Scotland.

**high–level language** a computer language that uses a number of everyday words such as *enter, add.*

**high·light** (hī′līt′) **1** the most interesting or most striking part, event, scene, etc.: *The highlight of our trip was the drive along the Cabot Trail.* **2** make prominent: *The new product was highlighted in all the company's brochures.* **3** the effect or representation of bright light. **4** a part of a painting, photograph, etc. in which light is represented as falling with full force. **5** emphasize a part of a painting, photograph, etc. with lighting, colour, etc.: *The photographer highlighted the child's curly hair.* 1, 3, 4 *n.*, 2, 5 *v.*, **high·light·ed, high·light·ing.**

**high·ly** (hī′lē) **1** in a high degree; very; very much. **2** favourably; with much approval; with great praise or honour. **3** at a high price. *adv.*

**high–mind·ed** (hī′mīn′did) having or showing high principles and feelings: *a high-minded person, a high-minded act of charity.* *adj.* —**high′-mind′ed·ly,** *adv.* —**high′-mind′ed·ness,** *n.*

**high·ness** (hī′nis) **1** being high; height. **2 Highness,** a title of honour given to members of royal families: *The Prince of Wales is addressed as "Your Highness" and spoken of as "His Royal Highness."* *n.*

**high noon** fully noon.

**high–pitched** (hī′picht′) **1** of high tone or sound; shrill: *a high-pitched whistle.* **2** of a roof, having a steep slope. **3** marked by or showing intense feeling; agitated: *the high-pitched excitement of the chase.* *adj.*

**high–pow·ered** (hī′pou′ərd) having much power or energy: *a high-powered car or rifle, a high-powered sales talk.* *adj.*

**high–pres·sure** (hī′presh′ər *for adjective,* hī′presh′ər *for verb*). **1** having, involving, or requiring the use of a relatively high pressure: *a high-pressure cylinder, a high-pressure laminate.* **2** having or showing a high barometric pressure: *There is a high-pressure area just to the south.* **3** *Informal.* using or involving a strong, insistent approach or argument, especially in selling: *a high-pressure sales pitch.* **4** persuade or influence by using such tactics: *He was high-pressured into buying the more expensive rug.* **5** involving a lot of emotional tension or strain: *She has a high-pressure job.* 1–3, 5 *adj.*, 4 *v.*, **high–pres·sured, high–pres·sur·ing.**

**high priest** **1** a chief priest. **2** in ancient times, the head of the Jewish priesthood.

**high relief** relief sculpture in which the modelled forms project well out from the background and parts may be undercut. See RELIEF for picture.

**high·rise** (hī′rīz′) **1** having many storeys: *highrise apartment buildings.* **2** a building having many storeys: *He lives in a highrise downtown.* 1 *adj.,* 2 *n.*

**high·road** (hī′rōd′) **1** a main road; highway. **2** a direct and easy way: *There is no highroad to success.* *n.*

**high school** a school that follows elementary or public school: *Some provinces have junior high schools, intermediate between elementary and high school.* —**high′-school′,** *adj.*
☛ *Usage.* Capitalize **high school** only when using it as part of a proper name to refer to a particular school: *She graduated from high school last year. I graduated from Collins Bay High School in 1990.*

**high seas** the open ocean: *The high seas are outside the authority of any country.*

**high–sound·ing** (hī′soun′ding) having an imposing or pretentious sound: *high-sounding words.* *adj.*

**high–spir·it·ed** (hī′spir′ə tid) having or showing a bold, proud, or energetic spirit: *a high-spirited horse. The team put up a high-spirited defence, even though they knew they were losing.* *adj.* —**high′-spir′it·ed·ly,** *adv.* —**high′-spir′it·ed·ness,** *n.*

**high spirits** happiness; cheerfulness; gaiety.

**high·stick** (hī′stik′) *Cdn.* in hockey and lacrosse, illegally strike or hinder an opposing player with one's stick raised above shoulder level. *v.*, **high·sticked, high·stick·ing.**

**high·stick·ing** (hī′stik′ing) *Cdn.* **1** in hockey and lacrosse, the act or practice of illegally striking or hindering an opposing player with one's stick carried above shoulder level: *He received a penalty for highsticking.* **2** ppr. of HIGHSTICK. 1 *n.,* 2 *v.*

**high–strung** (hī′strung′) very sensitive; easily excited; nervous. *adj.*

**high technology** electronic devices, especially computers and telecommunication systems: *The output of this factory was doubled by the latest high technology.*

**high–ten·sion** (hī′ten′shən) carrying a high voltage: *Hydro roped off the fallen high-tension wires.* *adj.*

**high–test** (hī′test′) **1** vaporizing at a low temperature: *High-test gasoline is used in automobiles during winter because it forms a vapour in the engine quickly.* **2** passing very difficult requirements and tests. *adj.*

**high tide** **1** the highest level of the tide. **2** the time when the tide is highest. **3** the highest point; a culminating point.

**high time** **1** the time just before it is too late: *It's high time that we got ready to go.* **2** *Informal.* a lively, jolly time at a party, etc.

**high–toned** (hī′tōnd′) **1** high in tone or pitch. **2** having a high character or high principles; dignified. **3** *Informal.* fashionable; stylish. *adj.*

**high treason** treason against one's ruler, state, or government.

**high water** **1** the highest level of water in a river or lake. **2** HIGH TIDE.

**high–water mark** **1** the highest level reached by a body of water. **2** any highest point.

**high·way** (hī′wā′) **1** a public road. **2** a main road or route. **3** a direct line or way to some end. *n.*

**high·way·man** (hī′wā′mən) formerly, a man, usually on horseback, who robbed travellers on a public road. *n., pl.* **high·way·men** (-mən).

**hi·jack** (hī′jak′) **1** stop a vehicle in transit by force or threat in order to steal it or its cargo: *The truck was hijacked about 70 kilometres out of the city.* **2** steal goods, etc. by force or threat while they are being transported: *Several shipments have been hijacked.* **3** seize control of an aircraft in flight by force or threat, in order to obtain money or some other concession: *The gang hijacked the plane and made the pilot fly to Algeria.* *v.*

**hi·jack·er** (hī′jak′ər) one who takes part in hijacking, especially of an aircraft. *n.*

**hike** (hīk) *Informal.* **1** take a long walk; tramp; march: *The scouts hiked into the hills.* **2** a long walk; a march or tramp: *We're going on a hike today.* **3** move, draw, or raise with a jerk: *He hiked himself up onto the platform.* **4** an increase: *a hike in prices.* 1, 3 *v.,* **hiked, hik·ing;** 2, 4 *n.* —**hik′er,** *n.*

**hi·lar·i·ous** (hə ler′ē əs) **1** very merry; noisily cheerful: *It was a hilarious party.* **2** very funny: *The joke was hilarious.* *adj.* —**hi·lar′i·ous·ly,** *adv.*

**hi·lar·i·ty** (hə lar′ə tē *or* hə ler′ə tē) great mirth; noisy gaiety. *n.*

**hill** (hil) **1** a raised part on the earth's surface, smaller than a mountain. **2** a heap, pile, or mound of earth, sand, etc.: *Moles had made hills all over the lawn. The potatoes were planted in hills.* **3** a plant or plants growing in a mound of earth: *a hill of corn.* **4** put a little heap of soil over and around: *to hill potatoes.* **5** form into a little heap. 1–3 *n.,* 4, 5 *v.*

**over the hill,** *Informal.* past one's prime.

**hill·ock** (hil′ək) a little hill. *n.*

**hill·side** (hil′sīd′) the side of a hill. *n.*

**hill·top** (hil′top′) the top of a hill. *n.*

**hill·y** (hil′ē) **1** having many hills: *hilly country.* **2** like a hill; steep: *a hilly slope.* *adj.*, **hill·i·er, hill·i·est.** —**hill′i·ness,** *n.*

**hilt** (hilt) the handle of a sword, dagger, etc. See SWORD for picture. *n.*
**up to the hilt,** thoroughly; completely.

**hi·lum** (hī′ləm) the mark or scar on a seed at the point of attachment to the seed vessel: *The eye of a bean is a hilum.* *n., pl.* **hi·la** (-lə).

**him** (him; *unstressed,* im) the objective form of HE: *Take him home. Go to him.* *pron.*
☞ **Hom.** HYMN.

**him·self** (him self′ *or, except when following a pause,* im self′) **1** a reflexive pronoun, the object of a reflexive verb with **he** as subject: *He cut himself. He asked himself what he really wanted.* **2** an intensive pronoun, used to emphasize the noun or pronoun it follows: *Did you see Roy himself?* **3** his usual self: *He feels himself again.* *pron.*

**hind**[1] (hīnd) back; rear: *The mule kicked up its hind legs.* *adj.*, **hind·er, hind·most** or **hind·er·most.**

**hind**[2] (hīnd) a female deer, usually a female red deer after its third year. *n., pl.* **hind** or **hinds.**

**hind·brain** (hīnd′brān′) the back of the brain, especially the part including the CEREBELLUM and the MEDULLA OBLONGATA. See BRAIN for picture. *n.*

**hin·der**[1] (hin′dər) keep or hold back; get in the way of; make difficult; stop; prevent: *She was hindered by deep snow. He made certain that nothing would hinder the completion of the project.* *v.*

**hin·der**[2] (hīn′dər) hind; back; rear. *adj.*

**hind·er·most** (hīn′dər mōst′) HINDMOST. *adj.*

**Hin·di** (hin′dē) the most widely spoken language of India, existing in several very different dialects as well as a literary, or written, form that is one of the official languages of India: *Hindi is an Indo-European language.* *n.*

**hind·most** (hīnd′mōst′) nearest the rear; last. *adj.*

**Hin·doo** (hin′dü) See HINDU. *n., pl.* **Hin·doos;** *adj.*

**hind·quar·ter** (hīnd′kwôr′tər) the hind leg and loin of a carcass of beef, lamb, etc. *n.*

**hin·drance** (hin′drəns) **1** a person or thing that hinders; obstacle: *The noise was a hindrance to our studying.* **2** the act of hindering. *n.*

**hind·sight** (hīnd′sīt′) the ability to see, after the event is over, what should have been done. *n.*

**Hin·du** (hin′dü) **1** a person who believes in HINDUISM. **2** formerly, a native or inhabitant of India. **3** of or having to do with HINDUISM. **1, 2** *n., pl.* **Hin·dus; 3** *adj.*

**Hin·du·ism** (hin′dü iz′əm) a religion and way of life that is practised mainly in India, having an ancient tradition characterized by the doctrine of transmigration of souls, the worship of many gods who are all thought of as aspects of the one God, and, formerly, the support of a system of hereditary social classes generally called castes. The three great gods of classical Hinduism are VISHNU, SHIVA, and SHAKTI. A fourth god, BRAHMA, was widely worshipped for a time as the highest god. *n.*

hat, āge, fär; let, ēqual, tėrm; it, īce
hot, ōpen, ôrder; oil, out; cup, pùt, rüle
əbove, takən, pencəl, lemən, circəs
ch, child; ng, long; sh, ship
th, thin; ᴛʜ, then; zh, measure

**Hin·du·sta·ni** (hin′dü stä′nē *or* hin′dü stan′ē) **1** a dialect of northern India that was used as a common language of trade throughout India for a century and a half until 1947, when India was divided: *Literary Hindi and Urdu both developed from Hindustani.* **2** of or having to do with Hindustan (India or northern India), its people, or the language Hindustani. **1** *n.,* **2** *adj.*

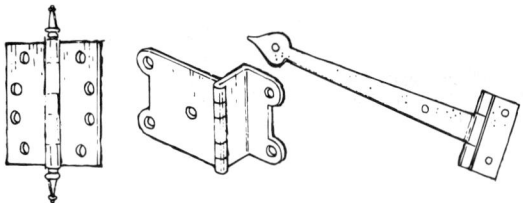

Three types of hinge

**hinge** (hinj) **1** a movable joint or mechanism by which a door, gate, cover, lid, etc. moves back and forth or up and down on its post, base, etc. **2** a natural joint that has a similar function: *the hinge of a clam shell.* **3** furnish with or attach by a hinge or hinges. **4** that on which something turns or depends; central principle or determining factor. **5** depend (*used with* **on** *or* **upon**): *The success of the enterprise will hinge on the dedication of the people involved.* **1, 2, 4** *n.,* **3, 5** *v.,* **hinged, hing·ing.**

**hint** (hint) **1** a slight indication; clue: *A small black cloud gave a hint of the coming storm.* **2** a statement or action implying something that the person prefers not to say directly; an indirect suggestion: *When she stood up, he took it as a hint that the interview was over.* **3** give a hint: *He tried to hint that he was tired by saying, "Do you often stay up this late?" The unsettled weather hinted at a storm.* **4** a very small amount or suggestion: *The soup has just a hint of garlic.* **5** a piece of practical information: *helpful hints for the traveller.* **1, 2, 4, 5** *n.,* **3** *v.* —**hint′er,** *n.*
**hint at,** give a hint of; suggest.

**hin·ter·land** (hin′tər land′) **1** the country or region behind a coast; the inland region. **2** a region remote from and outside the influence of major urban centres; backwater. *n.*

**hip**[1] (hip) **1** in human beings: **a** the projecting upper part of the pelvis on each side of the body; HIPBONE (def. 2). **b** the part on each side of the body between the waist and the upper thighs: *He has narrow hips.* **2** the corresponding part of an animal's body, where a hind leg joins the trunk. **3** Often, **hips,** *pl.* the measurement around a person's body at the level of the hips: *Her hips are 97 centimetres.* *n.* —**hip′like′,** *adj.*

**hip**[2] (hip) the pod containing the ripe seed of a rose bush. *n.*

**hip·bone** (hip′bōn′) **1** either of the large, irregular bones that form the main part of the pelvis in mammals: *The hipbone is composed of the ilium, ischium, and pubis, which are fused into one bone in adults.* See SOCKET for picture. **2** the rear, upper portion of either of these bones; ilium. See PELVIS for picture. *n.*

**hip·po** (hip′ō) *Informal.* HIPPOPOTAMUS. *n.*

**Hip·po·crat·ic** (hip′ə krat′ik) of or having to do with Hippocrates, the physician of ancient Greece who is called the father of medicine. *adj.*

**Hippocratic oath** a famous oath describing the duties and obligations of a physician, usually taken by those about to become physicians.

**hip·po·drome** (hip′ə drōm′) **1** in ancient Greece and Rome, an oval track for horse races and chariot races, surrounded by tiers of seats for spectators. **2** an arena or building for a circus, rodeo, etc. *n.*

A hippopotamus—about 140 cm high at the shoulder

**hip·po·pot·a·mus** (hip′ə pot′ə məs) a huge, thick-skinned, hairless mammal often weighing as much as four tonnes, found in and near the rivers of tropical Africa: *Hippopotamuses feed on plants and can stay under water for a long time.* *n., pl.* **hip·po·pot·a·mus·es** or **hip·po·pot·a·mi** (-mī′ *or* -mē′).
☛ *Etym.* Through Latin from Gk. *hippopotamos* 'the horse of the river', which was formed from *hippos* 'horse' + *potamos* 'river'. 16c.

**hip roof** a roof having sloping sides and ends. See ROOF for picture.

**hire** (hīr) **1** agree to pay for the temporary use of a thing or the work or services of a person: *He hired a car, and a man to drive it.* **2** take on as an employee; engage: *The manager hired two more clerks last week.* **3** payment for the use of a thing or the work or services of a person: *A good worker is worthy of his or her hire.* **4** give the use of a thing or the work or services of a person in return for payment. **5** a hiring. 1, 2, 4 *v.*, **hired, hir·ing;** 3, 5 *n.*
**for hire,** for use or work in return for payment.
**hire out,** give one's work in return for payment: *He hired out as a carpenter.*
**on hire,** for use or work in return for payment.

**hire·ling** (hīr′ling) a person available for hire, especially one who will follow anyone's orders and is interested only in the pay. *n.*

**hir·sute** (hėr′süt) hairy. *adj.*

**his** (hiz; *unstresssed,* iz) the possessive form of HE: **1** of, belonging to, or made or done by him or himself: *He shook his head. They attended his graduation. His novels are very good.* **2** that which belongs to him: *The writing is his. Those tapes are his.* 1 *adj.*, 2 *pron.*
☛ *Hom.* IS (for the unstressed pronunciation of **his**).

**hiss** (his) **1** make a sound like that of the *s* in *see*: *The snake hissed as we approached.* **2** such a sound: *There was a loud hiss as the water boiled over onto the hot stove.* **3** make this sound as a sign of disapproval: *The play was hissed by the audience.* **4** the sound of hissing to express disapproval: *The actor was upset by the hisses of the crowd.* **5** force or drive by hissing: *They hissed him off the stage.* **6** utter by hissing or as if by hissing: *"Sit down and be quiet!" she hissed.* 1, 3, 5, 6 *v.*, 2, 4 *n.*

**his·ta·mine** (his′tə mēn′) a substance released by the body in allergic reactions: *Histamine lowers the blood pressure.* *n.*

**his·tol·o·gy** (his tol′ə jē) **1** a branch of biology dealing with the structures of animal and plant tissues as seen through a microscope. **2** the tissue structure of an animal or plant. *n.*

**his·to·ri·an** (his tô′rē ən) **1** a person who has much knowledge of history, especially one who writes or lectures about history. **2** a person who records events; chronicler. *n.*

**his·tor·ic** (his tô′rik) **1** famous or important in history: *Halifax and Kingston are historic cities.* **2** HISTORICAL (defs. 1, 2 and 3). *adj.*

**his·tor·i·cal** (his tô′rə kəl) **1** of, or having to do with history: *a historical town.* **2** according to history; based on history: *a historical novel.* **3** known to be real or true; in history, not in legend: *historical facts.* **4** HISTORIC (def. 1). *adj.* —**his·tor′i·cal·ly,** *adv.*

**his·to·ry** (his′tə rē *or* his′trē) **1** a statement of what has happened. **2** the story of a person or a nation; a systematic written account. **3** a known past: *This ship has an interesting history.* **4** all past events considered together; the course of human affairs. **5** the branch of knowledge or study that deals with the recording and explaining of past events: *a course in history.* *n., pl.* **his·to·ries.**
**make history,** **a** influence or guide the course of history: *The Magna Charta made history.* **b** do something spectacular or worthy of remembrance: *Marilyn Bell made history when she became the first woman to swim across Lake Ontario.*

**his·tri·on·ic** (his′trē on′ik) **1** having to do with actors or acting. **2** theatrical; insincere. *adj.*

**his·tri·on·ics** (his′trē on′iks) **1** a dramatic representation; theatricals; dramatics. **2** a theatrical or insincere manner, expression, etc. *n. sing. or pl.*

**hit** (hit) **1** give a blow; strike; knock: *She hit the ball with the bat. He hit his head against the shelf.* **2** a blow; stroke. **3** get to what is aimed at: *Her second arrow hit the bull's-eye.* **4** a getting to what is aimed at. **5** discover, meet, or find, especially by chance or unexpectedly: *We happened to hit the right road in the dark.* **6** have a painful or distressing effect on: *The death of his sister hit him hard. The province was hard hit by the drought.* **7** occur suddenly: *As he lifted the heavy box, a sharp pain hit him in the back. An idea just hit me.* **8** reach a certain point or place: *Prices hit a new high. The temperature hit an all-time low yesterday.* **9** attack or criticize sharply: *The reviews hit the new play.* **10** a sharp attack or criticism: *The review ended with a hit at the producer.* **11** a very successful or popular person or thing: *My sister was a big hit at my party. That new play is sure to be a hit.* **12** a stroke of luck. **13** agree with; suit exactly: *This hits my fancy.* **14** in baseball, a successful hitting of the ball by a batter so that he or she can get at least to first base without the help of an error; base hit. **15** make such a hit: *She hit a double.* 1, 3, 5–9, 13, 15 *v.*, **hit, hit·ting;** 2, 4, 10–12, 14 *n.*
**hard hit,** affected deeply or painfully: *She was hard hit by the news of her mother's death.*
**hit back,** retaliate.
**hit it off,** *Informal.* agree or get along well with someone: *Geza hit it off well with his new neighbour.*
**hit on** or **upon,** discover by chance: *They've hit on a new idea for advertising the contest.*

**hit the books,** *Informal.* begin to study, especially very hard: *She decided it was time to hit the books.*

**hit the roof** or **ceiling,** *Informal.* react with a burst of anger: *When their father saw the condition of his car, he hit the roof.*

**hit-and-run** (hit′ən run′) **1** of or caused by a driver who runs into another person or vehicle and drives away without stopping. **2** of or suggesting any similar act: *a hit-and-run attack. adj.*

**hitch** (hich) **1** fasten with a hook, ring, rope, strap, etc.: *Olaf hitched his horse to a post.* **2** harness to a wagon, carriage, etc.: *She hitched up the team and drove to town.* **3** become fastened or caught; fasten; catch. **4** a fastening; catch: *The hitch joining the plough to the tractor is broken.* **5** move or pull with a jerk; move jerkily: *Pablo hitched his chair nearer the fire.* **6** a short, sudden pull or jerk; jerky movement: *The sailor gave his pants a hitch.* **7** limp; hobble. **8** an obstacle; hindrance; going wrong: *A hitch in their plans made them miss the train.* **9** a kind of knot used for temporary fastening: *She put a hitch in the rope.* **10** tie such a knot: *She hitched the rope around the spar.* **11** *Informal.* a period of time, especially a period of service in the armed forces. **12** *Informal.* obtain by hitchhiking: *They hitched a ride home.* 1–3, 5, 7, 10, 12 *v.*, 4, 6–9, 11 *n.*

**without a hitch,** smoothly, successfully.

**hitch·hike** (hich′hīk′) *Informal.* travel by asking for free rides from passing motorists: *They hitchhiked across the country last summer.* *v.*, **hitch·hiked, hitch·hik·ing.** —**hitch′hik′er,** *n.*

**hith·er** (hiTH′ər) **1** to or toward this place; here. **2** on this side; nearer. 1 *adv.,* 2 *adj.*
**hither and thither,** here and there.

**hith·er·to** (hiTH′ər tü′) up to this time; until now: *Hitherto they had always listened to him, so he was surprised when they ignored his suggestion. adv.*

**Hit·ler·ism** (hit′lə riz′əm) the policy and beliefs of Hitler and the Nazi party in Germany (1933 to 1945). *n.*

**hit-or-miss** (hit′ər mis′) showing a lack of care or planning; careless or haphazard: *Ali has always done his accounts in a hit-or-miss fashion. adj.*

**hit·ter** (hit′ər) especially in sports, a person who hits: *She's a good hitter, but not much of a catcher. n.*

**HIV** human immunovirus, a virus that destroys the body's capacity to protect itself from diseases, and so causes AIDS.

**hive** (hīv) **1** a house or box for bees to live in. **2** a large number of bees living together: *The hive was swarming.* **3** put bees in a hive. **4** of bees, enter a hive. **5** store up honey in a hive. **6** lay up for future use. **7** a busy place full of people: *On Saturdays, the department store is a hive.* **8** live close together as bees do. 1, 2, 7 *n.,* 3–6, 8 *v.,* **hived, hiv·ing.**

**hives** (hīvz) a condition in which the skin itches and shows slightly swollen patches: *Some people are allergic to strawberries and get hives when they eat them. n.*

**H.M.** His Majesty; Her Majesty.

**H.M.C.S.** His Majesty's Canadian Ship; Her Majesty's Canadian Ship: *H.M.C.S. St. Laurent.*

**H.M.S.** **1** His Majesty's Ship; Her Majesty's Ship. **2** His Majesty's Service; Her Majesty's Service.

hat, āge, fär; let, ēqual, tėrm; it, īce
hot, ōpen, ôrder; oil, out; cup, pút, rüle
əbove, takən, pencəl, lemən, circəs
ch, child; ng, long; sh, ship
th, thin; ᴛʜ, then; zh, measure

**ho** (hō) **1** an exclamation of surprise, joy, or scorn. **2** an exclamation used to attract attention: *Land ho! interj.*
☞ *Hom.* HOE.

**ho.** house.

**Ho** holmium.

**hoar** (hôr) HOARY. *adj.*
☞ *Hom.* WHORE.

**hoard** (hôrd) **1** save and store away: *A squirrel hoards nuts for the winter. The miser hoarded his money.* **2** what is saved and stored away; the things stored: *The squirrel kept its hoard in a tree.* 1 *v.,* 2 *n.* —**hoard′er,** *n.*
☞ *Hom.* HORDE.

**hoar·frost** (hôr′frost′) a film of tiny ice crystals that sometimes forms on a cold surface. *n.*

**hoar·hound** (hôr′hound′) See HOREHOUND. *n.*

**hoarse** (hôrs) **1** rough and deep in sound; husky: *Her voice was hoarse from shouting at the game.* **2** having a rough voice: *He's hoarse because of a cold.* *adj.,* **hoars·er, hoars·est.** —**hoarse′ly,** *adv.* —**hoarse′ness,** *n.*
☞ *Hom.* HORSE.

**hoar·y** (hô′rē) **1** of hair, grey or white. **2** having such hair, white or grey with age: *a hoary old man.* **3** very old; ancient. *adj.,* **hoar·i·er, hoar·i·est.** —**hoar′i·ness,** *n.*

**hoar·y-head·ed** (hô′rē hed′id) having white or grey hair. *adj.*

**hoary marmot** *Cdn.* a large grey marmot found in the mountains of western Canada; whistler: *The hoary marmot is the largest North American marmot.*

**hoax** (hōks) **1** a mischievous trick, especially a made-up story: *The report of an attack from Mars was a hoax.* **2** play a mischievous trick on; deceive. 1 *n.,* 2 *v.* —**hoax′er,** *n.*

**hob**¹ (hob) **1** a shelf at the back or side of a fireplace, used for keeping things warm. **2** a peg at which quoits, etc. are thrown. *n.*

**hob**² (hob) a HOBGOBLIN (def. 1); elf. *n.*
**play hob** or **raise hob,** *Informal.* cause trouble.

**hob·bit** (hob′ət) a member of an imaginary race of small, good-natured people about half as tall as human beings, having beardless faces, curly hair, and woolly, leathery-soled feet. *n.*
☞ *Etym.* Created by J.R.R. Tolkien (1892–1973) in his books *The Hobbit* and *Lord of the Rings.*

**hob·ble** (hob′əl) **1** walk or move awkwardly or unsteadily; limp: *She managed to hobble to the phone without using the crutches.* **2** cause to walk awkwardly or limp. **3** an awkward walk; limp. **4** put a strap, rope, etc. around the legs of an animal, especially a horse, so that it can move a little but not run away. **5** a rope or strap used to hobble a horse, etc. **6** hinder. 1, 2, 4, 6 *v.,* **hob·bled, hob·bling;** 3, 5 *n.*

**hob·ble·de·hoy** (hob′əl dē hoi′) a youth between boyhood and manhood, especially one who is clumsy or awkward. *n.*

**hob·by** (hob′ē) something a person especially likes to work at or study apart from his or her main business or occupation; any favourite pastime, topic of conversation, etc.: *Growing roses is her hobby. n., pl.* **hob·bies.**

**hob·by·horse** (hob′ē hôrs′) **1** a stick with a horse's head, used as a toy horse by children. **2** a rocking horse. **3** a favourite topic: *Father is again on his hobbyhorse of cutting costs. n.*

**hob·gob·lin** (hob′gob′lən) **1** a mischievous elf; goblin. **2** something imaginary that gives rise to fear. *n.*

**hob·nail** (hob′nāl′) a short nail with a large head: *Hobnails are used to protect the soles of boots.* *n.*

**hob·nob** (hob′nob′) *Informal.* **1** associate intimately; talk together on familiar terms: *Mikhail says that he hobnobs with royalty.* **2** drink together. *v.*, **hob·nobbed, hob·nob·bing.**

**ho·bo** (hō′bō) tramp. *n., pl.* **ho·bos** or **ho·boes.**

**Hob·son's choice** (hob′sənz) the choice of taking the thing offered or nothing.
☞ *Etym.* From *Hobson* (1540–1630) who owned stables in England. He rented out horses, allowing customers to take the one next to the door or none at all.

**hock** (hok) **1** the joint in the hind leg of a horse, cow, etc. above the fetlock joint. See HORSE for picture. **2** cripple by cutting the tendons of the hock; hamstring. **1** *n.*, **2** *v.*
☞ *Hom.* HAWK.

**hock·ey** (hok′ē) **1** a game played on ice by two teams of six players wearing skates and carrying hooked sticks with which they try to shoot a black rubber disk, the puck, into the opposing team's goal. **2** FIELD HOCKEY. *n.*

**ho·cus** (hō′kəs) **1** play a trick on; hoax; cheat. **2** stupefy with drugs. **3** put drugs in a drink. *v.* **ho·cussed** or **ho·cused, ho·cus·sing** or **ho·cus·ing.**

**ho·cus–po·cus** (hō′kəs pō′kəs) **1** sleight of hand; magic. **2** any meaningless or insincere talk or action designed to cover up a deception: *All her talk about our beautiful house and garden was just hocus-pocus.* **3** a typical formula for conjuring. **4** deceive; trick: *Don't try to hocus-pocus me.* **1–3** *n.*, **4** *v.*

A hod used to carry bricks

**hod** (hod) **1** a trough or tray with a long handle, used for carrying bricks, mortar, etc. on the shoulder. **2** COAL SCUTTLE. *n.*

**hodge·podge** (hoj′poj′) a disorderly mixture; a mess or jumble. *n.*

A hoe

**hoe** (hō) **1** an implement with a small blade set across the end of a long handle, used to loosen soil and cut weeds. **2** loosen, dig, or cut with a hoe: *There are a lot of weeds to hoe again.* **3** work with a hoe: *She spent all morning hoeing.* **1** *n.*, **2**, **3** *v.*, **hoed, hoe·ing.** —**ho′er,** *n.*
☞ *Hom.* HO.

**hoe·down** (hō′doun′) **1** a lively dance, especially a square dance. **2** the music for such a dance. **3** a party featuring hoedowns: *There's a hoedown Saturday night.* *n.*

**hog** (hog) **1** a domestic pig, especially a full-grown, castrated male raised for meat. **2** *Informal.* a selfish, greedy person. **3** *Informal.* take more than one's share of: *Don't hog the blanket.* **1, 2** *n.*, **3** *v.*, **hogged, hog·ging. go the whole hog,** *Informal.* go to the limit; do something thoroughly.

**hog·back** (hog′bak′) a low, sharp ridge having steep sides. *n.*

**hog·gish** (hog′ish) very selfish, greedy, or filthy. *adj.* —**hog′gish·ly,** *adv.* —**hog′gish·ness,** *n.*

**hog line** in curling, a line marked across the ice 7 yards (6.4 m) in front of each tee, the minimum distance for a rock to remain in play.

**hog·ma·nay** (hog′mə nā′) in Scotland, New Year's Eve, when children knock on doors to wish the inhabitants a Happy New Year in exchange for presents, cakes, etc. *n.*

**hogs·head** (hogz′hed′) **1** a large barrel or cask, especially one having a capacity of from 100 to 140 gallons (about 455 to 635 L). **2** a unit for measuring liquids, equal to 54 gallons (about 245 L). *n.*

**hog·wash** (hog′wosh′) any refuse given to pigs; swill. *n.*

**hoi pol·loi** (hoi′ pə loi′) *Greek.* ordinary people; the general populace.

**hoist** (hoist) **1** raise on high; lift up, often with ropes and pulleys: *to hoist sails, to hoist blocks of stone.* **2** a hoisting; lift: *She gave me a hoist up the wall.* **3** an elevator or other apparatus for hoisting heavy loads. See CAISSON for picture. **1** *v.*, **2, 3** *n.*

**hoi·ty–toi·ty** (hoi′tē toi′tē) **1** inclined to put on airs; haughty, or pompous. **2** flighty or silly. **3** hoity-toity behaviour. **4** an exclamation of annoyed surprise at a display of haughtiness or arrogance. **1, 2** *adj.*, **3** *n.*, **4** *interj.*

**hold**¹ (hōld) **1** take in the hands or arms and keep; not let go; keep from getting away: *Please hold my hat. Hold my watch while I play this game.* **2** the act of holding: *to release one's hold.* **3** something to hold by: *She looked for a hold on the smooth rock but couldn't find any.* **4** something to hold something else with. **5** keep in some position or condition; force to keep: *He will hold the paper steady while you draw.* **6** keep from falling; support: *He held his head in his hands.* **7** not break, loosen, or give

way: *The dike held during the flood.* **8** keep from acting; keep back: *Hold your breath.* **9** keep; retain: *This package will be held until called for.* **10** keep by force against an enemy; defend: *Hold the fort.* **11** keep or have within itself; contain: *This theatre holds 500 people.* **12** have and keep as one's own; possess; occupy: *to hold an office.* **13** have and take part in; carry on together: *Shall we hold a meeting of the club?* **14** keep or have in mind: *to hold a belief.* **15** think; consider: *People once held that the world was flat.* **16** remain faithful or firm: *She held to her promise.* **17** be true; be in force or effect: *The rule holds in all cases.* **18** keep on; continue: *The weather held warm.* **19** a controlling force or influence: *A habit has a hold on you.* **20** decide legally: *The court holds him guilty.* **21** in wrestling, a way of holding one's opponent. **22** in music, keep on singing or playing a note. **23** in music, a sign for a pause. **24** a prison. 1, 5–18, 20, 22 *v.*, **held, hold·ing**; 2–4, 19, 21, 23–24 *n.*
**hold against,** blame for.
**hold back,** keep back; keep from acting.
**hold down,** keep down; keep under control.
**hold forth,** a talk; preach (*often used disparagingly*). **b** offer.
**hold in,** a keep in; keep back. **b** restrain; control: *Mette was so angry she couldn't hold in her temper.*
**hold off,** keep at a distance; keep from acting or attacking.
**hold on,** *Informal.* **a** keep one's hold: *She held on to the overturned boat till help came.* **b** keep on; continue. **c** stop! wait a minute!
**hold one's own,** maintain one's strength or position.
**hold out,** a continue; last: *The water would not hold out much longer.* **b** keep resisting; not give in: *The company of soldiers held out for six days until help arrived.* **c** offer.
**hold over,** a keep longer than originally scheduled: *The movie was so popular that it was held over for another week.* **b** postpone: *The game has been held over until next week.*
**hold the fort,** be in charge, to see that nothing goes wrong.
**hold up,** a keep from falling; support. **b** display; show. **c** continue; last; endure. **d** stop: *The police officer held up the traffic.* **e** *Informal.* stop by force and rob.
**hold with,** a side with. **b** agree with. **c** approve of.
**lay** or **take hold of,** a seize; grasp. **b** get control or possession of.
**hold²** (hōld) the interior of a ship below the deck: *A ship's cargo is carried in its hold.* *n.*
**hold·back** (hōld′bak′) **1** something that holds back; restraint; hindrance. **2** an iron or strap on the shaft of a wagon, carriage, etc. to which the harness is attached enabling a horse to stop or to back the wagon, carriage, etc. *n.*
**hold·er** (hōl′dər) **1** a person who holds a bill, note, cheque, etc. and is legally entitled to receive payment on it. **2** a person who owns or occupies property. **3** a device for holding something (*usually used in compounds*): *a cigarette holder, a potholder.* **4** any person or thing that holds. *n.*
**hold·ing** (hōl′ding) **1** land, especially a piece of land rented from someone else. **2** in certain sports, the illegal hindering of an opponent's movements. **3** Usually, **holdings,** *pl.* property, especially in the form of stocks or bonds. **4** ppr. of HOLD. 1–3 *n.*, 4 *v.*
**holding company** a company that owns stocks or bonds of other companies and often controls them.
**hold·o·ver** (hōl′dō′vər) a person or thing that is held over from another time or place: *She was a holdover from last year's team.* *n.*

hold 571 holler

hat, āge, fär; let, ēqual, tėrm; it, īce
hot, ōpen, ôrder; oil, out; cup, püt, rüle
əbove, takən, pencəl, lemən, circəs
ch, child; ng, long; sh, ship
th, thin; ᴛʜ, then; zh, measure

**hold·up** (hōl′dup′) **1** *Informal.* the act of stopping by force and robbing. **2** stopping; delay: *She got out of her car to see what the holdup was.* *n.*
**hole** (hōl) **1** an opening in or through something, often a break or tear: *a hole in a stocking, a hole in a window. The calendar has a hole at the top to hang it up by.* **2** a hollow place; pit: *There's a hole in the lawn where the ground caved in.* **3** a place that is lower than the parts around it: *a hole in the road.* **4** burrow: *Rabbits live in holes.* **5** make a hole or holes in: *The side of the ship was holed by an iceberg.* **6** a small, dark, dreary, or dirty place: *I wouldn't want to live in that hole.* **7** *Informal.* a flaw or defect: *That argument has several holes.* **8** *Informal.* an embarrassing, awkward, or difficult position: *Sonia got herself into a hole, financially.* **9** in golf, a small round hole in a green, into which the golf ball is to be hit. **10** any of the sections of a golf course from a tee to a hole: *A regular golf course consists of 18 holes. She hit a hole in one.* **11** hit or drive into a hole. **12** a small, narrow indentation in a coastline, especially in a bay or harbour (*often used in place names*). 1–4, 6–10, 12 *n.*, 5, 11 *v.*, **holed, hol·ing.**
**burn a hole in one's pocket,** of money, make one want badly to spend; be easily spent: *Her birthday gift is burning a hole in her pocket.*
**hole out,** hit a golf ball into the hole.
**hole up,** a of animals, go into a hole. **b** *Informal.* go into hiding for a time: *The robbers holed up in an old cabin.*
**make a hole in,** use up a large amount of: *The new radio made quite a hole in my savings.*
**pick holes in,** find fault with; criticize.
☛ *Hom.* WHOLE.
**hol·ey** (hō′lē) having holes. *adj.*
☛ *Hom.* HOLI, HOLY, WHOLLY.
**Ho·li** (hō′lē) in Hinduism, a popular spring festival generally dedicated to Krishna. *n.*
☛ *Hom.* HOLEY, HOLY, WHOLLY.
**hol·i·day** (hol′ə dā′) **1** a day free of work; day for pleasure and enjoyment. **2** a day on which, either by law or custom, general business is suspended: *Labour Day and July 1st are both holidays as specified by law.* **3** suited to a holiday; festive: *in holiday spirits.* **4** a holy day; religious festival. **5** take or have a holiday: *They are holidaying in the tropics.* **6** Often, **holidays,** *pl.* vacation; period of rest or recreation: *the summer holidays. My mother gets three weeks of holidays a year.* 1–4, 6 *n.*, 5 *v.*
☛ *Etym.* From OE *hāligdæg* 'holy day'. In the Middle Ages days off work were given for the holy days, or feast days, of the Christian church.
**ho·li·ness** (hō′lē nis) **1** being holy. **2 Holiness,** a title used in speaking to or of the Pope. *n.*
**hol·lan·daise sauce** (hol′ən dāz′) a creamy sauce made from egg yolks, butter, lemon juice, and seasoning, served with fish, vegetables, etc.
**hol·ler** (hol′ər) *Informal.* **1** shout: *We hollered at her to come back.* **2** a loud cry or shout. 1 *v.*, 2 *n.*

**hol·low** (hol′ō) **1** having a hole or cavity inside; not solid: *A tube or pipe is hollow. Some plants have hollow stems.* **2** shaped like a bowl or cup; having an inward curve; concave or sunken: *There is a large hollow place in the lawn where the earth has settled.* **3** a hollow place; a wide, shallow hole: *a hollow in the road.* **4** make or become hollow. **5** make or form by hollowing (*usually used with* **out**): *He hollowed out a canoe from a log.* **6** a small valley: *They built their house in a hollow.* **7** sounding as if coming from something hollow; deep-toned and muffled: *a hollow voice, a hollow groan.* **8** lacking real worth, truth, or significance; worthless or false: *hollow promises, hollow joys, hollow victory.* **9** empty or hungry: *a hollow stomach.* **10** *Informal.* thoroughly or completely: *We beat their team hollow.* **11** deep and sunken: *A starving person has hollow eyes and cheeks.* 1, 2, 7–9, 11 *adj.*, 3, 6 *n.*, 4, 5 *v.*, 10 *adv.* —**hol′low·ly,** *adv.* —**hol′low·ness,** *n.*

**hol·low-eyed** (hol′ō īd′) **1** having eyes set deep in the head. **2** having dark shadows under the eyes: *hollow-eyed from lack of sleep.* *adj.*

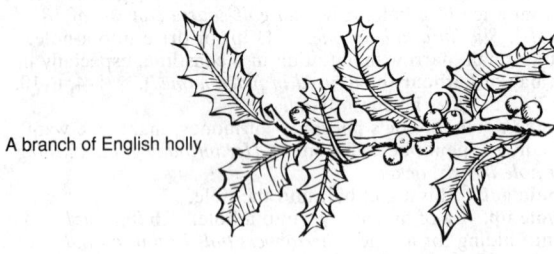
A branch of English holly

**hol·ly** (hol′ē) **1** any of a closely related group of trees and shrubs having thick, shiny leaves with spiny points along the edges, and clusters of bright-red berries. **2** the leaves and berries of holly, used as Christmas decorations: *a holly wreath.* **3** referring to the family of trees and shrubs that includes the hollies. *n., pl.* **hol·lies.**

**hol·ly·hock** (hol′ē hok′) a tall perennial plant of the MALLOW family native to China, but widely grown for its spikes of large, showy flowers: *Hollyhock flowers are usually white, pink, red, or yellow.* *n.*

**holm**[1] (hōm) **1** low, flat land by a stream. **2** a small island in a river or lake near a large island or the mainland. *n.*
☛ *Hom.* HOME.

**holm**[2] (hōm) HOLM OAK. *n.*
☛ *Hom.* HOME.

**hol·mi·um** (hōl′mē əm) a rare metallic chemical element belonging to the yttrium group. *Symbol:* Ho *n.*

**holm oak** an evergreen oak of southern Europe having leaves that look like holly.

**hol·o·caust** (hol′ə kost′) **1** a sacrificial offering, all of which is burned. **2** great or total destruction of life, especially by fire. **3 the Holocaust,** the wholesale slaughter of Jews, Poles, and other peoples by the Nazis during the Second World War. *n.*

**hol·o·gram** (hol′ə gram′) a three-dimensional photograph obtained by exposing a photographic plate near an object illuminated by a laser beam. *n.*

**hol·o·graph** (hol′ə graf′) **1** wholly written in the handwriting of the person in whose name it appears: *a holograph will.* **2** a holograph manuscript, letter, document, etc. 1 *adj.*, 2 *n.* —**hol′o·graph′ic,** *adj.*

**ho·log·ra·phy** (hə log′rə fē) a photographic process for making three-dimensional pictures by means of laser light. *n.*

**Hol·stein** (hōl′stīn *or* hōl′stēn) a breed of large black-and-white dairy cattle. *n.*

**hol·ster** (hōl′stər) a leather case for a pistol, usually attached to a belt. *n.*

**ho·ly** (hō′lē) **1** belonging to God; set apart for God's service; coming from God; sacred: *Most religions have a holy book.* **2** declared sacred by religious use and authority: *a holy day.* **3** like a saint; spiritually perfect; very good; pure in heart: *a holy woman.* **4** worthy of reverence: *The Tomb of the Unknown Soldier is a holy place.* **5** a holy place. 1–4 *adj.*, **ho·li·er, ho·li·est;** 5 *n., pl.* **ho·lies.**
☛ *Hom.* HOLEY, HOLI, WHOLLY.
☛ *Etym.* From OE *hālig*. See note at HALLOW.

**Holy City 1** a city considered sacred by the adherents of any religion: *Jerusalem, Rome, and Mecca are Holy Cities.* **2** heaven.

**Holy Communion** in the Christian church, the commemoration of Christ's Last Supper, in which bread and wine are consecrated and taken as the body and blood of Christ or as symbols of them; the Eucharist.

**holy day** a religious festival, especially one not occurring on Sunday: *Ash Wednesday and Good Friday are holy days.*

**Holy Grail** GRAIL.

**holy of holies 1** the inner shrine of the Jewish tabernacle and temple. **2** any place that is most sacred.

**Holy Roman Empire** an empire in western and central Europe regarded both as the continuation of the Roman Empire and as the temporal form of a universal dominion whose spiritual head was the Pope: *The Holy Roman Empire began in* A.D. *962 or, according to some, in* A.D. *800, and ended in 1806.*

**Holy See 1** the position or authority of the Pope. **2** the Pope's court.

**ho·ly·stone** (hō′lē stōn′) **1** a piece of soft sandstone used for scrubbing the wooden decks of ships. **2** scrub with a holystone. 1 *n.*, 2 *v.*, **ho·ly·stoned, ho·ly·ston·ing.**

**holy water** water blessed by a Christian priest.

**hom.** HOMONYM. *n.*

**hom·age** (hom′ij) **1** respect; reverence; honour: *Everyone paid homage to the great leader.* **2** in former times, a formal acknowledgment by a vassal that he owed loyalty and service to his lord. **3** anything done or given to show such acknowledgment. **4** a formal statement, or oath, of loyalty and service owed to one's sovereign. *n.*

**hom·bre** (om′brä *or* om′brē; *Spanish,* ōm′brä) a man. *n.*

**home** (hōm) **1** the place where a person or family lives; one's own house: *Her home is at 25 South Street.* **2** the place where a person was born or brought up; one's own town or country: *His home is Ottawa.* **3** a private house; a house, especially a new house built for occupation by one family: *There are some lovely homes for sale in the new subdivision.* **4** the place where an animal or plant lives: *A beaver makes its home at the water's edge.* **5** a place where a thing is very common: *The Canadian tundra is the home of the musk-ox.* **6** any place where a person can rest and be safe. **7** a place where people who are homeless, poor, old, sick, blind, etc. may live. **8** having to do with one's own home or country: *Write me all the home events.* **9** at, to, or toward one's own home or country: *Go home.* **10** the goal in many games. **11** in baseball, the home plate. **12** to the place where it belongs; to the thing aimed at: *to strike home.* **13** to the heart or centre; deep in: *to drive a nail home.* **14** effective; reaching its goal. **15** go home. **16** have a home. **17** furnish with a home. 1–7, 10, 11 *n.*, 8, 14 *adj.*, 9, 12, 13 *adv.*, 15–17 *v.* **homed, hom·ing.**
**at home, a** in one's own home or country. **b** in a friendly place or familiar condition; at ease; comfortable: *Tiiu felt completely at home with her next-door neighbour.* **c** ready to receive visitors. **d** reception.
**bring home,** make clear, emphatic, or realistic.
**come home to,** be understood or realized by.
**drive home, a** make secure with a hammer: *With the second blow, he drove the peg home.* **b** make someone realize: *He thumped the table to drive home his argument.*
**home in on,** be guided toward a goal or target by or as if by radar.
**see one home,** escort to one's home.
☛ **Hom.** HOLM.
☛ **Syn.** In general usage, **home** refers to a place that is the centre of family life; HOUSE refers to the place only as a building. In the advertising of real estate, etc., **home** is often used in place of **house** to suggest the comfort and happiness of family life.

**Home and School Association** an association of parents and teachers who meet from time to time in the interests of schoolchildren.

**home·bred** (hōm′bred′) **1** bred or reared at home; native; domestic. **2** not polished or refined; unsophisticated. *adj.*

**home·brew** (hōm′brü′) an alcoholic liquor made at home, especially beer. *n.*

**home·com·ing** (hōm′kum′ing) **1** a coming home. **2** an annual celebration held at many universities and colleges for alumni. *n.*

**home economics** the science and art that deals with the management of a household.

**home·land** (hōm′land′) the country that is one's home; one's native land. *n.*

**home·less** (hōm′lis) **1** having no home. **2** the homeless, people without homes. *adj.*
—**home′less·ness,** *n.*

**home·like** (hōm′līk′) like home; friendly; familiar; comfortable: *a homelike atmosphere.* *adj.*
—**home′like′ness,** *n.*

**home·ly** (hōm′lē) **1** not good-looking; plain: *His homely face lit up in a smile.* **2** suited to home life; simple; everyday: *homely pleasures, homely food.* **3** of plain manners; unpretending: *a simple, homely woman.* *adj.*, **home·li·er, home·li·est.** —**home′li·ness,** *n.*

**home·made** (hōm′mād′) made at home. *adj.*

**home·mak·er** (hōm′mā′kər) a person who manages a home, especially a woman who is a wife and mother. *n.*

**home·mak·ing** (hōm′mā′king) the art or practice of managing a home and looking after a family. *n.*

**ho·me·o·path** (hō′mē ə path′) a person who practises HOMEOPATHY. *n.*

**ho·me·op·a·thy** (hō′mē op′ə thē) a system of treating disease by giving very small doses of a drug that in large quantities would produce symptoms of the disease in healthy persons. Compare with ALLOPATHY. *n.*

**home plate** in baseball, the block or slab beside which a player stands to bat the ball, and to which he or she must return, after hitting the ball and rounding the bases, in order to score.

**hom·er** (hō′mər) *Informal.* in baseball, a home run. *n.*

**Homeric laughter** (hō mer′ik) loud, hearty laughter.

**home·room** (hōm′rüm′) **1** the classroom in a school where a given class meets first every day to be checked for attendance, hear announcements, etc. **2** the classroom in a school, especially an elementary school, where a given class is taught most subjects, usually by the same teacher. **3** the period during which a class meets in the homeroom. **4** the students of a given homeroom. **5** of or having to do with a homeroom or homerooms: *My homeroom teacher taught French.* *n.*

**home rule** the management of the affairs of a country, district, or city by its own people; local self-government.

**home run** in baseball, a run scored on a hit that enables the batter to run the entire circuit of the bases without a stop.

**home·sick** (hōm′sik′) ill or depressed because one is away from home; longing for home. *adj.*
—**home′sick′ness,** *n.*

**home·spun** (hōm′spun′) **1** spun or made at home. **2** cloth made of yarn spun at home. **3** a strong, loosely woven cloth similar to homespun. **4** not polished; plain, simple: *homespun manners.* 1, 4 *adj.*, 2, 3 *n.*

**home·stead** (hōm′sted′) **1** a house with its land and other buildings; farm with its buildings. **2** in western Canada, a parcel of public land, usually consisting of 160 acres (a quarter section, about 64 to 65 hectares), granted to a settler under certain conditions by the federal government. **3** settle on such land: *Her father homesteaded in Saskatchewan.* **4** settle and work a farm, land, etc.: *They homesteaded a quarter section west of the river.* 1, 2 *n.*, 3, 4 *v.*

**Homestead Act** the Act of 1872 under which settlers became homesteaders of the Canadian West.

**home·stead·er** (hōm′sted′ər) **1** a person who has a homestead. **2** a settler granted a homestead by the federal government. *n.*

**home stretch** **1** the part of a track over which the last part of a race is run. **2** the last part.

**home town** **1** the town or city where one grew up or spent most of one's early life. **2** the town or city of one's principal residence.

**home·ward** (hōm′wərd)   toward home: *to turn homeward, the homeward road.*   *adv., adj.*

**home·wards** (hōm′wərdz)   HOMEWARD.   *adv.*

**home·work** (hōm′wėrk′)   **1** a lesson or lessons to be studied or prepared outside the classroom.   **2** any work done at home.   *n.*

**hom·ey** (hō′mē) *Informal.*   like home; cosy and comfortable: *The old inn had a very homey atmosphere.*   *adj.*,   **hom·i·er, hom·i·est.**

**hom·i·cid·al** (hom′ə sī′dəl)   **1** of or having to do with HOMICIDE.   **2** murderous.   *adj.*

**hom·i·cide** (hom′ə sīd′)   the killing of one human being by another: *Intentional homicide is murder.*   *n.*

**hom·i·ly** (hom′ə lē)   **1** a sermon, usually on some part of the Bible.   **2** a serious moral talk or writing.   *n., pl.* **hom·i·lies.**

**homing pigeon**   a pigeon trained to fly home from great distances: *Homing pigeons are often used in racing or for carrying written messages.*

**hom·i·ny** (hom′ə nē)   dried, hulled corn: *Hominy grits is coarsely ground hominy that is boiled in water or milk for food.*   *n.*

**ho·mo** (hō′mō) *Informal.*   homogenized whole milk.   *n.*

**ho·mo·ge·ne·i·ty** (hō′mə jə nē′ə tē)   being HOMOGENEOUS.   *n.*

**ho·mo·ge·ne·ous** (hō′mə jē′nē əs)   **1** of the same kind; similar: *homogeneous interests.*   **2** composed of similar elements or parts; of uniform nature or character throughout: *a homogeneous rock, a homogeneous community.*   Compare with HETEROGENEOUS.   *adj.*
—**ho′mo·ge′ne·ous·ly,** *adv.*

**ho·mog·e·nize** (hə moj′ə nīz′)   **1** make HOMOGENEOUS.   **2** break up the fat globules of (whole milk) so that the fat remains emulsified and is distributed evenly throughout the milk: *In homogenized milk the fat does not rise to the top in the form of cream.*   *v.*, **ho·mog·e·nized, ho·mog·e·niz·ing.**

**hom·o·graph** (hom′ə graf′)   one of two or more words having the same spelling but different meanings, origins, or pronunciations: *Mail, meaning 'letters', and mail, meaning 'armour', are homographs.*   *n.*

**ho·mol·o·gous** (hō mol′ə gəs)   **1** corresponding in position, proportion, value, structure, etc.   **2** in biology, corresponding in type of structure and in origin but not necessarily in function: *The wing of a bird and the foreleg of a horse are homologous.*   *adj.*

**hom·o·logue** (hom′ə log′)   a HOMOLOGOUS thing, organ, or part.   *n.*

**ho·mol·o·gy** (hō mol′ə jē)   **1** a correspondence or similarity in position, proportion, value, structure, etc. **2** in biology, a correspondence in type or structure and in origin.   *n., pl.* **ho·mol·o·gies.**

**hom·o·nym** (hom′ə nim′)   **1** HOMOPHONE (def. 1). **2** one of two or more words having the same pronunciation and spelling but different meanings and origins: *Rose, past tense of the verb rise, and rose, meaning the flower, are homonyms.*   *n.*

**hom·o·phone** (hom′ə fōn′)   **1** one of two or more words having the same pronunciation but different meanings, origins, and, sometimes, spellings: *Pear, pair, and pare are homophones.*   **2** one of two or more letters or symbols representing the same sound. The letters *c* and *k* are homophones in the word *cork*.   *n.*

**ho·mop·ter·an** (hō mop′tə rən)   **1** a HOMOPTEROUS insect.   **2** of or referring to the order comprising these insects.   **1** *n.*, **2** *adj.*

**ho·mop·ter·ous** (hō mop′tə rəs)   of or having to do with an order (**Homoptera**) of sucking insects that feed on plants, including aphids, cicadas, and scale insects: *Most homopterous insects have two pairs of wings, with the front pair of the same thickness throughout, either all leathery or all thin and membranous; the wings at rest are usually sloped upward in a tentlike position over the body.*   *adj.*
☛ *Usage.*   See note at HETEROPTEROUS.

**Ho·mo sa·pi·ens** (hō′mō sā′pē enz′ *or* sap′ē enz′) *Latin.*   human being; the species including all existing races of humanity.

**ho·mo·sex·u·al** (hō′mə sek′shü əl)   **1** of, having to do with, or showing desire for one of the same sex. Compare with HETEROSEXUAL.   **2** a homosexual person. **1** *adj.*, **2** *n.*

**hon.**   **1** honorary.   **2** honourable.

**Hon.**   **1** Honourable.   **2** Honorary.   **3** Honours.

**hon·don** (hon don′)   the inner shrine of a Shinto temple which worshippers may not enter, and in which the chief treasure of the shrine is housed.   *n.*

**hone** (hōn)   **1** a fine-grained whetstone on which to sharpen cutting tools, especially razors.   **2** sharpen on a hone.   **3** make more precise, effective, etc.   **1** *n.*, **2, 3** *v.*, **honed, hon·ing.**

**hon·est** (on′ist)   **1** not lying, cheating, or stealing; fair and upright; truthful: *an honest person.*   **2** obtained by fair and upright means; without lying, cheating, or stealing: *honest profits.*   **3** not hiding one's real nature; frank, open: *honest opposition. I would like your honest opinion.*   **4** genuine; pure: *honest goods.*   *adj.*
—**hon′est·ly,** *adv.*

**hon·es·ty** (on′i stē)   **1** fairness and uprightness. **2** truthfulness.   **3** freedom from deceit or fraud.   *n.*

**hon·ey** (hun′ē)   **1** a thick, sweet liquid that bees make out of nectar they collect from flowers.   **2** the drop of sweet liquid found in many flowers; nectar: *Honey attracts bees to flowers.*   **3** sweetness.   **4** of or like honey; sweet. **5** lovable.   **6** dear.   **7** darling; dear: *I won't be long, honey.*   **8** *Informal.*   a person or thing that is attractive: *She's a honey. His new car is a honey.*   **9** sweeten with or as with honey.   **10** talk sweetly; flatter.   **1–3, 7, 8** *n., pl.* **hon·eys;**   **4–6** *adj.*, **9, 10** *v.*, **hon·eyed** *or* **hon·ied, hon·ey·ing.**   —**hon′ey-like′,** *adj.*

**hon·ey·bee** (hun′ē bē′)   a bee of a kind that makes honey and wax that can be used by people.   See BEE for picture.   *n.*

**hon·ey·comb** (hun′ē kōm′)   **1** a structure of wax containing rows of six-sided cells made by bees, in which they store honey, pollen, and their eggs.   See BEE for picture.   **2** anything like this.   **3** like a honeycomb: *a honeycomb weave of cloth, a honeycomb pattern in knitting.* **4** make like a honeycomb.   **5** pierce with many holes or tunnels: *The rock was honeycombed with passages.* **6** weaken or harm by spreading through: *That city is honeycombed with crime.*   **1–3** *n.*, **4–6** *v.*

**hon·ey·dew** (hun′ē dyü′ *or* hun′ē dü′)   **1** a sweet substance that oozes from the leaves of certain plants in hot weather. 2 a sweet, sticky substance deposited on leaves and stems, secreted by tiny insects called aphids. 3 a HONEYDEW MELON. *n.*

**honeydew melon** a variety of melon having sweet, green flesh and a smooth, whitish skin.

**hon·eyed** or **hon·ied** (hun′ēd) 1 sweetened with honey: *honeyed drinks.* 2 laden with honey. 3 sweet as honey: *honeyed words.* 4 pt. and pp. of HONEY. 1–3 *adj.*, 4 *v.*

**honey locust** a thorny North American tree having long, divided leaves and large, flat pods containing sweet pulp.

**hon·ey·moon** (hun′ē mün′) 1 the holiday spent together by a newly married couple. 2 the initial period of marriage. 3 the initial period of any new agreement, arrangement, etc., when things are harmonious and peaceful. 4 spend or have a honeymoon. 1–3 *n.*, 4 *v.* —**hon′ey·moon′er,** *n.*

**hon·ey·suck·le** (hun′ē suk′əl) 1 any of various upright or climbing shrubs or vines: *Some kinds of honeysuckle have fragrant, white, yellow, or red tubular flowers.* 2 any of various similar plants. *n.*

**hon·ied** (hun′ēd) 1 a pt. and a pp. of HONEY. 2 HONEYED. 1 *v.*, 2 *adj.*

**honk** (hongk) 1 the cry of the wild goose. 2 any similar sound: *the honk of a car horn.* 3 make the cry of a wild goose or similar sound: *We honked as we drove past their house.* 4 cause to make a sound similar to that of a goose: *to honk a horn.* 1, 2 *n.*, 3, 4 *v.* —**honk′er,** *n.*

**hon·or** (on′ər) See HONOUR. *n.*, *v.*

**hon·or·a·ble** (on′ə rə bəl) See HONOURABLE. *adj.*

**hon·o·rar·i·um** (on′ə rer′ē əm) an honorary fee for professional services on which no fixed price is set: *The guest speaker received an honorarium.* *n.*, *pl.* **hon·o·rar·i·ums** or **hon·o·rar·i·a** (-rer′ē ə).

**hon·or·ar·y** (on′ə rer′ē) 1 given or done as an honour: *an honorary membership.* 2 as an honour only; without pay or regular duties: *Some associations have honorary secretaries, etc. as well as those who are regularly employed.* *adj.*

**hon·or·if·ic** (on′ə rif′ik) 1 doing or giving honour; showing respect or deference. 2 a title of respect: *"Sir" is an honorific.* 1 *adj.*, 2 *n.*

**honor system** See HONOUR SYSTEM.

**hon·our** or **hon·or** (on′ər) 1 credit for acting well; good name: *It was greatly to her honour that she refused the reward.* 2 glory; fame; renown. 3 a source of credit; cause of honour: *She is an honour to her family and school.* 4 a nice sense of what is right or proper; sticking to action that is right or that is usual and expected. 5 great respect; high regard: *Our Queen is held in honour. We pay honour to heroes.* 6 an act of respect: *funeral honours.* 7 rank; dignity; distinction: *Knighthood is an honour.* 8 respect greatly; regard highly. 9 show respect to. 10 confer dignity upon; be an honour to; favour: *to be honoured by a royal visit.* 11 chastity; virtue. 12 accept and pay a bill, draft, note, etc. when due. 13 **honours** or **honors,** *pl.* a special favours or courtesies. b a special mention, grade, or credit given to a student by a school, college, or university for unusually excellent work. c in the game of bridge, the ace, king, queen, jack, and ten of trumps, or the four aces in no-trump. d a course of advanced studies for certain students. 14 **Honour** or **Honor,** a title used in speaking to or of a judge, mayor, etc. 1–7, 11, 13, 14 *n.*, 8–10, 12 *v.*

**honeydew melon**     **575**     **hoof**

hat, āge, fär; let, ēqual, tėrm; it, īce
hot, ōpen, ôrder; oil, out; cup, pút, rüle
əbove, takən, pencəl, lemən, circəs
ch, child; ng, long; sh, ship
th, thin; ᵺ, then; zh, measure

**do honour** or **honor to,** a show honour to; treat with great respect. b cause honour to; bring honour to. **do the honours** or **honors,** act as host or hostess. **upon** or **on one's honour** or **honor,** pledged to speak the truth and to do what is right.

**hon·our·a·ble** or **hon·or·a·ble** (on′ə rə bəl) 1 having or showing a sense of what is right and proper; honest; upright: *It was not honourable of her to cheat.* 2 causing honour; bringing honour to the one that has it; suffered under creditable circumstances: *honourable wounds.* 3 accompanied by honour or honours: *an honourable burial, an honourable discharge.* 4 worthy of honour; noble: *to perform honourable deeds.* 5 showing honour or respect. 6 having a title, rank, or position of honour. *adj.* —**hon′our·a·ble·ness** or **hon′or·a·ble·ness,** *n.* —**hon′our·a·bly** or **hon′or·a·bly,** *adv.*

**Hon·our·a·ble** or **Hon·or·a·ble** (on′ə rə bəl) in Canada, a title given to members of the Privy Council (which includes the Federal Cabinet), to the Speakers of both the House of Commons and the provincial legislative assemblies, and to certain senior judges. *adj.*

**honour system** or **honor system** a system of trusting people in schools and other institutions to obey the rules and do their work without being watched or forced.

**hood** (húd) 1 a soft, loose covering for the head and neck, either separate or as part of a cloak: *My raincoat has a hood.* 2 anything like a hood in shape or use. 3 a covering over the engine of an automobile. 4 in falconry, a cover for the head of a hawk, used to blind the hawk when not pursuing game. 5 cover with a hood. 6 a fold of cloth worn over an academic gown, having a band or bands of colour to indicate the degree held and the university or college of the wearer. 1–4, 6 *n.*, 5 *v.* —**hood′less,** *adj.* —**hood′like,** *adj.*

**–hood** a noun-forming suffix meaning: 1 the state or condition of being, as in *girlhood, likelihood.* 2 the character or nature of, as in *womanhood, sainthood.* 3 a group, body of, as in *priesthood, a sisterhood of noble women.*

**hood·ed** (húd′id) 1 having a hood attached: *a hooded coat.* 2 covered with or wearing a hood: *a hooded figure.* 3 shaped like a hood. 4 pt. and pp. of HOOD. 1–3 *adj.*, 4 *v.*

**hood·lum** (hü′dləm) *Informal.* 1 a young rowdy; street ruffian. 2 a criminal, especially one who uses force; gangster. *n.*

**hoo·doo** (hü′dü) 1 VOODOO. 2 *Informal.* a person or thing that brings bad luck. 3 a strangely shaped natural rock formation, found especially in western North America: *Hoodoos are common in the Alberta badlands. Hoodoos are caused by erosion.* 4 *Informal.* bad luck. 5 *Informal.* bring or cause bad luck to. 1–4 *n.*, *pl.* **hoo·doos;** 5 *v.*, **hoo·dooed, hoo·doo·ing.**

**hood·wink** (húd′wingk′) mislead by a trick; deceive. *v.* —**hood′wink′er,** *n.*
☛ *Etym.* From archaic *hoodwink,* meaning 'blindfold'.

**hoof** (hüf *or* húf) 1 a hard, horny covering on the feet

**hoofbeat** of horses, cattle, sheep, pigs, and some other animals. See HORSE for picture. **2** the whole foot of such animals. **3** *Informal.* walk: *We'll have to hoof it.* 1, 2 *n., pl.* **hoofs** or **hooves;** 3 *v.* —**hoof′less,** *adj.* —**hoof′like′,** *adj.*
**on the hoof,** of beef cattle, etc., alive; not killed and butchered.

**hoof·beat** (hüf′bēt′ *or* hüf′bēt′) the sound made by an animal's hoof. *n.*

**hoofed** (hüft *or* hüft) **1** having hoofs. **2** pt. and pp. of HOOF. 1 *adj.,* 2 *v.*

**hook** (hùk) **1** a piece of metal, wood, or other stiff material, curved or having a sharp angle for catching, holding, or fastening something or for hanging things on: *a fishhook, a clothes hook.* **2** attach or fasten with a hook or hooks: *Will you hook my dress for me?* **3** join; fit; be fastened: *This part hooks into the other part.* **4** a curved piece of wire, usually with a barb at the end, for catching fish. **5** catch or take hold of with a hook: *to hook a fish.* **6** catch fish with a hook. **7** give the form of a hook to. **8** anything curved or bent like a hook. **9** a large, curved knife for cutting down grass or grain. **10** a sharp bend: *a hook in the river.* **11** a point of land. **12** be curved or bent like a hook. **13** the act of hooking. **14** catch by a trick as if with a hook; entangle: *He's heard the group only once, but already he's hooked.* **15** *Informal.* steal. **16** make rugs, etc. by pulling loops of yarn or strips of cloth through canvas, burlap, etc. with a hook. **17** throw a ball so that it curves. **18** such a throw. **19** in sports, hit a ball so that it curves across the hitter. Compare with SLICE (def. 7). **20** such a hit. **21** in boxing, a short, swinging blow. **22** hit with such a blow. **23** in music, a line on the stem of certain notes. 1, 4, 8–11, 13, 18, 20, 21, 23 *n.,* 2, 3, 5–7, 12, 14–17, 19, 22 *v.* —**hook′like,** *adj.*
**by hook** or **by crook,** in any way at all; by fair means or foul.
**hook up, a** attach or fasten with a hook or hooks. **b** connect an electric light or appliance, or arrange and connect the parts of a radio set, telephone, etc.
**on one's own hook,** *Informal.* independently.

A hookah

**hook·ah** or **hook·a** (hùk′ə) a tobacco pipe with a long tube by which the smoke is drawn through water and cooled; water pipe. *n.*

**hook and eye** a fastener for a garment, etc., consisting of a loop or bar and a hook that catches on it.

**hooked** (hùkt) **1** curved or bent like a hook: *a hooked nose.* **2** having hooks: *a hooked fastening on a dress.* **3** made with a hook; made by hooking: *A hooked rug is made by pulling yarn or strips of cloth through canvas, etc. with a hook.* **4** addicted, especially to drugs. **5** pt. and pp. of HOOK. 1–4 *adj.,* 5 *v.*

**hook·up** (hùk′up′) the arrangement and connection of the parts of a radio or television set, telephone, broadcasting facilities, etc. *n.*

**hook·worm** (hùk′wėrm′) **1** a worm that gets into the intestines and causes a disease characterized by weakness and drowsiness. **2** the disease. *n.*

**hook·y** (hùk′ē) *n.*
**play hooky,** *Informal.* stay away from school without permission; play truant.

**hoo·li·gan** (hü′lə gən) one of a gang of street ruffians; HOODLUM. *n.*

**hoo·li·gan·ism** (hü′lə gə niz′əm) rough, noisy behaviour; lawless fun. *n.*

**hoop** (hüp) **1** a ring or flat band in the form of a circle: *a hoop for holding the staves of a barrel.* **2** bind or fasten together with a hoop or hoops. **3** a large wooden, metal, or plastic ring used as a toy by children: *The boy rolled his hoop along the ground.* **4** a circular frame formerly used to spread out a woman's skirt. **5** in croquet, one of the metal arches through which players try to hit the balls. **6** anything shaped like a hoop. 1, 3–6 *n.,* 2 *v.* —**hoop′like′,** *adj.*
☛ *Hom.* WHOOP (hüp).

A hoop skirt of 1860. The crinoline used to support the skirt is shown at the far left.

**hoop skirt** a skirt worn over a framework of connected flexible hoops that make it spread out.

**hoo·ray** (hü rā′) HURRAH. *interj., n., v.*

**hoot** (hüt) **1** the sound that an owl makes. **2** a sound like that made by an owl: *the hoot of an automobile horn.* **3** make the sound that an owl makes or one like it. **4** a sound to show disapproval or scorn. **5** a sound of merriment: *hoots of laughter.* **6** show disapproval, scorn, or enjoyment by hooting: *The audience hooted the speaker's words. We hooted with laughter.* **7** force or drive by hooting: *They hooted her off the platform.* **8** say or show by hooting: *They hooted their scorn.* **9** *Informal.* a tiny amount; a bit (used only in the negative): *She doesn't give a hoot what happens. That show wasn't worth a hoot.* 1, 2, 4, 5, 9 *n.,* 3, 6–8 *v.* —**hoot′er,** *n.*

**hoo·te·nan·ny** (hüt′nan′ē) an informal party or jamboree featuring folk-singing. *n., pl.* **hoo·te·nan·nies.**

**hooves** (hüvz *or* hùvz) a pl. of HOOF. *n.*

**hop¹** (hop) **1** spring or move by springing, on one foot. **2** spring, or move by springing, with both or all feet at once: *Many birds hop.* **3** jump over: *to hop a ditch.* **4** *Informal.* jump on a train, car, etc.: *I can just hop a bus and be there in 20 minutes.* **5** move or jump quickly onto, out of, etc.: *He hopped onto his bicycle and rode off. She hopped off the bus.* **6** a hopping; spring. **7** *Informal.* fly across in an aircraft. **8** *Informal.* a flight in an aircraft. **9** *Informal.* a dancing party: *the annual spring hop.* 1–5, 7 *v.,* **hopped, hop·ping;** 6, 8, 9 *n.*

**hop²** (hop) **1** a vine of the mulberry family having

flower clusters that look like small pine cones. **2** pick hops. **3** flavour with hops. **4 hops,** *pl.* the dried, ripe, flower clusters of the hop vine, used to flavour beer and other malt drinks. 1, 4 *n.*, 2, 3 *v.*, **hopped, hop·ping.**

**hope** (hōp) **1** a feeling that what one desires will happen: *His promise gave me hope.* **2** wish and expect: *She hopes to be able to travel to South America next year.* **3** a person or thing that gives or inspires hope: *She is the hope of the family.* **4** something hoped for: *Their one hope was to reach the shore before their pursuers saw them.* 1, 3 *n.*, 2 *v.*, **hoped, hop·ing.**
**hope against hope,** keep on hoping even though there is no good reason to have hope.

**hope chest** a chest in which a young lady collects articles that will be useful after she marries.

**hope·ful** (hōp′fəl) **1** feeling or showing hope: *a hopeful smile. They were all in a hopeful frame of mind by morning.* **2** giving or inspiring hope: *The lessening of the fever was a hopeful sign.* **3** a person who expects or is likely to achieve something: *The room was filled with young hopefuls waiting for auditions.* 1, 2 *adj.*, 3 *n.* —**hope′ful·ly,** *adv.* —**hope′ful·ness,** *n.*

**hope·ful·ly** (hōp′fùl ē) **1** in a hopeful manner: *The child followed hopefully to the fridge.* **2** *Informal.* it is to be hoped: *Hopefully, the weather will improve.*

**hope·less** (hō′plis) **1** feeling no hope: *He was disappointed so often that he became hopeless.* **2** giving no hope: *a hopeless illness.* *adj.* —**hope′less·ly,** *adv.* —**hope′less·ness,** *n.*

**hop·per** (hop′ər) **1** a person or thing that hops. **2** a grasshopper or other hopping insect. **3** a container, usually funnel-shaped, into which grain, corn, etc. is poured in order to be fed evenly into another container or a machine for grinding, mixing, etc.: *Some cement mixers are equipped with hoppers.* *n.*

**hop·scotch** (hop′skoch′) a children's game in which the players hop over the lines of a figure drawn on the ground. *n.*

**ho·ra** (hô′rə) **1** a Romanian and Israeli folk dance with a lively, syncopated rhythm. **2** the music for such a dance. *n.*

**horde** (hôrd) **1** a crowd or swarm: *hordes of grasshoppers.* **2** a wandering tribe or troop: *Hordes of Mongols and Turks invaded Europe in the Middle Ages.* *n.* ☛ *Hom.* HOARD.

**hore·hound** (hôr′hound′) **1** a plant of the same family as the mint, having woolly, whitish leaves and clusters of small, whitish flowers. **2** a bitter extract made from the leaves of this plant. **3** candy or cough medicine flavoured with it. *n.*

**ho·ri·zon** (hə rī′zən) **1** the line where the earth and sky seem to meet: *You cannot see beyond the horizon.* **2** Usually, **horizons,** *pl.* the limit of one's thinking, experience, interest or outlook: *She wanted to expand her horizons by travelling.* *n.*

**hor·i·zon·tal** (hôr′ə zon′təl) **1** parallel to the horizon; at right angles to a vertical line. **2** flat; level: *You need a horizontal surface to work on.* **3** placed, acting, or working wholly or mainly in a horizontal direction: *A helicopter has horizontal rotors.* **4** something that is horizontal, such as a line, plane, direction, or position. 1–3, *adj.*, 4 *n.* —**hor′i·zon′tal·ly,** *adv.*

**hor·mone** (hôr′mōn) **1** a substance, formed in certain parts of the body, that enters the blood stream and influences the activity of some organ: *Adrenalin and insulin are hormones.* **2** a similar substance carried in the sap of plants. **3** a synthetic substance that has the effect of a hormone. *n.*

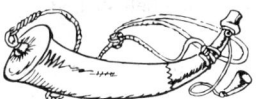 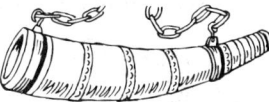

A powder horn    A hunting horn

**horn** (hôrn) **1** a hard growth, usually curved and pointed, on the heads of cattle, sheep, goats, and some other animals. **2** one of a pair of branching growths on the head of a deer, which fall off and grow afresh each year. **3** anything that sticks up on the head of an animal: *a snail's horns, an insect's horns.* **4** the tough fibrous material that horns are made of: *A person's fingernails, the beaks of birds, the hoofs of horses, and tortoise shells are all made of horn.* **5** something made, or formerly made, of horn. **6** a container made by hollowing out a horn: *a drinking horn, a powder horn.* **7** made of horn. **8** a musical instrument shaped like a horn and formerly made of horn, sounded by blowing into the smaller end: *The brass section of an orchestra includes several kinds of horn.* See FRENCH HORN for another picture. **9** a device sounded as a warning signal: *a foghorn, an automobile horn.* **10** anything that projects like a horn or is shaped like a horn: *a saddle horn, the horn of a bay.* See SADDLE for picture. **11** either pointed tip of a new or old moon, or of some other crescent. **12** hit or wound with horns; gore. 1–11 *n.*, 12 *v.* —**horn′less,** *adj.* —**horn′like′,** *adj.*
**draw** or **pull in one's horns,** **a** restrain oneself. **b** back down; withdraw.
**horn in,** *Informal.* meddle or intrude: *She kept trying to horn in on our conversation.*
**horns of a dilemma,** two unpleasant choices, one of which must be taken.

**horn·beam** (hôrn′bēm′) a tree or shrub of the same family as the birch, having very hard wood. *n.*

**horn·bill** (hôrn′bil′) a large bird having a very large bill with a horn or horny lump on it. *n.*

**horn·blende** (hôrn′blend′) a common black, dark-green, or brown mineral found in granite and other rocks. *n.*

**horn·book** (hôrn′bùk′) **1** a page with the alphabet, etc. on it, covered with a sheet of transparent horn and fastened in a frame with a handle, formerly used in teaching children to read. **2** an elementary treatise. *n.*

**horned** (hôrnd) **1** having a horn or horns. **2** pt. and pp. of HORN. 1 *adj.*, 2 *v.*

**horned toad** any of several closely related species of small insect-eating lizards of North America, having a broad, flat body, short tail, and many spines on the back and tail.

**hor·net** (hôr′nit) any of several large wasps, mostly dark-coloured, with white or yellow markings, that live in colonies above ground, in large roundish nests made of a papery material: *Hornets often build their nests under the eaves of buildings.* *n.*

**horn of plenty** CORNUCOPIA (def. 2).

**horn·pipe** (hôrn′pīp′) **1** a lively dance done by one person, formerly popular among sailors. **2** the music for such a dance. **3** a musical wind instrument of olden times, consisting of a wooden pipe with a bell-shaped end. *n.*

**horn·y** (hôr′nē) **1** made of horn or of a substance like it. **2** hard like horn: *The farmer's hands were horny from work.* **3** having a horn or horns. *adj.*, **horn·i·er, horn·i·est.**

**ho·rol·o·ger** (hō rol′ə jər) HOROLOGIST. *n.*

**ho·rol·o·gist** (hō rol′ə jist) a person skilled in HOROLOGY. *n.*

**ho·rol·o·gy** (hō rol′ə jē) **1** the science of measuring time. **2** the art of making timepieces. *n.*

**ho·ro·scope** (hô′rə skōp′) **1** the position of the planets and stars relative to each other at the hour of a person's birth, regarded as influencing life. **2** a diagram of the heavens at given times, used in telling fortunes by the planets and the stars. *n.*

**hor·ren·dous** (hō ren′dəs) horrible; terrible; frightful. *adj.* —**hor·ren′dous·ly,** *adv.*

**hor·ri·ble** (hôr′ə bəl) **1** causing horror; terrible; dreadful; frightful; shocking: *a horrible crime, a horrible disease.* **2** *Informal.* extremely unpleasant or amazing: *a horrible noise.* *adj.* —**hor′ri·ble·ness,** *n.* —**hor′ri·bly,** *adv.*

**hor·rid** (hôr′id) **1** terrible; frightful. **2** *Informal.* very unpleasant: *a horrid little boy, a horrid day.* *adj.* —**hor′rid·ly,** *adv.* —**hor′rid·ness,** *n.*

**hor·rif·ic** (hō rif′ik) producing horror; horrifying. *adj.*

**hor·ri·fy** (hôr′ə fī′) **1** cause to feel horror. **2** *Informal.* shock very much: *We were horrified by the wreck.* *v.*, **hor·ri·fied, hor·ri·fy·ing.**

**hor·ror** (hôr′ər) **1** a shivering, shaking fear and dislike; terror and disgust caused by something frightful or shocking. **2** a very strong dislike; very great disgust: *a horror of snakes and spiders.* **3** the quality of causing horror. **4** a cause of horror. **5** *Informal.* something very bad or unpleasant. *n.*

**hors de com·bat** (ôr də kôn bä′) *French.* out of the fight, disabled.

**hors d'oeu·vre** (ôr′dèrv′; *French,* ôr dœvr′) a relish or light food served before the regular courses of a meal: *Olives, celery, anchovies, etc. are often served as hors d'oeuvres.* *pl.* **hors d'oeu·vres** (-dèrvz′; *French,* ôr dœvr′).

Horses: a draft horse and a racehorse

**horse** (hôrs) **1** a large four-legged animal with solid hoofs and a mane and tail of long, coarse hair: *Horses have been used from very early times for riding and for carrying and pulling loads.* **2** a full-grown male horse. **3** soldiers on horses; cavalry: *a troop of horse.* **4** provide with a horse or horses. **5** put or go on horseback. **6** of or having to do with horses. **7** on horses. **8** a piece of gymnasium apparatus to jump or vault over. **9** a frame with legs to support something; a trestle. 1–3, 6–9 *n., pl.* **hors·es** or (*esp. collectively*) **horse**; 4, 5 *v.,* **horsed, hors·ing.**

**hold one's horses,** *Informal.* restrain oneself: *Hold your horses till we get there.*
**horse around,** *Informal.* fool around; get into mischief.
**horse of a different colour,** something different.
**on one's high horse,** *Informal.* behaving in an arrogant or pretentious way: *He got up on his high horse and said he wasn't used to being treated that way.*
**the horse's mouth,** the original source; a well-informed source: *news straight from the horse's mouth.*
☛ *Hom.* HOARSE.

**horse·back** (hôrs′bak′) **1** the back of a horse. **2** on the back of a horse. 1 *n.,* 2 *adv.*

**horse-boat** (hôrs′bōt′) formerly, a kind of ferry boat propelled by a paddle wheel that was turned by horses walking a treadmill on the boat: *Horse-boats were used in Canada in the 19th century.* *n.*

**horse·car** (hôrs′kär′) **1** a streetcar pulled by a horse or horses. **2** a car used for transporting horses. *n.*

**horse chestnut** **1** a large tree native to Europe and Asia, widely used in North America for ornament and shade, having showy spikes of white flowers and leaves made up of leaflets radiating out from the tip of the leaf stalk: *The shiny brown seeds of the horse chestnut resemble chestnuts, but they are bitter and poisonous.* **2** referring to the family of trees and shrubs that includes the horse chestnut and the buckeyes.

**horse·flesh** (hôrs′flesh′) **1** horses for riding, driving, and racing. **2** meat from horses. *n.*

**horse·fly** (hôrs′flī′) any of a family of large, two-winged flies that suck the blood of horses, cattle, etc. *n., pl.* **horse·flies.**

**horse·hair** (hôrs′her′) **1** the hair from the mane or tail of a horse. **2** a stiff fabric made of this hair. **3** made of or stuffed with horsehair: *a horsehair sofa.* *n.*

**horse·hide** (hôrs′hīd′) **1** the hide of a horse. **2** leather made from this hide. *n.*

**horse latitudes** two regions where there is often very calm weather and which extend around the world at about 30° north and 30° south of the equator.

**horse laugh** *Informal.* a loud, boisterous laugh; guffaw.

**horse·less** (hôr′slis) **1** without a horse. **2** not requiring a horse; self-propelled: *Automobiles used to be called horseless carriages.* *adj.*

**horse·man** (hôr′smən) **1** a man who rides on horseback. **2** a man skilled in riding or managing horses. *n., pl.* **horse·men** (-smən).

**horse·man·ship** (hôr′smən ship′) skill in riding or managing horses: *Jane is learning horsemanship.* *n.*

**horse·play** (hôr′splā′) rough, boisterous fun. *n.*

**horse·pow·er** (hôr′spou′ər) a unit of power equal to 746 watts, used for measuring the power of engines, motors, etc.: *One horsepower is about three-quarters of a kilowatt; therefore, a 40 hp outboard motor would be about equal to a 30 kW outboard motor.* Symbol: hp *n.*

**horse·rad·ish** (hôrs′rad′ish) **1** a tall plant having a white, hot-tasting root that is ground up and used as a relish with meat, oysters, etc. **2** a relish made of this root. *n.*

**horse sense** *Informal.* common sense; plain, practical good sense.

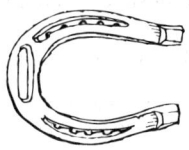 

Horseshoes

**horse·shoe** (hôrs′shü′ *or* hôrsh′shü′) **1** a U-shaped metal plate nailed to a horse's hoof to protect it. **2** put a horseshoe or horseshoes on. **3** anything shaped like a horseshoe: *a horseshoe of flowers.* **4 horseshoes,** game in which the players try to throw horseshoes over or near a stake 40 feet (about 12 m) away (*used with a singular verb*). 1, 3, 4 *n.,* 2 *v.,* **horse·shoed, horse·shoe·ing.**

**horseshoe crab** a crablike sea animal having a body shaped like a horseshoe and a long, spiny tail; king crab.

**horse·whip** (hôr′swip′ *or* hôrs′hwip′) **1** a whip for driving or controlling horses. **2** beat with a horsewhip. 1 *n.,* 2 *v.,* **horse·whipped, horse·whip·ping.**

**horse·wom·an** (hôr′swum′ən) **1** a woman who rides on horseback. **2** a woman skilled in riding or managing horses. *n., pl.* **horse·wom·en** (-swim′ən).

**hors·y** (hôr′sē) **1** having to do with horses. **2** fond of horses or horse racing. **3** dressing or talking like people who spend much time with horses. *adj.,* **hors·i·er, hors·i·est.**

**hor·ta·to·ry** (hôr′tə tô′rē) serving to urge or encourage; giving advice; exhorting. *adj.*

**hor·ti·cul·tur·al** (hôr′tə kul′chə rəl) of or having to do with the growing of flowers, fruits, vegetables, plants, etc.: *A flower show is a horticultural exhibit.* *adj.*

**hor·ti·cul·ture** (hôr′tə kul′chər) the art or science of growing flowers, fruits, vegetables, etc. *n.*

**hor·ti·cul·tur·ist** (hôr′tə kul′chə rist) a person skilled in HORTICULTURE. *n.*

**hose** (hōz) **1** stockings or socks. **2** an outer garment formerly worn by men, extending from the waist to the knees or to the toes and covering each leg separately: *Hose were attached to the doublet by laces or ribbons called points.* **3** a tube made of rubber, plastic, canvas, or other material that will bend, used to carry water or other liquids for short distances. See NOZZLE for picture. **4** put water on with a hose (*often used with* **down**): *She hosed down the lawn furniture.* 1–3 *n., pl.* **hos·es;** 4 *v.,* **hosed, hos·ing.**

**ho·sier** (hō′zhər) a person who makes or sells HOSIERY. *n.*

**ho·sier·y** (hō′zhə rē) **1** hose, stockings. **2** the business of a hosier. *n.*

**hos·pice** (hos′pis) **1** a house where travellers can lodge, especially such a house kept by monks: *the hospice of the monks of Saint Bernard in the Alps.* **2** a home to care for people who are terminally ill. *n.*
☞ *Etym.* See note at HOSPITAL.

**hos·pi·ta·ble** (hos′pi tə bəl *or* hos pit′ə bəl) **1** giving or liking to give a welcome, food and shelter, and friendly treatment to guests or strangers: *a hospitable family, reception, etc.* **2** willing and ready to consider; favourably receptive or open: *a person hospitable to new ideas.* *adj.* —**hos′pi·ta·bly,** *adv.*
☞ *Etym.* See note at HOSPITAL.

**hos·pi·tal** (hos′pi təl) an institution where sick or injured people are cared for or treated and where surgery is done. *n.*
☞ *Etym.* **Hospital,** HOSPICE, HOSPITABLE, HOSPITALITY, and HOSTEL all come through Old French from Latin words derived from L *hospes* 'host' or 'guest'. See the note at HOST[1]. See also the note at HOSTEL. HOSPITALIZE is a modern formation of **hospital** + *-ize.*

**hos·pi·tal·i·ty** (hos′pə tal′ə tē) friendly, generous reception and treatment of guests or strangers. *n., pl.* **hos·pi·tal·i·ties.**
☞ *Etym.* See note at HOSPITAL.

**hos·pi·tal·ize** (hos′pi tə līz′) put in a hospital to be treated or cared for: *The injuries were only minor and she did not have to be hospitalized.* *v.,* **hos·pi·tal·ized, hos·pi·tal·iz·ing.** —**hos′pi·tal·i·za′tion,** *n.*
☞ *Etym.* See note at HOSPITAL.

**host**[1] (hōst) **1** a person who receives another at his or her house as a guest. **2** the keeper of an inn or hotel. **3** a plant or animal in or on which a parasite lives: *The oak tree is the host of the mistletoe that grows on it.* **4** act as host. 1–3 *n.,* 4 *v.*
**reckon without one's host,** overlook the chances of one's plans going wrong.
☞ *Etym.* From OF *hoste,* which came from L *hospes, hospitem* 'host' or 'guest'. *Hospes* itself may have developed from L *hostis* 'stranger' or, possibly, both *hostis* and *hospes* developed from the same root. HOSTESS comes through OF from the same Latin source. See also the notes at HOSPITAL and HOST[2].

**host**[2] (hōst) **1** a large number; multitude: *a host of stars glittered in the sky.* **2** army. *n.*
☞ *Etym.* Through OF from Med. L. *hostis* 'army'. *Hostis* originally meant 'stranger', and then 'enemy', and so later (in the plural) 'army'. HOSTILE and HOSTILITY come from Latin words formed directly from *hostis.* See also the note at HOST[1].

**hos·tage** (hos'tij) **1** a person given up to another or held by an enemy as a pledge that certain promises, agreements, etc. will be carried out. **2** a pledge; security. *n.*
**give hostages to fortune,** have persons or things that one may lose.

**hos·tel** (hos'təl) **1** a lodging place, especially a supervised lodging place for young travellers. **2** an inn; hotel. *n.*
☞ *Etym.* **Hostel** is closely related to HOTEL. OF *hostel,* which gave us **hostel,** developed into *hôtel* and in this form came into English in the 17c. to give us **hotel.** See note at HOSPITAL.
☞ *Hom.* HOSTILE (hos'təl).

**hos·tel·ry** (hos'təl rē) an inn; hotel. *n., pl.* **hos·tel·ries.**

**host·ess** (hō'stis) **1** a woman who receives another person as her guest. **2** a woman who keeps an inn or hotel, or helps her husband to do so. **3** a woman who greets customers in a restaurant, night club, etc. and usually, shows them to a table. **4** FLIGHT ATTENDANT. **5** act as hostess. 1–4 *n.,* 5 *v.*
☞ *Etym.* See note at HOST¹.

**hos·tile** (hos'tīl *or* hos'təl) **1** of or relating to an enemy or enemies: *the hostile army.* **2** opposed; unfriendly: *a hostile look.* **3** unfavourable; harsh: *a hostile climate.* *adj.* —**hos'tile·ly,** *adv.*
☞ *Etym.* See note at HOST².
☞ *Hom.* HOSTEL (for the second pronunciation of **hostile**).

**hos·til·i·ty** (hos til'ə tē) **1** the feeling that an enemy has; the state of being an enemy; unfriendliness: *The mistreated child regarded everyone with hostility.* **2** the state of being at war. **3** opposition; resistance: *She showed signs of hostility to our plan.* **4 hostilities,** *pl.* acts of war; warfare; fighting. *n., pl.* **hos·til·i·ties.**
☞ *Etym.* See note at HOST².

**hos·tler** (os'lər *or* hos'lər) a person who takes care of horses at an inn or stable. *n.* Also, **ostler.**

**hot** (hot) **1** much warmer than the body; having much heat: *The fire is hot.* **2** having a relatively high temperature: *The food is too hot to eat.* **3** having a sharp, burning taste: *Pepper and mustard are hot.* **4** full of any strong feeling; passionate, violent, angry, etc.: *a hot temper, hot with rage.* **5** full of great interest or enthusiasm; very eager. **6** new; fresh: *a hot scent or trail.* **7** near or approaching an object or answer sought. **8** following closely: *in hot pursuit.* **9** charged with radio-activity; radio-active: *the hot debris left by a nuclear explosion.* **10** of swing music or jazz, played with variations from the score. **11** open and ready for instantaneous use: *the hot line between the White House and the Kremlin.* **12** in a hot manner: *The sun beats hot upon the sand.* 1–11 *adj.,* **hot·ter, hot·test;** 12 *adv.* —**hot'ly,** *adv.* —**hot'ness,** *n.*
**make it hot for,** *Informal.* make trouble for; make things unpleasant or uncomfortable for: *The police make it hot for counterfeiters.*

**hot·bed** (hot'bed') **1** a bed of earth covered with glass or plastic and kept warm for growing plants. **2** any place favourable to rapid growth: *These slums are a hotbed of crime.* *n.*

**hot–blood·ed** (hot'blud'id) **1** easily excited or angered. **2** rash; reckless. **3** passionate. *adj.*

**hot·box** (hot'boks') an overheated bearing on a shaft or axle. *n.*

**hot cake** GRIDDLECAKE.
**go** or **sell like hot cakes,** **a** be sold quickly. **b** be in great demand.

**hot dog** **1** a sandwich made of a hot frankfurter or wiener enclosed in a long roll and usually served with mustard, relish, etc. **2** a frankfurter or wiener.

**ho·tel** (hō tel') **1** a building where rooms may be rented and meals bought on a day-to-day basis. **2** *Cdn. Informal.* a place where beer and wine are sold for drinking on the premises; a beer parlour. *n.*
☞ *Etym.* See note at HOSTEL.

**hot·foot** (hot'fùt') *Informal.* **1** in great haste: *She went hotfoot up the stairs with me after her.* **2** go in great haste; hurry (usually used with **it**): *We hotfooted it out to the airport.* 1 *adv.,* 2 *v.*

**hot·head** (hot'hed') a hot-headed person. *n.*

**hot–head·ed** (hot'hed'id) **1** having a fiery temper; easily angered. **2** impetuous; rash. *adj.*
—**hot'head'ed·ly,** *adv.* —**hot'head'ed·ness,** *n.*

**hot·house** (hot'hous') a building with a transparent glass or plastic roof and sides, kept warm for growing plants; greenhouse. *n.*

**hot line** a direct means of communication for use in emergencies, especially between heads of state of different countries.

**hot–line** (hot'līn') of, having to do with, or referring to a radio or television show which broadcasts the comments of members of the public who phone in to express their views, especially on a controversial subject. *adj.*

**hot plate** **1** a small, portable gas or electric stove for cooking. **2** a heated metal plate for cooking food or keeping it hot.

**hot seat** **1** an embarrassing predicament. **2** the chair occupied by the victim of an aggressive type of interview.
**in the hot seat,** in a situation in which one is subject to aggressive and searching questioning.

**hot spot** **1** an exciting and fashionable nightclub, resort, etc. **2** a local place or region of potential or actual unrest or violence. **3** a local area showing significant radio-activity. **4** a point in the earth's crust, above a PLUME, where a volcano is likely to form. **5** the hottest place on a particular day.

**hot spring** Usually, **hot springs,** *pl.* a natural spring whose water has a higher temperature than the average temperature of its locality, especially one having water above 37° C.

**hot–tem·pered** (hot'tem'pərd) having a quick temper; easily angered. *adj.*

**hot war** a war involving actual fighting. Compare with COLD WAR.

**hot water** *Informal.* trouble: *I'll be in hot water with my parents if I'm not home soon.*

**hou·dah** (hou'də) See HOWDAH. *n.*

**hound** (hound) **1** a dog of any of various breeds, most of which hunt by scent and have large, drooping ears and short hair. **2** any dog. **3** keep on chasing or driving: *The police hounded the thief until they caught him.* **4** a contemptible person. **5** urge on continually or repeatedly; keep urging or pestering: *Rita's parents hounded her to do her homework.* 1, 2, 4 *n.,* 3, 5 *v.*
**follow the hounds** or **ride to hounds,** go hunting on horseback with hounds.

**hour** (our) **1** a unit used with the SI for measuring time, equal to 3600 seconds or 60 minutes: *There are 24 hours in a day.* Symbol: h  **2** one of the 12 points that measure time from noon to midnight and from midnight to noon: *Some clocks strike the hours and half-hours.*  **3** the time of day: *The hour is 7:30.*  **4** a particular or fixed time: *Our breakfast hour is at seven o'clock.*  **5** a short or limited space of time: *After his hour of glory, he was soon forgotten.*  **6** a period in a classroom, often less than a full hour.  **7** the present time.  **8** 15 degrees of longitude.  **9 hours,** *pl.*  **a** the time for work, study, etc.: *Our school hours are 9 to 12 and 1 to 4.*  **b** the usual times for going to bed and getting up.  **c** seven special times of day for Christian prayer and worship.  **d** the prayers or services for these times.  *n.*
**in an evil hour,** at a bad or unlucky time.
☛ *Hom.* OUR.

An hourglass

**hour·glass** (our′glas′)   a device for measuring time, requiring just an hour for its contents, usually sand, to go from a glass bulb or container on top to one on the bottom.  *n.*

**hou·ri** (hü′rē)   one of the young, eternally beautiful girls of the Moslem paradise.  *n., pl.* **hou·ris.**

**hour·ly** (our′lē)   **1** done, happening, or counted every hour: *There are hourly reports of the news on this radio station. Her hourly wage is now $12.90.*  **2** coming very often; frequent.  **3** every hour; hour by hour: *Give two doses of the medicine hourly.*  **4** very often; frequently: *Messages were coming hourly from the front.*  1, 2 *adj.*, 3, 4 *adv.*

**house** (hous *for noun,* houz *for verb*)   **1** a building designed for people to live in, especially one for a single family.  **2** the people living in a house; household: *The whole house was awake by 7 o'clock.*  **3** an abode or habitation.  **4** a building to hold anything: *an engine house.*  **5** an assembly for making laws and considering questions of government; lawmaking body: *the House of Commons.*  **6** the buildings in which such an assembly meets.  **7** a place of business.  **8** a business firm.  **9** a place of entertainment; theatre.  **10** an audience; attendance: *A large house heard the singer.*  **11** a family regarded as consisting of ancestors, descendants, and kindred, especially a noble or royal family: *He was a prince of the house of David.*  **12** in curling, the goal or target.  **13** put or receive into a house; provide with a house: *Where can we house all these children?*  **14** give shelter to; lodge.  **15** place in a secure or protected position: *The campers housed their provisions in a shack.*  **16** take shelter.  1–12 *n., pl.* **hou·ses** (hou′ziz);   13–16 *v.*, **housed, hous·ing.**
**bring down the house,** *Informal.* be loudly applauded.
**clean house,  a** set a house in order.  **b** get rid of bad conditions; set a business, institution, etc. in order.
**keep house,** manage a home and its affairs.
**on the house,** free; paid for by the owner of the business: *After visiting the candy factory, we were each given a box of chocolates on the house.*
**put** or **set one's house in order,** arrange one's affairs in good order.
☛ *Syn.* See note at HOME.

## hour 581 House of Lords

hat, āge, fär; let, ēqual, tėrm; it, īce
hot, ōpen, ôrder; oil, out; cup, pùt, rüle
above, takən, pencəl, lemən, circəs
ch, child; ng, long; sh, ship
th, thin; ᴛH, then; zh, measure

**house·boat** (hous′bōt′)   a boat that can be used as a place to live in.  *n.*

**house·bound** (hous′bound′)   confined to the house; not able to leave one's house: *He is housebound because of his arthritis.*  *adj.*

**house·break·er** (hous′brā′kər)   a person who breaks into a house to steal or commit some other crime.  *n.*

**house·break·ing** (hous′brā′king)   the act of breaking into a house to steal or commit some other crime.  *n.*

**house·bro·ken** (hous′brō′kən)   **1** of a pet such as a dog, cat, etc., trained to live cleanly indoors.  **2** made docile and easy to manage.  *adj.*

**house·coat** (hous′kōt′)   a woman's loose, informal garment, usually having a long skirt, for wearing at home.  *n.*

**house·fly** (hous′flī′)   a two-winged fly that lives around and in houses, feeding on food and garbage: *The larvae or maggots of the housefly develop in decaying organic matter.*  *n., pl.* **house·flies.**

**house·hold** (hous′hōld′)   **1** all the people living in a house; a family or a family and servants.  **2** a home and its affairs.  **3** of or having to do with a household; domestic: *household expenses, household cares.*  **4** common or familiar: *a household utensil.*  *n.*

**house·hold·er** (hous′hōl′dər)   **1** a person who owns or lives in a house.  **2** the head of a family.  *n.*

**household word**   any very familiar word or phrase.

**house·keep·er** (hou′skē′pər)   a person who manages a home and its affairs and does the housework, especially one hired to do so.  *n.*

**house·keep·ing** (hou′skē′ping)   **1** the managing of a home and its affairs.  **2** the internal operations and management of an organization or business.  *n.*

**house·maid** (hou′smād′)   a female servant who does housework.  *n.*

**housemaid's knee**   an inflammation near the knee, usually caused by much kneeling.

**house·moth·er** (hou′smuᴛH′ər)   a woman who supervises and takes care of a group of people living together as a family.  *n.*

**House of Assembly**   in Newfoundland, the provincial legislature, consisting of 36 elected members.

**House of Commons**   **1** in Canada, the elected representatives who meet in Ottawa to make laws and debate questions of government.  **2** the chamber in which the representatives, or members meet.  **3** in the United Kingdom, the elected members of Parliament.  **4** the buildings in which these members meet.

**House of Lords**   the upper, non-elective branch of the lawmaking body of the United Kingdom, composed of nobles and clergymen of high rank.

**House of Representatives** 1 the lower branch of the lawmaking body of the United States. 2 the chamber in which the representatives meet. 3 the lower branch of the lawmaking body of certain states of the United States. 4 the lower branch of the Parliament of Australia or of the General Assembly of New Zealand.

**house party** the entertainment of guests in a home, especially for a few days.

**house plant** a small plant in a pot or box, kept inside the house: *Ferns and African violets are often used as house plants.*

**house-sit** (hous′sit′) live in a house to look after it while the owners are away. *v.*, **house-sat, house-sit·ting.**

**house sparrow** ENGLISH SPARROW.

**house-to-house** (hou′stə hous′) from one house to the next, stopping at each in turn: *to sell house-to-house, a house-to-house campaign.* *adv., adj.*

**house·top** (hou′stop′) the top of a house; roof. *n.*

**house·warm·ing** (hou′swôr′ming) a party given when a person or family moves into a new residence. *n.*

**house·wife** (hou′swīf′ for 1, huz′if for 2) 1 HOMEMAKER. 2 a small case for needles, thread, etc. *n., pl.* **house·wives** (hous′wīvz′ for 1, huz′ifs for 2).

**house·work** (hou′swėrk′) the work to be done in housekeeping, such as washing, ironing, cleaning, and cooking. *n.*

**hous·ing**[1] (hou′zing) 1 the act of sheltering; providing houses as homes. 2 houses; dwellings: *That city does not have enough housing.* 3 a shelter or covering. 4 a frame or plate for holding together and protecting the parts of a machine. See DIFFERENTIAL for picture. 5 ppr. of HOUSE. 1–4 *n.*, 5 *v.*

**hous·ing**[2] (hou′zing) an ornamental covering for a horse: *Under the saddle was a housing of red velvet.* *n.*

**hove** (hōv) a pt. and a pp. of HEAVE: *The sailors hove at the ropes.* *v.*

**hov·el** (hov′əl *or* huv′əl) 1 a house that is small, crude, and unpleasant to live in. 2 an open shed for sheltering cattle, storing tools, etc. *n.*

**hov·er** (hov′ər *or* huv′ər) 1 stay in or near one place in the air: *The hummingbird hovered in front of the flower.* 2 stay in or near one place; wait nearby: *The dogs hovered around the kitchen door at mealtime.* 3 be in an uncertain condition; waver: *The sick woman hovered between life and death.* *v.*
**hover over,** threaten: *The fear of failure hovered over the young businessman.*

**hov·er·craft** (hov′ər kraft′ *or* huv′ər kraft′) a motorized vehicle capable of travelling just above the surface of water or land on a cushion of air held in a chamber beneath the vehicle. *n. pl.* **hov·er·craft.**

**how** (hou) 1 in what way; by what means: *Tell her how to do it.* 2 to what degree, extent, etc.: *How long will it take you to do this?* 3 at what price: *How do you sell these apples?* 4 in what state or condition: *Tell me how Mrs. Akisi is.* 5 for what reason; why: *How is it you are late?* 6 to what effect; with what meaning; by what name: *How do you mean?* 7 a way or manner of doing: *She considered all the hows and wherefores.* 1–6 *adv.,* 7 *n.*

**how come?** *Informal.* why? what is the reason or cause that?: *How come you didn't call me last night?*
**how now?** what does this mean?
**how so?** why is it so?
**how then?** what does this mean?

A howdah

**how·dah** (hou′də) a seat for persons riding on the back of an elephant. *n.* Also, **houdah.**

**how·ev·er** (hou ev′ər) 1 nevertheless; yet; in spite of that: *It is his; however, you may borrow it.* 2 to whatever extent, degree, or amount; no matter how: *However you do it, the effect will be the same.* 3 in whatever way; by whatever means: *However did you manage to get here?* 1 *conj.,* 2, 3 *adv.*

**how·itz·er** (hou′it sər) a short artillery piece for firing shells in a high curve. *n.*

**howl** (houl) 1 give a long, loud, mournful cry: *Dogs and wolves howl. The winter winds howled around our cabin.* 2 a long, loud, mournful cry. 3 give a long, loud cry of pain, rage, distress, etc. 4 a loud cry of pain, rage, etc. 5 a yell of scorn, amusement, etc. 6 yell; shout: *It was so funny that we howled with laughter.* 7 force or drive by howling: *The angry mob howled the speaker off the platform.* 8 *Informal.* something causing laughter: *The skit by the teachers was a howl.* 1, 3, 6, 7 *v.*, 2, 4, 5, 8 *n.*
**howl down,** drown out the words by howling: *The speaker was howled down by his opponents.*

**howl·er** (hou′lər) 1 a person or thing that howls. 2 *Informal.* a ridiculous mistake; stupid blunder. *n.*

**how·so·ev·er** (hou′sō ev′ər) 1 to whatever extent, degree, or amount. 2 in whatever way; by whatever means. *adv.*

**hoy·den** (hoi′dən) a boisterous, romping girl; tomboy. *n.*

**hoy·den·ish** (hoi′də nish) of or like a HOYDEN; boisterous; romping. *adj.*

**Hoyle** (hoil) a book of rules and instructions for playing card games. *n.*
**according to Hoyle,** according to the rules or customs; fair; correct.

**hp** horsepower.

**HP, H.P.,** or **h.p.** 1 high pressure. 2 horsepower.

**H.Q.** headquarters.

**hr.** hour; hours.

**h.r.** in baseball, home run.

**H.R.H.** His Royal Highness; Her Royal Highness.

**hrs.** hours.

**H.S.** or **HS** high school.

**ht.** **1** height. **2** heat.

**Hts.** Heights.

**hub** (hub) **1** the central part of a wheel. See WHEEL for picture. **2** any centre of interest, importance, activity, etc.: *London is the hub of England.* *n.*

**hub·bub** (hub′ub) a noisy tumult; uproar: *There was a hubbub when the crowd was told to move.* *n.*

**huck·a·back** (huk′ə bak′) a heavy, coarse, linen or cotton cloth, used for towels. *n.*

**huck·le·ber·ry** (huk′əl ber′ē) **1** a small berry similar to a blueberry, but having 10 hard seeds. **2** the shrub that it grows on. *n., pl.* **huck·le·ber·ries.**

**huck·ster** (huk′stər) **1** peddler. **2** a person who sells small articles. **3** a mean and unfair trader. **4** sell; peddle; haggle. 1–3 *n.*, 4 *v.*

**hud·dle** (hud′əl) **1** crowd close: *The sheep had huddled in a corner of the pen.* **2** crowd or put close together: *She huddled all four boys into one bed.* **3** curl oneself up: *The cat huddled on the cushion. The rescued swimmer sat huddled in a blanket by the fire.* **4** a confused heap or mass of people or things crowded together. **5** *Informal.* a secret conference. **6** in football, a grouping of players behind the line of scrimmage to receive signals, plan the next play, etc. **7** form such a group. 1–3, 7 *v.*, **hud·dled, hud·dling;** 4–6 *n.*
**go into a huddle,** *Informal.* confer secretly: *During the court recess, the lawyer went into a huddle with her partner.*

**Hudson's Bay Company** a trading company chartered by Charles II in 1670, as the Company of Adventurers of England trading into Hudson's Bay, to carry on the fur trade with the Indians of North America: *The Hudson's Bay Company has played a great part in the exploration and development of Canada's Northwest.*

**Hudson seal** MUSKRAT fur that is dyed and processed to look like seal.

**hue¹** (hyü) a colour; shade; tint: *There are flowers in our garden to match almost all the hues of the rainbow.* *n.*
☛ *Hom.* HEW.

**hue²** (hyü) *Archaic* (*except in* **hue and cry**). shouting. *n.*
**hue and cry, a** shouts of alarm or protest. **b** an outcry or alarm formerly raised to call people to pursue a criminal in which they were obliged by law to join. **c** the pursuit of a criminal in this way.
☛ *Hom.* HEW.

**huff** (huf) **1** a fit of anger or peevishness: *She has such a bad temper that she gets into a huff about nothing.* **2** make angry; offend. **3** puff; blow: *The old locomotive huffed along.* 1 *n.*, 2, 3 *v.*

**huff·y** (huf′ē) **1** offended; in a huff. **2** tending to be easily offended; touchy. *adj.*, **huff·i·er, huff·i·est.** —**huff′i·ly,** *adv.* —**huff′i·ness,** *n.*

**hug** (hug) **1** put the arms around and hold close, especially in affection; embrace: *The girl hugs her big doll.* **2** a tight clasp with the arms: *She gave her father a quick hug.* **3** squeeze tightly between the forelegs, as a bear does. **4** a tight squeeze with the arms; grip in wrestling. **5** cling firmly or fondly to: *They still hug their belief in his story.* **6** keep close to: *The boat hugged the shore.* 1, 3, 5, 6 *v.*, **hugged, hug·ging;** 2, 4 *n.*

hat, āge, fär; let, ēqual, tėrm; it, īce
hot, ōpen, ôrder; oil, out; cup, pút, rüle
əbove, tākən, pencəl, lemən, circəs
ch, child; ng, long; sh, ship
th, thin; ŦH, then; zh, measure

**huge** (hyüj) **1** extremely large in size, quantity, etc.: *A whale or an elephant is a huge animal.* **2** unusually great in extent, scope, degree, or capacity: *a huge undertaking.* *adj.*, **hug·er, hug·est.** —**huge′ly,** *adv.* —**huge′ness,** *n.*

**hug·ger–mug·ger** (hug′ər mug′ər) *Informal.*
**1** confusion; disorder. **2** confused; disorderly. **3** in a confused, disorderly manner. 1 *n.*, 2 *adj.*, 3 *adv.*

**huh** (hu) a sound made to express surprise, contempt, etc. or to ask a question. *interj.*

**hu·la** (hü′lə) **1** a native Hawaiian dance characterized by rhythmic movement of the hips and hand gestures that tell a story. **2** the music for this dance. *n.*

**hu·la–hu·la** (hü′lə hü′lə) HULA. *n.*

**hulk** (hulk) **1** the body of an old or worn-out ship. **2** a ship used as a prison. **3** a big, clumsy ship. **4** a big, clumsy person or thing. *n.*
☛ *Etym.* From OE *hulc* 'ship', especially a large cargo ship.

**hulk·ing** (hul′king) big and clumsy. *adj.*

**hull** (hul) **1** the body or frame of a ship: *Masts, sails, and rigging are not part of the hull.* **2** the main body or frame of a seaplane, airship, etc. **3** strike or pierce the hull of a ship with a shell, torpedo, etc. **4** the outer covering of a seed. **5** the calyx of some fruits: *We call the green leaves at the stem of a strawberry its hull.* **6** remove the hull or hulls from: *to hull strawberries, to hull grain.* **7** any outer covering. 1, 2, 4, 5, 7 *n.*, 3, 6 *v.*
—**hull′er,** *n.*
**hull down,** of ships, so far away that the hull is below the horizon.

**hul·la·ba·loo** (hul′ə bə lü′) a loud noise or disturbance; uproar. *n.*

**hum** (hum) **1** make a continuous murmuring sound like that of a bee or of a spinning top: *The sewing machine hums busily.* **2** a continuous murmuring sound: *the hum of the bees, the hum of a city street.* **3** make a low sound like that symbolized by the letter *m*, in hesitation, embarrassment, dissatisfaction, etc. **4** a low sound like that symbolized by the letter *m*, used to express hesitation, disagreement, etc. **5** sing with closed lips, not sounding words: *to hum a little tune.* **6** a singing in this way. **7** put or bring by humming: *She hummed her baby to sleep.* **8** *Informal.* be busy and active: *The new principal made things hum.* 1, 3, 5, 7, 8 *v.*, **hummed, hum·ming;** 2, 4, 6 *n.*, 4 *interj.* —**hum′mer,** *n.*

**hu·man** (hyü′mən) **1** of or belonging to all people: *Selfishness is a human weakness.* **2** being a person or persons; having the form or qualities of people: *Men, women, and children are human beings.* **3** having or showing qualities, good or bad, natural to people: *She is a very human person, warm and understanding and not too perfect.* **4** having to do with people; belonging to humanity: *human affairs. To know the future is beyond human power.* **5** a human being; person. 1–4 *adj.*, 5 *n.*

**human being** a man, woman, or child; person.

**hu·mane** (hyü mān′) **1** kind; merciful; not cruel or brutal: *We believe in the humane treatment of prisoners.*

**humanist** 584 **humorist**

2 tending to humanize and refine: *humane studies.* *adj.* —**hu·mane′ly,** *adv.* —**hu·mane′ness,** *n.*

**hu·man·ist** (hyü′mə nist) 1 a follower of any philosophy or field of study concerned with human interests and values. 2 a student of the humanities or of Latin and Greek culture. *n.*

**hu·man·i·tar·i·an** (hyü man′ə ter′ē ən) 1 helpful to humanity; philanthropic. 2 a person who is devoted to the welfare of all human beings. 1 *adj.,* 2 *n.*

**hu·man·i·tar·i·an·ism** (hyü man′ə ter′ē ə niz′əm) humanitarian principles or practices. *n.*

**hu·man·i·ty** (hyü man′ə tē) 1 human beings taken as a group; people: *Advances in science help all humanity.* 2 the fact of being human; human character or quality: *Humanity is a mixture of good and bad qualities.* 3 the fact of being humane; humane treatment; kindness; mercy: *Treat animals with humanity.* **4 the humanities, a** the Latin and Greek languages and literatures. **b** languages, literatures, philosophies, art, etc. **c** the branches of learning concerned with human ideas and their values. *n., pl.* **hu·man·i·ties.**

**hu·man·ize** (hyü′mə nīz′) 1 make human; give a human character or quality to. 2 make humane; cause to be kind or merciful. *v.,* **hu·man·ized, hu·man·iz·ing.**

**hu·man·kind** (hyü′mən kīnd′) human beings; people; the human race; mankind. *n.*

**hu·man·ly** (hyü′mən lē) 1 in a human manner. 2 by human means: *We will do all that is humanly possible.* 3 according to the feelings, knowledge, or experience of people. *adv.*

**hu·man·oid** (hyü′mə noid′) 1 having human characteristics; resembling a human being: *humanoid robots.* 2 one of the earliest ancestors of humankind. 3 any creature closely resembling a human being: *Science fiction often deals with humanoids from other planets.* 1 *adj.,* 2, 3 *n.*

**hum·ble** (hum′bəl) 1 low in position or condition; not important or grand: *A one-room log cabin is a humble place in which to live.* 2 having or showing a feeling that one is unimportant, weak, poor, etc.; modest in spirit; not proud: *Defeat and failure make people humble.* 3 deeply or courteously respectful: *in my humble opinion.* 4 make humble; bring down. 5 make lower in position, condition, or pride: *humbled by defeat.* 1–3 *adj.,* **hum·bler, hum·blest;** 4, 5 *v.,* **hum·bled, hum·bling.** —**hum′ble·ness,** *n.* —**hum′bly,** *adv.*

**hum·ble·bee** (hum′bəl bē′) BUMBLEBEE. *n.*

**humble pie** an inferior pie made of the inward parts of an animal. *Archaic* except in **eat humble pie, a** be forced to do something very disagreeable and humiliating. **b** admit one's mistake and say that one is sorry.
☞ *Etym.* From *umble pie,* a pie made of worthless bits of meat and formerly given to servants.

**hum·bug** (hum′bug′) 1 a person who pretends to be what he or she is not; fraud. 2 a cheat; sham. 3 nonsense; foolishness: *Mom says our argument is humbug.* 4 deceive with a sham; cheat. 5 a hard candy, usually brown with light stripes. 1–3, 5 *n.,* 4 *v.,* **hum·bugged, hum·bug·ging.**

**hum·drum** (hum′drum′) 1 without variety; commonplace; dull. 2 a humdrum routine. 1 *adj.,* 2 *n.*

**hu·mer·al** (hyü′mə rəl) 1 of or near the HUMERUS. 2 of or near the shoulder. *adj.*

**hu·mer·us** (hyü′mə rəs) the long bone in the upper part of the forelimb or arm, reaching from the shoulder to the elbow. See ARM¹ and COLLARBONE for pictures. *n., pl.* **hu·mer·i** (-mə rī′ or -mə rē′).
☞ *Hom.* HUMOROUS.

**hu·mid** (hyü′mid) moist; damp: *The air is very humid near the sea.* *adj.* —**hu′mid·ness,** *n.*

**hu·mi·dex** (hyü′mə deks′) *Cdn.* an index of discomfort resulting from a combination of humidity and heat. The humidex is calculated by adding a given value based on the dew point level to the temperature of the atmosphere. At a temperature of 20°C, the humidex is 21 when the dew point is 10° or 11°, and 26 when the dew point is 18°. With a humidex of 40 to 45, almost everyone feels uncomfortable. *n.*

**hu·mid·i·fi·ca·tion** (hyü mid′ə fə kā′shən) humidifying. *n.*

**hu·mid·i·fi·er** (hyü mid′ə fī′ər) a device for keeping the air moist. *n.*

**hu·mid·i·fy** (hyü mid′ə fī′) make moist or damp. *v.,* **hu·mid·i·fied, hu·mid·i·fy·ing.**

**hu·mid·i·ty** (hyü mid′ə tē) 1 the state of the atmosphere with respect to the amount of water vapour present in it. See RELATIVE HUMIDITY and ABSOLUTE HUMIDITY. 2 moistness; dampness: *The humidity today is worse than the heat.* *n.*

**hu·mi·dor** (hyü′mə dôr′) 1 a box, jar, etc. for keeping tobacco moist. 2 any similar device. *n.*

**hu·mil·i·ate** (hyü mil′ē āt′) lower the pride, dignity, or self-respect of; make ashamed: *We felt humiliated by our failure. He humiliated his parents by his rude behaviour.* *v.,* **hu·mil·i·at·ed, hu·mil·i·at·ing.** —**hu·mil′i·at′ing·ly,** *adv.*

**hu·mil·i·a·tion** (hyü mil′ē ā′shən) a lowering of pride, dignity, or self-respect; making or being made ashamed. *n.*

**hu·mil·i·ty** (hyü mil′ə tē) humbleness of mind; lack of pride; meekness. *n., pl.* **hu·mil·i·ties.**

Ruby-throated hummingbirds— about 10 cm long including the tail

**hum·ming·bird** (hum′ing bėrd′) a very small, brightly coloured bird of North and South America, having a long, narrow bill and narrow wings that move so rapidly they make a humming sound. *n.*

**hum·mock** (hum′ək) 1 a very small, rounded hill; knoll; hillock. 2 a bump or ridge in a field of ice. *n.*

**hu·mor** (hyü′mər) See HUMOUR. *n., v.*

**hu·mor·ist** (hyü′mə rist) 1 a person with a strong sense of humour. 2 a humorous talker or writer; a person who tells or writes jokes and funny stories. *n.*

**hu·mor·ous** (hyü′mə rəs) full of humour; funny; amusing: *Stephen Leacock was a humorous writer.* *adj.* —**hu′mor·ous·ly,** *adv.* —**hu′mor·ous·ness,** *n.*
☞ *Hom.* HUMERUS.

**hu·mour** or **hu·mor** (hyü′mər) **1** a funny or amusing quality: *I see no humour in your tricks.* **2** the ability to see or show the funny or amusing side of things: *Stephen Leacock was famous for his humour.* **3** a speech, writing, etc. showing this ability. **4** a state of mind; mood; disposition: *Success puts you in good humour.* **5** a fancy or whim. **6** give in to the fancies or whims of a person; indulge: *A sick person has to be humoured.* **7** adapt oneself to; act so as to agree with. **8** any of various body fluids formerly supposed to determine a person's health and disposition: *The four humours were blood, phlegm, choler (yellow bile), and melancholy (black bile).* 1–5, 8 *n.*, 6, 7 *v.* —**hu′mour·less** or **hu′mor·less,** *adj.*
**out of humour** or **humor,** angry; displeased; in a bad mood.
**sense of humour** or **humor,** the ability to see the amusing side of things.

**hump** (hump) **1** a rounded lump that sticks out: *Some camels have two humps on their backs.* **2** raise or bend up into a lump: *The cat humped its back when it saw the dog.* **3** a mound; hill. 1, 3 *n.*, 2 *v.* —**hump′like,** *adj.*
**over the hump,** past a difficult time or test.

**hump·back** (hump′bak′) **1** HUNCHBACK. **2** a back having a hump on it. **3** a large whale that has a humplike dorsal fin. **4** a species of Pacific salmon. *n*

**hump·backed** (hump′bakt′) HUNCHBACKED. *adj.*

**humph** (humpf) an exclamation expressing doubt, disgust, contempt, etc. *interj., n.*

**hump·y** (hum′pē) **1** full of humps. **2** humplike. *adj.*, **hump·i·er, hump·i·est.**

**hu·mus** (hyü′məs) the dark-brown or black part of soil formed from decayed leaves and other vegetable matter. *n.*

**Hun** (hun) **1** a member of an Asiatic people who, under the leadership of Attila, overran much of eastern and central Europe between about A.D. 375 and 450. **2** *Cdn., Informal.* HUNGARIAN PARTRIDGE. **3** Often, **hun,** a barbarous or destructive person. *n.*

**hunch** (hunch) **1** hump. **2** draw, bend, or form into a hump: *He sat hunched up with his chin on his knees.* **3** move, push, or shove by jerks. **4** *Informal.* a vague feeling or suspicion: *I had a hunch we would win the game.* 1–3 *v.*, 1, 4 *n.*

**hunch·back** (hunch′bak′) **1** a person with a crooked back that forms a hump at the level of the shoulders. **2** a crooked back that has a hump at the shoulders. *n.*

**hunch·backed** (hunch′bakt′) having a HUNCHBACK (def. 2). *adj.*

**hun·dred** (hun′drəd) **1** ten times ten; 100: *The audience numbered about two hundred. The equipment will cost at least a hundred dollars.* **2** a 100-dollar bill. **3 hundreds,** *pl.* the numbers between 100 and 999. 1–3 *n., pl.* **hun·dreds** or *(after a number)* **hun·dred;** 1 *adj.*

**hun·dred·fold** (hun′drəd fōld′) a hundred times as much or as many. *adj., adv., n.*

**hun·dredth** (hun′drədth) **1** next after the 99th; last in a series of 100: 100th. **2** one, or being one, of 100 equal parts. *adj., n.*

**hun·dred·weight** (hun′drəd wāt′) a non-metric unit

| hat, āge, fär; let, ēqual, tėrm; it, īce |
| hot, ōpen, ôrder; oil, out; cup, pút, rüle |
| əbove, takən, pencəl, lemən, circəs |
| ch, child; ng, long; sh, ship |
| th, thin; ᴛʜ, then; zh, measure |

for measuring mass, equal to 100 pounds (about 45 kg) in Canada and 112 pounds (about 50 kg) in the British Isles. *n., pl.* **hun·dred·weights** or *(after a numeral)* **hun·dred·weight.**

**hung** (hung) a pt. and a pp. of HANG: *He hung up his cap. A dress has hung here all day.* *v.*

**Hun·gar·i·an** (hung gerʹē ən) **1** of or having to do with Hungary, a country in central Europe, its people, or their language. **2** a native or inhabitant of Hungary. **3** a person of Hungarian descent. **4** the language of Hungary. 1 *adj.*, 2–4 *n.*

**Hungarian partridge** *Cdn.* a partridge introduced to North America from Europe as a game bird. Many of the first such birds to be brought over came from Hungary.

**hun·ger** (hungʹgər) **1** an uncomfortable or painful feeling or a weak condition caused by lack of food. **2** a desire or need for food. **3** feel hunger; be hungry. **4** a strong desire; longing: *a hunger for kindness.* **5** have a strong desire: *The lonely girl hungered for friends.* 1, 2, 4 *n.*, 3, 5 *v.*

**hunger strike** a refusal to eat until certain demands are granted.

**hung jury** a JURY that cannot agree on a verdict.

**hun·gry** (hungʹgrē) **1** feeling a desire or need for food: *Mother says that we always seem to be hungry.* **2** showing hunger: *a hungry look.* **3** having a strong desire or craving; eager: *hungry for knowledge.* **4** not rich or fertile: *hungry soil.* *adj.*, **hun·gri·er, hun·gri·est.** —**hunʹgri·ly,** *adv.* —**hunʹgri·ness,** *n.*

**hunk** (hungk) *Informal.* a big lump, piece, or slice: *a hunk of cheese.* *n.*

**hun·ker** (hungʹkər) squat on one's haunches. *v.*

**hunk·y–dor·y** (hungʹkē dôrʹē) *Informal.* fine; just right; satisfactory. *adj.*

**hunt** (hunt) **1** go after wild animals, game birds, etc. to catch them for zoos or kill them for food or sport. **2** search through a region in pursuit of game. **3** use horses or dogs in the chase. **4** the act of hunting: *Our gear for the duck hunt is all ready.* **5** a group of persons hunting together. **6** drive out or away; pursue; harry; persecute. **7** try to find: *to hunt a clue.* **8** look thoroughly; search carefully: *to hunt through drawers.* **9** an attempt to find something; thorough look; careful search. 1–3, 6–8, *v.*, 4, 5, 9 *n.*
**hunt down,** a hunt for until caught or killed. b look for until found.
**hunt out,** seek and find.
**hunt up,** a look carefully for. b find by search.

**hunt·er** (hunʹtər) **1** a person who hunts. **2** a horse or dog trained for hunting. **3** a gold pocket watch enclosed in a hinged case for protection. *n.*

**hunt·ing** (hunʹting) **1** the act of a person or animal that hunts, especially the pursuit of game: *They went hunting last weekend.* **2** ppr. of HUNT. 1 *n.*, 2 *v.*

**hunting ground** a place or region for hunting.

**happy hunting grounds,** a phrase applied by Europeans to their idea of what Amerindians considered to be a kind of 'heaven'.

**hunting horn** a horn used in a hunt. See HORN for picture.

**hunt·ress** (hun′tris) a woman who hunts. *n.*

**hunts·man** (hunt′smən) **1** HUNTER (def. 1). **2** the manager of a hunt. *n., pl.* **hunts·men** (-smən).

An athlete jumping a hurdle in a hurdle race

**hur·dle** (hėr′dəl) **1** in a race, a barrier for people or horses to jump over. **2** jump over: *The horse hurdled both the fence and the ditch.* **3** any obstacle or difficulty. **4** overcome an obstacle or difficulty. **5** a frame made of sticks used as a temporary fence. **6** enclose with such frames. **7 hurdles,** *pl.* a race in which the runners jump over hurdles. 1, 3, 5, 7 *n.*, 2, 4, 6 *v.*, **hur·dled, hur·dling.**

**hur·dler** (hėr′dlər) a person who jumps over hurdles in a race. *n.*

**hur·dy-gur·dy** (hėr′dē gėr′dē) **1** a hand organ played by turning a handle. **2** formerly, an instrument shaped like a guitar, played by turning a wheel. *n., pl.* **hur·dy-gur·dies.**

**hurl** (hėrl) **1** throw with much force: *The man hurled his spear at one bear. The dogs hurled themselves at the other.* **2** a forcible or violent throw. **3** speak with strong feeling; utter violently: *She hurled insults at me.* 1, 3 *v.*, 2 *n.* —**hurl′er,** *n.*

**hurl·y-burl·y** (hėr′lē bėr′lē) disorder and noise; tumult. *n., pl.* **hurl·y-burl·ies.**

**Hu·ron** (hyü′ron *or* hyü′rən) **1** a member of a First Nations people formerly living in the region between Lake Huron and Lake Ontario: *The Hurons were organized in a confederacy of four separate tribes.* **2** the Iroquoian language of the Hurons. **3** of or having to do with the Hurons or their language. 1, 2 *n., pl.* **Hu·rons** *or* **Hu·ron;** 3 *adj.*

**hur·rah** (hə rä′ *or* hə rȯ′) **1** a shout of joy, approval, etc. **2** shout hurrahs; cheer. 1 *interj., n.,* 2 *v.* Also, **hooray, hurray.**

**hur·ray** (hə rā′) HURRAH. *interj., n., v.*

**hur·ri·cane** (hėr′ə kān′) **1** a tropical cyclone that forms over the Atlantic Ocean, with winds of more than 120 kilometres per hour and, usually, very heavy rain: *Hurricanes sometimes move into temperate regions.* **2** any wind with a speed of more than 120 kilometres per hour. **3** a sudden, violent outburst or commotion: *a hurricane of cheers.* *n.*

**hur·ried** (hėr′ēd) **1** done or made in a hurry; hasty: *a hurried reply.* **2** forced to hurry. **3** *pt.* and *pp.* of HURRY. 1, 2 *adj.*, 3 *v.* —**hur′ried·ly,** *adv.*

**hur·ry** (hėr′ē) **1** drive, carry, send, or move quickly: *They hurried the sick child to the doctor.* **2** move or act with more than an easy or natural speed: *If you hurry, your work may be poor.* **3** a hurried movement or action: *In her hurry she dropped the eggs.* **4** an eagerness to have quickly or do quickly: *She was in a hurry to see her father.* **5** urge to act or move quickly; hasten; urge to great speed: *Don't hurry the driver.* **6** cause to go on or occur more quickly; hasten: *Please hurry dinner.* 1, 2, 5, 6 *v.*, **hur·ried, hur·ry·ing;** 3, 4 *n., pl.* **hur·ries.**

**hur·ry-scur·ry** *or* **hur·ry-skur·ry** (hėr′ē skėr′ē) *Informal.* **1** a hurrying and confusion. **2** hurried and confused. **3** with hurrying and confusion. 1 *n., pl.* **hur·ry-scur·ries** *or* **hur·ry-skur·ries;** 2 *adj.*, 3 *adv.*

**hurt** (hėrt) **1** cause pain, harm, or damage: *Falling on concrete hurts. My new shoes hurt.* **2** cause pain to; give a wound to; injure: *I hurt my arm when I fell.* **3** a wound or injury: *The hurt is almost healed.* **4** feel pain; suffer: *Pierre said he hurt all over after his fall. My sprained ankle hurts terribly.* **5** have a bad effect on; do damage or harm to: *Will it hurt this hat if it gets wet? The scandal has hurt her chances of getting elected.* **6** a bad effect; damage, harm, or injury: *The failure was a great hurt to her pride.* **7** grieve; distress: *He hurt his mother's feelings.* 1, 2, 4, 5, 7 *v.*, **hurt, hurt·ing;** 3, 6 *n.*

**hurt·ful** (hėrt′fəl) causing pain, harm, distress, or damage; injurious: *a mean and hurtful remark.* *adj.* —**hurt′ful·ly,** *adv.*

**hur·tle** (hėr′təl) **1** dash or drive violently; rush suddenly; come with a crash; fling: *The car hurtled across the road into a fence. The impact of the crash hurtled the driver against the windshield of the car.* **2** move with a clatter; rush noisily or violently: *The express train hurtled past.* **3** dash against; collide with. **4** the act or fact of hurtling; clash; clatter. 1–3 *v.*, **hur·tled, hur·tling;** 4 *n.*

**hus·band** (huz′bənd) **1** a married man. **2** manage carefully; be saving of: *A sick person must husband her strength.* 1 *n.*, 2 *v.*
☞ **Etym.** From OE *hūsbonda,* which came from ON *husbondi* 'master of a house', made up of *hus* 'house' + *bondi* 'residing, having a household'.

**hus·band·ry** (huz′bən drē) **1** farming. **2** careful management; thrift. *n.*

**hush** (hush) **1** stop making a noise; make or become silent or quiet: *The wind has hushed. Hush your dog.* **2** a stopping of noise; silence; quiet. **3** stop the noise! be silent! keep quiet! **4** soothe; calm. 1, 4 *v.*, 2 *n.*, 3 *interj.*

**hush up, a** keep from being told; stop discussion of. **b** *Informal.* be silent!

**hush money** *Informal.* money paid to keep a person from telling something.

**husk** (husk) **1** the dry outer covering of certain seeds or fruits: *The husk surrounding an ear of corn is made up of modified leaves.* **2** the dry or worthless outer covering of anything. **3** remove the husk from: *Husk the corn.* 1, 2 *n.*, 3 *v.* —**husk′er,** *n.*

**husk·y**[1] (hus′kē) **1** dry in the throat; hoarse; rough of voice: *A cold sometimes causes a husky cough.* **2** of, like, or having husks: *a husky covering.* **3** big and strong: *a husky young man.* *adj.*, **husk·i·er, husk·i·est.** —**husk′i·ly,** *adv.* —**husk′i·ness,** *n.*

**husk·y²** (hus′kē) **1** SIBERIAN HUSKY. **2** any northern work dog. *n., pl.* **husk·ies.**
☞ *Etym.* From a shortening of an early form of the word *Eskimo.* 19c. See also the note at ESKIMO.

**hus·sar** (hù zär′) **1** a light-armed cavalry soldier. **2** a member of certain armoured regiments. *n.*

**hus·sy** (huz′ē) **1** a bold or bad-mannered girl. **2** a woman who disregards moral conventions. *n., pl.* **hus·sies.**

**hus·tings** (hus′tingz) **1** a platform from which candidates for Parliament were formerly nominated and from which they addressed the voters. **2** a platform from which speeches are made in a political campaign. **3** the proceedings at an election. *n.pl. or sing.*

**hus·tle** (hus′əl) **1** hurry: *Mother hustled the boys to bed* (*v.*). *It was done with much hustle and bustle* (*n.*). **2** force hurriedly or roughly: *The police hustled the tramps out of town.* **3** push or shove roughly; jostle rudely: *The other boys hustled him along the street.* **4** a rough pushing or shoving; rude jostling. **5** *Informal.* go or work quickly or with tireless energy: *Anne had to hustle to earn enough money to support her family.* **6** *Informal.* tireless energy. 1–3, 5 *v.,* **hus·tled, hus·tling;** 1, 4, 6 *n.*
—**hus′tler,** *n.*

**hut** (hut) a small, roughly built house; small cabin: *The trappers built a hut deep in the woods.* *n.*
—**hut′like′,** *adj.*

**hutch** (huch) **1** a pen for rabbits, etc. **2** a box, chest, or bin. **3** a cupboard, open or with glass doors, having shelves for dishes, etc. and set on a buffet. **4** a high cupboard with usually open shelves on the upper part; china cabinet. *n.*

**Hut·ter·ite** (hut′ə rīt′) **1** a member of a religious group that came originally from Austria, now living mainly in Alberta and Manitoba. **2** of or having to do with the Hutterites: *Hutterite communities.* 1 *n.,* 2 *adj.*

**huz·za** (hə zä′) **1** a loud shout of joy, encouragement, or applause; hurrah. **2** shout huzzas; cheer. 1 *interj., n., pl.* **huz·zas;** 2 *v.,* **huz·zaed, huz·za·ing.**

**H.V., h.v.,** or **hv** high voltage.

Hyacinths

**hy·a·cinth** (hī′ə sinth′) **1** a plant of the same family as the lily, that grows from a bulb and has a spike of small, fragrant, bell-shaped flowers. **2** a reddish-orange gem, a variety of zircon. *n.*

**hy·a·line** (hī′ə lin *or* hī′ə līn′) **1** glassy; transparent: *A hyaline cartilage contains little fibre.* **2** something glassy or transparent. 1 *adj.,* 2 *n.*

**hy·a·lite** (hī′ə līt′) a colourless variety of opal, sometimes transparent like glass and sometimes whitish and translucent. *n.*

**hy·a·loid** (hī′ə loid′) glassy; transparent; crystalline. *adj.*

**hy·brid** (hī′brid) **1** the offspring of two animals or plants of different species, varieties, etc.: *Most garden roses are hybrids.* **2** anything of mixed origin: *A word formed of parts from different languages is a hybrid.* **3** bred from two different species, varieties, etc.: *A mule is a hybrid animal.* **4** of mixed origin. 1, 2 *n.,* 3, 4 *adj.*

**hy·brid·ism** (hī′bri diz′əm) the production of HYBRIDS. *n.*

**hy·brid·i·za·tion** (hī′bri də zā′shən *or* hī′bri dī zā′shən) the production of HYBRIDS; crossing of different species. *n.*

**hy·brid·ize** (hī′bri dīz′) **1** cause to produce HYBRIDS; crossbreed: *Botanists hybridize different kinds of plants to get new varieties.* **2** produce HYBRIDS. *v.,* **hy·brid·ized, hy·brid·iz·ing.**

**hy·dra** (hī′drə) **1** a kind of freshwater polyp, so called because when the tubelike body is cut into pieces, each piece forms a new individual. **2** any persistent evil; evil that is hard to overcome. *n., pl.* **hy·dras** or **hy·drae** (-drē *or* drī).
☞ *Etym.* Through Latin from Gk. *húdrā* 'water-serpent'. See also note at HYDRO-.

**hy·dran·gea** (hī drān′jə) a shrub with large, showy clusters of small white, pink, or blue flowers. *n.*

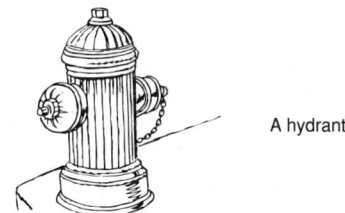
A hydrant

**hy·drant** (hī′drənt) a large upright pipe with a valve for drawing water directly from a water main: *Hydrants are used to get water to put out fires, to wash the streets, etc.* *n.*

**hy·drate** (hī′drāt) **1** a compound produced when any of certain other substances unite with water: *Washing soda is a hydrate.* **2** become or cause to become a hydrate; combine with water to form a hydrate: *Blue vitriol is hydrated copper sulphate.* 1 *n.,* 2 *v.,* **hy·drat·ed, hy·drat·ing.**

**hy·dra·tion** (hī drā′shən) the act or process of combining with water, especially to form a HYDRATE. *n.*

**hy·drau·lic** (hī drol′ik) **1** having to do with water or other liquid in motion. **2** operated by the pressure of water, or other liquid: *hydraulic brakes, a hydraulic press.* **3** hardening under water: *hydraulic cement.* **4** of or having to do with hydraulics: *a hydraulic engineer.* *adj.*
—**hy·drau′li·cal·ly,** *adv.*

**hy·drau·lics** (hī drol′iks) the branch of science dealing with water and other liquids in motion, their uses in engineering, the laws of their actions, etc. *n.* (used with a singular verb).

**hy·dride** (hī′drīd) a compound of hydrogen with another element or radical. *n.*

**hydro–** *combining form.* **1** of or having to do with water, as in *hydroplane*. **2** combined with hydrogen, as in *hydrochloric*.
☛ *Etym.* This combining form and all words beginning with **hydr-** came originally from forms or combinations of Gk. *húdōr* 'water'. Several such words came into English through Latin, while others are recent coinages created as part of our modern technical vocabulary.

**hy·dro** (hī′drō) *Cdn.* **1** HYDRO-ELECTRIC power: *Niagara Falls provides hydro for many factories.* **2** electricity as a utility distributed by a power company or commission: *The hydro was off for two hours during the storm.* **3 Hydro,** a company or commission producing and distributing electricity as a utility. *n.*

**hy·dro·car·bon** (hī′drō kär′bən) any of a class of organic compounds containing only hydrogen and carbon: *Methane, benzene, and acetylene are hydrocarbons. Gasoline is a mixture of hydrocarbons.* *n.*

**hy·dro·chlo·ric** (hī′drə klô′rik) containing hydrogen and chlorine. *adj.*

**hydrochloric acid** a very strong acid that is clear and colourless and has a strong, sharp odour: *Hydrochloric acid is present in a dilute form in the stomach juices.*

**hy·dro·cy·an·ic acid** (hī′drō sī an′ik) a weak acid that is a deadly poison with an odour like that of bitter almonds; prussic acid.

**hy·dro·dy·nam·ic** (hī′drō dī nam′ik) of or having to do with the force or motion of fluids, or with HYDRODYNAMICS. *adj.*

**hy·dro·dy·nam·ics** (hī′drō dī nam′iks) the branch of physics dealing with the forces that water and other liquids exert; hydraulics. *n.*

**hy·dro–e·lec·tric** (hī′drō i lek′trik) of or having to do with the generation of electricity by water power, or by the friction of water or steam: *There is a large hydro-electric plant on the St. Lawrence Seaway.* *adj.*

**hy·dro–e·lec·tric·i·ty** (hī′drō i lek′tris′ə tē) electricity produced from water power, etc. *n.*

**hy·dro·flu·or·ic** (hī′drō flü ô′rik) containing hydrogen and fluorine. *adj.*

**hydrofluoric acid** a colourless, corrosive, volatile liquid used for etching glass, treating metals, etc.

**hy·dro·foil** (hī′drō foil′) **1** one of a set of blades or fins attached to the hull of a boat at an angle so that the boat, when moving, is lifted just clear of the water: *Hydrofoils reduce friction and thus increase speed.* **2** a boat equipped with hydrofoils. *n.*

**hy·dro·gen** (hī′drə jən) a colourless, odourless gas that burns easily and weighs less than any other known element: *Hydrogen combines chemically with oxygen to form water.* Symbol: H *n.*

**hy·dro·gen·ate** (hī′drə jə nāt′) combine or treat with hydrogen; especially, combine an unsaturated organic compound with hydrogen: *Vegetable oils are hydrogenated to produce solid fats.* *v.,* **hy·dro·gen·at·ed, hy·dro·gen·at·ing.**

**hy·dro·gen·a·tion** (hī′drə jə nā′shən) the process of combining with hydrogen. *n.*

**hydrogen bomb** a bomb that uses the nuclear fusion of atoms to cause an explosion of tremendous force: *A hydrogen bomb is many times more powerful than an atomic bomb.*

**hydrogen peroxide** a colourless, unstable liquid often used in dilute solution as an antiseptic, as a bleaching agent, etc.

**hydrogen sulphide** or **sulfide** a flammable, poisonous gas having an odour like that of rotten eggs, found especially in mineral waters and decaying matter.

**hy·dro·graph·ic** (hī′drə graf′ik) of or having to do with HYDROGRAPHY. *adj.*
—**hy·dro·graph′i·cal·ly,** *adv.*

**hy·drog·ra·phy** (hī drog′rə fē) **1** the study, measurement and description of oceans, lakes, rivers, etc., especially with reference to their use for navigation and commerce. **2** oceans, lakes, rivers, etc., especially as dealt with on a map of a certain region, or in treatises or surveys: *the hydrography of northern Saskatchewan.* *n.*

**hydrologic cycle** the circular process in which water evaporates from the ocean, falling to earth as rain or snow, to return to the ocean from rivers fed by rain or melting snow.

**hy·drol·o·gy** (hī drol′ə jē) the branch of physical geography that deals with the laws, properties, distribution, etc. of water. *n.* —**hy·dro·log′ic,** *adj.*

**hy·drol·y·sis** (hī drol′ə sis) a chemical decomposition that changes a compound into a weak acid or base by taking up the elements of water. *n., pl.* **hy·drol·y·ses** (-sēz′).

**hy·dro·lyze** or **hy·dro·lyse** (hī′drə līz′) **1** decompose by HYDROLYSIS. **2** undergo HYDROLYSIS. *v.,* **hy·dro·lyzed** or **hy·dro·lysed, hy·dro·lyz·ing** or **hy·dro·lys·ing.**

**hy·drom·e·ter** (hī drom′ə tər) a graduated instrument for finding the specific gravities of liquids: *A hydrometer is used to test the battery of an automobile.* *n.*

**hy·dro·met·ric** (hī′drə met′rik) **1** of or having to do with HYDROMETRY. **2** of or having to do with a HYDROMETER. *adj.*

**hy·drom·e·try** (hī drom′ə trē) the determination of specific gravity, density, purity, etc. by means of a HYDROMETER. *n.*

**hy·dro·path·ic** (hī′drə path′ik) of or using HYDROPATHY. *adj.*

**hy·drop·a·thy** (hī drop′ə thē) the treatment of disease by using quantities of water externally and internally. *n.*

**hy·dro·pho·bi·a** (hī′drə fō′bē ə) **1** a morbid dread of water. **2** rabies, especially in human beings: *Rabies in people is called hydrophobia because one of the symptoms is a dislike and fear of water and other liquids.* *n.*

**hy·dro·plane** (hī′drə plān′) **1** a motorboat that glides on the surface of the water. **2** a finlike structure that lifts a motorboat or seaplane slightly above the level of the water; HYDROFOIL. **3** an aircraft that can take off from and land on water; seaplane. *n.*

**hy·dro·pon·ics** (hī′drə pon′iks) the growing of plants in water containing the necessary nutrients instead of in soil. *n.*

**hy·dro·sphere** (hī′drə sfēr′) **1** the water on the surface of the globe. **2** the water vapour in the atmosphere. Compare with ATMOSPHERE and LITHOSPHERE. *n.*

**hy·dro·stat** (hī′drə stat′) **1** any of various devices for preventing injury to a steam boiler from low water pressure. **2** an electrical device for detecting the presence of water from overflow, leakage, etc. *n.*

**hy·dro·stat·ic** (hī′drə stat′ik) of or having to do with HYDROSTATICS. *adj.*

**hy·dro·stat·ics** (hī′drə stat′iks) the branch of physics that deals with the equilibrium and pressure of water and other liquids. *n.*

**hy·dro·ther·a·py** (hī′drō ther′ə pē) the treatment of disease by means of water; hydropathy. *n.*

**hy·drot·ro·pism** (hī drot′rə piz′əm) TROPISM in response to water: *Hydrotropism causes roots to grow toward water.* *n.*

**hy·drous** (hī′drəs) containing water, usually in combination: *A hydrous salt is a crystalline compound.* *adj.*

**hy·drox·ide** (hī drok′sīd) any compound consisting of an element or radical combined with one or more HYDROXYL radicals: *Hydroxides of metals are bases; those of non-metals are acids.* *n.*

**hy·drox·yl** (hī drok′səl) a univalent radical, OH: *Hydroxyl is found in all hydroxides.* *n.*

**hy·dro·zo·an** (hī′drə zō′ən) any of a class of invertebrate water animals having a simple body consisting of two layers of cells and a mouth that opens into the body, including hydras, polyps, many jellyfishes, etc. *n.*

A spotted hyena—about 90 cm high at the shoulder

**hy·e·na** (hī ē′nə) a wild, wolflike, flesh-eating mammal of Africa and Asia. *n.*

**hy·giene** (hī′jēn) **1** the principles of keeping well and preventing disease; the science of health. **2** practices such as cleanliness that help to preserve health: *personal hygiene.* *n.*

**hy·gien·ic** (hī jē′nik *or* hī jen′ik) **1** healthful; sanitary. **2** having to do with health or HYGIENE. *adj.*

**hy·gien·ist** (hī′jē nist) a person trained in HYGIENE (def. 1), especially one who makes it his or her work. *n.*

**hy·grom·e·ter** (hī grom′ə tər) any of several kinds of instrument for determining the amount of moisture in the air. *n.*

**hy·gro·met·ric** (hī′grə met′rik) of or having to do with the measurement of moisture in the air. *adj.*

**hy·grom·e·try** (hī grom′ə trē) the measurement of the amount of moisture in the air. *n.*

**hy·gro·scope** (hī′grə skōp′) an instrument that shows changes in the humidity of the air. *n.*

**hy·gro·scop·ic** (hī′grə skop′ik) **1** having to do with or perceptible by the HYGROSCOPE. **2** absorbing or attracting moisture from the air. *adj.*

**hy·ing** (hī′ing) ppr. of HIE. *v.*

**hy·la** (hī′lə) any of a closely related group of tree frogs. *n.*

**hy·men** (hī′mən) a fold of mucous membrane extending partly across the opening of the vagina. *n.*

# hydrostatic 589 hyphenation

hat, āge, fär; let, ēqual, tėrm; it, īce
hot, ōpen, ôrder; oil, out; cup, pút, rüle
əbove, takən, pencəl, lemən, circəs
ch, child; ng, long; sh, ship
th, thin; ᴛʜ, then; zh, measure

**hy·me·ne·al** (hī′mə nē′əl) **1** having to do with marriage. **2** a wedding song. **1** *adj.*, **2** *n.*

**hy·me·nop·ter·ous** (hī′mə nop′tə rəs) belonging to an order of insects including ants, bees, and wasps: *Winged hymenopterous insects have four membranous wings.* *adj.*

**hymn** (him) **1** a song of praise to God, especially one sung as part of a religious service. **2** any song of praise. **3** praise or honour with a hymn. **1**, **2** *n.*, **3** *v.* —**hymn′like′**, *adj.*
☞ *Hom.* HIM.

**hy·oid** (hī′oid) **1** in human beings, the U-shaped bone at the root of the tongue. **2** in animals, a corresponding bone or group of bones. **3** referring to or having to do with this bone. **1**, **2** *n.*, **3** *adj.*

**hy·per·a·cid·i·ty** (hī′pər ə sid′ə tē) more than the normal amount of acid, especially in the stomach juices. *n.*

**hy·per·bo·le** (hī pėr′bə lē′) exaggeration for effect. *Example: Waves high as mountains broke over the reef.* *n.*

**hy·per·bol·ic** (hī′pər bol′ik) of, like, or using HYPERBOLE; exaggerated; exaggerating. *adj.*

**hy·per·crit·i·cal** (hī′pər krit′ə kəl) too critical. *adj.* —**hy′per·crit′i·cal·ly**, *adv.*

**hy·per·o·pi·a** (hī′pə rō′pē ə) far-sightedness. Compare with MYOPIA. *n.*

**hy·per·op·ic** (hī′pə rop′ik) far-sighted. Compare with MYOPIC. *adj.*

**hy·per·sen·si·tive** (hī′pər sen′sə tiv) excessively sensitive. *adj.* —**hy′per·sen′si·tive·ness**, *n.*

**hy·per·sen·si·tiv·i·ty** (hī′pər sen′sə tiv′ə tē) excessive sensitiveness. *n.*

**hy·per·ten·sion** (hī′pər ten′shən) an abnormally high blood pressure. *n.*

**hy·per·ton·ic** (hī′pər ton′ik) of a solution, having a higher concentration of solute than surrounding tissue: *A hypertonic solution has a higher concentration of solute than that of the cytoplasm, so that a cell loses water and volume by osmosis.* Compare with HYPOTONIC and ISOTONIC. *adj.*

**hy·per·tro·phy** (hī pėr′trə fē) **1** the enlargement of a part or organ; growing too big. **2** grow too big. **1** *n.*, *pl.* **hy·per·tro·phies**; **2** *v.*, **hy·per·tro·phied**, **hy·per·tro·phy·ing**.

**hy·phae** (hī′fē *or* hī′fā) fibrous structures that make up fungi. *n. pl.*

**hy·phen** (hī′fən) **1** a mark (-) used to join the parts of certain words such as *tail-less, radio-active, re-enter,* or the parts of a word divided at the end of a line of printing or writing, etc. **2** HYPHENATE. **1** *n.*, **2** *v.*

**hy·phen·ate** (hī′fə nāt′) connect by a HYPHEN; write or print with a hyphen. *v.*, **hy·phen·at·ed**, **hy·phen·at·ing**.

**hy·phen·a·tion** (hī′fə nā′shən) the act of connecting by or writing with a HYPHEN. *n.*

**hyp·no·sis** (hip nō′sis) a state resembling deep sleep, but more active, in which a person has little will and little feeling, and acts according to the suggestions of the person who brought about the hypnosis. *n., pl.* **hyp·no·ses** (-sēz).

**hyp·not·ic** (hip not′ik) **1** of, having to do with, or producing HYPNOSIS. **2** a person under HYPNOSIS or one who is easily hypnotized. **3** causing or tending to cause sleep: *the hypnotic monotone of his voice.* **4** a drug or other means of causing sleep. 1, 3 *adj.*, 2, 4 *n.*

**hyp·not·i·cal·ly** (hip not′i klē) in a HYPNOTIC manner. *adv.*

**hyp·no·tism** (hip′nə tiz′əm) **1** the inducing of HYPNOSIS; hypnotizing: *Hypnotism is sometimes used by doctors and dentists to inhibit pain.* **2** the study of hypnosis. *n.*

**hyp·no·tist** (hip′nə tist′) a person skilled in hypnotizing. *n.*

**hyp·no·tize** (hip′nə tīz′) **1** put into a hypnotic state; cause HYPNOSIS. **2** *Informal.* dominate or control the will of by suggestion. *v.*, **hyp·no·tized, hyp·no·tiz·ing.** —**hyp′no·tiz′a·ble,** *adj.* —**hyp′no·tiz′er,** *n.*

**hy·po**[1] (hī′pō) a colourless, crystalline salt, a sodium compound, used as a fixing agent in photography. *n., pl.* **hy·pos.**

**hy·po**[2] (hī′pō) *Informal.* HYPODERMIC (defs. 3, 4). *n., pl.* **hy·pos.**

**hy·po·chlo·rite** (hī′pə klô′rīt) a salt of HYPOCHLOROUS ACID. *n.*

**hy·po·chlo·rous acid** (hī′pə klô′rəs) a yellow solution with an irritating smell, used as a bleach, disinfectant, etc.

**hy·po·chon·dri·a** (hī′pə kon′drē ə) **1** an unnatural anxiety about one's health; imaginary illness. **2** low spirits without any real reason. *n.*

**hy·po·chon·dri·ac** (hī′pə kon′drē ak′) **1** a person suffering from HYPOCHONDRIA. **2** suffering from HYPOCHONDRIA. 1 *n.*, 2 *adj.*

**hy·poc·ri·sy** (hi pok′rə sē) **1** the act or fact of putting on a false appearance, especially of goodness or religion. **2** pretending to be what one is not; pretence. *n., pl.* **hy·poc·ri·sies.**

**hyp·o·crite** (hip′ə krit′) a person who pretends to be what he or she is not, especially one who puts on an appearance of goodness or religion. *n.*

**hyp·o·crit·i·cal** (hip′ə krit′ə kəl) of or like a HYPOCRITE; insincere. *adj.* —**hyp′o·crit′i·cal·ly,** *adv.*

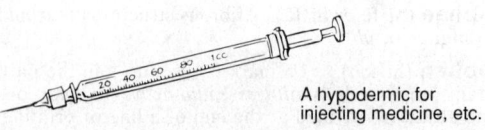
A hypodermic for injecting medicine, etc.

**hy·po·der·mic** (hī′pə dėr′mik) **1** under the skin. **2** for injecting under the skin: *The doctor used a hypodermic needle.* **3** a dose of medicine injected under the skin: *The doctor gave her a hypodermic to make her sleep.* **4** a syringe used to inject a dose of medicine under the skin. 1, 2 *adj.*, 3, 4 *n.*

**hy·po·der·mi·cal·ly** (hī′pə dėr′mi klē) by injection under the skin. *adv.*

**hy·poph·y·sis** (hī pof′ə sis) pituitary gland. *n., pl.* **hy·poph·y·ses** (-sēz′).

**hy·po·sul·phite** (hī′pə sul′fīt) a salt of HYPOSULPHUROUS ACID. *n.*

**hy·po·sul·phur·ous acid** (hī′pō sul′fə rəs) an unstable acid used as a reducing and bleaching agent. *adj.*

**hy·pot·e·nuse** (hī pot′ə nyüz′ *or* hī pot′ə nüz′, hī pot′ə nyüs′ *or* hī pot′ə nüs′) in mathematics, the side of a right-angled triangle opposite the right angle. *n.*

**hy·poth·e·cate** (hī poth′ə kāt′) pledge property, stock, etc. to a creditor as security for a loan or debt; mortgage. *v.*, **hy·poth·e·cat·ed, hy·poth·e·cat·ing.**

**hy·poth·e·ca·tion** (hī poth′ə kā′shən) **1** the act or fact of depositing as security. **2** a claim against property deposited as security. *n.*

**hy·poth·e·nuse** (hī poth′ə nyüz′ *or* hī poth′ə nüz′, hī poth′ə nyüs′ *or* hī poth′ə nüs′) See HYPOTENUSE. *n.*

**hy·po·ther·mi·a** (hī′pō thėr′mē ə) a body temperature greatly below normal: *Sailors shipwrecked in icy seas often die of hypothermia.* *n.*

**hy·poth·e·ses** (hī poth′ə sēz′) pl. of HYPOTHESIS. *n.*

**hy·poth·e·sis** (hī poth′ə sis) **1** something assumed because it seems likely to be a true explanation; theory: *Let us act on the hypothesis that she is honest.* **2** a proposition assumed as a basis for reasoning. *n., pl.* **hy·poth·e·ses** (-sēz′).

**hy·poth·e·size** (hī poth′ə sīz′) **1** make a HYPOTHESIS. **2** assume; suppose. *v.*, **hy·poth·e·sized, hy·poth·e·siz·ing.**

**hy·po·thet·ic** (hī′pə thet′ik) HYPOTHETICAL. *adj.*

**hy·po·thet·i·cal** (hī′pə thet′ə kəl) **1** of or based on a HYPOTHESIS; assumed; supposed. **2** fond of making hypotheses: *a hypothetical scientist.* *adj.* —**hy′po·thet′i·cal·ly,** *adv.*

**hy·po·ton·ic** (hī′pə ton′ik) of a solution, having a lower concentrate of solute than surrounding tissue: *A hypotonic solution has a lower concentrate of solute than that of the cytoplasm, so that a cell gains water and volume by osmosis.* Compare with HYPERTONIC and ISOTONIC. *adj.*

**hy·rax** (hī′raks) any of various small, timid, rabbitlike mammals of Asia and Africa. *n.*

**hys·sop** (his′əp) a fragrant, bushy plant of the same family as mint, used for medicine, flavouring, etc. *n.*

**hys·te·ri·a** (his tē′rē ə *or* his ter′ē ə) **1** a nervous disorder that causes violent fits of laughing and crying, imaginary or real illnesses, lack of self-control, etc. **2** senseless excitement. *n.*

**hys·ter·ic** (his ter′ik) HYSTERICAL. *adj.*

**hys·ter·i·cal** (his ter′ə kəl) **1** unnaturally excited. **2** showing extreme lack of control; unable to stop laughing, crying, etc.; suffering from HYSTERIA: *She was hysterical with grief.* *adj.* —**hys·ter′i·cal·ly,** *adv.*

**hys·ter·ics** (his ter′iks) a fit of HYSTERICAL laughing and crying. *n. pl.*

# I i  *I i*

**i** or **I**¹ (ī)   **1** the ninth letter of the English alphabet. **2** any speech sound represented by this letter.   **3** any person or thing considered as the ninth of a series.   **4 I**, the Roman numeral for 1.   *n., pl.* **i's** or **I's.**

**I²** (ī)   the person who is speaking or writing: *George said, "I am sixteen years old." I like my dog, and she likes me. pron., nom.* **I**, *poss.* **mine** or **my**, *obj.* **me;** *pl. nom.* **we**, *poss.* **ours** or **our**, *obj.* **us;** *n., pl.* **I's.**
☛ *Hom.* AYE, EYE.

**i.**   **1** island.   **2** interest.

**I**   iodine.

**I.**   **1** Island; Islands.   **2** Isle; Isles.

**–ial**   a suffix having the same meaning as **-al**, as in *adverbial, facial,* etc.

**i·am·bic** (ī am′bik)   **1** in poetry, of or referring to a metrical foot consisting basically of two syllables, the first one having a weak stress and the second a strong stress: *The iambic foot has been by far the commonest in English verse since the Middle Ages.*   **2** an iambic foot. *Example:*
The sún | that bríef | Decém | ber dáy
Rose cheér | less ó | ver hílls | of gréy.
1 *adj.,* 2 *n.*

**iambic pentameter**   a poetic metre based on five iambic feet in a line of verse: *Iambic pentameter was the standard metre for English verse from about the 15th century to the 19th.*

**–ian**   a form of the suffix **-an** used in certain words, such as *mammalian, Canadian,* etc.

**IATA**   International Air Transport Association.

**I·be·ri·an** (ī bē′rē ən)   **1** of or having to do with Iberia, a peninsula in southwestern Europe, or its people.   **2** an inhabitant of ancient Iberia, a region in Asia, south of the Caucasus: *The Basques are believed to be descended from the Iberians.*   **3** the language of ancient Iberia.   **4** a member of a people inhabiting a great part of southern Europe and parts of northern Africa.   1 *adj.,* 2–4 *n.*

**i·bex** (ī′beks)   a wild goat of Europe, Asia, or Africa: *The male ibex has very large horns.   n., pl.* **i·bex·es**, **ib·i·ces** (ib′ə sēz′ *or* ī′bə sēz′) or (*esp. collectively*) **i·bex.**

**ibid.**   an abbreviation for the Latin *ibidem,* meaning 'in the same place'.
☛ *Usage.* **Ibid.** is used in a footnote to refer to the book, article, etc. mentioned in the immediately preceeding footnote.

**i·bis** (ī′bis)   a long-legged wading bird resembling a heron: *The ancient Egyptians regarded the ibis as sacred. n., pl.* **i·bis·es** or (*esp. collectively*) **i·bis.**

**–ible**   an adjective-forming suffix meaning that can be _____ed, as in *convertible, perfectible, reducible.*

**–ic**   an adjective-forming suffix meaning:   **1** of or having to do with, as in *atmospheric, Icelandic.*   **2** having the nature of, as in *artistic, heroic.*   **3** constituting or being, as in *bombastic, monolithic.*   **4** characterized by; containing; made up of, as in *alcoholic, iambic.*   **5** made by; caused by, as in *photographic.*   **6** like; like that of; characteristic of, as in *meteoric, antagonistic, idyllic.*   **7** in chemical terms, -ic implies a smaller proportion of the element named than -ous implies, as in *boric, chloric, ferric, sulphuric.*
☛ *Usage.* Many words ending in -ic have two or more of the first six meanings.

**–ical**   an adjective-forming suffix with the meaning of -IC (defs. 1–6).
☛ *Usage.* Sometimes adjectives formed with -ical have quite different meanings from those formed with -IC: A historic city *means a city with a history*. A historical novel *means a novel based on history.*
☛ *Usage.* Adjectives ending in -al form adverbs by the addition of *-ly: critically, alphabetically, musically.* Adjectives ending in -ic form adverbs by the addition of *-ally: heroically, idiotically. Publicly* is the only exception.

**ICBM**   intercontinental ballistic missile, a ballistic missile of extreme range (up to 8000 km).

**ice** (īs)   **1** water made solid by cold; frozen water.   **2** a layer or surface of ice.   **3** of or having to do with ice.   **4** something that looks or feels like ice.   **5** cool with ice; put ice in or around.   **6** cover with ice.   **7** turn to ice; freeze.   **8** a frozen dessert usually made of sweetened fruit juice.   **9** cover with icing.   **10** ICING (def. 1).   **11** a frozen surface for skating, curling, hockey, etc.   **12** *Cdn.*   in hockey, shoot a puck from one's defensive zone past the red line at the opposite end of the rink: *No player may ice the puck when his team is at full strength.*   **13** *Cdn.*   put a hockey team into play: *Our town iced a good hockey team.*   **14 the ice,**   especially in Newfoundland, the edge of the Arctic ice fields where seal-hunting takes place.   1, 2, 4, 8, 10–11, 14 *n.,* 3 *adj.,* 5–7, 9, 12, 13 *v.,* **iced, ic·ing.** —**ice′less,** *adj.*
**break the ice,** *Informal.*   **a** make a beginning; start something dangerous or difficult.   **b** overcome first difficulties in talking or getting acquainted.
**on thin ice,**   in a dangerous or difficult position.

**ice age**   **1** any of the times when much of the earth was covered with glaciers.   **2** Often, **Ice Age**,   the most recent such time, when most of the Northern Hemisphere was covered with glaciers, beginning about 600 000 years ago.

**ice·berg** (īs′bėrg′)   a large mass of ice detached from a glacier and floating in the sea: *Only a small part of an iceberg projects above the surface of the water.   n.*
**tip of the iceberg,**   a small part of something much larger.
☛ *Etym.* From Dutch *ijsberg* 'mountain of ice'. 18c.

**ice·boat** (īs′bōt′)   **1** a light frame, often triangular, set on runners and fitted with sails or a propeller for skimming along the frozen surface of a lake, river, etc.   **2** ICEBREAKER.   *n.*

**ice·bound** (īs′bound′)   **1** held fast by ice; frozen in: *The ship was icebound for several weeks.*   **2** shut in or obstructed by ice: *The port at Churchill is icebound for about 10 months of the year.   adj.*

**ice–box** or **ice box** (īs′boks′)   **1** an insulated chest or box in which food is kept cool by ice.   **2** REFRIGERATOR.   *n.*

**ice·break·er** (īs′brā′kər) a ship designed for breaking a passage through ice. *n.*

**ice·cap** (ī′skap′) a permanent covering of ice over an area, sloping down on all sides from an elevated centre. *n.*

**ice cream** (ī′skrēm′ *or* ī′skrēm′) a frozen dessert made of cream or custard sweetened and flavoured.

**ice cube** a small chunk of ice, having six sides, used for chilling drinks or food.

**iced** (īst) **1** cooled with ice: *iced coffee.* **2** covered with ice. **3** covered with ICING (def. 1): *iced cookies. adj.*

**ice field** **1** a large sheet of ice floating in the sea, larger than a FLOE. **2** a large sheet of ice on land.

**ice fishing** *Cdn.* the act or practice of fishing through a hole or holes cut through ice.

**ice floe** FLOE.

**ice hockey** a game played on ice. See HOCKEY.

**ice·house** (īs′hous′) a building for storing ice. *n.*

**Ice·land·er** (ī′slan′dər *or* ī′slən dər) a native or inhabitant of Iceland, a large island in the northern Atlantic Ocean. *n.*

**Ice·lan·dic** (ī slan′dik) **1** of or having to do with Iceland, its people, or their language. **2** the language of Iceland. **1** *adj.*, **2** *n.*

**ice·man** (ī′sman′ *or* ī′smən) a person who sells, delivers, or handles ice. *n., pl.* **ice·men** (-smen′ *or* -smən).

**ice pack** **1** a large expanse of floating ice, consisting of many small FLOES packed together. **2** a bag containing ice for application to the body.

**ice pool** *Cdn.* a sweepstake, the winner being the person who makes the closest guess as to the date of the BREAK-UP (def. 1) in spring, as marked by the actual movement of the ice.

**ice sheet** a broad, thick sheet of ice covering a very large area for a long time.

**ice skate** a boot with a metal runner attached to the sole, for gliding over ice. See SKATE for pictures.

**ice–skate** (īs′skāt′) skate on ice. *v.,* **ice-skat·ed, ice-skat·ing.** —**ice′-skat′er,** *n.*

**ice storm** a freezing rain that covers exposed surfaces with a layer of glistening ice; SILVER THAW (def. 1).

**ice time** **1** in hockey, the time actually spent on the ice by a player during a game. **2** the time during which the ice at a rink is available to a team, group, or individuals.

**ice water** **1** water cooled with ice. **2** water from melted ice.

**ich·neu·mon** (ik nyü′mən *or* ik nü′mən) **1** a small brown mammal of Egypt, resembling the weasel. **2** ICHNEUMON FLY. *n.*

**ichneumon fly** an insect that looks like a wasp but does not sting. The larvae of this fly live as parasites in or on other insects.

**i·chor** (ī′kôr *or* ī′kər) an acrid, watery discharge from ulcers, wounds, etc. *n.*

☛ *Etym.* From the name of the fluid which, in Greek mythology, flowed in the veins of the gods.

**ich·thy·ol·o·gist** (ik′thē ol′ə jist) a person trained in ICHTHYOLOGY, especially one who makes it his or her work. *n.*

**ich·thy·ol·o·gy** (ik′thē ol′ə jē) the branch of zoology that deals with fish. *n.*

**ich·thy·o·saur** (ik′thē ə sôr′) any of an order of extinct sea reptiles having a fishlike body, four flippers, and a long snout. *n.*

**ich·thy·o·sau·rus** (ik′thē ə sô′rəs) ICHTHYOSAUR. *n., pl.* **ich·thy·o·sau·ri** (-sô′rī *or* -sô′rē).

**i·ci·cle** (ī′si kəl) a pointed, hanging stick of ice formed by the freezing of dripping water. *n.*

**ic·ing** (ī′sing) **1** a sweet, creamy mixture used to cover cakes, etc., made of sugar and some liquid, flavouring, sometimes the beaten whites of eggs, etc.: *Icing can be hard or soft.* **2** in hockey, the shooting of the puck from within one's own defensive zone across the opponent's goal line. **3** ppr. of ICE. **1, 2** *n.,* **3** *v.*

**i·con** or **i·kon** (ī′kon) **1** a sacred picture or image of Christ, an angel, a saint, etc. **2** any picture or image, such as a computer symbol of a function, procedure, etc. *n., pl.* **i·cons** or **i·kons, i·co·nes** or **i·ko·nes** (ī′kə nēz′).

**i·con·o·clast** (ī kon′ə klast′) **1** a person opposed to the use of images in religious worship. **2** a person who attacks cherished beliefs or institutions as wrong or foolish. *n.*

**i·con·o·clas·tic** (ī kon′ə klas′tik) of or having to do with ICONOCLASTS. *adj.*

**i·cy** (ī′sē) **1** like ice; very cold: *an icy blast of wind.* **2** having much ice; covered with ice: *an icy road.* **3** of ice. **4** without warm feeling; cold and unfriendly: *Robin gave her an icy stare. adj.,* **i·ci·er, i·ci·est.** —**i′ci·ly,** *adv.* —**i′ci·ness,** *n.*

**I'd** (īd) **1** I would: *I'd leave tomorrow if I could.* **2** I had: *I'd better get back to work.*

**ID card** IDENTIFICATION (def. 2) card.

**i·de·a** (ī dē′ə) **1** a picture or belief in the mind: *to have an idea how a thing looks.* **2** a thought; opinion: *She is always ready to express her ideas. I had an idea that everything would turn out well.* **3** a plan, scheme, or design: *She told them her idea for the publicity campaign.* **4** the point or purpose: *The idea of a vacation is to get a rest. n.* —**i·de′a-less,** *adj.*

**i·de·al** (ī dē′əl *or* ī dēl′) **1** a perfect type; model to be imitated; what one would wish to be: *Her mother is her ideal. Religion holds up high ideals for us to follow.* **2** just as one would wish; perfect: *A warm, sunny day is ideal for a picnic.* **3** existing only in thought: *A point without length, breadth, or thickness is an ideal object.* **4** not practical; visionary. **5** having to do with ideas; representing an idea. **1** *n.,* **2–5** *adj.* —**i·de′al-less,** *adj.*

**i·de·al·ism** (ī dē′ə liz′əm) **1** an acting according to one's ideals of what ought to be, regardless of circumstances or of the approval or disapproval of others. **2** a cherishing of fine ideals. **3** in art or literature, the representing of imagined types rather than an exact copy of any one person, instance, or situation: *Idealism is opposed to realism.* **4** in philosophy, the belief that all our knowledge is a knowledge of ideas and that it is impossible to know whether there really is a world of objects on which our ideas are based: *Idealism is opposed to materialism, which holds that objects really exist apart from our ideas. n.*

**i·de·al·ist** (ī dē′ə list) **1** a person who has high ideals and strives to act according to them. **2** a person who neglects practical matters in following ideals. **3** one who follows or practises idealism in art, literature, or philosophy. *n.*

**i·de·al·is·tic** (ī′dē ə lis′tik *or* ī dē′ə lis′tik) **1** having high ideals and acting according to them. **2** forgetting or neglecting practical matters in trying to follow out one's ideals; not practical. **3** of or having to do with idealism or idealists. *adj.*

**i·de·al·i·za·tion** (ī dē′ə lə zā′shən *or* ī dē′ə lī zā′shən) **1** idealizing or being idealized. **2** the result of idealizing. *n.*

**i·de·al·ize** (ī dē′ə līz′) make ideal; think of or represent as perfect rather than as is actually the case: *Douglas idealized his older sister and thought that everything she did was right.* *v.*, **i·de·al·ized, i·de·al·iz·ing.**

**i·de·al·ly** (ī dē′ə lē) **1** according to an ideal; perfectly. **2** in idea or theory. *adv.*

**i·den·ti·cal** (ī den′tə kəl) **1** the same: *Both events happened on the identical day.* **2** exactly alike: 122 mm and 12.2 cm *are identical amounts.* **3** of twins, coming from a single fertilized egg cell, as distinguished from FRATERNAL twins. *adj.* —**i·den′ti·cal·ly,** *adv.* —**i·den′ti·cal·ness,** *n.*

**i·den·ti·fi·ca·tion** (ī den′tə fə kā′shən) **1** an identifying or being identified. **2** something used to identify a person or thing: *She showed her driver's licence as identification.* *n.*

**i·den·ti·fy** (ī den′tə fī′) **1** recognize as being, or show to be, a certain person or thing; prove to be the same: *Chris identified the bag as hers by telling what it contained.* **2** make the same; treat as the same: *The good king identified his people's welfare with his own.* **3** connect closely; link; associate. *v.*, **i·den·ti·fied, i·den·ti·fy·ing.** —**i·den′ti·fi′a·ble,** *adj.* —**i·den′ti·fi′er,** *n.*

**i·den·ti·ty** (ī den′tə tē) **1** being oneself or itself and not another; who or what one is: *The writer concealed his identity under an assumed name.* **2** exact likeness; sameness: *The identity of the two crimes led the police to think that the same person committed them.* **3** the state or fact of being the same one: *to establish the identity of a person seen today with one seen yesterday.* *n., pl.* **i·den·ti·ties.**

**i·de·ol·o·gy** (ī′dē ol′ə jē *or* id′ē ol′ə jē) **1** a body of doctrines or concepts, especially about social, political, or economic systems. **2** the combined doctrines, assertions, and intentions of a social or political movement. **3** abstract speculation; especially, theorizing or speculation of a visionary or unpractical nature. **4** the study of ideas, their nature and origin. *n., pl.* **i·de·ol·o·gies.**

**ides** (īdz) in the ancient Roman calendar, the 15th day of March, May, July, and October, and the 13th day of the other months (*used with a singular or plural verb*). *n. pl.*

**id·i·o·cy** (id′ē ə sē) **1** the state of being an idiot. **2** an acting like an idiot. **3** very great stupidity or folly. *n., pl.* **id·i·o·cies.**

**id·i·om** (id′ē əm) **1** a phrase or expression whose meaning cannot be understood from the ordinary meanings of its individual words: *"How do you do?" and "I have caught a cold" are English idioms.* **2** dialect: *Zina speaks in the idiom of the Ottawa Valley.* **3** a people's way of expressing themselves: *In the French idiom, one can say "of a rapidity" for "rapid."* **4** an individual manner of expression in music, art, etc. *n.*

---

**idealist**     593     **idyll**

hat, āge, fär; let, ēqual, tėrm; it, īce
hot, ōpen, ôrder; oil, out; cup, pút, rüle
əbove, takən, pencəl, lemən, circəs

ch, child; ng, long; sh, ship
th, thin; ŦH, then; zh, measure

**id·i·o·mat·ic** (id′ē ə mat′ik) **1** using an idiom or idioms. **2** of or concerning idioms. **3** showing the individual character of a language; characteristic of a particular language. *adj.* —**id′i·o·mat′i·cal·ly,** *adv.*

**id·i·o·syn·cra·sy** (id′ē ə sing′krə sē) a personal peculiarity of taste, behaviour, opinion, etc.: *He was an eccentric person with many idiosyncrasies.* *n., pl.* **id·i·o·syn·cra·sies.**

**id·i·ot** (id′ē ət) **1** a person born with little ability to learn; a person who does not develop mentally. **2** a very stupid or foolish person: *He was an idiot to behave like that.* *n.*

**id·i·ot·ic** (id′ē ot′ik) of or like an idiot; very stupid or foolish: *We couldn't understand her idiotic behaviour.* *adj.* —**id′i·ot′i·cal·ly,** *adv.*

**i·dle** (ī′dəl) **1** doing nothing; not busy; not working: *idle hands.* **2** not willing to work; lazy: *The idle boy would not study.* **3** useless; worthless: *Luk wasted his time in idle pleasures.* **4** without any good reason, cause, or foundation: *idle fears, idle rumours.* **5** be idle; waste time; do nothing: *Are you going to spend your whole vacation just idling?* **6** run slowly without transmitting power: *The motor of a car idles when it is out of gear and running slowly.* **7** cause the motor of a car, etc., to idle: *Don't idle the motor too long.* 1–4 *adj.*, **i·dler, i·dlest;** 5–7 *v.*, **i·dled, i·dling.** —**i′dle·ness,** *n.*
**idle away,** spend wastefully: *She idled away many hours lying in the hammock.*
☞ *Hom.* IDOL, IDYLL (ī′dəl).

**i·dler** (ī′dlər) **1** a lazy person: *School is no place for idlers.* **2** a device allowing a motor to idle. *n.*

**i·dly** (ī′dlē) in an idle manner; doing nothing. *adv.*

**i·dol** (ī′dəl) **1** an image or other object worshipped as a god. **2** in the Bible, a false god. **3** a person or thing worshipped or loved very much; an object of extreme devotion: *The baby girl was the idol of her family.* *n.*
☞ *Hom.* IDLE, IDYLL (ī′dəl).

**i·dol·a·ter** (ī dol′ə tər) **1** a person who worships idols. **2** an admirer; adorer; devotee. *n.*

**i·dol·a·tress** (ī dol′ə tris) **1** a woman who worships idols. **2** an adorer; devotee. *n.*

**i·dol·a·trous** (ī dol′ə trəs) **1** worshipping idols. **2** having to do with IDOLATRY. **3** blindly adoring. *adj.* —**i·dol′a·trous·ly,** *adv.*

**i·dol·a·try** (ī dol′ə trē) **1** the worship of idols. **2** worship of a person or thing; great love or admiration; extreme devotion: *The queen was adored to the point of idolatry.* *n., pl.* **i·dol·a·tries.**

**i·dol·i·za·tion** (ī′də lə zā′shən *or* ī′də lī zā′shən) idolizing or being idolized. *n.*

**i·dol·ize** (ī′də līz′) **1** worship as an idol; make an idol of: *The boys idolized the hockey star.* **2** love or admire very much; be extremely devoted to: *The boy idolizes his little sister.* *v.*, **i·dol·ized, i·dol·iz·ing.**

**id·yll** or **id·yl** (ī′dəl *or* id′əl) **1** a short description in poetry or prose, or a depiction in music, of a simple and

**idyllic** 594 **illegality**

charming scene or event, especially one connected with country life.   2 a simple and charming scene or event suitable for such a description.   *n.*
☛ *Hom.*   IDLE, IDOL (for the first pronunciation of **idyll**).

**i·dyl·lic** (i dil′ik *or* ī dil′ik)   suitable for an idyll, simple and charming: *They lived an idyllic existence in their country home.*   *adj.*

**–ie**   a suffix meaning little or darling, as in *dearie, lassie.*

**i.e.**   an abbreviation of the Latin phrase *id est,* meaning that is or that is to say.

**if** (if)   1 supposing that; on condition that; in case that: *If you are going, leave now. I'll go if you will.*   2 whether: *I wonder if she will go.*   3 although; even though: *If he is little, he is strong.*   4 a condition or supposition.   1–3 *conj.,* 4 *n.*
**as if,**   as it would be if.

**IF, if,** or **i–f**   intermediate frequency.

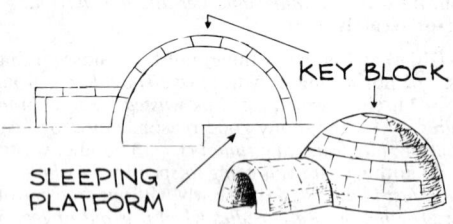
An igloo

**ig·loo** (ig′lü)   1 an Inuit dwelling, especially a domed structure, built of blocks of snow.   2 any structure resembling this in shape.   *n., pl.* **ig·loos.**
☛ *Etym.* From eastern Inuktitut *iglu* 'dwelling'.

**ig·ne·ous** (ig′nē əs)   1 of or having to do with fire. 2 in geology, referring to rock formed by the solidification of molten matter: *Granite is igneous rock.*   *adj.*

**ig·nis fat·u·us** (ig′nis fach′ü əs)   *Latin.*   1 a flitting phosphorescent light seen at night chiefly over marshy ground; WILL-O'-THE-WISP.   2 something deluding or misleading.   *pl.* **ig·nes fat·u·i** (ig′nēz fach′ü ī′ *or* fach′ü ē′).

**ig·nite** (ig nīt′)   1 set on fire: *The match was ignited by scraping it against the sidewalk.*   2 make intensely hot; cause to glow with heat.   3 take fire; begin to burn: *Gasoline ignites easily.*   *v.,* **ig·nit·ed, ig·nit·ing.** —**ig·nit′er,** *n.*

**ig·ni·tion** (ig nish′ən)   1 setting on fire: *The explosion was triggered by the ignition of a match.*   2 catching on fire.   3 the apparatus for igniting the explosive vapour in the cylinders of an INTERNAL-COMBUSTION ENGINE: *A spark plug is a part of the ignition of a gasoline engine.*   *n.*

**ig·no·ble** (ig nō′bəl)   1 mean; base; without honour: *To betray a friend is ignoble.*   2 not of noble birth or position; humble: *Their leader came from an ignoble family.*   *adj.*   —**ig·no′ble·ness,** *n.*   —**ig·no′bly,** *adv.*

**ig·no·min·i·ous** (ig′nə min′ē əs)   1 shameful; disgraceful; dishonourable; humiliating.   2 contemptible.   *adj.*   —**ig′no·min′i·ous·ly,** *adv.*

**ig·no·min·y** (ig′nə min′ē)   1 loss of one's good name; public shame and disgrace; dishonour.   2 shameful action or conduct.   *n., pl.* **ig·no·min·ies.**

**ig·no·ra·mus** (ig′nə rā′məs)   an ignorant person.   *n., pl.* **ig·no·ra·mus·es.**

**ig·no·rance** (ig′nə rəns)   a lack of knowledge; the quality or condition of being ignorant.   *n.*

**ig·no·rant** (ig′nə rənt)   1 knowing little or nothing; without knowledge: *A person who has not had much chance to learn may be ignorant without being stupid. People who live in the city are often ignorant of farm life.*   2 caused by or showing lack of knowledge: *an ignorant remark.*   3 uninformed; unaware: *He was ignorant of the fact that we had arrived.*   *adj.*   —**ig′no·rant·ly,** *adv.*

**ig·nore** (ig nôr′)   pay no attention to; disregard: *The teacher ignored the noise her pupils were making.*   *v.,* **ig·nored, ig·nor·ing.**

**i·gua·na** (i gwä′nə)   a large climbing lizard that has small scales and a fringelike crest of skin along the back, found in tropical America.   *n.*

**i·kon** (ī′kon)   See ICON.   *n.*

**il–**   a form of the prefix IN- occurring before the letter *l,* as in *illegal, illegible.*

**il·e·um** (il′ē əm)   the lowest part of the small intestine. See ALIMENTARY CANAL for picture.   *n.*
☛ *Hom.*   ILIUM.

**il·i·ac** (il′ē ak′)   1 of, having to do with, or near the ILIUM.   2 of or having to do with the ILEUM.   *adj.*

**il·i·um** (il′ē əm)   the broad, flat upper portion of the hipbone. See PELVIS for picture.   *n., pl.* **il·i·a** (il′ē ə).
☛ *Hom.*   ILEUM.

**ilk** (ilk)   *Informal.*   family; kind; sort.   *n.*
**of that ilk,** *Informal.*   **a** of the same place or name.   **b** of that kind or sort.

**ill** (il)   1 sick; having some disease; not well: *ill with a fever.*   2 a sickness or disease: *She told us about all the ills she had had.*   3 an evil; harm; trouble: *Poverty is an ill.* 4 bad; evil; harmful: *an ill deed.*   5 badly; harmfully: *work done ill.*   6 unfavourable; unfortunate: *an ill wind.* 7 unfavourably; unfortunately: *to fare ill.*   8 unkind; harsh; cruel: *an ill turn.*   9 in an unkind manner; harshly; cruelly: *He speaks ill of his former friends.*   10 scarcely; with trouble or difficulty: *You can ill afford to waste your money.*   1, 4, 6, 8 *adj.,* **worse, worst;**   2, 3 *n.,* 5, 7, 9, 10 *adv.*
**ill at ease,**   uncomfortable.

**ill.**   1 illustration.   2 illustrated.

**I'll** (īl)   1 I will.   2 I shall.
☛ *Hom.*   AISLE, ISLE.

**ill–ad·vised** (il′əd vīzd′)   acting or done without enough consideration; unwise.   *adj.*

**ill–bred** (il′bred′)   badly brought up; impolite; rude.   *adj.*

**ill breeding**   lack of good upbringing; bad manners; impoliteness; rudeness.

**ill–con·sid·ered** (il′kən sid′ərd)   not well considered; unwise; unsuitable.   *adj.*

**ill–dis·posed** (il′di spōzd′)   unfriendly; unfavourable. *adj.*

**il·le·gal** (i lē′gəl)   not lawful; against the law; forbidden by law: *illegal parking.*   *adj.*   —**il·le′gal·ly,** *adv.*

**il·le·gal·i·ty** (il′ē gal′ə tē)   1 unlawfulness.   2 an ILLEGAL act; an act contrary to law.   *n., pl.* **il·le·gal·i·ties.**

**il·leg·i·bil·i·ty** (i lej′ə bil′ə tē)   an ILLEGIBLE quality or condition.   *n., pl.* **il·leg·i·bil·i·ties.**

**il·leg·i·ble** (i lej′ə bəl)   very hard or impossible to read: *The ink had faded so that many words were illegible.*   *adj.* —**il·leg′i·ble·ness,** *n.*   —**il·leg′i·bly,** *adv.*
☛ *Usage.* Take care not to confuse **illegible** with ELIGIBLE.

**il·le·git·i·ma·cy** (il′i jit′ə mə sē)   being ILLEGITIMATE.   *n., pl.* **il·le·git·i·ma·cies.**

**il·le·git·i·mate** (il′i jit′ə mit)   **1** born of parents who are not married to each other.   **2** not according to the law or the rules.   **3** not logical; not properly deduced.   *adj.* —**il′le·git′i·mate·ly,** *adv.*

**ill–fat·ed** (il′fā′tid)   **1** sure to have a bad fate or end: *an ill-fated voyage.*   **2** bringing bad luck; unlucky: *an ill-fated decision.*   *adj.*

**ill–fa·voured** or **ill–fa·vored** (il′fā′vərd)   **1** not beautiful to look at; ugly.   **2** unpleasant; offensive.   *adj.*

**ill feeling**   dislike; mistrust: *There has been ill feeling between them ever since they quarrelled.*

**ill–found·ed** (il′foun′did)   without a good reason or sound basis.   *adj.*

**ill–got·ten** (il′got′ən)   acquired by evil or unfair means; dishonestly obtained: *ill-gotten riches.*   *adj.*

**ill–hu·moured** or **ill–hu·mored** (il′hyü′mərd)   cross; unpleasant.   *adj.*   —**ill′-hu′moured·ly** or **ill′-hu′mored·ly,** *adv.*

**il·lib·er·al** (i lib′ə rəl)   **1** not liberal; narrow-minded; prejudiced.   **2** stingy; miserly.   *adj.*

**il·lic·it** (i lis′it)   not permitted by law; forbidden: *illicit traffic in drugs.*   *adj.*   —**il·lic′it·ly,** *adv.* —**il·lic′it·ness,** *n.*
☛ *Hom.* elicit.

**il·lim·it·a·ble** (i lim′ə tə bəl)   limitless; boundless; infinite.   *adj.*   —**il·lim′it·a·bly,** *adv.*

**il·lit·er·a·cy** (i lit′ə rə sē)   **1** the quality or state of being ILLITERATE (defs. 1, 3), especially the inability to read or write.   **2** an error in speaking or writing, suggesting a lack of education or knowledge.   *n., pl.* **il·lit·er·a·cies.**

**il·lit·er·ate** (i lit′ə rit)   **1** unable to read or write.   **2** a person unable to read or write.   **3** showing a lack of education; not cultured: *He writes in a very illiterate way.*   **4** an uneducated person.   **1, 3** *adj.,* **2, 4** *n.* —**il·lit′er·ate·ly,** *adv.* —**il·lit′er·ate·ness,** *n.*

**ill–judged** (il′jujd′)   unwise; rash.   *adj.*

**ill–man·nered** (il′man′ərd)   having or showing bad manners; impolite.   *adj.*   —**ill′-man′nered·ly,** *adv.*

**ill–na·tured** (il′nā′chərd)   cross; disagreeable; spiteful.   *adj.*   —**ill-na′tured·ly,** *adv.*

**ill·ness** (il′nis)   **1** a sickness or disease: *Scarlet fever is a serious illness.*   **2** poor health; a sickly condition: *She suffered from long periods of illness.*   *n.*

**il·log·i·cal** (i loj′ə kəl)   **1** not according to the rules of logic.   **2** not reasonable; foolish: *an illogical fear of the dark.*   *adj.*   —**il·log′i·cal·ly,** *adv.* —**il·log′i·cal·ness,** *n.*

**ill–spent** (il′spent′)   spent badly; wasted.   *adj.*

hat, āge, fär; let, ēqual, tėrm; it, īce
hot, ōpen, ôrder; oil, out; cup, pùt, rüle
əbove, takən, pencəl, lemən, circəs
ch, child; ng, long; sh, ship
th, thin; ᴛʜ, then; zh, measure

**ill–starred** (il′stärd′)   unlucky; unfortunate: *The ill-starred ship struck an iceberg.*   *adj.*

**ill–suit·ed** (il′sü′tid)   poorly suited; unsuitable: *The job is ill-suited to a person of his temperament.*   *adj.*

**ill–tem·pered** (il′tem′pərd)   having or showing a bad temper; cross.   *adj.*   —**ill′-tem′pered·ly,** *adv.*

**ill–timed** (il′tīmd′)   done or happening at a bad time; inappropriate.   *adj.*

**ill–treat** (il′trēt′)   treat badly or cruelly; do harm to; abuse: *Dietrich would never ill-treat an animal.*   *v.*

**ill treatment**   bad or cruel treatment; harm; abuse.

**il·lu·mi·nant** (i lü′mə nənt)   something that gives light: *Electricity and oil are illuminants.*   *n.*

**il·lu·mi·nate** (i lü′mə nāt′)   **1** light up; make bright: *The room was illuminated by four large lamps.*   **2** make clear; explain: *Our interesting teacher could illuminate almost any subject we studied.*   **3** decorate with lights: *The streets were illuminated for the celebration.*   **4** decorate with gold, colours, pictures, and designs: *Some old books and manuscripts were illuminated.*   **5** enlighten; inform; instruct.   **6** make illustrious.   *v.,* **il·lu·mi·nat·ed, il·lu·mi·nat·ing.**

An illuminated initial letter from a Flemish manuscript of the Bible in Latin, dated A.D. 1148

**il·lu·mi·na·tion** (i lü′mə nā′shən)   **1** an illuminating; lighting up; making bright: *Illumination in this room is by four lamps.*   **2** the amount of light; light.   **3** making clear; explanation.   **4** a decoration with lights.   **5** the decoration of books and letters with gold, colours, pictures, and designs.   **6** enlightenment.   *n.*

**il·lu·mi·na·tive** (i lü′mə nə tiv *or* i lü′mə nā′tiv)   illuminating; tending to ILLUMINATE.   *adj.*

**il·lu·mine** (i lü′mən)   make or become bright; ILLUMINATE; light up: *A smile often illumines a homely face.*   *v.,* **il·lu·mined, il·lu·min·ing.**

**illus.**   **1** illustration.   **2** illustrated.

**ill–us·age** (il′yü′sij *or* il yü′zij)   bad, cruel, or unfair treatment.   *n.*

**ill–use** (il′yüz′ *for verb,* il′yüs′ *for noun*)   **1** treat badly, cruelly, or unfairly.   **2** bad, cruel, or unfair treatment.   **1** *v.,* **ill–used, ill–us·ing;**   **2** *n.*

Horizontal lines A and B are the same length but A appears shorter. The three figures are the same size, but the lines suggesting perspective make the ones on the right appear larger.

**il·lu·sion** (i lü′zhən) 1 an appearance or feeling that misleads because it is not real; something that deceives by giving a false idea: *an illusion of reality*. 2 a false impression or perception: *an optical illusion*. 3 a false idea, notion, or belief: *Many people have the illusion that wealth is the chief cause of happiness*. 4 a delicate silk net or gauze, often used for veils. *n*.
☞ *Hom.* ELUSION.
☞ *Usage.* Do not confuse **illusion** and ALLUSION. An **illusion** is a misleading appearance: *The large car she drives gives an illusion of wealth*. An **allusion** is an indirect reference or slight mention: *He made allusions to Spain so we gathered he had been there recently*.

**il·lu·sive** (i lü′siv) ILLUSORY. *adj*.
—**il·lu′sive·ly**, *adv*. —**il·lu′sive·ness**, *n*.
☞ *Hom.* ELUSIVE.

**il·lu·so·ry** (i lü′sə rē) due to or resulting in an illusion; unreal or misleading: *Their initial advantage proved to be illusory, as their opponents began to score points*. *adj*.
☞ *Hom.* ELUSORY.

**illust.** 1 illustration. 2 illustrated.

**il·lus·trate** (il′ə strāt *or* i lus′trāt) 1 make clear or explain by stories, examples, comparisons, etc.: *The way that a pump works was used to illustrate the action of the heart in circulating blood through the body*. 2 provide with pictures, diagrams, maps etc. that explain or decorate: *This book is well illustrated*. *v*., **il·lus·trat·ed**, **il·lus·trat·ing**.

**il·lus·tra·tion** (il′ə strā′shən) 1 a picture, diagram, map, etc. used to explain or decorate something: *Most books for children have many illustrations*. 2 a story, example, comparison, etc. used to make clear or explain something: *The teacher cut an apple into four equal pieces as an illustration of what* ¼ *means*. 3 the act or process of illustrating: *Illustration is used in teaching*. *n*.

**il·lus·tra·tive** (i lus′trə tiv *or* il′ə strā′tiv) illustrating; used to illustrate; helping to explain: *A good teacher uses many illustrative examples to explain hard ideas*. *adj*.
—**il·lus′tra·tive·ly**, *adv*.

**il·lus·tra·tor** (il′ə strā′tər) a person or thing that illustrates, especially an artist who makes illustrations for books, magazines, etc. *n*.

**il·lus·tri·ous** (i lus′trē əs) very famous; great; outstanding; eminent: *an illustrious statesman, an illustrious deed*. *adj*. —**il·lus′tri·ous·ly**, *adv*.
—**il·lus′tri·ous·ness**, *n*.

**ill will** unkind or unfriendly feeling; hostility; hate.

**I'm** (īm) I am.

**im-¹** a form of the prefix IN-¹ occurring before *b, m, p*, as in *imbalance, immoral, impatient*.

**im-²** a form of the prefix IN-² occurring before *b, m, p*, as in *imbibe, immure, impart*.

**im·age** (im′ij) 1 an artificial likeness, such as a painting or statue; idol: *The ancient Greeks and Romans worshipped images of their gods*. 2 a person or thing resembling another; counterpart: *She is the very image of her mother*. 3 a picture in the mind; idea: *Your memory or imagination forms images of people and things that you do not actually see*. 4 a description or figure of speech that helps the mind to form forceful or beautiful pictures: *Poetry often contains images*. 5 make or form an image of. See LENS for picture. 6 reflect as a mirror does: *The clouds were imaged in the still water*. 7 picture in one's mind; imagine. 1–4 *n*., 5–7 *v*., **im·aged, im·ag·ing**.

**im·age·ry** (im′ij rē) 1 pictures in the mind; things imagined. 2 descriptions and figures of speech that help the mind to form forceful or beautiful pictures. 3 images; statues. *n., pl.* **im·age·ries**.

**i·mag·i·na·ble** (i maj′ə nə bəl) that can be imagined; possible. *adj*. —**i·mag′i·na·bly**, *adv*.

**i·mag·i·nar·y** (i maj′ə ner′ē) existing only in the imagination; not real: *Elves are imaginary*. *The equator is an imaginary line circling the earth midway between the North and South Poles*. *adj*.

**i·mag·i·na·tion** (i maj′ə nā′shən) 1 imagining; the power of forming pictures in the mind of things not present to the senses: *The child's imagination filled the woods with strange animals*. 2 the ability to create new things or ideas or to combine old ones in new forms: *Poets, artists, and inventors make use of their imagination*. 3 a creation of the mind; fancy. *n*.

**i·mag·i·na·tive** (i maj′ə nə tiv *or* i maj′ə nā′tiv) 1 showing imagination: *an imaginative use of colour*. 2 having a good imagination; able to imagine well; fond of imagining: *The imaginative child made up fairy stories*. 3 of imagination. *adj*. —**i·mag′i·na·tive·ly**, *adv*.

**i·mag·ine** (i maj′ən) 1 picture in one's mind; form an image or idea of: *We can hardly imagine life without electricity*. 2 suppose; guess: *I cannot imagine what you mean*. 3 think; believe: *She imagined someone was watching her*. *v*., **i·mag·ined, i·mag·in·ing**.

**i·ma·go** (i mā′gō) an insect in the final adult, usually winged, stage. *n., pl.* **i·ma·gos** or **i·mag·i·nes** (i maj′ə nēz′).

**im·am** (i mäm′) in Islam: 1 in the Sunni tradition, a leader of worship in a mosque. 2 in the Shiite tradition, a spiritual leader whose authority derives directly from the prophet Mohammed. *n*.

**im·balm** (im bom′ *or* im bäm′) EMBALM. *v*.

**im·be·cile** (im′bə səl) 1 a person who has a weak mind and can learn to do only very simple tasks. 2 very weak in the mind. 3 a very stupid or foolish person: *Don't be an imbecile*. 4 very stupid or foolish: *an imbecile question*. 1, 3 *n*., 2, 4 *adj*.

**im·be·cil·i·ty** (im′bə sil′ə tē) 1 feebleness of mind; mental weakness. 2 great stupidity or dullness. 3 a very stupid or foolish action, remark, etc. *n., pl.* **im·be·cil·i·ties**.

**im·bed** (im bed′) EMBED. *v*., **im·bed·ded**, **im·bed·ding**.

**im·bibe** (im bīb′) 1 drink; drink in. 2 adsorb: *The roots of a plant imbibe moisture from the earth*. 3 take into one's mind: *Children often imbibe superstitions that last all their life*. *v*., **im·bibed, im·bib·ing**. —**im·bib′er**, *n*.

**im·bri·ca·tion** (im′brə kā′shən) **1** an overlapping like that of tiles, shingles, etc. **2** a decorative pattern in imitation of this. *n.*

**im·bro·glio** (im brō′lyō) **1** a complicated or difficult situation. **2** a complicated misunderstanding or disagreement. *n., pl.* **im·bro·glios.**

**im·brue** (im brü′) wet; stain: *His sword was imbrued with blood.* *v.*, **im·brued, im·bru·ing.**

**im·bue** (im byü′) **1** fill; inspire: *He imbued his daughter's mind with the ambition to succeed.* **2** fill with moisture or colour. *v.*, **im·bued, im·bu·ing.**

**im·i·ta·ble** (im′ə tə bəl) that can be imitated. *adj.*

**im·i·tate** (im′ə tāt′) **1** try to be or act like; follow the example of: *The little boy imitated his father.* **2** make or do something like; copy: *A parrot imitates the sounds it hears.* **3** act like, especially for amusement: *She made us laugh by imitating a bear.* **4** be like; look like; resemble: *Plastic is often made to imitate wood.* *v.*, **im·i·tat·ed, im·i·tat·ing.**

**im·i·ta·tion** (im′ə tā′shən) **1** an imitating: *We learn many things by imitation.* **2** a copy: *Give as good an imitation as you can of a rooster crowing.* **3** made to look like something better; not real: *imitation pearls, imitation leather.* **1, 2** *n.*, **3** *adj.*
**in imitation of,** in order to be or look like.

**im·i·ta·tive** (im′ə tā′tiv) **1** fond of imitating; likely or inclined to imitate others: *Monkeys are imitative.* **2** imitating; showing imitation: *"Bang" and "whiz" are imitative words.* **3** not real. *adj.*
—**im′i·ta′tive·ly,** *adv.* —**im′i·ta′tive·ness,** *n.*

**im·i·ta·tor** (im′ə tā′tər) a person or animal that imitates. *n.*

**im·mac·u·late** (i mak′yə lit) **1** without spot or stain; absolutely clean: *The newly washed shirts were immaculate.* **2** without fault; in perfect order: *His appearance was immaculate.* **3** without fault; pure: *Her behaviour was immaculate.* *adj.* —**im·mac′u·late·ly,** *adv.*
—**im·mac′u·late·ness,** *n.*

**im·ma·te·ri·al** (im′ə tē′rē əl) **1** not important; insignificant: *This error is immaterial.* **2** not material; spiritual rather than physical. *adj.*
—**im′ma·te′ri·al·ly,** *adv.* —**im′ma·te′ri·al·ness,** *n.*

**im·ma·ture** (im′ə chùr′ *or* im′ə tyùr′) not mature; not ripe or full-grown; not fully developed. *adj.*
—**im′ma·ture′ly,** *adv.*

**im·ma·tu·ri·ty** (im′ə chùr′ə tē *or* im′ə tyùr′ə tē) the state of being IMMATURE. *n.*

**im·meas·ur·a·ble** (i mezh′ə rə bəl) too vast to be measured; boundless; without limits. *adj.*
—**im·meas′ur·a·bly,** *adv.*

**im·me·di·a·cy** (i mē′dē ə sē) the state or condition of being IMMEDIATE. *n.*

**im·me·di·ate** (i mē′dē it) **1** coming at once; without delay: *an immediate reply.* **2** with nothing between: *in immediate contact.* **3** direct: *the immediate result.* **4** closest; nearest: *my immediate neighbour.* **5** close; near: *the immediate neighbourhood.* **6** having to do with the present: *our immediate plans.* *adj.*
—**im·me′di·ate·ness,** *n.*

**im·me·di·ate·ly** (i mē′dē it lē) **1** at once; without delay: *I need an answer immediately because I have to leave.* **2** with nothing between; next: *Immediately to his right was a newsstand.* **3** directly. *adv.*

---

# imbrication  597  immobilize

hat, āge, fär; let, ēqual, tėrm; it, īce
hot, ōpen, ôrder; oil, out; cup, pùt, rüle
əbove, takən, pencəl, lemən, circəs
ch, child; ng, long; sh, ship
th, thin; ᴛʜ, then; zh, measure

**im·me·mo·ri·al** (im′ə mô′rē əl) extending back beyond the bounds of memory; extremely old: *time immemorial.* *adj.* —**im′me·mo′ri·al·ly,** *adv.*

**im·mense** (i mens′) **1** very big; huge; vast: *An ocean is an immense body of water.* **2** very good; fine; excellent. *adj.* —**im·mense′ness,** *n.*

**im·mense·ly** (i men′slē) very greatly: *Grigor said he was immensely grateful.* *adv.*

**im·men·si·ty** (i men′sə tē) **1** very great or boundless extent; vastness: *the ocean's immensity.* **2** infinite space or existence. *n., pl.* **im·men·si·ties.**

**im·merse** (i mėrs′) **1** dip or lower into a liquid until covered by it. **2** baptize by dipping a person under water. **3** involve deeply; absorb: *immersed in business affairs, immersed in debts.* *v.*, **im·mersed, im·mers·ing.**

**im·mers·i·ble** (i mėr′sə bəl) that can be immersed without damage; especially, of an electric appliance, that can be immersed in water without damage to the electric element: *an immersible fry pan.* *adj.*

**im·mer·sion** (i mėr′zhən *or* i mėr′shən) **1** immersing or being immersed. **2** baptism by dipping a person under water. **3** *Cdn.* a method of teaching a foreign or additional language to a person by means of intensive exposure to and practice in the language. **4** *Cdn.* designating a course, school, etc. incorporating or employing such a method: *immersion French.* *n.*

**im·mi·grant** (im′ə grənt) **1** a person who comes into a country or region to live: *Canada has many immigrants from Europe.* **2** immigrating or recently immigrated: *an immigrant family.* **3** of or having to do with immigrants or immigration: *an immigrant visa.* **1** *n.*, **2, 3** *adj.*
☞ *Usage.* See note at EMIGRATE.

**im·mi·grate** (im′ə grāt′) come into a country or region to live. Compare with EMIGRATE. *v.*, **im·mi·grat·ed, im·mi·grat·ing.**
☞ *Usage.* See note at EMIGRATE.

**im·mi·gra·tion** (im′ə grā′shən) **1** coming into a country or region to live: *There has been immigration to Canada from most of the countries of Europe.* **2** immigrants: *The immigration of 1956 included many people from Hungary.* *n.* Compare with EMIGRATION.

**im·mi·nence** (im′ə nəns) **1** the state or fact of being IMMINENT. **2** something that is IMMINENT, especially something dangerous or evil. *n.*

**im·mi·nent** (im′ə nənt) likely to happen soon; about to occur: *The black clouds, thunder, and lightning show that a storm is imminent.* *adj.* —**im′mi·nent·ly,** *adv.*
☞ *Usage.* Do not confuse **imminent** with EMINENT.

**im·mo·bile** (i mō′bīl *or* i mō′bəl) **1** not movable; firmly fixed. **2** not moving; not changing; motionless. *adj.*

**im·mo·bil·i·ty** (im′ō bil′ə tē) being IMMOBILE. *n.*

**im·mo·bi·lize** (i mō′bə līz′) make IMMOBILE or almost immobile: *an immobilized truck. She has been immobilized by a severe back injury.* *v.*, **im·mo·bi·lized, im·mo·bi·liz·ing.**

**im·mod·er·ate** (i mod′ə rit) not moderate; too much; going too far; extreme; more than is right or proper: *His immoderate appetite embarrassed the other guests.* *adj.* —**im·mod′er·ate·ly,** *adv.* —**im·mod′er·ate·ness,** *n.*

**im·mod·est** (i mod′ist) **1** not modest; bold and rude. **2** indecent; improper. *adj.* —**im·mod′est·ly,** *adv.*

**im·mod·es·ty** (i mod′i stē) a lack of MODESTY. *n.*

**im·mo·late** (im′ə lāt) **1** kill as a sacrifice. **2** sacrifice. *v.*, **im·mo·lat·ed, im·mo·lat·ing.**

**im·mo·la·tion** (im′ə lā′shən) SACRIFICE (def. 1). *n.*

**im·mor·al** (i môr′əl) **1** wrong; wicked: *Lying and stealing are immoral.* **2** lewd; unchaste. *adj.* —**im·mor′al·ly,** *adv.*

**im·mo·ral·i·ty** (im′ə ral′ə tē) **1** wickedness; wrongdoing; vice. **2** lewdness; unchastity. **3** an immoral act. *n., pl.* **im·mo·ral·i·ties.**

**im·mor·tal** (i môr′təl) **1** living forever; never dying; everlasting. **2** a person living forever. **3** of or having to do with immortal beings or immortality; divine. **4** remembered or famous forever. **5** a person remembered or famous forever: *Shakespeare is one of the immortals.* **6 immortals,** *pl.* the gods of ancient Greek and Roman mythology. 1, 3, 4 *adj.*, 2, 5, 6 *n.* —**im·mor′tal·ly,** *adv.*

**im·mor·tal·i·ty** (im′ôr tal′ə tē) **1** endless life; living forever. **2** fame that is likely to last forever. *n.*

**im·mor·tal·ize** (i môr′tə līz′) **1** make immortal. **2** give everlasting fame to: *Great authors are immortalized by their works.* *v.*, **im·mor·tal·ized, im·mor·tal·iz·ing.**

**im·mor·telle** (im′ôr tel′) a plant whose flowers keep their shape and colour for a long time after the plant has entirely dried. *n.*

**im·mov·a·bil·i·ty** (i mü′və bil′ə tē) being IMMOVABLE. *n.*

**im·mov·a·ble** (i mü′və bəl) **1** that cannot be moved; firmly fixed. **2** not moving; not changing position; motionless: *immovable mountains.* **3** firm; steadfast; unyielding: *an immovable purpose.* **4** unfeeling; impassive. **5 immovables,** *pl.* land, buildings, and other property that cannot be carried from one place to another. 1–4 *adj.*, 5 *n.* —**im·mov′a·bly,** *adv.*

**im·mune** (i myün′) **1** protected from disease, poison, etc.; not susceptible; having IMMUNITY: *Some people are immune to poison ivy; they can touch it without getting a rash.* **2** exempt; being free from some duty or obligation, or from something unpleasant: *immune from taxes. Nobody is immune from criticism.* *adj.*

**im·mu·ni·ty** (i myü′nə tē) **1** resistance to disease, poison, etc.: *One attack of measles usually gives a person immunity to that disease for a number of years.* **2** freedom; protection: *The law gives schools immunity from taxation.* *n., pl.* **im·mu·ni·ties.**

**im·mu·ni·za·tion** (im′yə nə zā′shən *or* im′yə nī zā′shən) immunizing or being immunized: *Immunization against flu lasts about a year.* *n.*

**im·mu·nize** (im′yə nīz′) give IMMUNITY to; make immune: *Vaccination immunizes people against flu.* *v.*, **im·mu·nized, im·mu·niz·ing.** —**im′mu·ni·za′tion,** *n.*

**im·mu·nol·o·gy** (im′yə nol′ə jē) the branch of medicine dealing with the nature and causes of resistance to infection in human beings and animals. *n.*

**im·mure** (i myür′) **1** imprison. **2** confine closely. *v.*, **im·mured, im·mur·ing.** —**im·mure′ment,** *n.*

**im·mu·ta·bil·i·ty** (i myü′tə bil′ə tē) being IMMUTABLE. *n.*

**im·mu·ta·ble** (i myü′tə bəl) never changing; unchangeable. *adj.* —**im·mu′ta·bly,** *adv.*

**imp** (imp) **1** a young or small devil or demon. **2** a mischievous child. *n.*

**imp.** **1** imperative. **2** import; imported. **3** imperfect. **4** imperial.

**im·pact** (im′pakt) **1** a striking of one thing against another; collision: *The impact of the stone against the window shattered the glass.* **2** a forceful effect or influence: *Automobiles have had a strong impact on our lives.* *n.*

**im·pact·ed** (im pak′tid) **1** firmly wedged in place. **2** of a tooth, pressed between the jawbone and another tooth. **3** closely packed. *adj.*

**im·pair** (im per′) make worse; damage; weaken: *Poor food impaired her health.* *v.*

**im·paired** (im perd′) *Cdn.* **1** in law, being in control of a motor vehicle while under the influence of alcohol or narcotics: *She was charged with driving while impaired.* **2** pt. and pp. of IMPAIR. 1 *adj.*, 2 *v.*

**impaired driving** *Cdn.* in law, driving while the ability to drive is weakened by alcohol or narcotics: *He was fined $400 on a charge of impaired driving.*

**im·pair·ment** (im per′mənt) **1** impairing or being impaired. **2** an injury; damage. *n.*

**im·pa·la** (im pal′ə *or* im pä′lə) a medium-sized, slender, reddish-brown antelope of the savannah and bush country of S and E Africa, the adult males having long, slender horns that curve in an S, so that from the front the two horns form the outline of a lyre. *n., pl.* **im·pa·las** or (*esp. collectively*) **im·pa·la.**

**im·pale** (im pāl′) **1** pierce through with something pointed; fasten with something pointed: *The butterflies were impaled on small pins stuck in a sheet of cork.* **2** torture or punish by thrusting upon a pointed stake. **3** make helpless as if by piercing: *The teacher impaled the cheeky student with a look of ice.* *v.*, **im·paled, im·pal·ing.** —**im·pale′ment,** *n.*

**im·pal·pa·ble** (im pal′pə bəl) **1** that cannot be perceived by the sense of touch: *Sunbeams are impalpable. A thread of a spider's web is almost impalpable.* **2** very hard for the mind to grasp: *impalpable distinctions.* *adj.* —**im·pal′pa·bly,** *adv.*

**im·pan·el** (im pan′əl) **1** put on a list for duty on a jury. **2** select a jury from the list. *v.*, **im·pan·elled** or **im·pan·eled, im·pan·el·ling** or **im·pan·el·ing.** Also, **empanel.**

**im·part** (im pärt′) **1** give a part or share of; give: *The furnishings imparted an air of elegance to the room.* **2** communicate; tell: *The interviewer asked her to impart the secret of her success.* *v.*

**im·par·tial** (im pär′shəl) showing no more favour to one side than to the other; fair; just: *A judge should be impartial.* *adj.* —**im·par′tial·ly,** *adv.*

**im·par·ti·al·i·ty** (im pär′shē al′ə tē) fairness; justice: *The teacher was respected for his patience and impartiality.* *n.*

**im·pass·a·bil·i·ty** (im pas′ə bil′ə tē)   the condition of being IMPASSABLE.   *n.*

**im·pass·a·ble** (im pas′ə bəl)   not passable; so that one cannot go through or across: *Deep mud made the road impassable. adj.* —**im·pass′a·bly,** *adv.*
☛ Hom. IMPASSIBLE.

**im·passe** (im pas′ *or* im′pas)   **1** a position from which there is no escape; a problem with no apparent solution; deadlock.   **2** a road or way closed at one end; blind alley.   *n.*

**im·pas·si·ble** (im pas′ə bəl)   **1** unable to suffer or feel pain.   **2** that cannot be harmed.   **3** without feeling; IMPASSIVE (def. 1).   *adj.*
☛ Hom. IMPASSABLE.

**im·pas·sioned** (im pash′ənd)   full of strong feeling; ardent; rousing: *an impassioned speech.   adj.*

**im·pas·sive** (im pas′iv)   **1** not showing any feeling or emotion; unmoved: *She listened with an impassive face.*   **2** not feeling pain or injury; insensible: *The soldier lay as impassive as if he were dead.*   **3** incapable of being injured.   *adj.* —**im·pas′sive·ly,** *adv.*

**im·pas·siv·i·ty** (im′pa siv′ə tē)   the state or quality of being IMPASSIVE.   *n.*

**im·pa·tience** (im pā′shəns)   **1** the state or quality of being IMPATIENT.   **2** uneasiness and eagerness; restlessness.   *n.*
☛ Hom. IMPATIENS.

**im·pa·tiens** (im pā′shəns)   any of a closely related group of annual and biennial plants having spurred or pouch-shaped flowers and seed pods that burst open when ripe; especially, a common garden plant having bright red, pink, or white flowers.   *n.*
☛ Hom. IMPATIENCE.

**im·pa·tient** (im pā′shənt)   **1** not patient; not willing to bear delay, opposition, pain, bother, etc.: *It took him so long to make up his mind that the salesclerk began to get impatient.*   **2** restless; anxious: *They were impatient to see the new puppy.*   **3** caused by or showing lack of patience: *an impatient answer.   adj.* —**im·pa′tient·ly,** *adv.* —**im·pa′tient·ness,** *n.*
**impatient of,**   unwilling to endure.

**im·peach** (im pēch′)   **1** call in question; cast doubt on: *to impeach a person's honour, to impeach the testimony of a witness.*   **2** charge with wrongdoing; accuse.   **3** bring a public official to trial before a special court for wrong conduct during office: *The judge was impeached for taking a bribe.   v.*

**im·peach·a·ble** (im pē′chə bəl)   **1** liable to be IMPEACHED.   **2** likely to cause IMPEACHMENT: *an impeachable offence.   adj.*

**im·peach·ment** (im pēch′mənt)   IMPEACHing or being impeached: *We read of the judge's impeachment in the newspaper yesterday.   n.*

**im·pec·ca·bil·i·ty** (im pek′ə bil′ə tē)   an IMPECCABLE quality; faultlessness.   *n.*

**im·pec·ca·ble** (im pek′ə bəl)   **1** faultless.   **2** sinless. *adj.* —**im·pec′ca·bly,** *adv.*

**im·pe·cu·ni·ous** (im′pi kyü′nē əs)   having little or no money; penniless; poor.   *adj.* —**im′pe·cu′ni·ous·ly,** *adv.*

**im·pede** (im pēd′)   hinder; obstruct: *The deep snow impeded travel. v.,* **im·ped·ed, im·ped·ing.**

**im·ped·i·ment** (im ped′ə mənt)   **1** a hindrance or obstruction.   **2** a defect in speech: *Stuttering is an impediment.   n.*

**im·ped·i·men·ta** (im ped′ə men′tə)   **1** travelling equipment or baggage, especially the military supplies carried along with an army.   **2** any equipment, belongings, etc. that one carries and that obstruct one or hinder progress.   *n. pl.*

**im·pel** (im pel′)   **1** drive; force; cause: *Hunger impelled the lazy man to work.*   **2** cause to move; drive forward; push along: *The wind impelled the boat to shore.   v.,* **im·pelled, im·pel·ling.** —**im·pel′ler,** *n.*

**im·pend** (im pend′)   **1** be likely to happen soon; be ready to occur; be near: *When war impends, wise people try to prevent it.*   **2** hang; hang threateningly.   *v.*

**im·pend·ing** (im pen′ding)   **1** likely to happen soon; about to occur (*used especially of something unpleasant*): *She dreaded the impending exams.*   **2** overhanging: *Above her were impending cliffs.*   **3** ppr. of IMPEND.   1, 2 *adj.,* 3 *v.*

**im·pen·e·tra·bil·i·ty** (im pen′ə trə bil′ə tē)   being IMPENETRABLE.   *n.*

**im·pen·e·tra·ble** (im pen′ə trə bəl)   **1** that cannot be entered, pierced, or passed through: *A thick sheet of steel is impenetrable by an ordinary bullet.*   **2** not open to ideas, influences, etc.: *an impenetrable mind.*   **3** impossible to explain or understand; inscrutable: *an impenetrable mystery.   adj.* —**im·pen′e·tra·bly,** *adv.*

**im·pen·i·tence** (im pen′ə təns)   a lack of any sorrow or regret for doing wrong.   *n.*

**im·pen·i·tent** (im pen′ə tənt)   not PENITENT; feeling no sorrow or regret for having done wrong.   *adj.* —**im·pen′i·tent·ly,** *adv.*

**imper.**   imperative.

**im·per·a·tive** (im per′ə tiv)   **1** not to be avoided; urgent; necessary: *It is imperative that a very sick child stay in bed.*   **2** a command.   **3** in grammar, expressing a command: *"Go!"* and *"Stop, look, listen!"* are in the imperative mood.   **4** the imperative MOOD².   **5** a verb form in the imperative MOOD².   1, 3 *adj.,* 2, 4, 5 *n.* —**im·per′a·tive·ly,** *adv.* —**im·per′a·tive·ness,** *n.*

**imperative mood**   the form of a verb used to express a command.

**im·per·cep·ti·ble** (im′pər sep′tə bəl)   **1** very slight; gradual.   **2** that cannot be perceived or felt.   *adj.* —**im′per·cep′ti·bly,** *adv.*

**imperf.**   imperfect.

**im·per·fect** (im pėr′fikt)   **1** not perfect; having some defect or fault: *A crack in the cup made it imperfect.*   **2** not complete; lacking some part.   **3** in grammar, expressing continued or customary action in the past. **4** the imperfect tense: *English has no imperfect, but such forms as* was studying *and* used to study *have a function that is similar to the imperfect in other languages.*   **5** a verb form in this tense.   1–3 *adj.,* 4, 5 *n.* —**im·per′fect·ly,** *adv.* —**im·per′fect·ness,** *n.*

**im·per·fec·tion** (im′pər fek′shən)   **1** a lack of

perfection; imperfect condition or character. **2** a fault or defect: *The imperfections in the picture showed that it had been painted in a hurry.* *n.*

**im·pe·ri·al** (im pē′rē əl) **1** of or having to do with an empire or its ruler. **2** of or having to do with the rule or authority of one country over other countries and colonies. **3** having the rank of an emperor. **4** supreme; majestic; magnificent. **5** of larger size or better quality. **6** a small, pointed beard growing beneath the lower lip. See BEARD for picture. **7** according to the traditional British standard of weights and measures. **8** a size of paper, about 57 x 76 cm. 1–5, 7, 8 *adj.*, 6 *n.*
—**im·pe′ri·al·ly,** *adv.*

**imperial gallon** the traditional British and Canadian gallon, equal to 160 fluid ounces (about 4.55 dm³): *The imperial gallon is about 20 percent bigger than the United States gallon.*

**im·pe·ri·al·ism** (im pē′rē ə liz′əm) **1** the policy of extending the rule or authority of one country over other countries and territories. **2** an imperial system of government. *n.*

**im·pe·ri·al·ist** (im pē′rē ə list) **1** a person who favours IMPERIALISM. **2** IMPERIALISTIC. 1 *n.*, 2 *adj.*

**im·pe·ri·al·is·tic** (im pē′rē ə lis′tik) **1** of imperialism or imperialists. **2** favouring imperialism. *adj.*
—**im·pe′ri·al·is′ti·cal·ly,** *adv.*

**Imperial Order Daughters of the Empire** an organization of women founded in 1900, whose purpose is to stimulate patriotism and promote good citizenship.

**im·per·il** (im per′əl) put in danger: *Yussuf imperilled their lives by standing up and rocking the rowboat.* *v.*, **im·per·illed** or **im·per·iled, im·per·il·ling** or **im·per·il·ing.**

**im·pe·ri·ous** (im pē′rē əs) **1** haughty; arrogant; domineering; overbearing. **2** IMPERATIVE; necessary; urgent. *adj.* —**im·pe′ri·ous·ly,** *adv.*
—**im·pe′ri·ous·ness,** *n.*

**im·per·ish·a·bil·i·ty** (im per′i shə bil′ə tē) the quality or state of being IMPERISHABLE; enduring quality. *n.*

**im·per·ish·a·ble** (im per′i shə bəl) everlasting; not perishable; indestructible. *adj.*
—**im·per′ish·a·bly,** *adv.*

**im·per·me·a·bil·i·ty** (im pėr′mē ə bil′ə tē) an IMPERMEABLE quality or condition. *n.*

**im·per·me·a·ble** (im pėr′mē ə bəl) **1** that cannot be passed through; impassable. **2** not permitting the passage of fluid through the pores, interstices, etc. *adj.*

**impers.** impersonal.

**im·per·son·al** (im pėr′sə nəl) **1** referring to all or any persons, not to any special one: *"First come, first served"* is an impersonal remark. In the expression "One must do one's best," the word "one" is impersonal. **2** having no existence as a person: *Electricity is an impersonal force.* **3** of a verb, having an indefinite *it* for a subject. Example: rained in "It rained yesterday." *adj.*
—**im·per′son·al·ly,** *adv.*

**im·per·son·al·i·ty** (im pėr′sə nal′ə tē) the state or quality of being IMPERSONAL (defs. 1, 2); absence of personal quality. *n.*, *pl.* **im·per·son·al·i·ties.**

**im·per·son·al·ly** (im pėr′sə nə lē) in an IMPERSONAL (def. 1) manner; without personal reference or connection. *adv.*

**impersonal pronoun** any of the words *it, one, they,* or *you* when used to refer to a person or thing not named or identified: *It is cold today. One must do one's best. They say that life begins at forty. You should be careful in crossing the street.*

**im·per·son·ate** (im pėr′sə nāt′) **1** act the part of: *He impersonated Hamlet on the stage.* **2** pretend to be; mimic the voice, appearance, and manners of, especially in trying to deceive: *The thief impersonated a police officer.*
*v.*, **im·per·son·at·ed, im·per·son·at·ing.**

**im·per·son·a·tion** (im pėr′sə nā′shən) impersonating or being impersonated. *n.*

**im·per·son·a·tor** (im pėr′sə nā′tər) one who impersonates, especially an actor who impersonates particular persons or types; professional mimic. *n.*

**im·per·ti·nence** (im pėr′tə nəns) **1** impudence; insolence. **2** a lack of pertinence; irrelevance. **3** an impertinent act or speech. *n.*

**im·per·ti·nent** (im pėr′tə nənt) **1** saucy; impudent; insolent; rude: *Talking back to older people is impertinent.* **2** not pertinent; not to the point; out of place. *adj.*
—**im·per′ti·nent·ly,** *adv.*

**im·per·turb·a·bil·i·ty** (im′pər tėr′bə bil′ə tē) the state or quality of being IMPERTURBABLE; calmness. *n.*

**im·per·turb·a·ble** (im′pər tėr′bə bəl) **1** not capable of being excited or disturbed. **2** not easily excited; calm. *adj.* —**im′per·turb′a·bly,** *adv.*

**im·per·vi·ous** (im pėr′vē əs) **1** not letting things pass through; not allowing passage: *Rubber cloth is impervious to moisture.* **2** not open to or affected by argument, suggestions, etc.: *She is impervious to all the gossip about her.* *adj.* —**im·per′vi·ous·ness,** *n.*
—**im·per′vi·ous·ly,** *adv.*

**im·pe·ti·go** (im′pə tī′gō) an infectious skin disease causing pimples filled with pus. *n.*

**im·pet·u·os·i·ty** (im pech′ü os′ə tē) **1** sudden or rash energy; violence; ardour: *The impetuosity of the speaker stirred the audience.* **2** an IMPETUOUS action or impulse. *n.*, *pl.* **im·pet·u·os·i·ties.**

**im·pet·u·ous** (im pech′ü əs) **1** acting hastily, rashly, or with sudden feeling: *Children are usually more impetuous than adults.* **2** moving with great force or speed: *the impetuous rush of water over Niagara Falls.* *adj.* —**im·pet′u·ous·ly,** *adv.* —**im·pet′u·ous·ness,** *n.*

**im·pe·tus** (im′pə təs) **1** the force with which a moving body tends to maintain its velocity and overcome resistance: *the impetus of a moving automobile.* **2** a driving force; incentive: *Ambition is an impetus to working for success.* *n.*

**im·pi·e·ty** (im pī′ə tē) **1** lack of piety or reverence for God; wickedness. **2** lack of dutifulness or respect. **3** an IMPIOUS act. *n.*, *pl.* **im·pi·e·ties.**

**im·pinge** (im pinj′) **1** hit; strike: *Rays of light impinge on the eye.* **2** encroach; infringe. *v.*, **im·pinged, im·ping·ing.**

**im·pinge·ment** (im pinj′mənt) the act of impinging: *the effect of the impingement of modern technology upon a rural society.* *n.*

**im·pi·ous** (im′pē əs *or* im pī′əs) not pious; not having or not showing reverence for God; wicked; profane. *adj.*
—**im′pi·ous·ly,** *adv.* —**im′pi·ous·ness,** *n.*

**imp·ish** (imp′ish) of or like an imp; especially, mischievous: *an impish grin, an impish trick.* *adj.* —**imp′ish·ly,** *adv.* —**imp′ish·ness,** *n.*

**im·plac·a·bil·i·ty** (im plak′ə bil′ə tē) the state or quality of being IMPLACABLE. *n.*

**im·plac·a·ble** (im plak′ə bəl) that cannot be placated, pacified, or appeased; relentless: *an implacable enemy.* *adj.* —**im·pla′ca·bly,** *adv.*

**im·plant** (im plant′) 1 instil; fix deeply: *A good teacher implants high ideals in children.* 2 insert: *Teeth are implanted in the jaw.* 3 set in the ground; plant. 4 tissue or artificial support grafted into the body. 1–3 *v.*, 4 *n.*

**im·ple·ment** (im′plə mənt *for noun,* im′plə ment′ *for verb*) 1 a useful piece of equipment; tool; instrument; utensil: *Ploughs, axes, shovels, can openers, and brooms are all implements.* 2 provide with implements or other means. 3 provide the power and authority necessary to accomplish or put something into effect: *to implement an order.* 4 carry out; get done: *Do not undertake the project unless you can implement it.* 1 *n.*, 2–4 *v.*

**im·pli·cate** (im′plə kāt′) 1 show to have a part in or to be connected with a crime, fault, etc.; involve: *The thief's confession implicated two other people.* 2 involve as a consequence; imply. *v.* **im·pli·cat·ed, im·pli·cat·ing.**

**im·pli·ca·tion** (im′plə kā′shən) 1 an implying or being implied. 2 something implied; an indirect suggestion; hint: *There was no implication of dishonesty in her failure in business.* 3 an implicating or being implicated. *n.*

**im·plic·it** (im plis′it) 1 without doubting, hesitating, or asking questions; absolute: *implicit trust, implicit obedience.* 2 meant, but not clearly expressed or distinctly stated; implied: *Her silence gave implicit consent.* Compare with EXPLICIT. 3 involved as a necessary part or condition. *adj.*

**im·plic·it·ly** (im plis′i tlē) 1 unquestioningly: *They trusted her implicitly.* 2 by IMPLICATION. *adv.*

**im·plied** (im plīd′) 1 involved, indicated, suggested, or understood without a clear statement: *an implied contract, an implied rebuke.* 2 pt. and pp. of IMPLY. 1 *adj.*, 2 *v.*

**im·pli·ed·ly** (im plī′i dlē) by IMPLICATION. *adv.*

**im·plore** (im plôr′) 1 beg earnestly for: *The prisoner implored pardon.* 2 beg a person to do something: *She implored her mother to give permission for her to go on the trip.* *v.*, **im·plored, im·plor·ing.** —**im·plor′er,** *n.* —**im·plor′ing·ly,** *adv.*

**im·ply** (im plī′) 1 indicate without saying outright; express indirectly; suggest: *Silence often implies consent. Her smile implied that she had forgiven us.* 2 involve as a necessary part or condition: *Speech implies the existence of a speaker.* *v.*, **im·plied, im·ply·ing.**
☛ *Usage.* Do not confuse **imply** and INFER. A writer or speaker **implies** something in his or her words or manner: *She implied by the look in her eyes that she did not intend to keep the appointment.* A reader or listener **infers** something from what he or she reads, sees, hears, etc.: *They inferred from her smile that she knew he was lying.*

**im·po·lite** (im′pə līt′) not polite; having or showing bad manners; rude. *adj.* —**im′po·lite′ly,** *adv.* —**im′po·lite′ness,** *n.*

**im·pol·i·tic** (im pol′ə tik′) not POLITIC; not expedient; unwise: *It is impolitic to offend people who can help you.* *adj.*

**im·pon·der·a·ble** (im pon′də rə bəl) 1 that cannot be explained, or measured exactly: *Faith and love are imponderable forces.* 2 something imponderable. 1 *adj.*, 2 *n.* —**im·pon′der·a·bly,** *adv.*

**im·port** (im pôrt′ *or* im′pôrt *for verb,* im′pôrt *for noun*) 1 bring in from a foreign country for sale or use: *Canada imports coffee.* 2 anything imported: *Rubber is a useful import.* 3 an importing; importation: *The import of diseased animals is forbidden.* 4 mean; signify: *Tell me what your remark imports.* 5 meaning; significance: *What is the import of your remark?* 6 importance: *It is a matter of great import.* 7 be of importance or consequence; be significant. 8 *Cdn.* in professional football, a non-Canadian player who has played fewer than five years in Canada. 1, 4, 7 *v.*, 2, 3, 5, 6, 8 *n.*

**im·por·tance** (im pôr′təns) being important; consequence; significance; value: *Anybody can see the importance of good health.* *n.*

**im·por·tant** (im pôr′tənt) 1 meaning much; worth noticing or considering; having value or significance: *important business, an important occasion.* 2 having social position or influence: *The mayor is an important person in our town.* 3 acting as if important; seeming to be important; self-important: *He rushed around in an important manner, giving orders.* *adj.* —**im·por′tant·ly,** *adv.*

**im·por·ta·tion** (im′pôr tā′shən) 1 the act of importing. 2 something imported: *Her shawl is a recent importation from Mexico.* *n.*

**im·port·er** (im pôr′tər *or* im′pôr tər) a person or company whose business is importing goods. *n.*

**im·por·tu·nate** (im pôr′chə nit) asking repeatedly; annoyingly persistent; urgent. *adj.* —**im·por′tu·nate·ly,** *adv.*

**im·por·tune** (im′pôr tyün′ *or* im′pôr tün′) ask urgently or repeatedly; trouble with demands: *The boy importuned the teacher to raise his mark.* *v.*, **im·por·tuned, im·por·tun·ing.**

**im·por·tu·ni·ty** (im′pôr tyü′nə tē *or* im′pôr tü′nə tē) persistence in asking; the act of demanding again and again: *In spite of his importunity his request was refused.* *n., pl.* **im·por·tu·ni·ties.**

**im·pose** (im pōz′) 1 put a burden, tax, punishment, etc. on: *The judge imposed a fine of $500 on the convicted man.* 2 force or thrust one's authority or influence on another or others. 3 force or thrust oneself or one's company on another or others; obtrude; presume. 4 pass off a thing upon a person to deceive. 5 lay on hands in confirmation or ordination. 6 arrange pages of type for printing. *v.*, **im·posed, im·pos·ing.** —**im·pos′er,** *n.* **impose on** *or* **upon, a** take advantage of; use in a selfish way: *to impose on the good nature of others.* **b** deceive; cheat; trick.

**im·pos·ing** (im pō′zing) 1 impressive because of size, appearance, or dignity; commanding attention: *The Peace Tower of the Parliament Buildings is an imposing landmark.* 2 ppr. of IMPOSE. 1 *adj.*, 2 *v.* —**im·pos′ing·ly,** *adv.*

**im·po·si·tion** (im′pə zish′ən) 1 the act or fact of imposing: *A war requires the imposition of heavy taxes.* 2 a tax, duty, task, burden, etc. 3 an unfair tax, etc.

**4** an imposing upon a person by taking advantage of his good nature: *Would it be an imposition to ask you to mail this parcel?* **5** a deception; fraud; trick. **6** a ceremonial laying on of hands, as in confirmation. **7** the arrangement of pages of type for printing. *n.*

**im·pos·si·bil·i·ty** (im pos′ə bil′ə tē) **1** the quality of being impossible: *We all realize the impossibility of living long without food.* **2** something impossible. *n., pl.* **im·pos·si·bil·i·ties.**

**im·pos·si·ble** (im pos′ə bəl) **1** that cannot be reached, done, or fulfilled; hopeless: *an impossible task, an impossible plan.* **2** that cannot be or happen: *It is impossible for two and two to be six.* **3** that cannot be true: *an impossible story.* **4** not able to be tolerated; very objectionable: *an impossible person.* *adj.* —**im·pos′si·bly,** *adv.*

**im·post** (im′pōst) **1** a tax on goods brought into a country; customs duty: *There is an impost on wool imported from other countries.* **2** a tax; tribute. *n.*

**im·pos·tor** (im pos′tər) **1** a person who assumes a false name or character. **2** a deceiver; cheat. *n.*

**im·pos·ture** (im pos′chər) the act or practice of deceiving by assuming a false character or name. *n.*

**im·po·tence** (im′pə təns) lack of power; helplessness; the condition or quality of being IMPOTENT. *n.*

**im·po·tent** (im′pə tənt) not having power; helpless: *Without guns and ammunition the soldiers were impotent. The patient fell back in an impotent rage.* *adj.* —**im′po·tent·ly,** *adv.*

**im·pound** (im pound′) **1** shut up in a pen or pound: *to impound stray animals.* **2** shut up; enclose; confine: *A dam impounds water.* **3** put in the custody of a law court; confiscate: *The court impounded the documents to use as evidence.* *v.* —**im·pound′er,** *n.*

**im·pov·er·ish** (im pov′ə rish) **1** make very poor. **2** exhaust the strength, richness, or resources of: *to impoverish the soil.* *v.* —**im·pov′er·ish·er,** *n.* —**im·pov′er·ish·ment,** *n.*

**im·pov·er·ished** (im pov′ə risht) **1** very poor. **2** pt. and pp. of IMPOVERISH. 1 *adj.*, 2 *v.*

**im·pow·er** (im pou′ər) EMPOWER. *v.*

**im·prac·ti·ca·bil·i·ty** (im prak′tə kə bil′ə tē) **1** being IMPRACTICABLE. **2** something IMPRACTICABLE. *n., pl.* **im·prac·ti·ca·bil·i·ties.**

**im·prac·ti·ca·ble** (im prak′tə kə bəl) **1** that cannot be done without greater difficulty, expense, etc., than is wise or sensible; impossible to put into practice: *His suggestion was impracticable.* **2** very hard to manage: *an impracticable horse.* **3** that cannot be used: *an impracticable road.* *adj.* —**im·prac′ti·ca·bly,** *adv.*

**im·prac·ti·cal** (im prak′tə kəl) not PRACTICAL; unrealistic: *To build a bridge across the Atlantic Ocean is an impractical scheme.* *adj.* —**im·prac′ti·cal·ly,** *adv.*

**im·pre·cate** (im′prə kāt) call down curses, evil, etc.: *The prophet imprecated ruin on his enemies.* *v.*, **im·pre·cat·ed, im·pre·cat·ing.** —**im′pre·ca′tor,** *n.*

**im·pre·ca·tion** (im′prə kā′shən) **1** calling down curses, evil, etc. **2** a curse. *n.*

**im·preg·na·bil·i·ty** (im preg′nə bil′ə tē) the state or quality of being IMPREGNABLE. *n.*

**im·preg·na·ble** (im preg′nə bəl) **1** able to resist attack: *an impregnable fortress.* **2** not yielding to force, persuasion, etc.: *an impregnable argument.* *adj.* —**im·preg′na·bly,** *adv.*

**im·preg·nate** (im preg′nāt) **1** make pregnant. **2** in biology, fertilize: *to impregnate an egg cell.* **3** fill with; saturate: *Sea water is impregnated with salt.* **4** instil into the mind; inspire; imbue: *A great book impregnates the mind with new ideas.* **5** impregnated. 1–4 *v.*, **im·preg·nat·ed, im·preg·nat·ing;** 5 *adj.* —**im·preg′na·tor,** *n.*

**im·preg·na·tion** (im′preg nā′shən) **1** impregnating or being impregnated. **2** the thing, influence, etc. with which anything is impregnated. *n.*

**im·pre·sa·ri·o** (im′prə sä′rē ō′) an organizer or manager of an opera or concert company. *n., pl.* **im·pre·sa·ri·os.**

**im·press**¹ (im pres′ *for verb*, im′pres *for noun*) **1** have a strong effect on the mind or feelings of: *A hero impresses us with his courage.* **2** fix in the mind: *She repeated the list to impress it on her memory.* **3** an impression; a special mark or quality; stamp: *An author leaves the impress of his personality on his work.* **4** make marks by pressing or stamping: *to impress wax with a seal.* **5** imprint; stamp. 1, 2, 4, 5 *v.*, 3 *n.* —**im·press′er,** *n.*

**im·press**² (im pres′) **1** seize by force for public use: *The police impressed our car in order to pursue the escaping robbers.* **2** force men to serve in the navy or army. **3** bring in and use. *v.*, **im·pressed, im·press·ing.**

**im·pres·sion** (im presh′ən) **1** an effect produced on a person: *Punishment seemed to make little impression on the child.* **2** an idea or notion: *I have a vague impression that I left the house unlocked.* **3** something produced by pressure; mark, stamp, print, etc.: *The thief had left an impression of her feet in the garden.* **4** the act of impressing. **5** the state of being impressed. **6** the total number of copies of a book made at one time. **7** a printed copy. **8** an impersonation or mimicking of someone. *n.*

**im·pres·sion·a·bil·i·ty** (im presh′ə nə bil′ə tē) an IMPRESSIONABLE quality or condition. *n.*

**im·pres·sion·a·ble** (im presh′ə nə bəl) sensitive to impressions; easily impressed or influenced: *Children are more impressionable than adults.* *adj.*

**im·pres·sion·ism** (im presh′ə niz′əm) **1** a style in literature characterized by subjective impressions of reality presented in vivid, colourful scenes. **2** a style in music characterized by the use of unusual and rich harmonies, tonal qualities, etc. to suggest the composer's impressions of nature, emotions, etc. **3** Often, **Impressionism,** a school of painting developed by French painters of the late 19th century and characterized by the use of strong, bright, unmixed colours applied in small dabs to suggest natural reflected light. *n.*

**im·pres·sion·ist** (im presh′ə nist) **1** Usually, **Impressionist,** a painter of the 19th-century French school of IMPRESSIONISM (def. 3). **2** Often, **Impressionist,** a painter, writer, or composer who follows a style that presents subjective, often emotional, impressions of nature, etc. **3** an entertainer who does impersonations or IMPRESSIONS (def. 8), especially of famous persons.

**im·pres·sion·is·tic** (im presh′ə nis′tik) **1** giving only a general or hasty impression. **2** of or having to do with IMPRESSIONISM or IMPRESSIONISTS. *adj.*

**im·pres·sive** (im pres′iv) able to make an impression

on the mind, feelings, conscience, etc.: *an impressive sermon, an impressive storm, an impressive ceremony.* *adj.* —**im·pres′sive·ly**, *adv.* —**im·pres′sive·ness**, *n.*

**im·press·ment** (im pres′mənt) the act or practice of impressing men or property for public service or use. *n.*

**im·print** (im′print *for noun,* im print′ *for verb*) **1** a mark made by pressure; print: *the imprint of a foot in the sand.* **2** an impression or mark: *Suffering left its imprint on her face.* **3** a publisher's name, with the place and date of publication, on the title page or at the end of a book; a printer's name and address as printed on his or her work. **4** mark by pressing or stamping; print: *to imprint a postmark on an envelope, to imprint a letter with a postmark.* **5** press or impress: *to imprint a kiss on someone's cheek, a scene imprinted on the memory.* 1–3 *n.*, 4, 5 *v.* —**im·print′er**, *n.*

**im·pris·on** (im priz′ən) **1** put in prison. **2** confine closely; restrain. *v.*

**im·pris·on·ment** (im priz′ən mənt) **1** putting or keeping in prison. **2** being put or kept in prison. **3** close confinement; restraint. *n.*

**im·prob·a·bil·i·ty** (im prob′ə bil′ə tē) **1** being IMPROBABLE; unlikelihood. **2** something IMPROBABLE. *n., pl.* **im·prob·a·bil·i·ties**.

**im·prob·a·ble** (im prob′ə bəl) **1** not probable; not likely to happen: *It is improbable that they will win the most medals at the next Olympic games.* **2** not likely to be true: *an improbable story.* *adj.*

**im·prob·a·bly** (im prob′ə blē) with little or no PROBABILITY. *adv.*

**im·promp·tu** (im promp′tyü *or* im promp′tü) **1** without previous thought or preparation: *a speech made impromptu.* **2** unrehearsed; offhand: *an impromptu speech, an impromptu party.* **3** an impromptu speech, performance, etc.; improvisation. 1 *adv.*, 2 *adj.*, 3 *n.*

**im·prop·er** (im prop′ər) **1** not according to rules of conduct; not decent or polite: *improper language.* **2** not suitable for the purpose or in the circumstances; inappropriate: *improper clothing for a hike.* **3** incorrect: *an improper conclusion.* **4** not properly so called: *an improper fraction.* *adj.* —**im·prop′er·ly**, *adv.*

**improper fraction** a fraction greater than 1. Examples: ³/₂, ⁴/₃, ²⁷/₄.

**im·pro·pri·e·ty** (im′prə prī′ə tē) **1** a lack of PROPRIETY; the quality of being improper. **2** improper conduct. **3** an improper act, expression, etc.: *Using "learn" to mean "teach" is an impropriety.* *n., pl.* **im·pro·pri·e·ties**.

**im·prove** (im prüv′) **1** make better: *You could improve your handwriting if you tried.* **2** become better: *His health is improving.* **3** increase the value of land or property. **4** use well; make good use of: *Improve your time by studying.* *v.*, **im·proved, im·prov·ing**. —**im·prov′a·ble**, *adj.* —**im·prov′er**, *n.* **improve on,** make better; do better than.

**im·prove·ment** (im prüv′mənt) **1** making or becoming better: *Sean's schoolwork shows much improvement since last term.* **2** an increase in value. **3** a change or addition that increases the value: *An old house can be modernized by making improvements.* **4** a better condition; anything that is better than another; advance: *Travelling by automobile is an improvement over travelling by Red River cart.* *n.*

**im·prov·i·dence** (im prov′ə dəns) a lack of foresight

---

**impressment** 603 **impure**

hat, āge, fär; let, ēqual, tèrm; it, īce
hot, ōpen, ôrder; oil, out; cup, pùt, rüle
əbove, takən, pencəl, lemən, circəs
ch, child; ng, long; sh, ship
th, thin; ᴛʜ, then; zh, measure

---

or thrift; failure to look ahead; carelessness in providing for the future. *n.*

**im·prov·i·dent** (im prov′ə dənt) lacking foresight or thrift; not looking ahead; not careful in providing for the future. *adj.* —**im·prov′i·dent·ly**, *adv.*

**im·pro·vi·sa·tion** (im′prov ə zā′shən *or* im′prə vī zā′shən) **1** an improvising. **2** something improvised. *n.*

**im·pro·vise** (im′prə vīz′) **1** compose or sing, speak, recite, etc. without preparation: *Carl improvised a new stanza for the school song at the football game.* **2** perform without preparation or script: *Come and watch the children improvising.* **3** make or provide offhand, using whatever materials etc. happen to be available: *The girls improvised a tent out of two blankets and some long poles.* *v.*, **im·pro·vised, im·pro·vis·ing**. —**im′pro·vis′er**, *n.*

**im·pru·dence** (im prü′dəns) lack of PRUDENCE; imprudent behaviour. *n.*

**im·pru·dent** (im prü′dənt) not PRUDENT; rash; unwise: *an imprudent decision.* *adj.* —**im·pru′dent·ly**, *adv.*

**im·pu·dence** (im′pyə dəns) being IMPUDENT; insolence; great rudeness. *n.*

**im·pu·dent** (im′pyə dənt) rudely bold; insolent; forward: *The impudent girl made faces at the teacher.* *adj.* —**im′pu·dent·ly**, *adv.*

**im·pugn** (im pyün′) call in question; attack by words or arguments; challenge as false: *Do not impugn the umpire's fairness.* *v.* —**im·pugn′a·ble**, *adj.*

**im·pulse** (im′puls) **1** a sudden, driving force or influence; thrust; push: *the impulse of a wave, the impulse of hunger.* **2** the effect of a sudden, driving force or influence. **3** a sudden inclination or tendency to act: *A mob is influenced more by impulse than by reasoning.* **4** the stimulating force of desire or emotion: *The murderer acted on impulse.* **5** a change transmitted by nerve cells and muscles: *These impulses influence action in the muscular or nervous systems.* *n.*

**im·pul·sion** (im pul′shən) **1** an impelling; driving force: *The impulsion of hunger drove the man to steal.* **2** IMPULSE. **3** IMPETUS. *n.*

**im·pul·sive** (im pul′siv) **1** acting upon impulse; easily moved: *The impulsive child gave all her money to the beggar.* **2** coming from a sudden impulse: *an impulsive sneer.* **3** driving with sudden force; able to impel: *an impulsive force.* *adj.* —**im·pul′sive·ly**, *adv.* —**im·pul′sive·ness**, *n.*

**im·pu·ni·ty** (im pyü′nə tē) freedom from punishment, injury, or other unpleasant consequences: *If laws are not enforced, crimes are committed with impunity.* *n.*

**im·pure** (im pyúr′) **1** not pure; dirty; filthy; unclean: *The air in cities is often impure.* **2** mixed with something, especially a substance of lower value; adulterated: *The salt we use is slightly impure.* **3** not of one colour, style, etc.; mixed. **4** forbidden by religion as unclean. **5** bad; corrupt: *impure thoughts.* *adj.* —**im·pure′ly**, *adv.* —**im·pure′ness**, *n.*

**im·pu·ri·ty** (im pyü′rə tē)  1 a lack of purity; the state of being impure.  2 an impure thing or element; anything that makes something else impure: *Filtering the water removed some of its impurities.* *n., pl.* **im·pu·ri·ties.**

**im·pu·ta·tion** (im′pyə tā′shən)  1 the act of imputing. 2 a charge or hint of wrongdoing: *No imputation has ever been made against her good name.* *n.*

**im·pute** (im pyüt′)  consider as belonging; attribute; charge a fault, etc. to a person; blame: *I impute his failure to laziness.* *v.,* **im·put·ed, im·put·ing.**
—**im·put′a·ble,** *adj.*

**in** (in)  In expresses inclusion, situation, presence, existence, position, and action within limits of space, time, state, circumstances, etc.  1 inside; within: *in an hour, in the box.*  2 into: *She jumped in the water.*  3 with; having; by: *to wrap in paper, to be dressed in blue, to be in trouble, to cover a letter in an envelope.*  4 of; made of; using: *a table in mahogany.*  5 from among; out of: *one in a hundred.*  6 because of; for: *to act in self-defence.*  7 about; concerning: *a book in Canadian history.*  8 at; during; after: *in the present time. I will be back in one hour.*  9 while; when: *in crossing the street.*  10 in or into some place, position, condition, etc.: *to come in. A sheepskin coat has the woolly side in.*  11 present, especially in one's home or office: *The doctor is not in today.*  12 in fashion: *Short skirts are in again.*  13 that is in; being in: *Blue is the in colour.*  14 coming or going in: *Use the in door.* 1–9 *prep.,* 10–12 *adv.,* 13, 14 *adj.*
**in for,**  unable to avoid; sure to get or have: *We are in for a storm.*
**ins,**  people in office; the political party in power.
**ins and outs,**  **a** the turns and twists; nooks and corners: *the ins and outs of the road.* **b** the different parts; details: *The manager knows the ins and outs of the business better than the owner.*
**in with,**  **a** friendly with.  **b** partners with.
☞ *Hom.* **INN.**
☞ *Usage.* **In** generally shows location; **INTO** generally shows direction: *He was in the house. She came into the house. He was in a stupor. She fell into a deep sleep.* Informally, **in** is often used with certain words instead of **into**: *She fell in the creek.*

**In** indium.

**in–¹**  a prefix meaning not, the opposite of, or the absence of, as in *inexpensive, inattention, inconvenient.* Also, (before *l*) **il–,** (before *b, m, p*) **im–,** (before *r*) **ir–.**

**in–²**  a prefix meaning:  1 in, into, on, or upon, as in *inhale, inscribe.*  2 **in–** is also used to strengthen a meaning or change an intransitive verb to a transitive, or with little change in meaning. Also, (before *l*) **il–,** (before *b, m, p*) **im–,** (before *r*) **ir–.**

**in.**  inch; inches.

**in·a·bil·i·ty** (in′ə bil′ə tē)  a lack of ability, power, or means; being unable. *n.*

**in ab·sen·tia** (in ab sen′shə) *Latin*  while absent.

**in·ac·ces·si·bil·i·ty** (in′ək ses′ə bil′ə tē)  a lack of ACCESSIBILITY; being inaccessible. *n.*

**in·ac·ces·si·ble** (in′ək ses′ə bəl)  1 not ACCESSIBLE; that cannot be reached or entered.  2 hard to get at; hard to reach or enter: *The fort on top of the steep hill is inaccessible.*  3 that cannot be obtained; hard to obtain. *adj.* —**in′ac·ces′si·bly,** *adv.*

**in·ac·cu·ra·cy** (i nak′yə rə sē)  1 a lack of accuracy; being inaccurate: *The inaccuracy of the report was not hard to prove.*  2 an error or mistake: *There are several inaccuracies in the statistics.* *n., pl.* **in·ac·cu·ra·cies.**

**in·ac·cu·rate** (i nak′yə rit)  1 not accurate: *His aim was inaccurate and he missed the target.*  2 faulty; containing mistakes: *an inaccurate report.* *adj.*
—**in·ac′cu·rate·ly,** *adv.*

**in·ac·tion** (i nak′shən)  an absence of action; idleness: *Energetic people are not able to endure inaction calmly.* *n.*

**in·ac·tive** (i nak′tiv)  not active; idle; sluggish. *adj.*
—**in·ac′tive·ly,** *adv.*

**in·ac·tiv·i·ty** (in′ak tiv′ə tē)  an absence of activity; idleness; sluggishness. *n.*

**in·ad·e·qua·cy** (i nad′ə kwə sē)  being INADEQUATE. *n.*

**in·ad·e·quate** (i nad′ə kwit)  not adequate; not enough; not as much as is needed: *inadequate preparation for an examination.* *adj.* —**in·ad′e·quate·ly,** *adv.*

**in·ad·mis·si·bil·i·ty** (in′əd mis′ə bil′ə tē)  being INADMISSIBLE. *n.*

**in·ad·mis·si·ble** (in′əd mis′ə bəl)  1 not allowable: *The judge ruled the evidence inadmissible.*  2 not to be admitted. *adj.* —**in′ad·mis′si·bly,** *adv.*

**in·ad·vert·ence** (in′əd vėr′təns)  1 a lack of attention; carelessness.  2 an oversight; mistake. *n.*

**in·ad·vert·ent** (in′əd vėr′tənt)  1 not attentive; heedless; negligent.  2 not done on purpose; caused by oversight: *Mei's blunder was inadvertent, and we forgave it.* *adj.* —**in′ad·vert′ent·ly,** *adv.*

**in·ad·vis·a·bil·i·ty** (in′ad vī′zə bil′ə tē)  the condition of being INADVISABLE. *n.*

**in·ad·vis·a·ble** (in′əd vī′zə bəl)  not advisable; unwise; not prudent. *adj.* —**in′ad·vis′a·bly,** *adv.*

**in·a·lien·a·ble** (i nā′lē ə nə bəl *or* i nā′lyə nə bəl)  that cannot be given away or taken away: *Every person has the inalienable right of equality before the law.* *adj.*
—**in·al′ien·a·bly,** *adv.*

**in·ane** (i nān′)  silly or foolish; empty of meaning; senseless: *an inane thing to do, inane remarks.* *adj.*
—**in·ane′ly,** *adv.*

**in·an·i·mate** (i nan′ə mit)  1 not having life; not animate; lifeless: *the inanimate desert. Stones are inanimate.*  2 not animated; dull: *an inanimate face.* *adj.* —**in·an′i·mate·ly,** *adv.* —**in·an′i·mate·ness,** *n.*

**in·a·ni·tion** (in′ə nish′ən)  1 weakness and exhaustion from lack of food.  2 lack of vigour or spirit; lethargy. *n.*

**in·an·i·ty** (i nan′ə tē)  1 silliness; lack of sense.  2 a silly or senseless act, practice, remark, etc.  3 emptiness. *n., pl.* **in·an·i·ties.**

**in·ap·pli·ca·bil·i·ty** (i nap′lə kə bil′ə tē *or* in′ə plik′ə bil′ə tē)  being INAPPLICABLE. *n.*

**in·ap·pli·ca·ble** (i nap′lə kə bəl *or* in′ə plik′ə bəl)  not applicable; not appropriate; not suitable: *The name Tiny is inapplicable to that big dog.* *adj.*
—**in·ap′pli·ca·bly,** *adv.*

**in·ap·po·site** (i nap′ə zit)  not pertinent; not suitable; inappropriate. *adj.* —**in·ap′po·site·ly,** *adv.*

**in·ap·pre·ci·a·ble** (in′ə prē′shē ə bəl *or* in′ə prē′shə bəl)  too small to be noticed or felt; very slight. *adj.*
—**in′ap·pre′ci·a·bly,** *adv.*

**in·ap·pro·pri·ate** (in′ə prō′prē it) not APPROPRIATE; not suitable; not fitting: *Jokes are inappropriate at a funeral.* *adj.* —**in′ap·pro′pri·ate·ly,** *adv.* —**in′ap·pro′pri·ate·ness,** *n.*

**in·apt** (i napt′) **1** not APT; not suitable. **2** unskilful; awkward. *adj.* —**in·apt′ly,** *adv.* —**in·apt′ness,** *n.*
☛ *Syn.* **Inapt** and INEPT have similar meanings, but only **inept** (def. 3) means 'foolish, absurd'.

**in·ap·ti·tude** (i nap′tə tyüd′ *or* i nap′tə tüd′) **1** unfitness. **2** a lack of skill. *n.*

**in·ar·tic·u·late** (in′är tik′yə lit) **1** not distinct; not like regular speech: *an inarticulate mutter or groan.* **2** unable to speak in words; unable to say what one thinks; dumb: *Cats and dogs are inarticulate.* **3** not jointed: *A jellyfish's body is inarticulate.* *adj.* —**in′ar·tic′u·late·ly,** *adv.* —**in′ar·tic′u·late·ness,** *n.*

**in·ar·tis·tic** (in′är tis′tik) **1** not following the principles of art. **2** lacking talent in or appreciation of art. *adj.* —**in′ar·tis′ti·cal·ly,** *adv.*

**in·as·much as** (in′ə zmuch′) because; since; in view of the fact that: *Inasmuch as he was smaller than the other boys, he was given a head start in the race.*

**in·at·ten·tion** (in′ə ten′shən) a lack of attention; heedlessness; negligence: *That boy lost his job through inattention.* *n.*

**in·at·ten·tive** (in′ə ten′tiv) not ATTENTIVE; careless; heedless; negligent. *adj.* —**in′at·ten′tive·ly,** *adv.* —**in′at·ten′tive·ness,** *n.*

**in·au·di·ble** (i nod′ə bəl) that cannot be heard: *The street noises were almost inaudible at the back of the house.* *adj.* —**in·au′di·bly,** *adv.*

**in·au·gu·ral** (i nog′yə rəl) **1** of or for an INAUGURATION: *an inaugural address.* **2** an inaugural address or speech. **1** *adj.,* **2** *n.*

**in·au·gu·rate** (i nog′yə rāt′) **1** install in office with a ceremony: *The new mayor will be inaugurated at noon tomorrow.* **2** make a formal beginning of; begin: *The development of the airplane inaugurated a new era in transportation.* **3** open for public use with a ceremony or celebration: *The new playground was inaugurated with a parade and a ball game.* *v.,* **in·au·gu·rat·ed, in·au·gu·rat·ing.** —**in·au′gu·ra′tor,** *n.*

**in·au·gu·ra·tion** (i nog′yə rā′shən) **1** the act or ceremony of installing a person in office. **2** a beginning, especially a formal one. **3** the opening or bringing into use of public buildings etc. with a ceremony or celebration: *We were present at the inauguration of the new City Hall.* *n.*

**in·aus·pi·cious** (in′os pish′əs) with signs of failure; unfavourable; unlucky. *adj.* —**in′aus·pi′cious·ly,** *adv.* —**in′aus·pi′cious·ness,** *n.*

**in·board** (in′bôrd′) **1** inside the hull of a ship; in or toward the middle of a ship. **2** a motorboat having its motor inside the hull. **3** the motor itself. **1** *adv., adj.,* **2, 3** *n.*

**in·born** (in′bôrn′) born in a person; instinctive; natural: *an inborn sense of rhythm.* *adj.*

**in·bound** (in′bound′) inward bound. *adj.*

**in·bred** (in′bred′) **1** inborn; natural: *an inbred courtesy.* **2** bred for generations from ancestors closely related: *an inbred strain of horses.* **3** pt. and pp. of INBREED. **1, 2** *adj.,* **3** *v.*

**in·breed** (in′brēd′ *or* in brēd′) breed from closely related animals or plants. *v.,* **in·bred, in·breed·ing.**

## inappropriate 605 incarnate

hat, āge, fär; let, ēqual, tėrm; it, īce
hot, ōpen, ôrder; oil, out; cup, put, rüle
əbove, takən, pencəl, lemən, circəs
ch, child; ng, long; sh, ship
th, thin; ᴛʜ, then; zh, measure

**in·breed·ing** (in′brē′ding) **1** the practice of breeding from closely related stock in order to develop or preserve desirable characteristics. **2** ppr. of INBREED. **1** *n.,* **2** *v.*

**inc. 1** incorporated. **2** including. **3** included. **4** inclusive.

**in·cal·cu·la·ble** (in kal′kyə lə bəl) **1** too great in number to be counted; numerous: *The sands of the beach are incalculable.* **2** not to be reckoned beforehand: *A flood in the valley would cause incalculable losses.* **3** not to be relied on; uncertain. *adj.* —**in·cal′cu·la·bly,** *adv.*

**in·can·des·cence** (in′kən des′əns) the state or quality of being INCANDESCENT; glowing brightly with heat. *n.*

**in·can·des·cent** (in′kən des′ənt) **1** glowing with heat; red-hot or white-hot. **2** intensely bright; brilliant. **3** having to do with or containing a material that gives light by incandescence. An **incandescent lamp** is an electric lamp with a filament of very fine wire that becomes white-hot when current flows through it. *adj.*

**incandescent lamp** light bulb.

**in·can·ta·tion** (in′kan tā′shən) **1** a set of words spoken as a magic charm or to cast a magic spell: *"Double, double, toil and trouble, Fire burn and cauldron bubble"* is an incantation in Shakespeare's *Macbeth.* **2** the use of such words. *n.*

**in·ca·pa·bil·i·ty** (in kā′ pə bil′ə tē) INCAPACITY. *n.*

**in·ca·pa·ble** (in kā′pə bəl) without ordinary ability; not efficient; not competent. *adj.*
**incapable of, a** without the ability, power or fitness for: *Vilma's honesty made her incapable of lying.* **b** not legally qualified for: *Certain beliefs make a person incapable of serving on a jury.* **c** not susceptible to; not capable of receiving or admitting: *incapable of exact measurement. Gold is incapable of rusting.*

**in·ca·pac·i·tate** (in′kə pas′ə tāt′) **1** deprive of ability, power, or fitness; disable: *The man's injury incapacitated him for working.* **2** legally disqualify. *v.,* **in·ca·pac·i·tat·ed, in·ca·pac·i·tat·ing.** —**in′ca·pac′i·ta′tion,** *n.*

**in·ca·pac·i·ty** (in′kə pas′ə tē) **1** a lack of ability, power, or fitness; disability. **2** a legal disqualification. *n., pl.* **in·ca·pac·i·ties.**

**in·car·cer·ate** (in kär′sə rāt′) IMPRISON. *v.,* **in·car·cer·at·ed, in·car·cer·at·ing.**

**in·car·cer·a·tion** (in kär′sə rā′shən) IMPRISONMENT. *n.*

**in·car·na·dine** (in kär′nə dīn′ *or* in kär′nə din) **1** blood-red. **2** flesh-coloured. **3** make blood-red or flesh-coloured. **1, 2** *adj.,* **3** *v.,* **in·car·na·dined, in·car·na·din·ing.**

**in·car·nate** (in kär′nit *or* in kär′nāt *for adjective,* in kär′nāt *for verb*) **1** embodied in flesh, especially in human form: *The villain was a fiend incarnate.* **2** make incarnate; embody. **3** put into an actual form; realize: *The sculptor incarnated her vision in a beautiful statue.* **4** be the living embodiment of: *She incarnates all womanly*

**incarnation** virtues in her own person. 1 adj., 2–4 v., **in·car·nat·ed, in·car·nat·ing.**

**in·car·na·tion** (in′kär nā′shən) **1** a taking on of human form by a divine being. **2** embodiment. **3** a person or thing that represents some quality or idea: *A miser is an incarnation of greed.* *n.*

**in·case** (in kās′) **1** put into a case. **2** cover completely; enclose: *Armour incased the knight's body.* *v.*, **in·cased, in·cas·ing.** Also, **encase.**

**in·cau·tious** (in kôsh′əs) not CAUTIOUS; heedless; reckless; rash. *adj.* —**in·cau′tious·ly,** *adv.* —**in·cau′tious·ness,** *n.*

**in·cen·di·a·rism** (in sen′dē ə riz′əm) **1** the crime of setting fire to property. **2** the deliberate stirring up of strife or rebellion. *n.*

**in·cen·di·a·ry** (in sen′dē er′ē) **1** having to do with the setting of property on fire maliciously. **2** a person who maliciously sets fire to property. **3** causing fires; used to start a fire: *The enemy town was set on fire with incendiary shells and bombs.* **4** deliberately stirring up strife or rebellion: *The agitator was arrested for making incendiary speeches.* **5** a person who deliberately stirs up strife or rebellion. **6** a shell or bomb containing chemical agents that cause fire. 1, 3, 4 *adj.*, 2, 5, 6 *n.*, *pl.* **in·cen·di·ar·ies.**

**in·cense**[1] (in′sens) **1** a substance giving off a sweet smell when burned. **2** the perfume or smoke from it. **3** something sweet, such as the perfume of flowers, or the pleasure given by flattery or praise. *n.*

**in·cense**[2] (in sens′) make very angry; fill with rage: *Cruelty incenses kind people.* *v.*, **in·censed, in·cens·ing.**

**in·cen·tive** (in sen′tiv) something that urges a person on; the cause of action or effort; a motive or stimulus: *The fun of playing the game was a greater incentive than the prize.* *n.*

**in·cep·tion** (in sep′shən) a beginning; commencement. *n.*

**in·ces·sant** (in ses′ənt) never stopping; continued or repeated without interruption: *The roar of Niagara Falls is incessant. The incessant noise of the factory kept her awake all night.* *adj.* —**in·ces′sant·ly,** *adv.*

**in·cest** (in′sest) the crime of sexual intercourse between persons so closely related that their marriage is prohibited by law. *n.*

**in·ces·tu·ous** (in ses′chü əs) **1** involving incest. **2** guilty of incest. *adj.* —**in·ces′tu·ous·ly,** *adv.* —**in·ces′tu·ous·ness,** *n.*

**inch** (inch) **1** a unit for measuring length, equal to 1/12 of a foot (2.54 cm). *Symbol:* ″ **2** the smallest part, amount, or degree; very little bit (*used usually with negatives*): *She would not yield an inch.* **3** move slowly or little by little: *The worm inched along.* 1, 2 *n.*, 3 *v.* **by inches,** by degrees; gradually. **every inch,** in every way; completely: *He is every inch a soldier.* **inch by inch,** slowly; little by little. **within an inch of,** very near; very close to: *The man was within an inch of death.*

**in·cho·ate** (in kō′it) just begun; in an early stage; incomplete; undeveloped. *adj.* —**in·cho′ate·ly,** *adv.* —**in·cho′ate·ness,** *n.*

**inch·worm** (inch′wėrm′) a measuring worm; the larva of a GEOMETRID. *n.*

**in·ci·dence** (in′sə dəns) **1** the act or fact of coming in contact with, occurring, or influencing. **2** the manner, extent, or rate of occurrence or effect: *a high incidence of traffic accidents during the holiday weekend. In an epidemic, the incidence of a disease is widespread.* **3** in physics, the falling of a line, or of something moving in a line, on a surface. **4** the direction such a line, etc. takes in falling on a surface: *The angle of incidence of a ray of light falling on a surface is the angle between the ray and a line perpendicular to that surface.* See ANGLE OF INCIDENCE for picture. *n.*

**in·ci·dent** (in′sə dənt) **1** a happening; event. **2** an event that helps or adds to something else. **3** a distinct piece of action in a story, play, or poem. **4** liable to happen; belonging: *Hardships are incident to the life of an explorer.* **5** falling or striking upon: *rays of light incident upon a mirror.* 1–3 *n.*, 4, 5 *adj.*

**in·ci·den·tal** (in′sə den′təl) **1** happening or likely to happen along with something else more important: *Certain discomforts are incidental to camping out.* **2** occurring by chance: *an incidental encounter with a friend on the street.* **3** something incidental: *On our trip we spent $289 for meals, room, and bus fare, and $26.50 for incidentals such as candy, magazines, and stamps.* 1, 2 *adj.*, 3 *n.*

**in·ci·den·tal·ly** (in′sə den′tə lē *or* in′sə den′tlē) **1** in an INCIDENTAL manner; as an incident along with something else: *She mentioned incidentally that she had had no dinner.* **2** accidentally; by chance. *adv.*

**in·cin·er·ate** (in sin′ə rāt′) burn to ashes. *v.*, **in·cin·er·at·ed, in·cin·er·at·ing.** —**in·cin′er·a′tion,** *n.*

**in·cin·er·a·tor** (in sin′ə rā′tər) a furnace or other apparatus for burning garbage, trash, etc. to ashes. *n.*

**in·cip·i·ence** (in sip′ē əns) the very beginning; early stage. *n.*

**in·cip·i·ent** (in sip′ē ənt) just beginning; in an early stage: *The medicine stopped David's incipient cough.* *adj.* —**in·cip′i·ent·ly,** *adv.*

**in·cise** (in sīz′) **1** cut into. **2** carve; engrave. *v.*, **in·cised, in·cis·ing.**

**in·cised** (in sīzd′) **1** cut into. **2** carved; engraved: *Her ring had her name incised on the inside.* **3** having notches around the edge: *an incised leaf.* **4** pt. and pp. of INCISE. 1–3 *adj.*, 4 *v.*

**in·ci·sion** (in sizh′ən) **1** a cut made in something; gash: *The doctor made a small incision to remove all the glass from her foot.* **2** the act of incising. **3** an INCISIVE quality. *n.*

**in·ci·sive** (in sī′siv) sharp; penetrating; piercing; keen: *an incisive criticism.* *adj.* —**in·ci′sive·ly,** *adv.* —**in·ci′sive·ness,** *n.*

**in·ci·sor** (in sī′zər) a tooth having a sharp edge for cutting; one of the front teeth between the canine teeth in either jaw: *A human being has eight incisors in all.* See TEETH for picture. *n.*

**in·ci·ta·tion** (in′sī tā′shən) an inciting. *n.*

**in·cite** (in sīt′) urge on; stir up; rouse: *Their captain's example incited the men to bravery.* *v.*, **in·cit·ed, in·cit·ing.** —**in·cit′er,** *n.*

**in·cite·ment** (in sīt′mənt) **1** something that urges on, stirs up, or rouses: *Selfishness is an incitement to crime.* **2** the act of urging on, stirring up, or rousing. *n.*

**in·ci·vil·i·ty** (in′sə vil′ə tē) **1** rudeness; lack of courtesy; impoliteness. **2** a rude or impolite act. *n., pl.* **in·ci·vil·i·ties.**

**incl. 1** inclosure. **2** including. **3** inclusive.

**in·clem·en·cy** (in klem′ən sē) severity; harshness: *The inclemency of the weather kept us at home. n., pl.* **in·clem·en·cies.**

**in·clem·ent** (in klem′ənt) **1** rough and stormy: *inclement weather.* **2** severe; harsh: *an inclement ruler. adj.* —**in·clem′ent·ly,** *adv.*

**in·cli·na·tion** (in′klə nā′shən) **1** a preference or liking: *an inclination for sports.* **2** tendency: *Many older people have an inclination to become fat.* **3** a leaning; bending; bowing: *A nod is an inclination of the head.* **4** a slope or slant: *the inclination of a roof.* **5** the difference of direction of two lines, especially as measured by the angle between them. *n.*

**in·cline** (in klīn′ *for verb,* in′klīn *or* in klīn′ *for noun*) **1** be favourable to; willing; tend: *Dogs incline to eat meat as a food.* **2** make favourable or willing; influence: *The prisoner's plea failed to incline the judge to reduce his sentence.* **3** a slope or slant: *There is quite an incline to that roof.* **4** slope; slant: *That roof inclines steeply.* **5** a sloping surface: *The side of a hill is an incline.* **6** lean; bend; bow. **1, 2, 4, 6** *v.,* **in·clined, in·clin·ing; 3, 5** *n.* **incline one's ear,** listen favourably.

**in·clined** (in klīnd′) **1** disposed; willing; tending: *I am inclined to agree with you.* **2** sloping; slanting. **3** pt. and pp. of INCLINE. **1, 2** *adj.,* **3** *v.*

**inclined plane** a plank or other plane surface put at an oblique angle with a horizontal surface.

**in·close** (in klōz′) ENCLOSE. *v.,* **in·closed, in·clos·ing.**

**in·clo·sure** (in klō′zhər) ENCLOSURE. *n.*

**in·clude** (in klüd′) **1** put, hold, or enclose within limits: *The price includes both house and furniture.* **2** contain; comprise: *The farm includes about 65 hectares.* **3** put in a total, a class, etc.; reckon in a count: *All on board the ship were lost, including the captain. v.,* **in·clud·ed, in·clud·ing.** —**in·clud′a·ble,** *adj.*

**in·clu·sion** (in klü′zhən) **1** an including. **2** being included. **3** the thing included. *n.*

**in·clu·sive** (in klü′siv) **1** including in consideration; including; comprising: *"Read pages 10 to 20 inclusive" means "Read pages 10 and 20 and all those in between."* **2** including much; including everything concerned: *Make an inclusive list of your expenses. adj.* —**in·clu′sive·ly,** *adv.* —**in·clu′sive·ness,** *n.* **inclusive of,** including; taking in; counting on.

**incog.** incognito.

**in·cog·ni·to** (in kog′nə tō′ *or* in′kog nē′tō) **1** with one's name, character, rank, etc. concealed: *The princess travelled incognito to avoid crowds and ceremonies.* **2** a person who is incognito. **3** a disguised state or condition: *Iain's incognito was not successful and he was recognized almost immediately.* **1** *adj., adv.,* **2, 3** *n., pl.* **in·cog·ni·tos.**

**in·co·her·ence** (in′kō hē′rəns) **1** a failure to stick together; looseness. **2** a lack of logical connection. **3** disconnected thought or speech: *the incoherence of a madman. n.*

**in·co·her·ent** (in′kō hē′rənt) **1** not sticking together. **2** disconnected; confused. *adj.* —**in′co·her′ent·ly,** *adv.*

---

**incivility**     **607**     **incompletely**

hat, āge, fär; let, ēqual, tèrm; it, īce
hot, ōpen, ôrder; oil, out; cup, put, rüle
əbove, takən, pencəl, lemən, circəs
ch, child; ng, long; sh, ship
th, thin; ŦH, then; zh, measure

**in·com·bus·ti·ble** (in′kəm bus′tə bəl) **1** that cannot be burned; fireproof. **2** an incombustible substance. **1** *adj.,* **2** *n.*

**in·come** (in′kum) what comes in from property, business, work, etc.; receipts; returns: *A person's yearly income is all the money that is earned in a year. n.*

**income tax** a government tax on a person's income.

**in·com·ing** (in′kum′ing) **1** coming in: *The incoming tenant will pay a higher rent.* **2** a coming in: *the incoming of the tide.* **1** *adj.,* **2** *n.*

**in·com·men·su·ra·ble** (in′kə men′shə rə bəl *or* in′kə men′sə rə bəl) **1** that cannot be compared because not measurable in the same units or by the same scale: *Furniture and human life are incommensurable.* **2** having no common integral divisor except 1: *The numbers 8, 17, and 11 are incommensurable. adj.* —**in′com·men′su·ra·bly,** *adv.*

**in·com·men·su·rate** (in′kə men′shə rit *or* in′kə men′sə rit) **1** not in proportion; not adequate: *strength incommensurate to a task.* **2** having no common measure; INCOMMENSURABLE. *adj.* —**in′com·men′su·rate·ly,** *adv.*

**in·com·mode** (in′kə mōd′) inconvenience; trouble. *v.,* **in·com·mod·ed, in·com·mod·ing.**

**in·com·mu·ni·ca·ble** (in′kə myü′nə kə bəl) not capable of being communicated or told. *adj.*

**in·com·mu·ni·ca·do** (in′kə myü′nə kä′dō) deprived of communication with others: *The prisoner was being held incommunicado. adj.*

**in·com·pa·ra·ble** (in kom′pə rə bəl, in kom′ prə bəl *or* in′kəm per′ə bəl) **1** without equal; matchless: *Helen of Troy had incomparable beauty.* **2** not to be compared; unsuitable for comparison. *adj.* —**in·com′pa·ra·bly,** *adv.*

**in·com·pat·i·bil·i·ty** (in′kəm pat′ə bil′ə tē) **1** the quality of being INCOMPATIBLE; lack of harmony. **2** an INCOMPATIBLE thing, quality, etc. *n., pl.* —**in·com·pat·i·bil·i·ties.**

**in·com·pat·i·ble** (in′kəm pat′ə bəl) **1** not able to live or act together peaceably; opposed in character: *My cats and dogs are incompatible.* **2** inconsistent: *Late hours are incompatible with health. adj.* —**in′com·pat′i·bly,** *adv.*

**in·com·pe·tence** (in kom′pə təns) **1** a lack of ability, power, or fitness: *The workman was discharged for incompetence.* **2** a lack of legal qualification. *n.*

**in·com·pe·tent** (in kom′pə tənt) **1** not competent; lacking ability, power, or fitness. **2** not legally qualified. **3** an incompetent person: *There were so many incompetents in the group that the whole project failed.* **1, 2** *adj.,* **3** *n.* —**in·com′pe·tent·ly,** *adv.*

**in·com·plete** (in′kəm plēt′) not complete; lacking some part; unfinished. *adj.* —**in′com·plete′ness,** *n.*

**in·com·plete·ly** (in′kəm plē′tlē) not fully; imperfectly. *adv.*

**in·com·pre·hen·si·bil·i·ty** (in′kom pri hen′sə bil′ə tē) the fact or quality of being INCOMPREHENSIBLE. *n.*

**in·com·pre·hen·si·ble** (in′kom pri hen′sə bəl) impossible to understand. *adj.* —**in′com·pre·hen′si·bly**, *adv.*

**in·com·press·i·ble** (in′kəm pres′ə bəl) not capable of being squeezed into a smaller size. *adj.*

**in·con·ceiv·a·bil·i·ty** (in′kən sē′və bil′ə tē) being INCONCEIVABLE. *n.*

**in·con·ceiv·a·ble** (in′kən sē′və bəl) **1** impossible to imagine: *A circle without a centre is inconceivable.* **2** hard to believe; incredible: *The new jet can travel at an inconceivable speed. adj.*

**in·con·ceiv·a·bly** (in′kən sē′və blē) **1** in an INCONCEIVABLE manner. **2** to an INCONCEIVABLE degree. *adv.*

**in·con·clu·sive** (in′kən klü′siv) not convincing; not settling or deciding something doubtful: *The jury, finding the evidence against the prisoner inconclusive, acquitted him. adj.* —**in′con·clu′sive·ly**, *adv.* —**in′con·clu′sive·ness**, *n.*

**in·con·gru·i·ty** (in′kən grü′ə tē) **1** unfitness; inappropriateness; being out of place. **2** a lack of agreement or harmony; inconsistency. **3** something that is INCONGRUOUS. *n., pl.* **in·con·gru·i·ties.**

**in·con·gru·ous** (in kong′grü əs) **1** out of keeping; not appropriate; out of place: *Heavy walking shoes would be incongruous with a party dress.* **2** lacking in agreement or harmony; not consistent. *adj.* —**in·con′gru·ous·ly**, *adv.* —**in·con′gru·ous·ness**, *n.*

**in·con·nu** (in′kə nyü′ *or* in′kə nü′) *Cdn.* a species of whitefish found in fresh water in northern Canada. *n., pl.* **in·con·nu** or **in·con·nus.**

**in·con·se·quence** (in kon′sə kwens′) a lack of logic or logical sequence; irrelevance; the state of being INCONSEQUENT. *n.*

**in·con·se·quent** (in kon′sə kwent′) **1** not logical; not logically connected: *an inconsequent argument.* **2** not to the point; off the subject: *an inconsequent remark.* **3** apt to think or talk without logical connection. *adj.* —**in·con′se·quent·ly**, *adv.*

**in·con·se·quen·tial** (in′kon sə kwen′shəl) **1** unimportant; trifling. **2** INCONSEQUENT. *adj.*

**in·con·sid·er·a·ble** (in′kən sid′ə rə bəl) not worthy of consideration; not important. *adj.* —**in′con·sid′er·a·bly**, *adv.*

**in·con·sid·er·ate** (in′kən sid′ə rit) **1** not thoughtful of the rights and feelings of others. **2** thoughtless; heedless. *adj.* —**in′con·sid′er·ate·ly**, *adv.* —**in′con·sid′er·ate·ness**, *n.*

**in·con·sist·en·cy** (in′kən sis′tən sē) **1** a lack of agreement or harmony; variance. **2** a failure to keep to the same principles, course of action, etc.; changeableness. **3** a thing, act, etc. that is inconsistent. *n., pl.* **in·con·sist·en·cies.**

**in·con·sist·ent** (in′kən sis′tənt) **1** lacking in agreement or harmony; at variance: *The policewoman's failure to arrest the criminal was inconsistent with her duty.* **2** lacking harmony between its different parts; not uniform. **3** failing to keep to the same principles, course of action, etc.; changeable: *An inconsistent person's opinions change frequently without reason. adj.* —**in′con·sist′ent·ly**, *adv.*

**in·con·sol·a·ble** (in′kən sō′lə bəl) not to be comforted; broken-hearted: *May was inconsolable at the loss of her kitten. adj.* —**in′con·sol′a·bly**, *adv.*

**in·con·so·nant** (in kon′sə nənt) not harmonious; not in agreement or accord. *adj.* —**in·con′so·nant·ly**, *adv.*

**in·con·spic·u·ous** (in′kən spik′yü əs) not conspicuous; attracting little or no attention: *The woman's dress was an inconspicuous grey. adj.* —**in′con·spic′u·ous·ly**, *adv.* —**in′con·spic′u·ous·ness**, *n.*

**in·con·stan·cy** (in kon′stən sē) a lack of constancy; changeableness; fickleness. *n.*

**in·con·stant** (in kon′stənt) not constant; changeable; fickle. *adj.* —**in·con′stant·ly**, *adv.*

**in·con·test·a·ble** (in′kən tes′tə bəl) not to be disputed; unquestionable. *adj.* —**in′con·test′a·bly**, *adv.*

**in·con·ti·nence** (in kon′tə nəns) **1** a lack of self-restraint. **2** a lack of chastity. *n.*

**in·con·ti·nent** (in kon′tə nənt) **1** without self-restraint. **2** not chaste; licentious. *adj.* —**in·con′ti·nent·ly**, *adv.*

**in·con·tro·vert·i·ble** (in′kon trə vėr′tə bəl) that cannot be disputed; too clear or certain to be argued about; unquestionable. *adj.* —**in′con·tro·vert′i·bly**, *adv.*

**in·con·ven·ience** (in′kən vē′nē əns *or* in′kən vē′nyəns) **1** a lack of convenience or ease; trouble; bother. **2** a cause of trouble, difficulty, or bother. **3** cause trouble, difficulty, etc. to: *Will it inconvenience you to carry this package for me?* 1, 2 *n.*, 3 *v.*, **in·con·ven·ienced, in·con·ven·ienc·ing.**

**in·con·ven·ient** (in′kən vē′nē ənt *or* in′kən vē′nyənt) not CONVENIENT; causing trouble, difficulty, or bother; troublesome. *adj.* —**in′con·ven′ient·ly**, *adv.*

**in·con·vert·i·bil·i·ty** (in′kən vėr′tə bil′ə tē) the condition of being INCONVERTIBLE. *n.*

**in·con·vert·i·ble** (in′kən vėr′tə bəl) not CONVERTIBLE; incapable of being converted or exchanged: *Paper money is inconvertible when it cannot be exchanged for gold or silver. adj.*

**in·cor·po·rate** (in kôr′pə rāt′ *for verb,* in kôr′pə rit *for adjective*) **1** make something a part of something else; join or combine something with something else: *We shall incorporate your suggestion in this new plan.* **2** form into a corporation: *When the business became large, the owners incorporated it.* **3** form a corporation. **4** unite or combine so as to form one body. **5** embody; give material form to: *to incorporate one's thoughts in an article.* **6** united; combined; incorporated. 1–5 *v.*, **in·cor·po·rat·ed, in·cor·po·rat·ing;** 6 *adj.*

**in·cor·po·ra·tion** (in kôr′pə rā′shən) **1** an incorporating: *The incorporation of air bubbles in the glass spoiled it.* **2** being INCORPORATED (def. 2): *Incorporation gives a company the power to act as one person. n.*

**in·cor·po·re·al** (in′kôr pô′rē əl) not made of any material substance; spiritual. *adj.* —**in′cor·po′re·al·ly**, *adv.*

**in·cor·rect** (in′kə rekt′) **1** containing errors or mistakes; wrong; faulty. **2** not proper. *adj.* —**in′cor·rect′ly**, *adv.* —**in′cor·rect′ness**, *n.*

**in·cor·ri·gi·bil·i·ty** (in kô′rə jə bil′ə tē) the state or quality of being INCORRIGIBLE. *n.*

**in·cor·ri·gi·ble** (in kô′rə jə bəl) **1** so firmly fixed in bad ways, a bad habit, etc. that nothing else can be expected: *an incorrigible liar.* **2** so fixed that it cannot be changed or cured: *an incorrigible habit of wrinkling one's nose.* **3** an incorrigible person. 1, 2 *adj.*, 3 *n.*
—**in·cor′ri·gi·bly,** *adv.*

**in·cor·rupt·i·ble** (in′kə rup′tə bəl) **1** not to be corrupted; honest: *The incorruptible woman could not be bribed.* **2** not capable of decay: *Diamonds are incorruptible.* *adj.* —**in′cor·rupt′i·bly,** *adv.*

**in·crease** (in krēs′ *for verb*, in′krēs *for noun*) **1** make greater or more numerous; make richer, more prosperous, or more powerful: *The driver increased the speed of the car.* **2** become greater; grow in numbers, especially by propagation; advance in quality, success, power, etc.: *The danger increases. The flowers will increase every year.* **3** a gain in size, numbers, etc.; growth: *an increase in our family. There was a great increase in student enrolment last year.* **4** an addition; the result of increasing; increased product. **5** the production of offspring. **6** offspring. 1, 2 *v.*, **in·creased, in·creas·ing;** 3–6 *n.*
**on the increase,** increasing: *The movement of people to the cities is on the increase.*

**in·creas·ing·ly** (in krē′sing lē) more and more: *As we travelled south, the weather became increasingly warm.* *adv.*

**in·cred·i·bil·i·ty** (in kred′ə bil′ə tē) the fact or quality of being INCREDIBLE. *n.*

**in·cred·i·ble** (in kred′ə bəl) seeming too extraordinary to be possible; unbelievable: *incredible bravery. It seems incredible that anyone could be so stupid.* *adj.*
—**in·cred′i·bly,** *adv.*
☛ *Syn.* Do not confuse **incredible** and INCREDULOUS. **Incredible** means unbelievable: *His story of having seen a ghost seemed incredible to his family.* **Incredulous** means not ready to believe; showing a lack of belief: *He told his incredulous father that he would show him the evidence that night.*

**in·cre·du·li·ty** (in′krə dyü′lə tē *or* in′krə dü′lə tē) lack of belief; doubt. *n.*

**in·cred·u·lous** (in krej′ə ləs) **1** not willing or likely to believe; not credulous; doubting: *Most people are incredulous about ghosts and witches.* **2** showing a lack of belief: *an incredulous smile.* *adj.*
—**in·cred′u·lous·ly,** *adv.*
☛ *Syn.* See note at INCREDIBLE.

**in·cre·ment** (in′krə mənt *or* ing′krə mənt) **1** an increase; growth. **2** the amount by which something increases: *The wages are $160 a week with an increment of $15 for each year of service.* *n.*

**in·crim·i·nate** (in krim′ə nāt′) accuse of a crime; show to be guilty: *In his confession the thief incriminated two others who helped him steal.* *v.*, **in·crim·i·nat·ed, in·crim·i·nat·ing.** —**in·crim′i·na′tion,** *n.*

**in·crim·i·na·to·ry** (in krim′ə nə tô′rē) tending to INCRIMINATE. *adj.*

**in·crust** (in krust′) **1** cover with a crust or hard coating: *The inside of the kettle is incrusted with lime.* **2** form a crust; form into a crust: *The extremely cold weather during the night had incrusted the snow so that next morning it would bear our weight.* **3** decorate with a layer of costly material: *The gold crown was incrusted with precious gems.* *v.* Also, **encrust.**

**in·crus·ta·tion** (in′krus tā′shən) **1** an incrusting.

**2** being incrusted. **3** a crust or hard coating. **4** a decorative layer of costly material. *n.*

**in·cu·bate** (in′kyə bāt′ *or* ing′kyə bāt′) **1** sit on eggs in order to hatch them; brood. **2** keep eggs, bacteria, etc. at a certain temperature so that they will hatch or grow. *v.*, **in·cu·bat·ed, in·cu·bat·ing.**

**in·cu·ba·tion** (in′kyə bā′shən *or* ing′kyə bā′shən) **1** an incubating. **2** being incubated. **3** the stage of a disease from the time of infection until the appearance of the first symptoms. *n.*

**in·cu·ba·tor** (in′kyə bā′tər *or* ing′kyə bā′tər) **1** an apparatus for keeping eggs warm so that they will hatch: *An incubator has a box or chamber that can be kept at a certain temperature.* **2** a similar apparatus for protecting babies born very small or prematurely. **3** an apparatus in which bacterial cultures are developed. *n.*

**in·cu·bus** (in′kyə bəs *or* ing′kyə bəs) **1** an evil spirit supposed to descend upon sleeping persons. **2** nightmare. **3** an oppressive or burdensome thing: *This debt will be an incubus until I have paid it.* *n.*, *pl.* **in·cu·bi** (-bī′ *or* -bē′) *or* **in·cu·bus·es.**

**in·cu·des** (in kyü′dēz) *pl.* of INCUS. *n.*

**in·cul·cate** (in kul′kāt, in′kəl kāt′ *or* ing′kəl kāt′) impress by repetition; teach persistently: *Week after week she inculcated good manners in her pupils.* *v.*, **in·cul·cat·ed, in·cul·cat·ing.** —**in·cul′ca·tor,** *n.*

**in·cul·ca·tion** (in′kul kā′shən) the act or process of impressing principles, etc. on the mind by persistent urging or teaching. *n.*

**in·cul·pate** (in kul′pāt) **1** blame; accuse. **2** involve in responsibility for wrongdoing; incriminate. *v.*, **in·cul·pat·ed, in·cul·pat·ing.**

**in·cum·ben·cy** (in kum′bən sē) the holding of an office, position, etc. and performance of its duties; term of office: *During his incumbency as mayor, the city prospered.* *n.*, *pl.* **in·cum·ben·cies.**

**in·cum·bent** (in kum′bənt) **1** lying, leaning, or pressing on. **2** resting on a person as a duty: *She felt it incumbent upon her to answer the letter at once.* **3** a person holding an office, position, church living, etc. 1, 2 *adj.*, 3 *n.*

**in·cum·ber** (in kum′bər) ENCUMBER. *v.*

**in·cum·brance** (in kum′brəns) ENCUMBRANCE. *n.*

**in·cur** (in kėr′) run into or meet with something unpleasant; bring on oneself: *incur many expenses. The explorers incurred great danger when they tried to cross the rapids.* *v.*, **in·curred, in·cur·ring.**

**in·cur·a·bil·i·ty** (in kyü′rə bil′ə tē) being INCURABLE. *n.*

**in·cur·a·ble** (in kyü′rə bəl) **1** not capable of being cured or remedied: *an incurable disease.* **2** a person having an incurable disease: *That building is a home for incurables.* 1 *adj.*, 2 *n.* —**in·cur′a·bly,** *adv.*

**in·cur·sion** (in kėr′zhən) **1** an invasion; raid; sudden attack: *The pirates made incursions along the coast.* **2** a running or flowing in: *Dikes protected the lowland from incursions of the sea.* *n.*

**in·cur·sive** (in kėr′siv) making incursions. *adj.*

**in·curve** (in′kėrv′) a baseball pitched so that it curves toward the batter. *n.*

**in·cus** (ing′kəs) the middle one of a chain of three small bones in the middle ear of human beings and other animals: *The incus is shaped somewhat like an anvil.* See EAR[1] for picture. *n.*, *pl.* **in·cu·des** (in kyü′dēz).

**ind.** 1 independent. 2 indicative. 3 industrial. 4 index. 5 indirect.

**Ind.** 1 India. 2 Indian. 3 in politics, Independent.

**in·debt·ed** (in det′id) in debt; obliged; owing money or gratitude: *We are indebted to scientists for many of our comforts.* *adj.*

**in·debt·ed·ness** (in det′id nis) 1 the condition of being in debt. 2 the amount owed; debts. *n.*

**in·de·cen·cy** (in dē′sən sē) 1 lack of decency; being indecent. 2 an indecent act or word. *n.*, *pl.* **in·de·cen·cies**.

**in·de·cent** (in dē′sənt) 1 not decent; in very bad taste; improper: *He showed an indecent lack of gratitude to the woman who had saved his life.* 2 not modest; morally bad; disgusting; obscene. *adj.* —**in·de′cent·ly**, *adv.*

**in·de·ci·pher·a·ble** (in′di sī′fə rə bəl) incapable of being deciphered; illegible. *adj.*

**in·de·ci·sion** (in′di sizh′ən) a lack of decision; tendency to delay or to hesitate; tendency to put off deciding or to change one's mind. *n.*

**in·de·ci·sive** (in′di sī′siv) 1 having the habit of hesitating and putting off decisions. 2 not deciding or settling the matter: *an indecisive battle.* *adj.* —**in′de·ci′sive·ly**, *adv.* —**in′de·ci′sive·ness**, *n.*

**in·de·clin·a·ble** (in′di klī′nə bəl) not changing its spelling for changes in grammatical use: *"None" is an indeclinable pronoun.* *adj.*

**in·dec·o·rous** (in dek′ə rəs *or* in′di kô′rəs) not suitable; improper; unseemly. *adj.* —**in·dec′o·rous·ly**, *adv.* —**in·dec′o·rous·ness**, *n.*

**in·de·co·rum** (in′di kô′rəm) 1 a lack of DECORUM. 2 improper behaviour, speech, dress, etc. *n.*

**in·deed** (in dēd′) 1 in fact; really; truly; surely: *She is hungry; indeed, she is almost starving. War is indeed terrible.* 2 an expression of surprise, doubt, contempt, etc.: *Indeed! I would not have done it.* 1 *adv.*, 2 *interj.*

**indef.** indefinite.

**in·de·fat·i·ga·bil·i·ty** (in′di fat′ə gə bil′ə tē) the state or quality of being INDEFATIGABLE; tirelessness. *n.*

**in·de·fat·i·ga·ble** (in′di fat′ə gə bəl) never getting tired or giving up; tireless: *an indefatigable worker.* *adj.* —**in′de·fat′i·ga·bly**, *adv.*

**in·de·fea·si·ble** (in′di fē′zə bəl) not to be annulled or made void: *Kings were once believed to have an indefeasible right to rule.* *adj.* —**in′de·fea′si·bly**, *adv.*

**in·de·fen·si·ble** (in′di fen′sə bəl) 1 that cannot be defended: *an indefensible island.* 2 not justifiable: *an indefensible lie.* *adj.* —**in′de·fen′si·bly**, *adv.*

**in·de·fin·a·ble** (in′di fī′nə bəl) that cannot be defined. *adj.* —**in′de·fin′a·bly**, *adv.*

**in·def·i·nite** (in def′ə nit) 1 not clearly defined; not precise; vague: *"Maybe" is a very indefinite answer.* 2 not limited: *We have an indefinite time to finish this work.* 3 not specifying precisely: *An indefinite adjective, pronoun, etc. does not determine the person, thing, time, etc. to which it refers.* Some, many, *and* few *are often indefinite pronouns.* *adj.* —**in·def′i·nite·ly**, *adv.* —**in·def′i·nite·ness**, *n.*

**indefinite article** either of the articles **a** or **an**.
☛ *Usage.* A dog or *an* animal means *any* dog or *any* animal; *the* dog means *a certain or particular* dog.

**in·de·his·cent** (in′di his′ənt) not opening at maturity: *Acorns are indehiscent fruits.* *adj.*

**in·del·i·bil·i·ty** (in del′ə bil′ə tē) the fact or quality of being INDELIBLE; permanence. *n.*

**in·del·i·ble** (in del′ə bəl) 1 that cannot be erased or removed; permanent: *indelible ink, an indelible impression.* 2 capable of making an indelible mark: *an indelible pencil.* *adj.* —**in·del′i·bly**, *adv.*

**in·del·i·ca·cy** (in del′ə kə sē) a lack of delicacy; being INDELICATE. *n.*, *pl.* **in·del·i·ca·cies**.

**in·del·i·cate** (in del′ə kit) 1 not delicate; coarse; crude. 2 improper; immodest. *adj.* —**in·del′i·cate·ly**, *adv.*

**in·dem·ni·fi·ca·tion** (in dem′nə fə kā′shən) 1 an INDEMNIFYing. 2 being indemnified. 3 compensation; recompense. *n.*

**in·dem·ni·fy** (in dem′nə fī′) 1 repay; make good; compensate for damage, loss, or expense incurred: *She promised to indemnify me for my losses.* 2 secure against damage or loss; insure. *v.*, **in·dem·ni·fied**, **in·dem·ni·fy·ing**.

**in·dem·ni·ty** (in dem′nə tē) 1 the payment for damage, loss, or expense incurred: *Money demanded by a victorious nation at the end of a war as a condition of peace is an indemnity.* 2 a security against damage or loss; insurance. 3 in Canada, the remuneration of an MP or MLA. *n.*, *pl.* **in·dem·ni·ties**.

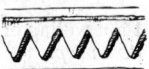 Indented moulding

**in·dent**[1] (in dent′ *for verb,* in′dent *or* in dent′ *for noun*) 1 make or form notches or jags in an edge, line, border, etc.: *an indented coastline. The rim of the plate was indented.* 2 a notch; indentation. 3 begin a line farther from the edge of a page than the other lines: *We usually indent the first line of a paragraph.* 1, 3 *v.*, 2 *n.*
☛ *Etym.* From Norman French *endenter* 'make a toothlike cut in'. Indenting was used for contracts or deeds that were made up in two or more copies, with each copy having an identical cut in the margin.

**in·dent**[2] (in dent′) 1 make a dent in; mark with a dent. 2 press in; stamp. *v.*

**in·den·ta·tion** (in′den tā′shən) 1 an INDENTing or being indented. 2 a dent; notch; cut. 3 INDENTION (defs 1, 2). *n.*

**in·den·tion** (in den′shən) 1 a beginning of one line farther from the edge of a page than the other lines. 2 the blank space left by doing this. 3 INDENTATION (defs. 1, 2). *n.*

**in·den·ture** (in den′chər) 1 a written agreement. 2 a contract by which a person is bound to serve someone else.   **3** bind by a contract to serve someone else: *Many persons came to the colonies indentured for several years.*   **4** INDENTATION (def. 2).   1, 2, 4 *n.*, 3 *v.*, **in·den·tured, in·den·tur·ing.**

**in·de·pend·ence** (in′di pen′dəns)   **1** freedom from the control, influence, support, or help of another: *Many African nations have recently achieved independence.*   **2** enough to live on.   *n.*

**Independence Day**   *U.S.*   the Fourth of July, a holiday in the United States, celebrating the adoption of the Declaration of Independence on July 4, 1776.

**in·de·pend·en·cy** (in′di pen′dən sē)   **1** INDEPENDENCE.   **2** an independent country.   *n., pl.* **in·de·pend·en·cies.**

**in·de·pend·ent** (in′di pen′dənt)   **1** not needing, wanting or getting help from others; not connected with others: *independent work, independent thinking.*   **2** not influenced by others; thinking or acting for oneself: *An independent person votes as he or she pleases.*   **3** guiding, ruling, or governing oneself; not under another's rule: *Canada is an independent member of the Commonwealth of Nations.*   **4** not depending on others: *Filippa Bauer has an independent fortune.*   **5** not resulting from another thing; not controlled or influenced by something else; separate; distinct.   **6** a person who is independent in thought or behaviour, especially one who votes without regard to party.   **7 Independent,** a person who stands for election to, or is an elected member of, a legislature without being a representative of any political party. 1–5 *adj.*, 6, 7 *n.*
**independent of,** apart from; without regard to: *independent of the feelings of others.*

**in·de·pend·ent·ly** (in′di pen′dən tlē)   in an INDEPENDENT manner.   *adv.*
**independently of,** apart from; without regard to.

**in·de·scrib·a·ble** (in′di skrī′bə bəl)   that cannot be described; beyond description: *a scene of indescribable beauty.*   *adj.*  —**in′de·scrib′a·bly,** *adv.*

**in·de·struct·i·bil·i·ty** (in′di struk′tə bil′ə tē)   being INDESTRUCTIBLE.   *n.*

**in·de·struct·i·ble** (in′di struk′tə bəl)   that cannot be destroyed: *Some toys are almost indestructible in ordinary use.*   *adj.*  —**in′de·struct′i·bly,** *adv.*

**in·de·ter·mi·na·ble** (in′di tėr′mə nə bəl)   **1** not capable of being settled or decided.   **2** not capable of being found out exactly.   *adj.*
—**in′de·ter′mi·na·bly,** *adv.*

**in·de·ter·mi·nate** (in′di tėr′mə nit)   not DETERMINED; not fixed; indefinite; vague.   *adj.*
—**in′de·ter′mi·nate·ly,** *adv.*

**in·de·ter·mi·na·tion** (in′di tėr′mə nā′shən)   **1** a lack of DETERMINATION.   **2** an unsettled state.   *n.*

**in·dex** (in′deks)   **1** a list of the contents of a book, giving page, paragraph, or section references for each of the subjects discussed: *The index is usually put at the end of a book and is arranged in alphabetical order.*   **2** provide with an index; make an index of.   **3** work at an index; prepare an index.   **4** enter in an index.   **5** something that points out or shows; a sign: *A man's face is often an index of his mood.*   **6** the index finger.   **7** pointer: *A dial or scale usually has an index.*   **8** in printing, a sign (☛) used to point out a particular note, paragraph, etc.   **9** in science, a number or formula expressing some property, ratio, etc.   **10** in mathematics, the number indicating the root: *In $\sqrt[3]{764}$ the index is 3.*   1, 5–10 *n., pl.* **in·dex·es** or **in·dic·es;** 2–4 *v.*

# independence 611 indicate

hat, āge, fär; let, ēqual, tėrm; it, īce
hot, ōpen, ôrder; oil, out; cup, pùt, rüle
əbove, takən, pencəl, lemən, circəs
ch, child; ng, long; sh, ship
th, thin; ᴛʜ, then; zh, measure

**index finger**   the finger next to the thumb; forefinger. See ARM¹ for picture.

**India ink**   **1** a black pigment consisting of lampblack mixed with a binding material and moulded into sticks or cakes: *India ink is made chiefly in China and Japan.*   **2** a liquid ink prepared from this pigment.

**In·di·an** (in′dē ən)   **1** a member of the race of people that was living in North and South America long before the Europeans came; an American Indian.   **2** of or having to do with American Indians: *Indian blankets, Indian sign language.*   **3** any one of the languages of the American Indians.   **4** made of INDIAN CORN or maize: *Indian pudding.*   **5** a native or inhabitant of India, a country in S. Asia, or of the East Indies, the islands of the Malay Archipelago.   **6** of, living in, or belonging to India or the East Indies: *Indian elephants, Indian temples.*   1, 3, 5 *n.*, 2, 4, 6 *adj.*

**Indian agent**   formerly, in Canada, an official of the federal government who looks after Indian affairs on a reservation, etc.

**Indian club**   a bottle-shaped wooden club that is swung for exercise.

**Indian corn**   **1** a variety of cereal grass first raised by American Indians; maize: *Various forms of Indian corn have been developed, such as sweet corn and popcorn.*   **2** grain or ears of this plant.

**Indian file**   single file.

**Indian ink**   INDIA INK.

**Indian paintbrush**   any of various wild plants having spikes of flowers and showy, bright scarlet or orange leaves just below the flowers.

**Indian pipe**   a leafless plant having a solitary flower that looks like a tobacco pipe.

**Indian summer**   a time of mild, dry, hazy weather in October or early November, after the first frosts of autumn.

**Indian tobacco**   a weed having small blue flowers and swollen capsules, used in medicine.

**Indian turnip**   JACK-IN-THE-PULPIT.

**India paper**   **1** a thin, tough paper, used for Bibles, prayer books, etc.   **2** a thin, soft paper, used for the first or finest impressions of engravings, etc.

**India rubber** or **india rubber**   a substance of great elasticity obtained from the coagulated, milky juice of various tropical plants; rubber.

**indic.**   indicative.

**Indic** (in′dik)   **1** of or having to do with India; Indian. **2** of or having to do with the Indian branch of the Indo-Iranian languages.   *adj.*

**in·di·cate** (in′də kāt′)   **1** point out; point to: *The arrow on the sign indicates the right way to go.*   **2** show; make known: *A thermometer indicates temperature.*   **3** be a sign or hint of: *Fever indicates sickness.*   **4** give a sign or hint of: *A dog indicates its feelings by growling, whining, barking* *or wagging its tail.* **5** show to be needed as a remedy or treatment. *v.*, **in·di·cat·ed, in·di·cat·ing.**

**in·di·ca·tion** (in′də kā′shən) **1** an indicating. **2** something that indicates; sign: *There was no indication of rain.* **3** the amount or degree indicated: *The speedometer indication was 80 km/h.* *n.*

**in·dic·a·tive** (in dik′ə tiv) **1** pointing out; showing; being a sign of; suggestive: *A headache is sometimes indicative of eye strain.* **2** of a verb, expressing or denoting a state, act, or happening as actual; asking a question of simple fact: *In "I go" and "Did I go?" the verbs are in the indicative mood.* **3** the indicative mood. **4** a verb form in this mood. 1, 2 *adj.*, 3, 4 *n.* —**in·dic′a·tive·ly**, *adv.*

**indicative mood** in grammar, the form of the verb used to show that something is a fact: *Close the door is in the imperative mood. You closed the door is in the indicative mood.*

**in·di·ca·tor** (in′də kā′tər) **1** a person or thing that indicates. **2** the pointer on the dial of an instrument that measures something. **3** a measuring or recording instrument. **4** a substance used to indicate chemical conditions or changes: *Litmus is an indicator.* *n.*

**in·di·ces** (in′də sēz′) a pl. of INDEX. *n.*

**in·dict** (in dīt′) **1** charge with an offence or crime; accuse. **2** of a grand jury, find enough evidence against an accused person to justify a trial. *v.* —**in·dict′er, in·dict′or,** *n.*
☛ *Hom.* INDITE.

**in·dict·a·ble** (indī′tə bəl) **1** making a person liable to be INDICTED: *an indictable offence.* **2** liable to be INDICTED. *adj.*

**indictable offence** a crime, such as armed robbery or murder, that is more serious than a SUMMARY OFFENCE: *A person charged with an indictable offence in Canada may be arrested without a warrant and may be fingerprinted and photographed for police records.*

**in·dict·ment** (in dīt′mənt) **1** a formal accusation, especially the legal accusation presented by a grand jury. **2** accusation. *n.*

**in·dif·fer·ence** (in dif′ə rəns *or* in dif′rəns) **1** a lack of interest or attention: *The boy's indifference to schoolwork worried his parents.* **2** little or no importance: *Where we ate was a matter of indifference.* *n.*

**in·dif·fer·ent** (in dif′ə rənt *or* in dif′rənt) **1** having no feeling for or against; having or showing no interest: *indifferent to an admirer. Rose enjoyed the trip but Sue was indifferent.* **2** impartial; neutral; without preference: *an indifferent decision.* **3** unimportant; not mattering much: *The time for starting is indifferent to me.* **4** not bad, but less than good; just fair: *an indifferent ballplayer.* **5** rather bad. **6** neutral chemically, magnetically, or electrically: *A substance that gives no acid or alkaline reaction is indifferent.* *adj.* —**in·dif′fer·ent·ly**, *adv.*

**in·di·gence** (in′də jəns) poverty. *n.*

**in·dig·e·nous** (in dij′ə nəs) **1** originating or produced in a particular country; growing or living naturally in a certain region, soil, climate, etc.; native: *Musk-ox are indigenous to Canada.* **2** innate; inherent. *adj.* —**in·dig′e·nous·ly**, *adv.*

**in·di·gent** (in′də jənt) poor; needy. *adj.* —**in′di·gent·ly**, *adv.*

**in·di·gest·i·bil·i·ty** (in′də jes′tə bil′ə tē) an INDIGESTIBLE nature or quality. *n.*

**in·di·gest·i·ble** (in′də jes′tə bəl) that cannot be properly digested; hard to DIGEST. *adj.*

**in·di·ges·tion** (in′də jes′chən) inability to digest food properly; pain resulting from difficulty in digesting food: *I ate too quickly and have been suffering from indigestion as a result.* *n.*

**in·dig·nant** (in dig′nənt) angry at something unworthy, unjust, or mean. *adj.* —**in·dig′nant·ly**, *adv.*

**in·dig·na·tion** (in′dig nā′shən) anger at something unworthy, unjust, or mean; anger mixed with scorn; righteous anger: *Cruelty to animals arouses indignation.* *n.*

**in·dig·ni·ty** (in dig′nə tē) an injury to dignity; lack of respect or proper treatment; insult. *n., pl.* **in·dig·ni·ties.**

**in·di·go** (in′də gō′) **1** a blue dye formerly obtained from certain plants, but now usually made artificially. **2** any plant from which indigo is obtained. **3** deep violet-blue. 1–3 *n., pl.* **in·di·gos** *or* **in·di·goes**; 3 *adj.*

**indigo bunting** a small North American finch. The male is a deep violet-blue; the female is brown.

**in·di·rect** (in′də rekt′ *or* in′dī rekt′) **1** not direct; not straight: *an indirect route.* **2** not directly connected; secondary: *Happiness is an indirect consequence of doing one's work well.* **3** not straightforward and to the point: *The witness gave an indirect answer to the lawyer's question instead of a frank "Yes" or "No."* **4** dishonest; deceitful: *indirect methods.* *adj.* —**in′di·rect′ly**, *adv.* —**in′di·rect′ness**, *n.*

**indirect discourse** the repetition of the substance of a person's speech without directly quoting it. *Example:* "*He said that he would come,*" instead of "*He said, 'I will come.'*" Compare with DIRECT DISCOURSE.

**in·di·rec·tion** (in′də rek′shən *or* in′dī rek′shən) **1** a roundabout act, means, or method. **2** dishonesty; deceit. *n.*

**indirect object** with verbs of saying, giving or showing, the person or thing to which something is said, given, or shown. The indirect object usually comes before the direct object and shows to whom or for whom something is done. *Example: In "I gave Lettie a book,"* Lettie *is the indirect object, and* book *is the direct object.* Compare with DIRECT OBJECT.

**indirect question** a question reported indirectly. *Example: She asked when they had arrived.* Compare with DIRECT QUESTION.

**indirect tax** a tax paid indirectly by the consumer and included in the price of an article.

**in·dis·cern·i·ble** (in′də sėr′nə bəl *or* in′də zėr′nə bəl) not DISCERNIBLE; imperceptible. *adj.*

**in·dis·creet** (in′di skrēt′) not discreet; not wise and judicious; imprudent: *The boy's indiscreet remark made the stranger feel insulted.* *adj.* —**in′dis·creet′ly**, *adv.* —**in′dis·creet′ness**, *n.*

**in·dis·cre·tion** (in′di skresh′ən) **1** being INDISCREET; lack of good judgment; imprudence. **2** an INDISCREET act. *n.*

**in·dis·crim·i·nate** (in′di skrim′ə nit) **1** confused: *Mervyn tipped everything out of his suitcase in an* *indiscriminate mass.* **2** not discriminating; not with feeling for differences: *She is an indiscriminate reader and likes both good books and bad ones.* *adj.* —**in′dis·crim′i·nate·ly**, *adv.*

**in·dis·pen·sa·bil·i·ty** (in′di spen′sə bil′ə tē) the state or quality of being INDISPENSABLE; absolute necessity. *n.*

**in·dis·pen·sa·ble** (in′di spen′sə bəl) absolutely necessary: *Air is indispensable to life.* *adj.*

**in·dis·pen·sa·bly** (in′di spen′sə blē) to an INDISPENSABLE degree; necessarily. *adv.*

**in·dis·pose** (in′di spōz′) **1** make unwilling; make averse: *Hot weather indisposes a person to work hard.* **2** make slightly ill. **3** make unfit or unable. *v.*, **in·dis·posed, in·dis·pos·ing.**

**in·dis·posed** (in′di spōzd′) **1** slightly ill. **2** unwilling; without inclination; averse: *The men were indisposed to work nights.* *adj.*

**in·dis·po·si·tion** (in′dis pə zish′ən) **1** a disturbance of health; slight illness. **2** an unwillingness; disinclination. *n.*

**in·dis·put·a·bil·i·ty** (in′di spyü′tə bil′ə tē *or* in dis′pyə tə bil′ə tē) being INDISPUTABLE. *n.*

**in·dis·put·a·ble** (in′di spyü′tə bəl *or* in dis′pyə tə bəl) not to be DISPUTEd; undoubtedly true; unquestionable. *adj.* —**in′dis·put′a·bly**, *adv.*

**in·dis·sol·u·bil·i·ty** (in′di sol′yə bil′ə tē) being INDISSOLUBLE; stability. *n.*

**in·dis·sol·u·ble** (in′di sol′yə bəl) not capable of being DISSOLVEd, undone, or destroyed; lasting; firm. *adj.* —**in′dis·sol′u·bly**, *adv.*

**in·dis·tinct** (in′di stingkt′) not DISTINCT; not clear to the eye, ear, or mind; confused: *an indistinct picture. We could hear an indistinct roar from the distant ocean.* *adj.* —**in′dis·tinct′ly**, *adv.* —**in′dis·tinct′ness**, *n.*

**in·dis·tin·guish·a·ble** (in′di sting′gwi shə bəl) that cannot be DISTINGUISHed: *Her writing is indistinguishable from her printing.* *adj.*

**in·dite** (in dīt′) put in words or writing; compose: *to indite a letter.* *v.*, **in·dit·ed, in·dit·ing.**
☛ Hom. INDICT.

**in·di·um** (in′dē əm) a rare metallic element that is soft, white, malleable, and easily fusible. Symbol: In *n.*

**in·di·vid·u·al** (in′də vij′ü əl) **1** person: *Joanna is a tall individual.* **2** one person, animal, or thing: *We saw a herd of giraffes containing 30 individuals.* **3** single; particular; separate: *an individual question.* **4** for one only: *We use individual salt-cellars.* **5** having to do with or peculiar to one person or thing: *individual tastes.* **6** marking off one person or thing specially: *Alice has an individual style of handwriting.* 1, 2 *n.*, 3–6 *adj.*
☛ Syn. See note at PERSON.

**in·di·vid·u·al·ism** (in′də vij′ü ə liz′əm) **1** a theory that individual freedom is as important as the welfare of the community or group as a whole. **2** any ethical, economic, or political theory that emphasizes the importance of individuals. **3** each for himself; the absence of co-operation; wanting a separate existence for oneself. **4** INDIVIDUALITY. *n.*

**in·di·vid·u·al·ist** (in′də vij′ü ə list) **1** one who goes his or her own way, independent of the views of others. **2** a supporter of INDIVIDUALISM. *n.*

**indispensability** 613 **indorse**

hat, āge, fär; let, ēqual, tėrm; it, īce
hot, ōpen, ôrder; oil, out; cup, pùt, rüle
əbove, takən, pencəl, lemən, circəs

ch, child; ng, long; sh, ship
th, thin; ᴛʜ, then; zh, measure

**in·di·vid·u·al·is·tic** (in′də vij′ü ə lis′tik) of INDIVIDUALISM or INDIVIDUALISTS. *adj.*

**in·di·vid·u·al·i·ty** (in′də vij′ü al′ə tē) **1** individual character; the sum of the qualities that make one person or thing different from another. **2** the condition of being individual; existence as an individual. **3** an individual person or thing. *n., pl.* **in·di·vid·u·al·i·ties.**

**in·di·vid·u·al·ize** (in′də vij′ü ə līz′) **1** make individual; cause to be different from others; give a distinctive character to. **2** consider as individuals; list one by one; specify. *v.*, **in·di·vid·u·al·ized, in·di·vid·u·al·iz·ing.**

**in·di·vid·u·al·ly** (in′də vij′ü ə lē) **1** personally; one at a time; as individuals: *The teacher helps us individually.* **2** each from the others: *People differ individually.* *adv.*

**in·di·vis·i·bil·i·ty** (in′də viz′ə bil′ə tē) the state or quality of being INDIVISIBLE. *n.*

**in·di·vis·i·ble** (in′də viz′ə bəl) **1** not capable of being divided. **2** not capable of being divided without a remainder. *adj.* —**in′di·vis′i·bly**, *adv.*

**In·do–Chi·nese** (in′dō chī nēz′) **1** a native or inhabitant of Indochina, a historical name for either the peninsula south of China that includes Burma, Thailand, Laos, Cambodia, and Vietnam, or the eastern part of this peninsula. **2** of or having to do with Indochina or the Indo-Chinese. 1 *n.*, 2 *adj.*

**in·doc·tri·nate** (in dok′trə nāt′) **1** teach a doctrine, belief, or principle to. **2** teach. *v.*, **in·doc·tri·nat·ed, in·doc·tri·nat·ing.** —**in·doc′tri·na′tion**, *n.*

**In·do–Eu·ro·pe·an** (in′dō yü′rə pē′ən) **1** of India and Europe. **2** of or having to do with a group of related languages spoken in India, western Asia, and Europe: *English, German, Latin, Greek, Persian, and Sanskrit are Indo-European languages.* *adj.*

**in·do·lence** (in′də ləns) laziness; dislike of work; idleness. *n.*

**in·do·lent** (in′də lənt) lazy; disliking work. *adj.* —**in′do·lent·ly**, *adv.*

**in·dom·i·ta·ble** (in dom′ə tə bəl) unconquerable; unyielding: *indomitable courage.* *adj.* —**in·dom′i·ta·bly**, *adv.*

**In·do·ne·sian** (in′dō nē′zhən *or* in′dō nē′shən) **1** a native or inhabitant of Indonesia, a country in SE Asia. **2** Bahasa Indonesia, the official language of Indonesia. **3** a member of a people supposed to have been dominant on the Malay Archipelago before the Malays. **4** of or having to do with Indonesia, its people, or their language. 1–3 *n.*, 4 *adj.*

**in·door** (in′dôr) **1** done, played, used, etc. in a house or building: *indoor tennis, indoor skating.* **2** that is indoors: *an indoor rink.* *adj.*

**in·doors** (in dôrz′) in or into a house or building: *to go indoors.* *adv.*

**in·dorse** (in dôrs′) ENDORSE. *v.*, **in·dorsed, in·dors·ing.**

**in·draft** (in′draft′) **1** a drawing in. **2** an inward flow or current of water, air, etc. *n.*

**in·du·bi·ta·ble** (in dyü′bə tə bəl *or* in dü′bə tə bəl) not to be doubted; certain: *Laziness was an indubitable cause of his failure.* *adj.* —**in·du′bi·ta·bly,** *adv.*

**in·duce** (in dyüs′ *or* in düs′) **1** lead on; influence; persuade: *Advertising induces people to buy.* **2** cause; bring about: *Some drugs induce sleep.* **3** produce an electric current, electric charge, or magnetic change without direct contact. **4** infer by reasoning from particular facts to a general rule or principle. *v.*, **in·duced, in·duc·ing.**

**in·duce·ment** (in dyü′smənt *or* in dü′smənt) something that influences or persuades; incentive: *Prizes are inducements to try hard to win.* *n.*

**in·duct** (in dukt′) **1** bring in; introduce into a place, seat, position, office, etc. **2** put formally into a position, office, etc.: *They proposed to induct him as secretary.* **3** *Esp. U.S.* take into the armed services. **4** INITIATE. *v.*

**in·duct·ance** (in duk′təns) the property of an electrical conductor or circuit that makes INDUCTION (def. 1) possible. *n.*

**in·duc·tion** (in duk′shən) **1** the process by which an object having electrical or magnetic properties produces similar properties in a nearby object, without direct contact. **2** the act of reasoning from particular facts to a general rule or principle. Compare with DEDUCTION (def. 3). **3** the conclusion reached in this way. **4** the act of inducting; act or ceremony of installing a person in office. *n.*

**induction coil** a device for producing a high, pulsating voltage from a current of low, steady voltage, such as from a battery.

**in·duc·tive** (in duk′tiv) **1** of or using INDUCTION (def. 2); reasoning by induction. **2** having to do with electrical or magnetic INDUCTION (def. 1). *adj.* —**in·duc′tive·ly,** *adv.*

**in·duc·tor** (in duk′tər) **1** a person who inducts another into office. **2** a part of an electrical apparatus that works or is worked by INDUCTION (def. 1). *n.*

**in·due** (in dyü′ *or* in dü′) ENDUE. *v.*, **in·dued, in·du·ing.**

**in·dulge** (in dulj′) **1** yield to the wishes of; humour: *We often indulge a sick person.* **2** give in to one's pleasures; let oneself have, use, or do what one wants: *He indulges in tobacco.* **3** give in to; let oneself have, use, or do: *She indulged her fondness for candy by eating a whole box.* *v.*, **in·dulged, in·dulg·ing.** —**in·dulg′ing·ly,** *adv.*

**in·dul·gence** (in dul′jəns) **1** yielding to the wishes of another or allowing oneself one's own desires. **2** something indulged in. **3** a favour or privilege. *n.*

**in·dul·gent** (in dul′jənt) **1** giving in to another's wishes or whims; too kind or agreeable: *The indulgent mother bought her boy everything he wanted.* **2** lenient; making allowances; not critical: *Our indulgent teacher praised every poem we wrote.* *adj.* —**in·dul′gent·ly,** *adv.*

**in·du·rate** (in′dyə rāt′ *or* in′dü rāt′ *for verb,* in′dyə rit *or* in′dü rit *for adjective*) **1** harden. **2** hardened. **3** make or become unfeeling. **4** unfeeling. 1, 3 *v.*, **in·du·rat·ed, in·du·rat·ing;** 2, 4 *adj.*

**in·dus·tri·al** (in dus′trē əl) **1** of or resulting from industry or productive labour: *industrial products.* **2** having to do with or connected with an industry or industries: *an industrial exhibition, industrial workers.* **3** of or having to do with the workers in industries: *industrial insurance.* *adj.* —**in·dus′tri·al·ly,** *adv.*

**in·dus·tri·al·ism** (in dus′trē ə liz′əm) a system of social and economic organization in which large industries are very important and industrial activities or interests prevail. *n.*

**in·dus·tri·al·ist** (in dus′trē ə list) **1** a person who conducts or owns an industrial enterprise. **2** an industrial worker. *n.*

**in·dus·tri·al·i·za·tion** (in dus′trē ə lə zā′shən *or* in dus′trē ə lī zā′shən) the development of large industries as an important feature in a country or a social or economic system. *n.*

**in·dus·tri·al·ize** (in dus′trē ə līz′) **1** make industrial. **2** organize as an industry. *v.*, **in·dus·tri·al·ized, in·dus·tri·al·iz·ing.**

**Industrial Revolution** the change from an agricultural to an industrial civilization that took place in England from about the middle of the 18th century to the middle of the 19th century, and later in other countries.

**in·dus·tri·ous** (in dus′trē əs) working hard and steadily: *An industrious student usually has good marks.* *adj.* —**in·dus′tri·ous·ly,** *adv.* —**in·dus′tri·ous·ness,** *n.*

**in·dus·try** (in′də strē) **1** any branch of business, trade, or manufacture: *the steel industry, the automobile industry.* **2** all such enterprises taken collectively: *Canadian industry is expanding.* **3** the production of goods; manufacturing in general: *He would rather be a professor than work in industry.* **4** systematic work or labour. **5** steady effort; close attention to work: *Industry and thrift favour success.* *n., pl.* **in·dus·tries.**

**in·dwell·ing** (in′dwel′ing) dwelling within. *adj.*

**in·e·bri·ate** (i nē′brē āt′ *for verb,* i nē′brē it *for noun and adjective*) **1** make drunk; intoxicate. **2** a habitual drunkard; intoxicated person. **3** intoxicated; drunk. 1 *v.*, **in·e·bri·at·ed, in·e·bri·at·ing;** 2 *n.*, 3 *adj.*

**in·e·bri·a·tion** (i nē′brē ā′shən) drunkenness; intoxication. *n.*

**in·e·bri·e·ty** (in′i brī′ə tē) drunkenness. *n.*

**in·ed·i·ble** (i ned′ə bəl) not fit to eat: *Some toadstools are inedible.* *adj.*

**in·ef·fa·ble** (i nef′ə bəl) not to be expressed in words; too great to be described in words: *the ineffable beauty of a sunset.* *adj.* —**in·ef′fa·bly,** *adv.*

**in·ef·face·a·ble** (in′ə fā′sə bəl) that cannot be rubbed out or wiped out. *adj.* —**in·ef·face′a·bly,** *adv.*

**in·ef·fec·tive** (in′ə fek′tiv) **1** not producing the desired effect; of little use: *An ineffective medicine fails to cure a disease or relieve pain.* **2** unfit for work; incapable. *adj.* —**in·ef·fec′tive·ly,** *adv.* —**in·ef·fec′tive·ness,** *n.*

**in·ef·fec·tu·al** (in′ə fek′chü əl) **1** failing to have the effect wanted; useless: *The searchlights were ineffectual in the fog.* **2** not able to produce the effect wanted; powerless. *adj.* —**in′ef·fec′tu·al·ly,** *adv.*

**in·ef·fi·ca·cious** (in′ef ə kā′shəs) not EFFICACIOUS; not able to produce the effect wanted. *adj.*

**in·ef·fi·ca·cy** (i nef′ə kə sē) a lack of EFFICACY; inability to produce the effect wanted. *n.*

**in·ef·fi·cien·cy** (in′ə fish′ən sē) a lack of EFFICIENCY; inability to get things done. *n.*

**in·ef·fi·cient** (in′ə fish′ənt) **1** not EFFICIENT; not able to produce an effect without waste of time, energy, etc.; wasteful: *A machine that uses too much power is inefficient.* **2** incapable; not able to get things done: *an inefficient housekeeper.* *adj.* —**in′ef·fi′cient·ly**, *adv.*

**in·e·las·tic** (in′i las′tik) not ELASTIC; stiff; inflexible; unyielding. *adj.*

**in·e·las·tic·i·ty** (in′i las tis′ə tē) a lack of ELASTICITY. *n.*

**in·el·e·gance** (i nel′ə gəns) **1** a lack of ELEGANCE; lack of good taste. **2** something that is not elegant or graceful. *n.*

**in·el·e·gant** (i nel′ə gənt) not elegant; not in good taste; crude; vulgar. *adj.* —**in·el′e·gant·ly**, *adv.*

**in·el·i·gi·bil·i·ty** (i nel′ə jə bil′ə tē) a lack of ELIGIBILITY; being INELIGIBLE. *n.*

**in·el·i·gi·ble** (i nel′ə jə bəl) **1** not suitable; not qualified: *Andrea's youth makes her ineligible for the post.* **2** a person who is not suitable or not qualified. **1** *adj.*, **2** *n.* —**in·el′i·gi·bly**, *adv.*

**in·ept** (i nept′) **1** not suitable; out of place: *He would be an inept choice as captain.* **2** awkward; clumsy; incompetent: *That was an inept performance.* **3** absurd; foolish: *inept ideas.* *adj.* —**in·ept′ly**, *adv.* —**in·ept′ness**, *n.*
☛ *Syn.* See note at INAPT.

**in·ept·i·tude** (i nep′tə tyüd′ *or* i nep′tə tüd′) **1** unfitness; foolishness. **2** a silly or inappropriate act or remark. *n.*

**in·e·qual·i·ty** (in′ē kwol′ə tē) **1** a lack of EQUALITY; being unequal in amount, size, value, rank, etc.: *the inequality between the salaries of a bank president and an office clerk.* **2** a lack of evenness, regularity, or uniformity. **3** a mathematical expression showing that two quantities are unequal, like $a > b$ or $c < d$. *n., pl.* **in·e·qual·i·ties.**

**in·e·qua·tion** (in′ē kwā′zhən) a statement of INEQUALITY between two quantities: *The statement $a > b$ ($a$ is greater than $b$) is an inequation.* *n.*

**in·eq·ui·ta·ble** (i nek′wə tə bəl) unfair; unjust. *adj.* —**in·eq′ui·ta·bly**, *adv.*

**in·eq·ui·ty** (i nek′wə tē) unfairness; injustice. *n., pl.* **in·eq·ui·ties.**

**in·e·rad·i·ca·ble** (in′i rad′ə kə bəl) that cannot be rooted out or got rid of. *adj.* —**in′e·rad′i·ca·bly**, *adv.*

**in·ert** (i nėrt′) **1** having no power to move or act; lifeless: *A stone is an inert mass of matter.* **2** inactive; slow; sluggish. **3** with few or no active properties: *Helium and neon are inert gases.* *adj.* —**in·ert′ly**, *adv.* —**in·ert′ness**, *n.*

**in·er·tia** (i nėr′shə) **1** a tendency to remain in the state one is in and not start changes: *The family talked about leaving Canada, but their inertia prevented them from actually moving.* **2** the tendency of all objects and matter in the universe to stay still if still or, if moving, to go on moving in the same direction unless acted on by some outside force. *n.*

**in·es·cap·a·ble** (in′is kā′pə bəl) that cannot be escaped or avoided. *adj.* —**in′es·cap′a·bly**, *adv.*

**in·es·ti·ma·ble** (i nes′tə mə bəl) too good, great,

---

**inefficiency** 615 **inexpressive**

hat, āge, fär; let, ēqual, tėrm; it, īce
hot, ōpen, ôrder; oil, out; cup, pùt, rüle
əbove, takən, pencəl, lemən, circəs
ch, child; ng, long; sh, ship
th, thin; ᴛʜ, then; zh, measure

---

valuable, etc. to be measured or estimated: *Freedom is an inestimable privilege.* *adj.* —**in·es′ti·ma·bly**, *adv.*

**in·ev·i·ta·bil·i·ty** (i nev′ə tə bil′ə tē) being INEVITABLE. *n.*

**in·ev·i·ta·ble** (i nev′ə tə bəl) not avoidable; sure to happen; certain to come. *adj.* —**in·ev′i·ta·bly**, *adv.*

**in·ex·act** (in′ig zakt′) not exact; with errors or mistakes; not just right. *adj.* —**in′ex·act′ly**, *adv.* —**in′ex·act′ness**, *n.*

**in·ex·cus·a·ble** (in′ik skyü′zə bəl) that ought not to be excused; that cannot be justified: *Joan's failure to thank her hostess when the party ended was inexcusable.* *adj.* —**in′ex·cus′a·bly**, *adv.*

**in·ex·haust·i·bil·i·ty** (in′ig zos′tə bil′ə tē) an INEXHAUSTIBLE nature or quality. *n.*

**in·ex·haust·i·ble** (in′ig zos′tə bəl) **1** that cannot be exhausted; very abundant: *The wealth of our country seems inexhaustible to many people.* **2** tireless: *an inexhaustible swimmer.* *adj.* —**in′ex·haust′i·bly**, *adv.*

**in·ex·o·ra·bil·i·ty** (i nek′sə rə bil′ə tē) an INEXORABLE nature or quality. *n.*

**in·ex·o·ra·ble** (i nek′sə rə bəl) relentless; unyielding; not influenced by prayers or entreaties: *The forces of nature are inexorable.* *adj.* —**in·ex′o·ra·bly**, *adv.*

**in·ex·pe·di·en·cy** (in′ik spē′dē ən sē) a lack of EXPEDIENCY; being inexpedient. *n.*

**in·ex·pe·di·ent** (in′ik spē′dē ənt) not EXPEDIENT; not practicable, suitable, or wise. *adj.*

**in·ex·pen·sive** (in′ik spen′siv) not expensive; cheap; low-priced. *adj.* —**in′ex·pen′sive·ly**, *adv.* —**in′ex·pen′sive·ness**, *n.*

**in·ex·pe·ri·ence** (in′ik spē′rē əns) a lack of experience or practice; lack of skill or wisdom gained from experience. *n.*

**in·ex·pe·ri·enced** (in′ik spē′rē ənst) not experienced; without practice; lacking the skill and wisdom gained by experience. *adj.*

**in·ex·pert** (i nek′spėrt *or* in′ek spėrt′) not expert; unskilled. *adj.* —**in·ex′pert·ly**, *adv.* —**in·ex′pert·ness**, *n.*

**in·ex·pi·a·ble** (i nek′spē ə bəl) that cannot be atoned for: *Murder is an inexpiable crime.* *adj.*

**in·ex·pli·ca·bil·i·ty** (in′ik splik′ə bil′ə tē *or* in ek′splə kə bil′ə tē) an unexplainable nature or quality. *n.*

**in·ex·plic·a·ble** (in′ik splik′ə bəl *or* i nek′splə kə bəl) impossible to explain or understand; mysterious: *an inexplicable fire.* *adj.* —**in·ex′pli·ca·bly**, *adv.*

**in·ex·press·i·ble** (in′ik spres′ə bəl) that cannot be expressed; beyond expression. *adj.* —**in′ex·press′i·bly**, *adv.*

**in·ex·pres·sive** (in′ik spres′iv) not expressive; lacking in expression. *adj.*

**in·ex·tin·guish·a·ble** (in′ik stiŋ′gwi shə bəl) that cannot be put out or stopped: *An inextinguishable fire keeps on burning.* *adj.* —**in′ex·tin′guish·a·bly,** *adv.*

**in·ex·tri·ca·ble** (i nek′strə kə bəl) **1** that one cannot get out of. **2** that cannot be disentangled or solved. *adj.* —**in·ex′tri·ca·bly,** *adv.*

**inf. 1** infantry. **2** infinitive. **3** inferior. **4** below (for L *infra*). **5** information.

**in·fal·li·bil·i·ty** (in fal′ə bil′ə tē) absolute freedom from error. *n.*

**in·fal·li·ble** (in fal′ə bəl) **1** free from error; that cannot be mistaken: *an infallible rule.* **2** absolutely reliable; sure: *infallible obedience.* *adj.* —**in·fal′li·bly,** *adv.*

**in·fa·mous** (in′fə məs) **1** deserving or causing a very bad reputation; shamefully bad; extremely wicked: *an infamous act.* **2** having a very bad reputation; in public disgrace: *an infamous traitor.* *adj.* —**in′fa·mous·ly,** *adv.*

**in·fa·my** (in′fə mē) **1** a very bad reputation; public disgrace: *His acts brought infamy to his family and himself.* **2** shameful badness; extreme wickedness: *Treason is an act of infamy.* *n., pl.* **in·fa·mies.**

**in·fan·cy** (in′fən sē) **1** the condition or time of being an infant; babyhood; early childhood. **2** an early stage; beginning of development: *Space travel is beyond its infancy.* *n., pl.* **in·fan·cies.**

**in·fant** (in′fənt) **1** a baby; very young child. **2** of or for an infant: *an infant dress, infant food.* **3** in an early stage; just beginning to develop: *an infant industry.* **4** a person under the legal age of responsibility; minor. 1, 4 *n.*, 2, 3 *adj.*
☞ *Etym.* Through OF *enfant* from L *infans, infantis* 'young child', literally '(one) unable to speak'.

**in·fan·ti·cide** (in fan′tə sīd′) the killing of a baby. *n.*

**in·fan·tile** (in′fən tīl′) **1** of an infant or infants; having to do with infants: *infantile diseases.* **2** like an infant; babyish; childish: *infantile behaviour.* **3** in an early stage; just beginning to develop. *adj.*

**infantile paralysis** POLIOMYELITIS; polio.

**in·fan·ti·lism** (in fan′tə liz′əm) an abnormal persistence or appearance of childish traits in adults. *n.*

**in·fan·tine** (in′fən tīn′) INFANTILE; babyish; childish. *adj.*

**in·fan·try** (in′fən trē) **1** soldiers trained, equipped and organized to fight on foot. **2** the branch of an army made up of such soldiers. *n., pl.* **in·fan·tries.**
☞ *Etym.* Through French from Italian *infanteria*, formed from *infante* 'young man' or 'foot soldier'. 16c. **Infantry** is, therefore, related to **infant**. See also the note at INFANT.

**in·fan·try·man** (in′fən trē mən) a soldier who fights on foot. *n., pl.* **in·fan·try·men** (-mən).

**in·fat·u·ate** (in fach′ü āt′ *for verb*, in fach′ü it *or* in fach′ü āt′ *for adjective*) **1** make foolish. **2** inspire with a foolish or extreme passion. **3** infatuated. 1, 2 *v.*, **in·fat·u·at·ed, in·fat·u·at·ing;** 3 *adj.*

**in·fat·u·at·ed** (in fach′ü ā′tid) **1** extremely adoring; foolishly in love. **2** pt. and pp. of INFATUATE. 1 *adj.*, 2 *v.*

**in·fat·u·a·tion** (in fach′ü ā′shən) **1** an infatuating; **2** being infatuated. **3** foolish love; unreasoning fondness. *n.*

**in·fect** (in fekt′) **1** cause disease in by introducing germs: *Dirt infects an open cut. Anyone with a bad cold may infect the people around her.* **2** influence in a bad way: *One criminal may infect his companions.* **3** influence, especially in feeling or mood, by spreading from one person to another: *The captain's courage infected his soldiers.* *v.*

**in·fec·tion** (in fek′shən) **1** a causing of disease in people, animals, and plants by the introduction of germs: *Air, water, clothing, and insects are all means of infection.* **2** a disease caused in this way: *Measles is an infection that spreads from one person to another.* **3** an influence, feeling, or idea spreading from one to another. **4** the fact or state of being infected. *n.*

**in·fec·tious** (in fek′shəs) **1** spread by infection: *Measles is an infectious disease.* **2** causing infection; liable to cause infection: *That disease is infectious.* **3** apt to spread from one to another: *an infectious laugh.* *adj.* —**in·fec′tious·ly,** *adv.* —**in·fec′tious·ness,** *n.*

**in·fec·tive** (in fek′tiv) INFECTIOUS. *adj.*

**in·fe·lic·i·tous** (in′fə lis′ə təs) **1** unsuitable; not appropriate. **2** unfortunate; unhappy. *adj.*

**in·fe·lic·i·ty** (in′fə lis′ə tē) **1** unsuitability; inappropriateness. **2** a misfortune; unhappiness. **3** something unsuitable; an inappropriate word, remark, etc. *n., pl.* **in·fe·lic·i·ties.**

**in·fer** (in fėr′) **1** find out by reasoning; conclude: *Seeing the frown on my face, the girl inferred that I was angry.* **2** be a sign or hint of; suggest indirectly. **3** draw inferences. *v.*, **in·ferred, in·fer·ring.**
☞ *Usage.* See note at IMPLY.

**in·fer·ence** (in′fə rəns) **1** the process of inferring: *What happened is only a matter of inference; no one saw the accident.* **2** that which is inferred; conclusion: *What inference do you draw from smelling smoke?* *n.*

**in·fer·en·tial** (in′fə ren′shəl) having to do with INFERENCE; depending on inference. *adj.*

**in·fe·ri·or** (in fē′rē ər) **1** low in quality; below average: *an inferior mind, an inferior grade of coffee.* **2** not so good; lower in quality; worse: *His grades are inferior this term.* **3** lower in position, rank, or importance: *an inferior officer.* **4** a person who is lower in rank or station: *A good leader gets along well with her inferiors.* **5** an inferior thing. 1–3 *adj.*, 4, 5 *n.*
**inferior to, a** below; lower than: *A lieutenant is inferior to a captain.* **b** not as good or as great as; worse than: *This cloth is inferior to silk.*

**in·fe·ri·or·i·ty** (in fē′rē ô′rə tē) an inferior condition or quality. *n.*

**inferiority complex** an abnormal or morbid feeling of being inferior to other people.

**in·fer·nal** (in fėr′nəl) **1** of hell; having to do with the lower world. **2** hellish; diabolical: *infernal heat. The heartless conqueror showed infernal cruelty.* **3** *Informal.* abominable; outrageous. *adj.* —**in·fer′nal·ly,** *adv.*

**in·fer·no** (in fėr′nō) **1** hell. **2** a place or thing that seems to be like hell: *Within half an hour of the start of the fire, the whole building was a raging inferno.* *n., pl.* **in·fer·nos.**

**in·fer·tile** (in fėr′tīl *or* in fėr′təl) not fertile; not fruitful; sterile: *It is not profitable to cultivate infertile ground.* *adj.*

**in·fer·til·i·ty** (in′fėr til′ə tē)  a lack of fertility; being INFERTILE.  *n.*

**in·fest** (in fest′)  trouble or disturb frequently or in large numbers: *Mosquitoes infest swamps. The mountains were infested with robbers.*  *v.*

**in·fes·ta·tion** (in′fes tā′shən)  **1** an infesting. **2** being infested.  *n.*

**in·fi·del** (in′fə dəl)  **1** a person who does not believe in religion.  **2** not believing in religion.  **3** a person who does not accept a particular faith.  **1, 3** *n.*, **2** *adj.*

**in·fi·del·i·ty** (in′fə del′ə tē)  **1** a lack of religious faith. **2** unfaithfulness, especially of husband or wife; disloyalty. **3** an unfaithful or disloyal act.  *n., pl.* **in·fi·del·i·ties.**

**in·field** (in′fēld′)  **1** the part of a baseball field within the base lines; DIAMOND (def. 5).  **2** the first, second, and third basemen and shortstop of a baseball team: *That team has a good infield.*  **3** the part of farm lands nearest the buildings.  *n.*

**in·field·er** (in′fēl′dər)  a baseball player of the INFIELD (def. 2).  *n.*

**in·fil·trate** (in fil′trāt *or* in′fil trāt′)  **1** pass into or through by, or as by, filtering: *Enemy troops infiltrated the front lines.*  **2** filter into or through; permeate.  *v.*, **in·fil·trat·ed, in·fil·trat·ing.**

**in·fil·tra·tion** (in′fil trā′shən)  **1** an infiltrating or being infiltrated.  **2** something that infiltrates.  **3** a method of attack in which small groups of men penetrate the enemy's lines at various weak points.  *n.*

**infin.** infinitive.

**in·fi·nite** (in′fə nit)  **1** without limits or bounds; endless: *the infinite extent of space.*  **2** extremely great: *Teaching little children takes infinite patience.*  **3** that which is infinite.  **1, 2** *adj.,* **3** *n.* —**in′fi·nite·ness,** *n.*

**in·fi·nite·ly** (in′fə nit lē)  to an infinite degree: *"I am infinitely pleased to see you," she said.*  *adv.*

**in·fin·i·tes·i·mal** (in′fi nə tes′ə məl)  **1** so small as to be almost nothing: *A millionth of a centimetre is an infinitesimal length.*  **2** an infinitesimal amount.  **1** *adj.,* **2** *n.* —**in′fi·ni·tes′i·mal·ly,** *adv.*

**in·fin·i·tive** (in fin′ə tiv)  a form of a verb not limited by person and number, and often preceded by *to.* *Examples: Let him* go. *We want to go* now.  Infinitives are used as nouns: *To swim across the English Channel is her ambition;* as adjectives: *He had money to burn;* as adverbs: *She went home to rest.*  *n.*

**in·fin·i·tude** (in fin′ə tyüd′ *or* in fin′ə tüd′)  **1** being infinite.  **2** an infinite extent, amount, or number.  *n.*

**in·fin·i·ty** (in fin′ə tē)  **1** the state of being infinite: *the infinity of space.*  **2** an infinite distance, space, time, or quantity.  **3** an infinite extent, amount, or number: *the infinity of a mother's love.*  *n., pl.* **in·fin·i·ties.** **to infinity,**  without limits or bounds; endlessly.

**in·firm** (in fėrm′)  **1** weak; feeble: *The woman was old and infirm.*  **2** weak in will or character; not steadfast: *The boy was infirm in his ambitions.*  **3** not firm; not stable.  *adj.* —**in·firm′ly,** *adv.* —**in·firm′ness,** *n.*

**in·fir·ma·ry** (in fėr′mə rē)  **1** a place for the care of the infirm, sick, or injured; hospital dispensary in a school or institution.  **2** any small hospital.  *n., pl.* **in·fir·ma·ries.**

**in·fir·mi·ty** (in fėr′mə tē)  **1** weakness; feebleness. **2** a sickness; illness.  **3** a moral weakness or failing.  *n., pl.* **in·fir·mi·ties.**

---

**infertility**     **617**     **inflict**

hat, āge, fär; let, ēqual, tėrm; it, īce
hot, ōpen, ôrder; oil, out; cup, pùt, rüle
əbove, takən, pencəl, lemən, circəs
ch, child; ng, long; sh, ship
th, thin; ᴛʜ, then; zh, measure

**in·flame** (in flām′)  **1** excite; make more violent: *Her stirring speech inflamed the crowd.*  **2** become excited with intense feeling.  **3** make or become unnaturally hot, red, sore, or swollen: *The smoke had inflamed the fireman's eyes.*  **4** become red or hot from disease, etc.  *v.,* **in·flamed, in·flam·ing.**

**in·flam·ma·bil·i·ty** (in flam′ə bil′ə tē)  an INFLAMMABLE quality or condition.  *n.*

**in·flam·ma·ble** (in flam′ə bəl)  **1** easily set on fire: *Paper and gasoline are inflammable.*  **2** easily excited or aroused: *an inflammable temper.*  **3** something inflammable.  **1, 2** *adj.,* **3** *n.* —**in·flam′ma·bly,** *adv.*
☞ *Usage.* See note at FLAMMABLE.

**in·flam·ma·tion** (in′flə mā′shən)  **1** a diseased condition of some part of the body, marked by heat, redness, swelling, and pain.  **2** inflaming.  **3** being inflamed.  *n.*

**in·flam·ma·to·ry** (in flam′ə tô′rē)  **1** tending to excite or arouse: *an inflammatory speech.*  **2** of, causing, or accompanied by inflammation: *an inflammatory condition of the tonsils.*  *adj.*

**in·flate** (in flāt′)  **1** blow out or swell with air or gas: *to inflate a balloon.*  **2** swell or puff out: *to inflate with pride.* **3** increase prices or currency beyond a reasonable or normal amount.  *v.,* **in·flat·ed, in·flat·ing.** —**in·flat′a·ble,** *adj.* —**in·flat′er, in·fla′tor,** *n.*

**in·fla·tion** (in flā′shən)  **1** a swelling with air, gas, pride, etc.  **2** a swollen state; too great expansion.  **3** an increase of the currency of a country by issuing much paper money.  **4** a sharp and sudden rise of prices resulting from too great an increase in the supply of paper money or bank credit.  *n.*

**in·fla·tion·ar·y** (in flā′shə ner′ē)  of or having to do with INFLATION (defs. 3, 4); tending to inflate.  *adj.*

**in·fla·tion·ist** (in flā′shə nist)  a person who favours INFLATION (defs. 3, 4).  *n.*

**in·flect** (in flekt′)  **1** change the tone or pitch of the voice.  **2** vary the form of a word to show case, number, gender, person, tense, mood, comparison etc.: *By inflecting "who," we get "whose" and "whom."*  **3** bend; curve.  *v.*

**in·flec·tion** (in flek′shən)  **1** a change in the tone or pitch of the voice: *We end certain questions with a rising inflection.*  **2** a variation in the form of a word to show case, number, gender, person, tense, mood, or comparison. **3** a bending or curving.  **4** a bend or curve.  *n.*

**in·flec·tion·al** (in flek′shə nəl)  of, having to do with, or showing grammatical INFLECTION.  *adj.*

**in·flex·i·bil·i·ty** (in flek′sə bil′ə tē)  a lack of flexibility; an INFLEXIBLE quality or condition.  *n.*

**in·flex·i·ble** (in flek′sə bəl)  **1** firm; unyielding; steadfast: *inflexible determination.*  **2** that cannot be changed; unalterable.  **3** not easily bent; stiff; rigid: *an inflexible rod.*  *adj.* —**in·flex′i·bly,** *adv.*

**in·flict** (in flikt′)  **1** cause to have or suffer; give a blow, wound, pain, etc.  **2** impose a burden, suffering, anything unwelcome, etc.: *to inflict a penalty. Mrs. Shapiro inflicted herself upon her relatives for a long visit.* *v.*

**in·flic·tion** (in flik′shən) **1** the act of inflicting: *The cruel man delighted in the infliction of pain.* **2** something inflicted; pain; suffering; burden; punishment. *n.*

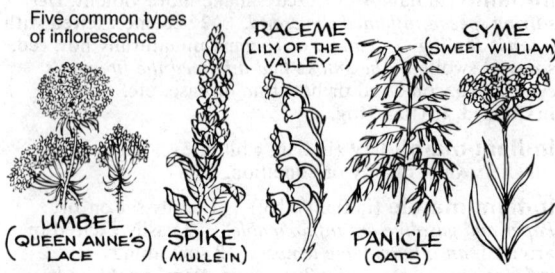

Five common types of inflorescence. UMBEL (QUEEN ANNE'S LACE), SPIKE (MULLEIN), RACEME (LILY OF THE VALLEY), PANICLE (OATS), CYME (SWEET WILLIAM)

**in·flo·res·cence** (in′flô res′əns) **1** of plants, the flowering stage. **2** the arrangement of flowers on the stem or axis. **3** a flower cluster. *n.*

**in·flo·res·cent** (in′flô res′ənt) showing INFLORESCENCE; flowering. *adj.*

**in·flow** (in′flō′) **1** a flowing in or into: *The discovery of gold in the Yukon caused an inflow of people.* **2** that which flows in. *n.*

**in·flu·ence** (in′flü əns) **1** the power of persons or things to act on others, seen only in its effects: *the influence of the moon on the tides.* **2** the power to produce an effect without using force: *A person may have influence because of her ability, personality, position, or wealth. Use your influence to persuade your friends to join our club.* **3** a person or thing that has such power: *His thoughtfulness for others made him a good influence throughout the school.* **4** have power over; change the nature or behaviour of: *The moon influences the tides.* 1–3 *n.,* 4 *v.* **in·flu·enced, in·flu·enc·ing**.

**in·flu·en·tial** (in′flü en′shəl) **1** having much INFLUENCE; having influence: *Influential friends got her a job.* **2** using INFLUENCE; producing results. *adj.*

**in·flu·en·za** (in′flü en′zə) an infectious disease, resembling a bad cold in its symptoms, but much more dangerous and exhausting; flu. *n.*

**in·flux** (in′fluks) a flowing in; steady flow: *the influx of immigrants into a country.* *n.*

**in·form** (in fôrm′) **1** give knowledge, facts, or news to; tell: *Report cards inform parents about a child's progress at school.* **2** give information to the police or some other authority: *One thief informed against the others who had escaped.* **3** inspire; animate: *The appeal informed their hearts with pity.* *v.*

**in·for·mal** (in fôr′məl) **1** not formal; not in the regular or prescribed manner: *informal proceedings.* **2** without ceremony; casual: *an informal party, informal clothes.* **3** used in general, everyday English, but not used in formal speech or writing: *Using the term* kids *in place of* children *or* students *is informal.* *adj.* —**in·for′mal·ly,** *adv.*

☞ *Usage.* **Informal** English is the kind of English used by educated people in everyday speaking and writing; it ranges in style from the familiar, or casual, to the careful and precise. FORMAL English is used in lectures, speeches, learned articles, legal documents, and so on. As a usage label in this dictionary, **Informal** is used more narrowly to mean "acceptable in everyday use, but not appropriate in situations requiring precise or formal language."

**in·for·mal·i·ty** (in′fôr mal′ə tē) **1** being INFORMAL; lack of ceremony. **2** an INFORMAL act. *n., pl.* **in·for·mal·i·ties.**

**in·form·ant** (in fôr′mənt) a person who gives information to another: *My informant saw it happen.* *n.*

**in·for·ma·tion** (in′fər mā′shən) **1** knowledge; facts; news: *A dictionary gives information about words. The general sent information of his victory.* **2** an informing: *A guidebook is for the information of travellers.* **3** an accusation or complaint against a person. *n.*

**in·for·ma·tion·al** (in′fər mā′shə nəl) giving INFORMATION; instructive. *adj.*

**information highway** all electronic media and communication systems.

**in·form·a·tive** (in fôr′mə tiv) giving INFORMATION; instructive. *adj.*

**in·form·er** (in fôr′mər) **1** a person who makes an accusation or complaint against others: *An informer told the police that the store was selling stolen goods.* **2** INFORMANT. *n.*

**in·frac·tion** (in frak′shən) a breaking of a law or obligation; violation: *Reckless driving is an infraction of the law.* *n.*

**in·fra–red** (in′frə red′) of or having to do with the long, invisible light waves just beyond the red end of the colour spectrum: *Most of the heat from sunlight, incandescent lamps, carbon arcs, resistance wires, etc. is from infra-red rays.* *adj.*

**in·fre·quence** (in frē′kwəns) INFREQUENCY. *n.*

**in·fre·quen·cy** (in frē′kwən sē) scarcity; rarity. *n.*

**in·fre·quent** (in frē′kwənt) not frequent; occurring seldom or far apart; scarce; rare. *adj.* —**in·fre′quent·ly,** *adv.*

**in·fringe** (in frinj′) **1** act contrary to or violate a law, obligation, right, etc.: *A false label infringes the laws relating to food and drugs.* **2** trespass; encroach: *to infringe upon the rights of another.* *v.,* **in·fringed, in·fring·ing.** —**in·fring′er,** *n.* —**in·fringe′ment,** *n.*

**in·fu·ri·ate** (in fyü′rē āt′) fill with anger; make furious; enrage: *The woman was infuriated when the dog snapped at her.* *v.,* **in·fu·ri·at·ed, in·fu·ri·at·ing.** —**in·fu′ri·at′ing·ly,** *adv.* —**in·fu′ri·a′tion,** *n.*

**in·fuse** (in fyüz′) **1** pour in; put in: *The captain infused his own courage into his soldiers.* **2** inspire: *She infused the survivors with her courage.* **3** steep or soak in a liquid to draw out flavour, minerals, etc. or to make a drink, drug, or other preparation: *We infuse tea leaves in hot water to make tea.* *v.,* **in·fused, in·fus·ing.**

**in·fu·si·ble** (in fyü′zə bəl) that cannot be fused or melted. *adj.*

**in·fu·sion** (in fyü′zhən) **1** the act or process of infusing. **2** something poured in or mingled; infused element. **3** a liquid extract obtained by steeping or soaking. *n.*

**–ing**[1] a suffix meaning: **1** the action, result, product, material, etc. of a verb, as in *hard thinking, the art of painting, a beautiful drawing, fine sewing, a blue lining, rich trimming.* **2** an action, result, product, material, etc. of some other part of speech, as in *lobstering, smoking, shirting.* **3** of one or more that _____: *The smoking habit is the habit of one who smokes.*

**–ing²** 1 a suffix that forms the present participle of verbs, as in *raining, staying, talking*. 2 a suffix meaning that _____s: *Lasting happiness is happiness that lasts*.

**in·ge·ni·ous** (in jē′nē əs *or* in jē′nyəs) 1 clever; skilful in planning or making: *The ingenious girl made a radio set.* 2 cleverly planned or made: *This mousetrap is an ingenious device.* *adj.* —**in·gen′ious·ly,** *adv.* —**in·gen′ious·ness,** *n.*
☞ *Usage.* Do not confuse **ingenious** and INGENUOUS. **Ingenious** means clever; skilful: *Fay is so ingenious that she is sure to think of some way of doing this work more easily.* **Ingenuous** means frank; sincere; simple: *The ingenuous child had never thought of being suspicious of what other people told him.*

**in·gé·nue** (on′zhə nü′; *French*, AN zhā NY′) 1 a simple, innocent girl or young woman, especially as represented on the stage. 2 an actress who plays such a part. *n.*, *pl.* **in·gé·nues.**

**in·ge·nu·i·ty** (in′jə nyü′ə tē *or* in′jə nü′ə tē) skill in planning, inventing, etc.; cleverness: *ingenuity in making toys. n., pl.* **in·ge·nu·i·ties.**

**in·gen·u·ous** (in jen′yü əs) 1 frank; open; sincere: *The honest girl gave an ingenuous account of her acts, concealing nothing.* 2 simple; natural; innocent. *adj.* —**in·gen′u·ous·ly,** *adv.* —**in·gen′u·ous·ness,** *n.*
☞ *Usage.* See note at INGENIOUS.

**in·gest** (in jest′) take food, etc. into the body for digestion. *v.*

**in·ges·tion** (in jes′chən) the act of taking food, etc. into the body for digesting. *n.*

**in·gle·nook** (ing′gəl nůk′) a corner by the fire. *n.*

**in·glo·ri·ous** (in glôr′ē əs) 1 bringing no glory; shameful; disgraceful. 2 having no glory; not famous. *adj.* —**in·glo′ri·ous·ly,** *adv.* —**in·glo′ri·ous·ness,** *n.*

**in·got** (ing′gət) a mass of metal, such as gold, silver, or steel, cast into a block or bar. *n.*

**in·graft** (in graft′) ENGRAFT. *v.*

**in·grain** (in grān′ *for verb,* in′grān′ *for adjective and noun*) 1 fix deeply and firmly; make an integral part of: *Certain habits are ingrained in one's nature.* 2 dye in the fibre before manufacture. 3 dyed before manufacture. 4 yarn, wool, etc. dyed before manufacture. 5 made of yarn dyed before weaving: *an ingrain rug.* 1, 2 *v.*, 3, 5 *adj.*, 4 *n.*

**in·grained** (in grānd′ *for verb;* in′grānd′ *for adjective and noun*) 1 deeply fixed; integrated: *ingrained characteristics.* 2 pt. and pp. of INGRAIN. 1 *adj.*, 2 *v.*

**in·grate** (in′grāt) a person who is ungrateful. *n.*

**in·gra·ti·ate** (in grā′shē āt′) bring oneself into favour: *He tried to ingratiate himself with the teacher by giving him presents. v.,* **in·gra·ti·at·ed, in·gra·ti·at·ing.** —**in·gra′ti·at′ing·ly,** *adv.*

**in·grat·i·tude** (in grat′ə tyüd′ *or* in grat′ə tüd′) a lack of gratitude or thankfulness; being ungrateful. *n.*

**in·gre·di·ent** (in grē′dē ənt) one of the parts of a mixture: *The ingredients of a cake usually include eggs, sugar, flour, and flavouring. n.*

**in·gress** (in′gres) 1 going in: *A high fence prevented ingress to the field.* 2 a way in; entrance. 3 a right to go in. *n.* Compare with EGRESS.

**in·grow·ing** (in′grō′ing) 1 growing within; growing inward. 2 growing into the flesh: *an ingrowing toenail. adj.*

hat, āge, fär; let, ēqual, tėrm; it, īce hot, ōpen, ôrder; oil, out; cup, půt, rüle əbove, takən, pencəl, lemən, circəs ch, child; ng, long; sh, ship th, thin; ᴛʜ, then; zh, measure

**in·grown** (in′grōn′) 1 grown within; grown inward. 2 grown into the flesh. *adj.*

**in·gulf** (in gulf′) ENGULF. *v.*

**in·hab·it** (in hab′it) 1 live in a place, region, house, cave, tree, etc.: *Fish inhabit the sea. Thoughts inhabit the mind.* 2 live; dwell. *v.*

**in·hab·it·a·ble** (in hab′ə tə bəl) 1 capable of being inhabited. 2 fit to live in; habitable. *adj.*

**in·hab·it·ant** (in hab′ə tənt) a person or animal that lives in a place. *n.*

**in·hab·it·ed** (in hab′ə tid) 1 lived in: *an inhabited house.* 2 pt. and pp. of INHABIT. 1 *adj.*, 2 *v.*

**in·hal·ant** (in hā′lənt) 1 a medicine to be inhaled. 2 an apparatus for inhaling it. 3 used for inhaling. 1, 2 *n.*, 3 *adj.*

**in·ha·la·tion** (in′hə lā′shən) 1 the act of inhaling. 2 a medicine to be inhaled. *n.*

**In·ha·la·tor** (in′hə lā′tər) an apparatus for inhaling anaesthetics, medicine, etc. *n.*

**in·hale** (in hāl′) draw into the lungs; breathe in air, fragrance, etc. *v.,* **in·haled, in·hal·ing.**

**in·hal·er** (in hā′lər) 1 an apparatus used in inhaling medicine, a gas, etc. 2 an apparatus for filtering dust, gases, etc. from air. 3 a person who inhales. *n.*

**in·har·mo·ni·ous** (in′här mō′nē əs) not HARMONIOUS; discordant; disagreeing. *adj.* —**in′har·mo′ni·ous·ly,** *adv.*

**in·here** (in hēr′) exist; belong to as a quality or attribute (used with **in**): *Greed inheres in human nature. Power inheres in that ruler. v.,* **in·hered, in·her·ing.**

**in·her·ence** (in hē′rəns *or* in her′əns) being INHERENT. *n.*

**in·her·ent** (in hē′rənt *or* in her′ənt) existing as a natural or basic quality of a person or thing: *inherent honesty, the inherent sweetness of sugar. adj.* —**in·her′ent·ly,** *adv.*

**in·her·it** (in her′it) 1 get or have after another person dies; receive as an heir: *Mrs. Chan's nephew inherited the farm.* 2 get or possess from one's ancestors through heredity: *Nicola inherits her father's blue eyes.* 3 receive anything as by succession from predecessors: *The new government inherited a financial crisis. v.*

**in·her·it·a·ble** (in her′ə tə bəl) 1 capable of being inherited. 2 capable of inheriting; qualified to inherit. *adj.*

**in·her·it·ance** (in her′ə təns) 1 the act of inheriting: *He obtained his house by inheritance from an aunt.* 2 the right of inheriting. 3 anything inherited: *Good health is a fine inheritance. n.*

**inheritance tax** a tax on inherited property; succession duty.

**in·her·i·tor** (in her′ə tər) one who inherits; HEIR. *n.*

**in·hib·it** (in hib′it) 1 check; hold back; hinder or

**in·hib·it** (in hib′it) **1** hold back; restrain: *The soldier's loyalty inhibited his impulse to run away.* **2** prohibit; forbid. *v.*

**in·hi·bi·tion** (in′ə bish′ən *or* in′hi bish′ən) **1** the act of inhibiting. **2** the state of being inhibited. **3** an idea, emotion, attitude, habit, or other inner force that restrains natural impulses. *n.*

**in·hib·i·tive** (in hib′ə tiv) INHIBITORY. *adj.*

**in·hib·i·to·ry** (in hib′ə tô′rē) inhibiting; tending to inhibit. *adj.*

**in·hos·pi·ta·ble** (in hos′pi tə bəl *or* in′hos pit′ə bəl) **1** not HOSPITABLE; not making visitors comfortable: *They were too inhospitable to offer us supper.* **2** providing no shelter; barren: *The colonists encountered a rocky, inhospitable shore. adj.* —**in·hos′pi·ta·bly,** *adv.*

**in·hos·pi·tal·i·ty** (in hos′pə tal′ə tē) a lack of HOSPITALITY; inhospitable behaviour. *n.*

**in·hu·man** (in hyü′mən) **1** without kindness; brutal; cruel. **2** not human; not having the qualities natural to a human being: *inhuman powers of endurance. adj.* —**in·hu′man·ly,** *adv.*

**in·hu·mane** (in′hyü mān′) not HUMANE; lacking in compassion, humanity, or kindness. *adj.* —**in′hu·mane′ly,** *adv.*

**in·hu·man·i·ty** (in′hyü man′ə tē) **1** an inhuman quality; lack of feeling; cruelty; brutality. **2** an inhuman, cruel, or brutal act. *n., pl.* **in·hu·man·i·ties.**

**in·im·i·cal** (i nim′ə kəl) **1** unfriendly; hostile. **2** adverse; unfavourable; harmful: *Lack of ambition is inimical to success. adj.* —**in·im′i·cal·ly,** *adv.*

**in·im·i·ta·ble** (i nim′ə tə bəl) that cannot be imitated or copied; matchless. *adj.* —**in·im′i·ta·bly,** *adv.*

**in·iq·ui·tous** (i nik′wə təs) very unjust; wicked. *adj.* —**in·iq′ui·tous·ly,** *adv.* —**in·iq′ui·tous·ness,** *n.*

**in·iq·ui·ty** (i nik′wə tē) **1** very great injustice; wickedness. **2** a wicked or unjust act. *n., pl.* **in·iq·ui·ties.**

**i·ni·tial** (i nish′əl) **1** occurring at the beginning; first; earliest: *The initial cost of the boat was low.* **2** the first letter of a word: *The initials N.S. stand for Nova Scotia.* **3** mark or sign with initials: *Juan Antonio Segovia initialled the note J.A.S.* **1** *adj.,* **2** *n.,* **3** *v.,* **i·ni·tialled** or **in·i·tialed, i·ni·tial·ling** or **i·ni·tial·ing.**

**i·ni·tial·ly** (i nish′ə lē) at the beginning. *adv.*

**i·ni·ti·ate** (i nish′ē āt′ *for verb,* i nish′ē it *or* i nish′ē āt′ *for noun and adjective*) **1** be the one to start; begin: *This year the school will initiate a series of free concerts.* **2** admit a person by special forms or ceremonies into mysteries, secret knowledge, or a society. **3** help to get a first understanding; introduce into the knowledge of some art or subject: *to initiate a person into business methods.* **4** a person who is initiated. **5** initiated. **1–3** *v.,* **i·ni·ti·at·ed, i·ni·ti·at·ing;** **4** *n.,* **5** *adj.* —**i·ni′ti·a′tor,** *n.*

**i·ni·ti·a·tion** (i nish′ē ā′shən) **1** the act or process of initiating; beginning: *the initiation of the free concerts.* **2** being initiated. **3** a formal admission into a group or society. **4** the ceremonies by which one is admitted to a group or society. *n.*

**i·ni·ti·a·tive** (i nish′ē ə tiv *or* i nish′ə tiv) **1** the active part in taking the first steps in any undertaking; the lead: *She is shy and does not take the initiative in making acquaintances.* **2** the readiness and ability to be the one to start something; enterprise: *A good leader must have initiative.* **3** the right to be the first to act, legislate, etc. *n.*

**i·ni·ti·a·to·ry** (i nish′ē ə tô′rē) **1** first; beginning; introductory. **2** of INITIATION. *adj.*

**in·ject** (in jekt′) **1** force liquid into a passage, cavity, or tissue: *inject penicillin into a muscle, inject fuel into an engine.* **2** fill a cavity, etc. with fluid forced in. **3** throw in; introduce: *The stranger injected a remark into their conversation. v.* —**in·jec′tor,** *n.*

**in·jec·tion** (in jek′shən) **1** the act or process of injecting: *Drugs are given by injection as well as through the mouth. They enjoyed the injection of the stranger's jokes into the dull discussion.* **2** something injected. *n.*

**in·ju·di·cious** (in′jü dish′əs) showing lack of judgment; unwise; not prudent. *adj.* —**in′ju·di′cious·ly,** *adv.* —**in′ju·di′cious·ness,** *n.*

**in·junc·tion** (in jungk′shən) **1** a command; order: *Injunctions of secrecy did not prevent the news from leaking out.* **2** a formal order issued by a law court ordering a person or group to do, or refrain from doing, something. *n.*

**in·jure** (in′jər) **1** do damage to; harm; hurt: *Do not injure the young trees. Dishonesty injures a business.* **2** be unfair to; do wrong to. *v.,* **in·jured, in·jur·ing.**

**in·ju·ri·ous** (in jü′rē əs) **1** causing injury; harmful: *Hail is injurious to crops.* **2** unfair; unjust; wrongful. *adj.* —**in·ju′ri·ous·ly,** *adv.* —**in·ju′ri·ous·ness,** *n.*

**in·ju·ry** (in′jə rē) **1** a hurt or loss caused to or endured by a person or thing; damage; harm: *She escaped from the train wreck without injury.* **2** a wound; hurt; an act that harms or damages: *He received a serious injury in the accident. The accident will certainly be an injury to the reputation of the airline.* **3** unfairness; injustice; wrong: *You did me an injury when you said I lied. n., pl.* **in·ju·ries.**

**in·jus·tice** (in jus′tis) **1** a lack of justice; being unjust. **2** an unjust act: *To send an innocent woman to jail is an injustice. n.*

**ink** (ingk) **1** a liquid used for writing, printing, or drawing. **2** a dark liquid thrown out for protection by cuttlefish, squids, etc. **3** put ink on; mark or stain with ink. **1, 2** *n.,* **3** *v.* —**ink′er,** *n.* —**ink′like′,** *adj.*
**ink in,** fill in an outline with ink.

**ink·ling** (ing′kling) a slight suggestion; vague notion; hint. *n.*

**ink·stand** (ingk′stand′) **1** a stand to hold ink and pens. **2** a container used to hold ink. *n.*

**ink·well** (ing′kwel′) a container used to hold ink on a desk or table. *n.*

**ink·y** (ing′kē) **1** dark; like ink; black: *inky shadows.* **2** covered with ink; marked or stained with ink. **3** of ink. *adj.,* **ink·i·er, ink·i·est.** —**ink′i·ness,** *n.*

**in·laid** (in′lād′) **1** set in the surface as a decoration or design: *The desk had an inlaid design of light wood in dark.* **2** decorated with a design or material set in the surface: *The box had an inlaid cover.* **3** pt. and pp. of INLAY. **1, 2** *adj.,* **3** *v.*

**in·land** (in′lənd *for adjective,* in′land′ *or* in′lənd *for noun and adverb*) **1** away from the coast or the border; having to do with or situated in the interior: *an inland sea.* **2** the interior of a country; land away from the border or the coast.   **3** in or toward the interior.   **4** domestic; not foreign: *inland trade.*   1, 4 *adj.*, 2 *n.*, 3 *adv.*

**in-law** (in′lo′) *Informal.*   a relative by marriage.   *n.*

**in·lay** (in′lā′)   **1** set as a decoration or design into a shallow recess in a surface: *to inlay strips of gold.*   **2** decorate with something set into the surface: *to inlay a wooden box with silver.*   **3** an inlaid decoration, design, or material.   **4** a shaped piece of gold, porcelain, etc. cemented in a tooth as a filling.   1, 2 *v.*, **in·laid**, **in·lay·ing**;   3, 4 *n.*

**in·let** (in′let′ *or* in′lət)   **1** a narrow strip of water extending from a larger body of water into the land or between islands: *The fishing village was on a small inlet of the sea.*   **2** entrance.   *n.*

**inline skates** (in′līn)   roller skates having four wheels in a single row, one behind the other.   —**inline skating.**

**in lo·co pa·ren·tis** (in′lō′kō pə ren′tis) *Latin.*   in the place of a parent; as a parent.

**in·mate** (in′māt′)   a person who lives with others in the same building, especially one in a prison, hospital, etc.   *n.*

**in me·mo·ri·am** (in′mə mô′rē əm) *Latin.*   in memory of; to the memory of.

**in·most** (in′mōst′)   **1** farthest in; deepest within: *the inmost depths of a mine.*   **2** most private or personal: *Her inmost desire was to be an astronaut.*   *adj.*

**inn** (in)   **1** a public house for lodging and caring for travellers: *Hotels have largely taken the place of the old inns.*   **2** tavern.   *n.*
☛ *Hom.* IN.

**in·nate** (i nāt′ *or* in′āt)   natural; inborn: *an innate talent for drawing. adj.*   —**in·nate′ly**, *adv.*
—**in·nate′ness**, *n.*

**in·ner** (in′ər)   **1** farther in; inside: *the inner bark of a tree, an inner room.*   **2** intimate or private; close to the central or most important part: *the inner circle of government. She kept her inner thoughts to herself.*   *adj.*

**inner city**   the older, central part of a large city, especially when it is densely populated and less affluent than the rest of the city.   —**in′ner-cit′y**, *adj.*

**inner ear**   the part of the ear which, in human beings, contains the organ that changes sound into nerve impulses and the organ for maintaining balance: *The inner ear is located behind the three bones of the middle ear.*   See EAR¹ for picture.

**in·ner·most** (in′ər mōst′)   farthest in; inmost: *the innermost parts. adj.*

**inner tube**   a separate rubber tube that fits inside some tires and is inflated with air.

**in·ning** (in′ing)   **1** in baseball, the period of play in which each team has a turn at bat. It ends when three players are out.   **2 innings**,   in cricket, the period of a game when one team is batting (*used with a singular verb*).   **3** Usually, **innings**,   the time when a person or group has a chance for action or accomplishment (*used with a singular verb*): *The girls are finally going to have their innings.*   *n.*

**inn·keep·er** (in′kē′pər)   a person who owns, manages, or keeps an inn.   *n.*

**in·no·cence** (in′ə səns)   **1** the state or quality of being free from sin or moral guilt, or from legal guilt for a particular offence: *The trial established his innocence.*

**in-law**   **621**   **inoffensive**

hat, āge, fär; let, ēqual, tėrm; it, īce
hot, ōpen, ôrder; oil, out; cup, put, rüle
əbove, takən, pencəl, lemən, circəs
ch, child; ng, long; sh, ship
th, thin; ᴛʜ, then; zh, measure

**2** the state or quality of being free from guile or cunning; simplicity: *the innocence of a child.*   **3** lack of worldly experience; naïvete: *In his innocence, he assumed that they meant it when they said, "You must come and see us sometime."*   *n.*

**in·no·cent** (in′ə sənt)   **1** free from wrongdoing: *An innocent bystander was hit in the shootout between police and the bank robbers.*   **2** not legally guilty of a particular offence: *The trial proved that the accused was innocent.*   **3** not wrong or bad; harmless: *innocent amusements.*   **4** without knowledge of evil, and therefore free from sin or wrong: *as innocent as a baby.*   **5** free from cunning or guile; simple and open; artless: *an innocent question.*   **6** naïve.   **7** a person who has no knowledge of evil or who is artless or naïve.   **8** lacking (*used with* **of**): *a bare, bleak room, innocent of all adornment.*   1–6, 8 *adj.*, 7 *n.*
—**in′no·cent·ly**, *adv.*

**in·noc·u·ous** (i nok′yü əs)   **1** harmless; not capable of causing damage or injury: *an innocuous medicine, an innocuous snake.*   **2** not likely to arouse hostility or strong feelings; not offensive or stimulating: *innocuous remarks.*   *adj.*

**in·no·vate** (in′ə vāt′)   make changes; bring in something new or do something in a new way.   *v.*,
**in·no·vat·ed**, **in·no·vat·ing**.

**in·no·va·tion** (in′ə vā′shən)   **1** a change made in the established way of doing things: *The new teacher has made many innovations.*   **2** the making of changes; bringing in new things or new ways of doing things: *He is strongly opposed to innovation.*   *n.*

**in·no·va·tor** (in′ə vā′tər)   a person who makes changes or introduces new methods.   *n.*

**in·nu·en·do** (in′yü en′dō)   **1** an indirect hint or reference.   **2** an indirect suggestion against somebody: *to spread scandal by innuendo.*   *n.*, *pl.* **in·nu·en·does.**

**In·nu·it** (in′ü it, in′yü it, *or* in′yə wit)   See INUIT.   *n.*, *adj.*

**in·nu·mer·a·ble** (i nyü′mə rə bəl *or* i nü′mə rə bəl)   too many to count; very many; countless: *innumerable stars. adj.*   —**in′nu·mer·a·ble·ness**, *n.*
—**in·nu′mer·a·bly**, *adv.*

**in·oc·u·late** (i nok′yə lāt′)   **1** infect a person or animal with organisms that will cause a very mild form of a disease, thus reducing the individual's chances of contracting the disease thereafter.   **2** use disease-producing organisms to prevent or cure diseases.   **3** put bacteria, serums, etc. into: *Farmers inoculate the soil with bacteria that will take nitrogen from the air and change it so that it can be used by plants.*   **4** fill a person's mind with ideas, opinions, etc.   *v.*, **in·oc·u·lat·ed**,
**in·oc·u·lat·ing**.   —**in·oc′u·la′tor**, *n.*

**in·oc·u·la·tion** (i nok′yə lā′shən)   the act or process of inoculating, especially in order to immunize against disease.   *n.*

**in·of·fen·sive** (in′ə fen′siv)   not offensive; harmless; not arousing objections.   *adj.*   —**in′of·fen′sive·ly**, *adv.*
—**in′of·fen′sive·ness**, *n.*

**in·op·er·a·ble** (i nop′ə rə bəl)   **1** not able to be cured by surgery: *an inoperable cancer.*   **2** not practicable; unworkable: *an inoperable plan.*   *adj.*

**in·op·er·a·tive** (i nop′ə rə tiv *or* i nop′ə rā′tiv)   not operative; not working; without effect.   *adj.*

**in·op·por·tune** (i nop′ər tyün′ *or* i nop′ər tün′)   not OPPORTUNE; coming at a bad time; inconvenient: *An inopportune call delayed us.*   *adj.*
—**in·op′por·tune′ly**, *adv.*   —**in·op′por·tune·ness**, *n.*

**in·or·di·nate** (i nôr′də nit)   much too great; excessive; immoderate: *She spends an inordinate amount of time tinkering with those old radios.*   *adj.*
—**in·or′di·nate·ly**, *adv.*

**in·or·gan·ic** (in′ôr gan′ik)   **1** composed of or referring to matter that is not animal or vegetable; not having the organized structure of animals or plants: *Minerals are inorganic.*   **2** of or referring to any chemical compound not classified as organic: *Most inorganic compounds are derived from minerals and do not contain carbon.*   **3** of or referring to the branch of chemistry that deals with inorganic compounds and elements.   *adj.*
—**in′or·gan′i·cal·ly**, *adv.*

**in·put** (in′pút′)   **1** what is put in or taken in.   **2** the power supplied to a machine.   **3** information fed into a computer or data processing system.   **4** feed (information) into a computer or data processing system. 1–3 *n.*, 4 *v.*   **in·put, in·put·ting.**

**in·quest** (in′kwest)   **1** a legal inquiry led by a coroner, usually with a jury, to determine the cause of a sudden death: *An inquest is held when there is a possibility that death was the result of a crime or of a situation that could be dangerous to other people.*   **2** a jury appointed to hold such an inquiry: *The inquest was told that a witness had been delayed.*   **3** any other investigation into the causes of an event, situation, etc.   *n.*

**in·quire** (in kwīr′)   **1** try to find out by questions; ask: *She telephoned the hotel to inquire about a room.*   **2** make an investigation or examination, especially by asking questions; search into: *to inquire into someone's past.*   *v.*, **in·quired, in·quir·ing.**   Also, **enquire.**   —**in·quir′er**, *n.*
—**in·quir′ing·ly**, *adv.*

**in·quir·y** (in kwī′rē *or* in′kwə rē)   **1** the act of inquiring.   **2** a question.   **3** an investigation or examination: *The authorities are conducting an inquiry into the cause of the explosion.*   *n., pl.* **in·quir·ies.**   Also, **enquiry.**

**in·qui·si·tion** (in′kwə zish′ən)   **1** an official investigation; judicial inquiry.   **2** any very severe or intensive questioning.   **3 the Inquisition,   a** a court established by the Roman Catholic Church in 1229 to discover and suppress heresy and to punish heretics. During the Renaissance, the powers of the Inquisition were tremendously enlarged, especially in Spain, Portugal, and parts of Italy. It was abolished in 1834.   **b** the activities of this court.   *n.*

**in·quis·i·tive** (in kwiz′ə tiv)   **1** curious; asking many questions: *Children are usually inquisitive.*   **2** too curious; prying into other people's affairs: *The old man is inquisitive about what his neighbours do.*   *adj.*
—**in·quis′i·tive·ly**, *adv.*   —**in·quis′i·tive·ness**, *n.*

**in·quis·i·tor** (in kwiz′ə tər)   **1** one who conducts an inquisition; official investigator; judicial inquirer.   **2** a person who conducts an inquiry in a very harsh or hostile manner.   **3 Inquisitor,**   a member of the INQUISITION (def. 3).   *n.*

**in·quis·i·to·ri·al** (in kwiz′ə tô′rē əl)   **1** of an INQUISITOR or INQUISITION.   **2** making searching inquiry; thorough.   **3** unduly curious.   *adj.*

**in·road** (in′rōd′)   an attack or raid; entry by force. **make inroads on** *or* **upon,**   an advance or penetration that destroys, injures, or lessens something: *The unusual expenses made serious inroads on her savings.*   *n.*

**in·rush** (in′rush′)   a rushing in; inflow: *The inrush of water soon filled the pool.*   *n.*

**ins.   1** inches.   **2** insurance.

**in·sane** (in sān′)   **1** not sane; mentally ill; crazy.   **2** extremely foolish; completely lacking in common sense: *an insane plan.*   *adj.*   —**in·sane′ly**, *adv.*
☛ Syn.   See note at MAD.

**in·san·i·tar·y** (in san′ə ter′ē)   unhealthful.   *adj.*
—**in·san′i·tar′i·ness**, *n.*

**in·san·i·ty** (in san′ə tē)   **1** the state of being insane; mental illness; madness.   **2** extreme folly.   *n., pl.* **in·san·i·ties.**

**in·sa·tia·ble** (in sā′shə bəl)   that cannot be satisfied; always wanting more: *The boy had an insatiable appetite for candy.*   *adj.*   —**in·sa′tia·bly**, *adv.*

**in·sa·ti·ate** (in sā′shē it)   never satisfied; INSATIABLE: *an insatiate desire for praise.*   *adj.*

**in·sa·ti·e·ty** (in′sə tī′i tē)   the quality of being never satisfied.   *n.*

**in·scribe** (in skrīb′)   **1** write or engrave on a surface: *Her initials were inscribed on the bracelet.*   **2** write on or engrave with words, letters, etc.: *How shall we inscribe the ring?*   **3** write a message in or informally dedicate a book, etc.: *The book was inscribed, "To Paula, with love from Dad."*   **4** impress deeply: *His mother's words are inscribed on his memory.*   **5** put in a list; enrol.   **6** in geometry, draw a figure inside another figure so that their boundaries touch in as many places as possible: *To inscribe a triangle in a circle, you must make all the points of the triangle touch the circle.*   *v.,* **in·scribed, in·scrib·ing.**
—**in·scrib′er**, *n.*

**in·scrip·tion** (in skrip′shən)   **1** something inscribed; words, letters, etc. written or engraved on stone, metal, paper, etc.: *A monument or a coin has an inscription on it.*   **2** an informal dedication in a book, on a picture, etc.   *n.*

**in·scru·ta·bil·i·ty** (in skrü′tə bil′ə tē)   **1** the quality of being INSCRUTABLE.   **2** something INSCRUTABLE.   *n.*

**in·scru·ta·ble** (in skrü′tə bəl)   that cannot be understood; so mysterious or obscure that one cannot make out its meaning; incomprehensible: *an inscrutable look.*   *adj.*   —**in·scru′ta·ble·ness**, *n.*
—**in·scru′ta·bly**, *adv.*

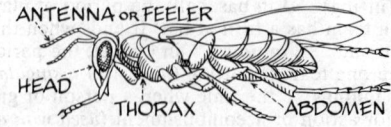

Insect (def. 1): a wasp

**in·sect** (in′sekt)   **1** any animal belonging to the class **Insecta,** a very large group of small invertebrate animals having the body divided into three well-defined parts (head, thorax, and abdomen), and having three pairs of legs and, usually, one or two pairs of wings: *Flies,* mosquitoes, grasshoppers, bees, and beetles are insects. **2** any similar small animal with its body divided into several parts, having several pairs of legs: *Spiders, centipedes, mites, and ticks are often called insects.* **3** an insignificant or contemptible person. *n.*

☛ *Etym.* From L *insectum,* formed from *insecare* 'to cut into, cut up'; an insect's body is divided into segments that make it look cut up.

**in·sec·ti·cide** (in sek′tə sīd′)   a substance for killing insects. *n.*

**in·sec·ti·vore** (in sek′tə vôr′)   **1** any of an order of mainly small mammals, most of which are active at night and feed largely on insects: *Moles, hedgehogs, and shrews are insectivores.* **2** any insect-eating animal or plant. *n.*

**in·sec·tiv·o·rous** (in′sek tiv′ə rəs)   **1** insect-eating; feeding mainly on insects. **2** of or belonging to the INSECTIVORES. *adj.*

**in·se·cure** (in′si kyùr′)   **1** not properly guarded or maintained; not safe from danger, failure, etc.: *insecure investments, an insecure position, an insecure marriage.* **2** liable to give way; not firm: *an insecure lock.* **3** lacking confidence; not sure of oneself; filled with fear and anxiety: *Hassan discovered that some of the people he had thought sophisticated were just as insecure as he was.* *adj.* —in′se·cure′ly, *adv.*

**in·se·cu·ri·ty** (in′si kyü′rə tē)   **1** a lack of security; being insecure. **2** something insecure. *n., pl.* in·se·cu·ri·ties.

**in·sem·i·nate** (in sem′ə nāt′)   **1** introduce semen into. **2** sow: *to inseminate seed.* **3** implant or instil ideas, etc.: *writings designed to inseminate new ideals.* *v.*   in·sem·i·nat·ed, in·sem·i·nat·ing. —in·sem′i·na′tion, *n.*

**in·sen·sate** (in sen′sāt)   **1** without sensation; inanimate: *the insensate stones.* **2** insensitive; unfeeling: *insensate cruelty.* **3** senseless; stupid: *insensate folly.* *adj.* —in·sen′sate·ly, *adv.*

**in·sen·si·bil·i·ty** (in sen′sə bil′ə tē)   the state or quality of being INSENSIBLE. *n., pl.* in·sen·si·bil·i·ties.

**in·sen·si·ble** (in sen′sə bəl)   **1** not having the power to perceive with the senses: *A blind person is insensible to colours.* **2** not able to respond emotionally: *We were thrilled by the view but Irene was insensible to it.* **3** not able to feel anything; unconscious: *The man hit by the truck was insensible.* **4** not easily felt or realized: *The room grew cold by insensible degrees.* **5** not aware: *The boys in the boat were insensible of the danger.* *adj.*

**in·sen·si·bly** (in sen′sə blē)   by imperceptible degrees; little by little. *adv.*

**in·sen·si·tive** (in sen′sə tiv)   **1** not responsive or susceptible to beauty, the thoughts or feelings of others, etc.; lacking feeling: *It was insensitive of her to laugh when he fell, because he had obviously hurt himself.* **2** not able to be affected by touch, light, etc.: *Dentists often give an injection to make a tooth insensitive so that the drilling does not hurt.* *adj.* —in·sen′si·tive·ness, *n.*

**in·sen·si·tiv·i·ty** (in sen′sə tiv′ə tē)   lack of SENSITIVITY. *n.*

**in·sep·a·ra·bil·i·ty** (in sep′ə rə bil′ə tē)   the state or quality of being INSEPARABLE. *n.*

**in·sep·a·ra·ble** (in sep′ə rə bəl)   **1** that cannot be separated or parted: *inseparable pals.* **2 inseparables,** *pl.* inseparable persons or things. **1** *adj.,* **2** *n.* —in·sep′a·ra·bly, *adv.*

**in·sert** (in sėrt′ *for verb,* in′sėrt *for noun*)   **1** thrust, fit,

---

**insecticide**    **623**    **insight**

hat, āge, fär; let, ēqual, tėrm; it, īce
hot, ōpen, ôrder; oil, out; cup, pùt, rüle
əbove, takən, pencəl, lemən, circəs
ch, child; ng, long; sh, ship
th, thin; ᴛʜ, then; zh, measure

or set in, into, between, etc.: *to insert elastic into the waistband of a skirt, to insert a lining. He inserted the key in the lock and turned it quietly.* **2** set or introduce something into written material, a newspaper, etc.: *to insert a missing letter into a word, to insert an advertisement in a newspaper.* **3** something set in or introduced: *Some magazines have a local insert for certain regions. The dress has lace inserts in the sleeves.* **1, 2** *v.,* **3** *n.*

**in·ser·tion** (in sėr′shən)   **1** the act or process of inserting: *the insertion of an ad in a newspaper.* **2** a single appearance of an advertisement in a newspaper, etc. **3** a band of lace or embroidery set into a cloth article for decoration: *The dress had a lace insertion near the neckline.* *n.*

**in·set** (in′set *for noun,* in set′ *or* in′set *for verb*)   **1** a small map, photograph, etc. set within the border of a larger one, to show some part in detail or to give extra information, etc. **2** a piece of lace or other material set into a dress, etc. for decoration; insert. **3** set or put in as an inset. **1, 2** *n.,* **3** *v.,* **in·set, in·set·ting.**

**in·shore** (in′shôr′ *for adjective,* in′shôr′ *for adverb*)   **1** near the shore: *inshore shoals.* **2** done or working near the shore: *the inshore fishery of Newfoundland, inshore fishermen.* **3** in toward the shore. **1, 2** *adj.,* **3** *adv.*

**in·side** (in′sīd′ *for noun and adjective,* in′sīd′ *for adverb and preposition*)   **1** the part within; the inner surface: *The inside of the box was lined with coloured paper.* **2** the contents: *The inside of the book was more interesting than the cover.* **3** being on the inside: *an inside seat.* **4** on or to the inside; within; in or into the inner part: *Please go inside.* **5** inside of; in: *The nut is inside the shell.* **6** private; secret; done or known by those inside: *The police needed inside information and questioned the maid.* **7** working within a group or company as an emissary or spy: *an inside man.* **8** indoor. **9** indoors. **10 insides,** *pl. Informal.* the parts inside the body; stomach and bowels. **1, 2, 10** *n.,* **3, 6–8** *adj.,* **4, 9** *adv.,* **5** *prep.*
**inside of,**   in; within the limits of: *He'll be back inside of an hour.*
**inside out,**   **a** so that what should be inside is outside; with the inside showing: *He turned his pockets inside out.* **b** completely: *Giulia learned her lessons inside out.*

**in·sid·er** (in′sī′dər)   a person who is recognized as being established within an organization, etc., especially someone who has power or access to important or confidential information: *an insider's report on the workings of Parliament.* *n.*

**in·sid·i·ous** (in sid′ē əs)   **1** wily; sly; crafty; tricky; treacherous: *an insidious plot.* **2** working secretly or subtly; developing gradually without attracting attention: *an insidious disease.* *adj.* —in·sid′i·ous·ly, *adv.* —in·sid′i·ous·ness, *n.*

**in·sight** (in′sīt)   **1** an understanding or awareness based on a seeing of the inside or inner nature of something: *Take the machine apart and get an insight into how it works.* **2** wisdom and understanding in dealing with people or with facts: *We study science to gain insight into natural laws.* *n.*

**in·sight·ful** (in′sīt′fəl) having or showing insight: *an insightful comment.* *adj.*

**in·sig·ni·a** (in sig′nē ə) **1** the emblems, badges, or other distinguishing marks of a high position, honour, military order, etc.: *The crown, orb, and sceptre are the insignia of monarchs.* **2** the distinguishing badges, crests, etc. of a team or society. *n., pl.* of **in·sig·ne** (in sig′nē).
☞ *Etym.* Insignia is a plural noun because it comes from the plural of L *insigne* 'badge'.

**in·sig·nif·i·cance** (in′sig nif′ə kəns) **1** unimportance. **2** meaninglessness. *n.*

**in·sig·nif·i·cant** (in′sig nif′ə kənt) **1** having little importance; trivial or trifling: *an insignificant error. Their losses in the first battle were insignificant.* **2** having little weight or influence: *The once thriving town had become an insignificant backwater. He has an insignificant position in a large company.* **3** having little or no meaning: *insignificant chatter.* *adj.* —**in′sig·nif′i·cant·ly,** *adv.*

**in·sin·cere** (in′sin sēr′) not sincere; not honest or candid; deceitful. *adj.* —**in′sin·cere′ly,** *adv.*

**in·sin·cer·i·ty** (in′sin ser′ə tē) a lack of SINCERITY; hypocrisy. *n., pl.* **in·sin·cer·i·ties.**

**in·sin·u·ate** (in sin′yü āt′) **1** suggest or hint indirectly, especially in an artful or scheming way: *She made no charge, but insinuated that the mayor had accepted bribes.* **2** get in or introduce by gradual, subtle, and stealthy means: *to insinuate doubt into a person's mind. The spy insinuated himself into the confidence of important army officers.* *v.,* **in·sin·u·at·ed, in·sin·u·at·ing.**

**in·sin·u·a·tion** (in sin′yü ā′shən) **1** the act or process of insinuating. **2** a hint or indirect suggestion, especially a sly, subtle, unpleasant one: *Her article contained an insinuation that their business deals were not as innocent as they appeared.* *n.*

**in·sip·id** (in sip′id) **1** without much taste: *A mixture of milk and water is an insipid drink.* **2** colourless and uninteresting; dull; lifeless: *insipid writing.* *adj.* —**in·sip′id·ly,** *adv.* —**in·sip′id·ness,** *n.*

**in·si·pid·i·ty** (in′sə pid′ə tē) **1** a lack of flavour; lack of interest. **2** something insipid. *n., pl.* **in·si·pid·i·ties.**

**in·sist** (in sist′) keep firmly to some demand, statement, or position; take a stand and refuse to give in: *to insist that something should be done, to insist on one's innocence.* *v.*

**in·sist·ence** (in sis′təns) **1** the act of insisting. **2** the quality of being INSISTENT. *n.*

**in·sist·ent** (in sis′tənt) **1** insisting; continuing to make a strong, firm demand or statement: *Although it was raining, she was insistent about going for a walk.* **2** compelling attention or notice; pressing; urgent: *An insistent knocking on the door woke us up.* *adj.* —**in·sist′ent·ly,** *adv.*

**in·snare** (in snēr′) ENSNARE. *v.,* **in·snared, in·snar·ing.**

**in·so·bri·e·ty** (in′sə brī′ə tē) intemperance; drunkenness. *n.*

**in·so·far** (in′sō fär′ *or* in′sə fär′) to such a degree or extent (*usually used with* **as**): *Rolf should be told the facts insofar as they concern him.* *adv.*

**in·sole** (in′sōl′) **1** the inner sole of a shoe or boot. **2** a shaped piece of warm or waterproof material laid on the sole inside a shoe or boot. *n.*

**in·so·lence** (in′sə ləns) bold rudeness; insulting behaviour or speech. *n.*

**in·so·lent** (in′sə lənt) boldly rude; insulting: *The insolent boy was punished for shouting at his mother.* *adj.* —**in′so·lent·ly,** *adv.*

**in·sol·u·bil·i·ty** (in sol′yə bil′ə tē) being INSOLUBLE. *n.*

**in·sol·u·ble** (in sol′yə bəl) **1** that cannot be dissolved: *Diamonds are insoluble. Fats are insoluble in cold water.* **2** that cannot be solved or explained: *an insoluble mystery.* *adj.* —**in·sol′u·bly,** *adv.*

**in·solv·a·ble** (in sol′və bəl) that cannot be solved. *adj.*

**in·sol·ven·cy** (in sol′vən sē) the condition of not being able to pay one's debts; bankruptcy. *n., pl.* **in·sol·ven·cies.**

**in·sol·vent** (in sol′vənt) **1** not able to pay one's debts; bankrupt. **2** an insolvent person. **1** *adj.,* **2** *n.*

**in·som·ni·a** (in som′nē ə) the inability to sleep, especially such a condition lasting a long time. *n.*

**in·so·much** (in′sō much′) to such an extent or degree; so (*usually used with* **as**). *adv.*

**in·sou·ci·ance** (in sü′sē əns) lack of concern; carelessness; indifference: *Edgar seemed to go through the whole trial with a smiling insouciance.* *n.*

**in·sou·ci·ant** (in sü′sē ənt) carefree; unconcerned: *an insouciant disposition.* *adj.*

**in·spect** (in spekt′) **1** look over carefully; examine: *A dentist inspects the children's teeth twice a year.* **2** examine officially: *The factory was inspected annually by a government official.* *v.*

**in·spec·tion** (in spek′shən) **1** inspecting: *An inspection of the roof showed no leaks.* **2** a formal or official examination: *The soldiers lined up for daily inspection by their officers.* *n.*

**in·spec·tor** (in spek′tər) **1** a person who inspects. **2** an officer or official appointed to inspect. **3** a police officer, usually ranking next below a superintendent. *n.*

**in·spi·ra·tion** (in′spə rā′shən) **1** the influence of thought and strong feelings on actions, especially on good or creative actions: *Some people get inspiration from speeches; some from poetry.* **2** a person or thing that arouses effort to do well: *The captain was an inspiration to his men.* **3** an idea that is inspired: *Many inventions are the result of inspiration.* **4** a suggestion to another; the act of causing something to be told or written by another. **5** a divine influence directly and immediately exerted upon the mind or soul of man or woman. **6** breathing in; the drawing of air into the lungs. *n.*

**in·spi·ra·tion·al** (in′spə rā′shə nəl) **1** inspiring: *The speech was instructive and inspirational.* **2** inspired. **3** of or having to do with INSPIRATION. *adj.*

**in·spire** (in spīr′) **1** put thought, feeling, life, force, etc. into: *The speaker inspired the crowd.* **2** cause thought or feeling: *The leader's courage inspired confidence in others.* **3** affect; influence; fill with a thought or feeling: *His sly ways inspire me with distrust.* **4** arouse or influence by a divine force. **5** suggest; cause to be told or written: *Gwen's enemies inspired false stories about her.*

6 breathe in; breathe in air.   *v.*, **in·spired, in·spir·ing.**
—**in·spir′er,** *n.*   —**in·spir′ing·ly,** *adv.*

**Inst.**   1 Institute.   2 Institution.

**in·sta·bil·i·ty** (in′stə bil′ə tē)   the quality or state of being UNSTABLE: *the instability of the dollar. His emotional instability made him a poor risk as an employee.*   *n.*

**in·stall** (in stol′)   1 place formally in a position, office, etc.: *to install a new judge.*   2 put in a place or position; settle: *The cat installed itself in an easy chair.*   3 put in position for use: *to install a telephone.*   *v.*
—**in·stall′er,** *n.*

**in·stal·la·tion** (in′stə lā′shən)   1 installing or being installed.   2 the thing installed; machinery placed in position for use: *They have requested new lighting installations.*   *n.*

**in·stal·ment**[1] or **in·stall·ment**[1] (in stol′mənt)   1 a part of a sum of money or of a debt to be paid at certain regular times: *The furniture cost $1500; we paid for it in instalments of $150 a month for ten months.*   2 any of several parts furnished or issued at successive times as part of a series: *The magazine has a serial story in six instalments.*   *n.*

**in·stal·ment**[2] or **in·stall·ment**[2] (in stol′mənt)   installing or being installed: *our instalment in our new home.*   *n.*

**instalment plan**   a system of paying for goods in instalments.

**in·stance** (in′stəns)   1 a person or thing serving as an example; case: *Her rude question was an instance of bad manners.*   2 refer to as an example: *He instanced the fly as a dirty insect.*   3 exemplify.   4 a stage or step in an action; occasion: *Markos said he preferred, in this instance, to remain where he was.*   5 a request or suggestion; urging: *She came at their instance.*   1, 4, 5 *n.*, 2, 3 *v.*,
**in·stanced, in·stanc·ing.**
**for instance,**   as an example: *Her many hobbies include, for instance, skating and stamp collecting.*

**in·stant** (in′stənt)   1 a particular moment: *Stop talking this instant!*   2 a moment of time: *She paused for an instant.*   3 immediate; without delay: *The medicine gave instant relief from pain.*   4 pressing; urgent: *When there is a fire, there is an instant need for action.*   5 prepared beforehand and requiring little or no cooking, mixing, or additional ingredients: *instant pudding, instant coffee.*
**the instant,**   just as soon as: *The instant he came in the door, everyone stopped talking.*   1, 2 *n.,* 3–5 *adj.*

**in·stan·ta·ne·ous** (in′stən tā′nē əs)   done, happening, or acting in an instant or without delay: *instantaneous applause. His reaction was instantaneous.*   *adj.*
—**in′stan·ta′ne·ous·ly,** *adv.*
—**in′stan·ta′ne·ous·ness,** *n.*

**in·stant·ly** (in′stənt lē)   in an instant; at once; immediately: *Instantly, she was gone.*   *adv.*

**in·stead** (in sted′)   in place of someone or something; as a substitute or equivalent: *If you cannot go, let him go instead.*   *adv.*
**instead of,**   rather than; in place of; as a substitute for: *Instead of studying, she read a story.*

**in·step** (in′step)   1 the upper surface of the human foot between the toes and the ankle. See LEG for picture.   2 the part of a shoe, stocking, etc. over the instep.   *n.*

**in·sti·gate** (in′stə gāt′)   1 stir up; set in motion, especially something undesirable: *Foreign agents instigated a rebellion.*   *v.*, **ins·ti·gat·ed, in·sti·gat·ing.**

**Inst.**   **625**   **institutionalism**

hat, āge, fär; let, ēqual, tėrm; it, īce
hot, ōpen, ôrder; oil, out; cup, pùt, rüle
əbove, takən, pencəl, lemən, circəs
ch, child; ng, long; sh, ship
th, thin; ᴛʜ, then; zh, measure

**in·sti·ga·tion** (in′stə gā′shən)   the act of instigating.   *n.*
**at the instigation of,**   instigated by.

**in·sti·ga·tor** (in′stə gā′tər)   a person who instigates; person who stirs up evil or trouble.   *n.*

**in·stil** or **in·still** (in stil′)   1 put in little by little; impart gradually: *Reading good books instils a love for fine literature.*   2 put in drop by drop: *to instil drops in the eye.*   *v.*, **in·stilled, in·still·ing.**

**in·stil·la·tion** (in′stə lā′shən)   1 instilling.   2 something instilled.   *n.*

**in·stinct**[1] (in′stingkt)   1 a natural feeling, knowledge, or power, such as guides animals; an inborn tendency to act in a certain way: *Birds do not learn to fly but fly by instinct.*   2 a natural tendency or ability; talent: *Even as a child, the artist had an instinct for colour.*   *n.*

**in·stinct**[2] (in stingkt′)   charged or filled with something: *The picture is instinct with life and beauty.*   *adj.*

**in·stinc·tive** (in stingk′tiv)   1 of or having to do with INSTINCT[1].   2 caused or done by INSTINCT[1]; independent of thought, will, or training: *She felt an instinctive distrust of the stranger. Climbing is instinctive in monkeys.*   *adj.*
—**in·stinc′tive·ly,** *adv.*

**in·sti·tute** (in′stə tyüt′ *or* in′stə tüt′)   1 an organization or society for the support or promotion of a particular cause: *an art institute, the Canadian National Institute for the Blind.*   2 the building used by such an organization: *We spent the afternoon at the Art Institute.*   3 an educational institution; school: *a collegiate institute.*   4 an established principle, law, or custom.   5 originate or set going; establish or begin: *The police instituted an inquiry into the causes of the accident.*   6 **institutes,** *pl.* especially in law, a collection or digest of established principles.   1–4, 6 *n.,* 5 *v.,* **in·sti·tut·ed, in·sti·tut·ing.**

**in·sti·tu·tion** (in′stə tyü′shən *or* in′stə tü′shən)   1 an organization or society established for some public or social purpose: *A church, school, college, hospital, or prison is an institution.*   2 a building used by such an organization or society.   3 an established law, custom, or system: *Giving presents for a birthday is an institution. Marriage is an institution among most peoples of the earth.*   4 a setting up; establishing; beginning: *Many people favour the institution of more clubs for young people.*   *n.*

**in·sti·tu·tion·al** (in′stə tyü′shə nəl *or* in′stə tü′shə nəl)
1 of, having to do with, like, or characteristic of INSTITUTIONS (def. 1): *She hated the institutional life of the boarding school. Institutional food is sometimes bland and boring.*   2 intended or designed for INSTITUTIONS (def. 1): *Their main business is in institutional sales rather than retail trade.*   *adj.*

**in·sti·tu·tion·al·ism** (in′stə tyü′shə nə liz′əm *or* in′stə tü′shə nə liz′əm)   1 belief in the importance of established organizations, especially religious institutions.   2 the care and maintenance in public institutions of people unable to care for themselves.   3 emphasis on the formal, impersonal aspects of the operation or maintenance of institutions: *She reacted against the institutionalism of education.* *n.*

**in·sti·tu·tion·al·iz·a·tion** (in′stə tyü′shə nə lə zā′shən *or* in′stə tyü′shə nə lī zā′shən, in′stə tü′shə nə lə zā′shən *or* in′stə tü′shə nə lī zā′shən) **1** the act or process of institutionalizing. **2** the state or condition of becoming institutionalized. *n.*

**in·sti·tu·tion·al·ize** (in′stə tyü′shə nə līz′ *or* in′stə tü′shə nə līz′) **1** make into or treat as an acceptable and established principle or custom: *to institutionalize gambling in the form of lotteries.* **2** make impersonal and formal: *She argued that charity had become too institutionalized.* **3** commit to a public institution for care or detention: *They decided not to institutionalize their mentally retarded son.* *v.*, **in·sti·tu·tion·al·ized**, **in·sti·tu·tion·al·iz·ing**.

**in·struct** (in strukt′) **1** teach; train; educate: *M. Paré instructs the class in French.* **2** give directions or orders to; order: *The owner instructed her agent to sell the property.* **3** inform; tell: *Her lawyer instructed her that the contract would be signed on March 1st.* *v.*

**in·struc·tion** (in struk′shən) **1** teaching or lesson: *instruction in boat building.* **2** Usually, **instructions**, *pl.* orders: *Their instructions were to be there at 7 o'clock.* **3 instructions**, *pl.* an outline of procedure, etc.; directions: *The kit includes complete instructions for assembling the airplane.* *n.*

**in·struc·tion·al** (in struk′shə nəl) of or for INSTRUCTION; educational. *adj.*

**in·struc·tive** (in struk′tiv) useful for INSTRUCTION; instructing; giving knowledge or information: *A trip around the world is an instructive experience.* *adj.* —**in·struc′tive·ly**, *adv.* —**in·struc′tive·ness**, *n.*

**in·struc·tor** (in struk′tər) **1** teacher. **2** in some colleges and universities, a teacher ranking below an assistant professor. *n.*

**in·struc·tress** (in struk′tris) a female instructor or teacher. *n.*

**in·stru·ment** (in′strə mənt) **1** a tool or mechanical device: *surgical instruments.* **2** a device for producing musical sounds: *wind instruments, stringed instruments.* **3** a device for measuring, recording, or controlling: *A thermometer is an instrument for measuring temperature.* **4** a person or thing by means of or through which something is done; agent or means. **5** a formal legal document, such as a contract, deed, or grant. *n.*

**in·stru·men·tal** (in′strə men′təl) **1** acting or serving as a means; useful; helpful: *His uncle was instrumental in getting him a job.* **2** performed on or written for a musical instrument: *an instrumental arrangement. She prefers instrumental music to choral music.* **3** of, having to do with, or done by a device or tool. *adj.* —**in′stru·men′tal·ly**, *adv.*

**in·stru·men·tal·ist** (in′strə men′tə list) a person who plays on a musical instrument. *n.*

**in·stru·men·tal·i·ty** (in′strə men tal′ə tē) **1** the quality or state of being INSTRUMENTAL (def. 1); usefulness or helpfulness. **2** agency; means. *n.*, *pl.* **in·stru·men·tal·i·ties**.

**in·stru·men·ta·tion** (in′strə men tā′shən) **1** the arrangement or composition of music for instruments. **2** the use of instruments; work done with instruments. *n.*

**instrument board** INSTRUMENT PANEL.

**instrument flying** the directing of an aircraft by instruments only, without being able to observe points or objects on the ground. Compare with CONTACT FLYING.

**instrument panel** on an aircraft, motor vehicle, or other machine, a panel displaying gauges, indicator lights, switches, etc., permitting the operator to check on and control specific functions of the machine.

**in·sub·or·di·nate** (in′sə bôr′də nit) **1** resisting authority; disobedient; unruly. **2** an insubordinate person. **1** *adj.*, **2** *n.*

**in·sub·or·di·na·tion** (in′sə bôr′də nā′shən) resistance to authority; active disobedience: *The private was put on charge for insubordination.* *n.*

**in·sub·stan·tial** (in′səb stan′shəl) **1** frail; flimsy; weak: *A cobweb is very insubstantial.* **2** unreal; not actual; imaginary: *Dreams and ghosts are insubstantial.* *adj.*

**in·suf·fer·a·ble** (in suf′ə rə bəl) intolerable; unbearable: *insufferable insolence.* *adj.* —**in·suf′fer·a·ble·ness**, *n.* —**in·suf′fer·a·bly**, *adv.*

**in·suf·fi·cien·cy** (in′sə fish′ən sē) too small an amount; lack; deficiency. *n.*

**in·suf·fi·cient** (in′sə fish′ənt) not enough; less than is needed: *Andrea was tired because she had had insufficient sleep.* *adj.* —**in′suf·fi′cient·ly**, *adv.*

**in·su·lar** (in′sə lər) **1** of or having to do with islands or islanders: *a moderate, insular climate.* **2** living or situated on an island: *an insular people.* **3** forming an island; standing alone like an island. **4** like or characteristic of people who live in isolation, especially when thought of as narrow-minded or ignorant: *an insular point of view, insular intolerance.* *adj.*

**in·su·lar·i·ty** (in′sə lar′ə tē *or* in′sə ler′ə tē) **1** the fact or condition of being an island or of living on an island. **2** narrow-mindedness or ignorance. *n.*

**in·su·late** (in′sə lāt′) **1** keep from losing or transferring electricity, heat, sound, etc., especially by covering or surrounding with a non-conducting material: *Wires are often insulated by a covering of rubber. Our heating bills are lower now that our house is better insulated.* **2** pack with material that will not burn, so as to prevent the spread of fire: *The builder insulated the wall between the garage and the house.* **3** set apart; separate from others; isolate. *v.*, **in·su·lat·ed**, **in·su·lat·ing**.

**in·su·la·tion** (in′sə lā′shən) **1** insulating or being insulated: *The electrician checked the insulation of the wiring.* **2** the material used in insulating: *Rock wool is often used as insulation against fire.* *n.*

**in·su·la·tor** (in′sə lā′tər) something that insulates, especially a material that prevents the passage of electricity or heat; a non-conductor: *Glass is an effective insulator.* *n.*

**in·su·lin** (in′sə lin) **1** a hormone secreted by the pancreas that enables the body to use sugar and other carbohydrates. **2** a preparation containing this hormone, used especially in the treatment of diabetes: *Insulin is obtained from the pancreas of slaughtered animals.* *n.*
☛ *Etym.* **Insulin** was isolated and named by the Canadian doctors F.G. Banting and C.H. Best in 1921.

**in·sult** (in sult′ *for verb*, in′sult *for noun*) **1** treat with scorn, abuse, and great rudeness: *The rebels insulted the flag by throwing mud on it. Such a question insults my intelligence.* **2** an insulting speech or action: *To be called a coward is an insult.* **1** *v.*, **2** *n.* —**in·sult′ing·ly**, *adv.*

**in·su·per·a·ble** (in sü′pə rə bəl)   that cannot be passed over or overcome: *an insuperable barrier.*   *adj.*   —**in·su′per·a·bly,** *adv.*

**in·sup·port·a·ble** (in′sə pôr′tə bəl)   **1** unbearable; unendurable; intolerable: *insupportable living conditions.* **2** that cannot be upheld or justified: *insupportable rudeness.*   *adj.*

**in·sur·a·ble** (in shü′rə bəl)   capable of being insured; fit to be insured.   *adj.*

**in·sur·ance** (in shü′rəns)   **1** an insuring of property, person, or life: *fire insurance, burglary insurance, accident insurance, life insurance, health insurance.*   **2** the business of insuring property, life etc.: *My aunt works in insurance.* **3** the amount of money for which a person or thing is insured: *He has $50 000 insurance.*   **4** the amount of money paid for insurance; PREMIUM: *She pays her insurance in two instalments.*   **5** any means of insuring or protecting: *Good health habits are an insurance against illness.*   *n.*

**in·sure** (in shür′)   **1** arrange for money payment in case of loss of property, profit, etc. or in case of accident, sickness, or death; take out or give insurance: *An insurance company will insure your property, person, or life if you pay a certain amount of money.*   **2** make safe or certain; ensure.   *v.,* **in·sured, in·sur·ing.**
☞ *Syn.* See note at ENSURE.

**in·sured** (in shürd′)   **1** a person whose life or property is insured.   **2** pt. and pp. of INSURE.   **1** *n.,* **2** *v.*

**in·sur·er** (in shü′rər)   a person or company that insures; one that sells insurance.   *n.*

**in·sur·gence** (in sėr′jəns)   a rising in revolt; rebellion.   *n.*

**in·sur·gent** (in sėr′jənt)   **1** a person who rises in revolt; rebel: *The insurgents captured the town.*   **2** rising in revolt; rebellious: *The insurgent forces captured the radio station.*   **1** *n.,* **2** *adj.*

**in·sur·mount·a·ble** (in′sər moun′tə bəl)   that cannot be overcome.   *adj.*   —**in′sur·mount′a·bly,** *adv.*

**in·sur·rec·tion** (in′sə rek′shən)   a rising against established authority; revolt.   *n.*

**in·sur·rec·tion·ar·y** (in′sə rek′shə ner′ē)   **1** having a tendency to revolt.   **2** having to do with revolt.   *adj.*

**in·sur·rec·tion·ist** (in′sə rek′shə nist)   a person who takes part in or favours an INSURRECTION; rebel.   *n.*

**in·sus·cep·ti·bil·i·ty** (in′sə sep′tə bil′ə tē)   the fact or quality of being INSUSCEPTIBLE.   *n.*

**in·sus·cep·ti·ble** (in′sə sep′tə bəl)   not SUSCEPTIBLE; not easily influenced.   *adj.*

**int.**   **1** interest.   **2** international.

**in·tact** (in takt′)   with no part missing or damaged; whole: *I checked the dishes when we unpacked them and found that they were all intact.*   *adj.*

**in·take** (in′tāk′)   **1** the place where water, air, gas, etc. enters a channel, pipe, or other narrow opening. **2** taking in.   **3** the amount or thing taken in: *The average daily intake from the water main was 10 m³.*   *n.*

**in·tan·gi·bil·i·ty** (in tan′jə bil′ə tē)   the state or quality of being INTANGIBLE.   *n.*

**in·tan·gi·ble** (in tan′jə bəl)   **1** not capable of being touched or felt: *Sound and light are intangible.*   **2** not easily grasped by the mind; vague: *She had that intangible quality called charm.*   **3** something intangible.   **1, 2** *adj.,* **3** *n.*   —**in·tan′gi·bly,** *adv.*

# insuperable   627   intelligence

hat, āge, fär; let, ēqual, tėrm; it, īce
hot, ōpen, ôrder; oil, out; cup, pùt, rüle
əbove, takən, pencəl, lemən, circəs
ch, child; ng, long; sh, ship
th, thin; ᴛʜ, then; zh, measure

**in·tar·si·a** (in tär′sē ə)   the art or technique of decorating a surface with or as if with inlaid wood: *Sweaters can be made in a pattern resembling intarsia.*

**in·te·ger** (in′tə jər)   **1** any positive or negative whole number or zero: *The numbers 4, −37, −8, 106, etc. are integers.*   **2** a thing complete in itself; something whole.   *n.*

**in·te·gral** (in′tə grəl)   **1** necessary to the completeness of the whole; essential: *Steel is an integral part of a modern skyscraper.*   **2** entire; complete.   **3** having to do with whole numbers; not fractional.   **4** a whole; a whole number.   **1–3** *adj.,* **4** *n.*

**in·te·grate** (in′tə grāt′)   **1** make more unified or harmonious: *The government should integrate its approach to unemployment.*   **2** bring parts together into a whole: *Let's integrate all these suggestions into one master plan.* **3** bring in individuals or groups as part of a larger group: *to integrate immigrants into Canadian society.*   **4** make facilities, institutions, etc. available to all people regardless of race, nationality, religion, etc.; desegregate: *to integrate a school.*   **5** become unified, brought together, or desegregated: *The three neighbouring cities have decided to integrate.*   *v.,* **in·te·grat·ed, in·te·grat·ing.**   —**in′te·gra′tor,** *n.*

**in·te·gra·tion** (in′tə grā′shən)   the act or process of integrating.   *n.*

**in·teg·ri·ty** (in teg′rə tē)   **1** firm attachment to moral or artistic principle; honesty and sincerity; uprightness: *People realized that he was a victim of circumstances, and did not question his integrity. Her poetry is too slick and commercial to have integrity.*   **2** wholeness; completeness: *The integrity of the country was guaranteed by treaty.*   **3** the condition of being unmarred or uncorrupted; the original, perfect condition: *Several scholars have questioned the integrity of the text of this poem.*   *n.*

**in·teg·u·ment** (in teg′yə mənt)   a natural outer covering of an animal or plant or of one of its parts: *The skin or shell of an animal and the husk of a seed or fruit are integuments.*   *n.*

**in·tel·lect** (in′tə lekt′)   **1** the power of knowing and understanding as distinguished from will and feeling: *Some people's actions are influenced more by feelings than by intellect.*   **2** great intelligence; high mental ability: *Sir Isaac Newton was a man of intellect.*   **3** a person having high mental ability: *Plato was one of the greatest intellects of all time.*   *n.*

**in·tel·lec·tu·al** (in′tə lek′chü əl)   **1** of or having to do with the intellect: *Thinking is an intellectual process.* **2** needing or involving the intellect: *an intellectual puzzle. Mathematics is an intellectual discipline.*   **3** inclined toward or favouring things that involve the intellect: *intellectual tastes, an intellectual person.*   **4** a person who is interested in intellectual things; an intellectual person: *a magazine designed for intellectuals.*   **1–3** *adj.,* **4** *n.*   —**in′tel·lect′u·al·ly,** *adv.*

**in·tel·li·gence** (in tel′ə jəns)   **1** the ability to learn and know; the ability to use the reason or intellect in dealing with a new situation, solving a problem, etc.

**2** knowledge or information: *The government received secret intelligence of the plans of the enemy.* **3** the getting or distributing of information, especially secret information: *She worked in intelligence during the war.* **4** a group or agency engaged in obtaining secret information: *Intelligence had informed them of the planned attack.* *n.*

**intelligence quotient** a number used to describe a person's relative intelligence in terms of certain thinking skills. It is computed by dividing his or her apparent mental age, as shown by a standardized test, by his or her actual age and multiplying by 100. *Abbrev.*: I.Q.

**intelligence test** a standardized test designed to measure a person's relative intelligence.

**in·tel·li·gent** (in tel′ə jənt) **1** having intelligence; rational: *Is there intelligent life on other planets?* **2** having or showing a high degree of intelligence; clever, perceptive, or bright: *an intelligent student, an intelligent remark.* **3** of a computer, having ARTIFICIAL INTELLIGENCE. *adj.* —**in·tel′li·gent·ly,** *adv.*

**in·tel·li·gent·si·a** (in tel′ə jent′sē ə *or* in tel′ə gent′sē ə) the persons representing, or claiming to represent, the superior intelligence or enlightened opinion of a country; the intellectuals. *n. pl.*

**in·tel·li·gi·bil·i·ty** (in tel′ə jə bil′ə tē) the fact or quality of being INTELLIGIBLE. *n.*

**in·tel·li·gi·ble** (in tel′ə jə bəl) capable of being understood; clear; comprehensible: *He was so upset that his account of the accident was hardly intelligible.* *adj.* —**in·tel′li·gi·bly,** *adv.*

**in·tem·per·ance** (in tem′pə rəns) **1** a lack of moderation or self-control; excess: *His intemperance in gambling cost him his job.* **2** the excessive drinking of intoxicating liquor, especially habitually. *n.*

**in·tem·per·ate** (in tem′pə rit) **1** not moderate; lacking in self-control; excessive: *an intemperate appetite, an intemperate anger.* **2** drinking too much intoxicating liquor. **3** not temperate; extreme in temperature; severe: *an intemperate climate.* *adj.* —**in·tem′per·ate·ly,** *adv.*

**in·tend** (in tend′) **1** have in mind as a purpose; plan: *We intend to go home soon. Gloria apologized and said she had intended no insult.* **2** mean for a particular purpose or use; design or destine: *That gift was intended for you.* *v.* —**in·tend′er,** *n.*

**in·tend·ant** (in ten′dənt; *French,* AN tän däN′) **1** the most important administrative office in New France, eventually responsible for the administration of finance, justice, and police in the colony. **2 Intendant,** an official who held this office: *Jean Talon was the first and greatest Intendant of New France.* *n.*

**in·tend·ed** (in ten′did) **1** meant; planned: *an intended insult. The medicine did not have the intended effect.* **2** prospective: *a woman's intended husband.* **3** *Informal.* a prospective husband or wife. **4** pt. and pp. of INTEND. 1, 2 *adj.*, 3 *n.*, 4 *v.*

**in·tense** (in tens′) **1** existing in or being of a very high degree; very strong; extreme: *intense pain, an intense colour, an intense light.* **2** of action, activity, etc., strenuous, eager, or ardent: *intense thought. She lived an intense life.* **3** having or showing strong feelings, purpose, etc.: *an intense face. He is an intense person.* *adj.* —**in·tense′ly,** *adv.*

**in·ten·si·fy** (in ten′sə fī) make or become intense or more intense; strengthen; increase: *Blowing on a fire intensifies the heat. Her first failure only intensified her desire to succeed.* *v.* —**in·ten′si·fied, in·ten′si·fy·ing.** —**in·ten′si·fi·ca′tion,** *n.* —**in·ten′si·fi′er,** *n.*

**in·ten·si·ty** (in ten′sə tē) **1** the quality or state of being intense; very great strength, force, etc.: *We had to close our eyes because of the intensity of the light.* **2** the amount or degree of strength of electricity, heat, light, sound, etc. per unit of area, volume, etc. *n., pl.* **in·ten·si·ties.**

**in·ten·sive** (in ten′siv) **1** very deep and thorough: *An intensive study of a few books is more valuable than a superficial reading of many.* **2** something that makes intense. **3** in grammar, giving force or emphasis; expressing intensity: *In "He himself said it,"* himself *is an intensive pronoun.* **4** an intensive word, prefix, etc. 1, 3 *adj.*, 2, 4 *n.* —**in·ten′sive·ly,** *adv.*

**intensive pronoun** a pronoun ending in *self* or *selves* used to emphasize the noun or pronoun it follows: *The explorer herself talked to our class. They themselves caused the problem.*

**in·tent**[1] (in tent′) **1** purpose; intention: *The thief shot with intent to kill.* **2** meaning; significance: *What is the intent of that sentence?* *n.*
**to** or **for all intents and purposes,** in almost every way; practically.

**in·tent**[2] (in tent′) **1** very attentive; having the eyes or thoughts earnestly fixed on something; earnest: *an intent look.* **2** earnestly engaged; much interested; determined: *She is intent on research.* *adj.* —**in·tent′ly,** *adv.*

**in·ten·tion** (in ten′shən) **1** the act or fact of having in mind as a purpose; determination to act in a certain way: *I'm sure she had no intention of hurting your feelings.* **2** what is intended; an object or purpose: *It wasn't my intention to start an argument.* **3 intentions,** *pl. Informal.* purpose with respect to marrying. *n.*

**in·ten·tion·al** (in ten′shə nəl) done on purpose; meant; planned; intended: *His insult was intentional; he wanted to hurt your feelings.* *adj.* —**in·ten′tion·al·ly,** *adv.*

**in·ter** (in tėr′) put a dead body into a grave or tomb; bury. *v.*, **in·terred, in·ter·ring.**
☞ *Usage.* Do not confuse **inter** 'bury' with INTERN 'confine in a certain place'. One **inters** a dead body: one **interns** a live person who might cause trouble.

**inter-** a prefix meaning: **1** together; one with the other: *Intercommunicate means communicate with each other.* **2** between: *Interpose means put between. Interface means place or be placed between surfaces.* **3** between or among a group: *Interscholastic means between or among schools.*

**in·ter·act** (in′tə rakt′) act on each other. *v.*

**in·ter·ac·tion** (in′tə rak′shən) action on each other: *The interaction of two chemicals may result in the formation of a new compound.* *n.*

**in·ter·ac·tive** (in′tə rak′tiv) involving direct communication between a computer system and a user. *adj.*

**in·ter·breed** (in′tər brēd′) breed by the mating of different kinds; breed by using different varieties or species of animals or plants. *v.*, **in·ter·bred, in·ter·breed·ing.**

**in·ter·cede** (in′tər sēd′) **1** plead or ask a favour in another's behalf: *Friends of the condemned man interceded with the authorities for a pardon.* **2** intervene in order to bring about an agreement; mediate. *v.*, **in·ter·ced·ed, in·ter·ced·ing.**

**in·ter·cel·lu·lar** (in′tər sel′yə lər) situated between or among cells. *adj.*

**in·ter·cept** (in′tər sept′) **1** take, seize, or stop a person, vehicle, etc. on the way from one place to another: *to intercept a messenger or a letter, to intercept an enemy aircraft, to intercept a pass in football.* **2** interrupt or stop motion, passage, progress, etc.: *to intercept the flight of a criminal.* **3** in mathematics, the distance from the origin to the point where a line crosses an axis on a graph. **1, 2** *v.*, **3** *n.* —**in′ter·cep′tion,** *n.*

**in·ter·cep·tor** (in′tər sep′tər) a person or thing that intercepts, especially a fighter aircraft or missile designed to stop enemy aircraft or missiles. *n.*

**in·ter·ces·sion** (in′tər sesh′ən) **1** the act or fact of interceding: *The judge's intercession saved the boy from a severe sentence.* **2** a prayer or petition in behalf of another person or persons. *n.*

**in·ter·ces·sor** (in′tər ses′ər) a person who INTERCEDES. *n.*

**in·ter·ces·so·ry** (in′tər ses′ə rē) making or relating to INTERCESSION; interceding. *adj.*

**in·ter·change** (in′tər chānj′ *for verb,* in′tər chānj′ *for noun*) **1** put each of two or more persons or things in the other's place: *Maria and Alicia interchanged dresses.* **2** the putting of each of two or more persons or things in the other's place: *The word team may be changed to meat by the interchange of the end letters.* **3** a road that permits traffic from one highway to change to another without crossing in front of other traffic; cloverleaf. **4** give and take; exchange: *to interchange gifts.* **5** a giving and taking; exchanging. **6** cause to happen by turns; alternate: *to interchange severity with indulgence.* **7** an alternation; alternate succession: *an interchange of hard work with rest.* **1, 4, 6** *v.*, **in·ter·changed, in·ter·chang·ing;** **2, 3, 5, 7** *n.*

**in·ter·change·a·bil·i·ty** (in′tər chān′jə bil′ə tē) being INTERCHANGEABLE. *n.*

**in·ter·change·a·ble** (in′tər chān′jə bəl) capable of being used in place of each other: *This saw has several interchangeable blades.* *adj.* —**in′ter·change′a·bly,** *adv.*

**in·ter·class** (in′tər klas′) between classes: *interclass swimming meets.* *adj.*

**in·ter·col·le·giate** (in′tər kə lē′jit) between high schools, colleges or universities: *intercollegiate football games.* *adj.*

**in·ter·co·lo·ni·al** (in′tər kə lō′nē əl) between colonies: *intercolonial trade.* *adj.*

**in·ter·com** (in′tər kom′) *Informal.* a system of radio or telephone communication between rooms of a building, parts of a ship or aircraft, etc. *n.*

**in·ter·com·mu·ni·cate** (in′tər kə myü′nə kāt′) communicate with each other. *v.*, **in′ter·com·mu·ni·cat·ed, in·ter·com·mu·ni·cat·ing.** —**in′ter·com·mu′ni·ca′tion,** *n.*

**in·ter·con·nect** (in′tər kə nekt′) connect with each other. *v.* —**in′ter·con·nec′tion,** *n.*

### intercede 629 interested

hat, āge, fär; let, ēqual, tėrm; it, īce
hot, ōpen, ôrder; oil, out; cup, pùt, rüle
əbove, takən, pencəl, lemən, circəs
ch, child; ng, long; sh, ship
th, thin; ᴛʜ, then; zh, measure

**in·ter·con·ti·nen·tal** (in′tər kon′tə nen′təl) **1** extending or carried on between or among continents: *intercontinental travel.* **2** capable of travelling between continents: *intercontinental ballistic missiles.* *adj.*

**in·ter·course** (in′tər kôrs′) **1** communication; dealings between people; exchange of thoughts, services, feelings, etc.: *Airplanes, good roads, and telephones make intercourse between different parts of the country far easier than it was fifty years ago.* **2** SEXUAL INTERCOURSE. *n.*

**in·ter·de·nom·i·na·tion·al** (in′tər di nom′ə nā′shə nəl) between or involving different religious denominations. *adj.*

**in·ter·de·part·men·tal** (in′tər dē′pärt men′təl) between departments: *an interdepartmental memo.* *adj.*

**in·ter·de·pend·ence** (in′tər di pen′dəns) dependence on each other; mutual dependence: *the interdependence of all living things.* *n.*

**in·ter·de·pend·ent** (in′tər di pen′dənt) dependent each upon the other. *adj.* —**in′ter·de·pend′ent·ly,** *adv.*

**in·ter·dict** (in′tər dikt′ *for noun,* in′tər dikt′ *for verb*) **1** an official prohibition; a formal, authoritative order forbidding something. **2** in the Roman Catholic church, a censure excluding a place or person from certain sacraments and privileges. **3** place under an interdict: *to interdict a parish.* **4** prohibit or forbid by authority: *to interdict trade with other countries.* **5** restrain by authority: *interdicted from buying alcoholic liquor.* **6** *Cdn.* a person forbidden to buy alcoholic liquor. **1, 2, 6** *n.*, **3–5** *v.*

**in·ter·dic·tion** (in′tər dik′shən) INTERDICTing or being interdicted. *n.*

**in·ter·est** (in′tə rist *or* in′trist) **1** a feeling of wanting to know, see, do, own, share in, or take part in: *She has no interest in sports.* **2** the power of arousing such a feeling: *A dull book lacks interest.* **3** make curious and hold the attention of: *An exciting story interests you.* **4** a share or part in property and actions: *She bought a half interest in the farm.* **5** cause a person to take a share or part in something: *The agent tried to interest us in buying a car.* **6** something in which a person has a share or part: *Any business, activity, or hobby can be an interest.* **7** a group of people having the same business, activity, etc.: *the farming interests, mining interests.* **8** advantage; benefit: *Each person should look after her own interest.* **9** money paid for the use of money, usually a percentage of the amount invested, borrowed, or loaned: *The interest on the loan was 12 percent a year.* **1, 2, 4, 6–9** *n.*, **3, 5** *v.*
**in the interest of,** for; to help.
**with interest,** with something extra given in return: *She returned our favour with interest.*

**in·ter·est·ed** (in′tə ris təd, in′tris təd, *or* in′tə res′təd) **1** feeling or showing interest: *He gave a demonstration before a crowd of interested spectators. Are you interested in running for class president?* **2** involved or concerned; having an interest or share: *A meeting will be held tonight for all interested parties.* **3** influenced by personal considerations; prejudiced: *interested motives.* **4** pt. and pp. of INTEREST. 1–3 *adj.*, 4 *v.* —**in′ter·est·ed·ly**, *adv.* —**in′ter·est·ed·ness**, *n.*

☛ *Usage.* The adjective **interested** has two opposites. UNINTERESTED is just its negative and means 'having no feeling about a matter': *He was uninterested in the outcome of the game.* DISINTERESTED means 'free from personal considerations; impartial; fair': *A disinterested onlooker offered to referee the game.*

**in·ter·est·ing** (in′tə ris ting, in′tris′ting, or in′tə res′ting) arousing interest; holding one's attention: *an interesting book. adj.* —**in′ter·est·ing·ly**, *adv.*

**in·ter·face** (in′tər fās′) **1** a surface that forms a common boundary between two regions, bodies, spaces, etc.: *the interface of air and water.* **2** an area or place where different systems, processes, etc. act on or influence each other: *Taxation is the most critical interface between government and business.* **3** the means by which different systems, processes, modes of thought, etc. interact: *serving as an interface between the two groups. The program sets up an interface between the two computers.* **4** serve as or form an interface: *There are problems where the two groups interface.* **5** bring into contact or interaction: *Can one interface programs in* BASIC *and in* FORTRAN? *To interface, computers must be compatible.* **6** add interfacing to: *to interface a collar.* **7** the program necessary to connect computers to each other or to other machines. 1–3, 7 *n.*, 4–6 *v.*, **in·ter·faced, in·ter·fac·ing.**

**in·ter·fac·ing** (in′tər fā′sing) **1** a relatively stiff material placed between two layers of fabric in a collar, cuff, etc. to give shape or body to it: *The interfacing is sewn or fused between the outside layer and the facing.* **2** ppr. of INTERFACE. 1 *n.*, 2 *v.*

**in·ter·fere** (in′tər fēr′) **1** come into opposition; come between in a way that obstructs or hinders: *I will come on Saturday if nothing interferes.* **2** disturb the affairs of others; meddle: *This has nothing to do with you, so don't interfere.* **3** take part for a purpose: *The police interfered to stop the riot.* **4** in sports, obstruct or hinder the action of an opposing player in an illegal way. **5** in physics, of waves, act upon one another in such a way as to increase, lessen, neutralize, etc. each other. *v.*, **in·ter·fered, in·ter·fer·ing.**
**interfere with,** prevent or obstruct: *The rain interfered with our plans.*

**in·ter·fer·ence** (in′tər fē′rəns) **1** the act or fact of interfering: *We resented his interference in our affairs.* **2** something that interferes: *After tripping over a fallen tree, we removed the interference and walked on.* **3** in physics, the effect that light or sound waves have on each other when their paths meet or cross, to intensify or neutralize each other, produce beats, etc. **4** in radio and television, confusion of radio signals, producing static, distortion of sound, etc. **5** something that produces such confusion. **6** in football, the legal blocking of an opposing player to clear the way for the ball carrier. **7** in sports, the illegal obstructing or hindering of an opposing player. *n.*
**run interference (for),** **a** in football, clear the way for the ball carrier. **b** act as a go-between or screen: *She never has to deal directly with the public because her secretary runs interference for her.*

**in·ter·fer·on** (in′tər fē′ron) a protein produced by the body to prevent the spread of viral infection. *n.*

**in·ter·fold** (in′tər fōld′) fold one within another; fold together. *v.*

**in·ter·fuse** (in′tər fyüz′) **1** be diffused through; permeate. **2** fuse together; blend. *v.*, **in·ter·fused, in·ter·fus·ing.** —**in′ter·fu′sion**, *n.*

**in·ter·im** (in′tə rim) **1** the meantime; time between: *The talks have been adjourned for three weeks and in the interim most of the delegates are returning home.* **2** for the meantime; temporary: *The investigation is not complete, but we have an interim report.* 1 *n.*, 2 *adj.*

**in·te·ri·or** (in tē′rē ər) **1** the inner surface or part; inside: *The interior of the house was beautifully decorated.* **2** on the inside; inner: *an interior wall.* **3** the part of a region or country away from the coast or border: *The interior of the island is sparsely populated.* **4** away from the coast or border: *the interior regions.* **5** having to do with affairs within a country; domestic. **6** private or secret: *interior longings.* **7** a picture or stage setting of the inside of a room, house, etc.: *The exhibit featured several landscapes and a few interiors.* 1, 3, 7 *n.*, 2, 4, 5, 6 *adj.*

**interior angle** **1** any of the four angles formed on the inner sides of two parallel lines by a straight line cutting through the parallel lines. **2** the angle formed on the inside of a polygon between two adjacent sides. Compare with EXTERIOR ANGLE.

**interj.** interjection.

**in·ter·ject** (in′tər jekt′) throw in between other things; insert abruptly: *Every now and then the speaker interjected some witty remark.* *v.*

**in·ter·jec·tion** (in′tər jek′shən) **1** the act of interjecting. **2** something interjected, such as a word or remark. **3** in grammar, an exclamation of surprise, sorrow, delight, etc.: *Oh!, Ah!, Ouch! and Whoops!* are used as interjections. *n.*

**in·ter·jec·tion·al** (in′tər jek′shə nəl) **1** of an interjection; used as an interjection. **2** containing an interjection. **3** interjected. *adj.*

**in·ter·lace** (in′tər lās′) **1** arrange or cross threads, strips, branches, etc. so that they go over and under each other; weave together; intertwine: *Baskets are made by interlacing reeds or fibres.* **2** cross in an intricate manner: *interlacing highways.* *v.*, **in·ter·laced, in·ter·lac·ing.**

**in·ter·lard** (in′tər lärd′) mix so as to give variety to; intersperse: *The speaker interlarded her long speech with amusing stories.* *v.*

**in·ter·leaf** (in′tər lēf′) a leaf of paper, usually blank, put between others for notes, to protect colour plates, etc. *n.*, *pl.* **in·ter·leaves.**

**in·ter·leave** (in′tər lēv′) insert a leaf or leaves of paper between the pages of. *v.*, **in·ter·leaved, in·ter·leav·ing.**

**in·ter·line** (in′tər līn′) **1** insert words, etc. between the lines of: *The document had been interlined in several places.* **2** write, print, or mark between the lines: *The teacher interlined corrections on the students' themes.* **3** provide with an INTERLINING: *to interline a coat for warmth.* *v.*, **in·ter·lined, in·ter·lin·ing.**

**in·ter·lin·e·ar** (in′tər lin′ē ər) inserted between the lines. *adj.*

**in·ter·lin·ing** (in′tər lī′ning) **1** an extra lining between the outer fabric of a garment and the lining: *The coat has a warm woollen interlining.* **2** ppr. of INTERLINE. 1 *n.*, 2 *v.*

**in·ter·link** (in′tər lingk′)   link together.   *v.*

**in·ter·lock** (in′tər lok′)   join or fit tightly together; lock together: *The two stags interlocked their horns.*   *v.*

**in·ter·loc·u·tor** (in′tər lok′yə tər)   a person who takes part in a conversation or dialogue.   *n.*

**in·ter·loc·u·to·ry** (in′tər lok′yə tô′rē)   **1** of or in conversation or dialogue.   **2** made during a lawsuit or other action; not final: *The judge granted an interlocutory decree after the hearing.*   *adj.*

**in·ter·lop·er** (in′tər lō′pər)   a person who intrudes on or meddles in others' affairs.   *n.*

**in·ter·lude** (in′tər lüd′)   **1** anything thought of as filling the time between two things; interval: *There were only a few interludes of fair weather during the rainy season.*   **2** a piece of music played between the parts of a song, church service, play, etc.   **3** an entertainment between the acts of a play.   *n.*

**in·ter·lu·nar** (in′tər lü′nər)   between the old moon and the new moon.   *adj.*

**in·ter·mar·riage** (in′tər mar′ij *or* in′tər mer′ij)   **1** marriage between members of different religious, social, or ethnic groups.   **2** marriage between close blood relations.   *n.*

**in·ter·mar·ry** (in′tər mar′ē *or* in′tər mer′ē)   of families, tribes, etc., become connected by marriage: *The people of this old town have intermarried for generations.*   *v.*, **in·ter·mar·ried, in·ter·mar·ry·ing.**

**in·ter·me·di·ar·y** (in′tər mē′dē er′ē)   **1** a person who deals with each side in settling a dispute, negotiating a business arrangement, etc., go-between: *She acted as intermediary in the land deal between the city and the developer.*   **2** acting between two persons or groups as an intermediary: *an intermediary agent.*   **3** being between; intermediate: *A chrysalis is an intermediary stage between caterpillar and butterfly.*   **1** *n., pl.* **in·ter·me·di·ar·ies;** 2, 3 *adj.*

**in·ter·me·di·ate** (in′tər mē′dē it)   **1** being or occurring between extremes or in a middle stage, place, or degree: *Grey is intermediate between black and white. The language school offers only beginning and intermediate courses in French.*   **2** anything intermediate.   **3** intermediary; go-between.   **4** act as intermediary; mediate.   **5** the second largest of the four basic sizes of automobile. Compare with SUBCOMPACT, COMPACT, and STANDARD.   **1** *adj.*, 2, 3, 5 *n.*, 4 *v.*, **in·ter·me·di·at·ed, in·ter·me·di·at·ing.**

**in·ter·ment** (in tėr′mənt)   the act of putting a dead body into a grave or tomb; burial.   *n.*

**in·ter·mez·zo** (in′tər met′sō *or* in′tər med′zō)   **1** a short dramatic, musical, or other entertainment of a light character between the acts of a drama or opera.   **2** in music:   **a** a short composition between the main divisions of an extended musical work.   **b** an independent composition of similar character.   *n., pl.* **in·ter·mezzos** or **in·ter·mez·zi** (-met′sē *or* -med′zē).

**in·ter·mi·na·ble** (in tėr′mə nə bəl)   endless or so long as to seem endless; very long and tiring: *an interminable speech.*   *adj.*   —**in·ter′mi·na·bly,** *adv.*

**in·ter·min·gle** (in′tər ming′gəl)   mix together; mingle: *The host encouraged his guests to intermingle.*   *v.*, **in·ter·min·gled, in·ter·min·gling.**

**in·ter·mis·sion** (in′tər mish′ən)   **1** a time between periods of activity; a pause, especially between acts of a play, a musical performance, etc.: *There were two fifteen-minute intermissions in the performance.*   **2** a stopping for a time; interruption: *The rain continued all day without intermission.*   *n.*

**in·ter·mit** (in′tər mit′)   stop for a time.   *v.*, **in·ter·mit·ted, in·ter·mit·ting.**

**in·ter·mit·tent** (in′tər mit′ənt)   stopping and beginning again; pausing at intervals: *The intermittent noise of passing trucks kept her awake.*   *adj.*   —**in′ter·mit′tent·ly,** *adv.*

**in·ter·mix** (in′tər miks′)   mix together; blend: *Oil and water do not intermix.*   *v.*

**in·ter·mix·ture** (in′tər miks′chər)   **1** mixing together.   **2** a mass of ingredients mixed together.   *n.*

**in·tern**[1] (in tėrn′)   confine within a country or place; force to stay in a certain place, especially during a war: *Aliens are sometimes interned in wartime.*   *v.*
☞ *Usage.* See note at INTER.

**in·tern**[2] (in′tėrn)   **1** a medical doctor working as an assistant in a hospital: *A doctor has to serve one year as an intern before she can practise medicine on her own.*   **2** act as an intern.   **1** *n.*, **2** *v.*

**in·ter·nal** (in tėr′nəl)   **1** inner; on the inside: *internal injuries.*   **2** to be taken inside the body: *internal remedies.*   **3** entirely inside; coming from within: *The date of the author's death is unknown, but events in the poem provide internal evidence that she was still alive in 1920.*   **4** having to do with affairs within a country; domestic: *internal politics.*   *adj.*   —**in·ter′nal·ly,** *adv.*

**internal–combustion engine**   an engine in which the pressure is produced by gas or vapour exploding inside a cylinder and against the piston: *Automobiles and some airplanes have internal-combustion engines.*

**in·ter·na·tion·al** (in′tər nash′ə nəl *or* in′tər nash′nəl)   **1** between or among nations: *international trade.*   **2** accepted by or agreed on by many or all nations: *an international driver's licence, an international unit of measure, international law.*   **3** for the use of all nations: *international waters.*   *adj.*, **in′ter·na′tion·al·ly,** *adv.*

**International Date Line**   DATE LINE (def. 1).

**In·ter·na·tio·nale** (in′tər nash′ə nal *or* in′tər nash′nal)   the anthem of the international socialist organizations of the late 19th and early 20th centuries.   *n.*

**in·ter·na·tion·al·ism** (in′tər nash′ə nə liz′əm *or* in′tər nash′nə liz′əm)   **1** the principle of international co-operation for the good of all nations.   **2** international quality, character, interests, etc.   *n.*

**in·ter·na·tion·al·ist** (in′tər nash′ə nə list *or* in′tər nash′nə list)   one who favours INTERNATIONALISM.   *n.*

**in·ter·na·tion·al·ize** (in′tər nash′ə nə līz′ *or* in′tər nash′nə līz′)   make international; bring territory under the control of several nations.   *v.*, **in·ter·na·tion·al·ized, in·ter·na·tion·al·iz·ing.**   —**in′ter·na′tion·al·iz·a′tion,** *n.*

**International Joint Commission** a committee set up by Canada and the United States to settle possible disputes concerning boundary waters.

**in·ter·ne·cine** (in′tər nē′sən or in′tər nē′sīn) 1 destructive to both sides. 2 deadly; destructive. *adj.*

**in·tern·ee** (in′tėr nē′) a person interned: *Prisoners of war, enemy aliens, etc. may be internees.* *n.*

**In·ter·net** (in′tər nėt) a huge and growing computer network that links many smaller computer networks around the world, providing access to information, e-mail, and many other services. Access to the Internet is through another network or by an independent service provider, usually for a fee. Also called **the Net**. *n.*
☛ *Usage.* **Internet** is usually preceded by **the**.

**in·tern·ment** (in tėrn′mənt) INTERNing[1] or being interned. *n.*

**in·tern·ship** (in′tėrn ship′) a position of or period of service as an INTERN[2]. *n.*

**in·ter·pen·e·trate** (in′tər pen′ə trāt′) penetrate thoroughly; permeate. *v.*, **in·ter·pen·e·trat·ed, in·ter·pen·e·trat·ing**. —**in′ter·pen·e·tra′tion**, *n.*

**in·ter·phase** (in′tər fāz′) the stage of a cell between periods of MITOSIS. *n.*

**in·ter·plan·e·tar·y** (in′tər plan′ə ter′ē) 1 existing or taking place between the planets; within the solar system, but outside the atmosphere of any of the planets or the sun: *interplanetary space.* 2 carried on between planets: *interplanetary travel.* *adj.*

**in·ter·play** (in′tər plā′) the action or influence of things on each other; interaction: *the interplay of light and shadow.* *n.*

**In·ter·pol** (in′tər pol′) International Criminal Police Commission; an organization that co-ordinates activities of police of participating nations to control international crime. *n.*

**in·ter·po·late** (in tėr′pə lāt′) 1 alter a book, passage, etc. by putting in new words or groups of words. 2 put in new words, passages, etc. *v.*, **in·ter·po·lat·ed, in·ter·po·lat·ing**.

**in·ter·po·la·tion** (in tėr′pə lā′shən) 1 the act of interpolating. 2 something interpolated: *an old manuscript with many interpolations of later date.* *n.*

**in·ter·pose** (in′tər pōz′) 1 put between; insert. 2 put forward; break in with; introduce as an interruption: *She interposed an objection.* 3 intervene in a dispute; mediate: *He quickly interposed between the angry children.* *v.*, **in·ter·posed, in·ter·pos·ing**. —**in′ter·pos′er**, *n.*

**in·ter·po·si·tion** (in′tər pə zish′ən) 1 an interposing. 2 the thing interposed. *n.*

**in·ter·pret** (in tėr′prit) 1 explain the meaning of: *to interpret a hard passage in a book, to interpret a dream.* 2 bring out the meaning of a dramatic part, a character, music, etc. 3 understand according to one's own judgment: *We interpreted your silence as consent.* 4 serve as an INTERPRETER; translate: *Juanita interprets for our Spanish visitors.* *v.*

**in·ter·pre·ta·tion** (in tėr′prə tā′shən) 1 an interpreting; explanation: *different interpretations of the same facts.* 2 a bringing out of the meaning of a dramatic part, music, etc.: *The critics praised the actor's interpretation of Hamlet.* 3 the explanation of the purpose and importance of national and provincial park systems and the influence of park visitors on the ecology of a park. 4 translation. *n.*

**in·ter·pre·ta·tive** (in tėr′prə tə tiv or in tėr′prə tā′tiv) 1 used for interpreting; explanatory. 2 of, having to do with, or referring to the interpretation of parks and park systems: *All national parks have interpretative programs.* *adj.*

**in·ter·pret·er** (in tėr′prə tər) a person who interprets, especially one whose work is translating a language orally, as in a conversation between people who do not understand each other's language: *The visiting dignitary spoke to government leaders through an interpreter.* *n.*

**in·ter·pre·tive** (in tėr′prə tiv) INTERPRETATIVE. *adj.*

**in·ter·pro·vin·cial** (in′tər prə vin′shəl) 1 between or among provinces: *interprovincial agreements.* 2 connecting two or more provinces: *an interprovincial highway.* *adj.*

**in·ter·ra·cial** (in′tər rā′shəl) between or involving different races. *adj.*

**in·ter·reg·num** (in′tər reg′nəm) 1 the time between the end of one ruler's reign and the beginning of the next one. 2 any time during which a nation is without its usual ruler or government. 3 a period of inactivity; pause. *n., pl.* **in·ter·reg·nums** or **in·ter·reg·na** (-nə).

**in·ter·re·late** (in′tər ri lāt′) relate to one another; connect: *The two proposals are interrelated.* *v.*, **in·ter·re·lat·ed, in·ter·re·lat·ing**.

**in·ter·re·la·tion** (in′tər ri lā′shən) a close connection with each other; mutual relationship. *n.*

**in·ter·ro·gate** (in ter′ə gāt′) 1 ask questions of, especially formally and systematically; examine by asking questions: *The lawyer took two hours to interrogate the witness.* 2 ask a series of questions. *v.*, **in·ter·ro·gat·ed, in·ter·ro·gat·ing**.

**in·ter·ro·ga·tion** (in ter′ə gā′shən) 1 a questioning: *The formal examination of a witness by asking questions is an interrogation.* 2 a question. *n.*

**interrogation mark** or **point** question mark (?).

**in·ter·rog·a·tive** (in′tə rog′ə tiv) 1 of or having the form of a question: *an interrogative look or tone of voice.* 2 in grammar, used in asking questions: *an interrogative pronoun.* 3 an interrogative word, especially a pronoun: *Who, why,* and *what* are interrogatives. 1, 2 *adj.*, 3 *n.*

**in·ter·ro·ga·tor** (in ter′ə gā′tər) questioner. *n.*

**in·ter·rog·a·to·ry** (in′tə rog′ə tô′rē) 1 questioning. 2 a formal question or set of questions. 1 *adj.*, 2 *n., pl.* **in·ter·rog·a·to·ries**.

**in·ter·rupt** (in′tə rupt′) 1 break in upon talk, work, rest, a person speaking, etc.; hinder; stop: *A fire drill interrupted the lesson.* 2 break the continuity of; obstruct: *A building interrupts the view from our window.* 3 cause a break; break in: *It is not polite to interrupt when someone is talking.* *v.* —**in′ter·rupt′er**, *n.*

**in·ter·rup·tion** (in′tə rup′shən) 1 interrupting or being interrupted: *The rain continued without interruption all day.* 2 something that interrupts: *It's hard to work when there are so many interruptions.* *n.*

**in·ter·scho·las·tic** (in′tər skə las′tik) between schools: *interscholastic competition.* *adj.*

**in·ter·sect** (in′tər sekt′) 1 cut or divide by passing

through or crossing. **2** cross each other: *Streets usually intersect at right angles.* *v.*

**in·ter·sec·tion** (in′tər sek′shən *or* in′tər sek′shən) **1** the act or process of intersecting: *the intersection of two lines. Bridges and overpasses are used to avoid the intersection of a railway and a highway.* **2** a point, line, or place where two or more things, such as roads, cross each other: *The light changed just before we got to the intersection.* **3** in mathematics, the set of points or other elements common to two or more given sets. *n.*

**in·ter·sperse** (in′tər spėrs′) **1** decorate or vary with other things put here and there: *The lawn was interspersed with beds of flowers.* **2** scatter or place here and there: *Lorna interspersed amusing anecdotes throughout her talk.* *v.*, **in·ter·spersed, in·ter·spers·ing.**

**in·ter·sper·sion** (in′tər spėr′zhən) an interspersing or being interspersed. *n.*

**in·ter·state** (in′tər stāt′) between states: *an interstate highway.* *adj.*

**in·ter·stel·lar** (in′tər stel′ər) **1** existing between or among the stars: *interstellar space.* **2** carried on between stars or star systems: *plans for interstellar travel.* *adj.*

**in·ter·stice** (in tėr′stis) a small or narrow space between things or parts; chink. *n.*, *pl.* **in·ter·sti·ces** (-stə sēz′).

**in·ter·trib·al** (in′tər trī′bəl) between tribes. *adj.*

**in·ter·twine** (in′tər twīn′) twine around each other; twist or become twisted together: *Two vines intertwined on the wall.* *v.*, **in·ter·twined, in·ter·twin·ing.**

**in·ter·twist** (in′tər twist′) twist, one with another. *v.*

**in·ter·ur·ban** (in′tər ėr′bən) between cities or towns: *an interurban railway.* *adj.*

**in·ter·val** (in′tər vəl) **1** the time or space between: *an interval of a week, intervals of freedom from pain. There are trees at intervals of 10 metres.* **2** in music, the difference in pitch between two tones. **3** INTERVALE. *n.*
**at intervals, a** now and then: *Stir the pudding at intervals.* **b** here and there: *We saw many lakes at intervals along the way.*
☞ *Etym.* From L *intervallum*, originally '(a space) between ramparts', from *inter-* 'between' + *vallum* 'wall, rampart'. INTERVALE developed in the 17c. from **interval**, being influenced by the word *vale* 'valley'.

**in·ter·vale** (in′tər vāl′) a low-lying area of rich land between hills or by a river. *n.*
☞ *Etym.* See note at INTERVAL.

**in·ter·vene** (in′tər vēn′) **1** come or be between: *A week intervenes between Christmas and the New Year.* **2** come in to help settle a dispute: *The prime minister intervened in the railway strike.* *v.*, **in·ter·vened, in·ter·ven·ing.** —**in′ter·ven′er,** *n.*

**in·ter·ven·tion** (in′tər ven′shən) **1** the act of intervening: *The strike was settled by the intervention of the federal government.* **2** interference, especially by one nation in the affairs of another. *n.*

**in·ter·view** (in′tər vyü′) **1** a meeting of people face to face, to talk over something special: *Father had an interview with the teacher about Regina's work.* **2** a meeting between a reporter, writer, radio or television commentator, etc. and a person from whom information is sought. **3** a printed report or broadcast of such a meeting. **4** meet and talk with, especially to obtain information: *Reporters interviewed the returning explorers.* 1–3 *n.*, 4 *v.* —**in′ter·view′er,** *n.*

---

**intersection** 633 **into**

hat, āge, fär; let, ēqual, tėrm; it, īce
hot, ōpen, ôrder; oil, out; cup, pùt, rüle
ə above, takən, pencəl, lemən, circəs
ch, child; ng, long; sh, ship
th, thin; ᴛʜ, then; zh, measure

**in·ter·weave** (in′tər wēv′) **1** weave together. **2** intermingle; blend; connect closely: *In his book Yu has interwoven the stories of two families.* *v.*, **in·ter·wove** or **in·ter·weaved, in·ter·wov·en, in·ter·wove** or **in·ter·weaved, in·ter·weav·ing.**

**in·ter·wove** (in′tər wōv′) a pt. and a pp. of INTERWEAVE. *v.*

**in·ter·wo·ven** (in′tər wō′vən) **1** woven together. **2** intermingled. **3** a pp. of INTERWEAVE. 1, 2 *adj.*, 3 *v.*

**in·tes·tate** (in tes′tāt) **1** having made no will. **2** a person who has died without making a will. **3** not disposed of by a will. 1, 3 *adj.*, 2 *n.*

**in·tes·ti·nal** (in tes′tə nəl) of or in the INTESTINES. *adj.* —**in·tes′ti·nal·ly,** *adv.*

**in·tes·tine** (in tes′tən) **1** either of the two parts of the alimentary canal extending from the stomach to the anus. Partially digested food passes from the stomach into the small intestine for further digestion and for absorption of nutrients by the blood, and into the large intestine for elimination. In grown people, the **small intestine** is about 640 cm long; the **large intestine** is about 165 cm long. See ALIMENTARY CANAL for picture. **2** within a country; internal: *Intestine strife is civil war.* **3 intestines,** *pl.* the intestine; the bowels. 1, 3 *n.*, 2 *adj.*

**in·thral** or **in·thrall** (in throl′) ENTHRAL. *v.*, **in·thralled, in·thrall·ing.**

**in·throne** (in thrōn′) ENTHRONE. *v.*, **in·throned, in·thron·ing.**

**in·ti·ma·cy** (in′tə mə sē) **1** deep friendship; close association; being intimate. **2** a familiar or intimate act. *n.*, *pl.* **in·ti·ma·cies.**

**in·ti·mate**[1] (in′tə mit) **1** very familiar; known very well: *an intimate friend.* **2** resulting from close familiarity; close: *an intimate knowledge.* **3** personal; private: *A diary is a very intimate book.* **4** a close friend: *Karel invited his intimates to a special dinner.* **5** far within; inmost: *The intimate recesses of the heart.* 1–3, 5 *adj.*, 4 *n.* —**in′ti·mate·ly,** *adv.*

**in·ti·mate**[2] (in′tə māt) **1** suggest indirectly; hint: *In his statement to the press, Werner intimated that an arrest would be made soon.* **2** announce; notify. *v.*, **in·ti·mat·ed, in·ti·mat·ing.** —**in′ti·mat′er,** *n.*

**in·ti·ma·tion** (in′tə mā′shən) **1** an indirect suggestion; hint: *Helga said nothing, but her frown was an intimation of disapproval.* **2** an announcement; notice. *n.*

**in·tim·i·date** (in tim′ə dāt′) frighten, especially in order to influence or force: *The banker told police that the men had tried to intimidate him by telling them they were holding his wife as hostage.* *v.*, **in·tim′i·dated, in·tim′i·dat·ing.** —**in·tim′i·da′tion,** *n.* —**in·tim′i·da′tor,** *n.*

**in·ti·tle** (in tī′təl) ENTITLE. *v.*, **in·ti·tled, in·ti·tling.**

**in·to** (in′tü; *before consonants, often* in′tə) **1** to the inside of; toward the inside; within: *to go into the house. I will look into the matter.* **2** to the condition of; to the form of: *to get into mischief, a house divided into ten rooms.*

Cold weather turns water into ice. **3** to a further time in: *She worked on into the night.* **4** against: *He wasn't watching and ran into the wall.* **5** in arithmetic, divided into: *Five into thirty is six.* **6** *Informal.* involved or concerned with: *She's really into philosophy these days.* *prep.*
☛ *Usage.* See note at IN.

**in·tol·er·a·bil·i·ty** (in tol′ə rə bil′ə tē) the state or quality of being INTOLERABLE. *n.*

**in·tol·er·a·ble** (in tol′ə rə bəl) unbearable; too much, too painful, etc. to be endured: *The toothache was almost intolerable.* *adj.* —**in·tol′er·a·bly,** *adv.*

**in·tol·er·ance** (in tol′ə rəns) **1** a lack of TOLERANCE; unwillingness to let others do and think as they choose, especially in matters of religion: *Religious intolerance has been the cause of many wars.* **2** being unable or unwilling to endure: *intolerance to penicillin, intolerance of popular music.* *n.*

**in·tol·er·ant** (in tol′ə rənt) **1** unwilling to let others do and think as they choose, especially in matters of religion. **2** unwilling to accept persons of different races, backgrounds, etc. as equals. *adj.*
—**in·tol′er·ant·ly,** *adv.*
**intolerant of,** not able or willing to endure: *intolerant of hot, humid weather.*

**in·tomb** (in tüm′) ENTOMB. *v.*

**in·to·na·tion** (in′tō nā′shən) **1** the act of intoning: *the intonation of a psalm.* **2** the opening phrase of a Gregorian chant. **3** the production of musical tones in tune: *Intonation is a problem for cellists.* **4** the manner of uttering or sounding words: *She has a monotonous intonation.* **5** the use of stress and pitch in speaking: *British intonation is quite different from standard Canadian intonation.* *n.*

**in·tone** (in tōn′) **1** read or recite in a singing voice; chant: *A priest intones part of the service.* **2** utter with a particular tone. **3** make musical sounds, especially in a slow, drawn-out manner. *v.,* **in·toned, in·ton·ing.**

**in to·to** (in′ tō′tō) *Latin.* as a whole; completely.

**in·tox·i·cant** (in tok′sə kənt) **1** something that intoxicates, especially alcoholic liquor. **2** intoxicating: *an intoxicant drug.* **1** *n.,* **2** *adj.*

**in·tox·i·cate** (in tok′sə kāt′) **1** make drunk: *Too much wine intoxicates people.* **2** excite greatly; exhilarate: *The early election returns intoxicated her supporters with thoughts of victory.* *v.,* **in·tox·i·cat·ed, in·tox·i·cat·ing.**
—**in·tox′i·cat′ing·ly,** *adv.*

**in·tox·i·cat·ed** (in tok′sə kā′tid) **1** drunk. **2** greatly excited. **3** pt. and pp. of INTOXICATE. 1, 2 *adj.,* 3 *v.*

**in·tox·i·ca·tion** (in tok′sə kā′shən) **1** drunkenness. **2** great excitement. **3** in medicine, poisoning. *n.*

**intr.** intransitive.

**intra-** a prefix meaning within, inside, or on the inside, as in *intravenous.*

**in·trac·ta·bil·i·ty** (in trak′tə bil′ə tē) being INTRACTABLE; stubbornness. *n.*

**in·trac·ta·ble** (in trak′tə bəl) hard to manage; stubborn. *adj.* —**in·trac′ta·bly,** *adv.*

**in·tra·mu·ral** (in′trə myü′rəl) within the walls; inside: *In intramural games, all the players belong to the same school.* *adj.*

**intrans.** intransitive.

**in·tran·si·gence** (in tran′sə jəns) being INTRANSIGENT; uncompromising hostility. *n.*

**in·tran·si·gen·cy** (in tran′sə jən sē) INTRANSIGENCE. *n.*

**in·tran·si·gent** (in tran′sə jənt) **1** unwilling to agree or compromise. **2** a person who is unwilling to agree or compromise. 1 *adj.,* 2 *n.* —**in·tran′si·gent·ly,** *adv.*

**in·tran·si·tive** (in tran′sə tiv) in grammar, not taking a direct object. *The verbs* belong, go, *and* seem *are intransitive verbs.* Compare with TRANSITIVE. *adj.*
—**in·tran′si·tive·ly,** *adv.*

**in·tra·ve·nous** (in′trə vē′nəs) **1** within a vein or the veins. **2** into a vein: *an intravenous injection.* *adj.*
—**in′tra·ve′nous·ly,** *adv.*

**in·treat** (in trēt′) ENTREAT. *v.*

**in·trench** (in trench′) ENTRENCH. *v.*

**in·trench·ment** (in trench′mənt) ENTRENCHMENT. *n.*

**in·trep·id** (in trep′id) fearless; dauntless; courageous; very brave: *an intrepid explorer.* *adj.*
—**in·trep′id·ly,** *adv.*

**in·tre·pid·i·ty** (in′trə pid′ə tē) fearlessness; dauntless courage; great bravery. *n.*

**in·tri·ca·cy** (in′trə kə sē) **1** the state or quality of being intricate; complexity: *They admired the delicacy and intricacy of the design.* **2** something intricate: *the intricacies of international diplomacy.* *n., pl.*
**in·tri·ca·cies.**

**in·tri·cate** (in′trə kit) **1** with many twists and turns; entangled or complicated: *an intricate knot, an intricate maze, an intricate plot.* **2** very hard to understand; obscure or puzzling: *an intricate problem.* *adj.*
—**in′tri·cate·ly,** *adv.* —**in′tri·cate·ness,** *n.*

**in·trigue** (in trēg′ *or* in′trēg *for noun,* in trēg′ *for verb*)
**1** underhand planning; secret scheming; plotting: *The royal palace was filled with intrigue.* **2** a crafty plot; secret scheme. **3** carry on an underhand plan; scheme secretly; plot. **4** excite the curiosity and interest of: *The book's unusual title intrigued me.* **5** interest in a pleasing way: *The actor's superb performance intrigued me.* **6** a secret love affair. **7** have a secret love affair. 1, 2, 6 *n.,* 3–5, 7 *v.,* **in·trigued, in·tri·guing.** —**in·tri′guing·ly,** *adv.*

**in·trin·sic** (in trin′sik *or* in trin′zik) belonging to a thing by its very nature; essential; inherent: *The intrinsic value of a five-dollar bill is only that of a piece of paper.* *adj.*

**in·trin·si·cal** (in trin′sə kəl *or* in trin′zə kəl) INTRINSIC. *adj.*

**in·trin·si·cal·ly** (in trin′si klē *or* in trin′zi klē) by its very nature; essentially; inherently. *adv.*

**intro-** a prefix meaning: inward or within, as in *introvert.*

**in·tro·duce** (in′trə dyüs′ *or* in′trə düs′) **1** bring in: *She introduced a new subject into the conversation.* **2** put in; insert: *The doctor introduced a long tube into the man's throat.* **3** bring into use, notice, knowledge, etc.: *to introduce a reform, to introduce a new word.* **4** make known: *The chairman introduced the speaker to the audience.* **5** bring to acquaintance with something: *I introduced my cousin to the city by showing her the sights.*

**6** bring forward: *to introduce a question for debate.* **7** begin; start: *Misha introduced his speech with a joke.* *v.*, **in·tro·duced, in·tro·duc·ing.** —**in′tro·duc′er,** *n.*

**in·tro·duc·tion** (in′trə duk′shən) **1** introducing or being introduced: *The introduction of steel made skyscrapers easy to build. She gave me an introduction to her aunt.* **2** something that introduces; the first part of a book, speech, piece of music, etc. leading up to the main part. **3** a first book for beginners. **4** something introduced; thing brought into use: *Radios are a later introduction than telephones.* *n.*

**in·tro·duc·to·ry** (in′trə duk′tə rē *or* in′trə duk′trē) used to introduce; serving as an introduction; preliminary: *introductory remarks, an introductory offer.* *adj.*

**in·tro·spec·tion** (in′trə spek′shən) an examination and analysis of one's own thoughts and feelings. *n.*

**in·tro·spec·tive** (in′trə spek′tiv) inclined to examine one's own thoughts and feelings. *adj.* —**in′tro·spec′tive·ly,** *adv.*

**in·tro·ver·sion** (in′trə vėr′zhən) a tendency to be more interested in one's own thoughts and feelings than in other persons or in what is going on around one. Compare with EXTROVERSION. *n.*

**in·tro·vert** (in′trə vėrt′) a person more interested in his or her own thoughts and feelings than in other persons or in what is going on around him or her; a person who is thoughtful rather than active or expressive. Compare with EXTROVERT. *n.*

**in·trude** (in trüd′) **1** thrust oneself in; come unasked and unwanted: *If you are busy, I will not intrude.* **2** give when not wanted; force in: *Do not intrude your opinions upon others.* *v.*, **in·trud·ed, in·trud·ing.** —**in·trud′er,** *n.*

**in·tru·sion** (in trü′zhən) the act of intruding; coming unasked and unwanted. *n.*

**in·tru·sive** (in trü′siv) **1** intruding; coming unasked and unwanted. **2** formed of rock in a molten state within the earth. Compare with EXTRUSIVE. *adj.* —**in·tru′sive·ly,** *adv.*

**in·trust** (in trust′) ENTRUST. *v.*

**in·tu·it** (in tyü′ət *or* in tü′ət) know or learn by INTUITION. *v.*

**in·tu·i·tion** (in′tyü ish′ən *or* in′tü ish′ən) **1** immediate perception or understanding of truths, facts, etc. without reasoning: *Carlo's intuition told him that the strangers were not what they appeared to be.* **2** something known or understood in this way. *n.*

**in·tu·i·tion·al** (in′tyü ish′ə nəl *or* in′tü ish′ə nəl) of, having to do with, or characterized by, INTUITION; based on intuition. *adj.*

**in·tu·i·tive** (in tyü′ə tiv *or* in tü′ə tiv) **1** perceiving by INTUITION: *intuitive power.* **2** acquired by INTUITION: *intuitive knowledge.* *adj.* —**in·tu′i·tive·ly,** *adv.*

**I·nu·it** (in′ü it, in′yü it, *or* in′yə wit) *Cdn.* **1** a people living mainly in northern Canada, Greenland, Alaska, and eastern Siberia, who are the original inhabitants of the Arctic; formerly the Eskimo people. **2** of or having to do with these people or their language: *Inuit games, an Inuit word.* **1** *n. pl.*, **2** *adj.*
☛ *Etym.* From Inuktitut *inuit* 'the people, men', the plural of *inuk* 'man'. Also from *inuk* come INUKSHUK, literally 'in the capacity of a man', a man-shaped cairn of piled stones, and INUKTITUT, literally 'as of a man, like that of a man', the Inuit's name for their language.

**introduction**    **635**    **invaluable**

hat, āge, fär; let, ēqual, tėrm; it, īce
hot, ōpen, ôrder; oil, out; cup, pùt, rüle
əbove, takən, pencəl, lemən, circəs
ch, child; ng, long; sh, ship
th, thin; ᴛʜ, then; zh, measure

☛ *Usage.* In Canada, *Inuit* is now the preferred term, although many people still use the term *Eskimos*.

**I·nuk** (in′ùk) *Cdn.* a member of the INUIT. *n.*, *pl.* **I·nu·it.**

**i·nuk·shuk** (i nùk′shùk) *Cdn.* a stone cairn having the rough outline of a human figure: *Inukshuks were traditionally built by the Inuit to serve as landmarks or, in some parts of the Arctic, in long rows to drive caribou toward waiting hunters.* *n.*, *pl.* **i·nuk·shuks** *or* **i·nuk·shu·it.** Also **inukshook.**
☛ *Etym.* See note at INUIT.

**I·nuk·ti·tuk** (i nùk′tə tùk′) *Cdn.* INUKTITUT. *n.*

**I·nuk·ti·tut** (i nùk′tə tùt′) *Cdn.* the language of the INUIT: *There are many dialects of Inuktitut.* *n.*
☛ *Etym.* See note at INUIT.

**in·un·date** (in′ən dāt′) **1** overflow; flood: *The water from the swollen river inundated the valley.* **2** overwhelm, as if by a flood: *The radio station was inundated by requests for the pamphlet.* *v.*, **in·un·dat·ed, in·un·dat·ing.**

**in·un·da·tion** (in′ən dā′shən) an overflowing; flood. *n.*

**in·ure** (i nyùr′) toughen or harden; accustom; habituate: *Many years in the wilderness had inured them to hardships.* *v.*, **in·ured, in·ur·ing.** —**in·ure′ment,** *n.*

**in·vade** (in vād′) **1** enter with force or as an enemy: *Soldiers invaded the country. Grasshoppers invade fields and eat the crops. Disease invades the body.* **2** enter as if to take possession: *Tourists invaded the city. Night invades the sky.* **3** interfere with; break in on; violate: *The law punishes people who invade the rights of others.* *v.*, **in·vad·ed, in·vad·ing.** —**in·vad′er,** *n.*

**in·va·lid**[1] (in′və lid) **1** a person who is weak because of sickness or injury: *An invalid cannot get about and do things.* **2** not well; disabled. **3** of or for an invalid or invalids: *an invalid chair.* **4** make weak or sick; disable. **5** remove from active service because of sickness or injury: *The wounded soldier was invalided home.* **1** *n.*, **2**, **3** *adj.*, **4, 5** *v.*
**invalid out,** release from service in the armed forces because of illness or injury.
☛ *Etym.* Both words spelled **invalid** came from L *invalidus* 'not strong'. The pronunciation of **invalid**[1] (in′və lid) was influenced by F *invalide*, as in *Les Invalides*, a famous hospital for disabled soldiers in Paris. 17c.

**in·val·id**[2] (in val′id) not VALID; without force or effect; worthless: *Unless a will is signed, it is invalid.* *adj.* —**in·val′id·ly,** *adv.*
☛ *Etym.* See note at INVALID[1]. 16c.

**in·val·i·date** (in val′ə dāt′) make valueless; deprive of force or effect: *A contract is invalidated if only one party signs it.* *v.*, **in·val·i·dat·ed, in·val·i·dat·ing.** —**in·val′i·da′tion,** *n.*

**in·val·id·ism** (in′və li diz′əm) the condition of being an INVALID[1]; prolonged ill health. *n.*

**in·va·lid·i·ty** (in′və lid′ə tē) a lack of VALIDITY, force, or effect; worthlessness. *n.*

**in·val·u·a·ble** (in val′yə bəl *or* in val′yü ə bəl)

priceless; very precious; valuable beyond measure: *her invaluable assistance, without which they would never have managed.* *adj.* —in·val′u·a·bly, *adv.*
—in·val′u·a·ble·ness, *n.*

**in·var·i·a·bil·i·ty** (in ver′ē ə bil′ə tē) unchangeableness; constancy; uniformity. *n.*

**in·var·i·a·ble** (in ver′ē ə bəl) always the same; unchangeable; unchanging: *After dinner it was her invariable habit to take a walk.* *adj.*
—in·var′i·a·bly, *adv.*

**in·va·sion** (in vā′zhən) 1 the act of invading: *There has been no invasion of England since 1066.* 2 an interference; encroachment; infringement: *She objected to the invasion of her privacy.* *n.*

**in·vec·tive** (in vek′tiv) a violent attack in words; abusive language. *n.*

**in·veigh** (in vā′) make a violent attack in words; complain bitterly (*used with* **against**): *She inveighed against the poor working conditions in the factory.* *v.*

**in·vei·gle** (in vā′gəl *or* in vē′gəl) win over by trickery; entice; lure: *The saleswoman inveigled the poor girl into buying four pairs of shoes.* *v.*, **in·vei·gled, in·vei·gling.**
—in·vei′gler, *n.*

**in·vent** (in vent′) 1 make for the first time; think out something new: *Alexander Graham Bell invented the telephone.* 2 make up; think up; fabricate: *to invent an excuse.* *v.*

**in·ven·tion** (in ven′shən) 1 the act or process of inventing: *The Chinese are credited with the invention of gunpowder.* 2 the thing invented: *Radio was a wonderful invention.* 3 the power of inventing; inventiveness: *To be a good novelist, a person needs invention.* 4 a made-up story, especially a falsehood: *Her account of the robbery was pure invention.* *n.*

**in·ven·tive** (in ven′tiv) 1 good at inventing; quick to invent things: *An inventive person thinks up ways to save time, money, and work.* 2 of invention. 3 showing power of inventing. *adj.* —in·ven′tive·ly, *adv.*
—in·ven′tive·ness, *n.*

**in·ven·tor** (in ven′tər) a person who invents: *Alexander Graham Bell was a great inventor.* *n.*

**in·ven·to·ry** (in′vən tô′rē) 1 a detailed list of articles with their estimated value. 2 a collection of articles that are or may be so listed; stock: *The storekeeper had a sale to reduce his inventory.* 3 make a detailed list of; enter in a list: *Some stores inventory their stock once a month.* 1, 2 *n.*, *pl.* **in·ven·to·ries;** 3 *v.*, **in·ven·to·ried, in·ven·to·ry·ing.**

**in·verse** (in vėrs′ *or* in′vėrs) 1 reversed in position, direction, or tendency; inverted: *DCBA is the inverse order of ABCD.* 2 something reversed: *The inverse of ³/₄ is ⁴/₃.* 3 direct opposite: *Evil is the inverse of good.* 1 *adj.*, 2, 3 *n.* —in·verse′ly, *adv.*

**in·ver·sion** (in vėr′zhən) 1 inverting or being inverted. 2 something inverted. *n.*

**in·vert** (in vėrt′) 1 turn upside down: *to invert a glass.* 2 turn the other way; reverse in position, direction, order, etc.: *If you invert "I can," you have "Can I?"* *v.*

**in·ver·te·brate** (in vėr′tə brāt′ *or* in vėr′tə brit) 1 without a backbone. 2 of or having to do with invertebrates: *invertebrate zoology.* 3 an animal without a backbone: *All animals except fish, amphibians, reptiles, birds, and mammals are invertebrates.* 1, 2 *adj.*, 3 *n.*

**in·vest** (in vest′) 1 use money to buy something that is expected to produce a profit, or income, or both: *Tiina invested her money in stocks, bonds, and land.* 2 invest money: *Learn to invest wisely.* 3 spend or put in time, energy, etc. for later benefit: *The volunteer group invested its energies in developing new playgrounds. A lot of time has already been invested in the project, so we can't quit now.* 4 clothe; cover; surround: *Darkness invests the earth by night.* 5 give power, authority, or right to: *He invested his lawyer with complete power to act for him.* 6 install in office with a ceremony: *A queen is invested by being crowned.* 7 surround with soldiers or ships; besiege: *The enemy invested the city and cut it off from our army.* *v.*

**in·ves·ti·gate** (in ves′tə gāt′) search into carefully; examine closely: *to investigate a complaint. Detectives investigate crimes.* *v.*, **in·ves·ti·gat·ed, in·ves·ti·gat·ing.**

**in·ves·ti·ga·tion** (in ves′tə gā′shən) a careful search; detailed or careful examination: *The police officer carried out an investigation of the accident.* *n.*

**in·ves·ti·ga·tor** (in ves′tə gā′tər) a person who INVESTIGATES. *n.*

**in·ves·ti·ture** (in ves′tə chür′) 1 a formal investing of a person with an office, dignity, power, right, etc. 2 clothing; apparel; covering. *n.*

**in·vest·ment** (in vest′mənt) 1 an investing; a laying out of money: *Getting an education is a wise investment of time and money.* 2 the amount of money invested: *Her investments amount to thousands of dollars.* 3 something that is expected to yield money as income or profit or both: *Canada Savings Bonds are a safe investment.* 4 the act of surrounding with soldiers or ships; siege.
5 INVESTITURE. *n.*

**in·ves·tor** (in ves′tər) one who invests money. *n.*

**in·vet·er·a·cy** (in vet′ə rə sē) a settled, fixed condition; habitualness. *n.*

**in·vet·er·ate** (in vet′ə rit) 1 confirmed in a habit, practice, feeling, etc.; habitual: *an inveterate smoker.* 2 long and firmly established: *Cats have an inveterate dislike of dogs.* *adj.* —in·vet′er·ate·ly, *adv.*

**in·vid·i·ous** (in vid′ē əs) likely to arouse ill will or resentment; giving offence because unfair or unjust: *Wise people avoid invidious rules.* *adj.* —in·vid′i·ous·ly, *adv.*
—in·vid′i·ous·ness, *n.*

**in·vig·or·ate** (in vig′ə rāt′) give vigour to; fill with life and energy: *The brisk weather was invigorating.* *v.*, **in·vig·or·at·ed, in·vig·or·at·ing.**
—in·vig′or·at′ing·ly, *adv.*

**in·vig·or·a·tion** (in vig′ə rā′shən) an invigorating or being invigorated. *n.*

**in·vin·ci·bil·i·ty** (in vin′sə bil′ə tē) the state or quality of being INVINCIBLE. *n.*

**in·vin·ci·ble** (in vin′sə bəl) impossible to overcome; unconquerable: *The champion wrestler seemed invincible.* *adj.* —in·vin′ci·bly, *adv.*

**in·vi·o·la·bil·i·ty** (in vī′ə lə bil′ə tē) the state or quality of being INVIOLABLE. *n.*

**in·vi·o·la·ble** (in vī′ə lə bəl) 1 that must not be violated or injured; sacred: *an inviolable vow, an inviolable sanctuary.* 2 that cannot be violated or injured: *The gods are inviolable.* *adj.* —in·vi′o·la·bly, *adv.*

**in·vi·o·late** (in vī′ə lit *or* in vī′ə lāt′) not violated; uninjured, unbroken; not profaned. *adj.*

**in·vis·i·bil·i·ty** (in viz′ə bil′ə tē) the state or quality of being INVISIBLE. *n.*

**in·vis·i·ble** (in viz′ə bəl) **1** not visible; not capable of being seen: *Thought is invisible.* **2** not in sight; hidden: *The queen kept herself invisible in her palace.* **3** too small to be perceived: *Germs are invisible to the naked eye.* **4 the invisible,** the unseen world. 1–3 *adj.*, 4 *n.*

**in·vis·i·bly** (in viz′ə blē) without being seen; so as not to be seen. *adv.*

**in·vi·ta·tion** (in′və tā′shən) **1** a request to come to some place or to do something: *Formal invitations are written or printed.* **2** the act of inviting. **3** temptation; inducement: *Leaving the keys in the car was an open invitation to theft.* *n.*

**in·vite** (in vīt′ *for verb,* in′vīt *for noun*) **1** ask someone politely to come to some place or to do something: *We invited her to join us.* **2** make a polite request for: *to invite an opinion.* **3** give a chance for; tend to cause: *The letter invites some questions. Carelessness invites trouble.* **4** attract; tempt; encourage: *The calm water invited swimming.* **5** *Informal.* INVITATION. 1–4 *v.*, **in·vit·ed, in·vit·ing;** 5 *n.*

**in·vit·ing** (in vī′ting) **1** attractive; tempting: *An iced drink is inviting on a hot day.* **2** ppr. of INVITE. 1 *adj.*, 2 *v.* —**in·vit′ing·ly,** *adv.*

**in·vo·ca·tion** (in′və kā′shən) **1** the act of calling upon in prayer; appeal for help or protection: *A church service often begins with an invocation to God.* **2** a calling forth of spirits by magic. **3** the set of magic words used to call forth spirits. *n.*

**in·voice** (in′vois) **1** a list of goods sent to a purchaser showing prices, amounts, shipping charges, etc. **2** make an invoice of; enter on an invoice. **3** a shipment of invoiced goods. **4** the form used for listing such goods. 1, 3, 4 *n.*, 2 *v.*, **in·voiced, in·voic·ing.**

**in·voke** (in vōk′) **1** call on in prayer; appeal to for help, protection, blessing, etc. **2** ask earnestly for; beg for: *The condemned criminal invoked the judge's mercy.* **3** call forth by magic: *Aladdin invoked the genie of the magic lamp.* *v.*, **in·voked, in·vok·ing.**

**in·vo·lu·cre** (in′və lü′kər) in botany, one or more circles of small leaves, called bracts, around the base of a flower, flower cluster, or fruit. See COMPOSITE for picture. *n.*

**in·vol·un·tar·y** (in vol′ən ter′ē) **1** not voluntary; not done of one's own free will; unwilling: *Jeanne was threatened until she gave involuntary consent to the plan.* **2** not done on purpose; not intended: *An accident is involuntary.* **3** not controlled by the will: *Breathing is mainly involuntary.* **4** done without a person's consent; forced: *involuntary commitment to a psychiatric hospital.* *adj.* —**in·vol′un·tar′i·ly,** *adv.* —**in·vol′un·tar′i·ness,** *n.*

**in·volve** (in volv′) **1** have as a necessary part, condition, or result; take in; include: *Housekeeping involves cooking, washing dishes, sweeping, and cleaning.* **2** have an effect on; affect: *These changes in the business involve the interests of all the owners.* **3** cause to be unpleasantly concerned; bring into difficulty, danger, etc.: *One foolish mistake can involve you in a good deal of trouble.* **4** entangle; complicate: *A sentence that is involved is often hard to understand.* **5** take up the attention of; occupy: *She was involved in working out a puzzle.* **6** wrap; enfold; envelop: *The outcome of the war is involved in doubt.*

**inviolate** 637 **ion**

hat, āge, fär; let, ēqual, tėrm; it, īce
hot, ōpen, ôrder; oil, out; cup, put, rüle
əbove, takən, pencəl, lemən, circəs
ch, child; ng, long; sh, ship
th, thin; ŦH, then; zh, measure

**7** wind spirally; coil: *The serpent involved its scaly folds.* *v.*, **in·volved, in·volv·ing.** —**in·volv′er,** *n.*

**in·volve·ment** (in volv′mənt) involving or being involved. *n.*

**in·vul·ner·a·bil·i·ty** (in vul′nə rə bil′ə tē) being INVULNERABLE. *n.*

**in·vul·ner·a·ble** (in vul′nə rə bəl) **1** that cannot be wounded or injured: *Achilles was invulnerable except for his heel.* **2** proof against attack; not easily assailable: *an invulnerable argument.* *adj.* —**in·vul′ner·a·bly,** *adv.*

**in·ward** (in′wərd) **1** toward the inside or centre: *a passage leading inward.* **2** placed within; internal: *the inward parts of the body.* **3** directed toward the inside: *an inward slant of the eyes.* **4** into the mind or soul: *Turn your thoughts inward.* **5** in mind or soul: *inward peace, inward happiness.* 1, 4 *adv.*, 2, 3, 5 *adj.*

**in·ward·ly** (in′wər dlē) **1** on the inside; within. **2** toward the inside or centre. **3** in the mind or soul. **4** not openly; secretly: *She was inwardly pleased but said nothing.* *adv.*

**in·ward·ness** (in′wərd nis) **1** inner nature or meaning. **2** spirituality. **3** earnestness. *n.*

**in·wards** (in′wərds *for adverb,* in′wərdz *or* in′ərdz *for noun*) **1** INWARD (defs. 1, 4). **2** the parts inside the body; stomach and intestines. 1 *adv.*, 2 *n. pl.*

**in·weave** (in wēv′) weave in; weave together; interweave. *v.*, **in·wove** *or* **in·weaved, in·wo·ven, in·wove,** *or* **in·weaved, in·weav·ing.**

**in·wove** (in wōv′) pt. or a pp. of INWEAVE. *v.*

**in·wo·ven** (in wō′vən) a pp. of INWEAVE. *v.*

**in·wreathe** (in rēŦH′) ENWREATHE. *v.*, **in·wreathed, in·wreath·ing.**

**in·wrought** (in rot′) **1** having a decoration worked in. **2** worked in. **3** mixed together; closely blended. *adj.*

**Io** ionium.

**I.O.D.E.** Imperial Order Daughters of the Empire.

**i·o·dide** (ī′ə dīd′) a compound of IODINE with another element or radical. *n.*

**i·o·dine** (ī′ə dīn′; *in chemistry,* ī′ə dēn′) **1** a non-metallic element usually obtained in the form of greyish-black crystals that give off a dense, violet-coloured vapour: *Iodine is used in medicine, in making dyes, in photography, etc.* Symbol: I **2** a brown liquid, **tincture of iodine,** used as an antiseptic. *n.*

**i·o·dize** (ī′ə dīz′) combine or impregnate with IODINE or an iodide: *iodized salt.* *v.*, **i·o·dized, i·o·diz·ing.** —**i′o·diz′er,** *n.*

**i·o·do·form** (ī ō′də fôrm′) a crystalline compound of IODINE, used as an antiseptic. *n.*

**IOF** *or* **I.O.F.** Independent Order of Foresters.

**i·on** (ī′ən *or* ī′on) **1** an atom or group of atoms having a negative or positive electric charge as a result of having lost or gained one or more electrons. **Positive ions**

(cations) are formed in ELECTROLYSIS by the loss of electrons. **Negative ions** (anions) are formed by the gain of electrons. **2** an electrically charged particle formed in a gas. *n.*

**–ion** a suffix meaning: **1** the act of _____ing, as in *attraction, calculation*. **2** the condition or state of being _____ed, as in *adoption, fascination*. **3** the result of _____ing, as in *abbreviation, collection, connection*.

**I·on·ic** (ī on′ik) **1** of or having to do with the second of three kinds of Greek architecture. The other two are Doric and Corinthian. See ORDER for picture. **2** of Ionia or its people. *adj.*

**i·on·ic** (ī on′ik) having to do with IONS. *adj.*

**i·o·ni·um** (ī ō′nē əm) a naturally occurring radio-active isotope of thorium, having a mass number of 230. *Symbol*: Io *n.*

**i·on·i·za·tion** (ī′ə nə zā′shən *or* ī′ə nī zā′shən) a separation into IONS; dissociation; formation of ions. *n.*

**i·on·ize** (ī′ə nīz′) separate into IONS; produce ions in: *Acids, bases, and salts ionize in solution. The gas in a neon light must be ionized before it can conduct an electric current.* *v.*, **i·on·ized, i·on·iz·ing.** —**i′on·iz′er,** *n.*

**i·on·o·sphere** (ī on′ə sfēr′) a region of ionized layers of air above the stratosphere. Low pressure and solar radiation in the ionosphere help to reflect radio waves so that they travel over long distances. *n.*

**i·o·ta** (ī ō′tə) **1** a very small quantity: *There is not an iota of truth in the prisoner's story.* **2** the ninth letter of the Greek alphabet (Ι or ι). *n.*

**IOU** or **I.O.U.** (ī′ō′ yü′) an informal note showing a debt: *Write me your IOU for ten dollars.*

**IPA** or **I.P.A.** **1** International Phonetic Alphabet. **2** International Phonetic Association.

**ip·e·cac** (ip′ə kak′) **1** a medicine made from the dried roots of a South American vine belonging to the madder family, used as an emetic or purgative. **2** the dried roots. **3** the vine. *n.*

**ip·so· fac·to** (ip′sō fak′tō) *Latin*. by that very fact; by the fact itself.

**IQ** or **I.Q.** intelligence quotient.

**Ir** iridium.

**ir-¹** a form of the prefix **in-¹** occurring before *r*, as in *irrational, irresolute*.

**ir-²** a form of the prefix **in-²** occurring before *r*, as in *irrigate, irradiate*.

**I·ra·ni·an** (i rā′nē ən) **1** of Iran, a country in southwestern Asia, its people, or their language. **2** a native or inhabitant of Iran. **1** *adj.*, **2** *n.*

**I·ra·qi** (i rä′kē) **1** a native or inhabitant of Iraq, a country in southwestern Asia. **2** of or having to do with Iraq or its people. **1** *n.*, **2** *adj.*

**i·ras·ci·bil·i·ty** (i ras′ə bil′ə tē) quickness of temper; irritability. *n.*

**i·ras·ci·ble** (i ras′ə bəl) **1** easily made angry; irritable. **2** showing anger. *adj.* —**i·ras′ci·bly,** *adv.*

**i·rate** (ī′rāt *or* ī rāt′) angry. *adj.* —**i′rate·ly,** *adv.*

**ire** (īr) anger; wrath. *n.*

**ire·ful** (īr′fəl) angry; wrathful. *adj.* —**ire′ful·ly,** *adv.*

**ir·i·des·cence** (ir′ə des′ns) a changing or play of colours, as in mother-of-pearl. *n.*

**ir·i·des·cent** (ir′ə des′nt) **1** displaying colours like those of the rainbow. **2** changing colours according to position. *adj.* —**ir′i·des′cent·ly,** *adv.*

**i·rid·i·um** (i rid′ē əm) a heavy, white, rare metallic element that resembles platinum. *Symbol*: Ir *n.*

An iris

**i·ris** (ī′ris) **1** any of a closely related group of perennial plants found in temperate regions of the Northern Hemisphere, having sword-shaped leaves and large, showy flowers: *There are many cultivated varieties of iris.* **2** the flower of an iris. **3** referring to a family of plants found in tropical and temperate regions, growing from an underground stem or a bulb: *Irises, crocuses, and gladioli belong to the iris family.* **4** the coloured part of the eye, having a round opening, called the pupil, in its centre: *The iris is a kind of diaphragm that controls the amount of light entering the eye.* See EYE for picture. **5** rainbow. *n.*

**iris diaphragm** a DIAPHRAGM (def. 4) that controls the aperture of a camera lens or of a microscope.

**I·rish** (ī′rish) **1** of or having to do with Ireland, a large island west of England, its people, or their language. **2 the Irish,** *pl.* the people of Ireland. **3** the Celtic language spoken in parts of Ireland; Irish Gaelic. **1** *adj.*, **2, 3** *n.*

**I·rish·man** (ī′rish mən) **1** a man who is a native or inhabitant of Ireland. **2** a man of Irish descent. *n., pl.* **I·rish·men** (-mən).

**Irish potato** the common white potato.

**Irish setter** a breed of large hunting dog having long, silky, reddish-brown hair.

**Irish terrier** a breed of small dog having wiry brown or reddish hair.

**Irish wolfhound** a breed of very large and powerful dog, formerly used in hunting wolves.

**I·rish·wom·an** (ī′rish wùm′ən) **1** a woman who is a native or inhabitant of Ireland. **2** a woman of Irish descent. *n., pl.* **I·rish·wom·en** (-wim′ən).

**irk** (ėrk) weary; disgust; annoy; bore: *It irks us to wait for people who are always late.* *v.*

**irk·some** (ėrk′səm) tiresome; tedious: *Washing dishes all day would be an irksome task.* *adj.* —**irk′some·ly,** *adv.* —**irk′some·ness,** *n.*

**i·ron** (ī′ərn) **1** a useful metal, from which tools, machinery, etc. are made: *Iron is a very hard, strong, silver-white chemical element.* *Symbol*: Fe **2** made of iron; having to do with iron: *an iron fence.* **3** a tool, instrument, or weapon made from this metal: *A tire iron is used to remove automobile tires.* **4** like iron; hard or strong; unyielding: *an iron will.* **5** great hardness and

strength; firmness: *men of iron.* **6** harsh or cruel: *the iron hand of fate.* **7** a tool with a flat surface which is heated for smoothing cloth or pressing clothes. **8** smooth or press cloth, etc. with a heated iron. **9** furnish or cover with iron. **10** a golf club with an iron or steel head. **11 irons,** *pl.* chains or bands of iron; handcuffs; shackles. *1, 3, 5, 7, 10, 11 n., 2, 4, 6 adj., 8, 9 v.*
**have too many irons in the fire,** try to do too many things at once.
**iron out,** straighten out; smooth away: *A tactful person can iron out many problems between people.*
**strike while the iron is hot,** act while conditions are favourable.

**Iron Age** a period of human culture characterized by the use of tools, weapons, etc. made of iron (in Europe begining about 1000 B.C.).

**i·ron·bound** (ī′ərn bound′) **1** bound with iron. **2** hard; rigid; unyielding: *an ironbound will, an ironbound code of ethics.* **3** rocky: *the ironbound coast of Newfoundland.* *adj.*

**i·ron·clad** (ī′ərn klad′) **1** protected with iron plates. **2** in former times, a warship protected with iron plates. **3** very hard to change or get out of: *An ironclad agreement must be kept. 1, 3 adj., 2 n.*

**Iron Curtain** an imaginary wall of secrecy or dividing line thought of as separating the former Soviet Union and the nations under its control or influence from the rest of the world.

**iron hand** a firm, strict manner.

**i·ron·ic** (ī ron′ik) **1** expressing one thing and meaning the opposite: *"Speedy" would be an ironic name for a snail.* **2** contrary to what would naturally be expected: *It was ironic that the woman was run over by her own car.* **3** using or having a habit of using irony: *an ironic person.* **4** showing irony: *an ironic statement.* *adj.*

**i·ron·i·cal** (ī ron′i kəl) IRONIC. *adj.*
—**i·ron′i·cal·ly,** *adv.*

**ironing board** a board covered with a smooth cloth, used for ironing clothes on: *An ironing board usually has folding legs.*

**iron lung** a device that gives artificial respiration by rhythmically alternating the air pressure in a chamber enclosing the patient's chest.

**iron–on** (ī′ərn on′) made of or coated on the reverse side with a substance that, when heated, as with an iron, will form a permanent bond with fabric: *iron-on interfacing.* *adj.*

**iron pyrites** pyrite; fool's gold.

**i·ron·stone** (ī′ərn stōn′) **1** any iron ore with clay or other impurities in it. **2** a hard variety of white ceramic ware. *n.*

**i·ron·ware** (ī′ərn wer′) articles made of iron, such as pots, kettles, tools, etc.; hardware. *n.*

**i·ron·weed** (ī′ərn wēd′) a plant of the same family as the aster, with flat-topped clusters of small tubular flowers, usually purple or red. *n.*

**i·ron·willed** (ī′ərn wild′) having an exceptionally firm will. *adj.*

**i·ron·wood** (ī′ərn wùd′) **1** any of various trees having very hard, heavy wood. **2** the wood itself. *n.*

**i·ron·work** (ī′ərn wėrk′) things made of iron. *n.*

**i·ron·work·er** (ī′ərn wėr′kər) **1** a person whose work

# Iron Age 639 irregular

hat, āge, fär; let, ēqual, tėrm; it, īce
hot, ōpen, ôrder; oil, out; cup, pùt, rüle
əbove, takən, pencəl, lemən, circəs
ch, child; ng, long; sh, ship
th, thin; ŦH, then; zh, measure

is making iron or iron articles. **2** a person whose work is building the framework of bridges, skyscrapers, etc. *n.*

**i·ron·works** (ī′ərn wėrks′) a place where iron is made or worked into iron articles (*often used with a singular verb*). *n. pl. or sing.*

**i·ro·ny** (ī′rə nē) **1** a method of expression in which the meaning intended is the opposite of that expressed: *Calling the thin girl "Fatty" was irony.* **2** an event or outcome contrary to what would naturally be expected: *It was an amusing irony when a fake diamond was stolen instead of the real one. It was the irony of fate that the great cancer doctor himself died of cancer. n., pl.* **i·ro·nies.**

**Ir·o·quois** (ir′ə kwo′ *or* ir′ə kwoi′) a member of a powerful group of First Nations and Native American tribes called the Five Nations (later, the Six Nations) living mostly in Quebec, Ontario, and New York State. *n., pl.* **Ir·o·quois.**

**ir·ra·di·ate** (i rā′dē āt′) **1** shine upon; make bright; illuminate. **2** shine. **3** radiate; give out. **4** treat with ultra-violet rays, X rays or radium. *v.,* **ir·ra·di·at·ed, ir·ra·di·at·ing.** —**ir·ra′di·a′tion,** *n.*

**ir·ra·tion·al** (i rash′ə nəl) **1** not rational; unreasonable: *It is irrational to be afraid of the number 13.* **2** unable to think and reason clearly. *adj.* —**ir·ra′tion·al·ly,** *adv.*

**ir·ra·tion·al·i·ty** (i rash′ə nal′ə tē) **1** the state or condition of being irrational. **2** something irrational; an absurdity. *n., pl.* **ir·ra·tion·al·i·ties.**

**irrational number** in mathematics, a number which cannot be expressed as a whole number or fraction. Its decimal expansion neither terminates nor repeats. *Examples:* $\pi$, $\sqrt{2}$.

**ir·re·claim·a·ble** (ir′i klā′mə bəl) that cannot be reclaimed. *adj.* —**ir′re·claim′a·bly,** *adv.*

**ir·rec·on·cil·a·ble** (i rek′ən sī′lə bəl *or* i rek′ən sī′ lə bəl) **1** that cannot be reconciled; that cannot be made to agree; opposed: *irreconcilable enemies.* **2** a person who refuses to compromise or collaborate: *The irreconcilables in the party made discussion of the proposal very difficult. 1 adj., 2 n.* —**ir·rec′on·cil′a·bly,** *adv.*

**ir·re·cov·er·a·ble** (ir′i kuv′ə rə bəl) **1** that cannot be regained or got back: *Wasted time is irrecoverable.* **2** that cannot be remedied: *irrecoverable sorrow.* *adj.*
—**ir′re·cov′er·a·bly,** *adv.*

**ir·re·deem·a·ble** (ir′i dē′mə bəl) **1** that cannot be bought back. **2** that cannot be exchanged for coin: *irredeemable paper money.* **3** beyond remedy; hopeless: *an irredeemable misfortune.* *adj.*
—**ir′re·deem′a·bly,** *adv.*

**ir·re·duc·i·ble** (ir′i dyü′sə bəl *or* ir′i dü′sə bəl) that cannot be reduced. *adj.* —**ir′re·duc′i·bly,** *adv.*

**ir·ref·u·ta·ble** (i ref′yə tə bəl *or* ir′i fyü′tə bəl) that cannot be refuted or disproved: *irrefutable arguments.* *adj.* —**ir·ref′u·ta·bly,** *adv.*

**ir·reg·u·lar** (i reg′yə lər) **1** not regular; not according to rule; out of the usual order or natural way: *irregular breathing.* **2** not even; not smooth; not straight; without symmetry: *irregular features, an irregular coastline.* **3** not according to law or morals: *irregular behaviour.* **4** not in the regular army. **5** a soldier not in the regular army. **6** of a word, not inflected in the usual way: *"Be" is an irregular verb.* 1–4, 6 *adj.*, 5 *n.* —**ir·reg′u·lar·ly,** *adv.*

**ir·reg·u·lar·i·ty** (i reg′yə lar′ə tē *or* i reg′yə ler′ə tē) **1** a lack of regularity; being irregular: *the irregularity of the coastline.* **2** something irregular: *There were a number of irregularities in the evidence.* **3** lack of regularity of bowel movements: *Do you suffer from irregularity? n., pl.* **ir·reg·u·lar·i·ties.**

**ir·rel·e·vance** (i rel′ə vəns) **1** being IRRELEVANT. **2** something IRRELEVANT. *n.*

**ir·rel·e·van·cy** (i rel′ə ven sē) IRRELEVANCE. *n.*

**ir·rel·e·vant** (i rel′ə vənt) not to the point; off the subject: *A question about economics is irrelevant in a music lesson. adj.* —**ir·rel′e·vant·ly,** *adv.*

**ir·re·li·gion** (ir′i lij′ən) **1** a lack of religion. **2** hostility to or disregard of religion. *n.*

**ir·re·li·gious** (ir′i lij′əs) **1** not religious; indifferent to religion. **2** contrary to religious principles; impious. *adj.* —**ir′re·li′gious·ly,** *adv.*

**ir·re·me·di·a·ble** (ir′i mē′dē ə bəl) that cannot be remedied; incurable. *adj.* —**ir′re·me′di·a·bly,** *adv.*

**ir·re·mov·a·ble** (ir′i mü′və bəl) that cannot be removed. *adj.* —**ir′re·mov′a·bly,** *adv.*

**ir·rep·a·ra·ble** (i rep′ə rə bəl) that cannot be repaired or made good: *Losing a leg is an irreparable injury. adj.* —**ir·rep′a·ra·bly,** *adv.*

**ir·re·place·a·ble** (ir′i plā′sə bəl) not replaceable; impossible to replace with another: *The old photographs were irreplaceable because the negatives had been lost long ago. adj.*

**ir·re·press·i·bil·i·ty** (ir′i pres′ə bil′ə tē) the condition of being IRREPRESSIBLE. *n.*

**ir·re·press·i·ble** (ir′i pres′ə bəl) that cannot be repressed or restrained. *adj.* —**ir′re·press′i·bly,** *adv.*

**ir·re·proach·a·ble** (ir′i prō′chə bəl) free from blame; faultless: *She had led an irreproachable life. adj.* —**ir′re·proach′a·bly,** *adv.*

**ir·re·sist·i·ble** (ir′i zis′tə bəl) that cannot be resisted; too great to be withstood; overwhelming: *an irresistible desire to laugh. adj.* —**ir′re·sist′i·bly,** *adv.*

**ir·res·o·lute** (i rez′ə lüt′) **1** unable to make up one's mind; not sure of what one wants; hesitating: *He stood there irresolute, not knowing which path to try.* **2** lacking in resoluteness: *An irresolute person makes a poor leader. adj.* —**ir·res′o·lute·ly,** *adv.* —**ir·res′o·lute·ness,** *n.*

**ir·res·o·lu·tion** (i rez′ə lü′shən) being irresolute; hesitation or a lack of resolution. *n.*

**ir·re·spec·tive** (ir′i spek′tiv) regardless: *Any person, irrespective of age, may join the club. adj.*

**ir·re·spon·si·bil·i·ty** (ir′i spon′sə bil′ə tē) a lack of responsibility; being IRRESPONSIBLE. *n.*

**ir·re·spon·si·ble** (ir′i spon′sə bəl) **1** not having or not showing a proper sense of responsibility: *It was irresponsible to leave the broken glass on the sidewalk.* **2** not responsible to any authority; that cannot be called to account: *A dictator is an irresponsible ruler. adj.* —**ir′re·spon′si·bly,** *adv.*

**ir·re·triev·a·bil·i·ty** (ir′i trē′və bil′ə tē) the quality or state of being IRRETRIEVABLE. *n.*

**ir·re·triev·a·ble** (ir′i trē′və bəl) that cannot be retrieved or recovered; that cannot be recalled or restored to its former condition. *adj.* —**ir′re·triev′a·bly,** *adv.*

**ir·rev·er·ence** (i rev′ə rəns) **1** a lack of reverence; disrespect. **2** an act showing irreverence. *n.*

**ir·rev·er·ent** (i rev′ə rənt) not reverent; disrespectful. *adj.* —**ir·rev′er·ent·ly,** *adv.*

**ir·re·vers·i·bil·i·ty** (ir′i vėr′sə bil′ə tē) the quality or state of being IRREVERSIBLE. *n.*

**ir·re·vers·i·ble** (ir′i vėr′sə bəl) not capable of being reversed. *adj.* —**ir′re·vers′i·bly,** *adv.*

**ir·rev·o·ca·bil·i·ty** (i rev′ə kə bil′ə tē) the fact or state of being IRREVOCABLE. *n.*

**ir·rev·o·ca·ble** (i rev′ə kə bəl) not to be recalled, withdrawn, or annulled: *an irrevocable decision. adj.* —**ir·rev′o·ca·bly,** *adv.*

**ir·ri·gate** (ir′ə gāt′) **1** supply land with water by means of ditches, sprinklers, etc.: *Farmers irrigate dry land to make crops grow better.* **2** in medicine, wash out or flush a wound, cavity in the body, etc. with a continuous flow of some liquid: *to irrigate the nose and throat with warm water.* **3** supply land, wounds, etc. thus: *Is it time to irrigate? v.,* **ir·ri·gat·ed, ir·ri·gat·ing.**

**ir·ri·ga·tion** (ir′ə gā′shən) irrigating or being irrigated: *Irrigation is needed to make crops grow in dry regions. n.*

**ir·ri·ta·bil·i·ty** (ir′ə tə bil′ə tē) **1** the state or quality of being IRRITABLE. **2** the response to a stimulus; the capacity of living things to react to changes in their environment. *n., pl.* **ir·ri·ta·bil·i·ties.**

**ir·ri·ta·ble** (ir′ə tə bəl) **1** easily made angry; impatient: *When the rain spoiled her plans, she was irritable for the rest of the day.* **2** of a part of the body, unnaturally sensitive or sore: *A baby's skin is often quite irritable. adj.* —**ir′ri·ta·ble·ness,** *n.* —**ir′ri·ta·bly,** *adv.*

**ir·ri·tant** (ir′ə tənt) **1** a thing that causes irritation: *A mustard plaster is an irritant.* **2** causing irritation. 1 *n.,* 2 *adj.*

**ir·ri·tate** (ir′ə tāt′) **1** make impatient or angry; annoy; provoke; vex: *The boy's foolish questions irritated his father. Flies irritate horses.* **2** make unnaturally sensitive or sore: *Too much sun irritates the skin. v.,* **ir·ri·tat·ed, ir·ri·tat·ing.** —**ir′ri·tat′ing·ly,** *adv.* —**ir′ri·ta′tor,** *n.*

**ir·ri·ta·tion** (ir′ə tā′shən) **1** the act or process of irritating; annoyance; vexation. **2** an irritated condition: *An irritation in Mei's nose made her sneeze. n.*

**ir·rup·tion** (i rup′shən) a breaking or bursting in; violent invasion: *The irruption of barbarians was one cause of the downfall of the Roman Empire. n.*

**is** (iz) third person singular, present indicative, of **be:** *The earth is round. He is at school. A child is loved by its mother and father. v.*

**as is,** as it is now; in its present condition.
☞ Hom. HIS (iz).

**Is.** **1** Island. **2** Isle.

**is·chi·um** (is′kē əm) the lower back and side portion of the hipbone. See PELVIS for picture. *n., pl.* **is·chi·a** (-is′kē ə).

**–ise** a form of the suffix -IZE.
☞ *Usage.* See note at -IZE.

**–ish** a suffix meaning: **1** somewhat, as in *oldish, sweetish*. **2** resembling; like, as in *a childish person*. **3** like that of; having the characteristics of, as in *a childish idea*. **4** of or having to do with; belonging to, as in *British, Spanish, Turkish*. **5** tending to; inclined to, as in *bookish, thievish*. **6** near, but usually somewhat past, as in *fortyish*.

**is·in·glass** (ī′zing glas′) **1** a kind of gelatin obtained from air bladders of sturgeon, cod, and similar fishes, used for making glue, clarifying liquors, etc. **2** mica, especially when split into thin, semi-transparent sheets. *n.*

**Is·lam** (is′ləm *or* i släm′) **1** the religion of Moslems, including belief in Allah as the one God and following the teachings of Mohammed as the prophet of Allah. **2** Moslems as a group. **3** the civilization of Moslem peoples. **4** all the countries in which Islam is the main religion. *n.*

**Is·lam·ic** (i slam′ik *or* i slä′mik) of or having to do with Islam; Moslem. *adj.*

**Is·lam·ism** (is′lə miz′əm) the faith or cause of Islam. *n.*

**is·land** (ī′lənd) **1** a body of land smaller than a continent and completely surrounded by water: *Cuba is a very large island. To reach the island, you go on a boat.* **2** something resembling this: *The city built a safety island at the busy intersection.* **3** a superstructure, especially of a battleship or aircraft carrier. **4** make into an island. 1–3 *n.*, 4 *v.* —**is′land·like′**, *adj.*
☞ *Etym.* From OE *īgland*. The *s* in the spelling came in the 16c. from a mistaken association with *isle, islet,* which came through OF *isle* and *islette* from forms of L *insula* 'island'.

**is·land·er** (ī′lən dər) a native or inhabitant of an island: *Newfoundlanders are islanders; so are Prince Edward Islanders. n.*

**isle** (īl) **1** a small island. **2** island. *n.*
☞ *Hom.* AISLE, I'LL.

**is·let** (ī′lit) a little island. *n.*
☞ *Hom.* EYELET.

**ism** (iz′əm) a distinctive doctrine, theory, system, or practice: *Capitalism, socialism, communism, and fascism are well-known isms. n.*

**–ism** a noun-forming suffix meaning: **1** an action; practice, as in *baptism, criticism*. **2** a doctrine; system; principle, as in *communism, socialism*. **3** a quality; characteristic; state; condition, as in *heroism, paganism*. **4** an illustration; case; instance, as in *colloquialism, witticism*. **5** an unhealthy condition caused by _____, as in *alcoholism, morphinism*.

**is·n't** (iz′ənt) is not.

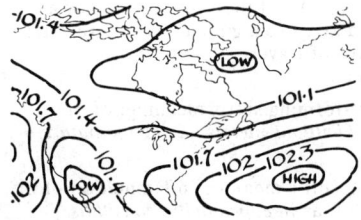
Isobars showing atmospheric pressures for an average July. The pressures are given in kilopascals.

**i·so·bar** (ī′sə bär′) a line on a weather map connecting places having the same average atmospheric pressure after allowance for height above sea level. *n.*

**i·soch·ro·nal** (ī sok′rə nəl) **1** equal or uniform in time. **2** performed or happening in equal periods of time. *adj.*

**i·soch·ro·nous** (ī sok′rə nəs) ISOCHRONAL. *adj.*

**i·so·hy·et** (ī′sō hī′ət) a line on a map or chart connecting places having the same average precipitation. *n.*

**i·so·late** (ī′sə lāt′) **1** place apart; separate from others; keep alone: *People with contagious diseases should be isolated.* **2** obtain a substance in a pure or uncombined form: *A chemist can isolate the oxygen from the hydrogen in water. v.*, **i·so·lat·ed, i·so·lat·ing.**

**i·so·la·tion** (ī′sə lā′shən) **1** setting apart or being set apart: *The isolation of infectious persons is essential.* **2** the state of being separated from other persons or things: *Robinson Crusoe lived in isolation for years. n.*
**in isolation,** without reference to related matter: *Considered in isolation, the whole thing assumes a less significant aspect.*

**i·so·la·tion·ism** (ī′sə lā′shə niz′əm) the principles or practice of ISOLATIONISTS. *n.*

**i·so·la·tion·ist** (ī′sə lā′shə nist) **1** one who objects to his country's participation in international affairs. **2** in Canada and the United States, a person who favours keeping his or her country out of European wars, etc. *n.*

**i·so·met·ric** (ī′sə met′rik) having to do with equality of measure; having equality of measure: *Isometric exercises are done without perceptible movement of body parts. adj.*

**i·sos·ce·les** (ī sos′ə lēz′) of a triangle, having two sides equal. See TRIANGLE for picture. *adj.*

**i·sos·ta·sy** (ī sos′stə sē) **1** a state in which each side bears equal pressure. **2** in geology, a state of balance in the earth's crust as it floats on the mantle. *n.*

**i·so·therm** (ī′sə thėrm′) a line on a weather map connecting places having the same average temperature. *n.*

**i·so·ther·mal** (ī′sə thėr′məl) **1** indicating equality of temperatures. **2** having to do with ISOTHERMS. *adj.*

**i·so·ton·ic** (ī′sə ton′ik) **1** in physiology and chemistry, having the same osmotic pressure. Compare with HYPERTONIC and HYPOTONIC. **2** in physiology, having to do with muscle contractions caused by minor, but constant, tension. **3** in music, characterized by equal tones. *adj.*

**i·so·tope** (ī′sə tōp′) any of two or more kinds of atom of a chemical element having the same number of protons and almost the same chemical properties, but having a different number of neutrons and different physical properties: *Most elements have naturally occurring isotopes; the known isotopes of hydrogen are ordinary hydrogen (sometimes called light hydrogen), deuterium, and tritium. n.*

**i·so·trop·ic** (ī′sə trop′ik) having the same properties such as elasticity or conduction, in all directions. *adj.*

**i·sot·ro·pous** (ī sot′rə pəs)  ISOTROPIC.  *adj.*

**Is·rae·li** (iz rā′lē)  **1** a native or inhabitant of modern Israel, a country between Jordan and the Mediterranean, established as a Jewish state in 1948.  **2** of or having to do with modern Israel or its people.  **1** *n.*, *pl.* **Is·rae·lis**; **2** *adj.*

**Is·sei** (ēs′sā′)  a first-generation Japanese living in Canada or the United States. A second-generation Japanese living in Canada or the United States is a NISEI. Compare with NISEI and SANSEI.  *n.*, *pl.* **Is·sei.**

**is·su·ance** (ish′ü əns)  an issuing; issue.  *n.*

**is·sue** (ish′ü)  **1** send out; put forth: *The government issues money and stamps.*  **2** something sent out; a quantity of bonds, stamps, copies of a magazine, etc. sent out at one time: *Did you read the last issue of our weekly paper?*  **3** a sending out; putting forth: *The next issue of new stamps will be on June 11.*  **4** come out; go out; proceed from: *Smoke was issuing from the chimney.*  **5** be published.  **6** publish; put into public circulation: *to issue a new edition of a book.*  **7** distribute; give out to a person or persons: *Heavy boots were issued to all the troops.*  **8** a coming forth; flowing out; discharge: *A nosebleed is an issue of blood from the nose.*  **9** a way out; outlet; exit.  **10** that which comes out.  **11** a profit; production.  **12** emerge.  **13** the result; outcome: *The issue of the game remained uncertain until the last moment.*  **14** result or end (*in*): *The game issued in a tie.*  **15** result (*from*).  **16** a point to be debated; problem: *political issues.*  **17** a child or children; offspring: *She died without issue.*  **18** be born, be descended; be derived.  **1, 4–7, 12, 14, 15, 18** *v.*, **is·sued, is·su·ing;**  **2, 3, 8–11, 13, 16, 17** *n.*  —**is′su·a·ble**, *adj.*  —**is′su·er**, *n.*

**at issue,**  in question; to be considered or decided.
**burning issue,**  a matter of great or topical importance.
**face the issue,**  admit the facts and do what must be done.
**join issue,**  take opposite sides in an argument.
**take issue,**  disagree: *I take issue with you on that point.*

**–ist**  a noun-forming suffix meaning:  **1** a person who does or makes, as in *theorist, tourist.*  **2** one who knows about or has skill with, as in *biologist, flutist.*  **3** one engaged in or busy with, as in *horticulturist, machinist.*  **4** one who believes in; adherent of, as in *abolitionist, idealist.*

**isth·mi·an** (is′mē ən)  **1** of or having to do with an ISTHMUS.  **2 Isthmian, a** of or having to do with the Isthmus of Panama.  **b** of or having to do with the Isthmus of Corinth in Greece: *The Isthmian games were national festivals of ancient Greece.*  *adj.*

**isth·mus** (is′məs)  a narrow strip of land having water on either side, connecting two larger bodies of land: *The Isthmus of Panama connects North America and South America.*  *n.*, *pl.* **isth·mus·es.**

**it** (it)  **1** a thing, part, animal, or person already spoken about.  **2** the subject of an impersonal verb: *It is raining.*  **3** an apparent subject of a clause when the logical subject comes later: *It is hard to believe that she is dead.*  **4** the antecedent to any relative pronoun when separated by the predicate: *It was a blue car that passed.*  **5** an object without definite force: *He lorded it over us.*  **6** in certain children's games, the player who must catch, find, guess, etc.  **7** something neither male or female: *If it's not a he or a she, it must be an it.*  **1–5** *pron.*, *nom.* **it,** *poss.* **its,** *obj.* **it;** *pl. nom.* **they,** *poss.* **their** or **theirs,** *obj.* **them;** **6, 7** *n.*

**ital.**  italic.

**I·tal·ian** (i tal′yən)  **1** of Italy, a country in southern Europe, its people, or their language.  **2** a native or inhabitant of Italy.  **3** a person of Italian descent.  **4** the language of Italy.  **1** *adj.*, **2–4** *n.*

**i·tal·ic** (i tal′ik)  **1** of or in type in which the letters slant to the right: *These words are in italic type.*  **2** an italic type, letter, or number.  **3 Italic,** a style of handwriting or calligraphy.  **4** Usually, **italics,** *pl.*  italic type or print: *Example sentences in this dictionary are in italics.*  **5 Italic,** of ancient Italy, its peoples, or their languages.  **1, 5** *adj.*, **2–4** *n.*
▶ *Etym.*  **Italic** type was introduced in the 17c. by an Italian printer of Venice; it was named **italic** to distinguish it from the upright letters of roman type.

**i·tal·i·ci·za·tion** (i tal′ə sə zā′shən *or* i tal′ə sī zā′shən)  the act or process of italicizing.  *n.*

**i·tal·i·cize** (i tal′ə sīz′)  **1** print in type in which the letters slant to the right: *This sentence is italicized.*  **2** underline with a single line to indicate italics: *We italicize words or expressions that are to be emphasized.*  **3** use italics.  *v.*, **i·tal·i·cized, i·tal·i·ciz·ing.**

**itch** (ich)  **1** a tickly, prickling feeling in the skin that makes one want to scratch.  **2** cause an itching feeling: *Mosquito bites itch.*  **3** have an itching feeling: *Wool makes me itch.*  **4** a restless, uneasy feeling, longing, or desire for anything: *an itch to get away and explore.*  **5** have such a desire: *She itched to know our secret.*  **6 the itch,**  a contagious disease of the skin caused by a tiny mite, accompanied by an itching feeling.  **1, 4, 6** *n.*, **2, 3, 5** *v.*

**itch·y** (ich′ē)  itching; like the itch.  *adj.*, **itch·i·er, itch·i·est.**  —**itch′i·ness,** *n.*

**–ite**  a noun-forming suffix meaning:  **1** a native or inhabitant of, as in *Canaanite.*  **2** a person associated with, as in *labourite.*  **3** a mineral species, or a rock substance, as in *hematite.*

**i·tem** (ī′təm)  **1** a separate thing or article: *The list contains twelve items.*  **2** a piece of news; a bit of information: *There were several interesting items in today's paper.*  **3** also; likewise (used in introducing each item of a list or series).  **1, 2** *n.*, **3** *adv.*

**i·tem·ize** (ī′tə mīz′)  give each item of; list by items: *to itemize the cost of a trip.*  *v.*, **i·tem·ized, i·tem·iz·ing.**

**it·er·ate** (it′ə rāt′)  repeat.  *v.*, **it·er·at·ed, it·er·at·ing.**  —**it′er·a′tion,** *n.*

**it·er·a·tive** (it′ə rə tiv *or* it′ə rā′tiv)  repeating; full of repetitions.  *adj.*

**i·tin·er·ant** (ī tin′ə rənt)  **1** travelling from place to place, especially on a regular route: *an itinerant salesperson.*  **2** a person who travels from place to place.  **1** *adj.*, **2** *n.*  —**i·tin′er·ant·ly,** *adv.*

**i·tin·er·ar·y** (ī tin′ə rer′ē)  **1** the route or plan of a journey.  **2** a travel diary.  **3** a guidebook for travellers.  **4** of travelling or routes of travel.  **1–3** *n.*, *pl.* **i·tin·er·ar·ies;**  **4** *adj.*

**–itious**  an adjective-forming suffix meaning: of or having the nature of: *Fictitious means having the nature of fiction.*

**–itis**  a noun-forming suffix meaning inflammation of or inflammatory disease of, as in *appendicitis, tonsillitis.*

**it'll** (it′əl)  it will.

**its** (its)   the possessive form of **it:**   **1** of, belonging to, or made or done by it or itself: *The dog hurt its paw. The report is important, and its delay now could cause problems.*   **2** that which belongs to it: *A dog's kennel is its and its alone.*   **1** *adj.*, **2** *pron.*

**it's** (its)   **1** it is: *It's my turn.*   **2** it has: *It's been a beautiful day.*

**it·self** (it self′)   **1** a reflexive pronoun, the object of a reflexive verb with **it** or a noun as subject: *The horse tripped and hurt itself.*   **2** an intensive pronoun, used to emphasize the neuter noun or pronoun it follows: *The land itself is worth more than they paid for the house.*   **3** its usual self: *After repairs, the car is itself again.*   *pron.*

**–ity**   a noun-forming suffix meaning condition or quality, as in *absurdity, activity, hostility, sincerity,* or an instance of any of these, as in *a monstrosity, an activity.*

**IU** or **I.U.**   international unit; international units.

**I've** (īv)   I have.

**i·vied** (ī′vēd)   covered or overgrown with ivy: *an ivied wall.*   *adj.*

**i·vo·ry** (ī′və rē *or* ī′vrē)   **1** a hard, white substance, a form of dentine, composing the tusks of elephants, walruses, etc.: *Ivory is easy to carve and is used for many kinds of ornament.*   **2** any substance like ivory.   **3** made of ivory.   **4** of or like ivory.   **5** creamy white: *The room has ivory walls and a white ceiling.*   1, 2, 5 *n., pl.* **i·vo·ries;**   3–5 *adj.*

**ivory black**   a fine-quality, deep-black pigment made from ivory that has been burned.

**ivory tower**   a condition of withdrawal from the world of action into a world of ideas and dreams.

**i·vy** (ī′vē)   **1** a climbing plant with smooth, shiny, evergreen leaves, also called English ivy.   **2** any of various other climbing plants that resemble the English ivy, such as *American ivy, Boston ivy, Japanese ivy, poison ivy.*   *n., pl.* **i·vies.**

**–ize**   a verb-forming suffix meaning:   **1** make, as in *legalize, centralize.*   **2** become, as in *crystallize, materialize.*   **3** engage in; be busy with; use, as in *apologize, theorize.*   **4** treat or combine with, as in *macadamize, oxidize.*   **5** other meanings, as in *alphabetize, colonize, criticize, memorize.*

☛ *Usage.* Both **-ize** and **-ise** have their origin in Greek, **-ise** being the Old French spelling. Some English verbs took the Old French ending: *surprise, exercise, supervise.* Others took the original Greek ending: *baptize, civilize.* The same Greek ending is used in creating new words: *winterize, customize, finalize.* A very few English words like *realize* and *realise* were formed with both endings. With such words, Canadian English prefers the **-ize** ending: *realize, criticize* as given in this dictionary.

hat, āge, fär; let, ēqual, tėrm; it, īce
hot, ōpen, ôrder; oil, out; cup, pùt, rüle
əbove, takən, pencəl, lemən, circəs
ch, child; ng, long; sh, ship
th, thin; ᴛʜ, then; zh, measure

# J j  *J j*

**j or J** (jā) **1** the tenth letter of the English alphabet. **2** any speech sound represented by this letter. **3** any person or thing considered as the tenth of a series. *n., pl.* **j's** or **J's.**

**J or J. 1** Judge. **2** Justice. **3** Journal.

**jab** (jab) **1** thrust with something pointed: *He jabbed his fork into the potato.* **2** poke roughly: *He jabbed her with his fist.* **3** pierce; stab: *I just jabbed myself with a pin.* **4** a thrust with a pointed thing, a fist, etc.: *She gave him a jab with her elbow.* 1–3 *v.,* **jabbed, jab·bing;** 4 *n.*

**jab·ber** (jab′ər) **1** talk very fast in a confused or senseless way; chatter. **2** very fast, confused, or senseless talk; chatter. 1 *v.,* 2 *n.* —**jab′ber·er,** *n.*

**ja·bot** (zha bō′ *or* zhab′ō) a ruffle or frill of lace or cloth, worn at the throat or down the front of a woman's dress or on a man's shirt. *n.*

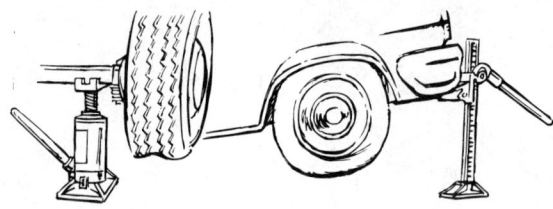

Two types of jack for automobiles

**jack** (jak) **1** a device for lifting or pushing up heavy weights a short distance: *Jacks are sometimes used to raise a house so that a cellar may be added.* **2** lift or push up with a jack. **3** a man or boy; fellow. **4** a playing card with a picture of a court page on it; knave. **5** jackstone; in a child's game, a pebble or piece of metal tossed up and caught. **6** a small ball for players to aim at in bowling. **8** a small flag used on a ship to show nationality or as a signal. **8** a device to turn roasting meat. **9** a male donkey. **10** a jack-rabbit. **11** an electrical device to receive a plug, as, a telephone or radio jack. **12** jacklight. **13** hunt or fish, especially illegally, by means of a jacklight. **14** Also, **Jack,** sailor. **15 jacks,** *pl.* jackstones; a child's game in which pebbles or pieces of metal are tossed up and caught or picked up in various ways. 1, 3–12, 14, 15 *n.,* 2, 13 *v.*
**every man jack,** everyone.
**jack up,** **a** lift up with a jack. **b** *Informal.* raise prices, wages, etc.: *Stores jacked up many prices this month.*

**jack·al** (jak′əl *or* jak′ol) **1** a wild animal of Asia, Africa and southeastern Europe, closely related to the dog: *Jackals hunt in packs at night and feed on small animals and carrion left by large animals.* **2** a person who does drudgery for another. *n.*

**jack·a·napes** (jak′ə nāps′) **1** an insolent, conceited fellow. **2** a saucy or mischievous child. *n.*

**jack·ass** (jak′as′) **1** a male donkey. **2** a very stupid person; fool. *n.*

**jack·boot** (jak′büt′) a heavy, leather, military boot reaching up to or above the knee. *n.*

**jack·daw** (jak′do′) a common black European bird closely related to the common crow, but smaller. *n.*

**jack·et** (jak′it) **1** an outer garment for the upper part of the body, having a front opening, sleeves, and, usually, a collar with lapels. **2** any of various kinds of outer covering such as the skin of a potato or the casing around a steampipe. **3** DUST JACKET. **4** put a jacket on; cover with a jacket. 1–3 *n.,* 4 *v.* —**jack′et·less,** *adj.*

**jack·fish** (jak′fish′) a common game fish of the pike family having a long, slender body and large head, found throughout most of Canada; northern pike. *n., pl.* **jack·fish** or **jack·fishes.**

**Jack Frost** frost or freezing cold weather, thought of as a person.

**jack-in-a-box** (jak′in ə boks′) JACK-IN-THE-BOX. *n.*

**jack-in-the-box** (jak′in ᴛʜə boks′) a toy figure that springs up from a box when the lid is unfastened. *n., pl.* **jack-in-the-boxes.**

**jack-in-the-pul·pit** (jak′in ᴛʜə pul′pit) a plant having a greenish, petal-like sheath arched up over a spike of tiny flowers; Indian turnip: *The jack-in-the-pulpit is found from Nova Scotia to Ontario.* See ARUM for picture. *n., pl.* **jack-in-the-pulpits.**

**jack-knife** (jak′nīf′) **1** a large, strong pocketknife. **2** a kind of headfirst dive in which the diver touches the feet with the hands while keeping the legs straight, and then straightens out again before touching the water. **3** double up like a jack-knife. **4** perform a jack-knife dive. **5** of railway cars, trailers, etc., double up at the connecting hitch when the vehicle is suddenly stopped or thrown off course. 1, 2 *n., pl.* **jack-knives;** 3–5 *v.,* **jack-knifed, jack-knif·ing.** Also, **jackknife.**

**jack·light** (jak′līt′) **1** a light used for hunting or fishing at night: *Fish or game are attracted by the jacklight so that they may be easily caught.* **2** hunt or fish, especially illegally, by means of a jacklight; jack. 1 *n.,* 2 *v.* —**jack′light·er,** *n.*

**jack·light·ing** (jak′lī′ting) the act or practice, often illegal, of hunting or fishing with a jacklight. *n.*

**jack of all trades** a person who can do many different kinds of work fairly well.

**jack-o'-lan·tern** (jak′ə lan′tərn) **1** a pumpkin hollowed out and cut to look like a face, used as a lantern at Halloween. **2** a will-o'-the-wisp; a moving light appearing at night over marshy places. *n.*

**jack pine** **1** a medium tall pine tree found throughout Ontario and Quebec and the forest regions of the Prairie Provinces, having stiff, sharp, light-green needles and cones that are often curved: *The wood of the jack pine is used in general construction and for pulp.* **2** any of several other species of pine, such as the lodgepole or ponderosa pine.

**jack·pot** (jak′pot′) **1** a large fund or pool of money that is competed for regularly and that increases as contestants fail to win it. **2** in poker, the stakes that accumulate until some player wins with a pair of jacks or something better. *n.*
**hit the jackpot,** **a** win a jackpot. **b** have a stroke of very good luck.

**jack-rab·bit** (jak′rab′it) a large hare of western North America, having very long ears and long back legs. *n.*

**jack·screw** (jak′skrü′) a tool or machine for lifting heavy masses short distances, operated by turning a screw. *n.*

**jack·stone** (jak′stōn′) **1** in a child's game, a pebble or piece of metal that is tossed up and caught. **2 jackstones**, *pl.* a child's game in which pebbles or pieces of metal are tossed up and caught or picked up in various ways; jacks. *n.*

**jack·straw** (jak′strò′) **1** a straw, strip of wood, bone, etc. used in a game. **2 jackstraws**, *pl.* a game played with a set of these thrown down in a confused pile and picked up one at a time without any of the rest of the pile being moved. *n.*

**Jack Tar** or **jack tar** sailor.

**Ja·cob's–lad·der** (jā′kəbz lad′ər) a common garden plant having ladderlike leaves. *n.*

**jade** (jād) **1** a hard stone, usually green or white, used for jewellery and ornaments. **2** green. 1, 2 *n.*, 2 *adj.*

**jad·ed** (jā′did) **1** worn out; tired; weary: *a jaded horse, a jaded appearance.* **2** dulled from continual use; surfeited; satiated: *a jaded appetite. adj.*

**jae·ger** or **jä·ger** (yā′gər) a sea bird like a gull, that pursues weaker birds and makes them disgorge their prey. *n.*

**jag** (jag) **1** a sharp point sticking out; pointed projection: *a jag of rock.* **2** make notches or indentations in. **3** cut or tear unevenly. 1 *n.*, 2, 3 *v.*, **jagged, jag·ging.**

**jag·ged** (jag′id) with sharp points sticking out; unevenly cut or torn: *We cut our bare feet on the jagged rocks. adj.* —**jag′ged·ly**, *adv.*

**jag·uar** (jag′wär or jag′yü är′) a fierce animal much like a leopard, but more heavily built: *Jaguars live in forests in the warmer parts of America. n.*

**jail** (jāl) **1** a prison, especially one for people awaiting trial or being punished for minor offences. **2** imprisonment. **3** put in jail; keep in jail. 1, 2 *n.*, 3 *v.* —**jail′-like′**, *adj.*
**break jail,** escape from jail.

**jail·bird** (jāl′bėrd′) *Informal.* **1** a prisoner in jail. **2** a person who has been in jail many times. *n.*

**jail·break** (jāl′brāk′) *Informal.* an escape from jail or prison. *n.*

**jail·er** or **jail·or** (jā′lər) **1** the keeper of a jail. **2** a person who keeps someone or something confined. *n.*

**Jain** (jān or jīn) a member or adherent of JAINISM. **2** of or having to do with the Jains or their religion. 1 *n.*, 2 *adj.*

**Jain·ism** (jā′niz əm or jī′niz əm) a religion of India founded about 500 B.C. and having Hindu and Buddhist elements. Its beliefs include non-violence, asceticism, and the transmigration of souls. *n.*

**jal·ou·sie** (zhal′ü zē′) a window blind or shutter made of horizontal slats of wood, metal, plastic, or glass, that can be adjusted to regulate the light or air entering a room. *n.*

**jam¹** (jam) **1** press; squeeze; hold; stick: *The ship was jammed between two rocks.* **2** crush; bruise: *to jam your fingers in the door.* **3** push or thrust a thing hard into a place; shove: *to jam one more book into the bookcase.* **4** fill up; block up: *The river was jammed with logs.* **5** stick fast or get caught so as not to work properly: *The window has jammed. Guns sometimes jam.* **6** make unworkable: *The key broke off and jammed the lock.* **7** a mass of people or things crowded together so that they cannot move freely: *a traffic jam.* **8** the act of jamming. **9** being jammed. **10** *Informal.* a difficulty or tight spot. **11** make radio signals, etc. unintelligible by sending out others of approximately the same frequency. 1–6, 11 *v.*, **jammed, jam·ming;** 7–10 *n.*
**jam on,** *Informal.* apply hastily: *jam on the brakes.*
☞ *Hom.* JAMB.

**jam²** (jam) a preserve made by boiling fruit with sugar until thick. *n.* —**jam′like′**, *adj.*
☞ *Hom.* JAMB.

**Ja·mai·can** (jə mā′kən) **1** of or having to do with Jamaica, an island country in the West Indies, or its people. **2** a native or inhabitant of Jamaica. 1 *adj.*, 2 *n.*

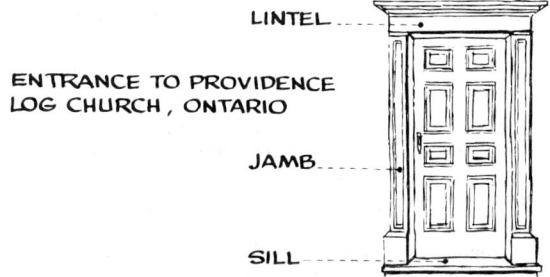

ENTRANCE TO PROVIDENCE LOG CHURCH, ONTARIO

**jamb** (jam) the upright piece forming the side of a doorway, window, fireplace, etc. See FRAME for another picture. *n.*
☞ *Hom.* JAM.

**jam·bo·ree** (jam′bə rē′) **1** *Informal.* a noisy party; lively entertainment. **2** a large rally or gathering of Boy Scouts. *n.*

**jam–packed** (jam′pakt′) *Informal.* filled to absolute capacity; packed tightly: *The arena was jam-packed for the final game. adj.*

**jam session** *Informal.* an informal gathering of jazz musicians at which they play improvisations.

**Jan.** January.

**jan·gle** (jang′gəl) **1** sound harshly; make a loud, clashing noise. **2** cause to make a hard, clashing sound: *She jangled a bell.* **3** a harsh sound; clashing noise or ring: *The jangle of the telephone woke him up.* **4** quarrel; dispute. **5** make tense or strained; upset: *Their continual complaints jangled her nerves.* 1, 2, 4, 5 *v.*, **jan·gled, jan·gling;** 3, 4 *n.* —**jan′gler**, *n.*

**jan·i·tor** (jan′ə tər) a person hired to take care of a building, offices, etc.; caretaker. *n.*

**jan·na** (jä′nə) in Islam, HEAVEN or PARADISE. *n.*

**jan·na·nam** (jä′nə nam) in Islam, HELL. *n.*

**Jan·u·ar·y** (jan′yə wer′ē or jan′yü er′ē) the first month of the year: *January has 31 days. n., pl.* **Jan·u·ar·ies.**

**Janus-faced** 646 **jealous**

☞ *Etym.* Through OF from L *Januarius*, which was based on the name of the god *Janus*, who had two faces—one looking forward and the other looking backward.

**Ja·nus–faced** (jā'nəs fāst') two-faced; double-dealing; deceitful. *adj.*
☞ *Etym.* From *Janus*, the Roman god of gates and doors, and of beginnings and endings, represented with two faces, one looking forward and the other looking backward.

**ja·pan** (jə pan') **1** a hard, glossy varnish: *Black japan is used on wood or metal.* **2** put japan on. **3** articles varnished and decorated in the Japanese manner. **4** a liquid used to make paint dry faster. 1, 3, 4 *n.*, 2 *v.*, **ja·panned, ja·pan·ning.**

**Japan current** a warm current in the Pacific Ocean.

**Jap·a·nese** (jap'ə nēz' *for adjective*, jap'ə nēz' *for noun*) **1** of or having to do with Japan, an island country off the east coast of Asia, its people, or their language: *Japanese art, Japanese writings, Japanese customs.* **2** a native or inhabitant of Japan. **3** a person of Japanese descent. **4** the language of Japan. 1 *adj.*, 2–4 *n.*, *pl.* (*for defs.* 2 *and* 3) **Jap·a·nese.**

**Japanese beetle** a small green-and-brown beetle that eats fruit, leaves and grasses.

**jape** (jāp) **1** joke; jest. **2** trick. 1 *n.*, 2 *v.*, **japed, jap·ing.** —**jap'er,** *n.*

**ja·pon·i·ca** (jə pon'ə kə) **1** CAMELLIA. **2** any of several closely related flowering shrubs of the rose family widely grown for ornament.

**jar**[1] (jär) **1** a deep container made of glass, earthenware, etc., with a wide mouth and a removable lid. **2** the amount that it holds: *George claims he can eat a whole jar of jelly at breakfast.* *n.*

**jar**[2] (jär) **1** cause to shake or rattle; vibrate: *The heavy footsteps jarred my desk so that I had trouble writing.* **2** a shake; rattle. **3** make a harsh, grating noise. **4** a harsh, grating noise. **5** have a harsh, unpleasant effect on; shock: *The children's playful screams jarred his nerves.* **6** a harsh, unpleasant effect; shock. **7** clash; quarrel: *Our opinions jar.* **8** a clash; quarrel. 1, 3, 5, 7 *v.*, **jarred, jar·ring;** 2, 4, 6, 8 *n.*

**jar·di·niere** (jär'də nēr'; *French*, zнaR dē nyeR') an ornamental pot or stand for flowers or plants. *n.*

**jar·gon** (jär'gən) **1** language that fails to communicate because it is full of long or unusual words, uses more words than necessary, and contains lengthy, awkward sentences. **2** a form of speech made up of features from two or more languages, used for communication between peoples whose native languages differ: *the Chinook jargon. Pidgin English is a jargon.* **3** the language of a special group, profession, etc.: *the jargon of sailors.* **4** formerly, any speech or language that is strange to one and therefore seems meaningless. **5** meaningless talk or chatter; gibberish. *n.*
☞ *Usage.* Definitions 2 and 3 carry no slur or criticism but are technical senses of **jargon** as used by linguists. They should not be confused with definition 1, which does suggest poor expression and muddled thinking.

**jas·mine** or **jas·min** (jas'mən) a shrub or vine having clusters of fragrant flowers: *There are yellow, white, and red jasmines.* *n.* Also, **jessamine.**

**jas·per** (jas'pər) **1** a coloured quartz, usually red, yellow, or brown. **2** a green precious stone. *n.*

**ja·to** (jā'tō) in aeronautics, a unit consisting of one or more jet engines, used to provide auxiliary propulsion for speeding up the take-off of an aircraft. *n.*
☞ *Etym.* Formed from *jet-assisted take-off.*

**jaun·dice** (jon'dis) **1** a disease that causes yellowness of the skin, eyes, and body fluids, and disturbed vision. **2** cause jaundice in. **3** a disturbed or unnaturally sour mental outlook, due to envy, jealousy, etc. **4** prejudice the mind and judgment of, by envy, discontent, etc.; sour the temper of. 1, 3 *n.*, 2, 4 *v.*, **jaun·diced, jaun·dic·ing.**

**jaunt** (jont) **1** a short pleasure trip or excursion. **2** take a short pleasure trip or excursion. 1 *n.*, 2 *v.*

**jaun·ty** (jon'tē) **1** easy and lively; sprightly; carefree: *The happy boy walked with jaunty steps.* **2** smart; stylish: *She wore a jaunty little hat.* *adj.*, **jaun·ti·er, jaun·ti·est.** —**jaun'ti·ly,** *adv.* —**jaun'ti·ness,** *n.*

**Jav·a·nese** (jav'ə nēz' *for adjective*, jav'ə nēz' *for noun*) **1** of Java, an island country in southeast Asia, its people, or their language. **2** a native or inhabitant of Java. **3** the language of Java. 1 *adj.*, 2, 3 *n.*, *pl.* (*for def.* 2) **Jav·a·nese.**

**jave·lin** (jav'lən) **1** a light spear thrown by hand. **2** a wooden or metal spear, thrown for distance in track and field contests. *n.*

**jaw** (jo) **1** either of the two bones, or sets of bones, that hold the teeth and together form the framework of the mouth in most vertebrates: *The lower jaw is usually movable; the upper jaw is fixed.* **2** the lower part of the face, especially the lower jaw: *She has a square jaw.* **3** find fault; scold. **4 jaws,** *pl.* **a** the mouth with its jawbones and teeth. **b** a narrow entrance to a valley, mountain pass, channel, etc. **c** the parts in a tool or machine that grip and hold: *A vise has jaws.* 1, 2, 4 *n.*, 3 *v.* —**jaw'less,** *adj.*

**jaw·bone** (jo'bōn') **1** the bone of either jaw. **2** the bone of the lower jaw. *n.*

**jay** (jā) any of several species of bird found in North America and Europe and related to the crow, often brightly coloured and often having a crest and a long tail: *Two kinds of jay found in Canada are the Canada jay and the bluejay.* *n.*

**jay·walk** (jā'wok') *Informal.* walk across a street at a place other than a regular crossing or without paying attention to traffic. *v.* —**jay'walk'er,** *n.*

**jazz** (jaz) **1** a style of music characterized by strong, often complex rhythms, improvisation of a basic melody, and unusual features of musical tone, such as long-drawn wavering or wailing sounds: *Jazz originated among black musicians in New Orleans in the rhythmic traditions of African music.* **2** of, having to do with, or playing jazz: *a jazz band.* **3** play or arrange music as jazz. **4** any popular dance music having a pronounced rhythm. 1, 2, 4 *n.*, 3 *v.*

**jaz·zy** (jaz'ē) **1** having the qualities of jazz. **2** *Informal.* loud, flashy, or unrestrained: *jazzy clothes.* *adj.*

**jct.** or **jctn.** junction.

**jeal·ous** (jel'əs) **1** fearful that a person one loves may love or prefer someone else: *One may be jealous of the person loved or of the rival.* **2** full of envy; envious: *She is jealous of Kim and of Kim's marks.* **3** watchful in keeping or guarding something; careful: *Each province is jealous of its rights within Confederation.* **4** close; watchful; suspicious: *The dog was a jealous guardian of the child.* *adj.* —**jeal'ous·ly,** *adv.* —**jeal'ous·ness,** *n.*

**jeal·ous·y** (jel′ə sē)  a jealous condition or feeling. *n., pl.* **jeal·ous·ies.**

**jeans** (jēnz)  **1** pants made of a strong, twilled cotton cloth, usually blue denim: *The cowboy wore blue jeans under his chaps.*  **2** overalls or trousers.  *n.*

**jeep** (jēp)  a small but powerful general-purpose automobile or truck in which power is transmitted to all four wheels: *Jeeps are used by soldiers, builders, farmers, etc.*  *n.*

**jeer** (jēr)  **1** make fun rudely or unkindly; mock; scoff: *Do not jeer at the mistakes or misfortunes of others.*  **2** a jeering remark; rude, sarcastic comment.  **1** *v.,* **2** *n.*

**jeer·ing·ly** (jē′ring lē)  in a jeering manner; with derision.  *adv.*

**Je·ho·vah** (ji hō′və)  in the Old Testament of the Bible, one of the names of God, according to Jewish belief.  *n.*

**je·june** (ji jün′)  **1** lacking nourishing qualities.  **2** flat and uninteresting.  *adj.*

**je·ju·num** (ji jü′nəm)  the middle portion of the small intestine, between the duodenum and the ileum.  See ALIMENTARY CANAL for picture.  *n.*

**jell** (jel)  **1** become jelly.  **2** *Informal.* take definite form; become fixed: *Our plans have jelled.*  *v.*

**jel·lied** (jel′ēd)  **1** turned into jelly; having the consistency of jelly.  **2** spread with jelly.  *adj*

**jel·ly** (jel′ē)  **1** a food that is liquid when hot but rather firm when cold: *Jelly can be made by boiling fruit juice and sugar together, or by cooking bones and meat in water, or by using some stiffening preparation like gelatin.*  **2** a jelly-like substance: *petroleum jelly.*  **3** become jelly; turn into jelly. **1, 2** *n., pl.* **jel·lies;**  **3** *v.,* **jel·lied, jel·ly·ing.** —**jel′ly·like′,** *adj.*

**jel·ly·bean** (jel′ē bēn′)  a small bean-shaped candy made of jellied sugar, coated in different colours.  *n.*

A jellyfish. It moves through the water by closing and opening like an umbrella.

**jel·ly·fish** (jel′ē fish′)  any of a group of invertebrate sea animals with a body formed of a mass of jelly-like tissue that is almost transparent: *Most jellyfish have long trailing tentacles that may have stinging hairs or feelers.*  *n., pl.* **jel·ly·fish** or **jel·ly·fish·es.**

**jen·ny** (jen′ē)  **1** SPINNING JENNY.  **2** the female of certain animals and birds: *jenny wren.*  *n., pl.* **jen·nies.**

**jeop·ard·ize** (jep′ər dīz′)  put in danger; risk; imperil: *Soldiers jeopardize their lives in war.*  *v.,* **jeop·ard·ized, jeop·ard·iz·ing.**

**jeop·ard·y** (jep′ər dē)  risk; danger; peril: *The firefighters put their lives in jeopardy when they entered the burning building.*  *n.*

**jer·bo·a** (jər bō′ə)  a small, jumping, mouselike mammal of Asia and N. Africa.  *n.*

**jer·e·mi·ad** (jer′ə mī′ad)  a mournful complaint; lamentation.  *n.*

hat, āge, fär; let, ēqual, tėrm; it, īce hot, ōpen, ôrder; oil, out; cup, pùt, rüle əbove, takən, pencəl, lemən, circəs ch, child; ng, long; sh, ship th, thin; ᴛʜ, then; zh, measure

**jerk¹** (jėrk)  **1** a sudden, sharp pull, twist, or start: *Her old car started with a jerk.*  **2** a pull or twist of the muscles that one cannot control; twitch.  **3** pull or twist suddenly: *If the water is unexpectedly hot, you jerk your hand out.*  **4** throw with a movement that stops suddenly. **5** move with a jerk: *the old wagon jerked along.*  **6** speak or say abruptly.  **1, 2** *n.,* **3–6** *v.*

**jerk²** (jėrk)  preserve meat by cutting it into long thin slices and drying it in the sun: *The Indians taught the early settlers in America how to jerk beef.*  *v.*

**jer·kin** (jėr′kən)  a short, close-fitting coat or jacket without sleeves: *Men used to wear leather jerkins in the 16th and 17th centuries.*  *n.*

**jerk·wa·ter** (jėr′kwot′ər) *Informal.*  **1** formerly, a train on a branch railway.  **2** not on the main line: *a jerkwater town.*  **3** insignificant.  **1** *n.,* **2, 3** *adj.*

**jerk·y¹** (jėr′kē)  with sudden starts and stops; with jerks: *The jerky motion of the old locomotive made father sick.* *adj.,* **jerk·i·er, jerk·i·est.**  —**jerk′i·ly,** *adv.* —**jerk′i·ness,** *n.*

**jerk·y²** (jėr′kē)  strips of dried beef.  *n.*

**jer·ry-built** (jer′ē bilt′)  built quickly and cheaply of poor materials; flimsy.  *adj.*

**jer·sey** (jėr′zē)  **1** a close-fitting sweater that is pulled on over the head.  **2** a woman's close-fitting knitted undergarment.  **3** a machine-knitted cloth.  **4** Jersey, a breed of small, fawn-coloured dairy cattle: *Jerseys give very rich milk.*  *n., pl.* **jer·seys.**
☞ *Etym.* Named for the island of *Jersey* in the English Channel, from which these cattle originally came. The knitted fabric and garments are named for the woollen sweaters traditionally worn by the fishermen of Jersey.

**Jerusalem artichoke**  **1** a kind of sunflower whose root is edible.  **2** the root of this plant.

**jes·sa·mine** (jes′ə min) JASMIN.  *n.*

**jest** (jest)  **1** joke.  **2** to joke; make a joke.  **3** make fun of; laugh at.  **4** the act of making fun of; mockery. **5** something intended to be mocked or laughed at.  **1, 4, 5** *n.,* **2, 3** *v.*  —**jest′ing·ly,** *adv.*
**in jest,**  in fun; not seriously: *Her words were spoken in jest.*

**jest·er** (jes′tər)  a person who jests: *In the Middle Ages kings often had jesters to amuse them.*  *n.*

**Je·sus** (jē′zəs)  the founder of the Christian religion. His birthday is celebrated by Christians every year on December 25th.  *n.*

**Jesus Christ** JESUS.

**jet¹** (jet)  **1** a stream of gas or liquid, sent with force, especially from a small opening: *A fountain sends up a jet of water.*  **2** a spout or nozzle for sending out a jet. **3** gush out; shoot forth in a jet or forceful stream.  **4** a jet-propelled aircraft.  **5** JET ENGINE.  **6** travel or carry by jet aircraft.  **7** of, having to do with, or involving the use of jet-propelled aircraft or jet propulsion: *the jet age, jet travel.*  **1, 2, 4, 5, 7** *n.,* **3, 6** *v.,* **jet·ted, jet·ting.**

**jet²** (jet)  **1** a hard, black variety of lignite that can be carved and polished to a high sheen: *Jet is used for making buttons, beads, etc.* **2** deep, glossy black: *Her hair is the colour of jet* (*n.*). **1, 2** *n.*, **2** *adj.*

**jet–black** (jet′blak′) very black. *adj.*

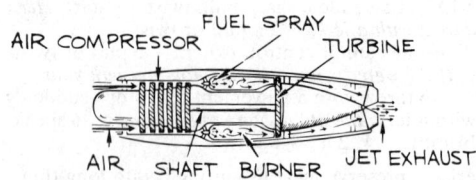

A jet engine. The air is sucked in through the front of the engine, compressed, and mixed with fuel. This mixture is burned in the burners, giving off gas that passes out in a powerful jet through the rear of the engine, pushing the aircraft forward.

**jet engine** an engine that produces motion by JET PROPULSION, especially an aircraft engine that moves the aircraft forward by the reaction to the discharge of heated gases from the combustion chamber through one or more exhaust nozzles at the rear: *Two types of jet engine are the turbojet and the ramjet.*

**jet lag** a delayed effect of fatigue and sleepiness after a long flight in a jet aircraft, especially when several time zones have been crossed.

**jet·lin·er** (jet′lī′nər) a large jet aircraft used for carrying passengers on commercial flights. *n.*

**jet plane** an aircraft that is driven by one or more JET ENGINES.

**jet–pro·pelled** (jet′prə peld′) **1** driven by JET PROPULSION. **2** moving very fast and energetically. *adj.*

**jet propulsion** propulsion in one direction by a jet of air, gas, etc. forced in the opposite direction.

**jet·sam** (jet′səm) **1** goods thrown overboard to lighten a ship in distress and often afterwards washed ashore. Compare with FLOTSAM. **2** anything tossed aside as useless. *n.*

**jet set** a wealthy social group, especially one whose members frequently visit fashionable resorts in various countries.

**jet stream** a current of air travelling at very high speed (often more than 350 km/h) from west to east at high altitudes (13 to 20 km): *Jet streams are often used by airplane pilots to gain extra speed when travelling in an easterly direction.*

**jet·ti·son** (jet′ə sən) **1** throw goods overboard to lighten a ship in distress. **2** the act of throwing goods overboard to lighten a ship in distress. **3** the goods thrown overboard; JETSAM. **4** throw away; discard. **1, 4** *v.*, **2, 3** *n.*

**jet·ty** (jet′ē) **1** a structure built out into the water to protect a harbour or to control the current or tide; breakwater. **2** a landing place; pier or dock. *n., pl.* **jet·ties.**

**Jew** (jü) **1** a person descended from the people led by Moses, who settled in Palestine and now live in Israel and many other countries; Hebrew. **2** a person whose religion is Judaism. *n.*

**jew·el** (jü′əl) **1** a precious stone; gem. **2** a valuable ornament to be worn, set with precious stones. **3** a person or thing that is very precious. **4** a gem or other piece of hard material used as a bearing in a watch. **5** set or adorn with jewels or with things like jewels: *a jewelled bracelet. The sky was jewelled with stars.* **1–4** *n.*, **5** *v.*, **jew·elled** or **jew·eled, jew·el·ling** or **jew·el·ing.** —**jew′el-like′,** *adj.*

**jewel case** a box or case to hold jewellery.

**jew·el·ler** or **jew·el·er** (jü′ə lər *or* jü′lər) a person who makes, sells, or repairs jewels, jewelled ornaments, watches, etc. *n.*

**jew·el·ler·y** or **jew·el·ry** (jü′əl rē *or* jül′rē) jewels and ornaments set with gems. *n.*

**jew·el·weed** (jü′əl wēd′) any of several species of wild impatiens having yellow or orange flowers; touch-me-not. *n.*

**Jew·ish** (jü′ish) **1** of, belonging to, or characteristic of the Jews: *Jewish customs.* **2** YIDDISH. **1** *adj.*, **2** *n.*

**Jew·ry** (jü′rē) Jews as a group; the Jewish people. *n.*

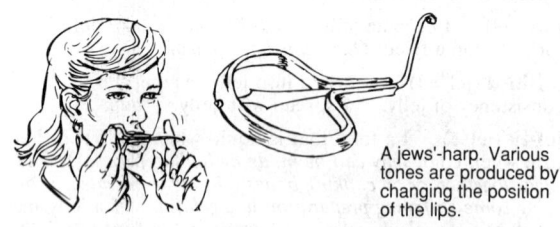

A jews'-harp. Various tones are produced by changing the position of the lips.

**jews'–harp** or **jew's–harp** (jüz′härp′) a simple musical instrument, held between the teeth and played by striking the free end of a flexible piece of metal with a finger. *n.*

**J.H.S.** Junior High School.

**jib**[1] (jib) on a ship or boat, a triangular sail in front of the foremast. See SCHOONER for picture. *n.*
**cut of one's jib,** *Informal.* one's outward appearance.

**jib**[2] (jib) JIBE[1]. *v.,* **jibbed, jib·bing.**

**jib**[3] (jib) move sideways or backward instead of forward; refuse to go ahead. *v.,* **jibbed, jib·bing.**
**jib at,** *Informal.* refuse to face or deal with: *The horse jibbed at the high fence. Management have jibbed at the strikers' latest proposals.*

**jib**[4] (jib) the projecting arm of a crane or derrick. *n.*

**jib boom** a spar extending out from a ship's bowsprit: *On a large sailing ship the jib is fastened to the jib boom.* See BOWSPRIT for picture.

**jibe**[1] (jīb) **1** shift a sail from one side of a ship to the other when sailing before the wind. **2** shift itself in this way: *Be careful or your mainsail will jibe.* **3** change the course of a ship so that the sails shift in this way. *v.,* **jibed, jib·ing.** Also, **jib.**

**jibe**[2] (jīb) See GIBE. *v.,* **jibed, jib·ing,** *n.* —**jib′er,** *n.*

**jibe**[3] (jīb) *Informal.* be in harmony; agree. *v.,* **jibed, jib·ing.**

**jif·fy** (jif′ē) *Informal.* a very short time; moment: *I'll be there in a jiffy.* *n., pl.* **jif·fies.**

**jig**[1] (jig) **1** any of several lively dances, often in triple time. **2** the music for a jig. **3** dance a jig. **4** move

jerkily; jerk up and down or back and forth.   1, 2 n., 3, 4 v., **jigged, jig·ging.**
**in jig time,**   quickly; rapidly.

**jig**[2] (jig)   **1** a fishing lure made of one or more fish-hooks, weighted with a bright metal or having a spoon-shaped piece of bone attached, for bobbing up and down or drawing through the water.   **2** fish with a jig.   **3** any of various mechanical contrivances or devices; especially, a guide in using a drill, file, etc.   1, 3 n., 2 v.

**jig·ger** (jig′ər)   **1** *Informal.*   some device, article, or part that one cannot name more precisely; gadget; contraption.   **2** a measure for liquor.   **3** JIG[2] (def. 1).   n.

**jig·gle** (jig′əl)   **1** shake or jerk slightly: *Please don't jiggle the desk when I'm trying to write.*   **2** a slight shake; light jerk.   1 v., **jig·gled, jig·gling;**   2 n.

**jig·saw** (jig′sô′)   a saw with a narrow blade mounted in a frame and worked with an up-and-down motion, used to cut curves or irregular lines.   n.

**jigsaw puzzle**   a picture cut into irregular pieces that can be fitted together again.

**ji·had** (ji häd′)   in Islam: **1** the duty to strive against the enemies of Islam.   **2** holy war; any crusade against rival beliefs.   n.

**jilt** (jilt)   **1** cast off a lover or sweetheart after giving encouragement.   **2** a woman who casts off a lover after encouraging him.   1 v., 2 n.   —**jilt′er,** n.

**jim·my** (jim′ē)   **1** a short crowbar used especially by burglars to force windows, doors etc. open.   **2** force open with or as if with a jimmy: *to jimmy a window.*   1 n., pl. **jim·mies;**   2 v., **jim·mied, jim·my·ing.**

**jim·son weed** or **Jim·son weed** (jim′sən)   a tall, coarse, bad-smelling weed having white flowers and poisonous, narcotic leaves.

**ji·na** (jin′ə)   in Jainism, one who has attained an eternal state of bliss.   n.

**jin·gle** (jing′gəl)   **1** a sound like that of little bells, or of coins or keys striking together.   **2** make a jingling sound: *The sleigh bells jingle as we ride.*   **3** cause to jingle: *He jingled the coins in his pocket.*   **4** a verse or song that repeats sounds or has a catchy rhythm: *She writes advertising jingles for radio and television.*   1, 4 n., 2, 3 v.   **jin·gled, jin·gling.**

**jin·gly** (jing′glē)   like a JINGLE.   adj.

**jinn** (jin)   in Moslem mythology:   **1** spirits that can appear in human or animal form and do good or harm to people.   **2** one of these spirits, JINNI: *The jinn turned the stone into gold.*   1 n., pl. of **jinni;**   2 n. sing., pl. **jinns.**   Also, **djinn.**

**jin·ni** or **jin·nee** (ji nē′)   one of the JINN.   n., pl. **jinn.**

**jin·rik·i·sha** or **jin·rick·sha** (jin rik′shə or jin rik′shô)   RICKSHAW.   n.

**jinx** (jingks) *Informal.*   **1** a person or thing that is believed to bring bad luck: *Eva must be a jinx; we've lost every game since she joined the team.*   **2** bring bad luck to.   1 n., 2 v.
☛ *Etym.*   From L. *iynx*, a bird once used in black magic.

**jit·ney** (jit′nē)   an automobile that carries passengers for a small fare: *A jitney usually travels along a regular route.*   n., pl. **jit·neys.**
☛ *Etym.*   From *jitney*, once used for a nickel.

**jit·ters** (jit′ərz)   extreme nervousness.   n. pl.

**jig**   **649**   **jodhpurs**

hat, āge, fär; let, ēqual, tėrm; it, īce
hot, ōpen, ôrder; oil, out; cup, put, rüle
əbove, takən, pencəl, lemən, circəs
ch, child; ng, long; sh, ship
th, thin; ᴛʜ, then; zh, measure

**jit·ter·y** (jit′ə rē)   nervous.   adj.

**jiu·jit·su** (jü jit′sü)   See JUJITSU.   n.

**jiu·jut·su** (jü jut′sü)   See JUJITSU.   n.

**ji·va** (jē′və)   in Jainism: **1** the individual and eternal soul of every living thing.   **2** the vital energy of life; the opposite of AJIVA.   n.

**job** (job)   **1** a piece of work: *Donna had the job of painting the boat.*   **2** a definite piece of work undertaken for a fixed price: *If you want your house painted, Mr. Huebert will do the job for $2000.*   **3** done by the job; hired for a particular piece of work.   **4** work; employment: *Mary's brother is hunting for a job.*   **5** anything a person has to do: *I'm not going to wash the dishes; that's your job.*   **6** *Informal.*   an affair; matter.   **7** manage a public matter for private gain in a dishonest way.   **8** a piece of public or official business managed dishonestly for private gain.   **9** buy goods from manufacturers in large quantities and sell to dealers in smaller lots.   **10** let out work to different contractors, workmen, etc.   **11** work at odd jobs.   1, 2, 4–6, 8 n., 3 adj., 7, 9–11 v., **jobbed, job·bing.**
**a good job,**   good work: *You did a good job on that flowerbed.*

**job·ber** (job′ər)   **1** a person who buys goods from manufacturers in large quantities and sells to retailers in smaller quantities.   **2** a person who manages public business dishonestly for private gain.   **3** a person who works by the job; pieceworker.   n.

**job·hold·er** (job′hōl′dər)   a person regularly employed.   n.

**job·less** (job′ləs)   **1** not having regular work; unemployed.   **2 the jobless,** pl.   all the people who are unemployed.   adj.   —**job′less·ness,** n.

**job lot**   a quantity of goods bought or sold together, usually containing several different kinds of things.

**jock·ey** (jok′ē)   **1** a person whose occupation is riding horses in races.   **2** ride a horse in a race.   **3** trick; cheat: *Swindlers jockeyed Mr. Moto into buying some worthless land.*   **4** manoeuvre to get advantage: *The crews were jockeying their boats to get into the best position for the race.*   1 n., pl. **jock·eys;**   2–4 v., **jock·eyed, jock·ey·ing.**
**jockey for,**   try to win by taking advantage: *Several entrants were jockeying for first place in the music competition.*

**joc·u·lar** (jok′yə lər)   funny; joking: *He spoke in a jocular way about his experiences as a policeman.*   adj.   —**joc′u·lar·ly,** adv.

**joc·u·lar·i·ty** (jok′yə lar′ə tē or jok′yə ler′ə tē)   **1** a jocular quality.   **2** jocular talk or behaviour.   **3** a jocular remark or act.   n., pl. **joc·u·lar·i·ties.**

**joc·und** (jok′ənd)   cheerful; merry: *a jocund manner.*   adj.   —**joc′und·ly,** adv.

**jo·cun·di·ty** (jō kun′də tē)   cheerfulness; merriment; gaiety.   n.

**jodh·purs** (jod′pərz)   breeches for horseback riding, loose above the knees and fitting closely below.   n. pl.

**jog¹** (jog) **1** shake with a push or jerk: *You may jog a person's elbow to get her attention.* **2** a shake, push, or nudge. **3** stir up with a hint or reminder: *to jog one's memory.* **4** a hint or reminder: *to give one's memory a jog.* **5** move up or down with a jerk or a shaking motion: *The old horse jogged along, and jogged me up and down on his back.* **6** go forward heavily and slowly. **7** run at a slow, steady rate: *My sister goes jogging every day for exercise.* **8** a slow walk or trot: *The riders went at a jog along the path.* 1, 3, 5–7 *v.*, **jogged, jog·ging;** 2, 4, 8 *n.* —**jog′ger,** *n.*

**jog²** (jog) **1** a part that sticks out or in; unevenness in a line or surface: *a jog in a wall.* **2** an abrupt, temporary change in direction: *There's a jog in the road where it goes around the poplar bluff.* **3** make or form a jog: *The road jogs to the left just before you get to our place.* 1, 2 *n.*, 3 *v.*

**jog·gle¹** (jog′əl) **1** shake or jolt slightly: *The milk spilled because you joggled my elbow.* **2** a slight shake or jolt. 1 *v.*, **jog·gled, jog·gling;** 2 *n.*

**jog·gle²** (jog′əl) **1** a projection on one of two joining surfaces, or a notch on the other, to prevent slipping. **2** a joint made in this way. **3** join or fasten with a joggle. 1, 2 *n.*, 3 *v.*, **jog·gled, jog·gling.**

**jog trot** **1** a slow, regular trot. **2** a routine or humdrum way of doing things.

**John Bull** **1** a supposedly typical Englishman often represented as stout and red-faced, in top hat and high boots. **2** a name for the English nation.
☞ *Etym.* Created in 1712 by John Arbuthnot, a Scottish writer.

**John Doe** a fictitious name used in legal forms or proceedings for the name of an unspecified person.

**John Do·ry** (dô′rē) an edible sea fish that has a high, flat body, spiny fins, and a large, black, yellow-ringed spot on each side. *pl.* **John Do·rys.**

**john·ny·cake** (jon′ē kāk′) corn bread in the form of a flat cake. *n.*

**Johnny Canuck** *Cdn.* **1** a Canadian, especially a member of the armed forces during the First or Second World War. **2** a personification of Canada: *Johnny Canuck can do a lot more than play hockey.*

**John·ny–jump–up** (jon′ē jum′pup′) WILD PANSY. *n.*

**join** (join) **1** bring or put together; connect; fasten: *to join hands, to join an island to a mainland by a bridge.* **2** come together; meet: *The two roads join here.* **3** meet and unite with: *The brook joins the river.* **4** make or become one; combine; unite: *to join in marriage.* **5** take part with others: *to join in a song.* **6** become a member of: *to join a club.* **7** come into the company of: *Go now, and I'll join you later.* **8** take or return to one's place in: *After a few days on shore, the sailor joined his ship.* **9** adjoin: *Her farm joins mine.* **10** a place or line of joining; seam. 1–9 *v.*, 10 *n.*
**join battle,** begin to fight.
**join forces,** give mutual support.
**join hands, a** shake or clasp hands. **b** agree.
**join in,** take part.

**join·er** (joi′nər) **1** a person or thing that joins. **2** a skilled worker who makes woodwork and furniture. *n.*

**join·er·y** (joi′nə rē) **1** the skill or trade of a JOINER (def. 2). **2** woodwork or furniture made by a JOINER (def. 2). *n.*

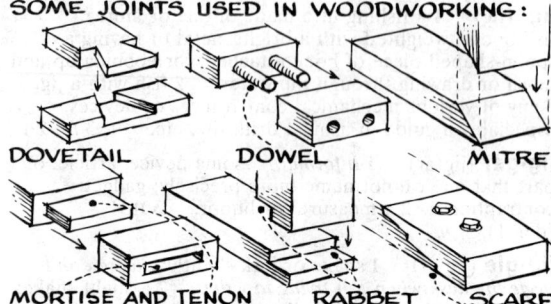
SOME JOINTS USED IN WOODWORKING: DOVETAIL, DOWEL, MITRE, MORTISE AND TENON, RABBET, SCARF

**joint** (joint) **1** the place at which two things or parts are joined together. **2** the way parts are joined: *a perfect joint.* **3** connect by a joint or joints. **4** in an animal, the joining of two bones in such a way as to allow movement. **5** one of the parts of which a jointed thing is made up: *the middle joint of the finger.* **6** the part of the stem from which a leaf or branch grows. **7** *Esp. Brit.* a large piece of meat for roasting. **8** divide at the joints: *I joint the chicken before frying it.* **9** shared or done by two or more persons: *By our joint efforts we managed to push the car back on the road.* **10** joined together; sharing: *My sister and I are joint owners of this dog.* 1, 2, 4–7 *n.*, 3, 8 *v.*, 9, 10 *adj.* —**joint′er,** *n.*
**out of joint, a** out of place at the joint. **b** out of order; in bad condition.

**joint·ly** (join′tlē) together; in common: *The two girls owned the boat jointly.* *adv.*

**joist** (joist) one of the parallel horizontal pieces of timber extending from wall to wall across a building, to which the boards of a floor or ceiling are fastened. See FRAME for picture. *n.*

**joke** (jōk) **1** something said or done to make somebody laugh; remark that is clever and amusing; something amusing; jest: *This was a good joke on me.* **2** make jokes; say or do something as a joke; jest. **3** a person or thing laughed at: *That car of hers is a joke. His being elected is a joke.* **4** something that is not in earnest or actually meant. 1, 3, 4 *n.*, 2 *v.*, **joked, jok·ing.** —**jok′ing·ly,** *adv.*
**no joke,** a serious matter: *That snowstorm was no joke.*

**jok·er** (jō′kər) **1** a person who tells funny stories or plays tricks on others. **2** *Informal.* any person; a fellow: *Who does that joker think he is?* **3** in some games, an extra playing card. **4** a trick for getting the better of someone. **5** *Informal.* a phrase or sentence hidden away in a law, contract, etc. to defeat its apparent purpose. *n.*

**jol·li·fi·ca·tion** (jol′ə fə kā′shən) festivity; merrymaking. *n.*

**jol·li·ty** (jol′ə tē) fun; merriment; festivity; gaiety. *n., pl.* **jol·li·ties.**

**jol·ly** (jol′ē) **1** full of fun; merry. **2** *Informal.* flatter a person to make him or her feel good or agreeable (*used with* **along**): *We jollied him along a bit.* 1 *adj.*, **jol·li·er, jol·li·est;** 2 *v.*, **jol·lied, jol·ly·ing.** —**jol′li·ly,** *adv.* —**jol′li·ness,** *n.*

**Jolly Rog·er** (roj′ər) a traditional pirates' flag, with a white skull and crossbones on a black background.

**jolt** (jōlt) **1** jar; shake up: *The wagon jolted us when the wheel went over a rock.* **2** move with a shock or jerk: *The* car jolted across the rough road.  **3** a jar; jerk: *She put her brakes on suddenly and the car stopped with a jolt.*  **4** a sudden surprise or shock: *The loss of the money was a severe jolt.*  **5** shock; surprise: *She was jolted out of complacency by news of the company's bankruptcy.*  1, 2, 5 *v.*, 3, 4 *n.*

**jolt·y** (jōl′tē)   jolting.   *adj.*

**jon·quil** (jong′kwəl)   **1** a plant having yellow or white flowers and long, slender leaves: *The jonquil is a kind of narcissus that is much like a daffodil.*  **2** the flower.   *n.*

**joss** (jos)   an image of a Chinese god; Chinese idol.   *n.*
☛ *Etym.*  From pidgin English, ultimately from Portuguese *deos*, 'a god'.

**joss house**   a Chinese temple.
☛ *Etym.*  See note at JOSS.

**joss stick**   a slender stick of dried, fragrant paste, burned by the Chinese as incense.
☛ *Etym.*  See note at JOSS.

**jos·tle** (jos′əl)   **1** crowd, shove, or push against; elbow roughly: *We were jostled by the big crowd at the circus entrance.*  **2** a jostling; push; knock.   1 *v.*, **jos·tled, jos·tling;**  2 *n.*   —**jos′tler,** *n.*

**jot** (jot)   **1** a little bit; a very small amount: *I do not care a jot.*  **2** write briefly or in haste (*often used with* **down**): *The clerk jotted down the order. He jotted notes on the back of an envelope.*  1 *n.*, 2 *v.*, **jot·ted, jot·ting.**   —**jot′ter,** *n.*

**joule** (jül)   an SI unit for measuring energy: *One joule is the amount of work done, or energy used, in applying one newton of force to move a body one metre in the direction of the force.*  Symbol: J   *n.*

**jounce** (jouns)   bounce; bump; jolt.   *v.*, **jounced, jounc·ing,**   *n.*

**jour·nal** (jėr′nəl)   **1** a daily record: *A diary, a ship's log, and a written account of what happens at each meeting of a society are all journals.*  **2** a book for keeping such a record.  **3** a newspaper or magazine.  **4** in bookkeeping, a book in which every item of business is written down so that the item can be entered under the proper account.  **5** the part of a shaft or axle that turns on a bearing.   *n.*
☛ *Etym.*  See note at DIARY.

**jour·nal·ese** (jėr′nə lēz′)   a careless or loose style of writing such as is sometimes used in newspapers, magazines, etc.: *Journalese is characterized by loose constructions, imprecise wording, and far-fetched or sensational expressions.*   *n.*

**jour·nal·ism** (jėr′nə liz′əm)   **1** the work of writing for, editing, managing, or publishing a newspaper or magazine.  **2** newspapers and magazines as a group.   *n.*

**jour·nal·ist** (jėr′nə list)   a person engaged in JOURNALISM: *Editors and reporters are journalists.*   *n.*

**jour·nal·is·tic** (jėr′nə lis′tik)   of or like JOURNALISM or JOURNALISTS.   *adj.*

**jour·ney** (jėr′nē)   **1** a trip, especially a fairly long one: *a journey around the world.*  **2** take a trip; travel: *to journey to New Brunswick.*  1 *n.*, *pl.* **jour·neys;**  2 *v.*, **jour·neyed, jour·ney·ing.**
☛ *Etym.*  From OF *journee* 'what is done or accomplished in a day', for example, a day's travel, a day's work. A JOURNEYMAN was originally one who had finished an apprenticeship in his trade and so was qualified to work for daily wages. OF *journee* developed from L *diurnus* 'of one day', from *dies* 'day'. See also the note at DIARY.

**jour·ney·man** (jėr′nē mən)   **1** a worker who knows a trade.  **2** a worker who has completed an apprenticeship

hat, āge, fär; let, ēqual, tėrm; it, īce
hot, ōpen, ôrder; oil, out; cup, put, rüle
above, takən, pencəl, lemən, circəs
ch, child; ng, long; sh, ship
th, thin; ᴛʜ, then; zh, measure

or is otherwise qualified to practise a trade, but is not an employer or master.   *n.*, *pl.* **jour·ney·men** (-mən).
☛ *Etym.*  See note at JOURNEY.

**joust** (joust, just, *or* jüst)   **1** a combat between two knights on horseback, armed with lances. See TILT for picture.  **2** fight with lances on horseback: *Knights used to joust with each other for sport.*  **3** jousts, pl. tournament.   1, 3 *n.*, 2 *v.*   —**joust′er,** *n.*

**jo·vi·al** (jō′vē əl)   good-hearted and full of fun; good-humoured and merry.   *adj.*   —**jo′vi·al·ly,** *adv.*   —**jo′vi·al·ness,** *n.*

**jo·vi·al·i·ty** (jō′vē al′ə tē)   jollity; merriment.   *n.*

**jowl**[1] (joul)   **1** the part under the jaw; jaw.  **2** the cheek.   *n.*

**jowl**[2] (joul)   a fold of flesh hanging from the jaw. See PORK for picture.   *n.*

**joy** (joi)   **1** a strong feeling of pleasure; gladness; happiness: *She jumped for joy when she saw the notice announcing the circus.*  **2** something that causes gladness or happiness: *"A thing of beauty is a joy forever."*  **3** an expression of happiness; outward rejoicing.   1–3 *n.*

**joy·ful** (joi′fəl)   **1** glad; happy: *a joyful heart.*  **2** causing joy: *joyful news.*  **3** showing joy: *a joyful look.*   *adj.*   —**joy′ful·ly,** *adv.*   —**joy′ful·ness,** *n.*

**joy·less** (joi′lis)   **1** without joy; sad; dismal.  **2** not causing joy: *a joyless prospect.*   *adj.*

**joy·ous** (joi′əs)   joyful; glad; gay: *a joyous song.*   *adj.*   —**joy′ous·ly,** *adv.*   —**joy′ous·ness,** *n.*

**joy ride**   *Informal.*   a ride in an automobile for pleasure, especially when the car is driven recklessly or is used without the owner's permission.

**joy–ride** (joi′rīd′)  *Informal.*   take a JOY RIDE.   *v.*, **joy-rode, joy-rid·den, joy-rid·ing.**   —**joy′-rid′er,** *n.*

**joy·stick** (joi′stik′)   a control mechanism for some computer games.   *n.*

**J.P.**   Justice of the Peace.

**Jr.** or **jr.**   Junior.

**ju·bi·lance** (jü′bə ləns)   rejoicing; great joy.   *n.*

**ju·bi·lant** (jü′bə lənt)   expressing or showing joy; rejoicing; exulting: *The people were jubilant when the war was over.*   *adj.*   —**ju′bi·lant·ly,** *adv.*

**ju·bi·la·tion** (jü′bə lā′shən)   **1** rejoicing.  **2** a joyful celebration.   *n.*

**ju·bi·lee** (jü′bə lē′)   **1** an anniversary thought of as a time of rejoicing: *a fiftieth wedding jubilee.*  **2** a time of rejoicing or great joy: *to have a jubilee in celebration of a victory.*  **3** rejoicing; great joy: *a day of jubilee.*   *n.*
☛ *Etym.*  From Hebrew *yōbēl* 'ram, ram's horn'; in the Old Testament a year of celebration was proclaimed by the Jews every fifty years by the blowing of a ram's horn, because mortgaged lands were made free from the mortgage.

**Ju·da·ic** (jü dā′ik)   of the Jews; Jewish.   *adj.*

**Ju·da·ism** (jü′dē iz′əm)   **1** the religion of the Jews, based on the teaching of Moses and the prophets as found in the Old Testament of the Bible. **2** the following of Jewish rules and customs. *n.*

**Ju·da·ize** (jü′dā īz′) conform to Jewish usages or ideas. *v.*, **Ju·da·ized, Ju·da·iz·ing.**

**Judas tree** a tree that has red, pink, or purplish flowers before the leaves come out.

**Ju·de·an** (jü dē′ən) **1** of Judea, the southern part of Palestine when it was a province of the Roman Empire. **2** of the Jews. *adj.*

**judge** (juj) **1** an official appointed to hear and decide cases in a law court. **2** hear and decide cases as a judge in a law court. **3** a person chosen to settle a dispute or decide who wins. **4** settle a dispute; decide who wins a race, contest, etc. **5** a person who can decide how good a thing is: *a good judge of cattle, a poor judge of poetry*. **6** form an opinion or estimate of: *to judge the merits of a book*. **7** think; suppose; conclude: *I judged that you had forgotten to come.* **8** criticize; condemn: *You had little cause to judge her so harshly.* **9** in ancient Israel, a ruler before the time of the kings. 1, 3, 5, 9 *n.*, 2, 4, 6–8 *v.*, **judged, judg·ing.** —**judg′er**, *n.*

**judge·ment** (juj′mənt) See JUDGMENT. *n.*

**judge·ship** (juj′ship) the position, duties, or term of office of a judge. *n.*

**judg·ment** or **judge·ment** (juj′mənt) **1** the act of judging. **2** a decision, decree, or sentence given by a judge or court. **3** a debt arising from a judge's decision. **4** an opinion or estimate: *It was a bad plan in her judgment.* **5** the ability to form sound opinions; good sense: *My grandmother was a woman of judgment.* **6** a decision made by anyone who judges. **7** criticism; condemnation: *Do not pass judgment on your neighbours.* **8** a misfortune considered as a punishment from God: *The neighbours considered his broken leg a judgment on him for staying away from church. n.*

**ju·di·ca·to·ry** (jü′də kə tô′rē) **1** of the administration of justice. **2** the administration of justice. **3** a court of justice. 1 *adj.*, 2, 3 *n.*, *pl.* **ju·di·ca·to·ries.**

**ju·di·cial** (jü dish′əl) **1** of or having to do with courts, judges, or the administration of justice. **2** ordered, permitted, or enforced by a judge or a court: *Mrs. Barnes got a judicial separation from her husband.* **3** of or suitable for a judge; impartial; fair: *A judicial mind considers both sides of a dispute before making a decision. adj.* —**ju·di′cial·ly,** *adv.*

**ju·di·ci·ar·y** (jü dish′ē er′ē *or* jü dish′ə rē) **1** the branch of government that administers justice; system of courts of justice of a country. **2** judges as a group. **3** of or having to do with courts, judges, or the administration of justice. 1, 2 *n.*, *pl.* **ju·di·ci·ar·ies;** 3 *adj.*

**ju·di·cious** (jü dish′əs) having, using, or showing good judgment; wise; sensible: *A judicious historian considers facts carefully and critically. adj.* —**ju·di′cious·ly,** *adv.*

**ju·do** (jü′dō) JUJITSU. *n.*

**jug** (jug) **1** a container for liquids: *A jug usually has a handle and either a spout or a narrow neck.* **2** put in a jug. **3** stew in an earthenware container: *jugged hare.* 1 *n.*, 2, 3 *v.*, **jugged, jug·ging.**

**jug·ger·naut** (jug′ər not′) something to which a person blindly devotes himself or herself, or is cruelly sacrificed. *n.*

**jug·gle** (jug′əl) **1** do tricks that require skill of hand or eye. **2** keep several objects in motion in the air at the same time by rapidly tossing them up in turn and catching them as they fall: *She can juggle three balls, keeping them all in the air at one time.* **3** change so as to deceive or cheat: *The bookkeeper juggled the company's accounts to hide her thefts.* **4** the act of juggling. 1, 2, 3 *v.*, **jug·gled, jug·gling;** 4 *n.*

**jug·gler** (jug′lər) **1** a person who can do juggling tricks. **2** a person who uses tricks, deception, or fraud. *n.*

**jug·gler·y** (jug′lə rē) **1** the skill or tricks of a juggler; sleight of hand. **2** trickery; deception; fraud. *n.*, *pl.* **jug·gler·ies.**

**jug·u·lar** (jug′yə lər) **1** of the neck or throat. **2** of the JUGULAR VEIN. **3** the JUGULAR VEIN. 1, 2 *adj.*, 3 *n.*

**jugular vein** one of the two large veins in the neck that return blood from the head to the heart.

**juice** (jüs) **1** the liquid in fruits, vegetables, and meats: *the juice of a lemon, meat juice.* **2** a fluid in the body: *The gastric juices of the stomach help to digest food. n.* —**juice′less,** *adj.*

**juic·er** (jü′sər) an apparatus for squeezing juice out of fruits or vegetables. *n.*

**juic·i·ness** (jü′sē nis) being juicy. *n.*

**juic·y** (jü′sē) **1** full of juice; having much juice. **2** full of interest; lively. *adj.*, **juic·i·er, juic·i·est.** —**juic′i·ly,** *adv.*

**ju·jit·su** (jü jit′sü) a Japanese method of wrestling or fighting without weapons that uses the strength and weight of an opponent to his or her disadvantage. *n.* Also, **jiujitsu, jujutsu, judo, jujutsu.**
☛ *Etym.* From Japanese *jūjutsu* (pronounced 'jujitsu'), made up of *jū* 'soft, yielding' + *jutsu* 'art'.

**ju·jube** (jü′jüb) **1** a lozenge or small tablet of gummy candy. **2** an edible datelike fruit of a shrub or tree, used to flavour this candy. *n.*

**ju·jut·su** (jü jit′sü) See JUJITSU. *n.*

**juke box** (jük) *Informal.* an automatic phonograph that plays a record when a coin is deposited in the slot.

**Jul.** July.

**ju·lep** (jü′ləp) a drink made of whisky or brandy, sugar, crushed ice, and fresh mint. *n.*

**Julian calendar** a calendar in which the average length of a year was 365¼ days: *The Julian Calendar was introduced by Julius Caesar in 46 B.C.*

**ju·li·enne** (jü′lē en′) **1** cut in thin strips or small pieces: *Julienne potatoes are cut in thin strips and fried.* **2** a clear soup containing vegetables cut into thin strips or small pieces. 1 *adj.*, 2 *n.*

**Ju·ly** (jü lī′) the seventh month of the year: *July has 31 days. n.*, *pl.* **Ju·lies.**
☛ *Etym.* Through OF from L *Julius,* named after *Julius Caesar* because he was born at this time of year.

**jum·ble** (jum′bəl) **1** mix; confuse: *She jumbled up everything in the drawer when she was hunting for her gloves.*

2 a confused mixture: *After I had studied history for two hours, my mind was a jumble of events.* 1 *v.*, **jum·bled, jum·bling;** 2 *n.*

**jum·bo** (jum′bō) *Informal.* 1 a big, clumsy person, animal, or thing; something unusually large of its kind. 2 very big: *a jumbo ice-cream cone.* 1 *n., pl.* **jum·bos;** 2 *adj.*
☛ *Etym.* From *Jumbo*, the name of a famous elephant in a 19th-century circus.

**jump** (jump) 1 spring from the ground; leap; bound: *to jump up and down.* 2 a spring from the ground; leap; bound. 3 leap over: *to jump a stream.* 4 cause to jump: *to jump a horse over a fence.* 5 the thing to be jumped over. 6 the distance jumped. 7 a contest in jumping: *Who won the broad jump?* 8 give a sudden start or jerk: *You made me jump.* 9 a sudden nervous start or jerk. 10 rise suddenly: *Prices jumped.* 11 a sudden rise: *a jump in the cost of living.* 12 in the game of checkers, a move made to capture an opponent's piece. 13 in checkers, pass over and capture an opponent's piece. 14 evade by running away: *to jump bail.* 15 get aboard a train by jumping. 1, 3, 4, 8, 10, 13–15 *v.*, 2, 5–7, 9, 11, 12 *n.*
**jump a claim,** seize a piece of land claimed by another.
**jump at,** accept eagerly and quickly: *jump at a chance; jump at an offer.*
**jump the track,** of a train, leave the rails suddenly.
**jump to conclusions,** make an unfair assumption.
**jump to it!** *Informal.* be quick!

**jump·er¹** (jum′pər) 1 a person or thing that jumps. 2 a simply constructed sleigh on low wooden runners. *n.*

**jump·er²** (jum′pər) 1 a sleeveless dress, usually worn over a blouse. 2 a loose jacket: *Jumpers are worn by workmen to protect their clothes and by sailors as part of their uniform.* 3 a loose blouse reaching to the hips. 4 **jumpers,** ROMPERS. *n.*

**jumping jack** a toy man or animal that can be made to jump by pulling a string.

**jump·mas·ter** (jump′mas′tər) the officer who controls the dropping of parachute troops and their equipment from an aircraft. *n.*

**jump·y** (jum′pē) 1 moving by jumps; making sudden, sharp jerks. 2 easily excited or frightened; nervous. *adj.*, **jump·i·er, jump·i·est.** —**jump′i·ly,** *adv.* —**jump′i·ness,** *n.*

**Jun.** 1 June. 2 Junior.

**jun·co** (jung′kō) any of several small North American finches often seen in flocks during the winter, including the snowbird. *n., pl.* **jun·cos.**

**junc·tion** (jungk′shən) 1 a joining or being joined: *the junction of two rivers.* 2 a place where things join or meet: *A railway junction is a place where railway lines meet or cross.* *n.*

**junc·ture** (jungk′chər) 1 a point of time. 2 the state of affairs. 3 crisis. 4 joint. 5 a joining or being joined. *n.*
**at this juncture,** when affairs are or were in this state: *At this juncture the doctor decided to operate.*

**June** (jün) the sixth month of the year: *June has 30 days.* *n.*
☛ *Etym.* Through OF from L *Junius, Junonius* '(the month) of the goddess Juno'.

**June beetle** JUNE BUG.

**June bug** a large, brown beetle that appears in June.

**jun·gle** (jung′gəl) 1 wild land thickly overgrown with bushes, vines, trees, etc. 2 a tangled mass. 3 a place characterized by vicious competition or struggle for survival: *She says the city is a jungle.* *n.*

**jungle fowl** any of several wild birds of India and Asia that are much like domestic fowl.

**jun·ior** (jü′nyər) 1 the younger, used of a son having the same name as his father: *John Parker, Junior, is the son of John Parker, Senior.* 2 a younger person: *Eva is her sister's junior by two years.* 3 of lower position, rank, or standing; of more recent appointment: *a junior officer, a junior partner.* 4 a person of lower rank or shorter service. 5 of or for students in grades 4–6: *junior school.* 6 of later date. 7 of or for young people: *a junior tennis match, a junior bed.* 1, 3, 5–7 *adj.*, 2, 4 *n.*

**junior college** a college giving only the first year or the first two years of a regular university degree program.

**junior high school** a school consisting of grades 7, 8, and 9; any school intermediate between elementary school and high school.

**ju·ni·per** (jü′nə pər) 1 any of about 40 closely related species of evergreen shrub or tree of the northern hemisphere, belonging to the cypress family, having tiny, scale-like, overlapping leaves, small, blue, berry-like cones and soft, fragrant wood that is used for lining closets and chests, etc.: *The four species of juniper native to Canada are the Rocky Mountain juniper, red juniper, dwarf or common juniper, and creeping juniper.* 2 the wood of the juniper. *n.*

**junk¹** (jungk) 1 old metal, paper, rags, etc. 2 *Informal.* rubbish; trash. 3 *Informal.* throw away or discard as junk: *We junked the old garden chairs last fall.* 4 a hard, salted meat eaten by sailors. 5 old rope used for making mats, oakum, etc. 1, 2, 4, 5 *n.*, 3 *v.*

A junk

**junk²** (jungk) a Chinese sailing ship. *n.*

**junk·er** (jung′kər) a worn-out automobile, usually one sold for scrap. *n.*

**Jun·ker** or **jun·ker** (yùng′kər) a member of the aristocratic, formerly privileged class in Prussia. *n.*

**jun·ket** (jung′kit) 1 curdled milk, sweetened and flavoured. 2 feast; picnic. 3 a pleasure trip. 4 go on a pleasure trip. 5 *Informal.* an unnecessary trip taken by an official at the expense of the government or the firm he or she works for. 1–3, 5 *n.*, 2, 4 *v.* —**jun′ket·er,** *n.*

**junk food** food, especially prepackaged snack food, characterized by a high carbohydrate content and little nutritive value.

**junk·man** (jungk′man′) a man who buys and sells old metal, paper, rags etc. *n., pl.* **junk·men** (-men′).

**jun·ta** (jun′tə *or* hùn′tə) **1** a group of persons forming a government, especially as the result of a revolution: *The country was ruled by a military junta.* **2** JUNTO. **3** especially in Spain or Latin-American countries, a legislative or administrative council. *n.*

**jun·to** (jun′tō *or* hùn′tō) a political faction; a group of plotters or partisans. *n., pl.* **jun·tos.**

**Ju·pi·ter** (jü′pə tər) the largest planet. *n.*
☞ *Etym.* Named after *Jupiter*, who, in Roman mythology, was the chief god, and ruler of the gods and people.

**ju·ral** (jü′rəl) **1** of law; legal. **2** having to do with rights and obligations. *adj.*

**ju·rid·i·cal** (jü rid′ə kəl) **1** having to do with the administration of justice. **2** of law; legal. *adj.* —**ju·rid′i·cal·ly,** *adv.*

**ju·ris·dic·tion** (jü′ris dik′shən) **1** the right or power of administering law or justice. **2** authority; power; control. **3** the extent of authority: *The judge ruled that the case was not within her jurisdiction.* **4** the territory over which authority extends. *n.*

**ju·ris·pru·dence** (jü′ris prü′dəns) **1** the science or philosophy of law. **2** a system of laws. **3** a branch of laws: *Medical jurisprudence deals with the application of medical knowledge to certain questions of law.* *n.*

**ju·rist** (jü′rist) **1** an expert in law. **2** a learned writer on law. *n.*

**ju·ris·tic** (jù ris′tik) of or having to do with jurists or jurisprudence; relating to law. *adj.*

**ju·ror** (jü′rər) a member of a jury. *n.*

**ju·ry**[1] (jü′rē) **1** a group of persons selected to hear evidence in a law court and sworn to give a decision in accordance with the evidence presented to it. **2** a group of persons chosen to give a judgment or to decide who is the winner in a contest: *The jury gave Helen's poem the first prize.* *n., pl.* **ju·ries.**

**ju·ry**[2] (jü′rē) for temporary use on a ship; makeshift. *adj.*

**ju·ry·man** (jü′rē mən) a member of a jury; juror. *n., pl.* **ju·ry·men** (-mən).

**just**[1] (just) **1** right; fair: *a just price.* **2** righteous: *a just life.* **3** deserved; merited: *a just reward.* **4** having good grounds; well-founded: *just anger.* **5** lawful: *a just claim.* **6** in accordance with standards or requirements; proper: *just proportions.* **7** true; correct: *a just description.* **8** exact: *just weights.* **9** exactly: *just a metre.* **10** very close; immediately: *There was a picture just above the fireplace.* **11** a very short while ago: *She has just gone.* **12** barely: *I just managed to catch the train.* **13** only; merely: *He is just an ordinary man.* **14** *Informal.* quite; truly; positively: *The weather is just glorious.* 1–8 *adj.,* 9–14 *adv.* —**just′ness,** *n.*
**just now, a** exactly at this moment; at present. **b** only a very short time ago: *I saw him just now.*

**just**[2] (just) JOUST. *v., n.*

**jus·tice** (jus′tis) **1** just conduct; fair dealing: *to have a sense of justice.* **2** being just; fairness; rightness; correctness: *to uphold the justice of our cause.* **3** rightfulness; lawfulness; well-founded reason: *She complained with justice of the bad treatment she had received.* **4** just treatment; deserved reward or punishment. **5** the exercise of power and authority to maintain what is just and right. **6** the administration of law; trial and judgment by process of law: *a court of justice.* **7** a judge. **8** a justice of the peace. *n.*
**bring a person to justice,** do what is necessary in order that a person shall be legally punished for his or her crime or crimes.
**do justice to, a** treat fairly. **b** see the good points of. **c** show proper appreciation for: *The crowd's applause did not do justice to his performance.*
**do oneself justice,** do as well as one really can do: *She did not do herself justice on the test.*

**justice of the peace** a local magistrate who tries minor cases, administers oaths, etc.

**jus·tice·ship** (jus′tis ship′) the position, duties, or term of office of a justice. *n.*

**jus·ti·fi·a·bil·i·ty** (jus′tə fī′ə bil′ə tē) being JUSTIFIABLE. *n.*

**jus·ti·fi·a·ble** (jus′tə fī′ə bəl) capable of being justified; that can be shown to be just and right; defensible: *Their bad behaviour was not justifiable even though they were provoked.* *adj.* —**jus′ti·fi′a·bly,** *adv.*

**jus·ti·fi·ca·tion** (jus′tə fə kā′shən) **1** justifying. **2** being justified. **3** the fact or circumstance that justifies; good reason: *What is your justification for being late?* **4** in printing and keyboarding, spacing adjusted to provide an even right-hand margin. *n.*

**jus·ti·fy** (jus′tə fī′) **1** show to be just or right; give a good reason for: *The fine quality of the cloth justifies its high price.* **2** clear of blame or guilt: *One is justified in shooting a man in self-defence.* **3** in printing or keyboarding, adjust spacing so that the lines are of even length. *v.,* **jus·ti·fied, jus·ti·fy·ing.** —**jus′ti·fi′er,** *n.*

**just·ly** (just′lē) **1** in a just manner: *The accused woman was tried justly.* **2** rightly: *You were justly angered by that insult.* *adv.*

**jut** (jut) **1** stick out; project: *The pier juts out from the shore into the water.* **2** a part that sticks out; projection. 1 *v.,* **jut·ted, jut·ting;** 2 *n.*

**jute** (jüt) a strong fibre used for making coarse sacks, burlap, rope, etc.: *Jute is obtained from two tropical plants.* *n.*

**ju·ve·nes·cence** (jü′və nes′əns) a renewal of youth; youthfulness. *n.*

**ju·ve·nes·cent** (jü′və nes′ənt) growing young again; youthful. *adj.*

**ju·ve·nile** (jü′və nīl′ *or* jü′və nəl) **1** young; youthful; immature: *juvenile behaviour.* **2** a young person. **3** of or for young people: *juvenile delinquency, juvenile books.* **4** a book for young people. **5** an actor who plays youthful parts. 1, 3 *adj.,* 2, 4, 5 *n.*

**juvenile court** a law court where cases involving boys and girls are heard.

**ju·ve·nil·i·ty** (jü′və nil′ə tē) a JUVENILE quality, condition, or manner. *n.*

**jux·ta·pose** (juk′stə pōz′) put close together; place side by side. *v.,* **jux·ta·posed, jux·ta·pos·ing.**

**jux·ta·po·si·tion** (juk′stə pə zish′ən) **1** putting close together; placing side by side. **2** a position close together or side by side. *n.*

# K k *K k*

hat, āge, fär; let, ēqual, tėrm; it, īce
hot, ōpen, ôrder; oil, out; cup, put, rüle
ə above, taken, pencəl, lemən, circəs
ch, child; ng, long; sh, ship
th, thin; ᴛʜ, then; zh, measure

**k or K** (kā) **1** the eleventh letter of the English alphabet. **2** any speech sound represented by this letter. **3** any person or thing identified as k, especially the eleventh in a series. *n., pl.* **k's** or **K's**.

**k** kilo- (an SI prefix).

**k.** karat.

**K¹** **1** potassium. **2** kelvin.

**K²** **1** one thousand. **2** a unit of computer memory. One K of computer memory is 1024 BYTES: *This home computer has a storage capacity of 64K*.

**Ka·a·ba** (kä′bə) the most sacred shrine of Islam, toward which Moslems face when praying. It is a cubelike granite building at the centre of the open-air mosque in Mecca. *n.* Also, **Caaba**.

**Kaf·fir** (kaf′ər) a member of any of several Bantu-speaking peoples of southern Africa. *n.*

**kaf·fir corn** (kaf′ər) a sorghum grown for grain and forage in dry regions: *Kaffir corn has a stout, short-jointed, leafy stalk.*

**kai·ser¹** (kī′zər) **1** the title of the rulers of Germany from 1871 to 1918. **2** the title of the rulers of Austria from 1804 to 1918. **3** the title of the rulers of the Holy Roman Empire from A.D. 962 to 1806. **4** emperor. *n.*

**kai·ser²** (kī′zər) a large, round, crusty bun used especially for sliced meat sandwiches. *n.* Also, **kaiser bun**.

**kale** (kāl) any of various kinds of cabbage that have loose leaves instead of a compact head. *n.*

**ka·lei·do·scope** (kə lī′də skōp′) **1** a tube containing bits of coloured glass and two or more mirrors: *As a kaleidoscope is turned, it reflects continually changing patterns.* **2** anything that changes continually; a continually changing pattern: *the kaleidoscope of current events. A circus is a kaleidoscope of activity.* *n.*
☛ *Etym.* Made up of Gk. *kalos* 'beautiful' + *eidos* 'shape', together with English -scope (also from Gk.) 'an instrument for viewing or observing'. 19c.

**ka·lei·do·scop·ic** (kə lī′də skop′ik) of or like a KALEIDOSCOPE; continually changing. *adj.*

**kal·ends** (kal′əndz) See CALENDS. *n.pl.*

**Kal·muck** or **Kal·muk** (kal′muk) **1** a member of any of the Mongol peoples. **2** their language. *n.*

**kal·so·mine** (kal′sə mīn′) See CALCIMINE. *n.*

**ka·mi** (kä′mē) in Shintoism, any divine spirit. *n., pl.* **ka·mi**.

**ka·mi·ka·ze** (kä′mi kä′zē) **1** in World War II, a member of a Japanese air corps that carried out suicide missions in which an aircraft loaded with explosives was deliberately crashed on a target by the pilot. **2** an aircraft used in such a mission. *n.*

**Kam·loops trout** (kam′lüps) *Cdn.* a subspecies of the steelhead trout, the most highly valued game and food fish of British Columbia's interior lakes and rivers: *The Kamloops trout varies greatly in colouring according to its environment, and because of this has acquired many different names, such as silver trout and rainbow trout.*

**Ka·nak·a** (kə nak′ə) **1** a native of Hawaii. **2** a South Sea islander. *n.*

**kan·ga·roo** (kang′gə rü′) a marsupial of Australia and New Guinea having small forelegs and very strong hind legs, which give it great leaping power: *The female kangaroo has a pouch in front in which she carries her young.* *n., pl.* **kan·ga·roos** or (*esp. collectively*) **kan·ga·roo**. —**kan′ga·roo′-like′**, *adj.*

**kangaroo court** an unauthorized or irregular court in which the law is deliberately disregarded or misinterpreted. A mock court held by convicts in prison is called a kangaroo court.

**kangaroo rat** any of a genus of small, mouselike, North American desert rodent having very long, strong hind legs adapted for leaping, a very long, tufted tail, and external fur-lined cheek pouches. Only one species is found in Canada, in the sand hills of southern Saskatchewan and Alberta.

**ka·o·lin** or **ka·o·line** (kā′ə lin) a fine white clay, used in making porcelain. *n.*

**ka·pok** (kā′pok) the silky fibres around the seeds of a tropical tree, used for stuffing pillows, etc. *n.*

**ka·put** (kä put′ *or* kə put′) *Informal.* ruined, broken, useless, etc. (*never used before a noun*) *adj.*

**kar·a·kul** (kar′ə kəl *or* ker′ə kəl) **1** a variety of Russian or Asiatic sheep. **2** fur with flat, loose curls; CARACUL. *n.*

**kar·at** (kar′ət *or* ker′ət) a unit used to specify the proportion of gold in an alloy; one of 24 equal parts: *An 18-karat gold ring is 18 parts pure gold and 6 parts alloy.* Symbol: k. *n.*
☛ *Hom.* CARAT, CARET, CARROT.

**ka·ra·te** (kə rä′tē) a Japanese system of self-defence without weapons, using studied hand and foot strokes capable of crippling or killing. *n.*

**kar·ma** (kär′mə) **1** in Buddhism and Hinduism, the totality of a person's thoughts, actions, etc. that are supposed to affect or determine his or her fate in his or her next incarnation. **2** destiny; fate. *n.*

**kart** (kärt) **1** GO-KART. **2** take part in a go-kart race. 1 *n.*, 2 *v.*

**kar·y·o·type** (kar′ē ō tīp′ *or* ker′ē ō tīp′) the appearance of the set of somatic chromosomes, giving number, size, and shape. *n.*

**ka·ty·did** (kā′tē did′) any of various large, green, long-horned grasshoppers. The male makes a shrill noise by rubbing its front wings together. *n.*
☛ *Etym.* The word **katydid** imitates the sound made by the male of this insect. 18c.

A kayak

**kay·ak** (kī′ak) 1 a light, narrow boat with pointed ends, made of skins, etc. stretched over a frame of wood or bone, leaving only a small opening in the middle for the user: *A kayak is propelled by a double-bladed paddle. Kayaks were traditionally used by the Inuit for hunting.* 2 any similar craft. *n.*

**ka·zoo** (kə zü′) a toy musical instrument made of a tube sealed off at one end with a membrane or paper that produces a buzzing sound when one hums into the tube. *n.*

**kc.** kilocycle; kilocycles.

**keel** (kēl) 1 the main timber or steel piece that extends the whole length of the bottom of a ship or boat. 2 a part, as on an aircraft, that is like a ship's keel. 3 turn upside down; upset. 1, 2 *n.*, 3 *v.*
**on an even keel,** a horizontal. b steady; properly balanced: *His business affairs are on an even keel again.*
**keel over,** a turn over or upside down; upset: *The sailboat keeled over in the storm.* b fall over suddenly. c *Informal.* faint.

**keen**[1] (kēn) 1 sharp enough to cut well: *a keen blade.* 2 sharp; piercing; cutting: *a keen wind, keen hunger, a keen wit, keen pain.* 3 strong; vivid: *keen competition.* 4 able to do its work quickly and accurately: *a keen mind, a keen sense of smell.* 5 full of enthusiasm; eager: *a keen player, keen about sailing. adj.* —**keen′ly,** *adv.*

**keen**[2] (kēn) *Irish.* 1 a wailing lament for the dead. 2 wail; lament. 1 *n.*, 2 *v.* —**keen′er,** *n.*

**keen·ness** (kēn′nis) 1 a keen or cutting quality; sharpness: *the keenness of an axe, the keenness of the cold wind, the keenness of a man's appetite.* 2 an interest in; enthusiasm for: *Her keenness for sports was easy to see. n.*

**keep** (kēp) 1 have for a long time or forever: *You may keep this book.* 2 have and not let go; hold; detain: *They were kept in prison.* 3 not reveal or divulge: *Will you promise to keep my secret?* 4 have and take care of: *My uncle keeps chickens. She was kept in hospital for ten days.* 5 take care of and protect: *The bank keeps money for people.* 6 have; hold: *Keep this in mind.* 7 hold back; prevent: *What is keeping her from coming?* 8 restrain oneself; refrain: *The little boy couldn't keep from crying when he fell down.* 9 maintain in good condition; maintain: *to keep a garden. Mother keeps house.* 10 be preserved; stay in good condition: *Butter will keep in a refrigerator.* 11 stay the same; continue to be: *keep awake. Keep going along this road for two kilometres.* 12 cause to continue in some stated place, condition, etc.; cause to stay the same: *to keep a light burning, to keep a student after school.* 13 make regular entries or records in: *keep books, keep a diary.* 14 do the right thing with; observe; celebrate: *to keep Thanksgiving as a holiday.* 15 be faithful to: *to keep a promise.* 16 provide for; support: *He is not able to keep himself, much less a family.* 17 food and a place to sleep: *She earns her keep.* 18 the strongest part of a castle or fort. See CASTLE for picture. 19 have habitually for sale: *That store keeps canned goods.* 1–16, 19 *v.,* **kept, keep·ing;** 17, 18 *n.*
**for keeps,** a for the winner to keep his or her winnings. b *Informal.* forever.
**keep in with,** *Informal.* keep acquaintance or friendship with.
**keep on,** continue; go on: *The girls kept on swimming in spite of the rain.*
**keep time,** go correctly; move at the right rate.
**keep up,** a continue; prevent from ending: *We kept up a small fire.* b maintain in good condition. c not fall behind; remain close or alongside.
**keep up with,** a not fall behind; go or move as fast as. b live or do as well as: *She tried hard to keep up with her wealthy neighbours.* c stay up to date with: *He keeps up with the news. Try to keep up with your reading.*

**keep·er** (kē′pər) 1 a person or thing that keeps. 2 a guard; watchman. 3 a guardian; protector: *The custodian of animals in a zoo is called a keeper.* 4 *Informal.* a fish large enough to be legally caught and kept. *n.*

**keep·ing** (kē′ping) 1 care; charge; maintenance: *The keeping of the orphaned children was paid for by their uncle.* 2 celebration; observance: *The keeping of Thanksgiving Day is an old North American custom.* 3 the fact or condition of being kept for future use; preservation. 4 ppr. of KEEP. 1–3 *n.*, 4 *v.*
**in keeping,** in agreement or harmony: *Their ideas are not in keeping.*

**keep·sake** (kēp′sāk′) something kept in memory of the giver: *My friend gave me her picture as a keepsake before going away. n.*

**keg** (keg) a small barrel or cask. *n.*

**kelp** (kelp) 1 a large, tough, brown seaweed. 2 ashes of seaweed: *Kelp contains iodine. n.*

**kel·pie** or **kel·py** (kel′pē) a water spirit, usually in the form of a horse, supposed to drown people or warn them of drowning. *n., pl.* **kel·pies.**

**Kelt** (kelt) CELT. *n.*

**Kelt·ic** (kel′tik) CELTIC. *adj., n.*

**kel·vin** (kel′vin) 1 an SI unit of temperature on the Kelvin scale: *One kelvin is equal to one degree Celsius. The kelvin is one of the seven base units in the SI.* Symbol: K 2 **Kelvin,** of, based on, or according to a scale of thermodynamic temperature used in science, on which 0 represents absolute zero, theoretically the coldest possible state: *Zero on the Kelvin scale is equal to −273.16 degrees Celsius. n.*
☞ *Etym.* Named after William Thomson, Lord *Kelvin* (1824–1907), the British scientist who developed this scale.

**ken** (ken) 1 the range of sight. 2 the range of knowledge: *What happens on Mars is beyond our ken. n.*

**ken·nel** (ken′əl) 1 a house for a dog or dogs: *We built a kennel for our dog.* 2 put or keep in a kennel. 3 take shelter or lodge in a kennel. 4 a pack of dogs. 5 Often, **kennels,** *pl.* a a place where dogs are bred: *Our puppy came from a well-known kennel near Ottawa.* b a place where dogs may be lodged and cared for. 1, 4, 5 *n.*, 2, 3 *v.,* **ken·nelled** or **ken·neled, ken·nel·ling** or **ken·nel·ing.**

**ke·pi** (kep′ē; *French,* kā pē′) a cap with a round, flat top, worn by French soldiers. See CAP for picture. *n., pl.* **kep·is.**

**kept** (kept) pt. and pp. of KEEP: *I gave him the book and he kept it. The juice was kept in bottles. v.*

**ker·a·tin** (ker′ə tin)   a complex protein, the chief constituent of horn, nails, hair, feather, etc.   *n.*

**ker·chief** (kėr′chif)   **1** a piece of cloth worn over the head or around the neck.   **2** HANDKERCHIEF.   *n.*

**kerf** (kėrf)   **1** a cut made by an axe, saw, etc.   **2** a piece cut off.   *n.*

**ker·nel** (kėr′nəl)   **1** the softer part inside the hard shell of a nut or inside the stone of a fruit: *The kernel of a peachstone resembles an almond.*   **2** a grain or seed like wheat or corn.   **3** the central or most important part: *the kernel of an argument.*   *n.*
☛ *Hom.* COLONEL.

**ker·o·sene** (ker′ə sēn′) *Cdn.*   a thin oil, a mixture of hydrocarbons, usually produced by distilling petroleum; coal oil: *Kerosene is used as a fuel in lamps, stoves, some types of engines, etc.*   *n.*

**ker·sey** (kėr′zē)   **1** a coarse, ribbed, woollen cloth with a cotton warp.   **2 kerseys,** *pl.*   trousers made of kersey.   *n., pl.* **ker·seys.**

**kes·trel** (kes′trəl)   a small European falcon.   *n.*

**ket·a** (kā′tə *or* kē′tə) *Cdn.*   a variety of Pacific salmon; chum.   *n., pl.* **ket·a.**

**ketch** (kech)   **1** a fore-and-aft-rigged sailing ship with a large mainmast toward the bow and a smaller mast toward the stern.   **2** formerly, a sturdy sailing vessel with two masts.   *n.*

**ketch·up** (kech′əp)   a sauce for use with meat, fish, etc.: *Tomato ketchup is made of tomatoes, onions, salt, sugar, and spices.*   *n.* Also, **catchup, catsup.**

**ket·tle** (ket′əl)   **1** a metal container for boiling liquids, cooking fruit, etc.   **2** TEA-KETTLE.   **3** in geology, a depression in glacial drift remaining after the melting of an isolated mass of buried ice.   *n.*
**kettle of fish,** *Informal.*   an awkward state of affairs; mess; muddle: *We were in a fine kettle of fish when I lost the keys to the car.*

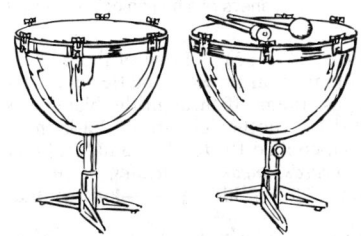
Kettledrums

**ket·tle·drum** (ket′əl drum′)   a drum consisting of a large hollow brass or copper hemisphere and a parchment top.   *n.*

**kew·pie doll**   a plastic or celluloid doll resembling a fat cherub with tiny wings and a curled topknot.

**key**[1] (kē)   **1** an instrument that locks and unlocks; something that turns the bolt in a lock: *I lost the key to the padlock on my bicycle.*   **2** anything like this in shape or use: *a key to open a tin.*   **3** lock.   **4** something that explains or answers: *the key to a puzzle. The key to an arithmetic book gives the answers to all the problems.*   **5** a place that commands or gives control of a sea, a district, etc. because of its position: *Gibraltar is the key to the Mediterranean.*   **6** controlling; very important: *the key industries of a nation.*   **7** an important or essential person, thing, etc.   **8** a pin, bolt, wedge, or other piece put in a hole or space to hold parts together.   **9** fasten or adjust with a key.   **10** a device to turn a bolt or nut: *Watches used to be wound with keys.*   **11** one of a set of parts pressed down by the fingers in playing a piano, in keyboarding, and in operating other instruments.   **12** in music, a scale or system of related tones based on a particular tone: *a song written in the key of B flat.*   **13** a tone of voice; style of thought or expression: *The poet wrote in a melancholy key.*   **14** regulate the pitch of: *to key a piano in preparation for a concert.*   **15** adjust a speech, etc. as if to a particular key: *a letter keyed to a tone of defiance.*   **16** a systematic explanation of abbreviations or symbols used in a dictionary, map, etc.: *There is a pronunciation key at the beginning of the dictionary.*   1, 2, 4, 5, 7, 8, 10–13, 16 *n., pl.* **keys;**   3, 9, 14, 15 *v.,* **keyed, key·ing;**   6 *adj.* —**key′less,** *adj.*
**key in,**   enter data, etc. in a word processor, computer, etc. by means of a keyboard: *The computer operator keyed in the numbers.*
**key up,**   raise the courage or nerve of: *The coach keyed up the team for the big game.*
☛ *Hom.* CAY (kē), QUAY.
☛ *Etym.* From OE *cæg.* Ultimate origin unknown.

**key**[2] (kē)   a low island; reef: *There are keys south of Florida.*   *n., pl.* **keys.**
☛ *Hom.* CAY (kē), QUAY.
☛ *Etym.* From late ME *key, keye,* older forms of **quay.** See also note at QUAY.

**key block**   a large conical block of snow, dropped into place at the centre of an igloo dome, serving to lock the structure firmly together.   See IGLOO for picture.

**key·board** (kē′bôrd′)   **1** the set of keys in a piano, typewriter, calculator, etc.   **2** operate the keyboard of a typewriter, word processor, or computer: *She was able to keyboard in the necessary information.*   1 *n.,* 2 *v.*

**key·board·ing** (kē′bôr′ding)   **1** skill in typing, word processing, and computer programming.   **2** ppr. of KEYBOARD.   1 *n.,* 2 *v.*

**keyed** (kēd)   **1** having keys: *a keyed flute or trombone.*   **2** in music, set or pitched in a particular key.   **3** fastened or strengthened with a key.   **4** constructed with a keystone.   **5** pt. and pp. of KEY.   1–4 *adj.,* 5 *v.*
**keyed up,**   excited or nervous.

**key·hole** (kē′hōl′)   an opening in a lock through which a key is inserted to turn the lock.   *n.*

**key·note** (kē′nōt′)   **1** in music, the note on which a scale or system of tones is based.   **2** the main idea or guiding principle: *World peace was the keynote of his speech.*   **3** give the KEYNOTE SPEECH of.   1, 2 *n.,* 3 *v.,* **key·not·ed, key·not·ing.**

**keynote speech**   a speech that presents the principal issues in which those present are interested.

**key·pad** (kē′pad′)   **1** that part of a computer keyboard that contains numbers and special keys.   **2** the keyboard of a KEY PUNCH.   *n.*

**key seat** part of a machine able to receive a key.

**key·seat** (kē′sēt′) make a machine have a KEY SEAT. *v.*

**key signature** the sharps or flats placed after the clef at the beginning of a staff of music to indicate the key.

**key·stone** (kē′stōn′) **1** the middle stone at the top of an arch, holding the other stones or pieces in place. See ARCH for picture. **2** the part on which other associated parts depend; essential principle: *Freedom is the keystone of our policy. n.*

**kg** kilogram; kilograms.

**khak·i** (kär′kē, kä′kē, *or* kak′ē) **1** dull yellowish-brown. **2** a stout twilled cloth of this colour, often used for soldiers' uniforms. **3** a uniform or uniforms made of this cloth: *Khakis will be worn for drill.* **1** *adj.*, **1–3** *n., pl.* **khak·is.**
☛ *Etym.* From Urdu *khākī* 'dusty', which came from Persian *khāk* 'dust'.

**kha·lif** (kā′lif *or* kal′if) See CALIPH. *n.*

**Khal·sa** (käl′sə) in Sikhism, the world-wide community of baptized members. *n.*

**khan**[1] (kän) **1** the title of a ruler among Tartar or Mongol tribes, or of the emperor of China during the Middle Ages. **2** a title of dignity in Iran, Afghanistan, India, etc. *n.*

**khan**[2] (kän) in Turkey and nearby countries, an inn without furnishings. *n.*

**khan·ate** (kä′nāt) **1** the territory ruled by a khan. **2** the position or authority of a khan. *n.*

**kha·tib** (kə tēb′) in Islam, the preacher—usually a mullah—who delivers the khutba, or sermon, in a mosque. *n.*

**kib·butz** (ki büts′) *Hebrew.* a communal settlement or farm co-operative in Israel. *n., pl.* **kib·butz·im** (ki büt sēm′).

**kibe** (kīb) a chapped or ulcerated sore, inflammation, or swelling on the heel caused by exposure to cold. *n.*

**kib·itz** (kib′its) *Informal.* look on as an outsider and offer unwanted advice. *v.*

**kib·itz·er** (kib′it sər) *Informal.* a person who gives unwanted advice; meddler. *n.*

**kick** (kik) **1** strike out with the foot: *That horse kicks when anyone comes near it.* **2** strike with the foot: *The horse kicked the girl.* **3** drive, force, or move by kicking: *to kick a ball.* **4** the act of kicking. **5** win by a kick: *to kick a goal in football.* **6** spring back when fired: *This shotgun kicks.* **7** the recoil of a gun when it is fired. **8** *Informal.* complain; object; grumble. **9** *Informal.* a complaint or objection. **10** *Informal.* excitement; a thrill: *She gets a kick out of gambling.* **11** *Informal.* the power of a drink, drug, etc. to intoxicate. **1–3, 5, 6, 8** *v.,* **4, 7, 9–11** *n.*
**kick back,** *Informal.* **a** spring back suddenly and unexpectedly. **b** return a stolen item to its owner. **c** return a portion of money received as a fee.
**kick off, a** put a football in play with a kick. **b** *Informal.* begin.
**kick out,** *Informal.* expel or turn out in a humiliating or disgraceful way: *She should be kicked out of our club.*

**kick·back** (kik′bak′) *Informal.* the amount or portion returned, especially as a fee: *He will expect a kickback for finding the money for you. n.*

**kick·er** (kik′ər) **1** a person, animal, or thing that kicks. **2** *Informal.* an outboard motor. *n.*

**kick·off** (kik′of′) **1** the start of a football game: *The kickoff is scheduled for 2:00 p.m.* **2** the start of any activity. *n.*

**kid**[1] (kid) **1** a young goat. **2** its flesh, used as food. **3** its skin, used as fur. **4** the leather made from the skin of young goats, used for gloves, shoes, etc. **5** *Informal.* child: *The kids went to the circus.* **6 kids,** *pl.* gloves or shoes made of kid. *n.*

**kid**[2] (kid) *Informal.* **1** tease playfully; talk jokingly; banter. **2** deceive; fool. *v.*, **kid·ded, kid·ding.** —**kid′der,** *n.*

**kid·nap** (kid′nap′) carry off and hold a person against his or her will by force or by fraud; abduct: *The banker's daughter was kidnapped and held for ransom. The gang planned to kidnap the movie star.* *v.*, **kid·napped** or **kid·naped, kid·nap·ping** or **kid·nap·ing.**

**kid·nap·per** or **kid·nap·er** (kid′nap′ər) a person who carries off and holds another by force: *The kidnappers demanded a ransom. n.*

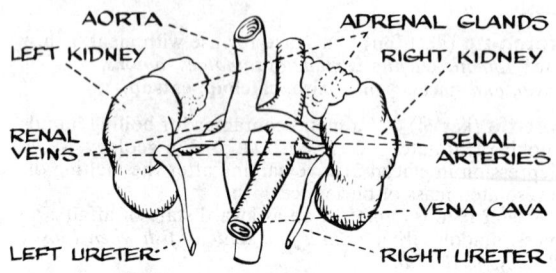

The kidneys of a human being, shown from the back

**kid·ney** (kid′nē) **1** one of the pair of organs in the body that separate waste matter and water from the blood and pass them off through the bladder as urine. See LIVER[1] for another picture. **2** a kidney or kidneys of an animal, cooked for food. **3** nature; kind; sort: *We don't like cowards, sneaks, tattletales, or any persons of that kidney.* *n., pl.* **kidneys.** —**kid′ney-like′,** *adj.*

**Ki·ku·yu** (ki kü′yü) **1** a member of a people living in the highlands of south central Kenya. **2** the Bantu language of these people. *n., pl.* **Ki·ku·yu** or **Ki·ku·yus.**

**kill** (kil) **1** put to death; cause the death of: *The blow from the axe killed him.* **2** cause death. **3** the act of killing. **4** the animal or animals killed. **5** put an end to; get rid of; destroy: *to kill odours, to kill rumours, to kill faith.* **6** cancel a word, paragraph, item, etc. **7** defeat or veto a legislative bill. **8** destroy or neutralize the active qualities of: *to kill land in farming.* **9** spoil the effect of: *One colour may kill another near it.* **10** use up time: *We killed an hour at the zoo.* **11** *Informal.* overcome completely: *My sore foot is killing me. Her jokes really kill me.* **1, 2, 5–11** *v.,* **3, 4** *n.*

**kill·dee** (kil′dē′) KILLDEER. *n., pl.* **kill·dees** or *(esp. collectively)* **kill·dee.**

**kill·deer** (kil'dēr') a small wading bird that has a loud, shrill cry, the largest and commonest plover of North America. *n., pl.* **kill·deers** or *(esp. collectively)* **kill·deer.**

**kill·er** (kil'ər) **1** a person, animal, or thing that kills. **2** a criminal who recklessly or wantonly kills others. **3** *Informal.* anything that is very difficult: *That climb is a killer.* *n.*

**killer whale** a dolphin that kills and eats large fish, seals, and even whales.

**kill·ing** (kil'ing) **1** deadly; destructive; fatal: *a killing frost.* **2** overpowering; exhausting: *She rode her horse at a killing pace.* **3** *Informal.* extremely funny. **4** *Informal.* a sudden great financial success: *to make a killing in the stock market.* **5** ppr. of KILL. 1–3 *adj.*, 4 *n.*, 5 *v.* —**kill'ing·ly,** *adv.*

**kill–joy** (kil'joi') a person who spoils other people's fun. *n.*

**kiln** (kiln *or* kil) **1** a furnace or oven for burning, baking, or drying something: *Limestone is burned in a kiln to make lime. Bricks are baked in a kiln.* **2** burn, bake, or dry in a kiln. 1 *n.*, 2 *v.*

**ki·lo** (kē'lō *or* kil'ō) KILOGRAM. *n., pl.* **ki·los.**

**kilo–** (kil'ə) an SI prefix meaning thousand: *One kilowatt is one thousand watts.* Symbol: k

**kil·o·cy·cle** (kil'ə sī'kəl) a thousand cycles, especially 1000 cycles per second: *Kilocycles have been replaced by kilohertz for expressing radio frequencies.* *n.* Symbol: kc.

**kil·o·gram** (kil'ə gram') an SI unit for measuring mass, equal to 1000 grams: *The kilogram is one of the seven base units in the SI.* Symbol: kg *n.* Also, **kilogramme.**

**kil·o·hertz** (kil'ə hėrts') an SI unit for measuring frequency of waves and vibrations, equal to 1000 hertz. Symbol: kHz *n., pl.* **kil·o·hertz.**

**kil·o·joule** (kil'ə jül') an SI unit for measuring energy, equal to 1000 joules. Symbol: kJ *n.*

**kil·o·li·tre** (kil'ə lē'tər) a unit used with the SI for measuring volume or capacity, equal to 1000 litres. Symbol: kL *n.* Also, **kiloliter.**

**kil·o·me·tre** (kil'ə mē'tər *or* kə lom'ə tər) an SI unit for measuring length or distance, equal to 1000 metres: *It takes about 12 minutes to walk one kilometre.* Symbol: km *n.* Also, **kilometer.**

**kil·o·pas·cal** (kil'ə pas'kəl) an SI unit for measuring pressure, equal to 1000 pascals: *The kilopascal is used in recording air pressure; the standard pressure of the atmosphere is about 101 kPa.* Symbol: kPa See ISOBAR for picture. *n.*

**kil·o·ton** (kil'ə tun') a unit for measuring explosive force, equal to 1000 tons of T.N.T. (about 907 tonnes). *n.*

**kil·o·watt** (kil'ə wot') an SI unit for measuring power, equal to 1000 watts. Symbol: kW *n.*

**kil·o·watt–hour** (kil'ə wot'our') a unit used with the SI for measuring electrical energy, defined as the number of kilowatts of electrical power used per hour: *One kilowatt-hour is equivalent to 3.6 megajoules.* Symbol: kW·h *n.*

hat, āge, fär; let, ēqual, tėrm; it, īce
hot, ōpen, ôrder; oil, out; cup, pùt, rüle
əbove, tākən, pencəl, lemən, circəs

ch, child; ng, long; sh, ship
th, thin; ᴛн, then; zh, measure

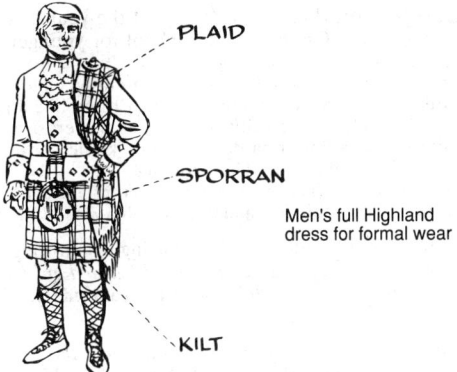

Men's full Highland dress for formal wear

**kilt** (kilt) **1** a pleated, knee-length skirt worn by men in the Scottish Highlands and by soldiers in Scottish and Irish regiments, including those in Canada. **2** a similar garment worn by women and girls. **3** *Scottish.* tuck up; fasten up. 1, 2 *n.*, 3 *v.* —**kilt'like',** *adj.*

**kil·ter** (kil'tər) *Informal.* good condition; order: *Our radio is out of kilter.* *n.*

A traditional Japanese kimono

**ki·mo·no** (kə mō'nə) **1** a loose outer garment held in place by a sash, worn by Japanese men and women. **2** a loose dressing gown. *n., pl.* **ki·mo·nos.**

**kin** (kin) **1** a person's family or relatives; kindred: *All our kin came to the family reunion.* **2** related: *My cousins are kin to me.* **3** family relationship; connection by birth or marriage: *What kin is she to you?* 1, 3 *n.*, 2 *adj.* —**kin'less,** *adj.*
**next of kin,** nearest living relative: *His next of kin is his mother.*
**of kin,** related.

**kind¹** (kīnd) **1** friendly; doing good: *kind words.* **2** gentle: *Be kind to animals.* **3** showing or characterized by kindness: *The dog had a kind mistress.* *adj.*

**kind²** (kīnd) **1** a class; sort; variety: *many kinds of candy. A kilt is a kind of skirt.* **2** a natural group; race. *n.*
**in kind, a** in goods or produce, not in money. **b** in something of the same sort. **c** in characteristic quality: *There is difference in kind, not merely in degree, between a hound and a terrier.*

**kind of,** *Informal.* nearly; almost; somewhat; rather: *The room was kind of dark.*
**of a kind,** **a** of the same kind; alike: *The cakes were all of a kind – chocolate.* **b** of a poor or mediocre quality: *Two boxes and a plank make a table of a kind.*

**kin·der·gar·ten** (kin′dər gär′tən) 1 the year of school that comes before Grade 1. 2 a school for younger children; a nursery school. *n.*
☞ *Etym.* From German *Kindergarten*, literally 'children garden'. This type of school is thought to be like a garden in which children are cultivated, just as flowers are cultivated in a flower garden. The first kindergarten was started in Blankenburg, Germany in 1840.
☞ *Pronunciation.* The pronunciation (as in German) with *t* in the final syllable is standard, though a *d* is often heard.

**kind–heart·ed** (kīnd′här′tid) having or showing a kind heart; kindly; sympathetic: *A kind-hearted girl helped me pick up my books.* *adj.* —**kind′-heart′ed·ly,** *adv.* —**kind′-heart′ed·ness,** *n.*

**kin·dle** (kin′dəl) 1 set on fire; light: *Light the paper with a match to kindle the wood.* 2 catch fire; begin to burn: *This damp wood will never kindle.* 3 arouse; stir up: *His cruelty kindled our anger.* 4 become stirred up or aroused. 5 light up; brighten: *The girl's face kindled as she told about the circus.* *v.,* **kin·dled, kin·dling.**

**kind·li·ness** (kīn′dlē nis) 1 a kindly feeling or quality. 2 a kindly act. *n.*

**kin·dling** (kin′dling) material, such as small pieces of wood, for starting a fire. *n.*

**kind·ly** (kīn′dlē) 1 kind; friendly: *kindly faces.* 2 in a kind or friendly way: *The children liked the old woman because she always treated them kindly.* 3 pleasant; agreeable: *a kindly shower.* 4 please: *Kindly pay the rent at the end of the month.* 1, 3 *adj.,* **kind·li·er, kind·li·est;** 2, 4 *adv.*
**take kindly to,** like or accept: *He does not take kindly to criticism.*

**kind·ness** (kīnd′nis) 1 a kind nature; being kind: *We admire her kindness.* 2 kind treatment: *Thank you for your kindness.* 3 a kind act: *He showed me many kindnesses.* *n., pl.* **kind·ness·es.**

**kin·dred** (kin′drid) 1 like; similar: *We are studying about dew, frost, and kindred facts of nature.* 2 related: *kindred tribes.* 3 one's family or relatives. 4 family relationship; connection by birth or marriage: *Does he claim kindred with you?* 5 a likeness; resemblance. 1, 2 *adj.,* 3–5 *n.*

**kin·e·mat·ics** (kin′ə mat′iks) the branch of mechanics dealing with the different kinds of motion that are possible for a body or system of bodies, without reference to mass or to the forces producing the motion. *n.*

**kin·e·scope** (kin′ə skōp′) 1 picture tube. 2 a record on film, which may be rebroadcast, made from images on a picture tube. *n.*
☞ *Etym.* From *Kinescope,* a trademark for a picture tube.

**kin·es·the·sia** (kin′əs thē′zhə) the sensation of movement in the muscles and joints. *n.*

**kin·es·thet·ic** (kin′əs thet′ik) having to do with sensations from the muscles and joints. *adj.*

**ki·net·ic** (ki net′ik) 1 of motion. 2 caused by motion. *adj.*

**kinetic energy** the energy of a given body depending on its motion.

**ki·net·ics** (ki net′iks) the branch of mechanics dealing with the effects of forces in causing or changing the motion of bodies: *Kinetics deals with laws for predicting the motion that will occur in a particular situation.* *n.*

**kin·folk** (kin′fōk′) KINSFOLK. *n. pl.*

**king** (king) 1 the male ruler of a nation; a male sovereign, with either absolute or limited power: *Richard the Lion-hearted was King of England.* 2 a person or animal or thing that is best or most important in a certain sphere or class: *The lion is called the king of the beasts. Babe Ruth was a king of baseball.* 3 in chess, the chief piece. 4 in checkers, a piece that has moved entirely across the board. 5 a playing card bearing a picture of a king. *n.* —**king′less,** *adj.*

**King Arthur** the central figure in a group of legends about the knights of the Round Table.

**king·bird** (king′bėrd′) a quarrelsome bird of the flycatcher family. *n.*

**king crab** HORSESHOE CRAB.

**king·craft** (king′kraft′) the art of ruling; royal statesmanship. *n.*

**king·dom** (king′dəm) 1 a country that is governed by a king or a queen. 2 a realm; domain; province: *The mind is the kingdom of thought.* 3 **a** one of the broad divisions of the natural world as animals, plants, and minerals. **b** in present-day biology, one of the five major divisions of living things: *animals, plants, fungi, protists, and monerans are kingdoms.* *n.*
☞ *Usage.* This dictionary follows the five-kingdom classification of living things in preference to the classification of the natural world into three kingdoms: animal, vegetable, and mineral.

**king·fish** (king′fish′) any of several large food fishes of the Atlantic or Pacific coast. *n., pl.* **king·fish** or **king·fish·es.**

A belted kingfisher—about 33 cm long including the tail

**king·fish·er** (king′fish′ər) a bright-coloured bird having a large head and a strong beak: *North American kingfishers eat fish; some of the European kinds eat insects.* *n.*

**king·let** (king′lit) 1 a petty king; ruler over a small country. 2 any of various small, greenish songbirds. *n.*

**king·ly** (king′lē) 1 of a king or kings; of royal rank. 2 fit for a king: *a kingly crown.* 3 like a king; royal; noble: *kingly pride.* 4 as a king does. 1–3 *adj.,* **king·li·er, king·li·est;** 4 *adv.* —**king′li·ness,** *n.*

**king salmon** the chinook salmon, a species found in the Pacific Ocean.

**King's Counsel** See QUEEN'S COUNSEL.

**King's English** See QUEEN'S ENGLISH.

**king's evil** scrofula, a disease that was supposed to be cured by the touch of a king.

**King's evidence** See QUEEN'S EVIDENCE.

**king·ship** (king′ship) **1** the position, rank, or dignity of a king. **2** the rule of a king; government by a king. *n.*

**king–size** (king′sīz′) **1** unusually large: *I made myself a king-size sandwich.* **2** longest or largest in a standard range of sizes: *king-size cigarettes. A king-size bed measures about 198 cm wide by 203 cm long.* **3** designed for use with a king-size bed: *king-size sheets. adj.*

**king's ransom** a very large amount of money.

**kink** (kingk) **1** a twist or curl in thread, rope, hair, etc. **2** form a kink or kinks; make kinks in: *The rope kinked as she rolled it up. Don't kink the clothesline.* **3** a pain or stiffness in the muscles of the neck, back, etc.; crick. **4** *Informal.* a mental twist; queer idea; odd notion; eccentricity; whim: *The old man had many kinks.* 1, 3, 4 *n.*, 2 *v.*

**kin·ka·jou** (king′kə jü′) a yellowish-brown mammal of Central and South America: *The kinkajou resembles a raccoon, but has a long prehensile tail. n.*

**kink·y** (king′kē) full of kinks; twisted; curly. *adj.*, **kink·i·er, kink·i·est.** —**kink′i·ness,** *n.*

**kin·ni·kin·ik** or **kin·ni·kin·nik** (kin′ə kə nik′) *Cdn.* **1** a smoking mixture made from the leaves or bark of various plants. **2** any of various shrubs from which the smoking mixture is made. *n.*

**kins·folk** (kinz′fōk′) a person's family; relatives; kin. *n. pl.*

**kin·ship** (kin′ship) **1** a family relationship: *Her kinship with the owner of the factory helped her to get a job.* **2** relationship. **3** resemblance: *Tennis and badminton have a kinship. n.*

**kins·man** (kinz′mən) a male relative: *Uncles are kinsmen. n., pl.* **kins·men** (-zmən).

**kins·wom·an** (kinz′wüm′ən) a female relative. *n., pl.* **kins·wom·en** (-zwim′ən).

**ki·osk** (kē′osk *or* kē osk′) a small building, usually with one or more sides open, used as a newsstand, bus shelter, telephone booth, etc. *n.*

**kip** (kip) **1** the hide of a young or undersized animal. **2** *Informal.* a sleep. **3** *Informal.* sleep. 1, 2 *n.*, 3 *v.*

**kip·per** (kip′ər) **1** salt and dry or smoke herring, salmon, etc. **2** a herring, salmon, etc. that has been kippered. **3** the male salmon or sea trout during or after the spawning season. 1 *v.*, 2, 3 *n.*

**kirk** (kėrk) *Scottish.* church. *n.*

**kis·met** (kiz′met *or* kis′met) fate; destiny. *n.*

**kiss** (kis) **1** touch with the lips as a sign of love, greeting, or respect. **2** touch gently: *A soft wind kissed the treetops.* **3** a gentle touch. **4** put, bring, take, etc. by kissing: *to kiss away tears.* **5** a piece of candy containing coconut, nuts, or the like and wrapped in a twist of paper: *Molasses kisses are a common Halloween treat.* **6** a fancy cake made of egg white and powdered sugar. 1, 2, 4 *v.*, 3, 5, 6 *n.* —**kiss′a·ble,** *adj.* —**kiss′er,** *n.*

**kit**[1] (kit) **1** a set of materials, supplies, or tools required for a particular job or purpose: *a first-aid kit, a sewing kit, a shaving kit.* **2** a set of parts intended to be put together to make a particular thing: *a radio kit, a model airplane kit.* **3** a set of printed materials issued for instruction and information: *a selling kit, a visitor's kit.* **4** the uniform or other clothing and personal equipment required for a certain activity: *a soldier's kit, skiing kit.* **5** *Informal.* any lot, set, or collection of persons or things. *n.*

**kit and caboodle,** *Informal.* the complete group; the lot: (*usually preceded by* **the whole**): *They met the children and their friends at the theatre and took the whole kit and caboodle out to supper.*

**kit**[2] (kit) **1** the young of certain fur-bearing wild animals. **2** KITTEN. *n.*

**Ki·tab–i–Aq·das** (ki tä′bē ak däs′) in Bahaism, the laws and teachings of Baha-ullah, the most sacred portion of the Bahai scriptures. *n.*

**kit–bag** (kit′bag′) a tall, rounded bag, usually made of canvas and closed at the top by a drawstring, for carrying personal belongings. *n.*

**kitch·en** (kich′ən) **1** a room where food is cooked or prepared. **2** the cooking department. **3** an outfit for cooking. *n.*

**kitch·en·ette** (kich′ə net′) **1** a very small, compactly arranged kitchen. **2** a part of a room fitted up as a kitchen. *n.* Also, **kitchenet.**

**kitchen midden** a mound of shells, bones, and other refuse at a place where prehistoric people lived.

**kitch·en·ware** (kich′ən wer′) kitchen utensils: *Pots, kettles, and pans are kitchenware. n.*

Kites flying

**kite** (kīt) **1** a light frame covered with paper, cloth, or plastic: *Kites are flown in the air on the end of a long string.* **2** *Informal.* fly like a kite; move rapidly and easily. **3** a hawk with long pointed wings. 1, 3 *n.*, 2 *v.*, **kit·ed, kit·ing.**

**fly a kite,** propose something simply to get a reaction from people.

**kith** (kith) friends. *n.*
**kith and kin,** friends and relatives.

**kit·ten** (kit′ən) a young cat. *n.*

**kit·ten·ish** (kit′ə nish) **1** like a kitten. **2** coquettish. *adj.*

**kit·ti·wake** (kit′ē wāk′) a medium-sized oceanic gull of North Atlantic coasts having mainly white plumage with black-tipped grey wings. Kittiwakes come ashore only to breed, at which time they nest in colonies on narrow cliff ledges. *n.*

**kit·ty**[1] (kit′ē) **1** kitten. **2** a pet name for a cat. *n., pl.* **kit·ties.**

**kit·ty²** (kit′ē)   1 the stakes in a poker game.   2 the money pooled by the players in other games for some special purpose: *The kitty goes to the winner.*   3 in certain card games, a number of cards which may be used by the person making the highest bid.   *n., pl.* **kit·ties.**

**kit·ty-cor·ner** (kit′ē kôr′nər)   1 diagonally opposite; on a diagonal line: *There is a small drugstore kitty-corner from the garage.*   2 diagonally: *She walked kitty-corner across the field.*   1 *adj.,* 2 *adv.*

**ki·wi** (kē′wē)   a flightless bird of New Zealand having shaggy feathers and a long, slender bill.   *n., pl.* **ki·wis.**

**kL**   kilolitre; kilolitres.

**klee·nex** (klē′neks)   1 a small piece of very soft, absorbent paper, or tissue, used as a handkerchief, for removing cosmetics, etc.: *She put two kleenexes in her pocket.*   2 a box or supply of such tissues: *We need more kleenex.*   *n.*
☞ *Etym.* From *Kleenex,* trademark, a brand of such tissues.

**klep·to·ma·ni·a** (klep′tə mā′nē ə)   an uncontrollable impulse to steal.   *n.*

**klep·to·ma·ni·ac** (klep′tə mā′nē ak′)   a person who has uncontrollable impulses to steal.   *n.*

**klieg light** (klēg)   a bright, hot arc light used in taking motion pictures.

**kludge** (kluj)   *Informal.*   a clumsy, improvised, patched-up adjustment made to a computer program, allowing it to function, at least temporarily.   *n.*

**km**   kilometre; kilometres.

**km/h**   kilometres per hour: *The top speed of this car is 120 km/h.*

**kn**   knot (unit of ship's or aircraft's speed).

**knack** (nak)   1 a special skill; power to do something easily: *The clown has the knack of making very funny faces.*   2 a trick; habit.   *n.*

A knapsack

**knap·sack** (nap′sak′)   a canvas or leather bag for carrying clothes, equipment, etc. on the back.   *n.*

**knap·weed** (nap′wēd′)   a perennial weed having light-purple flowers.   *n.*

**knave** (nāv)   1 a tricky, dishonest fellow; rogue; rascal.   2 the jack, a playing card with a picture of a servant or soldier on it.   *n.*
☞ *Hom.* NAVE.

**knav·er·y** (nā′və rē)   1 behaviour characteristic of a knave.   2 a tricky, dishonest act.   *n., pl.* **knav·er·ies.**

**knav·ish** (nā′vish)   tricky; dishonest.   *adj.*
—**knav′ish·ly,** *adv.*   —**knav′ish·ness,** *n.*

**knead** (nēd)   1 mix moist flour, clay, etc. into a dough or paste by pressing and stretching, usually with the hands: *A baker kneads dough.*   2 press and squeeze with the hands; massage: *Kneading the muscles in a stiff shoulder will sometimes take away the stiffness.*   3 make or shape by kneading.   *v.*
☞ *Hom.* NEED.

**knee** (nē)   1 the joint between the thigh and the lower leg. See LEG for picture.   2 any joint corresponding to the human knee or elbow.   3 anything like a bent knee in shape or position.   4 the part of pants, stockings, etc. covering the knee.   5 strike with the knee.   1–4 *n.,* 5 *v.,* **kneed, knee·ing.**
**bring to one's knees,**   force to yield.

**knee breeches**   breeches reaching to or just below the knees.

**knee·cap** (nē′kap′)   1 the flat, movable bone at the front of the knee; patella. See LEG for picture.   2 a covering to protect the knee.   *n.*

**kneel** (nēl)   1 go down on one's knee or knees: *She knelt down to pull a weed from the flower bed.*   2 remain in this position: *They knelt for several minutes.*   *v.,* **knelt** or **kneeled, kneel·ing.**   —**kneel′er,** *n.*

**knee·pad** (nē′pad′)   a pad worn around the knee for protection.   *n.*

**knell** (nel)   1 the sound of a bell rung slowly after a death or at a funeral.   2 ring slowly; toll.   3 a sign or warning of death, failure, etc.: *Their refusal rang the knell of our hopes.*   4 give such a warning sign.   5 a mournful sound.   6 make a mournful sound.   1, 3, 5 *n.,* 2, 4, 6 *v.*

**knelt** (nelt)   a pt. and a pp. of KNEEL: *He knelt to scrub the floor.*   *v.*

**knew** (nyü *or* nü)   pt. of KNOW: *Jean knew the right answer.*   *v.*
☞ *Hom.* GNU, NEW.

**knick·er·bock·ers** (nik′ər bok′ərz)   KNICKERS.   *n. pl.*

**knick·ers** (nik′ərz)   1 short, loose-fitting trousers gathered in at, or just below, the knee.   2 a woman's undergarment for the lower part of the body; briefs with legs.   *n. pl.*

**knick–knack** (nik′nak′)   a pleasing trifle; ornament; trinket.   *n.* Also, **nick-nack.**

**knife** (nīf)   1 a thin, flat blade, usually of metal, fastened in a handle so that it can be used to cut or spread.   2 any weapon having a short blade with a sharp edge and point, such as a dagger.   3 a cutting blade in a tool or machine: *The knives of a lawn mower cut grass.*   4 cut or stab with a knife.   5 pierce or cut as with a knife: *The wind knifed through her thin jacket.*   1–3 *n., pl.* **knives;**   4, 5 *v.,* **knifed, knif·ing.**   —**knife′like′,** *adj.*
**under the knife,** *Informal.*   undergoing a surgical operation.

**knight** (nīt)   1 in the Middle Ages, a man raised to an honourable military rank and pledged to do good deeds: *After serving as a page and squire, a man was made a knight by the king or a lord.*   2 in modern times, a man raised to an honourable rank because of personal achievement or because he has won distinction in some way: *A knight has the title Sir before his name.*   3 raise to the rank of knight: *He was knighted by the queen.*   4 a man devoted to the service or protection of a lady.   5 a piece in the game of chess.   1, 2, 4, 5 *n.,* 3 *v.*
☞ *Hom.* NIGHT.

**knight–er·rant** (nī′ter′ənt)   1 in the Middle Ages, a knight travelling in search of adventure.   2 a person of great chivalry.   *n., pl.* **knights-er·rant.**

**knight–er·rant·ry** (nī′ter′ən trē)   1 conduct or action

characteristic of a KNIGHT-ERRANT.  **2** quixotic conduct or action. *n., pl.* **knight·er·rant·ries.**

**knight·hood** (nīt′hud)  **1** the rank or dignity of a knight.  **2** the profession or occupation of a knight.  **3** the character or qualities of a knight.  **4** knights as a group or class: *All the knighthood of France came to the aid of the king. n.*

**knight·ly** (nīt′lē)  **1** of a knight; brave; generous; courteous; chivalrous.  **2** as a knight should do; bravely; generously; courteously.  1 *adj.*, 2 *adv.*
—**knight′li·ness,** *n.*
☞ *Hom.* NIGHTLY.

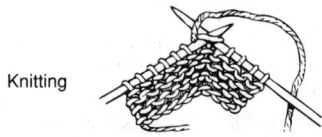
Knitting

**knit** (nit)  **1** make by looping yarn or thread together with long needles or by machinery which forms similar interlocking loops: *She is knitting a sweater.*  **2** make an article or fabric by looping yarn or thread together with long needles or by machinery: *Jersey is knitted cloth.*  **3** join closely and firmly together.  **4** grow together; be joined closely and firmly: *A broken bone knits.*  **5** draw the brows together in wrinkles.  *v.*, **knit·ted** or **knit, knit·ting.** —**knit′ter,** *n.*

**knit·ting** (nit′ing)  **1** knitted work.  **2** ppr. of KNIT. 1 *n.*, 2 *v.*

**knitting needle**  one of a pair of long needles used in knitting. See NEEDLE for picture.

**knives** (nīvz)  pl. of KNIFE.  *n.*

**knob** (nob)  **1** a rounded lump.  **2** the handle of a door, drawer, etc.  **3** a rounded hill or mountain.  *n.*
☞ *Hom.* NOB.

**knob·by** (nob′ē)  **1** covered with knobs: *Some kinds of squash have a knobby rind.*  **2** rounded like a knob. *adj.*, **knob·bi·er, knob·bi·est.** —**knob′bi·ness,** *n.*

**knock** (nok)  **1** hit; strike a blow with the fist, knuckles, or anything hard: *She knocked him on the head.*  **2** a hit: *The hard knock made him cry.*  **3** hit and cause to fall: *Marta ran against another girl and knocked her down.*  **4** make a noise by hitting: *to knock on a door.*  **5** a hit with a noise.  **6** make a noise, especially a rattling or pounding noise: *The engine is knocking.*  **7** *Informal.* criticize; find fault.  **8** the act of knocking.  **9** the sound of knocking: *She did not hear the knock at the door.*  **10** a pounding or rattling sound in an engine: *We learned that the knock was caused by loose parts.*  1, 3, 4, 6, 7 *v.*, 2, 5, 8–10 *n.*

**knock about,** *Informal.*  a wander from place to place.  **b** hit repeatedly.
**knock down,**  a sell an article to the highest bidder at an auction.  **b** take apart: *We knocked down the bookcase and packed it in the car.*  **c** strike down.
**knock off,** *Informal.*  a take off; deduct: *to knock off 50 cents from the price.*  **b** stop work: *We knock off at noon for lunch.*  **c** accomplish hastily; do quickly: *She knocked off a new poem in just a few minutes.*
**knock out,**  a hit so hard as to make helpless or unconscious.  **b** drive out of the contest; vanquish.
**knock together,**  make or put together hastily.
☞ *Hom.* NOCK.

**knock·a·bout** (nok′ə bout′)  **1** a small, easily handled

hat, āge, fär; let, ē·qual, tėrm; it, īce
hot, ō·pen, ôr·der; oil, out; cup, put, rüle
ə·bove, tak·ən, pen·cəl, lem·ən, cir·cəs
ch, child; ng, long; sh, ship
th, thin; ᴛH, then; zh, measure

sailboat having one mast, a mainsail, and a jib, but no bowsprit.  **2** suitable for rough use.  1 *n.*, 2 *adj.*

A door knocker

**knock·er** (nok′ər)  **1** a person or thing that knocks.  **2** a knob, ring, etc. fastened on a door for use in knocking.  *n.*

**knock–kneed** (nok′nēd′)  having legs curved inward so that the knees tend to touch when walking.  Compare with BOWLEGGED.  *adj.*

**knock·out** (nok′out′)  **1** the act of rendering unconscious or helpless by a punch: *He won the fight by a knockout.*  **2** the condition of being knocked out.  **3** a blow that knocks out.  **4** *Informal.*  a person or thing considered outstanding; a success: *The party was a knockout.*  **5** *Informal.*  that knocks out: *a knockout blow.*  1–4 *n.*, 5 *adj.*

**knoll** (nōl)  a small, rounded hill; mound: *The house stood on a wooded knoll.*  *n.*

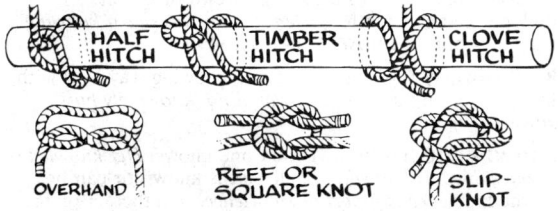

**knot¹** (not)  **1** a fastening made by tying or twining together pieces of rope, cord, string, etc.: *a square knot, a slip-knot.*  **2** tie or twine together in a knot.  **3** an accidental tying or twisting of rope, cord, string, etc.  **4** tangle in knots.  **5** make knots for a fringe.  **6** make a fringe by tying knots.  **7** a bow of ribbon, etc. worn as an ornament: *a shoulder knot.*  **8** a group; cluster: *A knot of people stood talking outside the door.*  **9** a hard mass of wood formed where a branch grows out from a tree, which shows as a roundish, cross-grained piece in a board.  **10** a hard lump: *A knot sometimes forms in a tired muscle.*  **11** form into a hard lump.  **12** a joint where leaves grow out on the stem of a plant.  **13** a unit for measuring the speed of a ship or aircraft; 1852 metres per hour: *The ship averaged 12 knots.*  Symbol: kn  **14** nautical mile (1852 metres).  **15** a difficulty or problem.  **16** unite closely or intricately; bind.  **17** something that unites closely or intricately.  1, 3, 7–10, 12–15, 17 *n.*, 2, 4–6, 11, 16 *v.*, **knot·ted, knot·ting.** —**knot′less,** *adj.*
☞ *Hom.* knot, NAUGHT, NOT, and NOUGHT are pronounced the same (to rhyme with **got**) by most Canadians.

**knot²** (not) a small sandpiper that breeds in the Canadian Arctic. *n.*
☞ *Hom.* See note at KNOT¹.

**knot·grass** (not′gras′) a weed whose stems have large joints. *n.*

**knot·hole** (not′hōl′) a hole in a board where a KNOT (def. 9) has fallen out. *n.*

**knot·ted** (not′id) **1** having a knot or knots; knotty. **2** pt. and pp. of KNOT. 1 *adj.*, 2 *v.*

**knot·ty** (not′ē) **1** full of knots: *knotty wood.* **2** difficult; puzzling: *a knotty problem. adj.*, **knot·ti·er**, **knot·ti·est**. —**knot′ti·ness**, *n.*
☞ *Hom.* NAUGHTY.

**know** (nō) **1** be sure of; have true information about: *She knows the facts of the case.* **2** have firmly in the mind or memory: *to know a lesson.* **3** be aware of; have seen or heard; have information about: *to know a person's name.* **4** be sure or certain because of experience or knowledge: *She does not have to guess; she knows.* **5** be acquainted with; be familiar with: *I know her.* **6** have an understanding of; have experience with; be skilled in: *She knows Canadian literature.* **7** recognize; identify: *You would hardly know her since her illness.* **8** tell apart from others; distinguish: *You will know her house by the stone chimney. v.*, **knew, known, know·ing.** —**know′er**, *n.*
**in the know**, *Informal.* having inside information.
**know what's what**, *Informal.* be well informed.
☞ *Hom.* NO.

**know·a·ble** (nō′ə bəl) capable of being known. *adj.*

**know–how** (nō′hou′) *Informal.* the ability to do something; the knowledge required to get something done. *n.*

**know·ing** (nō′ing) **1** having knowledge; well-informed. **2** clever; shrewd. **3** suggesting shrewd or secret understanding of matters: *Her only answer was a knowing look.* **4** ppr. of KNOW. 1–3 *adj.*, 4 *v.*

**know·ing·ly** (nō′ing lē) **1** in a knowing way. **2** with knowledge; on purpose: *She would not knowingly hurt anyone. adv.*

**knowl·edge** (nol′ij) **1** what one knows: *Her knowledge of the subject is limited.* **2** all that is known or can be learned: *Science is a part of knowledge.* **3** the act or fact of knowing: *a knowledge of the surrounding countryside. The knowledge of our victory caused great joy. n.*

**knowl·edge·a·ble** (nol′i jə bəl) *Informal.* well-informed, especially about a particular subject. *adj.*

**known** (nōn) **1** in the knowledge of everyone; widely recognized: *a known fact, a known artist.* **2** pp. of KNOW: *Champlain is known as an explorer.* 1 *adj.*, 2 *v.*

**know–noth·ing** (nō′nuth′ing) an ignorant person. *n.*

**knuck·le** (nuk′əl) **1** a finger joint, especially one of the joints between a finger and the rest of the hand. **2** press or rub with the knuckles. **3** put the knuckles on the ground in playing marbles. **4** the knee or hock joint of an animal used as food: *boiled pigs' knuckles.* 1, 4 *n.*, 2, 3 *v.*, **knuck·led**, **knuck·ling**.
**knuckle down**, **a** *Informal.* apply oneself earnestly; work hard. **b** *Informal.* submit; yield: *She would not knuckle down under their attack.*
**knuckle under**, *Informal.* submit, yield: *She refused to knuckle under to her enemies.*

**knuck·le·dust·er** (nuk′əl dus′tər) a piece of metal worn over the knuckles as a weapon. *n.*

**knurl** (nėrl) **1** knot; knob. **2** a small ridge, such as on the edge of a coin or round nut. *n.*

A koala with its young. Adult koalas are about 60 cm long.

**ko·a·la** (kō ä′lə) a furry grey marsupial of Australia that lives in trees and carries its young in a pouch: *Koalas belong to the same order as kangaroos. n.*

**Ko·di·ak bear** (kō′dē ak′) a subspecies of the brown bear, found on Kodiak Island. It is the largest living meat-eating animal.

**kohl·ra·bi** (kōl′rä′bē *or* kōl′rä′bē) a vegetable that resembles a turnip, and is related to the cabbage. *n., pl.* **kohl·ra·bies**.

**ko·ji·ki** (kō jē′kē) in Shintoism, one of the most highly revered of ancient texts, covering the history of Japan from the creation of the world to the middle of the 7th century. *n.*

**ko·ka·nee** (kō′kə nē′) *Cdn.* a permanent freshwater form of the sockeye salmon, common in British Columbia lakes and rivers. Compare with OUANANICHE. *n.*

**ko·la** (kō′lə) **1** a KOLA NUT. **2** a stimulant or tonic made from kola nuts. *n.*

**kola nut** a bitter, brownish nut of a tropical tree, containing about 3 percent caffeine.

**ko·ma·tik** (kō′mə tik′) *Cdn.* a large wooden dogsled used in the North, made of closely-spaced crossbars lashed to two broad runners. *n.*
☞ *Etym.* From eastern Inuktitut *qamutik*, the dual (meaning 'two') form of *qamut* 'sled runner'.

**ko·mo·do drag·on** (kə mō′dō) the largest living lizard, found in southeast Asia.

**koo·doo** (kü′dü) See KUDU. *n., pl.* **koo·doos**.

**kook·a·bur·ra** (kük′ə bėr′ə) a large Australian kingfisher noted for its cry that resembles loud, harsh laughter; laughing jackass: *The kookaburra feeds on lizards, snakes, insects, etc. n.*

**Ko·ran** (kô rän′ *or* kô ran′) the sacred book of Islam, consisting of reports of revelations made to the prophet Mohammed by Allah through the archangel Gabriel. *n.*

**Ko·re·an** (kə rē′ən *or* kô rē′ən) **1** of Korea, a small country in eastern Asia (since 1948 divided into North and South Korea), its people, or their language. **2** a native or inhabitant of Korea. **3** the language of Korea. 1 *adj.*, 2, 3 *n.*

**ko·sher** (kō′shər) **1** right or clean according to Jewish ritual law: *kosher meat.* **2** dealing in products that meet the requirements of Jewish ritual law: *a kosher butcher.* **3** prepare food according to the Jewish ritual law. **4** *Informal.* food thus prepared. **5** *Informal.* a shop selling such food. 1, 2 *adj.*, 3 *v.*, 4, 5 *n.*
☞ *Etym.* From Hebrew *kāsher*, 'proper, right'.

**kow·tow** (kou′tou′ *or* kō′tou′) **1** kneel and touch the ground with the forehead to show deep respect,

submission, or worship. **2** show slavish respect or obedience. **3** the act of kowtowing. 1, 2 *v.*, 3 *n.*
—**kow′tow′er,** *n.*

**kPa** kilopascal.

**Kr** krypton.

**kraal** (kräl) **1** a village of South African natives, protected by a fence. **2** a pen for cattle or sheep in South Africa. *n.*

**Krem·lin** (krem′lən) **1** the citadel of Moscow: *The chief offices of the Russian government are in the Kremlin.* **2** the government of Russia. *n.*

**kris** (krēs) a dagger with a wavy blade, used by the Malays. *n.* Also, **creese.**

**Krish·na** (krish′nə) a human form of the Hindu god Vishnu, occurring in many forms, but especially as the divine flute player, calling the human soul to God. *n.*

**Kriss Krin·gle** (kris′ kring′gəl) SANTA CLAUS.

**krul·ler** (krul′ər) See CRULLER. *n.*

**kryp·ton** (krip′ton) a rare inert gas, one of the chemical elements. *Symbol*: Kr *n.*

**kt.** knight.

**ku·dos** (kyü′dos) *Informal.* prestige; glory; fame. *n.*

**ku·du** (kü′dü) a large, greyish-brown African antelope having white stripes. *n.* Also, **koodoo.**

**kum·quat** (kum′kwot) **1** an orange-yellow fruit resembling a small orange and having a sour pulp and a sweet rind, used especially for preserves and candy. **2** any of several closely related trees or shrubs producing this fruit: *Kumquats are related to the orange.* *n.* Also, **cumquat.**

**kung fu** (kùng′fü′) a Chinese art of fighting similar to karate, that dates back to ancient times.

**Kurd** (kėrd) a member of a nomadic people living chiefly in Kurdistan, a mountainous region extending from eastern Turkey through northern Iraq and into western Iran. *n.*

**Kurd·ish** (kėr′dish) **1** the language of the Kurds, related to Persian. **2** of or having to do with the Kurds or their language. 1 *n.*, 2 *adj.*

**kV** kilovolt; kilovolts.

**kW** kilowatt; kilowatts.

**kW·h** kilowatt-hour; kilowatt-hours.

hat, āge, fär; let, ēqual, tėrm; it, īce
hot, ōpen, ôrder; oil, out; cup, pùt, rüle
əbove, takən, pencəl, lemən, circəs
ch, child; ng, long; sh, ship
th, thin; ᴛʜ, then; zh, measure

# L l L l

**l or L** (el) **1** the twelfth letter of the English alphabet. **2** any speech sound represented by this letter. **3** any person or thing identified as l, especially the twelfth in a series. **4** anything shaped like an L. **5** the Roman letter used as the numeral for 50. *n., pl.* **l's** or **L's.**

**l or l. 1** line. **2** league. **3** length. **4** left.

**L 1** Latin. **2** litre; litres. **3** pound (sterling). **4** Libra.

**L. 1** Latin. **2** low. **3** Licenciate. **4** Lake. **5** Law.

**la¹** (lä) in music: **1** the sixth tone of an eight-tone major scale. See DO² for picture. **2** the tone A. *n.*

**la²** (lä) an exclamation of surprise. *interj.*

**La** lanthanum.

**L.A.** Legislative Assembly.

**lab** (lab) *Informal.* LABORATORY. *n.*

**Lab.** Labrador.

**la·bel** (lā′bəl) **1** a slip of paper or other material attached to anything and marked to show what or whose it is, or where it is to go: *Can you read the label on the box?* **2** put or write a label on: *The bottle is labelled "Poison."* **3** a short phrase used to describe some person, thing, or idea: *"Land of Opportunity" is a label often given to Canada.* **4** describe as; call; name: *He labelled the boastful man a liar.* 1, 3 *n.*, 2, 4 *v.*, **la·belled** or **la·beled**, **la·bel·ling** or **la·bel·ing.** —**la′bel·ler** or **la′bel·er**, *n.*

**la·bi·al** (lā′bē əl) **1** of the lips. **2** a speech sound made by closing, nearly closing, or rounding the lips: *English labials are* b, p, m. **3** made in this way. 1, 3 *adj.*, 2 *n.*

**la·bi·um** (lā′bē əm) a lip or liplike part. *n., pl.* **la·bi·a** (-bē ə).

**la·bor** (lā′bər) See LABOUR. *n., v.*

**lab·o·ra·to·ry** (lab′rə tô′rē *or* lə bô′rə tô′rē) **1** a place where scientific work is done; a room or building fitted with apparatus for conducting scientific investigations, experiments, tests, etc. **2** a place fitted up for manufacturing chemicals, medicines, explosives, etc. *n., pl.* **lab·o·ra·to·ries.**

**la·bo·ri·ous** (lə bô′rē əs) **1** requiring much work; requiring hard work: *Climbing a mountain is laborious.* **2** willing to work hard; hard-working; industrious: *Bees and ants are laborious insects.* **3** showing signs of effort; not easy: *laborious breathing.* *adj.* —**la·bo′ri·ous·ly**, *adv.*

**la·bor·ite** (lā′bə rīt′) See LABOURITE (def. 1). *n.*

**la·bour** or **la·bor** (lā′bər) **1** the effort in doing or making something; work; toil: *Dan was well paid for his labour.* **2** a piece of work; task: *The king gave Hercules twelve labours to perform.* **3** work done by skilled and unskilled workers who are not clerks, managers, professional workers, or owners. **4** skilled and unskilled workers as a group: *Labour favours safe working conditions.* **5** do work; work hard; toil: *She laboured all day in the mill.* **6** elaborate with effort or in detail: *The speaker laboured the point so that we lost interest.* **7** move slowly and heavily: *The ship laboured in the high waves. The old car laboured as it climbed the steep hill.* **8** be burdened, troubled, or distressed: *to labour under a mistake.* **9** childbirth. **10** be in childbirth. 1–4, 9 *n.*, 5–8, 10 *v.*

**Labour Day** or **Labor Day 1** the first Monday in September, a legal holiday in Canada and the United States in honour of labour and labourers. **2** for or occurring on Labour Day: *a Labour Day parade.*

**la·boured** or **la·bored** (lā′bərd) **1** done with effort; forced; not easy or natural. **2** pt. and pp. of LABOUR. 1 *adj.*, 2 *v.*

**la·bour·er** or **la·bor·er** (lā′bə rər) **1** worker. **2** a person who does work requiring strength rather than skill or training. *n.*

**la·bour·ite** or **la·bor·ite** a member of a LABOUR PARTY. *n.*

**labour party** or **labor party** any political party organized to protect and promote the interests of workers.

**Labour Party** a British political party that claims especially to protect and advance the interests of working people.

**la·bour–sav·ing** or **la·bor–sav·ing** (lā′bər sā′ving) that takes the place of or lessens labour: *a labour-saving device.* *adj.*

**labour union** or **labor union** an association of workers to protect and promote their interests, and for dealing collectively with employers.

**Lab·ra·dor re·trie·ver** a breed of medium-sized retriever dog originating in Newfoundland but developed mainly in England, having a thick, short coat that is black, chocolate brown, or yellow.

**la·bur·num** (lə bėr′nəm) a small tree or shrub having hanging clusters of yellow flowers and poisonous seeds. *n.*

**lab·y·rinth** (lab′ə rinth′ *or* lab′rinth) **1** a place through which it is hard to find one's way; maze. **2** a confusing, complicated arrangement. **3** a confusing, complicated state of affairs. **4** the internal ear. *n.*
☛ *Etym.* From *Labyrinth*, in Greek mythology, the maze built by Daedalus for King Minos of Crete: *The Minotaur was kept in the Labyrinth.*

**lab·y·rin·thine** (lab′ə rin′thən *or* lab′ə rin′thēn) **1** of a LABYRINTH (defs. 1–3); forming a labyrinth. **2** intricate; confusing; complicated. *adj.*

**lac** (lak) a resinous substance deposited on trees in southern Asia by certain insects: *Lac is used in making sealing wax, varnish, red dye, etc.* *n.*
☛ *Hom.* LACK.

**lac·co·lith** (lak′ə lith) a bulge in strata such as on the outside of the crater of a volcano, formed by igneous rock which has not broken through to the surface. *n.*

**lace** (lās) **1** a delicate fabric woven in an open or netlike ornamental pattern. **2** trim with lace. **3** a cord, string, leather strip, etc. for pulling or holding together: *These shoes need new laces.* **4** put laces through; pull or hold together with a lace or laces. **5** be laced: *These shoes lace easily.* **6** gold or silver braid used for trimming: *Some uniforms have lace on them.* **7** adorn or trim with narrow braid: *His uniform was laced with gold.* **8** interlace; intertwine. **9** mark with streaks; streak: *a white petunia laced with pink.* **10** *Informal.* lash; beat; thrash. **11** mix coffee, etc. with liquor. **12** squeeze in the waist by a tight corset: *It was once fashionable to lace.* 1, 3, 6 *n.*, 2, 4, 5, 7–12 *v.*, **laced, lac·ing.** —**lace′like′**, *adj.* **lace into,** *Informal.* **a** attack. **b** criticize severely.

**lac·er·ate** (las′ə rāt′) **1** tear roughly; mangle: *The bear's claws lacerated her flesh.* **2** cause pain or suffering to; distress: *The coach's sharp words lacerated her feelings.* *v.*, **lac·er·at·ed, lac·er·at·ing.**

**lac·er·a·tion** (las′ə rā′shən) **1** the act of lacerating. **2** a rough tear; a mangled place; wound. *n.*

**lace·wing** (lā′swing′) an insect that has four lacelike wings. *n.*

**lace·work** (lā′swėrk′) **1** lace. **2** openwork like lace. *n.*

**lach·ry·mal** (lak′rə məl) **1** of tears, producing tears. **2** for tears. **3 lachrymals,** *pl.* glands that produce tears. 1, 2 *adj.*, 3 *n.* Also, **lacrimal.**

**lach·ry·mose** (lak′rə mōs′) tearful; mournful. *adj.* —**lach′ry·mose·ly,** *adv.*

**lac·ing** (lā′sing) **1** cord, string, etc. for pulling or holding something together. **2** gold or silver braid used for trimming. **3** *Informal.* a lashing; beating; thrashing. **4** ppr. of LACE. 1–3 *n.*, 4 *v.*

**lack** (lak) **1** have not enough; need: *A desert lacks water.* **2** a shortage; not having enough: *Lack of rest made her tired.* **3** be without: *A homeless person lacks a home.* **4** be absent or missing. **5** the fact or condition of being without: *Lack of a fire made him cold.* **6** the thing needed: *The campers' main lack was fuel for a fire.* 1, 3, 4 *v.*, 2, 5, 6 *n.*
**supply the lack,** supply what is needed.
☞ *Hom.* LAC.

**lack·a·dai·si·cal** (lak′ə dā′zə kəl) languid; listless; dreamy; weakly sentimental. *adj.* —**lack′a·dai′si·cal·ly,** *adv.*

**lack·ey** (lak′ē) **1** a male servant; footman. **2** a slavish follower. **3** wait on. **4** be slavish to. 1, 2 *n.*, *pl.* **lack·eys;** 3, 4 *v.*, **lack·eyed, lack·ey·ing.**

**lack·ing** (lak′ing) **1** not having enough; deficient: *A weak person is lacking in strength.* **2** absent; not present: *Water is lacking in a desert.* **3** without; not having: *Lacking anything better, use what you have.* **4** ppr. of LACK. 1, 2 *adj.*, 3 *prep.*, 4 *v.*

**lack·lus·tre** (lak′lus′tər) **1** not shining or bright; dull. **2** lacking vitality or interest: *a lacklustre production of a play.* *adj.* Also, **lackluster.**

**la·con·ic** (lə kon′ik) using few words; brief in speech or expression; concise. *adj.* —**la·con′i·cal·ly,** *adv.*

**lac·o·nism** (lak′ə niz′əm) **1** LACONIC brevity. **2** a LACONIC speech or expression. *n.*

**lac·quer** (lak′ər) **1** a varnish consisting of shellac dissolved in a solvent, used to give a protective coating or a shiny appearance to metals, wood, paper, etc. **2** a varnish made from the resin of a sumac tree of southeastern Asia: *Lacquer gives a high polish on wood.* **3** wooden articles coated with such varnish. **4** a nail polish. **5** coat with lacquer. 1–4 *n.*, 5 *v.*, —**lac′quer·er,** *n.*

**lac·ri·mal** (lak′rə məl) See LACHRYMAL. *adj.*, *n.*

**la·crosse** (lə kros′) *Cdn.* a game played, either indoors (**box lacrosse**) or outdoors (**field lacrosse**) by two teams of players equipped with LACROSSE STICKS, by means of which an India rubber ball is carried and passed from player to player in an attempt to score a goal. *n.*

A lacrosse stick and ball

**lacrosse stick** an L-shaped stick strung with leather thongs that form a kind of pouch for carrying the ball in the game of lacrosse.

**lac·tase** (lak′tās) a digestive enzyme in the intestinal glands which helps to break down carbohydrates into glucose. *n.*

**lac·tate** (lak′tāt) **1** any salt of LACTIC ACID. **2** secrete milk. 1 *n.*, 2 *v.*, **lac·tat·ed, lac·tat·ing.**

**lac·ta·tion** (lak tā′shən) **1** the act of suckling a baby. **2** the time during which a mother gives milk. **3** the secretion or formation of milk. *n.*

**lac·te·al** (lak′tē əl) **1** of milk; like milk; milky. **2** carrying CHYLE, a milky liquid formed from digested food. **3** any of the lymphatic vessels in the wall of the intestine that receive digested fats from the intestine and carry them to the bloodstream. 1, 2 *adj.*, 3 *n.*

**lac·te·ous** (lak′tē əs) milky. *adj.*

**lac·tic** (lak′tik) of milk; from milk. *adj.*

**lactic acid** a colourless, odourless acid formed in sour milk, in the fermentation of vegetable juices, etc.

**lac·to·fla·vin** (lak′tō flā′vən) RIBOFLAVIN. *n.*

**lac·tose** (lak′tōs) a crystalline sugar present in milk; milk sugar. *n.*

**la·cu·na** (lə kyü′nə) **1** an empty space; gap; blank: *There were several lacunas in her letter where words had been erased.* **2** a tiny cavity in bones or tissues. *n.*, *pl.* **la·cu·nas** or **la·cu·nae** (-nē *or* -nī).

**la·cus·trine** (lə kus′trin) **1** of lakes. **2** in lakes. *adj.*

**lac·y** (lā′sē) **1** of lace. **2** like lace; having an open pattern: *the lacy leaves of a fern.* *adj.*, **lac·i·er, lac·i·est.** —**lac′i·ness,** *n.*

**lad** (lad) **1** a boy; young man. **2** *Informal.* man. *n.*

A ladder

**lad·der** (lad′ər) **1** a set of rungs or steps fastened to two long sidepieces, for use in climbing. **2** a means of climbing higher: *Hard work is a ladder to success.* **3** a run in a knitted fabric, especially in a stocking. *n.* —**lad′der·like′,** *adj.*

**lad·der–back** (lad′ər bak′) of a chair, having a tall back designed like the rungs of a ladder: *a ladder-back chair.* *adj.*

**lade** (lād) **1** put a burden on; load. **2** dip; scoop; ladle. **3** take on cargo. *v.,* **lad·ed, lad·en** or **lad·ed, lad·ing.**

**lad·en** (lā′dən) **1** loaded; burdened: *The camels were laden with bundles of silk.* **2** a pp. of LADE. 1 *adj.,* 2 *v.*

**lad·ing** (lā′ding) **1** the act of loading. **2** a load; freight; cargo. **3** ppr. of LADE. 1, 2 *n.,* 3 *v.*

A ladle

**la·dle** (lā′dəl) **1** a large, cup-shaped spoon with a long handle, for dipping out liquids. **2** dip out and carry or serve in a ladle or other utensil: *The cook is ladling the soup.* 1 *n.,* 2 *v.,* **la·dled, la·dling.** —**la′dler,** *n.*
**ladle out,** *Informal.* give freely: *That teacher is too fond of ladling out punishments.*

**la·dy** (lā′dē) **1** a woman of refinement and courtesy. **2** a woman of high social position. **3** any woman: *Our teacher is a nice lady.* **4** a woman who has the rights or authority of a lord; a mistress of a household. **5** a noblewoman; woman who has the title of Lady. **6** a woman whom a man loves or is devoted to. **7** wife. **8 Lady,** in the United Kingdom, a title given to women of certain ranks of nobility. *n., pl.* **la·dies.**
☛ *Etym.* From OE *hlǣfdige* 'mistress of a household', originally 'bread kneader', made up of *hlāf* 'loaf' + *-dig-* 'to knead'. Compare note at LORD.
☛ *Usage.* In formal English, **lady** is used to mean a woman of high social position. Though **lady** is often used in everyday speech to refer to any woman (*lady cab driver, lady clerk*), the word is now usually considered rather affected. Many people would consider WOMAN the better word in all such cases.

**la·dy·bird** (lā′dē bėrd′) LADYBUG. *n.*

**la·dy·bug** (lā′dē bug′) a small beetle having a rounded back, usually red or orange with black spots: *Ladybugs eat harmful insects.* See METAMORPHOSIS and BEETLE for pictures.

**la·dy·fin·ger** (lā′dē fing′gər) a small sponge cake shaped rather like a finger. *n.*

**la·dy-in-wait·ing** (lā′dē in wā′ting) a lady who is an attendant of a queen or princess. *n., pl.* **la·dies-in-wait·ing.**

**la·dy·like** (lā′dē līk′) **1** like a lady. **2** suitable for a lady: *Her behaviour is invariably lady-like.* *adj.*

**La·dy·ship** (lā′dē ship′) *Brit.* a title used in speaking to or of a woman having the rank of Lady: *"your Ladyship," "her Ladyship."* *n.*

**la·dy–slip·per** (lā′dē slip′ər) LADY'S-SLIPPER. *n.*

Pink lady's-slippers

**la·dy's-slip·per** (lā′dēz slip′ər) any of several species of wild orchid found in the temperate regions of North America, having flowers whose shape suggests a slipper: *The pink lady's-slipper is the provincial flower of Prince Edward Island.* *n.*

**lag** (lag) **1** move too slowly; fall behind: *The child lagged because she was tired.* **2** the act of lagging. **3** the amount by which a person or thing lags. 1 *v.,* **lagged, lag·ging;** 2, 3 *n.*

**la·ger** (lä′gər) a light beer that is slowly fermented at a low temperature and stored from six weeks to six months before being used. *n.*

**lag·gard** (lag′ərd) **1** a person who moves too slowly or falls behind; backward person. **2** slow; falling behind; backward. 1 *n.,* 2 *adj.* —**lag′gard·ly,** *adv.*

**la·goon** (lə gün′) **1** a pond or small lake connected with a larger body of water. **2** shallow water separated from the sea by low sandbanks. **3** the water within a ring-shaped coral island. *n.*

**laid** (lād) **1** pt. and pp. of LAY¹: *He laid down the heavy bundle.* **2** marked with close parallel lines or watermarks: *laid paper.* 1 *v.,* 2 *adj.*
**laid up, a** stored up; put away for future use. **b** *Informal.* forced by illness or injury to stay indoors or in bed. **c** dismantled and put in dock.

**laid–back** (lād′bak′) **1** placed in a backward position or direction: *The horse had laid-back ears.* **2** *Informal.* very relaxed in manner. *adj.*

**lain** (lān) pp. of LIE²: *The snow has lain on the ground a week.* *v.*
☛ *Hom.* LANE.

**lair** (ler) the den or resting place of a wild animal. *n.*

**lais·sez faire** or **lais·ser faire** (les′ā fer′; *French,* le sā feʀ′) **1** the principle of letting people do as they please. **2** the absence of governmental regulation and interference in trade, business, industry, etc.

**lais·sez–faire** (les′ā fer′; *French,* le sā feʀ′) of or based on LAISSEZ FAIRE. *adj.*

**la·i·ty** (lā′ə tē) laymen; the people as distinguished from the clergy or from a professional class: *Doctors use many words that the laity do not understand.* *n., pl.* **la·i·ties.**

**lake¹** (lāk) **1** a large body of fresh water entirely, or almost entirely, surrounded by land. **2** a wide place in a river. *n.*

**lake²** (lāk) **1** a deep-red or purplish-red colouring matter. **2** an insoluble coloured compound formed from animal, vegetable, or coal tar colouring matters and metallic oxides. *n.*

**lake dweller** in prehistoric times, a person who lived in a house built on piles over a lake.

**lake dwelling** in prehistoric times, a house built on piles over a lake.

**lake·front** (lāk′frunt′) **1** land or land with buildings at the edge of a lake. **2** the part of a town or city next to a lake. **3** of or on a lakefront: *We have a lakefront cottage.*

**Lake·head** (lāk′hed′) the city of Thunder Bay, Ontario, and the surrounding region, on the northwest shore of Lake Superior. *n.*

**lake·side** (lāk′sīd′) beside a lake: *a lakeside cottage.* *adj.*

**lake trout** a large, grey trout of the lakes of North America: *The lake trout is an important food and game fish.*

**Lak·shmi** (luk′shmē) in Hinduism, the goddess of good fortune to whom the Festival of Lights is dedicated. *n.*

**la·ma** (lä′mə) a Buddhist priest or monk in Tibet and Mongolia. *n.*
☛ *Hom.* LLAMA (lä′mə).

**La·ma·ism** (lä′mə iz′əm) the religious system of the lamas in Tibet and Mongolia, a form of Buddhism. *n.*

**la·ma·ser·y** (lä′mə ser′ē) in Tibet and Mongolia, a building, or group of buildings, where lamas live, work, and worship. *n., pl.* **la·ma·ser·ies.**

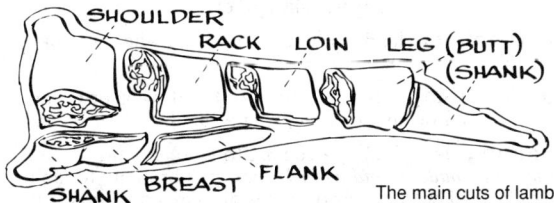
The main cuts of lamb

**lamb** (lam) **1** a young sheep. **2** the meat from a lamb: *roast lamb.* **3** lambskin. **4** give birth to a lamb or lambs. **5** a young, dear, or innocent person. *1–3, 5 n., 4 v.* —**lamb′like′**, *adj.*
**like a lamb, a** meekly; timidly. **b** easily fooled.

**lam·baste** (lam bāst′) *Informal.* **1** beat; thrash. **2** scold roughly. *v.*, **lam·bast·ed, lam·bast·ing.**

**lam·ben·cy** (lam′bən sē) a LAMBENT quality or condition. *n.*

**lam·bent** (lam′bənt) **1** moving lightly over a surface: *a lambent flame.* **2** playing lightly and brilliantly over a subject: *a lambent wit.* **3** softly bright: *Moonlight is lambent.* *adj.*

**lamb·kin** (lam′kin) **1** a little lamb. **2** a young or dear person. *n.*

**lamb·skin** (lam′skin′) **1** the skin of a lamb, especially with the wool on it. **2** leather made from the skin of a lamb. **3** parchment. *n.*

**lame** (lām) **1** not able to walk properly; having an injured leg or foot; crippled. **2** stiff and sore: *Her arm is lame from playing ball.* **3** make lame; cripple: *The accident lamed him for life.* **4** become lame; go lame. **5** poor; weak; unsatisfactory: *Sleeping too long is a lame excuse for being late.* *1, 2, 5 adj.,* **lam·er, lam·est;** *3, 4 v.,* **lamed, lam·ing.** —**lame′ly**, *adv.* —**lame′ness**, *n.*

**la·mé** (la mā′) a rich fabric made, wholly or partly, of metallic threads. *n.*

**lame duck** *Informal.* a disabled or helpless person or thing; someone unable or unwilling to perform a duty.

**la·mel·la** (lə mel′ə) a thin plate, scale, or layer,

especially of flesh or bone. *n., pl.* **la·mel·lae** (-lē *or* -lī) or **la·mel·las.**

**la·mel·lar** (lə mel′ər) having, consisting of, or arranged in LAMELLAE. *adj.*

**la·ment** (lə ment′) **1** feel or show grief for; mourn for: *to lament the dead.* **2** feel or show grief; weep. **3** an expression of grief; wail. **4** a poem, song, or tune that expresses grief. **5** regret: *We lamented his absence.* **6** a regret. *1, 2, 5 v., 3, 4, 6 n.* —**la·ment′er**, *n.* —**la·ment′ing·ly**, *adv.*

**lam·en·ta·ble** (lam′ən tə bəl) **1** to be regretted or pitied; giving cause for sorrow: *a lamentable accident. It was a lamentable day when our dog died.* **2** not so good; inferior: *The singer gave a lamentable performance.* *adj.* —**lam′en·ta·bly**, *adv.*

**lam·en·ta·tion** (lam′ən tā′shən) mourning; wailing; loud grief; cries of sorrow. *n.*

**lam·i·na** (lam′ə nə) **1** a thin plate, scale, or layer. **2** the flat, wide part of a leaf. *n., pl.* **lam·i·nae** (-nē′ *or* -nī′) or **lam·i·nas.**

**lam·i·nar** (lam′ə nər) having, consisting of, or arranged in thin layers, plates, or scales. *adj.*

**lam·i·nate** (lam′ə nāt′ *for verb,* lam′ə nāt′ *or* lam′ə nit *for adjective and noun*) **1** split into thin layers. **2** make by putting layer on layer: *Plywood is made by laminating thin sheets of wood.* **3** beat or roll metal into a thin plate. **4** cover with thin plates. **5** laminated; laminar. **6** a laminated plastic: *a bookcase of walnut-finished, high-pressure laminate on a core of hardwood.* *1–4 v.,* **lam·i·nat·ed, lam·i·nat·ing;** *5 adj., 6 n.*

**lam·i·na·tion** (lam′ə nā′shən) **1** the act of laminating. **2** being LAMINATEd. **3** a LAMINATEd structure; arrangement in thin layers. **4** a thin layer. *n.*

Lamps of ancient and modern times

**lamp** (lamp) **1** a device that provides artificial light: *a gas lamp, a street lamp, a floor lamp. An oil lamp holds oil and a wick by which the oil is burned.* **2** a similar device that gives heat: *a spirit lamp.* **3** a device for providing ultraviolet rays: *a sun lamp.* **4** an electric light bulb. *n.*

**lamp·black** (lamp′blak′) a fine black soot consisting of almost pure carbon that is deposited when oil, gas, etc. burn incompletely: *Lampblack is used as a colouring matter in paint and ink.* *n.*

**lamp·light** (lamp′līt′) the light from a lamp. *n.*

**lamp·light·er** (lamp′līt′ər) **1** a person who lights

**lampoon**    670    **landlubber**

street lamps. **2** a torch, twisted paper, etc. used to light lamps. *n.*

**lam·poon** (lam pün′) **1** a piece of writing that attacks and ridicules a person in a malicious or abusive way. **2** attack in a lampoon. **1** *n.*, **2** *v.* —**lam·poon′er**, *n.*

**lam·poon·ist** (lam pü′nist) a person who writes LAMPOONS. *n.*

**lamp·post** (lamp′pōst′) a post used to support a street lamp. *n.*

**lam·prey** (lam′prē *or* lam′prā) an eel-like fish having a large round mouth with horny teeth and no jaws: *Some species of lamprey attach themselves by their mouths to fish from which they suck body fluids.* *n.*, *pl.* **lam·preys.**

**LAN** local area network (def. 2).

**lance** (lans) **1** a long wooden spear with a sharp iron or steel head: *Knights used to carry lances.* **2** a soldier armed with a lance. **3** pierce with a lance. **4** any instrument like a soldier's lance. **5** LANCET. **6** cut open with a lancet: *The dentist lanced the gum so that the new tooth could come through.* **1, 2, 4, 5** *n.*, **3, 6** *v.*, **lanced, lanc·ing.**

**Lan·ce·lot** (lan′sə lot′) in the legends about King Arthur, the bravest of the knights of the Round Table: *Sir Lancelot was the lover of Queen Guinevere.* *n.*

**lanc·er** (lan′sər) a mounted soldier armed with a LANCE. *n.*

**lanc·ers** (lan′sərz) **1** a form of square dance. **2** the music for it. *n. pl.*

**lan·cet** (lan′sit) a small, sharp-pointed surgical knife, usually having two sharp edges: *Doctors use lancets for opening boils, abscesses, etc.* *n.*

**lance·wood** (lan′swūd′) **1** a tough, straight-grained, springy wood, used for fishing rods, cabinetwork, etc. **2** the tropical American tree that yields this wood. *n.*

**land** (land) **1** the solid part of the earth's surface: *dry land.* **2** ground, soil: *This is good land for a garden.* **3** ground used as property: *The farmer invested in land and machinery.* **4** a country; region: *mountainous land.* **5** the people of a country; nation: *Edith Fowke collected folk songs from all the land.* **6** come to land; bring to land: *The ship landed at the pier. The pilot landed the airplane in a field.* **7** put on land; set ashore: *The ship landed its passengers.* **8** go ashore: *The passengers landed.* **9** come to a stop; arrive: *The thief landed in jail. The car landed in the ditch.* **10** cause to arrive: *This boat will land you in London.* **11** *Informal.* catch; get: *to land a job, to land a fish.* **1–5** *n.*, **6–11** *v.*

**how the land lies,** what the state of affairs is.

An English landau of 1890

**lan·dau** (lan′do *or* lan′dou) **1** a four-wheeled carriage with two seats that face each other, and a top made in two parts that can be folded back. **2** an automobile with a similar top and seats. *n.*

**lan·dau·let** *or* **lan·dau·lette** (lan′də let′) **1** a small LANDAU (def. 1). **2** an automobile with a folding top. *n.*

**land breeze** a breeze blowing from the land toward the sea.

**land·ed** (lan′did) **1** owning land: *landed nobles.* **2** consisting of land: *Landed property is real estate.* **3** pt. and pp. of LAND. **1, 2** *adj.*, **3** *v.*

**landed immigrant** a person admitted to Canada as a settler and potential Canadian citizen.

**land·fall** (land′fol′) **1** a sighting of land. **2** the land sighted or reached after a voyage or flight: *The explorer's landfall was near the mouth of the St. Lawrence.* **3** an approach to land from the sea or air; landing. *n.*

**land·fill** (land′fil′) **1** the disposal of waste by burying it under a shallow layer of earth. **2** a place where waste is disposed of in this way. *n.*

**land·form** (land′fôrm′) the natural physical features of the land. *n.*

**land grant** a grant of land; a gift of land by the government for colleges, railways, etc.

**land·hold·er** (land′hōl′dər) a person who owns or occupies land. *n.*

**land·hold·ing** (land′hōl′ding) **1** that owns or occupies land. **2** an owning or occupying of land. **1** *adj.*, **2** *n.*

**land·ing** (lan′ding) **1** coming to land; coming ashore: *The army made a landing in France.* **2** bringing to land. **3** a place where persons or goods are landed from a ship, helicopter, etc.: *A wharf, dock, or pier is a landing for boats.* **4** a platform at the top of a flight of stairs. See BALUSTRADE for picture. **5** ppr. of LAND. **1–4** *n.*, **5** *v.*

**landing craft** any of various kinds of boats or ships used for landing troops or equipment on a shore, especially during an assault.

**landing field** a field large enough and smooth enough for aircraft to land on and take off from safely.

**landing gear** the wheels, pontoons, etc. under an aircraft: *When on land or water, an aircraft rests on its landing gear.* See AIRPLANE for picture.

**landing net** a small net for landing fish.

**landing stage** a floating platform used for loading and unloading people and goods.

**landing strip** a runway, often unpaved or temporary, for aircraft to take off from and land on.

**land·la·dy** (land′lā′dē) **1** a woman who owns buildings or land that she rents to others. **2** a woman who keeps a boarding house, lodging house, or inn. *n.*, *pl.* **land·la·dies.**

**land·less** (land′lis) without land; owning no land. *adj.*

**land·locked** (land′lokt′) **1** shut in, or nearly shut in, by land: *a landlocked harbour.* **2** living in waters shut off from the sea: *landlocked salmon.* *adj.*

**land·lord** (land′lôrd′) **1** a person who owns buildings or land that he rents to others. **2** the keeper of a boarding house, lodging house, or inn. *n.*

**land·lub·ber** (land′lub′ər) a person not used to being on ships; a person clumsy on ships. *n.*

**land·mark** (land′märk′) **1** something familiar or easily seen, used as a guide: *That tall tower makes a good landmark.* **2** an important fact or event; happening that stands out above others: *The inventions of the printing press, telephone, telegraph, and radio are landmarks in the history of communications.* **3** a stone or other object that marks the boundary of a piece of land. *n.*

**land mine** a container filled with explosives or chemicals, placed on the ground or lightly covered, and usually set off by the weight of vehicles or troops passing over it.

**land office** a government office that takes care of the business connected with public lands, and records sales, transfers, etc.

**Land of the Little Sticks** a region of stunted trees at the southern end of the Barren Ground in northern Canada.

**land·own·er** (land′ō′nər) one who owns land. *n.*

**land–poor** (land′pür′) **1** owning much land but needing ready money. **2** poor because of taxes, etc. on one's land. *adj.*

**land·scape** (land′skāp′ *or* lan′skāp′) **1** a view of scenery on land: *The two hills and the valley between them formed a beautiful landscape.* **2** a painting, etching, etc. showing such a view. **3** make land more pleasant to look at by arranging trees, shrubs, flowers, etc.: *The builder agreed to landscape the lot around the new house.* 1, 2 *n.*, 3 *v.*, **land·scaped, land·scap·ing.**

**landscape gardener** a person whose business is LANDSCAPE GARDENING.

**landscape gardening** an arrangement of trees, shrubs, flowers, and lawns to give a pleasing appearance to grounds, parks, etc.

**land·slide** (land′slīd′) **1** a sliding down of a mass of soil or rock on a steep slope. **2** a mass that slides down. **3** an overwhelming majority of votes for one political party or candidate. *n.*

**lands·man** (land′zmən) **1** a man who lives or works on land. **2** an inexperienced seaman. *n., pl.* **lands·men** (-zmən).

**land·ward** (land′wərd) toward the land. *adv., adj.*

**land·wards** (land′wərdz) LANDWARD. *adv.*

**land wind** a wind blowing from the land toward the sea.

**lane** (lān) **1** a narrow road or path, especially one between hedges, walls, or fences. **2** any narrow way: *The bride and groom walked down a lane formed by two lines of wedding guests. A highway is often marked off in lanes for separate lines of traffic.* **3** an alley between buildings. **4** a course or route used by ships or aircraft going in the same direction. **5** one of the narrow alleys on a track, marked by chalked lines, especially one in which a runner must stay during a race. **6** BOWLING ALLEY (def. 1). *n.*
☞ *Hom.* LAIN.

**lang.** language.

**lang syne** (lang′ sīn′ *or* lang′ zīn′) *Scottish.* long since; long ago.

**lan·guage** (lang′gwij) **1** human speech, spoken or written. **2** the distinct form of speech common to a people, nation, or group of peoples: *the French language.* **3** a form, style, or kind of speech or writing: *bad language, Shakespeare's language, the language of chemistry.* **4** the wording or words: *The lawyer explained the language of the contract to us.* **5** the expression of thoughts or feelings

---

**landmark** 671 **lantern**

hat, āge, fär; let, ēqual, tėrm; it, īce
hot, ōpen, ôrder; oil, out; cup, pùt, rüle
əbove, takən, pencəl, lemən, circəs
ch, child; ng, long; sh, ship
th, thin; ᴛʜ, then; zh, measure

---

otherwise than by words: *sign language. A dog's language is made up of barks, looks, and actions.* **6** a computer language such as COBOL or FORTRAN. *n.*
☞ *Etym.* See note at LINGUAL.

**language arts** a group of school subjects directly concerned with the study of language; especially, speaking, listening, reading, and writing.

**language laboratory** a room in a school, college, or university equipped with machines, usually tape-recorders, that enable students to practise speaking and listening to a language they are studying.

**lan·guid** (lang′gwid) **1** drooping; weak; weary; without energy: *A hot, sticky day makes a person feel languid.* **2** without interest or enthusiasm; indifferent: *She made a languid response to my suggestion.* **3** sluggish; dull; not brisk or lively. *adj.* —**lan′guid·ly,** *adv.*
—**lan′guid·ness,** *n.*

**lan·guish** (lang′gwish) **1** become weak or weary; lose energy; droop: *The flowers languished from lack of water.* **2** suffer for a long period under unfavourable conditions: *languish in poverty. Wild animals often languish in captivity.* **3** grow dull, slack, or less intense: *His vigilance never languished.* **4** long or pine for: *She languished for home.* **5** assume a soft, tender look for effect. *v.*
—**lan′guish·er,** *n.*

**lan·guish·ing** (lang′gwi shing) **1** drooping; pining; longing. **2** tender; sentimental; loving. **3** lasting; lingering. **4** ppr. of LANGUISH. 1–3 *adj.*, 4 *v.*
—**lan′guish·ing·ly,** *adv.*

**lan·guish·ment** (lang′gwi shmənt) **1** LANGUISHing; a drooping, pining condition. **2** a LANGUISHing look or manner. *n.*

**lan·guor** (lang′gər) **1** a lack of energy; weakness; weariness: *A long illness causes languor.* **2** a lack of interest or enthusiasm; indifference. **3** softness or tenderness of mood. **4** quietness; stillness: *the languor of a summer afternoon.* **5** lack of activity; sluggishness. *n.*

**lan·guor·ous** (lang′gə rəs) **1** LANGUID. **2** causing LANGUOR. *adj.* —**lan′guor·ous·ly,** *adv.*

**lan·gur** (lung gür′) a large, long-tailed, slender monkey of southern Asia. *n.*

**lan·iard** (lan′yərd) See LANYARD. *n.*

**lank** (langk) **1** long and thin; slender: *a lank boy.* **2** straight and flat; not curly or wavy: *lank hair.* *adj.*
—**lank′ly,** *adv.* —**lank′ness,** *n.*

**lank·i·ly** (lang′kə lē) in a LANKY condition or form. *adv.*

**lank·y** (lang′kē) awkwardly long and thin; tall and ungainly. *adj.,* **lank·i·er, lank·i·est.** —**lank′i·ness,** *n.*

**lan·o·lin** (lan′ə lin) fat or grease obtained from wool, used in ointments. *n.* Also, **lanoline.**

**lan·o·line** (lan′ə lin *or* lan′ə lēn′) LANOLIN. *n.*

**lan·tern** (lan′tərn) a case to protect a light from wind, rain, etc.: *A lantern has sides of glass or some other material through which the light can shine.* *n.*

**lan·than·ide** (lan'thə nīd')   having to do with the series of rare-earth elements.   *adj.*

**lan·tha·num** (lan'thə nəm)   a rare metallic element. *Symbol*: La   *n.*

**lan·yard** (lan'yərd)   a short rope or cord used on ships to fasten rigging: *Sailors sometimes use a lanyard to hang a knife around their necks.*   *n.* Also, **laniard**.

**Lao Tzu** (lou'dzu')   in Taoism, the greatest of the ancient masters, widely worshipped and considered to be the author of the Tao Te Ching.   *n.*

**lap¹** (lap)   **1** the front part from the waist to the knees of a person sitting down: *Mother holds the baby on her lap.* **2** the place where anything rests or is cared for: *the lap of the gods.*   **3** a loosely hanging edge of clothing; flap.   *n.* **in the lap of luxury,**   in luxurious circumstances.
☛ *Hom.* LAPP.

**lap²** (lap)   **1** place or be placed together, one partly over or beside another; overlap: *We lapped shingles on the roof.* **2** a lapping over.   **3** the amount of lapping over.   **4** the part that laps over.   **5** extend out beyond a limit: *The reign of Queen Elizabeth I (from 1558 to 1603) lapped over into the 17th century.*   **6** wind or wrap around; fold over or about: *He lapped the blanket around him.*   **7** enwrap; wrap up in: *He lapped himself in a warm, dry blanket.* **8** surround; envelop: *The young heiress was lapped in luxury.*   **9** one time around a race track.   **10** in a race, get a lap or more ahead of other racers.   **11** a part of any course travelled: *The last lap of our all-day hike was the toughest.*   1, 5–8, 10 *v.*, **lapped, lap·ping;**   2–4, 9, 11 *n.*
☛ *Hom.* LAPP.

**lap³** (lap)   **1** drink by lifting up with the tongue: *Cats and dogs lap water.*   **2** move or beat gently with a lapping sound; splash gently: *Little waves lapped against the boat.* **3** the act of lapping: *The cat took one lap of the sour milk and turned away.*   **4** the sound of lapping: *the lap of the waves against my boat.*   1, 2 *v.*, **lapped, lap·ping;**   3, 4 *n.* —**lap'per,** *n.*
**lap up,**   **a** drink by lapping.   **b** *Informal.*   consume or absorb eagerly: *The advanced students lapped up the new math course.*
☛ *Hom.* LAPP.

**lap dog**   a small pet dog.

**la·pel** (lə pel')   the part of the front of a coat that is folded back just below the collar.   *n.*

**lap·ful** (lap'fůl)   as much as a LAP¹ (def. 1) can hold. *n., pl.* **lap·fuls.**

**lap·i·dar·y** (lap'ə der'ē)   **1** a person who cuts, polishes, or engraves precious stones.   **2** having to do with cutting or engraving precious stones.   **3** engraved on stone. 1 *n., pl.* **lap·i·dar·ies;**   2, 3 *adj.*

**lap·in** (lap'ən)   **1** rabbit.   **2** rabbit fur.   *n.*

**lap·is laz·u·li** (lap'is laz'yü lē' *or* laz'yü lī')   **1** a deep-blue, opaque, semiprecious stone used for an ornament.   **2** deep blue.

**Lap·land·er** (lap'lan dər)   LAPP (def. 1).   *n.*

**Lapp** (lap)   **1** a member of a people having certain Mongoloid characteristics and living in Lapland, a region in northern Norway, Sweden, Finland, and northwestern Russia: *The Lapps are small and have short, broad heads.* **2** the language of the Lapps.   *n.*
☛ *Hom.* LAP.

**lap·pet** (lap'it)   **1** a small flap or fold.   **2** a loose fold of flesh or membrane.   **3** the lobe of the ear.   *n.*

**lap robe**   a blanket, fur robe, etc. used to keep the lap and legs warm when riding in an automobile, carriage, etc.

**lapse** (laps)   **1** a slight mistake or error: *A slip of the tongue, pen, or memory is a lapse.*   **2** make a slight mistake or error.   **3** a slipping or falling away from what is right: *a moral lapse.*   **4** slip or fall away from what is right.   **5** a slipping back; sinking down; slipping into a lower condition: *a lapse into savage ways.*   **6** slip back; sink down: *The house lapsed into ruin.*   **7** a slipping by; passing away: *A minute is a short lapse of time.*   **8** slip by; pass away: *The boy's interest in the story soon lapsed.* **9** the ending of a right or privilege because it was not renewed, not used, or otherwise neglected: *the lapse of a lease.*   **10** end in this way: *She allowed her driver's licence to lapse.*   1, 3, 5, 7, 9 *n.*, 2, 4, 6, 8, 10 *v.*, **lapsed, laps·ing.**

**lapse rate**   the rate at which temperature goes down as altitude increases.

**laptop computer**   a computer small enough to fit on a person's lap.

**lap·wing** (lap'wing')   a crested plover of Europe, Asia, and North Africa that has a slow, irregular flight and a peculiar wailing cry.   *n.*

**lar·board** (lär'bərd *or* lär'bôrd)   **1** the side of a ship to the left of a person looking from the stern toward the bow; port.   **2** on this side of a ship.   1 *n.*, 2 *adj.*

**lar·ce·nous** (lär'sə nəs)   **1** of or like LARCENY; characterized by larceny.   **2** thievish; guilty of LARCENY. *adj.*

**lar·ce·ny** (lär'sə nē)   theft.   *n., pl.* **lar·ce·nies.**

**larch** (lärch)   **1** any of a group of about ten closely related species of tree of the pine family found in the northern hemisphere, having small, upright cones and soft, flexible, needle-like leaves that are shed in the fall: *The three species of larch native to Canada are the tamarack, alpine larch, and western larch.*   **2** the hard wood of any of these trees.   *n.*

**lard** (lärd)   **1** the fat of pigs, melted down and made clear: *Lard is used in cooking.*   **2** insert strips of bacon or salt port in meat or poultry before cooking.   **3** put lard on or in; grease: *Lard the pan well.*   **4** give variety to; enrich: *to lard a long speech with stories.*   1 *n.*, 2–4 *v.*

**lar·der** (lär'dər)   **1** a pantry; place where food is kept. **2** a supply of food.   *n.*

**lar·es and pe·na·tes** (lä'rēz ənd pə nä'tēz)   **1** the household gods of the ancient Romans.   **2** the cherished possessions of a household.

**large** (lärj)   **1** of more than the usual size, amount, or number; big: *a large crowd, a large sum of money, a large animal. Canada is a large country.*   **2** of great scope or range; extensive; broad: *a man of large experience.*   **3** on a great scale: *a large employer of labour.*   *adj.*, **larg·er, larg·est.** —**large'ness,** *n.*

**at large,**   **a** at liberty; free: *Is the escaped prisoner still at*

large? **b** fully; in detail. **c** as a whole; altogether: *The people at large want peace.* **d** representing a whole area, business, group: *the firm's representative at large.*
**in large** or **in the large,** on a big scale.

**large–heart·ed** (lärj′här′tid) generous; liberal. *adj.*

**large intestine** the lower part of the intestines, between the small intestine and the anus. See ALIMENTARY CANAL for picture.

**large·ly** (lärj′lē) **1** to a great extent; mainly; for the most part: *This region consists largely of desert.* **2** in great quantity; much. *adv.*

**large–scale** (lärj′skāl′) **1** wide; extensive; involving many persons or things: *a large-scale disaster.* **2** made or drawn to a large SCALE³ (def. 4): *a large-scale map. adj.*

**lar·gesse** or **lar·gess** (lär′jis or lär jes′; French, lär zhes′) **1** generous giving. **2** a generous gift or gifts. *n.*

**larg·ish** (lär′jish) rather large. *adj.*

**lar·go** (lär′gō) in music: **1** slow and dignified; stately. **2** a slow, stately passage or piece of music. 1 *adj.*, 2 *n., pl.* **lar·gos.**

**lar·i·at** (lar′ē ət or ler′ē ət) **1** a long rope with a running noose at one end; lasso. **2** a rope for fastening horses, mules, etc. to a stake while they are grazing. *n.*
☛ *Etym.* From Spanish *la reata* 'the rope', originally the rope used to tie mules together.

**lark¹** (lärk) **1** a small songbird of Europe, Asia, and North Africa, having brown feathers and long hind claws: *One kind of lark, the skylark, sings while soaring in the air.* **2** any of several similar songbirds in America, such as the meadow lark or titlark. *n.*

**lark²** (lärk) *Informal.* **1** a merry or gay time; frolic: *What a lark we had at the picnic.* **2** have fun; play: *The boy was always larking.* 1 *n.,* 2 *v.*

**lark·spur** (lärk′spėr′) a plant whose flowers have a petal-like sepal shaped like a spur: *Larkspurs have clusters of blue, pink, or white flowers on tall stalks. n.*

**lar·ri·gan** (lar′ə gən or ler′ə gən) *Cdn.* an oiled leather moccasin. *n.*

**lar·va** (lär′və) **1** the early form of an insect from the time it leaves the egg until it becomes a pupa: *A caterpillar is the larva of a butterfly or moth. Maggots are the larvae of flies.* See METAMORPHOSIS for picture. **2** a young form of certain animals that is different in structure from the adult form: *A tadpole is the larva of a frog or toad. n., pl.* **lar·vae.**

**lar·vae** (lär′vē, lär′vī, or lär′və) pl. of LARVA. *n.*

**lar·val** (lär′vəl) **1** of or having to do with LARVAE. **2** characteristic of LARVAE. **3** in the form of a LARVA. *adj.*

**la·ryn·ge·al** (lə rin′jē əl) **1** of or having to do with the LARYNX. **2** in or produced in the LARYNX. **3** used on the LARYNX. *adj.*

**lar·yn·gi·tis** (lar′ən jī′tis or ler′ən jī′tis) inflammation of the LARYNX: *A person with laryngitis finds it difficult and even painful to talk. n.*

**lar·ynx** (lar′ingks or ler′ingks) **1** the cavity at the upper end of the human windpipe, containing the vocal cords and acting as a speech organ. See WINDPIPE for picture. **2** a similar organ in other mammals, or a corresponding structure in other animals. *n., pl.* **la·ryn·ges** (lə rin′jēz) or **lar·ynx·es.**

**la·sa·gna** (lə zä′nyə) a dish consisting of broad, flat,

hat, āge, fär; let, ēqual, tėrm; it, īce
hot, ōpen, ôrder; oil, out; cup, rüle
ə*bove, ta*kən, penc*ə*l, lem*ə*n, circ*ə*s
ch, child; ng, long; sh, ship
th, thin; ᴛʜ, then; zh, measure

pre-cooked noodles baked in layers with a sauce of ground meat, cheese, and tomatoes. *n.*

**las·car** (las′kər) a native sailor of the East Indies. *n.*

**las·civ·i·ous** (lə siv′ē əs) **1** feeling lust. **2** showing lust. **3** causing lust. *adj.* —**las·civ′i·ous·ly,** *adv.* —**las·civ′i·ous·ness,** *n.*

**la·ser** (lā′zər) a device for amplifying light waves, producing an intense, narrow beam of light: *Laser beams can cut through metal and have many potential uses in surgery, communications, etc. n.*
☛ *Etym.* From the first letters of *l*ight *a*mplification by *s*timulated *e*mission of *r*adiation.

**lash¹** (lash) **1** a whip, especially the rope, thong, etc. that is attached to the handle. **2** a stroke or blow with a whip, thong, etc. **3** beat or drive with a whip, etc.: *The driver of the team lashed her horses on.* **4** a sudden, swift movement. **5** wave or beat back and forth: *The lion lashed its tail. The wind lashes the sails.* **6** pour; rush violently: *The rain lashed against the windows.* **7** anything that hurts as a blow from a whip does. **8** strike violently; hit: *The horse lashed at him with its hoofs.* **9** attack severely with words; scold sharply: *The captain lashed the crew with his tongue.* **10** the hair on the edge of an eyelid; eyelash. 1, 2, 4, 7, 10 *n.*, 3, 5, 6, 8, 9 *v.* —**lash′er,** *n.*
**lash out, a** hit out; attack; strike. **b** attack severely in words; scold vigorously. **c** be lavish in giving or spending: *He really lashed out with his praise. She lashed out on the wedding.*

**lash²** (lash) tie or fasten with a rope, cord, etc.: *We lashed logs together to make a raft. v.*

**lash·ing¹** (lash′ing) **1** a whipping, especially as a punishment. **2** a severe attack in words; sharp scolding. **3 lashings,** *pl.* abundance; great plenty. **4** ppr. of LASH¹. 1–3 *n.*, 4 *v.*

**lash·ing²** (lash′ing) **1** rope, cord, etc. used in tying or fastening. **2** ppr. of LASH². 1 *n.*, 2 *v.*

**lass** (las) **1** a girl or young woman. **2** sweetheart. *n.*

**las·sie** (las′ē) **1** a young girl; lass. **2** sweetheart. *n.*

**las·si·tude** (las′ə tyüd′ or las′ə tüd′) lack of energy; weakness; weariness. *n.*

**las·so** (la sü′ or las′ü) **1** a long rope with a running noose at one end; lariat: *The cowboy threw a lasso over the steer's head and pulled the animal to the ground.* **2** catch with a lasso. 1 *n., pl.* **las·sos** or **las·soes;** 2 *v.,* **las·soed, las·so·ing.**

**last¹** (last) **1** coming after all others; being at the end; final: *the last page of the book.* **2** after all others; at the end; finally: *He arrived last.* **3** next before a specified point of time: *last night, last week, last year.* **4** on the latest or most recent occasion: *When did you last see him?* **5** previous; the one before this one: *The last movie we saw was much better than this western.* **6** most unlikely; least suitable: *That is the last thing one would expect.* **7** very great; extreme: *a paper of last importance.* **8** that remains: *Zoltan spent his last dollar.* **9** a person or thing

**last**      674      **latish**

that comes after all others: *She was the last in the line.* **10** the end: *You have not heard the last of this.* 1, 3, 5–8 *adj.*, 2, 4 *adv.*, 9, 10 *n.*
**at last,** at the end; after a long time; finally: *So you have come home at last.*
**breathe one's last,** die.
**see the last of,** not see again.

**last²** (last) **1** go on; hold out; continue to be; endure: *The storm lasted three days.* **2** continue in good condition, force, etc.: *I hope these shoes last a year.* *v.*

**last³** (last) **1** a block shaped like a person's foot, on which shoes and boots are formed or repaired. **2** form shoes and boots on a last. 1 *n.*, 2 *v.*
**stick to one's last,** pay attention to one's own work; mind one's own business.

**last·ing** (las′ting) **1** that lasts a long time; that lasts; that will last; permanent; durable: *The experience had a lasting effect on her.* **2** ppr. of LAST². 1 *adj.*, 2 *v.* —**last′ing·ly,** *adv.*

**last·ly** (las′tlē) finally; in conclusion: *Lastly, I want to thank all of you for your help.* *adv.*

**last name** surname; family name.

**last post** in the armed forces, the bugle call that gives the hour of retiring. It is sounded also at military funerals, Remembrance Day ceremonies, etc.

**last quarter** the period between second half moon and new moon; the phase of the moon represented by the half moon after full moon. See MOON for picture.

**last sleep** death.

**last straw** the last of a series of troublesome things that finally causes a collapse, outburst, etc.

**last word** **1** the last thing said. **2** *Informal.* the latest thing; the most up-to-date style. **3** *Informal.* something that cannot be improved.

**lat.** latitude.

A latch on a door

**latch** (lach) **1** a catch for fastening a door, gate, or window: *A latch consists of a movable piece of metal or wood that fits into a notch, opening, etc.* **2** fasten with a latch: *Latch the door.* 1 *n.*, 2 *v.*
**latch on,** *Informal.* understand.
**latch onto,** **a** seize. **b** get. **c** understand. **d** stick closely to a person or group of people.
**on the latch,** not locked; fastened only with a latch.

**latch·key** (lach′kē′) a key used to unfasten the latch on a door from the outside. *n.*

**latch·string** (lach′string′) a string used to unfasten the latch of a door. *n.*

**late** (lāt) **1** happening, coming, etc. after the usual or proper time: *We had a late dinner last night.* **2** after the usual or proper time: *She worked late.* **3** happening, coming, etc. at an advanced time: *success late in life.* **4** at an advanced time: *It rained late in the afternoon.* **5** recent: *The late storm did much harm.* **6** recently dead: *The late Harvey Todd was a fine man.* **7** gone out of or retired from office: *The late prime minister is still working actively.* **8** recently. **9** recently but no longer: *John Smith, late of Boston.* 1, 3, 5–7 *adj.*, **lat·er** or **lat·ter,** **lat·est** or **last;** 2, 4, 8, 9 *adv.*, **lat·er, lat·est** or **last.** —**late′ness,** *n.*
**of late,** lately; recently: *I haven't seen her of late.*

**la·teen** (la tēn′) having a LATEEN SAIL. *adj.*

**la·teen–rigged** (la tēn′rigd′) having a LATEEN SAIL. *adj.*

**lateen sail** a triangular sail held up by a long yard on a short mast.

**late·ly** (lāt′lē) a short time ago; recently: *He has not been looking well lately.* *adv.*

**la·ten·cy** (lā′tən sē) the condition or quality of being LATENT. *n.*

**la·tent** (lā′tənt) present or available but not used or brought to light; undeveloped: *a latent talent. The power of a seed to grow into a plant remains latent if it is not planted.* *adj.* —**la′tent·ly,** *adv.*

**lat·er·al** (lat′ə rəl) **1** of the side; at the side; from the side; toward the side: *A lateral branch of a family is a branch not in the direct line of descent.* **2** a lateral part or outgrowth. 1 *adj.*, 2 *n.*

**lat·er·al·ly** (lat′ə rə lē) **1** in a lateral direction; at the side; sideways. **2** from a lateral branch. *adv.*

**lat·er·ite** (lat′ə rīt) a soil formed by the decomposition of rocks, red in colour because of its content of ferric hydroxide. *n.*

**la·tex** (lā′teks) **1** a milky liquid in certain plants, such as milkweed, poppies, and plants yielding rubber. **2** an emulsion of rubber or a plastic and water, used in paint, adhesives, etc. *n., pl.* **lat·i·ces** (lat′ə sēz′ *or* lā′tə sēz′) *or* **la·tex·es** (lā′tek siz).

**lathe** (lāᴛʜ) a machine for holding pieces of wood, metal, etc. and turning them against a cutting tool that shapes them. *n.*

**lath·er** (laᴛʜ′ər) **1** the foam made from soap or detergent mixed in water. **2** put lather on: *Emilio lathers his face before shaving.* **3** form a lather: *This soap lathers well.* **4** foam formed in sweating: *the lather on a horse after a race.* **5** become covered with such foam. **6** *Informal.* beat; flog. 1, 4 *n.*, 2, 3, 5, 6 *v.*

**Lat·in** (lat′ən) **1** the language of the ancient Romans, considered classical in the form used by the best writers during the 2nd and 1st centuries B.C. **2** of Latin; in Latin: *Latin poetry, Latin grammar, a Latin scholar.* **3** a member of any of the peoples whose languages came from Latin: *The Italians, French, Spanish, Portuguese, and Romanians are Latins.* **4** of these peoples or their languages. 1, 3 *n.*, 2, 4 *adj.*

**Latin America** South America, Central America, Mexico, and much of the West Indies.

**Lat·in–A·mer·i·can** (lat′ən ə mer′ə kən) **1** of or having to do with Latin America. **2** a native or inhabitant of Latin America. 1 *adj.*, 2 *n.*

**Latin cross** a cross in which the upright is longer than the crossbeam. See CROSS for picture.

**lat·ish** (lā′tish) rather late. *adj., adv.*

hat, āge, fär; let, ēqual, tėrm; it, īce
hot, ōpen, ôrder; oil, out; cup, put, rüle
ǝbove, takǝn, pencǝl, lemǝn, circǝs
ch, child; ng, long; sh, ship
th, thin; ᴛʜ, then; zh, measure

**lat·i·tude** (lat′ǝ tyüd′ *or* lat′ǝ tüd′) **1** the distance north or south of the equator, measured in degrees: *On maps, lines parallel to the equator represent latitudes.* **2** a place or region having a certain latitude: *Polar bears live in the cold latitudes.* **3** room to act or think; scope; freedom from narrow rules: *An artist is allowed more latitude than a bricklayer.* *n.*

**lat·i·tu·di·nal** (lat′ǝ tyü′dǝ nǝl *or* lat′ǝ tü′dǝ nǝl) of or relating to LATITUDE. *adj.*

**la·trine** (lǝ trēn′) a toilet in a camp, factory, etc.; privy. *n.*

**lat·ter** (lat′ǝr) **1** later; more recent; nearer the end: *Friday comes in the latter part of the week.* **2 the latter**, the second of two: *Canada and the United States are in North America; the former lies north of the latter.* **1** *adj.*, **2** *n.*

**lat·ter·ly** (lat′ǝr lē) lately; recently. *adv.*

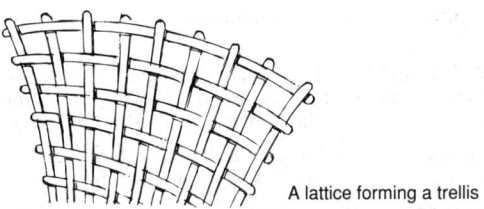

A lattice forming a trellis

**lat·tice** (lat′is) **1** a structure of crossed wooden or metal strips with open spaces between them. **2** a window, gate, etc. having a lattice. **3** form into a lattice; make like a lattice. **4** furnish with a lattice. **1, 2** *n.*, **3, 4** *v.*, **lat·ticed, lat·tic·ing.** —**lat′tice·like′**, *adj.*

**lat·tice·work** (lat′is wėrk′) a LATTICE (def. 1) or lattices. *n.*

**laud** (lod) **1** praise. **2** a song or hymn of praise. **1** *v.*, **1, 2** *n.*

**laud·a·bil·i·ty** (lod′ǝ bil′ǝ tē) praiseworthiness. *n.*

**laud·a·ble** (lod′ǝ bǝl) worthy of praise; commendable: *Unselfishness is laudable.* *adj.* —**laud′a·bly**, *adv.*

**lau·da·num** (lo′dǝ nǝm) a solution of opium in alcohol, used to lessen pain. *n.*

**lau·da·tion** (lo dā′shǝn) praise. *n.*

**laud·a·to·ry** (lod′ǝ tô′rē) expressing praise. *adj.*

**laugh** (laf) **1** make the sounds and movements of the face and body that show amusement or pleasure at humour or nonsense, etc.: *We all laughed at the joke.* **2** express with laughter: *to laugh a reply.* **3** drive, put, bring, etc. by or with laughing: *to laugh one's tears away.* **4** suggest the feeling of joy; be lively. **5** the act or sound of laughing: *a hearty laugh.* **1–4** *v.*, **5** *n.* —**laugh′er**, *n.*
**last laugh**, a victory: *When his old car won the race, Tom had the last laugh.*
**laugh at**, **a** make fun of; ridicule: *They laughed at me for believing in ghosts.* **b** disregard or make light of: *She laughed at danger.*
**laugh off**, pass off or dismiss with a laugh: *She laughed off my warning that the ice was not safe and walked to the middle of the pond.*
**laugh on the other side** or **wrong side of one's mouth**, *Informal.* be annoyed; be made sorry.
**laugh up one's sleeve**, laugh secretly or to oneself.

**laugh·a·ble** (laf′ǝ bǝl) such as to cause laughter; amusing: *a laughable mistake.* *adj.*
—**laugh′a·ble·ness**, *n.* —**laugh′a·bly**, *adv.*

**laugh·ing** (laf′ing) **1** that laughs or seems to laugh: *the laughing brook.* **2** accompanied by laughter. **3** laughter. **4** ppr. of LAUGH. **1, 2** *adj.*, **3** *n.*, **4** *v.*
—**laugh′ing·ly**, *adv.*
**no laughing matter**, a matter that is serious.

**laughing gas** NITROUS OXIDE, a colourless gas that makes one insensible to pain. This gas makes some people laugh and become excited.

**laughing jackass** KOOKABURRA.

**laugh·ing·stock** (laf′ing stok′) an object of ridicule; a person or thing that is made fun of. *n.*

**laugh·ter** (laf′tǝr) **1** the action of laughing. **2** a sound of laughing: *Laughter filled the room.* *n.*

**launch**[1] (lonch) **1** cause to slide into the water; set afloat: *A new ship is launched from the supports on which it has been built.* **2** the movement of a boat or ship from the land into the water. **3** push out or put forth on the water or into the air: *to launch a plane from an aircraft carrier.* **4** start; set going; set out: *His friends launched him in business by lending him money. He used the money to launch into a new business.* **5** throw; hurl; send out: *launch a rocket or missile. An angry person launches threats against enemies. A bow launches arrows into the air.* **6** the act of launching a rocket, ship, aircraft, etc.: *We watched the space launch on TV.* **7** burst; plunge: *The rebel launched into a violent attack on the government.* **1, 3–5, 7** *v.*, **2, 6** *n.* —**launch′er**, *n.*
**launch out**, begin; start.

**launch**[2] (lonch) **1** a motorboat used for pleasure trips. **2** the largest boat carried by a warship. *n.*

**launching pad** a surface or platform on which a rocket or a missile is prepared for launching and from which it is shot into the air.

**laun·der** (lon′dǝr) **1** wash and iron clothes, linens, etc. **2** be able to be washed; stand washing: *Cotton materials usually launder well.* *v.* —**laun′der·er**, *n.*

**laun·dress** (lon′dris) a woman whose work is washing and ironing clothes, linens, etc. *n.*

**laun·dro·mat** (lon′drǝ mat′) a self-service laundry having automatic washing machines and dryers, especially one having coin-operated machines. *n.*

**laun·dry** (lon′drē) **1** a room or building where clothes, linens, etc. are washed and ironed. **2** clothes, etc. washed or to be washed. **3** the washing and ironing of clothes, etc. *n., pl.* **laun·dries.**

**laun·dry·man** (lon′drē mǝn) **1** a man who works in a

**laun·dry.** 2 a man who collects and delivers laundry. *n., pl.* **laun·dry·men** (-mən).

**laun·dry·wom·an** (lon′drē wům′ən) LAUNDRESS. *n., pl.* **laun·dry·wom·en** (-wim′ən).

**lau·re·ate** (lô′rē it) **1** crowned with a laurel wreath as a mark of honour. **2** honoured; distinguished. **3** POET LAUREATE. 1, 2 *adj.*, 3 *n.*

**lau·re·ate·ship** (lô′rē it ship′) **1** the position of POET LAUREATE. **2** the time during which a poet is POET LAUREATE. *n.*

**lau·rel** (lô′rəl) **1** a large evergreen shrub or small tree native to southern Europe and northern Africa, having stiff, glossy, dark-green leaves: *The ancient Greeks wove laurel leaves into wreaths to crown victors and heroes.* **2** the foliage of the laurel: *wreaths of laurel.* **3** any of a closely related group of evergreen trees and shrubs including the European laurel. **4** referring to a family of evergreen shrubs and trees found mainly in tropical and subtropical regions: *The laurel family includes the laurels, cinnamon, avocado, etc.* **5 laurels,** *pl.* **a** a wreath of laurel for a crown. **b** honour, fame, or victory: *The laurels went to a young athlete who had not competed before.* *n.*
**look to one's laurels,** guard one's reputation or record from rivals.
**rest on one's laurels,** be satisfied with the honours that one has already won.

**lau·relled** or **lau·reled** (lô′rəld) **1** crowned with a laurel wreath. **2** honoured. *adj.*

**Lau·ren·tian** (lô ren′shən) of or having to do with the St. Lawrence River and neighbouring lands. *adj.*

**Laurentian Shield** the CANADIAN SHIELD.

**la·va** (lav′ə *or* lä′və) **1** the molten rock flowing from a volcano or fissure in the earth. **2** the rock formed by the cooling of this molten rock: *Some lavas, such as obsidian, are hard and glassy; others are light and porous.* *n.*

**lav·a·liere, lav·a·lier,** or **lav·al·ière** (lav′ə lēr′; *French,* lä vä lyeʀ′) an ornament hanging from a small chain, worn around the neck by women. *n.*

**lav·a·to·ry** (lav′ə trē *or* lav′ə tô′rē) **1** a room where a person can wash his or her hands and face. **2** a bowl or basin to wash in. **3** a toilet or washroom. *n., pl.* **lav·a·to·ries.**

**lav·en·der** (lav′ən dər) **1** pale purple. **2** a small shrub with spikes of fragrant pale-purple flowers yielding an oil much used in perfumes. **3** the dried flowers, leaves, and stalks of the lavender plant, used to perfume linens, clothes, etc. 1–3 *n.*, 1 *adj.*

**lav·ish** (lav′ish) **1** very free or too free in giving or spending; prodigal: *A very rich person can be lavish with money.* **2** very abundant; more than enough; given or spent too freely: *many lavish gifts.* **3** give or spend very freely or too freely: *It is a mistake to lavish kindness on ungrateful people.* 1, 2 *adj.*, 3 *v.* —**lav′ish·er,** *n.* —**lav′ish·ly,** *adv.* —**lav′ish·ness,** *n.*

**law** (lo) **1** a body of rules recognized by a country, state, province, municipality, or community as binding on its members: *international law. English law is different from French law.* **2** one of these rules: *a law against slavery. Good citizens obey the laws.* **3** the controlling influence of these rules, or the condition of society brought about by their observance: *to maintain law and order.* **4** law as a system: *courts of law.* **5** the department of knowledge or study concerned with these rules; jurisprudence: *to study law.* **6** a body of such rules concerned with a particular subject or derived from a particular source: *commercial law, criminal law.* **7** the legal profession: *to enter the law.* **8** legal action. **9** any act passed upon by the highest legislative body of a province, state, or nation: *a federal law.* **10** any rule or principle that must be obeyed: *the laws of hospitality, a law of grammar, the law of a game.* **11** legal authorities. **12** *Informal.* a police officer or detective. **13** a statement of a relation or sequence of phenomena invariable under the same conditions: *the law of gravitation, Mendel's law, Ohm's law.* **14** a divine rule or commandment. **15** a mathematical rule on which the construction of a curve, a series, etc. depends. *n.*
**go to law,** appeal to law courts; take legal action.
**lay down the law, a** give orders that must be obeyed. **b** give a scolding.
**read law,** study to be a lawyer.
**take the law into one's own hands,** take steps to gain one's rights or avenge a wrong without going to court.

**law-a·bid·ing** (lo′ə bī′ding) obedient to the law; peaceful and orderly: *Law-abiding citizens obey traffic regulations.* *adj.*

**law·break·er** (lob′rā′kər) a person who breaks the law. *n.*

**law·break·ing** (lob′rā′king) a breaking of the law. *n.*

**law court** a place where justice is administered; court of law.

**law·ful** (lof′əl) **1** according to law; done as the law directs: *lawful arrest.* **2** allowed by law; rightful: *lawful demands.* *adj.* —**law′ful·ly,** *adv.* —**law′ful·ness,** *n.*

**law·giv·er** (log′iv′ər) a person who prepares and puts into effect a system of laws for a people; lawmaker. *n.*

**law·less** (lol′is) **1** paying no attention to the law; breaking the law: *A thief leads a lawless life.* **2** hard to control; unruly: *a lawless mob.* **3** having no laws: *a lawless frontier town.* *adj.* —**law′less·ly,** *adv.* —**law′less·ness,** *n.*

**law·mak·er** (lom′ā′kər) a person who helps to make laws; a member of a legislature, parliament or congress; legislator. *n.*

**law·mak·ing** (lom′ā′king) **1** having the duty and power of making laws; legislative. **2** the making of laws; legislation. 1 *adj.*, 2 *n.*

**lawn**¹ (lon) land covered with grass kept closely cut, especially near or around a house or for recreational purposes. *n.*

**lawn**² (lon) a fine, sheer linen or cotton cloth. *n.*

**lawn bowling** a game played on a bowling green with a lopsided or unsymmetrically weighted wooden ball that is rolled toward a small, white target ball (the jack) that is stationary; bowls.

**lawn mower** a machine with revolving blades for cutting the grass on a lawn.

**lawn tennis** an outdoor game in which a ball is hit back and forth over a low net.

**law·ren·ci·um** (lô ren′sē əm) an artificial radio-active element. *Symbol:* Lr *n.*

**law·suit** (los′üt′) a case in a law court; an application to a court for justice: *Injustices are often remedied by lawsuits.* *n.*

**law·yer** (lo′yər *or* loi′ər)   a person whose profession is giving advice about the laws or acting for others in a law court.   *n.*

**lax** (laks)   **1** not firm or tight; slack: *The package was tied so loosely that the cord was lax.*   **2** not strict; careless: *lax behaviour. Don't let yourself become lax about doing your homework.*   **3** not exact; vague.   *adj.*   —**lax′ly**, *adv.* —**lax′ness**, *n.*

**lax·a·tive** (lak′sə tiv)   **1** a medicine that makes the bowels move.   **2** making the bowels move.   **1** *n.*, **2** *adj.*

**lax·i·ty** (lak′sə tē)   a lax condition or quality; slackness.   *n.*

**lay**¹ (lā)   **1** bring down, beat down: *A storm laid the crops low. A shower has laid the dust.*   **2** put down; place in a certain position: *Lay your hat on the table.*   **3** smooth down: *to lay the nap of cloth.*   **4** place in a lying-down position or a position of rest: *Lay the baby down gently.*   **5** place; put; set: *She lays great emphasis on good manners. The scene of the story is laid in Montreal. Lay aside the book for me. The mare laid her ears back.*   **6** place in proper position or in orderly fashion: *to lay bricks.*   **7** devise; arrange: *to lay plans.*   **8** put down as a bet; wager: *I lay five dollars that he comes.*   **9** make quiet or make disappear: *to lay a ghost.*   **10** impose a burden, penalty, etc.: *to lay a tax on property.*   **11** present; bring forward: *to lay claim to an estate.*   **12** impute; attribute: *The theft was laid to him.*   **13** produce an egg or eggs from the body: *Birds, fish, and reptiles lay eggs.*   **14** of hens, produce an egg or eggs: *All the hens are laying well. That hen hasn't laid yet this morning.*   **15** apply oneself vigorously: *The men laid to their oars.*   **16** the way or position in which a thing is laid or lies: *the lay of the ground.*   1–15 *v.*, **laid, lay·ing;**   16 *n.*
**lay about,**   hit out on all sides.
**lay aside, away,** *or* **by,**   **a** put away for future use; save: *I laid away five dollars a week toward buying a bicycle.*   **b** put away; put on one side.
**lay down,**   **a** declare; state: *The umpire laid down the conditions for settling the dispute.*   **b** give; sacrifice: *lay down one's life for the cause of freedom.*   **c** begin building: *We shall have to lay down a new floor.*   **d** store away for future use.   **e** bet.
**lay for,** *Informal.*   lie in wait for.
**lay in,**   provide; save; put aside for the future: *The trapper laid in enough supplies for the winter.*
**lay into,** *Informal.*   beat, thrash: *She laid into the vicious dog with a stick.*
**lay off,**   put aside.
**lay on,**   **a** apply.   **b** supply.   **c** strike; inflict.
**lay oneself out,** *Informal.*   make a big effort; take great pains: *Carlo laid himself out to be agreeable.*
**lay out,**   **a** spread out: *Supper was laid out on the table.*   **b** prepare a dead body for burial.   **c** arrange; plan: *to lay out a program.*   **d** mark off: *They laid out a tennis court.*   **e** spend: *They laid out two thousand dollars in repairs.*   **f** *Informal.*   make someone lose consciousness.
**lay to,**   **a** blame on; accuse of: *He lays his failure in business to the high cost of labour.*   **b** of ships, head into the wind and stand still.
**lay up,**   **a** put away for future use; save.   **b** cause to stay in bed or indoors because of illness or injury: *She was laid up with flu for a week.*   **c** put a ship in dock.
☛ *Usage.* Although the past tenses of **lay**¹ and LIE² are often confused, in standard English the two verbs are always kept distinct: **lie, lay, lain** and **lay, laid, laid.** *Lie* does not take an object: *He lay down for a rest. The village lies in a valley.* *Lay* always takes an object: *We laid a new floor in the kitchen. Lay the book on the table.*
☛ *Hom.* LEI.

---

**lawyer**   677   **l.c.**

hat, āge, fär; let, ēqual, tėrm; it, īce
hot, ōpen, ôrder; oil, out; cup, pút, rüle
əbove, takən, pencəl, lemən, circəs
ch, child; ng, long; sh, ship
th, thin; ŦH, then; zh, measure

**lay**² (lā)   pt. of LIE²: *After a long walk, I lay down for a rest.*   *v.*
☛ *Hom.* LEI.

**lay**³ (lā)   **1** of ordinary people; not of the clergy: *A lay sermon is one preached by a person who is not a clergyman.*   **2** of ordinary people; not of lawyers, doctors, or those learned in the profession in question: *The lay mind understands little of the causes of disease.*   *adj.*
☛ *Hom.* LEI.

**lay**⁴ (lā)   **1** a short poem to be sung; poem.   **2** a song; tune: *The blackbird whistles its lay.*   *n.*
☛ *Hom.* LEI.

**lay·er** (lā′ər)   **1** one thickness or fold: *A cake is often made of two or more layers put together.*   **2** one that lays: *That hen is a champion layer.*   *n.*

**lay·ette** (lā et′)   a set of clothes, bedding, etc. for a newborn baby.   *n.*

**lay·man** (lā′mən)   **1** a member of the church who is not a clergyman: *The priest and several laymen planned the church budget.*   **2** a person who is not a member of a particular profession: *It is hard for most laymen to understand doctors' prescriptions.*   *n., pl.* **lay·men** (-mən).

**lay·off** (lā′of′)   **1** a temporary dismissal of workers: *Because of a shortage of steel, there was a layoff at the plant.*   **2** the time during which such a dismissal lasts.   *n.*

**lay of the land**   **1** the nature of the place; the position of hills, water, woods, etc.: *Spies were sent out to find out the lay of the land.*   **2** the existing situation; condition of things.

**lay·out** (lā′out′)   **1** the act of laying out.   **2** an arrangement; plan: *This map shows the layout of the camp.*   **3** a plan or design for an advertisement, book, etc.   **4** a thing laid or spread out; display.   **5** an outfit; supply; set.   *n.*

**lay·o·ver** (lā′ō′vər)   a stopping for a time in a place.   *n.*

**laz·a·ret** *or* **laz·a·rette** (laz′ə ret′)   LAZARETTO.   *n.*

**laz·a·ret·to** (laz′ə ret′ō)   **1** a hospital for people having contagious or loathsome diseases; a pesthouse.   **2** a building or ship used for quarantine purposes.   **3** a place in some merchant ships, near the stern, in which supplies are kept.   *n., pl.* **laz·a·ret·tos.**

**laze** (lāz)   be lazy or idle.   *v.*, **lazed, laz·ing.**

**la·zi·ness** (lā′zē nis)   dislike of work; unwillingness to work or be active; being lazy.   *n.*

**la·zy** (lā′zē)   **1** not willing to work or be active: *She was too lazy to get up to turn off the TV.*   **2** moving slowly; not very active: *a lazy stream.*   *adj.*, **la·zi·er, la·zi·est.** —**la′zi·ly**, *adv.*

**lb.**   pound; pounds.

**LB**   Labrador.

**lbs**   pounds.

**l.c.**   lower case; in small letters, not capital letters.

**L.C.** Lower Canada.

**LCD, L.C.D.,** or **l.c.d.** least (or lowest) common denominator.

**LCM, L.C.M.,** or **l.c.m.** least common multiple.

**lea** (lē) a grassy field; meadow; pasture. *n.*
☛ *Hom.* LEE.

**leach** (lēch) **1** run water, etc. through slowly; filter. **2** dissolve out by running water through slowly: *Potash is leached from wood ashes.* **3** dissolve out soluble parts from ashes, etc. by running water through slowly. **4** lose soluble parts when water passes through. **5** a container for use in leaching. 1–4 *v.*, 5 *n.*

**lead¹** (lēd) **1** show the way by going along with or in front of: *He led the horses to the water.* **2** be first among: *She leads the class in spelling.* **3** guidance or direction; example: *Many scientists followed the lead of her research.* **4** guide or direct in action, policy, opinion, etc.; influence; persuade: *Such actions lead us to distrust them.* **5** be a way or road: *Hard work leads to success.* **6** pass or spend time in some special way: *He leads a quiet life in the country.* **7** go first; begin a game or other activity: *You may lead this time.* **8** be chief of; command; direct: *A general leads an army. A woman led the singing.* **9** the place of leader; place in front: *She always takes the lead when we plan to do anything.* **10** the right to go or begin first: *It is your lead this time.* **11** the distance, number of points, etc. that one is ahead: *He had a lead of three metres at the halfway mark.* **12** the principal part in a play, film, etc. **13** the actor or actress who plays the principal part in a play or film. **14** a guiding indication; clue: *Bjorn was not sure where to look for the information, but the librarian gave him some good leads.* **15** the first paragraph in a news story. 1, 2, 4–8 *v.*, led, lead·ing; 3, 9–15 *n.*
**lead astray, a** give false information to. **b** encourage to do wrong.
**lead nowhere,** have no effect.
**lead off,** begin; start.
**lead on, a** influence. **b** deceive.
**lead up to,** prepare the way for.
☛ *Usage.* The past tense is spelled **led,** not **lead**: *We lead a quiet life* (present tense). *We led the horse home* (past tense).

**lead²** (led) **1** a soft, heavy, bluish-grey metal having a low melting point: *Lead is a chemical element.* Symbol: Pb **2** something made of this metal or one of its alloys. **3** made of lead: *lead pipe.* **4** a weight on a line used to find out the depth of water; plummet. **5** bullets; shot: *a hail of lead.* **6** a long, thin piece of graphite or other substance in or for a pencil. **7** in printing, a metal strip for widening the space between lines. **8** insert leads between the lines of print. **9** cover, frame, or weight with lead. **10 leads,** *pl.* **a** strips of lead used to cover roofs. **b** the frames of lead in which panes of glass are set. 1, 2, 4, 5–7, 10 *n.*, 3 *adj.*, 8, 9 *v.*
☛ *Hom.* LED.

**lead dog** (lēd) the dog that leads a dogsled team; leader.

**lead·en** (led′ən) **1** made of lead: *a leaden coffin.* **2** heavy; hard to lift or move: *The tired runner could hardly lift his leaden legs.* **3** oppressive: *leaden air.* **4** dull; gloomy: *We had become a bit leaden by the time our team scored.* **5** bluish-grey: *leaden clouds. adj.*

**lead·er** (lē′dər) **1** a person or thing that leads: *an orchestra leader.* **2** a person who is well fitted to lead. **3** the horse harnessed at the front of a team. **4** the dog that leads a dogsled team: *The leader was a powerful husky.* **5** an important or leading article or editorial in a newspaper, magazine, etc. **6** a short length of nylon, wire, etc. used to attach the lure to a fishing line. **7** an article offered at a low price to attract customers. **8 leaders,** *pl.* a row of dots or dashes to guide the eye across a printed page. *n.* —**lead′er·less,** *adj.*

**lead·er·ship** (lē′dər ship′) **1** the state or position of being a leader. **2** the ability to lead: *Leadership is a great asset to a politician. n.*

**lead–in** (lēd′in′) **1** a wire that runs from an antenna to a radio or television receiver or transmitter. **2** introduction: *a lengthy lead-in. n.*

**lead·ing** (lē′ding) **1** the act of one who or that which leads; guidance; direction. **2** guiding; directing. **3** most important; chief; principal: *the leading lady in a play.* **4** ppr. of LEAD¹. 1 *n.*, 2, 3 *adj.*, 4 *v.*

**leading article** (lē′ding) an EDITORIAL.

**leading question** (lē′ding) a question so worded that it suggests the answer desired.

**lead pencil** (led) an ordinary pencil having a graphite lead.

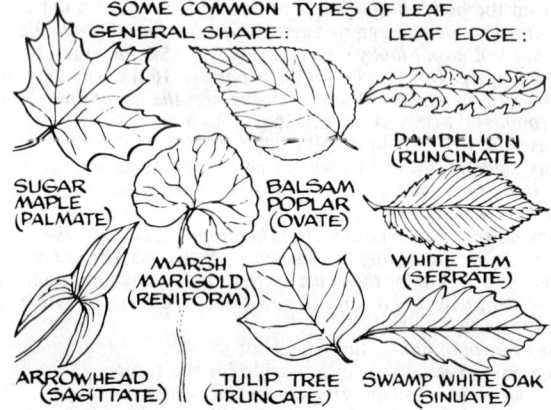

SOME COMMON TYPES OF LEAF
GENERAL SHAPE: SUGAR MAPLE (PALMATE), BALSAM POPLAR (OVATE), MARSH MARIGOLD (RENIFORM), ARROWHEAD (SAGITTATE), TULIP TREE (TRUNCATE)
LEAF EDGE: DANDELION (RUNCINATE), WHITE ELM (SERRATE), SWAMP WHITE OAK (SINUATE)

**leaf** (lēf) **1** one of the thin, flat, green parts that grow on the stem of a tree or other plant. **2** put forth leaves: *The trees along the river leaf earlier than those on the hill.* **3** a petal of a flower: *a rose leaf.* **4** a sheet of paper: *Each side of a leaf of a book is a page.* **5** turn the pages. **6** a very thin piece or sheet of metal, etc.: *gold leaf.* **7** the flat, movable piece of a table top. **8** the sliding, hinged, or movable part of a door, shutter, etc. 1, 3, 4, 6–8 *n.*, *pl.* **leaves;** 2, 5 *v.* —**leaf′like′,** *adj.*
**take a leaf from someone's book,** *Informal.* follow someone's example; copy someone's conduct.
**turn over a new leaf,** start all over again; try to do or be better in the future: *I promised to turn over a new leaf and study harder.*

**leaf·age** (lē′fij) leaves; foliage. *n.*

**leaf·i·ness** (lē′fē nis) a LEAFY condition. *n.*

**leaf·less** (lē′flis) having no leaves: *Maples, elms, and many other trees are leafless in winter. adj.*

**leaf·let** (lē′flit) **1** a small, flat or folded sheet of printed matter: *advertising leaflets.* **2** a small or young leaf. **3** one of the separate blades or divisions of a compound leaf. *n.*

**leaf·stalk** (lēf′stok′) the stalk by which a leaf is attached to a stem; PETIOLE. *n.*

**leaf·y** (lē′fē) **1** having many leaves; covered with leaves. **2** resembling a leaf: *We chose a fabric with a leafy design.* *adj.* **leaf·i·er, leaf·i·est.**

**league**[1] (lēg) **1** an association of persons, parties, or countries formed to help one another. **2** the persons, parties, or countries associated in a league. **3** associate in a league; form a league. **4** a group of teams which play a schedule of games against each other: *a hockey league, a bowling league.* 1, 2, 4 *n.,* 3 *v.,* **leagued, lea·guing.**
**in league,** united; in association: *They were in league against us. The suspected spies were thought to be in league with the enemy.*

**league**[2] (lēg) an old measure of distance, usually equal to about 5 km. *n.*

**League of Nations** an association of many countries, formed in 1919 and dissolved in April, 1946.

**lea·guer** (lē′gər) a member of a league. *n.*

**leak** (lēk) **1** a hole or crack, caused either by accident or by wear and tear, that lets something in or out: *a leak in a boat, a roof, a tire, etc.* **2** go in or out through a hole or crack. **3** let something in that should be kept out; let something out that should be kept in: *His boat leaks. Her teakettle leaks.* **4** let something pass in or out: *That pipe leaks gas.* **5** LEAKAGE. **6** a means of escape, loss, etc. **7** the escape or loss itself. **8** make or become known: *The secret leaked out. We think he leaked the story to some friends.* **9** come in or go out in a secret or stealthy way: *Spies somehow leaked into the city.* 1, 5–7 *n.,* 2–4, 8, 9 *v.*
☛ *Hom.* LEEK.

**leak·age** (lē′kij) **1** a leaking; entering or escaping through a leak. **2** that which leaks in or out. **3** the amount of leaking: *The leakage was estimated at 40 litres an hour.* *n.*

**leak·y** (lē′kē) leaking; having a leak or leaks. *adj.,* **leak·i·er, leak·i·est.** —**leak′i·ness,** *n.*

**lean**[1] (lēn) **1** stand slanting, not upright; bend: *A small tree leans over in the wind.* **2** rest in a sloping or slanting position: *Lean against me.* **3** set or put in a leaning position. **4** the act of leaning; inclination: *The old barn has more of a lean this year.* **5** depend; rely: *to lean on a friend's advice.* **6** tend or incline; show a preference (*used with* **to** *or* **toward**): *to lean toward mercy. Her favourite sport was tennis, but now she leans more to swimming.* 1–3, 5, 6 *v.,* **leaned** or **leant** (lent), **lean·ing;** 4 *n.*
**lean over backward,** *Informal.* be excessive in one direction so as to more than balance a tendency in the opposite direction.
☛ *Hom.* LIEN.

**lean**[2] (lēn) **1** with little or no fat: *a lean horse.* **2** meat having little fat. **3** producing little; scant: *a lean harvest, a lean diet.* 1, 3 *adj.,* 2 *n.* —**lean′ly,** *adv.* —**lean′ness,** *n.*
☛ *Hom.* LIEN.

**lean·ing** (lē′ning) **1** a tendency; inclination. **2** ppr. of LEAN[1]. 1 *n.,* 2 *v.*

**leant** (lent) a pt. and a pp. of LEAN[1]. *v.*

**leafstalk** 679 **learn**

hat, āge, fär; let, ēqual, tėrm; it, īce
hot, ōpen, ôrder; oil, out; cup, pùt, rüle
əbove, takən, pencəl, lemən, circəs
ch, child; ng, long; sh, ship
th, thin; ŦH, then; zh, measure

Lean-tos on the barn of a Quebec farm

**lean–to** (lēn′tü′) **1** a building attached to another, toward which its roof or supports slant. **2** having supports pitched against or leaning on an adjoining wall or building: *a lean-to roof.* **3** a crude shelter built or leaning against posts, trees, rock, etc.: *Hunters have a supply of wood in a lean-to here.* 1, 3 *n., pl.* **lean-tos;** 2 *adj.*

**leap** (lēp) **1** a jump or spring. **2** something to be jumped. **3** the distance covered by a jump. **4** jump: *A frog leaps.* **5** pass, come, rise, etc. as if with a leap or bound: *An idea leaped to her mind. A sudden breeze made the leaves leap.* **6** jump over: *to leap a fence.* 1–3 *n.,* 4–6 *v.,* **leaped** or **leapt** (lept), **leap·ing.**
**by leaps and bounds,** very fast and very much; swiftly.
**leap at,** *Informal.* take or accept with eagerness: *You should leap at such a chance.*
**leap in the dark,** an action taken without knowing what its results will be.

Girls playing leapfrog

**leap·frog** (lēp′frog′) **1** a game in which one player jumps over the bent back of another. **2** leap or jump as in this game. 1 *n.,* 2 *v.,* **leap·frogged, leap·frog·ging.**

**leapt** (lept) a pt. and a pp. of LEAP. *v.*

**leap year** a year having 366 days, the extra day being February 29: *A year is a leap year if its number can be divided exactly by four except years at the end of a century, which must be exactly divisible by 400; thus 1960 and 2000 are leap years, whereas 1900 and 1961 are not.*

**learn** (lėrn) **1** gain knowledge of a subject or skill in an art, trade, etc. by study, instruction, or experience: *to learn French, learn a new game.* **2** acquire knowledge, skill, etc.: *He learns easily.* **3** memorize: *She will learn the poem for a recitation at the concert.* **4** find out; come to know: *He tried to learn the details of the train wreck.* **5** become informed; hear: *I first learned of his illness from your letter.* **6** become able by study or practice: *to learn to fly an airplane.* *v.,* **learned** or **learnt, learn·ing.** —**learn′a·ble,** *adj.*
☛ *Usage.* Do not confuse **learn** with TEACH. Standard English keeps these two verbs completely distinct: *I learned how to play chess. He taught me how to play chess.*

**learn·ed** (lėr′nid) having, showing, or requiring much knowledge; scholarly: *a learned man, a learned book.* *adj.* —**learn′ed·ly,** *adv.*

**learn·er** (lėr′nər) 1 a person who is learning. 2 beginner. *n.*

**learn·ing** (lėr′ning) 1 the gaining of knowledge or skill. 2 the possession of knowledge gained by study; scholarship. 3 knowledge. 4 ppr. of LEARN. 1–3 *n.*, 4 *v.*

**learnt** (lėrnt) a pt. and a pp. of LEARN. *v.*

**lear·y** (lēr′ē) See LEERY. *adj.*

**lease** (lēs) 1 a contract, usually in the form of a written agreement, giving the right to use property for a certain length of time, usually by paying rent: *We refused to sign the lease.* 2 the length of time for which such an agreement is made: *They have a long lease on the property.* 3 give a lease on: *This dealer leases cars.* 4 rent: *We have leased an apartment for one year.* 5 be leased. 1, 2 *n.*, 3–5 *v.*, **leased, leas·ing.**
**new lease on life,** a chance to live longer, better, or more happily.

**lease·hold** (lēs′hōld′) 1 a holding by a LEASE (def. 1). 2 real estate held by a LEASE (def. 1). *n.*

**leash** (lēsh) 1 a strap, chain, etc. for holding or leading a dog or other animal in check. 2 fasten or hold with a leash; control. 3 a group of three animals: *a leash of hounds.* 1, 3 *n.*, 2 *v.*
**hold in leash,** control.

**least** (lēst) 1 less than any other; smallest; slightest: *The least bit of dirt in a watch may make it stop.* 2 the smallest amount or degree: *That is the least you can do.* 3 to the least extent, amount, or degree: *She liked that book least of all.* 1 *adj.*, 2 *n.*, 3 *adv.*
**at least** or **at the least,** a at the lowest estimate: *The temperature was at least 35°C.* b at any rate; in any case: *He may have been late, but at least he came.*
**not in the least,** not at all.

**least common multiple** the least quantity that contains two or more given quantities exactly: *12 is the least common multiple of 3, 4 and 6.*

**least·ways** (lēst′wāz′) *Informal.* LEASTWISE. *adv.*

**least·wise** (lēst′wīz′) *Informal.* at least; at any rate. *adv.*

**leath·er** (leᴛн′ər) 1 animal skin that has been prepared for use by removing all the flesh and hair from the skin and then tanning it. 2 made of or covered with leather: *leather gloves, a leather chair.* 3 something made of leather. 4 furnish or cover with leather. 5 *Informal.* beat with a strap; thrash. 1–3 *n.*, 4, 5 *v.*

**leath·er·ette** (leᴛн′ə ret′) imitation leather. *n.*

**leath·ern** (leᴛн′ərn) 1 made of leather. 2 like leather. *adj.*

**leath·er·y** (leᴛн′ər ē) like leather; tough: *Exposure to harsh weather had made his face leathery.* *adj.* —**leath′er·i·ness,** *n.*

**leave**[1] (lēv) 1 go away: *We leave tonight.* 2 go away from: *She left the house.* 3 stop living in, belonging to, or working at or for: *to leave the country, to leave a club.* 4 go without taking; let remain: *I left a book on the table.* 5 go away and let remain in a particular condition: *to leave a window open.* 6 let remain when one dies; bequeath: *He left a large fortune.* 7 give to be kept; deposit; give: *I left my suitcase in the station while I walked around the town.* 8 let a person, etc. alone to do something; let be: *Leave me to settle the matter.* 9 let remain for someone to do: *Leave the matter to me. I left the driving to my sister.* 10 let remain uneaten, unused, unremoved, etc.: *There is some wood left.* 11 not attend to: *I will leave my homework till tomorrow.* *v.*, **left, leav·ing.**
**leave off,** stop: *Continue the story from where I left off.*
**leave out,** not do, say, or put in; omit: *She left out two words when she read the sentence.*

**leave**[2] (lēv) 1 permission; consent: *They gave him leave to go.* 2 permission to be absent from duty. 3 the length of time that such permission lasts: *Their annual leave is thirty days.* *n.*
**leave of absence,** a permission to stay away. b the length of time that this lasts.
**on leave,** absent from duty with permission.
**take leave of,** say good-bye to.

**leave**[3] (lēv) put forth leaves: *Trees leave in the spring.* *v.*, **leaved, leav·ing.**

**leav·en** (lev′ən) 1 any substance, such as yeast, that will cause fermentation and make dough rise. 2 a small amount of fermenting dough kept for this purpose. 3 raise with a leaven; make dough light or lighter. 4 an influence that, spreading silently and strongly, changes conditions or opinions: *A leaven of hope brightened our despair.* 5 a modifying element: *The solemn speech had a leaven of humour.* 6 spread through and transform. 1, 2, 4, 5 *n.*, 3, 6 *v.*

**leav·en·ing** (lev′ə ning) 1 a thing that LEAVENS. 2 ppr. of LEAVEN. 1 *n.*, 2 *v.*

**leaves** (lēvz) 1 pl. of LEAF. 2 pl. of LEAVE[2]. *n.*

**leave–tak·ing** (lēv′tā′king) the act of taking leave; saying good-bye. *n.*

**leav·ings** (lē′vingz) leftovers; remnants. *n. pl.*

**lech·er** (lech′ər) a man who indulges in LECHERY. *n.*

**lech·er·ous** (lech′ə rəs) lewd; lustful. *adj.*

**lech·er·y** (lech′ə rē) gross indulgence of lust. *n.*

**lec·tern** (lek′tərn) reading desk, especially the desk in a church from which the lessons are read at daily prayer. *n.*

**lec·ture** (lek′chər) 1 a speech or planned talk on a chosen subject, usually for the purpose of instruction. 2 such a speech or talk written down or printed. 3 give a lecture. 4 instruct or entertain by a lecture. 5 a scolding: *My mother gives me a lecture when I come home late.* 6 scold; reprove. 1, 2, 5 *n.*, 3, 4, 6 *v.*, **lec·tured, lec·tur·ing.**

**lec·tur·er** (lek′chə rər) 1 a person who gives a lecture or lectures. 2 a teacher of junior rank at some universities. *n.*

**led** (led) pt. and pp. of LEAD[1]: *The policeman led the child across the street. That blind woman is led by her dog.* *v.*
☞ Hom. LEAD[2].

**L.E.D.** or **LED** (el′ē dē′) light-emitting diode: *Many digital watches have an L.E.D. time display.*

**ledge** (lej) 1 a narrow shelf: *a window ledge.* 2 a shelf or ridge of rock. 3 a layer or mass of metal-bearing rock. *n.*

**ledg·er** (lej′ər) a book of accounts in which a business keeps a record of all money transactions. *n.*

**lee** (lē) **1** shelter. **2** the side or part sheltered or away from the wind: *The wind was so fierce that we ran to the lee of the house.* **3** sheltered or away from the wind: *the lee side of a ship.* **4** the side away from the wind. **5** on the side away from the wind. **6** the direction toward which the wind is blowing. **7** in the direction toward which the wind is blowing. 1, 2, 4, 6 *n.*, 3, 5, 7 *adj.*
☞ Hom. LEA.

**lee·board** (lē′bôrd′) a large, flat board lowered into the water on the lee side of a sailboat to keep the boat from drifting sideways. *n.*

**leech**¹ (lēch) **1** a worm living in ponds and streams, that sucks the blood of animals: *Doctors formerly used leeches to suck blood from sick people.* **2** a person who persistently tries to get what he or she can out of others. *n.*

**leech**² (lēch) the edge of a sail not fastened to a rope or spar. *n.*

**leek** (lēk) a vegetable resembling an onion but having larger leaves, a smaller, cylindrical bulb, and a milder flavour: *The leek is the emblem of Wales.* *n.*
☞ Hom. LEAK.

**leer** (lēr) **1** a sly, sidelong look; evil glance. **2** give a sly, sidelong look; glance evilly. 1 *n.*, 2 *v.*
—**leer′ing·ly**, *adv.*

**leer·y** (lē′rē) *Informal.* **1** wary; suspicious: *We are leery of his advice.* **2** afraid. **3** sly; cunning and knowing. *adj.* Also, **leary**.

**lees** (lēz) dregs; sediment. *n. pl.*

**lee shore** the shore toward which the wind is blowing.

**lee·ward** (lē′wərd *or* lü′ərd) **1** on the side away from the wind. **2** the side away from the wind; lee. **3** in the direction toward which the wind is blowing. 1, 3 *adj., adv.*, 2 *n.*

**lee·way** (lē′wā′) **1** the side movement of a ship to LEEWARD, out of its course. **2** extra space at the side; more time, money, etc. than is needed; a margin of safety: *If you have $20 more than you need on a trip, you are allowing yourself a leeway of $20.* **3** convenient room or scope for action. *n.*

**left**¹ (left) **1** of the side that is toward the west when the main side faces north: *the left wing of an army. Make a left turn at the next light.* See RIGHT for picture. **2** when looking to the front, situated nearer the observer's or speaker's left hand than his or her right. **3** on or to the left side: *to turn left.* **4** the left side or hand: *She sat at my left.* **5** the part of a lawmaking body consisting of the groups favouring social and economic reform. **6** all the people and political parties that favour reform. 1, 2 *adj.*, 3 *adv.*, 4–6 *n.*

**left**² (left) pt. and pp. of LEAVE¹: *He left his hat in the hall. It was left there this morning. There is one apple left.* *v.*

**left face** turn to the left.

**left–hand** (left′hand′) **1** on or to the left. **2** of, for, or with the left hand. *adj.*

**left–hand·ed** (left′han′did) **1** using the left hand more easily and readily than the right. **2** done with the left hand. **3** made to be used with the left hand. **4** turning from right to left: *a left-handed screw.* **5** clumsy; awkward. **6** doubtful; insincere. A **left-handed compliment** is one that is very awkward or really not a compliment at all. *Example:* "You must have made that dress yourself." *adj.* —**left′-hand′ed·ly**, *adv.* —**left′-hand′ed·ness**, *n.*

**left·ist** (lef′tist) **1** a person who supports or favours the left in politics. **2** a member of an organization of the left. **3** *Informal.* tending to support or favour social and economic reform. 1, 2 *n.*, 3 *adj.*

**left·o·ver** (lef′tō′vər) **1** anything that is left: *Scraps of food from a meal are leftovers.* **2** that is left; remaining. 1 *n.*, 2 *adj.*

**left wing 1** the people supporting or favouring reform, especially the radical members of a political organization. **2** in hockey, lacrosse, etc., the playing position to the left of centre on a forward line. **3** the player in this position; LEFT WINGER.

**left winger** in hockey, lacrosse, etc., the player who occupies the position to the left of centre.

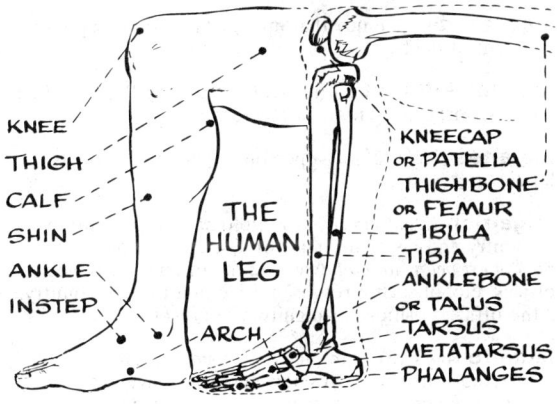

THE HUMAN LEG — KNEE, THIGH, CALF, SHIN, ANKLE, INSTEP, ARCH; KNEECAP OR PATELLA, THIGHBONE OR FEMUR, FIBULA, TIBIA, ANKLEBONE OR TALUS, TARSUS, METATARSUS, PHALANGES

**leg** (leg) **1** one of the limbs on which human beings and animals support themselves and walk. **2** the part of a garment that covers a leg. **3** anything shaped or used like a leg: *a table leg.* **4** one of the distinct portions or stages of any course: *the last leg of a trip.* **5** either of the sides adjacent to the right angle in a right triangle. **6** the course or run made by a sailing vessel on one tack. *n.*, —**leg′less**, *adj.*

**give a leg up**, *Informal.* help.

**have not a leg to stand on**, *Informal.* have no defence or reason.

**leg it**, *Informal.* walk or run.

**on one's last legs**, about to fall, collapse, die, etc.: *I feel as if I am on my last legs but a swim will revive me.*

**pull someone's leg**, *Informal.* fool, trick, or make fun of someone: *I didn't know he was pulling my leg until I heard you laugh.*

**stretch one's legs**, *Informal.* take a walk.
☞ *Etym.* From ON *leggr* 'limb'. This word replaced the native OE *sceanca* 'leg', which became more restricted in meaning and survives in modern English as SHANK.

**Leg.** *or* **leg. 1** legislature. **2** legislative. **3** legal. **4** legate. **5** legato.

**leg·a·cy** (leg′ə sē) **1** the money or other property left to a person by a will. **2** something that has been handed down from an ancestor or predecessor. *n., pl.* **leg·a·cies**.

**le·gal** (lē′gəl) **1** of law: *legal knowledge.* **2** of lawyers: *legal advice.* **3** according to law; lawful: *Hunting is legal only during certain seasons.* *adj.*

**le·gal·ism** (lē′gə liz′əm) strict adherence to law or prescription. *n.*

**le·gal·ist** (lē′gə list) a person who adheres strictly to laws or rules. *n.*

**le·gal·is·tic** (lē′gə lis′tik) adhering strictly to law or prescription. *adj.*

**le·gal·i·ty** (li gal′ə tē) accordance with law; lawfulness. *n., pl.* **le·gal·i·ties.**

**le·gal·ize** (lē′gə līz′) make legal; authorize by law; sanction. *v.,* **le·gal·ized, le·gal·iz·ing.** —**le′gal·i·za′tion,** *n.*

**le·gal·ly** (lē′gə lē) **1** in a legal manner. **2** according to law: *He is legally responsible for his wife's debts.* *adv.*

**legal tender** money that must, by law, be accepted in payment of debts.

**leg·ate** (leg′it) **1** a representative of the Pope. **2** an ambassador; representative; messenger. *n.*

**leg·a·tee** (leg′ə tē′) a person to whom a legacy is left. *n.*

**le·ga·tion** (li gā′shən) **1** a diplomatic representative of a country and his or her staff of assistants: *A legation ranks next below an embassy.* **2** the official residence, offices, etc. of such a representative in a foreign country. **3** the office, position, or dignity of a LEGATE. *n.*

**le·ga·to** (li gä′tō) in music: **1** smooth and connected; without breaks between successive tones: *Legato is the opposite of staccato.* **2** in a legato manner. 1 *adj.,* 2 *adv.*

**leg·end** (lej′ənd) **1** a story coming down from the past, which has been widely accepted: *The stories about King Arthur and his Knights of the Round Table are legends, not history.* **2** such stories as a group. **3** the inscription on a coin or medal. **4** the words, etc. accompanying a picture, map, or diagram; caption. *n.*
☛ *Syn.* **Legend** and MYTH have somewhat different meanings. A **legend** is a story relating to a people's past and usually glorifies a hero, saint, great event, etc.; it may contain an element of fact, or it may be wholly untrue. A **myth** is a story relating to a people's religion and is usually about a god, gods, or other superhuman beings; its original aim was to explain a religious belief or some aspect of life or nature.

**leg·end·ar·y** (lej′ən der′ē) of a legend or legends; like a legend; not historical: *Robin Hood is a legendary person.* *adj.*

**leg·er·de·main** (lej′ər də mān′) **1** sleight of hand; conjuring tricks; jugglery: *A common trick of legerdemain is to take rabbits from an apparently empty hat.* **2** trickery. *n.*

**legged** (legd *or* leg′id) having a leg or legs of a certain kind, number, etc. (*used only in compounds*): *two-legged, long-legged.* *adj.*

Leather leggings

**leg·gings** (leg′ingz) extra outer coverings of cloth or leather for the legs, for use out-of-doors; gaiters. *n. pl.*

**leg·gy** (leg′ē) **1** having long legs. **2** having awkwardly long legs. *adj.*

**leg·horn** (leg′hôrn *or* leg′ərn) **1** a hat made of flat, yellow, braided straw. **2** the braided straw from which such a hat is made. *n.*

**Leg·horn** (leg′hôrn *or* leg′ərn) a rather small kind of chicken. *n.*

**leg·i·bil·i·ty** (lej′ə bil′ə tē) a LEGIBLE condition or quality; clearness of print or writing. *n.*

**leg·i·ble** (lej′ə bəl) **1** that can be read. **2** easy to read; plain and clear: *legible handwriting.* *adj.* —**leg′ib·ly,** *adv.*

**le·gion** (lē′jən) **1** a large body of soldiers; army. **2** in the ancient Roman army, a body of soldiers consisting of 3000 to 6000 foot soldiers and 300 to 700 cavalrymen. **3** a great many; very large number: *a legion of difficulties, a legion of supporters.* **4 Legion,** ROYAL CANADIAN LEGION. *n.*

**le·gion·ar·y** (lē′jə ner′ē) **1** of or belonging to a LEGION. **2** a soldier of a LEGION. 1 *adj.,* 2 *n., pl.* **le·gion·ar·ies.**

**le·gion·naire** (lē′jə ner′) **1** a member of the ROYAL CANADIAN LEGION. **2** a soldier of a LEGION. *n.*

**Legion of Honour** or **Honor** an honorary society founded by Napoleon in 1802, in which membership is given as a reward for great services to France.

**leg·is·late** (lej′i slāt′) **1** make laws: *Parliament legislates for Canada.* **2** force by legislation: *The council legislated her out of office.* *v.,* **leg·is·lat·ed, leg·is·lat·ing.**

**leg·is·la·tion** (lej′i slā′shən) **1** the making of laws: *Parliament has the power of legislation.* **2** the laws made: *Important legislation is reported in today's newspaper.* *n.*

**leg·is·la·tive** (lej′i slə tiv *or* lej′i slā′tiv) **1** having to do with making laws: *legislative reforms.* **2** having the duty and power of making laws: *Parliament is a legislative body.* **3** ordered by law: *a legislative decree.* *adj.* —**leg′is·la′tive·ly,** *adv.*

**Legislative Assembly** in Canada, the group of representatives elected to the legislature of a province or territory.

**Legislative Council** formerly, in Quebec, the upper chamber of the LEGISLATURE, composed of 24 members appointed for life by the Lieutenant-Governor in Council: *The Legislative Council in Quebec was abolished in 1968.*

**leg·is·la·tor** (lej′i slā′tər) a lawmaker; member of a LEGISLATIVE body: *MP's and MLA's are legislators.* *n.*

**leg·is·la·ture** (lej′i slā′chər) **1** a group of persons having the duty and the power to make laws for a country, province, or state: *Each Canadian province has a legislature.* **2** the place where the LEGISLATORS meet. *n.*

**le·git·i·ma·cy** (lə jit′ə mə sē) a being legitimate or lawful; being recognized as lawful or proper. *n.*

**le·git·i·mate** (lə jit′ə mit *for adjective,* lə jit′ə māt′ *for verb*) **1** rightful; lawful: *The Prince of Wales is the legitimate heir to the throne of England.* **2** allowed; acceptable: *Sickness is a legitimate reason for absence from school.* **3** of, having to do with, or referring to drama acted on stage, as opposed to motion pictures and other stage entertainment such as vaudeville and burlesque: *the legitimate theatre.* **4** born of parents who are married. **5** make or declare lawful. **6** resting on, or ruling by, the principle of hereditary right: *the legitimate title to a throne, a legitimate heir.* **7** logical: *a legitimate conclusion.* 1–4, 6, 7 *adj.,* 5 *v.,* **le·git·i·mat·ed, le·git·i·mat·ing.** —**le·git′i·mate·ly,** *adv.*

**legitimate theatre** drama acted on the stage as opposed to motion pictures, vaudeville, burlesque, etc.

**le·git·i·mist** (lə jit′ə mist) a supporter of LEGITIMATE authority, especially of claims to rule based on direct descent. *n.*

**le·git·i·mize** (lə jit′ə mīz′) make or declare to be LEGITIMATE. *v.,* **le·git·i·mized, le·git·i·miz·ing.** —**le·git′i·mi·za′tion,** *n.*

**leg–of–mut·ton** (leg′əv mut′ən) having the shape of a leg of mutton; wide at one end and narrow at the other: *a leg-of-mutton sleeve. adj.*

**leg·ume** (leg′yüm *or* li gyüm′) **1** a plant having a number of seeds in a pod, such as beans, peas, etc. **2** the seed pod of such a plant. *n.*

**le·gu·mi·nous** (li gyü′mə nəs) **1** of or bearing LEGUMES. **2** having to do with or belonging to the pea family of plants. *adj.*

**leg warmers** coverings for the legs reaching from knee to ankle, used especially by dancers in preliminary or practice exercises.

**lei** (lā) in Hawaii, a wreath of flowers, leaves, etc. *n., pl.* **leis.**
☛ *Hom.* LAY.

**lei·sure** (lezh′ər *or* lē′zhər) **1** the time free from required work in which a person may rest, amuse himself or herself, and do the things he or she likes to do: *A busy woman hasn't much leisure for reading.* **2** free; not busy: *leisure hours.* **3** having leisure. *n.*
**at leisure, a** free; not busy. **b** without hurry; taking plenty of time.
**at one's leisure,** when one has leisure; at one's convenience.

**lei·sured** (lezh′ərd *or* lē′zhərd) **1** having LEISURE. **2** LEISURELY. *adj.*

**lei·sure·ly** (lezh′ər lē *or* lē′zhər lē) **1** without hurry; taking plenty of time: *He was a man of leisurely habits.* **2** in a leisurely manner: *He walked leisurely across the street.* 1 *adj.,* 2 *adv.* —**leis′ure·li·ness,** *n.*

**leit·mo·tif** or **leit·mo·tiv** (līt′mō tēf′) in music, a short theme or passage in a composition, repeated throughout the work and associated with a certain person, situation, or idea. *n.*

**lem·ming** (lem′ing) a small, mouselike arctic rodent having greyish or brownish fur, a short tail, and furry feet. *n.*

**lem·on** (lem′ən) **1** an acid-tasting, light-yellow citrus fruit growing in warm climates. **2** a thorny tree that bears this fruit. **3** pale yellow. **4** *Informal.* a thing or person that is considered inferior or disagreeable: *The last car he bought was a lemon.* 1–4 *n.,* 3 *adj.* —**lem′on·like′,** *adj.*

## legitimate 683 lenity

hat, āge, fär; let, ēqual, tėrm; it, īce
hot, ōpen, ôrder; oil, out; cup, pùt, rüle
əbove, takən, pencəl, lemən, circəs
ch, child; ng, long; sh, ship
th, thin; ŦH, then; zh, measure

**lem·on·ade** (lem′ə nād′) a drink made of lemon juice, sugar, and water. *n.*

**le·mur** (lē′mər) an animal related to the monkey, but having a foxlike face and woolly fur, found mainly in Madagascar. *n.*

**lend** (lend) **1** let another have or use for a time: *Will you lend me your bicycle for an hour?* **2** give the use of money for a fixed or specified amount of payment: *Banks lend money and charge interest.* **3** make a loan or loans: *A person who borrows should be willing to lend.* **4** give; contribute; add: *A lace curtain lends charm to a window. The Red Cross is quick to lend aid in time of disaster.* *v.,* **lent, lend·ing.** —**lend′er,** *n.*
**lend a hand,** help: *She lent a hand with the dishes.*
**lend itself to,** be suitable for: *The old engine lent itself to our purposes.*
**lend oneself to,** make oneself available for: *Don't lend yourself to foolish schemes.*

**length** (length *or* lengkth) **1** how long a thing is; a thing's measurement from end to end; the longest way a thing can be measured: *the length of your arm.* **2** the distance a thing extends: *The length of a race is the distance run.* **3** the extent in time; duration: *the length of a visit, the length of an hour.* **4** a long stretch or extent: *Quite a length of hair hung down in a braid.* **5** a piece or portion of cloth, pipe, rope, etc. of given length often either cut from a larger piece, or meant to be joined to another piece: *a length of rope, three lengths of pipe.* *n.*
**at full length,** with the body stretched out flat.
**at length, a** at last; finally: *At length, after many delays, the meeting started.* **b** with all the details; fully: *Giuseppe told of his adventures at length.*
**go to any length,** do everything possible.
**keep at arm's length,** discourage from being too familiar.

**length·en** (leng′thən *or* lengk′thən) **1** make longer: *A tailor can lengthen your trousers.* **2** become or grow longer: *Your legs have lengthened a great deal since you were five years old.* *v.*

**length·ways** (leng′thwāz′) LENGTHWISE. *adv., adj.*

**length·wise** (leng′thwīz′) in the direction of the length: *She cut the cloth lengthwise. adv., adj.*

**length·y** (leng′thē) long; too long: *His directions were so lengthy that everybody got confused. adj.,* **length·i·er, length·i·est.**

**le·ni·ence** (lē′nē əns *or* lē′nyəns) LENIENCY. *n.*

**le·ni·en·cy** (lē′nē ən sē *or* lē′nyən sē) mildness; gentleness; mercy. *n.*

**le·ni·ent** (lē′nē ənt *or* lē′nyənt) mild or gentle; merciful: *a lenient conqueror, a lenient punishment. adj.* —**len′ient·ly,** *adv.*

**len·i·ty** (len′ə tē) mildness; gentleness; mercifulness. *n., pl.* **len·i·ties.**

A lens. The kind of lens shown above bends light rays to produce a magnified image.

**lens** (lenz) **1** a piece of glass, or something like glass, that brings closer together or sends wider apart the rays of light passing through it: *The lens of a camera forms images. The lenses of a telescope make things look larger and nearer.* See CAMERA, CONCAVE, and CONVEX for other pictures. **2** a clear, oval structure in the eye directly behind the iris, that directs light rays upon the retina. See EYE for picture. *n., pl.* **lens·es.**

**lent** (lent) pt. and pp. of LEND: *I lent you my pencils. Hans had lent me his eraser.* *v.*

**len·til** (len′təl) **1** a plant of the pea family, whose pods contain two seeds shaped like double-convex lenses, growing mostly in southern Europe and Asia. **2** the edible seed of this plant. *n.*

**l'en·voi** or **l'en·voy** (len′voi *or* lon vwä′; French, län vwä′) a short stanza ending a poem. *n.*

**Le·o** (lē′ō) **1** in astronomy, a northern constellation thought of as having the shape of a lion. **2** in astrology, the fifth sign of the zodiac. The sun enters Leo about July 22. See ZODIAC for picture. **3** a person born under this sign. *n.*

**le·o·nine** (lē′ə nīn′) of or like a lion. *adj.*

**leop·ard** (lep′ərd) **1** a large fierce mammal of Africa and Asia having dull-yellowish fur spotted with black: *The leopard belongs to the cat family.* **2** any of various closely related animals, such as the jaguar. *n.*

**leop·ard·ess** (lep′ər dis) a female LEOPARD. *n.*

**le·o·tard** (lē′ə tärd′) **1** a one-piece, close-fitting garment worn by dancers, acrobats, etc. **2** leotards, *pl.* TIGHTS. *n.*

**lep·er** (lep′ər) a person who has LEPROSY. *n.*

**lep·i·dop·ter·an** (lep′ə dop′tə rən) any insect belonging to the order **Lepidoptera**, a very large group including the butterflies, moths, and skippers, having four broad, membranous wings covered with very tiny, often brightly coloured scales: *The larvae of lepidopterans are called caterpillars and have chewing mouth parts for feeding on plants; the adults have sucking mouth parts.* *n.*

**lep·i·dop·ter·ist** (lep′ə dop′tə rist) a person who studies the LEPIDOPTERANS.

**lep·i·dop·ter·ous** (lep′ə dop′tə rəs) of or having to do with the LEPIDOPTERANS. *adj.*

**lep·re·chaun** (lep′rə kon′) in Irish folklore, a sprite or goblin resembling a little old man. *n.*

**lep·ro·sy** (lep′rə sē) HANSEN'S DISEASE. *n.*

**lep·rous** (lep′rəs) **1** having LEPROSY: *a leprous person.* **2** of or like LEPROSY: *white leprous scales.* *adj.* —**lep′rous·ly,** *adv.*

**Les·bi·an** or **les·bi·an** (lez′bē ən) **1** a homosexual woman. **2** of or having to do with homosexuality in women. **1** *n.,* **2** *adj.*

**lese–maj·es·ty** (lēz′maj′i stē) a crime or offence against the sovereign power in a state; treason. *n.*

**le·sion** (lē′zhən) **1** an injury; hurt. **2** a diseased condition of tissue or an organ. *n.*

**less** (les) **1** smaller: *of less width, of less importance.* **2** not so much; not so much of: *to have less rain, to put on less butter, to eat less meat.* **3** fewer: *Five is less than seven.* **4** lower in age, rank, or importance: *no less a person than the Prince of Wales.* **5** a smaller amount or quantity: *She refused to take less than $5.* **6** to a smaller extent or degree: *less known.* **7** lacking; without; minus: *a year less two days.* 1–4 *adj.,* 5 *n.,* 6 *adv.,* 7 *prep.* **more or less, a** somewhat: *We are all more or less impatient.* **b** about; approximately: *The cost is fifty dollars, more or less.*
☞ *Syn.* See note at FEW.

**–less** an adjective-forming suffix meaning: **1** without; lacking, as in *homeless.* **2** that does not, as in *ceaseless.* **3** that cannot be _____ ed: *Countless* means that cannot be counted.

**les·see** (le sē′) a person who is granted a LEASE (def. 1). *n.*

**less·en** (les′ən) **1** grow less. **2** make less; decrease. **3** represent as less; minimize; belittle. *v.*
☞ *Hom.* LESSON.

**less·er** (les′ər) **1** less; smaller. **2** the less important of two. *adj.*

**les·son** (les′ən) **1** something learned or studied: *Children study many different lessons in school.* **2** a unit of learning or teaching; what is to be studied or practised at one time: *Our math text is divided into 20 lessons.* **3** a meeting of a student or class with a teacher to study a given subject: *She has gone for a piano lesson. There will be no lesson today.* **4** an instructive experience, serving to encourage or warn: *The accident was a lesson to me.* **5** give a lesson to. **6** a selection from the Bible or other sacred writings, read as part of a religious service. 1–4, 6 *n.,* 5 *v.*
☞ *Hom.* LESSEN.

**les·sor** (les′ôr) a person who grants a LEASE (def. 1). *n.*

**lest** (lest) **1** for fear that: *Be careful lest you fall from that tree.* **2** that: *They were afraid lest she should come too late to save them.* *conj.*

**let¹** (let) **1** allow; permit: *Let the dog have a bone.* **2** allow to pass, go, or come: *to let a person board a ship.* **3** rent; hire out: *to let a boat by the hour.* **4** be rented: *That apartment lets for $800 a month.* **5** *Let* is used in giving suggestions or giving commands: *"Let's go home"* means *"I suggest that we go home."* **6** suppose; assume: *Let the two lines be parallel.* *v.,* **let, let·ting.**
**let down, a** lower. **b** slow up: *As her interest in the work wore off, she began to let down.* **c** disappoint: *Don't let us down today; we're counting on you to help us.* **d** humiliate. **e** make clothes longer: *I shall have to let that skirt down, you're growing so fast.*
**let go, a** stop holding. **b** dismiss from a job.
**let in,** admit; permit to enter.
**let off, a** allow to go free; release: *let off with a warning.* **b** free from: *The teacher would not let us off homework.* **c** fire; explode: *let off a detonation.*
**let off steam,** give way to one's feelings: *He let off steam by shouting.*
**let on,** *Informal.* **a** allow to be known; reveal one's knowledge of: *He didn't let on his surprise at the news.* **b** pretend; make believe: *She let on that she didn't see me.*

**let oneself go, a** cease to restrain oneself. **b** cease to take care of one's appearance.
**let out, a** permit to go out. **b** make a garment larger. **c** rent: *Has the room been let out yet?* **d** *Informal.* dismiss or be dismissed. **e** make known; disclose.
**let up,** *Informal.* stop; pause: *They refused to let up in the fight.*

**let²** (let) in tennis and similar games, interference with the ball: *A let ball is one that strikes the top of the net.* *n.* **without let** or **hindrance,** with nothing to prevent, hinder, or obstruct.

**–let** a noun-forming suffix meaning: **1** little, as in *booklet, streamlet, wavelet, ringlet.* **2** a small thing worn as a band on, as in *anklet, armlet.*

**let·down** (let′doun′) **1** a slowing up. **2** *Informal.* disappointment. **3** humiliation. *n.*

**le·thal** (lē′thəl) causing death; deadly: *lethal weapons, a lethal dose.* *adj.*
☛ *Syn.* See note at FATAL.

**le·thar·gic** (lə thär′jik) **1** unnaturally drowsy; sluggish; dull: *A hot, humid day produces a lethargic condition.* **2** producing LETHARGY. *adj.*

**leth·ar·gy** (leth′ər jē) **1** drowsy dullness; lack of energy; sluggish inactivity. **2** a condition of unnatural drowsiness or prolonged sleep. *n., pl.* **leth·ar·gies.**

**let's** (lets) let us.

**let·ter** (let′ər) **1** a symbol or sign, used alone or combined, that represents speech sounds; a character of an alphabet: *Both* must *and* mask *have four letters.* **2** mark with letters. **3** inscribe something in letters. **4** make letters. **5** a written or printed message. **6** an official document granting some right or privilege. **7** the exact wording; actual terms: *He kept the letter of the law but not the spirit.* **8** a bit of metal type bearing a letter, used in printing. **9** a badge representing the initial letter of a school or college, given as an award for achievement, especially in athletics. **10 letters,** *pl.* **a** literature. **b** a knowledge of literature; literary culture. **c** the profession of an author. 1, 5–10 *n.*, 2–4 *v.*
—**let·ter·er,** *n.*
**to the letter,** very exactly; just as one has been told: *I carried out your order to the letter.*
☛ *Usage.* Sometimes a single sound is represented in spelling by a combination of letters. Thus, the two letters *sh,* as in *wish,* represent one sound. On the other hand, one combination of letters can stand for different sounds, as *ough* in *bough* and *through.*

**letter carrier** a person who collects or delivers mail: *My daughter was a letter carrier in Whitehorse.*

**let·tered** (let′ərd) **1** marked with letters. **2** able to read and write; educated. **3** knowing literature; having literary culture. **4** pt. and pp. of LETTER. 1–3 *adj.,* 4 *v.*

**let·ter·head** (let′ər hed′) **1** words printed at the top of a sheet of paper, usually a name and address. **2** a sheet of paper so printed. *n.*

**let·ter·ing** (let′ə ring) **1** letters drawn, painted, stamped, etc. **2** the making of letters. **3** ppr. of LETTER. 1, 2 *n.,* 3 *v.*

**let·ter-per·fect** (let′ər pèr′fikt) **1** knowing one's part or lesson perfectly: *René worked hard to learn his part in the play and was soon letter-perfect.* **2** correct in every detail: *The secretary's typing was letter-perfect.* *adj.*

**letters patent** (pat′ənt *or* pā′tənt) an official document giving a person or a corporation authority from a government to do some act or to have some right.

hat, āge, fär; let, ēqual, tėrm; it, īce
hot, ōpen, ôrder; oil, out; cup, put, rüle
əbove, takən, pencəl, lemən, circəs
ch, child; ng, long; sh, ship
th, thin; ᴛʜ, then; zh, measure

**let·tuce** (let′is) **1** any of a closely related group of annual plants of the COMPOSITE family, especially a common garden vegetable grown in several varieties, all having large, crisp, green leaves that grow out from a very short central stalk. **2** the leaves of garden lettuce: *Lettuce is usually eaten raw, in salads.* *n.*
☛ *Etym.* Through OF *laitues* from L *lactuca* 'lettuce', which developed from *lac, lactis* 'milk', with reference to the milky juice of the plant.

**let·up** (let′up′) *Informal.* a lessening or stopping: *They've been working since morning, without letup. After a slight letup, the rain started again, harder than ever.* *n.*

**leu·co·cyte** or **leu·ko·cyte** (lü′kə sīt′) any of the white or colourless cells that occur in the blood and help the body fight infection; white blood cell. *n.*

**leu·ke·mi·a** (lü kē′mē ə) a type of cancer occurring in several forms, characterized by the abnormal growth of white blood cells (LEUCOCYTES) in the bone marrow, lymphatic tissue, or spleen, usually resulting in an excess of these cells in the blood: *Leukemia may be a long-term or short-term disease.* *n.*

**Le·van·tine** (lə van′tin, lev′ən tīn′, *or* lev′ən tēn′) **1** of the Levant, the countries on the Mediterranean Sea east of Italy. **2** a person or ship of the Levant. 1 *adj.,* 2 *n.*

**lev·ee¹** (lev′ē) **1** an embankment built along a river to prevent flooding; dike. **2** a landing place for boats on the bank of a river. *n.*
☛ *Hom.* LEVY.

**lev·ee²** (lev′ē; *French,* lə vā′) a usually formal reception, especially one held during the day: *The regiment holds a levee on New Year's Day. She received an invitation to the Governor General's levee.* *n.*
☛ *Hom.* LEVY (for the first pronunciation of **levee**).

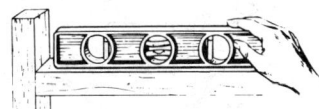

A level (def. 3). It has one or more glass tubes containing a liquid with an air bubble in it. The air bubble stays in the centre if the surface is level; if not, it moves to one side.

**lev·el** (lev′əl) **1** having the same height everywhere; completely flat and even, like the surface of still water: *level ground.* **2** not sloping; horizontal: *The floor is not quite level.* **3** an instrument for showing whether a surface is horizontal. **4** a measuring of differences in height or altitude between two points by means of such an instrument: *to take a level.* **5** a level condition or position: *The turntable should be placed on a level.* **6** a place or surface that is level: *The climbers stopped for breath when they reached the level.* **7** make level: *They used a bulldozer to level the ground.* **8** come to a level position or condition (*usually used with* **off**): *The path climbs for about 200 metres and then levels off.* **9** height: *We hung the picture at eye level. By evening the flood waters had risen to a level of three metres.* **10** of equal height or in the same plane: *The table is level with the window sill.*

**11** *Informal.* steady, calm, or sensible: *She's got a level head. He answered in a level voice.* **12** bring to the level of the ground; lay low; raze: *The tornado levelled every house in the village.* **13** raise and hold level for shooting; aim: *The soldier levelled his rifle.* **14** aim or direct words, intentions, etc.: *She levelled a stinging rebuke at the speaker.* **15** *Informal.* be honest and frank; tell the truth (*used with* **with**): *You can level with me; what really happened?* **16** degree, rate, or style: *The noise level in the library makes it hard to concentrate.* **17** a position or grade on a social, intellectual, or moral scale: *His work is not up to a professional level.* **18** equal or balanced in rank, degree, quality, etc.: *The two friends remained level in rank, but not in salary.* **19** of, suited to, or involving a particular rank, degree, etc. (used only in compounds): *High-level talks have begun between the major powers.* **20** bring to a common level or plane; remove or reduce differences: *Death levels all human ranks.* 1, 2, 10, 11, 18, 19 *adj.*, 3–6, 9, 16, 17 *n.*, 7, 8, 12–15, 20 *v.*, **lev′elled** or **lev′eled, lev′el·ling** or **lev′el·ing,** —**lev′el·ler** or **lev′el·er,** *n.* —**lev′el·ly,** *adv.* —**lev′el·ness,** *n.*

**find one's** or **its level,** arrive at the most natural or most appropriate position, rank, etc.: *After failing as a painter, Anton found his level as a successful cartoonist.*

**one's level best,** *Informal.* one's very best; as well or as much as one can do: *He said he had tried his level best but couldn't persuade them.*

**on the level,** *Informal.* **a** honest and straightforward: *Is that offer on the level?* **b** honestly and straightforwardly: *He always works on the level.*

☞ *Usage.* **Levels of usage** are different styles of language that are appropriate for different occasions. Two basic levels are **standard English** and **non-standard;** standard usage may be **formal** or **informal,** and other levels may be distinguished within these two. See also the notes at INFORMAL and STANDARD.

**level crossing** a place where a railway track crosses a road or another railway track at the same level.

**lev·el–head·ed** (lev′əl hed′id) having good common sense or good judgment; sensible. *adj.*

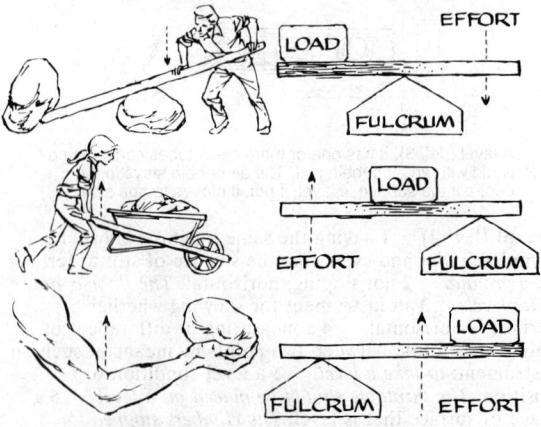

Lever (def. 3). The three classes of lever, with an example of each.

**le·ver** (lē′vər *or* lev′ər) **1** a bar used for moving or prying something: *A crowbar is a lever.* **2** anything used as a tool to influence or force: *He used his mother's name as a social lever.* **3** a simple machine consisting of a rigid bar supported and turning on a fixed point called the FULCRUM, using force, or effort, at a second point to move or lift a mass situated at a third point: *A wheelbarrow is one kind of a lever.* **4** pry, raise, or move with or as if with a lever: *She levered the rock out of the ground.* **5** use a lever or levers: *He levered for weeks and finally got the job.* 1–3 *n.*, 4, 5 *v.*

**lev·er·age** (lē′və rij *or* lev′ə rij) **1** the action of a lever. **2** the advantage or power gained by using a lever. **3** increased power of action. *n.*

**lev·er·et** (lev′ə rit) a young hare. *n.*

**le·vi·a·than** (lə vī′ə thən) **1** in the Bible, a huge sea animal. **2** a huge ship. **3** any great and powerful person or thing. *n.*

**lev·i·tate** (lev′ə tāt) **1** rise or float in the air. **2** cause to rise or float in the air. *v.,* **lev·i·tat·ed, lev·i·tat·ing.**

**lev·i·ta·tion** (lev′ə tā′shən) levitating. *n.*

**lev·i·ty** (lev′ə tē) lack of seriousness; lightness of spirit or mind, especially when excessive or not appropriate; frivolity: *The issue is a serious one and should not be treated with levity.* *n., pl.* **lev·i·ties.**

**lev·u·lose** (lev′yə lōs′) a form of sugar in honey, fruits, etc.; fruit sugar. *n.*

**lev·y** (lev′ē) **1** order to be paid: *The government levies taxes to pay its expenses.* **2** money collected by authority or force. **3** draft or enlist for an army: *to levy troops in time of war.* **4** the troops drafted or enlisted for an army. **5** seize by law for unpaid debts: *They levied on his property for unpaid rent.* **6** an act of levying. 1, 3, 5 *v.,* **lev·ied, lev·y·ing;** 2, 4, 6 *n., pl.* **lev·ies.**

**levy war on,** make war on; start a war against.

☞ *Hom.* LEVEE (lev′ē)

**lewd** (lüd) showing or designed to arouse sexual desire, especially in a coarse or offensive way; obscene: *a lewd glance, lewd pictures.* *adj.* —**lewd′ly,** *adv.* —**lewd′ness,** *n.*

**lex·i·cal** (lek′sə kəl) **1** of or having to do with words as separate units, rather than as elements of phrases, sentences, etc. **2** of or having to do with LEXICOGRAPHY or a LEXICON. *adj.*

**lex·i·cog·ra·pher** (lek′sə kog′rə fər) a person who compiles dictionaries. *n.*

**lex·i·co·graph·ic** (lek′sə kə graf′ik) LEXICOGRAPHICAL. *adj.*

**lex·i·co·graph·i·cal** (lek′sə kə graf′ə kəl) of or having to do with LEXICOGRAPHY. *adj.* —**lex′i·co·graph′i·cal·ly,** *adv.*

**lex·i·cog·ra·phy** (lek′sə kog′rə fē) the science or practice of compiling dictionaries; dictionary making. *n.*

**lex·i·con** (lek′sə kən) **1** a dictionary, especially of Greek, Latin, or Hebrew. **2** the total vocabulary of a particular speaker or writer or of a particular subject. **3** in linguistics, all the words and word elements of a language. *n.*

**Ley·den jar** (lī′dən) a device for collecting and storing an electric charge, consisting of a glass jar coated inside and outside with metal foil almost to the top, and having a conducting rod connected to the inner coating and passing up through an insulating stopper.

**LF, L.F.,** or **l.f.** low frequency.

**l.h.** or **L.H.** left hand.

**Li** lithium.

**li·a·bil·i·ty** (lī′ə bil′ə tē) **1** the state of being susceptible: *Insufficient rest can increase one's liability to disease.* **2** the state of being under obligation: *liability for damage. He refused to acknowledge any liability for his brother's debt.* **3** a person or thing that acts as a disadvantage: *Her short temper is a liability in dealing with people.* **4** Usually, **liabilities**, *pl.* debts: *The monthly statement shows the company's assets and liabilities.* *n.*, *pl.* **li·a·bil·i·ties.**

**li·a·ble** (lī′ə bəl) **1** likely, especially unpleasantly likely: *Glass is liable to break. One is liable to slip on ice.* **2** in danger of having, doing, etc.: *We are all liable to diseases.* **3** responsible; bound by law to pay: *The Post Office is not liable for damage to a parcel sent by mail unless it is insured.* **4** under obligation; subject: *Citizens are liable to jury duty.* *adj.*
☛ *Syn.* In formal English, **liable** (def. 1) is best used when the reference is to something happening to someone or something; LIKELY is the better word when the reference is to somebody doing something: *Amato is liable to be blamed for the accident. The other driver is likely to get off scot-free.*

**li·ai·son** (lē ā′zon) **1** communication in order to co-ordinate activities between parts of a whole, such as parts of a military unit, schools in a system, or departments within a government. **2** any close bond or connection. **3** an illicit love affair. **4** in speaking French, the pronouncing of a usually silent final consonant when it occurs before a word beginning with a vowel sound. The consonant is spoken as though it belonged to the second word. *Example: Comment allez-vous?* (kô mäɴ tä lä vü′). *n.*

**liaison officer** a person, especially an officer in the armed forces, who acts as a go-between to ensure proper co-operation between departments, units, etc.

**li·a·na** (lē ä′nə) a climbing vine with a woody stem: *Giant lianas wind around the trunks and climb from tree to tree in jungles.* *n.*

**li·ar** (lī′ər) a person who tells lies; a person who says what is not true. *n.*

**lib.** **1** librarian. **2** library.

**Lib.** Liberal.

**li·ba·tion** (lī bā′shən) **1** a pouring out of wine, water, etc. as an offering to a god. **2** the wine, water, etc. offered in this way. *n.*

**li·bel** (lī′bəl) **1** in law, a written or published statement, picture, etc. tending to damage a person's reputation. **2** write or publish a libel about. **3** the crime of writing or publishing a libel. **4** any false or damaging statement about a person. **5** make false or damaging statements about. 1, 3, 4 *n.*, 2, 5 *v.*, **li·belled** or **li·beled**, **li·bel·ling** or **li·bel·ing.**

**li·bel·ler** or **li·bel·er** (lī′bə lər) a person who LIBELS another. *n.*

**li·bel·lous** or **li·bel·ous** (lī′bə ləs) **1** containing a LIBEL. **2** spreading LIBELS: *a libellous tongue.* *adj.*

**lib·er·al** (lib′ə rəl *or* lib′rəl) **1** generous: *a liberal donation.* **2** plentiful; abundant: *He put in a liberal supply of wood for the winter.* **3** broad-minded; not narrow in one's ideas: *a liberal thinker.* **4** designed to broaden the mind in a general way; not professional or technical: *a liberal education.* **5** favouring or following the principles of LIBERALISM (def. 1). **6** a person who favours or follows such principles. **7** giving the general thought, not a word-for-word rendering: *a liberal*

interpretation of the speaker's ideas. 1–5, 7 *adj.*, 6 *n.*
—**lib′er·al·ly,** *adv.* —**lib′er·al·ness,** *n.*

**Lib·er·al** (lib′ə rəl *or* lib′rəl) **1** a member of the LIBERAL PARTY. **2** a person who supports the views and principles of the LIBERAL PARTY. **3** of or favouring the LIBERAL PARTY. 1, 2 *n.*, 3 *adj.*

**liberal arts** subjects such as literature, languages, history, and philosophy as distinct from technical or professional subjects.

**liberal education** an education in the LIBERAL ARTS, especially as distinct from a technical or professional education.

**lib·er·al·ism** (lib′ə rə liz′əm *or* lib′rə liz′əm) **1** a political philosophy that emphasizes belief in progress, individual freedom, and a democratic form of government. **2** the quality or state of being LIBERAL (def. 3). *n.*

**lib·er·al·ist** (lib′ə rə list *or* lib′rə list) a person who holds LIBERAL (defs. 3, 5) principles and ideas; believer in progress and reforms. *n.*

**lib·er·al·i·ty** (lib′ə ral′ə tē) **1** generosity; generous behaviour: *We were allowed to use the pool because of the liberality of the club members.* **2** gift. **3** broad-mindedness. **4** a tolerant and progressive nature: *The liberality of the class members helped them accept new pupils who looked different.* *n.*, *pl.* **lib·er·al·i·ties.**

**lib·er·al·ize** (lib′ə rə līz′ *or* lib′rə līz′) make or become LIBERAL. *v.*, **lib·er·al·ized, lib·er·al·iz·ing.** —**lib′er·al·i·za′tion,** *n.*

**Liberal Party** one of the principal political parties of Canada.

**lib·er·ate** (lib′ə rāt′) **1** set free: *to liberate a country, to liberate a slave.* **2** in chemistry, set free from combination: *liberate a gas.* *v.*, **lib·er·at·ed, lib·er·at·ing.** —**lib′er·a′tor,** *n.*

**lib·er·a·tion** (lib′ə rā′shən) setting free or being set free. *n.*

**Li·be·ri·an** (lī bē′rē ən) **1** of or having to do with Liberia, a country in West Africa, or its people. **2** a native or inhabitant of Liberia. 1 *adj.*, 2 *n.*

**lib·er·tine** (lib′ər tēn′) **1** a person who lives without regard to convention or accepted moral standards. **2** of, having to do with, or characteristic of a libertine. 1 *n.*, 2 *adj.*

**lib·er·tin·ism** (lib′ər tē niz′əm) the behaviour of a LIBERTINE (def. 1). *n.*

**lib·er·ty** (lib′ər tē) **1** freedom; independence: *The prisoner yearned for liberty. The colony finally won its liberty.* **2** the right or power to do as one pleases; power or opportunity to do something: *liberty of speech or action.* **3** the leave granted to a sailor to go ashore. **4** the right of being in, using, etc.: *We give our dog the liberty of the yard.* **5** a privilege or right granted by government. *n.*, *pl.* **lib·er·ties.**
**at liberty,** **a** free: *The escaped lion is still at liberty.* **b** allowed; permitted: *You are at liberty to make any choice*

*you please.* **c** not busy: *The principal will see you as soon as she is at liberty.*
**take liberties,** **a** be too familiar: *to take liberties with a person.* **b** treat too freely: *The author took liberties with the facts to make the story more interesting.*

**li·bi·do** (lə bē′dō) 1 sexual desire or instinct. 2 emotional or mental drive or energy in general. *n.*

**Li·bra** (lē′brə) 1 a southern constellation thought of as having the shape of a pair of scales. 2 in astrology, the seventh sign of the zodiac: *The sun enters Libra about September 23.* See ZODIAC for picture. 3 a person born under this sign. *n.*

**li·brar·i·an** (lī brer′ē ən) 1 a person trained in LIBRARY SCIENCE, especially one who makes it his or her work. 2 a person in charge of a library. *n.*

**li·brar·y** (lī′brer ē) 1 a room or building where a collection of books, periodicals, phonograph records, tapes, etc. is kept to be used, rented, or borrowed, but not sold: *Our town has a very good public library.* 2 a collection of books, periodicals, etc., especially a large collection that is systematically arranged: *They have an extensive library of rare books.* *n., pl.* **li·brar·ies.**

**library science** the principles and practice of library organization and management.

**li·bret·tist** (lə bret′ist) the writer of a LIBRETTO. *n.*

**li·bret·to** (lə bret′ō) 1 the words of an opera, oratorio, operetta, etc. 2 a book containing these words. *n., pl.* **li·bret·tos.**

**Lib·y·an** (lib′ē ən) 1 of or having to do with Libya, a country in northern Africa, or its people. 2 of or having to do with ancient Libya, which consisted of northern Africa west of Egypt. 3 a native or inhabitant of Libya. 4 the Berber language of ancient Libya. *1, 2 adj., 3, 4 n.*

**lice** (līs) *pl.* of LOUSE. *n.*

**li·cence** or **li·cense** (lī′səns) 1 permission given by law to do something. 2 the paper, card, plate, etc. showing such permission: *The barber hung his licence on the wall.* 3 the fact or condition of being permitted to do something. 4 freedom of action, speech, thought, etc. that is permitted or conceded: *Poetic licence is the freedom from rules that is permitted in poetry and art.* 5 too much liberty; disregard of what is right and proper; abuse of liberty: *The children were given licence to invade their neighbours' gardens.* *n.*

**li·cense** or **li·cence** (lī′səns) 1 give a LICENCE (def. 1) to: *to license a new driver.* 2 permit or authorize, especially by law: *A doctor is licensed to practise medicine.* *v.* **li·censed** or **li·cenced, li·cens·ing** or **li·cenc·ing.** —**li′cens·er** or **li′cen·cer,** *n.*

**li·censed** or **li·cenced** (lī′sənst) 1 holding a government LICENCE (def. 1) to sell alcoholic liquors for drinking on the premises: *a licensed restaurant. Beer parlours are licensed premises.* 2 holding any other kind of licence: *I am a licensed driver. He is a licensed hunter.* *adj.*

**li·cen·see** (lī′sən sē′) a person to whom a LICENCE (def. 1) is given. *n.*

**li·cen·tious** (lī sen′shəs) disregarding commonly accepted moral principles, especially in sexual behaviour; lewd. *adj.* —**li·cen′tious·ly,** *adv.* —**li·cen′tious·ness,** *n.*

**li·chee** (lē′chē) See LITCHI. *n.*

**li·chen** (lī′kən) a flowerless plant that resembles moss and grows in patches on trees, rocks, etc.: *A lichen consists of a fungus and an alga growing together so that they look like one plant.* *n.*
☞ *Hom.* LIKEN.

**lich–gate** (lich′gāt′) a roofed gateway to a churchyard where a coffin can be set down to await the clergyman's arrival. *n.* Also, **lych-gate.**

**lick** (lik) 1 pass the tongue over: *to lick a stamp.* 2 lap up with the tongue: *The cat licked the milk.* 3 make or bring by using the tongue: *The cat licked the plate clean.* 4 a stroke of the tongue over something: *She gave the ice-cream cone a big lick.* 5 pass about or play over like a tongue: *The flames were licking the roof.* 6 a place where natural salt is found and where animals go to lick it up. 7 *Informal.* a blow: *I lost the fight, but I got in a few good licks.* 8 *Informal.* beat; thrash: *Her dad will lick her if he finds out about the broken window.* 9 *Informal.* defeat or overcome; conquer: *So far we've licked every problem without help. I could lick him with one hand tied behind my back.* 10 a small quantity: *She didn't do a lick of work.* 11 *Informal.* a brief stroke of activity or effort: *a lick and a promise.* 12 *Informal.* speed; clip: *She came down the road at a great lick.* 13 *Informal.* **licks,** *pl.* opportunity; chance: *I'm sure you'll get your licks in later.* *1–3, 5, 8, 9 v., 4, 6, 7, 10–13 n.*
**lick into shape,** *Informal.* make presentable or usable.

**lick·e·ty–split** (lik′ə tē split′) *Informal.* at a great speed; headlong: *She was off down the sidewalk lickety-split before they could stop her.* *adv.*

**lick·ing** (lik′ing) *Informal.* 1 a thrashing or spanking. 2 a defeat or setback. 3 ppr. of LICK. *1, 2 n., 3 v.*

**lick·spit·tle** (lik′spit′əl) a contemptible flatterer. *n.*

**lic·o·rice** (lik′ə rish, lik′rish, *or* lik′ə ris) 1 a sweet, black, gummy extract obtained from the roots of a European plant, used as a flavouring. 2 candy flavoured with this extract. 3 the plant that yields licorice. 4 the dried root of this plant. *n.* Also, **liquorice.**
☞ *Etym.* Through OF from late L *liquiritia,* which came from Gk. *glukurrhiza,* made up of *glukus* 'sweet' (as in GLUCOSE) + *rhiza* 'root'.

**lic·tor** (lik′tər) in ancient Rome, an attendant on a public official, who punished offenders at the official's orders. See FASCES for picture. *n.*

**lid** (lid) 1 a movable cover or top: *the lid of a box.* 2 the cover of skin that is moved in opening and shutting the eye; eyelid. *n.*

**L.I.D.** Local Improvement District.

**lid·less** (lid′lis) 1 having no lid. 2 having no eyelids. *adj.*

**lie¹** (lī) 1 a false statement, known to be false by the person who makes it: *The naughty child told a lie to avoid punishment.* 2 something intended to give a false impression. 3 tell lies. 4 get, bring, put, etc. by lying: *to lie oneself out of a difficulty.* 5 make a false statement. *1, 2 n., 3, 4, 5 v.,* **lied, ly·ing.**
**give the lie to,** **a** call a liar; accuse of lying. **b** show to be false.
☞ *Hom.* LYE.

**lie²** (lī) 1 have one's body in a flat position along the ground or other surface: *to lie on the grass.* 2 assume such a position: *to lie down on a couch.* 3 be in a horizontal or flat position: *The book was lying on the table.*

**4** be kept or stay in a given position, state, etc.: *to lie idle.* **5** be; be placed: *The lake lies to the south of us.* **6** exist; be; have its place; belong: *The cure lies in education.* **7** be in the grave; be buried: *His body lies in Halifax.* *v.*, **lay, lain, ly·ing.**

**lie about** or **around,** **a** be lazy; do nothing. **b** be left: *Please don't leave your clothes lying around.*
**lie behind,** cause; be the reason for.
**lie down under,** suffer without complaint.
**lie in,** **a** be confined in childbirth. **b** stay in bed later than usual.
**lie off,** of a ship, etc., stay not far from.
**lie over,** be left waiting until a later time.
**lie to,** of a ship, etc., come almost to a stop, facing the wind: *During the storm, the sailing ship lay to.*
☛ *Hom.* LYE.
☛ *Usage.* See note at LAY¹.

**lied** (līd) pt. and pp. of LIE¹: *That boy lied about his work. He has lied before.* *v.*

**liege** (lēj) in the Middle Ages: **1** a lord having a right to the homage and loyal service of his vassals. **2** having a right to the homage and loyal service of VASSALS. **3** a VASSAL obliged to give homage and loyal service to his lord. **4** obliged to give homage and loyal service to a lord. 1, 3 *n.*, 2, 4 *adj.*

**liege lord** a feudal lord.

**liege·man** (lēj′mən) **1** VASSAL. **2** a faithful follower. *n., pl.* **liege·men** (-mən).

**lien** (lēn) in law, a claim placed on the property of another as a safeguard for payment of a debt in connection with that property. *n.*
☛ *Hom.* LEAN.

**lieu** (lü) *Archaic (except in* **in lieu of**). place; stead. *n.*
**in lieu of,** in place of; instead of: *During the hard times they gave the landlord produce in lieu of money for rent.*

**lieu·ten·an·cy** (lef ten′ən sē *or* lü ten′ən sē) the rank, commission, or authority of a LIEUTENANT (def. 2). *n., pl.* **lieu·ten·an·cies.**

**lieu·ten·ant** (lef ten′ənt *or* lü ten′ənt) **1** a person who acts for someone senior to him or her in authority: *The coach used the two boys as his lieutenants.* **2** a junior commissioned officer in the armed forces. *n.*
☛ *Etym.* From French, made up of *lieu* 'place' and *tenant* 'holding'; a lieutenant held the place of (or acted for) a captain who was absent. 16c.

**lieu·ten·ant–gov·er·nor** (lef ten′ənt guv′ər nər) the official head of a provincial government, appointed by the Governor General in Council, for a term of five years; the representative of the Crown in a province. *n.*

**life** (līf) **1** living or being alive; the quality that people, animals, and plants have and that rocks, dirt, and metals lack. **2** the time of being alive: *She enjoyed a long life.* **3** the time of existence or action; a period of being able to operate, etc.: *a machine's life.* **4** a living being; person: *Five lives were lost in the fire.* **5** living things considered together: *The desert island had almost no animal or vegetable life.* **6** a way of living: *a dull life.* **7** an account of a person's life: *a life of Helen Hogg.* **8** spirit; vigour: *Put more life into your work.* **9** a source of activity or liveliness. **10** a period of existence in the world of affairs or society: *The life of that administration was very short.* *n., pl.* **lives** (līvz).

hat, āge, fär; let, ēqual, tėrm; it, īce
hot, ōpen, ôrder; oil, out; cup, pùt, rüle
əbove, takən, pencəl, lemən, circəs
ch, child; ng, long; sh, ship
th, thin; ᴛн, then; zh, measure

**as large** or **as big as life,** **a** as big as the living person or thing. **b** in person.
**for dear life,** to save or as if to save one's life: *He ran for dear life.*
**for life,** **a** for the rest of one's life. **b** to save one's life.
**for the life of me,** *Informal.* even if my life depended on it (*used only in negative expressions*): *I can't for the life of me remember where I put my keys.*
**from life,** using a living model: *The drawing was made from life.*
**see life,** *Informal.* get experience, especially of the exciting features of human activities.
**take life,** kill.
**take one's own life,** kill oneself.
**to the life,** like the model; exactly; perfectly.
**true to life,** true to reality; as in real life: *Good novels are true to life.*

**life and limb** physical safety and survival: *The old bridge is a danger to life and limb.*

**life belt** a life preserver in the shape of a thick ring, worn around the chest and under the arms.

**life·blood** (līf′blud′) **1** blood necessary to life. **2** a source of strength and energy: *The young people became the lifeblood of the organization.* *n.*

**life·boat** (līf′bōt′) **1** a strong boat specially built for saving lives at sea or along the coast. **2** a boat carried on a ship for use by the passengers in an emergency. *n.*

**life buoy** a LIFE PRESERVER.

**life·guard** (līf′gärd′) a person who is responsible for the safety of swimmers and bathers at a public pool or beach. *n.*

**life insurance** insurance that provides for the payment of a specified amount of money to a particular person or persons on the death of the insured, or sometimes, to the insured when he or she reaches a certain age.

**life jacket** a life preserver in the form of a vest.

**life·less** (līf′lis) **1** not alive; without life: *a lifeless statue.* **2** dead: *lifeless bodies on the battlefield.* **3** having no living things: *a lifeless planet.* **4** dull: *a lifeless performance.* *adj.* —**life′less·ly,** *adv.* —**life′less·ness,** *n.*

**life·like** (līf′līk′) like life; looking as if alive; like the real thing: *a lifelike portrait.* *adj.* —**life′like·ness,** *n.*

**life line** **1** a rope for saving life, such as one thrown to a ship from shore. **2** a diver's signalling line. **3** anything that maintains or helps to maintain something that cannot exist by itself.

**life·long** (līf′flong′) lasting all one's life: *a lifelong friendship.* *adj.*

**life net** a strong net or sheet of canvas, used to catch people jumping from burning buildings.

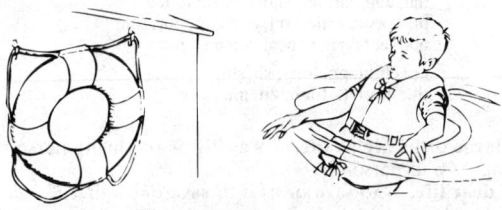
Two kinds of life preserver

**life preserver** a device made of buoyant or inflatable material, designed to keep a person afloat in water to prevent drowning. It may be in the form of a vest, a wide belt, or a thick ring.

**life raft** a raft for saving lives in a shipwreck or the wreck of an aircraft at sea.

**life·sav·er** (līf′sā′vər) **1** a person or thing that saves people from drowning, especially a lifeguard. **2** *Informal.* a person or thing that saves one from trouble, discomfort, embarrassment, etc.: *The interruption was a lifesaver, because I didn't know what to say to him any more.* *n.*

**life·sav·ing** (līf′sā′ving) **1** the skill, act, or practice of saving people's lives, especially by preventing drowning. **2** designed for or having to do with saving people's lives: *lifesaving classes, lifesaving equipment.* 1 *n.*, 2 *adj.*

**life-size** (līf′sīz′) having the same size as the living person, animal, etc.: *a life-size statue.* *adj.*

**life·style** (līf′stīl′) a way of life; the typical habits, pastimes, attitudes, etc. of a person or group: *a casual lifestyle. Their downtown apartment suits their lifestyle.* *n.*

**life·time** (līf′tīm′) **1** the length of time that someone is alive or that something exists or functions: *In his whole lifetime he had never been in an airplane.* **2** lasting for such a length of time: *a lifetime commitment.* *n.*

**life·work** (līf′fwėrk′) work that takes or lasts a whole lifetime; main work in life. *n.*

**lift** (lift) **1** raise; take up; raise into a higher position: *to lift a chair.* **2** hold up; display on high. **3** raise in rank, condition, estimation, etc.; elevate; exalt. **4** an elevating influence. **5** rise and go; go away: *The fog lifted at dawn.* **6** go up; yield to an effort to raise something: *This window will not lift.* **7** pull or tug upward. **8** the act of lifting. **9** the distance through which a thing is lifted. **10** a helping hand: *I gave him a lift with the heavy box.* **11** a ride in a vehicle given to a pedestrian or hiker; free ride: *She often gave the neighbour's boy a lift to school.* **12** send up loudly: *to lift a voice or cry.* **13** rise to view above the horizon. **14** *Informal.* pick or take up; steal: *to lift things from a store.* **15** pay off: *to lift a mortgage.* **16** *Esp. Brit.* elevator. **17** SKI LIFT. **18** one of the layers of leather in the heel of a shoe. **19** a rise in ground. **20** an improvement in spirits: *The promotion gave him a lift.* 1–3, 5–7, 12–15 *v.*, 4, 8–11, 16–20 *n.* —**lift′er**, *n.*

**lift off,** rise from the ground: *The spaceship will lift off in two hours.*

**lift lock** a canal or river lock in which each water-filled compartment itself is raised and lowered while the water level within the compartment remains the same.

**lift-off** (lif′tof′) the vertical take-off of an aircraft, rocket, etc.; the act or moment of rising from the ground or launching pad. *n.*

**lig·a·ment** (lig′ə mənt) **1** in anatomy, a band of strong tissue that connects bones or holds organs in place. **2** a tie or bond. *n.*

**lig·a·ture** (lig′ə chər *or* lig′ə chür′) **1** something used to bind or tie up, especially a thread, etc. used to tie up a bleeding artery, etc. **2** something that unites or connects; bond. **3** bind or tie up with a ligature. **4** a binding or tying up. **5** in music, a slur or a group of notes connected by a slur. **6** two or three letters joined in printing: Æ and ffl are ligatures. 1, 2, 4–6 *n.*, 3 *v.*, **lig·a·tured, lig·a·tur·ing.**

**light**[1] (līt) **1** that by which we see; the form of radiant energy that acts on the retina of the eye: *The sun gives light to the earth.* **2** having light or much light: *a light room.* **3** anything that gives light: *The sun, a lamp, or a lighthouse is called a light.* **4** a supply of light: *A tall building cuts off our light.* **5** cause to give light: *She lighted the lamp.* **6** give light to; provide with light: *The room is lighted by six windows.* **7** bright or clear: *It is as light as day.* **8** brightness; clearness; illumination: *a strong light, a dim light.* **9** a bright part: *light and shade.* **10** make bright: *Her face was lighted by a smile.* **11** become light: *The sky lights up at sunset.* **12** daytime; daylight: *The worker got up before light.* **13** dawn. **14** pale in colour; whitish: *light hair, light blue.* **15** a window or other means of letting in light. **16** show the way by giving light: *Her flashlight lighted us through the tunnel.* **17** something with which to start something else burning. **18** set fire to: *She lighted the candles.* **19** take fire. **20** knowledge; information; illumination of mind: *We need more light on this subject.* **21** public knowledge; open view. **22** the aspect in which a thing is viewed: *He put the matter in the right light.* **23** a shining figure; model; example: *The actor was a leading light in the theatre.* **24** favour; approval: *the light of his countenance.* 1, 3, 4, 8, 9, 12, 13, 15, 17, 20–24 *n.*, 2, 7, 14 *adj.*, 5, 6, 10, 11, 16, 18, 19 *v.*, **light·ed** or **lit, light·ing.**

**according to one's lights,** following one's own ideas, intelligence, etc. in the best way that one knows.

**bring to light,** reveal; expose: *Many facts were brought to light during the investigation.*

**come to light,** be revealed or exposed.

**in the light of,** **a** by considering. **b** from the standpoint of.

**see the light** or **see the light of day,** **a** be born. **b** be made public. **c** get the right idea.

**shed** or **throw light on,** explain; make clear.

**light**[2] (līt) **1** easy to carry; not heavy: *a light load.* **2** of little mass for its size: *a light metal.* **3** of less than usual mass: *light clothing.* **4** less than usual in amount, force, or strength: *a light meal, a light sleep, a light rain.* **5** easy to do or bear; not hard or severe: *light punishment, a light task.* **6** not looking heavy; graceful; delicate: *a light bridge, light carving.* **7** moving easily; nimble: *light on one's feet.* **8** cheerfully careless: *a light laugh, a light retort.* **9** not serious enough; fickle: *a light mind, light of purpose.* **10** aiming to entertain; not serious: *light reading.* **11** not important: *light losses.* **12** careless in morals. **13** not dense: *a light fog.* **14** porous; sandy: *light soil.* **15** containing little alcohol: *a light wine.* **16** lightly armed or equipped: *light cavalry, in light marching order.* **17** lightly. **18** with as little luggage as possible: *I like to travel light.* 1–16 *adj.*, 17, 18 *adv.*

**light in the head,** **a** dizzy. **b** silly; foolish. **c** crazy; out of one's head.

**make light of,** treat as of little importance.

**light**[3] (līt) **1** come down to the ground; alight: *He lighted from his horse.* **2** come down from flight: *A bird lighted on a twig.* **3** come by chance: *Her eye lighted on a* *crack.* **4** fall suddenly: *The blow lit on his ear.* *v.*, **light·ed** or **lit, light·ing.**

**light bulb** a glass bulb containing a filament of very fine wire that becomes white hot and gives off light when an electric current flows through it.

**light-e·mit·ting di·ode** (līˈtē mitˈing dīˈōd) a device that gives off light when electricity is applied. It is used especially for displays of numerals in calculators and digital clocks. *Abbrev.*: L.E.D. or LED.

**light·en**[1] (līˈtən) **1** make or become bright or brighter: *Dawn lightens the sky. The sky gradually lightened.* **2** make or become pale or paler in colour: *The summer sun lightened her hair.* **3** flash with lightning: *I just saw it lighten in the west.* *v.*

**light·en**[2] (līˈtən) **1** reduce the load of a ship; have the load reduced. **2** make or become less of a burden: *to lighten taxes.* **3** make or become more cheerful: *The good news lightened their hearts. His face lightened when he saw her.* *v.*

**light·er**[1] (līˈtər) a person or thing that starts something burning; especially a device used to light a cigarette, cigar, or pipe. *n.*

**light·er**[2] (līˈtər) **1** a flat-bottomed barge used for loading and unloading ships. **2** carry goods in a flat-bottomed barge. **1** *n.*, **2** *v.*

**light-fin·gered** (lītˈfingˈgərd) thievish; skilful at picking pockets. *adj.*

**light-foot·ed** (lītˈfutˈid) stepping lightly. *adj.*

**light-head·ed** (lītˈhedˈid) **1** dizzy or giddy: *The fever was gone, but she still felt a little light-headed.* **2** not sensible; silly; frivolous: *They're much too light-headed to take on a responsible job.* *adj.*

**light-heart·ed** (lītˈhärˈtid) carefree; cheerful; gay. *adj.* —**lightˈ-heartˈed·ly,** *adv.* —**lightˈ-heartˈed·ness,** *n.*

**light heavyweight** a boxer who weighs between 76 and 81 kilograms.

**light horse** cavalry that carries light weapons and equipment.

A lighthouse

**light·house** (lītˈhousˈ) a tower or framework with a bright light that shines far over the water: *Lighthouses are usually located at dangerous places to warn and guide ships.* *n.*

**light·ing** (līˈting) **1** the giving of light; providing with light. **2** the way in which lights are arranged. **3** light, and lighting equipment. **4** a starting to burn. **5** ppr. of LIGHT. **1–4** *n.*, **5** *v.*

**light·ly** (lītˈlē) **1** with little pressure, force, etc.; gently: *Her hand rested lightly on his arm. Janos held the bird lightly in his hand.* **2** to a small degree or extent: *lightly clad.* **3** quickly or easily: *She jumped lightly aside.* **4** cheerfully: *to take bad news lightly.* **5** indifferently or carelessly: *The issue is too important to be passed over lightly.* *adv.*

**light meter** a device for measuring the intensity of light, especially an exposure meter: *Some cameras have a built-in light meter.*

**light-mind·ed** (lītˈmīnˈdid) not serious; thoughtless and frivolous. *adj.* —**lightˈ-mindˈed·ly,** *adv.*

**light·ness**[1] (lītˈnis) **1** the quality or state of being bright or clear: *The lightness of the sky showed that the rain was over.* **2** the quality or state of being light in colour or pale: *Sven has to be careful in the sun because of the lightness of his skin.* *n.*

**light·ness**[2] (lītˈnis) **1** the quality or state of having little mass; not being heavy: *The lightness of the second load was a relief after the first one he had carried.* **2** lack of severity; leniency: *The lightness of the sentence surprised the defendant.* **3** a lack of pressure or force; delicacy: *the lightness of a touch.* **4** cheerfulness or gaiety: *lightness of spirits.* **5** gracefulness or nimbleness: *the lightness of a step.* **6** lack of proper seriousness: *Such lightness of conduct is not permitted in a courtroom.* *n.*

**light·ning** (lītˈning) **1** a flash of light in the sky caused by a discharge of electricity between clouds, or between a cloud and the earth's surface. **2** like lightning; very fast or sudden: *a lightning decision, a lightning change of mood.* *n.*

**lightning bug** FIREFLY.

**lightning rod** a metal rod fixed on a building or ship to conduct lightning into the earth or water to prevent fire.

**light pen** an electronic device to allow the user to control data on a computer terminal by pointing to it.

**light·proof** (lītˈprüfˈ) that will not let light in; sealed so that no light can enter: *A camera must be lightproof.* *adj.*

**light·ship** (lītˈshipˈ) a ship with a bright light that shines far over the water, anchored at a dangerous place to warn and guide ships. *n.*

**light·some** (lītˈsəm) **1** nimble and lively: *lightsome feet.* **2** carefree; cheerful: *a lightsome heart.* **3** frivolous. *adj.*

**light·weight** (lītˈwātˈ) **1** a person or thing of less than average mass. **2** having less than the average or usual mass: *a lightweight portable sewing machine.* **3** a boxer weighing between 58 and 60 kilograms. **4** a person of little importance or influence: *She is regarded as a lightweight in the literary world.* **5** of, having to do with, or characteristic of lightweights: *the lightweight boxing championship.* **1, 3, 4** *n.*, **2, 5** *adj.*

**light-year** (lītˈyērˈ) in astronomy, a unit of distance equal to the distance that light travels in one year in a vacuum, about 9 460 500 000 000 km: *The nearest star is more than four light-years away.* *n.*

**lig·ne·ous** (ligˈnē əs) of or like wood; woody. *adj.*

**lig·nite** (ligˈnīt) a very soft, brownish-black type of coal containing less carbon and more water than bituminous coal and often having a woody texture: *Lignite is a poor quality, imperfectly formed coal, intermediate between peat and bituminous coal.* *n.*

**lig·num vi·tae** (lig'nəm vī'tē *or* vē'tī)   **1** either of two closely related species of tropical American tree having very heavy, hard, olive-brown wood.   **2** the wood of any of these trees, highly valued for making pulleys, bearings, casters, etc.: *Lignum vitae is very resinous and so dense that it will not float in water.*   *n.*

**lik·a·ble** (lī'kə bəl)   having qualities that win good will or friendship; popular: *a likable person.*   *adj.*
—**lik'a·ble·ness,** *n.*   Also, **likeable**.

**like¹** (līk)   **1** having the characteristics of; resembling; similar to: *Myra is like her sister. I never saw anything like it.*   **2** in the same way as; in the manner of; similarly to: *She can run like a deer. He acted like a tyrant.*   **3** such as one would expect of; typical of: *Isn't that just like him?*   **4** of the same or nearly the same form, kind, appearance, amount, etc.; similar: *Suzanne's uncle promised her $50 if she could earn a like sum.*   **5** in the right state or frame of mind for doing or having: *She felt like working. I feel like a cup of coffee.*   **6** indicative or giving promise of: *It looks like rain.*   **7** such as; as for example: *They offer technical courses like mechanics, drafting, and plumbing.*   **8** *Informal.*   like as; as: *He reacted just like I did when I first saw it.*   **9** *Informal.*   as if: *It looks like we'll have to do it ourselves.*   **10** a person or thing like another; counterpart or equal; match: *We will not see her like again. They had never seen the like before.*   **11** *Informal.* probably: *Like enough it will rain.*   1–3, 5–7 *prep.,* 4 *adj.,* 8, 9 *conj.,* 10 *n.,* 11 *adv.*
**and the like,** and similar things; and so forth: *She studied music, painting, and the like.*
**like crazy, mad, etc.** *Informal.*   very much; to a great degree; with great speed, effort, or intensity: *She works like crazy.*
**nothing like,**   not nearly: *It's nothing like as cold as it was yesterday.*
**something like,**   about or almost like: *The tune goes something like this.*
☛ *Usage.* In standard written English, a distinction is made between the use of **like** and AS. **As** and AS IF are used as conjunctions to introduce clauses of comparison: *He still writes as he used to when he was a child. Act as if you were familiar with the place.* **Like** is used as a preposition in phrases of comparison: *She swims like a fish. He writes like a child.* In informal English, however, **like** is often used in place of **as** to introduce clauses: *He writes like he used to when he was a child.*

**like²** (līk)   **1** be pleased or satisfied with; enjoy: *Do you like milk? She likes the job but not the salary.*   **2** have a friendly feeling toward; feel an attraction toward: *They like their new math teacher.*   **3** wish for; want (*used with* would): *I would like a glass of milk, please. I'd like to get my hands on whoever took my bike.*   **4** be inclined; choose: *Come whenever you like.*   **5 likes,** *pl.* likings; preferences: *My mother knows most of my likes and dislikes.*   1–4 *v.,* **liked, lik·ing;** 5 *n.*

**–like**   an adjective-forming suffix meaning:   **1** like: *wolflike means like a wolf.*   **2** like that of; characteristic of: *childlike means like that of a child.*   **3** suited to; fit or proper for: *Businesslike means suited to business.*
☛ *Usage.* Words ending in a spoken vowel or diphthong, or the letter *l*, are followed by a hyphen before this suffix: *lily-like, day-like, hill-like.*

**like·a·ble** (lī'kə bəl)   See LIKABLE.   *adj.*
—**like'a·ble·ness,** *n.*

**like·li·hood** (līk'lē hüd')   probability: *Is there any likelihood of rain this afternoon?*   *n.*

**like·ly** (līk'lē)   **1** probable: *One likely result of the heavy rains is a flood.*   **2** probably: *I'll very likely be home all day.*   **3** to be expected: *It is likely to be hot in August.*   **4** suitable: *Is there a likely place to fish?*   **5** promising: *a likely boy.*   1, 3–5 *adj.,* **like·li·er, like·li·est;** 2 *adv.*
☛ *Syn.* See note at LIABLE.

**lik·en** (līk'ən)   represent or describe as like; compare: *The poet likens life to a dream.*   *v.*
☛ *Hom.* LICHEN.

**like·ness** (līk'nis)   **1** a resemblance; being alike: *There is a strong likeness between the girl and her mother.*   **2** something that is like; a copy or representation, especially a painting, drawing, or photograph: *The portrait is a good likeness of her.*   **3** the appearance or shape: *The wizard assumed the likeness of a very old man.*   *n.*

**like·wise** (līk'wīz')   **1** the same; in the same way: *See what I do. Now do likewise.*   **2** also; moreover; too: *He was a painter, a sculptor, and likewise a writer.*   *adv.*

**lik·ing** (līk'ing)   **1** a preference or taste: *She had a great liking for apples. The entertainment was not to his liking.*   **2** a fondness or kindly feeling: *She had a liking for children.*   **3** ppr. of LIKE.   1, 2 *n.,* 3 *v.*

**li·lac** (lī'lək *or* lī'lok)   **1** a shrub having clusters of tiny, fragrant flowers.   **2** the cluster of flowers: *Most lilacs are pale pinkish-purple, deep purple, or white.*   **3** pale pinkish-purple.   1–3 *n.,* 3 *adj.*

**Lil·li·pu·tian** (lil'ə pyü'shən)   **1** very small; tiny; petty.   **2** a very small person; dwarf.   1 *adj.,* 2 *n.*
☛ *Etym.* From *Lilliput,* an imaginary island described in *Gulliver's Travels,* by Jonathan Swift (1667–1745). The island was inhabited by tiny people about 15 cm tall.

**lilt** (lilt)   **1** sing or play a tune in a light, tripping manner.   **2** a lively song or tune with a swing.   **3** a way of speaking in which the pitch of the voice varies in a pleasing manner: *Brigid talks with an Irish lilt.*   **4** a lively, springy movement.   1 *v.,* 2–4 *n.*

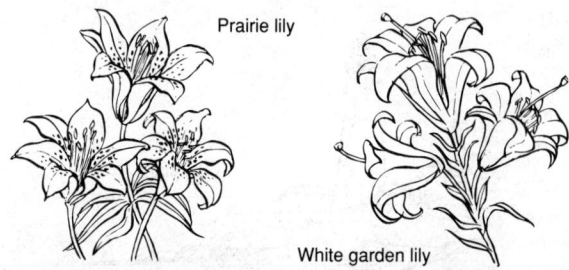

Prairie lily

White garden lily

**lil·y** (lil'ē)   **1** any of a closely related group of plants that grow from bulbs, having leafy stems and showy flowers: *The prairie lily is the provincial flower of Saskatchewan. The white garden lily is the provincial flower of Quebec.*   **2** any of various other plants of the same family having similar flowers: *The glacier lily is a common wildflower of the Rockies.*   **3** referring to the family of plants that includes the lilies: *Trilliums, hyacinths, tulips, onions, etc. also belong to the lily family.*   **4** any of various other plants having showy flowers, such as the calla lily and water lily. See WATER LILY for picture.   **5** the flower of a lily.   **6** like a lily in being white or pale, fragile, pure, etc.: *her lily hands.*   *n., pl.* **lil·ies,**
—**lil'y-like',** *adj.*

**gild the lily,** try to improve on something that is already excellent or completely satisfactory.

**lil·y–liv·ered** (lil′ē liv′ərd) cowardly. *adj.*

**lily of the valley** a low-growing perennial plant of the lily family having small, bell-shaped, fragrant, white flowers growing on short stems along a main stem. *pl.* **lilies of the valley.**

**lily pad** one of the large, round, floating leaves of a water lily.

**lima bean** (lī′mə) **1** a species of bean having broad pods that contain broad, flat, light-green seeds. **2** the seed of this plant, used as food.

**limb** (lim) **1** a leg, arm, or wing. **2** a large branch of a tree; bough: *They sawed off the dead limb.* **3** the part that projects: *the four limbs of a cross.* **4** a person or thing thought of as a part, branch, representative, etc.: *A police officer is a limb of the law.* *n.* —**limb′less,** *adj.*
**limb from limb,** completely apart; entirely to pieces.
**out on a limb,** in or into a dangerous or exposed position: *The producer of the play was left out on a limb when his backers suddenly withdrew their support.*
**tear limb from limb,** tear a body violently apart; dismember violently.
☞ *Hom.* LIMN.

**lim·ber¹** (lim′bər) **1** bending easily; flexible: *A pianist has to have limber fingers.* **2** make or become supple or more easily flexed (*used with* **up**): *We did some exercises to limber up before the game.* 1 *adj.,* 2 *v.*
—**lim′ber·ness,** *n.*

**lim·ber²** (lim′bər) the detachable front part of the carriage of a field gun. *n.*

**lim·bo¹** (lim′bō) **1** a condition or place of neglect or disregard: *The belief that the earth is flat belongs to the limbo of outworn ideas.* **2** an indefinite or intermediate condition or place: *Gregorio was left in limbo for some time before he was told he definitely had the job.* *n.*

**lim·bo²** (lim′bō) a dance that originated in the West Indies, in which dancers bend over backwards from the knees and pass under a low bar with only their feet touching the ground. The bar is brought lower for each pass a dancer makes. *n.*

**Lim·burg·er** (lim′bėr gər) a soft cheese having a strong smell. *n.*

**lime¹** (līm) **1** a white substance obtained by burning limestone, shells, bones, etc.; calcium oxide; quicklime: *Lime is used to make mortar and to improve soil.* **2** put lime on: *He drained the land and limed it.* **3** BIRDLIME. **4** smear branches, etc. with BIRDLIME. **5** catch birds with BIRDLIME. 1, 3 *n.,* 2, 4, 5 *v.,* **limed, lim·ing.**

**lime²** (līm) **1** a greenish-yellow citrus fruit that resembles a lemon, but is smaller and sourer. **2** the tree this fruit grows on. **3** a soft drink flavoured with lime juice. **4** greenish yellow. 1–4 *n.,* 4 *adj.*

**lime³** (līm) LINDEN, especially the European linden. *n.*

**lime·ade** (lī′mād′) a drink made of lime juice, sugar, and water. *n.*

**lime·kiln** (līm′kiln′ *or* līm′kil′) a furnace for making lime by burning limestone, shells, etc. *n.*

**lime·light** (līm′līt′) **1** an intense white light produced by heating LIME¹, formerly used as a stage spotlight in theatres. **2** the centre of public attention and interest: *Some politicians try to avoid the limelight.* *n.*

**lim·er·ick** (lim′ə rik) a kind of humorous poem

**lily-livered**     693     **limousine**

hat, āge, fär; let, ēqual, tėrm; it, īce
hot, ōpen, ôrder; oil, out; cup, pùt, rüle
əbove, takən, pencəl, lemən, circəs
ch, child; ng, long; sh, ship
th, thin; ҭн, then; zh, measure

consisting of five lines, with the first two lines rhyming with the last, and the third and fourth rhyming with each other. *n.* Example:
> There was a young lady from Lynn
> Who was so exceedingly thin
> That when she essayed
> To drink lemonade
> She slid down the straw and fell in.

**lime·stone** (līm′stōn′) rock formed mainly from organic remains, such as shells or coral, and consisting mostly of calcium carbonate, used for building and for making lime: *Marble is a kind of limestone.* *n.*

**lime·wa·ter** (līm′wot′ər) a solution of slaked lime (calcium hydroxide) in water, used to counteract an acid condition. *n.*

**lim·it** (lim′it) **1** the farthest point or edge; where something ends or must end: *the limit of one's vision. I have reached the limit of my patience.* **2** set a limit to; restrict: *We must limit our expenditure to $60.* **3** the largest amount or quantity allowed or accepted: *One helping of dessert is my limit. Yesterday they caught their limit of fish.* **4 limits,** *pl.* boundary; bounds: *Keep within the limits of the school grounds.* 1, 3, 4 *n.,* 2 *v.*
—**lim′it·a·ble,** *adj.* —**lim′it·er,** *n.*

**lim·i·ta·tion** (lim′ə tā′shən) **1** limiting or being limited. **2** something that limits; a limiting rule or circumstance; restriction: *The new government imposed limitations on the freedom of the press.* **3** in law, a period of time after which a claim, suit, etc. cannot be brought in court. A **statute of limitations** is a statute that fixes such a period of time. *n.*

**lim·it·ed** (lim′ə tid) **1** kept within limits; restricted: *a limited edition, a limited number of seats. He's having only limited success in his new business.* **2** of business organizations, restricted as to the amount of debt that any individual member is liable for. **3** travelling rapidly and making only a few stops: *a limited train or bus.* **4** a train, bus, etc. that travels rapidly and makes only a few stops. **5** *pt.* and *pp.* of LIMIT. 1, 2, 3 *adj.,* 4 *n.,* 5 *v.*

**limited edition** an edition of a book, etc. limited to a certain number of copies and often having a special format and binding.

**limited monarchy** a monarchy in which the ruler's powers are limited by the laws of the nation. Compare with ABSOLUTE MONARCHY.

**lim·it·less** (lim′it lis) without limits; boundless; infinite. *adj.*

**limn** (lim) **1** paint a picture. **2** portray in words. *v.*
☞ *Hom.* LIMB.

**lim·o** (lim′ō) *Informal.* LIMOUSINE. *n., pl.* **limos.**

**Li·moges** (li mōzh′; *French,* lē mōzh′) a kind of fine porcelain made at Limoges, France. *n.*

**lim·ou·sine** (lim′ə zēn′ *or* lim′ə zēn′) **1** a large, luxurious automobile, especially one driven by a chauffeur: *A limousine sometimes has a glass partition separating the passenger compartment from the driver's seat.* **2** a large automobile or small bus used to carry passengers to and from an airport, etc. *n.*

**limp¹** (limp) **1** a lame step or walk. **2** walk with a limp: *After falling down the stairs, she limped for several days.* 1 *n.*, 2 *v.* —**limp′er,** *n.*

**limp²** (limp) not stiff or firm; tending to bend or droop: *The lettuce had lost its crispness and was quite limp. I am so tired I feel as limp as a rag.* *adj.* —**limp′ly,** *adv.* —**limp′ness,** *n.*

**lim·pet** (lim′pit) any of various small sea MOLLUSCS having a single shell shaped like a squat cone and having a broad, fleshy foot by which they cling to rocks, etc. *n.*

**lim·pid** (lim′pid) clear; transparent: *limpid water, limpid eyes.* *adj.* —**lim′pid·ly,** *adv.*

**lim·pid·i·ty** (lim pid′ə tē) a LIMPID quality or condition. *n.*

**lim·y** (lī′mē) **1** of, containing, or resembling lime. **2** smeared with BIRDLIME. *adj.*, **lim·i·er, lim·i·est.**

**lin·age** (lī′nij) **1** the number of lines of printed or written matter on a page. **2** payment according to the number of lines. *n.* Also, **lineage.**

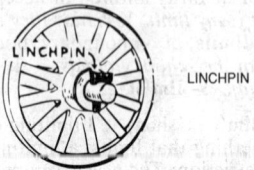
LINCHPIN

**linch·pin** (linch′pin′) a locking pin inserted through a hole in the end of an axle to keep the wheel on. *n.*

**lin·dane** (lin′dān) a benzene compound used as an insecticide. *n.*

**lin·den** (lin′dən) **1** any of a closely related group of trees native to the temperate regions of the Northern Hemisphere, having heart-shaped leaves and fragrant flowers: *Lindens are widely planted for ornament and shade.* **2** the soft, fine-grained, white wood of a linden. **3** referring to a small family of mainly tropical trees, shrubs, and a few herbs: *The linden family includes the lindens and jutes.* *n.*

**line¹** (līn) **1** a piece of rope, cord, or wire. **2** a cord for measuring, making level, etc. **3** a cord with a hook for catching fish. **4** a long, narrow mark: *Draw two lines along the margin.* **5** anything like such a mark: *the lines of the grain in the wood.* **6** mark with lines on paper, etc. **7** cover with lines: *a face lined by age.* **8** a wrinkle or crease: *the lines in his face. The fortune teller studied the lines on the palm of my hand.* **9** a straight line. **10** in geometry, the straight or curved path that a point may be imagined to make as it moves; CURVE (def. 7). **11** the use of lines in drawing: *clearness of line in an artist's work.* **12** an edge; limit; boundary: *That hedge marks our property line.* **13** a row of persons or things: *a line of cars.* **14** arrange in a line or row; align: *Line your shoes along the edge of the shelf.* **15** form or arrange a line along: *Cars lined the road for a kilometre.* **16** a row of words on a page or in a column: *a column of 40 lines.* **17** a short letter; note: *Drop me a line.* **18** a connected series of persons or things following one another in time: *The Stuarts were a line of English kings.* **19** family or lineage: *of noble line.* **20** a course; track; direction: *the line of march of an army.* **21** a course of action, conduct, or thought: *a line of policy.* **22** in warfare, the front. **23** a double row (front and rear rank) of soldiers. **24** troops or ships arranged abreast. **25** an arrangement of an army or fleet for battle. **26** take a position in a line; form a line; range. **27** a wire or wires connecting points or stations in a telegraph or telephone system. **28** the system itself. **29** any rope, wire, pipe, hose, etc. running from one point to another. **30** a single track of railway. **31** one branch of a system of transportation: *the main line of a railway.* **32** a whole system of transportation or conveyance: *the Cunard Line.* **33** a branch of business; a kind of activity: *the dry-goods line.* **34** a kind or brand of goods: *a good line of hardware.* **35** a single row of words in poetry. **36** in music, one of the horizontal lines that make a staff. **37** *Cdn.* in Ontario, CONCESSION ROAD: *He lives on the second line.* **38 the line, a** the equator. **b** the border between two countries, especially that between Canada and the United States. **c** the regular armed forces; the soldiers, ships, or aircraft that do the fighting. **39 lines,** *pl.* **a** outline or contour: *a ship of fine lines.* **b** the plan of construction: *The two books were written on the same lines.* **c** the words that an actor speaks in a play: *I forgot my lines and had to be prompted.* **d** reins. 1–5, 8–13, 16–25, 27–39 *n.*, 6, 7, 14, 15, 26 *v.*, **lined, lin·ing.**

**all along the line,** at every point; everywhere.
**bring into line,** cause to agree or conform: *She will bring the other members into line and the club will accept her plan.*
**come into line,** agree; conform.
**get** or **have a line on,** *Informal.* get or have information about.
**in line, a** in alignment. **b** in agreement. **c** ready.
**line up, a** form a line; form into a line. **b** arrange or provide. **c** in printing, make level with other lines.
**on a line,** even; level: *The lower edges of the pictures are not on a line.*
**on the line,** in between; neither one thing nor the other.
**out of line,** not in agreement; not suitable or proper: *Her last remark was out of line. He is always out of line with the rest of the club members.*
**read between the lines,** get more from the words than they say; find a hidden meaning.

**line²** (līn) **1** put a layer inside. **2** fill: *to line one's pocket with money.* **3** serve as a lining for: *This piece of satin would line the coat very nicely.* *v.*, **lined, lin·ing.**

**lin·e·age¹** (lin′ē ij) **1** one's descent in a direct line from an ancestor. **2** one's family or stock. *n.*

**line·age²** (lī′nij) See LINAGE. *n.*

**lin·e·al** (lin′ē əl) **1** in the direct line of descent: *A granddaughter is a lineal descendant of her grandfather.* **2** having to do with or derived from ancestors; hereditary: *The lands were his by lineal right.* **3** LINEAR. *adj.* —**lin′e·al·ly,** *adv.*

**lin·e·a·ment** (lin′ē ə mənt) a part or feature; a part or feature of a face with attention to its outline. *n.*

**lin·e·ar** (lin′ē ər) **1** of or having to do with a line or lines: *linear symmetry.* **2** made of lines; making use of lines: *a linear drawing, a linear arrangement of trees.* **3** in mathematics and physics, involving measurement in one dimension only: *linear measure.* **4** especially in botany, long, narrow, and even in width: *Grass has linear leaves.* **5** of length: *the linear dimensions of the building.* *adj.*

**linear accelerator** an accelerator in which charged particles are speeded up in a straight line by a series of electrical impulses along their flight path.

**linear equation** in mathematics, an equation whose graph is a straight line.

**linear measure** 1 measure of length. 2 a unit or system of units for measuring length.

**line·back·er** (līn′bak′ər) in football, a defensive player whose playing position is just behind the line of scrimmage. *n.*

**line·man** (līn′mən) 1 a person who sets up or repairs telegraph, telephone, or electric wires. 2 in football, a centre, guard, tackle, or end. 3 a person who inspects railway tracks. 4 in surveying, the person who carries the line or chain. *n., pl.* **line·men** (-mən).

**lin·en** (lin′ən) 1 thread or yarn spun from flax. 2 cloth made from flax thread or yarn: *Linen is very strong and is cool in summer.* 3 articles made of linen or of cotton, synthetics, or blends (*often used in the plural*): *Tablecloths and serviettes are called table linen; sheets, pillow cases, etc. are called bed linen.* 4 made of linen. 5 designed to hold or store linens: *a linen closet. n.*

**line of battle** soldiers or ships in battle formation.

**line of fire** 1 the path of a bullet, shell, etc. fired or about to be fired from a gun: *He threw himself on the ground to get out of the line of fire.* 2 any very dangerous or vulnerable position.

**line of force** in a field of electrical or magnetic force, the line that indicates the direction in which the force is acting.

**lin·er**[1] (lī′nər) 1 a ship or airplane belonging to a transportation system. 2 a person or thing that makes lines. 3 a baseball hit so that it travels not far above the ground. *n.*

**lin·er**[2] (lī′nər) something that serves as a lining: *a diaper liner, a hat liner. n.*

**lines·man** (līnz′mən) 1 LINEMAN. 2 in certain games, a person who watches the lines that mark out the field, rink, court, etc. and assists the umpire or referee. *n., pl.* **lines·men** (-zmən).

**line–up** or **line-up** (lī′nup′) 1 a number of persons arranged in a line; especially, a group including a suspected offender, lined up for identification by police or the victim of an offence. 2 in football, baseball, hockey, etc.: **a** the list of players on a team arranged according to position of play, etc. **b** the players on such a list. 3 any arrangement of persons or things in a line or as if in a line. 4 a queue of people waiting for something: *There was a long line-up for tickets. n.*

**ling** (ling) 1 a fish of northern Europe and Greenland, used for food. 2 a freshwater fish of North America. *n., pl.* **ling** or **lings**.

**ling.** linguistics.

**ling·cod** (ling′kod′) an edible fish of the Pacific coast. *n.*

**lin·ger** (ling′gər) 1 put off departure; stay on, especially because of reluctance to leave: *Several fans lingered at the stage door for some time after the actor had gone in.* 2 continue to stay or live, although gradually becoming less or dying: *Daylight lingers long in the summertime.* 3 go slowly; saunter; dally. *v.*

**lin·ge·rie** (lan′zhə rē′ *or* lon′zhə rā′) women's undergarments, nightgowns, etc. *n.*

**lin·go** (ling′gō) language, especially a dialect, jargon, etc. regarded as unintelligible or incomprehensible: *the lingo of sports writers, the lingo of medical people. n., pl.* **lin·goes**.

**lin·gual** (ling′gwəl) 1 of or having to do with the tongue: *a lingual defect.* 2 in phonetics, formed with the aid of the tongue: *a lingual sound.* 3 of or having to do with speech or languages; linguistic. *adj.*
☛ *Etym.* LINGO, **lingual**, LINGUIST and words derived from it, and also LANGUAGE, can all be traced back to L *lingua* 'tongue', from which also came F *langue* 'tongue'. **Lingo** came in the 17c. from the same word in Portuguese; **lingual** came into ME from Med.L *lingualis;* **linguist** was formed in English in the 16c., as were LINGUISTIC and LINGUISTICS in the 19c. **Language** came into ME from OF as *langage.*

**lin·guist** (ling′gwist) 1 a person skilled in a number of languages besides his or her own; polyglot. 2 a person trained in linguistics, especially one who makes it his or her work. 3 PHILOLOGIST. *n.*

**lin·guis·tic** (ling gwis′tik) of or having to do with language or the study of languages. *adj.*
—**lin·guis′ti·cal·ly**, *adv.*

**lin·guis·tics** (ling gwis′tiks) the study of human speech; the study of the structures, sounds, forms, functions, and varieties of language (*used with a singular verb*): *Linguistics also includes the historical development of language and languages.* Compare with PHILOLOGY. *n.*

**lin·i·ment** (lin′ə mənt) a liquid for rubbing on the skin to relieve soreness, sprains, bruises, etc. *n.*

**lin·ing** (lī′ning) 1 a layer of material covering the inner surface of something: *the lining of a coat, the lining of a stove.* 2 the material used for lining: *I bought satin lining for the coat.* 3 ppr. of LINE. *1, 2 n., 3 v.*

**link**[1] (lingk) 1 one ring or loop of a chain. 2 anything that joins as a link joins: *a cuff link.* 3 a fact or thought that connects others: *a link in a chain of evidence.* 4 join as a link does; unite or connect. 5 a unit of length used in surveying; one one-hundredth of a chain (about 20 cm). 6 one of a series of sausages in a chain. *1–3, 5 n., 4 v.*

**link**[2] (lingk) a torch formerly used for lighting people's way through the streets. *n.*

**link·age** (ling′kij) 1 linking or being linked. 2 an arrangement or system of links. *n.*

**linking verb** a verb (such as **be, become,** or **seem**) that does not express action and is not followed by an object. It links a subject with an adjective that modifies the subject or with a noun that stands for the same person or thing as the subject; copula: *Examples: I am sleepy. He turned pale. She is a doctor. They became friends.*
☛ *Usage.* Linking verbs are the only English verbs that can have as complement either an adjective or a noun or pronoun.

**links** (lingks) GOLF COURSE. *n. pl.*

**lin·net** (lin′it) a small songbird of Europe, Asia, and Africa. *n.*

**li·no·le·um** (lə nō′lē əm) 1 a durable, washable floor covering made by putting a hard surface of ground cork

mixed with oxidized linseed oil on a canvas or burlap back. **2** any similar floor covering. *n.*
☞ *Etym.* From *Linoleum,* a trademark for this kind of floor covering, coined from L *linum* 'flax'+*oleum* 'oil.'

**li·no·type** (līʹnə tīpʹ)  a typesetting machine that is operated like a typewriter and that casts each line of type in one piece. *n.*

**lin·seed** (linʹsēd)  the seed of FLAX. *n.*

**linseed oil**  a yellowish oil pressed from LINSEED, used especially in making paints, printing inks, and varnishes.

**lin·sey** (linʹzē)  LINSEY-WOOLSEY.  *n., pl.* **lin·seys.**

**lin·sey-wool·sey** (linʹzē wulʹzē)  a strong, coarse fabric made of linen and wool or of cotton and wool. *n., pl.* **lin·sey-wool·seys.**

**lint** (lint)  **1** a soft down or fleecy material obtained by scraping linen.  **2** fuzz or fluff consisting of tiny bits of fibre from yarn or cloth. *n.*

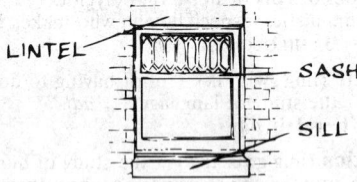

**lin·tel** (linʹtəl)  a horizontal beam or stone over a door, window, etc., that carries the weight of the wall above it. See JAMB for another picture. *n.*

**li·on** (līʹən)  **1** a large wild animal of the cat family, having a dull-yellow coat, a tufted tail, and, in the adult male, a heavy, shaggy, brown mane around the neck and shoulders: *Lions are native to Africa and southwestern Asia.* **2** a very brave or strong person.  **3** a famous or important person: *a literary lion.* *n.*  —**lionʹlike**ʹ, *adj.*
**beard the lion in his** or **her den,**  defy a person in his or her own home, office, etc.
**put one's head in the lion's mouth,**  put oneself in a dangerous position.

**li·on·ess** (līʹə nis)  a female lion. *n.*

**li·on-heart·ed** (līʹən härʹtid)  brave. *adj.*

**li·on·ize** (līʹə nīz)  treat as very important: *The visiting artist was lionized by the press.* *v.,* **li·on·ized, li·on·iz·ing.** —**liʹon·i·zaʹtion,** *n.*

**lion's share**  the biggest or best part: *She managed to get the lion's share of the cake before the rest of us got there.*

**lip** (lip)  **1** either of the two fleshy, movable edges of the mouth.  **2** touch with the lips.  **3** a folding or bent-out edge of any opening: *the lip of a pitcher.*  **4** the mouthpiece of a musical instrument.  **5** use the lips in playing a wind instrument.  **6** expressed in words, but not heartfelt or deep; only on the surface: *to pay lip service.*  **7** murmur.  **8** *Informal.* impudent talk.  **9** lips, *pl.* mouth.  1, 3, 4, 8, 9 *n.,* 2, 5, 7 *v.,* **lipped, lip·ping;** 6 *adj.*  —**lipʹlike**ʹ, *adj.*
**hang on the lips of,**  listen to with great attentiveness and admiration.
**keep a stiff upper lip,**  be brave and firm; show no fear or discouragement.

**li·pase** (līʹpās)  an enzyme occurring in the pancreatic juice, certain seeds, etc., capable of changing fats into fatty acids and glycerin. *n.*

**lip·id** (lipʹəd)  any of a large group of natural organic compounds, including fats, oils, waxes, and steroids, that are insoluble in water but soluble in certain organic solvents such as alcohol. Lipids, proteins, and carbohydrates are the main structural components of living organisms. *n.*

**lipped** (lipt)  **1** having lips of a certain kind (*used only in compounds*): *thin-lipped, tight-lipped.*  **2** pt. and pp. of LIP.  1 *adj.,* 2 *v.*

**lip-read** (lipʹrēd)  understand speech by LIP READING. *v.*  —**lipʹ-read·er,** *n.*

**lip reading**  interpret speech without hearing it by watching the lip movements and facial expression of the speaker.

**lip·stick** (lipʹstik)  **1** a smooth cosmetic paste for the lips, usually coloured and often in the form of a stick in a case.  **2** a case containing this cosmetic. *n.*

**liq.**  **1** liquid.  **2** liquor.

**liq·ue·fac·tion** (likʹwə fakʹshən)  **1** the process of changing into a liquid.  **2** the state of being a liquid. *n.*

**liq·ue·fy** (likʹwə fī)  change into a liquid; make or become liquid: *Liquefied air is extremely cold.* *v.,* **liq·ue·fied, liq·ue·fy·ing.**  —**liqʹue·fiʹa·ble,** *adj.* —**liqʹue·fiʹer,** *n.*

**li·ques·cence** (li kwesʹəns)  a LIQUESCENT condition. *n.*

**li·ques·cent** (li kwesʹənt)  becoming liquid; melting. *adj.*

**li·queur** (li kyurʹ *or* li kėrʹ)  a strong, sweet, highly flavoured alcoholic drink. *n.*

**liq·uid** (likʹwid)  **1** a substance that is neither a solid nor a gas; substance that flows freely like water.  **2** in the form of a liquid; melted: *liquid soap.*  **3** clear and bright like water.  **4** clear and smooth-flowing in sound: *the liquid notes of a bird.*  **5** easily turned into cash: *Canada Savings Bonds are a liquid investment.*  1 *n.,* 2–5 *adj.*

**liquid air**  the intensely cold, transparent liquid formed when air is very greatly compressed and then cooled: *Liquid air is used mainly as a refrigerant.*

**liquid assets**  things easily converted into cash: *Savings Bonds are liquid assets.*

**liq·ui·date** (likʹwə dātʹ)  **1** pay a debt.  **2** settle the accounts of a business, etc.; clear up the affairs of a bankrupt.  **3** get rid of an undesirable person or thing: *The Russian revolution liquidated the nobility.*  **4** kill ruthlessly; exterminate.  *v.,* **liq·ui·dat·ed, liq·ui·dat·ing.**  —**liqʹui·daʹtion,** *n.*

**li·quid·i·ty** (li kwidʹə tē)  **1** the state of being a liquid. **2** the state of having liquid assets. *n.*

**liquid measure**  **1** the measurement of liquids.  **2** unit or system of units for measuring liquids.

**liq·uor** (likʹər)  **1** an alcoholic drink, such as brandy, gin, rum, or whisky.  **2** any liquid, especially a liquid in which food is packaged, canned, or cooked: *Pickles are put up in a salty liquor.* *n.*

**liq·uo·rice** (likʹə rish, likʹrish, *or* likʹə ris)  See LICORICE. *n.*

**lisle** (līl)  **1** a fine, strong, linen or cotton thread, used for making stockings, gloves, etc.  **2** made of lisle. *n.*

**lisp** (lisp)  **1** use the sound of *th* instead of the sound of s or z in speaking: *A person who lisps might say "thing a thong" for "sing a song."* **2** the act, habit, or sound of speaking in this way: *She speaks with a lisp.* **3** speak imperfectly: *Babies are said to lisp.* 1, 3 *v.*, 2 *n.* —**lisp′er**, *n.*

**lis·some** or **lis·som** (lis′əm) **1** lithe; limber; supple. **2** nimble; active. *adj.*

**list**[1] (list) **1** a series of names, numbers, words, etc.: *a shopping list.* **2** make a list of; enter in a list: *I shall list my errands on a card.* 1 *n.*, 2 *v.*

**list**[2] (list) the woven edge of cloth, where the material is a little different; SELVAGE. *n.*

**list**[3] (list) **1** a tipping to one side; tilt: *the list of a ship.* **2** tip to one side; tilt: *The sinking ship was listing so that water lapped her decks.* 1 *n.*, 2 *v.*

**lis·ten** (lis′ən) **1** try to hear; pay attention so as to hear: *She listened for the sound of the car. I like to listen to music.* **2** give heed to advice, temptation, etc.; pay attention: *I don't know how to repair it because I did not listen.* *v.* —**lis′ten·er**, *n.*

**listen in**, **a** listen to others talking on a telephone: *I listened in on the extension.* **b** listen to the radio: *Listen in next week for another drama.*

**list·er** (lis′tər) a plough with a double mouldboard that throws the dirt to both sides of the furrow. *n.*

**list·less** (list′lis) seeming too tired to care about anything; not interested in things; not caring to be active: *a dull and listless mood.* *adj.* —**list′less·ly**, *adv.* —**list′less·ness**, *n.*

**list price** the price given in a catalogue or list.

**lists** (lists) **1** in the Middle Ages: **a** a place where knights fought in tournaments. **b** the barriers enclosing such a field. **2** any place or scene of combat. *n. pl.*

**enter the lists,** join in a contest; take part in a fight, argument, etc.

**lit** (lit) **1** a pt. and a pp. of LIGHT[1]: *She lit the lamp.* **2** a pt. and a pp. of LIGHT[3]: *His eye lit upon a word.* *v.*

**lit. 1** literature. **2** literal. **3** literally.

**lit·a·ny** (lit′ə nē) **1** a form of prayer for use in church services, consisting of a series of petitions recited by the clergy, alternating with fixed responses from the congregation. **2** any recital or account involving much repetition: *a litany of complaints.* *n.*

**li·tchi** (lē′chē) **1** a nut-shaped fruit having a hard, rough skin. **2** the tree that it grows on. *n.*, *pl.* **li·tchis.** Also, **lichee.**

**li·ter** (lē′tər) See LITRE. *n.*

**lit·er·a·cy** (lit′ə rə sē) the ability to read and write. *n.*

**lit·er·al** (lit′ə rəl *or* lit′rəl) **1** exact; following the exact words of the original: *a literal translation.* **2** taking words in their usual or basic meaning, actual: *a literal interpretation. When we say He flew down the stairs to meet them, we do not mean fly in the literal sense of the word.* **3** concerned mainly with facts; matter-of-fact: *a literal type of mind.* **4** true to fact; not exaggerated: *a literal account. The literal truth of the matter is that he was terrified.* **5** of, having to do with, or expressed by letters of the alphabet. *adj.*
☞ *Hom.* LITTORAL (for the first pronunciation of **literal**).

**lit·er·al·ism** (lit′ə rə liz′əm *or* lit′rə liz′əm) a keeping to the LITERAL meaning in translation or interpretation. *n.*

# lissome 697 lithography

hat, āge, fär; let, ēqual, tėrm; it, īce
hot, ōpen, ôrder; oil, out; cup, pùt, rüle
əbove, takən, pencəl, lemən, circəs
ch, child; ng, long; sh, ship
th, thin; ᴛʜ, then; zh, measure

**lit·er·al·ly** (lit′ə rə lē *or* lit′rə lē) **1** word for word: *to translate a passage literally.* **2** actually; without exaggeration: *I was literally penniless; I couldn't even buy a cup of coffee.* *adv.*

**lit·er·ar·y** (lit′ə rer′ē) **1** having to do with literature or the humanities: *a literary treatise.* **2** of or having to do with books: *a literary agent.* **3** of or having to do with writers, scholars, etc., or writing as a profession: *a literary journal.* **4** knowing much about and enjoying literature; fond of books and reading: *They are a very literary family.* *adj.*

**lit·er·ate** (lit′ə rit) **1** able to read and write. **2** a person who can read and write. **3** acquainted with literature; educated. **4** an educated person. 1, 3 *adj.*, 2, 4 *n.*

**lit·e·ra·ti** (lit′ə rä′tē) scholarly or literary people. *n. pl.*

**lit·er·a·ture** (lit′ə rə chür, lit′rə chər, *or* lit′ə rə chər) **1** the writings of a period or of a country, especially those kept alive by the excellence of style or thought: *Stephen Leacock is a famous name in Canadian literature.* **2** all the books and articles on a subject: *the literature of stamp collecting.* **3** the profession of a writer. **4** the study of literature: *I am going to take literature and mathematics this spring.* **5** *Informal.* printed matter of any kind: *Election campaign literature informs people about the candidates.* *n.*

**lith·arge** (lith′ärj) a yellow oxide of lead, used in making glass, glazes for pottery, and driers for paints and varnishes. *n.*

**lithe** (līᴛʜ) bending easily; supple: *lithe of body, a lithe willow.* *adj.* —**lithe′ly**, *adv.* —**lithe′ness**, *n.*

**lithe·some** (līᴛʜ′səm) LITHE. *adj.*

**lith·i·a** (lith′ē ə) a white crystalline oxide of LITHIUM. *n.*
☞ *Etym.* See note at LITHIUM.

**lith·i·um** (lith′ē əm) a soft, silver-white metallic element similar to sodium: *Lithium is the lightest of all metals.* Symbol: Li *n.*
☞ *Etym.* LITHIA, **lithium**, LITHOGRAPH and words formed from it, and LITHOSPHERE can all be traced back to Gk. *lithos* 'stone'. The first two were formed in the 19c. from scientific terms in modern Latin. **Lithograph** and **lithosphere** were formed in English from Gk. *lithos* + the English combining forms **-graph** and **-sphere**. The same root *lith* appears at the end of words like BATHOLITH, MEGALITH.

**lith·o·graph** (lith′ə graf′) **1** a picture, print, etc. made by LITHOGRAPHY. **2** produce or print by LITHOGRAPHY. 1 *n.*, 2 *v.*
☞ *Etym.* See note at LITHIUM.

**li·thog·ra·pher** (li thog′rə fər) a person trained in LITHOGRAPHY, especially one who makes it his or her work. *n.*

**lith·o·graph·ic** (lith′ə graf′ik) of, having to do with, or produced by LITHOGRAPHY. *adj.*

**li·thog·ra·phy** (li thog′rə fē) the art or process of

transferring an image onto paper from a flat surface such as a stone or metal plate, by preparing the surface so that certain parts receive ink while other parts repel it. *n.*

**lith·o·sphere** (lith′ə sfēr′)   the solid outer shell of the earth, including the crust and upper mantle, thought to be from about 70 to 150 kilometres thick: *Many scientists believe the lithosphere to consist of separate rigid plates that move on the softer rock of the lower mantle.*   Compare with ATMOSPHERE and HYDROSPHERE. *n.*
☛ *Etym.*   See note at LITHIUM.

**Lith·u·a·ni·an** (lith′yü ā′nē ən *or* lith′ù ā′nē ən)   **1** of or having to do with Lithuania, a republic in the western Soviet Union, its people, or their language.   **2** a native or inhabitant of Lithuania.   **3** the language of Lithuania. 1 *adj.*, 2, 3 *n.*

**lit·i·gant** (lit′ə gənt)   **1** a person engaged in a lawsuit. **2** engaging in a lawsuit.   1 *n.*, 2 *adj.*

**lit·i·gate** (lit′ə gāt′)   **1** engage in a lawsuit.   **2** contest in a lawsuit.   *v.*, **lit·i·gat·ed, lit·i·gat·ing.**
—**lit′i·ga′tor**, *n.*

**lit·i·ga·tion** (lit′ə gā′shən)   **1** the act of carrying on a lawsuit.   **2** going to law.   *n.*

**li·ti·gious** (lə tij′əs)   **1** having the habit of going to law. **2** offering material for a lawsuit; that can be disputed in a court of law.   **3** of lawsuits.   *adj.*

**lit·mus** (lit′məs)   a blue colouring matter obtained from lichens, that turns red in an acid solution and back to blue in an alkali solution: *Litmus is used to indicate whether a particular chemical solution is an acid or a base.*   *n.*
☛ *Etym.*   From Old Norwegian *litmosi*, formed from ON *litr* 'colour, dye' + *mosi* 'moss'.

**litmus paper**   paper treated with LITMUS, used to indicate whether a solution is an acid or a base.

**li·tre** (lē′tər)   a unit used with the SI for measuring volume or capacity, equal to one cubic decimetre: *One litre of water has a mass of one kilogram. The litre is used for measuring liquids and other products such as ice cream and fruit, and for measuring the capacity of containers such as gas tanks, cooking pots, jugs, and baskets.*   Symbol: L   *n.* Also, **liter**.
☛ *Usage.*   The international symbol for **litre** is the upright lower-case letter 'l'. However, the capital letter 'L' has been adopted as the official symbol in Canada because the lower-case letter can be confused in printing with the numeral '1'.

A litter (def. 10)

**lit·ter** (lit′ər)   **1** scattered rubbish; things scattered about or left in disorder: *Sedi should pick up her own litter.* **2** leave odds and ends lying around; scatter things about. **3** disorder; untidiness.   **4** make disordered or untidy:

*Joseph littered his room with books and papers, and his yard with bottles and cans.*   **5** the young animals born at the same time from one mother: *a litter of puppies.*   **6** give birth to young animals.   **7** straw, hay, etc. used as bedding for animals.   **8** make a bed for an animal with straw, hay, etc.   **9** a stretcher for carrying a sick or wounded person.   **10** a framework to be carried on men's shoulders or by beasts of burden, with a couch usually enclosed by curtains: *A litter usually carries one passenger.* 1, 3, 5, 7, 9, 10 *n.*, 2, 4, 6, 8 *v.*

**lit·ter·bug** (lit′ər bug′)   a person who leaves litter lying about in public places.   *n.*

**lit·tle** (lit′əl)   **1** not great or big; small: *A grain of sand is little.*   **2** not much; small in number, amount, degree, or importance: *little money, little hope, a little army.*   **3** in a small amount or degree; to a small extent; slightly: *They lived in a little-known town. She travels little.*   **4** a small amount, quantity, or degree: *to add a little.*   **5** short; brief: *She took a little walk.*   **6** a short time or distance: *to move a little to the left.*   **7** hardly at all: *He little knows what will happen.*   **8** mean and narrow in thought or feeling: *Only a little man would pinch a child. That little sneak stole my sweater.*   1, 2, 5, 8 *adj.*, **less** or **less·er,** **least**; or **lit·tler, lit·tlest**;   3, 7 *adv.*, **less, least**;   4, 6 *n.* —**lit′tle·ness**, *n.*
**in little**,   on a small scale.
**little by little**,   by a small amount at a time; slowly; gradually.
**make little of**,   treat or represent as of little importance: *She made little of her troubles.*
**not a little**,   much; very: *He was not a little upset by the accident.*
**think little of,**   **a** not value much; consider as unimportant or worthless.   **b** not hesitate about.

**Little Bear**   the northern constellation Ursa Minor.

**Little Dipper**   the seven principal stars in the constellation Ursa Minor, arranged in a form that suggests a dipper: *The star forming the end of the handle of the Little Dipper is the North Star.*   Compare with BIG DIPPER.   See DIPPER for picture.

**little finger**   the finger that is farthest from the thumb; the smallest finger: *She wears a ring on her little finger.*

**little theatre**   **1** a small theatre, usually amateur, that presents experimental plays.   **2** the drama produced by a little theatre.

**lit·to·ral** (lit′ə rəl)   **1** of or having to do with a shore, especially of the sea.   **2** found or growing on or near the shore.   **3** the region along a shore, especially the zone between the marks of high and low tide.   1, 2 *adj.*, 3 *n.* ☛ *Hom.*   LITERAL (lit′ə rəl).

**li·tur·gic** (lə tėr′jik)   LITURGICAL. *adj.*

**li·tur·gi·cal** (lə tėr′jə kəl)   of or having to do with LITURGY.   *adj.*   —**li·tur′gi·cal·ly,** *adv.*

**lit·ur·gy** (lit′ər jē)   **1** a form or ritual for public worship: *Different churches use different liturgies.* **2** Often, **Liturgy**,   the Eucharistic service, especially in the Eastern Orthodox Church.   *n., pl.* **lit·ur·gies.**

**liv·a·ble** (liv′ə bəl)   **1** fit to live in: *a livable house.* **2** easy to live with: *a livable person.*   **3** worth living; endurable.   *adj.*   Also, **liveable**.

**live**[1] (liv)   **1** have life; be alive; exist: *All creatures have an equal right to live.*   **2** remain alive; last; endure: *She managed to live through the war.*   **3** keep up life; support oneself: *to live on one's income.*   **4** feed or subsist:

Rabbits live mainly on grass. **5** pass life: *to live well, to live a life of ease.* **6** dwell: *My aunt lives in Victoria. Who lives in this house?* **7** carry out or show in life: *to live one's ideals.* **8** have a rich and full life: *Those people know how to live!* *v.,* **lived, liv·ing.**
**live down,** live so worthily that some fault or sin of the past is overlooked or forgotten: *He is determined to live down that disgrace.*
**live for,** take great interest in.
**live in,** live at the place where one works.
**live on, a** support oneself by. **b** use someone as a source of income or supplies. **c** continue to exist.
**live out, a** live away from where one works. **b** stay alive through; last through.
**live up to,** act according to; do what is expected or promised: *The car has not lived up to the salesman's description.*

**live²** (līv) **1** having life; alive: *a live dog.* **2** burning or glowing: *live coals.* **3** full of energy or activity: *She is a very live girl, always on the go.* **4** *Informal.* up-to-date: *live ideas.* **5** of present interest: *a live question.* **6** moving or imparting motion: *live wheels, a live axle.* **7** still in use or to be used: *live steam.* **8** carrying an electric current: *a live wire.* **9** charged with explosive: *a live cartridge.* **10** in the native state; not mined or quarried: *live metal, live rocks.* **11** in radio or television, broadcast as performed and not from a tape or film made beforehand: *a live television show.* **12** of recordings or broadcasts, made as performed before an audience: *The concert was recorded live.* 1–11 *adj.,* 12 *adv.*

**live·a·ble** (līv′ə bəl) See LIVABLE. *adj.*

**live·li·hood** (līv′lē hüd′) a means of living, that is, of obtaining the money necessary to buy food, clothing, and shelter; a means of supporting oneself; living (def. 4): *She writes for a livelihood. He earns his livelihood as a farmer.* *n.*

**live·li·ness** (līv′lē nis) a lively quality or condition; vigour; gaiety. *n.*

**live·long** (liv′long′) whole length of; whole; entire: *She is busy the livelong day.* *adj.*

**live·ly** (līv′lē) **1** full of life; active; vigorous; spirited: *A good night's sleep made us all lively again.* **2** exciting: *We had a lively time during the hurricane.* **3** bright; vivid: *lively colours.* **4** cheerful: *a lively conversation.* **5** bouncing well and quickly: *a lively tennis ball.* **6** in a lively manner. 1–5 *adj.,* **live·li·er, live·li·est;** 6 *adv.* —**live′li·ness,** *n.*

**liv·en** (līv′ən) make or become more lively or interesting (*often used with* **up**): *The show isn't bad, but they could liven it up a little.* *v.*

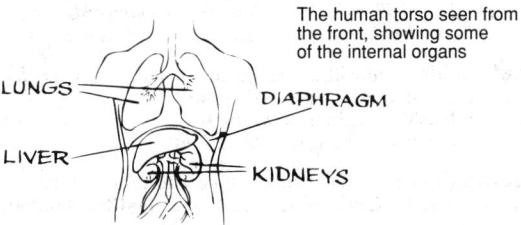
The human torso seen from the front, showing some of the internal organs
LUNGS
DIAPHRAGM
LIVER
KIDNEYS

**liv·er¹** (liv′ər) **1** in vertebrates, a large, reddish-brown organ that secretes bile and helps in the absorption of food: *The liver frees the blood of its waste matter and causes important changes in many of its substances.* **2** the liver of an animal used as food: *Liver is a good dietary source of iron and vitamins.* *n.*

hat, āge, fär; let, ēqual, tėrm; it, īce
hot, ōpen, ôrder; oil, out; cup, pùt, rüle
əbove, takən, pencəl, lemən, circəs
ch, child; ng, long; sh, ship
th, thin; ŦH, then; zh, measure

**liv·er²** (liv′ər) a person who lives in a certain way: *She is a wild liver.* *n.*

**liv·er·ied** (liv′ə rēd) clothed in a LIVERY (def. 1): *They had liveried attendants.* *adj.*

**liv·er·wort** (liv′ər wėrt′) **1** any of various plants that grow mostly on damp ground, the trunks of trees, etc.: *Liverworts are somewhat like mosses.* **2** HEPATICA. *n.*

**liv·er·wurst** (liv′ər wėrst′) a sausage consisting largely of ground liver. *n.*

**liv·er·y** (liv′ə rē *or* liv′rē) **1** any special uniform provided for the servants of a household, or adopted by any group or profession. **2** any characteristic dress, garb, or outward appearance. **3** the feeding, stabling, and care of horses for pay. **4** the keeping of cars, boats, bicycles, etc. for hire. **5** LIVERY STABLE. *n. pl.* **liv·er·ies.**

**liv·er·y·man** (liv′rē mən) **1** a person who owns or works in a LIVERY STABLE. **2** a person who wears or is entitled to wear LIVERY (defs. 1, 2). *n., pl.* **liv·er·y·men** (-mən).

**livery stable** a place where horses and vehicles are kept for hire or where horses are fed and stabled for a fee.

**lives** (līvz) pl. of LIFE. *n.*

**live·stock** (līv′stok′) farm animals: *Cows, horses, sheep, and pigs are livestock.* *n.*

**live wire** **1** a wire through which an electric current is flowing: *It is dangerous to touch an unprotected live wire.* **2** *Informal.* an energetic, wide-awake person: *He is such a live wire that he's always busy and active.*

**liv·id** (liv′id) **1** having a dull bluish or greyish colour, as from a bruise: *livid marks on an arm.* **2** very pale: *livid with shock.* **3** flushed; reddish: *livid with anger.* **4** *Informal.* very angry: *The insults made him livid.* *adj.*

**liv·ing** (liv′ing) **1** having life; being alive: *a living plant.* **2** the act or condition of being alive: *The old woman was filled with the joy of living.* **3** a means of obtaining what is needed to support life; livelihood: *Mr. Meyer earned his living as a grocer.* **4** a manner of life: *healthful living.* **5** full of life; vigorous; strong; active: *a living faith.* **6** in actual existence; still in use: *a living language.* **7** true to life; vivid; lifelike: *a living picture.* **8** of life; for living in: *good living conditions.* **9** sufficient to live on: *a living wage.* **10** a position in the church with the income attached; benefice. **11 the living,** *pl.* all the people who are alive. **12** ppr. of LIVE. 1, 5–9 *adj.,* 2–4, 10, 11 *n.,* 12 *v.*

**living quarters** a place to live.

**living room** a room in a house or apartment, used for the general leisure activities of the occupants, for entertaining guests, etc.

**living wage** a wage sufficient to enable a person or family to live in reasonable comfort and security.

A horned lizard—about 10 cm long including the tail

**liz·ard** (liz'ərd) **1** any of a large group of reptiles belonging to the same order as snakes, having external ears, eyes with movable lids, dry, scaly skin, and, in most species, a long, slender body with a long tail and four short legs: *Geckos, chameleons, and iguanas are lizards.* **2** any of various animals having a relatively long body, short legs, and a tail, such as salamanders, alligators, or dinosaurs. *n.* —**liz'ard·like'**, *adj.*

A llama—about 90 cm high at the shoulder

**lla·ma** (lä'mə *or* lam'ə) a domesticated animal of South America belonging to the same family as the camels, but smaller and having no humps: *Llamas have long been raised for their wool, milk, and meat and are also used as beasts of burden.* *n., pl.* **lla·mas** or (*esp. collectively*) **lla·ma**.
☛ *Hom.* LAMA (for the first pronunciation of **llama**).

**lm** lumen.

**lo** (lō) look! see! behold! *interj.*
☛ *Hom.* LOW.

**loach** (lōch) any of a family of small freshwater fishes of Asia and Europe having very small scales and having BARBELS around the mouth. *n.*

**load** (lōd) **1** whatever is being carried; a pack, cargo, burden, etc.: *The cart has a load of hay.* **2** the amount usually carried at one time; a more or less fixed quantity for a particular type of carrier (*often used in compounds*): *a planeload of tourists. Send us four loads of sand.* **3** place on or in a carrier of some kind: *The longshoremen are loading grain.* **4** put a load in or on: *to load a ship, to load a basket with groceries.* **5** take on a load: *The ship is still loading.* **6** something that weighs down or oppresses: *That's a load off my mind!* **7** oppress or burden (*often used with* **down**): *loaded down with debt. Don't load your mind with useless worry.* **8** supply amply or in excess: *They loaded her with compliments.* **9** in mechanics, the weight supported by a structure or part. **10** the external resistance overcome by an engine, dynamo, etc. under a given condition, measured by the power required. **11** add weight to: *to load dice.* **12** one charge of powder and shot for a gun. **13** put a charge in a gun. **14** place something needed to begin operation into a device: *to load a cassette into a videotape recorder, to load a camera.* **15 loads**, *pl. Informal.* a great quantity or number: *Don't worry; we have loads of food.* 1, 2, 6, 9, 10, 12, 15 *n.*, 3–5, 7, 8, 11, 13, 14 *v.* —**load'er**, *n.*

☛ *Etym.* From OE *lād* 'a way, journey, or carrying'. The meanings have been influenced by LADE which came from OE *hladan*.
☛ *Hom.* LODE.

**load·ed** (lō'did) **1** carrying a load: *a loaded truck.* **2** with a charge in it: *a loaded gun.* **3** weighted. **4** *Informal.* having plenty of money; rich. **5** *Informal.* full of half-hidden and unexpected meanings and suggestions: *Loaded questions are often intended to trap a person into saying more than she wants to say.* **6** *Informal.* equipped: *This new car is loaded with options.* **7** pt. and pp. of LOAD. 1–6 *adj.*, 7 *v.*

**load·star** (lōd'stär') See LODESTAR. *n.*

**load·stone** (lōd'stōn') See LODESTONE. *n.*

**loaf**[1] (lōf) **1** a quantity of bread baked as one piece in a more or less oblong or round shape: *Bread is usually sold by the loaf.* **2** any mass of food shaped like a loaf and baked: *a meat loaf, a salmon loaf.* **3** formerly, a cone-shaped mass of sugar. *n., pl.* **loaves**.

**loaf**[2] (lōf) spend time idly; do nothing: *I can loaf all day Saturday.* *v.*

**loaf·er** (lō'fər) **1** a person who LOAFS[2]; idler. **2** a shoe resembling a moccasin, but with sole and heel stitched to the upper. *n.*
☛ *Etym.* From *Loafer*, a trademark for this kind of shoe.

**loam** (lōm) **1** rich, fertile earth in which decaying and decayed plant matter is mixed with clay and sand. **2** a mixture of clay, sand, and straw, used to make moulds for large metal castings and to plaster walls, stop holes, etc. **3** cover or fill with loam. 1, 2 *n.*, 3 *v.*

**loam·y** (lō'mē) of or like LOAM (def. 1): *Loamy soil usually yields good crops.* *adj.*

**loan** (lōn) **1** the act of lending; the granting of temporary use: *She asked for the loan of his pen.* **2** anything that is lent, especially money: *He asked his sister for a loan.* **3** make a loan; lend: *His sister loaned him the money.* 1, 2 *n.*, 3 *v.* —**loan'er**, *n.*
**on loan**, lent or granted for temporary use or service: *Our department manager is on loan to another department for a week. The book was out on loan so I had to wait.*
☛ *Hom.* LONE.

**loan shark** *Informal.* a person who lends money at an extremely high or unlawful rate of interest.

**loan·word** (lōn'wėrd') a word taken into a language from another language and adopted as part of that language, often being slightly changed in the process: *Degree is a very old loanword that came into English from French about 700 years ago. More recent loanwords are* khaki, *from Hindi, and* intelligentsia, *from Russian.* *n.*

**loath** (lōth) unwilling; reluctant: *The little girl was loath to leave her mother.* *adj.* Also, **loth**.
**nothing loath**, willing or willingly: *They invited Pablo to stay for dinner, and he was nothing loath.*

**loathe** (lōᴛʜ) feel strong dislike and disgust for; abhor; hate: *We loathe rotten food.* *v.*, **loathed, loath·ing**.

**loath·ing** (lō'ᴛʜing) **1** strong dislike and disgust; intense aversion: *an intense loathing for spiders.* **2** ppr. of LOATHE. 1 *n.*, 2 *v.*

**loath·some** (lōᴛʜ'səm) disgusting; sickening: *a loathsome odour.* *adj.* —**loath'some·ly**, *adv.* —**loath'some·ness**, *n.*

**loaves** (lōvz) pl. of LOAF[1]. *n.*

**lob** (lob) **1** a tennis ball hit high to the back of the opponent's court. **2** hit a tennis ball high to the back of an opponent's court. **3** a slow underarm throw. **4** throw with a slow underarm movement. 1, 3 *n.*, 2, 4 *v.*, **lobbed, lob·bing.**

**lo·bar** (lō′bər) of or having to do with a LOBE or lobes. *adj.*

**lob·by** (lob′ē) **1** a large entrance hall or vestibule in an apartment building, theatre, hotel, etc.: *A lobby often has chairs or couches to sit on.* **2** a room or hall outside a legislative chamber: *the lobby of the House of Commons.* **3** a person or group that tries to influence legislators. **4** try to influence legislators: *The textile manufacturers are lobbying for a tax on imported fabrics.* 1–3 *n.*, *pl.* **lob·bies;** 4 *v.*, **lob·bied, lob·by·ing.**

**lob·by·ist** (lob′ē ist) a person who tries to influence legislators. *n.*

**lobe** (lōb) a rounded projecting part: *The lobe of the ear is the rounded lower end. The leaves of the white oak have deeply cut, narrow lobes.* *n.*

**lobed** (lōbd) having a LOBE or lobes. *adj.*

**lo·bel·ia** (lō bē′lē ə) any of various plants, both wild and cultivated, having blue, red, yellow, or white flowers. *n.*

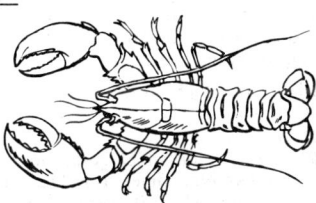

A North American lobster— about 25 to 50 cm long excluding the claws

**lob·ster** (lob′stər) **1** any of a family of edible sea crustaceans having eyes on stalks, a long body, and a pair of large pincers at the front with two pairs of much smaller pincers behind: *Lobsters are found along the coasts on both sides of the Atlantic.* **2** any of various similar crustaceans. **3** the flesh of a lobster used for food. *n.*

**lobster pot** a trap for lobsters.

**lob·stick** (lob′stik′) *Cdn.* in the North, a spruce or pine tree trimmed of all but the top branches: *Travellers often use lobsticks as landmarks.* *n.* Also, **lopstick.**

**lo·cal** (lō′kəl) **1** of or having to do with a certain place or places; limited to a certain place or places: *the local doctor, local politics, local news.* **2** of just one part of the body: *a local pain, local application of a remedy.* **3** making all, or almost all, stops: *a local train.* **4** a train, bus, etc. that stops at all of the stations on its route. **5** a branch or chapter of a labour union, fraternity, etc. **6** a newspaper item of interest to a particular place. **7** a telephone extension. 1–3 *adj.*, 4–7 *n.* —**lo′cal·ly,** *adv.*

**local area network** **1** a group of centrally organized services in a locality. **2** a network of computers able to share and exchange programs.

**local colour** or **color** the customs, peculiarities, etc. of a certain place or period, used in stories and plays to make them seem more real.

hat, āge, fär; let, ēqual, tėrm; it, īce hot, ōpen, ôrder; oil, out; cup, pùt, rüle əbove, takən, pencəl, lemən, circəs ch, child; ng, long; sh, ship th, thin; ᴛʜ, then; zh, measure

**lo·cale** (lō kal′) a location, site, or place, especially with reference to events or circumstances connected with it: *The locale of "Don Quixote" is Spain in the 16th century.* *n.*

**local government** **1** the system of administration of local affairs in a township, city, etc. by its own people. **2** the group elected for this purpose.

**local government district** LOCAL IMPROVEMENT DISTRICT.

**local improvement district** *Cdn.* in some provinces, a district administered by provincial officials because it is too thinly populated to have a municipal government of its own.

**lo·cal·ism** (lō′kə liz′əm) **1** a local practice, custom, etc. **2** a word or expression, etc. peculiar to a certain area: *"Outport," meaning an outlying fishing village, is a Newfoundland localism.* **3** PROVINCIALISM (def. 3). **4** attachment to a certain place. *n.*

**lo·cal·i·ty** (lō kal′ə tē) **1** a particular place, location, neighbourhood, etc.: *Are there any stores in this locality?* **2** situation; position: *A sense of locality enables one to find one's way.* *n.*, *pl.* **lo·cal·i·ties.**

**lo·cal·ize** (lō′kə līz′) make local; fix in, assign, or limit to a particular place or locality: *The infection seemed to be localized in the foot.* *v.*, **lo·cal·ized, lo·cal·iz·ing.** —**lo′cal·i·za′tion,** *n.*

**local option** the right of choice exercised by a minor political division, such as a county or city, especially as to whether the sale of liquor shall be permitted within its limits.

**lo·cate** (lō′kāt *or* lō kāt′) **1** establish in a place: *Takuk located his new store in Yellowknife.* **2** establish oneself in a place: *Early settlers located where there was water.* **3** find out the exact position of: *The general tried to locate the enemy's camp.* **4** state or show the position of: *Locate Regina on the map.* *v.*, **lo·cat·ed, lo·cat·ing.** —**lo′ca·tor,** *n.*
**be located,** be situated: *Ottawa is located on a river.*

**lo·ca·tion** (lō kā′shən) **1** locating or being located: *The scouts disputed about the location of the camp.* **2** a position or place: *The cottage was in a sheltered location.* **3** a plot of ground marked out by boundaries; lot: *a mining location.* **4** an area or place defined by lines of latitude and longitude: *Find the location of Toronto on the map.* *n.*
**on location,** at a place outside the studio for the purpose of filming a motion picture: *All the outdoor scenes were shot on location.*

**loch** (lok *or* loʜ) *Scottish.* **1** lake: *Loch Lomond.* **2** an arm of the sea partly shut in by land. *n.*
☛ *Hom.* LOCK (for the first pronunciation of **loch**).

**lo·ci** (lō′sī *or* lō′sē, lō′kī *or* lō′kē) pl. of LOCUS. *n.*

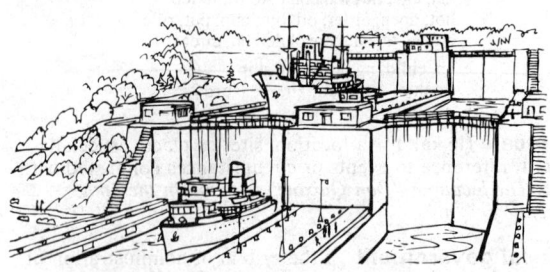

A set of locks in the Welland Canal, built to overcome the 99-metre difference in levels between Lake Ontario and Lake Erie. When a ship enters from above, the gates are closed and water is let out until the level is equal to that below the lock. Then the lower gates are opened. When a ship enters from below, the opposite process takes place.

**lock¹** (lok) **1** a means of fastening doors, boxes, etc. usually needing a key of special shape to open it. **2** fasten with a lock: *I forgot to lock the door.* **3** shut something in or out or up: *We lock up jewels in a safe.* **4** hold fast: *The ship was locked in ice. The secret was locked in her heart.* **5** an enclosed section of a canal, dock, etc. in which the level of the water can be changed by letting water in or out, to raise or lower ships. **6** go or pass by means of a lock; move a ship by means of a lock. **7** the part of a gun by which the charge is fired; gunlock. **8** a device to keep a wheel from turning: *A lock is used when a vehicle is going downhill.* **9** join, fit, jam, or link together: *The girls locked arms.* **10** become locked: *Two cars locked together in passing.* **11** an airtight chamber admitting to a compartment in which there is compressed air. **12** in wrestling, a kind of hold. 1, 5, 7, 8, 11, 12 *n.,* 2–4, 6, 9, 10 *v.*
**lock in,** invest money so that it cannot be taken out before a specified time.
**lock out,** refuse to give work to workers until they accept the employer's terms.
**lock, stock, and barrel,** *Informal.* completely; entirely.
**lock up,** lock a building for the night: *Be sure to lock up as you leave.*
**under lock and key,** locked up; in a place that is locked.
☛ *Hom.* LOCH (lok).

**lock²** (lok) **1** a curl or ringlet of hair. **2** a tuft of wool, cotton, etc. **3 locks,** *pl.* the hair of the head: *The child has curly locks.* *n.*
☛ *Hom.* LOCH (lok).

**lock·er** (lok′ər) **1** a chest, drawer, closet, or cupboard that can be locked. **2** a large refrigerated compartment for storing frozen food for a long time: *Lockers are usually rented from cold-storage plants.* **3** a person or thing that locks. *n.*

**lock·et** (lok′it) a small ornamental case of gold, silver, etc. for holding a picture or a lock of hair: *A locket is usually worn on a necklace.* *n.*

**lock·jaw** (lok′jo′) TETANUS. A characteristic symptom of the disease is a stiffness or spasm of the jaw muscles, which may become so severe that the jaws remain clamped shut. *n.*

**lock·out** (lok′out′) a refusal to give work to workers until they accept the employer's terms. *n.*

**lock·smith** (lok′smith′) a person who makes or repairs locks and keys. *n.*

**lock step** a way of marching in step very close together.

**lock stitch** a sewing-machine stitch in which two threads are fastened together at short intervals.

**lock·up** (lok′up′) *Informal.* JAIL. *n.*

**lo·co** (lō′kō) **1** LOCOWEED. **2** the disease caused by eating this weed. **3** poison with this weed. 1, 2 *n., pl.* **lo·cos;** 3 *v.,* **lo·coed, lo·co·ing.**

**lo·co·mo·tion** (lō′kə mō′shən) the act or power of moving from place to place: *Walking and flying are common forms of locomotion.* *n.*

**lo·co·mo·tive** (lō′kə mō′tiv) **1** an engine that runs on rails on its own power, used to move railway cars. **2** moving from place to place: *locomotive bacteria.* **3** of or having to do with the power to move from place to place. 1 *n.,* 2, 3 *adj.*

**lo·co·weed** (lō′kō wēd′) a plant of western North America that affects the brains of horses, sheep, etc. that eat it. *n.* Also, **loco.**

**lo·cus** (lō′kəs) a place. *n., pl.* **lo·ci** (-sī *or* -sē, -kī *or* -kē).

**lo·cust** (lō′kəst) **1** any of a family of grasshoppers having short antennae, especially any of several species that migrate in great swarms, often destroying all vegetation in the areas they pass through. **2** *Esp. U.S.* CICADA. **3** any of various hardwood trees of the pea family, such as the **black locust** and the **honey locust,** both tall North American trees often planted for ornament. **4** the hard, decay-resistant wood of a locust tree. *n.*

**lo·cu·tion** (lō kyü′shən) **1** style of speech. **2** a particular form of expression or phrasing, especially a word or expression characteristic of a particular region, group of people, etc. *n.*

**lode** (lōd) a vein of metal ore: *The miners struck a rich lode of copper.* *n.*
☛ *Hom.* LOAD.
☛ *Etym.* **Lode,** which is the first element of LODESTAR and LODESTONE, comes from OE *lād* 'a way, journey, or carrying', which is also the origin of LOAD. See note at LOAD.

**lode·star** (lōd′stär′) **1** a star that shows the way, especially the North Star. **2** a guiding principle. *n.* Also, **loadstar.**
☛ *Etym.* See note at LODE.

**lode·stone** (lōd′stōn′) **1** an oxide of iron that is highly magnetic. **2** anything that attracts strongly: *Gold was the lodestone that drew adventurers to the Yukon.* *n.*
☛ *Etym.* See note at LODE.

**lodge** (loj) **1** live in a place for a time. **2** provide with a place to live in or sleep in for a time: *Can you lodge us for the weekend?* **3** an inn, hotel, or motel. **4** a place to live in; small or temporary house; house: *My aunt rents a lodge in the mountains every summer.* **5** live in a rented room or rooms: *We are merely lodging at present.* **6** rent a room or rooms to. **7** get caught or stay in a place: *My kite lodged in the top of a tree.* **8** put or send into a place: *The hunter lodged a bullet in the lion's heart.* **9** put for safekeeping. **10** put before some authority: *We lodged a complaint with the police.* **11** put power, authority, etc. in a person or thing. **12** a branch of a club or society. **13** the place where such a group meets. **14** the den of an animal such as a beaver or otter. **15** a North American Indian dwelling. 1, 2, 5–11 *v.,* **lodged, lodg·ing;** 3, 4, 12–15 *n.*

**lodge·ment** (loj′mənt) See LODGMENT. *n.*

**lodge·pole pine** (loj′pōl′) *Cdn.* a pine tree found throughout British Columbia and western Alberta,

occurring in two quite distinct forms: a short, often crooked tree growing along the coast and a tall, straight, slender tree growing inland. The inland form is an important timber-producing tree. The coastal form is often called the **shore pine**.
☛ *Etym.* So called because it was used in building Canadian Indian LODGES (def. 15).

**lodg·er** (loj′ər) a person who lives in a rented room or rooms. *n.*

**lodg·ing** (loj′ing) **1** a place to live in for a time: *a lodging for the night.* **2 lodgings,** *pl.* a rented room or rooms in a house, not in a hotel. **3** ppr. of LODGE. 1, 2 *n.*, 3 *v.*

**lodging house** a house in which rooms are rented.

**lodg·ment** or **lodge·ment** (loj′mənt) **1** lodging or being lodged: *the lodgment of a complaint.* **2** something lodged or deposited: *a lodgment of earth on a ledge or rock. n.*

**lo·ess** (lō′is) a deposit of fine, yellowish-brown LOAM (def. 1) found in river valleys in North America, Europe, and Asia, believed to have been deposited by the wind: *Loess is very fertile when irrigated. n.*

**loft** (loft) **1** attic. **2** a room under the roof of a barn or stable; hayloft. **3** a gallery in a church or hall: *a choir loft.* **4** the upper floor of a business building or warehouse: *a studio loft.* **5** the backward slope of the face of a golf club. **6** a stroke that drives a golf ball upward. **7** hit a ball high up. 1–6 *n.*, 7 *v.*

**loft·y** (lôf′tē) **1** very high: *lofty mountains.* **2** high in character or spirit; exalted; noble: *lofty aims, lofty ideals.* **3** proud and haughty: *a lofty contempt for others. adj.*, **loft·i·er, loft·i·est.** —**loft′i·ly,** *adv.* —**loft′i·ness,** *n.*

**log**[1] (log) **1** a length of wood just as it comes from the tree. See PEAVEY for picture. **2** made of logs: *a log house.* **3** cut down trees, cut them into logs, and get them out of the forest. **4** cut trees into logs. **5** cut down trees on land. **6** the daily record of a ship's voyage. **7** enter in a ship's log. **8** enter the name and offence of a sailor in a ship's log. **9** the record of an airplane trip, performance of an engine, etc. **10** a float for measuring the speed of a ship. 1, 6, 9, 10 *n.*, 2 *adj.*, 3–5, 7, 8 *v.*, **logged, log·ging.** —**log′like**′, *adj.*
**log in** or **on,** be able to begin a session of work on a computer by entering a password or other identification.
**log off** or **out,** end a session of work on a computer by signing off.
**log out,** mark one's departure in a book.

**log**[2] (log) LOGARITHM. *n.*

**lo·gan** (lō′gən) *Cdn.* POKELOGAN. *n.*

**lo·gan·ber·ry** (lō′gən ber′ē) a large, purplish-red berry, a variety of blackberry, that grows mainly along the Pacific coast of North America. *n., pl.* **lo·gan·ber·ries.**
☛ *Etym.* Named after Judge J. H. *Logan* of California, who first grew the berry in 1881.

**log·a·rithm** (log′ə riᴛʜ əm) **1** the EXPONENT (def. 4) of the power to which a base, usually 10, must be raised in order to produce a given number: *If the base is 10, the logarithm of 1000 is 3; the logarithm of 10 000 is 4; the logarithm of 100 000 is 5.* **2** one of a system of such EXPONENTS (def. 4) used to shorten calculations in mathematics. *n.*

**log·a·rith·mic** (log′ə riᴛʜ′mik) of or having to do with LOGARITHM or logarithms. *adj.*

**log·a·rith·mi·cal** (log′ə riᴛʜ′mə kəl) LOGARITHMIC. *adj.*

**log·book** (log′bu̇k′) **1** a book containing a permanent record of all the details of the voyage of a ship or aircraft. **2** a traveller's diary. **3** any book containing a record of progress or performance over a period of time. *n.*

**loge** (lōj *or* lōzh) **1** a box in a theatre or opera house. **2** a balcony or mezzanine in a theatre, especially in the front part of such a balcony. *n.*

**log·ger** (log′ər) **1** a person whose work is felling trees and getting them to the mill; lumberjack. **2** a machine for loading or hauling logs. *n.*

**log·ger·head** (log′ər hed′) **1** any of various large-headed, meat-eating turtles of the western Atlantic. **2** an iron instrument having a long handle with a ball at the end that is heated for melting pitch, etc. *n.*
**at loggerheads,** disputing; in disagreement: *The council members are still at loggerheads over the housing issue.*

**log·gia** (loj′ə; *Italian,* lôd′jä) a gallery arcade open to the air on at least one side. *n., pl.* **log·gias** (lō′jəz), *Italian,* **log·gie** (lôd′jä).

**log·ging** (log′ing) **1** the work of cutting down trees, cutting them into logs, and removing them from the forest. **2** ppr. of LOG. 1 *n.*, 2 *v.*

**log·ic** (loj′ik) **1** the science of getting new and valid information by reasoning from facts that one already knows. **2** a book on logic. **3** reasoning; the use of argument: *The lawyer won her case because her logic was sound.* **4** reason; sound sense: *There is much logic in what you say. n.*

**log·i·cal** (loj′ə kəl) **1** having to do with or according to the principles of LOGIC: *logical reasoning.* **2** reasonable; reasonably expected: *Fatigue is a logical result of poor nutrition.* **3** reasoning correctly: *a clear and logical mind. adj.* —**log′i·cal·ly,** *adv.*

**lo·gi·cian** (lō jish′ən) a person trained in LOGIC. *n.*

**lo·gis·tic** (lō jis′tik) of or having to do with LOGISTICS. *adj.*

**lo·gis·tics** (lō jis′tiks) the art of planning and carrying out military movements, evacuation, and supply. *n.*

**log–jam** (log′jam′) **1** an accumulation of floating logs jammed together in the water. **2** any deadlock or blockage. **3** delay, block, or obstruct. 1, 2 *n.*, 3 *v.*, **log-jammed, log-jam·ming.**

**lo·go** (lō′gō *or* log′ō) an identifying symbol used as a trademark, in advertising, etc. *n.*

**LOGO** a computer language devised specially for children.
☛ *Etym.* From Gk. *logos,* 'word'.

**log–roll** (log′rōl′) take part in LOGROLLING. *v.* —**log′roll**′**er,** *n.*

**log–roll·ing** (log′rō′ling) **1** the act of rolling logs in water, especially by treading on them. **2** ppr. of LOGROLL. 1 *n.*, 2 *v.*

**log·wood** (log′wu̇d′) **1** the heavy, hard, brownish-red wood of a tropical American tree of the legume family, from which a dye is obtained that is used especially in biological stains. 2 the tree itself. 3 the dye. *n.*

**lo·gy** (lō′gē) heavy; sluggish; dull. *adj.*, **lo·gi·er, lo·gi·est.**

**–logy** *combining form.* 1 the account, doctrine, or science of, as in *biology.* 2 speaking; discussion, as in *eulogy.* 3 special meanings, as in *analogy, anthology.*

**loin** (loin) 1 a piece of meat from the part of the body between the ribs and the hips: *a loin of pork.* See BEEF, LAMB, PORK, and VEAL for pictures. 2 Usually, **loins,** *pl.* the part of the body between the ribs and the hips: *The loins are on both sides of the backbone.* *n.*
**gird up one's loins,** get ready for action.

**loin·cloth** (loin′kloth′) a piece of cloth fastened around the waist and covering the thighs: *The loincloth is worn by people of warm countries.* *n.*

**loi·ter** (loi′tər) 1 linger idly; stop and play along the way: *Mary loitered along daydreaming.* 2 spend time idly: *to loiter the hours away.* *v.* —**loi′ter·er,** *n.*

**loll** (lol) 1 recline or lean in a lazy manner: *to loll on a chesterfield.* 2 hang out loosely or droop: *A dog's tongue lolls out in hot weather.* 3 allow to hang out or droop: *A dog lolls out its tongue.* 4 a lolling. 1–3 *v.*, 4 *n.*

**lol·li·pop** or **lol·ly·pop** (lol′ē pop′) a piece of hard candy on the end of a small stick; sucker. *n.*

**Lombardy poplar** a variety of a European species of poplar tree having a narrow, spirelike crown and almost vertical branches, commonly grown in parts of Canada as an ornamental tree.

**Lon·don·er** (lun′də nər) a native or inhabitant of London. *n.*

**lone** (lōn) 1 having no company or companion; alone; solitary: *We met a lone traveller on our way.* 2 lonesome; lonely: *a lone life.* 3 standing apart; isolated: *a lone house on a hill.* *adj.*
☛ Hom. LOAN.

**lone·li·ness** (lōn′lē nis) being lonely; solitude. *n.*

**lone·ly** (lōn′lē) 1 feeling oneself alone and longing for company of friends: *He was lonely while his sister was away.* 2 without many people: *a lonely road.* 3 alone: *a lonely tree.* *adj.*, **lone·li·er, lone·li·est.** —**lone′li·ness,** *n.*

**lon·er** (lō′nər) *Informal.* a person who prefers to live or be alone. *n.*

**lone·some** (lōn′səm) 1 feeling lonely. 2 making one feel lonely: *a lonesome journey.* *adj.*, **lone·som·er, lone·som·est.**

**lone wolf** a person who prefers to work or live alone; loner.

**long¹** (long) 1 measuring much, or more than usual, from end to end in space or time: *a long distance, a long speech.* 2 having a specified length in space or time: *five metres long, two hours long.* 3 thin and narrow: *a long pole.* 4 far-reaching; extending to a great distance in space or time: *a long memory, long sight.* 5 throughout the whole length of: *all night long.* 6 for a long time: *a reform long advocated.* 7 a long time: *for long.* 8 at a point of time far distant from the time indicated: *long before, long since.* 9 in some languages, of vowels or syllables, taking a comparatively long time to speak. 10 a long sound. 11 well supplied with some commodity or stock. 12 depending on a rise in prices for profit.
1–4, 9, 11, 12 *adj.*, **long·er** (long′gər), **long·est** (long′gist); 5, 6, 8 *adv.*, 7, 10 *n.*
**a long face,** a sad expression.
**as long as** or **so long as,** provided that.
**before long,** soon; in a short time.
**in the long run,** over a long period of time; eventually.
**the long and short of it,** the sum total of something; substance: *He will never forgive you, and that is the long and short of it.*

**long²** (long) wish very much; have a strong desire: *He longed for his mother. She longed to see him.* *v.*

**long.** longitude.

**long·boat** (long′bōt′) the largest and strongest boat carried by a merchant sailing ship. *n.*

**long·bow** (long′bō′) a bow drawn by hand and shooting a long feathered arrow: *A longbow is usually between 170 and 185 cm long.* Compare with CROSSBOW.
**draw the longbow,** tell exaggerated stories.

**long–dis·tance** (long′dis′təns) 1 of or having to do with telephone service to another town, city, etc. 2 an operator or exchange that takes care of long-distance calls. 3 for or over great distances: *a long-distance moving van.* 1, 3 *adj.*, 2 *n.*

**long division** in arithmetic, division involving numbers containing usually two or more digits, and in which the steps of the process are written down in full. See DIVISION for picture.

**long dozen** thirteen.

**long–drawn** (long′dron′) lasting a long time; prolonged to great length: *the long-drawn howl of a coyote, a long-drawn speech.* *adj.*

**lon·gev·i·ty** (lon jev′ə tē) long life: *The old woman said she attributed her longevity to an active life.* *n.*

**long·hand** (long′hand′) ordinary writing, not shorthand or typewriting. *n.*

**long–head·ed** (long′hed′id) having foresight and good sense; shrewd. *adj.*

**long·horn** (long′hôrn′) a breed of cattle having very long horns, formerly common in the southwestern United States. *n.*

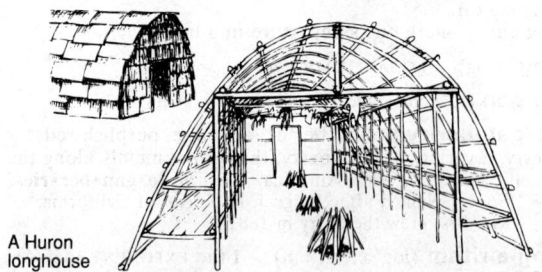

A Huron longhouse

**long·house** (long′hous′) a large dwelling of certain North American Indian peoples, especially the Iroquois and some west coast peoples, in which several families of a community lived together. *n.*

**long·ing** (long′ing) 1 an earnest desire: *a longing for home.* 2 having or showing earnest desire: *a child's longing look at a window full of toys.* 3 ppr. of LONG.
1 *n.*, 2 *adj.*, 3 *v.* —**long′ing·ly,** *adv.*

**long·ish** (long′ish) somewhat long. *adj.*

**lon·gi·tude** (lon′jə tyüd′ *or* lon′jə tüd′, long′gə tyüd′ *or* long′gə tüd′) **1** a distance east or west on the earth's surface, measured in degrees from a certain meridian: *On maps, lines running between the North and South Poles represent longitudes. Usually the meridian through Greenwich, England, is used to measure longitude, because it is the prime meridian.* See LATITUDE for picture. **2** *Informal.* length. *n.*

**lon·gi·tu·di·nal** (lon′jə tyü′də nəl *or* lon′jə tü′də nəl, long′gə tyü′də nəl *or* long′gə tü′də nəl) **1** of or having to do with length or the lengthwise dimension: *longitudinal measurements.* **2** running lengthwise; lengthways: *Our living room drapes have longitudinal stripes.* **3** of longitude. *adj.* —**lon′gi·tu′di·nal·ly,** *adv.*

**long jump** **1** an athletic event or contest in which contestants try to jump over as much ground as possible: *The long jump from a running start is one of the Olympic track and field events.* **2** a jump of this kind. **3 standing long jump,** a long jump from a standing start: *The standing long jump is often included in school field meets.*

**long–lived** (long′livd′ *or* long′līvd′) living or lasting a long time. *adj.*

**long measure** LINEAR MEASURE.

**long–play·ing** (long′plā′ing) of or referring to a microgroove phonograph record designed to be played at 33⅓ revolutions per minute. *adj.*

**long–range** (long′rānj′) **1** looking ahead; future: *long-range plans.* **2** capable of covering a great distance: *long-range missiles.* *adj.*

**long·shore·man** (long′shôr′mən) a person whose work is loading and unloading ships at a seaport. *n., pl.* **long·shore·men** (-mən).
☞ *Etym.* From *alongshoreman*, one who works on the shore.

**long shot** **1** *Informal.* a bet, or wager, against great odds, but which therefore carries great possible winnings. **2** *Informal.* any venture or undertaking involving great risk or only slight chance of success, but offering great rewards if successful. **3** in motion pictures and television, a scene photographed from a distance. **not by a long shot,** not at all; certainly not.

**long–sight·ed** (long′sī′tid) **1** far-sighted; focussing at more than the right distance. **2** having foresight; wise. *adj.* —**long′–sight′ed·ness,** *n.*

**long–stand·ing** (long′stan′ding) having lasted for a long time: *a long-standing feud.* *adj.*

**long–suf·fer·ing** (long′suf′ə ring) **1** enduring trouble, pain, or injury long and patiently. **2** long and patient endurance of trouble, pain, or injury. 1 *adj.*, 2 *n.*

**long suit** **1** in card games, the suit in which one has most cards. **2** something in which a person excels; a strong point: *Patience is not her long suit.*

**long–term** (long′tėrm′) **1** lasting or intended for a long time: *our long-term plans and ambitions.* **2** falling due in several years: *a long-term loan.* *adj.*

**long ton** the British ton, 2240 pounds (about 1.02 tonnes).

**long–tongued** (long′tungd′) **1** having a long tongue. **2** talking much or too much. *adj.*

**long·ways** (long′wāz′) LENGTHWISE; in the direction of the length. *adv.*

**long–wind·ed** (long′win′did) **1** capable of long effort without getting out of breath: *A long-distance runner must* be long-winded. **2** talking or writing at great lengths; tiresome: *a long-winded speaker.* *adj.* —**long′–wind′ed·ly,** *adv.* —**long′–wind′ed·ness,** *n.*

**long·wise** (long′wīz′) LENGTHWISE. *adv.*

**look** (lůk) **1** see; try to see; turn the eyes: *He looked this way.* **2** a glance; seeing: *She took a quick look at the magazine.* **3** search: *I looked through the drawer to see if I could find my keys.* **4** a search. **5** examine; pay attention (used with **at**): *You must look at all the facts.* **6** seem; appear: *She looks pale.* **7** appearance; aspect: *A deserted house has a desolate look.* **8** have a view; face: *Our house looks upon a garden.* **9** express or suggest by looks: *He said nothing, but looked his disappointment.* **10 looks,** **a** personal appearance: *Good looks means a good appearance.* **b** *Informal.* general appearance: *the looks of a situation.* 1, 3, 5, 6, 8, 9 *v.*, 2, 4, 7, 10 *n.*
—**look′er,** *n.*
**look after,** attend to; take care of.
**look alive,** hurry.
**look around** or **round,** consider many possibilities.
**look askance at,** treat with disfavour.
**look back,** recollect; think about the past.
**look bad,** seem improper.
**look black,** seem hopeless.
**look daggers at,** look at with hatred or anger.
**look down on,** despise; scorn.
**look for,** **a** seek or search for. **b** expect: *We'll look for you tonight.* **c** act so as to cause: *You're just looking for trouble.*
**look forward to,** expect, usually hopefully: *We look forward to seeing you. When the crops failed, they knew they had to look forward to a bad winter.*
**look in,** make a short visit: *She said she'd look in on her way back.*
**look into,** investigate: *She promised to look into the matter.*
**look on,** **a** watch without taking part: *The teacher conducted the experiment while we looked on.* **b** regard; consider: *I look on her as a very able person.*
**look oneself,** seem like oneself; look well: *She has been quite ill and still doesn't look herself.*
**look out,** be careful; watch out: *Look out for cars as you cross the street.*
**look out for,** take care of: *Ernie had always looked out for his little sister.*
**look over,** examine; inspect: *The police officer looked over the man's driver's licence.*
**look sharp** or **snappy,** *Informal.* be quick.
**look through,** examine.
**look to,** **a** attend to; take care of. **b** turn to for help.
**look up,** **a** find; refer to: *She looked up the word in the dictionary.* **b** *Informal.* call on; visit: *Look me up when you come to town.* **c** *Informal.* get better; improve.
**look up to,** respect; admire.

**look·er–on** (lůk′ə ron′) a person who watches without taking part; spectator. *n., pl.* **look·ers–on.**

**looking glass** mirror.

**look·out** (lůk′out′) **1** a careful watch: *Keep a good lookout for Mother. Be on the lookout for trouble.* **2** the person or group that keeps watch. **3** a place from which to watch, as for forest fires, etc.: *A crow's-nest is a lookout.* **4** what is seen ahead; outlook: *See those clouds! A poor lookout for our picnic.* **5** *Informal.* something to be cared for or worried about: *That is his lookout.* *n.*

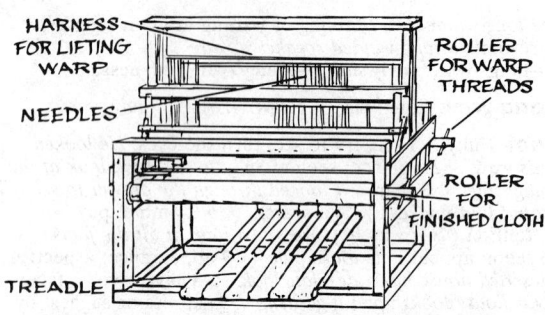

A loom

**loom¹** (lüm)   a machine for weaving cloth.   *n.*

**loom²** (lüm)   appear dimly or vaguely as a large, often threatening, shape: *A large iceberg loomed through the thick, grey fog.*   *v.*
**loom large,**   seem important.

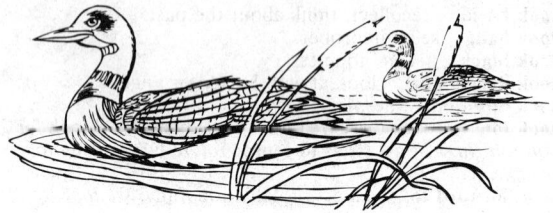

Common loons—about 80 cm long including the tail

**loon¹** (lün)   a large, web-footed diving bird that has a loud, wild cry.   *n.*
☛ *Hom.* LUNE.

**loon²** (lün)   a crazy or stupid person.   *n.*
☛ *Hom.* LUNE.

**loon·ie** (lü′nē) *Informal.*   a Canadian one-dollar coin.   *n., pl.* **loon·ies.** Also, **loony.**

**loop** (lüp)   **1** the shape of a curved string, ribbon, bent wire, etc. that crosses itself.   **2** a thing, bend, course, or motion shaped somewhat like this: *In handwriting, 'b,' 'g,' 'h,' and 'l' often have loops. The road makes a wide loop around the lake.*   **3** a fastening or ornament formed of cord, etc. bent and crossed.   **4** make a loop or loops in.   **5** a turn like the handwritten letter *l*, especially one made by an airplane.   **6** in a computer, a program or instruction that repeats continuously.   *1–3, 5, 6 n., 4 v.*
**loop the loop,**   turn over and over; make a loop in the air.

**loop·hole** (lüp′hōl′)   **1** a small opening in a wall to shoot through, look through, or let in light and air.   **2** a means of escape; especially, something in a law, contract, etc., that is ambiguous or unclear, which makes it possible to avoid the intent or consequences of the law, etc.   *n.*

**loose** (lüs)   **1** not firmly set or fastened: *a loose tooth, a loose thread.*   **2** not tight: *loose clothing.*   **3** not bound together: *loose papers.*   **4** not put up in a box, can, etc.: *loose coffee.*   **5** free; not shut in or up: *We leave the dog loose at night.*   **6** not close or solid; having spaces: *loose earth, cloth with a loose weave.*   **7** not strict or exact: *a loose translation from another language, loose thinking.*   **8** having or showing too little control or restraint: *loose conduct, a loose tongue.*   **9** lewd or unchaste.   **10** set free; let go: *They loosed the prisoners.*   **11** shoot an arrow, gun, etc.   **12** make loose; untie; unfasten: *to loose a knot.*   **13** relax.   **14** in a loose manner.   *1–9 adj.,* **loos·er, loos·est;** *10–13 v.,* **loosed, loos·ing;** *14 adv.*
—**loose′ly,** *adv.*   —**loose′ness,** *n.*
**break loose,**   **a** separate from anything; break a connection or relation.   **b** run away; free oneself.
**cast loose,**   unfasten; separate.
**cut loose,**   break loose.
**let loose,**   set free; release; let go.
**on the loose,** *Informal.*   **a** free; without restraint.   **b** on a spree.   **c** absent without leave.
**set** or **turn loose,**   set free; release; let go.

**loose end**   **1** something left hanging loose: *There's a loose end hanging from the hem.*   **2** an unfinished detail; a relatively minor thing that remains to be done: *We've finished the main job, but there are still a few loose ends to tie up.*
**at loose ends,**   **a** in an unsettled or disorganized condition or situation: *Lee has finished university, but is still at loose ends about what he wants to do.*   **b** unemployed.

**loose–joint·ed** (lüs′join′tid)   **1** having loose joints; loosely built.   **2** able to move very freely.   *adj.*

**loose–leaf** (lüs′lēf′)   of a notebook, etc., having pages or sheets that can be taken out and replaced.   *adj.*

**loos·en** (lü′sən)   **1** make loose or looser; untie; unfasten: *The doctor loosened the stricken man's collar.*   **2** become loose or looser: *Your ring will loosen when your fingers are cold.*   *v.*   —**loos′en·er,** *n.*
**loosen up,**   **a** warm up one's muscles with exercise.   **b** be more tolerant or relaxed.

**loose·strife** (lüs′strīf′)   **1** any of a closely related group of herbs, especially a common weed having long, showy spikes of purple flowers.   **2** referring to the family of mainly tropical plants that includes the purple loosestrife and henna.   **3** any of a closely related group of plants of the primrose family having leafy stems and spikes of yellow, white, or rose flowers.   *n.*

**loot** (lüt)   **1** spoils; plunder; booty: *loot taken by soldiers from a captured town, burglar's loot.*   **2** plunder; rob: *The jewellery store was looted by burglars.*   *1 n., 2 v.*
—**loot′er,** *n.*
☛ *Hom.* LUTE.

**lop¹** (lop)   **1** cut (usually used with **off**): *We lopped off a big chunk of cheese.*   **2** trim by cutting off branches, twigs, etc.: *to lop a tree.*   *v.,* **lopped, lop·ping.**

**lop²** (lop)   **1** hang loosely; droop.   **2** flop.   *v.,* **lopped, lop·ping.**

**lope** (lōp)   **1** run with a long, easy stride: *The coyote loped along the trail.*   **2** a long, easy stride.   *1 v.,* **loped, lop·ing;** *2 n.*   —**lop′er,** *n.*

**lop–eared** (lop′ērd′)   having ears that hang loosely or droop.   *adj.*

**lop·sid·ed** (lop′sī′did)   larger or heavier on one side than the other; unevenly balanced; leaning to one side.   *adj.*   —**lop′sid′ed·ly,** *adv.*   —**lop′sid′ed·ness,** *n.*

**lop·stick** (lop′stik′)   LOBSTICK.   *n.*

**lo·qua·cious** (lō kwā′shəs) talking much; fond of talking. *adj.* —**lo·qua′cious·ly,** *adv.*

**lo·quac·i·ty** (lō kwas′ə tē) an inclination to talk a great deal; talkativeness. *n.*

**lo·quat** (lō′kwot) **1** a small evergreen tree with small, yellow, edible, plumlike fruit, native to China and Japan. **2** the fruit. *n.*

**lo·ran** (lôr′ən) a device by which a ship or aircraft can determine its geographical position by utilizing signals sent out from two radio stations. *n.*
☛ *Etym.* From the first letters of *lo*ng *ra*nge *n*avigation.

**lord** (lôrd) **1** a ruler, master, or chief; a person who has the power. **2** rule proudly or absolutely: *He lorded it over us.* **3** a feudal superior. **4** in the United Kingdom, a man entitled by courtesy to the title of lord: *A baron is a lord.* **5** raise to the rank of lord. **6 Lord, a** in the United Kingdom, a titled nobleman or peer of the realm belonging to the House of Lords. **b** a title used in writing or speaking to or of noblemen of certain ranks: *Lord Beaverbrook was born in Ontario.* **c** a title given by courtesy to men holding certain positions: *Lord Chief Justice.* **7 the Lords,** HOUSE OF LORDS. **8 the Lord, a** God. **b** Christ. 1, 3, 4, 6–8 *n.*, 2, 5 *v.*
**lord it over,** domineer over.
☛ *Etym.* From OE *hlāford*, earlier *hlāfweard* 'bread keeper', made up of *hlāf* 'loaf' and *weard* 'guard, keeper'. Compare note at LADY.

**Lord Chamberlain** in the United Kingdom, a government officer and the official in charge of the royal household.

**lord·ling** (lôr′dling) a little or unimportant lord. *n.*

**lord·ly** (lôr′dlē) **1** like or suitable for a lord; grand; magnificent. **2** haughty; insolent; scornful: *His lordly airs annoyed many people.* **3** in a lordly manner. 1, 2 *adj.*, 3 *adv.* —**lord′li·ness,** *n.*
**lord·li·er, lord·li·est;**

**Lord Mayor** in the United Kingdom, the title of the mayors of London and of some other large cities.

**lord·ship** (lôrd′ship) **1** the rank or position of a lord. **2** rule; ownership: *His lordship over these lands is not questioned.* **3** Often, **Lordship,** *Brit.* a title used in speaking to or of a lord: *your Lordship, his Lordship.* *n.*

**lore** (lôr) **1** the facts and stories about a certain subject: *fairy lore, bird lore, Irish lore.* **2** learning; knowledge. *n.*

A lorgnette (def. 1)

**lor·gnette** (lôr nyet′) **1** eyeglasses mounted on a handle. **2** opera glasses mounted on a handle. *n.*

**lorn** (lôrn) forsaken; forlorn. *adj.*

**lor·ry** (lô′rē) **1** a long, flat wagon without sides. **2** *Brit.* motor truck. *n., pl.* **lor·ries.**
☛ *Hom.* LORY.

**lo·ry** (lō′rē) any of a number of small, brightly coloured parrots native to Australia, New Guinea, and nearby islands, most of which have a fringed, brushlike tongue tip for feeding on nectar and soft fruits. *n.*
☛ *Hom.* LORRY.

hat, āge, fär; let, ēqual, tėrm; it, īce
hot, ōpen, ôrder; oil, out; cup, put, rüle
əbove, takən, pencəl, lemən, circəs
ch, child; ng, long; sh, ship
th, thin; ᴛH, then; zh, measure

**lose** (lüz) **1** not have any longer; have taken away from one by accident, carelessness, gambling, parting, death, etc.: *to lose one's life.* **2** be unable to find: *to lose one's way, to lose a book.* **3** fail to keep or maintain; cease to have: *to lose patience, to lose all fear.* **4** miss; fail to get, catch, see, hear, or understand: *to lose a train, to lose a few words of what was said.* **5** fail to have, get, catch, etc.: *to lose a sale.* **6** fail to win: *to lose a bet.* **7** be defeated: *Our team lost.* **8** bring to destruction; ruin: *The ship and her crew were lost.* **9** let pass without use or profit; waste: *to lose an opportunity, to lose time.* **10** suffer loss: *to lose on a contract.* **11** be or become worse off in money, in numbers, etc.: *Because of the storm damage, the farmer lost heavily.* **12** cause the loss of: *Delay lost the battle.* **13** cause to lose: *That one act lost him his job.* **14** of a timepiece, run slow: *That clock loses five minutes a day.* *v.,* **lost, los·ing.** —**los′er,** *n.*
**lose oneself, a** let oneself go astray; become bewildered. **b** become absorbed.
**lose out,** fail; be unsuccessful.

**los·ing** (lü′zing) **1** that cannot win: *Karel's friends told him he was playing a losing game, but he wouldn't listen.* **2** ppr. of LOSE. 1 *adj.*, 2 *v.*

**los·ings** (lü′zingz) losses. *n. pl.*

**loss** (los) **1** losing or being lost: *The loss of one's health is serious but the loss of a pencil is not.* **2** the person or thing lost: *The fire was finally put out, but her house was a complete loss.* **3** the amount lost. **4** the harm or disadvantage caused by losing something: *Our losses by the fire amounted to $5000.* **5** a defeat: *Our team had two losses and one tie out of ten games played.* *n.*
**at a loss,** puzzled; not sure; uncertain; in difficulty: *She was at a loss for words.*
**at a loss to,** unable to.

**lost** (lost) **1** pt. and pp. of LOSE: *I lost my new pen. My glasses are lost, too.* **2** no longer had or kept: *lost friends.* **3** no longer to be found; missing: *lost articles.* **4** no longer visible: *She was soon lost in the crowd.* **5** attended with defeat: *a lost battle.* **6** not used to good purpose; wasted: *lost time.* **7** having gone astray. **8** destroyed or ruined: *a lost soul.* **9** bewildered: *She looked completely lost.* **10** absorbed; rapt; engrossed (*used with* **in**): *lost in thought.* 1 *v.,* 2–10 *adj.*
**lost on,** wasted on: *Sarcasm is lost on her.*
**lost to, a** no longer possible or open to. **b** no longer belonging to. **c** insensible to: *The deserting soldier was lost to all sense of duty to his country.*

**lost cause** an undertaking already defeated or one certain to be defeated.

**lost sheep** a person who has strayed from the right sort of conduct or religious belief.

**lot** (lot) **1** a large number or amount; a great many or a great deal: *a lot of books, a lot of money. There is a lot of truth in what she said.* **2** a number of persons or things considered as a group; collection or set: *This lot of ballots still has to be counted.* **3** a plot of ground, especially one having fixed boundaries, as a subdivision of a block in a town or city: *a vacant lot. Our house is on a corner lot.* **4** divide into lots. **5** a motion-picture studio together

with the surrounding property.   **6** an object used to decide something by chance: *We drew lots to decide who should be captain.*   **7** such a method of deciding: *to divide property by lot.*   **8** a choice made in this way: *The lot fell to me.*   **9** what one gets by lot; one's share.   **10** one's fate or fortune: *a happy lot.*   **11** an item or items for sale at an auction: *lot number 34.*   **12 lots**, *Informal.* a large number or amount: *She has lots of money. There were lots of people.*   **13 lots**, *Informal.*   much: *This table is lots nicer than that one.*   1–3, 5–12 *n.*, 13 *adv.*, 4 *v.*, **lot·ted, lot·ting.**
**a lot,**   much: *I feel a lot better. She skis a lot.*
**cast** or **draw lots,**   use lots to decide something.
**cast** or **throw in one's lot with,**   share the fate of; become a partner with.
☞ *Usage.* **Lots**, meaning 'a lot' is informal and is generally avoided in written English. In informal English, one might say, *She tried lots of different shots, but lost the game anyway.* In more formal English, one would say, *She tried a lot of different* (or *many different*) *shots.*

**loth** (lōth)   See LOATH.   *adj.*

**lo·tion** (lō′shən)   a liquid medicine or cosmetic which is applied to the skin: *Lotions are used to relieve pain, to heal, to cleanse, or to beautify the skin.*   *n.*

**lot·ter·y** (lot′ə rē)   a scheme for distributing prizes by lot or chance: *In a lottery many tickets are sold, only some of which win prizes.*   *n., pl.* **lot·ter·ies.**

**lot·to** (lot′ō)   a game played by drawing numbered disks from a bag or box and covering the corresponding numbers on cards; bingo.   *n.*

**lo·tus** (lō′təs)   **1** a water lily that grows in Egypt and Asia.   **2** a plant with red, pink, or white flowers, of the same family as the pea.   **3** a plant whose fruit was supposed to cause a dreamy and contented forgetfulness in those who ate it.   *n.*

**lo·tus–eat·er** (lō′tə sē′tər)   a person who leads a life of dreamy, indolent ease.   *n.*

**loud** (loud)   **1** strong in sound; noisy: *The music is too loud.*   **2** producing a loud sound; making a noise: *She has a very loud voice.*   **3** clamorous; insistent: *They were loud in their demands for higher pay.*   **4** *Informal.*   showy, flashy, or vulgar: *loud clothes.*   **5** in a loud manner: *She blew the bugle loud and long. Don't talk so loud.*   1–4 *adj.*, 5 *adv.* —**loud′ly,** *adv.* —**loud′ness,** *n.*
**out loud,**   loud enough to be heard; not to oneself or in a whisper; aloud: *She repeated her lines out loud to herself.*

**loud·hail·er** (loud′hā′lər)   a megaphone with an electric amplifier; bullhorn.   *n.*

**loud·ish** (lou′dish)   somewhat loud.   *adj.*

**lough** (loH) *Irish.*   **1** lake.   **2** an arm of the sea; bay or inlet.   *n.*

**lounge** (lounj)   **1** stand, stroll, sit, or lie at ease and lazily: *He lounged in an old chair.*   **2** the act or state of lounging.   **3** a comfortable and informal room in which one can lounge and be at ease: *a theatre lounge.*   **4** a couch or chesterfield.   1 *v.*, **lounged, loung·ing;**   2–4 *n.* —**loung′er,** *n.*

**lour** (lour)   See LOWER².   *v., n.*

**louse** (lous)   **1** a small, wingless insect that infests the hair or skin of people and animals, causing great irritation.   **2** any of various other insects that are parasitic on animals or plants.   *n., pl.* **lice.**

**lous·y** (lou′zē)   infested with lice.   *adj.*, **lous·i·er, lous·i·est.**

**lout** (lout)   an awkward, stupid fellow; boor: *The lout didn't even wipe his muddy boots when he came in.*   *n.*

**lout·ish** (lou′tish)   awkward and stupid; boorish.   *adj.*

**lou·vre** or **lou·ver** (lü′vər)   **1** a window or other opening covered with LOUVRE BOARDS.   **2** a ventilating slit.   *n.*

**louvre boards** or **louver boards**   horizontal strips of wood, glass, etc. set slanting in a window or other opening, so as to keep out rain or light but provide ventilation.

**lov·a·ble** (luv′ə bəl)   inspiring love; endearing.   *adj.* —**lov′a·ble·ness,** *n.* —**lov′a·bly,** *adv.*

**love** (luv)   **1** a deep feeling of fondness and friendship; great affection or devotion: *love of one's family, love for a sweetheart.*   **2** have such a feeling for: *She loves her mother. I love my country.*   **3** an instance of such feeling.   **4** this feeling as a subject for books, or as a personified influence.   **5** be in love with.   **6** be in love; fall in love.   **7** a loved one; sweetheart.   **8** a warm liking; fond or tender feeling.   **9** a strong liking: *a love of books.*   **10** like very much; take great pleasure in: *She loves music. Most people love ice cream.*   **11** *Informal.*   something charming or delightful.   **12** be fond of; hold dear.   **13** have affection: *He can hate but cannot love.*   **14** godly affection, devotion and brotherhood.   **15** in tennis and certain other games, no score.   1, 3, 4, 7–9, 11, 14, 15 *n.*, 2, 5, 6, 10, 12, 13 *v.*, **loved, lov·ing.**
**fall in love,**   begin to love; come to feel love.
**for love,**   **a** for nothing; without pay.   **b** for pleasure; not for money.
**for the love of,**   for the sake of; because of.
**in love,**   feeling love.
**make love,**   behave like lovers; do as lovers do; woo.
**not for love or money,**   not on any terms.

**love affair**   **1** a romantic relationship between two people who are not married to each other.   **2** a lively or intense interest in or enthusiasm about something.

**love apple**   an old name for the tomato.

**love·bird** (luv′bėrd′)   **1** any of various small parrots, often kept as cage birds, that appear to show great affection for their mates.   **2 lovebirds**, *pl.*   two people very obviously in love with each other.   *n.*

**love feast**   **1** a meal eaten together by the early Christians as a symbol of brotherly love.   **2** a religious ceremony imitating this.   **3** a banquet or other gathering to promote good feeling.

**love knot**   an ornamental knot or bow of ribbon as a token of love.

**love·less** (luv′lis)   **1** not loving.   **2** not loved.   *adj.*

**love–lies–bleed·ing** (luv′līz′blē′ding)   a species of AMARANTH that is a popular garden plant, having long, drooping, tassel-like spikes of dark-red flowers.   *n.*

**love·li·ness** (luv′lē nis)   the quality or state of being lovely.   *n.*

**love·lorn** (luv′lôrn′)   suffering because of love; forsaken by the person whom one loves.   *adj.*

**love·ly** (luv′lē)   **1** having beauty, harmony, or grace; inspiring admiration or affection: *a lovely woman. She is a lovely person.*   **2** *Informal.*   very pleasing; delightful: *We had a lovely holiday.*   *adj.*, **love·li·er, love·li·est.**

**lov·er** (luv′ər)   **1** a person who is in love with another.

**2** a person having a strong liking for something: *a lover of books.* **3 lovers,** *pl.* a man and a woman who are in love with each other. *n.* **—lov′er·like′,** *adj.*

**love seat** a small couch, or chesterfield, seating two persons.

**love·sick** (luv′sik′) languishing because of love. *adj.*

**lov·ing** (luv′ing) **1** feeling or showing love; affectionate; fond. **2** ppr. of LOVE. 1 *adj.*, 2 *v.* **—lov′ing·ly,** *adv.*

**loving cup** a large silver cup with handles, passed around for all to drink from; now given as a trophy in some sports.

**lov·ing–kind·ness** (luv′ing kīnd′nis) deep affection and tenderness. *n.*

**low¹** (lō) **1** not high or tall: *A low wall enclosed the garden. This stool is very low.* **2** of less than average or ordinary height, depth, amount, or degree: *The river is low this year.* **3** near the ground, floor, or base: *a low shelf, a low jump.* **4** lying or being below the general level: *low ground.* **5** almost used up; short: *Supplies were low. Our furnace oil is low.* **6** not loud; soft: *We heard a low sound.* **7** small in amount, degree, force, value, etc.: *a low price.* **8** at or to a low position, amount, rank, degree, pitch, etc.: *The lamp hangs too low. The sun sank low. Supplies are running low. He bowed low.* **9** not advanced in development, organization, complexity, etc.: *Bacteria are low organisms.* **10** lacking in dignity or elevation: *low thoughts.* **11** humble: *She rose from a low position to president of the company. He is of low birth.* **12** lacking health or strength; sick or weak: *Her mother is very low.* **13** unfavourable; poor: *He had a low opinion of their abilities.* **14** depressed or dejected: *low spirits. She has been feeling low.* **15** mean or base: *a low trick.* **16** coarse; vulgar: *low language, low company.* **17** near the horizon. **18** near the equator. **19** of a dress or its neckline, cut so as to leave the neck and part of the breast exposed. **20** deep: *a low bow.* **21** in music, not high in the scale; deep in pitch: *a low note.* **22** that which is low. **23** in automobiles and similar machines, an arrangement of the gears used for the lowest speed. **24** an area of low barometric pressure. **25** in a low manner. 1–8, 10–21 *adj.*, 8, 25 *adv.*, 22–24 *n.* **—low′ness,** *n.*
**lay low,** bring down; overthrow: *The first blow laid him low.*
**lie low,** *Informal.* stay hidden; keep still: *The robbers will lie low for a time.*
☛ *Hom.* LO.

**low²** (lō) **1** the sound that a cow makes; moo. **2** of cows, make this sound. **3** imitate this sound. 1 *n.*, 2, 3 *v.*
☛ *Hom.* LO.

**low·born** (lō′bôrn′) of humble birth; born into a family of low social rank. *adj.*

**low·boy** (lō′boi′) a chest or side table with drawers, about the height of a table and having fairly short legs. *n.*

**low·bred** (lō′bred′) coarse; rude; vulgar. *adj.*

**low·brow** (lō′brou′) *Informal.* **1** a person lacking in appreciation of intellectual or artistic things. **2** being a lowbrow; incapable of culture. **3** fit for lowbrows. 1 *n.*, 2, 3 *adj.*

**low–coun·try** (lō′kun′trē) of the Low Countries (the Netherlands, Belgium, and Luxembourg). *adj.*

**low–down** (lō′doun′) *Informal.* low; mean; nasty: *a low-down trick. adj.*

hat, āge, fär; let, ēqual, tėrm; it, īce
hot, ōpen, ôrder; oil, out; cup, put, rüle
əbove, takən, pencəl, lemən, circəs
ch, child; ng, long; sh, ship
th, thin; ᴛʜ, then; zh, measure

**low·er¹** (lō′ər) **1** let down or haul down: *to lower the flag.* **2** make lower: *to lower the volume of a radio.* **3** sink; become lower: *The sun lowered slowly.* **4** the comparative of LOW: *Prices were lower last year than this.* 1–3 *v.*, 4 *adj.*, *adv.*
**lower oneself,** **a** behave improperly. **b** do something unwillingly: *He could hardly lower himself to speak to us.*

**low·er²** (lou′ər) **1** become or appear dark and threatening: *a lowering sky.* **2** frown or scowl: *She sat there lowering at them.* **3** a frowning or threatening appearance or look. 1, 2 *v.*, 3 *n.* Also, **lour.**

**Lower Canada** **1** a traditional name for the province of Quebec. **2** the name of the present province of Quebec before 1841, when Upper and Lower Canada were united in the Province of Canada: *Lower Canada was lower down the St. Lawrence River than Upper Canada.*

**lower case** small letters, not capitals.
☛ *Etym.* From the printers' practice of keeping the individual characters of sets of metal type in two trays or cases, the lower one for small letters and the upper one for capitals.

**low·er–case** (lō′ər kās′) in small letters, not capitals. *adj.*

**Lower House** or **lower house** the more representative branch of a legislature that has two branches: *The members of the Lower House of a legislature are usually elected.*

**low·er·ing** (lou′ə ring) **1** dark and threatening. **2** frowning or scowling. **3** ppr. of LOWER². 1, 2 *adj.*, 3 *v.* **—low′er·ing·ly,** *adv.*

**Lower Lakes** the most southerly of the Great Lakes, Lakes Erie and Ontario.

**low·er·most** (lō′ər mōst′) lowest. *adj.*

**lower regions** hell.

**lower world** **1** hell. **2** earth.

**lowest terms fraction** a FRACTION whose NUMERATOR and DENOMINATOR have no factor in common.

**low frequency** the range of radio frequencies between 30 and 300 kilohertz: *Low frequency is the range next above very low frequency.* **—low′-fre′quen·cy,** *adj.*

**low–key** (lō′kē) played down; subdued or restrained: *a low-key attack on government policy.* *adj.*

**low·land** (lō′lənd) **1** land that is lower and flatter than the neighbouring country. **2** of or in the lowlands. **3** the Lowlands, *pl.* a low, flat region in southern and eastern Scotland. *n.*

**Low·land·er** (lō′lən dər) a native of the Lowlands of Scotland. *n.*

**low·ly** (lō′lē) **1** low in rank, station, or position: *a lowly servant, a lowly occupation.* **2** modest in feeling, behaviour, or condition; humble; meek: *He held a lowly opinion of himself.* **3** humbly; meekly. 1, 2 *adj.*, **low·li·er, low·li·est;** 3 *adv.* **—low′li·ness,** *n.*

**low-mind·ed** (lō′mīn′did) having or showing a low or vulgar mind. *adj.*

**low–necked** (lō′nekt′) of a dress, etc., cut low so as to show the neck, part of the bosom, and shoulders or back. *adj.*

**low–pitched** (lō′picht′) **1** having a deep tone: *a low-pitched musical instrument.* **2** having little slope; not steep: *a low-pitched roof. adj.*

**low–pres·sure** (lō′presh′ər) **1** having or using relatively little pressure: *a low-pressure laminate.* **2** having a low barometric pressure: *There is a low-pressure region to the south.* **3** not forceful; easygoing: *a low-pressure sales pitch. adj.*

**low relief** relief sculpture in which the modelled forms stand out only slightly from the background and no part of the forms is undercut; bas-relief. See RELIEF for picture.

**low–rise** (lō′rīz′) **1** of a building, having only a few storeys: *Only low-rise apartments are permitted in this area of the city.* **2** a low-rise building. 1 *adj.,* 2 *n.* Compare with HIGH-RISE.

**low–spir·it·ed** (lō′spir′ə tid) sad; depressed. *adj.*

**low spirits** sadness; depression.

**low tide 1** the lowest level of the tide: *At low tide there is a very wide beach.* **2** the time when the tide is lowest: *The boat must have left sometime after low tide.* **3** the lowest point of anything.

**low water 1** the lowest level of water in a lake or river. **2** LOW TIDE.

**low–water mark 1** a mark showing low water. **2** the lowest point of anything.

**lox¹** (loks) thinly sliced smoked salmon. *n.*

**lox²** (loks) liquid oxygen. *n.*

**loy·al** (loi′əl) **1** faithful to love, promise, or duty. **2** faithful to one's sovereign, government, or country: *a loyal citizen. adj.* —**loy′al·ly,** *adv.*

**loy·al·ist** (loi′ə list) a person who supports the existing government or sovereign, especially in time of revolt. *n.*

**Loy·al·ist** (loi′ə list) **1** a UNITED EMPIRE LOYALIST. **2** any American who favoured Britain at the time of the American Revolution. **3** a person loyal to the Republic during the Civil War in Spain from 1936 to 1939. *n.*

**Loyal Orange Association** a Protestant organization, named after William, Prince of Orange, who became King William III of England.

**loy·al·ty** (loi′əl tē) loyal feeling or behaviour; faithfulness. *n., pl.* **loy·al·ties.**

**loz·enge** (loz′inj) **1** a small tablet of medicine or a piece of candy: *Cough drops are sometimes called lozenges.* **2** a design or figure shaped like this ◊; diamond. *n.*

**L.P.P.** Labour Progressive Party, the former name of the Communist Party in Canada.

**Lr** lawrencium.

**LSD** lysergic acid diethylamide, a drug that can produce hallucinations and schizophrenic symptoms.

**Ltd.** or **ltd.** limited.

**Lu** lutetium.

**lub·ber** (lub′ər) **1** a big, clumsy, stupid fellow. **2** a clumsy sailor. *n.*

**lub·ber·ly** (lub′ər lē) **1** loutish; clumsy; stupid. **2** awkward in the work of a sailor. **3** in a lubberly manner. 1, 2 *adj.,* 3 *adv.*

**lu·bri·cant** (lü′brə kənt) **1** oil, grease, etc. for putting on surfaces that slide or move against one another, such as parts of machines, in order to reduce friction and make the surfaces move smoothly and easily. **2** lubricating. 1 *n.,* 2 *adj.*

**lu·bri·cate** (lü′brə kāt′) **1** put oil, grease, etc. on surfaces that slide or move against one another, such as parts of machines; put a lubricant on. **2** make slippery or smooth. *v.,* **lu·bri·cat·ed, lu·bri·cat·ing.**

**lu·bri·ca·tion** (lü′brə kā′shən) **1** lubricating or being lubricated. **2** oil, grease, etc. used for lubricating. *n.*

**lu·bri·ca·tor** (lü′brə kā′tər) a person or thing that lubricates, especially a lubricant or a device for applying a lubricant to machinery. *n.*

**lu·cent** (lü′sənt) **1** shining; luminous. **2** letting the light through; clear. *adj.* —**lu′cent·ly,** *adv.*

**lu·cerne** (lü sėrn′) ALFALFA. *n.*

**lu·cid** (lü′sid) **1** easy to understand: *a lucid explanation.* **2** shining bright. **3** sane: *Insane persons sometimes have lucid intervals.* **4** clear; transparent: *a lucid stream. adj.* —**lu′cid·ly,** *adv.* —**lu′cid·ness,** *n.*

**lu·cid·i·ty** (lü sid′ə tē) the quality or state of being LUCID (def. 1): *The critics admire the lucidity of her writing. n.*

**Lu·ci·fer** (lü′sə fər) the planet Venus when it is the morning star. *n.*

**luck** (luk) **1** that which seems to happen or come to one by chance; chance: *Luck was against the losers.* **2** good fortune: *Lots of luck to you. n.*
**down on one's luck,** *Informal.* having bad luck; unlucky.
**in luck,** having good luck; lucky: *I'm in luck today; I found a dollar.*
**luck out,** *Informal.* be lucky.
**out of luck,** having bad luck; unlucky.
**push** or **crowd one's luck,** take unnecessary chances when things are going favourably: *You've won every game so far, but don't push your luck.*
**try one's luck,** see what one can do: *Try your luck with this puzzle.*
**worse luck,** unfortunately.

**luck·i·ly** (luk′ə lē) by good luck; fortunately. *adv.*

**luck·i·ness** (luk′ē nis *or* luk′ə nis) the quality or state of being lucky. *n.*

**luck·less** (luk′lis) having or bringing bad luck; unlucky. *adj.* —**luck′less·ness,** *n.*

**luck·y** (luk′ē) **1** having good luck: *She was lucky to win the card game yesterday.* **2** bringing good luck: *a lucky day, a lucky charm.* **3** happening by good fortune; fortunate: *a lucky coincidence. adj.,* **luck·i·er, luck·i·est.**

**lu·cra·tive** (lü′krə tiv) bringing in money; profitable: *a lucrative business. adj.* —**lu′cra·tive·ly,** *adv.*

**lu·cre** (lü′kər) money: *filthy lucre. n.*

**lu·cu·bra·tion** (lü′kyə brā′shən) **1** study carried on late at night. **2** laborious study. **3** a learned or carefully written production, especially one that is laboured and dull. *n.*

**lu·di·crous** (lü′də krəs)  amusingly absurd; ridiculous. *adj.* —**lu′di·crous·ly,** *adv.*

**luff** (luf)  **1** turn the bow of a ship toward the wind. **2** the act of turning the bow of a ship toward the wind. **3** the forward edge of a fore-and-aft sail.  **1** *v.*, **2, 3** *n.* **luff the helm,** move the helm so that the bow of the ship turns toward the wind.

**lug**[1] (lug)  pull along or carry with effort; drag: *The children lugged home a big Christmas tree.* *v.*, **lugged, lug·ging.**

**lug**[2] (lug)  a projecting part used to hold or grip something. *n.*

**lug**[3] (lug)  LUGSAIL. *n.*

**luge** (lüzh)  a small sled which a person rides lying on his or her back, used in downhill races over snow or ice, often on a specially designed course. *n.*

**lug·gage** (lug′ij)  suitcases, bags, etc. used by a traveller for personal belongings; baggage. *n.*

**lug·ger** (lug′ər)  a boat with LUGSAILS. *n.*

**lugs** (lugz)  a cloth flap in certain kinds of caps, pulled down as protection for the ears in cold weather. *n.*

**lug·sail** (lug′sāl′ *or* lug′səl)  a four-cornered sail held by a yard that slants across the mast. *n.*

**lu·gu·bri·ous** (lü gü′brē əs)  sad; mournful, especially in an exaggerated or affected way. *adj.* —**lu·gu′bri·ous·ly,** *adv.*

**lug·worm** (lug′wėrm′)  a kind of worm that burrows in sand along the seashore. *n.*

**luke·warm** (lü′kwôrm′)  **1** of a liquid, neither hot nor cold; fairly warm.  **2** showing little enthusiasm; half-hearted: *a lukewarm greeting.* *adj.* —**luke′warm′ness,** *n.*

**lull** (lul)  **1** hush to sleep: *The mother lulled the crying baby.*  **2** make or become calm or more nearly calm: *The wind lulled.*  **3** a temporary period of less noise or activity; brief calm: *a lull in a storm.*  **4** set at rest: *to lull one's suspicions, to lull people into a false sense of security.* **1, 2, 4** *v.*, **3** *n.*

**lul·la·by** (lul′ə bī′)  **1** a song to lull a baby to sleep. **2** any soothing song or piece of music. *n., pl.* **lul·la·bies.**

**lum·ba·go** (lum bā′gō)  an injury of the muscles in the lower back producing pain, sometimes intense: *Lumbago can be caused by a sprain, lifting something that is too heavy, a sudden twisting movement, cold and damp, etc.* *n.*

**lum·bar** (lum′bər)  of, having to do with, or referring to the loins or a vertebra, artery, nerve, etc. in this part of the body. See SPINAL COLUMN for picture. *adj.* ☞ *Hom.* LUMBER.

**lum·ber**[1] (lum′bər)  **1** timber, logs, beams, boards, etc. roughly cut and prepared for use.  **2** cut and prepare lumber.  **3** household articles no longer in use; old furniture, etc. that takes up room.  **4** fill up or obstruct by taking space that is wanted for something else.  **1, 3** *n.*, **2, 4** *v.* **lumber with,** *Informal.* burden with. ☞ *Hom.* LUMBAR.

**lum·ber**[2] (lum′bər)  move along heavily and noisily: *The old stagecoach lumbered down the road.* *v.* —**lum′ber·ing·ly,** *adv.* ☞ *Hom.* LUMBAR.

**lum·ber·ing** (lum′bə ring)  **1** the business of cutting and preparing timber for use.  **2** ppr. of LUMBER. **1** *n.*, **2** *v.*

**lum·ber·jack** (lum′bər jak′) *Cdn.* CANADA JAY. *n.*

**lum·ber·man** (lum′bər mən)  **1** LOGGER. See PEAVEY for picture.  **2** a man whose business is buying and selling timber or LUMBER[1]. *n., pl.* **lum·ber·men** (-mən).

**lum·ber·yard** (lum′bər yärd′)  a place where LUMBER[1] is stored and sold. *n.*

**lu·men** (lü′mən)  an SI unit for the rate of emission or transmission of light rays from a given light source: *One lumen is the rate of emission in a cone of one steradian of a light source having an intensity of one candela.* Symbol: lm  *n.*

**lu·mi·nar·y** (lü′mə ner′ē)  **1** the sun, moon, or other light-giving body.  **2** a distinguished person, especially one who enlightens. *n., pl.* **lu·mi·nar·ies.**

**lu·mi·nes·cence** (lü′mə nes′əns)  an emission of light by a process other than INCANDESCENCE; any light produced at relatively low temperatures by chemical or electrical action, friction, etc.: *Luminescence includes phosphorescence, fluorescence, and the light produced by fireflies.* *n.*

**lu·mi·nes·cent** (lü′mə nes′ənt)  **1** of or having to do with LUMINESCENCE.  **2** producing or capable of producing light by LUMINESCENCE. *adj.*

**lu·mi·nos·i·ty** (lü′mə nos′ə tē)  **1** the quality or state of being LUMINOUS.  **2** something that is LUMINOUS. *n., pl.* **lu·mi·nos·i·ties.**

**lu·mi·nous** (lü′mə nəs)  **1** shining by its own light: *The sun and stars are luminous.*  **2** full of light; bright: *a luminous sunset.*  **3** treated with some substance that glows in the dark: *luminous paint.*  **4** easily understood; clear; enlightening: *She explained the method in a luminous way.* *adj.* —**lu′mi·nous·ly,** *adv.* —**lu′mi·nous·ness,** *n.*

**lum·mox** (lum′əks) *Informal.*  an awkward, stupid person. *n.*

**lump**[1] (lump)  **1** a solid mass of no particular shape: *a lump of coal.*  **2** a swelling; bump: *a lump on the head.* **3** make lumps of, on, or in.  **4** form into a lump or lumps: *The pudding lumped because it was not stirred.* **5** in lumps; in a lump.  **6** put together; deal with in a mass or as a whole: *We will lump all our expenses.*  **7** a small cube or oblong piece of sugar.  **8** a lot; mass. **9** *Informal.*  a dull or stupid person.  **10** a heavy, sturdy person; a fat person.  **1, 2, 7–10** *n.*, **3, 4, 6** *v.*, **5** *adj.* **a lump sum.**  **a** an amount of money that covers the entire cost of something when given in payment: *He paid for the car in a lump sum rather than by instalments.*  **b** an amount of money that covers the cost of a number of items. **in a lump,** as a whole or in one amount.

**lump**[2] (lump)  *v.* **lump it,** *Informal.*  put up with things; endure the situation: *If you don't like it, you can lump it.*

**lump·ish** (lum′pish)  **1** like a lump; heavy and clumsy. **2** stolid; stupid. *adj.*

**lump sugar** small blocks of sugar shaped like cubes or dominoes.

**lump·y** (lum′pē) 1 full of lumps: *lumpy gravy.* 2 covered with lumps: *lumpy ground.* 3 heavy and clumsy: *a lumpy animal.* 4 of water in a lake, etc., rough; having choppy waves. *adj.,* **lump·i·er, lump·i·est.** —**lump′i·ly,** *adv.* —**lump′i·ness,** *n.*

**lu·na·cy** (lü′nə sē) 1 insanity. 2 extreme folly. *n., pl.* **lu·na·cies.**

**luna moth** a large North American moth with light-green wings having crescent-shaped markings.

**lu·nar** (lü′nər) 1 of or having to do with the moon: *a lunar eclipse.* 2 like the moon in shape. 3 measured by the revolutions of the moon: *a lunar month.* 4 designed for use on the moon: *a lunar vehicle.* *adj.*
☞ *Etym.* From L *luna,* 'moon' (regarded as a supernatural being by the ancient Romans).

**lunar module** an independent unit designed for use on the moon: *A lunar module may be part of a lunar vehicle.*

**lunar month** the period of one complete revolution of the moon around the earth; the interval between one new moon and the next, about 29½ days.

**lunar vehicle** a vehicle designed for use on the moon.

**lu·nate** (lü′nāt) crescent-shaped. *adj.*

**lu·na·tic** (lü′nə tik′) 1 an insane person. 2 insane. 3 for insane people. 4 extremely foolish; idiotic: *a lunatic search for buried treasure.* 5 an extremely foolish person. 1, 5 *n.,* 2–4 *adj.*
☞ *Etym.* Through OF from L *lunaticus,* which comes from *luna* 'moon'. Insanity was once thought to be caused by the changes of the moon.

**lunch** (lunch) 1 a light meal between breakfast and dinner, or breakfast and supper: *We have lunch at noon.* 2 a light meal eaten at any time: *a lunch at bedtime.* 3 food for a lunch: *Leave your lunch in the locker.* 4 eat lunch. 1–3 *n.,* 4 *v.* —**lunch′er,** *n.*

**lunch·eon** (lun′chən) 1 LUNCH. 2 a formal meal taken at noon. 3 eat luncheon. 1, 2 *n.,* 3 *v.*

**lunch·eon·ette** (lun′chə net′) a restaurant that serves LUNCHes. *n.*

**lunch·room** (lunch′rüm′) 1 a public dining room; restaurant. 2 a room in a plant, school, etc. where employees, teachers, or students may eat the lunches they have brought. *n.*

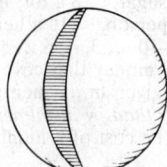
Lune (def. 2). The shaded area is a lune.

**lune** (lün) 1 anything shaped like a crescent or a half moon. 2 in geometry, a crescent-shaped figure formed on a sphere by two great semicircles intersecting at two points. *n.*
☞ *Hom.* LOON.
☞ *Etym.* See note at LUNAR.

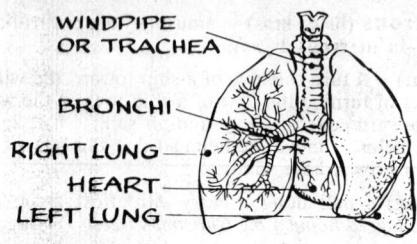
Human lungs seen from the front

**lung** (lung) 1 in vertebrates, one of the pair of breathing organs by means of which the blood receives oxygen and is relieved of carbon dioxide. See LIVER for another picture. 2 any of various similar organs in invertebrates. *n.*

**lunge¹** (lunj) 1 any sudden forward movement; thrust: *The catcher made a lunge toward the ball.* 2 move suddenly forward; thrust: *The dog lunged at the stranger.* 1 *n.,* 2 *v.,* **lunged, lung·ing.** —**lung′er,** *n.*

**lunge²** or **'lunge** (lunj) *Informal.* MUSKELLUNGE. *n.*

**lung·fish** (lung′fish′) a fish that can obtain oxygen by gulping air through the mouth as well as by passing water through its gills: *Lungfish are found in Australia, Africa, and South America.* *n., pl.* **lung·fish** or **lung·fish·es.**

**lung·wort** (lung′wėrt′) a European plant of the same family as borage, with blue flowers and spotted leaves. *n.*

**lup·in** or **lu·pine¹** (lü′pən) any of several plants of the same family as peas and beans, that have long spikes of flowers, radiating clusters of greyish, hairy leaflets, and flat pods with bean-shaped seeds. *n.*

**lu·pine²** (lü′pīn) of or like a wolf or wolves. *adj.*

**lurch¹** (lėrch) 1 a sudden leaning or roll to one side: *The car gave a lurch and overturned.* 2 make a lurch; stagger: *The wounded deer lurched forward.* 1 *n.,* 2 *v.*

**lurch²** (lėrch) in certain games, a condition in which one player scores nothing or is badly beaten. *n.*
**leave in the lurch,** leave in a helpless condition or in a difficult situation.

**lure** (lür) 1 attraction: *the lure of the sea.* 2 lead away or into something by awakening desire; attract; tempt: *Bees are lured by the scent of flowers.* 3 a decoy; bait. 4 attract with a bait. 1, 3 *n.,* 2, 4 *v.,* **lured, lur·ing.** —**lur′er,** *n.*

**lu·rid** (lü′rid) 1 lighted up with a red or fiery glare: *The sky was lurid with the flames of the burning city.* 2 causing horror; gruesome; terrible: *a lurid crime.* 3 sensational: *The newspaper carried a lurid account of the kidnapping.* 4 glaring in brightness or colour: *Her dress was a lurid yellow.* *adj.*

**lurk** (lėrk) 1 stay about without arousing attention; wait out of sight: *A tiger was lurking in the jungle.* 2 be hidden. *v.*

**lus·cious** (lush′əs) 1 delicious; richly sweet: *a luscious peach.* 2 very pleasing to the senses, especially those of taste and smell. *adj.* —**lus′cious·ly,** *adv.* —**lus′cious·ness,** *n.*

**lush** (lush) 1 tender and juicy; growing thick and green: *Lush grass grew along the river banks.* 2 characterized by abundant growth: *We passed many lush fields.* 3 abundant. 4 rich in ornament; flowery: *lush description.* *adj.* —**lush′ly,** *adv.* —**lush′ness,** *n.*

**lust** (lust) **1** sexual desire, especially when very intense. **2** any excessively strong desire; craving: *a lust for power, a lust for revenge.* **3** feel a very strong desire (*usually used with* **after** *or* **for**): *A miser lusts after gold.* 1, 2 *n.*, 3 *v.*

**lus·ter** (lus′tər) See LUSTRE. *n.*

**lust·ful** (lust′fəl) full of lust. *adj.* —**lust′ful·ly**, *adv.* —**lust′ful·ness**, *n.*

**lus·tral** (lus′trəl) of or used in ceremonial purification. *adj.*

**lus·trate** (lus′trāt) purify by a ceremonial method, such as washing, sacrifice, etc. *v.*, **lus·trat·ed, lus·trat·ing.**

**lus·tra·tion** (lu strā′shən) a ceremonial purification. *n.*

**lus·tre** (lus′tər) **1** a bright, even shine on the surface, without sparkle or glitter: *the lustre of pearls.* **2** brightness: *Her eyes lost their lustre.* **3** fame; glory; brilliance. **4** a kind of china or pottery that has a lustrous metallic, often iridescent, surface. **5** a thin fabric of cotton and wool that has a lustrous surface. *n.* Also, **luster.**

**lus·trous** (lus′trəs) having LUSTRE (def. 1); shining; glossy: *lustrous satin.* *adj.* —**lus′trous·ly**, *adv.*

**lus·ty** (lus′tē) strong and healthy; full of vigour: *a lusty boy.* *adj.*, **lust·i·er, lust·i·est.** —**lust′i·ly**, *adv.* —**lust′i·ness**, *n.*

A lute

**lute** (lüt) a stringed musical instrument like a large mandolin, much used in the 1500's and 1600's. *n.*
☛ *Hom.* LOOT.

**lu·te·ti·um** (lü tē′shē əm) a rare metallic element. Symbol: Lu *n.* Also, **lutecium.**

**lux** (luks) an SI unit for measuring illumination of a source of light per unit area on a surface: *One lux is the illumination of one lumen over an area of one square metre.* Symbol: lx *n., pl.* **lux.**

**lux·u·ri·ance** (lug zhü′rē əns) the quality or state of being LUXURIANT; rich abundance. *n.*

**lux·u·ri·ant** (lug zhü′rē ənt) **1** growing in a vigorous and healthy way; thick and lush: *In spring the grass on our lawn is luxuriant. She has a luxuriant head of hair.* **2** producing abundantly. **3** rich in ornament. *adj.* —**lux·u′ri·ant·ly**, *adv.*

**lux·u·ri·ate** (lug zhü′rē āt′) **1** indulge oneself luxuriously; take great delight; revel (*in*): *luxuriating in a hot bath.* **2** grow very abundantly. *v.*, **lux·u·ri·at·ed, lux·u·ri·at·ing.**

**lux·u·ri·ous** (lug zhü′rē əs) **1** fond of LUXURY; tending toward luxury; self-indulgent. **2** giving LUXURY; very comfortable and beautiful. *adj.* —**lux·u′ri·ous·ly**, *adv.* —**lux·u′ri·ous·ness**, *n.*

**lux·u·ry** (luk′shə rē *or* lug′zhə rē) **1** an abundance of the comforts and beauties of life: *After two weeks of being stranded in the wilderness, Sandor thought of his home as luxury.* **2** the use of the best and most costly food, clothes, houses, furniture, and amusements: *The movie star soon became accustomed to luxury.* **3** anything that one enjoys, usually something choice and costly: *She saves some money for luxuries such as fine paintings.* **4** something pleasant but not necessary: *Candy is a luxury.* *n., pl.* **lux·u·ries.**

**–ly**[1] an adverb-forming suffix meaning: **1** in a _____ manner: *Cheerfully means in a cheerful manner.* **2** in _____ ways or respects: *Financially means in financial respects.* **3** to a _____ degree or extent: *Greatly means to a great degree.* **4** in, to, or from a _____ direction: *Northwardly means to or from the north.* **5** in a _____ place: *Thirdly means in the third place.* **6** at a _____ time: *Recently means at a recent time.*

**–ly**[2] an adjective-forming suffix meaning: **1** like a _____: *A ghostly form means a form like a ghost.* **2** like that of a _____; characteristic of a _____: *A brotherly kiss means a kiss like that of a brother.* **3** suited to a _____; fit or proper for a _____: *Womanly kindness means kindness suited to a woman.* **4** of each or every _____; occurring once per _____: *Daily means of every day.* **5** being a _____; that is a _____: *A heavenly home means a home that is a heaven.*

**ly·ce·um** (lī sē′əm *or* lī′sē əm) **1** a lecture hall; a place where lectures are given. **2 Lyceum,** a grove and gymnasium near Athens, where Aristotle taught. *n.*

**lych–gate** (lich′gāt′) See LICH-GATE. *n.*

**ly·co·po·di·um** (lī′kə pō′dē əm) **1** any of a group of evergreen plants, including some creepers, that resemble mosses: *Club moss is a lycopodium.* **2** a fine yellow powder made from the spores of certain lycopodiums. *n.*

**lyd·dite** (lid′īt) a high explosive, consisting chiefly of PICRIC ACID. *n.*

**lye** (lī) any strong alkaline substance, especially sodium hydroxide or potassium hydroxide: *Lye is used in making soap and in cleaning.* *n.*
☛ *Hom.* LIE.

**ly·ing**[1] (lī′ing) **1** the telling of a lie; the habit of telling lies. **2** false; untruthful: *a lying report.* **3** ppr. of LIE[1]: *I was not lying; I told the truth.* 1 *n.*, 2 *adj.*, 3 *v.*

**ly·ing**[2] (lī′ing) ppr. of LIE[2]: *She was lying on the ground.*

**lymph** (limf) a nearly colourless liquid in the tissues of the body, resembling blood plasma and containing white blood cells but no red blood cells. *n.*

**lym·phat·ic** (lim fat′ik) **1** of LYMPH; carrying lymph. **2** a vessel that contains or carries LYMPH. **3** sluggish; lacking energy. 1, 3 *adj.*, 2 *n.*

**lymph gland** LYMPH NODE.

**lymph node** one of the rounded masses of tissue lying along the course of the lymphatic vessels, in which the LYMPH is purified and LYMPHOCYTES are formed.

**lym·pho·cyte** (lim′fə sīt′) one of the colourless cells of lymph produced in the LYMPH NODES, a variety of LEUCOCYTE. *n.*

**lynch** (linch)   kill, usually by hanging, through mob action and without a lawful trial.   *v.*   —**lynch′er,** *n.*

**lynch law**   the punishment of an accused person without a lawful trial, usually by putting him or her to death.
☛ *Etym.*   From *Lynch's law,* named after an American (Virginian) magistrate of the 18c.

A Canada lynx—about 80 cm long excluding the tail

**lynx** (lingks)   **1** any of a closely related group of medium-sized, wild members of the cat family found in North America, Europe, and Asia, having very short tails, ear tufts, and thick, silky, brownish or greyish fur with dark spots: *The two species of lynx found in North America are the Canada lynx and the bobcat.*   **2** CANADA LYNX.   *n., pl.* **lynx·es** or (*especially collectively*) **lynx.**
—**lynx′like′,** *adj.*

**lynx–eyed** (lingk′sīd′)   having sharp eyes; sharp-sighted.   *adj.*

**ly·on·naise** (lī′ə nāz′)   fried with pieces of onion: *lyonnaise potatoes.*   *adj.*

A lyre

**lyre** (līr)   an ancient stringed musical instrument resembling a small harp.   *n.*
☛ *Etym.*   **Lyre,** LYRIC, and LYRICAL can all be traced back to Gk. *lurā* 'lyre'. **Lyre** itself came into ME through OF *lire,* which developed from L *lyra.* **Lyric** came in the 16c. through French or Latin from Gk. *lurikos* 'of a lyre, suitable for a lyre'. **Lyrical** was formed in English from **lyric** in the 16c.

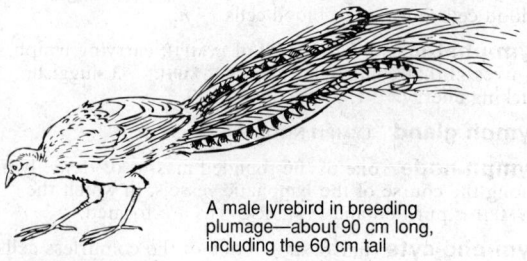

A male lyrebird in breeding plumage—about 90 cm long, including the 60 cm tail

**lyre·bird** (līr′bėrd′)   either of two closely related species of Australian songbird, the adult male having a long tail that resembles a lyre when spread out.   *n.*

**lyr·ic** (lir′ik)   **1** a short poem expressing personal emotion: *A love poem, a patriotic song, a lament, and a hymn are lyrics.*   **2** having to do with lyric poems: *a lyric poet.*   **3** characterized by a spontaneous expression of feeling.   **4** of or suitable for singing.   **5 lyrics,** *pl.* the words for a song.   1, 5 *n.,* 2–4 *adj.*
☛ *Etym.*   See note at LYRE.

**lyr·i·cal** (lir′ə kəl)   **1** showing or expressing great enthusiasm and emotion: *She was lyrical in her praise of the new auditorium.*   **2** LYRIC (def. 3).   *adj.*
—**lyr′i·cal·ly,** *adv.*
☛ *Etym.*   See note at LYRE.

**ly·sin** (lī′sən)   any of a class of substances that are developed in blood serum, and that are capable of causing the dissolution or destruction of bacteria, blood corpuscles, and other cellular elements.   *n.*

**ly·so·some** (lī′sə sōm′)   part of a cell which contains digestive enzymes capable of digesting living organisms such as bacteria, and which also helps to decompose the cell after death.   *n.*

# M m  *M m*

**m or M** (em) **1** the thirteenth letter of the English alphabet. **2** any speech sound represented by this letter. **3** any person or thing identified as m, especially the thirteenth in a series. **4** the Roman letter used as the numeral for 1000. *n., pl.* **m's** or **M's**.

**m 1** metre; metres. **2** milli- (an SI prefix). **3** mass.

**m. 1** minute. **2** masculine. **3** mile.

**M** mega- (an SI prefix).

**M or M. 1** Master. **2** Monsieur.

**ma** (mo, mä, ma) *Informal.* mamma; mother. *n.*

**ma'am** (mam) madam. *n.*

**ma·ca·bre** (mə käˊbrə *or* mə käˊbər) gruesome; horrible; ghastly. *adj.*

**ma·ca·co** (mə käˊkō) a black, short-tailed lemur of Asia and Africa. *n., pl.* **ma·ca·cos**.

**ma·cad·am** (mə kadˊəm) **1** material for making roads, consisting of small, broken stones of nearly uniform size which are mixed with a binding agent such as tar or asphalt: *Several layers of macadam are put down to make a road, each layer rolled until solid and smooth before the next layer is laid down.* **2** a road made with layers of macadam. *n.*
☞ *Etym.* Named after John L. *McAdam* (1756–1836), a Scottish engineer, who invented this process of road making.

**ma·cad·am·ize** (mə kadˊə mīz′) make or cover a road with MACADAM. *v.,* **mac·ad·am·ized, mac·ad·am·iz·ing**.

**ma·caque** (mə käkˊ) any of several closely related species of monkey of Asia, the East Indies, and Africa. *n.*

**mac·a·ro·ni** (makˊə rōˊnē) flour paste that has been dried, usually in the form of hollow tubes, to be cooked for food. *n., pl.* **mac·a·ro·nis** or **mac·a·ro·nies**.

**mac·a·roon** (makˊə rünˊ) a very sweet, chewy cookie, usually made of egg whites, sugar, and ground almonds or coconut. *n.*

**ma·caw** (mə kôˊ) any of several large parrots of South and Central America, characterized by long tails, brilliant feathers, and harsh voices. *n.*

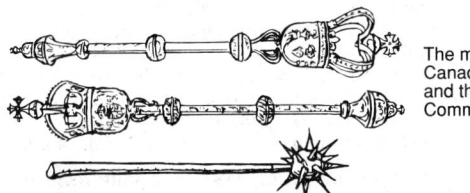

The maces of the Canadian Senate and the House of Commons

**mace¹** (mās) **1** a war club used in the Middle Ages. **2** a staff used as a symbol of authority. *n.*

**mace²** (mās) a spice made from the dried outer covering of nutmegs. *n.*

**mac·é·doine** (masˊə dwänˊ *or* masˊā dwänˊ) a mixture of vegetables or fruits, sometimes in jelly. *n.*

**mac·er·ate** (masˊə rāt′) **1** soften by soaking for some time: *Flowers are macerated to extract their perfume.* **2** break up or soften food by the digestive process. **3** grow or cause to grow thin. *v.,* **mac·er·at·ed, mac·er·at·ing**. —**mac·erˊaˊtion**, *n.*

**ma·chet·e** (mə chetˊē *or* mə shetˊē) a large, heavy knife, used as a tool and weapon in South America, Central America, and the West Indies. *n.*

**Mach·i·a·vel·li·an** (makˊē ə velˊē ən) **1** of Machiavelli, an Italian statesman and writer, or the political theory expounded by him. **2** characterized by subtle or unscrupulous cunning; crafty; wily; astute. **3** a follower of the crafty political methods described by Machiavelli. 1, 2 *adj.,* 3 *n.*

Machicolations

**ma·chic·o·la·tion** (mə chikˊə lāˊshən) an opening in the floor of a projecting gallery or parapet, or in the roof of an entrance, through which missiles, hot liquids, etc. might be dropped on attackers: *Machicolations were much used in medieval fortified structures.* *n.*

**mach·i·nate** (makˊə nāt′) plan or plot, especially with an evil purpose; intrigue. *v.,* **mach·i·nat·ed, mach·i·nat·ing**. —**machˊiˊnaˊtor**, *n.*

**mach·i·na·tion** (makˊə nāˊshən) **1** the act of machinating. **2** a secret or cunning scheme, especially one with an evil purpose (*usually used in the plural*): *He could not have been overthrown without the machinations of his enemies.* *n.*

**ma·chine** (mə shēnˊ) **1** a device consisting of an arrangement of interrelated fixed and moving parts powered mechanically, electrically, or electronically, designed to do a particular kind of work: *a sewing machine, a calculating machine.* **2** of or having to do with a machine or machines: *the machine age, machine action.* **3** make or finish by machine. **4** produced by or with a machine, not by hand: *machine printing.* **5** a device for transmitting power, energy, or motion, or changing its direction: *Levers and pulleys are simple machines.* **6** a coin-operated dispenser: *a coffee machine.* **7** a motor vehicle, aircraft, bicycle, etc. **8** a person or group that acts mechanically, without thinking or feeling. **9** a highly organized group of people, especially a group

**machine gun** controlling a political organization: *the Liberal machine.* 1, 2, 4–9 *n.*, 3 *v.*, **ma·chined, ma·chin·ing.**

**machine gun** a gun that fires small-arms ammunition automatically and can keep up a rapid fire of bullets.

**ma·chine–gun** (mə shēn′gun′) fire at with a MACHINE GUN. *v.*, **ma·chine-gunned, ma·chine-gun·ning.**

**machine language** a coding system that assigns storage locations in a computer and that allows the computer to operate immediately with no translation of words or numbers.

**machine readable** of data, which can be read and used by a computer.

**ma·chin·er·y** (mə shē′nə rē) **1** machines: *There is a lot of machinery in a shoe factory.* **2** the parts or works of a machine: *Paula examined the machinery of her watch.* **3** any combination of persons or things by which something is kept going or something is done: *Police officers, judges, courts, and prisons are the machinery of the law.* *n.*, *pl.* **ma·chin·er·ies.**

**machine shop** a workshop where machines or parts of machines are made or repaired.

**machine tool** an electrically or mechanically driven tool such as a lathe, drill, or punch press, used in manufacturing machinery.

**ma·chin·ist** (mə shē′nist) **1** a person skilled in using MACHINE TOOLS. **2** a person who runs a machine. **3** a person who makes and repairs machinery. *n.*

**Mach number** (mäk) a number representing the ratio of the speed of an object to the speed of sound in the same medium. Mach number 1 equals the speed of sound, Mach number 2 is twice the speed of sound, and Mach number 0.5 is half the speed of sound.

**ma·cho** (mä′chō) **1** robust and virile in an exaggerated way; proudly or aggressively masculine: *a macho swagger.* **2** a man who is proudly or aggressively masculine. **3** manhood; virility. 1 *adj.*, 2, 3 *n.*

**mac·in·tosh** (mak′ən tosh′) See MACKINTOSH. *n.*

**mack·er·el** (mak′ə rəl) a saltwater fish of the North Atlantic Ocean, much used for food. *n.*, *pl.* **mack·er·el** or **mack·er·els.**

**mackerel sky** a sky spotted with small, white, fleecy clouds.

**mack·i·naw** (mak′ə no′) **1** a kind of short coat made of heavy woollen cloth. **2** a kind of thick woollen blanket that often has bars of colour, used in the North and West by Indians, trappers, etc. **3** a large, heavy, flat-bottomed boat, formerly used in the region of the Upper Great Lakes. *n.*
☛ *Etym.* From the original name of Mackinac Island in Lake Huron: *Michilimackinac*, which came from an Ojibwa word meaning 'a large turtle', made up of *michi* 'great' and *mackinaw* 'turtle', since the centre of the island was thought to look from the side like a turtle's back.

**mack·in·tosh** (mak′ən tosh′) **1** a waterproof coat; raincoat. **2** waterproof cloth. *n.* Also, **macintosh.**
☛ *Etym.* Named after Charles *Macintosh* (1766–1843), a Scottish chemist who invented a method of waterproofing material.

**mac·ra·mé** (mak′rə mā′ *or* mak′rə mā′) **1** a heavy, coarse lace or fringe made by knotting twine or cord in decorative patterns: *Macramé is used for wall hangings, hangers for flower pots, furniture decoration, etc.* **2** the art of making such lace or fringe: *a course in macramé.* *n.*

**mac·ro–** (mak′rō) *combining form.* large. Compare with MICRO-.

**mac·ro·cosm** (mak′rə koz′əm) universe. *n.*

**ma·cron** (mak′ron *or* mā′kron) a short, horizontal line (¯) placed over a vowel letter to identify a sound differing from that represented by the same letter without such a mark. *Example:* (mak′ron *or* mā′kron). *n.*

**mac·ro·scop·ic** (mak′rə skop′ik) **1** that can be seen with the naked eye. **2** having to do with large groups. *adj.*

**mad** (mad) **1** out of one's head; insane; crazy: *A man must be mad to cut himself on purpose.* **2** *Informal.* very angry: *The insult made her mad.* **3** much excited; wild: *The dog made mad efforts to catch up with the automobile.* **4** foolish; unwise: *a mad undertaking.* **5** very lively: *a mad party.* **6** blindly and unreasonably fond: *Some teenagers are mad about going to dances.* **7** having RABIES, or hydrophobia: *A mad dog foams at the mouth and may bite people.* *adj.*, **mad·der, mad·dest.**
**like mad,** furiously; very hard or fast: *I ran like mad to catch the train.*
**mad as a hatter,** completely crazy.
☛ *Syn.* **Mad,** CRAZY, and INSANE have similar meanings. All three words have been commonly used at some time to describe someone who is mentally ill. **Insane** is the proper word to describe someone suffering from severe mental illness: *This man was so worried that he became insane.* **Mad** is used in the same way but often means just very reckless, or foolish: *Crossing the Pacific on a raft seems a mad thing to do.* **Crazy** suggests a more wild or disturbed state: *She was nearly crazy with fear.*

**mad·am** (mad′əm) **1** a polite or formal title used in speaking to a woman (used alone, not with a name): *The line is busy, madam; would you care to hold?* **2** a formal title for a woman used before the name of her rank or office: *Madam Chairman, Madam Prime Minister.* **3** a woman who runs a brothel. *n.*, *pl.* **mad·ams** or **mes·dames** (mā dam′).

**mad·ame** (mad′əm; *French*, mä däm′) **1** a French title for a married woman. **2** a title often used by female singers, artists, etc. *Abbrev.*: Mme. *n.*, *pl.* **mes·dames** (mā däm′).

**mad·cap** (mad′kap′) **1** impulsive, wild, or foolish: *a madcap escapade.* **2** a person who habitually does impulsive, wild, or foolish things. 1 *adj.*, 2 *n.*

**mad·den** (mad′ən) **1** make insane. **2** make very angry or excited. *v.*

**mad·der** (mad′ər) **1** a perennial vine native to Europe and Asia, having loose clusters of small, funnel-shaped, yellow flowers. **2** the root of this plant, formerly used for making a red dye. **3** the dye made from this root; ALIZARIN. **4** bright red. **5** referring to the family of mostly tropical and subtropical herbs, shrubs, and trees that includes the madder: *The gardenia, coffee tree, and cinchona also belong to the madder family.* 1–5 *n.*, 4 *adj.*

**made** (mād) **1** *pt.* and *pp.* of MAKE. **2** built; formed: *a strongly made swing.* **3** specially prepared: *made gravy, a made dish.* **4** artificially produced: *made land.* **5** invented. **6** *Informal.* certain of success; successful. 1 *v.*, 2–6 *adj.*
☛ *Hom.* MAID.

**mad·e·moi·selle** (mad′ə mə zel′; *French*, mäd mwä zel′)

a French title for an unmarried woman; Miss. *Abbrev.*: Mlle. *n., pl.* **mes·de·moi·selles** (mād mwä zel′).

**made–up** (mā′dup′) **1** put together; arranged. **2** invented; not real: *a made-up story.* **3** painted, powdered, etc.: *made-up lips.* *adj.*

**mad·house** (mad′hous′) **1** formerly, a hospital for the insane. **2** a place of uproar and confusion: *The arena was a madhouse after the home team won the championship game.* *n.*

**mad·ly** (mad′lē) **1** insanely. **2** furiously. **3** foolishly. *adv.*

**mad·man** (mad′man′ *or* mad′mən) a man who is insane or behaves like someone who is insane. *n., pl.* **mad·men** (-men′ *or* -mən).

**mad·ness** (mad′nis) **1** the state or condition of being mad; insanity; rage: *In his madness, he struck his best friend.* **2** folly: *It was madness to take a sailboat out in that storm.* *n.*

**ma·dra·sa** (mə dras′ə) a school for children or adults in which Islamic subjects are taught, especially the Koran, the Arabic language, the Hadith, and jurisprudence. *n.*

**mad·re·pore** (mad′rə pôr′) a tropical genus of stony corals that often form reefs. *n.*

**mad·ri·gal** (mad′rə gəl) **1** a short poem, often about love, that can be set to music. **2** a song with parts for several voices, sung without instrumental accompaniment. **3** any song. *n.*

**mael·strom** (māl′strəm) **1** a great or turbulent whirlpool. **2** a violent confusion of feelings, ideas, or conditions. *n.*
☛ *Etym.* From early modern Dutch *maelstrom*, formed from *maalen* 'grind, whirl around' + *stroom* 'stream'. 17c.

**mae·nad** (mē′nad) **1** a female follower of Bacchus; a female participant in the wild rites that were characteristic of the worship of Bacchus. **2** an extremely excited or frenzied woman. *n.*

**maes·tro** (mī′strō; *Italian,* mä es′trō) **1** a great composer, teacher, or conductor of music. **2** a master of any art. *n., pl.* **maes·tros** or (*Italian*) **ma·es·tri** (mä es′trē).

**Mae West** (mā′ west′) an inflatable vest worn as a life preserver by an aviator in flying over water.
☛ *Etym.* Named after *Mae West* (1892–1980), American actress.

**Ma·fi·a** (mä′fē ə) a world-wide secret organization of criminal elements engaged in racketeering, gambling, etc. *n.* Also, **mafia**.

**mag.** **1** magazine. **2** magnet. **3** magnetism. **4** in astronomy, magnitude.

**mag·a·zine** (mag′ə zēn′ *or* mag′ə zēn′) **1** a publication issued at regular intervals, especially weekly or monthly, which contains stories, articles, photographs, etc., by various contributors. **2** a room in a fort or warship for keeping gunpowder and other explosives. **3** a place for storing goods or supplies, such as a warehouse or military supply depot. **4** a holder in or on a repeating or automatic gun for the cartridges to be fed into the gun chamber. **5** a lightproof space in or container on a camera for holding film or plates. *n.*

**ma·gen·ta** (mə jen′tə) **1** a purplish-red aniline dye. **2** purplish red. **1, 2** *n.,* **2** *adj.*

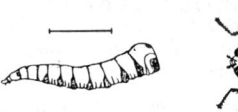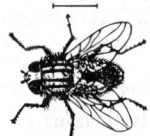

A maggot (at left) and an adult fly (at right). The lines above them show their actual length.

**mag·got** (mag′ət) a fly in the earliest, legless stage, just after leaving the egg: *Maggots often live in decaying matter.* *n.*

**mag·ic** (maj′ik) **1** the use of charms, spells, etc. to try to call up spirits or other occult powers and through them to control natural forces or change the normal course of events. **2** made or done by magic or as if by magic: *A magic palace stood in place of their hut.* **3** having supernatural powers: *a magic wand.* **4** something that produces results as if by magic; mysterious influence; unexplained power; enchantment: *the magic of music.* **5** producing a feeling of rapture or enchantment: *magic moments.* **1, 4** *n.,* **2, 3, 5** *adj.*

**mag·i·cal** (maj′ə kəl) **1** of, used in, or done by magic. **2** like magic; mysterious; unexplained. *adj.*
—**mag′i·cal·ly,** *adv.*

**ma·gi·cian** (mə jish′ən) **1** a person skilled in the use of magic, especially a sorcerer. **2** a person skilled in the use of sleight of hand to entertain: *The magician pulled three rabbits out of his hat.* *n.*

**mag·is·te·ri·al** (maj′i stē′rē əl) **1** of or suited to a MAGISTRATE: *A judge has magisterial rank.* **2** showing authority: *The captain spoke with a magisterial voice.* **3** imperious; domineering; overbearing. *adj.*
—**mag′is·te′ri·al·ly,** *adv.*

**mag·is·tra·cy** (maj′i strə sē) **1** the position, rank, or duties of a MAGISTRATE. **2** MAGISTRATES as a group. **3** a district under a MAGISTRATE. *n., pl.* **mag·is·tra·cies.**

**mag·is·trate** (maj′i strāt′) a government official appointed to hear and decide cases in a magistrate's court or similar lower court. *n.*

**magistrate's court** a court that has limited jurisdiction, dealing with minor civil and criminal cases: *In Canada, magistrate's courts are established by provincial legislation.*

**mag·ma** (mag′mə) the very hot, fluid substance that is found below the earth's crust and from which lava and igneous rocks are formed. *n., pl.* **mag·ma·ta** (mag′mə tə) or **magmas**.

**Mag·na Char·ta** or **Mag·na Car·ta** (mag′nə kär′tə) **1** the great charter guaranteeing the personal and political liberties of the people of England, forcibly secured from King John by the English barons at Runnymede on June 15, 1215. **2** any fundamental constitution guaranteeing civil and political rights.

**mag·na cum lau·de** (mag′nə kŭm′lou′dā) *Latin.* with high honours.

**mag·na·nim·i·ty** (mag′nə nim′ə tē) **1** a

MAGNANIMOUS nature or quality; nobility of soul or mind: *The soldiers showed magnanimity by treating their prisoners well.* **2** a MAGNANIMOUS act.  *n., pl.* **mag·na·nim·i·ties.**

**mag·nan·i·mous** (mag nan′ə məs)  **1** noble in soul or mind; generous in forgiving; free from mean or petty feelings or acts.  **2** showing or arising from a generous spirit: *a magnanimous attitude toward a conquered enemy.* *adj.* —**mag·nan′i·mous·ly,** *adv.*

**mag·nate** (mag′nāt)  an important or powerful person, especially in business or industry: *an oil magnate.* *n.*

**mag·ne·sia** (mag nē′zhə, mag nē′zē ə, *or* mag nē′shə)  **1** magnesium oxide, a white, tasteless powder, used in medicine as a laxative, and in making fertilizers and some building materials.  **2** MAGNESIUM.  *n.*
☛ *Etym.* See note at MAGNET.

**mag·ne·si·um** (mag nē′zē əm *or* mag nē′zhē əm)  a light, silver-white metallic element that burns with a dazzling white light.  *Symbol*: Mg  *n.*
☛ *Etym.* See note at MAGNET.

**mag·net** (mag′nit)  **1** a stone or piece of metal that attracts iron or steel to it.  **2** anything that attracts: *The rabbits in our backyard were a magnet that attracted all the children in the neighbourhood.* *n.*
☛ *Etym.* Through L *magneta* from a Gk. phrase meaning 'the stone of Magnesia', an ancient city in Asia Minor. MAGNESIA came through Med. L from a different form of the same phrase. MAGNESIUM was formed from **magnesia** in the 19c. MAGNETIC, MAGNETISM, MAGNETIZE, and MAGNETO were formed respectively in the 16th, 17th, 18th, and 19th centuries.

**mag·net·ic** (mag net′ik)  **1** having the properties of a magnet: *the magnetic needle of a compass.*  **2** of magnetism; producing magnetism.  **3** of the earth's magnetism: *the magnetic meridian.*  **4** capable of being magnetized or of being attracted by a magnet.  **5** attractive: *a magnetic personality.* *adj.*
—**mag·net′i·cal·ly,** *adv.*
☛ *Etym.* See note at MAGNET.

**magnetic disk**  a device containing or able to receive or store information in a computer: *Magnetic disks can be hard or floppy.*

**magnetic field**  **1** the region of magnetic influence, or force, around a magnet, a magnetic body such as the earth, or a body carrying an electric current.  **2** the magnetic forces present in such a region: *a strong magnetic field.*

**magnetic mine**  an underwater mine that is exploded by the action of the metal parts of an approaching ship upon a MAGNETIC NEEDLE.

**magnetic needle**  a slender bar of magnetized steel that forms the basic part of a compass. When mounted horizontally so that it can turn freely, it will show the direction of the magnetic field of the earth, pointing toward the magnetic poles, approximately north and south.

**magnetic pole**  **1** one of the two poles of a magnet.  **2** one of the two small, slightly shifting regions on the earth's surface where the lines of the earth's MAGNETIC FIELD converge and toward which a MAGNETIC NEEDLE points. The **north magnetic pole** is approximately in 71° North latitude and 95° West longitude. The **south magnetic pole** is approximately in 72° South latitude and 154° East longitude.

**magnetic tape**  a plastic ribbon coated on one side with a substance that magnetizes easily, such as particles of iron oxide, used for recording sounds, pictures, and other kinds of information by electromagnetic means: *Magnetic tape is used in computers, tape-recorders, and videotape recorders.*

**mag·net·ism** (mag′nə tiz′əm)  **1** the properties of a magnet; the manifestation of magnetic properties.  **2** the branch of physics dealing with magnets and magnetic properties.  **3** the power to attract or charm: *The hero's magnetism won him many friends and admirers.* *n.*
☛ *Etym.* See note at MAGNET.

**mag·net·ite** (mag′nə tīt′)  an important iron ore that is strongly attracted by a magnet; black iron oxide.  *n.*

**mag·net·ize** (mag′nə tīz′)  **1** give the properties of a magnet to: *An electric current in a coil around a bar of iron will magnetize the bar.*  **2** attract or influence like a magnet; charm: *Her beautiful voice magnetized the audience.* *v.*, **mag·net·ized, mag·net·iz·ing.**
—**mag′net·iz′a·ble,** *adj.* —**mag′net·i·za′tion,** *n.*
—**mag′net·iz′er,** *n.*
☛ *Etym.* See note at MAGNET.

**mag·ne·to** (mag nē′tō)  a small machine which uses a magnetic field to produce an electric current: *In some engines, a magneto supplies an electric spark to explode the gasoline vapour.* *n., pl.* **mag·ne·tos.**
☛ *Etym.* See note at MAGNET.

**mag·ne·to-e·lec·tric** (mag nē′tō i lek′trik)  of, referring to, or using electricity produced by magnetic means.  *adj.*

**mag·ne·tom·e·ter** (mag′nə tom′ə tər)  an instrument used to measure magnetic forces.  *n.*

**mag·ne·to·sphere** (mag nē′tə sfēr′)  **1** the region surrounding the earth in which ionized particles are controlled by the earth's magnetic field.  **2** a similar region around any other celestial body, such as a planet.  *n.*

**mag·ni·fi·ca·tion** (mag′nə fi kā′shən)  **1** the act of magnifying.  **2** a magnified condition.  **3** the power to magnify.  **4** a magnified copy, model, or picture.  *n.*

**mag·nif·i·cence** (mag nif′ə səns)  the quality or state of being MAGNIFICENT; grand beauty or splendour.  *n.*

**mag·nif·i·cent** (mag nif′ə sənt)  **1** richly coloured or decorated; splendid; grand; stately: *a magnificent palace.*  **2** impressive, noble, or exalted: *magnificent words, magnificent ideas.*  **3** extraordinarily fine; superb: *a magnificent view of the mountains.* *adj.*
—**mag·nif′i·cent·ly,** *adv.*

**mag·ni·fi·er** (mag′nə fī′ər)  a person or thing that magnifies, especially a lens or combination of lenses that makes things appear larger than they really are.  *n.*

**mag·ni·fy** (mag′nə fī′)  **1** cause to look larger than the real size; increase the apparent size of an object: *A microscope magnifies things to many times their real size.*  **2** make too much of; go beyond the truth in telling: *Maria not only tells tales on Tom, but she magnifies them.* *v.*, **mag·ni·fied, mag·ni·fy·ing.**

**magnifying glass**  a lens or combination of lenses that makes things look larger than they really are.

**mag·nil·o·quence** (mag nil′ə kwəns)  **1** a high-flown, lofty style of speaking or writing; the use of big and unusual words, elaborate phrases, etc.  **2** boastfulness.  *n.*

**mag·nil·o·quent** (mag nil′ə kwənt)  **1** using big and

unusual words; in high-flown language. **2** boastful. *adj.* —**mag·nil′o·quent·ly,** *adv.*

**mag·ni·tude** (mag′nə tyüd′ *or* mag′nə tüd′) **1** a greatness of size. **2** great importance or effect: *The peace brought new problems of very great magnitude to many nations.* **3** a measure of the brightness of a star: *Stars of the first magnitude are the brightest.* *n.*

A blossom and leaves of the southern magnolia, an evergreen tree native to the southeastern United States

**mag·no·lia** (mag nō′lē ə *or* mag nō′lyə) **1** any of a closely related group of shrubs and trees of North America and Asia having simple leaves and large, white, pink, or purple flowers that bloom in early spring: *In some magnolias, the flowers appear before the leaves.* **2** referring to a family of trees, shrubs, and a few vines that includes the magnolias and the tulip tree. *n.*
☛ *Etym.* Named after Pierre *Magnol* (1638–1715), a French botanist.

**mag·num o·pus** (mag′nəm ō′pəs) *Latin.* a great work of literature, music, or art, especially the greatest work of a particular artist or writer.

**mag·pie** (mag′pī) **1** a noisy, black-and-white bird having a long tail and short wings, related to the jays. **2** a person who chatters. *n.*

**Mag·yar** (mag′yär; *Hungarian,* mod′yor) **1** a member of a people that make up most of the population of Hungary. **2** the language of the Magyars; Hungarian: *Magyar is related to Finnish and Estonian.* **3** of or having to do with the Magyars or their language. 1, 2 *n.*, 3 *adj.*

**ma·ha·ra·jah** *or* **ma·ha·ra·ja** (mä′hə rä′jə) **1** formerly, the title of certain ruling princes in India. **2** a man holding this title. *n.*

**ma·ha·ra·ni** *or* **ma·ha·ra·nee** (mä′hə rä′nē) **1** the wife of a maharajah. **2** a woman holding in her own right a rank equal to that of a maharajah. *n.*

**ma·hat·ma** (mə hat′mə) in India, a wise and holy person who has extraordinary powers. *n.*

**Ma·ha·vi·ra** (mə hä′vē′rə) the chief founder of the Jain religion, and a contemporary of Buddha. *n.*

**Ma·ha·ya·na** (mä′hə yä′nə) a major branch of Buddhism, the "Northern School". It regards Buddha as divine. *n.*

**Mah·di** (mä′dē) **1** a leader expected by Moslems to come and establish a reign of righteousness. **2** a person claiming to be this leader. *n., pl.* **Mah·dis.**

**mah–jong** *or* **mah–jongg** (mä′jong′) a game of Chinese origin played with 144 domino-like pieces. *n.*

**ma·hog·a·ny** (mə hog′ə nē) **1** the hard, reddish-brown wood of a large evergreen tree growing in the West Indies and tropical America: *Because mahogany takes a high polish, it is much used in making furniture.* **2** the tree itself. **3** made of mahogany. **4** dark reddish-brown. 1, 2, 4 *n., pl.* **ma·hog·a·nies;** 3, 4 *adj.*

**Ma·hom·et** (mə hom′it) MOHAMMED. *n.*

**Ma·hom·et·an** (mə hom′ə tən) MOHAMMEDAN. *adj., n.*

## magnitude 719 mailer

hat, āge, fär; let, ēqual, tėrm; it, īce
hot, ōpen, ôrder; oil, out; cup, put, rüle
ə*bove,* tak*ə*n, penc*ə*l, lem*ə*n, circ*ə*s
ch, child; ng, long; sh, ship
th, thin; ᴛʜ, then; zh, measure

**ma·hout** (mə hout′) in India and the East Indies, the keeper and driver of an elephant. *n.*

**maid** (mād) **1** a young unmarried woman; girl. **2** a woman servant: *a kitchen maid.* **3** virgin. **4** See MAID OF HONOUR. **5 the Maid,** Joan of Arc (1412–1431), a French heroine who led armies against the invading English and saved the city of Orléans. Also, **the Maid of Orléans.** *n.*
☛ *Hom.* MADE.

**maid·en** (mā′dən) **1** a young unmarried woman; girl. **2** a virgin. **3** of, suited to, or characteristic of a maiden: *maiden grace, maiden blushes.* **4** unmarried: *a maiden aunt.* **5** first: *a ship's maiden voyage. The new MP delivered his maiden speech in Parliament.* **6** new or untried; fresh: *maiden ground.* 1, 2 *n.*, 3–6 *adj.*

**maid·en·hair** (mā′dən her′) any of a closely related group of ferns having very slender stalks and delicate, finely divided fronds. *n.* Also, **maidenhair fern.**

**maid·en·hood** (mā′dən hud′) **1** the condition of being a maiden. **2** the time of being a maiden. *n.*

**maid·en·ly** (mā′dən lē) **1** of a maiden or maidenhood. **2** like or suitable for a maiden; gentle; modest. *adj.* —**maid′en·li·ness,** *n.*

**maiden name** a woman's surname before her marriage: *Mrs. Oleksichuk's maiden name was Blake.*

**maid–in–waiting** (mā′din wā′ting) an unmarried young woman who attends a queen or princess. *n., pl.* **maids-in-waiting.**

**maid of honour** *or* **honor** **1** an unmarried woman who is the chief attendant of the bride at a wedding. **2** an unmarried lady who attends a queen or a princess.

**Maid of Orléans** a name for Joan of Arc.

**maid·serv·ant** (mād′sėr′vənt) a female servant. *n.*

**mail**[1] (māl) **1** letters, postcards, papers, parcels, or messages sent or to be sent by post or electronic means. **2** any system by which such items are sent or received. **3** all that comes by one post or delivery: *He opened the box to look for the mail.* **4** a train, boat, etc. that carries mail. **5** post; send by mail; put in a mailbox: *He mailed the letter.* **6** of mail. 1–4 *n.*, 5 *v.*, 6 *adj.*
☛ *Hom.* MALE.

**mail**[2] (māl) **1** flexible armour made of metal rings, loops of chain, or small plates linked together. See COAT OF MAIL for picture. **2** the hard, protective covering of some animals, such as turtles. **3** cover or protect with mail. 1, 2 *n.*, 3 *v.*
☛ *Hom.* MALE.

**mail·box** (māl′boks′) **1** a public box for depositing outgoing mail that is to be collected by the post office. **2** a private box outside a dwelling, where the occupant's mail is delivered. *n.*

**mailed** (māld) **1** covered or protected with MAIL[2]. **2** pt. and pp. of MAIL[1] *or* MAIL[2]. 1 *adj.*, 2 *v.*

**mail·er** (māl′ər) **1** a person who mails. **2** a mailing machine. **3** a boat carrying mail. **4** a container in which to mail things: *Cylindrical mailers are often used for maps, photographs, etc.* 5 a mail-order form. *n.*

**mail·man** (māl′man′) a person whose work is carrying or delivering mail; letter carrier. *n., pl.* **mail·men** (-men′).

**mail order** an order for goods sent by mail.

**mail–or·der** (māl′ôr′dər) of or having to do with mail orders or a business establishment that does business by mail. *adj.*

**maim** (mām) cause permanent damage to or loss of a part of the body; cripple; disable: *He lost two toes in the accident, but we were glad that he was not more seriously maimed.* *v.*

**main** (mān) 1 most important; largest: *the main street of a town.* 2 a large pipe for water, gas, etc. 1 *adj.*, 2 *n.*
**by main force** or **strength,** by using full strength.
**in the main,** for the most part; chiefly; mostly: *Her grades were excellent in the main.*
**with might and main,** with all one's force: *They argued with might and main.*
☞ *Hom.* MANE.

**main·frame** (mān′frām′) 1 of or referring to a type of central computer with large capacity, serving several terminals. 2 a mainframe computer. 1 *adj.*, 2 *n.*

**main·land** (mān′land′ *or* mān′lənd) the main part of a continent or land mass, apart from peninsulas and outlying islands. *n.*

**main·land·er** (mān′lan′dər *or* mān′lən dər) a person who lives on the mainland *n.*

**main·ly** (mān′lē) for the most part; chiefly; mostly: *He is interested mainly in sports and neglects his schoolwork.* *adv.*

**main·mast** (mān′mast′ *or* mān′məst) the principal mast of a sailing ship, usually the second one from the bow. See BRIG, MAST, SCHOONER, and YAWL for pictures. *n.*

**main·sail** (mān′sāl′ *or* mān′səl) the largest sail on the MAINMAST of a ship. See SCHOONER and YAWL for pictures. *n.*

**main·sheet** (mān′shēt′) a rope that controls the angle at which the MAINSAIL is set. *n.*

**main·spring** (mān′spring′) 1 the principal spring in a clock, watch, etc. 2 the main cause, motive, or influence. *n.*

**main·stay** (mān′stā′) 1 a supporting rope or wire extending from the maintop to the foot of the foremast. 2 the main support: *Sasha's friends were his mainstay through his time of trouble.* *n.*

**main·stream** (mān′strēm′) 1 the main current of a river, etc. 2 the main trend or direction of development of a fashion, body of opinion, activity, etc.: *She is not well known to the critics because her painting is outside the mainstream of modern art.* 3 integrate a handicapped child or children into a regular class. 1, 2 *n.*, 3 *v.*

**main·tain** (mān tān′) 1 keep; keep up; carry on: *to maintain a business, to maintain one's composure.* 2 keep from failing or declining; keep in good condition: *He employs a mechanic to maintain his fleet of trucks.* 3 pay the expenses of; provide for: *She maintains a family of four.* 4 uphold; argue for; keep to in argument or discussion: *to maintain an opinion. She maintains her innocence.* 5 declare to be true: *He maintained that he was innocent.* *v.* —**main·tain′er,** *n.*
☞ *Etym.* Through OF *maintenir* from a Latin phrase *manu tenere* 'hold by the hand'.

**main·te·nance** (mān′tə nəns) 1 maintaining or being maintained; support: *A government collects taxes to pay for its maintenance.* 2 keeping in good repair; upkeep: *The army devotes much time to the maintenance of its equipment.* 3 enough to support life; a means of living: *Her small farm provides a maintenance, but not much more.* 4 in law: **a** the payment of money by a person after divorce to his or her former spouse for the support of the former spouse and any children: *Maintenance is awarded by court order and usually stops if the supported person remarries.* Compare with ALIMONY. **b** the payment of money by a person for the support of children living apart from him or her, after separation or divorce of the parents. *n.*

**main·top** (mān′top′) a platform at the head of the MAINMAST of a square-rigged ship. See MAST for picture. *n.*

**main–top·mast** (mān′top′mast′ *or* mān′top′məst) the second section of the MAINMAST above the lower mainmast. See MAST for picture. *n.*

**main–top·sail** (mān′top′sāl′ *or* mān′top′səl) the sail above the MAINSAIL. *n.*

**main yard** the beam or pole fastened across the MAINMAST, used to support the MAINSAIL.

**maî·tre d'** (mā′tər dē′) *Informal.* headwaiter. *n., pl.* **maî·tre d's** (mā′tər dēz′).

**maî·tre d'hô·tel** (me tRə dō tel′) *French.* 1 a butler or steward; MAJOR-DOMO. 2 headwaiter. 3 of a sauce, etc., containing melted butter, chopped parsley, and lemon juice. *n., pl.* **maî·tres d'hô·tel** (met′Rə dō tel′).

**maize** (māz) 1 CORN (defs. 1 and 2); Indian corn. 2 yellow. 1, 2 *n.*, 2 *adj.*
☞ *Hom.* MAZE.

**ma·jes·tic** (mə jes′tik) grand; noble; dignified; stately. *adj.* —**ma·jes′ti·cal·ly,** *adv.*

**maj·es·ty** (maj′i stē) 1 grandeur; nobility; dignity; stateliness: *We were much impressed by the majesty of the coronation ceremony.* 2 the supreme power or authority: *Police officers and judges uphold the majesty of the law.* 3 **Majesty,** a title used in speaking to or of a king, queen, emperor, empress, etc.: *Your Majesty, His Majesty, Her Majesty.* *n., pl.* **maj·es·ties.**

**ma·jol·i·ca** (mə jol′ə kə) a kind of enamelled Italian pottery richly decorated in colours. *n.*

**ma·jor** (mā′jər) 1 larger; greater; more important: *Take the major share.* 2 of the first rank or order: *Margaret Atwood is a major poet.* 3 very serious or important: *a major disaster.* 4 a commissioned officer in the armed forces, senior to a captain and junior to a lieutenant-colonel. 5 of legal age. 6 a person of the legal age of responsibility. 7 the subject or course of study to which a student gives most of his or her time and attention. 8 in music: **a** of an interval, greater by a half step than the minor; having the difference of pitch which is found between the tonic and the second, third, sixth, or seventh tone (or step) of a major scale: *a major second, third, sixth, seventh.* **b** of a scale, key, or mode, in which the interval between the tonic and third step is a major third (two whole steps): *C major scale or key.* **c** of a chord, especially a triad, containing a major third (two whole steps) between the root and the second tone or note.   **9** a major interval, key, scale, chord, etc.: *The scale of C major has neither sharps nor flats.*   *1–3, 5, 8 adj.*, *4, 6, 7, 9 n.*

**major in,**   of a student, give most of one's time and attention to a subject or course of study: *to major in mathematics.*

**ma·jor–do·mo** (mā′jər dō′mō)   **1** the man in charge of a royal or noble household.   **2** a butler; steward.   *n., pl.* **ma·jor·do·mos.**

**ma·jor·ette** (mā jə ret′)   DRUM MAJORETTE.   *n.*

**ma·jor·i·ty** (mə jôr′ə tē)   **1** the larger number or greater part; more than half: *A majority of the students passed the test.*   **2** in a contest involving two or more candidates, the number of votes cast for one candidate when that number is more than half the total number of votes for all candidates: *If Xerri received 12 000 votes, Adams 7000, and Singh 3000, Xerri had a majority of 2000.*   **3** the legal age of responsibility: *A person who is 18 or 19 years old or over has reached his or her majority and may manage his or her own affairs.*   **4** the rank or position of major in the armed forces.   *n., pl.* **ma·jor·i·ties.**

**major league**   **1** either of the two chief leagues in American professional baseball.   **2** in hockey, the National Hockey League.

**major scale**   in music, a scale having eight tones, with half steps instead of whole steps after the third and seventh tones.   Compare with MINOR SCALE.

**make** (māk)   **1** bring into being; put together; build; form; shape: *to make a new dress, to make a poem, to make a boat, to make a medicine.*   **2** the way in which a thing is made; a style, build, or character: *Do you like the make of that coat?*   **3** a kind; brand: *What make of car is this?*   **4** the nature; character.   **5** the act of making.   **6** the amount made.   **7** have the qualities needed for: *Wood makes a good fire.*   **8** cause; bring about: *to make trouble, to make a noise.*   **9** cause to; force to: *He made me go.*   **10** cause to be or become; cause oneself to be: *to make a room warm, to make a fool of oneself.*   **11** turn out to be; become: *She will make a good legislator.*   **12** get ready for use; arrange: *to make a bed.*   **13** get; obtain; acquire; earn: *to make a fortune, to make one's living.*   **14** do; perform: *to make an attempt, to make a mistake.*   **15** amount to; add up to; count as: *Two and two make four.*   **16** think of as; figure to be: *I make the distance across the room 5 metres.*   **17** reach; arrive at: *The ship made port.*   **18** go; travel: *Some airplanes can make 2000 kilometres per hour.*   **19** cause the success of: *One big deal made the young businesswoman.*   **20** *Informal.*   get on; get a place on: *He made the football team.*   **21** in card games, win a trick or hand; state the trump, or bid.   **22** shuffle (cards).   **23** close an electric circuit.   *1, 7–23 v.,* **made, mak·ing,** *2–6 n.*

**make as if,**   pretend; act as if.

**make away with,**   **a** get rid of.   **b** kill.   **c** steal: *The treasurer made away with the club's funds.*

**make believe,**   pretend: *The girl liked to make believe she was a queen.*

**make fast,**   attach firmly.

**make for,**   **a** go toward: *Make for the hills!*   **b** rush at; attack.   **c** help bring about: *Careful driving makes for fewer accidents.*

**make fun of,**   mock; ridicule: *The boys made fun of the girl's pigtails.*

**make good,**   **a** succeed.   **b** prove: *Can you make your claims good?*

**make it,** *Informal.*   succeed.

**make off,**   run away.

**make off with,**   steal; take without permission: *He made off with some apples.*

hat, āge, fär; let, ēqual, tėrm; it, īce
hot, ōpen, ôrder; oil, out; cup, put, rüle
əbove, takən, pencəl, lemən, circəs
ch, child; ng, long; sh, ship
th, thin; ᴛʜ, then; zh, measure

**make or break,**   cause to succeed or fail.

**make out,**   **a** write out: *Yoshio made out his application for camp.*   **b** show to be; try to prove: *That makes me out most selfish.*   **c** understand: *The boy had a hard time making out the problem.*   **d** see with difficulty; distinguish: *I can barely make out three ships near the horizon.*   **e** *Informal.*   get along; manage: *We must try to make out with what we have.*

**make over,**   **a** alter; make different: *to make over a dress.*   **b** hand over; transfer ownership of: *Grandfather made over his farm to my mother.*

**make time,**   go with speed.

**make up,**   **a** put together: *to make up cloth into a dress.*   **b** invent: *to make up a story.*   **c** make satisfactory.   **d** become friends again after a quarrel.   **e** put paint, powder, etc. on the face.   **f** arrange type, pictures, etc. in the pages of a book, paper, or magazine: *to make up a page of type, to make up an edition of a newspaper.*   **g** complete; fill out: *We need two more eggs to make up a dozen.*   **h** comprise: *The committee is made up of women.*

**make up for,**   give or do in place of: *make up for lost time.*

**make up one's mind,**   decide.

**make up to,**   try to get the friendship of; flatter.

**on the make,** *Informal.*   trying for success, profit, etc.

**make–be·lieve** (māk′bi lēv′)   **1** pretence: *Goblins live in the land of make-believe.*   **2** pretended: *Children often have make-believe playmates.*   *1 n., 2 adj.*

**mak·er** (mā′kər)   **1** a person or thing that makes.   **2 Maker,**   God.   *n.*

**meet one's Maker,**   die: *He has gone to meet his Maker.*

**make·shift** (māk′shift′)   **1** something used for a time in the place of the proper thing; a temporary substitute: *When the power went off, we used candles as a makeshift.*   **2** used for a time instead of the proper thing: *The girls contrived a makeshift tent out of a blanket.*   *1 n., 2 adj.*

**make–up** (māk′kup′)   **1** the way of being put together; composition: *The make-up of a magazine is either the arrangement of type, illustrations, etc. or the kind of articles, stories, etc. used.*   **2** one's nature or disposition; constitution: *a nervous make-up.*   **3** the way in which an actor is dressed and painted to look his or her part.   **4** the paint, powder, wigs, etc. used by actors taking part in a play or film: *His make-up was so effective that we didn't recognize him.*   **5** the powder, rouge, lipstick, etc. put on the face; cosmetics.   *n.*

**mak·ing** (mā′king)   **1** cause of a person's success; means of advancement: *Early hardships were the making of him.*   **2** material needed.   **3** qualities needed: *I see in him the making of a hero.*   **4** something made.   **5** amount made at one time.   **6 makings,** *pl.*  ingredients; contributory factors.   **7** ppr. of MAKE.   *1–6 n., 7 v.*

**in the making,**   in the process of being made; not yet fully developed.

**mal·a·chite** (mal′ə kīt′)   a green mineral, copper carbonate, used as an ore of copper and as a stone for making ornamental objects.   *n.*

**mal·ad·just·ed** (mal′ə jus′tid)   badly adjusted;

especially, not in harmony with one's environment and conditions of life: *Maladjusted children often behave badly.* *adj.*

**mal·ad·just·ment** (mal′ə just′mənt) poor or unsatisfactory adjustment, especially to one's environment and conditions of life. *n.*

**mal·ad·min·is·ter** (mal′əd min′i stər) administer badly; manage inefficiently or dishonestly. *v.*

**mal·ad·min·is·tra·tion** (mal′əd min′i strā′shən) bad administration; inefficient or dishonest management. *n.*

**mal·a·droit** (mal′ə droit′) unskilful; awkward; clumsy. *adj.* —**mal′a·droit′ness,** *n.*

**mal·a·dy** (mal′ə dē) **1** a sickness or disease. **2** any unwholesome or disordered condition: *Poverty is a social malady.* *n., pl.* **mal·a·dies.**

**mal·ai·ka** (ma lä′ē kä′) in Islam, angels; the counterparts of the evil JINN. *n.*

**ma·laise** (ma lāz′) vague bodily discomfort. *n.*

**mal·a·mute** (mal′ə myüt′) a breed of large, powerful dog having a heavy grey, black, and white coat, erect ears, and a tail that curls over the back: *Malamutes have long been used as sled dogs in Alaska and the Canadian North.* *n.* Also called **Alaskan malamute.** Also, **malemute.**

**mal·a·prop·ism** (mal′ə pro piz′əm) **1** a ridiculous misuse of words, especially by confusing words that sound somewhat alike, as in *immortality* and *immorality* in *They believe in the immorality of souls.* **2** a misused word. *n.*
☛ *Etym.* From Mrs *Malaprop,* a character in *The Rivals,* a play by Richard Sheridan (1751–1816). Mrs. Malaprop was noted for her ridiculous misuse of words.

**ma·lar·i·a** (mə ler′ē ə) a disease characterized by periodic chills followed by fever and sweating: *Malaria is caused by minute parasitic animals in the red blood corpuscles, and is transmitted by the bite of anopheles mosquitoes that have bitten infected persons.* *n.*
☛ *Etym.* From Italian *mal′aria,* a shortening of *mala aria* 'bad air', since the disease was once thought to be caused by bad air coming from swamps.

**ma·lar·i·al** (mə ler′ē əl) **1** having or causing MALARIA. **2** of or like MALARIA. *adj.*

**ma·la·thi·on** (mal′ə thī′ən) a very powerful insecticide, recognizable by its pungent smell. *n.*

**Ma·lay** (Mā lā′ *or* mā′lā) **1** a member of a people living in the Malay peninsula, Borneo, and nearby islands. **2** the language of these people, consisting of various dialects: *Malay belongs to the same language family as Fijian, Hawaiian, and Javanese.* **3** of or having to do with the Malays or their language. 1, 2 *n.,* 3 *adj.*
☛ *Hom.* MELEE (mā′lā).

**Ma·lay·an** (mə lā′ən) MALAY. *adj.*

**Ma·lay·sian** (mə lā′zhən *or* mə lā′shən) **1** of or having to do with Malaysia, a country in S.E. Asia, its people, or their languages. **2** a native or inhabitant of Malaysia. 1 *adj.,* 2 *n.*

**mal·con·tent** (mal′kən tent′) **1** discontented or rebellious. **2** a discontented or rebellious person. 1 *adj.,* 2 *n.*

**male** (māl) **1** of, having to do with, or being the sex that produces the gametes, or sperm cells, that fertilize the eggs of a female to produce young: *the male organs.* **2** of, having to do with, or characteristic of men or boys: *a male voice.* **3** made up of men: *a male choir.* **4** an animal or plant that is male: *There were three puppies in the litter; two males and one female.* **5** referring to a part of a machine or a connection, etc. that fits into a corresponding hollow part: *a male pipe fitting.* 1–3, 5 *adj.,* 4 *n.*
☛ *Hom.* MAIL.

**Mal·e·cite** (mal′ə sēt′) **1** a member of a First Nations people living in New Brunswick and eastern Quebec: *The Malecites are an Algonquian people.* **2** of or having to do with these people. 1 *n., pl.* **Mal·e·cite** or **Mal·e·cites;** 2 *adj.*

**mal·e·dic·tion** (mal′ə dik′shən) the uttering of a curse; the calling down of evil on a person. *n.*

**mal·e·fac·tion** (mal′ə fak′shən) a crime or evil deed. *n.*

**mal·e·fac·tor** (mal′ə fak′tər) a criminal or evil-doer. *n.*

**mal·e·mute** (mal′ə myüt′) See MALAMUTE. *n.*

**ma·lev·o·lence** (mə lev′ə ləns) the wish that evil may happen to others; ill will; spite. *n.*

**ma·lev·o·lent** (mə lev′ə lənt) having or showing vicious ill will; spiteful; malicious: *a malevolent smile.* *adj.* —**ma·lev′o·lent·ly,** *adv.*

**mal·fea·sance** (mal fē′zəns) misconduct by a public official; violation of a public trust or duty: *A judge is guilty of malfeasance if he or she accepts a bribe.* *n.*

**mal·for·ma·tion** (mal′fôr mā′shən) an irregular, faulty, or abnormal shape or structure: *A hunchback is a malformation of the spine.* *n.*

**mal·formed** (mal fôrmd′) badly shaped; having an abnormal or faulty structure. *adj.*

**mal·func·tion** (mal′fungk′shən) **1** an improper functioning; failure to work or perform: *a malfunction of an organ of the body, a malfunction in a machine.* **2** function badly; work or perform improperly. 1 *n.,* 2 *v.*

**mal·ic acid** (mal′ik) an acid found in apples and numerous other fruits.

**mal·ice** (mal′is) **1** active ill will; a wish to hurt others; spite. **2** in law, an intent to commit an act which will result in harm to another person without justification. *n.*

**ma·li·cious** (mə lish′əs) showing active ill will; wishing to hurt others; spiteful: *a malicious telltale, malicious gossip.* *adj.* —**ma·li′cious·ly,** *adv.*

**ma·lign** (mə līn′) **1** speak evil of, often falsely; slander: *You malign him unjustly when you call him stingy, for he gives all he can afford to give.* **2** evil; injurious: *Gambling often has a malign influence.* **3** hateful; malicious. **4** harmful; threatening to be fatal. 1 *v.,* 2–4 *adj.*
—**ma·lign′er,** *n.*

**ma·lig·nance** (mə lig′nəns) MALIGNANCY. *n.*

**ma·lig·nan·cy** (mə lig′nən sē) **1** the quality or state of being MALIGNANT. **2** a MALIGNANT tendency, as of a tumour. **3** a MALIGNANT tumour. *n.*

**ma·lig·nant** (mə lig′nənt) **1** extremely evil, hateful, or malicious. **2** extremely harmful. **3** of a disease, very infectious and dangerous: *malignant cholera.* **4** of a tumour, cyst, etc., tending to grow and spread, causing harm to healthy tissues around it; cancerous. Compare with BENIGN (def. 3). *adj.* —**ma·lig′nant·ly,** *adv.*

**ma·lig·ni·ty** (mə lig′nə tē)   1 great malice; extreme hate.   2 great harmfulness; dangerous quality; deadliness.   3 a MALIGNANT act or feeling.   *n., pl.* **ma·lig·ni·ties.**

**ma·lin·ger** (mə ling′gər)   pretend to be sick in order to escape work or duty; shirk.   *v.* —**ma·lin′ger·er,** *n.*

**mall** (mol)   1 a shaded walk; public walk or promenade.   2 a walk lined with stores; a place to walk in a shopping centre.   3 SHOPPING MALL.   *n.*

**mal·lard** (mal′ərd)   a kind of wild duck: *The male mallard has a greenish-black head and a white band around his neck.* See DUCK¹ for picture.   *n., pl.* **mal·lards** or *(esp. collectively)* **mal·lard.**

**mal·le·a·bil·i·ty** (mal′ē ə bil′ə tē)   the quality or state of being MALLEABLE.   *n.*

**mal·le·a·ble** (mal′ē ə bəl)   1 capable of being hammered or pressed into various shapes without being broken: *Gold, silver, copper, and tin are malleable; they can be beaten into thin sheets.*   2 adaptable; yielding: *A malleable person is easily persuaded to change his or her plans.*   *adj.*

A rubber mallet and a wooden croquet mallet

**mal·let** (mal′it)   1 a hammer having a head of wood, rubber, or other fairly soft material.   2 a long-handled wooden mallet used to play croquet or polo.   *n.*

**mal·le·us** (mal′ē əs)   in mammals, the outermost of three small bones in the middle ear, shaped like a hammer. See EAR¹ for picture.   *n., pl.* **mal·le·i** (mal′ē ī).

**mal·low** (mal′ō)   1 any of a closely related group of herbs native to Europe, Asia, and northern Africa, having lobed leaves and usually large, showy flowers: *Many species of mallows have become naturalized in North America; a few are cultivated as garden flowers, while others, such as the common mallow, have become weeds.*   2 any of several other herbs or shrubs of the same family.   3 referring to a family of herbs, shrubs, and small trees found throughout the world, but especially in the tropics: *The cotton plant, hollyhock, mallows, and hibiscus belong to the mallow family.*   *n.*

**mal·nu·tri·tion** (mal′nyü trish′ən *or* mal′nü trish′ən)   poor nourishment; lack of nourishment: *Malnutrition may come from eating the wrong kinds of foods as well as from eating too little.*   *n.*

**mal·oc·clu·sion** (mal′ə klü′zhən)   failure of the upper and lower teeth to meet or close properly.   *n.*

**mal·o·dor·ous** (mal′ō′də rəs)   smelling bad.   *adj.*   —**mal′o·dor·ous·ly,** *adv.*

**mal·prac·tice** (mal′prak′tis)   1 criminal neglect or unprofessional treatment of a patient by a doctor.   2 wrong practice or conduct in any official or professional position.   *n.*

**malt** (molt)   1 barley or other grain that is soaked in water until it sprouts and is then dried and aged: *Malt has a sweet taste and is used in making beer and ale.*   2 change or be changed into malt.   3 prepare with malt.   4 beer or ale.   5 MALTED MILK.   1, 4, 5 *n.*, 2, 3 *v.*

**mal·tase** (mol′tās)   a digestive enzyme in the intestinal glands which hydrolyzes MALTOSE into sugar.   *n.*

**malted milk**   a sweet, cold drink made from dried milk and powdered malted cereal mixed with milk and, usually, ice cream and flavouring.

**Mal·tese** (mol tēz′)   1 a native or inhabitant of Malta, an island in the Mediterranean.   2 the language of Malta: *Maltese is a form of Arabic that contains many Italian words.*   3 of or having to do with Malta, its people, or their language.   4 a breed of toy dog usually weighing 2 to 3 kg, having long, silky, white hair, a black nose, and black eyes: *The Maltese is one of the oldest breeds of lap dog.*   5 MALTESE CAT.   1, 2, 4, 5 *n.*, *pl.* **Mal·tese;**   3 *adj.*

**Maltese cat**   a bluish-grey variety of short-haired domestic cat.

**Maltese cross**   a cross with arms that broaden out from the centre and are often indented at the ends. See CROSS for picture.

**malt·ose** (mol′tōs)   a white crystalline sugar made by the action of diastase on starch.   *n.*

**mal·treat** (mal trēt′)   treat roughly or cruelly; abuse: *Only vicious persons maltreat animals.*   *v.*

**mal·treat·ment** (mal trēt′mənt)   rough or cruel treatment; abuse: *Prisoners sometimes complain of maltreatment.*   *n.*

**malt sugar**   MALTOSE.

**ma·ma** or **mam·ma** (mom′ə *or* mä′mə) *Informal.* mother.   *n.*

**mam·bo** (mäm′bō *or* mam′bō)   1 a ballroom dance of Caribbean origin.   2 the music for such a dance.   *n.*

**mam·ma¹** (mom′ə *or* mä′mə)   See MAMA.   *n.*

**mam·ma²** (mam′ə)   a milk-giving gland in female mammals.   *n., pl.* **mam·mae** (mam′ē *or* mam′ī).

**mam·mal** (mam′əl)   any of a class of warm-blooded vertebrate animals the females of which have glands that produce milk for feeding their young: *Human beings, horses, dogs, rats, and whales are all mammals.*   *n.*

**mam·ma·li·an** (ma mā′lē ən)   1 of or having to do with MAMMALS.   2 a MAMMAL.   1 *adj.*, 2 *n.*

**mam·ma·ry** (mam′ə rē)   of or referring to the MAMMAE: *The mammary glands give milk.*   *adj.*

**Mam·mon** or **mam·mon** (mam′ən)   1 material wealth or possessions thought of as an object of worship.   2 material wealth or possessions thought of as evil; greed for wealth.   *n.*

**mam·moth** (mam′əth)   1 a large kind of elephant now extinct, having a hairy skin and long, curved tusks.   2 huge; gigantic: *Digging the St. Lawrence Seaway was a mammoth undertaking.*   1 *n.*, 2 *adj.*

**mam·my** (mam′ē)   1 a child's word for "mother."

**2** *U.S.* a black woman who took care of white children, especially in the South. *n., pl.* **mam·mies.**

**man** (man) **1** an adult male person. **2** a person; human being: *Death comes to all men.* **3** the human race; mankind: *Man has existed for thousands of years.* **4** men as a group; the average man: *The man of today likes to travel.* **5** a male follower, servant, or employee: *Robin Hood and his merry men.* **6** husband: *man and wife.* **7** one of the pieces used in games such as chess and checkers. **8** supply with a crew: *We can man ten ships.* **9** serve or operate; get ready to operate: *Man the guns.* **10** make oneself strong in anticipation; brace: *to man oneself for an ordeal.* **11** a man thought of as having all the best characteristics distinctive of manhood: *He was every inch a man.* 1–7, 11 *n., pl.* **men** (men); 8–10 *v.*, **manned, man·ning.**
**act the man,** be courageous.
**as a man,** from a human point of view.
**as one man,** with complete agreement; unanimously.
**be one's own man, a** be free to do as one pleases. **b** have complete control of oneself.
**man and boy,** from boyhood on; as a youth and as an adult.
**to a man,** every one, without an exception; all: *We accepted his idea to a man.*

**Man.** Manitoba.

**M.A.N.** *Cdn. French.* Membre de l'Assemblée nationale (Member of the National Assembly).

**man about town** a man who spends much of his time in fashionable clubs, theatres, etc.

**man·a·cle** (man′ə kəl) **1** a fetter for the hand; handcuff. **2** put manacles on: *The pirates manacled their prisoners.* **3** restrain. **4** any restraint. 1, 4 *n.*, 2, 3 *v.*, **man·a·cled, man·a·cling.**

**man·age** (man′ij) **1** control; conduct; handle; direct: *to manage a business, to manage a horse.* **2** conduct affairs. **3** succeed in accomplishing; contrive; arrange: *I finally managed to get the job done.* **4** get along: *to manage on one's income.* **5** make use of. **6** get one's way with a person by craft or by flattering. *v.*, **man·aged, man·ag·ing.**

**man·age·a·bil·i·ty** (man′i jə bil′ə tē) the condition or quality of being MANAGEABLE. *n.*

**man·age·a·ble** (man′i jə bəl) that can be managed. *adj.* —**man′age·a·ble·ness,** *n.* —**man′age·a·bly,** *adv.*

**man·age·ment** (man′ij mənt) **1** control; handling; direction: *The new store failed because of bad management.* **2** the persons that manage a business or an institution: *The management of the store decided to keep it open every evening.* *n.*

**man·ag·er** (man′i jər) **1** a person who manages. **2** a person skilled in managing affairs, time, money, etc.: *Mrs. Kielek is not much of a manager, but the family gets along somehow.* **3** a person in an executive position in a company, etc.; someone in charge: *the manager of the theatre.* **4** a person who directs the activities of a team, athlete, performer, etc. *n.*

**man·a·ge·ri·al** (man′ə jē′rē əl) of a manager; having to do with management. *adj.*

**ma·ña·na** (mä nyä′nä) *Spanish.* tomorrow; some time. *n., adv.*

**man–at–arms** (man′ə tärmz′) formerly, a soldier, especially one who was heavily armed and mounted on horseback. *n., pl.* **men–at–arms** (men′-).

**man·a·tee** (man′ə tē′) a sea cow, a large sea mammal with two flippers and a flat, oval tail, living in warm shallow water near coasts. *n.*

**Man·chu** (man′chü) **1** a member of an Asiatic people, the original inhabitants of Manchuria, who conquered China in 1644 and ruled it until 1912. **2** their language. **3** of the Manchus, their country, or their language. 1, 2 *n.*, 3 *adj.*

**Man·chu·ri·an** (man chü′rē ən) **1** of or having to do with Manchuria, an eastern Asian region that includes several Chinese provinces. **2** a native or inhabitant of Manchuria. 1 *adj.*, 2 *n.*

**man·da·rin** (man′də rin) **1** a kind of small, sweet orange having a thin, very loose, dark-orange peel. **2** the small, spiny citrus tree bearing this fruit: *The mandarin is native to China.* **3** in the Chinese Empire, an official of high rank. **4** a person of high position whose work is not publicized but who has, or is thought to have, considerable political or social influence: *the mandarins of Ottawa.* **5 Mandarin, a** formerly, in the Chinese Empire, the language of the court, government officials, and other educated people: *Mandarin was a northern dialect.* **b** the main language of modern China, the standard form being the one used in Beijing. *n.*

**man·date** (man′dāt *or* man′dit) **1** a command or official order. **2** an order from a higher court or official to a lower one. **3** a direction or authority given to a government by the votes of the people in an election: *The prime minister said he had a mandate to increase taxes.* **4** a commission given to one nation by a group of nations to administer the government and affairs of a territory, etc. **5** put a territory, etc. under the administration of another nation. **6** a mandated territory, etc. 1–4, 6 *n.*, 5 *v.*, **man·dat·ed, man·dat·ing.**

**man·da·to·ry** (man′də tô′rē) **1** of or like a mandate; giving a command or order. **2** required by a command or order. *adj.*

The head of a grasshopper, showing the parts of the mouth

**man·di·ble** (man′də bəl) **1** either member of the foremost pair of mouth parts of an insect, spider, lobster, etc., adapted for seizing and biting. **2** either the upper or lower part of the beak of a bird or of any other beaked animal, such as an octopus. **3** the jaw of a vertebrate, especially the lower jaw. *n.*

**man·do·lin** (man′də lin′ *or* man′də lin′) a musical instrument with a pear-shaped body, having metal strings and played with a plectrum. *n.*

**man·drake** (man′drāk) **1** a plant having a very short stem and a thick root, used in medicine. **2** the MAY APPLE. *n.*

**man·drel** or **man·dril** (man′drəl) **1** on a lathe, the spindle or bar that is inserted into a hole in a piece of work to support it while it is being turned. **2** a rod or core around which metal is shaped. *n.*
☞ *Hom.* MANDRILL.

**man·drill** (man′drəl) a large, fierce baboon of western

Africa: *The face of the male mandrill is marked with blue and scarlet.* *n.*
☞ Hom. MANDREL.

**mane** (mān) the long, heavy hair growing on the back or around the neck of a horse, lion, etc. *n.*
☞ Hom. MAIN.

**ma·nège** (mə nezh′) 1 the art of training or riding horses; horsemanship. 2 the movements of a trained horse. 3 a riding school. *n.*

**ma·neu·ver** (mə nü′vər) See MANOEUVRE. *n., v.*

**man·ful** (man′fəl) having or showing courage, resolution, etc.; manly. *adj.*, —**man′ful·ly**, *adv.* —**man′ful·ness**, *n.*

**man·ga·nese** (mang′gə nēz′) a hard, brittle, greyish-white metallic element: *Substances containing manganese are used in making steel, glass, paints, and medicines.* Symbol: Mn  *n.*

**mange** (mānj) an itchy skin disease of dogs, horses, cattle, etc., in which tiny skin sores form and the hair falls off in patches: *Mange is caused by a parasitic mite.* *n.*

**man·gel** (mang′gəl) a large, coarse variety of beet, used as a food for cattle. *n.*
☞ Hom. MANGLE.

**man·gel-wur·zel** (mang′gəl wėr′zəl) MANGEL. *n.*

**man·ger** (mān′jər) a box or trough in which hay or other food can be placed for horses or cows to eat. See STALL for picture. *n.*

**man·gle¹** (mang′gəl) 1 cut or tear roughly: *His arm was badly mangled in the accident.* 2 do or play badly; ruin: *The music was too difficult for her, and she mangled it.* *v.*, **man·gled, man·gling.**
☞ Hom. MANGEL.

**man·gle²** (mang′gəl) 1 a machine for pressing and smoothing cloth by passing it between rollers. 2 wringer. 3 press with a mangle; put through a mangle. 1, 2 *n.*, 3 *v.*, **man·gled, man·gling.**
☞ Hom. MANGEL.

**man·go** (mang′gō) 1 a tart, juicy fruit with a thick, yellowish-red or greenish rind: *Mangoes are eaten when ripe or pickled when green.* 2 the tropical tree this fruit grows on. *n., pl.* **man·goes** or **man·gos.**

**man·gold** (mang′gōld) MANGEL. *n.*

**man·grove** (man′grōv *or* mang′grōv) a tree having branches that send down many roots which look like new trunks or stems but twine together to make dense thickets: *Mangroves grow in the tropics in swamps and along the banks of rivers.* *n.*

**man·gy** (mān′jē) 1 having the MANGE; with the hair falling out: *a mangy dog.* 2 shabby and dirty: *a mangy house.* *adj.*, **man·gi·er, man·gi·est.** —**man′gi·ness**, *n.*

**man·han·dle** (man′han·dəl) 1 treat roughly; pull or push about. 2 move by human strength without mechanical appliances: *They manhandled the piano down the steps and into the truck.* *v.*, **man·han·dled, man·han·dling.**

**man–hole** (man′hōl′) a hole through which a worker may enter a sewer, steam boiler, etc. to inspect or repair it. *n.*

**man·hood** (man′hùd) 1 the condition or time of being a man. 2 courage; manliness. 3 men as a group: *the manhood of Canada.* *n.*

**man–hour** (man′our′) an hour of work by one person, used as a unit of time in industry. *n.*

# mane 725 manioc

hat, āge, fär; let, ēqual, tėrm; it, īce
hot, ōpen, ôrder; oil, out; cup, pùt, rüle
əbove, takən, pencəl, lemən, circəs
ch, child; ng, long; sh, ship
th, thin; ₮H, then; zh, measure

**ma·ni·a** (mā′nē ə) 1 a kind of mental illness characterized by great excitement and sometimes violence. 2 an excessive fondness; craze: *a mania for dancing.* *n.*

**ma·ni·ac** (mā′nē ak′) 1 a person affected by MANIA. 2 insane; raving. 1 *n.*, 2 *adj.*

**ma·ni·a·cal** (mə nī′ə kəl) insane; raving. *adj.* —**ma·ni′a·cal·ly**, *adv.*

**man·ic** (man′ik *or* mā′nik) 1 of or like MANIA (def. 1). 2 suffering from MANIA (def. 1). *adj.*

**man·ic-de·pres·sive** (man′ik di pres′iv) 1 having alternating attacks of MANIA (def. 1) and DEPRESSION (def. 2). 2 a person who has such attacks. 1 *adj.*, 2 *n.*

**man·i·cure** (man′ə kyùr′) 1 to care for the fingernails and hands; especially, to trim, clean, and polish the fingernails. 2 a treatment for the hands and fingernails: *She made an appointment for a manicure at the salon.* 3 trim closely and evenly: *a well-manicured lawn.* 1, 3 *v.*, **man·i·cured, man·i·cur·ing;** 2 *n.*

**man·i·cur·ist** (man′ə kyü′rist) a person whose work is manicuring: *Manicurists usually work in beauty salons.* *n.*

**man·i·fest** (man′ə fest′) 1 clear to the eye or to the mind; plain: *The thief left so many clues that his guilt was manifest.* 2 show plainly; reveal; display. 3 prove; put beyond doubt. 4 a list of a ship's cargo. 5 a list of passengers, freight, etc. on an airplane flight. 1 *adj.*, 2, 3 *v.*, 4, 5 *n.* —**man′i·fest′ly**, *adv.*

**man·i·fes·ta·tion** (man′ə fə stā′shən) 1 MANIFESTing or being manifested. 2 something that MANIFESTS: *A brave deed is a manifestation of courage.* 3 a public demonstration. *n.*

**man·i·fes·to** (man′ə fes′tō) a public declaration of intentions, purposes, or motives, especially of a political nature; proclamation. *n., pl.* **man·i·fes·toes.**

**man·i·fold** (man′ə fōld′) 1 of many kinds; many and various: *manifold duties.* 2 having many parts or forms: *The hero was praised for his manifold goodness.* 3 doing many things at the same time. 4 a pipe or chamber having several openings for connection with other pipes: *The manifold of an automobile conducts used gases to an exhaust pipe.* 5 one of many copies. 6 make many copies. 1–3 *adj.*, 4, 5 *n.*, 6 *v.*

**man·i·kin** (man′ə kin) 1 a little man; dwarf. 2 See MANNEQUIN. *n.* Also, **mannikin.**
☞ Hom. MANNEQUIN.

**ma·ni·la** or **ma·nil·la** (mə nil′ə) 1 MANILA HEMP. 2 MANILA PAPER. 3 MANILA ROPE. 4 made from MANILA PAPER or hemp: *a manila envelope.* *n.*

**Manila hemp** a strong fibre made from the leaves of a Philippine banana plant, used for making ropes and fabrics.

**Manila paper** a strong brown or brownish-yellow wrapping paper, made originally from MANILA HEMP.

**Manila rope** rope made from MANILA HEMP.

**man in the street** the average person.

**man·i·oc** (man′ē ok′) CASSAVA. *n.*

**ma·nip·u·late** (mə nip′yə lāt′)   1 handle or treat skilfully; handle: *The driver of an automobile manipulates the levers and pedals.*   2 manage by clever use of personal influence, especially unfair influence: *He so manipulated the ball team that he was elected captain.*   3 change for one's own purpose or advantage: *The bookkeeper manipulated the company's accounts to cover up her theft.*   *v.*, **ma·nip·u·lat·ed, ma·nip·u·lat·ing.**
—**ma·nip′u·la′tor,** *n.*

**ma·nip·u·la·tion** (mə nip′yə lā′shən)   1 skilful handling or treatment: *Chiropractors treat pain by manipulation of the spine.*   2 clever use of influence.   3 a change made for one's own purpose or advantage.   *n.*

**ma·nip·u·la·tive** (mə nip′yə lə tiv *or* mə nip′yə lā′tiv)   1 of or having to do with MANIPULATION.   2 done by MANIPULATION.   *adj.*

**man·i·to** (man′ə tō′)   MANITOU.   *n., pl.* **man·i·tos.**

A compound leaf of the Manitoba maple

**Manitoba maple** (man′ə tō′bə)   a species of medium-sized maple common on the Prairies, the only Canadian maple normally having compound leaves; box elder.

**Man·i·to·ban** (man′ə tō′bən)   1 a native or long-term resident of Manitoba, one of the Prairie Provinces.   2 of or having to do with Manitoba.   1 *n.*, 2 *adj.*

**man·i·tou** *or* **man·i·tu** (man′ə tü′)   in the traditional religion of the Algonquian peoples:   1 any of the spirits representing the power that dwells within all things in nature, both weak and strong, and having both good and evil influence.   2 the impersonal supreme being or supernatural force, author of life and all things; the chief of the manitous, called **gitche** (or **kitshi**) **manitou,** often translated as the Great Spirit.   *n.*   Also, **manito.**

**man·kind** (man′kīnd′ *for 1;* man′kīnd′ *for 2*)   1 the human race; all human beings.   2 men; men considered collectively: *Mankind and womankind both like praise.*   *n.*

**man·like** (man′līk′)   1 of an animal, having characteristics of a human being: *The chimpanzee is the most manlike of the apes.*   2 like or characteristic of a man or men.   3 suitable for a man; masculine.   *adj.*

**man·li·ness** (man′lē nis)   a manly quality; manly behaviour.   *n.*

**man·ly** (man′lē)   1 like a man; as a man should be.   2 suitable for a man; masculine: *Boxing is a manly sport.*   *adj.*, **man·li·er, man·li·est.**   —**man′li·ness,** *n.*

**man-made** (man′mād′)   made by humans; not occurring naturally; artificial or synthetic: *Nylon is a man-made fibre.*   *adj.*

**man·na** (man′ə)   1 food for the soul.   2 a much-needed thing that is unexpectedly supplied: *Winning the lottery was like manna from heaven for her.*   *n.*

**man·ne·quin** (man′ə kin)   1 a woman whose work is modelling clothes for designers, retail stores, etc.   2 a model of a human figure used by artists, tailors, stores, etc.: *Many clothing stores use mannequins for their window displays.*   *n.*
☛ *Hom.*   MANIKIN.

**man·ner** (man′ər)   1 the way something happens or is done: *The trouble arose in a curious manner.*   2 a way of acting or behaving: *She has a kind manner.*   3 a style or fashion: *He dresses in a strange manner.*   4 **manners,** *pl.*   **a** ways or customs: *Books and movies show us the manners of other times and places.*   **b** ways of behaving toward others: *bad manners.*   **c** polite behaviour: *It is nice to see a child with manners.*   *n.*
**all manner of,**   **a** all kinds of.   **b** many: *all manner of birds.*
**by all manner of means,**   most certainly.
**by no manner of means,**   not at all; under no circumstances.
**in a manner of speaking,**   as one might say.
**to the manner born,**   accustomed since birth to some way or condition.
☛ *Hom.*   MANOR.

**man·nered** (man′ərd)   1 having manners of a certain kind: *a well-mannered child.*   2 affected; artificial; having many mannerisms: *She has a very mannered style of writing.*   *adj.*

**man·ner·ism** (man′ə riz′əm)   1 too much use of some manner in speaking, writing, or behaving.   2 an odd little trick; queer habit; peculiar way of acting.   *n.*

**man·ner·less** (man′ər lis)   not MANNERLY (def. 1).   *adj.*

**man·ner·ly** (man′ər lē)   1 having or showing good manners; polite.   2 politely.   1 *adj.*, 2 *adv.*
—**man′ner·li·ness,** *n.*

**man·ni·kin** (man′ə kin)   See MANIKIN.   *n.*

**manning pool**   *Cdn.*   a central pool, or replacement depot, of seamen, airmen, etc.

**man·nish** (man′ish)   1 characteristic of a man: *a mannish way of holding a baby.*   2 generally associated with a man rather than a woman: *She has a mannish style of dress.*   *adj.*   —**man′nish·ly,** *adv.*

**ma·noeu·vre** (mə nü′vər)   1 a planned movement of troops or warships: *The army practises warfare by holding manoeuvres.*   2 perform manoeuvres.   3 cause to perform manoeuvres.   4 a skilful plan or movement; clever trick: *Her superior manoeuvres won the game.*   5 plan skilfully; use clever tricks; scheme: *He is always manoeuvring to gain some advantage over others.*   6 force by skilful plans; get by clever tricks: *She manoeuvred her mother into letting her have a party.*   7 move or manipulate skilfully: *He manoeuvred his car through the heavy traffic with ease.*   1, 4 *n.*, 2, 3, 5–7 *v.*, **ma·noeu·vred, ma·noeu·vring.**   Also, **maneuver.**
—**ma·noeu′vra·bil′i·ty,** *n.*   —**ma·noeu′vra·ble,** *adj.*

**man of letters**   1 writer.   2 a person who has a wide knowledge of literature.

**man of the world**   a man who has wide experience of different kinds of people and customs; a sophisticated and worldly-wise or practical man.

**ma·nom·e·ter** (mə nom′ə tər)   an instrument for measuring the pressure of gases or vapours.   *n.*

**man·or** (man′ər) **1** a feudal estate, part of which was set aside for the lord and the rest divided among his peasants: *In the Middle Ages, if the lord sold his manor, the peasants or serfs were sold with it.* **2** a large holding of land. **3** a large house on an estate, especially a MANOR HOUSE. *n.*
☞ *Hom.* MANNER.

**manor house** the house of the lord of a MANOR.

**ma·no·ri·al** (mə nô′rē əl) of, having to do with, or forming a MANOR. *adj.*

**man·pow·er** or **man power** (man′pou′ər) **1** the power supplied by the physical work of people. **2** strength thought of in terms of the number of people needed or available. **3 Manpower,** *Informal.* the Canadian federal labour exchange. *n.*

**man·sard** (man′särd) a four-sided roof having two slopes on each side, with the lower slope much steeper than the upper one. See ROOF for picture. *n.*

**man·sard·ed** (man′sär′dəd) of a roof, built with two slopes on each of four sides. *adj.*

**manse** (mans) a minister's house; parsonage. *n.*

**man·serv·ant** (man′sėr′vənt) a male servant. *n., pl.* **men·serv·ants.**

**man·sion** (man′shən) a large stately house. *n.*

**man·slaugh·ter** (man′slot′ər) **1** in law, the unlawful killing of another human being accidentally or without malice or premeditation: *The driver of a car that accidentally hits and kills a pedestrian while the pedestrian has the right of way may be charged with manslaughter.* **2** the killing of a human being or human beings. *n.*

**man·ta** (man′tə) DEVILFISH. *n.*

**manta ray** DEVILFISH.

**man·tel** (man′təl) **1** a shelf above a fireplace. See FIREPLACE for picture. **2** designed to rest on a mantel or similar surface: *a mantel radio.* **3** a decorative facing above and around a fireplace: *a mantel of tile.* *n.*
☞ *Etym.* **Mantel** comes from MANTLE. It developed in 15c. English as a separate word, influenced by the second meaning that had developed for the word in French. F *manteau* means both 'cloak' and 'mantelpiece'. See also note at MANTLE.
☞ *Hom.* MANTLE.

**man·tel·piece** (man′təl pēs′) a shelf above a fireplace; mantel. *n.*

**man·til·la** (man til′ə; *Spanish,* män tē′lyä) **1** a light scarf of lace, silk, etc. covering the hair and shoulders, worn especially by Spanish and Mexican women. **2** a short mantle or cape. *n.*

A praying mantis—body about 6 cm long

**man·tis** (man′tis) an insect that holds its forelegs doubled up as if praying. *n.*

**man·tis·sa** (man tis′ə) the decimal part of a logarithm: *In the logarithm 2.95424, the characteristic is 2 and the mantissa is .95424.* *n.*

**manor**     727     **manuscript**

hat, āge, fär; let, ēqual, tėrm; it, īce
hot, ōpen, ôrder; oil, out; cup, pùt, rüle
əbove, takən, pencəl, lemən, circəs
ch, child; ng, long; sh, ship
th, thin; ŦH, then; zh, measure

**man·tle** (man′təl) **1** a loose cloak with sleeves. **2** anything that covers or conceals like a mantle: *The ground had a mantle of snow.* **3** the part of the earth's interior between the crust and the core, beginning at about 8 to 35 km from the surface and extending to a depth of about 2880 km, and composed of very dense, solid rock believed to consist mainly of silicates of iron and magnesium. See CORE for picture. **4** clothe, cover, or conceal with or as if with a mantle: *mantled in a heavy fur coat, mountaintops mantled with snow, jealousy mantled in an outward friendliness.* **5** become covered with a coating or scum: *The pond has mantled.* **6** a netlike sheath fixed around the flame of a gas lamp, made of a substance that glows with an intense white light when it becomes hot. **7** redden; blush: *Her cheeks mantled.* 1–3, 6 *n.*, 4, 5, 7 *v.,* **man·tled, man·tling.**
☞ *Etym.* From OF *mantel* from L *mantellum* 'cloak'. See also note at MANTEL.
☞ *Hom.* MANTEL.

**man·tra** (man′trə) in many Eastern religions, a word or formula used as an aid to meditation. *n.*

**man·u·al** (man′yü əl) **1** of, having to do with, or using the hands: *manual labour. He has great manual dexterity.* **2** done or operated by hand, not automatically: *The car has a manual choke.* **3** a small book that helps its readers to understand or use something; handbook. **4** an organ keyboard played with the hands. 1, 2 *adj.,* 3, 4 *n.*
☞ *Etym.* The element *manu-* in **manual**, MANUFACTURE, MANUMIT, MANUSCRIPT, and words formed from them can be traced back to L *manus* 'hand'.

**man·u·al·ly** (man′yü ə lē) with or by means of the hand or hands; by using manual labour. *adv.*

**manual training** training in work done with the hands, especially in making things out of wood, metal, or plastic.

**man·u·fac·ture** (man′yə fak′chər) **1** make by hand or by machine: *A big factory manufactures goods in large quantities by using machines and dividing the work up among many people.* **2** the act of manufacturing. **3** the thing manufactured. **4** make into something useful. **5** invent; make up: *The dishonest lawyer manufactured evidence.* 1, 4, 5 *v.,* **man·u·fac·tured, man·u·fac·tur·ing;** 2, 3 *n.*
☞ *Etym.* See note at MANUAL.

**man·u·fac·tur·er** (man′yə fak′chə rər) a person whose business is manufacturing. *n.*

**man·u·mis·sion** (man′yə mish′ən) **1** freeing from slavery. **2** being freed from slavery. *n.*

**man·u·mit** (man′yə mit′) set free from slavery. *v.,* **man·u·mit·ted, man·u·mit·ting.**
☞ *Etym.* See note at MANUAL.

**ma·nure** (mə nyùr′ or mə nùr′) **1** a substance, especially animal waste, put in or on the soil as fertilizer: *The dung from a stable is a kind of manure.* **2** put manure in or on. 1 *n.,* 2 *v.,* **ma·nured, ma·nur·ing.**

**man·u·script** (man′yə skript′) **1** a book or paper written by hand or with a typewriter or computer. **2** handwritten or typewritten condition: *Her last book was*

three years in manuscript. **3** written by hand or with a typewriter or computer. 1–2 *n.*, 3 *adj.*
☞ *Etym.* See note at MANUAL.

**Manx** (mangks) **1** of the Isle of Man, an island off the west coast of England, its people, or their language. **2** the people of the Isle of Man. **3** their language, a Celtic tongue, now extinct. 1 *adj.*, 2, 3 *n.*

**Manx cat** a breed of cat that is tail-less and has a thick undercoat and a longer-haired outer coat.

**man·y** (men′ē) **1** in great number; numerous: *many people, many years ago.* **2** a large number of people or things: *There were many at the fair.* 1 *adj.*, **more, most;** 2 *n.*, *pron.*
**a good many,** a fairly large number.
**a great many,** a very large number.
**one too many for,** more than a match for.
**the many, a** most people. **b** people.

**man·y·plies** (men′ē plīz′) the third stomach of a cow or other ruminant; OMASUM. *n.*

**man·y-sid·ed** (men′ē sī′did) **1** having many sides. **2** having many interests or abilities. *adj.*

**Mao·ri** (mou′rē *or* mä′ō rē) **1** a member of a Polynesian people of New Zealand. **2** the language of these people. **3** of or having to do with the Maoris or their language. 1, 2 *n.*, *pl.* **Ma·o·ris** or **Ma·o·ri;** 3 *adj.*

**map** (map) **1** a drawing representing the earth's surface or part of it, usually showing countries, cities, rivers, seas, lakes, and mountains. **2** a drawing representing part of the sky, showing the position of the stars. **3** make a map of; show on a map. **4** plan; arrange in detail: *to map out the week's work.* 1, 2 *n.*, 3, 4 *v.*, **mapped, map·ping.**
☞ *Syn.* A **map** may refer especially to a plan of road or other routes on land, while CHART is used especially for plans showing air or sea routes. An ATLAS is a book of maps covering a large area or the whole world.

**ma·ple** (mā′pəl) **1** any of a large, closely related group of trees and shrubs found throughout the north temperate regions of the world, having usually lobed leaves that grow in opposite pairs and dry fruits with normally two winglike extensions, each containing a seed: *Two of the most common Canadian maples are the sugar maple and the Manitoba maple.* **2** the light-coloured, hard, close-grained wood of certain maples, valued for making furniture, flooring, etc. **3** referring to a family of trees and shrubs consisting of the maples and several trees of central and southern China: *All the trees of the maple family have winged seeds.* **4** made of or flavoured with maple sugar or syrup: *maple ice cream, maple candy.* *n.*
—**ma′ple-like′,** *adj.*

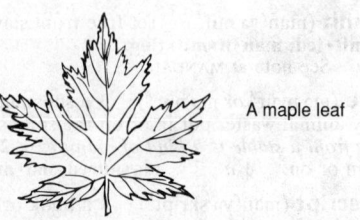
A maple leaf

**maple leaf 1** a leaf of the maple tree. **2** this leaf as a Canadian emblem: *A red maple leaf on a white background is in the centre of the Canadian flag. The song "The Maple Leaf Forever" was written in 1867 by Alexander Muir.*

**maple sugar** sugar made from the sap of the SUGAR MAPLE.

**maple syrup** syrup made from the sap of the SUGAR MAPLE.

**mar** (mär) spoil the beauty of; damage; injure: *The nails in the workmen's shoes have marred our newly finished floors.* *v.*, **marred, mar·ring.**

**mar.** **1** married. **2** marine. **3** maritime.

**Mar.** March.

**mar·a·bou** (mar′ə bü′ *or* mer′ə bü′) **1** a kind of large stork common in Africa and Asia. **2** a furlike trimming made from its soft, downy feathers. *n.*

**ma·ra·ca** (mə rä′kə *or* mə rak′ə) a percussion instrument resembling a rattle, made of a gourd or a gourd-shaped object containing seeds or pebbles: *Maracas are usually played in pairs.* *n.*

**mar·a·schi·no** (mar′ə skē′nō *or* mer′ə skē′nō; mar′ə shē′nō *or* mer′ə shē′nō) a strong, sweet cordial made from a kind of black cherry. *n.*

**maraschino cherries** cherries preserved in a syrup flavoured with MARASCHINO.

**mar·a·thon** (mar′ə thon′ *or* mer′ə thon′) **1** a long-distance foot race, officially measured at 42.195 km: *The marathon is an Olympic event.* **2** any long-distance race or endurance contest: *a marathon swim, a dance marathon.* *n.*
☞ *Etym.* Named after *Marathon,* where the Greeks defeated the Persians in 490 B.C. A Greek messenger ran 37 km from Marathon to Athens to bring news of the victory. The official distance for the Olympic marathon is from a decision by the British Olympic Committee at the 1908 London Games to make the race the distance from Windsor Castle to the royal box at the London Stadium.

**ma·raud** (mə rod′) go about in search of plunder; make raids on for booty. *v.* —**ma·raud′er,** *n.*

**mar·ble** (mär′bəl) **1** a hard limestone, white or coloured, capable of taking a beautiful polish. **2** made of marble. **3** like marble; white, hard, cold, or unfeeling. **4** colour in imitation of the patterns in marble: *The kitchen countertop had a marbled pattern.* **5** a small ball of clay, glass, stone, etc. used in games. **6 marbles, a** any game played with marbles. **b** a collection of sculptures. 1, 5, 6 *n.*, 2, 3 *adj.*, 4 *v.*, **mar·bled, mar·bling.**
—**mar′ble-like′,** *adj.*

**mar·ca·site** (mär′kə sīt′) white IRON PYRITES, a native iron disulphide, similar to and of the same composition as ordinary PYRITES: *Marcasite is often used in jewellery.* *n.*

**march**[1] (märch) **1** walk as soldiers do, with a regular beat and steps of the same length. **2** walk or proceed steadily: *The spy marched bravely to her death.* **3** cause to march or go: *The police officers marched the thief off to jail.* **4** the movement of troops: *The army is prepared for the march.* **5** the act or fact of marching: *The students' march was a great success and earned hundreds of dollars for charity.* **6** music for marching. **7** the distance marched. **8** a long, hard walk. **9** advance; progress: *History records the march of events.* 1–3 *v.*, 4–9 *n.*
—**march′er,** *n.*
**on the march,** moving forward; advancing.
**steal a march on,** gain an advantage over without being noticed.

**march²** (märch) **1** the land along the border of a country; frontier. **2 the Marches,** *pl.* the districts along the border between England and Scotland, or between England and Wales. *n.*

**March** (märch) the third month of the year: *March has 31 days.* *n.*
☛ *Etym.* Through OF from L *Martius* '(the month) of Mars', the Roman god of war.

**mar·chion·ess** (mär′shə nis *or* mär′shə nes′) **1** the wife or widow of a MARQUIS. **2** a lady equal in rank to a MARQUIS. *n.*

**march–past** (märch′past′) a display, especially a military parade, in which troops, etc. march past a reviewing stand. *n.*

**mare** (mer) **1** a female horse, donkey, etc. **2** a female horse that is five years old. *n.*

**mare′s–nest** (merz′nest′) **1** something supposed to be a great discovery that turns out to be a mistake or joke. **2** *Informal.* a situation that is disordered or confused. *n.*

**mare′s–tail** (merz′tāl′) **1** a water plant having many circles of narrow, hairlike leaves around the stems. **2** a high, white filmy cloud, shaped somewhat like a horse's tail: *Mare's-tails are a sign of wind.* *n.*

**mar·ga·rine** (mär′jə rin *or* mär′jə rēn′) a substitute for butter, usually made from vegetable oils; oleomargarine. *n.*

**mar·gin** (mär′jən) **1** an edge or border: *the margin of a lake.* **2** the blank space around the writing or printing on a page. **3** the blank space at the left-hand side, or sometimes on both sides, of a written or printed page: *Do not write in the margin.* **4** an extra amount; amount beyond what is necessary; difference: *a margin of 15 minutes in catching a train.* **5** the difference between the cost and selling price of stocks, etc. **6** the money or security deposited with a broker to protect him or her from loss on contracts undertaken for the real buyer or seller. **7** provide with a margin. 1–6 *n.*, 7 *v.*

**mar·gin·al** (mär′jə nəl) **1** written or printed in a MARGIN (def. 2). **2** of a MARGIN (def. 1), edge, or border: *marginal forests.* **3** barely useful, acceptable, or profitable: *marginal knowledge, marginal land.* *adj.*

**mar·gin·al·ly** (mär′jə nə lē) **1** in the MARGIN. **2** slightly: *She is marginally better today.* *adv.*

**mar·grave** (mär′grāv) **1** the title of certain princes of the Holy Roman Empire. **2** a German nobleman whose rank corresponds to that of a MARQUIS. **3** formerly, a German military governor of a border province. *n.*

**mar·gue·rite** (mär′gə rēt′) a kind of daisy having white or pale-yellow petals and a yellow centre. *n.*

**mar·i·gold** (mar′ə gōld′ *or* mer′ə gōld′) **1** a plant of the same family as the aster, with yellow, orange, or red flowers. **2** the flower of this plant. *n.*

**mar·i·jua·na** *or* **mar·i·hua·na** (mar′ə wä′nə *or* mer′ə wä′nə) **1** HEMP. **2** the dried leaves and flower clusters of the female HEMP plant, especially when smoked as a cigarette for its intoxicating effect. *n.*

march 729 maritime

hat, āge, fär; let, ēqual, tėrm; it, īce
hot, ōpen, ôrder; oil, out; cup, put, rüle
əbove, takən, pencəl, lemən, circəs
ch, child; ng, long; sh, ship
th, thin; ᴛʜ, then; zh, measure

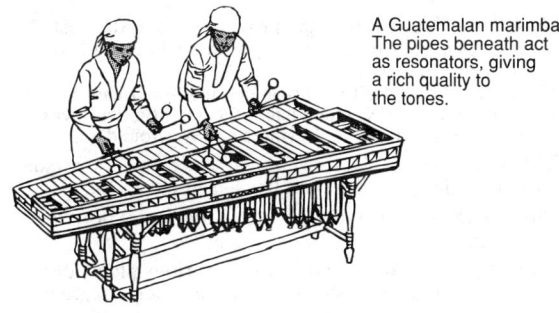

A Guatemalan marimba. The pipes beneath act as resonators, giving a rich quality to the tones.

**ma·rim·ba** (mə rim′bə) a musical instrument resembling a xylophone. *n.*

**ma·ri·na** (mə rē′nə) a place along a waterfront where boats may be moored and where fuel and equipment may be bought: *One can buy boats at some marinas.* *n.*
☛ *Etym.* See note at MARINE.

**mar·i·nade** (mar′ə nād′ *or* mer′ə nād′ *for noun,* mar′ə nād′ *or* mer′ə nād′ *for verb*) **1** a spiced vinegar or wine used to pickle meat or fish. **2** meat or fish pickled in this. **3** MARINATE. 1, 2 *n.*, 3 *v.*, **mar·i·nad·ed, mar·i·nad·ing.**

**mar·i·nate** (mar′ə nāt′ *or* mer′ə nāt′) **1** soak in brine or MARINADE (def. 1). **2** soak in oil and vinegar. *v.*, **mar·i·nat·ed, mar·i·nat·ing.**

**ma·rine** (mə rēn′) **1** of the sea; found in the sea; produced by the sea: *marine animals.* **2** of shipping: *marine law.* **3** of a navy: *marine power.* **4** for use at sea, on a ship: *marine supplies, marine engine.* **5** shipping; a fleet: *our merchant marine.* **6** a soldier formerly serving only at sea, now also participating in land and air action: *Canada has no marines.* **7** a picture showing a sea scene. 1–4 *adj.*, 5–7 *n.*
☛ *Etym.* MARINA, **marine,** MARINER, and MARITIME all come originally through Italian, French, or Latin forms, from L *mare* (mä′re) 'sea'.

**mar·i·ner** (mar′ə nər *or* mer′ə nər) a sailor or seaman; one who navigates a ship. *n.*
☛ *Etym.* See note at MARINE.

**mar·i·o·nette** (mar′ē ə net′ *or* mer′ē ə net′) a small doll or puppet made to imitate a person or an animal and moved by strings: *A marionette show is often given on a miniature stage.* See PUPPET for picture. *n.*

**Mar·i·po·sa lily** (mar′ə pō′sə *or* mer′ə pō′sə) **1** a plant having tuliplike flowers and growing in western North America. **2** the flower of this plant.

**mar·i·tal** (mar′ə təl *or* mer′ə təl) of marriage; having to do with marriage: *marital vows.* *adj.*
—**mar′i·tal·ly,** *adv.*

**mar·i·time** (mar′ə tīm′ *or* mer′ə tīm′) **1** on or near the sea: *Halifax is a maritime city.* **2** living near the sea: *Many maritime peoples live from fishing.* **3** of the sea; having to do with shipping and sailing: *Ships and sailors are governed by maritime law.* **4 Maritime,** of or having to do with the MARITIME PROVINCES. *adj.*
☛ *Etym.* See note at MARINE.

**Maritime Command** *Cdn.* the branch of the Canadian Armed Forces having to do with ships of war and their officers and men, formerly known as the Royal Canadian Navy.

**Maritime Provinces** the provinces along the east coast of Canada, especially New Brunswick, Nova Scotia, and Prince Edward Island.
☞ *Usage.* The **Maritime Provinces** and **Maritimes** do not usually include Newfoundland; the **Atlantic Provinces** include the Maritime Provinces and Newfoundland.

**Mar·i·tim·er** (mar′ə tī′mər *or* mer′ə tī′mər) a person born in or living in the MARITIME PROVINCES. *n.*

**Mar·i·times** (mar′ə timz′ *or* mer′ə tīmz′) MARITIME PROVINCES. *n.*

**mar·jo·ram** (mär′jə rəm) any of various plants of the mint family, especially **sweet marjoram**, whose fragrant leaves are used for flavouring in cooking. *n.*

**mark**¹ (märk) **1** a trace or impression made by some object on the surface of another: *A line, dot, spot, stain, or scar is a mark.* **2** make a mark on by stamping, cutting, writing, etc.: *Be careful not to mark the table.* **3** an object, arrow, line, dot, etc. put as a guide or sign: *a mark for pilots, the starting mark in a race, a question mark.* **4** show by means of a sign: *Mark all the large cities on this map. This post marks the city limits.* **5** something that indicates quality or characteristic; label: *Remove the price mark from your new suit. Courtesy is a mark of good breeding.* **6** put a sign on an article, as a tag, label, brand or seal, to show the price, quality, maker or owner. **7** show clearly; make plain: *A tall pine marks the beginning of the trail. A frown marked her displeasure.* **8** set off; give interest or importance to: *Many important inventions mark the last 150 years.* **9** a cross or other sign made by a person who cannot write, instead of signing his or her name: *Make your mark here.* **10** a letter or number to show how well one has done; grade or rating: *My mark in arithmetic was B.* **11** give grades to; rate: *The teacher marked our examination papers.* **12** something to be aimed at; target; goal: *Standing there, the lion was an easy mark.* **13** what is usual, proper, or expected; standard: *A tired person does not feel up to the mark.* **14** give attention to; notice; observe; see: *Mark how carefully she moves. Mark well my words.* **15** influence; impression: *A great woman leaves her mark on whatever she does.* **16** keep the score; record. **17** select as if by mark: *She was marked for promotion.* **18** PLIMSOLL MARK. 1, 3, 5, 9, 10, 12, 13, 15, 18 *n.*, 2, 4, 6–8, 11, 14, 16, 17 *v.*
**beside the mark,** a not hitting the thing aimed at. **b** not to the point; not relevant.
**hit the mark,** a succeed in doing what one tried to do. **b** be exactly right.
**make one's mark,** succeed; become famous.
**mark down,** a write down; note down. **b** mark for sale at a lower price.
**mark off** *or* **out,** make lines, etc. to show the position of or to separate.
**mark out for,** set aside for; select for.
**mark time,** a move the feet as in marching, but remaining in the same spot. **b** suspend progress temporarily. **c** go through motions without accomplishing anything.
**mark up,** a spoil the look of by making marks on: *Don't mark up the desks.* **b** mark for sale at a higher price. **c** prepare a manuscript for typesetting.
**miss the mark,** a fail to do what one tried to do. **b** be not exactly right.

**of mark,** important or famous: *That doctor is a woman of mark.*
**wide of the mark,** a missing the thing aimed at by a considerable margin. **b** irrelevant.

**marked** (märkt) **1** having a mark or marks on it. **2** very noticeable; very clear; easily recognized: *There is a marked difference between a grape and an orange.* **3** pt. and pp. of MARK. 1, 2 *adj.*, 3 *v.*

**mark·ed·ly** (mär′ki dlē) in a marked manner or degree; conspicuously; noticeably; plainly. *adv.*

**marked man** a person, such as a suspected criminal, who is picked out as someone to watch or take action against: *After he was reported as having been near the scene of the murder, John was a marked man.*

**mark·er** (mär′kər) **1** a person or thing that marks. **2** a person or thing that keeps the score in a game. **3** bookmark. *n.*

**mar·ket** (mär′kit) **1** a meeting of people for the purpose of buying and selling: *There is a fruit and vegetable market here every Saturday.* **2** a space or building in which provisions, cattle, etc. are shown for sale. **3** buy or sell in a market. **4** sell: *She cannot market the goods she makes.* **5** carry or send to market. **6** shop at a grocery store or supermarket; buy food. **7** a store for the sale of provisions: *a meat market.* **8** trade, especially as regards a particular article: *the wheat market.* **9** the opportunity to buy or sell: *to lose one's market.* **10** the demand for goods: *There was not enough cheese to supply the market.* **11** a region where goods can be sold: *China is a market for wheat.* 1, 2, 7–11 *n.*, 3–6 *v.*
—**mar′ket·er,** *n.*
**be in the market for,** be a possible buyer of: *She is in the market for a new bike.*
**play the market,** speculate on the stock exchange.

**mar·ket·a·bil·i·ty** (mär′ki tə bil′ə tē) the quality of being MARKETABLE. *n.*

**mar·ket·a·ble** (mär′ki tə bəl) that can be sold; salable. *adj.*

**market garden** a farm where vegetables are grown for market. —**market gardener,** *n.* —**market gardening,** *n.*

**mar·ket·place** (mär′kit plās′) **1** a place where a market is held. **2** the world of business and commerce. *n.*

**mark·ing** (mär′king) **1** a mark or marks. **2** the arrangement of marks: *I like the marking on your cat's coat.* **3** ppr. of MARK. 1, 2 *n.*, 3 *v.*

**marks·man** (märks′mən) a person who shoots, especially one who shoots well: *She is a noted marksman.* *n.*, *pl.* **marks·men** (-smən).

**marks·man·ship** (märks′mən ship′) skill in shooting. *n.*

**mark·up** (mär′kup′) the difference between the cost and the selling price of an article: *If a store buys a bicycle for $500 and adds a markup of $200, a customer will be able to buy the bicycle for $700.* *n.*

**marl** (märl) soil containing clay and calcium carbonate, used in making cement and as a fertilizer. *n.*

**mar·lin** (mär′lən) a large sea fish related to the sailfish. *n.*
☞ *Hom.* MARLINE.

**mar·line** (mär′lən) a small cord that sailors wind around the ends of a rope to keep it from fraying. *n.*
☞ *Hom.* MARLIN.

A marlinspike. The drawing at the right shows a marlinspike being used to separate strands of rope.

**mar·line·spike** or **mar·lin·spike** (mär′lən spīk′)   a pointed iron implement used by sailors to separate strands of rope in splicing, etc.   *n.*

**mar·ma·lade** (mär′mə lād′)   a preserve like jam, made of oranges or similar fruit: *In making marmalade, the peel is usually sliced and boiled with the fruit.*   *n.*

**mar·mo·re·al** (mär môr′ē əl)   **1** of marble.   **2** like marble; cold; smooth; white.   *adj.*

**mar·mo·set** (mär′mə set′ *or* mär′mə zet′)   a very small monkey having soft, thick fur: *Marmosets live in Central and South America.*   *n.*

**mar·mot** (mär′mət)   a rodent having a thick body and a bushy tail: *Groundhogs, or woodchucks, and prairie dogs are marmots.*   *n.*

**ma·roon**[1] (mə rün′)   dark brownish-red.   *adj., n.*

**ma·roon**[2] (mə rün′)   **1** put a person ashore in a lonely place and leave him or her there: *Pirates used to maroon people on desert islands.*   **2** leave in a lonely, helpless position.   *v.*

**mar·quee** (mär kē′)   **1** a large tent, often one put up for some outdoor entertainment.   **2** a rooflike shelter over an entrance.   *n.*

**mar·quess** (mär′kwis) *Esp. Brit.*   MARQUIS.   *n.*

**mar·quis** (mär′kwis *or* mär kē′)   a nobleman ranking below a duke and above an earl or count.   *n.* Also, **marquess.**

**mar·quise** (mär kēz′) *French.*   **1** the wife or widow of a MARQUIS.   **2** a woman equal in rank to a MARQUIS.   **3** a gem of a pointed oval shape, or a ring set with such a stone.   *n.*

**mar·riage** (mar′ij *or* mer′ij)   **1** married life; living together as husband and wife: *We wished the bride and groom a happy marriage.*   **2** the ceremony of being married; marrying; wedding.   **3** a close union: *the marriage of words and melody.*

**mar·riage·a·bil·i·ty** (mar′i jə bil′ə tē *or* mer′i jə bil′ə tē)   the state of being MARRIAGEABLE.   *n.*

**mar·riage·a·ble** (mar′i jə bəl *or* mer′i jə bəl)   fit for marriage; old enough to marry: *of marriageable age, a marriageable daughter.*   *adj.*

**marriage portion**   DOWRY.

**mar·ried** (mar′ēd *or* mer′ēd)   **1** living together as husband and wife.   **2** having a husband or wife.   **3** of marriage; of husbands and wives: *Married life has many duties.*   **4** closely united: *The painter was married to her art.*   **5** pt. and pp. of MARRY.   1–4 *adj.*, 5 *v.*
**married with,**   combined with: *The author's sensitivity is married with wit in this book.*

**mar·row** (mar′ō *or* mer′ō)   **1** the soft tissue that fills the cavities of most bones.   **2** the inmost or essential part: *The icy wind chilled me to the marrow.*   *n.*

**mar·row·bone** (mar′ō bōn′ *or* mer′ō bōn′)   **1** a bone containing MARROW[1] (def. 1).   *n.*

**mar·row·fat** (mar′ō fat′ *or* mer′ō fat′)   a kind of pea that has a large seed.   *n.*

**mar·ry** (mar′ē *or* mer′ē)   **1** join as husband and wife: *The minister married them.*   **2** take as husband or wife: *John planned to marry Grace.*   **3** become married; take a husband or wife: *She married late in life.*   **4** give in marriage (*often used with* **off**): *They married their daughter off to a young lawyer.*   **5** unite closely.   *v.*, **mar·ried, mar·ry·ing.**
☞ *Hom.*   MERRY (for the second pronunciation of **marry**).

**Mars** (märz)   the planet next beyond the earth: *Mars is the fourth planet in order from the sun.*   *n.*
☞ *Etym.*   From *Mars*, the Roman god of war.

**marsh** (märsh)   an area of wet, muddy land sometimes partly covered with water and having plant life that consists mainly of grasses and sedges.   *n.*

**mar·shal** (mär′shəl)   **1** any of various kinds of officer: *a fire marshal.*   **2** in certain armies, an officer of a high rank: *a field marshal.*   **3** a person who arranges the order of march in a parade: *a parade marshal.*   **4** arrange or order properly or effectively: *She spent a lot of time marshalling her arguments for the debate.*   **5** a person in charge of events or ceremonies.   **6** conduct with ceremony: *We were marshalled before the queen.*   1–3, 5 *n.*, 4, 6 *v.*, **mar·shalled** or **mar·shaled, mar·shal·ling** or **mar·shal·ing.**
☞ *Hom.*   MARTIAL.

**marsh gas**   METHANE.

**marsh·mal·low** (märsh′mal′ō *or* märsh′mel′ō)   **1** a soft, spongy confection originally made from the root of the MARSH MALLOW, now made from corn syrup, sugar, gelatin, and flavouring.   **2** a piece of this confection, covered with powdered sugar: *a bag of marshmallows.*   *n.*

**marsh mallow**   a perennial herb of the mallow family native to Europe, Asia, and northern Africa, found in marshy areas, having toothed leaves and pink flowers and a root that secretes a gummy substance originally used to make MARSHMALLOW: *The marsh mallow has become naturalized in eastern North America.*

**marsh marigold**   a plant of the buttercup family with yellow flowers and round leaves.

**marsh·y** (mär′shē)   **1** soft and wet like a marsh: *a marshy field.*   **2** having many marshes.   **3** of marshes.   *adj.*, **marsh·i·er, marsh·i·est.**   —**marsh′i·ness,** *n.*

**mar·su·pi·al** (mär sü′pē əl)   **1** an animal the female of which carries her young in a pouch: *Kangaroos and opossums are marsupials.*   **2** of marsupials.   **3** having a pouch for carrying the young.   1 *n.*, 2, 3 *adj.*

**mar·su·pi·um** (mär sü′pē əm)   a pouch or fold of skin on the abdomen of a female MARSUPIAL (def. 1), for carrying the young.   *n., pl.* **mar·su·pi·a** (-pē ə).

**mart** (märt)   a market; centre of trade: *Toronto and Vancouver are the great marts of Canada.*

**mar·ten** (mär′tən)   **1** any of several closely related species of small flesh-eating mammals related to the weasels, but larger, having a long, slender body and short legs: *Martens spend most of their time in trees and are active*

mainly at night. **2** the valuable fur of marten. *n., pl.* **mar·tens** or *(esp. collectively)* **mar·ten.**
☞ *Hom.* MARTIN.

**mar·tial** (mär′shəl) **1** of war; suitable for war: *martial music.* **2** fond of fighting; warlike; brave: *a man of martial spirit.* *adj.* —**mar′tial·ly,** *adv.*
☞ *Hom.* MARSHAL.

**martial law** rule by the army or militia with special military courts instead of by the usual civil authorities: *Martial law is declared during a time of trouble or war.* Compare with MILITARY LAW.

**Mar·tian** (mär′shən) **1** of the planet Mars. **2** a supposed inhabitant of the planet Mars. 1 *adj.,* 2 *n.*

**mar·tin** (mär′tən) any of various swallows, such as the **purple martin** of the Western Hemisphere, which has a forked tail and stout bill, the adult male having dark, glossy, purplish-blue plumage. *n.*
☞ *Hom.* MARTEN.

**mar·ti·net** (mär′tə net′) a person who enforces very strict discipline. *n.*

**mar·tin·gale** (mär′tən gāl′) **1** the strap of a horse's harness that prevents the horse from rising on its hind legs or throwing back its head. **2** a rope or spar that steadies the jib boom on a ship. See BOWSPRIT for picture. *n.*

**mar·tyr** (mär′tər) **1** a person who chooses to die or suffer rather than renounce his or her faith; a person who is put to death or made to suffer greatly for his or her religion or other beliefs: *Mrs. Pankhurst was a martyr for women's rights.* **2** put a person to death or torture because of his or her religion or other beliefs. **3** a person who suffers great pain or anguish. **4** cause to suffer greatly; torture. **5** a person who puts on a false appearance of suffering in order to attract sympathy or attention. 1, 3, 5 *n.,* 2, 4 *v.* —**mar′tyr·like′,** *adj.*

**mar·tyr·dom** (mär′tər dəm) **1** the death or suffering of a MARTYR (def. 1). **2** great suffering; torment. *n.*

**mar·vel** (mär′vəl) **1** something wonderful; an astonishing thing: *Television and the airplane are among the marvels of invention.* **2** be filled with wonder; be astonished: *She marvelled at the beautiful sunset.* 1 *n.,* 2 *v.,* **mar·velled** or **mar·veled, mar·vel·ling** or **mar·vel·ing.**

**mar·vel·lous** or **mar·vel·ous** (mär′və ləs) **1** causing wonder; extraordinary. **2** improbable; imaginative: *Children like hearing of marvellous events, such as those in the tale of Aladdin and his lamp.* **3** *Informal.* excellent; splendid; fine: *a marvellous time.* *adj.*
—**mar′vel·lous·ly** or **mar′vel·ous·ly,** *adv.*
—**mar′vel·lous·ness** or **mar′vel·ous·ness,** *n.*

**Marx·i·an** (märk′sē ən) **1** of Karl Marx or his theories. **2** MARXIST. 1 *adj.,* 2 *n.*

**Marx·ism** (märk′siz əm) the theories of Karl Marx. *n.*

**Marx·ist** (märk′sist) **1** a follower or disciple of Karl Marx. **2** a believer in Marxism. **3** of Karl Marx, his theories, or his followers. 1, 2 *n.,* 3 *adj.*

**mar·zi·pan** (mär′zə pan′) a paste of ground almonds and sugar, often moulded into various forms. *n.*

**masc.** masculine.

**mas·car·a** (mas kar′ə *or* mas ker′ə) a preparation used for colouring the eyelashes. *n.*

**mas·cot** (mas′kot) an animal, person, or thing supposed to bring good luck: *The girls kept the stray dog as a mascot.* *n.*

**mas·cu·line** (mas′kyə lin) **1** of men; male. **2** like a man; manly; strong; vigorous: *masculine courage.* **3** having qualities suited to a man; mannish. **4** in grammar, of the gender of male names: *King, ram, and bull are masculine nouns.* **5** the masculine gender. **6** a word or form in the masculine gender. 1–4 *adj.,* 5, 6 *n.*
—**mas′cu·line·ly,** *adv.*

**mas·cu·lin·i·ty** (mas′kyə lin′ə tē) a MASCULINE quality or condition. *n.*

**ma·ser** (mā′zər) a device for amplifying microwaves to produce a very narrow, intense beam of radiation. *n.*
☞ *Etym.* From the first letters of *m*icrowave *a*mplification by *s*timulated *e*mission of *r*adiation.

**mash** (mash) **1** a soft mixture; a soft mass. **2** beat into a soft mass; crush to a uniform mass. **3** a warm mixture of bran or meal and water for horses and other animals. **4** crushed malt or meal soaked in hot water for making beer. **5** a similar preparation of rye, corn, barley, etc., used to make whisky. **6** mix crushed malt or meal with hot water in brewing. 1, 3–5 *n.,* 2, 6 *v.*
—**mash′er,** *n.*

**mask** (mask) **1** a covering for the face, worn for disguise or in fun: *a Halloween mask.* **2** cover the face with a mask. **3** a masked person. **4** anything that hides or disguises: *a mask of friendship.* **5** hide; disguise: *A smile masked her disappointment.* **6** a covering for the face, worn for protection from cold, etc.: *a ski mask.* **7** a covering for the nose and mouth, worn for protection against infection: *a surgical mask.* **8** a device covering the nose and mouth, designed to aid breathing, purify air before it is inhaled, etc.: *a gas mask, an oxygen mask.* **9** a clay, wax, or plaster likeness of a person's face. 1, 3, 4, 6–9 *n.,* 2, 5 *v.* —**mask′er,** *n.*
☞ *Hom.* MASQUE.

**masked** (maskt) **1** wearing a mask: *a masked dancer.* **2** hidden or disguised; not apparent: *masked jealousy.* **3** pt. and pp. of MASK. 1, 2 *adj.,* 3 *v.*

**masked ball** a dance at which masks are worn.

**mas·kin·onge** (mas′kə nonj′) *Cdn.* MUSKELLUNGE. *n., pl.* **mas·kin·onge.**
☞ *Etym.* Through Cdn.F *masquinongé* from Cree *mashkkinonche* 'great pike'. Compare with note at MUSKELLUNGE.
☞ *Usage.* Maskinonge is the official Canadian name for this fish, though MUSKELLUNGE is now the more common term.

**mas·och·ism** (mas′ə kiz′əm *or* maz′ə kiz′əm) a tendency to experience pleasure from being hurt. *n.*

**ma·son** (mā′sən) a person whose work is building with stone, brick, or similar materials. *n.*

**Mason jar** a wide-mouthed glass jar with a top that screws on, used especially for home canning and preserving.
☞ *Etym.* Named after John L. *Mason,* a 19c. American inventor who patented such a jar.

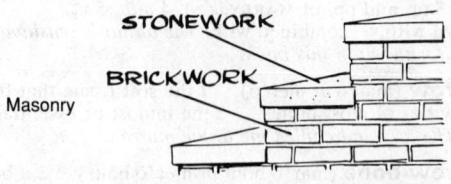
Masonry

**ma·son·ry** (mā′sən rē) **1** the work done by a mason;

stonework, brickwork, etc. **2** something constructed of stone, brick, etc., such as a chimney or wall. **3** the trade or skill of a mason. *n., pl.* **ma·son·ries**.

**masque** (mask) **1** an amateur dramatic entertainment in which fine costumes, scenery, music, and dancing are more important than the story: *Masques were often given in England in the 16th and 17th centuries, at court and at the homes of nobles.* **2** the play written for such an entertainment. **3** a masked ball; masquerade. *n.* ☛ *Hom.* MASK.

**mas·quer·ade** (mas′kə rād′) **1** a party or dance at which masks and fancy costumes are worn. **2** take part in a masquerade. **3** a false pretence; disguise. **4** disguise oneself; go about under false pretences: *The king masqueraded as a beggar to find out if his people really liked him.* 1, 3 *n.*, 2, 4 *v.*, **mas·quer·ad·ed**, **mas·quer·ad·ing**. —**mas′quer·ad′er**, *n.*

**mass**[1] (mas) **1** a lump: *a mass of dough.* **2** a large quantity together: *a mass of flowers.* **3** form or collect into a mass; assemble: *It would look better to mass the peonies behind the roses than to mix them.* **4** the majority; greater part: *The great mass of people consider themselves sensible.* **5** on a large scale: *mass buying.* **6** bulk; size: *the huge mass of an iceberg.* **7** in physics, a measure of the amount of matter a body contains: *The bigger the mass of an object, the more force is needed to give it a particular acceleration. The mass of water is not changed by freezing it or changing it into steam, even though the volume changes.* **8** a piece of metal having a specified mass, used to weigh something on a balance. **9 the masses**, the people; the general population: *Most television programs are entertainment for the masses.* 1, 2, 4–9 *n.*, 3 *v.*

**Mass** or **mass**[2] (mas) **1** the central service of worship in the Roman Catholic Church and in some other churches. **2** a piece of music written for or suggested by certain parts of the Mass. *n.*

**mas·sa·cre** (mas′ə kər) **1** a wholesale, pitiless slaughter of people or animals. **2** kill many people or animals needlessly or cruelly; slaughter in large numbers. 1 *n.*, 2 *v.*, **mas·sa·cred**, **mas·sa·cring**.

**mas·sage** (mə säzh′ *or* mə säj′) **1** a rubbing and kneading of the body to stimulate the circulation of blood and make the muscles and joints more supple: *A thorough massage relaxes tired muscles.* **2** give a massage to. 1 *n.*, 2 *v.*, **mas·saged**, **mas·sag·ing**.

**mas·sa·sau·ga** (mas′ə sog′ə) a small rattlesnake found in southern Ontario and the eastern United States. *n.*

**mas·seur** (ma sėr′) a man whose work is massaging: *Boxers and many other athletes use the services of a masseur regularly.* *n.*

**mas·seuse** (ma sėz′) a woman whose work is massaging. *n.*

**mas·sive** (mas′iv) **1** big and heavy; large and solid; bulky: *a massive wrestler.* **2** giving the impression of being large and broad: *a massive forehead.* **3** imposing; impressive. *adj.* —**mas′sive·ly**, *adv.* —**mas′sive·ness**, *n.*

**mass media** the various modern means of communication that reach a vast audience, such as television, radio, motion pictures, and the press.

**mass meeting** a large public gathering of people to hear or discuss some matter of common interest: *The school held a mass meeting to plan for a field day.*

**mass number** in physics and chemistry, the whole number that most closely indicates the mass of an isotope, equal to the sum of the protons and neutrons in the nucleus.

**mass–pro·duce** (mas′prə dyüs′ *or* mas′prə düs′) make or manufacture anything by MASS PRODUCTION. *v.*, **mass-pro·duced**, **mass-pro·duc·ing**.

**mass production** the making of goods in large quantities by machinery.

**mass·y** (mas′ē) MASSIVE. *adj.*, **mass·i·er**, **mass·i·est**. —**mass′i·ness**, *n.*

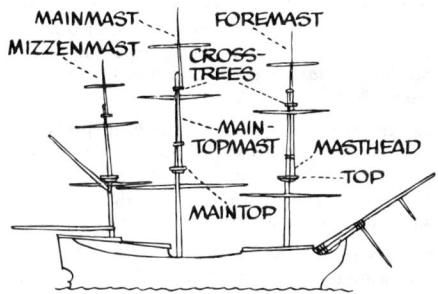

**mast**[1] (mast) **1** a long pole of wood or metal set upright on a ship to support the sails and rigging. **2** any upright pole: *a flag mast, a television mast.* *n.* —**mast′less**, *adj.* —**mast′like**, *adj.*

**before the mast**, serving as an ordinary sailor, because sailors (not officers) used to sleep in the forward part of the ship.

**mast**[2] (mast) acorns, chestnuts, beechnuts, etc. on the ground: *Pigs eat mast.* *n.*

**mas·ter** (mas′tər) **1** a person who has power or authority; one in control; employer; owner. **2** the man at the head of a household. **3** the captain of a merchant ship. **4** a male teacher, especially in private schools. **5** a great artist. **6** a picture or painting by a great artist: *an old master.* **7** a person who knows all about his or her work; expert. **8** a skilled worker, or craftsperson, qualified to teach apprentices. **9** a title of respect of a boy: *Master Henry Adams.* **10** of or by a master. **11** main; controlling: *a master switch, a master plan.* **12** See MASTER KEY. **13** become the master of; conquer: *Learn to master your temper.* **14** become expert in; become skilful at: *She has mastered riding her bicycle.* **15** victor. **16** a court officer appointed to assist the judge. **17** an initial recording, mould, stencil, etc. used for making duplications. 1–12, 15–17 *n.*, 13, 14 *v.*

**mas·ter-at-arms** (mas′tə rə tärmz′) in the navy, a police officer who keeps order on a ship and takes charge of prisoners. *n., pl.* **mas·ters-at-arms**.

**master builder** **1** a person skilled in planning buildings; architect. **2** a person who directs the construction of buildings; contractor.

**mas·ter·ful** (mas′tər fəl) **1** fond of power or authority; domineering. **2** expert; skilful; masterly: *The actor gave a masterful performance.* *adj.* —**mas′ter·ful·ly**, *adv.*

**master key** a key that opens all the different locks in a building, apartment block, etc.; passkey.

**mas·ter·ly** (mas′tər lē) expert; skilful: *Emily Carr was a masterly painter.* *adj.* —**mas′ter·li·ness,** *n.*

**mas·ter·mind** (mas′tər mīnd′) 1 a person who plans and directs a complex project. 2 plan and direct a complex project. 1 *n.*, 2 *v.*

**master of ceremonies** a person in charge of a ceremony or entertainment who announces the successive events and makes sure that they take place in the proper order.

**mas·ter·piece** (mas′tər pēs′) 1 anything done or made with wonderful skill; a perfect piece of art or workmanship. 2 a person's greatest work. *n.*

**master stroke** a very skilful act or achievement.

**mas·ter·y** (mas′tə rē) 1 power such as a master has; rule; control. 2 the upper hand; victory: *Two teams competed for mastery.* 3 great skill; expert knowledge: *Our teacher has a mastery of many subjects.* *n., pl.* **mas·ter·ies.**

**mast·head** (mast′hed′) 1 the top of a ship's mast: *A crow's-nest near the masthead of the lower mast is used as a lookout.* See MAST for picture. 2 the part of a newspaper or magazine that gives the title, the names of the owners and editors, and the publication address. *n.*

**mas·tic** (mas′tik) 1 a yellowish resin used in making varnish, chewing gum, and incense, and as an astringent. 2 any of various cements or mortars. *n.*

**mas·ti·cate** (mas′tə kāt′) CHEW (def. 1). *v.*, **mas·ti·cat·ed, mas·ti·cat·ing.** —**mas′ti·ca′tion,** *n.* —**mas′ti·ca′tor,** *n.*

**mas·ti·ca·to·ry** (mas′tə kə tô′rē) 1 of chewing; used in chewing. 2 a substance chewed to increase the flow of saliva. 1 *adj.*, 2 *n., pl.* **mas·ti·ca·to·ries.**

**mas·tiff** (mas′tif) a large, strong dog with drooping ears and hanging jowls. *n.*

**mas·to·don** (mas′tə don′) an extinct animal that resembled an elephant. *n.*

**mas·toid** (mas′toid) the projection of bone behind the ear. *n.*

**mas·toid·i·tis** (mas′toi dī′tis) inflammation of the MASTOID. *n.*

**mat¹** (mat) 1 a piece of coarse fabric like a rug, made of woven grass, straw, rope, etc. 2 a piece of material to put under a dish, vase, lamp, etc. 3 cover with mats. 4 anything packed or tangled thickly together: *a mat of weeds, a mat of hair.* 5 pack or tangle together like a mat: *The swimmer's wet hair was matted. The fur collar mats when it gets wet.* 6 a large, thick pad laid on the floor to protect wrestlers or gymnasts. 1, 2, 4, 6 *n.*, 3, 5 —*v.*, **mat·ted, mat·ting.**

**mat²** (mat) a border or background for a picture, between it and the frame. *n.*

**mat³** (mat) 1 dull; not shiny. 2 a dull surface or finish. 3 give a dull finish to. 1 *adj.*, 2 *n.*, 3 *v.*, **mat·ted, mat·ting.**

**mat·a·dor** (mat′ə dôr′) the chief performer in a bullfight: *The matador kills the bull with his sword.* *n.*

**match¹** (mach) 1 a short, slender piece of wood or pasteboard tipped with a mixture that takes fire when rubbed on a specially prepared surface. 2 a cord prepared to burn at a uniform rate, for firing guns and cannon. *n.*

**match²** (mach) 1 a person or thing equal to another: *A girl is not a match for a woman.* 2 be equal to; be a match for: *No one could match the unknown archer.* 3 a person or thing like another. 4 two persons or things that are alike and go well together: *Those two horses make a good match.* 5 be alike; go well together: *The rugs and the wallpaper match.* 6 be the same as. 7 find one like; get a match for. 8 make like; fit together. 9 a game or contest: *a boxing match, a tennis match.* 10 put in opposition; oppose: *Tom matched his strength against Dick's.* 11 marriage: *James and Ida made a match of it.* 12 marry: *The duke matched his daughter with the king's son.* 13 a person considered as a possible husband or wife: *That young man was considered a good match.* 1, 3, 4, 9, 11, 13 *n.*, 2, 5–8, 10, 12 *v.* —**match′er,** *n.*

**match·less** (mach′lis) so great or wonderful that it cannot be equalled. *adj.* —**match′less·ly,** *adv.*

**match·lock** (mach′lok′) an old type of gun fired by lighting the charge of powder with a wick or cord. *n.*

**match·mak·er** (mach′mā′kər) 1 a person who arranges, or tries to arrange, marriages for others. 2 a person who arranges contests, prize fights, races, etc. *n.*

**match·mak·ing** (mach′mā′king) 1 the practice of trying to arrange marriages. 2 having to do with matchmakers or matchmaking. 1 *n.*, 2 *adj.*

**match·wood** (mach′wùd′) 1 wood for making matches. 2 splinters; tiny pieces. *n.*

**mate¹** (māt) 1 one of a pair: *Where is the mate to this glove?* 2 either of two animals or birds (male and female) who have come together as a pair: *The eagle mourned her dead mate.* 3 put, bring, or come together as a pair: *Birds mate in the spring.* 4 a husband or wife. 5 marry. 6 a ship's officer next below the captain: *On large ships there is usually more than one mate: a first mate, a second mate, and, sometimes, a third mate.* 7 assistant: *cook's mate.* 8 a companion or fellow worker: *Ari and Rajiv were mates in the army.* 1, 2, 4, 6–8 *n.*, 3, 5 *v.*, **mat·ed, mat·ing.**

**mate²** (māt) in chess, checkmate; defeat. *n., v.*, **mat·ed, mat·ing.**

**ma·té** or **ma·te³** (mä′tā) 1 a kind of tea made from the dried leaves of a South American plant. 2 the plant. 3 its leaves. *n.*

**ma·te·ri·al** (mə tē′rē əl) 1 what is used to make or do something: *dress material, building materials, writing materials, the material of which history is made.* 2 of matter or things; physical: *the material world.* 3 of the body: *Food and shelter are material comforts.* 4 caring too much for the things of this world and neglecting spiritual needs: *a material point of view.* 5 that matters; important: *Hard work was a material factor in her success.* 6 written or printed material; information; documents. 1, 6 *n.*, 2–5 *adj.*

**ma·te·ri·al·ism** (mə tē′rē ə liz′əm) 1 the belief that all action, thought, and feeling can be explained by the movements and changes of matter. 2 a tendency to care too much for the things of this world and to neglect spiritual needs. *n.*

**ma·te·ri·al·ist** (mə tē′rē ə list) 1 a believer in MATERIALISM (def. 1). 2 a person who cares too much for the things of this world and neglects spiritual needs. *n.*

**ma·te·ri·al·is·tic** (mə tē′rē ə lis′tik) of MATERIALISM; of MATERIALISTS. *adj.* —**ma·te′ri·al·is′ti·cal·ly**, *adv.*

**ma·te·ri·al·ize** (mə tē′rē ə līz′) **1** become an actual fact; be realized: *Our plan for the party did not materialize.* **2** give material form to: *An inventor materializes her ideas by building a model.* **3** appear or cause to appear in material or bodily form: *A spirit materialized from the smoke of the magician's fire.* *v.*, **ma·te·ri·al·ized**, **ma·te·ri·al·iz·ing**. —**ma·te′ri·al·i·za′tion**, *n.*

**ma·te·ri·al·ly** (mə tē′rē ə lē) **1** with regard to material things; physically: *She improved materially and morally.* **2** considerably; greatly: *The tide helped the progress of the boat materially.* **3** in matter or substance; not in form. *adv.*

**ma·te·ri·a med·i·ca** (mə tē′rē ə med′ə kə) **1** drugs or other substances used in medicine. **2** the branch of medical science dealing with these drugs and substances.

**ma·té·ri·el** (mə tē rē el′) *French.* everything used by an army, organization, undertaking, etc.; equipment. *n.*

**ma·ter·nal** (mə tėr′nəl) **1** of or like a mother; motherly. **2** related on the mother's side of the family: *Everyone has two maternal grandparents and two paternal grandparents.* **3** received or inherited from a mother. *adj.* —**ma·ter′nal·ly**, *adv.*
☛ *Etym.* **Maternal,** MATRIARCH, MATRICIDE, MATERNITY, MATRIMONY, MATRIX, and MATRON can all be traced back to L *mater* 'mother'.

**ma·ter·ni·ty** (mə tėr′nə tē) **1** motherhood; being a mother. **2** motherliness; qualities of a mother. **3** for a woman soon to have a baby: *a maternity dress.* 1, 2 *n.*, 3 *adj.*
☛ *Etym.* See note at MATERNAL.

**maternity hospital** a hospital for women giving birth to children.

**math** (math) *Informal.* MATHEMATICS. *n.*

**math.** **1** mathematical. **2** mathematician.

**math·e·mat·i·cal** (math′ə mat′ə kəl) **1** of MATHEMATICS; having to do with mathematics: *mathematical problems.* **2** exact; accurate: *mathematical precision.* *adj.* —**math′e·mat′i·cal·ly**, *adv.*

**math·e·ma·ti·cian** (math′ə mə tish′ən) a person skilled in MATHEMATICS or whose work is mathematics. *n.*

**math·e·mat·ics** (math′ə mat′iks) the science dealing with the measurement, properties, and relationships of quantities (*used with a singular verb*): *Mathematics includes arithmetic, algebra, geometry, calculus, etc.* *n.*

**mat·i·née** or **mat·i·nee** (mat′ə nā′ *or* mat′ə nā′) a performance held in the afternoon, especially a dramatic or musical one. *n.*

**ma·tri·arch** (mā′trē ärk′) **1** a mother who is the ruler of a family or tribe. **2** a venerable old woman. *n.*
☛ *Etym.* See note at MATERNAL.

**ma·tri·ar·chal** (mā′trē är′kəl) **1** of a MATRIARCH or MATRIARCHY. **2** suitable for a MATRIARCH. *adj.*

**ma·tri·ar·chy** (mā′trē är′kē) a form of social organization in which the mother is the ruler of a family or tribe, descent being traced through the mother. *n.*, *pl.* **ma·tri·ar·chies**.

**ma·tri·ces** (mā′trə sēz′ *or* mat′rə sēz′) *pl.* of MATRIX. *n.*

**ma·tri·cid·al** (mat′rə sī′dəl *or* mat′rə sī′dəl) killing or tending to kill one's mother. *adj.*

---

**materialistic**     **735**     **matter**

hat, āge, fär; let, ēqual, tėrm; it, īce
hot, ōpen, ôrder; oil, out; cup, pùt, rüle
əbove, takən, pencəl, lemən, circəs
ch, child; ng, long; sh, ship
th, thin; ᴛʜ, then; zh, measure

**ma·tri·cide** (mā′trə sīd′ *or* mat′rə sīd′) the act of killing one's mother. *n.*
☛ *Etym.* See note at MATERNAL.

**ma·tric·u·late** (mə trik′yə lāt′) **1** enrol as a student in a college or university. **2** enrol as a candidate for a degree. *v.*, **ma·tric·u·lat·ed**, **ma·tric·u·lat·ing**.

**ma·tric·u·la·tion** (mə trik′yə lā′shən) an examination held at the end of secondary school or as a university entrance requirement. *n.*

**mat·ri·mo·ni·al** (mat′rə mō′nē əl) of marriage; having to do with marriage. *adj.*

**mat·ri·mo·ni·al·ly** (mat′rə mō′nē ə lē) **1** according to the custom or laws of MATRIMONY. **2** with regard to MATRIMONY. **3** by MATRIMONY. *adv.*

**mat·ri·mo·ny** (mat′rə mō′nē) **1** married life. **2** the act of marrying. **3** the relation between married persons. *n.*, *pl.* **mat·ri·mo·nies**.
☛ *Etym.* See note at MATERNAL.

**ma·trix** (mā′triks *or* mat′riks) **1** that which gives origin or form to something enclosed within it: *A mould for a casting or the rock in which gems are embedded is called a matrix.* **2** womb. *n.*, *pl.* **ma·tri·ces** *or* **ma·trix·es**.
☛ *Etym.* See note at MATERNAL.

**ma·tron** (mā′trən) **1** an older married woman or widow. **2** a woman who manages the household affairs or supervises the inmates of a school, hospital, or other institution. **3** a woman who is placed in charge of female prisoners in a jail, penitentiary, etc. *n.*
☛ *Etym.* See note at MATERNAL.

**ma·tron·ly** (mā′trən lē) like a MATRON; suitable for a matron; dignified. *adj.* —**ma′tron·li·ness**, *n.*

**matron of honour** or **honor** a married woman who is the chief attendant of the bride at a wedding.

**mat·ted** (mat′id) **1** formed into a mat; entangled in a thick mass: *a matted growth of shrubs.* **2** *pt.* and *pp.* of MAT. 1 *adj.*, 2 *v.*

**mat·ter** (mat′ər) **1** the material of which something is made or composed; substance. **2** the substance of the material world; the opposite of mind or spirit: *Matter occupies space.* **3** a concern or occasion: *business matters, a matter of life and death.* **4** what is said or written, thought of apart from the way in which it is said or written; content: *There was very little matter of interest in her speech.* **5** grounds or cause; basis: *If a person is robbed, she has matter for complaint to the police.* **6** an instance or case; a thing: *a matter of fact, a matter of record, a matter of business.* **7** things written or printed: *reading matter.* **8** an amount or quantity: *a matter of 20 kilometres.* **9** importance; significance: *Let it go since it is of no matter.* **10** be important: *Nothing seems to matter when you are very sick.* **11** mail: *Letters are first-class matter.* **12** pus. **13** form pus; discharge pus; suppurate. 1–9, 11, 12 *n.*, 10, 13 *v.*
**as a matter of fact,** actually; in reality.
**for that matter,** so far as that is concerned.
**matter of course,** something that is to be expected.

**no matter, a** it is not important; let it go. **b** regardless of: *She wants a bicycle, no matter what it costs.* **What is the matter?** What is wrong?

**mat·ter–of–fact** (mat′ər əv fakt′) dealing with facts; not imaginative or fanciful: *a matter-of-fact report.* *adj.*

**mat·ting** (mat′ing) **1** fabric of grass, straw, hemp, or other fibre, for covering floors, for mats, for wrapping material, etc. **2** ppr. of MAT. *1 n., 2 v.*

**mat·tock** (mat′ək) a tool like a pickaxe but having a flat blade on one side or flat blades on both sides, used for loosening soil and cutting roots. *n.*

**mat·tress** (mat′ris) a thick pad made of cotton, foam, rubber, hair, straw, or other material encased in a covering of strong cloth, and used on a bed or as a bed: *Many mattresses have springs inside.* *n.*

**mat·u·rate** (mach′ə rāt′) **1** discharge pus; suppurate. **2** ripen; mature. *v.*, **mat·u·rat·ed, mat·u·rat·ing.**

**mat·u·ra·tion** (mach′ə rā′shən) **1** a discharge of pus; suppuration. **2** a ripening; maturing. *n.*

**ma·ture** (mə chùr′ or mə tyùr′) **1** ripe or full-grown: *Grain is harvested when it is mature.* **2** come or bring to full growth; ripen: *The apples are maturing rapidly. We need more sun to mature the crops.* **3** of the body, mind, etc., come or bring to full development: *The experience has matured her understanding.* **4** having or showing full development of the body, mind, etc.: *a mature face, mature thinking.* **5** make or become ready or complete: *to mature a plan.* **6** fully worked out; carefully and completely thought out: *By next year we will have a mature plan for the subway.* **7** due; payable: *a mature loan.* **8** fall due; become payable: *The note to the bank matured yesterday.* *1, 4, 6, 7 adj., 2, 3, 5, 8 v.,* **ma·tured, ma·tur·ing.** —**ma·ture′ly,** *adv.*

**ma·tu·ri·ty** (mə chür′rə tē or mə tyü′rə tē) **1** a state of ripeness; full development: *She had reached maturity by the time she was twenty.* **2** being completed or ready: *When their plans reached maturity, they were able to begin.* **3** a falling due; the time a debt is payable. *n.*

**ma·tu·ti·nal** (mə tyü′tə nəl or mə tü′tə nəl) occurring in the morning; early in the day; having to do with the morning. *adj.*

**matz·o** (mä′tsō) a thin piece of unleavened bread, eaten by Jews especially during the Passover. *n. pl.* **matz·oth** (mät′sōth) or **matz·os.**

**maud·lin** (mod′lən) **1** sentimental in a weak, silly way: *Sympathy for criminals is often maudlin.* **2** sentimental and tearful because of drunkenness or excitement. *adj.*

**maul** (mol) **1** beat and pull about; handle roughly; injure: *The lion mauled its keeper badly.* **2** a very heavy hammer or mallet. *1 v., 2 n.*

**maun·der** (mon′dər) **1** talk in a rambling, foolish way: *People who maunder talk much but say little.* **2** move or act in an aimless, confused manner: *The sick woman maundered about in a daze.* *v.*

**mau·so·le·um** (mos′ə lē′əm or moz′ə lē′əm) a large, magnificent tomb. *n., pl.* **mau·so·le·ums** or **mau·so·le·a** (-lē′ə).
☛ *Etym.* Through Latin from Gk. *Mausōleion,* the tomb of King Mausolos of Caria, an ancient kingdom in Asia Minor; this magnificent tomb was erected in 353 B.C. and considered one of the seven wonders of the ancient world.

**mauve** (mōv *or* mov) delicate, pale purple. *n., adj.*

**mav·er·ick** (mav′ə rik) **1** a calf or other animal not marked with an owner's brand. **2** *Informal.* someone who refuses to affiliate with any one political party. **3** *Informal.* any person or organization that is unconventional or unwilling to conform; rebel. *n.*

**maw** (mo) **1** the mouth and throat of an animal, especially a meat-eating animal. **2** the stomach of an animal or bird. *n.*

**mawk·ish** (mok′ish) **1** sickening. **2** sickly sentimental; weakly emotional. *adj.* —**mawk′ish·ly,** *adv.* —**mawk′ish·ness,** *n.*

**max.** maximum.

**max·il·la** (mak sil′ə) **1** the jaw; jawbone; upper jawbone. **2** either of a pair of appendages just behind the mandibles of insects, crabs, etc. See MANDIBLE for picture. *n., pl.* **max·il·lae** (mak sil′ē *or* mak sil′ī).

**max·il·lar·y** (mak′sə ler′ē) **1** of or having to do with the jaw or jawbone. **2** MAXILLA. *1 adj., 2 n., pl.* **max·il·lar·ies.**

**max·il·li·ped** (mak sil′ə ped′) one of two additional jaws behind the mandibles in crabs and other similar crustaceans. *n.*

**max·im** (mak′səm) a short rule of conduct; a proverb; a statement of a general truth: *"Look before you leap" is a maxim.* *n.*

**max·i·ma** (mak′sə mə) a pl. of MAXIMUM. *n.*

**max·i·mum** (mak′sə məm) **1** the largest or highest amount; the greatest possible amount: *The speed limit is 60 kilometres an hour; drivers must not exceed this maximum.* **2** largest; highest; greatest possible: *The maximum score on this test is 100.* *1 n., pl.* **max·i·mums** or **max·i·ma;** *2 adj.*

**may** (mā) an auxiliary or helping verb used to express: **1** permission, opportunity, or possibility: *You may go now. You may if you can. She may have been the one.* **2** a wish or prayer: *May you be very happy.* **3** contingency, especially in clauses expressing condition, concession, purpose, result, etc.: *I write that you may know my plans.* *v., pt.* **might.**

**May** (mā) the fifth month of the year: *May has 31 days.* *n.*
☛ *Etym.* Through Old French from L *Maius* '(the month) of the goddess Maia'.

**Ma·ya** (mä′yə) **1** a member of any of a large group of Amerindian peoples mainly of Yucatán, Belize, and Guatemala, who speak Mayan languages. **2** a member of the branch of the Maya living in Yucatán: *The ancient Maya are famous for the remarkable civilization they developed, which flourished between about* A.D. *250 and 900.* See ARCHITECTURE for picture. **3** a Mayan language of the ancient Maya. *n., pl.* **Ma·ya** or **Ma·yas.**

**Ma·yan** (mä′yən) **1** a language family of Mexico and Central America. **2** MAYA (defs. 1 and 2). **3** of or having to do with the Maya or their languages. *1, 2 n., 3 adj.*

**May apple** **1** a North American plant having a large white flower. **2** its edible, yellowish, egg-shaped fruit.

**may·be** (mā′bē) possibly or perhaps; it may be so. *adv.*
☛ *Usage.* **Maybe** as an adverb is one word: *Maybe it will rain tomorrow.* **May be** as a verb phrase is two words: *He may be home soon.*

**May·day** (mā′dā′) an international signal of distress used in emergencies by ships and aircraft. *n.*

**May Day** May 1: *May Day is often celebrated by crowning the May queen and dancing around the Maypole. In some places, labour parades and meetings are held on May Day.*

**may·flow·er** (mā′flou′ər) **1** a plant or tree that flowers in May; trailing arbutus; hawthorn or cowslip. **2 Mayflower,** the ship on which the Pilgrims sailed to America in 1620. *n.*

**May fly** a slender insect, having the forewings much larger than the hind wings, that dies soon after reaching the adult stage; EPHEMERID.

**may·hem** (mā′hem) **1** the crime of intentionally maiming a person or injuring him or her so that he or she is less able to defend himself or herself. **2** confusion and willful violence. *n.*

**May·ing** (mā′ing) the celebration of MAY DAY; taking part in May festivities. *n.*

**may·n't** (mā′ənt *or* mānt) may not.

**may·on·naise** (mā′ə nāz′) a thick dressing for salads, made of egg yolks, vegetable oil, vinegar or lemon juice, and seasoning. *n.*

**may·or** (mā′ər) the person at the head of the government of a city, town, or village. *n.*

**may·or·al·ty** (mā′ə rəl tē *or* mer′əl tē) **1** the position of MAYOR. **2** a MAYOR's term of office. *n., pl.* **may·or·al·ties.**

**May·pole** or **may·pole** (mā′pōl′) **1** a high pole decorated with flowers or ribbons, around which merrymakers dance on MAY DAY. **2** in Canada, LOBSTICK. *n.*

**May queen** a girl crowned with flowers and honoured as queen on MAY DAY.

**May·time** (mā′tīm′) the month of May. *n.*

**maze** (māz) **1** a network of paths through which it is hard to find one's way: *A guide led us through a maze of caves.* **2** any complicated arrangement, as of streets, buildings, etc. **3** a state of confusion; a muddled condition: *Ella was in such a maze that she couldn't speak.* *n.*
☞ *Hom.* MAIZE.

**ma·zur·ka** or **ma·zour·ka** (mə zėr′kə *or* mə zür′kə) **1** a lively Polish dance. **2** the music for it. *n.*

**maz·y** (mā′zē) like a maze; intricate. *adj.,* **maz·i·er, maz·i·est.** —**maz′i·ness,** *n.*

**MB** Manitoba.

**mbar** millibar or millibars.

**M.C.** Master of Ceremonies.

**Mc·In·tosh** (mak′ən tosh′) a bright-red winter apple having crisp, white flesh.
☞ *Etym.* Named after John *McIntosh,* an Ontario farmer who found such an apple tree while clearing his farm in 1811.

**McIntosh Red** the MCINTOSH apple.

**Md** mendelevium.

**M.D.** **1** Doctor of Medicine. **2** Municipal District.

**mdse.** merchandise.

**me** (mē; *unstressed,* mi) the objective form of I: *The dog bit me. Give me a bandage.* *pron.*

---

**Mayday**     737     **mean**

hat, āge, fär; let, ēqual, tėrm; it, īce
hot, ōpen, ôrder; oil, out; cup, pút, rüle
əbove, takən, pencəl, lemən, circəs
ch, child; ng, long; sh, ship
th, thin; ᴛʜ, then; zh, measure

☞ *Usage.* In modern English, *It is I* is considered affected in speech. *It's me* is more frequent.

**M.E.** **1** Master of Engineering. **2** Mechanical Engineer. **3** Mining Engineer.

**mead** (mēd) an alcoholic drink made from fermented honey and water. *n.*

**mead·ow** (med′ō) **1** a piece of grassy land; a field where hay is grown. **2** low, grassy land near a stream. *n.*

A western meadow lark—about 25 cm long including the tail

**meadow lark** a North American songbird, about as big as a robin, having a black crescent on a yellow breast.

**mead·ow·sweet** (med′ō swēt′) a shrub of the same family as the rose, having dense clusters of small, fragrant, pink or white flowers. *n.*

**mead·ow·y** (med′ō ē) **1** like a MEADOW. **2** of MEADOWS. *adj.*

**mea·ger** (mē′gər) See MEAGRE. *adj.*

**mea·gre** (mē′gər) **1** poor or scanty: *a meagre meal.* **2** thin or lean: *a meagre face.* *adj.* Also, **meager.**
—**mea′gre·ness,** *n.*

**meal**[1] (mēl) **1** breakfast, lunch, dinner, supper, or tea. **2** the food served or eaten at any one time. *n.*

**meal**[2] (mēl) **1** ground grain, especially corn meal. **2** anything ground to a powder. *n.*

**meal·time** (mēl′tīm′) the usual time for eating a meal. *n.*

**meal·y** (mē′lē) **1** like meal; dry and powdery: *mealy potatoes.* **2** of meal. **3** covered with meal: *the miller's mealy hands.* **4** pale. **5** MEALY-MOUTHED. *adj.,* **meal·i·er, meal·i·est.** —**meal′i·ness,** *n.*

**meal·y-mouthed** (mē′lē mouᴛʜd′ *or* mē′lē moutht′) unwilling to tell the truth in plain words; using soft words insincerely. *adj.*

**mean**[1] (mēn) **1** refer to; signify; denote: *What does this word mean?* **2** intend to express or indicate: *"Keep out; that means you."* **3** convey; communicate: *What is that look supposed to mean?* **4** have as a purpose; have in mind; intend: *I do not mean to go.* **5** have intentions of some kind; be minded or disposed: *She means well.* **6** design for a definite purpose: *This toy is meant for young children.* **7** destine: *Fate meant us for each other. He was meant for a teacher.* *v.,* **meant, mean·ing.**
**mean well by,** have kindly feelings toward.
☞ *Hom.* MIEN.

**mean**[2] (mēn) **1** low in social position or rank; humble: *She was of mean birth.* **2** of little importance or value: *the meanest flower.* **3** of poor appearance; shabby: *a*

**mean** *house.* **4** small-minded; ignoble: *mean thoughts.* **5** stingy: *mean about money.* **6** *Informal.* humiliated; ashamed: *to feel mean.* **7** *Informal.* hard to manage; troublesome; bad-tempered: *a mean horse.* **8** *Informal.* in poor physical condition; unwell: *I feel mean today.* **9** *Informal.* good: *She still plays a mean guitar.* *adj.* —**mean′ly,** *adv.*

**no mean,** a very good: *He is no mean swimmer.*
☛ *Hom.* MIEN.

**mean³** (mēn) **1** halfway between the two extremes of a set of values; average: *The mean temperature for July in Yarmouth is 16.4°C.* **2** the average; arithmetic mean: *The grades this year have been consistently above the mean for the course.* **3** a condition, quality, or course of action halfway between two extremes or opposites; a medium: *the golden mean.* **4** intermediate in kind, quality, or degree: *She is trying to discover a mean course between the two extremes of telling nothing and telling everything.* **5** in mathematics, either of the two middle terms of a proportion of four terms: *The means in the proportion 8/4 = 4/2 are 4 and 4.* **6 means,** *pl.* in mathematics, all the terms between the first and last terms of an arithmetic progression. **7 means,** what a thing is done by; the method or methods or the agency by which something is brought about (*used with a singular or plural verb*): *by fair means. She thinks of her car as simply a means of transportation.* **8 means,** *pl.* **a** money resources: *to live within one's means.* **b** wealth; riches: *a woman of means.* 1, 4 *adj.*, 2, 3, 5–8 *n.*

**by all means,** without fail; certainly.
**by any means,** in any possible way; at any cost.
**by means of,** by the use of; through; with: *I found my dog by means of a notice in the paper.*
**by no means,** certainly not; not at all; under no circumstances; in no way: *This work is by no means easy.*
**means to an end,** a way of getting or doing something.
☛ *Hom.* MIEN.

**me·an·der** (mē an′dər) **1** follow a winding course: *A brook meanders through the meadow.* **2** a winding course. **3** wander aimlessly: *We meandered through the park.* **4** an aimless wandering. 1, 3 *v.*, 2, 4 *n.*

**mean·ing** (mē′ning) **1** what is meant or intended; significance: *The meaning of the sentence is clear.* **2** that means something; expressive: *a meaning look.* **3** ppr. of MEAN¹. 1 *n.*, 2 *adj.*, 3 *v.* —**mean′ing·ly,** *adv.*

**mean·ing·ful** (mē′ning fəl) full of meaning; having much meaning; significant. *adj.*
—**mean′ing·ful·ly,** *adv.*

**mean·ing·less** (mē′ning lis) without meaning; not making sense; not significant. *adj.*
—**mean′ing·less·ly,** *adv.*

**mean·ness** (mēn′nis) **1** being selfish in small things; stinginess. **2** being mean in grade or quality; poorness. **3** a mean act. *n.*

**means** (mēnz) See MEAN³ (defs. 6–8). *n.*

**meant** (ment) pt. and pp. of MEAN¹: *She explained what she meant. That sign was meant as a warning.* *v.*

**mean·time** (mēn′tīm) **1** the time between: *The carnival opens Friday; in the meantime we will make our costumes.* **2** in the time between; meanwhile: *Classes finish at 12 noon and begin again at 2 p.m.; meantime we can swim and have lunch.* 1 *n.*, 2 *adv.*

**mean·while** (mēn′wīl or mēn′hwīl) **1** in the time or period between: *Classes finish at 12 and start again at 2; meanwhile we can swim and have lunch.* **2** at the same time, especially in a different place. **3** MEANTIME (def. 1). 1, 2 *adv.*, 3 *n.*

**mea·sles** (mē′zəlz) **1** an infectious disease characterized by a bad cold, fever, and a breaking out of small red spots on the skin. **2** a similar but less severe disease, properly called GERMAN MEASLES. *n.*

**mea·sly** (mē′zlē) **1** of or like MEASLES. **2** having MEASLES. *adj.*, **mea·sli·er, mea·sli·est.**

**meas·ur·a·ble** (mezh′ə rə bəl) capable of being measured. *adj.*

**meas·ur·a·bly** (mezh′ə rə blē) to an amount or degree that can be measured; perceptibly. *adv.*

**meas·ure** (mezh′ər) **1** find out the extent, size, quantity, capacity, etc. of something: estimate by some standard: *to measure a room.* **2** the act or process of finding the extent, size, quantity, capacity, etc. of something, especially by comparison with a standard. **3** the size, dimensions, quantity, etc. thus ascertained: *Her waist measure is 60 cm.* **Short measure** means less than it should be; **full measure** means all it should be. **4** be of a certain size or amount: *This brick measures 5 × 10 × 20 centimetres.* **5** an instrument for measuring: *a litre measure.* **6** a system of measuring: *liquid measure, dry measure, square measure.* **7** a unit or standard of measuring: *Centimetre, kilogram, litre, and hour are common measures.* **8** any standard of comparison, estimation, or judgment. **9** get or take by measuring; mark off or out in metres, litres, etc.: *Measure off two metres of silk. Measure out a kilogram of potatoes.* **10** take measurements; find out sizes or amounts. **11** admit of measurement. **12** serve as a measure of. **13** compare: *The soldier measured his strength with that of his enemy in a hand-to-hand-fight.* **14** adjust: *to measure one's behaviour by the company one is in.* **15** a quantity or degree that should not be exceeded; reasonable limit: *angry beyond measure.* **16** quantity; extent; degree; proportion: *Accidents can in great measure be prevented. The measure of her courage was remarkable.* **17** rhythm in poetry or music: *the stately measures of blank verse.* **18** a metrical unit; foot of poetry. **19** a bar of music. See BAR for picture. **20** a dance or dance movement. **21** a course of action; procedure: *to take measures to relieve suffering.* **22** a legislative enactment. **23** in mathematics, a quantity contained in another some number of times without remainder. **24** a definite quantity measured out: *to drink a measure.* 1, 4, 9–14 *v.*, **meas·ured, meas·ur·ing;** 2, 3, 5–8, 15–24 *n.*
—**meas′ur·er,** *n.*

**beyond measure,** greatly; exceedingly.
**for good measure,** as something extra; as something not necessarily expected.
**full measure,** all it should be.
**in a measure,** to some degree; partly.
**measure one's length,** fall, be thrown, or lie flat on the ground.
**measure out, a** distribute by measuring. **b** distribute carefully.
**measure swords, a** fight with swords. **b** take part in a duel, battle, debate, etc.
**measure up,** have the necessary features; meet a required standard: *The party did not measure up to her expectations.*
**take measures,** do something; act.
**take someone's measure,** judge someone's character or abilities.

**meas·ured** (mezh′ərd) **1** regular; uniform: *the measured march of soldiers.* **2** rhythmical. **3** written in poetry, not in prose. **4** deliberate and restrained, not hasty or careless. **5** pt. and pp. of MEASURE. *1–4 adj., 5 v.*

**meas·ure·less** (mezh′ər lis) too great to be measured; unlimited; vast: *the measureless ocean.* *adj.*

**meas·ure·ment** (mezh′ər mənt) **1** measuring or finding the size, quantity, or amount: *The measurement of length by a metre-stick is easy.* **2** the size found by measuring: *The measurements of the room are 6 by 4.5 metres.* *n.*

**measuring worm** the larva of any GEOMETRID moth; inchworm: *The measuring worm moves by bringing the rear end of its body forward, forming a loop, and then advancing the front end.*

**meat** (mēt) **1** animal flesh used as food: *Fish is not usually called meat.* **2** food of any kind: *meat and drink.* **3** the part of anything that can be eaten: *the meat of a nut.* **4** the essential part or parts; substance; food for thought: *the meat of an argument, the meat of a book.* *n.*
—**meat′less**, *adj.*
☞ *Hom.* MEET, METE.

**meat packing** the business of slaughtering animals and preparing their meat for transportation and sale.

**meat·y** (mē′tē) **1** of meat; having the flavour of meat. **2** like meat. **3** full of meat. **4** full of substance; giving food for thought: *The speech was very meaty; it contained many valuable ideas.* *adj.*, **meat·i·er, meat·i·est.**

**Mec·ca** or **mec·ca** (mek′ə) **1** a place that many people visit: *a tourist mecca.* **2** a place that many people long for as a goal. *n.*
☞ *Etym.* From *Mecca*, a capital of Saudi Arabia, the birthplace of Mohammed and because of that birth, the holy city of Islam.

**me·chan·ic** (mə kan′ik) **1** a worker skilled with tools. **2** a worker who repairs machinery. *n.*

**me·chan·i·cal** (mə kan′ə kəl) **1** having to do with machinery or mechanisms: *a mechanical engineer.* **2** made or worked by machinery. **3** like a machine; like that of a machine; automatic; without expression: *Her reading is very mechanical.* **4** of, having to do with, or in accordance with, the science of mechanics. *adj.*
—**me·chan′i·cal·ly**, *adv.*

**mechanical drawing** drawing done with the help of rulers, scales, compasses, etc.

**me·chan·ics** (mə kan′iks) **1** the branch of physics dealing with motion and the effect of forces on bodies to produce motion or a state of balance: *Mechanics includes kinematics, kinetics, and statics.* **2** the application of the principles of mechanics to the design, construction, and operation of machinery. **3** the mechanical or technical part of something; technique: *the mechanics of playing the piano.* *n.*

**mech·a·nism** (mek′ə niz′əm) **1** a machine or its working parts: *Something must be wrong with the mechanism of our refrigerator.* **2** a system of parts working together as the parts of a machine do: *The bones and muscles are parts of the mechanism of the body.* **3** the means or way by which something is done: *Committees are a useful mechanism for getting things done.* **4** a mechanical part; technique. *n.*

**mech·a·nis·tic** (mek′ə nis′tik) of or having to do with MECHANISM, MECHANICS, or mechanical theories. *adj.*

**mech·a·ni·za·tion** (mek′ə nə zā′shən *or* mek′ə nī zā′shən) mechanizing or being MECHANIZED. *n.*

# measureless 739 median

hat, āge, fär; let, ēqual, tėrm; it, īce
hot, ōpen, ôrder, oil, out; cup, pùt, rüle
əbove, takən, pencəl, lemən, circəs

ch, child; ng, long; sh, ship
th, thin; ᴛʜ, then; zh, measure

**mech·a·nize** (mek′ə nīz′) **1** make mechanical. **2** do by machinery, rather than by hand: *Much housework can be mechanized.* **3** replace people or animals by machinery in a business, etc. **4** equip a military unit with armoured vehicles, tanks, and other machines. *v.*,
**mech·a·nized, mech·a·niz·ing.**

**med.** **1** medical. **2** medieval. **3** medium.
**Med.** medieval.

Canadian and Commonwealth medals

**med·al** (med′əl) a small, flat piece of metal stamped with a figure and an inscription to commemorate some event or as a mark of honour: *The captain won a medal for bravery. She won the gold medal for having the highest marks in the school. A medal was struck to commemorate the moon landing.* *n.*
☞ *Hom.* MEDDLE.

**med·al·ist** (med′ə list) **1** a person who designs or makes medals. **2** a person who has won a medal. *n.* Also, **medallist.**

**me·dal·lion** (mə dal′yən) **1** a large medal. **2** a round or oval design or ornament: *A design on a book or a pattern in lace may be called a medallion.* *n.*

**med·al·list** (med′ə list) See MEDALIST. *n.*

**med·dle** (med′əl) busy oneself with other people's things or affairs without being asked or needed: *Don't meddle with my books or my toys. That busybody has been meddling in my business.* *v.*, **med·dled, med·dling.**
☞ *Hom.* MEDAL.

**med·dler** (med′lər) a person who meddles. *n.*
☞ *Hom.* MEDLAR.

**med·dle·some** (med′əl səm) fond of meddling in other people's affairs; meddling. *adj.*

**me·di·a** (mē′dē ə) a pl. of MEDIUM (defs. 3–6). *Newspapers, magazines, billboards, television, and radio are important media for advertising.* *n.*
☞ *Usage.* See note at MEDIUM.

**me·di·ae·val** (mē′dē ē′vəl *or* med′ē ē′vəl) See MEDIEVAL. *adj.*

**me·di·al** (mē′dē əl) **1** in the middle. **2** having to do with a mathematical mean or average. **3** average; ordinary. *adj.* —**me′di·al·ly**, *adv.*

**me·di·an** (mē′dē ən) **1** middle. **2** the middle number of a series: *The median of 1, 3, 4, 8, 9 is 4.* **3** a measurement so chosen that half the numbers in the series are above it and half are below it: *The median of 1, 3, 9, 10 is 6.* **4** a line or point in the middle. **5** on a highway, a central strip of grass or pavement separating the lanes used by traffic proceeding in opposite directions. 1 *adj.*, 2–5 *n.*

**me·di·ate** (mē′dē āt′ *for verb*, mē′dē it *for adjective*) **1** be a go-between; act in order to bring about an agreement between persons or sides: *The mayor tried to mediate between the bus company and its employees.* **2** effect by intervening; settle by intervening. **3** be the medium for effecting a result, for conveying a gift, or for communicating knowledge. **4** connected, but not directly; connected through some other person or thing: *A vassal's relation to his king was mediate through the lord on whose estate he lived.* **5** intermediate. 1–3 *v.*, **me·di·at·ed, me·di·at·ing;** 4, 5 *adj.*

**me·di·a·tion** (mē′dē ā′shən) a mediating; effecting an agreement; friendly interference. *n.*

**me·di·a·tor** (mē′dē ā′tər) one who MEDIATES (def. 1): *Mother acts as mediator when John and I quarrel.* *n.*

**me·di·a·to·ry** (mē′dē ə tô′rē) mediating; having to do with MEDIATION. *adj.*

**med·ic** (med′ik) *Informal.* **1** physician. **2** a medical student. **3** a member of the medical branch of the armed forces. *n.*

**med·i·ca·ble** (med′ə kə bəl) capable of being cured or relieved by medical treatment. *adj.*

**med·i·cal** (med′ə kəl) **1** of or having to do with healing or with the science and art of medicine: *medical advice, medical schools, medical treatment.* **2** a medical examination. 1 *adj.*, 2 *n.* —**med′i·cal·ly,** *adv.*

**me·di·a·ment** (mə dik′ə mənt) a substance used to cure or heal; medicine. *n.*

**med·i·care** (med′ə ker′) a government-sponsored program of health insurance, usually covering hospital costs, doctors' fees, and other medical expenses. In Canada, T.C. Douglas, Premier of Saskatchewan, introduced medicare in 1962. *n.*

**med·i·cate** (med′ə kāt′) **1** treat with medicine. **2** put medicine on or in. *v.*, **med·i·cat·ed, med·i·cat·ing.**

**med·i·cat·ed** (med′ə kā′tid) **1** containing medicine: *medicated gauze.* **2** pt. and pp. of MEDICATE. 1 *adj.*, 2 *v.*

**med·i·ca·tion** (med′ə kā′shən) **1** treatment with medicine. **2** the putting of medicine on or in. **3** MEDICINE (def. 1). *n.*

**me·dic·i·nal** (mə dis′ə nəl) having value as medicine; healing; relieving. *adj.* —**me·dic′i·nal·ly,** *adv.*

**med·i·cine** (med′ə sən *or* med′sən) **1** any substance such as a drug, used to cure disease or improve health. **2** the art and science of curing disease or improving health: *The young woman decided to study medicine.* *n.* **take one's medicine,** do what one must; do something one dislikes to do.

**medicine ball** a large, heavy leather ball tossed from one person to another for exercise.

**medicine man** a man believed by North American Indians and some other aboriginal peoples to have magical power over diseases, evil spirits, and other things; SHAMAN.

**me·di·e·val** or **me·di·ae·val** (mē′dē ē′vəl *or* med′ē ē′vəl) **1** belonging to or having to do with the Middle Ages, the period from about A.D. 500 to about A.D. 1450: *medieval customs.* **2** like that of the Middle Ages. *adj.*

**me·di·o·cre** (mē′dē ō′kər *or* mē′dē ō′kər) neither good nor bad; average; ordinary, but less than satisfactory: *a mediocre cake, a mediocre student.* *adj.*

**me·di·oc·ri·ty** (mē′dē ok′rə tē) **1** MEDIOCRE quality. **2** MEDIOCRE ability or accomplishment. **3** a MEDIOCRE person. *n., pl.* **me·di·oc·ri·ties.**

**med·i·tate** (med′ə tāt′) **1** think quietly; reflect: *You should meditate on the lesson taught by the fable of the hare and the tortoise.* **2** think about; consider; plan; intend: *Our general was meditating an attack.* *v.*, **med·i·tat·ed, med·i·tat·ing.**

**med·i·ta·tion** (med′ə tā′shən) **1** continued thought; reflection. **2** contemplation on sacred or solemn subjects. *n.*

**med·i·ta·tive** (med′ə tā′tiv) **1** fond of meditating. **2** expressing meditation. *adj.* —**med′i·ta′tive·ly,** *adv.*

**Med·i·ter·ra·ne·an** (med′ə tə rā′nē ən *or* med′ə tə rā′nyən) of or having to do with the Mediterranean Sea or the lands around it. *adj.*

**me·di·um** (mē′dē əm) **1** having a middle position; moderate: *Eggs can be cooked hard, soft, or medium. 175 cm is a medium height for a man.* **2** that which is in the middle; neither one extreme nor the other; middle condition: *Life in a small town is a happy medium between city and country life.* **3** a substance or agent through which anything acts; a means: *Radio is a medium of communication.* **4** a means of artistic expression: *The sculptor did some carving in stone, but her favourite medium is wood.* **5** a substance in which something can live; environment: *Water is the medium in which most fish live.* **6** a liquid with which paints are mixed **7** a person through whom spirits of the dead can supposedly communicate with the living. 1 *adj.*, 2–7 *n., pl.* **me·di·ums** or **me·di·a.**
☛ *Usage.* **Mediums** is the only plural used when the reference is to persons (def. 7). **Media** is the only plural used for def. 3 and also is usual for defs. 4 and 5. Careful writers and speakers avoid using **media** as a singular or **medias** as a plural: *She gave up the medium of painting and took to other media instead.*

**medium frequency** the range of radio frequencies between 300 and 3000 kilohertz: *Medium frequency is the range next above low frequency.*

**me·di·um–sized** (mē′dē əm sīzd′) neither large nor small of its kind. *adj.*

**med·lar** (med′lər) **1** a fruit that looks like a small brown apple: *A medlar is eaten when partly decayed.* **2** the small, bushy tree, of the same family as the rose, that the fruit grows on. *n.*
☛ *Hom.* MEDDLER.

**med·ley** (med′lē) **1** a mixture of things that ordinarily do not belong together. **2** a piece of music made up of tunes or extracts from other pieces. **3** made up of parts that are not alike; mixed. 1, 2 *n., pl.* **med·leys;** 3 *adj.*

**me·dul·la** (mə dul′ə) **1** MEDULLA OBLONGATA. **2** the marrow of bones. **3** the inner substance of an organ or structure: *The medulla of the adrenal gland produces the hormone adrenaline.* **4** the pith of plants. *n., pl.* **me·dul·lae** (mə dul′ē *or* mə dul′ī).

**me·dul·la ob·lon·ga·ta** (mə dul′ə ob′long gä′tə) the lowest part of the brain, at the top end of the spinal cord. See BRAIN for picture.

**med·ul·lar·y** (med′ə ler′ē) of or like the MEDULLA or the MEDULLA OBLONGATA. *adj.*

**me·du·sa** (mə dyü′sə *or* mə dü′sə) JELLYFISH. *n., pl.* **me·du·sas** *or* **me·du·sae** (-sē *or* -sī).
☞ *Etym.* From the name of a horrible monster in Greek legend, one of the three Gorgons, the sight of whom turned the watcher to stone.

**meek** (mēk) **1** patient; not easily angered; mild; forbearing. **2** submitting tamely when ordered about or injured by others; yielding: *The girl was meek as a lamb when she was reproved. adj.* —**meek′ly,** *adv.* —**meek′ness,** *n.*

**meer·schaum** (mēr′shəm *or* mēr′shom) **1** a very soft, light stone used to make tobacco pipes. **2** a tobacco pipe made of this material. *n.*

**meet**[1] (mēt) **1** come face to face; come face to face with: *Their cars met on the narrow road.* **2** come together; come into contact or connection with: *Sword met sword in battle.* **3** join: *where the two streets meet.* **4** be united; join in harmony: *His is a nature in which courage and caution meet.* **5** come into company with; be together: *The hosts met their guests at the restaurant.* **6** keep an appointment with: *Meet me at one o'clock.* **7** be introduced to; become acquainted: *Have you met my sister?* **8** be present at the arrival of: *to meet a plane.* **9** satisfy; comply with: *to meet obligations, objections, etc.* **10** pay: *to meet bills, debts, etc.* **11** fight with; oppose; deal with. **12** fight. **13** face directly: *He met her glance with a smile.* **14** experience: *Dora met open scorn before she won fame.* **15** assemble: *Parliament will meet next month.* **16** a meeting; gathering; competition: *a racing meet, an athletic meet.* **17** the people at a meeting. **18** the place of meeting. 1–15 *v.*, **met, meet·ing;** 16–18 *n.*
**meet the eye** *or* **the ear,** be seen or heard.
**meet with, a** come across. **b** have or get: *The plan met with approval.* **c** talk with.
☞ *Hom.* MEAT, METE.

**meet**[2] (mēt) suitable; proper; fitting: *It is meet that you should help your friends. adj.*
☞ *Hom.* MEAT, METE.

**meet·ing** (mē′ting) **1** coming together: *He looked forward to the meeting with his sister.* **2** a coming together of a group of people to discuss or arrange business or action: *The club held a meeting.* **3** a coming together of people for worship. **4** the place where things meet; junction: *a meeting of roads.* **5** ppr. of MEET. 1–4 *n.*, 5 *v.*

**meeting house** **1** any place of worship; church. **2** a building used for meetings.

**mega–** combining form. **1** great; large, as in *megalith.* **2** an SI prefix meaning million: *A megavolt is one million volts.* Symbol: M
☞ *Etym.* From Gk. *megas* 'great'. Compare with MICRO–.

**meg·a·cy·cle** (meg′ə sī′kəl) MEGAHERTZ. *n.*

**meg·a·death** (meg′ə deth′) the death of one million persons. *n.*

**meg·a·hertz** (meg′ə hėrts′) an SI unit for measuring frequency, equal to 1 000 000 hertz. Symbol: MHz *n., pl.* **meg·a·hertz.**

**meg·a·lith** (meg′ə lith′) a stone of great size, especially in ancient construction work or in monuments left by people of prehistoric times. *n.*
☞ *Etym.* See note at MEGA–.

**meg·a·lo·ma·ni·a** (meg′ə lō mā′nē ə) insanity marked by delusions of greatness, wealth, etc. *n.*

**medullary** 741 **meld**

hat, āge, fär; let, ēqual, tėrm; it, īce
hot, ōpen, ôrder; oil, out; cup, pùt, rüle
əbove, takən, pencəl, lemən, circəs
ch, child; ng, long; sh, ship
th, thin; ᴛʜ, then; zh, measure

**meg·a·lo·ma·ni·ac** (meg′ə lō mā′nē ak′) a person who has MEGALOMANIA. *n.*

**meg·a·lop·o·lis** (meg′ə lop′ə lis) a heavily populated urban and industrial area made up of several cities. *n.*

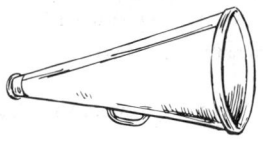
A megaphone

**meg·a·phone** (meg′ə fōn′) a large, funnel-shaped horn used to increase the loudness of the voice or the distance at which it can be heard. *n.*
☞ *Etym.* See note at MEGA–.

**meg·a·ton** (meg′ə tun′) a measure of atomic power equivalent to the energy released by one million tons of high explosive, specifically TNT. *n.*

**meg·ohm** (meg′ōm′) an SI unit for measuring electric resistance, equal to one million ohms. Symbol: MΩ *n.*

**mei·o·sis** (mī ō′sis) in biology, the division of the reproductive cells in sexually reproducing organisms to form germ cells, or GAMETES, in animals and spores in most plants: *In meiosis, the chromosome pairs of the dividing cell split up, with one of each pair going to each of the two daughter cells; the result is that each daughter cell has only half as many chromosomes as the parent cell.* Compare with MITOSIS. *n.*

**mel·an·cho·li·a** (mel′ən kō′lē ə) mental disorder characterized by great depression of spirits and gloomy fears. *n.* —**mel·an·cho′li·ac,** *n.*

**mel·an·chol·ic** (mel′ən kol′ik) **1** MELANCHOLY; gloomy. **2** suffering from MELANCHOLIA. *adj.*

**mel·an·chol·y** (mel′ən kol′ē) **1** sadness; low spirits; a tendency to be sad. **2** sad; gloomy. **3** causing sadness; depressing: *a melancholy scene.* **4** sober thoughtfulness; pensiveness. **5** soberly thoughtful; pensive. 1, 4 *n., pl.* **mel·an·chol·ies:** 2, 3, 5 *adj.*

**Mel·a·ne·sian** (mel′ə nē′zhən) **1** of or referring to a race of people that includes most of the peoples traditionally inhabiting Melanesia, a group of islands in the southwestern Pacific, especially New Guinea, New Britain, and the Solomon Islands. **2** a member of this race. **3** a native or inhabitant of Melanesia. **4** a group of languages widely spoken in Melanesia. **5** of or having to do with Melanesia or the people, cultures, or languages of Melanesia. 1, 5 *adj.*, 2–4 *n.*

**mé·lange** (mā länzh′) *French.* mixture; medley. *n.*

**mel·a·nin** (mel′ə nən) a dark-brown or black pigment present in the skin, hair, and eyes of humans and some animals. *n.*

**Mel·ba toast** (mel′bə) very thin, crisp toast.

**meld**[1] (meld) **1** in canasta, pinochle, etc., announce and show cards for a score. **2** the act of melding. **3** the cards which can be melded. 1, *v.*, 2, 3 *n.*

**meld²** (meld) **1** merge; blend; combine. **2** become merged, blended, or combined. **3** a blend or combination. 1, 2 v., 3 n.

**me·lee** or **mê·lée** (mel′ā or mā′lā; French, me lā′) **1** a confused fight; hand-to-hand fight among a number of fighters. **2** any similar state of hectic confusion. n.
☛ Hom. MALAY (for the second pronunciation of melee).

**mel·i·nite** (mel′ə nīt′) a powerful explosive containing PICRIC ACID. n.

**mel·io·rate** (mē′lyə rāt′) improve. v., **mel·io·rat·ed, mel·io·rat·ing.** —**mel′io·ra′tion,** n.

**mel·io·ra·tive** (mē′lyə rə tiv or mē′lyə rā′tiv) tending to improve. adj.

**mel·lif·lu·ence** (mə lif′lü əns) a sweet sound; smooth flow. n.

**mel·lif·lu·ent** (mə lif′lü ənt) MELLIFLUOUS. adj. —**mel·lif′lu·ent·ly,** adv.

**mel·lif·lu·ous** (mə lif′lü əs) sweetly or smoothly flowing: a mellifluous speech. adj. —**mel·lif′lu·ous·ly,** adv.

**mel·low** (mel′ō) **1** soft and full-flavoured from ripeness; sweet and juicy: a mellow apple. **2** fully matured: mellow wine. **3** soft and rich: a violin with a mellow tone, a mellow light in a picture, a mellow colour. **4** rich; loamy: mellow soil. **5** softened and made wise by age and experience. **6** make or become mellow: The apples mellowed after we picked them. **7** make mellow: Time had mellowed her youthful temper. **8** Informal. laid back; relaxed. 1–5, 8 adj., 6, 7 v. —**mel′low·ly,** adv. —**mel′low·ness,** n.

**me·lo·de·on** (mə lō′dē ən) a small reed organ in which air is sucked inward by a bellows. n.

**me·lod·ic** (mə lod′ik) **1** having to do with MELODY. **2** MELODIOUS. adj. —**me·lod′i·cal·ly,** adv.

**me·lo·di·ous** (mə lō′dē əs) **1** sweet-sounding; pleasing to the ear; musical: a melodious voice. **2** producing MELODY: a melodious bird. adj. —**me·lo′di·ous·ly,** adv. —**me·lo′di·ous·ness,** n.

**mel·o·dra·ma** (mel′ə dram′ə or mel′ə drä′mə) **1** a sensational drama with exaggerated appeal to the emotions and, usually, a happy ending: Shakespeare's play "The Merchant of Venice" is really a melodrama. **2** any sensational writing, speech, or action with exaggerated appeal to the emotions. n.

**mel·o·dra·mat·ic** (mel′ə drə mat′ik) of, like, or suitable for MELODRAMA; sensational and exaggerated. adj. —**mel′o·dra·mat′i·cal·ly,** adv.

**mel·o·dy** (mel′ə dē) **1** any agreeable succession of sounds. **2** musical quality: the melody of good speech. **3** in music, a succession of single tones, arranged in a rhythmical pattern; tune: Music has melody, harmony, and rhythm. **4** the main tune in harmonized music; air. n., pl. **mel·o·dies.**

**mel·on** (mel′ən) **1** a large, juicy fruit that grows on a vine: Watermelons and cantaloupes or muskmelons are common kinds of melon. **2** deep pink. 1, 2 n., 2 adj.

**melt** (melt) **1** change or be changed from solid to liquid by the action of heat: Ice becomes water when it melts. Great heat melts iron. **2** dissolve: Sugar melts in water. **3** disappear or cause to disappear gradually: As the sun came out, the clouds melted away. **4** blend or merge gradually: In the rainbow, the green melts into blue, the blue into violet. **5** soften; cause to become sympathetic: Pity for his wounded enemy melted his heart. v., **melt·ed, melt·ed** or **mol·ten, melt·ing.** —**melt′er,** n.

**melt·down** (melt′doun′) a situation in a nuclear reactor resulting from a failure of the cooling system so that heat generated by the reaction is not removed, and the metal holder for the bundles of fuel melts. If this happened, the reaction could no longer be controlled and would speed up, producing more heat and ending in a violent reaction, possibly an explosion. n.

**melting point** the temperature at which a solid substance melts.

**melting pot** **1** a pot or other vessel to melt something in. **2** a country or city thought of as a place in which various races or sorts of people are assimilated: America is often called a melting pot.

**melt·wa·ter** (melt′wot′ər) water from melting glaciers or snows. n.

**mem·ber** (mem′bər) **1** one belonging to a group: a member of our club. **2** a person elected to a legislative body: a Member of Parliament, a Member of the Legislative Assembly. **3** a constituent part of a whole: a member of an equation. **4** limb; a part of a human or animal body or of a plant, especially a leg, arm, wing, or branch. n.

**Member of Parliament** in Canada, a title given to each of the representatives elected to the Federal Parliament in Ottawa. Abbrev.: MP or M.P.

**Member of the House of Assembly** in Newfoundland, a member of the Legislative Assembly. Abbrev.: MHA or M.H.A.

**Member of the Legislative Assembly** a title given to each of the representatives elected to the legislatures of most Canadian provinces. Abbrev.: MLA or M.L.A.

**Member of the National Assembly** in Quebec, a title given to each of the representatives elected to the legislature. Abbrev.: MNA or M.N.A.

**Member of the Provincial Parliament** in Ontario, a Member of the Legislative Assembly. Abbrev.: MPP or M.P.P.

**mem·ber·ship** (mem′bər ship′) **1** the fact or state of being a member. **2** the members: The whole membership of the club was present. **3** the number of members: The membership of our club is over 30. n.

**mem·brane** (mem′brān) **1** a thin, soft sheet or layer of animal tissue, lining or covering some part of the body: One kind of membrane lines the stomach and another covers the front of the eyeball. **2** a similar layer of vegetable tissue. n.

**mem·bra·nous** (mem′brə nəs) **1** of or like membrane. **2** characterized by the formation of a membrane. In **membranous croup,** a membrane forms in the throat and hinders breathing. adj.

**me·men·to** (mə men′tō) something serving as a reminder, warning, or remembrance: These postcards are mementos of our trip abroad. n., pl. **me·men·tos** or **me·men·toes.**

**mem·o** (mem′ō) Informal. MEMORANDUM. n., pl. **mem·os.**

**mem·oir** (mem′wär) **1** biography. **2** a report of a scientific or scholarly study. n.

**mem·oirs** (mem′wärz) **1** a record of facts and events written from personal knowledge or special information.

**2** a record of a person's own experiences; autobiography: *The retired judge wrote her memoirs.* *n. pl.*

**mem·o·ra·bil·i·a** (mem′ə rə bil′ē ə)   things or events worth remembering.   *n. pl.*

**mem·o·ra·ble** (mem′ə rə bəl)   worth remembering; not to be forgotten; notable.   *adj.*   —**mem′o·ra·bly,** *adv.*

**mem·o·ran·da** (mem′ə ran′də)   a pl. of MEMORANDUM.   *n.*

**mem·o·ran·dum** (mem′ə ran′dəm)   **1** a short written statement for future use; a note to aid the memory: *Anna made a memorandum of her appointment with the dentist.* **2** an informal letter, note, or report.   *n., pl.* **mem·o·ran·dums** or **mem·o·ran·da** (mem′ə ran′də).

**me·mo·ri·al** (mə môr′ē əl)   **1** something that is a reminder of some event or person, such as a statue, an arch or column, a book, or a holiday.   **2** helping people to remember some person, thing, or event: *We have memorial services on Remembrance Day.*   **3** a statement sent to a government or person in authority, usually giving facts and asking that some wrong be corrected.   1, 3 *n.*, 2 *adj.*

**me·mo·ri·al·ize** (mə môr′ē ə līz′)   **1** preserve the memory of; COMMEMORATE.   **2** submit a memorial to; petition.   *v.*, **me·mo·ri·al·ized, me·mo·ri·al·iz·ing.**

**mem·o·rize** (mem′ə rīz′)   commit to memory; learn by heart: *to memorize the alphabet.*   *v.*, **mem·o·rized, mem·o·riz·ing.**   —**mem′o·ri·za′tion,** *n.* —**mem′o·riz′er,** *n.*

**mem·o·ry** (mem′ə rē)   **1** the ability to remember. **2** remembrance; remembering: *That vacation lives in her memory.*   **3** all that a person remembers.   **4** a person, thing, or event that is remembered: *His mother died when he was small; she is only a memory to him now.*   **5** the length of time during which the past is remembered: *This is the hottest summer within my memory.*   **6** reputation after death.   **7** the part of a computer that stores data. *n., pl.* **mem·ories.**
**in memory of,**   as a help in remembering; as a remembrance of: *On November 11 we observe a two-minute silence in memory of those who died for our country.*

**men** (men)   **1** pl. of MAN.   **2** human beings; people in general: *Men and animals have some things in common.*   *n. pl.*

**men·ace** (men′is)   **1** a threat: *In dry weather forest fires are a great menace.*   **2** threaten: *Floods menaced the valley towns with destruction.*   1 *n.*, 2 *v.*, **men·aced, men·ac·ing.** —**men′ac·ing·ly,** *adv.*

**mé·nage** or **menage** (mā näzh′)   *French.*   **1** a household; domestic establishment.   **2** housekeeping; management of a household.   *n.*

**me·nag·er·ie** (mə naj′ə rē)   **1** a collection of wild animals kept in cages for exhibition.   **2** the place where such animals are kept.   *n.*

**mend** (mend)   **1** put in good condition again; make whole; repair: *She mended the broken cup with cement.* **2** set right; improve: *He should mend his manners.*   **3** a place that has been mended: *The mend in your dress hardly shows.*   **4** get back one's health: *The child will soon mend if she has enough to eat.*   **5** a mending; improvement. 1, 2, 4 *v.*, 3, 5 *n.*
**on the mend,**   **a** improving.   **b** getting well.

**men·da·cious** (men dā′shəs)   **1** lying; untruthful: *a mendacious child.*   **2** false; untrue: *a mendacious rumour.* *adj.*   —**men·da′cious·ly,** *adv.*

---

**memorabilia**   743   **menopause**

hat, āge, fär; let, ēqual, tėrm; it, īce
hot, ōpen, ôrder; oil, out; cup, pùt, rüle
əbove, takən, pencəl, lemən, circəs
ch, child; ng, long; sh, ship
th, thin; ᴛʜ, then; zh, measure

**men·dac·i·ty** (men das′ə tē)   **1** the habit of telling lies; untruthfulness.   **2** a lie.   *n., pl.* **men·dac·i·ties.**

**men·de·le·vi·um** (men′də lā′vē əm *or* men′də lē′vē əm) a rare, radio-active, artificial element, produced as a by-product of nuclear fission.   *Symbol:* Md   *n.*

**Men·de·li·an** (men dē′lē ən)   **1** of Gregor Johann Mendel (1822–1884), an Austrian monk and botanist, who discovered the principles of genetics.   **2** inherited in accordance with MENDEL'S LAW.   *adj.*

**Mendel's Law**   a law describing the inheritance of many characteristics in animals and plants.

**men·di·can·cy** (men′də kən sē)   **1** the act of begging: *Since he was unable to work, he resorted to mendicancy.* **2** the state of being a beggar.   *n.*

**men·di·cant** (men′də kənt)   **1** begging: *Mendicant friars ask alms for charity.*   **2** beggar: *We were surrounded by mendicants asking for money.*   **3** a friar who begs. 1 *adj.*, 2, 3 *n.*

**men·folk** (men′fōk′)   **1** men.   **2** the male members of a family or other group.   *n. pl.*

**me·ni·al** (mē′nē əl)   **1** belonging to or suited to a servant; low; mean: *Cinderella had to do menial tasks.* **2** a servant who does the humblest and most unpleasant tasks.   1 *adj.*, 2 *n.*   —**me′ni·al·ly,** *adv.*

**me·nin·ges** (mə nin′jēz)   the three membranes that surround the brain and spinal cord.   *n., pl.* of **me·ninx** (mē′ningks).

**men·in·gi·tis** (men′in jī′tis)   a serious disease in which the MENINGES are inflamed.   *n.*

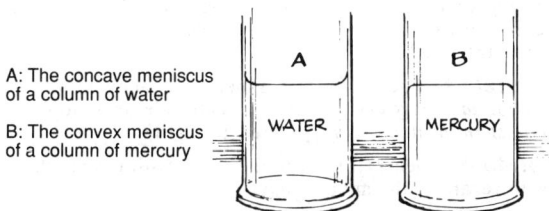

A: The concave meniscus of a column of water
B: The convex meniscus of a column of mercury

**me·nis·cus** (mə nis′kəs)   **1** the curved upper surface of a column of liquid: *The meniscus is concave when the walls of the container are made wet by the liquid and convex when they are not.*   **2** a lens that is concave on one side and convex on the other. See CONCAVE for picture.   **3** a crescent or crescent-shaped body.   *n., pl.* **me·nis·cus·es** or **me·nis·ci** (-nis′ī *or* -nis′ē).

**Men·non·ite** (men′ə nīt′)   a member of a Christian group that believes that the church should be separate from the government, that babies and young children do not need to be baptized, and that it is always wrong to go to war: *Some Mennonites wear very plain clothes and live simply. Mennonites have fine farms in western Canada and in Ontario.*   *n.*
☞ *Etym.*   Named after *Menno* Simons (1492–1559), an early Dutch leader of the group.

**men·o·pause** (men′ə poz′)   the period in a woman's

**menorah** life during which menstruation ceases permanently, usually between the ages of 45 and 55; change of life. *n.*

**men·o·rah** or **Men·o·rah** (mə nô′rə) a candelabrum used in Jewish worship: *The seven-branched menorah is used in temple services; the nine-branched one is used during Hanukkah.* *n.*

**men·ses** (men′sēz) MENSTRUATION. *n. pl.*

**men·stru·al** (men′strü əl) of or having to do with MENSTRUATION. *adj.*

**men·stru·ate** (men′strü āt′ *or* men′strāt) have a period; undergo MENSTRUATION. *v.*, **men·stru·at·ed, men·stru·at·ing.**

**men·stru·a·tion** (men′strü ā′shən *or* men strā′shən) the regular discharge of blood, secretions, and sloughed-off tissue from the uterus through the vagina, normally occurring about every four weeks in non-pregnant women from puberty to menopause. *n.*

**men·stru·um** (men′strü əm) a liquid that dissolves solids; solvent. *n., pl.* **men·stru·ums** or **men·stru·a** (-strü ə).

**men·su·ra·bil·i·ty** (men′shə rə bil′ə tē) the property of being MENSURABLE. *n.*

**men·su·ra·ble** (men′shə rə bəl) measurable. *adj.*

**men·su·ra·tion** (men′shə rā′shən) 1 the act, art, or process of measuring. 2 the branch of mathematics that deals with finding lengths, areas, and volumes. *n.*

**–ment** noun-forming suffix meaning: 1 the act or state or fact of _____ing, as in *enjoyment, management.* 2 the state or condition or fact of being _____ed, as in *amazement, astonishment.* 3 the product or result of _____ing, as in *pavement.* 4 a means or instrument for _____ing, as in *inducement.*

**men·tal** (men′təl) 1 of the mind: *a mental disease.* 2 for the mind; done by the mind: *mental arithmetic.* 3 having a mental disease or weakness. 4 for people who are mentally ill: *a mental hospital.* *adj.* —**men′tal·ly,** *adv.*

**men·tal·i·ty** (men tal′ə tē) 1 mental capacity; mind: *An idiot has a very low mentality.* 2 attitude or outlook: *the Eastern mentality.* *n., pl.* **men·tal·i·ties.**

**men·tal·ly** (men′tə lē) 1 in the mind; with the mind. 2 with regard to the mind. *adv.*

**mental reservation** an unexpressed qualification of a statement.

**mental telepathy** EXTRASENSORY PERCEPTION.

**men·thol** (men′thol) a white crystalline substance obtained from oil of peppermint and used in medicine. *n.*

**men·tho·lat·ed** (men′thə lā′tid) containing MENTHOL. *adj.*

**men·tion** (men′shən) 1 speak about; refer to: *Do not mention the accident to the children.* 2 a short statement about; reference to: *There was mention of the school party in the newspaper.* 1 *v.,* 2 *n.*
**make mention of,** speak of; refer to: *She made mention of her most famous pupil.*
**not to mention,** not even considering; besides.

**men·tor** (men′tər) a wise and trusted adviser. *n.*
▶ *Etym.* From *Mentor,* in Greek legend, a faithful friend of Ulysses: *Mentor was the teacher and advisor of Ulysses' son Telemachus.*

**men·u** (men′yü) 1 a list of the food served at a meal; bill of fare. 2 the food served. 3 in computer programs, a list of choices that allows the user to select a topic. *n.*

**me·ow** (mē ou′) 1 the sound made by a cat. 2 make this sound or one like it. 1 *n.,* 2 *v.* Also, **miaow, miaou.**

**me·phit·ic** (mi fit′ik) 1 having a nasty smell. 2 noxious; poisonous; pestilential. *adj.*

**me·phi·tis** (mi fī′tis) 1 a foul or nasty smell. 2 a poisonous or nasty vapour arising from the earth. *n.*

**mer·can·tile** (mėr′kən tīl′) of merchants or trade; commercial: *a mercantile firm, mercantile law.* *adj.*

**mercantile system** MERCANTILISM.

**mer·can·til·ism** (mėr′kən tī liz′əm) a theory or system of political economy that stressed the holding of gold and other precious metals, a greater volume of exports than imports, and the exploitation of colonies. *Mercantilism replaced feudalism.* *n.*

**mer·can·til·ist** (mėr′kən tī′list) a person who favours MERCANTILISM. *n.*

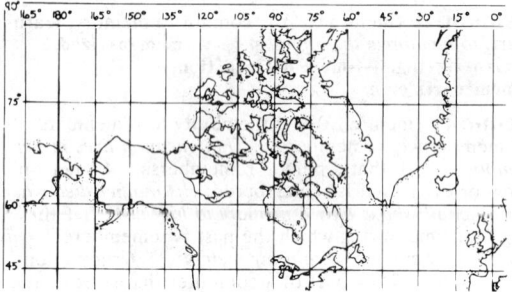

A Mercator projection of part of the Northern Hemisphere

**Mer·ca·tor projection** (mėr kā′tər) a method of drawing maps with straight instead of curved lines for latitude and longitude.

**mer·ce·nar·y** (mėr′sə ner′ē) 1 working for money only; acting with money as the motive. 2 done for money or gain. 3 a soldier serving for pay in a foreign army. 1, 2 *adj.,* 3 *n., pl.* **mer·ce·nar·ies.**

**mer·cer·ize** (mėr′sə rīz′) treat cotton thread or cloth with a chemical solution that strengthens it and makes it hold dyes better: *Mercerizing cotton gives it a silky lustre.* *v.,* **mer·cer·ized, mer·cer·iz·ing.**

**mer·chan·dise** (mėr′chən dīs′ or mėr′chən dīz′ for noun, mėr′chən dīz′ for verb) 1 goods for sale; wares; articles bought and sold. 2 buy and sell; trade. 1 *n.,* 2 *v.,* **mer·chan·dised, mer·chan·dis·ing.**
—**mer′chan·dis′er,** *n.*

**mer·chant** (mėr′chənt) 1 a person who buys and sells: *The business of some merchants is mostly with foreign countries.* 2 storekeeper. 3 trading; having to do with trade: *merchant ships.* 1, 2 *n.,* 3 *adj.*

**mer·chant·man** (mėr′chənt mən) a ship used in commerce. *n., pl.* **mer·chant·men** (-mən).

**merchant marine** 1 ships used in commerce. 2 the sailors who work on such ships, thought of as a group: *Jag's brother is in the merchant marine.*

**merchant vessel** a ship used in commerce.

**mer·ci·ful** (mėr′si fəl) having mercy; showing or feeling mercy; full of mercy. *adj.* —**mer′ci·ful·ly,** *adv.* —**mer′ci·ful·ness,** *n.*

**mer·ci·less** (mėr′si lis) without mercy; having no mercy; showing no mercy: *The invader's attack on the town was merciless. adj.* —**mer′ci·less·ly,** *adv.* —**mer′ci·less·ness,** *n.*

**mer·cu·ri·al** (mər kyü′rē əl) **1** sprightly; quick. **2** changeable; fickle. **3** caused by the use of mercury: *mercurial poisoning.* **4** containing mercury: *a mercurial ointment.* **5** a drug containing mercury. 1–4 *adj.*, 5 *n.* —**mer·cu′ri·al·ly,** *adv.*

**mer·cu·ric** (mər kyü′rik) of compounds, containing mercury with a valence of two. *adj.*

**mercuric chloride** a poisonous crystalline compound used as a disinfectant, for engraving metals, etc.

**mer·cu·rous** (mər kyü′rəs) of compounds, containing mercury with a valence of one. *adj.*

**mer·cu·ry** (mėr′kyə rē) **1** a heavy, silver-white metallic element that is liquid at ordinary temperatures. Symbol: Hg **2** the column of mercury in a thermometer or barometer. *n., pl.* **mer·cu·ries.**
☞ *Etym.* See note below.

**Mer·cu·ry** (mėr′kyə rē) the planet nearest the sun. *n.*
☞ *Etym.* Named after *Mercury*, in Roman mythology, the messenger of the gods, the god of commerce and of skill of hands, quickness of wit, and eloquence.

**mer·cy** (mėr′sē) **1** more kindness than justice requires; kindness beyond what can be claimed or expected: *The judge showed mercy to the young offender.* **2** kindly treatment; pity. **3** something to be thankful for; blessing: *It's a mercy that they arrived safely through the storm. n., pl.* **mer·cies.**
**at the mercy of,** in the power of: *Without shelter we were at the mercy of the storm.*

**mere** (mēr) nothing else than; only; simple: *The cut was a mere scratch. adj., superl.* **mer·est.**

**mere·ly** (mēr′lē) simply; only; and nothing more; and that is all. *adv.*

**mer·e·tri·cious** (mer′ə trish′əs) attractive in a showy way; alluring by false charms: *A wooden building painted to look like marble is meretricious. adj.* —**mer′e·tri′cious·ly,** *adv.* —**mer′e·tri′cious·ness,** *n.*

**mer·gan·ser** (mər gan′sər) any of several kinds of large ducks that have long, slender bills: *The male merganser has a crested head. n., pl.* **mer·gan·sers** or (*especially collectively*) **mer·gan·ser.**

**merge** (mėrj) **1** swallow up; absorb; combine: *The sisters decided to merge their two businesses.* **2** combine or blend: *Traffic on this road merges with eastbound traffic on the highway. The walker merged into the darkness.* **3** in computer science, combine two or more pieces of information. *v.*, **merged, merg·ing.**

**merg·er** (mėr′jər) the act of merging; combination: *One big company was formed by the merger of four small ones. n.*

**me·rid·i·an** (mə rid′ē ən) **1** an imaginary circle passing through any place on the earth's surface and through the North and South Poles. See LATITUDE for picture. **2** the half of such a circle from pole to pole: *All the places on the same meridian have the same longitude.* **3** the highest point that the sun or a star reaches in the sky. **4** the highest point; the time of greatest success and happiness: *The meridian of life is the prime of life.* **5** highest; greatest. 1–4 *n.*, 5 *adj.*

**Meridian, First** or **Principal** *Cdn.* the basic north-south line from which lands were surveyed in the Northwest Territories and are now surveyed in the Prairie Provinces: *The First Meridian is located just west of Winnipeg.*

**me·rid·i·o·nal** (mə rid′ē ə nəl) **1** southern; southerly; characteristic of the south or people living there, especially of southern France. **2** an inhabitant of the south, especially the south of France. **3** of, having to do with, or resembling a meridian. 1, 3 *adj.*, 2 *n.*

**me·ringue** (mə rang′) **1** a mixture of egg white and sugar, beaten until stiff: *Meringue is often spread on pies, puddings, etc. and lightly browned in the oven.* **2** a small cake, tart shell, etc. made of this mixture. *n.*

**me·ri·no** (mə rē′nō) **1** a kind of sheep having long, fine wool. **2** a soft yarn made from the wool of this sheep. **3** made of this wool, yarn, or cloth. *n., pl.* **me·ri·nos.**

**mer·it** (mer′it) **1** goodness; worth or value: *The council agreed that our plan for a community playground had merit. Each child will get a mark according to the merit of her work.* **2** anything that deserves praise or reward. **3** deserve: *A hardworking girl merits praise.* **4** Usually, **merits,** *pl.* actual facts or qualities, whether good or bad: *The judge will consider the case on its merits.* 1, 2, 4 *n.*, 3 *v.*

**mer·i·to·ri·ous** (mer′ə tô′rē əs) deserving reward or praise; having merit; worthy. *adj.* —**mer′i·to′ri·ous·ly,** *adv.* —**mer′i·to′ri·ous·ness,** *n.*

**mer·maid** (mėr′mād′) an imaginary sea maiden having the form of a fish from the waist down. *n.*

**mer·man** (mėr′man′ *or* mėr′mən) an imaginary man of the sea having the form of a fish from the waist down. *n., pl.* **mer·men** (-men′ *or* -mən).

**mer·ri·ment** (mer′ē mənt) laughter and gaiety; fun; mirth; merry enjoyment. *n.*

**mer·ri·ness** (mer′ē nis) being merry; laughter; fun. *n.*

**mer·ry** (mer′ē) **1** full of fun; loving fun. **2** happy; joyful: *a merry holiday. adj.*, **mer·ri·er, mer·ri·est.** —**mer′ri·ly,** *adv.*
**make merry,** laugh and be happy; have fun.
☞ *Hom.* MARRY (mer′ē).

**mer·ry-an·drew** (mer′ē an′drü) a clown or buffoon. *n.*

**mer·ry-go-round** (mer′ē gō round′) **1** a set of animal figures and seats on a platform that is driven round and round by machinery and that people ride for fun. **2** any whirl or rapid round: *a merry-go-round of parties. n.*

**mer·ry·mak·er** (mer′ē mā′kər) a person who is being merry; person engaged in merrymaking. *n.*

**mer·ry·mak·ing** (mer′ē mā′king) **1** laughter and

---

hat, āge, fär; let, ēqual, tėrm; it, īce
hot, ōpen, ôrder; oil, out; cup, pút, rüle
əbove, takən, pencəl, lemən, circəs
ch, child; ng, long; sh, ship
th, thin; ᴛн, then; zh, measure

gaiety; fun.   2 a happy festival; merry entertainment.   3 full of fun; engaged in merrymaking.   1, 2 *n.*, 3 *adj.*

**mé·sal·li·ance** (mā zal/ē əns; *French,* mā zä lyäns/)   misalliance; marriage with a person of lower social position.   *n.*

**mes·cal** (mes kal/)   1 an alcoholic drink made from the fermented juice of an agave plant.   2 the plant itself.   3 a small cactus whose buttonlike tops are dried and chewed as a stimulant by some American Indians.   *n.*

**mes·dames** (mā däm/)   pl. of MADAME.   *n.*

**mes·de·moi·selles** (mād mwä zel/)   pl. of MADEMOISELLE.   *n.*

**mesh** (mesh)   1 one of the open spaces of a net, sieve, or screen: *This net has one-centimetre meshes.*   2 cord, wire, etc., used in a net or screen: *We found an old fly swatter made of wire mesh.*   3 catch or be caught in a net.   4 engage or become engaged: *The teeth of gears mesh.*   5 agree: *Their ideas do not mesh.*   6 meshes,   a web; network: *Seaweed was caught in the meshes of the net.*   **b** snares.   1, 2, 6 *n.*, 3, 4, 5 *v.*
**in mesh,**   in gear; fitted together.

**mes·mer·ic** (mes mer/ik)   HYPNOTIC.   *adj.*

**mes·mer·ism** (mes/mə riz/əm)   HYPNOTISM.   *n.*

**mes·mer·ist** (mes/mə rist)   HYPNOTIST.   *n.*

**mes·mer·ize** (mes/mə rīz/)   HYPNOTIZE.   *v.*, **mes·mer·ized, mes·mer·iz·ing.**   —**mes/mer·iz/er,** *n.*
☛ Etym. Named after Franz *Mesmer* (1734–1815), an Austrian doctor who made hypnotism popular.

**mes·o·lith·ic** (mez/ə lith/ik *or* mes/ə lith/ik)   of or having to do with a period in the Stone Age between the PALEOLITHIC and NEOLITHIC periods.   *adj.*

**mes·on** (mes/on)   a highly unstable heavy electron found in cosmic rays; a particle having the same electric charge as an electron, but much greater mass: *In theory, mesons exert nuclear forces of attraction.*   *n.*

**mes·o·phyll** (mes/ə fil)   the soft tissue inside a leaf that aids PHOTOSYNTHESIS.   *n.*

**Mes·o·po·ta·mi·a** (mes/ə pə tā/mē ə)   an ancient country in southwestern Asia, between the Tigris and Euphrates rivers.   *n.*   —**Mes/o·po·ta/mi·an,** *adj., n.*

**mes·o·sphere** (mes/ə sfēr/)   the layer of the earth's atmosphere lying above the stratosphere, extending from about 50 km to about 85 km above the earth's surface, and characterized by a decrease in temperature with increasing altitude, to about -90°C. at the point where the thermosphere begins.   *n.*

**mes·o·tron** (mes/ə tron/)   MESON.   *n.*

**Mes·o·zo·ic** (mez/ə zō/ik *or* mes/ə zō/ik)   in geology:   1 of, having to do with, or referring to the era before the present era, beginning about 200 million years ago: *The Mesozoic era is the age of reptiles.*   See geological time chart in the Appendix.   2 of, having to do with, or referring to the system of rocks formed during this era.   3 the Mesozoic era or its rocks.   1, 2 *adj.*, 3 *n.*

**mes·quite** (mes kēt/ *or* mes/kēt)   a spiny tree or shrub of the legume family found in the southwestern United States and Mexico, bearing sugary pods of seeds used as fodder.   *n.*

**mess** (mes)   1 a dirty or untidy mass or group of things; a dirty or untidy condition: *There was a mess of dirty dishes in the sink.*   2 make dirty or untidy: *She messed up her book by scribbling on the pages.*   3 confusion or difficulty: *His affairs are in a mess.*   4 make a failure of; spoil: *He messed up his chances of winning the race.*   5 an unpleasant or unsuccessful affair or state of affairs: *She made a mess of her final examinations.*   6 a group of people who eat together regularly, especially such a group in the armed forces.   7 a meal for such a group: *The officers were at mess.*   8 take one's meals with.   9 an organization for social purposes in the armed forces: *He was secretary of the sergeants' mess.*   10 the dining-room, lounge, etc. used by members of such an organization: *He spent every Saturday evening at the mess.*   11 a portion of food, especially of soft food: *a mess of porridge, a mess of fish.*   12 food that does not look or taste good.   1, 3, 5–7, 9–12 *n.*, 2, 4, 8 *v.*
**mess about** or **mess around,**   busy oneself without seeming to accomplish anything.

**mes·sage** (mes/ij)   1 information or instructions sent from one person to another.   2 an official speech or writing: *On Christmas Day we listened to the Queen's message to the Commonwealth.*   3 a lesson or moral in a work or works of fiction, a motion picture, play, etc.   4 inspired words: *the message of a prophet.*   *n.*

**mes·sen·ger** (mes/ən jər)   1 a person who carries a message or goes on an errand.   2 any animal or thing thought of as carrying a message: *Each bullet was a messenger of death.*   3 a sign that something is coming; forerunner; herald: *Dawn is the messenger of day.*   *n.*

**mess hall**   in the armed forces, a place where a group of people eat together regularly.

**mes·sieurs** (mes/ərz; *French,* mā syœ/)   pl. of MONSIEUR.   *n.*

**mess·mate** (mes/māt/)   one of a group of people who eat together regularly.   *n*

**Messrs.** (mes/ərz)   pl. of MR.: *Messrs. Diefenbaker and Green.*   *n. pl.*

**mess·y** (mes/ē)   1 in a mess; untidy; dirty.   2 badly done.   *adj.*, **mess·i·er, mess·i·est.**   —**mess/i·ness,** *n.*

**met** (met)   pt. and pp. of MEET¹: *My father met us at ten. We were met at the gate by our dog.*   *v.*

**met.**   1 meteorological.   2 metronome.   3 metropolitan.

**met·a·bol·ic** (met/ə bol/ik)   having to do with METABOLISM.   *adj.*

**me·tab·o·lism** (mə tab/ə liz/əm)   the processes of building up food into living matter and of using living matter until it is broken down into simpler substances or waste matter, giving off energy.   *n.*

**met·a·car·pal** (met/ə kär/pəl)   1 of or having to do with the METACARPUS.   2 a metacarpal bone.   1 *adj.*, 2 *n.*

**met·a·car·pus** (met/ə kär/pəs)   1 the part of the hand between the wrist (the CARPUS) and the fingers (the PHALANGES), containing five long bones.   See ARM¹ for picture.   2 the corresponding part in the foreleg of an animal; the long bone or bones between the knee (the CARPUS) and the paw or hoof (the PHALANGES).   *n., pl.* **met·a·car·pi** (-pī *or* -pē).

**met·al** (met/əl)   1 a substance that is usually shiny, a good conductor of heat and electricity, and can be made into wire, or hammered into sheets: *Gold, silver, iron, copper, lead, tin, or aluminum are metals.*   2 an alloy or mixture of these, such as steel and brass.   3 made of metal or a mixture of metals: *a metal container, a metal*

coin. **4** any chemical element that can form a salt by replacing the hydrogen of an acid, or any mixture of such elements. **5** broken stone, cinders, etc. used for roads and roadbeds. **6** the melted material that becomes glass or pottery. **7** material; substance: *Cowards are not made of the same metal as heroes.* 1, 2, 4–7 *n.*, 3 *adj.*
☛ *Hom.* METTLE.

**me·tal·lic** (mə talʹik) **1** of or containing metal: *a metallic substance.* **2** like metal in lustre, hardness, etc.; that suggests metal: *a metallic cloth, a metallic voice. adj.*

**met·al·lif·er·ous** (metʹə lifʹə rəs)   containing or yielding metal: *metalliferous rocks.   adj.*

**met·al·lur·gic** (metʹə lėrʹjik; *also, esp. Brit.,* mə talʹər jik)   METALLURGICAL. *adj.*

**met·al·lur·gi·cal** (metʹə lėrʹjə kəl)   of or having to do with METALLURGY. *adj.*

**met·al·lur·gist** (metʹə lėrʹjist; *also, esp. Brit.,* mə talʹər jist)   a person who is trained in METALLURGY. *n.*

**met·al·lur·gy** (metʹə lėrʹjē; *also, esp. Brit.,* mə talʹər jē)   the science or art of working with metals, including the separating of them from their ores and refining them for use.   *n.*

**met·al·work** (metʹəl werkʹ)   **1** things made out of metal.   **2** the act of making things out of metal.   *n.*

**met·al·work·er** (metʹəl werʹkər)   a person who makes things out of metal.   *n.*

**met·al·work·ing** (metʹəl werʹking)   the process of making things out of metal.   *n.*

**met·a·mor·phic** (metʹə môrʹfik)   **1** characterized by change of form; having to do with change of form.   **2** in geology, referring to rock derived from either IGNEOUS or SEDIMENTARY rock that has undergone changes in composition, texture, or internal structure through the action of pressure, heat, moisture, etc.: *Slate is a metamorphic rock formed from shale.   adj.*

**met·a·mor·phism** (metʹə môrʹfiz əm)   **1** a change of form.   **2** a change in the structure of a rock caused by pressure, heat, etc.   *n.*

**met·a·mor·phose** (metʹə môrʹfōz)   change in form; transform: *The witch metamorphosed people into animals. v.,* met·a·mor·phosed, met·a·mor·phos·ing.

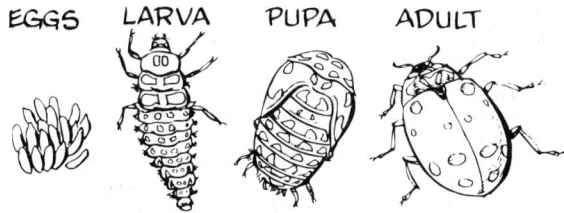

The four stages in the metamorphosis of a ladybug

**met·a·mor·pho·sis** (metʹə môrʹfə sis *or* metʹə môr fōʹsis)   **1** a change of form: *Tadpoles become frogs by metamorphosis; they lose their tails and grow legs.* **2** the changed form.   **3** a noticeable or complete change of character, appearance, or condition.   *n., pl.* met·a·mor·pho·ses (-sēzʹ).

**met·a·phase** (metʹə fāzʹ)   the second stage of MITOSIS, in which the nuclear membrane disintegrates, and the split chromosomes form a straight line.   *n.*

## metallic 747 meteor

hat, āge, fär; let, ēqual, tėrm; it, īce
hot, ōpen, ôrder; oil, out; cup, put, rüle
ə bove, tə ken, pencəl, lemən, circəs
ch, child; ng, long; sh, ship
th, thin; ᴛʜ, then; zh, measure

**met·a·phor** (metʹə fər *or* metʹə fôrʹ)   an implied comparison between two different things; a figure of speech in which a word or phrase that ordinarily means one thing is used of another thing in order to suggest a likeness between the two: *"A copper sky"* and *"a heart of stone" are metaphors.* Compare with SIMILE.   *n.*
**mix metaphors,**   confuse two or more metaphors in the same expression.
☛ *Syn.* Metaphors and SIMILES both make comparisons. A **metaphor** talks about one thing as if it were another: *Arrows of flame shot into the air.* A simile says that one thing is like another: *Flames shot into the air like arrows.*

**met·a·phor·i·cal** (metʹə fôrʹə kəl)   using METAPHORS; figurative.   *adj.* —**metʹa·phorʹi·cal·ly,** *adv.*

**met·a·phys·i·cal** (metʹə fizʹə kəl)   **1** of METAPHYSICS; about the real nature of things.   **2** highly abstract; hard to understand.   *adj.* —**metʹa·physʹi·cal·ly,** *adv.*

**met·a·phy·si·cian** (metʹə fə zishʹən)   a person skilled in or familiar with METAPHYSICS.   *n.*

**met·a·phys·ics** (metʹə fizʹiks)   the branch of philosophy that tries to explain reality and knowledge; the philosophical study of the real nature of the universe.   *n.*

**me·tas·ta·sis** (mə tasʹtə sis)   in medicine, the growth or spread of cells, especially of the diseased cells of a tumour or cancer, from one organ or part of the body to another.   *n., pl.* me·tas·ta·ses (-sēz).

**me·tas·ta·size** (mə tasʹtə sīzʹ)   undergo METASTASIS: *Has the cancer metastasized?*

**met·a·tar·sal** (metʹə tärʹsəl)   **1** of or having to do with the METATARSUS.   **2** a metatarsal bone: *The human foot has five metatarsals.* 1 *adj.*, 2 *n.*

**met·a·tar·sus** (metʹə tärʹsəs)   **1** the part of the foot between the heel and ankle (the TARSUS) and the toes (the PHALANGES), containing five long bones: *The metatarsus includes the instep and arch of the foot.* See LEG for picture.   **2** the corresponding part in the hind leg of an animal; the long bone or bones between the hock (the TARSUS) and the paw or hoof (the PHALANGES): *In a hoofed animal such as the horse, the metatarsus is called the cannon bone.   n., pl.* met·a·tar·si (-sī *or* -sē).

**met·a·zo·an** (metʹə zōʹən)   **1** any animal belonging to the Metazoa, a large zoological division made up of all animals having a body composed of many cells arranged into different tissues and organs with specialized functions. **2** of, having to do with, or referring to this group of animals.   1 *n.*, 2 *adj.*

**mete** (mēt)   give to each a share of; distribute; allot: *The judges will mete out praise and blame.   v.,* met·ed, met·ing.
☛ *Hom.* MEAT, MEET.

**met·emp·sy·cho·sis** (metʹəm sī kōʹsis)   the passing of the soul at death into a new body: *Some Oriental philosophies teach that by metempsychosis a person's soul lives again in an animal's body.   n., pl.* met·em·psy·cho·ses (-sēz).

**me·te·or** (mēʹtē ər)   a mass of stone or metal that comes toward the earth from outer space at enormous

**meteoric** / **metric system**

speed: *Meteors become so hot from hurtling through the air that they glow and usually burn up.* *n.*

**me·te·or·ic** (mē′tē ô′rik) **1** of METEORS: *a meteoric shower.* **2** flashing like a METEOR; brilliant and soon ended: *a singer's meteoric rise to fame.* **3** of the atmosphere: *Wind and rain are meteoric phenomena.* *adj.*

**me·te·or·ite** (mē′tē ə rīt′) a mass of stone or metal that has fallen to the earth from outer space; a fallen METEOR. *n.*

**me·te·or·oid** (mē′tē ə roid′) any of the solid bodies in outer space seen as meteors on entering the earth's atmosphere. *n.*

**me·te·or·o·log·ic** (mē′tē ə rə loj′ik) METEOROLOGICAL. *adj.*

**me·te·or·o·log·i·cal** (mē′tē ə rə loj′ə kəl) **1** having to do with the atmosphere and weather. **2** of or having to do with METEOROLOGY. *adj.*

**me·te·or·o·log·i·cal·ly** (mē′tē ə rə loj′i klē) in METEOROLOGICAL respects; by METEOROLOGY; according to meteorology. *adv.*

**me·te·or·ol·o·gist** (mē′tē ə rol′ə jist) a person trained in METEOROLOGY. *n.*

**me·te·or·ol·o·gy** (mē′tē ə rol′ə jē) the science of the atmosphere and weather: *Weather forecasting is a part of meteorology.* *n.*

**–meter** combining form. **1** a device for measuring, as in *speedometer, thermometer, barometer.* **2** having metrical feet, as in *pentameter.*

**me·ter**[1] (mē′tər) See METRE. *n.*

**me·ter**[2] (mē′tər) **1** a device that measures, or that measures and records: *a parking meter, a water meter.* **2** measure with a meter. **1** *n.,* **2** *v.*
☛ *Hom.* METRE.

**meth·ane** (meth′ān) a colourless, odourless, flammable gas, the simplest of the hydrocarbons: *Methane comes from marshes, petroleum wells, volcanoes, and coal mines.* *n.*

**meth·od** (meth′əd) **1** a way of doing something: *a method of teaching music. Roasting is one method of cooking meat.* **2** order or system in getting things done or in thinking: *If you used more method, you wouldn't waste so much time.* *n.*
**method in one's madness,** system and sense in what appears to be folly.

**me·thod·ic** (mə thod′ik) METHODICAL. *adj.*

**me·thod·i·cal** (mə thod′ə kəl) **1** done or arranged according to a method or order: *a methodical procedure.* **2** tending to act according to a method: *a methodical thinker.* *adj.* —**me·thod′i·cal·ly,** *adv.*
—**me·thod′i·cal·ness,** *n.*

**meth·od·ize** (meth′ə dīz) reduce to a method; arrange with method. *v.,* **meth·od·ized, meth·od·iz·ing.**

**meth·od·ol·o·gy** (meth′ə dol′ə jē) **1** a system or body of procedures, methods, and rules used in a particular field or discipline. **2** the branch of logic that deals with the analysis of such procedures and methods. *n.*

**meth·yl alcohol** (meth′əl) WOOD ALCOHOL.

**methylene blue** a blue analine dye used as a stain in isolating bacteria for microscopic examination.

**me·tic·u·lous** (mə tik′yə ləs) extremely or excessively careful about small details. *adj.*
—**me·tic′u·lous·ly,** *adv.*

**mé·tier** (mā tyā′) **1** a trade; profession. **2** the kind of work for which one has special ability. *n.*

**Mé·tis** or **Me·tis** (mā tē′, mā′tē, *or* mā tēs′) *Cdn.* **1** a person descended from Europeans, especially the French, and First Nations people who established themselves in the Red, Assiniboine, and Saskatchewan river valleys during the 19th century, forming a cultural group distinct from both Europeans and First Nations. **2** of or having to do with the Métis. **1** *n., pl.* **Mé·tis** or **Me·tis;** **2** *adj.*
☛ *Etym.* Through Canadian French from F *métis,* which developed from late Latin *misticius, mixticius* 'of mixed blood'.

**me·ton·y·my** (mə ton′ə mē) the use of the name of one thing for that of another which it naturally suggests. *Example: The pen (power of literature) is mightier than the sword (force).* *n.*

**me·tre**[1] (mē′tər) **1** any kind of poetic rhythm; the arrangement of beats or accents in a line of poetry: *The metre of "Jack and Jill went up the hill" is different from that of "O Canada."* **2** a musical rhythm; the arrangement of beats in music: *Three-four metre is waltz time.* *n.* Also, **meter.**
☛ *Hom.* METER.

**me·tre**[2] (mē′tər) an SI unit for measuring length: *A twin bed is about one metre wide. The metre is one of the seven base units in the SI.* *Symbol:* m *n.* Also, **meter.**
☛ *Hom.* METER.

**metre–stick** (mē′tər stik′) a measuring stick that is one metre long and is marked off in centimetres and millimetres. *n.*

**met·ric** (met′rik) **1** of the metre or the system of measurement based on it. **2** METRICAL. *adj.*

**met·ri·cal** (met′rə kəl) **1** of metre; having a regular arrangement of stresses or accents; written in verse, not in prose: *a metrical translation of Homer.* **2** of, having to do with, or used in, measurement. *adj.*

**met·ri·cal·ly** (met′ri klē) in METRE[1]; according to metre. *adv.*

**met·ri·cate** (met′rə kāt′) change into or express in a METRIC SYSTEM of measurement. *v.,* **met·ri·cat·ed, met·ri·cat·ing.**

**met·ri·ca·tion** (met′rə kā′shən) the act or process of converting from an existing system of measurement into a METRIC one. *n.*

**metric system** a decimal system of measurement, that is, one based on tens, traditionally using the metre as the basic unit of length, the kilogram as the basic unit of mass, and the litre as the basic unit of volume or capacity: *The metric system adopted by Canada is the new, simplified international version established in 1960, called the International System of Units (SI). It has a total of seven base units and two supplementary units from which all the other units are derived:*

| Quantity | Name | Symbol |
| --- | --- | --- |
| length | metre | m |
| mass | kilogram | kg |
| time | second | s |
| electric current | ampere | A |
| thermodynamic temperature | kelvin | K |
| amount of substance | mole | mol |
| luminous intensity | candela | cd |
| plane angle | radian | rad |
| solid angle | steradian | sr |

**metric ton** TONNE.

**met·ro** (met′rō) *Informal.* **1** a metropolitan government. **2** a metropolitan area. **3** a subway stystem, especially that of Montreal. *n.*

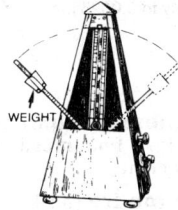

A metronome. The beat is regulated by the movable weight on the inverted pendulum. The higher the weight is moved, the slower the rate of swing of the pendulum and therefore, the slower the beat.

**met·ro·nome** (met′rə nōm′) a clocklike device with a pendulum that can be adjusted to tick at different speeds: *A metronome is used mainly by persons practising a musical instrument to help them keep time. n.*

**met·ro·nom·ic** (met′rə nom′ik) of or like a METRONOME. *adj.*

**me·trop·o·lis** (mə trop′ə lis) **1** the most important city of a country or region: *London is the metropolis of England.* **2** a large city; an important centre: *Montreal is a busy metropolis.* **3** the chief diocese of a church province. *n.*

**met·ro·pol·i·tan** (met′rə pol′ə tən) **1** of a large city; belonging to large cities: *metropolitan newspapers.* **2** a person who lives in a large city and knows its ways. **3** denoting a form of municipal government consisting of a type of federation of several municipalities within a metropolitan area. **4** the chief bishop who has authority over the bishops of a church province. **5** in the Eastern Church, a priest ranking above an archbishop and below a patriarch. 1, 3 *adj.,* 2, 4, 5 *n.*
**metropolitan area,** the area or region including a large city and its suburbs.

**met·tle** (met′əl) **1** disposition; spirit. **2** courage. *n.*
**on one's mettle,** ready to do one's best.
☛ *Hom.* METAL.

**met·tle·some** (met′əl səm) full of METTLE; spirited; courageous. *adj.*

**me·tump** (mə tump′) a broad strap or headband that is passed around the forehead and attached to a load carried on the back. See TUMPLINE for picture. *n.*

**Mev** (mev) a million electron volts. *n.*

**mew**[1] (myü) **1** the sound made by a cat or kitten. **2** make this sound: *Our kitten mews when it gets hungry.* 1 *n.,* 2 *v.*

**mew**[2] (myü) a sea gull; gull. *n.*

**mews** (myüz) *Esp. Brit.* **1** a set of stables built around a court or alley. **2** such stables converted into dwellings. *n.*

**Mex.** **1** Mexico. **2** Mexican.

**Mex·i·can** (mek′sə kən) **1** of or having to do with Mexico, a country in southern North America, or its people. **2** a native or inhabitant of Mexico. **3** a person of Mexican descent. 1 *adj.,* 2, 3 *n.*

**mez·za·nine** (mez′ə nēn′) **1** a partial storey between two main floors of a building: *Many hotels have a mezzanine between the ground floor and the next main floor up.* **2** in a theatre, the lowest balcony or its front section: *Tickets are $25.00 for seats in the mezzanine and $20.00 for the second balcony. n.*

---

**metric ton**     **749**     **micro-**

hat, āge, fär; let, ēqual, tėrm; it, īce
hot, ōpen, ôrder; oil, out; cup, put, rüle
əbove, takən, pencəl, lemən, circəs
ch, child; ng, long; sh, ship
th, thin; ᴛʜ, then; zh, measure

**mez·zo** (met′sō *or* mez′ō) **1** in music, middle; medium; half. **2** *Informal.* MEZZO-SOPRANO. 1 *adj.,* 2 *n.*

**mez·zo·for·te** (met′sō fôr′tā *or* mez′ō fôr′tā) in music, moderately loud; half as loud as FORTE. *adj., adv.*

**mez·zo–so·pran·o** (met′sō sə pran′ō *or* mez′ō sə pran′ō) **1** an adult female singing voice having an intermediate range between SOPRANO and ALTO. **2** a singer who has such a voice. **3** having to do with, having the range of, or designed for a mezzo-soprano. 1, 2 *n.,* pl. **mez·zo·so·pran·os;** 3 *adj.*

**mez·zo·tint** (met′sō tint′ *or* mez′ō tint′) **1** an engraving on copper or steel made by polishing and scraping away parts of a roughened surface. **2** a print made from such an engraving. **3** this method of engraving. **4** engrave in mezzotint. 1–3 *n.,* 4 *v.*

**mf.** or **mf** in music, moderately loud.

**mfg.** manufacturing.

**mfr.** manufacturer.

**Mg** magnesium.

**mg** milligram; milligrams.

**Mgr.** **1** Manager. **2** Monseigneur. **3** Monsignor.

**MHA** or **M.H.A.** *Cdn.* Member of the House of Assembly (in Newfoundland).

**MHz** megahertz.

**mi** (mē) in music: **1** the third tone of an eight-tone major scale. **2** the tone E. See DO[2] for picture. *n.*

**mi.** **1** mile; miles. **2** mill; mills.

**mi·aow** or **mi·aou** (mē ou′) See MEOW. *n., v.*

**mi·as·ma** (mī az′mə *or* mē az′mə) **1** poisonous vapour rising from the earth and infecting the air: *The miasma of swamps was formerly supposed to cause disease.* **2** an atmosphere or influence that infects or corrupts: *a miasma of evil thoughts. n., pl.* **mi·as·mas** *or* **mi·as·ma·ta** (-mə tə).

**mi·ca** (mī′kə) a mineral that divides into thin, partly transparent layers; isinglass: *Mica withstands heat and is used for insulation. n.*

**mice** (mīs) pl. of MOUSE. *n.*

**Mic·mac** or **Mi'k·maq** (mik′mak′) **1** a member of a First Nations people living in the Atlantic Provinces. **2** the Algonquian language of these people. **3** of or having to do with the Micmac or their language. 1, 2 *n.,* pl. **Micmac** or **Micmacs** or **Mi'kmaq** or **Mi'kmaqs;** 3 *adj.*

**micro–** combining form. **1** very small, as in *micro-organism, microfilm.* Compare with MACRO-. **2** done with or involving the use of a microscope, as in *microbiology.* **3** an SI prefix meaning one-millionth: *A microsecond is one one-millionth of a second.* Symbol: μ

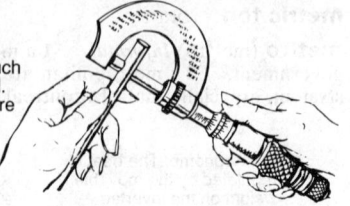

A micrometer calliper. It has a very finely threaded screw with a head that is graduated to show how much the screw has been moved. The instrument can measure accurately to 0.0025 mm.

☛ *Etym.* From Gk. *mikros* 'small'. Compare with MEGA- and MACRO-.

**mi·crobe** (mī′krōb)  1 a microscopic organism, usually one of vegetable nature; germ.  2 a bacterium, especially one causing disease.  *n.*

**mi·cro·bi·ol·o·gy** (mī′krō bī ol′ə jē)  the biology of MICRO-ORGANISMS.  *n.*

**mi·cro·chip** (mī′krō chip′)  a very small piece of semi-conducting material containing the information for a computer circuit.  *n.*

**mi·cro·cir·cuit** (mī′krō sėr′kit)  an electronic circuit consisting of miniature components, used in computers, etc.  *n.*

**mi·cro·coc·cus** (mī′krō kok′əs)  a spherical or egg-shaped bacterium: *Certain micrococci cause disease; others produce fermentation.*  *n., pl.* **mi·cro·coc·ci** (-kok′sī *or* -kok′sē).

**mi·cro·com·put·er** (mī′krō kəm pyü′tər)  a miniature, portable computer capable of carrying out only one operation at a time.  *n.*

**mi·cro·cop·y** (mī′krō kop′ē)  1 a copy made on MICROFILM.  2 make a copy on MICROFILM.  1 *n., pl.* **mi·cro·cop·ies;**  2 *v.,* **mi·cro·cop·ied, mi·cro·cop·y·ing.**

**mi·cro·cosm** (mī′krə koz′əm)  1 a little world; universe in miniature.  2 a human being thought of as a miniature representation of the universe.  *n.*

**mi·cro·dot** (mī′krō dot′)  a photograph of a document, etc., reduced to the size of a tiny dot.  *n.*

**mi·cro–e·lec·tron·ics** (mī′krō i lek tron′iks)  the branch of electronics that deals with the theory, manufacture, and use of electronic components of miniature size (*used with a singular verb*).  *n.*

**mi·cro·far·ad** (mī′krō far′əd *or* mī′krō fer′əd)  an SI unit for measuring electrical capacity, equal to one one-millionth of a farad.  Symbol: μF  *n.*

**mi·cro·fiche** (mī′krō fēsh′)  a single sheet of MICROFILM, usually the same size as a filing card, carrying microcopies of numerous pages of printed matter.  *n., pl.* **mi·cro·fiches** (-fēsh) *or* **mi·cro·fiche.**

**mi·cro·film** (mī′krō film′)  1 a film for making very small photographs of pages of a book, newspapers, records, etc. to preserve them in a very small space.  2 photograph on microfilm.  1 *n.,* 2 *v.*

**mi·cro·groove** (mī′krō grüv′)  a narrow groove used on long-playing phonograph records.  *n.*

**mi·cro·light** (mī′krō līt′)  a lightweight one-seater aircraft with a very small engine.  *n.*

**mi·crom·e·ter**[1] (mī krom′ə tər)  1 an instrument for measuring very small distances, angles, objects, etc.: *Certain kinds of micrometer are used with a microscope or telescope.*  2 MICROMETER CALLIPER.  *n.*

**mi·cro·me·ter**[2] (mī′krō mē′tər)  See MICROMETRE.  *n.*

**micrometer calliper** or **caliper**  a CALLIPER having a screw with a fine thread, used for very accurate measurement.

**mi·cro·me·tre** (mī′krō mē′tər)  an SI unit for measuring length, equal to one one-millionth of a metre: *The micrometre is used for measuring the size of bacteria and for other very precise measurements in technology, engineering, and science.*  Symbol: μm  *n.*  Also, **micrometer.**

**mi·cron** (mī′kron)  MICROMETRE.  *n., pl.* **mi·crons** or **mi·cra** (mī′krə).

**Mi·cro·ne·sian** (mī′krō nē′zhən)  1 of or referring to the race of people that includes the traditional inhabitants of Micronesia, a group of islands in the Pacific east of the Philippines and north of Australia.  2 a member of the Micronesian race: *Micronesians are most closely related to the Polynesians, but are smaller, and have dark skin and wavy or woolly hair.*  3 a native or inhabitant of Micronesia.  4 a group of languages spoken in Micronesia.  5 of or having to do with Micronesia or the people, cultures, or languages of Micronesia.  1, 5 *adj.,* 2–4 *n.*

**mi·cro–or·gan·ism** (mī′krō ôr′gə niz′əm)  any of a great number of one-celled organisms too small to be seen with the naked eye, most of which contain no chlorophyl, including the bacteria, viruses, yeasts, algae, fungi, and protozoans: *Because micro-organisms do not clearly show basic characteristics identifying them as either plants or animals, some scientists group them into a separate kingdom of living things.*  *n.*

**mi·cro·phone** (mī′krə fōn′)  an instrument for increasing the loudness of sounds or for transmitting sounds. Microphones change sounds into variations of an electric current and are used in recording and in radio and television broadcasting.  *n.*

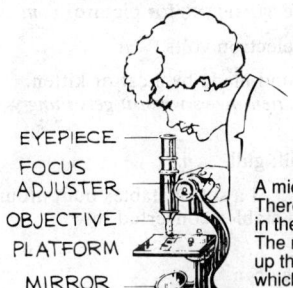

A microscope. There are magnifying lenses in the eyepiece and objective. The mirror reflects light up through the platform which has an opening in it.

**mi·cro·scope** (mī′krə skōp′)  an instrument with a lens or combination of lenses for magnifying objects so that one can see things not visible to the naked eye.  *n.*

**mi·cro·scop·ic** (mī′krə skop′ik)  1 that cannot be seen without using a MICROSCOPE; tiny.  2 like a MICROSCOPE; suggesting a microscope: *a microscopic eye for mistakes.*  3 of a MICROSCOPE; with a microscope: *Jean made a microscopic examination of a fly's wing.*  *adj.*

**mi·cro·scop·i·cal** (mī'krə skop'ə kəl) MICROSCOPIC. *adj.*

**mi·cro·scop·i·cal·ly** (mī'krə skop'i klē) **1** by the use of a MICROSCOPE. **2** as if with a MICROSCOPE; in great detail. *adv.*

**mi·cros·co·py** (mī kros'kə pē) the use of a MICROSCOPE; microscopic investigation. *n.*

**mi·cro·wave** (mī'krō wāv') **1** a very short electromagnetic wave, especially one having a wavelength between one and one hundred centimetres. **2** *Informal.* MICROWAVE OVEN. *n.*

**microwave oven** an oven in which food is cooked by means of the heat produced by microwaves penetrating the food.

**mid** (mid) in the middle of; middle. *adj.*

**mid–** a prefix meaning: **1** the middle point or part of. **2** of, in, or near the middle of.

**mid·air** or **mid–air** (mid'er') **1** the sky; air: *The parachute floated in midair.* **2** uncertainty; doubt: *With the contract still in midair, the board recessed.* **3** in midair: *a midair collision of two jets. n.*

**mid·brain** (mid'brān') the middle part of the brain. *n.*

**mid·chan·nel** (mid'chan'əl) the middle part of a channel. *n.*

**mid·day** (mid'dā') **1** the middle of the day; noon. **2** of or like midday: *the midday meal. n.*

**mid·den** (mid'ən) a KITCHEN MIDDEN. *n.*

**mid·dle** (mid'əl) **1** halfway in between; in the centre; at the same distance from either end or side: *the middle house in the row.* **2** the point or part that is the same distance from each end or side or other limit; the central part: *the middle of the road.* **3** the middle part of a person's body; waist. **4** in between; medium: *a woman of middle size.* **5** intermediate. **6** between old and modern: *Middle English.* 1, 4–6 *adj.*, 2, 3 *n.*

**middle age** the time of life between youth and old age.

**mid·dle–aged** (mid'əl lājd') between youth and old age, from about 40 to about 60 years of age. *adj.*

**Middle Ages** the period of European history between ancient and modern times, from about A.D. 500 to about A.D. 1450.

**middle C** in music, the note on the first added line below the treble staff and the first above the bass staff.

**middle class** people between the aristocracy or the very wealthy and the working class.

**middle ear** a cavity between the eardrum and the inner ear; tympanum: *In humans, the middle ear contains three bones: the malleus, incus, and stapes.* See EAR¹ for picture.

**Middle East** the region between the eastern Mediterranean and India: *Egypt, Israel, and Saudi Arabia are countries of the Middle East.*

**Middle English** **1** the period in the development of the English language between Old English and Modern English, lasting from about A.D. 1100 to about A.D. 1450. **2** the language of this period: *Chaucer wrote in Middle English.*

**mid·dle·man** (mid'əl man') a trader or merchant who buys goods from the producer and sells them to a retailer or directly to the consumer: *Co-operatives eliminate the*

hat, āge, fär; let, ēqual, tėrm; it, īce
hot, ōpen, ôrder; oil, out; cup, put, rüle
əbove, takən, pencəl, lemən, circəs
ch, child; ng, long; sh, ship
th, thin; ᴛʜ, then; zh, measure

*middleman by selling their produce directly to the consumer. n., pl.* **mid·dle·men** (-men').

**mid·dle·most** (mid'əl mōst') in the exact middle; nearest the middle; midmost. *adj.*

**mid·dle·weight** (mid'əl wāt') **1** a boxer weighing between 71 and 75 kg. **2** any person or thing of average mass. *n.*

**mid·dling** (mid'ling) **1** medium in size, quality, grade, etc. **2** *Informal or dialect.* moderately; fairly. 1 *adj.*, 2 *adv.*

**mid·dy** (mid'ē) *Informal.* a MIDSHIPMAN. *n., pl.* **mid·dies.**

**middy blouse** a loose blouse like a sailor's, having a collar with a broad flap at the back.

**midge** (mij) **1** a kind of tiny insect; gnat. **2** a very small person. *n.*

**midg·et** (mij'it) **1** a person very much smaller than normal. **2** anything much smaller than the usual size for its kind. **3** very small: *a midget submarine.* 1, 2 *n.*, 3 *adj.*
☞ *Syn.* See note at DWARF.

**mid·i·ron** (mid'ī'ərn) a golf club with a steel or iron head having a face of medium slope. *n.*

**mid·land** (mid'lənd) **1** the middle part of a country; the interior. **2** in or of the midland. 1 *n.*, 2 *adj.*

**mid·most** (mid'mōst') in the exact middle; nearest the middle. *adj.*

**mid·night** (mid'nīt') twelve o'clock at night; the middle of the night. *n.*
**burn the midnight oil,** work or study far into the night: *I'll have to burn the midnight oil again tonight if I want to get my project done.*

**midnight sun** the sun seen at midnight in the arctic and antarctic regions during summer.

**mid·point** (mid'point') a point at or near the centre or middle: *the midpoint of a line, the midpoint of a career. n.*

**mid·rib** (mid'rib') the central vein of a leaf. *n.*

**mid·riff** (mid'rif') the muscular wall separating the chest cavity from the abdomen; diaphragm. *n.*

**mid·ship** (mid'ship') in or of the middle of a ship. *adj.*

**mid·ship·man** (mid'ship'mən) **1** a junior officer training for a commission in a navy. **2** in former times, a boy who assisted the officers of a ship. *n., pl.* **mid·ship·men** (-mən).

**mid·ships** (mid'ships') AMIDSHIPS. *adv.*

**midst** (midst) **1** middle. **2** amidst; amid. 1 *n.*, 2 *prep.* Also (def. 2), **'midst.**
**in the midst of,** **a** in the middle of; among or surrounded by: *The bomb fell in the midst of the crowd.* **b** during: *The announcement was made in the midst of the program.*

**mid·stream** (mid′strēm′) the middle of a stream. *n.*

**mid·sum·mer** (mid′sum′ər) 1 the middle of summer. 2 the time around June 21. 3 in the middle of summer. 1, 2 *n.*, 3 *adj.*

**mid–Vic·to·ri·an** (mid′vik tô′rē ən) 1 in the United Kingdom, of the middle period of Queen Victoria's reign, or from about 1850 to 1890. 2 a person who lived during this period. 3 like this period; old-fashioned; strict in morals. 4 a person with mid-Victorian ideas and tastes. 1, 3 *adj.*, 2, 4 *n.*

**mid·way** (mid′wā′) 1 halfway; in the middle: *lying midway between the two towns* (*adv.*), *a midway point on the chart* (*adj.*). 2 a middle way or course. 3 at a fair or exhibition, the place for games, rides, and other amusements. 1 *adv., adj.*, 2, 3 *n.*

**mid·week** (mid′wēk′) 1 the middle of the week. 2 in the middle of the week. 1 *n.*, 2 *adj.*

**mid·wife** (mid′wīf′) a person who helps women in childbirth. *n., pl.* **mid·wives** (-wīvz′).

**mid·wife·ry** (mid′wī′fə rē *or* mid′wif′ə rē) the helping of women in childbirth. *n.*

**mid·win·ter** (mid′win′tər) 1 the middle of winter. 2 the time around December 21. 3 in the middle of winter. 1, 2 *n.*, 3 *adj.*

**mid·year** (mid′yēr′) 1 happening in the middle of the year. 2 **midyears**, *pl. Informal.* midyear examinations. 1 *adj.*, 2 *n.*

**mien** (mēn) one's manner of holding the head and body; a way of acting and looking: *The colonel had the mien of a soldier. n.*
☛ *Hom.* MEAN.

**miff** (mif) *Informal.* 1 a peevish fit; petty quarrel. 2 be offended; have a petty quarrel. 1 *n.*, 2 *v.*

**might**[1] (mīt) pt. of MAY: *Mother said that we might play in the barn. He might have done it when you were not looking. v.*
☛ *Hom.* MITE.
☛ *Usage.* **Might**, the pt. of MAY, is now used chiefly to express doubt or slight possibility: *It looks as if it might rain this afternoon.*

**might**[2] (mīt) great power; strength: *Work with all your might. n.*
**with might and main,** with all one's strength.
☛ *Hom.* MITE.

**might·i·ly** (mī′tə lē) 1 in a mighty manner; powerfully; vigorously. 2 very much; greatly: *We were mightily pleased at winning. adv.*

**might·i·ness** (mī′tē nis) power, strength. *n.*

**might·y** (mī′tē) 1 showing strength or power; powerful; strong: *a mighty ruler, a mighty force.* 2 very great: *a mighty famine.* 3 *Informal.* very; extremely: *a mighty cold day.* 1, 2 *adj.*, **might·i·er, might·i·est**; 3 *adv.*

**mi·gnon** (min′yon; *French,* mē nyôN′) small and pretty; dainty. *adj.*

**mi·gnon·ette** (min′yə net′) any of a closely related group of plants, especially an annual plant widely grown for its pointed clusters of fragrant, greenish-yellow flowers. *n.*

**mi·graine** (mī′grān) a type of severe headache, usually on one side only. *n.*

**mi·grant** (mī′grənt) 1 a person, animal, bird, or plant that migrates. 2 migrating; roving: *Crops of apples are picked by migrant workers.* 1 *n.*, 2 *adj.*

**mi·grate** (mī′grāt *or* mī grāt′) 1 move from one place to settle in another: *Pioneers from Ontario migrated to all parts of what are now the Prairie Provinces.* 2 go from one region to another with the change in the seasons: *Most birds migrate to warmer countries in the winter. v.*, **mi·grat·ed, mi·grat·ing.**

**mi·gra·tion** (mī grā′shən) 1 migrating. 2 a number of people or animals migrating together. *n.*

**mi·gra·to·ry** (mī′grə tô′rē) 1 migrating; that migrates: *migratory workers, migratory birds.* 2 of migration. 3 wandering: *a migratory pain. adj.*

**mi·ka·do** (mə kä′dō) the ancient title of the emperor of Japan. *n., pl.* **mi·ka·dos.**

**mike** (mīk) *Informal.* MICROPHONE. *n.*

**mil** (mil) a unit for measuring length, equal to 0.001 inch (25.4 micrometres): *The mil was used for measuring the diameters of wires. n.*

**mil.** 1 military. 2 militia. 3 mileage. 4 million.

**mil·age** (mī′lij) See MILEAGE. *n.*

**milch** (milch) giving milk; kept for the milk it gives: *a milch cow. adj.*

**mild** (mīld) 1 gentle; kind: *a mild old lady.* 2 warm; temperate; moderate; not harsh or severe: *a mild climate, a mild winter.* 3 soft or sweet to the senses; not sharp, sour, bitter, or strong in taste: *mild cheese, a mild cigar. adj.* —**mild′ly,** *adv.* —**mild′ness,** *n.*

**mil·dew** (mil′dyü *or* mil′dü) 1 a coating or discolouring caused by fungus that appears on paper, clothes, leather, etc. during damp weather: *Damp clothes left in a pile will show mildew in a few days.* 2 a plant disease in which a fungus grows on the plant: *Mildew killed the rosebuds in our garden.* 3 cover or become covered with mildew: *A pile of damp clothes in his closet mildewed.* 1, 2 *n.*, 3 *v.*

**mile** (mīl) 1 a unit for measuring distance or length on land, equal to about 1.609 kilometres; statute mile: *There are 5280 feet in a mile.* 2 NAUTICAL MILE. 3 **miles,** *pl.* a relatively great distance: *The sun went down, but we were still miles from home. From here you can see for miles. n.*

**mile·age** (mī′lij) 1 the total number of miles travelled: *What's the mileage on your car?* 2 the length, extent, or distance of a road, journey, etc., expressed in miles. 3 the distance a motor vehicle can go on a given amount of fuel: *We get good mileage on our new car.* 4 an allowance for travelling expenses at a fixed rate per unit of distance: *She gets mileage on trips she makes for the company.* 5 the profit or benefit a person is getting or can get out of something: *He's getting a lot of mileage out of that one joke. n.*

**mile·post** (mīl′pōst′) a post set up to show the distance in miles to a certain place. *n.*

**mile·stone** (mīl′stōn′) 1 a stone set up to show the distance in miles to a certain place. 2 an important event: *The invention of printing was a milestone in the progress of education. n.*

**mil·foil** (mil′foil) YARROW. *n.*

**mi·lieu** (mē lyœ′) *French.* surroundings; environment. *n.*

**mil·i·tan·cy** (mil′ə tən sē)   warlike behaviour or tendency; militant spirit or policy.   *n.*

**mil·i·tant** (mil′ə tənt)   **1** aggressive; fighting; warlike. **2** aggressively active in serving a cause or in spreading a belief: *a militant feminist.*   **3** a person aggressively active in serving a cause or in spreading a belief.   1, 2 *adj.*, 3 *n.* —**mil′i·tant·ly**, *adv.*

**mil·i·ta·rism** (mil′ə tə riz′əm)   **1** the policy of making military organization and power very strong.   **2** military spirit and ideals.   *n.*

**mil·i·ta·rist** (mil′ə tə rist)   **1** a person who believes in a powerful military organization.   **2** an expert in warfare and military matters.   *n.*

**mil·i·ta·ris·tic** (mil′ə tə ris′tik)   of or having to do with MILITARISTS or MILITARISM.   *adj.*

**mil·i·ta·rize** (mil′ə tə rīz′)   **1** make the military organization of a country very powerful.   **2** fill with military spirit and ideals.   *v.*, **mil·i·ta·rized, mil·i·ta·riz·ing.** —**mil′i·ta·ri·za′tion**, *n.*

**mil·i·tar·y** (mil′ə ter′ē)   **1** of soldiers or war: *military training, military history.*   **2** done by soldiers: *military manoeuvres.*   **3** fit for soldiers: *military discipline.* **4** suitable for war; warlike: *military valour.*   **5** belonging to the armed forces.   **6 the military**,   the armed forces; soldiers: *The military did rescue work during the flood.* 1–5 *adj.*, 6 *n.*   —**mil′i·tar′i·ly**, *adv.*

**military law**   a system of regulations governing the armed forces and others in military service.
☛ *Usage.* **Military law** is not to be confused with MARTIAL LAW, which replaces civil law in times of emergency, and applies to civilians as well as military personnel.

**military police**   soldiers who act as police for the army. *Abbrev.*: MP or M.P.

**Military Regime**   in Canada, the period of military rule between 1759 and 1764.

**mil·i·tate** (mil′ə tāt′)   act; work; operate (*against* or *in favour of*): *Bad weather militated against the success of the picnic.*   *v.*, **mil·i·tat·ed, mil·i·tat·ing.**

**mi·li·tia** (mə lish′ə)   a part of the army made up of citizens who are not regular soldiers but who undergo training for emergency duty or national defence; the reserve army.   *n.*

**mi·li·tia·man** (mə lish′ə mən)   a soldier in the MILITIA. *n.*, *pl.* **mi·li·tia·men** (-mən).

**milk** (milk)   **1** the white liquid secreted by female mammals for the nourishment of their young, especially that from cows.   **2** any kind of liquid resembling this, such as the white juice of a plant, tree, or nut: *coconut milk.*   **3** draw the milk from: *He used to milk twenty cows a day.*   **4** yield or produce milk.   **5** extract as if by milking; drain contents, strength, information, wealth, etc. from: *The dishonest treasurer milked the club treasury.* **6** draw juice, poison, etc. from: *to milk a snake.*   1, 2 *n.*, 3–6 *v.*   —**milk′er**, *n.*
**cry over spilt milk,**   waste sorrow or regret on what has happened and cannot be remedied.

**milk·ing** (mil′king)   **1** the amount of milk obtained at one time.   **2** ppr. of MILK.   1 *n.*, 2 *v.*

**milk leg**   a painful swelling of the leg caused by clots in the veins.

**milk·maid** (milk′mād′)   a woman whose job is to milk cows.   *n.*

**milk·man** (milk′man′)   a man who sells or delivers milk.   *n.*, *pl.* **milk·men** (-mən).

---

**militancy   753   milldam**

hat, āge, fär; let, ēqual, tėrm; it, īce
hot, ōpen, ôrder, oil, out; cup, pút, rüle
əbove, takən, pencəl, lemən, circəs
ch, child; ng, long; sh, ship
th, thin; ᴛʜ, then; zh, measure

**milk of human kindness**   natural sympathy and affection.

**milk of magnesia**   a milky-white medicine in water, used as a laxative and to counteract acidity.

**milk shake**   a drink consisting of milk, flavouring, and often ice cream, shaken or beaten until frothy.

**milk snake**   a small, harmless, grey snake of North America: *Milk snakes feed on small rodents, such as rats and mice.*

**milk sugar**   LACTOSE.

**milk tooth**   one of the first set of teeth; a temporary tooth of a young child or animal.

**milkweed** (mil′kwēd′)   a weed whose stem contains a white juice that looks like milk.   *n.*

**milk–white** (mil′kwīt′ *or* milk′hwīt′)   white as milk. *adj.*

**milk·y** (mil′kē)   **1** like milk; white as milk; whitish. **2** of milk; containing milk.   **3** mild; weak; timid.   *adj.*, **milk·i·er, milk·i·est.** —**milk′i·ness**, *n.*

**Milky Way**   **1** a broad band of faint light that stretches across the sky at night: *The Milky Way is made up of countless stars, too far away to see separately without a telescope.*   **2** the galaxy in which these countless stars are found: *The earth, sun, and all the planets around the sun are part of the Milky Way.*

An old-fashioned mill (def. 2)

**mill¹** (mil)   **1** a machine for grinding or crushing: *A flour mill grinds wheat into flour. A coffee mill grinds coffee beans.*   **2** a building containing a machine for grinding grain.   **3** grind: *Some wheat will be milled before it is exported.*   **4** a building where manufacturing is done: *A paper mill makes paper from wood pulp.*   **5** manufacture. **6** cut a series of fine notches or ridges on the edge of a coin: *A dime is milled.*   **7** move around in a confused way: *There were many people milling around after the parade.*   1, 2, 4 *n.*, 3, 5–7 *v.*
**go through the mill**, *Informal.*   **a** get a thorough training or experience.   **b** learn by hard or painful experience.
**put through the mill**, *Informal.*   **a** test; examine; try out. **b** teach by hard or painful experience.

**mill²** (mil)   $0.001, or ¹⁄₁₀ of a cent: *Mills are used in accounting but not as coins.*   *n.*

**mill·dam** (mil′dam′)   **1** a dam built in a stream to

**mil·le·ni·al** (mə len′ē əl) 1 of a thousand years. 2 like that of a MILLENNIUM; fit for the millennium. *adj.*

**mil·len·ni·um** (mə len′ē əm) 1 a period of a thousand years: *The world is many millenniums old.* 2 the period of a thousand years during which, according to the Christian Bible, Christ is expected to reign on earth. 3 a period of righteousness and happiness. *n., pl.* **mil·len·ni·ums** or **mil·len·ni·a** (mə len′ē ə).

**mil·le·pede** (mil′ə pēd′) See MILLIPEDE. *n.*

**mill·er** (mil′ər) 1 a person who owns or runs a mill, especially a flour mill. 2 a moth whose wings look as if they were powdered with flour. *n.*

**mil·les·i·mal** (mə les′ə məl) 1 thousandth. 2 consisting of thousandth parts. 3 a thousandth part. 1, 2 *adj.*, 3 *n.*

**mil·let** (mil′it) 1 a grain used for food in Europe, Asia, and Africa. 2 the plant that it grows on: *In North America millet is grown chiefly for hay.* *n.*

**milli–** (mil′ə *or* mil′ē) an SI prefix meaning one-thousandth: *A millilitre is one one-thousandth of a litre.* Symbol: m

**mil·li·am·pere** (mil′ē am′pēr) an SI unit for measuring electric current, equal to one one-thousandth of an ampere. Symbol: mA *n.*

**mil·liard** (mil′yərd *or* mil′yärd) a thousand millions (1 000 000 000). *n.*

**mil·li·bar** (mil′ə bär) a unit used with the SI for measuring pressure, equal to 0.1 kilopascals: *Atmospheric pressure readings are sometimes given in millibars.* Symbol: mbar *n.*

**mil·li·gram** (mil′ə gram′) an SI unit for measuring mass, equal to one one-thousandth of a gram: *The milligram is used for very small masses, such as the amount of vitamins and minerals contained in a serving of food.* Symbol: mg *n.* Also, **milligramme**.

**mil·li·li·tre** (mil′ə lē′tər) a unit used with the SI for measuring volume or capacity, equal to one one-thousandth of a litre: *Cooking measures are graduated in millilitres.* Symbol: mL *n.* Also, **milliliter**.

**mil·li·me·tre** (mil′ə mē′tər) an SI unit for measuring length, equal to one one-thousandth of a metre: *A dime is about one millimetre thick.* Symbol: mm *n.* Also, **millimeter**.

**mil·li·ner** (mil′ə nər) a person who makes, trims, or sells women's hats. *n.*

**mil·li·ner·y** (mil′ə ner′ē) 1 women's hats. 2 the business of making, trimming, or selling women's hats. *n.*

**mill·ing** (mil′ing) 1 the business or process of grinding grain in a mill. 2 manufacturing. 3 the business or process of cutting notches or ridges on the edge of a coin. 4 such notches or ridges. 5 ppr. of MILL. 1–4 *n.*, 5 *v.*

**mil·lion** (mil′yən) 1 one thousand thousand (1 000 000). 2 a very large number; very many: *Johann can always think of a million reasons for not helping with the dishes.* *n., adj.*

**mil·lion·aire** (mil′yə ner′) 1 a person who has a million or more dollars or owns property worth that amount. 2 a very wealthy person. *n.*

**mil·lion·fold** (mil′yən fōld′) a million times as much or as many. *adv., adj.*

**mil·lionth** (mil′yənth) 1 last in a series of a million. 2 one of a million equal parts. *adj., n.*

**mil·li·pede** (mil′ə pēd′) a small, wormlike arthropod that has two pairs of legs apiece for most of its segments. *n.* Also, **millepede**.

**mill·pond** (mil′pond′) a pond supplying water to drive a mill wheel. *n.*

**mill·race** (mil′rās′) 1 a current of water that drives a mill wheel. 2 the channel in which it flows to the mill. *n.*

**mill rate** a rate used for calculating municipal taxes. A mill rate of 45.6 means that a property owner pays a tax of 45.6 mills ($0.0456) for every dollar of the value of his or her property.

**mill·stone** (mil′stōn′) 1 either of a pair of round, flat stones used for grinding corn, wheat, etc. 2 a heavy burden. *n.*

**mill·stream** (mil′strēm′) the stream in a millrace. *n.*

**mill wheel** a wheel that is turned by water and supplies power for a mill. See MILL[1] for picture.

**mill·work** (mil′wėrk′) 1 doors, windows, mouldings, and other things made in a planing mill. 2 the work done in a mill. *n.*

**mill·wright** (mil′rīt′) 1 a person who designs, builds, or sets up mills or machinery for mills. 2 a mechanic who sets up and takes care of the machinery in a factory, etc. *n.*

**milque·toast** (milk′tōst′) an extremely timid person. *n.*

**milt** (milt) 1 the sperm cells of male fish with the milky fluid containing them. 2 the reproductive gland in male fish. *n.*

**mime** (mīm) 1 a form of drama in which the actors use movement and gestures but no words; pantomime. 2 communicating through gestures but without the use of words: *He told his story in mime.* 3 communicate in this way: *He mimed the story of his first date.* 4 an actor, especially in a pantomime. 5 in ancient Greece and Rome, a coarse farce using funny actions and gestures. 1, 2, 4, 5 *n.*, 3 *v.*, **mimed, mim·ing** —**mim′er**, *n.*

**mi·met·ic** (mi met′ik) 1 imitative: *mimetic gestures.* 2 mimic or make-believe. 3 having to do with or exhibiting protective mimicry. *adj.*

**mim·ic** (mim′ik) 1 make fun of by imitating: *We like to get him to mimic our old music teacher.* 2 a person or thing that imitates. 3 copy closely; imitate: *A parrot can mimic a person's voice.* 4 resemble closely: *Some insects mimic leaves.* 5 not real, but imitated or pretended for some purpose: *The soldiers staged a mimic battle for the visiting general.* 6 imitative. 1, 3, 4 *v.*, **mim·icked, mim·ick·ing;** 2 *n.*, 5, 6 *adj.*

**mim·ic·ry** (mim′i krē) a mimicking. *n., pl.* **mim·ic·ries.**

**mi·mo·sa** (mi mō′sə) a tree, shrub, or plant growing in tropical or warm regions, and usually having fernlike leaves and heads or spikes of small flowers: *The acacia and the sensitive plant are mimosas.* *n.*

**min** minute; minutes.

**min.** minimum.

**min·a·ret** (min′ə ret′ *or* min′ə ret′) a slender, high tower of a Moslem mosque, having one or more projecting balconies from which a crier calls the people to prayer. *n.*

**mince** (mins) **1** grind into very small pieces. **2** meat ground into very small pieces; ground beef, pork, or lamb. **3** made with MINCEMEAT: *mince pie.* **4** MINCEMEAT. **5** speak or move in a prim, affected way. **6** soften or moderate words, as when stating unpleasant facts: *The judge addressed the jury bluntly, without mincing words.* 1, 5, 6 *v.,* minced, minc·ing; 2–4 *n.*
**not to mince matters,** to speak plainly and frankly.

**mince·meat** (min′smēt′) a mixture of chopped suet, apples, raisins, currants, spices, etc., and sometimes meat, used as a filling for pies. *n.*

**minc·ing** (min′sing) **1** too polite or nice; affectedly elegant or dainty: *a mincing courtier.* **2** ppr. of MINCE. 1 *adj.,* 2 *v.* —**minc′ing·ly,** *adv.*

**mind** (mīnd) **1** that which knows, thinks, remembers, feels, and wills. **2** the intellect: *Mastering arithmetic requires a good mind.* **3** a person who has intelligence. **4** reason; sanity: *to be out of one's mind.* **5** a way of thinking and feeling: *to change one's mind.* **6** one's desire, purpose, intention, or will. **7** remembrance or recollection; memory: *Keep the rules in mind.* **8** bear in mind; give heed to: *Mind my words!* **9** take notice; observe. **10** be careful concerning: *Mind the step.* **11** be careful. **12** look after; take care of; tend: *Mind the baby.* **13** obey: *Mind your father and mother.* **14** feel concern about; object to: *We mind parting from a friend.* **15** feel concern; object. 1–7 *n.,* 8–15 *v.*
**bear in mind,** keep one's attention on; remember.
**be of one mind,** agree: *They were both of one mind.*
**call to mind,** **a** recall. **b** remember.
**give (someone) a piece of one's mind,** speak to angrily or without holding back.
**have a mind to,** intend to; think of favourably: *I have a mind to watch the hockey game tonight.*
**have half a mind,** be somewhat inclined.
**have in mind,** **a** remember. **b** think of; consider. **c** intend; plan.
**know one's mind,** know what one really thinks, wishes, or intends.
**make up one's mind,** decide; resolve.
**on one's mind,** in one's thoughts; troubling one.
**pass out of mind,** be forgotten.
**put in mind,** remind.
**set one's mind on,** want very much.
**speak one's mind,** give one's frank opinion.
**to one's mind,** in one's opinion; to one's way of thinking.

**mind·ed** (mīn′did) **1** having a certain kind of mind: *high-minded, strong-minded.* **2** inclined; disposed. **3** pt. and pp. of MIND. 1, 2 *adj.,* 3 *v.*

**mind·ful** (mīnd′fəl) being aware or careful: *Mindful of your advice, I went slowly.* *adj.* —**mind′ful·ly,** *adv.* —**mind′ful·ness,** *n.*

**mind·less** (mīnd′dlis) **1** without intelligence; stupid. **2** not taking thought; careless. *adj.* —**mind′less·ly,** *adv.*

**mind reader** a person who can guess the thoughts of others.

**mind's eye** imagination.

**mine**[1] (mīn) a possessive form of **I**; that which belongs to me: *The dog is mine. These are her records; mine are over there.* *pron.*

---

**min.** **755 mineral kingdom**

hat, āge, fär; let, ēqual, tėrm; it, īce
hot, ōpen, ôrder; oil, out; cup, pùt, rüle
əbove, takən, pencəl, lemən, circəs
ch, child; ng, long; sh, ship
th, thin; ᴛʜ, then; zh, measure

☛ *Usage.* See note at MY.

**mine**[2] (mīn) **1** a large hole or space dug in the earth to get out valuable minerals: *a coal mine, a gold mine.* **2** dig a mine; make a hole, space, passage, etc. below the earth. **3** dig into the earth, a hill, etc. for coal, ore, etc. **4** get metal, etc. from a mine. **5** a rich or plentiful source: *a mine of information.* **6** an underground passage in which an explosive is placed to blow up the enemy's forts, etc. **7** dig in; make passages, etc. by digging. **8** a container holding an explosive charge that is put under water and exploded by propeller vibrations (**acoustic** or **sonic mine**) or by magnetic attraction (**magnetic mine**), or laid on the ground or shallowly buried and exploded by contact with a vehicle, etc. (**land mine**). **9** put explosive mines in or under; lay explosive mines. **10** destroy secretly; ruin slowly; undermine. 1, 5, 6, 8 *n.,* 2–4, 7, 9, 10 *v.,* mined, min·ing.

**mine field** **1** an area throughout which explosive mines have been laid. **2** the pattern of mines in such an area.

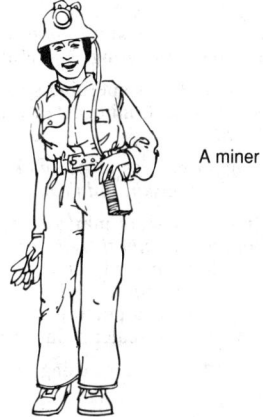

A miner

**min·er** (mī′nər) **1** a person who works in a mine: *a coal miner.* **2** a soldier who lays explosive mines. *n.*
☛ *Hom.* MINOR.

**min·er·al** (min′ə rəl) **1** a substance obtained by mining: *Coal is a mineral.* **2** any natural substance that is non-living, or inorganic: *Salt and sand are minerals.* **3** of minerals: *There are mineral deposits at the mouth of the river.* **4** containing minerals: *mineral water.* 1, 2 *n.,* 3, 4 *adj.*

**min·er·al·ize** (min′ə rə līz′) **1** convert into mineral substance; transform metal into an ore. **2** impregnate or supply with mineral substances. **3** search for minerals. *v.,* min·er·al·ized, min·er·al·iz·ing. —**min′er·al·i·za′tion,** *n.*

**mineral kingdom** one of the three broad divisions of the natural world, consisting of inorganic material and occurring naturally: *Minerals in the mineral kingdom have a distinctive internal structure, usually crystalline, as a diamond.* Compare with ANIMAL KINGDOM and PLANT KINGDOM.

**min·er·a·log·i·cal** (min′ə rə loj′ə kəl) of or having to do with MINERALOGY. *adj.*
—**min′er·a·log′i·cal·ly,** *adv.*

**min·er·al·o·gist** (min′ə ral′ə jist) a person trained in MINERALOGY, especially one who makes it his or her work. *n.*

**min·er·al·o·gy** (min′ə rol′ə jē *or* min′ə ral′ə jē) the science that deals with physical and chemical properties of minerals, their classification, and the form and structure of their crystals. *n.*

**mineral oil** any oil derived from a mineral substance, especially a colourless, odourless, tasteless oil obtained from petroleum, used as a laxative and as a base for cold creams, etc.

**mineral water** water containing mineral salts or gases: *People drink mineral water for its healthful properties.*

**min·e·stro·ne** (min′ə strō′nē) a thick soup containing vegetables, vermicelli, etc. *n.*

**mine sweeper** a warship equipped for dragging a harbour or the sea in order to remove enemy mines or make them harmless.

**Ming** (ming) 1 in China, the ruling dynasty from 1368 to 1644. 2 fine china made during this period. *n.*

**min·gle** (ming′gəl) 1 mix; blend: *Two rivers that join mingle their waters.* 2 associate: *to mingle with important people.* *v.,* **min·gled, min·gling.** —**min′gler,** *n.*

**min·i** (min′ē) *Informal.* something small, short, etc. for its kind, such as a miniskirt, minicar, or minibus: *She was wearing a mini.* *n.*

**mini–** *combining form.* small for its kind, very small, very short, etc., as in *miniskirt, minicar.*

**min·i·a·ture** (min′ē ə chər *or* min′ə chər) 1 a small model or copy: *In the museum there is a miniature of the ship "Victory."* 2 done or made on a very small scale; tiny: *She had miniature furniture for her doll house.* 3 a very small painting, usually a portrait. 1, 3 *n.,* 2 *adj.*
**in miniature,** on a small scale; reduced in size.

**miniature camera** a camera using narrow film (35 mm or less).

**min·i·bike** (min′ē bīk′) a small motorcycle. *n.*

**min·i·bus** (min′ē bus′) a small bus used for short runs, as between an airport and a hotel, etc. *n.*

**min·i·car** (min′ē kär′) a very small automobile, such as a small subcompact. *n.*

**min·i·com·pu·ter** (min′ē kəm pyü′tər) a computer midway between a MICROCOMPUTER and a MAINFRAME in size, cost, and power. *n.*

**min·im** (min′əm) 1 a unit for measuring liquids, equal to one sixtieth of a fluid dram (about 0.06 cm³): *The minim is the smallest unit in the imperial system of liquid measure.* 2 a very small amount. 3 something very small or insignificant. 4 in music, a half note. *n.*

**min·i·ma** (min′ə mə) a pl. of MINIMUM. *n.*

**min·i·mal** (min′ə məl) least possible; very small; having to do with a minimum: *The article claimed that the side effects of the drug were minimal.* *adj.*

**min·i·mize** (min′ə mīz′) 1 reduce to the least possible amount or degree: *The polar explorers took every precaution to minimize the dangers of their trip.* 2 state at the lowest possible estimate; make the least of: *An ungrateful person minimizes the help others have given her.* *v.,* **min·i·mized, min·i·miz·ing.** —**min′i·mi·za′tion,** *n.*
—**min′i·miz′er,** *n.*

**min·i·mum** (min′ə məm) 1 the least amount or smallest quantity possible or permitted: *I need a minimum of eight hours sleep a night.* 2 least possible; lowest: *a minimum rate. Eighteen is the minimum age for voting in federal elections.* *n., pl.* **min·i·mums** or **min·i·ma.**

**minimum wage** the lowest wage paid or allowed, especially the wage fixed by law as the lowest that can be paid to any employed person or to certain categories of employed persons.

**min·ing** (mī′ning) 1 the act, process, or business of digging coal, ore, etc. from mines. 2 of or having to do with this process or business: *a mining camp, a mining school.* 3 the act or process of laying explosive mines. 4 ppr. of MINE. 1–3 *n.,* 4 *v.*

**min·ion** (min′yən) 1 a person who is willing to do whatever he or she is ordered; a servile follower. 2 a darling; favourite. *n.*

**min·i·skirt** (min′ē skėrt′) a very short skirt ending well above the knees. *n.*

**min·is·ter** (min′i stər) 1 a member of the clergy serving a church; spiritual guide; pastor. 2 act as a servant or nurse; be of service: *She ministers to the sick man's wants.* 3 be helpful; give aid; contribute. 4 a member of the cabinet who is in charge of a government department: *the Minister of Finance.* 5 a person sent to a foreign country to represent his or her own government: *the British Minister to France.* 6 a person or thing employed in carrying out purpose, will, etc.: *The storm that killed the murderer seemed the minister of righteous vengeance.* 1, 4–6 *n.,* 2, 3 *v.*

**min·is·te·ri·al** (min′i stē′rē əl) 1 of, having to do with, or suitable for a minister of religion or the MINISTRY (def. 2). 2 of or having to do with a government minister or ministry. *adj.* —**min′is·te′ri·al·ly,** *adv.*

**minister plenipotentiary** a PLENIPOTENTIARY. *pl.* **ministers plenipotentiary.**

**minister without portfolio** a CABINET MINISTER who is not connected with any particular cabinet post or department.

**min·is·trant** (min′i strənt) 1 MINISTERing. 2 one who MINISTERS. 1 *adj.,* 2 *n.*

**min·is·tra·tion** (min′i strā′shən) the act or process of MINISTERing: *ministration to the sick.* *n.*

**min·is·try** (min′i strē) 1 the office, duties, or time of service of a minister. 2 the ministers of a church. 3 the ministers of a government. 4 in Canada, the United Kingdom, and Europe, a government department under a minister. 5 the offices of such a department. 6 ministering or serving. *n., pl.* **min·is·tries.**

**mink** (mingk) 1 a small animal, related to the weasel, that lives in water part of the time. 2 its valuable brown fur. 3 a coat, stole, etc. made of mink. *n.*
—**mink′like′,** *adj.*

**min·now** (min′ō) 1 any of a family of mostly very small freshwater fish, made up of more than 1000 species found in Africa and the North Temperate zone, used mainly as live bait for catching game fish: *The most common minnows native to Canada are the goldfish, chub, and dace.* 2 the young of any of various unrelated species of fish used as live bait. *n.*

**mi·nor** (mī′nər)   **1** smaller; lesser; less important: *a minor fault, a minor poet.*   **2** a person who is legally considered not an adult. In various provinces, minors are under 18 or 19 years of age: *While you are still a minor, you need the consent of a parent or guardian to marry and you cannot make legal contracts.*   **3** under legal age.   **4** in music:   **a** of an interval, less by a half step than the corresponding major interval.   **b** of or referring to a scale, mode, or key whose third tone is minor in relation to the fundamental tone.   **5** a minor musical interval, key, scale, chord, etc.: *the scale of A minor.*   **6** a subject or course of study to which a student gives much time and attention, but less than to his or her major subject.   1, 3, 4, *adj.*, 2, 5, 6 *n.*
**minor in,**   take as a minor subject of study.
☛ *Hom.* MINER.

**Mi·nor·ca** (mə nôr′kə)   a breed of large chicken originally developed in Spain.   *n.*

**mi·nor·i·ty** (mə nô′rə tē *or* mī nô′rə tē)   **1** the smaller number or part; less than half: *The minority must often do what the majority decides to do.*   **2** a group within a country, state, etc. that differs in race, religion, or national origin from the larger part of the population.   **3** of or constituting a minority: *a minority vote, group, etc.*   **4** belonging to a minority: *a minority opinion.*   **5** the condition or time of being under the legal age of responsibility.   *n., pl.* **mi·nor·i·ties.**

**minor league**   any professional sports league or association, especially in baseball or hockey, other than the major leagues.

**minor scale**   in music, a scale having eight tones with half steps instead of whole steps after the 2nd and 5th tones. Compare with MAJOR SCALE.

**min·ster** (min′stər) *Esp. Brit.*   **1** the church of a monastery.   **2** a large or important church; cathedral.   *n.*

**min·strel** (min′strəl)   **1** a medieval singer or musician who sang or recited poetry, often composed by himself, and accompanied himself on a harp or lute.   **2** formerly, a singer or musician in the household of the lord.   **3** any musician or poet.   *n.*

**min·strel·sy** (min′strəl sē)   **1** the art or practice of a MINSTREL.   **2** a collection of songs and ballads.   *n., pl.* **min·strel·sies.**

**mint**¹ (mint)   **1** any of about 25 closely related species of strongly scented herb, especially any of several species used for seasoning or flavouring food, such as peppermint or spearmint.   **2** any of several other plants of the same family.   **3** referring to a family mostly of herbs and shrubs found especially in the Old World, used in cooking and medicine since ancient times: *The mint family includes lavender, peppermint, sage, rosemary, savory, and thyme.*   **4** a piece of candy flavoured with mint, especially peppermint or spearmint.   *n.*

**mint**² (mint)   **1** a place where money is made by government authority: *Mints also often make special commemorative coins and medals.*   **2** make coins, medals, etc.: *This quarter was minted in 1938.*   **3** *Informal.* a large sum or amount, especially of money: *She made a mint when she sold her house.*   **4** a place where anything is made or fabricated.   **5** make or fabricate; originate.   1, 3, 4 *n.*, 2, 5 *v.*
**in mint condition,**   without a blemish; as good as new: *an old car in mint condition.*

**mint·age** (min′tij)   **1** minting; coinage.   **2** the product of minting; output of a mint.   **3** a charge for coining; cost of coining.   **4** a stamp or character impressed on a coin.   *n.*

**min·u·end** (min′yü end′)   a number or quantity from which another is to be subtracted: *In 100−23 = 77, the minuend is 100.*   See SUBTRACTION for picture.   *n.*

**min·u·et** (min′yü et′)   **1** a slow, stately dance, popular in the 1700's.   **2** the music for it.   *n.*

**mi·nus** (mī′nəs)   **1** decreased by; reduced by; less: *Five minus two is three.*   **2** the sign (−) meaning that the quantity following it is to be subtracted.   **3** showing subtraction: *The minus sign is −.*   **4** *Informal.* without or lacking: *a book minus its cover.*   **5** less than (never used before a noun): *A mark of B minus is not as high as B.*   **6** in mathematics, etc., less than zero; negative: *a minus quantity. The temperature this morning was minus thirteen degrees.*   1, 4 *prep.*, 2 *n.*, 3, 5, 6 *adj.*

**min·ute**¹ (min′it)   **1** a unit used with the SI for measuring time, equal to sixty seconds or one sixtieth of an hour.   Symbol: min   **2** any short period of time; moment: *It will only take me a minute to put the dishes away. She paused for a minute to listen.*   **3** a point in time: *Come here this minute.*   **4** a unit used with the SI for measuring plane angles, equal to sixty seconds or one sixtieth of a degree: *The minute and second are used mainly by geographers.*   Symbol: ′   **5 minutes,** *pl.* a written summary; the official record of the proceedings of a society, board, committee, etc.   *n.*
**up to the minute,**   up-to-date.

**mi·nute**² (mī nyüt′ *or* mī nüt′)   **1** very small; tiny: *a minute speck of dust.*   **2** going into or concerned with very small details: *a minute observer, minute instructions.*   *adj.*

**minute hand** (min′it)   on a watch or clock, the longer of the two hands, indicating the minutes: *The minute hand moves around the dial once every hour.*

**mi·nute·ly** (mī nyüt′lē *or* mī nü′tlē)   in minute manner, form, degree, or detail: *They examined the vase minutely but could find no flaws or cracks.*   *adv.*

**mi·nute·ness** (mī nyüt′nis *or* mī nüt′nis)   **1** extreme smallness.   **2** attention to very small details.   *n.*

**mi·nu·ti·ae** (mi nyü′shē ē′ *or* mi nü′shē ē′, mi nyü′shē ī′ *or* mi nü′shē ī′)   very small matters; trifling details.   *n. pl.*

**minx** (mingks)   a bold or impudent girl.   *n.*

**mir·a·cle** (mir′ə kəl)   **1** a wonderful happening that is contrary to or independent of the known laws of nature: *It would be a miracle if the earth stood still in space for an hour.*   **2** something marvellous; a wonder.   *n.*

**mi·rac·u·lous** (mə rak′yə ləs)   **1** contrary to or independent of the known laws of nature; suggesting a MIRACLE; supernatural.   **2** wonderful; marvellous: *Meeting you here is a miraculous good fortune.*   *adj.*
—**mi·rac′u·lous·ly,** *adv.*   —**mi·rac′u·lous·ness,** *n.*

**mi·rage** (mə räzh′)   **1** a misleading appearance in which some distant scene is viewed as being close and, often, upside down. In a mirage, the actual scene is reflected by layers of air of different temperatures. **2** an illusion; thing that does not exist. *n.*

**mire** (mīr) **1** soft, deep mud; slush. **2** a bog or swamp. **3** stick or cause to stick in mire: *He mired his car and had to go for help.* **4** soil with mud or mire. **5** hamper or hold back, as if in a mire; involve in difficulties: *She got mired in a traffic jam.* 1, 2 *n.*, 3–5 *v.*, **mired, mir·ing.**

**mirk** (mėrk) See MURK. *n.*

**mir·ror** (mir′ər, mē′rər, *or* mēr) **1** a looking glass; surface that reflects light. **2** reflect as a mirror does: *The still water mirrored the trees along the bank.* **3** whatever reflects or gives a true description: *This book is a mirror of Laurier's life.* **4** give a true description or picture of: *The book mirrored colonial life in Canada.* **5** a model or example: *That knight was a mirror of chivalry.* 1, 3, 5 *n.*, 2, 4 *v.* —**mir′ror·like′,** *adj.*

**mirth** (mėrth) merriment or gaiety accompanied by laughter: *Her sides shook with mirth.* *n.*

**mirth·ful** (mėrth′fəl) laughing and merry. *adj.* —**mirth′ful·ly,** *adv.* —**mirth′ful·ness,** *n.*

**mirth·less** (mėr′thlis) without mirth; joyless; gloomy. *adj.* —**mirth′less·ly,** *adv.* —**mirth′less·ness,** *n.*

**mir·y** (mī′rē) **1** muddy; swampy. **2** dirty; filthy. *adj.*, **mir·i·er, mir·i·est.** —**mir′i·ness,** *n.*

**mis–** a prefix meaning: **1** bad, as in *misgovernment.* **2** badly, as in *misbehave, mismanage.* **3** wrong, as in *mispronunciation.* **4** wrongly, as in *misapply, misunderstand.*

**mis·ad·ven·ture** (mis′əd ven′chər) **1** an unfortunate accident; an instance of bad luck: *We had several misadventures on our vacation.* **2** bad luck; misfortune: *By some misadventure, the letter got lost.* *n.*

**mis·al·li·ance** (mis′ə lī′əns) an unsuitable alliance or association, especially in marriage. *n.*

**mis·an·thrope** (mis′ən thrōp′) a hater of people; a person who dislikes or distrusts human beings. *n.*

**mis·an·throp·ic** (mis′ən throp′ik) of or like a MISANTHROPE. *adj.*

**mis·an·thro·pist** (mi san′thrə pist) MISANTHROPE. *n.*

**mis·an·thro·py** (mi san′thrə pē) a hatred, dislike, or distrust of human beings. *n.*

**mis·ap·pli·ca·tion** (mis′ap lə kā′shən) a wrong application; a MISAPPLYing or being misapplied. *n.*

**mis·ap·ply** (mis′ə plī′) apply wrongly; make a wrong application or use of. *v.*, **mis·ap·plied, mis·ap·ply·ing.**

**mis·ap·pre·hend** (mis′ap ri hend′) misunderstand. *v.*

**mis·ap·pre·hen·sion** (mis′ap ri hen′shən) a misunderstanding; wrong idea: *The belief that the earth was flat was a misapprehension.* *n.*

**mis·ap·pro·pri·ate** (mis′ə prō′prē āt) make use of for oneself without authority or right: *The treasurer had misappropriated the club funds.* *v.*, **mis·ap·pro·pri·at·ed, mis·ap·pro·pri·at·ing.**

**mis·ap·pro·pri·a·tion** (mis′ə prō′prē ā′shən) **1** a dishonest use of something as one's own. **2** any act of putting something to a wrong use. *n.*

**mis·be·came** (mis′bi kām′) pt. of MISBECOME. *v.*

**mis·be·come** (mis′bi kum′) be UNBECOMING to. *v.*, **mis·be·came, mis·be·come, mis·be·com·ing.**

**mis·be·got·ten** (mis′bi got′ən) **1** begotten unlawfully; illegitimate: *a misbegotten child.* **2** poorly done or conceived; pitiable: *She was ready to throw out the whole misbegotten plan.* *adj.*

**mis·be·have** (mis′bi hāv′) behave oneself badly: *The child was punished for misbehaving at the party.* *v.*, **mis·be·haved, mis·be·hav·ing.**

**mis·be·hav·iour** or **mis·be·hav·ior** (mis′bi hā′vyər) bad behaviour. *n.*

**mis·be·lief** (mis′bi lēf′) a false or erroneous belief, especially in religion. *n.*

**misc.** **1** miscellaneous. **2** miscellany.

**mis·cal·cu·late** (mis kal′kyə lāt′) calculate wrongly; judge or count wrongly: *His arrow fell short because he had miscalculated the distance.* *v.*, **mis·cal·cu·lat·ed, mis·cal·cu·lat·ing.** —**mis′cal·cu·la′tion,** *n.*

**mis·call** (mis kol′) call by a wrong name. *v.*

**mis·car·riage** (mis kar′ij *or* mis ker′ij) **1** failure: *Because a witness lied, the trial resulted in a miscarriage of justice.* **2** the involuntary expulsion of a fetus from the womb before it has developed enough to survive: *A pregnant woman might have a miscarriage because of an accident or illness.* **3** a failure to arrive: *the miscarriage of a letter.* *n.*

**mis·car·ry** (mis kar′ē *or* mis ker′ē) **1** go wrong: *Diane's plans miscarried, and she could not come.* **2** have a MISCARRIAGE (def. 2). **3** fail to arrive. *v.*, **mis·car·ried, mis·car·ry·ing.**

**mis·cast** (mis kast′) cast in an unsuitable role: *The young actress was badly miscast as a bank manager.* *v.*, **mis·cast, mis·cast·ing.**

**mis·ce·ge·na·tion** (mis′ə jə nā′shən) marriage or sexual relations between a man and woman of different races, especially between a white person and one of another race. *n.*

**mis·cel·la·ne·ous** (mis′ə lā′nē əs) **1** formed or consisting of different things or parts, not arranged in a particular pattern or system: *a miscellaneous collection of stamps. She writes a newspaper column of miscellaneous comments.* **2** having or showing various qualities, interests, etc.; many-sided: *a miscellaneous writer.* *adj.* —**mis′cel·la·ne·ous·ly,** *adv.* —**mis′cel·la·ne·ous·ness,** *n.*

**mis·cel·la·ny** (mis′ə lā′nē *or* mi sel′ə nē) **1** a MISCELLANEOUS collection; a mixture of various things. **2** **miscellanies,** *pl.* a collection of separate articles, etc. in one book. *n.*, *pl.* **mis·cel·la·nies.**

**mis·chance** (mis chans′) misfortune; bad luck: *By some mischance he didn't receive my telegram.* *n.*

**mis·chief** (mis′chif) **1** action or conduct that causes trouble or harm, often not intentionally: *A child's mischief with matches may cause a serious fire. She's always getting into mischief.* **2** merry teasing; playful mocking or fooling: *Her eyes were full of mischief.* **3** harm or injury, especially when done by a person: *He'll try to do you a mischief if you meddle.* **4** a person who causes annoyance, irritation, or harm: *He's a little mischief.* *n.*

**mis·chie·vous** (mis′chə vəs) **1** causing or tending to cause harm or annoyance: *mischievous gossip, mischievous behaviour.* **2** full of pranks and teasing fun: *mischievous*

children, a mischievous look. *adj.*
—**mis′chie·vous·ly**, *adv.* —**mis′chie·vous·ness**, *n.*

**mis·ci·ble** (mis′ə bəl) especially of liquids, capable of being mixed to form a substance having the same composition throughout: *Water and alcohol are miscible; water and oil are not.* *adj.*

**mis·con·ceive** (mis′kən sēv′) have wrong ideas about; misunderstand: *The reporter misconceived the speaker's meaning.* *v.*, **mis·con·ceived, mis·con·ceiv·ing.**

**mis·con·cep·tion** (mis′kən sep′shən) a mistaken idea or notion; wrong conception. *n.*

**mis·con·duct** (mis kon′dukt *for noun*, mis′kən dukt′ *for verb*) 1 bad or dishonest management, especially by a public or government official or a member of the military: *The ambassador was censured by the government for misconduct of diplomatic affairs.* 2 manage badly: *The sale of the deceased woman's property was misconducted.* 3 bad behaviour; improper conduct. 4 behave badly: *The report stated that the lawyer had misconducted himself in court.* 1, 3 *n.*, 2, 4 *v.*

**mis·con·struc·tion** (mis′kən struk′shən) the act or process of misconstruing or an instance of this; a taking in the wrong sense; misinterpretation: *Such vague and ambiguous statements are open to misconstruction.* *n.*

**mis·con·strue** (mis′kən strü′) take in a wrong sense; misinterpret: *Shyness is sometimes misconstrued as rudeness.* *v.*, **mis·con·strued, mis·con·stru·ing.**

**mis·count** (mis kount′ *for verb*, mis′kount′ *for noun*) 1 count wrongly. 2 a wrong count. 1 *v.*, 2 *n.*

**mis·cre·ant** (mis′krē ənt) 1 having very bad morals; depraved; base. 2 villain. 1 *adj.*, 2 *n.*

**mis·cue** (mis kyü′) 1 in billiards, a bad stroke in which the cue slips and does not hit the ball squarely. 2 make a miscue. 3 miss one's cue or signal or respond to a wrong cue. 4 *Informal.* mistake; slip-up. 1, 4 *n.*, 2, 3 *v.*, **mis·cued, mis·cu·ing.**

**mis·date** (mis dāt′) date wrongly; put a wrong date on or assign to a wrong date: *to misdate a document, to misdate an event.* *v.*, **mis·dat·ed, mis·dat·ing.**

**mis·deal** (mis dēl′ *for verb*, mis′dēl′ *for noun*) 1 deal wrongly at cards. 2 a wrong deal. 1 *v.*, **mis·dealt, mis·deal·ing;** 2 *n.*

**mis·dealt** (mis delt′) pt. and pp. of MISDEAL. *v.*

**mis·deed** (mis dēd′) a bad act; wicked deed. *n.*

**mis·de·mean·our** or **mis·de·mean·or** (mis′di mē′nər) 1 a wrong deed. 2 *Esp. U.S.* in law, a minor criminal offence, less serious than a felony: *A misdemeanour is similar to a summary conviction offence in Canada.* *n.*

**mis·did** (mis did′) pt. of MISDO. *v.*

**mis·di·rect** (mis′də rekt′) direct wrongly: *The thief left false clues to misdirect the police.* *v.*

**mis·di·rec·tion** (mis′də rek′shən) 1 misdirecting or being misdirected. 2 a wrong direction. *n.*

**mis·do** (mis dü′) do wrongly or improperly. *v.*, **mis·did, mis·done, mis·do·ing.** —**mis·do′er**, *n.*

**mis·do·ing** (mis dü′ing) 1 wrongdoing; misdeed. 2 ppr. of MISDO. 1 *n.*, 2 *v.*

**mis·done** (mis dun′) pp. of MISDO. *v.*

**mis·em·ploy** (mis′em ploi′) use wrongly or improperly. *v.* —**mis′em·ploy′ment**, *n.*

---

**miscible**     759     **Mishnah**

hat, āge, fär; let, ēqual, tėrm; it, īce
hot, ōpen, ôrder; oil, out; cup, pút, rüle
əbove, takən, pencəl, lemən, circəs
ch, child; ng, long; sh, ship
th, thin; ᴛн, then; zh, measure

**mi·ser** (mī′zər) a person who loves money for its own sake, especially one who lives poorly in order to save money and keep it: *A miser dislikes spending money.* *n.*

**mis·er·a·ble** (miz′ə rə bəl *or* miz′rə bəl) 1 unhappy; wretched: *A sick child is often miserable.* 2 causing trouble or unhappiness: *a miserable cold.* 3 poor; pitiful: *They live in a miserable, cold house.* *adj.*
—**mis′er·a·ble·ness**, *n.* —**mis′er·a·bly**, *adv.*

**mi·ser·ly** (mī′zər lē) of or like a miser; stingy. *adj.*
—**mi′ser·li·ness**, *n.*

**mis·er·y** (miz′ə rē *or* miz′rē) 1 a miserable, extremely unhappy state of mind: *Think of the misery of having no home or friends.* 2 poor, mean, or miserable conditions: *Some very poor people live in misery, without beauty or comfort around them.* *n., pl.* **mis·er·ies.**

**mis·fea·sance** (mis fē′zəns) in law, the wrongful performance of a lawful act; wrongful and injurious exercise of lawful authority. Compare with MALFEASANCE and NONFEASANCE. *n.*

**mis·fire** (mis fīr′) 1 of a firearm, missile, etc., fail to discharge or go off. 2 of an INTERNAL-COMBUSTION ENGINE, fail to ignite properly or at the right moment. 3 a failure to discharge or explode properly. 4 fail to have an intended effect; go wrong: *The robber's scheme misfired.* 1, 2, 4 *v.*, **mis·fired, mis·fir·ing;** 3 *n.*

**mis·fit** (mis′fit′) 1 a bad fit. 2 a person who is not suited to his or her environment or does not get along well with other people. *n.*

**mis·for·tune** (mis fôr′chən) 1 bad luck: *She had the misfortune to break her arm.* 2 a piece of bad luck; unlucky accident. *n.*

**mis·give** (mis giv′) cause to feel doubt, suspicion, or anxiety: *Eli's heart misgave him when he realized how far he still had to go.* *v.*, **mis·gave, mis·giv·en, mis·giv·ing.**

**mis·giv·en** (mis giv′ən) pp. of MISGIVE. *v.*

**mis·giv·ing** (mis giv′ing) 1 a feeling of doubt, suspicion, or anxiety: *We started off through the storm with some misgivings.* 2 ppr. of MISGIVE. 1 *n.*, 2 *v.*

**mis·gov·ern** (mis guv′ərn) govern or manage badly. *v.* —**mis·gov′ern·ment**, *n.*

**mis·guid·ance** (mis gī′dəns) bad or wrong guidance. *n.*

**mis·guide** (mis gīd′) lead into mistakes or wrongdoing; mislead. *v.*, **mis·guid·ed, mis·guid·ing.**

**mis·guid·ed** (mis gī′did) erring or misled in thought or action: *He mixed everything up in a well-meaning but misguided attempt to help.* *adj.*

**mis·han·dle** (mis han′dəl) 1 handle roughly or harshly; maltreat: *to mishandle a horse.* 2 manage badly or ignorantly: *to mishandle a business deal.* *v.*, **mis·han·dled, mis·han·dling.**

**mis·hap** (mis′hap) an unlucky accident. *n.*

**Mish·nah** or **Mish·na** (mish′nə) the collection of the traditional oral interpretations of the law of Moses, compiled about A.D. 200: *The Mishnah is the first part of the Talmud.* *n.*

**mis·in·form** (mis′in fôrm′) give wrong or misleading information to. *v.*

**mis·in·for·ma·tion** (mis′in fər mā′shən) wrong, inaccurate, or misleading information. *n.*

**mis·in·ter·pret** (mis′in tėr′prit) interpret wrongly; give a wrong meaning to: *She misinterpreted their signal to wait, and drove off before they were ready.* *v.*

**mis·in·ter·pre·ta·tion** (mis′in tėr′prə tā′shən) wrong interpretation; wrong explanation; misunderstanding. *n.*

**mis·judge** (mis juj′) 1 judge or estimate wrongly: *The archer misjudged the distance to the target and her arrow fell short.* 2 judge unfairly; have an unjust opinion: *The teacher soon discovered that he had misjudged the girl's capabilities.* *v.*, **mis·judged, mis·judg·ing.**

**mis·judg·ment** or **mis·judge·ment** (mis juj′mənt) a wrong or unjust judgment. *n.*

**mis·laid** (mis lād′) pt. and pp. of MISLAY: *She mislaid my books. I have mislaid my pen.* *v.*

**mis·lay** (mis lā′) put in a place and then forget where it is: *My mother is always mislaying her glasses.* *v.*, **mis·laid, mis·lay·ing.**

**mis·lead** (mis lēd′) cause to go in a wrong direction or to do or believe in something that is wrong: *Her cheerfulness misled us into believing that everything was all right. He was accused of misleading his followers.* *v.*, **mis·led, mis·lead·ing.** —**mis·lead′er,** *n.*

**mis·lead·ing** (mis lē′ding) 1 tending to mislead; deceptive or deceiving: *misleading advertising. The calmness of the sea was misleading.* 2 ppr. of MISLEAD. 1 *adj.*, 2 *v.*

**mis·led** (mis led′) pt. and pp. of MISLEAD: *The boy was misled by bad companions.* *v.*

**mis·man·age** (mis man′ij) manage badly. *v.*, **mis·man·aged, mis·man·ag·ing.**

**mis·man·age·ment** (mis man′ij mənt) bad management: *The collapse of the firm was due to years of mismanagement.* *n.*

**mis·match** (mis mach′ *for verb,* mis′mach *for noun*) 1 match incorrectly or unsuitably, or fail to match: *He was wearing a mismatched pair of socks.* 2 a poor or unsuitable match: *That marriage is definitely a mismatch.* 1 *v.*, 2 *n.*

**mis·mate** (mis māt′) mate unsuitably. *v.*, **mis·mat·ed, mis·mat·ing.**

**mis·name** (mis nām′) call by a wrong or unsuitable name: *The slow horse was misnamed 'Lightning'.* *v.*, **mis·named, mis·nam·ing.**

**mis·no·mer** (mis nō′mər) 1 a wrong or unsuitable name or term: *'Lightning' is a misnomer for that slow horse.* 2 an error in naming a person in a legal document. *n.*

**mi·sog·a·mist** (mi sog′ə mist) a person who hates marriage. *n.*

**mi·sog·a·my** (mi sog′ə mē) hatred of marriage. *n.*

**mi·sog·y·nist** (mi soj′ə nist) a hater of women. *n.*

**mi·sog·y·ny** (mi soj′ə nē) hatred of women. *n.*

**mis·place** (mis plās′) 1 put in the wrong place: *a misplaced adjective.* 2 *Informal.* put in a place and then forget where it is; mislay. 3 place one's affections, trust, etc. on an unworthy or unsuitable object. *v.*, **mis·placed, mis·plac·ing.** —**mis·place′ment,** *n.*

**mis·play** (mis plā′ *or* mis′plā *for noun,* mis plā′ *for verb*) 1 a wrong or unskilful play, as in a game: *A misplay in the last quarter almost cost us the game.* 2 play wrongly or unskilfully. 1 *n.*, 2 *v.*

**mis·print** (mis′print *for noun,* mis print′ *for verb*) 1 a mistake in printing. 2 print wrongly. 1 *n.*, 2 *v.*

**mis·pro·nounce** (mis′prə nouns′) pronounce in a way considered incorrect. *v.*, **mis·pro·nounced, mis·pro·nounc·ing.**

**mis·pro·nun·ci·a·tion** (mis′prə nun′sē ā′shən) an incorrect pronunciation. *n.*

**mis·quo·ta·tion** (mis′kwō tā′shən) an incorrect quotation. *n.*

**mis·quote** (mis kwōt′) quote incorrectly. *v.*, **mis·quot·ed, mis·quot·ing.**

**mis·read** (mis rēd′) 1 read wrongly: *I misread tapering as papering and got the whole sentence wrong.* 2 misinterpret; misunderstand: *She misread his silence as agreement.* *v.*, **mis·read** (-red′), **mis·read·ing.**

**mis·rep·re·sent** (mis′rep ri zent′) 1 represent falsely; give a wrong or untrue idea of, especially in order to deceive: *He misrepresented the car when he said it was in good running order.* 2 be a bad or inadequate representative of: *His new novel misrepresents his status as a writer.* *v.*

**mis·rep·re·sen·ta·tion** (mis′rep ri zen tā′shən) the action or an instance of MISREPRESENTing: *She obtained the part by misrepresentation. The report contains a serious misrepresentation of the facts.* *n.*

**mis·rule** (mis rül′) 1 bad or unwise rule. 2 rule badly; misgovern. 3 disorder. 1, 3 *n.*, 2 *v.*, **mis·ruled, mis·rul·ing.**

**miss¹** (mis) 1 fail to hit: *He fired twice, but both shots missed.* 2 fail to find, get, meet, attend, use, catch, hear, read, do, solve, etc.: *to miss a train.* 3 a failure to hit, attain, etc. 4 let slip by; not seize: *I missed my chance.* 5 escape or avoid: *I barely missed being hit.* 6 notice the absence of: *I did not miss my purse till I got home.* 7 feel keenly the absence of: *He missed his mother when she went away.* 8 fail to work properly; misfire: *The car was missing on two cylinders.* 9 leave out: *to miss a word in reading.* 1, 2, 4–8 *v.*, 3 *n.*
**a miss is as good as a mile,** a close miss has the same effect as a wide miss.

**miss²** (mis) 1 a girl or young woman. 2 **Miss,** a title put before a girl's or unmarried woman's name: *Miss Brown, the Misses Brown, the Miss Browns.* 3 a form of address used in place of the name of a girl or an unmarried woman: *I beg your pardon, Miss.* *n., pl.* **miss·es.**

**mis·shape** (mis shāp′) shape badly; deform; make in the wrong shape. *v.*, **mis·shaped, mis·shaped** or **mis·shap·en, mis·shap·ing.**

**mis·shap·en** (mis shā′pən) 1 badly shaped; deformed. 4 a pp. of MISSHAPE. 1 *adj.*, 2 *v.*

**mis·sile** (mis′īl *or* mis′əl) 1 an object that is thrown or shot at a target, such as a stone, arrow, bullet, etc. 2 a self-propelled rocket containing explosives: *Missiles can be launched from land, air, or water.* *n.*

**mis·sile·man** (mis′əl mən) *Esp. U.S.* a person whose

work is designing, building, or operating guided MISSILES (def. 2).   *n., pl.* **mis·sile·men** (-mən).

**miss·ing** (mis′ing)   **1** out of the usual or a known place; lost or gone: *The missing ring was found under the dresser.*   **2** absent: *Only two students were missing from class today.*   **3** lacking or wanting: *It was quite a good dinner, but there was something missing.*   **4** ppr. of MISS. 1–3 *adj.*, 4 *v.*

**mis·sion** (mish′ən)   **1** sending or being sent on some special work; errand: *An operation by one or more aircraft against the enemy is called a mission.*   **2** a group of persons sent on some special business: *She was one of a mission sent by our government to France.*   **3** the business on which a person or group is sent: *Their mission was to blow up the bridge.*   **4** the station or headquarters of a religious mission.   **5** the district assigned to a priest or pastor from a neighbouring parish.   **6** a place where persons may go for aid, such as food, clothing, shelter, or counsel.   **7** one's business or purpose in life; calling: *It seemed to be her mission to care for her brother's children.*   **8 missions,** *pl.*   an organized effort to spread the Christian religion.   *n.*

**mis·sion·ar·y** (mish′ə ner′ē)   **1** a person sent by a Christian church, etc. on a religious mission.   **2** a person who works to advance some cause or idea: *a missionary for science.*   **3** of, having to do with, or characteristic of missions or missionaries: *He spoke with missionary zeal of a new social order.*   *n., pl.* **mis·sion·ar·ies.**

**mis·sis** (mis′əz)   See MISSUS.   *n.*

**mis·sive** (mis′iv)   a written message; letter.   *n.*

**mis·spell** (mis spel′)   spell incorrectly.   *v.*, **mis·spelled** or **mis·spelt, mis·spell·ing.**

**mis·spell·ing** (mis spel′ing)   **1** an incorrect spelling. **2** ppr. of MISSPELL.   1 *n.*, 2 *v.*

**mis·spelt** (mis spelt′)   a pt. and a pp. of MISSPELL.   *v.*

**mis·spend** (mis spend′)   spend foolishly or wrongly; waste: *an old man regretting that he had misspent his youth.*   *v.*, **mis·spent, mis·spend·ing.**

**mis·spent** (mis spent′)   pt. and pp. of MISSPEND.   *v.*

**mis·state** (mis stāt′)   make wrong or misleading statements about.   *v.*, **mis·stat·ed, mis·stat·ing.**

**mis·state·ment** (mis stāt′mənt)   a wrong or erroneous statement: *The newspaper account of the game was full of misstatements.*   *n.*

**mis·step** (mis step′)   **1** a wrong step: *a single misstep would have plunged her into the abyss.*   **2** an error in judgment; blunder: *A misstep now could ruin his career.*   *n.*

**mis·sus** or **mis·sis** (mis′əz)   Often, **the missus,** *Informal.*   wife: *You'll have to ask the missus about that. Are you going to bring your missus along?*   *n.*
☛ *Usage.* See note at MRS.

**miss·y** (mis′ē) *Informal.*   little miss; miss.   *n., pl.* **miss·ies.**

**mist** (mist)   **1** a cloud of very fine drops of water in the air; fog.   **2** come down in mist; rain in very fine drops. **3** anything that dims, blurs, or obscures: *The ideas were lost in a mist of long words.*   **4** a haze before the eyes due to illness or tears.   **5** become covered with mist; become dim: *The windows are misting.*   **6** cover with a mist; put a mist before; make dim: *Tears misted her eyes.*   1, 3, 4 *n.*, 2, 5, 6 *v.*
**mist over** or **mist up,**   become covered with mist.

**mis·take** (mi stāk′)   **1** an error; blunder;

hat, āge, fär; let, ēqual, tėrm; it, īce
hot, ōpen, ôrder; oil, out; cup, pùt, rüle
əbove, takən, pencəl, lemən, circəs
ch, child; ng, long; sh, ship
th, thin; ᴛʜ, then; zh, measure

misunderstanding of the meaning or use of something: *I used your towel by mistake.*   **2** make a mistake; misunderstand what is seen or heard: *I was mistaken when I said she would not come.*   **3** take wrongly; take to be some other person or thing: *I mistook that stick for a snake.*   1 *n.*, 2, 3 *v.*, **mis·took, mis·tak·en, mis·tak·ing. and no mistake,**   without a doubt; surely.

**mis·tak·en** (mi stā′kən)   **1** wrong in opinion; having made a mistake: *A mistaken person should admit his error.* **2** wrong; wrongly judged; misplaced: *It was a mistaken kindness to give that boy more candy; it will make him sick.* **3** pp. of MISTAKE.   1, 2 *adj.*, 3 *v.*   **—mis·tak′en·ly,** *adv.*

**mis·ter** (mis′tər)   **1** *Informal.*   a title used in speaking to a man (used alone, not with a name): *Hey, Mister! You dropped your wallet.*   **2 Mister,**   the spoken form of MR., a title for a man, used before his last name or the name of his rank or office: *He always called his teacher 'Mister'.*   *n.*
☛ *Etym.* A weakened form of MASTER. The word **master,** when used before a title or name, gradually lost its stress and the vowel became weakened to an *i.* Moreover, because by the end of the 17c. the word was always abbreviated when used before a title or name, **Mr.** and **master** became two different words.
☛ *Usage.*   When used as a title before a name or office, the word **mister** is generally written in its abbreviated form. Compare with the note at MRS.

**mis·time** (mis tīm′)   **1** say or do at the wrong time. **2** misstate the time of.   *v.*, **mis·timed, mis·tim·ing.**

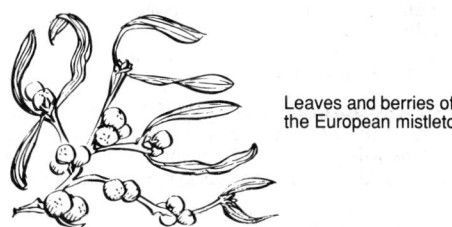

Leaves and berries of the European mistletoe

**mis·tle·toe** (mis′əl tō′)   **1** any of various related evergreen plants that grow as parasites on certain trees; especially, a European shrub often growing on apple trees, having yellow flowers and small, waxy, white berries, traditionally used as a Christmas decoration.   **2** referring to the family of parasitic plants that includes the mistletoes.   *n.*

**mis·took** (mi stůk′)   pt. of MISTAKE: *I mistook you for your sister yesterday.*   *v.*

**mis·tral** (mis′trəl *or* mi sträl′)   a cold, dry, northerly wind common in southern France and neighbouring regions.   *n.*

**mis·trans·late** (mis′tran slāt′ *or* mis′tran zlāt′, mis tran′slāt *or* mis tran′zlāt)   translate incorrectly.   *v.*, **mis·trans·lat·ed, mis·trans·lat·ing.**

**mis·trans·la·tion** (mis′tran slā′shən *or* mis′tran zlā′shən)   an incorrect translation.   *n.*

**mis·treat** (mis trēt′) treat badly; abuse: *That man mistreats his horses.* *v.*

**mis·treat·ment** (mis trēt′mənt) ill treatment. *n.*

**mis·tress** (mis′tris) **1** a woman who has power or authority, such as a female head of a household or institution. **2** a woman or girl as owner or possessor: *The dog was sitting outside the door, waiting for its mistress.* **3** a woman having a thorough knowledge or mastery: *mistress of the difficult art of fencing. She is mistress of the situation.* **4** a state or country that is in control or can rule: *Britain was mistress of the seas.* **5** a woman who has a continuing sexual relationship with a man without being legally married to him. **6** *Esp. Brit.* a female teacher: *the dancing mistress.* *n.*

**mis·tri·al** (mis trī′əl) **1** a trial declared to have no effect in law because of some error or serious misconduct in the proceedings. **2** a trial that is inconclusive because the jury has failed to reach a verdict. *n.*

**mis·trust** (mis trust′) **1** have no confidence or trust in; doubt: *She mistrusted her ability to learn to swim.* **2** lack of trust or confidence; distrust. 1 *v.*, 2 *n.*

**mis·trust·ful** (mis trust′fəl) lacking confidence; distrustful; doubting; suspicious. *adj.*

**mist·y** (mis′tē) **1** full of or covered with mist: *misty hills, misty air.* **2** not clearly seen or outlined: *The boys saw a misty shape in the graveyard.* **3** as if seen through a mist; vague; indistinct: *a misty idea.* *adj.*, **mist·i·er, mist·i·est.** —**mist′i·ly,** *adv.* —**mist′i·ness,** *n.*

**mis·un·der·stand** (mis′un dər stand′) **1** understand wrongly: *We misunderstood the directions and made a wrong turn.* **2** take in a wrong sense; give the wrong meaning to. *v.*, **mis·un·der·stood, mis·un·der·stand·ing.**

**mis·un·der·stand·ing** (mis′un dər stan′ding) **1** a failure to understand; a mistake as to meaning; a wrong understanding. **2** a disagreement: *After their misunderstanding, they scarcely spoke to each other for months.* **3** ppr. of MISUNDERSTAND. 1, 2 *n.*, 3 *v.*

**mis·un·der·stood** (mis′un dər stud′) **1** pt. and pp. of MISUNDERSTAND: *Kate misunderstood what the teacher said and so did the wrong thing.* **2** not understood or properly appreciated: *As a child, he had always felt misunderstood.* 1 *v.*, 2 *adj.*

**mis·us·age** (mis yü′sij) **1** a wrong or improper usage, especially of words. **2** ill usage; harsh treatment. *n.*

**mis·use** (mis yüz′ *for verb,* mis yüs′ *for noun*) **1** use for the wrong purpose: *He misuses his knife at the table by lifting food with it.* **2** abuse; ill-treat: *He misuses his sled dogs by driving them too hard.* **3** wrong or improper use: *the misuse of public funds, a misuse of words.* 1, 2 *v.*, **mis·used, mis·us·ing;** 3 *n.*

**mite** (mīt) **1** any of a large number of tiny animals of the same class as spiders, that are often parasites on plants or animals, and some of which carry diseases: *Some species of mite are so small they cannot be seen with the naked eye.* **2** any very small object or creature: *I'm not really hungry, but I'll have just a mite of toast. Our cat was just a mite when we got her.* **3** a tiny bit; very little: *I think she's a mite tired.* **4** a small coin or a small sum of money: *Though poor herself, she gave her mite to charity.* *n.*
☛ Hom. MIGHT.

**mi·ter** (mī′tər) See MITRE. *n., v.*

**mi·tered** (mī′tərd) See MITRED. *adj.*

**Mith·ras** (mith′räs) in Zoroastrianism, a mediator between Ahura Mazda and Angra Mainyu. He later acquired a cultic following throughout the Greco-Roman world. *n.*

**mit·i·gate** (mit′ə gāt′) make or become less severe, painful, or harsh; make or become mild or milder; soften or moderate: *to mitigate a person's anger, to mitigate pain, to mitigate the effects of war.* *v.*, **mit·i·gat·ed, mit·i·gat·ing.**

**mit·i·ga·tion** (mit′ə gā′shən) the action of mitigating or the fact or state of being MITIGATED. *n.*

**mi·to·chon·dri·on** (mī′tō kon′drē ən) any of the many organelles which provide the cell with energy through chemical reaction. *n., pl.* **mi·to·chon·dri·a** (-drē ə).

**mi·to·sis** (mi tō′sis *or* mī tō′sis) in biology, the process by which a plant or animal cell divides to produce two daughter cells that are identical to the parent: *In mitosis the pairs of chromosomes in the parent cell double, so that each daughter cell has the same number of chromosomes as the parent.* Compare with MEIOSIS. *n.*

**mitral valve** the valve between the left ATRIUM and the left VENTRICLE of the heart that prevents a flow of blood from going back to the atrium during SYSTOLE.

**mi·tre** (mī′tər) **1** a tall, pointed, folded cap worn by bishops and abbots during certain ceremonies as a symbol of office. **2** bestow a mitre on; make a bishop. **3** the official headdress of the ancient Jewish high priest. **4** a kind of joint or corner where two pieces of wood, etc. are fitted together at right angles, with the ends cut slanting, as at the corners of a picture frame. See JOINT for picture. **5** join thus; prepare for joining in a mitre joint. **6** the BEVEL on either of the pieces in a mitre joint. 1, 3, 4, 6 *n.*, 2, 5 *v.* Also, **miter.**

**mi·tred** (mī′tərd) **1** having a mitre joint. **2** wearing a bishop's mitre. **3** pt. and pp. of MITRE. 1, 2 *adj.*, 3 *v.*

**mitre joint** MITRE (def. 4).

**mitt** (mit) **1** MITTEN. **2** a padded, oversized mitten used for catching the ball in baseball, etc.: *a catcher's mitt.* **3** a knitted or lace hand covering that resembles a glove but does not cover the fingers. **4** a covering or pad worn over the hand, designed for a particular use: *a bath mitt, oven mitts.* *n.*

**mit·ten** (mit′ən) a kind of winter glove covering the four fingers together and the thumb separately. *n.*

**mix** (miks) **1** put together; stir well together: *to mix ingredients to make a cake.* **2** prepare by blending different things: *to mix a cake.* **3** an already mixed preparation: *a cake mix.* **4** join: *to mix business and pleasure.* **5** be mixed: *Milk and water mix.* **6** get along together; make friends easily: *She found it difficult to mix with strangers. He doesn't mix very well.* **7** mixture. **8** *Informal.* a mixed condition; mess. 1, 2, 4–6 *v.*, **mixed** or **mixt, mix·ing;** 3, 7, 8 *n.*
**mix up, a** confuse: *Don't mix me up; I'm trying to count.* **b** involve; concern: *He was mixed up in a plot to overthrow the queen.*

**mixed** (mikst) **1** put together or formed by mixing; composed of different parts or elements; of different kinds combined: *mixed candies, mixed emotions.* **2** of different classes, kinds, etc.; not exclusive: *a mixed company.* **3** of or for persons of both sexes: *She sings in the mixed chorus.* **4** a pt. and a pp. of MIX. 1–3 *adj.*, 4 *v.*

**mixed bag** *Informal.* a collection of different people

or things; assortment: *The people at the party were really a mixed bag.*

**mixed farming** raising crops and livestock on the same farm.

**mixed number** a whole number consisting of a whole number and a fraction, such as 1½, 16⅔.

**mix·er** (mik′sər) **1** an apparatus or appliance for mixing foods, etc. **2** a person whose work is mixing ingredients. **3** a person who gets along well with others, making friends easily: *She is a good mixer.* *n.*

**mix·ture** (mik′schər) **1** mixing or being mixed. **2** something made by mixing: *The mixture is put into a greased dish and baked. Green is a mixture of blue and yellow.* **3** in chemistry, a substance consisting of two or more ingredients that keep their individual chemical properties and can be separated by non-chemical means: *A sugar-and-water mixture can be separated by boiling off the water.* Compare with COMPOUND¹ (def. 2). *n.*

**mix–up** (mik′sup) *Informal.* **1** confusion; mess: *A misprint in the notice caused a mix-up over the date of the meeting.* **2** BRAWL (def. 1). *n.*

**miz·zen** (miz′ən) **1** a fore-and-aft sail on the MIZZENMAST. See YAWL for picture. **2** MIZZENMAST. *n.*

**miz·zen·mast** (miz′ən mast′ *or* miz′ən məst) the mast next behind the mainmast on a sailing ship or sailboat. See MAST and YAWL for pictures. *n.*

**mk.** mark.

**mkt.** market.

**mL** millilitre; millilitres.

**MLA** *or* **M.L.A.** Member of the Legislative Assembly.

**Mlle.** *or* **Mlle** Mademoiselle. *pl.* **Mlles.**

**mm** millimetre; millimetres.

**MM.** *or* **MM** Messieurs.

**Mme.** *or* **Mme** Madame. *pl.* **Mmes.**

**Mn** manganese.

**MNA** *or* **M.N.A.** Member of the National Assembly.

**mne·mon·ic** (ni mon′ik) **1** aiding or intended to aid memory: *a set of mnemonic symbols.* **2** of or having to do with memory: *He was a man of great mnemonic power.* **3** a device to aid the memory. *1, 2 adj., 3 n.*

**Mo** molybdenum.

**mo.** month; months.

**M.O.** **1** Money Order. **2** Medical Officer.

**moan** (mōn) **1** a long, low sound of suffering. **2** any similar sound: *the moan of the wind.* **3** make moans: *They heard the sick woman moan. The wind moaned in the trees.* **4** utter with a moan: *"I can't hang on any longer,"* he moaned. **5** complain about; complain: *He was always moaning about his luck.* **6** grieve or lament: *Julia moaned the loss of her friends.* *1, 2 n., 3–6 v.*
—**moan′ing·ly,** *adv.*
☞ *Hom.* MOWN.

**moat** (mōt) **1** a deep, wide ditch dug around a castle or town as a protection against enemies: *Moats were usually kept filled with water.* See CASTLE for picture. **2** a similar ditch used to separate areas in a zoo. **3** surround with a moat. *1, 2 n., 3 v.*
☞ *Hom.* MOTE.

**mob** (mob) **1** a large number of people; crowd: *There*

**mixed farming**    **763**    **mocha**

hat, āge, fär; let, ēqual, tėrm; it, īce
hot, ōpen, ôrder; oil, out; cup, pùt, rüle
əbove, takən, pencəl, lemən, circəs
ch, child; ng, long; sh, ship
th, thin; ᴛʜ, then; zh, measure

*was a great mob at the gate, waiting to get in.* **2** an uncontrollable crowd, easily moved to destructive or riotous action: *The crowd had turned into an ugly mob.* **3** attack with violence, as a mob does. **4** crowd around too closely in excessive eagerness, curiosity, etc.: *Autograph hunters mobbed the singer outside her hotel.* **5 the mob,** the masses (MASS, def. 9). *1–3, 5 n., 3, 4 v.,* **mobbed, mob·bing.**
☞ *Etym.* A shortening of *mobile* from the Latin phrase *mobile vulgus* 'mobile (or fickle) crowd'. 17c.

**mo·bile¹** (mō′bīl *or* mō′bəl) **1** capable of being moved easily; moving easily; movable: *The tongue is mobile. A car is a mobile machine.* **2** easily changed; quick to change from one position to another: *mobile features, a mobile mind.* *adj.*

**mo·bile²** (mō′bīl *or* mō′bēl) a decorative construction of small metal, plastic, wood, or paper shapes suspended from a balanced arrangement of horizontal bars so that the shapes will move in a current of air. *n.*

**mobile home** a large trailer used as a more or less permanent home.

**mo·bil·i·ty** (mō bil′ə tē) being MOBILE; ability or readiness to move or be moved. *n.*

**mo·bi·li·za·tion** (mō′bə lə zā′shən *or* mō′bə lī zā′shən) **1** mobilizing; calling troops, ships, etc. into active military service. **2** being MOBILIZED. *n.*

**mo·bi·lize** (mō′bə līz′) **1** call troops, warships, etc. into active military service; organize for war. **2** assemble and prepare for war: *The troops mobilized quickly.* **3** put into motion or active use: *to mobilize the wealth of a country.* *v.,* **mo·bi·lized, mo·bi·liz·ing.**
—**mo′bi·liz′a·ble,** *adj.*

Three traditional styles of moccasin

**moc·ca·sin** (mok′ə sən) **1** a soft, heel-less leather shoe or boot having the bottom and sides made of a single piece of leather which is joined in a puckered seam to the rounded piece forming the top: *Moccasins are the traditional footwear of many First Nations and Native American peoples.* **2** a shoe or slipper similar in construction or appearance. *n.*
☞ *Etym.* From an Algonquian word, possibly Ojibwa *makasin.*

**moccasin flower** any of several LADY'S-SLIPPERS, especially a species having pink or, sometimes, white flowers, found from Newfoundland to Alberta and south to Georgia and Alabama.

**mo·cha** (mō′kə) **1** a choice variety of coffee originally coming from Arabia.   2 a flavouring made from strong coffee or a mixture of coffee and cocoa or chocolate.   3 flavoured with mocha.   *n.*

**mock** (mok)   1 laugh at; make fun of.   2 make fun of by copying or imitating: *The thoughtless children mocked the limp of the disabled girl.*   3 imitate; copy.   4 not real; being an imitation: *a mock battle.*   5 an action or speech that mocks; mockery.   6 a person or thing scorned or deserving scorn.   7 scoff.   8 make light of; pay no attention to.   1–3, 7, 8 *v.*, 4 *adj.*, 5, 6 *n.*   —**mock′er,** *n.*
**make mock of,**   ridicule.

**mock·er·y** (mok′ə rē)   1 making fun; ridicule: *Their mockery of her hat hurt her feelings.*   2 a person or thing to be made fun of: *Through his foolishness he became a mockery in the village.*   3 a poor copy or imitation. 4 disregarding; setting at naught: *The unfair trial was a mockery of justice.*   *n.*, *pl.* **mock·er·ies.**
**make mockery of,**   ridicule.

**mock–he·ro·ic** (mok′hi rō′ik)   1 imitating or burlesquing what is heroic: *Pope's "Rape of the Lock" is a mock-heroic poem.*   2 an imitation or burlesque of what is heroic.   1 *adj.*, 2 *n.*

**mock·ing** (mok′ing)   1 that mocks; ridiculing or mimicking: *mocking laughter.*   2 ppr. of MOCK.   1 *adj.*, 2 *v.*   —**mock′ing·ly,** *adv.*

**mock·ing·bird** (mok′ing bėrd′)   a North American songbird belonging to the same family as the thrashers and famous for being able to imitate the songs of other birds: *The mockingbird is especially common in the southern United States.*   *n.*

**mock orange** or **mock–orange** (mok′ô′rinj)   any of a closely related group of shrubs having showy white, sometimes fragrant flowers: *Several species of mock orange are widely grown in temperate regions as ornamental shrubs.*   *n.*

**mock–up** (mok′up′)   a full-sized model of an aircraft, machine, piece of landscape, etc., built accurately to scale and used for display or for teaching or experimental purposes.   *n.*

**mo·dal** (mō′dəl)   1 in grammar: of, having to do with, or being a grammatical form that characteristically expresses action, state, or quality in terms of possibility, probability, power, etc. rather than simple fact: *Can, may, will, should, ought, etc. are modal verbs.*   2 a modal verb. 3 in music, of or referring to any of the various modes which preceded the modern diatonic scales.   1, 3 *adj.*, 2 *n.*

**modal auxiliary**   an auxiliary verb, such as *may, can, must, would,* and *should,* used with a verb expressing action, state, or quality to indicate possibility, probability, obligation, etc.

**mode**[1] (mōd)   1 the manner or way in which a thing is done: *Riding on a donkey is a slow mode of travel.*   2 in music, any of various arrangements of the tones of an octave.   3 in music, either of the two modern forms of scale: *minor mode.*   *n.*

**mode**[2] (mōd)   the style, fashion, or custom that prevails; the way most people are behaving, dressing, etc.: *Bobbed hair was the mode about 1920.*   *n.*

**mod·el** (mod′əl)   1 a small copy: *a model of a ship.* 2 a figure in clay or wax that is to be copied in marble, bronze, etc.: *a model for a statue.*   3 make; shape; fashion; design; plan: *to model a bird's nest in clay.*   4 in drawing or painting, show the effects of light and shade on objects or figures to make them appear three-dimensional. 5 make models; design: *to model in clay.*   6 a particular style or design of a thing: *Some car makers produce a new model every year. I want a dress like yours, for that model would suit me.*   7 a thing or person to be imitated: *The boy wrote so well that the teacher used his composition as a model for the class.*   8 follow as a model; form something after a particular model: *He modelled himself on his father.* 9 just right or perfect, especially in conduct: *a model child.* 10 a person who poses for artists, photographers, etc. 11 a person employed to help sell clothing by wearing it for customers to see.   12 be a model: *She models for advertisements on TV.*   13 show a dress, etc. for approval: *That girl usually models evening gowns.*   14 a figure of an item not yet made that serves as a plan for producing the finished item: *City Hall has displayed a model of what the new stadium will look like.*   1, 2, 6, 7, 10, 11, 14 *n.*, 3–5, 8, 12, 13 *v.*, **mod·elled** or **mod·eled, mod·el·ling** or **mod·el·ing;**   9 *adj.*

**mod·el·ling** or **mod·el·ing** (mod′ə ling)   1 the act or occupation of a person who models clothes: *She is interested in modelling.*   2 the making of solid forms or figures in clay, wax, etc. by pressing and shaping with the hands.   3 in drawing or painting, the showing of the effects of light and shade on objects or figures to give a three-dimensional appearance.   4 ppr. of MODEL.   1–3 *n.*, 4 *v.*

**mo·dem** (mō′dem′)   a device which enables a computer to receive and send data over telephone lines.   *n.*
☛ *Etym.*   From the initial letters of m*odulator and* dem*odulator.*

**mod·er·ate** (mod′ə rit *for adjective and noun,* mod′ə rāt′ *for verb*)   1 kept or keeping within proper bounds; not extreme: *moderate expenses, moderate styles.*   2 a person who holds moderate opinions.   3 make or become less extreme or violent: *The wind is moderating.*   4 fair; medium; not very large or good: *a moderate profit.*   5 act as MODERATOR (defs. 1, 2); preside over: *Our hockey coach will moderate a panel discussion on the plans for a sports program.*   1, 4 *adj.*, 2 *n.*, 3, 5 *v.*, **mod·er·at·ed, mod·er·at·ing.**   —**mod′er·ate·ly,** *adv.*

**mod·er·a·tion** (mod′ə rā′shən)   1 freedom from excess; proper restraint; temperance: *He still has to learn the value of moderation.*   2 a moderating or moving away from an extreme: *We all welcomed the moderation of the uncomfortably hot weather.*   3 calmness; lack of violence.   *n.*
**in moderation,**   within limits, not going to extremes: *She eats sweets in moderation.*

**mod·er·a·tor** (mod′ə rā′tər)   1 a presiding officer; chairman: *the moderator of a town meeting.*   2 an arbitrator; mediator.   3 the chief elected officer in some churches.   4 a material used in a REACTOR to slow down nuclear FISSION (def. 2).   *n.*

**mod·ern** (mod′ərn)   1 of the present time or times not long past: *Television is a modern invention.*   2 a person of the present time or of times not long past: *She is studying English dramatists, specializing in the moderns.*   3 using or involving recent techniques, ideas, etc.; up-to-date; not old-fashioned: *They bought the most modern style of kitchen range available.*   4 a person who has modern ideas and tastes.   1, 3 *adj.*, 2, 4 *n.*   —**mod′ern·ness,** *n.*

**Modern English**   the English language from about 1450 to the present.
☛ *Etym.*   Some scholars call the period from 1450 to the

middle of the 18th century Early Modern English. But the term Modern English as given here is acceptable.

**mod·ern·ism** (mod′ər niz′əm)  1 modern attitudes, methods, etc. or sympathy with what is modern.  2 a modern word or phrase.  *n.*

**mod·ern·ist** (mod′ər nist)  a person who holds modern views or follows modern techniques or ideas.  *n.*

**mod·ern·is·tic** (mod′ər nis′tik)  1 of or having to do with MODERNISM or MODERNISTS.  2 following modern styles, methods, etc., especially in art or music.  *adj.*

**mo·der·ni·ty** (mə dėr′nə tē)  1 being modern. 2 something modern.  *n., pl.* **mo·der·ni·ties.**

**mod·ern·i·za·tion** (mod′ər nə zā′shən or mod′ər nī zā′shən)  1 a modernizing or being modernized.  2 something MODERNIZEd; a modernized version.  *n.*

**mod·ern·ize** (mod′ər nīz′)  1 make modern; bring up to present ways or standards.  2 adopt modern ideas, techniques, etc.  *v.,* **mod·ern·ized, mod·ern·iz·ing.**

**mod·est** (mod′ist)  1 not thinking too highly of oneself; not vain; humble: *In spite of the honours he received, the scientist remained a modest man.*  2 bashful; not bold; shy.  3 having or showing a sense of what is fit and proper: *People liked the modest behaviour of the children.*  4 not too great; not asking too much: *a modest request.*  5 not gaudy; humble in appearance; quiet: *a modest little house.*  *adj.* —**mod′est·ly,** *adv.*

**mod·es·ty** (mod′i stē)  1 freedom from vanity; being modest or humble.  2 being shy or bashful.  3 decency of actions, thoughts, clothing, etc.  *n., pl.* **mod·es·ties.**

**mod·i·cum** (mod′ə kəm)  a small or moderate quantity: *Fred is so bright that even with a modicum of effort he does excellent work.*  *n.*

**mod·i·fi·ca·tion** (mod′ə fə kā′shən)  1 a slight or partial change in form: *a modification in plans.*  2 a reduction; making less; moderation.  3 a limitation or qualification of a statement.  4 a modified form or variety: *The most recent modification of the long-range missile performs flawlessly.*  5 in biology, a change in an animal or plant caused by environment and not inheritable.  *n.*

**mod·i·fi·er** (mod′ə fī′ər)  1 in grammar, a word or group of words that limits the meaning of another word or group of words. In "a very tight coat," the adjective *tight* is a modifier of *coat,* and the adverb *very* is a modifier of *tight.*  2 a person or thing that modifies.  *n.*

**mod·i·fy** (mod′ə fī′)  1 change somewhat: *to modify the terms of a lease.*  2 make less; reduce or moderate: *to modify one's demands.*  3 in grammar, limit the meaning of; qualify: *Adverbs modify verbs, adjectives, and other adverbs.*  4 in biology, make important structural changes in a part, usually resulting in a different function or orientation of the part: *The tusk of a narwhal is a modified tooth. In birds, the front limbs have become modified for flight.*  *v.,* **mod·i·fied, mod·i·fy·ing.** —**mod′i·fi′a·ble,** *adj.*

**mod·ish** (mō′dish)  fashionable; stylish: *a modish hat.*  *adj.* —**mod′ish·ly,** *adv.* —**mod′ish·ness,** *n.*

**mo·diste** (mō dēst′)  a maker of or dealer in women's clothes, hats, etc.; dressmaker or milliner.  *n.*

**Mo·dred** (mō′dred)  in the legends about King Arthur, Arthur's treacherous nephew.  *n.*

**mod·u·lar** (moj′ə lər)  1 of, having to do with, or based on a MODULE or MODULUS.  2 designed or constructed in standardized sizes or units that can be interchanged and fitted together in a variety of ways: *modular storage units, modular furniture.*  *adj.*

**mod·u·late** (moj′ə lāt′)  1 regulate; adjust; vary; soften; tone down.  2 alter the voice for expression: *Her speech is always beautifully modulated.*  3 in music, change from one key to another.  4 vary the frequency of electrical waves.  5 change a radio current by adding sound waves to it.  *v.,* **mod·u·lat·ed, mod·u·lat·ing.**

**mod·u·la·tion** (moj′ə lā′shən)  1 a modulating or being MODULATEd.  2 a change from one key to another in the course of a piece of music.  3 in electronics, varying the frequency of waves.  *n.*

**mod·u·la·tor** (moj′ə lā′tər)  a person or thing that MODULATES, especially a device for varying the range of frequency of a signal or wave in radio, television, etc.  *n.*

**mod·ule** (moj′ül)  1 a standard or unit for measuring. 2 the size of some part taken as a unit of measure.  3 a standardized piece or component.  4 an independent unit that forms part of a larger, complex structure, program, etc.: *The command module of a spacecraft can function independently.*  *n.*

**mod·u·lus** (moj′ə ləs)  in science, a quantity expressing the measure of some function, property, or the like, especially under conditions where the measure is unity.  *n., pl.* **mod·u·li** (-lī′ or lē′).

**mo·dus o·pe·ran·di** (mō′dəs op′ə ran′dī or op′ə ran′dē) *Latin.*  a method or manner of working.

**mo·dus vi·ven·di** (mō′dəs vi ven′dī or vi ven′dē) *Latin.*  a mode of living; way of getting along.

**mo·gul** (mō′gul)  1 an important or influential person; magnate.  2 **Mogul,** a Mongolian, especially one of the Mongol conquerors of India in the 16th century or one of their descendants.  *n.*

**M.O.H.**  Medical Officer of Health.

**mo·hair** (mō′her)  1 cloth or yarn made from the long, silky hair of the ANGORA GOAT.  2 the hair of the ANGORA GOAT.

**Mo·ham·med** (mō ham′id)  A.D. 570?– 632, a prophet and the founder of Islam, one of the world's great religions.  *n.*  Also, **Mahomet, Muhammad.**

**Mo·ham·med·an** (mō ham′ə dən)  1 of or having to do with Mohammed or Islam.  2 a western name for a Moslem.  1 *adj.,* 2 *n.*  Also, **Mahometan.**

**Mo·ham·med·an·ism** (mō ham′ə də niz′əm)  a western name for ISLAM.  *n.*  Also, **Mahometanism.**

**Mo·hawk** (mō′hok)  1 a member of a First Nations people now living mainly in southern Ontario and Quebec: *The Mohawk belonged to the Iroquois Confederacy.*  2 the language of these people: *Mohawk is an Iroquoian language.*  3 of or having to do with the Mohawk or their language.  1, 2 *n., pl.* **Mo·hawk** or **Mo·hawks;**  3 *adj.*

**moi·e·ty** (moi′ə tē)  1 half.  2 an indefinite part: *Only a moiety of high-school graduates go to college.*  *n., pl.* **moi·e·ties.**

**moil** (moil) **1** work hard; drudge. **2** hard work; drudgery. **3** trouble; confusion. *1 v., 2, 3 n.*

**moi·ré** or **moire** (mwä rā′, mwär, *or* mô rā′) **1** cloth having an irregular wavy finish; watered fabric. **2** having such a finish; watered: *moiré taffeta.* *1 n., 2 adj.*

**moist** (moist) **1** slightly wet; damp: *a moist towel.* **2** humid. **3** filled with tears: *His eyes were moist, but he did not cry.* *adj.* —**moist′ly,** *adv.* —**moist′ness,** *n.*

**moist·en** (moi′sən) make or become moist: *He moistened his dry lips. Her eyes moistened with tears.* *v.*

**mois·ture** (mois′chər) a slight wetness; water or other liquid spread in very small drops in the air or on a surface. *n.*

**mok·sha** (mōk′shə) in Indian religions, spiritual release and freedom from the ongoing cycle of death and rebirth; the final state of mystical bliss. *n.*

**mol** MOLE[4].

**mo·lar** (mō′lər) **1** a tooth with a broad surface for grinding: *A person's back teeth are molars.* See TEETH for picture. **2** pulverizing by friction; grinding or capable of grinding. **3** of or having to do with the molar teeth. *1 n., 2, 3 adj.*

**mo·las·ses** (mə las′iz) a sweet syrup obtained in making sugar from sugar cane. *n.*

**mold** (mōld) See MOULD. *n., v.*

**mold·board** (mōld′bôrd′) See MOULDBOARD. *n.*

**mold·er** (mōl′dər) See MOULDER. *v., n.*

**mold·ing** (mōl′ding) See MOULDING. *n., v.*

**mold·y** (mōl′dē) See MOULDY. *adj.,* **mold·i·er, mold·i·est.** —**mold′i·ness,** *n.*

**mole**[1] (mōl) a small, permanent spot on the skin, usually brown and slightly raised. *n.*

A star-nosed mole— about 13 cm long excluding the tail

**mole**[2] (mōl) **1** any of a family of small burrowing mammals that eat insects and have a thick body covered with soft fur, short legs with the front feet modified for digging, small, weak eyes, and a long, pointed snout. **2** *Cdn.* especially in the Prairie Provinces, POCKET GOPHER. *n.* —**mole′-like′,** *adj.*

**mole**[3] (mōl) **1** a barrier built of stone to break the force of the waves; breakwater. **2** a harbour formed by a mole. *n.*

**mole**[4] (mōl) an SI unit for measuring amounts of substances that take part in chemical reactions. One mole of an element, compound, etc. is the amount that contains as many elementary units (atoms, molecules, ions, etc.) as there are atoms in 0.012 kg of carbon 12. Symbol: mol *n.*

**mo·lec·u·lar** (mə lek′yə lər) of, having to do with, produced by, or consisting of MOLECULES. *adj.*

**mol·e·cule** (mol′ə kyül) **1** the smallest particle into which a substance can be divided without chemical change: *A molecule of an element consists of one or more atoms. A molecule of a compound consists of two or more atoms.* **2** any very small bit or particle. *n.*

**mole·hill** (mōl′hil′) a small mound or ridge of earth raised up by moles burrowing under the ground. *n.* **make a mountain (out) of a molehill,** give great importance to something which is really insignificant, especially a hindrance or obstacle.

**mo·lest** (mə lest′) **1** annoy, meddle with, or persecute, especially so as to injure: *It is cruel to molest animals.* **2** make improper sexual advances to. *v.* —**mo·lest′er,** *n.*

**mo·les·ta·tion** (mō′les tā′shən) MOLESTing or being molested. *n.*

**mol·li·fy** (mol′ə fī′) **1** soothe; appease: *The angry child refused all our attempts to mollify her.* **2** soften or mitigate: *Her anger was finally mollified.* *v.,* **mol·li·fied, mol·li·fy·ing.** —**mol′li·fi·ca′tion,** *n.*

**mol·lusc** or **mol·lusk** (mol′əsk) any animals belonging to the phylum **Mollusca,** a large group of invertebrate animals having soft, unsegmented bodies covered with a mantel that in most species produces a hard shell: *Abalones, chitons, clams, cockles, limpets, mussels, nautiluses, octopuses, oysters, scallops, slugs, snails, and whelks are molluscs.* *n.*

**mol·ly·cod·dle** (mol′ē kod′əl) **1** a person, especially a boy or man, accustomed to being fussed over and pampered; MILKSOP. **2** coddle; pamper. *1 n., 2 v.,* **mol·ly·cod·dled, mol·ly·cod·dling.**

**molt** (mōlt) See MOULT. *v., n.*

**mol·ten** (mōl′tən) **1** of metal, rock, etc., made liquid by heat; melted: *molten steel, molten lava.* **2** a pp. of MELT. *1 adj., 2 v.*

**mo·ly** (mō′lē) **1** a mythical herb with a milk-white flower and a black root, having magic properties: *Hermes gave Odysseus moly to counteract the spells of Circe.* **2** a European wild garlic. *n., pl.* **mo·lies.**

**mo·lyb·de·nite** (mə lib′də nīt′) a sulphide mineral that is the chief ore of MOLYBDENUM, occurring in soft, bluish-silver flakes resembling GRAPHITE. *n.*

**mo·lyb·de·num** (mə lib′də nəm) a silver-white metallic element of the CHROMIUM group. Symbol: Mo *n.*

**mom** (mom *or* mum) *Informal.* mother, mum. *n.*

**mo·ment** (mō′mənt) **1** a very short space of time: *In a moment, all was changed.* **2** a particular point of time: *We both arrived at the same moment.* **3** importance or significance: *a matter of moment.* **4** the tendency to cause rotation around a point or axis. *n.*

**mo·men·ta** (mō men′tə) a pl. of MOMENTUM. *n.*

**mo·men·tar·i·ly** (mō′mən ter′ə lē *or* mō′mən ter′ə lē) **1** for a moment: *to hesitate momentarily.* **2** at every moment; from moment to moment: *danger momentarily increasing.* **3** at any moment: *We expect her to arrive momentarily.* *adv.*

**mo·men·tar·y** (mō′mən ter′ē) lasting only a moment: *momentary hesitation.* *adj.* —**mo′men·tar′i·ness,** *n.*

**mo·men·tous** (mō men′təs) very important: *a momentous decision. His graduation was a momentous occasion.* *adj.* —**mo·men′tous·ly,** *adv.* —**mo·men′tous·ness,** *n.*

**mo·men·tum** (mō men′təm) **1** the force with which a body moves, the product of its mass and its velocity: *A* falling object gains momentum as it falls.   **2** the impetus resulting from movement: *The runner's momentum carried her far beyond the finish line.*   *n., pl.* **mo‧men‧tums** or **mo‧men‧ta** (-tə).

**Mon.** Monday.

**mo‧nad‧nock** (mə nad′nok)   an isolated hill or mass of rock left standing after the erosion of a surrounding plain.   *n.*

**mon‧arch** (mon′ərk)   **1** a king, queen, emperor, etc.; ruler.   **2** a person or thing like a monarch: *The lion has been called the monarch of the beasts.*   **3** a large orange-and-black butterfly.   *n.*

**mo‧nar‧chal** (mə när′kəl)   of, having to do with, characteristic of, or suitable for a MONARCH (def. 1); royal; regal.   *adj.*   —**mo‧nar′chal‧ly,** *adv.*

**mon‧ar‧chi‧al** (mə när′kē əl)   MONARCHAL.   *adj.*

**mon‧ar‧chic** (mə när′kik)   MONARCHICAL.   *adj.*

**mo‧nar‧chi‧cal** (mə när′kə kəl)   of, having to do with, or characteristic of a MONARCH (def. 1) or MONARCHY.   *adj.*

**mon‧ar‧chism** (mon′ər kiz′əm)   **1** the principles of MONARCHY.   **2** attachment to MONARCHY.   *n.*

**mon‧arch‧ist** (mon′ər kist)   a person who supports or favours government by a monarch.   *n.*

**mon‧ar‧chy** (mon′ər kē)   **1** government by or under a monarch.   **2** a nation governed or headed by a monarch.   *n., pl.* **mon‧ar‧chies.**

**mon‧as‧te‧ri‧al** (mon′ə stē′rē əl)   of, having to do with, or characteristic of a MONASTERY or monastic life.   *adj.*

**mon‧as‧ter‧y** (mon′ə ster′ē)   a building or buildings where monks or nuns live and work according to religious rules.   *n., pl.* **mon‧as‧ter‧ies.**
☛ *Usage.*   A monastery is the Christian equivalent of the LAMASERY of Lamaism.

**mo‧nas‧tic** (mə nas′tik)   **1** of monks or nuns: *monastic vows.*   **2** of monasteries.   **3** like that of monks or nuns: *He lives an almost monastic life.*   **4** monk.   1–3 *adj.,* 4 *n.*

**mo‧nas‧ti‧cal** (mə nas′tə kəl)   MONASTIC.   *adj.* —**mo‧nas′ti‧cal‧ly,** *adv.*

**mo‧nas‧ti‧cism** (mə nas′tə siz′əm)   the system or condition of living according to fixed rules and under religious vows, usually in a monastery or convent.   *n.*

**mon‧au‧ral** (mo nô′rəl)   in sound reproduction, having only one channel for transmission of sound: *a monaural recording.*   *adj.*

**Mon‧day** (mun′dā′ *or* mun′dē)   the second day of the week, following Sunday.   *n.*
☛ *Etym.*   From OE *mōnandæg* 'day of the moon'.

**mon‧er‧an** (mon′ə rən)   a member of the KINGDOM (def. 3) **monera** of living things: *Certain bacteria are monerans.*   *n.*

**mon‧e‧tar‧y** (mon′ə ter′ē)   **1** of or having to do with the currency of a country: *The monetary unit in Canada is the dollar.*   **2** of money: *a monetary reward.*   *adj.*

**mon‧e‧ti‧za‧tion** (mon′ə tə zā′shən *or* mon′ə tī zā′shən)   the act of monetizing.   *n.*

**mon‧e‧tize** (mon′ə tīz′)   **1** legalize as money.   **2** coin into money.   *v.,* **mon‧e‧tized, mon‧e‧tiz‧ing.**

**mon‧ey** (mun′ē)   **1** officially issued coins and paper notes used as a standard medium of exchange: *I have five dollars left in Canadian money.*   **2** a particular form or denomination of money.   **3** wealth: *She has a lot of money.*   **4 mon‧eys** or **mon‧ies,** *pl.*   **a** sums of money: *The treasurer was responsible for the moneys entrusted to her.*   **b** more than one kind of money: *He had a collection of the moneys issued by different countries.*   *n., pl.* **mon‧eys** or **mon‧ies.**   —**mon′ey‧less,** *adj.*
**for my money,** *Informal.*   for my choice; in my opinion; as I see it.
**make money,**   **a** earn or receive money.   **b** become rich.
☛ *Usage.*   Exact sums of money that are not round figures are usually written in figures: *72 cents, $4.98, $169.*   Round or approximate amounts are more likely to be written in words: *about two hundred dollars, a million and a half dollars.*

**mon‧ey‧chang‧er** (mun′ē chān′jər)   a person whose business is to exchange money, usually that of one country for that of another.   *n.*

**mon‧eyed** (mun′ēd)   **1** having money; wealthy: *a moneyed family.*   **2** consisting of or representing money or people having money: *moneyed resources, moneyed interests.*   *adj.*

**mon‧ey‧lend‧er** (mun′ē len′dər)   one whose business is lending money at interest.   *n.*

**money of account**   a MONETARY denomination used in reckoning, especially one not issued as a coin: *In Canada, the mill is a money of account but not a coin. The nickel is a coin, but not a money of account.*

**money order**   an order issued by a post office or bank for the payment of a particular amount of money by a post office or bank in another place: *You can buy a money order in one town and mail it to a person in another town, where that person can cash it.*

**Mon‧gol** (mong′gəl)   **1** a member of an Asiatic people now inhabiting Mongolia and nearby parts of China and Siberia.   **2** the language of these people; Mongolian.   **3** of or having to do with these people or their language.   **4** Asiatic.   1, 2, 4 *n.,* 3, 4 *adj.*

**Mon‧go‧li‧an** (mong gō′lē ən)   **1** of, having to do with, or referring to the Mongolian People's Republic, a country in central Asia, or to its people or their languages.   **2** of, having to do with, or referring to Mongolia, a vast region in Asia including the Mongolian People's Republic and part of China, or to its people or their languages.   **3** a native or inhabitant of the Mongolian People's Republic or Mongolia.   **4** the languages of the Mongolian People's Republic or Mongolia.   **5** MONGOLOID.   1, 2, 5 *adj.,* 3–5 *n.*

**Mon‧gol‧oid** (mong′gə loid′)   **1** belonging to or like the Mongols.   **2** a MONGOL (def. 1).   1 *adj.,* 2 *n.*

**mon‧goose** (mong′güs)   any of a closely related group of small meat-eating mammals of Africa and Asia, especially a slender, ferretlike animal of India, used for destroying rats, and noted for its ability to kill certain poisonous snakes without being harmed.   *n., pl.* **mon‧goos‧es.**

**mon·grel** (mung'grəl *or* mong'grəl) **1** an animal or plant of mixed breed, especially a dog. **2** of mixed breed, race, origin, nature, etc.: *He habitually used a mongrel speech that was half English and half French.* 1 *n.*, 2 *adj.*

**mon·ies** (mun'ēz) a pl. of MONEY. *n.*

**mon·ism** (mon'iz əm *or* mō'niz əm) the doctrine that the universe can be explained by one substance or principle by MATERIALISM (def. 1) or by IDEALISM (def. 4). *n.*

**mon·ist** (mon'ist *or* mō'nist) a person who accepts MONISM. *n.*

**mo·nis·tic** (mō nis'tik) of or having to do with MONISM. *adj.*

**mo·ni·tion** (mō nish'ən) **1** a warning or sign of danger. **2** a formal warning from a bishop or religious court to correct an offence. *n.*

**mon·i·tor** (mon'ə tər) **1** a pupil in school with special duties, such as helping to keep order and taking attendance. **2** a person who gives advice or warning. **3** something that reminds or gives warning. **4** act as a monitor. **5** any of a closely related group of mainly large, snakelike lizards of Africa, Australia, and southern Asia: *The monitors are distantly related to the iguanas.* **6** a device used for checking and listening to radio and television transmissions, telephone messages, etc., as they are being recorded or broadcast. **7** check and listen to by using such a device. **8** a device which provides a video display of a computer's output. 1–3, 5, 6, 8 *n.*, 4, 7 *v.*

**mon·i·to·ri·al** (mon'ə tô'rē əl) **1** of, having to do with, or using a MONITOR or monitors. **2** MONITORY. 1, 2 *adj.*, 2 *n.*

**mon·i·tor·ship** (mon'ə tər ship') the office, work, or period of service of a MONITOR (def. 1). *n.*

**mon·i·to·ry** (mon'ə tô'rē) **1** admonishing; warning. **2** a letter containing admonition. 1 *adj.*, 2 *n.*, *pl.* **mon·i·to·ries.**

**monk** (mungk) a man who has taken certain vows to live his life in a way prescribed by a religious brotherhood: *Monks usually live in monasteries.* *n.*

A capuchin monkey of South America—body excluding the tail about 33 cm long; tail about 43 cm long

**mon·key** (mung'kē) **1** any of the smaller, long-tailed members of the mammal order **Primates**, as contrasted with the apes, lemurs, and human beings. Monkeys are grouped into four main families, two native to the Old World and two native to the New World. **2** any primate, excluding the lemurs and human beings. **3** a person, especially a child, who is full of mischief. **4** *Informal.* play; fool; trifle: *Don't monkey with the TV set.* 1–3 *n.*,

*pl.* **mon·keys;** 4 *v.*, **mon·keyed, mon·key·ing.** —**mon'key-like'**, *adj.*

**monkey bars** **1** an open structure of vertical and horizontal pipes or bars, designed for children to climb and play on: *Many playgrounds have monkey bars.* **2** a structure of horizontal bars built against a wall, as in a gymnasium, used for climbing exercises.

**monkey business** *Informal.* **1** silly or mischievous acts: *Those kids are always full of monkey business.* **2** deceitful or treacherous acts: *There must have been some monkey business, because a few of the files were missing.*

**monkey jacket** a short, close-fitting jacket, formerly worn by sailors, now worn only as part of a military dress uniform.

**monkey wrench** a wrench with a movable jaw that can be adjusted to fit different sizes of nuts. See WRENCH for picture.

**monk·ish** (mung'kish) **1** of or having to do with monks. **2** like or characteristic of monks or their way of life. *adj.*

**monks·hood** (mungks'hůd') any of several species of ACONITE, having flowers shaped somewhat like the hoods worn by monks. *n.*

**mono–** *combining form.* one; single, as in *monochrome.*
☛ *Etym.* From Gk. *mono-*, the combining form of *monos* 'single, only'.

**mon·o·chro·mat·ic** (mon'ə krō mat'ik) **1** of one colour only, not counting black or white: *a monochromatic colour scheme in blue and white.* **2** consisting of only one wave length of light or other radiation. *adj.*

**mon·o·chrome** (mon'ə krōm') a painting, drawing, etc. in a single colour or shades of a single colour. *n.*

A monocle. It rests on the cheekbone and is held in place by the eyebrow muscle.

**mon·o·cle** (mon'ə kəl) an eyeglass for one eye. *n.*

**mon·o·cled** (mon'ə kəld) wearing a MONOCLE. *adj.*

**mon·o·cot·y·le·don** (mon'ə kot'ə lē'dən) any of a large group of seed plants having an embryo with only one COTYLEDON (seed leaf) and, usually, leaves with parallel veins: *Grasses, lilies, etc. are monocotyledons.* *n.*

**mo·noc·u·lar** (mə nok'yə lər) **1** of, involving, or affecting only one eye: *monocular vision.* **2** suitable for or adapted to only one eye: *a microscope with a monocular eyepiece.* *adj.*

**mo·nog·a·mist** (mə nog'ə mist) a person who practises or believes in MONOGAMY. *n.*

**mo·nog·a·mous** (mə nog'ə məs) **1** practising or advocating MONOGAMY: *a monogamous civilization.* **2** having to do with MONOGAMY. *adj.*

**mo·nog·a·my** (mə nog'ə mē) **1** the practice or condition of being married to only one person at a time. **2** in zoology, the habit of having only one mate. *n.*

**mon·o·gram** (mon'ə gram') a design made by combining letters, usually the initials of a person's name:

*Monograms are often used on notepaper, table linen, clothing, jewellery, etc.* *n.*

**mon·o·graph** (mon′ə graf′) a scholarly book or article on a small area of learning. *n.*

**mon·o·lin·gual** (mon′ə ling′gwal *or* mon′ə ling′gyə wəl) knowing or using only one language: *a monolingual person, a monolingual conversation.* *adj.*

**mon·o·lith** (mon′ə lith′) **1** a single large block of stone. **2** a monument, column, statue, etc. formed of a single large block of stone. **3** an organization that is massive, uniform, and therefore rigid and unyielding in its attitudes and policy. *n.*

**mon·o·lith·ic** (mon′ə lith′ik) **1** of or being a MONOLITH. **2** massively uniform: *a monolithic society, a monolithic state.* *adj.*

**mon·o·logue** (mon′ə log′) **1** a long speech by one person in a group. **2** an entertainment by a single speaker. **3** a scene or short play for one actor, often written to tell a story, to show character, or to describe a humorous or dramatic situation. **4** a part in a play in which a single actor speaks alone. *n.* Also, **monolog.**

**mon·o·logu·ist** (mon′ə log′ist) one who talks or acts in MONOLOGUE (defs. 2, 3), or delivers monologues. *n.*

**mon·o·ma·ni·a** (mon′ə mā′nē ə) **1** a form of mental disorder restricted to one idea or emotion only. **2** an interest or tendency so strong as to seem almost insane. *n.*

**mon·o·ma·ni·ac** (mon′ə mā′nē ak′) a person affected with MONOMANIA. *n.*

**mo·no·mi·al** (mō nō′mē əl) **1** consisting of a single word or term. **2** in biology, a name consisting of a single word: *phylum is a monomial.* **3** in mathematics, an expression consisting of a single term: $z$, $a^3b^4$, $3x$, and $m_1m_2$ are monomials. **1** *adj.*, **2, 3** *n.*

**mon·o·pho·nic** (mon′ə fon′ik) **1** MONAURAL. **2** in music, having a single melody, with no accompaniment. *adj.*

**mon·oph·thong** (mon′əf thong′) **1** a single vowel sound. **2** a letter representing a single vowel sound. *n.* Compare with DIPHTHONG.

**mon·o·plane** (mon′ə plān′) an airplane having one set of wings: *Most modern airplanes are monoplanes.* *n.*

**mo·nop·o·list** (mə nop′ə list) **1** a person who has a MONOPOLY. **2** one who favours MONOPOLY. *n.*

**mo·nop·o·lis·tic** (mə nop′ə lis′tik) **1** that MONOPOLIZES. **2** having to do with monopolies or MONOPOLISTS. *adj.*

**mo·nop·o·lize** (mə nop′ə līz′) **1** have or get exclusive possession or control of: *This firm nearly monopolizes the production of linen thread.* **2** occupy wholly; keep entirely to oneself: *The stranger tried to monopolize our conversation.* *v.*, **mo·nop·o·lized, mo·nop·o·liz·ing.** —**mo·nop′o·liz′er,** *n.*

**mo·nop·o·ly** (mə nop′ə lē) **1** control of a commodity or service for a particular market, with little or no competition: *The new dairy bought out the other two dairies in town and now has a monopoly on milk.* **2** such control granted by a government: *An inventor has a monopoly on the manufacture and sale of his invention for a certain number of years.* **3** a commodity or service that one company, etc. has a monopoly on: *In some provinces, the telephone service is a government monopoly.* **4** a company having a monopoly. **5** the exclusive possession or control

monograph 769 monster

hat, āge, fär; let, ēqual, tėrm; it, īce
hot, ōpen, ôrder; oil, out; cup, put, rüle
above, takən, pencəl, lemən, circəs
ch, child; ng, long; sh, ship
th, thin; ŦH, then; zh, measure

of something: *No one person has a monopoly on virtue.* *n., pl.* **mo·nop·o·lies.**

**mon·o·rail** (mon′ə rāl′) **1** a single rail serving as a complete track for a wheeled vehicle. **2** a railway in which cars run on a single rail. *n.*

**mon·o·sac·char·ide** (mon′ō sak′ə rīd) a simple sugar such as glucose or fructose, that cannot be decomposed by HYDROLYSIS. *n.*

**mon·o·syl·lab·ic** (mon′ə sə lab′ik) **1** having only one syllable. **2** consisting of a word or words of one syllable each: *"No, not now," is a monosyllabic reply.* *adj.*

**mon·o·syl·la·ble** (mon′ə sil′ə bəl) a word of one syllable: *"Yes" and "no" are monosyllables.* *n.*

**mon·o·the·ism** (mon′ə thē′iz əm) the doctrine or belief that there is only one God. *n.*

**mon·o·the·ist** (mon′ə thē′ist) a believer in only one God. *n.*

**mon·o·the·is·tic** (mon′ə thē is′tik) **1** believing in only one God. **2** having to do with belief in only one God. *adj.*

**mon·o·tone** (mon′ə tōn′) **1** sameness of tone, style of writing, colour, etc.: *Don't read in a monotone; use more expression.* **2** continuing on one tone; of one tone, style, or colour. **3** someone who is TONE-DEAF. *n.*

**mo·not·o·nous** (mə not′ə nəs) **1** continuing in the same tone: *She spoke in a monotonous voice.* **2** tedious or wearing because of lack of variety: *monotonous food, monotonous work.* *adj.* —**mo·not′o·nous·ly,** *adv.*

**mo·not·o·ny** (mə not′ə nē) **1** sameness of tone or pitch. **2** a wearisome sameness. *n.*

**mon·o·treme** (mon′ə trēm′) any of an order of lower mammals made up of the platypus and echidna. *n.*

**mon·o·type** (mon′ə tīp′) in biology, the only one of its group. *n.*

**mon·o·va·lent** (mon′ə vā′lənt) having a VALENCE of one. *adj.*

**mon·ox·ide** (mon ok′sīd) an oxide containing one oxygen atom in each molecule. *n.*

**Monroe Doctrine** the doctrine that European nations should not interfere with American nations or try to acquire more territory in America.

**Mon·sei·gneur** or **mon·sei·gneur** (môN se nyœr′) *French.* **1** a title of honour given to princes, bishops, and other persons of importance, usually used in front of a title of office. **2** a person bearing this title. *n., pl.* **Mes·sei·gneurs** or **mes·sei·gneurs** (mā se nyœr′).

**mon·sieur** (mə syœ′) *French.* Mr.; sir. *n., pl.* **mes·sieurs** (mā syœ′).

**mon·soon** (mon sün′) **1** a seasonal wind of the Indian Ocean and southern Asia, blowing from the southwest from April to October and from the northeast during the rest of the year. **2** a rainy season during which this wind blows from the southwest. *n.*

**mon·ster** (mon′stər) **1** any animal or plant that is out of the usual course of nature: *A two-headed cow would be a monster.* **2** an imaginary creature of strange appearance: *Mermaids and centaurs are monsters. The story was about monsters from Mars.* **3** a huge creature or thing. **4** huge. **5** a person who is extremely evil or cruel: *The man in charge of the slaves was a monster.* 1–3, 5 *n.*, 4 *adj.*

**mon·stros·i·ty** (mon stros′ə tē) **1** monster. **2** the state or character of being MONSTROUS. *n., pl.* **mon·stros·i·ties.**

**mon·strous** (mon′strəs) **1** huge; enormous. **2** unnaturally formed or shaped; like a monster. **3** shocking; horrible; dreadful. **4** *Informal.* very; extremely. 1–3 *adj.*, 4 *adv.* —**mon′strous·ly**, *adv.* —**mon′strous·ness**, *n.*

**Mont.** Montreal.

**mon·tage** (mon täzh′) **1** the combination of several distinct pictures to make a composite picture. **2** a composite picture so made. **3** in motion pictures or television, the use of a sequence of rapidly changing pictures to suggest an emotional reaction, a state of mind, etc. *n.*

**mon·te** (mon′tē) a Spanish and Spanish-American gambling game at cards. *n.*

**month** (munth) **1** one of the 12 parts into which the year is divided. **2** the period of time from any day of one month to the corresponding day of the next month: *It will take us about a month to finish the project.* *n.*

**month·ly** (mun′thlē) **1** of, for, or lasting a month: *a monthly supply.* **2** done, happening, payable, etc. once a month: *a monthly salary.* **3** once a month; every month. **4** a magazine published once a month. 1, 2 *adj.*, 3 *adv.*, 4 *n., pl.* **month·lies.**

**mon·u·ment** (mon′yə mənt) **1** something set up to keep a person or an event from being forgotten: *A monument may be a building, pillar, arch, statue, tomb, or stone.* **2** anything that keeps alive the memory of a person or an event. **3** an enduring or prominent instance or example: *The professor's writings were monuments of learning.* **4** something set up to mark a boundary. *n.*

**mon·u·men·tal** (mon′yə men′təl) **1** of or serving as a MONUMENT. **2** like a MONUMENT; weighty, lasting, and important: *monumental works of art. The Charter of Rights is a monumental document.* **3** very great: *monumental ignorance, a monumental achievement.* *adj.* —**mon′u·men′tal·ly**, *adv.*

**moo** (mü) **1** the sound made by a cow. **2** make this sound. 1 *n., pl.* **moos;** 2 *v.*, **mooed, moo·ing.**

**mood**[1] (müd) **1** a state of mind or feeling: *I am in the mood to play just now; I don't want to study.* **2** **moods**, *pl.* fits of depression or bad temper. *n.*

**mood**[2] (müd) in grammar, the form of a verb that shows whether the act or state expressed is thought of as fact, or as something else, such as command, possibility, or wish: *The indicative mood is used for statements of facts; the imperative mood is used for commands.* *n.*

**mood·y** (mü′dē) **1** likely to have changes of mood; temperamental: *He's a very moody person so it's hard to say how he'll react.* **2** often having gloomy moods: *She has been moody ever since she lost her job.* **3** sunk in sadness; gloomy; sullen: *Don sat in moody silence.* *adj.*,

**mood·i·er, mood·i·est.** —**mood′i·ly**, *adv.* —**mood′i·ness**, *n.*

WAXING CRESCENT  FIRST QUARTER  FULL MOON  LAST QUARTER  WANING CRESCENT

**moon** (mün) **1** a heavenly body that revolves around the earth from west to east once in approximately 29½ days: *The moon looks bright because it reflects the sun's light.* **2** the moon at a certain period of time: **new moon** (visible as a slender crescent), **half moon** (visible as a half circle), **full moon** (visible as a circle), **old moon** (waning). **3** a lunar month; about a month or 29 days: *The Indians counted time by moons.* **4** moonlight. **5** something shaped like the moon. **6** a natural or artificial satellite: *the moons of Jupiter.* **7** wander about or gaze idly or listlessly: *Don't moon when you have work to do.* 1–6 *n.*, 7 *v.* —**moon′like′**, *adj.*

**moon·beam** (mün′bēm′) a ray of moonlight. *n.*

**moon·calf** (mün′kaf′) a foolish or absent-minded person. *n.*

**moon·eye** (mü′nī) any of a closely related group of small, silvery, North American freshwater fishes, having strong, sharp teeth and a slender body. *n., pl.* **moon·eye** or **moon·eyes.**

**moon·less** (mün′lis) **1** lacking the light of the moon: *a moonless night.* **2** having no satellite: *a moonless planet.* *adj.*

**moon·light** (mün′līt′) **1** the light of the moon: *It is sometimes possible to read by moonlight.* **2** having the light of the moon: *a moonlight night.* **3** while the moon is shining; by night: *a moonlight swim.* **4** *Informal.* work at a second job, usually at night, in order to supplement the wages earned at a regular job. 1–3 *n.*, 4 *v.*

**moon·lit** (mün′lit′) lighted by the moon. *adj.*

**moon·rise** (mün′rīz′) **1** the rising of the moon above the horizon. **2** the time when the moon rises above the horizon. *n.*

**moon·shine** (mün′shīn′) **1** moonlight. **2** empty talk; empty show; nonsense. **3** *Informal.* intoxicating liquor made unlawfully, or smuggled. *n.*

**moon·shin·er** (mün′shī′nər) *Informal.* a person who makes or sells intoxicating liquor unlawfully. *n.*

**moon·stone** (mün′stōn′) a translucent whitish gem with a pearly lustre: *Moonstone is a variety of feldspar.* *n.*

**moon·struck** (mün′struk′) dazed; crazed. *adj.*

**moor**[1] (mur) **1** put or keep a ship, etc. in place by means of ropes or chains fastened to the shore or to anchors. **2** moor a ship. **3** be made secure by ropes, anchors, etc. *v.*

**moor**[2] (mur) *Brit.* open wasteland, usually hilly or high up and having low plant growth. *n.*

**moor cock** the male red GROUSE.

**moor·ing** (mü′ring) **1** a place where a ship or aircraft is made fast. **2** **moorings**, *pl.* the ropes, cables, anchors, etc. by which a ship, etc. is made fast. **3** ppr. of MOOR. 1, 2 *n.*, 3 *v.*

**moor·land** (mur′land′ or mur′lənd) *Brit.* an area of moors. *n.*

**moose** (müs) a large mammal of the same family as the deer, native to Canada and the northern United States. *n., pl.* **moose.**
☞ *Hom.* MOUSSE.

**moose·bird** (müs′bėrd′) *Cdn.* CANADA JAY. *n.*

**moot** (müt) **1** debatable; doubtful: *a moot point.* **2** argue. **3** bring forward a point, subject, case, etc. for discussion. **4** assembly. 1 *adj.*, 2, 3 *v.*, 4 *n.*

**moot court** a mock court held in a law school.

**mop** (mop) **1** a bundle of coarse yarn, rags, etc. fastened at the end of a stick, for cleaning floors, dishes, etc. **2** wash or wipe up; clean with a mop: *to mop the floor.* **3** wipe: *He mopped his brow with his handkerchief.* **4** something like a mop: *He is going to have his mop of hair cut before he goes for his interview.* 1, 4 *n.*, 2, 3 *v.*, **mopped, mop·ping.**
**mop up,** finish.

**mope** (mōp) **1** be dull, silent, and sad. **2** a person who mopes. 1 *v.*, **moped, mop·ing;** 2 *n.*

**mo·ped** (mō′ped) a motorized bicycle. *n.*

**mop·pet** (mop′it) child. *n.*

**mo·raine** (mə rān′) a mass or ridge of rocks, dirt, etc., deposited at the sides or end of a glacier after being carried down or pushed aside by the pressure of the ice. *n.*

**mor·al** (mô′rəl) **1** good in character or conduct; virtuous according to civilized standards of right and wrong; right; just: *a moral act, a moral person.* **2** capable of understanding right and wrong: *A little baby is not a moral being.* **3** having to do with character or with the difference between right and wrong: *a moral question.* **4** the lesson, inner meaning, or teaching of a fable, a story, or an event: *The moral of the story was "Look before you leap."* **5** teaching a good lesson; having a good influence: *a moral book.* **6** that encourages and gives confidence: *We gave moral support to the team by cheering loudly.* **7 morals,** *pl.* **a** character or behaviour in matters of right and wrong: *The girl's morals were excellent.* **b** one's principles in regard to conduct. 1–3, 5, 6 *adj.*, 4, 7 *n.*
☞ *Usage.* Do not confuse **moral** (a lesson) with MORALE (mental condition as regards courage, confidence, enthusiasm, etc.): *She understood the moral of the story. The coach was pleased with the morale of the team.*

**moral certainty** a probability so great that it might just as well be a certainty.

**mo·rale** (mə ral′ or mə räl′) mental condition or attitude as regards courage, confidence, enthusiasm, etc.: *The morale of the team was low after its defeat.* *n.*
☞ *Usage.* See note at MORAL.

**mor·al·ist** (mô′rə list) **1** a person who thinks much about moral duties, sees the moral side of things, and leads a moral life. **2** a person who teaches, studies, or writes about morals. **3** a person concerned with regulating or improving the morals of others. *n.*

**mor·al·is·tic** (mô′rə lis′tik) **1** moralizing; teaching the difference between right and wrong. **2** of or having to do with a moralist or moral teaching. *adj.*

**mo·ral·i·ty** (mə ral′ə tē) **1** the right or wrong of an action: *They argued about the morality of using animals for medical research.* **2** the doing of right; virtue: *She ranks very high in both intelligence and morality.* **3** a system of morals; set of rules or principles of conduct. **4** moral instruction; a moral lesson or precept. **5** a MORALITY PLAY. *n., pl.* **mo·ral·i·ties.**

**morality play** a form of drama popular during the 15th and 16th centuries, in which vices and virtues appear as real people.

**mor·al·ize** (mô′rə līz′) **1** think, talk, or write about questions of right and wrong. **2** point out the lesson or inner meaning of. **3** improve the morals of. *v.*, **mor·al·ized, mor·al·iz·ing.** —**mor′al·iz·a′tion,** *n.* —**mor′al·iz′er,** *n.*

**mor·al·ly** (mô′rə lē) **1** in a moral manner. **2** from a moral point of view; ethically: *What he did was morally wrong.* **3** practically; virtually: *I am morally sure that I locked the door.* *adv.*

**moral support** approval but not active help.

**moral victory** a defeat that has the effect on the mind that a victory would have.

**mo·rass** (mə ras′) **1** a piece of low, soft, wet ground; swamp. **2** a difficult situation; puzzling mess. *n.*

**mor·a·to·ri·um** (mô′rə tô′rē əm) **1** a legal authorization to delay payments of money due. **2** the period during which such authorization is in effect. **3** a temporary pause in action, negotiation, etc. on any issue. *n., pl.* **mor·a·to·ri·ums** or **mor·a·to·ri·a** (-rē ə).

**Mo·ra·vi·an** (mô rā′vē ən) **1** of or having to do with Moravia, a region in the former Czechoslovakia, its people, or their language. **2** a native or inhabitant of Moravia. **3** the Czech dialect spoken by Moravians. 1 *adj.*, 2, 3 *n.*

**mo·ray** (mô′rā) any of a number of related species of eel found in warm seas, having a heavy, often brilliantly coloured body and a large mouth with strong, sharp teeth. *n.*

**mor·bid** (môr′bid) **1** unhealthy; not wholesome: *His mother thinks his liking of horror movies is morbid.* **2** caused by disease; characteristic of disease; diseased: *Cancer is a morbid growth.* **3** horrible; frightful: *the morbid details of a murder.* *adj.* —**mor′bid·ly,** *adv.* —**mor′bid·ness,** *n.*

**mor·bid·i·ty** (môr bid′ə tē) **1** the quality or state of being MORBID. **2** the proportion of sickness in a certain group or locality: *Morbidity statistics show that tuberculosis is on the decline in Canada.* *n.*

**mor·dan·cy** (môr′dən sē) a MORDANT quality. *n.*

**mor·dant** (môr′dənt) **1** biting; cutting; sarcastic: *The mordant criticism hurt his feelings.* **2** a substance that fixes colours in dyeing. **3** that fixes colours in dyeing. **4** an acid that eats into metal. *1, 3 adj., 2, 4 n.*

**Mor·dred** (môr′dred) MODRED. *n.*

**more** (môr) **1** greater in number, quantity, amount, degree, or importance: *more women, more help.* **2** a greater number, quantity, amount, or degree: *The more they have, the more they want.* **3** in or to a greater extent or degree: *That hurts more.* **4** further; additional: *Take more time.* **5** an additional amount: *Tell me more.* **6** in addition; further; again: *Take one step more. Sing once more.* *1, 4 adj.* (used as comparative of MUCH and MANY, the superlative being MOST); *2, 5 n., 3, 6 adv.*
**be no more,** be dead.
**more or less, a** somewhat: *Most people are more or less selfish.* **b** nearly; approximately: *The distance is five kilometres, more or less.*
☞ *Usage.* **More** and **most** are often used before adjectives and adverbs to form comparatives and superlatives. **More** and **most** are put before all adjectives and adverbs of three syllables or more, and before some adjectives and most adverbs of two syllables. Other adjectives and adverbs, apart from a few irregular ones, use **-er** and **-est** to form the comparative and superlative.

**mo·rel** (mə rel′) any of several closely related species of edible fungus having a fleshy, pitted head on a stalk. *n.*

**more·o·ver** (mô rō′vər) also; besides; furthermore; in addition to that: *His power is absolute and, moreover, hereditary.* *adv.*

**mo·res** (mô′rēz) customs prevailing among a people or a social group that are accepted as right and obligatory; traditional rules; ways; manners. *n.pl.*

**mor·ga·nat·ic** (môr′gə nat′ik) referring to or having to do with a form of marriage in which a man of high rank marries a woman of lower rank with an agreement that neither she nor her children shall have any claim to his rank or property. *adj.*

**Morgan le Fay** (môr′gən lə fā′) King Arthur's half sister, a fairy, usually represented as harming him whenever she could.

**morgue** (môrg) **1** a place, usually in a police station or hospital, in which unclaimed bodies of dead persons are kept until they can be identified and taken away by their family or friends. **2** that part of a hospital where autopsies are performed. **3** in a newspaper office, the reference library. *n.*

**mor·i·bund** (mô′rə bund′) dying. *adj.*

**morn·ing** (môr′ning) **1** the early part of the day, ending at noon. **2** the first or early part of anything: *the morning of life.* **3** of or in the morning. *1, 2 n., 3 adj.*
☞ *Hom.* MOURNING.

**morn·ing–glo·ry** (môr′ning glô′rē) **1** any of a number of closely related species of twining plant having showy, trumpet-shaped, blue, mauve, pink, or white flowers and heart-shaped leaves. **2** referring to the family of herbs, shrubs, and trees that includes the morning-glories. *n., pl.* **morn·ing–glo·ries.**

**morning sickness** a feeling of nausea, often accompanied by vomiting, that occurs in the morning, especially during the early months of pregnancy.

**morning star** a planet, especially Venus, seen in the eastern sky before sunrise. Compare with EVENING STAR.

**Mo·roc·can** (mə rok′ən) **1** of or having to do with Morocco, a country in northwest Africa, or its people. **2** a native or inhabitant of Morocco. *1 adj., 2 n.*

**mo·roc·co** (mə rok′ō) **1** fine leather made from goatskin, used in binding books. **2** leather imitating this. *n., pl.* **mo·roc·cos.**

**mo·ron** (mô′ron) **1** a person who is unable to develop mentally to the normal level of an adult: *Moron was formerly used as a grade in a classification system for mentally retarded people.* **2** *Informal.* a stupid or annoyingly ignorant person; dullard; dunce. *n.*

**mo·rose** (mə rōs′) gloomy; sullen; ill-humoured: *She has a morose expression.* *adj.* —**mo·rose′ly,** *adv.* —**mo·rose′ness,** *n.*

**mor·pheme** (môr′fēm′) the smallest meaningful element of a language or dialect, such as *un-, -ing, do, make,* or *snow.* *n.*

**mor·phi·a** (môr′fē ə) MORPHINE. *n.*
☞ *Etym.* From the name of *Morpheus,* in Greek mythology, the god of dreams, popularly thought of as the god of sleep.

**mor·phine** (môr′fēn) an addictive drug made from opium, used to dull pain and to cause sleep. *n.*
☞ *Etym.* See note at MORPHIA.

**mor·pho·log·ic** (môr′fə loj′ik) MORPHOLOGICAL. *adj.*

**mor·pho·log·i·cal** (môr′fə loj′ə kəl) of or having to do with MORPHOLOGY; relating to form; structural. *adj.*

**mor·phol·o·gy** (môr fol′ə jē) **1** the branch of biology that deals with the forms and structure of animals and plants. **2** the branch of linguistics that deals with the forms of words. **3** the system of word-forming elements and processes of a language: *The morphology of English is very different from that of Japanese.* Compare with MORPHEME. *n.*

**Morse code** (môrs) a signalling system by which letters, numbers, etc. are represented by dots, dashes, and spaces or by long and short sounds or flashes of light.
☞ *Etym.* Named after Samuel F.B. Morse (1791–1872), American inventor of the telegraph.

**mor·sel** (môr′səl) **1** a small bite; mouthful. **2** a piece or fragment. *n.*

**mor·tal** (môr′təl) **1** sure to die sometime. **2** a being that is sure to die sometime: *All living creatures are mortals.* **3** of people; of mortals: *Mortal flesh has many pains and diseases.* **4** a person; human being: *No mortal could survive that storm.* **5** of death. **6** causing death of the soul. **7** causing death: *a mortal wound, a mortal illness.* **8** lasting until death: *a mortal enemy, a mortal battle.* **9** very great; deadly: *mortal terror.* *1, 3, 5–9 adj., 2, 4 n.*
☞ *Syn.* See note at FATAL.

**mor·tal·i·ty** (môr tal′ə tē) **1** mortal nature; the state of being sure to die sometime. **2** a loss of life on a large scale: *The mortality from automobile accidents is very serious.* **3** death rate; the number of deaths per thousand cases of a disease, or per thousand persons in the population: *The mortality from typhoid fever is decreasing.* *n.*

**mor·tal·ly** (môr′tə lē) **1** fatally; so as to cause death: *mortally wounded.* **2** very greatly; bitterly; grievously: *mortally offended.* *adv.*

**mor·tar**¹ (môr′tər) **1** a mixture of lime, cement, sand, and water, used for holding bricks or stones together. **2** plaster or fix with mortar. *1 n., 2 v.*

A mortar and pestle

**mor·tar**² (môr′tər) **1** a bowl of very hard material, in which substances may be pounded to a powder. **2** a very short artillery piece for shooting shells at high angles. *n.*

**mor·tar·board** (môr′tər bôrd′) **1** a board used by masons to hold mortar. **2** an academic cap with a close-fitting crown topped by a stiff, flat, cloth-covered square piece, worn by teachers and students in some schools and colleges on some occasions. *n.*

**mort·gage** (môr′gij) **1** a claim on property, given to a person, bank, or firm that has lent money in case the money is not repaid when due. **2** a document that gives such a claim. **3** give a lender a claim to one's property in case a debt is not paid when due. **4** put under some obligation; pledge: *Faust mortgaged his soul to the devil.* *1, 2 n., 3, 4 v.,* **mort·gaged, mort·gag·ing.**

**mort·ga·gee** (môr′gi jē′) the person, bank, or company to whom property is mortgaged. *n.*

**mort·gag·er** or **mort·ga·gor** (môr′gi jər) a person who mortgages his or her property. *n.*

**mor·tice** (môr′tis) See MORTISE. *n., v.,* **mor·ticed, mor·tic·ing.**

**mor·ti·cian** (môr tish′ən) UNDERTAKER. *n.*

**mor·ti·fi·ca·tion** (môr′tə fə kā′shən) **1** extreme embarrassment, shame, or humiliation: *The girl was overcome with mortification when she spilled milk on her host's suit.* **2** the cause of such feelings. **3** GANGRENE. **4** the control and subjection of one's physical desires and feelings through self-denial or endurance of pain. *n.*

**mor·ti·fy** (môr′tə fī′) **1** make ashamed or embarrassed; humiliate: *They were mortified by their cousin's rudeness to their friend.* **2** control or overcome one's physical desires and feelings through self-denial or the endurance of pain. **3** become affected with or cause GANGRENE. *v.,* **mor·ti·fied, mor·ti·fy·ing.** —**mor′ti·fi′er,** *n.*

**mor·tise** (môr′tis) **1** a hole in one piece of wood cut to receive a projection on another piece, called the tenon, so as to form a joint (**mortise and tenon joint**). See JOINT for picture. **2** fasten by a mortise: *Good furniture is mortised together, not nailed.* *1 n., 2 v.,* **mor·tised, mor·tis·ing.**

**mor·tu·ar·y** (môr′chü er′ē) **1** that part of a funeral parlour or of a cemetery where bodies of dead people await burial. **2** of death or burial. *1 n., pl.* **mor·tu·ar·ies;** *2 adj.*

**mos.** months.

A mosaic

**mo·sa·ic** (mō zā′ik) **1** a picture or design made of small pieces of stone, glass, wood, etc. of different colours, set together or inlaid: *Mosaics are used in floors, walls, ceilings, etc.* **2** the art or process of making such pictures or designs. **3** something made up of varied parts or elements, like a mosaic: *Canada is often called a cultural mosaic.* **4** of, having to do with, or used for mosaic or mosaics. *n.*

**mosaic disease** a plant disease caused by a virus, in which the leaves become mottled by small, brownish spots: *Mosaic disease occurs especially in tobacco, corn, and sugar cane.*

**Mos·lem** (moz′ləm) **1** a follower of Mohammed; a believer in Islam, the religion founded by Mohammed. **2** of or having to do with Mohammed or Islam. *1 n., 2 adj.* The spelling **Muslim** is becoming increasingly frequent.

**mosque** (mosk) a Moslem place of worship. *n.*

**mos·qui·to** (mə skē′tō) a small, slender insect: *The female mosquito can pierce the skin of people and animals and draw blood, causing a sting that itches.* *n., pl.* **mosqui·toes** or **mos·qui·tos.**

**moss** (mos) **1** any of various very small, soft, green or brown plants that grow close together like a carpet on the ground, on rocks, on trees, etc. **2** any of various similar plants. *n.* —**moss′like′,** *adj.*

**moss–bag** (mos′bag′) *Cdn.* a kind of bag of leather or cloth used by certain Indian tribes to carry a baby. Packed with dry moss, which serves as a diaper, it is laced up in front and usually carried strapped to a cradle-board. See CRADLE-BOARD for picture. *n.*

**moss rose** a cultivated rose having a mosslike growth on the calyx and stem.

**moss·y** (mos′ē) **1** covered with moss: *a mossy bank.* **2** like moss: *mossy green.* *adj.,* **moss·i·er, moss·i·est.** —**moss′i·ness,** *n.*

**most** (mōst) **1** greatest in quantity, amount, measure, degree, or number: *The winner gets the most money.* **2** the greatest quantity, amount, degree, or number: *She did most of the work.* **3** the majority of; almost all: *Most children like candy.* **4** in or to the greatest extent or degree: *Which movie did you like most?* **5** to a very great degree: *a most persuasive argument.* **6** *Informal.* almost; nearly: *We go there most every week.* *1, 3 adj.,* (used as superlative of MUCH and MANY, the comparative being MORE); *2 n., 4–6 adv.*

**at most** or **at the most,** not more than.

**for the most part,** mainly or usually.
**make the most of,** make the best use of.
☛ *Usage.* See note at MORE.

**–most** a suffix forming superlatives, meaning greatest in amount, degree, or number, as in *foremost, inmost, topmost, uttermost.*

**most·ly** (mōstlē) almost all; for the most part; mainly; chiefly. *adv.*

**mote** (mōt) a speck of dust. *n.*
☛ *Hom.* MOAT.

**mo·tel** (mō tel′) a kind of hotel consisting of a building or group of buildings having rooms that can be reached directly from an outdoor parking area. *n.*
☛ *Etym.* From *motor* + *hotel.*

**mo·tet** (mō tet′) in music, a polyphonic composition having a sacred theme, usually sung unaccompanied. *n.*

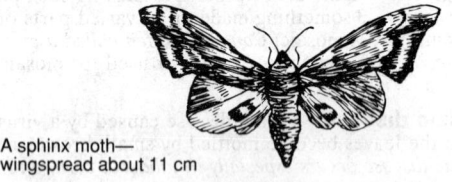
A sphinx moth—wingspread about 11 cm

**moth** (moth) any of a large group of mostly night-flying insects having broad wings that in most species are held flat on the back when at rest, feathery or threadlike antennae, usually a fairly stout body, and whose larvae are caterpillars that in most species feed on plants: *Clothes moths are small, yellowish moths whose larvae feed on wool, fur, or feathers. n., pl.* **moths** (moᴛHz *or* moths).

**moth·ball** (moth′bol′) a small ball made of naphthalene or some other strong-smelling substance, used for putting in garments or in clothes closets to keep moths away. *n.*

**moth–eaten** (moth′ē′tən) **1** eaten by moths; having holes made by moths. **2** worn-out; out-of-date. *adj.*

**moth·er**[1] (muᴛH′ər) **1** a female parent. **2** be mother of; act as mother to: *Ruth mothers her baby sister.* **3** acknowledge oneself mother of or assume as one's own. **4** the cause; source: *Necessity is the mother of invention.* **5** the head of a community of nuns. **6** a woman exercising control and responsibility like that of a mother. **7** a familiar name for an old woman. **8** that is a mother: *the mother church.* **9** like a mother. **10** of a mother. **11** belonging to one because of birth; native: *Scotland is my mother country and English is my mother tongue.* 1, 4–7 *n.*, 2, 3 *v.*, 8–11 *adj.* —**moth′er·less**, *adj.*

**moth·er**[2] (muᴛH′ər) a stringy, sticky substance, consisting of bacteria that is formed in vinegar or on the surface of liquids that are turning to vinegar. *n.*

**mother country** **1** the country where a person was born. **2** a country in relation to its colonies.

**moth·er·hood** (muᴛH′ər hůd′) **1** the state of being a mother: *The young wife was proud of her motherhood.* **2** mothers: *The motherhood of our city want more day nurseries. n.*

**Mother Hub·bard** (hub′ərd) **1** the subject of a well-known nursery rhyme beginning "Old Mother Hubbard went to the cupboard." **2** a full, loose gown for women.
☛ *Etym.* Def. 2 is named after the nursery rhyme because old illustrations of the woman showed her in such a gown.

**moth·er–in–law** (muᴛH′ə rin lo′) the mother of one's husband or wife. *n., pl.* **moth·ers-in-law.**

**moth·er·land** (muᴛH′ər land′) **1** one's native country. **2** the land of one's ancestors. *n.*

**mother lode** the main vein of ore in a mine.

**moth·er·ly** (muᴛH′ər lē) **1** of, suitable for, or characteristic of a mother: *motherly advice.* **2** like a mother; kindly: *She's a warm, motherly person. adj.* —**moth′er·li·ness**, *n.*

**moth·er–of–pearl** (muᴛH′ə rəv pėrl′) the hard, smooth, pearly lining of certain marine shells, such as that of the pearl oyster and abalone: *Mother-of-pearl is used to make buttons and ornaments. n.*

**mother superior** a woman who is the head of a convent of nuns.

**mother tongue** **1** one's native language. **2** a language to which other languages owe their origin.

**mother wit** natural intelligence; common sense.

**moth·proof** (moth′prüf′) **1** treated chemically so as to keep clothes moths away: *The carpet is mothproof.* **2** make mothproof: *a mothproofed fibre.* 1 *adj.*, 2 *v.*

**moth·y** (moth′ē) containing moths or having holes made by moths. *adj.*, **moth·i·er, moth·i·est.**

**mo·tif** (mō tēf′) **1** a subject for development or treatment in art, literature, or music; a principal idea or feature; motive: *This opera contains a love motif.* **2** a distinctive figure in a design. *n.* Also, **motive.**

**mo·tile** (mō′tīl *or* mō′təl) in biology, able to move about; capable of motion: *Barnacles are motile for the first two stages of their life. adj.*

**mo·til·i·ty** (mō til′ə tē) the quality of being MOTILE. *n.*

**mo·tion** (mō′shən) **1** the condition or state of moving; a movement or a change of position or place: *She swayed with the motion of the moving train. Everything is either in motion or at rest.* **2** make a movement, as of the hand or head, to show one's meaning: *She motioned to show us the way.* **3** show a person what to do by such a motion: *He motioned me out.* **4** a formal suggestion made in a meeting or court of law: *The motion to adjourn was carried.* 1, 4 *n.*, 2, 3 *v.*

**in motion,** moving; going.

**mo·tion·less** (mō′shən lis) not moving: *She stood perfectly motionless, watching the deer with its young. adj.* —**mo′tion·less·ly**, *adv.*

**motion picture** **1** a series of pictures on a continuous strip of film, projected on a screen in such rapid succession that the viewer gets the impression that the persons and things pictured are moving. **2** a story or drama told by means of this process; a moving picture; movie.

**motion sickness** nausea and dizziness caused by motion, such as the pitching and rolling of a ship or boat, the swaying, etc. of a train or car, or the swinging of a hammock.

**mo·ti·vate** (mō′tə vāt′) make someone want to act; provide with a MOTIVE: *Pride in his home motivated the boy to cut the lawn. v.*, **mo·ti·vat·ed, mo·ti·vat·ing.**

**mo·ti·va·tion** (mō′tə vā′shən) the act or process of furnishing with an incentive or inducement to action. *n.*

**mo·tive** (mō′tiv) **1** the thought or feeling that makes one act: *His motive in going away was a wish to travel.* **2** that makes something move: *Steam and electricity supply motive power.* **3** MOTIF. *1, 3 n., 2 adj.*

**motive power** **1** power used to impart motion to machinery; any source of mechanical energy: *The motive power of some trains is electricity.* **2** all the locomotives of a railway collectively.

**mot juste** (mō zhyst′) *French.* a word or phrase that exactly fits the case.

**mot·ley** (mot′lē) **1** made up of different colours and of different things; varied: *a motley collection of old books and toys.* **2** a suit of more than one colour worn by clowns: *At the party he wore motley.* *1 adj., 2 n., pl.* **mot·leys.**

**mo·tor** (mō′tər) **1** an engine that makes a machine go: *an electric motor.* **2** an INTERNAL-COMBUSTION ENGINE. **3** of, by, or by means of automobiles: *a motor tour.* **4** causing or having to do with motion or action; functioning like a motor: *Motor nerves arouse muscles to action.* **5** that which causes motion. *n.*

**mo·tor·bike** (mō′tər bīk′) *Informal.* a motorcycle, especially a small, lightweight one. *n.*

**mo·tor·boat** (mō′tər bōt′) a boat that is propelled by a motor. *n.*

**mo·tor·bus** (mō′tər bus′) bus. *n.*

**mo·tor·cade** (mō′tər kād′) a procession or long line of automobiles. *n.*

**mo·tor·cy·cle** (mō′tər sī′kəl) **1** a two-wheeled motor vehicle, sometimes having a sidecar with a third supporting wheel. **2** travel by motorcycle. *1 n., 2 v.,* **mo·tor·cy·cled, mo·tor·cy·cling.**

**mo·tor·cy·clist** (mō′tər sī′klist) a person who rides a MOTORCYCLE. *n.*

**motor generator** an apparatus consisting of a combination of motor and dynamo, used to lower voltage, etc.

**motor home** a large motor vehicle built on a truck chassis, having a completely enclosed body that is equipped for use as a travelling home. Compare with MOBILE HOME.

**motor hotel** or **inn** a hotel for accommodating motorists, somewhat more elaborate than a motel and usually consisting of several floors of rooms and suites.

**mo·tor·ist** (mō′tə rist) a person who drives or travels by automobile. *n.*

**mo·tor·ize** (mō′tə rīz) **1** furnish with a motor. **2** supply with motor-driven vehicles in place of horse and horse-drawn vehicles. **3** equip infantry with motor-driven transport vehicles, especially trucks. *v.,* **mo·tor·ized, mo·tor·iz·ing.** —**mo′tor·i·za′tion,** *n.*

**motor lodge** MOTEL.

**mo·tor·man** (mō′tər mən) the driver of a streetcar or subway train. *n., pl.* **mo·tor·men** (-mən).

**motor scooter** a light, two-wheeled motor vehicle steered by handlebars attached to the front wheel and having a seat for the rider with a broad footboard in front of it.

**motor truck** a truck with an engine and chassis made for carrying heavy loads.

**motivation** 775 **mouldy**

hat, āge, fär; let, ēqual, tėrm; it, īce
hot, ōpen, ôrder; oil, out; cup, put, rüle
əbove, takən, pencəl, lemən, circəs
ch, child; ng, long; sh, ship
th, thin; ᴛʜ, then; zh, measure

**motor vehicle** a vehicle that travels under its own power, having rubber-tired wheels and designed for use on roads and highways rather than rails; especially, an automobile, bus, or truck.

**mot·tle** (mot′əl) **1** mark with spots or streaks of different colours. **2** a mottled colouring and pattern. *1 v.,* **mot·tled, mot·tling;** *2 n.*

**mot·tled** (mot′əld) **1** spotted or streaked with different colours. **2** pt. and pp. of MOTTLE. *1 adj., 2 v.*

**mot·to** (mot′ō) **1** a brief sentence adopted as a rule of conduct: *"Think before you speak" is a good motto.* **2** a sentence, word, or phrase written or engraved on some object. *n., pl.* **mot·toes** or **mot·tos.**

**mouf·lon** or **mouf·flon** (mü′flon) **1** a wild sheep of the mountainous regions of Sardinia, Corsica, etc. **2** its wool, used as fur. *n.*

**mould¹** or **mold** (mōld) **1** a hollow shape in which anything is formed or cast: *Molten metal is poured into a mould to harden into shape.* **2** the shape or form which is given by a mould: *The moulds of ice cream were bells and bows.* **3** the model according to which anything is shaped: *The son is formed in his father's mould.* **4** form; shape: *to mould statues.* **5** something shaped in a mould: *a mould of pudding.* **6** make or form into shape: *We are moulding clay to make model animals. Her character was moulded by suffering.* **7** the nature or character of anything. **8** the shape or frame on or about which something is made. *1–3, 5, 7, 8 n., 4, 6 v.*

**mould²** or **mold** (mōld) **1** a woolly or furry growth of fungus that appears on food and other animal or vegetable substances when they are left too long in a warm, moist place. **2** any fungus that produces mould. **3** make or become covered with mould: *The boots moulded in the cellar.* *1, 2 n., 3 v.*

**mould³** or **mold** (mōld) soft, rich, crumbly soil; earth mixed with decaying leaves, manure, etc.: *Many wild flowers grow in the forest mould.* *n.*

**mould·board** or **mold·board** (mōld′bôrd′) a curved metal plate in a plough, that turns over the earth from the furrow. *n.*

**mould·er¹** or **mold·er** (mōl′dər) turn into dust by natural decay; crumble; waste away. *v.*

**mould·er²** or **mold·er** (mōl′dər) a person or thing that moulds, especially a person who shapes something or one who makes moulds for casting. *n.*

**mould·ing** or **mold·ing** (mōl′ding) **1** something produced by shaping or casting. **2** in architecture, a decorative shaping or contour given to a cornice along the top of a wall, to the jamb of a door or window, etc. **3** a shaped strip of wood or plaster, such as that often used around the upper walls of a room: *Mouldings may be simply ornamental, or they may be used to support pictures, to cover electric wires, etc.* See INDENT for picture. **4** ppr. of MOULD. *1–3 n., 4 v.*

**mould·y** or **mold·y** (mōl′dē) **1** covered with mould: *a mouldy crust of bread; mouldy cheese.* **2** musty or stale: *There was a mouldy smell in the deserted house.* *adj.,*

**mould·i·er** or **mold·i·er, mould·i·est** or **mold·i·est**. —**mould′i·ness** or **mold′i·ness,** *n*.

**moult** or **molt** (mōlt) **1** shed the feathers, fur, skin, shell, or horns periodically before a new growth: *Birds and snakes moult.* **2** shed: *We saw the snake moult its skin.* **3** the act or process of moulting. **1, 2** *v.,* **3** *n.*

**mound** (mound) **1** a bank or heap of earth or stones. **2** enclose with a mound. **3** heap up: *Gardeners mound the earth around a hill of corn.* **4** a small hill. **5** in baseball, the slightly elevated ground from which a pitcher pitches. **1, 4, 5** *n.,* **2, 3** *v.*

**mount**[1] (mount) **1** go up; ascend: *to mount stairs.* **2** move or proceed upwards: *A flush mounts to the brow.* **3** rise; increase; rise in amount: *The cost of living mounts steadily.* **4** get up on: *to mount a platform.* **5** get on a horse; get up on something: *to mount and ride away.* **6** put on a horse; furnish with a horse: *The police who patrol this park are mounted.* **7** a horse provided for riding: *The rider had an excellent mount.* **8** put in proper position or order for use: *The scientist mounted the sample on a slide for her microscope.* **9** fix in a proper setting, backing, support, etc.: *to mount a picture on cardboard.* **10** that on which anything is mounted, fixed, supported, or placed: *the mount for a picture.* **11** have or carry guns as a fortress or ship does: *The ship mounts eight guns.* **12** provide a play with scenery and costumes. **13** go on guard as a sentry or watch does. **14** plan and begin to carry out: *to mount a campaign to get elected.* **1–6, 8, 9, 11–14** *v.,* **7, 10** *n.*

**mount**[2] (mount) a mountain or high hill: *Mount Robson.* *n.*

**moun·tain** (moun′tən) **1** a very high hill: *the Rocky Mountains.* See PLATEAU for picture. **2** of, having to do with, or resembling a mountain or mountains: *mountain air.* **3** living, growing, or found on mountains: *mountain plants.* **4** a large heap or pile of anything: *a mountain of rubbish.* **5** a huge amount: *a mountain of difficulties.* **6 mountains,** *pl.* a series of very high hills: *You can see the mountains from here.* *n.*
**make a mountain (out) of a molehill,** give great importance to something which is really insignificant.

**mountain avens** (av′ənz) any of a small, closely related group of woody, evergreen plants of the rose family found especially in northern and mountainous regions, having horizontal branches, small, leathery leaves, and white or yellow, roselike flowers: *The white mountain avens is the flower of the Northwest Territories.*

**mountain chain** a connected series of mountains.

**moun·tain·eer** (moun′tə nēr′) **1** one skilled in mountain climbing. **2** a person who lives in the mountains. **3** climb mountains. **1, 2** *n.,* **3** *v.*

**mountain goat** the white antelope of the Rocky Mountains.

**mountain laurel** an evergreen shrub having glossy leaves and pale-pink or white flowers.

**mountain lion** COUGAR.

**moun·tain·ous** (moun′tə nəs) **1** covered with MOUNTAIN RANGES: *mountainous country.* **2** huge: *a mountainous wave.* *adj.*

**mountain range** a row of connected mountains; a series of mountains.

**moun·tain·side** (moun′tən sīd′) the side or face of a mountain: *The whole mountainside was covered with trees.* *n.*

**moun·te·bank** (moun′tə bangk′) **1** a person who sells quack medicines in public, appealing to his or her audience by tricks, stories, jokes, etc. **2** anybody who tries to deceive people by tricks, stories, and jokes. *n.*

**mount·ed** (moun′tid) **1** on horseback. **2** in a position for use: *a mounted gun.* **3** having a proper support or setting: *a mounted photograph.* **4** pt. and pp. of MOUNT. **1–3** *adj.,* **4** *v.*

**Mount·ie** or **mount·ie** (moun′tē) *Informal.* a member of the ROYAL CANADIAN MOUNTED POLICE, a force maintained by the government of Canada. *n., pl.* **Mount·ies** or **mount·ies.**

**mount·ing** (moun′ting) **1** a support, setting, or the like: *The mounting of a photograph is the paper or cardboard on which it is pasted.* **2** ppr. of MOUNT. **1** *n.,* **2** *v.*

**mourn** (môrn) **1** grieve. **2** feel or show sorrow over: *Sherri mourned her lost turtle.* *v.* —**mourn′er,** *n.*

**mourn·ful** (môrn′fəl) **1** full of grief; sad; sorrowful: *a mournful voice.* **2** gloomy; dreary: *a mournful occasion.* *adj.* —**mourn′ful·ly,** *adv.* —**mourn′ful·ness,** *n.*

**mourn·ing** (môr′ning) **1** the act of sorrowing; lamentation. **2** the wearing of black or some other colour (white in the Orient), or the draping of buildings, the flying of flags at half-mast, etc. as outward signs of sorrow for a person's death. **3** clothes, decorations, draperies, etc. worn or displayed to show such sorrow: *The widow was dressed in mourning.* **4** the period during which such signs of sorrow are shown. **5** of or used in mourning. **1–4** *n.,* **5** *adj.*
☛ *Hom.* MORNING.

**mourning dove** a wild dove of North America that makes a mournful sound.

A house mouse— about 10 cm long excluding the tail

**mouse** (mous; *sometimes,* mouz *for verb*) **1** a small rodent native to the Old World but now common throughout North America, having a pointed snout, large ears, and a long, scaly tail: *The mouse, also called the* **house mouse***, lives mainly in or near buildings.* **2** any of numerous other small rodents resembling the house mouse, but usually having a long tail more or less covered with hair; especially, any of a group belonging to the same family as voles and lemmings, such as the **deer mouse**. **3** hunt for mice; catch mice for food. **4** a shy, timid person. **5** an electronic hand-held device which enables the user to manipulate material on a computer screen. **1, 2, 4, 5** *n., pl.* **mice;** **3** *v.,* **moused, mous·ing.** —**mouse′like′,** *adj.*

**mous·er** (mou′sər *or* mou′zər) an animal that catches mice: *Our cat is a good mouser.* *n.*

**mouse·trap** (mous′trap′) a trap for catching mice. *n.*

**mousse** (müs) **1** a chilled or frozen dessert made with sweetened whipped cream or gelatin: *chocolate mousse.* **2** finely ground cooked meat or fish mixed with cream and

other ingredients and poached, steamed, or set with gelatin. **3** any other substance with a foamy texture, such as hair setting lotion. *n.*
☞ *Hom.* MOOSE.

**mous·tache** (mus′tash *or* mə stash′) See MUSTACHE. *n.*

**mous·y** (mou′sē) **1** resembling or suggesting a mouse in being timid, drab in colour, quiet, etc.: *My hair is mousy.* **2** infested with mice. *adj.*, **mous·i·er, mous·i·est.** Also, **mousey.**

**mouth** (mouth *for noun,* mouŦH *for verb*) **1** the opening through which a person or animal takes in food; the space in the head containing the tongue and teeth. **2** the part of the face around the mouth; the lips. **3** an opening suggesting a mouth: *the mouth of a cave.* **4** a part of a river, creek, etc. where its waters are emptied into some other body of water: *the mouth of the St. Lawrence River.* **5** utter words in an affected or pompous way: *I dislike actors who mouth their lines.* **6** speak oratorically. **7** grimace: *The boy made mouths at us* (n.). *We mouthed at him* (v.). **8** utter words without sincerity or understanding: *She mouthed an apology for her poor manners.* **9** form words with the lips without speaking. 1–4, 7 *n., pl.* **mouths** (mouŦHz); 5–9 *v.*
**down in the mouth,** *Informal.* in low spirits; discouraged.
**the horse's mouth,** the original source; the person who knows: *The news came straight from the horse's mouth.*

**–mouthed** (mouŦHd *or* moutht) having a mouth of a certain kind (*used only in compounds*): *big-mouthed, close-mouthed. adj.*

**mouth·ful** (mouth′fùl) **1** the amount the mouth can easily hold. **2** what is taken into the mouth at one time. **3** a small amount. *n., pl.* **mouth·fuls.**

**mouth organ** HARMONICA.

**mouth·piece** (mouth′pēs′) **1** the part of a musical instrument that is placed against or in the mouth of the player. **2** the part of a bit that goes in a horse's mouth. **3** a piece placed at or forming the mouth of something: *the mouthpiece of a telephone, the mouthpiece of a pipe.* **4** a person, newspaper, etc. used by other persons or groups to express their views: *That newspaper is just a mouthpiece for the government. n.*

**mouth–to–mouth** (mouth′tə mouth′) of, having to do with, or referring to a method of artificial resuscitation in which the rescuer places his or her mouth closely over the mouth of a person who has stopped breathing and forces his or her breath into the person's lungs. *adj.*

**mouth·wash** (mouth′wosh′) an antiseptic liquid for rinsing the inside of the mouth or gargling. *n.*

**mouth–wa·ter·ing** (mouth′wot′ə ring) very appealing, especially to the appetite; very appetizing: *a mouth-watering menu, a mouth-watering bowl of fruit. adj.*

**mouth·y** (mou′ŦHē *or* mou′thē) loud-mouthed; ranting; bombastic. *adj.*, **mouth·i·er, mouth·i·est.**

**mov·a·ble** (mü′və bəl) **1** that can be moved: *Our fingers are movable.* **2** that can be carried from place to place as personal possessions can. **3** changing from one date to another in different years: *Easter is a movable holy day.* **4** anything that can be carried from place to place: *The house was bare; all the furniture and other movables had been taken away.* **5 movables,** *pl.* in law, personal property. 1–3 *adj.*, 4, 5 *n.* Also, **moveable.**

**move** (müv) **1** change the place or position of: *Do not move your hand. I'm going to move that chair nearer the window.* **2** change place or position: *The child moved in his sleep.* **3** change one's place of living or working: *We move to the country next week.* **4** in chess or other games, the moving of a piece: *That was a good move.* **5** a player's turn to move: *It's your move now.* **6** put or keep in motion: *The wind moves the leaves.* **7** the act of moving; movement: *If you make a move, the dog will bark. We had nice weather for our move to the country.* **8** of the bowels, empty or cause to be emptied. **9** act: *The committee moved very slowly.* **10** an action taken to bring about some result: *a move to disconcert his opponents.* **11** impel; rouse; excite: *What moved you to do this?* **12** affect with emotion; excite to tender feeling: *The sad story moved her to tears.* **13** make a formal request, application, or proposal; propose: *Madam Chairman, I move that we adjourn.* **14** sell or be sold: *These pink dresses are moving slowly.* **15** make progress: *The train moved slowly.* **16** exist; be active: *to move in the best society.* **17** turn; swing; operate: *Most doors move on a hinge.* 1–3, 6, 8, 9, 11–17 *v.*, **moved, mov·ing;** 4, 5, 7, 10 *n.*
**move heaven and earth,** do everything possible.
**move in,** move oneself, one's family, one's belongings, etc., into a new place to live or work.
**move out,** move oneself, one's family, one's belongings, etc., out of a place where one has lived or worked.
**on the move,** moving about: *They are restless and always on the move.*

**move·a·ble** (mü′və bəl) See MOVABLE. *adj., n.*

**move·ment** (müv′mənt) **1** the act or fact of moving: *We run by movements of the legs.* **2** the moving parts of a machine; special groups of parts that move on each other: *The movement of a watch consists of many little wheels.* **3** in music, the kind of rhythm a piece has, its speed, etc.: *The movement of a waltz is very different from the movement of a march.* **4** one section of a long piece of music: *The program included only the first movement of the symphony.* **5** a program by a group of people to bring about some one thing: *the movement for peace.* **6** an emptying of the bowels. *n.*

**mov·er** (mü′vər) a person or thing that moves, especially a person whose work is moving furniture, etc. from one residence or place of work to another: *The movers will be here tomorrow. n.*

**mov·ie** (mü′vē) *Informal.* a motion picture. *n.*

**mov·ing** (mü′ving) **1** capable of or characterized by movement. **2** of or having to do with changing a place of residence or work: *a moving company, moving expenses.* **3** causing a strong emotional response; touching: *a moving story.* **4** ppr. of MOVE. 1–3 *adj.,* 4 *v.*
—**mov′ing·ly,** *adv.*

**moving picture** MOTION PICTURE.

**mow**[1] (mō) **1** cut down with a machine or a scythe: *to mow grass.* **2** cut down the grass or grain from: *to mow a field.* **3** cut down grass, etc.: *The men are mowing today.* **4** destroy at a sweep or in large numbers, as if by mowing: *The firing of the enemy mowed down our men like grass. v.,* **mowed, mowed** *or* **mown, mow·ing.**

**mow²** (mou *or* mō) **1** the place in a barn where hay, alfalfa, grain, or straw is piled or stored.  **2** a pile of hay, grain, etc. in a barn.  *n.*

**mow·er** (mō′ər)  a person or thing that mows: *a lawn mower.*  *n.*

**mow·ing** (mō′ing) **1** the act or process of cutting grass with a scythe or machine.  **2** a field in which grass is grown for hay.  **3** the hay mowed at one time.  **4** ppr. of MOW.  1–3 *n.,* 4 *v.*

**mown** (mōn)  a pp. of MOW¹: *New-mown hay is hay that has just been cut.*  *v.*
☞ *Hom.* MOAN.

**MP** or **M.P.**  **1** Member of Parliament.  **2** Military Police.  **3** Mounted Police.  **4** Metropolitan Police.

**MPP** or **M.P.P.**  Member of the Provincial Parliament.

**Mr.** or **Mr** (mis′tər)  a title for a man, used before his last name or the name of his rank or office: *Mr. Einola, Mr. Speaker, Mr. Chief Justice.*  *pl.* **Messrs.**
☞ *Etym.*  An abbreviation of **mister.** See also note at MISTER.
☞ *Usage.*  See note at MISTER.

**Mrs.** or **Mrs** (mis′iz)  a title for a married woman, used before her last name: *Mrs. Perlman.*
☞ *Etym.*  Originally an abbreviation of MISTRESS, the female equivalent of MASTER, when used as a title before a name. In this use, the spoken form of the word gradually became weakened to (mis′əz); and because the abbreviation **Mrs.** was used only before a name, it became a completely separate word, not thought of in connection with **mistress.**
☞ *Usage.*  Even when used in writing to represent conversation or to talk about the word itself, it is rarely written out in full: *"Did you say Miss Jarvis?" "No. Mrs." I think* Mrs. *sounds so formal.* The form MISSUS is used only for writing the word with its informal meaning of 'wife': *That's my missus over there.*

**Ms.** or **Ms** (miz)  a title used in front of the name of a woman or girl: *Ms. Jackson.*
☞ *Usage.*  **Ms.** is a form made up in the early 1950's to parallel MR. and MRS. Unlike them, it is not an abbreviation, but it imitates them in being followed by a period. Like **Mr.,** but unlike **Mrs.** or MISS, **Ms.** does not identify a woman as being married or unmarried.

**MS., MS, ms.,** or **ms**  manuscript.

**m'sieur** (mə syœ′)  MONSIEUR.  *n.*

**MSS., MSS, mss.,** or **mss**  manuscripts.

**Mt.**  **1** Mount: *Mt. Edith Cavell.*  **2** Mountain.

**mtg.**  **1** meeting.  **2** mortgage.

**Mtl.**  Montreal.

**Mtn.**  Mountain.

**much** (much)  **1** in great quantity, amount, or degree: *much money, much time.*  **2** to a great extent or degree: *much pleased, much better.*  **3** nearly; about: *This is much the same as the others.*  **4** a great deal: *Much of this is not true.*  **5** a great, important, or notable thing or matter: *The rain did not amount to much.*  1 *adj.,* **more, most;** 2, 3 *adv.,* **more, most;**  4, 5 *n.*
**make much of,**  treat, represent, or consider as of great importance.
**much of a size, height, etc.,**  nearly the same size, height, etc.
**not much of a,**  not a very good: *This is not much of a game.*
**too much for,**  more than a match for; more than one can cope with, stand, or bear: *The work is too much for her. Their team was too much for ours.*

**mu·ci·lage** (myü′sə lij)  **1** a sticky, gummy substance used to make things stick together.  **2** in plants, a substance like glue or gelatin.  *n.*

**mu·ci·lag·i·nous** (myü′sə laj′ə nəs)  **1** sticky; gummy.  **2** containing MUCILAGE.  *adj.*

**muck** (muk)  **1** dirt; filth.  **2** anything filthy, dirty, or disgusting.  **3** soil or make dirty.  **4** moist farmyard manure.  **5** in mining, dirt, gravel, and other waste material.  **6** put muck on.  **7** *Informal.* **a** mess; untidy condition.  **8** remove muck from.  1, 2, 4, 5, 7 *n.,* 3, 6, 8 *v.*
**muck about** or **around,**  waste time; putter or go about aimlessly: *She's mucking about in the basement.*
**muck out,**  clean out a stable, mine, etc.

**muck·rake** (muk′rāk′)  hunt out and expose real or imagined corruption or misconduct of prominent people, public officials, etc.  *v.,* **muck·raked, muck·rak·ing.**
—**muck′rak′er,** *n.*

**mu·cous** (myü′kəs)  **1** of or like MUCUS.  **2** containing or secreting MUCUS.  *adj.*
☞ *Hom.* MUCUS.

**mucous membrane**  the lining of the nose, throat, and other cavities of the body that are open to the air.

**mu·cus** (myü′kəs)  a slimy substance that is secreted by and moistens the MUCOUS MEMBRANES: *A cold in the head causes a discharge of mucus.*  *n.*
☞ *Hom.* MUCOUS.

**mud** (mud)  soft, sticky, wet earth: *mud on the ground after rain, mud at the bottom of a pond.*  *n.*
**clear as mud,**  incomprehensible; obscure.

**mud·dle** (mud′əl)  **1** mix or mess up; cause confusion or disorder in; bungle (often used with **up**): *to muddle a piece of work. She was trying to help, but she only muddled it up.*  **2** make confused or stupid; befog: *a mind muddled with alcohol. The more you talk the more you muddle me.*  **3** think or act in a confused, blundering way: *He is still muddling along, without accomplishing much.*  **4** a mess; disorder; confusion: *Everything is in a muddle.*  1–3 *v.,* **mud·dled, mud·dling;**  4 *n.*  —**mud′dler,** *n.*
**muddle through,**  manage somehow; succeed in one's object in spite of lack of skill or foresight: *Don't worry, I'll muddle through.*

**mud·dle–head·ed** (mud′əl hed′id)  confused or scatterbrained: *You're awfully muddle-headed today.*  *adj.*

**mud·dy** (mud′ē)  **1** full of or covered with mud: *a muddy sidewalk, muddy water.*  **2** of or like mud: *The dog left muddy footprints on the floor.*  **3** suggesting or resembling mud; dull, impure, etc.: *a muddy colour, a muddy flavour.*  **4** confused; not clear: *muddy thinking.*  **5** make or become muddy: *Don't muddy the water.*  1–4 *adj.,* **mud·di·er, mud·di·est;**  5 *v.,* **mud·died, mud·dy·ing.**
**muddy the water,**  confuse matters.

**mud·guard** (mud′gärd′)  a guard or shield so placed as to protect riders from the mud thrown up by the moving wheels of a vehicle: *My bicycle has two mudguards.*  *n.*

**mud hen**  the coot of North America.

**mud puppy**  a large North American salamander that

lives in mud under water: *The mud puppy has fluffy, red gills on either side of the head.*

**mud trout** BROOK TROUT.

**mud turtle** any of a closely related group of freshwater turtles of North America.

**mu·ez·zin** (myü ez′ən) a crier who, at certain hours, calls Moslems to prayer. *n.*

**muff** (muf) **1** a cylindrical covering of fur or other material into which the hands are thrust from both ends to keep them warm. **2** fail to catch and hold a ball when it comes into one's hands. **3** a clumsy failure to catch and hold a ball that comes into one's hands: *The catcher's muff allowed the runner to score.* **4** handle awkwardly; bungle: *My brother muffed his chance to get that job.* **5** awkward handling; bungling. 1, 3, 5 *n.*, 2, 4 *v.*

**muf·fin** (muf′ən) **1** a small, round kind of quick bread made of wheat flour, corn meal, etc. and egg, eaten with butter and usually served hot. **2** a small cake, with or without fruit: *bran muffin, blueberry muffin.* *n.*

**muf·fle** (muf′əl) **1** wrap or cover up in order to keep warm and dry: *She muffled her throat in a warm scarf.* **2** wrap oneself in garments, etc. **3** wrap or cover in order to soften or stop the sound: *A bell can be muffled with cloth.* **4** dull or deaden a sound. **5** a muffled sound. **6** something that muffles. 1–4 *v.*, **muf·fled**, **muf·fling**; 5, 6 *n.*

**muf·fler** (muf′lər) **1** a wrap or scarf worn around the neck for warmth. **2** a device attached to an automobile or similar engine in order to reduce the noise of the exhaust. **3** anything used to deaden sound. *n.*

**muf·ti** (muf′tē) ordinary clothes, not a uniform: *The retired general appeared in mufti.* *n.*
☞ *Etym.* From Arabic *mufti* 'judge' (apparently because of the informal costume traditional for the stage role of a mufti).

**mug** (mug) **1** a usually large and heavy earthenware or metal drinking cup with a handle, used without a saucer. **2** the amount a mug holds: *to drink a mug of milk.* **3** attack and rob a person. 1, 2 *n.*, 3 *v.*, **mugged**, **mug·ging**.

**mug·ger** (mug′ər) a person who attacks another person with intent to rob. *n.*

**mug·gy** (mug′ē) warm and humid; damp and close: *The weather was muggy.* *adj.*, **mug·gi·er**, **mug·gi·est.** —**mug′gi·ness**, *n.*

**Mu·ham·mad** (mü ham′əd) Mohammed. *n.*

**mu·jik** (mü zhik′) See MUZHIK. *n.*

**muk·luk** (muk′luk) *Cdn.* **1** a high waterproof boot, often made of sealskin, worn by Inuit and others in the North. **2** *Informal.* any similar boot, made of leather, canvas, etc. *n.*
☞ *Etym.* From Western Inuktitut *muklok* 'bearded seal'.

**mu·lat·to** (mə lat′ō or myü lat′ō) **1** a person having one white and one black parent. **2** a person having both European and African ancestors. *n., pl.* **mu·lat·toes.**

**mul·ber·ry** (mul′ber′ē) **1** any of a closely related group of trees and shrubs having edible, usually purple, berry-like fruit: *The leaves of the white mulberry of Europe and Asia are used for feeding silkworms.* **2** the fruit of a mulberry. **3** referring to a family of mainly tropical trees, shrubs, and herbs that includes the mulberry, fig and breadfruit trees, as well as the hop vine and hemp. **4** dark, reddish purple. 1–4 *n., pl.* **mul·ber·ries**; 4 *adj.*

## mud trout 779 multicellular

hat, āge, fär; let, ēqual, tėrm; it, īce
hot, ōpen, ôrder; oil, out; cup, pút, rüle
əbove, takən, pencəl, lemən, circəs
ch, child; ng, long; sh, ship
th, thin; ᴛʜ, then; zh, measure

**mulch** (mulch) **1** straw, leaves, loose earth, etc. spread on the ground around trees or plants: *Mulch is used to protect roots from cold or heat, to prevent evaporation of moisture from the soil, to control weeds, or to enrich the soil.* **2** cover with straw, leaves, etc. 1 *n.*, 2 *v.*

**mulct** (mulkt) **1** deprive of something by fraud or deceit; swindle: *He was mulcted of his money by a shrewd trick.* **2** punish by a fine. **3** a fine; penalty. 1, 2 *v.*, 3 *n.*

**mule**¹ (myül) **1** the offspring of the ass and horse, especially of a male ass and a mare: *The mule has the form and size of a horse, but the large ears, small hoofs, and tufted tail of an ass.* **2** *Informal.* a stubborn person. **3** a kind of spinning machine. *n.*

**mule**² (myül) a kind of slipper that leaves the heel uncovered. *n.*

**mule deer** a deer of western North America that has long ears and a white tail with a black tip: *The mule deer is larger than the white-tailed deer.*

**mu·le·teer** (myü′lə tēr′) a driver of mules. *n.*

**mul·ish** (myü′lish) like a mule; stubborn; obstinate. *adj.* —**mul′ish·ly**, *adv.* —**mul′ish·ness**, *n.*

**mull**¹ (mul) *Informal.* think about without making much progress: *She mulled over her problems.* *v.*

**mull**² (mul) make wine, beer, or cider into a hot drink, with sugar, spices, etc. *v.*

**mul·lah** (mul′ə) **1** in Islam, a title of respect for a Moslem who is learned in Islamic theology and the sacred law. **2** in the Shiite tradition, a scholar of religious law who also performs duties in the conduct of worship. *n.*

**mul·lein** or **mul·len** (mul′ən) any of a closely related group of plants related to the figworts, having coarse, woolly leaves and spikes of yellow, pink, or white flowers: *Some mulleins are common weeds; others are grown as garden flowers.* *n.*

**mul·let** (mul′it) **1** any of a family of important food fishes of small or medium size, having soft fins and a streamlined, rounded body: *Mullet are found in fresh and salt water.* Also called **grey mullet. 2** any of a family of bright-coloured, medium-sized saltwater fishes having BARBELS on the lower jaw. Some species are valued as food fish. Also called **red mullet.** *n., pl.* **mul·let** or **mul·lets.**

**mul·lion** (mul′yən) a vertical bar between the panes of a window, the panels in the wall of a room, or the like. *n.*

**mul·lioned** (mul′yənd) having MULLIONs. *adj.*

**multi–** combining form. **1** having or consisting of several or many: *multicoloured, multiform.* **2** involving or affecting many: *multinational.* **3** several or many times more than; several or many times over: *multimillionaire.*
☞ *Pronunciation.* See note at ANTI-.

**mul·ti·cel·lu·lar** (mul′tē sel′yə lər) having more than one cell. *adj.*

**mul·ti·col·oured** or **mul·ti·col·ored** (mul′tē kul′ərd) having many colours: *a multicoloured cotton print.* *adj.*

**mul·ti·cul·tur·al** (mul′tē kul′chə rəl) **1** of or having a number of distinct cultures existing side by side in the same country, province, etc.: *Canada is a multicultural country.* **2** designed for a country, province, etc. having a number of distinct cultures existing side by side: *multicultural programs.* *adj.*

**mul·ti·cul·tur·al·ism** (mul′tē kul′chə rə liz′əm) **1** the fact or condition of being MULTICULTURAL: *She wrote a report on multiculturalism in the schools.* **2** a policy supporting or promoting the existence of a number of distinct cultural groups side by side within a country, province, etc.: *Canada has a federal minister responsible for multiculturalism.* **3** the practice or support of such a policy: *Our city council's multiculturalism is too half-hearted.* *n.*

**mul·ti·far·i·ous** (mul′tə fer′ē əs) having many different kinds; extremely varied: *multifarious talents.* *adj.* —**mul′ti·far′i·ous·ly,** *adv.* —**mul′ti·far′ious·ness,** *n.*

**mul·ti·form** (mul′tə fôrm′) having many different shapes, forms, or kinds. *adj.*

**mul·ti·lat·er·al** (mul′tē lat′ə rəl) **1** having many sides. **2** involving two or more nations, parties, etc.: *a multilateral trade agreement.* *adj.*

**mul·ti·lin·gual** (mul′tē ling′gwəl *or* mul′tē ling′gyə wəl) **1** able to speak several languages well: *The company needs several multilingual sales representatives.* **2** expressed in or containing several languages: *a multilingual conversation, a multilingual dictionary.* *adj.* —**mul′ti·lin′gual·ly,** *adv.*

**mul·ti·lin·gual·ism** (mul′tē ling′gwə liz′əm *or* mul′tē ling′gyə wə liz′əm) the ability to speak several languages: *Multilingualism is common in Scandinavia.* *n.*

**mul·ti·me·di·a** (mul′tē mē′dē ə) **1** using, involving, or including several media together: *a multimedia presentation.* **2** making use of sound, graphics, scanned photos, text, etc. at the same time or within a single piece of software. *adj.*

**mul·ti·mil·lion·aire** (mul′tē mil′yə ner′) a person whose wealth amounts to many millions of dollars, pounds, etc. *n.*

**mul·ti·na·tion·al** (mul′tē nash′ə nəl *or* mul′tē nash′nəl) **1** of, having to do with, or involving several nations: *a multinational empire, a multinational agreement.* **2** of a business organization, having divisions in several nations: *a multinational food corporation.* **3** of or having to do with a multinational business organization. **4** a multinational company: *Several large multinationals have already located in this area.* 1–3 *adj.*, 4 *n.*

**mul·tip·a·rous** (mul tip′ə rəs) in biology, producing more than one offspring at a birth. *adj.*

**mul·ti·ple** (mul′tə pəl) **1** of, having, or involving many parts, elements, relations, etc.: *a woman of multiple interests.* **2** a number or quantity that contains another number or quantity a certain number of times without a remainder: *Twelve is a multiple of three. The kilometre is a multiple of the metre.* **3** SUB-MULTIPLE: *Ten is a multiple of one hundred.* 1 *adj.*, 2, 3 *n.*

**multiple sclerosis** a disease of the brain and spinal cord, that usually eventually results in permanent paralysis: *The cause of multiple sclerosis is unknown.*

**mul·ti·plex** (mul′tə pleks′) manifold; multiple: *Multiplex telegraphy is a system for sending more than two messages in opposite directions over the same wire at the same time.* *adj.*

**mul·ti·pli·cand** (mul′tə plə kand′) the number or quantity to be multiplied by another: *In 5 times 497, the multiplicand is 497.* *n.*

**mul·ti·pli·ca·tion** (mul′tə plə kā′shən) **1** MULTIPLYing or being multiplied. **2** the operation of MULTIPLYing one number by another. *n.*

**mul·ti·plic·i·ty** (mul′tə plis′ə tē) a manifold variety; great many: *a multiplicity of interests.* *n., pl.* **mul·ti·plic·i·ties.**

**mul·ti·pli·er** (mul′tə plī′ər) **1** the number by which another is to be multiplied: *In 5 times 83, the multiplier is 5.* **2** a person or thing that multiplies. *n.*

**mul·ti·ply** (mul′tə plī′) **1** increase in number or amount: *As we climbed up the mountain, the dangers and difficulties multiplied.* **2** take a number or quantity a given number of times: *To multiply 16 by 3 means to take 16 three times, making 48.* Symbol: x *v.*, **mul·ti·plied, mul·ti·ply·ing.**

**mul·ti·stage** (mul′tē stāj′) **1** of a rocket or missile, having several sections, each of which lifts it to a greater height before burning out and dropping off. **2** having a number of stages for the completion of a process: *a multistage investigation.* *adj.*

**mul·ti·tude** (mul′tə tyüd′ *or* mul′tə tüd′) **1** a great many; crowd. **2 the multitude,** the ordinary people. *n.*

**mul·ti·tu·di·nous** (mul′tə tyü′də nəs *or* mul′tə tü′də nəs) **1** forming a MULTITUDE; very numerous. **2** including many parts, elements, items, or features. *adj.* —**mul′ti·tu′di·nous·ly,** *adv.* —**mul′ti·tu′di·nous·ness,** *n.*

**mul·ti·va·lence** (mul′tə vā′ləns *or* mul tiv′ə ləns) the quality or state of being MULTIVALENT. *n.*

**mul·ti·va·lent** (mul′tə vā′lənt *or* mul tiv′ə lənt) **1** having a VALENCE of three or more. **2** having more than one degree of VALENCE. *adj.*

**mum**[1] (mum) **1** silent; saying nothing: *Keep mum about this, tell no one.* **2** be silent! say nothing! 1 *adj.*, 2 *interj.*
**mum's the word,** keep silent.

**mum**[2] (mum) *Informal.* mother. *n.*

**mum**[3] (mum) *Informal.* CHRYSANTHEMUM. *n.*

**mum·ble** (mum′bəl) **1** speak indistinctly, as a person does when his or her lips are partly closed. **2** chew as a person does who has no teeth. **3** mumbling. 1, 2 *v.*, **mum·bled, mum·bling;** 3 *n.* —**mum′bler,** *n.*

**Mum·bo Jum·bo** or **mum·bo jum·bo** (mum′bō jum′bō) **1** a foolish or meaningless ritual; ceremonial nonsense. **2** a BOGEY; any object foolishly worshipped or feared.

**mum·mer** (mum′ər) **1** a person who wears a mask, fancy costume, or disguise for fun: *Six mummers acted in a play at Christmas.* **2** actor. *n.*

**mum·mer·y** (mum′ər ē) **1** a performance of MUMMERS. **2** any useless or silly show or ceremony. *n., pl.* **mum·mer·ies.**

**mum·mi·fy** (mum′ə fī) **1** make a dead body into a MUMMY[1]. **2** dry or shrivel up. *v.*, **mum·mi·fied, mum·mi·fy·ing.**

An Egyptian mummy and coffin. The body was treated with chemicals and wrapped in linen.

**mum·my**[1] (mum′ē) **1** a dead body embalmed by the ancient Egyptians: *Egyptian mummies have lasted more than 3000 years.* **2** a dead human or animal body dried and preserved by nature. *n., pl.* **mum·mies.**
☛ *Etym.* Through French and Latin from Arabic *mūmiyā* 'embalmed body', which developed from Persian *mūm* 'wax'. Wax was used in embalming.

**mum·my**[2] (mum′ē) *Informal.* mother. *n., pl.* **mum·mies.**

**mumps** (mumps) a contagious disease caused by a virus, characterized especially by inflammation and swelling of the saliva glands below the ears and by difficulty in swallowing (*used with a singular verb*): *Mumps is generally a childhood disease.* *n.*

**munch** (munch) chew vigorously and steadily; chew noisily: *A horse munches its oats.* *v.*

**mun·dane** (mun′dān) **1** of this world, not of heaven; earthly. **2** ordinary; everyday; humdrum: *mundane matters of business.* *adj.*

**mung bean** an annual bean grown for forage or as a source of bean sprouts.

**mu·nic·i·pal** (myü nis′ə pəl) **1** of or having to do with the affairs of a city, town, or other municipality: *The provincial police assisted the municipal police.* **2** run by a MUNICIPALITY: *municipal affairs.* **3** having local self-government: *a municipal district.* *adj.*

**mu·nic·i·pal·i·ty** (myü nis′ə pal′ə tē) a city, town, county, district, township, or other area having local self-government. *n., pl.* **mu·nic·i·pal·i·ties.**

**mu·nic·i·pal·ly** (myü nis′i plē) by a city or town; with regard to a city or town or to municipal affairs. *adv.*

**mu·nif·i·cence** (myü nif′ə səns) very great generosity. *n.*

**mu·nif·i·cent** (myü nif′ə sənt) extremely generous. *adj.* —**mu·nif′i·cent·ly**, *adv.*

**mu·ni·tion** (myü nish′ən) **1** having to do with military supplies: *A munition plant is a factory for making munitions.* **2** provide with military supplies: *to munition a fort.* **3** Usually, **munitions**, *pl.* material used in war: *Munitions are military supplies, such as guns, powder, or bombs.* **1, 3** *n.*, **2** *v.*

**mu·ral** (myü′rəl) **1** on, in, or for a wall: *A mural painting is painted on a wall of a building.* **2** a picture painted on a wall. **3** of, having to do with, or like a wall. **1, 3** *adj.*, **2** *n.*

---

mummery 781 muscle

hat, āge, fär; let, ēqual, tėrm; it, īce
hot, ōpen, ôrder; oil, out; cup, pùt, rüle
əbove, takən, pencəl, lemən, circəs
ch, child; ng, long; sh, ship
th, thin; ᴛʜ, then; zh, measure

**mur·der** (mėr′dər) **1** the intentional and unlawful killing of a human being by another. **2** an instance of such a crime: *There has never been a murder in this town.* **3** kill a human being intentionally: *Manuel murdered his brother.* **4** *Informal.* something very hard, disagreeable, or dangerous: *The traffic was murder last night. The last part of the climb is murder.* **1, 2, 4** *n.*, **3** *v.* **murder will out, a** a murder cannot be hidden. **b** any great wrong will be found out.

**mur·der·er** (mėr′də rər) a person who is guilty of MURDER (defs. 1, 2). *n.*

**mur·der·ess** (mėr′də ris) a woman who is guilty of MURDER (defs. 1, 2). *n.*

**mur·der·ous** (mėr′də rəs) **1** able or likely to kill: *a murderous blow.* **2** ready or intending to MURDER (def. 3): *a murderous villain.* **3** causing MURDER (defs. 1, 2): *a murderous plot.* *adj.* —**mur′der·ous·ly**, *adv.*

**mu·rex** (myü′reks) a tropical shellfish formerly used as a source of purple dye. *n., pl.* **mu·rex·es** or **mu·ri·ces** (-sēz).

**mu·ri·at·ic acid** (myü′rē at′ik) the commercial name for HYDROCHLORIC ACID.

**murk** (mėrk) darkness; gloom. *n.* Also, **mirk**.

**murk·y** (mėr′kē) **1** dark or gloomy. **2** very thick and obscure; misty; hazy: *murky smoke.* *adj.*, **murk·i·er, murk·i·est.** —**murk′i·ly**, *adv.* —**murk′i·ness**, *n.*

**mur·mur** (mėr′mər) **1** a soft, low, indistinct sound that rises and falls a little but goes on without breaks: *the murmur of a stream, of little waves, or of voices in another room.* **2** make a soft, low, indistinct sound. **3** a sound in the heart or lungs, especially an abnormal sound due to a leaky valve in the heart. **4** a softly spoken word or speech. **5** utter in a murmur: *The girl murmured her thanks.* **6** a complaint made under the breath; not aloud. **7** complain under the breath; grumble. **1, 3, 4, 6** *n.*, **2, 5, 7** *v.* —**mur′mur·ing·ly**, *adv.*

**Murphy bed** (mėr′fē) a bed that may be folded or swung up into a wall cabinet when not in use.

**mur·rain** (mėr′ən) an infectious disease of cattle. *n.*

**mus. 1** music. **2** museum.

**mus·cat** (mus′kat) **1** a light-coloured grape with the flavour or odour of musk. **2** MUSCATEL wine. *n.*

**mus·ca·tel** (mus′kə təl′) **1** a strong, sweet wine made from MUSCAT grapes. **2** the MUSCAT grape. *n.*

**mus·cle** (mus′əl) **1** a kind of animal tissue consisting of long cells that contract and relax to produce movement. **2** an organ made up of a bundle of muscle tissue, attached at either end to a particular bone or joint, which moves or stops the movement of a part of the body. **3** strength: *It takes muscle to move a piano.* **4** *Informal.* power or influence, especially when based on force or the threat of force: *The organization has enough muscle to get their way with the city council.* **5** *Informal.* move or gain by using force or the threat of force: *He muscled his way past the doorman.* **1–4** *n.*, **5** *v.*, **mus·cled, mus·cling.** **not move a muscle,** keep perfectly still.

☛ Hom. MUSSEL.
☛ Etym. Both **muscle** and MUSSEL can be traced back to L *musculus*, originally 'little mouse'. **Muscle** came through French in the 16c. from the Latin word, which was used to mean 'muscle' since some muscles, when alternately tensed and relaxed, were thought to look like a running mouse. **Mussel**, on the other hand, comes from OE *muscelle*, from a late form of L *musculus* that meant 'mollusc', presumably because the humped shape of the shell resembled that of a mouse at rest.

**mus·cle–bound** (mus′əl bound′) having some of the muscles stiff or tight, usually as a result of too much exercise. *adj.*

**mus·co·vite** (mus′kə vīt′) the common light-coloured variety of MICA. *n.*

**Mus·co·vite** (mus′kə vīt′) **1** a native or inhabitant of Muscovy, a former grand duchy including Moscow and the surrounding territory, or of Moscow. **2** Russian. **3** of or having to do with Muscovy, Moscow, or Russia, or its inhabitants. 1, 2 *n.*, 2, 3 *adj.*

**mus·cu·lar** (mus′kyə lər) **1** of the MUSCLES: *a muscular strain, muscular activity.* **2** having well-developed MUSCLES; strong: *a muscular arm.* **3** consisting of MUSCLE. *adj.*

**muscular dys·tro·phy** (dis′trə fē) a disease in which the muscles gradually decay and become useless.

**mus·cu·lar·i·ty** (mus′kyə lar′ə tē *or* mus′kyə ler′ə tē) MUSCULAR development or strength. *n.*

**mus·cu·la·ture** (mus′kyə lə chər) a system or arrangement of MUSCLES. *n.*

**muse¹** (myüz) **1** think in a dreamy way; think; meditate: *The boy spent the whole afternoon in musing about being an astronaut.* **2** look thoughtfully. **3** say thoughtfully. *v.*, **mused, mus·ing.** —**mus′er,** *n.*

**muse²** (myüz) a spirit that inspires a poet or composer. *n.*
☛ Etym. From *Muse*, in Greek mythology, one of the nine goddesses of the fine arts and sciences.

**mu·se·um** (myü zē′əm) the building or rooms where a collection of objects illustrating science, history, art, or other subjects is kept and displayed. *n.*
☛ Etym. Through Latin from Gk. *mouseion* 'seat (or house) of the Muses'. 17c. See also notes at MUSE² and MUSIC.

**mush¹** (mush) **1** *Esp. U.S.* corn meal boiled in water. **2** any soft, thick mass: *The heavy rain made mush of the old dirt road.* **3** *Informal.* weak sentiment; silly talk. *n.*
☛ Etym. A variant of MASH.

**mush²** (mush) *Cdn.* **1** a command to advance, given to sled dogs. **2** urge sled dogs onward by shouting commands: *He mushed his dog team through the blinding storm.* **3** follow a dogsled on foot: *For six days he mushed across the Barren Lands.* **4** a journey made by dogsled, especially while driving the team from behind the sled. 1, 4 *n.*, 2, 3 *v.* —**mush′er,** *n.*
☛ Etym. From Cdn.F *marche (donc)* from *marcher* 'go, walk', used as a command to horses, sled dogs, etc.

Three kinds of mushroom

**mush·room** (mush′rüm) **1** the large, often umbrella-shaped fruiting body of any of a large number of fungi, especially the species that are edible. **2** anything shaped or growing like a mushroom. **3** of or like a mushroom in shape or rapid growth: *a mushroom town, growing out of control.* **4** grow very fast: *Her business mushroomed when she opened the new store.* **5** of a bullet, flatten at the end on impact against something very hard. 1–3 *n.*, 4, 5 *v.*

**mushroom cloud** a rapidly rising mushroom-shaped cloud of radio-active matter that follows a nuclear explosion.

**mush·y** (mush′ē) **1** like mush; pulpy. **2** *Informal.* weakly sentimental: *The children thought it a mushy story.* *adj.*, **mush·i·er, mush·i·est.** —**mush′i·ness,** *n.*

**mu·sic** (myü′zik) **1** the art of putting sounds together in beautiful, pleasing, or interesting arrangements. **2** such arrangements of sounds: *I like listening to music.* **3** a succession of pleasant sounds: *the music of streams, the music of the wind.* **4** written or printed signs for tones: *This book has the words and music for the song.* **5** an appreciation of, or responsiveness to, musical sounds. *n.* **face the music,** *Informal.* meet trouble boldly or bravely. **set to music,** provide the words of a poem with music.
☛ Etym. Through Old French and Latin from Gk. *mousikē (technē)* '(art) of a Muse or the Muses', applied later to music but originally referring to any or all of the arts. See also notes at MUSE² and MUSEUM.

**mu·si·cal** (myü′zə kəl) **1** of or having to do with music: *musical knowledge, musical instruments.* **2** like music; melodious and pleasant: *a musical voice.* **3** set to music or accompanied by music: *a musical comedy, the musical ride of the RCMP.* **4** fond of music. **5** skilled in music; talented as a musician. **6** a stage entertainment or motion picture in which a story is told through music, singing, and dancing as well as dialogue. 1–5 *adj.*, 6 *n.* —**mu′si·cal·ly,** *adv.*

**musical comedy** an amusing play in which plot and characterization are less important than singing, dancing, and costumes.

**musical instrument** **1** any stringed, wind, or percussion instrument, as a violin, trumpet, or drum, employed, or designed to be employed, in producing music or musical sounds. **2** an electronic instrument used to produce, not reproduce, musical sounds.

**music box** a box or case containing apparatus for producing music mechanically.

**music hall** *Esp. Brit.* **1** a theatre for singing, dancing, variety shows, etc.; VAUDEVILLE theatre. **2** VAUDEVILLE entertainment.

**mu·si·cian** (myü zish′ən) a person trained in music, especially one who earns a living by playing, conducting, composing, or singing music: *An orchestra is made up of many musicians.* *n.*

**mu·si·col·o·gy** (myü′zə kol′ə jē) the study of the forms, principles, literature, and history of music. *n.*

**music synthesizer** an electronic instrument capable of producing musical sounds.

**music video** a short videotape featuring a piece of music such as a rock song.

**mus·ing** (myü′zing) **1** dreamy; meditative; absorbed in thought. **2** ppr. of MUSE. 1 *adj.*, 2 *v.*

**musk** (musk) **1** a substance with a strong and lasting odour, used as a basis of perfumes: *Natural musk is obtained from a special gland in the male musk deer, but a similar substance can be produced synthetically.* **2** the odour of musk. *n.*

**musk deer** a small hornless deer of central Asia, the male of which has a gland containing MUSK.

**mus·keg** (mus′keg) *Cdn.* **1** a swamp or marsh. **2** an area of bog composed of decaying plant life, especially moss: *There are vast regions of muskeg in northern Alberta.* *n.*
☞ *Etym.* From an Algonquian word, possibly Cree *muskak* 'swamp'.

**mus·kel·lunge** (mus′kə lunj′) *Cdn.* a very large freshwater fish of the pike family: *The muskellunge is valued as a food and game fish.* *n., pl.* **mus·kel·lunge**.
☞ *Etym.* From an Algonquian word, probably an Ojibwa form corresponding to Cree *mashkkinonche*. See note at MASKINONGE.

**mus·ket** (mus′kit) a kind of old gun with a smooth bore and no spiral groove in the barrel: *Soldiers used muskets before rifles were invented.* *n.*

**mus·ket·eer** (mus′kə tēr′) a soldier armed with a MUSKET. *n.*

**mus·ket·ry** (mus′ki trē) **1** MUSKETS. **2** the act of shooting with MUSKETS or rifles. **3** soldiers armed with MUSKETS. *n.*

**mus·kie** (mus′kē) MUSKELLUNGE. *n.*

**musk·mel·on** (musk′mel′ən) a kind of sweet, juicy melon with a musky odour, having a thick, rough, netlike rind and orange pulp. *n.*

Musk-oxen—
about 150 cm high
at the shoulder

**musk-ox** or **musk·ox** (mus′koks′) *Cdn.* a large, shaggy-haired mammal of the same family as cattle, antelope, and sheep, native to northern Canada, Alaska, and northwestern Greenland: *The musk-ox has a strong, musky smell.* *n., pl.* **musk-ox** or **musk-ox·en**.

**musk·rat** (mus′krat′) **1** a water rodent of North America, resembling a rat, but larger and with webbed hind feet. **2** its valuable dark-brown fur. *n., pl.* **musk·rats** or (*esp. collectively*) **musk·rat**.
☞ *Etym.* See note at MUSQUASH.

**musk·y** (mus′kē) of, like, or having an odour of MUSK: *a musky perfume.* *adj.*, **musk·i·er**, **musk·i·est**.

**musicology   783   mustard seed**

hat, āge, fär; let, ēqual, tėrm; it, īce
hot, ōpen, ôrder, oil, out; cup, pùt, rüle
əbove, takən, pencəl, lemən, circəs
ch, child; ng, long; sh, ship
th, thin; ᴛʜ, then; zh, measure

**Mus·lim** (muz′ləm) MOSLEM. *n., adj.*

**mus·lin** (muz′lən) **1** a cotton cloth in a plain weave, made in a variety of weights ranging from sheer to coarse, and used for dresses, sheets, curtains, etc. **2** made of muslin. *n.*

**mus·quash** (mus′kwosh) *Cdn.* MUSKRAT. *n., pl.* **mus·quash**.
☞ *Etym.* From an Algonquian word, possibly Ojibwa *miskwasi*. 17 c. MUSKRAT came in the 18c. from this or a similar word, altered to suggest that it was made up of *musk* (from the smell) + *rat* (water rat).

**muss** (mus) *Informal.* **1** put into disorder; rumple: *The child's dress was mussed.* **2** disorder; untidiness; mess. 1 *v.*, 2 *n.*

**mus·sel** (mus′əl) **1** any of numerous edible saltwater MOLLUSCs resembling small clams, usually having dark, long, hinged shells. **2** any of numerous freshwater MOLLUSCs having usually wedge-shaped or pear-shaped shells that are often dark blue or brown on the outside and pearly inside: *The shells of freshwater mussels are used for making buttons.* *n.*
☞ *Hom.* MUSCLE.
☞ *Etym.* See note at MUSCLE.

**muss·y** (mus′ē) *Informal.* untidy; messy; rumpled: *Your hair is mussy.* *adj.*, **muss·i·er**, **muss·i·est**.

**must**[1] (must; *unstressed*, məst) **1** be obliged to; be forced to: *We must eat to live.* **2** ought to; should: *I must go home soon.* **3** be certain to be, do, etc.: *I must seem very rude.* **4** be supposed or expected to: *You must have that book.* **5** *Must* is sometimes used with its verb omitted: *We must to horse. We must away.* **6** something necessary; obligation: *This rule is a must.* **7** *Informal.* demanding attention or doing; necessary: *a must item, must legislation.* 1–5 auxiliary verb, *pt.* **must**; 6 *n.*, 7 *adj.*

**must**[2] (must) the unfermented juice of the grape; new wine. *n.*

**mus·tache** or **mous·tache** (mus′tash *or* mə stash′) **1** the hair that grows on a man's upper lip, especially when groomed and not shaved smooth. **2** the hairs or bristles growing near the mouth of an animal. *n.*

**mus·tang** (mus′tang) a small, wild or half-wild horse of the North American plains. *n.*

**mus·tard** (mus′tərd) **1** a yellow powder or paste used as seasoning to give food a pungent taste. **2** any of several plants of the mustard family, whose seeds are ground for this seasoning. **3** a dark-yellow colour. **4** referring to a family of plants having cross-shaped flowers and pointed pods: *Some plants of the mustard family are the mustards, cabbage, horseradish, radish, turnip, and broccoli.* *n.*

**mustard gas** a poison gas that causes burns, blindness, and death.

**mustard plaster** a poultice made of mustard and water, or of mustard, flour, and water.

**mustard seed** the seed of the mustard plant.

**mus·ter** (mus′tər) 1 assemble; gather together; collect. 2 an assembly or collection. 3 summon: *to muster up courage.* 4 a bringing together of men or troops for review or service. 5 the list of those mustered. 6 the number mustered. *1, 3 v., 2, 4–6 n.*
**muster in,** enlist.
**muster out,** discharge.
**pass muster,** be inspected and approved; come up to the required standards.

**must·n't** (mus′ənt) must not. *v.*

**mus·ty** (mus′tē) 1 having a smell or taste suggesting mould or damp; mouldy: *a musty room, musty crackers.* 2 stale; out-of-date: *musty laws. adj.,* **mus·ti·er, mus·ti·est.** —**mus′ti·ness,** *n.*

**mu·ta·bil·i·ty** (myü′tə bil′ə tē) the quality of being MUTABLE: *the mutability of species. n.*

**mu·ta·ble** (myü′tə bəl) 1 liable to change: *mutable customs.* 2 capable of or liable to undergo MUTATION. 3 fickle: *a mutable person. adj.*

**mu·tant** (myü′tənt) 1 of, having to do with, or produced by MUTATION (def. 2). 2 a new variety of plant or animal resulting from MUTATION (def. 2). *1 adj., 2 n.*

**mu·tate** (myü′tāt *or* myü tāt′) 1 change. 2 produce MUTATIONS (def. 3). *v.,* **mu·tat·ed, mu·tat·ing.**

**mu·ta·tion** (myü tā′shən) 1 a change; alteration. 2 a sudden change in the genetic structure of an animal or plant that produces a new feature or characteristic. 3 a new variety of animal or plant resulting from such a change. *n.*

**mute** (myüt) 1 silent; not making any sound: *The little girl stood mute.* 2 unable to speak. 3 a person who cannot speak. 4 a clip or some other device put on a musical instrument to soften the sound. 5 soften or deaden the sound of a musical instrument: *He muted the strings of his violin.* 6 not pronounced. The *e* in *mute* is mute. 7 a silent letter. *1, 2, 6 adj., 3, 4, 7 n., 5 v.*

**mu·ti·late** (myü′tə lāt′) 1 cut or tear off or destroy a part of a living body: *Many of the victims of the accident had been badly mutilated.* 2 tear, break, cut off, or remove some part of something as to damage or ruin it: *The book had been mutilated by someone who had torn some pages and written on others. The story had been mutilated by an editor. v.,* **mu·ti·lat·ed, mu·ti·lat·ing.**

**mu·ti·la·tion** (myü′tə lā′shən) mutilating or being MUTILATED. *n.*

**mu·ti·la·tor** (myü′tə lā′tər) a person or thing that MUTILATES. *n.*

**mu·ti·neer** (myü′tə nēr′) a person who takes part in a MUTINY. *n.*

**mu·ti·nous** (myü′tə nəs) 1 rebelling against authority, especially the authority of a superior officer or officers on a ship or in the armed forces: *a mutinous crew.* 2 of or having to do with MUTINY: *mutinous talk.* 3 unruly. *adj.* —**mu′ti·nous·ly,** *adv.*

**mu·ti·ny** (myü′tə nē) 1 an open rebellion against lawful authority, especially by sailors or soldiers against their officers. 2 take part in a mutiny; rebel. *1 n., pl.* **mu·ti·nies;** *2 v.,* **mu·ti·nied, mu·ti·ny·ing.**

**mutt** (mut) *Informal.* 1 a dog, especially a mongrel. 2 a stupid person. *n.*

**mut·ter** (mut′ər) 1 speak softly and indistinctly with lips partly closed: *He was muttering the numbers to himself as he counted.* 2 complain; grumble. 3 say in low and indistinct tones, especially when expressing secret anger or discontent: *"I'll get even with him," she muttered.* 4 the act of muttering. 5 muttered words. *1–3 v., 4, 5 n.* —**mut′ter·er,** *n.*

**mut·ton** (mut′ən) the meat from a mature sheep. *n.*

**mutton chop** 1 a CHOP¹ (def. 4) of mutton, usually from the ribs or loin, for broiling or frying. 2 **mutton chops,** *pl.* side whiskers shaped somewhat like mutton chops, extending from the ears to the side of the chin and leaving the chin bare.

**mu·tu·al** (myü′chü əl) 1 done, said, felt, etc. by each toward the other; given and received: *mutual promises, mutual dislike.* 2 each to the other: *mutual enemies.* 3 *Informal.* belonging to each of several: *our mutual friend. adj.* —**mu′tu·al·ly,** *adv.*

**mu·tu·al·ism** (myü′chü ə liz′əm) a form of SYMBIOSIS in which both species benefit. Compare with AMENSALISM, COMMENSALISM, and PARASITISM. *n.*

**muu·muu** (mü′mü′) a woman's long, loose, flowing gown that is gathered at the neckline. *n.*

**mu·zhik** (mü zhik′) a Russian peasant. *n.* Also, **mujik.**

A muzzle on a dog

**muz·zle** (muz′əl) 1 the nose, mouth, and jaws of a four-footed animal. 2 a cover of straps or wires for putting over an animal's head and mouth to keep it from biting or eating. 3 put a muzzle on. 4 compel to keep silent about something; prevent from expressing views: *The government muzzled the newspapers during the revolt.* 5 the open front end of a firearm. *1, 2, 5 n., 3, 4 v.,* **muz·zled, muz·zling.** —**muz′zler,** *n.*
**put a muzzle on,** prevent persons, newspapers, etc. from expressing free opinions.

**muz·zle-load·ing** (muz′əl lō′ding) of firearms, loaded by putting gunpowder in through the open front end and ramming it down. *adj.*

**my** (mī) 1 a possessive form of **I;** of, belonging to, of, made or done by me or myself: *I hurt my arm. Please hand me my coat. I'm getting a new watch for my graduation.* 2 a word used as part of certain formal titles: *The horses are ready, my lord.* 3 *Informal.* a word used before certain other words in addressing a person: *my boy, my dear fellow.* 4 *Informal.* a word used as an exclamation of surprise, often together with another word: *My! what a big cat! My, oh my! My word!* 5 *Informal.* A word used together with the name of some part of the body as an exclamation of disbelief or doubt: *Accident, my eye! It was plain carelessness.* *1–3 adj., 4, 5 interj.*

☛ *Usage.* **My** and MINE are possessive forms of **I. My** is a determiner and is always followed by a noun: *This is my hat.* **Mine** is a pronoun and stands alone: *This hat is mine.*

**myasthenia gravis** a chronic but treatable neurological disorder characterized by muscle weakness.

**my·ce·li·um** (mī sē′lē əm) the main part of a fungus, consisting of interwoven fibres. *n., pl.* **my·ce·li·a** (-lē ə).

**my·col·o·gist** (mī kol′ə jist) a person trained in MYCOLOGY.

**my·col·o·gy** (mī kol′ə jē) the branch of botany that deals with FUNGI. *n.*

**my·na** or **my·nah** (mī′nə) any of various starlings of Asia that can imitate human speech sounds. *n.*

**my·o·pi·a** (mī ō′pē ə) near-sightedness. Compare with HYPEROPIA. *n.*

**my·op·ic** (mī op′ik) NEAR-SIGHTED. Compare with HYPEROPIC. *adj.*

**myr·i·ad** (mir′ē əd) **1** originally, ten thousand. **2** a very great number: *There are myriads of stars.* **3** countless: *We saw myriad stars that summer night.* 1, 2 *n.*, 3 *adj.*

**myr·i·a·pod** (mir′ē ə pod′) any of a group of ARTHROPODS having a wormlike body with many segments and many legs: *Centipedes and millepedes are myriapods.* *n.*

**myrrh** (mėr) a fragrant, gummy substance with a bitter taste, used in medicines, perfumes, and incense: *Myrrh is obtained from a shrub that grows in the Arabian peninsula and in eastern Africa.* *n.*

**myr·tle** (mėr′tǝl) **1** an evergreen shrub of southern Europe having shiny leaves, fragrant white flowers, and black berries. **2** referring to a family of evergreen trees and shrubs: *The myrtle family includes the myrtle, pimento or allspice, clove, and eucalyptus.* **3** a low, creeping evergreen vine having blue flowers; periwinkle. *n.*

**my·self** (mī self′) **1** a reflexive pronoun, the object of a reflexive verb with **I** as subject: *I hurt myself. I told myself that it didn't really matter.* **2** an intensive pronoun used to emphasize the noun or pronoun it follows: *I will go myself.* **3** my usual self: *I'm sorry I shouted; I'm not myself today.* *pron.*, *pl.* **our·selves.**

**mys·te·ri·ous** (mis tē′rē əs) **1** full of mystery; hard to explain or understand; secret; hidden. **2** suggesting mystery: *a mysterious look.* *adj.* —**mys·te′ri·ous·ly**, *adv.* —**mys·te′ri·ous·ness**, *n.*

**mys·ter·y** (mis′tə rē *or* mis′trē) **1** a secret; something that is hidden or unknown. **2** secrecy; obscurity. **3** a story, play, etc. of suspense, telling of the development and solution of a crime or crimes, or about strange or secret events: *a writer of mysteries.* **4** something that is not explained or understood: *the mystery of the migration of birds.* **5** a religious idea or doctrine that human reason cannot understand. *n.*, *pl.* **mys·ter·ies.**

**mys·tic** (mis′tik) **1** MYSTICAL. **2** a person who believes that truth or God can be known through spiritual insight. 1 *adj.*, 2 *n.*

**mys·ti·cal** (mis′tə kəl) **1** having a spiritual meaning or reality that is beyond human understanding: *the mystical food of the sacrament.* **2** spiritually symbolic: *Many religions have mystical symbols.* **3** of or concerned with mystics or mysticism: *a mystical experience.* **4** of or having to do with secret rites open only to the initiated; cryptic. *adj.* —**mys′ti·cal·ly**, *adv.* —**mys′ti·cal·ness**, *n.*

**mys·ti·cism** (mis′tə siz′əm) **1** the beliefs or mode of thought of MYSTICS. **2** the doctrine that truth or God may be known through spiritual insight, independent of the mind. *n.*

**mys·ti·fi·ca·tion** (mis′tə fə kā′shən) **1** MYSTIFYing or being mystified; bewilderment; perplexity. **2** something that mystifies or is designed to do so. *n.*

hat, āge, fär; let, ēqual, tėrm; it, īce
hot, ōpen, ôrder; oil, out; cup, pùt, rüle
əbove, takən, pencəl, lemən, circəs
ch, child; ng, long; sh, ship
th, thin; ᴛʜ, then; zh, measure

**mys·ti·fy** (mis′tə fī′) **1** bewilder purposely; puzzle; perplex: *The magician's tricks mystified the audience.* **2** make mysterious; involve in mystery. *v.*, **mys·ti·fied, mys·ti·fy·ing.**

**mys·tique** (mis tēk′) **1** a MYSTICAL or peculiar way of interpreting reality. **2** an atmosphere of mystery associated with a particular person, institution, profession, etc. *n.*

**myth** (mith) **1** a legend or story about events in some supernatural world, often attempting to account for something in nature: *The myth of Proserpine is the ancient Greek explanation of summer and winter.* **2** any invented story. **3** an imaginary person or thing: *Her wealthy uncle was a myth invented to impress others.* *n.*
☞ *Syn.* See note at LEGEND.

**myth·i·cal** (mith′ə kəl) **1** of, like, or in myths: *a mythical interpretation of nature, mythical monsters.* **2** not real; made-up; imaginary: *Their wealth is merely mythical.* *adj.* —**myth′i·cal·ly**, *adv.*

**myth·o·log·i·cal** (mith′ə loj′ə kəl) of or having to do with MYTHOLOGY. *adj.* —**myth·o·log′i·cal·ly**, *adv.*

**my·thol·o·gist** (mi thol′ə jist) **1** a writer of MYTHS. **2** a person who knows much about MYTHOLOGY. *n.*

**my·thol·o·gy** (mi thol′ə jē) **1** a body of MYTHS relating to a particular people or person: *Greek mythology.* **2** MYTHS collectively. **3** the study of MYTHS. *n.*, *pl.* **my·thol·o·gies.**

# N n  *N n*

**n** or **N** (en)   1 the fourteenth letter of the English alphabet.   2 any speech sound represented by this letter.   3 a person or thing identified as n, especially the 14th in a series.   *n., pl.* **n's** or **N's.**

**N**   1 nitrogen.   2 North.   3 Northern.   4 newton.

**n**   1 in algebra, an indefinite number.   2 nano–.

**N.** or **N**   1 North.   2 Northern.   3 New.   4 Noon.

**n.**   1 born.   2 name.   3 noun.   4 neuter.   5 north.   6 northern.

**Na**   sodium.

**N.A.**   1 North America.   2 not applicable.

**nab** (nab) *Informal.*   1 catch or seize suddenly; grab.   2 arrest.   *v.,* **nabbed, nab·bing.**

**na·bob** (nā′bob)   1 a provincial governor under the Mogul empire in India.   2 a wealthy person, originally one who had returned to Europe after making a fortune in India.   *n.*

**na·celle** (nə sel′)   an enclosed part of an aircraft containing an engine or passengers.   *n.*

**na·cho** (nä′chō)   a highly flavoured, baked tortilla chip.   *n., pl.* **na·chos.**

**na·cre** (nā′kər)   mother-of-pearl.   *n.*

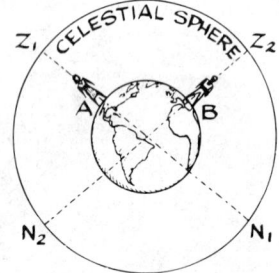

The zenith and nadir for observer A are $Z_1$ and $N_1$. For observer B, the zenith and nadir are $Z_2$ and $N_2$.

**na·dir** (nā′dər)   1 the point in the heavens directly beneath the place where one stands; the point opposite the ZENITH.   2 the lowest point.   *n.*

**NAFTA**   North American Free Trade Agreement.

**nag¹** (nag)   1 find fault or annoy by peevish complaints: *He's always nagging at me to walk faster. If you nag her too much she won't do anything.*   2 continue to cause annoyance, irritation, or pain: *a nagging headache. The thought kept nagging at the back of my mind that I had left the door unlocked.*   *v.,* **nagged, nag·ging.**

**nag²** (nag)   1 a horse, especially one that is old and worn out.   2 a small riding horse; pony.   *n.*

**nail** (nāl)   1 a slender piece of metal to be hammered into or through pieces of wood or other material to hold them together.   2 fasten with a nail or nails.   3 *Informal.* hold or keep fixed: *We should nail him to his promise.*   4 *Informal.* catch; seize.   5 the hard, horny substance covering the upper side of the end of a finger or toe.   1, 5 *n.,* 2–4 *v.*   —**nail′er,** *n.*

**hard as nails,**   a tough; physically fit.   b without pity; merciless.

**hit the nail on the head,** *Informal.*   guess or understand correctly; say or do something just right.

**nail down,**   a fix with nails: *The shingles were nailed down with a hammer.*   b *Informal.* win, settle, or get with certainty: *She nailed down first place in the singing competition.*

**on the nail,**   at once; immediately; without delay.

**nail·set** (nāl′set′)   a tool for driving nails beneath the surface.   *n.*

**nain·sook** (nān′sùk)   a very soft, fine, mercerized cotton cloth in a plain weave.   *n.*

**na·ïve** or **na·ive** (nī ēv′; *French,* nä ēv′)   1 simple in nature; like a child; artless.   2 not sophisticated; inexperienced; showing a lack of informed judgment: *The young woman's behaviour was naïve.*   *adj.*   —**na·ïve′ly** or **na·ive′ly,** *adv.*

**na·ïve·té** or **na·ive·te** (nī ēv′tā *or* nī ēv′ə tā′; *French,* nä ēf tā′)   1 the quality of being naïve; unspoiled freshness.   2 a naïve action, remark, etc.   *n.*

**na·ked** (nā′kid)   1 with no clothes on: *The boys enjoyed swimming naked.*   2 bare; not covered; stripped of usual cover: *The trees stood naked in the snow.*   3 not protected; exposed: *a naked sword.*   4 without addition of anything else; plain: *the naked truth.*   *adj.*   —**na′ked·ly,** *adv.*   —**na′ked·ness,** *n.*

**naked eye,**   the eye alone, not helped by any glass, telescope, or microscope.

**nam·a·ble** (nā′mə bəl)   that can be named.   *adj.*

**nam·by–pam·by** (nam′bē pam′bē)   1 weakly simple or sentimental; insipid: *That valentine is too namby-pamby.*   2 namby-pamby talk or writing.   3 a namby-pamby person.   1 *adj.,* 2, 3 *n., pl.* **nam·by–pam·bies.**

**name** (nām)   1 the word or words by which a person, animal, place, or thing is spoken of or to: *Our dog's name is Chippy. The name of our country is Canada.*   2 give a name to: *They named the baby Mary.*   3 call by name; mention by name: *Three persons were named in the report.*   4 give the right name for: *Can you name these flowers?*   5 a word or words applied descriptively; appellation, title, or epithet: *the name of a friend.*   6 persons grouped under one name; family; clan; tribe.   7 reputation: *Ihor made a name for himself as a writer.*   8 having a reputation that is known by a name: *The plumber buys all his supplies from name manufacturers.*   9 mention or speak of; state: *She named several reasons for her decision.*   10 specify or fix: *to name a price.*   11 nominate; appoint: *Jaime was named captain of the team.*   12 choose; settle on: *They named the day for their wedding.*   1, 5–8 *n.,* 2–4, 9–12 *v.,* **named, nam·ing.**

**call names,**   insult by using bad names; swear at.

**in name only,**   supposed to be, but not really so.

**in the name of,**   a on the authority of; acting for: *He bought the car in the name of his father.*   b for the sake of: *We did it in the name of charity.*

**know only by name,**   know only by hearing about.

**name after** or **for,**   give someone or something the same name as.

**to one's name,**   belonging to one.

**name day**   1 the feast day of the saint whose name one bears.   2 the day on which a child is named; baptismal day.

**name·less** (nām′lis)   1 having no name: *a nameless baby.*   2 not marked with a name: *a nameless grave.*

**3** not named; unknown: *a book by a nameless writer.* **4** that cannot be named or described: *a strange nameless longing.* **5** not fit to be mentioned. **6** unknown to fame; obscure. *adj.* —**name′less·ly,** *adv.* —**name′less·ness,** *n.*

**name·ly** (nām′lē) that is to say: *Only two students got a perfect mark—namely, Louella and Denise.* *adv.*

**name·sake** (nām′sāk′) a person having the same name as another, especially one named after another: *Wilfrid was proud to be the namesake of Sir Wilfrid Laurier.* *n.*

**nan·ny** (nan′ē) **1** *Informal.* a woman hired to look after the children of a family. **2** NANNY GOAT. *n., pl.* **nan·nies.**

**nan·ny goat** (nan′ē) a female goat.

**nano–** (nan′ə) an SI prefix meaning one-billionth: *A nanometre is one one-billionth of a metre.* Symbol: n

**nap**[1] (nap) **1** a short sleep: *Most babies have a nap in the afternoon.* **2** take a short sleep: *Grandfather naps in his armchair.* **1** *n.,* **2** *v.,* **napped, nap·ping. catch napping,** find off guard; take unprepared: *The test caught me napping.*

**nap**[2] (nap) the soft, short, woolly threads or hairs on the surface of cloth: *Velvet and flannelette have a nap.* *n.* —**nap′less,** *adj.*

**na·palm** (nā′pom′ or nā′päm′) **1** a chemical substance used to thicken gasoline for use in certain military weapons. **2** the thickened gasoline. **3** attack or destroy with napalm. **1, 2** *n.,* **3** *v.*

**nape** (nāp) the back of the neck. *n.*

**na·per·y** (nā′pə rē) tablecloths, serviettes, and doilies; table linen. *n.*

**naph·tha** (naf′thə or nap′thə) any of various colourless, often highly flammable liquids distilled from petroleum, coal tar, etc. used as a solvent, paint thinner, etc. *n.*

**naph·tha·lene** (naf′thə lēn′ or nap′thə lēn′) a white crystalline hydrocarbon, usually prepared from coal tar, used in mothballs and in the manufacture of organic compounds such as dyes. *n.*

**naph·thol** (naf′thol or nap′thol) a colourless crystalline substance obtained from NAPHTHALENE, used in making dyes, as an antiseptic, etc. *n.*

**nap·kin** (nap′kin) **1** a piece of cloth or paper used at meals for protecting the clothing or for wiping the lips or fingers; serviette. **2** a baby's diaper. **3** SANITARY NAPKIN. *n.*

**nap·pie** or **nap·py** (nap′ē) **1** a small dish used for serving fruit; a fruit dish. **2** *Esp. Brit.* a baby's diaper or napkin. *n., pl.* **nap·pies.**

**nar·cis·sus** (när sis′əs) a spring plant having yellow or white flowers and growing from a bulb: *Jonquils and daffodils are varieties of narcissus.* *n., pl.* **nar·cis·sus·es** or **nar·cis·si** (-ī or ē).

**nar·co·sis** (när kō′sis) a stupor or state of insensibility, brought about by NARCOTICS or other chemicals. *n.*

**nar·cot·ic** (när kot′ik) **1** a drug that produces drowsiness, sleep, dullness, or an insensible condition, and lessens pain by dulling the nerves: *Opium is a powerful narcotic.* **2** having the properties and effects of a narcotic. **1** *n.,* **2** *adj.*

# namely 787 nasalize

hat, āge, fär; let, ēqual, tėrm; it, īce
hot, ōpen, ôrder, oil, out; cup, put, rüle
above, takən, pencəl, lemən, circəs
ch, child; ng, long; sh, ship
th, thin; ŦH, then; zh, measure

**nar·es** (ner′ēz) the nostrils; nasal passages. *n., pl.* of **nar·is** (ner′is).

**nar·rate** (na rāt′ or nar′āt) **1** tell a story of. **2** tell stories, etc. *v.,* **nar·rat·ed, nar·rat·ing.**

**nar·ra·tion** (na rā′shən) **1** the act of telling. **2** the form of composition that relates an event or a story: *Novels, short stories, histories, and biographies are types of narration.* **3** the verbal accompaniment to certain kinds of films, television programs, etc.: *My sister read the narration for the travelogue.* *n.*

**nar·ra·tive** (nar′ə tiv or ner′ə tiv) **1** story: *His trip through the Far East made an interesting narrative.* **2** the art of narration; story-telling. **3** that narrates: *"Hiawatha" is a narrative poem.* **1, 2** *n.,* **3** *adj.*

**nar·ra·tor** (na rā′tər, nar′ā tər or ner′ā tər) a person who NARRATES. *n.*

**nar·row** (nar′ō or ner′ō) **1** not wide; having little width; of less than the specified, understood, or usual width: *narrow ribbon. A path 30 cm wide is narrow.* **2** limited in extent, space, amount, range, scope, opportunity, etc.: *She had only a narrow circle of friends.* **3** make or become narrow; decrease in width: *The road narrows here.* **4** close; with a small margin: *a narrow escape.* **5** lacking sympathy; not tolerant; prejudiced: *A person who says that all modern art is rubbish has a narrow mind about art.* **6** close; careful; minute: *a narrow scrutiny.* **7** with barely enough to live on: *to live in narrow circumstances.* **8** fix the limits of: *At last we could narrow our search to three places.* **9 narrows,** *pl.* the narrow part of a river, strait, sound, valley, pass, etc. **1, 2, 4–7** *adj.,* **3, 8** *v.,* **9** *n.* —**nar′row·ly,** *adv.* —**nar′row·ness,** *n.*

**nar·row-gauge** (nar′ō gāj′ or ner′ō gāj′) **1** having railway tracks less than 56½ inches (about 130 cm) apart. **2** NARROW-MINDED. *adj.*

**nar·row-mind·ed** (nar′ō mīn′did or ner′ō mīn′did) lacking understanding; blind to other points of view; prejudiced. *adj.* —**nar′row-mind′ed·ly,** *adv.* —**nar′row-mind′ed·ness,** *n.*

**nar·whal** (när′wəl or när′hwəl) a small toothed whale of the arctic seas. The male has a long tusk extending forward from a tooth in the upper jaw. *n.*

**na·sal** (nā′zəl) **1** of, in, or from the nose: *nasal bones, a nasal discharge, nasal passages.* **2** of speech sounds, given a nasal quality by keeping the VELUM lowered: *Three nasal sounds are represented by* m, n *and* ng. **3** a speech sound produced in this way: *A person whose nose is blocked by a cold cannot produce nasals.* **4** of a voice, characterized by resonance produced through the nose: *a nasal voice.* **1, 2, 4** *adj.,* **3** *n.* —**na′sal·ly,** *adv.*

**na·sal·i·ty** (nā zal′ə tē) of a voice or utterance, the quality of being NASAL. *n.*

**na·sal·ize** (nā′zə līz′) utter or speak with a NASAL sound: *Many vowels in French and Portuguese are nasalized.* *v.,* **na·sal·ized, na·sal·iz·ing.**

**nas·cent** (nas′ənt *or* nā′sənt)   in the process of coming into existence; just beginning to exist, grow, or develop: *a nascent tumour, nascent ideas of liberty.*   *adj.*

**nas·ti·ness** (nas′tē nis)   the quality or state of being NASTY: *We were surprised at the nastiness of his tone of voice.*   *n.*

**na·stur·tium** (nə stėr′shəm)   **1** any of a closely related group of plants having yellow, orange, or red flowers, and sharp-tasting seeds and leaves.   **2** the flower.   *n.*
☛ Etym.   From the Latin name, made up of L *nasus* 'nose' and *tortus* 'twisted' (pp. of *torquere* 'twist, torture'), because of the sharpness of the flower's odour. 17c.

**nas·ty** (nas′tē)   **1** disgustingly dirty; filthy: *a nasty room, a nasty word or story, a nasty mind.*   **2** very unpleasant: *nasty weather.*   **3** ill-natured; disagreeable to another: *a nasty temper.*   **4** rather serious; bad: *a nasty accident.*   *adj.*, **nas·ti·er, nas·ti·est.**   —**nas′ti·ly,** *adv.*

**nat.**   **1** national.   **2** native.   **3** natural.

**na·tal** (nā′təl)   of, having to do with, or present at birth: *a natal star. Your natal day is your birthday.*   *adj.*

**na·tant** (nā′tənt)   swimming; floating; represented as swimming.   *adj.*

**na·ta·to·ri·al** (nā′tə tô′rē əl)   having to do with, adapted for, or characterized by swimming: *Ducks are natatorial birds.*   *adj.* Also, **natatory.**

**na·ta·to·ri·um** (nā′tə tô′rē əm)   a swimming pool, especially an indoor one.   *n.*, *pl.* **na·ta·to·ri·ums** or **na·ta·to·ri·a** (-rē ə).

**na·tion** (nā′shən)   **1** a community of people occupying and possessing a defined territory and united under one government; especially, such a community that is politically independent; country; state.   **2** a people having the same descent and social and political history and, usually, sharing a common language; race or tribe: *The Scottish nation, the French-Canadian nation.*   **3 a** a confederacy of North American Indian peoples: *The Iroquois Nation included the Seneca, Mohawk, Oneida, Onondaga, and Cayuga tribes, and later the Tuscarora.*   **4** one of the peoples or tribes making up such a confederacy.   **5 the nation, a** the people of a community as in def. 1: *The prime minister appealed to the nation to support the government's policy of restraint.*   **b** the territory of such a community: *The entire nation experienced unusually cold weather over the weekend.*   *n.*
☛ Usage.   Def. 1, referring to people under an independent government, is the primary meaning of **nation** in English. But in Canadian English def. 2, referring to people with common ties of birth, language, and culture, has in recent years become more widely established. This use of the word has been reinforced by similar uses of the word *nation* in Canadian French.

**na·tion·al** (nash′ə nəl *or* nash′nəl)   **1** of a nation; affecting or belonging to a whole nation: *national laws, a national disaster.*   **2** a citizen of a nation: *Each year many nationals of Canada visit the United States.*   **3** strongly upholding one's own nation; patriotic; nationalistic.   1, 3 *adj.*, 2 *n.*

**National Assembly**   in Quebec, the group of representatives elected to the legislature.

**na·tion·al·ism** (nash′ə nə liz′əm *or* nash′nə liz′əm)   **1** patriotic feelings or efforts.   **2** the desire and plans for national independence.   **3** the desire of a people to preserve its own language, religion, traditions, etc.   *n.*

**na·tion·al·ist** (nash′ə nə list *or* nash′nə list)   **1** an upholder of nationalism; a person who believes in nationalism.   **2** NATIONALISTIC.   1 *n.*, 2 *adj.*

**na·tion·al·is·tic** (nash′ə nə lis′tik *or* nash′nə lis′tik)   **1** of or having to do with NATIONALISM or nationalists.   **2** supporting NATIONALISM: *a very nationalistic speech.*   *adj.*

**na·tion·al·i·ty** (nash′ə nal′ə tē *or* nash′nal′ə tē)   **1** the fact of belonging to a nation: *Ivan's passport showed that his nationality was Canadian.*   **2** the condition of being an independent nation; nationhood.   *n.*, *pl.* **na·tion·al·i·ties.**

**na·tion·al·ize** (nash′ə nə līz′ *or* nash′nə līz′)   **1** make national.   **2** bring land, industries, railways, etc. under the control or ownership of a nation.   **3** make into a nation.   *v.*, **na·tion·al·ized, na·tion·al·iz·ing.**
—**na′tion·al·i·za′tion,** *n.*

**na·tion·al·ly** (nash′ə nə lē *or* nash′nə lē)   **1** in a national manner; as a nation.   **2** throughout the nation: *The opposition leader's speech was broadcast nationally.*   *adv.*

**national park**   land owned by the federal government and kept for people to enjoy because of its beautiful scenery, historical interest, etc.

**na·tion·hood** (nā′shən hud′)   the condition or state of being a nation; the fact of having national existence.   *n.*

**na·tion–wide** (nā′shən wīd′)   extending throughout the nation: *a nation-wide election.*   *adj.*

**na·tive** (nā′tiv)   **1** a person born in a certain place or country: *She is a native of Montreal.*   **2** born in a certain place or country: *He is a native son of Canada.*   **3** belonging to one because of one's birth: *one's native land.*   **4** belonging to one because of one's country or the nation to which one belongs: *one's native language.*   **5** born in a person; natural: *native ability, native courtesy.*   **6** a member of a people who are the traditional inhabitants of a region or country, as contrasted with conquerors, settlers, visitors, etc.   **7** of, having to do with, or referring to people who are natives: *the native peoples of Canada, native customs.*   **8** an animal or plant living in the place where it originated.   **9** originating, grown, or produced in a certain place: *The Manitoba maple is native to Canada.*   **10** found pure in nature: *native copper.*   **11** found in nature; not produced: *Native salt is refined for use.*   1, 6, 8 *n.*, 2–5, 7, 9–11 *adj.*
—**na′tive·ly,** *adv.* —**na′tive·ness,** *n.*
**go native,**   of a conqueror, settler, visitor, etc., give up one's own culture and live as the natives do.

**na·tive–born** (nā′tiv bôrn′)   born in a particular town, country, etc.: *My father is a native-born Canadian, but my mother was born in Iceland.*   *adj.*

**na·tiv·i·ty** (nə tiv′ə tē)   birth.   *n.*, *pl.* **na·tiv·i·ties.**

**natl.**   national.

**NATO** (nā′tō)   North Atlantic Treaty Organization.

**nat·ter** (nat′ər)   **1** talk on at length; chatter: *We could hear her in the other room nattering away on the phone.*   **2** mutter discontentedly; fret.   *v.*

**nat·ty** (nat′ē)   trim and tidy; neatly smart in dress or appearance: *a natty uniform, a natty young officer.*   *adj.*
**nat·ti·er, nat·ti·est.**   —**nat′ti·ly,** *adv.*

**nat·u·ral** (nach′ə rəl *or* nach′rəl)   **1** produced by nature; based on some state of things in nature: *Scenery* has natural beauty. **2** not artificial: *Coal and oil are natural products.* **3** instinctive; inborn: *natural ability. It is natural for ducks to swim.* **4** coming or occurring in the ordinary course of events; normal: *a natural death.* **5** in accordance with the nature of things or the circumstances of the case: *a natural response.* **6** instinctively felt to be right and fair: *natural law, natural rights.* **7** like nature; true to nature: *The picture looked natural.* **8** free from affectation or restraint: *a natural manner.* **9** of or having to do with nature: *the natural sciences.* **10** concerned with natural science. **11** based on what is learned from nature: *natural religion.* **12** that which is natural. **13** in music, neither sharp nor flat; without sharps and flats. **14** neither sharped nor flatted: *C natural.* **15** in music, a natural tone or note. **16** a sign (♮) used to cancel the effect of a preceding sharp or flat. **17** having the pitch affected by the natural sign. **18** a white key on the piano. **19** a half-witted person. **20** by birth, but not legally recognized; illegitimate: *a natural son.* **21** *Informal.* a person who seems especially suited for something: *He's a natural for the football team.* 1–11, 13, 14, 17, 20 *adj.*, 12, 15, 16, 18, 19, 21 *n.* —**nat′u·ral·ness,** *n.*

**natural gas** a combustible gas commonly used as a fuel, that occurs dissolved in petroleum and is also found in separate natural deposits in the earth: *Natural gas consists of methane and other hydrocarbons.*

**natural history** **1** the study of animals, plants, minerals, and other things in nature. **2** a book or article on some aspect of nature.

**nat·u·ral·ism** (nach′ə rə liz′əm *or* nach′rə liz′əm) in art and literature, a style characterized by a realistic and objective portrayal of life, nature, etc. *n.*

**nat·u·ral·ist** (nach′ə rə list *or* nach′rə list) **1** a person who studies animals and plants; a field biologist. **2** a person who supports or practises NATURALISM. **3** naturalistic. 1, 2 *n.*, 3 *adj.*

**nat·u·ral·is·tic** (nach′ə rə lis′tik *or* nach′rə lis′tik) **1** of, having to do with, or characterized by NATURALISM: *a naturalistic painting.* **2** of natural history or naturalists. *adj.*

**nat·u·ral·ize** (nach′ə rə līz′ *or* nach′rə līz′) **1** grant the rights of citizenship to persons native to other countries; admit a foreigner to citizenship: *The government naturalizes many New Canadians every year. My father is a naturalized Canadian but my mother was born here.* **2** adopt a foreign word or custom: "*Chauffeur*" *is a French word that has been naturalized in English.* **3** introduce and make at home in another country: *The English sparrow has become naturalized in parts of Canada.* **4** make natural; free from conventional characteristics. **5** regard or explain as natural rather than supernatural. **6** become like a native. *v.*, **nat·u·ral·ized, nat·u·ral·iz·ing.** —**nat′u·ral·i·za′tion,** *n.*

**nat·u·ral·ly** (nach′ə rə lē *or* nach′rə lē) **1** in a natural way: *to speak naturally.* **2** by nature: *a naturally obedient child.* **3** as might be expected; of course: *Naturally, I accepted her gift.* *adv.*

**natural magnet** a piece of MAGNETITE; loadstone.

**natural number** any positive whole number: *The numbers 1 and 2 are natural numbers; −1 and −2 are not.*

**natural resource** a kind of material that is supplied by nature and is useful or necessary to people: *Minerals and water power are natural resources.*

---

**natural gas** 789 **nautical mile**

hat, āge, fär; let, ēqual, tėrm; it, īce
hot, ōpen, ôrder; oil, out; cup, put, rüle
ə*bove,* tak*ə*n, penc*ə*l, lem*ə*n, circ*ə*s
ch, child; ng, long; sh, ship
th, thin; ᴛʜ, then; zh, measure

**natural science** any of the sciences that deal with nature and the physical world, including biology, chemistry, physics, and geology.

**natural selection** the process by which animals and plants best adapted to their environment tend to survive.

**na·ture** (nā′chər) **1** the world; all things except those made by human beings. **2** the sum total of the forces at work throughout the universe: *the laws of nature.* **3** the instincts or inherent tendencies directing conduct: *It is against nature for a mother to kill her child.* **4** reality: *true to nature.* **5** a primitive, wild condition; condition of human beings before social organization. **6** the qualities or abilities with which a person or animal is born; character; way or manner: *It is the nature of birds to fly. She has a kind nature.* **7** sort; kind: *Books of a scientific nature do not interest Helen.* **8** physical being; vital powers: *food sufficient to sustain nature.* **9 Nature,** the personification of all natural facts and forces. *n.*
**by nature,** because of the essential character of the person or thing.
**of** or **in the nature of,** having the nature of; being a kind of.

**nature study** the study of animals, plants, and other things and events in nature.

**naught** (not) nothing: *All his work went for naught.* *n.*
☛ *Hom.* **Naught,** KNOT, NOT, and NOUGHT are pronounced the same (to rhyme with *got*) by most Canadians.

**naugh·ti·ness** (not′ē nis) bad behaviour; disobedience; mischief. *n.*

**naugh·ty** (not′ē) **1** bad; not obedient: *The naughty children strayed too far from home.* **2** somewhat improper: *a naughty story.* *adj.,* **naugh·ti·er, naugh·ti·est.** —**naugh′ti·ly,** *adv.* —**naugh′ti·ness,** *n.*
☛ *Hom.* KNOTTY.

**nau·se·a** (noz′ē ə *or* nosh′ə) **1** the feeling that one has when about to vomit. **2** extreme disgust; loathing. *n.*
☛ *Etym.* Through Latin from Gk. *nausia* 'seasickness' which, like NAUTICAL, developed from Gk. *naus* 'ship'. 16c. See also the note at NOISE.

**nau·se·ate** (noz′ē āt′ *or* nos′ē āt′) **1** cause NAUSEA in; make sick. **2** feel NAUSEA; become sick. **3** cause to feel loathing. *v.,* **nau·se·at·ed, nau·se·at·ing.**

**nau·se·ous** (noz′e əs *or* nosh′əs) **1** causing NAUSEA; sickening. **2** affected with nausea or disgust. *adj.*
—**nau′seous·ly,** *adv.*

**naut.** nautical.

**nau·ti·cal** (not′ə kəl) of or having to do with ships, sailors, or navigation. *adj.* —**nau′ti·cal·ly,** *adv.*
☛ *Etym.* Through Latin from Gk. *nautikos,* which developed from *naus* 'ship'. 16c. See also the notes at NAUSEA and NAVAL.

**nautical mile** a unit for measuring distance in air and sea navigation, equal to 1852 metres. *Abbrev.:* n.mi.

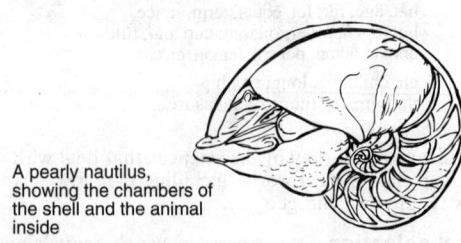
A pearly nautilus, showing the chambers of the shell and the animal inside

**nau·ti·lus** (nȯt′ə ləs)    either of two kinds of mollusc. See PEARLY NAUTILUS and PAPER NAUTILUS.   *n., pl.* **nau·ti·lus·es** or **nau·ti·li** (-lī′ or -lē′).

**Nav·a·ho** or **Nav·a·jo** (nav′ə hō′)    a member of a Native American people living in New Mexico, Arizona, and Utah.   *n., pl.* **Nav·a·ho** or **Nav·a·hos, Nav·a·jo** or **Nav·a·jos.**

**na·val** (nā′vəl)    **1** of or for warships or the navy: *a naval officer, naval supplies.*   **2** having a navy: *the naval powers.*   *adj.*   —**nav′al·ly,** *adv.*
☞ *Hom.* NAVEL.
☞ *Etym.*   **Naval,** NAVIGABLE, NAVIGATE and related words all developed from L *navis* 'ship', related to Gk. *naus.* NAVE comes from a special use of *navis* in Medieval Latin. See also notes at NAUSEA and NAUTICAL.

**nave** (nāv)    the main part of a church or cathedral between the side aisles. See BASILICA for picture.   *n.*
☞ *Hom.*   KNAVE.
☞ *Etym.*   See note at NAVAL.

**na·vel** (nā′vəl)    the small scar, usually a hollow, in the middle of the abdomen, marking the place where the umbilical cord was attached before and at birth.   *n.*
☞ *Hom.*   NAVAL.
☞ *Etym.*   From OE *nafela,* related to OE *nafu* 'hub of a wheel'.

**navel orange**    a seedless orange having a small growth that resembles a NAVEL in shape and contains a small secondary fruit.

**nav·i·ga·bil·i·ty** (nav′ə gə bil′ə tē)    the fact or quality of being NAVIGABLE.   *n.*

**nav·i·ga·ble** (nav′ə gə bəl)    **1** that ships can travel on: *The St. Lawrence River is deep enough to be navigable.* **2** seaworthy: *a ship in navigable condition.*   **3** that can be steered: *a navigable balloon.*   *adj.*
☞ *Etym.*   See note at NAVAL.

**nav·i·gate** (nav′ə gāt′)    **1** sail, manage, or steer a ship, aircraft, etc.   **2** sail on or over a sea, river, etc.: *Many ships navigate the St. Lawrence Seaway each year.*   **3** travel by water; sail.   **4** convey goods by water.   **5** sail through the air in an airship, etc.   **6** plot the position and course of a ship, aircraft, vehicle, etc.   **7** move; find one's way: *The old woman could hardly navigate along the icy streets.*   *v.,* **nav·i·gat·ed, nav·i·gat·ing.**
☞ *Etym.*   See note at NAVAL.

**nav·i·ga·tion** (nav′ə gā′shən)    **1** the act or process of navigating.   **2** the science of determining the position, course, and distance travelled of a ship, aircraft, or spacecraft.   *n.*

**nav·i·ga·tor** (nav′ə gā′tər)    **1** a person who is qualified to NAVIGATE: *The ship took on a special navigator to guide her through the dangerous waters. He served as a navigator in the air force.*   **2** a person who sails the seas as an explorer: *a story of one of the early navigators.*   *n.*

**nav·jo·te** (nav′jō tē′)    in Zoroastrianism, the initiation ceremony in which boys and girls, before puberty, are instructed concerning their religious duties and are received into full membership.   *n.*

**nav·vy** (nav′ē) *Brit.*    an unskilled labourer who works on canals, railways, roads, etc.   *n., pl.* **nav·vies.**

**na·vy** (nā′vē)    **1** all the ships of war of a country, with their personnel.   **2** in Canada, the function of a navy is served by the Maritime Command of the CANADIAN ARMED FORCES.   **3** the personnel of the navy.   **4** dark blue.   1–4 *n., pl.* **na·vies;**   4 *adj.*

**navy bean**    the common white bean, dried for use.

**navy blue**    dark blue.

**na·wab** (nə wob′)    **1** formerly in India, a title of a governor or nobleman.   **2** in Pakistan, a title of a distinguished Moslem.   *n.*

**Naw Ruz** (nä rüz′)    in Bahaism and Zoroastrianism, the New Year festival celebrated at the vernal equinox.   *n.*

**nay** (nā)    **1** not only that, but also: *We are willing, nay, eager to go.*   **2** no; a denial or refusal.   **3** a negative vote or voter: *The nays outnumbered the yeas.*   1 *adv.,* 2, 3 *n.*
☞ *Hom.*   NÉE, NEIGH.

**Nb**    niobium.

**NB**    New Brunswick.

**N.B.**    New Brunswick.

**N.B.** or **n.b.**    nota bene.

**N.C.O.**    non-commissioned officer.

**n.d.**    no date.

**Nd**    neodymium.

**NDP** or **N.D.P.**    New Democratic Party.

**Ne**    neon.

**N.E., NE,** or **n.e.**    **1** northeast.   **2** northeastern.

**Ne·an·der·thal man** (nē an′dər täl′ *or* nē an′dər thol′)    an extinct race or species, widespread in Europe in the early Stone Age.

**neap** (nēp)    **1** of, having to do with, or referring to a NEAP TIDE.   **2** NEAP TIDE.   1 *adj.,* 2 *n.*

**neap tide**    the tide that occurs when the difference in height between high and low tide is least; the lowest level of high tide: *Neap tide comes twice a month.*

**near** (nēr)    **1** close; not far: *My birthday is coming near.*   **2** closely: *tribes near allied.*   **3** close by; not distant; less distant: *The post office is quite near.*   **4** close to in space, time, condition, etc.: *Our house is near the river.*   **5** come or draw near; approach: *The ship neared the land.*   **6** intimate; familiar: *a near friend.*   **7** closely related: *a near relative.*   **8** *Informal.* all but; almost: *He was near crazy with fright.*   **9** approximating or resembling closely: *near silk, near beer.*   **10** left (opposed to *off,* or *right*): *The near horse and the off horse make a team.*   **11** short; direct: *Go by the nearest route.*   **12** stingy.   **13** by a close margin: *a near escape.*   1, 2, 8 *adv.,* 3, 6, 7, 9–13 *adj.,* 4 *prep.,* 5 *v.*   —**near′ness,** *n.*

**come near doing,**    almost do: *I came near forgetting my glasses.*

**near at hand,**    **a** within easy reach: *My pen is always near at hand.*   **b** not far in the future.

**near·by** (nēr′bī′ for adverb, nēr′bī′ for adjective) **1** near; close at hand: *They live in a nearby house.* **2** near; close at hand: *They live nearby.*   1 *adj.,* 2 *adv.*

**Near East** the countries of southwestern Asia (including Saudi Arabia, Lebanon, Iran, Israel, etc.) and Egypt.
☛ *Usage.* The term MIDDLE EAST, which often refers to a broader area, is now more commonly used than **Near East**.

**near·ly** (nēr′lē) **1** almost: *I nearly missed the train.* **2** closely: *a matter that concerns you very nearly.* *adv.*

**near–sight·ed** (nēr′sī′tid) having a condition of the eyes in which the visual images of distant objects come to a focus before they reach the retina, so that they are not clear: *A near-sighted person has better vision for nearby objects than for distant objects.* Compare with FAR-SIGHTED. *adj.* —**near′-sight′ed·ly,** *adv.* —**near′-sight′ed·ness,** *n.*

**neat** (nēt) **1** clean and in order: *a neat desk, a neat room, a neat dress.* **2** able and willing to keep things in order: *She's a very neat person.* **3** well-formed; in proportion: *a neat design.* **4** skilful; clever: *a neat trick.* **5** especially of alcoholic liquor, not having anything mixed in it; undiluted; straight: *He prefers his whisky neat.* *adj.* —**neat′ly,** *adv.* —**neat′ness,** *n.*

**neat·en** (nē′tən) make neat; tidy up. *v.*

**neat′s–foot oil** (nēts′fut′) an oil obtained especially from the feet and shinbones of cattle by boiling, and used to soften leather.

**neb·u·la** (neb′yə lə) a cloudlike cluster of stars or a mass of dust particles visible in the sky at night. *n., pl.* **neb·u·lae** (-lē or -lī) or **neb·u·las.**

**neb·u·lar** (neb′yə lər) of or concerning a NEBULA or nebulae. *adj.*

**nebular hypothesis** the hypothesis that the sun and planets developed from a luminous mass of gas.

**neb·u·los·i·ty** (neb′yə los′ə tē) **1** the quality or state of being NEBULOUS. **2** a cloudlike matter. *n., pl.* **neb·u·los·i·ties.**

**neb·u·lous** (neb′yə ləs) **1** hazy; vague; indistinct: *Our holiday plans are still somewhat nebulous.* **2** of, having to do with, or resembling a NEBULA; nebular. *adj.* —**neb′u·lous·ly,** *adv.*

**nec·es·sar·i·ly** (nes′ə ser′ə lē or nes′ə ser′ə lē) because of necessity; because it must be; invariably or inevitably: *Leaves are not necessarily green. War necessarily causes misery and waste.* *adv.*

**nec·es·sar·y** (nes′ə ser′ē) **1** that must be, be had, or be done; inevitable; required; indispensable: *Death is a necessary end.* **2** something essential; something that cannot be done without: *Food, clothing, and shelter are necessaries of life.* **1** *adj.,* **2** *n., pl.* **nec·es·sar·ies.**

**ne·ces·si·tate** (nə ses′ə tāt′) make necessary: *Her broken leg necessitated a surgical operation.* *v.,* **ne·ces·si·tat·ed, ne·ces·si·tat·ing.**

**ne·ces·si·tous** (nə ses′ə təs) **1** very poor; needy. **2** necessary; essential. **3** urgent. *adj.*

**ne·ces·si·ty** (nə ses′ə tē) **1** the fact of being necessary; extreme need: *the necessity of eating.* **2** the quality of being necessary. **3** anything that cannot be done without: *Water is a necessity.* **4** that which forces one to act in a certain way: *Necessity sometimes drives people to do disagreeable things.* **5** that which is inevitable: *Night follows day as a necessity.* **6** need; poverty: *a family in great necessity.* *n., pl.* **ne·ces·si·ties.**
**of necessity,** because it must be: *We left early of necessity; there is no bus service at night.*

hat, āge, fär; let, ēqual, tėrm; it, īce
hot, ōpen, ôrder; oil, out; cup, pùt, rüle
əbove, takən, pencəl, lemən, circəs
ch, child; ng, long; sh, ship
th, thin; ᴛʜ, then; zh, measure

**neck** (nek) **1** the part of the body that connects the head with the shoulders. **2** the part of a garment that fits around the neck. **3** any narrow part like a neck: *a neck of land, the neck of a vase.* **4** a narrow strip of land. **5** the slender part of a bottle, flask, retort, or other container. **6** the lowest part of the capital of a column. **7** the part of a tooth between the crown and the root. **8** in racing, the length of the neck of a horse or other animal as a measure. *n.*
**neck and neck, a** abreast. **b** being equal or even in a race or contest: *The two horses ran neck and neck for a kilometre.*
**neck or nothing,** venturing all.
**risk one's neck,** put oneself in a dangerous position; risk one's life.
**stick one's neck out,** *Informal.* put oneself in a dangerous or vulnerable position by foolish or zealous action.

**neck·er·chief** (nek′ər chif) a square of cloth worn around the neck. *n.*

**neck·lace** (nek′lis) a string of jewels, gold, silver, beads, etc. worn around the neck as an ornament. *n.*

**neck·line** (nek′līn′) the line formed by the neck opening of a garment: *a plain neckline, a low neckline.* *n.*

**neck·piece** (nek′pēs′) a separate article of clothing, such as a scarf, worn around the neck: *a fur neckpiece.* *n.*

**neck·tie** (nek′tī′) a TIE (def. 7). *n.*

**neck·wear** (nek′wer′) collars, ties, and other articles that are worn around the neck. *n.*

**nec·ro–** combining form. death, dead body, dead tissue.
☛ *Etym.* From the combining form of Gk. *nekros* 'corpse'.

**ne·crol·o·gy** (ni krol′ə jē) **1** a list of persons who have recently died. **2** a notice of a person's death; obituary. *n., pl.* **ne·crol·o·gies.**

**nec·ro·man·cer** (nek′rə man′sər) **1** a person who is supposed to foretell the future by communicating with the dead. **2** a magician; sorcerer; wizard. *n.*

**nec·ro·man·cy** (nek′rə man′sē) **1** a supposed foretelling of the future by communicating with the dead. **2** magic; enchantment; sorcery. *n.*

**ne·crop·o·lis** (ne krop′ə lis) CEMETERY. *n., pl.* **ne·crop·o·lis·es.**

**ne·cro·sis** (ni krō′sis) **1** the death or decay of body tissues. **2** a disease of plants characterized by small black spots of decayed tissue. *n., pl.* **ne·cro·ses** (-sēz).

**nec·tar** (nek′tər) **1** in Greek and Roman mythology, the drink of the gods. **2** any delicious drink. **3** a sweet liquid found in many flowers: *Bees gather nectar and make it into honey.* *n.* —**nec′tar·like′,** *adj.*

**nec·tar·ine** (nek′tə rēn′ or nek′tə rēn′) a kind of peach having no down on its skin. *n.*

**nec·ta·ry** (nek′tə rē) the part of a flower that secretes NECTAR (def. 3). *n., pl.* **nec·ta·ries.**

**née or nee** (nā) born. *Née* may be placed after the name of a married woman to indicate her maiden name: *Mrs. Tymchuk, née Adams.* *adj.*
☞ *Hom.* NAY, NEIGH.

**need** (nēd) **1** want; lack of a useful or desired thing: *The loss by our team showed the need of practice.* **2** a useful or desired thing that is lacking: *In the desert their need was water.* **3** have need of; want; require: *to need money.* **4** necessity; something that has to be; requirement: *There is no need to hurry.* **5** be necessary: *Something needs to be done to save it.* **6** must; should; have to; ought to: *He need not go. Need she go?* **7** a situation or time of difficulty: *a friend in need.* **8** extreme poverty: *This family's need was so great the children were underfed.* **9** be in want: *Give to those that need.* 1, 2, 4, 7, 8 *n.*, 3, 5, 6, 9 *v.*
**have need to,** must; should; have to; ought to.
**if need be,** if it has to be.
☞ *Hom.* KNEAD.

**need·ful** (nēd′fəl) needed; necessary: *a needful change.* *adj.* —**need′ful·ly,** *adv.*

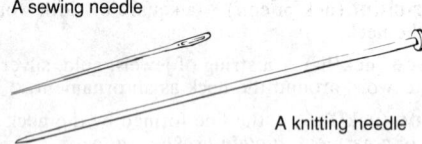
A sewing needle
A knitting needle

**nee·dle** (nē′dəl) **1** a slender tool, pointed at one end with a hole, or eye, at the other to pass a thread through, used in sewing. **2** a slender rod used in knitting. **3** a thin steel pointer on a compass or on electrical machinery. **4** a slender tube with a sharp point, used for injecting or extracting something: *The doctor jabbed the needle into my arm.* **5** an instrument resembling a needle, used in etching and engraving. **6** a phonograph needle; STYLUS (def. 2). **7** a slender, needle-shaped rod that controls the opening of a valve. **8** the needle-shaped leaf of the fir, pine, spruce, or larch. **9** a pillar; obelisk: *Cleopatra's needle.* **10** *Informal.* tease; goad or incite: *The boys needled him into losing his temper.* 1-9 *n.*, 10 *v.*,
**nee·dled, nee·dling.**

**nee·dle·fish** (nē′dəl fish′) any of a family of sea fishes having a long, pipelike body, a long snout, and many sharp teeth. *n.*

**nee·dle·point** (nē′dəl point′) **1** embroidery in even stitches made on coarse, stiff cloth and used for chair covers, footstools, etc. **2** of, having to do with, or made or decorated with such embroidery. *n.*

**need·less** (nēd′lis) not needed; unnecessary: *needless worry.* *adj.* —**need′less·ly,** *adv.* —**need′less·ness,** *n.*

**needle valve** a valve whose very small opening is controlled by a slender, needle-shaped rod.

**nee·dle·wom·an** (nē′dəl wùm′ən) a woman who does needlework, especially one who earns her living by sewing. *n., pl.* **nee·dle·wom·en** (-wim′ən).

**nee·dle·work** (nē′dəl wėrk′) work done with a needle, especially handwork such as embroidery, needlepoint, or fine hand sewing. *n.*

**need·n't** (nēd′ənt) need not.

**needs** (nēdz) because of necessity; necessarily: *A soldier needs must go where duty calls.* *adv.*

**need·y** (nēd′ē) very poor; not having enough to live on: *a needy family.* *adj.*, **need·i·er, need·i·est.** —**need′i·ness,** *n.*

**ne'er–do–well** (ner′dü wel′) **1** a worthless fellow; a good-for-nothing person. **2** worthless; good-for-nothing. 1 *n.*, 2 *adj.*

**ne·far·i·ous** (ni fer′ē əs) very wicked; villainous. *adj.* —**ne·far′i·ous·ly,** *adv.*

**ne·gate** (ni gāt′) deny; nullify. *v.*, **ne·gat·ed, ne·gat·ing.**

**ne·ga·tion** (ni gā′shən) **1** a denying; denial: *Shaking the head is a sign of negation.* **2** the absence or opposite of some positive thing or quality: *Darkness is the negation of light.* *n.*

**neg·a·tive** (neg′ə tiv) **1** saying no: *Her answer was negative.* **2** a word or statement that says no or denies: *"I won't" is a negative.* **3** say no to; deny; vote against: *Mother negatived our plan.* **4** the side that says no or argues against a question being debated; side opposing the AFFIRMATIVE. **5** disprove. **6** not positive or helpful: *Not being unkind is only negative kindness.* **7** a negative quality or characteristic. **8** minus; counting down from zero: *Three below zero is a negative quantity.* **9** a minus quantity, sign, etc. **10** having more electrons than protons: *a negative particle.* **11** of or having to do with the kind of electricity produced on resin when it is rubbed with silk. **12** the negative element in an electric cell. See DRY CELL for picture. **13** showing the lights and shadows reversed: *the negative image on a photographic plate.* **14** a photographic image in which the lights and shadows are reversed: *Prints are made from negatives.* **15** make useless; counteract; neutralize. **16** the right of veto. **17** showing an absence of the germs, symptoms, etc. of an illness. 1, 6, 8, 10, 11, 13, 17 *adj.*, 2, 4, 7, 9, 12, 14, 16 *n.*, 3, 5, 15 *v.*, **neg·a·tived, neg·a·tiv·ing.** —**neg′at·ive·ly,** *adv.*
**in the negative,** **a** in favour of denying a request, suggestion, etc. **b** expressing disagreement by saying no; denying: *Most of the replies were in the negative.*
☞ *Usage.* **Double negatives.** Two negatives should not be used in a sentence where only one is required. *She won't tell us nothing* should be corrected to *She'll tell us nothing* or *She won't tell us anything.* Double negatives were used in and before Shakespeare's time, but they are no longer accepted in standard English. See also note at HARDLY.

**neg·a·tiv·ism** (neg′ə ti viz′əm) a tendency to say or do the opposite of what is suggested. *n.*

**neg·lect** (ni glekt′) **1** give little care, respect, or attention to: *to neglect one's health. He neglected his lawyer's advice.* **2** leave undone; not attend to: *The maid neglected her work.* **3** omit; fail: *Don't neglect to water the plants.* **4** the act or fact of neglecting; disregard: *His neglect of the truth was astonishing.* **5** a want of attention to what should be done: *That car has been ruined by neglect.* **6** being neglected: *The children suffered from neglect.* 1-3 *v.*, 4-6 *n.* —**neg·lect′er,** *n.*

**neg·lect·ful** (ni glekt′fəl) careless; negligent: *A person who does not vote is neglectful of his or her duty.* *adj.* —**neg·lect′ful·ly,** *adv.*

**neg·li·gee** (neg′lə zhā′) a woman's loose, often sheer, dressing gown. *n.*

**neg·li·gence** (neg′lə jəns) **1** a lack of proper care or attention; neglect: *criminal negligence. Because of the owner's negligence, the house was in great need of repair.* **2** carelessness; indifference. *n.*

**neg·li·gent** (neg′lə jənt) 1 neglectful; given to neglect; showing neglect. 2 careless; indifferent: *His negligent behaviour resulted in an accident.* *adj.*
—**neg′li·gent·ly**, *adv.*

**neg·li·gi·ble** (neg′lə jə bəl) that can be disregarded; of little importance; trifling: *The difference in price between the two suits was negligible, so he was free to choose either one.* *adj.*

**ne·go·tia·bil·i·ty** (ni gō′shə bil′ə tē) being NEGOTIABLE. *n.*

**ne·go·ti·a·ble** (ni gō′shə bəl) 1 capable of being NEGOTIATED or sold; whose ownership can be transferred. 2 that can be got past or over. *adj.*

**ne·go·ti·ate** (ni gō′shē āt′) 1 talk over and arrange terms; parley; confer; consult: *The rebels negotiated for peace with the government.* 2 arrange for: *They finally negotiated a peace treaty. We negotiated the sale of our house.* 3 sell. 4 get past or over: *The driver negotiated the sharp curve by slowing down.* *v.*, **ne·go·ti·at·ed**, **ne·go·ti·at·ing**. —**ne·go′ti·a′tor**, *n.*

**ne·go·ti·a·tion** (ni gō′shē ā′shən) talking over and arranging; arrangement: *Negotiations for the new school are finished.* *n.*

**neigh** (nā) 1 the sound that a horse makes. 2 make this sound or one like it. 1 *n.*, 2 *v.*
☛ *Hom.* NAY, NÉE.

**neigh·bour** or **neigh·bor** (nā′bər) 1 a person who lives near another: *We asked our next-door neighbours to take in our mail while we were away. Their nearest neighbours are 20 kilometres away.* 2 a person or thing that is near another: *The big tree brought down several of its smaller neighbours as it fell.* 3 be near or next to; adjoin. 4 living or situated near or next to another; neighbouring. 5 a fellow human being: *One should be kind to one's neighbour.* 6 be friendly with. 1, 2, 4, 5 *n.*, 3, 6 *v.*

**neigh·bour·hood** or **neigh·bor·hood** (nā′bər hùd′) 1 the region near some place or thing: *She lives in the neighbourhood of the mill.* 2 a place; district: *Is your new house in an attractive neighbourhood?* 3 the people of a place or district: *The whole neighbourhood came to the party.* 4 neighbourly feeling or conduct. 5 of or having to do with a neighbourhood: *a neighbourhood newspaper.* 6 nearness. *n.*
**in the neighbourhood** or **neighborhood of**, somewhere near; about: *The car cost in the neighbourhood of $24 000.*

**neigh·bour·ing** or **neigh·bor·ing** (nā′bə ring) living or being near; bordering; adjoining: *We heard the bird calls from the neighbouring woods.* *adj.*

**neigh·bour·ly** or **neigh·bor·ly** (nā′bər lē) of, having to do with, or characteristic of neighbours who get along with each other; especially, sociable or kindly: *a neighbourly chat, a neighbourly atmosphere.* *adj.*
—**neigh′bour·li·ness** or **neigh·bor·li·ness**, *n.*

**nei·ther** (nē′ᴛHər *or* nī′ᴛHər) 1 not either: *Neither you nor I will go (conj.). Neither statement is true (adj.). Neither of the statements is true (pron.).* 2 nor yet; nor: *They didn't go; neither did we.* 1, 2 *conj.*, 1 *adj.*, 1 *pron.*

**nem·a·to·cyst** (nem′ə tə sist′ *or* nə mat′ə sist′) one of the tiny stinging organs of jellyfish, and other COELENTERATES: *Each nematocyst contains a coiled thread that can be projected as a sting.* *n.*

**nem·a·tode** (nem′ə tōd′) any of a class of worms having a long, unsegmented, round body: *Some nematodes,*

hat, āge, fär; let, ēqual, tėrm; it, īce
hot, ōpen, ôrder; oil, out; cup, pùt, rüle
əbove, takən, pencəl, lemən, circəs
ch, child; ng, long; sh, ship
th, thin; ᴛH, then; zh, measure

*such as hookworms, pinworms, and trichinae, are parasites in human beings and animals.* *n.*

**nem·e·sis** (nem′ə sis) 1 just punishment for evil deeds. 2 a person who punishes another for evil deeds; the agent of just punishment. 3 any person or thing that seems to have the power to defeat: *When he saw his opponent, he knew he had met his nemesis.* *n., pl.* **nem·e·ses** (-sēz′).
☛ *Etym.* From the name of *Nemesis*, the goddess of vengeance and retribution in Greek mythology; the punisher of excessive pride.

**neo**– a prefix meaning new or recent, as in *neophyte*.

**ne·o·dym·i·um** (nē′ō dim′ē əm) a rare metallic element found in certain rare minerals. Symbol: Nd *n.*

**ne·o·fas·cism** (nē′ō fash′iz əm) any movement to restore the former beliefs or principles of FASCISM. *n.*

**ne·o·lith·ic** (nē′ə lith′ik) of the later Stone Age, when polished stone weapons and tools were made and used: *neolithic man.* *adj.*

**ne·ol·o·gism** (nē ol′ə jiz′əm) a new word. *n.*

**ne·o·my·cin** (nē′ō mī′sən) an antibiotic or mixture of antibiotics produced by certain bacteria found in the soil. *n.*

**ne·on** (nē′on) an element that is a colourless, odourless gas, found in very small quantities in the atmosphere: *Neon is used in electric lights and signs because it gives off a glow when electricity is passed through it in a low-pressure tube.* Symbol: Ne *n.*

**ne·o·phyte** (nē′ə fīt′) 1 a new convert; one recently admitted to a religious body. 2 a beginner; novice. *n.*

**ne·o·prene** (nē′ə prēn′) a synthetic rubber made from chloroprene. *n.*

**ne·pen·the** (ni pen′thē) 1 a drug or potion used by the ancient Greeks to bring forgetfulness of trouble or sorrow. 2 anything that brings forgetfulness. *n.*

**neph·ew** (nef′yü) 1 a son of one's brother or sister. 2 a son of a brother or sister of one's spouse. *n.*

**ne·phrit·ic** (ni frit′ik) 1 of, having to do with, or located near the kidneys; renal. 2 of, having to do with, or affected with NEPHRITIS, a kidney disease. *adj.*

**ne·phri·tis** (ni frī′tis) acute or chronic inflammation of the kidney, caused by infection, degeneration of tissue, or disease of the blood vessels. *n.*

**neph·ron** (nef′ron) any of the minute tubular structures in the kidney, responsible for filtering out wastes from the blood. *n.*

**ne plus ul·tra** (nē plus′ ul′trə) *Latin.* the highest or furthest point attainable; height of excellence or achievement; culmination.

**nep·o·tism** (nep′ə tiz′əm) the showing of too much favour by someone in power to relatives, especially by giving them desirable appointments. *n.*

**Nep·tune** (nep′tyün *or* nep′tün) a large planet of the solar system, eighth in order from the sun: *Neptune is so*

far away from earth that it cannot be seen with the naked eye.  *n.*
☞ *Etym.* From *Neptune*, in Roman mythology, the god of the sea, corresponding to the Greek god Poseidon.

**nep·tu·ni·um** (nep tyü′nē əm *or* nep tü′nē əm)  a radio-active element chemically similar to uranium, obtained as a by-product in the production of plutonium. *Symbol:* Np  *n.*

**ner·va·tion** (nėr vā′shən)  the arrangement of veins or ribs in a leaf or an insect's wing.  *n.*

**nerve** (nėrv)  **1** a fibre or bundle of fibres connecting the brain or spinal cord with the eyes, ears, muscles, glands, etc.  **2** mental strength; courage: *The diver lost her nerve and wouldn't go off the high board.*  **3** strength; vigour; energy.  **4** put strength or courage in: *The soldiers nerved themselves for the battle.*  **5** *Informal.* rude boldness; impudence.  **6** a vein of a leaf.  **7** one of the thicker lines in an insect's wing.  **8 nerves**, *pl.*
**a** nervousness.  **b** an attack of nervousness.  1–3, 5–8 *n.*, 4 *v.*, **nerved, nerv·ing.**
**get on one's nerves**, *Informal.*  annoy or irritate one.
**strain every nerve**,  exert oneself to the utmost.

**nerve cell**  **1** the basic functional unit of nerve tissue, that conducts nervous impulses; NEURON.  **2** the cell body of a NEURON, excluding its fibres.  See NEURON for picture.

**nerve centre**  **1** a group of NERVE CELLS closely connected with one another and having a common function.  **2** a source of leadership or energy; a control centre or headquarters: *the economic nerve centre of the nation.*

**nerve fibre**  one of the long, threadlike fibres of a nerve cell that conduct impulses toward or away from the body of the nerve cell.

**nerve·less** (nėrv′lis)  **1** without strength or vigour; feeble; weak: *The gun dropped from his nerveless hand.*  **2** without courage or firmness.  **3** without NERVES (def. 8).  *adj.*  —**nerve′less·ly,** *adv.*

**nerve·wrack·ing** *or* **nerve–wrack·ing** (nėr′vrak ing)  trying to the limit of endurance; exasperating: *a nervewracking experience.*  *adj.*

**nerv·ous** (nėr′vəs)  **1** of the nerves: *The brain is a part of the nervous system.*  **2** having delicate or easily excited nerves.  **3** having or proceeding from nerves that are out of order: *a nervous patient, a nervous tapping of the fingers.*  **4** restless; uneasy; timid: *Worry and lack of sleep made Mother nervous. Alice is nervous about staying alone.*  **5** having nerves.  **6** strong; vigorous: *Tony painted with quick, nervous strokes.*  *adj.*  —**ner′vous·ly,** *adv.*  —**nerv′ous·ness,** *n.*

**nervous system**  the system in the body of an animal or human being that receives and interprets different stimuli and conducts impulses to the glands, muscles, etc. concerned: *In vertebrates, the nervous system includes the brain, spinal cord, ganglia nerves, and the parts of the sense organs that receive the stimuli.*

**ner·vure** (nėr′vyür)  **1** a vein of a leaf.  **2** a rib of an insect's wing.  *n.*

**nerv·y** (nėr′vē)  **1** rude and bold.  **2** showing courage or firmness.  **3** nervous.  *adj.*, **nerv·i·er, nerv·i·est.**

**nes·cience** (nesh′əns)  ignorance.  *n.*

**–ness**  a noun-forming suffix meaning the quality, state, or condition of being: *Preparedness means the state of being prepared.*

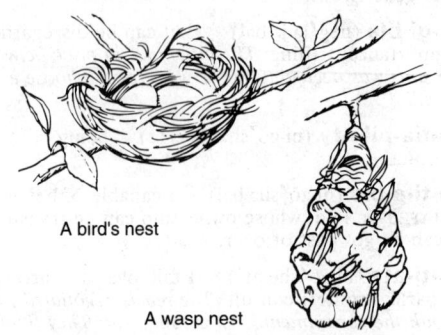

A bird's nest

A wasp nest

**nest** (nest)  **1** a structure or place used by birds for laying eggs and rearing young.  **2** a place used by insects, fish, turtles, rabbits, or the like, for depositing eggs or young.  **3** a snug abode, retreat, or resting place: *The little girl cuddled down in a nest among the sofa cushions.*  **4** a place where evil or harmful persons gather; a den: *a nest of thieves.*  **5** the birds, animals, or insects living in a nest.  **6** build and use a nest.  **7** place or fit together in a nest: *The chairs were nested and placed along the wall.*  **8** a set or series, often from large to small, such that each fits within another: *a nest of drinking cups.*  **9** hunt for birds' nests.  1–5, 8 *n.*, 6, 7, 9 *v.*

**nest egg**  **1** a natural or artificial egg left in a nest to induce a hen to continue laying eggs there.  **2** something, usually a sum of money, set aside as the beginning of a fund or as a reserve: *When he got married, he had already saved quite a nest egg.*

**nes·tle** (nes′əl)  **1** settle oneself or be settled comfortably and cosily: *nestle down in a big chair, a house nestling among trees.*  **2** press close in love or for comfort: *A mother nestles her baby in her arms.*  **3** make or have a nest; settle in a nest.  *v.*, **nes·tled, nes·tling** (nes′ling).  —**nes′tler,** *n.*

**nest·ling** (nes′tling)  a bird too young to leave the nest.  *n.*

**net**[1] (net)  **1** an open fabric made of string, cord, thread, or wire, knotted together in such a way as to leave holes regularly arranged: *Veils are made of very fine net.*  **2** a piece of netting used for some special purpose: *a fish net, a hair net, a tennis net.*  **3** anything like a net; set of things that cross each other.  **4** a lacelike cloth.  **5** a trap or snare: *The guilty boy was caught in a net of his own lies.*  **6** catch in a net: *to net a fish.*  **7** cover, confine, or protect with a net.  **8** make into net: *to net cord.*  **9** make with net: *to net a hammock.*  **10** in tennis, etc., a ball that hits the net. See LET[2] (def. 3).  **11** hit a ball into the net.  **12** INTERNET.  1–5, 10, 12 *n.*, 6–9, 11 *v.*, **net·ted, net·ting.**  —**net′like,** *adj.*

**net**[2] (net)  **1** real or actual; clear and free from deductions or additions: *A net gain or profit is the actual gain after all working expenses have been paid. The net weight of a glass jar of candy is the weight of the candy itself.*  **2** the net weight, profit, price, etc.  **3** gain: *The sale netted me a good profit.*  **4** final: *the net result.*  1, 4 *adj.*, 2 *n.*, 3 *v.*, **net·ted, net·ting.**

**neth·er** (neᴛн′ər)  lower: *nether garments, nether regions.*  *adj.*

**Neth·er·land·er** (neᴛн′ər lan′dər)  a native or

inhabitant of the Netherlands, a country in western Europe. *n.*

**neth·er·most** (neTH′ər mōst′) lowest. *adj.*

**net·ting** (net′ing) **1** a netted or meshed material: *mosquito netting, wire netting for window screens.* **2** the process of making a net. **3** ppr. of NET. 1, 2 *n.*, 3 *v.*

**net·tle** (net′əl) **1** any of a group of closely related plants of the nettle family having sharp hairs on the leaves and stems that sting the skin when touched. **2** any of various other prickly or stinging plants. **3** referring to a family of mainly tropical plants, most of which have stinging hairs. **4** sting the mind of; irritate; make angry: *She was nettled by the boy's frequent interruptions.* 1–3 *n.*, 4 *v.*, **net·tled, net·tling.**

**net·work** (net′wėrk′) **1** a netting; net. **2** any netlike combination or system of lines or channels: *a network of vines, a network of highways.* **3** group of radio or television stations, so connected that the same program may be broadcast by all: *the French network of CBC radio.* **4** a system of communication links interconnecting a set of computers and peripheral devices. **5** connect into a network. **6** meet with friends or colleagues to exchange ideas or further one's own interests. 1–4 *n.*, 5, 6 *v.*

**neu·ral** (nyü′rəl *or* nü′rəl) of or having to do with, or affecting a nerve or the nervous system. *adj.*

**neu·ral·gia** (nyü ral′jə *or* nü ral′jə) pain, usually sharp, along the course of a nerve. *n.*

**neu·ral·gic** (nyü ral′jik *or* nü ral′jik) of or having to do with NEURALGIA. *adj.*

**neu·ri·tis** (nyü rī′tis *or* nü rī′tis) inflammation of a nerve or nerves. *n.*

**neu·rol·o·gist** (nyü rol′ə jist *or* nü rol′ə jist) a person trained in NEUROLOGY, especially a physician who specializes in the diagnosis and treatment of diseases of the nervous system. *n.*

**neu·rol·o·gy** (nyü rol′ə jē *or* nü rol′ə jē) the study of the nervous system and its diseases. *n.*
—**neu·ro·log′ic·al,** *adj.*

**neu·ron** (nyü′ron *or* nü′ron) one of the conducting cells of which the brain, spinal cord, and nerves are composed: *The neuron is the basic functional unit of nervous tissue. It consists of a cell body, containing the nucleus, and its outgrowths, some of which may be very long.* *n.*

**neu·ro·sis** (nyü rō′sis *or* nü rō′sis) any of certain mental diseases or disorders. *n., pl.* **neu·ro·ses** (-sēz).

**neu·rot·ic** (nyü rot′ik *or* nü rot′ik) **1** of, having to do with, or suffering from a NEUROSIS. **2** *Informal.* having or showing a tendency toward erratic behaviour or obsession with certain unrealistic ideas. **3** a neurotic person. 1, 2 *adj.*, 3 *n.* —**neu·rot′i·cal·ly,** *adv.*
—**neu·rot′i·cism,** *n.*

**neut.** neuter.

**neu·ter** (nyü′tər *or* nü′tər) **1** of a word, neither masculine nor feminine: *"It" is a neuter pronoun.* **2** a neuter word or form. **3** the neuter gender. **4** having no sex organs or having sex organs that are not fully developed: *Worker bees are neuter.* **5** having neither stamens nor pistils. **6** an animal, plant, or insect that is neuter. **7** NEUTRAL (def. 1). 1, 4, 5, 7 *adj.*, 2, 3, 6 *n.*

**neu·tral** (nyü′trəl *or* nü′trəl) **1** not taking part in a quarrel, contest, or war: *Switzerland was neutral during the last two wars in Europe.* **2** a neutral person or country; one not taking part in a war. **3** of or belonging to a neutral country or neutral zone: *a neutral port.* **4** being neither one thing nor the other; indefinite. **5** having little or no colour; greyish. **6** neither acid nor alkaline. **7** of electricity, neither positive nor negative. **8** in biology, not developed in sex. **9** the position of gears when they do not transmit motion from the engine to the wheels or other working parts. 1, 3–8 *adj.*, 2, 9 *n.*

**neu·tral·ism** (nyü′trə liz′əm *or* nü′trə liz′əm) a policy, or the support of a policy, of remaining NEUTRAL (def. 1), especially in international conflicts. *n.*

**neu·tral·ist** (nyü′trə list *or* nü′trə list) **1** a person who practises or advocates NEUTRALISM. **2** practising or advocating NEUTRALISM: *a neutralist country.* *n.*

**neu·tral·i·ty** (nyü tral′ə tē *or* nü tral′ə tē) being NEUTRAL (def. 1); the policy of not taking part in a quarrel, contest, or war. *n.*

**neu·tral·ize** (nyü′trə līz′ *or* nü′trə līz′) **1** make neutral; keep from taking part in war: *There was talk of neutralizing Belgium.* **2** take away the power or effect of something by using an opposite power or force: *Bases neutralize acids. The dim light neutralizes the bright colours in this room.* *v.*, **neu·tral·ized, neu·tral·iz·ing.**
—**neu′tral·i·za′tion,** *n.* —**neu′tral·iz′er,** *n.*

**neutral vowel** SCHWA.

**neu·tri·no** (nyü trē′nō *or* nü trē′nō) in physics, an elementary particle that has no electric charge and is believed to have no mass, and that interacts only weakly with matter. *n.*

**neu·tron** (nyü′tron *or* nü′tron) in physics, an elementary particle having almost the same mass as a proton but having no electric charge, found in the nucleus of every kind of atom except that of hydrogen. *n.*

**neutron bomb** a nuclear bomb designed to explode with relatively little force but to produce intense radiation over a wide area, thus causing great loss of life but relatively little destruction of property.

**neutron star** a very dense, rapidly rotating star composed of the remains of a collapsed supernova.

**né·vé** (nā′vā′) **1** granular snow that is compacted and partly converted into ice, found on the surface of the upper part of a glacier. **2** a field of this snow. *n.*

**nev·er** (nev′ər) **1** not ever; at no time: *He never had to work for a living.* **2** in no case; not at all; to no extent or degree: *He was never the better for his experience. If we're careful, she'll be never the wiser.* *adv.*
**never mind,** **a** pay no attention to; forget about: *Never mind the noise. Never mind your coats.* **b** it doesn't matter! forget it!

**nev·er·more** (nev′ər môr′) never again. *adv.*

**nev·er·the·less** (nev′ər ᴛнə les′) however; none the less; for all that; in spite of it: *She was very tired; nevertheless she kept on working.* *adv.*

**new** (nyü *or* nü) **1** not existing before; having been made, grown, thought of, or produced only a short time ago: *a new invention, a new idea, a new house.* **2** now first used; not worn or used up: *a new path.* **3** beginning again: *The new moon is the moon when seen as a thin crescent.* **4** as if new; fresh: *to go on with new courage.* **5** different; changed: *After taking a shower, he felt a new man.* **6** not familiar: *a new country to me.* **7** not yet accustomed to: *new to the work.* **8** later; modern; recent: *a new dance.* **9** just come; having just reached the position: *a new arrival, a new president.* **10** being the later or latest of two or more things of the same kind: *New France.* **11** further; additional; more: *She sought new information on the subject.* **12** having been known only a short time, though existing before: *a new galaxy. The detective uncovered several new facts.* **13** recently gained or bought: *a new dress, a new car.* **14** newly; recently or lately: *new-mown hay, a new-found friend.* 1–13 *adj.*, 14 *adv.* —**new′ness,** *n.*
☛ *Hom.* GNU, KNEW.

**new·born** (nyü′bôrn′ *or* nü′bôrn′) **1** recently or only just born: *a newborn baby.* **2** ready to start a new life; born again. *adj.*

**New Bruns·wick·er** (brun′zwik ər) a native or long-term resident of New Brunswick. *n.*

**New Cal·e·do·ni·a** (kal′ə dō′nē ə) an early name for that part of British Columbia lying between the Rocky Mountains and the Coast Range.

**New Canadian** **1** a person who has recently arrived in Canada from another country and plans to become a Canadian citizen. **2** a person originally from another country who has recently become a Canadian citizen.

**New·cas·tle** (nyü′kas′əl *or* nü′kas′əl) *n.*
**carry coals to Newcastle,** **a** waste one's time, effort, etc. **b** take things to a place where they are already plentiful.

**new·com·er** (nyü′kum′ər *or* nü′kum′ər) a person who has just come or who came not long ago. *n.*

**New Democratic Party** a Canadian political party. It was formed in 1961 from the old CCF party with the assistance and support of the Canadian Labour Congress.

**new·el** (nyü′əl *or* nü′əl) **1** the post at the top or bottom of a stairway that supports the railing. See BALUSTRADE for picture. **2** the central post of a winding stairway. *n.*

**new·fan·gled** (nyü′fang′gəld *or* nü′fang′gəld) lately come into fashion; new; novel: *He's always coming up with newfangled ideas.* *adj.*

**new–fash·ioned** (nyü′fash′ənd *or* nü′fash′ənd) of a new fashion; lately come into style. *adj.*

**New·fie** (nyü′fē *or* nü′fē) *Cdn. Informal.*
**1** Newfoundlander. **2** of or having to do with Newfoundland or Newfoundlanders. 1 *n.*, 2 *adj.*, Also, **Newfy.**

A Newfoundland dog—
About 70 cm high at the shoulder

**New·found·land** (nyü′foun′dlənd *or* nü′foun′dlənd) a breed of very large, intelligent dog resembling a Saint Bernard, having a shaggy, usually black coat. *n.* Also, **Newfoundland dog.**
☛ *Etym.* This powerful swimming dog originated in Newfoundland, where it was trained to rescue people from drowning.

**New·found·land·er** (nyü′fən dlan′dər *or* nü′fən dlan′dər, nyü′fən dlan′dər *or* nü′fən dlan′dər, nyü′foun′dlən dər *or* nü′foun′dlən dər) a native or long-term resident of Newfoundland. *n.*

**New France** the name of the territory in North America belonging to France from 1609 to 1763. Among other regions, it included Quebec, Acadia, and the Louisiana Territory.

**New·fy** (nyü′fē *or* nü′fē) See NEWFIE. *n., adj.*

**new·ly** (nyü′lē *or* nü′lē) **1** lately; recently: *newly discovered.* **2** once again; anew: *newly painted walls.* *adv.*

**newly·wed** (nyü′lē wed′ *or* nü′lē wed′) a newly married person. *n.*

**new moon** **1** the phase of the moon when it is between the earth and the sun, so that its dark side is toward the earth and its face is invisible. **2** the thin crescent that appears at sunset two or three days after this phase, with the hollow side on the left. See MOON for picture.
**3** the time of the new moon.

**news** (nyüz *or* nüz) **1** something told as having just happened; information about something that has just happened or will soon happen (*used with a singular verb*): *The news that our teacher was leaving made us sad. The news from the various districts is sent to a central office.* **2** a report of a current happening or happenings in a newspaper, on television, radio, etc. (*used with a singular verb*): *We turned off the radio when the news was finished.* *n.*
**break the news,** make something known; tell something.

**news·boy** (nyüz′boi′ *or* nüz′boi′) a boy who sells newspapers. *n.*

**news·cast** (nyüz′kast′ *or* nüz′kast′) a radio or television program devoted to current events, news bulletins, etc. *n.* —**news′cast′er,** *n.*
☛ *Etym.* From *news* + *broadcast*.

**news·deal·er** (nyüz′dē′lər *or* nüz′dē′lər) a seller of newspapers and magazines. *n.*

**news·man** (nyü′zman′ *or* nü′zman′) **1** a man who sells or delivers newspapers. **2** a newspaperman or newscaster. *n., pl.* **news·men** (-men′).

**news·mon·ger** (nyü′zmung′gər *or* nü′zmung′gər) a person who gathers and spreads news; GOSSIP (def. 3). *n.*

**news·pa·per** (nyüz′pā′pər *or* nüz′pā′pər; nyü′spā′pər *or* nü′spā′pər) **1** a publication consisting of folded sheets of paper, usually printed daily or weekly and containing news stories and pictures, advertisements, and other reading matter, such as editorials, feature stories, weather reports, and comics. **2** the company or organization that

**publishes a newspaper:** *She used to work for a newspaper.* **3** the printed sheets making up a newspaper: *The plants were wrapped in newspaper.* *n.*

**news·pa·per·man** (nyüz′pā′pər man′ or nüz′pā′pər man′; nyü′spā′pər man′ or nü′spā′pər man′) a newspaper reporter, editor, etc. *n.*, *pl.* **news·pa·per·men** (-men′).

**news·print** (nyüz′print′ or nüz′print′; nyü′sprint′ or nü′sprint′) a soft, cheap, coarse paper made from wood pulp, the kind on which newspapers are usually printed. *n.*

**news·reel** (nyüz′rēl′ or nüz′rēl′) a motion picture showing current events. *n.*

**news·room** (nyüz′rüm′ or nüz′rüm′) a room or section of a newspaper office or radio or television station where news is collected and edited for publication or broadcasting. *n.*

**news·stand** (nyüz′stand′ or nüz′stand′) a place where newspapers and magazines are sold. *n.*

**news·wor·thy** (nyü′zwėr′ᴛнē or nü′zwėr′ᴛнē) having the qualities of news; interesting or important enough to the general public to be included in a newspaper or newscast: *The reporter tried to think of an angle that would make the basically ordinary story newsworthy.* *adj.*, **news·wor·thi·er, news·wor·thi·est.**

**news·y** (nyü′zē or nü′zē) *Informal.* **1** full of news. **2** a newsboy or newsman. **1** *adj.*, **news·i·er, news·i·est; 2** *n.*, *pl.* **news·ies.**

**newt** (nyüt or nüt) any of various small salamanders that live in water part of the time. *n.*

**new·ton** (nyü′tən or nü′tən) an SI unit for measuring force: *One newton is the force required to give an acceleration of one metre per second squared to a mass of one kilogram.* Symbol: N *n.*

**New·to·ni·an** (nyü tō′nē ən or nü tō′nē ən) of, having to do with, or according to Sir Isaac Newton or his discoveries: *Newtonian physics.* *adj.*

**New World 1** the Western Hemisphere; North America and South America. **2** of, having to do with, or found in the New World: *New World monkeys have tails adapted for grasping and holding on.* *n.*

**New Year** or **New Year's** the first day or days of the year.

**New Year's day** January 1, usually observed as a legal holiday.

**New Zea·land·er** (zē′lən dər) a native or inhabitant of New Zealand, a country of islands in the south Pacific Ocean.

**next** (nekst) **1** following at once; nearest: *We'll catch the next train.* **2** the first time after this: *On your next visit, bring your guitar.* **3** nearest to: *We live in the house next the church.* **4** in the place, time, or position that is nearest: *I am going to do my arithmetic problems next.* 1, 2 *adj.*, 3 *prep.*, 4 *adv.*

**next door to, a** in or at the house next to. **b** almost; very close to: *Cheating is an act next door to a crime.*

**next to, a** immediately following or adjacent to: *Who was the girl next to you?* **b** almost, nearly: *Chairs like these cost next to nothing. It was next to impossible to move in the crowd.*

**next–door** (nekst′dôr′) in or at the next house: *We get along well with our next-door neighbours.* *adj.*

**next of kin** the nearest blood relative or relative by marriage.

hat, āge, fär; let, ēqual, tėrm; it, īce hot, ōpen, ôrder; oil, out; cup, pùt, rüle
əbove, takən, pencəl, lemən, circəs
ch, child; ng, long; sh, ship
th, thin; ᴛн, then; zh, measure

**nex·us** (nek′səs) **1** a connection; link. **2** a connected series. *n.*, *pl.* **nex·us.**

**NF** Newfoundland.

**N.F. 1** Newfoundland. **2** New France.

**NFB** or **N.F.B.** National Film Board.

**Nfld.** Newfoundland.

**NHL** or **N.H.L.** National Hockey League.

**Ni** nickel.

**ni·a·cin** (nī′ə sin) NICOTINIC ACID. *n.*

**nib** (nib) **1** the point of a pen. **2** the point or tip of anything. **3** a bird's bill. *n.*

**nib·ble** (nib′əl) **1** eat away with quick, small bites, as a rabbit or a mouse does. **2** bite gently or lightly: *A fish nibbles at the bait.* **3** an act of nibbling: *We've been fishing all morning and haven't had a nibble.* **4** a small piece, especially of food: *I just want a nibble of the cake.* 1, 2 *v.*, **nib·bled, nib·bling;** 3, 4 *n.* —**nib′bler,** *n.*
**nibble at,** *Informal.* be interested in: *The management are nibbling at my suggestion.*

**Nic·a·ra·guan** (nik′ə rä′gwən or nik′ə rag′wən) **1** of or having to do with Nicaragua, a republic of Central America, or its people. **2** a native or inhabitant of Nicaragua. 1 *adj.*, 2 *n.*

**nice** (nīs) **1** pleasing; agreeable; satisfactory: *a nice day, a nice ride, a nice child.* **2** thoughtful; kind: *She was nice to us.* **3** fine; subtle; precise: *a nice distinction, a nice shade of meaning.* **4** delicately skilful; requiring care, skill, or tact: *a nice problem.* **5** exacting; particular; hard to please; fastidious; dainty: *nice in his eating.* **6** proper; suitable. **7** scrupulous: *too nice to be a crook.* **8** refined; cultured: *nice manners.* *adj.*, **nic·er, nic·est.** —**nice′ly,** *adv.* —**nice′ness,** *n.*
☛ **Hom.** GNEISS.

**ni·ce·ty** (nī′sə tē) **1** exactness; accuracy; delicacy: *Television sets require nicety of adjustment.* **2** a fine point; small distinction; detail: *I can paint, but I have not yet learned all the little niceties of composition.* **3** the quality of being particular; daintiness; refinement. **4** something dainty or refined. *n.*, *pl.* **ni·ce·ties.**
**to a nicety,** just right: *cakes browned to a nicety.*

**niche** (nich) **1** a recess or hollow in a wall for a statue, vase, etc. **2** a suitable place or position; place for which a person is suited: *Rod will find his niche in the world.* **3 a** the space occupied by an organism in its habitat. **b** the role of an organism or species including its behaviour, position in the food chain, etc. *n.*

**nick** (nik) **1** a place where a small bit has been cut or broken out; notch; groove: *He cut nicks in a stick to keep count of his score.* **2** make a nick or nicks in: *I nicked the edge of the plate while washing it.* **3** cut into or wound slightly: *The bullet just nicked his arm.* **4** hit, guess, catch, etc. exactly. 1 *n.*, 2–4 *v.*
**in the nick of time,** just in time; barely in time.

**nick·el** (nik′əl) **1** a hard, malleable, silvery-white metallic element that is resistant to rust, used mainly in alloys. Symbol: Ni **2** cover or coat with nickel. **3** a

**nickelodeon** 798 **nihilism**

five-cent piece. **4** five cents: *The paper costs a nickel a sheet.* 1, 3, 4 *n.*, 2 *v.*, **nick·elled** or **nick·eled**, **nick·el·ling** or **nick·el·ing**.

**nick·el·o·de·on** (nik′ə lō′dē ən) **1** in the early days of motion pictures, a place of amusement with motion-picture exhibitions, etc., to which the price of admission was only five cents. **2** a JUKE BOX. *n.*

**nickel plate** a thin coating of NICKEL (def. 1) deposited on a metal object to prevent rust, improve the appearance, etc.

**nickel silver** a hard, tough, silver-white alloy of copper, zinc, and NICKEL (def. 1) used to make utensils, wire, etc.

**nick·nack** (nik′nak′) See KNICK-KNACK.

**nick·name** (nik′nām′) **1** a short or familiar form of a proper name: *"The Alex" is a nickname for the Royal Alexandra Theatre. Elizabeth's nickname is "Betty."* **2** a name used instead of a proper name: *Roy's nickname was "Buzz."* **3** give a nickname to: *They nicknamed the short boy "Shorty."* 1, 2 *n.*, 3 *v.*, **nick·named, nick·nam·ing**.

**nic·o·tine** (nik′ə tēn′) a poison contained in tobacco. *n.*
☛ *Etym.* Named after Jacques *Nicot* (1530–1600), a French ambassador to Portugal, who introduced tobacco into France about 1560.

**nic·o·tin·ic acid** (nik′ə tin′ik) an acid of the vitamin B complex found in meat, eggs, wheat germ, etc.; niacin: *A deficiency of nicotinic acid can cause pellagra.*

**niece** (nēs) **1** a daughter of one's brother or sister. **2** a daughter of a brother or sister of one's spouse. *n.*

**Ni·ge·ri·an** (nī jē′rē ən) **1** of or having to do with Nigeria, a country in western Africa, or its people. **2** a native or inhabitant of Nigeria. 1 *adj.*, 2 *n.*

**nig·gard** (nig′ərd) **1** a stingy person. **2** stingy. 1 *n.*, 2 *adj.*

**nig·gard·ly** (nig′ər dlē) **1** stingy. **2** stingily. **3** meanly small or scanty: *a niggardly gift.* 1, 3 *adj.*, 2 *adv.* —**nig′gard·li·ness**, *n.*

**night** (nīt) **1** the period of darkness between evening and morning; the time between sunset and sunrise. **2** the darkness of night; the dark: *She went out into the night.* **3** the darkness of ignorance, sin, sorrow, old age, death, etc.: *Maureen sought one hope in the night of her despair.* **4** nightfall: *We expect to get back before night.* **5** of or having to do with night: *cold night winds.* **6** working or for use at night: *a night light.* **7** nights, regularly or habitually in the nighttime: *He works nights.* *n.*
**make a night of it,** celebrate until very late at night.
☛ *Hom.* KNIGHT.

**night blindness** a condition of the eyes in which the sight is normal in the day or in a strong light, but is abnormally poor or wholly gone at night or in a dim light.

**night·cap** (nīt′kap′) **1** a cap for wearing in bed: *Nightcaps are not much worn these days.* **2** *Informal.* a drink taken just before going to bed. *n.*

**night club** a place for dancing, eating, and entertainment, open only at night.

**night·fall** (nīt′fol′) the coming of night. *n.*

**night·gown** (nīt′goun′) **1** a loose garment worn in bed by girls and women. **2** NIGHTSHIRT. *n.*

**night·hawk** (nīt′hok′) **1** any of several birds related to the whip-poor-will; GOATSUCKER. **2** *Informal.* a person who stays up late at night. *n.*

**night·in·gale** (nī′tən gāl′ *or* nī′ting gāl′) **1** any of several thrushes of Europe and Asia noted for the sweet song of the male; especially, a small, reddish-brown bird having a varied song with loud and soft notes which it sings by night or day. **2** any of various other birds noted for their song. *n.*

**night latch** a door lock opened by a key from the outside or by a knob from the inside.

**night light** a small lamp that provides a dim light, used especially by the bed of a child or of a sick person at night.

**night·light·er** (nī′tlī′tər) a person who hunts game, often deer, illegally by means of a bright light; jacklighter. *n.*

**night·light·ing** (nī′tlī′ting) the practice of hunting game, often deer, illegally by means of a bright light; jacklighting. *n.*

**night·long** (nī′tlong′) **1** lasting all night: *a nightlong vigil, a nightlong celebration.* **2** through the whole night. 1 *adj.*, 2 *adv.*

**night·ly** (nīt′lē) **1** done, happening, or appearing every night. **2** every night: *Performances are given nightly except on Sunday.* **3** done, happening, or appearing at night: *nightly dew.* **4** at night; by night: *Many animals come out only nightly.* 1, 3 *adj.*, 2, 4 *adv.*
☛ *Hom.* KNIGHTLY.

**night·mare** (nīt′mer′) **1** a frightening dream: *Tom has nightmares about falling from a high roof.* **2** a very unpleasant or frightening experience: *The dust storm was a nightmare. The mountain climb was a nightmare adventure.* *n.*

**night·mar·ish** (nīt′mer′ish) like a nightmare; strange and horrifying. *adj.*

**night owl** *Informal.* a person who often stays up late.

**night school** a school held in the evening for persons who work during the day.

**night·shade** (nīt′shād′) **1** any of various related plants having berries that are often poisonous: *The common nightshade, also called bittersweet, and the deadly nightshade, also called belladonna, both have poisonous berries.* **2** referring to a family of mainly tropical herbs, shrubs, and trees having flowers in clusters and fruit in the form of a capsule or berry: *The tomato, potato, eggplant, peppers, and hemp belong to the nightshade family.* *n.*

**night·shirt** (nīt′shėrt′) a loose garment worn in bed by boys and men. *n.*

**night·time** (nīt′tīm′) the time between evening and morning. *n.*

**night watch 1** a watch or guard kept during the night. **2** the person or persons keeping such a watch. **3** a period or division of the night.

**night watchman** a person who guards a store, factory, etc. at night.

**ni·hil·ism** (nī′ə liz′əm) **1** the entire rejection of the usual beliefs in religion, morals, government, laws, etc. **2** in philosophy, the denial of all existence. **3** the beliefs of a former revolutionary party in Russia, which found nothing good in the old order of things and wished to clear it away to make place for a better state of society.

**4** the use of violent methods against a ruler. *n.*
☞ *Etym.* From L *nihil*, 'nothing'.

**ni·hil·ist** (nī′ə list) **1** a person who believes in some form of NIHILISM. **2** terrorist. *n.*

**ni·hil·is·tic** (nī′ə lis′tik) of NIHILISTS or NIHILISM. *adj.*

**Ni·hon Sho·ki** (nē′hon shō′kē) in Shintoism, an account of Japan's history and imperial ancestry from mythic origins to the 7th century. It is one of the highly revered texts of the Shinto religion. *n.*

**nil** (nil) nothing. *n.*

**nim·ble** (nim′bəl) **1** able to move lightly and quickly; agile: *Her nimble fingers flew over the piano keys.* **2** quick to understand; clever: *a nimble mind. adj.*, **nim·bler**, **nim·blest**. —**nim′ble·ness**, *n*. —**nim′bly**, *adv.*

**nim·bo·stra·tus** (nim′bō strā′təs *or* nim′bō strat′əs) a low, dark-grey layer of rain or snow cloud. *n., pl.* **nim·bo·stra·ti** (-tī *or* -tē).

**nim·bus** (nim′bəs) **1** a light disk or other radiance about the head of a divine or sacred person in a picture. **2** a bright cloud surrounding a god, person, or thing. **3** a rain cloud. *n., pl.* **nim·bus·es** *or* **nim·bi** (-bī *or* -bē).

**nin·com·poop** (nin′kəm püp′ *or* ning′kəm püp′) fool; simpleton. *n.*

**nine** (nīn) **1** one more than eight; 9: *We have nine; we need one more to make ten.* **2** the numeral 9: *The 9 is bigger than the other numerals.* **3** the ninth in a set or series; especially a playing card having nine spots: *the nine of clubs.* **4** being ninth in a set or series (*used mainly after the noun*): *Chapter Nine was very exciting.* **5** in baseball, a team of nine players. **6** in golf, the first or last nine holes of an 18-hole course. **7** any set or series of nine persons or things: *The band was called* The Intensely Vigorous College Nine. 1–3, 5–7 *n.*, 1, 4 *adj.*
**dressed to the nines**, *Informal.* very formally or elaborately dressed: *I showed up in my jeans and found out that everyone else was dressed to the nines.*
☞ *Etym.* From OE *nigon*, related to German *neun* and having the same Indo-European source as L *novem* (giving F *neuf*).

**nine·fold** (nīn′fōld′) **1** nine times as much or as great. **2** having nine parts. 1, 2 *adj.*, 1 *adv.*

**nine·pins** (nīn′pinz′) **1** a game in which nine large wooden pins are set up to be bowled down with a ball (*used with a singular verb*): *Ninepins resembles tenpins.* **2** the pins used in this game. *n. pl.*

**nine·teen** (nīn′tēn′) **1** nine more than ten; 19: *She got one question wrong and nineteen right. He lived there for nineteen years.* **2** the numeral 19: *The 19 is bigger than the other numbers.* **3** the nineteenth in a set or series. **4** being nineteenth in a set or series (*used after the noun*): *Chapter Nineteen.* **5** a set or series of nineteen persons or things. 1–3, 5 *n.*, 1, 4 *adj.*

**nine·teenth** (nīn′tēnth′) **1** next after the 18th; last in a series of 19; 19th. **2** one, or being one, of 19 equal parts. 1 *adj.*, 1, 2 *n.*

**nine·ti·eth** (nīn′tē ith) **1** next after the 89th; last in a series of 90; 90th. **2** one, or being one, of 90 equal parts. 1 *adj.*, 1, 2 *n.*

**nine·ty** (nīn′tē) **1** nine times ten; 90. **2** nineties, *pl.* the years from ninety through ninety-nine, especially of a century or of a person's life: *She was in her nineties when she died.* 1, 2 *n. pl.* **nine·ties**; 1 *adj.*

**nin·ny** (nin′ē) a fool. *n., pl.* **nin·nies**.

---

**nihilist** 799 **nitrate**

hat, āge, fär; let, ēqual, tėrm; it, īce
hot, ōpen, ôrder; oil, out; cup, pùt, rüle
əbove, takən, pencəl, lemən, circəs
ch, child; ng, long; sh, ship
th, thin; ᴛʜ, then; zh, measure

**ninth** (nīnth) **1** next after the eighth; last in a series of nine; 9th. **2** one, or being one, of nine equal parts. 1 *adj.*, 1, 2 *n.*

**ni·o·bi·um** (nī ō′bē əm) a rare, steel-grey metallic element that resembles tantalum in its chemical properties. *Symbol*: Nb  *n.*

**nip**[1] (nip) **1** squeeze tight and suddenly; pinch; bite: *The crab nipped my toe.* **2** a tight squeeze or pinch; sudden bite. **3** take off by biting, pinching, or snipping. **4** stop or spoil the growth, progress, or fulfilment of: *a new government policy designed to nip inflation.* **5** stinging cold; chill: *There was a nip in the air.* **6** injure or make numb with cold: *The cold wind nipped ours ears. The flowers were all nipped by frost.* **7** a strong, sharp flavour; tang: *cheese with a nip.* **8** a small bit. 1, 3, 4, 6 *v.*, **nipped**, **nip·ping**; 2, 5, 7, 8 *n.*
**nip and tuck**, *Informal.* in a race or contest, so evenly matched that the issue remains in doubt till the end.
**nip in the bud**, stop or spoil at the very beginning: *All his plans were nipped in the bud by the sudden death of his benefactor.*

**nip**[2] (nip) a small drink: *a nip of brandy. n.*

**nip·per** (nip′ər) **1** a person or thing that nips, especially a big claw of a lobster or crab. **2** *Informal.* a small boy. **3** nippers, *pl.* pincers, forceps, pliers, or any tool that nips. *n.*

**nip·ple** (nip′əl) **1** the small projection on a breast, etc., through which a baby or young animal gets its mother's milk. **2** the mouthpiece of a baby's bottle. **3** anything shaped or used like a nipple. *n.*

**Nip·pon·ese** (nip′ə nēz′) Japanese. *adj., n., pl.* **Nip·pon·ese**.

**nip·py** (nip′ē) **1** chilly; biting: *nippy weather.* **2** sharp; pungent: *nippy cheese. adj.*, **nip·pi·er**, **nip·pi·est**.

**nir·va·na** *or* **Nir·va·na** (nir vä′nə) **1** in Buddhism, the enlightened level of being of a person who has overcome the desires and the pain of worldly existence; a peaceful, pure, and deathless state which becomes complete and perfect when the body dies: *The desires of life are thought of as a fever and Nirvana is the extinguishing or cooling of this fever.* **2** blessed oblivion. *n.*

**Ni·sei** (nē′sā′) a native-born Canadian or United States citizen whose parents were Japanese immigrants. Compare with ISSEI *and* SANSEI. *n., pl.* **Ni·sei**.
☞ *Etym.* From Japanese *ni* 'two' and *sei* 'generation'.

**nit** (nit) the egg or the young of a louse or similar insect. *n.*

**ni·ter** (nī′tər) See NITRE. *n.*

**nit–pick** (nit′pik′) engage in NIT-PICKING. *v.* —**nit′-pick′er**, *n.*

**nit–pick·ing** (nit′pik′ing) criticizing and complaining in a petty manner; criticizing unimportant details; faultfinding: *You're being a little nit-picking in your criticism. n., adj.*

**ni·trate** (nī′trāt) **1** a salt or ester of NITRIC ACID. **2** potassium nitrate or sodium nitrate, used as a fertilizer.

**3** treat with NITRIC ACID or a nitrate. 1, 2 *n.*, 3 *v.*, **ni·trat·ed, ni·trat·ing. —ni·tra′tion,** *n.*

**ni·tre** (nī′tər) **1** a salt (potassium nitrate) obtained from potash, used in making gunpowder; saltpetre. **2** sodium nitrate, or Chile saltpetre, used in fertilizer. *n.* Also, **niter.**

**ni·tric** (nī′trik) of or containing nitrogen, especially with a higher VALENCE than in corresponding NITROUS compounds. *adj.*

**nitric acid** a clear, colourless liquid that eats into flesh, clothing, metal, and other substances: *Nitric acid is used as an oxidizing agent and in making dyes, fertilizers, and explosives.*

**ni·tride** (nī′trīd *or* nī′trid) a compound of nitrogen with a more electropositive element or radical, such as phosphorus, boron, or a metal. *n.*

**ni·trite** (nī′trīt) a salt or ester of nitrous acid. *n.*

**ni·tro·ben·zene** (nī′trō ben′zēn *or* nī′trō ben zēn′) a poisonous, yellowish liquid obtained from benzene by the action of NITRIC ACID. *n.*

**ni·tro·gen** (nī′trə jən) an element that is a colourless, tasteless, odourless gas and that makes up about four fifths of the air by volume: *Nitrogen occurs in combined form in all living tissues.* Symbol: N  *n.*

**ni·trog·e·nous** (nī troj′ə nəs) of or containing nitrogen or a compound of nitrogen. *adj.*

**ni·tro·glyc·er·in** or **ni·tro·glyc·er·ine** (nī′trə glis′ə rin) **1** a heavy, oily, explosive liquid made by treating glycerin with nitric and sulphuric acids: *Nitroglycerin provides the explosive power of dynamite.* **2** a medicine for treating angina pectoris. *n.*

**ni·trous** (nī′trəs) **1** of or containing nitrogen, especially with a lower VALENCE than in corresponding NITRIC compounds. **2** of or containing NITRE. *adj.*

**nitrous oxide** a colourless gas that causes laughing and inability to feel pain; laughing gas: *Nitrous oxide was formerly used as an anesthetic by dentists.*

**nit·ty-grit·ty** (nit′ē grit′ē) *Informal.* basic reality; actual fact or essence: *Let's get down to the nitty-gritty of who is going to pay for the broken window.* *n.*

**n. mi.** nautical mile.

**NNE** or **N.N.E.** north-northeast

**NNW** or **N.N.W.** north-northwest

**no** (nō) **1** a word used to deny, refuse, or disagree; the opposite of **yes**: *Will you come with us? No. Can a cow fly? No.* **2** not in any degree; not at all: *She is no better.* **3** not, chiefly in phrases like *whether or no.* **4** not any; not at all: *Dogs have no wings. He has no friends.* **5** a denial; refusal. **6** a negative vote or voter: *The noes won.* 1, 5, 6 *n., pl.* **noes;** 1–3 *adv.,* 4 *adj.*
☛ *Hom.* KNOW.

**No** nobelium.

**no.** number.

**No.** **1** north; northern. **2** number.

**no·bel·i·um** (nō bē′lē əm) an artificial radio-active element. Symbol: No  *n.*

**Nobel prize** (nō bel′) one of a group of prizes for physics, chemistry, physiology or medicine, literature, economic sciences, and the promotion of peace, established by Alfred B. Nobel to be given annually to the person or persons who have contributed most in each of these fields.

**no·bil·i·ty** (nō bil′ə tē) **1** people of noble rank: *Earls and counts belong to the nobility.* **2** noble birth; noble rank. **3** noble character or quality: *the nobility of an act.* *n., pl.* **no·bil·i·ties.**

**no·ble** (nō′bəl) **1** high and great by birth, rank, or title: *a noble family.* **2** a person high and great by birth, rank, or title: *A duchess is a noble.* **3** high and great in character; showing greatness of mind; illustrious; outstanding: *a noble person, a noble deed.* **4** excellent; fine; splendid; magnificent: *Niagara Falls is a noble sight.* 1, 3, 4 *adj.,* **no·bler, no·blest;** 2 *n.* **—no′ble·ness,** *n.*

**no·ble·man** (nō′bəl mən) a man who belongs to NOBILITY; a man of NOBLE rank or birth. *n., pl.* **no·ble·men** (-mən).

**no·blesse o·blige** (nō bles ô blēzh′) *French.* persons of noble rank should behave nobly.

**no·ble·wom·an** (nō′bəl wùm′ən) a woman who belongs to NOBILITY; a woman of NOBLE birth or rank. *n., pl.* **no·ble·wom·en** (-wim′ən).

**no·bly** (nō′blē) in a NOBLE manner, splendidly; as a noble person would do. *adv.*

**no·bod·y** (nō′bud′ē *or* nō′bod′ē) **1** no one; no person. **2** a person of no importance. 1 *pron.,* 2 *n., pl.* **no·bod·ies.**

**nock** (nok) **1** a notch on a bow or arrow for the bowstring. **2** make such a notch. **3** fit an arrow to the bowstring for shooting. 1 *n.,* 2, 3 *v.*
☛ *Hom.* KNOCK.

**noc·tur·nal** (nok tèr′nəl) **1** of, belonging to, or occurring at night: *a nocturnal journey. The stars are a nocturnal sight.* **2** of animals, active during the night instead of the day: *The owl is a nocturnal bird.* **3** of plants, having flowers that open only at night: *One species of cereus cactus is nocturnal.* *adj.*

**noc·tur·nal·ly** (nok tèr′nəl ē) **1** at night. **2** every night. *adv.*

**noc·turne** (nok′tèrn) **1** a dreamy or pensive musical piece. **2** a painting of a night scene. *n.*

**nod** (nod) **1** bow the head slightly and raise it again quickly. **2** show agreement by nodding: *I asked him if the baby was asleep and he nodded.* **3** express by bowing the head: *to nod consent.* **4** a nodding of the head: *She gave us a nod as she passed.* **5** let the head fall forward and bob about when sleepy or falling asleep. **6** be sleepy; become careless and dull: *She was beginning to nod before the meeting was halfway through.* **7** droop, bend, or sway back and forth: *Trees nod in the wind.* 1–3, 5–7 *v.,* **nod·ded, nod·ding;** 4 *n.*
**give someone the nod,** express consent.
**nod off,** fall asleep.

**nod·al** (nō′dəl) having to do with, located near, or being a NODE: *the nodal joints of a stem.* *adj.*

**node** (nōd) **1** a knot; knob; swelling. **2** a joint in a stem; the part of a stem from which leaves grow. See STEM for picture. **3** a central point in a system; point of concentration. *n.*

**nod·u·lar** (noj′ə lər) having NODULES. *adj.*

**nod·ule** (noj′ül) **1** a small knot, knob, or swelling. **2** a small, rounded mass or lump: *nodules of gold.* *n.*

**noise** (noiz) **1** a sound that is not musical or pleasant;

loud or harsh sound: *The noise kept me awake.* **2** any sound: *the noise of rain on the roof.* **3** a din of voices and movements; loud shouting; outcry; clamour. *n.*

☛ *Etym.* Through OF *noise* 'din, loud disturbance' from L *nausea* 'seasickness', because of the unpleasant din made by a shipful of seasick passengers.

**noise·less** (noi′zlis) making little or no noise: *a noiseless electric fan.* *adj.* —**noise′less·ly,** *adv.* —**noise′less·ness,** *n.*

**noise·mak·er** (noi′zmā′kər) a person or thing that makes noise, especially, a horn, rattle, etc. used to make noise at a party, sports event, etc. *n.*

**nois·i·ly** (noi′zə lē) in a noisy manner. *adv.*

**nois·i·ness** (noi′zē nis) noise; being noisy. *n.*

**noi·some** (noi′səm) **1** offensive; disgusting; smelling bad: *a noisome slum, a noisome sewer.* **2** harmful; injurious: *a noisome pestilence.* *adj.* —**noi′some·ly,** *adv.* —**noi′some·ness,** *n.*

☛ *Etym.* ME *noysome* from *noy* 'annoy or annoyance', which came from OF *enui, anoi* 'annoyance'.

**nois·y** (noi′zē) **1** making much noise: *a noisy girl, a noisy crowd, a noisy little clock.* **2** full of noise: *a noisy street, the noisy city.* **3** characterized by noise; having much noise with it: *a noisy quarrel, a noisy game.* *adj.,* **nois·i·er, nois·i·est.**

**nom.** nominative.

**no·mad** (nō′mad) **1** a member of a people that moves from place to place so as to have pasture for its cattle or to be near its own food or water supply: *The Inuit have traditionally been nomads.* **2** nomadic: *nomad peoples, a nomad way of life.* **3** wanderer. *n.*

**no·mad·ic** (nō mad′ik) of, having to do with, or referring to NOMADS or their ways of life: *The Sioux were one of many nomadic tribes of North American Indians.* *adj.* —**no·mad′i·cal·ly,** *adv.*

**no·mad·ism** (nō′ma diz′əm) the way that NOMADS live. *n.*

**no–man's–land** or **no man's land** (nō′man′zland′) **1** in war, the land or area between opposing armies. **2** a tract of land to which no one has a recognized or established claim. **3** any area of involvement or operation that is not clearly defined or is ambiguous or inconsistent: *a legal no-man's-land.* *n.*

**nom de guerre** (nôN′ də geR′) *French.* an assumed name under which to pursue a profession, undertaking, or the like.

**nom de plume** (nom′ də plüm′) a pen name; name used by a writer instead of his or her real name.

**no·men·cla·ture** (nō′mən klā′chər *or* nō men′klə chər) a system of names or terms used in a particular field of science, art, etc.: *the nomenclature of music, the international Latin nomenclature for animals and plants.* *n.*

**nom·i·nal** (nom′ə nəl) **1** existing in name only; not real: *The president is the nominal head of the club, but the secretary is the one who really runs its affairs.* **2** so small that it is not worth considering; unimportant compared

---

**noiseless**     **801**     **non-attendance**

hat, āge, fär; let, ēqual, tėrm; it, īce
hot, ōpen, ôrder; oil, out; cup, pùt, rüle
əbove, takən, pencəl, lemən, circəs
ch, child; ng, long; sh, ship
th, thin; ᴛʜ, then; zh, measure

with the real value: *We paid our friend a merely nominal rent for the cottage each summer–$50 a month.* **3** giving the name or names: *a nominal roll of the pupils in our room.* **4** of, having to do with, or being a name. **5** of, having to do with, or used as a noun. *Day is the nominal root of daily, daybreak, and Sunday.* **6** a word or group of words used as a noun. 1–5 *adj.,* 6 *n.*

**nom·i·nal·ly** (nom′ə nə lē) **1** in name; as a matter of form; in a NOMINAL way only. **2** by name. *adv.*

**nom·i·nate** (nom′ə nāt′) **1** name as candidate for an office; propose for an office: *Mrs. Conroy has been nominated as Liberal candidate in our riding.* **2** appoint to an office or duty: *The prime minister nominated him Secretary of State.* *v.,* **nom·i·nat·ed, nom·i·nat·ing.** —**nom′i·na′tor,** *n.*

**nom·i·na·tion** (nom′ə nā′shən) **1** the naming of someone as a candidate for an office or a prize: *The nominations for president of the club were written on the chalkboard.* **2** a selection for office or duty; appointment to office or duty: *Wesley was hopeful, but his friend got the nomination.* **3** being nominated: *Ellen's friends were pleased by her nomination.* *n.*

**nom·i·na·tive** (nom′ə nə tiv *or* nom′nə tiv) **1** of, having to do with, or being the grammatical case that in many languages shows that a noun, pronoun, or adjective is part of the subject of a sentence: *The English personal pronouns* I, he, she, we, *and* they *are in the nominative case.* **2** the nominative case. **3** a word in the nominative case. 1 *adj.,* 2, 3 *n.*

**nom·i·nee** (nom′ə nē′) a person nominated for an office or to be a candidate for election to an office. *n.*

**non–** a prefix meaning not; opposite of; lack of; as in *non-combatant, nonconformity, non-payment.*

**non–ac·cept·ance** (non′ak sep′təns) a failure or refusal to accept. *n.*

**non·age** (non′ij) **1** being under the legal age of responsibility; minority. **2** an early stage; period before maturity. *n.*

**non·a·ge·nar·i·an** (non′ə jə ner′ē ən) **1** a person who is 90 years old or between 90 and 100 years old. **2** 90 years old or between 90 and 100 years old. 1 *n.,* 2 *adj.*

**non–ag·gres·sion** (non′ə gresh′ən) a lack of aggression. *n.*

**non·a·gon** (non′ə gon′) a closed plane figure having nine interior angles and nine sides. *n.*

**non–al·co·hol·ic** (non′al kə hol′ik) containing no alcohol: *a non-alcoholic drink.* *adj.*

**non–at·tend·ance** (non′ə ten′dəns) failure to be present. *n.*

---

*In each of the words below* **non-** *means* not *or, for nouns,* no *or* not a.

non′-a·bra′sive    non′-ad·dic′tive    non′-ag·ri·cul′tur·al    non′-al·ler′gic    non′-ath·let′ic
non′-ab·sor′bent    non′-ad·min′is·tra·tive    non′-al·ler′gen·ic    non′-a·quat′ic    non′-au·thor′i·ta′tive
non′-ac·a·dem′ic    non′-ag·gres′sive

**non‧bel‧lig‧er‧ent** (non′bə lij′ə rənt)   1 not taking an active part in a war.   2 a non-belligerent nation or state. 1 *adj.*, 2 *n.*

**nonce** (nons) *Archaic* except in **for the nonce,** for the present time or occasion.   *n.*

**nonce word** a word created for use only once in order to describe something in a new and striking way.

**non‧cha‧lance** (non′shə lons′ *or* non′shə ləns)   cool unconcern or indifference: *Eleanor received the prize with pretended nonchalance.*   *n.*

**non‧cha‧lant** (non′shə lont′ *or* non′shə lənt)   coolly unconcerned or indifferent; without enthusiasm: *She remained quite nonchalant during all the excitement.*   *adj.* —**non′cha‧lant‧ly,** *adv.*

**non–com** (non′kom′) *Informal.* a NON-COMMISSIONED officer.   *n.*

**non‧com‧bat‧ant** (non′kəm bat′ənt *or* non′kom′bə tənt)   1 a person in the armed services who is not armed: *Surgeons, nurses, chaplains, etc. are non-combatants even though with the armed forces.*   2 a civilian in wartime.   3 not fighting.   4 having civilian status in wartime.   1, 2 *n.*, 3, 4 *adj.*

**non–com‧mis‧sioned** (non′kə mish′ənd)   without a commission; not commissioned: *Sergeants and corporals are non-commissioned officers.*   *adj.*

**non–com‧mit‧tal** (non′kə mit′əl)   not committing oneself; not saying yes or no: *"I will think it over" is a noncommittal answer.*   *adj.* —**non′com‧mit′tal‧ly,** *adv.*

**non–com‧pli‧ance** (non′kəm plī′əns)   the fact of not complying; a failure to comply.   *n.*

**non com‧pos men‧tis** (non′ kom′pəs men′tis) *Latin.* in law, mentally unable to manage one's own affairs; legally insane.

**non–con‧duct‧ing** (non′kən duk′ting)   not conducting; that is a NON-CONDUCTOR: *Rock wool is non-conducting of heat, electricity or sound.*   *adj.*

**non–con‧duc‧tor** (non′kən duk′tər)   a substance that does not readily allow heat, electricity, or sound to pass through it: *Rubber is a non-conductor of electricity.*   *n.*

**non‧con‧form‧ist** (non′kən fôr′mist)   a person who does not conform to accepted practices, conventions, etc.   *n.*

**non‧con‧form‧i‧ty** (non′kən fôr′mə tē)   a lack of conformity; failure or refusal to conform.   *n.*

**non–de‧liv‧er‧y** (non′di liv′ə rē)   failure to deliver.   *n.*

**non‧de‧script** (non′də skript′)   1 not easily classified; not of any one particular kind: *eyes of nondescript shade, neither brown, blue, nor grey.*   2 a nondescript person or thing.   1 *adj.*, 2 *n.*

**none** (nun)   1 not any: *We have none of that paper left.*   2 no one; not one: *None of these is a typical case.*   3 no persons or things: *None have arrived.*   4 no part; nothing: *She has none of her mother's beauty.*   5 to no extent; in no way; not at all: *Our supply is none too great.*   1–4 *pron.*, 5 *adv.*
**none the less,** nevertheless.
☛ Hom. NUN.
☛ Usage. **None, no one. None** is a single word, but **not one** or **no one** is often used instead of **none** for emphasis. **None** may be either singular or plural, and now is more common with the plural: *As only ten jurors have been chosen so far, none of the witnesses were called (or was called). She tried on ten hats, but none of them were attractive.*

**non‧en‧ti‧ty** (non en′tə tē)   1 a person or thing of little or no importance.   2 something that does not exist.   *n., pl.* **non‧en‧ti‧ties.**

**non–es‧sen‧tial** (non′ə sen′shəl)   1 not essential; not necessary.   2 a person or thing not essential.   1 *adj.*, 2 *n.*

**non–ex‧ist‧ence** (non′eg zis′təns)   1 the condition of not existing.   2 something having no existence.   *n.*

**non–ex‧ist‧ent** (non′eg zis′tənt)   having no existence.   *adj.*

**non‧fea‧sance** (non fē′zəns)   in law, the failure to perform some act that duty requires to be done. Compare with MALFEASANCE and MISFEASANCE.   *n.*

**non–fic‧tion** (non fik′shən)   prose literature that is not a novel, short story, or other form of writing based on imaginary people and events: *Biographies and histories are non-fiction.*   *n.*

**non–flam‧ma‧ble** (non flam′ə bəl)   not easily set on fire and not fast-burning if set on fire; not flammable.   *adj.*
☛ Usage. See note at FLAMMABLE.

**non–ful‧fil‧ment** or **non–ful‧fill‧ment** (non′fùl fil′mənt)   a failure to fulfil; failure to be fulfilled.   *n.*

**non–in‧ter‧ven‧tion** (non′in tər ven′shən)   1 a failure or refusal to intervene.   2 the systematic avoidance of any interference by a nation in the affairs of other nations or of its own states, etc.   *n.*

**non–in‧tox‧i‧cat‧ing** (non′in tok′sə kā′ting)   not producing intoxication; not alcoholic.   *adj.*

---

*In each of the words below* **non-** *means* not *or, for nouns,* no *or* not a.

| | | | | |
|---|---|---|---|---|
| non′‧be‧liev′er | non′‧com‧mu′ni‧ca‧ble | non–crit′i‧cal | non′–ex‧clu′sive | non‧gas′e‧ous |
| non′‧be‧liev′ing | non–com′mu‧nist | non′–de‧duct′i‧ble | non′–ex‧ist′ing | non′–he‧red′i‧tar′y |
| non–break′a‧ble | non′–com‧pet′ing | non′–de‧nom′i‧na′tion‧al | non′–ex‧plo′sive | non–hu′man |
| non–car′bon‧at′ed | non′–com‧pet′i‧tive | non′de‧struc′tive | non′–ex‧port′a‧ble | non′–in‧dict′a‧ble |
| non–car‧niv′o‧rous | non′–com‧pul′so‧ry | non′–dis‧tinc′tive | non–fac′tu‧al | non′–in‧dict′ment |
| non′–charge′a‧ble | non′–con‧fi‧den′tial | non′–dra‧mat′ic | non–fad′ing | non′–in‧dus′tri‧al |
| non–chem′i‧cal | non′–con‧form′ing | non–drink′er | non–fa′tal | non′–in‧fec′tious |
| non′–col‧laps′i‧ble | non′–con‧sec′u‧tive | non–driv′er | non–fat′ten‧ing | non′–in‧flam′ma‧ble |
| non′–col‧lect′a‧ble | non′–con‧ta′gious | non–dry′ing | non–fed′er‧al | non′–in‧her′it‧a‧ble |
| non′–col‧lect′i‧ble | non′–con‧vert′i‧ble | non–ed′u‧ca‧ble | non–fed′e‧rat′ed | non′–in‧sti‧tu′tion‧al |
| non–com′bat | non′–cor‧rod′ing | non′–ed‧u‧ca′tion‧al | non–fer′rous | non′–in′te‧grat′ed |
| non′–com‧bust′i‧ble | non′–cor‧ro′sive | non–e‧las′tic | non–flow′er‧ing | non′–in‧ter‧fer′ence |
| non′–com‧mer′cial | non′–crim′i‧nal | non′–e‧mo′tion‧al | non′–func′tion‧al | non′–in‧ter‧sect′ing |

**non·liv·ing** (non liv′ing) not living. *adj.*

**non·met·al** (non met′əl) a chemical element not having the character of a metal: *Carbon and nitrogen are non-metals.* *n.*

**non·me·tal·lic** (non′mə tal′ik) not a metal: *Carbon, oxygen, sulphur, and nitrogen are non-metallic chemical elements.* *adj.*

**non·pa·reil** (non′pə rel′) **1** having no equal. **2** a person or thing having no equal. 1 *adj.*, 2 *n.*

**non·par·ti·san** (non pär′tə zən *or* non pär′tə zan′) not partisan; especially, not controlled by or supporting any single faction or political party. *adj.*

**non·pay·ment** (non pā′mənt) a failure to pay; condition of not being paid. *n.*

**non·per·form·ance** (non′pər fôr′məns) the fact of not performing; failure to perform. *n.*

**non·plus** (non plus′ *or* non′plus) **1** puzzle completely; make unable to say or do anything: *We were nonplussed to see two roads leading off to the left where we had expected only one.* **2** a state of being nonplussed. 1 *v.*, **non·plussed** *or* **non·plused, non·plus·sing** *or* **non·plus·ing;** 2 *n.*

**non·poi·son·ous** (non poi′zə nəs) containing no poison. *adj.*

**non·po·lit·i·cal** (non′pə lit′ə kəl) not concerned with politics. *adj.*

**non·pro·duc·tive** (non′prə duk′tiv) **1** failing to produce; unproductive. **2** not directly connected with production. *adj.*

**non·prof·it** (non prof′it) not conducted for the purpose of making a profit: *a non-profit organization.* *adj.*

**non·re·new·able** (non′rē nyü′ə bəl *or* non′rē nü′ə bəl) **1** not able to be made new again. **2** that cannot be replaced: *Oil is a non-renewable resource because once extracted from an oil well and used up, it is gone forever.* *adj.*

**non·res·i·dent** (non rez′ə dənt) **1** living elsewhere; not living in a particular place. **2** not living where one's work, studies, official duties, etc. are carried on. **3** a non-resident person. 1, 2 *adj.*, 3 *n.*

**non·re·sist·ance** (non′ri zis′təns) **1** the state or condition of being non-resistant. **2** the principles or practice of not resisting established authority, even when it is unjust or tyrannical. *n.*

**non·re·sist·ant** (non′ri zis′tənt) **1** not resistant to the bad effects of something, such as an insecticide or disease-causing organism. **2** not resisting; practising

hat, āge, fär; let, ēqual, tėrm; it, īce
hot, ōpen, ôrder; oil, out; cup, put, rüle
əbove, takən, pencəl, lemən, circəs
ch, child; ng, long; sh, ship
th, thin; ᴛʜ, then; zh, measure

NON-RESISTANCE (def. 2). **3** a person who practises NON-RESISTANCE (def. 2). 1, 2 *adj.*, 3 *n.*

**non·re·stric·tive** (non′ri strik′tiv) **1** in grammar, adding descriptive detail: *Modifiers that do not limit the meaning of a noun but add a descriptive detail are non-restrictive modifiers.* **2** that does not restrict. *adj.*

**non·sec·tar·i·an** (non′sek ter′ē ən) not connected with any religious denomination. *adj.*

**non·sense** (non′səns) **1** words, ideas, or acts without meaning: *The magician talks nonsense as he is doing the tricks.* **2** foolish talk or doings; a plan or suggestion that is foolish: *It is nonsense to say that we can walk that far in an hour.* **3** impudent or silly behaviour or conduct: *She doesn't take any nonsense from her employees.* *n.*

**non·sen·si·cal** (non sen′sə kəl) foolish; absurd. *adj.*

**non sequi·tur** (non sek′wə tər) **1** a statement or reply that has no direct relationship with what has just been said. **2** in logic, an inference or conclusion that does not follow from the premises. 
☛ *Etym.* From L *non sequitur* 'it does not follow'.

**non·stand·ard** (non stan′dərd) **1** not conforming to regulations, accepted specifications, etc. **2** of language, differing from the standard usage of a group, especially by falling short of what is considered grammatical or acceptable by educated people: *Words like ain't and constructions like them books are considered non-standard.* *adj.*
☛ *Usage.* For non-standard English, see note at STANDARD.

**non·stop** (non′stop′ *for adjective;* non′stop′ *for adverb*) **1** without stopping: *We took a non-stop flight from Toronto to Rome.* **2** without a stop: *We flew non-stop from Regina to Montreal.* 1 *adj.*, 2 *adv.*

**non·suit** (non süt′) **1** a judgment given against a person beginning a lawsuit who neglects to prosecute or who fails to show a legal case, or who fails to bring sufficient evidence. **2** stop by a nonsuit. 1 *n.*, 2 *v.*

**non·sup·port** (non′sə pôrt′) failure to support, especially the failure to provide for someone for whom one is legally responsible. *n.*

**non·un·ion** (non yü′nyən) **1** not belonging to a trade union. **2** made by other than union labour. **3** not recognizing or favouring trade unions. *adj.*

---

*In each of the words below* **non-** *means* not *or, for nouns,* no *or* not a.

| | | | | |
|---|---|---|---|---|
| non′·ir′ri·tant | non′·op′e·rat·ing | non′·pro·fes′sion·al | non·sal′a·ble | non′·sys·tem·at′ic |
| non′·ir′ri·tat′ing | non′·op·e·ra′tion·al | non′·prof·i·teer′ing | non′·sci·en·tif′ic | non·tax′a·ble |
| non·lit′e·rar′y | non·or′tho·dox | non·ra′cial | non′·sea′son·al | non′·teach′a·ble |
| non·lit′er·ate | non·par′al·lel | non′·read′er | non′·se·lec′tive | non′·tech′ni·cal |
| non′·me·chan′i·cal | non′·par·lia·men′tar·y | non′·re·fill′a·ble | non′·sen′si·tive | non·tox′ic |
| non·mi′gra·to′ry | non·pa·ro′chi·al | non′·re·li′gious | non′·shrink′a·ble | non′·trans·fer′a·ble |
| non·mil′i·tant | non′·par·tic′i·pa′tion | non·smok′er | non·typ′i·cal |
| non·mil′i·tar′y | non·pay′ing | non′·re·mu′ne·ra·tive | non·smok′ing | non·ur′ban |
| non·nu′cle·ar | non·per′ma·nent | non′·re·new′a·ble | non′·spe′cial·ized | non·use′ |
| non·nu·tri′tious | non·po′rous | non′·res·i·den′tial | non′·stan′dard·ized | non·us′er |
| non′·o·blig′a·to′ry | non·preg′nant | non′·re·strict′ed | non·swim′mer | |
| non·oc·cur′rence | non′·pre·scrip′tive | non′·re·turn′a·ble | non′·sym·met′ri·cal | |
| | | non′·re·vers′i·ble | | |

**non·vi·o·lence** (non vī′ə ləns) **1** the absence of violence. **2** passive non-co-operation with authority, as opposed to mob violence, used as a means of gaining political ends. *n.*

**non–violent** (non vī′ə lənt) **1** free from violence: *a non-violent demonstration.* **2** supporting or practising NON-VIOLENCE (def. 2). *adj.*

**non–vot·er** (non vō′tər) **1** a person who does not vote. **2** a person who does not have the right to vote. *n.*

**noo·dles** (nü′dəlz) a food made of flour and water, or flour and eggs, resembling macaroni, but made in strips. *n.*

**nook** (nůk) **1** a cosy little corner. **2** a hidden spot; sheltered place: *There is a wonderful nook in the woods behind our house. n.*

**noon** (nün) **1** twelve o'clock in the daytime; the middle of the day. **2** of noon. *n.*

**noon·day** (nün′dā′) noon: *Lunch is our noonday meal. n.*

**no one** or **no-one** (nō′wun′) no person; nobody: *No one was hurt in the car accident. pron.*

**noon hour** lunch hour: *I'll see you at noon hour.*

**noon–hour** (nü′nour′) taking place at lunchtime: *There will be a noon-hour concert tomorrow. adj.*

**noon·tide** (nün′tīd′) noon. *n.*

**noon·time** (nün′tīm′) noon. *n.*

A noose

**noose** (nüs) **1** a loop with a slip-knot that tightens as the string or rope is pulled: *Nooses are used especially in lassos and snares.* **2** anything that restricts or snares like a noose. **3** catch in a noose or as if in a noose; snare. **4** make a noose with or in. **5 the noose,** death by hanging. 1, 2, 5 *n.*, 3, 4 *v.*, **noosed, noos·ing.**

**Noot·ka** (nüt′kə) **1** a member of a First Nations people living mainly on Vancouver Island. **2** the language of these people. **3** of or having to do with the Nootka or their language. 1, 2 *n., pl.* **Noot·ka** or **Noot·kas;** 3 *adj.*

**nor** (nôr) and not; or not; neither; and not either: *I have not been there, nor am I going. Nor is used with a preceding neither or negative: Not a boy nor a girl stirred. There is neither river nor stream in that desert. conj.*

**Nor·dic** (nôr′dik) **1** designating, belonging to, or having to do with a type of people characterized by tall stature, blond hair, blue eyes, and long heads. **2** a member of the Nordic people: *Many Scandinavians are Nordics.* 1 *adj.*, 2 *n.*

**Norfolk jacket** a loose-fitting, belted jacket having pleats at the front and back.

**norm** (nôrm) the standard for a certain group; type; model; pattern: *In arithmetic this class is above the norm for the eighth grade. n.*

**nor·mal** (nôr′məl) **1** of the usual standard or type; regular; usual: *The normal temperature of the human body is 37°C. It's normal for children to be energetic.* **2** in medicine and psychology, of average intelligence, mental or physical health, etc.; not diseased, defective, or disturbed. **3** the usual state or level: *two kilograms above normal.* 1, 2 *adj.*, 3 *n.*

**nor·mal·cy** (nôr′məl sē) a normal condition. *n.*

**nor·mal·i·ty** (nôr mal′ə tē) a normal condition. *n.*

**nor·mal·ize** (nôr′mə līz′) make normal. *v.*, **nor·mal·ized, nor·mal·iz·ing.** —**nor′mal·i·za′tion,** *n.*

**nor·mal·ly** (nôr′mə lē) in the normal way; regularly; if things are normal: *Normally I take the bus to school, but this morning my mother drove me. The tulips normally come up much later. adv.*

**normal school** formerly, a school where people were trained to be elementary school teachers.

**Nor·man** (nôr′mən) **1** a native or inhabitant of Normandy in France. **2** a member of the Scandinavian people who conquered Normandy in the 10th century A.D. **3** a member of the Norman-French people who conquered England in 1066. **4** of or having to do with the Normans or Normandy: *The rounded arch is characteristic of Norman architecture.* 1–3 *n.*, 4 *adj.*

**Norman Conquest** the conquest of England by the Normans in 1066, under the leadership of William the Conqueror.

**Norman French** **1** the dialect of French spoken by the medieval Normans, especially as spoken by the Norman conquerors of England. **2** a form of this dialect used as the language of law in England until the late 17th century. **3** the dialect of the modern-day inhabitants of Normandy.

**Norse** (nôrs) **1** of or having to do with ancient Scandinavia, its people, or their language. **2** the people of ancient Scandinavia; Norsemen. **3** of or having to do with Norway or its people. **4** the Norwegians. **5** the language of Norway. 1, 3 *adj.*, 2, 4 *n. pl.*, 5 *n. sing.*

**Norse·man** (nôr′smən) a member of a people that lived in ancient Scandinavia: *The Vikings were Norsemen.* *n., pl.* **Norse·men** (-smən).

**north** (nôrth) **1** the direction to which a compass needle points; the direction to the right as one faces the setting sun. See COMPASS for picture. **2** toward the north; farther toward the north: *Go north two blocks.* **3** originating in or coming from the north: *a north wind.* **4** in the north; living in the north; northern. **5** Also, **North,** the part of the world or a country or continent toward the north. **6 the North,** in Canada, the northern parts of the provinces from Quebec westward and the territories lying north of these provinces. 1, 5, 6 *n.*, 2, 4 *adv.*, 3 *adj.*

**north of,** farther north than.

**North American** **1** of or having to do with North America or its people. **2** a native or inhabitant of North America.

---

*In each of the words below* **non-** *means not or, for nouns, no or not a.*

| non-vis′u·al | non′-vo·cal′ic | non-vot′ing | non-white′ | non-wov′en |

**north·bound** (nôrth′bound′) going toward the north. *adj.*

**North Country** the North.

**north·east** (nôr′thēst′) **1** the direction or compass point halfway between north and east. **2** a place that is in the northeast part or direction. **3** of, at, in, to, toward, or from the northeast: *a northeast wind* (*adj.*). *They travelled northeast* (*adv.*). **1, 2** *n.*, **3** *adj., adv.*

**north·east·er** (nôr′thē′stər) a wind or storm from the northeast. *n.*

**north·east·er·ly** (nôr′thē′stər lē) **1** toward the northeast: *We're walking in a northeasterly direction.* **2** from the northeast: *the wind blew northeasterly.* **1** *adj.*, **2** *adv.*

**north·east·ern** (nôr′thē′stərn) of, at, in, to, toward, or from the northeast. *adj.*

**north·east·ward** (nôr′thē′stwərd) **1** toward the northeast: *The road turns northeastward here.* **2** northeast. **1, 2** *adv., adj.*, **2** *n.*

**north·east·ward·ly** (nôr′thē′stwər dlē) **1** toward the northeast. **2** of winds, from the northeast. **1, 2** *adj.*, **1** *adv.*

**north·east·wards** (nôr′thē′stwərdz) NORTHEASTWARD. *adv.*

**north·er** (nôr′ŦHər) a wind or storm from the north. *n.*

**north·er·ly** (nôr′ŦHər lē) **1** toward the north: *The windows face northerly.* **2** from the north: *a strong northerly wind.* **3** of the north. **1–3** *adj.*, **1, 2** *adv.*

**north·ern** (nôr′ŦHərn) **1** toward the north: *the northern side of a building.* **2** from the north: *a northern breeze.* **3** of or in the north: *She has travelled in northern countries.* **4** of or in the North of Canada: *Churchill is a northern port.* *adj.*

**north·ern·er** (nôr′ŦHər nər) **1** a native or inhabitant of the north. **2 Northerner**, *Cdn.* a native or inhabitant of the Far North. *n.*

**northern lights** the streamers and bands of light that appear in the northern sky at night; aurora borealis.

**north·ern·most** (nôr′ŦHərn mōst′) farthest north. *adj.*

**northern pike** a common game fish of the pike family having a long, slender body and large head, found throughout most of Canada.

**north·land** (nôr′thland′) **1** a northern region or country. **2** Usually, **Northland**, *Cdn.* the northern regions of Canada; the Far North. *n.*

**north·land·er** (nôr′thlən dər) an inhabitant of the northland. *n.*

**North·man** (nôr′thmən) NORSEMAN. *n., pl.* **North·men** (-thmən).

**north–north·east** (nôrth′nôr′thēst′) **1** a direction or compass point midway between north and northeast. **2** in, toward, or from this direction. **1** *n.*, **2** *adj., adv.*

**north–north·west** (nôrth′nôr′thwest′) **1** a direction or compass point midway between north and northwest. **2** in, toward, or from this direction. **1** *n.*, **2** *adj., adv.*

---

**northbound**     **805**     **nose**

hat, āge, fär; let, ēqual, tėrm; it, īce
hot, ōpen, ôrder; oil, out; cup, pùt, rüle
əbove, takən, pencəl, lemən, circəs
ch, child; ng, long; sh, ship
th, thin; ŦH, then; zh, measure

**North Pole** the northern end of the earth's axis. See LATITUDE for picture.

**north·ward** (nôr′thwərd) **1** toward the north; north: *Rocks lay northward of the ship's course* (*adv.*). *The orchard is on the northward slope of the hill* (*adj.*). **2** a northward part, direction, or point. **1** *adv., adj.*, **2** *n.*

**north·ward·ly** (nôr′thwər dlē) **1** toward the north. **2** of winds, coming from the north. **1, 2** *adj.*, **1** *adv.*

**north·wards** (nôr′thwərdz) NORTHWARD. *adv.*

**north·west** (nôr′thwest′) **1** the direction or compass point halfway between north and west. **2** a place that is in the northwest part or direction. **3** of, at, in, to, toward, or from the northwest: *a northwest wind* (*adj.*). *They travelled northwest* (*adv.*). **4 Northwest**, *Cdn.* the general region of Canada north and west of the Great Lakes. **1, 2, 4** *n.*, **3** *adj., adv.*

**North West Company** a group of fur-trading companies and individuals formed in Montreal during the late 1700's.

**north·west·er** (nôr′thwes′tər) **1** a wind or storm from the northwest. **2 Northwester**, *Cdn.* formerly, a wintering partner or employee of the NORTH WEST COMPANY. *n.*

**north·west·er·ly** (nôr′thwes′tər lē) **1** toward the northwest. **2** of winds, from the northwest. *adj., adv.*

**north·west·ern** (nôr′thwes′tərn) of, at, in, to, toward, or from the northwest. *adj.*

**North West Mounted Police** a former name of the ROYAL CANADIAN MOUNTED POLICE.

**Northwest Passage** a passage for ships from the Atlantic to the Pacific along the northern coast of North America.

**Northwest Rebellion** an armed uprising of Métis and Indians in Saskatchewan in 1885, springing from grievances similar to those that had led to the Red River Rebellion. Among other things, the Métis feared they would lose their farms, and the Indians were discontented at their loss of freedom to roam the plains and because of the extinction of the buffalo herds.

**north·west·ward** (nôr′thwes′twərd) **1** toward the northwest. **2** northwest. **1, 2** *adj., adv.*, **2** *n.*

**north·west·ward·ly** (nôr′thwes′twər dlē) **1** toward the northwest. **2** of winds, from the northwest. **1, 2** *adj.*, **1** *adv.*

**north·west·wards** (nôr′thwes′twərdz) NORTHWESTWARD. *adv.*

**Nor·we·gian** (nôr wē′jən) **1** of or having to do with Norway, a country in northern Europe, its people, or their language. **2** a native or inhabitant of Norway. **3** the language of Norway. **1** *adj.*, **2, 3** *n.*

**nor'west·er** (nôr wes′tər) a heavy, waterproof oilskin coat worn by seamen. *n.*

**Nos.** or **nos.** numbers.

**nose** (nōz) **1** the part of the face or head that stands

out just above the mouth in human beings, serving as an opening for breathing and as the organ of smell. **2** the muzzle or snout of an animal: *A collie has a long nose.* **3** the sense of smell: *A mouse has a good nose for cheese.* **4** discover by smelling; smell out. **5** smell; sniff at. **6** a faculty for perceiving or detecting: *A successful reporter must have a nose for news.* **7** rub with the nose: *The cat nosed her kittens.* **8** a forward end that stands out, especially the front of a ship, boat, or aircraft: *We saw the steamer's nose poking around the cliff.* **9** push with the nose or forward end: *The bulldozer nosed the great rock off the road.* **10** push one's way carefully: *The boat nosed along between the rocks.* **11** search (*for*); pry (*into*). 1–3, 6, 8 *n.*, 4, 5, 7, 9–11 *v.*, **nosed, nos·ing.**
**count noses,** find out how many people are present.
**follow one's nose, a** go straight ahead. **b** be guided by one's instinct. **c** be guided by one's sense of smell.
**lead by the nose,** have complete control over.
**look down one's nose at,** feel contempt for.
**nose out, a** find out by looking quietly or secretly: *The private detective nosed out the facts.* **b** in sports, defeat by a narrow margin.
**pay through the nose,** *Informal.* pay a great deal too much.
**poke one's nose into,** *Informal.* pry into, meddle in.
**put someone's nose out of joint,** *Informal.* **a** take a person's place in another's favour. **b** destroy another person's hopes, plans, etc.
**turn up one's nose at,** treat with contempt or scorn.
**under one's nose,** in plain sight; very easy to notice.

**nose·bleed** (nōz′blēd′) a flow of blood from the nose. *n.*

**nose cone** the front section of a missile, made to carry the payload and to withstand the intense heat met with in re-entering the earth's atmosphere.

**–nosed** (nōzd) having a nose of a certain kind (*used only in compounds*): *long-nosed.* *adj.*

**nose–dive** (nōz′dīv′) **1** a swift plunge straight downward by an aircraft. **2** a sudden, sharp drop: *The thermometer took a nose-dive the day before New Year's.* **3** of an aircraft, plunge swiftly downward. **4** take a sharp, sudden drop: *The price of beef nose-dived.* 1, 2 *n.*, 3, 4 *v.*, **nose-dived, nose-div·ing.**

**nose·gay** (nōz′gā′) a bunch of flowers; a small bouquet. *n.*

**nose·guard** (nōz′gärd′) the part of a football helmet that protects the nose. *n.*

**nose·piece** (nōz′pēs′) **1** the part of a helmet that covers and protects the nose. **2** the part of a bridle that goes over an animal's nose. **3** the bridge of a pair of eyeglasses. *n.*

**nos·ey** (nō′zē) *Informal.* too curious about other people's business; prying; inquisitive. *adj.,* **nos·i·er, nos·i·est.** Also, **nosy.**

**nos·tal·gia** (nos tal′jə *or* nos tal′jē ə) **1** homesickness. **2** a yearning for something in the past; sentimental longing for the return of a past period or of some former condition or circumstance: *She thought with nostalgia of how they used to go hiking in the hills.* *n.*

**nos·tal·gic** (nos tal′jik) of, having to do with, or characterized by NOSTALGIA: *A nostalgic film about the sixties.* *adj.* —**nos·tal′gi·cal·ly,** *adv.*

**nos·tril** (nos′trəl) either of the two openings in the nose: *Air is breathed into the lungs through the nostrils.* *n.*
☞ *Etym.* From OE *nosthyrl* 'nose hole', made up of *nosu* 'nose' + *thyrel* 'hole'.

**nos·trum** (nos′trəm) **1** a medicine of secret ingredients prepared and recommended by the same person, usually without scientific evidence of its effectiveness; patent medicine. **2** a pet scheme for producing wonderful results; a cure-all. *n.*

**nos·y** (nō′zē) See NOSEY. *adj.,* **nos·i·er, nos·i·est.**

**not** (not) a word used to make a negative statement: *Six and two do not make ten. He has not been here.* *adv.*
☞ *Hom.* **Not,** KNOT, NAUGHT, and NOUGHT are pronounced the same (to rhyme with *got*) by most Canadians.

**no·ta be·ne** (nō′tə bē′nē *or* ben′ē) *Latin.* note well; observe what follows; take notice. *Abbrev.:* N.B. *or* n.b.

**no·ta·bil·i·ty** (nō′tə bil′ə tē) **1** the quality of being NOTABLE; distinction. **2** a prominent person: *There were several notabilities at the reception.* *n., pl.* **no·ta·bil·i·ties.**

**no·ta·ble** (nō′tə bəl) **1** worthy of notice; striking; remarkable; important: *a notable event, a notable man, a notable book, a notable painter.* **2** an important or famous person: *Many notables attended the Governor General's levee.* 1 *adj.,* 2 *n.* —**no′ta·ble·ness,** *n.* —**no′ta·bly,** *adv.*

**no·ta·rize** (nō′tə rīz′) certify a contract, deed, will, etc. *v.,* **no·ta·rized, no·ta·riz·ing.**

**no·ta·ry** (nō′tə rē) **1** NOTARY PUBLIC. **2** in Quebec, a lawyer who has the same training as a barrister but who is not permitted to plead in court. *n., pl.* **no·ta·ries.**

**notary public** a person authorized to certify deeds and contracts, take oaths, and attend to certain other legal matters.

**no·ta·tion** (nō tā′shən) **1** a set of signs or symbols used to represent numbers, quantities, or other values: *In arithmetic we use the Arabic notation (1, 2, 3, 4, etc.).* **2** the representing of numbers, quantities, or other values by symbols or signs: *Music has a special system of notation, and so has chemistry.* **3** a note to assist memory; record; jotting: *She made a notation on the margin of the page.* **4** the act of noting. *n.*

**notch** (noch) **1** a V-shaped nick or cut made in an edge or on a curving surface: *Early peoples cut notches on a stick to keep count of numbers.* **2** make a notch or notches in. **3** record by notches; score; tally. **4** a deep, narrow pass or gap between mountains. **5** a grade; step; degree: *In this hot weather many people set their air conditioners several notches higher.* 1, 4, 5 *n.,* 2, 3 *v.*

Musical notes (def. 10)

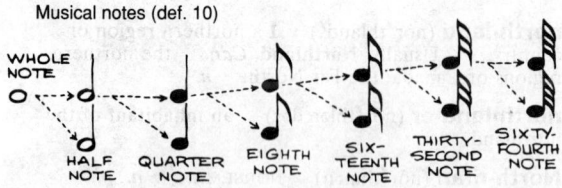

**note** (nōt) **1** a short sentence, phrase, or single word written down to remind one of what was in a book, a speech, an agreement, etc.; memorandum: *Her notes helped her remember what the speaker said.* **2** write down as a thing to be remembered. **3** observe carefully; give attention to; take notice of: *Now note what I do next.* **4** notice; heed; observation. **5** mention specially. **6** a comment or piece of information in a book, often added

to help students.  **7** a brief letter: *a note of thanks.*  **8** a formal letter from one government to another; diplomatic or official communication in writing: *England sent a note of protest to France.*  **9** a single sound of definite pitch made by a musical instrument or voice: *Let me hear that note again.*  **10** in music, a written sign to show the pitch and length of sound.  **11** a black or white key of a piano or other instrument.  **12** a bird's song or call.  **13** a song; melody; tune.  **14** a tone of voice or way of expression: *There was a note of anxiety in her voice.*  **15** a sign, token, or proof of genuineness; characteristic or distinguishing feature.  **16** distinction, importance, or consequence.  **17** a written promise to pay a certain sum of money at a certain time.  **18** a certificate of a government or bank that may be used as money.  1, 4, 6–18 *n.*, 2, 3, 5 *v.*, **not·ed, not·ing.** —**note′less,** *adj.* —**not′er,** *n.*
**compare notes,** exchange ideas or opinions.
**make a note of,** write down as something to be remembered.
**of note,** that is important, great, or notable: *Marie Curie was a person of note.*
**strike the right note,** say or do something suitable.
**take note of,** give attention to or notice: *Take note of the time, please; we must not be late.*
**take notes,** write down things to be remembered.

**note·book** (nōt′bůk′) **1** a book in which to write notes of things to be learned or remembered. **2** a small laptop computer. *n.*

**not·ed** (nō′tid) **1** especially noticed; conspicuous; well-known; celebrated; famous: *Shakespeare is a noted English author.* **2** pt. and pp. of NOTE. 1 *adj.*, 2 *v.*

**note·pa·per** (nōt′pā′pər) paper used for writing letters. *n.*

**note·wor·thy** (nōt′wėr′ᴛнē) worthy of notice; remarkable: *The first flight across the Atlantic was a noteworthy achievement.* *adj.* —**note′wor′thi·ness,** *n.*

**noth·ing** (nuth′ing) **1** not anything; no thing: *Nothing was said.* **2** something that does not exist: *to create a world out of nothing.* **3** a thing of no importance or value; a person of no importance: *People regard him as a nothing.* **4** zero; nought. **5** not at all: *She is nothing like her sister in looks.* 1–4 *n.*, 5 *adv.*
**make nothing of,** **a** be unable to understand. **b** fail to use or do. **c** treat as unimportant or worthless.
**nothing less than,** just the same as.
**think nothing of,** **a** consider as easy to do. **b** treat as unimportant or worthless.

**noth·ing·ness** (nuth′ing nis) **1** being nothing; non-existence. **2** being of no value; worthlessness. **3** an unimportant or worthless thing. **4** *Informal.* unconsciousness. *n.*

**no·tice** (nō′tis) **1** observation; heed; attention: *to escape one's notice. A sudden movement caught her notice.* **2** take notice of; see; give attention to; perceive: *I noticed a big difference at once.* **3** advance information; warning: *The whistle blew to give notice that the boat was about to leave.* **4** a written or printed sign; a paper posted in a public place: *We saw a notice of this week's movie outside the theatre.* **5** a warning or announcement that one is leaving a rented house or leaving a person's employ, or that one must leave the house one is living in or the position one is filling, at a certain time: *The servant gave notice.* **6** a paragraph or article about something: *The new book got a favourable notice.* **7** mention; refer to; speak of. 1, 3–6 *n.*, 2, 7 *v.*, **no·ticed, no·tic·ing.**
**serve notice,** give warning; inform; announce.
**take notice,** give attention; observe; see.

# notebook 807 nourish

hat, āge, fär; let, ēqual, tėrm; it, īce
hot, ōpen, ôrder; oil, out; cup, pùt, rüle
əbove, takən, pencəl, lemən, circəs
ch, child; ng, long; sh, ship
th, thin; ᴛн, then; zh, measure

**no·tice·a·ble** (nō′ti sə bəl) easily seen or noticed; discernible: *The class has made noticeable improvement.* *adj.* —**no′tice·a·bly,** *adv.*

**no·ti·fi·ca·tion** (nō′tə fə kā′shən) **1** a notifying. **2** a notice: *Have you received a notification of the meeting? n.*

**no·ti·fy** (nō′tə fī′) give notice to; let know; inform; announce to: *Our teacher notified us that there would be a test on Monday.* *v.*, **no·ti·fied, no·ti·fy·ing.**

**no·tion** (nō′shən) **1** an idea; understanding: *He has no notion of what I mean.* **2** an opinion; view; belief: *One common notion is that red hair goes with a quick temper.* **3** intention: *He has no notion of risking his money.* **4** an inclination; whim: *She had a notion to visit her grandmother.* **5 notions,** *pl.* small, useful articles such as pins, needles, thread, tape, etc. *n.*

**no·tion·al** (nō′shə nəl) **1** having to do with ideas or opinions. **2** in one's imagination or thought only; not real. *adj.*

**no·to·chord** (nō′tə kôrd′) **1** a rodlike structure that is the primitive cartilaginous backbone of the lowest vertebrates. **2** a similar structure in the embryos of higher vertebrates. *n.*

**no·to·ri·e·ty** (nō′tə rī′ə tē) **1** being famous for something bad; ill fame: *A crime or scandal brings much notoriety to those involved in it.* **2** the state of being widely known. **3** a well-known person. *n., pl.* **no·to·ri·e·ties.**

**no·to·ri·ous** (nō tô′rē əs) **1** well-known or commonly known because of something unfavourable or unpleasant; having a bad reputation: *The notorious criminal has been sent to prison.* **2** well-known: *Philip is a notorious crybaby.* *adj.* —**no·to′ri·ous·ly,** *adv.* —**no·to′ri·ous·ness,** *n.*

**no–trump** (nō′trump′) **1** without any trumps. **2** in bridge and certain other games, a declaration to play with no suit as trumps. 1 *adj.*, 2 *n.*

**not·with·stand·ing** (not′with stan′ding or not′wiᴛн stan′ding) **1** in spite of: *She bought it notwithstanding the high price.* **2** in spite of the fact that: *Notwithstanding there was need for haste, he still delayed.* **3** in spite of it; nevertheless: *It is raining but I shall go, notwithstanding.* 1 *prep.*, 2 *conj.*, 3 *adv.*

**nou·gat** (nü′gət *or* nü′gä) a kind of soft candy containing nuts. *n.*

**nought** (not) **1** zero; 0: *Two noughts after a six make six hundred.* **2** naught; nothing. *n.*
☞ *Hom.* **Nought,** KNOT, NAUGHT, and NOT are pronounced the same (to rhyme with *got*) by most Canadians.

**noun** (noun) **1** a word used as the name of a person, place, thing, quality, event, etc. Words like *John, table, school, kindness, skill* and *party* are nouns. **2** used as a noun. 1 *n.*, 2 *adj.*

**nour·ish** (nėr′ish) **1** make grow, or keep alive and well, with food; feed; nurture: *Milk nourishes a baby.* **2** maintain; foster; support; encourage: *to nourish a hope.* *v.*

**nour·ish·ment** (nėr′i shmənt) **1** food. **2** a nourishing or being nourished. *n.*

**nou·veau riche** (nü vō RēSH′) *French.* one who has recently become rich; often, one who makes a vulgar display of his or her wealth. *pl.* **nou·veaux riches** (nü vō RēSH′).

**Nov.** November.

**no·va** (nō′və) a star that suddenly becomes brighter and then gradually fades away. *n., pl.* **no·vae** (nō′vē or nō′vī) or **no·vas**.

**No·va Sco·tian** (skō′shən) **1** a native or long-term resident of Nova Scotia. **2** of or having to do with Nova Scotia. **1** *n.,* **2** *adj.*

**nov·el**[1] (nov′əl) **1** of a new kind or nature: *a novel experience.* **2** strikingly new; original: *Red snow is a novel idea to us.* *adj.*

**nov·el**[2] (nov′əl) a story with characters and a plot, long enough to fill one or more volumes: *Novels are usually about people and events such as might be met with in real life.* *n.*

**nov·el·ette** (nov′ə let′) a short NOVEL. *n.*

**nov·el·ist** (nov′ə list) a writer of NOVELS[2]. *n.*

**nov·el·is·tic** (nov′ə lis′tik) of or like NOVELS[2]. *adj.*

**nov·el·ty** (nov′əl tē) **1** newness; NOVEL[1] character: *After the novelty of washing dishes wore off, Mary lost interest in it.* **2** a new or unusual thing: *Staying up late was a novelty to the children.* **3 novelties,** *pl.* small, unusual articles such as toys, cheap jewellery, etc. *n., pl.* **nov·el·ties**.

**No·vem·ber** (nō vem′bər) the 11th month of the year: *November has 30 days.* *n.*
☞ *Etym.* Through OF *novembre* from L *November*, formed from *novem* 'nine'. November was the ninth month of the ancient Roman calendar.

**nov·ice** (nov′is) **1** one who is new to what he or she is doing; beginner: *Novices are likely to make some mistakes.* **2** a person who has been received into a religious group but has not yet taken final vows: *Before becoming a monk or a nun, a person is a novice.* *n.*

**no·vi·ti·ate** or **no·vi·ci·ate** (nō vish′ē it) **1** in a religious order, a period of preparation before taking final vows. **2** NOVICE (def. 2). **3** a house or rooms occupied by religious NOVICES. **4** the state or period of being a beginner in anything. *n.*

**now** (nou) **1** at the present time: *She is here now. Most people do not believe in ghosts now.* **2** by this time: *She must have reached the city now.* **3** the present; this time: *by now, until now, from now on.* **4** at once: *Do it now!* **5** then; next: *Now you see it; now you don't. We have signed the petition and it now goes to the school principal.* **6** at the time referred to: *The clock now struck three.* **7** under the present circumstances; as things are; as it is: *I would believe almost anything now.* **8** since; inasmuch as: *Now I am older, I have changed my mind.* **9** be careful! please! **10 Now** is also used to introduce, emphasize, or lessen the severity of a sentence: *Now what do you mean? Oh, come now! Now you knew that was wrong.* **1, 2, 4–7, 10** *adv.,* **3** *n.,* **8** *conj.,* **9** *interj.*

**just now,** only a few moments ago.

**now and again,** from time to time; once in a while.

**now and then,** from time to time; once in a while.

**now·a·days** (nou′ə dāz′) **1** at the present day; in these times: *Nowadays people travel in automobiles rather than in carriages.* **2** the present day; these times. **1** *adv.,* **2** *n.*

**no·where** (nō′wer or nō′hwer′) **1** in no place; at no place; to no place. **2** a nonexistent place. **1** *adv.,* **2** *n.*

**no·wise** (nō′wīz′) in no way; not at all. *adv.*

**nox·ious** (nok′shəs) **1** extremely harmful; poisonous: *Fumes from the exhaust of an automobile are noxious.* **2** morally hurtful; corrupting. *adv.* —**nox′ious·ly,** *adv.* —**nox′ious·ness,** *n.*

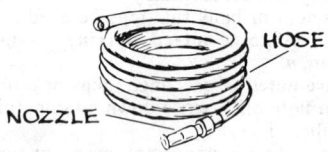

A garden hose with a nozzle attached

**noz·zle** (noz′əl) a tip or spout put on a hose, pipe, can, etc. to allow one to control the outward flow of liquid or gas, often made so that the user can adjust the force and shape of that flow: *He adjusted the nozzle so that the water came out in a fine spray.* *n.*

**Np** neptunium.

**nr.** near.

**NRC** or **N.R.C.** National Research Council.

**NS** or **N.S.** Nova Scotia.

**NSF** or **nsf** not sufficient funds.

**N.S.O.** or **NSO** northern service officer.

**NT** Northwest Territories.

**nth** (enth) last in the series 1, 2, 3, 4 ... n; being of the indefinitely large or small amount denoted by n. *adj.*
**to the nth degree** or **power,** **a** to any degree or power. **b** *Informal.* to the utmost: *He was dressed to the nth degree for the occasion.*

**nt. wt.** net weight.

**nu·ance** (nyü äns′ or nü äns′, nyü′äns or nü′äns) **1** a shade of expression, meaning, feeling, etc. **2** a shade of colour or tone. *n.*

**nub** (nub) **1** a knob; protuberance. **2** a lump or small piece. **3** *Informal.* the point or gist of anything. *n.*

**nub·bin** (nub′ən) **1** a small lump or piece. **2** a small or imperfect ear of corn. **3** an undeveloped fruit. *n.*

**nu·bile** (nyü′bīl or nü′bīl, nyü′bəl or nü′bəl) of a girl or young woman, old enough to be married, marriageable. *adj.*

**nu·cle·ar** (nyü′klē ər or nü′klē ər) **1** forming a NUCLEUS. **2** of or having to do with a NUCLEUS or the nuclei of atoms: *nuclear physics.* **3** of, having to do with, or using ATOMIC ENERGY: *nuclear age, nuclear submarine.* *adj.*

**nuclear energy** the energy contained in the nucleus of an atom; ATOMIC ENERGY.

**nuclear fission** FISSION (def. 2).

**nuclear fuel** a FISSILE substance that will sustain a chain reaction.

**nuclear fusion** FUSION (def. 4).

**nuclear physics** the branch of physics that is concerned with atoms and their nuclear structure.

**nuclear power** electrical or motive power from nuclear energy produced in a nuclear reactor: *Nuclear power has been developed as an alternative to hydro power.*

**nuclear reactor** a device for producing nuclear energy. Usually the nuclear energy is used to heat steam, which drives a generator that produces electricity.

**nuclear winter** a great cooling of the earth's temperature after a nuclear war, in which the sun's rays will be blocked by dense smoke and so all plant life will die, leading to human and animal starvation.

**nu·cle·i** (nyü′klē ī′ *or* nü′klē ī′)   pl. of NUCLEUS.  *n.*

**nu·cle·o·lus** (nyü klē′ə ləs *or* nü klē′ə ləs)   a small structure, usually round, found within the nucleus in most cells. See CELL for picture.  *n., pl.* **nu·cle·o·li** (-lī′ *or* -lē′).

**nu·cle·on** (nyü′klē on′ *or* nü′klē on′)   one of the atomic particles that make up the NUCLEUS of an atom, such as a neutron or proton.  *n.*

**nu·cle·on·ics** (nyü′klē on′iks *or* nü′klē on′iks)   the study and science of the characteristics of NUCLEONS.  *n.*

**nu·cle·us** (nyü′klē əs *or* nü′klē əs)   **1** a beginning to which additions are to be made: *Ella's ten-dollar bill became the nucleus of a flourishing bank account.*   **2** a central part or thing around which other parts or things are collected: *The family is the nucleus of our society.*   **3** in physics, a group of particles forming the central part of an atom and carrying a positive electric charge: *The nucleus of every kind of atom except hydrogen consists of protons and neutrons; the hydrogen nucleus has one proton but no neutrons.*   **4** in chemistry, the basic arrangement of atoms in a particular compound.   **5** in biology, a mass of protoplasm found in most plant and animal cells, without which a cell cannot grow and divide. See CELL for picture.   **6** the dense, central part of a comet's head.  *n., pl.* **nu·cle·i** *or* **nu·cle·us·es**.

**nude** (nyüd *or* nüd)   **1** with one's clothing removed; naked.   **2** in painting, sculpture, or photography, a naked figure.   **3 the nude,**   **a** the naked figure.   **b** a naked condition.   1 *adj.*, 2 *n.*, —**nude′ness,** *n.*
**in the nude,**   without clothes on; naked: *The boys went swimming in the nude.*

**nudge** (nuj)   **1** push slightly; jog with the elbow to attract attention, etc.: *Nudge me when you see the man we are looking for.*   **2** prod; stimulate: *nudge a person into action.*   **3** a slight push or jog: *When he gave me a nudge, I spilled the milk.*   1, 2 *v.*, **nudged, nudg·ing;**   3 *n.*

**nud·ism** (nyü′diz əm *or* nü′diz əm)   the practice of going naked, especially for the sake of one's health.  *n.*

**nud·ist** (nyü′dist *or* nü′dist)   **1** a person who practises NUDISM.   **2** of NUDISM or nudists.   1 *n.*, 2 *adj.*

**nu·di·ty** (nyü′də tē *or* nü′də tē)   **1** nakedness.   **2** something naked.  *n., pl.* **nu·di·ties.**

**nu·ga·to·ry** (nyü′gə tô′rē *or* nü′gə tô′rē)   **1** trifling; worthless.   **2** ineffective; useless.  *adj.*

**nug·get** (nug′it)   **1** a lump, especially a lump of gold in its natural state.   **2** anything valuable: *nuggets of wisdom.*   *n.*

**nui·sance** (nyü′səns *or* nü′səns)   a thing or person that annoys, troubles, offends, or is disagreeable; annoyance: *Flies are a nuisance.*   *n.*

---

hat, āge, fär; let, ēqual, tėrm; it, īce
hot, ōpen, ôrder; oil, out; cup, pùt, rüle
əbove, takən, pencəl, lemən, circəs
ch, child; ng, long; sh, ship
th, thin; ŦH, then; zh, measure

**nuisance ground**   *Cdn.*   a garbage dump; a place where worn-out and useless junk is thrown.

**nuisance tax**   a tax that is annoying because it is collected in very small amounts from the consumer.

**null** (nul)   **1** not binding; of no effect; as if not existing: *A promise obtained by force is legally null.*   **2** unimportant; useless; meaningless; valueless.   **3** not any; zero.  *adj.*
**null and void,**   without legal force or effect; worthless.

**nul·li·fi·ca·tion** (nul′ə fə kā′shən)   **1** a nullifying.   **2** being nullified: *the nullification of a treaty.*   *n.*

**nul·li·fy** (nul′ə fī′)   **1** make not binding or not the law; render void: *to nullify a law.*   **2** make unimportant, useless, or meaningless; destroy; cancel; wipe out: *The difficulties of the plan nullify its advantages.*   *v.*, **nul·li·fied, nul·li·fy·ing.**

**nul·li·ty** (nul′ə tē)   **1** futility; nothingness.   **2** a mere nothing: *The king's power in Denmark is almost a nullity.*   **3** something that is null, such as a nullified law or agreement.  *n., pl.* **nul·li·ties.**

**numb** (num)   **1** having lost the power of feeling or moving: *My fingers are numb with cold.*   **2** make numb.   **3** dull the feelings of: *The old lady was numbed with grief when her grandchild died.*   1 *adj.*, 2, 3 *v.* —**numb′ly,** *adv.* —**numb′ness,** *n.*

**num·ber** (num′bər)   **1** a word or symbol used in counting; numeral: *Two, fourteen, twenty-six, second, fourteenth, twenty-sixth, 2, 14, and 26 are all numbers.*   **2** mark with a number; assign a number to; distinguish with a number: *The pages of this book are numbered.*   **3** the amount of units; sum; total: *The number of your toes is ten.*   **4** be able to show; have: *This city numbers a million inhabitants.*   **5** amount to: *a crew numbering 20 men.*   **6** a large or small quantity: *a number of birds.*   **7** a collection or company: *the number of my acquaintances.*   **8** one of a numbered series, often a particular numeral or set of numerals identifying a person or thing: *a telephone number, a house number.*   Symbol: #   **9** include as one of a class or collection: *I number you among my best friends.*   **10** a single item on a program, etc.: *The program consisted of four musical numbers.*   **11** a song or other piece of music: *She sings many old numbers.*   **12** a single issue of a magazine.   **13** fix the number of; limit: *His days in office are numbered.*   **14** count.   **15** the property or feature of words that indicates whether they refer to one, or more than one, person or thing. *Boy, ox,* and *this* are in the singular number; *boys, oxen* and *these* are in the plural number.   **16** the form or group of forms indicating this.   **17 numbers,** *pl.*   **a** arithmetic.   **b** many: *Numbers were turned away.*   **c** numerical preponderance; being more: *to win a battle by force of numbers.*   **d** in music, a group of notes or measures.   1, 3, 6–8, 10–12, 15–17 *n.*, 2, 4, 5, 9, 13, 14 *v.* —**num′ber·er,** *n.*
**a number of,**   several; many.
**beyond number,**   too many to count.
**without number,**   too many to be counted: *stars without number.*

☞ **Usage.** Numbers up to and including ten are usually written out in full: *I bought three records today.* In formal writing, numbers of either one or two words are often written out in full: *There are twenty questions to be*

*answered. Now I have twenty-three records altogether.* In business or technical writing, however, figures may be used throughout: *We still have 14 units in stock, which is 70 percent of our original order.*
☛ *Usage.* See note at NUMERAL.

**number cruncher** *Informal.* **1** a very powerful computer. **2** a researcher who relies on statistics.

**number crunching** *Informal.* **1** carrying out long, complicated, tedious, repetitive, numerical calculations on the computer. **2** relying on statistics.

**num·ber·less** (num′bər lis) **1** very numerous; too many to count: *There are numberless fish in the sea.* **2** without a number. *adj.*

**number one** **1** *Informal.* oneself: *He worries too much about number one.* **2** the first or best in a series.

**numb·skull** (num′skul′) NUMSKULL. *n.*

**nu·mer·al** (nyü′mə rəl *or* nü′mə rəl) a word, figure, or a group of figures standing for a number. 2, 15 and 100 are Arabic numerals. II, XV, and C are Roman numerals for 2, 15, and 100. *n.*
☛ *Syn.* A **numeral** is a figure that stands for a number. A **number** is the idea of a quantity or amount. The numerals 15 and XV stand for the same number.

**nu·mer·ate** (nyü′mə rāt′ *or* nü′mə rāt′) **1** number; count; enumerate. **2** read an expression in numbers. *v.*, **nu·mer·at·ed, nu·mer·at·ing.**

**nu·mer·a·tion** (nyü′mə rā′shən *or* nü′mə rā′shən) **1** a numbering; counting; calculating. **2** a reading of numbers expressed in figures. *n.*

**nu·mer·a·tor** (nyü′mə rā′tər *or* nü′mə rā′tər) **1** in a fraction, the number above the line: *In ³⁄₈, 3 is the numerator and 8 is the denominator.* **2** a person or thing that makes a count, takes a census, etc. *n.*

**nu·mer·i·cal** (nyü mer′ə kəl *or* nü mer′ə kəl) **1** of or having to do with number or numbers; in numbers; by numbers. **2** shown by numbers, not by letters: *10 is a numerical quantity; bx is a literal or algebraic quantity.* *adj.* —**nu·mer′i·cal·ly,** *adv.*

**nu·mer·ous** (nyü′mə rəs *or* nü′mə rəs) **1** very many; several: *The child asked numerous questions.* **2** in great numbers: *She has a numerous acquaintance among politicians.* *adj.* —**nu′mer·ous·ly,** *adv.* —**nu′mer·ous·ness,** *n.*

**nu·mis·mat·ic** (nyü′miz mat′ik *or* nü′miz mat′ik) **1** of NUMISMATICS or numismatists. **2** of coins and medals. *adj.*

**nu·mis·mat·ics** (nyü′miz mat′iks *or* nü′miz mat′iks) the study of coins and medals. *n.*

**nu·mis·ma·tist** (nyü miz′mə tist *or* nü miz′mə tist) one who knows much about NUMISMATICS. *n.*

**num·skull** (num′skul′) *Informal.* a stupid person; blockhead. *n.*

**nun** (nun) a woman who is a member of a religious order and lives a life of service, prayer, and worship: *Some nuns teach; some nurse the sick.* *n.*
☛ *Hom.* NONE.

**Nu·na·vut** (nü′na vut′) an area in the central and eastern Northwest Terrritories, governed by the original peoples of Canada, including the First Nations and Inuit people. *n.*

**nun·cio** (nun′shē ō′) an ambassador from the Pope to a government. *n., pl.* **nun·ci·os.**

**nun·ner·y** (nun′ə rē) CONVENT. *n., pl.* **nun·ner·ies.**

**nup·tial** (nup′shəl *or* nup′chəl) **1** of marriage or weddings. **2** **nuptials,** *pl.* a wedding or the wedding ceremony. 1 *adj.,* 2 *n.*

**nurse** (nėrs) **1** a person who takes care of the sick, the injured, or the old, or is trained to do this. **2** be a nurse; act as a nurse; work as a nurse. **3** act as a nurse for; wait on or try to cure the sick; take care of sick, injured, or old people. **4** cure or try to cure by care: *She nursed a bad cold by going to bed.* **5** a woman who cares for and brings up the young children or babies of another person: *Mrs. Jones has hired a new nurse.* **6** take care of and bring up another's baby or young child. **7** one who feeds and protects. **8** make grow; nourish and protect: *to nurse a plant, to nurse a hatred in the heart.* **9** use or treat with special care: *He nursed his sore arm by using it very little.* **10** feed milk to a baby at the breast. **11** suck milk from the breast. 1, 5, 7 *n.,* 2–4, 6, 8–11 *v.,* **nursed, nurs·ing.**

**nurse·ling** (nėr′sling) See NURSLING. *n.*

**nurse·maid** (nėr′smād′) a maid employed to care for children. *n.*

**nurs·er·y** (nėr′sə rē) **1** a room set apart for the use of babies and children. **2** a DAY-CARE centre. **3** NURSERY SCHOOL. **4** a piece of ground or place where young plants are grown for transplanting or sale. **5** a place or condition that helps something to grow and develop: *Slums are often nurseries of disease.* *n., pl.* **nurs·er·ies.**

**nurs·er·y·maid** (nėr′sə rē mād′) NURSEMAID. *n.*

**nurs·er·y·man** (nėr′sə rē mən) a man who grows or sells young trees and plants. *n., pl.* **nurs·er·y·men** (-mən).

**nursery rhyme** a short poem for young children: *"Humpty Dumpty sat on a wall" is the beginning of a famous nursery rhyme.*

**nursery school** a school for children over three years and, usually, under five.

**nursing home** **1** a residence providing personal or nursing care for old, chronically ill, or disabled persons. **2** *Brit.* a private hospital.

**nurs·ling** (nėr′sling) **1** a baby that is being nursed. **2** any person or thing that is having tender care. *n.*

**nur·ture** (nėr′chər) **1** bring up; care for; rear: *She nurtured the child as if he had been her own.* **2** the act or process of raising or rearing; bringing up; training; education. **3** nourish: *Minerals in the soil nurture the plants.* **4** food; nourishment. 1, 3 *v.,* **nur·tured, nur·tur·ing;** 2, 4 *n.* —**nur′tur·er,** *n.*

**nu·sa** (nü sä′) a ceremonial wand waved by Shinto priests in purification rituals. *n.*

**nut** (nut) **1** a dry fruit or seed with a hard, woody or leathery shell and a kernel inside: *Some nuts, including walnuts, almonds, and pecans, are good to eat.* **2** the kernel of a nut. **3** gather nuts. **4** a small block, usually of metal, that screws on to a bolt to hold the bolt in place. See BOLT for picture. **5** a piece at the upper end of a violin, cello, etc. over which the strings pass. 1, 2, 4, 5 *n.,* 3 *v.,* **nut·ted, nut·ting.**
**hard nut to crack,** *Informal.* a difficult question, problem, or undertaking.

A nutcracker

**nut·crack·er** (nut′krak′ər)   **1** an instrument for cracking the shells of nuts.   **2** any of several birds, of the same family as the crow, that feed on nuts.   *v.*

**nut·gall** (nut′gol′)   a lump or ball that swells up on an oak tree where it has been injured by an insect; gall.   *n.*

**nut·hatch** (nut′hach′)   a small, sharp-beaked bird that feeds on small nuts, seeds, and insects.   *n.*

**nut·let** (nut′lit)   **1** a small nut.   **2** the stone of a peach, plum, cherry, etc.   *n.*

**nut·meat** (nut′mēt′)   the kernel of a nut.   *n.*

**nut·meg** (nut′meg′)   **1** a hard, spicy seed about as big as a marble, obtained from the fruit of an East Indian tree: *Nutmeg is grated and used for flavouring food.*   **2** the tree.

**nu·tri·a** (nyü′trē ə *or* nü′trē ə)   **1** the COYPU, an aquatic rodent native to South America but now widely bred for its fur.   **2** its valuable beaverlike fur.   *n.*

**nu·tri·ent** (nyü′trē ənt *or* nü′trē ənt)   **1** a nutritive substance.   **2** nourishing.   **1** *n.*, **2** *adj.*

**nu·tri·ment** (nyü′trə mənt *or* nü′trə mənt)   nourishment; food.   *n.*

**nu·tri·tion** (nyü trish′ən *or* nü trish′ən)   **1** food; nourishment: *A balanced diet gives good nutrition.*   **2** the series of processes by which food is changed to living tissue.   *n.*

**nu·tri·tion·al** (nyü trish′ə nəl *or* nü trish′ə nəl)   having to do with NUTRITION.   *adj.*   —**nu·tri′tion·al·ly,** *adv.*

**nu·tri·tious** (nyü trish′əs *or* nü trish′əs)   valuable as food; nourishing: *Oranges and cheese are nutritious.*   *adj.*   —**nu·tri′tious·ly,** *adv.*   —**nu·tri′tious·ness,** *n.*

**nu·tri·tive** (nyü′trə tiv *or* nü′trə tiv)   **1** having to do with foods and the use of foods: *Digestion is part of the nutritive process.*   **2** NUTRITIOUS.   *adj.*   —**nu′tri·tive·ness,** *n.*

**nut·shell** (nut′shel′)   the shell of a nut.   *n.*
**in a nutshell,**   in a very brief form; in a few words.

**nut·ting** (nut′ing)   **1** gathering or looking for nuts.   **2** ppr. of NUT.   **1** *n.*, **2** *v.*

**nut·ty** (nut′ē)   **1** containing many nuts: *nutty cake.*   **2** like nuts; tasting like nuts: *Some cereals have a nutty flavour.*   *adj.*, **nut·ti·er, nut·ti·est.**   —**nut′ti·ness,** *n.*

**nuz·zle** (nuz′əl)   **1** poke or rub with the nose; press the nose against: *The calf nuzzles its mother.*   **2** nestle; snuggle; cuddle.   *v.*, **nuz·zled, nuz·zling.**

**NW** or **N.W.**   northwest; northwestern.

**NWMP** or **N.W.M.P.**   North West Mounted Police.

**N.W.T.**   Northwest Territories.

**ny·lon** (nī′lon)   **1** an extremely strong and durable, plastic substance, used to make textiles, utensils, bristles, etc.   **2** made of nylon: *Many toothbrushes have nylon bristles.*   **3 nylons,** *pl.*   stockings made of nylon.   *n.*

**nymph** (nimf)   **1** a beautiful or graceful young woman.   **2** any of certain insects in the stage of development between larva and adult. It resembles the adult but has no wings.   *n.*   —**nymph·like,** *adj.*

**N.Z.**   New Zealand.

# Oo Oo

**o** or **O¹** (ō) **1** the fifteenth letter of the English alphabet. **2** any speech sound represented by this letter. **3** a person or thing identified as o, especially the 15th in a series. **4** zero. **5** anything shaped like an O. *n., pl.* **o's** or **O's**.
☞ *Hom.* OH, OWE.

**O²** See OH.
☞ *Hom.* OWE.
☞ *Usage.* **O** is usually used only before a name or something treated as a name: *O Canada. O Happy Day!* In other cases, the spelling generally used is **Oh**.

**O³** (ō) one of the four main blood groups.

**o'** (ə *or* ō) **1** OF: *will-o'-the-wisp.* **2** ON. *prep.*

**o** ohm.

**o. 1** octavo. **2** in baseball, out.

**O** oxygen.

**O.** Ocean.

**oaf** (ōf) **1** a very stupid child or person. **2** a clumsy person: *I felt like an oaf when I dropped my glass. n., pl.* **oafs**.

**oaf·ish** (ō′fish) very stupid; clumsy. *adj.*

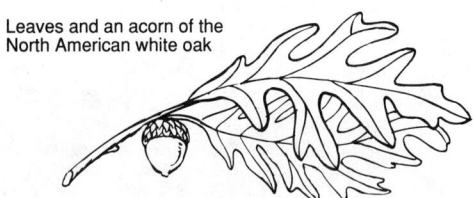
Leaves and an acorn of the North American white oak

**oak** (ōk) **1** a large tree with hard durable wood and nuts called acorns. **2** its wood: *The ship had timbers of oak.* **3** a tree or shrub resembling or suggesting an oak. **4** of an oak: *oak leaves.* **5** made of oak: *an oak table.* 1–3 *n.,* 4, 5 *adj.* —**oak′like,** *adj.*

**oak apple** a lump or ball on an oak leaf or stem, caused by injury by an insect.

**oak·en** (ō′kən) made of OAK wood: *the old oaken bucket. adj.*

**oa·kum** (ō′kəm) a loose fibre obtained by untwisting and picking apart old ropes, used for stopping up the seams or cracks in ships. *n.*

**oar** (ôr) **1** a long pole with a broad, flat blade at one end, used for rowing or steering a boat. See ROWBOAT for picture. **2** a person who rows: *She is the best oar in our crew.* **3** row. 1, 2 *n.,* 3 *v.*
**put one's oar in,** meddle; interfere.
**rest on one's oars,** stop working or trying and take a rest.
☞ *Hom.* OR, ORE.

**oar·lock** (ôr′lok′) a notch or U-shaped support for holding the OAR in place while rowing; rowlock. See ROWBOAT for picture. *n.*

**oars·man** (ôr′zmən) **1** a man who rows. **2** a man who rows well. *n., pl.* **oars·men** (-zmən).

**OAS** or **O.A.S.** Organization of American States.

**o·a·ses** (ō ā′sēz) pl. of OASIS. *n.*

**o·a·sis** (ō ā′sis) **1** a fertile spot in the desert: *Water is always available at an oasis.* **2** any fertile spot in a barren land; any pleasant place in a desolate region. *n., pl.* **o·a·ses**.

**oat** (ōt) **1** a tall cereal grass whose seeds are used in making oatmeal and as a food for horses. **2 oats,** *pl.* the seeds of the oat plant. *n.*
**feel one's oats,** *Informal.* **a** be lively or frisky. **b** feel pleased or important and show it.
**sow one's wild oats,** behave irresponsibly when young.

**oat·cake** (ōt′kāk′) a thin cake made of oatmeal. *n.*

**oat·en** (ō′tən) made of OATS or OATMEAL. *adj.*

**oath** (ōth) **1** a solemn promise or statement that something is true, especially such a promise made to a judge, coroner, etc.: *If a person tells lies after taking an oath he or she can be punished by the law.* **2** the name of some holy person or thing used as an exclamation to add force or to express anger. **3** a curse; a swear word. *n., pl.* **oaths** (ōTHz *or* ōths).
**take an oath** or **oaths,** certify or attest an oath: *A notary public is authorized to take oaths.*
**take oath,** make an oath; promise or state solemnly.
**under oath,** bound by an oath: *She gave her evidence under oath.*

**oat·meal** (ōt′mēl′) **1** oats made into meal; ground oats. **2** rolled oats. **3** porridge made from rolled oats or oatmeal. *n.*

**ob.** an abbreviation for the Latin *obiit,* meaning died.

**ob·bli·ga·to** (ob′lə gä′tō) **1** in music, accompanying a solo, but having a distinct character and independent importance. **2** an obbligato part or accompaniment. 1 *adj.,* 2 *n., pl.* **ob·bli·ga·tos.** Also, **obligato.**

**ob·du·ra·cy** (ob′dyə rə sē *or* ob′də rə sē) hardness of heart; stubbornness. *n.*

**ob·du·rate** (ob′dyə rit *or* ob′də rit) **1** stubborn; unyielding: *an obdurate refusal.* **2** hardened in feelings or heart; not repentant: *an obdurate criminal. adj.*
—**ob′du·rate·ly,** *adv.* —**ob′du·rate·ness,** *n.*

**o·be·di·ence** (ō bē′dē əns) the act or habit of doing what one is told; submission to authority or law: *Our puppy is already learning obedience. Soldiers act in obedience to orders. n.*

**o·be·di·ent** (ō bē′dē ənt) doing what one is told; willing to obey: *The obedient dog came at my command. adj.* —**o·be′di·ent·ly,** *adv.*

**o·bei·sance** (ō bā′səns *or* ō bē′səns) **1** a movement of the body expressing deep respect; deep bow: *The men made obeisance to the king.* **2** deference; HOMAGE: *acts of obeisance. n.*

An ancient Egyptian obelisk

hat, āge, fär; let, ēqual, tėrm; it, īce
hot, ōpen, ôrder; oil, out; cup, put, rüle
ə bove, takən, pencəl, lemən, circəs
ch, child; ng, long; sh, ship
th, thin; ŦH, then; zh, measure

**ob·e·lisk** (ob′ə lisk′)   a tapering, four-sided shaft of stone with a top shaped like a pyramid: *Obelisks were often put up as monuments in ancient Egypt.*   *n.*

**o·bese** (ō bēs′)   extremely fat.   *adj.*
—**o·bese′ness,** *n.*

**o·bes·i·ty** (ō bē′sə tē)   extreme fatness.   *n.*

**o·bey** (ō bā′)   **1** do what one is told: *The dog obeyed and went home.*   **2** follow the order of: *We obey our mother.*   **3** act in accordance with; comply with: *to obey the laws.*   **4** yield to the control of: *A car obeys the driver.*   *v.*

**ob·fus·cate** (ob′fə skāt′ *or* ob fus′kāt)   darken; obscure; confuse; STUPEFY (def. 1): *A person's mind may be obfuscated by liquor.*   *v.*, **ob·fus·cat·ed, ob·fus·cat·ing.**   —**ob′fus·ca′tion,** *n.*   —**ob′fus·ca′tor,** *n.*

An obi

**o·bi** (ō′bē)   a long, broad sash worn around the waist of a KIMONO (def. 1) by Japanese women and children.   *n.*

**ob·i·ter dic·tum** (ob′ə tər dik′təm) *Latin.*   **1** an incidental statement.   **2** in law, an incidental opinion given by a judge.   *pl.*, **ob·i·ter dic·ta** (dik′tə).

**o·bit·u·ary** (ō bich′ü er′ē)   **1** a notice of death, often with a brief account of the person's life.   **2** of a death; recording a death: *the obituary notices in the newspaper.*   1 *n.*, *pl.* **o·bit·u·ar·ies;**   2 *adj.*

**obj.**   **1** object.   **2** objective.   **3** objection.

**ob·ject** (ob′jikt *for noun,* əb jekt′ *for verb*)   **1** anything that can be seen or touched; thing; article: *What is that object by the fence? A dark object moved between me and the door.*   **2** a person or thing toward which feeling, thought, or action is directed: *an object of charity, an object of study.*   **3** something aimed at; end; purpose; goal: *My object in coming here was to get Mary's address.*   **4** a word or group of words used as the object of a transitive verb or a preposition: *In* "He threw the ball to his brother," *ball* is the object of *threw, and* brother *is the object of* to.   **5** make objections; be opposed; feel dislike: *I made my suggestion, but Lalia objected. Many people object to loud noise.*   **6** give as a reason against something; bring forward in opposition; oppose: *Mother objected that the weather was too wet to play outdoors.*   1–4 *n.*, 5, 6 *v.*   —**ob·ject′ing·ly,** *adv.*   —**ob·jec′tor,** *n.*

**object glass**   the lens or combination of lenses in a telescope, microscope, etc. that first receives light rays from the object and forms the image viewed through the eyepiece.

**ob·jec·ti·fy** (əb jek′tə fī′)   make OBJECTIVE (def. 2); externalize: *Experiments in chemistry objectify the teaching. Kind acts objectify kindness.*   *v.*, **ob·jec·ti·fied, ob·jec·ti·fy·ing.**

**ob·jec·tion** (əb jek′shən)   **1** something said in objecting; a reason or argument against something: *One of her objections to the plan was that it would cost too much.*   **2** a feeling of disapproval or dislike: *A lazy person has strong objections to working.*   *n.*

**ob·jec·tion·a·ble** (əb jek′shə nə bəl)   **1** likely to be OBJECTED (def. 6) to.   **2** unpleasant; disagreeable.   *adj.*   —**ob·jec′tion·a·bly,** *adv.*

**ob·jec·tive** (əb jek′tiv)   **1** something aimed at: *My objective this summer will be learning to play tennis better.*   **2** existing outside the mind as an actual object and not merely in the mind as an idea; real: *Buildings and landscapes are objective; ideas and feelings are subjective.*   **3** dealing with facts or objects, not with the thoughts and feelings of the speaker, writer, painter, etc.; impersonal: *A scientist must be objective in her experiments. The report was not objective, but was biassed in favour of the one firm.*   **4** something real and observable.   **5** of, having to do with, or being the grammatical form of an English pronoun that shows that it is an object of a verb or preposition. There are six English pronouns with special objective forms: *me, us, him, her, them,* and *whom.*   **6** the objective form: *Him is the objective of* he.   **7** a word in the objective case: *Me* and *whom are objectives.*   **8** the lens or set of lenses in a microscope or telescope that is nearest to the object being viewed and that forms the image of the object.   See MICROSCOPE for picture.   1, 4, 6–8 *n.*, 2, 3, 5 *adj.*   —**ob·jec′tive·ly,** *adv.*
☞ *Usage.* **Objective** and SUBJECTIVE are contrasted in two ways. First, in grammar, they mean basically 'of or having to do with an object' and 'of or having to do with a subject'. Second, **objective** (def. 3) means dealing with data in a factual, impersonal way, while **subjective** (def. 2) means reacting to data in terms of one's own feelings, preference, etc.: *The news report gave an objective account of the accident. The injured driver's account was more subjective, full of bitterness and anger.*

**ob·jec·tiv·i·ty** (ob′jek tiv′ə tē)   the state or quality of being OBJECTIVE (def. 3); intentness on objects external to the mind; external reality.   *n.*

**object lesson**   **1** instruction conveyed by means of material objects.   **2** a practical illustration of a principle: *Many street accidents are object lessons in the dangers of carelessness.*

**ob·jet d'art** (ôb zhe där′) *French.*   a small picture, vase, etc. of some artistic value.   *pl.* **ob·jets d'art** (ôb zhä där′).

**ob·jur·gate** (ob′jər gāt′)   reproach vehemently; UPBRAID violently; berate.   *v.*, **ob·jur·gat·ed, ob·jur·gat·ing.**

**ob·jur·ga·tion** (ob′jər gā′shən) vehement UPBRAIDING. *n.*

**ob·jur·ga·to·ry** (əb jėr′gə tô′rē) vehemently reproachful; UPBRAIDing; berating. *adj.*

**ob·late** (ob′lāt) flattened at the poles: *The earth is an oblate spheroid. adj.* —**ob′late·ness**, *n.*

**ob·li·gate** (ob′lə gāt′) bind morally or legally; pledge: *A witness in court is obligated to tell the truth. v.,* **ob·li·gat·ed, ob·li·gat·ing.**

**ob·li·ga·tion** (ob′lə gā′shən) **1** a duty under the law; duty due to a promise or contract; duty on account of social relationship or kindness received: *The man is under obligation to paint our house first. Taxes are an obligation on most citizens. A person's first obligation is to the people she loves.* **2** the binding power of a law, promise, sense of duty, etc.: *The one who did the damage is under obligation to pay for it.* **3** a binding legal agreement; bond; contract: *The firm was not able to meet its obligations.* **4** being in debt for a favour, service, or the like: *It was George's obligation to return Mary's favour by asking her to his birthday party.* **5** a service; favour; benefit: *An independent person likes to repay obligations. n.*

**ob·li·ga·to** (ob′lə gä′tō) See OBBLIGATO. *adj., n., pl.* **ob·li·ga·tos.**

**ob·lig·a·to·ry** (əb lig′ə tô′rē *or* ob′lə gə tô′rē) binding morally or legally; required: *Attendance at school is obligatory. adj.*

**o·blige** (ə blīj′) **1** bind by a promise, contract, duty, etc.; compel; force: *The law obliges parents to send their children to school.* **2** put under a debt of thanks for a favour or service: *She obliged us with a song.* **3** do a favour to: *Kindly oblige me by closing the door. v.,* **o·bliged, o·blig·ing.** —**o·blig′er,** *n.*

**be obliged,** be grateful to someone for a service: *I am obliged to you for letting me stay so long at your house.*

**o·blig·ing** (ə blī′jing) willing to do favours; helpful: *Anne's obliging good nature wins her friends. adj.* —**o·blig′ing·ly,** *adv.* —**o·blig′ing·ness,** *n.*

**ob·lique** (ə blēk′) **1** slanting; not straight up and down; not straight across: *An oblique angle is any angle that is not a right angle.* **2** not straightforward; indirect: *an oblique glance, an oblique movement. She made an oblique reference to her illness, but did not mention it directly.* **3** advance in an oblique manner; slant. 1, 2 *adj.,* 3 *v.,* **ob·liqued, ob·liqu·ing.** —**ob·lique′ly,** *adv.*

**oblique angle** an angle that is not a right angle. See ANGLE for picture.

**ob·liq·ui·ty** (ə blik′wə tē) **1** indirectness or crookedness of thought or behaviour, especially conduct that is not upright and moral. **2** being OBLIQUE (defs. 1, 2). *n., pl.* **ob·liq·ui·ties.**

**ob·lit·er·ate** (ə blit′ə rāt′) remove all traces of; blot out; destroy: *The heavy rain obliterated her footprints. v.,* **ob·lit·er·at·ed, ob·lit·er·at·ing.**

**ob·lit·er·a·tion** (ə blit′ə rā′shən) an obliterating or being OBLITERATEd; effacement. *n.*

**ob·liv·i·on** (ə bliv′ē ən) **1** the condition of being entirely forgotten: *Many ancient cities have long since passed into oblivion.* **2** the condition of being unaware of what is going on; forgetfulness: *Grandmother sat by the fire in peaceful oblivion. n.*

**ob·liv·i·ous** (ə bliv′ē əs) **1** forgetful; not mindful; unaware: *The book was so interesting that I was oblivious of my surroundings.* **2** bringing or causing forgetfulness: *an oblivious slumber. adj.* —**ob·liv′i·ous·ly,** *adv.* —**ob·liv′i·ous·ness,** *n.*

**ob·long** (ob′long) **1** longer than broad or round: *an oblong loaf of bread, an oblong tablecloth.* **2** of a plane figure, having four sides and four right angles, but not square; rectangular with adjacent sides unequal. **3** a rectangle that is not square. See QUADRILATERAL for picture. 1, 2 *adj.,* 3 *n.*

**ob·lo·quy** (ob′lə kwē) **1** public reproach; abuse; blame. **2** disgrace; shame. *n., pl.* **ob·lo·quies.**

**ob·nox·ious** (əb nok′shəs) very disagreeable; offensive; hateful: *His disgusting table manners made him obnoxious. adj.* —**ob·nox′ious·ly,** *adv.* —**ob·nox′ious·ness,** *n.*

**o·boe** (ō′bō) a wooden wind instrument in which a thin, poignant tone is produced by a double reed. *n.*
☛ *Etym.* From F *hautbois*, literally 'high wood', but the present spelling comes from Italian.

**obs.** obsolete; used formerly but not now.

**ob·scene** (əb sēn′ *or* ob sēn′) offending decency; impure; filthy: *We were annoyed by the man's obscene swearing at the hockey players. adj.* —**ob·scene′ly,** *adv.*

**ob·scen·i·ty** (əb sen′ə tē *or* əb sē′nə tē) **1** an OBSCENE quality. **2** OBSCENE language or behaviour; an obscene word or act. *n., pl.* **ob·scen·i·ties.**

**ob·scur·ant·ism** (əb skyü′rən tiz′əm *or* ob′skyə ran′tiz əm) opposition to progress and the spread of knowledge. *n.*

**ob·scur·ant·ist** (əb skyü′rən tist *or* ob′skyə ran′tist) **1** a person who is opposed to progress and the spread of knowledge. **2** of obscurantists or OBSCURANTISM. 1 *n.,* 2 *adj.*

**ob·scu·ra·tion** (ob′skyə rā′shən) **1** an obscuring. **2** being OBSCUREd. *n.*

**ob·scure** (əb skyür′) **1** not clearly expressed: *an obscure passage in a book.* **2** not expressing meaning clearly: *an obscure style of writing.* **3** not well-known; attracting no notice: *an obscure little village, an obscure poet, an obscure position in the government.* **4** not easily discovered; hidden: *an obscure path, an obscure meaning.* **5** not distinct; not clear: *an obscure form, obscure sounds, an obscure view.* **6** dark; dim: *an obscure corner.* **7** hide from view; make obscure; dim; darken: *Clouds obscure the sun.* 1–6 *adj.,* **ob·scur·er, ob·scur·est;** 7 *v.,* **ob·scured, ob·scur·ing.** —**ob·scure′ly,** *adv.* —**ob·scure′ness,** *n.* —**ob·scur′er,** *n.*

**ob·scu·ri·ty** (əb skyü′rə tē) **1** a lack of clearness; difficulty in being understood: *The obscurity of the passage makes several interpretations possible.* **2** something obscure; thing hard to understand; doubtful or vague meaning: *The movie had so many obscurities that we didn't enjoy it.* **3** the state or condition of being unknown: *The premier rose from obscurity to fame.* **4** a little known person or place. **5** a lack of light; dimness: *The dog hid in the obscurity of the thick bushes. n., pl.* **ob·scu·ri·ties.**

**ob·se·quies** (ob′sə kwēz) funeral rites or ceremonies; a stately funeral. *n. pl.*

**ob·se·qui·ous** (əb sē′kwē əs) polite or obedient from hope of gain or from fear; servile; FAWNing: *Obsequious courtiers greeted the queen. adj.* —**ob·se′qui·ous·ly,** *adv.* —**ob·se′qui·ous·ness,** *n.*

**ob·serv·a·ble** (əb zėr′və bəl) **1** that can be or is noticed; noticeable; easily seen. **2** that can be or is followed: *Laws are observable to preserve justice.* *adj.*

**ob·serv·a·bly** (əb zėr′və blē) so as to be observed; to an OBSERVABLE (def. 1) degree. *adv.*

**ob·serv·ance** (əb zėr′vəns) **1** the act of observing or keeping laws or customs: *the observance of polite behaviour.* **2** an act performed as a sign of worship or respect; religious ceremony. **3** a rule or custom to be observed. **4** an observation. *n.*

**ob·serv·ant** (əb zėr′vənt) **1** quick to notice; watchful; observing: *If you are observant in the fields and woods, you will find many flowers that others fail to notice.* **2** careful in observing a law, rule, custom, etc.: *observant of the traffic rules.* *adj.* —**ob·serv′ant·ly,** *adv.*

**ob·ser·va·tion** (ob′zər vā′shən) **1** the act, habit, or power of seeing and noting: *Her keen observation helped her to become a good scientist.* **2** the fact of being seen; being seen; notice: *The tramp escaped observation.* **3** something seen and noted: *The student of bird life kept a record of his observations.* **4** the act of watching for some special purpose; study: *The observation of nature is important in science.* **5** a remark or comment: *"Haste makes waste" was mother's observation when Gemma spilled the sugar.* *n.*

**ob·ser·va·tion·al** (ob′zər vā′shə nəl) of, having to do with, or founded on OBSERVATION, especially as contrasted with experiment. *adj.*

**ob·serv·a·to·ry** (əb zėr′və tô′rē) **1** a place or building equipped with a telescope, etc., for observing the stars and other heavenly bodies. See TELESCOPE for picture. **2** a place or building for observing facts or happenings of nature. **3** a high place or building giving a wide view. *n., pl.* **ob·serv·a·to·ries.**

**ob·serve** (əb zėrv′) **1** see and note; notice: *I observed nothing strange in her behaviour.* **2** examine for some special purpose; study: *An astronomer observes the stars.* **3** remark; comment: *"Bad weather," the captain observed.* **4** keep; follow in practice: *to observe silence, to observe a rule.* **5** show regard for; celebrate: *to observe her 80th birthday.* *v.,* **ob·served, ob·serv·ing.**

**ob·serv·er** (əb zėr′vər) **1** one who watches or examines. **2** one who follows or celebrates a rule, custom, etc.: *an observer of Remembrance Day.* **3** one who attends a meeting as a guest but can take no official part in it. *n.*

**ob·serv·ing** (əb zėr′ving) **1** observant; quick to notice. **2** ppr. of OBSERVE. 1 *adj.,* 2 *v.*

**ob·sess** (əb ses′) fill the mind of; keep the attention of; haunt: *Fear that someone might steal his money obsessed the old miser.* *v.*

**ob·ses·sion** (əb sesh′ən) **1** an obsessing or being obsessed; influence of a feeling, idea, or impulse that a person cannot escape. **2** the feeling, idea, or impulse itself. *n.*

**ob·sid·i·an** (ob sid′ē ən) a hard, dark, glassy rock that is formed when lava cools. *n.*

**ob·so·les·cence** (ob′sə les′əns) the condition or state of passing out of use; getting out-of-date; becoming OBSOLETE. *n.*

**ob·so·les·cent** (ob′sə les′ənt) passing out of use; tending to become out-of-date: *Horse carriages are obsolescent.* *adj.*

**ob·so·lete** (ob′sə lēt′) **1** no longer in use: *"Eft"*

## observable 815 obtrude

hat, āge, fär; let, ēqual, tėrm; it, īce
hot, ōpen, ôrder; oil, out; cup, put, rüle
əbove, takən, pencəl, lemən, circəs
ch, child; ng, long; sh, ship
th, thin; ᴛʜ, then; zh, measure

(meaning "again") is an obsolete word. *Wooden warships are obsolete.* **2** out-of-date: *We still use this machine though it is obsolete.* *adj.*

**ob·sta·cle** (ob′stə kəl) something that stands in the way or stops progress; hindrance: *A tree fallen across the road was an obstacle to our car. Blindness is an obstacle in most occupations.* *n.*

**ob·stet·ric** (ob stet′rik) having to do with the care of women in childbirth. *adj.*

**ob·ste·tri·cian** (ob′stə trish′ən) a physician whose specialty is OBSTETRICS. *n.*

**ob·stet·rics** (ob stet′riks) the branch of medicine and surgery concerned with caring for and treating women in, before, and after childbirth. *n.*

**ob·sti·na·cy** (ob′stə nə sē) **1** stubbornness; being obstinate: *Obstinacy drove the boy to repeat his statement even after he knew it was wrong.* **2** an obstinate act. *n., pl.* **ob·sti·na·cies.**

**ob·sti·nate** (ob′stə nit) **1** not giving in; stubborn: *The obstinate girl would go her own way, in spite of all warnings.* **2** hard to control or treat: *an obstinate cough.* *adj.* —**ob′sti·nate·ly,** *adv.*
☛ *Syn.* **Obstinate** (def. 1) and **stubborn** both mean fixed in purpose or opinion. **Obstinate** often suggests being unreasonable in refusing to give in. **Stubborn** suggests being firm enough not to give in. When used of animals or things, **stubborn** suggests being hard to handle: *The stubborn horse refused to jump.*

**ob·strep·er·ous** (əb strep′ə rəs) **1** noisy; boisterous: *Many children are naturally obstreperous.* **2** unruly; disorderly. *adj.* —**ob·strep′er·ous·ly,** *adv.* —**ob·strep′er·ous·ness,** *n.*

**ob·struct** (əb strukt′) **1** make hard to pass through; block up: *Fallen trees obstruct the road.* **2** be in the way of; hinder: *Trees obstruct our view of the ocean. A strike obstructed the work of the factory.* *v.*

**ob·struc·tion** (əb struk′shən) **1** anything that obstructs; something in the way; obstacle: *The soldiers had to get over such obstructions as ditches and barbed wire. Anger is an obstruction to clear thinking.* **2** a blocking; hindering: *the obstruction of progress by prejudices.* *n.*

**ob·struc·tion·ism** (əb struk′shə niz′əm) the hindering of the progress of business in a meeting, legislature, etc. *n.*

**ob·struc·tion·ist** (əb struk′shə nist) a person or procedure that hinders progress, legislation, reform, etc. *n.*

**ob·struc·tive** (əb struk′tiv) tending or serving to obstruct; blocking; hindering. *adj.*

**ob·tain** (əb tān′) **1** get or procure through diligence or effort; come to have: *She worked hard to obtain the prize. We study to obtain knowledge.* **2** be in use; be customary; prevail: *Different rules obtain in different schools.* *v.* —**ob·tain′a·ble,** *adj.*

**ob·trude** (əb trüd′) **1** put forward unasked and unwanted; force: *Don't obtrude your opinions on others.*

**obtrusion** 816 **ocean**

2 come unasked and unwanted; force oneself; intrude. 3 push out; thrust forward: *A turtle obtrudes its head from its shell.* *v.*, **ob·trud·ed, ob·trud·ing.** —**ob·trud′er,** *n.*

**ob·tru·sion** (əb trü′zhən) 1 an obtruding. 2 something OBTRUDED. *n.*

**ob·tru·sive** (əb trü′siv) inclined to obtrude; putting oneself forward; intrusive. *adj.* —**ob·tru′sive·ly,** *adv.* —**ob·tru′sive·ness,** *n.*

**ob·tuse** (əb tyüs′ *or* əb tüs′) 1 not sharp or acute; blunt. 2 having more than 90° of angle but less than 180°. See ANGLE for picture. 3 slow in understanding; stupid: *She was too obtuse to take the hint.* 4 not sensitive; dull: *One's hearing often becomes obtuse in old age.* *adj.* —**ob·tuse′ly,** *adv.*

**obtuse angle** an angle greater than 90° but less than 180°; an angle greater than a right angle. See ANGLE for picture.

**ob·verse** (ob′vėrs *for noun,* ob vėrs′ *or* ob′vėrs *for adjective*) 1 the side of a coin, medal, etc. that has the principal design. 2 the face of anything that is meant to be turned toward the observer; front. Compare with REVERSE (def. 5). 3 turned toward the observer. 4 a counterpart. 5 being a counterpart to something else. 1, 2, 4 *n.*, 3, 5 *adj.* —**ob·verse′ly,** *adv.*

**ob·vi·ate** (ob′vē āt′) meet and dispose of; clear out of the way; remove: *to obviate a difficulty, to obviate danger, to obviate objections.* *v.*, **ob·vi·at·ed, ob·vi·at·ing.** —**ob′vi·a′tion,** *n.*

**ob·vi·ous** (ob′vē əs) easily seen or understood; clear to the eye or mind; not to be doubted; plain: *It is obvious that two and two make four.* *adj.* —**ob′vi·ous·ly,** *adv.* —**ob′vi·ous·ness,** *n.*

**oc·a·ri·na** (ok′ə rē′nə) a musical instrument shaped like a sweet potato, with finger holes and a whistle-like mouthpiece. *n.*

**oc·ca·sion** (ə kā′zhən *or* ō kā′zhən) 1 a particular time: *We have met Ms. Nasahaki on several occasions.* 2 a special event: *The jewels were worn only on great occasions.* 3 a good chance; opportunity: *The trip gave us an occasion to get better acquainted.* 4 a cause; reason: *The dog that was the occasion of the quarrel had run away.* 5 cause; bring about: *Her strange behaviour occasioned talk.* 1–4 *n.*, 5 *v.*
**improve the occasion,** take advantage of an opportunity.
**on occasion,** now and then; once in a while.

**oc·ca·sion·al** (ə kā′zhə nəl) 1 happening or coming now and then, or once in a while: *We had fine weather except for an occasional thunderstorm.* 2 caused by or used for some special time or event: *She composed a piece of occasional music to be played at the opening concert in the new auditorium.* *adj.*

**oc·ca·sion·al·ly** (ə kā′zhə nə lē) now and then; once in a while; at times. *adv.*

**Oc·ci·dent** (ok′sə dənt) 1 the countries of Europe and America; the West: *The Occident and the Orient have many different ideals and customs.* 2 **occident,** the west. *n.*

**Oc·ci·den·tal** (ok′sə den′təl) 1 Western; of the Occident. 2 a native of the West: *Europeans are Occidentals.* 3 **occidental,** western. 1, 3 *adj.*, 2 *n.*

**oc·cip·i·tal** (ok sip′ə təl) 1 of or having to do with the back part of the head or skull. 2 the OCCIPITAL BONE. 1 *adj.*, 2 *n.*

**occipital bone** the compound bone forming the lower back part of the skull.

**oc·clude** (o klüd′) 1 stop up a passage, pores, etc.; close. 2 shut in, out, or off. 3 absorb and retain gases: *Platinum occludes hydrogen.* 4 meet closely: *The teeth in the upper jaw and those in the lower jaw should occlude.* 5 in meteorology, force (air) to rise, such as when a cold front overtakes and pushes under a warm front. *v.*, **oc·clud·ed, oc·clud·ing.**

**occluded front** in meteorology, the front created when a cold front overtakes a warm front, forcing the air up.

**oc·clu·sion** (o klü′zhən) an occluding or being OCCLUDED. *n.*

**oc·cult** (ə kult′ *or* ok′ult) 1 beyond the bounds of ordinary knowledge; mysterious. 2 outside the laws of the natural world; magical: *Astrology and alchemy are occult sciences.* 3 **the occult,** occult studies or beliefs. 1, 2 *adj.*, 3 *n.*

**oc·cul·ta·tion** (ok′əl tā′shən) 1 a hiding of one heavenly body by another passing between it and the observer: *the occultation of a star by the moon.* 2 a disappearance from view or notice. *n.*

**oc·cult·ism** (o kul′tiz əm *or* ok′əl tiz əm) 1 a belief in OCCULT powers. 2 the study or use of OCCULT sciences. *n.*

**oc·cu·pan·cy** (ok′yə pən sē) the act or fact of OCCUPYing; the holding of land, houses, etc. by being in possession: *The occupancy of the land by cattlemen was disputed by the farmers.* *n.*

**oc·cu·pant** (ok′yə pənt) 1 a person who occupies: *the occupant of the chair. The occupant of the shack was not at home.* 2 the person in actual possession of a house, office, etc. *n.*

**oc·cu·pa·tion** (ok′yə pā′shən) 1 one's business or employment; trade: *Teaching is a teacher's occupation.* 2 occupying or being occupied; possession: *the occupation of a town by the enemy.* *n.*

**oc·cu·pa·tion·al** (ok′yə pā′shə nəl) of or having to do with occupation, especially of or having to do with trades, callings, etc. *adj.*

**occupational therapy** the treatment of persons having physical or emotional disabilities through specific types of exercises, work, etc. to promote rehabilitation.

**oc·cu·py** (ok′yə pī′) 1 take up; fill: *The building occupies an entire block.* 2 keep busy; engage; employ: *Sports often occupy a girl's attention.* 3 take possession of: *The enemy occupied our fort.* 4 keep possession of; have; hold: *A judge occupies an important position. This seat is occupied.* 5 live in: *The owner and her daughter occupy the house.* *v.*, **oc·cu·pied, oc·cu·py·ing.** —**oc′cu·pi′er,** *n.*

**oc·cur** (ə kėr′) 1 take place; happen: *Storms often occur in winter.* 2 be found; exist: *"E" occurs in print more than any other English letter.* 3 come to mind; suggest itself: *Did it occur to you to close the window?* *v.*, **oc·curred, oc·cur·ring.**

**oc·cur·rence** (ə kėr′əns) 1 an OCCURRing: *The occurrence of storms delayed our trip.* 2 an event; happening: *an unexpected occurrence.* *n.*

**o·cean** (ō′shən) 1 the great body of salt water that covers almost three-fourths of the earth's surface; the sea; the main; the deep. 2 any of its four main divisions—the

Atlantic, Pacific, Indian, and Arctic oceans. **3** a vast expanse or quantity: *oceans of trouble*. *n.*

**o·cean·ar·i·um** (ō′shə ner′ē əm) a large saltwater aquarium for ocean fish and other animals. *n., pl.* **o·cean·ar·i·ums** or **o·cean·ar·i·a** (-ē ə).

**ocean bed** the bottom of the ocean.

**o·cean-go·ing** (ō′shən gō′ing) of, having to do with, or designed for travel on the ocean: *an ocean-going ship*. *adj.*

**o·ce·an·ic** (ō′shē an′ik) **1** of the ocean: *oceanic islands*. **2** living in the ocean: *oceanic fish*. **3** like the ocean; wide; vast. *adj.*

**o·cean·o·gra·pher** (ō shə nog′rə fər) a person skilled in OCEANOGRAPHY, especially one whose work it is.

**o·cean·o·gra·phy** (ō shə nog′rə fē) a branch of physical geography dealing with the oceans and ocean life. *n.*

**o·ce·lot** (ō′sə lot′ *or* os′ə lot′) a spotted wildcat resembling a leopard, found from Texas through South America. *n.*

**o·chre** (ō′kər) **1** any of the various clays ranging in colouring from pale yellow to orange, brown, and red, used as pigments. **2** brownish yellow. **1, 2** *n.*, **2** *adj.* Also, **ocher**.

**o'clock** (ə klok′) the time expressed in units of one hour: *five o'clock*.
☛ *Etym.* **O'clock** is a shortening of the older expression *of the clock*.

**Oct.** October.

**oc·ta·gon** (ok′tə gon′) a closed plane figure having eight interior angles and eight sides. See POLYGON for picture. *n.*
☛ *Etym.* Through Latin from Gk. *oktagōnos* 'eight-angled', made up of *oktō* 'eight' + *gōnia* 'angle'. Other words beginning with *oct-, octa-* and *octo-* developed from Gk. *oktō* or L *octo*, both meaning 'eight'.

**oc·tag·o·nal** (ok tag′ə nəl) having eight interior angles and eight sides. *adj.*

**oc·ta·he·dral** (ok′tə hē′drəl) having eight plane faces. *adj.*

**oc·ta·he·dron** (ok′tə hē′drən) a solid figure having eight plane faces or sides. *n., pl.* **oc·ta·he·drons** or **oc·ta·he·dra** (-drə).

**oc·tane** (ok′tān) a colourless, liquid HYDROCARBON that occurs in a PETROLEUM: *Good gasoline contains much octane*. *n.*

**octane number** the number indicating the quality of a motor fuel, based on its ANTIKNOCK properties.

An octave on the piano OCTAVE

**oc·tave** (ok′tiv *or* ok′tāv) **1** in music, the interval between a tone and another tone having twice or half as many vibrations per second: *From middle C to the C above is an octave*. **2** the eighth tone above or below a given tone, having twice or half as many vibrations per second. **3** the series of tones or of keys of an instrument, filling the interval between a tone and its octave. **4** the sounding together of a tone and its octave. **5** a group of eight. *n.*

**oc·ta·vo** (ok tā′vō *or* ok tav′ō) **1** the page size of a book in which each leaf is one eighth of a whole sheet of paper. **2** a book having this size, usually about 15 by 24 cm. *n., pl.* **oc·ta·vos**.

**oc·tet** or **oc·tette** (ok tet′) **1** a musical composition for eight voices or instruments. **2** eight singers or players. **3** a group of eight lines of verse. **4** any group of eight. *n.*

**oc·til·lion** (ok til′yən) **1** in Canada, the United States, and France, 1 followed by 27 zeros. **2** in the United Kingdom and Germany, 1 followed by 48 zeros. *n.*

**Oc·to·ber** (ok tō′bər) the tenth month of the year: *October has 31 days*. *n.*
☛ *Etym.* Through OF *octobre* from L *October*, formed from *octo* 'eight'. October was the eighth month of the ancient Roman calendar.

**oc·to·ge·nar·i·an** (ok′tə jə ner′ē ən) **1** a person who is 80 years old or between 80 and 90 years old. **2** 80 years old or between 80 and 90 years old. **1** *n.,* **2** *adj.*

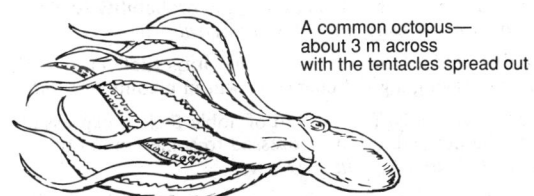
A common octopus— about 3 m across with the tentacles spread out

**oc·to·pus** (ok′tə pəs) **1** a sea MOLLUSC having a soft body and eight arms with suckers on them. **2** any person or thing that reaches out or grasps as an octopus does: *The octopus of organized crime threatens the business life of every major city*. **3** a powerful, grasping organization with far-reaching influence. *n., pl.* **oc·to·pus·es** or **oc·to·pi** (-pī).

**oc·to·roon** (ok′tə rün′) a person having one eighth African ancestry. *n.*

**oc·u·lar** (ok′yə lər) **1** of or having to do with the eye: *an ocular muscle*. **2** like an eye. **3** received by actual sight; seen: *ocular proof*. **4** the eyepiece of a telescope, microscope, etc. **1–3** *adj.,* **4** *n.*

**oc·u·list** (ok′yə list′) a doctor who examines eyes and treats diseases of the eyes; ophthalmologist. *n.*
☛ *Syn.* An **oculist**, an OPHTHALMOLOGIST, an OPTOMETRIST, and an OPTICIAN all have to do with the health of the eyes. An **oculist** or **ophthalmologist** is a physician who can treat diseases of the eye as well as recommending eyeglasses. An **optometrist** is not a physician but is trained to examine eyes and recommend eyeglasses. An **optician** supplies the lenses for eyeglasses and fits them into frames.

**O.D.** Officer of the Day.

**odd** (od) **1** left over: *Pay the bill with this money and keep the odd change*. **2** being one of a pair or set of which the rest is missing: *an odd stocking*. **3** extra;

occasional; casual: *odd jobs, odd moments, odd players.* **4** with some extra: *six hundred odd.* **5** of a number, leaving a remainder of 1 when divided by 2. **6** having an odd number: *the odd symphonies of Beethoven.* **7** strange; peculiar; queer: *It is odd that I cannot remember her name.* *adj.* —**odd′ness,** *n.*

**odd·i·ty** (od′ə tē) **1** strangeness; queerness; peculiarity: *the oddity of wearing a fur coat over a bathing suit.* **2** a strange, queer, or peculiar person or thing. *n., pl.* **odd·i·ties.**

**odd·ly** (od′lē) queerly; strangely. *adv.*

**odd·ment** (od′mənt) a thing left over; an extra bit. *n.*

**odd number** a number that has a remainder of 1 when divided by 2: *Three, five, and seven are odd numbers.*

**odds** (odz) **1** a difference in favour of one and against another; advantage: *The odds are in our favour, and we should win. In betting, odds of 3 to 1 mean that I will be paid if the bet is lost by the bettor, for every 3 that are received if the bet is won.* **2** in games, an extra allowance given to the weaker side. **3** things that are odd, uneven, or unequal. **4** difference: *It makes no odds when he goes.* *n. pl.* or *sing.*
**at odds,** quarrelling or disagreeing: *The two boys had been at odds for months.*
**odds and ends,** things left over; extra bits; odd pieces; scraps; remnants.
**the odds are,** the chances are; the probability is: *Since we are a better team, the odds are we will win.*

**odds–on** (od′zon′) having the ODDS (def. 1) in one's favour; having a good chance to win in a contest. *adj.*

**ode** (ōd) a lyric poem full of noble feeling expressed with dignity and, often, addressed to some person or thing: *Ode to a Nightingale.* *n.*

**o·di·ous** (ō′dē əs) very displeasing; hateful; offensive; detestable; repulsive: *odious behaviour.* *adj.* —**o′di·ous·ly,** *adv.* —**o′di·ous·ness,** *n.*

**o·di·um** (ō′dē əm) **1** hatred; dislike. **2** reproach; blame. *n.*

**o·dom·e·ter** (ō dom′ə tər) an instrument for measuring the distance a vehicle travels by counting the number of wheel revolutions. *n.*

**o·don·tol·o·gy** (ō′don tol′ə jē) the branch of anatomy dealing with the structure, development, and diseases of the teeth; dentistry. *n.*

**odor** (ō′dər) See ODOUR. *n.*

**o·dor·if·er·ous** (ō′də rif′ə rəs) giving forth an odour; fragrant. *adj.*

**o·dor·ous** (ō′də rəs) giving forth an odour; having an odour; sweet-smelling; fragrant: *Spices are odorous.* *adj.* —**o′dor·ous·ly,** *adv.* —**o′dor·ous·ness,** *n.*

**o·dour** or **o·dor** (ō′dər) **1** a smell or scent: *the odour of roses, the odour of garbage.* **2** repute: *They were in bad odour because of a suspected theft.* **3** a fragrance; perfume. *n.* —**o′dour·less** or **o′dor·less,** *adj.*

**Od·ys·sey** (od′ə sē) **1** a long Greek epic poem by Homer, describing the ten years of wandering of Ulysses after the Trojan War and his final return home. **2** any long series of wanderings and adventures. *n., pl.* **Od·ys·seys.**

**oe·soph·a·gus** (ē sof′ə gəs) See ESOPHAGUS. *n.*

**of** (uv *or* ov; *unstressed,* əv) **1** belonging to; associated with; forming a part of: *the children of a family, a friend of his boyhood, the news of the day, the captain of the ship, the cause of the quarrel.* **2** made from: *a house of bricks, a castle of sand.* **3** that has; containing; with: *a house of six rooms.* **4** that has as a quality: *a look of pity, a word of encouragement, a woman of good judgment.* **5** that is; named: *the city of Vancouver.* **6** away from; from: *north of Brandon, to shoot wide of the mark, to take leave of a friend.* **7** in regard to; concerning; about: *to think well of someone, to be fond of, to be hard of heart.* **8** that has a purpose: *the hour of prayer.* **9** by: *the writings of Shakespeare.* **10** as a result of; through: *to die of grief.* **11** out of: *We expect much of a new medicine. She came of a noble family.* **12** among: *a mind of the finest, a friend of mine.* **13** during: *of late years.* **14** in telling time, before: *ten minutes of six.* **15** in; as to: *She is sixteen years of age.* **16** *Of* connects nouns and adjectives having the meaning of a verb with what would be the object of the verb: *the eating of fruit, his drinking of milk, the love of truth, in search of a ball, a hall smelling of onions.* *prep.*
☛ *Usage.* In informal English *of* is sometimes used unnecessarily to make such double prepositions as *inside of, outside of.* This usage is usually avoided in formal writing. Using *of* after *off* is not acceptable in standard English: *She stepped off the sidewalk* (not *off of*).

**off** (of) **1** not in the usual or correct position on; not in the usual or correct condition of; not on: *A button is off her coat.* **2** from the usual or correct position, condition, etc.: *He took off his hat.* **3** from; away from; far from: *You are off the road.* **4** away; at a distance; to a distance: *to go off on a journey.* **5** distant in time: *My holiday is only five weeks off.* **6** so as to stop: *Turn the water off. The game was called off.* **7** no longer due to take place: *Our trip to Europe is off.* **8** not connected; stopped: *The electricity is off.* **9** without work: *an afternoon off (adv.). She pursues her hobby during off hours (adj.).* **10** in full; wholly: *Pay off the debt.* **11** in a specified condition in regard to money, property, etc.: *How well off are the Smiths?* **12** not very good; not up to average: *Bad weather made last summer an off season for fruit.* **13** possible but not likely: *I came on the off chance that I would find you.* **14** in error; wrong: *Your figures are way off.* **15** on one's way: *The train started, and we were off on our trip.* **16** go away! stay away! **17** more distant; farther: *the off side of a wall.* **18** on the right-hand side; right: *The near horse and the off horse make a team.* **19** of ships at sea, just away from: *The ship anchored off Victoria.* **20** seaward. **21** supported by; using the resources of: *He lived off his relatives.* **22** in cricket, the side opposite the batsman's batting hand. 1, 3, 19, 21 *prep.,* 2, 4–6, 9, 10, 15 *adv.,* 7–9, 11–14, 17, 18, 20 *adj.,* 16 *interj.,* 22 *n.*
**be off,** go away; leave quickly.
**off and on,** now and then: *She has lived in Europe off and on for ten years.*
**off with,** **a** take off. **b** away with!
**well off, badly off** or **comfortably off,** so situated, especially with regard to money or worldly goods.
☛ *Usage.* Avoid using the double preposition *off of.* See note at OF.

**off.** **1** office. **2** officer. **3** official.

**of·fal** (of′əl) **1** the waste parts of an animal killed for food. **2** garbage; refuse. *n.*
☛ *Hom.* AWFUL.

**off·beat** (of′bēt′) **1** in music, a beat that has relatively little stress. **2** of or having to do with offbeats. **3** *Informal.* unconventional; not usual; odd. **1** *n.,* **2, 3** *adj.*

**off-col·our** or **off-col·or** (of′kul′ər) **1** defective in colour. **2** somewhat improper: *an off-colour joke.* **3** not well: *She was feeling off-colour yesterday.* *adj.*

**of·fence** or **of·fense** (ə fens′ *or* ō fens′) **1** a breaking of the law; sin: *Offences against the law are punished by fines or imprisonment.* **2** something that offends or causes displeasure: *Rudeness is always an offence.* **3** the condition of being offended; hurt feelings; anger: *to cause offence.* **4** offending or hurting someone's feelings: *No offence was intended.* **5** the act of attacking: *The army proved weak in offence.* **6** an attacking team or force: *Our football team has a good offence.* *n.*
**give offence**, offend.
**take offence**, be offended.

**of·fend** (ə fend′) **1** hurt the feelings of; make angry; displease; pain: *My friend was offended.* **2** commit an offence; sin; do wrong: *In what way have I offended?* *v.*

**of·fend·er** (ə fen′dər) **1** a person who OFFENDS. **2** a person who does wrong or breaks a law. *n.*

**of·fense** (ə fens′ *or* ō fens′) See OFFENCE. *n.*

**of·fen·sive** (ə fen′siv) **1** giving offence; irritating; annoying: *"Shut up" is an offensive remark.* **2** unpleasant; disagreeable; disgusting: *Bad eggs have an offensive odour.* **3** ready to attack; attacking: *an offensive army.* **4** used for attack; having to do with attack: *offensive weapons, an offensive war for conquest.* **5** the position or attitude of attack: *The army took the offensive.* **6** an attack: *An offensive against polio was begun when the proper vaccine was developed by J.E. Salk.* **1–4** *adj.*, **5, 6** *n.* —**of·fen′sive·ly**, *adv.* —**of·fen′sive·ness**, *n.*

**of·fer** (of′ər) **1** hold out to be taken or refused; present; proffer: *to offer one's hand, to offer a gift. He offered us his help.* **2** present for sale: *offer suits at reduced prices.* **3** be willing; volunteer: *She offered to help us.* **4** propose; advance; suggest: *She offered a few ideas to improve the plan.* **5** present in worship: *to offer prayers.* **6** give; show: *The enemy offered resistance to the soldiers' attack.* **7** present itself; occur: *I will come if the opportunity offers.* **8** show intention; attempt; try: *The thieves offered no resistance to the police officers. He did not offer to hit back.* **9** bid as a price: *She offered twenty dollars for our old stove.* **10** the act of offering: *an offer of money, an offer to sing, an offer of marriage, an offer of $220 000 for a house.* **11** a thing that is offered. **1–9** *v.*, **10, 11** *n.*

**of·fer·ing** (of′ə ring *or* of′ring) **1** the giving of something as an act of worship. **2** a contribution or gift. **3** ppr. of OFFER. **1, 2** *n.*, **3** *v.*

**of·fer·to·ry** (of′ər tô′rē) **1** a collection at a religious service. **2** the verses said or the music sung or played while the offering is received. *n., pl.* **of·fer·to·ries.**

**off·hand** (of′hand′ *for adverb*, of′hand′ *for adjective*) **1** without previous thought or preparation; at once: *The carpenter could not tell offhand how much the work would cost.* **2** done or made on the spur of the moment, without previous thought or planning: *Her offhand remarks were often very funny.* **3** casual; informal. **4** impolite; without due courtesy: *The boy's offhand ways angered his mother.* **1** *adv.*, **2–4** *adj.*

**off·hand·ed** (of′han′did) OFFHAND. *adj.* —**off′hand·ed·ly**, *adv.* —**off′hand·ed·ness**, *n.*

**of·fice** (of′is) **1** the place in which the work of a business or profession is done; a room or rooms in which to do such work: *The executive offices were on the second floor.* **2** a position, especially in the public service: *The MP was appointed to the office of the Minister of Defence.* **3** the duty of one's position; one's job or work: *A teacher's office is teaching.* **4** the staff or persons carrying on work in an office: *Half the office is on vacation.* **5** an administrative department of a governmental organization. **6** an act of kindness or unkindness; a service or injury: *Through the good offices of a friend, she was able to get a job.* **7** a religious ceremony or prayer: *the communion office, last offices.* *n.*

**office boy** a boy whose work is doing odd jobs in an office.

**of·fice-hold·er** (of′is hōl′dər) a person who holds a public office; government official. *n.*

**of·fi·cer** (of′ə sər) **1** a person who commands others in the armed forces such as a colonel, a lieutenant, or a captain. **2** the captain of a ship or any of his or her chief assistants. **3** a person who holds an office in the government, the church, the public service, etc.: *a health officer, a police officer.* **4** the president, vice-president, secretary, treasurer, etc. of a company, club, society, etc. **5** provide with officers. **6** direct, conduct; manage. **7** in some societies, any member above the lowest rank. **1–4, 7** *n.*, **5, 6** *v.* —**of′fi·cer·less**, *adj.*

**Officer of the Day** in the armed services, an officer who has charge of the guards, internal security, and good order of a ship, garrison, air station, etc. for a given day.

**of·fi·cial** (ə fish′əl *or* ō fish′əl) **1** a person who holds a public position or who is in charge of some public work or duty: *Postmasters are government officials.* **2** a person holding office; officer: *bank officials.* **3** of or having to do with an office or officers: *Police officers wear an official uniform.* **4** having authority: *An official record is kept of the proceedings of our club.* **5** being an official: *an official representative.* **6** suitable for a person in office: *the official dignity of a judge.* **7** holding office. **1, 2** *n.*, **3–7** *adj.* —**of·fi′cial·ly**, *adv.*

**of·fi·cial·dom** (ə fish′əl dəm *or* ō fish′əl dəm) **1** the position or domain of officials. **2** officials collectively. *n.*

**of·fi·cial·ism** (ə fish′ə liz′əm *or* ō fish′ə liz′əm) **1** official methods or system. **2** excessive attention to official routine. *n.*

**of·fi·ci·ate** (ə fish′ē āt′ *or* ō fish′ē āt′) **1** perform the duties of any office or position: *The president officiates as chairman at meetings.* **2** perform the duties of a priest, minister, or rabbi: *The bishop officiated at the cathedral.* **3** serve as a referee or umpire in a sport. *v.*, **of·fi·ci·at·ed, of·fi·ci·at·ing.**

**of·fic·i·nal** (ə fis′ə nəl) **1** kept in stock by druggists. **2** a drug that is kept in stock. **3** recognized by the pharmacopoeia. **1, 3** *adj.*, **2** *n.*

**of·fi·cious** (ə fish′əs) too ready to offer services or advice; minding other people's business; fond of meddling: *Some officious person reported me for speeding.* *adj.* —**of·fi′cious·ly**, *adv.* —**of·fi′cious·ness**, *n.*

**off·ing** (of′ing) **1** the more distant part of the sea as seen from the shore. **2** a position at a distance from the shore. *n.*
**in the offing, a** just visible from the shore. **b** within

**off·ish** (of′ish) *Informal.* inclined to keep aloof; distant and reserved in manner. *adj.* —**off′ish·ness,** *n.*

**off-key** (of′kē′) **1** in music, not in the correct musical key; inharmonious. **2** *Informal.* improper; ill-timed. *adj.*

**off·set** (of′set′ *for verb,* of′set′ *for noun*) **1** make up for; counterbalance; compensate for: *The better roads offset the greater distance.* **2** balance one thing by another as an equivalent: *We offset the greater distance by the better roads.* **3** something that makes up for something else; compensation: *In football, his weight and strength were an offset to his slowness.* **4** a short side shoot from a main stem or root that starts a new plant. **5** any offshoot. **6** a printing process in which the inked impression is first made on a rubber roller and then on the paper, instead of directly on the paper. **7** form an offset. 1, 2, 7 *v.,* **off·set, off·set·ting;** 3–6 *n.*

**off·shoot** (of′shüt′) **1** a shoot or branch growing out from the main stem of a plant, tree, etc. **2** anything coming, or thought of as coming, from a main part, stock, race, etc.: *an offshoot of a mountain range.* *n.*

**off·shore** (of′shôr′ *for adv.,* of′shôr *for adj.*) **1** toward the water; from the shore: *The wind was blowing offshore.* **2** off or away from the shore: *an offshore wind, offshore fisheries.* 1 *adv.,* 2 *adj.*

**off·side** or **off-side** (of′sīd′; *in sport (soccer, hockey, etc.)* of′sīd′) **1** away from one's own or the proper side; being on the wrong side. **2** in many team sports, being in or moving into an illegal position, when play usually stops. *adj.*

**off·spring** (of′spring′) **1** the young of a person, animal, or plant; descendant: *Every one of Mrs. Kelly's offspring had red hair.* **2** a result; effect. *n.*

**off-stage** (of′stāj′) away from the part of the stage that the audience can see. *adj.*

**off-the-wall** (of′ᴛʜə wol′) *Informal.* unusual, strange, or eccentric: *an off-the-wall idea.* *adj.*

**of·ten** (of′ən *or* of′tən) in many cases; many times; frequently: *Blame is often misdirected. She comes here often.* *adv.*

**of·ten·times** (of′ən tīmz′ *or* of′tən tīmz′) OFTEN. *adv.*

**o·gle** (ō′gəl) **1** look at with desire; make eyes at. **2** look with desire; make eyes. **3** an ogling look. 1, 2 *v.,* **o·gled, o·gling;** 3 *n.* —**o′gler,** *n.*

**o·gre** (ō′gər) **1** in folklore and fairy tales, a giant or monster that supposedly eats people. **2** a dreaded or cruel person. *n.*

**oh** or **Oh** (ō) **1** a word used before names in addressing persons: *Oh Myra, look!* **2** an expression of surprise, joy, grief, pain and other feelings: *Oh, dear me! Oh! joy!* *interj.* Also, **O.**
☞ *Hom.* O, OWE.
☞ *Usage.* **Oh** is preferred to **O,** except before names: *Oh, what a lovely day!*

**O–Ha·rai** (ō′ha rī′) in Shinto, the purification ceremony observed in June and December, during which believers receive absolution from the sun goddess, Amaterasu. It is proclaimed traditionally by the emperor. *n.*

**ohm** (ōm) an SI unit for measuring the resistance of a conductor to an electric current sent through it: *A conductor has a resistance of one ohm if it takes one volt of pressure to send a current of one ampere through it.* Symbol: Ω *n.*

**o·ho** or **O·ho** (ō hō′) an exclamation expressing a taunt, surprise, or exultation. *interj.*

**oil** (oil) **1** any of several kinds of thick, fatty or greasy liquids that are lighter than water, that burn easily, and that dissolve in alcohol but not in water: *Mineral oils are used for fuel; animal and vegetable oils are used in cooking, medicine, and in many other ways. Essential or volatile oils, such as oil of peppermint, are distilled from plants, leaves, flowers, etc. and are thin and evaporate very quickly.* **2** petroleum. **3** olive oil. **4** any substance that resembles oil in some respect: *Sulphuric acid is called oil of vitriol.* **5** become oil: *Butter oils when heated.* **6** paint made by grinding colouring matter in oil: *The art class is now painting with oils.* **7** a painting in oils: *We like the oils of that artist better than her water colours.* **8** put oil on or in: *The repairman oiled the wheels.* **9** seek to persuade by bribery, flattery, etc. 1–4, 6, 7 *n.,* 5, 8, 9 *v.*
**pour oil on troubled waters,** make things calm and peaceful.
**strike oil,** **a** find oil by boring a hole in the earth. **b** find something very profitable.

**oil burner** **1** a furnace, ship, etc. that uses oil for fuel. **2** the part of such a furnace in which the fuel oil is atomized, mixed with air, and burned.

**oil·cloth** (oil′kloth′) **1** a cloth made waterproof and glossy on one side by coating it with a mixture of oil, clay, and colouring: *Oilcloth is used to cover shelves, tables, etc.* **2** OILSKIN. *n.*

**oil colour** or **color** **1** paint made by mixing pigment with oil. **2** a painting done in such colours.

**oil·er** (oi′lər) **1** a person or thing that oils. **2** a can with a long spout used in oiling machinery. **3** an oil tanker. **4 oilers,** *pl.* OILSKIN or other waterproof clothing. *n.*

**oil field** an area where PETROLEUM has been found.

**oil painting** **1** a picture painted with oil colours. **2** the art of painting with oil colours.

**oil·pa·per** (oil′pā′pər) paper treated with oil to make it transparent and waterproof. *n.*

**oil sand** any rock, especially SANDSTONE, that contains large deposits of oil.

**oil·skin** (oil′skin′) **1** cloth treated with oil to make it waterproof. **2 oilskins,** *pl.* a coat and trousers made of this cloth. *n.*

**oil·stone** (oil′stōn′) a fine-grained stone used for sharpening tools, the rubbing surface of which is oiled. *n.*

**oil well** a well drilled in the earth to get oil.

**oil·y** (oi′lē) **1** of oil: *an oily smell.* **2** containing oil: *oily salad dressing.* **3** covered or soaked with oil: *oily rags.* **4** like oil; smooth; slippery. **5** too smooth; suspiciously or disagreeably smooth: *an oily smile.* *adj.,* **oil·i·er, oil·i·est.** —**oil′i·ness,** *n.*

**oint·ment** (oint′mənt) a substance made from oil or fat, often containing medicine, used on the skin to heal or to make it soft: *Cold cream and salve are ointments.* *n.*

**O·jib·wa** or **O·jib·way** (ō jib′wä) **1** a member of a First Nations people living in the region around Lake Superior and westward: *The Ojibwa traditionally occupied an area stretching from the Ottawa Valley to the Prairies.* **2** an ALGONQUIAN (defs. 1–3) language spoken by the Ojibwa, Algonquins, Ottawas and Salteaux. *n., pl.* **O·jib·wa** or **O·jib·was, O·jib·way** or **O·jib·ways**.

**O.K.** or **OK** (ō′kā′) *Informal.* **1** all right; correct; approved: *The new schedule was O.K.* **2** endorse; approve. **3** approval: *The principal gave us her O.K.* **1** *adj., adv.,* **2** *v.,* **O.K.'d** or **OK'd, O.K.'ing** or **OK'ing;** **3** *n., pl.* **O.K.'s** or **OK's**. Also, **okay.**

**o·ka·pi** (ō kä′pē) an African mammal resembling the giraffe, but smaller and having a much shorter neck. *n., pl.* **o·ka·pis** or **o·ka·pi**.

**o·kay** (ō′kā′) See O.K. *adj., adv., v., n.*

**o·kra** (ō′krə) **1** a tall annual herb of the mallow family, a species of hibiscus, having heart-shaped lobed leaves and long, tapering seed pods: *The okra is native to Africa but is commonly cultivated in the United States and other countries.* **2** The unripe, tender pods of this plant, used as a vegetable and for thickening soups; gumbo. *n.*

**old** (ōld) **1** not young; having existed long; aged: *an old wall. We are old friends.* **2** of age; in age: *a year old.* **3** not new; not recent; made long ago; ancient: *an old excuse, an old tomb, an old debt, an old family.* **4** much worn by age or use: *old clothes.* **5** looking or seeming old; like an old person in wisdom, feebleness, etc.; mature: *old for her years.* **6** having much experience: *old in wrongdoing.* **7** former: *an old student.* **8** earlier or earliest: *Old English.* **9** time long ago: *the heroes of old.* **10** familiar; dear: *good old fellow.* **11** *Informal.* good; fine (used after some other adjective): *We had a high old time at the party.* **12** the old, old people: *a home for the old.* 1–8, 10, 11 *adj.,* **old·er** or **eld·er, old·est** or **eld·est;** 9, 12 *n.* —**old′ness,** *n.*
☛ *Syn.* See note at ELDERLY.
☛ *Usage.* **Elder** and **eldest** are used in formal English when describing persons of the same family: *The eldest daughter or the elder brother will get the fortune.* In informal English, **older** and **oldest** are more frequent.

**old age** the last part of life when a person is very old; the years of life from about 65 on.

**Old Country** the native land of persons living elsewhere: *To many New Canadians Britain is the Old Country.*

**Old English** the language of the English people up to about 1100 A.D.; ANGLO-SAXON (def. 2).

**old–fash·ioned** (ōld′fash′ənd) **1** of an old fashion; out-of-date in style, construction, etc.: *an old-fashioned dress.* **2** keeping to old ways, ideas, etc.: *an old-fashioned housekeeper.* *adj.*

**Old Guard** **1** the imperial guard of Napoleon I, which made the last French charge at Waterloo. **2** the conservative members of a country, community, organization, etc.

**old hand** an expert; very skilled or experienced person.

**old·ish** (ōl′dish) somewhat old. *adj.*

**old–line** (ōl′dlīn′) **1** keeping to old ideas and ways, conservative. **2** having a long history; established. *adj.*

**old maid** **1** a woman who has not married and seems unlikely to do so. **2** a prim, fussy person: *What an old maid he is!* **3** a very simple card game.

**old–maid·ish** (ōld′mā′dish) like, suggesting, or befitting an OLD MAID (defs. 1, 2); prim; fussy. *adj.*

**Old Man of the Sea** **1** in *The Arabian Nights,* a horrible old man who clung to the back of Sinbad. **2** a person or thing that is hard to get rid of.

**old master** **1** any great European painter who lived before 1800. **2** a painting by such a painter.

**old moon** the moon when seen as a thin crescent with the hollow side on the right.

**old school** any group of people who have old-fashioned or conservative ideas.

**old·ster** (ōld′stər) *Informal.* an old person. *n.*

**old–time** (ōld′tīm′) of former times; like old times. *adj.*

**old–tim·er** (ōld′tī′mər) *Informal.* **1** a person who has long been a resident, member, or worker in a place, group, or community. **2** a person who favours old ideas and ways. *n.*

**old wives' tale** a foolish story; silly belief.

**old–wom·an·ish** (ōl′dwùm′ə nish) like, suggesting, or befitting an old woman; fussy. *adj.*

**old–world** (ōl′dwėrld′) **1** of or having to do with the ancient world: *The mammoth was an old-world elephant.* **2** belonging to or characteristic of a former period: *old-world courtesy.* **3** of or having to do with the Eastern Hemisphere: *old-world folk songs.* *adj.*

**Old World** **1** Europe, Asia, and Africa. **2** of, having to do with, or found in the Old World: *Pythons are the Old World equivalent of the boas of the New World.* Compare with NEW WORLD.

**o·le·ag·i·nous** (ō′lē aj′ə nəs) OILY (defs. 1–4). *adj.*

**o·le·an·der** (ō′lē an′dər) a poisonous evergreen shrub having fragrant red, pink, or white flowers. *n.*

**o·le·ate** (ō′lē āt′) a salt of OLEIC ACID. *n.*

**o·le·ic acid** (ō′lē′ik) an oily liquid obtained by hydrolyzing various animal and vegetable oils and fats.

**o·le·in** (ō′lē in) an ESTER of oleic acid and glycerin: *Lard, olive oil, and cottonseed oil are mostly olein.* *n.*

**o·le·o·mar·ga·rine** (ō′lē ō mär′jə rin *or* ō′lē ō mär′jə rēn′) MARGARINE. *n.*

**o·le·o·res·in** (ō′lē ō rez′ən) a natural or prepared solution of RESIN in oil. *n.*

**ol·fac·tion** (ol fak′shən) **1** the act of smelling. **2** the sense of smell. *n.*

**ol·fac·to·ry** (ol fak′tə rē) **1** having to do with smelling; of smell: *The nose is an olfactory organ.* **2** an olfactory organ. 1 *adj.,* 2 *n., pl.* **ol·fac·to·ries**.

**ol·i·garch** (ol′ə gärk′) one of a small number of persons holding the ruling power in a state. *n.*

**ol·i·gar·chic** (ol′ə gär′kik) of an OLIGARCHY or oligarchs; having to do with rule by a few. *adj.*

**ol·i·gar·chi·cal** (ol′ə gär′kə kəl) OLIGARCHIC. *adj.*

**ol·i·gar·chy** (ol′ə gär′kē) **1** a form of government in which a few people have the power. **2** a country or state having such a government: *Ancient Sparta was really an oligarchy, though it had two kings.*   **3** the ruling few.   *n., pl.* **ol·i·gar·chies.**

**ol·ive** (ol′iv)   **1** a kind of evergreen tree with grey-green leaves that grows in southern Europe and other warm regions.   **2** the fruit of this tree: *Olives are eaten green or ripe. Olive oil is pressed from olives.*   **3** the wood of the olive tree.   **4** a wreath of olive leaves; olive branch.   **5** yellowish green: *The uniform was made of olive cloth.*   **6** yellowish brown: *The woman had an olive complexion.*   *1–6 n., 5, 6 adj.*

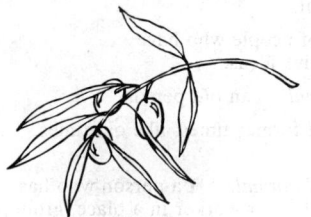
An olive branch with olives

The emblem of the United Nations, using olive branches as a symbol of peace

**olive branch**   **1** a branch of the olive tree long used as an emblem of peace.   **2** anything offered as a sign of peace.

**olive drab**   a dark greenish-yellow.

**olive oil**   oil pressed from olives, used in cooking, in medicine, etc.

**O·lym·pi·ad** or **o·lym·pi·ad** (ō lim′pē ad′)   **1** a period of four years reckoned from one celebration of the Olympic games to the next, by which Greeks computed time from 776 B.C.   **2** the celebration of the modern Olympic games.   *n.*
☛ *Etym.* From *Olympia,* in ancient Greece, a plain where games were held every four years in honour of Zeus.

**O·lym·pi·an** (ō lim′pē ən)   **1** having to do with Olympia in Greece or with Mount Olympus.   **2** like a god; heavenly.   **3** rather too gracious; magnificent; superior: *Olympian calm, Olympian manners.*   **4** one of the major Greek gods.   **5** a contender in the Olympic games.   *1–3 adj., 4, 5 n.*

**Olympian games**   OLYMPIC GAMES.

**O·lym·pic** (ō lim′pik)   **1** of or having to do with Olympia in ancient Greece: *the Olympic games.*   **2** of or having to do with Mount Olympus.   *adj.*

**Olympic games**   **1** contests in athletics, poetry, and music, held every four years by the ancient Greeks in honour of Zeus.   **2** modern athletic contests like the athletic contests of these games: *The Olympic games are held once every four years in a different country, and athletes from many nations compete in them.*

**Olym·pics** (ō lim′piks)   OLYMPIC GAMES.   *n.pl.*

**o·ma·sum** (ō mā′səm)   the third stomach of a cow or other ruminant: *The omasum receives the food when it is swallowed the second time.*   *n., pl.* **o·ma·sa** (-sə).

**om·buds·man** (om′bəd zmən *or* om bud′zmən)   a government official appointed to receive and investigate citizens' grievances against the government.   *n., pl.* **om·buds·men** (om′bəd zmən *or* om bud′zmən).

**o·me·ga** (ō meg′ə, ō mē′gə *or* ō′mi gə)   **1** the last letter of the Greek alphabet (Ω or ω).   **2** the last of any series; end.   *n.*

**om·e·lette** or **om·e·let** (om′ə lit *or* om′lit)   a food dish of eggs beaten with milk or water, cooked, and folded over: *Omelettes are sometimes filled with chopped meat, mushrooms, or some other filling.*   *n.*

**o·men** (ō′mən)   **1** a sign of what is to happen; object or event that is believed to mean good or bad fortune: *Spilling salt is said to be an omen of misfortune.*   **2** prophetic meaning: *Some people consider a black cat a creature of ill omen.*   **3** be a sign of; presage.   *1, 2 n., 3 v.*

**om·i·nous** (om′ə nəs)   of bad OMEN (defs. 1, 2); unfavourable; threatening: *The watchdog gave an ominous growl.*   *adj.*   —**om′i·nous·ly,** *adv.*   —**om′i·nous·ness,** *n.*

**o·mis·sion** (ō mish′ən)   **1** an omitting or being omitted: *the omission of a paragraph in copying a story.*   **2** anything omitted: *Her song was the only omission from the program.*   *n.*

**o·mit** (ō mit′)   **1** leave out: *to omit a letter in a word.*   **2** fail to do; neglect: *Shula omitted making her bed.*   *v.,* **o·mit·ted, o·mit·ting.**

**om·ni·bus** (om′nə bus′)   **1** a large vehicle with seats inside and sometimes also upstairs; bus.   **2** covering many things at once: *an omnibus law.*   **3** a collection in one volume of many stories, poems, etc. by the same author or on the same subject.   *1, 3 n., pl.* **om·ni·bus·es;**   *2 adj.*

**om·nip·o·tence** (om nip′ə təns)   complete power; unlimited power: *the omnipotence of God.*   *n.*

**om·nip·o·tent** (om nip′ə tənt)   **1** having all power; almighty: *an omnipotent ruler.*   **2 the Omnipotent,** God.   *adj.*   —**om·nip′o·tent·ly,** *adv.*

**om·ni·pres·ence** (om′nə prez′əns)   presence everywhere at the same time: *God's omnipresence.*   *n.*

**om·ni·pres·ent** (om′nə prez′ənt)   present everywhere at the same time.   *adj.*

**om·nis·cience** (om nis′ē əns *or* om nish′əns)   knowledge of everything; complete or infinite knowledge.   *n.*

**om·nis·cient** (om nis′ē ənt *or* om nish′ənt)   knowing everything; having complete or infinite knowledge.   *adj.*   —**om·nis′cient·ly,** *adv.*

**om·ni·vore** (om′ni vôr′)   a creature that eats every kind of food: *Human beings are omnivores.*   *n.*

**om·niv·o·rous** (om niv′ə rəs)   **1** eating every kind of food.   **2** eating both animal and vegetable food: *Rats are omnivorous animals.*   **3** taking in everything; fond of all kinds: *An omnivorous reader reads all kinds of books.*   *adj.*   —**om·niv′o·rous·ly,** *adv.*   —**om·niv′o·rous·ness,** *n.*

**on** (on)   **1** above and supported by: *The book is on the table.*   **2** touching so as to cover, be around, etc.: *There's new paint on the ceiling. Put the ring on her finger.*   **3** close to; along the edge of: *a house on the shore. She lives on the next street.*   **4** in the direction of; toward: *The soldiers marched on the capital.*   **5** against; upon: *The picture is on the wall.*   **6** on something: *The walls are up, and the roof is on.*   **7** to something: *Hold on, or you may fall.*   **8** toward something: *Some played; the others looked on.*   **9** farther: *March on.*   **10** by means of; by the use of: *This news is on good authority.*   **11** in the condition of; in the process of; in the way of: *on half pay, on purpose, on duty.*   **12** in or into a condition, process, manner, action, etc.:

*Turn the gas on.* **13** taking place: *The race is on.* **14** at the time of; during: *They greeted us on our arrival.* **15** not early or late in: *on time, on schedule.* **16** from a time; forward: *later on, from that day on.* **17** concerning; in relation to; in connection with: *a book on animals.* **18** for the purpose of: *She went on an errand.* **19** in addition to: *Defeat on defeat discouraged them.* **20** among: *I am on the committee.* 1–5, 10, 11, 14, 15, 17–20 *prep.*, 6–9, 12, 16 *adv.*, 13 *adj.*
**and so on,** and more of the same.
**on and off,** at some times and not others; now and then.
**on and on,** without stopping.
☞ *Usage.* **on to, onto.** See note at ONTO.
☞ *Hom.* AWN.

**ON** Ontario.

**once** (wuns) **1** one time: *She comes once a day.* **2** a single occasion: *Once is enough.* **3** at some one time in the past; formerly: *a once powerful nation.* **4** even a single time; ever: *If the facts once became known everybody would laugh at her.* **5** if ever; whenever; after: *Once you cross the river, you are safe.* **6** former: *a once friend.* 1, 3, 4 *adv.*, 2 *n.*, 5 *conj.*, 6 *adj.*
**at once** or **all at once,** **a** immediately: *Come at once.* **b** at the same time: *Everyone shouted at once.*
**for once,** for one time at least.
**once and again,** repeatedly.
**once and for all** or **once for all,** finally.
**once in a while,** now and then; at one time or another.
**once or twice,** a few times.
**once over,** a single time over.
**once upon a time,** long ago.

**once-o·ver** (wun′sō′vər) *Informal.* a quick look of appraisal: *He gave the stranger the once-over.* *n.*

**on·com·ing** (on′kum′ing) **1** approaching: *oncoming winter.* **2** approach: *the oncoming of the storm.* 1 *adj.*, 2 *n.*

**one** (wun) **1** the first and lowest whole number: 1. **2** the numeral 1: *What does the 1 in the margin mean?* **3** being a single unit or individual: *one apple.* **4** a single person or thing: *I gave him the one he wanted.* **5** some: *One day she will be sorry.* **6** some person or thing: *One of Bliss Carman's poems was selected for our new reader.* **7** any person or thing: *One must work hard to achieve success.* **8** the same: *They held one opinion.* **9** the same person or thing: *Dr. Jekyll and Mr. Hyde were one and the same.* **10** joined together; united: *They replied in one voice.* **11** the first in a set or series; especially, a playing card or side of a die having one spot; ace. **12** being the first in a set or series (*used mainly after the noun*): *We'll start with Chapter One.* **13** a certain: *One Jag Pharati was elected.* 1, 2, 4, 11 *n.*, 3, 5, 8, 10, 12, 13 *adj.*, 6, 7, 9 *pron.*
**all one,** a exactly the same: *They are all one in their love of hockey.* **b** making no difference: *It is all one to me whether you stay or go.*
**at one,** in agreement: *The two judges were at one about the winner.*
**make one,** **a** form or be one of a number, assembly, or party. **b** join together; unite in marriage.
**one and all,** everyone.
**one by one,** one after another.
**one or two,** a few.
☞ *Hom.* WON.
☞ *Etym.* From OE *ān*, related to German *ein* and having the same Indo-European source as L *unus.*

**one another** each of several in an action or relation that is common to all: *They struck at one another. They were in one another's way.*

**one-celled** (wun′seld′) having only one cell. *adj.*

---

**one-horse** (wun′hôrs′) **1** drawn or worked by a single horse: *a one-horse sleigh.* **2** using or having only a single horse: *a one-horse farmer.* **3** *Informal.* of little scope, capacity, or importance; minor: *a one-horse town.* *adj.*

**one·ness** (wun′nis) **1** the quality of being one in number or the only one of its kind; singleness. **2** the quality of being the same in kind; sameness. **3** the fact of forming one whole; unity. **4** agreement in mind, feeling, or purpose; harmony. *n.*

**on·er·ous** (on′ə rəs *or* ō′nə rəs) burdensome; oppressive: *an onerous task.* *adj.* —**on′er·ous·ly,** *adv.* —**on′er·ous·ness,** *n.*

**one·self** (wun self′) **1** a reflexive pronoun, the object of a reflexive verb with **one** as subject: *One might ask oneself if it is worth the trouble.* **2** an intensive pronoun used to emphasize the noun or pronoun it follows: *One has to do the real work oneself.* **3** one's usual self: *It's nice to be oneself again after an illness.* *pron.*

**one-sid·ed** (wun′sī′did) **1** seeing only one side of a question; partial; unfair; prejudiced: *The umpire seemed one-sided in her decisions.* **2** uneven; unequal: *If one team is much better than the other, a game is one-sided.* **3** having but one side. **4** on only one side. **5** having one side larger or more developed than the other. *adj.*

**one's self** ONESELF.

**one-step** (wun′step′) **1** a ballroom dance in 2/4 time, much like a quick walk. **2** the music for such a dance. **3** dance the one-step. 1, 2 *n.*, 3 *v.*, **one-stepped, one-step·ping.**

**one-time** (wun′tīm′) of the past; former. *adj.*

**one-track** (wun′trak′) **1** having only one track. **2** *Informal.* understanding or preoccupied with only one thing at a time: *a one-track mind.* *adj.*

**one-up·man·ship** (wun′up′mən ship′) *Informal.* the art or act of getting the better of someone else in business, social life, etc. *n.*

**one-way** (wun′wā′) moving or allowing movement in only one direction: *one-way traffic, a one-way ticket.* *adj.*

**on·go·ing** (on′gō′ing) actually going on; in process; continuing: *This is not an isolated crime, but part of an on-going social problem.* *adj.*

An onion bulb

**on·ion** (un′yən) **1** a commonly cultivated herb of the lily family having an edible bulb with a very sharp, strong taste and smell. **2** the bulb of this plant, used as a vegetable or seasoning: *Fried onions do not have the sharp taste of raw onions.* *n.* —**on′ion·like′,** *adj.*

**on·ion·skin** (un′yən skin′) **1** the thin, papery outer skin of an onion: *Onionskins can be used to make a yellow dye.* **2** a thin, glossy, translucent paper. *n.*

**on–line** (on′līn′) **1** involving or designating interactive processing done while directly connected to a computer: *Her flight to Winnipeg was booked through the on-line reservation system.* **2** by means controlled by a computer. 1 *adj.,* 2 *adv.*

**on·look·er** (on′lůk′ər) a person who watches without taking part; spectator. *n.*

**on·look·ing** (on′lůk′ing) watching; seeing; noticing. *adj., n.*

**on·ly** (ōn′lē) **1** by itself or themselves; one and no more; these and no more; sole, single, or few of the kind or class: *an only son. Those were the only clothes she owned. This is the only road along the shore.* **2** merely; just: *He sold only two. She was in Europe only one week.* **3** and no one or nothing more; and that is all: *Only he remained. I did it only through friendship.* **4** except that; but: *I would have gone only I didn't have the money.* **5** in a class by itself; best; finest: *As far as she is concerned, he is the only writer.* **6** but then; it must be added that: *We had camped right beside a stream, only the water was not fit to drink.* 1, 5 *adj.,* 2, 3 *adv.,* 4, 6 *conj.*
**if only,** I wish: *If only wars would cease!*
**only too,** very: *She was only too glad to help us.*
☞ *Usage.* To avoid uncertainty, **only** as an adverb should be placed immediately before the word or words it modifies. The following three sentences all have different meanings: *He only wrote to his parents last week* (He didn't telephone). *He wrote only to his parents last week* (not to anyone else). *He wrote to his parents only last week* (just last week).

**on·o·mat·o·poe·ia** (on′ə mat′ə pē′ə) **1** the naming of a thing or action by imitating the sound associated with it, as in *buzz, hum, cuckoo, slap, splash.* **2** the use of words whose sound suggests a particular meaning, especially for poetic effect, as in *"the murmurous haunt of flies on summer eves." n.*
☞ *Etym.* Through Late Latin from Gk. *onomatopoiia* 'word-making', made up of *onoma, onomatos* 'name, word' + *-poios* 'making' from *poiein* 'to make'. 16c. See also the note at POEM.

**on·rush** (on′rush′) a violent forward movement: *She was knocked down by the onrush of water.* *n.*

**on·set** (on′set′) **1** an attack: *The onset of the enemy took us by surprise.* **2** the beginning: *the onset of a disease. The onset of winter was marked by a severe snowstorm.* *n.*

**on·shore** (on′shôr′ *for adverb,* on′shôr′ *for adjective*) **1** toward the land: *The wind veered onshore.* **2** on the land: *an onshore patrol.* 1 *adv.,* 2 *adj.*

**on·side** (on′sīd′) in a position allowed by the rules of a game. *adj., adv.*

**on·slaught** (on′slot′) a vigorous attack: *The attackers were driven back by a sudden onslaught from within the city.* *n.*

**on stage** (on′stāj′) **1** being part of a scene: *the on stage characters.* **2** onto the stage: *He carried the sword on stage.*

**Ont.** Ontario.

**On·tar·i·an** (on ter′ē ən) **1** a native or long-term resident of Ontario. **2** of or having to do with Ontario. 1 *n.,* 2 *adj.*

**On·tar·i·o·an** (on ter′ē ō′ən) ONTARIAN. *n., adj.*

**on·to** (on′tü) **1** on to; to a position on: *to throw a ball onto the roof, to get onto a horse.* **2** *Informal.* familiar with or aware of: *Are you onto your new job yet? We're onto his tricks.* *prep.*
☞ *Usage.* **onto, on to.** Onto is a compound preposition and is written as one word: *The team skated onto the ice. They looked out onto the park.* When **on** is an adverb and **to** is a preposition (so that **on** is not part of the prepositional phrase), they are written as two words: *We drove on to the city.*

**on·tog·e·ny** (on toj′ə nē) the development of an individual organism. *n.*

**o·nus** (ō′nəs) a burden; responsibility: *Since she made the accusation, the onus is on her to prove it.* *n.*

**on·ward** (on′wərd) **1** toward the front; on or further on: *The army marched onward.* **2** forward: *She continued her onward course.* 1 *adv.,* 2 *adj.*

**on·wards** (on′wərdz) ONWARD (def. 1). *adv.*

**on·yx** (on′iks) a translucent variety of QUARTZ in layers of different colours: *Onyx is used as a semiprecious stone, especially for making cameos.* *n.*

**oo·dles** (ü′dəlz) *Informal.* large or unlimited quantities; heaps; loads: *oodles of money.* *n.pl.*

An Ookpik

**Ook·pik** (ůk′pik) *Cdn. Trademark.* a doll resembling an owl, invented by an unnamed Inuit artist in 1963, and soon adopted as a symbol of Canadian handicraft exhibits abroad. *n.*

**oo·li·chan** (ü′lə kən) *Cdn.* a small, oily fish of the smelt family, found on the Pacific coast; candlefish. *n., pl.* **oo·li·chan** or **oo·li·chans.** Also, **eulachon.**
☞ *Etym.* From Chinook jargon *ulakan.* 19c.

**o·o·lite** or **o·ö·lite** (ō′ə līt′) rock, usually LIMESTONE, consisting of small rounded grains cemented together. *n.*

**oo·long** (ü′long) tea made from leaves that have been partially fermented before being dried in ovens: *Oolong is greenish brown in colour.* *n.*

**oo·loo** (ü′lü) See ULU. *n.*

**oo·mi·ak** (ü′mē ak′) See UMIAK. *n.*

**ooze¹** (üz) **1** pass slowly through small openings: *Blood oozed from her scraped knee. The mud oozed into his boots.* **2** leak slowly and quietly: *The news of their failure oozed to the public.* **3** disappear or drain away: *Her courage oozed away as she waited.* **4** give out slowly: *The cut oozed blood.* **5** a slow flow. **6** something that oozes. 1–4 *v.,* **oozed, ooz·ing;** 5, 6 *n.*

**ooze²** (üz) a soft mud or slime, especially that at the bottom of a pond, lake, river, or ocean. *n.*

**oo·zy** (ü′zē) **1** containing ooze; muddy and soft; slimy. **2** leaking out; oozing. *adj.* —**oo′zi·ly,** *adv.*

**op.** **1** opus; opera. **2** opposite. **3** operation.

**O.P.** observation post.

**o·pac·i·ty** (ō pas′ə tē) **1** the quality or state of being OPAQUE: *Onionskin has less opacity than bond paper.* **2** something OPAQUE: *A cataract is an opacity of the lens of the eye.* *n., pl.* **o·pac·i·ties.**

**o·pal** (ō′pəl) a mineral, a form of SILICA that is softer and less dense than quartz, found in many varieties and colours, certain of which have a peculiar rainbow play of colours and are valued for gems. **Black opals** are green and blue with brilliant coloured lights; some are so dark as to seem almost black. **Milk opals** are milky white with rather pale lights. **Fire opals** are similar with more red and yellow lights. *n.*

**o·pal·esce** (ō′pə les′) exhibit a play of colours like that of the opal. *v.,* **o·pal·esced, o·pal·esc·ing.**

**o·pal·es·cence** (ō′pə les′əns) an exhibition of play of colours like an opal's. *n.*

**o·pal·es·cent** (ō′pə les′ənt) having a play of colours like an opal's. *adj.*

**o·pal·ine** (ō′pə līn′ *or* ō′pə lin) of or like opal. *adj.*

**o·paque** (ō pāk′) **1** not letting light through; not transparent: *Muddy water is opaque.* **2** not shining; dark; dull. **3** obscure; hard to understand. **4** stupid. **5** something opaque. 1–4 *adj.,* 5 *n.* —**o·paque′ness,** *n.*

**opaque projector** an apparatus for projecting written, drawn, or printed material onto a screen or wall: *An opaque projector projects images directly from paper or books rather than from transparencies.* Compare with OVERHEAD PROJECTOR.

**op art** (op) a style of drawing and painting that creates optical illusions of motion and depth by means of complex geometrical designs.

**op. cit.** in the book, article, etc. already referred to (an abbreviation of Latin *opere citato* 'in the work cited').

**o·pen** (ō′pən) **1** not shut; not closed; letting anyone or anything in or out: *Open windows let in the fresh air.* **2** not having its lid, cover, gate, etc. closed: *an open box, an open cage.* **3** cause to become open; move or remove so as to allow entry or exit: *Open the door. I can't open the vent. We opened the lid and looked in the box.* **4** open the lid, cover, etc. of: *to open a parcel, to open a cage.* **5** not closed in: *an open field.* **6** unfilled; not taken up: *have an hour open. The position is still open.* **7** that may be entered, used, shared, competed for, etc. by all: *an open meeting, an open market.* **8** accessible or available: *the only course still open.* **9** ready for business or for admission of the public: *The exhibition is now open.* **10** establish or set going: *She has opened a new store.* **11** begin; start: *School opens tomorrow.* **12** begin the proceedings of; initiate formally: *to open negotiations. The Queen opened Parliament.* **13** without restriction or prohibition: *open season for hunting deer.* **14** *Informal.* allowing liquor, gambling, etc.: *an open town.* **15** undecided; not settled: *an open question.* **16** have or make entrance; allow entry: *This hall opens into the bedrooms.* **17** become open or more open; become accessible: *The valley opens wide lower down.* **18** cause to be open or more open; make accessible: *Open a path through the woods.* **19** having no cover, roof, etc.; letting in air freely: *an open car.* **20** not covered or protected; exposed: *open to temptation.* **21** not obstructed: *an open view.* **22** unprejudiced; ready to consider new ideas: *an open mind.* **23** clear of obstructions; make a passage, etc. **24** exposed to general view, knowledge, etc.; not secret: *open disregard of rules.* **25** make or become accessible to knowledge, sympathy, etc.; enlighten or become enlightened: *to open a person's eyes.* **26** uncover; lay bare; expose to view; disclose; reveal; divulge.

**opacity** 825 **open-hearted**

hat, āge, fär; let, ēqual, tėrm; it, īce
hot, ōpen, ôrder; oil, out; cup, pu̇t, rüle
əbove, takən, pencəl, lemən, circəs
ch, child; ng, long; sh, ship
th, thin; ᴛʜ, then; zh, measure

**27** come to view. **28** having spaces or holes: *open ranks, cloth of open texture.* **29** expand, extend, or spread out; make or become less compact: *The ranks opened.* **30** of an organ pipe, not closed at the upper end. **31** of a string on a violin, cello, etc., not stopped by the finger. **32** of a note, produced by such a pipe or string, or without aid of slide, key, etc. **33** in phonetics, uttered with relatively wide opening between the tongue and the roof of the mouth: *an open vowel.* **34** unreserved, candid, or frank: *an open face.* **35** that is spread out; expanded: *an open flower, an open newspaper.* **36** generous; liberal: *to give with an open hand.* **37** cut into. **38** free from frost: *an open winter.* **39** free from hindrance, especially from ice: *open water on the lake, a river or harbour now open.* **40** of a city, town, etc., unfortified; protected from enemy attack under international law. **41 the open, a** the open country, air, sea, etc.: *I spent the afternoon out in the open and got badly sunburned.* **b** public view or knowledge: *It would be better to bring the problem out into the open.* 1, 2, 5–9, 13–15, 19–22, 24, 28, 30–36, 38–40 *adj.,* 3, 4, 10–12, 16–18, 23, 25–27, 29, 37 *v.,* 41 *n.* —**o′pen·ly,** *adv.*

**open to, a** ready to take; willing to consider: *open to suggestions.* **b** liable to: *open to criticism.* **c** to be had or used by.

**open up, a** make or become open. **b** unfold; spread out. **c** open a way to and develop: *The early settlers opened up the West.*

**open air** the OUT-OF-DOORS.

**o·pen–air** (ō′pə ner′) OUTDOOR: *an open-air concert. adj.*

**o·pen–and–shut** (ō′pə nən shut′) *Informal.* simple and direct; obvious; straightforward: *The Crown attorney was sure they had an open-and-shut case against the defendant. adj.*

**open door 1** freedom of access; unrestricted admission. **2** a policy of a country giving all other countries an equal chance to trade with it.

**o·pen–end·ed** (ō′pə nen′did) having no set boundary or limit; not rigidly defined or controlled; adaptable to a changing situation or need: *an open-ended agreement. The audience participated in an open-ended discussion after the speech. adj.*

**o·pen·er** (ō′pə nər *or* ōp′nər) **1** a person or thing that opens, especially a device for opening bottles, cans, letters, etc. **2** *Informal.* the first game of a scheduled series. *n.*

**for openers,** *Informal.* as a beginning.

**o·pen–eyed** (ō′pə nīd′) **1** having eyes wide open as in wonder. **2** having the eyes open; watchful or vigilant; observant. **3** done or experienced with the eyes open. *adj.*

**o·pen–hand·ed** (ō′pən han′did) generous; liberal. *adj.* —**op′en–hand′ed·ly,** *adv.* —**o′pen–hand′ed·ness,** *n.*

**o·pen–heart·ed** (ō′pən här′tid) **1** candid; frank; unreserved. **2** kindly; generous. *adj.* —**o′pen–heart′ed·ly,** *adv.* —**o′pen–heart′ed·ness,** *n.*

**o·pen-hearth** (ō′pən härth′) having an open hearth; using a furnace with an open hearth. *adj.*

**open-hearth process** a process of making steel in a furnace that reflects the flame from the roof onto the raw material.

**open house** 1 an informal social event that is open to all who wish to come: *They dropped in at their neighbour's open house before leaving for Christmas.* 2 an occasion when a school, university, factory, etc. is opened for inspection by the public: *The art college has an open house every spring to display student work and demonstrate the facilities of the college.* 3 a time when a house for sale is open to inspection by buyers and agents.

**o·pen·ing** (ō′pə ning *or* ōp′ning) 1 an open or clear space; gap; hole: *an opening in a wall, an opening in the forest.* 2 the first part; beginning: *the opening of a lecture.* 3 first; beginning: *the opening words of her speech.* 4 an official ceremony to mark the beginning of a new business, institution, etc.: *The opening of the new city hall was last week. Were you there for the opening?* 5 a job, place, or position that is open or vacant: *an opening for a teller in a bank.* 6 a favourable chance or opportunity: *He waited for an opening before asking to borrow the car.* 1, 2, 4–6 *n.*, 3 *adj.*

**open letter** a letter addressed to a particular person but published in a newspaper, magazine, etc.

**open mind** a mind ready to consider new arguments or ideas: *A politician ought to keep an open mind.*

**o·pen–mind·ed** (ō′pən mīn′did) having or showing a mind open to new arguments or ideas. *adj.* —**o′pen-mind′ed·ly,** *adv.* —**o′pen-mind′ed·ness,** *n.*

**o·pen-mouthed** (ō′pən mouŧHd′ *or* ō′pən moutht′) 1 having the mouth open. 2 gaping with surprise or astonishment. 3 greedy, ravenous, or rapacious. 4 vociferous or clamorous: *open-mouthed hounds.* 5 having a wide mouth: *an open-mouthed pitcher.* *adj.*

**o·pen·ness** (ō′pən nis) the quality or state of being open: *They like the new location because of its openness to the sea. Her openness to different opinions and ideas makes her a very popular politician.* *n.*

**open question** a matter that has not been decided and on which differences of opinion are accepted.

**open season** a period during which it is legal to hunt and kill fish or game that is protected by law at other times.

**open secret** a matter that is supposed to be secret but that everyone knows about: *It's an open secret that he has applied for another job.*

**open ses·a·me** (ses′ə mē) 1 in *The Arabian Nights,* the magic words that opened the door of the robbers' den in the story of Ali Baba. 2 anything that obtains easy access: *Her education was an open sesame to the job.*

**open shop** a factory, shop, or other establishment that will employ both union and non-union workers. Compare with CLOSED SHOP.

**open syllable** a syllable that ends with a vowel sound. *Examples: free* in *freedom, o* in *open.* Compare with CLOSED SYLLABLE.

**o·pen·work** (ō′pən wėrk′) ornamental work in cloth, metal, etc. that has openings in the material. *n.*

**op·er·a**[1] (op′ə rə *or* op′rə) 1 a kind of drama set to music, performed by a group of singers usually to an orchestral accompaniment. In an opera, the words are usually sung, rather than spoken: *"Faust" and "Lohengrin" are well-known operas.* 2 the art of creating or performing operas: *the history of opera.* 3 a performance of an opera. 4 a theatre where operas are performed. *n.*

**op·er·a**[2] (op′ə rə *or* op′rə) pl. of OPUS. *n.*

**op·er·a·ble** (op′ə rə bəl *or* op′rə bəl) 1 fit for, or admitting of, a surgical operation. 2 fit or able to be operated. *adj.*

**opera glasses** a small binocular telescope for use at the opera and in theatres: *Opera glasses are like field glasses, but smaller.*

**opera hat** a man's tall, collapsible hat worn with formal clothes.

**opera house** 1 a theatre where operas are presented. 2 any theatre.

**op·er·ate** (op′ə rāt′) 1 be at work; run: *The machinery operates night and day.* 2 keep at work; drive: *Who operates this elevator?* 3 direct the working of as owner or manager; manage: *That company operates factories in seven countries.* 4 take effect; produce an effect; work; act: *Several causes operated to bring in the war.* 5 go into action; become effective: *The medicine operated quickly.* 6 in medicine, treat the body, especially using instruments to remedy an injury, disease, etc.: *The doctor operated on the injured woman.* 7 carry on military movements. *v.,* **op·er·at·ed, op·er·at·ing.**

**op·er·at·ic** (op′ə rat′ik) of, having to do with, or like the opera: *operatic music.* *adj.* —**op′er·at′i·cal·ly,** *adv.*

**op·er·a·tion** (op′ə rā′shən) 1 working: *The operation of a railway requires many people.* 2 the way a thing works: *the operation of a machine.* 3 an action; activity: *the operation of brushing one's teeth.* 4 in medicine, a treatment, especially one in which instruments are used to cut into the body in order to remove, replace, or repair an organ or part: *She had her operation yesterday and is doing well.* 5 movements of soldiers, ships, supplies, etc.: *naval operations.* 6 in mathematics, something done to a number or quantity: *Addition, subtraction, multiplication, and division are the four commonest operations in arithmetic.* *n.*

**in operation,** a running; working; in action. b in use or effect.

**op·er·a·tion·al** (op′ə rā′shə nəl *or* op′ə rā′shnəl) 1 of or having to do with any kind of operation. 2 of equipment, in working order. 3 of a military operation, ready or equipped to perform a certain mission. *adj.* —**op′er·a′tion·al·ly,** *adv.*

**op·er·a·tive** (op′ə rə tiv *or* op′ə rā′tiv) 1 operating; effective: *the laws operative in a community.* 2 a person who operates a machine. 3 having to do with work or productiveness: *operative departments of a manufacturing establishment.* 4 of, concerned with, or resulting from a surgical operation. 5 a private detective or secret agent. 6 relevant; of note: *the operative word in a sentence.* 1, 3, 4, 6 *adj.*, 2, 5 *n.*

**op·er·a·tor** (op′ə rā′tər) 1 a person who operates something, especially a skilled worker who runs a machine, telephone exchange, telegraph, etc. 2 *Informal.* a person who is skilled in avoiding problems or restrictions or manipulating people for his or her own ends. *n.*

**op·er·cu·lum** (o pėr′kyü ləm) any one of the several

covering lids in plants and animals, such as the covering that protects the gills of a fish. *n.*

**op·er·et·ta** (op′ə ret′ə) a short, amusing opera with some words spoken rather than sung. *n., pl.* **op·er·et·tas.**

**o·phid·i·an** (ō fid′ē ən) 1 snake. 2 of, having to do with, or like snakes. 1 *n.*, 2 *adj.*

**oph·thal·mi·a** (of thal′mē ə) an acute infection of the membrane around the eye that may affect the eye, causing blindness. *n.*

**oph·thal·mic** (of thal′mik) 1 of or having to do with the eye. 2 having to do with or affected with OPHTHALMIA. *adj.*

**oph·thal·mol·o·gist** (of′thal mol′ə jist) a physician whose specialty is OPHTHALMOLOGY; OCULIST. *n.*
☛ Syn. See note at OCULIST.

**oph·thal·mol·o·gy** (of′thal mol′ə jē) a branch of medical science that deals with the structure, functions, and diseases of the eye. *n.*

**o·pi·ate** (ō′pē it *or* ō′pē āt) 1 any powerful drug containing opium or a derivative of opium (such as morphine) and used especially to dull pain or to bring sleep. 2 containing opium or a derivative. 3 anything that quiets. 4 bringing sleep or ease. 1, 3 *n.*, 2, 4 *adj.*

**o·pin·ion** (ə pin′yən *or* ō pin′yən) 1 what one thinks; a view or belief based on judgment rather than knowledge: *I try to learn the facts and form my own opinions.* 2 an impression; estimate: *Everyone has a poor opinion of a coward.* 3 a formal judgment made by an expert; professional advice: *She asked the doctor for an opinion about the new drug.* *n.*

**o·pin·ion·at·ed** (ə pin′yə nā′tid *or* ō pin′yə nā′tid) obstinate or conceited with regard to one's opinions; dogmatic: *Bill is too opinionated to listen to anybody else.* *adj.*

**o·pi·um** (ō′pē əm) 1 a powerful, addictive drug that causes sleep and eases pain: *Opium is made from a kind of poppy.* 2 anything that has a dulling or tranquillizing effect. *n.*

**o·pos·sum** (ə pos′əm) a small marsupial of the eastern United States that lives most of the time in trees and carries its young in a pouch; possum: *When an opossum is caught or frightened, it becomes unconscious and appears to be dead.* *n.*

**op·po·nent** (ə pō′nənt) 1 a person who is on the other side in a fight, game, or argument; a person fighting, struggling, or speaking against another: *Karl defeated his opponent in the election.* 2 opposing. 1 *n.*, 2 *adj.*

**op·por·tune** (op′ər tyün′ *or* op′ər tün′) fortunate; well-chosen; suitable; favourable: *You have come at a most opportune moment, for I need your advice.* *adj.*
—**op′por·tune′ly,** *adv.* —**op′por·tune′ness,** *n.*

**op·por·tun·ism** (op′ər tyü′niz əm *or* op′ər tü′niz əm) the policy or practice of taking advantage of opportunities and adapting thought and action to particular circumstances, especially with little regard for principles. *n.*

**op·por·tun·ist** (op′ər tyü′nist *or* op′ər tü′nist) a person who practises OPPORTUNISM: *She's just an opportunist, using the organization as a stepping-stone to political power.* *n.*

**op·por·tu·ni·ty** (op′ər tyü′nə tē *or* op′ər tü′nə tē) a good chance; favourable time; convenient occasion: *I had an opportunity to go to Europe. I have had no opportunity to* give Jan your message, because I have not seen him. *n., pl.* **op·por·tu·ni·ties.**

**op·pos·a·ble** (ə pō′zə bəl) 1 capable of being opposed or resisted. 2 capable of being placed opposite something else: *The thumb is opposable to the fingers.* *adj.*

**op·pose** (ə pōz′) 1 act, fight, or struggle against; try to hinder or stop; resist: *The residents opposed the widening of the street. The army's advance was fiercely opposed.* 2 put against as a defence, reply, or contrast: *Let us oppose good nature to anger.* 3 put in contrast: *to oppose European and North American culture.* 4 put in front of; cause to face: *to oppose one's finger to one's thumb.* *v.*, **op·posed, op·pos·ing.** —**op·pos′er,** *n.*

**op·posed** (ə pōzd′) 1 placed in opposition; contrary or contrasted: *The two brothers had strongly opposed characters.* 2 pt. and pp. of OPPOSE. 1 *adj.*, 2 *v.*
**as opposed to,** compared with: *I prefer fish as opposed to meat. We talked of the merits of train travel as opposed to air travel.*

**op·po·site** (op′ə zit) 1 placed face to face, back to back, or at the other end or side: *the opposite side of the street. The printing on the opposite side of the page shows through to this side.* 2 as different as can be; just contrary: *North and South are opposite directions. Sour is opposite to sweet.* 3 a thing or person that is opposite: *Black is the opposite of white.* 4 opposite to: *opposite the cinema. The map is opposite page 37.* 5 in a motion picture or play, acting as the leading lady or man of: *She played opposite a famous actor in her first starring role.* 1, 2 *adj.*, 3 *n.*, 4, 5 *prep.* —**op′po·site·ly,** *adv.* —**op′po·site·ness,** *n.*

**op·po·si·tion** (op′ə zish′ən) 1 action against; resistance: *The mob offered opposition to the police.* 2 contrast: *His views were in opposition to mine.* 3 the political party or parties not in power: *In parliament, the party having the second largest number of elected members is called the official opposition.* 4 any opponent or group of opponents: *Our team easily defeated the opposition.* 5 placing opposite: *the opposition of the thumb to the fingers.* 6 an opposite direction or position. 7 in astrology and astronomy, the position of two heavenly bodies when their longitude differs by 180 degrees. *n.*

**op·press** (ə pres′ *or* ō pres′) 1 govern harshly; keep down unjustly or by cruelty: *a good government will not oppress the poor.* 2 weigh down; lie heavily on; burden: *A fear of trouble ahead oppressed my spirits.* *v.*

**op·pres·sion** (ə presh′ən *or* ō presh′ən) 1 cruel or unjust treatment; tyranny; persecution; despotism: *The oppression of the people by the dictator caused the war. They fought against oppression.* 2 a heavy, weary feeling. *n.*

**op·pres·sive** (ə pres′iv *or* ō pres′iv) 1 harsh; severe; unjust: *Oppressive measures were taken to crush the rebellion.* 2 hard to bear; burdensome: *The great heat was oppressive.* *adj.* —**op·pres′sive·ly,** *adv.* —**op·pres′sive·ness,** *n.*

**op·pres·sor** (ə pres′ər *or* ō pres′ər) a person who is

cruel or unjust to people over whom he or she has authority or power. *n.*

**op·pro·bri·ous** (ə prō′brē əs) expressing scorn, reproach, or abuse: *Coward, liar, and thief are opprobrious names. adj.* —**op·pro′bri·ous·ly,** *adv.*

**op·pro·bri·um** (ə prō′brē əm) **1** disgrace or reproach caused by conduct considered shameful or vicious; infamy; scorn; abuse. **2** something that brings disgrace or scorn. *n.*

**op·so·nin** (op′sə nin) a substance in the blood SERUM (def. 1) that weakens bacteria and other foreign cells so that the white blood cells can destroy them more easily. *n.*

**opt** (opt) make a choice, especially in favour of something; decide (*usually used with* **for**): *The class opted for a field trip. v.*
**opt in,** choose to join.
**opt out (of),** decide to leave; choose to drop out of some activity or organization: *Several nations wanted to opt out of the alliance.*

**op·tic** (op′tik) **1** of the eye or the sense of sight. **2** *Informal.* eye. **1** *adj.*, **2** *n.*

**op·ti·cal** (op′tə kəl) **1** of or having to do with the eye or the sense of sight; visual: *an optical illusion. Being near-sighted is an optical defect.* See ILLUSION for picture. **2** made to assist sight or according to the principles of optics: *A microscope is an optical instrument. An optical telescope uses light waves, while a radio telescope uses radio waves.* **3** of or having to do with OPTICS. *adj.*
—**op′ti·cal·ly,** *adv.*

**optical microscope** a microscope using beams of light. Compare with ELECTRON MICROSCOPE.

**op·ti·cian** (op tish′ən) a maker or seller of eyeglasses and other optical instruments. *n.*
☛ *Syn.* See note at OCULIST.

**optic nerve** a nerve that goes from the eye to the brain: *The optic nerve conducts visual stimuli to the brain.* See EYE for picture.

**op·tics** (op′tiks) the science that deals with light and vision (*used with a singular verb*). *n.*

**op·ti·mal** (op′tə məl) most favourable or desirable; optimum. *adj.* —**op′ti·mal·ly,** *adv.*

**op·ti·mism** (op′tə miz′əm) **1** a tendency to look on the bright side of things and make the best of any situation or event as it comes about. **2** a belief that everything will turn out for the best. **3** a doctrine that the existing world is the best of all possible worlds. *n.* Compare with PESSIMISM.

**op·ti·mist** (op′tə mist) **1** a person who looks on the bright side of things. **2** a person who believes that everything in life will turn out for the best. *n.* Compare with PESSIMIST.

**op·ti·mis·tic** (op′tə mis′tik) **1** inclined to look on the bright side of things. **2** hoping for the best: *I am optimistic about winning the game.* **3** having to do with OPTIMISM. *adj.* Compare with PESSIMISTIC.
—**op′ti·mis′ti·cal·ly,** *adv.*

**op·ti·mize** (op′tə mīz′) make the most of; make as satisfactory or effective as possible: *She checked every detail of design to optimize the effect of the advertisement.* *v.*, **op·ti·mized, op·ti·miz·ing.**

**op·ti·mum** (op′tə məm) **1** the best or most favourable point, degree, amount, etc. for a particular purpose. **2** most favourable, desirable, or satisfactory; best: *an optimum temperature for growth.* **1** *n.*, *pl.* **op·ti·mums** or **op·ti·ma** (-mə); **2** *adj.*

**op·tion** (op′shən) **1** the right or power to choose: *We have the option of rejecting this offer and waiting for a better one.* **2** the act of choosing: *to make an option.* **3** something chosen or that may be chosen: *One of the options open to her was to accept a grant to study abroad. One of the options offered with this car model is air conditioning.* **4** a right to buy something at a certain price within a certain time: *to hold an option on land.* *n.*

**op·tion·al** (op′shə nəl) involving an option; not required or standard: *optional equipment on a car.* *adj.* —**op′tion·al·ly,** *adv.*

**op·tom·e·trist** (op tom′ə trist) a person who is qualified to practise OPTOMETRY: *An optometrist does not prescribe drugs or surgery.* *n.*
☛ *Syn.* See note at OCULIST.

**op·tom·e·try** (op tom′ə trē) the art or profession of examining the eyes for defects in vision and prescribing lenses or exercises to correct such defects. *n.*

**op·u·lence** (op′yə ləns) **1** wealth; affluence. **2** luxuriant abundance; lavishness. *n.*

**op·u·lent** (op′yə lənt) **1** wealthy; affluent. **2** abundant and luxuriant; lavish: *the opulent décor of the expensive hotel's lobby, an opulent musical style.* *adj.*

**o·pus** (ō′pəs) a literary work or musical composition: *The violinist played his own opus, No. 16.* *n.*, *pl.* **op·er·a** or **o·pus·es.**

**or** (ôr) **1** a word used to express a choice, alternative, difference, etc. or to connect words or groups of words of equal importance in a sentence: *You can go or stay. Is it sweet or sour?* **2** and if not; otherwise: *Either eat this or go hungry. Hurry, or you will be late.* **3** that is; being the same as: *This is the end or last part.* *conj.*
☛ *Hom.* OAR, ORE.

**-or** a suffix meaning: **1** a person or thing that _____s, as in *actor, accelerator, orator, survivor.* **2** an act, state, condition, quality, characteristic, etc., especially in words borrowed directly from Latin, such as in *error, horror, terror.*
☛ *Usage.* **-or, -our.** The suffix **-or** entered English directly from Latin: *horror, terror.* With a few words, the spelling **-our** was also introduced from French: *colour, labour, neighbour.* British English prefers **-our** in such words, but American English prefers **-or**. In Canada, both spellings are acceptable but **-our** is the more frequent, and is the variant given first in this dictionary.

**OR** or **O.R.** **1** operating room. **2** orderly room.

**or·a·cle** (ô′rə kəl) **1** in ancient times, an answer given by a god through a priest or priestess to some question: *An oracle often had a hidden meaning that was hard to understand.* **2** the place where the god gave answers: *A famous oracle was at Delphi.* **3** the priest, priestess, or other means by which the god's answer was given. **4** a person who gives wise advice. **5** something regarded as a reliable and sure guide. *n.*

**o·rac·u·lar** (ô rak′yə lər) **1** of or like an ORACLE. **2** with a hidden meaning that is difficult to make out. **3** very wise. *adj.* —**o·rac′u·lar·ly,** *adv.*

**o·ral** (ô′rəl) **1** spoken; using speech: *An oral agreement is not enough; we must have a written promise.* **2** of the mouth: *The oral opening in an earthworm is small.*

3 taken by the mouth: *oral medicine.* *adj.*
—**o′ral‧ly,** *adv.*

**or‧ange** (ô′rinj) 1 a round, reddish-yellow, edible citrus fruit having a bitter rind and a sweet or tangy, juicy pulp. 2 any of several closely related species of small evergreen tree growing in warm climates, that produce oranges: *The orange has fragrant white blossoms.* 3 any fruit or tree that suggests an orange. 4 of or like an orange. 5 the colour made by mixing red and yellow. 6 of or having this colour. 1–3, 5 *n.*, 4, 6 *adj.*
—**or′ange‧like′,** *adj.*

**or‧ange‧ade** (ô′rin jād′) a drink made of orange juice, sugar, and water. *n.*

**Orange Association** the LOYAL ORANGE ASSOCIATION.

**Or‧ange‧man** (ô′rinj mən) 1 a member of a secret society, formed in the north of Ireland in 1795, to uphold the Protestant religion and Protestant control in Ireland. 2 a member of the LOYAL ORANGE ASSOCIATION. *n., pl.* **Or‧ange‧men** (-mən).

**Orange Order** the LOYAL ORANGE ASSOCIATION.

**orange pekoe** (pē′kō) a black tea that comes from Sri Lanka or India.

**o‧rang‧ou‧tang** or **o‧rang–ou‧tang** (ô rang′ü tang′) ORANGUTAN. *n.*

**o‧rang‧u‧tan** or **o‧rang–u‧tan** (ô rang′ü tan′ *or* ô rang′ ə tan′) a large ape of the forests of Borneo and Sumatra, having very long arms and long, reddish-brown hair: *Orangutans live in trees much of the time and eat fruits and leaves.* *n.*
☛ *Etym.* From Malay *orang* 'man' + *utan* 'wild', originally applied to wild people of the forests and mistakenly applied to the ape by Europeans. 17c.

**o‧rate** (ô rāt′) *Informal.* make an ORATION; talk in a grand manner. *v.,* **o‧rat‧ed, o‧rat‧ing.**

**o‧ra‧tion** (ô rā′shən) a formal public speech delivered on a special occasion. *n.*

**or‧a‧tor** (ô′rə tər) 1 a person who makes an ORATION. 2 a person who can speak very well in public. *n.*

**or‧a‧tor‧i‧cal** (ô′rə tô′rə kəl) 1 of ORATORY¹; having to do with orators or oratory: *an oratorical contest.* 2 characteristic of orators or ORATORY¹: *an oratorical manner.* *adj.* —**or′a‧tor′i‧cal‧ly,** *adv.*

**or‧a‧to‧ri‧o** (ô′rə tô′rē ō′) a musical drama performed without action, costumes, or scenery, for solo voices, chorus, and orchestra: *Oratorios are usually based on Biblical or historical themes.* *n., pl.* **or‧a‧to‧ri‧os.**

**or‧a‧to‧ry¹** (ô′rə tô′rē) 1 the art of public speaking. 2 skill in public speaking; fine speaking. 3 language used in public speaking; words appropriate to fine speaking. *n.*

**or‧a‧to‧ry²** (ô′rə tô′rē) a small chapel; room set apart for prayer. *n., pl.* **or‧a‧to‧ries.**

**orb** (ôrb) 1 a sphere, especially a heavenly body such as the sun, moon, or a star. 2 a jewelled sphere, especially a symbol of royal power. 3 the eyeball or eye. 4 form into a circle or sphere. 1–3 *n.,* 4 *v.*
☛ *Etym.* From L *orbis* 'circle, disc'. 16c. ORBICULAR came in the 15c. directly from L *orbicularis.* ORBIT, which originally meant 'eye socket' came in the 16c. from a form of L *orbitus* 'circular'.

**or‧bic‧u‧lar** (ôr bik′yə lər) like a circle or sphere; rounded. *adj.*
☛ *Etym.* See note at ORB.

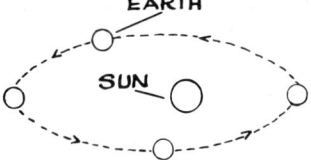

The orbit of the earth around the sun

**or‧bit** (ôr′bit) 1 the path of a heavenly body, planet, or satellite around another body in space: *the earth's orbit around the sun, the moon's orbit around the earth, the orbit of a weather satellite around the earth.* See ECLIPTIC for another picture. 2 travel in an orbit: *Many artificial satellites are orbiting the earth.* 3 put into an orbit: *They plan to orbit a new weather satellite.* 4 the regular course of life or experience. 5 the bony cavity or socket in which the eyeball is set. 1, 4, 5 *n.,* 2, 3 *v.*
☛ *Etym.* See note at ORB.

**or‧bit‧al** (ôr′bə təl) of an ORBIT. *adj.*

**or‧chard** (ôr′chərd) 1 a piece of ground on which fruit trees are grown. 2 the trees in an orchard. *n.*

**or‧ches‧tra** (ôr′ki strə) 1 a relatively large group of musicians, including especially players of violins and other stringed instruments, organized to perform music together. Compare with BAND. 2 all the instruments played together by the musicians in such a group. 3 the part of a theatre just in front of the stage, where the musicians sit to play. 4 the main floor of a theatre, especially the part near the front. *n.*

**or‧ches‧tral** (ôr kes′trəl) of, composed for, or performed by an ORCHESTRA (def. 1). *adj.*

**or‧ches‧trate** (ôr′ki strāt′) compose or arrange music for performance by an ORCHESTRA (def. 1). *v.,* **or‧ches‧trat‧ed, or‧ches‧trat‧ing.**

**or‧ches‧tra‧tion** (ôr′ki strā′shən) 1 an arrangement of music for an ORCHESTRA (def. 1). 2 the art of creating such an arrangement. *n.*

A variety of orchid grown in greenhouses and often used for corsages, etc.

**or‧chid** (ôr′kid) 1 any of a large family of perennial plants, some of which grow on other plants and obtain their food and moisture from the air: *Most orchids have showy, often brilliantly coloured flowers with three petals, one of which is large and shaped somewhat like a lip.* 2 the flower of an orchid: *Cultivated varieties of tropical orchids are much valued for corsages.* 3 light purple. 1–3 *n.,* 3 *adj.*

**or‧dain** (ôr dān′) 1 order or establish by law or by decree: *The law ordains that convicted murderers shall be* *imprisoned.* **2** officially appoint or consecrate as a member of the clergy. *v.*

**or·deal** (ôr dēl′) **1** a severe test or experience: *Written examinations were always an ordeal for her. The newspaper story described the ordeal of the survivors of the plane crash.* **2** in early times, an effort to decide the guilt or innocence of an accused person by making him or her do something dangerous such as putting his or her hand in a fire or taking poison: *It was supposed that an innocent person would not be harmed by such an ordeal.* *n.*

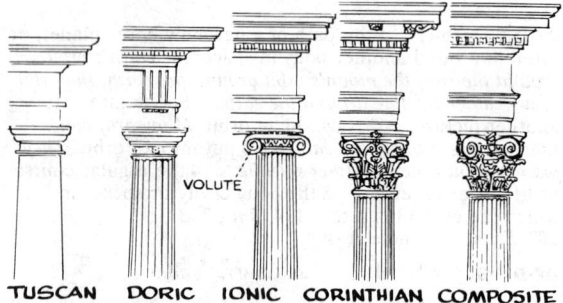

Order (def. 25): columns and entablatures illustrating the five orders of classical Greek and Roman architecture

**or·der** (ôr′dər) **1** the way one thing follows another: *in order of size, in alphabetical order.* **2** a condition in which every part or piece is in its right place: *to put a room in order.* **3** put in order; arrange: *to order one's affairs.* **4** a condition; state: *My affairs are in good order.* **5** the way the world works; way things happen: *the order of nature.* **6** the state or condition of things in which the law is obeyed and there is no trouble: *The police officer tried hard to keep order.* **7** the principles and rules by which a meeting is run. **8** a command; telling what to do: *The orders of the captain must be obeyed.* **9** tell what to do; command; bid: *The judge ordered the people in the courtroom to be quiet.* **10** give a request or directions for: *Please order dinner for me.* **11** a spoken or written request for goods that one wants to buy or receive: *a grocery order.* **12** the goods so requested: *Mother asked when they would deliver our order.* **13** the direction of a court or judge made in writing and not included in a judgment. **14** a paper saying that money is to be given or paid, or something handed over: *a money order.* **15** decide; will; determine: *The authorities ordered it otherwise.* **16** a kind or sort: *to have ability of a high order.* **17** in biology, a major category in the classification of plants and animals, more specific than a class and more general than a family: *Butterflies, moths, and skippers belong to the order of insects called Lepidoptera.* See classification chart in the Appendix. **18** a social rank, grade, or class: *all orders of society.* **19** a rank or position in the church: *the order of bishops.* **20** invest with clerical rank or authority. **21** a group of people banded together for some purpose or united by something they share in common: *the Franciscan order, the Imperial Order Daughters of the Empire.* **22** a society to which one is admitted as an honour: *the Order of the Golden Fleece.* **23** a fraternal group or society: *the Order of Freemasons.* **24** a badge worn by those belonging to an honorary order. **25** any of five types of column and entablature forming the basis of the five classical styles of architecture: *The five orders are Doric, Ionic, and Corinthian of ancient Greek origin, and Tuscan and Composite of ancient Roman origin.* **26** the regular form of worship for a given occasion. **27** a portion or serving of food served in a restaurant, etc.: *"I'd like one order of fish and chips, please."* **28** Usually, **orders**, **a** ORDINATION. **b** the rite of ordination; holy orders. 1, 2, 4–8, 11–14, 16–19, 21–28 *n.*, 3, 9, 10, 15, 20 *v.*
**by order,** according to an order given by the proper person: *by order of the premier.*
**call to order,** ask to be quiet and start work: *She called the meeting to order.*
**in holy orders,** being a member of the clergy.
**in order, a** in the right arrangement or condition: *Are all the pages in order?* **b** working properly. **c** allowed by the rules of a meeting, etc.
**in order that,** so that; with the purpose that.
**in order to,** as a means to; with a view to; for the purpose of: *She worked hard in order to win the prize.*
**in short order,** quickly: *They got the broken window replaced in short order.*
**on order,** having been ordered but not yet received.
**on the order of,** resembling; similar to: *a house on the order of ours.*
**order about** or **around,** send here and there; tell to do this and that: *Stop ordering me around.*
**out of order, a** in the wrong arrangement or condition: *These pages are out of order.* **b** not working properly: *The radio is out of order.* **c** against the rules of a meeting, etc.: *Your motion is out of order.*
**short-order,** of or having to do with the type of food cooked quickly in a fast-food restaurant: *a short-order cook.*
**take holy orders,** become a member of the clergy.
**to order,** according to the buyer's wishes: *They had the couch made to order.*

**or·der·ed** (ôr′dərd) **1** characterized by regular arrangement or order; systematic, harmonious, etc.: *They led a quiet, ordered existence. The window gave a wide view of ordered lawns and gardens.* **2** in mathematics, etc., having elements arranged in a specific order: *an ordered set of rules. A point in a plane can be identified by an ordered pair of numbers.* **3** pt. and pp. of ORDER. 1, 2 *adj.*, 3 *v.*

**Order in Council** a regulation made by a federal or provincial cabinet under the authority of the Governor General or Lieutenant-Governor.

**or·der·ly** (ôr′dər lē) **1** in order; with regular arrangement, method, or system: *an orderly arrangement, an orderly mind.* **2** keeping order; well-behaved or regulated: *an orderly class.* **3** in the armed forces, a person who attends a superior officer to carry messages, etc.: *The general's orderly delivered the message.* **4** concerned with carrying out orders; being on duty. **5** a hospital attendant who keeps things clean and in order. 1, 2, 4 *adj.*, 3, 5 *n.*, *pl.* **or·der·lies.** —**or′der·li·ness,** *n.*

**Orderly Officer** OFFICER OF THE DAY.

**or·di·nal** (ôr′də nəl) **1** showing order or position in a series. **2** ORDINAL NUMBER. **3** of or having to do with an order of animals or plants. **4** a book of special forms for certain church ceremonies. 1, 3 *adj.*, 2, 4 *n.*

**ordinal number** a number that shows order or position in a series. *First, second, third,* etc. are ordinal numbers; *one, two, three,* etc. are cardinal numbers. Compare with CARDINAL NUMBER.

**or·di·nance** (ôr′də nəns) **1** a rule or law made by authority; decree or regulation, especially a municipal regulation: *Many cities have ordinances against burning* leaves or garbage. **2** an established religious ceremony. *n.*

**or·di·nar·i·ly** (ôr′də ner′ə lē *or* ôr′də ner′ə lē)
**1** usually; regularly; commonly; normally: *We ordinarily go to the movies on Saturday.* **2** to the usual extent. *adv.*

**or·di·nar·y** (ôr′də ner′ē) **1** usual; regular; customary; normal: *Jack's ordinary supper consists of steak and onions.* **2** not special; common; everyday; average: *an ordinary person, an ordinary situation.* **3** somewhat below the average: *The speech was ordinary and tiresome.* **4** a person who has authority in his own right, especially a bishop or a judge. **5** a form of saying Mass. 1–3 *adj.*, 4, 5 *n.*, *pl.* **or·di·nar·ies.**
**in ordinary,** in regular service: *physician in ordinary to the queen.*
**out of the ordinary,** unusual; not regular or customary: *It wasn't anything out of the ordinary for her to jog 15 km.*

**or·di·na·tion** (ôr′də nā′shən) **1** the act or ceremony of admitting a person to the Christian ministry. **2** being admitted as a minister to the Christian church. *n.*

**ord·nance** (ôrd′nəns) **1** artillery; big guns or cannon. **2** military weapons and equipment of all kinds. *n.*

**ore** (ôr) a naturally occurring mineral containing a valuable substance such as metal: *Iron ore is mined and worked to extract the iron it contains.* *n.*
☞ *Hom.* OAR, OR.

**or·gan** (ôr′gən) **1** a large musical wind instrument consisting of sets of pipes of different diameters and lengths which are sounded by forcing air through them by means of keys and pedals; pipe organ. **2** an instrument in which a similar sound is produced by electronic means. **3** any of various other instruments such as a mouth organ or harmonium. **4** any structure in an animal or plant, such as an eye, lung, stamen or pistil, that is composed of different cells and tissues organized to perform some particular function. **5** a group or organization that performs a particular function within a larger group or organization: *A court is an organ of government.* **6** a means of giving information or expressing opinions; a newspaper or magazine that speaks for and gives the views of a political party or some other group or organization. *n.*

**or·gan·dy** or **or·gan·die** (ôr′gən dē) a very fine, thin, sheer cotton cloth with a crisp finish, woven in a plain weave with tightly twisted yarns: *Organdy is used for dresses, curtains, blouses, trimming, etc.* *n.*, *pl.* **or·gan·dies.**

**or·gan·elle** (ôr′gə nel′) a separate structure within a cell, such as a cilium or centriole. *n.*

**organ grinder** a person who plays a hand organ by turning a crank.

**or·gan·ic** (ôr gan′ik) **1** of, having to do with, or affecting a bodily organ: *an organic disease.* **2** of, having to do with, or characteristic of beings having organs or an organized physical structure; of, having to do with or characteristic of living things: *organic substances, organic nature.* **3** made up of related and co-ordinated parts; organized: *Every part of an organic whole depends on every other part.* **4** forming part of the basic structure of something fundamental: *The music is not just background but an organic part of the film.* **5** of, referring to, or containing compounds of carbon: *Organic compounds exist naturally as constituents of animals and plants.* **6** referring to the branch of chemistry dealing with such compounds. **7** obtained from animals or plants: *organic*

---

**ordinarily**    **831**    **orgy**

hat, āge, fär; let, ēqual, tėrm; it, īce
hot, ōpen, ôrder; oil, out; cup, pút, rüle
əbove, takən, pencəl, lemən, circəs
ch, child; ng, long; sh, ship
th, thin; ᴛH, then; zh, measure

*fertilizer.* **8** referring to a method of raising plants or animals without using chemical substances such as pesticides or growth hormones: *organic gardening.* **9** of vegetables, meat, etc. produced in this way: *organic beef.* *adj.* —**or·gan′i·cal·ly**, *adv.*

**organic chemistry** the branch of chemistry that deals with compounds of carbon.

**or·gan·ism** (ôr′gə niz′əm) **1** a living body having organs or an organized structure in which each part has a particular function but all depend on each other; an individual animal, plant, fungus, moneran or protist. **2** a very tiny living thing. **3** a complex structure made of related parts that work together and are dependent on each other and on the whole structure: *A community may be spoken of as a social organism.* *n.*

**or·gan·ist** (ôr′gə nist) a person who plays the organ, especially a skilled player. *n.*

**or·gan·i·za·tion** (ôr′gə nə zā′shən *or* ôr′gə nī zā′shən) **1** a group of persons united for some purpose: *Churches, clubs, and political parties are organizations.* **2** the act of organizing; the grouping and arranging of parts to form the whole: *The organization of a big picnic takes time and thought.* **3** the way in which a thing's parts are arranged to work together: *The organization of the human body is very complicated.* **4** something made up of related parts, each having a special duty: *A tree is an organization of roots, trunk, branches, leaves, and fruit.* *n.*

**or·ga·ni·za·tion·al** (ôr′gə nə zā′shə nəl *or* ôr′gə nī zā′shə nəl) of or having to do with organization or organizations. *adj.* —**or′ga·ni·za′tion·al·ly**, *adv.*

**Organization of American States** an association of the independent republics of North, Central, and South America, formed to promote mutual co-operation.

**or·gan·ize** (ôr′gə nīz′) **1** arrange to work or come together as a whole: *The general organized his soldiers into a powerful fighting force.* **2** plan and lead, get started, or carry out: *The explorer organized an expedition to the North Pole.* **3** arrange in a system: *She organized her thoughts. He organized his stamp collection.* **4** *Informal.* make oneself ready to do what is required: *Please wait—I'm not organized yet.* **5** bring into a labour union; form a labour union in or among; unionize. *v.*, **or·gan·ized**, **or·gan·iz·ing.** —**or′gan·iz′er**, *n.*

**organized labour** or **labor** the workers who belong to labour unions.

**or·gan·za** (ôr gan′zə) a silky cloth of silk, rayon, nylon, etc. that is more crisp and sheer than ORGANDY. *n.*

**or·gy** (ôr′jē) **1** wild, drunken or licentious revelry. **2** something resembling an orgy in lack of control, excessive indulgence in something: *an orgy of destruction, an orgy of bloodshed.* **3** Usually, **orgies**, *pl.* secret rites or ceremonies in the worship of certain Greek and Roman gods, especially Bacchus, the god of wine, celebrated with drinking, wild dancing, and singing. *n.*, *pl.* **or·gies.**

An oriel on the upper front wall of an early 20c. three-storey house in Toronto, Ontario

**o·ri·el** (ô′rē əl) a bay window projecting from a wall, usually in an upper storey, and supported by a bracket. *n.*

**o·ri·ent** (ô′rē ənt *for noun and adjective,* ô′rē ent′ *for verb*) **1** put or build facing east. **2** place or face in a certain position: *The building is oriented north and south.* **3** tend in a certain direction: *She is oriented toward a career in business.* **4** find the direction or position of. **5** lustrous; shining: *an orient pearl.* **6 the Orient, a** the Far East: *China, Japan, Korea, and Vietnam are in the Orient.* **b** formerly, the regions lying to the east of Europe and the Mediterranean Sea, including Asia Minor and the Indian subcontinent as well as the Far East. 1–4 *v.,* 5 *adj.,* 6 *n.*
**orient oneself,** bring into the right relationship with one's surroundings; adjust to a new situation: *It takes a while to orient yourself in a strange city.*

**O·ri·en·tal** (ô′rē en′təl) **1** a native or inhabitant of the Orient. **2** Sometimes, **oriental,** of, having to do with, or characteristic of the Orient or its inhabitants: *Oriental music.* 1 *n.,* 2 *adj.*

**O·ri·en·tal·ism** or **o·ri·en·tal·ism** (ô′rē en′tə liz′əm) **1** a custom, habit, etc. that is characteristic of Oriental peoples. **2** a knowledge of Oriental languages, literature, etc. *n.*

**O·ri·en·tal·ist** or **o·ri·en·tal·ist** (ô′rē en′tə list) a person who specializes in the study of Oriental languages, literature, cultures, history, etc. *n.*

**o·ri·en·tate** (ô′rē en tāt′ *or* ô′rē ən tāt′) ORIENT (defs. 1–4). *v.,* **o·ri·en·tat·ed, o·ri·en·tat·ing.**

**o·ri·en·ta·tion** (ô′rē en tā′shən *or* ô′rē ən tā′shən) **1** the act or process of orienting or the state of being oriented. **2** a general tendency or direction of interest or thought: *Her orientation toward the dramatic shows clearly in her dress designs. n.*

**or·i·en·teer** (ô′rē ən tēr′) **1** find one's way through unfamiliar territory by means of a map or compass or both. **2** a person who participates in the sport of ORIENTEERING. 1 *v.,* 2 *n.*

**or·i·en·teer·ing** (ô′rē ən tē′ring) the sport or practice of finding one's way through unfamiliar territory by means of a map or compass or both, usually involving a given starting and finishing point with a series of check points in between. *n.*

**or·i·fice** (ô′rə fis) an opening, such as a mouth, hole, or vent, through which something may pass. *n.*

**orig.** **1** origin. **2** originally.

**or·i·gam·i** (ô′ri gä′mē) a kind of paper sculpture developed by the Japanese in which paper is folded in a great variety of simple or intricate ways to make birds, flowers, etc. *n.*

**or·i·gin** (ô′rə jin) **1** the thing from which anything comes; source; beginning: *the origin of a quarrel, the origin of a disease.* **2** parentage; ancestry; birth: *The professor was a man of humble origin. The word beef is of French origin. n.*

**o·rig·i·nal** (ə rij′ə nəl) **1** belonging to the beginning; first; earliest: *the original settlers, a skirt marked down from its original price.* **2** fresh and unusual; novel: *She has written a very original story. They thought up several original games for the party.* **3** able to do, make, or think something new; inventive: *The inventor had an original mind.* **4** not copied, imitated, or translated from something else: *This is the original manuscript.* **5** the first version or actual thing from which something is copied, imitated, or translated: *This sculpture is a plaster copy; the original is in Rome.* **6** the language in which a book was first written: *She has read* War and Peace *in the original.* **7** an unusual or eccentric person. 1–4 *adj.,* 5–7 *n.*

**o·rig·i·nal·i·ty** (ə rij′ə nal′ə tē) **1** the quality or state of being original: *Several experts questioned the originality of the manuscript.* **2** freshness or novelty of style, etc.: *The furniture has a striking originality of design.* **3** the ability to do, make, or think up something new: *He is known for his originality in thinking up plots. n.*

**o·rig·i·nal·ly** (ə rij′ə nə lē) **1** by origin: *His family was originally Irish.* **2** at first; in the first place: *a house originally small.* **3** in an original manner: *The room was very originally decorated. adv.*

**o·rig·i·nate** (ə rij′ə nāt′) **1** cause to be; invent: *to originate a new style of painting.* **2** come into being; begin; arise: *Where did that story originate? v.,* **o·rig·i·nat·ed, o·rig·i·nat·ing.** —**o·rig′i·na′tor,** *n.*

**o·rig·i·na·tion** (ə rij′ə nā′shən) originating; ORIGIN. *n.*

**o·ri·ole** (ô′rē əl *or* ô′rē ōl′) **1** any of a closely related group of New World songbirds belonging to the same family as the bobolink, meadowlark, and blackbirds, the adult males having black and orange, yellow, or reddish-brown plumage, the females mainly yellowish. **2** any of a family of Old World songbirds, especially any of a closely related group that includes the yellow-and-black **golden oriole** of Europe and Asia: *The orioles of North America were given their name by early settlers from Britain because of their resemblance to the golden oriole. n.*

**O·ri·on** (ô rī′ən) a group of stars near the equator of the heavens, suggesting a man with a belt around his waist and a sword by his side. *n.*
☛ *Etym.* From *Orion,* in Greek and Roman mythology, a hunter loved by the goddess Diana, who was accidentally killed by her and placed among the stars after his death.

**or·na·ment** (ôr′nə mənt *for noun,* ôr′nə ment′ *for verb*) **1** something used to add beauty, especially a beautiful object or part that has no particular function in itself: *Jewellery and vases are ornaments.* **2** the use of ornaments, ornamentation: *Ornament played an important part in rococo architecture.* **3** a person or an act, quality, etc. that adds beauty, grace, or honour: *He was an ornament to his time.* **4** add beauty to; make more pleasing or attractive; decorate: *A single brooch ornamented her dress.* **5** Usually, **ornaments,** *pl.* things used in church services, such as the organ, bells, silver plate, etc. 1–3, 5 *n.,* 4 *v.*

**or·na·men·tal** (ôr′nə men′təl) **1** of or having to do with ornament. **2** used for ornament; decorative: *an ornamental staircase, ornamental plants. adj.*
—**or′na·men′tal·ly,** *adv.*

**or·na·men·ta·tion** (ôr′nə men tā′shən) 1 ornamenting or being ornamental.  2 decorations; ornaments: *She was dressed simply, with no ornamentation.* *n.*

**or·nate** (ôr nāt′) much adorned; much ornamented: *She liked ornate furniture.* *adj.* —**or·nate′ly,** *adv.* —**or·nate′ness,** *n.*

**or·ner·y** (ôr′nə rē) *Informal.* having an irritable or mean disposition; tending to be hard to get along with: *an ornery horse. He was born ornery.* *adj.* —**or′ner·i·ness,** *n.*

**or·ni·tho·log·i·cal** (ôr′nə thə loj′ə kəl) dealing with birds. *adj.*

**or·ni·thol·o·gist** (ôr′nə thol′ə jist) a person trained in ORNITHOLOGY, especially one who makes it his or her work. *n.*

**or·ni·thol·o·gy** (ôr′nə thol′ə jē) 1 a branch of ZOOLOGY dealing with birds.  2 an article or book on this subject. *n.*

**o·ro·tund** (ō′rə tund′) 1 strong, full, rich, and clear in voice or speech; sonorous.  2 POMPOUS; bombastic. *adj.*

**or·phan** (ôr′fən) 1 a child whose parents are dead or, sometimes, a child who has lost one parent.  2 of or for such children: *an orphan home.*  3 without a father or mother or both.  4 make an orphan of: *The war orphaned me at an early age.*  5 a word or line left alone at the top of a page.  1–3, 5 *n.,* 4 *v.*

**or·phan·age** (ôr′fə nij) 1 a home for orphans.  2 the condition of being an orphan. *n.*

**or·rer·y** (ôr′ə rē) a device showing various planets represented by balls that are moved by clockwork to illustrate motions of the solar system. *n., pl.* **or·rer·ies.**

**or·ris** (ô′ris) 1 ORRISROOT.  2 the plant that it grows on; a kind of iris. *n.*

**or·ris·root** (ô′ris rüt′) a fragrant rootstock of a variety of iris, used in making perfume, toothpaste, etc. *n.*

**ortho–** *combining form.* 1 straight: *Orthopterous* means straight-winged.  2 correct; accepted: *Orthodoxy* means correct doctrine.  3 correcting irregularities; making straight: *Orthodontics* deals with the straightening of teeth.

**or·tho·don·tics** (ôr′thə don′tiks) the branch of dentistry that deals with the straightening and adjusting of irregular or crooked teeth (*used with a singular verb*). *n.*

**or·tho·don·tist** (ôr′thə don′tist) a dentist who specializes in ORTHODONTICS. *n.*

**or·tho·dox** (ôr′thə doks′) 1 conforming to established doctrine, especially in religion: *orthodox views, an orthodox Jew.*  2 conforming to custom; conventional: *The orthodox Thanksgiving dinner is turkey and pumpkin pie.* *adj.*

**Orthodox Church** ORTHODOX EASTERN CHURCH.

**Orthodox Eastern Church** the common name for a Federation of independent Christian churches, mainly in Eastern Europe and the Near East, that recognize the Patriarch of Constantinople as their head.

**or·tho·dox·y** (ôr′thə dok′sē) the holding of correct or generally accepted beliefs; ORTHODOX practice, especially in religion; the state of being orthodox. *n., pl.* **or·tho·dox·ies.**

**or·tho·e·pist** (ôr thō′ə pist) a person who knows much about the pronunciation of words. *n.*

---

**ornamentation**    **833**    **Osage orange**

hat, āge, fär; let, ēqual, tėrm; it, īce
hot, ōpen, ôrder; oil, out; cup, pút, rüle
əbove, takən, pencəl, lemən, circəs
ch, child; ng, long; sh, ship
th, thin; ᴛʜ, then; zh, measure

**or·tho·e·py** (ôr thō′ə pē) 1 the standard pronunciation of a language.  2 the part of grammar that deals with pronunciation; PHONOLOGY. *n.*

**or·thog·ra·pher** (ôr thog′rə fər) a person skilled in ORTHOGRAPHY. *n.*

**or·tho·graph·ic** (ôr′thə graf′ik) 1 having to do with ORTHOGRAPHY.  2 correct in spelling. *adj.* —**or′tho·graph′i·cal·ly,** *adv.*

**or·tho·graph·i·cal** (ôr′thə graf′ə kəl) ORTHOGRAPHIC. *adj.*

**or·thog·ra·phy** (ôr thog′rə fē) 1 the spelling of a language; the representation of the sounds of a language by written symbols.  2 the art of using the correct, or standard, spelling.  3 the study of letters and spelling. *n., pl.* **or·thog·ra·phies.**

**or·tho·pe·dic** (ôr′thə pē′dik) of, having to do with or used in ORTHOPEDICS: *Orthopedic shoes are worn to help correct deformities of the feet.* *adj.*

**or·tho·pe·dics** (ôr′thə pē′diks) the branch of surgery that deals with deformities, diseases, and injuries of bones and joints (*used with a singular verb*). *n.*

**or·tho·pe·dist** (ôr′thə pē′dist) a surgeon who specializes in ORTHOPEDICS. *n.*

**or·thop·ter·an** (ôr thop′tə rən) 1 any insect belonging to the order **Orthoptera,** a large group of mostly plant-eating insects having two pairs of wings, the membranous hind wings covered by hard, narrow front wings or, in some species, having no wings at all: *Crickets, grasshoppers and cockroaches are orthopterans.*  2 of or referring to this order or an insect belonging to it.  1 *n.,* 2 *adj.*

**or·thop·ter·ous** (ôr thop′tə rəs) of or having to do with the ORTHOPTERANS or the order they belong to. *adj.*

**or·to·lan** (ôr′tə lən) a small European bird, a bunting whose meat is regarded as a specially delicate food. *n.*

**–ory** a suffix meaning: 1 _____ ing, as in *compensatory, contradictory.*  2 of or having to do with _____ ion, as in *admonitory, auditory.*  3 characterized by _____ ion, as in *adulatory.*  4 serving to _____, as in *expiatory.*  5 inclined to _____, as in *conciliatory.*  6 a place for _____ ing; establishment for _____ ing, as in *depository.*  7 other meanings, as in *conservatory, desultory.*

**o·ryx** (ô′riks) any of a closely related group of large African antelopes having long, nearly straight horns. *n., pl.* **o·ryx·es** (ô′rik siz) *or* (*esp. collectively*) **o·ryx.**

**Os** osmium.

**Osage orange** (ō′sāj) 1 a small, thorny, North American tree of the mulberry family having small, glossy, oval leaves and hard, orange wood: *The osage orange is* *often planted as an ornamental tree.* **2** the inedible, yellow fruit of this tree.

**os·cil·late** (os′ə lāt′) **1** swing to and fro like a pendulum. **2** move or travel to and fro between two points. **3** vary between opposing opinions, purposes, theories, etc. **4** in physics, vary regularly above and below a mean value, as an electric current. **5** cause to oscillate. *v.,* **os·cil·lat·ed, os·cil·lat·ing.**

**os·cil·la·tion** (os′ə lā′shən) **1** the fact or process of oscillating. **2** a single swing of an oscillating body. *n.*

**os·cil·la·tor** (os′ə lā′tər) a person or thing that oscillates, especially a device for producing the oscillations that give rise to an alternating electrical current. *n.*

**os·cil·la·to·ry** (os′ə lə tô′rē) oscillating. *adj.*

**os·cine** (os′in) **1** any bird belonging to the suborder **Passeres** (or **Oscines**), a large group of songbirds having well-developed, specialized vocal organs: *Most oscines sing. Larks, swallows, and finches are oscines.* **2** of or referring to this suborder. **1** *n.,* **2** *adj.*

**os·cu·late** (os′kyə lāt′) **1** kiss. **2** come into close contact. *v.,* **os·cu·lat·ed, os·cu·lat·ing.**

**os·cu·la·tion** (os′kyə lā′shən) **1** the act of kissing. **2** a kiss. **3** a contact: *the osculation between two curves in geometry.* *n.*

**os·cu·la·to·ry** (os′kyə lə tô′rē) **1** kissing. **2** coming into close contact. *adj.*

**o·sier** (ō′zhər) **1** any of various willows, especially a common willow of Europe and Asia having long, slender, straight branches used in making baskets, furniture, etc. **2** a branch or twig of an osier. **3** made of osier. **4** red-osier dogwood. *n.*

**os·mi·um** (oz′mē əm) a hard, heavy, greyish metallic element of the platinum group, used for electric light filaments, as a catalyst, and in hard alloys: *Osmium is the heaviest metal known.* Symbol: Os *n.*

**os·mo·sis** (oz mō′sis) **1** the tendency of a fluid separated from a more concentrated solution by a porous partition to pass through the partition until the concentration on each side is the same: *Nutrients dissolved in fluids pass in and out of plant and animal cells by osmosis.* **2** a process of gradual, often unconscious absorption that suggests osmosis: *He thought he could learn German by osmosis, without taking a course.* *n.*

**os·mot·ic** (oz mot′ik) of or having to do with OSMOSIS. *adj.*

**os·prey** (os′prē *or* os′prā) a large, long-winged, brown-and-white hawk that feeds on fish. *n., pl.* **os·preys.**

**os·se·ous** (os′ē əs) consisting of or resembling bone; bony. *adj.*

**os·si·fi·ca·tion** (os′ə fə kā′shən) **1** the process of developing or changing into bone. **2** a mass of tissue that has been ossified; a part that is ossified. **3** a tendency to settle into a conventional, rigid, or unimaginative condition. *n.*

**os·si·fy** (os′ə fī) **1** change into bone; become bone: *The soft parts of a baby's skull ossify as the baby grows older.* **2** harden; make or become fixed and rigid, or very conservative: *The once free and spontaneous exchange of ideas among the group members had ossified into mere ritual.* *v.,* **os·si·fied, os·si·fy·ing.**

**os·ten·si·ble** (os ten′sə bəl) apparent; pretended; professed: *They were sure that the ostensible reason for her resignation was not the true one.* *adj.*
—**os·ten′si·bly,** *adv.*

**os·ten·ta·tion** (os′tən tā′shən *or* os′ten tā′shən) a showing off; display intended to impress others: *the ostentation of a rich, vain man.* *n.*

**os·ten·ta·tious** (os′tən tā′shəs *or* os′ten tā′shəs) **1** done for display; intended to attract notice: *Nick rode his new bicycle up and down in front of Mike's house in an ostentatious way.* **2** showing off; liking to attract notice: *He was always an ostentatious boy.* *adj.*
—**os′ten·ta′tious·ly,** *adv.*

**os·te·o·path** (os′tē ə path′) a person who practises OSTEOPATHY. *n.*

**os·te·o·path·ic** (os′tē ə path′ik) of OSTEOPATHY or osteopaths. *adj.*

**os·te·op·a·thist** (os′tē op′ə thist) OSTEOPATH. *n.*

**os·te·op·a·thy** (os′tē op′ə thē) a system of medical practice based on the theory that the muscles and bones of the body are closely interrelated with all other parts of the body and that many diseases can be treated by manipulating the bones and muscles. *n.*

**ost·ler** (os′lər) HOSTLER. *n.*

**os·tra·cism** (os′trə siz′əm) **1** an ancient Greek method of banishing an unpopular or dangerous citizen for a number of years by popular vote, without a trial or formal accusation. **2** being shut out from society, from favour, from privileges, or from association with one's fellows. *n.*

**os·tra·cize** (os′trə sīz′) **1** banish by the ancient Greek method of OSTRACISM (def. 1). **2** shut out from society, from favour, from privileges, etc.: *The group finally ostracized her completely because of her inability to get along with people.* *v.,* **os·tra·cized, os·tra·ciz·ing.**

An ostrich—
about 2 m high
to the top of the head

**os·trich** (os′trich) a large bird of Africa and the Near East, that can run swiftly but cannot fly: *Ostriches have two toes and are the largest of existing birds.* *n.*

**oth·er** (uŦH′ər) **1** remaining: *Mei is here, but the other girls are at school.* **2** additional or further: *I have no other books with me.* **3** not the same as one or more already mentioned: *Come some other day.* **4** different: *I would not have him other than he is.* **5** the other one; not the same ones: *Each praises the other.* **6** another person or thing: *There are others to be considered.* **7** otherwise; differently: *I can't do other than go.* 1–4 *adj.,* 5, 6 *pron.,* 7 *adv.*

**every other,** every second; alternate: *She buys cream every other day.*

**none other than,** no one else but: *The presentation was made by none other than the prime minister.*
**no other than,** no one less than.
**of all others,** more than all others.
**the other day, night, etc.,** recently.

**oth·er·wise** (uŦH′ər wīz′) **1** in a different way; differently: *I could not do otherwise.* **2** different: *It might have been otherwise.* **3** in other ways: *He is noisy, but otherwise a very nice boy.* **4** under other circumstances; in a different condition: *She reminded me of what I should otherwise have forgotten.* **5** or else; if not: *Come at once; otherwise you will be too late.* 1, 3, 4 *adv.*, 2 *adj.*, 5 *conj.*

**oth·er·world·ly** (uŦH′ər wėrld′lē) of or devoted to another world, such as the world of mind or imagination, or the world to come: *She was a very withdrawn and otherworldly person.* *adj.* —**oth′er·world′li·ness,** *n.*

**o·ti·ose** (ō′shē ōs′ *or* ō′tē ōs′) **1** at leisure; lazy or idle: *an otiose individual sunning himself in the park.* **2** ineffective; futile: *otiose excuses.* **3** having no real function; superfluous: *The article was wordy and full of otiose comments and digressions.* *adj.*

**Ot·ta·wa** (ot′ə wo′ *or* ot′ə wä) **1** the capital city of Canada, in Ontario. **2** a member of a First Nations and Native American people living in southern Ontario and Michigan. **3** the ALGONQUIAN (def. 1–3) language of those people. **4** of or having to do with the Ottawas or their language. 1–3 *n., pl.* **Ot·ta·was** *or* **Ot·ta·wa;** 4 *adj.*

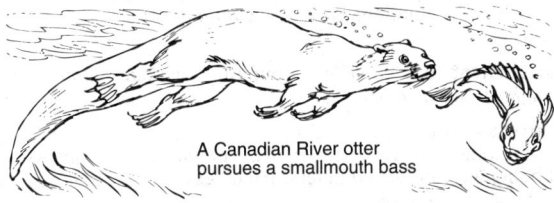
A Canadian River otter pursues a smallmouth bass

**ot·ter** (ot′ər) **1** any of several species of fish-eating water mammals of the weasel family having a long, lithe body, long neck, small ears, and webbed feet with claws. **2** the short, thick, glossy, brown fur of an otter. *n., pl.* **ot·ters** or (*esp. collectively*) **ot·ter.**

**ot·to·man** (ot′ə mən *or* ot′ə mən) **1** a low, cushioned seat without back or arms. **2** a cushioned footstool. **3** a heavy, corded fabric of silk or rayon, often with cotton or wool. *n., pl.* **ot·to·mans.**

**oua·na·niche** (wä′nə nish′) *Cdn.* a landlocked Atlantic salmon native to Lake St. John and some other freshwater lakes in Quebec and Ontario. Compare with KOKANEE. *n., pl.* **oua·na·niche.**
☞ *Etym.* Through Cdn. F from an Algonquian word *wananish* 'little salmon'. 19c.

**ou·bli·ette** (ü′blē et′) a secret dungeon having a trapdoor in the ceiling as its only entrance. *n.*

**ouch** (ouch) an exclamation expressing sudden pain. *interj.*

**ought¹** (ot) **1** have a duty; be obliged: *You ought to obey your parents.* **2** be right or suitable: *The theatre ought to allow children in free.* **3** be wise: *I ought to go before it rains.* **4** be expected: *At your age you ought to know better.* **5** be very likely: *The fastest one ought to win the race.* *v.*
☞ *Hom.* AUGHT.
☞ *Usage.* The forms *had ought* and *hadn't ought* are not used in careful English: *He ought* (not *had ought*) *to have won the race.*

☞ *Usage.* A verb following **ought** is always in the infinitive preceded by *to.*

**ought²** (ot) **1** aught; anything: *You may go for ought I care.* **2** in any way; to any degree; at all: *Help came too late to avail ought.* 1 *n.*, 2 *adv.*
☞ *Hom.* AUGHT.

**ought³** (ot) *Informal.* nought; zero; the cipher 0. *n.*
☞ *Hom.* AUGHT.

**ounce¹** (ouns) **1** a unit for measuring mass in the imperial system, one sixteenth of a pound (about 28 g) in avoirdupois and one twelfth of a pound (about 31 g) in troy weight. **2** a unit for measuring liquids, equal to one twentieth of a pint; fluid ounce (about 28 cm³). **3** a little bit; very small amount: *She hadn't an ounce of pity left.* *n.*

**ounce²** (ouns) a greyish, black-spotted wild cat that resembles a leopard. *n.*

**our** (our *or* är) a possessive form of **we**: of, belonging to, or made or done by us or ourselves: *Would you like to see our garden? We went to get our coats.* *adj.*
☞ *Hom.* HOUR (for the first pronunciation of **our**).
☞ *Usage.* **Our** and **ours** are possessive forms of **we**. **Our** is always followed by a noun: *This is our car.* **Ours** stands alone: *This car is ours.*

**ours** (ourz *or* ärz) a possessive form of **we**: that which belongs to us: *That car is ours. They got their tickets yesterday, but ours haven't come yet.* *pron.*
☞ *Usage.* See note at OUR.

**our·selves** (our selvz′ *or* är selvz′) **1** a reflexive pronoun, the object of a reflexive verb with **we** as subject: *We cannot see ourselves as others see us.* **2** an intensive pronoun, used to emphasize the noun or pronoun it follows: *We ourselves are responsible for what happened.* **3** our usual selves: *We weren't ourselves when we let them get away with that.* *pron.*

**-ous** an adjective-forming suffix meaning: **1** having; having much; full of, as in *joyous, perilous.* **2** characterized by, as in *blasphemous, parsimonious, zealous.* **3** having the nature of, as in *murderous, idolatrous.* **4** of or having to do with, as in *monogamous.* **5** like, as in *thunderous.* **6** committing or practising, as in *bigamous.* **7** inclined to, as in *amorous.* **8** in chemical terms, implying a larger proportion of the element indicated by the word than *-ic* implies. *Stannous* means containing tin in larger proportions than a corresponding *stannic* compound.

**oust** (oust) force out; drive out: *The sparrows have ousted the bluebirds from our birdhouse.* *v.*

**oust·er** (ou′stər) an ousting, especially an illegal forcing of a person out of his or her property. *n.*

**out** (out) **1** away; forth: *to rush out.* **2** not in or at a place, position, state, etc.: *That dress is out of fashion. The miners are going out on strike.* **3** into the open air: *He went out at noon.* **4** not in possession or control: *The Liberals are out, the Conservatives in.* **5** one who is out. **6** to or at an end: *Fight it out!* **7** from the usual place, condition, position, etc.: *Put the light out. The boy turned his pockets out.* **8** completely; effectively: *to fit out.*

**9** so as to project or extend: *to stand out.* **10** into or in existence, activity, or outward manifestation: *Fever broke out. Flowers are out.* **11** not in use, action, fashion, etc.: *The fire is out. Full skirts are out this season.* **12** aloud; loudly: *Speak out.* **13** to others: *Give out the books.* **14** from a number, stock, store, source, cause, material, etc.; from among others: *Pick out an apple for me. She picked out a new coat.* **15** in the wrong: *to be out in one's calculations.* **16** something wrong. **17** from a state of composure, satisfaction, or harmony: *to feel put out.* **18** at a money loss: *to be out ten dollars.* **19** without money, supplies, etc.: *"Have you any candies left?" "No, I'm right out."* **20** from out; forth from: *He went out the door.* **21** Informal. out along: *Drive out Main Street.* **22** be revealed; go or come out: *Murder will out.* **23** that which is omitted. **24** a defence or excuse: *to have an out for stealing.* **25** in baseball, etc., not in play, no longer at bat or on base: *We were soon out and the other team was at bat.* **26** in baseball, being out or putting out. **27** not having its inning: *The out side.* **28** external; exterior; outer; outlying: *an out island.* **29** not usual: *an out size.* 1–3, 6–10, 12–15, 17–19, 25 *adv.*, 4, 11, 27–29 *adj.*, 5, 16, 23, 24, 26 *n.*, 20, 21 *prep.*, 22 *v.*

**at outs** or **on the outs,** quarrelling; disagreeing: *to be on the outs with a friend.*
**out and away,** by far: *She is out and away the best player.*
**out and out,** thoroughly: *out and out discouraged.*
**out for,** looking for; trying to get: *We have a holiday and are out for a good time.*
**out of, a** from within: *He came out of the house.* **b** not within; away from; outside of; beyond: *out of town, sixty kilometres out of Calgary. The boat has gone out of sight.* **c** without; not having: *We are out of coffee.* **d** so as to take away: *She was cheated out of her money.* **e** from: *My dress is made out of silk.* **f** from among: *We picked our puppy out of that litter.* **g** because of: *I went only out of curiosity.*
**out of hand,** out of control: *The excited crowd soon got out of hand.*
**out to,** eagerly trying to: *Their team is out to make the finals.*

**out-** a prefix meaning: **1** outward; forth; away, as in *outburst, outgoing.* **2** outside; at a distance, as in *outbuilding, outfield, outlying.* **3** more than; longer than, as in *outbid, outlive, outnumber.* **4** better than, as in *outdo, outrun.*

**out-and-out** (ou′tən dout′ *or* ou′tə nout′) thorough; complete: *an out-and-out defeat, an out-and-out scoundrel.* *adj.*

**out·back** (out′bak′) **1** in Australia, the unsettled part of the interior; back country. **2** any similarly unsettled area. *n.*

**out·bal·ance** (out′bal′əns) **1** weigh more than. **2** exceed in value, importance, influence, etc. *v.*, **out·bal·anced, out·bal·anc·ing.**

**out·bid** (out′bid′) bid higher than someone else. *v.*, **out·bid, out·bid** or **out·bid·den, out·bid·ding.**

**out·board** (out′bôrd′) **1** outside the hull of a ship or boat. **2** away from the middle of a ship or boat. **3** a boat equipped with an OUTBOARD MOTOR. **4** the motor itself. 1, 2 *adj.*, 1, 2 *adv.*, 3, 4 *n.*

A boat with an outboard motor

**outboard motor** a portable INTERNAL-COMBUSTION ENGINE with an attached propeller, that is mounted on the outside of the stern of a small boat or canoe.

**out·bound** (out′bound′) outward bound: *an outbound ship.* *adj.*

**out·brave** (out′brāv′) **1** face bravely. **2** be braver than. *v.*, **out·braved, out·brav·ing.**

**out·break** (out′brāk′) **1** breaking out; a sudden occurrence or increase: *outbreaks of anger, an outbreak of flu.* **2** a riot; public disturbance. *n.*

**out·build·ing** (out′bil′ding) a shed or building built near a main building: *Barns are outbuildings on a farm.* *n.*

**out·burst** (out′bėrst′) a bursting forth: *an outburst of laughter, anger, smoke, etc.* *n.*

**out·cast** (out′kast′) **1** a person or animal cast out from home and friends: *Criminals are outcasts of society.* **2** being an outcast; homeless; friendless. 1 *n.*, 2 *adj.*

**out·class** (out′klas′) be of higher class than; be much better than: *He is a good runner, but his younger brother definitely outclasses him.* *v.*

**out·come** (out′kum′) a result or consequence: *The outcome of the election was in doubt until the very end.* *n.*

**out·crop** (out′krop′ *for noun,* out′krop′ *for verb*) **1** a coming to the surface of the earth: *the outcrop of a vein of coal.* **2** a part that comes to the surface: *The outcrop that we found proved to be very rich in gold.* **3** come to the surface; appear. 1, 2 *n.*, 3 *v.*, **out·crop·ped, out·crop·ping.**

**out·cry** (out′krī′) **1** crying out; a sudden cry or clamour. **2** a strong protest: *There was a public outcry against the proposal to widen the street into a four-lane highway.* *n., pl.* **out·cries.**

**out·dat·ed** (out′dā′tid) out-of-date; old-fashioned; obsolete: *The coal-oil lamp is outdated.* *adj.*

**out·did** (out′did′) pt. of OUTDO: *Their class outdid ours in raising money for the orchestra.* *v.*

**out·dis·tance** (out′dis′təns) leave behind; outstrip: *She outdistanced all the other runners and won the race.* *v.*, **out·dis·tanced, out·dis·tanc·ing.**

**out·do** (out′dü′) do more or better than; surpass: *You'll find it hard to outdo her performance.* *v.*, **out·did, out·done, out·do·ing.**

**out·done** (out′dun′) pp. of OUTDO: *He simply refused to be outdone and came back to finish first.* *v.*

**out·door** (out′dôr′) done, used, or living outdoors: *outdoor games.* *adj.*

**out·doors** (out′dôrz′) **1** out in the open air; not indoors: *The minute it stopped raining, we all went outdoors.* **2 the outdoors,** the world outside of buildings; the open air (*used with a singular verb*): *We spend most of the summer in the outdoors.* **1** *adv.*, **2** *n.*

**out·doors·man** (out′dôr′zmən) a person who enjoys the outdoors and spends much time in outdoor activities or sports. *n., pl.* **out·doors·men** (-zmən).

**out·door·sy** (out′dôr′zē) *Informal.* of, having to do with, or fond of the outdoors or outdoor activities: *She's an outdoorsy person, always going off on hikes.* *adj.*

**out·draw** (out′dro′) **1** be more popular than; attract more interest or a larger following than: *Hockey usually outdraws curling as a spectator sport in this town.* **2** draw a pistol or revolver more quickly than: *He could outdraw anyone in the territory.* *v.*, **out·drew, out·drawn, out·draw·ing.**

**out·drawn** (out′dron′) pp. of OUTDRAW. *v.*

**out·drew** (out′drü′) pt. of OUTDRAW. *v.*

**out·er** (ou′tər) **1** of or on the outside: *The outer door is locked.* **2** farther out; farther from the centre: *the outer suburbs of the city.* *adj.*

**outer ear** the outer, visible part of the ear that serves to direct sound waves toward the eardrum. See EAR¹ for picture.

**out·er·most** (ou′tər mōst′) farthest out. *adj.*

**outer space** **1** space immediately beyond the earth's atmosphere: *The moon is in outer space.* **2** space beyond the solar system or between the stars.

**out·face** (out′fās′) **1** face boldly; defy. **2** stare at a person until he or she stops staring back; abash. *v.*, **out·faced, out·fac·ing.**

**out·field** (out′fēld′) **1** the part of a baseball field beyond the diamond or infield. **2** the three players in the outfield. *n.*

**out·field·er** (out′fēl′dər) a baseball player stationed in the outfield. *n.*

**out·fit** (out′fit *for noun,* out′fit *or* out fit′ *for verb*) **1** all the articles necessary for any undertaking or purpose: *a sailor's outfit, the outfit for a camping trip.* **2** furnish with everything necessary for any purpose; equip: *Jo outfitted herself for camp.* **3** a group of people working together; an organization such as a military unit, business firm, or ranch: *They were in the same outfit during the war. He worked for the same outfit for five years.* **4** a set of clothes to be worn together; ensemble: *a bride's outfit, a summer outfit.* **5** supply: *The whole family was outfitted with new coats last winter.* 1, 3, 4 *n.*, 2, 5 *v.*, **out·fit·ted, out·fit·ting.** —**out′fit′ter,** *n.*

**out·flank** (out′flangk′) **1** go or extend beyond the flank of an opposing army, etc.; turn the flank of. **2** get the better of; circumvent: *They outflanked us and won the debate.* *v.*

**out·flow** (out′flō′) **1** flowing out: *the outflow from a waterpipe, an outflow of sympathy.* **2** that which flows out. *n.*

**out·fox** (out′foks′) get the better of; outsmart: *The escaped convict outfoxed his pursuers.* *v.*

**out·gen·er·al** (out′jən′ə rəl *or* out′jen′rəl) be a better general than; get the better of by superior strategy. *v.*, **out·gen·er·alled** or **out·gen·er·aled, out·gen·er·al·ling** or **out·gen·er·al·ing.**

**out·go** (out′gō′) what goes out; what is paid out; amount that is spent. *n., pl.* **out·goes.**

**out·go·ing** (out′gō′ing) **1** departing; outward bound: *outgoing ships, the outgoing mail.* **2** retiring or withdrawing from office: *A dinner was held for the outgoing president.* **3** friendly; sociable: *She is very outgoing and enjoys giving parties.* *adj.*

**out·grew** (out′grü′) pt. of OUTGROW. *v.*

**out·grow** (out′grō′) **1** grow too large for: *to outgrow one's clothes.* **2** grow beyond or away from; get rid of by growing older: *to outgrow early friends, to outgrow a babyish habit.* **3** grow or increase faster than: *She outgrew her twin sister. The population was rapidly outgrowing the food supply.* *v.*, **out·grew, out·grown, out·grow·ing.**

**out·grown** (out′grōn′) pp. of OUTGROW. *v.*

**out·growth** (out′grōth′) **1** a natural development, product, or result: *This big store is an outgrowth of the little shop Jane started ten years ago.* **2** an offshoot; something that has grown out of something else: *A corn is an outgrowth on a toe.* **3** a growing out or forth: *the outgrowth of leaves in the spring.* *n.*

**out·guess** (out′ges′) get the better of by anticipating a person's actions: *She outguessed her competitor and got her proposal accepted.* *v.*

**out·house** (out′hous′) **1** an outdoor toilet. **2** a separate building used in connection with a main building: *Near the farmhouse were sheds and other outhouses.* *n.*

**out·ing** (ou′ting) a short pleasure trip; walk or airing; holiday spent outdoors away from home: *On Sunday the family went on an outing to the beach.* *n.*

**out·land·ish** (ou′tlan′dish) **1** not familiar; strange or ridiculous: *an outlandish hairstyle.* **2** looking or sounding foreign. *adj.*

**out·last** (ou′tlast′) last longer than. *v.*

**out·law** (ou′tlo′) **1** a person outside the protection of the law; exile; outcast. **2** a lawless person; criminal. **3** make or declare a person an outlaw. **4** make or declare illegal: *A group of nations agreed to outlaw war.* **5** deprive of legal force: *An outlawed debt is one that cannot be collected because it has been due too long.* **6** an unbroken horse. 1, 2, 6 *n.*, 3–5 *v.*

**out·law·ry** (ou′tlo′rē) **1** being condemned as an outlaw; being outlawed: *Outlawry was formerly used as a punishment in England.* **2** the condition of being an outlaw. *n., pl.* **out·law·ries.**

**out·lay** (ou′tlā *for noun,* ou′tlā′ *for verb*) **1** spending; laying out of money, energy, etc.: *a large outlay for clothing.* **2** the amount spent. **3** expend: *to outlay money in improvements.* 1, 2 *n.*, 3 *v.*, **out·laid, out·lay·ing.**

**out·let** (ou′tlet′ *or* ou′tlit) **1** a means or place of letting out or getting out; way out; vent; opening; exit: *the outlet of a lake, an outlet for one's energies.* **2** a market for a product. **3** a store selling the products of a particular manufacturer: *The shoe manufacturer had several retail outlets.* **4** a place in a wall, etc. for inserting an electric plug to make connection with an electric circuit. *n.*

**out·line** (ou′tlīn) **1** the line that shows the shape of an object; line that bounds a figure: *We saw the outlines of the mountains against the evening sky.* **2** a drawing or style of drawing that gives only outer lines: *an outline of Canada.* **3** draw the outer line of: *Outline a map of Italy.* **4** a general plan; rough draft: *Make an outline before trying to write a composition.* **5** give a plan of; sketch: *She outlined their trip abroad.* 1, 2, 4 *n.*, 3, 5 *v.*, **out·lined, out·lin·ing.**
**in outline, a** with only the outline shown. **b** with only the main features.

**out·live** (ou′tliv′) live or last longer than; survive; outlast: *She outlived her older sister. The idea was good once, but it has outlived its usefulness.* *v.*, **out·lived, out·liv·ing.**

**out·look** (ou′tlùk′) **1** what one sees on looking out; view: *The room has a pleasant outlook.* **2** what seems likely to happen; prospect: *Because of the black clouds, the outlook for our picnic is not very good.* **3** a way of thinking about things; attitude of mind; point of view: *a gloomy outlook on life.* **4** a lookout; a tower or other high place to watch from. *n.*

**out·ly·ing** (ou′tlī′ing) lying outside the boundary; far from the centre; remote: *the outlying houses in the settlement.* *adj.*

**out·ma·noeu·vre** (out′mə nü′vər) **1** get the better of by skilful manoeuvring; outwit: *They were outmanoeuvred in the negotiations and lost the contract.* **2** surpass in being manoeuvrable: *This car can outmanoeuvre any other car of its size on the market.* *v.*, **out·ma·noeu·vred, out·ma·noeu·vring.** Also, **outmaneuver.**

**out·mod·ed** (out′mō′did) OUT-OF-DATE. *adj.*

**out·most** (out′mōst′) farthest out. *adj.*

**out·num·ber** (out′num′bər) be more than; exceed in number: *They outnumbered us three to one.* *v.*

**out–of–bounds** (ou′təv boundz′) **1** in sports, outside the boundary line. **2** outside the established limits of use or entry. *adj., adv.*

**out–of–date** (ou′təv dāt′) old-fashioned; not in present use: *A horse and buggy is an out-of-date means of travelling.* *adj.*

**out–of–door** (ou′təv dôr′) OUTDOOR. *adj.*

**out–of–doors** (ou′təv dôrz′ *for 1*, ou′təv dôrz′ *for 2*) **1** OUTDOOR. **2** OUTDOORS. 1 *adj.*, 2 *n., adv.*

**out–of–the–way** (ou′təv ᴛнə wā′) **1** remote; unfrequented; secluded: *an out-of-the-way cottage.* **2** seldom met with; unusual: *out-of-the-way bits of information.* *adj.*

**out·pa·tient** (out′pā′shənt) a patient receiving treatment at a hospital but not staying there. *n.*

**out·play** (out′plā′) play better than: *The visiting team outplayed us in every period.* *v.*

**out·point** (out′point′) **1** score more points than. **2** sail closer to the wind than. *v.*

**out·port** (out′pôrt′) *Cdn.* a small harbour, especially one of the isolated fishing villages along the coasts of Newfoundland. *n.*

**out·post** (out′pōst′) **1** a guard, or small number of soldiers, placed at some distance from an army or camp to prevent surprise attack. **2** the place where they are stationed. **3** a settlement or village in an outlying place: *an outpost in the North, a distant outpost of civilization.* **4** anything thought of as an outpost or advance guard. *n.*

**out·pour** (out′pôr′ *for noun,* out′pôr′ *for verb*) **1** a pouring out. **2** that which is poured out. **3** pour out. 1, 2 *n.*, 3 *v.*

**out·pour·ing** (out′pô′ring) **1** anything that is poured out. **2** an uncontrolled expression of thoughts or feelings. **3** ppr. of OUTPOUR. 1, 2 *n.*, 3 *v.*

**out·put** (out′pùt′) **1** the amount produced; the product or yield: *the daily output of automobiles. Last year's output surpassed anything she had written before.* **2** a putting forth: *With a sudden output of effort, Les moved the rock.* **3** information produced from the storage unit of a computer. *n.*

**out·rage** (ou′trāj′; *sometimes,* ou′trāj′ *for verb*) **1** an act showing no regard for the rights or feelings of others; an overturning of the rights of others by force; act of violence; offence; insult: *Hitler was guilty of many outrages.* **2** insult; offend greatly or arouse great anger in. **3** the hurt, angry feeling aroused by such treatment. **4** break the law, a rule of morality, etc. openly; treat as nothing at all: *She outraged all rules of behaviour.* 1, 3 *n.*, 2, 4 *v.*, **out·raged, out·rag·ing.**

**out·ra·geous** (ou trā′jəs) shocking; very bad or insulting: *an outrageous disregard for the rights of others, outrageous language, outrageous behaviour.* *adj.*
—**out·ra′geous·ly,** *adv.* —**out·ra′geous·ness,** *n.*

**out·ran** (ou′tran′) pt. of OUTRUN: *He outran me easily.* *v.*

**out·rank** (ou′trangk′) rank higher than: *A captain outranks a lieutenant.* *v.*

**out·reach** (ou′trēch′ *for verb,* ou′trēch′ *for noun*) **1** exceed or reach beyond: *Her accomplishments far outreached those of her predecessors.* **2** the act or fact of reaching out: *The social aid program has too little outreach into the community.* **3** the extent or limit of reach: *the outreach of the flood.* 1 *v.*, 2, 3 *n.*

**out·rid·den** (ou′trid′ən) pp. of OUTRIDE. *v.*

**out·ride** (ou′trīd′) **1** ride faster or better than. **2** of ships, last through a storm. *v.*, **out·rode, out·rid·den, out·rid·ing.**

**out·rid·er** (ou′trī′dər) a servant or attendant riding on a horse before or beside a carriage or wagon, etc.: *A chuckwagon team consists of a driver and his outriders.* *n.*

A Tahitian canoe with an outrigger

**out·rig·ger** (ou′trig′ər) **1** a framework ending in a float, extending outward from the side of a light boat or canoe to prevent upsetting. **2** a boat or canoe with an outrigger. **3** a bracket extending outward from either side of a boat to hold a rowlock. **4** a boat equipped with such brackets. **5** a projecting spar, framework, or part: *an outrigger from a ship's mast to extend a sail, an outrigger from an airplane to support the rudder.* *n.*

**out·right** (ou′trīt for adjective, ou′trīt′ or ou′trīt′ for adverb) **1** altogether; entirely; not gradually: *We paid for our car over two years but we wish we had bought it outright.* **2** openly; without restraint: *I laughed outright.* **3** complete; thorough: *an outright loss.* **4** downright; straightforward; direct: *an outright refusal.* **5** entire; total. **6** at once; on the spot: *She fainted outright.* 1, 2, 6 *adv.*, 3–5 *adj.*

**out·rode** (ou′trōd′) pt. of OUTRIDE. *v.*

**out·run** (ou′trun′) **1** run faster than. **2** leave behind; go beyond; pass the limits of: *His story outruns the facts.* *v.*, **out·ran, out·run, out·run·ning**.

**out·sell** (ou′sel′) **1** outdo in selling or salesmanship: *She can easily outsell any of the other sales reps.* **2** sell in greater amounts than; exceed in the number of items sold: *His second novel outsold his first by a wide margin.* *v.*, **out·sold, out·sell·ing**.

**out·set** (out′set′) start; beginning: *At the outset, it looked like a nice day.* *n.*

**out·shine** (out′shīn′) **1** shine more brightly than. **2** be more brilliant or excellent than; surpass. *v.*, **out·shone, out·shin·ing**.

**out·shoot** (out′shüt′ *for verb,* out′shüt′ *for noun*) **1** shoot better or farther than. **2** shoot forth. **3** projection. **4** an offshoot. 1, 2 *v.*, **out·shot, out·shoot·ing**; 3, 4 *n.*

**out·side** (out′sīd′; out′sīd′ or out′sīd′ for preposition) **1** the side or surface that is out; outer part: *The outside of the coat is stained.* **2** the external appearance. **3** on the outside; of or nearer the outside: *the outside leaves.* **4** on or to the outside; outdoors: *Run outside and play.* **5** a space or position without: *to ride on the outside of a bus.* **6** out of; beyond the limits of: *Stay outside the house.* **7** not belonging to a certain group, set, district, etc.: *Outside people tried to get control of the business.* **8** being, acting, done, or originating without or beyond a wall, boundary, etc.: *Outside noises disturbed the class.* **9** *Informal.* highest; largest; reaching the utmost limit: *an outside estimate of the cost.* **10** *Informal.* slight; small: *He had only an outside chance of winning the race.* **11** *Cdn.* the settled parts of Canada: *In the North, people refer to the rest of Canada as the outside.* 1, 2, 5, 11 *n.*, 3, 7–10 *adj.*, 4 *adv.*, 6 *prep.*
**at the outside**, *Informal.* at the most; at the limit: *I can do it in a week, at the outside.*
**outside in**, so that what should be outside is inside; with the outside not showing.
**outside of**, *Informal.* with the exception of: *Outside of Zelda, none of us liked the play.*

**out·sid·er** (out′sī′dər) **1** a person who does not belong to a particular group, company, party, etc. **2** *Cdn.* a person who does not live in the North: *The people of Whitehorse, Y.T., call the people of Edmonton outsiders.* **3** a person, horse, etc. that is not expected to win a competition. *n.*

**out·size** (out′sīz′) **1** larger than the usual size. **2** an article of clothing, etc. larger than the usual size. 1 *adj.*, 2 *n.*

**out·skirts** (out′skėrts′) the outer parts or edges of a town, district, etc.; outlying parts: *There is a ravine on the northern outskirts of town. We live on the outskirts.* *n. pl.*

# outright 839 outwit

hat, āge, fär; let, ēqual, tėrm; it, īce
hot, ōpen, ôrder; oil, out; cup, pùt, rüle
əbove, takən, pencəl, lemən, circəs
ch, child; ng, long; sh, ship
th, thin; ᴛʜ, then; zh, measure

**out·smart** (out′smärt′) *Informal.* outdo in cleverness: *By clever questioning the lawyer outsmarted the suspect.* *v.*

**out·sold** (out′sōld′) pt. and pp. of OUTSELL. *v.*

**out·spo·ken** (out′spō′kən) FRANK (defs. 1, 2); not reserved: *an outspoken person, outspoken criticism.* *adj.* —**out′spo′ken·ly**, *adv.* —**out′spo′ken·ness**, *n.*

**out·spread** (out′spred′ *for adjective,* out′spred′ *for verb*) **1** spread out; extended: *an eagle with outspread wings.* **2** spread out; extend. 1 *adj.*, 2 *v.*, **out·spread, out·spread·ing**.

**out·stand·ing** (out stan′ding) **1** standing out from others; well-known; important: *She is an outstanding basketball player.* **2** unpaid: *outstanding debts.* **3** needing attention: *outstanding letters.* **4** projecting. *adj.* —**out·stand′ing·ly**, *adv.*

**out·stay** (out′stā′) **1** stay beyond the limit of; overstay: *He outstayed his welcome.* **2** stay longer than; have more staying power than: *She outstayed all the other buyers. He outstayed the other guests.* *v.*

**out·stretched** (out′strecht′) stretched out; extended: *He welcomed his old friend with outstretched arms.* *adj.*

**out·strip** (out′strip′) **1** go faster than; leave behind in a race: *A horse can outstrip a man.* **2** do better than; excel: *Mario outstrips his friends in both sports and studies.* *v.*, **out·stripped, out·strip·ping**.

**out·talk** (out′tok′) talk better, faster, longer, or louder than; get the better of by talking. *v.*

**out·vote** (out′vōt′) defeat in voting: *The radical faction was outvoted on the issue.* *v.*, **out·vot·ed, out·vot·ing**.

**out·ward** (out′wərd) **1** going toward the outside; turned toward the outside: *an outward motion, an outward glance.* **2** toward the outside; away: *Porches extend outward from the house.* **3** outer: *to all outward appearances.* **4** on the outside: *She folded the coat with the lining outward.* **5** on the surface; external: *an outward transformation.* 1, 3, 5 *adj.*, 2, 4 *adv.*

**out·ward·ly** (ou′twər dlē) **1** on the outside or outer surface. **2** toward the outside. **3** as regards appearance or outward manifestation: *Though frightened, the boy remained outwardly calm.* *adv.*

**out·wards** (out′twərdz) OUTWARD (defs. 2, 4). *adv.*

**out·wash** (out′twosh′) in geology, rock fragments or other glacial debris carried beyond the glacier by meltwater. *n.*

**out·wear** (ou′twer′) **1** wear longer than: *Nylon will outwear cotton.* **2** wear out: *to outwear someone's patience.* **3** outgrow. *v.*, **out·wore, out·worn, out·wear·ing**.

**out·weigh** (ou′twā′) **1** weigh more than: *My older brother outweighs me by five kilograms.* **2** exceed in value, importance, influence, etc.: *The advantages of the plan outweigh its disadvantages.* *v.*

**out·wit** (ou′twit′) get the better of by being more

**out·work** (ou′twėrk′ *for noun,* ou′twėrk′ *for verb*)   1 a part of the fortifications of a place lying outside the main ones; a less important defence: *the outworks of a castle.*   2 surpass in working; work harder or faster than.   1 *n.,* 2 *v.*

**out·worn** (ou′twôrn′ *for adjective,* ou′twôrn′ *for verb*)   1 worn out: *outworn clothes.*   2 out-of-date; outgrown: *outworn opinions, outworn habits.*   3 pp. of OUTWEAR. 1, 2 *adj.,* 3 *v.*

**ou·zel** (ü′zəl)   1 a large European thrush having a white ring or bar on the neck and breast; also called **ring ouzel**.   2 any of several closely related diving birds, belonging to the same family as the thrushes, that dive into swift mountain streams in search of food; also called **water ouzel**. *n.*

**o·va** (ō′və)   pl. of OVUM. *n.*

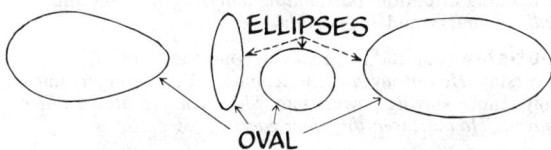

**o·val** (ō′vəl)   1 egg-shaped.   2 shaped like an ellipse.   3 something having an oval shape. See ELLIPSE for another picture.   1, 2 *adj.,* 3 *n.*

**o·val·ly** (ō′və lē)   in an oval form. *adv.*

**o·var·i·an** (ō ver′ē ən)   of or having to do with an OVARY. *adj.*

**o·va·ry** (ō′və rē)   1 in female animals, the reproductive organ that produces the egg cells and, in vertebrates, female sex hormones: *In mammals, there is one ovary on each side of the abdomen.*   2 in a seed-bearing plant, the part of the pistil that contains the young seeds, called ovules. See COMPOSITE and FLOWER for pictures.  *n., pl.* **o·va·ries**.

**o·vate** (ō′vāt)   egg-shaped: *an ovate leaf.* See LEAF for picture. *adj.*

**o·va·tion** (ō vā′shən)   an enthusiastic public welcome; burst of applause: *The dancer received a great ovation. n.*

**ov·en** (uv′ən)   1 a space in a stove or near a fireplace for baking food.   2 a small furnace for heating or drying. *n.*

**ov·en·bird** (uv′ən bėrd′)   1 any of several closely related, small, brown songbirds of South America that build a dome-shaped nest of clay and leaves or twigs, etc.: *The nest of an ovenbird has a side entrance and is often quite elaborate, with more than one chamber.*   2 a North American songbird of the wood warbler family that builds a dome-shaped nest of leaves and plant fibres on the forest floor: *This ovenbird's nest also has a side entrance. n.*

**o·ver** (ō′vər)   1 above in place or position: *the roof over one's head* (prep.). *The cliff hung over* (adv.).   2 above in authority, power, etc.: *We have a captain over us.*   3 upper; higher up: *the over crust of a pie.*   4 higher in authority, station, etc. (used chiefly in compounds), as in *overlord.*   5 on; upon: *a blanket lying over the bed.*   6 so as to cover the surface, or affect the whole surface: *Cover the tar over with sand until it has hardened.*   7 at all or various places on: *A blush came over her face. Farms were scattered over the valley.*   8 above and to the other side of; across: *to leap over a wall.*   9 on the other side of: *lands over the sea.*   10 from side to side; to the other side; across any intervening space: *Go over to the store for me.*   11 from one to another: *Hand the money over.*   12 on the other side; at some distance: *over in Europe, over by the hill.*   13 out and down from: *She fell over the edge of the cliff.*   14 down; out and down: *The ball went too near the edge and rolled over. When he lost his balance, he fell over.*   15 so as to bring the upper side or end down or under: *to turn over a page.*   16 again; in repetition: *ten times over. I'll have to do that assignment over.*   17 more than; beyond: *It costs over ten dollars.*   18 surplus; extra (used chiefly in compounds), as in *pay for overtime.*   19 too (used chiefly in compounds), as in *overnice.*   20 too much; too great (used chiefly in compounds), as in *overuse of drugs.*   21 here and there on or in; round about; all through: *We will be travelling over Europe.*   22 through a region, area, etc.: *to travel all over.*   23 from end to end of; along: *We drove over the new highway.*   24 from beginning to end: *to read a newspaper over.*   25 during; in the course of: *over many years.*   26 throughout or beyond a period of time: *Please stay over till Monday.*   27 more; besides; in excess or addition: *She spent seventy dollars and had thirty dollars over.*   28 at an end: *The play is over.*   29 in reference to; concerning; about: *He is troubled over his health.*   30 while engaged on or concerned with: *to fall asleep over one's work.*   31 by means of: *They spoke over the telephone.*   32 in cricket, the number of balls (usually six) delivered between successive changes of bowlers.   33 the part of a cricket game between such changes.   1, 2, 5, 7–9, 13, 17, 21, 23, 25, 29–31 *prep.,* 1, 6, 10–12, 14–16, 20, 22, 24, 26, 27 *adv.,* 3, 4, 18–20, 28 *adj.,* 32, 33 *n.*

**over again,**   once more: *Let's do that over again.*
**over against,**   **a** opposite to; in front of.   **b** so as to bring out a difference.
**over and above,**   besides; in addition to.
**over and over,**   again and again: *She keeps telling the same story over and over.*
**over with** or **over and done with,** *Informal.*   finished; completed: *I have to get this homework over with today.*

**over–**   a prefix meaning:   1 too; too much; too long, etc., as in *overcrowded, overfull, overburden, overpay, oversleep.*   2 extra, as in *oversize, overtime.*

**o·ver·act** (ō′və rakt′)   act to excess; overdo in acting; act a part in an exaggerated manner. *v.*

**o·ver·ac·tive** (ō′və rak′tiv)   too active; active to excess: *an overactive thyroid gland, an overactive child. adj.* —**o′ver·ac′tive·ly,** *adv.*

Farmers wearing overalls

**o·ver·all** (ō′və rol′ *for adjective and noun,* ō′və rol′ *for adverb*)   1 from one end to the other: *The overall length of the house is ten metres.*   2 including everything: *an overall estimate.*   3 as a whole; generally: *Overall, it was a successful meeting.*   4 *Esp. Brit.*   a loose-fitting smock, etc. worn over other clothes to protect them. **5 overalls,** *pl.* loose trousers of strong, usually cotton, cloth worn over clothes to keep them clean: *Overalls usually have a part that covers the chest.* *1, 2 adj., 3 adv., 4, 5 n.*

**o·ver·anx·ious** (ō′və rangk′shəs *or* ō′və rang′shəs) too anxious. *adj.*

**o·ver·arch** (ō′və rärch′) arch over; curve like an arch: *The street was overarched by elm trees.* *v.*

**o·ver·arm** (ō′və rärm′) with the arm raised above the shoulder; overhand: *an overarm stroke, to throw overarm.* *adj., adv.*

**o·ver·ate** (ō′və rāt′) pt. of OVEREAT. *v.*

**o·ver·awe** (ō′və ro′) overcome or restrain with awe: *She was overawed by the grandeur of the estate.* *v.,* **o·ver·awed, o·ver·aw·ing.**

**o·ver·bal·ance** (ō′vər bal′əns) **1** be greater than in weight, importance, value, etc.: *The gains overbalanced the losses.* **2** cause to lose balance: *As Jamie leaned over the side, his weight overbalanced the canoe and it upset.* **3** lose balance: *He overbalanced and fell.* *v.,* **o·ver·bal·anced, o·ver·bal·anc·ing.**

**o·ver·bear** (ō′vər ber′) **1** overcome by weight or force; oppress; master: *His mother overbore his objections.* **2** bear down by weight or force; overthrow; upset. *v.,* **o·ver·bore, o·ver·borne, o·ver·bear·ing.**

**o·ver·bear·ing** (ō′vər ber′ing) **1** inclined to dictate; forcing others to one's own will; domineering: *He was too overbearing to be a good leader.* **2** ppr. of OVERBEAR. *1 adj., 2 v.* —**o′ver·bear′ing·ly,** *adv.*

**o·ver·bid** (ō′vər bid′) **1** bid more than the value of something. **2** bid higher than another person. *v.,* **o·ver·bid, o·ver·bid** *or* **o·ver·bid·den, o·ver·bid·ding.**

**o·ver·blouse** (ō′vər blouz′ *or* ō′vər blous′) a blouse for women, designed to be worn outside a skirt or pants instead of tucked in: *An overblouse is usually slightly longer than a regular blouse.* *n.*

**o·ver·blown** (ō′vər blōn′) **1** of a flower, past its peak of beauty; too fully open. **2** inflated or pompous; pretentious: *His acceptance speech was filled with flowery, overblown sentiments.* *adj.*

**o·ver·board** (ō′vər bôrd′) from a ship or boat into the water: *She fell overboard. They threw the garbage overboard.* *adv.* **go overboard,** go too far in an effort because of extreme enthusiasm: *She went overboard and bought more than she needed.* **throw overboard,** *Informal.* get rid of; abandon or discard: *We had to throw all our plans overboard and start again from scratch.*

**o·ver·bold** (ō′vər bōld′) too bold. *adj.*

**o·ver·book** (ō′vər bùk′) issue tickets or reservations to more people than there is room for: *The airline had overbooked the flight and we had to wait for the next one.* *v.*

**o·ver·bore** (ō′vər bôr′) pt. of OVERBEAR. *v.*

**o·ver·borne** (ō′vər bôrn′) pp. of OVERBEAR. *v.*

**o·ver·bur·den** (ō′vər bėr′dən) load with too great a burden: *The overburdened donkey collapsed. She was overburdened with debts.* *v.*

**o·ver·came** (ō′vər kām′) pt. of OVERCOME. *v.*

**o·ver·cast** (ō′vər kast′) **1** cloudy; dark; gloomy: *The sky was overcast all day, but it did not rain.* **2** cover or be covered with clouds; darken. **3** sad; gloomy: *His face was*

**overanxious**    841    **overdraw**

hat, āge, fär; let, ēqual, tėrm; it, īce
hot, ōpen, ôrder; oil, out; cup, pùt, rüle
əbove, takən, pencəl, lemən, circəs
ch, child; ng, long; sh, ship
th, thin; ᴛʜ, then; zh, measure

*overcast.* **4** sew over and through the raw edges of a seam with long stitches to prevent ravelling. **5** sewn with overcast stitches. *1, 3, 5 adj., 2, 4 v.,* **o·ver·cast, o·ver·cast·ing.**

**o·ver·charge** (ō′vər chärj′ *for verb,* ō′vər chärj′ *for noun*) **1** charge too high a price: *The grocer overcharged you for the eggs.* **2** a charge that is too great. **3** load too heavily; fill too full: *The overcharged old musket burst.* **4** too heavy or too full a load. *1, 3 v.,* **o·ver·charged, o·ver·charg·ing;** *2, 4 n.*

**o·ver·cloud** (ō′vər kloud′) **1** cloud over; become clouded over; darken. **2** make or become gloomy. *v.*

**o·ver·coat** (ō′vər kōt′) a coat worn for warmth over regular clothing. *n.*

**o·ver·come** (ō′vər kum′) **1** get the better of; win the victory over; conquer; defeat: *to overcome an enemy, one's faults, all difficulties.* **2** make weak or helpless: *Weariness overcame her, and she fell asleep.* **3** confuse or overwhelm: *The girl was so overcome by the noise and the lights that she couldn't speak.* *v.,* **o·ver·came, o·ver·come, o·ver·com·ing.**

**o·ver·com·pen·sate** (ō′vər kom′pən sāt′) go too far in trying, consciously or unconsciously, to make up for or get rid of a feeling of not being good enough or worthy enough: *She overcompensated for her shyness at the party by insulting half the guests.* *v.*

**o·ver·com·pen·sa·tion** (ō′vər kom′pən sā′shən) the act or an instance of overcompensating. *n.*

**o·ver·con·fi·dence** (ō′vər kon′fə dəns) an excess of confidence; the quality or state of being OVERCONFIDENT. *n.*

**o·ver·con·fi·dent** (ō′vər kon′fə dənt) too confident. *adj.*

**o·ver·cook** (ō′vər kùk′) cook too much: *Meat loses its flavour when it is overcooked.* *v.*

**o·ver·crowd** (ō′vər kroud′) crowd too much; put in too many: *The boat sank because it was overcrowded.* *v.*

**o·ver·de·vel·op** (ō′vər di vel′əp) develop too much or too long: *If a photograph is overdeveloped, it will be too dark.* *v.*

**o·ver·do** (ō′vər dü′) **1** do or attempt too much: *She overdoes exercise. He overdid it and became tired.* **2** exaggerate: *The funny scenes in the play were overdone.* **3** exhaust; tire. *v.,* **o·ver·did, o·ver·done, o·ver·do·ing.**

**o·ver·done** (ō′vər dun′ *for verb,* ō′vər dun′ *for adjective*) **1** pt. of OVERDO: *You must have overdone your exercises.* **2** cooked too much: *overdone vegetables.* *1 v., 2 adj.*

**o·ver·dose** (ō′vər dōs′ *for noun,* ō′vər dōs′ *for verb*) **1** too big a dose. **2** give too large a dose to. *1 n., 2 v.,* **o·ver·dosed, o·ver·dos·ing.**

**o·ver·draft** (ō′vər draft′) **1** an overdrawing of a bank account. **2** the amount by which an account is overdrawn. *n.*

**o·ver·draw** (ō′vər dro′) **1** draw from a bank account more money than one has there: *He overdrew his account* by $24.00. **2** exaggerate: *The characters in the book were greatly overdrawn.* *v.,* **o‧ver‧drew, o‧ver‧drawn, o‧ver‧draw‧ing.**

**o‧ver‧dress** (ō′vər dres′ *for verb,* ō′vər dres′ *for noun*) **1** dress or decorate too formally or elaborately: *He decided not to wear his tuxedo because he did not want to risk being overdressed.* **2** a dress worn over another dress: *a sheer overdress.* 1 *v.,* 2 *n.*

**o‧ver‧drive** (ō′vər drīv′) an arrangement of gears whereby less power produces more speed than in high gear. *n.*

**o‧ver‧due** (ō′vər dyü′ *or* ō′vər dü′) **1** late coming or arriving: *The plane is overdue.* **2** due but not yet paid: *This bill is overdue.* *adj.*

**o‧ver‧eat** (ō′və rēt′) eat too much. *v.,* **o‧ver‧ate, o‧ver‧eat‧en, o‧ver‧eat‧ing.**

**o‧ver‧es‧ti‧mate** (ō′və res′tə māt′ *for verb,* ō′və res′tə mit *for noun*) **1** estimate at too high a value, amount, rate, etc. **2** an estimate that is too high. 1 *v.,* **o‧ver‧es‧ti‧mat‧ed, o‧ver‧es‧ti‧mat‧ing;** 2 *n.* —**o′ver‧es′ti‧ma′tion,** *n.*

**o‧ver‧ex‧cite** (ō′və rek sīt′) excite too much. *v.,* **o‧ver‧ex‧cit‧ed, o‧ver‧ex‧cit‧ing.** —**o′ver‧ex‧cit′able,** *adj.* —**o′ver‧ex‧cite′ment,** *n.*

**o‧ver‧ex‧ert** (ō′və reg zėrt′) put forth too much effort; exert too much (*usually used with a pronoun ending in* **-self**): *He hurt his back when he overexerted himself in gymnastics.* *v.*

**o‧ver‧ex‧er‧tion** (ō′və reg zėr′shən) the act or an instance of OVEREXERTing: *The injury was the result of overexertion.* *n.*

**o‧ver‧ex‧pose** (ō′və rek spōz′) expose to too much light or radiation: *She had sensitive skin and had to be careful not to overexpose herself to the sun. If you overexpose a film, the picture will be too light.* *v.,* **o‧ver‧ex‧posed, o‧ver‧ex‧pos‧ing.**

**o‧ver‧ex‧po‧sure** (ō′və rek spō′zhər) too much or too long an exposure: *He was suffering from overexposure to the sun. Several of my pictures were overexposures.* *n.*

**o‧ver‧ex‧tend** (ō′və rek stend′) extend too far; especially, commit oneself financially beyond what one can pay: *She overextended herself in her business and went bankrupt.* *v.*

**o‧ver‧feed** (ō′vər fēd′) feed too much: *Their puppy is so fat because they overfeed it.* *v.,* **o‧ver‧fed, o‧ver‧feed‧ing.**

**o‧ver‧fill** (ō′vər fil′) fill too full; fill so as to cause overflowing. *v.*

**o‧ver‧flow** (ō′vər flō′ *for verb,* ō′vər flō′ *for noun*) **1** flow over the bounds: *Rivers often overflow in the spring.* **2** cover; flood: *The river overflowed our garden.* **3** have the contents flowing over: *My cup is overflowing.* **4** flow over the top of: *The milk is overflowing the cup.* **5** extend out beyond; be too many for: *The crowd overflowed the little room and filled the hall.* **6** be very abundant: *an overflowing harvest, overflowing kindness.* **7** an overflowing: *The overflow from the glass ran into the sink.* **8** an excess: *We caught the overflow in a pail.* **9** an outlet or container for overflowing liquid. 1–6 *v.,* **o‧ver‧flowed, o‧ver‧flown, o‧ver‧flow‧ing;** 7–9 *n.*

**o‧ver‧flown** (ō′vər flōn′) **1** pp. of OVERFLOW. **2** pp. of OVERFLY. *v.*

**o‧ver‧fly** (ō′vər flī′) **1** fly in an airplane above: *Be careful not to overfly enemy territory.* **2** fly in an airplane beyond: *The plane overflew its destination because of snow on the runway.* *v.,* **o‧ver‧flew, o‧ver‧flown, o‧ver‧fly‧ing.**

**o‧ver‧gar‧ment** (ō′vər gär′mənt) an outer garment. *n.*

**o‧ver‧grow** (ō′vər grō′) **1** grow over: *The wall is overgrown with vines.* **2** grow too fast; become too big. **3** outgrow. *v.,* **o‧ver‧grew, o‧ver‧grown, o‧ver‧grow‧ing.**

**o‧ver‧grown** (ō′vər grōn′) **1** grown too big: *The trees on the boulevard were overgrown.* **2** pp. of OVERGROW. 1 *adj.,* 2 *v.*

**o‧ver‧growth** (ō′vər grōth′) **1** too great or too rapid growth. **2** growth overspreading or covering something. *n.*

**o‧ver‧hand** (ō′vər hand′) **1** with the hand raised above the shoulder: *an overhand throw* (*adj.*)*, to pitch overhand* (*adv.*)*.* **2** with the knuckles upward. **3** over and over; with stitches passing successively over an edge. **4** an overhand stroke or throw: *He's practising his overhand.* 1 *adv.,* 1–3 *adj.,* 4 *n.*

**o‧ver‧hang** (ō′vər hang′ *for verb,* ō′vər hang′ *for noun*) **1** hang over; project over: *Trees overhang the street to form an arch of branches.* **2** something that projects: *The overhang of the roof shaded the flower bed beneath.* **3** the amount of projecting. **4** hang over so as to darken, sadden, or threaten: *The threat of an invasion overhung the city.* 1, 4 *v.,* **o‧ver‧hung, o‧ver‧hang‧ing;** 2, 3 *n.*

**o‧ver‧haul** (ō′vər hol′ *for verb,* ō′vər hol′ *for noun*) **1** examine thoroughly and make any repairs or changes that are needed: *Once a year we overhaul our boat.* **2** gain upon; overtake: *The pirate's ship was overhauling ours.* **3** a thorough examination to find and make necessary repairs: *The engine needs an overhaul.* 1, 2 *v.,* 3 *n.*

**o‧ver‧head** (ō′vər hed′ *for adverb,* ō′vər hed′ *for adjective and noun*) **1** over the head; on high; above: *The plane flew overhead.* **2** being, working, or passing overhead: *overhead wires.* **3** applying to one and all; general. **4 overheads,** *pl.* general expenses of running a business, such as rent, lighting, heating, taxes, repairs. 1 *adv.,* 2, 3 *adj.,* 4 *n.*

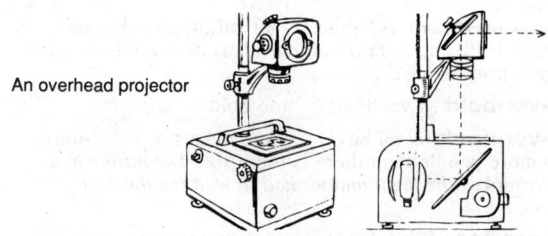

An overhead projector

**overhead projector** a projecting device in which transparencies are placed on a glass surface that is lit from below, the image being focussed and reflected onto a wall or screen by means of an overhead lens and mirror. Compare with OPAQUE PROJECTOR.

**o‧ver‧hear** (ō′vər hēr′) hear when one is not meant to hear: *They spoke so loudly that I could not help overhearing what they said.* *v.,* **o‧ver‧heard, o‧ver‧hear‧ing.**

**o‧ver‧heat** (ō′vər hēt′) heat too much; make too

warm or too hot: *They always overheat their house in winter.* v.

**o·ver·hung** (ō′vər hung′ *for adjective,* ō′vər hung′ *for verb*)  **1** hung from above: *an overhung door.*  **2** pt. and pp. of OVERHANG: *A big awning overhung the sidewalk.*  **1** *adj.,* **2** *v.*

**o·ver·in·dulge** (ō′və rin dulj′)  indulge too much.  *v.,* **o·ver·in·dulged, o·ver·in·dulg·ing.**

**o·ver·joyed** (ō′vər joid′)  filled with great joy: *She was overjoyed at finding them safe and sound.*  *adj.*

**o·ver·kill** (ō′vər kil′)  a capacity for destruction greater than that required to destroy a target or enemy.  *n.*

**o·ver·lad·en** (ō′vər lā′dən)  OVERLOADED.  *adj.*

**o·ver·laid** (ō′vər lād′)  pt. and pp. of OVERLAY¹: *The workers overlaid the dome with gold.*  *v.*

**o·ver·lain** (ō′vər lān′)  pp. of OVERLIE.  *v.*

**o·ver·land** (ō′vər land′ *or* ō′vər lənd)  on land; by land: *an overland route. We travelled overland from Halifax to Montreal.*  *adj., adv.*

**o·ver·lap** (ō′vər lap′ *for verb,* ō′vər lap′ *for noun*)  **1** lap over; place or be placed so that one piece covers part of the next: *Shingles are laid to overlap each other.*  **2** a lapping over.  **3** the part or amount that overlaps: *Allow for an overlap of ten centimetres.*  **1** *v.,* **o·ver·lapped, o·ver·lap·ping;**  **2, 3** *n.*

**o·ver·lay¹** (ō′vər lā′ *for verb,* ō′vər lā′ *for noun*)  **1** lay or place one thing over or upon another.  **2** cover, overspread, or surmount with something; especially, finish with a layer or applied decoration of something: *The dome is overlaid with gold.*  **3** weigh down.  **4** something laid over something else; covering.  **5** an ornamental layer: *The lid of the box had a gold overlay.*  **1–3** *v.,* **o·ver·laid, o·ver·lay·ing;**  **4, 5** *n.*

**o·ver·lay²** (ō′vər lā′)  pt. of OVERLIE.  *v.*

**o·ver·leap** (ō′vər lēp′)  leap over; pass beyond: *Her joy overleaped all bounds.*  *v.*

**o·ver·lie** (ō′vər lī′)  **1** lie over or upon.  **2** smother by lying on.  *v.,* **o·ver·lay, o·ver·lain, o·ver·ly·ing.**

**o·ver·load** (ō′vər lōd′ *for verb,* ō′vər lōd′ *for noun*)  **1** load too heavily: *to overload a boat.*  **2** too great a load: *The overload of electric current broke the circuit.*  **1** *v.,* **2** *n.*

**o·ver·look** (ō′vər lúk′)  **1** fail to see: *Here are the letters you overlooked.*  **2** pay no attention to; excuse: *His boss said he would overlook the mistake.*  **3** have a view of from above; be higher than: *This window overlooks half the city.*  **4** manage; look after and direct.  *v.*

**o·ver·lord** (ō′vər lôrd′)  **1** a person who is lord over another lord or other lords: *The duke was the overlord of barons and knights who held land from him.*  **2** a ruler with absolute or dictatorial powers; despot.  *n.*

**o·ver·ly** (ō′vər lē)  overmuch; excessively; too: *She's overly sensitive to criticism.*  *adv.*

**o·ver·mas·ter** (ō′vər mas′tər)  overcome; overpower: *She couldn't overmaster her desire to laugh.*  *v.*

**o·ver·match** (ō′vər mach′)  be more than a match for; surpass.  *v.*

**o·ver·much** (ō′vər much′)  too much.  *adj., adv., n.*

**o·ver·nice** (ō′vər nīs′)  too FASTIDIOUS.  *adj.*

**o·ver·night** (ō′vər nīt′ *for adverb,* ō′vər nīt′ *for adjective and noun*)  **1** for one night: *to stay overnight.*  **2** done, occurring, etc. from one day to the next: *an overnight stop.*

## overhung 843 overrule

hat, āge, fär; let, ēqual, tėrm; it, īce
hot, ōpen, ôrder; oil, out; cup, put, rüle
əbove, takən, pencəl, lemən, circəs
ch, child; ng, long; sh, ship
th, thin; ᴛʜ, then; zh, measure

**3** for use for one night: *An overnight bag contains articles needed for one night's stay.*  **4** on the night before: *Preparations were made overnight for an early start.*  **5** of or having to do with the night before.  **6** the previous evening.  **7** at once; immediately; in a very short time: *Change will not come overnight.*  **1, 4, 7** *adv.,* **2, 3, 5** *adj.,* **6** *n.*

**o·ver·pass** (ō′vər pas′ *for verb,* ō′vər pas′ *for noun*)  **1** a bridge over a road, railway, canal, etc.: *An overpass was built to replace the level crossing.*  **2** pass over, across, or beyond.  **3** overlook; disregard.  **1** *n.,* **2, 3** *v.,* **o·ver·passed** or **o·ver·past, o·ver·pass·ing.**

**o·ver·play** (ō′vər plā′)  **1** play a part, etc. in an exaggerated manner.  **2** overestimate the strength of one's position: *She overplayed her price advantage, failed to guarantee quick delivery, and lost the contract.*  *v.*

**o·ver·pow·er** (ō′vər pou′ər)  **1** overcome; master; overwhelm: *to overpower one's enemies. I was overpowered by the heat.*  **2** be so much greater than that nothing else is felt: *Sudden anger overpowered every other feeling.*  *v.*  —**o′ver·pow′er·ing·ly,** *adv.*

**o·ver·price** (ō′vər prīs′)  price too high: *His paintings aren't selling well because they're overpriced.*  *v.,* **o·ver·priced, o·ver·pric·ing.**

**o·ver·pro·duce** (ō′vər prə dyüs′ *or* ō′vər prə düs′)  produce more than there is a need or demand for.  *v.*

**o·ver·pro·duc·tion** (ō′vər prə duk′shən)  production of more than is needed or can be sold.  *n.*

**o·ver·pro·tect** (ō′vər prə tekt′)  protect too much; exercise more control over than is necessary or desirable in trying to shield from hurt, disappointment, etc.: *He had a hard time when he first left home because he had been overprotected as a child.*  *v.*

**o·ver·pro·tec·tive** (ō′vər prə tek′tiv)  having or showing a tendency to overprotect: *an overprotective parent.*  *adj.*

**o·ver·qual·i·fied** (ō′vər kwol′i fīd′)  having more education, training, or experience than a job calls for.  *adj.*

**o·ver·rate** (ō′vər rāt′)  rate or estimate too highly: *The movie was overrated; it really wasn't very good.*  *v.,* **o·ver·rat·ed, o·ver·rat·ing.**

**o·ver·reach** (ō′vər rēch′)  **1** reach over or beyond.  **2** reach too far.  **3** get the better of by cunning: *to overreach another in a bargain.*  **4** cheat.  *v.*  **overreach oneself, a** fail or miss by trying for too much.  **b** fail by being too crafty or tricky.

**o·ver·ride** (ō′vər rīd′)  **1** act in spite of: *to override advice or objections.*  **2** prevail over: *The new rule overrides all previous ones.*  **3** ride over; trample on.  **4** ride over a region, place, etc.  **5** tire out by riding; ride too much: *to override a horse.*  *v.,* **o·ver·rode, o·ver·rid·den, o·ver·rid·ing.**

**o·ver·rule** (ō′vər rül′)  **1** decide against an argument, objection, etc.; set aside: *The president overruled my plan.*  **2** be stronger than; prevail over: *The majority overruled me.*  *v.,* **o·ver·ruled, o·ver·rul·ing.**

**o·ver·run** (ō′vər run′) **1** spread over rapidly or in great numbers: *Weeds had overrun the old garden. The barn was overrun with rats.* **2** invade and conquer, occupy, or destroy: *Enemy troops overran most of the country.* **3** run or go beyond; exceed: *The speaker overran the time set for her.* *v.*, **o·ver·ran, o·ver·run, o·ver·run·ning.**

**o·ver·saw** (ō′vər sô′) pt. of OVERSEE. *v.*

**o·ver·sea** (ō′vər sē′ *for adverb,* ō′vər sē′ *for adjective*) OVERSEAS. *adv., adj.*
☞ *Hom.* OVERSEE (for the first pronunciation of **oversea**).

**o·ver·seas** (ō′vər sēz′ *for adverb,* ō′vər sēz′ *for adjective*) **1** across the sea; beyond the sea; abroad: *to travel overseas.* **2** done, used, or serving overseas: *overseas service.* **3** of countries across the sea; foreign: *overseas trade.* **4** of the armed forces, serving across the sea: *My grandfather was overseas during the war.* 1, 4 *adv.*, 2, 3 *adj.*

**o·ver·see** (ō′vər sē′) look after and direct work or workers; superintend; manage: *to oversee a factory.* *v.*, **o·ver·saw, o·ver·seen, o·ver·see·ing.**
☞ *Hom.* OVERSEA (ō′vər sē′).

**o·ver·se·er** (ō′vər sē′ər) one who oversees the work of others. *n.*

**o·ver·sell** (ō′vər sel′) sell to excess; sell more of than can be delivered. *v.*, **o·ver·sold, o·ver·sell·ing.**

**o·ver·shad·ow** (ō′vər shad′ō) **1** be or appear more important than: *The boy overshadowed his older brother as a hockey player.* **2** cast a shadow over. *v.*

**o·ver·shoe** (ō′vər shü′) a waterproof shoe or boot, often made of rubber, worn over another shoe to keep the foot dry and warm. *n.*

**o·ver·shoot** (ō′vər shüt′) **1** of an aircraft, pass beyond the limit of the runway or landing field when trying to land. **2** shoot or go beyond the target, mark, limit, etc. *v.*, **o·ver·shot, o·ver·shoot·ing.**

An overshot water wheel. The force and weight of the water falling on the blades make the wheel turn. Its axle is connected to machinery.

**o·ver·shot** (ō′vər shot′ *for adjective,* ō′vər shot′ *for verb*) **1** of a water wheel, driven by water flowing over it from above. **2** of the upper jaw, projecting beyond the lower. **3** pt. and pp. of OVERSHOOT. 1, 2 *adj.*, 3 *v.*

**o·ver·sight** (ō′vər sīt′) **1** a failure to notice or think of something; an unintentional mistake or omission: *Through an oversight, the kitten had no supper last night.* **2** watchful care: *While children are at school, they are under their teacher's oversight and direction.* *n.*

**o·ver·sim·pli·fi·ca·tion** (ō′vər sim′plə fə kā′shən) the act or fact of OVERSIMPLIFYing: *It is an oversimplification to say that her success is due to hard work.* *n.*

**o·ver·sim·pli·fy** (ō′vər sim′plə fī′) simplify too much; simplify to the point of distortion: *She has oversimplified the problem: there are several important factors she did not even consider.* *v.*

**o·ver·size** (ō′vər sīz′) **1** larger than the usual size; outsize. **2** too big. **3** something that is oversize. 1, 2 *adj.*, 3 *n.*

**o·ver·sleep** (ō′vər slēp′) sleep beyond the time set for waking; sleep too long; sleep in: *I was late for school this morning because I overslept.* *v.*, **o·ver·slept, o·ver·sleep·ing.**

**o·ver·spread** (ō′vər spred′) spread over: *A smile overspread her face.* *v.*, **o·ver·spread, o·ver·spread·ing.**

**o·ver·state** (ō′vər stāt′) state too strongly; exaggerate. *v.*, **o·ver·stat·ed, o·ver·stat·ing.** —**o′ver·state′ment,** *n.*

**o·ver·stay** (ō′vər stā′) stay beyond the time or limits of: *to overstay one's welcome.* *v.*

**o·ver·step** (ō′vər step′) go beyond; exceed: *He overstepped the limits of politeness by asking such personal questions.* *v.*, **o·ver·stepped, o·ver·step·ping.**

**o·ver·stock** (ō′vər stok′ *for verb,* ō′vər stok′ *for noun*) **1** stock or supply with more than is needed or can readily be used: *Stores often have sales when they're overstocked.* **2** too great a stock or supply. 1 *v.*, 2 *n.*

**o·ver·strung** (ō′vər strung′ *for 1,* ō′vər strung′ *for 2*) **1** too nervous or sensitive: *The young actress was overstrung.* **2** having the bass strings crossing the treble strings: *an overstrung piano.* *adj.*

**o·ver·stuff** (ō′vər stuf′) **1** stuff more than is necessary; stuff too much. **2** of furniture, upholster with very thick stuffing. *v.*

**o·ver·stuffed** (ō′vər stuft′) **1** of furniture, having very thick stuffing: *a large, comfortable, overstuffed armchair.* **2** pt. and pp. of OVERSTUFF. 1 *adj.*, 2 *v.*

**o·ver·sub·scribe** (ō′vər səb skrīb′) subscribe or subscribe for in excess of what is available or required. *v.*, **o·ver·sub·scribed, o·ver·sub·scrib·ing.**

**o·ver·sup·ply** (ō′vər sə plī′ *for verb,* ō′vər sə plī′ *for noun*) **1** supply with more than is needed. **2** too great a supply. 1 *v.*, **o·ver·sup·plied, o·ver·sup·ply·ing;** 2 *n.*

**o·vert** (ō′vėrt *or* ō vėrt′) open; evident; not hidden; public: *Hitting someone is an overt act.* *adj.* —**o′vert·ly** or **o·vert′ly,** *adv.*

**o·ver·take** (ō′vər tāk′) **1** come up with; catch up to: *If you hurry, you might be able to overtake her before she reaches her car.* **2** catch up with and pass: *They overtook us and arrived before we did.* **3** come upon suddenly: *A storm overtook the children.* *v.*, **o·ver·took, o·ver·tak·en, o·ver·tak·ing.**

**o·ver·task** (ō′vər task′) give too long or too hard tasks to. *v.*

**o·ver·tax** (ō′vər taks′) **1** tax too heavily. **2** put too heavy a burden on. *v.* —**o′ver·tax·a′tion,** *n.*

**o·ver·threw** (ō′vər thrü′) pt. of OVERTHROW. *v.*

**o·ver·throw** (ō′vər thrō′ *for verb,* ō′vər thrō′ *for noun*) **1** take away the power of; defeat: *to overthrow a government.* **2** put an end to; destroy: *to overthrow slavery.* **3** overturn; upset; knock down. **4** throw a ball over or past the player or place aimed for. **5** a defeat; upset: *The overthrow of her plans left her much discouraged.* **6** a ball thrown over or past the player or place aimed for. 1–4 *v.*, **o·ver·threw, o·ver·thrown, o·ver·throw·ing;** 5, 6 *n.*

**o·ver·thrown** (ō′vər thrōn′) pp. of OVERTHROW. *v.*

**o·ver·time** (ō′vər tīm′ *for noun, adverb, and adjective,* ō′vər tīm′ *for verb*) **1** extra time; time beyond the regular hours. **2** wages for this period. **3** beyond the regular hours: *She worked overtime.* **4** of or for overtime: *overtime work.* **5** give too much time to: *to overtime a camera exposure.* **6** in games, a period or periods beyond the normal game time. 1, 2, 6 *n.,* 3 *adv.,* 4 *adj.,* 5 *v.,* **o·ver·timed, o·ver·tim·ing.**

**o·ver·tone** (ō′vər tōn′) **1** in music, a tone heard along with the main or fundamental tone and whose rate of vibration is a multiple of the main tone; harmonic. **2** a hint or suggestion of something felt, believed, etc.: *an overtone of anger. n.*

**o·ver·took** (ō′vər tůk′) pt. of OVERTAKE. *v.*

**o·ver·top** (ō′vər top′) **1** rise above; be higher than: *The new building will overtop our apartment.* **2** surpass; excel. *v.,* **o·ver·topped, o·ver·top·ping.**

**o·ver·train** (ō′vər trān′) subject to or undergo excessive athletic training; train too hard or too much, with a resulting loss of proficiency. *v.*

**o·ver·ture** (ō′vər chùr′ *or* ō′vər chər) **1** a formal proposal or offer; the beginning of negotiations with another (*usually used in the plural*): *overtures for peace.* **2** a musical composition played by the orchestra as an introduction to an opera, oratorio, etc. **3** an independent composition of one movement in a similar style. *n.*

**o·ver·turn** (ō′vər tėrn′ *for verb,* ō′vər tėrn′ *for noun*) **1** turn upside down. **2** upset; fall down; fall over: *The boat overturned.* **3** make fall down; overthrow; defeat; destroy the power of: *The rebels overturned the government.* **4** an overturning. 1–3 *v.,* 4 *n.*

**o·ver·view** (ō′vər vyü′) a brief, general survey. *n.*

**o·ver·watch** (ō′vər woch′) watch over. *v.*

**o·ver·ween·ing** (ō′vər wē′ning) thinking too much of oneself; conceited; self-confident; presumptuous. *adj.*

**o·ver·weight** (ō′vər wāt′) **1** of a person or animal, having a mass that is too great in proportion to height and build: *He is overweight because he eats too many sweet things.* **2** totalling a greater mass than allowed by regulations: *overweight baggage.* **3** more mass than is needed, desired, or specified; extra or excessive mass: *The butcher gave us overweight on this roast.* 1, 2 *adj.,* 3 *n.*

**o·ver·whelm** (ō′vər welm′ *or* ō′vər hwelm′) **1** overcome completely; crush: *to overwhelm with grief.* **2** cover completely as a flood would: *A great wave overwhelmed the boat. v.*

**o·ver·whelm·ing** (ō′vər wel′ming *or* ō′vər hwel′ming) **1** too many, too great, or too much to be resisted; overpowering: *an overwhelming majority of votes.* **2** ppr. of OVERWHELM. 1 *adj.,* 2 *v.*

**o·ver·work** (ō′vər wėrk′ *for noun,* ō′vər wėrk′ *for verb*) **1** too much or too hard work: *A lazy person is not likely to die of overwork.* **2** work too hard or too long. **3** extra work. 1, 3 *n.,* 2 *v.*

**o·ver·wrought** (ō′vər rot′) **1** wearied or exhausted by too much excitement; overly excited: *overwrought nerves.* **2** decorated all over: *an overwrought platter.* **3** too elaborate. *adj.*
☞ *Etym.* See note at WROUGHT.

**o·vi·duct** (ō′və dukt′) the tube through which the ovum, or egg, passes from the ovary. *n.*

**o·vi·form** (ō′və fôrm′) egg-shaped. *adj.*

**o·vip·a·rous** (ō vip′ə rəs) producing eggs that are hatched after leaving the body: *Birds are oviparous.* Compare with VIVIPAROUS. *adj.*

**o·vi·pos·i·tor** (ō′və poz′ə tər) in certain insects, an organ at the end of the abdomen, by which eggs are deposited. *n.*

**o·void** (ō′void) **1** egg-shaped. **2** an egg-shaped object. 1 *adj.,* 2 *n.*

**o·vu·lar** (ō′vyə lər) of or being an OVULE. *adj.*

**o·vu·late** (ō′vyə lāt′) **1** produce an ovum. **2** discharge the ovum from an ovary. *v.,* **o·vu·lat·ed, o·vu·lat·ing.**

**o·vu·la·tion** (ō′vyə lā′shən) **1** the period when an ovum or female germ cell is produced or formed. **2** the discharge of an ovum from an ovary. *n.*

**o·vule** (ō′vyül) **1** a small ovum, especially one in an early stage of growth. **2** the part of a plant that develops into a seed. *n.*

**o·vum** (ō′vəm) a female GERM CELL; egg. *n., pl.* **o·va** (ō′və).

**owe** (ō) **1** have to pay; be in debt for: *I owe the grocer $20.* **2** be in debt: *He is always owing for something.* **3** be obliged or indebted for: *We owe a great deal to our parents. She owes her success to her own determination.* **4** be obliged to give or offer: *We owe friends our trust. v.,* **owed, ow·ing.**
☞ *Hom.* O, OH.

**ow·ing** (ō′ing) **1** due; owed: *to pay what is owing.* **2** ppr. of OWE. 1 *adj.,* 2 *v.*

**owing to,** on account of; because of; due to; as a result of: *The ball game was called off owing to rain.*
☞ *Usage.* See note at DUE.

A great grey owl— about 75 cm long including the tail

**owl** (oul) any of an order of birds of prey found throughout the world, having a very big head in proportion to the body, big eyes set in the front of the head, and a flexible neck which allows the head to be turned almost completely around to the back: *Most owls are active at night. n.*

**owl·et** (ou′lit) **1** a young owl. **2** a small owl. *n.*

**owl·ish** (ou′lish) like or characteristic of an owl, especially in having large, unblinking eyes or a seemingly wise expression: *He gave me an owlish look. adj.*

**own** (ōn) **1** of oneself or itself; belonging to oneself or itself: *We have our own troubles. The house is her own.* **2** in closest relationship: *Own brothers have the same parents.* **3** the one or ones belonging to oneself or itself: *They demanded their own and not a substitute.* **4** have; possess: *She owns much land.* **5** acknowledge; admit; confess: *He owned his guilt. She owns to many faults.* **6** acknowledge as one's own: *His father will not own him.* 1, 2 *adj.,* 3 *n.,* 4–6 *v.*
**come into one's own, a** get what belongs to one. **b** get the success or credit that one deserves.
**hold one's own,** keep one's position; not be forced back.
**of one's own,** belonging to oneself.
**on one's own,** *Informal.* on one's own account, responsibility, resources, etc.
**own up (to),** confess; admit: *The prisoner owned up to the crime.*

**own·er** (ō′nər) one who owns: *Owners of dogs have to buy licences for them. Home owners protested the increase in property taxes.* *n.* —**own′er·less,** *adj.*

**own·er·ship** (ō′nər ship′) the state of being an owner; the possessing of something; right of possession. *n.*

**ox** (oks) **1** a full-grown, castrated male of cattle, usually at least three or four years old: *Oxen are used as draft animals or for beef.* Compare with STEER. See YOKE for picture. **2** any of a subfamily of animals that includes cattle, the yak, and buffalo; BOVINE. *n., pl.* **ox·en.** —**ox′like′,** *adj.*

**ox·al·ic acid** (ok sal′ik) a poisonous organic acid that occurs in wood sorrel and various other plants, and that is used for bleaching, removing stains, making dyes, etc.

**ox·a·lis** (ok′sə lis) WOOD SORREL. *n.*

**ox·blood** (oks′blud′) deep red. *n., adj.*

**ox·bow** (oks′bō′) **1** a U-shaped frame of wood or iron that forms the lower part of a yoke for an ox: *The oxbow fits under and around the neck of the ox, with the upper ends inserted in the bar of the yoke.* See YOKE for picture. **2** a U-shaped bend in a river. **3** the land contained within such a bend. *n.*

**ox·cart** (oks′kärt′) a cart drawn by oxen. *n.*

**ox·en** (ok′sən) pl. of OX. *n.*

**ox–eyed** (oks′īd′) having large, full eyes like those of an ox. *adj.*

**ox–eye daisy** (oks′ī′) the common daisy of North America, having large flower heads composed of tiny yellow disk flowers surrounded by white ray flowers: *The ox-eye daisy was introduced to North America from Europe and has become a common weed.* See DAISY for picture.

**ox·ford** (oks′fərd) a kind of low shoe, laced over the instep. See SHOE for picture. *n.*

**Oxford blue** dark, sometimes purplish, blue.

**oxford cloth** a cotton cloth with a soft finish, in a plain or basket weave, used especially for shirts.

**Oxford grey** very dark grey.

**ox·i·da·tion** (ok′sə dā′shən) **1** the act or process of oxidizing; the combining of oxygen with another element to form one or more new substances: *Burning is one kind of oxidation.* **2** the state of being oxidized. *n.*

**ox·ide** (ok′sīd) a compound of oxygen with another element or a radical. *n.*

**ox·i·dize** (ok′sə dīz′) **1** combine with oxygen: *When a substance burns or rusts, it is oxidized. Water oxidizes some metals.* **2** rust. **3** lose or cause to lose hydrogen. **4** change to a higher positive VALENCE. *v.,* **ox·i·dized, ox·i·diz·ing.** —**ox′i·diz′er,** *n.*

**ox·lip** (ok′slip′) a primrose of Europe and Asia having clusters of pale-yellow flowers. *n.*

**oxy–** *combining form.* oxygen or containing oxygen, as in *oxyacetylene.*

**ox·y·a·cet·y·lene** (ok′sē ə set′ə lēn′) of, having to do with, or using a mixture of oxygen and ACETYLENE. *adj.*

**oxyacetylene torch** a device using a mixture of oxygen and ACETYLENE to produce a very hot flame for welding or cutting metals.

**ox·y·gen** (ok′sə jən) a colourless, odourless, tasteless gas that forms one fifth of the air and is also combined in water and most mineral and organic substances: *Oxygen is the most abundant of all elements and is essential to plant and animal life.* Symbol: O *n.*

**ox·y·gen·ate** (ok′sə jə nāt′) treat, combine, or supply with oxygen: *to oxygenate the blood.* *v.,* **ox·y·gen·at·ed, ox·y·gen·at·ing.** —**ox′y·gen·a′tion,** *n.*

**ox·y·gen·ize** (ok′sə jə nīz′) treat with oxygen; combine with oxygen. *v.,* **ox·y·gen·ized, ox·y·gen·iz·ing.** —**ox′y·gen·iz′a·ble,** *adj.*

**oxygen mask** a device worn over the nose and mouth through which oxygen is supplied from a storage tank: *Oxygen masks are used by athletes, hospitals, and climbers.*

**oxygen tent** a small, clear plastic tent or canopy that can be placed over the head of a patient lying in bed and provided with a measured flow of oxygen.

**O·yez** or **O·yes** (ō′yes) Hear! Attend! A cry uttered, usually three times, by a public or court crier to command silence and attention before a proclamation, etc. is made. *interj., n.*

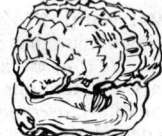

Common food oysters— usually about 5 to 12 cm long

**oys·ter** (oi′stər) **1** a kind of MOLLUSC much used as food, having a rough, irregular shell in two halves: *Oysters are found in shallow water along seacoasts. Some kinds of oysters yield pearls.* **2** one of the two oyster-shaped bits of dark meat found in the back of a fowl. *n.* —**oys′ter·like′,** *adj.*

**oyster bed** a place where oysters breed or are cultivated.

**oz.** ounce; ounces.

**o·zone** (ō′zōn) **1** a form of oxygen consisting of molecules composed of three atoms instead of the usual two, produced by electricity and present in the air, especially after a thunderstorm. Formula: $O_3$ **2** *Informal.* pure air that is refreshing. *n.*

**ozone layer** OZONOSPHERE.

**o·zo·nic** (ō zō′nik *or* ō zon′ik) of, having to do with, or containing OZONE. *adj.*

**o·zo·nif·er·ous** (ō zə nif′ə rəs) of, having to do with, or containing OZONE. *adj.*

**o·zo·no·sphere** (ō zō′nə sfēr′) a region of the upper stratosphere containing a relatively high concentration of OZONE that protects earth from excessive ultraviolet radiation from the sun. *n.* —**o·zo′no·spher′ic, o·zo′no·spher′ic·al,** *adj.*

# P p  *P p*

**p** or **P** (pē)   1 the sixteenth letter of the English alphabet.   2 any speech sound represented by this letter.   3 a person or thing identified as p, especially the sixteenth in a series.   *n., pl.* **p's** or **P's.**
**mind one's P's and Q's,**   be careful about what one says or does.

**p**   1 in music, piano.   2 in baseball, pitcher.   3 *Brit.* penny; pence.

*p*   pressure.

**p.**   1 page.   2 participle.   3 past.   4 population.   5 in baseball, pitcher.   6 *Brit.*   penny; pence.

**P**   phosphorus.

*P*   power.

**p.a.**   1 per annum.   2 participial adjective.

**Pa**   1 pascal.   2 protactinium.

**P.A.**   public address system.

**Pac.**   Pacific.

**pace** (pās)   1 a rate of speed; speed: *Harriet sets a fast pace in walking.*   2 set the pace for: *A motorboat will pace the boys training for the rowing match.*   3 a step.   4 walk over with regular steps: *to pace the floor.*   5 walk with regular steps: *The tiger paced up and down in its cage.*   6 the length of a step in walking, used as a unit for measuring length or distance; about 76 cm.   7 measure by paces: *We paced off the distance and found it to be 69 paces.*   8 a way of stepping: *The walk, trot, and canter are some of the paces of a horse.*   9 a particular pace of some horses in which both legs on one side are raised at the same time.   10 of a horse, move at a pace.   1, 3, 6, 8, 9 *n.*, 2, 4, 5, 7, 10 *v.*, **paced, pac·ing.**
**keep pace with,**   keep up with; go as fast as.
**put one through one's paces,**   try one out; find out what one can do.
**set the pace,**   **a** set a rate of speed for others to follow.   **b** be an example or model for others to follow.

**pace·mak·er** (pās'mā'kər)   1 a person or thing that sets the pace for another, as in a race.   2 the part of the heart in vertebrates that begins each contraction of the heart.   3 an electrical device that steadies or stimulates the heartbeat.   *n.*

**pac·er** (pā'sər)   a person or thing that paces, especially a horse that normally runs by raising both legs on the same side at the same time.   *n.*

**pace·set·ter** (pās'set'ər)   a person who leads the way or serves as a model for others in fashion, ideas, etc.   *n.*

**pach·y·derm** (pak'ə dėrm')   any of several large, thick-skinned, hoofed mammals, such as the elephant, hippopotamus or rhinoceros, that were formerly classified together.   *n.*

**pa·cif·ic** (pə sif'ik)   1 tending to make peace; making peace.   2 loving peace; not warlike: *a pacific nation.*   3 peaceful; calm; quiet: *a pacific nature, pacific weather.*   4 **Pacific,**   **a** of or having to do with the Pacific Ocean, the great ocean west of North and South America.   **b** on, in, over, or near the Pacific Ocean: *a Pacific airline.*   *adj.*
—**pa·cif'i·cal·ly,** *adv.*

**pac·i·fi·ca·tion** (pas'ə fə kā'shən)   PACIFYing or being pacified.   *n.*

**Pacific Rim**   the coastal areas and countries bordering the Pacific Ocean, especially with reference to trade and cultural relations, political agreements, etc.

**Pacific salmon**   any of a small, closely related group of important food and game fishes of the salmon and trout family, found in the Pacific Ocean: *The five species of Pacific salmon found along the North American coast are sockeye, chum, coho, pink, and spring.*

**pac·i·fi·er** (pas'ə fī'ər)   1 a person or thing that pacifies.   2 a rubber nipple or ring given to a baby to suck.   *n.*

**pac·i·fism** (pas'ə fiz'əm)   the principle or policy of opposing war or violence as a means of settling disputes; the refusal to take up arms or to resist violence by force.   *n.*

**pac·i·fist** (pas'ə fist)   1 of or having to do with PACIFISM or pacifists.   2 a person who is strongly opposed to conflict, especially war.   *n.*

**pac·i·fy** (pas'ə fī)   1 make calm; quiet down: *Can't you pacify that screaming baby?*   2 bring order to; make submissive: *Soldiers were sent to pacify the country.*   *v.*, **pac·i·fied, pac·i·fy·ing.**

**pack¹** (pak)   1 a bundle of things wrapped up or tied together for carrying: *The hiker carried a pack on his back.*   2 put together in a bundle, box, bale, etc.: *Pack your clothes in this bag.*   3 put things together in a bundle, box, bale, etc.: *Are you ready to pack?*   4 fill with things; put one's things into: *Pack your trunk.*   5 fit together closely; admit of storing and shipping: *These goods pack well.*   6 press or crowd closely together: *A hundred people were packed into one small room.*   7 become packed: *The theatre was packed.*   8 put into a container to be sold or stored: *Meat, fish, fruit, and vegetables are often packed in tins.*   9 the amount packed: *This year's pack of fish is larger than last year's.*   10 a set; lot; a number together: *a pack of thieves, a pack of nonsense, a pack of lies.*   11 a number of animals hunting together; a number of dogs kept together for hunting: *Wolves hunt in packs; foxes hunt alone.*   12 a complete set of playing cards, usually 52.   13 a large area of floating pieces of ice pushed together; ice pack: *A ship forced its way through the pack.*   14 something put on the body or skin as a treatment: *A cloth soaked in hot or cold water is often used as a pack.*   15 make tight with something that water, steam, air, etc. cannot leak through: *The plumber packed the joint between two sections of pipe.*   16 load an animal with a pack; burden.   17 *Informal.*   carry: *to pack a gun.*   18 carry in a pack: *She packed her supplies into the bush.*   19 *Informal.*   possess as a characteristic or power: *That guy packs quite a punch.*   20 a company or troop of Wolf Cubs or Brownies.   1, 9–14, 20 *n.*, 2–8, 15–19 *v.*
**pack off,**   send away: *The child was packed off to bed.*
**pack up,** *Informal.*   **a** stop working; cease operating; fail: *One of the aircraft's engines packed up.*   **b** die.
**send packing,**   send away abruptly.

**pack²** (pak)   arrange unfairly: *To pack a jury or a convention is to fill it unfairly with those who will favour one side.*   *v.*

**pack·age** (pak'ij)   1 a bundle of things packed or wrapped together; box with things packed in it; parcel.   2 a box, can, bottle, jar, case, or other receptacle for packing goods.   3 such a package with its contents, as offered for sale.   **4** put in a package.   1–3 *n.*, 4 *v.*, **pack·aged, pack·ag·ing.**

**package deal**   a bargain, sale, or business deal in which a number of items are presented as a single offer.

**package tour**   an arrangement for a holiday including airfare, hotel(s), and, sometimes, activities.

**pack·ag·ing** (pak′ə jing)   **1** the design and manufacture of packages.   **2** the process of putting goods into such packages.   **3** such packages collectively.   **4** ppr. of PACKAGE.   1–3 *n.*, 4 *v.*

**pack animal**   an animal used for carrying loads or packs.

**pack·er** (pak′ər)   a person or thing that packs; a person or company that packs meat, fruit, vegetables, etc. to be sold at wholesale: *a meat packer.*   *n.*

**pack·et** (pak′it)   a small package; parcel: *a packet of letters.*   *n.*

**pack horse**   a horse used to carry packs of goods.

**pack ice**   ice pushed by wind or current into a solid mass.

**pack·ing** (pak′ing)   **1** material used to pack or to make watertight, steamtight, etc.: *the packing around the valves of a radiator.*   **2** the business of preparing and packing meat, fish, fruit, vegetables, etc. to be sold.   **3** ppr. of PACK.   1, 2 *n.*, 3 *v.*

**packing house**   a place where meat, fruit, vegetables, etc. are prepared and packed to be sold.

**pack rat**   **1** a large, bushy-tailed wood rat found in the Rocky Mountains, having well developed cheek pouches: *Pack rats hoard food and often other objects they find.*   **2** *Informal.*   a person who has a tendency to hoard objects, especially useless ones.

**pack·sack** (pak′sak′)   a bag of canvas or leather for carrying gear, clothing, etc. when travelling on foot, usually worn strapped to the back; knapsack.   *n.*

**pack·saddle** (pak′sad′əl)   a saddle specially adapted for supporting the load on a pack animal.   *n.*

**pack train**   a line or group of animals carrying loads.

**pact** (pakt)   an agreement; compact: *The two nations signed a peace pact.*   *n.*

**pad¹** (pad)   **1** something soft used for comfort, protection, or stuffing; cushion: *We put a foam pad on top of the old mattress to make it more comfortable.*   **2** fill with something soft; stuff: *to pad a chair.*   **3** make a written paper or speech longer by using unnecessary words just to fill space: *Don't pad your compositions.*   **4** a soft, stuffed saddle.   **5** one of the cushionlike parts on the bottom side of the feet of dogs, foxes, and some other animals.   **6** the foot of such animals.   **7** a floating leaf of a water plant, especially a water lily.   **8** a number of sheets of paper fastened along an edge or edges; tablet: *a writing pad.*   **9** a cloth soaked with ink to use with a rubber stamp.   **10** the launching platform for a rocket or missile; LAUNCHING PAD: *The rocket rose from the pad at midday.*   1, 4–10 *n.*, 2, 3 *v.*, **pad·ded, pad·ding.**

**pad²** (pad)   **1** walk; tramp; trudge.   **2** walk or trot softly, with a muffled sound: *a wolf padding through the bush.*   **3** a dull or muffled sound, as of footsteps on the ground: *We heard the pad of hoofs on the path.*   **4** a slow horse for riding on a road.   1, 2 *v.*, **pad·ded, pad·ding;** 3, 4 *n.*

**pad·ding** (pad′ing)   **1** material used to pad with, such as foam rubber, cotton or synthetic fibre, or straw.

## package deal   849   pagan

hat, āge, fär; let, ēqual, tėrm; it, īce
hot, ōpen, ôrder; oil, out; cup, pùt, rüle
əbove, takən, pencəl, lemən, circəs
ch, child; ng, long; sh, ship
th, thin; ᴛʜ, then; zh, measure

**2** unnecessary words used to make a speech or a written paper longer.   **3** ppr. of PAD.   1, 2 *n.*, 3 *v.*

**pad·dle¹** (pad′əl)   **1** a short oar with a broad blade at one end or both ends, used without resting it against the boat.   **2** move a boat or canoe with a paddle or paddles.   **3** use a paddle to move a canoe.   **4** row gently.   **5** the act of paddling; a turn at the paddle.   **6** one of the broad boards fixed around a water wheel or a PADDLE WHEEL to push, or be pushed by, the water.   **7** a paddle-shaped piece of wood used for stirring, for mixing, for beating clothes, etc.   **8** *Informal.*   beat with a paddle or something similar; spank.   **9** a special handle with a wheel, by which the user can control the action in electronic games.   1, 5–7, 9 *n.*, 2–4, 8 *v.*, **pad·dled, pad·dling.**   —**pad′dler,** *n.*

**pad·dle²** (pad′əl)   **1** move the hands or feet about in water: *The children were paddling in the creek.*   **2** wade barefoot in water: *Children love to paddle at the beach.*   *v.*, **pad·dled, pad·dling.**   —**pad′dler,** *n.*

**pad·dle·fish** (pad′əl fish′)   either of two related species of large freshwater fish, one found in North America and the other in China, having a smooth, scaleless body and a very long, flat snout resembling a spatula: *Paddlefish catch food by swimming with the mouth open.*   *n., pl.* **pad·dle·fish** or **pad·dle·fish·es.**

**paddle wheel**   a wheel that propels a boat through the water by means of an arrangement of paddles.

**pad·dock** (pad′ək)   **1** a small field near a stable or house, used for exercising animals or as a pasture.   **2** a pen for horses at a race track.   *n.*

**pad·dy** (pad′ē)   **1** rice, especially before threshing or in the husk.   **2** a field of rice.   *n., pl.* **pad·dies.**

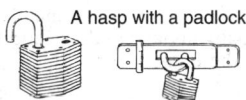

A hasp with a padlock

**pad·lock** (pad′lok′)   **1** a removable lock having a hinged bar that is passed through a loop or eye in the door, box, etc. to be locked and snapped shut.   **2** fasten with such a lock: *The gate is padlocked at night.*   1 *n.*, 2 *v.*

**pae·an** (pē′ən)   a song of praise, joy, or triumph.   *n.* Also, **pean.**

**pa·el·la** (pī el′ə; *Spanish,* pä ā′lyä *or* pä ā′yä)   a Spanish dish made of rice flavoured with saffron, chicken, shrimps, vegetables, etc.   *n.*

**pa·gan** (pā′gən)   **1** a person who is not a Christian, Jew, or Moslem; one who worships more than one god; heathen: *The ancient Greeks and Romans were pagans.*   **2** of or having to do with pagans: *pagan customs.*   **3** a person who has no religion.   **4** not religious.   1, 3 *n.*, 2, 4 *adj.*

☛ *Etym.* From *paganus* 'peasant, civilian', which came from L *pagus* 'country district, village'. The meaning 'heathen, non-believer' seems to have developed in the military world of Rome about A.D. 100 as a result of

Christians applying the sense 'civilian' to people who were not soldiers of Christ.

☛ *Usage.* Both **pagan** and HEATHEN have a basic connotation of 'unenlightened' or 'unbelieving'. People belonging to established religions other than Christian, Jewish, and Moslem object to being called pagan. **Heathen**, in particular, is sometimes used as a term of insult. The words, therefore, are best used in historical contexts: *Julius Caesar was a pagan. The Goths were heathen.*

**pa·gan·ism** ((pā′gə niz′əm)  **1** PAGAN beliefs and practices.  **2** a PAGAN religion.  **3** the quality or state of being a PAGAN.  *n.*

**page¹** (pāj)  **1** one side of a leaf or sheet of paper: *The book has 350 pages.*  **2** a leaf or sheet of paper, especially in a book, magazine, etc.: *The page was torn. Write on only one side of the page.*  **3** what is printed, written or pictured on one side of a leaf: *This page is hard to read.*  **4** a written record: *the pages of history.*  **5** an event or period worth recording: *a glorious page in the history of the country.*  **6** number the pages of: *Make sure you page your essay.*  1–5 *n.*, 6 *v.*,  **paged, pag·ing.**

**page²** (pāj)  **1** a servant, often a boy, who runs errands, carries hand luggage, etc. for guests at hotels, etc.: *The pages at hotels usually wear uniforms.*  **2** try to get a message to a person by means of an announcement, either by a page or on a PUBLIC ADDRESS SYSTEM.  **3** a person who carries messages, books, etc. for members of the House of Commons, the Senate, or a legislative assembly.  **4** a young man who attends a person of rank.  **5** in former times, a young man who was preparing to be a knight.  1, 3–5 *n.*, 2 *v.*,  **paged, pag·ing.**

**pag·eant** (paj′ənt)  **1** an elaborate spectacle; procession in costume; display: *The coronation of the new king was a splendid pageant.*  **2** a public entertainment that represents scenes from history, legend, or the like: *Our school gave a pageant of the coming of Jacques Cartier to Canada.*  **3** empty show, not reality.  *n.*

**pag·eant·ry** (paj′ən trē)  **1** a splendid show; gorgeous display; pomp.  **2** mere show; empty display.  *n., pl.* **pag·eant·ries.**

**page-boy** (pāj′boi′)  a girl's or woman's hair style in which the hair, usually about shoulder length, is curled smoothly under at the ends.  *n.*

**page-boy** (pāj′boi′)  PAGE² (def. 1).  *n.*

**pag·i·nate** (paj′ə nāt′)  number the pages of books, etc.  *v.*, **pag·i·nat·ed, pag·i·nat·ing.**

**pag·i·na·tion** (paj′ə nā′shən)  **1** the act of numbering the pages of books, etc.  **2** the figures with which pages are numbered.  *n.*

A pagoda in the Chinese style of architecture

**pa·go·da** (pə gō′də)  a temple having many storeys,
with a roof curving upward from each storey: *Pagodas are to be found in India, China, and Japan.*  *n.*

**paid** (pād)  **1** receiving money; hired.  **2** no longer owed; settled.  **3** cashed.  **4** pt. and pp. of PAY¹: *I have paid my bills. These bills are all paid.*  1–3 *adj.*, 4 *v.*

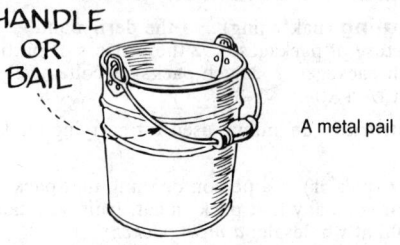

A metal pail

**pail** (pāl)  **1** a fairly large, usually round container for carrying liquids, having a wide top and a handle that is attached at each side and arches over the top.  **2** the amount a pail holds.  *n.*
☛ *Hom.* PALE.

**pail·ful** (pāl′fùl′)  the amount that fills a pail.  *n., pl.* **pail·fuls.**

**pain** (pān)  **1** an unpleasant sensation in the body or a particular part of it, due to some stimulus of the nerve endings from injury, disorder, or disease: *A cut usually causes pain. She felt a sharp pain in her back.*  **2** mental suffering; grief: *The memory still gave her pain.*  **3** cause to suffer, give rise to pain; ache: *His tooth was paining him a great deal.*  **4 pains,** *pl.*  **a** care; effort; trouble to do something: *He said he would not interfere, because he would get nothing but trouble for his pains.*  **b** the throes of childbirth; spasms of labour: *The pains had started.*  1, 2, 4 *n.*, 3 *v.*
**be at pains,**  make a conscientious effort: *She was at great pains to make them understand.*
**on** or **under pain of,**  as a way of avoiding the punishment or penalty of: *The traitor was ordered to leave the country on pain of death.*
**take pains,**  be careful: *She took pains to do a good job.*
☛ *Hom.* PANE.

**pain·ful** (pān′fəl)  **1** causing pain; unpleasant; hurting: *a painful illness, a painful duty.*  **2** difficult.  *adj.*
—**pain′ful·ly,** *adv.*  —**pain′ful·ness,** *n.*

**pain·less** (pān′lis)  causing or producing no pain: *The treatment is painless.*  *adj.*

**pains·tak·ing** (pānz′tā′king)  very careful; particular; scrupulous: *a painstaking painter.*  *adj.*
—**pains′tak′ing·ly,** *adv.*

**paint** (pānt)  **1** a mixture of a solid colouring matter and liquid that can be put on a surface to dry as a coloured coating.  **2** the solid colouring matter alone: *a box of paints.*  **3** cover or decorate with paint: *to paint a house.*  **4** use paint.  **5** represent an object, etc. in colours: *The artist painted the lights of the city.*  **6** make pictures: *She spends her weekends painting.*  **7** picture vividly in words: *The traveller painted an exciting picture of her trip to the Orient.*  **8** colouring matter put on the face or body.  **9** put on like paint: *The doctor painted iodine on the cut.*  1, 2, 8 *n.*, 3–7, 9 *v.*

**paint·brush** (pānt′brush′)  **1** a brush for putting on paint.  **2** any of a closely related group of plants belonging to the same family as the figworts, toad flax, and snapdragon, having spikes of small flowers surrounded by large, brightly coloured bracts: *Several species of paintbrush are common Canadian wildflowers.*  *n.*

**paint·er¹** (pān′tər)   1 a person who paints pictures; artist.   2 a person who paints houses, woodwork, etc.   *n.*

**paint·er²** (pān′tər)   a rope, usually fastened to the bow of a boat, for tying it to a ship, pier, etc.   *n.*

**paint·ing** (pān′ting)   1 something painted; a picture that has been painted.   2 the act of one who paints.   3 the art of representation, decoration, and creating beauty with paints.   4 ppr. of PAINT.   1–3 *n.*, 4 *v.*

**pair** (per)   1 a set of two; two that go together: *a pair of shoes, a pair of horses*.   2 arrange or be arranged in sets of two: *to pair stockings*.   3 a single thing consisting of two parts that cannot be used separately: *a pair of scissors, a pair of trousers*.   4 two people who are married or are engaged to be married.   5 join in love or marriage.   6 two animals that are mated.   7 mate.   8 two members on opposite sides who arrange not to vote on a certain question.   9 the arrangement thus made.   1, 3, 4, 6, 8, 9 *n.*, *pl.* **pairs** or (*sometimes after a numeral*) **pair**;   2, 5, 7 *v.*   **pair off**,   arrange in pairs; form into pairs: *The boys and girls paired off to learn the new dance.*
☛ *Hom.*   PARE, PEAR.

**pais·ley** (pāz′lē)   1 an elaborate, colourful fabric design of curving lines and figures: *silk paisley*.   2 made of fabric having a paisley design; having a design like paisley.   3 something made of fabric having such a design.   1, 3 *n.*, *pl.* **pais·leys**;   2 *adj.*

**pa·ja·mas** (pə jam′əz *or* pə jä′məz)   See PYJAMAS.   *n.*

**Pak·i·stan·i** (pak′i stan′ē)   1 of or having to do with Pakistan, a country in southern Asia, or its people.   2 a native or inhabitant of Pakistan.   1 *adj.*, 2 *n.*

The pa kua

**pa ku·a** (pä′kü ä′)   in Taoism, an ancient symbol made up of eight trigrams arranged within an octagon and around the yin-yang symbol.   *n.*

**pal** (pal)   1 a partner; chum; playmate; comrade.   2 associate as pals.   1 *n.*, 2 *v.*, **palled, pal·ling.**

**pal·ace** (pal′is)   1 the official home of a king, queen, bishop, or some other important person.   2 a very fine house or building.   *n.*

**pal·at·a·ble** (pal′ə təbəl)   agreeable to the taste; pleasing: *The lunch was not very palatable. I find your suggestion extremely palatable.*   *adj.*   —**pal′at·a·bly,** *adv.*

**pal·a·tal** (pal′ə təl)   1 of or having to do with the palate.   2 in phonetics, made with the tongue near or touching the hard palate. The *y* in *yet* is a palatal sound.   3 a palatal sound.   1, 2 *adj.*, 3 *n.*

**pal·a·tal·ize** (pal′ə tə līz′)   in phonetics, change into a palatal sound.   *v.*, **pal·a·tal·ized, pal·a·tal·iz·ing.**

**pal·ate** (pal′it)   1 the roof of the mouth: *The bony part in front is the hard palate; the fleshy part at the back is the soft palate.*   2 the sense of taste: *The new flavour pleased his palate.*   3 a liking.   *n.*
☛ *Hom.*   PALETTE, PALLET.

hat, āge, fär; let, ēqual, tėrm; it, īce
hot, ōpen, ôrder, oil, out; cup, pùt, rüle
əbove, takən, pencəl, lemən, circəs
ch, child; ng, long; sh, ship
th, thin; ᴛʜ, then; zh, measure

**pa·la·tial** (pə lā′shəl)   like or fit for a palace; magnificent: *a palatial apartment*.   *adj.*
—**pa·la′tial·ly,** *adv.*

**pal·a·tine** (pal′ə tīn′)   1 having royal rights in his own territory: *A count palatine was subject only to the emperor or king.*   2 a lord having royal rights in his own territory.   3 of a lord who has royal rights in his own territory.   4 palatial.   1, 3, 4 *adj.*, 2 *n.*

**Palatine Hill**   one of the seven hills on which the city of Rome was built.

**pa·lav·er** (pə lav′ər)   1 a parley or conference, especially between travellers or explorers and natives.   2 hold such a parley.   3 *Informal.*   smooth, persuading talk; fluent talk; flattery.   4 *Informal.*   talk fluently or flatteringly.   1, 3 *n.*, 2, 4 *v.*

**pale¹** (pāl)   1 without much colour; whitish: *When you have been ill, your face is often pale.*   2 not bright; dim: *pale blue. The street lamp gave a pale light in the fog.*   3 turn or cause to turn pale: *Helen's face paled at the bad news.*   1, 2 *adj.*, **pal·er, pal·est;**   3 *v.*, **paled, pal·ing.**
—**pale′ly,** *adv.*
☛ *Hom.*   PAIL.

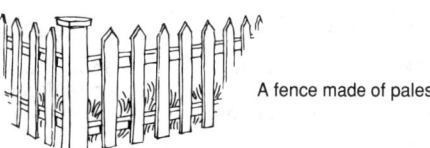
A fence made of pales

**pale²** (pāl)   1 a long, narrow board, pointed at the top, used for fences; picket.   2 a boundary, the limits within which one has a right to protection: *Murder is an act outside the pale of society.*   3 enclose with pales.   1, 2 *n.*, 3 *v.*, **paled, pal·ing.**
☛ *Hom.*   PAIL.

**pale·ness** (pāl′nis)   the quality or state of being pale.   *n.*

**pa·le·o·lith·ic** (pā′lē ə lith′ik)   of or having to do with the earlier part of the Stone Age: *Paleolithic tools were made from stone.*   *adj.*

**pa·le·on·tol·o·gist** (pā′lē on tol′ə jist)   a person trained in PALEONTOLOGY, especially one who makes it his or her work.   *n.*

**pa·le·on·tol·o·gy** (pā′lē on tol′ə jē)   the science that deals with the forms of life existing long ago in other geological periods, as known from fossil remains of animals and plants.   *n.*

**Pa·le·o·zo·ic** (pā′lē ə zō′ik)   in geology:   1 of, having to do with, or referring to the era before the Mesozoic era, beginning about 600 million years ago: *The Paleozoic era is the age of fishes.*   2 of, having to do with, or referring to the system of rocks formed during this era.   3 the Paleozoic era or its rocks.   1, 2 *adj.*, 3 *n.*   See geological time chart in the Appendix.

A palette

**pal·ette** (pal′it) **1** a thin board, usually oval or oblong, with a thumb hole at one end, used by painters to lay and mix colours on. **2** a set of colours on this board. **3** the range or quality of colour used by an artist: *He uses a wide palette.* *n.*
☞ Hom. PALATE, PALLET.

**pal·frey** (pol′frē) a gentle riding horse, especially one used by ladies. *n., pl.* **pal·freys.**

**pal·imp·sest** (pal′imp sest′) parchment or other writing material from which one writing has been erased to make room for another; a manuscript with one text written over another. *n.*

**pal·in·drome** (pal′in drōm′) a word, phrase, or sentence which reads the same backward or forward. The sentence "Madam, I'm Adam" is a palindrome. *n.*

**pal·ing** (pā′ling) **1** a fence of pales. **2** a pale in a fence. **3** ppr. of PALE. 1, 2 *n.*, 3 *v.*

**pal·i·sade** (pal′ə sād′) **1** a fence of stakes set firmly in the ground to enclose or defend. **2** furnish or surround with a palisade. **3** a long, strong wooden stake pointed at the top end. **4** Usually, **palisades**, *pl.* a line of high, steep cliffs. 1, 3, 4 *n.*, 2 *v.*, **pal·i·sad·ed, pal·i·sad·ing.**

**palisade layer** the palisade PARENCHYMA, a layer of cells shaped like cylinders below the upper epidermis of many leaves and serving to produce chlorophyll.

**pall¹** (pol) **1** a heavy cloth, often made of velvet, spread over a coffin, a hearse, or a tomb. **2** a dark, gloomy covering: *a pall of fog.* *n.*
☞ Etym. From OE *pæll*, which came from L *pallium* 'cloak'.

**pall²** (pol) **1** become distasteful or very tiresome because there has been too much: *Even the most tasty food palls if it is served day after day.* **2** cloy. *v.*
☞ Etym. A shortened form of APPAL. 14c.

**pal·la·di·um** (pə lā′dē əm) a rare, silver-white metallic element, harder than platinum. *Symbol:* Pd *n.*

**pall·bear·er** (pol′ber′ər) a person who accompanies or helps to carry the coffin at a funeral. *n.*

**pal·let¹** (pal′it) **1** a straw bed. **2** a small, hard, or inferior bed. *n.*
☞ Hom. PALATE, PALETTE.

**pal·let²** (pal′it) **1** an instrument with a flat wooden blade, used by potters, etc. **2** a portable platform on which goods can be stacked and transported from place to place in a factory, warehouse, etc. *n.*
☞ Hom. PALATE, PALETTE.

**pal·li·ate** (pal′ē āt) **1** lessen without curing; MITIGATE: *to palliate a disease.* **2** make appear less serious; excuse: *to palliate a fault.* *v.*, **pal·li·at·ed, pal·li·at·ing.**

**pal·li·a·tive** (pal′ē ə tiv *or* pal′ē ā′tiv) **1** useful to lessen or soften; mitigating; excusing. **2** something that lessens, softens, MITIGATES, or excuses. **3** serving to control pain: *Palliative care is given to people who are not likely to live.* 1, 3 *adj.*, 2 *n.*

**pal·lid** (pal′id) lacking colour; having less colour than normal or usual; pale: *a pallid face.* *adj.*

**pal·lor** (pal′ər) a lack of colour from fear, illness, death, etc.; paleness. *n.*

**palm¹** (pom *or* päm) **1** the inside of the hand between the wrist and the fingers. **2** the part of a glove or mitten that covers this. **3** the width of the hand as a unit for measuring length; about 10 cm. **4** conceal in the hand: *The magician palmed a loony.* 1, 2, 3 *n.*, 4 *v.*
**grease the palm of,** bribe.
**have an itching palm,** be greedy for money.
**palm off,** pass off or get accepted by fraud or deceit: *The book she palmed off on me turned out to have some pages missing.*

Coconut palms

**palm²** (pom *or* päm) **1** any of a family of mainly tropical and subtropical trees, shrubs, and vines, most species having a tall, pillarlike trunk crowned by very large, fan-shaped or feather-shaped leaves. **2** a leaf of a palm tree used as a symbol of victory or triumph. **3** a victory; triumph. *n.*
**bear** or **carry off the palm,** be the victor; win: *She bore off the palm both in tennis and swimming.*
**yield the palm to,** admit defeat by.

**pal·mate** (pal′māt) **1** shaped like a hand with the fingers spread out; having lobes radiating from a central point: *a palmate leaf.* See LEAF for picture. **2** of birds, having the front toes joined by a web; web-footed. *adj.*

**pal·met·to** (pal met′ō) any of a closely related group of palms found in the Caribbean, Central America, and the southeastern United States, having fan-shaped leaves. *n., pl.* **pal·met·tos** or **pal·met·toes.**

**palm·ist** (pom′ist *or* pä′mist) a person who practises PALMISTRY. *n.*

**palm·is·try** (pom′i strē *or* pä′mi strē) the art or practice of telling a person's future or reading his or her character from the lines and marks in the palm of the hand. *n.*

**palm leaf** a leaf of a palm tree, used for making hats, baskets, fans, etc.

**palm oil** an edible yellow fat obtained from the fruit of several species of palm tree, used especially to make soap and candles.

**palm·y** (pom′ē *or* pä′mē) **1** abounding in palms. **2** flourishing; prosperous; glorious: *palmy days of peace.* *adj.*, **palm·i·er, palm·i·est.**

**pal·o·mi·no** (pal′ə mē′nō) a type of horse of mainly Arabian stock, having a cream, golden, or tan coat and a white or ivory mane and tail. *n., pl.* **pal·o·mi·nos.**

**palp** (palp) PALPUS. *n.*

**pal·pa·bil·i·ty** (pal′pə bil′ə tē)   the state or quality of being PALPABLE.   *n.*

**pal·pa·ble** (pal′pə bəl)   **1** readily seen or heard and recognized; obvious: *a palpable error.*   **2** that can be touched or felt.   *adj.*

**pal·pa·bly** (pal′pə blē)   **1** plainly; obviously.   **2** to the touch.   *adv.*

**pal·pi** (pal′pī *or* pal′pē)   pl. of PALPUS.   *n.*

**pal·pi·tate** (pal′pə tāt′)   **1** beat very rapidly; throb: *Your heart palpitates when you are excited.*   **2** quiver; tremble: *Her body palpitated with terror.*   *v.*, **pal·pi·tat·ed, pal·pi·tat·ing.**

**pal·pi·ta·tion** (pal′pə tā′shən)   **1** very rapid beating of the heart.   **2** a quivering; trembling.   *n.*

**pal·pus** (pal′pəs)   a jointed feeler attached to a mouth part of insects, spiders, lobsters, etc.: *Palpi are organs of touch or taste.*   *n., pl.* **pal·pi** (-pī *or* -pē).

**pal·sied** (pol′zēd)   suffering from PALSY (def. 1).   *adj.*

**pal·sy** (pol′zē)   **1** PARALYSIS.   **2** paralyse.   **1** *n., pl.* **pal·sies;**   **2** *v.*, **pal·sied, pal·sy·ing.**

**pal·try** (pol′trē)   **1** almost worthless; trifling: *a paltry sum of money.*   **2** petty; mean: *Pay no attention to paltry gossip.*   *adj.*, **pal·tri·er, pal·tri·est.**   —**pal′tri·ly,** *adv.*   —**pal′tri·ness,** *n.*

**pam·pas** (pam′pəs; *Spanish*, päm′päs)   the vast, almost treeless plains of South America south of the Amazon and east of the Andes, especially in central Argentina.   *n.pl.*

**pam·pas grass** (pam′pəs)   a tall, reedlike grass of southern South America having silvery plumes.

**pam·per** (pam′pər)   indulge too much; allow too many privileges to: *to pamper a child, to pamper one's appetite.*   *v.*   —**pam′per·er,** *n.*

**pam·phlet** (pam′flit)   a short printed work, usually with no binding or having a stapled paper cover: *A pamphlet often deals with a question of current interest.*   *n.*

**pam·phlet·eer** (pam′fli tēr′)   **1** a writer of PAMPHLETS.   **2** write and issue PAMPHLETS.   **1** *n.*, **2** *v.*

**pan**[1] (pan)   **1** a dish for cooking and other household uses, usually broad, shallow, and with no cover. Compare with SAUCEPAN.   **2** anything like this: *Gold and other metals are sometimes obtained by washing ore in pans.*   **3** cook in a pan.   **4** wash in a pan: *to pan gold.*   **5** wash gravel, sand, etc. in a pan to get gold.   **6** yield gold.   **7** in old-fashioned guns, the hollow part of the lock that held a little gunpowder to set the gun off.   **8** hard subsoil.   **9** *Informal.* criticize severely: *The drama critic panned the new play.*   **10** *Cdn.* Also, **ice-pan**, a flat cake of drifting ice, often having upturned edges.   1, 2, 7, 8, 10 *n.*, 3–6, 9 *v.*, **panned, pan·ning.**
**pan out,** *Informal.*   turn out: *His scheme panned out well.*

**pan**[2] (pan)   in motion pictures or television, move a camera so as to take in a whole scene, follow a moving character or object, etc.   *v.*, **panned, pan·ning.**

**pan·a·ce·a** (pan′ə sē′ə)   a remedy for all diseases or ills; a cure-all.   *n.*

**pan·a·ma** (pan′ə mä)   a fine hat woven from the young leaves of a palmlike plant of Central and South America.   *n.*

**Pan·a·ma·ni·an** (pan′ə mā′nē ən)   **1** of or having to do with Panama, a country on the Isthmus of Panama, or its people.   **2** a native or inhabitant of Panama.   **1** *adj.*, **2** *n.*

---

**palpability**   853   **pander**

hat, āge, fär; let, ēqual, tėrm; it, īce
hot, ōpen, ôrder; oil, out; cup, pùt, rüle
əbove, takən, pencəl, lemən, circəs
ch, child; ng, long; sh, ship
th, thin; ŦH, then; zh, measure

**Pan–A·mer·i·can** (pan′ə mer′ə kən)   **1** including all the independent republics of North, Central, and South America.   **2** of all Americans.   *adj.*

**Pan–A·mer·i·can·ism** (pan′ə mer′ə kə niz′əm)   the principle or policy that all the countries in South America, Central America, and North America should co-operate for the improvement of their welfare.   *n.*

**pan·cake** (pan′kāk′)   **1** a thin, flat cake of batter, cooked in a pan or on a griddle.   **2** PANCAKE LANDING.   **3** make such a landing: *The pilot pancaked the damaged plane onto an open field.*   1, 2 *n.*, 3 *v.*, **pan·caked, pan·cak·ing.**

**pancake landing**   a quick landing in which an aircraft is levelled off at a higher altitude than for a normal landing, a manoeuvre that causes it to stall and drop almost straight down while remaining in a horizontal position.

**pan·chro·mat·ic** (pan′krō mat′ik)   sensitive to light of all colours: *a panchromatic photographic film.*   *adj.*

**pan·cre·as** (pan′krē əs *or* pang′krē əs)   a large gland near the stomach that secretes digestive enzymes into the small intestine and the hormone insulin into the blood: *The pancreas of animals, when used for food, is called sweetbread.*   *n.*

**pan·cre·at·ic** (pan′krē at′ik *or* pang′krē at′ik)   of the PANCREAS: *The pancreatic juice aids digestion.*   *adj.*

Giant pandas— about 120 cm long

**pan·da** (pan′də)   **1** a large black-and-white, bearlike mammal found in the bamboo forests of Tibet and China; giant panda: *Zoologists differ on whether the panda is more closely related to the bears or the raccoons.*   **2** a small, mainly reddish-brown mammal found in the Himalayas, having a bushy tail, white face with a reddish stripe on each side, and soft, thick fur: *This panda, also called the lesser, or common, panda, belongs to the same family as the raccoon.*   *n.*

**pan·de·mo·ni·um** (pan′də mō′nē əm)   **1** a scene or place of wild disorder and confusion.   **2** wild disorder and confusion; tumult.   *n.*
☛ *Etym.* From *Pandæmonium* '(the home of) all demons', the name given by the poet John Milton (1608–1674) in *Paradise Lost* to the capital city of Satan and his fallen angels, made up by Milton as a Latin word from Gk. *pan-* 'all' + *daimōn* 'demon, spirit'. 17c.

**pan·der** (pan′dər)   **1** a person who caters to or exploits the weaknesses of others; one who helps people indulge evil designs or base passions.   **2** act as a pander; supply material or opportunity for vices (used with **to**): *The* newspaper pandered to people's liking for sensational stories. 1 *n.*, 2 *v.*

**pane** (pān)   a single sheet of glass in a window, a door, or a sash.   *n.*
☞ *Hom.* PAIN.
☞ *Etym.* Through Old French from L *pannus* 'piece of cloth', which was the original meaning in Middle English. This first meaning survives in COUNTERPANE. The current meaning dates from the 15c.

**pan·e·gyr·ic** (pan'ə jir'ik *or* pan'ə jī'rik)   **1** something written or spoken in praise of a person or thing; eulogy. **2** enthusiastic or extravagant praise.   *n.*

**pan·e·gyr·ist** (pan'ə jir'ist *or* pan'ə jī'rist)   a person who praises enthusiastically or extravagantly.   *n.*

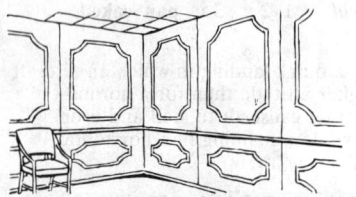
A wall with panels

A dress with a front panel

**pan·el** (pan'əl)   **1** a separate strip or surface that is usually set off in some way from what is around it: *Panels may be in a door or other woodwork, on large pieces of furniture, or made as parts of a dress.*   **2** arrange in panels; furnish or decorate with panels: *The room was panelled with oak.*   **3** a long, narrow picture, hanging, or design.   **4** a list of persons called as jurors; the members of a jury.   **5** a small group of persons selected for a special purpose, such as holding a discussion, judging a contest, or participating in a quiz: *The panel gave its opinion on the recent election.*   **6** a board containing the instruments, controls, or indicators used in operating an automobile, aircraft, computer, or other mechanism. 1, 3–6 *n.*, 2 *v.*, **pan·elled** *or* **pan·eled, pan·el·ling** *or* **pan·el·ing.**

**panel discussion**   the discussion of a particular issue by a selected group of people, usually experts.

**pan·el·ing** (pan'ə ling)   See PANELLING.   *n., v.*

**pan·el·ist** *or* **pan·el·list** (pan'ə list)   one of a group of persons making up a PANEL (def. 5).   *n.*

**pan·el·ling** *or* **pan·el·ing** (pan'ə ling)   **1** PANELS (def. 1) joined together to make a single surface, especially wooden panels forming a decorative wall surface: *We have pine panelling in the study.*   **2** ppr. of PANEL.   1 *n.*, 2 *v.*

**panel truck**   a small, light motor truck with a completely enclosed body.

**pan–fry** (pan'frī')   fry in a frying pan or skillet: *pan-fried fish.*   *v.*, **pan-fried, pan-fry·ing.**

**pang** (pang)   **1** a sudden, short, sharp pain: *the pangs of a toothache.*   **2** a sudden feeling of distress or anguish: *a pang of remorse.*   *n.*

**pan·go·lin** (pang gō'lən)   any of a small, closely related group of Asian and African mammals having a body covered with an armour of overlapping brownish scales, a long, toothless snout, and a long, wormlike tongue used for catching termites, ants, and other insects for food: *Pangolins curl up into a ball when they feel threatened.*   *n.*

**pan·han·dle**[1] (pan'han'dəl)   **1** the handle of a pan. **2** a narrow strip of land projecting like a handle: *the Alaska Panhandle.*   *n.*

**pan·han·dle**[2] (pan'han'dəl)   *Informal.*   beg, especially in the streets.   *v.*, **pan·han·dled, pan·han·dling.** —**pan'han'dler,** *n.*
☞ *Etym.* From the former custom of beggars who used a shallow pan to collect money or food.

**pan·ic** (pan'ik)   **1** a sudden fear that causes an individual or entire group to lose self-control; unreasoning fear: *When the theatre caught fire, there was a panic. When the stock market crashed, there was panic among investors.* **2** caused by panic; showing panic; unreasonable: *panic terror, panic haste.*   **3** lose control of oneself through fear: *The audience panicked when the fire broke out.*   **4** cause panic in.   1 *n.*, 2 *adj.*, 3, 4 *v.*, **pan·icked, pan·ick·ing.**
☞ *Etym.* Through French and modern Latin from Gk. *panikos* 'of or like Pan'. Pan was a Greek god of woods and fields whose presence was thought to cause terror. 17c.

**pan·ick·y** (pan'i kē)   **1** affected with panic; PANIC-STRICKEN: *She began to get panicky as the deadline approached.*   **2** liable to panic.   *adj.*

**pan·i·cle** (pan'ə kəl)   a loose, diversely branching flower cluster; a compound RACEME: *a panicle of oats.* See INFLORESCENCE for picture.   *n.*

**pan·ic–strick·en** (pan'ik strik'ən)   frightened out of one's wits; demoralized by fear.   *adj.*

A donkey carrying panniers

**pan·ni·er** (pan'ē ər)   a basket, especially one of a pair of considerable size, to be slung across the shoulders or across the back of a beast of burden.   *n.*

**pan·ni·kin** (pan'ə kin)   **1** a small pan.   **2** a metal cup or mug.   *n.*

**pan·o·plied** (pan'ə plēd)   covered with or dressed or arrayed in a PANOPLY.   *adj.*

**pan·o·ply** (pan'ə plē)   **1** a complete suit of armour. **2** complete equipment or covering: *a clown in panoply of comic dress and paint.*   *n., pl.* **pan·o·plies.**

**pan·o·ram·a** (pan'ə ram'ə)   **1** a wide, unbroken view of a surrounding region: *a panorama of beach and sea.*   **2** a complete survey of some subject: *a panorama of the development of the snowmobile.*   **3** a presentation of a landscape or other scene surrounding the spectator on all sides or gradually unrolled to pass continuously before the spectator's eyes.   **4** a continuously passing or changing scene: *the panorama of city life.*   *n.*

**pan·o·ram·ic** (pan'ə ram'ik)   of or like a PANORAMA: *a panoramic view.*   *adj.* —**pan'o·ram'i·cal·ly,** *adv.*

Pansies

hat, āge, fär; let, ēqual, tėrm; it, īce
hot, ōpen, ôrder; oil, out; cup, pu̇t, rüle
ǝbove, takǝn, pencǝl, lemǝn, circǝs
ch, child; ng, long; sh, ship
th, thin; ᴛʜ, then; zh, measure

**pan·sy** (pan′zē) **1** a common flowering garden plant of the violet family having large, showy flowers with velvety petals of several colours, usually combinations of blue, yellow, and white: *The pansy is a hybrid derived mainly from the wild pansy of Europe.* **2** the flower of this plant. *n., pl.* **pan·sies.**

**pant**[1] (pant) **1** breathe hard and quickly: *to pant from playing tennis. The dog panted in the heat.* **2** a short, quick breath. **3** speak with short, quick breaths: *"Come quick. Come quick," panted Jessica.* **4** long eagerly: *I am just panting for my turn.* **5** a throbbing or puffing sound: *the pant of an engine.* **6** throb; pulsate. *1, 3, 4, 6 v., 2, 5 n.*

**pan·ta·loon** (pan′tǝ lün′) **1** clown. **2 Pantaloon,** a character in traditional Italian comedy and in pantomime, a thin, foolish old man wearing spectacles, slippers, and pantaloons with stockings attached. **3 pantaloons,** *pl.* **a** wide breeches worn in England during the reign of Charles II. **b** close fitting trousers worn especially in the 19th century. *n.*

**pan·the·ism** (pan′thē iz′ǝm) **1** the belief that the universe is God. **2** the worship of the gods of all cultures together. *n.*

**pan·the·ist** (pan′thē ist) a person who believes in PANTHEISM. *n.*

**pan·the·is·tic** (pan′thē is′tik) of or having to do with PANTHEISM or pantheists. *adj.*

**pan·the·is·ti·cal·ly** (pan′thē is′ti klē) according to PANTHEISM; from a pantheist's point of view. *adv.*

**pan·the·on** (pan′thē on′ or pan′thē ǝn) **1** a temple dedicated to all the gods. **2** all the gods of a people, especially those that are officially recognized. **3** a public building containing tombs or memorials of the illustrious dead of a nation. **4** a group of illustrious people. **5 Pantheon,** in Rome, a temple for all the gods, built about 27 B.C. and later used as a Christian church. *n.*

**pan·ther** (pan′thǝr) any of several of the larger wild members of the cat family, such as the cougar, jaguar, or the black variety of leopard. *n., pl.* **pan·thers** or (*esp. collectively*) **pan·ther.**

**pan·tie** (pan′tē) PANTIES. *n.* Also, **panty.**

**pan·ties** (pan′tēz) **1** an undergarment worn by women and girls, covering the lower part of the body and having separate leg holes or short legs. **2** a similar undergarment for babies and young children. *n.pl.*

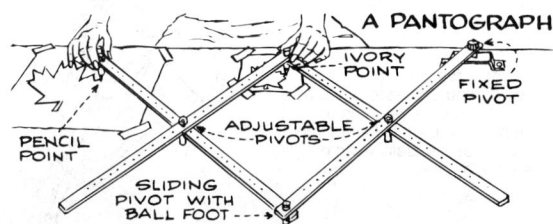
A PANTOGRAPH — IVORY POINT, FIXED PIVOT, ADJUSTABLE PIVOTS, PENCIL POINT, SLIDING PIVOT WITH BALL FOOT

**pan·to·graph** (pan′tǝ graf′) an instrument for copying plans, drawings, etc. to any scale desired. *n.*

**pan·to·mime** (pan′tǝ mīm′) **1** a play without words, in which the actors express themselves by gestures. **2** gestures without words. **3** express by gestures. *1, 2 n., 3 v.,* **pan·to·mimed, pan·to·mim·ing.**

**pan·to·mim·ic** (pan′tǝ mim′ik) of, in, or like PANTOMIME. *adj.*

**pan·to·mim·ist** (pan′tǝ mī′mist) an actor in a PANTOMIME. *n.*

**pan·to·then·ic acid** (pan′tǝ then′ik) an oily acid belonging to the VITAMIN B COMPLEX and found in all living tissues.

**pan·to·there** (pan′tǝ thėr′) an extinct mammal which lived during the Mesozoic Era: *Pantotheres may be the ancestors of marsupials. n.*

**pan·try** (pan′trē) **1** a small airy room used for storing food that must be kept cold. **2** a similar room in which food, dishes, silverware, table linen, etc. are kept. *n., pl.* **pan·tries.**

**pants** (pants) **1** trousers. **2** panties. *n.pl.*

**pant·suit** (pant′süt′) a suit for women, consisting of a jacket and long pants. *n.*

**pan·ty** (pan′tē) See PANTIE. *n.*

**panty hose** a garment for women, consisting of sheer stockings knitted in one piece with a pantie-like top of the same or slightly heavier material. Also, **pantyhose, panty-hose.**

**pan·zer** (pan′zǝr; *German*, pän′tsǝʀ) armoured, or mechanized and armoured: *A panzer division consists largely of tanks. adj.*

**pap** (pap) **1** soft food for infants or invalids. **2** ideas or facts watered down so that they have no force or value. *n.*

**pa·pa** (pop′ǝ *or* pä′pǝ) father; daddy. *n.*

**pa·pa·cy** (pā′pǝ sē) **1** the position, rank, or authority of the Pope. **2** the time during which a pope rules. **3** all the popes. **4** government by the Pope. *n., pl.* **pa·pa·cies.**

**pa·pal** (pā′pǝl) **1** of the Pope: *a papal letter.* **2** of the papacy. **3** of the Roman Catholic Church: *papal ritual. adj.*

**pa·paw** (pop′o) See PAWPAW. *n.*

**pa·pa·ya** (pǝ pä′yǝ) **1** a tropical American tree having a straight, palmlike trunk with a tuft of large leaves at the top and edible, melonlike fruit with yellowish pulp. **2** the fruit. *n.*

**pa·per** (pā′pǝr) **1** a material in the form of thin sheets made from wood pulp, rags, etc. and used for writing, printing, wrapping packages, and many other purposes: *This book is made of paper.* **2** a piece or sheet of paper. **3** a piece or sheet of paper with writing or printing on it; document: *Important papers were stolen.* **4** a wrapper, container, or sheet of paper containing something. **5** newspaper. **6** an article; essay: *Professor Smith read a paper on the teaching of English.* **7** a written examination. **8** a written promise to pay money; note.

**paperback**    856    **parachute**

**9** paper money.    **10** cover with paper, especially wallpaper: *to paper a room.*    **11** made of paper: *paper dolls.*    **12** like paper; thin: *almonds with paper shells.*    **13** existing only on paper: *When she tried to sell, her paper profits disappeared.*    **14** wallpaper.    **15 papers,** *pl.* documents telling who or what one is.    1–9, 14, 15 *n.,* 10 *v.,* 11–13 *adj.*    —**pa′per·er,** *n.*    —**pa′per·like′,** *adj.*
**on paper, a** in writing or in print. **b** in theory: *The plan looks all right on paper but it may not work.*
☛ *Etym.* Through OF *papier* from L *papyrus,* which came from Gk. *papūros* 'papyrus', a plant from which the ancient Egyptians made a material for writing on.

**pa·per·back** (pā′pər bak′)    a book with a flexible paper binding and cover, especially one that is smaller and less expensive than a hardcover edition.    *n.*

**pa·per·boy** (pā′pər boi′)    a boy who delivers or sells newspapers.    *n.*

**paper clip**    a flat clip of flexible bent wire, used to slip over the edge of a small bundle of loose sheets to hold them together.

**pa·per·girl** (pā′pər gėrl′)    a girl who delivers or sells newspapers.    *n.*

**pa·per·hang·er** (pā′pər hang′ər)    a person whose work is applying wallpaper.    *n.*

**paper knife**    a knife with a blade of metal, wood, ivory, etc., used to slit open letters or uncut pages of books.

**paper money**    money made of paper, not metal: *A five-dollar bill is paper money.*

**paper nautilus**    a small sea animal with eight arms, belonging to the same order as the octopus: *The female paper nautilus produces a very thin, paperlike shell in which the young are hatched and which the animal casts off afterwards.*

**paper profits**    PROFITS existing on paper, but not yet realized.

**pa·per·weight** (pā′pər wāt′)    a small, heavy object put on papers to keep them from being scattered.    *n.*

**pa·per·work** (pā′pər wėrk′)    work done on or with paper, such as writing, filing, or other clerical work: *She hates all the paperwork involved in her job.*    *n.*

**pa·per·y** (pā′pə rē)    thin like paper.    *adj.*

**pa·pier–mâ·ché** (pā′pər ma shā′; *French,* pä pyā mä shā′)    **1** a paper pulp mixed with some stiffener and used for modelling. It becomes hard and strong when dry.    **2** made of papier-mâché.    *n.*
☛ *Etym.* Made up in English from F *papier* 'paper' + *mâché* 'chewed'. 18c.

**pa·pil·la** (pə pil′ə)    **1** a small, nipple-like projection. **2** one of certain small protuberances concerned with the senses of touch, taste, or smell: *the papillae on the tongue.*    *n., pl.* **pap·il·lae** (-lē or -lī).

**pa·pil·lae** (pə pil′ē *or* pə pil′ī)    pl. of PAPILLA.    *n.*

**pap·il·lar·y** (pap′ə ler′ē *or* pə pil′ə rē)    **1** of or like a PAPILLA.    **2** having PAPILLAE.    *adj.*

**pa·poose** (pa püs′ *or* pə püs′)    a North American Indian baby.    *n.*
☛ *Etym.* From an Algonquian word meaning 'child'.

**pap·pi** (pap′ī *or* pap′ē)    pl. of PAPPUS.    *n.*

**pap·pus** (pap′əs)    an appendage to a seed, often made of down or bristles: *Dandelion and thistle seeds have pappi.*    *n., pl.* **pap·pi** (pap′ī *or* pap′ē).

**pap·ri·ka** (pap′rə kə *or* pa prē′kə)    **1** a kind of mild, red-coloured pepper made of the dried, ground-up pods of any of various sweet-pepper plants.    **2** a pod of pepper used for making paprika.    *n.*

**Pap·u·an** (pap′yü ən)    **1** any of a group of very different languages spoken in New Guinea, New Britain, and the Solomon Islands.    **2** a member of any of the Papuan-speaking peoples who live in this area.    **3** of or having to do with Papua, the peoples living there, or their languages.    1, 2 *n.,* 3 *adj.*

**pa·py·rus** (pə pī′rəs)    **1** a tall water plant of the Nile valley from which the ancient Egyptians, Greeks, and Romans made a kind of paper.    **2** a writing material made from its pith.    **3** an ancient record written on papyrus.    *n., pl.* **pa·py·ri** (-rī *or* -rē).
☛ *Etym.* See note at PAPER.

**par** (pär)    **1** equality; an equal level: *The gains and losses are about on a par. She is quite on a par with her sister in intelligence.*    **2** an average or normal amount, degree, or condition: *A sick person feels below par.*    **3** average; normal.    **4** the value of a bond, a note, a share of stock, etc. that is printed on it; face value: *That stock is selling above par.*    **5** the established normal value of the money of one country in terms of the money of another country. **6** of or at par.    **7** in golf, the number of strokes set as an expert score for a course or for any one hole.    1, 2, 4, 5, 7 *n.,* 3, 6 *adj.*

**par for the course,** *Informal.*    that which is normal or to be expected.

**par.**    **1** paragraph.    **2** parallel.    **3** parenthesis. **4** parish.

**para–¹**    a prefix meaning:    **1** beside, near, or beyond, as in *parathyroid, parapsychology.*    **2** functionally disordered, as in *paranoia.* Also, **par-.**

**para–²**    combining form.    that uses a parachute, as in *paratrooper.*

**para.**    paragraph.

**par·a·ble** (par′ə bəl *or* per′ə bəl)    a short, simple story used to teach a truth or moral lesson.    *n.*

**pa·rab·o·la** (pə rab′ə lə)    a curve formed by the intersection of a cone with a plane parallel to one side of the cone: *If there is no wind resistance, an arrow will travel in a parabola.*    See CONE for picture.    *n., pl.* **pa·rab·o·las.**

**par·a·bol·ic¹** (par′ə bol′ik *or* per′ə bol′ik)    having to do with or resembling a PARABOLA.    *adj.*

**par·a·bol·ic²** (par′ə bol′ik *or* per′ə bol′ik)    of, having to do with, or expressed in a PARABLE.    *adj.*

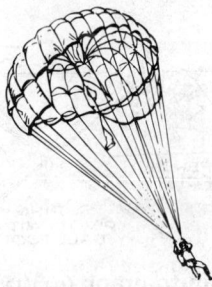

A woman descending by parachute. The parachute is fastened to a harness worn by the jumper. When not in use it is folded into a pack that is usually worn on the back or chest.

**par·a·chute** (par′ə shüt′ *or* per′ə shüt′)    **1** an

apparatus made to give a slow, gradual fall to a person or thing that jumps or is dropped from an aircraft: *The top of a parachute resembles that of an umbrella and is made from nylon or silk.* **2** come or send down by a parachute: *The pilot of the burning plane parachuted to the ground.* **1** *n.,* **2** *v.,* **par·a·chut·ed, par·a·chut·ing.**

**par·a·chut·ist** (par′ə shü′tist *or* per′ə shü′tist) a person who uses a parachute; a person skilled in making descents with a parachute. *n.*

**pa·rade** (pə rād′) **1** a march for display; procession: *The circus had a parade.* **2** march through with display: *The performers and animals paraded the streets.* **3** march in procession; walk proudly as if in a parade. **4** a group of people walking for display or pleasure. **5** a place where people walk for display or pleasure. **6** a great show or display: *A modest woman will not make a parade of her wealth.* **7** make a great show of. **8** a military display or review of troops. **9** come together in military order for review or inspection. **10** assemble troops for review. **11** a parade ground or parade square. 1, 4–6, 8, 11 *n.,* 2, 3, 7, 9, 10 *v.,* **pa·rad·ed, pa·rad·ing.** —**pa·rad′er,** *n.*

**parade square** the area where troops parade, drill, etc.

**par·a·digm** (par′ə dīm′ *or* per′ə dīm′, par′ə dim′ *or* per′ə dim′) **1** a pattern; example. **2** an example of a noun, verb, pronoun, etc. in all its inflections. *n.* —**pa′ra·dig·mat′ic,** *adj.*

**par·a·dise** (par′ə dīs′ *or* per′ə dīs′) **1** heaven. **2** a place or condition of great happiness. **3** a place of great beauty. **4** the garden of Eden. *n.*
☞ *Etym.* From Old French *paradis,* which came originally from Gk. *paradeisos* 'an enclosed private park (such as those of wealthy Persians)', which came from Old Persian *pairidaēza,* made up of *pairi* 'around' (related to *peri*-) + *daēza* 'wall', from *diz* 'mould (with clay), smear, knead'. See also note at LADY.

**par·a·dox** (par′ə doks′ *or* per′ə doks′) **1** a statement that may be true but seems to say two opposite things: *"More haste, less speed"* and *"The child is father of the man"* are paradoxes. **2** a statement that is false because it says two opposite things. **3** a person or thing that seems to be full of contradictions. *n.*

**par·a·dox·i·cal** (par′ə dok′sə kəl *or* per′ə dok′sə kəl) **1** of or involving a PARADOX. **2** having the habit of using PARADOXes. *adj.* —**par′a·dox′i·cal·ly,** *adv.*

**par·af·fin** (par′ə fin *or* per′ə fin) **1** a flammable, white, waxy substance that is a mixture of HYDROCARBONS obtained especially from petroleum or shale, used for making candles or for coating or sealing. **2** treat with paraffin. 1 *n.,* 2 *v.*

**par·a·gon** (par′ə gon′ *or* per′ə gon′) a model of excellence or perfection. *n.*

**par·a·graph** (par′ə graf′ *or* per′ə graf′) **1** a group of sentences relating to the same idea or topic and forming a distinct part of a chapter, letter, or other piece of writing: *Paragraphs usually begin on a new line and may be indented.* **2** divide into paragraphs. **3** a separate note or item of news in a newspaper. **4** write paragraphs about. **5** a sign (¶) used to show where a paragraph begins or should begin: *The paragraph sign is used mostly in correcting written work.* 1, 3, 5 *n.,* 2, 4 *v.* —**par′a·graph′er,** *n.*

**Par·a·guay·an** (par′ə gwā′ən *or* par′ə gwā′ən, par′ə gwī′ən *or* per′ə gwī′ən) **1** of or having to do with Paraguay, a country in central South America, or its inhabitants. **2** a native or inhabitant of Paraguay. 1 *adj.,* 2 *n.*

**par·a·keet** (par′ə kēt′ *or* per′ə kēt′) any of various small parrots, most of which have slender bodies and long tails. *n.*

Parallax. The trees appear to be in different positions in relation to the building when viewed from different points.

**par·al·lax** (par′ə laks′ *or* per′ə laks′) the apparent change or amount of change in the direction or position of an object as seen from two different points. *n.*

**par·al·lel** (par′ə lel′ *or* per′ə lel′) **1** at or being the same distance apart everywhere, like the two rails of a railway track. **2** a parallel line or surface. **3** any of the imaginary circles around the earth parallel to the equator, marking degrees of latitude: *The 49th parallel marks much of the boundary between Canada and the United States.* See LATITUDE for picture. **4** the markings on a map that represent these circles. **5** to be at the same distance from throughout the length: *The street parallels the railway.* **6** cause to be or run parallel to. **7** similar; corresponding: *parallel points in the characters of different men.* **8** something like or similar to another: *Her experience was an interesting parallel to ours.* **9** be like; be similar to: *Your story closely parallels what she told me.* **10** find a case that is similar or parallel to: *Can you parallel that for friendliness?* **11** a comparison to show likeness: *to draw a parallel between this winter and last winter.* **12** compare in order to show likeness. **13** an arrangement of the wiring of batteries, lights, etc. in which electric current can run along two or more alternative paths. Compare with SERIES. 1, 7 *adj.,* 2–4, 8, 11, 13 *n.,* 5, 6, 9, 10, 12 *v.,* **par·al′lelled** *or* **par·al′leled, par·al′lel·ling** *or* **par·al′lel·ing.**

**par·al·lel·ism** (par′ə le liz′əm *or* per′ə le liz′əm) **1** the quality or state of being PARALLEL. **2** a likeness; similarity; correspondence; agreement. **3** in writing, a balance between parts of a sentence or paragraph, obtained by echoing structure or style. *n.*

**par·al·lel·o·gram** (par′ə lel′ə gram′ *or* per′ə lel′ə gram′) a four-sided plane figure having opposite sides parallel and equal: *Squares, rhombuses, and rhomboids are parallelograms.* See QUADRILATERAL for picture. *n.*

**par·a·lyse** *or* **par·a·lyze** (par′ə līz′ *or* per′ə līz′) **1** affect with a lessening or loss of the power of motion or feeling in a part of the body: *Her left arm was paralysed after the accident.* **2** make powerless or ineffective;

# paralysis — pardon

cripple: *The whole project was paralysed when the funds were cut off.* **3** stun or deaden: *paralysed with fear.* *v.*, **par·a·lysed** or **par·a·lyzed, par·a·lys·ing** or **par·a·lyz·ing.**

**pa·ral·y·sis** (pə ral′ə sis) **1** a lessening or loss of the power of motion or sensation in any part of the body: *The accident left her with paralysis of the legs.* **2** a condition of powerlessness or helpless inactivity; crippling: *The war caused a paralysis of trade.* *n., pl.* **pa·ral·y·ses** (-sēz′).

**par·a·lyt·ic** (par′ə lit′ik *or* per′ə lit′ik) **1** of, having to do with, or like paralysis. **2** having paralysis: *a paralytic limb.* **3** person who has paralysis. 1, 2 *adj.*, 3 *n.*

**par·a·lyze** (par′ə līz′ *or* per′ə līz′) See PARALYSE. *v.*

**par·a·me·ci·um** (par′ə mē′sē əm *or* per′ə mē′sē əm) any of a closely related group of free-swimming, one-celled creatures shaped somewhat like the sole of a slipper, completely covered with cilia and having a groove along one side leading into the mouth cavity. *n., pl.* **par·a·me·ci·a** (-sē ə *or* -shē ə).

**par·a·med·ic** (par′ə med′ik *or* per′ə med′ik) a person trained in PARAMEDICAL work. *n.*

**par·a·med·i·cal** (par′ə med′ə kal *or* per′ə med′ə kəl) of, having to do with, or referring to auxiliary medical personnel such as medical technicians, X-ray technicians, or midwives, or the work they do. *adj.*

**pa·ram·e·ter** (pə ram′ə tər) **1** in mathematics, a quantity that is constant in a particular calculation or case but varies in other cases. **2** any of a set of measurable features or properties that determine the characteristics or behaviour of something: *parameters of space and time.* **3** any limiting or defining element or feature: *She found the parameters of her life too restricting.* *n.*

**par·a·mount** (par′ə mount′ *or* per′ə mount′) chief in importance; above others; supreme: *Truth is of paramount importance.* *adj.*

**par·a·mour** (par′ə mür′ *or* per′ə mür′) a person who takes the place of a husband or wife illegally. *n.*

**par·a·noi·a** (par′ə noi′ə *or* per′ə noi′ə) a serious mental illness characterized by the firm belief that one is being persecuted, or by delusions of grandeur. *n.*

**pa·ra·noi·ac** (par′ə noi′ak *or* per′ə noi′ak) PARANOID. *adj., n.*

**par·a·noid** (par′ə noid′ *or* per′ə noid′) **1** of, like, or showing PARANOIA. **2** having an extreme tendency to mistrust people and suspect them of ill will or bad intentions. **3** a person suffering from PARANOIA. 1, 2 *adj.*, 3 *n.*

**par·a·pet** (par′ə pet′ *or* per′ə pet′) **1** a low wall or mound of stone, earth, etc. to protect soldiers. **2** a low wall at the edge of a balcony, roof, bridge, etc. See FORT for picture. *n.*

**par·a·pher·nal·ia** (par′ə fə nā′lē ə *or* per′ə fə nā′lē ə, par′ə fər nā′lyə *or* per′ə fər nā′lyə) **1** personal belongings: *All her paraphernalia was out in the hall, ready to be shipped.* **2** equipment; outfit: *Military paraphernalia includes guns, rifles, and ammunition.* *n. sing. or pl.*

**par·a·phrase** (par′ə frāz′ *or* per′ə frāz′) **1** state the meaning of a passage in other and different words. **2** an expression of the meaning of a passage in other words. 1 *v.*, **par·a·phrased, par·a·phras·ing**; 2 *n.*

**par·a·ple·gi·a** (par′ə plē′jē ə *or* per′ə plē′jē ə) paralysis of the legs and the lower part of the trunk. *n.*

**par·a·ple·gic** (par′ə plē′jik *or* per′ə plē′jik, par′ə plej′ik *or* per′ə plej′ik) **1** a person afflicted with PARAPLEGIA. **2** having to do with, or afflicted with, PARAPLEGIA. 1 *n.*, 2 *adj.*

**par·a·psy·chol·o·gy** (par′ə sī kol′ə jē *or* per′ə sī kol′ə jē) the study of mental phenomena not explainable in terms of known physical laws, such as clairvoyance, telepathy, and psychokinesis. *n.*

**par·a·site** (par′ə sīt′ *or* per′ə sīt′) **1** an animal or plant that lives on or in another, from which it gets its food: *Lice and tapeworms are parasites. Mistletoe is a parasite on oak trees.* **2** a person who lives on others without making any useful and fitting return; hanger-on: *The lazy woman was a parasite on her family.* *n.*

**par·a·sit·ic** (par′ə sit′ik *or* per′ə sit′ik) of or like a PARASITE; living on others. *adj.*
—**par′a·sit′i·cal·ly,** *adv.*

**par·a·sit·ism** (par′ə si tiz′əm *or* per′ə si tiz′əm) a form of SYMBIOSIS in which one organism lives in or on another organism. Compare with AMENSALISM, COMMENSALISM, and MUTUALISM. *n.*

**par·a·sol** (par′ə sol′ *or* per′ə sol′) a light umbrella used as a protection from the sun. *n.*
☛ *Etym.* Through French from Italian *parasole,* made up of *para-,* from *parare* 'to defend or shelter from', + *sole* 'sun'.

**par·a·thy·roid gland** (par′ə thī′roid *or* per′ə thī′roid) any of usually four small glands situated near or imbedded in the THYROID GLAND and producing a hormone that regulates the level of calcium in the body: *The hormone of the parathyroid gland is necessary for life.*

**par·a·troop·er** (par′ə trü′pər *or* per′ə trü′pər) a soldier trained to use a parachute for descent from an aircraft into a battle area. *n.*

**par·a·troops** (par′ə trüps′ *or* per′ə trüps′) troops moved by air and landed by parachutes in a battle area. *n. pl.*

**par·boil** (pär′boil′) **1** boil till partly cooked: *to parboil beans before baking them.* **2** overheat. *v.*

**par·cel** (pär′səl) **1** a bundle of things wrapped or packed together; package: *The lady had her arms filled with parcels of gifts.* **2** a container with things packed in it: *Put your shirts in this parcel.* **3** a piece: *a parcel of land.* **4** a group; lot; pack: *a parcel of liars.* **5** make a parcel of. 1–4 *n.*, 5 *v.*, **par·celled** or **par·celed, par·cel·ling** or **par·cel·ing.**

**parcel out,** divide into portions or distribute in portions.

**parcel post 1** a class of postal service for sending heavy or large parcels. **2** mail handled by this service.

**parch** (pärch) **1** make hot and dry or thirsty: *The fever parched her.* **2** become dry, hot, or thirsty: *She was parched with the heat.* **3** dry by heating; roast slightly: *Corn is sometimes parched.* *v.*

**parch·ment** (pärch′mənt) **1** the skin of sheep, goats, etc. prepared for use as writing material. **2** a manuscript or document written on parchment. **3** a kind of paper that looks like parchment. *n.*

**par·don** (pär′dən) **1** forgiveness; excuse: *I beg your pardon but I'm afraid I am late.* **2** forgive; excuse: *She pardoned his bad manners.* **3** set free from punishment:

*The Governor General pardoned the criminal.* **4** a setting free from punishment. **5** a legal document setting a person free from punishment. *1, 4, 5 n., 2, 3 v.*

**par·don·a·ble** (pär′də nə bəl)  that can be pardoned; excusable.  *adj.* —**par′don·a·bly,** *adv.*

**par·don·er** (pär′də nər)  a person who pardons.  *n.*

**pare** (per)  **1** trim by cutting away irregular bits: *to pare a corn.*  **2** cut or shave off the outer skin or layer of; peel: *to pare an apple.*  **3** cut away or lessen little by little: *We're trying to pare expenses.* *v.,* **pared, par·ing.** ☞ *Hom.* PAIR, PEAR.

**par·e·gor·ic** (par′ə gôr′ik *or* per′ə gô′rik)  **1** a soothing medicine containing camphor and a little opium. **2** soothing.  *1 n., 2 adj.*

**paren.** parenthesis.

**pa·ren·chy·ma** (pə reng′kə mə)  **1** in botany, the tissue that makes up much of the substance of the softer parts of leaves, the pulp of fruits, the pith of stems, etc., composed of thin-walled, unspecialized, living cells.  **2** in anatomy, the essential, functional tissue of an animal organ, as distinguished from its connective or supporting tissue.  *n.*

**par·ent** (per′ənt)  **1** a father or mother.  **2** any living thing that produces offspring or seed.  **3** a source; cause: *Danger is the parent of fear.*  **4** take care of a child or children: *Parenting classes are often given in high school.* *1–3 n., 4 v.*

**par·ent·age** (per′ən tij)  descent from parents; family line; ancestry: *a child of unknown parentage.*  *n.*

**pa·ren·tal** (pə ren′təl)  of or having to do with a parent or parents; like a parent's: *parental advice.*  *adj.* —**pa·ren′tal·ly,** *adv.*

**pa·ren·the·ses** (pə ren′thə sēz′)  pl. of PARENTHESIS.  *n.*

**pa·ren·the·sis** (pə ren′thə sis)  **1** a word, phrase, or sentence, inserted within a sentence to explain or qualify something, and usually set off by brackets, commas, or dashes: *A parenthesis is not grammatically essential to the sentence it is in.*  **2** either or both of two curved lines ( ) used to set off such an expression; bracket.  *n., pl.* **pa·ren·the·ses.**

**par·en·thet·ic** (par′ən thet′ik *or* per′ən thet′ik) **1** qualifying; explanatory.  **2** put in parentheses. **3** using parentheses.  *adj.* —**par′en·thet′i·cal·ly,** *adv.*

**par·en·thet·i·cal** (par′ən thet′ə kəl *or* per′ən thet′ə kəl) PARENTHETIC.  *adj.*

**pa·rent·hood** (per′ənt hud′)  the state of being a parent.  *n.*

**Parent–Teacher Association**  an organization made up of parents and teachers who meet from time to time in the interests of schoolchildren.  *Abbrev.:* PTA or P.T.A.

**pa·re·sis** (pə rē′sis)  **1** an incomplete paralysis that affects the ability to move, but does not affect ability to feel.  **2** a disease of the brain that gradually causes general paralysis.  *n.*

**pa·ret·ic** (pə ret′ik *or* pə rē′tik)  **1** of, having to do with, or caused by PARESIS.  **2** a person having PARESIS. *1 adj., 2 n.*

**par ex·cel·lence** (pä rek sə läns′; *French,* pä Rek se läns′)  beyond comparison; above all others of the same sort.

---

# pardonable 859 park

hat, āge, fär; let, ēqual, tèrm; it, īce
hot, ōpen, ôrder; oil, out; cup, pủt, rüle
əbove, takən, pencəl, lemən, circəs
ch, child; ng, long; sh, ship
th, thin; ᴛн, then; zh, measure

**par·fait** (pär fā′; *French,* päR fe′)  **1** ice cream with syrup or crushed fruit and whipped cream, served in a tall glass.  **2** a rich ice cream, containing eggs and whipped cream, frozen unstirred.  *n.*

**par·he·li·on** (pär hē′lē ən)  a bright, circular spot on a solar halo.  *n., pl.* **par·he·li·a** (-hē′lē ə).

**pa·ri·ah** (pə rī′ə)  **1** outcast.  **2** a member of a low CASTE in southern India and Burma.  *n.*

**pa·ri·e·tal** (pə rī′ə təl)  in anatomy:  **1** of the wall of the body or of one of its cavities.  **2** either of two bones that form part of the sides and top of the skull.  *1 adj., 2 n.*

**par·i–mu·tu·el** (par′ē myü′chü əl *or* per′ē myü′chü əl) **1** a system of betting on horse races in which those who have bet on the winning horses divide the money lost by the losers.  **2** a machine for recording such bets.  *n.*

**par·ing** (per′ing)  **1** a part pared off; skin; rind: *apple parings.*  **2** ppr. of PARE.  *1 n., 2 v.*

**Paris green**  a very poisonous, emerald-green powder used as an INSECTICIDE and pigment: *Paris green is a compound of copper, arsenic, and acetic acid.*

**par·ish** (par′ish *or* per′ish)  **1** a district that has its own church and minister or priest.  **2** the people of a parish. **3** the members of the congregation of a particular church. **4** in New Brunswick, a political unit similar to a township. **5** in Quebec, a civil district; a municipality similar to a township and related to a religious parish.  **6** in the United Kingdom, a civil district.  *n.*
☞ *Hom.* PERISH (for the second pronunciation of **parish**).

**pa·rish·ion·er** (pə rish′ə nər)  a member of a PARISH.  *n.*

**Pa·ri·sian** (pə rizh′ən)  **1** of or having to do with Paris, the capital of France, or its people.  **2** a native or inhabitant of Paris.  *1 adj., 2 n.*

**par·i·ty** (par′ə tē *or* per′ə tē)  **1** equality; similarity or close correspondence with regard to state, position, condition, value, quality, degree, etc.  **2** the balance between the market prices for a farmer's commodities and his or her own gross expenditures.  *n.*

**park** (pärk)  **1** a piece of land in or near a city, town, etc. set apart for public recreation: *Let's have a picnic in the park.*  **2** a large area of land kept in a natural state as a recreation area (for camping, picnicking, hiking, canoeing, etc.) and as a refuge for wildlife: *Canada has fine national and provincial parks.*  **3** the grounds around a fine house.  **4** leave an automobile, etc. for a time in a certain place.  **5** a place to leave an automobile, etc. for a time.  **6** a space where army vehicles, supplies, and artillery are put when an army camps.  **7** arrange army vehicles, artillery, etc. in a park.  **8** *Informal.* place, put, or leave: *Just park your books on the table.*  **9** a commercially operated recreation area with facilities for picnicking, swimming, etc.  *1–3, 5, 6, 9 n., 4, 7, 8 v.*

A traditional Inuit parka

A style of parka commonly worn in most parts of Canada in winter

**par·ka** (pär′kə)   1 a fur jacket with a hood, worn in the North.   2 a long, warm jacket with a hood, worn in winter.   *n.*

**parking lot**   an area used for parking motor vehicles.

**parking meter**   a device containing a coin-operated clock mechanism for indicating the amount of parking time that has been bought for a vehicle.

**park·land** (pärk′land′)   1 the region between the foothills of the Rockies and the prairie.   2 the wooded region between the Barrens and the prairie.   3 land kept free from buildings, factories, etc. and maintained as a public park: *Parklands are intended to preserve the scenic beauty of the countryside.   n.*

**park·way** (pärk′wā′)   a broad road through an area kept up as a park, made attractive by grass, trees, flowers, etc.: *There is a beautiful parkway running through Ottawa.   n.*

**par·lance** (pär′ləns)   a way of speaking; idiom: *The will was written in legal parlance.   n.*

**par·lay** (pär′lā *or* pär′lē)   1 risk an original bet and its winnings on another bet.   2 build up by taking risks: *She parlayed a few hundred dollars into a fortune.*   3 a series of bets made by parlaying.   1, 2 *v.,* 3 *n.*
☛ *Hom.* PARLEY (for the second pronunciation of **parlay**).

**par·ley** (pär′lē)   1 a conference or informal talk, especially one with an enemy, to discuss terms of surrender, exchange of prisoners, etc.   2 discuss terms, especially with an enemy.   1 *n., pl.* **par·leys;**   2 *v.,* **par·leyed, par·ley·ing.**
☛ *Hom.* PARLAY (pär′lā).

**par·lia·ment** (pär′lə mənt)   1 the highest law-making body in certain countries.   2 **Parliament, a** the national lawmaking body of Canada: *Parliament consists of the Senate and the House of Commons.*   **b** the national lawmaking body of the United Kingdom: *Parliament consists of the House of Lords and the House of Commons.*   **c** the lawmaking body of a country or colony having the British system of government.   *n.*

**par·lia·men·tar·i·an** (pär′lə men ter′ē ən)   a person skilled in PARLIAMENTARY (def. 2) procedure or debate.   *n.*

**par·lia·men·ta·ry** (pär′lə men′tə rē)   1 of a PARLIAMENT: *parliamentary authority.*   2 according to the rules and customs of a PARLIAMENT or other lawmaking body: *Our debating society is run by the rules of parliamentary procedure.*   3 done by a PARLIAMENT.   4 having a PARLIAMENT: *a parliamentary democracy.*   *adj.*

**par·lor** (pär′lər)   See PARLOUR.   *n.*

**par·lour** *or* **par·lor** (pär′lər)   1 a room for receiving or entertaining guests; sitting room or living room.   2 a room or rooms specially furnished or equipped for a certain kind of business: *a beauty parlour, a funeral parlour.*   3 a place where refreshments of various kinds are sold: *an ice-cream parlour, a beer parlour.   n.*

**parlour car** *or* **parlor car**   formerly, a CLUB CAR.

**Par·me·san** (pär′mə zan′)   a very hard, dry Italian cheese with a sharp flavour, usually used in grated form.   *n.*

**pa·ro·chi·al** (pə rō′kē əl)   1 of or in a PARISH: *parochial affairs.*   2 narrow; limited: *a parochial viewpoint.   adj.*

**pa·ro·chi·al·ism** (pə rō′kē ə liz′əm)   a parochial character, spirit, or tendency; narrowness of interests or views.   *n.*

**parochial school**   a school maintained by a church.

**par·o·dist** (par′ə dist *or* per′ə dist)   a writer of parodies.   *n.*

**par·o·dy** (par′ə dē *or* per′ə dē)   1 a humorous imitation of a serious writing: *A parody follows the form of the original, but changes its sense to nonsense, thus making fun of the characteristics of the original.*   2 any work of art that makes fun of another.   3 make fun of by imitating; make a parody on.   4 a poor imitation.   5 imitate poorly.   1, 2, 4 *n., pl.* **par·o·dies;**   3, 5 *v.,* **par·o·died, par·o·dy·ing.**

**pa·role** (pə rōl′)   1 a conditional release from prison or jail before the full term is served: *The prisoner was released on parole.*   2 give a parole: *The girls were paroled on condition that they report to the judge every three months.*   3 conditional freedom allowed in place of imprisonment.   4 word of honour: *The prisoner of war gave his parole not to try to escape.*   1, 3, 4 *n.,* 2 *v.,* **pa·roled, pa·rol·ing.**

**pa·rot·id** (pə rot′id)   1 near the ear. The **parotid glands,** one in front of each ear, supply saliva to the mouth through the **parotid ducts.**   2 a parotid gland.   1 *adj.,* 2 *n.*

**par·ox·ysm** (par′ək siz′əm *or* per′ək siz′əm)   1 a sudden attack or increase of symptoms of a disease; convulsion: *a paroxysm of coughing.*   2 a sudden violent emotion, etc.: *a paroxysm of rage.   n.*

**par·ox·ys·mal** (par′ək siz′məl *or* per′ək siz′məl)   of, like, or having PAROXYSMS.   *adj.*

**par·quet** (pär kā′ *or* pär ket′)   1 a flooring made of inlaid pieces of wood, often of different kinds, fitted together to form a pattern.   2 furnish with a parquet floor: *to parquet a room.*   3 the main floor of a theatre, especially from the orchestra pit to the part under the balconies; ORCHESTRA (def. 4).   1, 3 *n.,* 2 *v.,* **par·quetted** *or* **par·queted, par·quet·ting** *or* **par·quet·ing.**

Parquetry

**par·quet·ry** (pär′ki trē)   woodwork of small pieces of wood, often in different shapes and of different kinds, arranged in a geometric pattern: *Parquetry is used especially for floors.   n., pl.* **par·quet·ries.**

**parr** (pär)   a young salmon before it leaves fresh water and enters the sea.   *n., pl.* **parr** *or* **parrs.**

**par·ra·keet** (par′ə kēt′ *or* per′ə kēt′)   See PARAKEET.   *n.*

**par·ri·cid·al** (par′ə sī′dəl or per′ə sī′dəl) of or having to do with PARRICIDE. *adj.*

**par·ri·cide** (par′ə sīd′ or per′ə sīd′) **1** the crime of killing one's parent or a close relative. **2** a person who kills his or her parent. *n.*

Grey parrots—about 30 cm long including the tail

**par·rot** (par′ət or per′ət) **1** any of a family of birds of the tropics and southern temperate regions, having a stout, hooked bill and, usually, brightly coloured plumage: *Parrots are excellent mimics.* **2** a person who repeats words or acts without understanding them. **3** repeat without understanding: *The small child parroted the words of the song.* 1, 2 *n.*, 3 *v.* —**par′rot·like′,** *adj.*

**par·ry** (par′ē or per′ē) **1** ward off; turn aside a thrust, stroke, weapon, etc.: *He parried the sword with his dagger.* **2** dodge; counter: *She parried our question by asking us one.* **3** the act of warding off or avoiding. 1, 2 *v.*, **par·ried, par·ry·ing;** 3 *n., pl.* **par·ries.**

**parse** (pärs) **1** analyse a sentence grammatically, telling its parts of speech and their uses in the sentence. **2** describe a word grammatically, telling what part of speech it is, its form, and its use in a sentence. *v.,* **parsed, pars·ing.**

**Par·see** or **Par·si** (pär′sē) in India, a member of a ZOROASTRIAN sect descended from Persians who settled there early in the 8th century A.D. *n.*

**par·si·mo·ni·ous** (pär′sə mō′nē əs) too economical; stingy. *adj.* —**par′si·mo′ni·ous·ly,** *adv.*

**par·si·mo·ny** (pär′sə mō′nē) **1** carefulness in using money; thrift. **2** extreme carefulness in using money; stinginess. *n.*

**pars·ley** (pär′slē) a garden plant having finely divided, fragrant leaves, used to flavour food and to garnish platters of meat, etc. *n., pl.* **pars·leys.**

**pars·nip** (pär′snip) **1** a vegetable that is the long, tapering, whitish root of a plant belonging to the same family as the carrot. **2** the plant. *n.*

**par·son** (pär′sən) **1** a minister in charge of a parish; rector. **2** any member of the clergy; minister. *n.*

**par·son·age** (pär′sə nij) the house provided for a minister by his or her church. *n.*

**part** (pärt) **1** something less than the whole: *What part of the chicken do you like best?* **2** each of several equal quantities into which a whole may be divided; fraction: *A dime is a tenth part of a dollar.* **3** anything that helps to make up a whole: *A radio has many parts.* **4** a share: *Everyone must do his or her part.* **5** a side in a dispute or contest: *Amelia always takes her sister's part.* **6** a character in a play, motion picture, etc.; role: *She played the part of Juliet.* **7** the words spoken by a character: *An actor has to learn his part quickly.* **8** divide into two or more pieces. **9** force apart; divide: *The policewoman on horseback parted the crowd.* **10** go apart; separate: *The friends parted in anger.* **11** a dividing line left in combing one's hair. **12** comb the hair away from a dividing line. **13** in music, one of the voices or instruments: *The four parts in singing are soprano, alto, tenor, and bass.* **14** the music for one voice or instrument. **15** less than the whole: *part-time.* **16** in part; partly; in some measure or degree. **17** ability; talent: *a man of parts.* **18** a region; district; place: *She has travelled much in foreign parts.* 1–7, 11, 13, 14, 17, 18 *n.*, 8–10, 12 *v.*, 15 *adj.*, 16 *adv.*
**for one's part,** as far as one is concerned.
**for the most part,** mostly: *The attempts were for the most part unsuccessful.*
**in good part,** in a friendly or gracious way: *She took the teasing in good part.*
**in part,** in some measure or degree; to some extent; partly.
**on the part of one** or **on one's part,** **a** as far as one is concerned. **b** by one.
**part and parcel,** a necessary or essential part: *Practising is part and parcel of learning to play the piano.*
**part from,** go away from; leave.
**part with,** give up; let go.
**take part,** take or have a share.

**part.** **1** participle. **2** particular.

**par·take** (pär tāk′) **1** eat or drink some; take some: *We are eating lunch. Will you partake?* **2** take or have a share or part: *Will you partake of this cake? v.,* **par·took, par·tak·en, par·tak·ing.** —**par·tak′er,** *n.*
**partake of,** have to some extent the nature or character of: *Her graciousness partakes of condescension.*

**par·tak·en** (pär tā′kən) pp. of PARTAKE. *v.*

**Parth·i·an shot** (pär′thē ən) a sharp parting remark or action.

**par·tial** (pär′shəl) **1** not complete; not total: *Mother has made a partial payment on our new car.* **2** inclined to favour one side more than another; favouring unfairly; biassed: *A father should not be partial to any one of his children.* **3** having a liking; favourably inclined (used with *to*): *She is partial to sports. adj.*

**par·ti·al·i·ty** (pär′shē al′ə tē) **1** a favouring of one more than another or others; the quality or state of being PARTIAL (def. 2). **2** a particular liking; fondness; preference; bent: *Children often have a partiality for candy. n., pl.* **par·ti·al·i·ties.**

**par·tial·ly** (pär′shə lē) **1** in part; not generally or totally; partly. **2** in a PARTIAL (def. 2) manner; with undue bias. *adv.*

**par·tic·i·pant** (pär tis′ə pənt) **1** a person who shares or participates. **2** participating. 1 *n.*, 2 *adj.*

**par·tic·i·pate** (pär tis′ə pāt′) have a share; take part: *The teacher participated in the children's games. v.,* **par·tic·i·pat·ed, par·tic·i·pat·ing.** —**par·tic′i·pa·tor,** *n.* —**par·tic′i·pa·to·ry,** *adj.*

**par·tic·i·pa·tion** (pär tis′ə pā′shən) a participating; taking part. *n.*

**par·ti·cip·i·al** (pär′tə sip′ē əl) in grammar, of, having to do with, or formed from a PARTICIPLE; as, a **participial adjective** (a *masked* man, a *becoming* dress), a **participial noun** (in *training* dogs, the fatigue of *marching*). *adj.* —**par′ti·cip′i·al·ly,** *adv.*

**par·ti·ci·ple** (pär′tə sip′əl) in grammar, the PAST PARTICIPLE or PRESENT PARTICIPLE of a verb. *Examples:* the girl *writing* sentences at the blackboard, the man *waiting* for a train, the silver *stolen* recently, Julia *having missed* the boat. In these phrases, *writing* and *waiting* are PRESENT PARTICIPLES; *stolen* and *missed* are PAST PARTICIPLES. They can also be used with an auxiliary verb to form various tenses, as in *I am talking, I have talked.* *n.*
☞ *Usage.* In English, the present participle ends in *-ing* (*walking*) and the past participle of most verbs ends in *-ed* (*walked*) or *-en* (*risen*). Participles may be used as adjectives.

**par·ti·cle** (pär′tə kəl) **1** a very little bit: *I have a particle of dust in my eye.* **2** a prefix or suffix. *Un-* and *-ment* are particles. **3** a part of speech, short and without inflections, used to show syntactical relationships: *The definite and indefinite articles, prepositions, and conjunctions are particles.* *n.*

**particle board** a kind of board used in building, furniture-making, etc., made of sawdust or small pieces of wood pressed together with a synthetic resin or similar binding agent.

**par·ti–col·oured** or **par·ti–col·ored** (pär′tē kul′ərd) coloured differently in different parts; partly of one colour or tint, partly of another or others. *adj.*

**par·tic·u·lar** (pər tik′yə lər) **1** apart from others; considered separately; single: *That particular chair is already sold.* **2** belonging to some one person, thing, group, occasion, etc.: *A particular characteristic of a skunk is its smell.* **3** different from others; unusual; special: *a particular friend.* **4** hard to please; wanting everything to be just right; very careful: *She is very particular; nothing but the best will do.* **5** giving details; full of details: *a particular account of the game.* **6** an individual part; item; point: *The work is complete in every particular.* 1–5 *adj.*, 6 *n.*
**in particular,** especially: *We drove around, going nowhere in particular.*

**par·tic·u·lar·i·ty** (pər tik′yə lar′ə tē or par tik′yə ler′ə tē) **1** a detailed quality; minuteness. **2** special carefulness. **3** attentiveness to details. **4** a particular characteristic, feature, or trait. **5** the quality of being hard to please. **6** the quality or fact of being particular. *n., pl.* **par·tic·u·lar·i·ties.**

**par·tic·u·lar·ize** (pər tik′yə lə rīz′) **1** mention particularly or individually; treat in detail; specify. **2** mention individuals; give details. *v.*, **par·tic·u·lar·ized, par·tic·u·lar·iz·ing.**
—**par·tic′u·lar·i·za′tion,** *n.*

**par·tic·u·lar·ly** (pər tik′yə lər lē) **1** in a high degree; especially: *The teacher praised Ruth particularly.* **2** in a particular manner; in detail; minutely: *The inspector examined the machine particularly.* *adv.*

**part·ing** (pär′ting) **1** a departure; going away; taking leave. **2** given, taken, spoken, done, etc. on going away: *a parting gift, a parting request, a parting shot.* **3** departing. **4** dividing; separating: *the parting of the ways.* **5** a division; separation. **6** a place of division or separation: *Her hair is arranged with a side parting.* **7** ppr. of PART. 1, 4–6 *n.*, 2, 3 *adj.*, 7 *v.*

**Parti Québecois** (pär tē′kā bek wä′) *Cdn.* a major political party in Quebec, formed as a separatist party in 1968.

**par·ti·san** (pär′tə zan′ or pär′tə zən) **1** a strong supporter of a person, party, or cause, especially one whose support is based on feeling rather than on reason. **2** a member of a party of light, irregular troops, often working behind enemy lines; guerrilla. **3** of or like a partisan. 1, 2 *n.*, 3 *adj.* Also, **partizan.**

**par·ti·san·ship** (pär′tə zən ship′) **1** strong loyalty to a party or cause. **2** the act of taking sides. *n.*

**par·ti·tion** (pär tish′ən) **1** a division into parts: *the partition of a man's wealth when he dies.* **2** divide into parts: *The empire was partitioned after the emperor's death.* **3** one of the parts of a whole. **4** something that separates, especially a thin inside dividing wall or membrane. **5** separate by a partition (often used with **off**): *A corner of the basement was partitioned off for a washroom.* 1, 3, 4 *n.*, 2, 5 *v.*

**par·ti·tive** (pär′tə tiv) in grammar: **1** a word or phrase meaning a part of a collective whole. *Some, few,* and *any* are partitives. **2** expressing a part of a collective whole: *a partitive adjective.* 1 *n.*, 2 *adj.*
—**par′ti·tive·ly,** *adv.*

**par·ti·zan** (pär′tə zan′ or pär′tə zən) See PARTISAN. *n., adj.*

**part·ly** (pärt′lē) in part; in some measure or degree: *She is partly to blame.* *adv.*

**part·ner** (pärt′nər) **1** a member of a PARTNERSHIP (def. 1). **2** associate or colleague: *The thief climbed through the window while his partner watched the street.* **3** spouse. **4** either person of a couple dancing together. **5** in games such as cards or tennis, either of two players playing together against another pair. **6** one who shares: *My sister was the partner of my walks.* **7** be a partner of. 1–6 *n.*, 7 *v.*

**part·ner·ship** (pärt′nər ship′) **1** a legal association of two or more persons in a business enterprise: *The members of a partnership share the risks and profits of their business.* **2** the people associated in a partnership. **3** the state of being a partner; association: *the partnership of marriage.* *n.*

**part of speech** one of the following classes into which words are grouped according to their use or function in sentences: noun, pronoun, adjective, verb, adverb, preposition, conjunction, and interjection.
☞ *Usage.* Many words in English can function as more than one part of speech. In *I can run fast* the word *run* is a verb; in *I am going for a run* the same word is a noun.

**par·took** (pär tůk′) pt. of PARTAKE: *She partook of food and drink.* *v.*

**par·tridge** (pär′trij) **1** any of numerous related species of medium-sized game bird native to the Old World: *The Hungarian partridge was introduced to Canada from Europe early in this century.* **2** any of various North American game birds resembling the partridges, such as the ruffed grouse or the quail. *n., pl.* **par·tridg·es** or (*esp. collectively*) **par·tridge.**

**par·tridge·ber·ry** (pär′trij ber′ē) **1** a North American trailing evergreen plant of the madder family having fragrant white flowers and scarlet berries. **2** the edible but almost tasteless berry of this plant. *n., pl.* **par·tridge·ber·ries.**

**part song** a song consisting of parts for two or more voices in harmony, with one voice carrying the melody: *Part songs are usually sung without accompaniment.*

**part–time** (pärt′tīm′) **1** using or working only part of the standard or usual number of hours: *a part-time job,* *part-time employees.* **2** for only part of the usual number of hours: *She's working part-time this year.* **1** *adj.,* **2** *adv.*

**part time** part of the time.

**par·tu·ri·ent** (pär tyü′rē ənt *or* pär tü′rē ənt)
**1** bringing forth young; about to give birth to young.
**2** of or having to do with PARTURITION. **3** about to produce an idea, literary work, etc. *adj.*

**par·tu·ri·tion** (pär′tyə rish′ən *or* pär′tə rish′ən) the act or process of giving birth to young. *n.*

**par·ty** (pär′tē) **1** a group of people doing something together: *a sewing party, a dinner party.* **2** a gathering for pleasure: *On her birthday she had a party and invited her friends.* **3** a group of people having similar political aims and opinions, organized together to gain influence and control: *the Liberal, Conservative, or New Democratic Party.* **4** of or having to do with a party. **5** one who takes part in, aids, or knows about: *She was a party to our plot.* **6** each of the persons or sides in or affected by a contract, lawsuit, etc. **7** *Informal.* a person: *Old Billy Mudd was a strange party. He lent the book to a third party.* **8** any one of two or more persons or families using the same telephone line. 1–3, 5–8 *n., pl.* **par·ties;** 4 *adj.*

**party line** **1** a telephone line by which two or more subscribers are connected with the exchange by one circuit. **2** the official policy or policies of a political party: *The members of parliament were not expected to vote along party lines on the issue.*

**par·ty–lin·er** (pär′tē lī′nər) a person who follows closely the officially adopted policies of his or her political party. *n.*

**pa·ru·sha·na** (pä′rü shä′nə) a communal act of confession and repentance observed on the last day of the year in the Jain calendar. *n.*

**par value** the value of a stock, bond, note, etc. printed on it; face value.

**par·ve·nu** (pär′və nyü′ *or* pär′və nü′) **1** a person who has risen quickly to a position of wealth or power, but is not yet socially accepted in this new position; upstart. **2** like or characteristic of a parvenu. 1 *n.,* 2 *adj.*

**pas·cal** (pas′kəl) an SI unit for measuring pressure or stress, equal to the pressure produced by the force of one newton applied to an area of one square metre.
Symbol: Pa *n.*
☞ *Hom.* PASCHAL.

**PASCAL** (pas′kəl) a computer language. *n.*
☞ *Etym.* Named for *Pascal,* a French mathematician, who built the first mechanical calculator.

**pas·chal** (pas′kəl) **1** of or having to do with Passover. **2** of or having to do with Easter; used in Easter celebrations. *adj.*
☞ *Hom.* PASCAL.

**pasque–flow·er** (pask′flou′ər) any of several species of ANEMONES having mauve or white flowers, especially the prairie crocus. *n.*

**pass** (pas) **1** go by; move past: *The parade passed. We passed the big truck.* **2** move on; go: *The salesman passed from house to house.* **3** go from one to another: *Her estate passed to her children.* **4** cause to go from one to another; hand around: *Please pass the butter. The old coin was passed around for everyone to see.* **5** get through or by: *We passed the dangerous section of the road successfully.* **6** go across or over: *The horse passed the stream.* **7** put or direct a rope, string, etc.: *He passed a rope around his waist for support.* **8** go away; depart: *The time for action had already passed.* **9** cause to go, onward, or proceed: *to pass troops in review.* **10** discharge from the body. **11** be successful in an examination, a course, etc.: *Kee passed arithmetic.* **12** success in an examination, etc.; the passing of an examination but without honours. **13** the act of passing; passage: *The invading army made a swift pass through the country.* **14** cause or allow to go through something; sanction or approve: *to pass accounts as correct.* **15** ratify or enact: *to pass a bill or law.* **16** be approved by a lawmaking body, etc.: *The new law passed the City Council.* **17** come to an end; die: *King Arthur passed in peace.* **18** go beyond; exceed; surpass: *Her strange story passes belief.* **19** use; spend: *We passed the days pleasantly.* **20** change: *Water passes from a liquid to a solid state when it freezes.* **21** take place; happen: *Tell me all that passed.* **22** go about; circulate: *Money passes from person to person.* **23** give approval to: *The inspector passed the item after examining it.* **24** express; pronounce: *A judge passes sentence on guilty persons.* **25** give a judgment or opinion: *The judges passed on each contestant.* **26** go without notice: *She was rude, but let that pass.* **27** let go without action. **28** leave out; omit. **29** a note, licence, etc. allowing one to do something: *He needed a pass to enter the fort.* **30** free ticket: *a pass to the circus.* **31** state; condition: *Things have reached a strange pass when children give orders to their parents.* **32** a motion of the hands. **33** a sleight-of-hand motion; manipulation; trick. **34** a narrow road, path, way, channel, etc.; narrow passage through mountains. **35** in football, hockey, and other games, transfer the ball, etc. **36** in football, hockey, etc., a transference of a ball, puck, etc. **37** in card playing, give up a chance to bid or to play a hand. **38** thrust. **39** in fencing, make a thrust. **40** a thrust in fencing. **41** *Informal.* an attempt to kiss or otherwise flirt. **42** promise: *to pass one's word.*
1–11, 14–28, 35, 37–39, 42 *v.,* **passed, pass·ing;** 12, 13, 29–34, 36, 40, 41 *n.,* **—pass′er,** *n.*
**bring to pass,** accomplish; cause to be.
**come to pass,** take place; happen.
**pass as** or **for,** be accepted as: *Use silk, or a material that will pass as silk. She could pass for twenty.*
**pass away,** come to an end; die.
**pass by, a** move past. **b** fail to notice; overlook; disregard.
**pass off, a** go away. **b** take place; be done. **c** get accepted; pretend to be.
**pass on,** a pass from one person to another. **b** die.
**pass out, a** faint; lose consciousness. **b** hand out or circulate: *The teacher passed out the report cards.*
**pass over,** a fail to notice; overlook; disregard: *The teacher passed over my mistake.* **b** die.
**pass up,** a give up; renounce: *to pass up a chance to go to college.* **b** fail to take advantage of.

**pass.** 1 passive. 2 passenger.

**pass·a·ble** (pas′ə bəl) **1** fairly good; tolerable; mediocre: *a passable performance. Her French is passable, but not good.* **2** that can be crossed or travelled on: *The roads are just barely passable.* **3** that can be freely circulated; current; valid: *passable coin. adj.*

**pass·a·bly** (pas′ə blē) fairly; moderately. *adv.*

**pas·sage** (pas′ij) **1** a hall or way through a building; passageway. **2** a means of passing; way through: *to ask* for passage through a crowd. 3 right, liberty, or leave to pass: *The guard refused us passage.* 4 passing: *the passage of time.* 5 a piece from a speech, writing, or musical composition: *a passage from the first symphony of Beethoven.* 6 a journey, especially by sea: *We had a stormy passage across the Atlantic.* 7 making into law by vote of a legislature: *the passage of a bill.* 8 what passes between persons. 9 an exchange of blows: *a passage of arms.* 10 a an alley or narrow lane. b a tube in the body for carrying liquid, etc. *n.*

**passage of arms** an exchange of blows; quarrel.

**pas·sage·way** (pas′ij wā′) a way along which one can pass; passage: *Halls and alleys are passageways.* *n.*

**pas·sé** (pa sā′; *French,* pä sā′) 1 past one's prime. 2 no longer useful or fashionable; out-of-date: *That expression is very passé.* *adj.*

**pas·sen·ger** (pas′ən jər) a traveller in a train, motor vehicle, boat, or airplane who has nothing to do with its operation: *The driver and one of the passengers were hurt in the accident.* *n.*

**pass·er-by** (pas′ər bī′) a person who passes by: *The robbery was seen by a passer-by who called the police.* *n.,* *pl.* **pass·ers-by.**

**pas·ser·ine** (pas′ə rīn′ *or* pas′ə rin) 1 of, having to do with, or referring to the bird order **Passeriformes,** the largest order, including more than half of all the existing bird species in the world: *Passerine birds are also called songbirds because most of them sing.* 2 a bird belonging to this order. 1 *adj.,* 2 *n.*

**pas·sim** (pas′im) *Latin.* here and there; in various places. *adv.*

**pass·ing** (pas′ing) 1 that passes. 2 the act of one that passes; going by; departure: *the passing of summer.* 3 not lasting; fleeting: *a passing idea, a passing fashion.* 4 cursory; incidental: *a passing fancy.* 5 that is now happening: *the passing scene.* 6 a means or place of passing. 7 allowing one to pass an examination or test: *a passing mark.* 8 ppr. of PASS. 1, 3–5, 7 *adj.,* 2, 6 *n.,* 8 *v.* **in passing,** a as one proceeds or passes. b by the way; incidentally: *In passing, I'd like to compliment you on your excellent work.*

**pas·sion** (pash′ən) 1 very strong feeling: *Love and hate are passions.* 2 a violent anger; rage: *She flew into a passion.* 3 intense love or sexual desire. 4 a very strong liking or devotion: *a passion for music.* 5 the object of a passion: *Music is her passion.* *n.*

**pas·sion·ate** (pash′ə nit) 1 affected with or easily moved to strong emotion, especially anger or indignation: *a passionate believer in freedom, a passionate person.* 2 caused by or showing strong emotion: *a passionate defence of the accused man.* 3 affected with or influenced by sexual desire. *adj.*
—**pas′sion·ate·ly,** *adv.*

**pas·sion·flow·er** (pash′ən flou′ər) any of a closely related group of mainly tropical vines having showy red, purple, white, or yellow flowers and, in some species, edible fruit. *n.*

**pas·sive** (pas′iv) 1 not acting in return; being acted on without itself acting: *a passive mind or disposition.* 2 not resisting; yielding or submitting to the will of another: *The slaves gave passive obedience to their master.* 3 in grammar, the PASSIVE VOICE. 4 a verb form in the passive voice, consisting of a form of the verb **be** followed by a PAST PARTICIPLE. 5 of or referring to the PASSIVE VOICE or containing a passive verb form: *a passive sentence.* 1, 2, 5 *adj.,* 3, 4 *n.* —**pas′sive·ly,** *adv.*

**passive resistance** resistance to a government or other authority, especially by non-violent refusal to co-operate.

**passive voice** in grammar, the form of the verb that shows the subject as being acted on rather than acting. In *She broke the window,* broke is in the active voice; in *The window was broken,* was broken is in the passive voice.

**pas·siv·i·ty** (pa siv′ə tē) the state or quality of being PASSIVE; lack of action; non-resistance. *n.*

**pass·key** (pas′kē) 1 a key for opening several locks; master key. 2 a private key. *n.*

**Pass·o·ver** (pas′ō′vər) an annual Jewish holiday in memory of the escape of the Hebrews from Egypt, where they had been slaves. It is so called because, according to the Bible, a destroying angel "passed over" the houses of the Hebrews when it killed the first-born male child in every Egyptian home. *n.*

**pass·port** (pas′pôrt′) 1 an official document identifying and giving the citizenship of the holder, and giving the holder permission to leave and return to the country issuing the document, and to travel abroad under the protection of its government. 2 anything that gives one admission or acceptance: *An interest in gardening was a passport to my aunt's favour.* *n.*

**pass·word** (pas′wėrd′) 1 a secret word or phrase that identifies a person speaking it and allows him or her to pass. 2 a personal code which enables its possessor to use a computer by keying in the code. *n.*

**past** (past) 1 gone by; ended: *Summer is past. Our troubles are past.* 2 just gone by: *The past year was full of trouble.* 3 time gone by; time before: *Life began far back in the past.* 4 a past life or history: *Our country has a glorious past.* 5 a person's past life, especially if hidden or unknown: *He was a man with a past; no one knew that he had been in prison.* 6 beyond; farther on than: *The arrow went past the mark.* 7 after; later than: *half past two. It is past noon.* 8 so as to pass by or beyond: *The bus goes past once an hour.* 9 beyond in number, amount, or degree. 10 beyond the ability, range, scope, etc. of: *absurd fancies that are past belief.* 11 having served a term in office: *a past president.* 12 indicating time gone by, or former action or state: *the past tense, a past participle.* 13 the PAST TENSE or a verb form in it. 1, 2, 11, 12 *adj.,* 3–5, 13 *n.,* 6, 7, 9, 10 *prep.,* 8 *adv.*
☛ *Usage.* Past should never be used as a verb. The past tense of the verb PASS should always be spelled **passed.**

**pas·ta** (pas′tə *or* pä′stə) 1 a type of flour paste used to make foods such as spaghetti, macaroni, ravioli, noodles, etc. 2 food or foods made of this paste. *n.*

**paste** (pāst) 1 a mixture, such as flour and water, that will stick paper together, stick it to a wall, etc. 2 stick with paste: *paste a label on a box.* 3 cover by pasting: *paste a door over with notices.* 4 dough for pastry. 5 a soft, dough-like mixture: *Pottery is made from a paste of clay and water.* 6 a hard, glassy material used in making imitations of precious stones. 7 a soft, jelly-like candy. 8 a mixture of meat, fish, etc. used for spreading on sandwiches: *liver paste, chicken paste, shrimp paste, salmon paste.* 1, 4–7, 8 *n.,* 2, 3 *v.,* **past·ed, past·ing.**
—**past′er,** *n.*

**paste·board** (pāst′bôrd′) 1 a stiff material made of

sheets of paper pasted together or of paper pulp pressed and dried.   2 flimsy; sham.   *n.*

**pas·tel** (pas tel′)   **1** a kind of crayon made of ground colouring matter and gum, used in drawing.   **2** a drawing made with such crayons.   **3** a soft, pale shade of some colour.   **4** soft and pale: *pastel pink, pastel shades.*   1–3 *n.*, 4 *adj.*

**pas·tern** (pas′tərn)   **1** the part of a horse's foot between the fetlock and the hoof.   See HORSE for picture.   **2** a corresponding part in other animals.   *n.*

**pas·teur·i·za·tion** (pas′chə rə zā′shən or pas′chə rī zā′shən)   **1** the process of pasteurizing.   **2** the fact or state of being PASTEURIZED.   *n.*

**pas·teur·ize** (pas′chə rīz′)   heat milk, beer, etc. to a prescribed temperature and chill it quickly to destroy harmful bacteria without causing a major chemical change to the substance itself.   *v.*, **pas·teur·ized, pas·teur·iz·ing.**
☛ *Etym.*   Named after Louis *Pasteur* (1822–1895), a French chemist who discovered this way of destroying bacteria.

**pas·tille** (pas tēl′)   **1** a flavoured or medicated lozenge.   **2** a small roll or cone of aromatic paste, burnt as a disinfectant, incense, etc.   *n.*

**pas·time** (pas′tīm)   something that causes the time to pass pleasantly; a form of amusement or recreation: *Games and sports are pastimes.*   *n.*

**past master**   **1** one who has filled the office of master in a society, lodge, etc.   **2** a person who has much experience in any profession, art, etc.

**pas·tor** (pas′tər)   a member of the clergy in charge of a church; spiritual guide.   *n.*

**pas·tor·al** (pas′tə rəl)   **1** of shepherds or country life.   **2** a pastoral play, poem, music, or picture.   **3** simple or naturally beautiful like the country: *a pastoral scene.*   **4** of a PASTOR or his or her duties.   **5** a letter from a bishop to his or her clergy or to the people of his or her church district.   1, 3, 4 *adj.*, 2, 5 *n.*

**past participle**   a PARTICIPLE that indicates time gone by, or a former action or state.   *Played* and *thrown* are past participles in *She has played all day,* and *The ball should have been thrown to me.*

**past perfect**   **1** a verb form employing the PRETERITE of the verb **have** with a past participle and showing that an event was completed before a given past time. In *She had learned to read before she went to school, had learned* is the past perfect of *learn. Past perfect* and *pluperfect* mean the same.   **2** the past perfect tense or a verb form in it.

**pas·tra·mi** (pə strä′mē)   smoked and highly seasoned beef, especially from a shoulder cut.   *n.*

**pas·try** (pā′strē)   **1** a paste, or dough, of flour and lard, butter, or shortening, used to make pie crusts, tarts, and certain other foods: *Pastry has a flaky texture when it is baked.*   **2** food made wholly or partly of this paste: *She eats too much pastry.*   **3** a piece of pastry; a tart, turnover, etc.   *n.*, *pl.* **pas·tries.**

**past tense**   in grammar:   **1** a tense expressing time gone by, or a former action or state.   **2** a verb form in the past tense. In the sentence *I went to bed early last night, went* is in the past tense.

**pas·tur·age** (pas′chə rij)   **1** the growing grass and other plants that cattle, sheep, or horses feed on.   **2** pasture land.   *n.*

**pas·ture** (pas′chər)   **1** a grassy field or hillside; grasslands on which cattle, sheep, or horses can feed.

hat, āge, fär; let, ēqual, tėrm; it, īce
hot, ōpen, ôrder; oil, out; cup, pùt, rüle
əbove, takən, pencəl, lemən, circəs
ch, child; ng, long; sh, ship
th, thin; ŦH, then; zh, measure

**2** grass and other growing plants: *These lands afford good pasture.*   **3** put cattle, sheep, etc. out to pasture.   **4** feed on growing grass, etc.   1, 2 *n.*, 3, 4 *v.*, **pas·tured, pas·tur·ing.**

**past·y**[1] (pā′stē)   of or like paste in appearance or texture; especially, pale and flabby.   *adj.*, **past·i·er, past·i·est.**   —**past′i·ness,** *n.*

**pas·ty**[2] (pas′tē)   a pie filled with game, fish, etc.: *a venison pasty.*   *n.*, *pl.* **pas·ties.**

**pat** (pat)   **1** strike or tap lightly with something flat: *She patted the dough into a flat cake.*   **2** tap lightly with the hand as a sign of sympathy, approval, or affection: *to pat a dog.*   **3** a light stroke or tap with the hand or with something flat.   **4** the sound made by patting.   **5** a small mass, especially of butter.   **6** apt; suitable; to the point: *a pat reply.*   **7** aptly; exactly; suitably.   **8** ready-made without much thought: *The minister merely gave a pat answer to a very difficult question.*   1, 2 *v.*, **pat·ted, pat·ting;**   3, 4, 5 *n.*, 6, 8 *adj.*, 7 *adv.*
**have down pat** or **know down pat,** *Informal.*   have perfectly; know thoroughly: *Keira has the history lesson down pat.*
**pat on the back,** praise or compliment.
**stand pat,** *Informal.*   keep the same position; hold to things as they are and refuse to change: *Many people were angry with the government but the prime minister stood pat.*

**Pat·a·go·ni·an** (pat′ə gō′nē ən)   **1** of or having to do with Patagonia, a region in the extreme south of South America, or its people.   **2** a native or inhabitant of Patagonia.   **3** a member of a tribe of very tall Indians living in Patagonia.   1 *adj.*, 2, 3 *n.*

**patch** (pach)   **1** a piece of some material put on to mend a hole or a tear, or to stengthen a weak place.   **2** a protective pad for placing over an injured eye: *The doctor ordered him to wear a patch over his right eye.*   **3** put on a patch; mend, protect, or cover with a patch or patches: *to patch a sleeve. These clothes are so old that I spend all my time patching.*   **4** a small piece of cloth, especially one used for patchwork.   **5** a tiny bit of black cloth that women used to wear on their faces to hide a blemish or to set off their fair skin.   **6** a small area different from that around it: *a patch of brown on the skin.*   **7** a piece of ground: *a garden patch.*   **8** piece together; make hastily.   1, 2, 4–7 *n.*, 3, 8 *v.*   —**patch′er,** *n.*
**patch up, a** put an end to; settle: *to patch up a quarrel.*   **b** put right hastily or for a time: *to patch up a leaking tap.*   **c** put together hastily or poorly: *to patch up a costume for Halloween.*

**patch·work** (pach′wėrk′)   **1** pieces of cloth of various colours or shapes sewn together: *a bedspread of patchwork.*   **2** sewing things in this way: *She enjoys patchwork.*   **3** made in this way: *a patchwork quilt.*   **4** anything like this: *From the airplane, we saw a patchwork of fields and woods.*   *n.*

**patch·y** (pach′ē)   **1** abounding in or characterized by patches: *a patchy lawn.*   **2** occurring in, forming, or resembling patches.   **3** not consistent or regular; not uniform in quality, etc.: *a patchy performance.*   *adj.*, **patch·i·er, patch·i·est.**   —**patch′i·ness,** *n.*

**pate** (pāt) the top of the head; head: *a bald pate.* *n.*

**pâ·té** (pä tā′) *French.* **1** a pastry case filled with chicken, sweetbreads, oysters, etc.; patty. **2** a meat paste, usually highly seasoned. *n.*

**pâté de foie gras** (pä tā də fwä grä′) *French.* a paste made with livers of specially fattened geese.

**pa·tel·la** (pə tel′ə) **1** kneecap. See LEG for picture. **2** a small pan or shallow vessel. **3** in biology, a panlike or cuplike formation. *n., pl.* **pa·tel·las** or **pa·tel·lae** (-tel′ē or -tel′ī).

**pa·tel·lar** (pə tel′ər) of or having to do with the kneecap. *adj.*

**pat·ent** (pat′ənt or pā′tənt for 1–5, pā′tənt for 6) **1** a right given by a government to a person by which he or she is the only one allowed to make, use, or sell a new invention for a certain number of years. **2** protected by a patent: *a patent lock.* **3** get a patent for: *The inventor patented many inventions.* **4** an invention that is protected by a patent. **5** an official document from a government giving a right or privilege. **6** evident; plain: *She smiled at the patent ineptness of their scheme.* 1, 4, 5 *n.,* 2, 6 *adj.,* 3 *v.* —**pat′ent·a·ble,** *adj.*

**pat·ent·ee** (pat′ən tē′) a person to whom a patent is granted. *n.*

**patent leather** leather with a very glossy, smooth surface, usually black.

**pa·tent·ly** (pā′tənt lē or pat′ən tlē) **1** plainly; clearly; obviously. **2** openly. *adv.*

**patent medicine** a medicine sold under a trademark and not requiring a doctor's prescription.

**Patent Office** a government office that issues patents.

**pa·ter·fa·mil·i·as** (pat′ər fə mil′ē əs or pā′tər fə mil′ē əs) a father or head of a family. *n.*

**pa·ter·nal** (pə tėr′nəl) **1** of, having to do with, or like a father; fatherly. **2** related on the father's side of the family: *Everyone has two paternal grandparents and two maternal grandparents.* **3** received or inherited from one's father: *Mary's blue eyes were a paternal inheritance.* *adj.* —**pa·ter′nal·ly,** *adv.*

**pa·ter·nal·ism** (pə tėr′nə liz′əm) the principle or practice of managing the affairs of a country or group of people as a father manages the affairs of his children. *n.*

**pa·ter·nal·is·tic** (pə tėr′nə lis′tik) of, having to do with, or characterized by PATERNALISM: *He has a paternalistic attitude toward his employees.* *adj.*

**pa·ter·ni·ty** (pə tėr′nə tē) **1** the fact or state of being a father; fatherhood. **2** paternal origin: *King Arthur's paternity was unknown.* *n.*

**path** (path) **1** a track made by people or animals walking: *A path is usually too narrow for cars or wagons.* **2** a way made to walk upon or to ride horses, bicycles, etc. upon: *She laid stone for a garden path.* **3** a line or route along which a person or thing moves; track: *The moon has a regular path through the sky.* **4** a way of acting or behaving; way of life: *"Some choose paths of glory, some choose paths of ease."* *n., pl.* **paths** (pa<small>TH</small>z). —**path′less,** *adj.*

**pa·thet·ic** (pə thet′ik) **1** arousing pity and compassion; pitiful: *A lost child is a pathetic sight.* **2** arousing contempt; pitifully inadequate or unsuccessful: *a pathetic attempt to be funny.* *adj.*

**pa·thet·i·cal** (pə thet′ə kəl) PATHETIC. *adj.*

**pa·thet·i·cal·ly** (pə thet′i klē) in a PATHETIC way; pitifully: *He was crying pathetically.* *adv.*

**path·find·er** (path′fīn′dər) a person who finds a path or way, especially through a wilderness. *n.*

**path·o·gen** (path′ə jen′) a disease-causing agent. *n.*

**path·o·gen·ic** (path′ə jen′ik) having to do with PATHOGENY; producing disease. *adj.*

**pa·thog·e·ny** (pə thoj′ə nē) the production of disease. *n.*

**path·o·log·ic** (path′ə loj′ik) PATHOLOGICAL. *adj.*

**path·o·log·i·cal** (path′ə loj′ə kəl) **1** of PATHOLOGY; dealing with diseases or concerned with diseases. **2** due to disease or accompanying disease: *a pathological condition of the blood cells.* **3** caused or controlled by an obsession; compulsive: *a pathological hatred of cats. He's a pathological liar.* *adj.* —**path′o·log′i·cal·ly,** *adv.*

**pa·thol·o·gist** (pə thol′ə jist) a person trained in PATHOLOGY, especially one who makes it his or her work. *n.*

**pa·thol·o·gy** (pə thol′ə jē) **1** the study of the nature and causes of disease and of the changes in the body caused by them. **2** unhealthy conditions and processes caused by a disease. *n., pl.* **pa·thol·o·gies.**

**pa·thos** (pā′thos) a quality in experience or events, or in literature, art, or music that arouses a feeling of pity or sadness. *n.*

**path·way** (path′wā′) PATH. *n.*

**–pathy** combining form. **1** a feeling, as in *antipathy.* **2** a disorder or disease, as in *neuropathy.* **3** the treatment of disease, as in *osteopathy.*

**pa·tience** (pā′shəns) **1** the ability to accept calmly things that trouble or annoy, or that require long waiting or effort: *The cat showed patience in watching the mousehole.* **2** long, hard work; steady effort: *This carving shows the skill and patience of the artist.* **3** a card game played by one person; solitaire. *n.*

**pa·tient** (pā′shənt) **1** having or showing patience: *patient suffering.* **2** with steady effort or long, hard work: *patient research.* **3** a person who is being treated by a doctor, dentist, etc. 1, 2 *adj.,* 3 *n.* —**pa′tient·ly,** *adv.*

**pat·i·na** (pat′ə nə) **1** a film or incrustation, usually green, formed naturally over time on the surface of copper or bronze. **2** a smooth surface appearance produced by age and exposure on other substances such as wood or stone: *The old table had a beautiful glossy patina.* *n.*

**pat·i·o** (pat′ē ō) **1** an inner court or yard open to the sky: *Houses in Spanish countries are often built around patios.* **2** a terrace for outdoor meals, lounging, etc. *n., pl.* **pat·i·os.**

**pat·ois** (pat′wä; *French,* pä twä′) **1** a dialect different from the standard language of a country or district, especially one spoken in rural areas. **2** the special language characteristic of a particular group; jargon. *n., pl.* **pat·ois** (pat′wäz; *French,* pä twä′).

**pa·tri·arch** (pā′trē ärk′) **1** the father and ruler of a family or tribe. **2** a person thought of as the father or founder of something. **3** a venerable old man. **4** in the early Christian church, a bishop of the highest rank. **5** a high-ranking bishop in certain churches, especially the

Roman Catholic Church and the Eastern Orthodox Church. *n.*

**pa·tri·ar·chal** (pā′trē är′kəl) **1** having to do with or suitable for a PATRIARCH. **2** under the rule of a PATRIARCH: *a patriarchal society.* *adj.*

**pa·tri·ar·chy** (pā′trē är′kē) **1** a form of social organization in which the father is head of the family and in which descent is reckoned in the male line, the children belonging to the father's clan. **2** a family, community, or tribe governed by a patriarch or the eldest male. *n., pl.* **pa·tri·ar·chies.**

**pa·tri·ate** (pā′trē āt′ *or* pat′rē āt′) *Cdn.* bring (government, decision-making powers, etc.) under the direct control of the people of a given region, nation, etc.: *The British parliament voted in 1982 to patriate the Canadian constitution.* *v.* **pat·ri·a·ted, pa·tri·a·ting.** —**pa′tri·a′tion,** *n.*

**pa·tri·cian** (pə trish′ən) **1** in ancient Rome, a member of the nobility. Compare with PLEBEIAN (def. 1). **2** a person of noble birth or high social rank; aristocrat. **3** of or having to do with patricians. **4** noble; aristocratic. 1, 2 *n.*, 3, 4 *adj.*

**pat·ri·cide** (pat′rə sīd′) the crime of killing one's father. *n.*

**pat·ri·mo·ni·al** (pat′rə mō′nē əl) having to do with a PATRIMONY; inherited from one's father or ancestors. *adj.*

**pat·ri·mo·ny** (pat′rə mō′nē) **1** property inherited from one's father or ancestors. **2** property belonging to a church, monastery, or convent. **3** any heritage. *n., pl.* **pat·ri·mo·nies.**

**pa·tri·ot** (pā′trē ət *or* pat′rē ət) a person who loves and loyally supports the interests and rights of his or her country. *n.*

**pa·tri·ot·ic** (pā′trē ot′ik *or* pat′rē ot′ik) inspired by love and loyal support for one's country: *a patriotic speech. She is very patriotic.* *adj.* —**pa′tri·ot′i·cal·ly,** *adv.*

**pa·tri·ot·ism** (pā′trē ə tiz′əm *or* pat′rē ə tiz′əm) love and loyal support for the interests and rights of one's country. *n.*

**pa·trol** (pə trōl′) **1** go the rounds as a watchman or a police officer does. **2** go around a town, camp, etc. to watch or guard. **3** the persons who patrol: *The patrol was changed at midnight.* **4** a going of the rounds to watch or guard: *She was on patrol last night.* **5** a group of soldiers, ships, or airplanes, sent out to find out all they can about the enemy. **6** one of the subdivisions of a troop of Boy Scouts or a company of Girl Guides: *There are eight people in a patrol, including a patrol leader and a second.* 1, 2 *v.*, **pa·trolled, pa·trol·ling.** 3–6 *n.*

**patrol car** a police car used for patrolling roads or districts: *The patrol car caught him speeding.*

**pa·trol·man** (pə trōl′mən) a person who patrols, especially a police officer who patrols a certain district. *n., pl.* **pa·trol·men** (-mən).

**patrol wagon** a closed van or truck used by the police for carrying prisoners.

**pa·tron** (pā′trən) **1** one who buys regularly at a given store or goes regularly to a given restaurant, hotel, etc. **2** a person, especially one having social or political influence, who sponsors or supports another person or a cause, institution, etc.: *a patron of the arts.* **3** a guardian saint or god; protector. **4** in ancient Rome, an influential man who took certain persons under his protection. **5** guarding; protecting: *a patron saint.* 1–4 *n.*, 5 *adj.*

**pa·tron·age** (pā′trə nij *or* pat′rə nij) **1** the regular business given to a store, hotel, etc. by customers. **2** the favour, encouragement, or support given by a patron. **3** favour, kindness, etc. given in a haughty, superior way: *an air of patronage.* **4** the power to give jobs or favours: *the patronage of a premier, mayor, or reeve.* **5** political jobs or favours. *n.*

**pa·tron·ess** (pā′trə nis *or* pat′rə nis) **1** a woman, especially one having social or political influence, who sponsors or supports another person or a cause, institution, etc. **2** a woman who is a guardian saint or a goddess. *n.*

**pa·tron·ize** (pā′trə nīz′ *or* pat′rə nīz′) **1** be a regular customer of; give regular business to: *We patronize our neighbourhood stores.* **2** act as a patron toward; support or protect: *to patronize the ballet.* **3** treat in a haughty, condescending way: *Children do not like being patronized by adults.* *v.* **pa·tron·ized, pa·tron·iz·ing.** —**pa′tron·iz′ing·ly,** *adv.*

**pat·ro·nym·ic** (pat′rə nim′ik) a name derived from the name of a father or ancestor: *Williamson, meaning "son of William" is a patronymic.* *n.*

**pat·ter**[1] (pat′ər) **1** make rapid taps: *bare feet pattering along the floor. The rain pattered against the window.* **2** move or run with light, rapid steps: *She pattered down the stairs.* **3** a series of quick taps or the sound they make: *the patter of hail on the roof.* 1, 2 *v.*, 3 *n.*

**pat·ter**[2] (pat′ər) **1** rapid and easy talk, such as that of a magician, comedian, or circus barker. **2** talk or say rapidly and easily, without much thought: *to patter a prayer.* **3** the specialized vocabulary of a certain group, especially thieves, etc.; cant. **4** rapid speech, usually for comic effect, introduced into a song. 1, 3, 4 *n.*, 2 *v.*

**pat·tern** (pat′ərn) **1** an arrangement of forms and colours; design: *the patterns of wallpaper, rugs, cloth, and jewellery.* **2** model or guide for something to be made: *Mother used a paper pattern in cutting out her new dress.* **3** a fine example; model to be followed: *The captain was a pattern of manliness.* **4** make according to a pattern. **5** work or decorate with a pattern. **6** any arrangement of characteristics, actions, etc. that does not normally change: *behaviour pattern, speech pattern.* **7** use as an example: *He patterned himself after his favourite hockey star.* 1–3, 6 *n.*, 4, 5, 7 *v.*

**pat·ty** (pat′ē) **1** a hollow shell of pastry filled with chicken, oysters, etc. **2** a small, flat, usually round cake of chopped food: *hamburger or chicken patties.* **3** a small, round, flat piece of candy: *a peppermint patty.* *n., pl.* **pat·ties.**

**pau·ci·ty** (pos′ə tē) **1** small number; fewness. **2** a small amount; scarcity; lack. *n.*

**paunch** (ponch) **1** the belly; abdomen. **2** a large, protruding belly; potbelly. **3** the first stomach of a cud-chewing animal; rumen. *n.*

**paunch·y** (pon′chē) having a big PAUNCH. *adj.* —**paunch′i·ness,** *n.*

**pau·per** (pop′ər) 1 a very poor person. 2 a person supported by charity or by public welfare. *n.*

**pau·per·ism** (pop′ə riz′əm) the state of being very poor; poverty. *n.*

**pau·per·ize** (pop′ə rīz′) make a PAUPER of. *v.*, **pau·per·ized, pau·per·iz·ing.** —**pau′per·i·za′tion,** *n.*

**pause** (pöz) 1 stop for a time; wait: *The dog paused when she heard me.* 2 a moment of silence; brief stop; rest. 3 dwell; linger: *to pause upon a word.* 4 a brief stop in speaking or reading: *She made a short pause and then went on reading.* 5 any punctuation mark used to indicate such a stop. 6 in music, a sign (⌒ or ⌣) above or below a note or rest, meaning that it is to be held for a longer time. 1, 3 *v.*, **paused, paus·ing;** 2, 4–6 *n.*

**pave** (pāv) cover a street, sidewalk, etc. with PAVEMENT (def. 1). *v.*, **paved, pav·ing.**
**pave the way,** make preparation; make something smooth or easy: *She paved the way for me by doing careful work.*

**pave·ment** (pāv′mənt) 1 a covering, or surface, for streets, sidewalks, etc., made of stones, gravel, concrete, asphalt, etc. 2 a paved road, etc. *n.*

**pa·vil·ion** (pə vil′yən) 1 a building, usually open-sided, used for shelter, pleasure, etc.: *an amusement pavilion, the cricket pavilion.* 2 a large tent, often luxurious, for entertainment or shelter. 3 any building that houses an exhibition at a fair. 4 a part of a building higher or more decorated than the rest. 5 one of a group of buildings forming a hospital. 6 furnish with a pavilion; enclose or shelter in a pavilion. 1–5 *n.*, 6 *v.*

**pav·ing** (pā′ving) 1 the material for pavement. 2 pavement. 3 ppr. of PAVE. 1, 2 *n.*, 3 *v.*

**paw** (pö) 1 the foot of an animal having claws: *Cats and dogs have paws.* 2 strike at or touch with a paw: *The kitten pawed the ball of yarn.* 3 scrape or strike with or as if with a hoof: *The horse was pawing the ground, eager to go.* 4 *Informal.* a hand, especially when large or clumsy. 5 handle or touch awkwardly, rudely, or too intimately. 6 grab at or for wildly: *She pawed the air in an effort to keep herself from falling.* 1, 4 *n.*, 2, 3, 5, 6 *v.*

**pawl** (pol) a pivoted bar arranged to catch in the teeth of a ratchet wheel or the like so as to allow rotation in only one direction. See RATCHET WHEEL for picture. *n.*

**pawn¹** (pon) 1 give something as security that borrowed money will be repaid: *She pawned her watch to buy food until she could get work.* 2 something left as security. 3 a pledge. 1 *v.*, 2, 3 *n.*
**in pawn,** in another's possession as security: *Her watch is in pawn to the man who lent her money.*

**pawn²** (pon) 1 in chess, one of the 16 pieces of lowest value. 2 a person or thing used by someone to further his or her own purposes: *She used her friends and colleagues as pawns in her race for political power.* *n.*
☛ *Etym.* **Pawn,** PEON, and PIONEER can all be traced back to Med. L *pedo(ne)* 'a person going on foot, foot soldier', which developed from L *pes, pedis* 'foot'. **Pawn** came into Middle English from a Norman form of OF *peon*. **Peon** was borrowed in the 17c. (in India) from Portuguese *peão* and in the 19c. (in South America) from Spanish *peón*. **Pioneer,** originally *pionner,* came in the 16c. from F *pionnier* 'a soldier who goes ahead of an army to prepare the route', which itself came from OF *peon.*

**pawn·bro·ker** (pon′brō′kər) a person who lends money at interest on articles that are left with him or her as security for the loan. *n.*

**pawn·shop** (pon′shop′) a PAWNBROKER's shop. *n.*

**paw·paw** or **pa·paw** (pö′pö) 1 a small tropical American tree bearing oblong, yellowish, edible fruit with many beanlike seeds. 2 the fruit of this tree. 3 PAPAYA. *n.*

**pay¹** (pā) 1 give a person what is due for goods, services, work, etc.: *She paid the sales-clerk.* 2 money or equivalent given for goods, services, or work; wages; salary: *Anna gets her pay every Saturday.* 3 give money for: *Pay your way.* 4 hand over money owed; hand over the amount of: *to pay a debt.* 5 give what is due: *She owes it and must pay.* 6 give; make; offer: *to pay attention, to pay compliments, to pay a visit.* 7 be profitable; be worthwhile to: *It pays me to keep that stock. It wouldn't pay me to take that job.* 8 yield as a return: *That stock pays me fifteen percent.* 9 be profitable: *It paid her to be patient.* 10 a source of payment. 11 a return for favours or hurts: *Dislike is the pay for being mean.* 12 reward or punish: *She paid them for their insults by causing them trouble.* 13 suffer; undergo: *to pay a penalty.* 14 let out a rope, etc. 15 fall off to leeward. 16 requiring a cash payment or the insertion of coins or tokens: *a pay telephone, pay television.* 1, 3–9, 12–15 *v.*, **paid** or (for def. 14) **payed, pay·ing;** 2, 10, 11, 16 *n.*
**in the pay of,** paid by and working for.
**pay as you go,** pay or discharge obligations as they are incurred.
**pay back,** **a** return borrowed money. **b** give the same treatment as received: *I'll pay her back for her hospitality by inviting her for dinner.* **c** take revenge on: *I'll pay you back yet!*
**pay off,** **a** give all the money that is owed; pay in full. **b** get even with; get revenge on.
**pay up,** pay; pay in full.

**pay²** (pā) cover a ship's bottom, seams, rope, etc. with tar, pitch, or another waterproof substance. *v.*, **payed, pay·ing.**

**pay·a·ble** (pā′ə bəl) 1 required to be paid; due: *accounts payable.* 2 that may or can be paid. 3 of a mine, etc., profitable. *adj.*

**pay·day** (pā′dā′) a day on which wages are paid. *n.*

**pay dirt** 1 earth, ore, etc. containing enough metal to be worth mining. 2 *Informal.* something that yields a profit or beneficial result.

**pay·ee** (pā ē′) a person to whom money is paid or is to be paid. *n.*

**pay·er** (pā′ər) one who pays; one who is to pay. *n.*

**pay·load** (pā′lōd′) 1 the part of a vehicle's load that produces revenue. 2 the warhead, instruments, etc. carried by a missile or rocket. *n.*

**pay·mas·ter** (pā′mas′tər) a person whose job is to pay wages. *n.*

**pay·ment** (pā′mənt) 1 the act or fact of paying; compensation. 2 the amount paid: *a monthly payment of $90.* 3 reward or punishment: *She said her child's good health was payment enough.* *n.*

**pay·mis·tress** (pā′mis′tris) a woman whose job is to pay wages. *n.*

**pay-off** (pā′of′) **1** a paying of wages. **2** the time of such payment. **3** returns from an enterprise, specific action, etc. **4** *Informal.* a dividing of the returns from some undertaking among those having an interest in it. *n.*

**pay phone** a coin-operated telephone.

**pay·roll** (pā′rōl′) **1** a list of persons to be paid and the amounts that each one is to receive. **2** the total amount to be paid to them. *n.*

**pay TV** **1** a television service for which extra payment is made. **2** a coin-operated television set.

**payt.** payment.

**Pb** lead.

**PBX** Private Branch (Telephone) Exchange.

**p.c.** **1** percent. **2** postcard. **3** petty cash.

**P.C.** or **PC** **1** personal computer. **2** Police Constable. **3** politically correct. **4** Privy Council. **5** Privy Councillor.

**PCB** polychlorinated biphenyl, one of a family of chemical compounds regarded as highly toxic and possibly carcinogenic pollutants.

**pct.** percent.

**pd.** paid.

**p.d.** **1** per diem. **2** potential difference.

**Pd** palladium.

**P.D.** **1** Police Department. **2** per diem. **3** Postal District.

**PE** Prince Edward Island (*used especially in computerized address systems*).

**P.E.** Petroleum Engineer.

**pea** (pē) **1** an annual vine grown in many varieties for its smooth, round, protein-rich seeds borne in pods. See POD for picture. **2** the seed of this plant, used as a vegetable when green or for soups, etc. when ripened and dried. **3** any of various plants that are related to or resemble the garden pea (*usually used in compounds*): *chick-pea, sweet pea.* **4** referring to a very large family of herbs, climbing plants, shrubs, and trees found throughout the world, having usually compound leaves and bearing fruit in the form of oblong pods that split open evenly along the middle when ripe and in which the seeds are arranged in rows: *The bean, pea, clover, alfalfa, wisteria, and rosewood are some members of the pea family.* **5** especially in the West Indies, the fresh or dried seed of a legume, especially any of various beans or peas: *Rice and peas is a common West Indian dish.* **6** something resembling a pea. *n., pl.* **peas.**
**as like as two peas,** exactly alike.

**peace** (pēs) **1** freedom from war or strife of any kind: *to work for world peace.* **2** public quiet, order, and security. **3** an agreement between contending parties to end a war: *to sign the peace, the Peace of Paris.* **4** quiet; calm; stillness: *peace of mind.* **5** keep still! stay quiet! be silent! 1–4 *n.*, 5 *interj.*
**at peace,** **a** not in a state of war. **b** not quarrelling. **c** in a state of quietness; quiet; peaceful.
**hold** or **keep one's peace,** be silent; keep still.
☛ *Hom.* PIECE.

**peace·a·ble** (pē′sə bəl) **1** liking peace; keeping peace: *Peaceable people keep out of quarrels.* **2** peaceful: *a peaceable reign.* *adj.* —**peace′a·ble·ness,** *n.*
—**peace′a·bly,** *adv.*

hat, āge, fär; let, ēqual, tèrm; it, īce
hot, ōpen, ôrder; oil, out; cup, pùt, rüle
əbove, takən, pencəl, lemən, circəs
ch, child; ng, long; sh, ship
th, thin; ᴛʜ, then; zh, measure

**peace·ful** (pēs′fəl) **1** free of turmoil, commotion, or conflict; quiet; calm: *a peaceful day, a peaceful scene.* **2** keeping peace: *peaceful neighbours.* **3** of or having to do with peace or a time of peace: *peaceful uses for nuclear energy.* **4** without violence or force: *to settle a dispute by peaceful means.* *adj.* —**peace′ful·ly,** *adv.*
—**peace′ful·ness,** *n.*

**peace·keep·ing** (pēs′kē′ping) the preserving of peace, especially the enforcement of peace between hostile nations by means of an international body: *a peacekeeping force.* *n.* —**peace′keep′er,** *n.*

**peace·mak·er** (pēs′māk′ər) a person who makes peace, especially by reconciling conflicts or quarrels between individuals or groups. *n.*

**peace offering** **1** an offering made to obtain peace. **2** in old Jewish custom, an offering of thanksgiving to God.

**peace officer** a person responsible for preserving public peace, such as a mayor, magistrate, or police officer.

**peace pipe** a pipe smoked by North American Indians as a token or pledge of peace; calumet.

**Peace River Block** a settled region in northern British Columbia and Alberta, lying in the fertile valley of the Peace River: *The Peace River Block is often called the Peace River Country.*

**peace·time** (pēs′tīm′) **1** a time of peace. **2** of or having to do with a time of peace: *peacetime policies.* *n.*

**peach** (pēch) **1** a juicy, roundish fruit having a soft, pinkish-yellow, fuzzy skin and sometimes a rough stone, or pit: *Peaches are grown in temperate climates.* **2** the small tree, a member of the rose family, on which peaches grow. **3** yellowish pink. 1–3 *n.*, 3 *adj.*

**peach·y** (pē′chē) like a peach, as in colour or texture. *adj.*, **peach·i·er, peach·i·est.** —**peach′i·ness,** *n.*

A peacock and peahen. The male is about 180 cm long including the 120 cm tail.

**pea·cock** (pē′kok′) **1** an adult male peafowl, a large bird with beautiful green, blue, and gold feathers: *The peacock's tail feathers have spots resembling eyes and can be spread out and held upright like a fan.* **2** a person who is vain and fond of showing off. **3** strut like a peacock. **4** bright blue-green. 1, 2, 4 *n., pl.* **pea·cocks** or (*esp. collectively*) **pea·cock;** 3 *v.*, 4 *adj.*

**pea·fowl** (pē′foul′) a peacock or peahen, a large pheasant of Asia and Africa: *Peafowl are commonly kept in public gardens or parks.* *n.*

**pea·hen** (pē′hen′) an adult female peafowl. *n.*

**pea jacket** a short coat of thick woollen cloth, worn especially by sailors.

**peak** (pēk) **1** the pointed top of a mountain or hill: *snowy peaks.* **2** a mountain that stands alone. **3** the highest point: *to reach the peak of one's profession.* **4** any pointed end or top: *the peak of a beard, the peak of a roof.* **5** the front part or the brim of a cap. **6** the narrow part of a ship's hold at the bow or the stern. **7** the upper rear corner of a sail. **8** raise straight up; tilt up. *1–7 n., 8 v.*
☛ *Hom.* PEEK.

**peaked**[1] (pēkt *or* pē′kid) having a peak; pointed: *a peaked hat.* *adj.*

**peak·ed**[2] (pē′kid) sickly in appearance; wan; thin. *adj.*

**peal** (pēl) **1** a loud, long sound: *a peal of thunder, peals of laughter.* **2** the loud ringing of bells. **3** a set of bells; chimes. **4** ring out; ring: *The bells pealed forth their message of joy.* *1–3 n., 4 v.*
☛ *Hom.* PEEL.

**pe·an** (pē′ən) See PAEAN. *n.*

**pea·nut** (pē′nut′) **1** a plant of the same family as the pea, whose pods ripen underground and contain large seeds that are used as nuts when roasted, and that also yield an oil used in cooking. **2** one of these pods containing seeds. **3** one of these seeds. **4 peanuts,** *Informal.* something of little value, especially a small amount of money: *It costs peanuts to run this car.* *n.*

**peanut butter** a spread made from ground peanuts, used as a filling for sandwiches, etc.

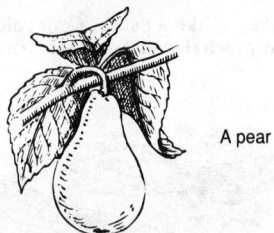
A pear

**pear** (per) **1** a sweet, juicy, edible fruit rounded at one end and smaller toward the stem end. **2** the tree that bears this fruit: *The pear is a member of the rose family.* **3** *Informal.* especially in the West Indies, AVOCADO. *n.*
☛ *Hom.* PAIR, PARE.

**pearl** (pėrl) **1** a white or nearly white gem that has a soft shine like satin: *Pearls are formed inside the shell of a kind of oyster, or in other similar shellfish.* **2** a similar gem made artificially. **3** anything that looks like a pearl, such as a dewdrop or a tear. **4** a very fine one of its kind: *She is a pearl among women.* **5** very pale, clear bluish grey. **6** hunt or dive for pearls. **7** formed into small, round pieces: *pearl tapioca.* **8** MOTHER-OF-PEARL. *1–5, 8 n., 5, 7 adj., 6 v.*
**cast pearls before swine,** give something very fine to a person who cannot appreciate it.
☛ *Hom.* PURL.

**pearl grey** a soft, pale bluish grey.

**pearl·y** (pėr′lē) **1** like a pearl; having the colour or lustre of pearls: *pearly teeth.* **2** like MOTHER-OF-PEARL. *adj.* **pearl·i·er, pearl·i·est.** —**pearl′i·ness,** *n.*

**pearly nautilus** any of a closely related group of sea animals belonging to the same class as octopuses and squids, having a smooth spiral shell composed of a series of chambers and with a pearly lining: *A pearly nautilus has about 90 small, suckerless tentacles with which it captures shrimps and other prey.* See NAUTILUS for picture.

**peas·ant** (pez′ənt) **1** in parts of Europe or Asia, a person who lives in the country and works on the land, especially a farm labourer or tenant farmer. **2** of peasants: *peasant labour.* *1 n., 2 adj.*

**peas·ant·ry** (pez′ən trē) PEASANTS collectively. *n.*

**pea·shoot·er** (pē′shü′tər) a toy blowgun through which to blow dried peas and other small objects. *n.*

**peat** (pēt) vegetable matter consisting of mosses and other plants that have decomposed in water and become partly carbonized, used as fertilizer and as a fuel when dried. *n.*

**peat bog** a bog composed of PEAT.

**peat moss** any of a closely related group of mosses that grow only in wet acid areas; sphagnum: *Peat moss forms peat when it dies and decomposes together with other plants.*

A logger using a peavey to move a log

**pea·vey** (pē′vē) a strong pole tipped with an iron or steel point and having a hinged hook near the end: *Loggers use peaveys in managing logs.* *n., pl.* **pea·veys.**

**peb·ble** (peb′əl) **1** a small stone, usually worn smooth and round by being rolled about by water. **2** a rough, uneven surface on leather, paper, etc. **3** prepare leather so that it has a grained surface. *1, 2 n., 3 v.,* **peb·bled, peb·bling.** —**peb′ble·like′,** *adj.*

**peb·bly** (peb′lē) having many pebbles; covered with pebbles. *adj.*

**pe·can** (pē′kan *or* pi kan′) **1** an olive-shaped, edible nut with a smooth, thin shell, that grows on a kind of hickory tree common in the southern United States. **2** the tree that it grows on. **3** the wood of the pecan tree. *n.*

**pec·ca·dil·lo** (pek′ə dil′ō) a slight sin or fault. *n., pl.* **pec·ca·dil·loes** *or* **pec·ca·dil·los.**

**pec·ca·ry** (pek′ə rē) either of two closely related species of small, piglike animal of North and South America having sharp tusks, small, erect ears, and a very short tail: *The peccaries make up a family of mammals and are distantly related to pigs.* *n., pl.* **pec·ca·ries** or (*esp. collectively*) **pec·ca·ry.**

**peck**[1] (pek) **1** a non-metric unit of measure for volume, equal to eight quarts or one fourth of a bushel (about 9.1 dm³): *The peck was used for measuring grain, fruit, etc.* **2** a container for measuring, holding just a peck. **3** a great deal: *a peck of trouble.* *n.*

**peck**[2] (pek) **1** strike and pick with the beak or with something like a beak. **2** a stroke made with the beak: *The hen gave me a peck.* **3** make by striking with the beak or with something pointed: *Woodpeckers peck holes in trees.* **4** a hole or mark made by pecking: *The bark of the tree was riddled with pecks.* **5** aim with a beak; make a pecking motion. **6** strike at and pick up with the beak: *A hen pecks corn.* **7** *Informal.* a hurried or casual kiss: *She gave him a peck on the cheek as she hurried out the door.* **8** find fault. 1, 3, 5, 6, 8 *v.*, 2, 4, 7 *n.*
**peck at, a** try to peck. **b** *Informal.* eat only a little, bit by bit: *She just pecked at her food.* **c** keep criticizing.

**peck·er** (pek′ər) a person or thing that pecks, especially a bird such as a woodpecker. *n.*

**pec·ten** (pek′tən) a comblike part; especially, a membrane in the eyes of birds and reptiles that has parallel folds suggesting the teeth of a comb. *n.*
☞ *Hom.* PECTIN.

**pec·tin** (pek′tən) a substance that is found in ripe fruits and is used to stiffen fruit jelly. *n.*
☞ *Hom.* PECTEN.

**pec·to·ral** (pek′tə rəl) **1** of, in, or on the breast or chest. **2** good for diseases of the lungs. **3** a medicine for the lungs. **4** something, such as an ornament, worn on the breast. 1, 2 *adj.*, 3, 4 *n.*

**pectoral fin** one of the two fins behind the head of a fish.

**pec·u·late** (pek′yə lāt′) steal money or goods entrusted to one; embezzle. *v.*, **pec·u·lat·ed, pec·u·lat·ing.** —**pec·u·la′tion**, *n.* —**pec·u·la′tor**, *n.*

**pe·cul·iar** (pi kyü′lyər) **1** strange; odd; unusual: *It was peculiar that the fish market had no fish last Friday. A woman's hat on a man's head looks peculiar.* **2** belonging to one person or thing and not to another; special; particular: *This old book has a peculiar value. Some minerals are peculiar to the Canadian Shield.* *adj.* —**pe·cul′iar·ly**, *adv.*

**pe·cu·li·ar·i·ty** (pi kyü′lē ar′ə tē or pi kyü′lē er′ə tē) **1** the quality or state of being peculiar; strangeness; oddness; unusualness: *We noticed the peculiarity of his manner at once.* **2** some little thing that is strange or odd; oddity or quirk: *One of his peculiarities is that his two eyes are not the same colour.* **3** a peculiar or characteristic quality. *n., pl.* **pe·cu·li·ar·i·ties.**

**pe·cu·ni·ar·y** (pi kyü′nē er′ē) of or having to do with money; in the form of money. *adj.*

**ped·a·gog** (ped′ə gog′) See PEDAGOGUE. *n.*

**ped·a·gog·ic** (ped′ə goj′ik) of teachers or teaching; of PEDAGOGY. *adj.* —**ped′a·gog′i·cal·ly**, *adv.*

**ped·a·gog·i·cal** (ped′ə goj′ə kəl) PEDAGOGIC. *adj.*

**ped·a·gogue** (ped′ə gog′) a narrow-minded or pedantic teacher. *n.* Also, **pedagog.**

**ped·a·go·gy** (ped′ə goj′ē or ped′ə gō′jē) **1** the profession of teaching. **2** the science or art of teaching. *n.*

**ped·al** (ped′əl) **1** a lever worked by the foot; the part on which the foot is placed to move any kind of machinery: *Organs have pedals for producing deep notes.* **2** work or use the pedals of; move by pedals: *She pedalled her bicycle slowly up the hill.* **3** work pedals. **4** in biology, of or having to do with the foot. 1 *n.*, 2, 3 *v.*, **ped·alled** or **ped·aled, ped·al·ling** or **ped·al·ing;** 4 *adj.*
☞ *Hom.* PEDDLE.

**ped·al·fer** (pə dal′fər) soil lacking calcium and magnesium because of high humidity. *n.*

**ped·ant** (ped′ənt) **1** a person who displays his or her knowledge in an unnecessary or tiresome way. **2** a teacher or scholar who places too much emphasis on detail and precision in the use or presentation of knowledge. *n.*

**pe·dan·tic** (pi dan′tik) **1** displaying one's knowledge more than is necessary. **2** tediously learned; scholarly in a dull and narrow way. *adj.* —**pe·dan′ti·cal·ly**, *adv.*

**ped·ant·ry** (ped′ən trē) **1** a PEDANTIC way of presenting or applying knowledge. **2** an example or instance of pedantry: *The author's many pedantries make the book difficult to read.* *n., pl.* **ped·ant·ries.**

**ped·dle** (ped′əl) **1** carry from place to place and sell: *to peddle fruit.* **2** sell or deal out in small quantities: *to peddle newspapers, to peddle gossip.* **3** travel about with things to sell: *She peddles for a living.* *v.*, **ped·dled, ped·dling.**
☞ *Hom.* PEDAL.

**ped·dler** (ped′lər) a person who travels about selling things that he or she carries in a pack, in a cart, or on a truck. *n.* Also, **pedlar.**

**ped·es·tal** (ped′i stəl) **1** the base supporting a column or pillar. **2** a base on which a statue, tall vase, lamp, etc. stands. **3** any foundation or support. *n.*
**put** or **set on a pedestal,** regard as extremely admirable or important; idolize.

**pe·des·tri·an** (pə des′trē ən) **1** a person who goes on foot; walker. **2** going on foot; walking: *Pedestrian traffic is not permitted on this bridge.* **3** without imagination; dull; slow: *a pedestrian style in writing.* 1 *n.*, 2, 3 *adj.*

**pe·di·a·tri·cian** (pē′dē ə trish′ən) a medical doctor who specializes in PEDIATRICS. *n.*

**pe·di·at·rics** (pē′dē at′riks) the branch of medicine dealing with children's diseases and the care and development of babies and children (*used with a singular or plural verb*). *n.*

**ped·i·cab** (ped′i kab′) a tricycle with a roofed cab for one or two passengers, pedalled by the driver: *Pedicabs are common in the Far East.* *n.*

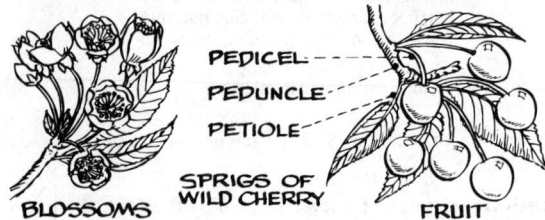

**ped·i·cel** (ped′ə səl) on a plant, a stalk that supports a single flower or spore-bearing organ. See STEM for another picture. *n.*

**ped·i·cure** (ped′ə kyūr′) 1 a treatment for the feet, toes, and toenails, especially a cosmetic treatment including trimming and polishing of the toenails. 2 the care of the feet, toes, and toenails. *n.*

**ped·i·gree** (ped′ə grē′) 1 the list of the ancestors of a person or animal; family tree. 2 ancestry; line of descent. *n.*

**ped·i·greed** (ped′ə grēd′) having a known PEDIGREE: *Molly's dog is pedigreed. Horses, cows, dogs, and other animals of known and recorded ancestry are called pedigreed stock.* *adj.*

**ped·i·ment** (ped′ə mənt) 1 in classic architecture, a low, triangular part forming the front of a building with a two-pitched roof: *A pediment is like a gable.* See PORTICO for picture. 2 a similar form used as a decoration on any building, piece of furniture, etc. *n.*

**ped·lar** (ped′lər) See PEDDLER. *n.*

**ped·o·cal** (ped′ə kəl) soil high in calcium and magnesium because of low humidity. *n.*

**pe·dom·e·ter** (pi dom′ə tər) an instrument for recording the number of steps taken and thus measuring the distance travelled. *n.*

**pe·dun·cle** (pi dung′kəl) on a plant, a stalk that supports a flower or a flower cluster. See PEDICEL for picture. *n.*

**peek** (pēk) 1 look quickly or secretively: *He pretended to have his eyes covered, but I could see he was peeking between his fingers. She peeked around the corner.* 2 a quick, secretive look: *We took a peek at the Christmas presents.* 3 look through a small narrow hole or crack: *I peeked through the hole in the fence.* 4 a look through a hole or crack; a quick look: *to take a peek into the refrigerator.* 1, 3 *v.,* 2, 4 *n.*
☞ *Hom.* PEAK.

**peel** (pēl) 1 the rind or outer covering of fruit or vegetables. 2 strip the skin, rind, or bark from: *to peel an orange, to peel a potato.* 3 strip: *The Indians peeled the bark from trees to make canoes.* 4 come off: *When I was sunburnt, my skin peeled.* 1 *n.,* 2–4 *v.*
**keep one's eyes peeled,** *Informal.* be on the alert: *Keep your eyes peeled for cars turning off the highway here.*
☞ *Hom.* PEAL.

**peel·ing** (pē′ling) 1 a piece or strip, as of rind or skin, peeled or pared off: *potato peelings.* 2 ppr. of PEEL. 1 *n.,* 2 *v.*

**peep¹** (pēp) 1 look through a small or narrow hole or crack. 2 a look through a crack or hole; little look; peek. 3 a small hole or crack to look through. 4 look secretly. 5 a secret look: *to take a peep into the pantry.* 6 look out, as if peeping: *Violets peeped among the leaves.* 7 come partly out; show slightly: *Her toe peeped through the hole in her stocking.* 8 the first looking or coming out: *at the peep of day.* 1, 4, 6, 7 *v.,* 2, 3, 5, 8 *n.*

**peep²** (pēp) 1 a short, high sound such as that made by a baby bird; cheep: *the peeps of newly hatched chicks.* 2 make such a sound; chirp. 3 speak in a small, weak voice. 4 a slight, feeble utterance, especially of protest: *I don't want to hear another peep out of you.* 1, 4 *n.,* 2, 3 *v.*

**peep·er** (pē′pər) 1 a person or thing that peeps. 2 any of certain frogs that make peeping noises. 3 *Informal.* eye. *n.*

**peep·hole** (pēp′hōl′) a hole through which one may peep. *n.*

**peer¹** (pēr) 1 a person of the same rank, ability, age, etc. as another; equal: *a jury of one's peers. He is so fine a man that it would be hard to find his peer.* 2 a member of the PEERAGE; a noble: *Dukes, marquises, earls, counts, viscounts, and barons are British peers.* *n.*
☞ *Hom.* PIER.

**peer²** (pēr) 1 look closely to see clearly, as a near-sighted person does: *She peered at the tag to read the price.* 2 come out slightly; peep out: *The sun was peering from behind a cloud.* *v.*
☞ *Hom.* PIER.

**peer·age** (pēr′ij) 1 all the titled persons of a country; the body of PEERS (def. 2). 2 the rank or dignity of a PEER (def. 2). 3 a book giving a list of PEERS (def. 2) of a country with their genealogy, titles, etc. *n.*

**peer·ess** (pēr′is) 1 a woman who is a member of the PEERAGE; noblewoman. 2 the wife or widow of a PEER (def. 2). *n.*

**peer group** the people of approximately the same age, social status, etc. within a culture or community: *As a boy, he was heavily influenced by his peer group at school.*

**peer·less** (pēr′lis) without an equal; matchless: *She was a peerless leader of our country.* *adj.*

**peer pressure** pressure to conform, exerted by one's equals.

**peeve** (pēv) *Informal.* 1 make cross; annoy. 2 an annoyance. 1 *v.,* **peeved, peev·ing;** 2 *n.*

**pee·vish** (pē′vish) cross; fretful; complaining: *A peevish child is unhappy and makes others unhappy.* *adj.*
—**pee′vish·ly,** *adv.* —**pee′vish·ness,** *n.*

**pee·wee** (pē′wē) 1 a very small person or thing. 2 in boys' or girls' sports, a player aged between 8 and 12. *n.* Also, PEWEE.
☞ *Hom.* PEWEE.

**peg** (peg) 1 a pin or small bolt of wood, metal, etc. used to fasten parts together, to hang things on, to stop a hole, to make fast a rope or string, to mark the score in a game, etc. 2 fasten or hold with pegs: *to peg down a tent.* 3 mark with pegs: *The girls pegged out the spaces for parking bicycles.* 4 work hard and steadily: *She pegged away at her studies so that she would get high marks.* 5 a step; degree. 6 CLOTHESPEG. 1, 5, 6 *n.,* 2–4 *v.,* **pegged, peg·ging.**
**take someone down a peg,** lower the pride of; humble.

**peg·board** (peg′bôrd′) a board with evenly spaced holes in which pegs or hooks are inserted to hold tools, displays, etc. *n.*

**peg leg** 1 a wooden leg. 2 *Informal.* a person who has a wooden leg.

**P.E.I.** Prince Edward Island.

**Pe·kin·ese** (pē'ki nēz') PEKINGESE. *n., adj.*

**Pe·king·ese** (pē'ki nēz' *for 1,* pē'king ēz' *for 2-4*) **1** a breed of small dog with long, soft hair and a broad, flat nose, originally developed in China. **2** a native or inhabitant of Peking. **3** the Chinese dialect of Peking. **4** of or having to do with Peking, its people, or their language. *1–3 n., pl.* **Pe·king·ese;** *4 adj.*
☛ *Usage.* Peking is now officially spelled **Beijing.**

**pe·koe** (pē'kō) a kind of black tea. *n.*

**pel·age** (pel'ij) the hair, fur, wool, or other soft covering of a mammal. *n.*

**pe·lag·ic** (pə laj'ik) of, having to do with or living in the ocean or the open sea. *adj.*

**pelf** (pelf) money or riches, thought of as bad or degrading. *n.*

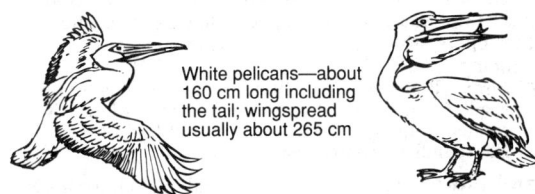

White pelicans—about 160 cm long including the tail; wingspread usually about 265 cm

**pel·i·can** (pel'ə kən) a large fish-eating water bird having a huge bill with a pouch on the underside for scooping up and holding food. *n.*

**pe·lisse** (pə lēs') **1** a coat lined or trimmed with fur. **2** a woman's long cloak. *n.*
☛ *Hom.* POLICE.

**pel·la·gra** (pə lag'rə) a disease marked by eruption on the skin, a nervous condition, and sometimes insanity. It is caused by lack of vitamin B in the diet. *n.*

**pel·let** (pel'it) **1** a little ball of paper, mud, medicine, compressed food for animals, etc. **2** bullet. **3** a piece of small shot. *n.*

**pell–mell** or **pell·mell** (pel'mel') **1** in a rushing, tumbling mass or crowd: *The children dashed pell-mell down the beach and into the waves.* **2** in headlong haste. **3** headlong; tumultuous. **4** violent disorder or confusion. *1, 2 adv., 3 adj., 4 n.*

**pel·lu·cid** (pə lü'sid) **1** transparent; clear: *a pellucid stream.* **2** clearly expressed; easy to understand: *pellucid language. adj.*

**Pel·o·pon·ne·sian** (pel'ə pə nē'shən) **1** of or having to do with the Peloponnesus, a peninsula in southern Greece, or its people. **2** a native or inhabitant of the Peloponnesus. *1 adj., 2 n.*

**pe·lo·ta** (pə lō'tə) a game of Basque or Spanish origin played on a walled court with a hard ball that is struck with a kind of curved wicker racket fastened to a glove on the hand. *n.*

**pelt¹** (pelt) **1** throw things at; attack; assail: *The boys were pelting the dog with stones.* **2** beat heavily: *The rain came pelting down.* **3** throw: *The clouds pelted rain upon us.* **4** pelting. **5** hurry. **6** speed: *The horse is coming at full pelt. 1–3, 5 v., 4, 6 n.*

**pelt²** the skin of a fur-bearing animal before it has been dressed or tanned. *n.*

**pel·vic** (pel'vik) of, having to do with, or located in or near the PELVIS. *adj.*

hat, āge, fär; let, equal, tèrm; it, īce
hot, ōpen, ôrder; oil, out; cup, pùt, rüle
əbove, takən, pencəl, lemən, circəs
ch, child; ng, long; sh, ship
th, thin; ᴛʜ, then; zh, measure

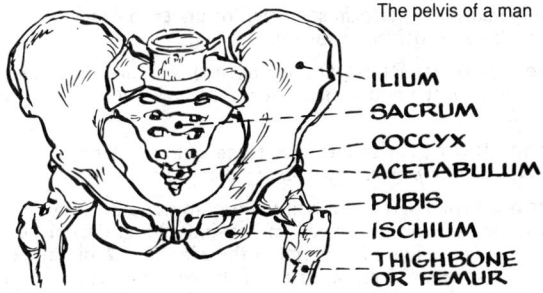

The pelvis of a man
- ILIUM
- SACRUM
- COCCYX
- ACETABULUM
- PUBIS
- ISCHIUM
- THIGHBONE OR FEMUR

**pel·vis** (pel'vis) **1** the basin-shaped structure in many vertebrates formed by the hipbones and the end of the backbone. **2** the cavity of the pelvis. *n., pl.* **pel·ves** (-vēz).

**pem·mi·can** (pem'ə kən) *Cdn.* dried, lean meat pounded into a paste with melted fat: *Pemmican was the usual food of the voyageurs because it would keep for a long time under almost any conditions. n.*
☛ *Etym.* From Cree *pimii* 'fat' + *-kan* 'prepared'.

**pen¹** (pen) **1** a writing instrument supplying a continuous flow of ink, such as a fountain pen, ball-point, or felt-tip pen. **2** a small metal instrument with a split point used with a holder, for writing in ink. **3** such an instrument together with its holder. **4** writing or a style of writing: *She makes her living with her pen.* **5** write: *He penned a few lines to his mother. 1–4 n., 5 v.,* **penned, pen·ning.** —**pen'like',** *adj.*
☛ *Etym.* Through OF from L *penna* 'feather', since the first pens were made from feathers, or quills.

**pen²** (pen) **1** a small, closed yard for cows, sheep, pigs, chickens, etc. **2** the animals in a pen. **3** any small place of confinement. **4** shut in a pen. **5** confine closely: *I kept the dog penned in a corner while they hunted for the leash. 1–3 n., 4, 5 v.,* **penned** or **pent, pen·ning.** —**pen'like',** *adj.*

**pen³** (pen) a female swan. *n.*

**Pen.** or **pen.** peninsula.

**pe·nal** (pē'nəl) **1** of, having to do with, or given as punishment: *penal laws, penal labour.* **2** liable to be punished: *Robbery is a penal offence.* **3** used as a prison or place of punishment: *a penal colony. adj.*

**pe·nal·ize** (pē'nə līz' *or* pen'ə līz') **1** declare punishable by law or by rule; set a penalty for: *Fouls are penalized in many games.* **2** inflict a penalty on; punish: *Our team was penalized five yards. v.,* **pe·nal·ized, pe·nal·iz·ing.**

**pen·al·ty** (pen'əl tē) **1** a punishment for breaking a law or rule: *Her penalty for speeding was a fine of eighty dollars.* **2** a disadvantage imposed on a side or player for breaking the rules of a sport or game. **3** a disadvantage attached to some act or condition: *the penalties of old age.* **4** a handicap. *n., pl.* **pen·al·ties.**

**penalty box** *Cdn.* in hockey or lacrosse, a special bench where players awarded penalties spend their time off the ice or field.

**pen·ance** (pen′əns) 1 a punishment borne to show sorrow for sin, to make up for a wrong done, and to obtain pardon from the church for sin. 2 the sacrament of the Roman Catholic Church that includes contrition, confession, satisfaction, and absolution. *n.*
**do penance,** perform some act, or undergo some penalty, in satisfaction for sin.

**pe·na·tes** or **Pe·na·tes** (pə nā′tēz) in ancient Rome, the gods of the household. See LARES AND PENATES. *n. pl.*

**pen·chant** (pen′chənt) a strong taste or liking; inclination: *a penchant for taking long walks.* *n.*

**pen·cil** (pen′səl) 1 a pointed tool to write or draw with, usually made of wood and having a long, thin piece of black or coloured material in the centre. 2 an object of like shape. 3 mark, write, or draw with a pencil. 4 a stick of colouring matter. 5 an artist's paintbrush. 6 a set of lines, light rays, or the like coming to a point or extending in different directions from a point. 7 the skill or style of an artist. 1, 2, 4–7 *n.,* 3 *v.,* **pen·cilled** or **pen·ciled, pen·cil·ling** or **pen·cil·ing.**

**pend·ant** (pen′dənt) 1 a hanging ornament, especially one attached to an earring, necklace, or bracelet. 2 an ornament hanging down from a ceiling or roof: *Pendants were common in late Gothic architecture.* 3 PENDENT. 1, 2 *n.,* 3 *adj.*
☞ *Hom.* PENDENT.

**pend·ent** (pen′dənt) 1 hanging: *the pendent branches of a willow.* 2 overhanging. 3 pending. 4 a PENDANT. 1–3 *adj.,* 4 *n.*
☞ *Hom.* PENDANT.

**pend·ing** (pen′ding) 1 waiting to be decided or settled: *while the agreement was pending.* 2 while waiting for; until: *Pending his return, let us get everything ready.* 3 during: *pending the investigation.* 1 *adj.,* 2, 3 *prep.*

**pen·du·lous** (pen′jə ləs or pen′dyə ləs) 1 hanging downward: *pendulous jowls.* 2 suspended so as to swing freely. *adj.* —**pen′du·lous·ly,** *adv.* —**pen′du·lous·ness,** *n.*

**pen·du·lum** (pen′jə ləm or pen′dyə ləm) a body or mass hung from a fixed point so as to swing freely to and fro under the forces of gravity and momentum: *The movement of the works of a tall clock is often timed by a pendulum.* See ESCAPEMENT for picture. *n.*

**pen·e·tra·bil·i·ty** (pen′ə trə bil′ə tē) the capability of being PENETRATED. *n.*

**pen·e·tra·ble** (pen′ə trə bəl) that can be PENETRATED. *adj.*

**pen·e·trate** (pen′ə trāt′) 1 pass into or through: *The bullet penetrated five centimetres into the wall.* 2 pierce through: *Our eyes could not penetrate the darkness.* 3 make a way: *Even where the trees were thickest the sunshine penetrated.* 4 soak through; spread through: *The damp penetrated the whole house.* 5 see into; understand: *I could not penetrate the mystery.* *v.,* **pen·e·trat·ed, pen·e·trat·ing.**

**pen·e·trat·ing** (pen′ə trā′ting) 1 sharp; piercing: *a penetrating scream.* 2 acute or keen: *a penetrating insight.* 3 that can penetrate: *a penetrating medication, penetrating oil.* 4 ppr. of PENETRATE. 1–3 *adj.,* 4 *v.* —**pen′e·trat′ing·ly,** *adv.*

**pen·e·tra·tion** (pen′ə trā′shən) 1 the act or power of penetrating. 2 the act of entering a country and gaining influence there. 3 the depth to which something penetrates. 4 the ability to understand deeply: *a mind of great acuteness and penetration.* *n.*

**pen·e·tra·tive** (pen′ə trā′tiv) penetrating; piercing; acute, or keen. *adj.*

Emperor penguins— about 120 cm high

**pen·guin** (pen′gwin or peng′gwin) any of numerous related species of flightless sea bird native to the cold areas of the Southern Hemisphere, having wings modified into flippers, which are used for diving and swimming. *n.*
☞ *Etym.* Probably from a Breton word meaning 'white head'. Compare Welsh *pen* 'head' + *gwyn* 'white', first applied to the great auk, a now extinct bird of the Newfoundland coasts. 16c.

**pen·hold·er** (pen′hōl′dər) a stand or rack for a pen or pens. *n.*

**pen·i·cil·lin** (pen′ə sil′ən) any of several antibiotic acids that are produced by moulds or synthetically: *Penicillin is used especially for destroying certain kinds of bacteria.* *n.*

**pen·i·cil·li·um** (pen′ə sil′ē əm) any of a certain kind of fungus: *The mould on cheese is a penicillium.* *n., pl.* **pen·i·cil·li·ums** or **pen·i·cil·li·a** (-ē ə).

**pen·in·su·la** (pə nin′sə lə or pə nin′syə lə) a piece of land almost surrounded by water, or extending far out into the water: *Nova Scotia is a peninsula.* *n.*

**pen·in·su·lar** (pə nin′sə lər or pə nin′syə lər) of, in, or like a PENINSULA. *adj.*

**pe·nis** (pē′nis) the male sex organ, which, in mammals, is also the organ through which urine is excreted. *n., pl.* **pe·nis·es** (-nis iz) or **pe·nes** (-nēz).

**pen·i·tence** (pen′ə təns) sorrow for sinning or doing wrong; repentance. *n.*

**pen·i·tent** (pen′ə tənt) 1 sorry for sinning or doing wrong; repenting: *The penitent child promised never to cheat again.* 2 a person who is sorry for sin or wrongdoing. 3 a person who confesses and does penance for his or her sins under the direction of a church. 1 *adj.,* 2, 3 *n.* —**pen′i·tent·ly,** *adv.*

**pen·i·ten·tial** (pen′ə ten′shəl) 1 of, showing, or having to do with PENITENCE: *The penitential psalms express remorse for sin.* 2 of or having to do with PENANCE. *adj.*

**pen·i·ten·tia·ry** (pen′ə ten′shə rē) 1 a prison, especially a federal prison for persons convicted of serious crimes. 2 making one liable to punishment in a prison: *a penitentiary offence.* 3 used for punishment, discipline, and reformation: *penitentiary measures.* 4 of PENANCE; penitential. 1 *n., pl.* **pen·i·ten·tia·ries;** 2–4 *adj.*

**pen·knife** (pen′nīf′) a small folding pocketknife. *n., pl.* **pen·knives.**

**pen·man** (pen′mən) 1 a person whose handwriting is good. 2 a person who writes; author. *n., pl.* **pen·men** (-mən).

**pen·man·ship** (pen′mən ship′)   1 skill in writing with pen, pencil, etc.: *We admired the teacher's penmanship.* 2 a style of handwriting.   *n.*

**pen name**   a name used by a writer instead of his or her real name.

**pen·nant** (pen′ənt)   1 a flag, usually long and narrow and tapering to a point or swallowtail, used on ships for signalling, as a school banner, etc.   2 a flag or other trophy competed for in an athletic contest: *Our team won the baseball pennant.*   *n.*

**pen·ni·less** (pen′i lis)   having no money, very poor. *adj.*

**Penn·syl·van·ia Dutch** (pen′səl vā′nē ə)   1 the descendants of 17th and 18th century immigrants to southeastern Pennsylvania from southern Germany and Switzerland.   2 people of this stock who settled in Upper Canada after the American Revolution.   3 the dialect of German spoken by these people.

**pen·ny** (pen′ē)   1 a piece or sum of money: *I wouldn't give him a penny.*   2 in Canada and the United States, cent.   *n., pl.* **pen·nies.**
**a pretty penny,** *Informal.*   a large sum of money.
**turn an honest penny,**   earn money honestly.

**pen·ny·roy·al** (pen′ē roi′əl)   1 a European herb having a strong scent, closely related to spearmint and peppermint.   2 a strong scented North American plant of the same family.   3 an oil obtained from either of these plants, traditionally used in medicine.   *n.*

**pen·ny·weight** (pen′ē wāt′)   a former unit for measuring mass, equal to 24 grains or one twentieth of an ounce in troy weight (about 1.56 g).   *n.*

**pen·ny–wise** (pen′ē wīz′)   thrifty in regard to small sums.   *adj.*
**penny-wise and pound-foolish,**   thrifty in small expenses and wasteful in big ones.

**pen·ny·worth** (pen′ē wėrth′)   as much as can be bought for a penny.   *n.*

**pe·nol·o·gy** (pē nol′ə jē)   the study of the treatment of criminals and the management of prisons: *Penology is a branch of criminology.*   *n.*

**pen·sion**[1] (pen′shən)   1 money other than wages paid regularly to a person under certain conditions: *Pensions are paid to people who have retired from regular work because of old age, sickness, or injury, or for long service or special merit.*   2 give a pension to.   1 *n.*, 2 *v.*
**pension off,**   retire from service with a pension.

**pen·sion**[2] (päN syôN′) *French.*   1 boarding house. 2 accommodation; board and lodging.   3 boarding school.   *n.*

**pen·sion·er** (pen′shə nər)   a person who receives or lives on a pension, especially an old-age pension.   *n.*

**pen·sive** (pen′siv)   1 thoughtful in a serious or sad way: *She was in a pensive mood, and sat staring out of the window.*   2 melancholy.   *adj.*   —**pen′sive·ly,** *adv.* —**pen′sive·ness,** *n.*

**pent** (pent)   1 closely confined; shut (used with **in** or **up**): *She was pent up in the house most of the winter because of illness.*   2 pt. and a pp. of PEN[2].   1 *adj.*, 2 *v.*

**penta–**   *combining form.*   five: *A pentagon is a plane figure with five angles.* Also, **pent-**.
☞ *Etym.*   From the combining form of Gk. *pente* 'five'.

**pen·ta·cle** (pen′tə kəl)   a symbol, frequently in the shape of a five-pointed star, formerly used in magic.   *n.*

# penmanship   875   peonage

hat, āge, fär; let, ēqual, tėrm; it, īce
hot, ōpen, ôrder; oil, out; cup, pùt, rüle
above, takən, pencəl, lemən, circəs
ch, child; ng, long; sh, ship
th, thin; ᴛʜ, then; zh, measure

**pen·ta·gon** (pen′tə gon′)   1 a plane figure having five sides and five interior angles. See POLYGON for picture.
2 **the Pentagon,**   **a** in the United States, a building that is the headquarters of the Department of Defense, just outside Washington, D.C.   **b** the United States Department of Defense, its policies, etc.   *n.*

**pen·tag·o·nal** (pen tag′ə nəl)   having five sides and five interior angles.   *adj.*

**pen·ta·he·dron** (pen′tə hē′drən)   a solid figure having five faces.   *n., pl.* **pen·ta·he·drons** or **pen·ta·he·dra** (-drə).

**pen·tam·e·ter** (pen tam′ə tər)   1 a line of verse consisting of five metrical feet. *Example: A lit│tle learn│ing is│ a dan│ g'rous thing.*   2 consisting of five metrical feet.   *n.*

**pen·tath·lete** (pen tath′lēt)   an athlete who competes in the PENTATHLON.   *n.*

**pen·tath·lon** (pen tath′lən)   an athletic contest consisting of five different events, in which the person having the highest total score wins.   *n.*

**Pen·te·cost** (pen′tə kost′)   1 the seventh Sunday after Easter, a Christian festival in memory of the descent of the Holy Ghost upon the Apostles. Also called **Whitsunday.**   2 a Jewish harvest festival, observed about seven weeks after the Passover.   *n.*

**pent·house** (pent′hous′)   1 an apartment or house built on the top of a building.   2 a sloping roof projecting from a building.   3 a shed with a sloping roof attached to a building.   *n.*

**pent–up** (pent′up′)   shut up; closely confined: *Her pent-up feelings could no longer be restrained, and she burst into tears.*   *adj.*

**pe·nult** (pi nult′ *or* pē′nult)   the next to the last syllable in a word.   *n.*

**pe·nul·ti·mate** (pi nul′tə mit)   1 next to the last. 2 of or having to do with the PENULT.   3 PENULT.   1, 2 *adj.*, 3 *n.*

**pe·num·bra** (pi num′brə)   1 the partial shadow outside of the complete shadow formed by the sun, moon, etc. during an eclipse. See ECLIPSE for picture.   2 the greyish outer part of a sunspot.   *n., pl.* **pe·num·brae** (-brē *or* -brī) or **pe·num·bras.**

**pe·nu·ri·ous** (pi nyü′rē əs *or* pi nü′rē əs) 1 characteristic of or suffering from penury; poor: *penurious surroundings, penurious times.*   2 mean about spending or giving money; stingy.   *adj.* —**pe·nu′ri·ous·ly,** *adv.*   —**pe·nu′ri·ous·ness,** *n.*

**pen·u·ry** (pen′yə rē)   very great poverty.   *n.*

**pe·on** (pē′on)   1 in Spanish America, a person doing work which requires little skill.   2 any of various workers, etc. in India or Sri Lanka, such as a foot soldier, attendant, or unskilled labourer.   *n.*
☞ *Etym.*   See note at PAWN.

**pe·on·age** (pē′ə nij)   the condition or service of a PEON.   *n.*

**pe·o·ny** (pē'ə nē)   1 a perennial garden plant having large, showy red, pink, or white flowers.   2 its flower. *n., pl.* **pe·o·nies.**

**peo·ple** (pē'pəl)   1 men, women, and children; persons: *There were ten people present.*   2 a race or nation: *the Canadian people, the peoples of Asia.*   3 the body of citizens of a state; the public: *People are funny.*   4 the persons of a place, class, or group: *city people, prairie people.*   5 the common people; lower classes: *The French nobles oppressed the people.*   6 persons in relation to a superior: *A queen rules over her people.*   7 *Informal.* family; relatives: *Tiiu has many friends, but she likes her own people best.*   8 fill or provide with people; populate: *Canada is peopled very largely by Europeans.*   1-7 *n., pl.* **peo·ple** or (for def. 2) **peo·ples;**   8 *v.,* **peo·pled, peo·pling.**

**pep** (pep) *Informal.*   1 spirit; energy; vim or enthusiasm.   2 fill or inspire with energy, etc.; put new life into (used with **up**): *to pep up a party.*   1 *n.,* 2 *v.,* **pepped, pep·ping.**

A dress with a peplum

**pep·lum** (pep'ləm)   1 a short flared, gathered, or pleated piece of material attached to the waistline of a jacket, blouse, or dress and extending to the hips.   2 a full garment worn by women in ancient Greece. *n.*

**pep·per** (pep'ər)   1 a seasoning with a hot taste, made from the ground-up berries of a tropical woody vine. See BLACK PEPPER and WHITE PEPPER.   2 any of a closely related group of tropical climbing shrubs having fragrant leaves; especially, the plant bearing the red berries from which white and black pepper are made.   3 the hollow, fleshy-walled, sweet, red or green fruit of a New World capsicum. Sweet red and green peppers are eaten as vegetables, either raw, cooked, or pickled.   4 the small, hot, red or green fruit of any of several capsicums; cayenne; chili.   5 a capsicum bearing sweet or hot peppers.   6 season or sprinkle with black, white, or red pepper.   7 sprinkle thickly: *Her face is peppered with freckles.*   8 hit with small objects sent thick and fast: *They peppered the enemy with bullets.*   9 a small container for pepper: *silver salts and peppers.*   1-5, 9 *n.,* 6-8 *v.*

**pep·per·corn** (pep'ər kôrn')   one of the dried berries of the pepper plant that are ground up to make black pepper. *n.*

**pep·per·grass** (pep'ər gras')   any of a closely related group of plants of the mustard family, especially garden cress. *n.*

**pep·per·mint** (pep'ər mint')   1 a common herb, a species of mint closely related to spearmint, yielding a sweet-smelling oil used in medicine and as a flavouring for candy.   2 the oil of this herb.   3 candy flavoured with peppermint oil. *n.*

**pep·per·o·ni** (pep'ə rō'nē)   a spicy Italian sausage, often put on a PIZZA. *n.*

**pep·per·y** (pep'ə rē)   1 of, like, or full of pepper: *a peppery stew.*   2 sharp; pungent.   3 having a hot temper; easily made angry. *adj.* —**pep'per·i·ness,** *n.*

**pep·py** (pep'ē) *Informal.*   full of pep; energetic; lively: *Scotch terriers are peppy dogs. adj.,* **pep·pi·er, pep·pi·est.** —**pep'pi·ness,** *n.*

**pep rally** *Informal.*   a meeting organized to stimulate support and enthusiasm for a team, cause, campaign, etc.

**pep·sin** (pep'sən)   1 an enzyme in the gastric juice of the stomach that helps to digest meat, eggs, cheese, and other proteins.   2 a medicine to help digestion, containing this enzyme. *n.*

**pep talk** *Informal.*   a short, emotional talk intended to encourage a person or group in some activity: *The coach gave us a pep talk before the game.*

**pep·tic** (pep'tik)   1 promoting digestion; digestive.   2 of or having to do with PEPSIN.   3 having to do with or caused by the action of digestive juices: *a peptic ulcer. adj.*

**pep·tone** (pep'tōn)   any of a class of diffusible, soluble substances into which meat, eggs, cheese, and other proteins are changed by the action of PEPSIN in digestion. *n.*

**Pé·quiste** (pā kēst')  *Cdn.*   a member or supporter of the PARTI QUÉBÉCOIS. *n.*

**per** (pər; *stressed,* pėr)   1 for each: *We need 125 grams of ground beef per person.*   2 by; through; by means of: *The letter was sent per messenger.*   3 according to: *a payment calculated per number of children in the family. The order was sent out as per instructions. prep.*

**per·am·bu·late** (pə ram'byə lāt')   1 walk through, over, etc.: *perambulating the street.*   2 walk about from place to place.   3 walk through and inspect. *v.,* **per·am·bu·lat·ed, per·am·bu·lat·ing.** —**per·am'bu·la'tion,** *n.*

**per·am·bu·la·tor** (pə ram'byə lā'tər)   1 a small carriage in which a baby is pushed about; pram.   2 a person who PERAMBULATES. *n.*

**per an·num** (pə ran'əm)   yearly; for each year: *Her salary was $34 000 per annum.*

**per·cale** (pər kāl')   a smooth, firm cotton cloth in a plain weave made in different grades: *High-grade percale with a very close weave and a lustrous finish is used for bed linen. n.*

**per cap·i·ta** (pər kap'ə tə)   for each person: *$40 for eight people amounts to $5 per capita.*

**per·ceive** (pər sēv')   1 be aware of through the senses; see, hear, taste, smell, or feel: *Did you perceive the colour of that bird?*   2 take in with the mind; observe: *I perceived that I could not make her change her mind. v.,* **per·ceived, per·ceiv·ing.**

**per·cent** or **per cent** (pər sent')   1 hundredths; parts in each hundred: *Five percent is 5 out of 100, or* $^5/_{100}$ *of the whole. Five percent (5%) of 40 is 2.* Symbol: %   2 for each hundred; in each hundred: *Seven percent of the children failed. n.*
☞ *Etym.* **Per cent** came into English in the 16c. as a shortening of Italian *per cento* or Late Latin *per centum.* However, it is not treated as an abbreviation and so is not normally followed by a period. The one-word form **percent** is now more common than **per cent**, possibly through the influence of PERCENTAGE and PERCENTILE.

**per·cent·age** (pər sen'tij)   1 the rate or proportion of each hundred; part of each hundred: *What percentage of* *children were absent?* **2** a part or proportion: *A large percentage of schoolbooks now have pictures.* **3** an allowance, commission, discount, rate of interest, etc. figured by percent. *n.*

**per·cen·tile** (pər sen′tīl) any value in a series of points on a scale arrived at by dividing a group into a hundred equal parts: *A pupil at the fiftieth percentile is at a point half way between the top and the bottom of his or her group.* *n.*

**per·cept** (pėr′sept) **1** that which is perceived. **2** understanding that is the result of perceiving. *n.*

**per·cep·ti·bil·i·ty** (pər sep′tə bil′ə tē) the fact, quality, or state of being PERCEPTIBLE. *n.*

**per·cep·ti·ble** (pər sep′tə bəl) that can be PERCEIVEd: *The other ship was barely perceptible in the fog.* *adj.*

**per·cep·ti·bly** (pər sep′tə blē) in a PERCEPTIBLE way or amount; to a perceptible degree. *adv.*

**per·cep·tion** (pər sep′shən) **1** the act of perceiving: *Her perception of the change came in a flash.* **2** the power of perceiving: *a keen perception.* **3** the understanding that is the result of perceiving: *Having a clear perception of what was wrong, she soon corrected it.* *n.*

**per·cep·tive** (pər sep′tiv) **1** having to do with perception. **2** having the power of perceiving. *adj.* —**per·cep′tive·ly,** *adv.* —**per·cep′tive·ness,** *n.*

**Per·ce·val** (pėr′sə vəl) in the legends about King Arthur, one of only three Knights of the Round Table who see the Holy Grail: *In the earliest legends about the Quest for the Holy Grail, Perceval is the main hero.* *n.*

**perch**¹ (pėrch) **1** a bar, branch, or anything else on which a bird can come to rest. **2** alight and rest: *A robin perched on our porch railing.* **3** a rather high place or position. **4** sit, especially on something high: *She perched on a stool.* **5** place high up: *The village was perched on a high hill.* **6** a unit for measuring length; rod (about 5.03 m). **7** a unit for measuring area; square rod (about 25.3 m²). 1, 3, 6, 7 *n.*, 2, 4, 5 *v.* —**perch′er,** *n.*

**perch**² (pėrch) **1** any of a closely related group of small freshwater food fishes, especially the **yellow perch** of North America or a similar European species. **2** referring to a family of freshwater fishes including the perches and the walleye: *Fishes of the perch family have two dorsal fins, the first having spiny rays and the second having soft rays.* **3** any of various other freshwater or saltwater fishes. *n., pl.* **perch** or **perch·es.**

**Per·che·ron** (pėr′chə ron′) a breed of large, strong draft horse originally developed in France. *n.*

**per·cip·i·ent** (pər sip′ē ənt) **1** capable of perceiving, especially quickly or keenly; discerning. **2** a person who PERCEIVEs. 1 *adj.*, 2 *n.*

**per·co·late** (pėr′kə lāt) **1** drip or drain through small holes or spaces. **2** filter through; permeate: *Water percolates sand.* **3** make coffee in a percolator. *v.,* **per·co·lat·ed, per·co·lat·ing.**

**per·co·la·tor** (pėr′kə lā′tər) a kind of coffee pot in which boiling water continually bubbles up through a tube and drips down through ground coffee. *n.*

**per·cus·sion** (pər kush′ən) **1** the striking of one object against another with force; stroke; blow: *Caps are exploded by percussion.* **2** the shock made by the striking of one object against another with force. **3** the striking of sound upon the ear. **4** in medicine, the technique of tapping a part of the body to find out the condition of the

---

## percentile 877 perfectionism

hat, āge, fär; let, ēqual, tėrm; it, īce
hot, ōpen, ôrder; oil, out; cup, pùt, rüle
əbove, takən, pencəl, lemən, circəs
ch, child; ng, long; sh, ship
th, thin; ŦH, then; zh, measure

internal organs by the resulting sound. **5** the section of an orchestra playing PERCUSSION INSTRUMENTS. *n.*

**percussion cap** a small cap containing powder that explodes when struck by the hammer of the gun.

**percussion instrument** a musical instrument played by striking it, such as a drum or cymbal.

**per di·em** (pər dē′əm *or* pər dī′əm) *Latin.* **1** per day; for each day. **2** an allowance of so much every day.

**per·di·tion** (pər dish′ən) **1** the loss of one's soul and the joys of heaven. **2** hell. *n.*

**per·e·gri·nate** (per′ə grə nāt′) travel; journey. *v.,* **per·e·gri·nat·ed, per·e·gri·nat·ing.**

**per·e·gri·na·tion** (per′ə grə nā′shən) a journey; travel. *n.*

**per·e·grine** (per′ə grin *or* per′ə grēn) a large falcon, formerly much used in Europe for hawking. *n.*

**per·emp·to·ry** (pə remp′tə rē) **1** IMPERIOUS; positive: *a peremptory teacher.* **2** allowing no denial or refusal: *a peremptory command.* **3** leaving no choice; decisive; final; absolute: *a peremptory decree.* *adj.* —**per·emp′to·ri·ly,** *adv.* —**per·emp′to·ri·ness,** *n.*

**per·en·ni·al** (pə ren′ē əl) **1** lasting through the whole year: *a perennial stream.* **2** lasting for a very long time; enduring: *the perennial beauty of the hills.* **3** having underground parts that live more than two years: *perennial garden plants.* **4** a perennial plant: *Roses are perennials.* 1–3 *adj.,* 4 *n.* —**per·en′ni·al·ly,** *adv.*

**perf.** **1** perfect. **2** perforated.

**per·fect** (pėr′fikt *for adjective and noun,* pər fekt′ *for verb*) **1** without defect; not spoiled at any point; faultless: *a perfect spelling paper. Perfect work shows great care.* **2** remove all faults from; make perfect; improve; add the finishing touches to: *to perfect an invention. The artist was perfecting her picture.* **3** completely skilled; expert: *a perfect golfer.* **4** having all its parts; complete: *The set was perfect; nothing was missing or broken.* **5** carry through; complete: *to perfect a plan.* **6** entire; utter: *a perfect stranger to us.* **7** in grammar, showing an action or state thought of as being completed: *There are three perfect tenses: present perfect, past perfect, and future perfect.* **8** one of the PERFECT TENSES. **9** a verb form in this tense. *Have eaten* is the perfect of *eat.* **10** exact: *a perfect copy.* 1, 3, 4, 6, 7, 10 *adj.,* 2, 5 *v.,* 8, 9 *n.* —**per·fect′er,** *n.* —**per′fect·ness,** *n.*

**per·fect·i·bil·i·ty** (pər fek′tə bil′ə tē) the capability of becoming, or of being made, perfect. *n.*

**per·fect·i·ble** (pər fek′tə bəl) capable of becoming, or of being made, perfect. *adj.*

**per·fec·tion** (pər fek′shən) **1** a perfect condition; faultlessness; highest excellence. **2** a perfect person or thing: *Her work is always perfection.* **3** a making complete or perfect: *The perfection of our plans will take another week.* *n.*
**to perfection,** perfectly: *He played the violin concerto to perfection.*

**per·fec·tion·ism** (pər fek′shə niz′əm) **1** a striving for absolute perfection in what one does. 2 a doctrine that a state of freedom from sin can and should be achieved on earth. *n.*

**per·fec·tion·ist** (pər fek′shə nist) 1 a person who is not content with anything that is not perfect or nearly perfect. 2 a person who believes it possible to lead a sinless life. *n.*

**per·fect·ly** (per′fik tlē) 1 in a perfect manner or degree; completely and faultlessly: *a perfectly drawn circle.* 2 to an adequate extent: *This skirt is still perfectly good. adv.*

**perfect participle** a PAST PARTICIPLE, preceded by a form of the verb *have*, expressing action completed before the time of speaking or acting. In *Having written the letter, she mailed it*, *having written* is a perfect participle.

**perfect tense** the form of a verb which shows that the action is completed now (PRESENT PERFECT); was completed in the past (PAST PERFECT); is to be completed in the future (FUTURE PERFECT).

**per·fer·vid** (pər fer′vid) very FERVID. *adj.*

**per·fid·i·ous** (pər fid′ē əs) deliberately faithless; treacherous. *adj.* —**per·fid′i·ous·ly**, *adv.*

**per·fi·dy** (per′fə dē) breaking faith; base treachery; being false to a trust. *n., pl.* **per·fi·dies.**

**per·fo·rate** (per′fə rāt) 1 make a hole or holes through: *His bullets perforated the target.* 2 make a series of small holes through in order to make separation easier: *Sheets of postage stamps are perforated. v.*, **per·fo·rat·ed, per·fo·rat·ing.**

**per·fo·ra·tion** (per′fə rā′shən) 1 a hole or series of holes bored or punched through something: *She removed the coupon by tearing along the perforation.* 2 perforating or being perforated. *n.*

**per·force** (pər fôrs′) by necessity; necessarily. *adv.*

**per·form** (pər fôrm′) 1 do; carry out: *Perform your duties well. The surgeon performed an operation.* 2 put into effect; fulfil: *Perform your promise.* 3 go through; render: *to perform a piece of music.* 4 act, play, sing, or entertain in public. *v.*

**per·form·ance** (pər fôr′məns) 1 the act of carrying out or doing: *in the performance of one's regular duties.* 2 the thing performed; act; deed: *The child's kicks and screams made a disgraceful performance.* 3 the giving of a play, circus, or other show: *The evening performance is at 8 o'clock. n.*

**per·form·er** (pər fôr′mər) a person who performs, especially one who performs for the entertainment of others; player. *n.*

**per·fume** (per′fyüm *or* pər fyüm′ *for noun*, pər fyüm′ *for verb*) 1 the scent of something that smells sweet: *the perfume of flowers.* 2 a substance having a sweet smell, especially a liquid prepared from essences of flowers or from synthetic substances and applied to the skin or clothes to produce a pleasant scent. 3 fill with a sweet odour: *Flowers perfumed the air.* 4 put a sweet-smelling liquid on. 1, 2 *n.*, 3, 4 *v.*, **per·fumed, per·fum·ing.**

**per·fum·er** (pər fyü′mər) a maker or seller of perfumes. *n.*

**per·fum·er·y** (pər fyü′mə rē) 1 the products made by a perfumer; perfumes. 2 the art or process of making perfumes. 3 a place where perfumes are made or sold. *n., pl.* **per·fum·er·ies.**

**per·func·to·ry** (pər fungk′tə rē) 1 done merely for the sake of getting rid of the duty; done from force of habit; mechanical; indifferent: *The little girl gave her face a perfunctory washing.* 2 acting in a perfunctory way: *The new employee was perfunctory; she did not really care about her work. adj.* —**per·func′to·ri·ly**, *adv.* —**per·func′to·ri·ness**, *n.*

A pergola

**per·go·la** (per′gə lə) an arbour formed by vines, etc. growing over an open roof of latticework or rafters supported by posts. *n.*

**per·haps** (pər haps′) maybe; possibly: *Perhaps she'll do it if you ask her. It would perhaps be better to wait. adv.*

**peri–** a prefix meaning: 1 around; surrounding, as in *periphery, periscope.* 2 near, as in *perigee, perihelion.* ☛ *Etym.* From Gk. *peri* 'around, about'.

**per·i·anth** (per′ē anth) the envelope of a flower, including the CALYX and the COROLLA. *n.*

**per·i·car·di·al** (per′ə kär′dē əl) 1 of or having to do with, or affecting the PERICARDIUM. 2 around the heart. *adj.*

**per·i·car·di·um** (per′ə kär′dē əm) the membranous sac enclosing the heart and the roots of the great blood vessels. *n., pl.* **per·i·car·di·a** (-dē ə).

**per·i·carp** (per′ə kärp′) the walls of a ripened ovary or fruit, sometimes consisting of three layers; a SEED VESSEL. *n.*

**per·i·cra·ni·um** (per′ə krā′nē əm) the membrane covering the bones of the skull. *n., pl.* **per·i·cra·ni·a** (-nē ə).

**per·i·gee** (per′ə jē′) the point in the orbit of a satellite of the earth or an orbiting vehicle where it comes closest to the earth. Compare with APOGEE. *n.*

**per·i·he·li·on** (per′ə hē′lē ən) the point in its orbit where a heavenly body comes closest to the sun. Compare with APHELION. *n., pl.* **per·i·he·li·a** (-lē ə).

**per·il** (per′əl) 1 a chance of harm; exposure to danger or the risk of being injured or destroyed: *This bridge is not safe; cross it at your peril.* 2 put in danger; expose to risk. 1 *n.*, 2 *v.*, **per·illed** *or* **per·iled, per·il·ling** *or* **per·il·ing.**

**per·il·ous** (per′ə ləs) dangerous; full of peril: *a perilous journey. adj.* —**per′il·ous·ly**, *adv.*

**pe·rim·e·ter** (pə rim′ə tər) 1 the outer boundary of a plane figure or an area: *the perimeter of a circle. A fence marks the perimeter of a field.* 2 the distance around such a boundary: *The perimeter of a square equals four times the length of one side. n.*

**pe·ri·od** (pē′rē əd) 1 a portion of time, having certain features or conditions: *the period of the Great War. She visited us for a short period.* 2 a portion of time marked off by events that happen again and again; time after which the same things begin to happen again: *A month,* from new moon to new moon, is a period. **3** a subdivision of a geological ERA. **4** the portion of a game during which there is actual play: *There are three twenty-minute periods in a hockey game.* **5** one of the portions of time into which a school day is divided. **6** the time needed for a disease to run its course. **7** an occurence of MENSTRUATION. **8** a mark (.) of punctuation, marking the end of statements or showing an abbreviation. *Examples: Mrs., Dec.* **9** the pause at the end of a sentence. **10** a complete sentence: *The orator spoke in stately periods.* **11** characteristic of a certain period of time: *period furniture.* **12** the length of time it takes a planet to orbit the sun. *n.*

**pe·ri·od·ic** (pē′rē od′ik) **1** occurring, appearing, or done again and again at regular intervals: *periodic attacks of malaria.* **2** happening every now and then: *a periodic fit of clearing up one's desk.* **3** having to do with a period: *The coming of the new moon is a periodic occurrence.* **4** expressed in PERIODIC SENTENCES. *adj.*

**pe·ri·od·i·cal** (pē′rē od′ə kəl) **1** a magazine that appears regularly: *Maclean's is a Canadian periodical.* **2** of or having to do with periodicals. **3** published at regular intervals, less often than daily. **4** PERIODIC. **1** *n.*, **2–4** *adj.*

**pe·ri·od·i·cal·ly** (pē′rē od′i klē) **1** at regular intervals. **2** every now and then: *My aunt visits us periodically.* *adv.*

**pe·ri·o·dic·i·ty** (pē′rē ə dis′ə tē) a periodic character; tendency to happen at regular intervals. *n., pl.* **pe·ri·o·dic·i·ties.**

**periodic law** in chemistry, the law stating that, when the chemical elements are arranged in the order of their atomic numbers, the elements with similar chemical properties appear at regular intervals.

**periodic sentence** a complex sentence with the MAIN CLAUSE at the end. In *When he was ready, he left the room*, *he left the room* is the main clause.

**periodic table** a table in which the chemical elements, arranged in the order of their atomic weights, are shown in related groups. See chart in the Appendix.

**per·i·os·te·um** (per′ē os′tē əm) the dense fibrous membrane closely covering the surface of bones except at the joints. *n., pl.* **per·i·os·te·a** (-tē ə).

**per·i·pa·tet·ic** (per′ə pə tet′ik) walking about; travelling from place to place; itinerant. *adj.*

**pe·riph·er·al** (pə rif′ər əl) **1** having to do with, situated in, or forming an outside boundary: *The wall marks the peripheral limits of the yard. The doctor checked my peripheral vision.* **2** in computing science, having to do with hardware that is connected to a computer to make up a computer system: *Printers, monitors, and disk drives are peripheral devices.* *adj.* —**pe·riph′er·al·ly,** *adv.*

**peripheral nervous system** all the nerves in the body outside the brain and spinal cord. Compare with CENTRAL NERVOUS SYSTEM.

**peripheral vision** the area of vision outside the line of direct sight; the outer part of the field of vision.

**pe·riph·er·y** (pə rif′ə rē) **1** an outside boundary; perimeter: *The periphery of a circle is called the circumference.* **2** an area outside the centre or main area; outer parts: *the periphery of a city.* **3** in anatomy, the area surrounding a nerve ending, such as a sense organ or muscle. *n., pl.* **pe·riph·er·ies.**

**pe·riph·ra·sis** (pə rif′rə sis) a roundabout way of speaking or writing; circumlocution: *The wife of your* father's brother *is a periphrasis for* your aunt. *n., pl.* **pe·riph·ra·ses** (-sēz′).

hat, āge, fär; let, ēqual, tėrm; it, īce
hot, ōpen, ôrder; oil, out; cup, put, rüle
əbove, takən, pencəl, lemən, circəs
ch, child; ng, long; sh, ship
th, thin; ŦH, then; zh, measure

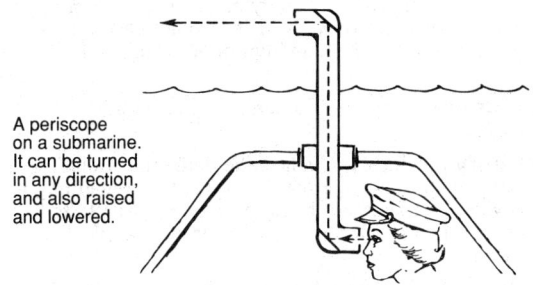

A periscope on a submarine. It can be turned in any direction, and also raised and lowered.

**per·i·scope** (per′ə skōp′) an instrument consisting of a tube with an arrangement of mirrors or prisms that permits a person to see things that are otherwise out of sight: *Periscopes are used to get a view of the surface from a trench or a submerged submarine, to see around a corner or over the heads of people in a crowd, etc.* See SUBMARINE for another picture. *n.*

**per·i·scop·ic** (per′ə skop′ik) giving distinct vision obliquely as well as in a direct line. *adj.*

**per·ish** (per′ish) **1** die or be destroyed: *Ships perish in storms. People perish in war.* **2** decay; become spoiled: *Fruit will perish quickly in hot weather.* *v.*
☛ Hom. PARISH (per′ish).

**per·ish·a·ble** (per′i shə bəl) **1** liable to spoil or decay: *Fresh fruit is perishable.* **2** Usually, **perishables,** *pl.* things that are liable to spoil or decay, especially fresh food: *We put the perishables into the refrigerator right away, but left the canned goods in the bag.* **1** *adj.,* **2** *n.* —**per′ish·a·ble·ness,** *n.*

**per·i·stal·sis** (per′ə stal′sis) the successive wavelike contractions of the alimentary canal or other hollow muscular organ by which its contents are propelled onward. *n., pl.* **per·i·stal·ses** (-sēz).

**per·i·stal·tic** (per′ə stal′tik) of or having to do with PERISTALSIS. *adj.*

**per·i·style** (per′ə stīl′) **1** a row of columns surrounding a building, court, etc. **2** a space or court so enclosed. *n.*

**per·i·to·ne·al** (per′ə tə nē′əl) of or having to do with the PERITONEUM. *adj.*

**per·i·to·ne·um** (per′ə tə nē′əm) the smooth, transparent MEMBRANE that lines the walls of the abdomen of a mammal and covers the organs in it. *n., pl.* **per·i·to·ne·a** (-nē′ə).

**per·i·to·ni·tis** (per′ə tə nī′tis) inflammation of the PERITONEUM. *n.*

**per·i·wig** (per′ə wig′) WIG. *n.*

**per·i·win·kle**[1] (per′ə wing′kəl) a low, trailing evergreen plant with blue flowers: *The North American periwinkle is called myrtle. n.*

**per·i·win·kle²** (pėr'ə wing'kəl) a sea snail having a thick, cone-shaped, spiral shell, used for food in Europe. *n.*

**per·jure** (pėr'jər) make oneself guilty of PERJURY; swear falsely; lie when on oath (*used with a pronoun ending in* -**self**): *The witness perjured herself at the trial.* *v.*, **per·jured, per·jur·ing.**

**per·jured** (pėr'jərd) **1** guilty of PERJURY: *a perjured witness.* **2** characterized by or involving PERJURY: *perjured evidence.* **3** pt. and pp. of PERJURE. 1, 2 *adj.*, 3 *v.*

**per·jur·er** (pėr'jə rər) a person who commits PERJURY. *n.*

**per·ju·ry** (pėr'jə rē) in law, the deliberate violation of an oath or affirmation, either by saying that something is true which one knows to be false or by omitting to tell something that one has promised to tell. *n., pl.* **per·ju·ries.**

**perk¹** (pėrk) **1** move, lift the head, or act briskly or saucily. **2** raise smartly or briskly: *The sparrow perked up its tail.* **3** make trim or smart: *She is all perked out in her best clothes.* **4** put oneself forward briskly or assertively. *v.*
**perk up,** brighten up; become lively and vigorous: *We all perked up after a good lunch.*

**perk²** (pėrk) *Informal.* **1** percolate: *to perk a pot of coffee. We could hear the coffee perking.* **2** be in a state of activity; go well: *a new tax measure to keep the economy perking.* *v.*

**perk³** (pėrk) *Informal.* PERQUISITE: *enjoying perks such as free theatre tickets.* *n.*

**perk·y** (pėr'kē) smart; brisk; saucy; pert: *a perky squirrel.* *adj.*, **perk·i·er, perk·i·est.** —**perk'i·ly,** *adv.* —**perk'i·ness,** *n.*

**perm** (pėrm) *Informal.* a PERMANENT WAVE. *n.*

**per·ma·frost** (pėr'mə frost') *Cdn.* ground or subsoil that is permanently frozen: *Where the permafrost extends to the surface of the ground, nothing can grow.* *n.*

**per·ma·nence** (pėr'mə nəns) the state or condition of being PERMANENT; a lasting quality or condition. *n.*

**per·ma·nen·cy** (pėr'mə nən sē) **1** PERMANENCE. **2** something that is permanent. *n., pl.* **per·ma·nen·cies.**

**per·ma·nent** (pėr'mə nənt) **1** lasting; intended to last; not for a short time only: *a permanent filling in a tooth. After doing odd jobs for a week, she got a permanent position as office girl.* **2** a PERMANENT WAVE. 1 *adj.*, 2 *n.* —**per'ma·nent·ly,** *adv.*

**permanent tooth** one of the second set of teeth in a mammal that follow the baby teeth, or milk teeth.

**permanent wave** a wave produced in the hair by chemicals or heat, that lasts even after the hair is washed many times.

**per·me·a·bil·i·ty** (pėr'mē ə bil'ə tē) the quality or state of being PERMEABLE. *n.*

**per·me·a·ble** (pėr'mē ə bəl) that can be PERMEATED: *A sponge is permeable by water.* *adj.*

**per·me·ate** (pėr'mē āt') **1** spread through the whole of; penetrate throughout; pass into or through and affect all of: *Smoke permeated the house. Water will not permeate this fabric.* **2** spread or diffuse itself: *Anger permeated through the crowd.* *v.*, **per·me·at·ed, per·me·at·ing.**

**per·me·a·tion** (pėr'mē ā'shən) permeating or being PERMEATED. *n.*

**per·mis·si·ble** (pər mis'ə bəl) that may be permitted; allowable. *adj.* —**per·mis'si·bly,** *adv.*

**per·mis·sion** (pər mish'ən) consent; leave; the act of permitting or allowing: *She asked the teacher's permission to go early. My father gave me permission to use his camera.* *n.*

**per·mis·sive** (pər mis'iv) **1** not strict in discipline; allowing a great deal of freedom; lenient; indulgent: *a permissive society, permissive parents.* **2** permitting; giving permission: *a permissive statute.* *adj.* —**per·mis'sive·ly,** *adv.* —**per·mis'sive·ness,** *n.*

**per·mit** (pər mit' *for verb,* pėr'mit *or* pər mit' *for noun*) **1** allow a person, etc. to do something: *His parents permitted him to borrow the car when he was seventeen.* **2** let something be done or occur: *The law does not permit smoking in this store.* **3** a formal written order giving permission to do something: *a permit to fish or hunt.* **4** PERMISSION. 1, 2 *v.*, **per·mit·ted, per·mit·ting;** 3, 4 *n.*

**per·mu·ta·tion** (pėr'myə tā'shən) **1** an alteration. **2** in mathematics, a changing of the order of a set of things; arranging in different orders. **3** such an arrangement or group. The permutations of *a, b,* and *c* are *abc, acb, bac, bca, cab, cba.* *n.*

**per·mute** (pər myüt') alter the order or arrangement of; especially, alter in all possible ways. *v.*, **per·mut·ed, per·mut·ing.**

**per·ni·cious** (pər nish'əs) **1** that will destroy or ruin; causing great harm or damage; injurious: *pernicious habits.* **2** fatal. *adj.* —**per·ni'cious·ly,** *adv.*

**pernicious anemia** a severe disease in which the number of RED CORPUSCLES in the blood decreases.

**per·o·gy** (pə rog'ē) pastries with a meat, cheese, or other filling; pyrohy. *n. pl.*

**per·o·rate** (per'ə rāt') speak at length; make a long or majestic speech. *v.*, **per·o·rat·ed, per·o·rat·ing.**

**per·o·ra·tion** (per'ə rā'shən) the last part of an oration or discussion, summing up what has been said. *n.*

**per·ox·ide** (pə rok'sīd) **1** an oxide of a given element or radical that contains the greatest, or an unusual amount of, oxygen. **2** HYDROGEN PEROXIDE. **3** bleach hair by applying HYDROGEN PEROXIDE. 1, 2 *n.*, 3 *v.*, **per·ox·id·ed, per·ox·id·ing.**

**per·pen·dic·u·lar** (pėr'pən dik'yə lər) **1** upright; standing straight up: *a perpendicular cliff.* **2** at right angles to a given line, plane, or surface: *One line is perpendicular to another when it makes a square corner with another. The floor of a room is perpendicular to the side walls, and parallel to the ceiling.* **3** a perpendicular line, plane, or position. **4 Perpendicular,** of the style of English GOTHIC (def. 1) architecture of the 14th to 16th centuries. See ARCHITECTURE for picture. 1, 2 *adj.*, 3, 4 *n.*

**per·pe·trate** (pėr'pə trāt') do or commit crime, fraud, or anything bad or foolish: *to perpetrate a murder, to perpetrate a hoax.* *v.*, **per·pe·trat·ed, per·pe·trat·ing.**

**per·pe·tra·tion** (pėr'pə trā'shən) **1** the act of perpetrating. **2** the thing PERPETRATEd. *n.*

**per·pe·tra·tor** (pėr′pə trā′tər)  a doer; a person who does something bad or foolish.  *n.*

**per·pet·u·al** (pər pech′ü əl)  **1** lasting forever; eternal: *the perpetual hills.*  **2** lasting throughout life: *a perpetual income.*  **3** continuous; never ceasing: *a perpetual stream of visitors, perpetual motion.*  *adj.*

**perpetual calendar**  a calendar or table that allows one to find out the day of the week for any given date over a wide range of years.

**per·pet·u·al·ly** (pər pech′ü ə lē)  forever.  *adv.*

**per·pet·u·ate** (pər pech′ü āt′)  make PERPETUAL; cause to last indefinitely: *attempts to perpetuate a species. The Brock Monument was built to perpetuate the memory of a great man.*  *v.,* **per·pet·u·at·ed, per·pet·u·at·ing.** —**per·pet′u·a′tion,** *n.* —**per·pet′u·a′tor,** *n.*

**per·pe·tu·i·ty** (pėr′pə tyü′ə tē *or* pėr′pə tü′ə tē)  the state of being PERPETUAL; endless time.  *n., pl.* **per·pe·tu·i·ties.**
**in perpetuity,**  forever.

**per·plex** (pər pleks′)  trouble with doubt; make unable to think about clearly or logically; puzzle: *The problem is hard enough to perplex even the teacher.*  *v.* —**per·plex′ing·ly,** *adv.*

**per·plexed** (pər plekst′)  **1** not knowing what to do or how to act; puzzled and confused: *She was greatly perplexed by her friend's strange manner.*  **2** pt. and pp. of PERPLEX.  **1** *adj.,* **2** *v.*

**per·plex·ed·ly** (pər plek′sə dlē)  in a PERPLEXED manner.  *adv.*

**per·plex·i·ty** (pər plek′sə tē)  **1** a perplexed condition; the state of being puzzled or of not knowing what to do or how to act: *Her perplexity was so great that she had to ask for advice.*  **2** something that perplexes: *There are many perplexities in that job.*  *n., pl.* **per·plex·i·ties.**

**per·qui·site** (pėr′kwə zit)  **1** anything desirable received in addition to regular pay and that results directly from one's position, especially something promised or expected: *Included in the secretary's perquisites was membership in the golf club.*  **2** a tip.  *n.*

**per se** (pėr sā′ *or* pėr sē′)  Latin.  in itself; intrinsically.

**per·se·cute** (pėr′sə kyüt′)  **1** treat badly; do harm to again and again; oppress, especially for religious, racial, or political reasons: *The child was persecuted by other children in the neighbourhood because she seemed different.*  **2** annoy: *persecuted with endless questions.*  *v.,* **per·se·cut·ed, per·se·cut·ing.** —**per′se·cu′tor,** *n.*
☞ *Usage.* Both **persecute** and PROSECUTE come from the same Latin word *sequi,* meaning 'follow' or 'pursue'. But **persecute** means to pursue or harass a person (or other creature) with the idea of doing him or her harm, while **prosecute** means to bring someone before a court of law or to pursue a plan, a job, or idea in the sense of carrying it out or bringing it to completion.

**per·se·cu·tion** (pėr′sə kyü′shən)  **1** treating badly; oppressing: *The boy's persecution of the kitten was cruel.*  **2** being treated badly or harmed again and again: *The boy's sister didn't take part in the kitten's persecution.*  *n.*

**per·se·ver·ance** (pėr′sə vē′rəns)  a sticking to a purpose or an aim; never giving up what one has set out to do; persistence: *By perseverance the lame girl learned to swim.*  *n.*

**per·se·vere** (pėr′sə vēr′)  continue steadily in doing something hard; persist.  *v.,* **per·se·vered, per·se·ver·ing.** —**per′se·ver′ing·ly,** *adv.*

## perpetrator 881 personage

hat, āge, fär; let, ēqual, tėrm; it, īce
hot, ōpen, ôrder; oil, out; cup, pút, rüle
əbove, takən, pencəl, lemən, circəs
ch, child; ng, long; sh, ship
th, thin; ŦH, then; zh, measure

**Per·sian** (pėr′zhən)  **1** of or having to do with Persia (or Iran), a country in southwestern Asia, its people, or their language.  **2** a native or inhabitant of Persia (or Iran).  **3** the language of Persia (or Iran).  **1** *adj.,* **2, 3** *n.*

**Persian cat**  a breed of cat having a chunky build and long, glossy fur.

**Persian lamb**  the curly fur of lambs from Iran and parts of central Asia.

**per·si·flage** (pėr′sə fläzh′)  light, joking talk; banter.  *n.*

**per·sim·mon** (pər sim′ən)  **1** a North American plumlike fruit, containing one to ten seeds, that is bitter when green but sweet and tasty when ripe.  **2** the hardwood tree that bears this fruit.  *n.*

**per·sist** (pər sist′)  **1** continue firmly; refuse to stop or be changed: *He persists in eating with his fingers. She persisted till she had solved the difficult problem.*  **2** last; stay; endure, especially past a usual, normal, or expected time: *The cold weather will persist for some time.*  **3** say again and again; maintain: *She persisted that she was innocent of the crime.*  *v.*

**per·sist·ence** (pər sis′təns)  **1** a being PERSISTENT: *the persistence of a fly buzzing around one's head.*  **2** the continuing existence: *The persistence of her cough was annoying.*  *n.*

**per·sist·ent** (pər sis′tənt)  **1** persisting; having lasting qualities, especially in the face of dislike, disapproval, or difficulties: *a persistent worker, a persistent beggar.*  **2** lasting; going on; continuing: *a persistent headache.*  *adj.* —**per·sist′ent·ly,** *adv.*

**per·son** (pėr′sən)  **1** a man, woman, or child; human being: *Any person who wishes may come to the fair.*  **2** a human body: *The person of the king was well guarded.*  **3** bodily appearance: *He kept his person neat and trim.*  **4** in grammar, a change in a pronoun or verb to show the person speaking (**first person**), the person spoken to (**second person**), or the person or thing spoken of (**third person**). *I* and *we* are used for the first person; *thou* and *you,* for the second person; *he, she, it,* and *they,* for the third person.  **5** a form of a pronoun or verb giving such indication. *Comes* is third person singular of *come.*  *n.*
**in person,**  **a** with or by one's own action or presence; personally: *Come in person; do not phone.*  **b** really present, not merely thought of.
☞ *Syn.* **Person,** INDIVIDUAL. **Person** is the ordinary word for a human being of either sex: *A well-known person came into the room.* **Individual** emphasizes the person's uniqueness: *A strange individual came into the room.* Unlike **person, individual** can also be applied to animals and objects: *Our cat is a fascinating individual.* The phrase *a person* is often used instead of the impersonal pronoun *one: Exercise makes a person hungry.* It is, as a rule, awkward and pretentious to use **individual** in this way.

**per·son·a·ble** (pėr′sə nə bəl)  having a pleasing appearance and personality; attractive: *a personable young man.*  *adj.*

**per·son·age** (pėr′sə nij)  **1** a person of importance.  **2** a person.  **3** a character in a book, play, etc.  *n.*

**per·son·al** (pėr′sə nəl) 1 individual; private: *a personal letter.* 2 done in person; directly by oneself, not through others or by letter: *a personal visit.* 3 of the body or bodily appearance: *personal beauty.* 4 about or against a person or persons: *personal abuse.* 5 inclined to make remarks to or ask questions of others about their private affairs: *Don't be too personal.* 6 a short paragraph in a newspaper about a particular person or persons. 7 in grammar, showing person. *I, we, thou, you, he, she, it,* and *they* are the PERSONAL PRONOUNS. 8 of or having to do with possessions that can be moved, not land or buildings. 1–5, 7, 8 *adj.*, 6 *n.*
☛ *Usage.* Do not confuse **personal** and PERSONNEL. **Personal** is usually an adjective and is stressed on the first syllable. **Personnel** is a noun and is stressed on the last syllable.

**personal effects** personal belongings normally worn or carried, such as clothing, cosmetics, etc.

**per·son·al·i·ty** (pėr′sə nal′ə tē) 1 the personal or individual quality that makes one person be different or act differently from another: *Her personality makes her a lady to be admired.* 2 the pleasing or attractive qualities of a person: *Donna is developing a fine personality.* 3 a remark made about or against one particular person: *Tactful people avoid personalities.* 4 a person of importance or renown; personage: *personalities of the stage and screen.* 5 a person who regularly faces the public in his or her work, such as a television announcer. *n., pl.* **per·son·al·i·ties.**

**per·son·al·ize** (pėr′sə nə līz′) make personal or individual; especially, mark with one's name, etc.: *Personalized stationery has the owner's monogram, name, or name and address on it. v.,* **per·son·al·ized, per·son·al·iz·ing.**

**per·son·al·ly** (pėr′sə nə lē) 1 in person; not by the aid of others: *The hostess personally greeted her guests.* 2 as far as oneself is concerned: *Personally, I like fruit better than nuts.* 3 as a person: *We like him personally, but we dislike his way of living.* 4 as being meant for oneself: *He intended no insult to you; do not take what he said personally. adv.*

**personal pronoun** the person or persons speaking (*I, we*); the person or persons being spoken about (*he, she, they, it*); the person or persons addressed (*thou, you*).

**personal property** property that is not land, buildings, mines, or forests; movable possessions.

**per·so·na non gra·ta** (pər sō′nə non′ grä′tə or pər sō′nə non′ grat′ə) *Latin.* a person who is not acceptable.

**per·son·ate** (pėr′sə nāt′) 1 act the part of a character in a play, etc. 2 give a personality or personal characteristics to; PERSONIFY (def. 1). 3 pretend to be someone else, especially for purposes of fraud; impersonate. *v.,* **per·son·at·ed, per·son·at·ing.**

**per·son·i·fi·ca·tion** (pər son′ə fə kā′shən) 1 representation of a thing or idea as a person or as having human qualities: *Personification is a common figure of speech. The expression* Duty calls us *involves a personification of the idea of duty.* 2 a person, creature, or divinity representing a thing or idea: *Satan is the personification of evil.* 3 a person or thing seen as a striking example or embodiment of a quality, etc.: *A miser is the personification of greed. n.*

**per·son·i·fy** (pər son′ə fī′) 1 regard or represent as a person or as having human qualities: *The sea is often personified in poetry.* 2 be a type of; embody: *She personifies kindness. v.,* **per·son·i·fied, per·son·i·fy·ing.**

**per·son·nel** (pėr′sə nel′) persons employed in any work, business, or service: *All personnel are invited to the office party. n.*
☛ *Usage.* See note at PERSONAL.

**per·spec·tive** (pər spek′tiv) 1 the art of picturing objects on a flat surface so as to give the appearance of distance. 2 drawn so as to show the proper perspective. 3 the effect of distance on the appearance of objects: *Railway tracks seem to meet at the horizon because of perspective.* 4 the effect that the distance of events has on the mind: *Many happenings of last year seem less important when viewed in perspective.* 5 a view of things or facts in which they are in the right relations: *a lack of perspective.* 6 a view in front; distant view. 1, 3–6 *n.*, 2 *adj.*

**per·spi·ca·cious** (pėr′spə kā′shəs) keen in observing and understanding; discerning. *adj.*
—**per′spi·ca′cious·ly,** *adv.*

**per·spi·cac·i·ty** (pėr′spə kas′ə tē) keen perception; discernment; wisdom and understanding in dealing with people or with facts: *Our teacher's perspicacity makes her a good judge of people. n.*

**per·spi·cu·i·ty** (pėr′spə kyü′ə tē) clearness in expression; ease in being understood: *The premier was noted for the perspicuity of his speeches. n.*

**per·spic·u·ous** (pər spik′yü əs) clear; easily understood: *a perspicuous argument. adj.*

**per·spi·ra·tion** (pėr′spə rā′shən) 1 sweat: *Her forehead was damp with perspiration.* 2 a sweating or perspiring. *n.*

**per·spire** (pər spīr′) sweat: *We perspire when we work hard on a hot day. v.,* **per·spired, per·spir·ing.**

**per·suade** (pər swād′) 1 cause a person to do something by urging, arguing, etc.; prevail upon: *I knew that I should have studied, but he persuaded me to go to the movies.* 2 cause a person to believe something by urging, arguing, etc.; convince: *They finally persuaded her of the truth of the rumour. We tried to persuade her that we had known all along what she was up to. v.,* **per·suad·ed, per·suad·ing.**

**per·sua·sion** (pər swā′zhən) 1 persuading: *All our persuasion was of no use; she would not come.* 2 the power of persuading: *a man of great persuasion.* 3 a firm belief; conviction: *He and his brother were of different political persuasions.* 4 a religious belief; creed: *All people are not of the same persuasion. n.*

**per·sua·sive** (pər swā′siv or pər swā′ziv) able to persuade; effective in persuading: *The salesman had a very persuasive way of talking. adj.* —**per·sua′sive·ly,** *adv.*
—**per·sua′sive·ness,** *n.*

**pert** (pėrt) too forward or free in speech or action; saucy; bold: *a pert answer. adj.* —**pert′ly,** *adv.*
—**pert′ness,** *n.*

**per·tain** (pər tān′) 1 belong or be connected as a part, possession, etc.: *We own the house and the land pertaining to it.* 2 refer; be related: *The phrase* pertaining to school *means having to do with school.* 3 be appropriate: *We had turkey and everything else that pertains to Thanksgiving Day. v.*

**per·ti·na·cious** (pėr′tə nā′shəs) holding firmly to a

purpose, action, or opinion; very persistent; stubborn: *A bulldog is a pertinacious fighter.* *adj.* —**per′ti·na′cious·ly,** *adv.*

**per·ti·nac·i·ty** (pėr′tə nas′ə tē) great persistence; holding firmly to a purpose, action, or opinion. *n.*

**per·ti·nence** (pėr′tə nəns) fitness; being to the point; relevance: *The pertinence of the girl's replies showed that she was not stupid.* *n.*

**per·ti·nent** (pėr′tə nənt) having to do with what is being considered; relating to the matter in hand; to the point: *If your question is pertinent, I will answer it.* *adj.* —**per′ti·nent·ly,** *adv.*

**per·turb** (pər tėrb′) disturb greatly; make uneasy or troubled: *The management was perturbed at the possibility of another strike.* *v.*

**per·tur·ba·tion** (pėr′tər bā′shən) 1 PERTURBing or being perturbed. 2 something that PERTURBS. *n.*

Perukes. On the left is a French peruke of 1690; on the right is an English peruke of 1730.

**pe·ruke** (pə ruk′) a wig, especially a style of wig commonly worn by European men in the 17th and 18th centuries. *n.*

**pe·rus·al** (pə rü′zəl) perusing; reading: *the perusal of a letter.* *n.*

**pe·ruse** (pə rüz′) 1 read thoroughly and carefully. 2 read. *v.,* **pe·rused, pe·rus·ing.**

**Pe·ru·vi·an** (pə rü′vē ən) 1 of or having to do with Peru, a country on the western coast of South America, or its people. 2 a native or inhabitant of Peru. 1 *adj.,* 2 *n.*

**Peruvian bark** a bark from which quinine is obtained; CINCHONA.

**per·vade** (pər vād′) go or spread throughout; be throughout: *The odour of pines pervades the air.* *v.,* **per·vad·ed, per·vad·ing.** —**per·vad′er,** *n.*

**per·va·sion** (pər vā′zhən) pervading or being PERVADED; permeation. *n.*

**per·va·sive** (pər vā′siv *or* pər vā′ziv) tending to PERVADE. *adj.* —**per·va′sive·ness,** *n.*

**per·verse** (pər vėrs′) 1 contrary and willful; stubborn: *The perverse child did just what we told her not to do.* 2 persistent in wrong. 3 wicked. 4 not correct; wrong: *perverse reasoning.* *adj.* —**per·verse′ly,** *adv.* —**per·verse′ness,** *n.*

**per·ver·sion** (pər vėr′zhən) a turning or being turned to what is wrong; a change to what is unnatural, abnormal, or wrong: *A tendency to eat sand is a perversion of appetite.* *n.*

**per·ver·si·ty** (pər vėr′sə tē) 1 the quality of being PERVERSE. 2 a PERVERSE character or conduct. *n., pl.* **per·ver·si·ties.**

**per·vert** (pər vėrt′ *for verb,* pėr′vėrt *for noun*) 1 lead or turn from the right way or from the truth: *Reading comic books often perverts our taste for good books.* 2 give a wrong meaning to: *His enemies perverted his friendly remark and made it into an insult.* 3 use for wrong purposes or in a wrong way: *A clever criminal perverts his talents.* 4 change from what is natural or normal. 5 a perverted person. 1–4 *v.,* 5 *n.* —**per·vert′er,** *n.*

**per·vi·ous** (pėr′vē əs) 1 giving passage or entrance; permeable: *Sand is easily pervious to water.* 2 open to influence, argument, etc.; accessible: *pervious to reason.* *adj.*

**Pe·sach** (pā′säH) PASSOVER. *n.*

**pes·ky** (pes′kē) *Informal.* troublesome; annoying: *a pesky cold, pesky mosquitoes.* *adj.,* **pes·ki·er, pes·ki·est.**

**pes·si·mism** (pes′ə miz′əm) 1 a tendency to look on the dark side of things or to see difficulties and disadvantages. 2 a belief that things naturally tend to evil, or that life is not worthwhile. *n.* Compare with OPTIMISM.

**pes·si·mist** (pes′ə mist) 1 a person inclined to see all the difficulties and disadvantages or to look on the dark side of things. 2 a person who thinks that life holds more evil than good, and so is not worth living. *n.* Compare with OPTIMIST.

**pes·si·mis·tic** (pes′ə mis′tik) 1 of, having to do with, or characterized by PESSIMISM: *a pessimistic outlook on life. I was beginning to feel pessimistic about the whole trip because so many things were going wrong.* 2 having to do with PESSIMISM. *adj.* Compare with OPTIMISTIC. —**pes′si·mis′ti·cal·ly,** *adv.*

**pest** (pest) any thing or person that causes trouble, injuries, or destruction; nuisance: *Flies and mosquitoes are pests.* *n.*

**pes·ter** (pes′tər) 1 annoy; trouble; vex: *If we sit outside we'll be pestered by flies.* 2 bother with repeated requests or demands; keep after: *He kept pestering his older sister till she gave in and took him along.* *v.*

**pes·ti·cide** (pes′tə sīd′) any chemical agent or other substance used to destroy plant or animal pests. *n.*

**pes·tif·er·ous** (pes tif′ə rəs) 1 bringing disease or infection: *Rats are pestiferous.* 2 bringing moral evil: *the pestiferous influence of a bad example.* 3 *Informal.* troublesome; annoying. *adj.*

**pes·ti·lence** (pes′tə ləns) 1 a fatal infectious or contagious epidemic disease, especially bubonic plague. 2 anything that is extremely destructive or deadly in its effect. *n.*

**pes·ti·lent** (pes′tə lənt) 1 often causing death: *Bubonic plague is a pestilent disease.* 2 harmful to morals; destroying peace: *a pestilent den of vice, the pestilent effects of war.* 3 troublesome; annoying. *adj.*

**pes·ti·len·tial** (pes′tə len′shəl) 1 of, having to do with, or causing PESTILENCE. 2 morally or socially harmful. 3 irritating. *adj.*

**pes·tle** (pes′əl) 1 a tool for pounding or crushing substances into a powder in a mortar. See MORTAR for picture. 2 pound or crush with a pestle. 1 *n.,* 2 *v.,* **pes·tled, pes·tling.**

**pet**[1] (pet) 1 an animal kept as a favourite and treated with affection. 2 darling; favourite: *teacher's pet.*

**3** treated as a pet: *a pet rabbit.* **4** showing affection: *a pet name.* **5** *Informal.* particular; special: *a pet aversion, a pet theory.* **6** treat as a pet. **7** stroke; pat; touch lovingly and gently: *Helen is petting the new kitten.* 1, 2 *n.*, 3–5 *adj.*, 6, 7 *v.*, **pet·ted, pet·ting.**

**pet²** (pet) a fit of peevishness; fretful discontent: *When he didn't get his way, he jumped on his bicycle and rode off in a pet. n.*

**pet·al** (pet′əl) one of the parts of a flower that are usually coloured; one of the leaves of a COROLLA: *A daisy has many petals.* See COMPOSITE and FLOWER for pictures. *n.* —**pet′al·like′,** *adj.*

**pet·alled** or **pet·aled** (pet′əld) having petals: *six-petalled. adj.*

**pe·tard** (pi tärd′) an explosive device formerly used in warfare to break down a door or gate or to breach a wall: *The petard was fastened to the gate or wall and ignited. n.* **hoist with** or **by one's own petard,** injured or destroyed by one's own scheme or device for the ruin of others.

**pet·cock** (pet′kok′) a small tap. *n.*

**pe·ter** (pē′tər) *Informal.* gradually fail or come to an end; give out or become exhausted (*used with* **out**): *We were forced to ration our food as supplies began to peter out. v.*

**pet·i·ole** (pet′ē ōl′) the slender stalk by which a leaf is attached to the stem. See PEDICEL and STEM for pictures. *n.*

**pe·tite** (pə tēt′) little, of small size; tiny, especially with reference to a woman or girl. *adj.*

**pe·ti·tion** (pə tish′ən) **1** a formal request to a superior or to one in authority for some privilege, right, benefit, etc.: *The people signed a petition asking the city council for a new sidewalk.* **2** ask earnestly; make a petition to: *They petitioned the mayor to use his influence with the city council.* **3** prayer. **4** pray. **5** that which is requested or prayed for. 1, 3, 5 *n.*, 2, 4 *v.* —**pe·ti′tion·er,** *n.*

**pet·it jury** (pet′ē) a group of persons chosen to decide a case in court; trial jury.

**pet·it point** (pet′ē point′) **1** a fine needlepoint stitch. **2** embroidery, such as a picture, made with this stitch.

**pet·rel** (pet′rəl) any of various sea birds, especially a small, black-and-white bird having long, pointed wings. *n.*
☞ *Hom.* PETROL.
☞ *Etym.* From the name of St. *Peter,* which comes from Gk. *petra* 'rock'. St. Peter walked on the water and petrels were named after him because they appear to walk on the sea as they feed on sea organisms and refuse. See also note at PETROLEUM.

**Pe·tri dish** or **pe·tri dish** (pā′trē *or* pē′trē) a round, shallow glass container with a loose cover, used in laboratories to hold bacteria cultures.

**pet·ri·fac·tion** (pet′rə fak′shən) **1** PETRIFYing or being petrified. **2** something petrified. *n.*

**pet·ri·fy** (pet′rə fī) **1** replace animal or vegetable cells with mineral deposits; turn into stone: *The girls found a piece of petrified wood.* **2** paralyse with fear, horror, or surprise: *They heard a footstep upstairs and stopped, petrified. v.*, **pet·ri·fied, pet·ri·fy·ing.**

**pet·ro·chem·i·cal** (pet′rō kem′ə kəl) **1** any of various important chemicals made from petroleum or natural gas, used in the manufacture of plastics, synthetic fibres, paints, etc. **2** of or having to do with petrochemicals or PETROCHEMISTRY. 1 *n.*, 2 *adj.*

**pet·ro·chem·is·try** (pet′rō kem′i strē) **1** the branch of chemistry dealing with petroleum and PETROCHEMICALS. **2** the chemistry of rocks. *n.*

**pet·ro·glyph** (pet′rə glif′) a carving or inscription on rock, especially a prehistoric one: *There are some interesting petroglyphs depicting animals on the shores of Lake Ontario. n.*

**pe·trog·ra·phy** (pi trog′rə fē) the branch of geology that deals with the description and classification of rocks. *n.*

**pet·rol** (pet′rəl) *Esp. Brit.* GASOLINE. *n.*
☞ *Hom.* PETREL.
☞ *Etym.* See note at PETROLEUM.

**pe·tro·le·um** (pə trō′lē əm) a combustible, usually dark-coloured liquid, a kind of oil that occurs in deposits within the rock strata of many parts of the world and consists of a complex mixture of HYDROCARBONS and small amounts of many other substances: *Petroleum is processed to produce gasoline, fuel oils, kerosene, paraffin, lubricants, etc. n.*
☞ *Etym.* From Med. L *petroleum,* a combination of L *petra* (from Gk. *petra* 'rock') and L *oleum* 'oil'. Petroleum was also commonly called "rock oil" in England in the Middle Ages. **Petrol,** meaning 'gasoline', came from F *petrol,* which also came from Med. L *petroleum.*

**petroleum jelly** a smooth, greasy, odourless, and tasteless substance obtained from PETROLEUM, used as an ointment and as a lubricant.

**pe·trol·o·gy** (pi trol′ə jē) the science of rocks, including their origin, structure, changes, etc. *n.*

**pet·ti·coat** (pet′ē kōt′) **1** a skirt worn beneath a dress or outer skirt by women and girls. **2** skirt. *n.*

**pet·ti·fog·ger** (pet′ē fog′ər) **1** a lawyer who uses petty, underhanded, or dishonest methods; shyster. **2** any person who uses petty, underhanded, or dishonest methods. **3** a person who quibbles over small details. *n.*

**pet·ti·fog·ging** (pet′ē fog′ing) **1** petty, underhanded, or dishonest. **2** quibbling. *adj.*

**pet·ti·ness** (pet′ē nis) **1** the quality or state of being PETTY; petty nature or behaviour. **2** something PETTY. *n.*

**pet·tish** (pet′ish) peevish; cross: *a pettish reply, a pettish child. adj.* —**pet′tish·ly,** *adv.*

**pet·ty** (pet′ē) **1** having little importance or value; small: *She insisted on telling me all her petty troubles.* **2** spiteful; mean; narrow-minded. **3** lower in rank or importance; subordinate: *My sister is a petty official in that big company. adj.*, **pet·ti·er, pet·ti·est.**

**petty jury** a PETIT JURY.

**petty officer** a non-commissioned officer in the navy.

**pet·u·lance** (pech′ə ləns) peevishness; bad humour; being irritated by trifles. *n.*

**pet·u·lant** (pech′ə lənt) peevish; subject to little fits of bad temper; irritable over trifles. *adj.*
—**pet′u·lant·ly,** *adv.*

**pe·tu·ni·a** (pə tyü′nē ə *or* pə tü′nē ə) **1** a plant having funnel-shaped flowers of various colours. **2** the flower. *n.*

**pew** (pyü) in a church, a bench for people to sit on,

having a back and often fastened to the floor: *In some churches the pews are separated by partitions.* *n.*

**pe·wee** (pē′wē) **1** a small North American bird having an olive-coloured or grey back. **2** PEEWEE. *n.*
☛ *Hom.* PEEWEE.

**pew·ter** (pyü′tər) **1** any of various ALLOYS (def. 1) composed mainly of tin; especially, a dull alloy containing lead, formerly used for eating and cooking utensils. **2** dishes or other utensils made of this ALLOY (def. 1). **3** made of pewter. *n.*

**pfd.** preferred.

**pg.** page.

**pH** a symbol used to express acid or alkaline content, used in testing water and soils, for various applications in industry, etc. A pH of 14 denotes high alkaline content, and a pH of 0 indicates high acidity; pH 7 is taken as neutral.

**pha·e·ton** (fā′ə tən) **1** a light, four-wheeled carriage with or without a top. **2** an open automobile of the touring-car type. *n.*

**phag·o·cyte** (fag′ə sīt′) a white blood corpuscle, or leucocyte, capable of absorbing and destroying waste or harmful material, such as disease microbes. *n.*

**pha·lan·ges** (fə lan′jēz) a plural of PHALANX (defs. 1, 4): *The bones of the fingers and toes are called the phalanges.* See ARM¹ and LEG for pictures. *n.*

**phal·anx** (fal′angks *or* fā′langks) **1** in ancient Greece, a special battle formation of infantry fighting in close ranks with their shields joined and long spears overlapping each other. **2** a compact or closely massed body of persons, animals, or things: *a phalanx of trees. The speaker could not get past the phalanx of angry residents.* **3** a number of persons united for a common purpose: *They were opposed in the debate by a phalanx of Conservative MP's.* **4** any one of the bones of the fingers or toes. *n., pl.* **pha·lanx·es** *or* **pha·lan·ges** (fə lan′jēz) (for def. 1), **pha·lanx·es** (for def. 2 and 3), **pha·lan·ges** (for def. 4).

**phal·a·rope** (fal′ə rōp′) any of three species, constituting a family of shorebirds resembling sandpipers, having a long, slender bill and lobed toes adapted for swimming. Phalaropes are noted for their reversal of the typical male and female roles: the female is larger and more brightly coloured than the male; the male rears the young. *n., pl.* **phal·a·rope**.

**phan·tasm** (fan′taz əm) **1** a thing seen only in one's imagination; unreal fancy: *the phantasms of a dream.* **2** a supposed appearance of an absent person, living or dead. **3** a deceiving likeness of something. *n.*

**phan·tas·ma·go·ri·a** (fan taz′mə gô′rē ə) **1** a shifting scene of real things, illusions, imaginary fancies, deceptions, and the like: *the phantasmagoria of a dream.* **2** a show of optical illusions in which figures increase or decrease in size, fade away, and pass into each other. *n.*

**phan·tas·mal** (fan taz′məl) of, having to do with, or being a PHANTASM; unreal; imaginary. *adj.*

**phan·ta·sy** (fan′tə sē *or* fan′tə zē) See FANTASY. *n., pl.* **phan·ta·sies**.

**phan·tom** (fan′təm) **1** an image in the mind which seems to be real: *phantoms of a dream.* **2** a vague, dim, or shadowy appearance; ghost. **3** like a ghost; unreal: *a phantom ship.* **4** a mere show; appearance with no substance: *a phantom of a government.* *n.*

pewee 885 phase

hat, āge, fär; let, ēqual, tėrm; it, īce
hot, ōpen, ôrder; oil, out; cup, pùt, rüle
above, takən, pencəl, lemən, circəs
ch, child; ng, long; sh, ship
th, thin; ᴛʜ, then; zh, measure

**Phar·aoh** (fer′ō) a title given to the kings of ancient Egypt. *n.*
☛ *Hom.* FARO, FARROW (fer′ō).

**phar·i·sa·ic** (far′ə sā′ik *or* fer′ə sā′ik) **1** making an outward show of religion or morals without the real spirit. **2** thinking oneself more moral than others; hypocritical. *adj.* —**phar′i·sa′i·cal·ly**, *adv.*

**Phar·i·see** (far′ə sē′ *or* fer′ə sē′) a member of an ancient Jewish sect that was very strict in keeping to tradition and the laws of its religion. *n.*

**phar·i·see** (far′ə sē′ *or* fer′ə sē′) **1** a person who makes a show of religion rather than following its spirit. **2** a person who considers himself or herself much better than other people. *n.*

**phar·ma·ceu·tic** (fär′mə sü′tik) PHARMACEUTICAL. *adj.*

**phar·ma·ceu·ti·cal** (fär′mə sü′tə kəl) **1** of or having to do with PHARMACY or pharmacists. **2** a medicinal drug. **1** *adj.*, **2** *n.*

**phar·ma·ceu·tics** (fär′mə sü′tiks) PHARMACY (def. 1) (used with a singular verb). *n.*

**phar·ma·cist** (fär′mə sist) a person who is qualified to prepare and dispense medicinal drugs; druggist. *n.*

**phar·ma·col·o·gist** (fär′mə kol′ə jist) a person trained in PHARMACOLOGY, especially one who makes it his or her work. *n.*

**phar·ma·col·o·gy** (fär′mə kol′ə jē) the science of drugs, including their sources and properties, and their preparation, uses, and effects. *n.*

**phar·ma·co·poe·ia** (fär′mə kə pē′ə) **1** a book containing an official list and description of drugs and medicines. **2** a stock or collection of drugs. *n.*

**phar·ma·cy** (fär′mə sē) **1** the art or practice of preparing and dispensing drugs and medicines. **2** drugstore. **3** the department of a hospital where drugs, medicine, etc. are prepared. *n., pl.* **phar·ma·cies**.

**pha·ryn·ge·al** (fə rin′jəl *or* far′in jē′əl) **1** having to do with the PHARYNX. **2** located or produced in the region of the PHARYNX. *adj.*

**phar·yn·gi·tis** (far′in jī′tis *or* fer′in jī′tis) an inflammation of the mucous membrane of the PHARYNX. *n.*

**phar·ynx** (far′ingks *or* fer′ingks) the muscular tube connecting the mouth cavity with the esophagus, or, in simpler creatures, directly with the digestive system: *The human pharynx is part of the alimentary canal.* See WINDPIPE for picture. *n., pl.* **phar·ynx·es** *or* **pha·ryn·ges** (fə rin′jēz).

**phase** (fāz) **1** one of the changing states or stages of development of a person or thing: *The pupa is a phase in the life cycle of the moth.* **2** one side, part, or view of a subject: *a phase of arithmetic.* **3** the shape of the moon or of a planet as it is seen at a given time: *The last quarter*

*is a phase of the moon.* See MOON for picture. *n.*
☞ Hom. FAZE.

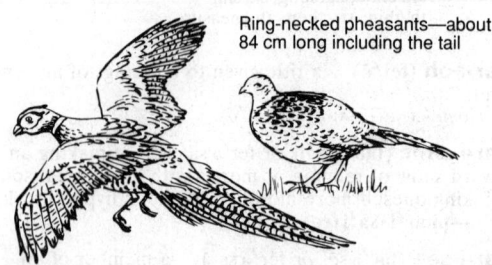
Ring-necked pheasants—about 84 cm long including the tail

**pheas·ant** (fez′ənt) a game bird related to the domestic fowl and the peacock, having a long tail and brilliant feathers: *Wild pheasants are found in many parts of Europe and America. n., pl.* **pheas·ants** or (*esp. collectively*) **pheas·ant**.

**phe·no·bar·bi·tal** (fē′nō bär′bə tol′) a white crystalline barbiturate drug used as a hypnotic or sedative. *n.*

**phe·nol** (fē′nol *or* fē′nōl) CARBOLIC ACID. *n.*

**phe·nol·phthal·ein** (fē′nolf thal′ēn) a white or yellowish crystalline compound used in testing acidity, making dyes, and as a laxative: *Phenolphthalein is brilliant red in an alkali solution and colourless in an acid solution. n.*

**phe·nom·e·na** (fə nom′ə nə) pl. of PHENOMENON. *n.*

**phe·nom·e·nal** (fə nom′ə nəl) 1 of or having to do with a PHENOMENON or phenomena. 2 having the nature of a PHENOMENON. 3 extraordinary: *a phenomenal memory. adj.* —**phe·nom′e·nal·ly,** *adv.*

**phe·nom·e·non** (fə nom′ə non′) 1 a fact, event, or circumstance that can be observed: *Lightning is an electrical phenomenon. Fever and inflammation are phenomena of disease.* 2 something or someone extraordinary or remarkable: *An eclipse is an interesting phenomenon. n., pl.* **phe·nom·e·na** or (especially for def. 2) **phe·nom·e·nons**.

**phe·no·type** (fē′nə tīp′) 1 the physical, especially visible, characteristics or properties of an organism as determined by the interaction of its genetic inheritance (GENOTYPE) and its environment. 2 a group of organisms sharing such characteristics or properties. *n.*

**phew** (fyü′) an exclamation of disgust, impatience, relief, surprise, etc. *interj.*

**phi·al** (fī′əl) a small bottle; vial. *n.*

**phi·lan·der** (fə lan′dər) make love without serious intentions; flirt. *v.,* —**phi·lan′der·er,** *n.*

**phil·an·throp·ic** (fil′ən throp′ik) of, having to do with, or characterized by PHILANTHROPY; charitable; benevolent. *adj.* —**phil′an·throp′i·cal·ly,** *adv.*

**phil·an·throp·i·cal** (fil′ən throp′ə kəl) PHILANTHROPIC. *adj.*

**phil·an·thro·pist** (fə lan′thrə pist) a person who practises PHILANTHROPY, especially a wealthy person who supports charitable organizations, etc. *n.*

**phi·lan·thro·py** (fə lan′thrə pē) 1 love of people, especially as shown by practical kindness and active efforts to help humanity: *Charitable institutions appeal to one's philanthropy.* 2 a philanthropic act, institution, etc. *n., pl.* **phi·lan·thro·pies**.

**phil·a·tel·ic** (fil′ə tel′ik) of or having to do with PHILATELY. *adj.*

**phi·lat·e·list** (fə lat′ə list) a person whose hobby is PHILATELY; stamp collector. *n.*

**phi·lat·e·ly** (fə lat′ə lē) the collecting and studying of postage stamps and, often, envelopes or postcards with postmarked stamps on them; stamp collecting. *n.*

**–phile** *combining form.* a lover of _____; a person who is fond of _____: *A discophile is a person who is fond of records, or discs.*

**phil·har·mon·ic** (fil′här mon′ik) 1 devoted to music; loving music: *A musical club is often called a philharmonic society.* 2 given by a philharmonic society: *a philharmonic concert.* 3 a philharmonic society or concert. 1, 2 *adj.,* 3 *n.*

**Phil·ip·pine** (fil′ə pēn′) of or having to do with the Philippines, a country consisting of about 7000 islands in the western Pacific Ocean, or its inhabitants. *adj.* Also, **Filipine, Filipino**.

**Phi·lis·ti·a** (fə lis′tē ə) 1 the land of the ancient Philistines, in ancient southwestern Palestine. 2 a place inhabited or frequented by people with uncultured tastes. *n.*

**Phi·lis·tine** (fə lis′tən, fil′ə stīn′, *or* fil′ə stēn′) 1 in the Bible, one of the warlike people in southwestern Palestine who repeatedly attacked the Israelites. 2 of the Philistines. 3 Sometimes, **philistine**, a person having commonplace ideas and tastes and indifferent to or contemptuous of artistic or intellectual values. 4 Usually, **philistine**, smugly commonplace and uncultured. 1, 3 *n.,* 2, 4 *adj.*

**phi·lis·tin·ism** (fə lis′tə niz′əm *or* fil′ə sti niz′əm) the character, habits, or views of persons indifferent to artistic or intellectual values. *n.* Also, **Philistinism**.

**phil·o·den·dron** (fil′ə den′drən) any of a closely related group of tropical plants of the arum family that are cultivated for their thick, glossy leaves: *Philodendrons are popular house plants because they thrive with little care. n.*

**phil·o·log·i·cal** (fil′ə loj′ə kəl) of or having to do with PHILOLOGY. *adj.*

**phi·lol·o·gist** (fə lol′ə jist) a person trained in PHILOLOGY. *n.*

**phi·lol·o·gy** (fə lol′ə jē) the historical and comparative study of languages, especially through literature and written documents. Compare with LINGUISTICS. *n.*

**phi·los·o·pher** (fə los′ə fər) 1 a person who studies philosophy. 2 a person who has a system of philosophy. 3 a person who shows the calmness of philosophy under hard conditions, accepting life and making the best of it. *n.*

**philosophers' stone** an imaginary stone, substance, or chemical preparation sought for by ALCHEMISTS in the belief that it had the power to change base metals into gold or silver.

**phil·o·soph·ic** (fil′ə sof′ik) 1 of or having to do with philosophers or philosophy. 2 devoted to or skilled in philosophy: *a philosophic society.* 3 like a philosopher, especially in being wise or in taking a calm, patient

**attitude in the face of trouble; philosophical:** *a philosophic person.* *adj.* —**phil‧o‧soph′i‧cal‧ly,** *adv.*

**phil‧o‧soph‧i‧cal** (fil′ə sof′ə kəl) PHILOSOPHIC; like a philosopher. *adj.*

**phi‧los‧o‧phize** (fə los′ə fīz′) think or reason as a philosopher does; try to understand and explain things: *philosophizing about life and death.* *v.,* **phi‧los‧o‧phized, phi‧los‧o‧phiz‧ing.** —**phi‧los′o‧phiz′er,** *n.*

**phi‧los‧o‧phy** (fə los′ə fē) **1** the study of the truth or principles underlying all knowledge; study of the most general causes and principles of the universe. **2** an explanation or theory of the universe. **3** a system for guiding life, such as a body of principles of conduct, religious beliefs, or traditions. **4** the broad general principles of a particular subject: *the philosophy of history.* **5** a calm and reasonable attitude; the practice of accepting things as they are and making the best of them. *n., pl.* **phi‧los‧o‧phies.**

**phil‧tre** (fil′tər) **1** a potion, drug, or charm supposed to arouse sexual love, especially toward a particular person. **2** any magic drink. *n.* Also, **philter.**
☞ *Hom.* FILTER.

**phle‧bi‧tis** (fli bī′tis) the inflammation of a vein. *n.*

**phlegm** (flem) **1** the thick discharge from the nose and throat during a cold or other respiratory disease. **2** sluggishness or indifference. **3** coolness or calmness. *n.*

**phleg‧mat‧ic** (fleg mat′ik) **1** sluggish; indifferent. **2** cool; calm: *Joanne is phlegmatic; she never gets excited about anything.* *adj.* —**phleg‧mat′i‧cal‧ly,** *adv.*

**phleg‧mat‧i‧cal** (fleg mat′ə kəl) PHLEGMATIC. *adj.*

**phlo‧em** or **phlo‧ëm** (flō′əm) in botany, the soft tissue in the vascular system of plants or trees that transports and stores food materials and helps to support the plant: *The phloem consists mainly of sieve tubes and parenchyma cells.* Compare with XYLEM. *n.*

**phlox** (floks) **1** a garden plant with clusters of showy flowers in various colours. **2** the flower. *n.*

**pho‧bi‧a** (fō′bē ə) an irrational, exaggerated fear of or aversion to a particular thing or situation. *n.*

**-phobia** *combining form.* hatred or fear of _____: *Claustrophobia* means fear of being in an enclosed or confined space.

**phoe‧be** (fē′bē) a small North American bird with a greyish-brown back, a yellowish-white breast, and a low crest on the head. *n.*

**Phoe‧ni‧cian** (fə nish′ən) **1** of or having to do with Phoenicia, an ancient country in western Syria, its people, or their language. **2** a native or inhabitant of Phoenicia. **3** the language of Phoenicia. **1** *adj.,* **2, 3** *n.*

**phoe‧nix** (fē′niks) a mythical bird, the only one of its kind, said to live 500 or 600 years, to burn itself to ashes on a funeral pyre, and to rise again from the ashes, fresh and beautiful, for another long life. *n.*

**phone**[1] (fōn) *Informal.* telephone. *n., v.,* **phoned, phon‧ing.**

**phone**[2] (fōn) any speech sound. *n.*

**-phone** *combining form.* sound: *Telephone* means *sounding at a distance.*

**pho‧neme** (fō′nēm) a PHONE[2] used to distinguish the meaning of a word from that of another word: *In* cat, bat, *and* sat, /k/, /b/ *and* /s/ *are phonemes.* *n.*

---

**philosophical** 887 **phosgene**

hat, āge, fär; let, ēqual, tėrm; it, īce
hot, ōpen, ôrder; oil, out; cup, pùt, rüle
əbove, takən, pencəl, lemən, circəs
ch, child; ng, long; sh, ship
th, thin; ᴛʜ, then; zh, measure

**pho‧nem‧ics** (fə nēm′iks) the description of the PHONES[2] of a language that are used to distinguish word meanings. Compare with PHONETICS. *n.*
☞ *Usage.* Used with a singular verb.

**pho‧net‧ic** (fə net′ik) **1** of or having to do with sounds made with the voice: *phonetic laws.* **2** representing the sounds of speech. In this dictionary, the phonetic symbol (ə) stands for the vowel sound in the second syllable of *taken, pencil, lemon,* and *circus.* *adj.*

**pho‧net‧i‧cal‧ly** (fə net′i klē) in a phonetic manner; as regards the sound and not the spelling of words. *adv.*

**pho‧ne‧ti‧cian** (fō′nə tish′ən) a person trained in PHONETICS, especially one who makes it his or her work. *n.*

**pho‧net‧ics** (fə net′iks) the description of the production of PHONES[2] as consonants and vowels: *Phonetics describes all the phones*[2] *of a language but does not explain their use in distinguishing meanings.* Compare with PHONEMICS. *n.*
☞ *Usage.* Used with a singular verb.

**phon‧ic** (fon′ik *or* fō′nik) **1** of, or having to do with sound; acoustic. **2** of sounds made in speech; phonetic. **3** of or having to do with PHONICS. *adj.*

**phon‧ics** (fon′iks *or* fō′niks) **1** a method of teaching people to read or pronounce words by learning the relationship between the sounds of the language and the letters or groups of letters used to represent them. **2** the science of sound; acoustics. *n.*
☞ *Usage.* Used with a singular verb.

**phono-** *combining form.* sound or sounds: *Phonology* means the study of sounds used in speech.

**pho‧no‧gram** (fō′nə gram′) a symbol representing a single speech sound, syllable, or word. *n.*

**pho‧no‧graph** (fō′nə graf′) record player. *n.*

**pho‧no‧graph‧ic** (fō′nə graf′ik) **1** for, having to do with, or produced by a phonograph. **2** of or having to do with PHONOGRAPHY. *adj.*
—**pho′no‧graph′i‧cal‧ly,** *adv.*

**pho‧nog‧ra‧phy** (fō nog′rə fē *or* fə nog′rə fē) the art of writing according to sound; phonetic spelling. *n.*

**pho‧nol‧o‧gist** (fə nol′ə jist) a person trained in PHONOLOGY. *n.*

**pho‧nol‧o‧gy** (fō nol′ə jē *or* fə nol′ə jē) **1** the study of human speech sounds, especially of their systems and historical changes in particular languages. **2** the sounds and systems of sounds used in a given language at a particular time. *n.*

**pho‧ny** (fō′nē) *Informal.* **1** not genuine; counterfeit; fake: *a phony smile, a phony $20 bill.* **2** a fake; pretender: *He's a phony.* **1** *adj.,* **pho‧ni‧er, pho‧ni‧est; 2** *n., pl.* **pho‧nies.** —**pho′ni‧ness,** *n.*
☞ *Etym.* From *fawny,* a thieves' name for a cheap ring sold as genuine gold to people.

**phos‧gene** (fos′jēn) a colourless, poisonous gas, a compound of carbon monoxide and chlorine. *n.*

**phos·phate** (fos′fāt) 1 a salt or ester of an acid containing phosphorus: *Bread contains phosphates.* 2 a fertilizer containing such salts. 3 a drink of carbonated water flavoured with fruit syrup and containing a little PHOSPHORIC ACID. *n.*

**phos·phide** (fos′fīd) a compound of PHOSPHORUS with another element or a radical. *n.*

**phos·phite** (fos′fīt) a salt or ester of PHOSPHOROUS ACID. *n.*

**phos·pho·res·cence** (fos′fə res′əns) 1 the act or process of giving out light without burning or by very slow burning that seems not to give out heat: *the phosphorescence of fireflies.* 2 such light. *n.*

**phos·pho·res·cent** (fos′fə res′ənt) showing PHOSPHORESCENCE. *adj.*

**phos·phor·ic** (fos fô′rik) of, having to do with, or containing PHOSPHORUS, especially with a higher valence than in phosphorous compounds. *adj.*

**phosphoric acid** a colourless, odourless acid containing PHOSPHORUS, used especially in preparing phosphates for fertilizers, in rustproofing metals, and in flavouring soft drinks.

**phos·pho·rous** (fos′fə rəs) of, having to do with, or containing PHOSPHORUS, especially with a lower valence than in phosphoric compounds. *adj.*
☞ *Hom.* PHOSPHORUS.

**phosphorous acid** a colourless, unstable acid used especially in making compounds and as a chemical reducing agent.

**phos·pho·rus** (fos′fə rəs) a solid, non-metallic element existing in two forms: one yellow, poisonous, flammable, and luminous in the dark; the other red, non-poisonous, and less flammable. *Symbol:* P *n.*
☞ *Hom.* PHOSPHOROUS.

**pho·to** (fō′tō) *Informal.* photograph. *n., pl.* **pho·tos**.

**photo–** *combining form.* 1 light, as in *photometry.* 2 photographic or photograph, as in *photocopy.*

**pho·to·chem·i·cal** (fō′tō kem′ə kəl) 1 of, having to do with, or resulting from the chemical action of light or other radiant energy. 2 of or having to do with PHOTOCHEMISTRY: *photochemical studies.* *adj.*

**pho·to·chem·is·try** (fō′tō kem′i strē) the branch of chemistry dealing with the chemical changes produced by light and other electromagnetic radiation. *n.*

**pho·to·cop·i·er** (fō′tō kop′ē ər) a machine that makes photocopies. *n.*

**pho·to·cop·y** (fō′tō kop′ē) 1 a photographic reproduction of a document or other printed matter. 2 make a photocopy. 1 *n., pl.* **pho·to·cop·ies**; 2 *v.*, **pho·to·cop·ied, pho·to·cop·y·ing.**

**pho·to·e·lec·tric** (fō′tō i lek′trik) 1 having to do with the electricity or electrical effects produced by light. 2 noting or having to do with an apparatus for taking photographs by electric light. *adj.*

**photo–electric cell** a cell or vacuum tube that produces variations in an electric current in accordance with variations in the light falling upon it; electric eye: *Photo-electric cells can be used to open doors automatically, set off alarms, etc.*

**pho·to–en·grav·ing** (fō′tō en grā′ving) 1 a process by which plates to print from are produced with the aid of photography. 2 a plate so produced. 3 a picture printed from it. *n.*

**photo finish** in racing, a finish so close that a photograph is required to decide the winner.

**pho·to·flood lamp** (fō′tō flud′) an electric lamp that gives very bright, sustained light for taking pictures.

**pho·to·gen·ic** (fō′tō jen′ik) 1 looking or likely to look attractive in photographs or motion pictures: *a photogenic face. Julia is very photogenic.* 2 phosphorescent; LUMINESCENT: *Certain bacteria are photogenic.* *adj.*

**pho·to·graph** (fō′tə graf′) 1 a picture made with a camera: *A photograph is made by the action of light rays from the thing pictured coming through the lens of the camera onto a piece of film.* 2 take a photograph of. 3 take photographs. 4 look clear, natural, etc. in a photograph: *She does not photograph well.* 1 *n.*, 2–4 *v.*

**pho·tog·ra·pher** (fə tog′rə fər) 1 a person who takes photographs. 2 a person whose business is taking photographs. *n.*

**pho·to·graph·ic** (fō′tə graf′ik) 1 of or like photography: *photographic accuracy.* 2 used in or produced by photography: *photographic plates, a photographic record of a trip.* *adj.*
—**pho′to·graph′i·cal·ly,** *adv.*

**pho·tog·ra·phy** (fə tog′rə fē) the art or process of making photographs. *n.*

**pho·to·gra·vure** (fō′tō grə vyùr′) a picture printed from a metal plate on which a photograph has been engraved. *n.*

**pho·tom·e·ter** (fō tom′ə tər) an instrument for measuring the intensity of light or the relative illuminating power of different lights. *n.*

**pho·to·met·ric** (fō′tō met′rik) having to do with PHOTOMETRY or a photometer. *adj.*

**pho·tom·e·try** (fō tom′ə trē) the branch of physics dealing with the measurement of the intensity of light. *n.*

**pho·to·mi·cro·graph** (fō′tō mī′krə graf′) a photograph of an object as seen through a microscope. *n.*

**pho·ton** (fō′ton) in physics, a QUANTUM or unit particle of light, having a momentum equal to its energy and moving with the velocity of light. *n.*

**pho·to·play** (fō′tō plā′) a motion-picture play or scenario. *n.*

**pho·to·sen·si·tive** (fō′tō sen′sə tiv) sensitive to light; easily stimulated by light or other radiant energy. *adj.*

**pho·to·sphere** (fo′tō sfēr′) 1 the dazzling surface of the sun as seen from the earth. 2 a sphere of light or radiance. *n.*

**pho·to·syn·the·sis** (fō′tə sin′thə sis) the process by which plant cells make sugar from carbon dioxide and water in the presence of chlorophyl and light. *n.*

**pho·tot·rop·ism** (fō tot′rə piz′əm *or* fō′tō trō′piz əm) a tendency of plants to turn in response to light. *n.*

**phrasal verb** a verb used in combination with an adverb or preposition, or both, whose meaning cannot be obtained from the meanings of the separate words. In *She looked up the word, looked up* is a phrasal verb, but in *She looked up the stairs, looked up* is not.

**phrase** (frāz) **1** a combination of words: *She spoke in phrases that children could understand.* **2** a short, often used expression. *Call up* is the common phrase for *make a telephone call to.* **3** a short, striking expression. Examples: *a war to end wars; from sea to sea; atoms for peace.* **4** express in a particular way: *She phrased her excuse politely.* **5** a group of words not containing a subject and predicate and used as a unit in a clause or sentence. In *He went to the house,* the words *to the house* form a prepositional phrase. **6** a short part of a piece of music, often containing four measures. **7** mark off or bring out the phrases of a piece of music. 1–3, 5, 6 *n.*, 4, 7 *v.*, **phrased, phras·ing.**

**phra·se·ol·o·gy** (frā′zē ol′ə jē) the selection and arrangement of words; the particular way in which a person expresses himself or herself in language: *scientific phraseology. n., pl.* **phra·se·ol·o·gies.**

**phras·ing** (frā′zing) **1** the style of wording or verbal expression; phraseology. **2** the grouping of spoken words by pauses. **3** in music, a grouping or dividing into phrases. **4** the playing of phrases. **5** ppr. of PHRASE. 1–4 *n.*, 5 *v.*

**phre·net·ic** (frə net′ik) See FRENETIC. *adj.*

**phren·o·log·i·cal** (fren′ə loj′ə kəl) of or having to do with PHRENOLOGY. *adj.*

**phre·nol·o·gist** (frə nol′ə jist) a person who professes to tell a person's character from the shape of his or her skull. *n.*

**phre·nol·o·gy** (frə nol′ə jē) a theory that the shape of the skull shows what sort of mind and character a person has; the practice of reading character from the shape of the skull. *n.*

**phy·lac·ter·y** (fə lak′tə rē) **1** either of two small leather cases containing texts from the Jewish law, worn by orthodox Jews during prayer to remind them to keep the law. **2** reminder. **3** a charm worn as a protection. *n., pl.* **phy·lac·ter·ies.**

**phy·lo·ge·net·ic** (fī′lō jə net′ik) of or having to do with PHYLOGENY. *adj.*

**phy·lo·gen·ic** (fī′lō jen′ik) of or having to do with PHYLOGENY. *adj.*

**phy·log·e·ny** (fī loj′ə nē) **1** racial history. **2** the origin and development of anything, especially of an animal or plant. *n., pl.* **phy·log·e·nies.**

**phy·lum** (fī′ləm) in biology, a major category in the classification of animals, more general than a class. It corresponds to a division in the classification of plants. See classification chart in the Appendix. *n., pl.* **phy·la** (-lə).

**phys·i·cal** (fiz′ə kəl) **1** of the body: *physical exercise.* **2** of matter; material: *The tide is a physical force.* **3** according to the laws of nature: *It is a physical impossibility to stop the earth's movement around the sun.* **4** of the science of physics. **5** *Informal.* a medical examination: *my annual physical.* 1–4 *adj.*, 5 *n.* —**phys′i·cal·ly,** *adv.*

**physical education** instruction in how to exercise and take care of the body, especially as a course at school or college.

**physical geography** the study of land forms, climate, winds, and all other physical features of the earth.

**physical science** **1** PHYSICS. **2** physics, chemistry, geology, astronomy, and other sciences dealing with inanimate matter.

**physical training** the practice of doing exercises of various kinds so as to keep the body in good physical condition.

**phy·si·cian** (fə zish′ən) a doctor of medicine. *n.*

**phys·i·cist** (fiz′ə sist) a person trained in PHYSICS, especially one who makes it his or her work. *n.*

**phys·ics** (fiz′iks) the science that deals with matter and energy and their relationships, excluding chemical and biological change (*used with a singular verb*): *Physics deals with mechanics, heat, light, sound, electricity, etc. n.*

**phys·i·og·no·my** (fiz′ē og′nə mē) **1** the kind of features or type of face one has; one's face: *a kindly physiognomy.* **2** the art of estimating character from the features of the face or the form of the body. **3** the general aspect or looks of a countryside, a situation, etc. *n., pl.* **phys·i·og·no·mies.**

**phys·i·og·ra·pher** (fiz′ē og′rə fər) a person trained in PHYSIOGRAPHY. *n.*

**phys·i·o·graph·ic** (fiz′ē ə graf′ik) having to do with PHYSIOGRAPHY. *adj.*

**phys·i·og·ra·phy** (fiz′ē og′rə fē) physical geography. *n.*

**phys·i·o·log·i·cal** (fiz′ē ə loj′ə kəl) having to do with PHYSIOLOGY: *Digestion is a physiological process. adj.* —**phys′i·o·log′i·cal·ly,** *adv.*

**phys·i·ol·o·gist** (fiz′ē ol′ə jist) a person trained in PHYSIOLOGY. *n.*

**phys·i·ol·o·gy** (fiz′ē ol′ə jē) **1** the science dealing with the normal functions of living things or their parts: *animal physiology, plant physiology.* **2** all the functions and activities of a living thing or of one of its parts. *n.*

**phys·i·o·ther·a·pist** (fiz′ē ō ther′ə pist) a person trained in PHYSIOTHERAPY. *n.*

**phys·i·o·ther·a·py** (fiz′ē ō ther′ə pē) the treatment of sprained muscles and broken bones by physical remedies, such as massage or electricity (rather than by drugs). *n.*

**phy·sique** (fə zēk′) the body; bodily structure, organization, or development: *Hercules was a man of strong physique. n.*

**pi**[1] (pī) the ratio of the circumference of any circle to its diameter, equal to about 3.141 592: *the circumference of a circle equals pi times the diameter of the circle ($C = \pi d$).* Symbol: $\pi$ *n., pl.* **pis.**
☛ *Hom.* PIE.

**pi**[2] (pī) **1** printing types all mixed up. **2** mix up type. **3** any confused mixture. 1, 3 *n.*, 2 *v.*, **pied, pi·ing.**
☛ *Hom.* PIE.

**pi·a ma·ter** (pī′ə mā′tər) the innermost of three membranes enveloping the brain and spinal cord.

**pi·a·nis·si·mo** (pē′ə nis′ə mō′) in music: **1** very soft. **2** very softly. 1 *adj.*, 2 *adv.*

**pi·an·ist** (pē an′ist *or* pē′ə nist) a person who plays the piano, especially a skilled player. *n.*

A grand piano

**pi·an·o** (pē an'ō)   a large musical instrument having strings that sound when struck by hammers operated by the keys on a keyboard.  *n., pl.* **pi·an·os.**
☛ *Etym.*   Short for **pianoforte**, which came from Italian and was made up of *piano* 'soft' and *forte* 'loud.'

**piano accordion**   an accordion having a keyboard for the right hand and buttons on the other side for producing chords with the left hand.

**pi·an·o·for·te** (pē an'ə fôr'tē)   PIANO.  *n.*

**pi·az·za** (pē at'sə *for 1,* pē az'ə *for 2*)   **1** in Italy, an open public square in a town.   **2** a large porch or veranda along one or more sides of a house.  *n.*

**pi·broch** (pē'brok)   music, usually warlike or sad, played on the bagpipe.  *n.*

**pi·ca** (pī'kə)   **1** a size of type, 12 point.
This sentence is in pica.
**2** this size of type used as a measure; about 4 mm.  *n.*
☛ *Hom.*   PIKA.

**pic·a·dor** (pik'ə dôr')   one of the horsemen who begin a bullfight by irritating the bull with pricks of their lances.  *n.*

**pic·a·resque** (pik'ə resk')   dealing with wandering rogues and their questionable adventures: *a picaresque novel.  adj.*

**pic·a·yune** (pik'ə yün')   small; petty; mean.  *adj.*

**pic·ca·lil·li** (pik'ə lil'ē)   a relish made of chopped pickles, onions, tomatoes, etc. and hot spices.  *n.*

**pic·co·lo** (pik'ə lō')   a small flute, sounding an octave higher than the ordinary flute.  *n., pl.* **pic·co·los.**

**pick** (pik)   **1** choose; select: *I picked a winning horse at the races.*   **2** a choice or selection: *This red rose is my pick.*   **3** the best or most desirable part: *We got a high price for the pick of our peaches.*   **4** pull away with the fingers; gather: *We pick fruit and flowers.*   **5** the amount of a crop gathered at one time.   **6** pierce, dig into, or break up with something pointed: *to pick ground, rocks, etc.*   **7** use something pointed to remove things from: *to pick one's teeth, to pick a bone.*   **8** PICKAXE.   **9** a sharp-pointed tool: *Ice is broken into pieces with a pick.*   **10** prepare for use by removing feathers, waste parts, etc.: *to pick a chicken.*   **11** pull apart: *The woollen stuffing in the pillow needs to be picked, as it has matted.*   **12** use the fingers on with a plucking motion: *to play a banjo by picking its strings.*   **13** something held in the fingers and used to pluck the strings of a musical instrument.
**14** seek and find occasion for; look for and hope to find: *to pick a quarrel, to pick flaws.*   1, 4, 6, 7, 11, 12, 14 *v.*, 2, 3, 5, 8, 9, 13 *n.*

**pick a lock,**   open a lock with a pointed instrument, wire, etc.

**pick a pocket,**   steal from a person's pocket.

**pick at,**   **a** pull on with the fingers: *The sick woman picked at the blankets.*   **b** eat only a little at a time.   **c** *Informal.*   find fault with; nag.

**pick off,**   shoot one at a time.
**pick on,**   **a** *Informal.*   find fault with: *The teacher picked on him for always being late.*   **b** *Informal.*   annoy; tease: *The bigger boys picked on the new boy during recess.*   **c** bully; take advantage of.   **d** select: *Why did he pick on you first?*
**pick out,**   **a** choose; select: *Pick out a dress you would like to wear.*   **b** distinguish a thing from surroundings: *Can you pick me out in this group picture?*   **c** make out the sense or meaning.
**pick over,**   **a** look over carefully.   **b** prepare for use.
**pick up,**   **a** take up: *The boy picked up a stone. She picked up the chance to make some money by baby-sitting.*   **b** summon courage, etc.   **c** get by chance: *to pick up a bargain.*   **d** learn without being taught: *She picks up games easily.*   **e** take up into a vehicle or ship: *The bus picked up passengers at every other corner.*   **f** *Informal.* improve; recover: *He seemed to pick up quickly after his fever.*   **g** regain; find again.   **h** go faster; increase in speed.   **i** become acquainted with without being introduced.   **j** tidy up; put in order.

**pick·a·back** (pik'ə bak')   on the back or shoulders; piggyback.  *adv.*

A pickaxe

**pick·axe** (pik'aks')   a heavy metal tool that is pointed at one or both ends and has a long wooden handle, used for breaking up dirt, rocks, etc.; pick.  *n.*   Sometimes, **pickax.**

**picked** (pikt)   **1** with waste parts removed and ready for use.   **2** specially chosen or selected for merit: *a crew of picked men.*   **3** pt. and pp. of PICK. 1, 2 *adj.*, 3 *v.*
☛ *Hom.*   PICT.

**pick·er** (pik'ər)   **1** a person who gathers, picks, or collects.   **2** a tool for picking anything.  *n.*

**pick·er·el** (pik'ə rəl)   **1** any of several species of fish of the pike family.   **2** WALLEYE.  *n., pl.* **pick·er·el** or **pick·er·els.**

**pick·er·el·weed** (pik'ə rəl wēd')   a plant having blue flowers and heart-shaped leaves, growing in shallow water.  *n.*

**pick·et** (pik'it)   **1** a pointed stake or peg placed upright to make a fence, to tie a horse to, etc.   **2** enclose with pickets; fence.   **3** tie to a picket: *Picket your horse here.*
**4** a small body of troops, or a single man, posted at some place to watch for the enemy and guard against surprise attacks.   **5** a person stationed by a labour union near a place of work where there is a strike: *Pickets try to prevent employees from working or customers from buying.*
**6** station pickets at or near: *to picket a factory during a strike.*   **7** act as a picket.   1, 4, 5 *n.*, 2, 3, 6, 7 *v.*

**picket fence**   a fence made of pickets.

**picket line**   a group or line of people picketing a business, etc.

**pick·ings** (pik'ingz)   **1** the amount picked.   **2** things left over; scraps.   **3** things stolen or received dishonestly.  *n.pl.*

**pick·le** (pik′əl) **1** a cucumber or other vegetable preserved in salt water, vinegar, or some other liquid. **2** preserve in pickle: *to pickle beets.* **3** the liquid in which foods can be preserved. **4** *Informal.* trouble; difficulty: *I got in a bad pickle today.* **5** an acid bath for cleaning metal castings, etc. **6** clean with acid. 1, 3–5 *n.,* 2, 6 *v.,* **pick·led, pick·ling.**

**pick·pock·et** (pik′pok′it) a person who steals from people's pockets. *n.*

**pick·up** (pik′up′) **1** a picking up: *the daily pickup of mail.* **2** an acceleration; going faster; increase in speed. **3** *Informal.* an acquaintance made without an introduction. **4** a catching or hitting of a ball very soon after it has bounced on the ground. **5** the reception of sounds for radio broadcasting. **6** an apparatus for such reception. **7** the place where it occurs. **8** in television, the reception of images and their conversion into electric waves. **9** an apparatus that does this. **10** on a record player, a device that transforms into electrical current the vibrations set up in a phonograph needle by variations in the grooves of a record. **11** a small truck for collecting and delivering light loads. *n.*

**Pick·wick·i·an** (pik wik′ē ən) **1** of, having to do with, or characteristic of Samuel Pickwick, the kindly, genial hero of Dickens's *Pickwick Papers,* or his club. **2** given a special meaning for the occasion: *words used in a Pickwickian sense.* *adj.*

**pic·nic** (pik′nik) **1** a pleasure trip with a meal in the open air. **2** go on a picnic: *Our family often picnics at the beach.* **3** eat in picnic style. 1 *n.,* 2, 3 *v.,* **pic·nicked, pic·nick·ing.**

**pic·nick·er** (pik′ni kər) a person who PICNICS. *n.*

**pi·cot** (pē′kō) **1** one of a number of fancy loops in embroidery, tatting, etc. or along the edge of lace, ribbon, etc. **2** trim with picots. 1 *n.,* 2 *v.*

**pic·ric acid** (pik′rik) an intensely bitter acid used as a dye and in explosives.

**Pict** (pikt) a member of a people of disputed origin, formerly living in Scotland, especially northern Scotland. *n.*
☛ *Hom.* PICKED.

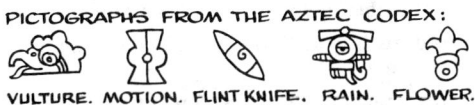

Pictographs from the Aztec calendar stone

**pic·to·graph** (pik′tə graf′) **1** a picture or symbol used to represent a word or idea. **2** a chart or graph on which symbols are used to represent quantities such as population or production of goods. *n.*

**pic·to·graph·ic** (pik′tə graf′ik) of PICTOGRAPHS. *adj.*

**pic·to·ri·al** (pik tô′rē əl) **1** having to do with pictures; expressed in pictures: *A photograph album is a pictorial record.* **2** making a picture for the mind; vivid: *a pictorial way of writing.* **3** illustrated by pictures: *a pictorial history.* **4** a magazine in which pictures are an important feature. **5** having to do with painters or painting: *pictorial skill.* 1–3, 5 *adj.,* 4 *n.* —**pic·to′ri·al·ly,** *adv.*

**pic·ture** (pik′chər) **1** a drawing, painting, portrait, or photograph; a print of any of these: *The book contains a good picture of Laura Secord.* **2** a scene: *The trees and brook make a lovely picture.* **3** something beautiful: *She was a picture in her new dress.* **4** draw, paint, etc.; make into a picture: *The artist pictured the family.* **5** an image; likeness: *He is the picture of his father.* **6** form a picture of in the mind; imagine: *It is hard to picture life a hundred years ago.* **7** a mental image; idea: *I have a clear picture of the problem.* **8** an example; embodiment: *She was the picture of despair.* **9** a vivid description. **10** show by words; describe vividly: *The speaker pictured the suffering of the poor.* **11** a motion picture. **12** an image on a television screen. **13** *Informal.* state of affairs; condition; situation: *the employment picture.* 1–3, 5, 7–9, 11–13 *n.,* 4, 6, 10 *v.,* **pic·tured, pic·tur·ing.**

**pic·tur·esque** (pik′chə resk′) **1** quaint or interesting enough to be used as the subject of a picture: *a picturesque old mill.* **2** making a picture for the mind; vivid: *picturesque language.* *adj.*
—**pic′tur·esque′ly,** *adv.* —**pic′tur·esque′ness,** *n.*

**picture writing** **1** the recording of events or expressing of ideas by pictures. **2** pictures used to record events or express ideas.

**pid·dle** (pid′əl) *Informal.* **1** do anything in a trifling or ineffective way. **2** urinate. *v.,* **pid·dled, pid·dling.**
—**pid′dler,** *n.*

**pid·dling** (pid′ling) *Informal.* **1** trifling; petty. **2** ppr. of PIDDLE. 1 *adj.,* 2 *v.*

**pid·gin** (pij′ən) a mixed jargon, combining simplified grammatical forms and vocabulary from two different languages, used for trade or communication between different peoples or groups. *n.*
☛ *Hom.* PIGEON.

**pidgin English** one of several forms of English, with reduced grammatical structure and vocabulary, used in western Africa, Australia, Melanesia, and formerly in China, as a trade or communication jargon.

**pie**[1] (pī) a food consisting of fruit, meat, etc. set in a shell of pastry, fine crumbs, etc. and sometimes covered with pastry, and baked or chilled: *apple pie, chicken pie.* *n.*
☛ *Hom.* PI.

**pie**[2] (pī) MAGPIE. *n.*
☛ *Hom.* PI.

**pie·bald** (pī′bold′) **1** spotted in two colours, especially black and white. **2** a spotted animal, especially a horse. 1 *adj.,* 2 *n.*

**piece** (pēs) **1** one of the parts into which a thing is divided or broken; bit: *a piece of wood. The cup broke in pieces.* **2** a portion; limited part; small quantity: *a piece of land containing two hectares, a piece of bread.* **3** a single thing of a set or class: *a piece of luggage. This set of china has 144 pieces.* **4** coin: *A nickel is a five-cent piece.* **5** an example; instance: *Sleeping with a light on in the room is a piece of nonsense.* **6** a single work of art: *a piece of music, a piece of poetry.* **7** a gun or cannon. **8** the quantity in which goods are made: *She bought the whole piece of muslin.* **9** the amount of work done: *paid by the piece.* **10** a figure, disk, block, etc. used in playing checkers, chess, and other games. **11** make or repair by adding or joining pieces: *to piece a quilt.* **12** join the

**pieces of.** 13 a 90-pound (about 40.8 kg) package that was the standard load carried by the fur brigades. *1–10, 13 n., 11, 12 v.*, **pieced, piec·ing.** —**piec′er,** *n.*
**go to pieces,** a fall apart; break up: *Another ship had gone to pieces on the rocks.* b break down; collapse: *When his business failed, he went completely to pieces.*
**of a piece,** of the same kind; in keeping: *The plan is of a piece with the rest of his silly suggestions.*
**piece of one's mind,** *Informal.* a candid opinion. b a scolding: *He gave the boy a piece of his mind for coming late.*
☞ *Hom.* PEACE.

**pièce de ré·sis·tance** (pyez də Rā zē stäns′) *French.* 1 the chief dish of a meal. 2 the main article in any collection.

**piece·meal** (pē′smēl′) 1 piece by piece; a little at a time: *work done piecemeal.* 2 piece from piece; to pieces; into fragments. 3 done piece by piece. *1, 2 adv., 3 adj.*

**piece of eight** in former times, a Spanish dollar.

**piece·work** (pē′swėrk′) work paid for by the amount done, not by the time it takes. *n.*

**piece·work·er** (pē′swėr kər) a person who does PIECEWORK. *n.*

**pie crust** pastry used for the bottom or top of a pie.

**pied** (pīd) 1 having patches of two or more colours; many-coloured. 2 spotted. 3 wearing a costume of two or more colours. *adj.*

**Pie·gan** (pē′gan) a member of a First Nations people of the Plains, one of the three Algonquian tribes of the BLACKFOOT CONFEDERACY. *n., pl.* **Pie·gan** or **Pie·gans.**

**pier** (pēr) 1 a structure supported on columns extending into the water, used as a walk or a landing place for ships. 2 BREAKWATER. 3 one of the solid supports on which the arches of a bridge rest; pillar. 4 the solid part of a wall between windows, doors, etc. *n.*
☞ *Hom.* PEER.

**pierce** (pērs) 1 make a hole in; bore into or through: *A nail pierced the tire of our car.* 2 go into; go through: *A tunnel pierces the mountain.* 3 force a way; force a way through or into: *A sharp cry pierced the air.* 4 make a way through with the eye or mind: *to pierce a disguise, to pierce a mystery.* 5 affect sharply with some feeling: *Her heart was pierced with grief.* *v.,* **pierced, pierc·ing.**

**pierc·ing** (pēr′sing) 1 that pierces; penetrating; sharp; keen: *piercing cold, a piercing look.* 2 ppr. of PIERCE. *1 adj., 2 v.* —**pierc′ing·ly,** *adv.*

**Pi·e·ri·an spring** (pī ē′rē ən) the supposed fountain of knowledge and poetic inspiration.

Pierrot in traditional costume

**Pi·er·rot** (pē′ər ō) a clown who is a frequent character in French pantomimes: *Pierrot has his face whitened and wears white pantaloons and usually a white jacket with big buttons.* *n.*

**pi·e·ty** (pī′ə tē) 1 being pious or having reverence for God; devotion to religion; holiness. 2 a dutiful regard for one's parents. 3 a pious act, remark, belief, etc. *n., pl.* **pi·e·ties.**

**pif·fle** (pif′əl) *Informal.* silly talk; nonsense. *n.*

**pig** (pig) 1 a cloven-hoofed mammal having a long snout and a stout, heavy body, especially one that is raised for its meat. 2 pork. 3 *Informal.* a person who seems or acts like a pig; one who is greedy, dirty, dull, sullen, or stubborn. 4 an oblong mass of metal that has been run into a mould while hot. *n.*

**pi·geon** (pij′ən) 1 any of a family of birds having a stout body and small head: *There are many domesticated varieties of pigeon bred from the wild pigeons, or rock doves, of Europe.* 2 CLAY PIGEON. *n.*
☞ *Hom.* PIDGIN.

**pigeon hawk** a pigeon-sized falcon which breeds in northern North America.

**pi·geon·hole** (pij′ən hōl′) 1 a small place, built, usually as one of a series, for a pigeon to nest in. 2 one of a set of boxlike compartments for holding papers and other articles in a desk, a cabinet, etc. 3 put in a pigeonhole; put away. 4 classify and lay aside in memory where one can refer to it. 5 put aside with the idea of dismissing, forgetting, or neglecting: *to pigeonhole a request.* *1, 2 n., 3–5 v.,* **pi·geon·holed, pi·geon·hol·ing.**

**pi·geon–toed** (pij′ən tōd′) having the toes or feet turned inward. *adj.*

**pig·gish** (pig′ish) like a pig; greedy; filthy. *adj.*

**pig·gy** (pig′ē) a little pig. *n., pl.* **pig·gies.**

**pig·gy·back** (pig′ē bak′) 1 on the back or shoulders. 2 a carrying or being carried on the back or shoulders: *She gave the child a piggyback.* 3 the act or process of transporting loaded truck trailers on railway flatcars. 4 by this means: *The goods will be sent piggyback to Edmonton.* 5 carry by piggyback. *1, 4 adv., 2, 3 n., 5 v.*

**piggy bank** 1 a small container in the shape of a pig, with a slot in the top for coins. 2 any coin bank.

**pig·head·ed** (pig′hed′id) stupidly obstinate or stubborn. *adj.*

**pig iron** crude iron as it first comes from the blast furnace or smelter, usually cast into oblong masses called pigs.

**pig latin** a children's jargon in which the syllable *-ay* (ā) is added to the end of a word, any initial consonant being placed immediately before this ending. *Examples: oodgay=good, orfay=for, ordway=word.* Also, **pig Latin.**

**pig·ment** (pig′mənt) 1 a colouring matter: *Paint is made by mixing pigments with liquid.* 2 in animals or plants, the natural colouring matter of a cell or tissue. *n.*

**pig·men·tar·y** (pig′mən ter′ē) of or containing PIGMENT. *adj.*

**pig·men·ta·tion** (pig′mən tā′shən) 1 a deposit of pigment in the tissue of a living animal or plant, causing colouration or discolouration. 2 the colouring of an animal or plant resulting from pigment in the tissues. *n.*

**pig·my** (pig′mē) See PYGMY. *n.*

**pig·nut** (pig′nut′) 1 the nut of the brown hickory of

North America. **2** the tree itself. **3** the tuber of a certain European plant, a kind of earthnut. *n.*

**pig·pen** (pig′pen′) **1** a pen where pigs are kept. **2** a filthy place. *n.*

**pig·skin** (pig′skin′) **1** the skin of a pig. **2** leather made from it. **3** *Informal.* football. *n.*

**pig·sty** (pig′stī′) PIGPEN. *n., pl.* **pig·sties.**

**pig·tail** (pig′tāl′) **1** a braid of hair hanging from the back of the head. **2** a twist of tobacco. *n.*

**pig·weed** (pig′wēd′) **1** any of several North American amaranths that are troublesome weeds. **2** a tall annual plant of the goosefoot family, native to Asia but now a common Canadian weed, especially in the Prairies. *n.*

**pi·ka** (pī′kə) a small rabbitlike mammal found in mountainous regions of Asia and North America. *n.*
☞ *Hom.* PICA.

**pike**[1] (pīk) a weapon having a long wooden handle and a pointed metal head, once carried by foot soldiers; spear. *n.*

**pike**[2] (pīk) a sharp point; spike. *n.*

**pike**[3] (pīk) **1** a large, long freshwater food and game fish having a long, narrow, pointed head with many sharp teeth. Also called **northern pike.** **2** referring to a family of freshwater food and game fishes found in North America, Europe, and Asia: *The pike family includes the pike, muskellunge, and pickerel.* **3** PICKEREL. **4** WALLEYE. *n.*

**pike**[4] (pīk) TURNPIKE. *n.*

**pike·man** (pīk′mən) a soldier armed with a PIKE[1]. *n., pl.* **pike·men** (-mən).

**pike·staff** (pīk′staf′) **1** the staff or shaft of a pike or spear. **2** a staff with a metal point or spike, used by travellers. *n., pl.* **pike·staves** (-stāvz′).

**pi·laf** or **pi·laff** (pi läf′) PILAU. *n.*

A pilaster

**pi·las·ter** (pə las′tər) a rectangular pillar, especially when it forms part of a wall from which it projects somewhat. *n.*

**pi·lau** or **pi·law** (pi lo′) an Oriental dish consisting of rice boiled with mutton, fowl, etc. and flavoured with spices, raisins, etc. *n.*

**pil·chard** (pil′chərd) **1** sardine. **2** a small sea fish resembling a sardine. *n.*

**pile**[1] (pīl) **1** many things lying one upon another in a more or less orderly way: *a pile of wood.* **2** a heap; a mass like a hill or mound: *a huge pile of dirt.* **3** make into a pile; heap evenly; heap up: *Pile the blankets in a corner.* **4** gather or rise in piles: *Snow piled against the fences.* **5** a heap of wood on which a dead body or

# pigpen 893 pillage

hat, āge, fär; let, ēqual, tėrm; it, īce
hot, ōpen, ôrder; oil, out; cup, put, rüle
әbove, takәn, pencәl, lemәn, circәs
ch, child; ng, long; sh, ship
th, thin; ᴛʜ, then; zh, measure

sacrifice is burned. **6** a large structure or mass of buildings. **7** cover with large amounts. **8** a large amount: *a pile of work, a pile of dishes.* **9** *Informal.* a large amount of money; fortune. **10** in nuclear physics, REACTOR. **11** a series of plates of different metals, arranged alternately with cloth or paper wet with acid between them, for producing an electric current. **12** any similar arrangement for producing an electric current; battery. 1, 2, 5, 6, 8–12 *n.*, 3, 4, 7 *v.*, **piled, pil·ing.**
**pile in** or **out,** go in or out in a confused rush: *to pile out into the street.*
**pile up,** heap up, collect together.

**pile**[2] (pīl) **1** a heavy beam driven upright into the earth, often under water, to support a bridge, wharf, building, etc. **2** furnish with piles; drive piles into. 1 *n.*, 2 *v.*, **piled, pil·ing.**

**pile**[3] (pīl) **1** the surface of certain fabrics woven with loops of yarn which may be uncut, as towelling, or cut, as velvet, carpeting, etc. **2** the loops that form the surface. **3** soft, fine hair or down. *n.*

**pile driver** a machine for driving down PILES[2] or stakes, usually a tall framework in which a heavy weight is raised and then allowed to fall upon the pile.

**piles** (pīlz) a swelling of blood vessels at the anus, often painful; hemorrhoids. *n.pl.*

**pile–up** (pīl′up′) a vehicle crash. *n.*

**pil·fer** (pil′fər) steal in small quantities; steal: *The tramp pilfered some apples from the barrel.* *v.*

**pil·grim** (pil′grәm) **1** a person who goes on a journey to a sacred or holy place as an act of religious devotion: *In the Middle Ages, many people went as pilgrims to Jerusalem and to holy places in Europe.* **2** a traveller; wanderer. **3 Pilgrim,** one of the Puritan settlers of Plymouth Colony in 1620: *The Pilgrims crossed the Atlantic in the "Mayflower."* *n.*

**pil·grim·age** (pil′grә mij) **1** a pilgrim's journey; journey to some sacred place as an act of religious devotion: *Moslems make pilgrimages to Mecca.* **2** a long journey, especially one to see or visit a special place, etc. **3** life thought of as a journey. *n.*

**pil·ing** (pī′ling) **1** PILES[2] or heavy beams driven into the ground, etc. **2** a structure made of PILES[2]. **3** ppr. of PILE. 1, 2 *n.*, 3 *v.*

**pill** (pil) **1** medicine made up into a tiny ball, tablet, or capsule, to be swallowed whole. **2** something unpleasant that has to be endured: *Our defeat was a bitter pill.* **3** a very small ball of anything. **4** of knitted or brushed woven fabric, become matted into small balls: *This sweater is pilling badly.* **5 the pill** or **the Pill,** any of various pills for contraception; an oral contraceptive. 1–3, 5 *n.*, 4 *v.*

**pil·lage** (pil′ij) **1** rob with violence; plunder: *Pirates pillaged the towns along the coast.* **2** plunder; robbery. 1 *v.*, **pil·laged, pil·lag·ing;** 2 *n.* —**pil′lag·er,** *n.*

**pil·lar** (pil′ər) **1** a slender, upright structure; column: *Pillars are usually made of stone, wood, or metal and used as supports or ornaments for a building.* **2** anything slender and upright like a pillar: *a pillar of smoke.* **3** an important support or supporter: *She is a pillar of the community.* *n.*
**from pillar to post,** from one thing or place to another without any definite purpose.
**pillar of society,** an influential and dependable member of the community.

**pil·lared** (pil′ərd) **1** having pillars. **2** formed into pillars. *adj.*

**pill·box** (pil′boks′) **1** a box, usually shallow and often round, for holding pills. **2** a small, low fortress with very thick walls and roof, having machine guns, antitank weapons, etc. **3** a small, round brimless hat with a low, flat crown: *Royal Military College cadets wear pillboxes.* *n.*

**pil·lion** (pil′yən) a pad attached behind a saddle on a horse or motorcycle for a passenger to sit on. *n.*

A pillory

**pil·lo·ry** (pil′ə rē) **1** a frame of wood with holes through which a person's head and hands were put: *In former times the pillory was used as a punishment, being set up in a public place where the crowd could make fun of the offender.* **2** put in the pillory. **3** expose to public ridicule, contempt, or abuse: *The newspaper pilloried the cruel father.* **1** *n., pl.* **pil·lo·ries;** **2, 3** *v.,* **pil·lo·ried, pil·lo·ry·ing.**

**pil·low** (pil′ō) **1** a bag or case filled with feathers, down, or some other soft material, usually used to support the head when resting or sleeping. **2** rest on or as if on a pillow: *She pillowed her head on a pile of leaves.* **3** be a pillow for. **1** *n.,* **2, 3** *v.* **—pil′low·like′,** *adj.*

**pil·low·case** (pil′ō kās′) a removable cotton or linen cover for a pillow. *n.*

**pil·low·slip** (pil′ō slip′) PILLOWCASE. *n.*

**pi·lose** (pī′lōs) covered with soft hair; hairy. *adj.*

**pi·lot** (pī′lət) **1** a person who operates the controls of an aircraft in flight. **2** a person who steers a ship. **3** a person whose business is steering ships in or out of a harbour or through dangerous waters: *A ship takes on a pilot before coming into a strange harbour.* **4** act as the pilot of; steer: *The businesswoman pilots her own plane.* **5** a guide or leader. **6** guide; lead: *The manager piloted us through the big factory.* **7** a device that controls the action of one part of a machine, motor, etc. **8** serving as an advance or experimental version or sample of some action, operation, device, etc.: *a pilot project, a pilot film.* **1–3, 5, 7, 8** *n.,* **4, 6** *v.*

**pi·lot·age** (pī′lə tij) **1** piloting. **2** a pilot's art or duties. **3** the fee paid for a pilot's service. *n.*

**pilot biscuit** or **bread** a ship biscuit; a large, flat cracker.

**pilot fish** a small, bluish fish found in warm seas, often accompanying sharks.

**pilot house** an enclosed place on the deck of a ship, sheltering the steering wheel and helmsman.

**pilot light** a small flame kept burning all the time and used to light a main burner whenever desired. Gas stoves and gas water heaters have pilot lights.

**pi·men·to** (pə men′tō) **1** a variety of sweet red pepper, the fruit of a cultivated capsicum, used as a relish and as stuffing for green olives: *Pimentos are dried and ground up to make paprika.* **2** a small evergreen tree of the myrtle family native to the West Indies. **3** a spice made from the dried berries of the West Indian pimento; allspice. *n., pl.* **pi·men·tos.**

**pi·mien·to** (pi myen′tō) PIMENTO (def. 1). *n., pl.* **pi·mien·tos.**

**pim·per·nel** (pim′pər nel′) **1** a small scarlet, purple, or white flower that closes in bad weather. **2** the plant that it grows on. *n.*

**pim·ple** (pim′pəl) a small inflamed swelling in the skin, containing pus: *A pimple is a small abscess.* *n.*

**pim·pled** (pim′pəld) having PIMPLES. *adj.*

**pim·ply** (pim′plē) having PIMPLES. *adj.,* **pim·pli·er, pim·pli·est.**

**pin** (pin) **1** a short, slender piece of wire with a point at one end and a head at the other, used for fastening things together. **2** a kind of badge with a pin or clasp to fasten it to the clothing: *She wore her class pin.* **3** a brooch. **4** a peg made of wood, metal, or plastic used to fasten things together, hold something, hang things on, etc.: *a clothespin.* **5** a BELAYING PIN. **6** a peg that holds an oar in place. **7** a peg in a violin, etc. to which a string is fastened. **8** fasten with a pin or pins; put a pin through. **9** fasten or attach firmly to or on; tack; fasten as if with pins. **10** hold fast in one position: *When the tree fell, it pinned his shoulder to the ground.* **11** bind to an undertaking or pledge. **12** anything that fastens or keeps something in place: *a bobbypin, a safety pin.* **13** a bottle-shaped piece of wood used in the game of ninepins, tenpins, etc. **14** something small or worthless. **15** the stick for the flag marking a hole on a golf course. **16 pins,** *pl. Informal.* legs. **1–7, 12–16** *n.,* **8–11** *v.,* **pinned, pin·ning.** **—pin′like′,** *adj.*
**on pins and needles,** very anxious or uneasy.
**pin down,** hold or bind to an undertaking or pledge.
**pin on,** *Informal.* fix blame, responsibility, etc. on: *The police could not pin the crime on him.*

**PIN** personal identification number, a specific number assigned by a bank to let a person gain access to banking services, including making a deduction or withdrawal from an account.

**pin·a·fore** (pin′ə fôr′) **1** a garment like a full apron worn by children or women to protect other clothes. **2** *Esp. Brit.* a sleeveless dress usually worn over a blouse or sweater; jumper. *n.*

**pi·ña·ta** (pē nyä′tə) a Mexican papier-mâché or clay figure, usually of an animal such as a donkey, filled with candies: *Children, blindfolded, hit the piñata with sticks to get at the candy.* *n.*

**pin·ball** (pin′bol′) a game in which a ball rolls down a board, which is studded with pins or pegs, into numbered compartments. *n.*

**pince–nez** (pans′nā′ *or* pins′nā′; *French,* paNs nā′) eyeglasses kept in place by a spring that pinches the nose. *n.*

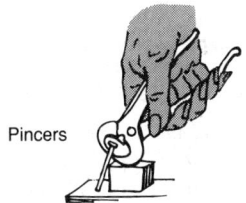
Pincers

**pin·cer** (pin′sər) **1** a claw of a crab, lobster, etc., used to pinch or nip; a pair of claws. **2** a military operation in which the enemy is surrounded and crushed by the meeting of columns driven on each side of them. **3 pincers,** *pl.* a tool for gripping and holding tight, made like scissors but with jaws instead of blades. *n.* Also, **pincher.**

**pinch** (pinch) **1** squeeze between two hard edges; squeeze with thumb and forefinger: *He pinched his little sister's arm.* **2** squeeze or press so as to hurt; get squeezed: *He pinched his finger in the door.* **3** sharp pressure that hurts; squeeze: *the pinch of tight shoes.* **4** as much as can be taken up with the tips of finger and thumb: *a pinch of salt.* **5** sharp discomfort or distress: *the pinch of hunger.* **6** cause sharp discomfort or distress to. **7** cause to shrink or become thin: *a face pinched by hunger.* **8** a time of special need; emergency: *We will ask for help in a pinch.* **9** limit closely; stint: *to be pinched for space.* **10** be stingy. **11** be stingy with: *The miser knew how to pinch pennies.* 1, 2, 6, 7, 9–11 *v.,* 1, 3–5, 8 *n.* —**pinch′er,** *n.*

**pinch·er** (pin′chər) PINCER. *n.*

**pinch–hit** (pinch′hit′) **1** in baseball, bat for another player, especially when a hit is badly needed. **2** take another's place in an emergency: *The pianist is ill and our teacher will pinch-hit for her at the concert tonight.* *v.,* **pinch-hit, pinch-hit·ting.**

**pinch hitter** one who PINCH-HITS for another.

**pin·cush·ion** (pin′kush′ən) a small cushion to stick pins in until they are needed. *n.*

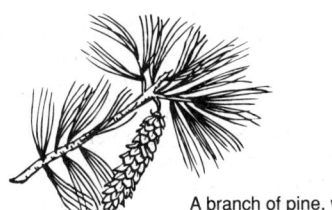
A branch of pine, with a cone

**pine¹** (pīn) **1** any of a group of about 90 species of evergreen tree found in many parts of the Northern Hemisphere, having long, needle-like leaves growing in tufts from the stems. **2** the wood of any of these trees. **3** made of the wood of any of these trees: *pine furniture.* **4** referring to a family of coniferous trees: *The pine family includes the pines, spruces, firs, larches, and true cedars.* *n.* —**pine′like′,** *adj.*

**pine²** (pīn) **1** long eagerly; yearn: *The mother was pining to see her son.* **2** waste away with pain, hunger, grief, or desire. *v.,* **pined, pin·ing.**

**pin·e·al** (pin′ē əl) **1** resembling a pine-cone in shape. **2** having to do with the PINEAL BODY. *adj.*

**pineal body** or **gland** a small body present in the brain of vertebrates, whose function has not been definitely established.

A pineapple

**pine·ap·ple** (pī′nap′əl) **1** a large, edible, tropical fruit resembling a large pine-cone. **2** the plant the pineapple grows on. *n.*

**pine–cone** (pīn′kōn′) a cone of a pine tree or of any of various other members of the pine family, such as spruce or fir. *n.*

**pine marten** MARTEN.

**pine needle** the very slender, needle-like leaf of a pine tree or of other members of the pine family, such as spruce or fir.

**pine siskin** a small North American finch having streaky, greyish-brown and yellowish plumage. It is found in coniferous and mixed forests from southern Alaska, across Canada, and south to Mexico.

**pine tar** a brownish-black, semisolid tar obtained by distilling pine wood and used especially in roofing materials, paints, and varnishes, and as an antiseptic.

**pin·feath·er** (pin′feTH′ər) an undeveloped feather just emerging through the skin: *A pinfeather looks like a small stub.* *n.*

**pin·fold** (pin′fōld′) **1** a place where stray animals, especially cattle, are kept. **2** confine in a pinfold. 1 *n.,* 2 *v.*

**ping** (ping) **1** a very short ringing sound like that of the sound produced when striking a very hard object, or that of a desk bell. **2** produce a ping. 1 *n.,* 2 *v.*

**pin·go** (ping′gō) *Cdn.* a cone-shaped or dome-shaped mound or hill of peat or soil, usually with a core of ice, found in tundra regions and produced by the pressure of water or ice accumulating underground and pushing upward. *n.*

**pin·head** (pin′hed′) **1** the head of a pin. **2** something very small or unimportant. **3** *Informal.* a very stupid person. *n.*

**pin·head·ed** (pin′hed′əd) *Informal.* very stupid or silly: *That was a pinheaded thing to do.* *adj.*

**pin·hole** (pin′hōl′) **1** a tiny hole made by or as if by a pin. **2** a hole made for a pin or peg to go into. *n.*

**pin·ion**¹ (pin′yən) **1** the outermost segment of a bird's wing. **2** any one of the stiff flying feathers of the wing. **3** cut off or tie the pinions of a bird to prevent its flying. **4** bind: *His arms were pinioned behind his back.* **5** bind the arms of or bind to something: *The thieves pinioned him securely. She was pinioned to the chair.* 1, 2 *n.*, 3–5 *v.*
☛ *Hom.* PIÑON (pin′yən).

**pin·ion**² (pin′yən) a small gear with teeth that fit into those of a larger gear or rack. See DIFFERENTIAL and RACK for pictures. *n.*
☛ *Hom.* PIÑON (pin′yən).

**pink**¹ (pingk) **1** a colour made by mixing red and white: *Pink may vary from a very pale, light colour to a vivid, almost red colour.* **2** of or having this colour: *a pink flower.* **3** any of a closely related group of plants native to Europe, Asia, and Africa, having long, slender leaves, stems with swollen joints, sepals joined together to form a tube below the petals, and white, pink, red, or purple, often fragrant flowers: *Many species of pink are cultivated for their flowers, including the garden pink, carnation, and sweet william.* **4** referring to a family of annual or perennial herbs having flowers with four or five petals, simple leaves, and stems with swollen joints: *Pinks, chickweeds, and baby's-breath belong to the pink family.* **5** the highest degree or condition of excellence: *An athlete needs to be in the pink of health.* 1, 3, 5 *n.*, 2, 4 *adj.*

**pink**² (pingk) **1** prick or pierce with a sword, spear, or dagger. **2** cut the edge of cloth in small scallops or notches: *Cloth is pinked to prevent fraying.* **3** ornament with small, round holes. **4** adorn. *v.*

**pink·eye** (ping′kī′) **1** a contagious disease characterized by inflammation and soreness of the membrane that lines the eyelids and covers the eyeball: *Pinkeye is a kind of conjunctivitis.* *n.*

**pink·ie** (ping′kē) *Informal.* the smallest finger. *n.*

**pinking shears** shears for PINKing² (def. 2) cloth.

**pink·ish** (ping′kish) somewhat pink. *adj.*

**pink salmon** *Cdn.* the smallest species of Pacific salmon, found along the coast of British Columbia and neighbouring coastal areas of the United States: *The pink salmon is blue and silver in colour and has pink flesh.*

**pin money** **1** money set aside for buying extra or minor things. **2** formerly, an allowance of money given to a wife for her own use.

**pin·na** (pin′ə) **1** in biology, a projecting body part such as a feather, wing, or fin. **2** the upper part of the external ear. **3** one of the main divisions of a pinnate leaf; leaflet. *n., pl.* **pin·nae** (pin′ē *or* pin′ī) *or* **pin·nas.**

**pin·nace** (pin′is) **1** a ship's boat. **2** a very small schooner. *n.*

**pin·na·cle** (pin′ə kəl) **1** in architecture, a slender turret or spire, used especially in Gothic buildings at the top of a buttress. **2** a high peak or point of rock. **3** the highest point of development or achievement: *at the pinnacle of her fame.* **4** put on a pinnacle. **5** furnish with pinnacles. 1–3 *n.*, 4, 5 *v.*, **pin·na·cled, pin·na·cling.**

**pin·nate** (pin′āt) **1** like a feather, especially in having parts arranged on opposite sides of an axis. **2** of a leaf, consisting of leaflets arranged on opposite sides of the leaf stalk: *The Manitoba maple has pinnate leaves.* *adj.*
—**pin′nate·ly,** *adv.*

**pi·noch·le** *or* **pi·noc·le** (pē′nuk′əl) **1** a game played with 48 cards, in which points are scored according to the value of certain combinations of cards. **2** a combination of the jack of diamonds and the queen of spades in this game. *n.*

**piñ·on** (pin′yən *or* pē′nyōn) **1** a small pine of the Rocky Mountains in the southwestern United States and northern Mexico, producing large, edible, nutlike seeds. **2** the seed of this tree. *n.*
☛ *Hom.* PINION (for the first pronunciation of **piñon**).

**pin·point** (pin′point′) **1** the point of a pin. **2** something very small or sharp: *We could see a pinpoint of light through a hole in the blind.* **3** aim at or locate precisely: *to pinpoint the heart of the problem.* **4** extremely accurate or precise: *pinpoint bombing.* 1, 2 *n.*, 3 *v.*, 4 *adj.*

**pint** (pīnt) **1** a unit for measuring liquids, equal to half a quart (about 0.57 dm³). **2** a container holding a pint: *They bought a pint of cream.* *n.*

**pin·tail** (pin′tāl′) **1** a slender North American duck having grey, white, and brown plumage, the adult male having a white stripe running up each side of the neck just behind the head and two long, black feathers in the centre of the tail. **2** a common GROUSE of the Prairies, having a pointed tail. *n.*

**pin·tle** (pin′təl) a pin or bolt, especially an upright one upon which something turns, as in a hinge. *n.*

**pin·to** (pin′tō) **1** spotted in two or more colours; pied. **2** a pinto horse. 1 *adj.*, 2 *n., pl.* **pin·tos.**

**pint–sized** (pīnt′sīzd′) *Informal.* small. *adj.*

**pin–up** (pin′up′) **1** a picture of a very attractive person, pinned up on a wall, usually by admirers who have not met the person. **2** a very attractive person. **3** very attractive. 1, 2 *n.*, 3 *adj.*

**pin·wheel** (pin′wēl′ *or* pin′hwēl′) **1** a toy made of a wheel fastened to a stick by a pin so that it revolves in the wind. **2** a kind of firework that revolves when lighted. *n.*

**pin·worm** (pin′wėrm′) any of various small, threadlike worms that are intestinal parasites in vertebrates, especially a worm that infests the rectum and large intestine of human beings, most commonly children. *n.*

**pin·y** (pī′nē) **1** abounding in or covered with pine trees: *piny mountains.* **2** having to do with or suggesting pine trees: *a piny fragrance.* *adj.*, **pin·i·er, pin·i·est.**

**pi·o·neer** (pī′ə nēr′) **1** a person who settles in a region that has not been settled before. **2** a person who goes first or does something and so prepares a way for others. **3** prepare or open up for others; take the lead: *Astronauts are pioneering in exploring outer space.* **4** one of a group of soldiers whose job it is to go in advance of other troops, preparing camps, roads, trenches, etc.; engineer; sapper. 1, 2, 4 *n.*, 3 *v.*
☛ *Etym.* See note at PAWN.

**pi·ous** (pī′əs) **1** having or showing reverence for God; religious: *a pious person, a pious act.* **2** showing religious scruples in a smug or ostentatious way, especially when not sincere: *pious platitudes about work and duty.* *adj.*
—**pi′ous·ly,** *adv.* —**pi′ous·ness,** *n.*

**pip**¹ (pip) the seed of an apple, orange, etc. *n.*

**pip²** (pip) **1** a contagious disease of poultry, etc. characterized by thick mucus in the mouth and throat and, often, a scale or crust on the tongue. **2** *Informal.* any slight, unspecified illness of human beings. *n.*
**give one the pip,** *Informal.* make one sick; disgust one; irritate one: *That man's nasty way of talking gives me the pip.*

**pip³** (pip) **1** one of the spots on playing cards, dominoes, or dice. **2** in the British army, etc., one of the stars of rank worn on the shoulders of certain officers: *A captain wears three pips, a lieutenant two.* *n.*

**pip⁴** (pip) **1** peep; chirp. **2** of a young bird, break through the shell. *v.*, **pipped, pip·ping.**

**pipe** (pīp) **1** a tube through which a liquid or gas flows. **2** carry by means of a pipe or pipes. **3** supply with pipes: *Our street is being piped for gas.* **4** transmit music, speech, etc. from one room or part of a building to another by means of an electric or electronic system (*used with* **in**): *The background music for the reception will be piped in.* **5** a tube with a bowl of clay, wood, etc. at one end, for smoking. **6** the quantity of tobacco a pipe will hold. **7** a musical instrument with a single tube into which the player blows. **8** anything shaped like a tube. **9** play on a pipe. **10** any one of the tubes in an organ. **11** make a shrill noise; sing or speak in a shrill voice. **12** sing; utter. **13** a shrill sound, voice, or song: *the pipe of the lark.* **14** a boatswain's whistle. **15** give orders, signals, etc. with a boatswain's whistle. **16** summon by a pipe: *All hands were piped on deck.* **17** trim a dress, etc. with a cordlike fold. **18 pipes,** *pl.* **a** a set of musical tubes: *the pipes of Pan.* **b** bagpipe. 1, 5–8, 10, 13, 14, 18 *n.*, 2–4, 9, 11, 12, 15–17 *v.*, **piped, pip·ing.**

**pipe dream** *Informal.* an impractical idea.

**pipe·ful** (pīp'fúl) the quantity sufficient to fill the bowl of a pipe. *n., pl.* **pipe·fuls.**

**pipe·line** (pīp'plīn') **1** a line of pipes for carrying gas, oil, or other liquids: *Some pipelines are hundreds of kilometres long.* **2** a direct channel for supplying information, etc.: *She's got a pipeline into the manager's office and always knows what's going on.* **3** carry by a pipeline. **4** provide with a pipeline. 1, 2 *n.*, 3, 4 *v.*, **pipe·lined, pipe·lin·ing.**

**pipe organ** a large musical wind instrument consisting of sets of pipes of different diameters and lengths which are sounded by forcing air through them by means of keys and pedals: *Pipe organs usually have two or more keyboards for producing many different varieties of sound.*

**pip·er** (pī'pər) a person who plays on a pipe or bagpipe, especially one who goes about the country playing at different places. *n.*
**pay the piper,** pay for one's pleasure; bear the consequences (from the proverb *He who pays the piper calls the tune,* meaning 'the one who pays has the right to be in control').

**pi·pette** (pi pet' *or* pī pet') a slender pipe or tube for transferring or measuring liquids: *Pipettes are used especially in chemical laboratories.* *n.*

**pipe wrench** an adjustable wrench for gripping and turning pipes, used by plumbers, etc. See WRENCH for picture.

**pip·ing** (pī'ping) **1** a quantity or system of pipes: *We have installed new copper piping throughout the house.* **2** material that can be used for pipes. **3** the music of a pipe. **4** a shrill sound or call: *the piping of frogs in the spring.* **5** shrill. **6** a narrow band of material, sometimes containing a cord, used for trimming along edges and seams of clothing, curtains, etc. **7** ornamental lines of icing, meringue, etc. **8** ppr. of PIPE. 1–4, 6, 7 *n.*, 5 *adj.*, 8 *v.*
**piping hot,** very hot.

**pip·it** (pip'it) any of a closely related group of songbirds found in open country, having streaked brownish or greyish plumage, a slender bill, very long hind toenails, and a fairly long tail that the bird habitually wags up and down when perching: *Pipits resemble larks.* *n.*

**pip·pin** (pip'ən) any of several kinds of apple, such as the **Newtown pippin,** the **white pippin.** *n.*

**pip·sis·se·wa** (pip sis'ə wə) *Cdn.* a small plant whose evergreen leaves are used in medicine as a tonic, astringent, etc. *n.*

**pip·squeak** (pip'skwēk') *Informal.* a small or insignificant person or thing. *n.*

**pi·quan·cy** (pē'kən sē) the quality or state of being PIQUANT. *n.*

**pi·quant** (pē'kənt) **1** sharp or pungent in an agreeable way; pleasantly stimulating to the taste: *a piquant sauce.* **2** pleasantly stimulating to the mind, etc.; intriguing: *a piquant bit of news.* *adj.* —**pi'quant·ly,** *adv.*

**pique** (pēk) **1** a feeling of anger at being slighted; wounded pride: *She left the party in a pique.* **2** cause a feeling of anger or resentment in; wound the pride of: *It piqued her that they had gone ahead with their plans without consulting her.* **3** arouse; stir up: *Our curiosity was piqued by the locked trunk.* 1 *n.*, 2, 3 *v.*, **piqued, pi·quing.**
**pique oneself on** *or* **upon,** feel proud about.

**pi·qué** (pē kā') a cloth, usually cotton or cotton blend, woven with raised, narrow lengthwise ribs or cords, sometimes also having a honeycomb, waffle, or bird's-eye pattern. *n.*

**pi·ra·cy** (pī'rə sē) **1** robbery on the high seas. **2** the act of publishing, reproducing, or using a book, play, piece of music, etc. without permission. *n., pl.* **pi·ra·cies.**

**pi·ra·nha** (pi rä'nyə *or* pi ran'ə) a small freshwater fish of tropical America, noted for its voraciousness. Schools of piranha will attack and devour human beings or large animals. *n.*

**pi·rate** (pī'rit) **1** one who attacks and robs ships; a robber on the high seas. **2** be a pirate; plunder; rob. **3** publish, reproduce, or use without permission. **4** a person who publishes, reproduces, or uses a book, play, musical composition, computer software, etc. without permission. 1, 4 *n.*, 2, 3 *v.*, **pi·rat·ed, pi·rat·ing.**

**pi·rat·i·cal** (pī rat'ə kəl) of or like PIRATES or piracy. *adj.* —**pi·rat'i·cal·ly,** *adv.*

**pi·rogue** (pə rōg') **1** a canoe hollowed from the trunk of a tree; dugout. **2** any canoe. *n.*

**pi·rosh·ki** *or* **pi·rozh·ki** (pir'əsh kē') small pastry turnovers filled usually with a ground beef mixture. *n.pl.*

**pir·ou·ette** (pir'ü et') **1** a whirling about on one foot or on the toes, as in dancing. **2** whirl in this way. 1 *n.*, 2 *v.*, **pir·ou·et·ted, pir·ou·et·ting.**

**pis·ca·to·ri·al** (pis′kə tô′rē əl)  of or having to do with fishermen or fishing.  *adj.*

**pis·ca·to·ry** (pis′kə tô′rē)  PISCATORIAL.  *adj.*

**Pis·ces** (pī′sēz, pis′ēz, *or* pis′kēz)  (*used with a singular verb*)  **1** in astronomy, a northern constellation thought of as having the shape of two fishes with a ribbon connecting their tails.  **2** in astrology, the twelfth sign of the zodiac. The sun enters Pisces about February 21. See ZODIAC for picture.  **3** a person born under this sign.  *n.*

**pis·ta·chi·o** (pis tash′ē ō′ *or* pis tä′shē ō′)  **1** the greenish, edible seed of a small tree of the cashew family that grows in warm climates: *Pistachios have a flavour similar to almonds.*  **2** the tree it grows on.  **3** the flavour of the pistachio nut.  **4** light, yellowish green. 1–4 *n.*, *pl.* **pis·ta·chi·os;**  4 *adj.*

**pis·til** (pis′təl)  the part of a flower that produces seeds, consisting of a base section called the ovary, a thinner middle section, the style, and, at the top, the stigma: *A simple pistil, like that of the pea, consists of one carpel; a compound pistil, like that of the iris, consists of several carpels fused together.* See FLOWER for picture.  *n.*
☛ *Hom.* PISTOL.

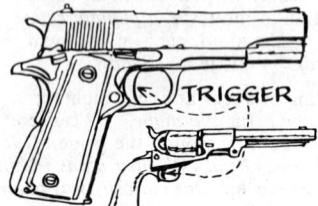
Pistols: an automatic pistol (above) and a revolver (below)

**pis·tol** (pis′təl)  a small, short gun capable of being held and fired with one hand: *A revolver is a kind of pistol.*  *n.*
☛ *Hom.* PISTIL.

**pis·ton** (pis′tən)  **1** in an engine, pump, etc., a short cylinder, or a flat, round piece of wood or metal, fitting closely inside a tube or hollow cylinder in which it is moved back and forth by the force of exploding vapour or steam: *A piston receives or transmits motion by means of the piston rod that is attached to it.*  See CYLINDER and STEAM ENGINE for pictures.  **2** in a wind instrument, a sliding valve that, when pressed by the fingers, lowers the pitch.  *n.*

**piston ring**  a metal ring split so it can expand, put around a PISTON (def. 1) to ensure a tight fit.

**piston rod**  a rod that moves or is moved by a PISTON (def. 1).

**pit¹** (pit)  **1** a hole or cavity in the ground: *Deep pits are used to trap wild animals. A mine or the shaft of a mine is a pit.*  **2** a hollow on the surface of the body: *the armpit.*  **3** a little hole or scar in the skin, such as is left by smallpox; pockmark.  **4** mark with small pits or scars.  **5** an unsuspected danger; a trap or snare.  **6** *Brit.* the rear part of the main floor of a theatre, where the seats are cheap.  **7** *Brit.* the people who sit there.  **8** the part of the floor of an exchange where a particular kind of trading is done: *the wheat pit.*  **9** an enclosed place where animals or birds are made to fight each other.  **10** set to fight or compete; match: *The man pitted his brains against the strength of the bear.*  **11** an area in a garage, often below floor level, for repairing and servicing automobiles.  **12** an area alongside an automobile race track where cars are serviced or repaired during a race.  1–3, 5–9, 11, 12 *n.*, 4, 10 *v.*, **pit·ted, pit·ting.**

**pit²** (pit)  **1** the hard seed of a cherry, peach, plum, date, etc.; stone.  **2** remove pits from fruit.  1 *n.*, 2 *v.*, **pit·ted, pit·ting.**

**pi·ta** (pē′tə)  a Mediterranean form of bread having a pocket which can be stuffed with meat, vegetables, etc.  *n.*

**pit·a·pat** (pit′ə pat′)  **1** with a quick succession of beats or taps: *She went pitapat down the stairs. Her heart was going pitapat.*  **2** the movement or sound of something going pitapat.  1 *adv.*, 2 *n.*

**pitch¹** (pich)  **1** throw; fling; hurl; toss: *The men were pitching horseshoes. She pitched a penny in the pail.*  **2** throw a baseball, etc. for the batter to hit.  **3** erect or set up: *to pitch a tent, to pitch camp.*  **4** take up a position; settle.  **5** fall or plunge forward: *The man lost his balance and pitched down the cliff.*  **6** plunge with the bow rising and then falling: *The ship pitched about in the storm.*  **7** a point or position; degree: *The poor woman has reached the lowest pitch of bad fortune.*  **8** the highness or lowness of a sound: *The pitch of a sound is determined by the frequency of the waves producing the sound; a sound with a low pitch has a lower frequency than one with a high pitch.*  **9** set at a certain point, degree, or level.  **10** determine the key of a tune, etc.  **11** height: *the pitch of an arch.*  **12** the act or manner of pitching.  **13** that which is pitched.  **14** the amount of slope.  **15** slope.  **16** the distance between the successive teeth of a cogwheel.  **17** the distance between two things in a machine.  **18** the distance between the centres of any two successive threads of a screw.  **19** the piece of ground on which certain games are played: *a cricket pitch, a horseshoe pitch.*  **20** *Informal.*  a talk, argument, offer, plan, etc. used to persuade, as in selling, or to promote an idea, product, etc.: *a sales pitch.*  1–6, 9, 10, 15 *v.*, 7, 8, 11–14, 16–20 *n.*
**pitch in,** *Informal.*  work or begin to work vigorously: *All the girls pitched in to get the job done.*
**pitch into,** *Informal.*  attack.
**pitch on** *or* **upon,**  choose; select.

**pitch²** (pich)  **1** a black, sticky substance obtained from the distillation of tar, petroleum, etc., used to waterproof the seams of ships, cover roofs, make pavements, etc.  **2** BITUMEN.  **3** cover or smear with pitch.  **4** resin obtained from various evergreens, often used as medicine.  **5** any of various artificial mixtures resembling pitch. 1, 2, 4, 5 *n.*, 3 *v.*

**pitch–black** (pich′blak′)  very dark or black.  *adj.*

**pitch·blende** (pich′blend′)  a mineral consisting largely of uranium oxide, occurring in black, pitchlike masses: *Pitchblende is a source of radium, uranium, and actinium.*  *n.*

**pitch–dark** (pich′därk′)  very dark; with no light at all: *It was pitch-dark in the room when the heavy curtains were pulled shut.*  *adj.*

**pitched battle**  **1** a planned battle with lines of troops, etc. arranged beforehand.  **2** an intense battle involving close combat.

**pitch·er¹** (pich′ər)  **1** a container for holding and pouring liquids, with a lip on one side and a handle on the other; jug.  **2** the amount that a pitcher holds.  *n.*

**pitch·er²** (pich′ər)   the player on a baseball team who throws the ball to the batter.   *n.*

**pitch·er·ful** (pich′ər fùl′)   the quantity sufficient to fill a pitcher.   *n., pl.* **pitch·er·fuls.**

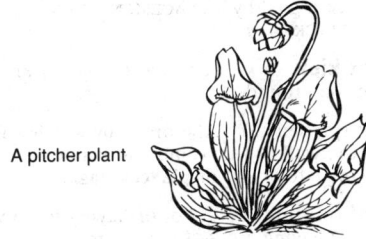
A pitcher plant

**pitcher plant**   **1** any of a closely related group of plants found in the bogs and peat barrens of northern and eastern Canada and the eastern United States, having leaves modified into pitchers in which insects are trapped, to be digested by the plant by means of an enzyme secreted by the leaves: *The pitcher plant is the provincial flower of Newfoundland.*   **2** referring to a family of insect-eating plants of North and South America that includes the pitcher plants.   **3** any of various plants having pitcher-shaped or trumpet-shaped leaves that trap and digest insects.

A pitchfork

**pitch·fork** (pich′fôrk′)   **1** a large fork with a long handle and two or three slightly curved prongs, used for lifting and throwing hay or straw.   **2** lift and throw with a pitchfork.   **1** *n.*, **2** *v.*

**pitch pipe**   a small musical pipe having one or more fixed tones, used to give the desired musical pitch for singing or for tuning an instrument.

**pitch·y** (pich′ē)   **1** full of PITCH².   **2** like PITCH².   **3** black.   *adj.*, **pitch·i·er, pitch·i·est.**

**pit·e·ous** (pit′ē əs)   to be pitied; moving the heart; deserving PITY: *The starving children in the village were a piteous sight.*   *adj.*   —**pit′e·ous·ly,** *adv.*   —**pit′e·ous·ness,** *n.*

**pit·fall** (pit′fol′)   **1** a hidden pit to catch animals in.   **2** any trap or hidden danger: *Life is full of pitfalls.*   *n.*

**pith** (pith)   **1** the central, spongy tissue in the stems of certain plants.   **2** a similar tissue occurring in other parts of plants, as that lining the skin of an orange.   **3** the soft inner substance of a bone, feather, etc.   **4** an important or essential part: *the pith of a speech.*   **5** strength; energy.   *n.*

**Pith·e·can·thro·pus** (pith′ə kan thrō′pəs)   a type of extinct, prehistoric apelike person, whose existence is assumed from remains found in Java in 1891 and 1892.   *n., pl.* **Pith·e·can·thro·pi** (-pī *or* -pē).

**pith·y** (pith′ē)   **1** full of substance, meaning, force, or vigour: *pithy phrases, a pithy speaker.*   **2** of or like PITH.   **3** having much PITH: *a pithy orange.*   *adj.*, **pith·i·er, pith·i·est.**   —**pith′i·ly,** *adv.*   —**pith′i·ness,** *n.*

**pit·i·a·ble** (pit′ē ə bəl)   **1** to be pitied; moving the heart; deserving PITY.   **2** deserving contempt; mean; to be scorned: *His half-hearted attempts to help were pitiable.*   *adj.*   —**pit′i·a·bly,** *adv.*

**pit·i·ful** (pit′ē fəl)   **1** to be pitied; arousing PITY: *The deserted children were a very pitiful sight.*   **2** deserving contempt; mean; to be scorned: *a pitiful performance.*   *adj.*   —**pit′i·ful·ly,** *adv.*

**pit·i·less** (pit′ē lis)   showing no pity or mercy: *a pitiless tyrant, a pitiless act.*   *adj.*   —**pit′i·less·ly,** *adv.*

**pit·tance** (pit′əns)   **1** a small allowance or wage.   **2** a small amount or share.   *n.*

**pi·tu·i·tar·y** (pə tyü′ə ter′ē *or* pə tü′ə ter′ē)   **1** having to do with the PITUITARY GLAND.   **2** the PITUITARY GLAND.   **3** medicine made from it.   **1** *adj.*, **2, 3** *n.*

**pituitary gland**   a small, oval ENDOCRINE GLAND situated at the base of the brain. It secretes hormones that promote growth, stimulate other glands, and regulate many other basic bodily functions.   See BRAIN for picture.

**pit·y** (pit′ē)   **1** sympathy; sorrow for another's suffering or distress; a feeling for the sorrows of others.   **2** feel pity for.   **3** a cause for pity or regret; something to be sorry for: *It is a pity to be kept in the house in good weather.*   **1, 3** *n., pl.* **pit·ies;   2** *v.,* **pit·ied, pit·y·ing.**   —**pit′y·ing·ly,** *adv.*
**have** *or* **take pity on,**   show pity for.

**piv·ot** (piv′ət)   **1** a shaft, pin, or point on which something turns.   See PANTOGRAPH for picture.   **2** mount on, attach by, or provide with a pivot.   **3** turn on a pivot or something like a pivot: *to pivot on one's heel.*   **4** that on which something turns, hinges, or depends; central point: *Her ability to lead made her the pivot of the team.*   **1, 4** *n.*, **2, 3** *v.*

**piv·ot·al** (piv′ə təl)   of, having to do with, or serving as a PIVOT; being that on which something turns, hinges, or depends; very important: *The Liberals will have to win the by-election in this pivotal riding.*   *adj.*

**pix·el** (pik′səl)   any of the many tiny dots, which can be dark or bright, which make up an image on a computer or television screen.   *n.*

**pix·ie** *or* **pix·y** (pik′sē)   a fairy or elf.   *n., pl.* **pix·ies.**

**piz·za** (pē′tsə)   an open pie, usually made of a thin layer of bread dough covered with a savoury mixture of tomatoes, cheese, olives, etc. and baked.   *n.*

**pizza pie**   PIZZA.

**piz·zi·ca·to** (pit′sə kä′tō)   in music:   **1** played by plucking the strings of a musical instrument with the finger instead of using the bow.   **2** in a pizzicato manner.   **3** a note or passage so played.   **1** *adj.*, **2** *adv.*, **3** *n., pl.* **piz·zi·ca·ti** (-tē).

**pk.**   **1** peck.   **2** peak.   **3** park.   **4** pack.

**pkg.**   package.

**pl.** 1 plural. 2 place. 3 plate.

**pla·ca·ble** (plak′ə bəl *or* plā′kə bəl) forgiving; easily quieted; mild. *adj.*

**plac·ard** (plak′ärd *for noun,* plə kärd′ *or* plak′ärd *for verb*) 1 a notice to be posted in a public place; poster. 2 put placards on or in: *The circus placarded the city with advertisements.* 1 *n.*, 2 *v.*

**pla·cate** (plak′āt, plā′kāt *or* plə kāt′) soothe or satisfy the anger of; make peaceful: *to placate a person one has offended.* *v.*, **pla·cat·ed, pla·cat·ing.**

**place** (plās) 1 a particular part of space: *This would be a good place for a picnic.* 2 a city, town, village, district, etc.: *What place do you come from?* 3 a building or spot used for a certain purpose: *A temple is a place of worship. A store or office is a place of business.* 4 a house or dwelling: *We all went to my place for supper after skating. They have a beautiful place in the country.* 5 a part or spot in something: *There's a sore place on my leg where I bumped into the table.* 6 the proper or natural position: *books in place on shelves.* 7 a position in time: *The performance went too slowly in several places.* 8 a space or seat for a person: *Keep a place for me if you reach the boat first.* 9 put in a spot, position, condition, or relation: *The orphan was placed in a good home. The people placed confidence in their leader.* 10 give the place, position, or condition of; identify: *I remember his name, but I cannot place him.* 11 a situation; post or office; official employment or position: *to get a place in a store.* 12 appoint a person to a post or office; find a situation, etc. for. 13 duty; business: *It is not my place to find fault.* 14 a step or point in order of proceeding: *In the first place, the room is too small; in the second place, it is too dirty.* 15 in arithmetic, the position of a figure in a number or series: *in the third decimal place.* 16 a position among the leaders at the finish of a race: *Alicia won first place.* 17 be among the leaders at the finish of a race or competition: *He failed to place in the first race and was eliminated.* 18 a short street or court. 19 an open space or square in a city, town, etc. 1–8, 11, 13–16, 18, 19 *n.*, 9, 10, 12, 17 *v.*, **placed, plac·ing.**
**give place, a** make room. **b** yield; give in: *His anger gave place to remorse.*
**in place of,** instead of: *Use water in place of milk in that recipe.*
**know one's place,** act according to one's position in life.
**out of place, a** not in the proper or usual place. **b** inappropriate or ill-timed.
**put in one's place,** tell or show someone that he or she is unduly conceited.
**take place,** happen; occur.
☛ *Hom.* PLAICE.

**pla·ce·bo** (plə sē′bō) in medicine, a pill, etc. containing no drug but given to humour or satisfy a patient, or to serve as a control in an experiment to test a new drug. *n., pl.* **pla·ce·bos** *or* **pla·ce·boes.**

**place card** a small card with a person's name on it, to indicate where he or she is to sit at the table.

**place holder** in mathematics, the symbol zero when used to indicate the place value of another digit: *In the number 40, the 0 is a place holder indicating that the 4 is in the tens place.*

**place in the sun** a favourable position; as favourable a position as any occupied by others.

**place mat** a small, usually oblong, mat of cloth, paper, plastic, etc. that serves as an individual table cover for a person at a meal.

**place·ment** (plās′mənt) 1 a placing or being placed; location; arrangement. 2 the finding of work or a job for a person. 3 a placing of a football on the ground for an attempt to kick a goal by a PLACEMENT KICK. 4 PLACEMENT KICK. *n.*

**placement kick** a kick given a football after it has been put on the ground.

**pla·cen·ta** (plə sen′tə) the organ by which a fetus is attached to the wall of the womb and is nourished. *n., pl.* **pla·cen·tae** (-tē *or* -tī) *or* **pla·cen·tas.**

**pla·cen·tal** (plə sen′təl) 1 of or having to do with the PLACENTA. 2 having a PLACENTA. *adj.*

**plac·er**[1] (plā′sər) a person or thing that places. *n.*

**plac·er**[2] (plas′ər) a deposit of sand and gravel containing gold or other valuable minerals in particles that can be washed out. *n.*

**placer mining** (plas′ər) the process of washing loose sand or gravel for gold or other minerals: *Placer mining was a common practice in the Klondike.*

**place setting** the dishes and cutlery required to set one person's place at a table.

**place value** the value of a digit according to its position in a number: *In 582, the place values are 5×100, 8×10, 2×1.*

**plac·id** (plas′id) calm; peaceful; quiet: *a placid lake, a placid face.* *adj.* —**plac′id·ly,** *adv.* —**plac′id·ness,** *n.*

**pla·cid·i·ty** (plə sid′ə tē) calmness; peace; tranquillity. *n.*

**plack·et** (plak′it) an opening or slit at the top of a skirt, the side or back of a dress, etc. to make it easy to put on. *n.*

**pla·gia·rism** (plā′jə riz′əm) 1 the act of plagiarizing; taking and using as one's own the idea, writing, invention, etc. of another. 2 an idea, expression, plot, etc. taken from another and used as one's own. *n.*

**pla·gia·rist** (plā′jə rist) a person who PLAGIARIZES. *n.*

**pla·gia·rize** (plā′jə rīz′) take and use as one's own the thoughts, writings, inventions, etc. of another; especially, take and use a passage, plot, etc. from the work of another writer. *v.*, **pla·gia·rized, pla·gia·riz·ing.** —**pla′gia·riz′er,** *n.*

**plague** (plāg) 1 a very dangerous disease that spreads rapidly and often causes death: *bubonic plague.* 2 any epidemic disease; pestilence. 3 a punishment thought to be sent from God. 4 cause to suffer from a disease or calamity. 5 anything or anyone that torments, vexes, annoys, troubles, offends, or is disagreeable: *My hay fever is a plague this year.* 6 vex; annoy; bother: *Stop plaguing me for money.* 1–3, 5 *n.*, 4, 6 *v.*, **plagued, pla·guing.**

**pla·guy** (plā′gē) *Informal.* troublesome; annoying. *adj.*

**plaice** (plās) 1 a red-and-brown European flounder that is a commercially important food fish. 2 a reddish or brownish fish of the western North Atlantic belonging to the same family. *n., pl.* **plaice** *or* **plaic·es.**
☛ *Hom.* PLACE.

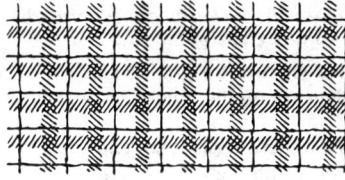
Cloth woven in a plaid design

**plaid** (plad) **1** a pattern consisting of a repeated design of broad and narrow unevenly spaced stripes crossing each other at right angles. **2** such a pattern as the distinctive identification of a Scottish clan or other group; tartan. **3** cloth woven or printed with a plaid. **4** having such a pattern: *a plaid dress.* **5** an oblong length of woollen cloth, usually woven with a tartan design, worn over the left shoulder as part of the traditional dress of the Scottish Highlanders. See KILT for picture. *n.*
☛ *Etym.* From Scots Gaelic *plaide* 'blanket'. There is a related modern Irish word *ploid*, but the original source of the Gaelic word is unknown.

**plaid·ed** (plad'id) **1** made of PLAID; having a plaid pattern. **2** wearing a PLAID. *adj.*

**plain** (plān) **1** easy to understand; easily seen or heard; clear: *The meaning is plain.* **2** in a plain manner; clearly: *Speak it plain.* **3** without ornament or decoration; simple: *a plain dress.* **4** without figured pattern, varied weave, or variegated colour: *a plain blue fabric.* **5** not rich or highly seasoned: *plain food.* **6** common; ordinary; simple in manner: *They're plain people.* **7** not good-looking: *a plain face.* **8** not very hard; easy. **9** frank and honest; straightforward: *plain speech. She believes in plain dealing.* **10** a knitting stitch which raises a ridge on the back of the knitted fabric. Compare with PURL² (defs. 1, 2). **11** Often, **plains,** *pl.* a large, more or less flat and treeless stretch of land: *Buffalo used to roam the North American plains.* See PLATEAU for picture. 1, 3–9 *adj.,* 2 *adv.,* 10, 11 *n.* —**plain'ly,** *adv.* —**plain'ness,** *n.*
☛ *Hom.* PLANE.

**plain–clothes man** or **woman** a police officer or detective wearing ordinary clothes, not a uniform, when on duty.

**plain sailing 1** sailing in a straightforward course. **2** a clear, simple course of action; easy, unobstructed progress: *We had some problems at first but after that it was plain sailing.*

**plains·man** (plānz'mən) an inhabitant of the plains. *n., pl.* **plains·men** (-mən).

**Plains of A·bra·ham** (ā'brə ham') a plain outside and just west of Quebec City, the site of the battle of 1759 that gave the British supremacy in North America.

**plain·song** (plān'song') vocal music used in the Christian church from very early times, sung in unison and unaccompanied, and using a limited musical scale and free rhythm. *n.*

**plain–spo·ken** (plān'spō'kən) plain or frank in speech. *adj.*

**plaint** (plānt) COMPLAINT. *n.*

**plain·tiff** (plān'tif) a person who begins a lawsuit. *n.*

**plain·tive** (plān'tiv) mournful; sad: *a plaintive song. adj.* —**plain'tive·ly,** *adv.* —**plain'tive·ness,** *n.*

**plait** (plāt *or* plat) **1** a braid: *She wore her hair in a plait.* **2** braid: *She plaits her hair.* **3** pleat. 1, 3 *n.,* 2, 3 *v.*
☛ *Hom.* PLATE (for the first pronunciation of **plait**); PLAT (for the second pronunciation).

# plaid 901 plane angle

hat, āge, fär; let, ēqual, tėrm; it, īce
hot, ōpen, ôrder; oil, out; cup, pùt, rüle
əbove, takən, pencəl, lemən, circəs
ch, child; ng, long; sh, ship
th, thin; ᴛʜ, then; zh, measure

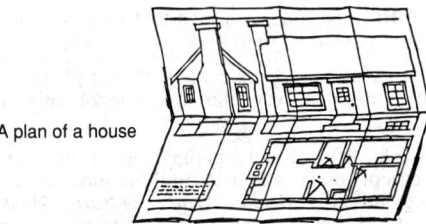
A plan of a house

**plan** (plan) **1** a way of making or doing something that has been worked out beforehand; a scheme or method for achieving an end: *He explained his plan for attracting more tourists to the area.* **2** think out beforehand how something is to be made or done; design, scheme, or devise: *to plan a program.* **3** goal; aim: *Her plan was to have the business firmly established by the end of the year.* **4** make plans. **5** have in mind as a purpose; intend: *We are planning to take a long vacation this year.* **6** a drawing or diagram made on a flat surface, especially one showing how a floor of a building is arranged and the relative size of all its rooms, etc. **7** a large-scale, detailed map of a small area such as a town or district. **8** make a drawing or diagram of. 1, 3, 6, 7 *n.,* 2, 4, 5, 8 *v.,* **planned, plan·ning.**

**pla·nar·i·an** (plə ner'ē ən) any of a family of freshwater flatworms having three-branched intestines, soft, flat bodies, and the power of growing again when cut apart. *n.*

**plane¹** (plān) **1** any flat or level surface. **2** flat; level. **3** a level of development, thought, conduct, achievement, etc.: *the intellectual plane. He keeps his work on a high plane.* **4** a thin, flat or curved supporting surface of an airplane. **5** airplane. **6** glide as an airplane does. **7** of a speedboat, etc., rise slightly out of the water while moving; skim over the water. **8** in geometry, a surface such that if any two points on it are joined by a straight line, the line will be contained wholly in the surface. **9** being wholly in a plane: *Rectangles and circles are plane figures.* **10** of or having to do with such figures: *plane geometry.* 1, 3–5, 8 *n.,* 2, 9, 10 *adj.,* 6, 7 *v.,* **planed, plan·ing.**
☛ *Hom.* PLAIN.

A carpenter's plane. The blade is set crosswise, projecting at a set angle through a slot in the bottom plate. The blade can be raised or lowered to shave more or less wood at each stroke.

**plane²** (plān) **1** a carpenter's tool with a blade for smoothing or shaping wood. **2** make smooth or level by means of a plane; use a plane on. **3** remove with a plane. 1 *n.,* 2, 3 *v.,* **planed, plan·ing.**
☛ *Hom.* PLAIN.

**plane³** (plān) PLANE-TREE. *n.*

**plane angle** an angle formed by two straight lines lying on the same plane.

**plane figure** in geometry, a figure which lies in a single PLANE¹ (def. 8); a flat figure.

**plane geometry** a branch of geometry dealing with plane figures.

**plane-load** (plān'lōd') a load that fills an airplane: *a planeload of supplies.* *n.*

**plan·er** (plā'nər) a person or thing that planes, especially a machine for planing wood or for finishing flat surfaces on metal. *n.*

**plan·et** (plan'it) **1** in astronomy, one of the heavenly bodies (except comets and meteors) that move around the sun in regular paths: *Mercury, Venus, the Earth, Mars, Jupiter, Saturn, Uranus, Neptune, and Pluto are planets.* **2** in astrology, a heavenly body, including the sun and the moon, thought to influence people's lives. *n.*

**plan·e·tar·i·um** (plan'ə ter'ē əm) **1** an apparatus that shows the movements of the sun, moon, planets, and stars by projecting lights on the inside of a dome. **2** a room or building with such an apparatus. *n., pl.* **plan·e·tar·i·a** (-ē ə) or **plan·e·tar·i·ums.**

**plan·e·tar·y** (plan'ə ter'ē) **1** of, having to do with, or being a planet: *planetary influence, planetary motion.* **2** wandering; erratic. **3** of, having to do with, or belonging to the earth; terrestrial. **4** having to do with a form of transmission for varying the speed in automobiles. *adj.*

**plan·e·tes·i·mal** (plan'ə tes'ə məl) of or having to do with minute bodies in space that, according to a certain hypothesis, move in planetary orbits and gradually unite to form the planets of a given planetary system. *adj.*

**plan·et·oid** (plan'ə toid') a small planet revolving around the sun; asteroid. *n.*

**plane–tree** or **plane tree** (plān'trē') any tree of a closely related group making up a family of trees native to North America, Europe, and Asia, having large, broad, lobed leaves, spreading branches, and small fruits hanging in ball-shaped clusters from long stems; sycamore. *n.*

**plank** (plangk) **1** a long, flat piece of sawed timber thicker than a board. **2** cover or furnish with planks. **3** cook and serve on a board: *Steak is sometimes planked.* **4** an item or feature of the platform of a political party, etc.: *The main plank of the party's election platform was a proposal to stimulate economic growth.* **5** *Informal.* put or set with force (*used with* **down**): *She planked down the package.* **6** *Informal.* pay at once; pay on the spot (*used with* **down** *or* **out**): *She planked her money down.* 1, 4 *n.*, 2, 3, 5, 6 *v.*
**walk the plank,** be forced to walk off a plank extending from a ship's side over the water: *Pirates used to make their prisoners walk the plank.*

**plank·ing** (plang'king) **1** the act of laying or covering with PLANKS. **2** a quantity of PLANKS together: *They bought planking for the floor of the shed.* **3** ppr. of PLANK. 1, 2 *n.*, 3 *v.*

**plank·ton** (plangk'tən) the mass of very small or microscopic animal or plant life that floats or drifts near the surface of bodies of salt and fresh water, providing food for fish and other water animals: *Plankton contains algae, protozoans, fish in a larval stage, etc.* *n.*

**plan·ner** (plan'ər) a person who plans, especially one whose job is planning things: *Most cities have a city planner who looks after the arrangement of parks, residential and business areas, etc. of the city.* *n.*

**pla·no–con·cave** (plā'nō kon'kāv) flat on one side and concave on the other. See CONCAVE for picture. *adj.*

**pla·no–con·vex** (plā'nō kon'veks) flat on one side and convex on the other. See CONVEX for picture. *adj.*

**plant** (plant) **1** any living thing that is not an animal, moneran, protist, or fungus: *Trees, shrubs, herbs, etc. are plants.* **2** a living thing that has leaves, roots, and a soft stem, and is small in contrast with a tree or shrub: *a tomato plant, a house plant.* **3** a young tree, shrub, vine, or herb ready to be planted: *The farmer set out 100 cabbage plants.* **4** put or set in the ground to grow: *to plant seeds, to plant a sapling.* **5** provide with seed or plants; stock; put seed in: *We planted our garden last weekend.* **6** deposit young fish, spawn, oysters in a river, lake, etc. **7** set firmly; put; place: *She planted her feet firmly apart and pulled hard.* **8** establish or set up a colony, city, etc. **9** implant principles, doctrines, etc.: *Parents try to plant ideals in their children.* **10** the buildings, machinery, etc. used in manufacturing: *an aluminum plant.* **11** buildings, equipment, etc. for any purpose: *a college plant.* **12** *Informal.* a person or thing placed or devised so as to trap, lure, or deceive: *She claimed that the money found in her room was a plant.* **13** *Informal.* place a person or thing so as to trap, lure, or deceive: *The evidence was planted.* 1–3, 10–12 *n.*, 4–9, 13 *v.*

**Plan·tag·e·net** (plan taj'ə nit) a member of the royal family that ruled England from 1154 to 1485: *The English kings from Henry II through Richard III were Plantagenets.* *n.*

**plan·tain¹** (plan'tān) **1** a tree-like plant closely related to the banana, yielding an edible fruit similar to the common banana. **2** the fruit of this plant, larger and starchier than a banana: *Plantains are not eaten raw; they are boiled or fried and also dried and ground up into meal or flour.* *n.*

**plan·tain²** (plan'tān) any of a closely related group of plants having spikes of tiny, greenish flowers and usually broad leaves that spread out from the base of the stem: *Several species of plantain are common Canadian weeds.* *n.*

**plan·ta·tion** (plan tā'shən) **1** a large farm or estate especially in a tropical or semitropical country, on which cotton, tobacco, sugar, etc. are grown: *The work on a plantation is done by labourers who live there.* **2** a large group of trees or other plants that have been planted: *a rubber plantation.* **3** a colony; settlement: *Plantations were established in Newfoundland in the early 1600's.* *n.*

**plant·er** (plan'tər) **1** a person who owns or runs a plantation: *a cotton planter.* **2** a machine for planting: *a corn planter.* **3** a person who plants. **4** an early settler; colonist. **5** an enclosure in which flowers are planted alongside a building. **6** a box, stand, or pot used for growing plants indoors, on a patio or balcony, etc. **7** *Cdn.* in Newfoundland, a small trader; a person who hires others to fish for him or her, advancing their supplies and taking a share of the catch. *n.*

**plan·ti·grade** (plan'tə grād') walking on the whole sole of the foot: *A bear is a plantigrade animal.* *adj.*

**plant kingdom 1** one of the broad divisions of the natural world, ranging from small plants to large trees: *Members of this kingdom make use of photosynthesis to produce sugars for nourishment.* **2** in present-day biology, one of the five divisions of living things. Compare with

ANIMAL KINGDOM and MINERAL KINGDOM. See also PROTIST, FUNGUS, and MONERAN.

**plant louse** APHID.

**plaque** (plak) **1** an ornamental inscribed tablet of metal, porcelain, etc. **2** a flat, thin ornament or badge. **3** a thin film of saliva, mucus, etc., together with bacteria, that forms on the teeth: *Plaque hardens into calculus, or tartar, if not removed.* *n.*

**plash** (plash) SPLASH. *v., n.*

**plasm** (plaz′əm) PLASMA. *n.*

**plas·ma** (plaz′mə) **1** the liquid part of blood or lymph, as distinguished from the corpuscles. **2** the watery part of milk, as distinguished from the globules of fat. *n.*

**plas·mo·di·um** (plaz·mō′dē·əm) a one-celled parasite found in red blood corpuscles, including the type that produces malaria. *n.*

**plas·mol·y·sis** (plaz·mol′ə·sis) a reduction in volume of a plant cell as a result of loss of water by OSMOSIS. *n.*

**plas·ter** (plas′tər) **1** a soft mixture of lime, sand, and water that hardens in drying, used for covering walls or ceilings. **2** PLASTER OF PARIS. **3** cover walls, ceilings, etc. with plaster. **4** spread with anything thickly: *My shoes were plastered with mud.* **5** make smooth and flat: *He plastered his wet hair down.* **6** a medical substance spread on cloth, which will stick to the body and protect cuts, relieve pain, etc.: *A mustard plaster was once a common remedy for a chest cold.* **7** apply a plaster to. **8** apply like a plaster. 1, 2, 6 *n.*, 3–5, 7, 8 *v.*

**plas·ter·board** (plas′tər·bôrd′) a thin board made of a layer of plaster between layers of pressed felt, covered with paper and used for walls and partitions. *n.*

**plaster cast 1** a rigid casing made of layers of gauze soaked in wet PLASTER OF PARIS and formed around an arm or other part of the body to keep a broken bone in place. **2** a sculptor's model of a statue made of PLASTER OF PARIS.

**plas·ter·er** (plas′tə·rər) a person who PLASTERS walls, etc. *n.*

**plas·ter·ing** (plas′tə·ring) **1** a covering of PLASTER on walls, etc. **2** ppr. of PLASTER. 1 *n.*, 2 *v.*

**plaster of Paris** a mixture of powdered gypsum and water, which hardens quickly and is used for making moulds, cheap statuary, casts, etc.

**plas·tic** (plas′tik) **1** any of various materials that harden and retain their shape after being moulded or shaped when subjected to heat, pressure, etc.: *Glass, celluloid, vulcanite, and nylon are all plastics.* **2** such a substance produced in a laboratory from raw materials such as petroleum, urea, phenol, or glycerin; a synthetic plastic: *Plastics may be rigid or soft and are often used in place of natural substances such as glass, leather, wood, or metal. Some of the most widely used plastics are polyethylene, vinyl, styrene, and polyester.* **3** artificial or phony; not natural or real: *a plastic hero, plastic food.* **4** made of plastic: *plastic cups.* **5** moulding or giving shape to material. **6** concerned with moulding or modelling: *Sculpture is a plastic art.* **7** easily moulded or shaped: *Clay, wax, and plaster are plastic substances.* **8** easily influenced; impressionable. **9 plastics,** the branch of chemistry that deals with the production and use of plastics (used with a singular verb): *Plastics is a fascinating branch of chemistry.* 1, 2, 9 *n.*, 3–8 *adj.*

**plas·tic·i·ty** (plas·tis′ə·tē) the quality or state of being plastic, especially the capacity for being moulded. *n.*

**plant louse** 903 **plateau**

hat, āge, fär; let, ēqual, tėrm; it, īce
hot, ōpen, ôrder; oil, out; cup, put, rüle
əbove, takən, pencəl, lemən, circəs
ch, child; ng, long; sh, ship
th, thin; ᴛʜ, then; zh, measure

**plas·ti·cize** (plas′tə·sīz′) **1** make or become PLASTIC. **2** treat with a PLASTIC: *a plasticized fabric for raincoats.* *v.*

**plastic surgeon** a medical doctor who specializes in PLASTIC SURGERY.

**plastic surgery** a branch of surgery concerned with repairing or restoring parts of the body that are deformed or have been lost or injured, or with improving the outward appearance, especially of the face.

**plas·tid** (plas′tid) any of the structures found in some plant cells in which proteins and colouring matter are stored. *n.*

**plat** (plat) braid; plait. *n., v.,* **plat·ted, plat·ting.**
☞ *Hom.* PLAIT (plat).

**plate** (plāt) **1** a dish, usually round, that is almost flat: *The main course of a meal is usually served on a dinner plate.* **2** the contents of such a dish: *a plate of meat and potatoes.* **3** the dishes and food served to one person at a meal: *The dinner will cost $30 a plate.* **4** a tray or other container similar to a plate: *A plate is passed in church to receive the collection.* **5** dishes or utensils made of or covered with a thin layer of silver or gold: *The family plate included a silver pitcher, candlesticks, and the usual knives, forks, and spoons.* **6** cover with a thin layer of silver, gold, or other metal. **7** a thin, flat sheet or piece of metal: *The warship was covered with steel plate.* **8** armour made of such pieces of metal. **9** cover with metal plates for protection. **10** a part, organ, or structure resembling such metal plates: *Some animals and fish have a covering of horny or bony plates.* **11** a thin, flat piece of metal, plastic, etc. on which something is engraved: *Plates are used for printing pictures.* **12** something printed from such a piece of metal. **13** a metal copy of a page of type. **14** make a plate from type for printing. **15** a thin sheet of glass coated with chemicals that are sensitive to light: *Plates are sometimes used in taking photographs.* **16** in geology, one of the enormous segments of which the crust of the earth appears to be composed, that float and move on the softer mantle below. **17** in baseball, the place where the batter stands to hit a pitched ball; home base. **18** the part of a set of false teeth that fits to the gums, and in which the teeth are fixed: *a partial plate, an upper plate.* **19** a thin cut of beef from the lower end of the ribs. See BEEF for picture. **20** the anode of an electron tube, especially when flat. 1–5, 7, 8, 10–13, 15–20 *n.*, 6, 9, 14 *v.,* **plat·ed, plat·ing.**
☞ *Hom.* PLAIT (plāt).

**pla·teau** (plat·ō′) **1** a large level or mainly level area of land in the mountains or rising sharply from the sea or a lowland area: *Many plateaus have a very dry climate.* **2** a level of progress or achievement, especially the level at which something is stabilized for a time: *Our volleyball* team *improved rapidly and then reached a plateau.* *n., pl.* **pla·teaus** or **pla·teaux** (-tōz′).

**plate·ful** (plāt′fůl) as much or as many as a plate will hold: *a plateful of cookies.* *n., pl.* **plate·fuls.**

**plate glass** thick sheet glass that has been ground and polished to make it very smooth and clear: *Plate glass is used for mirrors, large windows, etc.*

**plate·let** (plāt′lət) one of the very tiny, colourless disks found in the blood of vertebrates, that assist in blood clotting. *n.*

**plat·en** (plat′ən) **1** in a printing press, a flat metal plate that presses the paper against the inked type. **2** the roller against which the paper rests in a typewriter. *n.*

**plate tectonics** the study of the structure of the earth's crust on the basis of the theory that the crust is made up of huge segments, called plates, that float on the mantle below, and whose individual movement is responsible for continental drift, mountain building, etc.

**plat·form** (plat′fôrm) **1** a raised, level surface: *There is usually a platform beside the track at a railway station. A hall usually has a platform for speakers.* **2** a plan of action or statement of principles of a group: *A political party is said to have a platform.* *n.*

**platform rocker** a rocking chair that rocks on a stable platform.

**plat·ing** (plā′ting) **1** a thin layer of silver, gold, or other metal. **2** a covering of metal plates. **3** ppr. of PLATE. 1, 2 *n.*, 3 *v.*

**plat·i·num** (plat′ə nəm) a heavy, precious, metallic chemical element that looks like silver or white gold and does not tarnish or melt easily: *Platinum is used as a catalyst, in jewellery, etc.* Symbol: Pt *n.*

**plat·i·tude** (plat′ə tyüd *or* plat′ə tüd′) **1** a dull or commonplace remark, especially one given out solemnly as if it were fresh and important: *"Better late than never" is a platitude.* **2** flatness; triteness; dullness. *n.*

**plat·i·tu·di·nous** (plat′ə tyü′də nəs *or* plat′ə tü′də nəs) characterized by, using, or being a PLATITUDE. *adj.*

**Pla·ton·ic** (plə ton′ik) **1** of or having to do with Plato (427?–347? B.C.), a Greek philosopher, or his philosophy. **2** idealistic or impractical: *a Platonic scheme for international disarmament.* **3** Usually, **platonic, a** having to do with or referring to love or affection between a man and woman that has a purely spiritual or intellectual character, free from sexual desire or activity. **b** feeling or declaring such love. *adj.* —**pla·ton′i·cal·ly,** *adv.*

**pla·toon** (plə tün′) **1** one of the formations of soldiers making up a company: *A platoon is smaller than a company and larger than a section.* **2** a small group of people sharing an activity or interest. *n.*

**plat·ter** (plat′ər) a large, often oval or oblong plate, used especially for holding or serving a main dish such as meat or fish. *n.*
**on a platter,** *Informal.* involving no effort: *The position was practically handed to her on a platter.*

**plat·y** (plat′ē) a small, brightly coloured tropical fish, often kept in a home aquarium. *n., pl.* **plat·ies** or **plat·ys.**

A platypus

**plat·y·pus** (plat′ə pəs) a small, egg-laying water mammal of Australia and Tasmania having a broad, flat, rubbery snout resembling a duck's bill, thick fur, four webbed feet, and a broad, flat tail: *The platypus and the echidna make up a separate mammal family, called* **monotreme.** *n., pl.* **plat·y·pus·es** or **plat·y·pi** (-pī′ or -pē′).
☛ **Etym.** From Gk. *platupous* 'flat-footed' made up of *platus* 'broad, flat' + *pous* 'foot'. The animal's webbed feet are broad and flat.

**plau·dit** (plod′it) **1** a round of applause. **2** Usually, **plaudits,** *pl.* enthusiastic expression of approval or praise: *She basked in the plaudits of the critics.* *n.*

**plau·si·bil·i·ty** (ploz′ə bil′ə tē) **1** the quality or state of being PLAUSIBLE. **2** something PLAUSIBLE. *n.*

**plau·si·ble** (ploz′ə bəl) **1** appearing true, reasonable, or fair: *His story sounded plausible to us.* **2** apparently worthy of confidence but often not really so: *a plausible liar.* *adj.* —**plau′si·bly,** *adv.*

**play** (plā) **1** fun; sport; recreation; something done to amuse oneself: *The children are happy at play.* **2** have fun; do something in sport; take part in a game: *The kitten plays with its tail.* **3** do or perform for amusement or to deceive, make fun of, etc.: *to play a joke on someone. He played a mean trick.* **4** take part in a game: *Children play tag and ball.* **5** take part in a game against: *Our team played the grade nine team.* **6** put in the game; cause to play in a game: *Each coach played his best goalie.* **7** a turn, move, or act in a game: *It is your play next.* **8** the act of carrying on a game: *Play was slow in the first half of the game.* **9** a way of carrying on a game. **10** a story written for or presented as a dramatic performance; drama: *"Peter Pan" is a charming play.* **11** act on a stage, or as if on a stage; act a part: *to play in a tragedy.* **12** act the part of a character in a play, etc. **13** give theatrical performances in: *to play the larger cities.* **14** act in a specified way: *to play sick.* **15** action: *foul play, fair play.* **16** make believe; pretend in fun: *Let's play the hammock is a boat.* **17** make music. **18** produce music on an instrument: *to play a tune.* **19** perform on a musical instrument: *to play a piano.* **20** of a musical instrument, radio, etc., produce sound: *We could hear the piano playing in the next apartment.* **21** move lightly or quickly: *A breeze played on the water.* **22** a light, quick movement: *the play of sunlight on leaves, the play of colour in an opal.* **23** freedom for action, movement, etc.: *The girl gave her fancy full play in telling what she could do with a million dollars.* **24** movement in operation: *There is too much play in the front wheel.* **25** cause to act, move, or work; direct in a constant manner over an area: *to play a hose on a burning building.* **26** put into action in a game: *Play your ten of hearts.* **27** operate with continued or repeated action: *A fountain played in the garden.* **28** allow a hooked fish to exhaust itself by pulling on the line.
**29** do something foolishly or pointlessly; trifle: *Do not play with your food. Don't play with matches.* **30** gambling.
**31** gamble; bet. **32** bet on: *She plays the horses.*
1, 7–10, 15, 22–24, 30 *n.*, 2–6, 11–14, 16–21, 25–29, 31, 32 *v.*

**in play,** in sports, of a ball, in a position or condition to be legally played.
**out of play,** in sports, of a ball, not in a position to be legally played.
**play down,** make unimportant or less important; avoid or reduce emphasis on: *The government tried to play down the unfavourable results of the opinion poll.*
**played out, a** exhausted. **b** finished; done with.
**play into someone's hands,** act so as to give a person the advantage.
**play off, a** hold a competition in which players or teams are pitted against each other to decide the championship. **b** play an extra game or round to settle a tie.
**play on** or **upon,** take advantage of; make use of: *She played on her mother's good nature.*
**play out,** play drama to the end; bring to end.
**play up,** make the most of; exploit: *The singer's agent played up her extensive background in classical music.*

**play·a·ble** (plā′ə bəl) 1 that can be played. 2 fit to be played on. *adj.*

**play–act** (plā′akt′) 1 pretend; make believe: *We used to enjoy play-acting when we were little.* 2 perform in a play. *v.*

**play·back** (plā′bak′) a replaying of a tape recording or videotape, especially when it has just been made: *We noticed several weak spots when we listened to the playback.* *n.*

**play·bill** (plā′bil′) 1 a handbill or placard announcing a play. 2 the program of a play. *n.*

**play·boy** (plā′boi′) a man, usually rich, who devotes his time to the pursuit of pleasure. *n.*

**play–by–play** (plā′bī plā′) giving each event or action as it happens or happened: *a play-by-play broadcast of a hockey game. She gave us a play-by-play account of the whole silly misunderstanding.* *adj.*

**play·down** (plā′doun′) PLAYOFF. *n.*

**play·er** (plā′ər) 1 a person who plays a game: *a baseball player.* 2 in the theatre, an actor. 3 a person who plays a musical instrument; musician. 4 a device that plays: *a record player.* *n.*

**player piano** a piano played by machinery.

**play·fel·low** (plā′fel′ō) PLAYMATE. *n.*

**play·ful** (plā′fəl) 1 full of fun; fond of playing: *a playful kitten.* 2 joking; not serious: *a playful remark.* *adj.* —**play′ful·ly,** *adv.* —**play′ful·ness,** *n.*

**play·go·er** (plā′gō′ər) a person who goes often to the theatre. *n.*

**play·ground** (plā′ground′) 1 a place for outdoor play, especially an area equipped with swings, slides, etc. for children. 2 a popular or, sometimes, notorious place for leisure activity, such as a resort area: *The Riviera is a playground of the wealthy.* *n.*

**play·house** (plā′hous′) 1 a small house for children to play in. 2 theatre. *n.*

**playing card** one of a set of small, oblong plastic or paper cards used in games, having one side marked with numbers and symbols for rank and group, or suit: *Most sets, or decks, of playing cards consist of 52 cards with 13 cards in each of 4 suits.*

**play·mate** (plā′māt′) a person who plays with another; a playing companion. *n.*

**play·off** (plā′of′) 1 an extra game or round played to settle a tie. 2 one of a series of games played by the top teams in a league to determine the winner of the championship, of a special trophy, etc. *n.*

**play on words** PUN.

**play·pen** (plā′pen′) a small portable enclosure for very young children to play in. *n.*

**play·room** (plā′rüm′ or plā′rum′) a room for children to play in. *n.*

**play·thing** (plā′thing′) a thing to play with; toy. *n.*

**play·time** (plā′tīm′) time for playing. *n.*

**play·wright** (plā′rīt′) a writer of plays; dramatist. *n.*
☛ *Etym.* See note at WRIGHT.

**pla·za** (plaz′ə *or* plä′zə) 1 a shopping centre. 2 a public square in a city or town. *n.*

**plea** (plē) 1 a request or appeal; asking: *a plea for pity.* 2 an excuse: *The man's plea was that he had not seen the signal.* 3 the answer made by a defendant to a charge against him or her in a law court: *The defendant entered a plea of not guilty.* *n.*

**plead** (plēd) 1 offer reasons for or against; argue: *She pleaded the cause of the evicted tenants.* 2 ask earnestly; make an earnest appeal: *He pleaded for more time to finish his paper.* 3 offer as an excuse: *The woman who stole pleaded poverty.* 4 in law: **a** act as counsel for; speak for: *She had a good lawyer to plead her case.* **b** conduct a case in court: *Who is pleading for the defence?* **c** answer to a charge in court: *Do you plead guilty or not guilty?* *v.*, **plead·ed** or **pled** (pled), **plead·ing,** —**plead′ing·ly,** *adv.*

**plead·er** (plē′dər) a person who PLEADS, especially in a law court. *n.*

**pleas·ant** (plez′ənt) 1 pleasing; agreeable; giving pleasure: *a pleasant swim on a hot day.* 2 easy to get along with; friendly. 3 fair; not stormy: *pleasant weather.* *adj.* —**pleas′ant·ly,** *adv.* —**pleas′ant·ness,** *n.*

**pleas·ant·ry** (plez′ən trē) 1 a good-natured joke, a witty remark: *Her speech was full of pleasantries.* 2 lively, good-humoured talk; banter. *n., pl.* **pleas·ant·ries.**

**please** (plēz) 1 give enjoyment to; be agreeable to: *Toys please children.* 2 be agreeable; satisfy: *Such a fine meal cannot fail to please.* 3 wish; think fit: *Do what you please.* 4 be the will of: *It pleased her to remain anonymous.* 5 may it please you (*now used merely as a polite addition to requests or commands*): *Come here, please. Could you please tell me the time? Two orders of fish and chips, please. Please come in.* *v.,* **pleased, pleas·ing.**
**be pleased, a** be moved to pleasure: *She was pleased at the good news.* **b** be disposed; like; choose: *I will be pleased to go.*
**if you please,** if you like; with your permission.

**pleas·ing** (plē′zing) 1 giving PLEASURE; pleasant: *a pleasing manner.* 2 ppr. of PLEASE. 1 *adj.,* 2 *v.*
—**pleas′ing·ly,** *adv.*

**pleas·ur·a·ble** (plezh′ə rə bəl) PLEASANT; agreeable. *adj.* —**pleas′ur·a·bly,** *adv.*

**pleas·ure** (plezh′ər) 1 a feeling of being pleased;

enjoyment; delight; joy: *The girl's pleasure in the gift was good to see.* **2** something that pleases; cause of joy or delight: *It would be a pleasure to see you again.* **3** anything that amuses; sport; play: *He takes his pleasure in riding and hunting.* **4** one's will, desire, or choice: *What is your pleasure in the matter?* *n.*

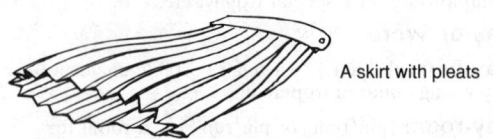
A skirt with pleats

**pleat** (plēt) **1** a flat, usually narrow, fold made by doubling material on itself. **2** fold or arrange in pleats: *a pleated skirt.* **1** *n.,* **2** *v.*

**ple·be·ian** (pli bē′ən) **1** in ancient Rome, one of the common people. Compare with PATRICIAN (def. 1). **2** of or having to do with the plebeians. **3** one of the common people. **4** belonging or having to do with the common people. **5** a common, vulgar person. **6** common; vulgar. **1, 3, 5** *n.,* **2, 4, 6** *adj.*

**ple·be·ian·ism** (pli bē′ə niz′əm) PLEBEIAN character or ways. *n.*

**pleb·i·scite** (pleb′ə sīt′ *or* pleb′ə sit) a direct vote by the qualified voters of a country, province, municipality, etc. on a particular question. *n.*

**plec·trum** (plek′trəm) a small piece of ivory, horn, metal, etc. used for plucking the strings of a mandolin, lyre, zither, etc. *n., pl.* **plec·trums** *or* **plec·tra** (-trə).

**pled** (pled) a pt. and a pp. of PLEAD: *The man pled for mercy.* *v.*

**pledge** (plej) **1** a solemn promise: *He signed a pledge never to drink again.* **2** promise solemnly: *They pledged $100 to the United Way. We pledge loyalty to our country.* **3** cause to promise solemnly; bind by a promise: *The conspirators were pledged to secrecy.* **4** something that secures or makes safe; security: *I left my watch as pledge for the money I borrowed.* **5** give as security. **6** the condition of being held as security. **7** a person who has promised to join an organization but is serving a probationary period before being granted membership. **8** something given to show favour or as a promise of something to come; sign; token: *He gave her a brooch as a pledge of his friendship.* **9** the drinking of a health or toast. **10** drink a health to; drink in honour of someone and wish him or her well: *The knights rose from the banquet table to pledge the king.* **1, 4, 6–9** *n.,* **2, 3, 5, 10** *v.,* **pledged, pledg·ing.** —**pledg′er,** *n.*
**take the pledge,** *Informal.* promise not to drink alcoholic liquor.

**pledg·ee** (plej ē′) a person with whom something is deposited as a PLEDGE (def. 4). *n.*

**Plei·ad** (plē′ad) any of the PLEIADES. *n.*

**Ple·ia·des** (plē′ə dēz′ *or* plī′ə dēz′) a group of hundreds of stars in the constellation Taurus, including six that can normally be seen with the naked eye. *n.pl.*
☞ *Etym.* From *Pleiades,* in Greek mythology, the seven daughters of Atlas who were turned into a group of stars.

**ple·na·ry** (plē′nə rē *or* plen′ə rē) **1** full; complete; entire; absolute. **2** attended or to be attended by all qualified members: *a plenary session.* *adj.* —**ple′na·ri·ly,** *adv.*

**plen·i·po·ten·ti·ar·y** (plen′ə pə ten′shē er′ē) **1** a diplomatic agent having full power or authority. **2** having or giving full power and authority. **1** *n., pl.* **plen·i·po·ten·ti·ar·ies;** **2** *adj.*

**plen·i·tude** (plen′ə tyüd′ *or* plen′ə tüd′) **1** fullness; completeness: *in the plenitude of health and vigour.* **2** abundance: *They consumed a plenitude of food and drink in the course of the evening.* *n.*

**plen·ti·ful** (plen′ti fəl) more than enough; abundant: *a plentiful supply of gasoline for the trip, a plentiful harvest.* *adj.* —**plen′ti·ful·ly,** *adv.* —**plen′ti·ful·ness,** *n.*

**plen·ty** (plen′tē) **1** a full supply; all that one needs; a large enough number or quantity: *You have plenty of time to catch the train.* **2** the quality or condition of being plentiful; abundance: *years of peace and plenty.* **3** enough; plentiful; abundant: *Six potatoes will be plenty.* **4** *Informal.* quite; fully: *plenty good enough.* **1, 2** *n., pl.* **plen·ties;** **3** *adj.,* **4** *adv.*

**ple·o·nasm** (plē′ə naz′əm) **1** the use of more words than are necessary to express an idea; redundancy; tautology. *Examples: The two twins* arrived together (*twins are always two*). *The realization of his dream* came true. (*His dream came true is sufficient.*) **2** an instance of pleonasm. *n.*

**ple·o·nas·tic** (plē′ə nas′tik) characterized by or using PLEONASM; redundant. *adj.*

**ple·si·o·saur** (plē′sē ə sôr′) any of a group of water reptiles, now extinct, having a small head, long neck, and four flippers instead of legs: *The plesiosaurs lived during the age of the dinosaurs.* *n.*

**pleth·o·ra** (pleth′ə rə) excessive abundance or fullness; too much: *a plethora of helpful friends and neighbours.* *n.*

**ple·thor·ic** (ple thô′rik *or* pleth′ə rik) too full; overstocked, overloaded, or swollen. *adj.*

**pleu·ra** (plü′rə) in mammals, either of the thin membranes lining the two halves of the thorax and folded back over the surface of the lung on the same side. *n., pl.* **pleu·rae** (plü′rē *or* plü′rī).

**pleu·ral** (plü′rəl) of or having to do with the PLEURA. *adj.*
☞ *Hom.* PLURAL.

**pleu·ri·sy** (plü′rə sē) inflammation of the PLEURA, in which varying amounts of fluid from the inflamed membrane enter the chest cavity: *Pleurisy is usually accompanied by severe pain in breathing.* *n.*

**pleu·rit·ic** (plü rit′ik) of, causing, or having PLEURISY. *adj.*

**plex·us** (plek′səs) **1** a network of nerves, blood vessels, etc. The **solar plexus** is a collection of nerves behind the stomach. **2** an interwoven combination of parts in a system; network. *n., pl.* **plex·us·es** *or* **plex·us.**

**pli·a·bil·i·ty** (plī′ə bil′ə tē) the quality or state of being PLIABLE. *n.*

**pli·a·ble** (plī′ə bəl) **1** easily bent; flexible; supple: *Willow twigs are very pliable.* **2** easily influenced; yielding: *She is too pliable to be a good leader.* *adj.*

**pli·an·cy** (plī′ən sē) the state or condition of being easily bent or influenced; being PLIANT. *n.*

**pli·ant** (plī′ənt) **1** bending easily; flexible; supple;

**pliable:** *pliant leather.* **2** easily influenced; yielding: *a pliant nature.* *adj.* —**pli′ant·ly,** *adv.*

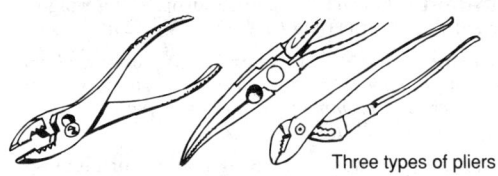
Three types of pliers

**pli·ers** (plī′ərz) small pincers with long jaws used for bending or cutting wire, holding small objects, etc. (used with a plural or singular verb). See TOGGLE JOINT for another picture. *n.*

**plight¹** (plīt) a condition or state, especially a bad one: *He was in a sad plight, ill and penniless.* *n.*

**plight²** (plīt) **1** pledge; promise solemnly: *to plight one's loyalty.* **2** a solemn promise; pledge. 1 *v.*, 2 *n.*

**Plim·soll mark** or **line** (plim′səl) a mark or line painted on a ship's hull to show how heavily it may safely be loaded.

**plinth** (plinth) **1** the lowest, square part of the base of a column. See COLUMN for picture. **2** any square base, as of a pedestal, etc. *n.*

**plod** (plod) **1** walk heavily; trudge: *The old man plods wearily along the road.* **2** walk slowly or heavily along: *We plodded the mountain path.* **3** proceed in a slow or dull way; work patiently with effort: *Dan plods away at his lessons until he learns them.* *v.*, **plod·ded, plod·ding.** —**plod′der,** *n.*

**plop** (plop) **1** a sound like that of a flat object striking water without a splash. **2** fall or drop with such a sound: *The stone plopped into the water.* **3** a fall that makes such a sound. **4** allow oneself to fall heavily: *She plopped into the first soft chair she came to.* **5** with a plop: *My lunch fell plop into the puddle.* 1, 3 *n.*, 2, 4 *v.*, **plopped, plop·ping;** 5 *adv.*

**plot** (plot) **1** a secret plan, especially to do something wrong: *Two men formed a plot to rob the bank.* **2** plan secretly with others; plan: *The rebels plotted against the government.* **3** the plan or main story of a play, novel, poem, etc.: *The story has a very exciting plot.* **4** a small piece of ground: *a garden plot.* **5** divide land into plots: *The farm was plotted into house lots.* **6** a map or diagram. **7** make a map or diagram of. **8** mark something on a map or diagram: *The nurse plotted the patient's temperature over several days.* 1, 3, 4, 6 *n.*, 2, 5, 7, 8 *v.*, **plot·ted, plot·ting.** —**plot′less,** *adj.*

**plot·ter** (plot′ər) **1** one who plots. **2** in computer science, a computer-controlled device to produce diagrams and pictures on paper. *n.*

A plough

**plough** or **plow** (plou) **1** a farm implement used for cutting the soil and turning it over. **2** turn over soil with a plough: *to plough a field.* **3** use a plough: *He was*

hat, āge, fär; let, ēqual, tėrm; it, īce
hot, ōpen, ôrder; oil, out; cup, pu̇t, rüle
əbove, takən, pencəl, lemən, circəs
ch, child; ng, long; sh, ship
th, thin; ŦH, then; zh, measure

*ploughing yesterday.* **4** move as a plough does; advance slowly and with effort: *The ship ploughed through the waves. The girl ploughed through two books to get material for her essay.* **5** a machine for removing snow; snowplough. **6** remove with a plough or as if with a plough: *to plough up old roots.* **7** furrow: *wrinkles ploughed in one's face by time.* **8** cut the surface of water: *The ship ploughed the waves.* 1, 5 *n.*, 2–4, 6–8 *v.* —**plough′er** or **plow′er,** *n.*

**plough back,** reinvest profits in the same business.
**plough into,** *Informal.* **a** hit hard or at speed and travel into: *The car went out of control and ploughed into the building.* **b** undertake a job, project, etc. with energy and determination.
**plough under,** **a** plough into the ground to enrich the soil. **b** defeat; destroy; overwhelm.

**plough·boy** or **plow·boy** (plou′boi′) **1** a boy who guides the horses drawing a plough. **2** a country boy. *n.*

**plough·man** or **plow·man** (plou′mən) **1** a man who guides a plough. **2** a farm worker. *n.*, *pl.* **plough·men** or **plow·men** (-mən).

**plough·share** or **plow·share** (plou′sher′) the part of a plough that cuts the soil. See FURROW for picture. *n.*

**plov·er** (pluv′ər *or* plō′vər) **1** any of a number of related shore birds having a plump, compact body with brownish or greyish plumage, a fairly short bill and tail, long wings, and, usually, no hind toes: *The killdeer is a plover.* **2** UPLAND PLOVER. *n.*

**plow** (plou) See PLOUGH. *n., v.*

**plow·boy** (plou′boi′) See PLOUGHBOY. *n.*

**plow·man** (plou′mən) See PLOUGHMAN. *n.*

**plow·share** (plou′sher′) See PLOUGHSHARE. *n.*

**pluck** (pluk) **1** pull off; pick: *to pluck flowers. She plucked a bit of lint from the blanket.* **2** pull or pull at; tug: *The little girl plucked at her sleeve.* **3** the act of picking or pulling. **4** pick or pull at the strings of a musical instrument: *to pluck a banjo, to pluck the strings of a violin for a pizzicato passage.* **5** pull off the feathers or hair from: *to pluck a chicken, to pluck one's eyebrows.* **6** courage; boldness and spirit: *It took pluck to stand up to that bully.* **7** the heart, liver, and lungs of an animal as food. 1, 2, 4, 5 *v.*, 3, 6, 7 *n.*

**pluck up one's spirits, courage,** etc., take courage: *She plucked up her spirits and carried on.*

**pluck·y** (pluk′ē) having or showing courage: *a plucky fellow.* *adj.*, **pluck·i·er, pluck·i·est.** —**pluck′i·ly,** *adv.* —**pluck′i·ness,** *n.*

**plug** (plug) **1** a piece of wood or some other substance used to stop up a hole. **2** a disk of rubber or metal for stopping the drain of a sink, basin, bathtub, etc. **3** stop up or fill with a plug. **4** a device to make an electrical connection. **5** insert the plug of an electrical appliance or device into an outlet (used with **in** or **into**): *Where can I plug in the hair dryer?* **6** of an electrical appliance or device, able to be connected to a certain type of outlet (used with **into**): *They got a coffee maker that plugs into the* cigarette lighter of the car.   **7** a place where a hose can be attached; hydrant.   **8** SPARK PLUG. See CYLINDER for picture.   **9** *Informal.*   work steadily; plod: *She plugged away at her homework.*   **10** *Informal.*   recommend or advertise, especially on a radio or television program: *to plug a new product.*   **11** *Informal.*   an advertisement or recommendation: *The interview was mainly a plug for her latest book. I'll put in a plug for you when I talk to her.*   **12** a cake of pressed tobacco or a piece of this cut off for chewing.   **13** *Informal.*   a worn-out or inferior horse.   **14** a lure for catching fish.   1, 2, 4, 7, 8, 11–14 *n.*, 3, 5, 6, 9, 10 *v.*, **plugged, plug·ging.** —**plug′ger,** *n.*

**plug-in** (plug′in′)   **1** a receptacle in a wall, etc. designed to receive a plug attached to an electrical appliance in order to complete the circuit and operate the appliance; electrical outlet: *There are only two plug-ins in the bedroom.*   **2** designed to operate by being plugged into an electric outlet: *a plug-in light fixture.*   1 *n.*, 2 *adj.*

**plum** (plum)   **1** any of several closely related trees and shrubs of the rose family producing roundish or oval, edible fruit with a smooth skin, juicy flesh, and a somewhat flat, oblong stone or pit.   **2** the fruit of any of these trees or shrubs: *Plums may be purple, red, green, or yellow when ripe.*   **3** any of various other trees bearing edible fruit resembling plums.   **4** the fruit of any of these trees.   **5** a raisin when used in a pudding, cake, etc.: *plum pudding.*   **6** something very good or desirable: *His new job is a fine plum.*   **7** dark, reddish purple.   1–7 *n.*, 7 *adj.* —**plum′like,** *adj.*
☛ Hom. PLUMB.

**plum·age** (plü′mij) · the feathers of a bird: *Many parrots have bright plumage.*   *n.*

**plumb** (plum)   **1** a small weight used on the end of a line to find the depth of water or to see if a wall is vertical.   **2** vertical: *The wall is not quite plumb.*   **3** vertically.   **4** test or adjust by a plumb line; test; sound: *Our line was not long enough to plumb the depths of the lake.*   **5** get to the bottom of: *No one could plumb the mystery.*   **6** *Informal.*   completely; thoroughly: *My horse is plumb worn out.*   1 *n.*, 2 *adj.*, 3, 6 *adv.*, 4, 5 *v.*
**out of plumb** or **off plumb,**   not vertical.
☛ Hom. PLUM.

**plum·ba·go** (plum bā′gō)   GRAPHITE.   *n.*

**plumb bob**   the weight attached to the end of a PLUMB LINE; PLUMB (def. 1).

**plumb·er** (plum′ər)   a person whose work is putting in, maintaining, and repairing water pipes and fixtures in buildings.   *n.*

**plumb·ing** (plum′ing)   **1** the work or trade of a PLUMBER.   **2** the water pipes and fixtures in a building: *the bathroom plumbing.*   **3** ppr. of PLUMB.   1, 2 *n.*, 3 *v.*

**plumb line**   a line with a PLUMB (def. 1) at the end, used to find the depth of water or to see if a wall is vertical.

**plume** (plüm)   **1** a large, long feather; feather.   **2** a feather, bunch of feathers, or tuft of hair worn as an ornament on a hat, helmet, etc.   **3** something resembling a plume, as on a plant or animal.   **4** furnish with plumes.   **5** smooth or arrange the feathers of: *The eagle plumed its wing.*   **6** a moving column of something such as smoke or snow: *Snow rose in a plume from the snowblower.*   **7** a narrow, jetlike flow of hot material from deep in the earth's mantle.   1–3, 6, 7 *n.*, 4, 5 *v.*, **plumed, plum·ing.**

**plume oneself on,**   be proud of; show pride concerning: *She plumed herself on her skill in dancing.*

**plum·met** (plum′it)   **1** plunge; drop.   **2** a weight fastened to a line; PLUMB (def. 1).   1 *v.*, 2 *n.*

**plum·my** (plum′ē)   **1** like or full of plums: *a plummy flavour, a plummy cake.*   **2** *Informal.*   good; desirable: *She got herself a plummy part in the new play.*   **3** of a voice, rich and full in tone.   *adj.*

**plu·mose** (plü′mōs)   **1** having feathers or plumes; feathered.   **2** feathery; like a plume.   *adj.*

**plump¹** (plump)   **1** rounded out; full; attractively fat: *A healthy baby has plump cheeks.*   **2** make plump; become plump: *He plumped the pillows on the bed.*   1 *adj.*, 2 *v.*
—**plump′ness,** *n.*

**plump²** (plump)   **1** fall or drop heavily or suddenly: *All out of breath, she plumped down on a chair.*   **2** *Informal.* a sudden plunge; heavy fall.   **3** *Informal.*   the sound made by a plunge or fall.   **4** heavily or suddenly: *She ran plump into me.*   **5** directly; bluntly.   **6** direct; downright; blunt: *a plump denial.*   1 *v.*, 2, 3 *n.*, 4, 5 *adv.*, 6 *adj.*
**plump for,** *Informal.*   give one's complete support to; champion vigorously: *to plump for lower taxes.*

**plum pudding**   a rich, cooked pudding containing raisins, currants, spices, etc., and, originally, plums.

**plu·mule** (plü′myül)   **1** the bud of a plant embryo that becomes the growing stem tip.   **2** a small, soft feather; a down feather.   *n.*

**plum·y** (plü′mē)   **1** having plumes or feathers.   **2** adorned with a plume or plumes.   **3** like a plume; feathery.   *adj.*

**plun·der** (plun′dər)   **1** rob by force; rob: *The pirates plundered the ship.*   **2** things taken in plundering; booty; loot: *They carried off the plunder in their ships.*   **3** the act of plundering; pillaging or robbing by force: *The invading army abstained from plunder.*   1 *v.*, 2, 3 *n.*
—**plun′der·er,** *n.*

**plunge** (plunj)   **1** throw or thrust with force into something, especially a liquid: *He plunged his hand into the water to rescue the watch.*   **2** throw suddenly or violently into a certain condition: *plunge the world into war, plunge the room into darkness.*   **3** throw oneself into water, danger, a fight, etc.: *Sergio plunged into the river and saved Paula.*   **4** move or act recklessly or in great haste: *She plunged into the crowd.*   **5** pitch or lurch suddenly and violently: *The ship plunged about in the storm.*   **6** the act of plunging.   **7** a dive into the water.   **8** a place for diving.   **9** *Informal.*   gamble heavily.   1–5, 9 *v.*, **plunged, plung·ing;**   6–8 *n.*
**take the plunge,** *Informal.*   dare to do something which requires courage.

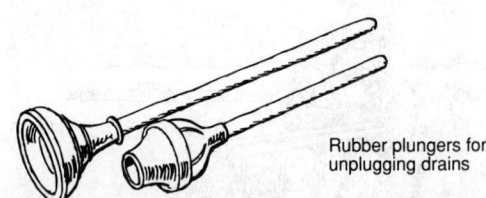
Rubber plungers for unplugging drains

**plung·er** (plun′jər)   **1** a part of a machine that acts with a plunging motion, such as a piston. See CAM for picture.   **2** a rubber suction cup on a long stick, used for unplugging stopped-up drains, toilets, etc.   **3** *Informal.* a reckless gambler or speculator.   **4** any person or thing that plunges.   *n.*

**plunk** (plungk)  **1** hit or pluck so as to produce a short hollow metallic sound: *to plunk a banjo string.*  **2** put down or drop heavily or suddenly: *She plunked her books on the table.*  **3** the act or sound of plunking.  **4** with a thud or twang: *He sat down plunk on the ground.*  *1, 2 v., 3 n., 4 adv.*

**plu·per·fect** (plü′pėr′fikt)   PAST PERFECT.  *n., adj.*

**plupf.**  pluperfect.

**plur.**  **1** plural.  **2** plurality.

**plu·ral** (plü′rəl)  **1** more than one: *plural citizenship.*  **2** in grammar, indicating or implying more than one: *the plural ending -s, the plural noun oxen.*  **3** a form of a word to show that it means more than one or refers to more than one: *Books is the plural of book; these is the plural of this.*  *1, 2 adj., 3 n.*
☞ *Hom.* PLEURAL.

**plu·ral·i·ty** (plü ral′ə tē)  **1** in a contest involving more than two candidates, the number of votes cast for one candidate when that number is more than for any other one, but not more than half the total number of votes for all candidates: *She won by only a plurality, not a majority.*  **2** a greater number of votes cast for a candidate than for an opposing candidate.  **3** a number that is greater than another.  **4** a large number; multitude.  **5** the state or fact of being plural or numerous.  *n., pl.* **plu·ral·i·ties.**

**plu·ral·ize** (plü′rə līz′)   make PLURAL or express in the plural form.  *v.,* **plu·ral·ized, plu·ral·iz·ing.**

**plu·ral·ly** (plü′rə lē)   in the plural number; so as to express or imply more than one.  *adv.*

**plus** (plus)  **1** added to: *Three plus two equals five.*  **2** and also: *The work of an engineer requires intelligence plus experience.*  **3** and more: *I reread the whole thing; plus, I had to check all the other reports.*  **4** showing addition: *the plus sign.*  **5** the plus sign (+).  **6** *Informal.* additional; extra: *a plus value.*  **7** an added quantity; something extra; a gain.  **8** positive; positively electrified.  **9** a positive quantity.  *1, 2 prep., 3 conj., 4, 6, 8 adj., 5, 7, 9 n.*
**be plus,** *Informal.*  have in addition: *We are plus a puppy.*

**plus fours**   loose, baggy men's knickers that come down below the knee: *Plus fours are normally made four inches longer than ordinary knickers.*

**plush** (plush)  **1** cloth of silk, wool, cotton, etc. having a softer and longer pile than velvet.  **2** of, resembling, or made of plush: *plush toys, plush upholstery.*  **3** luxurious and showy: *plush surroundings.*  *1 n., 2, 3 adj.*

**plush·y** (plush′ē)  **1** like or covered with plush.  **2** luxurious; rich-looking: *a plushy apartment.*  *adj.*

**Plu·to** (plü′tō)   the planet farthest from the sun.  *n.*
☞ *Etym.* From the name of *Pluto*, in Greek mythology, the god of the lower world.

**plu·toc·ra·cy** (plü tok′rə sē)  **1** a system of government in which the rich rule.  **2** a ruling class of wealthy people.  *n., pl.* **plu·toc·ra·cies.**

**plu·to·crat** (plü′tə krat′)  **1** a person who has power or influence because of his or her wealth.  **2** any wealthy person.  *n.*

**plu·to·crat·ic** (plü′tə krat′ik)  **1** having power and influence because of wealth.  **2** of or having to do with PLUTOCRATS or PLUTOCRACY.  *adj.*

**plu·to·ni·um** (plü tō′nē əm)   a radio-active metallic element formed from neptunium that is chemically similar to uranium and is used in nuclear weapons and reactors.  *Symbol:* Pu  *n.*

hat, āge, fär; let, ēqual, tėrm; it, īce
hot, ōpen, ôrder; oil, out; cup, pùt, rüle
əbove, takən, pencəl, lemən, circəs
ch, child; ng, long; sh, ship
th, thin; ᴛʜ, then; zh, measure

**plu·vi·al** (plü′vē əl)  **1** of or having to do with rain.  **2** characterized by much rain.  **3** in geology, caused or formed by the action of rain.  *adj.*

**ply¹** (plī)  **1** work with; use: *The dressmaker plies her needle.*  **2** work steadily or busily at or on something: *a carpenter plying his trade. For three hours we plied the water with our paddles.*  **3** set upon forcefully: *The messenger was plied with questions.*  **4** supply with in a pressing manner: *to ply a person with food or drink.*  **5** go back and forth regularly between certain places: *Boats ply the river. A bus plies between the airport and the hotel.*  *v.*, **plied, ply·ing.**
☞ *Etym.*  Shortened form of APPLY. 14c.

**ply²** (plī)   a thickness; layer; fold; strand; twist: *Three-ply rope is made up of three twists.*  *n., pl.* **plies.**
☞ *Etym.*  Through OF *plier* from L *plicare* 'to fold'.

**Ply·mouth Rock** (plim′əth)   a breed of medium-sized, white, grey, or grey-and-black chicken.

**ply·wood** (plī′wüd′)   a kind of board made of several thin layers of wood glued together, with the grain in adjacent layers running at right angles to each other: *Plywood can be bought in large sheets.*  *n.*

**Pm**  promethium.

**p.m.** (pē′em′)   post mortem.

**p.m.** or **P.M.**   post meridiem; the time from noon to midnight (*used especially to refer to a particular time after noon and before midnight*): *The show starts at 8 p.m.*

**P.M.**  **1** Prime Minister.  **2** Postmaster.  **3** Provost Marshal.  **4** Police Magistrate.  **5** Paymaster or Paymistress.

**pneu·mat·ic** (nyü mat′ik *or* nü mat′ik)  **1** worked by air pressure: *a pneumatic drill.*  **2** filled with air; containing air: *a pneumatic tire.*  **3** having to do with air and other gases.  *adj.* —**pneu·mat′i·cal·ly,** *adv.*

**pneu·mat·ics** (nyü mat′iks *or* nü mat′iks)   the branch of physics that deals with the pressure, elasticity, mass, etc. of air and other gases (*used with a singular verb*).  *n.*

**pneu·mo·nia** (nyü mō′nyə *or* nü mō′nyə)   a disease in which the lungs are inflamed.  *n.*

**Po**  polonium.

**P.O.**  **1** Post Office.  **2** Petty Officer.  **3** Pilot Officer.  **4** postal order.

**poach¹** (pōch)  **1** trespass on another's land, especially to hunt or fish.  **2** take game or fish without any right.  *v.*

**poach²** (pōch)  **1** cook an egg by breaking it into boiling water.  **2** cook an egg in a very small pan over boiling water.  **3** cook fish, etc. by simmering in water, milk, or wine.  *v.*

**poach·er** (pō′chər)   a person who hunts or fishes on another's land without any right.  *n.*

**pock** (pok)  **1** a PUSTULE in the skin caused by a disease or accident.  **2** any mark or spot suggesting such a PUSTULE.  **3** pockmark.  **4** mark or pit with pocks.  *1–3 n., 4 v.*

**pock·et** (pok′it) **1** a small, flat bag or pouch sewn into or onto clothing for carrying small articles such as a handkerchief, pocket watch, comb, or money. **2** put in one's pocket: *She pocketed her change.* **3** small enough to go in a pocket. **4** a pouch attached to the inside of a suitcase, car door, etc. **5** one of the bags at each corner and on each side of a pool or billiard table. **6** a hollow place: *She hid in a pocket in the side of the hill. A pocket of air in the snowbank saved his life.* **7** in geology, a cavity in the earth containing ore, oil, water, etc. **8** a small deposit of ore: *The miner struck a pocket of silver.* **9** shut in or hem in. **10** hold back; suppress; hide: *He pocketed his pride and said nothing.* **11** take and endure, without doing anything about it: *She pocketed the insult.* **12** take secretly or dishonestly: *Tomaso pocketed all the profits.* **13** any current or condition in the air that causes an aircraft to drop suddenly; air pocket. 1, 3–8, 13 *n.*, 2, 9–12 *v.*
**be out of pocket, a** spend or lose money. **b** be a loser.
**in pocket,** having or gaining money.

**pock·et·book** (pok′it bůk′) **1** a small case for carrying money, papers, etc. in a pocket. **2** financial resources: *The dress was just too expensive for her pocketbook.* **3** Often, **pocket book,** a small, inexpensive, paper-covered edition of a book; paperback. *n.*

**pock·et·ful** (pok′it fůl′) as much as a pocket will hold. *n., pl.* **pock·et·fuls.**

**pocket gopher** any of several related species of rat-sized rodent found on the North American plains, having fur-lined, external cheek pouches, a heavy body, a broad, flat head, short legs, and a short tail.

**pock·et·knife** (pok′it nīf′) a small knife with one or more blades that fold into the handle. *n., pl.* **pock·et·knives.**

**pocket money** money for occasional or minor personal expenses.

**pock·et-size** (pok′it sīz′) **1** small enough to go in a pocket: *a pocket-size radio, camera, etc.* **2** *Informal.* small for its kind: *a pocket-size country.* *adj.*

**pock·mark** (pok′märk′) **1** a scar or pit in the skin such as those left by chicken pox or an accident. **2** any small hollow suggesting such a scar. **3** cover or scar with pockmarks. 1, 2 *n.*, 3 *v.*

**pock-marked** (pok′märkt′) having POCKMARKS. *adj.*

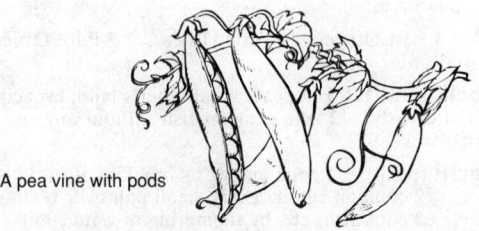
A pea vine with pods

**pod¹** (pod) **1** the shell or case in which plants like beans and peas grow their seeds. **2** produce pods. **3** fill out into a pod. **4** a streamlined cover over anything carried externally, especially on the wings or fuselage of an aircraft: *a gun pod, a missile pod.* **5** a part of a spacecraft that can be detached from the main part. 1, 4, 5 *n.*, 2, 3 *v.*, **pod·ded, pod·ding.**

**pod²** (pod) **1** a small flock of birds. **2** a small herd of whales, seals, etc. *n.*

**po·di·a·trist** (pə dī′ə trist) CHIROPODIST. *n.*

**po·di·a·try** (pə dī′ə trē) CHIROPODY. *n.*

**po·di·um** (pō′dē əm) a small raised platform, especially a platform used by an orchestra conductor. *n., pl.* **po·di·a** (-dē ə).

**po·em** (pō′əm) **1** a piece of writing that uses language that is more figurative than in most prose or ordinary speech, in which the words and phrases have a controlled rhythm and are usually arranged in lines to produce pattern, with or without rhyme. **2** a composition showing great beauty or nobility of language or thought. **3** something very beautiful: *The dancer was a poem in motion.* *n.*
☛ *Etym.* Through Old French and Latin from Gk. *poēma* 'poem, fiction, something made', which came from *poein, poiein* 'to make'. POET, POETIC, POETRY, etc. came through L *poeta* from Gk. *poētēs, poiētēs,* which also came from *poein, poiein* 'to make'.

**po·et** (pō′it) **1** a person who writes poetry. **2** a person, especially a creative artist, who has great ability to feel and express beauty, emotion, etc.: *She is a poet with her paintbrush.* *n.*
☛ *Etym.* See note at POEM.

**po·et·as·ter** (pō′i tas′tər) a writer of poor poetry. *n.*

**po·et·ic** (pō et′ik) **1** of, having to do with, or characteristic of poets or poetry: *poetic imagery.* **2** written in verse: *Her poetic compositions are all very short.* **3** showing beautiful or noble language, imagery, or thought: *a poetic description of a scene.* *adj.*
—**po·et′i·cal·ly,** *adv.*
☛ *Etym.* See note at POEM.

**po·et·i·cal** (pō et′ə kəl) POETIC. *adj.*

**poetic justice** ideal justice, with the proper distribution of rewards and punishments.

**poetic licence** a freedom traditionally granted to poets to violate certain grammatical rules or to alter fact or history for effect within a poetic work.

**po·et·ics** (pō et′iks) the theory or study of poetry (*used with a singular verb*). *n.*

**poet lau·re·ate** (lô′rē it) **1** in England, a poet appointed by the king or queen to write poems in celebration of court and national events. **2** the official or most respected poet of any country, state, etc. *pl.* **poets laureate.**

**po·et·ry** (pō′i trē) **1** poetical works; poems: *a book of poetry.* **2** the art or theory of writing poems: *Poetry uses many effects of sound, imagery, and vocabulary to achieve a heightened, intensive form of expression.* **3** a poetic quality; poetic spirit or feeling: *Her skating is pure poetry.* *n.*
☛ *Etym.* See note at POEM.

**po·go stick** (pō′gō) a stick used in playing to hop from place to place by jumping up and down on the spring-supported footrests.

**po·grom** (pō grom′ *or* pō′grəm) an organized, often officially sanctioned massacre, especially of Jews. *n.*

**poign·an·cy** (poi′nyən sē *or* poi′nən sē) **1** the quality or state of being POIGNANT: *They were moved by the poignancy of his appeal for help.* **2** an instance of poignancy. *n.*

**poign·ant** (poi′nyənt *or* poi′nənt) **1** deeply affecting;

causing sympathy; touching: *a poignant cry, a poignant story.*   **2** painfully sharp to the feelings; piercing: *poignant suffering.*   **3** stimulating; keen or intense: *a subject of poignant interest.*   **4** sharp in taste or smell.   *adj.*
—**poign′ant·ly,** *adv.*

**poin·set·ti·a** (poin set′ē ə *or, sometimes,* poin set′ə)   a plant having a small flower surrounded by large, scarlet leaves resembling petals.   *n.*
☛ *Etym.*   Named after Joel R. *Poinsett* (1779–1851), an American diplomat who discovered the plant in Mexico.

**point** (point)   **1** a sharp end; something having a sharp end: *the point of a needle.*   **2** a tiny, round mark; dot: *A period is a point. Use a point to set off decimals.*   **3** mark with dots; punctuate.   **4** in mathematics, something that has position but not extension: *Two lines meet or cross at a point.*   **5** a particular place or spot: *This is the point where we turned around and went back.*   **6** a particular time or moment: *At this point he lost interest in the game.*   **7** a particular or definite position, state, condition or degree; stage: *boiling point.*   **8** an item; detail: *She answered my questions point by point.*   **9** a distinguishing mark or quality: *one's good points.*   **10** a physical characteristic or feature of an animal.   **11** the main idea; the important or essential thing: *I missed the point of his talk.*   **12** give force to speech, action, etc.: *He told a story to point his advice.*   **13** force; effectiveness: *The story gave point to her advice.*   **14** a particular aim, end, or purpose: *What was your point in asking for an adjournment? What's the point of going on when we don't know if we can get more funds?*   **15** aim; tend: *Her work points to success.*   **16** indicate position or direction, or direct attention with, or as if with, the finger: *point at a house.*   **17** show with the finger; call attention to.   **18** direct a finger, weapon, etc.: *Don't point a gun at anybody. It's rude to point your finger.*   **19** have or face a specified direction: *The signboard points north.*   **20** each of the 32 positions indicating direction marked at the circumference of the card of a compass.   **21** the interval between any two adjacent points of a compass; 11 degrees 15 minutes.   **22** a piece of land with a sharp end sticking out into the water; cape.   **23** a unit of scoring or measuring: *We're three points ahead. The stock has gone up half a point.*   **24** in printing, a unit for measuring type; $1/12$ of a pica (about 0.33 mm).   **25** *Informal.*   a hint; suggestion.   **26** of a dog, show the presence of game by standing rigid and looking toward it.   **27** fill joints of brickwork with mortar or cement.   **28** lace made with a needle.   **29** *Brit.*   a railway-switch.   **30** of an abscess, come to a head.   **31** in hockey, a position at the opponents' blueline, taken by an offensive player when the puck is within their defensive zone, especially during a power play.   **32** in lacrosse, one of the defencemen playing out in front of the goalie.   **33** sharpen: *to point a pencil.*   1, 2, 4–11, 13, 14, 20–25, 28, 29, 31, 32 *n.*, 3, 12, 15–19, 26, 27, 30, 33 *v.*
**at the point of,**   very near to; on the verge of: *at the point of death.*
**beside the point,**   having little or nothing to do with the subject; not appropriate.
**in point,**   apt or relevant: *the case in point.*
**in point of,**   as regards.
**in point of fact,**   as a matter of fact: *In point of fact, she never left the house at all.*
**make a point of,**   be particular about: *She always makes a point of being on time.*
**make one's point,**   convince a person that an idea or argument is reasonable or correct: *He is not a very good speaker, but he made his point.*
**on the point of,**   just about; on the verge of: *She was on the point of going out when a neighbour came in.*
**point off,**   mark off with points or dots.

**point out,**   show or call attention to: *Please point out my mistakes.*
**point up,**   show clearly: *Synonym notes in this dictionary point up the differences between similar words.*
**strain** or **stretch a point,**   **a** exceed the reasonable limit.   **b** make a special exception.
**to the point,**   apt; appropriate: *Her speech was brief and to the point.*

**point–blank** (point′blangk′ *for adjective,* point′blangk′ *for adverb*)   **1** aimed straight at the mark, without allowing for the bullet, shell, etc. dropping from the original line of flight.   **2** straight at the mark: *She spoke point-blank.*   **3** plain and blunt; direct: *a point-blank question.*   **4** plainly and bluntly; directly: *One boy gave excuses, but the other refused point-blank.*   **5** close range: *He fired the gun from point-blank range.*   **6** from close range: *The shells went point-blank toward the enemy.*   1, 3, 5 *adj.*, 2, 4, 6 *adv.*

**point blanket**   *Cdn.*   a Hudson's Bay Company blanket.

**point·ed** (poin′tid)   **1** having or as if sharpened to a point or points: *a pointed pencil, a pointed arch.*   **2** sharp; piercing: *a pointed wit.*   **3** directed; aimed: *a pointed remark.*   **4** emphasized; conspicuous: *a pointed refusal.*   **5** pt. and pp. of POINT.   1–4 *adj.*, 5 *v.*
—**point′ed·ly,** *adv.*   —**point′ed·ness,** *n.*

**point·er** (poin′tər)   **1** a person or thing that points.   **2** a long, tapering stick used in pointing things out on a map, chalkboard, etc.   **3** a hand of a clock, meter, etc.   **4** a short-haired hunting dog trained to show where game is by standing rigid and looking toward it.   **5** *Informal.*   a useful hint or suggestion: *She gave him some pointers on improving his tennis.*   *n.*

**point·less** (poin′tlis)   **1** without a point; blunt.   **2** without force or meaning: *a pointless question.*   **3** in a game, not having scored a point.   *adj.*

**point of departure**   in a discussion, etc., a starting point.

**point of honour** or **honor**   a matter that seriously affects a person's honour or principles: *It was a point of honour with her to give every applicant equal time.*

**point of no return**   a stage in an action or event after which there is no turning back, so that one is obliged to continue.

**point of order**   a question raised as to whether proceedings are according to the rules.

**point of view**   **1** a position from which objects are considered.   **2** an attitude of mind: *Farmers and campers sometimes have different points of view about rain.*

**points of the compass**   the 32 directions marked on a compass: *North, south, east, and west are the four main, or cardinal, points of the compass.*

**poise** (poiz)   **1** mental balance, composure, or self-possession: *She has perfect poise and never seems embarrassed.*   **2** the way in which the body, head, etc. are held; carriage: *He admired the major's poise.*   **3** balance: *Poise yourself on your toes.*   **4** hold or carry evenly or steadily: *The athlete poised the weight in the air before throwing it.* **1, 2** *n.*, **3, 4** *v.*, **poised, pois·ing.**

**poi·son** (poi′zən) **1** a drug or other substance that is very dangerous to health and capable of causing death: *Strychnine and opium are poisons.* **2** kill or harm by poison. **3** put poison in or on: *to poison arrows.* **4** poisonous. **5** anything dangerous or deadly: *Hate becomes a poison in the mind.* **6** have a dangerous or harmful effect on: *Lies poison the mind. He poisoned his friend's mind against the girl.* **1, 5** *n.*, **2, 3, 6** *v.*, **4** *adj.* —**poi′son·er,** *n.*

Poison ivy

**poison ivy** **1** a North American woody vine or shrub of the cashew family having greenish flowers, white berries, and leaves composed of three leaflets, and producing a toxic oil in its leaves, flowers, fruit, and bark that causes a severe rash on contact with the skin. **2** any of several closely related plants.

**poison oak** **1** a plant of the sumac family closely related to poison ivy, found along the Pacific coast of North America: *The poison oak has leaflets shaped like oak leaves.* **2** POISON SUMAC.

**poi·son·ous** (poi′zə nəs) **1** containing poison; very harmful to health and capable of causing death: *The rattlesnake's bite is poisonous.* **2** having a harmful effect: *a poisonous lie.* *adj.* —**poi′son·ous·ly,** *adv.* —**poi′son·ous·ness,** *n.*

**poison sumac** a shrub growing in swamps having leaves composed of seven to thirteen leaflets and bearing white berry-like fruit: *Poison sumac causes a severe rash on most people if they touch it.*

**poke**¹ (pōk) **1** push against with something pointed; jab: *He poked me in the ribs with his elbow.* **2** thrust; push: *She poked her head in the kitchen window.* **3** stir a fire with a poker. **4** a poking; thrust; push. **5** *Informal.* punch: *He threatened to poke his brother in the nose.* **6** *Informal.* a punch. **7** pry: *She's always poking into other people's business.* **8** make by poking: *He accidentally poked a hole in the tablecloth with his pencil.* **9** go lazily; loiter: *Tom pokes along on his way to school.* **10** a slow, lazy person. **11** a projecting brim on the front of a POKE BONNET, or the bonnet itself. **1–3, 5, 7–9,** *v.*, **poked, pok·ing;** **4, 6, 10, 11** *n.*

**poke**² (pōk) *Dialect (except in* **buy a pig in a poke**). a bag or sack. *n.*
**buy a pig in a poke,** buy something without seeing it first.

**poke·ber·ry** (pōk′ber′ē) **1** the berry of the POKEWEED. **2** POKEWEED. *n., pl.* **poke·ber·ries.**

**poke bonnet** a bonnet with a projecting brim at the front.

**poke check** in hockey, a quick thrust or jab with one's stick at the puck in order to get it away from an opponent.

**poke–check** (pōk′chek′) **1** carry out a POKE CHECK. **2** administer a POKE CHECK to (an opposing player). *v.*

**poke·lo·gan** (pō′klō′gən) *Cdn.* a small stagnant backwater in a stream; logan. *n.*

**pok·er**¹ (pō′kər) a person or thing that pokes, especially a metal rod for stirring a fire. *n.*

**pok·er**² (pō′kər) any of several card games in which a player bets that the value of the cards he or she holds is greater than that of the cards held by the other players. *n.*

**poker face** *Informal.* **1** a face or facial expression that does not show one's thoughts or feelings. **2** a person having such a face or facial expression.

**poke·weed** (pōk′wēd′) a tall weed of North America having juicy, purple berries and poisonous roots. *n.*

**pok·ey** or **pok·y** (pō′kē) **1** puttering; dull; stupid. **2** moving, acting, etc. slowly; slow. **3** small; mean: *a pokey room.* **4** shabby. *adj.*, **pok·i·er, pok·i·est.**

**po·lar** (pō′lər) **1** of, having to do with, or coming from the North or South Pole or the region around it: *the polar wastes, a polar wind.* **2** passing over the North or South Pole: *a satellite in polar orbit. We flew the polar route to Europe last year.* **3** of or having to do with the poles of a magnet, battery, etc. **4** directly opposite in character, like the poles of a magnet: *Good and evil are polar elements.* *adj.*

A polar bear— about 2.5 m long excluding the tail

**polar bear** a large, white bear living in the arctic regions.

**Po·lar·is** (pō ler′is) the NORTH STAR; polestar. *n.*

**po·lar·i·ty** (pō lar′ə tē *or* pō ler′ə tē) **1** the possession of two opposed poles: *A magnet or battery has polarity.* **2** a positive or negative polar condition, as in electricity. **3** the possession or exhibition of two opposite or contrasted principles or tendencies. *n.*

**po·lar·i·za·tion** (pō′lə rə zā′shən *or* pō′lə rī zā′shən) **1** the production or acquisition of polarity. **2** the process by which gases produced during electrolysis are deposited on one or both electrodes of a cell, giving rise to a reverse electromotive force. **3** the division of a complex but continuous group into two opposite extremes: *the polarization of the electorate on the issue of free trade.* *n.*

**po·lar·ize** (pō′lə rīz′) give polarity to; cause POLARIZATION in. *v.*, **po·lar·ized, po·lar·iz·ing.**

**pole**¹ (pōl) **1** a long, slender, usually round piece of wood, metal, etc.: *a telephone pole, a flagpole, a ski pole.* **2** push or make something go with a pole: *to pole a raft. We poled down the river.* **3** a unit for measuring length, equal to a rod or perch (about 5.03 m). **4** a unit for measuring area, equal to a square rod (about 25.3 m²). **1, 3, 4** *n.*, **2** *v.*, **poled, pol·ing.**
☞ *Hom.* POLL.

**pole**² (pōl) **1** either end of the earth's axis: *The North*

Pole and the South Pole are opposite each other. **2** either of two parts or points where opposite forces are strongest: *A magnet or battery has both a positive pole and a negative pole.* **3** either end of the axis of any sphere. **4** either of two opinions, forces, etc. considered as being opposite extremes. *n.*
**poles apart,** very much different; in strong disagreement: *The two bargaining parties are still poles apart and there is no sign of a settlement.*
☛ Hom. POLL.

**Pole** (pōl) **1** a native or inhabitant of Poland, a country in central Europe. **2** a person of Polish descent. *n.*
☛ Hom. POLL.

**pole·cat** (pōl′kat′) **1** a small, dark-brown, carnivorous European mammal of the weasel family. **2** *Esp. U.S.* the North American skunk. *n.*

**po·lem·ic** (pə lem′ik) **1** a strong argument against or attack on an idea, belief, or opinion: *The book is nothing but a long polemic against communism.* **2** of, having to do with, or actively engaged in controversy or disagreement: *a polemic writer.* **3** Usually, **polemics,** the art or practice of argument or controversy (*used with a singular or plural verb*): *This is not the time to indulge in polemics.* 1, 3 *n.*, 2 *adj.* —**po·lem′i·cal·ly,** *adv.*

**po·lem·i·cal** (pə lem′ə kəl) POLEMIC. *adj.*

**pole·star** (pōl′stär′) **1** the NORTH STAR, formerly much used as a guide by sailors. **2** a guiding principle; guide. **3** a centre of attraction, interest, or attention. *n.*

**pole vault 1** an athletic event or contest in which contestants jump, or vault, over a high, horizontal bar, with the aid of a long, flexible pole: *The pole vault is one of the Olympic track and field events.* See VAULT² for picture. **2** a vault of this kind.

**pole–vault** (pōl′volt′) make a POLE VAULT. *v.* —**pole′-vault′er,** *n.*

**po·lice** (pə lēs′) **1** the civil force of a community, province, or state whose duty is to guard people's lives and property, to preserve peace and order, and to arrest those who commit crimes. **2** the people who carry out this duty for a community: *The police arrived within 10 minutes.* **3** guard to keep order in: *to police the streets, to police an army camp.* 1, 2 *n.*, 3 *v.*, **po·liced, po·lic·ing.**
☛ Hom. PELISSE.

**police dog 1** a dog trained for use in police work: *German shepherds, Doberman pinschers, and Airedales are often used as police dogs.* **2** GERMAN SHEPHERD.

**police force** the law-enforcing body of a community.

**po·lice·man** (pə lēs′mən) a male member of a POLICE FORCE. *n.*, *pl.* **police·men** (-smən).

**police officer** a member of a POLICE FORCE.

**police state** a nation strictly controlled by governmental authority, especially with the aid of a secret police organization.

**police station** the headquarters of the POLICE of a particular area or district in a city, or of the local police force of a small community.

**po·lice·wom·an** (pə lēs′swum·ən) a woman who is a member of a POLICE FORCE. *n.*, *pl.* **po·lice·wom·en** (-swim′ən).

**pol·i·cy**¹ (pol′ə sē) **1** a plan of action; a course or method of action that has been deliberately chosen and that guides or influences future decisions: *It is poor policy to promise more than you can give. The candidate explained*

**Pole**      913      **political science**

hat, āge, fär; let, ēqual, tėrm; it, īce
hot, ōpen, ôrder; oil, out; cup, put, rüle
əbove, takən, pencəl, lemən, circəs
ch, child; ng, long; sh, ship
th, thin; ᴛʜ, then; zh, measure

*her party's policy.* **2** practical wisdom; prudence. *n.*, *pl.* **pol·i·cies.**

**pol·i·cy**² (pol′ə sē) a written agreement about insurance: *Our fire-insurance policy expires in October. n.*, *pl.* **pol·i·cies.**

**pol·i·cy·hold·er** (pol′ə sē hōl′dər) the owner of an insurance policy. *n.*

**po·li·o** (pō′lē ō′) *Informal.* POLIOMYELITIS. *n.*

**po·li·o·my·e·li·tis** (pō′lē ō mī′ə lī′tis) **1** an acute infectious disease caused by a virus, characterized by symptoms ranging from fever, headaches, vomiting, etc. to extensive permanent paralysis of muscles. **2** any inflammation of the grey matter of the spinal cord. *n.*

**pol·ish** (pol′ish) **1** make smooth and shiny: *to polish shoes.* **2** become smooth and shiny: *This leather polishes well.* **3** remove by smoothing (*used with* **off** *or* **away**). **4** put into a better condition; improve (*often used with* **up**): *to polish a manuscript, to polish up one's French.* **5** a substance used to give smoothness or shine: *silver polish.* **6** shininess; smoothness: *The table has a high polish.* **7** make elegant; refine: *to polish one's manners.* **8** culture; elegance; refinement: *She was a woman of breeding and polish.* **9** the act or process of polishing: *I gave the table a quick polish.* 1–4, 7 *v.*, 5, 6, 8, 9 *n.* —**pol′ish·er,** *n.*
**polish off,** *Informal.* get done with; finish.

**Pol·ish** (pō′lish) **1** of or having to do with Poland, a country in central Europe, its people, or their language. **2** the language of Poland. **3** **the Polish,** *pl.* the people of Poland. 1 *adj.*, 2, 3 *n.*

**Po·lit·bu·ro** (pə lit′byü rō or pol′it byü′rō) an executive committee of the Communist Party that controlled policy in the former Soviet Union. *n.*

**po·lite** (pə līt′) **1** having or showing good manners; behaving properly: *The polite boy gave the lady his seat on the bus.* **2** refined; elegant: *She wished to learn all the customs of polite society.* *adj.* —**po·lite′ly,** *adv.* —**po·lite′ness,** *n.*

**pol·i·tic** (pol′ə tik′) **1** characterized by prudence and practical wisdom; sensible and expedient: *It was not politic to arouse his irritation.* **2** scheming; crafty: *playing a politic game with an enemy.* *adj.* —**pol′i·tic·ly,** *adv.*

**po·lit·i·cal** (pə lit′ə kəl) **1** of or concerned with politics. **2** having to do with public affairs or government: *Treason is a political offence.* **3** of politicians or their methods. **4** having a definite system of government. *adj.* —**po·lit′i·cal·ly,** *adv.*

**political economy** a social science dealing with the ways in which political and economic processes are related to each other; the study of the economic problems of government.

**political party** a group of people that tries to have its members elected to a legislature or government. Members of a political party have similar ideas about the running of business, industry, education, health care, social issues, etc.

**political science** a social science dealing with political institutions and processes, especially with the principles and conduct of government.

**pol·i·ti·cian** (pol'ə tish'ən) 1 a person holding a political office. 2 a person active in politics, especially one seeking political office. *n.*

**pol·i·tick** (pol'ə tik') take part in political activity, especially in order to directly or indirectly solicit votes: *She's politicking in the Maritimes this week.* *v.* —**pol'i·tick'er**, *n.*

**pol·i·tics** (pol'ə tiks') 1 the management of public affairs: *She was engaged in politics for many years.* 2 political ideas or opinions: *My father's politics were strongly against rule by any one person.* 3 political methods or manoeuvres. 4 the science and art of government. *n. sing. or pl.*

**pol·i·ty** (pol'ə tē) 1 political organization; government. 2 a particular form or system of government. 3 a community with a government; state. *n., pl.* **pol·i·ties**.

**pol·ka** (pōl'kə *or* pō'kə) 1 a kind of lively dance. 2 the music for this dance. 3 dance a polka. 1, 2 *n.*, 3 *v.*, **pol·kaed, pol·ka·ing**.

**polka dot** 1 a dot or round spot repeated to form a regular pattern on cloth. 2 a pattern or fabric with such dots. —**pol'ka-dot** *or* **pol·ka-dot'ted**, *adj.*

**poll** (pōl) 1 a voting; collection of votes: *The class took a poll to decide where the picnic would be held.* 2 the number of votes cast: *If it rains on election day, there is often a light poll.* 3 the results of these votes. 4 a list of persons, especially a list of voters. 5 the place where votes are cast or counted: *The polls will be open till 8 o'clock tonight.* 6 receive as votes: *The mayor polled a record vote.* 7 vote; cast a vote. 8 take or register the votes of. 9 a survey of public opinion concerning a particular subject. 10 the head, especially the part of it on which the hair grows. 11 cut off or cut short the hair, wool, horns, branches, etc. of. 1–5, 9, 10 *n.*, 6–8, 11 *v.* ☛ *Hom.* POLE.

**pol·lack** (pol'ək) See POLLOCK. *n.*

**pol·len** (pol'ən) a fine, yellowish powder formed in the anthers of flowers, consisting of tiny grains that are the male sex cells which fertilize the ovules. *n.*

**pollen basket** an area surrounded by stiff hairs on each hind leg of a honeybee, in which the bee collects POLLEN to carry back to the hive.

**pol·li·nate** (pol'ə nāt') carry POLLEN from stamens to pistils of; shed pollen on: *Many flowers are pollinated by bees.* *v.*, **pol·li·nat·ed, pol·li·nat·ing**. —**pol'li·na'tion**, *n.*

**polling booth** in a POLLING STATION, a screened or otherwise enclosed space where a voter marks his or her ballot in privacy.

**polling station** during an election, a room or building set up as a place where the people living nearby may vote.

**pol·li·wog** (pol'ē wog') TADPOLE. *n.* Also, **pollywog**.

**pol·lock** (pol'ək) 1 an important food fish of the cod family found in the northern Atlantic Ocean, especially off the coast of Nova Scotia, having a deep-green back and pale belly, a long body, and a small barbel under the jaw. 2 a related fish of the northern Pacific Ocean having little value as a food fish. *n., pl.* **pollock** *or* **pollocks**. Also, **pollack**.

**poll tax** a tax on every person, or on every person of a specified class, especially as a prerequisite to the right to vote in public elections.

**pol·lu·tant** (pə lü'tənt) something that POLLUTES: *Automobile exhaust is a major air pollutant.* *n.*

**pol·lute** (pə lüt') 1 make physically impure or unclean; especially, contaminate the air, water, soil, etc. with synthetic waste materials: *the polluted air of cities. The lake has been polluted with waste from a large factory.* 2 make morally impure; defile. *v.*, **pol·lut·ed, pol·lut·ing**. —**pol·lut'er**, *n.*

**pol·lu·tion** (pə lü'shən) 1 polluting or being POLLUTED. 2 something that POLLUTES; pollutant: *That's not fog, that's pollution.* *n.*

**Pol·lux** (pol'əks) one of the two brightest stars in the constellation Gemini. *n.*
☛ *Etym.* From *Pollux*, in Greek mythology, one of the twin sons of Zeus.

**Pol·ly·an·na** (pol'ē an'ə) one who is always cheerful, or overly cheerful, and always sees good in everything, even in the face of disaster. *n.*
☛ *Etym.* From *Pollyanna*, the heroine of stories by Eleanor H. Porter (1868–1920).

**pol·ly·wog** (pol'ē wog') See POLLIWOG. *n.*

A polo player on horseback

**po·lo** (pō'lō) a game played by two teams of players on horseback, who use long-handled mallets to drive a wooden ball through the opposing team's goal. *n.*

**pol·o·naise** (pol'ə nāz' *or* pō'lə nāz') 1 a slow, stately dance in three-four time. 2 the music for such a dance. *n.*

**po·lo·ni·um** (pə lō'nē əm) a radioactive element that occurs in pitchblende. Symbol: Po *n.*

**pol·ter·geist** (pol'tər gīst') a ghost or spirit supposedly responsible for unexplained happenings and noises such as door slamming, chain rattling, or rapping sounds on walls or tables. *n.*

**poly–** *combining form.* 1 more than one; many; extensive, as in *polyangular.* 2 polymeric; polymerized, as in *polyethylene, polystyrene.*
☛ *Etym.* From Gk. *polu-*, the combining form of *polus, polu* 'many, much'.

**pol·y·an·drous** (pol'ē an'drəs) having to do with or practising POLYANDRY. Compare with POLYGAMOUS. *adj.*

**pol·y·an·dry** (pol'ē an'drē) the practice or condition of having more than one husband at the same time. Compare with POLYGAMY. *n.*

**pol·y·an·thus** (pol′ē an′thəs) 1 OXLIP. 2 a kind of narcissus bearing clusters of small yellow or white flowers. *n.*

**pol·y·chro·mat·ic** (pol′i krō mat′ik) having a variety of colours. *adj.*

**pol·y·chrome** (pol′i krōm′) 1 having to do with, or made or decorated with, several colours. 2 a work of art in several colours, especially a painted statue. 3 a combination of many colours. 1 *adj.*, 2, 3 *n.*

**pol·y·clin·ic** (pol′i klin′ik) a clinic or hospital treating many different diseases. *n.*

**pol·y·es·ter** (pol′ē es′tər) 1 any of a group of synthetic organic POLYMERS usually formed from glycols and certain acids, prepared in the form of plastics, fibres, etc. 2 thread, yarn, or fabric made of a polyester. *n.*

**pol·y·eth·y·lene** (pol′ē eth′ə lēn′) any of various very strong, lightweight synthetic POLYMERS of ethylene that are good insulators and are resistant to chemicals and moisture: *Polyethylenes are used for insulation and a wide variety of moulded containers and also in the form of thin films or sheets for packaging, etc.* *n.*

**po·lyg·a·mist** (pə lig′ə mist) a person who practises or favours POLYGAMY. *n.*

**po·lyg·a·mous** (pə lig′ə məs) 1 having to do with or practising POLYGAMY. Compare with POLYANDROUS. 2 in biology, having more than one mate: *Baboons are polygamous.* *adj.*

**po·lyg·a·my** (pə lig′ə mē) the practice or condition of having more than one wife or, sometimes, husband, at one time. Compare with POLYANDRY. *n.*

**pol·y·glot** (pol′i glot′) 1 knowing several languages; multilingual. 2 a person who knows several languages. 3 written in several languages. 4 a book written in several languages. 1, 3 *adj.*, 2, 4 *n.*

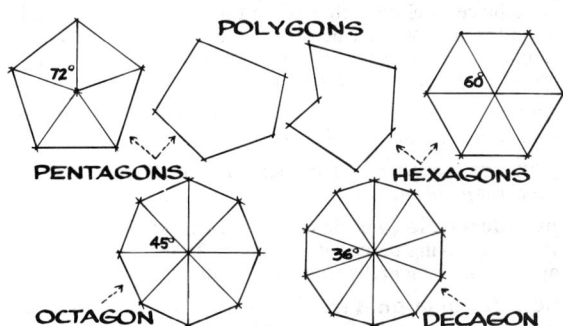

**pol·y·gon** (pol′i gon′) a closed plane figure having three or more interior angles and straight sides. *n.*

**po·lyg·o·nal** (pə lig′ə nəl) having three or more angles and sides. *adj.*

**pol·y·he·dral** (pol′i hē′drəl) 1 of or having to do with a POLYHEDRON. 2 having many faces: *A cut diamond is polyhedral.* *adj.*

**pol·y·he·dron** (pol′i hē′drən) a solid figure formed by four or more faces. See SOLID for picture. *n., pl.* **pol·y·he·drons** or **pol·y·he·dra** (-drə).

**pol·y·mer** (pol′i mər) any of a large number of natural or synthetic, organic or inorganic compounds composed of very large molecules that are made up of many light, simple molecules chemically linked together:

hat, āge, fär; let, ēqual, tėrm; it, īce
hot, ōpen, ôrder; oil, out; cup, put, rüle
əbove, takən, pencəl, lemən, circəs
ch, child; ng, long; sh, ship
th, thin; ᴛʜ, then; zh, measure

*Cellulose and proteins are naturally occurring polymers; concrete, plastics, and glass are synthetic polymers.* *n.*

**pol·y·mer·ic** (pol′i mer′ik) of, having to do with, or being a POLYMER: *a polymeric compound.* *adj.*

**pol·y·mer·i·za·tion** (pol′i mə rə zā′shən or pol′i mə rī zā′shən) the chemical union of many small, simple molecules into very large molecules to form a polymer: *The molecules produced in polymerization contain repeating structural units of the simple molecules in the form of a chain or network.* *n.*

**pol·y·morph** (pol′i môrf′) a POLYMORPHIC organism. *n.*

**pol·y·mor·phic** (pol′i môr′fik) having, assuming, or passing through many of various forms, stages, etc. *adj.*

**pol·y·mor·phism** (pol′i môr′fiz əm) 1 in biology, the occurrence of different forms or colour types in an individual organism or in different individuals of one species. 2 in chemistry, the property of a compound of crystallizing in at least two distinct forms. *n.*

**pol·y·mor·phous** (pol′i môr′fəs) POLYMORPHIC. *adj.*

**Pol·y·ne·sian** (pol′ə nē′zhən) 1 of or referring to a race of mankind that includes most of the peoples traditionally inhabiting Polynesia, a large group of islands in the eastern Pacific, extending from Hawaii south to New Zealand and east to Easter Island: *The Polynesian race includes the Hawaiians, Maoris, Samoans, and Tahitians.* 2 a member of this race: *Polynesians are usually tall and have light or medium brown skin.* 3 a related group of languages widely spoken in Polynesia. 4 of or having to do with Polynesia or the people, cultures, or languages of Polynesia. 1, 4 *adj.*, 2, 3 *n.*

**pol·y·no·mi·al** (pol′i nō′mē əl) 1 in algebra, an expression consisting of a number of terms. $ab+x^2y$ and $pq-p^2+q$ are polynomials. 2 consisting of two or more terms: *polynomial equations.* 1 *n.*, 2 *adj.*

**pol·yp** (pol′ip) any of various small water animals typically having a tubelike body that is closed at one end and has at the other end a mouthlike opening surrounded by tentacles for gathering in food: *Polyps often grow in colonies, with their bases connected. Corals and sea anemones are polyps.* *n.*

**pol·y·phon·ic** (pol′i fon′ik) of, having to do with, or characterized by POLYPHONY: *polyphonic music.* *adj.*

**po·lyph·o·ny** (pə lif′ə nē) the combination of two or more independent melodies or musical parts so that they relate harmonically to each other; COUNTERPOINT. *n.*

**pol·y·sac·cha·ride** (pol′i sak′ə rīd′) any of a large group of natural carbohydrates, including starch, cellulose, and glycogen, whose molecules consist of two or more molecules of simple sugars linked together. *n.*

**pol·y·sty·rene** (pol′i stī′rēn) a synthetic organic POLYMER formed from styrene. It is a rigid, colourless, thermoplastic resin resistant to acids, alkalis, and many solvents, and having excellent insulating properties: *Polystyrene is used as an insulator and for many moulded products such as dishes, toys, etc.* *n.*

**pol·y·syl·lab·ic** (pol′i sə lab′ik) having more than three syllables. *adj.*

**pol·y·syl·la·ble** (pol′i sil′ə bəl) a word of more than three syllables: *Politician is a polysyllable.* *n.*

**pol·y·tech·nic** (pol′i tek′nik) **1** having to do with or giving instruction in many technical arts or applied sciences. **2** a polytechnic school. 1 *adj.*, 2 *n.*

**pol·y·the·ism** (pol′i thē′iz əm) belief in more than one god: *The religion of the ancient Greeks was polytheism.* *n.*

**pol·y·the·ist** (pol′i thē′ist) a person who believes in more than one god. *n.*

**pol·y·the·is·tic** (pol′i thē is′tik) having to do with or characterized by belief in many gods. *adj.*

**pol·y·ur·e·thane** (pol′ē yü′rə thān′) any of a group of synthetic organic POLYMERS that may be rubbery, resinous, or fibrous: *Polyurethanes are most often made in the form of flexible foams used for mattresses, cushions, etc. and rigid foams used for insulation, lightweight cores for aircraft wings, etc.* *n.*

**pom·ace** (pum′is) **1** apple pulp or similar fruit pulp before or after the juice has been pressed out. **2** the crushed matter that is left after oil has been pressed out of fish, seeds, etc. *n.*
☛ *Hom.* PUMICE.

**po·ma·ceous** (pə mā′shəs) of, having to do with, or resembling apples or similar fruits. *adj.*

**po·made** (pom ād′ *or* pom äd′) a perfumed ointment for the scalp and hair. *n.*

**pome** (pōm) an apple or any fruit like it; fruit consisting of firm, juicy flesh surrounding a core that contains several seeds: *Apples, pears, and quinces are pomes.* *n.*

Pomegranates. The one on the right is cut open showing the seeds.

**pome·gran·ate** (pom′gran′it *or* pom′ə gran′it) **1** a fruit with a thick, leathery, red or brownish-yellow skin, juicy red pulp, and many seeds: *The pulp of a pomegranate has a pleasant tart taste.* **2** the small tropical tree or bush that bears this fruit. *n.*

**Pom·er·a·ni·an** (pom′ə rā′nē ən) **1** of or having to do with Pomerania, a region in central Europe on the Baltic Sea, or its people. **2** a native or inhabitant of Pomerania. **3** a breed of small dog having a sharp nose, pointed ears, and long, thick, silky hair. 1 *adj.*, 2, 3 *n.*

**pom·mel** (pom′əl *or* pum′əl *for noun,* pum′əl *for verb*) **1** the part of a saddle that sticks up at the front. See SADDLE for picture. **2** a rounded knob on the hilt of a sword, dagger, etc. **3** PUMMEL. 1, 2 *n.*, 3 *v.*, **pom·melled** *or* **pom·meled, pom·mel·ling** *or* **pom·mel·ing.**

☛ *Hom.* PUMMEL (for the second pronunciation of *pommel*).

**po·mol·o·gy** (pə mol′ə jē) the science or practice of fruit growing. *n.*

**pomp** (pomp) **1** a stately display; splendour; magnificence: *The queen was crowned with great pomp.* **2** an excessively showy display. *n.*

**pom·pa·dour** (pom′pə dôr′) **1** a woman's hairstyle in which the hair is puffed high over the forehead and turned under in a roll. **2** a man's hairstyle in which the hair is brushed straight up and back from the forehead. *n.*

**pom·pa·no** (pom′pə nō′) **1** a saltwater food fish of the West Indies and neighbouring coasts of North America having a deep body, no teeth, and a forked tail. **2** any of several related fishes. *n.*

**Pom·pei·an** (pom pā′ən) **1** of or having to do with Pompeii, a city in ancient Italy, or its people: *Many Pompeian houses were beautifully decorated.* **2** a native or inhabitant of Pompeii. 1 *adj.*, 2 *n.*

**pom-pom** (pom′pom) **1** an ornamental ball or tuft of yarn, feathers, etc. used especially on clothing, hats, shoes, etc. **2** any of several varieties of chrysanthemum or dahlia having small, rounded flower heads. *n.*

**pom·pon** (pom′pon) POMPOM. *n.*

**pom·pos·i·ty** (pom pos′ə tē) **1** the quality of being POMPOUS; pompous behaviour, speech, etc.: *He is a good speaker, except for his tendency toward pomposity.* **2** a POMPOUS act, gesture, remark, etc. *n., pl.* **pom·pos·i·ties.**

**pom·pous** (pom′pəs) **1** having or showing a tendency to display oneself in an overly grand or self-important way: *a pompous speech. The band leader bowed in a pompous way.* **2** marked by pomp; splendid; magnificent. *adj.* —**pom′pous·ly,** *adv.* —**pom′pous·ness,** *n.*

**pon·cho** (pon′chō) **1** a cloak consisting basically of a large piece of cloth with a slit in the middle for the head to go through, worn especially in Latin America. **2** a similar garment, especially one that is waterproof, worn by cyclists, hikers, etc. as a raincoat. *n., pl.* **pon·chos.**

**pond** (pond) a body of still water, smaller than a lake: *a duck pond, a mill pond.* *n.*

**pon·der** (pon′dər) consider carefully; think over: *to ponder a problem.* *v.*

**pon·der·a·ble** (pon′də rə bəl) **1** capable of being weighed; having perceptible mass. **2** capable of being appraised, or mentally weighed. *adj.*

**pon·de·ro·sa pine** (pon′də rō′sə) **1** a large pine tree found from southern British Columbia to California, usually 25 to 30 metres tall but sometimes reaching a height of about 50 metres, having very long needles and large cones with prickles; yellow pine: *The ponderosa pine is one of the main timber-producing trees of western North America.* **2** its yellowish wood.

**pon·der·os·i·ty** (pon′də ros′ə tē) the quality of being PONDEROUS; ponderousness. *n.*

**pon·der·ous** (pon′də rəs) **1** very heavy: *a great ponderous oak door.* **2** heavy and clumsy: *Slowly he lifted his ponderous bulk from the chair.* **3** overly serious and laboured: *a ponderous way of speaking.* *adj.*
—**pon′der·ous·ly,** *adv.* —**pon′der·ous·ness,** *n.*

**pond lily** WATER LILY.

**pond·weed** (pon′dwēd′) any of a large group of water plants that grow in quiet water: *Most pondweeds* have oval leaves that grow on the surface of the water and grasslike leaves under water.  *n.*

**pon·gee** (pon jē′)   a kind of soft, plain-woven silk, usually left in a natural brownish-yellow colour.  *n.*

**pon·iard** (pon′yərd)   DAGGER.  *n.*

**pon·tiff** (pon′tif)   **1** Pope.  **2** bishop.  **3** a high priest; chief priest.  *n.*

**pon·tif·i·cal** (pon tif′ə kəl)   **1** of or having to do with the Pope; papal.  **2** of or having to do with a bishop.  **3** pompous.  **4** Usually, **pontificals,** *pl.*   the vestments and marks of dignity used by cardinals and bishops at certain ecclesiastical functions or ceremonies.   **1, 2, 3** *adj.,* **4** *n.*  —**pon·tif′i·cal·ly,** *adv.*

**pon·tif·i·cate** (pon tif′ə kit *or* pon tif′ə kāt′ *for noun,* pon tif′ə kāt′ *for verb*)   **1** the office or term of office of a PONTIFF.  **2** officiate as a PONTIFF, especially at Mass.  **3** speak dogmatically and pompously: *He loved to pontificate on the virtues of thrift.*  **1** *n.,* **2, 3** *v.,* **pon·tif·i·cat·ed, pon·tif·i·cat·ing.**

Pontoons supporting a bridge

**pon·toon** (pon tün′)   **1** a low, flat-bottomed boat.  **2** such a boat, or some other floating structure, used as one of the supports of a temporary bridge.  **3** a boat-shaped float on an aircraft, used for coming down on or taking off from water.  See AMPHIBIAN for picture.  *n.*

**pontoon bridge**   a temporary bridge supported by low, flat-bottomed boats or other floating structures.

**po·ny** (pō′nē)   **1** a very small horse, especially any of several breeds of very small, stocky, gentle horse, usually less than 130 cm high.  **2** *Informal.*  something that is small for its kind, especially a small liqueur glass or the amount it will hold.  *n., pl.* **po·nies.**

**pooch** (pùch) *Informal.*  dog.  *n.*

A standard poodle— about 48 cm high at the shoulder

**poo·dle** (pü′dəl)   a breed of intelligent, active dog having thick, wool-like hair that is not shed and that is often clipped in any of several standard patterns.  *n.* —**poo′dle-like′,** *adj.*

☛ *Etym.*   From German *Pudel,* short for *Pudelhund* 'splash dog', made up of *pudeln* 'to splash in water' + *Hund* 'dog', so-called because it was used by hunters to bring game from water.

**pool¹** (pül)   **1** a small body of still water; a small pond.  **2** a still, deep place in a stream: *Trout are often found in the pools of a brook.*  **3** a puddle of water or any other liquid: *There was a pool of oil under the car. The water stood in pools in the garden after the rain.*  **4** a large tank made of concrete, plastic, etc. for swimming or bathing in; swimming pool.  *n.*

**pool²** (pül)   **1** a game played on a special table with six pockets: *In pool, the players try to drive balls into the pockets with long sticks called cues.*  See BILLIARDS for picture.  **2** put things or money together for common advantage: *The three girls pooled their savings for a year to buy a boat.*  **3** the things or money put together by different persons for common advantage.  **4** *Cdn.*  in the West, a co-operative grain-marketing organization among farmers.  **5** a group of people, usually having the same skills, who are drawn upon as needed: *a secretarial pool.*  **6** an arrangement between business firms to create a monopoly in order to control prices.  **7** CAR POOL.  **8** form a pool.  **9** the persons who form a pool.  **10** the stake played for in some games.   **1, 3–7, 9, 10** *n.,* **2, 8** *v.*

**pool·room** (pül′rüm′ *or* pül′rum′)   a room or place in which the game of pool is played.  *n.*

**pool train**   *Cdn.*  a train that is operated over a line of track by more than one railway company: *A pool train used to run between Toronto and Montreal.*

**poop¹** (püp)   **1** a deck at the stern above the ordinary deck, often forming the roof of a cabin.  **2** of a wave, break over the stern of a ship.  **1** *n.,* **2** *v.*

**poop²** (püp) *Informal.*   make or become exhausted: *All of us were pooped after the climb. That last dance pooped me out.*  *v.*

**poor** (pùr)   **1** not having enough income to maintain a standard of living regarded as normal in the community in which one lives: *They were poor, but never destitute.*  **2** not favourable: *a poor chance for recovery.*  **3** not good in quality; lacking something needed: *poor soil, a poor crop, a poor cook, poor health.*  **4** needing pity; unfortunate: *This poor child has hurt himself.*  **5 the poor,** *pl.*   persons who are needy.   **1–4** *adj.,* **5** *n.*  —**poor′ness,** *n.*

**poor·ly** (pùr′lē)   **1** in a poor manner; not enough; badly: *A desert is poorly supplied with water. Tomasina did poorly in the test.*  **2** *Informal.*  in bad health; somewhat ill: *I feel poorly today.*   **1** *adv.,* **2** *adj.*

**poor–spir·it·ed** (pùr′spir′ə tid)   having or showing a poor, cowardly, or abject spirit: *a poor-spirited wretch.*  *adj.*

**pop¹** (pop)   **1** make a short, quick, explosive sound: *The firecrackers popped in bunches.*  **2** a short, quick, explosive sound: *the pop of a cork.*  **3** with a pop; suddenly.  **4** move, go, or come suddenly or unexpectedly: *Our neighbour popped in for a short call.*  **5** thrust or put suddenly: *She popped her head out through the window.*  **6** put a question suddenly.  **7** *Informal.*  shoot.  **8** a shot from a gun, etc.  **9** burst open with a pop: *The chestnuts were popping in the fire.*  **10** heat or roast popcorn until it bursts with a pop.  **11** bulge: *The surprise made her eyes pop out.*  **12** in baseball, hit a short, high ball over the infield.  **13** a non-alcoholic carbonated drink: *strawberry pop.*  **1, 4–7, 9–12** *v.,* **popped, pop·ping;**   **2, 8, 13** *n.,* **3** *adv.*

**pop the question,** *Informal.* propose marriage.

**pop²** (pop) *Informal.* **1** popular. **2** a piece of popular music. **3** POP ART. 1 *adj.*, 2, 3 *n.*

**pop³** (pop) *Informal.* papa; father. *n.*

**pop. 1** population. **2** popular.

**pop art** an art style, especially in painting and sculpture, that is based on the style of advertising art, comic strips, etc., and uses commonplace objects such as hamburgers or soup cans as subject matter.

**pop·corn** (pop′kôrn′) **1** a variety of corn whose kernels burst open and puff out in a white mass when heated. **2** the white, puffed-out kernels, usually eaten salted and buttered. *n.*

**Pope** or **pope** (pōp) the supreme head of the Roman Catholic Church: *the Pope, the last three popes.* *n.*

**pop·gun** (pop′gun′) a toy gun that shoots with a popping sound. *n.*

**pop·in·jay** (pop′in jā′) a vain, overtalkative person; a conceited, silly person. *n.*

**pop·lar** (pop′lər) **1** any of a closely related group of slender, fast-growing trees found mainly in north temperate regions, having oval or heart-shaped leaves, flowers in drooping catkins, and light, soft wood. **2** the wood of a poplar: *Poplar is used for veneer, boxes, barrels, etc.* *n.*

**poplar bluff** *Cdn.* in the Prairies, a grove of poplar trees: *The farmhouse nestled in the shady poplar bluff.*

**pop·lin** (pop′lən) a strong, plain-woven fabric with a crosswise rib, used for sportswear, raincoats, etc. *n.*

**pop·o·ver** (pop′ō′vər) a very light and hollow muffin. *n.*

**pop·per** (pop′ər) a person or thing that pops, especially a wire basket or metal pan used for popping popcorn. *n.*

**pop·py** (pop′ē) **1** any of a closely related group of annual, perennial, or biennial plants having lobed leaves, a milky sap, showy flowers, and seeds in a capsule: *Opium is made from the juice in the seed capsule of one species of poppy; other species are cultivated as garden plants.* **2** the flower of a poppy. **3** bright orange-red. 1–3 *n.*, 3 *adj.*

**pop·py·cock** (pop′ē kok′) *Informal.* nonsense; bosh. *n., interj.*

**pop·u·lace** (pop′yə ləs) the people in general; the masses. *n.*
☛ *Hom.* POPULOUS.

**pop·u·lar** (pop′yə lər) **1** liked by most acquaintances or associates: *She was always popular with her co-workers.* **2** liked by a great many people: *The song quickly became popular.* **3** intended to appeal to the current tastes of the general public: *popular music, popular science.* **4** within the means of the average person: *popular prices.* **5** of or by the people; representing the people: *Canada has a popular government.* **6** widespread among many people; of people in general: *It is a popular belief that exercise is beneficial.* *adj.*

**pop·u·lar·i·ty** (pop′yə lar′ə tē *or* pop′yə ler′ə tē) the quality or state of being liked by most people. *n.*

**pop·u·lar·ize** (pop′yə lə rīz′) **1** change, especially by simplifying and presenting in an interesting form, so as to appeal to a great number of people instead of a special group: *history in a popularized form.* **2** cause to be generally liked: *to popularize a tune.* *v.*, **pop·u·lar·ized, pop·u·lar·iz·ing.** —**pop′u·lar·i·za′tion,** *n.* —**pop′u·lar·iz′er,** *n.*

**pop·u·lar·ly** (pop′yə lər lē) **1** by the people as a whole; in general: *The defendant was popularly believed to have been guilty, though she was acquitted.* **2** in a popular manner. *adv.*

**popular vote** the number of votes cast as distinct from seats won.

**pop·u·late** (pop′yə lāt′) **1** inhabit: *This city is densely populated.* **2** furnish with inhabitants: *Europeans populated much of the Canadian West.* *v.*, **pop·u·lat·ed, pop·u·lat·ing.**

**pop·u·la·tion** (pop′yə lā′shən) **1** the people of a city or a country: *The population was up in arms.* **2** the total number of such people. **3** a part of the inhabitants distinguished in any way from the rest: *the urban population, the Inuit population.* **4** the act or process of furnishing with inhabitants: *Are scientists seriously considering the population of the moon?* **5** the total number of animals, birds, etc. of a region: *the deer population of North America.* *n.*

**pop·u·lous** (pop′yə ləs) heavily populated; inhabited by many people: *a populous region.* *adj.*
☛ *Hom.* POPULACE.

**por·ce·lain** (pôr′sə lin *or* pôr′sə lən) very fine, hard, translucent EARTHENWARE having a transparent glaze: *Porcelain consists basically of a fine white clay, quartz, and feldspar and is fired at a high temperature.* *n.*

The porch on the front of Alexander Graham Bell's house in Brantford, Ontario

**porch** (pôrch) **1** a covered, sometimes enclosed, entrance to a building. **2** veranda. **3** stoop; a platform at the entrance to a house. *n.*

**por·cine** (pôr′sīn) of, having to do with, or like pigs. *adj.*

A North American porcupine—about 90 cm long including the tail

**por·cu·pine** (pôr′kyə pīn′) any of a number of large, heavy-set, short-legged rodents having long, sharp, barbed spines mixed in with the coarse hair of the back and tail. Porcupines make up two families of rodents: the New World tree-dwelling porcupines and the Old World ground-dwelling porcupines. *n.*

☛ *Etym.* From OF *porc espin*, which came from an earlier compound made up of L *porcus* 'pig' + *spinus* 'spine'.

**porcupine fish** any of various marine fishes having a spine-covered body that the fish can inflate into a ball as a means of defence when disturbed.

**pore**¹ (pôr) **1** study long and steadily (*used with* **over**): *She pored over the magnificent old book for hours.* **2** meditate or ponder intently (*used with* **over**): *to pore over a problem.* *v.*, **pored, por·ing.** —**por′er,** *n.*
☛ *Hom.* POUR.

**pore**² (pôr) a very tiny opening through which fluids may pass; especially, one of the openings in the skin of people or animals or in the leaves of plants through which fluids are absorbed or excreted: *Sweat comes through the pores of our skin.* See EPIDERMIS for picture. *n.*
☛ *Hom.* POUR.

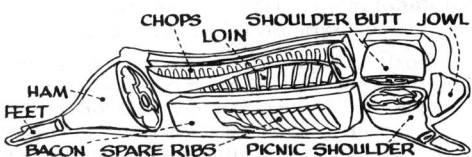

The main cuts of pork

**pork** (pôrk) the flesh of a pig used for food. *n.*

**pork·er** (pôr′kər) a pig, especially one fattened for meat. *n.*

**por·nog·ra·pher** (pôr nog′rə fər) a person who produces PORNOGRAPHY. *n.*

**por·no·graph·ic** (pôr′nə graf′ik) of, having to do with, or being PORNOGRAPHY. *adj.*

**por·nog·ra·phy** (pôr nog′rə fē) writings, pictures, films, etc. depicting sexual activity, especially when connected with violence and abuse. *n.*

**po·ros·i·ty** (pô ros′ə tē) the quality or state of being POROUS. *n.*

**po·rous** (pô′rəs) full of pores or tiny holes; permeable by water, air, etc.: *Cloth, blotting paper, and ordinary red clay flowerpots are porous.* *adj.* —**po′rous·ness,** *n.*

**por·phy·ry** (pôr′fə rē) **1** a hard rock quarried in ancient Egypt, consisting of white or red feldspar crystals embedded in a fine-grained, dark red or purplish base. **2** any IGNEOUS rock in which crystals are scattered through a mass of fine-grained minerals. *n., pl.* **por·phy·ries.**

**por·poise** (pôr′pəs) **1** any of several small whales found especially in the northern Atlantic and Pacific oceans, having a blunt snout and flattened, spade-shaped teeth: *Some authorities classify porpoises as belonging to the same family as dolphins; others place them in a separate family.* **2** DOLPHIN. *n., pl.* **por·pois·es** or (*esp. collectively*) **por·poise.**

**por·ridge** (pô′rij) a food made of oatmeal or other cereal boiled in water or milk until it thickens. *n.*

**por·rin·ger** (pô′rən jər) a small dish from which soup, porridge, bread and milk, etc. can be eaten. *n.*

**port**¹ (pôrt) **1** a harbour; place where ships and boats can take shelter from storms. **2** a city or town with a harbour where ships and boats may take on or unload cargo. *n.*

**port**² (pôrt) **1** an opening in the side of a ship for letting in light and air; porthole. **2** an opening in a wall, ship's side, etc. through which guns may be fired. **3** the cover for such an opening. **4** an opening in machinery for steam, air, water, etc. to pass through. **5** a device for connecting a computer to other hardware. *n.*

**port**³ (pôrt) **1** the left side of a ship or aircraft when facing forward. See AFT for picture. **2** on the left side of a ship. **3** turn or shift to the left side (*used mainly as a command*). 1 *n.*, 2 *adj.*, 3 *v.*

**port**⁴ (pôrt) **1** a way of holding one's head and body; bearing. **2** bring, hold, or carry a rifle or sword across and close to the body with the barrel or blade near the left shoulder. **3** the position of a weapon when ported. 1, 3 *n.*, 2 *v.*

**port**⁵ (pôrt) a strong, sweet wine that is dark-red or tawny. *n.*

**port·a·ble** (pôr′tə bəl) **1** capable of being carried; easily carried: *a portable typewriter.* **2** a portable radio, phonograph, etc. **3** a temporary building on the grounds of an overcrowded school, used as an extra classroom. 1 *adj.*, 2, 3 *n.*

**por·tage** (pôr tāzh′ *or* pôr′tij) **1** a carrying of boats, canoes, provisions, etc. overland from one stretch of water to another: *She found the last portage the most difficult.* **2** carry canoes, etc. from one stretch of water to another: *He had to portage five times during the trip.* **3** a place where such carrying takes place: *The hunters pitched camp at the portage.* **4** the act of carrying. **5** the cost of carrying. **6** an instance of such a carrying: *She made the canoe trip without a single portage.* 1, 3–6 *n.*, 2 *v.*, **por·taged, por·tag·ing.**

**por·tal** (pôr′təl) a door, gate, or entrance, especially an imposing one. *n.*

**port authority** a commission appointed to manage a port.

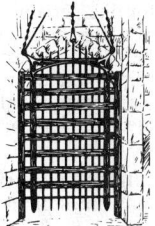

A portcullis

**port·cul·lis** (pôrt kul′is) a strong gate or grating of iron sliding up and down in grooves, used to close the gateway of an ancient castle or fortress. *n.*

**por·tend** (pôr tend′) indicate beforehand; be a portent of: *Black clouds portend a storm.* *v.*

**por·tent** (pôr′tent) **1** a significant sign of something to come; omen: *The scandal was regarded as a portent of worse things to come.* **2** prophetic significance: *an event of great portent.* *n.*

**por·ten·tous** (pôr ten′təs) **1** of, having to do with, or being a PORTENT: *an event of portentous significance.* **2** amazing; extraordinary: *a portentous effort of will.*

**3** self-important; pompous: *With a portentous clearing of the throat, she began to speak.* *adj.* —**por‧ten′tous‧ly,** *adv.* —**por‧ten′tous‧ness,** *n.*

**por‧ter**[1] (pôr′tər) **1** a person employed to carry things, especially one who carries luggage for patrons at a hotel, airport, etc. **2** an attendant in a parlour car or sleeping car of a railway train. *n.*

**por‧ter**[2] (pôr′tər) **1** a person who guards a door or entrance; doorkeeper. **2** janitor. *n.*

**por‧ter**[3] (pôr′tər) a heavy, dark-brown beer made from browned or charred malt. *n.*

**por‧ter‧house** (pôr′tər hous′) a choice beefsteak containing the tenderloin. *n.*

**port‧fo‧li‧o** (pôrt fō′lē ō′) **1** a briefcase; portable case for loose papers, drawings, etc. **2** the position and duties of a cabinet member or a minister of state: *The Minister of Labour resigned her portfolio.* **3** holdings in the form of stocks, bonds, etc. *n., pl.* **port‧fo‧li‧os.**

**port‧hole** (pôrt′hōl′) **1** an opening in a ship's side to let in light and air. **2** an opening in a wall, ship's side, etc. through which guns may be fired. *n.*

A portico

**por‧ti‧co** (pôr′tə kō′) a porch or covered walk having the roof supported by columns. *n., pl.* **por‧ti‧coes** or **por‧ti‧cos.**

**por‧tiere** or **por‧tière** (pôr tyer′) a curtain hung at a doorway. *n.*

**por‧tion** (pôr′shən) **1** a part or share: *A portion of each school day is devoted to arithmetic.* **2** the quantity of food served for one person: *Each child ate her portion. The restaurant serves large portions.* **3** divide into parts or shares. **4** the part of an estate that goes to an heir; property inherited. **5** dowry. **6** give a thing to a person as a share; give a portion, inheritance, dowry, etc. to. **7** one's lot; fate. 1, 2, 4, 5, 7 *n.*, 3, 6, *v.* —**por′tion‧less,** *adj.*

**Port‧land cement** (pôrt′lənd) a kind of cement made by burning limestone and clay in a kiln.

**port‧ly** (pôrt′lē) **1** stout; corpulent. **2** stately; dignified. *adj.*, **port‧li‧er, port‧li‧est.** —**port′li‧ness,** *n.*

**port‧man‧teau** (pôrt man′tō) *Esp. Brit.* a travelling bag, especially a stiff, oblong one with two compartments opening like a book. *n., pl.* **port‧man‧teaus** or **port‧man‧teaux** (-tōz).

**por‧trait** (pôr′trit *or* pôr′trāt) **1** a picture, especially a painting of a person. **2** a picture in words; description. *n.*

**por‧trait‧ist** (pôr′trā tist) a person who paints PORTRAITS. *n.*

**por‧trai‧ture** (pôr′trə chər *or* pôr′trə chür′) **1** the act of PORTRAYing. **2** the art of making PORTRAITS. **3** a portrait or portraits. *n.*

**por‧tray** (pôr trā′) **1** describe or picture in words: *The book* Black Beauty *portrays the life of a horse.* **2** make a likeness of in a drawing or painting; make a picture of. **3** represent on the stage; impersonate; act. *v.* —**por‧tray′er,** *n.*

**por‧tray‧al** (pôr trā′əl) **1** a portraying by pictures or in words. **2** a picture or description. *n.*

**Por‧tu‧guese** (pôr′chù gēz′ *for noun,* pôr′chù gēz′ *for adjective*) **1** a native or inhabitant of Portugal, a country in southwestern Europe. **2** a person of Portuguese descent. **3** the language of Portugal and Brazil. **4** of or having to do with Portugal, its people, or their language. **5 the Portuguese,** *pl.* the people of Portugal. 1–3, 5 *n., pl.* **Por‧tu‧guese;** 4 *adj.*

**por‧tu‧lac‧a** (pôr′chə lak′ə) a low plant having thick, fleshy leaves and variously coloured flowers. *n.*

**pose**[1] (pōz) **1** a position of the body; way of holding the body: *That snapshot shows her in an attractive pose.* **2** hold a position: *She posed an hour for her portrait.* **3** put in a certain position: *The artist posed him before painting his picture.* **4** an attitude assumed for effect; pretence; affectation: *She takes the pose of being an invalid when really she is well and strong.* **5** pretend; make a pretence, especially for effect: *He posed as a rich man though he owed more than he owned.* **6** put forward; state: *to pose a question.* 1, 4 *n.*, 2, 3, 5, 6 *v.*, **posed, pos‧ing.**

**pose**[2] (pōz) puzzle completely. *v.*, **posed, pos‧ing.**

**pos‧er**[1] (pō′zər) a person who POSES. *n.*

**pos‧er**[2] (pō′zər) a very puzzling problem: *The last question on the test was a real poser.* *n.*

**po‧seur** (pō zėr′; *French,* pō zœR′) an affected person; one who poses to impress others. *n.*

**posh** (posh) *Informal.* smart; stylish; elegant: *They have a very posh apartment in a new highrise downtown.* *adj.*

**pos‧it** (poz′it) lay down or assume as a fact or principle; affirm. *v.*

**po‧si‧tion** (pə zish′ən) **1** a place where a thing or person is: *The house is in a sheltered position.* **2** a way of being placed: *Sit in a more comfortable position.* **3** the proper place. **4** a condition with reference to place or circumstances: *The army manoeuvred for position before attacking.* **5** job: *She has a position in a bank.* **6** a rank; standing, especially high standing: *She was raised to the position of captain.* **7** a way of thinking; set of opinions: *What is your position on this question?* **8** the place held by a player on a team: *My position on the hockey team was defence.* **9** put in position; place: *The riders positioned their horses at the starting gate.* **10** a relationship with other people: *Your careless remark put me in an awkward position.* 1–8, 10 *n.*, 9 *v.*

**po‧si‧tion‧al** (pə zish′ə nəl) of, having to do with, or dependent on position or context. *adj.*

**pos‧i‧tive** (poz′ə tiv) **1** admitting of no question; without doubt; sure: *We have positive knowledge that the earth moves around the sun.* **2** too sure; too confident: *Her positive manner annoys people.* **3** definite; emphatic: *a positive refusal.* **4** affirmative or approving: *Do you think we can expect a positive answer? You should take a more positive attitude.* **5** that can be thought of as real and present: *Light is a positive thing; darkness is only the absence of light.* **6** showing that a particular disease, condition, germ, etc. is present. **7** that definitely does something or adds something; practical: *Don't just make criticisms; give us some positive help.* **8** tending in the direction thought of as that of increase or progress: *Motion in the direction that the hands of a clock move is positive.* **9** greater than zero; plus: *Positive numbers are used to count things. Five above zero is a positive quantity.* **10** a positive degree or quantity. **11** of the kind of electrical charge produced on glass by rubbing it with silk; lacking or losing electrons. See DRY CELL for picture. **12** in photography, showing light and shadow or colour as in the subject photographed. **13** a positive photograph or a print made from a negative. **14** the simple form of an adjective or adverb, as distinct from the comparative and superlative. *Fast* is the positive; *faster* is the comparative; *fastest* is the superlative. **15** of the simple form of an adjective or adverb. 1–9, 11, 12, 15 *adj.*, 10, 13, 14 *n.* —**pos′i·tive·ly**, *adv.* —**pos′i·tive·ness**, *n.*

**pos·i·tron** (poz′ə tron′) a particle having the same mass and magnitude of charge as an ELECTRON, but exhibiting a positive charge; positive electron. *n.*

**poss.** **1** possessive. **2** possession.

**pos·se** (pos′ē) **1** a group of persons summoned by a law officer to help him or her, especially in an emergency: *Posses were often formed to capture criminals during frontier days in the American West.* **2** *Cdn.* in western Canada, a troop of horses and riders trained for special exercises and drills, often giving exhibitions at rodeos and stampedes. *n.*

**pos·sess** (pə zes′) **1** own; have: *The general possessed great wisdom.* **2** hold as property; hold; occupy. **3** control; influence strongly: *Sarah was possessed by the desire to be rich.* **4** control by a spirit: *She fought like one possessed.* **5** maintain; keep: *Possess your soul in patience.* *v.*

**pos·ses·sion** (pə zesh′ən) **1** a possessing; holding: *Our soldiers fought hard for possession of the hilltop.* **2** ownership: *At his mother's death he came into possession of a million dollars.* **3** something possessed; property: *She put most of her possessions in storage before she left.* **4** a territory under the rule of a country: *Ascension Island is a possession of the United Kingdom.* **5** domination by a particular feeling, idea, etc. **6** self-control. **7** control by a spirit: *He was in a state of possession.* *n.*

**pos·ses·sive** (pə zes′iv) **1** of or having to do with possession: *the possessive instinct.* **2** having or showing a strong desire to own or dominate: *a possessive manner. That girl has a possessive nature. She is very possessive.* **3** of, having to do with, or being the form of an English noun or pronoun that shows that it refers to the possessor or source of something or to a part of a larger whole: *My is the possessive form of I in my books; bird's is the possessive form of bird in a bird's wing.* **4** the possessive form: *The English possessive is also called the genitive case.* **5** a word or word group in the possessive form: *their and woman's are possessives.* 1–3 *adj.*, 4, 5 *n.* —**pos·ses′sive·ly**, *adv.* —**pos·ses′sive·ness**, *n.*

**possessive adjective** the possessive pronoun used with a noun: *In my friend was late, my is a possessive adjective.*
☛ *Usage.* Many grammarians use the term POSSESSIVE PRONOUN to include possessive adjectives as well. That is, they will call both **my** and **mine** possessive pronouns.

**possessive pronoun** a pronoun in the possessive form: *In the book is hers and my friend was late, hers and my are possessive pronouns.*
☛ *Usage.* Because a possessive pronoun frequently serves as a modifier of a noun, as an adjective does, it can be called a possessive adjective.

hat, āge, fär; let, ēqual, tėrm; it, īce
hot, ōpen, ôrder; oil, out; cup, pút, rüle
əbove, takən, pencəl, lemən, circəs
ch, child; ng, long; sh, ship
th, thin; ᴛʜ, then; zh, measure

**pos·ses·sor** (pə zes′ər) one that occupies, owns, or controls: *the possessor of a lease. She is the proud possessor of a grand piano.* *n.*

**pos·set** (pos′it) a hot drink made of milk with ale, wine, etc., and spices. *n.*

**pos·si·bil·i·ty** (pos′ə bil′ə tē) **1** the condition of being POSSIBLE: *There is a possibility that the train may be late.* **2** any thing or event that is POSSIBLE; a person considered as a possible choice: *He would be a good possibility for captain. A whole week of rain is a possibility.* *n., pl.* **pos·si·bil·i·ties.**

**pos·si·ble** (pos′ə bəl) **1** that can happen or be done: *If it's at all possible, they'll come. It is possible to cure tuberculosis.* **2** that may be true or a fact: *It is possible that he left by the rear exit.* **3** that can be done, chosen, etc. properly: *the only possible candidate.* *adj.*

**pos·si·bly** (pos′ə blē) **1** by any possibility; no matter what happens: *I cannot possibly go.* **2** perhaps: *Possibly you are right.* *adv.*

**pos·sum** (pos′əm) OPOSSUM. *n.*
**play possum,** pretend to be dead or asleep.

**post**[1] (pōst) **1** a length of timber, metal, or the like, set upright, usually as a support: *the posts of a door or bed, a hitching post.* **2** fasten a notice up in a place where it can easily be seen: *The list of winners will be posted soon.* **3** make known by, or as if by, a posted notice; offer publicly: *to post a reward.* **4** announce in a posted notice: *Her train is posted as on time.* **5** cover a wall, etc. with notices or bills. **6** put up notices warning people to keep out of: *That farmer posts her land.* **7** the post, line, etc. where a race starts or ends. 1, 7 *n.*, 2–6 *v.*

**post**[2] (pōst) **1** a place where a soldier, police officer, etc. is stationed; place where one is supposed to be when on duty. **2** a place where soldiers are stationed; a military station, fort, etc. **3** send to a station or post: *We posted guards at the door.* **4** in the armed forces, appoint to a post, unit, etc. **5** a job or position: *She has a new post as district manager.* **6** a trading station, especially in unsettled country: *a Hudson's Bay Company post.* **7** *Esp. U.S.* a local branch of a veterans' organization. 1, 2, 5–7 *n.*, 3, 4 *v.*

**post**[3] (pōst) **1** an established system for carrying letters, papers, packages, etc.; the mail: *to send by post.* **2** a single delivery of mail; the letters, etc. thus delivered: *this morning's post.* **3** send by post; mail: *to post a letter.* **4** post office. **5** a MAILBOX (def. 1). **6** formerly, one of a series of fixed stations along a route for furnishing relays of men and horses for carrying letters, etc. and supplying service to travellers by post horse, post chaise, etc. **7** formerly, travel with post horses or by post chaise. **8** travel with haste; hurry. **9** by post; speedily. **10** rise and fall in the saddle in rhythm with the horse's trot. **11** supply with up-to-date information; inform: *She keeps posted on current events.* **12** in bookkeeping, transfer an entry from journal to ledger; enter an item in due place and form; make all requisite entries in a ledger, etc. **13** a size of paper, about 40 × 50 cm. 1, 2, 4–6, 13 *n.*, 3, 7, 8, 10–12 *v.*, 9 *adv.*

**post–** a prefix meaning after, as in *postgraduate, postmortem, postscript*.

**post·age** (pō′stij) the amount paid on anything sent by mail. *n.*

**postage stamp** an official stamp for use on mail to show that postage has been paid.

**post·al** (pō′stəl) of or having to do with mail or the post office: *postal regulations*. *adj.*

**postal code** *Cdn.* a part of an address that uses a system of alternating letters and numerals to identify a particular postal delivery route or point: *The system of postal codes is designed to speed the processing of machine-sorted mail. The postal code of the CN Tower in Toronto is M5V 2T6.*

**postal station** one of several branch POST OFFICES (def. 1) in a large community.

**post bel·lum** (pōst′bel′əm) *Latin.* after the war.

**post box** a box into which letters, parcels, etc. are put for collection and delivery by the Post Office; mailbox.

**post·boy** (pōst′boi′) 1 a boy or man who carries mail. 2 a man who rides one of the horses drawing a carriage or coach; postilion. *n.*

**post·card** (pōst′kärd′) a card used without an envelope for sending a short message by mail: *Most postcards have a picture on one side.* *n.*

**post chaise** a hired carriage that was used for travelling before there were railways.

**post·date** (pōst′dāt′) 1 give to a letter, cheque, etc. a later date than the actual date of writing. 2 follow in time. *v.*, **post·dat·ed, post·dat·ing.**

**post·ed** (pō′stid) 1 having posts. 2 informed. 3 pt. and pp. of POST. 1, 2 *adj.*, 3 *v.*

**post·er** (pō′stər) 1 a large printed advertisement, or notice, often illustrated, put up in some public place; placard. 2 a person who posts notices, etc. 3 a large printed picture or message, used for room decoration. *n.*

**pos·te·ri·or** (pos tē′rē ər) 1 situated behind; back; rear; hind. 2 later; coming after. 3 *Informal.* the buttocks; rump. 1, 2 *adj.*, 3 *n.*

**pos·ter·i·ty** (pos ter′ə tē) 1 the generations of the future: *Posterity may travel to distant planets.* 2 all of a person's descendants. *n.*

**post·grad·u·ate** (pōst′graj′ü it) 1 a student who continues university studies at a level beyond that of a bachelor's degree. 2 taking a course of study at such a level. 3 of or for postgraduates. 1 *n.*, 2, 3 *adj.*

**post·haste** (pōst′hāst′) very speedily; in great haste. *adv.*

**post horse** formerly, a horse hired for use in travelling by relay, each horse being changed for a fresh one after a certain distance.

**post·hu·mous** (pos′chu məs) 1 happening after death: *posthumous fame.* 2 published after the death of the author: *a posthumous book.* 3 born after the death of the father: *a posthumous son.* *adj.*

**post·hu·mous·ly** (pos′chu mə slē) after death. *adv.*

**pos·til·ion** or **pos·til·lion** (pō stil′yən *or* pos til′yən) a person who rides one of the horses drawing a carriage. *n.*

**post·lude** (pōst′lüd) 1 a closing piece of music, especially a composition played at the end of a church service. 2 a final or concluding phase: *the postlude of an era.* *n.* Compare with PRELUDE.

**post·mark** (pōst′märk′) 1 an official mark stamped on mail to cancel the postage stamp and record the place and date of mailing. 2 stamp with a postmark. 1 *n.*, 2 *v.*

**post·mas·ter** (pōst′mas′tər) a person in charge of a post office. *n.*

**post·me·rid·i·an** (pōst′mə rid′ē ən) occurring after noon; of or having to do with the afternoon. *adj.*

**post me·rid·i·em** (pōst′mə rid′ē əm) p.m. or P.M.

**post·mis·tress** (pōst′mis′tris) a woman in charge of a post office. *n.*

**post–mor·tem** (pōst′môr′təm) 1 after death: *A post-mortem examination showed that the woman had been poisoned.* 2 an examination of a dead body; AUTOPSY: *The coroner ordered a post-mortem to determine the cause of death.* 1 *adj.*, 2 *n.*
☛ *Etym.* From L *post mortem* 'after death'. Though originally a Latin phrase, **post-mortem** is now fully accepted as an English word. The noun has a regular plural (**post-mortems**).

**post·na·tal** (pōst′nā′təl) having to do with or for the mother of a newborn baby: *postnatal care, postnatal depression.* *adj.*

**post office** 1 a local office where mail is received and sorted for delivery or placement in individual boxes, and where stamps and money orders are sold, mail is registered or insured, etc. 2 a small office, located in a drug store, etc., where stamps and money orders are sold and mail can be registered or insured, etc., but that does not function as a distribution centre for mail.

**post–op·er·a·tive** (pō stop′ər ə tiv *or* pō stop′ə rā′tiv) of or occurring in the period immediately following a surgical operation: *a post-operative infection.* *adj.*

**post·paid** (pōst′pād′) with the postage paid for. *adj.*

**post·pone** (pō spōn′ *or* pōst pōn′) put off till later; put off to a later time; delay: *The ball game was postponed because of rain.* *v.*, **post·poned, post·pon·ing.**

**post·pone·ment** (pō spōn′mənt *or* pōst pōn′mənt) putting off till later; delay: *The postponement of the ball game disappointed many people.* *n.*

**post·pran·di·al** (pōst′pran′dē əl) after-dinner: *postprandial speeches.* *adj.*

**post·rid·er** (pō′strī′dər) formerly, a person, especially one carrying mail, travelling by means of relays of horses. See POST HORSE. *n.*

**post road** 1 a road or route over which mail is or was carried. 2 formerly, a road with stations providing post horses.

**post·script** (pōst′skript) 1 an addition to a letter, written after the writer's name has been signed. 2 a supplementary part appended to any composition or literary work. *n.*

**post–test** (pōst′test) a test taken after instruction to test what has been learned. Compare with PRETEST. *n.*

**pos·tu·lant** (pos′chə lənt) a candidate, especially for admission to a religious order. *n.*

**pos·tu·late** (pos′chə lit *for noun,* pos′chə lāt′ *for verb*)
**1** something taken for granted or assumed as a basis for reasoning; a fundamental principle; necessary condition: *One postulate of geometry is that a straight line may be drawn between any two points.* **2** take for granted; assume without proof as a basis of reasoning; require as a fundamental principle or necessary condition: *Geometry postulates certain things as a basis for its reasoning.* **3** require; demand; claim.   1 *n.,* 2, 3 *v.,* **pos·tu·lat·ed, pos·tu·lat·ing.**

**pos·tur·al** (pos′chə rəl)   of or having to do with POSTURE. *adj.*

**pos·ture** (pos′chər)   **1** the position of the body; way of holding the body: *Good posture is important for health.* **2** take a certain posture: *The dancer postured before the mirror, bending and twisting her body.* **3** put in a certain position.   **4** pose for effect.   **5** a condition; situation; state: *In the present posture of public affairs, it is difficult to invest money safely.*   **6** a mental or spiritual attitude. 1, 5, 6 *n.* 2–4 *v.,* **pos·tured, pos·tur·ing.**

**post·war** (pō′stwôr′)   **1** of, having to do with, or happening during the period immediately following a war: *a postwar construction boom. adj.*

**po·sy** (pō′zē)   **1** flower.   **2** a bunch of flowers; bouquet.   **3** a motto or line of poetry engraved within a ring.   *n., pl.* **po·sies.**

**pot** (pot)   **1** a deep container made of metal, earthenware, glass, etc.: *a cooking pot, a flower pot, a coffee pot.*   **2** a pot and what is in it; the amount a pot can hold: *a pot of beans.*   **3** put into a pot: *We potted young tomato plants.*   **4** cook and preserve in a pot.   **5** a basket used to catch fish, lobsters, etc.   **6** *Informal.*   a large sum of money.   **7** *Informal.*   all the money bet at one time.   **8** take a pot shot at; shoot.   1, 2, 5–7 *n.,* 3, 4, 8 *v.,* **pot·ted, pot·ting.**
**go to pot,** *Informal.*   go to ruin: *After losing his job he took to drinking and went to pot.*
**keep the pot boiling,** *Informal.*   **a** make a living.   **b** keep things going in a lively way.

**po·ta·ble** (pō′tə bəl)   **1** fit for drinking.   **2** potables, *pl.* anything drinkable.   1 *adj.,* 2 *n.*

**pot·ash** (pot′ash′)   **1** any of several substances made from wood ashes and used in soap, fertilizers, etc.: *Potash is mainly impure potassium carbonate.*   **2** any of several POTASSIUM salts mined and processed for use in agriculture and industry.   **3** POTASSIUM.   *n.*

**po·tas·si·um** (pə tas′ē əm)   a soft, silver-white metallic element, occurring in nature only in compounds. Symbol: K   *n.*

**potassium bromide**   a white crystalline compound with a salty taste, used in medicine, photography, etc.

**potassium carbonate**   a white crystalline compound that forms a strongly alkaline solution and is used especially in making glass and soap.

**potassium chlorate**   a colourless crystalline compound used as an oxidizing agent in explosives, matches, etc.

**potassium chloride**   a crystalline compound that occurs naturally as a mineral, used in fertilizers and as a salt substitute.

**potassium cyanide**   a very poisonous white crystalline compound used for removing gold from ore, for electroplating, etc.

**potassium hydroxide**   a very strong alkali used especially in making soap and as a reagent; caustic potash.

hat, āge, fär; let, ēqual, tėrm; it, īce
hot, ōpen, ôrder; oil, out; cup, pùt, rüle
əbove, takən, pencəl, lemən, circəs
ch, child; ng, long; sh, ship
th, thin; ŦH, then; zh, measure

**potassium nitrate**   a colourless crystalline compound used as an oxidizing agent, in gunpowder, in explosives, etc.; nitre; saltpetre.

**po·ta·tion** (pō tā′shən)   **1** the act of drinking.   **2** a drink, especially of alcoholic liquor.   *n.*

**po·ta·to** (pə tā′tō)   **1** a hard, starchy tuber of a cultivated plant, a vegetable most widely used in Europe and North America; white potato; Irish potato.   **2** the plant producing these tubers.   **3** sweet potato.   *n., pl.* **po·ta·toes.**

**potato beetle**   a beetle having black and yellow stripes, which damages potato plants.

**potato bug**   POTATO BEETLE.

**potato chip**   **1** a crisp, thin, dry slice of potato that has been fried in deep fat: *We each took a soft drink and a bag of potato chips.*   **2** French fry: *Potato chips are often eaten with fried fish.*

**pot·bel·lied** (pot′bel′ēd)   **1** having a POTBELLY. **2** shaped like a POTBELLY: *a potbellied stove. adj.*

**pot·bel·ly** (pot′bel′ē)   a large, protruding belly; paunch.   *n.*

**pot·boil·er** (pot′boi′lər) *Informal.*   a work of literature or art produced merely to make a living.   *n.*

**po·ten·cy** (pō′tən sē)   **1** the quality or state of being potent; power; strength: *the potency of an argument, the potency of a drug.*   **2** the power or capacity to develop; potentiality.   *n., pl.* **po·ten·cies.**

**po·tent** (pō′tənt)   **1** having power or effectiveness in action; effective: *a potent remedy for a disease.*   **2** of a drink, etc., strong: *potent tea.*   **3** powerful or mighty: *a potent leader. adj.*   —**po′tent·ly,** *adv.*

**po·ten·tate** (pō′tən tāt′)   a ruler having great power: *the potentates of ancient India. The Roman emperors were potentates.   n.*

**po·ten·tial** (pə ten′shəl)   **1** possible as opposed to actual; capable of coming into being or action: *a potential danger.*   **2** something potential; possibility.   **3** the amount of electrification of a point with reference to some standard: *A current of high potential is used in transmitting electric power over long distances.*   1 *adj.,* 2, 3 *n.*

**potential energy**   the energy that something has that is due to its position or its structure, not to motion: *A tightly coiled spring or a raised weight has potential energy.*

**po·ten·ti·al·i·ty** (pə ten′shē al′ə tē)   **1** a potential state or quality; possibility as opposed to actuality; latent power or capacity.   **2** something potential; a possibility.   *n., pl.* **po·ten·ti·al·i·ties.**

**po·ten·tial·ly** (pə ten′shə lē)   possibly, but not yet actually.   *adv.*

**pot·ful** (pot′fùl′)   **1** as much or as many as a pot will hold: *a potful of potatoes.*   **2** a large amount: *She made a potful of money on that deal.*   1 *adj.,* 2 *n.*

**pot·herb** (pot′ėrb′ *or* pot′hėrb′)   **1** any plant whose leaves and stems are boiled as a vegetable, such as spinach.   2 any plant used as seasoning in cooking: *Sage and parsley are potherbs.*   *n.*

**pot·hold·er** (pot′hōl′dər)   a small pad used for protecting one's hands when handling hot pots, etc.   *n.*

**pot·hole** (pot′hōl′)   1 a deep, round hole, especially one made in the rocky bed of a river by stones and gravel being spun around in the current.   2 a hole in the surface of a road.   *n.*

**pot·hook** (pot′hůk′)   1 an S-shaped hook for hanging a pot or kettle over an open fire.   2 a rod with a hook for lifting hot pots, etc.   *n.*

**pot·hunt·er** (pot′hun′tər)   1 a person who shoots anything he or she comes upon regardless of the rules of sport.   2 a person who takes part in contests merely to win prizes.   3 a person who hunts just for food or for profit.   *n.*

**po·tion** (pō′shən)   a drink, especially one that is used as a medicine or poison, or in magic.   *n.*

**pot·latch** (pot′lach′) *Cdn.*   1 formerly, among North American Indian peoples of the West Coast, a large gathering to celebrate some event, at which the host would present costly gifts to his guests: *Because potlatches were thought to have become too extravagant, they were outlawed in 1884.*   2 a present-day festival and ceremony that is a modified version of the historical one, involving races, dancing, games, etc.   3 *Informal.*   a party or celebration.   *n.*

**pot·luck** (pot′luk′)·   1 whatever food happens to be ready or on hand for a meal: *Come into the house and take potluck with us.*   2 a meal to which all present have contributed: *a potluck lunch.*   *n.*

**pot marigold**   a popular garden flower, a species of calendula having huge, double yellow or orange flowers: *The flowers of the pot marigold were once used for flavouring in cakes, soups, etc.*

**pot·pie** (pot′pī′)   1 a baked meat and vegetable pie.   2 a stew with dumplings.   *n.*

**pot·pour·ri** (pō′pü rē′)   1 a musical or literary medley.   2 a fragrant mixture of dried flower petals and spices.   *n.*

**pot roast**   a large piece of meat, usually beef, cooked slowly with a little water in a deep, heavy, tightly covered dish.

**pot·sherd** (pot′shėrd′)   a broken piece of EARTHENWARE.   *n.*

**pot shot**   1 a shot taken at game just to provide a meal, with little regard to the rules of sport.   2 a quick shot at something from close range without careful aim.

**pot·tage** (pot′ij)   a thick soup.   *n.*

**pot·ted** (pot′id)   1 put into a pot.   2 cooked and preserved in pots or cans.   3 pt. and pp. of POT.   1, 2 *adj.*, 3 *v.*

**pot·ter**[1] (pot′ər)   a person who makes pottery.   *n.*

**pot·ter**[2] (pot′ər)   PUTTER[1].   *v.*   —**pot′terer,** *n.*

**potter's field**   a burial ground for paupers, unknown persons, etc.

**potter's wheel**   a rotating horizontal disk upon which clay is moulded into dishes, etc.

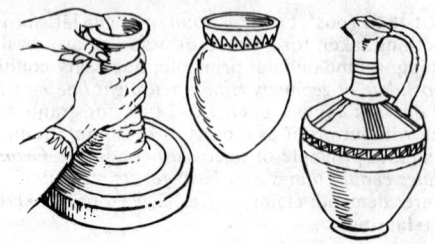
Pottery. The drawing at the left shows a vase being formed by hand on a potter's wheel

**pot·ter·y** (pot′ə rē)   1 pots, dishes, vases, or other EARTHENWARE, especially as distinct from porcelain or stoneware: *Pottery is not as strong as stoneware and not as fine as porcelain.*   2 the art or craft of making pottery.   3 a place where pottery is made.   *n., pl.* **pot·ter·ies.**

**pouch** (pouch)   1 a bag; sack: *a letter carrier's pouch.*   2 in biology, a baglike cavity or receptacle, such as that on the abdomen of a female kangaroo, in which the young are carried.   3 a loose fold of skin: *pouches under the eyes.*   4 a large bag that can be locked, used for transporting mail or government dispatches: *a diplomatic pouch.*   5 form a pouch or form into a pouch.   1–4 *n.,* 5 *v.*   —**pouch′like′,** *adj.*

**pouf** (püf)   1 a woman's hairstyle popular in the 18th century and consisting of high rolls or puffs of hair.   2 a loose roll of hair.   3 a puffed or gathered part of a dress.   4 a soft hassock or ottoman.   *n.* Also, **pouff** or **pouffe.**

**poul·tice** (pōl′tis)   1 a soft, moist mass of mustard, herbs, etc. applied to the body as a medicine.   2 put a poultice on.   1 *n.,* 2 *v.* **poul·ticed, poul·tic·ing.**

**poul·try** (pōl′trē)   birds raised for their meat or eggs, such as chickens, turkeys, geese, ducks, etc.   *n.*

**pounce** (pouns)   1 come down with a rush and seize: *The cat pounced upon the mouse.*   2 dash, come, or jump suddenly: *The actor pounced onto the stage.*   3 a sudden swoop or pouncing.   4 a claw or talon of a bird of prey.   1, 2 *v.,* **pounced, pounc·ing;**   3, 4 *n.*

**pound**[1] (pound)   1 a unit for measuring mass. In the avoirdupois system, formerly in general use in English-speaking countries, one pound equals 16 ounces (about 454 g). In the troy system, used for precious metals and gems, one pound equals 12 troy ounces (about 373 g).   2 a unit of money of the United Kingdom, equal to 100 pence; pound sterling: *A pound was formerly equal to 20 shillings or 240 pence.*   Symbol: £   3 a unit of money of Cyprus, Egypt, Ireland, Israel, Lebanon, Malta, Sudan, Syria, and Turkey.   4 a coin or note worth one pound.   *n., pl.* **pounds** or (*esp. collectively*) **pound.**

**pound**[2] (pound)   1 hit hard again and again; hit heavily: *He pounded the door with his fist.*   2 beat hard; throb: *After running fast, you can feel your heart pound.*   3 crush to powder or pulp by beating.   4 move heavily: *Jemima pounded down the hill to catch the bus.*   5 the act of pounding.   6 a heavy or forcible blow.   7 the sound of a blow.   8 produce sound by pounding or as if by pounding: *We could hear drums pounding in the distance.*   1–4, 8 *v.,* 5–7 *n.*

**pound**[3] (pound)   1 an enclosed place for keeping stray or unlicensed animals, especially dogs, cats, etc. until claimed by the owners: *Most cities and towns have a pound.*   2 a place for keeping automobiles or other personal property until redeemed by the owners.   3 an enclosure for keeping or trapping animals.   4 any place of confinement.   *n.*

**pound·age** (poun′dij)   1 mass, or weight, in pounds.   2 a tax or commission of so much per pound sterling.   3 a charge of so much per pound of weight.   *n.*

**pound·al** (poun′dəl)   a unit for measuring force, equal to about 0.138 newtons.   *n.*

**pound cake**   a rich butter cake containing equal amounts of the principal ingredients: *The original recipe for pound cake required one pound each of sugar, flour, and butter.*

**pound·er**[1] (poun′dər)   a person or thing that pounds, especially an instrument such as a pestle for pounding or crushing.   *n.*

**pound·er**[2] (poun′dər)   a person or thing weighing, having, or associated with a particular number of pounds (*used in compounds*): *We caught a ten-pounder in the lake yesterday.*   *n.*

**pound–foolish** (pound′fü′lish)   foolish or careless in regard to large sums of money.   *adj.*
**penny-wise and pound-foolish,**   thrifty in small expenses and wasteful in big ones.

**pour** (pôr)   1 cause to flow in a steady stream: *I poured the milk from the bottle.*   2 flow in a steady stream: *The crowd poured out of the cinema. The rain poured down.*   3 pouring.   4 pour tea or coffee at a formal reception: *Mrs. Brandt poured at the tea.*   1, 2, 4 *v.*, 3 *n.*
—**pour′er,** *n.*
☞ *Hom.* PORE.

**pout** (pout)   1 thrust or push out the lips, as a displeased or sulky child does.   2 a pushing out of the lips when displeased or sulky.   1 *v.*, 2 *n.*

**pout·er** (pou′tər)   1 a person who pouts.   2 a breed of domestic pigeon that has the ability to inflate its crop, producing a puffed-up breast.   *n.*

**pout·y** (pou′tē) *Informal.*   inclined to POUT.   *adj.*

**pov·er·ty** (pov′ər tē)   1 the condition of being poor or needy; the condition of not having enough income to maintain a standard of living regarded as normal in a community: *She died in poverty.*   2 the renunciation of the right to own property as an individual: *A person joining any of certain religious orders takes a vow of poverty.*   3 a lack of what is needed; inadequacy: *The poverty of the soil in this region makes farming difficult.*   4 scarcity; dearth: *a poverty of ideas.*   *n.*

**pov·er·ty–strick·en** (pov′ər tē strik′ən)   extremely poor.   *adj.*

**P.O.W.** or **POW**   prisoner of war.

**pow·der** (pou′dər)   1 a solid reduced to dust by pounding, crushing, or grinding.   2 make into powder.   3 become powder.   4 something made or prepared as powder: *face powder, powders taken as medicine.*   5 sprinkle or cover with powder: *to powder a cake with sugar.*   6 apply powder to the face, etc.: *to powder one's nose.*   7 sprinkle: *The ground was powdered with snow.*   8 gunpowder. See CARTRIDGE for picture.   1, 4, 8 *n.*, 2, 3, 5–7 *v.*

**powder blue**   pale blue.

**powder burn**   a burn on the skin resulting from the explosion of gunpowder at close range.

**powder flask**   formerly, a flask or case of horn, metal, or leather for carrying gunpowder.

**powder horn**   a POWDER FLASK made of an animal's horn.   See HORN for picture.

**powder keg**   1 a small cask for holding gunpowder or blasting powder.   2 something that is liable to explode: *The whole country was a powder keg after the death of the dictator.*

**powder magazine**   a place where gunpowder is stored.

**powder puff**   a soft puff or pad for applying cosmetic powder to the skin.

**pow·der·y** (pou′də rē)   1 of, like, or in the form of powder: *powdery snow.*   2 easily made into powder; crumbling: *powdery topsoil.*   3 covered with powder or as if with powder.   *adj.*

**pow·er** (pou′ər)   1 strength; might; force: *a medicine of great power. Bulldozers have great power.*   2 the ability to do or act: *I will give you all the help in my power.*   3 a particular ability: *She has great powers of concentration.*   4 control; authority; influence; right: *Parliament has power to declare war.*   5 any person, thing, body, or nation having authority or influence: *Five powers held a peace conference.*   6 energy or force that can do work, such as electricity: *Running water produces power to run mills. Turn on the power. We had a power cut.*   7 a simple machine.   8 the capacity for exerting mechanical force, as measured by the rate at which it is exerted or at which the work is done: *In the SI, all power is expressed in watts or in multiples or sub-multiples of the watt.*   9 provide with power or energy: *a boat powered by an outboard motor.*   10 operated by a motor; equipped with its own motor: *power tools, power steering.*   11 the product of a number multiplied by itself: *16 is the 4th power of 2.*   12 the capacity of an instrument to magnify: *The higher the power of a telescope or microscope, the more details you can see.*   1–8, 11, 12 *n.*, 9 *v.*, 10 *adj.*
**in power,**   having control or authority: *the government in power.*
**the powers that be,**   those who have control or authority.

**pow·er·boat** (pou′ər bōt′)   a boat propelled by an engine on board; motorboat.   *n.*

**power brakes**   in a motor vehicle, a braking system that uses power produced by the engine to increase the effect of pressure on the brake pedal: *It takes very little pressure to stop a car that has power brakes.*

**power dive**   in aeronautics, a dive of an aircraft speeded up by the power of the engine.

**pow·er–dive** (pou′ər dīv′)   make a POWER DIVE.   *v.*, **-dived** or **-dove, -dived, -div·ing.**

**pow·er·ful** (pou′ər fəl)   having great power or force; mighty; strong: *a powerful man, a powerful medicine, a powerful speech, a powerful nation, a powerful emotion.*   *adj.*

**pow·er·ful·ly** (pou′ər fə lē)   strongly; with power.   *adv.*

**pow·er·house** (pou′ər hous′)   1 a building containing boilers, engines, dynamos, etc. for generating electric power.   2 *Informal.*   a person or group having great power, energy, drive, etc.: *That new teacher is a real powerhouse.*   *n.*

**pow·er·less** (pou′ər lis) without power; helpless: *The mouse was powerless in the cat's claws.* *adj.*

**power loom** a LOOM¹ worked by steam, electricity, water power, etc., not by hand.

**power mower** a lawn mower powered by a motor.

**power of attorney** a written statement giving one person legal power to act for another.

**power plant** 1 a building with machinery for generating power. 2 a motor; engine.

**power play** *Cdn.* in hockey, a special combination of players put on the ice when the opposition is short-handed.

**power politics** international political strategy that uses the threat of superior military or economic power to advance national interests (*used with a singular or plural verb*).

**power saw** a saw powered by a motor.

**power squadron** an organization for promoting safe boating and good seamanship, etc. among operators of powerboats, yachts, etc.

**power station** POWERHOUSE (def. 1).

**power steering** in a motor vehicle, a steering mechanism that uses power from the engine to increase the effect of the force used in turning the steering wheel: *It requires little effort to turn the steering wheel of a car with power steering.*

**pow·wow** (pou′wou′) 1 among North American Indian peoples, a celebration or ceremony, usually featuring feasting and dancing and certain rites, held before an expedition, hunt, council, or conference. 2 the hubbub and noise accompanying such a celebration. 3 a council or conference of or with a North American Indian people. 4 *Informal.* any conference or meeting. 5 hold a powwow. 6 among some North American Indian peoples, a medicine man. 1–4, 6 *n.*, 5 *v.*
☛ *Etym.* From an Algonquian word meaning 'he dreams', originally referring to a 'medicine man' because he was thought to have learned his craft from dreams. The word was later applied by the Algonquians to a meeting or ceremony involving medicine men's rites. 17c.

**pox** (poks) 1 any of several diseases that are characterized by pustules, or pocks (*used especially in compounds*): *chicken pox*. 2 SYPHILIS. *n.*

**pp.** 1 pages. 2 past participle. 3 in music, pianissimo.

**p.p.** past participle.

**P.P.** Parcel Post.

**ppd.** 1 postpaid. 2 prepaid.

**ppr.** or **p.pr.** present participle.

**P.P.S.** or **p.ps.** an abbreviation for Latin *post postscriptum* meaning a second postscript.

**PQ** 1 Province of Quebec. 2 Parti Québécois.

**P.Q.** Province of Quebec.

**pr.** 1 pair. 2 price. 3 present.

**Pr.** praseodymium.

**P.R.** or **PR** public relations.

**prac·ti·ca·bil·i·ty** (prak′tə kə bil′ə tē) the quality of being PRACTICABLE; feasibility. *n.*

**prac·ti·ca·ble** (prak′tə kə bəl) 1 that can be done; capable of being put into practice: *a practicable idea.* 2 that can be used: *a practicable road.* *adj.*
—**prac′ti·ca·bly**, *adv.*

**prac·ti·cal** (prak′tə kəl) 1 having to do with action or practice rather than thought or theory: *Earning a living is a practical matter.* 2 able to be put into practice: *a practical plan.* 3 useful in practice: *His legal knowledge was not very practical when he became a chemist.* 4 having good sense: *a practical person.* 5 engaged in actual practice or work: *A practical farmer runs a farm.* 6 being such in effect; virtual: *So many of our soldiers were killed that our victory was a practical defeat.* *adj.*
—**prac′ti·cal·ness**, *n.*

**prac·ti·cal·i·ty** (prak′tə kal′ə tē) 1 the quality of being PRACTICAL; practical usefulness; practical habit of mind. 2 a PRACTICAL matter: *She finds it hard to face the practicalities of earning a living.* *n., pl.* **prac·ti·cal·i·ties.**

**practical joke** a kind of trick that depends for its effect or humour on a person being put at a disadvantage or embarrassed or abused in some way.

**prac·ti·cal·ly** (prak′ti klē) 1 almost; nearly; virtually: *We are practically home. They practically ran the show.* 2 in a practical way: *reacting very practically to the emergency.* *adv.*

**practical nurse** a nurse whose occupation is to care for the sick, but who has not the hospital training required of a registered nurse.

**prac·tice** (prak′tis) 1 an action done many times over in order to gain skill: *Practice makes perfect.* 2 the skill gained by experience or exercise: *He was out of practice at batting.* 3 the action or process of doing or being something: *Her plan is good in theory, but not in actual practice.* 4 the usual way; custom: *It is the practice at the factory to blow a whistle at noon.* 5 the working at or following of a profession or occupation: *engaged in the practice of law.* 6 the business of a doctor, dentist, or lawyer: *Dr. Adams has sold his practice to a younger doctor.* 7 in law, the established method of conducting legal proceedings. 8 a period set aside for practising: *He went to hockey practice last night.* *n.*
☛ *Usage.* **Practice** is one of the two words (the other is LICENCE) that in Canadian English are usually spelled differently as nouns and verbs. The preferred spelling for the noun is **practice** and for the verb **practise**. For this reason the noun and verb are entered separately in this dictionary.

**prac·tise** or **prac·tice** (prak′tis) 1 do something again and again so as to learn to do it well: *to practise playing the piano.* 2 do as a rule; make a custom of; follow, observe, or use day after day: *to practise moderation. Practise what you preach.* 3 work at or follow as a profession, art, or occupation: *to practise medicine, to practise architecture.* 4 practise a profession, especially law, medicine, or dentistry: *My aunt practises in Thunder Bay.* 5 give training to; drill. 6 take advantage of. *v.*, **prac·tised** or **prac·ticed, prac·tis·ing** or **prac·tic·ing.** —**prac′tis·er** or **prac′tic·er**, *n.*

**prac·tised** or **prac·ticed** (prak′tist) 1 experienced; skilled; expert; proficient: *a practised musician.* 2 acquired or perfected through practice: *a practised skill.* 3 pt. and pp. of PRACTISE. 1, 2 *adj.*, 3 *v.*

**prac·tis·ing** or **prac·tic·ing** (prak′tə sing) 1 actively engaged in a particular profession or career: *a practising lawyer.* 2 ppr. of PRACTISE. 1 *adj.*, 2 *v.*

**prac·ti·tion·er** (prak tish′ə nər) a person engaged in the practice of a profession: *She was a medical practitioner for ten years; later she taught medicine.* *n.*

**prae·tor** (prē′tər *or* prē′tôr) in ancient Rome, a magistrate or judge, ranking next below a consul. *n.*

**prae·to·ri·an** (prē tô′rē ən) **1** of or having to do with a PRAETOR. **2** a man having the rank of a PRAETOR. **3** having to do with or forming the bodyguard of a Roman commander or emperor. **4** a soldier of this bodyguard. 1, 3, *adj.*, 2, 4 *n.*

**prag·mat·ic** (prag mat′ik) **1** of or concerned with practical results or values, not with theories or ideals: *She is a very pragmatic person.* **2** of, or having to do with the philosophy of PRAGMATISM. *adj.*
—**prag·mat′i·cal·ly**, *adv.*

**prag·ma·tism** (prag′mə tiz′əm) **1** the quality or condition of being PRAGMATIC, or practical and matter-of-fact. **2** a philosophy that tests the value and truth of ideas by their practical consequences. *n.*

**prag·ma·tist** (prag′mə tist) a person who believes in PRAGMATISM. *n.*

**prai·rie** (prer′ē) **1** a large area of level or rolling land with grass but very few or no trees. **2 the Prairies,** *pl.* the great, almost treeless, plain that covers much of central and southern Manitoba, Saskatchewan, and Alberta. *n.*

**prairie chicken** **1** a GROUSE found on the Prairies, especially in southern Saskatchewan, but now becoming rare. **2** SHARP-TAILED GROUSE.

**prairie crocus** a small wildflower of the central North American plains; CROCUS (def. 2): *The prairie crocus is the provincial flower of Manitoba.* See CROCUS for picture.

**prairie dog** any of several North American burrowing rodents found especially on the central plains, related to and resembling ground squirrels, but somewhat larger and stouter and having a shorter tail: *Prairie dogs live in colonies often called "towns"; in Canada, they live only in extreme southern Saskatchewan.*
☛ *Etym.* Named for its call, which resembles the bark of a dog.

**prairie lily** a North American wild lily found in dry or wet places on the prairies and in open woods from Quebec to British Columbia and south to New Mexico: *The prairie lily is the provincial flower of Saskatchewan.* See LILY for picture.

**Prairie Provinces** Manitoba, Saskatchewan, and Alberta.

**prairie schooner** a large covered wagon formerly used on the plains of North America, especially by American settlers.

**prairie wolf** COYOTE.

**praise** (prāz) **1** the act of saying that a thing or person is good; words that tell the worth or value of a thing or person: *When he won the race, his friends heaped praise upon him.* **2** express approval or admiration of: *Everyone praised the winning team for its fine play.* **3** worship in words or song: *to praise God.* **4** words or song setting forth the glory and goodness of God. 1, 4 *n.*, 2, 3 *v.*, **praised, prais·ing.** —**prais′er**, *n.*
**damn with faint praise,** praise with so little enthusiasm as to condemn.
**sing the praise** or **praises of,** praise with enthusiasm.

**praise·wor·thy** (prā′zwėr′ᵺē) worthy of praise; deserving approval: *a praiseworthy act.* *adj.*
—**praise′wor′thi·ly,** *adv.* —**praise′wor′thi·ness,** *n.*

hat, āge, fär; let, ēqual, tėrm; it, īce
hot, ōpen, ôrder; oil, out; cup, pu̇t, rüle
əbove, takən, pencəl, lemən, circəs
ch, child; ng, long; sh, ship
th, thin; ᵺ, then; zh, measure

**pra·line** (prä′lēn) a small cake of brown candy made of sugar and nuts, usually pecans or almonds. *n.*

**prance** (prans) **1** spring about on the hind legs: *Horses prance when they feel lively.* **2** ride on a horse doing this. **3** move gaily or proudly; swagger: *The children pranced about in their Halloween costumes.* **4** caper; dance. **5** a prancing. 1–4 *v.*, **pranced, pranc·ing.** 5 *n.*

**prank** (prangk) a piece of mischief; playful trick: *On April Fool's Day people play pranks.* *n.*

**prank·ish** (prang′kish) **1** full of PRANKS; fond of pranks. **2** like a PRANK. *adj.* —**prank′ish·ness,** *n.*

**prank·ster** (prangk′stər) a person who plays PRANKS. *n.*

**pra·se·o·dym·i·um** (prā′zē ō dim′ē əm) a rare metallic element of the same group as cerium. *Symbol:* Pr *n.*

**prate** (prāt) **1** talk a great deal in a foolish way; prattle; chatter. **2** empty or foolish talk. 1 *v.*, **prat·ed, prat·ing.** 2 *n.*

**prat·tle** (prat′əl) **1** talk as a child does; tell freely and carelessly. **2** talk or tell in a foolish way; prate. **3** foolish or childish talk. **4** sound like baby talk; babble. **5** a sound like baby talk; babble: *the prattle of a brook.* 1, 2, 4 *v.*, **prat·tled, prat·tling;** 3, 5 *n.* —**prat′tler,** *n.*

**prawn** (pron) any of several edible shellfish resembling shrimp but larger. *n.*

**pray** (prā) **1** speak to God in worship; enter into spiritual communion with God; offer worship. **2** make earnest request to God or to any other object of worship: *to pray for help, to pray for one's family.* **3** ask earnestly: *They prayed the kidnappers to let them go.* **4** ask earnestly for: *to pray one's forgiveness.* **5** bring or get by praying. **6** please: *Pray come with me.* *v.* —**pray′er,** *n.*
☛ *Hom.* PREY.

**prayer** (prer) **1** an earnest request, especially one made to God. **2** the act of praying: *She was at prayer.* **3** the thing prayed for: *Our prayers came true.* **4** a form of words to be used in praying: *a book of prayers.* **5** a form of worship; religious service consisting mainly of prayers: *They always have morning prayers.* *n.*

**prayer·ful** (prer′fəl) **1** having the custom of praying often; devout. **2** like a prayer; earnest. *adj.*
—**prayer′ful·ly,** *adv.* —**prayer′ful·ness,** *n.*

**prayer rug** a small rug used by Moslems to kneel on when praying.

**prayer shawl** a shawl with a fringe traditionally worn over the head and shoulders by Jewish men for morning prayers.

**praying mantis** MANTIS.

**pre–** a prefix meaning: before in place, time, order, or rank, as in *prepay, preheat, prewar, premolar, pre-eminent.*

**preach** (prēch) **1** speak publicly on a religious subject. **2** deliver a sermon. **3** make known by preaching; proclaim: *to preach the Gospel.* **4** advise or recommend strongly; urge: *The coach was always preaching exercise and* fresh air. **5** give earnest advice: *My older sister is forever preaching about good table manners.* *v.*

**preach·er** (prē′chər) a person who preaches; clergyman; minister. *n.*

**preach·i·fy** (prē′chə fī′) *Informal.* preach or moralize too much. *v.*, **preach·i·fied, preach·i·fy·ing.**

**preach·ing** (prē′ching) **1** what is preached; a sermon. **2** ppr. of PREACH. 1 *n.*, 2 *v.*

**preach·y** (prē′chē) *Informal.* having or showing too great an inclination to preach or moralize: *Don't be so preachy; I know it was a stupid thing to do. The film was quite good, but a little too preachy about ecology.* *adj.*, **preach·i·er, preach·i·est.**

**pre·am·ble** (prē′am′bəl) **1** a preliminary statement; introduction to a speech or a writing: *The reasons for a law and its general purpose are often stated in a preamble.* **2** a preliminary or introductory fact or circumstance. *n.*

**pre·ar·range** (prē′ə rānj′) arrange beforehand: *a prearranged meeting place, a prearranged signal.* *v.*, **pre·ar·ranged, pre·ar·rang·ing.**
—**pre′ar·range′ment,** *n.*

**pre·as·signed** (prē′ə sīnd′) assigned beforehand: *The seats at the conference table were preassigned.* *adj.*

**prec.** preceding.

**Pre·cam·bri·an** or **Pre-Cam·bri·an** (prē′kam′brē ən) **1** of, having to do with, or referring to the earliest era of geological time, including all the time before the Paleozoic era, or the rocks formed during this time: *The Canadian Shield consists of Precambrian rock.* **2 the Precambrian,** the Precambrian era. 1 *adj.*, 2 *n.* See geological time chart in the Appendix.

**pre·car·i·ous** (pri ker′ē əs *or* pri kar′ē əs) not safe or secure; uncertain; dangerous; risky: *A bush pilot leads a precarious life. Her hold on the branch was precarious.* *adj.* —**pre·car′i·ous·ly,** *adv.* —**pre·car′i·ous·ness,** *n.*

**pre·cau·tion** (pri kosh′ən) **1** something done beforehand to prevent harm or to secure good results: *Locking the door of a house is a precaution against theft.* **2** taking care beforehand; foresight: *Proper precaution is necessary when taking a trip by car in winter.* *n.*

**pre·cau·tion·ar·y** (pri kosh′ə ner′ē) of or using PRECAUTION: *precautionary measures against catching a cold.* *adj.*

**pre·cede** (prē sēd′) **1** go or come before: *The rain was preceded by a violent windstorm. A band preceded the first float in the parade.* **2** be higher than in rank or importance: *A major precedes a captain.* *v.*, **pre·ced·ed, pre·ced·ing.**
☞ *Usage.* Do not confuse **precede** 'go or come before' with PROCEED 'move forward': *January precedes February. The year proceeds slowly.*

**prec·e·dence** (pres′ə dəns *or* prē′sə dəns) **1** a coming before in time or order. **2** a higher position or rank; greater importance: *This work takes precedence over all other work.* **3** the right to precede others in ceremonies or social affairs; social superiority: *A duchess takes precedence over a countess.* *n.*

**prec·e·den·cy** (pres′ə dən sē *or* prē sē′dən sē) PRECEDENCE. *n.*, *pl.* **prec·e·den·cies.**

**prec·e·dent** (pres′ə dənt *or* prē′sə dənt *for noun,* prē sē′dənt *or* pres′ə dənt *for adjective*) **1** a case that may serve as an example or reason for a later case: *He refused his assistant's request for time off because he didn't want to set a precedent.* **2** preceding. 1 *n.*, 2 *adj.*

**pre·ced·ing** (prē sē′ding) **1** going or coming before; previous: *the preceding page, the preceding year.* **2** ppr. of PRECEDE. 1 *adj.*, 2 *v.*

**pre·cen·tor** (pri sen′tər) a person who leads and directs the singing of a church choir or congregation. *n.*

**pre·cept** (prē′sept) a general rule of action or behaviour; maxim: *"If at first you don't succeed, try, try again" is a familiar precept.* *n.*

**pre·cep·tor** (pri sep′tər) an instructor; teacher. *n.*

**pre·cinct** (prē′singkt) **1** a boundary or limit. **2** *U.S.* a district within certain boundaries, for administrative or other purposes: *a police precinct.* **3** Usually, **precincts,** *pl.* a space enclosed by walls, a fence, etc.: *the school precincts.* *n.*

**pre·ci·os·i·ty** (presh′ē os′ə tē) too much refinement; affectation. *n.*, *pl.* **pre·ci·os·i·ties.**

**pre·cious** (presh′əs) **1** worth much; valuable: *Gold, platinum, and silver are often called the precious metals.* **2** much loved; dear: *a precious child.* **3** too nice; overrefined; affected. **4** *Informal.* very great; thoroughgoing: *a precious mess.* **5** *Informal.* very: *precious little money.* 1–4 *adj.*, 5 *adv.*
—**pre′cious·ness,** *n.*

**pre·cious·ly** (presh′ə slē) **1** at great cost. **2** in a valuable manner or degree. **3** extremely. **4** with extreme care in matters of detail. *adv.*

**precious metal** a valuable metal such as gold, silver, or platinum.

**precious stone** a jewel; gem: *Diamonds, rubies, and sapphires are precious stones.*

**prec·i·pice** (pres′ə pis) **1** a very steep cliff; almost vertical slope; the face of a cliff. **2** a very dangerous situation; the brink of disaster. *n.*

**pre·cip·i·tance** (pri sip′ə təns) headlong haste; rashness. *n.*

**pre·cip·i·tant** (pri sip′ə tənt) **1** a substance that causes another substance in solution in a liquid to be deposited in solid form; a precipitating agent. **2** PRECIPITATE (defs. 2, 3). 1 *n.*, 2 *adj.* —**pre·cip′i·tant·ly,** *adv.*

**pre·cip·i·tate** (pri sip′ə tāt′ *for verb,* pri sip′ə tāt′ *or* pri sip′ə tit *for adjective and noun*) **1** hasten the beginning of; bring about suddenly: *to precipitate a war.* **2** very hurried; sudden: *A cool breeze caused a precipitate drop in the temperature.* **3** with great haste and force; plunging or rushing; hasty; rash: *precipitate actions.* **4** throw headlong; hurl: *to precipitate a rock down a cliff, to precipitate oneself into a struggle.* **5** a substance, usually crystalline, separated out from a solution as a solid. **6** separate a substance out from a solution as a solid. **7** condense moisture from vapour in the form of rain, dew, etc. **8** be condensed in this way. 1, 4, 6–8 *v.*, **pre·cip·i·tat·ed, pre·cip·i·tat·ing;** 2, 3 *adj.*, 5 *n.*
—**pre·cip′i·tate·ly,** *adv.*

**pre·cip·i·ta·tion** (pri sip′ə tā′shən) **1** the depositing of moisture in the form of rain, dew, or snow. **2** something that is precipitated, such as rain, dew, or snow. **3** the amount that is precipitated. **4** the act or state of precipitating; throwing down or falling headlong. **5** hastening or hurrying. **6** a sudden bringing on: *the precipitation of a war without warning.* **7** unwise or rash speed; sudden haste. **8** the separating out of a substance from a solution as a solid. **9** the substance separated out from a solution as a solid. *n.*

**pre·cip·i·tous** (pri sip′ə təs) **1** like a precipice; very steep: *precipitous cliffs.* **2** hasty; rash: *Running away was a precipitous action.* *adj.* —**pre·cip′i·tous·ness,** *n.*

**pré·cis** (prā′sē) summary. *n., pl.* **pré·cis** (-sēz).

**pre·cise** (pri sīs′) **1** exact; accurate; definite: *The precise sum was $31.28.* **2** careful: *precise handwriting. She is precise in her manners.* **3** strict; scrupulous: *precise orders to be home at six.* *adj.* —**pre·cise′ness,** *n.*

**pre·cise·ly** (pri sīs′lē) in a precise manner; exactly: *Do precisely as the directions say.* *adv.*

**pre·ci·sion** (pri sizh′ən) **1** the quality or state of being precise; exactness: *the precision of a machine. The precision of her calculations was amazing.* **2** the degree of refinement or exactness obtained. **3** designed for or marked by precision: *precision instruments, precision drawing.* *n.*

**pre·clude** (pri klüd′) shut out; make impossible; prevent: *Buying a house now would preclude any possibility of a holiday trip for the next few years.* *v.,* **pre·clud·ed, pre·clud·ing.**

**pre·clu·sion** (pri klü′zhən) precluding or being PRECLUDed. *n.*

**pre·clu·sive** (pri klü′siv) tending or serving to PRECLUDE. *adj.* —**pre·clu′sive·ly,** *adv.*

**pre·co·cious** (pri kō′shəs) **1** developed much earlier than normal in knowledge, skill, etc.: *She was so precocious that she was composing music at the age of six.* **2** of a plant, developing or maturing very early. *adj.* —**pre·co′cious·ly,** *adv.* —**pre·co′cious·ness,** *n.*

**pre·coc·i·ty** (pri kos′ə tē) PRECOCIOUS development; early maturity: *Macaulay's precocity was extraordinary; when he was only four years old, he began to write a history of the world.* *n.*

**pre·con·ceive** (prē′kən sēv′) form an idea or opinion of before having any actual experience or knowledge: *Her first sea voyage didn't fit any of her preconceived notions of what it would be like.* *v.,* **pre·con·ceived, pre·con·ceiv·ing.**

**pre·con·cep·tion** (prē′kən sep′shən) an idea or opinion formed beforehand. *n.*

**pre·con·cert** (prē′kən sėrt′) arrange beforehand: *At a preconcerted signal the police rushed in.* *v.*

**pre·con·di·tion** (prē′kən dish′ən) **1** something that must be fulfilled before something else can come about; prerequisite. **2** prepare or condition in advance. **1** *n.,* **2** *v.*

**pre·cur·sor** (pri kėr′sər) a forerunner: *A severe cold may be the precursor of pneumonia.* *n.*

**pre·cur·so·ry** (pri kėr′sə rē) indicative of something to follow; introductory. *adj.*

**pred.** predicate.

**pre·date** (prē′dāt′) **1** come before in time: *Sonia's teaching career predated her entry into politics.* **2** assign something to a date before its actual date: *She predated her letter to make it look as if she had written it a week earlier.* *v.,* **pre·dat·ed, pre·dat·ing.**

**pred·a·tor** (pred′ə tər) **1** an animal that lives by killing and eating other animals. **2** a person who lives by exploiting or preying on others. *n.*

**pred·a·to·ry** (pred′ə tô′rē) **1** of or inclined to

## precipitous 929 predigest

hat, āge, fär; let, ēqual, tėrm; it, īce
hot, ōpen, ôrder; oil, out; cup, pùt, rüle
əbove, tākən, pencəl, lemən, circəs
ch, child; ng, long; sh, ship
th, thin; ᴛʜ, then; zh, measure

plundering or robbery: *Predatory tramps infested the highways.* **2** living by preying upon other animals: *Hawks and owls are predatory birds.* *adj.*

**pred·e·ces·sor** (prē′də ses′ər *or* pred′ə ses′ər) **1** a person holding a position or office before another: *Elaine was the predecessor of the present supervisor.* **2** something that came before another. *n.*

**pre·des·ti·na·tion** (prē′des tə nā′shən) **1** an ordaining beforehand; destiny; fate. **2** an action of God in deciding beforehand what shall happen. *n.*

**pre·des·tine** (prē des′tən) determine or settle beforehand, especially by predestination; foreordain: *predestined to failure and disappointment, predestined to rule.* *v.,* **pre·des·tined, pre·des·tin·ing.**

**pre·de·ter·mine** (prē′di tėr′mən) **1** determine or decide beforehand: *The time for the meeting was predetermined.* **2** direct or impel beforehand to something. *v.,* **pre·de·ter·mined, pre·de·ter·min·ing.**

**pred·i·ca·ble** (pred′ə kə bəl) that can be predicated or affirmed. *adj.*

**pre·dic·a·ment** (pri dik′ə mənt) an unpleasant, difficult, or dangerous situation: *Kim was in a predicament when she missed the last train home.* *n.*

**pred·i·cate** (pred′ə kit *for noun and adjective,* pred′ə kāt′ *for verb*) **1** in grammar, a word or words expressing what is said about the subject; the part of a sentence or clause that contains the verb. *Examples:* Women **work**. *The committee* **has organized a fund-raising drive**. *The men are* **musicians**. **2** in grammar, belonging to the predicate. In *Horses are strong,* **strong** is a **predicate adjective. 3** found or base a statement, action, etc. on something. **4** declare, assert, or affirm to be real or true: *Most religions predicate life after death.* **5** declare to be an attribute or quality of some person or thing: *We predicate determination of those we admire, and obstinacy of those we dislike.* **1** *n.,* **2** *adj.,* **3–5** *v.,* **pred·i·cat·ed, pred·i·cat·ing.**

**pred·i·ca·tion** (pred′ə kā′shən) predicating; affirming; assertion. *n.*

**pred·i·ca·tive** (pred′ə kā′tiv *or* pri dik′ə tiv) **1** predicating; expressing predication. **2** acting as a PREDICATE. *adj.*

**pred·i·ca·tive·ly** (pred′ə kā′tiv lē *or* pri dik′ə ti vlē) as a PREDICATE. *adv.*

**pre·dict** (pri dikt′) tell beforehand; prophesy: *The weather bureau predicts rain for tomorrow. She predicted that the novel would be a bestseller.* *v.* —**pre·dic′tor,** *n.*

**pre·dict·a·ble** (pri dik′tə bəl) that can be PREDICTed. *adj.* —**pre·dict′a·bly,** *adv.*

**pre·dic·tion** (pri dik′shən) **1** the act of PREDICTing. **2** something PREDICTed; prophecy: *Two newspapers are filled with predictions on the outcome of the federal election.* *n.*

**pre·di·gest** (prē′dī jest′ *or* prē′di jest′) **1** cause food to be partly digested beforehand by a natural or artificial process: *Predigested food is sometimes used for persons who* are ill or whose digestion is impaired. **2** simplify to make easier to use: *a predigested edition of* Gulliver's Travels *for children.* *v.*

**pre·di·ges·tion** (prē′dī jes′chən *or* prē′di jes′chən) partial digestion beforehand. *n.*

**pre·di·lec·tion** (prē′də lek′shən *or* pred′ə lek′shən) a liking; preference: *She had always had a predilection for ornate furniture.* *n.*

**pre·dis·pose** (prē′di spōz′) give an inclination or tendency to; make liable or susceptible (*used with* **to**): *A cold predisposes a person to other diseases.* *v.*, **pre·dis·posed, pre·dis·pos·ing.**

**pre·dis·po·si·tion** (prē′di spə zish′ən) a previous inclination or tendency; susceptibility or liability: *She has a predisposition to look on the dark side of things.* *n.*

**pre·dom·i·nance** (pri dom′ə nəns) the quality or state of being PREDOMINANT: *the predominance of weeds in the deserted garden.* *n.*

**pre·dom·i·nant** (pri dom′ə nənt) **1** having more power, authority, or influence than others; superior: *Which will be the predominant nation in Europe in 50 years?* **2** prevailing; most noticeable or frequent: *Green was the predominant colour in the room.* *adj.* —**pre·dom′i·nant·ly,** *adv.*

**pre·dom·i·nate** (pri dom′ə nāt′) be greater in power, strength, influence, or numbers: *Kindness finally predominated over their decision.* *v.*, **pre·dom·i·nat·ed, pre·dom·i·nat·ing.**

**pre·dom·i·na·tion** (pri dom′ə nā′shən) PREDOMINANCE. *n.*

**pree·mie** (prē′mē) *Informal.* a baby born prematurely. *n.*

**pre-em·i·nence** (prē em′ə nəns) the quality or state of being PRE-EMINENT; superiority: *the pre-eminence of Edison among the inventors of his day.* *n.*

**pre-em·i·nent** (prē em′ə nənt) standing out above all others; superior to others in some quality: *a pre-eminent scientist.* *adj.* **pre-em′i·nent·ly,** *adv.*

**pre-empt** (prē empt′) **1** secure before someone else can; acquire or take possession of beforehand: *The cat had pre-empted the comfortable chair.* **2** take the place of: *The regular programs were pre-empted by the Grey Cup telecast.* *v.*

**pre-emp·tion** (prē emp′shən) PRE-EMPTing or being pre-empted. *n.*

**preen** (prēn) **1** of birds, smooth or arrange the feathers with the beak. **2** arrange or dress up one's hair, clothing, etc. in a fussy, self-satisfied way: *She preened in front of the mirror for fifteen minutes. He's always preening himself.* *v.* **preen oneself on,** show pride and self-satisfaction in an achievement or skill: *He preens himself on his dancing skill.*

**pre-ex·ist** (prē′eg zist′) exist beforehand, or before something else: *Dinosaurs pre-existed elephants.* *v.*

**pre-exist·ence** (prē′eg zis′təns) a previous existence. *n.*

**pre-ex·ist·ent** (prē′eg zis′tənt) existing previously. *adj.*

**pref.** **1** preface. **2** prefix. **3** preferred.

**pre·fab** (prē fab′ *or* prē′fab) *Informal.* a prefabricated structure, especially a building. *n.*

**pre·fab·ri·cate** (prē fab′rə kāt′) **1** make all standardized parts of at a factory, so that construction at the site consists mainly of assembling the various sections: *a prefabricated house.* **2** put together or prepare in advance, especially in an artificial way: *a prefabricated excuse.* *v.*, **pre·fab·ri·cat·ed, pre·fab·ri·cat·ing.** —**pre′fab·ri·ca′tion,** *n.*

**pref·ace** (pref′is) **1** an introduction to a book, writing, or speech: *A preface sometimes explains how a book came to be written.* **2** introduce by written or spoken remarks; give a preface to. **3** be a preface to; begin. **1** *n.*, **2, 3** *v.*, **pref·aced, pref·ac·ing.**

**pref·a·to·ry** (pref′ə tô′rē) of, like, or given as a preface; introductory; preliminary. *adj.*

**pre·fect** (prē′fekt) **1** in ancient Rome, etc., a title of various military and civil officers. **2** the chief administrative official of a department of France. **3** in some schools, a senior student who has some authority over other students; monitor. *n.*

**pre·fec·ture** (prē′fek chər) the office, jurisdiction, territory, or official residence of a PREFECT (defs. 1, 2). *n.*

**pre·fer** (pri fėr′) **1** like better; choose rather: *I will come later, if you prefer. She prefers reading to sewing. I would prefer to go home.* **2** put forward; present or submit: *They decided not to prefer charges against the boy because he had returned the car. She preferred her claim to the inheritance.* *v.*, **pre·ferred, pre·fer·ring.**

**pref·er·a·ble** (pref′ə rə bəl *or* pref′rə bəl) to be preferred; more desirable: *She decided that going along was preferable to staying home alone.* *adj.* —**pref′er·a·bly,** *adv.*

**pref·er·ence** (pref′ə rəns *or* pref′rəns) **1** liking better; the favouring of one above another: *A teacher should not show preference for any one student.* **2** something preferred; first choice: *Her preference in reading is historical novels.* *n.*

**pref·er·en·tial** (pref′ə ren′shəl) of, having to do with, or showing PREFERENCE: *She was given preferential treatment at the hotel because her father had once been the manager.* *adj.* —**pref′er·en′tial·ly,** *adv.*

**pre·fer·ment** (pri fėr′mənt) **1** advancement; promotion: *Captain White seeks preferment in the army.* **2** a position, office, or honour to which a person is advanced: *a sought-after preferment.* **3** the act of putting forward a charge or claim. *n.*

**preferred stock** STOCK (def. 9) that is guaranteed priority over COMMON STOCK in the payment of dividends and, usually, in the distribution of assets.

**pre·fig·u·ra·tion** (prē′fig ə rā′shən *or* prē′fig yə rā′shən) **1** prefiguring or being PREFIGUREd. **2** that in which something is PREFIGUREd; prototype. *n.*

**pre·fig·u·ra·tive** (prē′fig′ə rə tiv *or* prē′fig′yə rə tiv) of, having to do with, or showing by PREFIGURATION. *adj.*

**pre·fig·ure** (prē fig′ər *or* prē fig′yər) **1** show or suggest beforehand by a figure or type. **2** imagine to oneself beforehand; foresee. *v.*, **pre·fig·ured, pre·fig·ur·ing.**

**pre·fix** (prē′fiks *for noun*, prē′fiks *or* prē fiks′ *for verb*) **1** in grammar, a syllable, syllables, or word put at the beginning of a word to change its meaning or to form a new word, as in *pre*paid, *under*line, *un*like. **2** put before: *We prefix "Mr." to a man's name.* **1** *n.*, **2** *v.*

**preg·na·ble** (preg′nə bəl) open to attack; assailable. *adj.*

**preg·nan·cy** (preg′nən sē) the state or condition of being PREGNANT (def. 1). *n., pl.* **preg·nan·cies.**

**preg·nant** (preg′nənt) **1** having an embryo or embryos developing in the uterus; being with child or young. **2** filled; teeming; abounding: *a mind pregnant with ideas, a scheme pregnant with possibilities.* **3** filled with meaning; very significant: *a pregnant pause. Most proverbs are pregnant sayings.* *adj.*

**pre·heat** (prē hēt′) heat beforehand; especially, of an oven, heat to a particular temperature before placing something in it to cook. *v.*

**pre·hen·sile** (pri hen′sīl *or* pri hen′səl) adapted for seizing, grasping, or holding on: *New World monkeys have prehensile tails; Old World monkeys do not.* *adj.*

**pre·his·tor·ic** (prē′hi stôr′ik) of, having to do with, or existing in periods before recorded history: *Fossils and artifacts provide us with information about prehistoric people and animals.* *adj.*

**pre·his·tor·i·cal** (prē′hi stôr′ə kəl) PREHISTORIC. *adj.*

**pre·his·tor·i·cal·ly** (prē′hi stôr′i klē) before recorded history. *adv.*

**pre·judge** (prē juj′) judge beforehand; judge without knowing all the facts. *v.*, **pre·judged, pre·judg·ing.**

**prej·u·dice** (prej′ə dis) **1** an opinion or judgment based on irrelevant considerations or inadequate knowledge, especially an unfavourable opinion or judgment: *a prejudice against doctors.* **2** unreasonable hostility toward a particular person, group, race, nation, etc.: *the battle against prejudice. She was accused of prejudice.* **3** cause prejudice in: *The unpleasant experience prejudiced her against lawyers.* **4** injury or disadvantage resulting from another's action or judgment that ignores one's rights: *They feel that the new bylaw works to the prejudice of apartment dwellers.* **5** injure or damage: *She was careful to say nothing that might prejudice their interests.* **1, 2, 4** *n.*, **3, 5** *v.*, **prej·u·diced, prej·u·dic·ing.**

**prej·u·diced** (prej′ə dist) **1** having or showing a PREJUDICE for or, more often, against a person, group, idea, or thing: *a prejudiced report. She is very prejudiced.* **2** pt. and pp. of PREJUDICE. **1** *adj.*, **2** *v.*

**prej·u·di·cial** (prej′ə dish′əl) causing PREJUDICE or disadvantage; hurtful. *adj.* —**prej·u·di′cial·ly,** *adv.*

**prelim.** preliminary.

**pre·lim·i·nar·y** (pri lim′ə ner′ē) **1** coming before the main business; leading to something more important: *After preliminary remarks by the principal, the school play began.* **2** a preliminary step; something preparatory: *A physical examination is a preliminary to joining the armed forces.* **1** *adj.*, **2** *n., pl.* **pre·lim·i·nar·ies.**

**prel·ude** (prel′yüd *or* prē′lüd) **1** anything serving as an introduction: *Their meeting was a prelude to a long friendship.* Compare with POSTLUDE. **2** be a prelude or introduction to. **3** a piece of music, or part of it, that introduces another piece or part. Compare with POSTLUDE. **4** an independent instrumental composition, usually short. **5** a composition played at the beginning of a church service. **6** introduce with a prelude. **1, 3–5** *n.*, **2, 6** *v.*, **prel·ud·ed, prel·ud·ing.**

**pre·ma·ture** (prē′mə chùr′ *or* prem′ə chùr′) **1** born at

# pregnable 931 premonition

hat, āge, fär; let, ēqual, tèrm; it, īce
hot, ōpen, ôrder; oil, out; cup, pùt, rüle
əbove, takən, pencəl, lemən, circəs
ch, child; ng, long; sh, ship
th, thin; ŦH, then; zh, measure

less than 40 weeks of pregnancy. **2** before the proper time; too soon: *His premature arrival spoiled our plan to surprise him.* *adj.* —**pre′ma·ture·ly,** *adv.*

**pre·med·i·cal** (prē med′ə kəl) preparing for the study of medicine: *a premedical student.* *adj.*

**pre·med·i·tat·ed** (prē med′ə tā′təd) thought out or planned beforehand; characterized by conscious forethought and intent: *It looked more like accidental death than premeditated murder.* *adj.*

**pre·med·i·ta·tion** (prē′med ə tā′shən) previous deliberation or planning. *n.*

**pre·mier** (prē′mēr, prē′myər, *or* pri mēr′) **1** in Canada, the chief executive officer of a provincial government; the head of a provincial cabinet: *The ten premiers are attending a conference with the prime minister in Ottawa.* **2** the chief officer of any government; prime minister: *The term* premier *is sometimes used in the United Kingdom to refer to the prime minister.* **3** first in rank or quality: *a novel of premier importance.* **4** first in time; earliest. **1, 2** *n.*, **3, 4** *adj.*

**pre·mière** *or* **pre·miere** (pri mēr′ *or* prə myer′) **1** the first public performance or showing: *Many dignitaries attended the première of the latest play.* **2** give a first public performance or showing of: *The theatre group is premièring a new play by a Winnipeg playwright.* **3** have a first public performance: *The film is premièring at the festival tonight.* **4** appear for the first time as a star: *She premièred last year in a musical comedy.* **5** the leading actress in a theatrical cast or company. **1, 5** *n.*, **2–4** *v.*, **pre·mièred** *or* **pre·miered, pre·mièr·ing** *or* **pre·mier·ing.**

**prem·ise** (prem′əs *for noun*, pri mīz′ *or* prem′əs *for verb*) **1** in logic, a statement assumed to be true and used to draw a conclusion. Example: Major premise: *Children should go to school.* Minor premise: *He is a child.* Conclusion: *He should go to school.* **2** give as an introduction or explanation; mention beforehand. **3 premises,** *pl.* **a** a house or building with its grounds. **b** in law, things mentioned previously, such as the names of the parties concerned, a description of the property, the price, etc. **c** in law, the property forming the subject of a document. **1, 3** *n.*, **2** *v.*, **pre·mised, pre·mis·ing.**

**pre·mi·um** (prē′mē əm) **1** a reward; prize: *Some magazines give premiums for obtaining new subscriptions.* **2** something more than the ordinary price or wages; an extra payment or charge: *Her contract allows for premiums such as overtime pay. They had to pay a considerable premium to get first-quality goods.* **3** money paid regularly for an insurance policy: *He pays his life insurance premium in two instalments.* **4** the excess value of one form of money over another of the same nominal value. **5** an unusually high value: *The company puts a premium on accuracy of work.* *n.*
**at a premium,** much valued and in demand: *Good housing is at a premium these days.*

**pre·mo·lar** (prē mō′lər) **1** one of the permanent teeth in front of the molars; BICUSPID. **2** having to do with or being the premolars. **1** *n.*, **2** *adj.*

**pre·mo·ni·tion** (prē′mə nish′ən *or* prem′ə nish′ən)

**premonitory** 1 a feeling that something bad is about to happen; foreboding. 2 a forewarning. *n.*
**pre·mon·i·to·ry** (pri mon′ə tô′rē) giving warning beforehand. *adj.*
**pre·na·tal** (prē nā′təl) 1 having to do with or for a woman who is expecting a child: *prenatal classes, prenatal care.* 2 before birth: *a prenatal diagnosis of defects.* *adj.*
**pre·oc·cu·pa·tion** (prē ok′yə pā′shən) preoccupying or being preoccupied; especially, complete absorption of the mind in something. *n.*
**pre·oc·cu·pied** (prē ok′yə pīd′) 1 lost in thought; with thoughts elsewhere: *He stood in the middle of the room, looking about him with a preoccupied air.* 2 pt. and pp. of PREOCCUPY. 1 *adj.*, 2 *v.*
**pre·oc·cu·py** (prē ok′yə pī′) 1 take up all the attention of; engross the mind of: *The question of getting to Vancouver preoccupied her mind.* 2 occupy or take possession of beforehand or before others: *Our favourite seats had been preoccupied.* *v.*, **pre·oc·cu·pied, pre·oc·cu·py·ing.**
**pre·or·dain** (prē′ôr dān′) decide or settle beforehand; foreordain. *v.*
**pre·or·di·na·tion** (prē′ôr də nā′shən) PREORDAINing or being preordained. *n.*
**prep** (prep) *Informal.* preparatory. *adj.*
**prep.** 1 preposition. 2 preparatory.
**pre·paid** (prē pād′) pt. and pp. of PREPAY: *Send this shipment prepaid.* *v.*
**prep·a·ra·tion** (prep′ə rā′shən) 1 a preparing or making ready: *She was studying in preparation for a test.* 2 a state of being prepared; readiness. 3 anything done to get ready: *André made careful preparations for his holidays.* 4 a medicine, food, or other substance made by a special process: *The preparation included alum.* *n.*
**pre·par·a·tive** (pri par′ə tiv *or* pri per′ə tiv) 1 PREPARATORY. 2 something that helps to prepare. 1 *adj.*, 2 *n.*
**pre·par·a·to·ry** (pri par′ə tô′rē *or* pri per′ə tô′rē) of or for preparation; making ready; serving to prepare; introductory: *a short preparatory note. Some jobs require one to take preparatory courses. Preparatory schools fit students for college.* *adj.*
**pre·pare** (pri per′) 1 put together or make from ingredients or parts: *They prepared a delicious meal for us. The witch prepared a magic brew.* 2 make or get ready for some purpose: *to prepare for school, to prepare someone for bad news.* 3 work out the details of; plan: *to prepare an adequate defence.* *v.*, **pre·pared, pre·par·ing.** —**pre·par′er,** *n.*
**pre·par·ed·ness** (pri per′id nis) 1 being prepared; readiness. 2 the state of having adequate military forces and defences to meet threats or outbreaks of war. *n.*
**pre·pay** (prē pā′) pay or pay for in advance: *They prepaid the charges.* *v.*, **pre·paid, pre·pay·ing.** —**pre·pay′ment,** *n.*
**pre·pon·der·ance** (pri pon′də rəns) 1 a greater power, importance, or influence: *the preponderance of good over evil.* 2 a greater number or quantity: *a preponderance of oaks in the woods.* *n.*
**pre·pon·der·ant** (pri pon′də rənt) 1 having greater power, importance, or influence: *Greed is a miser's preponderant characteristic.* 2 having greater number or quantity; being prevalent: *Mixed farms are preponderant in the region.* *adj.* —**pre·pon′der·ant·ly,** *adv.*
**pre·pon·der·ate** (pri pon′də rāt′) be the chief, most important, or most numerous element; predominate: *Oak and maple preponderate in our eastern woods.* *v.*, **pre·pon·der·at·ed, pre·pon·der·at·ing.**
**prep·o·si·tion** (prep′ə zish′ən) in grammar, a word that shows relationships of time, direction, position, etc. between other words. *With, for, by,* and *in* are prepositions in the sentence "A man *with* rugs *for* sale walked *by* our house *in* the morning." *n.*
**prep·o·si·tion·al** (prep′ə zish′ə nəl) having to do with, containing, or having the nature or function of a PREPOSITION: *prepositional usage, a prepositional phrase.* *adj.* —**prep′o·si′tion·al·ly,** *adv.*
**pre·pos·sess** (prē′pə zes′) 1 fill with a favourable feeling or opinion: *We were prepossessed by the girl's modest behaviour.* 2 fill with a feeling or opinion. *v.*
**pre·pos·sess·ing** (prē′pə zes′ing) 1 making a favourable first impression; attractive; pleasing: *prepossessing manners.* 2 ppr. of PREPOSSESS. 1 *adj.*, 2 *v.*
**pre·pos·ses·sion** (prē′pə zesh′ən) a bias; prejudice; favourable feeling or opinion formed beforehand: *A well-written letter applying for a position will create a prepossession in the writer's favour.* *n.*
**pre·pos·ter·ous** (pri pos′tə rəs) contrary to nature, reason, or common sense; absurd; senseless: *It would be preposterous to shovel snow with a teaspoon.* *adj.* —**pre·pos′ter·ous·ly,**
**prep·py** (prep′ē) *Informal.* 1 a student or graduate of a preparatory school. 2 of or like such a student or graduate; tending to be smart and self-opinionated. 1 *n.*, *pl.* **prep·pies;** 2 *adj.*, **prep·pi·er, prep·pi·est.**
**pre·puce** (prē′pyüs) FORESKIN. *n.*
**pre·req·ui·site** (prē rek′wə zit) 1 something that is necessary to achieve an end; something required as a condition before something else can be considered: *A high-school course is the usual prerequisite to college work.* 2 required beforehand. 1 *n.*, 2 *adj.*
**pre·rog·a·tive** (pri rog′ə tiv) 1 a right or privilege that nobody else has: *The government has the prerogative of coining money.* 2 having or exercising a prerogative. 1 *n.*, 2 *adj.*
**pres.** present.
**Pres.** President.
**pres·age** (pres′ij *for noun,* pri sāj′ *for verb*) 1 something that foreshadows a future event; portent; omen: *a sure presage of evil.* 2 give warning of; foreshadow: *Some people think that a circle around the moon presages a storm.* 3 a feeling that something is about to happen; presentiment. 4 of a person, predict or have a presentiment of: *He presaged disaster from the experiment.* 1, 3 *n.*, 2, 4 *v.*, **pre·saged, pre·sag·ing.**
**pre·school** (prē′skül′) 1 of, for, or being the period in a child's life after infancy and before the child begins elementary school: *the preschool years, preschool activities.* 2 of, for, or referring to a child of this age. *adj.*
**pre·school·er** (prē′skü′lər) a child who is too young to go to elementary school; especially, one between the

ages of two and five: *This game is designed for preschoolers.* *n.*

**pre·sci·ence** (prē′shē əns *or* presh′ē əns) a knowledge of things before they exist or happen; foreknowledge; foresight. *n.*

**pre·sci·ent** (prē′shē ənt *or* presh′ē ənt) knowing beforehand; foreseeing. *adj.*

**pre·scribe** (pri skrīb′) **1** lay down as a rule or guide; order; direct: *to do what the law prescribes. There are two prescribed texts for this course.* **2** order as a remedy or treatment: *The doctor prescribed quinine.* **3** give medical advice. *v.,* pre·scribed, pre·scrib·ing.

**pre·scrip·tion** (pri skrip′shən) **1** an order; direction. **2** a written direction or order for preparing and using a medicine: *a prescription for a cough.* Symbol: ℞ **3** medicine that has been prescribed: *Did you use up the whole prescription?* **4** the possession or use of a thing long enough to give a right or title to it. **5** the right or title. *n.*

**pre·scrip·tive** (pri skrip′tiv) **1** that PRESCRIBES. **2** depending or based on legal PRESCRIPTION. **3** established by long use or custom. *adj.*

**pres·ence** (prez′əns) **1** the fact or condition of being present in a place: *I knew of her presence in the other room.* **2** the place where a person is: *The messenger was admitted to the leader's presence.* **3** a formal attendance upon a person of very high rank: *The knight retired from the royal presence.* **4** appearance; bearing: *a man of noble presence.* **5** something present, especially a ghost, spirit, etc. *n.*
**in the presence of,** in the sight or company of: *Mette signed her name in the presence of two witnesses.*

**presence of mind** the ability to think calmly and quickly when taken by surprise. Compare with ABSENCE OF MIND.

**pres·ent**[1] (prez′ənt) **1** being in a proper or expected place; at hand, not absent: *Every member of the class was present.* **2** at this time; being or occurring now: *the present ruler, present prices.* **3** the present time: *At present people need courage.* **4** in grammar, denoting action now going on or a state now existing. *They go* is the present tense; *they went* is the past tense. **5** the present tense or a verb form in that tense. 1, 2, 4 *adj.*, 3, 5 *n.*
**by these presents,** by these words; by this document.

**pre·sent**[2] (pri zent′ *for verb,* prez′ənt *for noun*) **1** give formally: *They presented flowers to the singer after the performance.* **2** make a formal gift to (used with **with**): *The company presented him with a silver tray.* **3** something given; gift: *I got the record player as a birthday present.* **4** bring before the mind; offer for consideration: *He presented reasons for his action.* **5** offer to view or notice: *The new City Hall presents a fine appearance.* **6** bring before the public; perform: *Our school presented a play.* **7** set forth in words: *The speaker presented arguments for her side.* **8** hand or send in: *The grocer presented his bill.* **9** introduce socially: *Ms. Janzen, may I present Mr. Bindon?* **10** bring before a person of high rank: *She was presented to the Governor General.* **11** direct, point, or turn in a particular direction: *The handsome actor presented his profile to the camera.* 1, 2, 4–11 *v.,* 3 *n.*
**present arms,** bring a rifle, etc. to a vertical position in front of the body.

**pre·sent·a·ble** (pri zen′tə bəl) **1** fit to be introduced or go into company; suitable in appearance, dress, manners, etc.: *It took him an hour to make himself presentable again after cleaning the basement.* **2** suitable to be offered or given: *That is a very presentable gift. Make the essay more presentable before you hand it in.* *adj.*
—**pre·sent′a·bly,** *adv.*

**pres·en·ta·tion** (prez′ən tā′shən) **1** the act of giving or delivering: *the presentation of a gift or a speech.* **2** gift. **3** a proposal for consideration. **4** an offering to be seen; showing; exhibition: *the presentation of a play.* **5** a formal introduction, especially to somebody of high rank: *the presentation of a lady to the Queen.* *n.*

**pres·ent–day** (prez′ənt dā′) of the present time: *present-day living standards, present-day attitudes.* *adj.*

**pre·sen·ti·ment** (pri zen′tə mənt) a feeling or impression that something is about to happen; premonition. *n.*
☞ *Usage.* Do not confuse **presentiment** with PRESENTMENT.

**pres·ent·ly** (prez′ən tlē) **1** before long; soon: *The clock will strike presently.* **2** at present; now: *The prime minister is presently in Ottawa.* *adv.*

**pre·sent·ment** (pri zent′mənt) **1** bringing forward; offering to be considered. **2** showing; offering to be seen. **3** a representation on the stage or by a portrait. *n.*
☞ *Usage.* Do not confuse **presentment** with PRESENTMENT.

**present participle** a participle that can be used with an auxiliary verb to show that an action is continuing, or as a modifier of a noun. *Examples: In* They are reading, reading *is the present participle. In* running water, running *is a present participle used as an adjective.*
☞ *Usage.* In modern English the present participle always ends in **-ing**.

**present perfect** **1** a tense that expresses action or a state that is completed at the time of speaking. It is formed in English with the present tense of *have* plus a past participle, as in *They have gone.* **2** a verb form in the present perfect.

**present tense** a tense that expresses time that is now or that is treated as if it were now. *Examples: She reads. The earth is round.*

**pre·serv·a·ble** (pri zėr′və bəl) that can be PRESERVEd. *adj.*

**pres·er·va·tion** (prez′ər vā′shən) preserving or being PRESERVEd: *the preservation of one's health. The artifacts were in an excellent state of preservation.* *n.*

**pre·serv·a·tive** (pri zėr′və tiv) **1** any substance that will prevent decay or injury: *Paint is a preservative for wood surfaces. Salt is a preservative for meat.* **2** that preserves. 1 *n.,* 2 *adj.*

**pre·serve** (pri zėrv′) **1** keep from harm or change; keep safe; protect. **2** keep up; maintain. **3** keep from spoiling: *Ice helps to preserve food.* **4** prepare food to keep it from spoiling: *Boiling with sugar, salting, smoking, and pickling are different ways of preserving food.* **5** an area or region where wild animals, fish, or trees and plants are protected. **6** Usually, **preserves**, *pl.* fruit cooked with sugar and sealed from the air: *plum preserves.* 1–4 *v.*, **pre·served, pre·serv·ing;** 5, 6 *n.* **—pre·ser′ver,** *n.*

**pre·side** (pri zīd′) **1** hold the place of authority; have charge of a meeting: *Our principal will preside at our election of school officers.* **2** have authority; have control: *The manager presides over the business of the store.* *v.*, **pre·sid·ed, pre·sid·ing.**

**pres·i·den·cy** (prez′ə dən sē) **1** the office of president: *Helen was elected to the presidency of the Athletic Club.* **2** the time during which a president is in office: *Her presidency of the club lasted two years.* **3 Presidency,** the office or time of office of a President of the United States. *n., pl.* **pres·i·den·cies.**

**pres·i·dent** (prez′ə dənt) **1** the chief officer of a company, university, society, club, etc. **2** Often, **President,** the highest executive officer of a republic. *n.*

**pres·i·dent–e·lect** (prez′ə dən ti lekt′) a president who has been elected but has not yet taken office. *n.*

**pres·i·den·tial** (prez′ə den′shəl) of, having to do with, or belonging to a president or presidency: *a presidential election, a presidential candidate.* *adj.* **—pres′i·den′tial·ly,** *adv.*

**pre·sid·i·um** (pri sid′ē əm) a permanent executive committee at a high level of government in Communist countries. *n.*

**press¹** (pres) **1** use force or weight steadily against; push with steady force: *Press the button to ring the bell.* **2** squeeze; squeeze out: *Press all the juice from the oranges.* **3** use force steadily. **4** clasp; hug: *Mother pressed the baby to her.* **5** make smooth; flatten: *to press clothes with an iron.* **6** put a crease in: *My father pressed my trousers.* **7** a crease. **8** a pressing; pressure; push: *the press of ambition. The press of many duties keeps me busy.* **9** a pressed condition. **10** any of various machines for exerting pressure. **11** a machine for printing; printing press. **12** an establishment for printing books, etc. **13** the process or art of printing. **14** newspapers, magazines, and the people who work for them: *Our school picnic was reported by the press.* **15** a notice given in newspapers or magazines. **16** push forward; keep pushing: *The boy pressed on in spite of the wind.* **17** move by pushing steadily up, down, against, etc. **18** urge onward; cause to hurry. **19** a crowd or throng: *The little boy was lost in the press.* **20** a pressing forward or together; crowding. **21** urge a person; keep asking; entreat: *Because it was so stormy, we pressed our guest to stay all night.* **22** lay stress upon; insist on. **23** constrain; compel; force: *The government pressed people into its service.* **24** urge for acceptance. **25** harass; oppress; trouble. **26** weigh heavily upon the mind, a person, etc. **27** demand prompt action; be urgent. **28** urgency; hurry. **29** a cupboard for clothes, books, etc. 1–6, 16–18, 21–27 *v.*, 7–15, 19, 20, 28, 29 *n.* **go to press,** begin to be printed: *The newspaper goes to press at midnight.*

**press²** (pres) **1** force into service, usually naval or military. **2** an impressment into service, usually naval or military. **3** an order for such impressment. **4** seize and use. 1, 4 *v.*, 2, 3 *n.*

**press agent** an AGENT in charge of publicity for a person, organization, etc.

**press gang** in former times, a group of men whose job it was to obtain men, often by force, for service in the navy or army.

**press·ing** (pres′ing) **1** requiring immediate action or attention; urgent. **2** the act of creasing or pressing with an iron: *That dress needs a good pressing.* **3** ppr. of PRESS. 1 *adj.*, 2 *n.*, 3 *v.* **—press′ing·ly,** *adv.*

**press·man** (pres′mən) a person who operates or has charge of a PRINTING PRESS. *n., pl.* **press·men** (-mən).

**pres·sure** (presh′ər) **1** the continued action of a weight or force: *The pressure of the wind filled the sails of the boat.* **2** the force per unit of area: *The tires of a 3-speed bicycle need a pressure of about 300 kPa.* **3** a state of trouble or strain: *the pressure of poverty.* **4** a compelling force or influence: *Pressure was brought to bear on Sif to make her do better work.* **5** force or urge by exerting pressure: *The salesman tried to pressure my mother into buying the car.* **6** the need for prompt or decisive action; urgency: *the pressure of business.* **7** electromotive force. **8** ATMOSPHERIC PRESSURE. 1–4, 6–8 *n.*, 5 *v.*, **pres·sured, pres·sur·ing.**

**pressure cooker** an airtight apparatus for cooking with steam under pressure.

**pressure group** any business, professional, or labour group that attempts to further its interests in the federal or provincial legislatures or elsewhere.

**pres·sur·ize** (presh′ə rīz′) keep the ATMOSPHERIC PRESSURE inside the cabin of an aircraft at a normal level in spite of the altitude. *v.*, **pres·sur·ized, pres·sur·iz·ing.**

**press·work** (pres′wėrk′) **1** the working or management of a PRINTING PRESS. **2** the work done by a PRINTING PRESS. *n.*

**pres·ti·dig·i·ta·tion** (pres′tə dij′ə tā′shən) SLEIGHT OF HAND. *n.*

**pres·ti·dig·i·ta·tor** (pres′tə dij′ə tā′tər) a person skilled in SLEIGHT OF HAND; conjurer. *n.*

**pres·tige** (pres tēzh′ *or* pres tēj′) reputation, influence, or distinction based on what is known of one's abilities, achievements, opportunities, associations, etc.: *His success in the courts gave him great prestige as a lawyer.* *n.*

**pres·to** (pres′tō) **1** quickly. **2** quick. **3** a quick part in a piece of music. 1 *adv.*, 2 *adj.*, 3 *n., pl.* **pres·tos.**

**pre–stressed concrete** (prē′strest′) concrete that has been cast around steel cables which are under tension. The tension of the cables compresses the concrete, thus increasing its strength. The cables can also be bent to exert force in any direction in order to counteract the effect of the pressure of a load on the concrete.

**pre·sum·a·ble** (pri zü′mə bəl *or* pri zyü′mə bəl) that can be presumed or taken for granted; probable; likely: *the presumable time of their arrival.* *adj.* **—pre·sum′a·bly,** *adv.*

**pre·sume** (pri züm′ *or* pri zyüm′) **1** take for granted without proving; suppose: *The law presumes innocence until guilt is proved.* **2** take upon oneself; venture; dare: *May I presume to tell you what to do?* **3** take an unfair advantage (*used with* **on** *or* **upon**): *Don't presume on her good nature by borrowing from her every week.* *v.*, **pre·sumed, pre·sum·ing.**

☛ *Syn.* **Presume, ASSUME. Presume** implies that something is true because there is no evidence against it. **Assume** implies that something is accepted simply as a basis for an action or idea, without evidence for or against.

**pre·sum·ed·ly** (pri zü′mi dlē or pri zyü′mi dlē) as is or may be supposed. *adv.*

**pre·sump·tion** (pri zump′shən) **1** the act of presuming. **2** something taken for granted; a conclusion based on good evidence: *Since he had the stolen jewels, the presumption was that he was the thief.* **3** a cause or reason for presuming; probability. **4** unpleasant boldness: *It is presumption to go to a party when one has not been invited.* *n.*

**pre·sump·tive** (pri zump′tiv) **1** based on likelihood; presumed. **2** giving ground for presumption or belief: *The man's running away was regarded as presumptive evidence of his guilt.* *adj.*

**pre·sump·tive·ly** (pri zump′ti vlē) by PRESUMPTION; presumably. *adv.*

**pre·sump·tu·ous** (pri zump′chü əs) acting without permission or right; too bold; forward. *adj.* —**pre·sump′tu·ous·ly,** *adv.* —**pre·sump′tu·ous·ness,** *n.*

**pre·sup·pose** (prē′sə pōz′) **1** take for granted in advance; assume beforehand: *Let us presuppose that she wants more money.* **2** require as a necessary condition; imply: *A fight presupposes fighters.* *v.,* **pre·sup·posed, pre·sup·pos·ing.**

**pre·sup·po·si·tion** (prē′sup ə zish′ən) **1** a presupposing. **2** the thing PRESUPPOSEd: *The detective acted upon the presupposition that the thief knew the value of the jewels.* *n.*

**pret.** preterite.

**pre·tence** (pri tens′ or prē′tens) **1** a false appearance: *Under pretence of picking up the handkerchief, she took the money.* **2** a false claim: *The girl made a pretence of knowing the answer.* **3** a claim. **4** a pretending; make-believe: *His anger was all pretence.* **5** showing off; display: *Her manner is free from pretence.* **6** anything done to show off. *n.* Also, **pretense.**

**pre·tend** (pri tend′) **1** make believe. **2** claim falsely: *She pretended to like the meal so she wouldn't offend the hostess.* **3** claim falsely to have: *She pretended illness.* **4** claim: *I don't pretend to be a musician.* **5** lay claim without just right: *James Stuart pretended to the English throne.* **6** venture; attempt; presume: *I cannot pretend to judge between them.* *v.*

**pre·tend·ed** (pri ten′did) **1** claimed falsely; asserted falsely. **2** pt. and pp. of PRETEND. **1** *adj.,* **2** *v.* —**pre·tend′ed·ly,** *adv.*

**pre·tend·er** (pri ten′dər) **1** a person who pretends. **2** a person who makes claims to a throne without just right. *n.*

**pre·tense** (pri tens′ or prē′tens) See PRETENCE. *n.*

**pre·ten·sion** (pri ten′shən) **1** a claim: *The young prince has pretensions to the throne.* **2** a putting forward of a claim. **3** the practice of doing things for show or to make a fine impression; showy display: *People were often annoyed by her pretensions.* *n.*

**pre·ten·tious** (pri ten′shəs) **1** making claims to excellence or importance: *a pretentious person, book, or speech.* **2** doing things for show or to make a fine appearance; showy: *a pretentious style of entertaining guests.* *adj.* —**pre·ten′tious·ly,** *adv.* —**pre·ten′tious·ness,** *n.*

**pret·er·ite** or **pret·er·it** (pret′ə rit) **1** a verb form that expresses occurrence in the past; past tense. *Obeyed* is the preterite of *obey; spoke,* of *speak;* and *saw,* of *see.* **2** expressing past time. **1** *n.,* **2** *adj.*

**pre·ter·nat·u·ral** (prē′tər nach′ə rəl or prē′tər nach′rəl)

hat, āge, fär; let, ēqual, tėrm; it, īce
hot, ōpen, ôrder; oil, out; cup, pút, rüle
əbove, takən, pencəl, lemən, circəs
ch, child; ng, long; sh, ship
th, thin; ᴛʜ, then; zh, measure

**1** out of the ordinary course of nature; abnormal. **2** due to something above or beyond nature; supernatural. *adj.* —**pre′ter·nat′u·ral·ly,** *adv.*

**pre-test** (prē′test) a test taken before instruction, to determine the existing level of knowledge. Compare with POST-TEST. *n.*

**pre·text** (prē′tekst) a false reason concealing the real reason; pretence; excuse: *He used his sore finger as a pretext for not going to school.* *n.*

**pret·ti·fy** (prit′ə fī′) make pretty. *v.,* **pret·ti·fied, pret·ti·fy·ing.**

**pret·ty** (prit′ē) **1** attractive or pleasing: *a pretty face, a pretty dress, a pretty tune.* **2** not at all pleasing: *a pretty mess.* **3** too dainty or delicate. **4** a pretty person or thing. **5** *Informal.* considerable in amount or extent. **6** fairly; rather: *It is pretty late.* 1–3, 5 *adj.,* **pret·ti·er, pret·ti·est;** 4 *n., pl.* **pret·ties;** 6 *adv.* —**pret′ti·ly,** *adv.* —**pret′ti·ness,** *n.*

**sitting pretty,** *Informal.* well off; in a good position.

**pret·zel** (pret′səl) a hard biscuit, usually made in the shape of a loose knot and salted on the outside. *n.*
☛ *Etym.* Through German *Brezel* from Med. L *brachiatellum,* a word for such a biscuit meaning, literally, something in the shape of crossed arms. The Latin word was formed from *brachium* 'arm'.

**pre·vail** (pri vāl′) **1** exist in many places; be in general use: *That custom still prevails.* **2** be the most usual or strongest: *Sadness prevailed in our minds.* **3** be the stronger; win the victory; succeed: *The knights prevailed against their foe.* **4** be effective. *v.*

**prevail on, upon,** or **with,** persuade: *Can't I prevail upon you to stay for dinner?*

**pre·vail·ing** (pri vā′ling) **1** that prevails; having superior force or influence; victorious. **2** in general use; most common: *a prevailing style.* **3** ppr. of PREVAIL. 1, 2 *adj.,* 3 *v.* —**pre·vail′ing·ly,** *adv.*

**prev·a·lence** (prev′ə ləns) widespread occurrence; general use: *the prevalence of complaints about the weather.* *n.*

**prev·a·lent** (prev′ə lənt) widespread; general; common: *Colds are prevalent in the winter.* *adj.*

**pre·var·i·cate** (pri var′ə kāt′ or pri ver′ə kāt′) turn aside from the truth in speech or act; lie. *v.,* **pre·var·i·cat·ed, pre·var·i·cat·ing.**

**pre·var·i·ca·tion** (pri var′ə kā′shən or pri ver′ə kā′shən) the act of prevaricating; a departure from the truth; a lie. *n.*

**pre·var·i·ca·tor** (pri var′ə kā′tər or pri ver′ə kā′tər) a person who turns aside from the truth in speech or action; liar. *n.*

**pre·vent** (pri vent′) **1** keep (*from*): *Illness prevented him from doing his work.* **2** keep from happening: *Rain prevented the game.* **3** hinder: *I'll meet you if nothing prevents.* *v.* —**pre·vent′er,** *n.*

**pre·vent·a·ble** (pri ven′tə bəl) that can be prevented. *adj.* Also, **preventible.**

**pre·ven·ta·tive** (pri ven′tə tiv) PREVENTIVE. *adj., n.*

**pre·vent·i·ble** (pri ven′tə bəl) PREVENTABLE. *adj.*

**pre·ven·tion** (pri ven′shən) 1 preventing: *the prevention of fire.* 2 something that prevents. *n.*

**pre·ven·tive** (pri ven′tiv) 1 that prevents: *preventive measures against disease.* 2 something that prevents: *Vaccination is a preventive against polio.* 1 *adj.*, 2 *n.*

**pre·view** (prē′vyü) 1 a previous view, inspection, survey, etc. 2 view beforehand. 3 an advance showing of scenes from a motion picture, play, television program, etc. 1, 3 *n.*, 2 *v.*

**pre·vi·ous** (prē′vē əs) 1 coming or going before; that came before; earlier: *She did better in the previous lesson.* 2 *Informal.* quick; hasty; premature: *Don't be too previous about refusing.* *adj.*
**previous to,** before: *Previous to her departure she gave a party.*

**pre·vi·ous·ly** (prē′vē ə slē) at a PREVIOUS time: *I had not met him previously.* *adv.*

**pre·vi·sion** (prē vizh′ən) 1 foresight; foreknowledge. 2 a prophetic vision or perception: *Some prevision warned the explorer of trouble.* *n.*

**pre·war** (prē′wôr′) before the war: *Prewar prices seem incredibly low today.* *adj.*

**prey** (prā) 1 an animal hunted or seized for food, especially by another animal: *Mice and birds are the prey of cats.* 2 a person or thing injured; victim: *to be a prey to fear or disease.* *n.*
**birds of prey** and **beasts of prey,** birds and animals, such as hawks and lions, that hunt and kill other animals for food.
**prey on** or **upon,** a hunt or kill for food: *Cats prey on mice.* b be a strain upon; injure; irritate: *Worry about her many debts preys upon her mind.* c rob; plunder.
☞ Hom. PRAY.

**price** (prīs) 1 the amount for which a thing is sold or can be bought; the cost to the buyer: *The price of these gloves is $20.98.* 2 put a price on; set the price of. 3 *Informal.* ask the price of; find out the price of: *to price a rug.* 4 a reward offered for the capture of a person alive or dead: *Every member of the gang has a price on his head.* 5 what must be given, done, undergone, etc. to obtain a thing: *We paid a heavy price for the victory, for we lost ten thousand soldiers.* 6 value; worth. 1, 4–6 *n.*, 2, 3 *v.*, **priced, pric·ing.**
**at any price,** at any cost, no matter how great: *She wanted to win at any price.*
**beyond** or **without price,** so valuable that it cannot be bought or be given a value in money.

**price·less** (prī′slis) beyond price; extremely valuable: *a priceless painting.* *adj.* —**price′less·ness,** *n.*

**prick** (prik) 1 a sharp point. 2 a little hole or mark made by a sharp point. 3 make a little hole in with a sharp point: *I pricked the map with a pin to show our route.* 4 mark with a sharp point. 5 a pricking. 6 a sharp pain. 7 cause sharp pain to: *The cat pricked me with its claws.* 8 cause or feel a sharp pain. 1, 2, 5, 6 *n.*, 3, 4, 7, 8 *v.* —**prick′er,** *n.*
**kick against the pricks,** make useless resistance that only hurts oneself.
**prick up,** point upward.
**prick up the ears,** a point the ears upward: *The dog pricked up its ears.* b give sudden attention; listen carefully: *The boy pricked up his ears when the teacher started talking about a trip.*

**prick·le** (prik′əl) 1 a small, sharp point; thorn; spine. 2 feel a prickly or smarting sensation: *Her skin prickled when she saw the big snake.* 3 such a sensation. 4 cause such a sensation in. 1, 3 *n.*, 2, 4 *v.* **prick·led, prick·ling.**

**prick·ly** (prik′lē) 1 having many sharp points like thorns: *a prickly rosebush, the prickly porcupine.* 2 sharp and stinging; itching: *a prickly feeling. Heat sometimes causes a prickly rash on the skin.* 3 hard to deal with; likely to raise problems, controversy, etc.: *a prickly question.* 4 quick to take offence; easily angered: *He is a prickly individual.* *adj.*, **prick·li·er, prick·li·est.** —**prick′li·ness,** *n.*

**prickly heat** a red itching rash on the skin caused by inflammation of the sweat glands.

**prickly pear** 1 a pear-shaped, edible fruit of a certain kind of cactus. 2 the plant that it grows on.

**prickly rose** a common North American wild rose found along roadsides, on grassy slopes, and in clearings from Quebec to Alaska and south to Colorado, having large pink flowers and leaves usually consisting of five leaflets. See ROSE for picture.

**pride** (prīd) 1 a high opinion of one's own worth or possessions: *Pride in our city should make us help to keep it clean.* 2 pleasure or satisfaction in something concerned with oneself: *take pride in a hard job well done.* 3 something that one is proud of: *Her youngest child is her great pride.* 4 too high an opinion of oneself. 5 acting as if better than others; scorn of others. 6 the best part; most flourishing period: *in the pride of manhood.* 7 a group or company of lions. *n.*
**pride oneself on,** be proud about; indulge in pride about: *He prides himself on his mathematical ability.*

**pride·ful** (prīd′fəl) PROUD. *adj.* —**pride′ful·ly,** *adv.*

**pries** (prīz) pl. of PRY.
☞ Hom. PRIZE.

**priest** (prēst) 1 a special servant of a god: *a priest of Apollo.* 2 a clergyman or minister of certain Christian churches. 3 a clergyman authorized to administer the sacraments and pronounce absolution. 4 a minister of any religion: *a Buddhist priest.* *n.*

**priest·ess** (prē′stis) a woman who serves at an altar or in sacred rites: *a priestess of the goddess Diana.* *n.*

**priest·hood** (prēst′hùd) 1 the position or rank of PRIEST: *He was admitted to the priesthood.* 2 PRIESTS as a group: *the priesthood of Spain.* *n.*

**priest·ly** (prēs′tlē) 1 of or having to do with a PRIEST: *priestly duties.* 2 like a priest; suitable to a PRIEST. *adj.*, **priest·li·er, priest·li·est.**

**prig** (prig) someone who is smug and thinks he or she is a better person than others. *n.*

**prig·ger·y** (prig′ə rē) the conduct or character of a PRIG. *n., pl.* **prig·ger·ies.**

**prig·gish** (prig′ish) too particular about doing right in things that show outwardly; priding oneself on being better than others. *adj.* —**prig′gish·ness,** *n.*

**prim** (prim) stiffly precise, neat, proper, or formal: *a prim appearance.* *adj.*, **prim·mer, prim·mest.** —**prim′ly,** *adv.* —**prim′ness,** *n.*

**pri·ma·cy** (prī′mə sē) 1 the condition of being first in order, rank, importance, etc. 2 the position or rank of a church PRIMATE.   **3** in the Roman Catholic Church, the supreme power of the Pope.   *n., pl.* **pri·ma·cies.**

**pri·ma don·na** (prē′mə don′ə)   the principal woman singer in an opera.   *pl.* **pri·ma don·nas.**

**pri·ma fa·ci·e** (prī′mə fā′shē ē *or* prī′mə fā′shē) *Latin.* at first view; before investigation.

**pri·mal** (prī′məl)   **1** of early times; first; primeval. **2** chief; fundamental.   *adj.* —**pri′mal·ly,** *adv.*

**pri·ma·ri·ly** (prī′mer′ə lē *or* prī mer′ə lē)   **1** chiefly; principally: *Napoleon was primarily a general.*   **2** at first; originally.   *adv.*

**pri·ma·ry** (prī′mer′ē *or* prī′mə rē)   **1** first in time; first in order.   **2** anything that is first in order, rank, or importance.   **3** from which others have come; original; fundamental.   **4** a PRIMARY COLOUR.   **5** first in importance; chief: *The primary reason for the party is to celebrate her birthday.*   **6** *U.S.*   a meeting or gathering of the voters of a political party in an election district to choose candidates for office: *Primaries are held before the regular election.*   **7** noting or having to do with the inducing circuit, coil, or current in an induction coil or the like.   **8** a primary coil or circuit.   **1**, **3**, **5**, **7** *adj.*, **2**, **4**, **6**, **8** *n., pl.* **pri·mar·ies.**

**primary accent**   PRIMARY STRESS.

**primary colour** or **color**   one of three colours that can be mixed together to make any other colour: *Red, yellow, and blue are the primary colours in pigments; in the spectrum, they are red, green, and blue.*

**primary election**   *U.S.*   an election to choose candidates for office from a certain political party.

**primary school**   the first three or four grades of the elementary school.

**primary stress**   **1** the strongest stress or accent in the pronunciation of a word. In *tel′e·phone′* there is primary stress on the first syllable and secondary stress on the third syllable.   **2** the mark (′) used to show where this stress falls.

**pri·mate** (prī′mit *or* prī′māt)   **1** an archbishop or bishop ranking above all other bishops in a country or church province.   **2** any of the highest order of mammals, including human beings, apes, and monkeys.   *n.*

**prime**[1] (prīm)   **1** first in rank; chief: *Her prime object was to lower the tax rate.*   **2** first in time or order; fundamental: *the prime causes of war.*   **3** first in quality; first-rate; excellent: *prime ribs of beef.*   **4** the best time; best condition: *A man of forty is in the prime of life.*   **5** the best part.   **6** the first part; beginning.   **7** springtime.   **8** early manhood or womanhood; youth. **9** that cannot be divided without a remainder by any whole number except itself and 1: *7, 11, and 13 are prime numbers.*   **10** having no common divisor but 1: *2 is prime to 7.*   **11** a PRIME NUMBER.   **12** one of the sixty minutes in a degree.   **13** the mark (′) indicating such a part. **1–3**, **9**, **10** *adj.*, **4–8**, **11–13** *n.* —**prime′ness,** *n.*

**prime**[2] (prīm)   **1** prepare by putting something in or on. **2** supply a gun with powder.   **3** prime a firearm. **4** cover a surface with a first coat of paint or oil so that the finishing coat of paint will not soak in.   **5** equip a person with information, words, etc.   **6** pour water into a pump to start action.   *v.*, **primed, prim·ing.**

**prime meridian**   the meridian from which the longitude east and west is measured: *The prime meridian passes through Greenwich, England, and its longitude is 0°.*   See LATITUDE for picture.

hat, āge, fär; let, ēqual, tėrm; it, īce
hot, ōpen, ôrder; oil, out; cup, pút, rüle
әbove, takәn, pencәl, lemәn, circәs
ch, child; ng, long; sh, ship
th, thin; ŦH, then; zh, measure

**prime minister**   the chief minister in certain governments; the head of the cabinet: *The prime minister of Canada is the first minister of the federal government at Ottawa.*

**prime number**   a number not exactly divisible by any whole number other than itself and 1; prime: *2, 3, 5, 7, and 11 are prime numbers; 4, 6, and 9 are composite numbers.*

**prim·er**[1] (prīm′ər)   **1** a first book in reading.   **2** a beginner's book: *a primer of chemistry.*   *n.*

**prim·er**[2] (prīm′ər)   **1** a person or thing that PRIMES[2]. **2** a cap or cylinder containing a little gunpowder, used for firing a charge of dynamite, etc.   **3** a first coat of paint, etc.   *n.*

**prime time**   in radio and television, the period of the day when the largest audience can be expected, usually the early evening hours.

**pri·me·val** (prī mē′vәl)   **1** of or having to do with the earliest time: *In its primeval state the earth was without any form of life.*   **2** ancient: *primeval forests untouched by the axe.*   *adj.* —**pri·me′val·ly,** *adv.*

**prim·ing** (prī′ming)   **1** powder or other material used to set fire to an explosive.   **2** a first coat of paint, sizing, etc.   **3** ppr. of PRIME[2].   **1**, **2** *n.*, **3** *v.*

**prim·i·tive** (prim′ә tiv)   **1** of early times; of long ago: *Primitive people often lived in caves.*   **2** first of the kind. **3** very simple; such as people had early in human history; crude: *A primitive way of making fire is by rubbing two sticks together.*   **4** original; primary.   **5** an artist belonging to an early period, especially before the Renaissance.   **6** an artist who imitates early painters, or who paints with directness and simplicity.   **7** a picture by such an artist.   **8** old-fashioned: *The farmer drove a primitive buggy.*   **1–4**, **8** *adj.*, **5–7** *n.* —**prim′i·tive·ly,** *adv.*

**pri·mo·gen·i·tor** (prī′mō jen′ə tər)   **1** an ancestor; forefather.   **2** the earliest ancestor.   *n.*

**pri·mo·gen·i·ture** (prī′mō jen′ə chər *or* prī′mō jen′ə chür′)   **1** the state, condition, or fact of being the first-born of the children of the same parents: *Primogeniture grants certain rights.*   **2** in law, the right or principle of inheritance or succession by the first-born, especially the inheritance of a family estate by the eldest son.   *n.*

**pri·mor·di·al** (prī môr′dē əl)   **1** existing at the very beginning; primitive.   **2** original; elementary.   *adj.*

**primp** (primp)   dress oneself or arrange one's hair or clothing in a fussy or careful way, to make oneself look smart or showy.   *v.*

**prim·rose** (prim′rōz)   **1** any of a closely related group of perennial plants having large leaves and showy flowers of many different colours: *Primroses are very popular garden plants.*   **2** the flower of any of these plants. **3** referring to a family of plants found mainly in the Northern Hemisphere, having leaves that grow from the base of the plant and flowers growing in clusters: *The primrose family includes the primroses, cyclamens, and* *loosestrife.* **4** pale yellow, the colour of the common European primrose. 1, 2, 4 *n.*, 3, 4 *adj.*

**primrose path** a pleasant way; path of pleasure.

**prin.** **1** principally. **2** principle.

**prince** (prins) **1** a male member of a royal family; especially, in the United Kingdom, a son or grandson of a king or queen. **2** sovereign. **3** a ruler of a small state subordinate to a king or emperor. **4** in certain countries, a high-ranking member of the nobility. **5** the greatest or best of a group; chief: *a merchant prince, a prince of artists. n.*

**prince consort** a prince who is the husband of a queen or empress ruling in her own right.

**prince·dom** (prins′dəm) **1** the territory ruled by a prince. **2** the position, rank, or dignity of a prince. *n.*

**Prince Edward Islander** a native or long-term resident of Prince Edward Island.

**prince·ling** (prin′sling) a young, little, or petty prince. *n.*

**prince·ly** (prin′slē) **1** of a prince or his rank; royal. **2** like a prince; noble. **3** fit for a prince; magnificent: *He earns a princely salary.* *adj.* **prince·li·er, prince·li·est.** —**prince′li·ness,** *n.*

**prince of the blood** a prince of a royal family.

**Prince of Wales** in the United Kingdom, a title conferred on the eldest son, or heir apparent, of the sovereign: *Prince Charles was named Prince of Wales in 1956.*

**prince royal** the oldest son of a king or queen.

**prin·cess** (prin′sis *or* prin′ses) **1** a daughter of a king or queen or of a king's or queen's son. **2** the wife or widow of a prince. **3** a woman having the same rank as a prince. *n.*

**princess royal** the oldest daughter of a king or queen.

**prin·ci·pal** (prin′sə pəl) **1** most important; main; chief: *St. John's is the principal city of Newfoundland.* **2** a chief person; one who gives orders. **3** the head, or one of the heads, of a school, college, etc. **4** a sum of money on which interest is paid. **5** the money or property from which income is received. **6** a person who hires another person to act for him or her: *Ms. Olu does the business of renting the houses for Mr. Bauer, her principal.* **7** a person directly responsible for a crime. **8** a person responsible for the payment of a debt that another person has endorsed. 1 *adj.*, 2–8 *n.*
☛ *Hom.* PRINCIPLE.
☛ *Usage.* Do not confuse **principal** with PRINCIPLE. **Principal** means 'chief, chief person' and can be a noun or an adjective. **Principle** means 'a basic fact, rule, belief, or method' and is always a noun.

**prin·ci·pal·i·ty** (prin′sə pal′ə tē) **1** a small state or country ruled by a prince. **2** a country from which a prince gets his title. **3** a supreme power. *n., pl.* **prin·ci·pal·i·ties.**

**prin·ci·pal·ly** (prin′sə plē *or* prin′sə pə lē) for the most part; above all; chiefly. *adv.*

**principal parts** the main parts of a verb, from which the rest can be derived. In English the principal parts are the present infinitive, preterite, and past participle.

Examples: *go, went, gone; do, did, done; drive, drove, driven; push, pushed, pushed.*

**prin·ci·pal·ship** (prin′sə pəl ship′) the position or office of a PRINCIPAL (def. 3). *n.*

**prin·ci·ple** (prin′sə pəl) **1** a fact or belief on which other ideas are based: *Science is based on the principle that things can be explained.* **2** a rule of action or conduct: *I make it a principle to save some money each week.* **3** uprightness; honour: *Joseph Howe was a man of principle.* **4** a rule of science explaining how things act: *the principle of the lever.* **5** the method of operation. **6** a source; origin; first cause or force. **7** one of the elements that compose a substance, especially one that gives some special quality or effect: *the bitter principle in a drug.* *n.*
**in principle,** as regards the general truth or rule: *to approve something in principle.*
**on principle,** **a** according to a certain principle. **b** for reasons of right conduct.
☛ *Hom.* PRINCIPAL.
☛ *Usage.* See note at PRINCIPAL.

**prink** (pringk) PRIMP. *v.* —**prink′er,** *n.*

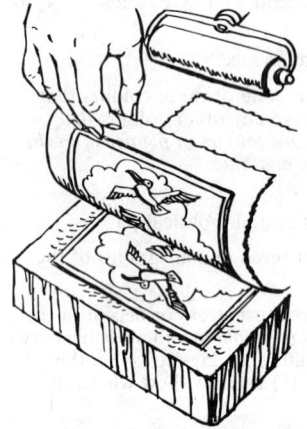

A print (def. 12) being pulled off a wooden block into which a design has been cut. For this kind of print, the background of the design is cut away and the raised parts that are left are covered with ink. A sheet of paper is then pressed onto the inked block. When the paper is pulled off, it shows the block design in reverse.

**print** (print) **1** use type, blocks, plates, etc. and ink or dye to reproduce words, pictures, designs, etc. on paper or some other surface: *Who prints this newspaper?* **2** reproduce letters, words, etc. on with type, etc. and ink. **3** cause to be printed; publish: *to print books.* **4** produce books, newspapers, etc. by printing press. **5** printed words, letters, etc.: *This book has clear print.* **6** a printed condition. **7** a printed publication; newspaper or magazine. **8** an edition or impression of a book, etc. made at one time. **9** make words or letters the way they look in print instead of in writing. **10** make with such letters: *Print your name clearly.* **11** stamp with designs, patterns, pictures, etc.: *Machines print wallpaper, cloth, etc.* **12** a picture or design printed from an engraved block, plate, etc. **13** cloth with a pattern printed on it: *Amy has two dresses made of print.* **14** a mark made by pressing or stamping: *the print of a foot.* **15** stamp; produce marks or figures by pressure; impress. **16** something that prints; stamp; DIE². **17** something that has been marked or shaped by pressing or stamping: *a print of butter.* **18** fix: *The scene is printed on my memory.* **19** take an impression from type, etc. **20** a photograph produced from a negative. **21** produce a photograph by transmission of light through a negative. 1–4, 9–11, 15, 18, 19, 21 *v.*, 5–8, 12–14, 16, 17, 20 *n.*
**in print,** of books, etc., still available for purchase from the publisher.
**out of print,** no longer sold by the publisher.

**print·a·ble** (prin′tə bəl) 1 capable of being printed. 2 capable of being printed from. 3 fit to be printed. *adj.*

**print·er** (prin′tər) 1 a person whose business or work is printing or setting type. 2 a machine or device used for printing, such as the part of a computer that produces printouts. *n.*

**printer's devil** a young helper or errand boy in a printing shop.

**print·ing** (prin′ting) 1 the producing of books, newspapers, etc. by stamping in ink or dye from movable type, plates, etc. 2 printed words, letters, etc. 3 all the copies of a book, pamphlet, etc. printed at one time. 4 letters made like those in print. 5 ppr. of PRINT. 1–4 *n.*, 5 *v.*

**printing press** a machine for printing from movable type, plates, etc.

**print·out** (prin′tout′) a typewritten or printed record of the output of a computer, produced automatically. *n.*

**print·wheel** (prin′twēl *or* print′hwēl′) a circular device containing characters for printing on a computer printer; daisy wheel. *n.*

**pri·or**[1] (prī′ər) coming before; earlier: *I can't go with you because I have a prior engagement.* *adj.*

**prior to,** coming before in time, order, or importance; earlier than; before.

**pri·or**[2] (prī′ər) the head of a priory or monastery for men: *Priors usually rank below abbots.* *n.*

**pri·or·ess** (prī′ə ris) the head of a convent or priory for women: *Prioresses usually rank below abbesses.* *n.*

**pri·or·i·ty** (prī ô′rə tē) 1 the fact of being earlier in time: *The priority in the invention of the telephone to that of television is a known fact.* 2 a coming before in order of importance: *Fire engines and ambulances have priority over other traffic.* 3 a governmental rating giving right of way to persons or things important in national defence, essential affairs of state, etc. in order of importance. *n.*, *pl.* **pri·or·i·ties.**

**pri·o·ry** (prī′ə rē) a monastery, convent, etc. governed by a prior or prioress: *A priory is often, but not necessarily, dependent on an abbey.* *n.*, *pl.* **pri·o·ries.**

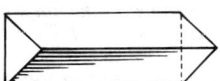 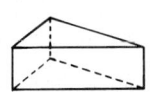

Prisms (def. 2)

**prism** (priz′əm) 1 a solid whose bases or ends have the same size and shape and are parallel to one another, and each of whose sides has two pairs of parallel edges: *A six-sided pencil before it is sharpened has the shape of one kind of prism.* 2 a transparent prism, usually with three-sided ends, that separates white light passing through it into the colours of the spectrum. See ANGLE OF DEVIATION for another picture. *n.*

**pris·mat·ic** (priz mat′ik) 1 of or like a PRISM. 2 formed by a transparent PRISM. 3 varied in colour. *adj.*

**pris·mat·i·cal·ly** (priz mat′i klē) by, or as if by, a PRISM. *adv.*

**prismatic colours** *or* **colors** the colours formed when white light is passed through a prism; red, orange, yellow, green, blue, indigo, and violet; the colours of the rainbow.

---

printable 939 privilege

hat, āge, fär; let, ēqual, tėrm; it, īce
hot, ōpen, ôrder; oil, out; cup, pùt, rüle
əbove, takən, pencəl, lemən, circəs
ch, child; ng, long; sh, ship
th, thin; ᴛʜ, then; zh, measure

**pris·on** (priz′ən) 1 a public building in which criminals are confined: *Lawbreakers are confined in prison.* 2 any place where a person or animal is shut up against his or her will: *The small apartment was a prison to the big dog from the farm.* 3 imprison. 1, 2 *n.*, 3 *v.*

**pris·on·er** (priz′ə nər *or* priz′nər) 1 a person who is under arrest or held in a jail or prison. 2 a person who is confined against his or her will or who is not free to move. *n.*

**prisoner of war,** a person taken by the enemy in war.

**pris·sy** (pris′ē) 1 too precise and fussy. 2 too easily shocked; overnice. *adj.*, **pris·si·er, pris·si·est.**

**pris·tine** (pris′tēn) as it was in its earliest time or state; original; primitive: *The colours of the paintings inside the pyramid had kept their pristine freshness in spite of their age.* *adj.*

**pri·va·cy** (prī′və sē) 1 the condition of being private; being away from others: *in the privacy of one's home.* 2 an absence of publicity; secrecy: *Veznu told me her reasons in strict privacy.* *n.*, *pl.* **pri·va·cies.**

**pri·vate** (prī′vit) 1 not for the public; for just a few special people or for one: *a private car, a private house, a private letter.* 2 not public; individual; personal: *the private life of a queen, my private opinion.* 3 secret; confidential: *a private drawer.* 4 secluded: *some private corner.* 5 having no public office: *a private citizen.* 6 in Canada, a person holding the lowest rank in any of the three parts (sea, land, or air) of the Canadian Armed Forces. 1–5 *adj.*, 6 *n.* —**pri′vate·ly,** *adv.* —**pri′vate·ness,** *n.*

**in private,** a not publicly: *My mother spoke to the principal in private.* b secretly: *We met in private to plan her surprise birthday party.*

**private enterprise** the production and sale of goods, etc. by industries under private control and ownership rather than under government control or ownership.

**pri·va·teer** (prī′və tēr′) 1 an armed ship owned by private persons and holding a government commission to attack and capture enemy ships. 2 the commander or one of the crew of a privateer. 3 cruise as a privateer. 1, 2 *n.*, 3 *v.*

**pri·va·teers·man** (prī′və tēr′zmən) an officer or member of the crew of a PRIVATEER. *n.*, *pl.* **pri·va·teers·men** (-zmən).

**private sector** business and industry.

**pri·va·tion** (prī vā′shən) 1 the lack of the comforts or necessities of life: *Many children were hungry or homeless because of privation during the war.* 2 loss; absence; the state of being deprived. *n.*

**priv·et** (priv′it) any of several shrubs much used for hedges. *n.*

**priv·i·lege** (priv′ə lij *or* priv′lij) 1 a special right, advantage, or favour: *Ms. Sikorski has given us the privilege of using her television set.* 2 give a privilege to: *You are privileged to belong to this university.* 1 *n.*, 2 *v.*, **priv·i·leged, priv·i·leg·ing.**

**priv·i·leged** (priv′ə lijd) **1** having a privilege or privileges: *the privileged classes of society.* **2** not having to be revealed in a court of law: *Communication between a lawyer and client is privileged.* **3** pt. and pp. of PRIVILEGE. 1, 2 *adj.*, 3 *v.*

**priv·i·ly** (priv′ə lē) in a private manner; secretly. *adv.*

**priv·y** (priv′ē) **1** private. **2** a small outhouse used as a toilet. 1 *adj.*, 2 *n., pl.* **priv·ies.**
**privy to,** having secret or private knowledge of.

**privy council** a group of personal advisers to a ruler.

**Privy Council** in Canada, the body of advisers to the Governor General, made up of the ministers of the federal cabinet and all former CABINET MINISTERS.

**Privy Councillor** a member of the PRIVY COUNCIL: *Privy Councillors hold office for life, but can advise the Governor General only while they are cabinet ministers.*

**privy seal** in Britain, the seal affixed to grants, etc. that are afterwards to receive the GREAT SEAL, and to documents that do not require the great seal.

**prix fixe** (prē fēks′) *French.* a fixed price for a complete meal.

**prize**[1] (prīz) **1** a reward won or offered in a contest or competition: *Prizes will be given for the three best stories.* **2** given as a prize. **3** that has won a prize. **4** worthy of a prize: *prize vegetables.* **5** a reward worth working for. 1, 5 *n.*, 2–4 *adj.*
☛ *Hom.* PRIES.

**prize**[2] (prīz) a thing or person taken or captured in war, especially an enemy's ship and its cargo taken at sea. *n.*
☛ *Hom.* PRIES.

**prize**[3] (prīz) **1** value highly: *She prizes her best china.* **2** estimate the value of. *v.*, **prized, priz·ing.**
☛ *Hom.* PRIES.

**prize**[4] (prīz) PRY. *v.*, **prized, priz·ing.**
☛ *Hom.* PRIES.

**prize court** a court that makes decisions concerning ships and other property captured at sea during a war.

**prize fight** a boxing match fought for money.

**prize fighter** a person who fights boxing matches for money.

**prize fighting** the fighting of boxing matches for money.

**prize money** **1** the money obtained by the sale of ships and other property captured at sea in the course of a war, sometimes divided among those who made the capture. **2** the money offered as a prize in races, contests, etc.

**prize ring** **1** a square space enclosed by ropes, used for PRIZE FIGHTS. **2** PRIZE FIGHTING.

**pro**[1] (prō) **1** in favour of; for: *They voted pro, and won.* **2** a reason in favour of: *The pros and cons of a question are the arguments for and against it.* 1 *adv.*, 2 *n., pl.* **pros.**

**pro**[2] (prō) *Informal.* a professional, such as a professional athlete or actor. *n., pl.* **pros;** *adj.*

**pro–** a prefix meaning: **1** forward, as in *proceed, project.* **2** forth; out, as in *prolong, proclaim.* **3** on the side of; in favour of; in behalf of, as in *pro-British.* **4** in place of; acting as, as in *pronoun, proconsul.*

**prob·a·bil·i·ty** (prob′ə bil′ə tē) **1** the quality or fact of being likely or PROBABLE; a good chance: *There is a probability that school will close a week earlier than usual.* **2** something likely to happen: *A storm is one of the probabilities for tomorrow.* *n., pl.* **prob·a·bil·i·ties.**
**in all probability,** probably.

**prob·a·ble** (prob′ə bəl) **1** likely to happen: *Cooler weather is probable after rain.* **2** likely to be true: *Something she ate is the probable cause of her pain.* *adj.*

**prob·a·bly** (prob′ə blē) more likely than not. *adv.*

**pro·bate** (prō′bāt) **1** in law, the official proving of a will as genuine. **2** of or concerned with the probating of wills: *a probate court.* **3** prove by legal process the genuineness of a will. **4** a true copy of a will with a certificate that it has been proved genuine. 1, 4 *n.*, 2 *adj.*, 3 *v.*, **pro·bat·ed, pro·bat·ing.**

**pro·ba·tion** (prō bā′shən) **1** a trial or testing of conduct, character, qualifications, etc.: *Sophie was admitted to the sixth grade on probation. After a period of probation a trainee becomes a nurse.* **2** the time of trial or testing. **3** the system of letting young offenders against the law, or first offenders, go free under the supervision of a PROBATION OFFICER. **4** the time that a first offender against the law is kept under supervision by a probation officer. *n.*

**pro·ba·tion·ar·y** (prō bā′shə ner′ē) **1** of or having to do with PROBATION. **2** on PROBATION. *adj.*

**pro·ba·tion·er** (prō bā′shə nər) a person who is on PROBATION. *n.*

**probation officer** an officer appointed by a court of law to supervise offenders who have been placed on PROBATION (def. 3).

**pro·ba·tive** (prō′bə tiv) **1** giving proof or evidence. **2** for a trial or test. *adj.*

**probe** (prōb) **1** search into; examine thoroughly; investigate: *Teresa probed her thoughts and feelings to find out why she acted as she did.* **2** search; penetrate: *to probe into the causes of crime.* **3** a thorough examination; investigation. **4** an investigation, usually by a legislative body, in an effort to discover evidences of law violation. **5** a slender instrument with a rounded end for exploring the depth or direction of a wound, a cavity in the body, etc. **6** an instrument, often electronic, used to test or explore: *A Geiger counter uses a probe to detect the amount of radiation in radioactive matter, such as rock.* **7** a spacecraft carrying scientific instruments to record or report back information about planets, etc.: *a lunar probe.* **8** examine with a probe: *The doctor probed the wound to find the pieces of glass.* 1, 2, 8 *v.*, **probed, prob·ing;** 3–7 *n.*

**pro·bi·ty** (prō′bə tē) uprightness; honesty; high principle. *n.*

**prob·lem** (prob′ləm) **1** a question, especially a difficult question. **2** a matter of doubt or difficulty. **3** something to be worked out: *a problem in arithmetic.* **4** that causes difficulty: *a problem child.* *n.*

**prob·lem·at·ic** (prob′lə mat′ik) having the nature of a problem; doubtful; uncertain; questionable: *What the weather will be is often problematic.* *adj.*
—**prob′lem·at′i·cal·ly,** *adv.*

**prob·lem·at·i·cal** (prob′lə mat′ə kəl) PROBLEMATIC. *adj.*

**pro bo·no pu·bli·co** (prō′ bō′nō pub′lə kō′) *Latin.* for the public welfare.

**pro·bos·cis** (prō bos′is) **1** an elephant's trunk. **2** a long, flexible snout. **3** the mouth parts of some insects, developed to great length for sucking: *the proboscis of a fly or a mosquito.* **4** *Informal.* a person's nose. *n., pl.* **pro·bos·cis·es** (-sēz) or **pro·bos·ci·des** (-ki dēz)

**pro·car·y·ote** (prō kar′ē ət *or* prō ker′ē ət) a cell without a visible nucleus: *A procaryote has genetic material in a streptococcic or chainlike configuration, but no nuclear membrane.* *n.* Also, **prokaryote**.
—**pro·car·y·ot·ic**, *adj.*

**pro·ce·dure** (prə sē′jər) **1** a way of proceeding; method for doing things: *What is the procedure for nominating a candidate?* **2** the customary manners or ways of conducting business: *parliamentary procedure, legal procedure.* *n.*

**pro·ceed** (prə sēd′ *or* prō sēd′) **1** go on after having stopped; move forward: *Please proceed with your story.* **2** be carried on; take place: *The trial may proceed.* **3** carry on any activity: *He proceeded to polish his shoes.* **4** come forth; issue; go out; emanate: *Heat proceeds from fire.* **5** begin and carry on an action at law. *v.*
—**pro·ceed′er**, *n.*
☛ *Usage.* See note at PRECEDE.

**pro·ceed·ing** (prə sē′ding *or* prō sē′ding) **1** action; conduct; what is done: *What a strange and unheard-of proceeding!* **2 proceedings**, *pl.* **a** action in a case in a law court. **b** a record of what was done at the meetings of a society, club, etc. **3** ppr. of PROCEED. 1, 2 *n.*, 3 *v.*

**pro·ceeds** (prō′sēdz) the money obtained from a sale, etc.: *The proceeds from the school play will be used to buy a new curtain for the stage.* *n. pl.*

**pro·cess** (pros′es *or* pros′əs) **1** a set of actions or changes in a special order: *By what process or processes is cloth made from wool?* **2** treat or prepare by some special method: *This cloth has been processed to make it waterproof.* **3** treated or prepared by some special method. **4** a part that grows out or sticks out: *the process of a bone.* **5** a written command or summons to appear in a law court. **6** start legal action against. 1, 4, 5 *n.*, 2, 6 *v.*, 3 *adj.*
**in process**, **a** in the course or condition: *In process of time the house will be finished.* **b** in the course or condition of being done: *The author has just finished one book and has another in process.*

**pro·ces·sion** (prə sesh′ən) **1** something that moves forward; persons marching or riding: *A funeral procession filled the street.* **2** an orderly moving forward: *We formed lines to march in procession onto the platform.* *n.*

**pro·ces·sion·al** (prə sesh′ə nəl) **1** of a PROCESSION. **2** used or sung in a PROCESSION. **3** PROCESSIONAL music: *The choir and clergy marched into the church singing the processional.* **4** a book containing hymns, etc., for use in religious PROCESSIONS. 1, 2 *adj.*, 3, 4 *n.*

**pro·ces·sor** (pros′e sər *or* pros′ə sər) **1** a kitchen appliance that performs many functions in the processing of food, such as chopping, mixing, blending, and extracting juice. **2** a computer or the part of a computer that processes data. **3** any person or thing that processes. *n.*

**pro·claim** (prə klām′) make known publicly and officially; declare publicly: *War was proclaimed. The people proclaimed her queen.* *v.*

**proc·la·ma·tion** (prok′lə mā′shən) an official announcement; a public declaration: *A proclamation was issued to announce the forthcoming election.* *n.*

---

**proboscis**     **941**     **prodigious**

hat, āge, fär; let, ēqual, tėrm; it, īce
hot, ōpen, ôrder; oil, out; cup, pùt, rüle
əbove, takən, pencəl, lemən, circəs
ch, child; ng, long; sh, ship
th, thin; ŦH, then; zh, measure

**pro·cliv·i·ty** (prō kliv′ə tē) a tendency; inclination. *n., pl.* **pro·cliv·i·ties**.

**pro·con·sul** (prō kon′səl) in the ancient Roman empire, the governor or military commander of a province, with duties and powers like those of a CONSUL. *n.*

**pro·cras·ti·nate** (prō kras′tə nāt′) put things off until later; delay; delay repeatedly: *Lazy people tend to procrastinate.* *v.*, **pro·cras·ti·nat·ed**, **pro·cras·ti·nat·ing**. —**pro·cras′ti·na′tor**, *n.*

**pro·cras·ti·na·tion** (prō kras′tə nā′shən) the act or habit of putting things off till later; delay. *n.*

**pro·cre·ate** (prō′krē āt′) **1** become parent to; beget. **2** produce offspring. **3** bring into being; produce. *v.*, **pro·cre·at·ed**, **pro·cre·at·ing**.

**pro·cre·a·tion** (prō′krē ā′shən) **1** begetting; a becoming a parent. **2** a production. *n.*

**Pro·crus·te·an** (prō krus′tē ən) tending to produce conformity by violent or arbitrary means. *adj.*
☛ *Etym.* From the name of *Procrustes*, in Greek legend, a robber who stretched his victims or cut off their legs to make them fit the length of his bed.

**proc·tor** (prok′tər) **1** an official in a university or school who keeps order. **2** a person employed to manage another's case in a law court. *n.*

**proc·to·ri·al** (prok tô′rē əl) of or having to do with a PROCTOR. *adj.*

**pro·cum·bent** (prō kum′bənt) lying face down; prone; prostrate. Compare with SUPINE. *adj.*

**proc·u·ra·tor** (prok′yə rā′tər) **1** a person employed to manage the affairs of another; a person authorized to act for another; agent. **2** in the ancient Roman empire, a financial agent or administrator of a province.

**pro·cure** (prə kyür′) **1** obtain by care or effort; get: *A friend procured a position in the bank for my daughter.* **2** bring about; cause: *to procure a person's death.* *v.*, **pro·cured**, **pro·cur·ing**. —**pro·cur′a·ble**, *adj.*

**pro·cure·ment** (prə kyür′mənt) a procuring. *n.*

**prod** (prod) **1** poke or jab with something pointed: *to prod an animal with a stick.* **2** stir up; urge on: *to prod a lazy girl to action by threats and entreaties.* **3** a poke or thrust: *That prod in the ribs hurt.* **4** a sharp-pointed stick; goad. 1, 2 *v.*, **prod·ded**, **prod·ding**; 3, 4 *n.*
—**prod′der**, *n.*

**prod.** **1** product. **2** produced.

**prod·i·gal** (prod′ə gəl) **1** spending too much; wasting money or other resources; wasteful: *Do not be prodigal of your wealth.* **2** abundant; lavish. **3** a person who is wasteful or extravagant; spendthrift. 1, 2 *adj.*, 3 *n.*
—**prod′i·gal·ly**, *adv.*

**prod·i·gal·i·ty** (prod′ə gal′ə tē) **1** wasteful or reckless extravagance. **2** rich abundance; profuseness. *n., pl.* **prod·i·gal·i·ties**.

**pro·di·gious** (prə dij′əs) **1** very great; huge; vast: *The ocean contains a prodigious amount of water.*

**2** wonderful; marvellous: *It was a prodigious achievement.* *adj.* —**pro·di′gious·ly,** *adv.* —**pro·di′gious·ness,** *n.*

**prod·i·gy** (prod′ə jē)  **1** a marvel; wonder: *An infant prodigy is a child remarkably brilliant in some respect.*  **2** a marvellous example: *The warriors performed prodigies of valour.*  *n., pl.* **prod·i·gies.**

**pro·duce** (prə dyüs′ *or* prə düs′ *for verb,* prod′yüs *or* prō′düs *for noun*)  **1** make; bring into existence: *This factory produces stoves.*  **2** bring about; cause: *Hard work produces success.*  **3** bring forth or yield offspring, crops, products, dividends, interest, etc.  **4** bring forth; supply; create: *Hens produce eggs. The tree produced only a few apples this year.*  **5** bring forward; show; present: *Produce your proof.*  **6** bring a play, etc. before the public.  **7** what is produced; yield: *Vegetables are a garden's produce.*  **8** fruit and vegetables: *She owns a produce market.*  1–6 *v.,* **pro·duced, pro·duc·ing;** 7, 8 *n.*

**pro·duc·er** (prə dyü′sər *or* prə dü′sər)  **1** one who produces.  **2** a person who grows or makes things that are to be used or consumed by others.  **3** a person in charge of presenting a play, a motion picture, a television program, etc.  *n.*

**pro·duc·i·ble** (prə dyü′sə bəl *or* prə dü′sə bəl)  capable of being PRODUCEd.  *adj.*

**prod·uct** (prod′əkt)  **1** that which is produced; result of work or of growth: *factory products, farm products.*  **2** a number or quantity resulting from multiplying: *The product of 5 and 8 is 40.*  See MULTIPLICATION for picture.  *n.*

**pro·duc·tion** (prə duk′shən)  **1** the act of producing; creation; manufacture: *Her business is the production of automobiles.*  **2** something that is produced: *The school play was a fine production.*  **3** the total amount produced.  *n.*

**pro·duc·tive** (prə duk′tiv)  **1** capable of producing or bringing forth: *fields now productive only of weeds, hasty words that are productive of quarrels.*  **2** producing food or other articles of commerce: *Farming is productive labour.*  **3** producing abundantly; fertile: *a productive farm, writer, etc.*  *adj.* —**pro·duc′tive·ly,** *adv.* —**pro·duc′tive·ness,** *n.*

**pro·duc·tiv·i·ty** (prō′duk tiv′ə tē)  the power to PRODUCE; productiveness.  *n.*

**Prof.**  professor.

**prof·a·na·tion** (prof′ə nā′shən)  the act of showing contempt or disregard toward something holy; the mistreatment of something sacred.  *n.*

**pro·fane** (prə fān′ *or* prō fān′)  **1** not sacred; worldly: *Mozart wrote both religious and profane music.*  **2** with contempt or disregard for God or holy things: *profane language.*  **3** treat holy things with contempt or disregard: *Rebels profaned the church by stabling horses there.*  **4** put to wrong or unworthy use.  1, 2 *adj.,* 3, 4 *v.,* **pro·faned, pro·fan·ing.** —**pro·fane′ly,** *adv.* —**pro·fane′ness,** *n.*

**pro·fan·i·ty** (prə fan′ə tē)  **1** the use of profane language; swearing.  **2** being profane; a lack of reverence.  *n., pl.* **pro·fan·i·ties.**

**pro·fess** (prə fes′)  **1** lay claim to; claim: *She professed the greatest respect for the law. I don't profess to be an expert.*  **2** declare openly: *She professed her loyalty to her country.*  **3** declare one's belief in: *She professed*

eclecticism.  **4** have as one's profession or business: *to profess law.*  *v.*

**pro·fessed** (prə fest′)  **1** alleged; pretended.  **2** avowed or acknowledged; openly declared.  **3** having taken the vows of, or been received into, a religious order.  **4** pt. and pp. of PROFESS.  1–3 *adj.,* 4 *v.*

**pro·fess·ed·ly** (prə fes′i dlē)  **1** AVOWEDLY.  **2** ostensibly.  *adv.*

**pro·fes·sion** (prə fesh′ən)  **1** an occupation requiring special education and training, such as law, medicine, teaching, or nursing.  **2** the people engaged in such an occupation: *The medical profession favours this law.*  **3** the act of professing; open declaration: *I welcomed her profession of friendship.*  **4** a declaration of belief in a religion.  **5** the religion or faith professed.  **6** the act of taking the vows and entering a religious order.  *n.*

**pro·fes·sion·al** (prə fesh′ə nəl)  **1** of or having to do with a profession; appropriate to a profession: *professional skill, a professional manner.*  **2** engaged in a profession: *A lawyer or a doctor is a professional person.*  **3** making a business or trade of something that others do for pleasure: *a professional ballplayer.*  **4** a person who does this.  **5** undertaken or engaged in by professionals rather than amateurs: *a professional ball game.*  **6** making a business of something not properly to be regarded as a business: *a professional politician.*  1–3, 5, 6 *adj.,* 4 *n.*

**pro·fes·sion·al·ism** (prə fesh′ə nə liz′əm)  **1** PROFESSIONAL character, spirit, or methods.  **2** the standing, practice, or methods of a PROFESSIONAL, as distinguished from those of an amateur.  *n.*

**pro·fes·sion·al·ly** (prə fesh′ə nə lē)  in a PROFESSIONAL manner; in professional matters; because of one's profession.  *adv.*

**pro·fes·sor** (prə fes′ər)  **1** a teacher of the highest rank in a college or university.  **2** *Informal.* any teacher at a college or university.  **3** a person who professes.  **4** a person who declares his or her belief in a religion.  *n.*

**pro·fes·so·ri·al** (prof′ə sô′rē əl *or* prō′fə sô′rē əl)  of, having to do with, or characteristic of a PROFESSOR (def. 1).  *adj.* —**prof′es·so′ri·al·ly,** *adv.*

**pro·fes·sor·ship** (prə fes′ər ship′)  the position, rank or term of office of a PROFESSOR (def. 1).  *n.*

**pro·fi·cien·cy** (prə fish′ən sē)  being proficient; knowledge; skill; expertness.  *n., pl.* **pro·fi·cien·cies.**

**pro·fi·cient** (prə fish′ənt)  advanced in any art, science, or subject; skilled; expert: *She was very proficient in music.*  *adj.* —**pro·fi′cient·ly,** *adv.*

Profile of the Blackfoot leader Crowfoot

**pro·file** (prō′fīl)  **1** a side view, especially of the human face.  **2** outline.  **3** a drawing of a transverse vertical section of a building, bridge, etc.  **4** draw a profile of.  **5** a concise description of a person's abilities, character, or career: *The magazine carried an interesting profile of the Lieutenant-Governor.*  1–3, 5 *n.,* 4 *v.,* **pro·filed, pro·fil·ing.**

**prof·it** (prof′it)  **1** the gain from a business; what is left

when the cost of goods and of carrying on the business is subtracted from the amount of money taken in: *The profits in this business are not large.* **2** make such a gain; make a profit. **3** advantage; benefit: *What profit is there in worrying?* **4** get advantage; gain; benefit: *A wise person profits by mistakes.* **5** be an advantage or benefit to. 1, 3 *n.*, 2, 4, 5 *v.* —**prof′it·less**, *adj.*
☛ *Hom.* PROPHET.

**prof·it·a·ble** (prof′ə bəl) **1** providing a PROFIT in money: *a profitable sale.* **2** giving a gain or benefit; useful: *We spent a profitable afternoon in the library.* *adj.* —**prof′it·a·ble·ness**, *n.* —**prof′it·a·bly**, *adv.*

**prof·it·eer** (prof′ə tēr′) **1** a person who makes an unfair PROFIT by taking advantage of public necessity. **2** seek to make excessive PROFITS by taking advantage of public necessity. 1 *n.*, 2 *v.*

**profit sharing** the sharing of PROFITS between employer and employees.

**prof·li·ga·cy** (prof′lə gə sē) **1** great wickedness; vice. **2** reckless extravagance. *n.*

**prof·li·gate** (prof′lə git) **1** very wicked; shamelessly bad. **2** recklessly extravagant. **3** a person who is very wicked or extravagant. 1, 2 *adj.*, 3 *n.* —**prof′li·gate·ly**, *adv.*

**pro·found** (prə found′) **1** very deep: *a profound sigh, a profound sleep.* **2** deeply felt; very great: *profound despair, profound sympathy.* **3** having or showing great depth of knowledge or understanding: *a profound book, a profound thinker.* **4** low; carried far down; going far down: *a profound bow.* *adj.* —**pro·found′ly**, *adv.* —**pro·found′ness**, *n.*

**pro·fun·di·ty** (prə fun′də tē) **1** being profound; great depth. **2** a very deep thing or place. *n., pl.* **pro·fun·di·ties.**

**pro·fuse** (prə fyüs′) **1** very abundant: *profuse thanks.* **2** spending or giving freely; lavish; extravagant: *Olga was so profuse with her money that she is now poor.* *adj.* —**pro·fuse′ly**, *adv.* —**pro·fuse′ness**, *n.*

**pro·fu·sion** (prə fyü′zhən) **1** a great ABUNDANCE: *There was a profusion of gulls on the breakwater.* **2** extravagance; lavishness. *n.*

**Prog.** Progressive.

**pro·gen·i·tor** (prō jen′ə tər) an ancestor in the direct line; forefather. *n.*

**prog·e·ny** (proj′ə nē) children; offspring; descendants: *Kittens are a cat's progeny.* *n., pl.* **prog·e·nies.**

**prog·na·thous** (prog′nə thəs *or* prog nā′thəs) of a skull or a person, having the jaws protruding beyond the upper part of the face. *adj.*

**prog·no·sis** (prog nō′sis) **1** a forecast of the probable course of a disease. **2** an estimate of what will probably happen. *n., pl.* **prog·no·ses** (-sēz).

**prog·nos·tic** (prog nos′tik) **1** indicating something in the future. **2** indication; sign. **3** forecast; prediction. 1 *adj.*, 2, 3 *n.*

**prog·nos·ti·cate** (prog nos′tə kāt′) predict from facts; forecast. *v.*, **prog·nos·ti·cat·ed**, **prog·nos·ti·cat·ing**. —**prog·nos′ti·ca′tion**, *n.* —**prog·nos′ti·ca′tor**, *n.*

**pro·gram** or **pro·gramme** (prō′gram) **1** a list of items or events; list of performers, players, etc.: *a theatre program.* **2** the items composing an entertainment: *The entire program was delightful.* **3** a plan of what is to be done: *a school program, a business program, a government*

**profitable   943   progressive jazz**

hat, āge, fär; let, ēqual, tėrm; it, īce
hot, ōpen, ôrder; oil, out; cup, pùt, rüle
əbove, takən, pencəl, lemən, circəs
ch, child; ng, long; sh, ship
th, thin; ᵺ, then; zh, measure

*program.* **4** arrange or enter in a program. **5** draw up a program or plan for. **6** a set of instructions fed into a computer outlining the steps to be performed by the machine in a specific operation. **7** prepare a set of instructions for a computer. **8** in education, a unit of subject matter arranged in a series of small steps for PROGRAMMED LEARNING. **9** arrange in a series of small steps for PROGRAMMED LEARNING. **10** in education, a set of courses: *Each graduate student has an individual program.* **11** a presentation or performance, especially a radio or television show: *We listened to a radio program about mysteries.* 1–3, 6, 8, 10, 11 *n.*, 4, 5, 7, 9 *v.*, **pro·grammed, pro·gram·ming.**

**programmed learning** a method of study by which a person works step by step through a series of problems, checking the correctness of his or her response to each step before proceeding to the next.

**pro·gram·mer** (prō′gram ər) a person who prepares a program or programs, especially for a computer or other automatic machine. *n.*

**programming language** a system of words and codes, like a language, which allows a person to put instructions into a computer in a form that the computer can recognize and process.

**prog·ress** (prō′gres *or* prog′res *for noun*, prə gres′ *for verb*) **1** an advance; growth; development; improvement: *the progress of science.* **2** get better; advance; develop: *We progress in learning step by step.* **3** moving forward; going ahead: *to make rapid progress on a journey.* **4** move forward; go ahead: *The building of the city hall has progressed a great deal this week.* 1, 3 *n.*, 2, 4 *v.*

**pro·gres·sion** (prə gresh′ən) **1** a moving forward; going ahead: *Creeping is a slow method of progression.* **2** in mathematics, a succession of quantities in which there is always the same relation between each quantity and the one succeeding it: *2, 4, 6, 8, 10 are in arithmetical progression. 2, 4, 8, 16 are in geometrical progression.* *n.*

**pro·gres·sive** (prə gres′iv) **1** making progress; advancing to something better; improving: *a progressive nation.* **2** favouring progress; wanting improvement or reform in government, business, etc. **3** a person who favours improvement and reform in government, business, etc.: *She is a progressive in her beliefs.* **4** moving forward; developing: *a progressive disease.* **5** going from one to the next; involving shifts of players or guests from one table to another: *a game of progressive bridge.* **6** in grammar, showing the action as going on. *Is reading, was reading,* and *has been reading* are progressive forms of *read.* 1, 2, 4–6 *adj.*, 3 *n.* —**pro·gres′sive·ly**, *adv.* —**pro·gres′sive·ness**, *n.*

**Progressive Conservative** **1** a member of the PROGRESSIVE CONSERVATIVE PARTY. **2** a person who supports the policies of this party. **3** of or having to do with this party: *the Progressive Conservative policy.*

**Progressive Conservative Party** one of the principal political parties of Canada.

**progressive jazz** in music, a style of jazz that evolved

**progressive tense** — in the late 1940's and early 1950's, characterized by very complex and subtle harmonies and rhythms.

**progressive tense** the form of a verb which shows that an action is continuing. *Example: She is still reading the same book.*

**pro·hib·it** (prō hib′it) **1** forbid by law or authority: *Picking flowers in this park is prohibited.* **2** prevent: *The high price prohibits my buying the bicycle.* *v.*

**pro·hi·bi·tion** (prō′ə bish′ən) **1** the act of prohibiting or forbidding: *The prohibition of swimming in the city's reservoirs is sensible.* **2** a law or order that prohibits. **3** a law or laws against making or selling alcoholic liquors: *The United States had prohibition from 1920 to 1933.* *n.*

**pro·hi·bi·tion·ist** (prō′ə bish′ə nist) one who favours laws against the manufacture and sale of alcoholic liquors. *n.*

**pro·hib·i·tive** (prō hib′ə tiv) prohibiting; preventing: *The price of a new car was prohibitive.* *adj.*

**pro·hib·i·to·ry** (prō hib′ə tô′rē) PROHIBITIVE. *adj.*

**pro·ject** (prō′jekt *or* proj′ekt *for noun,* prə jekt′ *for verb*) **1** a plan; scheme: *Flying in a heavy machine was once thought an impossible project.* **2** plan; scheme. **3** an undertaking; enterprise: *She is busy with several projects.* **4** stick out: *The rocky point projects far into the water.* **5** cause to stick out or protrude. **6** throw or cast forward: *A catapult projects stones.* **7** cause to fall on a surface: *Motion pictures are projected on the screen. The tree projects a shadow on the grass.* **8** draw lines through a point, line, figure, etc. and reproduce it on a surface. 1, 3 *n.*, 2, 4–8 *v.*

**pro·jec·tile** (prə jek′tīl *or* prə jek′təl) **1** any object that is thrown, hurled, or shot, such as a rocket, stone, or bullet. **2** capable of being thrown, hurled, or shot: *Bullets and arrows are projectile weapons.* **3** forcing forward; impelling: *a projectile force.* 1 *n.*, 2, 3 *adj.*

**pro·jec·tion** (prə jek′shən) **1** a part that projects or sticks out: *rocky projections on the face of a cliff.* **2** a sticking out: *The projection of these nails is dangerous.* **3** a throwing or casting forward: *the projection of a shell from a field gun.* **4** in geometry, the projecting of a figure, etc. upon a surface. **5** a representation, upon a flat surface, of all or part of the surface of the earth. See MERCATOR PROJECTION for picture. **6** a forming of projects or plans. **7** a forecast. *n.*

**pro·jec·tor** (prə jek′tər) **1** an apparatus for projecting a picture on a screen. See OPAQUE PROJECTOR and OVERHEAD PROJECTOR. **2** a person who forms projects; schemer. *n.*

**pro·kar·y·ote** (prō′kar′ē ət *or* prō ker′ē ət) See PROCARYOTE. *n.*

**prol.** prologue.

**pro·le·tar·i·an** (prō′lə ter′ē ən) **1** of or belonging to the PROLETARIAT. **2** a person belonging to the PROLETARIAT. 1 *adj.*, 2 *n.*

**pro·le·tar·i·at** (prō′lə ter′ē ət) **1** the lowest class in economic and social status: *The proletariat includes unskilled labourers, casual labourers, and tramps.* **2** in Europe, the labouring class. *n.*

**pro·lif·ic** (prə lif′ik) **1** producing offspring abundantly: *prolific animals.* **2** producing much: *a prolific garden, a prolific imagination, a prolific writer.* *adj.* —**pro·lif′i·cal·ly**, *adv.*

**pro·lif·i·ca·cy** (prə lif′ə kə sē) the quality or state of being PROLIFIC. *n.*

**pro·lix** (prō liks′ *or* prō′liks) using too many words; too long; tedious. *adj.* —**pro·lix′ness**, *n.*

**pro·lix·i·ty** (prō lik′sə tē) too great length; tedious length of speech or writing. *n.*

**pro·logue** (prō′log) **1** a speech or poem addressed to the audience by one of the actors at the beginning of a play, opera, etc. **2** an introduction to a novel, poem, or other literary work. **3** any introductory act or event. *n.* Also, **prolog**.

**pro·long** (prə long′) make longer; draw out; stretch; protract: *Good care may prolong life. The lonesome dog uttered prolonged howls.* *v.*

**pro·lon·ga·tion** (prō′long gā′shən) **1** an extension; lengthening in time or space: *the prolongation of one's university days by graduate study.* **2** an added part. *n.*

**prom** (prom) *Informal.* a dance or ball given by a college or high-school class. *n.*

**prom·e·nade** (prom′ə nād′ *or* prom′ə näd′) **1** a walk for pleasure or display: *The Easter promenade is well known as a fashion show.* **2** walk about or up and down for pleasure or for display: *She promenaded back and forth on the ship's deck.* **3** a public place for such a walk: *Toronto has a famous promenade called the "Boardwalk."* **4** walk through. **5** take on a promenade. **6** a dance; ball. **7** a march of all the guests at the opening of a formal dance. 1, 3, 6, 7 *n.*, 2, 4, 5 *v.*, **prom·e·nad·ed, prom·e·nad·ing**. —**prom′e·nad′er**, *n.*

**pro·me·thi·um** (prə mē′thē əm) a rare metallic element. *Symbol:* Pm *n.*

**prom·i·nence** (prom′ə nəns) **1** the quality or fact of being PROMINENT, distinguished, or conspicuous: *the prominence of athletics in some schools.* **2** something that juts out or projects, especially upward: *A hill is a prominence.* *n.*

**prom·i·nent** (prom′ə nənt) **1** well-known; important: *a prominent citizen.* **2** easy to see: *A single tree in a field is prominent.* **3** standing out; projecting: *Some insects have prominent eyes.* *adj.* —**prom′i·nent·ly**, *adv.*

**prom·is·cu·i·ty** (prom′is kyü′ə tē) the fact, state, or condition of being PROMISCUOUS. *n.*

**pro·mis·cu·ous** (prə mis′kyü əs) **1** mixed and in disorder: *a promiscuous heap of clothing on your closet floor.* **2** making no distinctions; not discriminating, especially in sexual relationships: *promiscuous friendships, a promiscuous woman.* *adj.* —**pro·mis′cu·ous·ly**, *adv.*

**prom·ise** (prom′is) **1** the words that bind a person to do or not to do something: *A man of honour always keeps his promise.* **2** make a promise of something to a person, etc.: *to promise help.* **3** give one's word; make a promise: *She promised to stay till we came.* **4** an indication of what may be expected: *The clouds give promise of rain.* **5** an indication of future excellence; something that gives hope of success: *a young scholar who shows promise.* **6** give indication of; give hope of; give grounds for expectation: *The rainbow promises fair weather. The dark clouds promise rain.* 1, 4, 5 *n.*, 2, 3, 6 *v.*, **prom·ised, prom·is·ing**.

**prom·is·ing** (prom′i sing) **1** likely to turn out well: *a promising violinist.* **2** ppr. of PROMISE. 1 *adj.*, 2 *v.* —**prom′is·ing·ly**, *adv.*

**prom·is·so·ry** (prom′ə sôr′ē) containing a promise. *adj.*

**promissory note** a written promise to pay a stated sum of money to a certain person at a certain time.

A promontory

**prom·on·to·ry** (prom′ən tô′rē) a high point of land extending from the coast into the water; headland. *n., pl.* **prom·on·to·ries.**

**pro·mote** (prə mōt′) 1 raise in rank, condition, or importance: *Those who pass the test will be promoted to the next higher grade.* 2 help to grow or develop; help to success: *The United Nations has done much to promote peace.* 3 help to organize; start: *Several bankers promoted the new company.* 4 further the sale of an article by advertising: *to promote a new product.* *v.*, **pro·mot·ed, pro·mot·ing.**

**pro·mot·er** (prə mō′tər) 1 a person or thing that PROMOTES: *Good humour is a promoter of friendship.* 2 one who organizes new companies and secures capital for them. *n.*

**pro·mo·tion** (prə mō′shən) 1 an advance in rank or importance: *The clerk was given a promotion and an increase in salary.* 2 helping to grow or develop; helping along to success: *The doctors were busy in the promotion of a health campaign.* 3 publicity; advertising. *n.*

**prompt** (prompt) 1 on time; quick: *Be prompt to obey.* 2 done at once; made without delay: *I expect a prompt answer.* 3 cause someone to do something: *Her curiosity prompted her to ask questions.* 4 give rise to; suggest; inspire: *A kind thought prompted the gift.* 5 remind a learner, speaker, actor, etc. of the words or actions needed: *Rosemary will prompt you if you forget your lines in the play.* 6 in computer science, a message on the screen requesting input. 7 request input through a message on the screen. 1, 2 *adj.*, 3–5, 7 *v.*, 6 *n.* —**prompt′ly,** *adv.* —**prompt′ness,** *n.*

**promp·ter** (promp′tər) a person who tells actors, speakers, etc. what to say when they forget. *n.*

**promp·ti·tude** (promp′tə tyüd′ or promp′tə tüd′) promptness; readiness in acting or deciding. *n.*

**pro·mul·gate** (prom′əl gāt′ or prō mul′gāt) 1 proclaim formally; announce officially: *The queen promulgated a decree.* 2 spread far and wide: *Schools try to promulgate knowledge and good habits.* *v.*, **pro·mul·gat·ed, pro·mul·gat·ing.**

**pro·mul·ga·tion** (prō′mul gā′shən or prom′əl gā′shən) 1 promulgating. 2 being PROMULGATED. *n.*

**pron.** 1 pronoun. 2 pronunciation.

**prone** (prōn) 1 inclined; liable (*to*): *prone to evil. He was prone to believe the worst of everyone.* 2 very likely to have (*used in compounds*): *She is accident-prone.* 3 lying face downwards. Compare with SUPINE. 4 lying flat. *adj.*

**prone·ness** (prōn′nis) 1 an inclination; tendency; preference: *Because of a proneness to pneumonia she tries to avoid colds.* 2 a PRONE position. *n.*

**prong** (prong) 1 one of the pointed ends of a fork, antler, etc. 2 pierce or stab with a prong. 1 *n.*, 2 *v.*

hat, āge, fär; let, ēqual, tėrm; it, īce
hot, ōpen, ôrder; oil, out; cup, put, rüle
əbove, takən, pencəl, lemən, circəs
ch, child; ng, long; sh, ship
th, thin; ᴛʜ, then; zh, measure

**pronged** (prongd) 1 having PRONGS. 2 pt. and pp. of PRONG. 1 *adj.*, 2 *v.*

**prong·horn** (prong′hôrn′) a mammal like an antelope, found on the plains of western North America. See ANTELOPE for picture. *n., pl.* **prong·horns** or (*esp. collectively*) **prong·horn.**

**pro·nom·i·nal** (prō nom′ə nəl) of or having to do with PRONOUNS; having the nature of a pronoun. *adj.*

**pro·nom·i·nal·ly** (prō nom′ə nə lē) like a PRONOUN. *adv.*

**pro·noun** (prō′noun) a word used instead of a noun. Examples: *I, we, you, he, it, they, who, whose, which, this, mine, whatever.* *n.*

**pro·nounce** (prə nouns′) 1 make the sounds of; speak: *Pronounce your words clearly.* 2 pronounce words. 3 give an opinion or decision: *Only an expert should pronounce on this case.* 4 declare a person or thing to be: *The doctor pronounced her cured.* 5 declare formally or solemnly: *The judge pronounced sentence on the criminal.* *v.*, **pro·nounced, pro·nounc·ing.** —**pro·nounce′a·ble,** *adj.*

**pro·nounced** (prə nounst′) 1 strongly marked; decided: *She held pronounced opinions on gambling.* 2 pt. and pp. of PRONOUNCE. 1 *adj.*, 2 *v.* —**pro·nounc′ed·ly** (prə noun′si dlē), *adv.*

**pro·nounce·ment** (prə nouns′mənt) 1 a formal statement; declaration. 2 an opinion; decision. *n.*

**pron·to** (pron′tō) *Informal.* promptly; quickly; right away. *adv.*

**pro·nun·ci·a·tion** (prə nun′sē ā′shən) 1 the way of pronouncing: *Most dictionaries give the pronunciation of each entry word.* 2 a pronouncing. *n.*

**proof** (prüf) 1 a way or means of showing beyond doubt the truth of something: *Is what you say a guess or have you proof?* 2 establishment of the truth of anything. 3 the act of testing; trial: *That box looks big enough; but let us put it to the proof.* 4 the condition of having been tested and approved. 5 a trial impression from type: *A book is first printed in proof so that errors can be corrected.* 6 a trial print of an etching, photographic negative, etc. 7 of tested value against something: *Now we know that we are proof against being taken by surprise.* 1–6 *n.*, 7 *adj.*

**–proof** an adjective-forming suffix meaning: protected against; safe from, as in *fireproof, waterproof, bombproof.*

**proof·read** (prüf′rēd′) read printers' proofs, etc. and mark errors to be corrected. *v.*, **proof·read** (-red′), **proof·read·ing.** —**proof′read′er,** *n.*

**prop¹** (prop) 1 hold up by placing a support under or against (*usually used with* **up**): *Prop up the clothesline with a stick.* 2 support; sustain: *to prop a failing cause.* 3 a support; thing or person used to support another: *Many branches are heavy with apples and need a prop.* 1, 2 *v.*, **propped, prop·ping;** 3 *n.*

**prop²** (prop) *Informal.* any article, such as a table or a weapon, used in staging a play: *Prop is short for property.* See PROPERTY (def. 5). *n.*

**prop.** proprietor.

**prop·a·gan·da** (prop′ə gan′də) 1 systematic efforts to spread opinions or beliefs, especially by distortion and deception: *The Nazis were experts in propaganda.* 2 any plan or method for spreading opinions or beliefs: *The life insurance companies engaged in health propaganda.* 3 the opinions or beliefs thus spread. *n.*
☛ *Etym.* From Modern Latin *Propaganda*, a short name for the Roman Catholic *Congregatio de propaganda fide* 'Congregation for the Propagation of the Faith', a committee of the Church responsible for foreign missions. Though **propaganda** (as in def. 2) may still be used for honest efforts to spread beliefs or opinions that are accepted as worthwhile, the word usually refers nowadays to unscrupulous methods of spreading beliefs or opinions that are judged to be misguided or distasteful.

**prop·a·gan·dist** (prop′ə gan′dist) 1 a person who gives time, effort, etc. to the spreading of PROPAGANDA. 2 of PROPAGANDA or propagandists. *n.*

**prop·a·gan·dize** (prop′ə gan′dīz) 1 propagate or spread doctrines, etc. by PROPAGANDA. 2 carry on PROPAGANDA. *v.*, **prop·a·gan·dized, prop·a·gan·diz·ing.**

**prop·a·gate** (prop′ə gāt′) 1 produce offspring; reproduce. 2 increase in number; multiply: *Trees propagate themselves by seeds.* 3 cause to increase in number by the production of young: *Cows and sheep are propagated on farms.* 4 spread news, knowledge, etc.: *Don't propagate unkind reports.* 5 pass on; send further: *Sound is propagated by vibrations.* *v.*, **prop·a·gat·ed, prop·a·gat·ing.**

**prop·a·ga·tion** (prop′ə gā′shən) 1 the breeding of plants or animals. 2 spreading or getting more widely believed; making more widely known: *the propagation of the principles of science.* 3 passing on; sending further; spreading or extending: *the propagation of the shock of an earthquake.* *n.*

**pro·pane** (prō′pān) a gaseous HYDROCARBON; a heavy, colourless gas used for fuel, refrigeration, etc. *n.*

**pro·pel** (prə pel′) drive forward; force ahead: *to propel a boat by oars, a person propelled by ambition.* *v.*, **pro·pelled, pro·pel·ling.**

**pro·pel·lant** (prə pel′ənt) 1 something that PROPELS, such as the fuel of a missile or the explosive charge of a shell. 2 a person who PROPELS. *n.*

**pro·pel·lent** (prə pel′ənt) 1 propelling; driving forward. 2 PROPELLANT. 1 *adj.*, 2 *n.*

A steamship's propellers     An airplane propeller

**pro·pel·ler** (prə pel′ər) 1 a device with revolving blades, for propelling boats and aircraft. See AIRPLANE for another picture. 2 a person or thing that PROPELS. *n.*

**pro·pen·si·ty** (prə pen′sə tē) a natural inclination or bent; inclination: *Most children have a propensity for playing with water.* *n.*, *pl.* **pro·pen·si·ties.**

**prop·er** (prop′ər) 1 correct; right; fitting: *Night is the proper time to sleep, and bed the proper place.* 2 strictly so called; in the strict sense of the word: *The population of Vancouver proper does not include that of the suburbs.* 3 decent; respectable: *proper conduct.* 4 referring to a particular person, place, institution, etc.: *Sandra is a proper name.* 5 *Informal.* complete; thorough; fine; excellent. 6 belonging exclusively or distinctively: *qualities proper to a substance.* *adj.*

**proper fraction** a fraction less than 1. Examples of proper fractions are ²/₃, ¹/₈, ³/₄, and ¹⁹⁹/₂₀₀.

**prop·er·ly** (prop′ər lē) 1 in a proper, correct, or fitting manner: *This job must be done properly.* 2 rightly; justly: *The policewoman was properly indignant at the offer of a bribe.* 3 strictly: *Properly speaking, a whale is not a fish.* *adv.*

**proper noun** in grammar, a noun that identifies one particular person, place, organization, period of time, etc.; a name used to identify an individual: *Sarah, Calgary, and Renaissance* are proper nouns. Compare with COMMON NOUN.

**prop·er·tied** (prop′ər tēd) owning PROPERTY (defs. 1, 2). *adj.*

**prop·er·ty** (prop′ər tē) 1 any thing or things owned; possession or possessions: *This house is Mrs. Berg's property.* 2 a piece of land or real estate: *She owns some property out West.* 3 ownership; the people who own land, etc.: *the demands of property for lower taxes.* 4 a quality or power belonging specially to something: *Soap has the property of removing dirt.* 5 **properties,** *pl.* the furniture, weapons, etc. used in staging a play, motion picture, or television scene. *n.*, *pl.* **prop·er·ties.**

**pro·phase** (prō′fāz) the first stage of MITOSIS, in which changes take place in the nucleus of a cell. *n.*

**proph·e·cy** (prof′ə sē) 1 a telling of what will happen; the foretelling of future events: *She claims to have the gift of prophecy.* 2 something told about the future. 3 a divinely inspired utterance, revelation, writing, etc. *n.*, *pl.* **proph·e·cies.**

**proph·e·sy** (prof′ə sī′) 1 tell what will happen. 2 foretell; predict: *The sailor prophesied a severe storm.* 3 speak when or as if divinely inspired. 4 utter in prophecy. *v.*, **proph·e·sied, proph·e·sy·ing.**

**proph·et** (prof′it) 1 a person who tells what will happen. 2 a person who believes his or her preaching to be inspired by God: *Every religion has its prophets.* 3 **the Prophet,** among Moslems, Mohammed. 4 **the Prophets,** books of the Old Testament written by prophets. *n.*
☛ *Hom.* PROFIT.

**proph·et·ess** (prof′i tis) a woman PROPHET. *n.*

**pro·phet·ic** (prə fet′ik) 1 belonging to a PROPHET; such as a prophet has: *prophetic power.* 2 containing prophecy: *a prophetic saying.* 3 giving warning of what is to happen; foretelling: *Thunder is prophetic of rain.* *adj.*
—**pro·phet′i·cal·ly,** *adv.*

**pro·phy·lac·tic** (prō′fə lak′tik *or* prof′ə lak′tik) 1 protecting from disease. 2 a medicine or treatment that protects against disease. 3 protective; preservative; precautionary. 4 precaution. 1, 3 *adj.*, 2, 4 *n.*

**pro·phy·lax·is** (prō′fə lak′sis *or* prof′ə lak′sis) 1 protection from disease. 2 treatment to prevent disease. *n.*

**pro·pin·qui·ty** (prō ping′kwə tē) 1 nearness in place, especially personal nearness. 2 nearness of blood; kinship. *n.*

**pro·pi·ti·ate** (prə pish′ē āt′) prevent or reduce the anger of; win the favour of; appease or conciliate. *v.*, **pro·pi·ti·at·ed, pro·pi·ti·at·ing.** —**pro·pi′ti·a′tor,** *n.*

**pro·pi·ti·a·tion** (prə pish′ē ā′shən) the act of propitiating. *n.*

**pro·pi·ti·a·to·ry** (prə pish′ē ə tô′rē) intended to PROPITIATE; making propitiation; conciliatory: *a propitiatory offering. adj.*

**pro·pi·tious** (prə pish′əs) 1 favourable: *It seemed propitious weather for our trip.* 2 favourably inclined; gracious: *The ancient Romans used to consult the omens to see if the gods were propitious to their plans. adj.* —**pro·pi′tious·ly,** *adv.* —**pro·pi′tious·ness,** *n.*

**pro·po·nent** (prə pō′nənt) 1 one who makes a proposal or proposition. 2 a favourer; supporter. *n.*

**pro·por·tion** (prə pôr′shən) 1 the relation in size, number, amount, or degree of one thing compared to another: *Each woman's pay will be in proportion to her work.* 2 a proper relation between parts: *Her short legs were out of proportion with her long body.* 3 fit one thing to another so that they go together: *The designs in that rug are well-proportioned.* 4 a part or share: *A large proportion of British Columbia is mountainous.* 5 an equality of ratios. *Example:* 4 is to 2 as 10 is to 5. 6 a method of finding the fourth term of such a proportion when three are known. 7 **proportions,** *pl.* **a** size; extent: *Canada has forests of huge proportions.* **b** dimensions: *The proportions of the furniture are wrong for this small room.* 1, 2, 4–6 *n.*, 3 *v.* —**pro·por′tion·ment,** *n.*

**pro·por·tion·a·ble** (prə pôr′shə nə bəl) being in due proportion; PROPORTIONAL. *adj.*

**pro·por·tion·al** (prə pôr′shə nəl) 1 in the proper PROPORTION; corresponding: *The increase in price is proportional to the improvement in the car.* 2 one of the terms of a proportion in mathematics. 1 *adj.*, 2 *n.*

**pro·por·tion·al·ly** (prə pôr′shə nə lē) in PROPORTION. *adv.*

**proportional representation** an electoral system in which the number of seats that each party or group is given is proportional to its share of the total number of votes cast.

**pro·por·tion·ate** (prə pôr′shə nit) in the proper PROPORTION; proportioned; proportional: *The money obtained by the bazaar was really not proportionate to the effort we put into it. adj.*

**pro·por·tion·ate·ly** (prə pôr′shə ni tlē) in PROPORTION: *The money the girls earned was divided proportionately to the time each worked. adv.*

**pro·por·tioned** (prə pôr′shənd) 1 adjusted in PROPORTION. 2 pt. and pp. of PROPORTION. 1 *adj.*, 2 *v.*

**pro·pos·al** (prə pō′zəl) 1 what is proposed; plan; scheme; suggestion: *The club welcomed our member's proposal.* 2 an offer of marriage. 3 the act of proposing: *Her proposal for a new committee was interrupted by several members. n.*

**pro·pose** (prə pōz′) 1 put forward for consideration, discussion, acceptance, etc.; suggest: *I propose that we take turns at the swing.* 2 present the name of someone for office, membership, etc. 3 present as a toast to be drunk. 4 intend; plan: *She proposes to save half of all she* earns. 5 make an offer of marriage. *v.*, **pro·posed, pro·pos·ing.**

**prop·o·si·tion** (prop′ə zish′ən) 1 what is offered to be considered; a proposal: *The tailor made a proposition to buy out his rival's business.* 2 a statement; assertion. *Example: The earth is round.* 3 a statement of the subject of a debate. *Example: Resolved. That our school should have a bank.* 4 a problem to be solved: *a proposition in geometry.* 5 a business enterprise; an undertaking: *a paying proposition.* 6 *Informal.* a person or thing to be dealt with. 7 *Informal.* propose a scheme, plan, or action to, often an improper one. 1–6 *n.*, 7 *v.*

**pro·pound** (prə pound′) put forward; propose: *to propound a theory, a question, or a riddle. v.* —**pro·pound′er,** *n.*

**pro·pri·e·tar·y** (prə prī′ə ter′ē) 1 belonging to a proprietor. 2 holding property. 3 owner. 4 a group of owners. 5 ownership; the holding of property. 6 owned by a private person or company; belonging to or controlled by a private person as property: *A proprietary medicine is a patent medicine, that is, one which can be made and sold only by some one person or certain persons.* 7 in former times, the owner or group of owners of a grant from a king of England. 1, 2, 6 *adj.*, 3–5, 7 *n.*, *pl.* **pro·pri·e·tar·ies.**

**pro·pri·e·tor** (prə prī′ə tər) an owner, especially of a business; manager. *n.*

**pro·pri·e·tor·ship** (prə prī′ə tər ship′) ownership. *n.*

**pro·pri·e·tress** (prə prī′ə tris) a woman owner or manager. *n.*

**pro·pri·e·ty** (prə prī′ə tē) 1 the quality of being proper; fitness. 2 proper behaviour: *She acted with propriety.* 3 **proprieties,** *pl.* the conventional standards or requirements of proper behaviour: *The proprieties require that a boy stand up when he is introduced to a lady. n.*, *pl.* **pro·pri·e·ties.**

**pro·pul·sion** (prə pul′shən) 1 a driving forward or onward. 2 a propelling force or impulse: *the propulsion of jet engines. n.*

**pro·pul·sive** (prə pul′siv) propelling; driving forward or onward. *adj.*

**pro ra·ta** (prō rā′tə *or* prō rä′tə) *Latin.* in proportion; according to the share, interest, etc. of each.

**pro·rate** (prō rāt′) distribute or assess proportionally: *We prorated the money according to the number of days each had worked. v.*, **pro·rat·ed, pro·rat·ing.**

**pro·ro·ga·tion** (prō′rə gā′shən) the discontinuance of the meetings of a lawmaking body without dissolving it. *n.*

**pro·rogue** (prō rōg′) discontinue the regular meetings of a lawmaking body for a time. *v.*, **pro·rogued, pro·rogu·ing.**

**pro·sa·ic** (prō zā′ik) like prose; matter-of-fact; ordinary; not exciting: *The new play was rather prosaic. adj.* —**pro·sa′i·cal·ly,** *adv.*

---

propinquity 947 prosaic

hat, āge, fär; let, ēqual, tėrm; it, īce
hot, ōpen, ôrder; oil, out; cup, pùt, rüle
əbove, takən, pencəl, lemən, circəs
ch, child; ng, long; sh, ship
th, thin; ᴛʜ, then; zh, measure

**pro·sce·ni·um** (prō sē′nē əm) 1 the part of the stage in front of the curtain. 2 the curtain and the framework that holds it. 3 the stage of an ancient theatre or of a modern theatre having no curtains. *n., pl.* **pro·sce·ni·a** (-nē ə).

**pro·scribe** (prō skrīb′) 1 prohibit as wrong or dangerous; condemn: *In earlier days, the church proscribed dancing and cardplaying.* 2 put outside the protection of the law; outlaw. 3 forbid to come into a certain place; banish. *v.*, **pro·scribed, pro·scrib·ing.**

**pro·scrip·tion** (prō skrip′shən) 1 proscribing. 2 being PROSCRIBEd. *n.*

**prose** (prōz) 1 the ordinary form of spoken or written language. 2 language not arranged in poetic metre: *This writer's prose is better than her poetry. Milton and Samuel Johnson are masters of English prose.* 3 of prose; in prose. 4 dull, ordinary talk. 5 lacking imagination; matter-of-fact; commonplace. 6 talk or write in a dull, commonplace way. 1–5 *n.*, 6 *v.*, **prosed, pros·ing.**

**pros·e·cute** (pros′ə kyüt′) 1 bring before a court of law: *Reckless drivers will be prosecuted.* 2 bring a case before a law court. 3 carry out; follow up: *She prosecuted an inquiry into reasons for the company's failure.* 4 carry on a business or occupation. *v.*, **pros·e·cut·ed, pros·e·cut·ing.**
☛ *Usage.* See note at PERSECUTE.

**pros·e·cu·tion** (pros′ə kyü′shən) 1 the carrying on of a lawsuit: *The prosecution will be abandoned if the stolen money is returned.* 2 the side that starts action against another in a law court: *The prosecution makes certain charges against the defence.* 3 a carrying out; following up: *In prosecution of her plan, she stored away a supply of food. n.*

**pros·e·cu·tor** (pros′ə kyü′tər) 1 a lawyer who represents the state in the conducting of proceedings in a court of law against persons accused of crime. In Canada, such a person is a **Crown prosecutor,** who is a full-time or part-time officer of the court. 2 any person who carries on legal proceedings against another or others. *n.*

**pros·e·lyte** (pros′ə līt′) 1 a person who has been converted from one opinion, religious belief, etc. to another. 2 convert from one opinion, religious belief, etc. to another. 1 *n.*, 2 *v.*, **pros·e·lyt·ed, pros·e·lyt·ing.**

**pros·e·lyt·ize** (pros′ə lə tīz′ *or* pros′ə lī tīz′) make converts; proselyte. *v.*, **pros·e·lyt·ized, pros·e·lyt·iz·ing.**

**pros·o·dy** (pros′ə dē) the science of poetic metres and versification. *n.*

**pros·pect** (pros′pekt) 1 anything expected or looked forward to: *good prospects in business.* 2 the act of looking forward; expectation: *The prospect of a vacation is pleasant.* 3 outlook for the future. 4 a person who may be a customer, candidate, etc.; prospective customer: *The saleswoman had several prospects in mind.* 5 a view; scene: *The prospect from the mountain was grand.* 6 in mining, search: *to prospect for gold, to prospect a region for silver.* 1–5 *n.*, 6 *v.*
**in prospect,** expected; looked forward to.

**pro·spec·tive** (prə spek′tiv) 1 probable; expected: *a prospective client.* 2 looking forward to the future: *a prospective suggestion. adj.* —**pro·spec′tive·ly,** *adv.*

**pros·pec·tor** (pros′pek tər) a person who explores or examines a region for gold, silver, etc. *n.*

**pro·spec·tus** (prə spek′təs) a printed statement describing and advertising something. *n.*

**pros·per** (pros′pər) 1 be successful; have good fortune; flourish: *That man prospers in everything he attempts.* 2 make successful. *v.*

**pros·per·i·ty** (pros per′ə tē) a PROSPEROUS condition; good fortune; success. *n., pl.* **pros·per·i·ties.**

**pros·per·ous** (pros′pə rəs) 1 successful; thriving; doing well; fortunate: *A prosperous person is one who is happy, healthy, paying her way, and getting on well in her work.* 2 favourable; helpful: *prosperous weather for growing wheat. adj.* —**pros′per·ous·ly,** *adv.* —**pros′per·ous·ness,** *n.*

**pros·tate** (pros′tāt) 1 a large gland surrounding the male urethra in front of the bladder. 2 designating or having to do with this gland. 1 *n.*, 2 *adj.*

**pros·the·sis** (pros′thə sis *or* pros thē′sis) 1 the addition of a false tooth, artificial leg, etc. to the body. 2 the part itself. *n., pl.* **pros·the·ses** (-sēz′).

**pros·thet·ics** (pros thet′iks) the branch of dentistry or surgery pertaining to PROSTHESIS. *n.*

**pros·ti·tute** (pros′tə tyüt′ *or* pros′tə tüt′) 1 a girl or woman who accepts money to engage in sexual acts with men. 2 any person who accepts payment for sexual acts: *a male prostitute.* 3 offer oneself or another person for hire to commit sexual acts. 4 give up oneself or one's talents to an unworthy cause: *He has prostituted his art by selling paintings that he knows are not well done.* 5 a person who gives up himself or herself or his or her talents to an unworthy cause. 1, 2, 5 *n.*, 3, 4 *v.*, **pros·ti·tut·ed, pros·ti·tut·ing.**

**pros·ti·tu·tion** (pros′tə tyü′shən *or* pros′tə tü′shən) 1 the act or business of offering oneself or another person for hire to engage in sexual acts. 2 the act of giving up oneself or one's talents to an unworthy cause: *Churning out those cheap romances is a prostitution of her talents as a writer. n.*

**pros·trate** (pros′trāt) 1 lay down flat; cast down: *The captives prostrated themselves before the conqueror.* 2 lying flat, with the face downward. 3 lying flat. 4 make very weak or helpless; exhaust: *Sickness often prostrates people.* 5 helpless; overcome: *a prostrate enemy.* 1, 4 *v.*, **pros·trat·ed, pros·trat·ing;** 2, 3, 5 *adj.*

**pros·tra·tion** (pros trā′shən) 1 the act of prostrating; bowing down low or lying face down in submission, respect, or worship. 2 exhaustion; dejection; the state or condition of being very much worn out in body or mind. *n.*

**pros·y** (prō′zē) like PROSE; commonplace; dull; tiresome. *adj.*, **pros·i·er, pros·i·est.** —**pros′i·ness,** *n.*

**prot·ac·tin·i·um** (prō′tak tin′ē əm) a rare radioactive metallic element. *Symbol:* Pa *n.*

**pro·tag·o·nist** (prō tag′ə nist) 1 the main character in a play, story, or novel. 2 a person who takes a leading part; an active supporter. *n.*

**pro·te·an** (prō′tē ən) readily assuming different forms or characters; exceedingly variable. *adj.*

**pro·tect** (prə tekt′) 1 shield from harm or danger; shelter; defend; guard: *Protect yourself from danger. Protect the baby's eyes from the sun.* 2 guard home industry against foreign goods by taxing any that are brought into the country. *v.*

**pro·tect·ing·ly** (prə tek′ting lē)   so as to protect. *adv.*

**pro·tec·tion** (prə tek′shən)   **1** the act of protecting; condition of being kept from harm; defence: *We have police officers for our protection.*   **2** a thing or person that prevents damage: *This apron is my protection against paint splatters.*   **3** the system of taxing foreign goods so that people are more likely to buy goods made in their own country; the opposite of FREE TRADE.   **4** something that assures safe passage through a region; passport.   *n.*

**pro·tec·tion·ism** (prə tek′shə niz′əm)   the economic system or theory of PROTECTION (def. 3).   *n.*

**pro·tec·tion·ist** (prə tek′shə nist)   **1** a person who favours PROTECTIONISM.   **2** of PROTECTIONISM or protectionists.   *n.*

**pro·tec·tive** (prə tek′tiv)   **1** being a defence; protecting: *a protective helmet.*   **2** preventing injury to those around: *a protective device on a machine.*   **3** guarding against foreign-made goods by putting a high tax or duty on them: *a protective tariff.*   *adj.*
—**pro·tec′tive·ly,** *adv.*   —**pro·tec′tive·ness,** *n.*

**protective colouring** or **coloring**   a colouring some animals have that makes them hard to distinguish from the things they live among, and so hides them from their enemies.

**protective mimicry**   a close resemblance of an animal to its surroundings, or to some different animal, that prevents its enemies from attacking it.

**pro·tec·tor** (prə tek′tər)   **1** a person or thing that protects; defender.   **2** the head of a kingdom when the king or queen cannot rule: *Oliver Cromwell was Lord Protector of England from 1653 to 1658.*   *n.*

**pro·tec·tor·ate** (prə tek′tə rit)   **1** a weak country under the protection and partial control of a strong country.   **2** such protection and control.   **3** the position or term of a PROTECTOR (def. 2).   **4** government by a PROTECTOR (def. 2).   *n.*

**pro·tec·tress** (prə tek′tris)   a woman protector.   *n.*

**pro·té·gé** (prō′tə zhā′)   a person under the patronage or protection of another.   *n.*

**pro·té·gée** (prō′tə zhā′)   a woman PROTÉGÉ.   *n.*

**pro·tein** (prō′tēn *or* prō′tē in)   a complex compound containing nitrogen, etc., a necessary part of the cells of animals and plants: *Meat, fish, milk, cheese, eggs, and beans contain protein.*   *n.*

**pro·test** (prō′test *for noun,* prə test′ *for verb*)   **1** a statement that denies or objects strongly: *They yielded only after much protest.*   **2** make objections; object: *The boys protested against having girls in the game.*   **3** object to: *to protest a decision.*   **4** a solemn declaration: *The accused man was judged guilty in spite of his protest of innocence.*   **5** declare solemnly; assert: *The accused man protested his innocence.*   **6** a written statement by a NOTARY PUBLIC that a bill, note, cheque, etc. has been presented to someone who has refused to pay it or accept it.   **7** state that a cheque, note, bill, etc. has not been paid.   1, 4, 6 *n.*, 2, 3, 5, 7 *v.*
**under protest,**   unwillingly; though objecting: *The prisoner obeyed under protest.*

**Prot·es·tant** (prot′i stənt)   **1** a member or adherent of certain Christian churches that have developed after the break with the Roman Catholic Church in the 16th century.   **2** of Protestants or their religion.   1 *n.*, 2 *adj.*

**Prot·es·tant·ism** (prot′i stən tiz′əm)   **1** the religion of PROTESTANTS.   **2** their principles and beliefs.   **3** PROTESTANTS or Protestant churches as a group.   *n.*

**prot·es·ta·tion** (prot′i stā′shən)   **1** a solemn declaration; PROTESTing: *to make a protestation of one's innocence.*   **2** a PROTEST.   *n.*

**pro·tist** (prō′tist)   any of the **Protista** that include algae, yeasts, bacteria, etc.   *n.*

**pro·to·col** (prō′tə kol′)   **1** a first draft or record from which a document, especially a treaty, is prepared.   **2** the rules of etiquette of the diplomatic corps.   *n.*

**pro·ton** (prō′ton)   in physics, an elementary particle carrying one unit of positive electric charge, found in the nucleus of every kind of atom: *Each kind of atom has a different number of protons; for instance, the nucleus of a hydrogen atom has one proton; that of an oxygen atom has eight.*   *n.*

**pro·to·plasm** (prō′tə plaz′əm)   living matter; a colourless substance somewhat like soft jelly or egg white that is the living substance of all plant and animal cells.   *n.*

**pro·to·plas·mic** (prō′tə plaz′mik)   of PROTOPLASM; having to do with protoplasm.   *adj.*

**pro·to·type** (prō′tə tīp′)   the first or primary type of anything; the original or model: *A modern ship has its prototype in the hollowed log used by primitive peoples.*   *n.*

**Pro·to·zo·a** (prō′tə zō′ə)   PROTOZOANS.   *n.pl.*

**pro·to·zo·an** (prō′tə zō′ən)   **1** a microscopic animal that consists of a single cell.   **2** belonging or having to do with the single-celled animals.   1 *n.*, 2 *adj.*

**pro·tract** (prō trakt′)   **1** draw out; lengthen in time: *to protract a visit.*   **2** slide out; thrust out; extend.   **3** draw by means of a scale and PROTRACTOR (def. 1).   *v.*

**pro·tract·ed** (prō trak′tid)   **1** lengthened.   **2** pt. and pp. of PROTRACT.   1 *adj.*, 2 *v.*

**pro·trac·tile** (prō trak′tīl *or* prō trak′təl)   capable of being lengthened out, or of being thrust forth: *The turtle has a protractile head.*   *adj.*

**pro·trac·tion** (prō trak′shən)   **1** the act of drawing out; extension.   **2** a drawing that has exactly the same proportions as the thing it represents.   *n.*

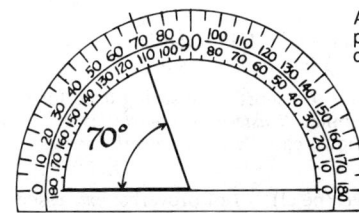

A protractor. The middle part of the instrument is cut out or transparent.

**pro·trac·tor** (prō trak′tər)   **1** an instrument in the form

**pro·trude** (prō trüd′ *or* prə trüd′) 1 thrust forth; stick out: *The saucy child protruded her tongue.* 2 be thrust forth; project: *Her teeth protrude too far.* *v.*, **pro·trud·ed, pro·trud·ing.**

**pro·tru·sion** (prō trü′zhən *or* prə trü′zhən) 1 a protruding or being protruded: *Starvation caused the protrusion of the poor cat's bones.* 2 a projection; something that sticks out: *A protrusion of rock gave us shelter from the storm.* *n.*

**pro·tru·sive** (prō trü′siv *or* prə trü′siv) sticking out; projecting. *adj.*

**pro·tu·ber·ance** (prō tyü′bə rəns *or* prō tü′bə rəns) a part that sticks out; bulge; swelling. *n.*

**pro·tu·ber·ant** (prō tyü′bə rənt *or* prō tü′bə rənt) bulging; sticking out; prominent. *adj.* —**pro·tu′ber·ant·ly,** *adv.*

**proud** (proud) 1 thinking well of oneself: *He was too proud to cry when he cut himself.* 2 feeling or showing pleasure or satisfaction: *I am proud to call him my friend.* 3 having a becoming sense of what is due to oneself, one's position, or character. 4 thinking too well of oneself; haughty; arrogant: *She was too proud to share a taxi with a stranger.* 5 such as to make a person proud; highly honourable, creditable, or gratifying: *a proud moment.* 6 proceeding from pride; due to pride: *a proud smile.* 7 imposing; stately; majestic; magnificent: *proud cities.* *adj.* —**proud′ly,** *adv.* —**proud′ness,** *n.*
**proud of,** thinking well of; being well satisfied with; proud because of: *be proud of oneself, be proud of one's family.*

**proud flesh** the formation of too many grainlike particles of flesh during the healing of a wound or sore.

**prov.** 1 province. 2 provincial. 3 provisional. 4 provost.

**Prov.** 1 Province. 2 Provost.

**prove** (prüv) 1 establish as true; make certain: *Can you prove his guilt in court?* 2 establish the genuineness or validity of, especially of a will. 3 be found to be: *This book proved interesting.* 4 try out; test; subject to some testing process: *The test pilot spent months proving the new plane.* *v.*, **proved, proved** *or* **proven, prov·ing.** —**prov′a·ble,** *adj.*
**prove oneself,** show oneself to be: *He proved himself honest.*

**prov·en** (prü′vən) a pp. OF PROVE. *v.*

**Pro·ven·çal** (prov′ən sal′; *French,* prô vän säl′) 1 a native or inhabitant of Provence, a region in southeastern France. 2 the language of Provence. 3 of or having to do with Provence, its people, or their language. 1, 2 *n.*, 3 *adj.*

**prov·en·der** (prov′ən dər) 1 dry food for animals, such as hay or corn. 2 *Informal.* food. *n.*

**prov·erb** (prov′ėrb) 1 a short, wise saying used for a long time by many people: *"Haste makes waste" is a proverb.* 2 a well-known case: *He is a proverb for carelessness.* *n.*

**pro·ver·bi·al** (prə vėr′bē əl) 1 of proverbs; expressed in a proverb; like a proverb: *proverbial brevity, proverbial wisdom, a proverbial saying.* 2 that has become a proverb: *the proverbial stitch in time.* 3 well-known: *the proverbial loyalty of dogs.* *adj.* —**pro·ver′bi·al·ly,** *adv.*

**pro·vide** (prə vīd′) 1 supply; furnish: *Sheep provide us with wool.* 2 supply means of support; arrange to supply means of support: *Parents provide for their children.* 3 take care for the future: *to provide for old age.* 4 state as a condition beforehand: *Our club's rules provide that dues must be paid monthly.* 5 get ready; prepare: *They provided a good dinner.* *v.*, **pro·vid·ed, pro·vid·ing.** —**pro·vid′er,** *n.*

**pro·vid·ed** (prə vī′did) 1 on the condition that; if: *She will go provided her friends can go also.* 2 pt. and pp. of PROVIDE. 1 *conj.*, 2 *v.*

**prov·i·dence** (prov′ə dəns) 1 God's care and help. 2 an instance of God's care and help. 3 care for the future; good management: *Greater providence on the parents' part would have kept the children from poverty.* *n.*

**prov·i·dent** (prov′ə dənt) 1 having or showing foresight; careful in providing for the future: *Provident parents lay aside money for their families.* 2 economical; frugal. *adj.* —**prov′i·dent·ly,** *adv.*

**prov·i·den·tial** (prov′ə den′shəl) 1 fortunate: *Our delay seemed providential, for the train we had planned to take was wrecked.* 2 of or proceeding from divine power or influence. *adj.*

**pro·vid·ing** (prə vī′ding) 1 on the condition that: *I shall go providing it doesn't rain.* 2 ppr. of PROVIDE. 1 *conj.*, 2 *v.*

**prov·ince** (prov′əns) 1 in Canada, one of the ten main political divisions: *Newfoundland became the tenth province on April 1, 1949.* 2 in certain other countries, a main political or administrative division. 3 proper work or activity: *Teaching spelling is not within the province of a college.* 4 a division; department: *the province of science, the province of literature.* 5 an ancient Roman territory outside Italy, ruled by a Roman governor. 6 a large church district governed by an archbishop. 7 **provinces,** *pl.* the parts of a country at a distance from the capital or the largest cities: *She was accustomed to city life and did not like living in the provinces.* *n.*

**pro·vin·cial** (prə vin′shəl) 1 of a province. 2 a person born or living in the provinces. 3 belonging or peculiar to some particular province or provinces rather than to the whole country; local: *provincial England, provincial customs.* 4 having the manners, speech, dress, point of view, etc. of people living in the provinces. 5 lacking refinement or polish; narrow: *a provincial point of view.* 6 a provincial person. 1, 3–5 *adj.*, 2, 6 *n.* —**pro·vin′cial·ly,** *adv.*

**pro·vin·cial·ism** (prə vin′shə liz′əm) 1 provincial manners, habits of thought, etc. 2 narrow-mindedness. 3 a word, expression, or way of pronunciation peculiar to a district of a country; localism. *n.*

**pro·vin·ci·al·i·ty** (prə vin′shē al′ə tē) 1 a provincial quality or character. 2 a provincial characteristic or trait. *n., pl.* **pro·vin·ci·al·i·ties.**

**provincial park** *Cdn.* a tract of land established by a provincial government as a preserve for wildlife and as a holiday area: *Algonquin Park in Ontario is a well-known provincial park.*

**provincial parliament** *Cdn.* the legislative assembly of a province.

**pro·vi·sion** (prə vizh′ən) 1 a statement making a condition: *A provision of the lease is that the rent must be paid promptly.* 2 taking care for the future. 3 care

taken for the future; an arrangement made beforehand: *There is a provision for making the building larger if necessary.* **4** that which is made ready; supply; stock, especially of food; food. **5** supply with provisions. **6 provisions,** *pl.* a supply of food and drink. 1–4, 6 *n.*, 5 *v.*
**make provision,** take care for the future; make arrangements beforehand.

**pro·vi·sion·al** (prə vizh′ə nəl) for the time being; temporary: *a provisional agreement, a provisional government.* *adj.*

**pro·vi·sion·al·ly** (prə vizh′ə nə lē) **1** for the time being; temporarily. **2** conditionally. *adv.*

**pro·vi·so** (prə vī′zō) a sentence or part of a sentence in a contract, or other agreement, that states a condition; condition: *Aino was admitted to the eighth grade with the proviso that she was to be put back if she failed any subject.* *n., pl.* **pro·vi·sos** or **pro·vi·soes.**

**pro·vi·so·ry** (prə vī′zə rē) **1** containing a PROVISO; conditional. **2** provisional. *adj.*

**prov·o·ca·tion** (prov′ə kā′shən) **1** the act of provoking. **2** something that stirs one up; cause of anger: *Their insulting remarks were a provocation.* *n.*

**pro·voc·a·tive** (prə vok′ə tiv) **1** irritating; vexing. **2** tending or serving to call forth action, thought, laughter, anger, etc.: *a remark provocative of mirth.* **3** something that rouses or irritates. 1, 2 *adj.*, 3 *n.*
—**pro·voc′a·tive·ly,** *adv.* —**pro·voc′a·tive·ness,** *n.*

**pro·voke** (prə vōk′) **1** make angry; vex: *She provoked him by her teasing.* **2** stir up; excite: *An insult provokes a person to anger.* **3** call forth; bring about; start into action; cause: *The prime minister's speech provoked much discussion.* *v.,* **pro·voked, pro·vok·ing.**

**pro·vok·ing** (prə vō′king) **1** that provokes; irritating: *The habit of being late for meals is provoking to the cook.* **2** ppr. of PROVOKE. 1 *adj.,* 2 *v.* —**provok′ing·ly,** *adv.*

**prov·ost** (prov′əst) **1** a person appointed to superintend, maintain discipline, or preside, such as the head of certain colleges or churches. **2** in Scotland, the chief magistrate of a town. *n.*

**pro·vost marshal** (prō′vō) **1** in the army and air force, an officer acting as head of police in a camp or district, and charged with the maintenance of order, etc. **2** in the navy, an officer charged with the safekeeping of prisoners until their trial by court-martial.

**prow** (prou) **1** the front part of a ship or boat; bow. **2** the projecting front part of anything: *the prow of an aircraft.* *n.*

**prow·ess** (prou′is) **1** bravery; daring. **2** brave or daring acts. **3** unusual skill or ability: *Her prowess as a skater was widely recognized.* *n.*

**prowl** (proul) **1** go about slowly and secretly hunting for something to eat or steal: *Many wild animals prowl at night.* **2** wander: *He got up and prowled about his room.* **3** the act of prowling. 1, 2 *v.,* 3 *n.* —**prowl′er,** *n.*
**on the prowl,** prowling about.

**prowl car** a police car that patrols roads and streets and maintains contact with headquarters by radio telephone; squad car; cruiser.

**prox·i·mate** (prok′sə mit) **1** next; nearest. **2** near the exact amount; approximate. *adj.*

**prox·im·i·ty** (prok sim′ə tē) nearness; closeness: *She and her cat enjoy proximity to the fire.* *n.*

**provisional** 951 **P.S.**

hat, āge, fär; let, ēqual, tėrm; it, īce
hot, ōpen, ôrder; oil, out; cup, put, rüle
ə above, taken, pencəl, lemən, circəs
ch, child; ng, long; sh, ship
th, thin; ᴛʜ, then; zh, measure

**prox·y** (prok′sē) **1** the action of a deputy or substitute: *In marriage by proxy, someone is substituted for the absent bride or bridegroom at the marriage service.* **2** person authorized to act for another: *Rita acted as proxy for the child's godmother at the christening.* **3** a written statement authorizing a proxy to act or vote for a person. **4** the vote so given. *n., pl.* **prox·ies.**

**prude** (prüd) a person who appears to be too proper or too modest; a person who puts on extremely proper or modest airs. *n.*

**pru·dence** (prü′dəns) **1** careful thought before taking action; good judgment or discretion. **2** good management; economy. *n.*

**pru·dent** (prü′dənt) **1** planning carefully ahead of time; taking no chances; sensible; discreet: *A prudent man saves part of his wages.* **2** characterized by good judgment or good management: *a prudent policy.* *adj.* —**pru′dent·ly,** *adv.*

**pru·den·tial** (prü den′shəl) of, marked by, or showing prudence. *adj.* —**pru·den′tial·ly,** *adv.*

**prud·er·y** (prü′də rē) **1** extreme modesty or propriety, especially when not genuine. **2** a prudish act or remark. *n., pl.* **prud·er·ies.**

**prud·ish** (prü′dish) like a prude; extremely proper or modest; too modest. *adj.* —**prud′ish·ness,** *n.*

**prune**¹ (prün) a kind of dried, sweet plum. *n.*

**prune**² (prün) **1** cut out useless or undesirable parts from: *The editor pruned the needless words from the writer's manuscript.* **2** cut superfluous or undesirable twigs or branches from a bush, tree, etc. **3** cut off or out: *Prune all the dead branches.* *v.,* **pruned, prun·ing.**

**pruning hook** an implement with a hooked blade, used for pruning vines, etc.

**pru·ri·ence** (prü′rē əns) being PRURIENT. *n.*

**pru·ri·ent** (prü′rē ənt) having lustful thoughts or wishes. *adj.* —**pru′ri·ent·ly,** *adv.*

**Prus·sian** (prush′ən) **1** of or having to do with Prussia, a former state in northern Germany, its people, or their language. **2** a native or inhabitant of Prussia. **3** the dialect of German spoken in Prussia. 1 *adj.,* 2, 3 *n.*

**Prussian blue** a deep-blue pigment, essentially a cyanogen compound of iron.

**prus·sic acid** (prus′ik) a deadly poison that smells like bitter almonds; HYDROCYANIC ACID.

**pry**¹ (prī) **1** look with curiosity; peep: *She likes to pry into others' affairs.* **2** an inquisitive person. 1 *v.,* **pried, pry·ing;** 2 *n., pl.* **pries.**

**pry**² (prī) **1** raise or move by force: *Pry up that stone with your pickaxe.* **2** a lever for prying. **3** get with much effort: *We finally pried the secret out of him.* 1, 3 *v.,* **pried, pry·ing;** 2 *n., pl.* **pries.**

**pry·ing** (prī′ing) **1** looking or searching curiously; inquisitive. **2** ppr. of PRY¹ or PRY². 1 *adj.,* 2 *v.*

**P.S.** **1** postscript. **2** privy seal. **3** public school.

**psalm** (som *or* säm) a sacred song or poem.

**psalm·ist** (som'ist *or* sä'mist) the author of a PSALM or psalms. *n.*

**psalm·o·dy** (som'ə dē *or* sä'mə dē) **1** the act, practice, or art of singing psalms or hymns. **2** psalms or hymns. *n., pl.* **psalm·o·dies.**

Two styles of psaltery, as shown in manuscript illuminations. The one on the left is from the 15th century; the other is from the 14th century.

**psal·ter·y** (sol'tə rē) an ancient musical instrument played by plucking the strings. *n., pl.* **psal·ter·ies.**

**pseud.** pseudonym.

**pseu·do** (sü'dō) **1** false; sham; pretended. **2** having only the appearance of. *adj.*

**pseu·do·nym** (sü'də nim') a name used by an author instead of his or her real name: *Mark Twain is a pseudonym for Samuel Langhorne Clemens.* *n.*

**pseu·do·pod** (sü'də pod') any false limb, such as the extensions on an amoeba or the unsegmented legs of certain caterpillars, used for movement or to catch prey. *n.*

**p.s.f.** pounds per square foot.

**psit·ta·co·sis** (sit'ə kō'sis) a contagious disease of parrots and other birds, communicable to people. *n.*

**psych.** **1** psychology. **2** psychological.

**psy·che** (sī'kē) **1** the human soul or spirit. **2** the mind. *n.*

**psy·che·del·ic** (sī'kə del'ik) **1** of, having to do with, or referring to drugs that can produce abnormal changes in the mind, including intensified awareness of light, sound, colour, etc., often accompanied by hallucinations or delusions: *LSD is a psychedelic drug.* **2** produced by such a drug: *a psychedelic experience.* **3** suggesting or imitating the intensified or bizarre colours, sounds, etc. produced by psychedelic drugs: *a psychedelic pink, psychedelic music.* **4** a psychedelic drug. **5** a person who uses psychedelic drugs. 1–3 *adj.*, 4, 5 *n.*

**psy·chi·at·ric** (sī'kē at'rik) of or having to do with the treatment of mental diseases. *adj.*

**psy·chi·a·trist** (sī kī'ə trist) a doctor who treats mental disorders. *n.*

**psy·chi·a·try** (sī kī'ə trē) the study and treatment of mental disorders. *n.*

**psy·chic** (sī'kik) **1** of the soul or mind; mental: *illness due to psychic causes.* **2** outside the known laws of physics; supernatural: *A psychic force or influence is believed by spiritualists to explain second sight, telepathy, table moving, tappings, etc.* **3** especially susceptible to psychic influences. **4** a person supposed to be specially sensitive or responsive to psychic force or spiritual influences; medium. 1–3 *adj.*, 4 *n.*

**psy·chi·cal** (sī'kə kəl) PSYCHIC (def. 2). *adj.*

**psy·cho·act·i·vate** (sī'kō ak'ti vāt') have a pronounced effect on the mind: *Some medicines are psychoactivating.* *v.*, **psy·cho·act·i·vat·ed, psy·cho·act·i·vat·ing.**

**psy·cho·an·a·lyse** or **psy·cho·an·a·lyze** (sī'kō an'ə līz') examine by PSYCHOANALYSIS. *v.*, **psy·cho·an·a·lysed** or **psy·cho·an·a·lyzed, psy·cho·an·a·lys·ing** or **psy·cho·an·a·lyz·ing.** —**psy·cho·an'a·lys'er** or **psy·cho·an'a·lyz'er,** *n.*

**psy·cho·an·a·ly·sis** (sī'kō an nal'ə sis) the minute examination of a mind or minds to discover the underlying mental causes producing certain mental and nervous disorders; analysis of mind and personality. *n.*

**psy·cho·an·a·lyst** (sī'kō an'ə list) a person who is trained in or practises PSYCHOANALYSIS. *n.*

**psy·cho·an·a·lyze** (sī'kō an'ə līz') See PSYCHOANALYSE. *v.*

**psy·cho·kin·e·sis** (sī'kō kī nē'sis) the claimed ability to move objects using only mental powers. *n.*

**psy·cho·log·i·cal** (sī'kə loj'ə kəl) **1** of the mind. **2** of PSYCHOLOGY or psychologists. *adj.*

**psy·cho·log·i·cal·ly** (sī'kə loj'i klē) **1** in a PSYCHOLOGICAL manner. **2** in PSYCHOLOGICAL respects. *adv.*

**psychological moment** the psychologically favourable moment.

**pyschological warfare** systematic efforts to affect morale, loyalty, etc., especially of large national groups.

**pys·chol·o·gist** (sī kol'ə jist) a person trained in PSYCHOLOGY (def. 1), especially one who makes it his or her work. *n.*

**psy·chol·o·gy** (sī kol'ə jē) **1** the study of the mind and the ways of thought: *Psychology tries to explain why people act, think, and feel as they do.* **2** the mental states and processes of a person or persons; mental nature and behaviour: *Mrs. O'Reilly knew her husband's psychology well.* *n., pl.* **psy·chol·o·gies.**

**psy·chom·e·try** (sī kom'ə trē) the ability to deduce facts about the history of an object or about its owner by touching or being near the object. *n.*

**psy·cho·neu·ro·sis** (sī'kō nyü rō'sis *or* sī'kō nü rō'sis) a NEUROSIS of psychic origin. *n., pl.* **psy·cho·neu·ro·ses** (-sēz).

**psy·cho·path** (sī'kə path') one who is suffering from severe mental illness. *n.*

**psy·cho·path·ic** (sī'kə path'ik) **1** of or having to do with mental diseases. **2** having a mental disease. **3** likely to become insane. *adj.*

**psy·chop·a·thy** (sī kop'ə thē) **1** mental disease. **2** mental eccentricity or instability so extreme as to border on insanity. *n.*

**psy·cho·sis** (sī kō'sis) any severe form of mental disturbance or disease. *n., pl.* **psy·cho·ses** (-sēz).

**psy·cho·so·mat·ic** (sī'kō sə mat'ik) **1** of or having to do with both mind and body. **2** of or having to do with physical disorders caused by mental or emotional disturbances. *adj.*

**psy·cho·ther·a·py** (sī'kō ther'ə pē) the mental treatment of disorders of the mind or body. *n.*

**psy·chot·ic** (sī kot′ik) 1 of or having to do with PSYCHOSIS; unstable or mentally ill. 2 an unstable or mentally ill person. 1 *adj.*, 2 *n.*

**pt.** 1 pint. 2 part. 3 point. 4 past tense. 5 preterite. 6 port.

**Pt.** platinum.

**P.T.** physical training.

**PTA** or **P.T.A.** Parent-Teacher Association.

A willow ptarmigan—about 40 cm long including the tail

**ptar·mi·gan** (tär′mə gən) any of several kinds of GROUSE that have feathered feet and are found in mountainous and cold regions. *n., pl.* **ptar·mi·gans** or (*especially collectively*) **ptar·mi·gan**.

**PT boat** a small, fast motorboat that carries torpedoes, depth charges, etc.
☛ *Etym.* A shortened form of *P*atrol *T*orpedo boat.

**pter·i·do·phyte** (ter′ə dō fīt′) any of the highest group of seedless plants having roots, stems, and leaves: *Ferns, horsetails, and club mosses are pteridophytes. n.*

**pter·o·dac·tyl** (ter′ə dak′təl) an extinct flying reptile that had wings resembling those of a bat. *n.*

**P.T.O.** or **p.t.o.** please turn (the page) over.

**Ptol·e·ma·ic** (tol′ə mā′ik) 1 of or having to do with the astronomer Ptolemy (2nd century A.D.). The **Ptolemaic system** of astronomy taught that the earth was the fixed centre of the universe, around which the heavenly bodies moved. 2 of or having to do with the Ptolemies, who were rulers of Egypt from 323 B.C. to 30 B.C. *adj.*

**pto·maine** or **pto·main** (tō′mān) any of several alkaloid substances produced in decaying matter. *n.*

**ptomaine poisoning** food poisoning caused by bacteria or poisons found in decaying food.

**pts.** 1 pints. 2 parts. 3 points.

**pty·a·lin** (tī′ə lin) an enzyme contained in the saliva of humans and of certain other animals. It possesses the property of converting starch into dextrin and maltose, thus aiding digestion. *n.*

**Pu** plutonium.

**pub** (pub) *Informal.* a beer parlour; tavern. *n.*

**pu·ber·ty** (pyü′bər tē) the physical beginning of manhood and womanhood: *Puberty usually comes at about 14 in boys and about 12 in girls. n.*

**pu·bic** (pyü′bik) having to do with the PUBIS: *pubic hair. adj.*

**pu·bis** (pyü′bis) the lower, front portion of the hipbone. See PELVIS for picture. *n., pl.* **pu·bes** (-bēz).

**pub·lic** (pub′lik) 1 of, belonging to, or concerning the people as a whole: *public affairs, public buildings.* 2 done, made, acting, etc. for the people as a whole: *public relief.* 3 open to all the people; serving all the people: *a public park, public meetings.* 4 of or engaged in the affairs or service of the people: *a public official.* 5 known to many or all; not private: *The fact became*

hat, āge, fär; let, ēqual, tėrm; it, īce
hot, ōpen, ôrder; oil, out; cup, pút, rüle
ə above, takən, pencəl, lemən, circəs
ch, child; ng, long; sh, ship
th, thin; ᴛʜ, then; zh, measure

*public.* 6 a particular section of the people: *A popular actress has a large public.* 7 international: *public law.* 8 **the public**, **a** the people in general; all the people: *The public is not likely to accept more restraints.* **b** a particular group of people sharing an interest, etc.: *the reading public.* 1-5, 7 *adj.*, 6, 8.
**in public,** not in private or secretly; publicly; openly.

**public address system** an arrangement of loudspeakers used to carry speeches, messages, music, etc. to an audience in a large room, in different rooms of one building, or in the open air. *Abbrev.:* P.A. system.

**pub·li·can** (pub′lə kən) 1 *Brit.* a keeper of a PUBLIC HOUSE. 2 in ancient Rome, a tax collector. *n.*

**pub·li·ca·tion** (pub′lə kā′shən) 1 a book, newspaper, or magazine; anything that is published: *This magazine is a weekly publication.* 2 the printing and selling of books, newspapers, magazines, etc. 3 the act of making known; the fact or state of being made known: *There is prompt publication of any important news over the radio. n.*

**public domain** the lands belonging to the government. **in the public domain,** of works, material, etc., available for unrestricted use because unprotected by copyright or patent.

**public enemy** one who is a menace to the public.

**public funds** money provided by the government: *Public funds are used to pay for defence.*

**public house** 1 *Brit.* a place where alcoholic liquor is sold to be drunk; beer parlour; tavern. 2 an inn; hotel.

**pub·li·cist** (pub′lə sist) 1 a person trained in law or in public affairs. 2 a writer on law, politics, or public affairs. *n.*

**pub·lic·i·ty** (pub lis′ə tē) 1 the fact of being brought to public notice by special effort, through newspapers, signs, radio, etc. 2 public notice: *the publicity that actors desire.* 3 the measures used for getting, or the process of getting, public notice: *a campaign of publicity for a new automobile.* 4 being public; being seen by or known to everybody: *in the publicity of the street. n.*

**pub·li·cize** (pub′lə sīz′) give PUBLICITY to. *v.*, **pub·li·cized, pub·li·ciz·ing.**

**pub·lic·ly** (pub′li klē) 1 in a public manner; openly. 2 by the public. *adv.*

**public opinion** the opinion of the people in a country, community, etc.: *to make a survey of public opinion.*

**public relations** the activities of an organization that are concerned with giving the general public a better understanding of its policies and purposes, by giving out news through the newspapers, magazines, radio, television, motion pictures, etc. *Abbrev.:* P.R. or PR

**public school** 1 in Canada and the United States, a free school maintained by taxes. 2 in Great Britain, an endowed private boarding school.

**public servant** a member of the PUBLIC SERVICE (def. 1); civil servant.

**public service** 1 CIVIL SERVICE. 2 employment by any level of government: *School teachers are in the public service.* 3 the business of supplying a service or commodity to a community, especially one subsidized by public funds or administered by public servants: *Bus service is a public service in most cities.* 4 a service given for the benefit of the community: *That church runs a drop-in centre as a public service.* 5 **public-service,** of or being a public service: *a public-service announcement.*

**pub·lic–spir·it·ed** (pub′lik spir′ə tid) having or showing an unselfish desire for the public good. *adj.*

**public utility** a company formed or chartered to render services to the public, such as a company furnishing electricity or gas, a railway, a streetcar or bus line, etc.

**public works** things built by the government at public expense and for public use, such as roads, bridges, docks, canals, and waterworks.

**pub·lish** (pub′lish) 1 prepare and offer a book, paper, map, piece of music, etc. for sale or distribution. 2 make publicly or generally known: *Don't publish family secrets.* *v.* —**pub′lish·a·ble,** *adj.*

**pub·lish·er** (pub′lish ər) a person or company whose business is to PUBLISH books, newspapers, magazines, etc. *n.*

**PUC** or **P.U.C.** Public Utilities Commission.

**puce** (pyüs) purplish or dark brown. *n., adj.*

**puck**[1] (puk) 1 a mischievous spirit; goblin. 2 **Puck,** a mischievous fairy in English folklore, who appears in Shakespeare's play *A Midsummer Night's Dream.* *n.*

**puck**[2] (puk) a hard, black rubber disk used in the game of ice hockey. *n.*

**puck–car·ri·er** (puk′kar′ē ər *or* puk′ker′ē ər) the hockey player in possession of the puck. *n.*

**puck·er** (puk′ər) 1 draw into wrinkles or irregular folds: *to pucker one's brow, to pucker cloth in sewing. The baby's lips puckered just before he began to cry.* 2 an irregular fold; wrinkle: *There are puckers at the shoulders of this ill-fitting coat.* 1 *v.*, 2 *n.*

**puck·ish** (puk′ish) mischievous; impish. *adj.*

**pud·ding** (pud′ing) 1 a soft cooked food, usually sweet: *Rice pudding is nourishing.* 2 a cakelike dessert, usually steamed or baked: *plum pudding.* 3 a kind of sausage. 4 anything soft like a pudding. *n.*

**pud·dle** (pud′əl) 1 a small pool of water, especially dirty water: *a puddle of rain water.* 2 make wet or muddy. 3 a small pool of any liquid: *a puddle of ink.* 4 wet clay and sand stirred into a paste. 5 mix up wet clay and sand into a thick paste. 6 use such a mixture to stop water from running through: *Puddle up that hole.* 7 stir melted iron with an oxidizing agent to make wrought iron. 1, 3, 4 *n.*, 2, 5–7 *v.*, **pud·dled, pud·dling.**

**pud·dling** (pud′ling) 1 the act or process of converting PIG IRON into WROUGHT IRON by stirring the molten metal with an oxidizing agent. 2 ppr. of PUDDLE. 1 *n.*, 2 *v.*

**pud·dly** (pud′lē) 1 full of puddles: *The streets are usually puddly after a shower.* 2 like a puddle. *adj.*

**pudg·y** (puj′ē) short and fat or thick: *a child's pudgy hand, a pudgy little man.* *adj.*, **pudg·i·er, pudg·i·est.** —**pudg′i·ness,** *n.*

**pu·er·ile** (pyü′rīl *or* pyü′rəl) foolish for a grown person to say or do; childish: *Hiding the carpenter's hammer was a puerile trick.* *adj.*

**pu·er·il·i·ty** (pyü ril′ə tē) 1 childishness; foolishness. 2 a foolish act, idea, or statement. *n., pl.* **pu·er·il·i·ties.**

**Puer·to Ri·can** (pwer′tə rē′kən) 1 a native or inhabitant of Puerto Rico, a country in the West Indies. 2 having to do with Puerto Rico or its inhabitants. 1 *n.*, 2 *adj.*

**puff** (puf) 1 blow with short, quick blasts: *The bellows puffed on the fire.* 2 a short, quick blast: *a puff of wind.* 3 a small quantity of air, smoke, etc. blown out in short, quick blasts. 4 breathe quickly and with difficulty: *She puffed as she climbed the stairs.* 5 a quick, hard breath. 6 give out puffs; move with puffs: *The engine puffed out of the station.* 7 move or come in puffs: *Smoke puffed out of the chimney.* 8 smoke: *to puff a cigar.* 9 swell with air or pride: *He puffed out his cheeks.* 10 the act or process of swelling. 11 arrange in soft, round masses. 12 a soft, round mass: *a puff of hair.* 13 a small pad for putting powder on the skin, etc. 14 a light pastry filled with whipped cream, jam, etc.: *a cream puff.* 15 praise in exaggerated language: *They puffed him to the skies.* 16 extravagant praise. 17 a portion of material gathered and held down at the edges but left full in the middle, as in a sleeve of a dress. 1, 4, 6–9, 11, 15 *v.*, 2, 3, 5, 10, 12–14, 16, 17 *n.*

**puff adder** a large and poisonous African snake that puffs up the upper part of its body when excited.

**puff·ball** (puf′bol′) a ball-shaped FUNGUS resembling a mushroom: *When suddenly broken, a ripe puffball gives off a cloud of tiny spores.* *n.*

**puffed–up** (puf′tup′) 1 bloated; swollen. 2 conceited; vain. 3 inflated with air. *adj.*

**puff·er** (puf′ər) 1 one that puffs. 2 any of various fishes capable of inflating the body, such as a globefish. *n.*

A common puffin— about 30 cm long including the tail

**puf·fin** (puf′ən) a sea bird of the northern Atlantic Ocean, having a high, narrow, furrowed, parti-coloured bill. *n.*

**puff·y** (puf′ē) 1 puffed out; swollen: *Her eyes are puffy from crying.* 2 puffed up; vain. 3 blowing or breathing in puffs. *adj.*, **puff·i·er, puff·i·est.** —**puff′i·ness,** *n.*

**pug** (pug) 1 a small, tan dog with a curly tail and a short, turned-up nose. 2 a PUG NOSE. *n.*

**pu·gi·lism** (pyü′jə liz′əm) the art of fighting with the fists; boxing. *n.*

**pu·gi·list** (pyü′jə list) a person who fights with the fists; boxer. *n.*

**pu·gi·lis·tic** (pyü′jə lis′tik) of or having to do with PUGILISM or pugilists. *adj.*

**pug·na·cious** (pug nā′shəs) having the habit of fighting; fond of fighting; quarrelsome: *a pugnacious young*

man. *adj.* —**pug·na′cious·ly,** *adv.*
—**pug·na′cious·ness,** *n.*

**pug·nac·i·ty** (pug nas′ə tē)   a fondness for fighting; quarrelsomeness.   *n.*

**pug nose**   a short, turned-up nose.

**pug–nosed** (pug′nōzd′)   having a PUG NOSE.  *adj.*

**pul·chri·tude** (pul′krə tyüd′ *or* pul′krə tüd′)
beauty.  *n.*

**pule** (pyül)   cry in a thin voice, as a sick child does; whimper; whine.   *v.*, **puled, pul·ing.**

**pull** (pùl)   **1** move something by grasping it and drawing toward oneself: *to pull a trigger. Pull the door open; don't push it.*   **2** take hold of and tug: *He pulled at his tie.*   **3** move by tugging, usually with effort or force: *to pull a sleigh uphill. I pulled ahead of the others in the race.*   **4** the act or effort of pulling; a tug: *The girl gave a pull on the rope.*   **5** pick; pluck: *to pull flowers.*   **6** tear; rip: *The baby pulled the toy to pieces.*   **7** stretch too far; strain: *The football player pulled a ligament in his leg.*   **8** row: *Pull for the shore.*   **9** be provided or rowed with: *The boat pulls eight oars.*   **10** a difficult climb, journey, or other effort: *It was a hard pull to get up the hill.*   **11** a handle, rope, ring, or other thing to pull by: *a curtain pull.*   **12** drink.   **13** suck: *to pull at a cigar.*   **14** the act of sucking: *a pull at a cigar.*   **15** hold back, especially to keep from winning: *to pull one's punches in a fight.*   **16** a force that attracts: *magnetic pull.*   **17** *Informal.* perform; carry through: *Don't pull any tricks.*   **18** in golf, hit a ball so that it curves to the left.   **19** such a hit.   **20** in printing, take an impression or proof.   **21** *Informal.* influence; advantage.   1–3, 5–9, 12, 13, 15, 17, 18, 20 *v.*, 4, 10, 11, 14, 16, 19, 21 *n.*   —**pull′er,** *n.*
**pull apart,**   **a** separate into pieces by pulling.   **b** be severely critical of: *to pull apart a term paper.*
**pull for,** *Informal.*   give help to: *to pull for the underdog.*
**pull in,**   **a** stop; check.   **b** *Informal.* arrest: *She was pulled in for speeding.*   **c** arrive: *He pulled in this morning.*
**pull off,**   successfully complete.
**pull oneself together,**   gather one's faculties, energy, etc.
**pull out,**   **a** withdraw from a venture, undertaking, etc.   **b** leave: *The train pulled out of the station.*
**pull through,**   get through a difficult or dangerous situation.
**pull together,**   work in harmony; get on together.
**pull up,**   **a** tear up; uproot.   **b** remove utterly.   **c** bring or come to a halt; stop.

**pul·let** (pùl′it)   a young hen, usually less than a year old.   *n.*

**pul·ley** (pùl′ē)   **1** a wheel with a grooved rim in which a rope, belt, or wire can run, making it possible to change the direction of the pull.   See BLOCK AND TACKLE for picture.   **2** a set of such wheels used to increase the power applied.   **3** a wheel used to transfer power by driving a belt or being driven by a belt that moves some other part of the machine.   See GENERATOR for picture.   *n., pl.* **pul·leys.**

**pull·o·ver** (pùl′ō′vər)   a sweater put on by pulling it over the head.   *n.*

**pul·mo·nar·y** (pul′mə ner′ē)   **1** of or having to do with the lungs: *Tuberculosis and pneumonia are pulmonary diseases.*   **2** having lungs.   *adj.*

**pulp** (pulp)   **1** the soft part of any fruit or vegetable.   **2** of a tooth, the soft inner part containing blood vessels and nerves.   **3** a soft, moist mixture of ground-up wood, rags, or other material, from which paper is made.   **4** any soft, wet mass.   **5** referring to a type of magazine or book printed usually on rough, cheap paper and often containing sensational stories or articles.   **6** reduce to pulp.   **7** remove pulp from.   1–5 *n.*, 6, 7 *v.*

**pul·pit** (pùl′pit)   **1** a platform or raised structure in a church from which the minister preaches.   **2** ministers or their sermons: *the influence of the pulpit.*   *n.*

**pulp·wood** (pulp′wùd′)   **1** a wood reduced to pulp for making paper.   **2** any soft wood suitable for making paper: *Canada's forests produce large quantities of pulpwood.*   *n.*

**pulp·y** (pul′pē)   of pulp; like pulp; soft.   *adj.*, **pulp·i·er, pulp·i·est.**

**pul·sar** (pul′sär)   a body or mass of energy in space that emits regular, rapid, pulsating radio waves.   *n.*

**pul·sate** (pul′sāt)   **1** beat; throb: *The patient's heart was pulsating rapidly.*   **2** vibrate; quiver.   *v.*, **pul·sat·ed, pul·sat·ing.**

**pul·sa·tion** (pul sā′shən)   **1** a beating; throbbing.   **2** a beat; throb.   **3** a vibration; quiver.   *n.*

**pulse**[1] (puls)   **1** the beating of the arteries caused by the rush of blood into them after contraction of the heart.   **2** the rate of this beating: *The nurse took the woman's pulse by holding her wrist and counting the beats.*   **3** any regular, measured beat: *the pulse in music, the pulse of an engine.*   **4** beat; throb; vibrate: *Her heart pulsed with excitement.*   **5** feeling; sentiment: *the pulse of the nation.*   1–3, 5 *n.*, 4 *v.*, **pulsed, puls·ing.**

**pulse**[2] (puls)   the edible seeds of peas, beans, lentils, etc.   *n.*

**pulse-jet** (puls′jet′)   a type of JET ENGINE into which the air necessary for the burning of the fuel is admitted in spurts by valves.   *n.*

**pul·ver·ize** (pul′və rīz′)   **1** grind to powder or dust.   **2** become dust.   **3** break to pieces; demolish.   *v.*, **pul·ver·ized, pul·ver·iz·ing.**

**pu·ma** (pyü′mə)   a large North American wildcat; cougar.   *n.*

**pum·ice** (pum′is)   **1** a light, spongy stone thrown up from volcanoes, used for cleaning, smoothing, and polishing: *Rub your hands with pumice to remove the ink.*   **2** clean, smooth, or polish with pumice.   1 *n.*, 2 *v.*, **pum·iced, pum·ic·ing.**
☛ *Hom.* POMACE.

**pum·mel** (pum′əl)   beat; beat with the fists; pommel.   *v.*, **pum·melled** *or* **pum·meled, pum·mel·ling** *or* **pum·mel·ing.**   Also, **pommel.**
☛ *Hom.* POMMEL (pum′əl).

# pump 956 pungency

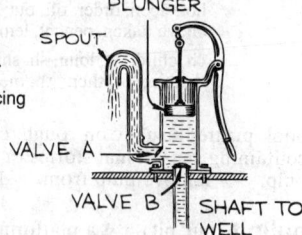

A water pump. As the handle is pushed down, the plunger is raised, pulling water upward through valve B from the shaft. As the handle is raised, the plunger moves downward, forcing water through valve A and out of the spout.

**pump**[1] (pump) **1** an apparatus or machine for forcing liquids or gases into or out of things: *a water pump, an oil pump.* **2** remove liquids, air, etc. by a pump: *Pump water from the well into a pail.* **3** blow air into: *Pump up the car's tires.* **4** remove water, etc. from by a pump: *Pump the well dry.* **5** work a pump. **6** work as a pump does. **7** move up and down like a pump handle. **8** move by, or as if by, a pump handle: *She pumped my hand.* **9** draw, force, etc. as if from a pump. **10** *Informal.* get information out of; try to get information out of: *Don't let him pump you.* 1 *n.*, 2–10 *v.*

**pump**[2] (pump) a low-cut shoe with no laces, straps, or other fastenings. See SHOE for picture. *n.*

**pum·per·nick·el** (pum'pər nik'əl) a slightly sour bread made of unsifted rye flour. *n.*

A pumpkin

**pump·kin** (pump'kin) **1** a large, roundish, orange-yellow fruit of a trailing vine, used for making pies, as a vegetable, and as food for stock: *The girl made a pumpkin jack-o'-lantern for Halloween.* **2** the vine that this fruit grows on. *n.*

**pun** (pun) **1** a humorous use of a word where it can have different meanings; play on words. Example: Humpty Dumpty had a great fall, but the winter was rough. **2** make puns. 1 *n.*, 2 *v.*, **punned, pun·ning.**

**punch**[1] (punch) **1** hit with the fist: *They punched each other like boxers.* **2** a quick thrust or blow. **3** *Informal.* vigorous force or effectiveness: *This story lacks punch.* **4** herd or drive cattle: *He punched cows for a living.* 1, 4 *v.*, 2, 3 *n.* —**punch'er,** *n.*

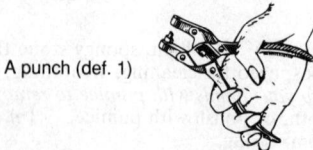

A punch (def. 1)

**punch**[2] (punch) **1** a tool for making holes. **2** make a hole with a punch or any pointed instrument: *The train conductor punched our tickets.* **3** a tool or apparatus for piercing, perforating, or stamping materials, impressing a design, forcing nails beneath a surface, driving bolts out of holes, etc. **4** pierce, cut, stamp, force, or drive with a punch: *to punch metal.* 1, 3 *n.*, 2, 4 *v.* —**punch'er,** *n.*

**punch**[3] (punch) a drink made of different liquids mixed together. *n.*

**Punch** (punch) a hook-nosed, hump-backed doll who quarrels violently with his wife Judy in the puppet show *Punch and Judy.* *n.*
**pleased as Punch,** very much pleased.

**punch card** card on which information is recorded by means of holes punched according to a code, for use in processing data by machine, electronic computer, etc.

**punch–drunk** (punch'drunk') **1** suffering from slight brain damage as a result of repeated blows to the head received in boxing. **2** *Informal.* behaving as if punch-drunk; appearing bewildered or dazed. *adj.*

**pun·cheon**[1] (pun'chən) **1** a slab of timber, or a piece of a split log, with the face roughly smoothed. **2** a short, upright piece of wood in the frame of a building. **3** a punching or stamping tool used by goldsmiths, etc. *n.*

**pun·cheon**[2] (pun'chən) a large cask for liquor. *n.*

**pun·chi·nel·lo** (pun'chə nel'ō) clown. *n., pl.* **pun·chi·nel·los** or **pun·chi·nel·loes.**

**punching bag** a leather bag filled with air or stuffed, to be hung up and punched with the fist for exercise.

**punch line** a telling phrase, sentence, etc. that makes the point of a joke, story, or other narrative.

**punc·til·i·o** (pungk til'ē ō) **1** a detail of honour, conduct, ceremony, etc.: *The knight observed every punctilio.* **2** care in attending to such details. *n., pl.* **punc·til·i·os.**

**punc·til·i·ous** (pungk til'ē əs) **1** very careful and exact: *A nurse should be punctilious in obeying the doctor's orders.* **2** paying strict attention to details of conduct and ceremony. *adj.* —**punc·til'i·ous·ly,** *adv.*

**punc·tu·al** (pungk'chü əl) prompt; on time: *She is punctual to the minute.* *adj.* —**punc'tu·al·ly,** *adv.*

**punc·tu·al·i·ty** (pungk'chü al'ə tē) promptness; the act, fact, or habit of being on time. *n.*

**punc·tu·ate** (pungk'chü āt') **1** use periods, commas, and other marks in writing or printing to help make the meaning clear. **2** put punctuation marks in. **3** interrupt now and then: *a speech punctuated with cheers.* **4** give point or emphasis to: *She punctuated her remarks with gestures.* *v.,* **punc·tu·at·ed, punc·tu·at·ing.**

**punc·tu·a·tion** (pungk'chü ā'shən) **1** the use of periods, commas, and other marks to help make the meaning of a sentence clear: *Punctuation does for writing and printing what pauses and changes in the pitch of the voice do for speech.* **2** PUNCTUATION MARKS. *n.*

**punctuation marks** marks used in writing or printing to help make the meaning of a sentence clear: *Periods, commas, question marks, colons, semi-colons, quotation marks, and exclamation marks are punctuation marks.*

**punc·ture** (pungk'chər) **1** a hole made by something pointed. **2** make such a hole in. **3** have or get a puncture. **4** the act or process of puncturing. **5** reduce, spoil, or destroy as if by a puncture: *A sharp voice punctured my dreams.* 1, 4 *n.*, 2, 3, 5 *v.*, **punc·tured, punc·tur·ing.**

**pun·dit** (pun'dit) a learned person; expert; authority. *n.*

**pun·gen·cy** (pun'jən sē) a PUNGENT quality: the

pungency of pepper, the pungency of ammonia, the pungency of wit. *n.*

**pun·gent** (pun′jənt) **1** sharply affecting the organs of taste and smell: *a pungent pickle, the pungent smell of burning leaves.* **2** sharp; biting: *pungent criticism.* **3** stimulating to the mind; keen; lively: *a pungent wit.* *adj.* —**pun′gent·ly**, *adv.*

**Pu·nic** (pyü′nik) **1** of or having to do with ancient Carthage or its inhabitants. **2** treacherous; faithless. *adj.*

**pun·ish** (pun′ish) **1** cause a person pain, loss, or discomfort for some fault or offence: *The government punishes criminals.* **2** cause pain, loss, or discomfort for: *The law punishes crimes.* **3** *Informal.* deal with severely, roughly, or greedily. *v.* —**pun′ish·er**, *n.*

**pun·ish·a·ble** (pun′i shə bəl) **1** liable to punishment: *First-degree murder is punishable by life imprisonment.* **2** deserving punishment: *a punishable offence.* *adj.*

**pun·ish·ment** (pun′ish mənt) **1** a punishing; being punished. **2** pain, suffering, or loss. **3** *Informal.* severe or rough treatment. *n.*

**pu·ni·tive** (pyü′nə tiv) **1** concerned with punishment. **2** inflicting punishment: *a punitive military expedition.* *adj.*

**punk¹** (pungk) **1** a preparation that burns very slowly, often used to light fireworks. **2** decayed wood used as tinder. *n.*

**punk²** (pungk) *Informal.* **1** poor or bad in quality. **2** a young, inexperienced person. **3** a hoodlum or petty gangster. **4** a style associated with PUNK ROCK music that is characterized by outrageous and grotesque clothing, make-up, and hair styles. 1 *adj.*, 2–4 *n.*

**punk rock** a form of hard-driving ROCK² (def. 5) music that expresses anger and discontent.

**pun·ster** (pun′stər) a person fond of making PUNS. *n.*

**punt¹** (punt) **1** kick a football before it touches the ground after being dropped from the hands. **2** such a kick: *The punt went over the goal line.* 1 *v.*, 2 *n.* —**punt′er**, *n.*

**punt²** (punt) **1** a shallow, flat-bottomed boat having square ends, usually moved by pushing with a pole against the bottom of a river, etc. **2** propel a boat by pushing with a pole against the bottom of a river, pond, etc. **3** use a punt; travel by punt: *We loved to punt on the river.* 1 *n.*, 2, 3 *v.* —**punt′er**, *n.*

**pu·ny** (pyü′nē) **1** of less than usual size and strength; weak. **2** petty; not important. *adj.*, **pu·ni·er**, **pu·ni·est.** —**pu′ni·ness**, *n.*

**pup** (pup) **1** a young dog; puppy. **2** a young fox, wolf, seal, etc. **3** a silly, conceited young man. *n.*

**pu·pa** (pyü′pə) **1** a stage between the larva and the adult in the development of many insects. **2** the form of an insect in this stage: *A chrysalis is a pupa. Most pupae are inactive and some, such as those of many moths, are enclosed in a tough case or cocoon.* See METAMORPHOSIS for picture. *n., pl.* **pu·pae** (-pē or -pī) or **pu·pas.**

**pu·pal** (pyü′pəl) of, having to do with, or in the form of a PUPA. *adj.*
☞ *Hom.* PUPIL.

**pu·pil¹** (pyü′pəl) a person who is learning in school or being taught by someone. *n.*
☞ *Hom.* PUPAL.

**pungent** 957 **pure**

hat, āge, fär; let, ēqual, tėrm; it, īce
hot, ōpen, ôrder; oil, out; cup, pùt, rüle
əbove, takən, pencəl, lemən, circəs
ch, child; ng, long; sh, ship
th, thin; ᴛʜ, then; zh, measure

**pu·pil²** (pyü′pəl) the opening in the centre of the iris of the eye which looks like a black spot: *The pupil, which is the only place where light can enter the eye, expands and contracts, thus controlling the amount of light that strikes the retina.* *n.*
☞ *Hom.* PUPAL.

Two kinds of puppet. The hand puppet on the left is moved with the fingers. The marionette on the right is moved by means of strings; one set moves the head and arms and another moves the legs.

**pup·pet** (pup′it) **1** a small doll. **2** a figure made to look like a person or animal and moved by wires, strings, or the hands. **3** anybody who is not independent, who waits to be told how to act, or who does what somebody else says. *n.* —**pup′pet·like′**, *adj.*

**pup·pe·teer** (pup′ə tēr′) a person who designs or makes puppets or who manipulates puppets in puppet shows. *n.*

**pup·pe·try** (pup′i trē) the art of making and manipulating puppets. *n.*

**pup·py** (pup′ē) **1** a young dog. **2** a young fox, wolf, etc. **3** a silly, conceited young man. *n., pl.* **pup·pies.**
☞ *Etym.* From OF *poupée* 'doll, plaything', which came from L *pupa* 'doll'.

**puppy love** sentimental love that often exists briefly between adolescent girls and boys.

**pur·blind** (pėr′blīnd′) **1** nearly blind. **2** slow to discern or understand. *adj.* —**pur′blind′ness**, *n.*

**pur·chas·a·ble** (pėr′chə sə bəl) that can be bought. *adj.*

**pur·chase** (pėr′chəs) **1** get by paying a price; buy: *We purchased a new car.* **2** the act of buying: *the purchase of a new car.* **3** the thing bought: *That coat was a good purchase.* **4** get in return for something: *to purchase safety at the cost of happiness.* **5** a firm hold to help move something or to keep from slipping: *Wind the rope twice around the tree to get a better purchase.* **6** a device for obtaining such a hold. 1, 4 *v.*, **pur·chased**, **pur·chas·ing**; 2, 3, 5, 6 *n.* —**pur′chas·er**, *n.*

**pur·dah** (pėr′də) among some Hindus and Moslems: **1** a curtain serving to screen women from the sight of men or strangers. **2** a veil worn by women to hide the face. **3** the condition of being kept hidden from men or strangers. *n.*

**pure** (pyùr) **1** not mixed with anything else;

unadulterated; genuine: *pure gold.* **2** perfectly clean; spotless: *pure hands.* **3** perfect; correct; without defects: *pure articulation in speech.* **4** nothing else than; mere; sheer: *pure accident.* **5** with no evil; without sin; chaste: *a pure mind.* **6** abstract or theoretical (opposed to APPLIED): *pure mathematics.* **7** keeping the same qualities, characteristics, etc. from generation to generation; of unmixed descent: *a pure Indian family.* **8** that which is pure. 1–7 *adj.*, **pur·er, pur·est;** 8 *n.* —**pure′ness,** *n.*

**pure·bred** (pyür′bred′) **1** denoting an animal or plant whose ancestors are known to have belonged to one breed and that will itself breed true to type: *purebred Holstein cows.* **2** an animal or plant of this type. 1 *adj.*, 2 *n.*

**pu·rée** (pyü rā′ *or* pyü′rā) **1** food boiled soft and put through a sieve or blender. **2** a thick soup. **3** make into a purée. 1, 2 *n.*, 3 *v.*, **pu·réed, pu·rée·ing.**

**pure·ly** (pyür′lē) **1** in a pure manner. **2** exclusively; entirely. **3** merely: *She scored the goal purely by chance.* **4** innocently; chastely. *adv.*

**pur·ga·tion** (pər gā′shən) purging; cleansing. *n.*

**pur·ga·tive** (pėr′gə tiv) **1** a medicine that empties the bowels: *Castor oil is a purgative.* **2** purging. 1 *n.*, 2 *adj.*

**pur·ga·to·ri·al** (pėr′gə tô′rē əl) of, like, or having to do with PURGATORY. *adj.*

**pur·ga·to·ry** (pėr′gə tô′rē) **1** in Roman Catholic belief, a temporary condition or place in which the souls of those who have died penitent are, by punishment, purified from sin or the effects of sin. **2** any condition or place of temporary suffering or punishment. *n.*, *pl.* **pur·ga·to·ries.**

**purge** (pėrj) **1** wash away all that is not clean from; make clean. **2** become clean. **3** the act of purging. **4** clear of any undesired thing or person, such as air in a water pipe or opponents in a nation. **5** the elimination of undesired persons from a nation or party. **6** empty the bowels. **7** a medicine that purges. 1, 2, 4, 6 *v.*, **purged, purg·ing;** 3, 5, 7 *n.*

**pu·ri·fi·ca·tion** (pyü′rə fə kā′shən) PURIFYing; being purified. *n.*

**pu·ri·fy** (pyü′rə fī′) **1** make pure: *Filters are used to purify water. Gold is purified by fire.* **2** become pure. *v.*, **pu·ri·fied, pu·ri·fy·ing.** —**pu′ri·fi′er,** *n.*

**pur·ism** (pyü′riz əm) an insistence on purity and correctness, especially in language and art. *n.*

**pur·ist** (pyü′rist) a person who is very careful or too careful about purity and correctness, especially in language: *A purist dislikes slang and all expressions that are not formally correct.* *n.*

**pu·ris·tic** (pyü ris′tik) very careful or too careful about purity and correctness, especially in language. *adj.*

**Pu·ri·tan** (pyü′rə tən) **1** during the 16th and 17th centuries, a member of a group in the Church of England who wanted simpler forms of worship and stricter morals: *Many Puritans settled in New England.* **2** of the Puritans. **3 puritan,** a person who is very strict in morals and religion. **4 puritan,** very strict in morals and religion. 1, 3 *n.*, 2, 4 *adj.*

**pu·ri·tan·ic** (pyü′rə tan′ik) PURITANICAL. *adj.*

**pu·ri·tan·i·cal** (pyü′rə tan′ə kəl) of or like a puritan; very strict or too strict in morals or religion. *adj.*

**pu·ri·ty** (pyü′rə tē) **1** freedom from dirt or mixture; clearness; cleanness: *the purity of drinking water.* **2** freedom from evil; innocence: *No one doubts the purity of Joan of Arc's motives.* **3** freedom from foreign or inappropriate elements; correctness: *purity of style.* *n.*

**purl¹** (pėrl) **1** flow with rippling motions and a murmuring sound: *A shallow brook purls.* **2** a purling motion or sound. 1 *v.*, 2 *n.*
☛ *Hom.* PEARL.

**purl²** (pėrl) **1** knit with inverted stitches. **2** an inversion of stitches in knitting. Compare with PLAIN (def. 10). **3** border material with small loops. **4** a loop or chain of small loops along the edge of lace, braid, ribbon, etc. **5** a thread of twisted gold or silver wire. 1, 3 *v.*, 2, 4, 5 *n.*
☛ *Hom.* PEARL.

**pur·lieu** (pėr′lü) **1** a piece of land on the border of a forest. **2** one's haunt or resort; one's bounds. **3** any bordering, neighbouring, or outlying region or district. *n.*

**pur·loin** (pər loin′) steal: *The hungry tramp purloined a chicken.* *v.*

**pur·ple** (pėr′pəl) **1** a colour made by mixing red and blue. **2** of or having this colour. **3** in ancient times, crimson. **4** make or become purple. **5** purple cloth or clothing, especially as worn by emperors, kings, etc. to indicate high rank. **6** an imperial, royal, or high rank. **7** imperial; royal. **8** the rank or position of a cardinal. **9** brilliant; gorgeous. 1, 3, 5, 6, 8 *n.*, 2, 3, 7, 9 *adj.*, 4 *v.*, **pur·pled, pur·pling.**
**born to the purple,** born in a royal or imperial family: *The prince was born to the purple.*

**pur·plish** (pėr′plish) somewhat purple. *adj.*

**pur·port** (pər pôrt′ *for verb*, pėr′pôrt *for noun*) **1** claim; profess: *The document purported to be official.* **2** have as its main idea; mean. **3** the meaning; main idea: *The purport of her letter was that she could not come.* 1, 2 *v.*, 3 *n.*

**pur·pose** (pėr′pəs) **1** something one intends to get or do; plan; aim; intention: *His purpose was to pass his exams.* **2** the object or end for which a thing is made, done, used, etc.: *What is the purpose of this machine?* **3** plan; aim; intend. 1, 2 *n.*, 3 *v.*, **pur·posed, pur·pos·ing.**
**on purpose,** with a purpose; not by accident: *He tripped me on purpose.*
**to good purpose,** with good results.
**to little** or **no purpose,** with few or no results.

**pur·pose·ful** (pėr′pəs fəl) having a PURPOSE: *She worked with purposeful movements.* *adj.*
—**pur′pose·ful·ly,** *adv.* —**pur′pose·ful·ness,** *n.*

**pur·pose·less** (pėr′pəs slis) lacking a PURPOSE. *adj.*
—**pur′pose·less·ly,** *adv.* —**pur′pose·less·ness,** *n.*

**pur·pose·ly** (pėr′pəs slē) on purpose; intentionally. *adv.*

**purr** (pėr) **1** a low, murmuring sound such as a cat makes when pleased. **2** make this sound. 1 *n.*, 2 *v.*

**purse** (pėrs) **1** a bag or case for carrying money, usually carried in a handbag or pocket. **2** handbag: *She put the keys and gloves in her purse.* **3** money; resources; treasury: *The family purse cannot afford a vacation.* **4** a sum of money offered as a prize or gift: *A purse was made up for the victims of the fire.* **5** draw together; press into folds or wrinkles: *Grace pursed her lips and frowned.* 1–4 *n.*, 5 *v.*, **pursed, purs·ing.**

**purse–proud** (pėr'sproud') proud of being rich. *adj.*

**purs·er** (pėr'sər) an officer who keeps the accounts of a ship or airplane, pays wages, and attends to other matters of business. *n.*

**purse strings** control of the money.

**purs·lane** (pėr'slān) 1 a common plant that has small, yellow flowers and small, thick leaves. 2 any of several plants like purslane. *n.*

**pur·su·ance** (pər sü'əns) a following; carrying out; pursuit: *In pursuance of his duty, the policeman risked his life.* *n.*

**pur·su·ant** (pər sü'ənt) following; carrying out; according. *adj.* **pursuant to,** following; acting according to; in accordance with.

**pur·sue** (pər sü') 1 follow to catch or kill; chase. 2 proceed along; follow in action; follow: *She pursued a wise course by taking no chances.* 3 strive for; try to get; seek: *to pursue pleasure.* 4 carry on; keep on with: *She pursued the study of French for four years.* 5 continue to annoy or trouble: *to pursue a person with questions.* *v.*, **pur·sued, pur·su·ing.** —**pur·su'a·ble,** *adj.* —**pur·su'er,** *n.*

**pur·suit** (pər süt') 1 the act of pursuing; chase: *The dog was in hot pursuit of the cat. The pursuit of the escaped convict continued all night.* 2 an occupation or pastime: *Fishing is his favourite pursuit.* *n.*

**pursuit plane** a fighter aircraft that has high speed, a high rate of climb, and can be manoeuvred with ease.

**pu·ru·lence** (pyü'rə ləns *or* pyür'yə ləns) the formation or discharge of pus; suppuration. *n.*

**pu·ru·lent** (pyü'rə lənt *or* pyür'yə lənt) full of pus; discharging pus; like pus: *a purulent sore.* *adj.*

**pur·vey** (pər vā') supply food or provisions; provide; furnish: *to purvey meat for an army.* *v.*

**pur·vey·ance** (pər vā'əns) 1 a purveying. 2 provisions; supplies. *n.*

**pur·vey·or** (pər vā'ər) 1 a person who supplies provisions. 2 a person who supplies anything. *n.*

**pur·view** (pėr'vyü) range of operation, activity, concern, etc.; scope; extent. *n.*

**pus** (pus) a liquid formed by inflammation of infected tissue in the body, that consists of white blood cells, bacteria, serum, etc. *n.*

**push** (pùsh) 1 move something away by pressing against it: *Push the door; don't pull it.* 2 move up, down, back, forward, etc. by pressing: *Push him outdoors.* 3 thrust: *Trees push their roots down into the ground.* 4 press hard: *to push with all one's might.* 5 go forward by force: *to push on at a rapid pace.* 6 force one's way: *We had to push our way through the crowd.* 7 make go forward; urge: *He pushed his plans cleverly.* 8 continue with; follow up: *to push a claim.* 9 extend: *Alexander pushed his conquests still farther east.* 10 *Informal.* urge the use, sale, etc. of. 11 *Informal.* force; energy; the power to succeed: *She has plenty of push.* 12 the act of pushing. 13 a hard effort; determined advance. 1–10 *v.*, 11–13 *n.*

**push around,** *Informal.* treat roughly or with contempt; bully.

**purse-proud** 959 **put**

hat, āge, fär; let, ēqual, tėrm; it, īce
hot, ōpen, ôrder; oil, out; cup, pùt, rüle
əbove, takən, pencəl, lemən, circəs
ch, child; ng, long; sh, ship
th, thin; ŦH, then; zh, measure

**push off,** a move from shore: *We pushed off in the boat.* b *Informal.* go away; depart.

**push·ball** (pùsh'bol') 1 a game played with a large, heavy ball, usually about 180 cm in diameter: *In pushball, two teams try to push the ball toward opposite goals.* 2 the ball used in this game. *n.*

**push button** a small button or knob that is pushed to close or open an electric circuit.

**push-but·ton** (pùsh'but'ən) operated by means of a PUSH BUTTON or buttons: *a push-button telephone.* *adj.*

**push·cart** (pùsh'kärt') a light cart pushed by hand. *n.*

**push·er** (pùsh'ər) 1 a person or thing that pushes. 2 an airplane with propeller behind instead of in front. 3 *Informal.* a dealer in illegal drugs. *n.*

**push-o·ver** (pùsh'ō'vər) *Informal.* 1 something very easy to do. 2 a person very easy to beat in a contest. *n.*

**push-up** or **push·up** (pùsh'up') an exercise performed in a prone position facing the floor, in which the person alternately raises and lowers his or her body by straightening and bending the arms while keeping the body and legs straight. *n.*

**push·y** (pùsh'ē) offensively forceful and aggressive. *adj.*

**pu·sil·la·nim·i·ty** (pyü'sə lə nim'ə tē) cowardliness; timidity. *n.*

**pu·sil·lan·i·mous** (pyü'sə lan'ə məs) cowardly; mean-spirited; faint-hearted: *The pusillanimous man avoided the fight.* *adj.* —**pu'sil·lan'i·mous·ly,** *adv.*

**puss** (pùs) cat. *n.*

**puss·y** (pùs'ē) 1 cat. 2 catkin. *n., pl.* **puss·ies.**

**puss·y·foot** (pùs'ē fùt') 1 *Informal.* move softly and cautiously to avoid being seen. 2 be cautious and timid about revealing one's opinions or committing oneself. 3 a person who pussyfoots. 1, 2 *v.*, 3 *n., pl.* **puss·y·foots.**

**pussy willow** a small WILLOW with silky catkins.

**pus·tu·lar** (pus'chə lər) of, like, or having to do with PUSTULES; characterized by pustules. *adj.*

**pus·tu·la·tion** (pus'chə lā'shən) the formation of PUSTULES. *n.*

**pus·tule** (pus'chül) 1 a pimple containing pus. 2 any swelling like a pimple or blister, such as the pustules of chicken pox. *n.*

**put** (pùt) 1 cause to be in some place or position; place; lay: *I put sugar in my tea. Put away your toys.* 2 cause to be in some state, condition, position, relation, etc.: *The murderer was put to death. Put your room in order.* 3 express: *The teacher puts things clearly.* 4 propose or submit for answer, consideration, deliberation, etc.: *He put several questions before me.* 5 take one's course; go; turn; proceed: *The ship put out to sea.* 6 throw or cast with an overhand motion from the shoulder: *to put the shot.* 7 a throw or cast. 8 set at a particular place, point, amount,

etc. in a scale of estimation; appraise: *She puts the distance at five kilometres.* **9** apply: *A doctor puts his or her skill to good use.* **10** impose: *to put a tax on gasoline.* 1–6, 8–10 *v.,* **put, put·ting;** 7 *n.*
**put about,** **a** put a ship on the opposite tack. **b** change direction.
**put across,** *Informal.* **a** carry out successfully. **b** get accepted.
**put aside** or **by,** save for future use.
**put away,** **a** lay aside for future use: *I've always put my winter clothes away during the summer.* **b** *Informal.* commit to a prison, mental hospital, etc.: *The judge put him away for ten years.*
**put down,** **a** put an end to; suppress. **b** write down. **c** pay as a down payment. **d** *Informal.* have a pet or other domestic animal put to death to prevent suffering, etc.: *We had to put our dog down after she was hit by a car.* **e** *Informal.* insult; belittle.
**put forth,** **a** grow; sprout; issue: *to put forth buds.* **b** use fully; exert: *to put forth effort.*
**put in,** **a** *Informal.* spend time doing; do; accomplish: *She always puts in a good day's work.* **b** enter port. **c** enter a place for supplies, etc.: *The ship put in at Vancouver.* **d** make a claim, plea, or offer: *She put in for a loan.*
**put off,** **a** lay aside; postpone: *Don't put off going to the dentist.* **b** go away; start out: *The ship put off for England.* **c** bid or cause to wait. **d** get rid of. **e** *Informal.* annoy; irritate.
**put on,** **a** clothe or adorn oneself with; don: *She put on her new hat.* **b** assume or take on, especially as a pretence: *She put on an air of innocence.* **c** add to; increase: *The driver put on speed.* **d** apply or exert: *to put on pressure.* **e** advance; move ahead: *to put the clock on.* **f** present on a stage; produce: *The class put on a play.*
**put out,** **a** extinguish. **b** confuse; embarrass. **c** distract, disturb, or interrupt. **d** destroy an eye, etc. **e** cause to be out in a game. **f** dislocate: *I put out my knee when I fell.* **g** publish. **h** offend; provoke: *Don't put out your friends by rude behaviour.*
**put over,** *Informal.* carry out successfully.
**put someone up to something,** *Informal.* incite: *Who put you up to this?*
**put through,** carry out successfully.
**put to it,** force to a course; put in difficulty.
**put up,** **a** offer; give; show: *to put up a house for sale.* **b** make. **c** build: *to put up a monument.* **d** lay aside. **e** put in its usual place. **f** prepare or pack up food for later use. **g** preserve fruit, vegetables, etc. **h** give lodging or food to. **i** make available: *He put up the money for the car.* **j** *Informal.* plan beforehand craftily.
**put upon,** impose upon; take advantage of; victimize.
**put up with,** bear with patience; tolerate.

**pu·ta·tive** (pyü′tə tiv) supposed; reputed: *the putative author of a book.* *adj.*

**put-down** (pùt′doun′) *Informal.* **1** a slighting or belittling of a person or thing. **2** a comment, reply, etc., intended to snub or belittle. *n.*

**pu·tre·fac·tion** (pyü′trə fak′shən) decay; rotting. *n.*

**pu·tre·fac·tive** (pyü′trə fak′tiv) **1** causing PUTREFACTION. **2** characterized by or having to do with PUTREFACTION. *adj.*

**pu·tre·fy** (pyü′trə fī) rot; decay: *The putrefying meat has a bad smell.* *v.,* **pu·tre·fied, pu·tre·fy·ing.**

**pu·tres·cence** (pyü tres′əns) a PUTRESCENT condition. *n.*

**pu·tres·cent** (pyü tres′ənt) **1** becoming PUTRID; rotting. **2** having to do with PUTREFACTION. *adj.*

**pu·trid** (pyü′trid) **1** rotten; foul: *putrid meat.* **2** thoroughly corrupt or depraved; extremely bad. *adj.* —**pu′trid·ly,** *adv.* —**pu′trid·ness,** *n.*

**pu·trid·i·ty** (pyü trid′ə tē) **1** a PUTRID condition. **2** PUTRID matter. *n.*

**putt** (put) **1** strike a golf ball gently and carefully in an effort to make it roll into the hole. **2** the stroke itself. 1 *v.,* 2 *n.*

**put·tee** (put′ē *or* pu tē′) **1** a long narrow strip of cloth wound round the leg from ankle to knee, formerly worn by soldiers, sportsmen, etc. **2** a GAITER (def. 1) of cloth or leather reaching from ankle to knee, worn by soldiers, riders, etc. *n.*
☛ *Hom.* PUTTY (for the first pronunciation of **puttee**).

**put·ter**[1] (put′ər) keep busy in a rather aimless way: *Petra spends the day puttering in the garden.* *v.* Also, **potter.** —**put′ter·er,** *n.*

**putt·er**[2] (put′ər) **1** a person who putts. **2** a golf club used in putting. *n.*

**putt·ing green** (put′ing) that part of a golf course within about 18 metres of a hole, except the hazards; the smooth turf around a golf hole.

**put·ty** (put′ē) **1** a soft mixture of WHITING[2] and linseed oil, used mainly for fastening panes of glass into window frames. **2** stop up or cover with putty: *He puttied up the holes in the woodwork before painting it.* 1 *n., pl.* **put·ties;** 2 *v.,* **put·tied, put·ty·ing.**
☛ *Hom.* PUTTEE (put′ē).

**put–up** (pùt′up′) *Informal.* planned beforehand, or deliberately, in a secret or crafty manner: *A put-up attempt to get rid of him failed.* *adj.*

**puz·zle** (puz′əl) **1** a hard problem: *How to get all my things into one trunk is a puzzle.* **2** a problem or task to be done for fun: *This puzzle has seventy pieces of wood to fit together.* **3** make unable to answer, solve, or understand something; perplex: *How the cat got out puzzled us.* **4** exercise one's mind on something hard: *I puzzle over arithmetic every night.* **5** a puzzled condition. 1, 2, 5 *n.,* 3, 4 *v.,* **puz·zled, puz·zling.** —**puz′zler,** *n.*
**puzzle out,** find out by thinking or trying hard: *to puzzle out the meaning of a sentence.*
**puzzle over,** think hard about; try hard to do or work out: *They puzzled over their arithmetic.*

**puz·zled** (puz′əld) **1** not understanding; unable to find an answer or solve a problem: *We could see by the frown on his face that he was puzzled.* **2** pt. and pp. of PUZZLE. 1 *adj.,* 2 *v.* —**puz′zled·ly,** *adv.*

**puz·zle·ment** (puz′əl mənt) a PUZZLED condition. *n.*

**pwt.** pennyweight.

**py·e·mi·a** or **py·ae·mi·a** (pī ē′mē ə) a form of BLOOD POISONING caused by bacteria that produce pus. *n.*

**pyg·my** (pig′mē) **1** a very short or insignificant person. **2** anything that is unusually small for its kind; dwarf. **3** unusually or abnormally small or insignificant. **4 Pygmy,** a member of a small people of equatorial Africa, usually less than 150 cm tall. 1, 2, 4 *n., pl.* **pyg·mies;** 3 *adj.* Also, **pigmy.**
☛ *Syn.* See note at DWARF.

**py·ja·mas** or **pa·ja·mas** (pə jam′əz or pə jä′məz) **1** garments for sleeping or lounging in, consisting of a loose jacket and a pair of loose pants fastened at the waist. **2** loose trousers worn in the Orient, especially by Moslem men and women. *n. pl.*
☞ *Etym.* From Hindi *pāējāmah*, made up of Persian *pāē* 'leg' + *jāmah* 'garment'.

The outer pylon of an ancient Egyptian temple at Karnak, Egypt

**py·lon** (pī′lon) **1** a post or tower for guiding aircraft pilots. **2** a tall steel framework used to carry high-tension wires across country. **3** either of a pair of high supporting structures marking an entrance at either end of a bridge. **4** a gateway, particularly of an ancient Egyptian temple. *n.*

**py·lor·ic** (pī lô′rik) of or having to do with the PYLORUS. *adj.*

**py·lo·rus** (pī lô′rəs) the opening that leads from the stomach into the intestine. *n., pl.* **py·lo·ri** (-rī or -rē).

**py·or·rhe·a** or **py·or·rhoe·a** (pī′ə rē′ə) a disease of the gums in which pockets of pus form about the teeth, the gums shrink, and the teeth become loose. *n.*

One of the huge stone pyramids of Egypt

**pyr·a·mid** (pir′ə mid′) **1** in geometry, a solid figure having triangular sides meeting at a point. See SOLID for picture. **2** any thing or things having the form of a pyramid. **3** be or put in the form of a pyramid. **4** raise or increase costs, wages, etc. gradually. **5 Pyramids,** *pl.* the huge, massive stone pyramids, serving as royal tombs, built by the ancient Egyptians. 1, 2, 5 *n.*, 3, 4 *v.*

**py·ram·i·dal** (pə ram′ə dəl) shaped like a PYRAMID. *adj.*

**pyre** (pīr) a pile of wood on which a dead body is burned as a funeral rite. *n.*

**py·ret·ic** (pī ret′ik) **1** of or having to do with fever. **2** producing fever. **3** feverish. *adj.*

**pyr·i·dox·ine** (pir′ə dok′sēn) vitamin B₆, essential to human nutrition, found in wheat germ, fish, liver, etc. *n.*

**py·rite** (pī′rīt) a common mineral consisting of iron sulphide, having a yellow colour and a metallic glitter that suggests gold; fool's gold. *n.*

**py·ri·tes** (pī rī′tēz or pī′rīts) any of various compounds of sulphur and a metal: *Pyrite is the commonest pyrites.* *n., pl.* **py·ri·tes.**

**py·ro·hy** (per′ō hä′ or pir′ō hē′) PEROGY. *n. pl.*

hat, āge, fär; let, ēqual, tèrm; it, īce
hot, ōpen, ôrder; oil, out; cup, put, rüle
əbove, takən, pencəl, lemən, circəs
ch, child; ng, long; sh, ship
th, thin; ᴛʜ, then; zh, measure

**py·ro·ma·ni·a** (pī′rə mā′nē ə) an uncontrollable desire to set things on fire. *n.*

**py·ro·ma·ni·ac** (pī′rə mā′nē ak′) a person who has PYROMANIA. *n.*

**py·ro·tech·nic** (pī′rə tek′nik) **1** of or having to do with fireworks. **2** resembling fireworks; brilliant; sensational: *pyrotechnic eloquence.* *adj.*

**py·ro·tech·ni·cal** (pī′rə tek′nə kəl) PYROTECHNIC. *adj.*

**py·ro·tech·nics** (pī′rə tek′niks) **1** the making of fireworks. **2** use of fireworks. **3** a display of fireworks. **4** a brilliant or sensational display. *n.*

**py·rox·y·lin** (pī rok′sə lin) any of various substances made by nitrating certain forms of cellulose: *Pyroxylins are used in celluloid, collodion, etc.* *n.*

**Pyrrhic victory** a victory won at too great cost, so named after Pyrrhus, King of Epirus, who won a battle with an enormous loss of life.

**Py·thag·o·re·an** (pī thag′ə rē′ən or pə thag′ə rē′ən) **1** of or having to do with Pythagoras, a Greek philosopher and mathematician, 582–507 B.C., his teachings, or his followers. **2** a follower of Pythagoras. 1 *adj.*, 2 *n.*

**Pythagorean theorem** in geometry, the theorem that the square of the hypotenuse of a right-angled triangle is equal to the sum of the squares of the other two sides.

**py·thon** (pī′thon) **1** any of several large snakes of Asia, Africa, and Australia that are related to the boas and kill their prey by crushing: *Pythons usually live in trees near water.* **2** any large boa. *n.*

**pyx** (piks) **1** a box in which the consecrated Host is kept or carried. **2** a box at the British mint in which specimen coins are kept to be tested for weight and purity. *n.*

**pyx·id·i·um** (pik sid′ē əm) a SEED VESSEL that bursts open transversely into a top part and a bottom part, the top part acting as a lid. *n., pl.* **pyx·id·i·a** (-ē ə).

# Q q  Q q

**q or Q** (kyü) 1 the seventeenth letter of the English alphabet. 2 any speech sound represented by this letter. 3 a person or thing identified as q, especially as the seventeenth of a series. *n., pl.* **q's** or **Q's**.

**q.** 1 quart; quarts. 2 quarterly.

**Q** 1 Queen. 2 question; query.

**Q.C.** Queen's Counsel.

**Q.E.D.** which was to be proved (an abbreviation of the Latin phrase *quod erat demonstrandum*).

**qr.** 1 quarter. 2 quire. 3 quarterly.

**Q.R.** Queen's Regulations.

**qt.** 1 quart; quarts. 2 quantity.

**qu.** 1 quart. 2 quarterly. 3 question.

**quack¹** (kwak) 1 the sound a duck makes. 2 any similar sound. 3 make the sound of a duck or one like it. 1, 2 *n.*, 3 *v.*

**quack²** (kwak) 1 person who practises as a doctor but lacks professional training. 2 an ignorant pretender to knowledge or skill: *Don't pay a quack to tell your fortune.* 3 used by quacks. 4 not genuine. 1, 2 *n.*, 3, 4 *adj.*

**quack·er·y** (kwak′ə rē) the practices or methods of a QUACK². *n., pl.* **quack·er·ies**.

**quack grass** a coarse, perennial grass that is a common, very troublesome weed; couch grass.

**quad¹** (kwod) *Brit. Informal.* a QUADRANGLE of a college. *n.*

**quad²** (kwod) *Informal.* QUADRUPLET. *n.*

**quad·ran·gle** (kwod′rang′gəl) 1 a four-sided space or court wholly or nearly surrounded by buildings. 2 the buildings around a quadrangle. 3 a QUADRILATERAL (def. 2). *n.*

**quad·ran·gu·lar** (kwod rang′gyə lər) like a QUADRANGLE; having four corners or angles. *adj.*

Quadrants (def. 1)

**quad·rant** (kwod′rənt) 1 a quarter of a circle or of its circumference. 2 an instrument used in astronomy, navigation, etc. for measuring altitudes. *n.*

**quad·rat·ic** (kwod rat′ik) 1 involving a square or squares, but no higher powers. 2 QUADRATIC EQUATION. 1 *adj.*, 2 *n.*

**quadratic equation** an equation involving a square or squares, but no higher powers of the unknown quantity or quantities. Example: $x^2 + 3x + 2 = 12$.

**quad·rat·ics** (kwod rat′iks) the branch of algebra that deals with QUADRATIC EQUATIONS. *n.*

**quad·ren·ni·al** (kwod ren′ē əl) 1 occurring every four years: *a quadrennial election.* 2 of or for four years. *adj.*

**quad·ren·ni·al·ly** (kwod ren′ē ə lē) once in four years. *adv.*

QUADRILATERALS
TRAPESIUM (NO SIDES PARALLEL)
TRAPEZOID (TWO SIDES PARALLEL)
PARALLELOGRAMS (OPPOSITE SIDES PARALLEL)
RECTANGLES
SQUARE   OBLONG   RHOMBUS   RHOMBOID

**quad·ri·lat·er·al** (kwod′rə lat′ə rəl) 1 having four sides and four interior angles. 2 a plane figure having four sides and four interior angles. 1 *adj.*, 2 *n.*

**qua·drille** (kwə dril′) 1 a square dance for four couples that has five parts or movements. 2 the music for such a dance. *n.*

**quad·ril·lion** (kwod ril′yən) 1 in Canada, the United States, and France, 1 followed by 15 zeros. 2 in the United Kingdom and Germany, 1 followed by 24 zeros. *n., adj.*

**quad·ri·no·mi·al** (kwod′rə nō′mē əl) 1 consisting of four terms. 2 an algebraic expression having four terms. Example: $a^2 - ab + 4a - b^2$. 1 *adj.*, 2 *n.*

**quad·roon** (kwo drün′) a person having one fourth African ancestry. *n.*

**quad·ru·ped** (kwod′rə ped′) 1 an animal, especially a mammal, that has four feet. 2 having four feet. 1 *n.*, 2 *adj.*

**quad·ru·ple** (kwod′rə pəl *or* kwo drü′pəl) 1 fourfold; consisting of four parts; including four parts or parties. 2 four times; four times as great. 3 a number, amount, etc. four times as great as another: *80 is the quadruple of 20.* 4 make or become four times as great. 5 in music, having four beats to each measure, with the first and third beats accented. 1, 2, 5 *adj.*, 2 *adv.*, 3 *n.*, 4 *v.*, **quad·ru·pled, quad·ru·pling**.

**quad·ru·plet** (kwo drü′plit *or* kwod′rə plit) 1 one of four children born at the same time from the same mother. 2 a group of four. *n.*

**quaes·tor** (kwes′tər) in ancient Rome: 1 an official in charge of the public funds; treasurer. 2 a public prosecutor in certain criminal cases. *n.*

**quaff** (kwof *or* kwaf) 1 drink in large drafts; drink deeply and freely. 2 an act of quaffing. 1 *v.*, 2 *n.*

**quag·mire** (kwag′mīr′) 1 soft, muddy ground; a boggy or miry place. 2 a difficult situation. *n.*

**qua·hog** (kwo′hog *or* kwə hog′) an edible clam of the Atlantic coast of North America, having a hard, thick, rounded shell. *n.* Also, **quahaug**.

**quail¹** (kwāl) any of numerous related species of fowl-like game birds resembling partridges: *The bobwhite is a New World quail. n., pl.* **quails** or (*especially collectively*) **quail**.

**quail²** (kwāl) be afraid; lose courage; shrink back in fear: *They quailed in face of danger. v.*

**quaint** (kwānt) strange or odd in an interesting, pleasing, or amusing way: *Old photographs seem quaint to us today.* *adj.* —**quaint′ly,** *adv.* —**quaint′ness,** *n.*

**quake** (kwāk) **1** shake; tremble: *She quaked with fear.* **2** a shaking; trembling. **3** EARTHQUAKE. **1** *v.*, **quaked, quak·ing;** **2, 3** *n.*

**qual·i·fi·ca·tion** (kwol′ə fə kā′shən) **1** anything that makes a person fit for a job, task, office, etc.: *Good eyesight is a necessary qualification for a pilot.* **2** that which limits, changes, or makes less free and full: *Her enjoyment of the trip had one qualification; her friends could not enjoy it, too.* **3** a modification; limitation; restriction: *The statement was made without any qualification.* *n.*

**qual·i·fied** (kwol′ə fīd′) **1** having the desirable or required qualifications; fitted; adapted: *He is fully qualified for his job.* **2** modified; limited; restricted: *Her qualified answer was, "I will go, but only if you will come with me."* *adj.*

**qual·i·fi·er** (kwol′ə fī′ər) **1** a person or thing that qualifies. **2** a word that qualifies another word: *Adjectives and adverbs are qualifiers.* *n.*

**qual·i·fy** (kwol′ə fī′) **1** make fit or competent: *to qualify oneself for a job.* **2** furnish with legal power; make legally capable. **3** become fit; show oneself fit: *Can you qualify for the Boy Scouts?* **4** in sports, gain the right to compete in a race, contest, or tournament: *She qualified for the tennis tournament.* **5** make less strong; change somewhat; limit; modify: *Qualify your statement that dogs are loyal by adding "usually."* *v.*, **qual·i·fied, qual·i·fy·ing.**

**qual·i·ta·tive** (kwol′ə tə tiv *or* kwol′ə tā′tiv) concerned with QUALITY or qualities. *adj.* —**qual′i·ta′tive·ly,** *adv.*

**qualitative analysis** the process of determining the chemical components of a substance.

**qual·i·ty** (kwol′ə tē) **1** something special about an object that makes it what it is: *One quality of iron is hardness; one quality of sugar is sweetness.* **2** a characteristic; attribute: *She has many fine qualities.* **3** grade of excellence; degree of worth: *That is a poor quality of cloth.* **4** nature; disposition; temper: *Trials often test a person's quality.* **5** character; position; relation: *Dr. Burak was present, but in the quality of a friend, not of a physician.* **6** fineness; merit; excellence: *Look for quality rather than quantity.* **7** high rank; good or high social position. **8** people of high rank. **9** the character of sounds aside from pitch and volume or intensity. *n.*, *pl.* **qual·i·ties.**

**qualm** (kwom *or* kwäm) **1** a sudden disturbing feeling in the mind; uneasiness; misgiving; doubt: *I tried the test with some qualms.* **2** a disturbance or scruple of conscience: *She felt some qualms at staying away from school.* **3** a momentary feeling of faintness or sickness, especially of NAUSEA. *n.*

**qualm·ish** (kwom′ish *or* kwä′mish) **1** inclined to have QUALMS. **2** having QUALMS. *adj.*

**quan·da·ry** (kwon′də rē *or* kwon′drē) a state of perplexity or uncertainty; dilemma. *n.*, *pl.* **quan·da·ries.**

**quan·ti·ta·tive** (kwon′tə tə tiv *or* kwon′tə tā′tiv) **1** concerned with QUANTITY. **2** that can be measured. *adj.* —**quan′ti·ta′tive·ly,** *adv.*

**quantitative analysis** testing of something to find out not only what chemical substances are in it, but also how much there is of each substance.

**quan·ti·ty** (kwon′tə tē) **1** amount: *Equal quantities of* nuts and raisins were used in the cake. **2** a large amount; large number: *The baker buys flour in quantity. She owns quantities of books.* **3** something that is measurable. **4** in music, the length of a note. **5** in speech, the length of a vowel or consonant sound or syllable. *n.*, *pl.* **quan·ti·ties.**

**quan·tum** (kwon′təm) in physics: **1** the smallest amount of energy capable of existing independently. **2** this amount of energy regarded as a unit. *n.*, *pl.* **quan·ta** (-tə).

**quantum leap** or **jump** **1** a sudden change of an atom, electron, etc. from one discrete energy level or state to another. **2** any sudden major change or advance: *a quantum leap in electronic technology.*

**quantum mechanics** the branch of physics dealing with the interpretation of the behaviour of atoms and elementary particles, such as electrons, on the basis of the QUANTUM THEORY.

**quantum theory** the theory that whenever energy is transferred, the transfer occurs in pulsations or stages rather than continuously, and that the amount of energy transferred during each stage is of a definite quantity.

**quar·an·tine** (kwô′rən tēn′) **1** isolate from others, especially to prevent the spread of an infectious disease: *People with yellow fever were quarantined.* **2** the state of being quarantined: *Our house was in quarantine when I had scarlet fever.* **3** detention, isolation, and other measures taken to prevent the spread of an infectious disease. **4** a place where people, animals, plants, ships, etc. are held until it is sure that they have no infectious diseases, insect pests, etc. **1** *v.*, **quar·an·tined, quar·an·tin·ing;** **2–4** *n.*

**quark** (kwôrk *or* kwärk) one of the hypothetical basic building blocks of the fundamental particles, thought to combine with the electron, neutron, and proton to form the nucleus of an atom: *Quarks have never been isolated in a free state.* *n.*

**quar·rel**[1] (kwô′rəl) **1** any angry dispute or disagreement; a breaking off of friendly relations: *The children had a quarrel over the division of the candy.* **2** dispute or disagree angrily; break off friendly relations: *The children were quarrelling when Mother came home.* **3** a cause for a dispute or disagreement; reason for breaking off friendly relations: *A bully likes to pick quarrels. He said he had no quarrel with the government.* **4** find fault: *It is useless to quarrel with fate.* **1, 3** *n.*, **2, 4** *v.*, **quar·relled** *or* **quar·reled, quar·rel·ling** *or* **quar·rel·ing.**

**quar·rel**[2] (kwô′rəl) **1** a bolt or arrow used with a crossbow. **2** a small, square or diamond-shaped pane of glass, used in latticed windows. **3** a stone-mason's chisel. *n.*

**quar·rel·ler** *or* **quar·rel·er** (kwô′rə lər) one who QUARRELS. *n.*

**quar·rel·some** (kwô′rəl səm) too ready to QUARREL; fond of fighting and disputing. *adj.* —**quar′rel·some·ness,** *n.*

**quar·ry¹** (kwôr′ē)   **1** a place where stone is dug, cut, or blasted out for use in building, road making, etc. **2** obtain from a quarry: *We watched the workers quarry a huge block of stone.*   1 *n., pl.* **quar·ries;**   2 *v.,* **quar·ried, quar·ry·ing.** —**quar′ri·er,** *n.*

**quar·ry²** (kwôr′ē)   **1** an animal chased in a hunt; game; prey.   **2** anything hunted or eagerly pursued.   *n., pl.* **quar·ries.**

**quart** (kwôrt)   **1** a unit for measuring volume or capacity, equal to one fourth of a gallon or one eighth of a peck (about 1.14 dm³): *a quart of milk, a quart of blueberries.*   **2** a container holding a quart.   *n.*
☞ *Etym.* **Quart** and QUARTER came through Old French from forms derived from L *quartus* 'fourth'. QUARTET came in the 18c. from F *quartette,* which can also be traced back to L *quartus.*

**quar·ter** (kwôr′tər)   **1** one fourth; half of a half; one of four equal or corresponding parts: *a quarter of an apple.* **2** divide into quarters: *She quartered the apple.*   **3** one fourth of a dollar; 25 cents.   **4** in Canada or the United States, a coin worth 25 cents.   **5** one fourth of an hour; 15 minutes; a moment marking this period.   **6** one fourth of a year; 3 months.   **7** one of the four phases of the moon: *The quarters of the moon are four periods of about seven days each.* See MOON for picture.   **8** one fourth of a unit of measure.   **9** being one of four equal parts; being equal to only about one fourth of full measure. **10** a region; place.   **11** a section; district: *The French quarter is on the south side of the town.*   **12** a certain part of a community, group, etc.: *The bankers' theory was not accepted in other quarters.*   **13** a point of the compass; direction: *In what quarter is the wind?*   **14** give a place to live in: *Soldiers were quartered in all the houses of the town.* **15** live or stay in a place.   **16** mercy shown a defeated enemy in sparing his or her life: *They gave no quarter.* **17** one of four parts into which an animal's carcass is divided: *a quarter of lamb.*   **18** the leg and its adjoining parts.   **19** cut the body of a person or animal into quarters.   **20** the part of a ship's side near the stern. **21** of the wind, blow on a ship's quarter.   **22** in heraldry, one of four or more parts into which a shield is divided by lines at right angles.   **23** the emblem occupying the upper right fourth of a shield.   **24** place or bear COATS OF ARMS in quarters of a shield.   **25** the part of a boot or shoe above the heel and below the top of either side of the foot from the middle of the back to the vamp.   **26** one of four equal periods of play in football, basketball, etc.
**27 quarters,** *pl.*   **a** a place to live or stay: *servants' quarters, officers' quarters. The baseball team has winter quarters in Florida.*   **b** proper position or station. 1, 3–8, 10–13, 16–18, 20, 22, 23, 25–27 *n.,* 2, 14, 15, 19, 21, 24 *v.,* 9 *adj.*
**at close quarters,** at close range; close together: *The two families lived at close quarters until a second apartment was found.*
☞ *Etym.* See note at QUART.

**quar·ter·back** (kwôr′tər bak′)   in football, the player whose position is immediately behind the centre of the line of scrimmage: *The quarterback usually directs the team's play in the field.*   *n.*

**quar·ter·deck** (kwôr′tər dek′)   the part of the upper deck between the mainmast and the stern, used especially by the officers of a ship.   *n.*

**quar·tered** (kwôr′tərd)   **1** divided into QUARTERS. **2** furnished with rooms or lodging.   **3** in heraldry, divided or arranged in quarters.   **4** QUARTERSAWED.   **5** pt. and pp. of QUARTER.   1–4 *adj.,* 5 *v.*

**quarter horse**   a strong horse originally bred for racing on quarter-mile (.4 km) tracks.

**quar·ter–hour** (kwôr′tər our′)   **1** fifteen minutes. **2** the point one fourth or three fourths of the way through an hour.   *n.*

**quar·ter·ing** (kwôr′tə ring)   **1** the act of dividing into fourths.   **2** the act of assigning QUARTERS, especially for soldiers.   **3** of a wind, blowing on a ship's side near the stern.   **4** the division of a shield into quarters or parts. **5** one of such parts.   **6** the COAT OF ARMS on a quartering.   **7** ppr. of QUARTER.   1, 2, 4–6 *n.,* 3 *adj.,* 7 *v.*

**quar·ter·ly** (kwôr′tər lē)   **1** happening, done, etc. four times a year: *to make quarterly payments on one's insurance.*   **2** once each quarter of a year: *to pay one's insurance premiums quarterly.*   **3** a magazine published four times a year: *The Queen's Quarterly.*   1 *adj.,* 2 *adv.,* 3 *n., pl.* **quar·ter·lies.**

**quar·ter·mas·ter** (kwôr′tər mas′tər)   **1** an army officer who has charge of providing QUARTERS (def. 27), clothing, fuel, transportation, etc. for troops.   **2** a navy officer who has charge of the steering, the compasses, signals, etc. on a ship.   *n.*

**quarter note**   in music, a note equal to one fourth of a whole note. See NOTE for picture.

**quarter rest**   in music, a rest lasting as long as a QUARTER NOTE. See REST¹ for picture.

**quar·ter·saw** (kwôr′tər sô′)   saw a log lengthwise into quarters and then into boards.   *v.,* **quar·ter·sawed, quar·ter·sawed** or **quar·ter·sawn, quar·ter·saw·ing.**

**quarter section**   a piece of land, usually square, containing 160 acres (about 65 hectares).

**quarter sessions**   **1** an English court, held QUARTERLY, that has limited criminal jurisdiction and certain other powers.   **2** any of various other courts held QUARTERLY.

**quar·ter·staff** (kwôr′tər staf′)   an old English weapon consisting of a stout pole 2 to 3 metres long, tipped with iron.   *n., pl.* **quar·ter·staves.**

**quar·ter·staves** (kwôr′tər stāvz′)   *pl.* of QUARTERSTAFF.   *n.*

**quar·tet** or **quar·tette** (kwôr tet′)   **1** a group of four musicians (singers or players).   **2** a piece of music for four voices or instruments.   **3** any group of four.   *n.*
☞ *Etym.* See note at QUART.

**quar·to** (kwôr′tō)   **1** the page size of a book in which each leaf is one fourth of a whole sheet of paper. **2** having this size.   **3** a book having this size.   *n., pl.* **quar·tos.**

**quartz** (kwôrts)   a very hard mineral composed of silica: *Common quartz crystals are colourless and transparent, but amethyst, jasper, and many other coloured stones are quartz.* See CRYSTAL for picture.   *n.*

**quartz·ite** (kwôrt′sīt)   a granular rock consisting mostly of QUARTZ.   *n.*

**qua·sar** (kwā′sär *or* kwā′zär)   any of various starlike bodies that are very distant from the earth and give off strong light and radio waves.   *n.*
☞ *Etym.* From *quasi*–stellar radio source.

**quash¹** (kwosh)   put down completely; crush: *to quash a revolt.*   *v.*

**quash²** (kwosh)   make void; annul: *The judge quashed the charges against the prisoner.*   *v.*

**qua·si** (kwā′sē, kwā′zē, *or* kwos′ē)   **1** seeming; not real; halfway: *quasi humour.*   **2** seemingly; not really; partly; almost.   **1** *adj.*, **2** *adv.*

**quasi–**   a prefix meaning the same as QUASI, used in combination, as in *quasi-official.*

**quas·sia** (kwosh′ə)   **1** a bitter drug obtained from the wood of a tropical American tree, used as a tonic and as an insecticide.   **2** the wood.   **3** the tree.   *n.*

**Qua·ter·na·ry** (kwə tėr′nə rē)   **1** the geological period beginning 600 000 years ago, that includes the Recent Epoch. See geological time chart in the Appendix.   **2** deposits of rock made in this period.   **3** of this period or these deposits.   **1, 2** *n.*, **3** *adj.*

**quat·rain** (kwot′rān)   a stanza or poem of four lines.   *n.*

**quat·re·foil** (kat′ər foil *or* kat′rə foil′)   **1** a leaf or flower composed of four leaflets or petals: *The four-leaf clover is a quatrefoil.*   **2** an architectural ornament having four lobes.   See CINQUEFOIL for picture.   *n.*
☛ *Etym.* From OF *quatre* 'four' (from L *quattuor*) + *feuil* 'leaf' (from L *folium*).

**qua·ver** (kwā′vər)   **1** shake tremulously; tremble: *The old man's voice quavered.*   **2** a shaking or trembling, especially of the voice.   **3** sing or say in trembling tones.   **4** trill in singing or in playing on a musical instrument.   **5** in music, an EIGHTH NOTE.   **1, 3, 4** *v.*, **2, 5** *n.*   —**qua′ver·ing·ly,** *adv.*

**qua·ver·y** (kwā′və rē)   QUAVERing.   *adj.*

**quay** (kē)   a solid landing place where ships load and unload, often built of stone.   *n.*
☛ *Hom.* CAY (kē), KEY.
☛ *Etym.* **Quay** is historically the same word as KEY². Originally late ME *key, keye* from OF *kai*, which came from Celtic. The spelling **quay** was introduced in the 17c. to match the modern French form *quai.*

**Que.** Province of Quebec.

**quea·sy** (kwē′zē)   **1** inclined to nausea; easily upset: *a queasy stomach.*   **2** tending to unsettle the stomach.   **3** uneasy; uncomfortable.   **4** squeamish; fastidious.   *adj.*, **quea·si·er, quea·si·est.**   —**quea′si·ly,** *adv.*   —**quea′si·ness,** *n.*

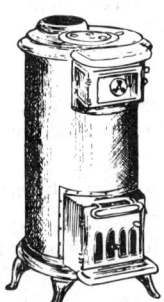

A Quebec heater

**Quebec heater** (kwi bek′ *or* kā bek′)   a kind of stove for heating rooms.

**Que·beck·er** (kwi bek′ər *or* kā bek′ər)   a native or long-term resident of the province of Quebec.   *n.*

**Qué·béc·ois** (kā bā kwä′) *French.*   a person from Quebec.   *n., pl.* **Qué·béc·ois.**

**quash**   965   **quench**

hat, āge, fär; let, ēqual, tėrm; it, īce
hot, ōpen, ôrder; oil, out; cup, pùt, rüle
əbove, takən, pencəl, lemən, circəs
ch, child; ng, long; sh, ship
th, thin; ŦH, then; zh, measure

**Qué·béc·oise** (kā bā kwäz′) *French.*   a female from Quebec.   *n., pl.* **Qué·béc·oises.**

**queen** (kwēn)   **1** the wife of a king.   **2** a female ruler of a nation: *Queen Elizabeth II.*   **3** a woman judged to be first in importance or best in beauty or some other quality: *the queen of society, the queen of the May.*   **4** act like a queen.   **5** in a colony of bees, ants, etc., a female that lays eggs: *There is usually only one queen in a hive of bees.*   **6** a playing card bearing a picture of a queen.   **7** a piece in chess that can move in any straight or diagonal row.   **8** the chief, best, finest, etc.: *the rose, queen of flowers.*   **1–3, 5–8** *n.*, **4** *v.*   —**queen′like′,** *adj.*

**Queen Anne's lace**   the wild carrot.

**Queen City**   **1** Toronto.   **2** Regina.

**queen consort**   the wife of a reigning king.

**queen·dom** (kwēn′dəm)   **1** the realm of a queen.   **2** the position or dignity of a queen.   *n.*

**queen dowager**   the widow of a king.

**queen·ly** (kwēn′lē)   **1** of a queen; fit for a queen.   **2** like a queen; like a queen's.   **3** in a queenly manner; as a queen does.   **1, 2** *adj.*, **queen·li·er, queen·li·est;**   **3** *adv.*   —**queen′li·ness,** *n.*

**queen mother**   the widow of a former king and mother of a reigning king or queen.

**queen regent**   **1** a queen ruling in place of an absent or unfit king.   **2** a queen ruling in her own right.

**Queen's Counsel**   a lawyer or barrister who may serve as counsel to the crown.

**Queen's English**   the English that is recognized as correct and standard in Britain.

**Queen's evidence**   **1** EVIDENCE (def. 2) brought forward by the government in a criminal case.   **2** testimony given in court by a criminal against his or her associates in a crime.
**turn Queen's evidence,**   testify in court against one's associates in a crime.

**Queen's Highway**   in Canada, a main road, usually surfaced, that is the responsibility of the provincial government for maintenance, etc.

**queer** (kwēr)   **1** different from what is normal or usual; strange; odd; peculiar: *a queer remark, a queer noise, a queer reaction.*   **2** *Informal.* eccentric or mildly crazy: *She's a little bit queer.*   **3** not as it should be; causing doubt or suspicion: *There's something queer going on here.*   **4** not well; faint or giddy: *I started to feel queer and had to sit down.*   *adj.*   —**queer′ly,** *adv.*

**queer·ness** (kwēr′nis)   **1** queer nature or behaviour.   **2** something strange or odd; peculiarity.   *n.*

**quell** (kwel)   **1** put down disorder, rebellion, etc.   **2** put an end to; overcome: *to quell one's fears.*   *v.*

**quench** (kwench)   **1** put an end to; stop: *to quench a thirst.*   **2** drown out; put out: *Water quenched the fire.*   **3** cool suddenly by plunging into water or other liquid: *Hot steel is quenched to harden it.*   *v.*

**quench·less** (kwench′lis) that cannot be quenched; inextinguishable. *adj.*

**quer·u·lous** (kwer′ə ləs *or* kwer′yə ləs) **1** complaining; faultfinding. **2** fretful; peevish: *a querulous voice.* *adj.* —**quer′u·lous·ly,** *adv.*

**que·ry** (kwē′rē) **1** a question; inquiry. **2** put as a question; ask: *"How long will that be?" she queried.* **3** ask questions of: *They queried him about his future plans.* **4** ask questions about; inquire into, especially to express doubt: *She queried the wisdom of accepting the first offer.* **5** a doubt: *There was a query in his mind about the whole procedure.* **6** QUESTION MARK. 1, 5, 6 *n., pl.* **que·ries;** 2–4 *v.,* **que·ried, que·ry·ing.**

**quest** (kwest) **1** a hunt; search: *Mary went to the library in quest of something to read.* **2** search or seek for; hunt. **3** an expedition or journey in search of something noble, ideal, or holy: *There are many stories about the quest for the Holy Grail.* **4** an object or place sought for. 1, 3, 4 *n.,* 2 *v.*

**ques·tion** (kwes′chən) **1** something asked; a sentence in interrogative form, addressed to someone to get information; inquiry. **2** ask in order to get information; seek information from: *The police questioned the witness to the accident.* **3** ask; inquire. **4** a judicial examination or trial; interrogation. **5** a matter of doubt or dispute; controversy: *A question arose about the ownership of the property.* **6** doubt; dispute: *I question the truth of his story.* **7** a matter to be talked over, investigated, considered, etc.; problem: *the question of prohibition.* **8** a proposal to be voted on. **9** the taking of a vote on a proposal: *The president asked if the club members were ready for the question.* 1, 4, 5, 7–9 *n.,* 2, 3, 6 *v.* —**ques′tion·er,** *n.* —**ques′tion·ing·ly,** *adv.*
**beside the question,** off the subject.
**beyond** or **without question,** without doubt; not to be disputed: *The statements in that book are true beyond question. She is without question the brightest student in the school.*
**call in question,** dispute; challenge.
**in question,** **a** under consideration or discussion. **b** in dispute.
**out of the question,** not to be considered; impossible.

**ques·tion·a·ble** (kwes′chə nə bəl) **1** open to question or dispute; doubtful; uncertain: *a questionable statement, calculations of questionable accuracy.* **2** of doubtful propriety, honesty, morality, respectability, or the like: *questionable motives.* *adj.*

**question mark** a mark (?) put after a question or used to express doubt about something written or printed.

**ques·tion·naire** (kwes′chə ner′) **1** a set of questions designed for obtaining statistical information: *The questionnaire was quite straightforward.* **2** a form containing such questions, usually having spaces for answers: *to fill out a questionnaire.* *n.*

**quet·zal** (ket säl′) a Central American bird having brilliant golden-green and scarlet plumage: *The male quetzal has long, flowing tail feathers.* *n.*

**queue** (kyü) **1** a line of people, automobiles, etc.; a line-up: *There was a long queue in front of the theatre.* **2** form or stand in a line while waiting to be served, etc. (*usually used with* **up**): *We had to queue up to get tickets.* **3** a braid of hair hanging down the back. 1, 3 *n.,* 2 *v.,* **queued, queu·ing.**
☞ *Hom.* CUE.

☞ *Etym.* Through F *queue* from L *cauda* 'tail'. 16c. CODA (a "tail" added to a musical composition) comes from Italian *coda,* which also came from L *cauda.*

**quib·ble** (kwib′əl) **1** an evasion of the main point, especially a petty one or one that depends on words that are vague or have a double meaning: *a legal quibble.* **2** a minor criticism or objection: *The meeting was delayed for several minutes because of a quibble about procedure.* **3** use quibbles; resort to petty objections or evasions: *This is no time to quibble about a few cents in change.* 1, 2 *n.,* 3 *v.,* **quib·bled, quib·bling.**

**quiche** (kēsh) a kind of pie usually served as a main dish, consisting of a pastry shell filled with an egg and cream mixture together with any of various other ingredients, such as ham, bacon, cheese, or seafood. *n.*

**quiche Lor·raine** (kēsh′lô rān′) a quiche containing bacon and, usually, cheese.

**quick** (kwik) **1** fast and sudden; swift: *a quick turn.* **2** begun and ended in a very short time: *a quick visit.* **3** coming soon; prompt: *a quick reply.* **4** not patient; hasty: *a quick temper.* **5** brisk: *a quick fire.* **6** acting quickly; ready; lively: *a quick wit.* **7** understanding or learning quickly: *a child who is quick in school.* **8** tender, sensitive flesh, especially the flesh under a fingernail or toenail: *The child bit his nails down to the quick.* **9** the tender, sensitive part of one's feelings: *Their insults cut her to the quick.* **10** living; *Archaic* except in: *the quick and the dead.* **11** quickly: *Come quick!* 1–7 *adj.,* 8–10 *n.,* 11 *adv.* —**quick′ness,** *n.*

**quick bread** bread, biscuits, etc., made with a leavening agent that does not require the dough to be left to rise before baking.

**quick·en** (kwik′ən) **1** make or become more rapid; accelerate: *He quickened his pace. His pulse quickened.* **2** make or become stimulated or animated: *Her interest quickened when the discussion turned to travel.* **3** cause to burn brighter: *to quicken hot ashes into flames.* **4** make or become alive. *v.*

**quick–freeze** (kwik′frēz′) freeze food quickly in preparation for storage, so that the ice crystals formed during the freezing process are too small to rupture the cells, thus preserving the natural juices and flavour of the food. *v.,* **quick-froze, quick-fro·zen, quick-freez·ing.**

**quick·hatch** (kwik′hach′) *Cdn.* WOLVERINE. *n.*

**quick·ie** (kwik′ē) *Informal.* something made or done very quickly or superficially: *His last film was just a quickie. Let's stop for coffee; we've got time for at least a quickie.* *n.*

**quick·lime** (kwik′līm′) a white alkaline substance usually obtained by burning limestone and used for making mortar, cement, etc. *n.*

**quick·ly** (kwik′lē) with haste or speed: *They walked quickly. The wound healed quickly.* *adv.*

**quick march** in the armed forces, an order to begin marching in QUICK TIME.

**quick·sand** (kwik′sand′) **1** soft, wet sand that will not support a heavy weight: *The horse was swallowed by the quicksand.* **2** an expanse of such sand. *n.*

**quick·sil·ver** (kwik′sil′vər) MERCURY. *n.*

**quick·step** (kwik′step′) **1** a lively dance step. **2** music in a brisk march rhythm, as that used to accompany marching in QUICK TIME. **3** a step used in marching in QUICK TIME. *n.*

**quick–tem·pered** (kwik′tem′pərd) easily angered. *adj.*

**quick time** a marching rate of 120 paces per minute, or about 5.5 km/h.

**quick–wit·ted** (kwik′wit′id) having a quick mind; mentally alert. *adj.*

**quid** (kwid) **1** a piece to be chewed. **2** a bite of chewing tobacco. *n.*

**quid pro quo** (kwid′ prō kwō′) *Latin.* meaning 'which for what'; compensation; one thing in return for another.

**qui·es·cence** (kwī es′əns *or* kwē es′əns) absence of activity; quietness; stillness; motionlessness. *n.*

**qui·es·cent** (kwī es′ənt *or* kwē es′ənt) inactive; quiet; still; motionless. *adj.* —**qui′es′cent·ly**, *adv.*

**qui·et** (kwī′ət) **1** moving very little; still: *a quiet river.* **2** with no or little noise: *quiet footsteps, a quiet room.* **3** peaceful; gentle; unobtrusive: *a quiet mind, quiet manners.* **4** at rest; not active: *a quiet evening at home.* **5** a state of rest; stillness; freedom from disturbance; peace: *to read in quiet.* **6** make quiet: *The father quieted his frightened child.* **7** become quiet: *The wind quieted down.* **8** not showy or bright: *Grey is a quiet colour.* **9** in a quiet manner. 1–4, 8 *adj.*, 5 *n.*, 6, 7 *v.*, 9 *adv.*, —**qui′et·er**, *n.* —**qui′et·ly**, *adv.* —**qui′et·ness**, *n.*

**qui·et·en** (kwī′ə tən) **1** cause to become quiet; make still or peaceful: *The mother quietened her excited child.* **2** become quiet (usually used with **down**): *The wind finally quietened down.* *v.*

**qui·e·tude** (kwī′ə tyüd′ *or* kwī′ə tüd′) quietness; stillness; calmness. *n.*

**qui·e·tus** (kwī ē′təs) **1** final settlement or release from an obligation or debt. **2** final release from life; death. **3** anything that ends, settles, or kills: *The arrival of the militia gave the riot its quietus.* *n.*

**quill** (kwil) **1** a large, stiff feather. **2** the hollow stem of a feather. **3** anything made from the hollow stem of a feather, such as a pen or toothpick. **4** one of the stiff sharp spines of a porcupine or hedgehog. *n.*

**quilt** (kwilt) **1** a bed covering made of two layers of cloth with a filling between them that is held in place by lines of stitching, often in decorative patterns: *Quilts are filled with down or feathers or a batting of wool, cotton, or a synthetic fibre.* **2** any thick bed covering. **3** fill or pad like a quilt: *to quilt a jacket.* **4** stitch with lines or patterns through layers of cloth: *to quilt a traditional design.* **5** stitch in layers with a padding between: *I bought some quilted material for a vest.* **6** make quilts: *They enjoy quilting.* 1, 2 *n.*, 3–6 *v.* —**quilt′er**, *n.*

**quilt·ing** (kwil′ting) **1** QUILTED work. **2** material that is QUILTed or used for making quilts. **3** ppr. of QUILT. 1, 2 *n.*, 3 *v.*

**quince** (kwins) **1** a hard, yellowish, acid fruit, used for preserves and jelly. **2** the tree it grows on, a member of the rose family. **3** JAPONICA. *n.*

**qui·nine** (kwī′nīn *or* kwi nēn′) **1** a bitter, colourless crystalline drug made from CINCHONA bark, used in medicine. **2** any of various compounds of quinine that are used as medicine. *n.*

**quin·quen·ni·al** (kwing kwen′ē əl) **1** occurring every five years. **2** of or for five years. *adj.* —**quin·quen′nial·ly**, *adv.*

**quin·que·reme** (kwing′kwə rēm′) in former times, a GALLEY (def. 1) with five tiers of oars. *n.*

**quick-tempered 967 quirt**

hat, āge, fär; let, ēqual, tėrm; it, īce
hot, ōpen, ôrder; oil, out; cup, pùt, rüle
əbove, takən, pencəl, lemən, circəs
ch, child; ng, long; sh, ship
th, thin; ŦH, then; zh, measure

**quin·sy** (kwin′zē) an ABSCESS behind the tonsils, usually caused by a severe case of tonsillitis. *n.*

**quint** (kwint) *Informal.* QUINTUPLET. *n.*

**quin·tal** (kən′təl) **1** *Cdn.* in Newfoundland: **a** a unit used for weighing fish, especially cod, equal to 112 pounds (about 50.8 kg). **b** a quantity of fish weighing one quintal: *The first day they got 50 quintals of cod.* **c** a container holding one quintal, used for packing and shipping dried, salted cod. **2** a unit for measuring mass, equal to 100 pounds (about 45.4 kg). **3** a unit for measuring mass, equal to 10 kg. *n.*

**quin·tes·sence** (kwin tes′əns) **1** the essence of a thing in its purest form. **2** the best example or representative of something: *He was the quintessence of goodness.* *n.*
☛ *Etym.* Through F from L *quinta essentia* 'fifth essence', referring in medieval science to an unidentified basic substance beyond the four elements of earth, air, fire, and water. 15c.

**quin·tes·sen·tial** (kwin′tə sen′shəl) having the nature of a quintessence; of the purest or most perfect kind: *the quintessential detective of modern fiction.* *adj.* —**quin′te·sen′tial·ly**, *adv.*

**quin·tet** *or* **quin·tette** (kwin tet′) **1** a group of five musicians who perform together. **2** a piece of music for five voices or instruments. **3** any group of five. *n.*
☛ *Etym.* Quintet, QUINTILLION, and QUINTUPLE came through French from forms derived from L *quintus* 'fifth'. QUINTUPLET was formed in the 19c. from **quintuple** on the pattern of TRIPLET and QUADRUPLET. See also note at QUINTESSENCE.

**quin·til·lion** (kwin til′yən) **1** in Canada and the United States, a number represented by 1 followed by 18 zeros. **2** in the United Kingdom, France, and Germany, 1 followed by 30 zeros. *n.*

**quin·tu·ple** (kwin tyü′pəl, kwin tü′pəl, *or* kwin tup′əl) **1** fivefold; consisting of five parts. **2** five times as great or as many. **3** make five times as great or as many: *He quintupled his investment.* **4** become five times as great or as many: *His investment quintupled.* **5** a number, amount, etc. five times as great as another. 1, 2 *adj.*, 3, 4 *v.*, **quin·tu·pled, quin·tu·pling**; 5 *n.*

**quin·tu·plet** (kwin tyü′plit, kwin tü′plit, kwin tup′lit, *or* kwin′tə plit) **1** one of five offspring born at one birth from the same mother. **2** any group or combination of five. *n.*

**quip** (kwip) **1** a clever or witty saying, especially one made on the spur of the moment. **2** a sharp, cutting remark. **3** make quips. 1, 2 *n.*, 3 *v.*, **quip·ped, quip·ping.**

**quire** (kwīr) 24 or 25 sheets of paper of the same stock and size; one twentieth of a ream. *n.*
☛ *Hom.* CHOIR.

**quirk** (kwėrk) **1** a peculiar trait; an odd mannerism or way of behaving: *She has some irritating quirks.* **2** an unexpected or sudden happening, action, etc.: *a quirk of fate.* **3** a sudden turn or curve, such as a flourish in writing. *n.*

**quirt** (kwėrt) **1** a riding whip with a short, stout handle and a lash of braided leather.   2 strike with a quirt.   1 *n.*, 2 *v.*

**quis·ling** (kwiz′ling)   a person who collaborates with an enemy occupying his or her country, especially by serving in a puppet government.   *n.*
☛ *Etym.*   From Vidkun *Quisling* (1887–1945), a Norwegian army officer and politician, who co-operated with the Germans when they invaded Norway during World War II.

**quit** (kwit)   1 stop: *The men quit work when the whistle blew.*   2 stop working: *It will soon be time to quit.*   3 leave: *He quit his room in anger.*   4 give up; let go.   5 pay back; pay off a debt.   6 free; clear; rid: *I gave him money to be quit of him.*   1–5 *v.*, **quit** or **quit·ted**, **quit·ting**;   6 *adj.*

**quit·claim** (kwit′klām′)   1 the giving up of a claim, especially to land or property.   2 a document stating that somebody gives up a claim.   3 give up claim to a right or title.   1, 2 *n.*, 3 *v.*

**quite** (kwīt)   1 completely; wholly; entirely: *That's not quite true. I'm afraid it's quite impossible for me to go.*   2 really; positively: *It's quite the thing these days.*   3 to a considerable extent or degree: *This dress is quite nice but I like the other one better. He plays the piano quite well.*   *adv.*
**quite a**,   **a** a considerable number, amount, size, etc.: *There are quite a few left. It cost quite a lot. We waited quite a while.*   **b** *Informal.*   impressive or unusual: *That's quite a ring you have. He's quite a guy.*

**quit·rent** (kwit′rent′)   under a feudal system, rent paid in money, instead of by services rendered.   *n.*

**quits** (kwits)   on even terms by repayment or retaliation (*never used before a noun*): *After the book was returned undamaged, the boys were quits.*   *adj.*
**call it quits**,   stop doing something: *The mosquitoes got so bad that we finally had to call it quits and go home.*
**cry quits**,   admit that things are now even; agree to stop quarrelling, etc.

**quit·ter** (kwit′ər) *Informal.*   a person who gives up too easily.   *n.*

**quiv·er¹** (kwiv′ər)   1 shake; shiver; tremble: *His voice quivered. The dog quivered with excitement.*   2 shaking or trembling: *A quiver of his mouth showed that he was about to cry.*   1 *v.*, 2 *n.*

**quiv·er²** (kwiv′ər)   1 a case to hold arrows. See ARCHERY for picture.   2 the arrows in a quiver.   *n.*

**qui vive?** (kē vēv′) *French.*   who goes there?
**on the qui vive**,   watchful; alert.
☛ *Etym.*   From a French sentry's challenge meaning 'Long live who?'; that is, 'whose side are you on?' the appropriate answer being *Vive le roi!* 'Long live the king!'.

**Qui·xo·te** (kē hō′tē *or* kwik′sət; *Spanish,* kē Hō′tä)   See DON QUIXOTE.   *n.*

**quix·ot·ic** (kwik sot′ik)   characterized by very high but impractical ideals or extravagant chivalry.   *adj.*
—**quix·ot′i·cal·ly**, *adv.*

**quiz** (kwiz)   1 a short or informal test: *a quiz in geography.*   2 give such a test to: *to quiz a class in history.*   3 question; interrogate: *The lawyer quizzed the witness.*   1 *n.*, *pl.* **quiz·zes**;   2, 3 *v.*, **quizzed, quiz·zing**.

**quiz·mas·ter** (kwiz′mas′tər)   the person who asks questions of the contestants in a QUIZ SHOW.   *n.*

**quiz show**   a radio or television program in which contestants are given prizes for answering questions correctly.

**quiz·zi·cal** (kwiz′ə kəl)   1 odd; queer; comical.   2 that suggests making fun of others; teasing: *a quizzical smile.*   *adj.* —**quiz′zi·cal·ly**, *adv.*

**quoit** (kwoit)   1 a heavy, flattish ring of iron or circle of rope, rubber, etc., used in a game in which it is thrown at a peg stuck in the ground to encircle it or come as close to it as possible.   2 **quoits**,   the game in which quoits are thrown at a peg (*used with a singular verb*): *Quoits is similar to horseshoes.*   *n.*

**quon·dam** (kwon′dəm)   that once was; former: *The quondam servant is now master.*   *adj.*

**quo·rum** (kwô′rəm)   the number of members of any society or assembly that must be present if the business done is to be legal or binding: *In our club twenty-five people make a quorum.*   *n.*

**quot.**   quotation.

**quo·ta** (kwō′tə)   1 a share or proportion that is required of or due to a person or group: *Each club member was given his or her quota of tickets to sell for the banquet.*   2 a quantity or proportion that is allowed: *a government quota on imports.*   *n.*

**quot·a·ble** (kwō′tə bəl)   suitable for or worth quoting: *The opposition leader made some quotable comments in her speech.*   *adj.*

**quo·ta·tion** (kwō tā′shən)   1 somebody's words repeated exactly by another person; a passage quoted from a book, speech, etc.: *From what author does this quotation come?*   2 quoting: *Quotation is a habit of some teachers.*   3 the stating of the current price of stock, commodity, etc.   4 the price so stated: *today's quotation on wheat.*   *n.*

**quotation mark**   one of a pair of marks used to indicate the beginning and end of a quotation. The usual marks are (" ") for a single quotation and (' ') for a quotation within a quotation.

**quote** (kwōt)   1 repeat the exact words of; give words or passages from: *to quote Shakespeare. He often quotes his grandchildren.*   2 repeat exactly the words of another or a passage from a book: *The minister quoted from the Charter of Rights.*   3 bring forward as an example or authority; cite: *The judge quoted various cases in support of his opinion.*   4 give a price: *to quote a price on a home.*   5 QUOTATION (def. 1).   6 QUOTATION MARK.   1–4 *v.*, **quot·ed, quot·ing**;   5, 6 *n.*   —**quot′er**, *n.*

**quo·tient** (kwō′shənt)   the number obtained by dividing one number by another: *In* $26 \div 2 = 13$, *13 is the quotient.* See DIVISION for picture.   *n.*

**quo war·ran·to** (kwō′wə ran′tō) *Latin.*   1 a writ commanding a person to show by what authority he or she holds a public office, privilege, franchise, etc.   2 the legal proceedings taken against such a person as distinct from a private citizen.

**q.v.**   see this word (an abbreviation of Latin *quod vide* 'which see').

# R r  R r

hat, āge, fär; let, ēqual, tėrm; it, īce
hot, ōpen, ôrder; oil, out; cup, put, rüle
əbove, takən, pencəl, lemən, circəs
ch, child; ng, long; sh, ship
th, thin; ŦH, then; zh, measure

**r or R** (är)  **1** the eighteenth letter of the English alphabet.  **2** any speech sound represented by this letter.  **3** a person or thing identified as r, especially as the eighteenth of a series.  *n., pl.* **r's** or **R's.**
**the three R's,** the basic elements of an education; reading, writing, and arithmetic.

**r**  **1** ratio.  **2** radius.

**r.**  **1** railway.  **2** rod.

**R.**  **1** River.  **2** Royal.  **3** Railway; Railroad.  **4** King (an abbreviation of Latin *rex* 'king').  **5** Queen (an abbreviation of Latin *regina* 'queen').  **6** Rabbi.

**Ra**  radium.

**rab·bet** (rab′it)  **1** a groove, slot, or recess made on the edge or surface of a board, etc. to receive the end or edge of another piece of wood shaped to fit it.  **2** a joint so made, also called a **rabbet joint.** See JOINT for picture.  **3** cut or form a rabbet in.  **4** join with a rabbet.  1, 2 *n.*, 3, 4 *v.*, **rab·bet·ed, rab·bet·ing.**
☞ *Hom.* RABBIT.

**rab·bi** (rab′ī)  **1** a teacher or scholar of the Jewish law.  **2** a Jewish religious leader, especially the spiritual head of a congregation.  *n., pl.* **rab·bis.**
☞ *Etym.* Through Old French and Latin from Hebrew *rabbī* 'my master'.

**rab·bin·i·cal** (rə bin′ə kəl)  of or having to do with RABBIS, their learning, writings, etc.  *adj.*

**Rab·bin·ic Hebrew** (rə bin′ik)  the Hebrew language as used by RABBIS of the Middle Ages in their writings.

A cottontail rabbit—about 32 cm long excluding the tail

**rab·bit** (rab′it)  **1** a burrowing mammal with soft fur, long ears, and long hind legs.  **2** its fur.  *n.*
—**rab′bit·like′,** *adj.*
☞ *Hom.* RABBET.

**rabbit ears**  *Informal.*  a small indoor television antenna consisting of two rods of adjustable length attached to a small base in such a way that they can be swivelled apart to form a wide or narrow V.

**rab·ble** (rab′əl)  **1** a disorderly crowd; mob: *The noisy rabble protesting outside the building disturbed the meeting.*  **2 the rabble,** the lowest class of people.  *n.*

**rab·ble–rous·er** (rab′əl rou′zər)  a person who tries to stir up groups of people to violence, as a form of social or political protest.  *n.*

**rab·id** (rab′id)  **1** unreasonably extreme; fanatical; violent: *The rebels are rabid idealists.*  **2** furious; raging: *rabid with anger.*  **3** having RABIES; mad: *a rabid dog.*  **4** of RABIES.  *adj.*  —**rab′id·ly,** *adv.*  —**rab′id·ness,** *n.*

**ra·bies** (rā′bēz)  an acute, usually fatal, infectious disease of the central nervous system that can be transmitted to any warm-blooded animal, including humans, by the bite of an animal that has the disease: *The usual symptoms of rabies are wild excitement and aggressiveness, followed by paralysis and death.*  *n.*

A raccoon—about 60 cm long excluding the tail

**rac·coon** (ra kün′)  **1** a small, greyish-brown mammal with a bushy, ringed tail and a dark patch around the eyes: *Most of the time raccoons live in trees and are active at night.*  **2** its fur: *a raccoon coat.*  *n.*  Also, **racoon.**

**race**¹ (rās)  **1** a contest of speed, as in running, driving, riding, sailing, etc.  **2** engage in a contest of speed: *Our horse will race tomorrow.*  **3** try to beat in a contest of speed; run a race with: *I'll race you to the corner.*  **4** cause to run in a race.  **5** a series of horse races run at a set time over a regular course.  **6** any contest that suggests a race: *a political race.*  **7** run, move, or go swiftly: *The fire engine raced to the scene of the fire.*  **8** cause to run, move, or go swiftly.  **9** of a motor, wheel, etc., run too fast when load or resistance is lessened without corresponding lessening of power.  **10** onward movement: *the race of life.*  **11** a strong or fast current of water: *a mill race.*  **12** the channel of a stream.  **13** a channel leading water to or from a place where its energy is utilized.  **14** a track, groove, etc. for a sliding or rolling part of a machine.  1, 5, 6, 10–14 *n.*, 2–4, 7–9 *v.*, **raced, rac·ing.**

**race**² (rās)  **1** in anthropology, a major grouping of human beings, distinguished biologically mainly by such hereditary traits as dominant blood types and resistance to particular diseases and also by skin colour, body proportions, etc.: *The three major races now generally recognized are the Caucasoid, Mongoloid, and Negroid.*  **2** sometimes, a variety of certain animals or plants: *the race of hunting dogs, the race of flowering shrubs.*  **3** sometimes, ancestry: *Her speech reveals her to be of the Irish race.*  **4** the state or condition of belonging to a particular race: *Intelligence does not depend on race.*  *n.*
**the human race,** all the people of the world.
☞ *Usage.* Because **race**² has several meanings, some scholars prefer *ethnic group* or *stock* instead of *race.*

**race·course** (rās′kôrs′)  a course or track for racing; RACE-TRACK.  *n.*

**race·horse** (rās′hôrs′)  a horse bred or kept for racing. See HORSE for picture.  *n.*

**ra·ceme** (rā sēm′ *or* rə sēm′)  a simple flower cluster having its flowers on short stalks along a stem, the lower flowers blooming first: *The lily of the valley, the currant, and the chokecherry have racemes. A raceme is a kind of inflorescence.*  See INFLORESCENCE for picture.  *n.*

**rac·er** (rā′sər)  **1** a person who races or an animal,

vehicle, boat, or aircraft that is used for racing. **2** any of several harmless North American snakes that can move very fast, especially the blacksnake. *n.*

**race riot** an outbreak of violence resulting from hostility or hatred between RACES².

**race–track** (rā′strak′) a track or course, usually oval in shape, on which races with horses or vehicles are run. *n.*

**ra·chis** (rā′kis) **1** the stem from which the individual flowers of a flower cluster or the leaflets of a compound leaf grow. **2** the shaft of a feather. **3** SPINAL COLUMN. *n., pl.* **ra·chis·es** or **rach·i·des** (rak′ə dēz′ or rā′kə dēz′).

**ra·chit·ic** (rə kit′ik) having to do with or affected with RICKETS; rickety. *adj.*

**ra·chi·tis** (rə kī′tis) RICKETS. *n.*

**ra·cial** (rā′shəl) **1** of, having to do with, or characteristic of a RACE²: *racial traits.* **2** occurring between or involving two or more RACES²: *racial tensions, racial harmony.* *adj.*

**ra·cial·ly** (rā′shə lē) in respect to RACE². *adv.*

**rac·i·ness** (rā′sē nis) the quality of being RACY. *n.*

**rac·ism** (rā′siz əm) **1** prejudice or discrimination against a person or group because of a difference of RACE². **2** prejudice or discrimination against a person or group because of a difference of cultural or ethnic background. **3** belief in the superiority of a particular RACE², based on the out-of-date theory that human abilities, character, etc. are determined by race. *n.*

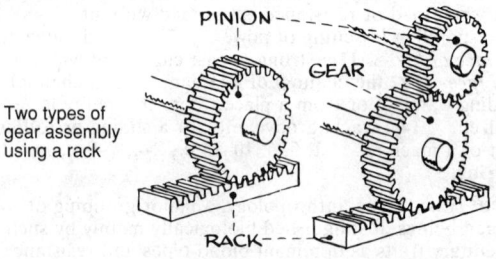

Two types of gear assembly using a rack

**rack¹** (rak) **1** a frame with bars, shelves, or pegs to hold, arrange, or keep things on: *a towel rack, a hat rack, a baggage rack.* **2** a frame of bars to hold hay and other food for cattle. **3** a framework set on a wagon for carrying hay, straw, etc. **4** formerly, an instrument used for torturing people by stretching them. **5** torture on the rack. **6** hurt very much: *racked with grief. A toothache racked her jaw.* **7** a cause or condition of great suffering in body or mind. **8** stretch; strain. **9** a bar with pegs or teeth on one edge, into which teeth on the rim of a wheel can fit. **10** a piece of lamb prepared for cooking. See LAMB for picture. 1–4, 7–10 *n.*, 5, 6, 8 *v.*
**on the rack,** in great pain; suffering very much.
**rack one's brains,** think as hard as one can.
☛ *Hom.* WRACK.

**rack²** (rak) wreck; destruction: *Over the years, the vacant house went to rack and ruin.* *n.*
☛ *Hom.* WRACK.

**rack³** (rak) SINGLE-FOOT. *n., v.*
☛ *Hom.* WRACK.

**rack·et¹** (rak′it) **1** loud noise or talking; uproar; din: *Who's making all the racket?* **2** a dishonest scheme for getting money from people, especially by threatening violence. **3** *Informal.* any dishonest or fraudulent scheme or activity. *n.*

Rackets for tennis, badminton, and squash

**rack·et²** or **rac·quet** (rak′it) **1** a light, wide bat used in games like tennis, badminton, and squash, consisting of a network of nylon, gut, etc. stretched in an open oval or round frame attached to a handle. **2** Usually, **racquets**, a game for two or four players with a ball and rackets, played in a walled court (*used with a singular verb*). *n.*

**rack·et·eer** (rak′ə tēr′) **1** a person who operates a RACKET¹ (def. 2), especially one who extorts money by threatening violence or by blackmail. **2** obtain money by such means. 1 *n.*, 2 *v.*

**rack·et·eer·ing** (rak′ə tē′ring) the business of a RACKETEER. *n.*

**rac·on·teur** (rak′on tėr′) a person who is skilful at telling stories, anecdotes, etc. *n.*

**ra·coon** (ra kün′) See RACCOON. *n.*

**rac·quet** (rak′it) See RACKET². *n.*

**rac·quet·ball** (rak′it bol′) an indoor game similar to handball, played by two or four players in a walled court, using a short racket and a hollow rubber ball about the size of a tennis ball. *n.*

**rac·y** (rā′sē) **1** vigorous; lively. **2** having the distinctive quality characteristic of something in its best or original form: *racy flavour.* **3** risqué; suggestive; slightly indecent: *a racy novel.* *adj.*, **rac·i·er, rac·i·est.**

**ra·dar** (rā′där) **1** a system for determining the distance, direction, speed, etc. of unseen objects by the reflection of high-frequency radio waves. **2** an instrument used for this. *n.*
☛ *Etym.* From the first letters of *ra*dio *d*etection *a*nd *r*anging.

**radar trap** an apparatus, usually located in a hidden or unexpected place, that uses RADAR to detect road vehicles travelling faster than the speed limit.

**ra·di·al** (rā′dē əl) **1** arranged like or in radii or rays from a centre: *The petals of a daisy and the spokes of a wagon wheel have a radial form.* **2** of, having to do with, or near the bone called the RADIUS (def. 3). **3** RADIAL TIRE. 1, 2 *adj.*, 3 *n.*

**ra·di·al·ly** (rā′dē ə lē) like the spokes of a wheel; in rays; like radii or rays. *adv.*

**radial tire** an automobile tire in which the plies of cord extending to the edges of the tire are at right angles to the centre line of the tread.

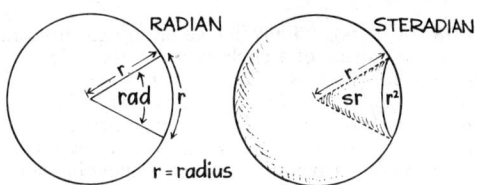

**ra·di·an** (rā′dē ən) an SI unit for measuring plane angles, equal to the angle formed between two radii of a circle that cuts off an arc on the circumference equal in length to the radius: *There are two pi (2π) radians in a circle. The radian, which is used especially in mathematics, is one of the two supplementary units in the SI.* Symbol: rad    *n.*

**ra·di·ance** (rā′dē əns) the quality or state of being RADIANT; vivid brightness: *the radiance of the sun, the radiance of a smile.*    *n.*

**ra·di·ant** (rā′dē ənt) **1** shining; bright; beaming: *a radiant smile.* **2** sending out rays of light or heat: *The sun is a radiant body.* **3** sent off in rays from some source; radiated: *We get radiant energy from the sun.*    *adj.* —**ra′di·ant·ly,** *adv.*

**radiant energy** a form of energy that is transmitted by electromagnetic waves and is perceived as heat, light, X rays, etc.: *The sun is our main source of radiant energy.*

**ra·di·ate** (rā′dē āt) **1** give out rays of: *The sun radiates light and heat.* **2** give out rays; shine. **3** issue in rays: *Heat radiates from those hot steam pipes.* **4** give out; send forth: *Her face radiates joy.* **5** spread out from or as if from a centre: *Roads radiate from the city in every direction.* **6** having rays: *A daisy is a radiate flower.* **7** radiating from a centre.    1–5 *v.,* **ra·di·at·ed, ra·di·at·ing;** 6, 7 *adj.*

**ra·di·a·tion** (rā′dē ā′shən) **1** the act or process of giving out light, heat, or other RADIANT ENERGY. **2** the energy radiated. **3** a RADIO-ACTIVE ray or rays: *Radiation is harmful to living tissues. The radiation from an atomic bomb is dangerous to life.* **4** the process of treating disease by radiation from a RADIO-ACTIVE material such as radium.    *n.*

**radiation sickness** a disease resulting from an overdose of RADIATION from radio-active materials: *Radiation sickness is usually characterized by internal bleeding and changes in tissue structure.*

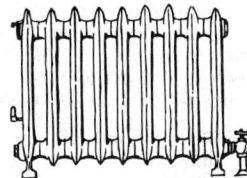
A radiator

**ra·di·a·tor** (rā′dē ā′tər) **1** a heating device consisting of a set of pipes through which steam or hot water passes. **2** a device for circulating water: *The radiator of an automobile gives off heat very quickly and so cools the water inside it.* **3** any person or thing that radiates, or transmits something.    *n.*

**rad·i·cal** (rad′ə kəl) **1** going to the root; fundamental: *If she wants to lose weight, she must make a radical change in her diet.* **2** favouring extreme changes or reforms; extreme. **3** a person who favours extreme changes or reforms, especially in politics; person with extreme opinions. **4** an atom or group of atoms acting as a unit in chemical reactions: *Ammonium (NH₄) is a radical in NH₄OH and NH₄Cl.* **5** the mathematical sign (√) put before an expression to show that some root of it is to be extracted. **6** in grammar, a root. **7** of or from the root or roots. **8** anything fundamental or basic. 1, 2, 7 *adj.,* 3–6, 8 *n.* —**rad′i·cal·ly,** *adv.* —**rad′i·cal·ness,** *n.*  *Hom.* RADICLE.

**rad·i·cal·ism** (rad′ə kə liz′əm) the principles or practices of radicals; extreme views.    *n.*

**rad·i·ces** (rad′i sēz′) a plural of RADIX.    *n.*

**rad·i·cle** (rad′ə kəl) **1** the part of a seed that develops into the main root. **2** a small root; rootlet.    *n.*  *Hom.* RADICAL.

**ra·di·i** (rā′dē ī′) a pl. of RADIUS.    *n.*

**ra·di·o** (rā′dē ō′) **1** the sending and receiving of sound in the form of electric signals by means of electric waves without connecting wires. **2** an apparatus for receiving and making audible the sounds so sent. **3** of, having to do with, used in, or sent by radio: *a radio set, radio speeches.* **4** transmit or send out by radio: *The ship radioed a call for help.* **5** *Informal.* a message sent by radio. **6** of or having to do with electric frequencies higher than 10 000 per second.    1, 2, 5 *n., pl.* **ra·di·os;** 3, 6 *adj.,* 4 *v.,* **ra·di·oed, ra·di·o·ing.**

**radio–** *combining form.* **1** having to do with RADIO: *Radiotelegraphy means telegraphing by radio. Radio-controlled means controlled from a distance by radio.* **2** having to do with rays or RADIATION: *A radiograph is a picture produced by X rays.* **3** having to do with RADIO-ACTIVITY: *A radio-isotope is a radio-active isotope.* **4** of or having to do with a RADIUS: *Radio-symmetrical means radially symmetrical; that is, symmetrical around a central point.*

**ra·di·o–ac·tive** or **ra·di·o·ac·tive** (rā′dē ō ak′tiv) giving off RADIANT ENERGY in the form of alpha, beta, or gamma rays as a result of the breaking up of atoms: *Radium, uranium, and thorium are radio-active elements.*    *adj.*

**ra·di·o–ac·tiv·i·ty** (rā′dē ō ak tiv′ə tē) **1** the property of being RADIO-ACTIVE. **2** the radiation given off.    *n.*

**radio astronomy** the branch of ASTRONOMY that studies objects in space by analysing radio waves given off by or reflected from them.

**radio beacon** a radio transmitter that sends out special radio signals to help ships, aircraft, etc. determine their position or come in safely when visibility is poor.

**ra·di·o·car·bon** (rā′dē ō kär′bən) radio-active carbon, especially CARBON 14, used in finding out the age of ancient organic materials: *The amount of radiocarbon in a fossil, etc. is an indication of how old it is.*    *n.*

**radio control** control by means of radio signals: *Our garage door is operated by radio control.*

**ra·di·o–con·trolled** (rā′dē ō kən trōld′) controlled from a distance by means of radio signals: *a radio-controlled model airplane.*    *adj.*

**radio frequency** any frequency of electromagnetic

waves between about 10kHz and 300 000 MHz, used especially in transmitting radio and television signals.

**ra·di·o·gram** (rā′dē ō gram′) 1 a message transmitted by RADIOTELEGRAPHY. 2 RADIOGRAPH. *n.*

**ra·di·o·graph** (rā′dē ō graf′) 1 a picture produced by X rays or gamma rays on a photographic plate, commonly called an X-ray picture. 2 make a radiograph of. 1 *n.*, 2 *v.*

**ra·di·o–iso·tope** (rā′dē ō ī′sə tōp′) a radio-active ISOTOPE. *n.*

**ra·di·ol·o·gist** (rā′dē ol′ə jist) a person trained in RADIOLOGY. *n.*

**ra·di·ol·o·gy** (rā′dē ol′ə jē) the science that deals with RADIO-ACTIVE rays or X rays. *n.*

**ra·di·o·phone** (rā′dē ō fōn′) RADIOTELEPHONE. *n.*

**ra·di·o·sonde** (rā′dē ō sond′) a miniature radio transmitter carried up in a balloon to broadcast information about atmospheric humidity, temperature, pressure, etc. at various altitudes. *n.*

**ra·dio·sym·met·ri·cal** (rā′dē ō sə met′ri kəl) radially SYMMETRICAL; symmetrical about a central point. See SYMMETRY for picture. *adj.*

**ra·di·o·tel·e·graph** (rā′dē ō tel′ə graf′) 1 a telegraph worked by radio. 2 telegraph by radio. 1 *n.*, 2 *v.*

**ra·di·o·te·leg·ra·phy** (rā′dē ō tə leg′rə fē) the system of telegraphing by radio. *n.*

**ra·di·o·tel·e·phone** (rā′dē ō tel′ə fōn′) 1 a radio transmitter using voice communication. 2 telephone by radio. 1 *n.*, 2 *v.*, **ra·di·o·tel·e·phoned, ra·di·o·tel·e·phon·ing.**

The main radio telescope at the National Research Council's radio astrophysical observatory near Penticton, B.C.

**radio telescope** an apparatus for making observations of bodies in outer space by detecting and recording radio waves coming from them or radar waves reflected from them: *Some radio telescopes have a large, parabola-shaped antenna.*

**ra·di·o·ther·a·py** (rā′dē ō ther′ə pē) the treatment of disease by means of RADIATION. *n.*

**radio wave** an electromagnetic wave of radio frequency (between about 10 kHz and 300 000 MHz).

**rad·ish** (rad′ish) 1 a small, crisp root with a red or white skin, used as a relish and in salads. 2 the plant. *n.*

**ra·di·um** (rā′dē əm) a radio-active, silvery-white metallic element found in very small amounts in uranium ores such as pitchblende: *Radium is used in treating cancer and in making luminous paint. Radium atoms are constantly breaking up and in this process give off alpha, beta, and gamma rays.* Symbol: Ra *n.*

**ra·di·us** (rā′dē əs) 1 any line going straight from the centre to the outside of a circle or a sphere. See CIRCLE and RADIAN for pictures. 2 a circular area measured by the length of its radius: *The explosion could be heard within a radius of ten kilometres.* 3 in a human being, that one of the two bones of the forearm which is on the thumb side. See ARM¹ for picture. 4 a corresponding bone in the forelimb of other vertebrates. *n., pl.* **ra·di·i** or **ra·di·us·es.**

**ra·dix** (rā′diks) 1 a root; radical; source or origin. 2 in mathematics, a number taken as the base of a system of numbers, logarithms, or the like: *The radix of the decimal system is ten.* *n., pl.* **rad·i·ces** (rad′ə sēz′ or rā′də sēz′) or **ra·dix·es.**

**ra·don** (rā′don) a heavy, radio-active gas that is a rare element given off by RADIUM. Symbol: Rn *n.*

**RAF** or **R.A.F.** Royal Air Force.

**raf·fi·a** (raf′ē ə) 1 a fibre from the leafstalks of a species of palm tree native to Madagascar, used in making baskets, mats, etc. 2 the tree from which this fibre is obtained. *n.*

**raf·fle** (raf′əl) 1 a lottery, often held for charity, in which many people each pay a small sum for a chance to win a prize. 2 sell an article by a raffle (*often used with* **off**): *to raffle off a quilt.* 1 *n.*, 2 *v.*, **raf·fled, raf·fling.**

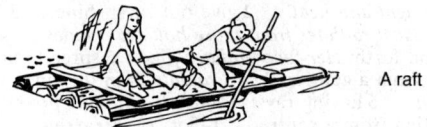

A raft

**raft¹** (raft) 1 platform made of logs, boards, etc. fastened together and used for transportation or support on water. 2 in lumbering, pieces of timber lashed together for floating downstream, as to a mill. 3 send by or carry on a raft. 4 make into a raft. 1, 2 *n.*, 3, 4 *v.*

**raft²** (raft) *Informal.* a large number; abundance: *He's got a whole raft of essays to mark.* *n.*

**raft·er¹** (raf′tər) a supporting beam, often slanting, of a roof. See FRAME for picture. *n.*

**raft·er²** (raf′tər) a person who rafts timber. *n.*

**rag** (rag) 1 a torn or waste piece of cloth: *Use clean rags to polish this mirror.* 2 a small piece of cloth. 3 a small piece of anything of no value: *The meat was boiled to rags.* 4 made from rags: *a rag doll, a rag rug.* 5 **rags,** *pl.* tattered or worn-out clothes. *n.* —**rag′like′,** *adj.* **in rags,** torn or worn-out: *His clothing was in rags.*

**rag·a·muf·fin** (rag′ə muf′ən) a ragged, dirty person, especially a child. *n.*

**rage** (rāj) 1 a state of violent anger: *to quiver with rage.* 2 a fit of violent anger: *to be in a rage.* 3 be furious with anger. 4 speak or move with furious anger: *Be calm, don't rage.* 5 violence: *the rage of a tiger.* 6 act violently; move, proceed, or continue with great violence: *A storm is raging.* 7 a movement, idea, or fashion that is popular for a short time: *Red ties are all the rage this year.* 8 a great enthusiasm. 1, 2, 5, 7, 8 *n.*, 3, 4, 6 *v.*, **raged, rag·ing.**

**rag·ged** (rag′id) 1 worn or torn into rags. 2 wearing torn or badly worn-out clothing: *a ragged beggar.* 3 not straight and tidy; rough: *an Airedale's ragged coat, a ragged garden.* 4 having loose shreds or bits: *a ragged wound.* 5 having rough or sharp points; uneven; jagged: *ragged*

rocks.   6 harsh: *a ragged voice.*   *adj.*   —**rag′ged·ly,** *adv.*
—**rag′ged·ness,** *n.*

**rag·lan** (rag′lən)   **1** an overcoat having sleeves that continue up to the neckline so that there is no seam at the top of the arm.   **2** having such sleeves.   *n.*

A coat with raglan sleeves

**raglan sleeve**   a sleeve that is cut to continue up to the neckline instead of ending at the shoulder.

**rag·man** (rag′man′)   a man who gathers, buys, or sells rags.   *n., pl.* **rag·men** (-men′).

**ra·gout** (ra gü′)   a highly seasoned stew of meat and vegetables.   *n.*

**rag·time** (rag′tīm′)   in music, an early style of jazz characterized by a strong, regular rhythm.   *n.*

**rag·weed** (rag′wēd′)   any of several coarse weeds of the same family as the aster, whose pollen is one of the most common causes of hay fever.   *n.*

**rag·wort** (rag′wėrt′)   any of various plants having irregularly lobed leaves and yellow flowers.   *n.*

**rah** (rä)   HURRAH.   *interj., n.*

**raid** (rād)   **1** an attack, especially a sudden attack.   **2** a sudden attack by a small force having no intention of holding the territory invaded.   **3** an entering and seizing what is inside: *The hungry girls made a raid on the refrigerator.*   **4** attack suddenly: *The enemy raided our camp.*   **5** force a way into; enter and seize what is in: *The police raided the gaming house.*   **6** engage in a raid.   1–3 *n.,* 4–6 *v.*   —**raid′er,** *n.*

A fence of wooden rails    Steel rails of a train track

**rail**[1] (rāl)   **1** a horizontal or slanting bar of wood or metal extending between supports or posts and used as a barrier or guard: *a stair rail. She leaned against the top rail of the fence.*   **2** a steel bar or series of bars forming a continuous track for a train, etc.   **3** RAILWAY: *They shipped their car by rail.*   **4** supply or furnish with rails or a railing.   **5** the upper part of the bulwarks of a ship.   1–3, 5 *n.,* 4 *v.*

**rail**[2] (rāl)   complain bitterly; use violent and abusive language (*usually used with* **at**): *Danylo railed at his hard luck.*   *v.*   —**rail′er,** *n.*

**rail**[3] (rāl)   **1** any of numerous related small or medium-sized wading birds having short wings and tail, a narrow body, and strong legs with very long toes that allow them to run over the mud of marshes and swamps: *Rails have a harsh cry.*   **2** referring to the family of birds that includes the rails and gallinules.   *n., pl.* **rails** or (*esp. collectively*) **rail**.

# raglan    973    rain check

hat, āge, fär; let, ēqual, tėrm; it, īce
hot, ōpen, ôrder; oil, out; cup, pùt, rüle
əbove, takən, pencəl, lemən, circəs
ch, child; ng, long; sh, ship
th, thin; ᴛн, then; zh, measure

**rail·ing**[1] (rā′ling)   **1** a barrier made of RAILS[1], especially along the side of a staircase, the edge of a balcony, etc.   **2** material for making RAILS[1].   **3** RAILS[1] collectively: *A pile of railing lay by the barn.*   **4** ppr. of RAIL[1].   1–3 *n.,* 4 *v.*

**rail·ing**[2] (rā′ling)   **1** harsh complaints or reproaches.   **2** ppr. of RAIL[2].   1 *n.,* 2 *v.*

**rail·ler·y** (rā′lə rē)   **1** good-humoured ridicule; joking; teasing.   **2** a bantering remark.   *n., pl.* **rail·ler·ies.**

**rail·road** (rāl′rōd′)   **1** RAILWAY.   **2** send or carry on a RAILWAY.   **3** work on a RAILWAY: *He has been railroading all his life.*   **4** *Informal.* rush through or into hastily, especially so as to prevent fair and careful consideration: *to railroad a bill through a committee.*   1 *n.,* 2–4 *v.*
—**rail′road′er,** *n.*

**rail·road·ing** (rāl′rō′ding)   **1** the construction or operation of RAILWAYS.   **2** *Informal.* the act or process of hurrying a thing or person along hastily and unfairly.   **3** ppr. of RAILROAD.   1, 2 *n.,* 3 *v.*

**rail·way** (rāl′wā′)   **1** a road or track for trains, consisting of parallel steel rails along which the wheels of the locomotives and cars go: *The rails of a railway are supported on heavy wooden crosswise beams called ties.* See TRESTLE for picture.   **2** tracks, stations, trains, and other property of a system of transportation that uses rails, together with the people who manage them: *One of Canada's railways is owned by the government.*   *n.*

**rai·ment** (rā′mənt)   clothing; garments.   *n.*

**rain** (rān)   **1** water falling in drops from the clouds: *Rain is formed from moisture condensed from water vapour in the atmosphere.*   **2** the fall of such drops: *There was a light rain this morning.*   **3** fall in drops of water: *It rained all day.*   **4** a thick, fast fall of anything: *a rain of bullets.*   **5** fall like rain: *Tears rained down his cheeks. Sparks rained down from the fire.*   **6** send or give like rain: *The crowds rained praises on the victorious legions. The angry child rained blows with her fists on the door.*   **7 the rains,** *pl.* the rainy season, as in tropical climates.   1, 2, 4, 7 *n.,* 3, 5, 6 *v.*
**rain cats and dogs,** *Informal.*   rain very hard.
**rained out,**   of an outdoors sports event, etc., cancelled because of rain: *The first game of the season was rained out.*
☛ *Hom.*   REIGN, REIN.

**rain·bow** (rān′bō′)   an arch of coloured light, showing the different colours of the spectrum, that is seen in the sky when the sun's rays are seen through rain, mist, or spray: *The colours of the rainbow are red, orange, yellow, green, blue, indigo, violet.*   *n.*

**rainbow trout**   any TROUT having black spots and a pinkish or reddish band along its sides: *The steelhead trout changes colour when it moves into fresh water, and is then called a rainbow trout.* See FISH for picture.

**rain check**   **1** a ticket for future use, given to spectators at a baseball game or other outdoor performance stopped by rain.   **2** *Informal.* an understanding that an invitation which cannot presently be accepted will be renewed later: *May I take a rain check on your invitation to dinner?*   **3** *Informal.* a promise by a store to honour a special price for goods which have run out.

**rain·coat** (rān′kōt′) a waterproof or water-repellent coat worn for protection from rain. *n.*

**rain·drop** (rān′drop′) a drop of rain. *n.*

**rain·fall** (rān′fol′) **1** a shower of rain: *There was a light rainfall during the night.* **2** the amount of water in the form of rain that falls in a particular area over a certain period of time: *Rainfall is measured in millimetres.* *n.*

**rain forest** a large, densely wooded region where there is very heavy rainfall throughout the year, usually but not always in tropical climates.

**rain gauge** an instrument for measuring rainfall.

**rain·mak·er** (rān′mā′kər) a person who tries to produce rain. *n.*

**rain·proof** (rān′prüf′) that will not let rain through; proof against rain: *The roof of our cottage isn't rainproof any more.* *adj.*

**rain·storm** (rān′stôrm′) a storm with much rain. *n.*

**rain·wa·ter** (rān′wot′ər) water that has been collected from rain, not taken from a well, etc.: *Rainwater is soft water.* *n.*

**rain·wear** (rān′wer′) clothing to be worn in the rain, such as rubbers, raincoats, etc. *n.*

**rain·y** (rā′nē) **1** having rain, especially much rain: *rainy weather, the rainy season.* **2** wet with rain: *rainy streets.* **3** of clouds or winds, bringing in rain. *adj.*, **rain·i·er, rain·i·est.**

**rainy day** a time of need in the future: *to save for a rainy day.*

**raise** (rāz) **1** lift up: *to raise one's hand.* **2** set upright: *Raise the overturned lamp.* **3** cause to rise: *to raise a cloud of dust.* **4** put or take into a higher position; make higher or nobler: *to raise a saleswoman to manager.* **5** a raised place. **6** increase in degree, amount, price, pay, etc.: *to raise the rent.* **7** an increase in amount, price, pay, etc. **8** the amount of such an increase. **9** make louder or of higher pitch: *I cannot hear you; please raise your voice.* **10** in games, bid or bet more than an opponent. **11** gather together; collect; manage to get: *The leader raised a band of firefighters.* **12** breed; grow: *The farmer raises crops and cattle.* **13** cause; bring about: *A funny remark raises a laugh.* **14** bring forward; mention: *The speaker raised an interesting point.* **15** build; create; produce; start; set up: *to raise a monument.* **16** rouse; stir up: *The dog raised a rabbit from the underbrush.* **17** bring up; rear: *Parents raise their children.* **18** cause to become light: *Yeast raises bread.* **19** bring back to life: *to raise the dead.* **20** put an end to: *Our soldiers raised the siege of the fort by driving away the enemy.* **21** come in sight of: *After a long voyage, the ship raised land.* 1–4, 6, 9–21 *v.*, **raised, rais·ing;** 5, 7, 8 *n.*
☛ *Hom.* RAZE.

**rais·er** (rā′zər) a person who grows or raises things: *a cattle raiser.* *n.*
☛ *Hom.* RAZOR.

**rai·sin** (rā′zən) a sweet dried grape. *n.*

**rai·son d'être** (Re zôn detR′) *French.* reason for being; justification.

**raj** (räj) formerly in India, sovereignty; dominion: *the British raj.* *n.*

**ra·ja** (rä′jə) a member of a hereditary class of noblemen and rulers in countries of southern Asia, including Malaysia and, formerly, India. *n.* Also, **rajah.**

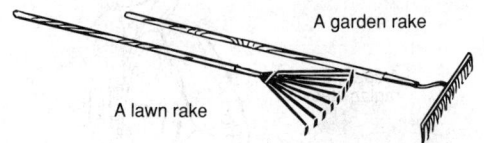
A garden rake
A lawn rake

**rake¹** (rāk) **1** a long-handled tool having a bar at one end with teeth in it: *A rake is used for smoothing the soil or gathering together loose leaves, hay, or straw.* **2** move with a rake: *Rake the leaves off the grass.* **3** make clear, clean, smooth, etc. with a rake, or as if with a rake: *Rake the yard.* **4** use a rake. **5** gather; gather together (used with **up** or **together**): *She raked up enough money to rent a canoe.* **6** search carefully: *She raked the newspapers for descriptions of the accident.* **7** fire guns along the length of a ship, line of soldiers, etc. 1 *n.*, 2–7 *v.*, **raked, rak·ing.**

**rake²** (rāk) a PROFLIGATE or dissolute man: *That young rake is always drinking and gambling.* *n.*

**rake³** (rāk) **1** a slant; slope: *A ship's smokestacks have a slight backward rake.* **2** have a slant: *The masts raked backwards.* 1 *n.*, 2 *v.*, **raked, rak·ing.**

**rak·ish¹** (rā′kish) **1** smart; jaunty; dashing: *a hat set at a rakish angle.* **2** suggesting dash and speed: *He owns a rakish boat.* *adj.*

**rak·ish²** (rā′kish) of, having to do with, or like a RAKE²; immoral; dissolute; licentious. *adj.*

**ral·ly¹** (ral′ē) **1** bring together; bring together again; get in order again: *The commander was able to rally the fleeing troops.* **2** pull together; revive: *Ali rallied all his energy for one last effort.* **3** come together in a body for a common purpose or action: *The children rallied to help clean up the school after the fun fair.* **4** come to help a person, party, or cause: *Paula rallied to the side of her injured friend.* **5** recover health and strength: *The sick woman may rally now.* **6** the act of rallying; recovery. **7** coming together; mass meeting: *a political rally.* **8** a meeting or assembly of many people for a common purpose or action: *a sports-car rally.* **9** hitting the ball back and forth several times in tennis and similar games. **10** take part in such a rally. 1–5, 10 *v.*, **ral·lied, ral·ly·ing;** 6–9 *n.*, *pl.* **ral·lies.**

**ral·ly²** (ral′ē) make fun of or tease in a good-natured way. *v.*, **ral·lied, ral·ly·ing.**

**ram** (ram) **1** a male sheep. **2** butt against; strike head on; strike violently: *One ship rammed the other.* **3** push hard; drive down or in by heavy force or effect: *He rammed the bolt into the wall.* **4** a machine or part of a machine that strikes heavy blows: *The ram on a pile driver is the weight that drives the piles into the ground.* **5** BATTERING RAM. **6** the beak at the bow of a warship, used to break the sides of enemy ships. **7** a ship with such a beak. **8** the plunger of a force pump. **9** a pump in which the force of a descending column of water raises some of the water above its original level. 1, 4–9 *n.*, 2, 3 *v.*, **rammed, ram·ming.**

**RAM** Random Access Memory, the part of a computer's memory in which information can be changed or erased.

**Ram·a·dan** (ram′ə dän′) in Islam, the ninth month of the Islamic calendar—the holy month—during which Moslems practise fasting, abstinence, and self-examination daily from dawn to dusk. *n.*

**ram·ble** (ram′bəl) **1** wander about for pleasure: *We rambled here and there through the woods.* **2** a walk for pleasure, not to go to any special place. **3** talk or write about first one thing and then another with no clear connection between them. **4** grow or spread irregularly in various directions: *Vines rambled over the wall.* 1, 3, 4 *v.*, **ram·bled, ram·bling;** 2 *n.*

**ram·bler** (ram′blər) **1** a person or thing that rambles. **2** any of various climbing roses. *n.*

**ram·bling** (ram′bling) **1** wandering about. **2** going from one thing to another without clear connection; moving from one subject to another: *a rambling speech.* **3** climbing: *rambling roses.* **4** extending irregularly in various directions; not planned in an orderly way: *a rambling old farmhouse.* **5** ppr. of RAMBLE. 1–4 *adj.*, 5 *v.*

**ram·bunc·tious** (ram bungk′shəs) uncontrollably exuberant; boisterous and unruly: *The kids were very rambunctious after travelling all day.* *adj.*

**ram·i·fi·ca·tion** (ram′ə fə kā′shən) **1** a dividing or spreading out into branches or parts. **2** a branch; part. **3** something that springs out like a branch; a result, consequence, extension, etc.: *the ramifications of an idea.* *n.*

**ram·i·fy** (ram′ə fī) divide or spread out into branchlike parts. *v.*, **ram·i·fied, ram·i·fy·ing.**

**ram·jet** (ram′jet′) a type of JET ENGINE in which the fuel is fed into air that is compressed by the forward speed of the aircraft, missile, etc., instead of by means of a mechanical compressor: *The ramjet is the simplest type of jet engine.* *n.*

**ram·mer** (ram′ər) a person or thing that rams, especially a device for driving or compacting something. *n.*

**ra·mose** (rā′mōs) consisting of or having many branches; branching. *adj.*

**ra·mous** (rā′məs) **1** RAMOSE. **2** of or like a branch. *adj.*

A ramp onto an expressway

**ramp** (ramp) **1** a sloping walk or roadway connecting two different levels of a building, road, etc. **2** a stairway for going into or out of aircraft. *n.*

**ram·page** (ram′pāj *for noun,* ram pāj′ *or* ram′pāj *for verb*) **1** a spell of violent behaviour often accompanied by rushing about wildly; wild outbreak: *The mad elephant went on a rampage and killed its keeper.* **2** rush wildly about; behave violently; rage. 1 *n.*, 2 *v.*, **ram·paged, ram·pag·ing.**

**ramp·ant** (ram′pənt) **1** growing without any check: *The vines ran rampant over the fence.* **2** passing beyond restraint or usual limits; unchecked: *Anarchy was rampant after the dictator died.* **3** angry; excited; violent. **4** in heraldry, standing up on the hind legs. *adj.*
—**ramp′ant·ly,** *adv.*

hat, āge, fär; let, ēqual, tėrm; it, īce
hot, ōpen, ôrder; oil, out; cup, pùt, rüle
əbove, takən, pencəl, lemən, circəs
ch, child; ng, long; sh, ship
th, thin; ᴛʜ, then; zh, measure

**ram·part** (ram′pärt) **1** a wide bank of earth, often with a wall on top, built around a fort to help defend it. See FORT for picture. **2** anything that defends; a defence; protection. *n.*

**ram·pike** (ram′pīk′) *Cdn.* a tall, dead tree, especially one that has been blackened and stripped of its branches by fire. *n.*

**ram·rod** (ram′rod′) **1** a rod for ramming down the charge in a gun that is loaded from the muzzle. **2** a rod for cleaning the barrel of a gun. *n.*

**ram·shack·le** (ram′shak′əl) loose and shaky; likely to come apart: *ramshackle old buildings.* *adj.*

**ran** (ran) pt. of RUN: *The dog ran after the cat.* *v.*

**ranch** (ranch) **1** a large farm with grazing land, for raising cattle, sheep, or horses in large numbers. **2** any farm, especially one used to raise one kind of animal or crop: *a mink ranch, a fruit ranch.* **3** the persons working or living on a ranch. *The entire ranch was at the party.* **4** work on or operate a ranch. 1–3 *n.*, 4 *v.*

**ranch·er** (ran′chər) a person who owns or operates a RANCH. *n.*

**ranch hand** *Cdn.* a person employed on a RANCH, especially a cattle ranch.

**ranch house** **1** the main building on a RANCH. **2** on the West coast, a large communal dwelling or house of the Indians. **3** a long, low, spacious, one-storey house.

**ranch·man** (ranch′mən) RANCHER. *n., pl.* **ranch·men** (-mən).

**ran·cid** (ran′sid) **1** stale; spoiled: *rancid butter.* **2** tasting or smelling like stale fat or butter: *a rancid odour.* *adj.*

**ran·cid·i·ty** (ran sid′ə tē) the quality or state of being RANCID. *n.*

**ran·cor** (rang′kər) See RANCOUR. *n.*

**ran·cor·ous** (rang′kə rəs) spiteful; bitterly malicious. *adj.* —**ran′cor·ous·ly,** *adv.*

**ran·cour** or **ran·cor** (rang′kər) a deep-seated, bitter resentment or ill will; extreme hatred or spite. *n.*

**ran·dom** (ran′dəm) by chance; with no plan: *Because Leona was not listening, she had to give a random answer to the teacher's question.* *adj.*
**at random,** by chance; with no plan or purpose: *She took a book at random from the shelf.*

**random access** the capability of a computer memory to store data so that the location is independent of the content, giving the user immediate and direct access to any part of it, without working through the body of data from the beginning.

**ra·nee** (rä′nē) the wife of a RAJA. *n.* Also, **rani.**

**rang** (rang) pt. of RING². *The telephone rang.* *v.*

**range** (rānj) **1** the distance between certain limits; an extent: *a range of prices from 5 cents to 25 dollars.* **2** vary within certain limits: *prices ranging from $5 to $10.* **3** the distance a gun can shoot. **4** the distance from a gun, etc.

to an object aimed at. **5** a place to practise shooting or other skill: *a driving range.* **6** land for grazing. **7** of or on land for grazing. **8** wander; rove; roam. **9** wander over: *Buffalo once ranged these plains. Our talk ranged over all that had happened on our holidays.* **10** the act of wandering or moving about. **11** a row or line of mountains. **12** a row; line. **13** a line of direction: *The two barns are in direct range with the house.* **14** put in a row or rows: *Range the books by size.* **15** put in groups or classes. **16** put in a line on someone's side: *Loyal citizens ranged themselves with the queen.* **17** a rank, class, or order. **18** a district in which certain plants or animals live. **19** run in a line; extend: *a boundary ranging east and west.* **20** be found; occur: *a plant ranging from Canada to Mexico.* **21** a stove for cooking: *At our summer cottage we cook on a wood range.* 1, 3–6, 10–13, 17, 18, 21 *n.*, 2, 8, 9, 14–16, 19, 20 *v.*, **ranged, rang·ing;** 7 *adj.*

**range finder** an instrument for determining the distance between an object or target and an observer, camera, gun, etc.

**rang·er** (rān′jər) **1** a person employed to guard a tract of forest. **2** a person or thing that ranges; rover. **3** a soldier of certain regiments originally organized for fighting in the North American forests: *the Queen's Rangers.* **4 Ranger, a** a member of the senior branch of the Girl Guides, for girls over 16 years of age. **b** *Cdn.* in the North, an Indian or Inuit who acts as a volunteer military scout or observer. *n.*

**rang·ette** (rān jet′) a cooking stove smaller than a range. *n.*

**rang·y** (rān′jē) **1** fitted for ranging or moving about. **2** slender and long-limbed: *a rangy horse, a rangy youth.* *adj.*, **rang·i·er, rang·i·est.**

**ra·ni** (rä′nē) See RANEE. *n.*

**rank¹** (rangk) **1** a row or line of people or things, especially soldiers. **2** arrange in a row or line. **3** a position; grade; class: *the rank of colonel.* See table of ranks in the Appendix. **4** a high position: *A duchess is a woman of rank.* **5** have a certain place or position in relation to other persons or things: *Bill ranked low in the test.* **6** an orderly arrangement or array. **7** put in some special order in a list: *Rank the continents in order of size.* **8** be more important than; outrank: *A major ranks a captain.* **9 ranks,** *pl.* a private soldiers and junior non-commissioned officers: *He came up through the ranks.* **b** RANK AND FILE. 1, 3, 4, 6, 9 *n.*, 2, 5, 7, 8 *v.* —**rank′er,** *n.*

**rank²** (rangk) **1** large and coarse: *rank grass.* **2** growing richly. **3** producing a dense but coarse growth: *rank swampland.* **4** having a strong, unpleasant smell or taste: *rank meat, rank tobacco.* **5** strongly marked; extreme: *rank ingratitude, rank nonsense.* **6** coarse; not decent. *adj.* —**rank′ly,** *adv.* —**rank′ness,** *n.*

**rank and file 1** an armed force excluding its officers. **2** the members of an organization, society, or other groups, excluding the leaders: *The union leaders were in favour of the offer but it was rejected by the rank and file.*

**ran·kle** (rang′kəl) cause anger, bitterness, or irritation: *Even after all those years, the memory of the insult still rankled.* *v.*, **ran·kled, ran·kling.**

**ran·sack** (ran′sak *or* ran sak′) **1** search thoroughly through: *I ransacked the whole closet, but couldn't find the belt.* **2** plunder or rob: *When they returned they found the house had been ransacked and their silver and jewellery were gone.* *v.*

**ran·som** (ran′səm) **1** the price paid or demanded before a captive is set free: *The robbers held the travellers as prisoners for ransom.* **2** obtain the release of a captive by paying a price. **3** redeem. **4** the act of ransoming. 1, 4 *n.*, 2, 3 *v.*

**rant** (rant) **1** speak wildly, extravagantly, violently, or noisily. **2** an extravagant, violent, or noisy speech. 1 *v.*, 2 *n.* —**rant′er,** *n.*

**rap¹** (rap) **1** a quick, light blow; a light, sharp knock: *a rap at the door.* **2** knock sharply; tap: *The chairman rapped on the table for order.* **3** say sharply: *to rap out an answer.* 1 *n.*, 2, 3 *v.*, **rapped, rap·ping.**
**take the rap,** *Informal.* pay the penalty; take the blame.
☛ *Hom.* WRAP.

**rap²** (rap) *Informal.* the least bit: *I don't care a rap.* *n.*
☛ *Hom.* WRAP.

**ra·pa·cious** (rə pā′shəs) **1** seizing by force; plundering: *rapacious pirates.* **2** grasping; greedy; voracious: *a rapacious miser.* **3** of animals, living by the capture of prey; predatory. *adj.* —**ra·pa′cious·ly,** *adv.* —**ra·pa′cious·ness,** *n.*

**ra·pac·i·ty** (rə pas′ə tē) the quality of being RAPACIOUS. *n.*

**rape¹** (rāp) **1** the crime of an individual having sexual intercourse with another person forcibly and without his or her consent. **2** force an individual to have sexual intercourse; commit rape on a person. **3** any forcible or outrageous interference or violation: *the rape of a country's natural resources.* 1, 3 *n.*, 2 *v.*, **raped, rap·ing.**

**rape²** (rāp) a small plant whose leaves are used as food for sheep or hogs. *n.*

**rape oil** an oil made from RAPESEED and used mainly as a lubricant and food.

**rape·seed** (rāp′sēd′) the seed of the RAPE² plant. *n.*

**rapeseed oil** RAPE OIL.

**rap·id** (rap′id) **1** quick; swift; moving, acting, or doing with speed: *a rapid worker.* **2** going on or forward at a fast rate: *rapid growth.* **3 rapids,** *pl.* a part of a river's course where the water rushes quickly, often over rocks near the surface: *The boat overturned in the rapids.* 1, 2 *adj.*, 3 *n.* —**rap′id·ly,** *adv.* —**rap′id·ness,** *n.*

**rap·id–fire** (rap′id fīr′) **1** firing or adapted for firing shots in quick succession. **2** rapid and lively; done or carried on quickly or sharply: *a rapid-fire style of speaking.* *adj.*

**ra·pid·i·ty** (rə pid′ə tē) quickness; swiftness; speed. *n.*

**rapid transit** a system of fast public transportation by railway in urban areas, often underground.

**ra·pi·er** (rā′pē ər) a light, straight, two-edged sword used for thrusting. See SWORD for picture. *n.* —**ra′pi·er·like′,** *adj.*

**rap·ine** (rap′ēn) a seizing by force and carrying off; plundering. *n.*

**rap·port** (ra pôrt′; *French,* RÄ pÔR′) a connection or relationship, especially a harmonious or agreeable one: *He has no rapport with his students. There was good rapport among the leaders throughout the negotiations.* *n.*

**en rapport** (äN Rä pôR′) *French.* in close relation, accord, or harmony.

**rap·proche·ment** (Rä pRôsh mäN′) *French.* the establishment or renewal of friendly relations. *n.*

**rap·scal·lion** (rap skal′yən) a rascal; scamp; rogue. *n.*

**rapt** (rapt) **1** lost in delight; completely entranced or absorbed: *We listened to the story with rapt attention.* **2** caused by or showing rapture or delight: *a rapt smile.* *adj.* —**rapt′ly,** *adv.*
☛ Hom. WRAPT.

**rap·to·ri·al** (rap tô′rē əl) **1** adapted for seizing prey; having a hooked beak and sharp claws suited for seizing prey. **2** belonging to or having to do with an order of birds of prey, such as the eagles, hawks, etc. *adj.*

**rap·ture** (rap′chər) **1** a strong feeling that absorbs the mind; very great joy: *The mother gazed with rapture at her newborn baby.* **2** an expression of great joy. *n.*

**rap·tur·ous** (rap′chə rəs) full of RAPTURE; expressing or feeling rapture. *adj.* —**rap′tur·ous·ly,** *adv.*

**rare¹** (rer) **1** seldom seen or found; uncommon: *The whooping crane has become very rare.* **2** not happening often; unusual: *a rare event.* **3** unusually good or great: *Edison had rare powers as an inventor.* **4** thin; not dense: *The higher you go, the rarer the air is.* *adj.*, **rar·er, rar·est.**

**rare²** (rer) of meat, not cooked much; cooked so that the inside is still red: *She prefers her steak rare.* *adj.*, **rar·er, rar·est.**

**rare·bit** (rer′bit) WELSH RABBIT. *n.*

**rare–earth element** or **metal** any of the rare metallic elements that have atomic numbers from 57 to 71.

**rar·e·fac·tion** (rer′ə fak′shən) RAREFYing or being rarefied. *n.*

**rar·e·fy** (rer′ə fī′) **1** make less dense: *The air high in the mountains is rarefied.* **2** become less dense. **3** refine; purify. *v.*, **rar·e·fied, rar·e·fy·ing.**

**rare·ly** (rer′lē) **1** seldom; not often. **2** unusually; unusually well: *a rarely carved panel.* *adv.*

**rar·ing** (rer′ing) *Informal.* very eager: *raring to go, raring for a fight.* *adj.*

**rar·i·ty** (rer′ə tē) **1** something rare: *A thirty-year-old car is a rarity.* **2** the quality or state of being rare or scarce; scarcity: *The value of diamonds is partly due to their rarity.* **3** a lack of density; thinness: *the rarity of the air in the mountains.* *n.*, *pl.* **rar·i·ties.**

**ras·cal** (ras′kəl) **1** a dishonest person; rogue. **2** a mischievous person or animal: *Come back here with my slipper, you rascal!* *n.*

**ras·cal·i·ty** (ras kal′ə tē) **1** the character or actions of a RASCAL. **2** a rascally act. *n.*, *pl.* **ras·cal·i·ties.**

**ras·cal·ly** (ras′kə lē) mean or dishonest; bad: *To steal the poor girl's lunch was a rascally trick.* *adj.*

**rash¹** (rash) too hasty or too bold; reckless; impetuous; taking too much risk: *It is rash to cross the street without looking both ways.* *adj.* —**rash·ly,** *adv.*

**rash²** (rash) **1** a breaking out of many small red spots on the skin: *Perfumed soaps give me a rash.* **2** a sudden appearance of a large number of instances or cases of something unpleasant or unhappy: *There was a rash of angry letters following the publication of the article.* *n.*

hat, āge, fär; let, ēqual, tėrm; it, īce
hot, ōpen, ôrder; oil, out; cup, put, rüle
əbove, takən, pencəl, lemən, circəs
ch, child; ng, long; sh, ship
th, thin; ᴛʜ, then; zh, measure

**rash·er** (rash′ər) a thin slice of bacon or ham for frying or broiling. *n.*

**rash·ness** (rash′nis) unwise boldness; recklessness. *n.*

**rasp** (rasp) **1** make a harsh, grating sound: *The file rasped on the scythe blade.* **2** a harsh, grating sound: *the rasp of crickets, a rasp in a person's voice.* **3** utter with a grating sound: *to rasp out a command.* **4** have a harsh or irritating effect on; grate on. **5** scrape with a rough instrument. **6** a coarse file with pointlike teeth. 1, 3–5 *v.*, 2, 6 *n.*

Raspberries

**rasp·ber·ry** (raz′ber′ē) **1** a small fruit that grows on brambles: *Raspberries are usually red or black, but some kinds are white or yellow.* **2** the bramble that it grows on. **3** made of or flavoured with raspberry: *raspberry pie.* **4** purplish red. **5** *Informal.* a sound of disapproval or contempt made with the tongue and lips. 1, 2, 4, 5 *n.*, *pl.* **rasp·ber·ries;** 3, 4 *adj.* —**rasp′ber′ry-like′,** *adj.*

**rat** (rat) **1** any of a number of long-tailed RODENTs native to the Old World, related to and resembling the Old World mouse, but larger: *Rats are now common disease-carrying pests in communities throughout the Western Hemisphere.* **2** any of various other RODENTs, such as the wood rat of North America. **3** hunt for or catch rats. **4** *Cdn.* MUSKRAT. **5** a small pad over which a woman's hair is arranged to make it look thicker. 1, 2, 4, 5 *n.*, 3 *v.*, **rat·ted, rat·ting.**
**smell a rat,** *Informal.* suspect a trick or scheme: *I smelled a rat when none of the others showed up.*

**ratch·et** (rach′it) **1** a wheel or bar with teeth that strike against a catch so fixed that motion is permitted in one direction but not in the other. **2** the catch. **3** the entire device, wheel and catch or bar and catch: *Some wrenches and screwdrivers have ratchets.* *n.*

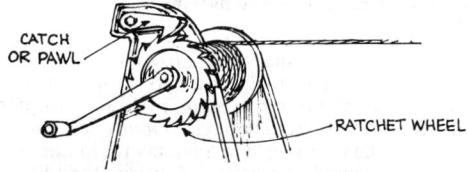

**ratchet wheel** a wheel with teeth and a catch that permits motion in only one direction.

**rate¹** (rāt) **1** a quantity, amount, or degree measured in proportion to something else: *The rate of interest is 12 cents on the dollar. The car was going at the rate of 85*

kilometres per hour. **2** price: *We pay the regular rate.* **3** put a value on: *We rated the house as worth $250 000.* **4** consider; regard: *She was rated as one of the richest women in town.* **5** a class; grade; rating: *the top rate, second rate.* **6** put in a certain class or grade. **7** be regarded; be classed; rank: *She rates high as a musician.* **8** *Informal.* have value; be worthy of: *He doesn't rate. She rates the best seat in the house.* **9** a local tax, often on property. 1, 2, 5, 9 *n.*, 3, 4, 6–8 *v.*, **rat·ed, rat·ing.** —**rat′er,** *n.*
**at any rate,** in any case; under any circumstances.
**at that** or **this rate,** in that or this case; under such circumstances.

**rate²** (rāt) scold. *v.*, **rat·ed, rat·ing.**

**rate·pay·er** (rāt′pā′ər) a person who pays municipal taxes. *n.*

**rath·er** (raŦH′ər *or* räŦH′ər) **1** more readily; more willingly: *I would rather go than stay.* **2** more properly or justly; with better reason: *This is rather for your mother to decide than for you.* **3** more precisely; more truly: *It was last Monday night, or, rather, early Tuesday morning.* **4** with verbs, in some degree: *She rather felt that this was unwise.* **5** to some extent; somewhat; more than a little: *rather good.* **6** on the contrary: *The sick man is no better today; rather he is worse.* *adv.*
**had rather,** would more willingly; prefer to.

**rat·i·fi·ca·tion** (rat′ə fə kā′shən) formal approval and sanction: *the ratification of a treaty by Parliament.* *n.*

**rat·i·fy** (rat′ə fī′) approve formally; confirm; authorize: *The two countries will ratify the agreement made by their representatives.* *v.*, **rat·i·fied, rat·i·fy·ing.**
—**rat′i·fi′er,** *n.*

**rat·ing** (rā′ting) **1** a class; grade. **2** a position in a class or grade: *the rating of a seaman, the rating of a ship according to tonnage.* **3** an amount fixed as a rate or grade: *a rating of 80% in English.* **4** a sailor in the navy of the same rank as a private in the army; an ordinary seaman: *Three officers and ten ratings were lost in the battle.* **5** a level of popularity or merit as established by a survey, especially of television programs. **6** a credit rating. **7** ppr. of RATE. 1–6 *n.*, 7 *v.*

**ra·ti·o** (rā′shē ō′ *or* rā′shō) **1** the relative magnitude. *She has sheep and cows in the ratio of 10 to 3 means that she has ten sheep for every three cows, or 3⅓ times as many sheep as cows.* **2** a quotient: *The ratio between two quantities is the number of times one contains the other. The ratio of 6 to 10 is 6:10. The ratio of 10 to 6 is 10:6.* *n., pl.* **ra·ti·os.**

**ra·ti·oc·i·nate** (rash′ē os′ə nāt′ *or* rat′ē os′ə nāt′) carry on a process of reasoning; reason. *v.*, **ra·ti·oc·i·nat·ed, ra·ti·oc·i·nat·ing.**
—**ra′ti·oc′i·na′tion,** *n.*

**ra·tion** (rash′ən *or* rā′shən) **1** a fixed allowance of food; daily allowance of food for a person or animal. **2** supply with rations: *to ration an army.* **3** a portion of anything dealt out; share; allotment: *rations of sugar, of coal, etc.* **4** allow only certain amounts to: *to ration citizens when supplies are scarce.* **5** distribute in limited amounts: *Food was rationed to the public in wartime.* 1, 3 *n.*, 2, 4, 5 *v.*

**ra·tion·al** (rash′ə nəl *or* rash′nəl) **1** sensible; reasonable; reasoned out: *When very angry, people seldom act in a rational way.* **2** able to think and reason clearly: *As children grow older, they become more rational.* **3** of reason; based on reasoning: *There is a rational explanation for thunder and lightning.* **4** in mathematics, expressible in finite terms; involving no root that cannot be extracted. *adj.* —**ra′tion·al·ly,** *adv.*

**ra·tion·ale** (rash′ə nal′) the whys and wherefores; the fundamental reason. *n.*

**ra·tion·al·ism** (rash′ə nə liz′əm *or* rash′nə liz′əm) the principle or habit of accepting reason as the supreme authority in matters of opinion, belief, or conduct. *n.*

**ra·tion·al·ist** (rash′ə nə list *or* rash′nə list) a person who accepts reason as the supreme authority in matters of opinion, belief, or conduct. *n.*

**ra·tion·al·is·tic** (rash′ə nə lis′tik *or* rash′nə lis′tik) of or having to do with RATIONALISM or rationalists. *adj.*

**ra·tion·al·i·ty** (rash′ə nal′ə tē *or* rash′nal′ə tē) the possession of reason; reasonableness: *Mr. Wallace is somewhat strange, but no one doubts his rationality.* *n.*

**ra·tion·al·ize** (rash′ə nə līz′ *or* rash′nə līz′) **1** make rational or conformable to reason. **2** treat or explain in a rational manner. **3** find (often unconsciously) an explanation or excuse for: *She rationalizes her gluttony by thinking, "I must eat to keep up my strength."* **4** find excuses for one's desires. *v.*, **ra·tion·al·ized, ra·tion·al·iz·ing.** —**ra′tion·al·i·za′tion,** *n.*

**rational number** in mathematics, any number that can be expressed as an integer or as a ratio between two integers, excluding zero as a denominator. 2, 5, and ½ are rational numbers.

**rat·line** or **rat·lin** (rat′lən) one of the small ropes that cross the shrouds of a ship, used as steps for going aloft. See SHROUD for picture. *n.*

**rat race** *Informal.* a fierce frantic scramble or struggle, especially with reference to competing and keeping one's place in the business world.

**rats·bane** (rats′bān′) any poison for rats. *n.*

**rat·tan** (ra tan′) **1** any of several species of climbing palm having very long, jointed, pliable stems. **2** the stems of such palm trees, used for wickerwork, canes, etc. **3** a cane or switch made from a piece of such a stem. *n.*

**rat·ter** (rat′ər) an animal or, sometimes, a person that catches rats: *Our terrier is a good ratter.* *n.*

**rat·tle** (rat′əl) **1** make a number of short, sharp sounds: *The window rattled in the wind.* **2** cause to rattle: *She rattled the dishes.* **3** a number of short, sharp sounds: *the rattle of empty bottles.* **4** a sound in the throat, occurring in some diseases of the lungs and also often just before death. **5** a racket; uproar. **6** move with short, sharp sounds: *The cart rattled down the street.* **7** a toy, instrument, etc. that makes a noise when it is shaken: *The baby shakes her rattle.* **8** a series of horny pieces at the end of a rattlesnake's tail. **9** talk quickly, on and on. **10** say quickly. **11** *Informal.* confuse; upset: *She was so rattled that she forgot her speech.* 1, 2, 6, 9–11 *v.*, **rat·tled, rat·tling;** 3–5, 7, 8 *n.*

**rat·tle·brain** (rat′əl brān′) a giddy, thoughtless person. *n.*

**rat·tler** (rat′lər) *Informal.* RATTLESNAKE. *n.*

**rat·tle·snake** (rat′əl snāk′) a poisonous snake with a thick body and a broad, triangular head, that makes a rattling noise with its tail. *n.*

**rat·tle·trap** (rat′əl trap′) something shaky, rickety, or rattling, especially an old, worn-out car. *n.*

**rat·tling** (rat′ling) ppr. of RATTLE. *v.*

**rat–trap** (rat′trap′) **1** a trap to catch rats. **2** a dirty, run-down building. **3** a desperate situation. *n.*

**rat·ty** (rat′ē) **1** of or like rats. **2** full of rats. **3** *Informal.* angry or irritable. *adj.*, **rat·ti·er, rat·ti·est.**

**rau·cous** (rok′əs) hoarse; harsh-sounding: *the raucous caw of a crow. adj.* —**rau′cous·ly,** *adv.*

**rav·age** (rav′ij) **1** lay waste; damage greatly; destroy: *The fire ravaged huge areas of forest.* **2** violence; destruction; great damage: *War causes ravage.* **1** *v.*, **rav·aged, rav·ag·ing;** **2** *n.* —**rav′ag·er,** *n.*

**rave** (rāv) **1** talk wildly: *An excited, angry person raves; so does a madman.* **2** talk with too much enthusiasm: *She raved about her food.* **3** howl; roar; rage: *The wind raved about the lighthouse.* **4** *Informal.* unrestrained praise, especially a highly enthusiastic review of a play, film, etc.: *The play got raves in the local press.* **1–3** *v.*, **raved, rav·ing;** **4** *n.*

**rav·el** (rav′əl) **1** separate the threads of; fray. **2** fray out; separate into threads: *The sweater has ravelled at the wrist.* **3** an unravelled thread or fibre. **4** make plain or clear; UNRAVEL (def. 3). **5** become tangled, involved, or confused. **6** tangle; involve; confuse. **1, 2, 4–6** *v.*, **rav·elled** or **rav·eled, rav·el·ling** or **rav·el·ing;** **3** *n.*

**rav·el·ling** or **rav·el·ing** (rav′ə ling) **1** something ravelled, a thread drawn from a woven or knitted fabric. **2** ppr. of RAVEL. **1** *n.*, **2** *v.*

**ra·ven** (rā′vən) **1** a large black bird, resembling a crow but larger. **2** deep, glossy black: *She has raven hair.* **1** *n.*, **2** *adj.*

**rav·en·ing** (rav′ə ning) **1** seeking eagerly for prey: *ravening wolves.* **2** greedy and hungry; voracious. *adj.*

**rav·en·ous** (rav′ə nəs) **1** very hungry; famished: *The hikers were all ravenous by the time they stopped to eat.* **2** very eager or greedy: *ravenous hunger. He was ravenous for praise.* **3** RAPACIOUS. *adj.* —**rav′en·ous·ly,** *adv.*

**ra·vine** (rə vēn′) a long, deep, narrow gorge worn by running water or by the action of glaciers. *n.*

**rav·ing** (rā′ving) **1** that raves; delirious; frenzied; raging. **2** delirious, incoherent talk. **3** *Informal.* remarkable; extraordinary: *The talent night was a raving success. She's a raving beauty.* **4** ppr. of RAVE. **1, 3** *adj.*, **2** *n.*, **4** *v.* —**rav′ing·ly,** *adv.*

**rav·i·o·li** (rav′ē ō′lē) small, thin cases of pasta filled with chopped meat, cheese, etc., cooked in water and usually served with a highly seasoned tomato sauce. *n.*

**rav·ish** (rav′ish) **1** fill with delight; charm; enrapture: *ravished by the beauty of the scene.* **2** commit RAPE on. *v.*

**rav·ish·ing** (rav′i shing) **1** very delightful; enchanting: *jewels of ravishing beauty.* **2** ppr. of RAVISH. **1** *adj.*, **2** *v.* —**rav′ish·ing·ly,** *adv.*

**rav·ish·ment** (rav′i shmənt) **1** the act of RAVISHing. **2** rapture; ecstasy. *n.*

**raw** (ro) **1** not cooked: *raw oysters.* **2** in the natural state; not manufactured, treated, or prepared: *raw materials. Raw milk is milk that has not been pasteurized.* **3** not experienced; not trained: *a raw recruit.* **4** unpleasantly damp or cold: *raw weather.* **5** with the skin off; sore: *a raw spot.* **6** *Informal.* harsh; unfair: *a raw deal.* **7 the raw,** a raw or sore place or condition. **1–6** *adj.*, **7** *n.* —**raw′ly,** *adv.* —**raw′ness,** *n.*

hat, āge, fär; let, ēqual, tėrm; it, īce
hot, ōpen, ôrder; oil, out; cup, put, rüle
əbove, takən, pencəl, lemən, circəs
ch, child; ng, long; sh, ship
th, thin; ŦH, then; zh, measure

**in the raw,** **a** naked: *to sleep in the raw.* **b** in an unrefined or crude state: *experiencing life in the raw.*

**raw–boned** (rob′ōnd′) **1** having little flesh on the bones; gaunt. **2** having a heavy, large, somewhat bony frame: *She was tall and raw-boned. adj.*

**raw·hide** (ro′hīd′) **1** the untanned skin of cattle. **2** a rope or whip made of this skin. **3** whip or drive with a rawhide. **1, 2** *n.*, **3** *v.*, **raw·hid·ed, raw·hid·ing.**

**raw material** a substance in its natural state, before being manufactured, treated, or prepared.

**ray¹** (rā) **1** a line or beam of light: *rays of the sun.* **2** a line or stream of RADIANT ENERGY in the form of heat, electricity, light, etc.: *X rays.* **3** a thin line like a ray, coming out from a centre. **4** any part like a ray: *The petals of a daisy and the arms of a starfish are rays.* **5** a slight trace; faint gleam: *Not a ray of hope pierced our gloom.* **6** send forth in rays; radiate. **7** treat with rays. **8** in geometry, a straight line extending from a point. **1–5, 8** *n.*, **6, 7** *v.*
☞ *Hom.* RE¹.

**ray²** (rā) any of several species of fish related to the sharks, that have broad, flat bodies with very broad pectoral fins: *The electric ray has organs with which it shocks or kills its prey. n.*
☞ *Hom.* RE¹.

**ray flower** one of the petal-like flowers forming the outside of the flower head of a COMPOSITE plant: *The flower head of a daisy consists of central disk flowers surrounded by ray flowers.* See COMPOSITE and DAISY for pictures.

**ray·on** (rā′on) any of several types of fibre or fabric made from cellulose treated with chemicals. *n.*

**raze** (rāz) tear down; destroy completely; demolish: *The old school was razed and a new one was built in the same place. v.*, **razed, raz·ing.**
☞ *Hom.* RAISE.

**ra·zor** (rā′zər) a cutting instrument used for shaving or cutting hair: *an electric razor, a safety razor. n.*
☞ *Hom.* RAISER.

**ra·zor·back** (rā′zər bak′) **1** a kind of thin, half-wild mongrel hog with a ridged back: *Razorbacks are common in the southern United States.* **2** a finback whale; rorqual. **3** a sharp ridge on a hill, mountain, etc. *n.*

**Rb** rubidium.

**R.C.** **1** Roman Catholic. **2** Red Cross.

**RCAF** or **R.C.A.F.** Royal Canadian Air Force.

**RCMP** or **R.C.M.P.** Royal Canadian Mounted Police.

**RCN** or **R.C.N.** Royal Canadian Navy.

**rd.** **1** road. **2** rod; rods.

**Rd.** Road.

**re¹** (rā) in music: **1** the second tone of an eight-tone major scale. See DO² for picture. **2** the tone D. *n.*
☞ *Hom.* RAY.

**re²** (rē) with reference to; in the matter or case of; about; concerning. *prep.*

**Re** rhenium.

**re-** a prefix meaning: **1** again; anew; once more, as in *reappear, rebuild, reheat, reopen, re-enter.* **2** back, as in *recall, repay, replace.*
☞ *Usage.* Most words beginning with **re-** are not hyphenated: *rearm, refine, remit.* However, a hyphen is often used if the letter following the **re-** is also *e*: *re-entry, re-establish.* In addition, a hyphen is always used to distinguish a word in which **re-** means 'again' from another word that would otherwise have the same spelling: *recover* 'get back, get better', *re-cover* 'cover again'; *reform* 'make better, improve', *re-form* 'make or shape again'.

**reach** (rēch) **1** get to; come to; arrive at: *to reach the top of a hill, the end of a book, an agreement, etc.* **2** stretch; stretch out: *to reach toward a book.* **3** extend in space, time, operation, effect, influence, etc. (*to*): *The power of Rome reached to the ends of the known world.* **4** extend to: *Radio reaches millions.* **5** get or come; function: *farther than the eye can reach.* **6** get in touch with by anything extended, cast, etc.; touch: *The anchor reached bottom.* **7** make a stretch of a certain length with the hand, etc.: *I cannot reach to the top of the wall.* **8** make a stretch in a certain direction: *The man reached for his gun.* **9** get at; influence: *People are reached by flattery.* **10** amount to; be equal to: *The cost of the war reached billions.* **11** *Informal.* take or pass with the hand: *Please reach me the sugar.* **12** a stretching out; reaching: *By a long reach, the drowning woman grasped the rope.* **13** the extent or distance of reaching: *out of one's reach.* **14** range; power; capacity: *the reach of the mind.* **15** a continuous stretch or extent: *a reach of woodland.* **16** a part of a river between bends. **17** a part of a canal between locks. **18** sail on course with the wind forward of the beam. **19** the distance sailed on one tack. 1–11, 18 *v.*, 12–17, 19 *n.*

**re·act** (rē akt′) **1** act back; have an effect on the one that is acting: *Unkindness often reacts on the unkind person.* **2** act in response: *Dogs react to kindness by showing affection. Some people react against fads.* **3** act chemically; undergo a reaction: *Acids react on metals.* **4** return to a previous state, level, etc. *v.*

**re-act** (rē akt′) act over again: *to re-act a scene in a play.* *v.*

**re·act·ance** (rē ak′təns) in electricity, that part of the impedance of an alternating-current circuit which is due to inductance or capacitance or both. It is expressed in OHMS. *n.*

**re·act·ion** (rē ak′shən) **1** a result which is the opposite of the cause: *Fever is a common reaction from a chill.* **2** in politics, economics, etc., a tendency toward a previous state of affairs. **3** an action in response to some influence or force: *Our reaction to a joke is to laugh. The doctor carefully observed her patient's reactions to certain tests.* **4** the chemical action of two substances on each other which results in the formation of one or more additional substances: *The reaction between nitrogen and hydrogen produces ammonia.* *n.*

**re·ac·tion·ar·y** (rē ak′shə ner′ē) **1** having to do with, marked by, or favouring REACTION (def. 2): *The bad results of the revolution brought about a reactionary feeling.* **2** a person who favours REACTION (def. 2), especially in politics. 1 *adj.*, 2 *n.*, *pl.* **re·ac·tion·ar·ies**.

**re·ac·tor** (rē ak′tər) **1** a device, such as a coil, having low resistance and high inductance, used to introduce reactance into an alternating-current circuit. **2** a person or animal that reacts, especially one that reacts positively to a medical test for a disease, allergy, etc. **3** NUCLEAR REACTOR. *n.*

**read¹** (rēd) **1** distinguish and understand the meaning of symbols such as those used in writing or printing: *read a book. The blind read with their fingers.* **2** learn from writing or printing: *We read of heroines of other days.* **3** speak printed or written words; say aloud the words one sees, or touches: *Read this story to me.* **4** show by letters, figures, signs, etc.: *The thermometer reads 30 degrees.* **5** give as the word or words in a particular passage: *For "fail," a misprint, read "fall."* **6** study: *to read law.* **7** get the meaning of; understand: *As I read her intention, she means to resign.* **8** give the meaning of; interpret: *A prophet reads the future.* **9** introduce something not expressed or directly indicated by one's manner of understanding or interpreting: *to read a hostile intent in a friendly letter.* **10** produce a certain impression when read; mean; be in effect when read: *This does not read like a child's composition.* **11** admit of being read or interpreted: *A rule that reads two ways.* **12** bring or put by reading: *Mario reads himself to sleep.* *v.*, **read** (red), **read·ing**.
**read between the lines,** find a meaning not actually expressed in the writing or print.
**read into,** interpret in a certain way, often attributing more than intended: *She read into the statement a deep insult.*
**read out,** **a** read aloud: *She read out her answer to the class.* **b** produce a READOUT (def. 2) of.
**read out of,** expel from a political party, etc.
☞ *Hom.* REED.

**read²** (red) **1** having knowledge gained by reading; informed: *a well-read woman.* **2** pt. and pp. of READ¹: *I read that book last year. Joanne has read it too.* 1 *adj.*, 2 *v.*
☞ *Hom.* RED.

**read·a·bil·i·ty** (rē′də bil′ə tē) the quality or condition of being READABLE. *n.*

**read·a·ble** (rē′də bəl) **1** interesting or enjoyable to read: *Her novels are very readable.* **2** easy to read; legible: *readable handwriting.* *adj.*
—**read′·a·ble·ness,** *n.*

**re·ad·dress** (rē′ə dres′) **1** put a new address on: *We had to readdress several of the letters because we found out that the people had moved.* **2** speak to again. **3** apply oneself anew. *v.*

**read·er** (rē′dər) **1** a person who reads: *She is an avid reader. They are both poor readers.* **2** a person employed to read manuscripts and estimate their fitness for publication. **3** a book for learning and practising reading. *n.*

---

*In each of the words below* **re-** *means* again *or* anew; *the pronunciation of the main part of each word is not changed.*

re′ab·sorb′        re′ac·quaint′        re′ac·quain′tance        re′a·dapt′

**read·i·ly** (red′ə lē) **1** without reluctance; willingly: *She answered our questions readily. He doesn't readily accept advice.* **2** without difficulty; easily: *The parts fitted together readily.* *adv.*

**read·i·ness** (red′ē nis) **1** being ready; preparedness. **2** quickness; promptness. **3** ease; facility. **4** willingness. *n.*

**read·ing** (rē′ding) **1** the act or process of getting the meaning of writing or printing. **2** a speaking out loud of written or printed words; public recital. **3** the study of books, etc. **4** written or printed matter read or to be read: *There's good reading in this magazine.* **5** the information shown by letters, figures, or signs on a gauge or the scale of an instrument: *The reading on the thermometer was 38 degrees.* **6** the interpreting of symbols, designs, plans, etc. **7** the form of a given word or passage in a particular edition of a book: *No two editions have the same reading for that passage.* **8** an interpretation: *Each actor gave the lines a different reading.* **9** that reads. **10** used in or for reading: *reading glasses.* **11** the extent to which one has read; literary knowledge. **12** ppr. of READ. 1–8, 11 *n.*, 9, 10 *adj.*, 12 *v.*

**reading room** a special room for reading in a library, club, etc.

**re·ad·just** (rē′ə just′) adjust again; arrange again. *v.* —**re′ad·just′ment**, *n.*

**Read Only Memory** that part of a computer's memory that cannot be erased: *The Read Only Memory usually contains the programming language.*

**read·out** (rē′dout′) **1** the process of retrieving information from a computer storage or memory device and displaying it in understandable form, such as words or numerals. **2** the information so displayed. *n.*

**read·y** (red′ē) **1** prepared for immediate action or use; prepared: *ready for the exam.* **2** willing: *The knights were ready to die for their lords.* **3** quick; prompt: *a ready welcome.* **4** quick in thought or action; dexterous: *a ready wit.* **5** apt; likely; liable: *She is too ready to find fault.* **6** immediately available: *ready money.* **7** make ready; prepare. **8** the condition of being ready for action: *The hunters walked through the forest with their guns at the ready.* 1–6 *adj.*, **read·i·er, read·i·est;** 7 *v.*, **read·ied, read·y·ing;** 8 *n.*
**make ready,** prepare.

**read·y–made** (red′ē mād′) **1** of clothes, made beforehand in standard sizes; not made to order. **2** not original; commonplace: *a magazine article filled with ready-made ideas.* **3** already established and available: *The postal strike provided her with a ready-made excuse for not writing.* *adj.*

**re·a·gent** (rē ā′jənt) a substance used to detect the presence of other substances by the chemical reactions it causes. *n.*

**re·al** (rē′əl *or* rēl) **1** existing as a fact; not imagined or made up; actual; true: *a real experience.* **2** genuine: *a real diamond.* **3** in law, noting or having to do with immovable property: *Lands and houses are called real property.* **4** in mathematics, either rational or irrational, not imaginary. **5** *Informal.* really; very: *He talked real loud.* 1–4 *adj.*, 5 *adv.*

**in real life,** in reality; actually: *He plays a gangster in the TV series, but in real life he's a very gentle man.*
☛ **Usage.** The use of **real** as an adverb (as in *It was real good*) is common in familiar speech but should be avoided in writing.
☛ **Hom.** REEL (for the second pronunciation of **real**).

**real estate** land, together with the buildings, fences, trees, water, and minerals that belong with it.

**real estate agent** a person dealing in REAL ESTATE.

**re·al·ism** (rē′ə liz′əm) **1** practical tendency: *Jag's realism made him dislike fanciful schemes.* **2** in art and literature, the picturing of life as it actually is. *n.*

**re·al·ist** (rē′ə list) **1** a person interested in what is real and practical rather than what is imaginary or theoretical. **2** a writer or artist who represents things as they are in real life. *n.*

**re·al·is·tic** (rē′ə lis′tik) **1** like the real thing; lifelike. **2** in literature or art, representing life as it actually is. **3** seeing things as they really are; practical. **4** having to do with realists or realism. *adj.*
—**re′al·is′ti·cal·ly,** *adv.*

**re·al·i·ty** (rē al′ə tē) **1** the quality or state of being real: *Kurt was convinced of the reality of what he had seen.* **2** a real thing, fact, or event: *the terrible realities of war. Her dream became a reality.* **3** actual existence; the true state of affairs: *They said his writing was just an attempt to escape from reality.* *n., pl.* **re·al·i·ties.**
**in reality,** really; actually; in fact; truly: *We thought she was joking, but in reality she was serious.*

**re·al·i·za·tion** (rē′ə lə zā′shən *or* rē′ə lī zā′shən) **1** the action of realizing or the state of being REALIZED: *The explorers had a full realization of the dangers they might face. For years they saved, waiting for the realization of their hopes.* **2** something that is REALIZED: *The farm was the realization of all her dreams.* *n.*

**re·al·ize** (rē′ə līz′) **1** understand clearly; be fully aware of: *She realizes how hard you worked.* **2** make real; bring into actual existence: *Her uncle's present made it possible for her to realize her dream of going to college.* **3** cause to seem real. **4** change property into money: *Before going to England to live, he realized all his Canadian property.* **5** obtain as a return or profit: *He realized $10 000 from his investment.* **6** bring as a return or profit. *v.*, **re·al·ized, re·al·iz·ing.**

**re·al·ly** (rē′ə lē *or* rē′lē) **1** actually; in fact: *things as they really are. She really didn't know who it was.* **2** without question; truly: *a really magnificent house.* **3** an expression of surprise, disbelief, or disapproval: *Really, Don? I don't believe it!* *adv.*

**realm** (relm) **1** kingdom. **2** range; domain: *the realm of science. Such an occurrence is outside the realm of possibility.* *n.*

---

*In each of the words below,* **re-** *means* **again** *or* **anew;** *the pronunciation of the main part of each word is not changed.*

re′ad·mit′  re′af·firm′

**real number** in mathematics, a member of the set of numbers which includes all the RATIONAL NUMBERS (e.g., ³/₄, 0.777..., -⁴/₁) and all the IRRATIONAL NUMBERS (e.g., pi, square root of 2, e).

**re·al·ty** (rē′əl tē *or* rēl′tē)   REAL ESTATE.  *n.*

**ream¹** (rēm)   1 about 500, sometimes 480–516, sheets of paper of the same stock and size.   2 Usually, **reams,** *pl.* a very large quantity: *He took reams of notes.*   *n.*
☞ *Etym.* Through OF *raime* from Arabic *rismah* 'a bundle', which came from *rasama* 'make into a bundle'.

**ream²** (rēm)   1 enlarge or shape a hole.   2 remove with a REAMER.   *v.*
☞ *Etym.* From ME dialect *remen,* related to OE *rȳman* 'widen, make roomy', which was itself related to OE *rūm* 'room'.

A reamer for removing burrs from the inside of a cut pipe

**ream·er** (rē′mər)   1 a tool for enlarging or shaping a hole.   2 a utensil for squeezing the juice out of oranges, lemons, etc.   *n.*

**re·an·i·mate** (rē an′ə māt′)   restore to life; give fresh spirit, vigour, activity, etc. to: *to reanimate discouraged troops, to reanimate trade.*   *v.,* **re·an·i·mat·ed, re·an·i·mat·ing.**

**reap** (rēp)   1 cut grain.   2 gather a crop.   3 cut grain or gather a crop from: *to reap fields.*   4 get as a return or reward: *Kind acts often reap happy smiles.*   5 get a return.   *v.*

**reap·er** (rē′pər)   a person or machine that cuts grain or gathers a crop.   *n.*

**re·ap·pear** (rē′ə pēr′)   appear again.   *v.*

**re·ap·pear·ance** (rē′ə pē′rəns)   reappearing.   *n.*

**rear¹** (rēr)   1 the back part; the part opposite the front; back: *the rear of the house.*   2 at the back; in the back: *the rear door of the car.*   3 the space or position at the back: *She moved toward the rear.*   4 the last part of an army, fleet, etc.; the part farthest from the battlefront.   1, 3, 4 *n.,* 2 *adj.*
**at** *or* **in the rear of,**   behind.
**bring up the rear,**   come or be last: *We filed through the woods, with me bringing up the rear.*

**rear²** (rēr)   1 make grow; help to grow; bring up: *The mother was very careful in rearing her children.*   2 set up; build: *to rear a temple.*   3 raise; lift up: *to rear one's head.*   4 especially of a horse, rise on the hind legs, rise: *The horse reared as the fire engine dashed past.*   5 extend to a great height: *Mountain peaks reared up behind the valley.*   *v.*

**rear guard**   that part of an army that protects the rear.

**re·arm** (rē ärm′)   especially of a nation or a military force, arm again with new or better weapons.   *v.*

**re·ar·ma·ment** (rē är′mə mənt)   REARMing or being rearmed.   *n.*

**rear·most** (rēr′mōst)   farthest in the rear; last.   *adj.*

**re·ar·range** (rē′ə rānj′)   1 arrange in a new or different way: *to rearrange furniture.*   2 arrange again.   *v.,* **re·ar·ranged, re·ar·rang·ing.**

**re·ar·range·ment** (rē′ə rānj′mənt)   a new or different arrangement.   *n.*

**rear·view mirror** (rēr′vyü′)   a mirror on an automobile, etc. attached so as to give a view of the area to the rear.

**rear·ward** (rēr′wərd)   toward or in the rear.   *adv., adj.*

**rea·son** (rē′zən)   1 a cause or motive for an action, feeling, etc.; ground: *I have my own reasons for doing this.*   2 a justification; explanation: *What is your reason for doing such poor work?*   3 the ability or power to think and draw conclusions.   4 think; think logically: *People can reason.*   5 draw conclusions or inferences from facts or premises.   6 right thinking; good sense: *The stubborn child was at last brought to reason.*   7 sanity: *That poor old man has lost his reason.*   8 consider; discuss; argue: *Reason with Helen and try to make her change her mind.*   1–3, 6, 7 *n.,* 4, 5, 8 *v.*   —**rea′son·er,** *n.*
**bring to reason,**   cause to be reasonable.
**by reason of,**   on account of; because of.
**in reason,**   within reasonable and sensible limits.
**stand to reason,**   be reasonable and sensible: *It stands to reason that he would resent your insults.*
☞ *Usage.* **The reason is, the reason was,** etc. should be followed by **that,** not by **because.** Instead of *His reason for being late is because his car would not start,* say: *His reason for being late is that his car would not start.* Or avoid the word *reason* and say: *He was late because his car would not start.*
☞ *Syn.* **Reason** and **cause** have similar meanings, but they must not be confused. A **reason** explains why or how something happens: *His reason for being late was that his car would not start.* A **cause** is what makes something happen: *The cause of his car not starting was a cracked distributor cap.*

**rea·son·a·ble** (rē′zə nə bəl)   1 according to reason; not absurd: *a reasonable explanation, a reasonable theory.*   2 fair or moderate; not extreme: *a reasonable request, a reasonable price.*   3 not high in price; inexpensive: *I expected the dress to be expensive, but it was really very reasonable.*   4 ready to listen to reason; sensible: *She's a reasonable person. Be reasonable; it can't possibly work that way.*   5 having the ability to reason.   *adj.*
—**rea′son·a·ble·ness,** *n.*   —**rea′son·a·bly,** *adv.*

**rea·son·ing** (rē′zə ning)   1 the process of drawing conclusions from facts.   2 reasons, arguments, etc. resulting from or used in this process: *I didn't understand her reasoning.*   3 ppr. of REASON.   1, 2 *n.,* 3 *v.*

**re·as·sem·ble** (rē′ə sem′bəl)   1 come or bring together again: *We shall reassemble here after the coffee break.*   2 assemble something that has been taken apart:

---

*In each of the words below,* **re-** *means* again *or* anew; *the pronunciation of the main part of each word is not changed.*

| re′ap·ply′ | re′ap·point′ment | re′ap·prais′al | re′as·cend′ | re′as·sess′ |
| re′ap·point′ | re′ap·por′tion | re′ap·praise′ | re′as·sert′ | re′as·sign′ |

*We reassembled the old clock piece by piece.* *v.*, **re·as·sem·bled, re·as·sem·bling.**

**re·as·sur·ance** (rē′ə shùr′əns) **1** reassuring or being REASSURED. **2** REINSURANCE. *n.*

**re·as·sure** (rē′ə shùr′) **1** restore to confidence: *The captain's confidence during the storm reassured the passengers.* **2** assure again or anew: *We reassured him that we would get there on time.* **3** insure again. *v.*, **re·as·sured, re·as·sur·ing.**

**re·bate** (rē′bāt) **1** the return of part of the money paid; partial refund; discount. **2** give as a rebate. **1** *n.*, **2** *v.*, **re·bat·ed, re·bat·ing.**

A rebec

**re·bec** or **re·beck** (rē′bek) a musical instrument resembling a violin, used in the Middle Ages. *n.*

**reb·el** (reb′əl *for noun,* ri bel′ *for verb*) **1** a person who opposes or takes up arms against a government or ruler. **2** of, having to do with, or made up of persons who take up arms against a government or ruler: *a rebel stronghold, a rebel army.* **3** use force or arms to oppose a government or an authority: *The people rebelled when the new tax was imposed. The troops rebelled against their commander.* **4** a person who resists authority or control: *She always was a rebel; her family never understood her.* **5** resist authority or control: *He rebelled against his parents.* **6** feel or express a great dislike: *We rebelled at the thought of having to stay home all weekend.* **1, 2, 4** *n.*, **3, 5, 6** *v.*, **re·belled, re·bel·ling.**

**re·bel·lion** (ri bel′yən) **1** organized resistance against the authority of a government; a revolt: *Louis Riel led a rebellion in Saskatchewan in 1885.* **2** an act of resistance against any authority; a revolt or fight against any restriction. *n.*

**re·bel·lious** (ri bel′yəs) **1** defying authority; acting like a rebel: *rebellious troops.* **2** hard to manage; hard to treat; disobedient. *adj.* —**re·bel′lious·ly,** *adv.* —**re·bel′lious·ness,** *n.*

**re·bind** (rē bīnd′) bind again or anew: *This book with the broken back needs rebinding.* *v.*, **re·bound, re·bind·ing.**

**re·birth** (rē′bėrth′ *or* rē bėrth′) **1** being born again; reincarnation. **2** a new spiritual life; spiritual renewal. **3** revival; reawakening: *the rebirth of nationalism, the rebirth of hope.* *n.*

**re·born** (rē bôrn′) born again, renewed, or revived: *Our hopes for a win were reborn when we heard she would be playing after all.* *adj.*

hat, āge, fär; let, ēqual, tėrm; it, īce
hot, ōpen, ôrder; oil, out; cup, pùt, rüle
əbove, takən, pencəl, lemən, circəs
ch, child; ng, long; sh, ship
th, thin; ᴛʜ, then; zh, measure

**re·bound** (ri bound′ *for verb,* rē′bound′ *for noun*) **1** spring back. **2** springing back: *You hit the ball on the rebound in handball.* **3** resound. **4** in basketball, a ball that bounds off the backboard when a scoring attempt has been missed. **1, 3** *v.*, **2, 4** *n.*
**on the rebound,** in a state of shock caused by the abrupt ending of a love affair.

**re·broad·cast** (rē brod′kast′) **1** broadcast again at a later time or date: *The interview with the prime minister will be rebroadcast Sunday afternoon.* **2** relay a television or radio program as it is being received from another station. **3** a relayed or repeated television or radio broadcast. **1, 2** *v.*, **re·broad·cast** or **re·broad·cast·ed, re·broad·cast·ing;** **3** *n.*

**re·buff** (ri buf′) **1** a blunt or sudden rejection of a person or animal that makes advances, offers help or sympathy, makes a request, etc.; snub: *Ruth's offer to help Mona met with the rebuff, "Let me alone."* **2** give a rebuff to: *The friendly dog was rebuffed by a kick.* **1** *n.*, **2** *v.*

**re·build** (rē′bild′) build again: *The snowman fell down and the children are trying to rebuild it.* *v.*, **re·built, re·build·ing.**

**re·built** (rē′bilt′) pt. and pp. of REBUILD. *v.*

**re·buke** (ri byük′) **1** express disapproval of; reprove. **2** an expression of disapproval; scolding: *The child feared the teacher's rebuke.* **1** *v.*, **re·buked, re·buk·ing;** **2** *n.*

**re·bus** (rē′bəs) a representation of a word or phrase by pictures suggesting the syllables or words: *A picture of a cat on a log is a rebus for "catalogue."* *n.*

**re·but** (ri but′) contradict or oppose by formal argument presenting evidence on the other side; try to disprove: *Each team in the debate was given two minutes to rebut the other's arguments.* *v.*, **re·but·ted, re·but·ting.**

**re·but·tal** (ri but′əl) rebutting. *n.*

**rec. 1** receipt. **2** recipe. **3** record. **4** recorder.

**re·cal·ci·trance** (ri kal′sə trəns) a refusal to submit, conform, or comply. *n.*

**re·cal·ci·trant** (ri kal′sə trənt) resisting authority or control; disobedient. *adj.*

**re·call** (ri kol′; *usually,* rē′kol′ *for noun*) **1** call back to mind; remember. **2** a recalling to mind. **3** call back; order back: *The ambassador was recalled.* **4** a calling back; ordering back. **5** a signal used in calling back forces, ships, etc. **6** bring back: *recalled to life.* **7** take back; withdraw: *The order has been given and cannot be recalled.* **8** taking back; revocation; annulment. **9** the removal of a public official from office by vote of the people: *There is no longer provision for recall in Canada.* **1, 3, 6, 7** *v.*, **2, 4, 5, 8, 9** *n.*

---

*In each of the words below,* **re-** *means* again *or* anew; *the pronunciation of the main part of each word is not changed.*

re′as·sign′ment    re′at·tach′    re′au′dit    re′a·wak′en    re′bap·tize′

**re·cant** (ri kant′) **1** take back formally or publicly; withdraw or renounce a statement, opinion, purpose, etc. **2** renounce an opinion or allegiance: *Though he was tortured to make him change his religion, the prisoner would not recant.* *v.*

**re·can·ta·tion** (rē′kan tā′shən) a RECANTing. *n.*

**re·cap**[1] (rē′kap′ *or* rē′kap′ *for verb,* rē′kap′ *for noun*) **1** put a strip of rubber or similar material on a worn surface of an automobile tire, by using heat and pressure to make a firm union. **2** a tire repaired in this manner. **3** put a cap or lid on again: *to recap a bottle of ginger ale.* 1, 3 *v.*, **re·capped, re·cap·ping;** 2 *n.*

**re·cap**[2] (rē′kap′ *or* rē′kap′ *for verb,* rē′kap′ *for noun*) *Informal.* **1** RECAPITULATE: *Can we just recap what's been agreed on?* **2** RECAPITULATION: *a recap of the discussion.* 1 *v.*, **re·capped, re·cap·ping;** 2 *n.*

**re·ca·pit·u·late** (rē′kə pich′ə lāt′) repeat or recite the main points of; tell briefly; sum up. *v.,* **re·ca·pit·u·lat·ed, re·ca·pit·u·lat·ing.**

**re·ca·pit·u·la·tion** (rē′kə pich′ə lā′shən) a brief statement of the main points; summary. *n.*

**re·cap·ture** (rē kap′chər) **1** capture or take again. **2** a taking or being taken again. **3** bring back; recall: *The picture album recaptured the days of the horse and buggy.* 1, 3 *v.*, **re·cap·tured, re·cap·tur·ing;** 2 *n.*

**re·cast** (rē kast′ *for verb,* rē′kast′ *for noun*) **1** cast again or anew: *to recast a bell, to recast a play.* **2** make over; remodel: *to recast a sentence.* **3** a recasting. 1, 2 *v.,* **re·cast, re·cast·ing;** 3 *n.*

**recd.** *or* **rec'd.** received.

**re·cede** (ri sēd′) **1** move back or away: *Houses and trees seem to recede as you ride past in a train.* **2** slope backward: *He has a chin that recedes.* **3** withdraw: *She receded from the agreement.* *v.*, **re·ced·ed, re·ced·ing.**

**re·ceipt** (ri sēt′) **1** a written statement that money, a package, a letter, etc. has been received. **2** write on or stamp a bill, etc. to indicate that something has been received or paid for: *Pay the bill and ask the grocer to receipt it.* **3** the act or fact of receiving or being received: *The goods will be sent on receipt of payment. She wrote to acknowledge receipt of the package.* **4** Usually, **receipts,** *pl.* money, etc. received: *The expenses were greater than the receipts.* 1, 3, 4 *n.*, 2 *v.*

**re·ceiv·a·ble** (ri sē′və bəl) **1** fit for acceptance: *Gold is receivable all over the world.* **2** on which payment is to be received: *Bills receivable is the opposite of bills payable.* **3** to be received. *adj.*

**re·ceive** (ri sēv′) **1** take something offered or sent; take into one's hands or possession: *to receive gifts.* **2** have something bestowed, conferred, etc.: *to receive a name.* **3** be given; get: *to receive a letter from home.* **4** take, accept, admit, or get something: *We received your greetings.* **5** take; support; bear; hold: *The boat received a heavy load.* **6** take or let into the mind: *to receive new ideas.* **7** accept as true or valid: *a theory widely received.* **8** agree to listen to: *to receive confession.* **9** experience; suffer; endure: *to receive a blow.* **10** let into one's house, society, etc.: *The people of the neighbourhood were glad to receive the new couple.* **11** admit to a place; give shelter to: *to receive strangers.* **12** admit to a state or condition: *to receive a person into the association.* **13** be at home to friends and visitors: *She receives on Tuesdays.* **14** in radio or television, change electromagnetic waves into sound or picture signals. *v.*, **re·ceived, re·ceiv·ing.**
**be on the receiving end,** *Informal.* be in the position of victim; bear the brunt of something unpleasant.

☛ *Syn.* Both **receive** and ACCEPT mean to take something that is given or offered. **Receive** suggests taking or getting without any act of will or decision: *She received a strange parcel.* **Accept** always suggests a definite wish or decision to take what is offered: *She accepted his unusual present gracefully. They considered the offer but decided not to accept it.*

**re·ceiv·er** (ri sē′vər) **1** a person who receives. **2** anything that receives. **3** the part of a telephone held to the ear. **4** a device that changes electromagnetic waves into sound or picture signals: *a radio or television receiver.* **5** one appointed by law to take charge of the property of others: *Mr. Takahasi will act as a receiver for the bankrupt firm.* *n.*

**re·ceiv·er·ship** (ri sē′vər ship′) **1** the position of a RECEIVER (def. 5) in charge of the property of others. **2** the condition of being in the control of a RECEIVER (def. 5). *n.*

**receiving blanket** a small, lightweight blanket for wrapping a newborn baby.

**receiving line** a group of people who stand in a row at wedding receptions or other formal occasions in order to welcome each guest individually.

**re·cen·cy** (rē′sən sē) the fact or condition of being RECENT. *n.*

**re·cent** (rē′sənt) **1** done, made, or happening not long ago: *recent events.* **2** not long past; modern: *a recent period in history.* **3** **Recent,** of, having to do with, or being the most recent geological epoch, including the present time. See geological time chart in the Appendix. *adj.* —**re′cent·ness,** *n.*

**re·cent·ly** (rē′sən tlē) lately; not long ago. *adv.*

**re·cep·ta·cle** (ri sep′tə kəl) **1** any container or place used to put things in to keep them conveniently: *Bags, baskets, and vaults are all receptacles.* **2** in botany, the base of the flower to which all the parts of the flower are attached. See FLOWER for picture. *n.*

**re·cep·tion** (ri sep′shən) **1** the act of receiving: *calm reception of bad news.* **2** the fact of being received: *Helen's reception as a club member pleased her.* **3** a manner of receiving: *a warm reception.* **4** a gathering to receive and welcome people: *Our school gave a reception to our new principal.* **5** the quality of the sound in a radio or of the sound and picture signals in a television set. *n.*

**re·cep·tion·ist** (ri sep′shə nist) a person employed in an office to welcome visitors, direct them where to go, give out information, etc. *n.*

**re·cep·tive** (ri sep′tiv) able, quick, or willing to receive ideas, suggestions, or impressions, etc.: *a receptive mind, a receptive audience.* *adj.* —**re·cep′tive·ly,** *adv.*

**re·cep·tive·ness** (ri sep′tiv nəs) the ability or readiness to RECEIVE. *n.*

**re·cep·tiv·i·ty** (rē′sep tiv′ə tē) the ability or readiness to RECEIVE. *n.*

**re·cep·tor** (ri sep′tər) a cell or group of cells sensitive to stimuli; sense organ. *n.*

**re·cess** (rē′ses *or* ri ses′ *for noun,* ri ses′ *for verb*) **1** a time during which work stops: *There will be a short recess before the next meeting.* **2** take a recess: *The convention recessed until afternoon.* **3** a part in a wall or other surface set back from the rest; alcove; niche. **4** put in a recess; set back. **5** make a recess in. **6** an inner place or part; quiet, secluded place: *the recesses of a cave, the recesses of one's secret thoughts.* 1, 3, 6 *n.*, 2, 4, 5 *v.*

**re·ces·sion** (ri sesh′ən) **1** going backward; moving backward. **2** sloping backward. **3** withdrawal. **4** a period of temporary business decline, shorter and less extreme than a depression. *n.*

**re·ces·sive** (ri ses′iv) **1** tending to go back; receding. **2** in biology, of or referring to a gene in one of a pair of chromosomes that is dominated by the corresponding gene in the other chromosome and is therefore latent and not expressed as a trait in an organism. Compare with DOMINANT. *adj.*

**re·cher·ché** (rə sher′shā; *French,* Rə sheR shā′) **1** sought out or devised with care; rare; choice. **2** too studied; far-fetched. *adj.*

**rec·i·pe** (res′ə pē) **1** a set of directions for preparing something to eat: *I'd like to try this recipe for oatmeal cookies.* **2** a set of directions for preparing anything by combining various ingredients: *Grandmother's recipe for making soap was highly prized.* **3** a means of reaching some state or condition: *a recipe for happiness.* *n.*

**re·cip·i·ent** (ri sip′ē ənt) **1** a person or thing that receives something: *The recipients of the prizes had their names printed in the paper.* **2** receiving; willing to receive; receptive. 1 *n.*, 2 *adj.*

**re·cip·ro·cal** (re sip′rə kəl) **1** in return: *Although I gave her many presents, I had no reciprocal gifts from her.* **2** MUTUAL: *reciprocal liking, reciprocal distrust.* **3** expressing MUTUAL action or relation. *Example: In "The two children like each other," each other is a reciprocal pronoun.* **4** a number so related to another that when multiplied together they give 1: *The reciprocal of 3 is ⅓, and the reciprocal of ⅓ is 3.* **5** something that is reciprocal. 1–3 *adj.*, 4, 5 *n.*

**re·cip·ro·cal·ly** (ri sip′rə kə lē *or* ri sip′rə klē) in a RECIPROCAL way; each to the other; mutually. *adv.*

**re·cip·ro·cate** (ri sip′rə kāt′) **1** give, do, feel, or show in return: *She likes me, and I reciprocate her liking. He said he appreciated what they had done for him and wanted to reciprocate.* **2** interchange: *to reciprocate favours.* **3** move or cause to move with an alternating backward and forward motion: *a reciprocating valve.* *v.*, **re·cip·ro·cat·ed, re·cip·ro·cat·ing.**

**reciprocating engine** an engine in which the back-and-forth motion of a piston is converted into a circular motion of the crankshaft by means of a connecting rod: *Most internal-combustion engines are reciprocating engines.*

**re·cip·roc·a·tion** (ri sip′rə kā′shən) the act of reciprocating; return: *a reciprocation of a favour received.* *n.*

**receptor**    **985**   **reclaim**

hat, āge, fär; let, ēqual, tėrm; it, īce
hot, ōpen, ôrder; oil, out; cup, put, rüle
ə*bove,* ta*k*ən, penc*ə*l, lem*ə*n, circ*ə*s
ch, child; ng, long; sh, ship
th, thin; ᴛʜ, then; zh, measure

**rec·i·proc·i·ty** (res′ə pros′ə tē) **1** a RECIPROCAL state; mutual action, influence, or dependence. **2** a mutual exchange; especially, an exchange of special privileges in regard to trade between two countries, institutions, etc. *n.*

**re·cit·al** (ri sī′təl) **1** the act of reciting; a telling of facts in detail: *Her recital of her experiences in the hospital bored her hearers.* **2** a story or account. **3** a program of music or dance given by a single performer or several individual performers, or by a small ensemble. **4** a public performance given by a number of music or dance pupils to show their skill. *n.*

**rec·i·ta·tion** (res′ə tā′shən) **1** reciting; a telling of facts in detail. **2** a repeating of something from memory, especially before an audience. **3** a piece repeated from memory. *n.*

**rec·i·ta·tive** (res′ə tə tēv′) **1** a style of music halfway between speaking and singing: *Operas often contain long passages of recitative.* **2** a passage, part, or piece in this style. *n.*

**re·cite** (ri sīt′) **1** tell in detail: *She recited the day's adventures.* **2** mention in order; enumerate: *They recited a long list of grievances.* **3** repeat a poem, etc. before an audience. *v.*, **re·cit·ed, re·cit·ing.**

**reck·less** (rek′lis) rash; heedless; careless: *Reckless of consequences, the boy played truant. Reckless driving causes many automobile accidents.* *adj.* —**reck′less·ly,** *adv.* —**reck′less·ness,** *n.*

**reck·on** (rek′ən) **1** find the number or value of; count: *Reckon the cost before you decide.* **2** consider; judge; account: *She is reckoned the best speller in the class.* **3** *Informal.* think; suppose. **4** depend; rely: *You can reckon on our help.* **5** settle; settle accounts. *v.* —**reck′on·er,** *n.*
**reckon on,** count on, take into account: *He didn't reckon on breaking his leg when he decided to try skiing.*
**reckon with,** take into account; face: *We are going to have to reckon with higher prices for food.*

**reck·on·ing** (rek′ə ning) **1** the act or an instance of computing; a count or calculation: *By my reckoning, we still have about seven kilometres to go.* **2** the settlement of an account: *a day of reckoning.* **3** a bill, especially at an inn or tavern. **4** the calculation of the position of a ship. **5** the position calculated. **6** ppr. of RECKON. 1–5 *n.*, 6 *v.*
**day of reckoning,** a time when one must account for or be punished for one's actions: *There will be a day of reckoning for your foolish behaviour.*

**re·claim** (ri klām′) **1** make available for cultivation, etc.: *to reclaim a swamp.* **2** rescue or bring back from wrong conduct, vice, etc.; reform. **3** recover from discarded or waste products: *to reclaim tin from tin cans.*

---

*In each of the words below,* **re-** *means* again *or* anew; *the pronunciation of the main part of each word is not changed.*

| re·chan′nel | re·char′ter | re·chew′ | re·cir′cle | re·cir′cu·late′ |
| re·chart′ | re·check′ | re·chris′ten | | |

**re-claim** / **reconnoitre**

**4** demand or obtain the return of: *The library sent a notice reclaiming the book.* *v.* —**re·claim′a·ble,** *adj.* —**re·claim′er,** *n.*

**re–claim** (rē klām′) claim back or again: *He had trouble re-claiming the money.* *v.*

**rec·la·ma·tion** (rek′lə mā′shən) RECLAIMing or being reclaimed: *the reclamation of deserts by irrigation.* *n.*

**re·cline** (ri klīn′) **1** lean back or lie down: *to recline on a couch.* **2** lay back or down: *Mohammed reclined his head on the pillow.* *v.,* **re·clined, re·clin·ing.**

**rec·luse** (rek′lüs *or* ri klüs′ *for noun,* ri klüs′ *for adjective*) **1** a person who lives shut up or withdrawn from the world. **2** shut up or apart from the world: *a recluse life.* **1** *n.,* **2** *adj.*

**re·clu·sive** (ri klü′siv) having or showing a tendency to withdraw from society: *She became reclusive in her old age and rarely had any visitors.* *adj.*

**rec·og·ni·tion** (rek′əg nish′ən) **1** a knowing again; recognizing; being recognized: *By a good disguise he escaped recognition.* **2** an acknowledgment: *We insisted on complete recognition of our rights.* **3** notice. **4** favourable notice: *The actor soon won recognition from the public.* **5** formal approval or sanction. *n.*

**rec·og·niz·a·ble** (rek′əg nī′zə bəl) capable of being recognized. *adj.* —**rec′og·niz′a·bly,** *adv.*

**re·cog·ni·zance** (ri kog′nə zəns) **1** a bond binding a person to do some particular act. **2** the sum of money to be forfeited if the act is not performed. *n.*

**rec·og·nize** (rek′əg nīz′) **1** know again: *I could scarcely recognize my old friend.* **2** identify: *to recognize a person from a description.* **3** acknowledge acquaintance with; greet: *recognize a person on the street.* **4** acknowledge; accept; admit: *He recognized his duty to defend his country.* **5** take notice of: *Those who wish to speak in a public meeting should stand up and wait till the chairman recognizes them.* **6** show appreciation of. **7** acknowledge and agree to deal with: *For some years certain nations did not recognize the new government.* *v.,* **rec·og·nized, rec·og·niz·ing.**

**re·coil** (ri koil′ *for verb,* ri koil′ *or* rē′koil *for noun*) **1** draw back; shrink back: *Most people would recoil at seeing a snake in their path.* **2** spring back: *The gun recoiled after I fired.* **3** react: *Revenge often recoils on the avenger.* **4** the act or action of recoiling. **5** the distance or force with which a gun, spring, etc., springs back. **1–3** *v.,* **4, 5** *n.*

**rec·ol·lect** (rek′ə lekt′) call back to mind; remember. *v.*

**re–col·lect** (rē′kə lekt′) **1** collect again. **2** recover control of oneself. *v.*

**rec·ol·lec·tion** (rek′ə lek′shən) **1** the act or power of recalling to mind. **2** memory; remembrance: *This has been the hottest summer within my recollection.* **3** something remembered: *Father's recollections of his boyhood are of great interest to us.* *n.*

**re·com·bine** (rē′kəm bīn′) COMBINE again or anew. *v.,* **re·com·bined, re·com·bin·ing.**

**rec·om·mend** (rek′ə mend′) **1** speak in favour of; suggest favourably: *They recommended Janet for the job.* **2** advise: *The doctor recommended that she stay in bed.* **3** make pleasing or attractive: *The location of the camp recommends it as a summer home.* **4** hand over for safe-keeping: *The orphan was recommended to the care of her aunt.* *v.*

**rec·om·men·da·tion** (rek′ə men dā′shən) **1** the act of recommending. **2** something that recommends a person or thing or that expresses praise: *She got a very good recommendation from her former boss.* **3** something recommended: *The doctor's recommendation was that the child stay in bed for a few days.* *n.*

**re·com·mit** (rē′kə mit′) **1** COMMIT again. **2** refer again to a committee. *v.,* **re·com·mit·ted, re·com·mit·ting.**

**re·com·mit·ment** (rē′kə mit′mənt) recommitting or being recommitted. *n.*

**rec·om·pense** (rek′əm pens′) **1** pay a person; pay back; reward. **2** make a fair return for an action, anything lost, damage done, hurt received, etc.: *The insurance company recompensed him for the loss of his car.* **3** a payment or reward: *He asked for fair recompense for the work he had done.* **4** a return for anything lost, damaged, etc.; amends: *He demanded recompense for the broken window.* **1, 2** *v.,* **re·com·pensed, rec·om·pens·ing; 3, 4** *n.*

**rec·on·cil·a·bil·i·ty** (rek′ən sī′lə bil′i tē) the quality of being RECONCILABLE. *n.*

**rec·on·cil·a·ble** (rek′ən sī′lə bəl) capable of being RECONCILEd: *The two points of view are not reconcilable.* *adj.*

**rec·on·cile** (rek′ən sīl′) **1** make friends again: *The children had quarrelled but were soon reconciled.* **2** settle a quarrel, disagreement, etc. **3** make agree; bring into harmony: *It is impossible to reconcile his story with the facts.* **4** make satisfied or content with: *It is hard to reconcile oneself to being sick for a long time.* *v.,* **rec·on·ciled, rec·on·cil·ing.**

**rec·on·cile·ment** (rek′ən sīl′mənt) RECONCILIATION. *n.*

**rec·on·cil·i·a·tion** (rek′ən sil′ē ā′shən) reconciling or being RECONCILEd: *the reconciliation of opposite points of view. They had hopes of a reconciliation between the sisters.* *n.*

**rec·on·dite** (rek′ən dīt′) **1** hard to understand; profound. **2** little known, obscure. *adj.*

**re·con·di·tion** (rē′kən dish′ən) restore to a good or satisfactory condition by repairing or replacing parts, etc.: *The motor has been completely reconditioned.* *v.*

**re·con·nais·sance** (ri kon′ə səns) an examination or survey, especially for military purposes. *n.*

**rec·on·noi·tre** (rek′ə noi′tər *or* rē′kə noi′tər) **1** approach and examine or observe in order to learn something; make a survey of the enemy, the enemy's strength or position, a region, etc. in order to gain

---

*In each of the words below,* **re-** *means* **again** *or* **anew;** *the pronunciation of the main part of each word is not changed.*

re·clothe′  re·con′quer  re′con′quest  re′con′se·crate′  re′con·se·cra′tion
re′com·mence′

information for military purposes. **2** approach a place and make a first survey of it: *It seemed wise to reconnoitre before entering the town.* *v.*, **rec·on·noi·tred**, **rec·on·noi·tring**. Also, **reconnoiter**.

**re·con·sid·er** (rē′kən sid′ər) consider again with a view to changing or reversing a position or decision: *The assembly voted to reconsider the bill. They have said they won't go, but we're hoping they will reconsider.* *v.* —**re′con·sid′er·a′tion**, *n.*

**re·con·sti·tute** (rē kon′stə tyüt′ *or* rē kon′stə tüt′) constitute anew; especially, restore a condensed or dehydrated substance to its original liquid state by adding water: *reconstituted orange juice.* *v.*, **re·con·sti·tut·ed**, **re·con·sti·tut·ing**.

**re·con·struct** (rē′kən strukt′) **1** construct again; rebuild; make over. **2** go back over and organize all the information or evidence on an event to try to discover exactly what happened: *When the police reconstructed the crime, they realized who the murderer must be.* *v.*

**re·con·struc·tion** (rē′kən struk′shən) **1** the act of RECONSTRUCTing. **2** the thing RECONSTRUCTed. *n.*

**re·cord** (ri kôrd′ *for verb,* rek′ərd *for noun*) **1** set down in writing so as to keep for future use: *Listen to the speaker and record what she says.* **2** put in some permanent form; keep for remembrance: *History is recorded in books.* **3** the thing written or kept. **4** an official written account. *The secretary kept a record of what was done at the meeting.* **5** a thin, flat disc with narrow spiral grooves on its surface that reproduces sounds when played on a record player. **6** put on a phonograph disc, on magnetic tape, or on compact disc. **7** tell; indicate: *The thermometer records temperatures.* **8** the known facts about what a person, animal, ship, etc. has done: *She has a fine record at school.* **9** a criminal record. **10** a remarkable performance or event, going beyond others of the same kind, especially the best achievement in a sport: *to hold the record for the high jump.* **11** unequalled; greater, higher, better, etc. than ever before: *a record wheat crop.* **12** a recording or being recorded: *What happened is a matter of record.* **13** a set of information fields treated as a unit in a database. 1, 2, 6, 7 *v.*, 3–5, 8–13 *n.*
**break a record,** improve on a record previously set in some athletic event, etc.
**go on record,** state publicly.
**off the record,** not to be recorded or quoted: *The prime minister was speaking off the record.*
**on record,** written down, printed, or otherwise made available: *The facts of the murder are now on record.*
☛ *Etym.* Through OF *record* 'remembrance' and *recorder* 'remember' from L *recordare* 'have in mind, bring back to mind', made up of *re-* 'back' + *cor, cordis* 'heart, mind'. The original English meaning of the verb was 'learn by heart'.

**record club** a business organization that regularly supplies selected records to its subscribers.

A recorder

**re·cord·er** (ri kôr′dər) **1** a person whose business is to

# reconsider 987 recreancy

hat, āge, fär; let, ēqual, tėrm; it, īce
hot, ōpen, ôrder; oil, out; cup, pùt, rüle
əbove, takən, pencəl, lemən, circəs
ch, child; ng, long; sh, ship
th, thin; ᴛH, then; zh, measure

make and keep records. **2** a machine that records: *The recorder of a cash register adds up and prints the amount of sales made.* **3** TAPE-RECORDER. **4** a title given to certain judges in some cities. **5** a wooden or plastic musical instrument having a tone similar to that of a flute. *n.*

**re·cord·ing** (ri kôr′ding) **1** a sound record made on a disc or tape: *I bought their new recording yesterday.* **2** the original transcription of any sound or combination of sounds: *to make a recording of birdsong.* **3** ppr. of RECORD. 1, 2 *n.*, 3 *v.*

**record player** an instrument that plays back sounds that have been recorded on discs; phonograph.

**re·count¹** (ri kount′) tell in detail; give an account of: *He recounted all the happenings of the day.* *v.*

**re·count²** (rē′kount′) a second count, as of votes: *The vote was so close that we asked for a recount.* *n.*

**re–count** (rē′kount′) count again: *We re-counted the ballots to make sure the result was accurate.* *v.*

**re·coup** (ri küp′) **1** make up for: *He recouped his losses.* **2** repay: *I will recoup you for any money you spend.* *v.*

**re·course** (rē′kôrs *or* ri kôrs′) **1** an appealing; turning to somebody or something for help or protection: *Our recourse in illness is to a doctor.* **2** a person or thing appealed to or turned to for help or protection: *A child's great recourse in trouble is its mother.* *n.*
**have recourse to,** appeal to; turn to for help: *When we do not know what a word means, we have recourse to a dictionary.*

**re·cov·er** (ri kuv′ər) **1** get back something lost, taken away, or stolen: *to recover one's temper or health, to recover a lost purse.* **2** make up for something lost or damaged: *to recover lost time.* **3** bring back to life, health, one's senses, or normal condition. **4** get well; get back to a normal condition. **5** get back to the proper position or condition: *He started to fall but recovered himself.* **6** obtain by judgment in a law court. **7** obtain judgment in one's favour in a law court. **8** rescue; deliver. **9** regain in usable form; reclaim. *v.* —**re·cov′er·er**, *n.*

**re–cov·er** (rē′kuv′ər) cover again or anew: *We re-covered our chesterfield in navy-blue corduroy.* *v.*

**re·cov·er·y** (ri kuv′ə rē) **1** a recovering. **2** a coming back to health or normal condition. **3** the getting back of something that was lost, taken away, or stolen. **4** a getting back to a proper position or condition: *He started to fall, but made a quick recovery.* **5** the act of locating and repossessing a missile, nose cone, etc. after a flight in space. *n.*, *pl.* **re·cov·er·ies**.

**rec·re·an·cy** (rek′rē ən sē) **1** cowardice. **2** unfaithfulness or treason. *n.*

---

*In each of the words below,* **re-** *means* again *or* anew; *the pronunciation of the main part of each word is not changed.*

re′con·vene′         re′cook′         re′cop′y

**rec·re·ant** (rek′rē ənt) 1 cowardly. 2 coward. 3 disloyal or traitorous. 4 traitor. 1, 3 *adj.*, 2, 4 *n.*

**rec·re·ate** (rek′rē āt′) 1 refresh with games, pastimes, exercises, etc. 2 take RECREATION. *v.*, **rec·re·at·ed, rec·re·at·ing.**

**re–cre·ate** (rē′krē āt′) create anew. *v.*, **re-cre·at·ed, re-cre·at·ing.**

**rec·re·a·tion** (rek′rē ā′shən) 1 a refreshing of the body and spirit after working, through play or amusement. 2 a form of play or amusement that serves as recreation: *Her favourite recreation is tennis.* *n.*

**rec·re·a·tion·al** (rek′rē ā′shə nəl) of or having to do with RECREATION. *adj.*

**recreation room** 1 in a hotel, apartment building, community centre, etc., a room for recreation such as playing games, lounging, dancing, and other informal activities. 2 in a private home, a family room; REC ROOM.

**rec·re·a·tive** (rek′rē ā′tiv) refreshing; restoring. *adj.*

**re·crim·i·nate** (ri krim′ə nāt′) accuse someone in return: *Rose said Harry had lied, and Harry recriminated by saying Rose had lied too.* *v.*, **re·crim·in·at·ed, re·crim·i·nat·ing.**

**re·crim·i·na·tion** (ri krim′ə nā′shən) an accusing in return; counter accusation: *The quarrelling children indulged in many recriminations.* *n.*

**re·crim·i·na·to·ry** (ri krim′ə nə tô′rē) of or involving RECRIMINATION: *recriminatory statements.* *adj.*

**rec room** (rek) *Informal.* a room in a house, often in the basement, used for recreation and relaxation; a family room.

**re·cru·des·cence** (rē′krü des′əns) breaking out afresh after a period of being inactive or dormant; renewed activity: *a sudden recrudescence of a disease epidemic.* *n.*

**re·cruit** (ri krüt′) 1 a newly enlisted member of the armed forces. 2 get people to join one of the armed forces. 3 strengthen or supply an army, navy, etc. with new men and women. 4 a new member of any group or class. 5 get new members: *to recruit volunteers, to recruit teachers.* 6 increase or maintain the number of. 7 renew health, strength, or spirits. 8 renew; get a sufficient number or amount of; replenish. 1, 4 *n.*, 2, 3, 5–8 *v.* —**re·cruit′er,** *n.* —**re·cruit′ment,** *n.*

**rec·tal** (rek′təl) of or having to do with the RECTUM. *adj.*

**rec·tan·gle** (rek′tang′gəl) 1 a four-sided plane figure with four right angles; a right-angle parallelogram: *Squares and oblongs are rectangles.* See QUADRILATERAL for picture. 2 a rectangle that is not square; oblong. *n.*

**rec·tan·gu·lar** (rek tang′gyə lər) shaped like a RECTANGLE. *adj.* —**rec·tan′gu·lar·ly,** *adv.*

**rec·ti·fi·ca·tion** (rek′tə fə kā′shən) the act or process of making right. *n.*

**rec·ti·fi·er** (rek′tə fī′ər) 1 a person or thing that makes right, corrects, adjusts, etc. 2 a device for changing alternating current into direct current. *n.*

**rec·ti·fy** (rek′tə fī′) 1 make right; put right; adjust; remedy: *The storekeeper was willing to rectify his error.* 2 in electricity, change an alternating current into a direct current. 3 purify; refine: *to rectify a liquor by distilling it several times.* *v.*, **rec·ti·fied, rec·ti·fy·ing.**

**rec·ti·lin·e·ar** (rek′tə lin′ē ər) 1 in, moving in, or forming a straight line. 2 bounded or formed by straight lines. 3 characterized by straight lines. *adj.*

**rec·ti·tude** (rek′tə tyüd′ or rek′tə tüd′) upright conduct or character; honesty; righteousness. *n.*

**rec·tor** (rek′tər) in some schools, colleges, or universities, the head or principal. *n.*

**rec·tum** (rek′təm) the lowest part of the large intestine. See ALIMENTARY CANAL for picture. *n.*

**re·cum·ben·cy** (ri kum′bən sē) a RECUMBENT position or condition. *n.*

**re·cum·bent** (ri kum′bənt) lying down, reclining, or leaning. *adj.*

**re·cu·per·ate** (ri kü′pə rāt′ or ri kyü′pə rāt′) 1 get back to a former state or condition, especially, recover from sickness or exhaustion: *She is at home, recuperating from surgery.* 2 get back; regain: *to recuperate one's health. He worked hard to recuperate his losses after the fire.* *v.*, **re·cu·per·at·ed, re·cu·per·at·ing.**

**re·cu·per·a·tion** (ri kü′pə rā′shən or ri kyü′pə rā′shən) a recovery from sickness, exhaustion, loss, etc. *n.*

**re·cu·per·a·tive** (ri kü′pə rə tiv or ri kü′pə rā′tiv, ri kyü′pə rə tiv or ri kyü′pə rā′tiv) 1 of or having to do with RECUPERATION: *She has remarkable recuperative powers.* 2 aiding RECUPERATION; helping to restore health, strength, etc. *adj.*

**re·cur** (ri kėr′) 1 come up again; occur again; be repeated: *Dawn recurs daily.* 2 return in thought or speech: *Old memories recurred to him. She recurred to the matter of cost.* *v.*, **re·curred, re·cur·ring.**

**re·cur·rence** (ri kėr′əns) an occurring again; repetition; return: *More care in the future will prevent recurrence of the mistake.* *n.*

**re·cur·rent** (ri kėr′ənt) 1 recurring; occurring again and again; repeated: *recurrent attacks of hay fever.* 2 in anatomy, turned back so as to run in the opposite direction: *a recurrent nerve.* *adj.* —**re·cur′rent·ly,** *adv.*

**re·cy·cle** (rē sī′kəl) reprocess waste material so that it can be used again: *Old cars can be recycled and the steel used again.* *v.*, **re·cy·cled, re·cy·cling.**

**re·cyc·ling** (rē sī′kling) the reprocessing of waste material so that it can be used again. *n.*

**red** (red) 1 the colour of blood; the colour of the spectrum having the longest light waves. 2 any shade of that colour. 3 of or having the colour of blood; being like it; suggesting it: *red ink, red hair, a red fox.* 4 a red pigment or dye. 5 red cloth or clothing. 6 a red or

---

*In each of the words below,* **re-** *means* again *or* anew; *the pronunciation of the main part of each word is not changed.*

**re·cross′**   **re·crys′tal·lize′**   **re·cut′**

reddish person, animal, or thing. **7** sore; inflamed: *red eyes.* **8** blushing. **9** radical; revolutionary. 1, 2, 4–6 *n.*, 3, 7, 8, 9 *adj.*, **red·der, red·dest.**
**in the red,** operating at a loss; in debt: *We'll be in the red soon if we don't cut down our expenses.*
**see red,** *Informal.* become very angry: *She sees red as soon as you mention the new by-law.*
☛ *Hom.* READ².

**red alert** the final stage of alert, when an attack by an enemy is expected at any moment.

**red·bird** (red'bėrd') **1** a CARDINAL bird. **2** a SCARLET TANAGER. **3** a European BULLFINCH. *n.*

**red blood cell** one of the cells found in the blood of vertebrates that carry oxygen to the tissues of the body: *Red blood cells contain hemoglobin and give blood its red colour.*

**red–blood·ed** (red'blud'id) full of life and spirit; vigorous; lusty. *adj.*

**red·breast** (red'brest') ROBIN. *n.*

**red·bud** (red'bud') a tree that has many small, pink, budlike flowers early in the spring. *n.*

**red·cap** (red'kap') a porter at a railway station, bus station, etc., usually wearing a red cap as part of the uniform. *n.*

**red carpet** a carpet, traditionally red, laid out at formal receptions for royalty or other important persons.
**roll out the red carpet,** welcome royally and treat with special consideration.

**red–car·pet** (red'kär'pət) *Informal.* showing special courtesy: *They got the red-carpet treatment.* *adj.*

**red cedar** **1** the WESTERN RED CEDAR, a species of arborvitae. **2** either of two species of JUNIPER found in Canada, the ROCKY MOUNTAIN JUNIPER or the RED JUNIPER.

**Red Chamber** *Cdn.* a name sometimes given to the Canadian Senate because of the colour of the rugs, draperies, etc. of the room in which the Senate meets.

**red clover** a variety of clover that has ball-shaped heads of reddish-purple flowers, cultivated as food for horses, cattle, etc.

**red·coat** (red'kōt') **1** in former times, a British soldier. **2** *Informal. Cdn.* a member of the RCMP. *n.*

**red corpuscle** RED BLOOD CELL.

**Red Cross** **1** a group of societies in over 100 countries, that work to relieve human suffering in time of war or peace. Each national society has its own program, but international co-operation takes place through the League of Red Cross Societies. The badge of most societies is a red cross on a white background, but societies in Muslim countries have a red crescent, and are called Red Crescent societies. **2** a national society that is a branch of this organization: *the Canadian Red Cross.* **3 red cross,** a red Greek cross on a white ground, the emblem of the Red Cross. It is the Swiss flag with the colours reversed, because the Red Cross was founded in Geneva.

**red deer** **1** a deer of Europe, Asia, and northern Africa, about 120–135 cm tall at the shoulder, having a smooth, reddish coat, a buff-coloured patch on the rump, and a mane of dark, shaggy hair around the neck and shoulders. **2** the white-tailed deer of North America, especially in its reddish summer coat.
☛ *Usage.* The name **red deer** was also used by English explorers to Western Canada for the North American elk, or wapiti, which many authorities consider to belong to the same species as the European red deer.

**red·den** (red'ən) **1** make or become red: *The sky was just beginning to redden when we left home.* **2** blush: *She reddened with embarrassment.* *v.*

**red·dish** (red'ish) somewhat red. *adj.*

**re·deem** (ri dēm') **1** buy back: *The property on which the money was lent was redeemed when the loan was paid back.* **2** pay off: *We redeemed the mortgage.* **3** carry out; make good; fulfil: *Carl will have to redeem his promise.* **4** set free; rescue; save; liberate; deliver; release: *redeemed from bankruptcy.* **5** make up for; balance: *A good feature will sometimes redeem several bad ones.* *v.*

**re·deem·a·ble** (ri dē'mə bəl) **1** capable of being redeemed. **2** that will be redeemed or paid: *bonds redeemable in 1998.* *adj.*

**re·deem·er** (ri dē'mər) a person who REDEEMS. *n.*

**re·demp·tion** (ri demp'shən) **1** an act of redeeming. **2** being redeemed. **3** a deliverance or rescue. **4** deliverance from sin; salvation. *n.*

**re·demp·tive** (ri demp'tiv) serving to REDEEM. *adj.*

**Red Ensign** **1** until 1965, the distinctive flag of Canada. **2** the ensign used by British merchant ships, a red flag with a Union Jack in the upper corner next to the staff.

**re·de·ploy** (rē'di ploi') change the position of troops from one theatre of war to another. *v.*
—**re'de·ploy'ment,** *n.*

**red fire** a chemical that burns with a red light, used in fireworks, signals, etc.

**red flag** **1** a symbol of rebellion, revolution, etc. **2** a sign of danger. **3** anything that stirs up anger.

**red fox** **1** the common reddish fox of Europe. **2** a related fox of North America. See FOX for picture. **3** the reddish fur of a fox.

**red giant** a star in an intermediate stage of development, characterized by large volume and reddish colouring. Compare with WHITE DWARF.

**red grouse** a reddish-brown northern grouse of the British Isles.

---

*In each of the words below,* **re-** *means* again *or* anew; *the pronunciation of the main part of each word is not changed.*

re'de·fine'      re'de·liv'er      re'de·liv'er·y      re'de·pos'it      re'de·vel'op

**red-hand·ed** (red′han′did) **1** having hands red with blood. **2** in the very act of crime: *a robber caught red-handed.* *adj.* —**red′-hand′ed·ly,** *adv.*

**red·head** (red′hed′) **1** a person having red hair. **2** a kind of duck resembling the canvasback but having a red head. *n.*

**red·head·ed** (red′hed′id) **1** having red hair. **2** having a red head. *adj.*

**red herring** **1** the common smoked herring. **2** something used to draw attention away from the real issue.

**red hot** *Informal.* HOT DOG.

**red-hot** (red′hot′) **1** red with heat; very hot: *red-hot iron.* **2** very enthusiastic; excited; violent: *a red-hot fanatic.* **3** fresh from the source: *red-hot rumours.* *adj.*

**re·di·rect** (rē′də rekt′ *or* rē′dī rekt′) **1** direct again or anew: *redirect a letter.* **2** give a new direction to: *redirect the activities of an organization.* *v.* —**re′di·rec′tion,** *n.*

**re·dis·count** (rē dis′kount) **1** discount again. **2** an act of rediscounting. **3** *Informal.* a cheque, note, or draft that has been rediscounted. **1** *v.*, **2, 3** *n.*

**re·dis·trib·ute** (rē′dis trib′yüt) change the distribution of. *v.*, **re·dis·trib·ut·ed, re·dis·trib·ut·ing.**

**re·dis·tri·bu·tion** (rē′dis trə byü′shən) **1** a distribution made again or anew. **2** the revision, made every ten years, of the number of seats in the Canadian House of Commons to which each province is entitled on the basis of its population. *n.*

**red juniper** a small, pyramid-shaped evergreen tree, a species of JUNIPER found in southern Ontario and the eastern United States: *Red juniper wood was formerly much used for making pencils.*

**red lead** red oxide of lead, used in paint, and in making glass.

**red-let·ter** (red′let′ər) **1** marked by red letters. **2** memorable; especially happy: *The day we won the cup for hockey was a red-letter day.* *adj.*

**red light** *Informal.* any warning signal or instruction to stop, exercise caution, etc.

**red line** either of two red lines drawn across the ice at each end of a hockey rink as an extension of the goal line.

**red mullet** any of a group of reddish fishes valued as food.

**red·ness** (red′nis) the quality of being red; red colour. *n.*

**re·do** (rē dü′) do again; do over. *v.*

**red·o·lence** (red′ə ləns) the quality of being REDOLENT. *n.*

**red·o·lent** (red′ə lənt) **1** having a pleasant smell; fragrant. **2** smelling strongly; giving off an odour: *a house redolent of fresh paint.* **3** suggesting thoughts or feelings: *"Ivanhoe" is a name redolent of romance.* *adj.*

**red-o·sier dogwood** (red′ō′zhər) *Cdn.* a species of dogwood, a shrub found all across Canada, having bright-red twigs and branchlets, white flowers, and whitish fruit.

**re·dou·ble** (rē dub′əl) **1** double again. **2** increase greatly; double: *When he saw land ahead, the swimmer redoubled his speed.* **3** repeat; echo. **4** double back: *The fox redoubled on its trail to escape the hunters.* *v.*, **re·dou·bled, re·dou·bling.**

**re·doubt** (ri dout′) a small fort standing alone. *n.*

**re·doubt·a·ble** (ri dou′tə bəl) deserving to be feared or dreaded: *a redoubtable warrior, a redoubtable debater.* *adj.* —**re·doubt′a·bly,** *adv.*

**re·dound** (ri dound′) come back as a result; contribute: *The number of scholarships we gained redound to the honour of our school.* *v.*

**red pepper** **1** a seasoning having a very strong, burning taste, made from the dried, ground fruit of any of various varieties of CAPSICUM. **2** a CAPSICUM bearing pungent, red fruits used to make red pepper. **3** the fruit itself.

**red pine** a medium-tall pine found from the Atlantic coast to southeastern Manitoba, having long needles and egg-shaped cones without prickles: *The wood of the red pine is used especially for poles, piles, and railway ties.*

**red·poll** (red′pōl′) any of several kinds of small finches: *Male redpolls have crimson heads.* *n.*

**re·draft** (rē draft′ *for verb,* rē′draft′ *for noun*) **1** draft again or anew. **2** a second draft. **1** *v.*, **2** *n.*

**re·dress** (ri dres′ *for verb,* rē′dres *or* ri dres′ *for noun*) **1** set right; repair; remedy: *King Arthur tried to redress wrongs in his kingdom.* **2** a setting right; reparation; relief: *Any person who has been treated unfairly deserves redress.* **1** *v.*, **2** *n.*

**Red River cart** *Cdn.* a strong two-wheeled cart pulled by oxen or horses: *Red River carts were much used during pioneer days in the West.*

**Red River Rebellion** the uprising in 1869–70 of mainly Métis settlers in the Red River region against the takeover of their territory by the government of Canada from the Hudson's Bay Company. The Métis' main objection was that it was done without consultation with the Red River settlers or assurance that their rights and way of life would be protected.

**Red River Settlement** the colony that was founded on the Red River by Lord Selkirk in 1812: *The Red River Settlement was made up of Scottish and Irish settlers.*

**red salmon** *Cdn.* SOCKEYE.

**red shift** in astronomy, a movement of light from distant galaxies to the red end of the spectrum, which has longer wavelengths.

**red spruce** **1** a medium-sized spruce tree found mainly in the Maritimes and southern Quebec, having narrow, egg-shaped cones and shiny, yellowish-green, often curved needles. **2** the soft, light wood of this tree.

**red squirrel** the common North American squirrel, having reddish fur.

**red·start** (red′stärt′) **1** a flycatching warbler of North

---

*In each of the words below,* **re-** *means* again *or* anew; *the pronunciation of the main part of each word is not changed.*

re′di·gest′      re′di·ges′tion      re′dis·cov′er      re′dis·till′      re·draw′

America. **2** a small European bird with a reddish tail. *n.*

**red tape** strict attention to form and detail, especially in government business, causing delay and irritation.
☛ *Etym.* So called because official documents used to be tied with red tape.

**red tide** *Cdn.* **1** an area of sea water having a reddish colouration due to the presence of large numbers of micro-organisms that are constituents of plankton and that in large numbers are poisonous to many forms of marine life. **2** a population of such micro-organisms.

**re·duce** (ri dyüs′ *or* ri düs′) **1** make less; make smaller; decrease: *to reduce expenses, to reduce one's weight.* **2** bring down; lower: *Misfortune reduced that poor woman to begging.* **3** bring to a certain state, form, or condition; change: *The teacher soon reduced the noisy class to order. I was reduced to tears by the cruel words.* **4** change to another form: *to reduce a statement to writing.* **5** conquer; subdue: *The army reduced the fort by a sudden attack.* **6** restore to its proper place or normal condition: *A doctor can reduce a fracture or dislocation.* **7** combine with hydrogen. **8** remove oxygen from. **9** change a compound so that the VALENCE of the positive element is lower. *v.*, **re·duced, re·duc·ing.**

**re·duc·i·ble** (ri dyü′sə bəl *or* ri dü′sə bəl) that can be REDUCED: $4/8$ *is reducible to* $1/2$. *adj.*

**reducing agent** any chemical substance that reduces or removes the oxygen in a compound.

**re·duc·ti·o ad ab·sur·dum** (ri duk′tē ō *or* ri duk′shē ō ad′ab sėr′dəm) *Latin.* a reduction to absurdity; a method of proving something false by showing that conclusions to which it leads are absurd.

**re·duc·tion** (ri duk′shən) **1** a reducing or being REDUCED. **2** the amount by which a thing is REDUCED. **3** a form of something produced by reducing; a copy of something on a smaller scale. *n.*

**re·dun·dance** (ri dun′dəns) REDUNDANCY. *n.*

**re·dun·dan·cy** (ri dun′dən sē) **1** more than is needed. **2** a REDUNDANT thing, part, or amount. **3** the use of too many words for the same idea. *n., pl.* **re·dun·dan·cies.**

**re·dun·dant** (ri dun′dənt) **1** extra; not needed. **2** that says the same thing again; using too many words for the same idea; wordy: *"We two both had an apple each" is a redundant sentence. adj.* —**re·dun′dant·ly,** *adv.*

**re·du·pli·cate** (ri dyü′plə kāt′ *or* ri dü′plə kāt′ *for verb,* ri dyü′plə kit *or* ri dü′plə kit *for adjective*) **1** double; repeat. **2** doubled or repeated. **1** *v.,* **2** *adj.*

**re·du·pli·ca·tion** (ri dyü′plə kā′shən *or* ri dü′plə kā′shen) **1** reduplicating or being reduplicated; doubling; repetition. **2** something resulting from repeating; a duplicate; copy: *To the prisoner, each day seemed a reduplication of the preceding day. n.*

**re·du·pli·ca·tive** (ri dyü′plə kə tiv *or* ri dyü′plə kā′tiv, ri dü′plə kə tiv *or* ri dü′plə kā′tiv) tending to reduplicate; having to do with or marked by REDUPLICATION. *adj.*

**red·wing** (red′wing′) **1** a North American blackbird, the male of which has a scarlet patch on each wing:

**red tape**      **991**      **reel**

hat, āge, fär; let, ēqual, tėrm; it, īce
hot, ōpen, ôrder; oil, out; cup, pùt, rüle
əbove, takən, pencəl, lemən, circəs
ch, child; ng, long; sh, ship
th, thin; ŦH, then; zh, measure

*Redwings live in marshy places.* **2** a European thrush that has reddish colour on the under side of the wings. *n.*

**red–winged blackbird** REDWING (def. 1).

**red·wood** (red′wùd′) **1** an evergreen tree that sometimes grows to a height of 90 metres. **2** its brownish-red wood. *n.*

**reed** (rēd) **1** a kind of tall grass that grows in wet places and has a hollow, jointed stalk. **2** such stalks. **3** a thing made from the stalk of a reed or anything like it. **4** a thin piece of wood, metal, or plastic in a musical instrument that produces sound when a current of air moves it. **5** producing tones by means of reeds: *a reed organ.* 1–4 *n.,* 5 *adj.*
☛ *Hom.* READ¹.

**reed·bird** (rēd′bėrd′) BOBOLINK. *n.*

**reed instrument** a musical instrument that produces sound by means of a vibrating reed or reeds: *Oboes, clarinets, and saxophones are reed instruments.*

**reed organ** a musical instrument producing tones by means of small metal reeds: *Two common forms of reed organ are the harmonium, in which the air is forced outward through the reeds, and the American organ, in which the air is sucked inward.*

**reed·y** (rē′dē) **1** full of reeds. **2** made of a reed or reeds. **3** like a reed or reeds. **4** sounding like a REED INSTRUMENT: *a thin, reedy voice. adj.,* **reed·i·er, reed·i·est.**

**reef¹** (rēf) **1** a narrow ridge of rocks or sand at or near the surface of the water: *The ship was wrecked on a hidden reef.* **2** a vein or lode in mining. *n.*

**reef²** (rēf) **1** the part of a sail that can be rolled or folded up to reduce its size. **2** reduce the size of a sail by rolling or folding up a part of it. **3** reduce the length of a topmast, bow-sprit, etc. by lowering, etc. 1 *n.,* 2, 3 *v.*

**reef·er** (rē′fər) **1** a person who REEFS². **2** a short coat of thick cloth, worn especially by sailors and fishermen. *n.*

**reef knot** a SQUARE KNOT. See KNOT for picture.

**reek** (rēk) **1** a strong, unpleasant smell; vapour: *We noticed the reek of rotting vegetables as we entered the cottage.* **2** send out vapour or a strong, unpleasant smell: *She reeked of cheap perfume.* **3** be wet with sweat or blood. 1 *n.,* 2, 3 *v.*
☛ *Hom.* WREAK.

**reel¹** (rēl) **1** a frame turning on an axis, for winding thread, a fishing line, rope, wire, etc. **2** a spool; roller. **3** something wound on a reel: *two reels of motion-picture film.* **4** wind on a reel. **5** draw with a reel or by winding: *to reel in a fish.* 1–3 *n.,* 4, 5 *v.*
**off the reel,** *Informal.* quickly and easily.

---

*In each of the words below,* **re-** *means* again *or* anew; *the pronunciation of the main part of each word is not changed.*

re·dye′      re·ed′it      re·ed′u·cate′      re·ed′u·ca′tion

**reel off,** say, write, or make in a quick, easy way: *My grandfather can reel off stories by the hour.*
☞ Hom. REAL (rēl).

**reel²** (rēl) **1** sway, swing, or rock under a blow, shock, etc. **2** sway in standing or walking. **3** be in a whirl; be dizzy. **4** a reeling or staggering movement. **5** go with swaying or staggering movements: *The drunkard reeled down the street.* **6** sway; stagger; waver: *Our regiment reeled when the cavalry attacked.* 1–3, 5, 6 *v.,* 4 *n.*
☞ Hom. REAL (rēl).

**reel³** (rēl) **1** a lively dance: *the Highland reel, the Virginia reel.* **2** the music for a reel. *n.*
☞ Hom. REAL (rēl).

**re–e·lect** (rē′i lekt′) elect again. *v.*
—**re′-e·lec′tion,** *n.*

**re–en·force** (rē′en fôrs′) See REINFORCE. *v.,* **re–en·forced, re–en·forc·ing.**

**re–en·force·ment** (rē′en fôr′smənt) See REINFORCEMENT. *n.*

**re–en·ter** (rē en′tər) enter again; go in again. *v.*

**re–en·try** (rē en′trē) an entering again or returning, especially of a rocket or spacecraft into the earth's atmosphere after flight in outer space. *n., pl.* **re·en·tries.**

**reeve** (rēv) **1** *Cdn.* in Ontario and in some parts of the western provinces, the elected head of a rural municipal council; in Ontario, also the head of a village or township council. **2** formerly, a bailiff; steward; overseer. *n.*

**ref.** **1** referee. **2** reference. **3** referred.

**re·fec·tion** (ri fek′shən) **1** refreshment by food or drink. **2** a meal; repast. *n.*

**re·fec·to·ry** (ri fek′tə rē) a room for meals, especially in a monastery, convent, or school. *n., pl.* **re·fec·to·ries.**

**re·fer** (ri fėr′) **1** direct attention to or speak about: *May I refer to the minutes of the last meeting?* **2** relate; apply: *The rule refers only to special cases.* **3** send or direct for information, help, or action: *We referred him to the boss.* **4** turn for information or help: *Writers often refer to a dictionary.* **5** hand over; submit: *Let's refer the dispute to the umpire.* **6** consider as belonging or due; assign: *Many people refer their failures to bad luck instead of to poor work.* *v.,* **re·ferred, re·fer·ring.**

**ref·er·ee** (ref′ə rē′) **1** a judge of play in certain games and sports, including hockey, football, and boxing. **2** a person to whom something is referred for decision or settlement. **3** act as referee; act as referee in. 1, 2 *n.,* 3 *v.,* **ref·er·eed, ref·er·ee·ing.**

**ref·er·ence** (ref′ə rəns) **1** referring or being referred. **2** a directing of the attention: *This history contains many references to larger histories.* **3** a statement, book, etc. to which the attention is directed: *You will find that reference on page 16.* **4** something used for information or help: *A dictionary is a book of reference.* **5** used for information or help: *a reference library.* **6** a person who can give information about another person's character or ability: *Janie gave her principal as a reference.* **7** a statement about someone's character or ability: *The boy had excellent references from men for whom he had worked.* **8** relation; respect; regard: *This test is to be taken by all pupils without reference to age or grade.* 1–4, 6–8 *n.,* 5 *adj.*
**in** or **with reference to,** about; concerning.
**make reference to,** mention.

**ref·er·en·dum** (ref′ə ren′dəm) **1** the process of submitting a law already passed by the lawmaking body to a direct vote of the citizens for approval or rejection: *British Columbia and Alberta have provision for a referendum.* **2** the submitting of any matter to a direct vote. *n., pl.* **ref·er·en·dums** or **ref·er·en·da** (-də).

**re·fill** (rē fil′ *for verb,* rē′fil′ *for noun*) **1** fill again. **2** something to refill a thing. 1 *v.,* 2 *n.*
—**re·fill′a·ble,** *adj.*

**re·fine** (ri fīn′) **1** make free from impurities: *Sugar, oil, and metals are refined before being used.* **2** make or become fine, polished, or cultivated: *Reading good books helped to refine her speech.* **3** change or remove by polishing, purifying, etc. **4** make very fine, subtle, or exact. *v.,* **re·fined, re·fin·ing.**
**refine on** or **upon,** **a** improve. **b** excel.

**re·fined** (ri fīnd′) **1** freed from impurities: *refined sugar.* **2** freed or free from grossness, coarseness, crudeness, vulgarity, or the like: *refined tastes.* **3** having or showing nice feeling, taste, manners, etc.; polished; cultivated: *a refined voice, refined manners.* **4** fine; subtle: *refined distinctions.* **5** minutely precise: *refined measurements.* **6** pt. and pp. of REFINE. 1–5 *adj.,* 6 *v.*

**re·fine·ment** (ri fīn′mənt) **1** fineness of feeling, taste, manners, or language: *Good manners and correct speech are marks of refinement.* **2** the act or result of refining: *Gasoline is produced by the refinement of petroleum.* **3** improvement. **4** a fine point; subtle distinction. **5** an improved, higher, or extreme form of something. *n.*

**re·fin·er·y** (ri fī′nə rē) a building and machinery for purifying metal, sugar, petroleum, or other crude materials. *n., pl.* **re·fin·er·ies.**

**re·fit** (rē fit′ *for verb,* rē′fit *for noun*) **1** fit, prepare, or equip for use again: *to refit an old ship.* **2** get fresh supplies. **3** a fitting, preparing, or equipping for use again: *The ship went to the dry dock for a refit.* 1, 2 *v.,* **re·fit·ted, re·fit·ting;** 3 *n.*

**re·flect** (ri flekt′) **1** turn back or throw back light, heat, sound, etc.: *The sidewalks reflect heat on a hot day.* **2** give back an image; give back a likeness or image of: *A mirror reflects your face and body.* **3** reproduce or show like a mirror: *The newspaper reflected the owner's opinions.* **4** think; think carefully: *Take time to reflect before doing important things.* **5** cast blame, reproach, or discredit: *Bad behaviour reflects on home training.* **6** serve to cast or bring: *A brave act reflects credit on the person who performs it.* *v.*

---

*In each of the words below,* **re-** *means* again *or* anew; *the pronunciation of the main part of each word is not changed.*

| | | | | |
|---|---|---|---|---|
| re′em·bark′ | re′em·pha·size′ | re′e·quip′ | re′ex·ca·va′tion | re·fas′ten |
| re′e·merge′ | re′em·ploy′ | re′e·val′u·ate′ | re′ex·change′ | re·film′ |
| re′e·mer′gence | re′en·act′ | re′e·val′u·a′tion | re′ex·port′ | re·fil′ter |
| re·em′i·grate′ | re′en·act′ment | re′e·vap′o·rate′ | re′ex·por·ta′tion | re·fi′nance |
| re′em·pha·sis′ | re′en·gage′ | re′ex·ca·vate′ | re·fash′ion | |

**reflecting telescope** a type of optical telescope in which the light rays entering it are brought to a focus by means of a concave mirror. Compare with REFRACTING TELESCOPE.

A reflection of a tree in water

**re·flec·tion** (ri flek′shən) 1 reflecting or being reflected. 2 something reflected. 3 a likeness; image: *You can see your reflection in a mirror.* 4 thinking; careful thinking: *On reflection, the plan seemed too dangerous.* 5 an idea or remark resulting from careful thinking; idea; remark. 6 a remark, action, etc. that casts blame or discredit. *n.*

**re·flec·tive** (ri flek′tiv) 1 REFLECTING: *the reflective surface of polished metal.* 2 thoughtful: *a reflective look.* *adj.*

**re·flec·tor** (ri flek′tər) any thing, surface, or device that reflects light, heat, sound, etc.; especially, a piece of glass or metal, usually concave, for reflecting light in a required direction. *n.*

**re·flex** (rē′fleks *for noun and adjective,* ri fleks′ *for verb*) 1 not voluntary; not controlled by the will; coming as a direct response to a stimulation of some sensory nerve cells: *Sneezing is a reflex act.* 2 an automatic action in direct response to a stimulation of certain nerve cells: *Sneezing and shivering are reflexes.* 3 something reflected; image; reflection: *A law should be a reflex of the will of the people.* 4 bend back; turn back. 5 bent or turned back. 1, 5 *adj.,* 2, 3 *n.,* 4 *v.*

**re·flex·ive** (ri flek′siv) in grammar: a REFLEXIVE VERB or PRONOUN. *Example: In* The boy hurt himself, hurt *and* himself *are reflexives.* *n.* —**re·flex′ive·ly,** *adv.*

**reflexive pronoun** a pronoun that is the direct object of a REFLEXIVE VERB.

**reflexive verb** a verb, the subject and direct object of which refer to the same person or thing: *He cut himself. The cat washed itself.*

**ref·lu·ent** (ref′lü ənt) flowing back; ebbing. *adj.*

**re·flux** (rē′fluks) flowing back; the ebb of a tide. *n.*

**re·for·est** (rē fô′rist) replant with trees. *v.*,

**re·for·es·ta·tion** (rē fô ri stā′shən) replanting or being replanted with trees. *n.*

**re·form** (ri fôrm′) 1 make better; improve by removing faults: *Prisons should try to reform criminals instead of just punishing them.* 2 correct one's own faults; improve one's behaviour: *The girl promised to reform if given another chance.* 3 an improvement, especially one made by removing faults or abuses; a change to improve conditions: *The new government put through many reforms.* 1, 2 *v.,* 3 *n.* —**re·form′a·ble,** *adj.*

**re–form** (rē fôrm′) 1 form again. 2 take a new shape. *v.*

**ref·or·ma·tion** (ref′ər mā′shən) 1 a reforming or being reformed; change for the better; improvement. 2 **Reformation,** the 16th-century religious movement in Europe that began with the aim of reforms in the Roman Catholic Church and ended with the establishment of the Protestant church. *n.*

**re·form·a·tive** (ri fôr′mə tiv) tending toward or inducing REFORM. *adj.*

**re·form·a·to·ry** (ri fôr′mə tô′rē) 1 serving to REFORM; intended to reform. 2 an institution for REFORMing young offenders against the laws; prison for juveniles. 1 *adj.,* 2 *n., pl.* **re·form·a·to·ries.**

**re·form·er** (ri fôr′mər) a person who REFORMS, or tries to reform, some state of affairs, custom, etc.; supporter of reforms. *n.*

**Reform Party** 1 in the 19th century, the party that opposed Tory rule in Upper Canada and the Maritimes: *Joseph Howe was a prominent leader of the Reform Party.* 2 in western Canada, a modern political party to promote the interests of the West.

**re·fract** (ri frakt′) bend a ray from a straight source: *Water refracts light.* *v.*

**refracting telescope** a type of optical telescope having one lens that bends light rays to a focus and a second lens that acts as an eyepiece. Compare with REFLECTING TELESCOPE.

The refraction of light rays entering the water makes the straw appear to be broken at the water line.

**re·frac·tion** (ri frak′shən) the turning or bending of a ray of light, sound waves, a stream of electrons, etc., when passing obliquely from one medium into another of different density. See ANGLE OF REFRACTION for picture. *n.*

**re·frac·tive** (ri frak′tiv) 1 having power to REFRACT. 2 having to do with or caused by REFRACTION. *adj.*

**re·frac·tor** (ri frak′tər) 1 anything that REFRACTS. 2 a REFRACTING TELESCOPE. *n.*

**re·frac·to·ry** (ri frak′tə rē) 1 hard to manage; stubborn; obstinate: *Mules are refractory.* 2 not yielding readily to treatment: *She had a refractory cough.* 3 hard

---

*In each of the words below,* **re-** *means* again *or* anew; *the pronunciation of the main part of each word is not changed.*

re·fo′cus      re·fold′      re·for′mu·late′      re·for′ti·fy′

to melt, reduce, or work: *Some ores are more refractory than others.* *adj.* —**re·frac′to·ri·ly**, *adv.* —**re·frac′to·ri·ness**, *n.*

**re·frain¹** (ri frān′) hold oneself back: *Refrain from crime.* *v.*

**re·frain²** (ri frān′) **1** a phrase or verse repeated regularly in a song or poem; chorus. **2** the music for a refrain. *n.*

**re·fran·gi·bil·i·ty** (ri fran′jə bil′ə tē) **1** the property of being REFRANGIBLE. **2** the amount of REFRACTION of light rays, etc. that is possible. *n.*

**re·fran·gi·ble** (ri fran′jə bəl) capable of being REFRACTed: *Rays of light are refrangible.* *adj.*

**re·fresh** (ri fresh′) make fresh again; renew: *He refreshed his memory by a glance at the book. She refreshed herself with a cup of tea.* *v.*

**re·fresh·er** (ri fresh′ər) **1** helping to renew knowledge or abilities, or to bring a person new needed knowledge. **2** a person or thing that refreshes. *1 adj., 2 n.*

**re·fresh·ing** (ri fresh′ing) **1** that refreshes. **2** welcome as a pleasing change. **3** ppr. of REFRESH. *1, 2 adj., 3 v.* —**re·fresh′ing·ly**, *adv.*

**re·fresh·ment** (ri fresh′mənt) **1** refreshing or being refreshed. **2** anything that refreshes. **3 refreshments,** *pl.* food or drink: *to serve refreshments at a party.* *n.*

**re·frig·er·ant** (ri frij′ə rənt) **1** refrigerating; cooling. **2** reducing bodily heat or fever. **3** something that cools, etc.: *Ice is a refrigerant.* *1, 2 adj., 3 n.*

**re·frig·er·ate** (ri frij′ə rāt′) make or keep cold or cool: *Milk and meat must be refrigerated to prevent spoiling.* *v.*, **re·frig·er·at·ed, re·frig·er·at·ing.**

**re·frig·er·a·tion** (ri frij′ə rā′shən) the act or process of cooling or keeping cold: *Refrigeration delays the spoiling of food.* *n.*

**re·frig·er·a·tor** (ri frij′ə rā′tər) an appliance, closet, or room equipped for keeping things, especially food and drink, cool. *n.*

**re·fu·el** (rē fyü′əl) **1** supply with fuel again. **2** take on a fresh supply of fuel. *v.*

**ref·uge** (ref′yüj) **1** a shelter or protection from danger, trouble, etc.; safety; security: *The cat took refuge in a tree.* **2** any person or thing giving safety, security, or comfort. *n.*

**ref·u·gee** (ref′yü jē′ *or* ref′yə jē′) a person who flees for refuge or safety, especially to a foreign country, in time of persecution, war, etc.: *Many refugees came from Europe to Canada.* *n.*

**re·ful·gence** (ri ful′jəns) radiance; brightness. *n.*

**re·ful·gent** (ri ful′jənt) shining brightly; radiant; splendid: *a refulgent sunrise.* *adj.*

**re·fund¹** (ri fund′ *for verb,* rē′fund *for noun*) **1** pay back: *If these shoes do not wear well, the shop will refund your money.* **2** the return of money paid. **3** the money paid back. *1 v., 2, 3 n.*

**re·fund²** (rē′fund′) change a debt, loan, etc. into a new form. *v.*

**re·fur·bish** (rē fėr′bish) polish up again; do up anew; brighten; renovate. *v.*

**re·fus·al** (ri fyü′zəl) **1** the act of refusing: *Her refusal to play provoked the others.* **2** the right to refuse or take a thing before it is offered to others: *Give me the refusal of the car till tomorrow. I had first refusal on the bicycle.* *n.*

**re·fuse¹** (ri fyüz′) **1** decline to accept; reject: *to refuse an offer.* **2** deny a request, demand, invitation; decline to give or grant: *to refuse admittance.* **3** decline to do something: *to refuse to discuss the question.* **4** decline to accept or consent: *She is free to refuse.* *v.*, **re·fused, re·fus·ing.**

**ref·use²** (ref′yüs) **1** useless stuff; waste; rubbish: *The street-cleaning department took away all refuse from the streets.* **2** rejected as worthless or of little value; discarded: *Some refuse material can be recycled.* *1 n., 2 adj.*

**ref·u·ta·ble** (ref′yə tə bəl *or* ri fyü′tə bəl) able to be REFUTED. *adj.*

**ref·u·ta·tion** (ref′yə tā′shən) disproof of a claim, opinion, or argument. *n.*

**re·fute** (ri fyüt′) prove a claim, opinion, or argument to be false or incorrect: *How would you refute the statement that the cow jumped over the moon?* *v.*, **re·fut·ed, re·fut·ing.** —**re·fut′er**, *n.*

**reg. 1** register. **2** registered. **3** regular. **4** regularly. **5** region.

**re·gain** (ri gān′) **1** get again; recover: *to regain health.* **2** get back to; reach again: *to regain the shore.* *v.*

**re·gal** (rē′gəl) **1** belonging to a king or queen; royal. **2** kinglike or queenlike; fit for a king or queen; stately; splendid; magnificent: *It was a regal banquet.* *adj.*

**re·gale** (ri gāl′) **1** entertain agreeably; delight with something pleasing: *The old sailor regaled the boys with sea stories.* **2** entertain with a choice repast; feast: *The children regaled themselves with ice cream and candy.* *v.*, **re·galed, re·gal·ing.**

**re·ga·li·a** (ri gā′lē ə *or* ri gā′lyə) **1** the emblems of royalty: *Crowns, sceptres, etc. are regalia.* **2** the emblems or decorations of any society, order, etc. *n. pl.*

**re·gal·i·ty** (rē gal′ə tē) **1** royalty; sovereignty; kingship. **2** a right or privilege having to do with a king or queen. **3** kingdom. *n., pl.* **re·gal·i·ties.**

**re·gard** (ri gärd′) **1** consider; think of: *He is regarded as the best doctor in town.* **2** show thought or consideration for; care for; respect: *She always regards her parents' wishes.* **3** heed: *None regarded her screams.* **4** consideration; thought; care: *Have regard for the feelings of others.* **5** look at; look closely at; watch: *He regarded me sternly.* **6** look closely. **7** a look; steady look: *His regard seemed fixed upon some distant object.* **8** esteem; favour; good opinion: *He has high regard for Fred's ability.* **9** a point; particular matter. **10 regards,** *pl.* good wishes; an expression of esteem. *1–3, 5, 6 v., 4, 7–10 n.* **as regards,** as for; concerning; relating to: *As regards money, I have enough.* **in** *or* **with regard to,** about; concerning; relating to. **without regard to,** not considering.

---

*In each of the words below,* **re-** *means* again *or* anew; *the pronunciation of the main part of each word is not changed.*

**re·freeze′**         **re·fur′nish**

**re·gard·ful** (ri gärd′fəl) **1** heedful; observant; mindful. **2** considerate; respectful. *adj.*

**re·gard·ing** (ri gär′ding) **1** with regard to; concerning; about: *a prophecy regarding the future.* **2** ppr. of REGARD. **1** *prep.*, **2** *v.*

**re·gard·less** (ri gär′dlis) **1** with no heed; careless: *Regardless of grammar, she said, "Me and him has went."* **2** in spite of what happens: *We plan to leave on Monday, and we will leave then, regardless.* **1** *adj.*, **2** *adv.* —**re·gard′less·ly,** *adv.* —**re·gard′less·ness,** *n.*
☛ *Usage.* The form *irregardless* is not logical since it literally means 'not regardless'. As a result, it is generally considered to be non-standard and should be avoided in both speech and writing.

**re·gat·ta** (ri gat′ə) **1** a boat race. **2** a series of boat races: *the annual regatta of the yacht club.* *n.*

**re·gen·cy** (rē′jən sē) **1** the position, office, or function of a REGENT or group of regents: *The Queen Mother held the regency till the young king came of age.* **2** a body of REGENTS. **3** a government consisting of REGENTS. **4** the time during which there is a regency. **5 Regency,** in the United Kingdom, the period from 1811 to 1820 during which George, Prince of Wales, acted as REGENT for King George III. *n., pl.* **re·gen·cies.**

**re·gen·er·a·cy** (ri jen′ə rə sē′) a REGENERATE state. *n.*

**re·gen·er·ate** (ri jen′ə rāt′ *for verb,* ri jen′ə rit *for adjective*) **1** give a new and better spiritual life to. **2** improve the moral condition of; put new life and spirit into. **3** reform. **4** grow again; form new tissue, a new part, etc. to replace what is lost: *If a young crab loses a claw, it can regenerate a new one.* **5** in electronics, amplify by transferring a portion of the power from the output back to the input. **6** born again spiritually. **7** made over in better form; formed anew morally. 1–5 *v.*, **re·gen·er·at·ed, re·gen·er·at·ing;** 6, 7 *adj.*

**re·gen·er·a·tion** (ri jen′ə rā′shən) regenerating or being REGENERATEd. *n.*

**re·gen·er·a·tive** (ri jen′ə rə tiv *or* ri jen′ə rā′tiv) regenerating; tending to REGENERATE. *adj.*

**re·gent** (rē′jənt) **1** a person who rules in the name of a sick or absent sovereign or a sovereign who is not yet grown up: *The regent ruled for seven years until the boy king came of age.* **2** a member of a governing board: *Many universities have regents.* **3** acting as a regent (*used after a noun*): *a queen regent.* 1, 2 *n.,* 3 *adj.*

**re·gent·ship** (rē′jənt ship′) the position of a REGENT. *n.*

**reg·gae** (reg′ā) a style of music that developed in Jamaica in the mid 1970's, that is a blend of rock rhythms and traditional West Indian folk song. *n.*

**reg·i·cide** (rej′ə sīd′) **1** the crime of killing a king or queen. **2** a person who kills a king or queen. *n.*

**re·gime** or **ré·gime** (ri zhēm′ *or* rā zhēm′) **1** a system of government or rule: *a dictatorial regime.* **2** a prevailing system: *Under the old regime women could not vote.* **3** a system of living; REGIMEN (def. 1): *Baby's regime includes two naps a day.* *n.*

**reg·i·men** (rej′ə mən) **1** a set of rules or habits of diet, exercise, or manner of living followed to improve health, reduce weight, etc. **2** the act of governing; government; rule. *n.*

**reg·i·ment** (rej′ə mənt *for noun,* rej′ə ment′ *for verb*) **1** a unit of an army, consisting of several companies of soldiers organized into one large group, usually commanded by a colonel: *A regiment is larger than a battalion and smaller than a brigade.* **2** a large number. **3** form into a regiment or organized group. **4** assign to a regiment or group. **5** treat in a strict or uniform manner: *A totalitarian state regiments its citizens.* 1, 2 *n.,* 3–5 *v.*

**reg·i·men·tal** (rej′ə men′təl) **1** of a REGIMENT; having to do with a regiment. **2 regimentals,** *pl.* military uniform. 1 *adj.,* 2 *n.* —**reg′i·men′tal·ly,** *adv.*

**reg·i·men·ta·tion** (rej′ə men tā′shən) **1** a formation into organized or uniform groups. **2** making uniform. **3** a subjection to control: *In time of war there may be regimentation of our work, play, food, and clothing.* *n.*

**re·gion** (rē′jən) **1** any large part of the earth's surface: *the region of the equator.* **2** a place; space; area: *an unhealthful region.* **3** a part of the body: *the region of the heart.* **4** a sphere; domain: *the region of art, the region of imagination.* **5** *Cdn.* in Ontario, a geographical division for purposes of government, having wider powers than those of a county: *Regions were established in 1973 in some parts of the province by combining counties and townships to provide for more effective planning.* *n.*

**re·gion·al** (rē′je nəl) of or in a particular REGION: *a regional storm.* *adj.* —**re′gion·al·ly,** *adv.*

**reg·is·ter** (rej′i stər) **1** a list; record: *A register of attendance is kept in our school.* **2** a book in which a list or record is kept: *a hotel register.* **3** write in a list or record: *to register the names of the new members.* **4** have one's name written in a list or record: *You must register if you want to attend the conference.* **5** anything that records: *A cash register shows the amount of money taken in.* **6** indicate; record: *The thermometer registers 25 degrees.* **7** a registration or registry. **8** REGISTRAR. **9** show surprise, joy, anger, etc. by the expression on one's face or by actions. **10** an opening in a wall or floor with an arrangement to regulate the amount of cooled or heated air that passes through. **11** the range of a voice or an instrument. **12** in printing, the exact fit or correspondence of lines, columns, colours, etc. **13** make lines, columns, colours, etc. fit or correspond exactly. **14** have a letter, parcel, etc. recorded in a post office, paying extra postage for special care in delivery. 1, 2, 5, 7, 8, 10–12 *n.,* 3, 4, 6, 9, 13, 14 *v.*

**registered mail** a postal service that provides proof that a letter or parcel has been sent and delivered and also guarantees compensation if the mail is not delivered: *Every article of registered mail is recorded at the post office where it is mailed and must be signed for by the receiver.*

**reg·is·trar** (rej′i strär′) **1** an official who keeps a REGISTER; official recorder. **2** in some universities, colleges, etc., the officer in charge of admissions, examinations, and general regulations. *n.*

**reg·is·tra·tion** (rej′i strā′shən) **1** the act of

REGISTERing.   2 an entry in a REGISTER.   3 the number of people REGISTEREd: *Registration for camp is higher this year than last.*   4 a document certifying an act of REGISTERing.   *n.*

**reg·is·try** (rej′i strē)   1 REGISTERing; registration.   2 a place where a REGISTER is kept; office of registration.   3 a book in which a list or record is kept.   *n., pl.* **reg·is·tries.**

**re·gress** (ri gres′ *for verb,* rē′gres *for noun*)   1 go back; move in a backward direction.   2 return to an earlier or less advanced state.   3 going back; movement backward.   1, 2 *v.,* 3 *n.*

**re·gres·sion** (ri gresh′ən)   1 the act of going back; backward movement.   2 in biology, the reversion of offspring toward a more average condition.   *n.*

**re·gret** (ri gret′)   1 feel regret about: *We regretted her absence.*   2 feel sorry; mourn: *He wrote, regretting that he could not visit us.*   3 the feeling of being sorry; sorrow; a sense of loss.   4 **regrets,** *pl.*   a polite reply declining an invitation: *She could not come to the meeting but she sent regrets.*   1, 2 *v.,* **re·gret·ted, re·gret·ting;** 3, 4 *n.*

**re·gret·ful** (ri gret′fəl)   feeling or expressing REGRET.   *adj.*   —**re·gret′ful·ly,** *adv.*   —**re·gret′ful·ness,** *n.*

**re·gret·ta·ble** (ri gret′ə bəl)   that should be or is regretted.   *adj.*   —**re·gret′ta·bly,** *adv.*

**re·group** (rē′grüp′)   1 form into a new arrangement or grouping: *to regroup military forces. You can regroup two bags of six oranges each to make three bags of four oranges each.*   2 in subtraction, decrease the digit in one column of the minuend by 1 in order to increase the value in the column on the right by 10: *To subtract 8 from 64, regroup 64 as 5 tens and 14 ones.*   *v.*

**Regt.**   1 regent.   2 regiment.

**reg·u·lar** (reg′yə lər)   1 fixed by custom or rule; usual; normal: *Six o'clock was her regular hour of rising.*   2 following some rule or principle; according to rule: *A period is the regular ending for a sentence.*   3 coming, acting, or done again and again at the same time: *Saturday is a regular holiday.*   4 steady; habitual: *A regular customer trades often at the same store.*   5 even in size, spacing, or speed; well-balanced: *regular features.*   6 SYMMETRICAL.   7 having all its angles equal and all its sides equal.   8 having all the same parts of a flower alike in shape and size.   9 orderly; methodical: *to lead a regular life.*   10 properly fitted or trained: *The maid did the cooking while the regular cook was sick.*   11 in grammar, having the usual changes of form to show tense, number, person, etc.: *Ask is a regular verb.*   12 *Informal.* thorough; complete: *a regular bore.*   13 fine; agreeable; all right: *He's a regular fellow.*   14 permanently organized: *The regular army is under the direct control of the federal government.*   15 a full-time member of a group: *The fire department was made up of regulars and volunteers.*   16 of or belonging to the permanent armed forces of a country.   17 a person who makes the armed forces a full-time career.   18 belonging to a religious order bound by certain rules: *The regular clergy live in religious communities.*   19 a person belonging to a religious order bound by certain rules.   20 in sports, a player who plays in all or most of a team's games.   21 in mathematics: **a** of a polygon, having all its sides and all its angles equal.   **b** of a polyhedron (a solid figure), having identical regular polygons as faces.   1–14, 16, 18, 21 *adj.,* 15, 17, 19, 20 *n.*   —**reg′u·lar·ly,** *adv.*

**reg·u·lar·i·ty** (reg′yə lar′ə tē *or* reg′yə ler′ə tē)   order; system; steadiness; the state or condition of being regular.   *n.*

**reg·u·late** (reg′yə lāt′)   1 control by rule, principle, or system: *Good schools regulate the behaviour of students.*   2 put in condition to work properly.   3 keep at some standard: *A thermostat regulates temperature.*   *v.,* **reg·u·lat·ed, reg·u·lat·ing.**

**reg·u·la·tion** (reg′yə lā′shən)   1 control by rule, principle, or system.   2 a rule or law: *traffic regulations.*   3 according to or required by a regulation; standard: *Soldiers wear a regulation uniform.*   1, 2 *n.,* 3 *adj.*

**reg·u·la·tive** (reg′yə lə tiv *or* reg′yə lā′tiv)   regulating.   *adj.*

**reg·u·la·tor** (reg′yə lā′tər)   1 a person or thing that REGULATES.   2 a device in a clock or watch to make it go faster or slower.   3 a very accurate clock used as a standard of time.   *n.*

**reg·u·la·to·ry** (reg′yə lə tô′rē)   regulating.   *adj.*

**re·gur·gi·tate** (rē gėr′jə tāt′)   1 of liquids, gases, undigested foods, etc., rush, surge, or flow back.   2 throw up: *The baby regurgitated food from her stomach.*   *v.,* **re·gur·gi·tat·ed, re·gur·gi·tat·ing.**

**re·gur·gi·ta·tion** (rē gėr′jə tā′shən)   regurgitating.   *n.*

**re·ha·bil·i·tate** (rē′hə bil′ə tāt′)   1 restore to a good condition; make over in a new form: *The old house is to be rehabilitated.*   2 restore to former standing, rank, rights, privileges, reputation, etc.: *The former criminal completely rehabilitated himself and was trusted and respected by all.*   *v.,* **re·ha·bil·i·tat·ed, re·ha·bil·i·tat·ing.**   —**re′ha·bil′i·ta′tion,** *n.*

**re·hash** (rē hash′ *for verb,* rē′hash *for noun*)   1 deal with again; work up old material in a new form: *The question had been rehashed again and again.*   2 an act of rehashing.   3 something old put in a different form: *That composition is simply a rehash of an article in the encyclopedia.*   1 *v.,* 2, 3 *n.*

**re·hears·al** (ri hėr′səl)   1 the act of rehearsing.   2 a performance beforehand for practice or drill.   *n.*

**re·hearse** (ri hėrs′)   1 practise a play, part, music, etc. for a public performance: *We rehearsed our parts for the school play.*   2 drill or train a person, etc. by repetition.   3 tell in detail; repeat: *She rehearsed all the happenings of the day from beginning to end.*   *v.,* **re·hearsed, re·hears·ing.**

**reign** (rān)   1 the period of power of a monarch: *Queen Victoria's reign lasted sixty-four years.*   2 be a monarch; have royal power: *A king reigns over his kingdom.*   3 the royal power; rule: *The reign of a wise ruler benefits his or her country.*   4 exist everywhere; prevail: *Silence reigned*

---

*In each of the words below,* **re-** *means* again *or* anew; *the pronunciation of the main part of each word is not changed.*

| re·glaze′ | re·grow′ | re·hard′en | re·heat′ | re·ig·nite′ |
| re·glue′ | | | | |

on the lake, except for the sound of our paddles in the water. **5** existence everywhere; prevalence. 1, 3, 5 *n*., 2, 4 *v*.
☛ *Hom*. RAIN, REIN.

**re·im·burse** (rē′im bėrs′) pay back: *His employer reimbursed him for his travelling expenses.* *v*., **re·im·bursed, re·im·burs·ing.** —**re′im·burse′ment,** *n*.

**rein** (rān) **1** a long, narrow strap or line fastened to the bit of a bridle, by which to guide and control an animal: *A driver or rider of a horse holds the reins in his or her hands.* See HARNESS for picture. **2** check or pull with reins. **3** a means of control and direction: *to seize the reins of government.* **4** guide and control: *Rein your tongue.* 1, 3 *n*., 2, 4 *v*.
**draw rein,** **a** tighten the reins. **b** slow down; stop.
**give rein to,** let move or act freely, without guidance or control: *give rein to one's feelings.*
**keep a tight rein on,** keep under close supervision and control.
**rein in** or **up,** cause to stop or to go slower.
☛ *Hom*. RAIN, REIGN.

**re·in·car·nate** (rē′in kär′nāt) give a new body to a soul. *v*., **re·in·car·nat·ed, re·in·car·nat·ing.**

**re·in·car·na·tion** (rē′in kär nā′shən) **1** a rebirth of the soul in a new body. **2** a new incarnation or embodiment. *n*.

**rein·deer** (rān′dēr′) a kind of large deer with branching antlers living in northern regions: *The caribou is a North American reindeer.* *n*., *pl*. **rein·deer.**

**re·in·force** (rē′in fôrs′) **1** strengthen with new force or materials: *to reinforce an army or a fleet, to reinforce a garment with an extra thickness of cloth, to reinforce a wall or a bridge.* **2** strengthen: *to reinforce an argument, a plea, an effect, a stock, a supply, etc.* *v*., **re·in·forced, re·in·forc·ing.** Also, **re-enforce.**

**reinforced concrete** concrete with metal embedded in it to make the structure stronger.

**re·in·force·ment** (rē′in fôr′smənt) **1** the act of reinforcing. **2** being REINFORCEd. **3** something that REINFORCEs. **4 reinforcements,** *pl*. extra people and equipment, especially troops, warships, military aircraft, etc. *n*. Also, **re-enforcement.**

**re·in·state** (rē′in stāt′) restore to a former position or condition; establish again. *v*., **re·in·stat·ed, re·in·stat·ing.** —**re′in·state′ment,** *n*.

**re·in·sur·ance** **1** renewed insurance. **2** the transfer of insurance from one person to another. *n*.

**re·in·sure** (rē′in shủr′) insure again; insure under a contract by which a first insurer relieves himself or herself from the risk and transfers it to another insurer. *v*.

**re·in·te·grate** (rē in′tə grāt′) **1** make whole again; restore to a perfect state; renew or re-establish. **2** become whole again; be renewed. *v*., **re·in·te·grat·ed, re·in·te·grat·ing.** —**re′in·te·gra′tion,** *n*.

**re·it·er·ate** (rē it′ə rāt′) say or do several times; repeat an action, demand, etc. again and again: *The boy did not move, though the teacher reiterated her command.* *v*., **re·it·er·at·ed, re·it·er·at·ing.** —**re·it′er·a′tion,** *n*.

## reimburse 997 relation

hat, āge, fär; let, ēqual, tėrm; it, īce
hot, ōpen, ôrder; oil, out; cup, pụt, rüle
əbove, takən, pencəl, lemən, circəs
ch, child; ng, long; sh, ship
th, thin; ᴛH, then; zh, measure

**re·ject** (ri jekt′ *for verb,* rē′jekt *for noun*) **1** refuse to take, use, believe, consider, grant, etc.: *She rejected our help. He tried to join the army but was rejected.* **2** throw away as useless or unsatisfactory: *Reject all apples with soft spots.* **3** a rejected person or thing: *The rejects were sold at a lower price.* **4** vomit. 1, 2, 4 *v*., 3 *n*.
—**re·ject′er,** *n*.

**re·jec·tion** (ri jek′shən) **1** an act of REJECTing. **2** being REJECTed. **3** the thing REJECTed. *n*.

**re·joice** (ri jois′) **1** be glad; be filled with joy. **2** make glad; fill with joy. *v*., **re·joiced, re·joic·ing.**

**re·joic·ing** (ri joi′sing) **1** the feeling or expression of joy. **2** ppr. of REJOICE. 1 *n*., 2 *v*.

**re·join**[1] (rē join′) **1** join again; unite again: *The members of our family will rejoin at Thanksgiving.* **2** join the company of again. *v*.

**re·join**[2] (ri join′) answer; reply: *"Not on your life,"* she rejoined. *v*.

**re·join·der** (ri join′dər) an answer to a reply; response. *n*.

**re·ju·ve·nate** (ri jü′və nāt′) make young or vigorous again; give youthful qualities to: *The long rest and new clothes have rejuvenated Mrs. Werner.* *v*., **re·ju·ve·nat·ed, re·ju·ve·nat·ing.** —**re·ju′ve·na′tion,** *n*. —**re·ju′ve·na′tor,** *n*.

**re·kin·dle** (rē kin′dəl) set on fire again; kindle anew. *v*., **re·kin·dled, re·kin·dling.**

**re—laid** (rē lād′) pt. and pp. of RE-LAY. *v*.

**re·lapse** (ri laps′ *for verb, usually* rē′laps *for noun*) **1** fall or slip back into a former state, way of acting, etc.: *After one cry of surprise, she relapsed into silence.* **2** falling or slipping back into a former state, way of acting, etc.: *He seemed to be getting over his illness but had a relapse.* 1 *v*., **re·lapsed, re·laps·ing;** 2 *n*.

**re·late** (ri lāt′) **1** give an account of; tell: *The traveller related her adventures.* **2** connect in thought or meaning: *"Better" and "best" are related to "good."* **3** be connected in any way: *We are interested in what relates to ourselves.* *v*., **re·lat·ed, re·lat·ing.**

**re·lat·ed** (ri lā′tid) **1** connected. **2** belonging to the same family; connected by a common origin: *Cousins are related.* **3** pt. and pp. of RELATE. 1, 2 *adj*., 3 *v*.
—**re·lat′ed·ness,** *n*.

**re·la·tion** (ri lā′shən) **1** a connection in thought or meaning: *Your answer has no relation to the question.* **2** connections or dealings between persons, groups, countries, etc.: *The relation of mother and child is a very close one.* **3** a person who belongs to the same family as another, such as a father, brother, aunt, etc.; relative.

---

*In each of the words below,* **re-** *means* again *or* anew; *the pronunciation of the main part of each word is not changed.*

| re′im·plant′ | re′im·pris′on | re′in·fest′ | re′in·ter′pret | re·is′sue |
| re′im·port′ | re′in·duc′tion | re′in·fes·ta′tion | re′in·tro·duce′ | re·judge′ |
| re′im·por·ta′tion | re′in·fect′ | re′in·sert′ | re′in·tro·duc′tion | re·la′bel |
| re′im·pose′ | re′in·fec′tion | re′in·ter′ | | |

**4** reference; regard: *We must plan with relation to the future.* **5** the act of telling; account: *We were amused by his relation of his adventures.* **6 relations,** *pl.* dealings; affairs: *Our firm has business relations with his firm.* *n.*
**in** or **with relation to,** about; concerning; having to do with: *We must plan in relation to the future.*

**re·la·tion·al** (ri lā′shə nəl) **1** that relates. **2** having to do with RELATIONS. *adj.*

**re·la·tion·ship** (ri lā′shən ship′) **1** connection: *What is the relationship of clouds to rain?* **2** the condition of belonging to the same family. *n.*

**rel·a·tive** (rel′ə tiv) **1** a person who belongs to the same family as another, such as father, brother, aunt, etc. **2** related or compared to each other: *Before ordering our dinner, we considered the relative merits of chicken and roast beef.* **3** depending for meaning on a relation to something else: *East is a relative term; for example, Regina is east of Vancouver but west of Toronto.* **4** introducing a subordinate clause; referring to another person or thing. Example: In "The woman *who* wanted it is gone," *who is a relative pronoun, and* who wanted it *is a relative clause.* **5** a relative pronoun. 1, 5 *n.*, 2–4 *adj.*
**relative to,** **a** about; concerning: *a letter relative to my proposal.* **b** in proportion to: *Dinu is strong relative to his size. This subject is little understood relative to its importance.*

☞ *Usage.* **Relative clauses.** A relative clause is an adjective clause introduced by a relative pronoun, **that, which,** or **who,** or a relative adverb, **where, when,** or **why:** *The ball that had been lost was found by the caddy. Mike's plane, which was lost in the storm, landed safely in a field. They asked for a student who could volunteer to play Santa Claus. That is the place where he lived.*

☞ *Usage.* **Relative pronouns.** The relative pronouns are **that, which** (**of which, whose**) and **who** (**whose, whom**). They introduce relative clauses and refer to an antecedent in the main clause: *A man who was there gave us the details. Our team, which scored first, had the advantage.* **Who** refers to persons; **which,** to animals or things; and **that,** to persons, animals, or things.

**relative density** the ratio of the DENSITY of any substance to the density of a particular substance used as a standard. For solids and liquids, the standard is water and for gases, it is air.

**relative humidity** the ratio between the amount of water vapour actually present in the air and the amount it would take to saturate the air at the same temperature, expressed as a percentage: *At 15°C, if the air contains 10 grams of water vapour per cubic metre, its relative humidity is about 80%; at 30°C with the same amount of water vapour, the air has a relative humidity of about 33%, because warmer air can hold more water vapour.* Compare with ABSOLUTE HUMIDITY.

**rel·a·tive·ly** (rel′ə ti vlē) in a relative manner; in relation to something else; comparatively: *a relatively small difference.* *adv.*

**rel·a·tiv·i·ty** (rel′ə tiv′ə tē) **1** being relative. **2** in physics, the character of being relative rather than absolute, as ascribed to motion or velocity. **3** a theory expressed in a certain equation by Einstein. See EINSTEIN EQUATION. According to this theory, the only velocity we can measure is velocity relative to some body; observers on any celestial body may regard that body as motionless except for its rotation and acceleration and obtain the same observations as they would on any other celestial body, thus obtaining always the same value for the velocity of light; the mass of a moving body increases in dependence on its velocity; in a certain sense, space is curved. *n.*

**re·la·tor** (ri lā′tər) a person who relates or narrates. *n.*

**re·lax** (ri laks′) **1** loosen up; make or become less stiff or firm: *Relax your muscles to rest them.* **2** make or become less strict or severe; lessen in force: *Discipline is relaxed on the last day of school.* **3** relieve or be relieved from work or effort; give or take recreation or amusement: *Take a vacation and relax.* **4** weaken: *Don't relax your efforts until the game is over.* *v.*

**re·lax·a·tion** (rē′lak sā′shən) **1** a loosening: *the relaxation of the muscles.* **2** a lessening of strictness, severity, force, etc.: *the relaxation of discipline.* **3** a relief from work or effort; recreation; amusement: *Walking and reading were the only relaxations permitted on Sunday.* **4** the state or condition of being relaxed. *n.*

**re·lax·ed·ly** (ri lak′si dlē) in a RELAXED manner. *adv.*

**re·lay** (rē′lā *for noun,* ri lā′ or rē′lā *for verb*) **1** a fresh supply: *New relays of men were sent to the disaster area.* **2** take and carry farther: *Messengers will relay your message.* **3** a RELAY RACE. **4** one part of a RELAY RACE. **5** an electromagnetic device in which a weak current controls a stronger current: *A relay is used in transmitting telegraph or telephone messages over long distances.* **6** transmit by an electrical relay. **7** receive and then pass to another: *to relay a phone message, to relay a thrown ball.* 1, 3–5 *n.*, 2, 6, 7 *v.*

**re–lay** (rē lā′) lay again. *v.*, **re·laid, re·lay·ing.**

**re·lay race** (rē′lā) a race in which each member of a team runs, swims, etc. only a certain part of the distance.

**re·lease** (ri lēs′) **1** let go; let loose: *The prisoner was released.* **2** letting go; setting free: *a petition for the release of the prisoner.* **3** set free; relieve: *The nurse is released from duty at seven o'clock.* **4** freedom; relief: *release from pain.* **5** a device for releasing a part or parts of a mechanism. **6** a legal surrender of right, estate, etc., to another. **7** give up legal right, claim, etc.; make over property, stock, etc. to another. **8** a document that does this. **9** permit to be published, shown, sold, etc. **10** an authorization for the publication, exhibition, sale, etc. **11** an article, statement, etc. distributed for publication. 1, 3, 7, 9 *v.*, **re·leased, re·leas·ing;** 2, 4–6, 8, 10, 11 *n.*

**rel·e·gate** (rel′ə gāt′) **1** send away, usually to a lower position or condition: *to relegate a dress to the rag bag.* **2** send into exile; banish. **3** hand over a matter, task, etc. *v.*, **rel·e·gat·ed, rel·e·gat·ing.** —**rel′e·ga′tion,** *n.*

**re·lent** (ri lent′) become less harsh or cruel; be more tender and merciful: *After hours of questioning the suspect, the police relented and allowed him to rest.* *v.*

**re·lent·less** (ri len′tlis) without pity; unyielding;

---

*In each of the words below,* **re-** *means* **again** *or* **anew;** *the pronunciation of the main part of each word is not changed.*

**re·learn′**

harsh: *The storm raged with relentless fury.* *adj.*
—re·lent′less·ly, *adv.*

**rel·e·vance** (rel′ə vəns)   being to the point, being RELEVANT: *The relevance of his question was doubtful.* *n.*

**rel·e·vant** (rel′ə vənt)   bearing upon or connected with the matter in hand; to the point: *relevant questions.* *adj.*

**re·li·a·bil·i·ty** (ri lī′ə bil′ə tē)   the quality of being RELIABLE; trustworthiness; dependability: *A machine has perfect reliability if it always does its work.* *n.*

**re·li·a·ble** (ri lī′ə bəl)   worthy of trust; that can be depended on: *reliable sources of news.* *adj.*
—re·li′a·bly, *adv.*

**re·li·ance** (ri lī′əns)   **1** trust; dependence: *A child has reliance on his or her mother.* **2** confidence. *n.*

**re·li·ant** (ri lī′ənt)   **1** relying; trusting or depending. **2** confident. *adj.*

**rel·ic** (rel′ik)   **1** a thing, custom, etc. that remains from the past: *This ruined bridge is a relic of pioneer days.* **2** something belonging to a holy person, kept as a sacred memorial.   **3** an object having interest because of its age or its associations with the past; keepsake; souvenir. **4 relics,** *pl.* remains; ruins.   *n.*

Reliefs (def. 9). The picture on the left is a detail from an ancient Greek sculpture in high relief; the picture on the right is a detail from an ancient Indic sculpture in low relief.

**re·lief** (ri lēf′)   **1** the lessening of, or freeing from, a pain, burden, difficulty, etc.   **2** something that lessens or frees from pain, burden, difficulty, etc.; aid; help: *Relief was quickly sent to the sufferers from the great fire.*   **3** help, in the form of money or food, given to poor people. **4** something that makes a pleasing change or lessens strain.   **5** a release from a post of duty, often by the coming of a substitute: *This nurse is on duty from seven in the morning until seven at night, with only two hours' relief.* **6** a change of persons on duty.   **7** a person or persons relieving others from duty: *The sentry was waiting for his relief.*   **8** the projection of figures and designs from a flat surface in sculpture, drawing, painting, etc.   **9** a figure or design standing out from the surface from which it is cut, shaped, or stamped.   **10** the appearance of standing out given to a drawing or painting by use of shadow, shading, colour, or line.   **11** differences in height between the summits and lowlands of a region.   **12** a strong, clear manner; distinctness: *Beulah's noble nature stood out in relief from the evil of her surroundings.*   *n.*
**in relief,**   standing out from a surface.
**on relief,**   receiving money to live on from public funds.

**relief map**   a map that shows the different heights of a surface by using shading, colours, etc., or solid materials such as clay.

**re·lieve** (ri lēv′)   **1** make less; make easier; reduce the pain or trouble of: *This pill will relieve a headache.*   **2** set free: *Your coming relieves me of the bother of writing a long letter.*   **3** bring aid to; help: *Soldiers were sent to relieve the fort.*   **4** give variety or a pleasing change to: *The black dress was relieved by red trimming.*   **5** free a person on duty by taking his or her place.   **6** make stand out more clearly.   *v.*, re·lieved, re·liev·ing.

**re·li·gion** (ri lij′ən)   **1** belief in or worship of God or gods.   **2** a matter of conscience: *She makes a religion of keeping her house neat.*   **3** a particular system of religious belief and worship: *the Christian religion, the Islamic religion.*   *n.*

**re·li·gi·os·i·ty** (ri lij′ē os′ə tē)   the affectation of religious feeling.   *n.*

**re·li·gious** (ri lij′əs)   **1** of religion; connected with religion: *religious meeting, religious books, religious differences.*   **2** much interested in religion; devoted to the worship of God or gods: *Nora is very religious and goes to church every day.*   **3** belonging to an order of monks, nuns, friars, etc.   **4** a monk, nun, friar, etc.; a member of a religious order: *There are six religious at this college.* **5** such persons collectively.   **6** of or connected with such an order.   **7** strict; very careful: *We paid religious attention to the doctor's orders.*   1–3, 6, 7 *adj.*, 4, 5 *n.*, *pl.* re·li·gious.   —re·li′gious·ly, *adv.*   —re·li′gious·ness, *n.*

**re·lin·quish** (ri ling′kwish)   give up; let go: *The small dog relinquished his bone to the big dog. She has relinquished all hope of going abroad this year.*   *v.*

**re·lin·quish·ment** (ri ling′kwi shmənt)   giving up; abandonment; surrender.   *n.*

**rel·i·quar·y** (rel′ə kwer′ē)   a small box or other receptacle for a RELIC (def. 2) or relics.   *n.*, *pl.* rel·i·quar·ies.

**rel·ish** (rel′ish)   **1** a pleasant taste; good flavour: *Hunger gives relish to simple food.*   **2** something to add flavour to food: *Olives and pickles are relishes.*   **3** a kind of pickle made of chopped cucumbers, etc.   **4** a slight dash of something.   **5** a liking; appetite; enjoyment: *The hungry girl ate with a great relish. The teacher has no relish for John's jokes.*   **6** like; enjoy: *A cat relishes cream. He did not relish the prospect of staying after school.*   1–5 *n.*, 6 *v.*

**re·luc·tance** (ri luk′təns)   **1** a reluctant feeling or action; unwillingness.   **2** slowness in action because of unwillingness: *She took part in the game with reluctance because she was tired.*   *n.*

**re·luc·tant** (ri luk′tənt)   **1** unwilling; showing unwillingness.   **2** slow to act because unwilling: *Werner was very reluctant to give his money away.*   *adj.*
—re·luc′tant·ly, *adv.*

**re·ly** (ri lī′)   depend; trust: *Rely on your own efforts.* *v.*, re·lied, re·ly·ing.

---

*In each of the words below,* **re-** *means* again *or* anew; *the pronunciation of the main part of each word is not changed.*

re·light′     re·line′     re·lock′

**re·main** (ri mān′) **1** continue in a place; stay: *We remained at the lake till September.* **2** continue; last; keep on: *The town remains the same year after year.* **3** be left: *A few apples remain on the trees.* **4 remains,** *pl.* **a** what is left. **b** a dead body. **c** a writer's works not yet published at the time of his or her death. *1–3 v., 4 n.*

**re·main·der** (ri mān′dər) **1** the part left over; the rest: *After studying for an hour, she spent the remainder of the afternoon in play.* **2** in arithmetic: **a** a number left over after subtracting one number from another: *In 9–2, the remainder is 7.* **b** a number left over after dividing one number by another: *In 14 ÷ 3, the quotient is 4 with a remainder of 2.* See DIVISION for picture. *n.*

**re·make** (rē māk′ *for verb,* rē′māk *for noun*) **1** make anew; make over. **2** something made over or anew: *The movie was a remake of an earlier one.* *1 v.,* **re·made, re·mak·ing;** *2 n.*

**re·mand** (ri mand′) **1** send back. **2** send back a prisoner or an accused person into custody. **3** the act of remanding. *1, 2 v., 3 n.*

**re·mark** (ri märk′) **1** say; speak; comment: *Mother remarked that Bill's hands would be better for a wash.* **2** something said in a few words; short statement: *The president made a few remarks.* **3** observe or notice: *Did you remark that oddly shaped cloud?* **4** the act of noticing; observation. *1, 3 v., 2, 4 n.*

**re·mark·a·ble** (ri mär′kə bəl) worthy of notice; unusual. *adj.* —**re·mark′a·bly,** *adv.*

**re·mar·ry** (rē mar′ē *or* rē mer′ē) marry again. *v.,* **re·mar·ried, re·mar·ry·ing.**

**re·me·di·a·ble** (ri mē′dē ə bəl) that can be remedied or cured. *adj.* —**re·me′di·a·bly,** *adv.*

**re·me·di·al** (ri mē′dē əl) intended as a remedy or cure; curing; helping. *adj.* —**re·me′di·al·ly,** *adv.*

**rem·e·di·less** (rem′ə dē lis) without remedy; incurable; irreparable. *adj.*

**rem·e·dy** (rem′ə dē) **1** anything used to cure or relieve illness: *Honey and chicken broth are two traditional cold remedies.* **2** anything intended to put right something bad or wrong: *The free movie was a remedy for the children's bad spirits.* **3** put right; make right; cure: *A thorough cleaning remedied the trouble.* *1, 2 n., pl.* **rem·e·dies;** *3 v.,* **rem·e·died, rem·e·dy·ing.**

**re·mem·ber** (ri mem′bər) **1** have something come into the mind again; call to mind; recall: *Then I remembered where I was.* **2** recall something. **3** keep in mind; take care not to forget: *Remember my birthday.* **4** have memory: *Dogs remember.* **5** make a gift to; reward: *My aunt remembered us in her will.* **6** mention a person as sending friendly greetings; recall to the mind of another: *Ruth asked to be remembered to Ann.* *v.*

**re·mem·brance** (ri mem′brəns) **1** the power to remember; act of remembering; memory. **2** a state of being remembered. **3** a keepsake; any thing or action that makes one remember a person, place, or event; souvenir. **4 remembrances,** *pl.* greetings. *n.*

**Remembrance Day** November 11, the day set aside to honour the memory of those killed in World Wars I and II.

**re·mind** (ri mīnd′) make one think of something; cause to remember. *v.*

**re·mind·er** (ri mīn′dər) something to help one remember. *n.*

**rem·i·nisce** (rem′ə nis′) talk or think about past experiences or events. *v.,* **rem·i·nisced, rem·i·nisc·ing.**

**rem·i·nis·cence** (rem′ə nis′əns) **1** remembering; the recalling of past happenings, etc. **2** an account of something remembered; recollection: *reminiscences of the war.* *n.*

**rem·i·nis·cent** (rem′ə nis′ənt) **1** recalling past events, etc.: *reminiscent talk.* **2** awakening memories of something else; suggestive: *a manner reminiscent of a statelier age.* *adj.* —**rem′i·nis′cent·ly,** *adv.*

**re·miss** (ri mis′) careless; slack; neglectful; negligent: *A police officer who fails to report a crime is remiss in his or her duty.* *adj.* —**re·miss′ness,** *n.*

**re·mis·sion** (ri mish′ən) **1** a letting off from debt, punishment, etc.: *The bankrupt man sought remission of his debts.* **2** pardon; forgiveness: *Remission of sins is promised to those who repent.* **3** a lessening of pain, force, labour, etc. **4** a cessation, temporary or permanent, of a disease: *Her cancer is in remission.* *n.*

**re·mit** (ri mit′) **1** send money to a person or place: *Enclosed is our bill; please remit the amount due.* **2** send money due. **3** refrain from carrying out; refrain from exacting; cancel: *The queen remitted the prisoner's punishment.* **4** pardon; forgive: *power to remit sins.* **5** make less; decrease: *After we had rowed the boat into calm water, we remitted our efforts.* **6** become less. **7** send back a case to a lower court for further action. *v.,* **re·mit·ted, re·mit·ting.** —**re·mit′ter,** *n.*

**re·mit·tal** (ri mit′əl) REMISSION. *n.*

**re·mit·tance** (ri mit′əns) **1** the act of sending money to someone at a distance. **2** the money that is sent. *n.*

**remittance man** someone who lives abroad on money sent from relatives at home.

**rem·nant** (rem′nənt) **1** a small part left: *This town has only a remnant of its former population.* **2** a piece of cloth, ribbon, lace, etc. left after the rest has been used or sold: *She bought a remnant of silk at a bargain.* *n.*

**re·mod·el** (rē mod′əl) **1** model again. **2** make over; change or alter: *The old barn was remodelled into a house.* *v.,* **re·mod·elled** *or* **re·mod·eled, re·mod·el·ling** *or* **re·mod·el·ing.**

**re·mon·strance** (ri mon′strəns) a protest; complaint. *n.*

**re·mon·strant** (ri mon′strənt) **1** remonstrating; protesting. **2** a person who REMONSTRATES. *1 adj., 2 n.*

**re·mon·strate** (ri mon′strāt *or* rem′ən strāt′) speak, reason, or plead in complaint or protest: *The lawyer remonstrated with the judge against the sentence.* *v.,* **re·mon·strat·ed, re·mon·strat·ing.**

---

*In each of the words below,* **re-** *means* again *or* anew; *the pronunciation of the main part of each word is not changed.*

**re′man·u·fac′ture**   **re·melt′**

**re·mon·stra·tion** (rē′mon strā′shən or rem′ən strā′shən)   an act of remonstrating.   *n.*

**re·mon·stra·tive** (ri mon′strə tiv)   remonstrating.   *adj.*

**rem·o·ra** (rem′ə rə)   any of a family of fishes of warm seas having the front dorsal fin modified into a flat sucking disk on the head, by means of which they attach themselves to larger fish or to ships, rocks, etc.   *n.*

**re·morse** (ri môrs′)   deep, painful regret for having done wrong: *Because he felt remorse for his crime, the thief confessed.*   *n.*

**re·morse·ful** (ri môr′sfəl)   feeling or expressing REMORSE.   *adj.*  —**re·morse′ful·ly,** *adv.*

**re·morse·less** (ri môr′slis)   without REMORSE; pitiless; cruel: *The remorseless villain hit and kicked his dog.*   *adj.*  —**re·morse′less·ly,** *adv.*

**re·mote** (ri mōt′)   **1** far away from a given place or time: *Dinosaurs lived in remote ages.*   **2** out of the way; secluded: *a remote village.*   **3** distantly related or connected: *a remote relative.*   **4** slight; faint: *I haven't the remotest idea what you mean.*   *adj.*, **re·mot·er, re·mot·est.**  —**re·mote′ly,** *adv.*

**remote control**   **1** control from a distance, usually by electrical impulses or radio signals: *Some model airplanes can be flown by remote control.*   **2** the device used for operating a remote control system.

**re·mount** (rē mount′ *for verb,* rē′mount *for noun*)   **1** mount again: *The fallen rider remounts his horse. The troops remounted the hill.*   **2** furnish with fresh horses.   **3** a fresh horse, or a supply of fresh horses, for use.   1, 2 *v.*, 3 *n.*

**re·mov·al** (ri mü′vəl)   **1** a removing; taking away: *We paid twenty dollars for garbage removal.*   **2** a change of place: *The store announced its removal to larger quarters.*   **3** a dismissal from an office or position.   *n.*

**re·move** (ri müv′)   **1** move from a place or position; take off; take away: *Remove your hat.*   **2** get rid of; put an end to: *to remove all doubt.*   **3** dismiss from an office or position: *to remove an official for taking bribes.*   **4** go away; move oneself to another place.   **5** a moving away.   **6** a step or degree of distance: *His cruelty was only one remove from crime.*   1–4 *v.*, **re·moved, re·mov·ing;** 5, 6 *n.*  —**re·mov′a·ble,** *adj.*  —**re·mov′er,** *n.*

**re·moved** (ri müvd′)   **1** distant; remote.   **2** separated by one or more steps or degrees of relationship.   **3** pt. and pp. of REMOVE.   1, 2 *adj.*, 3 *v.*

**re·mu·ner·ate** (ri myü′nə rāt′)   pay for work, services, trouble, etc.; reward: *The boy who returned the lost jewels was remunerated. The harvest will remunerate the labourers for their toil.*   *v.*, **re·mu·ner·at·ed, re·mu·ner·at·ing.**

**re·mu·ner·a·tion** (ri myü′nə rā′shən)   a reward; pay; payment.   *n.*

**re·mu·ner·a·tive** (ri myü′nə rə tiv *or* ri myü′nə rā′tiv)   paying; profitable.   *adj.*

**ren·ais·sance** (ren′ə säns′ *or* ren′ə säns′)   a revival; new birth.   *n.*

**Ren·ais·sance** (ren′ə säns′ *or* ren′ə säns′)   **1** the great

## remonstration 1001 renege

hat, āge, fär; let, ēqual, tėrm; it, īce
hot, ōpen, ôrder; oil, out; cup, pút, rüle
əbove, takən, pencəl, lemən, circəs
ch, child; ng, long; sh, ship
th, thin; ᴛʜ, then; zh, measure

revival of art and learning in Europe during the 14th, 15th, and 16th centuries.   **2** the period of time when this revival occurred.   **3** the style of art, architecture, etc. of this period.   *n.*

**re·nal** (rē′nəl)   **1** of or having to do with the kidneys.   **2** near the kidneys: *the renal arteries.*   See KIDNEY for picture.   *adj.*

**re·name** (rē nām′)   give a new name to; name again.   *v.*, **re·named, re·nam·ing.**

**re·nas·cence** (ri nas′əns *or* ri nā′səns)   **1** a new birth; revival; renewal: *a renascence of religion.*   **2** being RENASCENT.   *n.*

**re·nas·cent** (ri nas′ənt *or* ri nā′sənt)   being born again; reviving; springing again into being or vigour.   *adj.*

**rend** (rend)   **1** pull apart violently; tear: *Wolves will rend a lamb.*   **2** split: *Lightning rent the tree.*   **3** disturb violently: *Her mind was rent by doubt.*   *v.*, **rent, rend·ing.**

**ren·der** (ren′dər)   **1** cause to become; make: *An accident has rendered him helpless.*   **2** give; do: *She rendered us a great service by her help.*   **3** offer for consideration, approval, payment, etc.; hand in; report: *The treasurer rendered an account of all the money spent.*   **4** give in return: *Render thanks for your blessings.*   **5** pay as due: *The conquered rendered tribute to the conqueror.*   **6** bring out the meaning of; represent; perform: *The actor rendered the part of Hamlet well.*   **7** play or sing music.   **8** change from one language to another; translate: *Render that Latin proverb in English.*   **9** give up; surrender: *The knights rendered their swords to the victors.*   **10** melt fat, etc.; clarify or extract by melting: *Fat from pigs is rendered for lard.*   *v.*

**ren·der·ing** (ren′də ring)   **1** an interpretation in music or painting.   **2** ppr. of RENDER.   1 *n.*, 2 *v.*

**ren·dez·vous** (ron′də vü′; *French,* ʀäɴ dä vü′)   **1** an appointment or engagement to meet at a fixed place or time; meeting by agreement.   **2** a meeting place; gathering place: *The family had two favourite rendezvous, the library and the garden.*   **3** a place agreed on for a meeting at a certain time, especially of troops or ships.   **4** meet at a rendezvous.   1–3 *n., pl.* **ren·dez·vous** (-vüz′); 4 *v.*, **ren·dez·voused** (-vüd′), **ren·dez·vous·ing** (-vü′ing).

**ren·di·tion** (ren dish′ən)   **1** an act of RENDERing.   **2** the RENDERing of music, a dramatic part, etc. as to bring out the meaning.   **3** translation.   *n.*

**ren·e·gade** (ren′ə gād′)   **1** a deserter from a religious faith, a political party, etc.; traitor.   **2** an outlaw.   **3** deserting; disloyal; like a traitor.   *n.*

**re·nege** (ri neg′, ri nāg′, *or* ri nig′)   **1** fail to play a card of the suit that is led, although you have one; REVOKE (def. 3): *It is against the rules of card games to renege.*   **2** in card playing, failure to follow suit when able to do so;

---

*In each of the words below,* **re-** *means* again *or* anew; *the pronunciation of the main part of each word is not changed.*

**re·mould′**

**REVOKE** (def. 2). **3** *Informal.* back out; fail to keep a promise. 1, 3 *v.*, **re·neged, re·neg·ing;** 2 *n.*

**re·new** (ri nyü′ *or* ri nü′) **1** make new again; make like new; restore. **2** make spiritually new. **3** begin again; get again; say, do, or give again: *to renew an attack, one's youth, one's vows, one's efforts.* **4** replace by new material or a new thing of the same sort; fill again: *He renewed the sleeves of his jacket. The well renews itself no matter how much water is taken away.* **5** give or get for a new period: *We renewed our lease for two years.* *v.*
—**re·new′a·ble,** *adj.*

**re·new·al** (ri nyü′əl *or* ri nü′əl) RENEWing or being renewed. *n.*

**re·new·ed·ly** (ri nyü′i dlē *or* ri nü′i dlē) ANEW. *adv.*

**ren·i·form** (ren′ə fôrm′) shaped like a kidney. See LEAF for picture. *adj.*

**ren·net** (ren′it) a substance containing RENNIN, used for making cheese and junket. *n.*

**ren·nin** (ren′ən) an enzyme in the gastric juice that coagulates or curdles milk. *n.*

**re·nounce** (ri nouns′) **1** declare that one gives up; give up: *He renounced his claim to the money.* **2** make formal surrender. **3** cast off; refuse to recognize as one's own: *He renounced his wicked son.* *v.*, **re·nounced, re·nounc·ing.** —**re·nounce′ment,** *n.*

**ren·o·vate** (ren′ə vāt′) make new again; make like new; restore to good condition: *to renovate a garment or a house.* *v.*, **ren·o·vat·ed, ren·o·vat·ing.**
—**ren′o·va·tor,** *n.*

**ren·o·va·tion** (ren′ə vā′shən) a restoration to good condition; RENEWAL. *n.*

**re·nown** (ri noun′) the condition of being widely known; fame. *n.*

**re·nowned** (ri nound′) FAMED. *adj.*

**rent¹** (rent) **1** a payment, especially when made regularly, for the right to occupy or use another's land, buildings, goods, etc. **2** pay at regular times for the use of property: *We rent a house from Mr. Lee.* **3** receive regular pay for the use of property: *She rents several other houses.* **4** be leased or let for rent: *This house rents for $1200 a month.* 1 *n.*, 2–4 *v.* —**rent′er,** *n.*
**for rent,** available in return for rent paid: *That vacant apartment is for rent.*

**rent²** (rent) **1** a torn place; tear; split. **2** torn; split. **3** pt. and pp. of REND: *The tree was rent by the wind.*
1 *n.*, 2 *adj.*, 3 *v.*

**rent·al** (ren′təl) **1** an amount received or paid as rent: *The monthly rental of her house is $1200.* **2** something rented or able to be rented. **3** of or in rent. **4** that is rented: *a rental car.* 1, 2, 3, 4 *adj.*

**re·nun·ci·a·tion** (ri nun′sē ā′shən) a giving up of a right, title, possession, etc.; renouncing. *n.*

**re·o·pen** (rē ō′pən) **1** open again. **2** bring up again for discussion: *The matter is settled and cannot be reopened.* *v.*

**re·or·der** (rē ôr′dər) **1** put in order again; rearrange. **2** give a second or repeated order for goods; order again. **3** a second or repeated order for goods. 1, 2 *v.*, 3 *n.*

**re·or·gan·i·za·tion** (rē ôr′gə nə zā′shən *or* rē ôr′gə nī zā′shən) **1** reorganizing. **2** being REORGANIZED. *n.*

**re·or·gan·ize** (rē ôr′gə nīz′) **1** organize anew; form again; arrange in a new way: *Classes will be reorganized after the first four weeks.* **2** form a new company to operate a business in the hands of a RECEIVER (def. 5). *v.*, **re·or·gan·ized, re·or·gan·iz·ing.**
—**re·or′gan·iz′er,** *n.*

**rep** *Informal.* REPRESENTATIVE: *The company has hired several new sales reps.* *n.*

**rep.** **1** report. **2** reported. **3** reporter. **4** representative.

**Rep.** **1** Representative. **2** Republican. **3** Republic.

**re·paid** (ri pād′) pt. and pp. of REPAY: *Louis repaid the money he had borrowed. All debts should be repaid.* *v.*

**re·pair¹** (ri per′) **1** put in a good condition again; mend: *He repairs shoes.* **2** the act or work of repairing: *Repairs on the school building are made during the summer.* **3** an instance or piece of repairing. **4** a condition fit to be used: *Keeping highways in repair is the responsibility of the provinces.* **5** a condition with regard to the need for repairs: *The house was in bad repair.* **6** make up for: *How can I repair the harm done?* 1, 6 *v.*, 2–5 *n.*
—**re·pair′a·ble,** *adj.* —**re·pair′er,** *n.*

**re·pair²** (ri per′) go to a place: *After dinner we repaired to the porch.* *v.*

**re·pair·man** (ri per′man′ *or* ri per′mən) a person whose work is repairing machines, etc. *n., pl.* **re·pair·men** (-men′ *or* -mən).

**rep·a·ra·ble** (rep′ə rə bəl) that can be repaired or remedied. *adj.*

**rep·a·ra·tion** (rep′ə rā′shən) **1** the giving of satisfaction or compensation for wrong or injury done. **2** a compensation for wrong or injury. **3** a repairing or being repaired; restoration to good condition. **4 reparations,** *pl.* compensation demanded from a defeated enemy for the devastation of territory during war: *England and France demanded reparations from Germany after World War I.* *n.*

**rep·ar·tee** (rep′ər tē′) **1** a witty reply or replies. **2** talk characterized by clever and witty replies. **3** cleverness and wit in making replies. *n.*

**re·pass** (rē pas′) **1** pass back. **2** pass again. *v.*

**re·past** (ri past′) a meal; food. *n.*

**re·pa·tri·ate** (rē pā′trē āt′ *or* rē pat′rē āt′ *for verb,* rē pā′trē it *or* re pat′rē it *for noun*) **1** send back or restore to one's own country: *After peace was declared, refugees and prisoners of war were repatriated.* **2** a person who is sent back to his or her own country. 1 *v.*, **re·pa·tri·at·ed, re·pa·tri·at·ing;** 2 *n.*
—**re·pa′tri·a′tion,** *n.*

---

In each of the words below, **re-** means *again* or *anew;* *the pronunciation of the main part of each word is not changed.*

| | | | | |
|---|---|---|---|---|
| re·nom′i·nate | re·oc′cu·pa′tion | re·oc·cur′rence | re·o′ri·en·ta′tion | re·paint′ |
| re·nom′i·na′tion | re·oc′cu·py′ | re·of′fer | re·pack′ | re·pa′per |
| re·num′ber | re·oc·cur′ | re·o′ri·ent | re·pack′age | re·pave′ |

**re·pay** (ri pā′) **1** pay back; give back: *Elsie repaid the money she had borrowed.* **2** make return for: *No thanks can repay such kindness.* **3** make return to: *The boy's success repaid the teacher for her efforts.* *v.*, **re·paid, re·pay·ing.** —**re·pay′ment,** *n.*

**re·peal** (ri pēl′) **1** take back; withdraw; do away with: *A law may be repealed by act of Parliament.* **2** the act of repealing; withdrawal; abolition: *She voted for the repeal of that law.* **1** *v.*, **2** *n.*

**re·peat** (ri pēt′) **1** do or make again: *to repeat an error.* **2** say again: *to repeat a word for emphasis.* **3** say over; recite: *to repeat a poem from memory.* **4** say after another says: *Repeat the oath after me.* **5** tell to another or others: *I promised not to repeat the secret.* **6** an act of repeating. **7** a thing repeated: *We saw the repeat on television.* **8** in music, a passage to be repeated. **9** a sign indicating this, usually a row of dots. **10** vote more than once in an election. **1–5, 10** *v.*, **6–9** *n.* **repeat oneself,** say what one has already said.

**re·peat·ed** (ri pē′tid) **1** said, done, made, or happening a number of times: *Her repeated efforts at last won success.* **2** pt. and pp. of REPEAT. **1** *adj.*, **2** *v.*

**re·peat·ed·ly** (ri pē′ti dlē) again and again; more than once. *adv.*

**re·peat·er** (ri pē′tər) **1** a gun that fires several shots without reloading. **2** a watch or clock that, if a spring is pressed, strikes again the hour it struck last. **3** any person or thing that repeats. **4** *Informal.* a person who is repeatedly sent to prison or a reformatory; habitual criminal. *n.*

**re·pel** (ri pel′) **1** force back; drive back; drive away: *They repelled the enemy.* **2** keep off or out; fail to mix with: *Oil and water repel each other. This tent repels moisture.* **3** force apart or away by some inherent force: *Particles with similar electric charges repel each other.* **4** be displeasing to; cause disgust in: *Spiders and worms repel me.* **5** reject. *v.*, **re·pelled, re·pel·ling.**

**re·pel·lent** (ri pel′ənt) **1** unattractive; disagreeable: *He has a cold, repellent manner.* **2** repelling; driving back. **3** anything that REPELS: *We sprayed an insect repellent on our arms and legs to keep the mosquitoes away.* **1, 2** *adj.*, **3** *n.*

**re·pent** (ri pent′) **1** feel sorry for doing evil: *Jean repented after he had done wrong.* **2** feel sorry for; regret: *to repent one's choice.* *v.* —**re·pent′er,** *n.*

**re·pent·ance** (ri pen′təns) **1** sorrow for doing wrong. **2** sorrow; regret. *n.*

**re·pent·ant** (ri pen′tənt) repenting; feeling repentance or regret; sorry for wrongdoing. *adj.* —**re·pent′ant·ly,** *adv.*

**re·peo·ple** (rē pē′pəl) **1** fill with people again. **2** restock with animals. *v.*, **re·peo·pled, re·peo·pling.**

**re·per·cus·sion** (rē′pər kush′ən) **1** an indirect influence or reaction from an event. **2** a sound flung back; echo. **3** springing back; rebound; recoil. *n.*

**rep·er·toire** (rep′ər twär′) the list of plays, operas, parts, pieces, etc. that a company, an actor, a musician, or a singer is prepared to perform. *n.*

hat, āge, fär; let, ēqual, tėrm; it, īce
hot, ōpen, ôrder; oil, out; cup, pùt, rüle
ə bove, takən, pencəl, lemən, circəs
ch, child; ng, long; sh, ship
th, thin; ᴛʜ, then; zh, measure

**rep·er·to·ry** (rep′ər tô′rē) **1** a catalogue or list of things; repertoire. **2** a store or stock of things ready for use. **3** storehouse. *n.*, *pl.* **rep·er·to·ries.**

**repertory theatre 1** a theatre in which a company of actors, singers, or dancers presents a repertoire of productions for a season. **2** a theatre in which one company presents a different production at regular intervals, such as every week, every two weeks, or every month.

**rep·e·ti·tion** (rep′ə tish′ən) **1** the act of repeating; doing again; saying again: *Repetition helps learning. Any repetition of the offence will be punished.* **2** the thing repeated. *n.*

**rep·e·ti·tious** (rep′ə tish′əs) full of repetitions; repeating in a tiresome way. *adj.* —**rep′e·ti′tious·ness,** *n.*

**re·pet·i·tive** (ri pet′ə tiv) of or characterized by repetition. *adj.*

**re·phrase** (rē frāz′) phrase again; phrase in a new or different way: *to rephrase a speech, to rephrase a melody.* *v.*, **re·phrased, re·phras·ing.**

**re·place** (ri plās′) **1** fill or take the place of. **2** get another in place of: *I will replace the cup I broke.* **3** put back; put in place again: *Replace the books on the shelf.* *v.*, **re·placed, re·plac·ing.**

**re·place·ment** (ri plās′mənt) **1** an act of replacing or being replaced. **2** something or someone that replaces. **3** a person who takes the place of another. *n.*

**re·plant** (rē plant′) plant again. *v.*

**re·plen·ish** (ri plen′ish) fill again; provide a new supply for: *Her wardrobe needs replenishing. You had better replenish the fire.* *v.* —**re·plen′ish·er,** *n.*

**re·plen·ish·ment** (ri plen′i shmənt) **1** an act of replenishing or being replenished. **2** a fresh supply. *n.*

**re·plete** (ri plēt′) abundantly supplied; filled. *adj.*

**re·ple·tion** (ri plē′shən) fullness; excessive fullness. *n.*

**rep·li·ca** (rep′lə kə) a copy; reproduction: *The artist made a replica of her picture.* *n.*

**re·ply** (ri plī′) **1** answer by words or action; answer: *Has she replied to your letter? The rebels replied with a burst of gunfire.* **2** give as an answer: *He replied, "I have no intention of going."* **3** a response or answer. **1, 2** *v.*, **re·plied, re·ply·ing;** **3** *n.*, *pl.* **re·plies.**

**re·port** (ri pôrt′) **1** an account or statement of facts: *a news report.* **2** an account officially expressed, generally in writing: *an annual report.* **3** make a report of; announce: *to report the news.* **4** give a formal account of; state officially: *Our treasurer reports that all dues are paid up.* **5** take down in writing; write an account of. **6** make a report. **7** act as reporter. **8** repeat or give an

---

*In each of the words below,* **re-** *means* again *or* anew; *the pronunciation of the main part of each word is not changed.*

re·phase′      re·pho′to·graph′      re·pop′u·late′

account of; describe; tell: *The radio reports the news and weather.* **9** present; present oneself: *Report for duty at 9 a.m.* **10** announce as a wrongdoer; denounce: *to report someone to the police.* **11** the sound of a shot or an explosion: *the report of a gun.* **12** common talk; rumour: *Report has it that our neighbours are leaving town.* **13** reputation. 1, 2, 11–13 *n.*, 3–10 *v.*

**re·port·a·ble** (re pôr′tə bəl) capable of being reported; worth reporting. *adj.*

**report card** a report sent regularly by a school to parents or guardians, showing the quality of a student's work.

**re·port·er** (ri pôr′tər) **1** a person who reports. **2** a person who gathers news for a newspaper, magazine, radio or television station, etc. *n.*

**re·pose**¹ (ri pōz′) **1** rest or sleep: *Do not disturb her repose.* **2** lie at rest: *The cat reposed upon the cushion.* **3** lie in a grave. **4** rest from work or toil; take a rest. **5** quietness; ease: *She has repose of manner.* **6** peace; calmness. **7** be supported. **8** depend; rely on. 1, 5, 6 *n.*, 2–4, 7, 8 *v.*, **re·posed, re·pos·ing.**

**re·pose**² (ri pōz′) put; place: *We repose complete confidence in her honesty.* *v.*, **re·posed, re·pos·ing.**

**re·pose·ful** (ri pōz′fəl) calm; quiet. *adj.*

**re·pos·i·to·ry** (ri poz′ə tô′rē) **1** a place or container where things are stored or kept: *The box was the repository for old magazines.* **2** a person to whom something is confided or entrusted. *n.*, *pl.* **re·pos·i·to·ries.**

**re·pos·sess** (rē′pə zes′) possess again; get possession of again. *v.*

**re·pos·ses·sion** (rē′pə zesh′ən) an act of REPOSSESSing. *n.*

**rep·re·hend** (rep′ri hend′) reprove; rebuke; blame. *v.*

**rep·re·hen·si·ble** (rep′ri hen′sə bəl) deserving reproof, rebuke, or blame: *Cheating is a reprehensible act.* *adj.* —**rep′re·hen′si·bly,** *adv.*

**rep·re·hen·sion** (rep′ri hen′shən) reproof; rebuke; blame. *n.*

**rep·re·sent** (rep′ri zent′) **1** stand for; be a sign or symbol of: *The stars on this map represent cities.* **2** act in place of; speak and act for: *People are elected to represent us in the government.* **3** act the part of: *Each child will represent an animal at the party.* **4** show in a picture, statue, carving, etc.; give a likeness of; portray: *This painting represents the Fathers of Confederation.* **5** be a type of; be an example of: *A log represents a very simple kind of boat.* **6** describe; set forth: *She represented the plan as safe.* **7** bring before the mind; make one think of: *His fears represented the undertaking as impossible.* *v.*

**rep·re·sen·ta·tion** (rep′ri zen tā′shən) **1** an act of representing. **2** being represented: *"Taxation without representation is tyranny."* **3** representatives considered as a group. **4** a likeness; picture; model. **5** a symbol; sign. **6** a performance of a play; presentation: *A representation of Robin Hood will be given in the auditorium today.* **7** the process of forming mental images or ideas. **8** a protest; complaint. **9** an account; statement: *They deceived us by false representations.* *n.*

**rep·re·sent·a·tive** (rep′ri zen′tə tiv) **1** a person appointed or elected to act or speak for others: *She is the club's representative at the convention.* **2** having its citizens represented by chosen persons: *a representative government.* **3** representing: *Images representative of animals were made by the children.* **4** a typical example; type: *The tiger is a representative of the cat family.* **5** serving as an example of; typical: *Oak, birch, and maple are representative North American hardwoods.* **6 Representative,** in the United States, a member of the House of Representatives. 1, 4, 6 *n.*, 2, 3, 5 *adj.*

**re·press** (ri pres′) **1** prevent from acting; check: *She repressed her desire to laugh.* **2** keep down; put down; suppress: *The dictator repressed the revolt.* *v.* —**re·press′er,** *n.*

**re·press·i·ble** (ri pres′ə bəl) that can be REPRESSed. *adj.*

**re·pres·sion** (ri presh′ən) **1** an act of REPRESSING: *The repression of a laugh made Anton choke.* **2** the state of being REPRESSed: *Repression made her behave worse.* *n.*

**re·pres·sive** (ri pres′iv) tending to REPRESS; having power to repress. *adj.*

**re·prieve** (ri prēv′) **1** delay the execution of a person condemned to death. **2** a delay in carrying out a punishment, especially of the death penalty. **3** the order giving authority for such delay. **4** a temporary relief from any hardship or trouble: *We had a reprieve of two days, and then the rain started again.* **5** give relief from any hardship or trouble. 1, 5 *v.*, **re·prieved, re·priev·ing;** 2–4 *n.*

**rep·ri·mand** (rep′rə mand′) **1** a severe or formal reproof. **2** reprove severely or formally. 1 *n.*, 2 *v.*

**re·print** (rē print′ *for verb,* rē′print′ *for noun*) **1** print again; print a new impression of. **2** a reprinting; a new impression of printed work. 1 *v.*, 2 *n.*

**re·pris·al** (ri prī′zəl) **1** any measure, economic or military, taken in retaliation by one nation against another. **2** any act of retaliation by one person against another. *n.*

**re·proach** (ri prōch′) **1** blame. **2** disgrace: *A coward is a reproach to a regiment.* **3** any object of blame, censure, or disapproval. **4** an expression of blame, censure, or disapproval. 1–4 *n.*, 1 *v.*

**re·proach·ful** (ri prōch′fəl) full of REPROACH; expressing reproach. *adj.* —**re·proach′ful·ly,** *adv.*

**re·proach·less** (ri prōch′lis) without REPROACH; irreproachable. *adj.*

**rep·ro·bate** (rep′rə bāt′) **1** an unprincipled scoundrel. **2** morally abandoned; unprincipled: *reprobate acts.* **3** disapprove; condemn; censure. 1 *n.*, 2 *adj.*, 3 *v.*, **rep·ro·bat·ed, rep·ro·bat·ing.**

**rep·ro·ba·tion** (rep′rə bā′shən) disapproval; condemnation; censure. *n.*

**re·pro·duce** (rē′prə dyüs′ *or* rē′prə düs′) **1** produce again: *A radio reproduces sounds.* **2** make a copy of: *She took the picture to the printer to be reproduced.* **3** produce offspring: *Most plants reproduce by seeds.* *v.*, **re·pro·duced, re·pro·duc·ing.**

**re·pro·duc·i·ble** (rē′prə dyü′sə bəl *or* rē′prə dü′sə bəl) that can be REPRODUCEd. *adj.*

**re·pro·duc·tion** (rē′prə duk′shən) **1** an act of reproducing or being reproduced. **2** a copy. **3** the process by which offspring are produced. *n.*

**re·pro·duc·tive** (rē′prə duk′tiv) **1** that REPRODUCES. **2** for or concerned with REPRODUCTION. *adj.* —**re′pro·duc′tive·ly,** *adv.* —**re′pro·duc′tive·ness,** *n.*

**re·proof** (ri prüf′) words of blame or disapproval; blame. *n.*

**re·prov·al** (ri prü′vəl) a reproving or REPROOF. *n.*

**re·prove** (ri prüv′) find fault with; blame: *Reprove the boy for teasing the cat.* *v.*, **re·proved, re·prov·ing.**

**rep·tile** (rep′tīl) **1** any of the group of cold-blooded animals that creep or crawl: *Snakes, lizards, turtles, alligators, and crocodiles are reptiles.* **2** of or like a reptile; crawling; creeping. **3** a low, mean person. **4** low; mean. 1, 3 *n.*, 2, 4 *adj.*

**rep·til·i·an** (rep til′ē ən) **1** of REPTILES; having to do with reptiles. **2** like a REPTILE; base; mean. **3** a REPTILE. 1, 2 *adj.*, 3 *n.*

**re·pub·lic** (ri pub′lik) a nation or state in which the citizens elect representatives to manage the government, which is usually headed by a president rather than by a monarch: *The United States and Mexico are republics.* *n.*

**re·pub·li·can** (ri pub′lə kən) **1** of a REPUBLIC; like that of a republic. **2** favouring a REPUBLIC. **3** a person who favours a REPUBLIC. **4 Republican,** *U.S.* of or having to do with the REPUBLICAN PARTY. **5 Republican,** *U.S.* a member of the REPUBLICAN PARTY. 1, 2, 4 *adj.*, 3, 5 *n.*

**re·pub·li·can·ism** (ri pub′lə kə niz′əm) **1** REPUBLICAN government. **2** REPUBLICAN principles; adherence to republican principles. **3 Republicanism,** *U.S.* the principles or policies of the REPUBLICAN PARTY. *n.*

**Republican Party** one of the two main political parties in the United States.

**re·pub·li·ca·tion** (rē′pub lə kā′shən) **1** publication anew. **2** a book, etc. published again. *n.*

**re·pu·di·ate** (ri pyü′dē āt) **1** refuse to accept; reject: *to repudiate a doctrine.* **2** refuse to acknowledge or pay: *to repudiate a debt.* **3** cast off; disown: *to repudiate a son.* *v.*, **re·pu·di·at·ed, re·pu·di·at·ing.**

**re·pu·di·a·tion** (ri pyü′dē ā′shən) the act of repudiating; fact or condition of being REPUDIATEd. *n.*

**re·pug·nance** (ri pug′nəns) strong dislike, distaste, or aversion: *a repugnance for snakes.* *n.*

**re·pug·nant** (ri pug′nənt) **1** distasteful; disagreeable; offensive: *Work is repugnant to lazy people.* **2** objecting; averse; opposed: *We are repugnant to every sort of dishonesty.* *adj.*

**re·pulse** (ri puls′) **1** drive back; repel. **2** a driving back; being driven back: *After the second repulse, the enemy surrendered.* **3** refuse to accept; reject: *She coldly repulsed him.* **4** a refusal; rejection. 1, 3 *v.*, **re·pulsed, re·puls·ing.** 2, 4 *n.*

**re·pul·sion** (ri pul′shən) **1** a strong dislike or aversion. **2** a REPULSE; repelling or being repelled. *n.*

**re·pul·sive** (ri pul′siv) **1** causing strong dislike or aversion: *Snakes are repulsive to some people.* **2** tending to drive back or repel. *adj.* —**re·pul′sive·ness,** *n.*

hat, āge, fär; let, ēqual, tėrm; it, īce
hot, ōpen, ôrder; oil, out; cup, pùt, rüle
əbove, takən, pencəl, lemən, circəs
ch, child; ng, long; sh, ship
th, thin; ᴛH, then; zh, measure

**rep·u·ta·ble** (rep′yə bəl) having a good reputation; well thought of; in good repute. *adj.* —**rep′u·ta·bly,** *adv.*

**rep·u·ta·tion** (rep′yə tā′shən) **1** what people think and say the character of a person or thing is; character in the opinion of others; name: *She had a reputation for honesty.* **2** a good name; high standing in the opinion of others: *The scandal ruined his reputation.* **3** fame: *She has an international reputation.* *n.*

**re·pute** (ri pyüt′) **1** REPUTATION: *This is a district of bad repute on account of many robberies.* **2** a good REPUTATION: *a man of repute.* **3** generally suppose to be; consider; suppose: *He is reputed the richest man in the city.* 1, 2 *n.*, 3 *v.*, **re·put·ed, re·put·ing.**

**re·put·ed** (ri pyü′tid) **1** accounted or generally supposed to be such: *the reputed author of a book.* **2** pt. and pp. of REPUTE. 1 *adj.*, 2 *v.*

**re·put·ed·ly** (ri pyü′ti dlē) by repute; supposedly. *adv.*

**re·quest** (ri kwest′) **1** ask for; ask as a favour: *She requested a loan from the bank.* **2** ask: *He requested her to go with him.* **3** the act of asking: *She did it at our request.* **4** what is asked for: *He granted my request.* **5** the state of being asked for or sought after: *She is such a good dancer that she is in great request.* 1, 2 *v.*, 3–5 *n.*
**by request,** in response to a request: *The school remained open all evening by request of the principal.*

**Requi·em** or **requi·em** (rek′wē əm or rē′kwē əm) **1** Mass for the dead; a sung or played church service for the dead. **2** the music for this service. *n.*

**re·qui·es·cat in pa·ce** (rek′wē es′kat in pä′chä) *Latin.* "May he (or she) rest in peace," a wish or prayer for the dead. *Abbrev.*: R.I.P.

**re·quire** (ri kwīr′) **1** have need for; need; want: *The government requires more money.* **2** command; order; demand: *The rules require us all to be present.* *v.*, **re·quired, re·quir·ing.**

**re·quire·ment** (ri kwīr′mənt) **1** a need; something needed: *Patience is a requirement in teaching.* **2** a demand; something demanded: *She has filled all requirements for graduation.* *n.*

**req·ui·site** (rek′wə zit) **1** required by circumstances; needed; necessary; indispensable: *the qualities requisite for a leader, the number of votes requisite for election.* **2** the thing needed: *Food and air are requisites for life.* 1 *adj.*, 2 *n.* —**req′ui·site·ly,** *adv.* —**req′ui·site·ness,** *n.*

**req·ui·si·tion** (rek′wə zish′ən) **1** the act of requiring. **2** a demand made, especially a formal written demand: *the requisition of supplies for troops.* **3** demand or take by authority: *to requisition supplies or labour.* **4** make demands upon: *The army requisitioned the village for food.* **5** the state of being required for use or called into service:

---

*In each of the words below,* **re-** *means* again *or* anew; *the pronunciation of the main part of each word is not changed.*

re·pub′lish   re·pur′chase   re·quick′en

*The car was in constant requisition for errands.* **6** an essential condition; requirement. 1, 2, 5, 6 *n.*, 3, 4 *v.*

**re·quit·al** (ri kwīt′əl) a repayment; payment; return: *What requital can we make for all her kindness to us?* *n.*

**re·quite** (ri kwīt′) **1** pay back; make return for: *I was brought up to requite evil with good.* **2** make return to: *The knight requited the girl for her warning.* *v.*, **re·quit·ed, re·quit·ing.**

**re·read** (rē′rēd′) read again: *She reread the letter several times.* *v.*, **re·read** (-red′), **re·read·ing.**

**rere·dos** (rēr′dos) a screen or a decorated part of the wall behind an altar. *n.*

**re·route** (rē rüt′ *or* rē rout′) send by a new or different route: *Buses will be rerouted while the parade is on.* *v.*, **re·rout·ed, re·rout·ing.**

**re·run** (rē run′ *for verb,* rē′run′ *for noun*) **1** run again. **2** a running again. **3** a television program or motion-picture film that is shown again. 1 *v.*, **re·ran, re·run·ning;** 2, 3 *n.*

**re·sale** (rē′sāl′ *or* rē sāl′) the act of selling again. *n.*

**re·scind** (ri sind′) deprive of force; repeal; cancel: *to rescind a law.* *v.*

**re·script** (rē′skript) **1** a written answer to a question or petition. **2** an edict; decree; official announcement. **3** a rewriting. *n.*

**res·cue** (res′kyü) **1** save from danger, capture, harm, etc.; free; deliver: *Searchers rescued the boy lost in the mountains.* **2** the act of saving or freeing from danger, capture, harm, etc.: *The fireman was praised for his brave rescue of the children in the burning house. A dog was chasing our cat when Mary came to the rescue.* **3** in law, take a person forcibly or unlawfully from a jail, police officer, etc.; take property unlawfully from legal custody. **4** in law, the forcible or unlawful taking of a person or thing from the care of the law. 1, 3 *v.*, **res·cued, res·cu·ing;** 2, 4 *n.* —**res′cu·er,** *n.*

**re·search** (ri sėrch′ *or* rē′sėrch′) **1** a careful hunting for facts or truth; inquiry; investigation: *Medical research has done much to lessen disease.* **2** carry out research. 1 *n.*, 2 *v.*

**re·search·er** (ri sėr′chər *or* rē′sėr′chər) a person who carries out research; investigator. *n.*

**re·sem·blance** (ri zem′bləns) a similar appearance; likeness: *Twins often show great resemblance.* *n.*

**re·sem·ble** (ri zem′bəl) be like; be similar to; have likeness to in form, figure, or qualities. *v.*, **re·sem·bled, re·sem·bling.**

**re·sent** (ri zent′) feel injured and angry at; feel indignation at: *Our cat seems to resent having anyone sit in its chair.* *v.*

**re·sent·ful** (ri zent′fəl) feeling resentment; injured and angry; showing resentment. *adj.* —**re·sent′ful·ly,** *adv.* —**re·sent′ful·ness,** *n.*

**re·sent·ment** (ri zent′mənt) the feeling that one has at being injured or insulted; indignation. *n.*

**res·er·va·tion** (rez′ər vā′shən) **1** a keeping back; hiding in part; something not expressed: *She outwardly approved of the plan with the mental reservation that she would change it to suit herself.* **2** a limiting condition: *The committee accepted the plan with reservations plainly stated.* **3** land set aside for a special purpose: *a forest reservation.* **4** an arrangement to keep a thing for a person; securing of accommodations, etc.: *We made reservations in advance for rooms at a hotel, seats at a theatre or stadium, etc.* **5** something reserved. **6** in Canada, the provision made for the withholding of royal assent to a bill, federal or provincial, until it has been re-examined. **7** *U.S.* land set apart, usually by treaty, for the exclusive use of Indians. *n.*

**re·serve** (ri zėrv′) **1** keep back; hold back: *to reserve criticism.* **2** set apart: *time reserved for recreation.* **3** save for use later: *Reserve enough money for your fare home.* **4** the actual cash in a bank or assets that can be turned into cash quickly: *Banks must keep a reserve of money.* **5** a body of soldiers kept ready to help the main army in battle. **6** land set apart by the government for a special purpose: *a forest reserve.* **7** land set apart, usually by treaty, for the exclusive use of Indians. **8** a person kept in reserve or available as a substitute: *He is a reserve for the basketball team.* **9** anything kept back for future use. **10** the act of keeping back or holding back: *You may speak here without reserve.* **11** the fact, state, or condition of being kept, set apart, or saved for use later. **12** set aside for the use of a particular person or persons: *Reserve a table.* **13** kept in reserve; forming a reserve. **14** the act of keeping one's thoughts, feelings, and affairs to oneself; self-restraint; lack of friendliness. **15** an exception or qualification to the acceptance of some idea, belief, etc. **16** a quiet, aloof manner that keeps people from making friends easily. **17 reserves,** *pl.* members of the armed forces not in active service but ready to serve if needed. 1–3, 12 *v.*, **re·served, re·serv·ing;** 4–11, 13–17 *n.*

**re·served** (ri zėrvd′) **1** kept in reserve; kept by special arrangement: *reserved seats.* **2** set apart. **3** self-restrained in action or speech. **4** disposed to keep to oneself: *A reserved boy does not make friends easily.* **5** pt. and pp. of RESERVE. 1–4 *adj.*, 5 *v.*

**re·serv·ed·ly** (ri zėr′vi dlē) in a RESERVED manner. *adv.*

**re·serv·ist** (ri zėr′vist) a member of the armed forces not in active service but available if needed. *n.*

**res·er·voir** (rez′ər vwär′) **1** a place where water is collected and stored for use: *This reservoir supplies the entire city.* **2** anything to hold a liquid: *A fountain pen has an ink reservoir.* **3** a place where anything is collected and stored: *Her mind was a reservoir of facts.* **4** a great supply: *a reservoir of food.* *n.*

**re·set** (rē set′ *for verb,* rē′set′ *for noun*) **1** set again: *The diamonds were reset in platinum. Paul's broken arm had to*

---

In each of the words below, **re-** means *again* or *anew; the pronunciation of the main part of each word is not changed.*

| | | | | |
|---|---|---|---|---|
| re·read′ | re′re·vise′ | re·sched′ule | re·seed′ | re·send′ |
| re′re·cord′ | re·roll′ | re·score′ | re′seg′re·gate′ | re·set′tle |
| re·reg′is·ter | re·sad′dle | re·screen′ | re′seg·re·ga′tion | re·set′tle·ment |
| re′reg·is·tra′tion | re·sail′ | re·seal′ | re·sell′ | re·sew′ |
| re′re·lease′ | re·say′ | | | |

be reset. **2** an act of resetting. **3** the thing reset. **1** *v.*, **re·set, re·set·ting;** **2, 3** *n.*

**re·shape** (rē shāp′) shape anew; form into a new or different shape. *v.*, **re·shaped, re·shap·ing.**

**re·side** (ri zīd′) **1** live in or at for a long time; dwell. **2** be in; exist in: *Her charm resides in her happy smile.* *v.*, **re·sid·ed, re·sid·ing.** **—re·sid′er,** *n.*

**res·i·dence** (rez′ə dəns) **1** a house; home; place where a person lives. **2** residing; living; dwelling: *Long residence in France made him very fond of the French.* **3** a period of residing in a place. **4** a building in which students, nurses, etc. live. *n.*
**in residence,** living in an institution while on duty or doing active work: *a doctor in residence.*

**res·i·dent** (rez′ə dənt) **1** a person living in a place, not a visitor. **2** staying; dwelling in a place: *A resident owner lives on his or her property.* **3** living in a place while on duty or doing active work: *Dr. Bauer is a resident physician at the hospital.* **4** a physician in residence. **5** an official sent to live in a foreign land to represent his or her country. **6** not migratory: *English sparrows are resident birds.* **1, 4, 5** *n.*, **2, 3, 6** *adj.*

**res·i·den·tial** (rez′ə den′shəl) **1** of, having to do with, or fitted for homes or RESIDENCES: *They live in a good residential district.* **2** having to do with RESIDENCE: *The city government is considering a residential qualification for schoolteachers.* *adj.*

**re·sid·u·al** (ri zij′ü əl) of or forming a RESIDUE; remaining; left over. *adj.*

**res·i·due** (rez′ə dyü′ *or* rez′ə dü′) what remains after a part is taken; a remainder: *Mrs. Kovac's will directed that, after the payment of all debts, the residue of her property should go to her son. The syrup had dried up, leaving a sticky residue.* *n.*

**re·sid·u·um** (ri zij′ü əm) what is left at the end of any process; residue; remainder. *n., pl.* **re·sid·u·a** (-ü ə).

**re·sign** (ri zīn′) **1** take oneself out of a job, position, etc.; leave; depart (*often used with* **from**): *He resigned in a fit of rage. She has resigned from the club.* **2** give up: *She resigned her seat in Parliament.* **3** give in or yield; often unwillingly, but without complaint (*used with a pronoun ending in* **self**): *He had to resign himself to a week in bed when he hurt his back.* *v.*

**res·ig·na·tion** (rez′ig nā′shən) **1** the act of RESIGNing. **2** a written statement giving notice that one RESIGNS. **3** patient acceptance; quiet submission: *She bore the pain with resignation.* *n.*

**re·signed** (ri zīnd′) **1** showing or feeling resignation; accepting often unwillingly; submissive: *resigned to an unhappy fate.* **2** pt. and pp. of RESIGN. **1** *adj.*, **2** *v.*

**re·sign·ed·ly** (ri zī′ni dlē) in a RESIGNED manner; with resignation. *adv.*

**re·sil·i·ence** (ri zil′ē əns) **1** the power of springing back; elasticity; a resilient quality or nature: *Rubber has resilience.* **2** buoyancy; cheerfulness. *n.*

**re·sil·i·ent** (ri zil′ē ənt) **1** springing back; returning to the original form or position after being bent, compressed,

hat, āge, fär; let, ēqual, tėrm; it, īce
hot, ōpen, ôrder; oil, out; cup, pùt, rüle
əbove, tākən, pencəl, lemən, circəs
ch, child; ng, long; sh, ship
th, thin; ᴛʜ, then; zh, measure

or stretched: *resilient steel, resilient turf.* **2** buoyant; cheerful: *a resilient nature that throws off trouble.* *adj.*

**res·in** (rez′ən) **1** a sticky, yellow or brown substance that flows from certain plants and trees, especially the pine and fir: *Resin is used in medicine and varnish. The harder portion of resin remaining after heating is called rosin. Compare with* ROSIN. **2** any similar substance that is made synthetically: *Artificial resins are used in the manufacture of plastics.* *n.*

**res·in·ous** (rez′ə nəs) **1** of RESIN. **2** like RESIN. **3** containing RESIN; full of resin. *adj.*

**re·sist** (ri zist′) **1** act against; strive against; oppose: *The window resisted his efforts to open it.* **2** act against something; oppose something: *Do not resist.* **3** strive successfully against; keep from: *I could not resist laughing.* **4** withstand the action or effect of an acid, storm, etc.: *A healthy body resists disease.* *v.* **—re·sist′er,** *n.*

**re·sist·ance** (ri zis′təns) **1** the act of resisting: *The bank clerk made no resistance to the robbers.* **2** the power to resist: *She has little resistance to germs and so is often ill.* **3** a thing or act that resists; opposing force; opposition: *An airplane can overcome air resistance and go in any desired direction, but a balloon simply drifts.* **4** the property of a conductor that opposes the passage of an electric current and changes electric energy into heat: *The elements of electric stoves have high resistance. Copper has a low resistance.* **5** a conductor, coil, etc. that offers resistance. **6** Usually, **Resistance,** people in a country occupied or controlled by another country who secretly organize and fight for their freedom: *the French Resistance in World War II.* *n.*

**re·sist·ant** (ri zis′tənt) RESISTing. *adj.*

**re·sist·i·bil·i·ty** (ri zis′tə bil′ə tē) the quality of being RESISTIBLE. *n.*

**re·sist·i·ble** (ri zis′tə bəl) capable of being RESISTed. *adj.*

**re·sist·less** (ri zis′tlis) that cannot be RESISTed: *A resistless impulse made him wander over the earth.* *adj.*

**re·sole** (rē sōl′) put a new sole on a shoe, etc. *v.*, **re·soled, re·sol·ing.**

**re·sol·u·ble** (ri zol′yü bəl) capable of being RESOLVed. *adj.*

**res·o·lute** (rez′ə lüt′) determined; firm; bold: *Roberta was resolute in her attempt to climb to the top of the mountain.* *adj.* **—res′o·lute·ly,** *adv.*

**res·o·lu·tion** (rez′ə lü′shən) **1** something decided on or determined: *She made a resolution to get up early.* **2** an act of resolving or determining. **3** the power of holding firmly to a purpose; determination: *The man's firm resolution overcame the handicap of poverty.* **4** a formal

---

*In each of the words below,* **re-** *means* again *or* anew; *the pronunciation of the main part of each word is not changed.*

| re·ship′ | re·show′ | re·sil′ver | re·smooth′ | re·soak′ |
| re·shoot′ | | | | |

**resolve**     1008     **respiration**

expression of opinion: *The club passed a resolution thanking Mr. Kay for his help throughout the year.*    **5** a breaking into parts.    **6** an act or result of solving; solution: *the resolution of a problem.*    *n.*

**re·solve** (ri zolv′)    **1** make up one's mind; determine; decide: *She resolved to do better work in the future.*    **2** the thing determined on: *Ala kept her resolve to do better.*    **3** firmness in carrying out a purpose; determination: *The president was a man of great resolve.*    **4** break into parts; break up: *The compound can be made to resolve into its parts.*    **5** answer and explain; solve: *His letter resolved all our doubts.*    **6** decide by vote: *It was resolved that our school have a uniform.*    **7** present for a decision by voting.    **8** change: *The assembly resolved itself into a committee.*    1, 4–8 *v.*, **re·solved, re·solv·ing;**    2, 3 *n.*

**re·solved** (ri zolvd′)    **1** determined; resolute.    **2** pt. and pp. of RESOLVE.    1 *adj.*, 2 *v.*

**re·solv·ed·ly** (ri zol′vi dlē)    in a determined manner; with resolution.    *adv.*

**res·o·nance** (rez′ə nəns)    **1** a resounding quality; being resonant: *the resonance of an organ.*    **2** a reinforcing and prolonging of sound by reflection or by vibration of other objects: *The sounding board of a piano gives it resonance.*    **3** the condition of an electrical circuit adjusted to allow the greatest flow of current at a certain frequency: *A radio set must be in resonance to receive music or speech from a radio station.*    *n.*

**res·o·nant** (rez′ə nənt)    **1** resounding; continuing to sound; echoing: *a resonant tone.*    **2** tending to increase or prolong sound: *A guitar has a resonant body.*    **3** of or in resonance.    *adj.*    —**res′o·nant·ly,** *adv.*

**res·o·nate** (rez′ə nāt′)    resound; exhibit RESONANCE.    *v.*, **res·o·nat·ed, res·o·nat·ing.**

**res·o·na·tor** (rez′ə nā′tər)    something that produces RESONANCE; an appliance for increasing sound by resonance.    *n.*

**res·or·cin** (rez ôr′sən)    RESORCINOL.    *n.*

**res·or·cin·ol** (rez ôr′sə nol′)    a colourless crystalline substance that is used in medicine as an antiseptic, and in making dyes, drugs, etc.    *n.*

**re·sort** (ri zôrt′)    **1** go; go often: *Many people resort to the beaches in hot weather.*    **2** an assembling; going to often: *A park is a place of popular resort in good weather.*    **3** a place people go to, usually for relaxation or recreation: *There are many holiday resorts in the mountains.*    **4** turn for help: *to resort to violence.*    **5** an act of turning for help: *Any resort to force is forbidden in this school.*    **6** a person or thing turned to for help: *Books are her resort when she is lonely. Friends are the best resort in trouble.*    1, 4 *v.*, 2, 3, 5, 6 *n.*

**re·sound** (ri zound′)    **1** give back sound; echo: *The hills resounded when we shouted.*    **2** sound loudly: *Radios resound from every house.*    **3** be filled with sound: *The room resounded with our shouts.*    **4** repeat loudly: *to resound a hero's praise.*    **5** be much talked about: *The news of the first space flight resounded all over the world.*    *v.*    —**re·sound′ing·ly,** *adv.*

**re·source** (ri zôrs′, ri sôrs′, *or* rē′zôrs′)    **1** any supply that will meet a need: *We have resources of money, of quick wit, and of strength.*    **2** any means of getting success or getting out of trouble: *Climbing a tree is a cat's resource when chased by a dog.*    **3** skill in meeting difficulties, getting out of trouble, etc.    **4 resources,** *pl.* the actual and potential wealth of a country; natural resources.    *n.*

**re·source·ful** (ri zôr′sfəl *or* ri sôr′sfəl)    good at thinking of ways to do things; quick-witted.    *adj.*    —**re·source′ful·ly,** *adv.*    —**re·source′ful·ness,** *n.*

**resp.** respectively.

**re·spect** (ri spekt′)    **1** honour; esteem: *Children should show respect to those who are older and wiser.*    **2** feel or show honour or esteem for: *We respect an honest person.*    **3** consideration; regard: *Show respect for other people's property.*    **4** show consideration for: *Respect the ideas and feelings of others.*    **5** a point; matter; detail: *The plan is unwise in many respects.*    **6** relation; reference: *We must plan in respect to the future.*    **7** relate to; refer to; be connected with.    **8 respects,** *pl.* expressions of respect; regards: *We must pay our respects to the mayor.*    1, 3, 5, 6, 8 *n.*, 2, 4, 7 *v.*    —**re·spect′er,** *n.*

**in respect of,** with reference or comparison to.
**in respect that,** because of the fact that; since.
**with respect to,** with relation, reference, or regard to something: *We must plan with respect to the future.*

**re·spect·a·bil·i·ty** (ri spek′tə bil′ə tē)    **1** the quality or condition of being RESPECTABLE.    **2** RESPECTABLE social standing.    *n.*, *pl.* **re·spect·a·bil·i·ties.**

**re·spect·a·ble** (ri spek′tə bəl)    **1** worthy of respect; having a good reputation: *Respectable citizens obey the laws.*    **2** having fair social standing; honest and decent: *Her parents were poor but respectable people.*    **3** fairly good; moderate in size or quality: *Pieter's record in school was respectable but not brilliant.*    **4** good enough to use; fit to be seen: *That dirty dress is not respectable.*    *adj.*    —**re·spect′a·bly,** *adv.*

**re·spect·ful** (ri spekt′fəl)    showing respect; polite.    *adj.*    —**re·spect′ful·ly,** *adv.*    —**re·spect′ful·ness,** *n.*

**re·spect·ing** (ri spek′ting)    **1** regarding; about; concerning: *A discussion arose respecting the merits of different automobiles.*    **2** ppr. of RESPECT.    1 *prep.*, 2 *v.*

**re·spec·tive** (ri spek′tiv)    belonging to each; particular; individual: *The classes went to their respective rooms.*    *adj.*

**re·spec·tive·ly** (ri spek′ti vlē)    as regards each one in turn or in the order mentioned: *Helga, Johan, and Bols are 16, 18, and 20 years old respectively.*    *adv.*

**re·spell** (rē′spel′)    spell over again, especially in a phonetic alphabet or in the alphabet or writing system of another language.    *v.*

**res·pi·ra·tion** (res′pə rā′shən)    **1** the act of inhaling and exhaling; breathing: *Her bad cold hinders respiration.*    **2** the process by which an animal, plant, or living cell obtains oxygen from the air or water, distributes it, combines it with substances in the tissues, and gives off carbon dioxide.    *n.*

---

*In each of the words below,* **re-** *means* again *or* anew; *the pronunciation of the main part of each word is not changed.*

**re·sow′**

**res·pi·ra·tor** (res′pə rā′tər)  1 a device worn over the nose and mouth to prevent inhaling harmful substances.  2 a device used to help a person to breathe: *Respirators are used by underwater swimmers and in giving artificial respiration.*  *n.*

**res·pi·ra·to·ry** (res′pə rə tô′rē)  having to do with or used for breathing: *The lungs are respiratory organs.*  *adj.*

**re·spire** (ri spīr′)  inhale and exhale; breathe: *The sick child respired at an abnormally rapid rate.*  *v.*, **re·spired, re·spir·ing.**

**res·pite** (res′pit *or* res′pīt)  1 a time of relief and rest; lull: *A thick cloud brought a respite from the glare of the sun.*  2 a putting off; delay, especially in carrying out a sentence of death; reprieve.  3 give a respite to.  1, 2 *n.*, 3 *v.*, **res·pit·ed, res·pit·ing.**

**re·splend·ence** (ri splen′dəns)  splendour; great brightness; gorgeous appearance.  *n.*

**re·splend·ent** (ri splen′dənt)  very bright; shining; splendid: *The queen was resplendent with jewels.*  *adj.*  —**re·splend′ent·ly,** *adv.*

**re·spond** (ri spond′)  1 answer; reply.  2 act in answer; react: *A dog responds to kind treatment by loving its owner.*  *v.*

**re·spond·ent** (ri spon′dənt)  1 answering; responding.  2 a person who responds.  3 a defendant, especially in a divorce case.  1 *adj.*, 2, 3 *n.*

**re·sponse** (ri spons′)  1 an answer by word or act: *Her response to my letter was prompt. Ruth stuck out her tongue in response to Tom's teasing.*  2 a set of words said or sung by the congregation or choir in answer to the minister.  3 in psychology and physiology, the reaction of mind or body to stimulus.  *n.*

**re·spon·si·bil·i·ty** (ri spon′sə bil′ə tē)  1 being responsible; obligation: *A little child does not feel much responsibility.*  2 something for which one is responsible: *Keeping accounts and preparing reports are her responsibilities.*  *n.*, *pl.* **re·spon·si·bil·i·ties.**

**re·spon·si·ble** (ri spon′sə bəl)  1 obliged or expected to account for; accountable; answerable: *Each student is responsible for the care of the books given him or her.*  2 deserving credit or blame: *The bad weather is responsible for the small attendance.*  3 trustworthy; reliable: *A responsible person should take care of the money.*  4 involving obligation or duties: *The prime minister holds a very responsible position.*  5 able to tell right from wrong; able to think and act reasonably: *Insane people are not responsible.*  *adj.*  —**re·spon′si·ble·ness,** *n.*  —**re·spon′si·bly,** *adv.*

**re·spon·sive** (ri spon′siv)  1 making answer; responding: *a responsive glance.*  2 easily moved; responding readily: *to have a responsive nature, to be responsive to kindness.*  3 using or containing responses: *responsive reading in church, in which minister and congregation read in turn.*  *adj.*  —**re·spon′sive·ly,** *adv.*  —**re·spon′sive·ness,** *n.*

**respirator    1009    restaurant**

hat, āge, fär; let, ēqual, tėrm; it, īce
hot, ōpen, ôrder; oil, out; cup, pút, rüle
əbove, takən, pencəl, lemən, circəs
ch, child; ng, long; sh, ship
th, thin; ŦH, then; zh, measure

Musical rests (def. 21). A whole rest has the same duration as a whole note, a half rest the same as a half note, and so on.

**rest**[1] (rest)  1 sleep; repose: *a good night's rest.*  2 be still; sleep: *Lie down and rest.*  3 ease after work or effort; freedom from activity: *Allow an hour for rest.*  4 freedom from anything that tires, troubles, disturbs, or pains; respite: *The medicine gave the sick woman a short rest from pain.*  5 be free from work, trouble, pain, etc.: *He was able to rest during his holidays.*  6 the absence of motion: *The driver brought the car to rest.*  7 stop moving; cause to stop moving: *The ball rested at the bottom of the hill.*  8 give rest to; refresh by rest: *Stop and rest your horse.*  9 lie, recline, sit, lean, etc., for ease: *He spent the whole day resting in a chair.*  10 be supported: *The ladder rests against the wall.*  11 be fixed: *Our eyes rested on the open book.*  12 be at ease: *Don't let Mrs. White rest until she promises to visit us.*  13 become inactive; let remain inactive: *Let the matter rest. Rest the matter there.*  14 place for support; lay; lean: *to rest one's head in one's hands.*  15 a support: *a rest for a billiard cue.*  16 a place of rest: *a rest for sailors.*  17 rely on; trust in; depend; be based: *Our hope rests on you.*  18 cause to rely or depend; base: *We rest our hope on you.*  19 be found; be present: *In a democracy, government rests with the people.*  20 in music, a period of silence.  21 a mark to show a period of silence.  22 in reading, a pause.  23 death; the grave.  24 be dead; lie in the grave: *The old man rests with his forefathers.*  25 end voluntarily the introduction of evidence in a case at law: *The lawyer rested her case.*  1, 3, 4, 6, 15, 16, 20–23 *n.*, 2, 5, 7–14, 17–19, 24, 25 *v.*
**at rest,**  **a** asleep.  **b** not moving: *The lake was at rest.*  **c** free from pain, trouble etc.: *The gravely injured man is now at rest.*  **d** dead.
**lay to rest,**  bury: *Lay his bones to rest.*
☞ **Hom.** WREST.

**rest**[2] (rest)  1 what is left; those that are left: *The sun was out in the morning but it rained for the rest of the day. One horse was running ahead of the rest.*  2 continue to be: *You may rest assured that I will keep my promise.*  1 *n.*, 2 *v.*
☞ **Hom.** WREST.

**re·state** (rē stāt′)  1 state again or anew.  2 state in a new way.  *v.*, **re·stat·ed, re·stat·ing.**

**re·state·ment** (rē stāt′mənt)  1 a statement made again.  2 a new statement.  *n.*

**res·tau·rant** (res′tə ront *or* res′tront)  a place to buy and eat a meal.  *n.*

---

*In each of the words below,* **re-** *means* again *or* anew; *the pronunciation of the main part of each word is not changed.*

| re·spray′ | re·staff′ | re·stage′ | re·stamp′ | re·start′ |
| re·sprin′kle | | | | |

**res·tau·ra·teur** (res′tə rə tėr′) the owner or manager of a restaurant. *n.*

**rest·ful** (rest′fəl) **1** full of rest; giving rest: *She had a restful nap.* **2** quiet; peaceful: *From this window you have a restful view of field and hills.* *adj.* —**rest′ful·ly**, *adv.* —**rest′ful·ness**, *n.*

**res·ti·tu·tion** (res′tə tyü′shən *or* res′tə tü′shən) **1** the giving back of what has been lost or taken away. **2** the act of making good any loss, damage, or injury: *It is only fair that those who do the damage should make restitution.* *n.*

**res·tive** (res′tiv) **1** restless; uneasy. **2** hard to manage. **3** refusing to go ahead; balky. *adj.* —**res′tive·ly**, *adv.* —**res′tive·ness**, *n.*

**rest·less** (res′tlis) **1** unable to rest; uneasy: *The dog seemed restless as if it sensed some danger.* **2** without rest or sleep; not restful: *The sick child passed a restless night.* **3** rarely or never still or quiet; always moving: *That nervous boy is very restless.* *adj.* —**rest′less·ly**, *adv.* —**rest′less·ness**, *n.*

**res·to·ra·tion** (res′tə rā′shən) **1** an act of restoring or being restored; bringing back to a former condition: *the restoration of health, the restoration of a king.* **2** something restored: *The house we slept in was a restoration of a Loyalist mansion.* **3 Restoration**, in England: **a** the re-establishment of the monarchy in 1660 under Charles II. **b** the period from 1660 to 1688. *n.*

**re·stor·a·tive** (ri stôr′ə tiv) **1** capable of restoring; tending to RESTORE health or strength. **2** something that RESTORES health and strength. **1** *adj.*, **2** *n.*

**re·store** (ri stôr′) **1** bring back; establish again: *to restore order.* **2** bring back to a former condition or to a normal condition: *The old house has been restored.* **3** give back; put back: *The thief was forced to restore the money to its owner.* *v.*, **re·stored, re·stor·ing.** —**re·stor′er**, *n.*

**re·strain** (ri strān′) **1** hold back; keep down; keep in check; keep within limits: *She could not restrain her curiosity. He restrained the excited dog when guests came.* **2** keep in prison; confine. *v.* —**re·strain′a·ble**, *adj.* —**re·strain′er**, *n.*

**re·strain·ed·ly** (ri strā′ni dlē) in a RESTRAINed manner; with restraint. *adv.*

**re·straint** (ri strānt′) **1** RESTRAINing or being restrained. **2** a means of RESTRAINing: *A horse's bridle is a restraint.* **3** control of natural feeling; reserve: *Joel was very angry, but he spoke with restraint.* *n.*

**restraint of trade** the limitation or prevention of free competition in business.

**re·strict** (ri strikt′) **1** keep within limits; confine: *Our club membership is restricted to twelve artists.* **2** put limitations on: *restrict the meaning of a word.* *v.*

**re·strict·ed** (ri strik′tid) **1** limited; kept within limits: *She is on a very restricted diet, and can have no sweets.* **2** having restrictions or limiting rules: *Factories may not be built in this restricted residential section.* **3** pt. and pp. of RESTRICT. **1, 2** *adj.*, **3** *v.*

**re·stric·tion** (ri strik′shən) **1** something that restricts; limiting condition or rule: *The restrictions on the use of the playground are no fighting and no damaging property.* **2** restricting or being restricted: *This park is open to the public without restriction.* *n.*

**re·stric·tive** (ri strik′tiv) restricting; limiting: *Some laws are prohibitive; some are only restrictive.* *adj.* —**re·stric′tive·ly**, *adv.*

**re·string** (rē string′) put a new string or new strings on. *v.*, **re·strung, re·string·ing.**

**rest room** a room providing toilet facilities in a public building, theatre, store, service station, etc.; washroom.

**re·sult** (ri zult′) **1** that which happens as the outcome of something: *The result of the fall was a broken leg.* **2** a good or useful end or outcome: *We want results, not talk.* **3** be a result; follow as a consequence: *Sickness often results from eating too much.* **4** have as a result; end: *Eating too much often results in sickness.* **5** in mathematics, a quantity, value, etc. obtained by calculation. **6** an outcome: *We were happy at the result of the hockey game.* **1, 2, 5, 6** *n.*, **3, 4** *v.*

**re·sult·ant** (ri zul′tənt) **1** RESULTing. **2** RESULT. **3** in physics, any force that has the same effect as two or more forces acting together. **1** *adj.*, **2, 3** *n.*

**re·sume** (ri züm′ *or* ri zyüm′) **1** begin again; go on: *Resume reading where we left off.* **2** get or take again: *Those standing may resume their seats.* *v.*, **re·sumed, re·sum·ing.** —**re·sum′a·ble**, *adj.*

**rés·u·mé** (rez′ù mā′; *French*, RĀ ZY MĀ′) **1** a short account of a person's education, employment history, etc., prepared for submission with a job application. **2** summary: *a brief résumé of the news.* *n.*

**re·sump·tion** (ri zump′shən) the act of resuming: *the resumption of duties after absence.* *n.*

**re·sur·face** (rē sėr′fis) provide with a new or different surface. *v.*, **re·sur·faced, re·sur·fac·ing.**

**re·surge** (ri sėrj′) rise again. *v.*, **re·surged, re·surg·ing.**

**re·sur·gence** (ri sėr′jəns) rising again. *n.*

**re·sur·gent** (ri sėr′jənt) rising or tending to rise again. *adj.*

**res·ur·rect** (rez′ə rekt′) **1** raise from the dead; bring back to life. **2** bring back to sight or into use: *to resurrect an old custom.* *v.*

**res·ur·rec·tion** (rez′ə rek′shən) **1** a coming to life again; rising from the dead. **2** a restoration from decay, disuse, etc.: *the resurrection of an old plan for rebuilding the city.* **3 Resurrection**, in Christian theology, the rising again of Christ after His death and burial. *n.*

**re·sus·ci·tate** (ri sus′ə tāt′) bring or come back to life or consciousness; revive: *The doctor resuscitated the woman who was overcome by gas.* *v.*, **re·sus·ci·tat·ed, re·sus·ci·tat·ing.** —**re·sus′ci·ta′tion**, *n.* —**re·sus′ci·ta′tor**, *n.*

**re·sus·ci·ta·tive** (ri sus′ə tə tiv *or* ri sus′ə tā′tiv) helping to RESUSCITATE. *adj.*

---

*In each of the words below,* **re-** *means* again *or* anew; *the pronunciation of the main part of each word is not changed.*

| re·stitch′ | re·struc′ture | re·stuff′ | re′sub·mit′ | re′sur·vey′ |
| re·stock′ | re·stud′y | re·style′ | re′sur·face | re′swal′low |

**ret.** 1 retain. 2 retired. 3 return.

**re·tail** (rē′tāl *for 1–5, 7,* ri tāl′ *for 6*) 1 the sale of goods in small quantities directly to the final consumer: *Most stores sell at retail.* 2 in small lots or quantities: *The retail price of this jewellery is 70 percent higher than the wholesale price.* 3 selling in small quantities to the final consumer: *the retail trade, a retail merchant.* 4 sell in small quantities. 5 be sold in small quantities: *a dress retailing at $70.00.* 6 tell over again: *She retails everything she hears about her acquaintances.* 7 from a retail merchant or dealer: *He has to buy his supplies retail.* 1 *n.,* 2, 3 *adj.,* 4–6 *v.,* 7 *adv.*

**re·tail·er** (rē′tā lər) a retail merchant or dealer. *n.*

**re·tain** (ri tān′) 1 continue to have or hold; keep: *China dishes retain heat longer than metal pans do.* 2 keep in mind; remember: *She retained the tune but not the words of the song.* 3 employ by payment of a fee: *He retained the best lawyer in the city.* *v.*

**re·tain·er**[1] (ri tā′nər) a person who serves a person of rank; vassal; attendant; follower: *The king had many retainers.* *n.*

**re·tain·er**[2] (ri tā′nər) a fee paid to secure services: *This lawyer receives a retainer before he begins work on a case.* *n.*

**re·take** (rē tāk′ *for verb,* rē′tāk′ *for noun*) 1 take again. 2 take back. 3 retaking: *a retake of a scene in a movie.* 1, 2 *v.,* **re·took, re·tak·en, re·tak·ing;** 3 *n.*

**re·tal·i·ate** (ri tal′ē āt′) pay back wrong, injury, etc.; return like for like: *If we insult them, they will retaliate.* *v.,* **re·tal·i·at·ed, re·tal·i·at·ing.**

**re·tal·i·a·tion** (ri tal′ē ā′shən) the paying back of a wrong, injury, etc. *n.*

**re·tal·i·a·tive** (ri tal′ē ə tiv *or* ri tal′ē ā′tiv) disposed to RETALIATE; retaliatory. *adj.*

**re·tal·i·a·to·ry** (ri tal′ē ə tô′rē) returning like for like. *adj.*

**re·tard** (ri tärd′) make slow; delay the progress of; keep back; hinder: *Bad roads retarded the car.* *v.* —**re·tard′er,** *n.*

**re·tar·da·tion** (rē′tär dā′shən) 1 the act of RETARDing. 2 that which RETARDs; a hindrance. *n.*

**re·tard·ed** (ri tär′dəd) 1 limited in mental development; backward. 2 pt. and pp. of RETARD. 1 *adj.,* 2 *v.*

**retch** (rech) make efforts to vomit; make movements like those of vomiting. *v.*
☛ **Hom.** WRETCH.

**ret'd.** 1 returned. 2 retired.

**re·tell** (rē tel′) tell again. *v.,* **re·told, re·tell·ing.**

**re·ten·tion** (ri ten′shən) 1 RETAINing. 2 being RETAINed. 3 the power to RETAIN. 4 the ability to remember. *n.*

**re·ten·tive** (ri ten′tiv) 1 able to hold or keep. 2 able to remember. *adj.* —**re·ten′tive·ness,** *n.*

**re·ten·tiv·i·ty** (rē′ten tiv′ə tē) 1 the power to RETAIN; retentiveness. 2 the power of RETAINing magnetization after the magnetizing force has ceased to operate. *n.*

---

**ret.** 1011 **retold**

hat, āge, fär; let, ēqual, tėrm; it, īce
hot, ōpen, ôrder; oil, out; cup, pu̇t, rüle
əbove, takən, pencəl, lemən, circəs
ch, child; ng, long; sh, ship
th, thin; ᴛʜ, then; zh, measure

**ret·i·cence** (ret′ə səns) a tendency to be silent or say little; reserve in speech. *n.*

**ret·i·cent** (ret′ə sənt) disposed to keep silent or say little; not speaking freely; reserved in speech. *adj.* —**ret′i·cent·ly,** *adv.*

**re·tic·u·lar** (ri tik′yə lər) 1 netlike. 2 intricate; entangled. *adj.*

**re·tic·u·late** (ri tik′yə lit *or* ri tik′yə lāt′ *for adjective,* ri tik′yə lāt′ *for verb*) 1 netlike; covered with a network: *Reticulate leaves have the veins arranged like the threads of a net.* 2 cover or mark with a network. 3 form a network. 1 *adj.,* 2, 3 *v.,* **re·tic·u·lat·ed, re·tic·u·lat·ing.**

**re·tic·u·la·tion** (ri tik′yə lā′shən) 1 a reticulated formation, arrangement, or appearance; network. 2 one of the meshes of a network. *n.*

**re·tic·u·lum** (ri tik′yə ləm) 1 a network; any reticulated system or structure. 2 the second stomach of cud-chewing mammals. *n., pl.* **re·tic·u·la** (-lə).

**ret·i·na** (ret′ə nə) the layer of cells at the back of the eyeball, which is sensitive to light and receives the images of things looked at. See EYE for picture. *n., pl.* **ret·i·nas** *or* **ret·i·nae** (-nē′ *or* -nī′).

**ret·i·nal** (ret′ə nəl) of or on the RETINA. *adj.*

**ret·i·nue** (ret′ə nyü′ *or* ret′ə nü′) a group of attendants or retainers; following: *the queen's retinue.* *n.*

**re·tire** (ri tīr′) 1 give up an office, occupation, etc.: *The teacher expects to retire at 65.* 2 remove from an office, occupation, etc. 3 go away, especially to be quiet: *She retired to a convent.* 4 withdraw; draw back; send back: *The government retires worn or torn five-dollar bills from use.* 5 go back; retreat: *The enemy retired before the advance of our troops.* 6 go to bed: *We retire early.* 7 take up and pay off bonds, loans, etc. 8 in baseball and cricket, put out a batter, side, etc.: *The pitcher retired three batters in a row.* *v.,* **re·tired, re·tir·ing.**

**re·tired** (ri tīrd′) 1 withdrawn from one's occupation: *a retired sea captain.* 2 reserved; retiring: *a shy, retired nature.* 3 secluded; shut off; hidden: *a retired spot.* 4 pt. and pp. of RETIRE. 1–3 *adj.,* 4 *v.*

**re·tire·ment** (ri tīr′mənt) 1 the act of retiring or being retired; withdrawal: *The teacher's retirement from service was regretted by the school.* 2 the state of being thus withdrawn: *My grandfather is enjoying his retirement.* 3 a quiet way or place of living: *She lives in retirement, neither making nor receiving visits.* *n.*

**re·tir·ing** (ri tī′ring) 1 shrinking from society or publicity; reserved; shy: *a retiring nature.* 2 ppr. of RETIRE. 1 *adj.,* 2 *v.*

**re·told** (rē tōld′) pt. and pp. of RETELL. *v.*

---

*In each of the words below,* **re-** *means* again *or* anew; *the pronunciation of the main part of each word is not changed.*

| re·tai′lor | re·test′ | re·think′ | re·thread′ | re·tie′ |
| re·teach′ | re·thatch′ | | | |

**re·took** (rē tūk′) pt. of RETAKE. *v.*

**re·tort**[1] (ri tôrt′) **1** reply quickly or sharply. **2** a sharp or witty reply. **3** return in kind; turn back on: *to retort insult for insult or blow for blow.* 1, 3 *v.*, 2 *n.*

**re·tort**[2] (ri tôrt′) a container used for distilling or decomposing substances by heat. See STILL[2] for picture. *n.*

**re·touch** (rē tuch′) improve a photographic negative, etc. by making slight changes. *v.*

**re·trace** (ri trās′) go back over: *We retraced our steps to where we started.* *v.*, **re·traced, re·trac·ing.**
—**re·trace′a·ble,** *adj.*

**re–trace** (rē trās′) trace over again: *Re-trace these drawings.* *v.*, **re-traced, re-trac·ing.**

**re·tract** (ri trakt′) **1** draw back or in: *The kitten retracted her claws and purred when I petted her.* **2** withdraw; take back: *to retract an offer or an opinion.* *v.*

**re·trac·tile** (ri trak′tīl *or* ri trak′təl) capable of being drawn back or in. *adj.*

**re·trac·tion** (ri trak′shən) **1** a drawing or being drawn back or in. **2** a taking back; withdrawal of a promise, statement, etc.: *The boy who accused Freda of cheating made a retraction of the charge.* **3** retractile power. *n.*

**re·trac·tor** (ri trak′tər) **1** a person or thing that draws back something. **2** a muscle that retracts an organ, protruded part, etc. *n.*

**re·tread** (rē tred′ *for verb*, rē′tred′ *for noun*) **1** put a new tread on. **2** a retreaded tire. 1 *v.*, **re·tread·ed, re·tread·ing;** 2 *n.*

**re·treat** (ri trēt′) **1** go back; move back; withdraw: *Seeing the big dog, the tramp retreated rapidly. He retreated to his cottage for the weekends.* **2** the act of going back or withdrawing: *The army's retreat was orderly.* **3** a signal for retreat: *The drums beat a retreat.* **4** a signal on a bugle or drum, given in the army at sunset: *The flag is lowered at retreat.* **5** a safe, quiet place; place of rest or refuge: *He found his cottage an ideal retreat.* 1 *v.*, 2–5 *n.*
**beat a retreat,** run away; retreat: *We dropped the apples and beat a hasty retreat when the farmer shouted at us.*

**re·trench** (ri trench′) **1** cut down in order to save. **2** reduce expenses: *In hard times, we must retrench.* *v.*

**re·trench·ment** (ri trench′mənt) **1** a reduction of expenses. **2** cutting down; cutting off. *n.*

**re·tri·al** (rē trī′əl) a second trial; new trial. *n.*

**ret·ri·bu·tion** (ret′rə byü′shən) a deserved punishment; return for evil done or, sometimes, for good done. *n.*

**re·trib·u·tive** (ri trib′yə tiv) paying back; bringing or inflicting punishment in return for some evil, wrong, etc. *adj.*

**re·trieve** (ri trēv′) **1** get again; recover: *to retrieve a lost pocketbook.* **2** bring back to a former or better condition; restore: *to retrieve one's fortunes.* **3** make good; make amends for; repair: *to retrieve a mistake, to retrieve a loss or defeat.* **4** find and bring to a person: *A dog can be trained to retrieve game.* **5** find and bring back killed or wounded game. *v.*, **re·trieved, re·triev·ing.**

**re·triev·er** (ri trē′vər) a dog trained to find killed or wounded game and bring it to a hunter. *n.*

**retro–** a prefix meaning: back or backwards, as in *retroflex, retro-rocket, retrospect.*

**ret·ro·ac·tive** (ret′rō ak′tiv) acting back; having an effect on what is past: *A retroactive law applies to events that occurred before the law was passed.* *adj.*

**ret·ro·cede** (ret′rə sēd′) CEDE back territory, etc. *v.*, **ret·ro·ced·ed, ret·ro·ced·ing.**

**ret·ro·flex** (ret′rə fleks′) bent backward. *adj.*

**ret·ro·flex·ion** (ret′rə flek′shən) bending backward. *n.*

**ret·ro·grade** (ret′rə grād′) **1** moving backward; retreating. **2** move or go backward. **3** becoming worse. **4** fall back toward a worse condition; grow worse; decline. 1, 3 *adj.*, 2, 4 *v.*, **ret·ro·grad·ed, ret·ro·grad·ing.**

**ret·ro·gress** (ret′rə gres′ *or* ret′rə gres′) **1** move backward; go back. **2** become worse. *v.*

**ret·ro·gres·sion** (ret′rə gresh′ən) **1** a backward movement. **2** a becoming worse; falling off; decline. *n.*

**ret·ro·gres·sive** (ret′rə gres′iv) **1** moving backward. **2** becoming worse. *adj.* —**ret′ro·gres′sive·ly,** *adv.*

**ret·ro–rock·et** (ret′rō rok′it) on a space ship, artificial satellite, etc., a rocket that fires in a direction opposite to that of the motion of the craft, thus acting as a brake. *n.*

**ret·ro·spect** (ret′rə spekt′) **1** a survey of past time, events, etc.; thinking about the past. **2** think of something past. 1 *n.*, 2 *v.*
**in retrospect,** when looking back.

**ret·ro·spec·tion** (ret′rə spek′shən) a looking back on things past; a survey of past events or experiences. *n.*

**ret·ro·spec·tive** (ret′rə spek′tiv) **1** looking back on things past; surveying past events or experiences. **2** applying to the past; retroactive. **3** an art exhibition reviewing the work of an artist or group of artists over a number of years. 1, 2 *adj.*, 3 *n.*
—**ret′ro·spec′tive·ly,** *adv.*

**ret·rous·sé** (ret′rü sā′; *French,* Rə tRü sā′) turned up: *a retroussé nose.* *adj.*

**re·try** (rē trī′) try again: *The murder case was retried in a higher court.* *v.*, **re·tried, re·try·ing.**

**re·turn** (ri tėrn′) **1** go back; come back: *My sister will return this summer.* **2** bring, give, send, hit, put, or pay back: *Return that book to the library.* **3** a going or coming back; happening again: *We look forward all winter to our return to the country. We wish you many happy returns of your birthday.* **4** something returned. **5** a bringing back; giving back; sending back; hitting back; putting back: *a poor return for kindness.* **6** yield; provide: *The concert returned about $150 over expenses.* **7** a report; account: *election returns.* **8** report or announce officially: *The jury returned a verdict of guilty.* **9** reply: *"No!" she returned crossly.* **10** elect to a lawmaking body. **11** of or having

---

*In each of the words below,* **re-** *means* **again** *or* **anew;** *the pronunciation of the main part of each word is not changed.*

**re·train′**   **re′trans·late′**   **re′trans·mit′**   **re·turf′**

to do with a return: *a return ticket.* **12** sent, given, done, etc. in return: *a return game.* **13** in card games, lead the suit led by one's partner. **14** Often, **returns**, *pl.* a profit; an amount received: *The returns from the sale were more than a hundred dollars.* 1, 2, 6, 8–10, 13 *v.*, 3–5, 7, 9, 14 *n.*, 11, 12 *adj.*

**in return,** as a return: *If you lend me your skates now, I'll lend you my tennis racket next summer in return.*

**re·turn·a·ble** (ri tėr′nə bəl) **1** that can be returned. **2** meant or required to be returned. *adj.*

**returned man** *Cdn.* a war veteran.

**re·turn·ee** (ri tėr′nē′) a person who has returned, especially one who has returned to his or her own country after capture in a war or service abroad. *n.*

**returning officer** in Canada, the official who is responsible for the entire election procedure in a particular constituency, from preparing the voters' list and the ballots to the proclamation of the winning candidate: *In federal elections, returning officers are appointed by the Governor General in Council.*

**return trip** a trip to a place and back again; a round trip.

**re·tuse** (ri tyüs′ *or* ri tüs′) of a leaf, etc., having an obtuse or rounded apex with a shallow notch. *adj.*

**re·un·ion** (rē yü′nyən) **1** a coming together again: *the reunion of parted friends.* **2** a social gathering of persons who have been separated or who have interests in common: *a family reunion.* *n.*

**re·u·nite** (rē′yü nīt′) **1** bring together again: *Mother and child were reunited after years of separation.* **2** come together again. *v.*, **re·u·nit·ed, re·u·nit·ing.**

**rev** (rev) *Informal.* **1** a revolution of an engine or motor. **2** increase the speed of an engine or motor. 1 *n.*, 2 *v.*, **revved, rev·ving.**

**rev.** **1** revenue. **2** reverse. **3** review. **4** revised. **5** revision. **6** revolution.

**Rev.** Reverend.

**re·val·ue** (rē val′yü) value again or anew. *v.*, **re·val·ued, re·val·u·ing.**

**re·vamp** (rē vamp′) patch up; repair. *v.*

**re·veal** (ri vēl′) **1** make known something hidden, secret, or mysterious: *Never reveal my secret.* **2** display; show: *Her smile revealed her even teeth.* *v.* —**re·veal′er,** *n.*

**rev·eil·le** (rə val′ē) a signal on a bugle or drum to waken military personnel in the morning: *The bugler blows reveille.* *n.*
☛ Pronunciation. The pronunciation (rev′ə lē) is American.

**rev·el** (rev′əl) **1** take great pleasure (*in*): *The children revel in country life.* **2** a noisy good time; merrymaking. **3** make merry. 1, 3 *v.*, **rev·elled** *or* **rev·eled, rev·el·ling** *or* **rev·el·ing;** —**rev′el·ler** *or* **rev′el·er,** *n.*

**rev·e·la·tion** (rev′ə lā′shən) **1** the act of making known something hidden, secret, or mysterious: *The revelation of the thieves' hiding place resulted in their capture.* **2** the thing made known: *Her true nature was a revelation to me.* *n.*

hat, āge, fär; let, ēqual, tėrm; it, īce hot, ōpen, ôrder; oil, out; cup, pùt, rüle
above, taken, pencəl, lemən, circəs
ch, child; ng, long; sh, ship
th, thin; ᴛH, then; zh, measure

**rev·el·ry** (rev′əl rē) a boisterous revelling or festivity; wild merrymaking: *the sound of revelry.* *n.*, *pl.* **rev·el·ries.**

**re·venge** (ri venj′) **1** harm done in return for a wrong; vengeance; a returning of evil for evil: *a blow struck in revenge.* **2** do harm in return for: *His family vowed to revenge his death.* **3** a desire for vengeance: *She said nothing but there was revenge in her heart.* **4** take vengeance. **5** a chance to win in a return game after losing a game. 1, 3, 5 *n.*, 2, 4 *v.*, **re·venged, re·veng·ing.** **be revenged,** get revenge: *He swore to be revenged on his brother's murderers.*
**revenge oneself on,** take revenge: *I'll revenge myself on her for that insult.*

**re·venge·ful** (ri venj′fəl) feeling or showing a strong desire for REVENGE. *adj.* —**re·venge′ful·ly,** *adv.*

**rev·e·nue** (rev′ə nyü′ *or* rev′ə nü′) money coming in; income: *The government gets revenue from taxes.* *n.*

**revenue stamp** a stamp to show that money has been paid to the government as a tax on something.

**re·ver·ber·ate** (ri vėr′bə rāt′) **1** echo back: *Her voice reverberates from the high ceiling.* **2** cast or be cast back; reflect light or heat. *v.*, **re·ver·ber·at·ed, re·ver·ber·at·ing.**

**re·ver·ber·a·tion** (ri vėr′bə rā′shən) **1** an echoing back of sound; echo. **2** a reflection of light or heat. *n.*

**re·ver·ber·a·to·ry** (ri vėr′bə rə tô′rē) characterized by or produced by REVERBERATIONS; deflected. *adj.*

**re·vere** (ri vēr′) love and respect deeply; honour greatly; show reverence for: *People revered the great statesman.* *v.*, **re·vered, re·ver·ing.**

**rev·er·ence** (rev′ə rəns) **1** a feeling of deep respect, mixed with wonder, awe, and love. **2** regard with reverence. **3** a deep bow. **4 Reverence,** in the Christian church, a title used in speaking of or to a member of the clergy. 1, 3, 4 *n.*, 2 *v.*, **rev·er·enced, rev·er·enc·ing.**

**rev·er·end** (rev′ə rənd) **1** worthy of great respect. **2** *Informal.* member of the clergy. **3 Reverend,** in the Christian church, a title for members of the clergy: *the Reverend Thomas A. Johnson.* 1 *adj.*, 2, 3 *n.*

**rev·er·ent** (rev′ə rənt) feeling REVERENCE (def. 1); showing reverence. *adj.* —**rev′er·ent·ly,** *adv.*

**rev·er·en·tial** (rev′ə ren′shəl) REVERENT. *adj.* —**rev′er·en′tial·ly,** *adv.*

**rev·er·ie** (rev′ə rē) dreamy thoughts; dreamy thinking of pleasant things: *She loved to indulge in reveries about the future.* *n.* Also, **revery.**

**re·vers** (rə vėr′ *or* rə ver′) a part of a garment that is turned back to show the lining or facing. *n.*, *pl.* **re·vers** (rə vėrz′ *or* rə verz′).

---

*In each of the words below,* **re-** *means* again *or* anew; *the pronunciation of the main part of each word is not changed.*

re·type′   re′up·hol′ster   re·val′u·ate′   re·ver′i·fy′

**re·ver·sal** (ri vėr′səl) a change to the opposite; a reversing or being reversed. *n.*

**re·verse** (ri vėrs′) **1** the opposite or contrary: *She did the reverse of what I ordered.* **2** turned backward; opposite or contrary in position or direction: *the reverse side of a phonograph record.* **3** acting in a manner opposite or contrary to that which is usual. **4** causing an opposite or backward movement. **5** turn the other way: *Reverse that gun; don't point it at me.* **6** turn inside out: *Your raincoat is reversed.* **7** turn upside down: *She reversed the hourglass.* **8** turn in a direction opposite to the usual one while dancing. **9** the gear or gears that reverse the movement of machinery: *an automobile in reverse.* **10** the position of such a gear or gears: *Put the car in reverse to drive out of the garage.* **11** change to the opposite; repeal: *The court reversed its decree of imprisonment, and the man went free.* **12** a change to bad fortune; check; defeat: *He used to be rich, but he met with reverses.* **13** the back: *Her name is on the reverse of the medal.* 1, 9, 10, 12, 13 *n.*, 2–4 *adj.*, 5–8, 11 *v.*, **re·versed, re·vers·ing.**

**re·verse·ly** (ri vėrs′lē) **1** in a reverse position, direction, or order. **2** on the other hand; on the contrary. *adv.*

**re·vers·i·bil·i·ty** (ri vėr′sə bil′ə tē) the fact or quality of being REVERSIBLE. *n.*

**re·vers·i·ble** (ri vėr′sə bəl) **1** that can be reversed; that can reverse. **2** of a fabric or garment, finished on both sides so that either can be used as the right side. *adj.* —**re·vers′i·bly,** *adv.*

**re·ver·sion** (ri vėr′zhən) **1** a return to a former condition, practice, belief, etc.; return. **2** the return of property to the grantor or his or her heirs. *n.*

**re·ver·sion·al** (ri vėr′zhə nəl) of, having to do with, or involving a REVERSION. *adj.*

**re·vert** (ri vėrt′) go back; return: *If a person dies without heirs, his or her property reverts to the government.* *v.*

**rev·er·y** (rev′ə rē) See REVERIE. *n.*, *pl.* **rev·er·ies.**

**re·view** (ri vyü′) **1** study again; look at again: *She reviewed the scene of the crime.* **2** studying again: *Before the examinations, we have a review of the term's work.* **3** look back on: *Before falling asleep, Helen reviewed the day's happenings.* **4** looking back on; survey: *A review of the trip was pleasant.* **5** examine again; look at with care; examine: *A superior court may review decisions of a lower court.* **6** a re-examination. **7** an examination; inspection: *A review of the scouts will be held during the leader's visit to the camp.* **8** inspect formally: *The admiral reviewed the fleet.* **9** a critical account of a book, play, etc., giving its merits and faults: *That magazine contains good reviews of the new movies.* **10** a magazine containing articles on subjects of current interest, including accounts of books, etc.: *a law review, a motion-picture review.* **11** examine to give an account of: *Ms. Moro reviews books for a living.* **12** review books, etc. **13** REVUE. 1, 3, 5, 8, 11, 12 *v.*, 2, 4, 6, 7, 9, 10, 13 *n.*

**re·view·er** (ri vyü′ər) **1** a person who REVIEWS. **2** a person who writes articles discussing books, plays, etc. *n.*

**reviewing stand** a raised platform for those REVIEWing (def. 8) a formal parade.

**re·vile** (ri vīl′) call bad names; abuse with words: *The tramp reviled the woman who drove him off.* *v.*, **re·viled, re·vil·ing.**

**re·vile·ment** (ri vīl′mənt) **1** the act of reviling. **2** reviling speech. *n.*

**re·vise** (ri vīz′) **1** read carefully and correct or improve; look over and change: *She has revised the poem she wrote.* **2** change; alter: *to revise one's opinion.* **3** the process of revising. **4** a revised form or version. 1, 2 *v.*, **re·vised, re·vis·ing;** 3, 4 *n.* —**re·vis′er,** *n.*

**re·vi·sion** (ri vizh′ən) **1** the act or work of revising. **2** a REVISED form: *a revision of a book.* *n.*

**re·vi·so·ry** (ri vī′zə rē) of or having to do with REVISION. *adj.*

**re·viv·al** (ri vī′vəl) **1** a bringing or coming back to life or consciousness. **2** a restoration to vigour or health. **3** a bringing or coming back to style, use, activity, etc.: *the revival of a play of years ago.* **4** an awakening or increase of interest: *a revival of learning.* **5** special efforts made to awaken or increase interest: *a revival of democracy.* *n.*

**re·viv·al·ist** (ri vī′və list) a person who holds special services to awaken interest in religion. *n.*

**re·vive** (ri vīv′) **1** bring back or come back to life or consciousness: *to revive a half-drowned person.* **2** bring or come back to a fresh, lively condition: *Flowers revive in water.* **3** make or become fresh; restore: *Hot coffee revived the cold, tired man.* **4** bring back or come back to notice, use, fashion, memory, activity, etc.: *to revive an old song. An old play is sometimes revived on the stage.* *v.*, **re·vived, re·viv·ing.**

**rev·o·ca·ble** (rev′ə kə bəl) that can be repealed, cancelled, or withdrawn. *adj.*

**rev·o·ca·tion** (rev′ə kā′shən) a repeal; cancelling; withdrawal: *the revocation of a law.* *n.*

**rev·o·ca·to·ry** (rev′ə kə tô′rē) revoking; recalling; repealing. *adj.*

**re·voke** (ri vōk′) **1** take back; repeal; cancel; withdraw: *The government revoked the bill before it was voted on.* **2** in cards, a failure to follow suit when one can and should; RENEGE (def. 2). **3** in cards, fail to follow suit when one can and should; RENEGE (def. 1). 1, 3 *v.*, **re·voked, re·vok·ing;** 2 *n.*

**re·volt** (ri vōlt′) **1** the act or state of rebelling: *The town is in revolt.* **2** turn away from and fight against a leader; rise against the government's authority: *The people revolted against the dictator.* **3** turn away with disgust: *to revolt at a bad smell.* **4** cause to feel disgust: *Violence in movies revolts many people.* 1 *n.*, 2–4 *v.* —**re·volt′er,** *n.*

**re·volt·ing** (ri vōl′ting) **1** disgusting; repulsive. **2** ppr. of REVOLT. 1 *adj.*, 2 *v.*

**rev·o·lu·tion** (rev′ə lü′shən) **1** a complete, often violent, overthrow of an established government or political system: *The French Revolution from 1789 to 1799 changed France from a kingdom to a republic.* **2** a complete change: *Plastics have brought about a revolution*

---

*In each of the words below,* **re-** *means* again *or* anew; *the pronunciation of the main part of each word is not changed.*

**re·vis′it**

in industry. **3** movement in a circle or curve around some point: *One revolution of the earth around the sun takes a year.* **4** the act or fact of turning round a centre or axis; rotation: *The revolution of the earth causes day and night.* **5** a single complete turn around a centre: *The wheel of the motor turns at a rate of more than one thousand revolutions a minute.* **6** the time or distance of one revolution. **7** a complete cycle or series of events: *The revolution of the four seasons completes a year.* *n.*

**rev·o·lu·tion·ar·y** (rev′ə lü′shə ner′ē) **1** of a REVOLUTION (defs. 1, 2); connected with a revolution. **2** bringing or causing great changes. **3** REVOLUTIONIST. **1, 2** *adj.*, **3** *n., pl.* **rev·o·lu·tion·ar·ies.**

**Revolutionary War** in the United States, the war from 1775 to 1783 by which the thirteen colonies gained independence from the United Kingdom.

**rev·o·lu·tion·ist** (rev′ə lü′shə nist) a person who advocates, or takes part in, a REVOLUTION (def. 1). *n.*

**rev·o·lu·tion·ize** (rev′ə lü′shə nīz′) change completely; produce a very great change in: *Mechanization revolutionized farm life.* *v.*, **rev·o·lu·tion·ized, rev·o·lu·tion·iz·ing.**

**re·volve** (ri volv′) **1** move in a circle; move in a curve around a point: *The moon revolves around the earth.* **2** turn round a centre or axis; rotate: *The wheels of a moving car revolve.* **3** cause to move round. **4** move in a complete cycle or series of events: *The seasons revolve.* *v.*, **re·volved, re·volv·ing.**

**re·volv·er** (ri vol′vər) a pistol with a revolving cylinder in which the cartridges are contained. It can be fired several times without reloading. *n.*

**re·vue** (ri vyü′) a theatrical entertainment with singing, dancing, parodies of recent plays, humorous treatments of happenings and fads of the year, etc. *n.* Also, **review.**

**re·vul·sion** (ri vul′shən) **1** a strong feeling of disgust or distaste: *The stench of rotting vegetables filled us with revulsion.* **2** a sudden, violent change of feeling: *He suddenly felt a revulsion from the long solitude.* *n.*

**re·ward** (ri wôrd′) **1** a return made for something done. **2** a money payment given or offered for capture of criminals, the return of lost property, etc. **3** give a reward to. **4** give a reward for. **1, 2** *n.*, **3, 4** *v.*

**re·wire** (rē wīr′) **1** put new wires on or in. **2** telegraph again. *v.*, **re·wired, re·wir·ing.**

**re·word** (rē wėrd′) put into other words. *v.*

**re·write** (rē rīt′ *for verb,* rē′rīt *for noun*) **1** write again; write in a different form; revise. **2** write a news story from material supplied in a form that cannot be used as copy. **3** something revised or written again. **1, 2** *v.*, **re·wrote, re·writ·ten, re·writ·ing;** **3** *n.*

**Rf** rutherfordium.

**RF, R.F.,** or **r.f.** radio frequency.

**r.h.** **1** right hand. **2** relative humidity.

**Rh** **1** Rh factor. **2** rhodium.

**rhap·sod·i·cal** (rap sod′ə kəl) of, having to do with, or characteristic of RHAPSODY; extravagantly enthusiastic; ecstatic. *adj.* —**rhap·sod′i·cal·ly,** *adv.*

## revolutionary 1015 rheumy

hat, āge, fär; let, ēqual, tėrm; it, īce
hot, ōpen, ôrder; oil, out; cup, put, rüle
ə·bove, taken, pencəl, lemən, circəs
ch, child; ng, long; sh, ship
th, thin; ᴛʜ, then; zh, measure

**rhap·so·dize** (rap′sə dīz′) talk or write with extravagant enthusiasm. *v.*, **rhap·so·dized, rhap·so·diz·ing.**

**rhap·so·dy** (rap′sə dē) **1** an utterance or writing marked by extravagant enthusiasm: *She went into rhapsodies over the garden.* **2** in music, an instrumental composition irregular in form: *Liszt's Hungarian Rhapsodies.* *n., pl.* **rhap·so·dies.**

**rhe·a** (rē′ə) any of several large birds of South America that resemble the ostrich but are smaller and have three toes instead of two. *n.*

**rhe·ni·um** (rē′nē əm) a rare, hard, greyish metallic element that has chemical properties similar to those of manganese. Symbol: Re *n.*

**rhe·o·stat** (rē′ə stat′) an instrument for regulating the strength of an electric current by introducing different amounts of resistance into the circuit. *n.*

**rhe·sus** (rē′səs) a small, yellowish-brown monkey with a short tail, found in India. *n.*

**Rhesus factor** (rē′səs) RH FACTOR.

**rhet·o·ric** (ret′ə rik) **1** the art of using words effectively in speaking or writing. **2** a book about this art. **3** mere display in language. *n.*

**rhe·tor·i·cal** (ri tôr′ə kəl) **1** of or having to do with RHETORIC. **2** using RHETORIC. **3** intended especially for display; artificial. **4** ORATORICAL. *adj.* —**rhe·tor′i·cal·ly,** *adv.*

**rhetorical question** a question asked only for effect, not for information.

**rhet·o·ri·cian** (ret′ə rish′ən) **1** a person skilled in RHETORIC. **2** a person given to display in language. *n.*

**rheum** (rüm) **1** a watery discharge, such as mucus, tears, or saliva. **2** catarrh; a cold. *n.*
☛ *Hom.* ROOM.

**rheu·mat·ic** (rü mat′ik) **1** of RHEUMATISM. **2** having RHEUMATISM; liable to have rheumatism. **3** causing RHEUMATISM. **4** caused by RHEUMATISM. **5** a person who has RHEUMATISM. **6 rheumatics,** *pl. Informal.* RHEUMATISM. **1–4** *adj.*, **5, 6** *n.*

**rheumatic fever** an acute disease occurring usually in children, characterized by fever, swelling, pain in the joints, and inflammation of the heart.

**rheu·ma·tism** (rü′mə tiz′əm) any of various painful conditions of the joints, muscles, or connective tissue, characterized by inflammation, stiffness, etc.: *Bursitis and arthritis are forms of rheumatism.* *n.*

**rheum·y** (rü′mē) **1** full of RHEUM. **2** causing RHEUM; damp and cold. *adj.*
☛ *Hom.* ROOMY.

---

In each of the words below, **re-** means *again* or *anew;* the pronunciation of the main part of each word is not changed.

| re·vote′ | re·wash′ | re·wax′ | re·weld′ | re·wind′ |
| re·warm′ | re·wa′ter | re·weigh′ | re·win′ | |

**Rh factor** a substance often found in the blood of human beings and the higher mammals. Blood containing this substance (**Rh positive**) does not combine favourably with blood lacking it (**Rh negative**). Also, **Rhesus factor.**

**rhi·nal** (rī′nəl) of or having to do with the nose; nasal. *adj.*

**rhine·stone** (rīn′stōn′) an imitation diamond, made of glass. *n.*

**rhi·ni·tis** (rī nī′tis) inflammation of the nose or its mucous membrane. *n.*

**rhi·no** (rī′nō) RHINOCEROS. *n., pl.* **rhi·nos.**

A black rhinoceros of Africa— about 175 cm high at the shoulder and about 3 m long

**rhi·noc·er·os** (rī nos′ə rəs) a large, thick-skinned mammal of Africa and Asia, having one or two upright horns on the snout. *n., pl.* **rhi·noc·er·os·es** or (*esp. collectively*) **rhi·noc·er·os.**
☛ *Etym.* Through Latin from Gk. *rhīnokerōs* made up of *rhīs, rhīno-* 'nose' + *keras* 'horn'. 13c.

**rhi·zoid** (rī′zoid) rootlike. *adj.*

Rhizomes of three different plants: from left to right, Solomon's-seal, trillium, and jack-in-the-pulpit

**rhi·zome** (rī′zōm) a rootlike stem lying along or under the ground, that usually produces roots below and shoots from the upper surface; rootstock. *n.*

**rhi·zo·pod** (rī′zə pod′) any of a group of one-celled animals that form temporary projections of protoplasm for moving about and taking in food: *Amoebas are rhizopods. n.*

**Rhodes Scholar** (rōdz) a holder of any of a number of scholarships awarded annually to outstanding students from certain Commonwealth countries, South Africa, and the United States for study at Oxford University in England.
☛ *Etym.* Named for Cecil I. *Rhodes* (1853–1902), a British statesman, who provided for these scholarships in his will.

**rho·di·um** (rō′dē əm) a greyish-white metallic element, forming salts that give rose-coloured solutions: *Rhodium is similar to aluminum.* Symbol: Rh *n.*

**rho·do·den·dron** (rō′də den′drən) any of a very large, closely related group of shrubs and small trees of the heath family, found mainly in the cooler regions of the Northern Hemisphere and the mountains of southern Asia, having showy, bell-shaped or funnel-shaped flowers and evergreen or deciduous leaves: *There are more than 800 species of rhododendron including about 70 azaleas; some are widely cultivated as garden plants. n.*

**rhomb** (rom *or* romb) RHOMBUS. *n.*

**rhom·bic** (rom′bik) 1 having the form of a RHOMBUS. 2 having a RHOMBUS as base or cross section. 3 bounded by RHOMBUSES. *adj.*

**rhom·boid** (rom′boid) 1 a parallelogram with equal opposite sides that is not a rectangle. See QUADRILATERAL for picture. 2 shaped like a RHOMBUS or rhomboid. 1 *n.,* 2 *adj.*

**rhom·boi·dal** (rom boi′dəl) RHOMBOID. *adj.*

**rhom·bus** (rom′bəs) a parallelogram with equal sides, having two obtuse angles and two acute angles; diamond. See QUADRILATERAL for picture. *n., pl.* **rhom·bus·es** or **rhom·bi** (-bī *or* bē).

**rhu·barb** (rü′bärb) 1 a garden plant having very large poisonous leaves, whose sour stalks are used for making sauce, pies, etc. 2 the stalks of this plant. 3 the sauce made of the stalks. *n.*

**rhyme** (rīm) 1 sound alike in the last part: *Long and song rhyme. Go to bed rhymes with sleepy head.* 2 an agreement in the final sounds of words or lines. 3 put or make into rhyme: *to rhyme a translation.* 4 a word or line having the same last sound as another: *Cat is a rhyme for mat.* 5 verses or poetry with some of the lines ending in similar sounds. 6 make rhymes: *She enjoys rhyming.* 7 use a word with another that rhymes with it: *We rhyme* love *and* dove. 1, 3, 6, 7 *v.,* **rhymed, rhym·ing;** 2, 4, 5 *n.* Also, **rime.** —**rhym′er,** *n.*
**without rhyme** *or* **reason,** having no system or sense.
☛ *Hom.* RIME.

**rhyme·ster** (rīm′stər) a maker of rather poor rhymes or verse. *n.* Also, **rimester.**

**rhythm** (riŦH′əm) 1 a movement having a regular repetition of a beat, accent, stress, rise and fall, etc.: *the rhythm of dancing, skating, or swimming, the rhythm of the tides, the rhythm of one's heartbeats.* 2 the repetition of an accent; arrangement of beats in a line of poetry: *The rhythms of "The Rime of the Ancient Mariner" and "O Canada" are different.* 3 a grouping by accents or beats: *triple rhythm.* 4 any sequence of regularly recurring events: *visual rhythm. n.*

**rhyth·mic** (riŦH′mik) RHYTHMICAL. *adj.*

**rhyth·mi·cal** (riŦH′mə kəl) having RHYTHM; of or having to do with rhythm. *adj.* —**rhyth′mi·cal·ly,** *adv.*

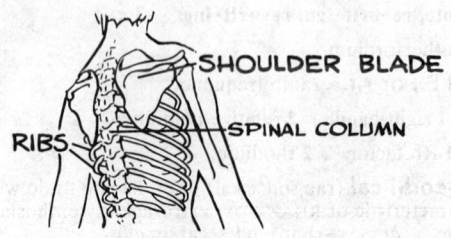

**rib** (rib) 1 one of the curved bones extending from the backbone and enclosing the upper part of the body. See COLLARBONE for another picture. 2 one of a number of similar pieces forming a frame: *An umbrella has ribs.* 3 a cut of meat containing a rib used for food: *ribs of beef.*

See BEEF for picture. **4** a thick vein of a leaf. **5** furnish or strengthen with ribs. **6** a ridge in cloth, knitting, etc. **7** mark with riblike ridges. **8** *Informal.* tease. 1–4, 6 *n.*, 5, 7, 8 *v.*, **ribbed, rib·bing.**

**rib·ald** (rib′əld) offensive in speech; coarsely mocking; irreverent; indecent; obscene. *adj.*

**rib·ald·ry** (rib′əl drē) RIBALD language. *n.*

**ribbed** (ribd) **1** having ribs or ridges. **2** pt. and pp. of RIB. 1 *adj.*, 2 *v.*

**rib·bing** (rib′ing) **1** ribs collectively; a group or arrangement of ribs. **2** *Informal.* a teasing. **3** ppr. of RIB. 1, 2 *n.*, 3 *v.*

**rib·bon** (rib′ən) **1** a strip or band of silk, satin, velvet, etc. **2** anything like such a strip: *a typewriter ribbon.* **3** a small badge or cloth worn as a sign of membership in an order, decoration for bravery, etc.: *the ribbon of the Victoria Cross.* **4 ribbons,** *pl.* torn pieces; shreds: *Her dress was torn to ribbons by thorns and briars.* *n.* —**rib′bon·like′,** *adj.*

**ri·bo·fla·vin** (rī′bō flā′vən) a constituent of the vitamin B complex, present in liver, eggs, milk, spinach, etc.; lactoflavin: *Riboflavin is sometimes called vitamin G or B₂. Persons who lack riboflavin are retarded in growth.* *n.*

**ri·bo·nu·cle·ic acid** (rī′bō nyü klē′ik *or* rī′bō nü klē′ik) an acid found in the nuclei and other parts of cells that helps promote the synthesis of cell proteins.

**ri·bo·some** (rī′bə sōm′) an organelle occurring in large numbers in the cytoplasm of a cell, concerned with the manufacture of protein. *n.*

**rice** (rīs) **1** the starch seeds or grain of a plant grown in warm climates: *Rice is an important food in India, China, and Japan.* **2** the plant itself. **3** reduce to a form like rice: *to rice potatoes.* 1, 2 *n.*, 3 *v.*, **riced, ric·ing.**

**rich** (rich) **1** having much money or property: *a rich man.* **2** well supplied; abounding: *Canada is rich in oil and nickel.* **3** producing or yielding abundantly; fertile: *rich soil, a rich mine.* **4** valuable; having great worth: *a rich harvest.* **5** costly; elegant: *a rich dress.* **6** of food, made with plenty of butter, eggs, flavouring, etc. **7** of colours, sounds, smells, etc., deep; full; vivid: *a rich red, a rich tone.* **8** *Informal.* very amusing; ridiculous. **9** of a fuel, containing a high proportion of fuel to air. **10 the rich,** rich people. 1–9 *adj.*, 10 *n.* —**rich′ly,** *adv.* —**rich′ness,** *n.*

**rich·es** (rich′iz) wealth; abundance of property; much money, land, goods, etc. *n. pl.*

**Rich·ter scale** (rik′tər) a scale for measuring the intensity of an earthquake in terms of the vibrations produced at its centre. Each whole number on the scale, beginning with 1, represents a magnitude 10 times greater than the preceding one. An earthquake of magnitude 1 can be detected only by instruments; a magnitude of 7 indicates a major earthquake: *The most powerful earthquake so far recorded registered 8.6 on the Richter scale.* ☛ *Etym.* Named after Charles F. *Richter,* an American scientist, born in 1900.

**rick** (rik) a stack of hay, straw, etc., especially one made so that the rain will run off it. *n.*

**rick·ets** (rik′its) a disease of childhood, caused by lack of vitamin D or calcium, that results in softening and, sometimes, bending of the bones; rachitis. *n.*

**rick·et·y** (rik′ə tē) **1** liable to fall or break down; shaky: *a rickety old chair.* **2** having RICKETS; suffering from rickets. **3** feeble in the joints. *adj.* —**rick′et·i·ness,** *n.*

**rick·shaw** *or* **rick·sha** (rik′shô) a small, two-wheeled hooded carriage pulled by one or more men: *Rickshaws were originally used in Japan.* *n.*

**ric·o·chet** (rik′ə shā′) **1** the skipping or jumping motion of an object as it goes along a flat surface: *the ricochet of a stone thrown along the surface of water.* **2** move with a skipping or jumping motion: *The bullets struck the ground and ricochetted through the grass.* 1 *n.*, 2 *v.*, **ric·o·chet·ted** *or* **ric·o·cheted** (-shād′), **ric·o·chet·ting** *or* **ric·o·chet·ing** (-shā′ing).

**rid¹** (rid) make free from: *What will rid a house of rats?* *v.*, **rid** *or* **rid·ded, rid·ding.**
**be rid of,** be freed from.
**get rid of, a** get free from: *I can't get rid of this cold.* **b** do away with: *Poison will get rid of the rats in the barn.*

**rid·dance** (rid′əns) a clearing away or out; removal. *n.*
**good riddance,** an exclamation expressing relief that something or somebody has been removed.

**rid·den** (rid′ən) pp. of RIDE: *The horsewoman had ridden all day.* *v.*

**rid·dle¹** (rid′əl) **1** a puzzling question, statement, problem, etc. *Example: When is a door not a door? Answer: When it's ajar.* **2** a person or thing that is hard to understand, explain, etc. **3** speak in riddles. 1, 2 *n.*, 3 *v.*, **rid·dled, rid·dling.**

**rid·dle²** (rid′əl) **1** make many holes in: *The door of the fort was riddled with bullets.* **2** a coarse sieve. **3** sift: *to riddle gravel.* 1, 3 *v.*, **rid·dled, rid·dling;** 2 *n.*

**ride** (rīd) **1** sit on a horse, camel, etc. and make use of it for transport. **2** be a passenger or a driver of a bicycle, car, etc. **3** admit of being ridden: *a horse that rides easily.* **4** ride over, along, or through: *He likes to ride the mountain trail.* **5** be carried along by anything: *to ride on a train.* **6** be mounted on; be carried on: *The eagle rides the winds.* **7** a trip on the back of a horse, in a car, train, boat, etc.: *On Sundays, we take a ride into the country.* **8** a path, road, etc. made for riding. **9** do or perform: *to ride a race.* **10** move on; float; float along: *The ship rode the waves.* **11** *Informal.* make fun of; tease. **12** cause to ride or be carried: *to ride a small child on one's shoulders.* **13** control, dominate, or tyrannize over: *to be ridden by foolish fears.* **14** a mechanical amusement, such as a merry-go-round, Ferris wheel, etc. **15** a turn on a merry-go-round, Ferris wheel, roller coaster, etc. 1–6, 9–13 *v.*, **rode, rid·den, rid·ing;** 7, 8, 14, 15 *n.*
**let ride,** leave undisturbed or inactive: *Let the matter ride until the next meeting.*
**ride down, a** knock down. **b** overcome. **c** overtake by riding. **d** exhaust by riding.
**ride high,** succeed; do very well.
**ride out, a** withstand a gale, etc. without damage. **b** endure successfully.
**ride up,** slide up out of place: *That coat rides up at the back.*

**Ri·deau Hall** (rē′dō) the official residence of the Governor General of Canada, situated in Ottawa.

**rid·er** (rī′dər) 1 a person who rides: *The Calgary Stampede is famous for the riders who perform there.* 2 anything added to a record, document, legislative bill, or statement after it was considered to be completed. *n.* —**rid′er·less**, *adj.*

**ridge** (rij) 1 the long and narrow upper part of something: *the ridge of an animal's back.* 2 the line where two upward sloping surfaces meet: *the ridge of a roof.* 3 a long, narrow chain of hills or mountains. 4 any raised, narrow strip: *the ridges on corduroy cloth, the ridges in ploughed ground.* 5 form or make into ridges. 6 cover with ridges; mark with ridges. 1–4 *n.*, 5, 6 *v.*, **ridged, ridg·ing.**

**ridge·pole** (rij′pōl′) the horizontal timber along the top of a roof or tent. See FRAME for picture. *n.*

**rid·i·cule** (rid′ə kyül′) 1 laugh at; make fun of: *Boys should not ridicule their sisters' friends.* 2 laughter in mockery; words or actions that make fun of somebody or something: *Silly mistakes and strange clothes invite ridicule.* 1 *v.*, **rid·i·culed, rid·i·cul·ing;** 2 *n.*

**ri·dic·u·lous** (ri dik′yə ləs) deserving ridicule; absurd; laughable: *His attempts to be the life of the party were ridiculous. adj.* —**ri·dic′u·lous·ly,** *adv.* —**ri·dic′u·lous·ness,** *n.*

**rid·ing** (rī′ding) 1 *Cdn.* a political division represented by a Member of Parliament or a Member of the Legislative Assembly; a constituency: *She votes in the riding of South York.* 2 *Brit.* formerly, an administrative division, smaller than a county: *the West Riding of Yorkshire. n.*

**riding boot** a high boot worn by riders.

**riding crop** a short whip with a loop on one end instead of a lash.

**riding habit** a dress or suit worn by riders.

**Ri·el Rebellions** (rē el′) the RED RIVER REBELLION and the NORTHWEST REBELLION.

**rife** (rīf) 1 happening often; common; numerous; widespread. 2 well supplied; full; abounding: *The land was rife with rumours of war. adj.*

**rif·fle** (rif′əl) 1 a shoal or other object in a stream causing a ripple or a stretch of choppy water. 2 the ripple itself; a rapid. 3 shuffle cards by bending the edges slightly so that the two divisions of the deck slide into each other. 4 the act of shuffling cards in this way. 5 leaf through the pages of a book quickly. 1, 2, 4 *n.*, 3, 5 *v.*, **rif·fled, rif·fling.**

**riff·raff** (rif′raf′) 1 worthless people. 2 trash. 3 worthless. 1, 2 *n.*, 3 *adj.*

**ri·fle¹** (rī′fəl) 1 a gun having spiral grooves in its barrel to spin the bullet as it is fired. 2 such a gun that is fired from the shoulder. 3 cut spiral grooves in a gun. 1, 2 *n.*, 3 *v.*, **ri·fled, ri·fling.**

**ri·fle²** (rī′fəl) 1 search and rob; ransack and rob. 2 steal; take away. 3 strip bare: *The bad boys rifled the apple tree. v.*, **ri·fled, ri·fling.** —**ri′fler,** *n.*

**ri·fle·man** (rī′fəl mən) 1 a soldier armed with a rifle. 2 a man who uses a rifle. *n., pl.* **ri·fle·men** (-mən).

**ri·fling** (rī′fling) 1 the act or process of cutting spiral grooves in a gun barrel. 2 the system of spiral grooves in a rifle. 3 *ppr.* of RIFLE. 1, 2 *n.*, 3 *v.*

**rift** (rift) 1 a split; cleft; break; crack: *a rift in the clouds.* 2 a breach in relations between individuals, groups, or nations. *n.*

**rig¹** (rig) 1 equip a ship with masts, sails, ropes, etc.: *The sailor rigged a toy boat for the little boy.* 2 the arrangement of masts, sails, ropes, etc. on a ship: *A schooner has a fore-and-aft rig; that is, the sails are set lengthwise on the ship.* 3 move a shroud, boom, stay, etc. to its proper place. 4 equip (used with **out**): *to rig out a football team.* 5 *Informal.* clothe; dress (usually used with **out** or **up**): *On Halloween the children rig themselves up in queer clothes.* 6 *Informal.* clothing or costume, especially when unusual, showy, etc.: *Jon's rig consisted of a silk hat and overalls.* 7 an outfit; equipment: *a drilling rig. A large truck with attached trailer is a rig.* 8 get ready for use. 9 put together in a hurry or by using odds and ends (often used with **up**): *The girls rigged up a tent, using a rope and a blanket.* 10 *Informal.* a carriage, with its horse or horses. 1, 3–5, 8, 9 *v.*, **rigged, rig·ging;** 2, 6, 7, 10 *n.*

**rig²** (rig) arrange dishonestly for one's own advantage: *to rig a race. v.*, **rigged, rig·ging.**

**rigged** (rigd) 1 having a certain kind of rigging (used only in compounds): *square-rigged.* 2 *pt.* and *pp.* of RIG. 1 *adj.*, 2 *v.*

**rig·ger** (rig′ər) 1 a person who rigs. 2 a person who rigs ships, or works with hoisting tackle, etc.: *an oil rigger.* 3 *Informal.* a person who manipulates something fraudulently. *n.*
☛ *Hom.* RIGOUR.

**rig·ging** (rig′ing) 1 the ropes, chains, etc. used to support and work the masts, yards, sails, etc. on a ship. 2 tackle; equipment. 3 *ppr.* of RIG. 1, 2 *n.*, 3 *v.*

**right** (rīt) 1 good; just; lawful: *Jacqueline did the right thing when she told the truth.* 2 in a way that is good, just, or lawful: *He acted right when he told the truth.* 3 that which is right: *Do right, not wrong.* 4 a just claim, title, or privilege: *the right to vote.* 5 correct; true: *the right answer.* 6 correctly; truly: *She guessed right.* 7 proper; fitting: *Learn to say the right thing at the right time.* 8 properly; well: *It's faster to do a job right the first time.* 9 favourable: *If the weather is right, we'll go.* 10 favourably: *to turn out right.* 11 healthy; normal: *My head doesn't feel right.* 12 in a good or suitable condition: *Put things right.* 13 meant to be seen; most important: *the right side of cloth.* 14 make correct: *to right errors.* 15 do justice to: *to right the oppressed.* 16 fair treatment; justice. 17 get or put into proper position: *The ship righted as the wave passed.* 18 of the side that is turned to the east when the main side faces north; opposite left: *You have a right hand and a left hand. The right bank of a river is the one to the right as one faces downstream.* 19 the right side or hand: *Turn to your right. The school is on the right.* 20 on or to the right hand: *Turn right.* 21 a blow struck with the right hand. 22 in politics, a person, party, etc. that tends to oppose political

and social change.   **23** of or having to do with a person, party, etc. that tends to oppose political and social change.   **24** the part of a lawmaking body, made up of conservative or reactionary political groups, that sits on the right of the presiding officer.   **25** all the people and parties having conservative or reactionary views.   **26** exactly; just; precisely: *Put it right here.*   **27** at once; immediately: *Stop playing right now.*   **28** used in some titles, very: *Right Honourable.*   **29** in a straight line; directly: *Look me right in the eye.*   **30** straight: *a right line.*   **31** completely: *Her hat was knocked right off.*   **32** formed by a line drawn to another line or surface by the shortest course: *a right angle, a right cone.*   **33** the privilege of subscribing for a stock or bond.   **34** a certificate granting such a privilege.   **35** yes; very well: *"Come at once," his mother called. "Right," he replied.*   1, 5, 7, 9, 11, 13, 18, 23, 30, 32 *adj.*, 2, 6, 8, 10, 12, 20, 26–29, 31, 35 *adv.*, 3, 4, 16, 19, 21, 22, 24, 25, 33, 34 *n.*, 14, 15, 17 *v.*   —**right′ness,** *n.*
**by right** or **by rights,** rightly; properly; correctly.
**in the right,** right.
**right about!** turn in the opposite direction.
**right away,** at once; immediately: *She promised to do it right away.*
**right now,** immediately; at the present time: *Stop that right now! They're playing in the yard right now.*
**right off,** at once; immediately.
**to rights,** *Informal.* in or into proper condition, order, etc.
☛ *Hom.* RITE, WRIGHT, WRITE.

**right angle**   an ANGLE of 90 degrees.   See ANGLE for picture.

**right-an·gled** (rī′tang′gəld)   containing a RIGHT ANGLE or right angles; rectangular.   *adj.*

**right·eous** (rī′chəs)   **1** doing right; virtuous; behaving justly.   **2** morally right or justifiable: *righteous indignation.*   *adj.*   —**right′eous·ly,** *adv.*

**right·eous·ness** (rī′chəs nis)   upright conduct; virtue; the state or condition of being right and just.   *n.*

**right·ful** (rīt′fəl)   **1** according to law; by rights: *the rightful owner of this dog.*   **2** just and right; proper.   *adj.*   —**right′ful·ly,** *adv.*   —**right′ful·ness,** *n.*

**right-hand** (rīt′hand′)   **1** on or to the right.   **2** of, for, or with the right hand.   **3** most helpful or useful: *one's right-hand man.*   *adj.*

**right-hand·ed** (rīt′han′did)   **1** using the right hand more easily and readily than the left.   **2** done with the right hand.   **3** made to be used with the right hand.   **4** turning from left to right: *a right-handed screw.*   *adj.*

**Right Honourable**   a title given to all members of the United Kingdom Privy Council. The prime minister of Canada has this title.

**right·ist** (rī′tist)   **1** a person who has conservative or reactionary ideas in politics.   **2** having conservative or reactionary ideas in politics.   1 *n.*, 2 *adj.*

**right·ly** (rīt′lē)   **1** justly; fairly.   **2** correctly: *She rightly guessed that I was safe.*   **3** properly; suitably.   *adv.*

**right-mind·ed** (rīt′mīn′did)   having right opinions or principles.   *adj.*

**right of way**   **1** the right to go first; precedence over all others: *Car drivers must give firetrucks and ambulances right of way.*   **2** the right to pass over property belonging to someone else.   **3** a strip of land on which a road, railway, power line, etc. is built.

**right triangle**   a triangle one of whose angles is a RIGHT ANGLE.

hat, āge, fär; let, ēqual, tėrm; it, īce
hot, ōpen, ôrder; oil, out; cup, pùt, rüle
above, takən, pencəl, lemən, circəs
ch, child; ng, long; sh, ship
th, thin; ᴛʜ, then; zh, measure

**right whale**   any of several whales having large heads and long, toothlike whalebones on the sides of the mouth.

**right wing**   **1** the people opposing reform, especially the conservative or reactionary members of a political organization.   **2** in hockey, lacrosse, etc., the playing position to the right of centre on a forward line.   **3** the player in this position.

**right winger**   in hockey, lacrosse, etc., the player who occupies the position to the right of centre.

**rig·id** (rij′id)   **1** stiff; firm; not bending: *a rigid support.*   **2** strict; not changing: *Our club has a few rigid rules.*   **3** severely exact; rigorous: *a rigid examination.*   *adj.*   —**rig′id·ly,** *adv.*   —**rig′id·ness,** *n.*

**ri·gid·i·ty** (ri jid′ə tē)   **1** stiffness; firmness.   **2** strictness; severity.   *n.*

**rig·ma·role** (rig′mə rōl′)   foolish talk; words without meaning; nonsense.   *n.*

**rigor** (rig′ər)   See RIGOUR.   *n.*

**rig·or mor·tis** (rig′ər môr′tis) *Latin.*   the stiffening of the muscles after death.

**rig·or·ous** (rig′ə rəs)   **1** very severe; strict: *the rigorous discipline in the army.*   **2** harsh: *a rigorous climate.*   **3** thoroughly logical and scientific; exact: *the rigorous methods of science.*   *adj.*   —**rig′or·ous·ly,** *adv.*

**rig·our** or **rig·or** (rig′ər)   **1** strictness; severity.   **2** harshness: *the rigour of a long, cold winter.*   **3** logical exactness: *the rigour of scientific method.*   **4** stiffness; rigidity.   **5** a chill caused by illness.   *n.*
☛ *Hom.* RIGGER.

**rile** (rīl)   **1** make water, etc. muddy by stirring up sediment.   **2** disturb; irritate; vex.   *v.,* **riled, ril·ing.**

**rill** (ril)   a tiny stream; little brook.   *n.*

**rim** (rim)   **1** an edge, border, or margin on or around anything: *the rim of a wheel, the rim of a cup.*   See WHEEL for picture.   **2** form or put a rim around: *Wildflowers and grasses rimmed the little pool.*   1 *n.,* 2 *v.,* **rimmed, rim·ming.**   —**rim′less,** *adj.*

**rime**[1] (rīm)   See RHYME.   *v.,* **rimed, rim·ing;** *n.*

**rime**[2] (rīm)   **1** white frost; hoarfrost.   **2** cover with rime.   1 *n.,* 2 *v.,* **rimed, rim·ing.**
☛ *Hom.* RHYME.

**rime·ster** (rīm′stər)   See RHYMESTER.   *n.*

**rind** (rīnd)   the hard or firm outer covering of oranges, melons, cheeses, etc.   *n.*

**ring**[1] (ring)   **1** a circle: *One can tell the age of a tree by counting the rings in a cross-section of its trunk; one ring grows every year.*   **2** a thin circle of metal or other material: *a napkin ring, rings on her fingers.*   **3** the outer edge or border of a coin, plate, wheel, or anything round.   **4** put a ring around; enclose; form a circle around.   **5** toss a horseshoe ring, etc. around a certain mark or post.   **6** provide with a ring.   **7** put a ring in the nose of.   **8** form a ring or rings.   **9** an enclosed space for races, games, circus performances, showing livestock, etc.: *The ring for a boxing match is square.*   **10** professional boxing.

**ring** 1020 **ripple**

**11** a competition; rivalry; contest: *in the ring for election to the House.* **12** a group of people combined for a selfish or bad purpose: *A ring of crooks controlled the smuggling operation.* **13** cut away the bark in a circle around a tree or branch. **14** an enclosed area for the showing and judging of livestock. 1–3, 9–12, 14 *n.*, 4–8, 13 *v.*, **ringed, ring·ing.**
☞ *Hom.* WRING.

**ring²** (ring) **1** give forth a clear sound, as a bell does. **2** cause to give forth a clear, ringing sound: *Ring the bell.* **3** cause a bell or buzzer to sound: *Did you ring?* **4** make a sound by ringing: *The bells rang a joyous peal.* **5** call to church, prayers, etc. by ringing bells. **6** announce or proclaim by ringing; usher; conduct: *Ring out the old year; ring in the new.* **7** proclaim or repeat loudly everywhere: *to ring a person's praises.* **8** resound; sound loudly: *The room rang with shouts of laughter.* **9** echo; give back sound: *The mountains rang with the roll of thunder.* **10** be filled with report or talk. **11** sound: *Her words rang true.* **12** have a sensation as of sounds of bells: *My ears ring.* **13** the act of ringing. **14** the sound of a bell or buzzer: *Did you hear a ring?* **15** a sound like that of a bell: *the ring of one glass against another.* **16** a characteristic sound or quality: *a ring of sincerity.* **17** call on the telephone. **18** a telephone call. 1–12, 17 *v.*, **rang, rung, ring·ing;** 13–16, 18 *n.*
**ring for,** summon by a bell.
**ring in,** *Informal.* bring in dishonestly or trickily.
**ring off,** end a telephone call.
**ring up, a** record a specified amount on a cash register. **b** call on the telephone.
☞ *Hom.* WRING.

**ringed** (ringd) **1** having or wearing a ring or rings. **2** marked or decorated with a ring or rings. **3** surrounded by a ring or rings. **4** formed of or with rings; ringlike. *adj.*

**ring·er¹** (ring′ər) **1** a person or thing that encircles, surrounds with a ring, etc. **2** a quoit, horseshoe, etc. thrown so as to fall over a peg. *n.*
☞ *Hom.* WRINGER.

**ring·er²** (ring′ər) **1** a person or thing that rings; a device for ringing a bell. **2** *Informal.* a person or thing very like another. *n.*
☞ *Hom.* WRINGER.

**ring·lead·er** (ring′lē′dər) a person who leads others in opposition to authority or law: *the ringleaders of the mutiny.* *n.*

Ringlets (def. 1)

**ring·let** (ring′lit) **1** a long curl: *She wears her hair in ringlets.* **2** a little ring: *Drops of rain made ringlets in the pond.* *n.*

**ring·mas·ter** (ring′mas′tər) a person in charge of the performances in the ring of a circus. *n.*

**ring·side** (ring′sīd′) **1** a place just outside the ring at a circus, boxing match, etc. **2** a place giving a close view. *n.*

**ring·worm** (ring′wėrm′) a contagious skin disease, caused by fungi and characterized by ring-shaped patches. *n.*

**rink** (ringk) **1** a sheet of ice for playing hockey or for pleasure skating. **2** a smooth floor for roller skating. **3** a sheet of ice for curling. **4** a curling team of four players: *Some of Canada's best rinks curled in the bonspiel.* **5** a building in which there is a rink; arena: *This rink has 800 seats.* *n.*

**rinse** (rins) **1** wash with clean water: *Rinse the soap out of your hair.* **2** the act of washing in clean water. **3** wash lightly: *Rinse your mouth with water.* **4** a light washing. **5** a preparation to add temporary lustre or colour to the hair. 1, 3 *v.*, **rinsed, rins·ing;** 2, 4, 5 *n.*

**ri·ot** (rī′ət) **1** a wild, violent public disturbance; disorder caused by an unruly crowd or mob: *The guards stopped several riots in the prison.* **2** behave in a wild, disorderly way. **3** loose living; wild revelling. **4** REVEL. **5** a bright display: *a riot of colour.* **6** *Informal.* a very amusing person or performance: *She was a riot at the party.* 1, 3, 5, 6 *n.*, 2, 4 *v.*, —**ri′ot·er,** *n.*
**read the riot act, a** give orders for disturbance to cease. **b** reprimand severely.
**run riot, a** act without restraint. **b** of plants, grow wildly or luxuriantly: *The weeds have run riot in our garden.* **c** run wild.

**ri·ot·ous** (rī′ə təs) **1** taking part in a riot. **2** boisterous; disorderly: *riotous conduct, riotous glee.* *adj.* —**ri′ot·ous·ly,** *adv.*

**rip¹** (rip) **1** cut roughly; tear apart; tear off: *Rip the cover off this box.* **2** become torn apart. **3** cut or pull out the stitches in the seams of a garment. **4** a torn place. **5** a seam unstitched in a garment: *Please sew up this rip in my sleeve.* **6** saw wood along the grain, not across the grain. **7** *Informal.* move fast or violently. **8** *Informal.* speak or say with violence: *He ripped out an angry oath.* 1–3, 6–8 *v.*, **ripped, rip·ping;** 4, 5 *n.*
**rip into,** *Informal.* attack violently.

**rip²** (rip) **1** a stretch of rough water made by cross currents meeting. **2** a swift current made by the tide. *n.*

**R.I.P.** requiescat in pace.

**ri·par·i·an** (rə per′ē ən *or* rī per′ē ən) of or on the bank of a river, a lake, etc.: *riparian rights, riparian property.* *adj.*

**rip cord** a cord which, when pulled, opens a parachute.

**ripe** (rīp) **1** full-grown and ready to be gathered and eaten: *ripe fruit.* **2** resembling ripe fruit in ruddiness and fullness. **3** fully developed; mature: *a ripe cheese, ripe in knowledge.* **4** ready to break or be lanced: *a ripe boil.* **5** ready: *ripe for mischief.* **6** far enough along. **7** advanced in years. *adj.*, **rip·er, rip·est.**
—**ripe′ness,** *n.*

**rip·en** (rī′pən) **1** become ripe. **2** make ripe. *v.*

**ri·poste** (rə pōst′) **1** in fencing, a quick thrust given after parrying a lunge. **2** a quick, sharp reply or return. **3** make a riposte; reply; retaliate. 1, 2 *n.*, 3 *v.*, **ri·post·ed, ri·post·ing.**

**rip·per** (rip′ər) **1** one that rips. **2** a tool for ripping. *n.*

**rip·ple** (rip′əl) **1** a very little wave: *Throw a stone into still water and watch the ripples spread in rings.* **2** anything that seems like a little wave: *ripples in cardboard.* **3** a sound that reminds one of little waves: *a ripple of laughter in the crowd.* **4** make a sound like rippling water. **5** form or have little waves. **6** flow with little waves on the surface.   **7** make little waves on: *A breeze rippled the quiet water.*   1–3 *n.*, 4–7 *v.*, **rip·pled, rip·pling.**

**rip·ply** (rip′lē)   characterized by RIPPLES; rippling. *adj.*

**rip·saw** (rip′sô′)   a saw for cutting wood along the grain, not across the grain.   *n.*

**rip·tide** (rip′tīd′)   a strong current of churning water caused by one tide meeting another.   *n.*

**rise** (rīz)   **1** get up from a lying, sitting, or kneeling position: *to rise from a chair.*   **2** get up from sleep or rest: *to rise at dawn.*   **3** go up; come up; move up; ascend: *The kite rises in the air.*   **4** extend upward: *The tower rises to a height of 30 metres.*   **5** an upward movement; ascent: *the rise of a balloon.*   **6** the coming of a fish to the surface of the water to seize bait, etc.   **7** slope upward: *Hills rise in the distance.*   **8** an upward slope: *The rise of that hill is gradual.*   **9** a piece of rising or high ground; hill.   **10** the vertical height of a step, slope, arch, etc.   **11** cause to rise; cause to rise above the horizon by approaching nearer to it.   **12** go higher; increase: *Prices are rising. His anger rose at the remark.*   **13** an increase.   **14** an advance in rank, power, etc.   **15** advance to a higher level of action, thought, feeling, expression, rank, position, etc.: *He rose from errand boy to president.*   **16** become louder or of a higher pitch.   **17** an increase in loudness or pitch.   **18** appear above the horizon: *The sun rises in the morning.*   **19** a coming above the horizon.   **20** start; begin: *The river rises from a spring. Quarrels often rise from trifles.*   **21** come into being or action: *The wind rose rapidly.*   **22** an origin; beginning; start: *the rise of a river, the rise of a storm, the rise of a new problem.*   **23** be built up, erected, or constructed: *Houses are rising on the edge of town.*   **24** become more animated or more cheerful: *Her spirits rose.*   **25** revolt; rebel: *The peasants rose against their masters.*   **26** grow larger and lighter: *Yeast makes dough rise.*   **27** come to life again.   **28** end a meeting or session; adjourn: *The House rose for July and August.*   1–4, 7, 11, 12, 15, 16, 18, 20, 21, 23–28 *v.*, **rose, ris·en, ris·ing;**   5, 6, 8–10, 13, 14, 17, 19, 22 *n.*
**get a rise out of somebody,**   cause a person to react in a way expected to some question or situation deliberately put or arranged: *We can always get a rise out of him with an attack on hockey.*
**give rise to,**   start; begin; cause; bring about: *The circumstances of her disappearance gave rise to the fear that she might have been kidnapped.*
**rise to,**   be equal to; be able to deal with: *They rose to the occasion.*

**ris·en** (riz′ən)   pp. of RISE: *The sun has risen.*   *v.*

**ris·er** (rī′zər)   **1** a person or thing that rises: *an early riser.*   **2** the vertical part of a step.   *n.*

**ris·i·bil·i·ty** (riz′ə bil′ə tē)   **1** an ability or inclination to laugh.   **2** risibilities, *pl.* desire to laugh; sense of humour.   *n., pl.* **ris·i·bil·i·ties.**

**ris·i·ble** (riz′ə bəl)   **1** able or inclined to laugh.   **2** of laughter; used in laughter.   **3** causing laughter; amusing; funny.   *adj.*

**ris·ing** (rī′zing)   **1** the act of ascending; coming up: *the rising of the sun.*   **2** getting up: *Seven o'clock is my hour for rising.*   **3** a fight against the government; revolt.   **4** that rises; advancing in power, influence, etc.; growing.   **5** ppr. of RISE.   1–3 *n.*, 4 *adj.*, 5 *v.*

**risk** (risk)   **1** a chance of harm or loss; danger: *Jeanne rescued the dog at the risk of her own life. If you drive carefully, there is no risk of being fined.*   **2** expose to the chance of harm or loss: *A climber risks his or her life.*   **3** take the risk of: *They risked getting wet.*   **4** a person or thing described with reference to the chance of loss from insuring him, her, or it: *Very fat people and alcoholics are not good risks.*   **5** a person or thing that cannot be relied on: *An old car and a lazy student are both poor risks.*   1, 4, 5 *n.*, 2, 3 *v.*
**run a risk** or **take a risk,**   expose oneself to the chance of harm or loss.

**risk·y** (ris′kē)   **1** full of risk; dangerous.   **2** somewhat improper; risqué.   *adj.* **risk·i·er, risk·i·est.** —**risk′i·ly,** *adv.*   —**risk′i·ness,** *n.*

**ris·qué** (ris kā′)   suggestive of indecency; somewhat improper: *a risqué situation in a play.*   *adj.*

**rit.** or **ritard.**   ritardando.

**ri·tar·dan·do** (rē′tär dän′dō)   **1** in music, becoming gradually slower.   **2** gradually more slowly.   **3** a gradual decrease in tempo.   1 *adj.*, 2 *adv.*, 3 *n.*

**rite** (rīt)   **1** a solemn ceremony: *Most religions have rites for baptism, marriage, and burial. Secret societies have their special rites.*   **2** a particular form or system of ceremonies: *This synagogue uses the Orthodox rite.*   *n.*
☛ *Hom.* RIGHT, WRIGHT, WRITE.

**rit·u·al** (rich′ü əl)   **1** a form or system of rites: *The rites of baptism, marriage, and burial are parts of the ritual of most religions.*   **2** a book containing rites or ceremonies.   **3** of or having to do with rites; done as a rite: *a ritual dance.*   **4** the carrying out of rites.   1, 2, 4 *n.*, 3 *adj.*

**rit·u·al·ism** (rich′ü ə liz′əm)   **1** a fondness for RITUAL; insistence upon ritual.   **2** the study of RITUAL practices or religious rites.   *n.*

**rit·u·al·ist** (rich′ü ə list)   **1** a person who practises or advocates observance of RITUAL.   **2** a person who studies or knows much about RITUAL practices or religious rites.   *n.*

**rit·u·al·is·tic** (rich′ü ə lis′tik)   **1** having to do with RITUAL or ritualism.   **2** fond of RITUAL.   *adj.*

**rit·u·al·ly** (rich′ü ə lē)   with or according to a RITUAL.   *adv.*

**ri·val** (rī′vəl)   **1** a person who wants and tries to get the same thing as another; one who tries to equal or do better than another; competitor.   **2** wanting the same thing as another; competing: *The rival store tried to get the other's trade.*   **3** try to equal or outdo: *The stores rival each other in beautiful window displays.*   **4** equal; match: *The sunset rivalled the sunrise in beauty.*   **5** a thing that will bear comparison with something else; equal; match: *Her beauty has no rival.*   1, 5 *n.*, 2 *adj.*, 3, 4 *v.*, **ri·valled** or **ri·valed, ri·val·ling** or **ri·val·ing.**
☛ *Etym.* From L *rivalis*, originally meaning 'one who uses the same stream as another', which came from *rivus* 'stream'.

**ri·val·ry** (rī′vəl rē)   the action, position, or relation of a rival or rivals; competition: *There is rivalry among business firms for trade.*   *n., pl.* **ri·val·ries.**

**rive** (rīv)   tear apart; split; cleave.   *v.*, **rived, rived** or **riv·en, riv·ing.**

**riv·en** (riv′ən) 1 torn apart; split. 2 a pp. of RIVE. 1 *adj.*, 2 *v.*

**riv·er** (riv′ər) 1 a large, natural stream of water that flows into a lake, ocean, etc. 2 any abundant stream or flow: *rivers of blood.* *n.*

**river basin** land that is drained by a river and its tributaries.

**riv·er·head** (riv′ər hed′) the source of a river. *n.*

**riv·er·side** (riv′ər sīd′) 1 the bank of a river. 2 on the bank of a river: *The riverside path is much used.* *n.*

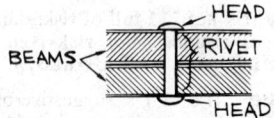

A rivet in place, holding two steel beams together

**riv·et** (riv′it) 1 a metal bolt having a head at one end, the other end made to be hammered into a head once it is in position. 2 fasten with a rivet or rivets. 3 flatten the end of a bolt so as to form a head. 4 fasten firmly; fix firmly: *Their eyes were riveted on the speaker.* 1 *n.*, 2–4 *v.* —**riv′et·er,** *n.*

**riv·u·let** (riv′yə lit) a very small stream. *n.*

**rm.** 1 room. 2 ream.

**R.M.** Rural Municipality.

**Rn** radon.

**RN** or **R.N.** 1 registered nurse. 2 Royal Navy.

**RNA** RIBONUCLEIC ACID.

**roach¹** (rōch) COCKROACH. *n.*

**roach²** (rōch) 1 a European freshwater fish related to the carp. 2 any of various similar fishes, such as the North American sunfish. *n., pl.* **roach** or **roach·es.**

**road** (rōd) 1 a highway between places; way made for trucks or automobiles to travel on: *The road from here to the city is being paved.* 2 a way or route: *Our road went through the woods.* 3 a way: *the road to ruin, a road to peace.* 4 railway. 5 Also, **roads,** a place near the shore where ships can ride at anchor. *n.*
**on the road,** a travelling, especially as a salesperson. b of a theatre company, etc., on tour.
**take to the road,** a go on the road; begin to travel. b formerly, become a highwayman.
☛ *Hom.* RODE.

**road allowance** land reserved by the government as public property to be used for roads: *The road allowance includes the road and a certain amount of land on either side of it.*

**road·bed** (rōd′bed′) the foundation of a road or of a railway. *n.*

**road·block** (rōd′blok′) 1 an obstacle placed across a road: *The police set up a roadblock to stop the car thief.* 2 any obstacle to progress. *n.*

**road hog** *Informal.* a driver who obstructs traffic by keeping his or her vehicle in the middle of the road, refusing to let other vehicles pass.

**road runner** a long-tailed bird of the deserts of the southwestern United States that is related to the cuckoo. It usually runs instead of flying.

**road·side** (rōd′sīd′) 1 the side of a road. 2 beside a road: *a roadside inn.* 1 *n.,* 2 *adj.*

**road·stead** (rōd′sted) ROAD (def. 5). *n.*

**road·ster** (rōd′stər) 1 an open automobile with one seat. 2 a horse for riding or driving on the roads. *n.*

**road·way** (rōd′wā) 1 ROAD (def. 1). 2 the part of a road used by vehicles: *Walk on the path, not in the roadway.* *n.*

**roam** (rōm) 1 go about with no special plan or aim; wander: *to roam through the fields.* 2 wander over. 3 a walk or trip with no special aim; wandering. 1, 2 *v.,* 3 *n.* —**roam′er,** *n.*

**roan** (rōn) 1 yellowish-brown or reddish-brown sprinkled with grey or white. 2 an animal, especially a horse, of this colour. 1 *adj.,* 2 *n.*

**roar** (rôr) 1 make a loud, deep sound; make a loud noise: *The lion roared.* 2 a loud, deep sound; loud noise: *a roar of applause.* 3 utter loudly: *to roar out an order.* 4 make or put by roaring: *The crowd roared itself hoarse. The audience roared the actor off the stage.* 5 laugh loudly. 6 move with a roar: *The express train roared past us.* 1, 3–6 *v.,* 2 *n.* —**roar′er,** *n.*

**roast** (rōst) 1 cook by dry heat; cook in an oven, before or over an open fire, or in embers; bake. 2 a piece of roasted meat; piece of meat to be roasted. 3 roasted: *roast beef.* 4 prepare by heating: *to roast coffee, to roast a metal ore.* 5 make or become very hot. 6 be baked. 7 an informal outdoor meal, at which some food is cooked over an open fire: *a wiener roast.* 8 *Informal.* make fun of; ridicule. 9 a special dinner for a well-known public figure who is ridiculed by the other guests. 10 reprove; criticize severely. 1, 4–6, 8, 10 *v.,* 2, 7, 9 *n.,* 3 *adj.*

**roast·er** (rō′stər) 1 a pan used in roasting. 2 a chicken, young pig, etc. fit to be roasted. 3 one that roasts. *n.*

**rob** (rob) 1 take away from by force or threats: *The old lady was robbed of all her money. Bandits robbed the bank.* 2 steal: *They said they would not rob again.* 3 take away some characteristic; keep from having or doing: *The disease has robbed him of his strength.* *v.,* **robbed, rob·bing.**

**rob·ber** (rob′ər) a person who robs. *n.*

**rob·ber·y** (rob′ə rē) an act of robbing; theft. *n., pl.* **rob·ber·ies.**

**robe** (rōb) 1 a long, loose outer garment. 2 a garment that shows rank, office, etc.: *a judge's robe, the queen's robes of state.* 3 a covering or wrap: *Put a robe over you when you go on the sleigh ride.* 4 a bathrobe or dressing gown. 5 put a robe on; dress. 1–4 *n.,* 5 *v.,* **robed, rob·ing.**

Robins—about 25 cm long including the tail

**rob·in** (rob′ən) 1 a large North American thrush with a reddish breast. 2 a small European bird with a yellowish-red breast. *n.*

**robin run** the first run of maple syrup. Compare with BUD RUN and FROG RUN.

**ro·bot** (rō′bot or rō′bət) **1** a machine-made person; mechanical device that does some of the work of human beings. **2** a person who acts or works in a dull, mechanical way. *n.*
☞ *Etym.* From Czech *robota* 'forced labour' and *robotnik* 'serf'. The term was used by the Czech playwright Karel Capek (1890–1938) in his play *R.U.R.* (Rossum's Universal Robots).

**ro·bot·ics** (rō bot′iks) the development and use of ROBOTS to perform tasks normally done by people. *n.*

**ro·bust** (rō bust′ or rō′bust) **1** strong and healthy; sturdy: *a robust person, a robust mind.* **2** suited to or requiring bodily strength: *robust exercises.* **3** rough; rude. *adj.* —**ro·bust′ly**, *adv.* —**ro·bust′ness**, *n.*

**Ro·chelle salt** (rō shel′) a colourless crystalline compound, potassium sodium tartrate, used as a laxative.

**rock**[1] (rok) **1** a large mass of stone: *The ship was wrecked on the rocks.* **2** any piece of stone; a stone. **3** the mass of mineral matter of which the earth's crust is made up. **4** a particular layer or kind of such matter. **5** something firm like a rock; support; defence: *My grandmother was a rock when I most needed support.* **6** anything that suggests or acts as a rock: *The division of the money was the rock on which the thieves split.* **7** a curling stone. *n.* **on the rocks, a** wrecked; ruined. **b** *Informal.* bankrupt. **c** of alcoholic drinks, with ice but without water or mixes: *whisky on the rocks.*

**rock**[2] (rok) **1** move backward and forward, or from side to side; sway: *My chair rocks. The waves rocked the ship.* **2** move or shake violently: *The earthquake rocked the houses.* **3** put to sleep, rest, etc. with swaying movements. **4** a rocking movement. **5** a kind of lively popular music with a very heavy, regular beat and much repetition, usually played with electronically amplified instruments: *Rock often has elements of jazz or country and folk music.* **6** *Informal.* disturb; shake; upset: *The family was rocked by the news.* 1–3, 6 *v.*, 4, 5 *n.*

**rock–and–roll** (rok′ən rōl′) **1** a style of popular music with a heavy beat, an early form of ROCK[2] (def. 5). **2** a lively style of dancing to such music, characterized by improvisation and exaggerated movements. *n.* Also, **rock 'n' roll.**

**rock bottom** the very bottom; lowest level.

**rock–bot·tom** (rok′bot′əm) down to the very bottom; lowest. *adj.*

**rock–bound** (rok′bound′) surrounded by rocks; rocky. *adj.*

**rock candy** sugar in the form of large hard crystals.

**Rock Cornish** a chicken that is a cross between a Cornish chicken and a white Plymouth Rock: *Rock Cornish chickens are usually killed young and eaten as broilers.*

**rock crystal** a colourless, transparent variety of quartz that is often used for jewellery, ornaments, etc.

**rock·er**[1] (rok′ər) **1** one of the curved pieces on which a cradle, rocking chair, etc. rocks. **2** a ROCKING CHAIR. *n.*

**rock·er**[2] (rok′ər) **1** a ROCK (def. 5) singer or musician. **2** a fan of rock music. *n.*

**rock·er·y** (rok′ə rē) an ornamental garden consisting of an arrangement of rocks and earth for growing plants

hat, āge, fär; let, ēqual, tėrm; it, īce hot, ōpen, ôrder; oil, out; cup, pụt, rüle ȧbove, takən, pencəl, lemən, circəs ch, child; ng, long; sh, ship th, thin; ᴛʜ, then; zh, measure

and flowers; a rock garden: *Rockeries are often built on slopes.* *n.*, *pl.* **rock·er·ies.**

A large rocket which uses liquid fuel

**rock·et** (rok′it) **1** a projectile consisting of a tube open at one end and filled with some substance that burns rapidly, creating expanding gases that propel the tube and whatever is attached to it at great speed: *Rockets are used for fireworks, for signalling, for propelling weapons, and for carrying satellites into outer space.* **2** a spacecraft, missile, etc., propelled by such a projectile. **3** go like a rocket; rise or move extremely fast. 1, 2 *n.*, 3 *v.*

**rock·et·ry** (rok′i trē) the designing and firing of rockets, missiles, etc. *n.*

**rock garden** ROCKERY.

**rock·hound** (rok′hound′) *Informal.* a person who collects rocks as a hobby. *n.*

**Rock·ies** (rok′ēz) ROCKY MOUNTAINS. *n. pl.*

A rocking chair

**rocking chair** a chair mounted on rockers, or on springs, so that it can rock back and forth.

**rocking horse** a toy horse on rockers, or sometimes springs, for children to ride.

**rock 'n' roll** (rok′ən rōl′) See ROCK-AND-ROLL.

**rock–ribbed** (rok′ribd′) **1** having ridges of rock. **2** unyielding. *adj.*

**rock salt** common salt as it occurs in the earth in large crystals.

**rock·weed** (rok′wēd′) any of various coarse seaweeds growing on rocks near the shore. *n.*

**rock wool** wool-like fibres made from rock or slag and used for insulation and soundproofing.

**rock·y**[1] (rok′ē) **1** full of rocks: *a rocky shore.* **2** made of rock. **3** like rock; hard; firm. *adj.*, **rock·i·er, rock·i·est.**

**rock·y**[2] (rok′ē) **1** likely to rock; shaky: *That table is a bit rocky; put a piece of wood under the short leg.* **2** unpleasantly uncertain. **3** *Informal.* sickish; weak;

**dizzy.** *adj.*, **rock·i·er, rock·i·est.** —**rock'i·ly,** *adv.* —**rock'i·ness,** *n.*

**Rocky Mountain juniper** a small, bushy, evergreen tree, a species of JUNIPER found in southern Alberta and British Columbia and the western United States.

**Rocky Mountains** a range of mountains lying in Alberta and British Columbia, and the western United States.

**ro·co·co** (rō kō′kō) a style of architecture and decoration with elaborate ornamentation, combining shellwork, scrolls, foliage, etc., much used in the early 18th century. *n.*

**rod** (rod) **1** a thin, straight bar of metal or wood. See STEAM ENGINE for picture. **2** a thin, straight stick, either growing or cut off. **3** anything like a rod in shape. **4** a stick used to beat or punish. **5** punishment. **6** a long, light pole. **7** a long, springy, tapered piece of wood, metal, plastic, etc. to which a reel may be attached, used for fishing: *His father gave him a rod and reel for his birthday.* **8** a unit for measuring length, equal to 5½ yards (about 5.03 metres). **9** a stick used to measure with. **10** a staff or wand carried as a symbol of one's position. **11** power; authority; tyranny. **12** a rod-shaped cell in the retina of the eye, sensitive to light. Compare with CONE. *n.*
**spare the rod,** fail to punish.

**rode** (rōd) pt. of RIDE: *We rode ten kilometres today.* *v.*
☛ *Hom.* ROAD.

**ro·dent** (rō′dənt) **1** any of a group of mammals having teeth especially adapted for gnawing wood and similar material: *Rats, mice, and squirrels are rodents.* **2** gnawing. **3** of or like a rodent. **1** *n.*, **2, 3** *adj.*

**ro·de·o** (rō′dē ō *or* rō dā′ō) a contest or exhibition of skill in roping cattle, riding horses, etc. *n., pl.* **ro·de·os.**

**roe**[1] (rō) fish eggs. *n.*
☛ *Hom.* ROW[1,2].

**roe**[2] (rō) a small deer of Europe and Asia, having forked antlers. *n., pl.* **roes** or (*esp. collectively*) **roe.**
☛ *Hom.* ROW[1,2].

**roe·buck** (rō′buk′) a male roe deer. *n.*

**roent·gen** (rent′gən; *German,* rœnt′gən) the unit for measuring the effect of X rays or gamma rays. *n.*

**Roentgen rays** X RAYS.

**rog·er** (roj′ər) *Informal.* message received and understood. *interj.*

**rogue** (rōg) **1** a tricky, dishonest, or worthless person; rascal. **2** a mischievous person: *The little rogue has his grandma's glasses on.* **3** an animal with a savage nature that lives apart from the herd: *An elephant that is a rogue is very dangerous.* *n.*

**ro·guer·y** (rō′gə rē) **1** the conduct of rogues; dishonest trickery; rascality. **2** playful mischief. *n., pl.* **ro·guer·ies.**

**rogues' gallery** a collection of photographs of known criminals.

**ro·guish** (rō′gish) **1** dishonest; rascally; having to do with or like rogues. **2** playfully mischievous: *with a roguish twinkle in her eyes.* *adj.* —**ro′guish·ly,** *adv.* —**ro′guish·ness,** *n.*

**roil** (roil) RILE. *v.*

**rois·ter** (rois′tər) be boisterous; revel noisily; swagger. *v.*

**role** or **rôle** (rōl) **1** a performer's part in a play, opera, etc.: *the leading role.* **2** a part played in real life: *She played an important role in Canadian history.* *n.*
☛ *Hom.* ROLL.
☛ *Etym.* From F *rôle,* earlier *roule,* originally the roll of paper, etc. on which an actor's part was written. 17c.

**role model** someone who offers his or her own example as an inspiration for younger people to imitate.

**role–play** (rōl′plā′) act as oneself or another in an imaginary situation for therapeutic or other purposes: *to role-play an interview.* *v.*

**roll** (rōl) **1** move along by turning over and over: *A ball rolls.* **2** wrap around on itself or on some other thing: *Roll the string into a ball.* **3** something rolled up; a cylinder formed by rolling, often forming a definite measure: *rolls of paper.* **4** a more or less rounded, cylindrical, or rolled-up mass. **5** move or be moved on wheels: *The car rolled along.* **6** move smoothly; sweep along: *Waves roll in on the beach. The years roll on.* **7** turn around; revolve. **8** of a heavenly body, etc., perform a periodical revolution in an orbit. **9** move from side to side: *The ship rolled in the waves.* **10** continued motion up and down, or from side to side. **11** turn over, or over and over: *The horse rolled in the dust.* **12** walk with a swaying gait. **13** rise and fall again and again: *rolling country.* **14** make flat or smooth with a roller; spread out with a rolling pin, etc.: *Rolling the grass makes a smooth lawn. I like to roll the dough for cookies.* **15** put ink on with a roller. **16** make deep, loud sounds: *Thunder rolls.* **17** beat a drum with rapid continuous strokes. **18** a rapid continuous beating on a drum. **19** a deep, loud sound: *the roll of thunder.* **20** utter with full, flowing sound: *The organ rolled out the stirring tune.* **21** utter with a trill: *to roll one's r's.* **22** the act of rolling. **23** a motion like that of waves; undulation. **24** a record; list; list of names: *Call the roll.* **25** a kind of bread or cake: *a sweet roll.* **26** *Informal.* have more than enough: *to be rolling in money.* **27** cast dice. **28** turn up a number on a dice: *roll a five.* **1, 2, 5–9, 11–17, 20, 21, 26–28** *v.*, **3, 4, 10, 18, 19, 22–25** *n.*
**roll up,** increase; pile up or become piled up: *Bills roll up fast.*
**strike off the rolls,** expel from membership.
☛ *Hom.* ROLE.

**roll call** the calling of a list of names, as of soldiers, pupils, etc. to find out those who are present.

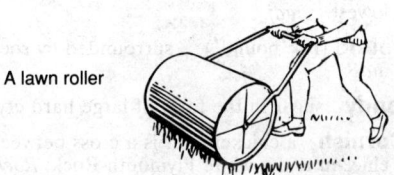

A lawn roller

**roll·er** (rōl′ər) **1** anything that rolls; a cylinder on which something is rolled along or rolled up. **2** a cylinder of metal, stone, wood, etc. used for smoothing, pressing, crushing, etc.: *A heavy roller was used to smooth the tennis court.* **3** a long rolled bandage. **4** a long, swelling wave: *Huge rollers broke on the sandy beach.* **5** a person who rolls something. **6** a kind of canary that has a trilling voice. **7** a kind of tumbler pigeon. *n.*

**roller bearing** a bearing in which the shaft turns on rollers to lessen friction.

**roller coaster** a railway built for amusement, on which small cars roll up and down steep inclines, round sharp corners, etc.

A roller skate

**roller skate** a skate equipped with small wheels: *Roller skates are used on special rinks.*

**roll·er–skate** (rō′lər skāt′) move on roller skates: *The children roller-skated in the park.* *v.*, **roll·er–skat·ed, roll·er–skat·ing.**

**rol·lick** (rol′ik) frolic; be merry; enjoy oneself in a free, hearty way. *v.*

**rol·lick·ing** (rol′i king) **1** frolicking; jolly; lively: *I had a rollicking time at the picnic.* **2** ppr. of ROLLICK. **1** *adj.* **2** *v.*

**rol·lick·some** (rol′ik səm) ROLLICKING. *adj.*

**roll·ing** (rō′ling) **1** the action, motion, or sound of anything that rolls or is being rolled: *the rolling of a ball, the rolling of thunder.* **2** that rolls: *Rolling land rises and falls in gentle slopes. A person with a rolling gait sways from side to side. A rolling collar turns back or folds over.* **3** ppr. of ROLL. **1** *n.*, **2** *adj.*, **3** *v.*

**rolling mill** **1** a factory where metal is rolled into sheets and bars. **2** a machine for rolling metal.

**rolling pin** a cylinder of wood, porcelain, plastic, etc. for rolling out dough.

**rolling stock** the locomotives and cars of a railway.

**roll–top** (rōl′top′) having a top that rolls back: *a roll-top desk.* *adj.*

**ro·ly–po·ly** (rō′lē pō′lē) **1** short and plump. **2** a short, plump person or animal. **3** a pudding made of jam or fruit spread on a rich dough, rolled up and cooked. **1** *adj.*, **2, 3** *n.*, *pl.* **ro·ly–po·lies.**

**ROM** Read Only Memory.

**rom.** in printing, roman (type).

**ro·maine** (rō mān′) a variety of lettuce having long, green leaves with crinkly edges, which are joined loosely at the base. *n.*

**Ro·man** (rō′mən) **1** of or having to do with ancient or modern Rome or its people. **2** a native or inhabitant of Rome. **3** of or having to do with the Roman Catholic Church. **4** Also, **roman,** the style of type most used in printing and typewriting: *Most of this dictionary is in roman; this sentence is in italic.* **5 roman,** of or in roman type. **1, 3, 5** *adj.*, **2, 4** *n.*

**Roman candle** a kind of firework consisting of a tube that shoots out balls of fire, etc.

**Roman Catholic** **1** a member of the Christian church that recognizes the Pope as its supreme head. **2** of or having to do with this church. *Abbrev.*: R.C.

**Roman Catholicism** the doctrines, faith, practices, and system of government of the Roman Catholic Church.

**ro·mance** (rō mans′ *or* rō′mans *for noun,* rō mans′ *for verb*) **1** a love story. **2** a story of adventure: *The Arabian Nights and Treasure Island are romances.* **3** a story or poem telling of heroes: *Have you read the romances about King Arthur and his knights?* **4** real events or conditions that are like such stories, full of love, excitement, or noble deeds; the character or quality of such events or conditions: *The explorer's life was filled with romance.* **5** an interest in adventure and love. **6** a love affair. **7** a false or extravagant story: *Nobody believes her romances about the wonderful things that have happened to her.* **8** make up stories or adventures. **9** think or talk in a romantic way: *Some children romance because of their lively imaginations.* **10** exaggerate; lie. **1–7** *n.*, **8–10** *v.*, **ro·manced, ro·manc·ing.**

**Romance languages** French, Italian, Spanish, Portuguese, Romanian, Provençal, Catalan, and other languages that developed from Latin, the language of the Romans.

**ro·manc·er** (rō man′sər) **1** a writer of romance. **2** a person who makes up false or extravagant stories. *n.*

**Ro·man·esque** (rō′mə nesk′) **1** a style of architecture using round arches and vaults, popular in Europe during the early Middle Ages, between the periods of Roman and Gothic architecture. See ARCHITECTURE for picture. **2** of, in, or having to do with this style of architecture. **1** *n.*, **2** *adj.*

**Ro·ma·ni·an** (rō mā′nē ən) **1** of or having to do with Romania, a country in central Europe, its inhabitants, or their language. **2** a native or inhabitant of Romania. **3** the Latin language of Romania. **1** *adj.*, **2, 3** *n.* Also, **Roumanian, Rumanian.**

**Roman law** the laws of the ancient Romans: *Roman law is the basis of civil law in many countries.*

**Roman nose** a nose having a prominent bridge.

**Roman numerals** a system of numerals used by the ancient Romans, for example, numerals like XXIII, LVI, and MDCCLX, in which I=1, V=5, X=10, L=50, C=100, D=500, and M=1000.

**ro·man·tic** (rō man′tik) **1** characteristic of romances or romance; appealing to fancy and the imagination: *She likes romantic tales of love and war.* **2** having ideas or feelings suited to romance: *The romantic schoolgirl's mind was full of handsome heroes, jewels, balls, and fine clothes.* **3** suited to a romance: *What a romantic wood! Fairies might live here!* **4** fond of making up fanciful stories. **5** in literature, music, and art, appealing to the emotions and the imagination in subject and style; not classical: *Jane Eyre and Chopin's music are romantic. Romantic writing usually tells about the unusual and adventurous aspects of life and uses complete freedom of form and expression.* *adj.* —**ro·man′ti·cal·ly,** *adv.*

**ro·man·ti·cism** (rō man′tə siz′əm) **1** a romantic spirit or tendency. **2** in art and literature, a style or movement that prevailed in western Europe in the late 18th and early 19th centuries, characterized by a highly imaginative and emotional treatment of life, nature, and the supernatural. *n.*

**ro·man·ti·cist** (rō man′tə sist) a follower of

ROMANTICISM in literature or art: *Scott and Wordsworth were romanticists.* *n.*

**ro·man·ti·cize** (rō man′tə sīz′) **1** make ROMANTIC; give a romantic character to. **2** be ROMANTIC; act, talk, or write in a romantic manner. *v.*, **ro·man·ti·cized, ro·man·ti·ciz·ing.**

**Rom·a·ny** (rom′ə nē) **1** GYPSY. **2** the language of the Gypsies. **3** belonging or having to do with the Gypsies, their customs, or their language. 1, 2 *n., pl.* **Rom·a·nies;** 3 *adj.*

**Ro·me·o** (rō′mē ō′) **1** the hero of Shakespeare's play *Romeo and Juliet,* who died for love. **2** any young and romantic lover. *n.*

**romp** (romp) **1** play in a rough, boisterous way; rush, tumble, and punch in play. **2** a rough, lively play or frolic: *A pillow fight is a romp.* **3** run or go quickly and easily. **4** a swift but effortless victory in which all the others are left behind, as in racing: *win in a romp.* 1, 3 *v.,* 2, 4 *n.* —**romp′er,** *n.*

**romp·ers** (romp′ərz) a loose outer garment, worn by young children. *n., pl.*

**ron·do** (ron′dō *or* ron do′) in music, a composition or movement having one principal theme to which return is made after the introduction of each subordinate theme. *n., pl.* **ron·dos.**

**Rönt·gen** (rent′gən; *German,* rœnt′gən) ROENTGEN. *n.*

**rood** (rüd) **1** a unit for measuring land area, equal to ¼ acre (about 1012 m²). **2** a representation of the cross; crucifix. *n.*
☛ *Hom.* RUDE.

GABLE ROOF: AN 18c HOUSE IN ONTARIO
GAMBREL ROOF: AN 18c HOUSE IN NOVA SCOTIA
HIP ROOF: AN EARLY 20c HOUSE IN MANITOBA
MANSARD ROOF: A CONTEMPORARY HOUSE, QUE.

**roof** (rüf) **1** the top covering of a building. **2** something that in form or position resembles the roof of a building: *the roof of a cave, the roof of a car, the roof of the mouth.* **3** cover with a roof; form a roof over. 1, 2 *n., pl.* **roofs** *or* **rooves;** 3 *v.*
**raise the roof,** *Informal.* make a disturbance; create an uproar or confusion.

**roof·er** (rü′fər) a person who makes or repairs roofs. *n.*

**roof garden 1** a garden on the flat roof of a building. **2** the roof or top storey of a building, ornamented with plants, etc. and used for a restaurant, theatre, etc.

**roof·ing** (rü′fing) **1** material used for roofs. **2** ppr. of ROOF. 1 *n.,* 2 *v.*

**roof·less** (rü′flis) **1** having no roof. **2** having no home or shelter. *adj.*

**roof·tree** (rüf′trē′) the horizontal timber along the top of the roof. *n.*

**rook¹** (ruk) a European crow that often nests in trees near buildings. *n.*

**rook²** (ruk) one of the pieces with which the game of CHESS is played, also called a castle. *n.*

**rook·er·y** (rük′ə rē) **1** a breeding place for ROOKS¹; colony of ROOKS¹. **2** a breeding place or colony where other birds or animals are crowded together: *a rookery of seals.* **3** a crowded, dirty, and poor tenement house or group of such houses. *n., pl.* **rook·er·ies.**

**rook·ie** (rük′ē) *Informal.* a beginner, such as a recruit or a new player on a team. *n.*

**room** (rüm) **1** a part of a house, or other building, with walls separating it from the rest of the building of which it is a part. **2** the people in a room. **3** the space occupied by, or available for, something: *There is little room to move in a crowd.* **4** scope; opportunity: *room for improvement, room for advancement.* **5** rent a room; lodge: *The two girls roomed together.* **6** provide with a room. **7 rooms,** *pl.* LODGINGS. 1–4, 7 *n.,* 5, 6 *v.*
☛ *Hom.* RHEUM.

**room·er** (rü′mər) a person who lives in a rented room or rooms in another's house. *n.*
☛ *Hom.* RUMOUR.

**room·ette** (rü met′) a small private bedroom in some railway cars. *n.*

**room·ful** (rüm′fùl) **1** enough to fill a room. **2** the people or things in a room. *n., pl.* **room·fuls.**

**rooming house** a house with rooms to rent.

**room–mate** (rüm′māt′) a person who shares a room with another or others. *n.*

**room·y** (rü′mē) having plenty of room; large; spacious. *adj.*, **room·i·er, room·i·est.**
—**room′i·ness,** *n.*
☛ *Hom.* RHEUMY.

**roost** (rüst) **1** a bar, pole, or perch on which birds rest or sleep. **2** sit as birds do on a roost; settle for the night. **3** a place for birds to roost in. **4** a place to rest or stay: *a robber's roost in the mountains.* 1, 3, 4 *n.,* 2 *v.*
**rule the roost,** *Informal.* be master.

**roost·er** (rü′stər) a male domestic fowl; cock. *n.*

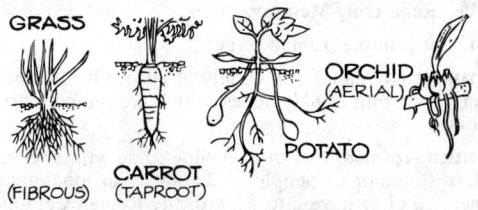

GRASS (FIBROUS)  CARROT (TAPROOT)  POTATO  ORCHID (AERIAL)

Examples of the four main types of root

**root¹** (rüt) **1** the part of a plant that grows downward, usually into the ground, to hold the plant in place, absorb water and mineral foods from the soil, and often to store food material. **2** any underground part of a plant. **3** something like a root in shape, position, use, etc.: *the root of a tooth, the roots of the hair.* **4** a thing from which other things grow and develop; cause; source: *"The love of money is the root of all evil."* **5** send out roots and begin to grow; become fixed in the ground: *Some plants root more quickly than others.* **6** fix firmly: *She was rooted to the spot by surprise.* **7** become firmly fixed. **8** the essential part; base: *to get to the root of a problem.* **9** the

quantity that produces another quantity when multiplied by itself a certain number of times: 2 *is the square root of* 4 *and the cube root of* 8 (2 × 2 = 4, 2 × 2 × 2 = 8).   **10** the quantity that satisfies an equation when substituted for an unknown quantity: *In the equation* $x^2 + 2x - 3 = 0$, 1 *and* -3 *are the roots*.   **11** a word or word element from which others are derived. *Example:* Room *is the root of* roominess, roomer, room-mate, *and* roomy.   **12** in music, the fundamental note of a chord.   1-4, 8-12 *n*., 5-7 *v*.
—**root′like**, *adj*.
**root out** or **up**,   get rid of completely: *root out corruption in government*.
**take root**,   **a** send out roots and begin to grow.   **b** become firmly fixed.
☞ *Hom.* ROUTE (rüt).

**root²** (rüt)   **1** dig with the snout: *Pigs like to root in gardens*.   **2** poke; pry; search.   *v*.
☞ *Hom.* ROUTE (rüt).

**root³** (rüt) *Informal.*   cheer or support a contestant, etc. enthusiastically.   *v*.
☞ *Hom.* ROUTE (rüt).

**root beer**   a soft drink flavoured with the juice of the roots of certain plants, such as SARSAPARILLA and SASSAFRAS.

**root cellar**   the part of a house or barn below ground level, used for storing root vegetables such as carrots by keeping them cool.

**root·er¹** (rü′tər)   **1** an animal that digs with its snout.   **2** a machine that digs or uproots stumps, trees, etc.   *n*.

**root·er²** (rü′tər) *Informal.*   a person who cheers or supports enthusiastically.   *n*.

**root hair**   a hairlike outgrowth from a root, that absorbs water and dissolved minerals from the soil.

**root·let** (rü′tlit)   a little root; small branch of a root.   *n*.

**root·stock** (rüt′stok′)   RHIZOME.   *n*.

**rooves** (rüvz)   a pl. of ROOF.   *n*.

**rope** (rōp)   **1** a strong, thick line or cord made by twisting smaller cords together.   **2** tie, bind, or fasten with a rope.   **3** enclose or mark off with a rope.   **4** a lasso.   **5** catch a horse, calf, etc. with a lasso.   **6** a number of things twisted or strung together: *a rope of pearls, a rope of onions*.   **7** a cord or noose for hanging a person.   **8** death by being hanged.   **9** a sticky, stringy mass: *Molasses candy forms a rope*.   **10** form a sticky, stringy mass: *Cook the syrup until it ropes when you lift it with a spoon*.   1, 4, 6-9 *n*., 2, 3, 5, 10 *v*., **roped, rop·ing**.
**give someone rope**, *Informal.*   let someone act freely.
**know the ropes**,   **a** know the various ropes of a ship.   **b** *Informal.*   know about a business or activity.
**rope in**, *Informal.*   get or lead in by tricking.
**the end of one's rope**,   the end of one's resources, activities, etc.

**rope·danc·er** (rōp′dan′sər)   a person who dances, walks, etc. on a rope hung high above the floor or ground.   *n*.

**rope·walk** (rōp′wok′)   a place where ropes are made: *A ropewalk is usually a long, low shed*.   *n*.

**rope·walk·er** (rōp′wok′ər)   a person who walks on a rope hung high above the floor or ground.   *n*.

**rop·y** (rō′pē)   **1** forming sticky threads; stringy.   **2** like a rope or ropes.   *adj*., **rop·i·er, rop·i·est**.
—**rop′i·ness**, *n*.

**roque** (rōk)   a form of croquet played on a hard, rolled court and modified from ordinary croquet so as to demand greater skill.   *n*.

**Roque·fort** (rōk′fərt)   a strongly flavoured French cheese made of goats' milk, veined with mould.   *n*.

**ror·qual** (rôr′kwəl)   any of the whalebone whales having a dorsal fin; any finback.   *n*.

**ro·sa·ceous** (rō zā′shəs)   **1** belonging to the same family as the rose.   **2** like a rose.   **3** rose-coloured.   *adj*.

**ro·sa·ry** (rō′zə rē)   **1** a string of beads for keeping count in saying a series of prayers.   **2** a series of prayers.   **3** a rose garden; rose bed.   *n*., *pl*. **ro·sa·ries**.

The prickly rose, a common wild rose

**rose¹** (rōz)   **1** any of a closely related group of shrubs of the Northern Hemisphere, having compound leaves, showy flowers, and, usually, prickly stems: *There are many cultivated species and varieties of rose. Wild roses have flowers with five petals*.   **2** the flower of any of these shrubs.   **3** referring to a large family of herbs, shrubs, and trees, found especially in temperate regions, that includes some of the most important fruit-bearing and ornamental shrubs and trees: *Raspberries, strawberries, cherries, plums, peaches, hawthorns, brambles, and roses belong to the rose family*.   **4** pinkish red.   **5** make rosy: *The cold rosed her cheeks*.   **6** a perfume made from roses.   **7** something shaped like a rose or suggesting a rose, such as a rosette, the compass card, or a gem cut out with faceted top and flat base.   **8** a woman of great beauty, loveliness, or excellence.   1, 2-4, 6-8 *n*., 4 *adj*., 5 *v*., **rosed, ros·ing**.   —**rose′like**, *adj*.
**under the rose**,   in secret; privately.

**rose²** (rōz)   pt. of RISE: *The man rose and bowed*.   *v*.

**ro·se·ate** (rō′zē it *or* rō′zē āt′)   **1** rose-coloured; rosy.   **2** cheerful; optimistic.   *adj*.

**rose·bud** (rōz′bud′)   the bud of a rose.   *n*.

**rose·bush** (rōz′bush′)   a shrub or vine that bears roses.   *n*.

**rose-col·oured** or **rose-col·ored** (rōz′kul′ərd)   **1** pinkish-red.   **2** bright; cheerful; optimistic.   *adj*.

**rose geranium**   a kind of geranium having fragrant, narrowly divided leaves and small, pinkish flowers.

**rose leaf**   a petal of a rose.

**rose mallow**   **1** any of several species of hibiscus, especially a herb native to marshy areas of the eastern United States, from which many cultivated varieties have been derived: *The rose mallow has large red, pink, or white flowers*.   **2** hollyhock.

**rose·mary** (rōz′mer ē) an evergreen shrub whose leaves yield a fragrant oil used in making perfume: *Rosemary is a symbol of remembrance.* *n., pl.* **rose·mar·ies.**

**rose of Sharon** (shar′ən *or* sher′ən) a shrub or small tree native to Asia, commonly cultivated for its large bell-shaped, usually rose, purple, or white flower.

**Ro·set·ta stone** (rō zet′ə) a slab of black basalt found in 1799 near the mouth of the Nile. A decree carved on it in two kinds of ancient Egyptian writing and in Greek provided the most important key to the understanding of Egyptian hieroglyphics. It is in the British Museum in London.

**ro·sette** (rō zet′) an ornament, object, or arrangement shaped like a rose: *Rosettes made of ribbon are given as prizes at livestock shows. Carved or moulded rosettes are used in architecture.* *n.*

**rose water** water made fragrant with oil of roses.

**rose window** an ornamental circular window, especially one with a pattern of small sections that radiate from a centre.

**rose·wood** (rōz′wu̇d) **1** a beautiful reddish wood used in fine furniture. **2** the tropical tree that it comes from. *n.*

**Rosh Ha·sha·na** (rosh′hə shä′nə) the Jewish New Year, falling usually in late September or early October.

**ro·shi** (rō′shē) in Zen Buddhism, a term of respect for a wise teacher, the head of a monastery, or the chief priest of a temple. *n.*

**ros·i·ly** (rō′zə lē) **1** with a rosy tinge or colour. **2** brightly; cheerfully. *adv.*

**ros·in** (roz′ən) **1** a hard, yellow substance that remains when turpentine is evaporated from pine resin: *Rosin is rubbed on violin bows and on the shoes of acrobats and boxers to keep them from slipping.* Compare with RESIN. **2** cover or rub with rosin. **1** *n.,* **2** *v.*

**ros·ter** (ros′tər) **1** a list of people's names and the duties assigned to them. **2** any list. *n.*

**ros·tral** (ros′trəl) of or having to do with a ROSTRUM. *adj.*

**ros·trum** (ros′trəm) **1** a platform for public speaking. **2** the beak of an ancient war galley. **3** a beaklike part. *n., pl.* **ros·trums** or **ros·tra** (-trə).

**ros·y** (rō′zē) **1** like a rose; rose-red; pinkish-red. **2** made of roses. **3** bright; cheerful: *a rosy future.* *adj.,* **ros·i·er, ros·i·est.** —**ros′i·ness,** *n.*

**rot** (rot) **1** decay; spoil. **2** cause to decay. **3** the process of rotting; decay. **4** rotten matter. **5** moisten or soak flax, etc. in order to soften. **6** a disease of plants and animals, especially of sheep. **7** lose vigour; degenerate. **8** *Informal.* nonsense; rubbish. **1, 2, 5, 7** *v.,* **rot·ted, rot·ting;** **3, 4, 6, 8** *n.*
☛ *Hom.* WROUGHT.

**ro·ta·ry** (rō′tə rē) **1** turning like a top or a wheel; rotating. **2** having parts that rotate. **3** a traffic circle. **4** a system in schools by which students move to different rooms and teachers for different subjects: *All classes are on rotary this year.* **5** of an airplane engine, having radially arranged cylinders that revolve about a common fixed crankshaft. **1, 2, 5** *adj.,* **3, 4** *n.*

**ro·tate** (rō′tāt *or* rō tāt′) **1** move around a centre or axis; turn in a circle; revolve: *Wheels, tops, and the earth rotate.* **2** change in a regular order; take turns or cause to take turns: *The officials will rotate. Farmers rotate crops.* *v.,* **ro·tat·ed, ro·tat·ing.**

**ro·ta·tion** (rō tā′shən) **1** the act or process of moving around a centre or axis; a turning in a circle; revolving: *The earth's rotation causes night and day.* **2** a change in a regular order. **3** a system of taking turns; changing in regular succession: *The job of classroom roll call is done in rotation.* *n.*

**ro·ta·tion·al** (rō tā′shə nəl) of or with ROTATION. *adj.*

**rotation of crops** varying the crops grown in the same field to keep the soil from losing its fertility.

**ro·ta·tor** (rō′tā tər) **1** a person or thing that ROTATES. **2** a muscle that turns a part of the body. *n.*

**ro·ta·to·ry** (rō′tə tô′rē) **1** rotating; rotary. **2** causing ROTATION. **3** passing or following from one to another in a regular order: *a rotatory office in a club.* *adj.*

**rote** (rōt) a set, mechanical way of doing things. *n.*
**by rote,** by memory without thought of the meaning: *to learn a lesson by rote.*
☛ *Hom.* WROTE.

**rot·hole** (rot′hōl′) *Cdn.* a soft place in the ice over a lake, river, etc. *n.*

**ro·ti·fer** (rō′tə fər) any of a group of complex, microscopic water animals that have one or more rings of CILIA on a disk at one end of the body. *n.*

**ro·tis·se·rie** (rō tis′ə rē) a rotating spit used in an oven, under a broiler, or over an open fire, for roasting meat or fowl. *n.*

**ro·to·gra·vure** (rō′tə grə vyu̇r′) **1** a process of printing from an engraved copper cylinder on which the pictures, letters, etc. have been depressed instead of raised. **2** a print or section of a newspaper made by this process. *n.*

**ro·tor** (rō′tər) **1** the rotating part of a machine or apparatus. See GYROSCOPE for picture. **2** a system of rotating blades by which a helicopter is enabled to fly. *n.*

**rot·ten** (rot′ən) **1** decayed; spoiled: *a rotten egg.* **2** foul; disgusting: *rotten air.* **3** not in good condition; unsound; weak: *rotten ice.* **4** corrupt; dishonest: *rotten government.* **5** *Informal.* bad; nasty: *rotten luck, to feel rotten.* *adj.* —**rot′ten·ly,** *adv.* —**rot′ten·ness,** *n.*

**ro·tund** (rō tund′) **1** round; plump. **2** sounding rich and full; full-toned: *a rotund voice.* *adj.*
—**ro·tund′ly,** *adv.*

**ro·tun·da** (rō tun′də) **1** a circular building or part of a building, especially one with a dome. **2** a large circular room with a high ceiling. **3** a large room with a high ceiling, such as the lobby of a hotel or the concourse of a railway station. *n.*

**ro·tun·di·ty** (rō tun′də tē) **1** roundness; plumpness. **2** something round. **3** rounded fullness of tone. *n., pl.* **ro·tun·di·ties.**

**rou·é** (rü ā′ *or* rü′ā) a dissipated man; rake. *n.*

**rouge** (rüzh) **1** a red or reddish powder, paste, or liquid for colouring the cheeks or lips. **2** colour with rouge. **3** a red powder, chiefly ferric oxide, used for polishing metal, jewels, etc. **4** *Cdn.* in Canadian football, a point scored when a ball kicked into the end zone is not run back into the playing area by the

defending team.   **5** *Cdn.*   make a point in this way.
**6** *Cdn.*   tackle a defending player in the end zone so as to score a rouge: *Jones rouged Sumush on the last play.* 1, 3, 4 *n.*, 2, 5, 6 *v.*, **rouged, roug·ing.**

**rough** (ruf)   **1** not smooth, not level, not even: *rough boards, rough bark.*   **2** without polish or fine finish: *rough diamonds.*   **3** without luxury and ease: *rough life in camp.* **4** not completed or perfected; done as a first try; without details: *a rough drawing, a rough idea.*   **5** coarse and tangled: *a dog with a rough coat of hair.*   **6** likely to hurt others; harsh; rude; not gentle: *rough manners.*
**7** disorderly; riotous: *a rough crowd.*   **8** *Informal.* unpleasant; hard; severe: *She was in for a rough time.*
**9** requiring merely strength rather than intelligence or skill: *rough work.*   **10** stormy: *rough weather.*
**11** violently disturbed or agitated: *a rough sea.*   **12** a coarse, violent person.   **13** make rough; roughen.
**14** become rough.   **15** treat roughly.   **16** shape or sketch roughly: *rough out a plan, rough in the outlines of a face.*
**17** in rough manner; roughly: *Those boys play too rough for me.*   **18** rough ground.   **19** a rough thing or condition.
**20** harsh, sharp, or dry to the taste: *rough wines.*
**21** ground where there is long grass, etc. on a golf course: *I lost my ball in the rough.*   1–11, 20 *adj.*, 12, 18, 19, 21 *n.*, 13–16 *v.*, 17 *adv.*   —**rough**′**ness,** *n.*
**in the rough,**   not polished or refined; coarse; crude.
**rough it,**   live without comforts and conveniences.
☛ *Hom.* RUFF.

**rough·age** (ruf′ij)   **1** rough or coarse material.   **2** the coarser parts or kinds of food which stimulate the movement of food and waste products through the intestines: *Bran, fruit skins, and certain fruits are roughage.*   *n.*

**rough–and–read·y** (ruf′ən red′ē)   **1** rough and crude, but good enough for the purpose; roughly effective.
**2** showing rough vigour rather than refinement.   *adj.*

**rough–and–tum·ble** (ruf′ən tum′bəl)   showing confusion and violence; with little regard for rules; roughly vigorous; boisterous.   *adj.*

**rough·en** (ruf′ən)   **1** make rough.   **2** become rough.   *v.*

**rough–hew** (ruf′hyü′)   **1** hew timber, stone, etc. roughly or without smoothing or finishing.   **2** shape roughly; give crude form to.   *v.*, **rough–hewed, rough–hewed** or **rough–hewn, rough–hew·ing.**

**rough·house** (ruf′hous′) *Informal.*   **1** rough play; rowdy conduct; disorderly behaviour.   **2** act in a rough or disorderly way.   **3** disturb by such conduct.   1 *n.*, 2, 3 *v.*, **rough·housed, rough·hous·ing.**

**rough·ing** (ruf′ing)   **1** the rough treatment of another player in hockey, football, and other games: *He got a penalty for roughing.*   **2** ppr. of ROUGH.   1 *n.*, 2 *v.*

**rough·ly** (ruf′lē)   **1** in a rough manner.
**2** approximately: *From Quebec City to Vancouver is roughly five thousand kilometres.*   *adv.*

**rough·neck** (ruf′nek′) *Informal.*   **1** a rough, bad-mannered person; a rowdy.   **2** a member of an oil-drilling crew.   *n.*

**rough·rid·er** (ruf′rī′dər)   **1** a person used to rough, hard riding.   **2** a person who breaks in and rides rough, wild horses.   *n.*

**rough·shod** (ruf′shod′)   having horseshoes with sharp CALKS[2] to prevent slipping.   *adj.*
**ride roughshod over,**   domineer over; show no consideration for; treat roughly.

**rough** **1029** **round**

hat, āge, fär; let, ēqual, tėrm; it, īce
hot, ōpen, ôrder; oil, out; cup, put, rüle
ə *above,* ə *taken,* ə *pencil,* ə *lemon,* ə *circus*
ch, child; ng, long; sh, ship
th, thin; ᴛʜ, then; zh, measure

**rou·lette** (rü let′)   **1** a gambling game in which the players bet on the turn of a wheel.   **2** a small wheel with sharp teeth for making lines of marks, dots, or perforations.   *n.*

**Rou·ma·ni·an** (rü mā′nē ən)   ROMANIAN.   *adj.*, *n.*

**round** (round)   **1** shaped like a ball, a ring, a cylinder, or the like; having a circular or curved outline or surface: *a round hoop.*   **2** anything shaped like a ball, circle, cylinder, or the like: *The rungs of a ladder are sometimes called rounds.*   **3** plump: *Her figure was short and round.*
**4** make or become round: *The carpenter rounded the corners of the table.*   **5** making or requiring a circular movement: *The waltz is a round dance.*   **6** in a circle; with a whirling motion: *Wheels go round.*   **7** on all sides; in every direction: *The travellers were compassed round by dangers.*   **8** on all sides of: *Bullets whistled round him, but he was not hit.*   **9** in circumference: *The pumpkin measures ninety centimetres round.*   **10** go wholly or partly around: *They rounded the island. The ship rounded Cape Horn.*   **11** take a circular course; make a complete or partial circuit: *The car rounded the corner.*   **12** so as to encircle or surround: *They built a fence round the yard.*
**13** so as to make a turn to the other side of: *She walked round the corner.*   **14** by a longer road or way: *We went round by the candy store on our way home.*   **15** to all or various parts of: *We took our cousins round the town.*
**16** turn around; wheel about: *The bear rounded and faced the hunters.*   **17** a fixed course ending where it begins: *The watchman makes his rounds of the building every hour.*
**18** a movement in a circle or about an axis: *the earth's yearly round.*   **19** from one to another: *A report is going round that the stores will close.*   **20** through a round of time: *Summer will soon come round again.*   **21** about; around: *She doesn't look fit to be round* (*adv.*). *Stand still and look round you* (*prep.*).   **22** here and there in: *There are boxes for mail all round the city.*   **23** here and there: *I am just looking round.*   **24** for all: *There is just enough cake to go round.*   **25** a series of duties, events, etc.; routine: *a round of pleasures, a round of duties.*   **26** the distance between any limits; range; circuit: *the round of human knowledge.*   **27** a section of a game or sport: *a round in a boxing match, a round of cards.*   **28** the firing of a number or group of rifles, guns, etc. at the same time.
**29** the bullets, powder, etc. for such a shot: *Only three rounds of ammunition were left.*   **30** a single bullet, artillery shell, etc.   **31** an action that a number of people do together: *a round of applause, a round of cheers.*   **32** a dance in which the dancers move in a circle.   **33** a short song, sung by several persons or groups beginning one after the other: *"Three Blind Mice" is a round.*   **34** full; complete: *a round dozen.*   **35** large: *a good round sum of money.*   **36** general; approximate; to the nearest unit, ten, hundred, etc.: *The cost of the whole trip should be $500 in round figures. 3974 in round numbers would be 4000.*
**37** fill out; complete: *to round out a paragraph, to round out a career.*   **38** plainly expressed; plain-spoken; frank: *The boy's mother scolded him in good round terms.*
**39** with a full tone: *a mellow, round voice.*   **40** vigorous; brisk: *a round trot.*   **41** utter a vowel with a circular opening of the lips.   **42** a form of sculpture in which the figures are apart from any background.   **43** a cut of beef just above the hind leg.   See BEEF for picture.   1, 3, 5,

**34–36, 38–40** *adj.*, **2, 17, 18, 25–33, 42, 43** *n.*, **4, 10, 11, 16, 37, 41** *v.*, **6, 7, 9, 14, 19–21, 23, 24** *adv.*, **8, 12, 13, 15, 21, 22** *prep.* —**round′ness,** *n.*
**get** or **come round a person,** **a** outwit him or her. **b** wheedle him or her.
**go the round,** be passed, told, shown, etc. by many people from one to another.
**round and about,** in various places.
**round in,** in nautical use, haul in.
**round off,** **a** make or become round. **b** finish; complete: *round off a meal with a light dessert.* **c** make a number more simple or less exact by expressing it in the nearest unit, ten, hundred, etc.; generalize a number: *The total was 361, but she rounded it off to 350. Please round the answer off to two decimal places.*
**round on,** **a** turn so as to attack. **b** reprimand.
**round out,** complete: *round out a paragraph, round out a career.*
**round to,** in nautical use, come head up to the wind.
**round up,** draw or drive together.

**round·a·bout** (round′ə bout′) **1** indirect: *a roundabout route. I heard about it in a roundabout way.* **2** an indirect way, course, or speech. **3** a short, tight jacket for men or boys. **4** *Brit.* a MERRY-GO-ROUND. **1** *adj.*, **2–4** *n.*

**round dance** **1** a dance performed by couples and characterized by circular or revolving movements. **2** formerly, a dance performed by dancers in a circle.

**round·house** (round′hous′) **1** a circular building for storing or repairing locomotives, that is built about a turntable. **2** a cabin on the after part of a ship's deck. *n.*

**round·ish** (roun′dish) somewhat round. *adj.*

**round·ly** (roun′dlē) plainly; bluntly; severely: *to refuse roundly, to scold roundly.* *adv.*

**round number** **1** a whole number without a fraction. **2** a number in even tens, hundreds, thousands, etc.: *3874 in round numbers would be 3900 or 4000.*

**round robin** **1** a petition, protest, etc. with the signatures written in a circle, so that it is impossible to tell who signed first. **2** petition. **3** a system of scheduling a number of games in hockey, football, etc., in which every competing player or team is matched with every other one.

**round–shoul·dered** (round′shōl′dərd) having the shoulders bent forward. *adj.*

**round steak** a cut of beef just above the hind leg. See BEEF for picture.

**round table** a group of persons assembled for an informal discussion, etc.

**Round Table** **1** the table around which King Arthur and his knights sat. **2** King Arthur and his knights.

**round trip** a trip to a place and back again.

**round·up** (roun′dup′) **1** the act of driving or bringing cattle or horses together from long distances. **2** the people and horses that take part in a roundup. **3** a gathering together of people or things: *a roundup of criminals, a roundup of late news, a roundup of old friends.* *n.*

**round·worm** (roun′dwėrm′) any of a group of unsegmented worms that have long, round bodies: *The hookworm and trichina are roundworms.* *n.*

**roup** (rüp) **1** either of two diseases of poultry characterized by hoarseness and a discharge of catarrh from the eyes, nostrils, and throat: *A contagious form of roup is often fatal.* **2** hoarseness or huskiness. *n.*

**rouse** (rouz) **1** arouse; wake up: *I was roused by the telephone.* **2** stir up; excite: *She was roused to anger by the insult.* *v.*, **roused, rous·ing.** —**rous′er,** *n.*

**roust·a·bout** (rou′stə bout′) *Informal.* an unskilled labourer on wharves, ships, ranches, circuses, etc. *n.*

**rout**[1] (rout) **1** the flight in disorder of a defeated army: *The enemy's retreat soon became a rout.* **2** put to flight: *Our soldiers routed the enemy.* **3** a complete defeat: *The Battle of Waterloo was a complete rout.* **4** defeat completely: *The team routed its opponents by a score of ten to one.* **5** a group of followers. **6** a noisy, disorderly crowd; mob; rabble. **7** a riot; disturbance. **1, 3, 5–7** *n.*, **2, 4** *v.*
☞ *Hom.* ROUTE (rout).

**rout**[2] (rout) **1** dig out; get by searching. **2** put out; force out: *The farmer routed her sons out of bed at five o'clock.* **3** dig with the snout: *The pigs were routing for nuts under the trees.* **4** poke; search; rummage. *v.*
☞ *Hom.* ROUTE (rout).

**route** (rüt *or* rout) **1** a way to go; road: *Will you go to the coast by the northern route?* **2** a fixed, regular course or area assigned to a person making deliveries, sales, etc.: *a newspaper route, a milk route.* **3** arrange the route for. **4** send by a certain route: *The bus was routed by way of the detour.* **1, 2** *n.*, **3, 4** *v.*, **rout·ed, rout·ing.**
☞ *Hom.* ROOT (for the first pronunciation of **route**); ROUT (for the second pronunciation).

**rout·er** (rou′tər) a tool or machine for cutting grooves in or hollowing out wood or metal. *n.*

**rou·tine** (rü tēn′) **1** a fixed, regular method of doing things; habitual doing of the same things in the same way: *Getting up and going to bed are parts of your daily routine.* **2** using routine: *routine methods, a routine operation.* **3** average or ordinary; run-of-the-mill: *a routine show with routine performances.* **1** *n.*, **2, 3** *adj.*

**rove** (rōv) wander; wander about; roam; ramble; range: *She loved to rove over the fields and woods.* *v.*, **roved, rov·ing.**

**rov·er**[1] (rō′vər) **1** a wanderer or roamer. **2** a player in a lacrosse team who holds no special position but who may rove over the entire field. *n.*

**rover**[2] (rō′vər) **1** pirate. **2** a pirate ship. *n.*

**Rov·er** (rō′vər) a member of the senior branch of the BOY SCOUTS for boys over 17 years. *n.*

**row**[1] (rō) **1** a line of people or things: *The children stood in a row in front of the row of chairs.* **2** a street with a line of buildings on either side. *n.*
**hard row to hoe,** a difficult thing to do.
☞ *Hom.* ROE, ROW[2].

**row**[2] (rō) **1** move a boat by means of oars: *Row to the island.* **2** cause a boat, etc. to move by the use of oars. **3** carry in a rowboat: *We were rowed to the shore.* **4** perform a race, etc. by rowing. **5** the act of using oars. **6** a trip in a rowboat: *We went for a row at sunset.* **1–4** *v.*, **5, 6** *n.* —**row′er,** *n.*
☞ *Hom.* ROE, ROW[1].

**row**[3] (rou) **1** a noisy quarrel, disturbance; clamour: *The three children had a row over the bicycle.* **2** *Informal.* a squabble. **3** *Informal.* quarrel noisily; make noise. **4** *Informal.* scold. **1, 2** *n.*, **3, 4** *v.*

**row·an** (rou′ən *or* rō′ən)   **1** the mountain ash.   **2** its red, berry-like fruit.   *n.*

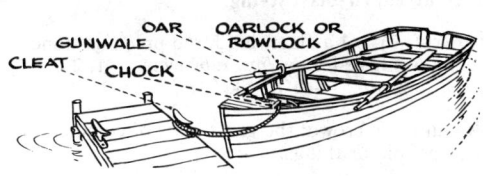

**row·boat** (rō′bōt′)   a small boat moved by oars.   *n.*

**row·dy** (rou′dē)   **1** a rough, disorderly, quarrelsome person.   **2** rough; disorderly; quarrelsome.   **1** *n.*, *pl.* **row·dies**;   **2** *adj.*, **row·di·er, row·di·est**.   —**row′di·ness**, *n.*

**row·dy·ish** (rou′dē ish)   like a rowdy; rough and disorderly; quarrelsome.   *adj.*

**row·dy·ism** (rou′dē iz′əm)   disorderly, quarrelsome conduct; rough, noisy behaviour: *rowdyism at Halloween.*   *n.*

**row·el** (rou′əl)   **1** a small wheel having sharp points, attached to the end of a spur. See SPUR for picture.   **2** use a rowel on.   **1** *n.*, **2** *v.*, **row·elled** *or* **row·eled**, **row·el·ling** *or* **row·el·ing**.

**row house**   one of several houses built together in a ROW¹ and constituting one building.

**row·lock** (rō′lok′)   a notch, metal support, etc, in which the oar rests in rowing; oarlock.   See ROWBOAT for picture.   *n.*

**roy·al** (roi′əl)   **1** of kings and queens, princes and princesses: *the royal family.*   **2** belonging to a king or queen: *royal power.*   **3** favoured or encouraged by a king or queen; serving a king or queen: *the Royal Academy.*   **4** from or by a king or queen: *a royal command.*   **5** of a kingdom or its government.   **6** appropriate for a king or queen; splendid: *a royal welcome.*   **7** like a king or queen; noble; majestic: *The lion is a royal beast.*   **8** fine; excellent.   **9** rich and bright: *royal blue.*   **10** *Informal.* a member of a royal family.   **11** a small mast or sail set above the topgallant.   1–9 *adj.*, 10, 11 *n.* —**roy′al·ly**, *adv.*

**royal assent**   in Canada, the signature of the Governor General or lieutenant-governor giving approval to a bill that has been passed by Parliament or by a legislative assembly: *A bill does not become law until royal assent has been given.*

**Royal Canadian Air Force**   formerly, the branch of the CANADIAN ARMED FORCES having to do with land-based aircraft.   *Abbrev.*: RCAF or R.C.A.F.

**Royal Canadian Legion**   an organization of Canadian former military personnel, especially war veterans, and nowadays also the families of such personnel. It sponsors numerous community services and undertakes welfare work for veterans and their families.

**Royal Canadian Mounted Police**   the federal police force of Canada: *In some provinces the Royal Canadian Mounted Police act as provincial police.*   *Abbrev.*: RCMP or R.C.M.P.

**Royal Canadian Navy**   formerly, the branch of the CANADIAN ARMED FORCES having to do with ships of war.   *Abbrev.*: RCN or R.C.N.

**royal commission**   **1** any investigation by a person or persons commissioned by the Crown to inquire into some matter on behalf of the federal or a provincial government

and to make a report recommending appropriate action.   **2** the person or persons so commissioned.

**roy·al·ist** (roi′ə list)   a supporter of a king or queen, or of a royal government: *The Royalists supported Charles I of England while the Puritans opposed him.*   *n.*

**roy·al·ty** (roi′əl tē)   **1** a royal person; royal persons: *Kings, queens, royal dukes and duchesses, princes, and princesses are royalty.*   **2** the rank or dignity of a king or queen; royal power: *The crown is the symbol of royalty.*   **3** kingliness or queenliness; royal quality; nobility.   **4** a royal right or privilege.   **5** a share of the receipts or profits paid to an owner of a patent or copyright; payment for the use of any of various rights: *An author receives royalties from the sale of his or her books.*   *n., pl.* **roy·al·ties**.

**rpm** *or* **r.p.m.**   revolutions per minute.

**rps** *or* **r.p.s.**   revolutions per second.

**R.R.**   **1** Rural Route: *Her address is R.R. 1, Kingston, Ontario.*   **2** Railroad.

**RRSP**   Registered Retirement Savings Plan.

**R.S.V.P.** *or* **r.s.v.p.**   please answer.

**rt.**   right.

**Rt. Hon.**   Right Honourable.

**Ru**   ruthenium.

**rub** (rub)   **1** move one thing back and forth against another; move two things together: *Rub your hands to warm them.*   **2** move one's hand or an object over the surface of; push and press along the surface of: *The nurse rubbed my lame back.*   **3** press as it moves: *That door rubs on the floor.*   **4** make or bring to some condition by rubbing: *to rub silver bright, to rub one's skin off.*   **5** clean, smooth, or polish by moving one thing firmly against another: *Rub that out and do it over.*   **6** admit of rubbing.   **7** the act of rubbing: *Give the silver a rub with this cloth.*   **8** something that rubs or hurts the feelings: *She didn't like his mean rub at her slowness.*   **9** a rough spot due to rubbing.   **10** irritate or make sore by rubbing: *The new shoes rubbed her heels.*   **11** a difficulty: *The rub came when both girls wanted to sit with the driver.*   **12** *Informal.* keep going with difficulty: *Money is scarce, but we shall rub along.*   1–6, 10, 12 *v.*, **rubbed, rub·bing**;   7–9, 11 *n.*
**rub down**,   rub the body; massage.
**rub it in**, *Informal.*   keep on mentioning something unpleasant.
**rub off**,   **a** remove by rubbing.   **b** be removed by rubbing.
**rub the right way**,   please; pacify.
**rub the wrong way**,   annoy; irritate.

**rub·ber**¹ (rub′ər)   **1** an elastic substance obtained from the milky juice of various tropical plants, or by various chemical processes: *Rubber will not let air or water through.*   **2** something made from this or a similar substance: *Pencils often have rubbers for erasing pencil marks.*   **3** made of rubber: *a rubber tire.*   **4** a person or thing that rubs.   **5** **rubbers**, *pl.*   **a** partial overshoes.   **b** *Informal.* waterproof boots for children.   1, 2, 4, 5 *n.*, 3 *adj.* —**rub′ber·like′**, *adj.*

**rub·ber²** (rub′ər) 1 a series of two games out of three, or three games out of five, won by the same side. 2 the deciding game in such a series: *If each side has won two games, the fifth game will be the rubber.* *n.*

**rubber band** a circular strip of RUBBER¹, used to hold things together.

**rubber boa** a small BOA in southern British Columbia.

**rub·ber·ize** (rub′ə rīz′) cover or treat with RUBBER¹. *v.*, **rub·ber·ized, rub·ber·iz·ing.**

**rubber plant** 1 any plant yielding RUBBER¹. 2 an ornamental house plant with oblong, shining, leathery leaves.

**rubber stamp** 1 a stamp made of RUBBER¹, used with ink for printing dates, signatures, etc. 2 *Informal.* a person or group that approves or endorses something without thought or without power to refuse.

**rub·ber–stamp** (rub′ər stamp′) 1 print or sign with a RUBBER STAMP. 2 *Informal.* approve or endorse a policy, bill, etc. without thought or without power to refuse. *v.*

**rub·ber·y** (rub′ə rē) like RUBBER¹; elastic; tough. *adj.*

**rub·bing** (rub′ing) 1 an image of an engraved or textured surface, such as a brass inscription or rock carving, made by rubbing charcoal, graphite, etc. over a piece of paper placed on top of the surface. 2 ppr. of RUB. 1 *n.*, 2 *v.*

**rub·bish** (rub′ish) 1 worthless or useless stuff, waste; trash; litter; debris: *After the picnic be sure to gather up the rubbish.* 2 silly words and thoughts; nonsense. *n.*

**rub·ble** (rub′əl) 1 rough, broken stones, bricks, etc., especially from collapsed or demolished buildings. 2 masonry made of this: *The house was built of rubble and plaster.* *n.*

**rub–down** (rub′doun′) a rubbing of the body; massage. *n.*

**Ru·bi·con** (rü′bə kon′) *n.*
**cross the Rubicon,** make an important decision from which one cannot turn back.
☛ *Etym.* From *Rubicon*, a small river in eastern Italy, in ancient times forming a boundary between the Roman republic and its provinces. By crossing the Rubicon into the republic in 49 B.C., Julius Caesar started the civil war that made him master of Rome.

**ru·bi·cund** (rü′bə kund′) reddish; ruddy: *The jolly captain had a rubicund face.* *adj.*

**ru·bi·cun·di·ty** (rü′bə kun′də tē) a RUBICUND quality or state. *n.*

**ru·bid·i·um** (rü bid′ē əm) a silver-white metallic element resembling potassium. Symbol: Rb *n.*

**ru·bric** (rü′brik) 1 a title or heading of a chapter, a law, etc. written or printed in red or in special lettering. 2 a direction for the conducting of religious services inserted in a prayer book, ritual, etc. 3 any heading, rule, or guide. *n.*

**ru·bri·cal** (rü′brə kəl) 1 red; marked with red; printed or written in special lettering. 2 of, having to do with, or according to religious rubrics. *adj.*

**ru·bri·cate** (rü′brə kāt′) 1 mark or colour with red. 2 furnish with rubrics. 3 regulate by rubrics. *v.*, **ru·bri·cat·ed, ru·bri·cat·ing.**

**ru·by** (rü′bē) 1 a clear, hard, red precious stone. 2 deep, glowing red: *ruby lips, ruby wine.* 1, 2 *n., pl.* **ru·bies;** 2 *adj.* —**ru′by-like′,** *adj.*

**ruck** (ruk) a crowd; the great mass of common or inferior people or things. *n.*

**ruck·sack** (ruk′sak′) a kind of knapsack, usually of canvas with two shoulder straps. *n.*

**ruck·us** (ruk′əs) *Informal.* a noisy disturbance or uproar; row. *n.*

**ruc·tion** (ruk′shən) *Informal.* a disturbance; quarrel; row. *n.*

A small sailboat, showing the rudder and tiller

TILLER
RUDDER

**rud·der** (rud′ər) 1 a hinged, flat piece of wood or metal at the stern of a boat or ship, by which it is steered. 2 a similar piece in an airplane, dirigible, etc., hinged vertically for right-and-left steering. See AIRPLANE for picture. *n.* —**rud′der·less,** *adj.*

**rud·dy** (rud′ē) 1 red or reddish: *a ruddy glow.* 2 rosy and glowing, as with good health: *After skiing all afternoon the girls had ruddy cheeks.* *adj.*, **rud·di·er, rud·di·est.** —**rud′di·ness,** *n.*

**rude** (rüd) 1 impolite; not courteous: *It is rude to stare at people.* 2 roughly made or done; without finish or polish; coarse: *rude tools, a rude cabin.* 3 rough in manner or behaviour; violent; harsh: *Rude hands seized the child and threw him into the car.* 4 harsh to the ear; unmusical. 5 not having learned much; uncivilized; rather wild; barbarous. 6 belonging to the poor or to uncultured people; simple; without luxury or elegance. 7 not fully or properly developed. *adj.* **rud·er, rud·est.** —**rude′ly,** *adv.*, —**rude′ness,** *n.*
☛ *Hom.* ROOD.

**ru·di·ment** (rü′də mənt) 1 a part to be learned first; beginning: *the rudiments of music.* 2 something in an early stage of development. 3 an organ or part incompletely developed in size or structure: *the rudiments of wings on a baby chick.* 4 an organ or part, such as the appendix, that does not develop completely and has no function. *n.*

**ru·di·men·ta·ry** (rü′də men′tə rē or rü′də men′trē) 1 to be learned or studied first; elementary: *rudimentary facts.* 2 in an early stage of development; undeveloped: *The wings on a baby chick are only rudimentary.* *adj.*

**rue¹** (rü) be sorry for; regret: *She will rue the day she insulted her friend.* *v.*, **rued, ru·ing.**

**rue²** (rü) a plant with yellow flowers and leaves that have a strong smell and a bitter taste. *n.*

**rue·ful** (rü′fəl) 1 sorrowful; unhappy; mournful: *a rueful expression.* 2 causing sorrow or pity: *a rueful sight.* *adj.* —**rue′ful·ly,** *adv.* —**rue′ful·ness,** *n.*

A ruff

**ruff** (ruf) **1** a deep frill, stiff enough to stand out, worn around the neck by men and women in the 16th century. **2** a collarlike growth of long or specially marked feathers or hairs on the neck of a bird or animal. *n.*
☛ *Hom.* ROUGH.

**ruffed** (ruft) having a RUFF. *adj.*

**ruffed grouse** a North American game bird having a tuft of feathers on each side of the neck. See GROUSE for picture.

**ruf·fi·an** (ruf′ē ən) **1** a rough, brutal, or cruel person; bully; rowdy; hoodlum. **2** rough; brutal; cruel. **1** *n.*, **2** *adj.*

**ruf·fi·an·ism** (ruf′ē ə niz′əm) brutal conduct; RUFFIANLY conduct or character. *n.*

**ruf·fi·an·ly** (ruf′ē ən lē) like a RUFFIAN; violent; lawless. *adj.*

Ruffles on a dress

**ruf·fle**[1] (ruf′əl) **1** make rough or uneven; wrinkle: *A breeze ruffled the lake. The hen ruffled her feathers at the sight of the dog.* **2** a roughness or unevenness in some surface; wrinkling. **3** a strip of cloth, ribbon, or lace gathered along one edge and used for trimming. **4** gather into a ruffle. **5** trim with ruffles. **6** disturb; annoy: *Nothing can ruffle her calm temper.* **7** become ruffled. **8** a disturbance; annoyance. **9** disorder; confusion. **10** shuffle playing cards. **1, 4–7, 10** *v.*, **ruf·fled, ruf·fling**. **2, 3, 8, 9** *n.*

**ruf·fle**[2] (ruf′əl) **1** a low, steady beating of a drum. **2** beat a drum in this way. **1** *n.*, **2** *v.*, **ruf·fled, ruf·fling**.

**rug** (rug) **1** a heavy floor covering: *Oriental rugs, scatter rugs.* **2** a thick, warm cloth used as covering: *The sick woman wrapped her woollen rug around her.* *n.*

**rug·by** (rug′bē) **1** in Canada, a game played by teams of twelve players who carry, pass, or kick an oval ball toward the opposing team's goal; football. **2** RUGGER. *n.*
☛ *Etym.* Named after *Rugby*, a famous school for boys in Rugby, England, where the game was first played. 19c.

**rug·ged** (rug′id) **1** rough; wrinkled; uneven: *rugged ground.* **2** strong; vigorous; sturdy: *The pioneers were rugged people.* **3** strong and irregular: *rugged features.* **4** harsh; stern; severe: *rugged times.* **5** rude; unpolished; unrefined: *rugged manners.* **6** stormy: *rugged weather.* *adj.* —**rug′ged·ly**, *adv.* —**rug′ged·ness**, *n.*

**rug·ger** (rug′ər) a game played by teams of fifteen players who kick or pass an oval ball toward the opposing team's goal. *n.*

hat, āge, fär; let, ēqual, tėrm; it, īce
hot, ōpen, ôrder; oil, out; cup, pút, rüle
əbove, takən, pencəl, lemən, circəs
ch, child; ng, long; sh, ship
th, thin; ᴛʜ, then; zh, measure

**ru·in** (rü′ən) **1** a building, wall, etc. that has fallen to pieces: *That ruin was once a famous castle.* **2** very great damage; destruction; overthrow; decay: *His enemies planned the duke's ruin.* **3** a condition of destruction, decay, or downfall: *The house had gone to ruin and neglect.* **4** the cause of destruction, decay, or downfall: *Drink was his ruin.* **5** bring to ruin; destroy; spoil. **6** be destroyed; come to ruin. **7** BANKRUPTCY. **8** make bankrupt. **9 ruins**, *pl.* that which is left after destruction, decay, or downfall, especially of a building, wall, etc. that has fallen to pieces: *the ruins of an ancient city.* **1–4, 7, 9** *n.*, **5, 6, 8** *v.*

**ru·in·a·tion** (rü′ə nā′shən) ruin; destruction; downfall. *n.*

**ru·in·ous** (rü′ə nəs) **1** bringing ruin; causing destruction. **2** fallen into ruins; ruined: *a building in ruinous condition.* *adj.* —**ru′in·ous·ly**, *adv.*

**rule** (rül) **1** a statement of what to do and not to do; a law; principle governing conduct, action, arrangement, etc. **2** an order by a law court, based upon a principle of law. **3** a set of rules; code: *A religious order lives under a certain rule.* **4** make a rule; decide. **5** make a formal decision: *The judge ruled against them.* **6** exercise highest authority; control; govern; direct: *She tries to rule her family as a dictator rules a nation.* **7** control; government: *In a democracy the people have the rule.* **8** a period of power of a ruler; reign: *The BNA Act was passed during the rule of Queen Victoria.* **9** a regular method; what usually happens or is done; what is usually true: *Fair weather is the rule in summer.* **10** prevail; be current: *Prices of wheat and corn ruled high all the year.* **11** RULER (def. 2). **12** mark with lines: *She used a ruler to rule the paper.* **13** mark off. **14** a thin, type-high strip of metal, for printing a line or lines. **1–3, 7, 8, 9, 11, 14** *n.*, **4–6, 10, 12, 13** *v.*, **ruled, rul·ing**. —**rul′a·ble**, *adj.*
**as a rule**, usually.
**rule out**, decide against, exclude.

**rule book** a book of rules, especially those of some game or sport: *the NHL Rule Book.*

**rule of three** a method of finding the fourth term in a mathematical proportion when three are given.

**rule of thumb** **1** a rule based on experience or practice rather than on scientific knowledge. **2** a tough, practical method of procedure.

**rul·er** (rü′lər) **1** a person who RULES. **2** a straight strip of wood, metal, etc., marked in units, such as centimetres, used in drawing lines or in measuring. *n.*

**rul·ing** (rü′ling) **1** a decision of a judge or court. **2** that rules; governing; controlling. **3** predominating; prevalent. **4** ruled lines. **5** ppr. of RULE. **1, 4** *n.*, **2, 3** *adj.*, **5** *v.*

**rum** (rum) an alcoholic liquor made from sugar cane, molasses, etc. *n.*

**Ru·ma·ni·an** (rü mā′nē ən) ROMANIAN. *adj., n.*

**rum·ba** (rum′bə) **1** a dance in quadruple time, that originated among the black people of Cuba. **2** the music for such a dance. *n.*

**rum·ble** (rum′bəl) **1** make a deep, heavy, continuous sound. **2** a deep, heavy, continuous sound: *We heard the far-off rumble of thunder.* **3** move with such a sound. **4** utter with such a sound. **5** the rear part of an automobile or carriage, containing an extra seat or a place for baggage. 1, 3, 4 *v.*, **rum·bled, rum·bling;** 2, 5 *n.*

**rumble seat** in certain old-fashioned types of automobile, an extra, open seat behind the enclosed driver's seat.

**ru·men** (rü′mən) **1** the first stomach of an animal that chews the cud. **2** the cud of such an animal. *n., pl.* **ru·mi·na** (rü′mə nə).

**ru·mi·nant** (rü′mə nənt) **1** an animal that chews the cud: *Cows, sheep, and camels are ruminants.* **2** belonging to the group of ruminants. **3** meditative; reflective. 1 *n.*, 2, 3 *adj.*

**ru·mi·nate** (rü′mə nāt′) **1** chew food for a second time; chew the cud. **2** chew again: *A cow ruminates its food.* **3** ponder; meditate: *She ruminated on the strange events of the past week.* *v.*, **ru·mi·nat·ed, ru·mi·nat·ing.**

**ru·mi·na·tion** (rü′mə nā′shən) **1** the act or process of chewing the cud. **2** meditation; reflection. *n.*

**ru·mi·na·tive** (rü′mə nə tiv *or* rü′mə nā′tiv) meditative; inclined to ruminate. *adj.*

**rum·mage** (rum′ij) **1** search thoroughly by moving things about: *I rummaged in my drawer for a pair of gloves.* **2** pull from among other things; bring to light. **3** a rummaging search. 1, 2 *v.*, **rum·maged, rum·mag·ing;** 3 *n.*

**rummage sale** a sale of odds and ends, old clothing, etc., usually held to raise money for charity.

**rum·my** (rum′ē) a kind of card game in which points are scored by forming sets of three or four cards of the same rank, or sequences of three or more of the same suit. *n.*

**ru·mour** *or* **ru·mor** (rü′mər) **1** a story or statement talked of as news without any proof that it is true: *The rumour spread that a new school would be built here.* **2** vague, general talk: *Rumour has it that Bill will marry Joan.* **3** tell or spread by rumour. 1, 2 *n.*, 3 *v.*
☛ Hom. ROOMER.

**rump** (rump) **1** the hind part of the body of an animal, where the legs join the back. **2** a cut of beef or veal from this part: *a rump steak.* See BEEF and VEAL for pictures. **3** the corresponding part of the human body; buttocks. **4** an unimportant or inferior part; remnant. *n.*

**rum·ple** (rum′pəl) **1** crumple; crush; wrinkle: *If you play in your best dress, you'll rumple it.* **2** a wrinkle; crease. 1 *v.*, **rum·pled, rum·pling;** 2 *n.*

**rum·pus** (rum′pəs) *Informal.* a noisy disturbance or uproar; row. *n.*

**rumpus room** REC ROOM.

**run** (run) **1** move the legs quickly; go faster than walking: *A horse can run faster than a person.* **2** go hurriedly; hasten: *Run for help.* **3** flee: *Run for your life.* **4** cause to run; cause to move: *to run a horse up and down.* **5** perform by, or as by, running: *to run errands.* **6** go; move; keep going: *This train runs to Calgary.* **7** go on; proceed: *Prices of shoes in that shop run as high as $180.00.* **8** creep; trail; climb: *Vines run along the sides of the road.* **9** go along a way, path, etc.: *to run the course until the end.* **10** pursue; chase game, etc.: *to run a fox.* **11** pass or cause to pass quickly: *A thought ran through my mind. Time runs on.* **12** trace; draw: *Run that report back to its source.* **13** stretch; extend: *Shelves run along the walls.* **14** drive; force; thrust: *She ran a splinter into her hand.* **15** flow; flow with: *The streets ran oil after an oil truck overturned.* **16** discharge fluid, mucus, or pus: *My nose is running.* **17** get; become: *Never run into debt. The well ran dry.* **18** have a specified character, quality, form, size, etc.: *These potatoes run large.* **19** spread: *The colour ran when the dress was washed.* **20** continue; last: *a lease to run two years.* **21** have currency or be current; occur: *The story runs that school will close early today.* **22** have legal force. **23** take part in a race or contest. **24** be a candidate for election. **25** expose oneself to: *to run a risk.* **26** move easily, freely, or smoothly; keep operating: *A rope runs in a pulley.* **27** cause to move easily, freely, or smoothly; cause to keep operating: *to run a machine.* **28** be worded or expressed: *How does the first verse run?* **29** the act of running: *to set out at a run.* **30** a spell or period of causing a machine, etc. to operate; amount of anything produced in such a period: *During a run of eight hours the factory produced a run of 100 cars.* **31** a spell of causing something liquid to run or flow, or the amount that runs: *the run of sap from maple trees.* **32** a trip, especially a journey over a certain route: *The ship reached port after a six weeks' run.* **33** conduct; manage: *to run a business.* **34** in baseball or cricket, the unit of score. **35** a period; a continuous spell or course; continuous extent: *a run of bad luck.* **36** a succession of performances: *This play has had a two-year run.* **37** an onward movement; progress; course; trend: *the run of events.* **38** a continuous series or succession of something; succession of demands: *a run on the bank to draw out money.* **39** in music, a rapid succession of tones. **40** the usual kind: *the common run of people.* **41** freedom to go over or through, or to use: *We were given the run of the house.* **42** go about without restraint; grow without restraint: *We are not allowed to run about the streets.* **43** a flow or rush of water; small stream. **44** a number of fish moving together, especially a periodic movement to spawning grounds: *a run of salmon.* **45** a way; track; trough; pipe: *a ski run.* **46** a stretch or enclosed space for animals: *a chicken run.* **47** drop stitches; ravel: *Nylon stockings often run.* **48** a place where stitches have slipped out or become undone: *a run in a stocking.* **49** sew by pushing a needle in or out with even stitches in a line. **50** get past or through: *Enemy ships tried to run the blockade.* **51** smuggle: *to run rum.* **52** a landing of smuggled goods. **53** publish an advertisement, story, etc. in a newspaper: *She ran an ad in the evening paper.* **54** soften; become liquid; melt: *The wax ran when the candles were lit.* **55** shape by melting: *to run bullets through a mould.* **56** the extreme after part of a ship's bottom. 1–28, 33, 42, 47, 49–51, 53–55 *v.*, **ran, run, run·ning;** 29–32, 34–41, 43–46, 48, 52, 56 *n.*

**a run for one's money, a** strong competition.
**b** satisfaction for one's efforts.
**in the long run,** on the whole; in the end.
**on the run, a** hurrying: *The butcher had so many orders that he was on the run all day.* **b** in retreat or rout: *Victory is ours; the enemy are on the run.*
**run across,** meet by chance.
**run a fever,** have a body temperature higher than normal.
**run away with,** do far better than others in.
**run down, a** cease to go; stop working. **b** pursue till caught or killed; hunt down. **c** knock down by running against. **d** speak evil against. **e** decline or reduce in vigour or health. **f** fall off, diminish, or decrease. **g** in

baseball, put a base runner out after tagging him or her between bases.
**run for it,** run for safety.
**run in, a** *Informal.* arrest and put in jail. **b** pay a short visit.
**run into, a** meet by chance. **b** crash into; collide with.
**run off, a** cause to be run or played: *to run off a tennis tournament.* **b** print; duplicate. **c** run away; flee.
**run out,** come to an end; become exhausted.
**run out of,** use up; have no more: *I can't bake a cake because we have run out of sugar.*
**run over, a** ride or drive over: *The car ran over some glass.* **b** overflow: *Coffee ran over into the saucer.* **c** go through quickly: *Please run over these figures to check my addition.*
**run through, a** consume or spend rapidly or recklessly: *The spendthrift ran through his inheritance in a year.* **b** pierce. **c** review; rehearse: *The teacher ran through the homework assignment a second time.*
**run up,** *Informal.* **a** make quickly. **b** collect; accumulate: *Don't run up a big bill.* **c** raise; hoist: *to run up a flag.*

**run·a·bout** (run′ə bout′) 1 a light automobile or carriage with a single seat. 2 a small motorboat. 3 a person who travels about from place to place. *n.*

**run·a·round** (run′ə round′) *Informal.* avoidance; evasion: *She gave us the runaround by making excuses and side-stepping our questions.* *n.*

**run·a·way** (run′ə wā′) 1 a person, horse, etc. that runs out of control. 2 a running away; eloping. 3 running with nobody to guide or stop it; out of control: *a runaway horse, a runaway car.* 4 done by runaways: *a runaway marriage.* 5 easily won: *a runaway victory.* 1, 2 *n.*, 3–5 *adj.*

**run·ci·nate** (run′sə nit *or* run′sə nāt′) of a leaf, having large lobes or teeth pointing toward the base: *Dandelion leaves are runcinate.* See LEAF for picture. *adj.*

**run·down** (run′doun′) 1 tired; sick. 2 falling to pieces; partly ruined: *a run-down building.* 3 that has stopped going or working. 4 in baseball, the act of putting a base runner out after tagging him or her between bases. 1–3 *adj.*, 4 *n.*

**run·down** (run′doun′) an account; summary: *Give me a rundown on what happened.* *n.*

Letters of the Anglo-Saxon runic alphabet

**rune**¹ (rün) 1 any letter of an ancient Germanic alphabet. 2 a mark that looks like a rune and has some mysterious, magic meaning. *n.*

**rune**² (rün) an old Scandinavian poem or song. *n.*

**rung**¹ (rung) pp. of RING². *The bell has rung.* *v.*
☛ *Hom.* WRUNG.

**rung**² (rung) 1 a round rod or bar used as a step of a ladder. 2 a crosspiece set between the legs of a chair or as part of the back or arm of a chair. 3 a spoke of a wheel. 4 a bar of wood having a shape and use similar to those of a spoke. *n.*
☛ *Hom.* WRUNG.

hat, āge, fär; let, ēqual, tėrm; it, īce
hot, ōpen, ôrder; oil, out; cup, pùt, rüle
əbove, takən, pencəl, lemən, circəs
ch, child; ng, long; sh, ship
th, thin; ᴛʜ, then; zh, measure

**ru·nic** (rü′nik) consisting of RUNES; written in runes; marked with runes. *adj.*

**run–in** (run′in′) *Informal.* a sharp disagreement; argument; quarrel. *n.*

**run·nel** (run′əl) a small stream or brook. *n.*

**run·ner** (run′ər) 1 a person or animal that runs. 2 messenger: *a runner for a bank.* 3 a person who runs or works a machine, etc. 4 either of the narrow pieces on which a sleigh or sled slides. 5 a blade of a skate. 6 a long, narrow strip: *We have a runner of carpet in our hall, and runners of linen and lace on our dressers.* 7 a smuggler; a person or ship that tries to evade somebody: *a blockade runner.* 8 a slender stem that grows along the ground and takes root, thus producing new plants; STOLON: *runner beans. Strawberry plants spread by runners.* See STOLON for picture. 9 a ravelled place. *n.*

**run·ner–up** (run′ə rup′) the person, player, or team that takes second place in a contest. *n.*

**run·ning** (run′ing) 1 the act of a person or thing that runs. 2 a flow of liquid; a discharge. 3 cursive: *a running hand.* 4 discharging matter: *a running sore.* 5 flowing. 6 liquid. 7 going or carried on continuously: *a running commentary.* 8 current: *the running month.* 9 repeated continuously: *a running pattern.* 10 following in succession: *for three nights running.* 11 prevalent. 12 moving or proceeding easily or smoothly. 13 moving when pulled or hauled: *a running rope.* 14 slipping or sliding easily: *a running knot or noose.* 15 of plants, creeping or climbing. 16 that is measured in a straight line. 17 of the normal run of a train, bus, etc.: *the running time between towns.* 18 performed with or during a run: *a running leap.* 19 ppr. of RUN: *The machines are running.* 1, 2 *n.*, 3–18 *adj.*, 19 *v.*
**be in the running,** have a chance to win.
**be out of the running,** have no chance to win.

**running board** formerly, a metal step along the side of an automobile.

**running gear** the wheels and axles of an automobile, locomotive, or other vehicle.

**running knot** a knot made to slip along the rope or cord around which it is tied; slip-knot.

**running mate** a candidate running jointly with another, but for a less important office, such as a candidate for vice-president.

**run·ny** (run′ē) having a tendency to run: *a runny nose. The pie filling is a bit runny.* *adj.*

**run–off** (run′of′) 1 something that runs off. 2 the running off of water as during the spring thaw or after a heavy rain. 3 a final deciding race or contest. *n.*

**run–of–the–mill** (run′əv ᴛʜə mil′) average or commonplace; ordinary: *a run-of-the-mill design.* *adj.*

**run–on entry** in a dictionary, a word or phrase that is given at the end of the entry word from which it is derived.

**runt** (runt) 1 an animal, person, or plant which is

smaller than the usual size. 2 an ox or cow of a small breed. *n.*

**runt·y** (run′tē) stunted; dwarfish. *adj.*, **runt·i·er, runt·i·est.**

**run·way** (run′wā′) 1 a strip having a level surface on which aircraft land and take off. 2 a channel, track, groove, trough, etc. along which something moves, slides, etc. 3 the beaten track of deer or other animals. 4 an enclosed place for animals to run in. *n.*

**Rupert's Land** the name given to the territories granted to the Hudson's Bay Company by Charles II in 1670: *Rupert's Land, so named because Prince Rupert was the first governor of the company, included all land watered by rivers flowing into Hudson Bay.*

**rup·ture** (rup′chər) 1 the tearing apart of body tissue: *the rupture of a muscle or blood vessel.* 2 HERNIA. 3 a breaking off of friendly relations; especially, a break between nations that threatens to lead to war. 4 any breaking apart or break of relations: *the rupture of a marriage.* 5 burst or break: *A heart muscle has ruptured. She ruptured her spleen.* 6 suffer or cause to suffer a breaking apart of friendly relations: *Their friendship has ruptured. She ruptured the family peace.* 1–4 *n.*, 5, 6 *v.*, **rup·tured, rup·tur·ing.**

**ru·ral** (rü′rəl) in, of, having to do with, or like the country or the people who live in the country: *a rural upbringing, a rural riding. adj.*

**rural municipality** *Cdn.* in certain provinces, a municipal district in a rural area, administered by an elected reeve and council.

**rural route** 1 a postal service by which mail is delivered by car or truck to the mailboxes of individual farms or country residences or businesses from a local post office. 2 any one route or circuit in this service: *There are four rural routes from this post office.* Abbrev.: R.R.

**ruse** (rüz *or* rüs) a trick; stratagem. *n.*

**rush**[1] (rush) 1 move with speed or force: *We rushed along.* 2 attack with much speed and force: *They rushed the enemy.* 3 come, go, pass, act, etc. with speed and haste: *She rushes into things without knowing anything about them.* 4 send, push, force, etc. with speed or haste: *Rush this order, please.* 5 the act of rushing: *the rush of the flood.* 6 busy haste; hurry: *the rush of city life.* 7 a great or sudden effort of many people to go somewhere or get something: *the holiday rush. Few people got rich in the Klondike gold rush.* 8 an eager demand; pressure: *a rush on steel stocks. A sudden rush of business kept everyone working hard.* 9 requiring haste: *A rush order must be filled at once.* 10 *Informal.* lavish much and frequent attention on: *He rushed the girl all summer.* 11 in football, an attempt to carry the ball through the opposing line. 12 **rushes,** *pl.* the first prints made of film shot for a motion picture. 1–4, 10 *v.*, 5–8, 11, 12 *n.*, 9 *adj.* —**rush′er,** *n.*
**with a rush,** suddenly, quickly.

**rush**[2] (rush) 1 any of a closely related group of marsh plants having round, pithy stems, grasslike leaves, and clusters of tiny, greenish or brownish flowers: *The stems of some rushes are widely used for chair bottoms, mats, baskets, etc. The pith of the stems was also formerly used for wicks in candles.* 2 referring to the family of perennial flowering marsh plants that includes these rushes, found in temperate and cold regions, and having slender leaves that are either grasslike or round and clusters of small flowers. 3 any of various other flowering marsh plants having round stems or hollow, stemlike leaves often used to make chair bottoms, mats, etc. 4 the stem or hollow leaf of a rush, used for baskets, etc. 5 made of or with rushes. *n.* —**rush′like′,** *adj.*

**rush hour** a time of day when traffic is very heavy and when trains, buses, etc. are very crowded.

**rush–hour** (rush′our′) of or describing the rush hour: *rush-hour traffic. adj.*

**rush·y** (rush′ē) 1 abounding in or covered with RUSHES[2]. 2 made of RUSHES[2]. *adj.* **rush·i·er, rush·i·est.**

**rusk** (rusk) 1 a piece of bread or cake toasted in the oven. 2 a kind of light, soft, sweet biscuit. *n.*

**rus·set** (rus′it) 1 reddish brown. 2 a coarse, russet-coloured cloth: *The peasants used to make and wear russet.* 3 a kind of apple having a rough, brownish skin. 1 *adj.*, 1–3 *n.*

**Rus·sia leather** a fine, smooth leather, usually dyed dark red, made from skins treated with birch bark oil: *Russia leather is used especially for bookbinding.*

**Rus·sian** (rush′ən) 1 of or having to do with Russia, its people, or their language. 2 a native or inhabitant of Russia, especially a member of the dominant Slavic peoples of Russia. 3 a person of Russian descent. 4 the language of Russia. 1 *adj.*, 2–4 *n.*

**Russian thistle** a common annual weed introduced to North America from Europe and Asia, having very narrow leaves ending in a sharp point and tiny flowers that grow from the leaf AXILS: *When a Russian thistle plant is mature, the leaves become very stiff and prickly and the nearly ball-shaped plant breaks off at ground level and is rolled by the wind, scattering its seed as it goes.*

**Russian wolfhound** BORZOI.

**rust** (rust) 1 the reddish-brown or orange coating that forms on iron or steel when exposed to air or moisture; ferric oxide. 2 any film or coating on any other metal due to oxidization, etc. 3 become covered with rust: *Don't let your tools rust.* 4 coat with rust. 5 spoil by not using. 6 become spoiled by not being used: *Don't let your mind rust during vacation.* 7 a harmful growth, habit, influence, or agency. 8 a plant disease that spots leaves and stems. 9 have or cause to have the disease rust. 10 reddish brown or orange. 1, 2, 7, 8, 10 *n.*, 3–6, 9 *v.*, 10 *adj.*

**rus·tic** (rus′tik) 1 belonging to or suitable for the country; rural: *rustic furnishings.* 2 simple; plain: *His rustic speech and ways made him uncomfortable in the city school.* 3 rough; awkward. 4 a country person: *The rustics gathered at the country fair.* 5 made of branches with the bark still on them: *rustic arches in a garden.* 1–3, 5 *adj.*, 4 *n.* —**rus′ti·cal·ly,** *adv.*

**rus·ti·cate** (rus′tə kāt′) 1 go to or live in the country. 2 send to the country. *v.*, **rus·ti·cat·ed, rus·ti·cat·ing.**

**rus·ti·ca·tion** (rus′tə kā′shən) 1 the act of rusticating or being RUSTICATEd. 2 residence in the country. *n.*

**rus·tic·i·ty** (rus tis′ə tē) 1 a RUSTIC quality or characteristic. 2 rural life. *n.*, *pl.* **rus·tic·i·ties.**

**rust·i·ly** (rus′tə lē) in a RUSTY state; in such a manner as to suggest rustiness. *adv.*

**rus·tle** (rus′əl) 1 a light, soft sound of things gently rubbing together, such as leaves make when moved by the wind. 2 make this sound: *Leaves rustled in the breeze.*

**3** move or stir something so that it makes such a sound: *We could hear her rustling papers in the next room.* **4** *Informal.* steal cattle. **5** *Informal.* act, do, or get with energy or speed: *We'll have to rustle if we want to finish in time.* 1 *n.*, 2-5 *v.*, **rus·tled, rus·tling.**
**rustle up,** **a** gather; find. **b** get ready; prepare: *The cook rustled up some food.*

**rus·tler** (rus′lər) **1** *Informal.* a cattle thief. **2** an active and energetic person. *n.*

**rust·less** (rus′tlis) free from rust; resisting rust. *adj.*

**rust·proof** (rust′prüf′) **1** resisting rust: *The tools have a rustproof finish.* **2** treat with a preparation that resists rust: *to rustproof a car.* 1 *adj.*, 2 *v.*

**rust·y** (rus′tē) **1** covered with rust; rusted: *a rusty knife.* **2** make by rust: *a rusty spot.* **3** coloured like rust. **4** faded: *a rusty black.* **5** weakened from lack of use or practice: *My mother says her biology is rusty.* **6** out of practice. *adj.*, **rust·i·er, rust·i·est.**
—**rust′i·ness,** *n.*

**rut**[1] (rut) **1** a track made in the ground, especially by a wheel. **2** make a rut or ruts in: *The road to the cottage was deeply rutted.* **3** a channel or groove in which something runs. **4** a fixed or established way of acting, especially a dull routine: *She decided to change jobs because she felt she was getting into a rut.* 1, 3, 4 *n.*, 2 *v.*, **rut·ted, rut·ting.**

**rut**[2] (rut) **1** sexual excitement of deer, goats, sheep, etc., occurring at regular intervals. **2** the period during which this excitement lasts. **3** be in rut. 1, 2 *n.*, 3 *v.*, **rut·ted, rut·ting.**

**ru·ta·ba·ga** (rü′tə bā gə *or* rü′tə bag′ə) a species of turnip with a very large yellowish root. *n.*

**ru·the·ni·um** (rü thē′nē əm) a hard, brittle, greyish metallic element of the platinum group. Symbol: Ru *n.*

**ruth·er·for·di·um** (ruTH′ər fôr′dē əm) an artificially produced radio-active element. Symbol: Rf *n.*

**ruth·less** (rü′thlis) having no pity; showing no mercy; cruel. *adj.* —**ruth′less·ly,** *adv.* —**ruth′less·ness,** *n.*

**rut·ty** (rut′ē) full of RUTS[1]. *adj.*, **rut·ti·er, rut·ti·est.** —**rut′ti·ness,** *n.*

**Ry.** railway.

**-ry** a noun-forming suffix meaning: **1** the occupation or work of a _____, as in *dentistry, chemistry.* **2** the act of a _____, as in *mimicry.* **3** the quality, state, or condition of a _____, as in *rivalry.* **4** a group of _____s, considered collectively, as in *jewellery, peasantry.*

**rye** (rī) **1** a cereal grass widely grown in northern Europe and northern North America for grain and straw. **2** the seeds, or grain, of this plant, used for bread or for fodder. **3** flour made from this grain. **4** bread made from rye flour: *He ordered a corned beef on rye.* **5** whisky made from rye. **6** in Canada, a blended whisky made from rye and other grains; Canadian whisky. *n.*
☛ *Hom.* WRY.

**rye–grass** (rī′gras′) any of several closely related grasses native to Europe and northern Africa, widely cultivated as a pasture grass in western Europe, Britain, New Zealand, and along the Atlantic and Pacific coasts of North America. *n.*

hat, āge, fär; let, ēqual, tėrm; it, īce
hot, ōpen, ôrder; oil, out; cup, pút, rüle
above, takən, pencəl, lemən, circəs
ch, child; ng, long; sh, ship
th, thin; ᴛʜ, then; zh, measure

# S s S s

**s or S** (es) **1** the nineteenth letter of the English alphabet. **2** any speech sound represented by this letter. **3** a person or thing identified as s, especially the nineteenth of a series. **4** anything shaped like the letter S: *an s-curve.*  *n., pl.* **s's** or **S's.**

**–s**[1] a suffix used to form the plural of most nouns, as in *hats, boys, dogs, houses, monkeys, taxis, handfuls.*

**–s**[2] a suffix used to form the third person singular, present tense, of verbs, as in *asks, lies, sees, tells, drives, loses.*

**s.**   **1** son.   **2** south.   **3** southern.   **4** singular.
**S**   **1** South.   **2** sulphur.   **3** siemens.
**S.**   **1** south.   **2** southern.   **3** School.   **4** Saturday. **5** Sunday.
**S.A.**   **1** South America.   **2** South Africa.   **3** South Australia.

**Sab·bath** (sab′əth) **1** the seventh day of the week, Saturday, observed as a day of rest and worship by Jews and members of some Christian denominations. **2** Sunday, observed as a day of rest and worship by most Christians. **3** of or belonging to the Sabbath. **4** sabbath, any day or period of rest.  *n.*
☞ *Usage.* Christians have generally accepted Sunday as the Sabbath because of their belief that Christ rose from the dead on the first day of the week.

**sab·bat·ic** (sə bat′ik) SABBATICAL.  *adj.*

**sab·bat·i·cal** (sə bat′ə kəl) **1** of, having to do with, or suitable for the SABBATH: *sabbatical laws.* **2** of or having to do with SABBATICAL LEAVE. **3** SABBATICAL LEAVE. 1, 2 *adj.,* 3 *n.*

**sabbatical leave** a leave of absence for a year or half year given to teachers, usually in a university and especially once in seven years, for study and travel.

**sa·ber** (sā′bər) See SABRE.  *n., v.,* **sa·bered, sa·ber·ing.**

**sa·ble** (sā′bəl) **1** a small, flesh-eating mammal of the forests of northern Asia, closely related to the martens, having glossy, dark-brown or black fur. **2** the fur of the sable, one of the most costly furs. **3** any of various animals related to the sable. **4** the fur of any of these animals.  *n.*

**sab·ot** (sab′ō or sab′ət; *French,* sä bō′) **1** a shoe hollowed out of a single piece of wood, worn by peasants in France, Belgium, etc. **2** a coarse leather shoe with a thick wooden sole.  *n.*

**sab·o·tage** (sab′ə täzh′) **1** the destruction of machinery or tools, a hindering of a manufacturing process, waste of materials, etc. as a threat or act of protest against an employer. **2** damage or destruction by civilians or enemy agents to interfere with a military operation or war effort: *Sabotage may be carried out by civilians against conquerors of their country or by enemy agents or by sympathizers within a country at war.* **3** any destruction or damage intended to hinder or hurt. **4** commit sabotage on; damage or destroy deliberately: *The group was accused of trying to sabotage the negotiations for a new labour contract.* 1–3 *n.,* 4 *v.,* **sab·o·taged, sab·o·tag·ing.**

**sab·o·teur** (sab′ə tėr′) a person who practises SABOTAGE.  *n.*

**sa·bre** (sā′bər) **1** a heavy, curved sword having a sharp point and cutting edge. See SWORD for picture. **2** a light sword used in fencing or duelling, having a tapering, flexible blade with a full cutting edge along one side: *A sabre is heavier than a foil.* **3** strike, wound, or kill with a sabre. 1, 2 *n.,* 3 *v.,* **sa·bred, sa·bring.** Also, **saber.**

**sabre saw** a hand-held power saw for light work, having a narrow blade that moves back and forth at high speed.

**sabre-toothed tiger** any of a number of extinct tigerlike mammals of the cat family having very long, curved upper canine teeth.

**sac** (sak) a baglike part in an animal or plant, often containing liquids: *the sac of a honeybee.*  *n.* —**sac′like**′, *adj.*
☞ *Hom.* SACK, SACQUE.

**sac·cha·rin** (sak′ə rin) a very sweet substance obtained from coal tar, used as a calorie-free substitute for sugar: *Saccharin is very much sweeter than cane sugar.*  *n.*
☞ *Hom.* SACCHARINE.

**sac·cha·rine** (sak′ə rin) **1** of, like, or containing sugar: *a saccharine taste.* **2** too sweet. **3** unpleasantly friendly or agreeable; ingratiating: *a saccharine smile.*  *adj.* —**sac′cha·rine·ly,** *adv.*
☞ *Hom.* SACCHARIN.

**sa·chem** (sā′chəm) **1** among Algonquian peoples, a ruler or chief, especially the chief of a confederacy of tribes: *The position of sachem was a hereditary one.* **2** any North American Indian leader or chief.  *n.*

**sa·chet** (sa shā′ or sash′ā) **1** a small bag or pad containing perfumed powder, used especially for scenting linens and clothes. **2** a small packet of shampoo, etc.  *n.*

**sack**[1] (sak) **1** a large bag, usually made of coarse cloth: *Sacks are used for holding grain, flour, potatoes, and coal.* **2** such a bag with what is in it: *She bought two sacks of potatoes.* **3** put into a sack or sacks: *to sack corn.* **4** a woman's loose-fitting dress. **5** *Informal.* discharge from employment; fire. **6 the sack,** *Informal.* dismissal from a job, etc.: *He got the sack for always coming to work late.* 1, 2, 4, 6 *n.,* 3, 5 *v.*
**hold the sack,** *Informal.* be left empty-handed.
☞ *Hom.* SAC, SACQUE.

**sack**[2] (sak) **1** plunder or pillage: *The invaders sacked the town.* **2** a plundering of a captured city: *the sack of Rome by the barbarians.* 1 *v.,* 2 *n.* —**sack′er,** *n.*
☞ *Hom.* SAC, SACQUE.

**sack**[3] (sak) sherry or other strong, light-coloured wine.  *n.*
☞ *Hom.* SAC, SACQUE.

**sack·but** (sak′but′) **1** a musical wind instrument of the Middle Ages, the ancestor of the trombone. **2** an ancient harplike stringed instrument: *The English name sackbut is the result of a mistranslation of an Aramaic word.*  *n.*

**sack·cloth** (sak′kloth′) **1** coarse cloth for making sacks. **2** a garment of such cloth worn as a sign of mourning or penance.  *n.*

**sack coat**  a man's loose-fitting jacket or suit coat having a straight-cut back.

**sack·ful** (sak′fŭl)  enough to fill a sack: *a sackful of potatoes.* *n., pl.* **sack·fuls.**

**sack·ing** (sak′ing)  **1** coarse cloth, such as burlap, for making sacks, etc.  **2** ppr. of SACK.  **1** *n.,* **2** *v.*

**sac·ra·ment** (sak′rə mənt)  **1** in Christian churches, any of certain formal religious ceremonies established or recognized by Jesus, considered especially sacred: *Baptism is a sacrament.*  **2** something especially sacred; a sacred sign, token, or symbol.  **3** a solemn promise; oath.  **4** Often, **Sacrament,**  the elements of the EUCHARIST; the consecrated bread and wine or the bread alone.  *n.*

**sac·ra·men·tal** (sak′rə men′təl)  **1** of or having to do with, or used in a SACRAMENT: *sacramental wine.*  **2** especially sacred.  **3** in the Roman Catholic Church, a ceremony similar to, but not included among, the SACRAMENTS: *The use of holy water is a sacramental.*  **1, 2** *adj.,* **3** *n.* —**sac·ra·men′tal·ly,** *adv.*

**sa·cred** (sā′krid)  **1** belonging to or dedicated to God or a god; holy: *the sacred altar, a sacred building.*  **2** connected with religion; religious: *sacred writings, sacred music.*  **3** worthy of reverence: *the sacred memory of a dead hero.*  **4** dedicated to some person, object, or purpose: *This monument is sacred to the memory of the Unknown Soldier.*  **5** that must not be violated or disregarded: *sacred oaths.* *adj.* —**sa′cred·ly,** *adv.* —**sa′cred·ness,** *n.*

**sacred cow**  a person or thing so highly regarded as to be beyond criticism.

**sac·ri·fice** (sak′rə fīs′)  **1** the act of offering to a god.  **2** the thing offered: *The ancient Hebrews killed animals on altars as sacrifices to God.*  **3** give or offer to a god.  **4** a giving up or destroying of one thing for the sake of something else: *the sacrifice of one's life for an ideal, the sacrifice of an ideal for commercial gain.*  **5** the thing given up or destroyed.  **6** give up, suffer the loss of, or injure or destroy for a particular belief or purpose: *to sacrifice one's life for another person, to sacrifice business for pleasure. We decided to sacrifice part of the garden for a patio.*  **7** a loss from selling something below its value: *Juanita will sell her house at a sacrifice because she needs the money.*  **8** sell at a loss.  **9** in baseball, a bunt or fly that helps the runner to advance although the batter is put out.  **10** help a runner to advance by such a bunt or fly.  **1, 2, 4, 5, 7, 9** *n.,* **3, 6, 8, 10** *v.,* **sac·ri·ficed, sac·ri·fic·ing.**

**sac·ri·fi·cial** (sak′rə fish′əl)  of, having to do with, involving, or used in a SACRIFICE.  *adj.* —**sac·ri·fi′cial·ly,** *adv.*

**sac·ri·lege** (sak′rə lij)  an intentional injury to anything sacred; disrespectful treatment of anyone or anything sacred: *Robbing the temple was a sacrilege.*  *n.*

**sac·ri·le·gious** (sak′rə lij′əs)  injurious or insulting to sacred persons or things; involving SACRILEGE.  *adj.* —**sac·ri·le′gious·ly,** *adv.*

**sac·ro·il·i·ac** (sak′rō il′ē ak′)  **1** of, or having to do with, or referring to the part of the body where the SACRUM and ILEUM meet.  **2** the joint or part of the body where the SACRUM and ILEUM meet. See PELVIS for picture.  **1** *adj.,* **2** *n.*

**sac·ro·sanct** (sak′rō sangkt)  **1** most holy or sacred; not to be violated.  **2** *Informal.*  very much revered; not to be scorned or laughed at: *That old car of his is sacrosanct to him.*  *adj.*

**sac·ro·sanc·ti·ty** (sak′rō sangk′tə tē)  the fact or state of being SACROSANCT; an especial sacredness.  *n.*

**sa·crum** (sā′krəm *or* sak′rəm)  the triangular bone at the lower end of the spine, that is formed by the joining of several VERTEBRAe and which makes the back of the pelvis. See PELVIS and SPINAL COLUMN for pictures.  *n., pl.* **sa·cra** (-krə) *or* **sa·crums.**

**sad** (sad)  **1** not happy; full of sorrow or grief: *a sad look, a sad child.*  **2** causing sorrow; distressing: *a sad disappointment.*  **3** dark or dull in colour; not cheerful-looking: *She always dressed in sad greys and browns.*  **4** *Informal.*  shocking; hopeless; pitiable: *This is a sad mess.*  *adj.,* **sad·der, sad·dest.** —**sad′ly,** *adv.*

**sad·den** (sad′ən)  make or become sad: *It saddened him to think that he might never see them again.*  *v.*

A western saddle   An English saddle

**sad·dle** (sad′əl)  **1** a seat, usually padded and leather-covered, for a rider on an animal such as a horse.  **2** a seat for a rider on a bicycle, etc.  **3** the part of a harness that holds the shafts, or to which a checkrein is attached. See HARNESS for picture.  **4** a coloured marking on the back of an animal: *a brown dog with a black saddle and black ears.*  **5** anything shaped or used like a saddle.  **6** a ridge between two mountain peaks.  **7** put a saddle on: *to saddle a horse.*  **8** burden: *He is saddled with a big house that he does not need or want.*  **9** a cut of meat consisting of the upper back portion of an animal, including both loins: *a saddle of venison.*  **1–6, 9** *n.,* **7, 8** *v.,* **sad·dled, sad·dling.**

**in the saddle,** *Informal.*  in a position of control.

**sad·dle·bag** (sad′əl bag′)  **1** one of a pair of bags laid over an animal's back behind the saddle.  **2** a similar bag hanging over the rear wheel of a bicycle or motorcycle.  *n.*

**sad·dle·bow** (sad′əl bō′)  the front part of a saddle, which sticks up.  *n.*

**sad·dle·cloth** (sad′əl kloth′)  a cloth put between an animal's back and the saddle.  *n.*

**saddle horse**  a horse for riding.

**sad·dler** (sad′lər)  a person who makes or sells saddles and harness.  *n.*

**sad·dler·y** (sad′lə rē)  **1** the work of a saddler.  **2** the shop of a saddler.  **3** saddles, harness, and other equipment for horses.  *n., pl.* **sad·dler·ies.**

**sad·dle·tree** (sad′əl trē′)  the frame of a saddle.  *n.*

**Sad·du·cee** (saj′ù sē′)  one of a Jewish sect, of the time of Christ, that denied the resurrection of the dead and the existence of angels, but believed in immortality.  *n.*

**sa·dhu** (sä′dü)   a Hindu holy man.   *n.*

**sad·i·ron** (sad′ī′ərn)   a heavy, solid flatiron pointed at both ends, used for ironing clothes.   *n.*

**sa·dism** (sā′diz əm *or* sad′iz əm)   delight in cruelty; getting pleasure from inflicting physical or mental pain on another person or on an animal.   *n.*

**sa·dist** (sā′dist *or* sad′ist)   a person who practises SADISM.   *n.*

**sa·dis·tic** (sə dis′tik)   of, having to do with, or showing SADISM: *a sadistic streak, a sadistic act.*   *adj.*

**sad·ness** (sad′nis)   sorrow; grief.   *n.*

**sa·fa·ri** (sə fä′rē)   **1** a journey or hunting expedition, especially in eastern Africa.   **2** any long trip or expedition.   *n., pl.* **sa·fa·ris.**

**safe** (sāf)   **1** free from harm or danger: *Keep money in a safe place.*   **2** not harmed: *He returned from war safe and sound.*   **3** out of danger; secure: *We feel safe with the dog in the house.*   **4** put beyond power of doing harm: *a criminal safe in prison.*   **5** careful: *a safe guess, a safe move.*   **6** that can be depended on: *a safe guide.*   **7** a box or place that can be locked, used for keeping things safe; especially, a heavy steel or iron chest or room for money, jewels, documents, etc.   1-6 *adj.,* **saf·er, saf·est;** 7 *n.*   —**safe′ly,** *adv.*   —**safe′ness,** *n.*
☛ *Etym.* Through OF *sauf* from L *salvus* 'whole, intact'. SAFETY comes through F *sauveté,* which also comes from L *salvus.* SALVAGE and SALVATION come from related words in early French; both can be traced back to L *salvare* 'save'. See also notes at SALUTE and SAVE.

**safe–con·duct** or **safe conduct** (sāf′kon′dukt)   **1** the privilege of passing safely through a region, especially in time of war: *The messenger was promised safe-conduct through the enemy camp.*   **2** a paper granting this privilege.   *n.*

**safe·crack·er** (sāf′krak′ər)   a thief who specializes in SAFECRACKING.   *n.*

**safe·crack·ing** (sāf′krak′ing)   the act or practice of breaking open safes and stealing the contents.   *n.*

**safe·guard** (sāf′gärd′)   **1** keep safe; guard against hurt or danger; protect: *Pure food laws safeguard our health.*   **2** a protection; defence: *Keeping clean is a safeguard against disease.*   **3** guard; convoy.   1, 3 *v.,* 2, 3 *n.*

**safe·keep·ing** (sāf′kē′ping)   protection; keeping safe; care: *Put your money in the bank for safekeeping.*   *n.*

**safe·ty** (sāf′tē)   **1** the quality or state of being safe; freedom from harm or danger: *They did not stop running until they had reached safety.*   **2** a device on a firearm, machine, etc. designed to prevent injury through accidental or careless operation.   **3** designed to give extra safety; designed to protect against harm through accident or misuse: *a safety lamp, safety glass, a safety belt.*   **4** in football, a SAFETY TOUCH.   *n., pl.* **safe·ties.**
☛ *Etym.* See note at SAFE.

**safety belt**   **1** SEAT BELT.   **2** a strap used by window cleaners, loggers, linemen, etc. to prevent falling.

**safety deposit box**   a box in the vault of a bank, etc. for the storage of valuables, such as original documents, bonds, jewellery, etc.

**safety glass**   glass that resists shattering, made of two or more layers of glass joined together by a layer of transparent plastic.

**safety island**   a marked area or a platform built in a thoroughfare for the convenience of pedestrians boarding and getting off buses, streetcars, etc.: *The city built safety islands at all busy intersections.*

**safety lamp**   **1** a miner's lamp in which the flame is kept from setting fire to explosive gases by a piece of wire gauze.   **2** an electric lamp similarly protected.

Safety pins, shown open and closed

**safety pin**   a pin bent back on itself to form a spring and having a guard that covers the point in order to prevent injury or accidental unfastening.

**safety razor**   a razor having a replaceable blade that is protected to reduce the risk of the shaver cutting his or her skin.

**safety touch**   in football, the act of putting a ball down behind one's own goal line after a player on one's own team has sent it there. It counts two points for the other team.

**safety valve**   **1** a valve in a steam boiler, etc. that opens and lets steam or fluid escape when the pressure becomes too great.   **2** something that helps a person get rid of anger, nervousness, etc. in a harmless way.

**saf·flow·er** (saf′lou′ər)   **1** an annual herb of the COMPOSITE family having large, red or orange flower heads yielding a red dye and seeds that are rich in oil.   **2** a red dye prepared from the flower heads.   *n.*

**safflower oil**   an edible oil obtained from SAFFLOWER seeds.

**saf·fron** (saf′rən)   **1** the dried orange-coloured stigmas of a species of crocus, used to flavour and colour candy, drinks, etc.   **2** the purple-flowered autumn crocus from which saffron is obtained.   **3** medium orange or orange yellow.   1-3 *n.,* 3 *adj.*

**sag** (sag)   **1** sink under weight or pressure; bend down in the middle.   **2** hang down unevenly: *Your dress sags in the back.*   **3** become less firm or elastic; yield through weakness, weariness, or lack of effort; droop; sink: *Our courage sagged.*   **4** decline in price.   **5** the act, state, or degree of sagging.   **6** the place where anything sags.   1-4 *v.,* **sagged, sag·ging;** 5, 6 *n.*

**sa·ga** (sä′gə *or* sag′ə)   **1** a type of prose story of heroic deeds written in Iceland or Norway in the Middle Ages.   **2** any extended story of adventure or heroic deeds.   *n.*
☛ *Etym.* From ON *saga* 'tale, story'. See also note at SAY.

**sa·ga·cious** (sə gā′shəs)   **1** wise in a keen, practical, farsighted way; shrewd.   **2** resulting from or showing wisdom or SAGACITY: *a sagacious decision.*   *adj.*
—**sa·ga′cious·ly,** *adv.*   —**sa·ga′cious·ness,** *n.*

**sa·gac·i·ty** (sə gas′ə tē)   keen, sound judgment; mental acuteness; shrewdness.   *n.*

**sag·a·more** (sag′ə môr′)   **1** among Algonquian peoples, an elected ruler or chief of a tribe, especially one subordinate to a SACHEM.   **2** SACHEM.   *n.*

**sage**[1] (sāj)   **1** wise: *a sage adviser.*   **2** showing wisdom or good judgment: *a sage reply.*   **3** a very wise person:

*The sage gave advice to the young man.* **1, 2** adj., **sag·er, sag·est; 3** n. —**sage′ly,** adv. —**sage′ness,** n.

**sage²** (sāj) **1** any of a closely related group of plants of the mint family; especially, **scarlet sage,** grown for its brilliant red flowers, and **garden sage,** grown for its aromatic leaves. **2** the dried leaves of the garden sage, used mainly as a seasoning for meats. n.

**sage·brush** (sāj′brush′) any of several closely related shrubs of the COMPOSITE family native to the dry plains of western North America: *Common sagebrush has greyish-green leaves and a smell like sage.* n.

**sage grouse** a very large GROUSE common on the plains of western North America.

**sage hen** SAGE GROUSE.

**Sag·it·tar·i·us** (saj′ə ter′ē əs) **1** in astronomy, a southern constellation thought of as having the shape of a centaur drawing a bow. **2** in astrology, the ninth sign of the zodiac: *The sun enters Sagittarius about November 23.* See ZODIAC for picture. **3** a person born under this sign. n.

**sag·it·tate** (saj′ə tāt′) shaped like an arrowhead: *Calla lilies have sagittate leaves.* See LEAF for picture. adj.

**sa·go** (sā′gō) a kind of starch obtained from the pith of a SAGO PALM and used in making puddings and as a stiffening for fabrics. n., pl **sa·gos.**

**sago palm** any of various species of palm that yield SAGO.

**said** (sed) **1** pt. and pp. of SAY: *Kim finally said she would come. Earlier, she had said "No" every time.* **2** named or mentioned before: *the said witness, the said sum of money.* **1** v., **2** adj.

**sail** (sāl) **1** a piece of cloth spread to the wind to make a ship move through the water. **2** sails: *Our ship had all sail spread.* **3** something like a sail, such as the part of an arm of a windmill that catches the wind. **4** a ship; ships: *a fleet numbering 30 sail.* **5** a trip on a boat with a sail or sails: *Let's go for a sail.* **6** travel on water by the action of wind on sails. **7** travel on a ship of any kind: *She is sailing to Europe on the Queen Elizabeth II.* **8** move smoothly like a ship with sails: *The eagle sailed by. Mrs. Grand sailed into the room.* **9** sail upon, over, or through: *to sail the seas.* **10** manage a ship or boat: *The boys are learning to sail.* **11** manage or navigate: *to sail a schooner.* **12** begin a trip by water: *We sail at 2 p.m.* **13** travel through the air: *The football sailed over the goal post.* 1–5 n., 6–13 v.
**in sail,** in a ship with sails.
**make sail, a** spread out the sails of a ship. **b** begin a trip by water.
**sail into,** *Informal.* **a** attack; beat. **b** criticize; scold.
**set sail,** begin a trip by water.
**take in sail, a** lower or lessen the sails of a ship. **b** lessen one's hopes, ambitions, etc.
**under sail,** moving with the sails spread out.
☛ *Hom.* SALE.

**sail·board** (sāl′bôrd′) a long, narrow board, usually of plastic, with provision for a sail, used in BOARDSAILING. n.

**sail·boat** (sāl′bōt′) a boat that is moved by a sail or sails. See SCHOONER and SLOOP for pictures. n.

**sail·cloth** (sāl′klôth′) **1** canvas or other material used for making sails. **2** a similar material used in making clothes, curtains, etc. n.

# sage 1041 sajjada

hat, āge, fär; let, ēqual, tėrm; it, īce
hot, ōpen, ôrder; oil, out; cup, pu̇t, rüle
above, takən, pencəl, lemən, circəs
ch, child; ng, long; sh, ship
th, thin; ŦH, then; zh, measure

**sail·er** (sāl′ər) a ship with reference to its sailing power: *the best sailer in the fleet, a fast sailer.* n.
☛ *Hom.* SAILOR.

**sail·fish** (sāl′fish′) a large saltwater fish belonging to the same family as the marlins, having a long, high, sail-like fin on its back. n., pl. **sail·fish** or **sail·fish·es.**

**sail·or** (sāl′ər) **1** a person whose work is handling a sailboat or other vessel. **2** a member of a ship's crew, not an officer. **3** one who sails for pleasure; yachtsman: *She's a born sailor.* **4** a person serving in the navy. **5** like that of a sailor: *a sailor collar.* **6** a flat-brimmed hat modelled after the kind of hat sailors used to wear years ago. n. —**sail′or·like′,** adj.
**a good sailor,** a person who does not get seasick.
☛ *Hom.* SAILER.

**sail·or·ly** (sāl′ər lē) like or suitable for a SAILOR. adj.

**saint** (sānt) **1** a very holy person; true Christian. **2** a person who has gone to heaven. **3** a person declared a saint by the Roman Catholic Church. **4** a person who is very humble, patient, etc., like a saint. **5** make a saint of; canonize. **6** call or consider a saint. **7** angel. **8 Saint,** holy or sacred (*used as a title before the name of a canonized person or an archangel*): *St. Teresa, St. Michael.* 1–4, 7, 8 n., 5, 6 v. —**saint′like′,** adj.
☛ *Usage.* Most names beginning with "Saint" are commonly written with the abbreviation **St.** Entries beginning with this abbreviation, such as **St. Elmo's fire** or **St. Vitus's dance** are found in this dictionary in their alphabetical place after **St.**

A Saint Bernard— about 75 cm high at the shoulder

**Saint Ber·nard** (bər närd′ or bėr′nərd) a breed of big, powerful working dog, often tan and white, having a large head: *Saint Bernards were formerly much used in helping to rescue travellers lost in the snow of the Swiss mountains.*

**saint·ed** (sān′tid) **1** declared to be a saint. **2** thought of as a saint; gone to heaven. **3** sacred; very holy. **4** SAINTLY. **5** pt. and pp. of SAINT. 1–4 adj., 5 v.

**saint·hood** (sānt′hu̇d) **1** the character or status of a saint. **2** saints as a group. n.

**Saint–Jean Bap·tiste Society** (saN zhäN bä tēst′) *Cdn.* an organization in the Province of Quebec that is dedicated to the preserving and fostering of French culture in Canada.

**saint·ly** (sānt′lē) like a saint; very holy or very good. adj., **saint′li·er, saint′li·est.** —**saint′li·ness,** n.

**saint·ship** (sānt′ship) SAINTHOOD. n.

**saj·ja·da** (sə jä′də) in Islam, the PRAYER RUG upon

which worshippers kneel and bow during daily prayers. *n.*

**sake**¹ (sāk)   **1** benefit; account; interest: *Don't go to any trouble just for my sake. For your own sake, drive carefully.*  **2** purpose; aim: *She moved to the country for the sake of peace and quiet. For the sake of argument, let us suppose that the Tories win the election.*   *n.*
**for goodness'** (or **Pete's, Heaven's, gosh,** etc.) **sake,** *Informal.*   an exclamation of impatience, annoyance, surprise, etc.
**for old times' sake,**   in memory of former days.

**sa·ke**² (sä′kē)   a Japanese fermented alcoholic drink made from rice.   *n.*

**sal** (sal)   SALT: *Sal is used especially in druggists' terms, such as* SAL VOLATILE.   *n.*

**sa·laam** (sə läm′)   **1** a salutation or greeting used especially among Moslems, meaning literally, "Peace."  **2** a very low bow, made with the palm of the right hand placed on the forehead.   **3** any ceremonial or respectful greeting or bow.   **4** greet with a salaam.   **5** make a salaam.   1–3 *n.*, 4, 5 *v.*

**sal·a·bil·i·ty** (sā′lə bil′ə tē)   a SALABLE condition or quality.   *n.*

**sal·a·ble** (sā′lə bəl)   that can be sold; fit to be sold; easily sold: *This dress is not salable because it is torn.* *adj.*  Also, **saleable.**

**sa·la·cious** (sə lā′shəs)   **1** lustful; lewd.   **2** of writings, pictures, etc., obscene; tending to arouse sexual desire. *adj.*   —**sa·la′cious·ly,** *adv.*   —**sa·la′cious·ness,** *n.*

**sal·ad** (sal′əd)   **1** raw, leafy, green vegetables, such as lettuce, spinach, endive, etc., often mixed with other raw vegetables such as tomatoes, celery, sweet peppers, mushrooms, etc. and served with a dressing.   **2** a similar cold dish made with cooked meat, fish, vegetables, eggs, potatoes, or fruits, etc., served with a dressing.   **3** any leafy, green vegetable eaten raw, especially lettuce.   *n.*
☛ *Etym.* Through OF *salade* from a Romance form such as *salata,* literally meaning 'salted', which developed from Latin *sal* 'salt'.

**salad days**   days of youthful inexperience.

**salad dressing**   a sauce used in or on a salad.

**sal·al** (sə lal′)   *Cdn.*   **1** a small evergreen shrub native to the Pacific coast, having glossy leaves, showy white flowers, and edible purplish berries: *Salal is closely related to wintergreen.*   **2** the berry of this shrub.   *n.*

A spotted salamander—about 15 cm long including the tail

**sal·a·man·der** (sal′ə man′dər)   **1** any of a group of amphibians with tails, resembling lizards, but having a moist, smooth, scale-less skin and breathing by gills in the larva stage: *The order that comprises salamanders includes newts and mud puppies.*   **2** in myths and legends, a reptile able to live in fire.   **3** in ancient Greek philosophy, the spirit that inhabited fire, which was one of the four elements.   *n.*

**sa·la·mi** (sə lä′mē)   a highly seasoned sausage of pork and beef or beef alone, often flavoured with garlic: *Salami may be eaten dried or fresh.*   *n.*

**sal·a·ried** (sal′ə rēd *or* sal′rēd)   receiving a SALARY. *adj.*

**sal·a·ry** (sal′ə rē *or* sal′rē)   fixed pay for regular work, usually paid every two weeks or monthly.   Compare with WAGE.   *n.*, *pl.* **sal·a·ries.**
☛ *Etym.* Through Norman French from L *salarium* 'an allowance paid to soldiers for them to buy salt', derived from L *sal* 'salt'.
☛ *Syn.* **Salary** and **wages** both refer to a fixed amount paid for regular work. **Salary** is used more for professional and office work, and for pay spoken of as covering a long period of time: *The young engineer was paid a salary of $60 000.* **Wages** is used more for manual and physical work, and for pay spoken of as covering an hour, day, or week: *The minimum wage was fixed at $5 an hour.*

**sa·lat** (sə lät′)   in Islam, ritual prayer offered five times daily to Allah.   *n.*

**sale** (sāl)   **1** the act of selling; exchange of goods for money: *Did she make the sale? That was the last sale of the day.*   **2** the chance to sell; demand; market: *There is a large sale for antiques these days.*   **3** a selling at lower prices than usual: *This store is having a sale of suits.*   **4** an auction.   **5 sales,** *pl.*   the amount sold; gross receipts: *Today's sales were larger than yesterday's.*   **6 sales,** the work involved in selling (*used with a singular verb*): *Her first job was in sales.*   *n.*
**for sale,**   to be sold; available for buying: *There are several nice houses for sale in this area.*
**on sale,**   **a** offered at a reduced price: *All the winter boots are on sale now.*   **b** for sale: *Tickets for the concert will be on sale here on Monday.*
☛ *Hom.* SAIL.

**sale·a·ble** (sā′lə bəl)   See SALABLE.   *adj.*

**sal·e·ra·tus** (sal′ə rā′təs)   SODIUM BICARBONATE or potassium bicarbonate used as a LEAVENing agent in cooking.   *n.*

**sales·clerk** (sālz′klėrk′)   a person whose work is selling in a store.   *n.*

**sales·girl** (sālz′gėrl′)   SALESWOMAN.   *n.*

**sales·la·dy** (sālz′lā′dē)   SALESWOMAN.   *n.*, *pl.* **sales·la·dies.**

**sales·man** (sālz′mən)   **1** a man whose work is selling goods in a store; salesclerk.   **2** a person employed as a representative of a company to sell its goods or services in a certain territory.   *n.*, *pl.* **sales·men** (-zmən).

**sales·man·ship** (sālz′mən ship′)   the skill or technique of selling.   *n.*

**sales·per·son** (sālz′pėr′sən)   **1** SALESCLERK. **2** SALES REPRESENTATIVE.   *n.*

**sales representative**   a person employed as a representative of a company to sell its goods or services in a certain territory.

**sales tax**   a TAX based on the amount received for articles sold.

**sales·wom·an** (sālz′wùm′ən)   a woman whose work is selling, especially in a store.   *n.*, *pl.* **sales·wom·en** (-zwim′ən).

**sal·i·cin** (sal′ə sin)   a bitter, white, crystalline compound of GLUCOSE, obtained from the bark of various willows and poplars: *Salicin is used in medicine as a tonic and to reduce fever.*   *n.*

**sal·i·cyl·ate** (sal′ə sil′āt) a salt or ester of SALICYLIC ACID. *n.*

**sal·i·cyl·ic acid** (sal′ə sil′ik) a white, crystalline compound used as a mild antiseptic and preservative, and as a medicine for rheumatism, gout, etc.

**sa·li·ence** (sā′lē əns) **1** the quality or state of being SALIENT. **2** a striking part or feature. *n.*

**sa·li·ent** (sā′lē ənt *or* sā′lyənt) **1** standing out; easily seen or noticed; prominent; striking: *the salient features in a landscape, the salient points in a speech.* **2** pointing outward; projecting: *a salient angle.* **3** a salient angle or part. **4** the part of a fort or line of trenches that projects toward the enemy. 1, 2 *adj.*, 3, 4 *n.*

**sa·line** (sā′līn *or* sā′lēn) **1** of or like salt; salty: *a saline taste.* **2** containing common salt or any other salts: *a saline solution.* **3** a salt spring, well, or marsh. **4** a substance containing common salt or any other salts. 1, 2 *adj.*, 3, 4 *n.*

**sa·lin·i·ty** (sə lin′ə tē) saltiness; saline quality. *n.*

**sa·li·va** (sə lī′və) the liquid that the salivary glands secrete into the mouth to keep it moist, to aid in chewing, and to start digestion. *n.*

**sal·i·var·y** (sal′ə ver′ē) of or producing SALIVA: *the salivary glands.* *adj.*

**salivary gland** any of various glands that secrete SALIVA into the mouth: *The salivary glands of human beings and most other vertebrates are digestive glands that secrete saliva containing enzymes, salts, albumin, etc.*

**sal·i·vate** (sal′ə vāt′) **1** secrete SALIVA, especially an excessive amount. **2** produce an excessive flow of SALIVA in. *v.*, **sal·i·vat·ed, sal·i·vat·ing.**

**sal·i·va·tion** (sal′ə vā′shən) **1** the secretion of SALIVA. **2** an abnormally large flow of SALIVA. *n.*

**sal·low** (sal′ō) **1** of or having a pallid, yellowish complexion: *a sallow face. Mette still looks quite sallow after her illness.* **2** make or become yellow. 1 *adj.*, 2 *v.* —**sal′low·ness,** *n.*

**sal·low·ish** (sal′ō ish) rather SALLOW. *adj.*

**sal·ly** (sal′ē) **1** a sudden attack on an enemy made from a defensive position; sortie: *The men in the fort made a brave sally and returned with many prisoners.* **2** go suddenly from a defensive position to attack an enemy. **3** a sudden rushing forth. **4** rush forth suddenly; go out: *We sallied forth at dawn.* **5** a going forth; trip; excursion. **6** set out briskly. **7** go on an excursion or trip. **8** of things, issue forth. **9** a sudden start into activity. **10** an outburst. **11** a witty remark: *She continued her story undisturbed by the merry sallies of her hearers.* 1, 3, 5, 9–11 *n., pl.* **sal·lies;** 2, 4, 6–8 *v.*, **sal·lied, sal·ly·ing.**

**Sal·ly Lunn** (sal′ē lun′) a slightly sweetened tea cake, served hot with butter.

**sal·ma·gun·di** (sal′mə gun′dē) **1** a dish of chopped meat, anchovies, eggs, onions, oil, etc. **2** any mixture or medley of things, qualities, etc. *n.*

**sal·mi** (sal′mē) a highly seasoned stew, especially of game. *n.*

**salm·on** (sam′ən) **1** any of various related saltwater and freshwater fishes that are highly prized as food and game fish, especially the Atlantic salmon of the northern Atlantic coasts or any of the closely related group of fishes of the northern Pacific, called Pacific salmon. **2** yellowish pink. 1, 2 *n., pl.* **salm·on** or **salm·ons;** 2 *adj.*

---

**salicylate**     **1043**     **salt-chuck**

hat, āge, fär; let, ēqual, tėrm; it, īce
hot, ōpen, ôrder; oil, out; cup, pút, rüle
əbove, takən, pencəl, lemən, circəs
ch, child; ng, long; sh, ship
th, thin; ŦH, then; zh, measure

**salm·on·ber·ry** (sam′ən ber′ē) **1** a showy shrub of the Pacific coast closely related to the raspberry, having red flowers and edible, salmon-coloured, raspberry-like fruit. **2** the fruit of the salmonberry. *n.*

**salmon trout** LAKE TROUT.

**sa·lon** (sə lon′ *or* sal′on) **1** a large room for receiving or entertaining guests. **2** an assembly of guests in such a room. **3** a place used to exhibit works of art. **4** an exhibition of works of art. **5** a business establishment that provides services such as hairdressing and manicuring. *n., pl.* **sa·lons.**

**sa·loon** (sə lün′) **1** a place where alcoholic drinks are sold and drunk; bar. **2** a large room for general or public use: *Concerts were often held in the saloon of the steamship. The ship's passengers ate in the dining saloon.* *n.*

**sa·loon·keep·er** (sə lün′kē′pər) a person who keeps a SALOON (def. 1). *n.*

**sal·si·fy** (sal′sə fē′) **1** a European biennial plant of the composite family having a long, fleshy, edible root. **2** the root of this plant, eaten as a vegetable: *Salsify has an oysterlike flavour.* *n.*

**sal soda** washing soda; crystallized SODIUM CARBONATE.

**salt** (solt) **1** a white substance found in the earth and in sea water; sodium chloride: *Salt is used to season and preserve food.* **2** containing salt. **3** tasting like salt. **4** overflowed with or growing in salt water: *salt marshes, salt grass.* **5** mix or sprinkle with salt. **6** cure or preserve with salt. **7** cured or preserved with salt. **8** provide or feed with salt: *to salt cattle.* **9** SALT-CELLAR. **10** season; make pungent: *conversation salted with wit.* **11** sharp; pungent; to the point; lively: *salt speech.* **12** that which gives liveliness, piquancy, or pungency to anything. **13** a compound derived from an acid by replacing the hydrogen wholly or partly by a metal or an electropositive radical: *Baking soda is a salt.* **14** in chemical processes, treat with any salt. **15** *Informal.* sailor: *an old salt.* **16** **salts,** *pl.* **a** a medicine that causes movements of the bowels. **b** SMELLING SALTS. 1, 9, 12, 13, 15, 16 *n.,* 2–4, 7, 11 *adj.,* 5, 6, 8, 10, 14 *v.*
**above** or **below the salt,** in a superior or inferior position.
**eat a person's salt,** be his or her guest.
**salt a mine,** put ore, gold dust, etc. into it to create a false impression of value.
**salt away** or **down,** **a** pack with salt to preserve: *The fish were salted down in a barrel.* **b** store away: *The miser salted a lot of money away.*
**salt of the earth,** a person, or people, considered to be especially fine, noble, etc.
**with a grain of salt,** with some reservation or allowance: *The police officer took their story with a grain of salt.*
**worth one's salt,** worth one's support, wages, etc.

**salt–cel·lar** (solt′sel′ər) a shaker or dish for holding salt, used on the table. *n.*

**salt–chuck** (solt′chuk) *Cdn.* on the west coast and in the Northwest, the sea; salt water.

**Sal·teaux** (sal'tō or sol'tō)  1 a member of an Algonquian people, a western branch of the Ojibwa. 2 of or having to do with the Salteaux.  *n., pl.* **Sal·teaux.**

**salt·ine** (sol tēn')  a thin, crisp, salted cracker. *n.*

**salt lick**  1 a place where salt occurs naturally on the surface of the ground and where animals go to lick it up. 2 a block of salt placed in a pasture for cattle, etc. to lick.

**salt·pe·tre** (solt'pē'tər)  1 a salty, white mineral, used in making gunpowder, in preserving meat, and in medicine; POTASSIUM NITRATE; nitre.  2 a kind of fertilizer; SODIUM NITRATE. *n.* Also, **saltpeter.**

**salt pork**  fatty pork that has been cured in salt.

**salt·shak·er** (solt'shā'kər)  a container for salt, having a perforated top for sprinkling the salt. *n.*

**salt·wa·ter** (solt'wot'ər)  1 of, containing, or having to do with salt water or the sea: *a saltwater solution, saltwater fishing.* 2 living or found in the sea: *saltwater fish. adj.*

**salt·y** (sol'tē)  1 containing or tasting of salt: *Sweat and tears are salty. The soup is too salty.* 2 to the point; witty and a bit improper: *a salty remark.* 3 suggesting the sea or nautical life: *a salty breeze. adj.,* **salt·i·er, salt·i·est.**

**sa·lu·bri·ous** (sə lü'brē əs)  HEALTHFUL. *adj.*
☞ *Etym.* See note at SALUTE.

**sal·u·tar·y** (sal'yə ter'ē)  1 beneficial: *The teacher gave the girl salutary advice.* 2 good for the health; wholesome: *Walking is a salutary exercise. adj.*
☞ *Etym.* See note at SALUTE.

**sal·u·ta·tion** (sal'yə tā'shən)  1 greeting; saluting: *The man raised his hat in salutation.* 2 something uttered, written, or done to salute: *Most letters begin with a salutation, such as* Dear Sir *or* Dear Mrs. Ing. *n.*

**sa·lu·ta·to·ry** (sə lü'tə tô'rē)  expressing greeting; welcoming. *adj.*

**sa·lute** (sə lüt')  1 honour or show respect in a formal manner by raising the hand to the head, by firing guns, by dipping flags, etc.: *The soldier saluted the officer.* 2 meet with kind words, cheers, a bow, a kiss, etc.; greet: *She saluted her cousin with a kiss.* 3 make a bow, gesture, etc. to.  4 come to; meet: *Shouts of welcome saluted their ears.* 5 make a salute.  6 the act of saluting.  7 a sign of welcome, farewell, or honour: *The queen gracefully acknowledged the salutes of the crowds.* 8 the position of the hand, gun, etc. in saluting.  1–5 *v.,* **sa·lut·ed, sa·lut·ing;**  6–8 *n.*
☞ *Etym.* **Salute** and SALUTARY come from a Latin verb and adjective (*salutare, salutaris*) derived from L *salus* 'health, well-being', which also meant 'a wish for well-being', and so 'a greeting'. SALUBRIOUS comes from L *saluber* 'healthy', also derived from *salus*, which was itself related to *salvus* 'whole, intact'. See note at SAFE.

**Sal·va·do·ran** (sal'və dôr'ən)  1 of or having to do with El Salvador, a country in Central America, or its people.  2 a native or inhabitant of El Salvador.  1 *adj.,* 2 *n.*

**sal·vage** (sal'vij)  1 the act or process of saving or rescuing a ship or its cargo from wreck, capture, etc. 2 payment made or due for such saving or rescuing. 3 the property saved or rescued.  4 the act of saving or rescuing anything from wreckage, destruction, etc. 5 anything saved or rescued for use, such as scrap metal, wood, etc.: *They used mostly salvage to build their cabin.* 6 save or rescue from wreckage, destruction, etc.: *We salvaged quite a few parts from the engine of the old car.* 7 save or rescue from harm or ruin: *to salvage one's dignity.* 8 the act of saving or rescuing from harm or ruin.  1–5, 8 *n.,* 6, 7 *v.* **sal·vaged, sal·vag·ing.**
☞ *Etym.* See note at SAFE.

**sal·va·tion** (sal vā'shən)  1 a saving or being saved. 2 a person or thing that saves.  3 a saving of the soul; deliverance from wrong and from punishment for wrong. *n.*
☞ *Etym.* See note at SAFE.

**salve¹** (sav)  1 a soft, greasy ointment put on wounds and sores to soothe or heal them.  2 put salve on. 3 something soothing; balm: *The kind words were a salve to her hurt feelings.*  4 soothe; smooth over: *He salved his conscience by the thought that his lie harmed no one.*  1, 3 *n.,* 2, 4 *v.,* **salved, salv·ing.**

**salve²** (salv)  save from loss or destruction; SALVAGE. *v.,* **salved, salv·ing.**

**sal·ver** (sal'vər)  tray. *n.*

**sal·vi·a** (sal'vē ə)  any of a large, closely related group of herbs and shrubs of the mint family, especially a popular garden plant, also called scarlet sage, having showy spikes of scarlet flowers: *Common sage is also a salvia. n.*

**sal·vo** (sal'vō)  1 the discharge of several guns at the same time as a broadside or as a salute.  2 a load of bombs or missiles released at the same time from an aircraft.  3 a round of cheers or applause.  *n., pl.* **sal·vos** or **sal·voes.**

**sal vo·la·ti·le** (sal'və lat'ə lē)  1 an aromatic solution of ammonium carbonate and alcohol, used to relieve faintness, etc.  2 ammonium carbonate. *n.*
☞ *Etym.* From modern L *sal volatile* 'volatile salt'.

**sam·aj** (sə mäj')  in Hinduism:  1 a religious association or society.  2 any assembly of Hindu worshippers: *"Hindu Prarthana Samaj" is the name of Toronto's oldest Hindu temple. n.*

A samara of a maple

**sam·a·ra** (sam'ə rə)  any dry fruit that has a winglike extension and does not split open when ripe: *The fruit of the maple tree is a double samara with one seed in each half. n.*

**Sa·mar·i·tan** (sə mar'ə tən or sə mer'ə tən)  1 a native or inhabitant of Samaria, a district in the northern part of ancient Palestine.  2 of or having to do with Samaria or its people.  3 a person who helps another in trouble or distress.  1, 3 *n.,* 2 *adj.*

**sa·mar·i·um** (sə mer'ē əm)  a rare, lustrous, grey metallic element used especially in alloys that form permanent magnets.  *Symbol:* Sm  *n.*

**sam·ba** (sam'bə)  1 a Brazilian dance of African origin. 2 the music for this dance.  3 dance the samba.  1, 2 *n.,* 3 *v.*

**Sam Browne belt** (sam' broun')  a military belt having a supporting piece passing over the right shoulder, worn by officers.

**same** (sām)  1 not another; identical: *We came back the*

same way we went. 2 just alike; not different: *Her name and mine are the same.* 3 unchanged: *She is the same kind old woman.* 4 just spoken of; aforesaid: *The boys were talking about a strange man; this same man wore his hair very long and always dressed in white.* 5 the same person or thing: *The situation is the same as before.* 1–4 *adj.,* 5 *pron.*
**all the same,** notwithstanding; nevertheless.
**just the same, a** in the same manner. **b** nevertheless.
**the same,** in the same manner: *"Sea" and "see" are pronounced the same.*

**same·ness** (sām′nis) 1 the state of being the same; an exact likeness; identity or uniformity. 2 a lack of variety; tiresomeness; monotony. *n.*

**sam·gha** (säng′ə) in Jainism, the world-wide "four-fold" congregation consisting of monks, nuns, laymen and lay women. *n.*

**Sa·mi·an** (sā′mē ən) 1 of or having to do with Samos, a Greek island in the Aegean Sea. 2 a native or inhabitant of Samos. 1 *adj.,* 2 *n.*

**sam·i·sen** (sam′i sen′) a Japanese musical instrument resembling a banjo, having three strings and played with a PLECTRUM. *n.*

**sam·ite** (sam′īt) a heavy, rich silk fabric, sometimes interwoven with gold, worn in the Middle Ages. *n.*

**Sa·mo·an** (sə mō′ən) 1 of or having to do with Samoa, a group of islands in the South Pacific, or its people. 2 a native or inhabitant of Samoa. 3 the Polynesian language of the Samoans. 1 *adj.,* 2, 3 *n.*

A samovar

**sam·o·var** (sam′ə vär′) a metal urn with a tap, used for heating water for tea. *n.*

A sampan

**sam·pan** (sam′pan) a type of small boat sculled by one or more oars at the stern, usually having a single sail and a cabin made of mats: *Sampans are used in the rivers and coastal waters of China, southeast Asia, and Japan.* *n.*

**sam·ple** (sam′pəl) 1 a part or single item taken to represent a larger whole or a group; a part or item shown or presented as evidence of what the rest is like: *The display samples are not for sale. We sent a sample of the soil to the university for testing.* 2 serving as a sample: *a sample copy.* 3 take a sample of, especially in order to test quality, etc.: *We sampled the cake and found it very good.* 1, 2 *n.,* 3 *v.,* **sam·pled, sam·pling.**

**sam·pler** (sam′plər) 1 a person who samples. 2 a

# sameness 1045 sanctuary

hat, āge, fär; let, ēqual, tėrm; it, īce
hot, ōpen, ôrder; oil, out; cup, pu̇t, rüle
ə*bove, ta*k*ən, penc*ə*l, lem*ə*n, circ*ə*s
ch, child; ng, long; sh, ship
th, thin; ᴛʜ, then; zh, measure

piece of cloth embroidered with letters, verses, etc. in various stitches to show skill in needlework. *n.*

**sam·pling** (sam′pling) 1 a small part or number selected for the purpose of testing or analysing. 2 ppr. of SAMPLE. 1 *n.,* 2 *v.*

**sam·sa·ra** (səm sä′rə) in Hinduism and Sikhism, the ongoing cycle of death and rebirth in the world; the belief that the soul is normally subject to transmigration at death. *n.*

**sam·u·rai** (sam′u̇ rī′) 1 in feudal Japan, the military class, consisting of the retainers of the great nobles. 2 a member of this class. *n., pl.* **sam·u·rai.**

**san·a·tive** (san′ə tiv) healing; having power to cure. *adj.*

**san·a·to·ri·um** (san′ə tô′rē əm) 1 an establishment for the treatment of the sick, especially persons with long-term or chronic diseases, such as tuberculosis. 2 a health resort. *n., pl.* **san·a·to·ri·ums** or **san·a·to·ri·a** (-ē ə).

**sanc·ti·fi·ca·tion** (sangk′tə fə kā′shən) a sanctifying or being sanctified; consecration; purification from sin. *n.*

**sanc·ti·fied** (sangk′tə fīd′) 1 consecrated. 2 sanctimonious. 3 pt. and pp. OF SANCTIFY. 1, 2 *adj.,* 3 *v.*

**sanc·ti·fy** (sangk′tə fī′) 1 make holy: *A life of sacrifice had sanctified her.* 2 set apart as sacred; observe as holy: *This building is sanctified for all religions to use.* 3 make free from sin. 4 justify; make right. *v.,* **sanc·ti·fied, sanc·ti·fy·ing.**

**sanc·ti·mo·ni·ous** (sangk′tə mō′nē əs) making a show of holiness; putting on airs of sanctity; pretending to be pious. *adj.* —**sanc′ti·mo′ni·ous·ly,** *adv.* —**sanc′ti·mo′ni·ous·ness,** *n.*

**sanc·ti·mo·ny** (sangk′tə mō′nē) a show of holiness; airs of sanctity; religious hypocrisy. *n.*

**sanc·tion** (sangk′shən) 1 permission with authority; support; approval: *We have the sanction of the law to play ball in this park.* 2 authorize; approve; allow: *Her conscience does not sanction stealing.* 3 a solemn ratification. 4 confirm. 5 a provision of a law enacting a penalty for disobedience to it or a reward for obedience. 6 the penalty or reward. 7 an action by several nations toward another, such as a blockade, economic restrictions, etc., intended to force it to obey international law. 8 a consideration that leads one to obey a rule of conduct. 9 binding force. 1, 3, 5–9 *n.,* 2, 4 *v.* —**sanc′tion·er,** *n.*

**sanc·ti·ty** (sangk′tə tē) 1 holiness; saintliness; godliness. 2 the fact or quality of being inviolable or sacred; being hallowed: *the sanctity of a church, the sanctity of the home.* 3 **sanctities,** *pl.* sacred obligations, feelings, etc. *n., pl.* **sanc·ti·ties.**

**sanc·tu·ar·y** (sangk′chü er′ē) 1 a sacred place: *A church is a sanctuary.* 2 the part of a Christian church around the altar. 3 a place of refuge or protection: *This island is maintained as a bird sanctuary.* 4 refuge or protection: *The lost travellers found sanctuary in a deserted hut.* n., pl. **sanc·tu·ar·ies.**

**sanc·tum** (sangk′təm) **1** a sacred place. **2** a private room or office where a person can be undisturbed. n., pl. **sanc·tums** or (rare) **sanc·ta** (-tə).

**sanc·tum sanc·to·rum** (sangk′təm sangk tô′rəm) Latin. **1** holy of holies. **2** an especially private place.

**sand** (sand) **1** tiny grains of worn-down or disintegrated rock finer than gravel but coarser than silt: *Sand is found along seashores and in deserts.* **2** the sand in an hourglass thought of as moments or particles of time: *The sands of time will run out.* **3** sprinkle with sand: *The front walk is icy and should be sanded.* **4** fill up or cover with sand. **5** clean, smooth, or polish by rubbing with an abrasive such as sandpaper. **6** very light greyish brown. **7 sands,** pl. a tract or region composed mainly of sand: *the sands of the desert.* 1, 2, 6, 7 n., 3–5 v., 6 adj.

Sandals

**san·dal** (san′dəl) a kind of open shoe consisting of a sole kept on the foot by means of any of various arrangements of straps over the toes or instep and often around the heel and ankle. n.

**san·dalled** or **san·daled** (san′dəld) wearing SANDALS. adj.

**san·dal·wood** (san′dəl wud′) **1** a fragrant wood used for making boxes, fans, etc. and burned as incense. **2** the tree that this wood comes from. n.

**sand·bag** (sand′bag′) **1** a bag filled with sand: *Sandbags are used to form temporary dams, protective walls for trenches used in battle, and as ballast on balloons.* **2** furnish with sandbags. **3** a small bag of sand used as a club. **4** hit or stun with a sandbag. 1, 3 n., 2, 4 v., **sand·bagged, sand·bag·ging.**

**sand·bank** (sand′bangk′) a ridge of sand. n.

**sand bar** a ridge of sand in a river or along a shore formed by the action of tides or currents.

**sand·blast** (sand′blast′) **1** a blast of air or steam containing sand, used to clean, grind, cut, or decorate hard surfaces, such as glass, stone, or metal. **2** the apparatus used to apply such a blast: *A sandblast is often used in cleaning the outside of buildings.* **3** use a sandblast on. 1, 2 n., 3 v.

**sand·box** (sand′boks′) a box for holding sand, especially for children to play in. n.

**sand cherry 1** any of several closely related North American shrubs of the rose family, especially common in the Prairie Provinces. **2** the edible, purplish or black berry of any of these shrubs.

**sand dollar** a small, flat, round sea urchin that lives on sandy parts of the ocean floor.

**sand·er** (san′dər) **1** a truck having a device for spreading sand on icy roads. **2** the device itself. **3** a tool or machine for cleaning, smoothing, or polishing by means of sandpaper or some similar material. **4** any person or thing that sands. n.

**sand flea** a flea found in sandy places.

**sand·glass** (sand′glas′) HOURGLASS. n.

**sand·hill crane** (sand′hil′) a crane of central and eastern North America, mainly bluish grey with a bare, reddish patch on the forehead and upper face: *The sandhill crane resembles the great blue heron.* See CRANE for picture.

**sand·hog** (sand′hog′) a person who works under compressed air in underground or underwater construction, as in a caisson or tunnel. n.

**sand·man** (sand′man′) in folk tales, a man said to make children sleepy by sprinkling sand on their eyes. n.

**sand·pa·per** (sand′pā′pər) **1** a strong paper with a layer of sand or some other rough material glued on it, used for smoothing, cleaning, or polishing. **2** smooth, clean, or polish with sandpaper. 1 n., 2 v.

**sand·pip·er** (sand′pī′pər) **1** any of numerous related species of small or medium-sized shore bird having slender legs and long toes, a long, slender bill, and spotted or streaked, brownish or greyish plumage. **2** referring to a family of shore birds found throughout the world: *The sandpiper family includes the sandpipers, curlews, snipes, and woodcocks.*

**sand·stone** (sand′stōn′) a kind of SEDIMENTARY rock consisting of grains of sand held together by a natural cementing material. n.

**sand·storm** (sand′stôrm′) a storm of wind that carries clouds of sand. n.

**sand·wich** (san′dwich) **1** two or more slices of bread with meat, jelly, cheese, or some other filling between them. **2** something formed by similar arrangement: *an ice-cream sandwich.* **3** put or squeeze (between): *When she went to get her car, she found it sandwiched between two trucks.* 1, 2 n., 3 v.
☞ *Etym.* Named after the Earl of *Sandwich* (1718–1792), who is said to have invented it so that he would not have to stop playing cards for meals.

**sandwich board** a pair of signboards, usually hinged at the top, designed to be hung from a person's shoulders with one board in front and the other behind, and used for advertising or picketing.

**sand·wort** (sand′wėrt′) any of a closely related group of herbs of the pink family that grow in low tufts or mats in sandy soil and have many very small, white or purplish flowers. n.

**sand·y** (san′dē) **1** containing, consisting of, or covered with sand: *Most of the shore is rocky, but there is a sandy beach.* **2** of the colour of sand: *sandy hair.* **3** like sand in texture, etc. adj., **sand·i·er, sand·i·est.**
—**sand′i·ness,** n.

**sane** (sān) **1** having a healthy mind; especially, in law, able to make rational judgments and to appreciate the effects of one's actions. **2** showing good sense; reasonable or sensible: *a sane foreign policy.* adj., **san·er, san·est.** —**sane′ly,** adv. —**sane′ness,** n.
☞ *Hom.* SEINE.

**sang** (sang) pt. of SING: *The bird sang.* v.

**San·gat** (sung′gət) in Sikhism, a congregation, community, or assembly of worshippers: *The Sangat assembles each Sunday for worship.* n.

**sang–froid** (sän frwä′) *French.* coolness of mind; calmness; composure. *n.*

**san·gha** (sang′gə) **1** in Buddhism, the entire world-wide community of ordained monks and nuns. **2** in Buddhism and Jainism, any religious community or monastic order. *n.*

**san·gui·nar·y** (sang′gwə ner′ē) **1** with much blood or bloodshed; bloody: *a sanguinary battle.* **2** delighting in bloodshed; bloodthirsty. *adj.* —**san′gui·nar′i·ness,** *n.*

**san·guine** (sang′gwin) **1** cheerful and hopeful; optimistic; confident: *a sanguine disposition. They were sanguine of success.* **2** having a healthy red colour; ruddy: *a sanguine complexion.* **3** in the physiology of the Middle Ages, having a temperament in which blood predominates over other humours; having an active circulation, ruddy complexion, and a cheerful and ardent disposition. *adj.*

**san·guin·e·ous** (sang gwin′ē əs) **1** of or like blood; bloody. **2** blood-red. **3** sanguinary; bloodthirsty. *adj.*

**san·i·tar·i·um** (san′ə ter′ē əm) *esp. Brit.* SANATORIUM. *n., pl.* **san·i·tar·i·ums** or **san·i·tar·i·a** (-ē ə).

**san·i·tar·y** (san′ə ter′ē) **1** of or having to do with health and the conditions that affect health: *The city is looking for a more sanitary method of waste disposal.* **2** free from dirt or anything bad for health: *The top of the picnic table was not very sanitary.* *adj.* —**san′i·tar′i·ness,** *n.*

**sanitary napkin** or **pad** a disposable absorbent pad worn on the outside of the body to absorb the discharge from menstruation.

**san·i·ta·tion** (san′ə tā′shən) the working out and practical application of sanitary measures, such as disposal of garbage and government inspection of food. *n.*

**san·i·tize** (san′i tīz′) make SANITARY by cleaning, sterilizing, etc.: *The lining of these shoes has been sanitized.* *v.,* **san·i·tized, san·i·tiz·ing.**

**san·i·ty** (san′ə tē) **1** soundness of mind; especially, in law, the ability to make rational judgments and appreciate the effects of one's actions. **2** soundness of judgment; sensibleness; reasonableness. *n.*

**sank** (sangk) a pt. of SINK: *The ship sank.* *v.*

**San·sei** (san′sā′) a native-born Canadian or United States citizen whose grandparents were Japanese immigrants; an offspring of Nisei parents. Compare with ISSEI and NISEI. *n., pl.* **San·sei** or **San·seis.**

**San·skrit** (san′skrit) the ancient literary language of India. *n.*

**sans–serif** (sanz′ser′if) in printing, any style of type having no SERIFS. *n., adj.*

**sans sou·ci** (sän sü sē′) *French.* without care or worry.

**San·ta** (san′tə *for noun,* san′tə *or* sän′tä *for adjective*) **1** SANTA CLAUS. **2** a Spanish or an Italian word meaning *holy* or *saint,* used in combinations, as in *Santa Maria.* **1** *n.,* **2** *adj.*

**San·ta Claus** (san′tə klôz′) Saint Nicholas, the spirit or saint of Christmas giving; according to modern conception, a jolly old man with a white beard, dressed in a fur-trimmed red suit.

**sap**[1] (sap) **1** the liquid that circulates through a plant as blood does in animals: *Rising sap carries water and salt from the roots; sap travelling downward carries sugar, gums,*

hat, āge, fär; let, ēqual, tėrm; it, īce
hot, ōpen, ôrder; oil, out; cup, put, rüle
əbove, takən, pencəl, lemən, circəs
ch, child; ng, long; sh, ship
th, thin; ᴛʜ, then; zh, measure

*resins, etc.* **2** any body fluid essential to life or health. **3** vital spirit; health and vigour: *the sap of youth.* *n.*

**sap**[2] (sap) **1** weaken or use up; undermine: *The extreme heat sapped their strength.* **2** dig under or wear away the foundation of: *The walls of the boathouse had been sapped by the waves.* **3** the making of trenches to approach a besieged place or an enemy's position. **4** a trench protected by the earth dug up; a trench dug to approach the enemy's position. **5** dig protected trenches. **6** approach the enemy's position by means of such trenches. **7** make a tunnel under. **1, 2, 5–7** *v.,* **sapped, sap·ping; 3, 4** *n.*

**sa·pi·ence** (sā′pē əns *or* sap′ē əns) WISDOM. *n.*

**sa·pi·ent** (sā′pē ənt *or* sap′ē ənt) wise; sage. *adj.* —**sa′pi·ent·ly,** *adv.*

**sap·less** (sap′lis) **1** without sap; withered. **2** without energy or vigour. *adj.*

**sap·ling** (sap′ling) **1** a young tree. **2** a young person. *n.*

**sa·pon·i·fi·ca·tion** (sə pon′ə fə kā′shən) SAPONIFYing or being saponified. *n.*

**sa·pon·i·fy** (sə pon′ə fī′) **1** make a fat or oil into soap by treating it with an alkali. **2** be saponified; become soap. *v.,* **sa·pon·i·fied, sa·pon·i·fy·ing.**

**sap·per** (sap′ər) a soldier employed in the construction of trenches, fortifications, etc. *n.*

**sap·phire** (saf′īr) **1** a transparent, bright-blue or colourless precious stone that is a variety of CORUNDUM. **2** bright blue: *a sapphire sky.* **1, 2** *n.,* **2** *adj.*

**sap·py** (sap′ē) **1** full of sap. **2** vigorous; energetic. *adj.,* **sap·pi·er, sap·pi·est.** —**sap′pi·ness,** *n.*

**sap·ro·phyte** (sap′rō fīt′) an organism that lives on decaying organic matter; especially, any of several species of fungus. *n.*

**sap·ro·phyt·ic** (sap′rō fit′ik) of or like a SAPROPHYTE; living on dead organic matter. *adj.*

**sap·suck·er** (sap′suk′ər) either of two species of North American woodpecker that drill holes in trees to feed on sap and insects. *n.*

**sap weather** *Cdn.* spring weather, with cold nights and warm days, that in sugar maples makes the sap run ready for collecting.

**sap·wood** (sap′wud′) the sap-carrying tissue between the bark and the heartwood of most trees: *The sapwood is softer and usually lighter in colour than the heartwood.* *n.*

**sar·a·band** (sar′ə band′ *or* ser′ə band′) **1** a slow and stately Spanish dance. **2** the music for this dance. *n.*

**Sar·a·cen** (sar′ə sən *or* ser′ə sən) **1** especially in the Middle Ages, a Moslem, either Arab or Turkish. **2** in earlier times, an Arab. **3** of or having to do with the Saracens. **1, 2** *n.,* **3** *adj.*

**Sar·a·cen·ic** (sar′ə sen′ik *or* ser′ə sen′ik) of or having to do with the SARACENS. *adj.*

**sa·ran** (sə ran′) a synthetic polymer of vinyl chloride

and a radical derived from ethylene, manufactured as a thin, flexible sheet or film or as a textile fibre: *Saran is highly resistant to rotting, soiling, and damage and is used in clothing, automobile seat covers, insect screens, etc.* *n.*

**sar·casm** (sär′kaz əm) **1** a sneering or cutting remark; an ironical taunt. **2** the act of making fun of a person to hurt his or her feelings; bitter irony: *With obvious sarcasm she called the scared boy a hero.* *n.*

**sar·cas·tic** (sär kas′tik) **1** characterized by SARCASM: *a sarcastic remark.* **2** using or tending to use SARCASM: *She gets sarcastic when her feelings are hurt.* *adj.*
—**sar·cas′ti·cal·ly**, *adv.*

**Sar·cee** (sär′sē) **1** a member of a First Nations people formerly living in the region of the upper Athabasca River in Alberta, now living mainly near Calgary. **2** the Athapascan language of these people. **3** of or having to do with the Sarcee or their language. 1, 2 *n.*, *pl.* **Sar·cee** or **Sar·cees;** 3 *adj.*

**sar·co·ma** (sär kō′mə) a cancerous tumour that develops in connective tissue, bone, or muscle. *n.*, *pl.* **sar·co·mas** or **sar·co·ma·ta** (-mə tə).

**sar·coph·a·gus** (sär kof′ə gəs) a stone coffin, especially one ornamented with sculpture or inscriptions. *n.*, *pl.* **sar·coph·a·gi** (-jī *or* jē′) or **sar·coph·a·gus·es.**

**sard** (särd) a deep-brownish-red variety of CHALCEDONY, a quartz mineral used as a gem stone since ancient times: *Sard is traditionally classified as a variety of carnelian.* *n.*

**sar·dine** (sär dēn′) **1** any of various food fishes of the herring family: *Some species of small or young sardines are commonly preserved and canned in oil.* **2** such a fish or any of various other small, herringlike fishes when preserved and canned in oil. *n.*, *pl.* **sar·dines** or (*esp.* collectively) **sar·dine.**
**packed like sardines,** very much crowded.

**Sar·din·i·an** (sär din′ē ən) **1** of or having to do with Sardinia, a large island off the southwestern coast of Italy, its people, or their language. **2** a native or inhabitant of Sardinia. **3** the Romance language of Sardinia. 1 *adj.*, 2, 3 *n.*

**sar·don·ic** (sär don′ik) bitterly mocking or cynical and disdainful: *She listened to their naïve proposal with a sardonic smile.* *adj.* —**sar·don′i·cal·ly,** *adv.*

**sar·don·yx** (sär′də niks) a variety of onyx containing layers of SARD. *n.*

**sar·gas·so** (sär gas′ō) any of a group of brown seaweeds that have berry-like air bladders and float in large masses. *n.*

A sari

**sa·ri** (sä′rē) a garment worn by women especially in India and Pakistan, consisting of a long piece of light fabric, usually cotton or silk, draped around the body so that one end forms a long skirt and the other end hangs loosely over the shoulder or is draped over the head. *n.*, *pl.* **sa·ris.**

A sarong

**sa·rong** (sə rong′) a rectangular piece of cloth, usually a brightly coloured printed material, worn as a skirt by men and women in the Malay Archipelago, Sri Lanka, and some parts of India. *n.*

**sar·sa·pa·ril·la** (sas′pə ril′ə *or* sär′sə pə ril′ə) **1** a tropical American climbing or trailing plant or its root. **2** a medicine or cooling drink made from the root. *n.*

**sar·to·ri·al** (sär tô′rē əl) of tailors, tailoring, or tailored clothes: *His clothes were a sartorial triumph.* *adj.*

**sash¹** (sash) a long, broad strip of cloth or ribbon, worn as an ornament round the waist or over one shoulder. *n.*

**sash²** (sash) **1** the frame which holds the glass in a window or door. See LINTEL for picture. **2** the frame together with its pane or panes of glass, usually forming a movable part of a window: *She raised the sash to let in the spring air.* **3** furnish with a sash. 1, 2 *n.*, 3 *v.*

**sa·shay** (sa shā′) *Informal.* move or walk casually in a bold or swaggering manner: *He sashayed up to the front door as if he owned the place.* *v.*
☞ *Etym.* An alteration of the word *chassé*, which refers to a sliding step used in many kinds of dance. *Chassé* is a F word formed from the past participle of *chasser* 'to chase'.

**sa·shi·mi** (sä shē′mē) very thin slices of raw fish, used as food in Japan. *n.pl.*

**Sask.** Saskatchewan.

**Sas·katch·e·wan·i·an** (səs kach′ə won′ē ən) **1** a native or long-term resident of Saskatchewan. **2** of or having to do with Saskatchewan. 1 *n.*, 2 *adj.*

**sas·ka·toon** (sas′kə tün′) *Cdn.* **1** a North American shrub of the rose family found from western Ontario to the Yukon and south to Colorado, having tiny white flowers that bloom in May and edible purple berries. **2** the sweet, juicy berry of this shrub: *Saskatoons are harvested wild in western Canada and used especially in pies and preserves.* *n.*
☞ *Etym.* From Cree *misāskwatomin* 'fruit of the tree of many branches'.

**Sas·quatch** (sas′kwoch) *Cdn.* a wild, hairy monster of subhuman appearance, supposed to inhabit certain western mountain regions. *n.*

**sas·sa·fras** (sas′ə fras′) **1** a slender American tree that has fragrant, yellow flowers and bluish-black fruit. **2** the aromatic, dried bark of its root, used in medicine and to flavour candy, soft drinks, etc. **3** the flavour. *n.*

**sat** (sat) pt. and pp. of SIT: *Yesterday I sat in a train all day. The cat has sat at that mouse hole for hours.* *v.*

**Sat.** Saturday.

**Sa·tan** (sā′tən)   Lucifer; the Devil.   *n.*

**sa·tan·ic** (sā tan′ik)   **1** of or having to do with SATAN: *satanic magic.*   **2** showing extreme viciousness or cruelty; very wicked: *a satanic act of revenge.*   *adj.*

**Sa·tan·ism** (sā′tə niz′əm)   **1** devil worship, especially a French cult of the 1890's that professed worship of Satan.   **2** the beliefs or rites of devil worship.   **3** wickedness; a malicious or diabolical disposition.   *n.*

**Sa·tan·ist** (sā′tə nist)   **1** an adherent of the cult of SATANISM (def. 1).   **2** of or having to do with SATANISM. 1 *n.*, 2 *adj.*

**Sa·tan·ist·ic** (sā′tə nis′tik)   of or having to do with SATANISM.   *adj.*

**satch·el** (sach′əl)   a small bag, often having a shoulder strap, for carrying books, clothes, etc.   *n.*

**sate** (sāt)   **1** satisfy fully any appetite or desire: *A long drink slaked her thirst.*   **2** supply with more than enough, so as to disgust or weary.   *v.*, **sat·ed, sat·ing.**

**sa·teen** (sa tēn′)   a fabric, usually cotton, woven in a satin weave and having a smooth, lustrous face.   *n.*

**sat·el·lite** (sat′ə līt′)   **1** a small planet that revolves around a larger planet, especially around one of the nine major planets of the solar system.   **2** an artificial object or vehicle sent into an orbit around the earth or other heavenly body.   **3** a follower or attendant upon a person of importance.   **4** a subservient follower.   **5** a country that is nominally independent but is actually under the control of a more powerful country; especially, a country under Soviet control.   *n.*

**sa·ti·ate** (sā′shē āt′)   **1** feed fully; satisfy fully. **2** supply with too much; weary or disgust with too much: *Alice was so satiated with bananas that she would not even look at one.*   *v.*, **sa·ti·at·ed, sa·ti·at·ing.**

**sa·ti·e·ty** (sə tī′ə tē)   the feeling of having had too much; disgust or weariness caused by excess; a satiated condition.   *n.*

**sat·in** (sat′ən)   **1** a soft fabric, usually of silk or rayon, woven in a satin weave, having a smooth, lustrous face and a dull back.   **2** of or like satin; smooth and glossy.   **3** a smoothness or glossiness like that of satin: *the satin of the silver bowl.*   1, 3 *n.*, 2 *adj.*

**satin stitch**   an embroidery stitch using long stitches placed closely together, producing a solid embroidered surface resembling the smooth finish of satin.   See EMBROIDERY for picture.

**satin weave**   a weave in which the crosswise threads alternately cross over a number of lengthwise threads and under a single thread, producing a soft, luxurious fabric with a smooth, glossy surface.   See WEAVE for picture.

**sat·in·wood** (sat′ən wüd′)   **1** the beautiful, smooth wood of an East Indian tree, used to ornament furniture, etc.   **2** the tree itself.   *n.*

**sat·in·y** (sat′ə nē)   like satin in smoothness and gloss.   *adj.*

**sat·ire** (sat′īr)   **1** the use of biting, often bitter wit, especially in the form of irony or sarcasm, to attack vice or foolishness: *Satire implies or states a moral judgment.*   **2** a poem, essay, story, etc. that attacks or ridicules in this way.   *n.*

**sa·tir·ic** (sə tir′ik)   **1** of or having to do with SATIRE: *satiric verse.*   **2** SATIRICAL.   *adj.*

**sa·tir·i·cal** (sə tir′ə kəl)   **1** containing, showing, or reflecting SATIRE: *a satirical smile, a satirical letter.* **2** fond of using SATIRE: *a satirical columnist.*   *adj.* —**sa·tir′i·cal·ly,** *adv.*

**sat·i·rist** (sat′ə rist)   a writer of SATIRES; a person who uses satire: *The follies and vices of their own times are the chief subjects of satirists.*   *n.*

**sat·i·rize** (sat′ə rīz′)   criticize or ridicule by means of SATIRE: *Her novel satirizes Canadian attitudes toward the United States.*   *v.*, **sat·i·rized, sat·i·riz·ing.**

**sat·is·fac·tion** (sat′is fak′shən)   **1** a fulfilment; satisfying: *The satisfaction of hunger requires food.*   **2** the condition of being satisfied or pleased and contented: *Mariette felt satisfaction at winning a prize.*   **3** anything that makes us feel pleased or contented: *It is a great satisfaction to have things turn out just the way you want.* **4** the payment of debt; discharge of obligation; making up for wrong or injury done.   *n.*
**give satisfaction,**   satisfy.

**sat·is·fac·to·ry** (sat′is fak′tə rē *or* sat′is fak′trē)   satisfying; good enough to satisfy; pleasing; adequate; sufficient.   *adj.*   —**sat′is·fac′to·ri·ly,** *adv.* —**sat′is·fac′to·ri·ness,** *n.*

**sat·is·fy** (sat′is fī)   **1** give enough to; fulfil desires, hopes, demands, etc.; put an end to needs, wants, etc.: *We satisfy hunger by eating.*   **2** fully meet an objection, doubt, demand, etc.   **3** make contented; please: *Are you satisfied now?*   **4** give satisfaction.   **5** pay; make right: *After the accident, he satisfied all claims for damage.*   **6** set free from doubt; convince: *She was satisfied that it was an accident.*   **7** make up for a wrong or injury.   *v.*, **sat·is·fied, sat·is·fy·ing.**   —**sat′is·fi′er,** *n.* —**sat′is·fy′ing·ly,** *adv.*

**sa·to·ri** (sə tô′rē)   in Zen Buddhism, the state of enlightenment, especially as attained through sudden flashes of intuition.   *n.*

**sat·u·ra·ble** (sach′ə rə bəl)   that can be SATURATEd.   *adj.*

**sat·u·rate** (sach′ə rāt′)   **1** soak thoroughly; fill full: *During the fog, the air was saturated with moisture. Saturate the moss with water before planting the bulbs in it.* **2** cause a substance to unite with the greatest possible amount of another substance: *a saturated solution of sugar, salt, etc. is one that cannot dissolve any more sugar, salt, etc.*   **3** load or fill anything to capacity: *The manufacturers are not making any more of these toys for a while, for their competitors have saturated the market.*   *v.*, **sat·u·rat·ed, sat·u·rat·ing.**

**sat·u·ra·tion** (sach′ə rā′shən)   **1** the act or process of saturating.   **2** the degree of purity of a colour: *The saturation of a colour increases as the amount of white in it is decreased.*   *n.*

**saturation point**   **1** the point at which a substance can absorb no more of another substance.   **2** the stage beyond which no more can be accepted, endured, etc.

**Sat·ur·day** (sat′ər dā *or* sat′ər dē)   the seventh day of the week, following Friday.   *n.*

☛ **Etym.** From OE *Sæterdæg*, a translation of L *Saturni dies* 'day of Saturn'.

**Sat·urn** (sat′ərn) the second largest planet and the sixth in distance from the sun: *Saturn is encircled by many rings composed of fine particles of matter.* *n.*
☛ **Etym.** From the name of *Saturn*, in Greek mythology, the god of agriculture.

**Sat·ur·na·li·a** (sat′ər nā′lē ə) **1** the ancient Roman festival of Saturn, celebrated in December with much feasting and merrymaking. **2 saturnalia,** a period of unrestrained revelry and licence. 1 *n. pl.,* 2 *n. sing.* or *pl.*

**Sat·ur·na·li·an** (sat′ər nā′lē ən) **1** of or having to do with the Roman SATURNALIA. **2 saturnalian,** riotously merry; revelling without restraint. *adj.*

**sat·ur·nine** (sat′ər nīn′) gloomy, grave, or taciturn: *His saturnine disposition made him somewhat difficult to get along with.* *adj.* —**sat′ur·nine·ly,** *adv.*

**sat·yr** (sat′ər *or* sā′tər) **1** in Greek mythology, any of a class of minor gods of the woods, usually pictured as having the head, arms, and body of a man and the legs and tail of a goat, and with horns and pointed ears. **2** a lecherous man. *n.*

**sauce** (sos) **1** something, usually a liquid, served with food to make it taste better: *We eat mint sauce with lamb, egg sauce with fish, and many different sauces with puddings.* **2** stewed fruit: *cranberry sauce, applesauce.* **3** prepare with sauce; season. **4** something that adds interest or relish. **5** give interest or flavour to. **6** *Informal.* sauciness: *I don't like Mary's sauce.* **7** *Informal.* be saucy to. 1, 2, 4, 6 *n.,* 3, 5, 7 *v.,* **sauced, sauc·ing.**

**sauce·pan** (sos′pan′) a deep cooking utensil of metal, glass, ceramic, etc., usually having a lid and a long handle at the side, and used for cooking on top of the stove. *n.*

**sau·cer** (sos′ər) **1** a shallow dish to set a cup on. **2** any small, round, shallow dish, such as a dish put under a flowerpot to catch excess water. **3** something round and shallow like a saucer. *n.* —**sau′cer·like′,** *adj.*

**sau·cy** (sos′ē) **1** showing lack of respect; rude. **2** pert; smart: *a saucy hat.* *adj.,* **sau·ci·er, sau·ci·est.** —**sau′ci·ly,** *adv.* —**sau′ci·ness,** *n.*

**sauer·kraut** (sour′krout′) cabbage cut fine, salted, and allowed to ferment; cabbage pickled in brine. *n.*

**sault** (sü) *Cdn.* a waterfall or rapids (*now used mainly in place names*). *n.*
☛ **Hom.** SIOUX, SUE.

**sau·na** (son′ə *or* sou′nə) **1** a steam bath in which the steam is usually produced by pouring water over hot stones. **2** a house or other structure used for such baths. *n.*

**saun·ter** (son′tər) **1** walk along slowly and quietly; stroll: *People sauntered through the park.* **2** a leisurely or careless gait. **3** a stroll: *They went for a saunter along the river.* 1 *v.,* 2, 3 *n.* —**saun′ter·er,** *n.*

**sau·ri·an** (sô′rē ən) **1** any reptile belonging to the suborder **Sauria,** commonly known as lizards: *Geckos, horned toads, chameleons, etc. are saurians.* **2** any of various reptiles resembling the lizards, such as the crocodiles. **3** of, referring to, or like lizards. 1, 2 *n.,* 3 *adj.*

**sau·ry** (sô′rē) a small fish having jaws that resemble a beak. *n.,* *pl.* **sau·ry** *or* **sau·ries.**
☛ **Hom.** SORRY.

**sau·sage** (sos′ij) chopped pork, beef, or other meats, seasoned and stuffed into a thin casing, or skin. *n.*

**sau·té** (sō tā′ *or* sot ā′) **1** fried quickly in a little fat, over a high heat. **2** a dish of food prepared in this way. **3** fry quickly in a little fat. 1 *adj.,* 2 *n.,* 3 *v.,* **sau·téed, sau·té·ing.**

**sau·terne** (sō tėrn′) **1** a French white table wine. **2** any wine of the same type. *n.*

**sav·age** (sav′ij) **1** of animals, not tamed or under human control; wild and fierce: *savage beasts of the jungle.* **2** of geographical features, wild and rugged: *savage mountain scenery.* **3** ferocious or brutal: *She was the victim of a savage attack by a mugger.* **4** a fierce, brutal, or cruel person. **5** a crude or boorish person. **6** not having an advanced or complex culture; uncivilized; primitive: *a savage people.* **7** attack fiercely or brutally: *The child was savaged by a dog.* 1–3, 6 *adj.,* 4, 5 *n.,* 7 *v.,* **sav·aged, sav·ag·ing.** —**sav′age·ly,** *adv.* —**sav′age·ness,** *n.*
☛ **Usage.** The use of **savage** to refer to people of different societies is no longer considered proper.

**sav·age·ry** (sav′ij rē) **1** the quality or condition of being savage: *The savagery of their attack took the enemy by surprise.* **2** an act of cruelty or brutality. **3** a primitive state: *a people living in savagery.* *n.,* *pl.* **sav·age·ries.**

**sa·van·na** *or* **sa·van·nah** (sə van′ə) **1** a treeless plain. **2** a region of tropical or subtropical grassland having a scattering of trees. **3** especially in the Maritimes, a swamp or tract of peat bog; MUSKEG. *n.*

**sa·vant** (sə vänt′ *or* sav′ənt) a person of learning. *n.*

**save**[1] (sāv) **1** make safe from harm, danger, loss, etc.; rescue: *to save a drowning woman.* **2** keep safe from harm, danger, hurt, loss, etc.; protect: *to save one's honour.* **3** lay aside; store up: *She saves pieces of string.* **4** keep from spending or wasting: *Save your strength.* **5** avoid expense or waste: *She saves in every way she can.* **6** prevent; make less: *to save work, to save trouble, to save expense.* **7** treat carefully to lessen wear, weariness, etc.: *Large print saves one's eyes.* **8** set free from sin and its results: *The Christian church teaches that Christ came to save the world.* **9** the act of saving, especially by preventing an opponent from scoring. 1–8 *v.,* **saved, sav·ing;** 9 *n.* —**sav′er,** *n.*
☛ **Etym.** Through Norman French *sauver* and OF *salver* from Late Latin *salvare* 'save', which came from L *salvus* 'safe'. See also note at SAFE.

**save**[2] (sāv) except; but: *She works every day of the week save Sunday.* *prep.*

**sav·ing** (sā′ving) **1** that saves. **2** tending to save up money; avoiding waste; economical. **3** making a reservation: *a saving clause.* **4** an act or way of saving money, time, etc.: *It will be a saving to take this short cut.* **5** that which is saved. **6** save; except: *Saving a few crusts, we had eaten nothing all day.* **7** with all due respect to or for: *Saving your beliefs, you are wrong.* **8 savings,** *pl.* money saved. **9** *ppr.* of SAVE. 1–3 *adj.,* 4, 5, 8 *n.,* 6, 7 *prep.,* 9 *v.*

**saving grace** a redeeming quality or feature.

**savings account** an account in a bank, trust company, or credit union on which interest is paid.

**sav·iour** or **sav·ior** (sā′vyər) 1 a person who saves or rescues. 2 **the Saviour** or **the Savior,** Jesus Christ. *n.*

**sa·voir–faire** (sav′wär fer′) the knowledge of just the right thing to do or say, especially in social situations. *n.*
☞ *Etym.* From F *savoir-faire* 'knowledge of what to do; ability or skill'.

**sa·vor·y** (sā′və rē) any of a closely related group of fragrant herbs of the mint family, used for seasoning food; especially, **summer savory**. *n., pl.* **sa·vor·ies.**
☞ *Hom.* SAVOURY.

**sa·vour** or **sa·vor** (sā′vər) 1 a taste or smell; flavour: *The soup has a savour of onion.* 2 taste or smell (*of*): *That sauce savours of lemon.* 3 enjoy the savour of; perceive or appreciate by taste or smell: *She savoured the soup with pleasure.* 4 give flavour to; season. 5 a distinctive quality; a noticeable trace: *There is a savour of conceit in everything he says.* 6 have the quality or nature (*of*): *a request that savours of a command.* 1, 5 *n.*, 2–4, 6 *v.* —**sa′vour·er** or **sa′vor·er,** *n.* —**sa′vour·less** or **sa′vor·less,** *adj.*

**sa·vour·y** or **sa·vor·y** (sā′və rē) 1 pleasing in taste or smell especially because of the seasoning: *The savoury smell of roasting turkey greeted us as we entered the house.* 2 having a salt or piquant flavour and not a sweet one: *There were both sweet and savoury relishes on the table.* 3 a small portion of highly seasoned food served at the beginning or end of a dinner to stimulate the appetite or digestion. 4 morally acceptable: *His reputation was not particularly savoury.* 1, 2, 4 *adj.*, **sa·vour·i·er** or **sa·vor·i·er, sa·vour·i·est** or **sa·vor·i·est;** 3 *n., pl.* **sa·vour·ies** or **sa·vor·ies.**
☞ *Hom.* SAVORY.

**sa·voy** (sə voi′) a variety of cabbage having a compact head and wrinkled leaves. *n.*

**Sa·voy·ard** (sə voi′ərd) 1 a native or inhabitant of Savoy, a region in eastern France. 2 an actor, producer, or warm admirer of Gilbert and Sullivan's operas, many of which were first produced at the Savoy Theatre, London, England. 3 of Savoy or its people. 1, 2 *n.* 3 *adj.*

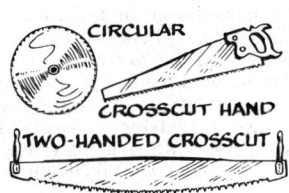

Three common types of saw. The circular saw is mounted in a frame and turned by a motor. The other two are used by hand.

**saw**[1] (so) 1 a tool for cutting hard material such as wood or metal, consisting of a blade or disk with sharp teeth on the edge, especially one operated by hand. 2 a device or machine that includes such a tool. 3 cut with a saw. 4 make with a saw: *Boards are sawed from logs.* 5 use a saw: *Can you saw straight?* 6 be sawed: *Pine saws more easily than oak.* 7 cut as if with a saw; move through as if sawing. 1, 2 *n.*, 3–7 *v.*, **sawed, sawed** or **sawn, saw·ing.**

**saw**[2] (so) pt. of SEE[1]: *I saw a robin today.* *v.*

**saw**[3] (so) a wise saying; proverb: *"A stitch in time saves nine" is a familiar saw.* *n.*
☞ *Etym.* From OE *sagu* 'a saying'. See also note at SAY.

**saw·buck** (sob′uk′) 1 SAWHORSE. 2 a ten-dollar bill. *n.*

**saw·dust** (sod′ust′) tiny particles of wood produced in sawing. *n.*

**sawed–off** (sod′of′) referring to a shotgun with the end of the barrel cut off. *adj.*

**saw·fish** (sof′ish′) a fish like a shark, having a long, flat snout like a saw. *n., pl.* **saw·fish** or **saw·fish·es.**

**saw·fly** (sof′lī′) any of a large family of insects belonging to the same order as ants, bees, and wasps, the adult female having a saw-like part on its egg-laying organ which it uses to cut slits in plants, depositing its eggs in these openings: *Adult sawflies can be distinguished from bees and wasps by their thick bodies.* *n., pl.* **saw·flies.**

SAWHORSES

**saw·horse** (so′hôrs′) a frame on which wood is placed for sawing. *n.*

**saw·mill** (som′il′) 1 a place where timber is sawed into planks, boards, etc. by power-driven machines. 2 a large machine for sawing. *n.*

**sawn** (son) a pp. of SAW[1]. *v.*

**saw·yer** (soi′yər *or* so′yər) a person whose work is sawing timber. *n.*

**sax·horn** (saks′hôrn′) any of a family of trumpetlike, valved brass instruments ranging from soprano to bass, used especially in military-style brass bands. *n.*

**sax·i·frage** (sak′sə frij) 1 any of several closely related, low-growing plants having rosettes of thick, fleshy leaves growing from near the base of the plant and clusters of white, pink, yellow, or purple flowers: *Some saxifrages are popular plants for rock gardens.* 2 referring to a family of herbs, shrubs, or small trees found mainly in north temperate and subarctic regions: *Saxifrages, currants, gooseberries, and mock oranges belong to the saxifrage family.* *n.*

**Sax·on** (sak′sən) 1 a member of an ancient Germanic people of northwestern Germany: *Saxons invaded Britain in the 5th and 6th centuries* A.D., *settling in western and southern England.* 2 the language of the Saxons. 3 of or having to do with the early Saxons or their language. 4 Anglo-Saxon. 5 English. 6 a native of Saxony in modern Germany. 7 of or having to do with Saxony. 1, 2, 4, 6 *n.*, 3–5, 7 *adj.*

A saxophone

**sax·o·phone** (sak′sə fōn′) any of a group of musical wind instruments ranging from soprano to bass, having a curved metal body, keys for the fingers, and a single-reed mouthpiece. *n.*
☛ *Etym.* Named after Adolphe *Sax* (1814–1894), its Belgian inventor, + Gk. *phōnē* 'sound'.

**sax·o·phon·ist** (sak′sə fō′nist) a person who plays the SAXOPHONE, especially a skilled player. *n.*

**sax·tu·ba** (sak′styü′bə *or* sak′stü′bə) a bass SAXHORN. *n.*

**say** (sā) 1 speak: *What did you say?* 2 put into words; express; declare: *Say what you think. What does that sign say?* 3 recite; repeat: *Say the poem.* 4 suppose; take as an estimate: *You can learn in, say, ten lessons.* 5 express an opinion: *It is hard to say which dress is prettier.* 6 what a person says or has to say: *I have had my say.* 7 the chance to say something: *We will all have our say before the meeting ends.* 8 power; authority: *Who has the say in this matter?* 1–5 *v.*, **said, say·ing;** 6–8 *n.* —**say′er,** *n.*
**go without saying,** be extremely obvious: *It goes without saying that she will be furious when she gets the bill.*
**that is to say,** that is; in other words.
**to say nothing of,** without mentioning: *The hotel itself cost a lot, to say nothing of the meals.*
☛ *Etym.* From OE *secgan* 'say', which came from the same Germanic source as ON *saga* 'saga' and OE *sagu* 'SAW³'.

**say·ing** (sā′ing) 1 something said, especially a wise statement that is often repeated: *I remember a saying of my mother's. "Haste makes waste" is a saying.* 2 ppr. of SAY. 1 *n.*, 2 *v.*

**says** (sez) third person singular, present tense of SAY. *v.*

**say-so** (sā′sō′) *Informal.* 1 an unsupported statement: *Don't do it just on his say-so; he might not know what he's talking about.* 2 authority or power to decide; say: *She has no say-so in the matter.* *n.*

**sb.** substantive.
**Sb** antimony.
**sc.** 1 scene. 2 science.
**Sc** scandium.
**Sc.** 1 Scotch. 2 Scottish. 3 Scotland.
**S.C.** Social Credit.

**scab** (skab) 1 the crust that forms over a sore or wound during healing: *A scab formed on the spot where Joe was vaccinated.* 2 a skin disease in animals, especially sheep. 3 any of several fungous diseases of plants, usually producing dark, crustlike spots. 4 become covered with a scab: *The scrape on your knee will scab by tomorrow.* 1–3 *n.*, 4 *v.*, **scabbed, scab·bing.**

**scab·bard** (skab′ərd) a sheath or case for the blade of a sword, dagger, etc. See SWORD for picture. *n.*

**scab·by** (skab′ē) 1 covered with SCABS: *scabby skin.* 2 having the disease SCAB: *scabby potatoes.* 3 *Informal.* low; mean: *a scabby trick.* *adj.*, **scab·bi·er, scab·bi·est.**
—**scab·bi·ness,** *n.*

**sca·bies** (skā′bēz) the itch; a disease of the skin caused by mites that live as parasites under the skin and cause itching. *n.*

**sca·bi·o·sa** (skā′bē ō′sə) SCABIOUS. *n.*

**sca·bi·ous** (skā′bē əs) a plant having long, tough stems and dense flower heads of various colours. *n.*

**sca·brous** (skā′brəs) 1 rough with very small points or projections: *a scabrous leaf.* 2 full of difficulties; harsh. 3 hard to treat with decency; indelicate. *adj.*

**scaf·fold** (skaf′əld) 1 a temporary structure for holding workers when working at a height above the ground or floor during the construction, repair, etc. of a building. 2 a raised platform used as a base for a gallows or guillotine. 3 any raised framework or platform. 4 furnish or support with a scaffold. 1–3 *n.*, 4 *v.*

**scaf·fold·ing** (skaf′əl ding) 1 a SCAFFOLD or system of scaffolds. 2 materials for building SCAFFOLDS. 3 ppr. of SCAFFOLD. 1, 2 *n.*, 3 *v.*

**scal·a·wag** (skal′ə wag′) *Informal.* a good-for-nothing person; scamp; rascal. *n.*

**scald** (skold) 1 burn with hot liquid or steam. 2 a burn caused by hot liquid or steam: *The scald on her hand came from lifting a pot cover carelessly.* 3 pour boiling liquid over; use boiling liquid on: *They scalded the bottles to sterilize them.* 4 heat or be heated almost to boiling, but not quite: *to scald milk.* 1, 3, 4 *v.*, 2 *n.*
☛ *Hom.* SKALD.

**scale¹** (skāl) 1 one of the thin, flat, hard plates forming the outer covering of some fishes, snakes, and lizards. 2 a thin layer or piece like a scale: *Scales of skin peeled off after she had scarlet fever.* 3 a thin piece of metal or other material. 4 a coating on the inside of a boiler, etc. 5 remove scales from: *He scaled the fish with a sharp knife.* 6 remove tartar, or scale, from: *He had his teeth scaled by the dentist.* 7 come off in thin pieces or a thin layer: *The paint is starting to scale.* 8 remove in thin layers. 9 cover with scale. 10 become coated with scale. 11 SCALE LEAF. 12 SCALE INSECT. 1–4, 11, 12 *n.*, 5–10 *v.*, **scaled, scal·ing.** —**scale′-less,** *adj.*
☛ *Etym.* ME from OF *escale,* which came from a Germanic word related to SCALE².

**scale²** (skāl) 1 either of the two dishes or pans of a balance. 2 have as one's mass; weigh: *He scales 80 kilograms.* 3 weigh in scales: *The produce is scaled and packaged on the premises.* 4 Usually, **scales,** *pl.* **a** a balance. **b** any instrument for weighing. 1, 4 *n.*, 2, 3 *v.*, **scaled, scal·ing.**
**tip the scales at,** have as one's mass; weigh: *She tips the scales at 65 kilograms.*
**tip** or **turn the scale** or **scales,** be the deciding factor; decide: *His year of experience tipped the scales in his favour and he got the job.*
☛ *Etym.* ME from ON *skāl* 'bowl', first used in England for a drinking bowl and then for a bowl or dish used on a balance.

**scale³** (skāl) 1 a series of steps and degrees; scheme of graded amounts: *The scale of wages in this factory ranges from fifty dollars to ninety dollars a day.* 2 a series of marks made along a line at regular distances, to use in

measuring: *A thermometer has a scale.* **3** an instrument marked in this way, used for measuring, etc. **4** the size of a plan, map, drawing, or model compared with what it represents: *a map drawn to the scale of one centimetre for each 100 kilometres.* **5** relative size or extent: *to entertain on a large scale.* **6** a system of numbering: *The decimal scale counts by tens, as in cents, dimes, dollars.* **7** in music, a specific series of tones ascending or descending in pitch. See DO² for picture. **8** climb: *They scaled the wall by ladders.* **9** change according to a certain proportion: *All prices were scaled down ten percent.* **10** make according to a scale. 1–7 *n.*, 8–10 *v.*, **scaled, scal·ing.**
**to scale,** following a set of measurements that is used as the equivalent of another, usually larger, set: *This map is not to scale; five centimetres are given as representing one kilometre, but they really represent two.*
☛ Etym. ME from L *scalae* 'steps, ladder'. 14c.

**scale insect** any of various small insects, the females of which mostly have the body and eggs covered by a scale or shield formed by a secretion from the body: *Scale insects feed on and often destroy plants.*

**scale leaf** one of the leaf parts that unite to cover a bud in winter.

**scale model** a model of a building, ship, etc., which uses a set of small measurements to represent larger ones: *The architect showed a scale model of the new arena, with one centimetre representing one metre.*

**sca·lene** (skā lēn′ *or* skā′lēn′) **1** of a triangle, having three unequal sides. See TRIANGLE for picture. **2** of a cone or cylinder, having its axis not perpendicular to the base. *adj.*

**scal·lion** (skal′yən) **1** a young, green onion with a small, undeveloped bulb. **2** SHALLOT. *n.*

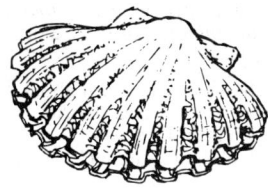
A scallop (def. 1)

Scallops (def. 7) on a collar

**scal·lop** (skol′əp *or* skal′əp) **1** a shellfish resembling a clam but having a fan-shaped shell with ridges that form a wavy edge around the shell. **2** in certain species, the large, edible muscle that opens and closes the shell. **3** this muscle, used as food. **4** one of the two parts of the shell: *Pilgrims returning from Palestine formerly wore scallops as the sign of their pilgrimage.* **5** a small dish or scallop shell in which fish or other food is baked and served. **6** in cooking, bake with sauce, bread crumbs etc. in a scallop shell or other low dish; escallop: *scalloped oysters.* **7** one of a series of semicircular curves on an edge of a dress, etc. **8** make with a series of such curves on: *She scalloped the hems of the pillowcases.* 1–5, 7 *n.*, 6, 8 *v.* Also, **scollop.**

**scalp** (skalp) **1** the skin on the top and back of the head, usually covered with hair. **2** part of this skin with the hair attached, taken from a conquered enemy and kept as a token of victory: *The taking of scalps was formerly practised among certain Amerindian and European peoples.* **3** any trophy or token of victory. **4** cut or tear the scalp from. **5** *Informal.* buy and sell stocks, etc. to make small, quick profits. **6** *Informal.* buy tickets to theatre productions, games, etc. and resell at greatly increased prices. 1–3 *n.*, 4–6 *v.*

**scal·pel** (skal′pəl) a small, sharp, straight knife used in surgery. *n.*

**scalp·er** (skal′pər) *Informal.* one who SCALPS, especially one who scalps stocks, tickets, etc. *n.*

**scal·y** (skā′lē) **1** having scales like a fish. **2** covered or encrusted with a layer of something like scales: *This iron pipe is scaly with rust.* **3** like or suggesting scales. *adj.*, **scal·i·er, scal·i·est.**

**scaly anteater** PANGOLIN.

**scamp¹** (skamp) **1** a rascal; rogue; worthless person. **2** a mischievous person, especially a child. *n.*

**scamp²** (skamp) do work, etc. in a hasty, careless manner. *v.*

**scam·per** (skam′pər) **1** run or move away quickly: *The mice scampered when the cat came.* **2** run about playfully: *The dogs were scampering in the yard.* **3** a playful running about: *Let the dog out for a scamper.* 1, 2 *v.*, 3 *n.*

**scam·pi** (skam′pē *or* skäm′pē) large shrimps or prawns, especially when used in Italian dishes. *n.pl.*

**scan** (skan) **1** look at closely; examine with care: *His mother scanned his face to see if he was telling the truth.* **2** *Informal.* glance at; look over hastily: *She took a few minutes to scan the newspaper headlines.* **3** find or test the metre of a poem by marking the lines off into feet. Example: Tíger!| Tíger!| búrning| bríght| ín the| fórests| óf the| níght.| **4** read or recite poetry so as to emphasize the metre. **5** fit a particular metrical pattern: *Your poem is good, but this line does not scan.* **6** in television, pass over a scene, picture, etc. with a rapidly moving electron beam so as to transmit an image made up of lines showing qualities of light and shade. *v.*, **scanned, scan·ning.**

**Scand. 1** Scandinavia. **2** Scandinavian.

**scan·dal** (skan′dəl) **1** a shameful action, condition, or event that brings disgrace or offends public opinion: *It was a scandal for the city official to take tax money for his own use.* **2** damage to someone's reputation; disgrace. **3** public talk about a person that will hurt his or her reputation; evil gossip; slander; defamation. *n.*
**be the scandal of,** scandalize.

**scan·dal·ize** (skan′də līz′) offend by doing something thought to be wrong or improper; shock: *She scandalized the neighbours by neglecting her children.* *v.*, **scan·dal·ized, scan·dal·iz·ing.**

**scan·dal·mon·ger** (skan′dəl mung′gər *or* skan′dəl mong′gər) a person who spreads scandal and evil gossip. *n.*

**scan·dal·ous** (skan′də ləs) **1** bringing disgrace; shameful; shocking: *scandalous behaviour.* **2** consisting of or spreading scandal or slander; slandering: *a scandalous piece of gossip.* *adj.* —**scan′dal·ous·ly,** *adv.*

**scandal sheet** a newspaper or periodical that features sensational stories and malicious gossip.

**Scan·di·na·vi·an** (skan′də nā′vē ən) **1** of or having to do with Scandinavia, a region including Denmark, Norway, Sweden, and, often, Iceland, or its people, or their languages. **2** a native or inhabitant of Scandinavia. **3** a person of Scandinavian descent. **4** the group of northern Germanic languages spoken in Scandinavia. *1 adj., 2–4 n.*
☞ *Usage.* The terms **Scandinavian** and **Scandinavia** have sometimes been used to include Finland, but Finland is historically distinct from the Scandinavian countries, having a very different language and different cultural traditions.

**scan·di·um** (skan′dē əm) a rare metallic element. *Symbol:* Sc *n.*

**scanner** (skan′ər) **1** any device that scans, such as in a radar system. **2** an input device for a computer that reads printed numbers, codes, or other visible information: *The cashier rang up my purchase using a scanner to read the price on the label.* *n.*

**scan·sion** (skan′shən) the analysis of the metre of a poem or poetry. *n.*

**scant** (skant) **1** not enough in size, amount, or quantity: *making do with scant provisions.* **2** scarcely full or complete; not coming quite up to a particular measure: *He takes a scant teaspoon of sugar in his tea. You have a scant hour in which to pack.* **3** make scant; limit or cut down; stint: *Don't scant the butter if you want a rich cake.* *1, 2 adj., 3 v.*
**scant of,** having not enough: *scant of breath.*

**scant·ling** (skan′tling) **1** a small beam or piece of timber, especially one used as an upright piece in the frame of a building. **2** the dimensions of stone or timber used in building: *timber of small scantling.* **3** the set of standard dimensions of parts of a structure, especially a ship: *The two ships were built to the same scantling.* *n.*

**scant·y** (skan′tē) **1** not enough: *Her scanty clothing did not keep out the cold.* **2** barely enough; meagre: *a scanty harvest.* *adj.,* **scant·i·er, scant·i·est.** **—scant′i·ly,** *adv.* **—scant′i·ness,** *n.*

**scape·goat** (skāp′gōt′) **1** a person or thing made to bear the blame for the mistakes or sins of others. **2 make a scapegoat of.** *1 n., 2 v.*
☞ *Etym.* From *scapegoat,* in the Bible, a goat on which the sins of the people were laid by the ancient Jewish high priests. The goat was then driven into the wilderness.

**scape·grace** (skāp′grās′) a reckless, good-for-nothing person; scamp. *n.*

**scap·u·la** (skap′yə lə) SHOULDER BLADE. See RIB for picture. *n., pl.* **scap·u·lae** (-lē′ *or* -lī′) *or* **scap·u·las.**

**scap·u·lar** (skap′yə lər) **1** of the shoulder or shoulder blade. **2** in the Roman Catholic Church, a loose, sleeveless cloak hanging from the shoulders, worn by certain religious orders. **3** a symbol of devotion or association with a religious order, consisting of two small pieces of cloth joined by shoulder pieces and worn to hang down over the chest and back. *1 adj., 2, 3 n.*

**scar** (skär) **1** the mark left by a healed cut, wound, burn, or sore. **2** any mark like this: *A fallen leaf leaves a scar where it joined the stem. There is a small scar from a cigarette burn on the tabletop.* **3** a lasting effect from grief, etc.: *War leaves deep scars on the minds of those who endure it.* **4** of a wound, etc., form a scar; heal over. **5** make a scar on: *The door was badly scarred by the fire.* *1–3 n., 4, 5 v.,* **scarred, scar·ring.**

**scar·ab** (skar′əb *or* sker′əb) **1** a beetle, especially the sacred beetle of the ancient Egyptians. **2** an image of this beetle: *Scarabs were much used in ancient Egypt as charms or ornaments.* *n.*

**scar·a·mouch** (skar′ə mouch′ *or* sker′ə mouch′, skar′ə müsh′ *or* sker′ə müsh′) **1** braggart. **2** rascal. *n.*

**scarce** (skers) **1** hard to get; rare: *Good cooks are always scarce.* **2** scarcely. *1 adj.,* **scarc·er, scarc·est;** *2 adv.*
**make oneself scarce,** *Informal.* **a** go away. **b** stay away.
**scarce as hen's teeth,** *Informal.* very scarce.

**scarce·ly** (skers′lē) **1** only just; barely; hardly: *scarcely old enough for school. We could scarcely see through the fog.* **2** decidedly not: *He could scarcely have said that.* **3** very probably not: *I will scarcely pay that much.* *adv.*
☞ *Usage.* See note at HARDLY.

**scar·ci·ty** (sker′sə tē) too small a supply; a lack; rarity: *There is a scarcity of nurses.* *n., pl.* **scar·ci·ties.**

**scare** (sker) **1** make or become frightened: *The dog's barking scared the children. She doesn't scare easily.* **2** a fright: *I got a real scare when the lights went out.* **3** a state of alarm or panic: *There was a polio scare last summer. The flight was delayed because of a bomb scare.* *1 v.,* **scared, scar·ing;** *2, 3 n.*
**scare up,** *Informal.* get or get together quickly: *We made camp and then tried to scare up some food.*

**scare·crow** (sker′krō′) **1** an object, usually a figure of a man dressed in old clothes, set in a field to frighten birds away from crops. **2** a person who is thin and gaunt or who dresses like a scarecrow. **3** anything that fools people into being frightened. *n.*

**scared** (skerd) **1** filled with fear; afraid: *He is scared of heights. Were you scared during the thunderstorm?* **2** pt. and pp. of SCARE. *1 adj., 2 v.*

**scarf**[1] (skärf) **1** a piece of silk, wool, etc. worn about the neck, shoulders, head, or waist. **2** a necktie with hanging ends. **3** a long strip of cloth used as a decorative cover for a dresser, table, etc.; runner. *n., pl.* **scarves** or, sometimes, **scarfs.**

**scarf**[2] (skärf) **1** a joint made by cutting away part of the ends of beams, etc. so that they overlap and fit tightly together without increasing the overall thickness. See JOINT for picture. **2** an end cut this way. **3** join by a scarf. *1, 2 n., pl.* **scarfs;** *3 v.*

**scarf·pin** (skärf′pin′) an ornamental pin worn in a scarf or necktie. *n.*

**scarf·skin** (skärf′skin′) EPIDERMIS. *n.*

**scar·i·fi·ca·tion** (skar′ə fə kā′shən *or* sker′ə fə kā′shən) **1** SCARIFYing. **2** a scratch or scratches made by SCARIFYing. *n.*

**scar·i·fy** (skar′ə fī′ *or* sker′ə fī′) **1** in surgery, make scratches or cuts in the surface of the skin, etc. **2** criticize severely; hurt the feelings of. *v.,* **scar·i·fied, scar·i·fy·ing.** **—scar′i·fi′er,** *n.*

**scar·la·ti·na** (skär′lə tē′nə) SCARLET FEVER. *n.*

**scar·let** (skär′lit) **1** light, brilliant red with a slight tinge of orange. **2** cloth or clothing having this colour: *The Mounties look fine in their scarlets.* *1, 2 n., 1 adj.*

**scarlet fever** a contagious disease characterized by a scarlet rash, sore throat, and fever.

**scarlet sage** a popular garden salvia having spikes of scarlet flowers.

**scarlet tanager** a TANAGER of central and eastern North America, the adult male having a bright red body with black wings and tail in spring and summer, the red changing to olive green in fall and winter. The female is mainly olive green and pale yellow.

**scarp** (skärp) **1** a steep slope. **2** the inner slope or side of a ditch surrounding a fortification. **3** make into a steep slope; slope steeply. 1, 2 *n.*, 3 *v.*

**scarves** (skärvz) a pl. of SCARF¹. *n.*

**scar·y** (sker′ē) *Informal.* **1** causing fright or alarm: *a scary movie.* **2** easily frightened. **3** frightened. *adj.*, **scar·i·er, scar·i·est.**

**scat**¹ (skat) *Informal.* **1** an impatient exclamation used especially to drive away an animal. **2** beat it; get away quickly: *She told the boys to scat.* 1 *inter.*, 2 *v.*, **scat·ted, scat·ting.**

**scat**² (skat) in music: **1** jazz singing with meaningless syllables instead of words: *In scat, the voice is used as an instrument.* **2** sing scat. 1 *n.*, 2 *v.*, **scat·ted, scat·ting.**

**scathe** (skāŦH) hurt; harm. *Archaic except in* SCATHELESS. *n.*

**scathe·less** (skā′ŦHlis) without harm; unhurt. *adj.*

**scath·ing** (skā′ŦHing) extremely severe: *scathing criticism.* *adj.* —**scath′ing·ly,** *adv.*

**scat·ter** (skat′ər) **1** throw here and there; sprinkle: *Scatter ashes on the icy sidewalk.* **2** separate and drive off in different directions: *The police scattered the mob.* **3** separate and go in different directions: *The hens scattered.* **4** the act or fact of scattering. **5** a small number occurring or distributed irregularly or here and there: *a scatter of houses in the valley.* 1–3 *v.*, 4, 5 *n.* —**scat′ter·er,** *n.*

**scat·ter·brain** (skat′ər brān′) a thoughtless, frivolous person. *n.*

**scat·ter·brained** (skat′ər brānd′) frivolous; thoughtless; not able to think steadily. *adj.*

**scat·tered** (skat′ərd) **1** not occurring together or in great numbers; few and far apart: *scattered instances of violence. We heard scattered shouts in the distance.* **2** pt. and pp. of SCATTER. 1 *adj.*, 2 *v.*

**scat·ter·ing** (skat′ə ring) **1** a small number or quantity occurring or situated at irregular intervals: *a scattering of cheers, a scattering of villages.* **2** widely separated; occurring here and there. **3** ppr. of SCATTER. 1 *n.*, 2 *adj.*, 3 *v.*

**scatter rug** a small rug.

**scaup** (skop) either of two species of diving duck closely related to the canvasback, the adult male having black-and-white plumage and the female brownish plumage: *Both species of scaup are found in Canada.* *n.*

**scav·enge** (skav′ənj) **1** salvage something usable from discarded materials, rubbish, etc.: *to scavenge usable wood scraps. He makes a living by scavenging.* **2** of an animal, feed on garbage or other dead or decaying matter. **3** expel exhaust gas from the cylinder of an INTERNAL-COMBUSTION ENGINE. **4** chemically remove impurities from molten metal. *v.*

**scav·en·ger** (skav′ən jər) **1** an animal that feeds on dead animals or other decaying matter: *Vultures and jackals are scavengers.* **2** a person who searches through discarded material for something of value. *n.*

hat, āge, fär; let, ēqual, tėrm; it, īce hot, ōpen, ôrder; oil, out; cup, pùt, rüle ∂bove, tak∂n, penc∂l, lem∂n, circ∂s ch, child; ng, long; sh, ship th, thin; ŦH, then; zh, measure

**sce·nar·i·o** (si ner′ē ō′) **1** an outline of a motion picture, giving the main facts about the scenes, persons, and acting. **2** an outline of any play, opera, etc. **3** an outline of a course of action or sequence of events, proposed as a possible outcome of a real or imagined situation: *In our worst-case scenario, interest rates will continue to rise.* *n.*, *pl.* **sce·nar·i·os.**

**sce·nar·ist** (si ner′ist) a person who writes SCENARIOS. *n.*

**scene** (sēn) **1** the time, place, circumstances, etc., of a play or story: *The scene of the novel is laid in Quebec City in the year 1759.* **2** the place where anything is carried on or takes place: *the scene of an accident, the scene of my childhood.* **3** the painted screens, hangings, etc. used in a theatre to represent places: *The scene represents a city street.* **4** a part of an act of a play: *The king comes to the castle in Act I, Scene 2.* **5** a particular incident of a play: *the trial scene in* The Merchant of Venice. **6** an action, incident, situation, etc., occurring in reality or represented in literature or art: *He has painted a series of pictures called "Scenes of My Boyhood."* **7** a view; picture: *The white sailboats in the blue water made a pretty scene.* **8** a show of strong feeling in front of others; exhibition; display: *The child kicked and screamed and made such a scene that her mother was ashamed of her.* *n.*
**behind the scenes,** **a** out of sight of the audience. **b** privately; secretly, not publicly: *A lot of planning for the Festival was done behind the scenes.*
☞ *Hom.* SEEN.
☞ *Etym.* Through L *scena* from Gk. *skēnē* 'tent, stage', originally the tent where actors changed their costumes.

**scen·er·y** (sē′nə rē *or* sēn′rē) **1** the painted hangings, fittings, etc. used in a theatre to represent places. **2** the general appearance of the natural features of a place: *mountain scenery.* *n.*, *pl.* **scen·er·ies.**

**sce·nic** (sē′nik *or* sen′ik) **1** of or having to do with natural scenery; having much fine scenery: *a scenic highway. The scenic splendours of Lake Louise are famous.* **2** belonging to the stage of a theatre; of or having to do with stage effects: *The production of the musical comedy was a scenic triumph.* **3** in art, representing an action, incident, situation, etc.: *a scenic painting.* *adj.*

**scent** (sent) **1** a smell, especially an agreeable one: *the scent of new-mown hay, the scent of roses.* **2** become aware of through smell: *The dog immediately scented the rabbit and dashed off after it.* **3** the sense of smell: *Bloodhounds have a keen scent.* **4** hunt by using the sense of smell: *The dog scented about till it found the trail.* **5** use the sense of smell on: *to scent the air for signs of rain.* **6** a smell left in passing: *The dogs followed the scent of the fox.* **7** any means by which a person or thing can be traced: *The police picked up the thief's scent again where he had stopped for gas.* **8** perfume: *She uses too much scent.* **9** apply perfume to: *She scented her handkerchief. This tobacco has been scented.* **10** fill with odour: *Lilacs scented the air.* **11** get or have a suspicion, or inkling, of: *They scented trouble and left quickly.* 1, 3, 6–8 *n.*, 2, 4, 5, 9–11 *v.*
☞ *Hom.* CENT, SENT.

**scent·less** (sen′tlis) having no smell. *adj.*

**scep·ter** (sep′tər) See SCEPTRE. *n., v.*, **scep·tered, scep·ter·ing.**

**scep·tered** (sep′tərd) See SCEPTRED. *adj., v.*

**scep·tic** or **skep·tic** (skep′tik) **1** a person who questions the truth of a particular theory or apparent fact; doubter. **2** a person who doubts or questions the possibility or certainty of our knowledge of anything. **3** a person who doubts the truth of religious doctrines. *n.*

**scep·ti·cal** or **skep·ti·cal** (skep′tə kəl) having to do with, characteristic of, or marked by SCEPTICISM: *They showed him all their data, but he remained sceptical about the plan. adj.* —**scep′ti·cal·ly** or **skep′ti·cal·ly,** *adv.*

**scep·ti·cism** or **skep·ti·cism** (skep′tə siz′əm) **1** a sceptical attitude; a general tendency to doubt or doubt about a particular idea or thing. **2** doubt or unbelief with regard to religion. **3** the doctrine that nothing can be proved absolutely. *n.*

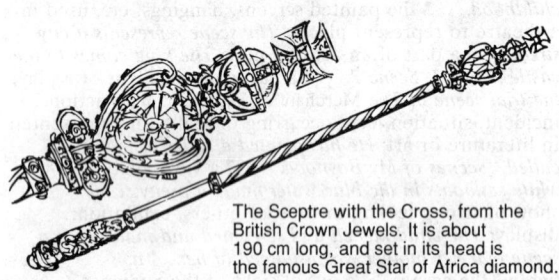

The Sceptre with the Cross, from the British Crown Jewels. It is about 190 cm long, and set in its head is the famous Great Star of Africa diamond.

**scep·tre** (sep′tər) **1** the rod or staff carried by a ruler as a symbol of royal power or authority. **2** furnish with a sceptre. **3** royal or imperial power or authority. 1, 3 *n.*, 2 *v.*, **scep·tred, scep·tring.** Also, **scepter.**

**scep·tred** (sep′tərd) **1** furnished with or bearing a SCEPTRE. **2** invested with regal authority; regal. **3** pt. and pp. of SCEPTRE. 1, 2 *adj.*, 3 *v.* Also, **sceptered.**

**sch.** school.

**sched·ule** (skej′ül *or* shej′ül) **1** a written or printed statement of details; list: *A timetable is a schedule of the coming and going of trains.* **2** a listing of the games to be played by the teams in a league: *a hockey schedule.* **3** make a schedule of; enter in a schedule. **4** plan or arrange something for a definite time or date: *Schedule the convention for the fall.* **5** the time or times fixed for doing something, arrival at a place, etc.: *The bus was an hour behind schedule.* 1, 2, 5 *n.*, 3, 4 *v.*, **sched·uled, sched·ul·ing.**

**sche·ma** (skē′mə) an outline, synopsis, plan, or scheme. *n., pl.* **sche·ma·ta** (-mə tə).

**sche·mat·ic** (skē mat′ik) having to do with or having the nature of a diagram, plan, or scheme; diagrammatic. *adj.* —**sche·mat′i·cal·ly,** *adv.*

**sche·ma·tize** (skē′mə tīz′) reduce to or represent as a formula or SCHEME: *to schematize the metre of a poem. v.*, **sche·ma·tized, sche·ma·tiz·ing.**

**scheme** (skēm) **1** a program of action; plan: *She has a scheme for extracting gold from sea water.* **2** a plot: *a scheme to cheat the government.* **3** plan or plot: *Those men were scheming to bring the jewels into the country without paying duty.* **4** a system of connected things, parts, thoughts, etc.; design: *The colour scheme of the room is blue and gold.* **5** a diagram, outline, or table. 1, 2, 4, 5 *n.*, 3 *v.*, **schemed, schem·ing.**

**schem·ing** (skē′ming) **1** given to forming sly or tricky schemes; deceitful and crafty. **2** ppr. of SCHEME. 1 *adj.*, 2 *v.*

**scher·zo** (sker′tsō) in music, a light and playful composition or part of a sonata, concerto, or symphony. *n., pl.* **scher·zos** or **scher·zi** (-tsē).

**Schick test** (shik) a test to determine whether a person is immune to diphtheria, made by injecting a diluted diphtheria toxin under the skin. If the skin becomes inflamed as a result, the person is not immune to the disease.

**schism** (siz′əm, shiz′əm, *or* skiz′əm) **1** a division because of some difference of opinion about religion. **2** a division into hostile groups. **3** the offence of causing or trying to cause a religious schism. **4** a sect or group formed by a schism within a church. *n.*

**schis·mat·ic** (siz mat′ik, shiz mat′ik, *or* skiz mat′ik) **1** causing or likely to cause SCHISM. **2** inclined toward, or guilty of, SCHISM. **3** a person who tries to cause a SCHISM or takes part in a schism. 1, 2 *adj.*, 3 *n.*

**schist** (shist) a kind of crystalline rock that splits easily into layers. *n.*

**schist·ose** (shis′tōs) of or like SCHIST; having the structure of schist. *adj.*

**schiz·o·carp** (skiz′ə karp′) in botany, a dry compound fruit that splits when ripe into two or more closed parts containing one seed each. *n.*

**schiz·oid** (skit′soid) **1** characterized by, tending toward, or resulting from SCHIZOPHRENIA: *schizoid tendencies. He's a bit schizoid.* **2** a schizoid person. 1 *adj.*, 2 *n.*

**schiz·o·phre·ni·a** (skit′sə frē′nē ə) a mental disorder characterized by dissociation from environment and deterioration of personality. *n.*

**schiz·o·phren·ic** (skit′sə fren′ik) **1** of, having to do with, or suffering from SCHIZOPHRENIA. **2** a person suffering from SCHIZOPHRENIA. 1 *adj.*, 2 *n.*

**schnapps** or **schnaps** (shnäps) any of various distilled liquors, especially a kind of gin made in the Netherlands. *n.*

**schnau·zer** (shnou′zər *or* shnou′tsər) any of three breeds of terrier originally developed in Germany, having a short, wiry coat, small ears, bushy eyebrows, and a beard: *The three breeds of schnauzer are the* **standard schnauzer, giant schnauzer,** *and* **miniature schnauzer.** *n.*

**schol·ar** (skol′ər) **1** a learned person; a person having much knowledge: *Professor Lodge was a famous Latin scholar.* **2** a pupil at school; learner. **3** a student who is given money by some institution to help him or her continue studies; the holder of a scholarship: *a Rhodes scholar. n.*

**schol·ar·ly** (skol′ər lē) **1** of, like, or fit for a scholar: *scholarly habits.* **2** having much knowledge; learned. **3** fond of learning; studious. **4** thorough and orderly in methods of study: *a scholarly book.* **5** in a scholarly manner. 1–4 *adj.*, 5 *adv.* —**schol′ar·li·ness,** *n.*

**schol·ar·ship** (skol′ər ship′) **1** the possession of knowledge gained by study; quality of learning and knowledge: *Good scholarship is more important than athletics.* **2** money or other aid to help a student continue his or her studies. *n.*

**scholarship fund,** a fund to provide this money.

**scho·las·tic** (skə las′tik) **1** of schools, scholars, or education; academic: *scholastic achievements or methods, scholastic life.* **2** of or like SCHOLASTICISM. **3** a person who favours SCHOLASTICISM. **4** in the Middle Ages, a theologian and philosopher. 1, 2 *adj.*, 3, 4 *n.*

**scho·las·ti·cal·ly** (skə las′ti klē) in a SCHOLASTIC way or manner; in scholastic respects. *adv.*

**scho·las·ti·cism** (skə las′tə siz′əm) **1** in the Middle Ages, a system of theological and philosophical teaching, based chiefly on the authority of the church fathers and of Aristotle, and characterized by a formal method of discussion. **2** an adherence to the teachings of the schools or to traditional doctrines and methods. *n.*

**school¹** (skül) **1** a place for learning and teaching: *Children go to school to learn.* **2** a regular course of meetings of teachers and pupils for instruction. **3** a session of such a course: *summer school.* **4** those who are taught and their teachers. **5** any place, situation, experience, etc. as a source of instruction or training: *the school of adversity.* **6** a group of people holding the same beliefs or opinions: *the Dutch school of painting, a gentleman of the old school.* **7** a particular department or group in a university: *a medical school, a law school.* **8** a room, rooms, building, or group of buildings in a university, set apart for the use of one department. **9** educate in a school; teach. **10** a place of training or discipline: *a reform school.* **11** train; discipline: *School yourself to control your temper.* **12** of or having to do with a school or schools: *school administration, school tax.* 1–8, 10, 12 *n.*, 9, 11 *v.*

**school²** (skül) **1** a large group of the same kind of fish or water animals swimming together: *a school of mackerel, a school of whales.* **2** swim together in a school. 1 *n.*, 2 *v.*

**school age** **1** the age at which a child begins to go to school. **2** the years during which going to school is compulsory or customary.

**school board** a group of people, usually elected, who manage the schools in a certain area.

**school·book** (skül′bůk′) a book for study in schools. *n.*

**school·boy** (skül′boi′) a boy attending school. *n.*

**school·child** (skül′chīld′) a child who goes to school. *n.*, *pl.* **school·chil·dren**.

**school·fel·low** (skül′fel′ō) a companion at school. *n.*

**school·girl** (skül′gėrl′) a girl attending school. *n.*

**school guard** **1** a member of a SCHOOL PATROL. **2** a person whose job is to escort school children across busy streets near schools.

**school·house** (skül′hous′) a small building used as a school, especially in a village. *n.*

**school·ing** (skül′ing) **1** instruction in school; the education received at school. **2** the cost of instruction. **3** *ppr.* of SCHOOL. 1, 2 *n.*, 3 *v.*

**school·ma'am** (skül′mäm or skül′mam′) SCHOOLMARM. *n.*

**school·man** (skül′mən) in the Middle Ages, a teacher in a university; medieval theologian. *n.*, *pl.* **school·men** (-mən).

**school·marm** (skül′märm) *Informal.* **1** a female schoolteacher, especially in a rural or village school. **2** a

## scholastic 1057 sciatic nerve

hat, āge, fär; let, ēqual, tėrm; it, īce
hot, ōpen, ôrder; oil, out; cup, pùt, rüle
əbove, takən, pencəl, lemən, circəs
ch, child; ng, long; sh, ship
th, thin; ᴛʜ, then; zh, measure

very strict conservative teacher or similar person of either sex. *n.*

**school·mas·ter** (skül′mas′tər) a man who teaches in or manages a school. *n.*

**school·mate** (skül′māt′) a companion at school. *n.*

**school·mis·tress** (skül′mis′tris) a woman who teaches in or manages a school. *n.*

**school patrol** a group of older school children who escort younger ones across busy streets.

**school·room** (skül′rüm′) a room in which pupils are taught. *n.*

**school·teach·er** (skül′tē′chər) a person who teaches in a school. *n.*

**school·yard** (skül′yärd′) a piece of ground around or near a school, used for play, games, etc. *n.*

**school year** that part of the year during which school is in session.

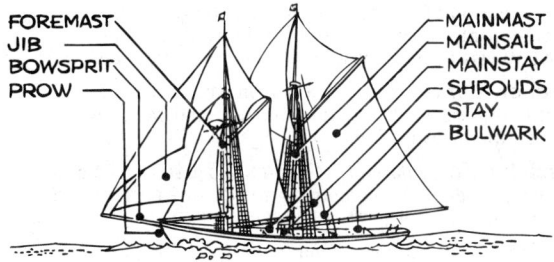

The *Bluenose*, a famous Canadian schooner

**schoon·er** (skü′nər) **1** a ship with two or more masts and fore-and-aft sails. **2** a large glass of beer. *n.*

**schoon·er–rigged** (skü′nər rigd′) having fore-and-aft sails. *adj.*

**schot·tische** (shot′ish *or* shot ēsh′) **1** a dance resembling the polka. **2** the music for such a dance. *n.*

**schuss** (shùs) in skiing: **1** a straight, downhill run at high speed. **2** make such a run. **3** a straight, downhill course for making such a run. 1, 3 *n.*, 2 *v.*

**schwa** (shwä) **1** an unstressed vowel sound such as that of the *a* in *about*, the *u* in *circus*, or the *o* in *lemon*; neutral vowel. **2** the symbol (ə) used to represent this sound. *n.*

**sci.** **1** science. **2** scientific.

**sci·at·ic** (sī at′ik) **1** of, having to do with, or in the region of a hip. **2** of, having to do with, or caused by SCIATICA. *adj.*

**sci·at·i·ca** (sī at′ə kə) pain along the path of the SCIATIC NERVE and its branches; neuralgia of the hips or legs. *n.*

**sciatic nerve** a large nerve that begins in the pelvis and runs down along the back of the thigh.

**sci·ence** (sī′əns) **1** knowledge of general facts, laws and relationships that is obtained through systematic observation and experiment, especially as applied to the physical world and the phenomena associated with it: *new discoveries in science, natural science.* **2** a branch of such knowledge: *Biology and chemistry are sciences.* **3** any branch of knowledge arranged in an orderly system and considered as an object of study: *Economics is a social science.* **4** a technique, skill, etc. that can be studied in a systematic way: *the science of boxing. Photography is both an art and a science.* *n.*

**science fiction** a type of FICTION based on actual or fanciful elements of science: *Science fiction stories are often about life in the future or on other galaxies and make much use of the latest discoveries of science.*

**sci·en·tif·ic** (sī′ən tif′ik) **1** using the facts and laws of SCIENCE: *a scientific method, a scientific farmer.* **2** of or having to do with SCIENCE; used in science: *scientific books, scientific instruments.* *adj.*

**sci·en·tif·i·cal·ly** (sī′ən tif′i klē) in a SCIENTIFIC manner; according to the facts and laws of science. *adv.*

**scientific method** the principles and procedures of scientific investigation, including (1) the recognition and description of a particular problem, (2) the collection of data related to this problem, through observation and experimentation, (3) the interpretation of the data and formulation of a hypothesis to describe the event, law, or relationship discovered, and (4) the testing of the hypothesis by more observation and experimentation.

**sci·en·tist** (sī′ən tist) a person who is trained in SCIENCE, especially a natural science, and whose work is scientific investigation. *n.*

**sci–fi** (sī′fī′) *Informal.* **1** SCIENCE FICTION. **2** of, having to do with, or referring to SCIENCE FICTION: *sci-fi fans. She has a huge sci-fi collection.* *n.*

**scim·i·tar** (sim′ə tər *or* sim′ə tär′) a short, curved sword having a cutting edge on the convex side, used mainly by Arabs and Turks. See SWORD for picture. *n.*

**scin·til·la** (sin til′ə) a spark or trace: *There is not a scintilla of evidence against him.* *n.*

**scin·til·late** (sin′tə lāt′) sparkle; flash: *The snow scintillates in the sun like diamonds. Brilliant wit scintillates.* *v.,* scin·til·lat·ed, scin·til·lat·ing.

**scin·til·la·tion** (sin′tə lā′shən) **1** a sparkling; flashing. **2** a spark; flash. *n.*

**sci·o·lism** (sī′ə liz′əm) superficial knowledge. *n.*

**sci·o·list** (sī′ə list) a person who pretends to have more knowledge than he or she really has. *n.*

**sci·on** (sī′ən) **1** a bud or branch cut for GRAFTing or planting. **2** descendant. *n.*

**scis·sion** (sizh′ən) the act of cutting, dividing, or splitting; division; separation. *n.*

**scis·sor** (siz′ər) **1** cut, cut off, or cut out with SCISSORS. **2** SCISSORS. 1 *v.,* 2 *n.*

**scis·sors** (siz′ərz) **1** a tool or instrument for cutting that has two sharp blades so fastened that their edges slide against each other (*usually used with a plural verb*): *My embroidery scissors are very sharp.* **2** in gymnastics, a forward and backward movement of the legs suggesting the action of scissors (*used with a singular or plural verb*).

**3** in wrestling, a hold in which the opponent's body or head is held with the legs (*used with a singular verb*). *n.*

**scler·a** (skler′ə) the tough, fibrous, white outer membrane covering all of the eyeball except the part covered by the cornea. See EYE for picture. *n.*

**scle·ro·sis** (sklə rō′sis) a hardening of a tissue or part of the body by an increase of connective tissue or the like at the expense of more active tissue. *n., pl.* scle·ro·ses (-sēz).

**scle·rot·ic** (sklə rot′ik) **1** having to do with or being the SCLERA. **2** SCLERA. **3** of, having to do with, or affected with SCLEROSIS. 1, 3 *adj.,* 2 *n.*

**scoff** (skof) **1** make fun to show one does not believe something; mock: *We scoffed at the idea of drowning in ten centimetres of water. He scoffs at religion.* **2** mocking words or acts. **3** something ridiculed or mocked. 1 *v.,* 2, 3 *n.* —**scoff′er,** *n.* —**scoff′ing·ly,** *adv.*

**scold** (skōld) **1** find fault with and criticize severely or angrily; rebuke with severe or angry words: *His mother scolded him for tearing his jacket.* **2** find fault; talk angrily: *He's always scolding.* **3** a person who makes a habit of scolding. 1, 2 *v.,* 3 *n.* —**scold′er,** *n.*

**scol·lop** (skol′əp) SCALLOP. *n., v.*

**sconce** (skons) a bracket projecting from a wall, used to hold a candle or other light. *n.*

**scone** (skon *or* skōn) a thick, flat cake cooked on a griddle or in an oven. *n.*

**scoop** (sküp) **1** a tool like a small shovel, having a short handle and a deeply concave blade for dipping out or shovelling up things. **2** the part of a dredge, shovel, etc. that holds coal, sand, etc. **3** the amount taken up at one time by a scoop. **4** a place hollowed out. **5** take up or out with a scoop, or as a scoop does: *Scoop out a kilogram of sugar. The children scooped up the snow with their hands to make a snowman.* **6** hollow out; dig out; make by scooping: *The children scooped holes in the sand.* **7** the action or process of scooping. **8** *Informal.* the publishing of a piece of news before a rival newspaper does. **9** *Informal.* the piece of news so published. **10** *Informal.* publish a piece of news before a rival newspaper does. 1–4, 7–9 *n.,* 5, 6, 10 *v.*

**scoop·ful** (sküp′fúl) enough to fill a SCOOP. *n., pl.* scoop·fuls.

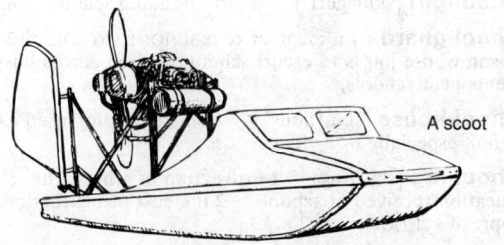

A scoot

**scoot** (sküt) **1** *Informal.* go quickly; dart: *She scooted out of the side door just as I came in the front.* **2** *Informal.* the act of scooting. **3** *Cdn.* a strong-hulled, flat-bottomed boat, driven by an aircraft propeller on an engine mounted toward the stern, designed for travelling on water, through slob ice, or over ice or snow. 1 *v.,* 2, 3 *n.*

A child's scooter

hat, āge, fär; let, ēqual, tėrm; it, īce
hot, ōpen, ôrder; oil, out; cup, put, rüle
ǝbove, takǝn, pencǝl, lemǝn, circǝs
ch, child; ng, long; sh, ship
th, thin; ŦH, then; zh, measure

**scoot·er** (skü′tǝr) 1 a child's vehicle consisting of a long footboard with a wheel at the front and the back, steered by raised handlebars and moved by pushing against the ground with one foot. 2 a light, two-wheeled motor vehicle having a footboard and handlebars somewhat like a child's scooter and equipped with a seat; motor scooter. 3 a sailboat with runners, for use on either water or ice. 4 go or travel by scooter. 1–3 *n.*, 4 *v.*

**scope** (skōp) 1 the amount the mind can take in; extent of one's view: *Very hard words are not within the scope of a child's understanding.* 2 the area over which any activity extends: *This subject is not within the scope of our investigation.* 3 space; opportunity: *Football gives scope for courage and quick thinking.* *n.*

**–scope** combining form. an instrument or other means for viewing or examining, as in *stethoscope, telescope.* ☛ *Etym.* From Med. L *-scopium* and Gk. *-skopion,* which came from Gk. *skopein* 'observe, look at'.

**sco·pol·a·mine** (skō pol′ǝ mēn′) a drug obtained from the roots of certain plants of the nightshade family, used as a sedative or truth serum or, with morphine, to relieve pain. *n.*

**scor·bu·tic** (skôr byü′tik) 1 having to do with or of the nature of SCURVY. 2 affected with SCURVY. *adj.*

**scorch** (skôrch) 1 burn slightly; burn on the outside: *The cake tastes scorched. I scorched the shirt when I ironed it.* 2 a slight burn. 3 parch with intense heat; dry up; wither: *grass scorched by the sun.* 4 criticize with harsh or sarcastic words. 1, 3, 4 *v.*, 2 *n.*

**scorched–earth policy** (skôrcht′tėrth′) a military policy of destroying all crops, buildings, etc. in the course of a retreat, so as to leave nothing useful for the enemy.

**scorch·er** (skôr′chǝr) 1 *Informal.* a very hot day. 2 a scathing criticism. 3 any person or thing that SCORCHES. *n.*

**score** (skôr) 1 the record of points made in a game, contest, test, etc.: *The score was 9 to 2 in our favour.* 2 in a game, contest, test, etc., make as points. 3 achieve a success; succeed: *She had difficulty getting a job but scored at last.* 4 keep a record of the number of points made in a game, contest, etc. 5 make as an addition to the score; gain; win: *He scored a touchdown in the last minute of the game.* 6 an amount owed; debt; account: *He paid his score at the inn.* 7 keep a record of as an amount owed; mark; set down: *The innkeeper scored on a slate the number of meals each person had.* 8 a group or set of twenty; twenty: *A score or more were present at the party.* 9 a written or printed piece of music arranged for different instruments or voices: *the score of a musical comedy.* 10 arrange a piece of music for different instruments or voices. 11 a cut; scratch; stroke; mark; line. 12 make a partial cut: *Score the cardboard with a knife before bending.* 13 an account; reason; ground: *Don't worry on that score.* 14 cut; scratch; mark; line: *Mistakes are scored in red ink.* 15 *Informal.* blame or scold severely. 16 **scores,** *pl.* a large number, but less than hundreds: *Scores died in the epidemic.* 17 **the score,** *Informal.* the truth about anything or things in general; the facts: *The new man doesn't know what the score is yet.* 1, 6, 8, 9, 11, 13, 16, 17 *n.*, 2–5, 7, 10, 12, 14, 15 *v.*, **scored, scor·ing.** —**score′less,** *adj.* —**scor′er,** *n.*
**on the score of,** because of; on account of.
**pay off** or **settle a score,** get even for an injury or wrong.

**score·board** (skôr′bôrd′) a large board for posting the score and, sometimes, other details of a game or other sporting event. *n.*

**score·card** (skôr′kärd′) a card for keeping the score of a game, match, etc. *n.*

**sco·ri·a** (skô′rē ǝ) 1 refuse left from ore after the metal has been melted out; slag. 2 cinderlike lava. *n.*, *pl.* **sco·ri·ae** (-ē ē′ or -ē ī′).

**scorn** (skôrn) 1 look down upon; think of as mean or low; despise: *He scorned their attempts at reconciliation. She scorns her critics as being out-of-date and incompetent.* 2 reject or refuse as low or wrong: *The judge scorned to take a bribe.* 3 a feeling that a person, animal, or act is mean or low; contempt: *We feel scorn for a traitor.* 4 an object of contempt: *His betrayal of his friends made him the scorn of the school.* 1, 2 *v.*, 3, 4 *n.* —**scorn′er,** *n.*

**scorn·ful** (skôrn′fǝl) showing contempt; mocking; full of SCORN: *a scornful laugh. She was very scornful of his beliefs.* *adj.* —**scorn′ful·ly,** *adv.* —**scorn′ful·ness,** *n.*

**Scor·pi·o** (skôr′pē ō′) 1 in astronomy, a southern CONSTELLATION thought of as having the shape of a scorpion. 2 in astrology, the eighth sign of the zodiac: *The sun enters Scorpio about October 24.* See ZODIAC for picture. 3 a person born under this sign. *n.*

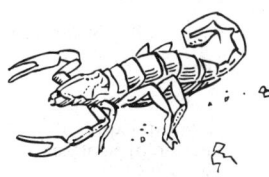
A scorpion—the different species range in size from 1.3 to 18 cm long

**scor·pi·on** (skôr′pē ǝn) 1 any of an order of small animals having six pairs of legs, the first two pairs adapted for grasping and tearing apart prey, and having a segmented abdomen that tapers to form a tail with a poisonous stinger at the tip: *Scorpions are arachnids.* 2 **Scorpion,** SCORPIO. *n.*

**Scot** (skot) 1 a native or inhabitant of Scotland, a division of Great Britain. 2 a person of Scottish descent. *n.*

**Scot.** 1 Scotland. 2 Scottish. 3 Scotch.

**scotch** (skoch) 1 wound so as to cripple or make temporarily harmless: *to scotch a snake without killing it.* 2 stamp out; stifle; crush: *to scotch a rumour.* 3 cut; score; gash. *v.*

**Scotch** (skoch) 1 a kind of whisky made in Scotland. 2 SCOTTISH. 1, 2 *n.,* 2 *adj.*

**Scotch–I·rish** (skoch′ī′rish) 1 of or having to do with a part of the population of Ulster descended from Scottish settlers. 2 of both Scottish and Irish descent. 3 a person of both Scottish and Irish descent. 1, 2 *adj.,* 3 *n.*

**Scotch·man** (skoch′mən) SCOT. *n., pl.* **Scotch·men** (-mən).

**Scotch pine** 1 a pine tree native to northern Europe but now widely planted in Canada, having spreading branches and short, twisted, bluish-green needles. 2 the hard, yellowish wood of this tree, valuable for timber. Also, **Scots pine.**

**Scotch terrier** SCOTTISH TERRIER.

**sco·ter** (skō′tər) any of several species of diving sea duck found along the northern coasts and large lakes and rivers of North America and Europe, the adult male having mostly black plumage, the female mostly brown. *n.*

**scot–free** (skot′frē′) completely free from injury, punishment, penalty, etc.: *His partner was convicted of fraud but he got off scot-free. adj., adv.*
☞ *Etym.* The word *scot* in **scot-free** means payment or tax. It is originally from ON *skot* 'contribution, payment'.

**Scot·land Yard** (skot′lənd) in England: 1 the headquarters of the London police, properly called **New Scotland Yard.** 2 the London police, especially the department that does detective work.
☞ *Etym.* Named for the building in which the London police headquarters was formerly located, in Great Scotland Yard.

**Scots** (skots) 1 any of the dialects of English spoken in Scotland. 2 of, having to do with, or characteristic of Scotland, its people, or their language; Scottish. 1 *n.,* 2 *adj.*

**Scots–Gael·ic** (skots′gā′lik; *also, esp. in Scotland,* skots′gä′lik) the Celtic language of the Scottish Highlanders. *n.*

**Scots·man** (skot′smən) SCOT. *n., pl.* **Scots·men** (-smən).

**Scots pine** SCOTCH PINE.

**Scot·ti·cism** (skot′ə siz′əm) a word, expression, pronunciation, etc. that is characteristic of Scottish English. *n.*

**Scot·tish** (skot′ish) 1 of or having to do with Scotland, its people, or their language. 2 **the Scottish,** *pl.* **a** the people of Scotland. **b** people of Scottish descent. 3 SCOTS (def. 1) 1 *adj.,* 2, 3 *n.*

**Scottish deerhound** DEERHOUND.

**Scottish terrier** an old Scottish breed of short-legged terrier having rough, wiry hair and pointed, standing ears.

**scoun·drel** (skoun′drəl) a mean or wicked person; a person without principles; villain: *The scoundrels who set fire to the barn have been caught. n.*

**scoun·drel·ly** (skoun′drə lē) 1 having the character of a SCOUNDREL: *a scoundrelly fellow.* 2 having to do with or characteristic of a SCOUNDREL: *a scoundrelly act. adj.*

**scour¹** (skour) 1 clean or polish by vigorous rubbing: *Scour the frying pan with cleanser.* 2 remove dirt and grease by washing: *Raw wool is usually scoured before it is made into yarn.* 3 clear of dirt, weeds, etc.: *The current scoured mud and sand out of the channel.* 4 dig or dig out by the action of running water: *The stream had scoured a channel.* 5 the act of scouring. 1–4 *v.,* 5 *n.,* —**scour′er,** *n.*

**scour²** (skour) 1 move quickly over: *People scoured the country round about for the lost child.* 2 go swiftly in search or pursuit. *v.*

**scourge** (skėrj) 1 a whip. 2 any means of punishment. 3 whip severely; flog. 4 some thing or person that causes great trouble or misfortune: *In former times, an outbreak of disease was called a scourge.* 5 punish severely. 6 put great hardship or suffering on; afflict or oppress: *War scourged the country for eight years.* 1, 2, 4 *n.,* 3, 5, 6 *v.,* **scourged, scourg·ing.**

**scour·ings** (skou′ringz) 1 dirt or other material removed by scouring or cleaning. 2 the lowest level or class of society; rabble: *the scourings of the slums. n.pl.*

**scout¹** (skout) 1 a person sent to find out what the enemy is doing: *A scout wears a uniform; a spy does not.* 2 a warship, airplane, etc. used to find out what the enemy is doing. 3 a person sent out to get information especially about one's opponents, competitors, etc. 4 a person who looks for promising recruits for a film studio, sports team, etc. 5 act as a scout; hunt around to find something: *Go and scout for firewood for the picnic.* 6 observe or examine to get information. 7 the act of scouting. 8 *Informal.* a fellow; person: *He's a good scout.* 9 **Scout,** a member of the BOY SCOUTS. 1–4, 7–9 *n.,* 5, 6 *v.* —**scout′er,** *n.*

**scout²** (skout) 1 refuse to believe in; reject with scorn: *She scouted the idea of a dog with two tails.* 2 scoff at. *v.*

**Scout·er** (skou′tər) an adult who is associated in some way with the BOY SCOUTS or WOLF CUBS. *n.*

**scout·ing** (skou′ting) 1 the activities of the BOY SCOUTS. 2 ppr. of SCOUT. 1 *n.,* 2 *v.*

**scout·mas·ter** (skout′mas′tər) the man in charge of a troop of BOY SCOUTS. *n.*

**scow** (skou) a large, flat-bottomed boat, used to carry freight, and usually either towed or pushed with a pole, like a raft: *The scow was loaded with sand. n.*

**scowl** (skoul) 1 draw the eyebrows down and together and tighten the mouth, especially as an expression of anger or sullenness; frown: *She scowled at us and asked what we were doing there.* 2 an angry or sullen look. 3 express with a scowl: *She scowled her displeasure.* 1, 3 *v.,* 2 *n.* —**scowl′er,** *n.*
☞ *Syn.* See note at FROWN.

**scrab·ble** (skrab′əl) 1 scratch or scrape about with hands, claws, etc.; scramble. 2 struggle or scramble feverishly, desperately, etc.: *to scrabble for scraps of food, scrabble for a living.* 3 scrawl; scribble. 4 a scraping; scramble. 1–3 *v.,* **scrab·bled, scrab·bling;** 4 *n.*

**scrag** (skrag) 1 a lean, skinny person or animal: *An old, bony horse is a scrag.* 2 a lean, bony cut of meat, especially the lean end of a neck of mutton or veal. *n.*

**scrag·gly** (skrag′lē) rough, irregular, or ragged: *a scraggly garden. The child's hair was scraggly and matted.* *adj.*, **scrag·gli·er, scrag·gli·est.**

**scrag·gy** (skrag′ē) **1** lean; thin. **2** scraggly. *adj.*, **scrag·gi·er, scrag·gi·est.**

**scram** (skram) *Informal.* go away: *Scram! You're in the way here. She told the kids to scram.* *v.*, **scrammed, scram·ming.**

**scram·ble** (skram′bəl) **1** make one's way by climbing, crawling, etc.: *It took us half an hour to scramble up the rocky hill.* **2** a climb or walk over rough ground: *It was a long scramble through bushes and over rocks to the top of the hill.* **3** struggle with others for something: *The boys scrambled to get the football.* **4** a struggle to possess: *the scramble for wealth.* **5** any disorderly struggle or activity: *The pile of boys on the football seemed a wild scramble of arms and legs.* **6** collect in a hurry or without method. **7** mix together in a confused way. **8** cook eggs with the whites and yolks mixed together. **9** in telecommunications, break up or mix a message or signal so that it cannot be received and understood without special equipment. 1, 3, 6–9 *v.*, **scram·bled, scram·bling;** 2, 4, 5 *n.*

**scrap**¹ (skrap) **1** a small discarded or leftover piece of food: *The cook gave the scraps to the dog.* **2** a small detached or separated bit or piece: *scraps of paper, fabric scraps.* **3** a bit of something written, printed, etc.: *She read out scraps from the letter. She saves pictures and other scraps from the local newspaper.* **4** material or articles discarded as useless and fit only to be broken down, melted, etc. and reprocessed: *a yard full of iron scrap.* **5** in the form of scraps or scraps: *She buys scrap metal.* **6** throw aside as worn out or useless: *They decided to scrap their old chesterfield. The army scrapped the old tanks.* **7** condemn or abandon as useless, not worth the effort, etc.: *The missile project was scrapped.* **8 scraps,** *pl.* CRACKLINGS. 1–5, 8 *n.*, 6, 7 *v.*, **scrapped, scrap·ping.**

**scrap**² (skrap) *Informal.* **1** a fight or quarrel: *Our dog got into a scrap with the neighbour's cat again.* **2** have a scrap; fight or quarrel: *Those kids are always scrapping.* 1 *n.*, 2 *v.*, **scrapped, scrap·ping.**

**scrap·book** (skrap′buk′) a book in which pictures or clippings are pasted and kept. *n.*

**scrape** (skrāp) **1** rub with something sharp or rough; make smooth or clean thus: *Scrape your muddy shoes with this old knife.* **2** remove by rubbing with or against something sharp or rough: *I scraped some paint off the table as I pushed it through the doorway.* **3** scratch or graze by rubbing against something rough: *She fell and scraped her knee on the sidewalk.* **4** the act of scraping. **5** a scraped place. **6** rub with a harsh sound; rub harshly: *Don't scrape your feet on the floor. The branch of the tree scraped against the window.* **7** give a harsh sound; grate. **8** a harsh, grating sound: *the scrape of a saw.* **9** dig: *The child scraped a hole in the sand.* **10** collect with difficulty or a little at a time: *Emil has scraped together enough money for his first year at college.* **11** a position hard to get out of; difficulty: *Katie is always getting her friends into scrapes.* **12** bow with a drawing back of the foot. 1–3, 6, 7, 9, 10, 12 *v.*, **scraped, scrap·ing;** 4, 5, 8, 11 *n.*
**scrape acquaintance,** take the trouble to get acquainted.
**scrape along, through,** or **by,** barely get through or manage with difficulty: *That family can just scrape along but never asks for charity. She scraped through the examination.*

# scraggly 1061 scrawl

hat, āge, fär; let, ēqual, tėrm; it, īce
hot, ōpen, ôrder; oil, out; cup, pùt, rüle
above, taken, pencəl, lemən, circəs
ch, child; ng, long; sh, ship
th, thin; ŦH, then; zh, measure

Scrapers: one for cleaning mud off boots and the other for removing paint, etc.

**scrap·er** (skrā′pər) an instrument or tool for scraping: *We removed the loose paint with a scraper.* *n.*

**scrap·ing** (skrā′ping) **1** the act of a person or thing that scrapes. **2** the sound produced by this: *We could hear the scraping of the shovel against the sidewalk.* **3** Usually, **scrapings,** *pl.* that which is scraped off, together, or up: *Put the scrapings into this box.* *n.*

**scrap iron** or **metal** broken or waste pieces of old iron or other metal collected for reworking: *He buys scrap iron.*

**scrap·per** (skrap′ər) *Informal.* a person or animal that fights readily or effectively: *The way she took on that bully showed that she was a scrapper.* *n.*

**scrap·py**¹ (skrap′ē) made up of odds and ends; fragmentary; disconnected. *adj.*, **scrap·pi·er, scrap·pi·est.**

**scrap·py**² (skrap′ē) *Informal.* fond of fighting. *adj.*, **scrap·pi·er, scrap·pi·est.**

**scratch** (skrach) **1** mark or cut slightly with something sharp or rough: *Your shoes have scratched the chair.* **2** a mark made by scratching. **3** tear or dig with the nails or claws: *The cat scratched her.* **4** a very slight cut on the skin. **5** rub or scrape to relieve itching: *He scratched his head.* **6** rub with a harsh noise; rub: *She scratched a match on the wall.* **7** the sound of scratching: *the scratch of a pen.* **8** write in a hurry or carelessly. **9** strike out; draw a line through; cancel. **10** withdraw from a race or contest. **11** the starting place of a race or contest. **12** gather by effort; scrape. **13** any act of scratching. **14** made up from whatever is on hand: *a scratch meal, a scratch football team.* 1, 3, 5, 6, 8–10, 12 *v.*, 2, 4, 7, 11, 13 *n.*, 14 *adj.*
**from scratch,** with no advantages; from the beginning: *She lost her notes and so had to start her project again from scratch.*
**up to scratch,** up to standard; in good condition.

**scratch hit** in baseball, a poorly hit ball that is credited as a base hit.

**scratch pad** a pad of paper used for rough work or casual writing.

**scratch·y** (skrach′ē) **1** that scratches or scrapes: *a scratchy rosebush.* **2** giving a prickly feeling; irritating: *This woollen dress is scratchy.* **3** making a scratching noise: *a scratchy pen.* **4** consisting of or made with scratches: *a scratchy drawing.* *adj.*, **scratch·i·er, scratch·i·est.** —**scratch′i·ly,** *adv.* —**scratch′i·ness,** *n.*

**scrawl** (skrol) **1** write or draw poorly, carelessly, or hastily: *She scrawled a note on the back of an envelope.*

**scrawny** (skrôn′ē) *Informal.* lean; thin; skinny: *Turkeys have scrawny necks.* *adj.*, **scraw·ni·er, scraw·ni·est.**

**scream** (skrēm) **1** make a loud, sharp, piercing cry: *She screamed when she saw the child fall.* **2** a loud, sharp, piercing cry: *a scream of rage, screams of laughter.* **3** any loud, sharp, piercing noise: *the scream of a siren.* **4** make such a noise. **5** utter or speak very loudly: *"That's wet paint!" he screamed. We had to scream to hear each other above the music.* **6** laugh loudly or uncontrollably: *The audience screamed at his antics.* **7** *Informal.* something or somebody extremely funny: *She was a scream at the party.* **8** produce an extremely startling effect: *"War declared!" the headlines screamed.* 1, 4–6, 8 *v.*, 2, 3, 7 *n.*

**scream·er** (skrē′mər) **1** a person or thing that screams. **2** any of three species of large South American marsh bird having a plump body with mainly grey or black plumage, spurs on the front edge of the wings, and a very loud, trumpeting call: *Screamers make up a separate family of birds whose closest relatives are ducks, geese, and swans.* *n.*

**scream·ing** (skrē′ming) **1** that screams. **2** evoking screams of laughter: *a screaming farce.* **3** startling: *screaming headlines, screaming colours.* **4** ppr. of SCREAM. 1–3 *adj.*, 4 *v.*

**scream·ing·ly** (skrē′ming lē) to an extreme degree: *screamingly funny.* *adv.*

**screech** (skrēch) scream; shriek. *v., n.* —**screech′er,** *n.*

**screech owl** any of several small, closely related New World owls having hornlike tufts of feathers on the head: *Screech owls have a mournful, wailing, whistling call.*

**screech·y** (skrē′chē) SCREECHing. *adj.*, **screech·i·er, screech·i·est.**

**screed** (skrēd) **1** a long speech or piece of writing. **2** a strip of plaster or wood of the proper thickness, applied to the wall as a guide in plastering. *n.*

**screen** (skrēn) **1** a covered frame that hides, protects, or separates. **2** wire woven together with small openings in between the strands: *We have screens at our windows to keep out flies.* **3** an ornamental partition. **4** anything like a screen: *A screen of trees hides our house from the road.* **5** shelter, protect, or hide with, or as with, a screen: *She screened her face from the fire with her hand. The mother tried to screen her guilty son.* **6** a surface on which motion pictures, television images, etc. appear or are shown. **7** show a motion picture on a screen. **8** photograph with a motion-picture camera. **9** motion pictures; films. **10** adapt a story, etc. for reproduction as a motion picture. **11** be suitable for reproducing on a motion-picture screen. **12** a sieve for sifting sand, gravel, coal, seed, etc. **13** sift with a screen: *to screen sand.* **14** examine or test very carefully: *Applicants for this job must be carefully screened.* 1–4, 6, 9, 12 *n.*, 5, 7, 8, 10, 11, 13, 14 *v.* —**screen′a·ble,** *adj.* —**screen′er,** *n.* —**screen′like′,** *adj.*

**screen·ings** (skrē′ningz) the matter separated out by sifting through a sieve or screen. *n.pl.*

**screen·play** (skrēn′plā′) a story or play written for production as a motion picture, including description of characters and scenes, dialogue, action, etc. *n.*

**screen test** a short film sequence made to test a person's ability as an actor in motion pictures.

 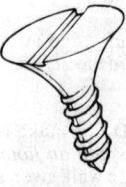 

A screw-topped jar    A screw (def. 1) for wood    A screw (def. 2) for use with a nut

**screw** (skrü) **1** a fastening device like a nail but having a ridge twisted evenly round its length and often a groove across the head: *Turn the screw to the right to tighten it.* **2** a simple machine consisting of a spiral ridge around a cylinder that acts to exert pressure in any of various ways: *Certain kinds of jack use a screw as the means for exerting the force to raise an object.* **3** a part into which this cylinder fits and advances. **4** any thing that turns like a screw or looks like one. **5** a turn of a screw; screwing motion. **6** turn as one turns a screw; twist: *Screw the lid on the jar.* **7** turn like a screw; be fitted for being put together or taken apart by a screw or screws. **8** wind; twist; contort: *His face was screwed up with fear.* **9** fasten or tighten with a screw or screws: *The carpenter screwed the hinges to the door.* **10** force, press, or stretch tight by using screws. **11** force to do something; force prices down; force people to tell or to give up; force people to tell or give up something. **12** gather for an effort: *She finally screwed up enough courage to try to dive.* **13** a propeller that moves a boat. 1–5, 13 *n.*, 6–12 *v.*
**put the screws on,** *Informal.* use pressure or force to get something.

**screw·driv·er** (skrü′drī′vər) a tool for putting in or taking out screws by turning them. *n.*

**screw propeller** a device consisting of a revolving hub with radiating, slightly twisted blades, used for propelling a steamship, aircraft, etc.

**screw thread** the spiral ridge of a screw.

**scrib·ble** (skrib′əl) **1** write or draw carelessly or hastily. **2** make marks that do not mean anything. **3** something scribbled. 1, 2 *v.*, **scrib·bled, scrib·bling;** 3 *n.*

**scrib·bler** (skrib′lər) **1** a person who scribbles. **2** a pad of paper or a book in which to make notes, do rough work, etc. **3** an author of little or no importance. *n.*

**scribe** (skrīb) **1** a person who copies manuscripts: *Before printing was invented, there were many scribes.* **2** a teacher of the Jewish law. **3** a writer; author. **4** a public clerk or secretary. **5** mark or cut with something sharp. 1–4 *n.*, 5 *v.*, **scribed, scrib·ing.**

**scrim** (skrim) lightweight, loosely woven cotton or linen fabric having a mesh weave, used for curtains. *n.*

**scrim·mage** (skrim′ij) **1** a rough fight or struggle. **2** take part in a rough fight or struggle. **3** in football, a play that takes place when the two teams are lined up and the ball is snapped back. **4** take part in such a play. 1, 3 *n.*, 2, 4 *v.*, **scrim·maged, scrim·mag·ing.**

**scrimp** (skrimp) **1** be very economical; stint; skimp: *They had to scrimp for several years to save enough for a good down payment on a house.* **2** make too small, short, or scant; be very sparing of: *to scrimp food.* **3** treat stingily or very economically. *v.*

**scrimp·y** (skrim′pē) too small; too little; scanty; meagre. *adj.*, **scrimp·i·er, scrimp·i·est.**
—**scrimp′i·ly,** *adv.* —**scrimp′i·ness,** *n.*

**scrip** (skrip) **1** a receipt, certificate, or other document showing a right to something, especially a certificate entitling the holder to a fraction of a share of stock. **2** a short piece of writing, such as a certificate, prescription, or schedule. *n.*

**script** (skript) **1** written letters, figures, signs, etc.; handwriting: *German script.* **2** a style of type that looks like handwriting. **3** the written text of a play, an actor's part, a radio or television broadcast, etc. *n.*

**scrip·to·ri·um** (skrip tô′rē əm) a writing room; especially, a room in a medieval monastery set apart for writing or copying manuscripts. *n., pl.* **scrip·to·ri·ums** or **scrip·to·ri·a** (-ē ə).

**scrip·tur·al** or **Scrip·tur·al** (skrip′chər əl) of, according to, contained in, or based on the SCRIPTURES. *adj.* —**scrip′tur·al·ly,** *adv.*

**Scrip·ture** (skrip′chər) **1** the Bible. **2 the Scriptures** or **the Holy Scriptures,** *pl.* the Bible. **3** *scripture*, any sacred writing. *n.*

**scrod** (skrod) a young COD, especially one split for cooking. *n.*

**scrof·u·la** (skrof′yə lə) a form of TUBERCULOSIS characterized by the enlargement of the lymphatic glands, especially those in the neck. *n.*

**scrof·u·lous** (skrof′yə ləs) **1** of or having to do with SCROFULA. **2** having SCROFULA. *adj.*

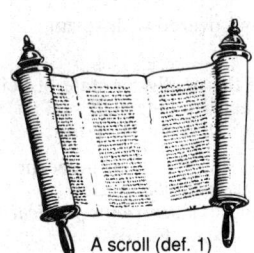 

A scroll (def. 1)   A border design using scrolls (def. 2)

**scroll** (skrōl) **1** a roll of parchment or paper, especially one with writing on it: *He slowly unrolled the scroll as he read from it.* **2** an ornament resembling a partly unrolled sheet of paper, or having a spiral or coiled form. **3** the curved head of a violin, etc. See VIOLIN for picture. **4** in computing, move the lines of writing on the screen of a computer's video display upward, down, or across, to allow room for a new line to be added. 1–3 *n.,* 4 *v.*
—**scroll′-like′,** *adj.*

**scroll·work** (skrōl′wėrk′) **1** decorative work in which SCROLLS (def. 2) are much used. **2** ornamental work in wood, cut out with a special saw. *n.*

**Scrooge** (skrüj) **1** in Dickens's story *A Christmas Carol,* an embittered old miser. **2** any mean or stingy person. *n.*

**scro·tum** (skrō′təm) in most male mammals, the pouch of skin that contains the TESTICLES. *n., pl.* **scro·ta** (-tə) or **scro·tums.**

**scrounge** (skrounj) *Informal.* **1** find or collect by hunting around: *They're out scrounging kindling for the fire.* **2** get by begging; mooch; cadge: *He was always scrounging*

---

# scrimpy 1063 scrutineer

hat, āge, fär; let, ēqual, tėrm; it, īce
hot, ōpen, ôrder; oil, out; cup, pùt, rüle
əbove, takən, pencəl, lemən, circəs
ch, child; ng, long; sh, ship
th, thin; ŦH, then; zh, measure

*cigarettes.* **3** take without permission; pilfer: *to scrounge bricks from a construction site.* **4** look around for something; forage: *She scrounged around in the drawer, looking for a pencil.* *v.,* **scrounged, scroung·ing.**
—**scroung′er,** *n.*

**scrub**[1] (skrub) **1** wash or clean by rubbing hard with a brush or cloth: *to scrub the kitchen floor.* **2** remove dirt, a spot, etc. by rubbing with a brush or cloth: *Paolo scrubbed the ink off his fingers.* **3** rub hard in cleaning: *He had to scrub to get the ink off.* **4** *Informal.* call off, especially at the last minute: *The launching was scrubbed.* **5** a scrubbing: *She gave her hands a good scrub.* 1–4 *v.,* **scrubbed, scrub·bing;** 5 *n.*

**scrub**[2] (skrub) **1** low, stunted trees or shrubs. **2** anything small, or below the usual size: *He is a little scrub of a man.* **3** small; poor; inferior: *A scrub ball team is made up of inferior, substitute, or untrained players.* **4** a player not on the regular team, etc. **5** of or for players not on the regular team. 1, 2, 4 *n.,* 3, 5 *adj.*

**scrub·by** (skrub′ē) **1** low; stunted; small; below the usual size: *scrubby trees.* **2** covered with scrub: *scrubby land.* **3** shabby; mean. *adj.,* **scrub·bi·er, scrub·bi·est.**

**scruff** (skruf) the back of the neck or the skin at the back of the neck: *She picked up the kitten by the scruff of the neck.* *n.*

**scruf·fy** (skruf′ē) unkempt, slovenly, or shabby: *That scruffy little kid is Anna's sister.* *adj.*

**scrump·tious** (skrump′shəs) *Informal.* splendid; first-rate: *a scrumptious meal.* *adj.*

**scrunch** (skrunch) **1** crunch, crush, or crumple: *He scrunched the paper into a tiny ball.* **2** hunch or squeeze: *We scrunched down behind the fence and waited.* **3** move with or make a scrunching sound: *They scrunched over the snow.* *v.*

**scru·ple** (skrü′pəl) **1** a feeling of doubt about what one ought to do: *No scruple ever holds her back from prompt action.* **2** a feeling of uneasiness that keeps a person from doing something that might be morally or ethically wrong: *She had scruples about playing cards for money.* **3** hesitate or be unwilling to do something: *A dishonest man does not scruple to deceive others.* **4** have scruples. **5** a unit of mass used by druggists, equal to 20 grains (about 1.3 g): *Three scruples make one dram.* **6** a very small amount. 1, 2, 5, 6 *n.,* 3, 4 *v.,* **scru·pled, scru·pling.**

**scru·pu·los·i·ty** (skrü′pyə los′ə tē) the quality or state of being SCRUPULOUS; scrupulousness. *n., pl.* **scru·pu·los·i·ties.**

**scru·pu·lous** (skrü′pyə ləs) **1** having or showing a strict regard for what is right; having moral integrity: *Indira was scrupulous in her dealings with customers.* **2** very careful or exact; painstaking: *scrupulous attention to detail. She worked out the plan with scrupulous care.* *adj.*
—**scru′pu·lous·ly,** *adv.*

**scru·pu·lous·ness** (skrü′pyə ləs nəs) the quality or state of being SCRUPULOUS. *n.*

**scru·ti·neer** (skrü′tə nėr′) **1** a person who represents the interests of a particular candidate or party at a polling station on election day in order to ensure that the voting procedure and counting of ballots are properly carried out.   **2** act as a scrutineer.   *1 n., 2 v.*

**scru·ti·nize** (skrü′tə nīz′)   examine closely; inspect carefully: *The jeweller scrutinized the diamond for flaws.* *v.,* **scru′ti·nized, scru′ti·niz·ing.** —**scru′ti·niz′ing·ly,** *adv.*

**scru·ti·ny** (skrü′tə nē)   a close examination; careful inspection: *His work looks all right at first glance, but it will never bear scrutiny.*   *n., pl.* **scru·ti·nies.**

**scu·ba** (skü′bə)   a portable apparatus used for breathing while swimming underwater or diving. See SKINDIVER for picture.   *n.*
☛ **Etym.** From the first letters of *s*elf-*c*ontained *u*nderwater *b*reathing *a*pparatus.

**scuba diver**   a person who uses SCUBA gear to breathe while swimming underwater or diving.

**scud** (skud)   **1** run or move swiftly: *Clouds scudded across the sky, driven by the high wind.*   **2** the action of scudding.   **3** clouds or spray driven by the wind.   *1 v.,* **scud·ded, scud·ding;**   *2, 3 n.*

**scuff** (skuf)   **1** walk without lifting the feet; shuffle. **2** wear or injure the surface of by hard use: *to scuff one's shoes.*   **3** the act of scuffing.   **4** the noise made by scuffing.   **5** a slipper having a toe piece but no covering for the heel.   *1, 2 v., 3–5 n.*

**scuf·fle** (skuf′əl)   **1** struggle or fight in a rough, confused manner, but not violently: *The children scuffled for first place in the lineup.*   **2** a confused, rough struggle or fight: *The boy lost his hat in the scuffle.*   **3** SHUFFLE. *1, 3 v.,* **scuf·fled, scuf·fling;**   *2, 3 n.*

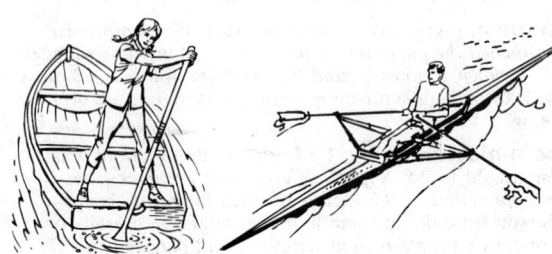

A girl sculling a boat        A man in a racing scull

**scull** (skul)   **1** an oar worked with a side twist over the end of a boat to make it go.   **2** one of a pair of oars used, one on each side, by a single rower.   **3** propel a boat by a scull or by sculls.   **4** the act of propelling by sculls.   **5** a light racing boat for one or more rowers using sculls; sculler.   *1, 2, 4, 5 n., 3 v.*
☛ **Hom.** SKULL.

**scull·er** (skul′ər)   **1** a person who SCULLS.   **2** a boat propelled by SCULLing.   *n.*

**scul·pin** (skul′pin)   any of several kinds of scale-less saltwater fish.   *n.*

**sculpt** (skulpt)   carve; sculpture: *to sculpt a statue.*   *v.*

**sculp·tor** (skulp′tər)   a person who makes figures by carving, modelling, casting, etc.; artist in SCULPTURE: *Sculptors work in marble, wood, bronze, etc.*   *n.*

**sculp·tress** (skulp′tris)   a woman who sculptures; a female artist in sculpture.   *n.*

**sculp·tur·al** (skulp′chə rəl)   of, having to do with, or like sculpture: *The fine use of light and shadow gave the painting a sculptural quality.*   *adj.* —**sculp′tur·al·ly,** *adv.*

**sculp·ture** (skulp′chər)   **1** the art or process of carving, modelling, or welding hard or plastic substances into solid figures: *Sculpture includes the cutting of statues from blocks of marble or wood, casting in bronze, and modelling in clay or wax.*   **2** carve, model, or weld into a three-dimensional work of art.   **3** sculptured work; a piece of such work: *They have a large sculpture in their living room.*   **4** change or shape by erosion: *snowbanks sculptured into strange shapes by the wind.*   **5** decorate with sculpture.   *1, 3 n., 2, 4, 5 v.,* **sculp·tured, sculp·tur·ing.**

**sculp·tured** (skulp′chərd)   **1** carved, moulded, cast, etc., in sculpture.   **2** covered or ornamented with sculpture.   **3** pt. and pp. of SCULPTURE.   *1, 2 adj., 3 v.*

**scum** (skum)   **1** a surface film formed when certain liquids are boiled: *The scum had to be skimmed from the top of the boiling maple syrup.*   **2** the layer of algae or other matter that forms on the top of still water: *Green scum floated on the water.*   **3** form scum; become covered with scum.   **4** low, worthless people; rabble.   *1, 2, 4 n., 3 v.,* **scummed, scum·ming.**

**scum·my** (skum′ē)   **1** consisting of or covered with SCUM.   **2** low; worthless.   *adj.,* **scum·mi·er, scum·mi·est.**

**scup·per** (skup′ər)   an opening in the side of a ship to let water run off the deck.   *n.*

**scurf** (skėrf)   **1** small scales of dead skin; dandruff. **2** any scaly matter on a surface.   *n.*

**scurf·y** (skėr′fē)   of, like, or covered with SCURF. *adj.,* **scurf·i·er, scurf·i·est.**

**scur·ril·i·ty** (skə ril′ə tē)   **1** the quality or state of being SCURRILOUS.   **2** indecent or abusive language.   **3** an indecent or coarse remark.   *n., pl.* **scur·ril·i·ties.**

**scur·ri·lous** (skėr′ə ləs)   **1** using coarse or indecent language; foulmouthed: *a scurrilous rabble-rouser.* **2** containing obscenities and abuse: *a scurrilous political pamphlet, a scurrilous attack.*   *adj.* —**scur′ri·lous·ly,** *adv.*   —**scur′ri·lous·ness,** *n.*

**scur·ry** (skėr′ē)   **1** run quickly; hurry: *We could hear the mice scurrying about in the walls.*   **2** a hasty running; hurrying: *With much fuss and scurry, we finally got underway.*   *1 v.,* **scur·ried, scur·ry·ing;**   *2 n., pl.* **scur·ries.**

**S–curve** (es′kėrv′)   a curve in the shape of the letter S.   *n.*

**scur·vy** (skėr′vē)   **1** a disease characterized by swollen and bleeding gums, livid spots on the skin, and prostration, due to lack of vitamin C in the diet: *Scurvy used to be common among sailors when they had little to eat except bread and salt meat.*   **2** low; mean; contemptible: *a scurvy fellow, a scurvy trick.*   *1 n., 2 adj.,* **scur·vi·er, scur·vi·est.**

**scut** (skut)   a short tail, especially that of a rabbit or deer.   *n.*

**scutch** (skuch)   **1** separate flax or cotton fibre from woody parts by beating; make fibre ready for use by beating.   **2** SCUTCHER.   *1 v., 2 n.*

**scutch·eon** (skuch′ən)   ESCUTCHEON.   *n.*

**scutch·er** (skuch′ər) an implement for SCUTCHing. *n.*

**scut·tle**[1] (skut′əl) a kind of bucket for holding or carrying coal. *n.*

**scut·tle**[2] (skut′əl) scamper; scurry. *v.*, **scut·tled, scut·tling.** —**scut′tler,** *n.*

**scut·tle**[3] (skut′əl) **1** a small opening with a lid or cover, especially in the deck or side of a ship. **2** the lid or cover for any such opening. **3** cut a hole or holes through the bottom or sides of a ship to sink it: *After the pirates captured the ship, they scuttled it.* **4** cut a hole or holes in the deck of a ship to salvage the cargo. 1, 2 *n.*, 3, 4 *v.*, **scut·tled, scut·tling.**

**scut·tle·butt** (skut′əl but′) **1** a drinking fountain or cask containing drinking water on a ship. **2** *Informal.* rumour and stories not based on fact. *n.*

**scu·tum** (skyü′təm) a shieldlike part of bone, shell, etc., as on the body of certain reptiles or insects. *n.*, *pl.* **scu·ta** (-tə).

A scythe

**scythe** (sīᴛʜ) **1** an implement used for cutting grass, grain, etc., consisting of a long, slightly curved blade set at an angle on the end of a long handle. **2** cut with a scythe. 1 *n.*, 2 *v.*, **scythed, scyth·ing.**

**S.D.** School District.

**Se** selenium.

**SE, S.E.,** or **s.e.** **1** southeast. **2** southeasterly.

**sea** (sē) **1** the great body of salt water that covers almost three fourths of the earth's surface; the ocean. **2** any large body of salt water, smaller than an ocean, partly or wholly enclosed by land: *the North Sea, the Mediterranean Sea.* **3** a large lake of fresh water. **4** a large, heavy wave: *A high sea swept away the ship's masts.* **5** the swell of the ocean. **6** an overwhelming amount or vast expanse: *a sea of trouble, a sea of faces.* *n.*
**at sea,** **a** out on the sea. **b** *Informal.* puzzled; confused: *Her complicated explanation left me even more at sea about the problem.*
**follow the sea,** be a sailor.
**go to sea,** **a** become a sailor. **b** begin a voyage.
**put to sea,** begin a voyage.
☛ *Hom.* SEE.

**sea anemone** any of numerous flowerlike, often bright-coloured polyps found especially in warm seas, having a fleshy, cylinder-shaped body with a mouth opening at the upper end surrounded by many tentacles.

**sea bass** **1** a common food fish of the Atlantic coast having a peculiar tail fin. **2** any of various similar fishes.

**sea bird** any bird that spends most of its time on or near the open sea: *Gulls, cormorants, murres, and puffins are sea birds.*

hat, āge, fär; let, ēqual, tėrm; it, īce
hot, ōpen, ôrder; oil, out; cup, put, rüle
əbove, tāken, pencəl, lemən, circəs
ch, child; ng, long; sh, ship
th, thin; ᴛʜ, then; zh, measure

**sea·board** (sē′bôrd′) **1** the land near the sea; seacoast; seashore: *the Atlantic seaboard.* **2** bordering on the sea. 1 *n.*, 2 *adj.*

**sea bread** hardtack; SHIP BISCUIT.

**sea bream** any of certain fishes belonging to the family that includes scups, porgies, etc.

**sea breeze** a breeze blowing from the sea toward the land.

**sea cadet** a person under military age who is undertaking basic naval training in an organization subsidized by the armed forces.

**sea·coast** (sē′kōst′) land along the sea. *n.*

**sea cow** **1** a manatee, dugong, or any similar mammal living in the sea. **2** walrus.

**sea cucumber** any of a group of small ECHINODERMS, most of which have flexible bodies that resemble cucumbers.

**sea dog** **1** a sailor having long experience at sea. **2** any of various seals.

**sea elephant** a kind of very large seal, the male of which has a trunklike snout.

**sea·far·er** (sē′fer′ər) a traveller on the sea, especially a sailor. *n.*

**sea·far·ing** (sē′fer′ing) **1** going, travelling, or working on the sea: *He had been a seafaring man all his life.* **2** the calling or profession of a sailor. **3** the act or fact of travelling by sea. 1 *adj.*, 2, 3 *n.*

**sea·food** (sē′füd′) edible saltwater fish and shellfish. *n.*

**sea-go·ing** (sē′gō′ing) **1** going by sea; seafaring. **2** fit for going to sea: *a sea-going merchant ship.* *adj.*

**sea green** light bluish-green.

**sea gull** any of various large gulls, especially the herring gull.

Atlantic sea horses—about 10 cm long

**sea horse** **1** any of a number of small, related sea fishes found in warm seas, having rings of scales around the body, a forward-curled tail and a horselike head set at an angle to the body: *Sea horses swim in an upright position.* **2** walrus. **3** in old stories, a sea animal with the foreparts of a horse and the hind parts of a fish.

**seal**[1] (sēl) **1** a design stamped on a piece of wax, etc. to show ownership or authenticity; a paper, circle, mark, etc. representing it: *The official seal is attached to important government papers.* **2** a stamp marking things with such a

# seal

design: *a seal with one's initials on it.* **3** a piece of wax, paper, metal, etc. on which the design is stamped. **4** mark a document with a seal; make binding or certify by affixing a seal: *The treaty was signed and sealed by both governments.* **5** close tightly; shut; fasten: *Seal the letter before mailing it. She sealed the jars of fruit. Her promise sealed her lips.* **6** close up the cracks of: *They sealed the log cabin with clay.* **7** a thing that fastens or closes something tightly. **8** something that secures; a pledge: *under seal of secrecy.* **9** something that settles or determines: *the seal of authority.* **10** settle; determine: *The judge's words sealed the prisoner's fate.* **11** give a sign that something is true: *to seal a promise with a kiss. They sealed their bargain by shaking hands.* **12** a mark; sign. **13** set apart; destine; decide beyond recall: *The king's fate was sealed.* **14** a special kind of stamp: *Christmas seals, Easter seals.* **15 the seals,** *pl.* the symbols of public office. 1–3, 7–9, 12, 14, 15 *n.,* 4–6, 10, 11, 13 *v.* —**seal′a·ble,** *adj.*
**seal off,** restrict access to by means of a seal or something acting as a seal: *The police sealed off the road.*
**set one's seal to,** **a** put one's seal on. **b** approve.

A ringed seal—about 140 cm long

**seal²** (sēl) **1** any of numerous carnivorous water mammals found especially in cold seas, having a streamlined, fur-covered body, limbs modified into flippers, and a thick layer of fat, or blubber, under the skin that provides insulation, acts as food reserve, and makes the animals more buoyant. **2** the skin or fur of a seal. **3** the leather made from the skin of a seal. **4** hunt seals. 1–3 *n., pl.* **seals** or **seal;** 4 *v.*

**sea legs** *Informal.* legs accustomed to walking steadily on a rolling or pitching ship.
**get one's sea legs,** become accustomed to the motion of a ship, especially after an initial period of seasickness.

**seal·er¹** (sē′lər) **1** something that seals, especially a substance applied to a porous surface such as wood to prevent paint or varnish from soaking in. **2** a glass jar that can be sealed, usually one holding about a litre or half a litre, used for home preserving of food. **3** an official appointed to inspect and test weights and measures. *n.*

**seal·er²** (sē′lər) **1** a person who hunts seals. **2** a ship used for hunting seals. *n.*

**sea level** the level of the surface of the sea, especially when halfway between mean high and low water. Mountains, plains, ocean beds, etc. are measured as so many metres above or below sea level. See PLATEAU for picture.

**sea lily** any of a group of crinoids that are attached to the sea bottom by a long stalk. See CRINOID for picture.

**sealing wax** a substance used for sealing letters, etc., consisting of a mixture of resin, shellac, turpentine, and pigment that is hard at normal temperatures but becomes soft when heated.

**sea lion** a large seal of the Pacific coast.

**seal·skin** (sēl′skin′) **1** the pelt or fur of a fur seal, prepared for use. **2** a garment made of this fur. *n.*

**Sea·ly·ham** (sē′lē ham′ *or* sē′lē əm) a breed of small terrier originally developed in Wales, having short legs, a rough, shaggy coat, and a square jaw. *n.*

**seam** (sēm) **1** the join formed when two pieces of cloth, canvas, leather, etc. are sewn together: *the seams of a coat, the seams of a sail.* **2** any join where edges come together: *The seams of the boat must be filled in if they leak. The seams of the carpet hardly show.* **3** join by sewing or as if by sewing. **4** any mark or line like a seam. **5** mark with lines or wrinkles: *Years of exposure to the harsh climate had seamed her face.* **6** a layer; stratum: *a seam of coal.* **7** develop cracks or fissures. 1, 2, 4, 6 *n.,* 3, 5, 7 *v.* —**seam′less,** *adj.*
☛ Hom. SEEM.

**sea·man** (sē′mən) **1** a sailor, especially one who sails the ocean. **2** a sailor who is not an officer. *n., pl.* **sea·men** (-mən).
☛ Hom. SEMEN.

**sea·man·like** (sē′mən līk′) like or fit for a good SEAMAN; having or showing seamanship. *adj.*

**sea·man·ship** (sē′mən ship′) skill in handling and navigating a ship. *n.*

**sea·mark** (sē′märk′) **1** a lighthouse, beacon, or other landmark that can be seen from the sea, used as a guide for a ship's course. **2** a line on the shore that shows the limit of the tide. *n.*

**sea·men** (sē′mən) *pl.* of SEAMAN. *n.*

**sea mew** SEA GULL.

**sea mile** NAUTICAL MILE (about 1.85 km).

**seam·stress** (sēm′stris) a woman who sews, especially one whose occupation is sewing. *n.*

**seam·y** (sē′mē) **1** least attractive or pleasant; sordid or squalid: *the seamy side of life.* **2** showing seams; especially, showing the rough edges of the seams on the inside of a garment, etc. *adj.,* **seam·i·er, seam·i·est.**

**sé·ance** (sā′äns; *French,* sā äNs′) **1** a meeting of people trying to communicate with spirits of the dead by the help of a medium. **2** any session or meeting of an organization. *n.*

**sea otter** a large marine otter of the northern Pacific coastal waters having large, flipperlike hind feet and a thick, reddish-brown or dark-brown coat. It was hunted almost to extinction for its fur and is now a rare and protected species.

A seaplane

**sea·plane** (sē′plān′) an airplane that can take off from and come down on water. *n.*

**sea·port** (sē′pôrt′) a port or harbour on the seacoast; a city or town with a harbour that ships can reach from the sea. *n.*

**sea purse** the horny case or pouch produced by certain species of fish, such as some sharks, to protect their eggs and anchor them to rocks, weeds, etc.

**sear** (sēr) **1** burn or char the surface of: *The hot iron seared his flesh.* **2** a mark made by searing. **3** make hard or unfeeling: *Years of cruelty had seared his heart.* **4** dry up; wither. **5** become dry, burned, or hard. *1, 3, 4, 5 v., 2 n.*
☛ *Hom.* SEER, SERE.

**search** (sėrch) **1** try to find by looking; seek; look for: *We searched all day for the lost cat.* **2** look through; go over carefully; examine, especially for something concealed: *The police searched the thief to see if he had a gun.* **3** the act of searching; examination: *I found my cap after a long search.* **4** look carefully at: *She searched his face for clues as to what he was thinking.* *1, 2 v., 3 n.*
**in search of,** trying to find; looking for: *They went in search of buried treasure.*
**search out,** find by searching.

**search·ing** (sėr′ching) **1** examining carefully; thorough: *a searching gaze or look, a searching examination.* **2** piercing; penetrating: *a searching wind.* **3** ppr. of SEARCH. *1, 2 adj., 3 v.* —**search′ing·ly,** *adv.*

**search·light** (sėrch′līt′) **1** a device that can throw a bright, far-reaching beam of light in any direction desired. **2** the beam of light. *n.*

**search–mas·ter** (sėrch′mas tər) the person in charge of a search-and-rescue operation. *n.*

**search warrant** a legal document authorizing the search of a house or building for stolen or contraband goods, persons wanted by the police, etc.

**sea robin** a sea fish with a large head, thickly scaled cheeks, and three pectoral rays, especially certain reddish North American species.

**sea room** space at sea free from obstruction, in which a ship can easily sail, tack, turn around, etc.

**sea rover** **1** pirate. **2** a pirate ship.

**sea·scape** (sē′skāp′) **1** a picture, often a painting, of the sea and, often, the shore. **2** a view of the sea. *n.*

**Sea Scout** a BOY SCOUT enrolled in a program of training in SEAMANSHIP.

**sea serpent** **1** a huge, snakelike sea monster often reported as having been seen in the sea, but never proven to exist. **2** a poisonous SEA SNAKE having a finlike tail.

**sea–shell** (sē′shel′) the shell of any sea mollusc, such as an oyster, conch, abalone, etc. *n.*

**sea·shore** (sē′shôr′) the land along the sea; the beach at the seaside. *n.*

**sea·sick** (sē′sik′) suffering from SEASICKNESS. *adj.*
**sea·sick·ness** (sē′sik′nis) **1** nausea and dizziness caused by the pitching and rolling of a ship at sea. **2** *Informal.* nausea and dizziness caused by any similar motion, as when travelling in a motor vehicle or aircraft or swinging in a hammock; motion sickness. *n.*

**sea·side** (sē′sīd′) **1** the land along the sea; seacoast; seashore. **2** beside the sea: *a seaside inn. n.*

**sea snake** any of a family of poisonous aquatic snakes having a laterally compressed, rudderlike tail, found in tropical seas, especially in the Indian and western Pacific oceans.

**sea·son** (sē′zən) **1** one of the four periods of the year; spring, summer, autumn, or winter. **2** any period of time marked by something special: *the holiday season, the harvest season.* **3** the time when something is occurring, active, at its best, or in fashion: *the baseball season.* **4** a period of time: *a season of rest.* **5** the period of the year

## sear 1067 seat

hat, āge, fär; let, ēqual, tėrm; it, īce
hot, ōpen, ôrder; oil, out; cup, pu̇t, rüle
əbove, takən, pencəl, lemən, circəs
ch, child; ng, long; sh, ship
th, thin; ᴛʜ, then; zh, measure

when a place is most frequented or active: *the Ottawa season.* **6** a suitable or fit time: *the duck-hunting season, the spawning season.* **7** add flavour to: *to season soup with salt.* **8** give interest or character to: *to season conversation with wit.* **9** make fit for use by a period of keeping or treatment: *Wood is seasoned for building by being dried and hardened.* **10** become fit for use. **11** accustom; make used: *Soldiers are seasoned to battle by experience in war.* **12** make less severe; soften: *Season justice with mercy.* *1–6 n., 7–12 v.* —**sea′son·er,** *n.*
**for a season,** for a time.
**in good season,** early enough.
**in season, a** at the right or proper time. **b** in the time or condition for eating, hunting, etc. **c** early enough.
**in season and out of season,** at all times.
**out of season,** not in season.
☛ *Usage.* The names of the seasons—*spring, summer, fall* (or *autumn*), and *winter*—are not normally capitalized: *We are going to move next spring. We shall all relax when summer comes.*

**sea·son·a·ble** (sē′zə nə bəl) **1** suitable to the season: *Hot weather is seasonable in July.* **2** coming at the right or proper time: *The second expedition brought seasonable aid to the men who had survived the first.* *adj.* —**sea′son·a·ble·ness,** *n.* —**sea′son·a·bly,** *adv.*

**sea·son·al** (sē′zə nəl) **1** of, having to do with, or occurring in a particular season: *seasonal variations in the weather, seasonal rains.* **2** depending on or affected by the season: *seasonal unemployment, a seasonal worker.* *adj.* —**sea′son·al·ly,** *adv.*

**sea·son·ing** (sē′zə ning) **1** something that is added to food to give extra flavour: *Salt, pepper, spices, and herbs are used as seasonings.* **2** anything that adds interest or character. **3** ppr. of SEASON. *1, 2 n., 3 v.*

**season ticket** a ticket that gives its holder the right to attend a series of games or entertainments, or to make a certain daily trip on a railway for a stated period of time, etc.

**sea squirt** a small, soft-bodied sea animal that squirts water when it contracts.

**seat¹** (sēt) **1** something to sit on. **2** a place to sit. **3** a place in which one has the right to sit: *We have reserved seats in the first balcony.* **4** a right to sit as a member of a legislature, city council, stock exchange, etc.: *The Liberals lost ten seats in the last election.* **5** that part of a chair, bench, stool, etc. on which one sits: *This bench has a broken seat.* **6** that part of the body on which one sits, or the clothing covering it: *The seat of his trousers was patched.* **7** a manner of sitting on horseback: *That rider has a good seat.* **8** that on which anything rests; base. **9** set or place on a seat: *to seat a person on a chair.* **10** have seats for a specified number: *Our school auditorium seats one thousand pupils.* **11** provide with a seat or seats. **12** put a seat on. *1–8 n., 9–12 v.*
**be seated, a** sit down. **b** be sitting. **c** be situated.

**seat²** (sēt) **1** an established place or centre: *A university is a seat of learning. Canada's seat of government is in Ottawa.* **2** the throne of a king, etc.; authority or dignity of a king, etc. **3** a residence; home: *The family seat of*

**the Howards is in Kent.** **4** fix in a particular or proper place; settle; locate. 1–3 *n.*, 4 *v.*

**seat belt** in an automobile or aircraft, a belt or arrangement of straps designed to hold an occupant in the seat in case of a crash, jolt, bump, etc.

**sea trout** **1** any of various species of trout found in salt water. **2** any of several WEAKFISHES.

**sea urchin** any of a group of small, round sea animals having spiny shells.

**sea wall** a strong wall or embankment made to prevent the waves from wearing away the shore, to act as a breakwater, etc.

**sea·ward** (sē′wərd) **1** toward the sea: *a seaward view (adj.). Our house faces seaward (adv.).* **2** the direction toward the sea: *The island lies one kilometre to seaward.* 1 *adv., adj.,* 2 *n.*

**sea·wards** (sē′wərdz) SEAWARD (def. 1). *adv.*

**sea·way** (sē′wā′) **1** a way or route over the ocean. **2** the progress of a ship through the waves. **3** a rough sea. **4** an inland waterway that connects with the sea and is deep enough to permit ocean shipping: *Ocean liners reach Toronto by passing through the St. Lawrence Seaway.* *n.*

**sea·weed** (sē′wēd′) any plant or plants growing in the sea, especially a sea alga such as kelp. *n.*

**sea·wor·thy** (sē′wėr′ᴛнē) fit for sailing on the sea; able to stand storms at sea: *a seaworthy ship.* *adj.*

**se·ba·ceous** (si bā′shəs) **1** of, having to do with, or being fat; fatty. **2** producing SEBUM: *sebaceous glands.* See EPIDERMIS for picture. *adj.*

**se·ba·go** (si bā′gō) a kind of Atlantic salmon found in freshwater lakes in New Brunswick and Nova Scotia. *n.*

**se·bum** (sē′bəm) the oily substance produced by the sebaceous glands to lubricate the skin and hair. *n.*

**sec.** **1** secretary. **2** second; seconds. **3** section; sections.

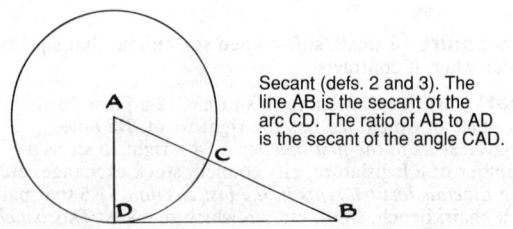

Secant (defs. 2 and 3). The line AB is the secant of the arc CD. The ratio of AB to AD is the secant of the angle CAD.

**se·cant** (sē′kənt) **1** in geometry, a line that intersects a curve at two or more points. **2** a straight line drawn from the centre of a circle through one extremity of an arc to the tangent from the other extremity of the same arc. **3** the ratio of the length of this line to the length of the radius of the circle. **4** the ratio of the length of the hypotenuse of a right-angled triangle to the length of the side adjacent to an acute angle. See SINE for picture. **5** intersecting. 1–4 *n.,* 5 *adj.*

**se·cede** (si sēd′) withdraw formally from an organization, especially a church or a political federation. *v.,* **se·ced·ed, se·ced·ing.**

**se·ces·sion** (si sesh′ən) a formal withdrawing from an organization or nation. *n.*

**se·ces·sion·ism** (si sesh′ə niz′əm) the principles or policy of those in favour of SECESSION. *n.*

**se·ces·sion·ist** (si sesh′ə nist) **1** a person who believes that SECESSION is a right. **2** a person who takes part in a SECESSION. *n.*

**se·clude** (si klüd′) shut off or keep apart from others; isolate: *Moranna has secluded herself and no longer accepts visitors.* *v.,* **se·clud·ed, se·clud·ing.**

**se·clud·ed** (si klü′did) **1** shut off from others; undisturbed: *a secluded cottage, a secluded life.* **2** pt. and pp. of SECLUDE. 1 *adj.,* 2 *v.*

**se·clu·sion** (si klü′zhən) **1** a keeping apart or being shut off from others; retirement: *She lives in seclusion apart from her friends.* **2** a secluded place. *n.*

**se·clu·sive** (si klü′siv) **1** fond of SECLUSION. **2** tending to SECLUDE. *adj.* —**se·clu′sive·ness,** *n.*

**sec·ond**[1] (sek′ənd) **1** next after the 1st; 2nd: *the second seat from the front.* **2** next below the first in rank, authority, etc.: *the second officer on a ship.* **3** another; other: *Napoleon has been called a second Caesar.* **4** in the second group, division, rank, etc.; secondly. **5** a person or thing that is second. **6** a person who supports or aids another; backer: *The prize fighter had a second.* **7** support; back up; assist: *to second another person's idea.* **8** express approval or support of: *One member made a motion to adjourn the meeting, and another seconded it.* **9** in music, lower in pitch. **10** rendering a part lower in pitch: *second soprano.* **11** the second, or lower, part in a composition. **12** a voice or instrument rendering such a part. **13** a tone on the next degree from a given tone. **14** the interval between the two tones. **15** the harmonic combination of such tones. **16** the second note in a scale. **17** in automobiles and similar machines, the forward gear or speed next above first. **18** inferior: *cloth of second quality.* **19** seconds, *pl.* articles below first quality: *Seconds have some defect.* 1–3, 9, 10, 18 *adj.,* 4 *adv.,* 5, 6, 11–17, 19 *n.,* 7, 8 *v.* —**sec′ond·er,** *n.*

**sec·ond**[2] (sek′ənd) **1** an SI unit for measuring time: *There are sixty seconds in one minute, sixty minutes in one hour, and twenty-four hours in one day. The second is one of the seven base units in the SI. Symbol:* s **2** any short period of time: *I'll be with you in a second.* **3** a unit used with the SI for measuring plane angles: *There are sixty seconds in one minute and sixty minutes in one degree. Symbol:* ″ *n.*

**sec·ond·ar·y** (sek′ən der′ē) **1** next after the first in order, place, time, etc. **2** not main or chief; having less importance: *Reading quickly is secondary to reading well.* **3** a person or thing that is secondary, second in importance, or subordinate. **4** not original; derived. **5** a coil or circuit in which a current is produced by induction. **6** noting or having to do with such a coil or circuit. 1, 2, 4, 6 *adj.,* 3, 5 *n., pl.* **sec·ond·ar·ies.** —**sec′ond·ar′i·ly,** *adv.*

**secondary accent** SECONDARY STRESS.

**secondary colour** a colour produced by mixing two or more primary colours. Compare with PRIMARY COLOUR.

**secondary school** a school attended after elementary or junior high school; a high school or collegiate institute.

**secondary stress** **1** a stress that is weaker than the strongest stress in a word (primary stress), but stronger than weak stress: *The second syllable of* ab′bre′vi·a′tion *has*

a *secondary stress.* **2** a mark, such as ('), used to show where this stress falls.
☛ *Usage.* In this dictionary, primary and secondary stresses are shown, but unstressed syllables are not marked.

**second childhood** a period or state of mental decline associated with old age; DOTAGE.

**sec·ond–class** (sek′ənd klas′) **1** of, having to do with, or belonging to a class ranking next below the first or highest. **2** having to do with or referring to the grade of travel accommodation next below the best: *a second-class ticket, a second-class cabin.* **3** with second-class accommodation: *to travel second-class.* **4** of inferior quality or grade: *Their products are definitely second-class.* **5** not enjoying the full rights of the majority: *second-class citizens.* **6** referring to a mail classification that includes newspapers and periodicals sent to subscribers. 1, 2, 4–6 *adj.*, 3 *adv.*

**second growth** **1** a crop of grass or hay that comes up after the first crop has been cut. **2** a new growth of trees in an area where virgin forest has been cut or burned.

**sec·ond–guess** (sek′ənd ges′) *Informal.* solve a problem, criticize, etc., by using HINDSIGHT. *v.*

**second hand** a hand on a clock or watch, pointing to the seconds.

**sec·ond–hand** (sek′ənd hand′) **1** not original; obtained from another: *second-hand information.* **2** not new; used already by someone else: *second-hand clothes. adj.*

**sec·ond·ly** (sek′ən dlē) in the second place. *adv.*

**second mortgage** additional funding lent on the security of property such as a house. It has second claim on the property, the first mortgage having the prior claim.

**second nature** a habit, quality, knowledge, etc. that a person has acquired and had for so long that it seems to be almost a part of his or her nature.

**second person** the form of a pronoun or verb used to indicate the person spoken to. *You, your* and *yours* are the second person.

**sec·ond–rate** (sek′ən drāt′) of inferior quality or value; mediocre: *a second-rate diamond, a second-rate author. adj.*

**second sight** the power to see distant objects or future events; clairvoyance.

**second wind** **1** a recovery or renewal of breath and energy following the initial feeling of exhaustion during an effort, as in running a race. **2** any recovery or renewal of energy: *The rise in steel production faltered in early spring and then got its second wind.*

**se·cre·cy** (sē′krə sē) **1** being secret: *The outcome remains a secrecy.* **2** being kept secret: *It needs no secrecy.* **3** the act or habit of keeping things secret: *They relied on her secrecy. n., pl.* **se·cre·cies.**

**se·cret** (sē′krit) **1** kept from the knowledge of others: *a secret marriage.* **2** keeping to oneself what one knows: *Be as secret as you can.* **3** known only to a few: *a secret society.* **4** kept from sight; hidden: *a secret drawer.* **5** retired; secluded: *a secret place.* **6** working or acting in secret: *a secret agent, secret police.* **7** very hard to understand or discover. **8** something secret or hidden; mystery. **9** something known only to a few. **10** a hidden cause or reason. 1–7 *adj.*, 8–10 *n.*
—**se′cret·ly**, *adv.*
**in secret,** in private; not openly.

**sec·re·tar·i·al** (sek′rə ter′ē əl) of a secretary; having

# second childhood     1069     sectarian

hat, āge, fär; let, ēqual, tėrm; it, īce
hot, ōpen, ôrder; oil, out; cup, pùt, rüle
əbove, takən, pencəl, lemən, circəs
ch, child; ng, long; sh, ship
th, thin; ŦH, then; zh, measure

to do with a secretary: *She learned keyboarding, filing, and other secretarial work. adj.*

**sec·re·tar·i·at** (sek′rə ter′ē it) **1** the office or position of secretary. **2** the administrative unit controlled by a secretary or secretary-general: *the United Nations Secretariat.* **3** a group of secretaries. **4** a place where a secretary transacts business. *n.*

**sec·re·tar·y** (sek′rə ter′ē) **1** someone who writes letters, keeps records, etc. for a person, company, club, etc.: *The secretary of our club keeps the minutes of the meeting.* **2** in some countries, a person who administers a department of the government. **3** a writing desk with a set of drawers, often having shelves for books. *n., pl.* **sec·re·tar·ies.**

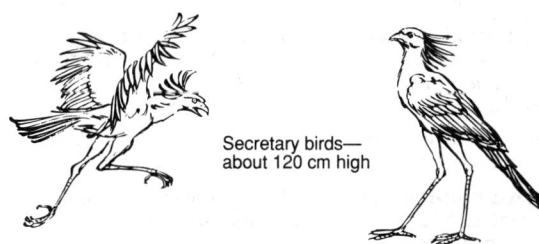
Secretary birds— about 120 cm high

**secretary bird** a large, long-legged African bird of prey that feeds on reptiles, so-called because its crest suggests pens stuck over the ear.

**sec·re·tar·y–gen·er·al** (sek′rə ter′ē jen′ə rəl) the chief or senior secretary; the administrator or head of a SECRETARIAT (def. 2): *the Secretary-General of the United Nations. n., pl.* **sec·re·tar·ies–gen·er·al.**

**se·crete** (si krēt′) **1** keep secret; hide. **2** produce and release: *Glands in the mouth secrete saliva. v.*, **se·cret·ed, se·cret·ing.**

**se·cre·tion** (si krē′shən) **1** a substance that is secreted by some part of an animal or plant: *Bile is the secretion of the liver.* **2** the producing and releasing of such a substance. **3** the act of concealing; hiding. *n.*

**se·cre·tive** (sē′krə tiv *or* si krē′tiv *for 1,* si krē′tiv *for 2*) **1** having the habit of secrecy; not frank and open. **2** causing or aiding SECRETION. *adj.*
—**se·cre′tive·ly,** *adv.* —**se·cre′tive·ness,** *n.*

**secret society** an association of which some ceremonies and activities are known only to members.

**secs.** **1** seconds. **2** sections.

**sect** (sekt) **1** a group of people having the same principles, beliefs, or opinions. **2** a group of people that forms part of a larger religious body but rejects some of the larger body's beliefs or customs: *The Protestant church used to have many different sects. The Shiites are an Islamic sect. n.*

**sect.** **1** section. **2** sectional.

**sec·tar·i·an** (sek ter′ē ən) **1** of or having to do with a SECT. **2** characteristic of one SECT only; strongly prejudiced in favour of a certain sect. **3** a devoted

**sectarianism** member of a SECT, especially a narrow-minded or strongly prejudiced member. **4** a member of a religious group separated from an established church. *1, 2 adj., 3, 4 n.*

**sec·tar·i·an·ism** (sek ter′ē ə niz′əm) the spirit or tendencies of SECTARIANS; adherence or too great devotion to a particular sect. *n.*

**sec·tion** (sek′shən) **1** a part; division; slice: *Divide the cake into sections. Her section of the family estate was larger than her sister's.* **2** a division of a book: *Chapter X has seven sections.* **3** a region; part of a country, city, etc.: *The city has a business section and a residential section.* **4** the act of cutting. **5** cut into sections; divide into sections: *to section an orange.* **6** a view of a thing as it would appear if cut straight through; cross section. **7** a district or tract of land one mile square; 640 acres (about 260 ha): *She farms two sections near Regina.* **8** a part of a railway line kept up by one group of workmen. **9** a part of a sleeping car containing an upper and a lower berth. **10** a small formation of soldiers: *A section is smaller than a platoon and is usually commanded by a corporal.* *1–4, 6–10 n., 5 v.*

**sec·tion·al** (sek′shə nəl) **1** having to do with a particular SECTION (def. 3); local. **2** made of SECTIONS (def. 1): *a sectional bookcase.* *adj.* —**sec′tion·al·ly,** *adv.*

**sec·tion·al·ism** (sek′shə nə liz′əm) too great regard for sectional interest; sectional prejudice or hatred. *n.*

**sec·tion·al·ize** (sek′shə nə līz′) **1** make sectional. **2** divide into sections. *v.,* **sec·tion·al·ized, sec·tion·al·iz·ing.**

**sec·tor** (sek′tər) **1** the part of a circle between two radii and the included arc. **2** a clearly defined military area that a given military unit protects or covers with fire; the part of a front held by a military unit. **3** an instrument consisting of two rulers connected by a joint: *A sector is used in measuring or drawing angles.* *n.*

**sec·u·lar** (sek′yə lər) **1** worldly, not religious or sacred: *secular music, a secular education.* **2** living in the world; not belonging to a religious order: *the secular clergy, a secular priest.* **3** a secular priest. **4** occurring once in an age; lasting for an age or century. **5** lasting through long ages; going on from age to age. *1, 2, 4, 5 adj., 3 n.* —**sec′u·lar·ly,** *adv.*

**sec·u·lar·ism** (sek′yə lə riz′əm) **1** SCEPTICISM in regard to religion. **2** opposition to the introduction of religion into public schools or other public affairs. *n.*

**sec·u·lar·ist** (sek′yə lə rist) a believer in SECULARISM. *n.*

**sec·u·lar·i·ty** (sek′yə lar′ə tē *or* sek′yə ler′ə tē) a SECULAR spirit or quality; worldliness. *n.*

**sec·u·lar·ize** (sek′yə lə rīz′) **1** make secular or worldly; separate from religious connection or influence: *to secularize the schools.* **2** transfer property from the possession of the church to that of the government. *v.,* **sec·u·lar·ized, sec·u·lar·iz·ing.** —**sec′u·lar·i·za′tion,** *n.*

**se·cure** (si kyúr′) **1** safe against loss, attack, escape, etc.: *This is a secure hiding place. Land in a growing city is a secure investment. Keep the prisoner secure within his cell.* **2** make safe; protect: *Every loan was secured by bonds or mortgages.* **3** make oneself safe; be safe: *We must secure against the dangers of the coming storm.* **4** sure; certain; that can be counted on: *We know in advance that our victory is secure.* **5** make something sure or certain. **6** free from care or fear: *She hoped for a secure old age.* **7** firmly fastened; not likely to give way: *The boards of this bridge do not look secure.* **8** make firm or fast: *Secure the locks on the windows.* **9** get; obtain: *Secure your tickets early.* *1, 4, 6, 7 adj., 2, 3, 5, 8, 9 v.,* **se·cured, se·cur·ing.** —**se·cur′a·ble,** *adj.* —**se·cure′ly,** *adv.*

**se·cu·ri·ty** (si kyür′ə tē) **1** freedom from danger, care, or fear; feeling or condition of being safe: *You may cross the street in security when a police officer holds up her hand.* **2** certainty. **3** carelessness; overconfidence. **4** something that secures or makes safe: *My watchdog is a security against burglars.* **5** something given as a guarantee that a person will be able to pay back a loan or fulfil some duty, promise, etc.: *A life-insurance policy may serve as security for a loan.* **6** a person who agrees to be responsible for another: *Mother was security for Ms. Visanji.* **7 securities,** *pl.* bond or stock certificates: *These railway securities can be sold for $5000.* *n., pl.* **se·cu·ri·ties.**

**secy.** secretary.

**se·dan** (si dan′) **1** a closed automobile seating four or more persons. **2** SEDAN CHAIR. *n.*

A sedan chair

**sedan chair** a covered chair carried on two poles by two men: *Sedan chairs were used in the 17th and 18th centuries.*

**se·date** (sə dāt′) **1** quiet; calm; serious: *She is very sedate for a child and would rather read or sew than play.* **2** make calm, as with a drug: *The grieving widow had to be sedated.* *1 adj., 2 v.,* **se·dat·ed, se·dat·ing.** —**se·date′ly,** *adv.* —**se·date′ness,** *n.*

**se·da·tion** (sə dā′shən) in medicine: **1** the producing of a relaxed state by means of a SEDATIVE; treatment with sedatives. **2** a relaxed or painless state produced by SEDATIVES. *n.*

**sed·a·tive** (sed′ə tiv) **1** a medicine that lessens pain or excitement. **2** lessening pain or excitement. **3** anything soothing or calming. **4** soothing; calming. *1, 3 n., 2, 4 adj.*

**sed·en·tar·y** (sed′ən ter′ē) **1** used to sitting still much of the time: *Sedentary people get little physical exercise.* **2** that keeps one sitting still much of the time: *Bookkeeping is a sedentary occupation.* **3** moving little and rarely. **4** fixed to one spot. **5** not migratory: *Pigeons are sedentary birds.* *adj.* —**sed′en·tar′i·ly,** *adv.* —**sed′en·tar′i·ness,** *n.*

**Se·der** (sā′dər) the religious rites and feast held in Jewish homes on the first two nights of PASSOVER. *n., pl.* **Se·ders** *or* **Se·dar·im** (se dä rēm′ *or* se də rēm′).

**sedge** (sej) any of a large family of grasslike plants that grow in marshes, bogs, and shallow water, having solid, often triangular, stems, long, narrow leaves, and spikelets of tiny, petal-less flowers: *Bulrushes are sedges.* *n.*

**sedg·y** (sej′ē) **1** abounding in or covered with SEDGE; bordered with sedge: *a sedgy brook.* **2** like SEDGE. *adj.*

**sed·i·ment** (sed′ə mənt) **1** matter that settles to the bottom of a liquid; dregs. **2** earth, stones, etc., deposited by water, wind, or ice: *Each year the Nile overflows and deposits sediment on the land.* *n.*

**sed·i·mental** (sed′ə men′təl) SEDIMENTARY. *adj.*

**sed·i·men·ta·ry** (sed′ə men′tə rē) **1** of SEDIMENT; having to do with sediment. **2** in geology, referring to rock that is made up of SEDIMENT, fragments of older rock, or organic materials: *Shale is a kind of sedimentary rock.* *adj.*

**sed·i·men·ta·tion** (sed′ə men tā′shən) a depositing of SEDIMENT. *n.*

**se·di·tion** (si dish′ən) speech or action causing discontent or rebellion against the government; incitement to discontent or rebellion. *n.*

**se·di·tion·ar·y** (si dish′ə ner′ē) **1** having to do with or involving SEDITION. **2** one guilty of SEDITION. 1 *adj.*, 2 *n.*

**se·di·tious** (si dish′əs) **1** stirring up discontent or rebellion. **2** taking part in SEDITION; guilty of sedition. **3** having to do with SEDITION. *adj.* —se·di′tious·ly, *adv.*

**se·duce** (si dyüs′ *or* si düs′) **1** tempt to wrongdoing; persuade to do wrong: *The traitor was seduced by the offer of great wealth to betray his country.* **2** lead away from virtue; lead astray; beguile. **3** entice to a surrender of chastity. *v.*, se·duced, se·duc·ing. —se·duc′er, *n.*

**se·duc·tion** (si duk′shən) **1** the act of seducing; the fact or condition of being SEDUCEd. **2** something that SEDUCES; temptation; attraction. *n.*

**se·duc·tive** (si duk′tiv) alluring; captivating; charming. *adj.* —se·duc′tive·ly, *adv.* —se·duc′tive·ness, *n.*

**se·du·li·ty** (si dyü′lə tē *or* si dü′lə tē) the quality of being SEDULOUS; diligent application or care. *n.*

**sed·u·lous** (sej′ə ləs) hard-working; diligent; painstaking. *adj.* —sed′u·lous·ly, *adv.* —sed′u·lous·ness, *n.*

**se·dum** (sē′dəm) any of a large group of fleshy plants, most of which have clusters of yellow, white, or pink flowers. *n.*

**see**[1] (sē) **1** perceive with the eyes; look at: *See that black cloud.* **2** use the eyes to see things: *to see a tennis match.* **3** have the power of sight: *The blind do not see.* **4** perceive with the mind; understand: *I see what you mean.* **5** find out; learn: *I will see what needs to be done.* **6** take care; make sure: *See that you lock the back door.* **7** have knowledge or experience of: *That coat has seen hard wear.* **8** attend; escort; go with: *to see a girl home.* **9** meet; have a talk with; call on: *She wishes to see you alone. I went to see a friend.* **10** receive a visit from: *She is too ill to see anyone.* **11** visit; attend: *We saw the Canadian National Exhibition.* **12** in poker, etc., meet a bet by staking an equal sum. *v.*, saw, seen, see·ing.
**see fit,** consider to be reasonable: *They saw fit to accept.*
**see into,** understand the real character or hidden purpose of.
**see off,** go with to the starting place of a journey.
**see out,** go through with; finish.
**see through, a** understand the real character or hidden purpose of. **b** go through with; finish. **c** watch over or help through a difficulty: *June's mother saw her through her illness.*

hat, āge, fär; let, ēqual, tėrm; it, īce hot, ōpen, ôrder; oil, out; cup, pút, rüle
əbove, takən, pencəl, lemən, circəs
ch, child; ng, long; sh, ship
th, thin; ŦH, then; zh, measure

**see to,** look after; take care of.
☞ *Hom.* SEA.

**see**[2] (sē) **1** the position or authority of a bishop. **2** the district under a bishop's authority; diocese; bishopric. *n.*
☞ *Hom.* SEA.

**seed** (sēd) **1** the thing from which a flower, vegetable, or other plant grows; small, grainlike fruit: *Farmers often save part of a crop for the seeds.* **2** a bulb, sprout, or any part of a plant from which a new plant will grow. **3** of or containing seeds; used for seeds. **4** sow with seeds; scatter seeds over: *The farmer seeded his field with corn.* **5** sow seeds. **6** produce seeds; shed seeds. **7** remove the seeds from: *She seeded the grapes for the salad.* **8** the source or beginning of anything: *seeds of trouble.* **9** children; descendants: *We are all the seed of our parents.* **10** semen; sperm. **11** in tournaments, arrange the names of players according to a preliminary ranking so that the best players do not meet in the early matches. **12** scatter chemicals into clouds from an airplane in an effort to produce rain artificially. **13** a player of high ranking in a tennis tournament. **14** give a tennis player high ranking. 1, 2, 8–10, 13 *n.*, *pl.* **seeds** *or* **seed;** 3 *adj.*, 4–7, 11, 12, 14 *v.* —seed′less, *adj.* —seed′like, *adj.*
**go to seed, a** come to the time of yielding seeds: *Dandelions go to seed when their heads turn white.* **b** come to the end of vigour, usefulness, prosperity, etc.: *After the mines closed, the town went to seed.*
☞ *Hom.* CEDE.

**seed·case** (sēd′kās′) any pod, capsule, or other dry, hollow fruit that contains seeds. *n.*

**seed coat** the outer layer protecting the seed from damage and water loss.

**seed·er** (sē′dər) **1** one that seeds. **2** a machine or device for planting seeds. **3** a machine or device for removing seeds. *n.*
☞ *Hom.* CEDAR.

**seed·i·ness** (sē′dē nis) a SEEDY condition. *n.*

**seed leaf** the embryo leaf in the seed of a plant; COTYLEDON.

**seed·ling** (sēd′ling) **1** a young plant grown from a seed. **2** a young tree less than one metre high. *n.*

**seed pearl** a very small pearl.

**seed plant** any plant that bears seeds: *Most seed plants have flowers and produce seeds in fruits; some, such as the pines, form seeds on cones.*

**seeds·man** (sēdz′mən) **1** a sower of seed. **2** a dealer in seed. *n.*, *pl.* **seeds·men** (-zmən).

**seed vessel** any pod, capsule, or other hollow fruit that contains seeds; PERICARP.

**seed·y** (sē′dē) **1** full of seed. **2** gone to seed. **3** *Informal.* shabby; no longer fresh or new: *seedy clothes.* *adj.*, **seed·i·er, seed·i·est.** —seed′i·ly, *adv.*

**see·ing** (sē′ing) **1** in view of the fact; considering: *Seeing it is 10 o'clock, we will wait no longer.* **2** ppr. of SEE. 1 *conj.*, 2 *v.*

**Seeing Eye** an organization that breeds and trains dogs as guides for blind people.

**seeing–eye dog** a dog trained as a guide for blind people.

**seek** (sēk) **1** try to find; look for: *We are seeking a home.* **2** hunt; search: *to seek for something lost.* **3** try to get: *Friends sought her advice.* **4** try; attempt: *She seeks to make peace.* **5** go to: *He sought his bed early.* *v.,* **sought, seek·ing.**
☛ *Hom.* SIKH.

**seem** (sēm) **1** appear; appear to be: *He seemed a very old man.* **2** appear to oneself: *I still seem to hear the music.* **3** appear to exist: *There seems no need to wait longer.* **4** appear to be true or to be the case: *It seems likely to rain. This, it seems, is your idea of cleaning a room.* *v.*
☛ *Hom.* SEAM.

**seem·ing** (sē′ming) **1** apparent; that appears to be: *a seeming advantage.* **2** appearance: *It was worse in its seeming than in reality.* **3** ppr. of SEEM. 1 *adj.*, 2 *n.*, 3 *v.*

**seem·ing·ly** (sē′ming lē) apparently; as far as appearances go: *This hill is, seemingly, the highest around here.* *adv.*

**seem·li·ness** (sēm′li nis) fitness; suitability; propriety; decorum. *n.*

**seem·ly** (sēm′lē) **1** suitable; proper: *Some old people do not consider modern dances seemly.* **2** having a pleasing appearance. **3** properly; becomingly; fittingly: *Try to behave seemly.* 1, 2 *adj.*, **seem·li·er, seem·li·est;** 3 *adv.*

**seen** (sēn) pp. of SEE¹: *Have you seen Joanna?* *v.*
☛ *Hom.* SCENE.

**seep** (sēp) ooze; trickle; leak: *Water seeps through sand.* *v.*

**seep·age** (sē′pij) **1** a seeping; slow leakage. **2** moisture or liquid that seeps: *We found a centimetre of seepage in the cellar.* *n.*

**seer** (sēr) a person who foresees or foretells future events; prophet. *n.*
☛ *Hom.* SEAR, SERE.

**seer·suck·er** (sēr′suk′ər) cloth with alternate stripes of plain and crinkled material. *n.*

**see·saw** (sē′so′) **1** TEETER-TOTTER. **2** move up and down or back and forth. **3** moving up and down or back and forth: *the seesaw of a pitching ship.* 1, 3 *n.*, 1, 2 *v.*

**seethe** (sēᴛʜ) **1** be excited; be disturbed: *The pirate crew was seething with discontent and ready for mutiny.* **2** bubble and foam: *Water seethed under the falls.* **3** soak; steep. **4** boil. *v.,* **seethed, seeth·ing.**

**seg·ment** (seg′mənt) **1** a part cut, marked, or broken off; division; section: *Some oranges are easily pulled apart into segments.* **2** in geometry, a part of a circle, sphere, etc. cut off by a line or plane: *A segment of a circle is an area that is bounded or cut off by a chord.* **3** divide into segments. 1, 2 *n.*, 3 *v.*

**seg·men·tal** (seg men′təl) **1** composed of SEGMENTS. **2** of or having to do with SEGMENTS. **3** having the form of a SEGMENT of a circle. *adj.* —**seg·men′tal·ly,** *adv.*

**seg·men·ta·tion** (seg′mən tā′shən) **1** a division into SEGMENTS. **2** the growth and division of a cell into two, four, eight cells, and so on. *n.*

**seg·re·gate** (seg′rə gāt′ *for verb,* seg′rə git *or* seg′rə gāt′ *for adjective*) **1** separate from others; set apart; isolate: *The doctor segregated the child with mumps to protect the other patients.* **2** separate from the rest and collect in one place. **3** separate or keep apart one racial group from another or from the rest of society especially in schools, public facilities, etc. **4** segregated. 1–3 *v.,* **seg·re·gat·ed, seg·re·gat·ing;** 4 *adj.*

**seg·re·ga·tion** (seg′rə gā′shən) **1** a separation from others; setting apart; isolation: *the segregation of lepers.* **2** the separation of one racial group from another or from the rest of society, especially in schools, theatres, etc. **3** something separated or set apart; an isolated part, group, etc. *n.*

**seg·re·ga·tion·ist** (seg′rə gā′shə nist) one who believes in the separation of racial groups, especially of black people from white people. *n.*

**seg·re·ga·tive** (seg′rə gā′tiv) **1** tending to SEGREGATE. **2** keeping apart from others; unsociable. *adj.*

**seiche** (sāsh) a random movement in a body of water produced by earthquake, wind, etc., and causing variation in the water level. *n.*

**sei·gneur** or **seign·ior** (sē nyėr′; *French,* se nyœʀ′) **1** in French Canada, a person granted a SEIGNEURY; landowner. **2** a feudal lord or landowner. A **grand seigneur** was a person of high rank, or one who behaved as a person of high rank should. *n.*

**sei·gneur·y** or **seign·ior·y** (sē′nyə rē; *French,* se nyœ ʀē′) in French Canada, a tract of land or an estate originally granted to an individual by the King of France. *n., pl.* **seign·eur·ies** or **sei·gnior·ies.**

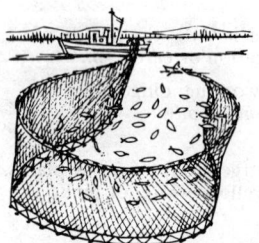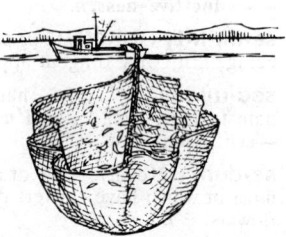

A purse seine, used for commercial fishing

**seine** (sān) **1** a fishing net that hangs straight down in the water: *A seine has floats at the upper edge and sinkers at the lower.* **2** fish or catch with a seine: *to seine for herring.* 1 *n.*, 2 *v.,* **seined, sein·ing.**
☛ *Hom.* SANE.

**sein·er** (sā′nər) **1** a fishing boat equipped with a SEINE. **2** a person who fishes with a SEINE. *n.*

**seis·mic** (sīz′mik) **1** of earthquakes; having to do with an earthquake. **2** caused by an earthquake. *adj.*

**seis·mo·gram** (sīz′mə gram′) a record of an earthquake obtained on a SEISMOGRAPH. *n.*

**seis·mo·graph** (sīz′mə graf′) an instrument for recording the direction, intensity, and duration of earthquakes. *n.*

**seis·mo·graph·ic** (sīz′mə graf′ik) **1** of a SEISMOGRAPH. **2** of SEISMOGRAPHY. *adj.*

**seis·mog·ra·phy** (sī zmog′rə fē) the art of using the SEISMOGRAPH in recording earthquakes. *n.*

**seis·mo·log·i·cal** (sī′zmə loj′ə kəl) of or having to do with SEISMOLOGY. *adj.*

**seis·mol·o·gist** (sī zmol′ə jist) a person who is trained in SEISMOLOGY. *n.*

**seis·mol·o·gy** (sī zmol′ə jē) the study of earthquakes and other movements of the earth's crust. *n.*

**seize** (sēz) 1 take hold of suddenly; clutch; grasp: *When she lost her balance, she seized his arm.* 2 grasp with the mind: *to seize an idea, the point, etc.* 3 take possession of by force: *The soldiers seized the city.* 4 take possession of or come upon suddenly: *A fever seized her.* 5 take possession of by legal authority. 6 bind; lash; make fast: *to seize one rope to another.* *v.,* **seized, seiz·ing.**
**seize on** or **upon,** **a** take hold of suddenly. **b** take possession of.

**seiz·ing** (sē′zing) 1 a binding, lashing, or fastening together with several turns of small rope, cord, etc. 2 a fastening made in this way: *nautical seizings.* 3 a small rope, cord, etc. used for making such fastenings. 4 ppr. of SEIZE. 1–3 *n.,* 4 *v.*

**sei·zure** (sē′zhər) 1 the act of seizing. 2 the condition of being seized. 3 a short period of unconsciousness which occurs suddenly and is accompanied by a general more or less violent contraction of the muscles. 4 any sudden onset of disease: *heart seizure.* *n.*

**sel·dom** (sel′dəm) rarely; not often: *She is seldom ill.* *adv.*

**se·lect** (si lekt′) 1 choose; pick out: *Select the book you want.* 2 picked as best; chosen specially: *A few select officials were admitted to the conference.* 3 choice; superior: *That store carries a very select line of merchandise.* 4 careful in choosing; particular as to friends, company, etc.: *She belongs to a very select club.* 1 *v.,* 2–4 *adj.*
—**se·lect′ness,** *n.*

**se·lec·tion** (si lek′shən) 1 the act of selecting; choice: *Carol's selection of a gift took a long time.* 2 a person, thing, or group chosen: *The plain blue suit was Jane's selection.* 3 a range of things from which one may select: *The shop offered a very good selection of clothes.* 4 the process of selecting animals or plants to survive, especially the process of NATURAL SELECTION. *n.*

**se·lec·tive** (si lek′tiv) 1 selecting; having the power to select. 2 having to do with selection. 3 responding to oscillations of a certain frequency only: *When a selective radio is tuned to one station, those on other wavelengths are excluded.* *adj.*

**se·lec·tiv·i·ty** (si lek tiv′ə tē) 1 the quality of being selective. 2 the property of a circuit, instrument, etc. by virtue of which it responds to electric oscillations of a particular frequency; especially the ability of a radio receiving set to receive certain frequencies or waves to the exclusion of others. *n.*

**se·lec·tor** (si lek′tər) 1 a person who selects. 2 a mechanical or electrical device that selects. *n.*

**sel·e·nite** (sel′ə nīt′ *or* sə lē′nīt) a variety of GYPSUM, found in transparent crystals and foliated masses. *n.*

**se·le·ni·um** (sə lē′nē əm) a non-metallic element resembling sulphur in chemical properties: *Because its electrical resistance varies with the amount of light, selenium is used in photo-electric cells.* Symbol: Se *n.*

**self** (self) 1 one's own person: *her very self.* 2 one's own welfare, interests, etc.: *A selfish person puts self first.* 3 the nature, character, etc. of a person or thing: *She does not seem like her former self.* 4 being the same throughout; all of one kind, quality, colour, material, etc.: *A coat with a self collar is one with a collar of the same material and colour as the coat.* 1–3 *n.,* 4 *adj.*

**self–** a prefix meaning: 1 of oneself, etc., as in *self-consciousness, self-control.* 2 by or in oneself, etc., as in *self-inflicted, self-evident.* 3 to or for oneself, etc., as in *self-addressed, self-respect.* 4 automatic; automatically, as in *self-starter, self-winding.*

**self–act·ing** (self′ak′ting) working of itself: *a self-acting machine.* *adj.*

**self–ad·dressed** (self′ə drest′) addressed to oneself: *a self-addressed envelope.* *adj.*

**self–as·ser·tion** (self′ə sėr′shən) an insistence on one's own wishes, opinions, claims, etc. *n.*

**self–as·ser·tive** (self′ə sėr′tiv) putting oneself forward; insisting on one's own wishes, opinions, etc. *adj.*

**self–as·sur·ance** (self′ə shü′rəns) SELF-CONFIDENCE. *n.*

**self–as·sured** (self′ə shürd′) SELF-CONFIDENT; sure of oneself. *adj.*

**self–cen·tred** or **self–cen·tered** (self′sen′tərd) 1 occupied with one's own interests and affairs. 2 selfish. 3 being a fixed point around which other things move. *adj.*

**self–com·mand** (self′kə mand′) control of oneself. *n.*

**self–com·pla·cence** (self′kəm plā′səns) SELF-COMPLACENCY. *n.*

**self–com·pla·cen·cy** (self′kəm plā′sən sē) the state of being self-satisfied. *n.*

**self–com·pla·cent** (self′kəm plā′sənt) pleased with oneself; self-satisfied. *adj.*
—**self′–com·pla′cent·ly,** *adv.*

**self–con·ceit** (self′kən sēt′) conceit; too much pride in oneself or one's ability. *n.*

**self–con·fi·dence** (self′kon′fə dəns) a belief in one's own ability, power, judgment, etc.; confidence in oneself. *n.*

**self–con·fi·dent** (self′kon′fə dənt) believing in one's own ability, power, judgment, etc. *adj.*
—**self′–con′fi·dent·ly,** *adv.*

**self–con·scious** (self′kon′shəs) made conscious of how one is appearing to others; embarrassed, especially by the presence of other people and their attitude toward one; shy. *adj.* —**self′–con′scious·ly,** *adv.*
—**self′con′scious·ness,** *n.*

**self–con·se·quence** (self′kon′sə kwəns) a sense of one's own importance. *n.*

**self–con·sist·ent** (self′kən sis′tənt) consistent with

oneself or itself; having its parts or elements in agreement. *adj.*

**self–con·tained** (self′kən tānd′) **1** saying little; reserved. **2** containing in oneself or itself all that is necessary; independent of what is external. **3** having all its working parts contained in one case, cover, or framework: *A watch is self-contained. adj.*

**self–con·tra·dic·tion** (self′kon′trə dik′shən) **1** a contradiction of oneself or itself. **2** a statement containing elements that are contradictory. *n.*

**self–con·tra·dic·to·ry** (self′kon′trə dik′tə rē) contradicting oneself or itself. *adj.*

**self–con·trol** (self′kən trōl′) control of one's own actions, feelings, etc. *n.*

**self–de·cep·tive** (self′di sep′tiv) deceiving oneself. *adj.*

**self–de·fence** or **self–de·fense** (self′di fens′) a defence of one's own person, property, reputation, etc. *n.*

**self–de·ni·al** (self′di nī′əl) a sacrifice of one's own desires and interests; going without things one wants; austerity. *n.*

**self–de·ny·ing** (self′di nī′ing) unselfish; sacrificing one's own wishes and interests. *adj.*

**self–de·struct** (self′di strukt′) destroy itself or oneself: *The atomic warhead is designed to self-destruct if any part of its program fails. v.*

**self–de·struct·ing** (self′di struk′ting) **1** designed to destroy itself. **2** ppr. of SELF-DESTRUCT. 1 *adj.*, 2 *v.*

**self–de·ter·mi·na·tion** (self′di tėr′mə nā′shən) **1** direction from within only, without influence or force from without. **2** the deciding by the people of a nation what form of government they are to have, without reference to the wishes of any other nation. *n.*

**self–de·vo·tion** (self′di vō′shən) SELF-SACRIFICE. *n.*

**self–dis·ci·pline** (self′dis′ə plin) careful control and training of oneself. *n.*

**self–ed·u·cat·ed** (sel′fej′ú kā′tid) self-taught; educated by one's own efforts. *adj.*

**self–ef·face·ment** (sel′fə fā′smənt) the act or habit of modestly keeping oneself in the background. *n.*

**self–em·ployed** (sel′fem ploid′) not employed by others; working for oneself: *Doctors, lawyers, and farmers are usually self-employed. adj.*

**self–es·teem** (sel′fə stēm′) **1** thinking well of oneself; self-respect. **2** thinking too well of oneself; conceit. *n.*

**self–ev·i·dent** (sel′fev′ə dent) evident by itself; needing no proof. *adj.*

**self–ex·plan·a·to·ry** (sel′fek splan′ə tô rē) explaining itself; that needs no explanation; obvious. *adj.*

**self–ex·pres·sion** (sel′fek spresh′ən) an expression of one's personality. *n.*

**self–fill·ing** (self′fil′ing) that can fill itself. *adj.*

**self–gov·ern·ing** (self′guv′ər ning) that governs itself. *adj.*

**self–gov·ern·ment** (self′guv′ərn ment or self′guv′ər mənt) **1** government of a group by its own members: *self-government through elected representatives.* **2** SELF-CONTROL. *n.*

**self–heal** (self′hēl′) a weed with blue or purple flowers, formerly supposed to heal wounds. *n.*

**self–help** (self′help′) a helping oneself; getting along without assistance from others. *n.*

**self–help group** an organization of people sharing a similar problem, for mutual aid.

**self–im·por·tance** (sel′fim pôr′təns) a having or showing too high an opinion of one's own importance; conceit; behaviour showing conceit. *n.*

**self–im·por·tant** (sel′fim pôr′tənt) having or showing too high an opinion of one's own importance. *adj.* —**self′–im·por′tant·ly**, *adv.*

**self–im·posed** (sel′fim pōzd′) imposed on oneself by oneself. *adj.*

**self–im·prove·ment** (sel′fim prüv′mənt) an improvement of one's character, mind, etc. by one's own efforts. *n.*

**self–in·duced** (sel′fin dyüst′ or sel′fin düst′) **1** induced by itself; induced by oneself. **2** produced by SELF-INDUCTION. *adj.*

**self–in·duc·tion** (sel′fin duk′shən) the inducing of an electric current in a circuit by a varying current in that circuit. *n.*

**self–in·dul·gence** (sel′fin dul′jəns) a gratification of one's own desires, passions, etc., with too little regard for the welfare of others. *n.*

**self–in·dul·gent** (sel′fin dul′jənt) characterized by SELF-INDULGENCE. *adj.* —**self′–in·dul′gen·tly**, *adv.*

**self–in·flict·ed** (sel′fin flik′tid) inflicted on oneself by oneself. *adj.*

**self–in·ter·est** (sel′fin′trist or sel′fin′tə rist) **1** an interest in one's own welfare with too little care for the welfare of others; selfishness. **2** personal advantage. *n.*

**self·ish** (sel′fish) **1** caring too much for oneself; caring too little for others: *a selfish child.* **2** showing care solely or chiefly for oneself: *selfish motives. adj.* —**self′ish·ly**, *adv.* —**self′ish·ness**, *n.*

**self·less** (sel′flis) having no regard or thought for self; unselfish. *adj.*

**self–love** (sel′fluv′) **1** love for oneself; selfishness. **2** CONCEIT. *n.*

**self–made** (self′mād′) **1** made by oneself. **2** successful through one's own efforts: *A self-made person is one who succeeds in business, etc., without the usual formal training or education. adj.*

**self–pit·y** (self′pit′ē) pity for oneself. *n.*

**self–pos·sessed** (self′pə zest′) having or showing control of one's feelings and acts; not excited, embarrassed, or confused; calm. *adj.*

**self–pos·ses·sion** (self′pə zesh′ən) the control of one's feelings and actions; composure; calmness. *n.*

**self–praise** (self′prāz′) praise of oneself. *n.*

**self–pres·er·va·tion** (self′prez′ər vā′shən) the preservation of oneself from harm or destruction. *n.*

**self–pro·pelled** (self′prə peld′) propelled by an engine, motor, etc., within itself: *a self-propelled missile. adj.*

**self-reg·is·ter·ing** (self'rej'is tə ring *or* self'rej'i string) registering automatically. *adj.*

**self-reg·u·lat·ing** (self'reg'yə lā'ting) regulating oneself or itself. *adj.*

**self-re·li·ance** (self'ri lī'əns) a reliance on one's own acts, abilities, etc. *n.*

**self-re·li·ant** (self'ri lī'ənt) having or showing SELF-RELIANCE. *adj.* —**self'-re·li'ant·ly,** *adv.*

**self-re·proach** (self'ri prōch') blame by one's own conscience. *n.*

**self-re·spect** (self'ri spekt') respect for oneself; proper pride. *n.*

**self-re·spect·ing** (self'ri spek'ting) having SELF-RESPECT; properly proud. *adj.*

**self-re·straint** (self'ri strānt') SELF-CONTROL. *n.*

**self-right·eous** (self'rī'chəs) thinking that one is more moral than others. *adj.* —**self'-right'eous·ly,** *adv.* —**self'-right'eous·ness,** *n.*

**self-sac·ri·fice** (self'sak'rə fīs') the sacrifice of one's own interests and desires, for one's duty, another's welfare, etc. *n.*

**self-sac·ri·fic·ing** (self'sak'rə fī'sing) unselfish; giving up something for someone else. *adj.*

**self·same** (self'sām') the very same: *We study the selfsame books that you do. adj.*

**self-sat·is·fac·tion** (self'sat'i sfak'shən) a satisfaction with oneself. *n.*

**self-sat·is·fied** (self'sat'is fīd') pleased with oneself; complacent. *adj.*

**self-seek·er** (self'sē'kər) a person who seeks his or her own interests too much. *n.*

**self-seek·ing** (self'sē'king) 1 SELFISH. 2 SELFISHNESS. 1 *adj.,* 2 *n.*

**self-serv·ice** (self'sèr'vis) the act or process of serving oneself in a restaurant, store, etc.: *a self-service cafeteria. n.*

**self-start·er** (self'stär'tər) 1 an electric motor or other device used to start an engine automatically. 2 *Informal.* a person who has initiative. *n.*

**self-styled** (self'stīld') called by oneself: *a self-styled leader whom no one follows. adj.*

**self-suf·fi·cien·cy** (self'sə fish'ən sē) 1 the ability to supply one's own needs. 2 conceit; SELF-ASSURANCE. *n.*

**self-suf·fi·cient** (self'sə fish'ənt) 1 asking and needing no help; independent. 2 having too much confidence in one's own resources, powers, etc.; conceited. *adj.*

**self-suf·fic·ing** (self'sə fī'sing) sufficing in or for oneself or itself; self-sufficient. *adj.*

**self-sup·port** (self'sə pôrt') unaided support of oneself. *n.*

**self-sup·port·ing** (self'sə pôr'ting) earning one's expenses; getting along without help. *adj.*

**self-sus·tain·ing** (self'sə stā'ning) SELF-SUPPORTING. *adj.*

**self-taught** (self'tot') taught by oneself without aid from others. *adj.*

**self-will** (self'wil') insistence on having one's own way. *n.*

**self-willed** (self'wild') insisting on having one's own way; objecting to doing what others ask or command. *adj.*

**self-wind·ing** (self'wīn'ding) that is wound automatically. *adj.*

**sell** (sel) 1 exchange for money or other payment: *to sell a house.* 2 deal in; keep for sale: *The butcher sells meat.* 3 be given in exchange; be on sale; be sold; get sold: *Strawberries sell at a high price in January.* 4 give up; betray: *The traitor sold his country for money.* 5 cause to be accepted, approved, or adopted by representations and methods characteristic of salesmanship: *to sell an idea to the public.* 6 *Informal.* win acceptance, approval, or adoption: *This is an idea that will sell.* *v.,* **sold, sell·ing; be sold on,** *Informal.* be convinced of the value, truth, etc., of: *For a time she was sold on folk music.*
**sell off,** dispose of by sale.
**sell someone on,** inspire someone with the desire to buy or possess something: *She has sold me on a convertible as opposed to a sedan.*
**sell out, a** sell all that one has of; get rid of by selling. **b** *Informal.* betray by a secret bargain.
☞ *Hom.* CELL.

**sell·er** (sel'ər) 1 a person who sells. 2 a thing considered with reference to its sale: *This book is a best seller. n.*
☞ *Hom.* CELLAR.

**seller's market** an economic situation in which the seller has the advantage because goods are scarce and prices tend to be high. Compare with BUYER'S MARKET.

**sell-out** (sel'out') 1 *Informal.* a selling out. 2 *Informal.* a performance of a play, sports event, etc. for which all seats are sold. *n.*

**selt·zer** (selt'sər) 1 a bubbling MINERAL WATER containing salt, sodium, calcium, and magnesium carbonates. 2 an artificial water of similar composition. *n.*

**sel·vage** or **sel·vedge** (sel'vij) the edge of a fabric finished off to prevent ravelling; border; edge. *n.*

**selves** (selvz) pl. of SELF: *She had two selves—a friendly self and a shy self. n.*

**se·man·tic** (sə man'tik) having to do with meaning. *adj.*

**se·man·tics** (sə man'tiks) the scientific study of the meanings and the history of changes in the meanings of words and sentences. *n.*

RED LIGHT STOP    YELLOW LIGHT CAUTION    GREEN LIGHT PROCEED

Railway semaphores

**sem·a·phore** (sem'ə fôr') 1 an apparatus for

**semblance** 1076 **semitrailer**

signalling; upright post or structure with movable arms, an arrangement of lanterns, flags, etc. used in railway signalling. **2** signal by semaphore. **3** a system of signals for sending messages by using different positions of the arms or flags, or by using other mechanical devices: *Many Girl Guides learn semaphore.* 1, 3 *n.*, 2 *v.*, **sem·a·phored, sem·a·phor·ing.**

**sem·blance** (sem′bləns) **1** the outward appearance: *His story had the semblance of truth, but was really false.* **2** likeness: *These clouds have the semblance of a face.* *n.*

**se·men** (sē′mən) the thick, whitish fluid produced by the male reproductive organs and containing the male reproductive cells, or sperm. *n.*
☛ *Hom.* SEAMAN.

**se·mes·ter** (sə mes′tər) a half of a school year. *n.*

**sem·i** (sem′ē *or* sem′ī) *Informal.* SEMITRAILER. *n.*

**semi–** a prefix meaning: **1** half: *Semicircle means half circle.* **2** partly; incompletely: *Semiconscious means partly conscious.* **3** partial; incomplete: *Semidarkness means partial darkness.* **4** twice. *Semi _____ ly* means in each half of a _____, or twice in a _____: *Semi-annually means every half year, or twice a year.*
☛ *Pronunciation.* See note at ANTI-.
☛ *Usage.* **Semi-** is usually hyphenated before a vowel and before proper nouns and proper adjectives: *semi-annual, semi-French.* In other cases a hyphen is not required.

**sem·i·an·nu·al** (sem′ē an′yü əl) **1** occurring every half year. **2** lasting a half year. *adj.*

**sem·i·an·nu·al·ly** (sem′ē an′yü ə lē) twice a year. *adv.*

**sem·i–ar·id** (sem′ē ar′id *or* sem′ē er′id) having very little rainfall. *adj.*

**sem·i·breve** (sem′ē brēv′) in music, the longest note in common use; a WHOLE NOTE. *n.*

**sem·i·cir·cle** (sem′ē sėr′kəl) half a circle: *We sat in a semicircle around the fire.* *n.*

**sem·i·cir·cu·lar** (sem′ē sėr′kyə lər) having the form of half a circle. *adj.*

**semicircular canal** any of three curved, tubelike canals in the inner part of the ear that help us keep our balance. See EAR for picture.

**sem·i·civ·i·lized** (sem′ē siv′ə līzd′) partly civilized. *adj.*

**sem·i·co·lon** (sem′ē kō′lən) a mark of punctuation (;) that shows a separation less marked than that shown by a period: *A semicolon is used to separate two main clauses if one or both contain a comma.* *n.*

**sem·i·con·duc·tor** (sem′ē kən duk′tər) any of a group of solids, such as silicon and germanium, that are poor conductors at low temperatures, but good conductors at high temperatures. *n.*

**sem·i·con·scious** (sem′ē kon′shəs) half conscious; not fully conscious. *adj.* —**sem′i·con′scious·ly,** *adv.* —**sem′i·con′scious·ness,** *n.*

**sem·i·dark·ness** (sem′ē därk′nəs) partial darkness. *n.*

**sem·i·de·tached** (sem′ē di tacht′) partly detached, used especially of either of two houses joined by a common wall but separated from other buildings. *adj.*

**sem·i·de·vel·oped** (sem′ē di vel′əpt) not fully developed. *adj.*

**sem·i·fi·nal** (sem′ē fī′nəl *for noun*, sem′ē fī′nəl *for adjective*) **1** one of the two rounds, matches, etc. that settles who will play in the final one, which follows. **2** designating or having to do with such a round, match, etc.: *a semifinal score.* 1 *n.*, 2 *adj.*

**sem·i·for·mal** (sem′ē fôr′məl *for adjective*, sem′ē fôr′məl *for noun*) **1** designed for or referring to a somewhat formal social occasion: *a semiformal gown, a semiformal dinner party.* **2** a semiformal gown. 1 *adj.*, 2 *n.*

**sem·i·month·ly** (sem′ē munth′lē *for adjective*, sem′ē munth′lē *for adverb and noun*) **1** occurring or appearing twice a month. **2** twice a month. **3** something that occurs or appears twice a month; a magazine or paper published twice a month. 1 *adj.*, 2 *adv.*, 3 *n., pl.* **sem·i·month·lies.**

**sem·i·nal** (sem′ə nəl) **1** of or having to do with SEMEN or seed. **2** containing SEMEN or seed. **3** having to do with reproduction. **4** like seed; having the possibility of future development: *a seminal theory.* *adj.*

**sem·i·nar** (sem′ə när′) **1** a group of college or university students doing research under direction. **2** a course of study or work for such a group. *n.*

**sem·i·nar·y** (sem′ə ner′ē) **1** a school, especially one beyond high school. **2** an academy or boarding school, especially for young women. **3** a school or college for training students to be priests, ministers, etc. **4** a place for instruction, training, or development. *n., pl.* **sem·i·nar·ies.**

**sem·i·na·tion** (sem′ə nā′shən) a sowing; propagation; dissemination. *n.*

**sem·i·nif·er·ous** (sem′ə nif′ə rəs) **1** bearing or producing seed. **2** conveying or containing SEMEN. *adj.*

**sem·i–of·fi·cial** (sem′ē ə fish′əl *or* sem′ē ō fish′əl) partly official; having some degree of authority. *adj.*

**sem·i·pre·cious** (sem′ē presh′əs) having value but not sufficient value to rank as gems: *Amethysts and garnets are semiprecious stones; diamonds and rubies are precious stones.* *adj.*

**sem·i·qua·ver** (sem′ē kwā′vər) in music, a SIXTEENTH NOTE. *n.*

**sem·i·skilled** (sem′ē skild′) partly skilled. *adj.*

**sem·i·sol·id** (sem′ē sol′id) **1** partly solid. **2** a partly solid substance. 1 *adj.*, 2 *n.*

**Sem·ite** (sem′īt *or* sē′mīt) a member of the linguistic family that includes the Hebrews, Arabs, Maltese, Syrians, Phoenicians, Assyrians, etc. *n.*

**Se·mit·ic** (sə mit′ik) **1** of or having to do with the Semites or their languages. **2** a group of languages including Hebrew, Arabic, Maltese, Aramaic, Phoenician, and Assyrian. 1 *adj.*, 2 *n.*

**Sem·i·tism** (sem′ə tiz′əm *or* sē′mə tiz′əm) **1** SEMITIC character, especially the ways, ideas, influence, etc. of the Jews. **2** a SEMITIC word or idiom. *n.*

**sem·i·tone** (sem′ē tōn′) in music, one of the smaller intervals of the modern scale; a half tone; HALF STEP. *n.*

**sem·i·trail·er** (sem′ē trā′lər) a large trailer used for carrying freight, having wheels at the back but supported in front by the truck tractor to which it is hitched. *n.*

**sem·i·trop·i·cal** (sem′ē trop′ə kəl)   halfway between tropical and temperate: *Florida is a semitropical state.* *adj.*

**sem·i·vow·el** (sem′ē vou′əl)   **1** a sound that is produced like a vowel but cannot form a syllable: *English semivowels are* y *and* w.   **2** a letter or character representing such a sound. The letters *w* and *y* are semivowels in *win* and *yet*.   *n.*

**sem·i·week·ly** (sem′ē wē′klē *for adjective,* sem′ē wē′klē *for adverb and noun*)   **1** occurring or appearing twice a week.   **2** twice a week.   **3** something that occurs or appears twice a week; a magazine or paper published twice a week.   **1** *adj.*, **2** *adv.*, **3** *n., pl.* **sem·i·week·lies.**

**sem·o·li·na** (sem′ə lē′nə)   the coarsely ground hard parts of wheat remaining after the fine flour has been sifted through, used in making puddings, macaroni, etc.   *n.*

**sem·pi·ter·nal** (sem′pi tėr′nəl)   everlasting; eternal. *adj.*

**Sen.**   **1** Senate.   **2** Senator.   **3** Senior.

**sen·ate** (sen′it)   **1** a governing or lawmaking assembly: *the senate of a university. The highest council of state in ancient Rome was called the senate.*   **2** the upper and smaller branch of an assembly or parliament that makes laws.   *n.*
☞ *Hom.* SENNIT.

**Sen·ate** (sen′it)   the upper and smaller branch of a parliament or legislature: *The Canadian Senate, which consists of 104 members, is made up of representatives from each province and territory.*   *n.*
☞ *Hom.* SENNIT.

**sen·a·tor** (sen′ə tər)   a member of a SENATE.   *n.*

**sen·a·to·ri·al** (sen′ə tô′rē əl)   **1** of or befitting a SENATOR or senators.   **2** consisting of SENATORS.   **3** entitled to elect a SENATOR: *a senatorial district.*   *adj.*

**sen·a·tor·ship** (sen′ə tər ship′)   the position, duties, etc. of a SENATOR.   *n.*

**send** (send)   **1** cause to go from one place to another: *send a child on an errand.*   **2** cause to be carried: *to send a letter.*   **3** cause to come, occur, be, etc.: *Send help at once. The earthquake sent destruction to the village.*   **4** send a message or messenger: *to send for a doctor.*   **5** drive; impel; throw: *to send a ball. The volcano sent clouds of smoke into the air.*   **6** transmit radio signals, etc. *v.*, **sent, send·ing.** —**send′er,** *n.*
**send around,**   have something circulate.
**send away for,**   mail a request for.
**send off,**   say goodbye to someone beginning a journey.
**send out for,**   order food, etc. by telephone to be delivered to one's home or office.
**send packing,**   send away or force to leave quickly.
**send under,**   defeat.
**send up,** *Informal.*   make fun of by imitating and exaggerating.

**send–off** (sen′dof′)   **1** a friendly demonstration in honour of a person setting out on a journey, course, career, etc.   **2** *Informal.*   a start given to a person or thing: *a good send-off for the idea.*   *n.*

**Sen·e·ca** (sen′ə kə)   **1** a member of a Native American tribe living mainly in New York State: *The Seneca belonged to the Iroquois Confederacy.*   **2** the Iroquoian language of the Seneca.   **3** of or having to do with the Seneca or their language.   **1, 2** *n., pl.* **Sen·e·ca** or **Sen·e·cas;** **3** *adj.*

**Sen·e·gal·ese** (sen′ə gə lēz′)   **1** of or having to do with Senegal, a country in western Africa, or its people.   **2** a native or inhabitant of Senegal.   **1** *adj.,* **2** *n., pl.* **Sen·e·gal·ese.**

**se·nes·cence** (sə nes′əns)   the fact or condition of growing old.   *n.*

**se·nes·cent** (sə nes′ənt)   growing old; beginning to show old age.   *adj.*

**se·nile** (sen′īl *or* sē′nīl)   **1** of old age.   **2** showing the weakness of old age.   **3** caused by old age.   *adj.*

**se·nil·i·ty** (sə nil′ə tē)   **1** old age.   **2** the physical and mental weakening associated with old age.   *n.*

**sen·ior** (sē′nyər)   **1** older or elderly: *a senior citizen.*   **2** the older; designating a father whose son has the same given name: *John Parker, Senior.*   **3** an older person: *Paul is his brother's senior by two years.*   **4** higher in rank or longer in service: *Mr. Etmos is the senior member of the firm of Etmos and Brown.*   **5** a person of higher rank or longer service.   **6** a member of the graduating class of a high school or college.   **7** of or having to do with the graduating class.   **1, 2, 4, 7** *adj.,* **3, 5, 6** *n.*

**senior citizen**   a person who is 65 years of age or older.

**senior high school**   a school attended after junior high school.

**sen·ior·i·ty** (sē nyôr′ə tē)   **1** superiority in age or standing; the state or fact of being older: *Harriet felt that two years' seniority gave her the right to advise her sister.*   **2** priority or precedence in office or service: *A captain has seniority over a lieutenant.*   *n., pl.* **sen·ior·i·ties.**

**sen·na** (sen′ə)   **1** a laxative extracted from the dried leaves of any of several CASSIA plants.   **2** the dried leaves of any of these plants.   **3** the CASSIA plant, or a plant similar to it.   *n.*

**sen·nit** (sen′it)   a kind of flat, braided cordage used on shipboard, formed by plaiting strands of rope yarn or other fibre.   *n.*
☞ *Hom.* SENATE.

**sen·sa·tion** (sen sā′shən)   **1** the action of the senses; power to see, hear, feel, taste, smell, etc.: *A dead body is without sensation.*   **2** a feeling: *Ice gives a sensation of coldness; sugar, of sweetness.*   **3** a strong or excited feeling: *The news of war caused a sensation throughout the nation.*   **4** the cause of such feeling: *The first manned orbit of the earth was a great sensation.*   *n.*

**sen·sa·tion·al** (sen sā′shə nəl)   **1** arousing strong or excited feeling: *The player's sensational catch made the crowd cheer wildly.*   **2** trying to arouse strong or excited feeling: *a sensational newspaper story.*   **3** of the senses; having to do with sensation.   *adj.*
—**sen·sa′tion·al·ly,** *adv.*

**sen·sa·tion·al·ism** (sen sā′shə nə liz′əm)   **1** SENSATIONAL methods; sensational writing, language, etc.   **2** the philosophical theory or doctrine that all ideas are derived solely through SENSATION.   *n.*

**sen·sa·tion·al·ist** (sen sā′shə nə list)   **1** a sensational writer, speaker, etc.; one who tries to make a SENSATION. **2** a believer in philosophical SENSATIONALISM. *n.*

**sense** (sens) **1** one of the special powers of the body by which people and animals become aware of the world around them and of changes within themselves: *Sight, hearing, touch, taste, and smell are the five senses.* **2** a sensation felt through one of these senses: *a sense of pain.* **3** a mental feeling: *The extra lock on the door gave her a sense of security.* **4** be aware; feel: *She sensed that he was tired.* **5** an understanding; appreciation: *Everyone thinks Janet has a sense of humour.* **6** *Informal.* understand. **7** judgment; intelligence: *She had the good sense to keep out of foolish quarrels. Common sense would have prevented the accident.* **8** the ability to perceive or judge things: *a sense of direction, a sense of beauty.* **9** a meaning: *He was a gentleman in every sense of the word.* **10** the general opinion: *The sense of the assembly was clear even before the vote.* **11** Usually, **senses**, *pl.* normal, sound condition of mind: *He must be out of his senses to act so.* 1–3, 5, 7–11 *n.*, 4, 6 *v.*, **sensed, sens·ing.**
**in a sense,** in some respects, to some degree.
**make sense,** have a meaning; be understandable; be reasonable: *Cow cat bless Monday does not make sense.*

**sense·less** (sen'slis) **1** unconscious: *A blow on the head knocked him senseless.* **2** foolish; stupid: *That senseless dog is chasing cars again.* **3** meaningless: *senseless words.* *adj.* —**sense'less·ly,** *adv.* —**sense'less·ness,** *n.*

**sense organ** the eye, ear, or other part of the body by which a person or an animal receives sensations of colours, sounds, smells, etc.

**sen·si·bil·i·ty** (sen'sə bil'ə tē) **1** the ability to feel or perceive: *Some drugs lessen a person's sensibilities.* **2** sensitiveness. **3** fineness of feeling: *She has an unusual sensibility for colours.* **4** a tendency to feel hurt or offended too easily. **5** awareness; consciousness. **6** Usually, **sensibilities,** *pl.* sensitive feelings. *n., pl.* **sen·si·bil·i·ties.**

**sen·si·ble** (sen'sə bəl) **1** having or showing good judgment; wise: *She is much too sensible to do anything so foolish.* **2** aware; conscious: *I am sensible of your kindness.* **3** that can be noticed: *There is a sensible difference between yellow and orange.* **4** that can be perceived by the senses. **5** SENSITIVE. *adj.* —**sen'si·bly,** *adv.*

**sen·si·tive** (sen'sə tiv) **1** receiving impressions readily: *The eye is sensitive to light.* **2** easily affected or influenced: *The mercury in the thermometer is sensitive to changes in temperature.* **3** easily hurt or offended: *She is sensitive to the least hint of disapproval.* **4** of or connected with the senses or sensation. *adj.* —**sen'si·tive·ly,** *adv.* —**sen'si·tive·ness,** *n.*

**sensitive plant** **1** a tropical American plant whose leaflets fold together when touched. **2** any of various other plants showing sensitiveness to touch.

**sen·si·tiv·i·ty** (sen'sə tiv'ə tē) the state or quality of being SENSITIVE. *n., pl.* **sen·si·tiv·i·ties.**

**sen·si·tize** (sen'sə tīz') make SENSITIVE: *Camera films have been sensitized to light.* *v.*, **sen·si·tized, sen·si·tiz·ing.** —**sen'si·tiz'er,** *n.*

**sen·sor** (sen'sər) a device for receiving and transmitting a physical stimulus such as heat, light, or pressure: *Sensors were applied to the astronaut's body to record his pulse, temperature, etc.* *n.*
☛ *Hom.* CENSER, CENSOR.

**sen·so·ri·al** (sen sô'rē əl) SENSORY. *adj.*

**sen·so·ry** (sen'sə rē) **1** of or having to do with SENSATION or the senses: *The eyes and ears are sensory organs.* **2** of nerves, ganglia, etc., conveying an impulse from the sense organs to a nerve centre. *adj.*

**sen·su·al** (sen'shü əl) **1** having to do with the bodily senses rather than with the mind or soul: *Gluttons derive sensual pleasure from eating.* **2** caring too much for the pleasures of the senses. **3** lustful; lewd. **4** of or having to do with the senses or sensation. *adj.* —**sen'su·al·ly,** *adv.*
☛ *Syn.* **Sensual** and SENSUOUS both relate to pleasure coming from the senses. **Sensual** emphasizes an appeal to the bodily senses and desires often suggesting excess or lust: *She was told to give up her sensual pleasures.* **Sensuous,** a more favourable term, suggests a refinement of feeling and a sensitivity to beauty: *She found sensuous delight in the smells of the forest.*

**sen·su·al·ism** (sen'shü ə liz'əm) SENSUALITY. *n.*

**sen·su·al·ist** (sen'shü ə list) a person who indulges too much in the pleasures of the senses: *Gluttons and drunkards are sensualists.* *n.*

**sen·su·al·i·ty** (sen'shü al'ə tē) **1** a sensual nature. **2** an excessive indulgence in the pleasures of the senses. **3** lewdness. *n., pl.* **sen·su·al·i·ties.**

**sen·su·al·ize** (sen'shü ə līz') make SENSUAL. *v.*, **sen·su·al·ized, sen·su·al·iz·ing.**

**sen·su·ous** (sen'shü əs) **1** of or derived from the senses; having an effect on the senses; perceived by the senses: *the sensuous thrill of a warm bath, a sensuous love of colour.* **2** enjoying the pleasures of the senses. *adj.* —**sen'su·ous·ly,** *adv.* —**sen'su·ous·ness,** *n.*
☛ *Syn.* See note at SENSUAL.

**sent** (sent) pt. and pp. of SEND: *They sent the trunks last week. Nancy was sent on an errand.* *v.*
☛ *Hom.* CENT, SCENT.

**sen·tence** (sen'təns) **1** a word or group of words making a grammatically complete statement, question, request, command, or exclamation: *Boys and girls is not a sentence. The boys and girls are here is a sentence.* **2** a complete idea expressed in mathematical symbols. $4 + 2 = 6$ is a closed sentence which is true. $x + 2 = 6$ is an open sentence which may be true or false according to the value assigned to $x$. **3** a decision by a judge on the punishment of a criminal. **4** the punishment itself. **5** pronounce punishment on: *The judge sentenced the thief to five years in prison.* **6** a short wise saying; proverb. 1–4, 6 *n.*, 5 *v.*, **sen·tenced, sen·tenc·ing.**

**sen·ten·tial** (sen ten'shəl) **1** having to do with or of the nature of a judicial SENTENCE (def. 3). **2** having to do with a grammatical SENTENCE (def. 1). *adj.*

**sen·ten·tious** (sen ten'shəs) **1** full of meaning; saying much in few words. **2** speaking as if one were a judge settling a question. **3** inclined to make wise sayings; abounding in proverbs. *adj.* —**sen·ten'tious·ly,** *adv.* —**sen·ten'tious·ness,** *n.*

**sen·tience** (sen'shəns *or* sen'shē əns) a capacity for feeling: *Some people believe in the sentience of flowers.* *n.*

**sen·tient** (sen'shənt *or* sen'shē ənt) **1** that can feel; having feeling. **2** one that feels. 1 *adj.*, 2 *n.*

**sen·ti·ment** (sen'tə mənt) **1** a mixture of thought and feeling: *Admiration, patriotism, and loyalty are sentiments.*

2 feeling, especially refined or tender feeling. 3 a thought or saying that expresses feeling. 4 a mental attitude. 5 a personal opinion. *n.*

**sen·ti·men·tal** (sen′tə men′təl) 1 having or showing much tender feeling: *sentimental poetry.* 2 likely to act from feelings rather than from logical thinking. 3 of sentiment; dependent on sentiment: *She values her mother's gift for sentimental reasons.* 4 having too much sentiment. *adj.* —**sen′ti·men′tal·ly**, *adv.*

**sen·ti·men·tal·ism** (sen′tə men′tə liz′əm) 1 a tendency to be influenced by sentiment rather than reason. 2 an excessive indulgence in sentiment. 3 a feeling expressed too openly or commonly or sentimentally. *n.*

**sen·ti·men·tal·ist** (sen′tə men′tə list) a sentimental person; one who indulges in SENTIMENTALITY. *n.*

**sen·ti·men·tal·i·ty** (sen′tə men tal′ə tē) 1 a tendency to be influenced by sentiment rather than reason. 2 an excessive indulgence in sentiment. 3 a feeling expressed too openly or sentimentally. *n., pl.* **sen·ti·men·tal·i·ties.**

**sen·ti·men·tal·ize** (sen′tə men′tə līz′) 1 indulge in sentiment; affect sentiment. 2 make sentimental. 3 be sentimental about. *v.,* **sen·ti·men·tal·ized, sen·ti·men·tal·iz·ing.**

**sen·ti·nel** (sen′tə nəl) 1 a person stationed to keep watch and guard against surprise attack. 2 a person or thing that watches, or stands as if watching, like a sentinel: *The tree stood like a sentinel against the sky.* 3 stand or place on guard. 1, 2 *n.,* 3 *v.* **sen·ti·nelled** or **sen·ti·neled, sen·ti·nel·ling** or **sen·ti·nel·ing. stand sentinel,** act as a sentinel; keep watch.

**sen·try** (sen′trē) a person, especially a soldier, stationed at a place to keep watch and guard against surprise attacks, etc. *n., pl.* **sen·tries.**
**stand sentry,** watch; guard: *We stood sentry over the sleepers.*

**sentry box** a small building for sheltering a SENTRY.

**sep.** 1 sepal; sepals. 2 separate.

**Sep.** September.

**se·pal** (sē′pəl) one of the leaflike divisions of the calyx, or outer covering, of a flower. In a carnation, the sepals make a green cup at the base of the flower. In a tulip, the sepals are coloured like the petals. See FLOWER for picture. *n.*

**sep·a·ra·ble** (sep′ə rə bəl *or* sep′rə bəl) that can be SEPARATED. *adj.* —**sep′a·ra·bly,** *adv.*

**sep·a·rate** (sep′ə rāt′ *for verb,* sep′ə rit *or* sep′rit *for adjective and noun*) 1 be between; keep apart; divide: *The Atlantic Ocean separates the Americas from Europe.* 2 take apart; part; disjoin: *to separate church and state.* 3 live apart or cause to live apart: *A husband and wife may be separated by agreement or by order of a court.* 4 divide into parts or groups; divide or part a mass, compound, or whole into elements, sizes, etc.: *to separate a tangle of string.* 5 draw, come, or go apart; become disconnected or disunited; part company: *After school the children separated in all directions. The rope separated under the strain.* 6 put apart; take away: *Separate your books from mine.* 7 apart from others; divided; not joined; individual; single: *separate clubs. These are two separate questions. Our teeth are separate.* 8 something separate. 1–6 *v.,* **sep·a·rat·ed, sep·a·rat·ing.** 7 *adj.,* 8 *n.*
—**sep′a·rate·ly,** *adv.*

**separate school** 1 *Cdn.* a school for children belonging to a religious minority in a particular district,

**sentimental**     **1079**     **septicemia**

hat, āge, fär; let, ēqual, tėrm; it, īce
hot, ōpen, ôrder; oil, out; cup, put, rüle
əbove, takən, pencəl, lemən, circəs
ch, child; ng, long; sh, ship
th, thin; ŦH, then; zh, measure

receiving taxes imposed by its own school board as well as grants from the provincial Department (or Ministry) of Education. 2 a Roman Catholic parochial school. 3 sometimes, a school that is not part of the public school system; a private or independent school.

**sep·a·ra·tion** (sep′ə rā′shən) 1 the act of separating; dividing; taking apart. 2 the condition of being separated. 3 the line or point where things separate: *They soon came to the separation of the path into two tracks.* 4 the living apart of husband and wife by agreement or by order of a court. *n.*

**sep·a·ra·tism** (sep′ə rə tiz′əm *or* sep′rə tiz′əm) 1 a principle or policy for separation, secession, or segregation. 2 in Canada, **Separatism,** advocacy or support for the withdrawal of Quebec from Confederation. *n.*

**sep·a·ra·tist** (sep′ə rə tist *or* sep′rə tist) 1 an advocate or supporter of SEPARATISM. 2 in Canada, **Separatist,** an advocate or supporter of the withdrawal of Quebec from Confederation. *n.*

**sep·a·ra·tor** (sep′ə rā′tər) a person or thing that separates, especially a machine for separating cream from milk, wheat from chaff or dirt, etc. *n.*

**se·pi·a** (sē′pē ə) 1 brown paint or ink prepared from the inky fluid of cuttlefish. 2 dark brown. 3 done in sepia: *a sepia print.* 1, 2 *n.,* 3 *adj.*

**se·poy** (sē′poi) formerly, a native of India who was a soldier in the British army. *n.*

**sep·sis** (sep′sis) a poisoning of the blood stream caused by disease-producing bacteria in festering wounds, certain micro-organisms, etc. *n.*

**Sept.** September.

**sep·ta·gon** (sep′tə gon′) a closed plane figure having seven interior angles and seven sides. *n.*

**sep·tal** (sep′təl) of or having to do with a SEPTUM. *adj.*

**Sep·tem·ber** (sep tem′bər) the ninth month: *September has 30 days.* *n.*
☞ *Etym.* Through OF *septembre* from L *September,* formed from *septem* 'seven'. September was the seventh month in the ancient Roman calendar.

**sep·te·nar·y** (sep′tə ner′ē *or* sep ten′ə rē) 1 of or having to do with the number seven. 2 the number seven. 3 forming a group of seven. 4 a group or set of seven things. 5 SEPTENNIAL. 6 a period of seven years. 1, 3, 5 *adj.,* 2, 4, 6 *n., pl.* **sep·te·nar·ies.**

**sep·ten·ni·al** (sep ten′ē əl) 1 lasting seven years. 2 occurring every seven years. *adj.*
—**sep·ten′ni·al·ly,** *adv.*

**sep·tet** or **sep·tette** (sep tet′) 1 a musical composition for seven voices or instruments. 2 seven singers or players. 3 any group of seven. *n.*

**sep·tic** (sep′tik) 1 causing infection or putrefaction. 2 caused by infection or putrefaction. *adj.*

**sep·ti·ce·mi·a** or **sep·ti·cae·mi·a** (sep′tə sē′mē ə)

**septic tank** 1080 **sergeant**

blood poisoning, especially a form in which micro-organisms as well as their toxins are absorbed by the blood. *n.*

**septic tank** a tank in which sewage is acted on by bacteria.

**sep·til·lion** (sep til′yən) **1** in Canada, the United States and France, 1 followed by 24 zeros. **2** in the United Kingdom, 1 followed by 42 zeros. *n.*

**sep·tu·a·ge·nar·i·an** (sep′chü ə jə ner′ē ən) **1** of the age of 70 years, or between 70 and 80 years old. **2** a person who is 70, or between 70 and 80, years old. 1 *adj.*, 2 *n.*

**sep·tum** (sep′təm) a dividing wall; partition: *There is a septum of bone and cartilage between the nostrils. The inside of a green pepper is divided into chambers by septa.* *n.*, *pl.* **sep·ta** (-tə).

**sep·tu·ple** (sep tyü′pəl, sep tü′pəl, sep tup′əl, *or* sep′tə pəl) **1** seven times as great; sevenfold. **2** make seven times as great. 1 *adj.*, 2 *v.*, **sep·tu·pled, sep·tu·pling.**

**sep·ul·cher** (sep′əl kər) See SEPULCHRE. *n.*, *v.*, **sep·ul·chered, sep·ul·cher·ing.**

**se·pul·chral** (sə pul′krəl) **1** of SEPULCHRES or tombs. **2** of burial: *sepulchral ceremonies.* **3** deep and gloomy; dismal; suggesting a tomb: *a sepulchral voice.* *adj.*

**sep·ul·chre** or **sep·ul·cher** (sep′əl kər) **1** a place of burial; tomb. **2** bury a dead body in a sepulchre. 1 *n.*, 2 *v.*, **sep·ul·chred** or **sep·ul·chered, sep·ul·chring** or **sep·ul·cher·ing.**

**seq.** the following (an abbreviation of Latin *sequentia*).

**se·quel** (sē′kwəl) **1** that which follows; a continuation. **2** something that follows as a result of some earlier happening; a result; consequence; outcome: *Famine is often the sequel to war.* **3** a complete story continuing an earlier one about the same people. *n.*

**se·quence** (sē′kwəns) **1** the coming of one thing after another; succession; order of succession: *Arrange the names in alphabetical sequence.* **2** a connected series: *a sequence of lessons on one subject.* **3** something that follows; result: *Crime has its sequence of misery.* **4** in card playing, a set of three or more cards of the same suit following one after another in order of value. **5** part of a motion picture consisting of an episode without breaks. **6** in music, a series of melodic or harmonic phrases repeated three or more times at successive pitches upward or downward. *n.*

**se·quent** (sē′kwənt) **1** following; SUBSEQUENT. **2** following in order; CONSECUTIVE. **3** following as a result; CONSEQUENT. **4** that which follows; result; CONSEQUENCE. 1–3 *adj.*, 4 *n.*

**se·quen·tial** (si kwen′shəl) **1** SEQUENT (defs. 1–3). **2** forming a sequence or connected series; characterized by a regular sequence of parts. *adj.*

**se·ques·ter** (si kwes′tər) **1** remove or withdraw from public use or from public view: *The shy old lady sequestered herself from all strangers.* **2** take away property for a time from an owner until a debt is paid or some claim is satisfied. **3** seize by authority; take and keep: *The soldiers sequestered food from the people they conquered.* *v.*

**se·ques·trate** (si kwes′trāt) CONFISCATE. *v.*, **se·ques·trat·ed, se·ques·trat·ing.**

**se·ques·tra·tion** (sē′kwe strā′shən) **1** the seizing and holding of property until legal claims are satisfied. **2** a forcible or authorized seizure; CONFISCATION. **3** a separation or withdrawal from others; SECLUSION. *n.*

**se·quin** (sē′kwin) **1** a small spangle used to ornament dresses, scarves, etc. **2** a former Italian gold coin, worth about $2.25. *n.*

**se·quoi·a** (si kwoi′ə) either of two kinds of very tall evergreen trees of California. *n.*
☛ *Etym.* Named after *Sequoya* (1770?–1843), a Cherokee Indian scholar who invented a writing system for his own language.

**se·ra·pe** (sə rä′pē) a shawl or blanket, often having bright colours, worn by Indians in Spanish-American countries. *n.*

**Serb** (sėrb) a native or inhabitant of Serbia, a region in eastern Yugoslavia. *n.*

**Ser·bi·an** (sėr′bē ən) **1** of or having to do with Serbia, its people, or their language. **2** the Slavic language spoken by the Serbs, very closely related to Croatian. **3** SERB. 1 *adj.*, 2, 3 *n.*

**Ser·bo–Cro·a·tian** (sėr′bō krō ā′shən) **1** the Slavic language of the Serbs and Croats, consisting of Serbian, written with the Cyrillic alphabet, and Croatian, written with the Latin alphabet. **2** of or having to do with this language or the people who speak it. 1 *n.*, 2 *adj.*

**sere** (sēr) dried up; withered. *adj.*
☛ *Hom.* SEAR, SEER.

**ser·e·nade** (ser′ə nād′) **1** music played or sung outdoors at night, especially by a lover under his lady's window. **2** a piece of music suitable for such a performance. **3** sing or play a serenade to. **4** sing or play a serenade. 1, 2 *n.*, 3, 4 *v.*, **ser·e·nad·ed, ser·e·nad·ing.**

**ser·en·dip·i·ty** (ser′ən dip′ə tē) the faculty of accidentally making fortunate discoveries; happening upon things, information, etc. by chance. *n.*
—**ser′en·dip′i·tous,** *adj.*
☛ *Etym.* Coined by Horace Walpole from *Serendip* in the title of the Persian fairy tale *The Three Princes of Serendip*, whose heroes make many fortunate discoveries accidentally. 18c.

**se·rene** (sə rēn′) **1** peaceful; calm: *a serene smile.* **2** clear; bright; not cloudy: *a serene sky.* *adj.*
—**se·rene′ly,** *adv.*

**se·ren·i·ty** (sə ren′ə tē) **1** peace; calmness. **2** clearness; brightness. *n.*, *pl.* **se·ren·i·ties.**

**serf** (sėrf) **1** formerly, a person who worked on a feudal estate and passed with the land from one owner to another. **2** a person treated almost like a slave; a person who is mistreated, underpaid, etc. *n.* —**serf′like′,** *adj.*
☛ *Hom.* SURF.

**serf·dom** (sėrf′dəm) **1** the condition of a SERF. **2** the custom of having SERFs: *Serfdom existed all over Europe in the Middle Ages and lasted in Russia till the middle of the 19th century.* *n.*

**serge** (sėrj) a kind of cloth having slanting lines or ridges on its surface. *n.*

**ser·geant** (sär′jənt) **1** a non-commissioned officer in the Canadian Forces ranking next above a master corporal and below a warrant officer. *Abbrev.*: Sgt.   **2** a police officer, especially one senior to a constable.   **3** a SERGEANT AT ARMS.   *n.*

**sergeant at arms** or **ser·geant–at–arms** (sär′jən tə tärmz′)   an officer who keeps order in a legislature, law court, etc.   *n., pl.* **sergeants at arms** or **ser·geants-at-arms.**

**se·ri·al** (sē′rē əl)   **1** a story presented one part at a time in a magazine or newspaper or on radio or television.   **2** published, broadcast, or televised one part at a time: *a serial publication, a serial story.*   **3** of a series; arranged in a series; making a series: *Arrange volumes 1 to 5 on the shelf in serial order.*   **1** *n.*, **2, 3** *adj.*
☛ *Hom.* CEREAL.

**se·ri·al·ly** (sē′rē ə lē)   **1** in a SERIES.   **2** as a SERIAL.   *adv.*

**serial number**   an individual number given to a person, article, etc., as a means of easy identification.

**se·ri·ate** (sē′rē it *or* sē′rē āt′)   arranged or occurring in one or more SERIES.   *adj.*

**se·ri·a·tim** (sē′rē ā′tim)   in a series; one after the other.   *adv.*

**se·ries** (sē′rēz′)   **1** a number of similar things in a row: *A series of rooms opened off the long hall.*   **2** a number of things placed one after another: *Our names were listed in an alphabetical series.*   **3** a number of things, events, etc. coming one after the other: *A series of rainy days spoiled their vacation.*   **4** an arrangement of appliances, batteries, etc. connected to form part of one continuous path of electricity.   Compare with PARALLEL.   *n., pl.* **se·ries.**

**ser·if** (ser′if)   in printing, a thin or smaller line used to finish off a main stroke of a letter, as at the top and bottom of M.   *n.*   Compare with SANS-SERIF.

**se·ri·o–com·ic** (sē′rē ō kom′ik)   partly serious and partly comic.   *adj.*

**se·ri·ous** (sē′rē əs)   **1** thoughtful; grave: *a serious face.*   **2** in earnest; not joking; sincere: *She was serious about the subject.*   **3** needing thought; important: *Choice of one's life work is a serious matter.*   **4** important because it may do much harm; dangerous: *The badly injured woman was in serious condition.*   *adj.*   —**se′ri·ous·ly,** *adv.*   —**se′ri·ous·ness,** *n.*
☛ *Hom.* CEREUS.

**ser·mon** (sèr′mən)   **1** a public talk on religion or something connected with religion: *Ministers preach sermons in church.*   **2** a serious talk, often long and tiresome, about morals, conduct, duty, etc.: *After the guests left, the boy got a sermon on table manners from his mother.*   *n.*

**ser·mon·ize** (sèr′mə nīz′)   **1** give a sermon; preach.   **2** preach or talk seriously to; lecture.   *v.,* **ser·mon·ized, ser·mon·iz·ing.**   —**ser′mon·iz′er,** *n.*

**se·rol·o·gy** (si rol′ə jē)   the study of the use of SERUMS in curing or preventing disease.   *n.*

**se·rous** (sē′rəs)   **1** of SERUM; having to do with serum.   **2** like SERUM; watery: *Tears are drops of a serous fluid.*   *adj.*

**ser·pent** (sèr′pənt)   **1** a snake, especially a big snake.   **2** a sly, treacherous person.   *n.*

**ser·pen·tine** (sèr′pən tīn′ *or* sèr′pən tēn′)   **1** of or like a serpent.   **2** winding; twisting: *the serpentine course of a creek.*   **3** cunning; sly; treacherous: *a serpentine suggestion.*   **4** a mineral consisting chiefly of a hydrous silicate of magnesium, usually green, and sometimes spotted like a snakeskin.   **1–3** *adj.*, **4** *n.*

**ser·rate** (ser′āt *or* ser′it)   of a leaf, having saw-like notches pointing toward the tip.   See LEAF for picture.   *adj.*

**ser·rat·ed** (ser′ā tid)   SERRATE.   *adj.*

**ser·ra·tion** (se rā′shən)   **1** a SERRATED edge or formation.   **2** one of its series of notches.   *n.*

**ser·ried** (ser′ēd)   crowded closely together.   *adj.*

**ser·ru·late** (ser′yə lāt′)   very finely notched: *a serrulate leaf.*   *adj.*

**se·rum** (sē′rəm)   **1** a clear, pale-yellow, watery part of the blood that separates from the clot when blood coagulates.   **2** a liquid used to prevent or cure a disease, usually obtained from the blood of an animal that has been made immune to the disease: *Diphtheria antitoxin is a serum.*   **3** any watery animal liquid: *Lymph is a serum.*   **4** WHEY.   *n., pl.* **se·rums** or **se·ra** (sē′rə).

**ser·val** (sèr′vəl)   an African wild cat that has a brownish-yellow coat with black spots.   *n.*

**serv·ant** (sèr′vənt)   **1** a person employed in a household.   **2** a person employed by another: *Police officers and firefighters are public servants.*   **3** a person devoted to any service: *Doctors are often called the servants of humanity.*   *n.*   —**ser′vant·less,** *adj.*

**serve** (sèrv)   **1** be a servant of; work for or in: *A maid serves her employer.*   **2** be a servant; give service; work; perform official duties: *He served as butler. The soldier served three years in the army.*   **3** wait on at table; bring food or drink to: *The waiter served us.*   **4** put food or drink on the table: *The maid served the first course.*   **5** supply; furnish; supply with something needed: *The dairy serves us with milk. The men were served with a round of ammunition.*   **6** supply enough for: *One pie will serve six persons.*   **7** help; aid: *Let me know if I can serve you in any way.*   **8** be useful; be what is needed; be of use: *Boxes served as seats.*   **9** be useful to; fulfil: *This will serve my purpose.*   **10** be favourable or suitable; be favourable or suitable to; satisfy: *The ship will sail when the wind and tide serve.*   **11** treat: *The prisoner was poorly served.*   **12** pass; spend: *The thief served a term in prison.*   **13** deliver an order from a court, etc.; present with an order from a court, etc.: *He was served with a notice to appear in court.*   **14** in tennis and similar games, put the ball in play by hitting it.   **15** the act or way of serving a tennis ball.   **16** in tennis, a player's turn to serve.   **17** operate a gun, etc.   **18** in nautical use, bind or wind a rope, etc. with small cord to strengthen or protect it.   **1–14, 17, 18** *v.*, **served, serv·ing;**   **15, 16** *n.*
**serve one right,**   be just what one deserves: *The punishment served him right.*

**serv·er** (sèr′vər)   **1** a person who serves.   **2** a tray for dishes.   *n.*

**serv·ice** (sèr′vis)   **1** a helpful act or acts; aid; conduct that is useful to others: *She performed many services for her country.*   **2** supply; arrangements for supplying something useful or necessary: *The bus service was good.*   **3** occupation or employment as a servant: *to go into*

**service.** **4** work done for others; performance of duties; work: *Mrs. Weiss no longer needs the services of a doctor.* **5** advantage; benefit; use: *This coat has given me great service. Every available truck was pressed into service.* **6** a department of government or public employment; the persons engaged in it. **7** duty in the armed forces: *to be on active service.* **8** a religious meeting, ritual, or ceremony: *We attend church services once a week.* **9** regard; respect; devotion. **10** the manner of serving food; the food served: *The service in this restaurant is excellent.* **11** a set of dishes, etc.: *a solid silver tea service.* **12** in law, the serving of a process or writ upon a person. **13** in tennis, etc., the act or manner of putting the ball in play. **14** the ball as put into play. **15** a turn at starting the ball in play. **16** a small cord wound about a rope, etc. to strengthen or protect it. **17** make fit for service; keep fit for service: *The mechanic serviced our automobile.* **18 services, a** work done in the service of others; helpful labour, as opposed to production, manufacturing, construction work, etc.: *goods and services.* **b** arrangements or installations for public use, such as electricity, water supply, and sewers. **19 the service** or **services,** the navy, army, or air force: *We entered the service together.* 1–16, 18, 19 *n.,* 17 *v.,* **serv·iced, serv·ic·ing.**
**at someone's service,** ready to do what someone wants.
**in service,** in working order; functioning: *We'll call you as soon as the line is in service again. Is their telephone in service?*
**of service,** helpful, useful.
**out of service,** not in working order; not functioning: *This elevator is out of service.*

**serv·ice·a·bil·i·ty** (sėr′vi sə bil′ə tē) being SERVICEABLE. *n.*

**serv·ice·a·ble** (sėr′vi sə bəl) **1** useful for a long time; able to stand much use: *You will find this heavy coat quite serviceable.* **2** capable of giving good service; useful: *He should make a serviceable goalkeeper.* *adj.* —**serv′ice·a·ble·ness,** *n.* —**serv′ice·a·bly,** *adv.*

**serv·ice·ber·ry** (sėr′vis ber′ē) **1** a bush or small tree bearing white flowers and large, sweet, purple berries. In the West, the serviceberry is often called the saskatoon and, in the Maritimes, shadbush. **2** the fruit of this bush. *n.*

**service centre** a stopping area adjoining an expressway, consisting of a service station, restaurant, toilet facilities, etc.

**serv·ice·man** (sėr′vi sman′ or sėr′vi smən) **1** a member of the armed forces. **2** a person whose job it is to maintain and repair machines, appliances, etc. *n., pl.* **serv·ice·men** (-smen′ or -smən).

**service road 1** ACCESS ROAD. **2** a road, generally paralleling an expressway, to carry local traffic and to provide access to adjoining property.

**service station 1** a place for supplying automobiles with gasoline, oil, water, etc. **2** a place where repairs, parts, adjustments, etc. can be obtained for automobiles.

**ser·vi·ette** (sėr′vē et′) a piece of cloth or paper used at meals for protecting the clothing or for wiping the lips or fingers. *n.*

**ser·vile** (sėr′vīl or sėr′vəl) **1** like that of slaves; mean; base: *servile flattery.* **2** of or having to do with slaves: *a servile revolt, servile work.* **3** fit for a slave. **4** yielding through fear, lack of spirit, etc.: *An honest judge cannot be servile to public opinion.* *adj.* —**ser′vile·ly,** *adv.* —**ser′vile·ness,** *n.*

**ser·vil·i·ty** (sėr vil′ə tē) an attitude or behaviour fit for a slave; servile yielding. *n., pl.* **ser·vil·i·ties.**

**serv·ing** (sėr′ving) portion of food served to a person at one time; helping. *n.*

**ser·vi·tor** (sėr′və tər) a servant; attendant. *n.*

**ser·vi·tude** (sėr′və tyüd′ or sėr′və tüd′) **1** slavery; bondage. **2** forced labour as punishment: *The criminal was sentenced to five years' servitude.* *n.*

**ses·a·me** (ses′ə mē) **1** an Oriental plant. **2** its seeds, used for food and in medicine. **3** See OPEN SESAME. *n.*

**ses·qui·cen·ten·ni·al** (ses′kwi sen ten′ē əl) **1** a 150th anniversary or its celebration. **2** having to do with, or marking the completion of, a period of a century and a half. 1 *n.,* 2 *adj.*

**ses·qui·pe·da·li·an** (ses′kwi pə dā′lē ən) **1** of a word, very long; containing many syllables. **2** using long words. *adj.*

**ses·sile** (ses′īl or ses′əl) **1** attached by the base instead of by a stem: *a sessile leaf.* **2** fixed to one spot; not able to move around: *Barnacles and sponges are sessile.* *adj.*

**ses·sion** (sesh′ən) **1** a sitting or meeting of a court, council, legislature, etc.: *a session of Parliament.* **2** a series of such sittings. **3** the term or period of such sittings: *This year's session of Parliament was unusually long.* **4** a period of meetings, classes, etc.: *Our school has two sessions, one in the morning and one in the afternoon. She attended the university during the summer session.* *n.*
**in session,** meeting: *The teachers were in session all Saturday morning.*
☛ *Hom.* CESSION.

**ses·sion·al** (sesh′ə nəl) **1** of a SESSION; having to do with sessions. **2** occurring every SESSION. *adj.*

**sessional indemnity** in certain provinces of Canada, the remuneration paid each session to a MEMBER OF THE LEGISLATIVE ASSEMBLY.

**ses·tet** (ses tet′) **1** a musical SEXTET. **2** the last six lines of certain sonnets. *n.*

**set** (set) **1** put in some place; put; place: *Set the box on its end.* **2** put in the right place, position, or condition: *to set a broken bone.* **3** arrange the hair when damp to make it take a certain position. **4** adjust according to a standard: *to set a clock.* **5** put in some condition or relation: *A spark set the woods on fire. The slaves were set free.* **6** put a price, etc.; fix the value of a certain amount or rate: *She set the value of the watch at $500.* **7** put as the measure of esteem of a person or thing: *to set great store by a thing.* **8** post, appoint, or station for the purpose of performing some duty: *to set a detective on a person.* **9** fix; arrange; appoint: *to set a time limit for taking an examination.* **10** fixed or appointed beforehand; established: *a set time, set rules.* **11** provide for others to follow: *to set a good example.* **12** put in a fixed, rigid, or settled state: *to set one's teeth.* **13** fixed; rigid: *a set smile. He has set opinions.* **14** become fixed; make or become firm or hard: *Jelly sets as it cools.* **15** firm; hard. **16** put in a frame or other thing that holds: *to set a diamond in gold.* **17** adorn; ornament: *a bracelet set with diamonds.* **18** go down; sink: *The sun sets in the west.* **19** put a hen to sit on eggs to hatch them; place eggs under a hen to be hatched. **20** of a hen, sit on eggs. **21** of a dog, indicate the position of

game by standing stiffly and pointing with the nose. **22** a dog's pointing in the presence of game. **23** a number of things or persons belonging together: *a set of dishes.* **24** in mathematics, a specified collection of elements, especially a collection having some feature or features in common: *the set of all right triangles, the set of even integers.* **25** the complete scenery for a play, act, scene, etc. **26** a device for receiving or sending by radio, television, telephone, telegraph, etc. **27** the way a thing is put or placed; form; shape: *His jaw had a stubborn set.* **28** hang or fit in a particular manner: *That coat sets well.* **29** a direction; tendency; course; drift: *The set of opinion was toward building a new bridge.* **30** have a direction; tend: *The current sets to the south.* **31** begin to move. **32** make an attack. **33** encourage to attack; cause to be hostile. **34** begin to apply; begin to apply oneself: *Have you set to work?* **35** a warp; bend; displacement: *a set to the right.* **36** a slip or shoot for planting. **37** a young fruit just formed from a blossom. **38** form fruit in the blossom. **39** in music, adapt; fit: *to set words to music.* **40** arrange music for certain voices or instruments. **41** in printing, put type in the order required. **42** make (a colour of fabrics, etc.) fast. **43** the act or manner of setting. **44** resolved; determined: *She is set on going today.* **45** *Informal.* stubbornly fixed; obstinate. **46** in tennis, a group of six or more games: *To win a set, one side must win at least six games, and two more games than the other side.* **47** in square dancing, a group of four couples. **48** the figures of a square dance. 1–9, 11, 12, 14, 16 21, 28, 30 34, 38 42 *v.*, **set, set·ting** 10, 13, 15, 44, 45 *adj.*, 22–27, 29, 35–37, 43, 46–48 *n.*
**set about,** start work upon; begin: *Set about your washing.*
**set against, a** make unfriendly toward. **b** balance; compare.
**set aside, a** put to one side. **b** put by for later use. **c** discard, dismiss, or leave out; reject; annul: *Sometimes a higher court sets aside the decision in a lawsuit.*
**set back, a** stop; hinder; check: *The job was set back because of the accident.* **b** *Informal.* cost a person so much: *The new car set her back a lot of money.*
**set bread,** mix batter or dough and leave it to rise.
**set down, a** deposit or let alight; put down: *set down a suitcase. The bus set him down near the town.* **b** put down in writing or printing. **c** consider; ascribe: *Your failure in the test can be set down to too much haste.*
**set forth, a** make known; express; declare. **b** start out: *We set forth on our trip.*
**set in, a** begin. **b** blow or flow toward the shore.
**set off, a** explode. **b** start to go: *set off for home.* **c** emphasize or enhance by contrast: *The green dress set off her red hair.* **d** balance; compensate: *His losses were set off by some gains.* **e** mark off; separate from the others: *One sentence was set off from the rest by quotation marks.*
**set on** or **set upon, a** attack: *The dog set on him.* **b** urge to attack.
**set out, a** start to go. **b** spread out to show, sell, or use. **c** plant. **d** plan; intend to do something.
**set to, a** begin: *Set to work.* **b** begin fighting: *The two boys set to.*
**set up, a** build. **b** begin; start. **c** put up; raise in place, position, power, pride, etc. **d** claim; pretend. **e** ready; prepare; arrange. **f** establish.
**set up for,** claim or pretend to be.
☞ *Usage.* **Set,** meaning 'to place', should not be confused with SIT: *He set a book on the stool. He sat on the stool. A builder sets his bricks carefully. An old man sits carefully.*

**se·ta** (sē′tə) any slender, stiff, bristle-like structure: *Earthworms have two pairs of setae in each segment.* *n.*, *pl.* **se·tae** (sē′tē or sē′tī).

**seta** 1083 **settle**

hat, āge, fär; let, ēqual, tėrm; it, īce
hot, ōpen, ôrder; oil, out; cup, pút, rüle
əbove, takən, pencəl, lemən, circəs
ch, child; ng, long; sh, ship
th, thin; ᴛʜ, then; zh, measure

Setback (def. 2)

**set·back** (set′bak′) **1** a check to progress; reverse. **2** a steplike setting back of the outside wall of a tall building in order to give better light and air in the street. **3** a lessening in the thickness of a wall. **4** a flat, plain projection of a wall. *n.*

**set·off** (set′of′) **1** a setting off on a trip; start; departure. **2** a thing used to set off or adorn; ornament; decoration. **3** a compensation; offset; something that counterbalances or makes up for something else. *n.*

**set·tee** (se tē′) a sofa or long bench with a back and, usually, arms. *n.*

**set·ter** (set′ər) **1** a person who sets or arranges things: *a setter of type, a setter of jewels.* **2** a long-haired hunting dog, trained to stand motionless and point the nose toward the game that it scents. *n.*

**set·ting** (set′ing) **1** a frame or other thing in which something is set: *The mounting of a jewel is its setting.* **2** the scenery of a play; a set. **3** the place, time, etc. of a play or story. **4** the surroundings; background: *a scenic mountain setting.* **5** the music composed to go with a story, poem, etc. **6** the eggs that a hen sets on for hatching. **7** the act of one that sets. **8** the dishes or cutlery required to set one place at a table. **9** ppr. of SET. 1–8 *n.*, 9 *v.*

**set·tle**[1] (set′əl) **1** determine; decide; agree upon: *to settle on a time for leaving.* **2** put or be put in order; arrange: *to settle all one's affairs before going away.* **3** pay; arrange payment: *to settle a bill.* **4** take up residence in a new country or place: *to settle in Manitoba.* **5** establish colonies or communities in: *The French settled Quebec.* **6** set or be in a fairly permanent position, place, or way of life: *We are settled in our new home.* **7** put or come to rest in a particular place; put in or come to a definite condition: *Eva's cold settled in her lungs.* **8** arrange in or come to a desired or comfortable position: *The cat settled herself in the chair.* **9** make or become quiet: *Rest will settle your nerves.* **10** go down; sink: *The end of that wall has settled five centimetres.* **11** of liquid, make or become clear: *Cold water will settle coffee.* **12** of dregs, sink or cause to sink to the bottom. **13** make or become firm and compact: *to settle the contents of a barrel.* *v.*, **set·tled, set·tling.**
**settle down, a** live a more regular life. **b** direct steady effort or attention. **c** calm down; become quiet.

**settle upon** or **on**, give property, etc. to by law.

**set·tle²** (set′əl) a long, wooden bench with arms and a high back. *n.*

**set·tle·ment** (set′əl mənt) **1** the act of settling or state of being settled. **2** establishment in life. **3** a deciding; determining: *settlement of a date.* **4** a putting in order; arrangement: *No settlement of the dispute is possible unless each side yields some point.* **5** a payment: *Settlement of all claims against the firm will be made shortly.* **6** the settling of persons in a new region: *The settlement of the English along the Atlantic coast of North America gave England claim to that section.* **7** a region settled in this way: *England had many settlements along the Atlantic coast.* **8** a group of buildings and the people living in them: *The explorers spent the night in an Indian settlement.* **9** a place in a poor, neglected neighbourhood where work for its improvement is carried on: *The Scott Mission is a famous settlement in Toronto.* **10** the settling of property upon someone: *She received $200 000 by a marriage settlement.* **11** the amount so given. *n.*

**set·tler** (set′lər) **1** a person who SETTLES. **2** a person who SETTLES in a new region: *The early settlers in Canada faced many hardships. n.*

**set·tlings** (set′lingz) the things in a liquid which settle to the bottom; sediment. *n.pl.*

**set-to** (set′tü′) *Informal.* a fight; dispute. *n., pl.* **set-tos.**

**set-up** (set′up′) **1** an arrangement of apparatus, machinery, etc. **2** the arrangement of an organization: *I dislike the set-up of the committee.* **3** one's manner of holding the head and body; carriage; bearing. *n.*

**sev·en** (sev′ən) **1** one more than six; 7: *Ten minus three equals seven. They stayed seven days.* **2** the numeral 7: *This 7 looks like a 1.* **3** the seventh in a set or series; especially, a playing card having seven spots: *She smiled with a seven of spades.* **4** being seventh in a set or series (*used mainly after the noun*): *Lesson Seven was boring.* **5** a set or series of seven persons or things: *She arranged the cards in sevens.* 1–3, 5 *n.*, 1, 4 *adj.*
☛ *Etym.* From OE *seofon*, related to German *sieben* and having the same Indo-European source as L *septem* (giving F *sept*) and Gk. *hepta*.

**sev·en·fold** (sev′ən fōld′) **1** seven times as much or as many. **2** having seven parts. **3** seven times as much or as often; in the proportion of seven to one. 1, 3 *adv.*, 1, 2 *adj.*

**seven seas** all the seas and oceans of the world, traditionally believed to be the Arctic, Antarctic, North Atlantic, South Atlantic, North Pacific, South Pacific, and Indian oceans: *to sail the seven seas.*

**sev·en·teen** (sev′ən tēn′) **1** seven more than ten; 17: *Seventeen plus three is twenty. It cost about seventeen dollars.* **2** the numeral 17: *I think it's a 17, not an 11.* **3** the seventeenth in a set or series. **4** being seventeenth in a set or series (*used after the noun*): *Chapter Seventeen looks interesting.* **5** a set or series of seventeen persons or things. 1–3, 5 *n.*, 1, 4 *adj.*

**sev·en·teenth** (sev′ən tēnth′) **1** next after the 16th; last in a series of 17; 17th. **2** one, or being one, of 17 equal parts. *adj., n.*

**sev·enth** (sev′ənth) **1** next after the sixth; last in a series of 7; 7th. **2** one, or being one, of 7 equal parts. **3** in music, the interval between two tones that are seven degrees apart. **4** the combination of two such tones. 1, 2 *adj.*, 1–4 *n.*

**seventh heaven** **1** the highest part of heaven. **2** the highest place or condition of joy and happiness.

**sev·enth·ly** (sev′ən thlē) in the seventh place. *adv.*

**sev·en·ti·eth** (sev′ən tē ith) **1** next after the 69th; last in a series of 70; 70th. **2** one, or being one, of 70 equal parts. *adj., n.*

**sev·en·ty** (sev′ən tē) **1** seven times ten; 70. **2 seventies,** *pl.* the years from seventy through seventy-nine, especially of a century or of a person's life: *He was still skiing regularly well into his seventies.* 1, 2 *n., pl.* **sev·en·ties;** 1 *adj.*

**sev·er** (sev′ər) **1** cut apart; cut off: *to sever a rope. The axe severed his head from his body.* **2** part; divide; separate: *a party severed into two factions. The rope severed and the swing fell down.* **3** break off: *The two countries severed friendly relations.* v. —**sev′er·a·ble,** *adj.*

**sev·er·al** (sev′ər əl *or* sev′rəl) **1** being more than two or three but not many; some; a few: *to gain several kilograms.* **2** more than two or three but not many; some; a few: *Several had given their consent.* **3** individual; different: *The boys went their several ways, each concerned with his own business.* **4** considered separately; single: *The several steps in the process of making paper were shown in a movie.* 1, 3, 4 *adj.*, 2 *n.*

**sev·er·al·ly** (sev′ə rə lē *or* sev′rə lē) **1** separately; singly; individually: *Consider these points, first severally and then collectively.* **2** RESPECTIVELY. *adv.*

**sev·er·al·ty** (sev′ə rəl tē *or* sev′rəl tē) the state of being SEPARATE or distinct. *n., pl.* **sev·er·al·ties.**

**sev·er·ance** (sev′ə rəns *or* sev′rəns) **1** a severing or being severed; separation; division. **2** a breaking off: *the severance of diplomatic relations between two countries. n.*

**severance pay** additional pay granted to employees who are leaving a business, company, etc., based on seniority.

**se·vere** (sə vēr′) **1** very strict; stern; harsh: *The judge imposed a severe sentence on the criminal.* **2** sharp; violent: *a severe criticism, a severe storm.* **3** serious; grave: *a severe manner, a severe illness.* **4** very plain or simple; without ornament: *Her severe dress made her look old.* **5** difficult: *The new gun had to pass a series of severe tests.* **6** rigidly exact, accurate, or methodical: *severe reasoning.* *adj.*, **se·ver·er, se·ver·est.** —**se·vere′ly,** *adv.* —**se·vere′ness,** *n.*

**se·ver·i·ty** (sə ver′ə tē) **1** strictness; sternness; harshness: *The children feared their father because of his severity.* **2** violence; sharpness: *the severity of storms, pain, disease, grief, etc.* **3** a simplicity of style or taste; plainness: *The severity of her dress is becoming.* **4** seriousness. **5** accuracy; exactness. **6** something severe. *n., pl.* **se·ver·i·ties.**

**sew** (sō) **1** work with needle and thread. **2** fasten with stitches. *v.*, **sewed, sewn** or **sewed, sew·ing.** **sew up, a** close with stitches: *The doctor sewed up the wound.* **b** *Informal.* make certain of.
☛ *Hom.* so, sow¹.

**sew·age** (sü′ij) the waste matter that passes through sewers. *n.*

**sew·er¹** (sü′ər) a pipe or channel to carry off waste water and refuse: *Sewers are usually underground. n.*

**sew·er²** (sō′ər) a person or thing that sews. *n.*

**sew·er·age** (sü′ə rij) **1** the removal of waste matter by

**sewers.** 2 a system of sewers. 3 the waste matter that passes through sewers; sewage. *n.*

**sew·ing** (sō′ing) 1 work done with a needle and thread. See NEEDLE for picture. 2 something to be sewn. 3 for sewing; used in sewing: *a sewing room.* 4 ppr. of SEW. 1, 2 *n.*, 3 *adj.*, 4 *v.*

**sewing circle** a group of people, usually women, who meet regularly to sew for charity, etc.

**sewing machine** a machine for sewing or stitching cloth.

**sewn** (sōn) a pp. of SEW. *v.* ☞ Hom. SOWN.

**sex** (seks) 1 either of the two categories, male and female, into which human beings, animals, and plants are divided, according to their function in the reproductive process: *Men, bulls, and roosters are of the male sex; women, cows, and hens are of the female sex.* 2 the fact or condition of being male or female: *People were admitted without regard to age or sex.* 3 sexual attraction between people. 4 behaviour resulting from or motivated by this attraction. 5 SEXUAL INTERCOURSE. 6 of or having to do with sex: *sex education.* *n.* —**sex′less**, *adj.*

**sex·a·ge·nar·i·an** (sek′sə jə ner′ē ən) 1 of the age of 60 years, or between 60 and 70 years old. 2 a person who is 60, or between 60 and 70, years old. 1 *adj.*, 2 *n.*

**sex appeal** sexual attractiveness.

**sex·ism** (sek′siz əm) prejudice or discrimination against a person or group of persons on the basis of sex. *n.*

**sex·ist** (sek′sist) 1 characterized by prejudice or discrimination on the basis of sex: *a sexist attitude, a sexist statement.* 2 a person who has such an attitude. 1 *adj.*, 2 *n.*

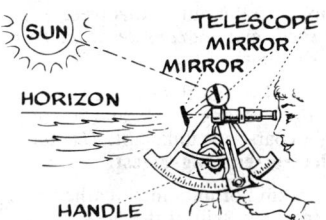

A sextant. It is held so that the horizon is seen in mirror A. The arm is then moved until the sun or a star is reflected from mirror B into mirror A. The number of degrees marked off by the arm is the altitude of the sun or star.

**sex·tant** (sek′stənt) 1 an instrument used by navigators, surveyors, etc. for measuring the angular distance between two objects: *Sextants are used at sea to measure the altitude of the sun, a star, etc. in order to determine latitude and longitude.* 2 one sixth of a circle. *n.*

**sex·tet** or **sex·tette** (sek stet′) 1 a musical composition for six voices or instruments. 2 six singers or players. 3 any group of six. *n.*

**sex·til·lion** (sek stil′yən) 1 in Canada, the United States and France, 1 followed by 21 zeros. 2 in the United Kingdom, 1 followed by 36 zeros. *n.*

**sex·ton** (sek′stən) a person who takes care of a church building: *A sexton's duties sometimes include ringing the bell, digging graves, etc.* *n.*

**sex·tu·ple** (sek styü′pəl, sek stü′pəl, sek stup′əl, or sek′stə pəl) 1 consisting of six parts; sixfold. 2 six times as great. 3 a number or amount six times as great as another. 4 make or become six times as great. 5 in music, characterized by six beats to the measure. 1, 2, 5 *adj.*, 3 *n.*, 4 *v.*, **sex·tu·pled, sex·tu·pling.**

**sex·tu·plet** (sek styü′plit or sek stü′plit, sek stup′lit or sek′stə plit′) 1 one of six children, animals, etc. born of the same mother at the same time. 2 a group of six things. *n.*

**sex·u·al** (sek′shü əl) 1 of or having to do with sex or the sexes: *sexual distinctions.* 2 of or having to do with relations between the sexes: *sexual morality.* *adj.*

**sexual intercourse** any act between people that involves genital contact and the sexual organs of male or female.

**sex·u·al·i·ty** (sek′shü al′ə tē) 1 sexual character; possession of sex. 2 awareness of or interest in sex. 3 sexual drive or capability. *n.*

**sex·u·al·ly** (sek′shü ə lē) 1 by means of sex. 2 in regard to sex. *adv.*

**sex·y** (sek′sē) *Informal.* 1 sexually provocative or stimulating: *a sexy dress, sexy young men.* 2 especially concerned with sexual functions: *a sexy novel.* *adj.*, **sex·i·er, sex·i·est.**

**s.g.** specific gravity.

**sh** or **'sh** (sh) a shortening of **hush**, used to urge silence. *interj.*

**shab·by** (shab′ē) 1 much worn: *a shabby suit.* 2 wearing old or much worn clothes. 3 poor or neglected; run-down: *a shabby old house.* 4 not generous; mean; unfair: *It is shabby not to speak to an old friend because he is poor.* *adj.*, **shab·bi·er, shab·bi·est.** —**shab′bi·ly**, *adv.* —**shab′bi·ness**, *n.*

**shack** (shak) 1 a roughly built hut or cabin: *The girls made a shack in the backyard.* 2 a house in bad condition: *There are a lot of shacks in that part of town.* *n.*

**shack·le** (shak′əl) 1 a metal band fastened around the ankle or wrist of a prisoner, slave, etc.: *Shackles are usually fastened to each other, the wall, floor, etc. by chains.* 2 the link fastening together the two rings for the ankles and wrists of a prisoner. 3 put shackles on. 4 anything that prevents freedom of action, thought, etc. 5 restrain; hamper. 6 something for fastening or coupling. 7 fasten or couple with a shackle. 8 **shackles**, *pl.* fetters; chains. 1, 2, 4, 6, 8 *n.*, 3, 5, 7 *v.*, **shack·led, shack·ling.** —**shack′ler**, *n.*

**shad** (shad) any of several saltwater fishes, related to the herrings, that ascend rivers in the spring to spawn: *The shad common on the northern Atlantic coast is a valuable food fish.* *n.*, *pl.* **shad** or **shads.**

**shad·ber·ry** (shad′ber ē) 1 the fruit of the SHADBUSH. 2 the SHADBUSH. *n.*, *pl.* **shad·ber·ries.**

**shad·blos·som** (shad′blos əm) SHADBUSH. *n.*

**shad·bush** (shad′bush′) in the Maritimes, SERVICEBERRY. *n.*

**shad·dock** (shad′ək) 1 a pear-shaped fruit like a

# shade — shake

coarse, dry, inferior grapefruit. **2** the tree that it grows on. *n.*

**shade** (shād) **1** a partly dark place, not in the sunshine: *He sat in the shade of a big tree.* **2** a slight darkness or coolness afforded by something that cuts off light: *Big trees cast shade.* **3** a place or condition of comparative obscurity. **4** something that shuts out light; a blind: *Pull down the shades of the windows.* **5** screen from light; darken: *A big hat shades the eyes.* **6** lightness or darkness of colour: *silks in all shades of blue.* **7** the dark part of a picture. **8** make darker than the rest. **9** a very small difference, amount, or degree: *a shade too long.* **10** a darkening look, feeling, etc.; shadow; cloud: *A shade of doubt troubled her.* **11** make dark or gloomy. **12** show small differences; change little by little: *This scarf shades from deep rose to pale pink.* **13** lessen slightly: *Can't you shade the price for me?* **14** a ghost; spirit: *the shades of departed heroes.* **15** in drawing and painting, mark with various degrees of darkness: *The artist shaded the picture of the ball to make it look more real.* **16 the shades,** the darkness of evening or night. 1–4, 6, 7, 9, 10, 14, 16 *n.,* 5, 8, 11–13, 15 *v.,* **shad•ed, shad•ing.** —**shade′less,** *adj.* **in** or **into the shade, a** out of the light. **b** in or into a condition of being unknown or unnoticed.

**shad fly 1** any of various kinds of tiny, winged insects that appear in swarms during the spring. **2** an artificial lure shaped like a shad fly and used for fishing.

**shad•i•ness** (shā′dē nis) the quality or state of being SHADY. *n.*

**shad•ing** (shā′ding) **1** a covering from the light. **2** the use of black or colour to give the effect of shade or depth in a picture. **3** a slight variation or difference of colour, character, etc. **4** ppr. of SHADE. 1–3 *n.,* 4 *v.*

**shad•ow** (shad′ō) **1** the shade made by some person, animal, or thing: *Sometimes a person's shadow is much longer than she is, and sometimes much shorter.* **2** shade; darkness; partial shade. **3** the dark part of a place or picture. **4** protect from light; shade: *The grass is shadowed by huge oaks.* **5** cast a shadow on. **6** a little bit; small degree; slight suggestion: *There's not a shadow of a doubt about his guilt.* **7** ghost. **8** a faint image or likeness: *You look worn to a shadow.* **9** represent faintly. **10** a reflected image. **11** protection; shelter. **12** follow closely and secretly: *The detective shadowed the suspect.* **13** a person who follows another closely and secretly. **14** a constant companion; follower. **15** sadness; gloom. **16** make sad or gloomy. **17** obscurity. **18** a gloomy or troubled look or expression. **19** represent in a prophetic way. **20 the shadows,** darkness after sunset. 1–3, 6–8, 10, 11, 13–15, 17, 18, 20 *n.,* 4, 5, 9, 12, 16, 19 *v.* **under** or **in the shadow of,** very near to.

**shad•ow•box•ing** (shad′ō bok′sing) boxing before a mirror or with an imaginary opponent for exercise or training. *n.*

**shad•ow•less** (shad′ō lis) having or casting no shadow. *adj.*

**shad•ow•y** (shad′ō ē) **1** having much shadow or shade; shady: *We went out of the hot sunshine into the cool, shadowy room.* **2** like a shadow; dim, faint, or slight: *She saw a shadowy outline on the window curtain.* **3** not real; ghostly. *adj.* —**shad′ow•i•ness,** *n.*

**shad•y** (shā′dē) **1** in the shade; shaded. **2** giving shade. **3** *Informal.* of doubtful honesty, character, etc.: *He has engaged in rather shady occupations.* *adj.* **shad•i•er, shad•i•est.** **on the shady side of,** older than; beyond the age of: *on the shady side of thirty.*

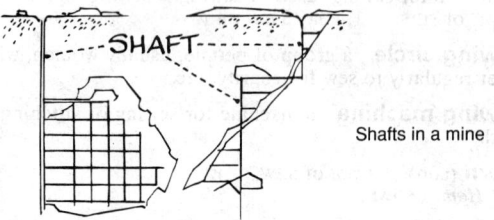
Shafts in a mine

**shaft** (shaft) **1** in a machine, a cylindrical bar that rotates or supports rotating parts. See CAM and DIFFERENTIAL for pictures. **2** a deep passage sunk in the earth: *The entrance to a mine is called a shaft.* **3** a well-like passage; deep, narrow space: *an elevator shaft.* **4** the long, slender stem of an arrow, spear, lance, etc. **5** an arrow, spear, lance, etc. **6** something aimed at a person as one might aim an arrow or spear: *shafts of ridicule.* **7** a ray or beam of light. **8** a wooden pole by means of which a horse is harnessed to a carriage, etc. **9** COLUMN. **10** the main part of a column. See COLUMN for picture. **11** flagpole. **12** the long, straight handle of a hammer, axe, golf club, etc. **13** a stem; stalk. **14** the rib of a feather. *n.* —**shaft′like′,** *adj.*

**shag** (shag) **1** rough, matted hair, wool, etc. **2** a mass of this material: *the shag of a dog.* **3** the long, rough nap of some kinds of cloth. **4** cloth having such a nap. **5** a coarse tobacco cut into shreds. *n.*

**shag•a•nap•pi** (shag′ə nap′ē) *Cdn.* **1** thongs, straps, lines, or cords made from rawhide. **2** a kind of pony. *n.*

**shag•bark** (shag′bärk′) **1** a hickory tree whose rough bark peels off in long strips. **2** the nut of this tree: *Shagbarks have fairly thin shells and are considered the best hickory nuts.* *n.* Also, **shellbark.**

**shag•gy** (shag′ē) **1** covered with a thick, rough mass of hair, wool, etc.: *a shaggy dog.* **2** long, thick, and rough: *shaggy eyebrows.* **3** rough, coarse, or unkempt: *The dog had shaggy hair.* *adj.,* **shag•gi•er, shag•gi•est.**

**sha•green** (shə grēn′) a kind of untanned leather with a granular surface, made from the skin of the horse, ass, shark, seal, and other animals. *n.*

**Shah** (shä) formerly, a title of the monarch of Iran. *n.*

**Shai•tan** (shī tän′) SATAN. *n.*

**shake** (shāk) **1** move quickly backward and forward, up and down, or from side to side: *to shake a rug.* **2** bring, throw, force, rouse, scatter, etc. by such movement: *to shake snow off one's clothes.* **3** be shaken: *Sand shakes off easily.* **4** clasp hands in greeting, congratulating, etc. another: *to shake hands.* **5** tremble: *He is shaking with cold.* **6** make tremble: *The explosion shook the town.* **7** totter; waver: *His courage began to shake.* **8** cause to totter or waver: *to shake the very foundations of society.* **9** disturb; make less firm: *His lie shook my faith in his honesty.* **10** the act or fact of shaking: *a shake of the head.* **11** *Informal.* EARTHQUAKE. **12** a drink made by shaking ingredients together: *a milk shake.* **13** *Informal.* movement: *I'll be there in two shakes.* **14** trill. **15** in music, a rapid alternation of a note with a tone above or below it; a trill. **16** a crack in a growing tree; fissure. **17** *Informal.* get rid of: *Can't you shake*

him? **18** mix dice before throwing. 1–9, 14, 17, 18 *v.*, shook, shak·en, shak·ing; 10–13, 15, 16 *n.*
**no great shakes,** *Informal.* not unusual, extraordinary, or important.
**shake down, a** bring or throw down by shaking. **b** cause to settle down. **c** bring into working order.
**shake off,** get rid of.
**shake up, a** shake hard. **b** stir up. **c** jar in body or nerves: *He was somewhat shaken up by the experience.*

**shak·en** (shā′kən) pp. of SHAKE. *v.*

**shak·er** (shā′kər) **1** a person who shakes something. **2** a machine or utensil used in shaking. **3** a container for pepper, salt, etc., having a perforated top. *n.*

**Shake·spear·e·an** or **Shake·sper·e·an** (shāk spē′rē ən) **1** of, having to do with, or suggestive of Shakespeare or his works. **2** a specialist in the study of the works of Shakespeare. 1 *adj.*, 2 *n.*

**Shake·spear·i·an** or **Shake·sper·i·an** See SHAKESPEAREAN. *adj., n.*

**shake–up** (shā′kup′) *Informal.* a sudden and complete change; drastic rearrangement of policy, personnel, etc.: *a shake-up in the government.* *n.*

**shak·i·ly** (shā′kə lē) in a shaky manner. *adv.*

**shak·i·ness** (shā′kē nis) a shaky condition. *n.*

**shak·o** (shak′ō) a high, stiff military hat with a plume or other ornament. See HAT for picture. *n., pl.* **shak·os.**

**Shak·ti** (shuk′tē) one of the three great gods of classical Hinduism, the mother goddess who stands for nature in all its aspects, the main object of worship among Hindus in northeastern India. *n.*

**shak·y** (shā′kē) **1** shaking: *a shaky voice.* **2** liable to break down; weak: *a shaky porch.* **3** not to be depended on; not reliable: *a shaky firm, a shaky knowledge of art.* *adj.*, **shak·i·er**, **shak·i·est.**

**shale** (shāl) a fine-grained sedimentary rock formed from clay that has been subjected to great pressure: *Shale splits easily into thin layers.* *n.*

**shall** (shal; *unstressed* shəl) a word used: **1** in questions to ask what one is to do: *Shall we go? Shall I wait?* **2** in statements with "you," "he," "she," or "they" to show that a person has to do something: *You shall pay attention. He shall stay in his room for an hour.* **3** with "I" and "we" to indicate simple future time: *I shall go tomorrow if I cannot make it today.* *v.*, **should** (def. 3).
☞ *Usage.* Many people make no distinction between the verbs **shall** and WILL, using both to express future time. However, in formal English, the following distinction is made between the two verbs. To express simple future, use **shall** with *I* and *we: I shall leave tomorrow* but use **will** with *you, he, she, they: He (you, they) will leave tomorrow.* To express determination, use **will** with *I or we: I (we) will go no matter what you say* but use **shall** with *he, she, you, they: She (you, they) shall finish the work no matter how long it takes.*

**shal·lop** (shal′əp) a small, light, open boat propelled by sail or oars. *n.*

**shal·lot** (shə lot′) **1** a small plant related to and resembling the onion, but having a bulb composed of sections or cloves. **2** a bulb or clove of this plant. **3** a small brown onion. *n.*

**shal·low** (shal′ō) **1** not deep: *shallow water, a shallow dish.* **2** lacking depth of thought, knowledge, feeling, etc.: *a shallow mind.* **3** become less deep. **4** make less deep. **5** Usually, **shallows,** *pl.* a shallow place: *The girls splashed in the shallows of the pond.* 1, 2 *adj.*, 3, 4 *v.*, 5 *n.* —**shal′low·ness,** *n.*

**shal·y** (shā′lē) of, like, or containing SHALE. *adj.*

**sham** (sham) **1** a pretence; fraud. **2** a counterfeit; imitation. **3** pretended; feigned; being an imitation: *The soldiers fought a sham battle for practice.* **4** pretend; feign: *He shammed sickness so he wouldn't have to work.* 1, 2 *n.*, 3 *adj.*, 4 *v.*, **shammed, sham·ming.**

**sha·man** (shä′mən, shā′mən, *or* sham′ən) a medicine man, woman, or priest believed to have the power to influence spirits for good or evil. *n.*

**sham·ble** (sham′bəl) **1** walk awkwardly or unsteadily: *The tired old man shambles.* **2** a shambling walk. 1 *v.*, **sham·bled, sham·bling;** 2 *n.*

**sham·bles** (sham′bəlz) **1** slaughterhouse. **2** a place of butchery or of great bloodshed. **3** *Informal.* confusion; mess; general disorder: *The careless children made a shambles of their room.* *n.pl.* or *sing.*

**shame** (shām) **1** a painful feeling of having done something wrong, improper, or silly: *to blush with shame.* **2** cause to feel shame: *My silly mistake shamed me.* **3** drive or force by shame: *Bill was shamed into combing his hair.* **4** a disgrace; dishonour: *That young man's arrest has brought shame to a fine family.* **5** bring disgrace upon. **6** a fact to be sorry about: *It is a shame to be so wasteful.* **7** a person or thing to be ashamed of; cause of disgrace. **8** a sense of what is decent or proper. 1, 4, 6–8 *n.*, 2, 3, 5 *v.*, **shamed, sham·ing.**
**for shame!** shame on you!
**put to shame, a** disgrace; make ashamed. **b** surpass; make dim by comparison: *Her careful work put all the rest to shame.*

**shame·faced** (shām′fāst′) **1** bashful; shy. **2** showing shame and embarrassment. *adj.*

**shame·ful** (shām′fəl) causing shame; bringing disgrace. *adj.* —**shame′ful·ly,** *adv.* —**shame′ful·ness,** *n.*

**shame·less** (shām′lis) **1** without shame. **2** not modest. *adj.* —**shame′less·ly,** *adv.* —**shame′less·ness,** *n.*

**sham·my** (sham′ē) CHAMOIS. *n., pl.* **sham·mies.**

**sham·poo** (sham pü′) **1** wash (the hair, the scalp, a rug, etc.) with a soapy preparation. **2** a washing of the hair, the scalp, a rug, etc. with such a preparation. **3** a preparation used for shampooing. 1 *v.*, **sham·pooed, sham·poo·ing;** 2, 3 *n.*

Shamrocks

**sham·rock** (sham′rok) **1** a bright-green leaf of certain clovers, composed of three parts, and thought to bring good luck: *The shamrock is the national emblem of the Irish*

Republic. **2** any of various plants that have leaves like this, such as white clover, wood sorrel, etc. *n.*

**Shan·gri–La** or **Shan·gri·la** (shang′grĭ lä′) an idyllic earthly paradise. *n.*

**shank** (shangk) **1** the part of the leg between the knee and the ankle. **2** the corresponding part in animals. See BEEF, LAMB, and VEAL for pictures. **3** the whole leg. **4** any part like a leg, stem, or shaft: *The shank of a fish-hook is the straight part between the hook and the loop.* See ANCHOR for picture. **5** the narrow part of a shoe, connecting the broad part of the sole with the heel. **6** the latter end or part of anything. *n.*
**go** or **ride on shanks' mare,** walk.
☛ *Etym.* From OE *sceanca* 'leg'. See also note at LEG.

**shan't** (shant) shall not. *v.*

**shan·tung** (shan′tŭng *or* shan tung′) **1** a heavy PONGEE, a kind of soft silk. **2** a similar fabric of cotton, rayon, etc. *n.*

**shan·ty**[1] (shan′tē) **1** a roughly built hut or cabin. **2** the log-built living quarters of a gang of loggers. *n., pl.* **shan·ties.**
☛ *Etym.* From Cdn. F *chantier* 'logger's headquarters', originally, in F, 'timber yard, dock'.

**shan·ty**[2] (shan′tē) a song sung by sailors in rhythm with the motions made during their work. *n., pl.* **shan·ties.** Also, **chantey, chanty.**
☛ *Etym.* A variant of *chantey*, which came from F *chanter* 'to sing'.

**shape** (shāp) **1** the outward contour or outline; the form of a person or thing; figure: *the shape of a triangle. All circles have the same shape; rectangles have different shapes.* **2** form into a shape: *The child shapes clay into balls.* **3** take shape; assume form: *Her plan is shaping well.* **4** adapt in form: *That hat is shaped to your head.* **5** an assumed appearance: *A witch was supposed to take the shape of a cat.* **6** something seen, or thought to be seen, though having no definite or describable form: *A white shape stood at his bedside.* **7** condition: *Exercise keeps one in good shape.* **8** a definite form; proper arrangement; order: *Take time to get your thoughts into shape.* **9** give definite form or character to: *events that shape people's lives.* **10** direct; plan; devise; aim: *to shape one's course in life.* **11** express in words: *to shape a question.* **12** a kind; sort: *adventures of every shape.* **13** mould; pattern. **14** something shaped; jelly, pudding, etc., shaped in a mould; metal of any of various shapes. 1, 5–8, 12–14 *n.,* 2–4, 9–11, 13 *v.,* **shaped, shap·ing.**
—**shap′er,** *n.*
**shape up,** **a** take on a certain form or appearance; develop. **b** show a certain tendency. **c** perform well: *Shape up or ship out.*
**take shape,** have or take on a definite form.

**shape·less** (shāp′lis) **1** without definite shape. **2** having an unattractive shape. *adj.*
—**shape′less·ly,** *adv.* —**shape′less·ness,** *n.*

**shape·ly** (shāp′lē) having a pleasing shape; well-formed. *adj.* **shape·li·er, shape·li·est.**
—**shape′li·ness,** *n.*

**shape–up** (shāp′ŭp′) *Informal.* a system of hiring longshoremen whereby the men line up each workday to be selected for work by the foreman. *n.*

**shard** (shärd) **1** a broken piece; fragment. **2** a piece of broken earthenware or pottery. **3** the hard case that covers a beetle's wing. *n.* Also, **sherd.**

**share**[1] (sher) **1** a part belonging to one individual; portion; part: *Do your share of the work.* **2** a part of anything owned in common with others: *One of the boys offered to sell his share in the boat.* **3** each of the parts into which the ownership of a company or corporation is divided: *The ownership of this company is divided into several million shares.* **4** use together; enjoy together; have in common: *The sisters share a room.* **5** divide into parts, each taking a part: *The child shared his candy with his sister.* **6** have a share; take part: *Everyone shared in making the picnic a success.* 1–3 *n.,* 4–6 *v.,* **shared, shar·ing.**
**go shares,** share in something.
**on shares,** sharing in the risks and profits.

**share**[2] (sher) PLOUGHSHARE. *n.*

**share·crop** (sher′krop′) farm or raise a crop as a SHARECROPPER. *v.,* **share·cropped, share·crop·ping.**

**share·crop·per** (sher′krop′ər) a person who farms land for the owner in return for part of the crops. *n.*

**share·hold·er** (sher′hōl′dər) a person owning shares of STOCK (def. 9). *n.*

A white shark—about 6 m long including the tail

**shark**[1] (shärk) any of a group of fishes, mostly marine, certain kinds of which are large and ferocious, destructive to other fishes, and sometimes dangerous to people. *n.* —**shark′like′,** *adj.*

**shark**[2] (shärk) *Informal.* a dishonest person who preys on others: *a loan shark.* *n.*

**shark·skin** (shärk′skin′) cloth made from fine threads of wool, rayon, or cotton, used in suits. *n.*

**sharp** (shärp) **1** having a thin cutting edge or a fine point: *a sharp knife, a sharp pencil.* **2** having a point; not rounded: *a sharp nose, a sharp corner on a box.* **3** with a sudden change of direction: *a sharp turn.* **4** very cold: *sharp weather, a sharp morning.* **5** severe; biting: *sharp words.* **6** causing a sensation like a cut or pinprick; affecting the senses keenly: *a sharp taste, a sharp noise, a sharp pain.* **7** clear; distinct: *the sharp contrast between black and white.* **8** quick; brisk: *a sharp walk or run.* **9** fierce; violent: *a sharp struggle.* **10** keen; eager: *a sharp desire, a sharp appetite.* **11** being aware of things quickly: *a sharp eye, sharp ears.* **12** watchful; wide-awake: *a sharp watch.* **13** quick in mind; clever: *a sharp boy.* **14** shrewd; artful; almost dishonest: *sharp practice. She is sharp at a bargain.* **15** promptly; exactly: *Come at one o'clock sharp.* **16** high in pitch; shrill. **17** in music, **a** above the true pitch. **b** raised a half step in pitch: *F sharp.* **18** of a key, having sharps in the signature. **19** a tone one HALF STEP, or half note, above a given tone. **20** the sign (♯) that stands for such a tone. **21** in a sharp manner; in an alert manner; keenly: *Look sharp!* **22** suddenly: *to pull a horse up sharp.* **23** *Informal.* a swindler; SHARPER. **24** *Informal.* attractive; striking in looks, value, etc.: *a sharp car. His new suit looks sharp.* **25 sharps,** *pl.* the hard part of wheat requiring a second grinding. 1–14, 16–18, 24 *adj.*, 15, 21, 22 *adv.*, 19, 20, 23, 25 *n.* —**sharp′ly,** *adv.* —**sharp′ness,** *n.*

**sharp·en** (shär′pən) **1** make sharp: *to sharpen a pencil. Sharpen your wits.* **2** become sharp: *Her voice sharpened as she became angry.* *v.* —**sharp′en·er,** *n.*

**sharp·er** (shär′pər) **1** a swindler; cheat. **2** a gambler who makes a living by cheating at cards, etc. *n.*

**sharp·ie** (shär′pē) a long, flat-bottomed boat having one or two masts, each rigged with a triangular sail. *n.*

**sharp·shoot·er** (shärp′shü′tər) a person who shoots very well, especially with a rifle. *n.*

**sharp–sight·ed** (shärp′sī′tid) **1** having sharp sight. **2** sharp-witted. *adj.*

**sharp–tailed grouse** (shärp′tāld′) a GROUSE of western Canada and the United States, so called because of its short, pointed tail.

**sharp–wit·ted** (shärp′pwit′id) having or showing a quick, keen mind. *adj.*

**Shas·ta daisy** (shas′tə) **1** a flower like a large common daisy. **2** the plant that produces it.

**shat·ter** (shat′ər) **1** break into pieces: *A stone shattered the window.* **2** disturb greatly; destroy: *shattered hopes.* **3 shatters,** *pl.* fragments. 1, 2 *v.*, 3 *n.*

**shave** (shāv) **1** remove hair with a razor; cut hair from the face, chin, etc. with a razor: *He shaves every day.* **2** the cutting off of hair with a razor. **3** cut off hair with a razor: *The actor shaved his head for the movie.* **4** cut off in thin slices; cut in thin slices: *shaved roast beef.* **5** a tool for shaving, scraping, removing thin slices, etc. **6** a shaving; thin slice. **7** cut very close. **8** come very close to; graze: *The car shaved the corner.* **9** a narrow miss or escape: *The shot missed him, but it was a close shave.* 1, 3, 4, 7, 8 *v.*, **shaved, shaved** or **shav·en, shav·ing;** 2, 5, 6, 9 *n.*

**shav·en** (shā′vən) **1** SHAVED. **2** closely cut. **3** tonsured. **4** a pp. of SHAVE. 1–3 *adj.*, 4 *v.*

**shav·er** (shā′vər) **1** a person who shaves. **2** an instrument for shaving. **3** *Informal.* a youngster; small boy. *n.*

**shav·ing** (shā′ving) **1** a very thin piece or slice: *Shavings of wood are cut off by a plane.* **2** the act or process of cutting hair with a razor. **3** ppr. of SHAVE. 1, 2 *n.*, 3 *v.*

**shawl** (shol′) a square or oblong piece of cloth to be worn about the shoulders or head. See FRINGE for picture. *n.*

**Shaw·nee** (shô nē′) **1** a member of a tribe of Algonquin Indians now living in Oklahoma. **2** their language. *n., pl.* **Shaw·nee** or **Shaw·nees.**

**she** (shē) **1** the girl, woman, or female animal already referred to and identified: *My sister says she likes to read.* **2** any girl, woman, or female animal: *Is it a he or a she?* **1** *pron., sing. nom.* **she,** *poss.* **her** or **hers,** *obj.* **her;** *pl. nom.* **they,** *poss.* **their** or **theirs,** *obj.* **them;** **2** *n., pl.* **she's.**

**sheaf** (shēf) **1** a bundle of cut grain bound in the middle for drying, loading, and stacking. **2** any bundle of things that are alike: *a sheaf of notes.* *n., pl.* **sheaves.**

**shear** (shēr) **1** cut with shears or scissors. **2** cut the wool or fleece from: *The farmer sheared her sheep.* **3** cut close; cut off; cut. **4** to strip or deprive as if by cutting: *The assembly had been shorn of its legislative powers.* **5** the act or process of shearing. **6** that which is taken off by shearing. **7** one blade of a pair of SHEARS. **8** a pair of SHEARS. **9** a force causing two parts or pieces to slide on each other in opposite directions. **10** break by a force causing two parts or pieces to slide on each other in opposite directions: *Too much pressure on the handles of the scissors sheared off the rivet holding the blades together.* 1–4, 10 *v.*, **sheared, sheared** or **shorn, shear·ing;** 5–9 *n.* —**shear′er,** *n.*
☞ Hom. SHEER.

**shears** (shērz) **1** large scissors. **2** any cutting instrument resembling scissors: *grass shears, tin shears.* *n.pl.*

**sheath** (shēth) **1** a case or covering for the blade of a sword, knife, etc. **2** any similar covering, especially on an animal or plant. **3** a woman's dress, having a fitted bodice and straight skirt, usually unbelted. *n., pl.* **sheaths** (shēᴛHz).

**sheathe** (shēᴛH) **1** put into a SHEATH. **2** enclose in a case or covering: *a mummy sheathed in linen, doors sheathed in metal.* *v.*, **sheathed, sheath·ing.**

**sheath·ing** (shē′ᴛHing) **1** a casing; covering: *The first covering of boards on a house is sheathing.* **2** ppr. of SHEATHE. 1 *n.*, 2 *v.*

**sheath knife** a knife carried in a sheath.

**sheave**[1] (shēv) gather and tie into a SHEAF or sheaves. *v.*, **sheaved, sheav·ing.**

**sheave**[2] (shēv *or* shiv) a wheel with a grooved rim; the wheel of a pulley. *n.*

**sheaves** (shēvz for 1, shēvz *or* shivz for 2) **1** pl. of SHEAF. **2** pl. of SHEAVE[2]. *n.*

**she·bang** (shə bang′) *Informal.* **1** an outfit; concern. **2** an affair; event. *n.*

**shed**[1] (shed) a building used for shelter, storage, etc., usually having only one storey: *a tool shed.* *n.*

**shed**[2] (shed) **1** pour out; let fall: *He shed his blood for his country. The girl shed tears.* **2** throw off; cast aside: *The snake sheds its skin. The umbrella sheds water.* **3** throw off a covering, hair, etc.: *That snake has just shed.* **4** scatter abroad; give forth: *The sun sheds light. Flowers shed perfume on the air.* **5** cause to flow: *He shed his enemy's blood.* *v.*, **shed, shed·ding.**
**shed blood,** destroy life; kill.
**shed one's own blood,** sacrifice one's life.

**she'd** (shēd; *unstressed,* shid) **1** she had. **2** she would.

**sheen** (shēn) brightness; lustre: *Satin and polished silver have a sheen.* *n.*

**sheen·y** (shē′nē) bright; lustrous: *Her gown was made of some sheeny material.* *adj.*

A domestic sheep: a Shropshire ram— usually about 90 cm high at the shoulder

**sheep** (shēp) **1** a cud-chewing mammal raised for wool,

meat, and skin. 2 a person who is weak, timid, or easily led. n., pl. sheep. —sheep′like′, adj.
make sheep's eyes, give a longing, loving look.

**sheep·cote** (shēp′kōt′) a shelter for sheep. n.

**sheep dog** a collie or other dog trained to help a shepherd watch and tend sheep.

**sheep·fold** (shēp′fōld′) a pen for sheep. n.

**sheep·herd·er** (shēp′hėr′dər) a person who watches and tends large numbers of sheep while they are grazing on unfenced land. n.

**sheep·hook** (shēp′huk′) a shepherd's staff. n.

**sheep·ish** (shē′pish) 1 awkwardly bashful or embarrassed: a sheepish smile. 2 like a sheep; timid; weak; stupid. adj. —sheep′ish·ly, adv. —sheep′ish·ness, n.

**sheep·man** (shēp′man′) 1 a person who owns and raises sheep. 2 SHEEPHERDER. n., pl. sheepmen (-men′).

**sheep range** a tract of land on which sheep are pastured.

**sheep·skin** (shēp′skin′) 1 the skin of a sheep, especially with wool on it. 2 leather or parchment made from the skin of a sheep. 3 Informal. diploma. n.

**sheer¹** (shēr) 1 very thin; almost transparent: a sheer white dress. 2 a dress or curtain of transparent material. 3 unmixed with anything else; complete: sheer weariness. 4 straight up or down; steep: From the top there was a sheer drop of 50 metres to the water below. 5 completely; quite. 6 very steeply: The cliff rose sheer from the river's edge. 1, 3, 4 adj., 2 n., 5, 6 adv. —sheer′ness, n.
☞ Hom. SHEAR.

**sheer²** (shēr) 1 turn from a course; turn aside; swerve. 2 a turning of a ship from its course. 3 the upward curve of a ship's deck or lines from the middle toward each end. 4 the position in which a ship at anchor is placed to keep it clear of the anchor. 1 v., 2–4 n.
☞ Hom. SHEAR.

**sheer·ly** (shēr′lē) absolutely; thoroughly; quite. adv.

**sheet¹** (shēt) 1 a large piece of cloth, usually cotton or partly cotton, used to sleep on or under. 2 a broad, thin piece of anything: a sheet of glass. 3 a single piece of paper. 4 newspaper. 5 a broad, flat surface: a sheet of water. 6 furnish or cover with a sheet. 7 Poetic. a sail. 1–5, 7 n., 6 v.

**sheet²** (shēt) a rope that controls the angle at which a sail is set. n.

**sheet home,** stretch a square sail as flat as possible by pulling hard on the sheets fastened to it.

**sheet anchor** 1 a large anchor used only in emergencies. 2 the chief support or source of security.

**sheet·ing** (shē′ting) 1 cotton or linen cloth for bed sheets. 2 a lining or covering of timber or metal, used to protect a surface. 3 ppr. of SHEET. 1, 2 n., 3 v.

**sheet iron** iron in sheets or thin plates.

**sheet lightning** lightning reflected from clouds in broad flashes.

**sheet metal** metal in thin pieces or plates.

**sheet music** music printed on unbound sheets of paper.

**sheets** (shēts) the space at the bow or stern of an open boat. n.pl.

**Shef·field plate** (shef′ēld) an especially durable silver plate made by rolling out sheets of copper and silver fused together.

**shel·drake** (shel′drāk′) 1 any of various large ducks of Europe and Asia, many of which have variegated plumage. 2 any merganser. n., pl. shel·drakes or (esp. collectively) shel·drake.

**shelf** (shelf) 1 a thin, flat piece of wood or other material fastened to a wall or frame to hold things, such as books, dishes, etc. 2 anything like a shelf: The ship hit a shelf of coral. n., pl. shelves.
**on the shelf,** put aside as no longer useful or desirable.

**shelf life** the length of time that a perishable product such as a food or drug can be expected to remain fresh and fit for use.

An artillery shell

**shell** (shel) 1 a hard outside covering of an animal: Oysters, turtles, and beetles have shells. 2 the hard outside covering of a nut, seed, fruit, etc. 3 the hard outside covering of an egg. 4 take out of a shell: to shell peas. 5 separate the grains of corn from a cob. 6 the outer part or appearance; outward show: Her behaviour is just the shell of sincerity. 7 something like a shell: The frame of a house, a light racing boat, and a hollow pastry case are called shells. 8 a cartridge used in a rifle or shotgun. 9 a metal projectile filled with explosives that is fired by artillery and explodes on impact. 10 fire cannon at; bombard with shells: to shell a town. 1–3, 6–9 n., 4, 5, 10 v. —shell′-like′, adj.
**come out of one's shell,** stop being shy or reserved; join in conversation, etc. with others.
**retire into one's shell,** become shy and reserved; refuse to join in conversation, etc. with others.
**shell out,** Informal. a give something away: On Halloween the children cry, "Shell out!" b hand over money; pay up: He shelled out $25 for the roses.

**she'll** (shēl; unstressed, shil) 1 she will. 2 she shall.

**shel·lac** (shə lak′) 1 a liquid for coating wood, metal, etc.: Shellac hardens to a smooth, shiny finish. 2 the resinous substance used. 3 put shellac on; cover or fasten with shellac. 4 Informal. defeat completely. 1, 2 n., 3, 4 v., shel·lacked, shel·lack·ing.

**shell·bark** (shel′bärk′) SHAGBARK. n.

**shell·er** (shel′ər) 1 a person who shells something. 2 a tool or machine used in shelling. n.

**shell·fire** (shel′fīr′) bombardment by explosive shells or projectiles. n.

**shell·fish** (shel′fish′) a water animal (not a fish in the ordinary sense) having a shell: Oysters, clams, crabs, and lobsters are shellfish. n., pl. shell·fish or shell·fish·es.

**shell·proof** (shel′prüf′) secure against shells, bombs, etc. adj.

**shell·y** (shel′ē) 1 abounding in shells. 2 consisting of a shell or shells. 3 shell-like. adj., shell·i·er, shell·i·est.

**shel·ter** (shel′tər) 1 something that covers or protects from weather, danger, or attack: Trees are a shelter from the sun. 2 protect; shield; hide: to shelter refugees. 3 protection; refuge: We took shelter from the storm in a *barn.* **4** find shelter; take shelter: *The sheep sheltered from the hot sun in the shade of the haystack.* 1, 3 *n.*, 2, 4 *v.* —**shel′ter·less,** *adj.*

**shelter tent** a small tent, usually made of pieces of waterproof cloth that fasten together.

**shelve** (shelv) **1** put on a shelf. **2** lay aside: *Let us shelve that argument.* **3** furnish with shelves. **4** slope gradually: *The sandy bottom of the lake shelves down to rock in the middle.* *v.*, **shelved, shelv·ing.**

**shelves** (shelvz) pl. of SHELF. *n.*

**shelv·ing** (shel′ving) **1** wood, metal, etc. for shelves. **2** shelves collectively. **3** ppr. of SHELVE. 1, 2 *n.*, 3 *v.*

**she·nan·i·gans** (shə nan′ə gənz) *Informal.* mischief or trickery. *n.pl.*

**shep·herd** (shep′ərd) **1** a person who takes care of sheep. **2** take care of: *He will shepherd his flock.* **3** guide; direct: *The teacher shepherded the children safely out of the burning building.* **4** a person who cares for and protects. **5** a spiritual guide; pastor. 1, 4, 5 *n.*, 2, 3 *v.*

**shepherd dog** SHEEP DOG.

**shep·herd·ess** (shep′ər dis) a woman who takes care of sheep. *n.*

**shep·herd's–purse** (shep′ərdz pėrs′) a weed that has small white flowers and purselike pods. *n.*

**sher·bet** (shėr′bət) a frozen dessert made of fruit juice, sugar, water, gelatin, and, sometimes, milk or egg white. *n.*
☞ *Etym.* See note at SYRUP.

**sherd** (shėrd) SHARD. *n.*

**she·reef** (shə rēf′) See SHERIF. *n.*

**she·rif** (shə rēf′) **1** a descendant of Mohammed through his daughter Fatima. **2** an Arab prince or ruler; especially, the sovereign of Morocco or the chief magistrate of Mecca. *n.* Also, **shereef.**

**sher·iff** (sher′if) **1** in Canada, an official whose job is to enforce certain court orders, such as evicting persons for failure to pay rent and escorting convicted persons to prison. **2** in the United States, the most important law-enforcing officer of a county. *n.*

**sher·ry** (sher′ē) **1** a strong wine made in southern Spain: *Sherry varies in colour from pale yellow to brown.* **2** any similar wine. *n., pl.* **sher·ries.**

**she's** (shēz; *unstressed*, shiz) **1** she is. **2** she has.

**Shet·land** (shet′lənd) **1** a county of northeast Scotland, consisting of a group of islands. **2** SHETLAND PONY. **3** SHETLAND WOOL. *n.*

**Shetland pony** a small, sturdy, rough-coated pony, originally from the Shetland Islands.

**Shetland sheep** a breed of sheep from Shetland, noted for its fine wool.

**Shetland wool** a fine, hairy, strong worsted spun from the wool of Shetland sheep, widely used in knitting fine shawls, garments, etc.

**Shi·ah** (shē′ə) **1** one of the two major branches of the Islamic religion. **2** a member of this group. Compare with SUNNI. *n.*

**shib·bo·leth** (shib′ə lith) **1** any peculiarity of speech, habit, or custom considered distinctive of a particular group, class, etc. **2** any test word, password, watchword, or pet phrase of a political party, class, sect, etc. *n.*

**shied** (shīd) pt. and pp. of SHY. *v.*

## shelter tent     1091     shimmy

hat, āge, fär; let, ēqual, tėrm; it, īce
hot, ōpen, ôrder; oil, out; cup, pùt, rüle
əbove, takən, pencəl, lemən, circəs
ch, child; ng, long; sh, ship
th, thin; ᴛʜ, then; zh, measure

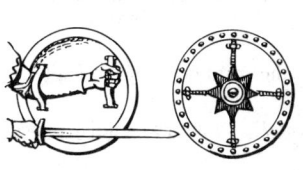
An Anglo-Saxon shield

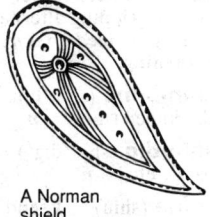
A Norman shield

**shield** (shēld) **1** a piece of armour carried on the arm to protect the body in battle. **2** any person or thing that protects: *She held up a newspaper as a shield against the sun.* **3** something shaped like a shield. **4** be a shield to; protect; defend: *His mother shielded him from punishment.* **5** serve as a shield. **6 the Shield,** the CANADIAN SHIELD. 1–3, 6 *n.*, 4, 5 *v.*

**shift** (shift) **1** change from one place, position, person, sound, etc. to another; change: *The wind has shifted to the southeast. He shifted the heavy bag from one hand to the other.* **2** a change of direction, position, attitude, etc.: *a shift of the wind, a shift in policy.* **3** a group of workers who work during the same period of time: *This man is on the night shift.* **4** the time during which such a group works. **5** a way of getting on; scheme; trick: *The lazy girl tried every shift to avoid doing her work.* **6** be rather dishonest; scheme. **7** manage to get along; contrive: *When his parents died, Tomas had to shift for himself.* **8** a woman's dress having straight, loose-fitting lines. **9** get rid of. **10** change the position of the gears of an automobile. **11** a change in the arrangement of players before a football is put into play. 1, 6, 7, 9, 10 *v.*, 2–5, 8, 11 *n.* —**shift′er,** *n.*
**make shift, a** manage to get along. **b** manage with effort or difficulty. **c** do as well as one can.

**shift·less** (shif′tlis) lazy; inefficient. *adj.* —**shift′less·ly,** *adv.* —**shift′less·ness,** *n.*

**shift·y** (shif′tē) tricky; sly; not straightforward. *adj.*, **shift·i·er, shift·i·est.** —**shift′i·ly,** *adv.* —**shift′i·ness,** *n.*

**Shi·ite** (shē′īt) SHIAH (def. 2). *n.*

**shil·le·lagh** or **shil·la·lah** (shə lā′lē) *Irish.* a stick to hit with; cudgel. *n.*

**shil·ly–shal·ly** (shil′ē shal′ē) **1** vacillating; wavering; hesitating; undecided. **2** be undecided; vacillate; hesitate. **3** an inability to decide; hesitation. 1 *adj.*, 2 *v.*, **shil·ly-shal·lied, shil·ly-shal·ly·ing;** 3 *n.*

**shi·ly** (shī′lē) See SHYLY. *adv.*

**shim** (shim) **1** a thin strip of metal or wood used to fill up space, make something level, etc. **2** put a shim or shims in. 1 *n.*, 2 *v.*, **shimmed, shim·ming.**

**shim·mer** (shim′ər) **1** gleam faintly: *The satin shimmers.* **2** a faint gleam or shine: *The pearls have a beautiful shimmer.* 1 *v.*, 2 *n.*

**shim·mer·y** (shim′ə rē) shimmering; gleaming softly. *adj.*

**shim·my** (shim′ē) **1** an unusual shaking or vibration,

especially of the front wheels of a car, truck, etc. **2** shake; vibrate. *1 n., 2 v.*

**shin** (shin) **1** the front part of the leg from the knee to the ankle. See LEG for picture. **2** the lower part of the foreleg in beef cattle. **3** climb up or down a rope, pole, etc. by gripping alternately with the hands and feet: *He quickly shinned up a tree.* *1, 2 n., 3 v.,* **shinned, shin·ning.**

**shin·bone** (shin′bōn′) the front bone of the leg below the knee; TIBIA. *n.*

**shin·dig** (shin′dig′) *Informal.* a merry or noisy dance, party, etc. *n.*

**shine** (shīn) **1** send out light; be bright with light; reflect light; glow: *The sun shines.* **2** a light; brightness: *the shine of a lamp.* **3** a lustre; polish; gloss, as of silk. **4** fair weather; sunshine: *rain or shine.* **5** do very well; be brilliant; excel: *Carmen shines in school.* **6** make bright; polish: *to shine shoes.* **7** polish put on shoes. **8** cause to shine: *to shine a light.* **9** *Informal.* a fancy; liking. *1, 5, 6, 8 v.,* **shone** or (especially for def. 6) **shined, shin·ing;** *2–4, 7, 9 n.*

**shin·er** (shī′nər) **1** a person or thing that shines. **2** a small North American freshwater fish having glistening scales. *n.*

Roof shingles

**shin·gle**¹ (shing′gəl) **1** a thin piece of wood, etc. used to cover roofs, walls, etc.: *Shingles are laid in overlapping rows with the thicker ends exposed.* **2** cover with shingles: *to shingle a roof.* **3** *Informal.* a small signboard, especially for a doctor's or lawyer's office. *1, 3 n., 2 v.,* **shin·gled, shin·gling.**
**hang out one's shingle,** *Informal.* of lawyers, doctors, and dentists, etc., open an office.

**shin·gle**² (shing′gəl) **1** loose stones or pebbles such as lie on the seashore; coarse gravel. **2** a beach or other place covered with this. *n.*

**shin·gles** (shing′gəlz) a virus disease that causes painful irritation of a group of nerves and an outbreak of itching spots or blisters. *n. sing. or pl.*

**shin·gly** (shing′glē) consisting of or covered with small, loose stones or pebbles. *adj.*

**shin·ing** (shī′ning) **1** that shines; bright. **2** brilliant; outstanding. **3** ppr. of SHINE. *1, 2 adj., 3 v.*
—**shin′ing·ly,** *adv.*

**shin·ny**¹ (shin′ē) **1** a simple kind of hockey, played on the ice with skates, or without skates on the street or in a field. **2** *Informal.* the game of ice hockey. **3** play shinny. *1, 2 n., pl.* **shin·nies;** *3 v.,* **shin·nied, shin·ny·ing.**

**shin·ny**² (shin′ē) *Informal.* shin; climb. *v.,* **shin·nied, shin·ny·ing.**

**shin splints** a painful strain of the lower leg muscles, which often occurs after prolonged running.

**Shin·to** (shin′tō) **1** the main religion of Japan, primarily a system of nature worship and ancestor worship. **2** an adherent of this religion. **3** of or having to do with Shinto. *1, 2 n., 3 adj.*

**Shin·to·ism** (shin′tō iz′əm) the SHINTO religion. *n.*

**shin·y** (shī′nē) **1** shining; bright: *a shiny new nickel.* **2** worn to a glossy smoothness: *a coat shiny from hard wear.* *adj.,* **shin·i·er, shin·i·est.** —**shin′i·ness,** *n.*

**ship** (ship) **1** any large vessel for travel on water, such as a steamship, frigate, or galley. **2** a large sailing vessel, especially one with three or more masts. **3** an airship, airplane, spacecraft, etc. **4** the officers and crew of a vessel. **5** put, take, or receive on board a ship. **6** go on board a ship. **7** travel on a ship; sail. **8** send or carry from one place to another by a ship, train, truck, etc.: *Did he ship it by express or by freight?* **9** engage for service on a ship: *to ship a new crew.* **10** take a job on a ship: *He shipped as cook.* **11** take in water over the side, as a vessel does when the waves break over it. **12** fix in a ship or boat in its proper place for use: *to ship a rudder.* *1–4 n., 5–12 v.,* **shipped, ship·ping.**
**about ship!** turn the ship around! Put the ship on the other tack!
**when one's ship comes home** or **in,** when one's fortune is made; when one has money.

**–ship** a suffix meaning: **1** the office, position, or occupation of _____, as in *authorship, kingship.* **2** the quality, state, or condition of being _____ as in *kinship, partnership.* **3** the act, acts, power, or skill of _____, as in *horsemanship, workmanship.* **4** the relation between _____ s, as in *comradeship.*

**ship biscuit** a kind of hard biscuit used on shipboard; hardtack.

**ship·board** (ship′bôrd′) ship. *n.*
**on shipboard,** on or inside a ship.

**ship·build·er** (ship′bil′dər) a person who designs or constructs ships. *n.*

**ship·build·ing** (ship′bil′ding) **1** the designing or building of ships. **2** the art of building ships. **3** of or used in shipbuilding; having to do with shipbuilding. *n.*

**ship canal** a canal wide and deep enough for ships.

**ship·load** (ship′lōd′) a full load for a ship. *n.*

**ship·mas·ter** (ship′mas′tər) a master, commander, or captain of a ship. *n.*

**ship·mate** (ship′māt′) a fellow sailor on a ship. *n.*

**ship·ment** (ship′mənt) **1** the act of shipping goods. **2** goods sent at one time to a person, firm, etc.: *We received two shipments from Calgary.* *n.*

**ship of the desert** CAMEL.

**ship·own·er** (ship′ō′nər) a person who owns a ship or ships. *n.*

**ship·per** (ship′ər) a person who ships goods. *n.*

**ship·ping** (ship′ing) **1** the act or business of sending goods by water, rail, etc. **2** ships collectively: *There is a lot of shipping in the harbour.* **3** their total tonnage. **4** the ships of a nation, city, or business. **5** ppr. of SHIP. *1–4 n., 5 v.*

**shipping clerk** a person whose work is to see to the packing and shipping of goods.

**ship·shape** (ship′shāp′)  **1** in good order; trim.  **2** in a trim, neat manner.  *1 adj., 2 adv.*

**ship·worm** (ship′wėrm′)  any of various molluscs having small valves and long wormlike bodies, that burrow into the timbers of ships.  *n.*

**ship·wreck** (ship′rek′)  **1** the destruction or loss of a ship: *Only two people were saved from the shipwreck.*  **2** a wrecked ship.  **3** destruction; ruin: *The shipwreck of his plans discouraged him.*  **4** wreck; ruin; destroy.  **5** suffer shipwreck.  *1–3 n., 4, 5 v.*

**ship·wright** (ship′rīt′)  a person who builds or repairs ships.  *n.*
☛ *Etym.* See note at WRIGHT.

**ship·yard** (ship′yärd′)  a place near the water where ships are built or repaired.  *n.*

**shire** (shīr)  one of the counties into which Great Britain is divided.  *n.*

**shirk** (shėrk)  avoid or get out of doing work, a duty, etc.: *Dev lost his job because he shirked his work.*  *v.* —**shirk′er,** *n.*

**shirr** (shėr)  **1** draw up or gather cloth on parallel threads.  **2** a shirred arrangement of cloth, etc.  **3** bake eggs in a shallow dish with butter, etc.  *1, 3 v., 2 n.*

**shirt** (shėrt)  **1** a garment for the upper part of the body.  **2** an undergarment for the upper part of the body.  **3** SHIRTWAIST.  *n.* —**shirt′less,** *adj.*
☛ *Etym.* **Shirt** comes from OE *scyrte*, while SKIRT comes from ON *skyrte*. Both forms came from a Germanic word meaning 'shirt' or 'short garment'.

**shirt·band** (shėrt′band′)  the neckband or other band of a shirt.  *n.*

**shirt·ing** (shėr′ting)  cloth for shirts.  *n.*

**shirt–sleeve** (shėrt′slēv′) *Informal.*  INFORMAL: *shirt-sleeve diplomacy.*  *adj.*

**shirt·waist** (shėr′twāst′)  **1** a woman's tailored blouse, worn with a separate skirt or pants.  **2** a tailored dress having a bodice similar to that of such a blouse.  *n.*

**shish ke·bab** (shish′ kə bob′)  cubes of lamb, beef, or other meat, marinated and cooked with mushrooms, tomatoes, onions, etc. on a skewer or spit.

**shi·va** (shē′və)  the period of mourning—normally seven days—traditionally observed in a Jewish home following the funeral of a family member or close relative.  *n.*

**Shi·va** (shē′və)  SIVA.  *n.*

**shiv·a·ree** (shiv′ə rē′)  **1** a celebration held to do honour to a newly married couple; charivari.  **2** a noisy serenade for a newly married couple, often performed in a spirit of mockery.  *n.*

**shiv·er**[1] (shiv′ər)  **1** shake with cold, fear, etc.: *He crept shivering into bed.*  **2** a shaking from cold, fear, etc.  *1 v., 2 n.* —**shiv′er·er,** *n.*

**shiv·er**[2] (shiv′ər)  **1** break into small pieces: *She shivered the mirror with a hammer.*  **2** a small piece; splinter: *shivers of glass.*  *1 v., 2 n.*

**shiv·er·y** (shiv′ə rē)  **1** quivering from cold, fear, etc.; shivering.  **2** inclined to shiver from cold.  **3** chilly.  **4** causing shivers.  *adj.*

**shoal**[1] (shōl)  **1** a place in a sea, lake, or stream where the water is shallow.  **2** a sandbank or sand bar that makes the water shallow: *The ship was wrecked on the shoals.*  **3** shallow.  **4** become shallow.  *1, 2 n., 3 adj., 4 v.*

**shoal**[2] (shōl)  **1** a large number; crowd: *We saw a shoal of fish in the water.*  **2** form into a shoal; crowd together.  *1 n., 2 v.*

**shoal·y** (shō′lē)  full of shoals or shallow places.  *adj.*

**shoat** (shōt)  a young pig able to feed itself.  *n.* Also, **shote.**

**shock**[1] (shok)  **1** a sudden, violent shake, blow, or crash: *Earthquake shocks are often felt in Japan. The two trains collided with a terrible shock.*  **2** strike together violently.  **3** a sudden, violent, or upsetting disturbance to the mind or feelings: *Ernst's death was a great shock to his family.*  **4** cause to feel surprise, horror, or disgust: *That child's bad language shocks everyone.*  **5** collide with a shock.  **6** condition of physical collapse or depression, together with a sudden drop in blood pressure, often resulting in unconsciousness: *Shock may set in after a severe injury, great loss of blood, or a sudden emotional disturbance. The operation was successfully performed, but the patient suffered from shock.*  **7** *Med.* paralysis; a sudden attack of illness that makes a person senseless or takes away the power to move or speak.  **8** a disturbance produced by an electric current passing through the body.  **9** give an electric shock to.  **10** *Informal.* a SHOCK ABSORBER (def. 2).  *1, 3, 6–8, 10 n., 2, 4, 5, 9 v.* —**shock′er,** *n.*

**shock**[2] (shok)  STOOK.  *n., v.*

**shock**[3] (shok)  a thick, bushy mass: *He has a shock of red hair.*  *n.*

**shock absorber**  **1** anything that absorbs or lessens shocks.  **2** a device used on automobiles to absorb or lessen the shocks caused by rough roads.

**shock–head·ed** (shok′hed′id)  having a thick, bushy mass of hair.  *adj.*

**shock·ing** (shok′ing)  **1** causing intense and painful surprise: *shocking news.*  **2** offensive; disgusting; revolting: *a shocking sight.*  **3** *Informal.* very bad: *shocking manners.*  *adj.* —**shock′ing·ly,** *adv.*

**shock therapy**  ELECTRO-CONVULSIVE THERAPY.

**shock troops**  troops chosen and specially trained for making attacks.

**shock wave**  **1** a disturbance of the atmosphere created by the movement of an aircraft, rocket, etc. at velocities greater than that of sound.  **2** a similar effect caused by an explosion or earthquake.

**shod** (shod)  pt. and pp. of SHOE: *The blacksmith shod the horses. The children were all well shod.*  *v.*

**shod·dy** (shod′ē)  **1** an inferior kind of wool made of woollen waste, old rags, yarn, etc.  **2** made of woollen waste.  **3** cloth made of woollen waste.  **4** anything inferior made to look like what is better.  **5** pretending to be better than it is: *a shoddy necklace.*  **6** mean; shabby: *shoddy treatment, a shoddy trick.*  **7** of poor quality: *shoddy workmanship.*  *1, 3, 4 n., pl.* **shod·dies;** *2, 5–7 adj.,* **shod·di·er, shod·di·est.** —**shod′di·ness,** *n.*

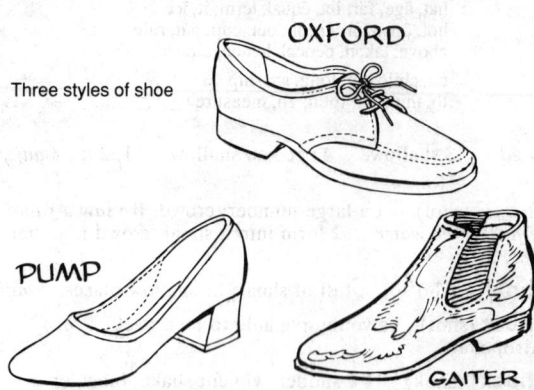

Three styles of shoe: OXFORD, PUMP, GAITER

**shoe** (shü) **1** an outer covering, usually of leather, for a person's foot. **2** anything like a shoe in shape or use. **3** HORSESHOE. **4** a FERRULE; metal band, etc. to protect the end of a staff, pole, etc. **5** the part of a brake that presses on a wheel. **6** the outer case of an automobile tire. **7** a sliding plate or contact by which an electric car takes current from the third rail. **8** furnish with a shoe or shoes: *A blacksmith shoes horses.* **9** protect or arm at the point; edge or face with metal: *a stick shod with steel.* 1–7 *n., pl.* **shoes;** 8, 9 *v.,* **shod, shoe·ing.**
—**shoe′less,** *adj.*
**fill another's shoes,** take another person's place.
**in another's shoes,** in another's place, situation, or circumstances: *I wouldn't like to be in the murderer's shoes right now.*
**where the shoe pinches,** where the real trouble or difficulty lies.
☞ *Hom.* SHOO.

**shoe·black** (shü′blak′) a person who cleans and polishes shoes to earn money. *n.*

**shoe·horn** (shü′hôrn′) a piece of metal, horn, etc. inserted at the heel of a shoe to make it slip on easily. *n.*

**shoe·lace** (shü′lās′) a cord, braid, or leather strip for fastening a shoe. *n.*

**shoe·mak·er** (shü′mā′kər) a person who makes or repairs shoes. *n.*

**shoe·shine** (shü′shīn′) **1** the shining or polishing of shoes. **2** the polished look of shined shoes. *n.*

**shoe·string** (shü′string′) **1** SHOELACE. **2** *Informal.* a very small amount of money used to start or carry on a business, investment, etc. *n.*

**shoe tree** a device with a shaped front for keeping a shoe in shape when it is not being worn.

**shone** (shon) a pt. and a pp. of SHINE: *The sun shone all last week. It has not shone since.* *v.*

**shoo** (shü) **1** an exclamation used to scare away hens, birds, etc. **2** scare or drive away: *Shoo those flies away from the sugar.* **3** call "Shoo!" 1 *interj.,* 2, 3 *v.,* **shooed, shoo·ing.**
☞ *Hom.* SHOE.

**shoo-in** (shü′in′) *Informal.* **1** a person who will win easily; sure winner. **2** a contest or match considered easy to win. *n.*

**shook** (shuk) pt. of SHAKE: *They shook hands.* *v.*

**shoot** (shüt) **1** hit, wound, or kill with a bullet, arrow, etc.: *to shoot a rabbit.* **2** send with force or swiftly at or as if at a target: *He shot question after question at us.* **3** fire or use a weapon, such as a gun, bow, catapult, etc. **4** of a gun, etc., send a bullet: *This gun shoots straight.* **5** shooting practice. **6** kill game in or on: *to shoot a farm.* **7** a trip, party, or contest for shooting. **8** move suddenly and swiftly: *A car shot by us. Flames shot up from the burning house. Pain shot up her arm. He shot back the bolt.* **9** pass quickly along, through, over, or under: *to shoot Niagara Falls in a barrel.* **10** hurt sharply from time to time. **11** a new part growing out; young bud or stem: *The rosebush is putting out new shoots.* **12** come forth from the ground; grow; grow rapidly: *Buds shoot forth in the spring. The corn is shooting up in the warm weather.* **13** take a picture with a camera; photograph. **14** project sharply: *a cape that shoots out into the sea.* **15** a sloping trough for conveying coal, grain, etc.; chute. **16** dump; empty out. **17** vary with some different colour, etc.: *Her dress was shot with threads of gold.* **18** measure the altitude of: *to shoot the sun.* **19** send a ball, etc. toward the goal, pocket, etc. 1–4, 6, 8–10, 12–14, 16–19 *v.,* **shot, shoot·ing;** 5, 7, 11, 15 *n.*
**shoot at** or **for,** *Informal.* aim at; aspire to.
**shoot up,** grow tall or large quickly, as a plant, building, young person, etc.
☞ *Hom.* CHUTE.

**shooting gallery** a long room or deep booth fitted with targets for practice in shooting.

**shooting star** **1** a meteor resembling a star seen falling or darting through the sky. **2** a plant that has a cluster of rose, purple, or white flowers whose petals and sepals turn backward.

**shop** (shop) **1** store. **2** visit stores to look at or to buy things: *We shopped all morning for a coat.* **3** a place where things are made or repaired: *a carpenter's shop.* **4** a place where a certain kind of work is done: *a barber shop.* 1, 3, 4 *n.,* 2 *v.,* **shopped, shop·ping.**
**set up shop,** start work or business.
**shut up shop,** give up work or business.
**talk shop,** talk about one's work or occupation.

**shop·girl** (shop′gėrl′) a girl who works in a shop or store. *n.*

**shop·keep·er** (shop′kē′pər) a person who carries on business in a shop or store. *n.*

**shop·lift·er** (shop′lif′tər) one who steals goods from a store while pretending to be a customer. *n.*

**shop·lift·ing** (shop′lif′ting) the act of stealing goods from a store while pretending to be a customer. *n.*

**shop·per** (shop′ər) a person who visits stores to look at or buy things. *n.*

**shop·ping** (shop′ing) **1** the buying of groceries, clothes, etc.: *Our family likes to do the shopping together.* **2** ppr. of SHOP. 1 *n.,* 2 *v.*
**go shopping,** go to the store or stores in order to buy groceries, clothes, etc.

**shopping centre** a concentration of retail stores, usually in a suburban residential district, built as a unit and having ample parking, spacious walks, etc.

**shopping mall** a large SHOPPING CENTRE, especially one that is roofed and contains one or more department stores.

**shopping plaza** *Cdn.* SHOPPING CENTRE.

**shop·talk** (shop′tok′) **1** the informal language of an occupation. **2** the discussion of business or professional matters, especially outside of office hours. *n.*
► *Usage.* **Shoptalk** (def. 1) is a less formal term for JARGON (def. 3) and refers to a private or restricted aspect of language. It is appropriate to use shoptalk when writing for and about people in a particular walk of life. In speaking or writing for a wider audience, shoptalk terms can be useful for the sake of realism if their meaning is explained or clear from the context. Otherwise, they should be avoided.

**shop·worn** (shop′wôrn′) soiled by being displayed or handled in a store. *adj.*

**shore¹** (shôr) **1** the land at the edge of a sea, lake, etc. **2** the land near a sea: *There is good farmland on the western shore of the island.* **3** in law, the land between high-water and low-water marks. **4 shores,** *pl.* land: *foreign shores.* *n.*
**in shore,** in or on the water, near to the shore or nearer to the shore.
**off shore,** in or on the water, not far from the shore.

Shores supporting a ship frame in a dry dock

**shore²** (shôr) **1** a prop placed against or beneath something to support it. **2** prop up or support with shores. 1 *n.*, 2 *v.*, **shored, shor·ing.** *v.*

**shore bird** any of various birds, such as sandpipers and plovers, that spend much of their time on the shores of oceans and lakes.

**shore·less** (shôr′lis) **1** having no shore. **2** boundless. *adj.*

**shore·line** (shôr′līn′) the line where shore and water meet. *n.*

**shore pine** a form of the LODGEPOLE PINE found along the Pacific coast.

**shore·ward** (shôr′wərd) toward the shore. *adv., adj.*

**shor·ing** (shô′ring) the shores or props for supporting a building, ship, etc. *n.*

**shorn** (shôrn) **1** a pp. of SHEAR: *The sheep was shorn of its wool.* **2** SHEARed. **3** deprived. 1 *v.*, 2, 3 *adj.*

**short** (shôrt) **1** not long; of small extent from end to end: *a short distance, a short time, a short street.* **2** not long for its kind: *a short tail, short hair.* **3** not tall: *a short man, short grass.* **4** not coming up to the right amount, measure, standard, etc.: *The cashier is short in his accounts.* **5** not having enough; scanty: *The prisoners were kept on short allowance of food.* **6** so brief as to be rude: *She was so short with me that I felt hurt.* **7** abruptly; suddenly: *The horse stopped short.* **8** briefly. **9** of vowels or syllables, said to be occupying a relatively short time in utterance: *The vowels are considered short in fat, net, pin, not, up.* **10** something short. **11** on the near side of an intended or particular point: *to stop short of actual crime.* **12** a SHORT CIRCUIT. **13** SHORT-CIRCUIT. **14** breaking or crumbling easily: *Pastry is made short with lard or butter.* **15** not possessing at the time of sale the stocks or commodities that one sells. **16** noting or having to do with sales of stocks or commodities that the seller does not possess. **17** a person who has sold short; a sale made by selling short; stock, etc. sold short. **18** depending for profit on a decline in prices. **19** without possessing at the time the stocks, etc. which are sold: *It is risky to sell short.* 1–6, 9, 14–16, 18 *adj.*, 7, 8, 11, 19 *adv.*, 10, 12, 17 *n.*, 13 *v.*
—**short′ness,** *n.*
**cut short,** end suddenly.
**fall short, a** fail to reach. **b** be insufficient.
**for short,** to make shorter.
**in short,** briefly.
**make short work of,** deal with quickly.
**run short, a** not have enough. **b** not be enough.
**short of, a** not up to; less than: *Nothing short of your best work will satisfy me.* **b** not having enough of. **c** on the near side of.

**short·age** (shôr′tij) **1** too small an amount; a lack; deficiency: *There is a shortage of grain because of poor crops.* **2** the amount by which something is deficient. *n.*

**short·bread** (shôrt′bred′) a rich cake or cookie that crumbles easily. *n.*

**short·cake** (shôrt′kāk′) **1** a cake made of rich biscuit dough, covered or filled with berries or other fruit. **2** a sweet cake filled or spread with fruit. **3** SHORTBREAD. *n.*

**short–change** (shôrt′chānj′) *Informal.* **1** give less than the right change to. **2** cheat. *v.*, **short-changed, short-chang·ing.**

**short circuit** an electrical circuit, formed accidentally or intentionally, that by-passes the main circuit: *An accidental short circuit, in which worn or faulty wires touch each other, may blow a fuse or cause a fire.*

**short–cir·cuit** (shôrt′sėr′kit) **1** make a SHORT CIRCUIT in. **2** make a SHORT CIRCUIT. *v.*

**short·com·ing** (shôrt′kum′ing) a fault; defect: *Rudeness is a serious shortcoming.* *n.*

**short·cut** (shôrt′kut′) **1** a quicker or less distant route: *We took a shortcut through the field.* **2** a method, procedure, etc. that is simpler or quicker than the standard one: *shortcuts in cooking.* **3** use or take a shortcut. 1, 2 *n.*, 3 *v.*, **short·cut, short·cut·ting.**

**short division** in arithmetic, division using a divisor containing only one digit, and in which the steps of the process are not written down in full.

**short·en** (shôr′tən) **1** make shorter; cut off: *The new highway shortens the trip.* **2** become shorter. **3** make rich with butter, lard, etc. **4** take in sail. *v.*
—**short′en·er,** *n.*

**short·en·ing** (shôr′tə ning) **1** butter, lard, or other fat used in baking to make pastry, cake, etc. crisp or crumbly. **2** ppr. of SHORTEN. 1 *n.*, 2 *v.*

Examples of three systems of shorthand. Each says, "Your letter was received today."

**short·hand** (shôrt′hand′) **1** a method of rapid writing which uses symbols or a combination of letters and symbols to represent sounds. **2** writing done in such symbols. *n.*

**short–hand·ed** (shôrt′han′did) **1** not having enough workers or helpers. **2** in hockey and certain other games, playing without the services of one or more players as a result of penalties. **3** playing with less than a full side because of injuries. *adj.*

**short·horn** (shôrt′hôrn′) **1** a breed of beef cattle having short horns. **2** an animal of this breed. *n.*

**short·ish** (shôr′tish) rather short. *adj.*

**short–lived** (shôr′tlivd′ *or* shôr′tlīvd′) living only a short time; lasting only a short time. *adj.*

**short·ly** (shôrt′lē) **1** in a short time; before long; soon: *I will be with you shortly.* **2** in a few words; briefly. **3** briefly and rudely. *adv.*

**short–range** (shôr′trānj′) not reaching far. *adj.*

**shorts** (shôrts) **1** short, loose-fitting pants that reach no lower than the knees: *Shorts are worn by players in such games as tennis and basketball. Many people wear shorts in hot weather.* **2** a pair of short underpants worn by men or boys. **3** a baby's short clothes. **4** a mixture of bran and coarse meal. *n.pl.*

**short shrift** **1** short time for confession and absolution. **2** little mercy, respite, or delay.

**short–sight·ed** (shôrt′sī′tid) **1** near-sighted; not able to see far. **2** lacking in foresight; not prudent: *a short-sighted plan.* *adj.* —**short**′-**sight**′ed·ly, *adv.* —**short**′-**sight**′ed·ness, *n.*

**short–staffed** (shôrt′staft′) not having enough staff; short of the regular or necessary number of people. *adj.*

**short–stop** (shôrt′stop′) in baseball, a player stationed between second base and third base. *n.*

**short story** a prose story with a full plot, but of much less length than a novel: *As a rule, short stories develop one central theme and have relatively few characters.*

**short–tem·pered** (shôrt′tem′pərd) easily made angry; quick-tempered. *adj.*

**short–term** (shôrt′tėrm′) **1** lasting or intended for a short period of time: *our short-term plans.* **2** falling due in a short time: *a short-term loan.* *adj.*

**short ton** 2000 pounds avoirdupois; about 0.9 tonnes.

**short–waist·ed** (shôr′twā′stid) short from neck to waistline. *adj.*

**short wave** a high-frequency radio wave having a WAVELENGTH of 60 metres or less.

**short–wave** (shôr′twāv′) transmit by SHORT WAVES: *The prime minister's speech was short-waved overseas.* *v.*, **short-waved, short-wav·ing.**

**short·wind·ed** (shôr′twin′did) getting out of breath too quickly; having difficulty in breathing. *adj.*

**shot**[1] (shot) **1** the discharge of a gun or cannon: *She heard two shots.* **2** the act of shooting. **3** small pellets of lead or steel that make up the charge of a shotgun cartridge. **4** a single ball of lead for a gun or cannon. **5** load with shot. **6** an attempt to hit by shooting: *That was a good shot.* **7** the distance a weapon can shoot; range: *We were within rifle shot of the fort.* **8** a person who shoots: *My daughter is a good shot.* **9** the act of sending, directing, or propelling with force or swiftly: *His shot is hard for a goalie to stop.* **10** *Informal.* injection of a vaccine or drug: *a polio shot, a tetanus shot.* **11** a remark aimed at some person or thing. **12** an attempt; try: *to make a shot at the job.* **13** a heavy metal ball thrown in athletic contests. **14** a single picture taken with a camera or a motion-picture record of a single scene or subject. **15** *Informal.* a drink: *a shot of whisky.* **16** in mining, a blast. **17** an amount due or to be paid: *Mother paid the shot.* 1–4, 6–17 *n.*, *pl.* **shots** or (for def. 3) **shot**; 5 *v.*, **shot·ted, shot·ting.**
**a long shot,** an attempt at something difficult.
**not by a long shot,** not at all.
**put the shot,** in athletics, heave a heavy metal ball as far as one can with one throw.

**shot**[2] (shot) **1** pt. and pp. of SHOOT: *Many years ago he shot a rival and was himself shot in revenge.* **2** woven so as to show a play of colours: *blue silk shot with gold.* 1 *v.*, 2 *adj.*
**shot through with,** full of.

**shote** (shōt) See SHOAT. *n.*

**shot·gun** (shot′gun′) a large firearm having a long barrel with a smooth bore and firing cartridges filled with SHOT (def. 3). *n.*

**shot–put** (shot′pŭt′) a contest in which a person sends a heavy metal ball as far as he or she can with one throw. *n.*

**shot silk** silk woven so that the warp appears to be one colour and the woof another.

**should** (shůd; *unstressed,* shəd) a word used: **1** to mean that one ought to do something: *Everyone should learn to swim. I really should do my homework before I go out.* **2** to suggest that the speaker is uncertain about a thing or unwilling to believe something: *I don't see why you should think that. It's strange that they should be so late.* **3** to express a possible action in the future: *The statement I will be there in an hour is a promise; I should be there in an hour means that the speaker is not sure and therefore is not willing to promise.* **4** to express a belief: *She should be there by now.* **5** to express the pt. of SHALL. *v.*

**shoul·der** (shōl′dər) **1** the part of the body to which an arm of a human being, a foreleg of an animal, or a wing of a bird is attached. **2** the part of a garment covering this. **3** the foreleg and adjoining parts of a slaughtered animal. See LAMB and PORK for pictures. **4** take upon or support with the shoulder or shoulders: *to shoulder a tray.* **5** bear a burden, blame, etc.; assume responsibility, expense, etc.: *Aunt Ethel shouldered the responsibility of sending Jim to college.* **6** a shoulderlike part or projection: *the shoulder of a hill.* **7** the edge of a road or highway, often unpaved: *Do not drive on the shoulder.* **8** push with the shoulders: *He shouldered his way through the crowd.* **9 shoulders**, *pl.* the two shoulders and the upper part of the back. 1–3, 6, 7, 9 *n.*, 4, 5, 8 *v.*

**put one's shoulder to the wheel,** make a great effort.
**shoulder arms,** hold a rifle almost upright with the barrel resting in the hollow of the shoulder and the butt in the hand.
**shoulder to shoulder,** **a** side by side; together. **b** with united effort.
**straight from the shoulder,** frankly; directly.
**turn** or **give a cold shoulder to,** shun; avoid; show dislike for.

**shoulder blade** the flat triangular bone in the upper back behind either shoulder; scapula. See COLLARBONE and RIB for pictures.

**shoulder knot** a knot of ribbon or lace worn on the shoulder.

**shoulder strap** a strap worn over the shoulder to hold a garment up.

**should·n't** (shud'ənt) should not. *v.*

**shout** (shout) **1** call or cry loudly and vigorously: *Olga shouted for help. Somebody shouted, "Fire!"* **2** a loud, vigorous call or cry: *Shouts of joy rang through the halls.* **3** talk or laugh very loudly. **4** a loud outburst of laughter. **5** express by a shout or shouts: *The officer shouted his commands.* 1, 3, 5 *v.*, 2, 4 *n.* —**shout′er,** *n.*
**shout a person down,** silence a person by very loud talk.

**shove** (shuv) **1** push; move forward or along by the application of force from behind. **2** push roughly or rudely; jostle: *The people shoved to get on the crowded bus.* **3** a push: *Freda gave the boat a shove that sent it far out into the water.* 1, 2 *v.*, **shoved, shov·ing;** 3 *n.* —**shov′er,** *n.*
**shove off,** push away from the shore; row away.

A snow shovel

**shov·el** (shuv'əl) **1** a tool with a longish handle and broad, concave blade, used to lift and throw loose matter: *a snow shovel.* **2** a part of a machine having a similar use. **3** lift and throw with a shovel. **4** make with a shovel: *They shovelled a path through the snow.* **5** work with a shovel. **6** shovelful. **7** throw in large quantities: *The hungry man greedily shovelled the food into his mouth.* **8** a SHOVEL HAT. 1, 2, 6, 8 *n.*, 3–5, 7 *v.*, **shov·elled** or **shov·eled, shov·el·ling** or **shov·el·ing.**

**shov·el·er** (shuv'ə lər *or* shuv'lər) SHOVELLER. *n.*

**shov·el·ful** (shuv'əl ful') as much as a shovel can hold. *n., pl.* **shov·el·fuls.**

**shovel hat** a hat having a broad brim turned up at the sides and projecting with shovel-like curves in front and behind.

**shov·el·ler** or **shov·el·er** (shuv'ə lər *or* shuv'lər) **1** a person or thing that shovels. **2** a kind of freshwater duck with a broad, flat bill. *n.*

**show** (shō) **1** let be seen; put in sight; display: *She showed her new computer.* **2** reveal; manifest; disclose: *He showed himself a generous man by giving charity.* **3** be in sight; appear; be seen: *Anger showed in his face.* **4** point out: *She showed us the way to town.* **5** direct; guide: *Show him out.* **6** make clear to; explain to: *Show us how to do the problem.* **7** prove: *She showed that it was true.* **8** grant; give: *to show mercy, to show favour.* **9** a display: *The jewels made a fine show.* **10** display for effect: *He put on a show of learning to impress us.* **11** any kind of public exhibition or display: *a horse show.* **12** a showing: *The club voted by a show of hands.* **13** an appearance: *There is some show of truth in his excuse.* **14** a false appearance: *He hid his treachery by a show of friendship.* **15** a trace; indication: *a show of oil in a region.* **16** of a list, instrument, etc., indicate: *a watch showing twelve o'clock.* **17** *Informal.* an entertainment, such as a stage play or motion picture: *a motion-picture show.* **18** *Informal.* a theatre or motion-picture theatre: *I'll meet you in front of the show.* **19** in sports, finish among the first three in a race. **20** finish third in a race or competition. Compare with WIN (def. 2) and PLACE (def. 18). **21** third place in a race: *win, place, and show.* **22** an object of scorn; something odd; queer sight: *Don't make a show of yourself.* **23** a chance; opportunity. 1–8, 16, 19, 20 *v.*, **showed, shown** or **showed, show·ing;** 9–15, 17, 18, 21–23 *n.*
**for show,** for effect; to attract attention: *Some houses are furnished for show, not comfort.*
**show off,** **a** make a show of; display; act or talk for effect: *He was showing off his new bike.* **b** make a vain display; act in such a way as to attract attention: *That girl is always showing off.*
**show up,** **a** expose. **b** stand out: *He is very tall and shows up in any crowd.* **c** *Informal.* put in an appearance: *The prime minister showed up at the first concert.*

**show bill** a poster, placard, etc. advertising a show.

**show·boat** (shō'bōt') a steamboat with a theatre for plays: *Showboats carry their own actors and make frequent stops to give performances.* *n.*

**show·case** (shō'kās') **1** a glass case to display and protect articles in stores, museums, etc. **2** anything that displays: *Quebec City is a showcase of Canadian history.* *n.*

**show·down** (shō'doun') *Informal.* a forced disclosure of facts, purposes, methods, etc. *n.*

**show·er** (shou'ər) **1** a brief fall of rain. **2** rain for a short time. **3** wet with a shower; spray; sprinkle. **4** anything like a fall of rain: *a shower of hail, a shower of tears, a shower of sparks from an engine.* **5** come or fall in a shower. **6** send in a shower; pour down: *They showered gifts upon her.* **7** a party for giving presents to a woman or couple about to be married, or on some other special occasion. **8** a bath in which water is sprayed over the body from above in small jets. **9** the apparatus or enclosure for taking a shower. **10** take a shower. 1, 4, 7, 8, 9 *n.*, 2, 3, 5, 6, 10 *v.*

**shower bath** **1** a bath in which water pours down on the body from above in small jets. **2** the apparatus for such a bath.

**show·er·y** (shou'ə rē) **1** raining in showers. **2** having many showers. **3** like a shower. *adj.*

**show·man** (shō'mən) **1** a person who manages a show. **2** a person skilled in presenting things in a dramatic and exciting way. *n., pl.* **show·men** (-mən).

**show·man·ship** (shō′mən ship′) 1 the management of shows. 2 skill in managing shows or publicity. *n.*

**shown** (shōn) a pp. of SHOW: *The clerk has shown the girl many bicycles. We were shown many tricks.* *v.*

**show–off** (shō′ôf′) 1 a showing off. 2 *Informal.* a person who shows off; a person who is always calling attention to himself or herself. *n.*

**show–piece** (shō′pēs′) anything displayed as an outstanding example of its kind. *n.*

**show·place** (shō′plās′) any place considered worth exhibiting because of its superior beauty, interest, etc. *n.*

**show·room** (shō′rüm′) a room used for the display of goods or merchandise. *n.*

**show·y** (shō′ē) 1 making a display; striking; conspicuous: *A peony is a showy flower.* 2 too bright and gaudy to be in good taste. 3 ostentatious. *adj.*, **show·i·er, show·i·est.** —**show′i·ly,** *adv.* —**show′i·ness,** *n.*

**shrank** (shrangk) a pt. of SHRINK: *That woollen shirt shrank in the wash.* *v.*

**shrap·nel** (shrap′nəl) 1 a shell filled with fragments of metal and powder, set to explode in the air and scatter the fragments over a wide area. 2 the fragments scattered by such a shell: *He showed us the scars made when he was hit by shrapnel.* *n.*
☛ *Etym.* Named after Henry *Shrapnel* (1761–1842), a British general who invented this type of shell. 19c.

**shred** (shred) 1 a very small piece torn off or cut off; very narrow strip; scrap: *The wind tore the sail to shreds.* 2 a particle; fragment; bit: *There's not a shred of evidence that he took the money.* 3 tear or cut into small pieces. 1, 2 *n.,* 3 *v.,* **shred·ded** or **shred, shred·ding.**

**shred·der** (shred′ər) a machine for destroying documents by tearing them into shreds. *n.*

**shrew** (shrü) 1 a small, mouselike mammal having a long snout and brownish fur: *Shrews are fierce fighters and will attack animals much larger than themselves.* 2 a bad-tempered, quarrelsome woman. *n.*

**shrewd** (shrüd) 1 having a sharp, practical mind; showing a keen wit; clever: *She is a shrewd businesswoman.* 2 keen; sharp. *adj.* —**shrewd′ly,** *adv.* —**shrewd′ness,** *n.*
**shrewd turn,** a mean trick; mischievous act.

**shrew·ish** (shrü′ish) scolding; bad-tempered. *adj.* —**shrew′ish·ly,** *adv.* —**shrew′ish·ness,** *n.*

**shriek** (shrēk) 1 a loud, sharp, shrill sound: *We heard the shriek of the engine's whistle.* 2 make such a sound: *People sometimes shriek because of terror, anger, pain, or amusement.* 3 utter loudly and shrilly. 4 a loud, shrill laugh. 1, 4 *n.,* 2, 3 *v.*

**shrike** (shrīk) a bird that has a strong, hooked beak and feeds on large insects, frogs, and sometimes on other birds. *n.*

**shrill** (shril) 1 having a high pitch; high and sharp in sound; piercing: *Crickets, locusts, and katydids make shrill noises.* 2 full of shrill sounds. 3 make a shrill sound: *to shrill a reply.* 4 sound sharply: *the whistle shrilled.* 5 a shrill sound. 6 with a shrill sound: *She sang shrill and loud.* 1, 2 *adj.,* 3, 4 *v.,* 5 *n.,* 6 *adv.* —**shrill′ness,** *n.* —**shrill′ly,** *adv.*

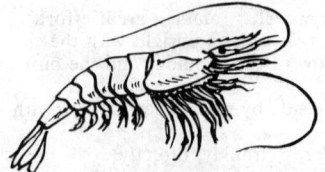
A shrimp—the different species range in size from 2.5 to 20 cm long

**shrimp** (shrimp) 1 a small, long-tailed shellfish, used for food. 2 a small or insignificant person. *n., pl.* **shrimp** or **shrimps.** —**shrimp′like′,** *adj.*

**shrine** (shrīn) 1 a case, box, etc. holding a holy object. 2 the tomb of a saint, etc. 3 a place of worship: *a wayside shrine.* 4 a place or object considered as sacred because of its memories, history, etc. 5 enclose in a shrine or something like a shrine. 1–4 *n.,* 5 *v.,* **shrined, shrin·ing.**

**shrink** (shringk) 1 draw back: *The dog shrank from the whip. A shy person shrinks from making new acquaintances.* 2 become smaller: *Her wool sweater shrank when it was washed.* 3 make smaller; cause to contract: *Cloth is often shrunk with water before being made up.* 4 a shrinking. 1–3 *v.,* **shrank** or **shrunk, shrunk** or **shrunk·en, shrink·ing;** 4 *n.* —**shrink′a·ble,** *adj.* —**shrink′er,** *n.*

**shrink·age** (shring′kij) 1 the fact or process of shrinking. 2 the amount or degree of shrinking: *a shrinkage of five centimetres in the length of a sleeve.* *n.*

**shriv·el** (shriv′əl) 1 dry up; wither; shrink and wrinkle: *The hot sunshine shrivelled the grass.* 2 waste away; become useless. 3 make helpless or useless. *v.,* **shriv·elled** or **shriv·eled, shriv·el·ling** or **shriv·el·ing.**

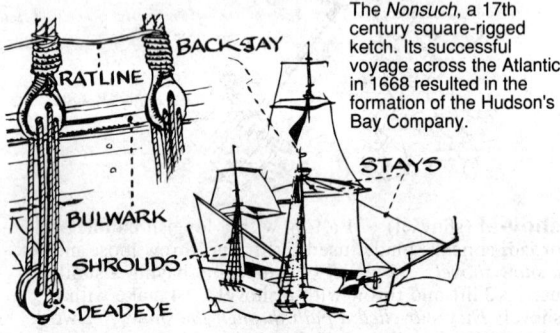
The *Nonsuch*, a 17th century square-rigged ketch. Its successful voyage across the Atlantic in 1668 resulted in the formation of the Hudson's Bay Company.

**shroud** (shroud) 1 a cloth or garment in which a dead person is wrapped for burial. 2 wrap for burial. 3 something that covers, conceals, or veils: *The fog was a shroud over the city.* 4 cover; conceal; veil: *The earth is shrouded in the darkness of night.* 5 one of the ropes from a mast to the side of a ship: *Shrouds help to support the mast.* See SCHOONER for another picture. 1, 3, 5 *n.,* 2, 4 *v.*

**shrub** (shrub) a woody plant smaller than a tree, usually with many separate stems starting from or near the ground; bush: *A lilac bush is a shrub.* *n.* —**shrub′like′,** *adj.*

**shrub·ber·y** (shrub′ə rē) 1 shrubs collectively. 2 a place planted with shrubs. *n., pl.* **shrub·ber·ies.**

**shrub·by** (shrub′ē) 1 like shrubs. 2 covered with shrubs. 3 consisting of shrubs. *adj.* **shrub·bi·er, shrub·bi·est.**

**shrug** (shrug) 1 raise the shoulders as an expression of dislike, doubt, indifference, impatience, etc.: *She shrugged* and walked away. **2** a raising of the shoulders in this way. **1** *v.*, **shrugged, shrug·ging;** **2** *n.*

**shrunk** (shrungk) a pt. and a pp. of SHRINK. *v.*

**shrunk·en** (shrung′kən) **1** grown smaller; shrivelled. **2** a pp. of SHRINK. **1** *adj.*, **2** *v.*

**shru·ti** (shrüt′ē) the collective term for all sacred Hindu scriptures. *n.*

**shuck** (shuk) **1** a husk; pod. **2** remove the shucks from: *Please shuck the corn.* **1** *n.*, **2** *v.* —**shuck′er,** *n.*

**shucks** (shuks) *Informal.* an exclamation of disgust, regret, impatience, etc. *interj.*

**shud·der** (shud′ər) **1** tremble with horror, fear, cold, etc.: *She shudders at the sight of a snake.* **2** a trembling; quivering. **1** *v.*, **2** *n.* —**shud′der·ing·ly,** *adv.*

**shuf·fle** (shuf′əl) **1** walk without lifting the feet: *The old man shuffles feebly along.* **2** scrape or drag the feet. **3** a scraping or dragging movement of the feet. **4** dance with a shuffle. **5** change the order of cards, officials, etc. **6** a shuffling of cards or officials, etc.: *a cabinet shuffle.* **7** the right or turn to shuffle cards. **8** put on with clumsy haste: *He shuffled on his clothes and ran out of the house.* **9** move this way and that: *to shuffle a stack of papers.* **10** a movement this way and that: *After a hasty shuffle through her papers, the speaker began to talk.* **11** put, bring, come about, or answer in a tricky way; dodge; equivocate; quibble. **12** a trick; unfair act; evasion: *Through some legal shuffle he secured a new trial.* **1, 2, 4, 5, 8, 9, 11** *v.*, **shuf·fled, shuf·fling;** **3, 6, 7, 10, 12** *n.* —**shuf′fler,** *n.*
**shuffle off,** get rid of.

**shuf·fle·board** (shuf′əl bôrd′) a game played by pushing large wooden or iron disks along a surface to numbered squares. *n.*

**shun** (shun) keep away from; avoid: *She was lazy and shunned work.* *v.*, **shunned, shun·ning.** —**shun′ner,** *n.*

**shunt** (shunt) **1** move out of the way; turn aside. **2** a turning aside; shift. **3** sidetrack; put aside; get rid of. **4** switch a train from one track to another. **5** a railway switch. **6** a wire or other conductor joining two points in an electric circuit and forming a path through which a part of the current will pass. **7** carry a part of a current by means of a shunt. **1, 3, 4, 7** *v.*, **2, 5, 6** *n.* —**shunt′er,** *n.*

**shut** (shut) **1** close a receptacle or opening by pushing or pulling a lid, door, or other such part into place: *to shut a box, to shut a window.* **2** close the eyes, a knife, a book, etc. by bringing parts together. **3** close tight; close securely; close doors or other openings of: *After Thanksgiving, we shut our cottage up for the winter.* **4** become shut; be closed. **5** closed; fastened up; enclosed. **6** enclose; confine: *The criminal was shut in prison.* **1–4, 6** *v.*, **shut, shut·ting;** **5** *adj.*
**shut down,** **a** close by lowering. **b** close a factory or the like for a time; stop work. **c** settle down so as to cover or envelop. **d** *Informal.* put a stop or check (on).
**shut in,** keep from going out.
**shut off,** close; obstruct; check; bar; turn off: *Shut off the radio.*
**shut out,** **a** keep from coming in: *The curtains shut out the light.* **b** defeat a team without allowing it to score.
**shut up,** **a** shut the doors and windows of. **b** *Informal.* stop talking. **c** keep from going out.

**shut–down** (shut′doun′) a shutting down; a closing of a factory, etc. for a time. *n.*

**shut–in** (shut′in′) **1** confined. **2** a person who is kept from going out by sickness, weakness, etc. **1** *adj.*, **2** *n.*

**shut–out** (shut′out′) **1** the defeat of a team without allowing it to score. **2** a LOCKOUT. *n.*

**shut·ter** (shut′ər) **1** a movable cover for a window: *When we shut up our cottage for the winter, we put shutters on all the windows.* **2** a movable cover, slide, etc. for closing an opening: *The device that opens and closes in front of the film in a camera is the shutter.* See CAMERA for picture. **3** put a shutter or shutters on or over. **4** a person or thing that shuts. **1, 2, 4** *n.*, **3** *v.*

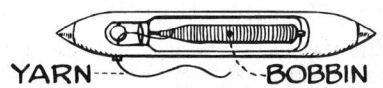
A shuttle used in weaving

**shut·tle** (shut′əl) **1** in weaving, a device that carries the thread from one side of the web to the other. **2** a similar device on which thread is wound: *Shuttles are used in tatting, a kind of lacemaking.* **3** something that goes back and forth: *The shuttle in a sewing machine is the sliding holder for the lower thread.* **4** move quickly to and fro. **5** a bus, train, airplane, etc. that runs back and forth regularly over a short distance. **1–3, 5** *n.*, **4** *v.* **shut·tled, shut·tling.**

**shut·tle·cock** (shut′əl kok′) **1** a cone of feathers or light plastic with a cork or similar base, used in the game of badminton. **2** a cork with feathers stuck in one end, which is hit back and forth by a small racket, called a battledore, in the game of battledore and shuttlecock. *n.*

**shuttle service** a train, bus, or other form of transport that provides fast service back and forth over short distances.

**shy¹** (shī) **1** uncomfortable in company; bashful: *Sonia is shy and dislikes parties.* **2** easily frightened away; timid: *A deer is a shy animal.* **3** cautious; wary. **4** start back or aside suddenly: *The horse shied at the fence.* **5** a sudden start to one side. **6** not having enough; short; scant: *This store is shy on children's clothing.* **7** draw back; shrink. **1–3, 6** *adj.*, **shy·er** or **shi·er, shy·est** or **shi·est,** **4, 7** *v.*, **shied, shy·ing;** **5** *n.*, *pl.* **shies.** —**shy′ness,** *n.*
**fight shy of,** keep away from; avoid.
**shy of,** *Informal.* having little; lacking.

**shy²** (shī) throw; fling: *The boy shied a stone at the tree.* *v.*, **shied, shy·ing;** *n.*, *pl.* **shies.**

**shy·ly** (shī′lē) in a shy manner. *adv.* Also, **shily.**

**shy·ster** (shī′stər) *Informal.* a person who uses improper or questionable methods in his or her business or profession. *n.*

**si** (sē) in music, TI. *n.*

**Si** silicon.

**SI** Système international d'unités (International System of Units), the system adopted by Canada as the official system of measurement. See METRIC SYSTEM.

**Si·a·mese** (sī′ə mēz′)  1 of or having to do with Thailand, its people, or their language.  2 a breed of cat having pale fur, dark tips to the ears, tail, and feet, and often blue eyes.  1 *adj.*, 2 *n.*

**Siamese twins**  1 twin Siamese boys, 1811–1874, who were born joined by a band of flesh between their chests.  2 any twins joined together at birth.

**sib** (sib)  1 related by blood; closely related; akin.  2 a kinsman or relative.  3 one's kin.  4 a brother or sister; sibling.  1 *adj.*, 2–4 *n.*

**Si·be·ri·an** (sī bē′rē ən)  of or having to do with Siberia, a part of Russia extending across northern Asia.  *adj.*

**Siberian husky**  a breed of dog much used in the North.

**sib·i·lance** (sib′ə ləns)  a hissing.  *n.*

**sib·i·lant** (sib′ə lənt)  1 hissing.  2 a hissing sound, letter, or symbol: *The sounds represented by* s *and* sh *are sibilants.*  1 *adj.*, 2 *n.*  —**sib′i·lant·ly,** *adv.*

**sib·ling** (sib′ling)  a brother or sister.  *n.*

**sic**[1] (sik) *Latin.*  so; thus. *Sic* is often used in square brackets to show or emphasize the fact that something has been copied just as it was in the original.  *adv.*
☞ *Hom.* SICK.

**sic**[2] (sik)  See SICK[2].  *v.*, **sicced, sic·cing.**

**sic·ca·tive** (sik′ə tiv)  1 drying.  2 a drying substance, especially a drier used in painting.  1 *adj.*, 2 *n.*

**Si·cil·ian** (sə sil′yən)  1 of or having to do with Sicily, an island region of Italy, its people, or their dialect.  2 a native or inhabitant of Sicily.  3 the dialect of Italian spoken in Sicily.  1 *adj.*, 2, 3 *n.*

**sick**[1] (sik)  1 in poor health; having some disease; ill.  2 *Informal.*  vomiting; inclined to vomit; feeling nausea.  3 for a sick person; connected with sickness: *a sick room.*  4 showing sickness: *a sick look.*  5 weary; tired: *She is sick of school.*  6 disgusted.  7 affected with sorrow or longing: *sick at heart.*  8 not in the proper condition.  9 pale; wan.  10 morbid; sadistic; cruel: *a sick joke, sick humour.*  11 **the sick,** sick people.  1–10 *adj.*, 11 *n.*
☞ *Hom.* SIC.

**sick**[2] or **sic**[2] (sik)  1 set upon or attack.  2 incite to set upon or attack (*used with* **on**).  *v.*, **sicced, sic·cing.**
☞ *Hom.* SIC.

**sick bay**  1 a place used as a hospital on a ship.  2 a room or rooms set apart for the care of the sick or injured: *There is a sick bay in the students' residence.*

**sick·bed** (sik′bed′)  the bed of a sick person.  *n.*

**sick·en** (sik′ən)  1 become sick: *The bird sickened when kept in the cage.*  2 make sick.  *v.*

**sick·en·ing** (sik′ə ning)  1 making sick; causing nausea, faintness, disgust, or loathing.  2 becoming sick.  3 *ppr.* of SICKEN.  1, 2 *adj.*, 3 *v.*  —**sick′en·ing·ly,** *adv.*

**sick headache**  a headache accompanied by nausea; migraine.

**sick·ish** (sik′ish)  1 somewhat sick.  2 somewhat sickening.  *adj.*  —**sick′ish·ly,** *adv.*  —**sick′ish·ness,** *n.*

A sickle

**sick·le** (sik′əl)  1 a tool consisting of a short, curved blade on a short handle, used for cutting grass, etc.  2 mow or cut with a sickle.  1 *n.*, 2 *v.*

**sick·ly** (sik′lē)  1 often sick; not strong; not healthy.  2 of or having to do with sickness: *Her skin is a sickly yellow.*  3 causing sickness: *That place has a sickly climate.*  4 faint; weak; pale.  5 weak; mawkish: *sickly mentality.*  6 in a sick manner.  1–5 *adj.*, **sick·li·er, sick·li·est;**  6 *adv.*  —**sick′li·ness,** *n.*

**sick·ness** (sik′nis)  1 the condition of being sick; illness; disease.  2 nausea; vomiting.  *n.*

**sick parade**  in the armed forces, the coming together of persons requiring medical attention: *Sick parade is at 10 a.m. daily.*

**side** (sīd)  1 a surface or line bounding a thing: *the sides of a square.*  2 one of the surfaces of an object that is not the front, back, top, or bottom: *There is a door at the side of the house.*  3 either of the two surfaces of paper, cloth, etc.: *Write only on one side of the paper.*  4 a particular surface: *the outer and inner sides of a hollow ball, the side of the moon turned toward the earth.*  5 either the right or the left part of the body of a person or an animal: *a pain in one's side.*  6 a slope of a hill or bank.  7 either the right or the left part of a thing; either part or region beyond a central line: *the east side of a city, our side of the street, turn to one side.*  8 a bank or shore of a river.  9 an aspect or view of someone or something: *the better side of one's nature, the bright side of a difficulty.*  10 a group of persons opposed to another group: *Both sides are ready for the contest.*  11 team: *The girls chose sides for a game of softball.*  12 the position, course, attitude, or part of one person or party against another: *It is pleasant to be on the winning side of a dispute.*  13 a part of a family; line of descent: *The man is English on his mother's side.*  14 at one side; on one side: *the side aisles of a theatre.*  15 from one side: *a side view.*  16 toward one side: *a side glance.*  17 less important: *a side issue.*  18 (*used with* **with**) take the part of; favour one among opposing or differing groups or persons: *The sisters always side with each other.*  1–13 *n.*, 14–17 *adj.*, 18 *v.*, **sid·ed, sid·ing.**
**by one's side,**  near one.
**on the side,** *Informal.*  in addition to one's ordinary duties.
**side by side,**  beside one another.
**split one's sides,**  laugh very hard.
**take sides,**  place oneself with one person or group against another.

**side arms**  weapons such as a sword, revolver, bayonet, etc. carried at the side or in the belt.

**side·board** (sīd′bôrd′)  a piece of dining-room furniture; a buffet: *A sideboard has drawers and shelves for holding silver and linen, and space on top for dishes.*  *n.*

**side·burns** (sīd′bėrnz′)  hair growing down in front of the ears, especially when the chin is shaved.  *n.pl.*
☞ *Etym.*  Originally called *burnsides*, after Ambrose Burnside (1824–1881), an American general who wore such whiskers.

**side·car** (sīd′kär′) a small, one-wheeled car for a passenger, baggage, etc. attached to the side of a motorcycle. *n.*

**–sided** an adjective-forming suffix meaning: having a side or sides, as in *three-sided*.

**side effect** 1 a secondary result or effect of a course of action, treatments, etc., especially an undesirable reaction to a drug: *The pills stopped me sneezing but had the side effect of making me sleepy.* 2 any unpleasant incidental effect.

**side light** 1 light coming from the side. 2 incidental information about a subject. 3 either of two lights carried by a moving ship at night, a red one on the port side and a green one on the starboard side. 4 a window or other opening for light in the side of a building, ship, etc. 5 a window at the side of a door or of another window.

**side·line** (sīd′līn′) 1 a line at the side of something. 2 a line that marks the limit of play on the side of the field in football, etc. 3 an additional line of goods or of business. 4 put on the sidelines; make inactive. 5 Often, **sidelines**, *pl.* the space just outside the lines of a football field: *The spectators watched the game from the sidelines.* 1–3, 5 *n.*, 4 *v.*
**on the sidelines,** inactive; not taking an active part in a game, enterprise, etc.

**side·long** (sīd′lông′) to one side; toward the side: *a sidelong glance.* *adj., adv.*

**side·piece** (sīd′pēs′) a piece forming a side or part of a side, or fixed at the side of something. *n.*

**si·de·re·al** (sī dē′rē əl) 1 of or having to do with the stars. 2 measured by the apparent daily motion of the stars: *A sidereal day is about four minutes shorter than a mean solar day.* *adj.*

**sid·er·ite** (sid′ə rīt′) an iron ore composed of iron carbonate: *Siderite occurs in various colours.* *n.*

**side road** 1 *Cdn.* in Ontario, a road running at right angles to a concession road or main road. 2 any road that is not a main road.

**side·sad·dle** (sīd′sad′əl) 1 a woman's saddle so made that both of the rider's legs are on the same side of the horse. 2 on a sidesaddle; as on a sidesaddle. *n.*

**side show** a small show in connection with a principal one: *the side shows of a circus.*

**side·slip** (sīd′slip′) 1 slip or skid to one side. 2 the slipping of an aircraft to one side and downward. 1, 2 *n.*, 1 *v.*, **side·slipped, side·slip·ping.**

**side step** 1 a step or stepping to one side. 2 a step at the side of a ship, vehicle, etc.

**side–step** (sīd′step′) 1 step aside. 2 avoid by stepping aside; evade: *to side-step a responsibility.* *v.*, **side-stepped, side-step·ping.** —**side′-step′per,** *n.*

**side street** a less important street than a main road; a street leading off a main road.

**side·swipe** (sīd′swīp′) 1 hit with a sweeping blow along the side. 2 a sweeping blow along the side. 1 *v.*, **side·swiped, side·swip·ing;** 2 *n.*

**side·track** (sīd′trak′) 1 a railway SIDING. 2 switch a train, etc. to a SIDING. 3 put aside; turn aside: *The teacher refused to be sidetracked by questions on other subjects.* 1 *n.*, 2, 3 *v.*

**side·walk** (sīd′wok′) a place to walk at the side of a street: *Sidewalks are usually paved.* *n.*

---

# sidecar 1101 sieve

hat, āge, fär; let, ēqual, tėrm; it, īce
hot, ōpen, ôrder; oil, out; cup, pùt, rüle
əbove, takən, pencəl, lemən, circəs
ch, child; ng, long; sh, ship
th, thin; ᴛʜ, then; zh, measure

**side·ward** (sīd′wərd) toward one side. *adj., adv.*

**side·wards** (sīd′wərdz) SIDEWARD. *adv.*

**side·way** (sīd′wā′) 1 SIDEWAYS. 2 a side street, not a main road; byway. 3 a sidewalk. 1 *adv., adj.,* 2, 3 *n.*

**side·ways** (sīd′wāz′) 1 toward one side: *to walk sideways.* 2 from one side: *a sideways glimpse.* 3 with one side toward the front: *to stand sideways, to place a book sideways on a shelf.* 1, 3 *adv.,* 2 *adj.*

**side–wheel** (sīd′wēl′ *or* sīd′hwēl′) having a paddle wheel on each side. *adj.*

**side·wise** (sīd′wīz′) SIDEWAYS. *adv., adj.*

**sid·ing** (sī′ding) 1 a short railway track to which cars can be switched from a main track. 2 *Cdn.* a place in the country along a secondary railway line, having a grain elevator with a residence for the agent and, sometimes, a few other houses, stores, etc. 3 the boards, shingles, etc. forming the outside walls of a building. 4 ppr. of SIDE. 1–3 *n.,* 4 *v.*

**si·dle** (sī′dəl) 1 move sideways. 2 move sideways, especially shyly or stealthily: *The little boy shyly sidled up to the visitor.* 3 a movement sideways. 1, 2 *v.,* **si·dled, si·dling;** 3 *n.*

**siege** (sēj) 1 the surrounding of a fortified place by an army trying to capture it; a besieging or being besieged: *Troy was under a siege for ten years.* 2 any long or persistent effort to overcome resistance; any long-continued attack: *a siege of illness.* 3 besiege. 1, 2 *n.,* 3 *v.,* **sieged, sieg·ing.**
**lay siege to,** **a** besiege: *to lay siege to a city.* **b** attempt to win or get by long and persistent effort: *to lay siege to someone's affections.*

**sie·mens** (sē′mənz) an SI unit for measuring electrical conductance: *One siemens is the conductance between two points of a conductor when a current of one ampere produces one volt of electromotive force.* Symbol: S *n.*

**si·en·na** (sē en′ə) 1 a yellowish-brown colouring matter (**raw sienna**) made from earth containing iron. 2 a reddish-brown colouring matter (**burnt sienna**) made by roasting earth containing iron. 3 yellowish brown or reddish brown. 1–3 *n.,* 3 *adj.*

**si·er·ra** (sē er′ə) a chain of hills or mountains having jagged peaks. *n.*
☛ *Etym.* From Spanish *sierra* 'a saw'. The line of jagged peaks was thought to resemble the teeth of a saw.

**si·es·ta** (sē es′tə) a nap or rest taken at noon or in the afternoon. *n.*

Sieves

**sieve** (siv) 1 a utensil having holes that let liquids and small pieces pass through, but not large pieces. **2** put through a sieve. 1 *n.*, 2 *v.*, **sieved, siev·ing.**

**sif·fleur** (sē flėr′) *Cdn.* HOARY MARMOT. *n.*

**sift** (sift) **1** separate large pieces from small by shaking in a sieve: *Sift the gravel and put the larger stones in another pile.* **2** put through a sieve: *Sift sugar onto the top of the cake.* **3** use a sieve. **4** fall through, or as if through, a sieve: *The snow sifted softly down.* **5** examine very carefully: *The jury sifted the evidence to decide if the woman was guilty.* *v.* —**sift′er,** *n.*

**sigh** (sī) **1** draw in or let out a very long, deep, loud breath because one is sad, tired, relieved, etc. **2** the act or sound of sighing: *a sigh of regret, a sigh of relief.* **3** say or express with a sigh. **4** make a sound like a sigh: *The wind sighed in the treetops.* **5** wish very much; long: *She often sighed for home and friends.* **6** lament with sighing: *to sigh over one's unhappy fate.* 1, 3–6 *v.*, 2 *n.* —**sigh′er,** *n.* —**sigh′ing·ly,** *adv.*

**sight** (sīt) **1** the power of seeing; vision: *Birds have better sight than dogs.* **2** the act or fact of seeing; look: *love at first sight.* **3** the range or field of vision: *Land was in sight.* **4** the thing seen; view; glimpse: *I caught a sight of her.* **5** something worth seeing: *to see the sights of the city.* **6** something that looks bad or odd: *Her clothes were a sight.* **7** see: *At last Columbus sighted land.* **8** a device on a gun, surveying instrument, etc., used in taking aim or observing: *a bomb sight.* **9** an observation taken with a telescope or other instrument; aim with a gun, etc. **10** take a sight or observation of. **11** aim by means of sights: *The hunter sighted very carefully before firing his gun.* **12** adjust the sight of a gun, etc. **13** provide with sights. **14** a way of looking or thinking; regard: *Dolls are precious in a little girl's sight.* **15** *Informal.* a considerable quantity; a great deal. 1–6, 8, 9, 14, 15 *n.*, 7, 10–13 *v.*
**at sight,** as soon as seen: *She reads music at sight.*
**catch sight of,** see: *I caught sight of him.*
**in sight of,** where one can see or be seen by: *We live in sight of the school.*
**know by sight,** know sufficiently to recognize when seen: *I've never met him but I know him by sight.*
**on sight,** as soon as seen; at sight.
**out of sight of,** **a** where one cannot see: *out of sight of land.* **b** where one cannot be seen by: *out of sight of the neighbours.*
**sight unseen,** not seen beforehand: *She bought the radio sight unseen.*
☛ *Hom.* CITE, SITE.

**sight draft** a written order from one bank to another, requiring a certain amount of money to be paid on demand.

**sight·less** (sīt′lis) blind. *adj.*

**sight·ly** (sīt′lē) **1** pleasing to the sight. **2** affording a fine view. *adj.*, **sight·li·er, sight·li·est.** —**sight′li·ness,** *n.*

**sight·read** (sīt′trēd′) play an instrument or sing by reading music not previously seen. *v.*

**sight·read·ing** (sīt′trē′ding) **1** the act of playing an instrument or singing from music not previously seen. **2** ppr. of SIGHTREAD. 1 *n.*, 2 *v.*

**sight·see·ing** (sīt′sē′ing) **1** the act of going around to see objects or places of interest: *a weekend of sightseeing.* **2** of or having to do with sightseeing: *a sightseeing tour.* 1 *n.*, 2 *adj.*

**sight·se·er** (sīt′sē′ər) a person who goes around to see objects or places of interest. *n.*

**sig·moid** (sig′moid) **1** shaped like the letter S. The **sigmoid flexure** of the COLON is its last curve before the rectum. **2** having to do with the sigmoid flexure of the COLON. **3** shaped like the letter C. *adj.*

**sign** (sīn) **1** any mark used to mean, represent, or point out something: *The signs for addition, subtraction, multiplication, and division are +, −, ×, ÷.* **2** attach one's name to: *Sign this letter.* **3** attach one's name to show authority, agreement, obligation, etc.; write one's name: *Sign on the dotted line.* **4** write: *Sign your initials here.* **5** hire by a written agreement: *to sign a new player.* **6** accept employment: *They signed for three years.* **7** a motion or gesture used to mean, represent, or point out something: *A nod is a sign of agreement. We talked to the deaf man by signs.* **8** give a sign to; signal: *to sign someone to enter.* **9** communicate by gesture: *to sign assent.* **10** communicate by means of SIGN LANGUAGE. **11** mark with a sign. **12** an inscribed board, space, etc. serving for advertisement, information, etc.: *The sign reads, "Keep out."* **13** an indication; trace; evidence: *signs of life. The hunter found signs of deer.* **14** an indication of a coming event: *a sign of spring.* **15** in astrology, any of the twelve divisions of the ZODIAC. 1, 7, 12–15 *n.*, 2–6, 8–11 *v.* —**sign′er,** *n.*
**sign away,** assign.
**sign in,** indicate by signing a register, etc. that one is present: *Everyone at the office had to sign in each morning.*
**sign off, a** in radio and television, stop broadcasting. **b** bring a letter, speech, lecture, etc. to a close.
**sign on** or **sign up,** **a** accept a job by putting one's name to an agreement: *Ten men signed on with the company last week.* **b** hire in this way: *The company signed up twenty new men.* **c** enlist in the armed services.
**sign out,** indicate by signing a register, etc. that one will not be present: *Ms. Appelt signed out an hour ago.*
**sign over,** hand over by signing one's name.
☛ *Hom.* SINE.

**sig·nal** (sig′nəl) **1** a sign giving notice of something: *A red light is a signal of danger.* **2** a wave, current, impulse, etc., serving to convey sounds and images in communications by radio, television, etc. **3** make a signal or signals to: *He signalled the car to stop by raising his hand.* **4** make known by a signal or signals: *A bell signals the end of a school period.* **5** used as a signal or in signalling: *a signal flag.* **6** remarkable; striking; notable: *The aircraft carrier was a signal invention.* **7** in card games, a bid or play that gives information to one's partner. 1, 2, 7 *n.*, 3, 4 *v.*, **sig·nalled** or **sig·naled, sig·nal·ling** or **sig·nal·ing,** 5, 6 *adj.* —**sig′nal·ler** or **sig′nal·er,** *n.*

**signal fire** a fire used in giving a signal.

**signal flag** a flag used in giving a signal.

**Signal Hill** the hill overlooking the entrance to St. John's harbour in Newfoundland, where Marconi received the first transatlantic radio signal in 1901.

**sig·nal·ing** (sig′nə ling) SIGNALLING. *n., v.*

**sig·nal·ize** (sig′nə līz′) make stand out; make notable: *Many great inventions signalize the last 150 years. The year 1945 was signalized by the end of World War II.* *v.*, **sig·nal·ized, sig·nal·iz·ing.**

**sig·nal·ler** or **sig·nal·er** (sig′nə lər) **1** a soldier in the infantry, artillery, etc. who looks after communications within the regiment. **2** SIGNALMAN. *n.*

**sig·nal·ling** or **sig·nal·ing** (sig′nə ling) **1** the act of

using, making, or controlling signals.   2 ppr. of SIGNAL.
1 n., 2 v.

**sig·nal·ly** (sig′nə lē)   remarkably; strikingly; notably. *adv.*

**sig·nal·man** (sig′nəl mən *or* sig′nəl man′)   1 a man in charge of the signals of a railway, in the armed services, etc.   2 a private soldier in a signals regiment.   *n., pl.* **sig·nal·men** (-mən *or* -men′).

**sig·na·to·ry** (sig′nə tô′rē)   1 a signer of a document.   2 signing: *signatory delegates.*   1 *n., pl.* **sig·na·to·ries**; 2 *adj.*

**sig·na·ture** (sig′nə chər)   1 a person's name written by himself or herself.   2 a writing of one's name.   3 in music, the signs printed at the beginning of a staff to show the key and time of a piece of music.   4 in printing, a sheet folded into pages, forming a section of a book.   5 a tune, song, or slogan used to identify a radio or television program.   *n.*

**sign·board** (sīn′bôrd′)   a board having a sign, notice, advertisement, inscription, etc. on it.   *n.*

**sig·net** (sig′nit)   a small SEAL¹ (def. 1): *The order was sealed with the king's signet.*   *n.*

**signet ring**   a finger ring containing a SIGNET.

**sig·nif·i·cance** (sig nif′ə kəns)   1 importance; consequence: *The teacher wanted to see her on a matter of significance.*   2 the meaning: *Do you understand the significance of H₂0?*   3 expressiveness; significant quality: *the significance of her smile.*   *n.*

**sig·nif·i·cant** (sig nif′ə kənt)   1 full of meaning; important; of consequence: *July 1, 1867, is a significant date for Canadians.*   2 having a meaning; expressive: *Smiles are significant of pleasure.*   3 having or expressing a hidden or special meaning: *A significant nod warned him to be silent.*   *adj.* —**sig·nif′i·cant·ly,** *adv.*

**sig·ni·fi·ca·tion** (sig′nə fə kā′shən)   1 the meaning; sense.   2 the act or process of SIGNIFYING: *Signification relies largely upon words and gestures.*   *n.*

**sig·nif·i·ca·tive** (sig nif′ə kə tiv *or* sig nif′ə kā′tiv)   1 serving to signify; having a meaning.   2 significant or suggestive.   *adj.*

**sig·ni·fy** (sig′nə fī)   1 be a sign of; mean: *Oh! signifies surprise.*   2 make known by signs, words, or actions: *Marc signified his consent with a nod.*   3 have importance; be of consequence; matter: *What a fool says does not signify.*   *v.,* **sig·ni·fied, sig·ni·fy·ing.**

**sign language**   language in which motions, especially of the hands, stand for words, ideas, etc.: *Sign language is used especially by the hearing and voice impaired.*

**sign·post** (sīn′pōst′)   a post having a sign, notice, or direction on it; guidepost.   *n.*

**Sikh** (sēk)   1 a follower of SIKHISM.   2 of or having to do with SIKHISM or the Sikhs.   1 *n.,* 2 *adj.*
☞ *Hom.* SEEK.

**Sikh·ism** (sē′kiz′əm)   a religion founded in northwest India in the early 16th century. It has retained from Hinduism the belief in Karma and reincarnation, while rejecting the caste system and worship of idols. It has adopted from Islam the belief in one God.   *n.*

**si·lage** (sī′lij)   green fodder for farm animals, preserved and stored in a silo; ensilage.   *n.*

**si·lence** (sī′ləns)   1 the absence of sound or noise; stillness.   2 a state of keeping still; not talking.   3 the omission of mention: *His silence about the hockey game

**signally**      1103      silicic

hat, āge, fär; let, ēqual, tėrm; it, īce
hot, ōpen, ôrder; oil, out; cup, pùt, rüle
əbove, takən, pencəl, lemən, circəs
ch, child; ng, long; sh, ship
th, thin; ᴛн, then; zh, measure

*was surprising.*   4 stop the speech or noise of; make silent; quiet: *The nurse silenced the baby's crying.*   5 make silent by restraint or prohibition; repress: *silence the press, silence an uprising.*   6 be silent!   1–3 *n.,* 4, 5 *v.,* **si·lenced, si·lenc·ing**;   6 *interj.*
**in silence,**   without saying anything: *Janice passed over his foolish remarks in silence.*

**si·lenc·er** (sī′lən sər)   1 a person or thing that silences.   2 a muffler on an INTERNAL-COMBUSTION ENGINE.   3 a device for deadening the sound of a gun.   *n.*

**si·lent** (sī′lənt)   1 quiet; still; noiseless: *a silent house, the silent hills.*   2 not speaking; saying little or nothing: *a silent person.*   3 not spoken; not said out loud: *a silent prayer. The "l" in "folk" is a silent letter.*   4 not active; taking no open or active part: *A silent partner has no share in managing a business.*   5 omitting mention of something, as in a narrative.   *adj.* —**si′lent·ly,** *adv.* —**si′lent·ness,** *n.*

**si·lex** (sī′leks)   1 SILICA.   2 a strong glass that is mostly quartz and resists heat.   *n.*

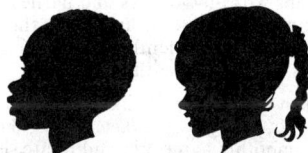
Silhouettes of children's heads

**sil·hou·ette** (sil′ü et′)   1 an outline portrait cut out of black paper or filled in with some single colour.   2 a dark image outlined against a lighter background.   3 show in outline: *The mountain was silhouetted against the sky.*   1, 2 *n.,* 3 *v.,* **sil·hou·et·ted, sil·hou·et·ting.**
**in silhouette,**   shown in outline, or in black against a white background.
☞ *Etym.* Named after Etienne de *Silhouette* (1709–1767), a French minister of finance, who was scorned for doing such drawings.

**sil·i·ca** (sil′ə kə)   silicon dioxide, a compound that occurs in crystalline form as in quartz and non-crystalline form as in opal, and that also forms the main ingredient of sand.   *n.*

**silica gel**   a non-crystalline form of SILICA resembling sand, but having many fine pores that make it highly absorbent: *Silica gel is used as a drying and deodorizing agent in air conditioners, etc.*

**sil·i·cate** (sil′ə kit *or* sil′ə kāt)   any of many insoluble compounds of silicon, oxygen, and a metal or metals, that make up the largest class of minerals: *Silicates are found widely in rocks of the earth and are used in building materials such as glass, bricks, and cement.*   *n.*

**si·li·ceous** *or* **si·li·cious** (sə lish′əs)   of, having to do with, containing, or resembling SILICA or a SILICATE.   *adj.*

**si·lic·ic** (sə lis′ik)   of, having to do with, or derived from SILICA or SILICON.   *adj.*

**sil·i·con** (sil′ə kən) a non-metallic element that occurs naturally only in compounds and is the most abundant element, next to oxygen, in the earth's crust: *Silicon combines with oxygen to form silica. Silicon is used for making electronic chips for computers.* Symbol: Si *n.*

**sil·i·cone** (sil′i kōn′) any of a large group of organic SILICON compounds that are water-resistant and are good insulators for heat, cold, or electricity: *Silicones are used to make lubricants, synthetic rubber, waterproof polishes, etc. n.*

**silicone rubber** a synthetic rubber made from certain SILICONES, having great tensile strength and elasticity over a wide range of temperatures.

**sil·i·co·sis** (sil′ə kō′sis) a disease of the lungs caused by continually breathing air filled with dust from quartz or silicates. *n.*

**silk** (silk) **1** a fine, soft, tough protein fibre produced by silkworms for their cocoons and used to make textiles. **2** any of various similar fibres produced by other insect larvae, usually for cocoons. **3** thread, yarn, or cloth made from the silk produced by silkworms. **4** silklike fibre, thread, or cloth made artificially. **5** a garment of silk or silklike cloth, such as the gown worn by a King's or Queen's Counsel. **6** anything like silk in softness, lustre, etc.: *corn silk.* **7** of, like, or having to do with silk: *silk thread, a silk finish.* **8** PARACHUTE. **9 silks,** the blouses and caps worn by jockeys and harness race drivers and the coverings sometimes draped over their horses which, by their colouring, identify the owner of these horses; colours. *n.* —**silk′like′,** *adj.*

**silk·en** (sil′kən) **1** made of silk: *a silken dress.* **2** like silk; smooth, soft, and glossy: *silken hair.* **3** of a voice, manner, etc., smoothly agreeable and polite, especially when suggesting insincerity: *He spoke in silken tones.* **4** clothed in silk: *silken legs. adj.*

**silk–screen** (silk′skrēn′) **1** a method of colour printing in which a screen of silk or similar material is prepared as a stencil and the colouring matter is forced through the mesh in all the areas of the design to be printed. **2** produce a print by means of silk-screen. 1 *n.,* 2 *v.*

**silk·worm** (silk′wėrm′) **1** the hairless, yellowish caterpillar of an Asiatic moth that produces the silk used for textiles: *The silkworm feeds mainly on mulberry leaves.* **2** any of various other moth caterpillars that spin cocoons of silk. *n.*

**silk·y** (sil′kē) **1** of or like silk; smooth, soft, glossy, etc.: *Some cats have silky fur.* **2** of a voice, manner, etc., smooth and extremely polite, especially so as to suggest insincerity or an ulterior motive: *a silky voice describing the features of a new luxury-model car. adj.,* **silk·i·er, silk·i·est.** —**silk′i·ness,** *n.*

**sill** (sil) **1** a horizontal piece of wood, block of stone, etc. that forms the bottom of a window or door frame. See JAMB and LINTEL for pictures. **2** in geology, a mass or sheet of IGNEOUS rock that has come between layers of other rock while molten and has solidified there. *n.*

**sil·li·ness** (sil′ē nis) **1** foolishness; being silly. **2** a silly act, thing, etc. *n.*

**sil·ly** (sil′ē) **1** having or showing a lack of sense or reason; foolish or ridiculous; nonsensical: *The movie was just too silly to be funny. Don't be silly; you can't possibly swim that far.* **2** *Informal.* stunned; dazed: *The blow knocked him silly. I was scared silly.* **3** a foolish person. 1, 2 *adj.,* **sil·li·er, sil·li·est;** 3 *n.*

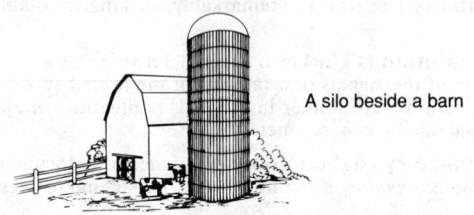
A silo beside a barn

**si·lo** (sī′lō) **1** an airtight building or pit in which green fodder for farm animals is stored. **2** a vertical underground shaft in which missiles, nuclear rockets, etc. are housed ready for launching. *n., pl.* **si·los.**

**silt** (silt) **1** very fine earth, sand, etc. carried by moving water and deposited as sediment: *The river mouth is being choked up with silt.* **2** make or become choked or filled with silt or mud. 1 *n.,* 2 *v.*

**silt·stone** (silt′stōn′) a kind of fine-grained sedimentary rock formed from SILT that has been subjected to great pressure. *n.*

**silt·y** (sil′tē) of, like, or full of SILT. *adj.,* **silt·i·er, silt·i·est.**

**Si·lu·ri·an** (sə lür′ē ən) **1** of, having to do with, or referring to a very early period in the formation of the earth's rocks: *The earliest vertebrates appeared near the end of the Silurian period.* **2** the SILURIAN PERIOD. 1 *adj.,* 2 *n.*

**Silurian period** the period, 435 million years ago, when the first small land plants appeared, and mountains formed in northwestern Europe. See geological time chart in the Appendix.

**sil·va** (sil′və) the forest trees of a particular region. *n.*

**sil·van** (sil′vən) See SYLVAN. *adj.*

**sil·ver** (sil′vər) **1** a white metallic element that is a precious metal. It takes a high polish, it can be moulded, stretched, hammered, or drawn thin without breaking, and it is the best conductor of heat and electricity: *Silver is used for jewellery, cutlery, dishes, coins, etc.* Symbol: Ag **2** coins, especially those made of silver or having a silvery colour: *Do you have any silver?* **3** cutlery, dishes, etc. made of or plated with silver; silverware: *I spent half an hour polishing the silver.* **4** made of, plated with, or containing silver: *a silver spoon, silver thread.* **5** of, having to do with, or resembling silver: *a silver sheen, silver shoes. The back of a mirror has a silver coating.* **6** cover or coat with silver or something like silver: *to silver a spoon, to silver a mirror.* **7** yielding silver: *a silver mine.* **8** soft, lustrous, light grey or white: *silver hair. She wore a gown of silver.* **9** give a sheen to, like that of silver: *Moonlight silvered the lake.* **10** make or become white or very light grey: *Her hair had silvered since he had last seen her.* **11** having a clear, melodious, ringing sound, like the sound of silver when struck. **12** eloquent: *a silver tongue.* 1–3, 8 *n.,* 4, 5, 7, 8, 11, 12 *adj.,* 6, 9, 10 *v.*

**sil·ver·fish** (sil′vər fish′) a small, wingless insect having silvery scales on its body and a bristly tail, often found in houses, where it does damage to paper and certain fabrics. *n.*

**silver fox** **1** a variety of North American red fox having white-tipped black fur. **2** the fur of a silver fox.

**silver leaf** silver beaten into very thin sheets.

**silver lining** the brighter side of a sad or unfortunate situation.

**silver maple** a species of maple found especially in southern central and eastern Canada, having deeply lobed leaves that are light green above and silvery underneath: *The silver maple is a popular shade and ornamental tree.*

**silver nitrate** a white crystalline salt obtained by treating silver with nitric acid, used in medicine as an antiseptic, in photography, dyeing, etc.

**silver paper** paper covered or coated on one side with a metallic layer resembling silver: *Silver paper is used as decoration in greeting cards, as a wrapping for chocolate bars, etc.*

**silver plate** 1 dishes, cutlery, etc. made of silver or of copper, etc. plated with silver. 2 a plating of silver.

**sil·ver-plate** (sil′vər plāt′) coat with silver, especially by electroplating. *v.*

**silver screen** 1 a screen with a silverlike coating on which motion pictures are shown. 2 motion pictures: *stars of the silver screen.*

**sil·ver·smith** (sil′vər smith′) an artisan or craftsperson who makes and repairs articles of silver. *n.*

**silver thaw** *Cdn.* 1 a storm of quick-freezing rain. 2 the thin, glittering coat of ice found after such a rain, encrusting trees, rocks, and other surfaces.

**sil·ver-tongued** (sil′vər tungd′) ELOQUENT. *adj.*

**sil·ver·ware** (sil′vər wer′) articles, especially cutlery or dishes, made of or plated with silver. *n.*

**silver wedding** the 25th anniversary of a wedding.

**sil·ver·y** (sil′və rē) 1 having a lustre or sheen like that of silver: *silvery moonbeams, a silvery gown.* 2 having a soft, clear resonance; melodious: *silvery laughter, a silvery voice.* *adj.* —**sil′ver·i·ness,** *n.*

**sim·i·an** (sim′ē ən) 1 of, having to do with, or like apes or monkeys. 2 an ape or monkey. 1 *adj.*, 2 *n.*

**sim·i·lar** (sim′ə lər) 1 having characteristics in common; much the same as; like or alike: *A creek and a brook are similar. Your desk is similar to mine.* 2 in geometry, of figures, having the same shape but not necessarily the same size: *similar triangles.* *adj.* —**sim′i·lar·ly,** *adv.*

**sim·i·lar·i·ty** (sim′ə lar′ə tē *or* sim′ə ler′ə tē) the state of being similar; a likeness; resemblance. *n., pl.* **sim·i·lar·i·ties.**

**sim·i·le** (sim′ə lē) an expressed comparison of two different things or ideas. *Examples: a face like marble, a girl as brave as a lioness.* Compare with METAPHOR. *n.* ☞ *Syn.* See note at METAPHOR.

**si·mil·i·tude** (sə mil′ə tyüd′ *or* sə mil′ə tüd′) a similarity or likeness: *similitude of structure.* *n.*

**sim·mer** (sim′ər) 1 keep or stay at or just below the boiling point: *The stew should be simmered for two hours.* 2 a degree of heat at or just below the boiling point: *Keep the sauce at a simmer.* 3 be on the point of bursting or breaking out; be in an inner turmoil: *She simmered with indignation, but said nothing.* 1, 3 *v.*, 2 *n.*
**simmer down,** calm down; cool down: *She told the excited child to simmer down.*

**si·mo·ni·a·cal** (sī′mə nī′ə kəl) 1 guilty of SIMONY. 2 of, having to do with, or involving SIMONY. *adj.*

**si·mon-pure** (sī′mən pyür′) *Informal.* real; genuine; authentic: *simon-pure maple sugar.* *adj.*

hat, āge, fär; let, ēqual, tėrm; it, īce
hot, ōpen, ôrder; oil, out; cup, put, rüle
əbove, taken, pencəl, lemən, circəs
ch, child; ng, long; sh, ship
th, thin; ŦH, then; zh, measure

**si·mo·ny** (sī′mə nē *or* sim′ə nē) the buying or selling of ecclesiastical positions, promotions, etc. *n.*

**si·moom** (sə müm′) a hot, suffocating, dust-laden wind of the deserts of the Arabian peninsula and northern Africa. *n.*

**si·moon** (sə mün′) SIMOOM. *n.*

**sim·per** (sim′pər) 1 smile in a silly, affected way. 2 express by a simper; say with a simper. 3 a silly, affected smile. 1, 2 *v.*, 3 *n.*

**sim·ple** (sim′pəl) 1 easy to do or understand: *a simple problem, simple language.* 2 not divided into parts; single; not compound: *An oak leaf is a simple leaf. "Jon called his dog" is a simple sentence.* 3 having few parts; not complex; not involved; elementary: *a simple one-celled animal.* 4 with nothing added; bare; mere: *My answer is the simple truth.* 5 without ornament; not rich or showy; plain: *simple clothes.* 6 natural; not affected; not showing off: *a simple manner.* 7 honest; sincere: *a simple heart.* 8 not subtle; not sophisticated; innocent; artless: *a simple child.* 9 common; ordinary: *a simple citizen.* 10 dull; stupid; weak in mind. 11 a foolish, stupid person. 12 something simple. 13 a plant used in medicine; medicine made from it. 1–10 *adj.*, **sim·pler, sim·plest;** 11–13 *n.* —**sim′ple·ness,** *n.*

Simple closed curves

**simple closed curve** in geometry, a closed plane curve that does not cross itself.

**simple fraction** a fraction in which both the numerator and the denominator are whole numbers. Examples: $\frac{1}{3}$, $\frac{3}{4}$, $\frac{219}{125}$. Compare with COMPLEX FRACTION.

**sim·ple-heart·ed** (sim′pəl här′tid) having or showing a simple, unaffected, sincere nature. *adj.*

**simple interest** interest paid only on the principal of a loan, etc., as opposed to COMPOUND INTEREST which is paid on the principal and other interest already added to it.

**simple machine** any of the elementary devices or mechanical powers on which other machines are based: *The lever, wedge, pulley, wheel and axle, inclined plane, and screw are often called the six simple machines.*

**sim·ple-mind·ed** (sim′pəl mīn′did) 1 natural and inexperienced; artless; unsophisticated: *a simple-minded approach to a complex problem.* 2 foolish or feeble-minded. *adj.*

**simple sentence** a sentence consisting of one main CLAUSE (def. 1). Examples: *The whistle blew. We got back yesterday.*

**sim·ple·ton** (sim′pəl tən) a silly person; fool. *n.*

**sim·plic·i·ty** (sim plis′ə tē) **1** the state or quality of being simple in form or structure; freedom from complexity: *the simplicity of a design. They appreciated the simplicity of the directions he had given them.* **2** absence of luxury, ornamentation, etc.; plainness: *simplicity of dress, the simplicity of a lifestyle.* **3** absence of show or pretence; sincerity or naturalness: *The old man answered all their questions with simplicity.* **4** lack of shrewdness; ignorance or dullness: *His simplicity made him easy to fool.* *n., pl.* **sim·plic·i·ties.**

**sim·pli·fi·ca·tion** (sim′plə fə kā′shən) **1** the act or process of SIMPLIFYing: *The simplification of the plan will take some time.* **2** something that has been simplified: *This is a simplification of an earlier model.* *n.*

**sim·pli·fy** (sim′plə fī′) make simple or simpler; make plainer, easier, or more streamlined: *to simplify a design. The plot of your story is a little confusing, and should be simplified.* *v.*, **sim·pli·fied, sim·pli·fy·ing.**
—**sim′pli·fi′er,** *n.*

**sim·plis·tic** (sim plis′tik) simplified to such an extent as to be misleading; given a false simplicity by ignoring some important aspects: *Her interpretation of the issue of international disarmament is biassed and simplistic.* *adj.*

**sim·plis·tic·al·ly** (sim plis′ti klē) in a SIMPLISTIC manner. *adv.*

**sim·ply** (sim′plē) **1** in a simple manner: *to dress simply. She explained the procedure simply and clearly.* **2** merely; only: *The baby did not simply cry; she yelled. He thinks of his car as simply a means of transportation.* **3** really; absolutely: *simply perfect.* *adv.*

**sim·u·la·cra** (sim′yə lā′krə) a pl. of SIMULACRUM. *n.*

**sim·u·la·crum** (sim′yə lā′krəm) **1** a faint, shadowy, or unreal likeness; mere semblance: *The dictator permitted only a simulacrum of democracy.* **2** an image. *n., pl.* **sim·u·la·cra** or **sim·u·la·crums.**

**sim·u·late** (sim′yə lāt′) **1** pretend; feign: *Anne simulated interest to please her friend.* **2** act like; look like; imitate: *Certain insects simulate leaves.* *v.*, **sim·u·lat·ed, sim·u·lat·ing.** —**sim′u·la′tor,** *n.*

**sim·u·lat·ed** (sim′yə lā′təd) **1** made to look genuine or real: *simulated pearls.* **2** pt. and pp. of SIMULATE. 1 *adj.*, 2 *v.*

**sim·u·la·tion** (sim′yə lā′shən) **1** a pretence; feigning: *a simulation of enjoyment.* **2** an imitation; an acting or looking like: *a harmless insect's simulation of a poisonous one.* *n.*

**sim·u·la·tive** (sim′yə lə tiv or sim′yə lā′tiv) simulating; pretending; imitating. *adj.*

**sim·ul·cast** (sim′əl kast′ or sī′məl kast′) **1** broadcast a program over radio and television at the same time or over more than one radio and television station at the same time: *CBC FM Radio and Television will simulcast the concert live from the civic auditorium.* **2** a broadcast made in this way. 1 *v.*, **sim·ul·cast** or **sim·ul·cast·ed, sim·ul·cast·ing;** 2 *n.*

**sim·ul·ta·ne·ous** (sim′əl tā′nē əs or sī′məl tā′nē əs) existing, done, or happening at the same time. *adj.*

**sim·ul·ta·ne·ous·ly** (sim′əl tā′nē ə slē or sī′məl tā′nē ə slē) at once; at the same time; together. *adv.*

**sin** (sin) **1** a breaking of the law of God deliberately. **2** break the law of God. **3** any act regarded as immoral or bad; wrongdoing: *It's a sin to waste food.* **4** do wrong. 1, 3 *n.*, 2, 4 *v.*, **sinned, sin·ning.**

**SIN** (sin) *Cdn.* Social Insurance Number.

**Sin·bad** (sin′bad) a sailor in the *Arabian Nights*, who had seven extraordinary voyages. *n.*

**since** (sins) **1** from a past time continuously till now: *The package has been ready since noon.* **2** in the course of the period following the time when: *He has written home only once since he left us.* **3** continuously or counting from the time when: *Charles has worked hard since he left school.* **4** at any time between some past time or event and the present: *We have not seen her since Saturday.* **5** from then till now: *She got sick last Saturday and has been in bed ever since.* **6** at some time between a particular past time and the present: *At first he refused but has since accepted.* **7** before now; ago: *I heard that old joke long since.* **8** because: *Since you feel tired, you should rest.* 1, 4 *prep.*, 2, 3, 8 *conj.*, 5–7 *adv.*

**sin·cere** (sin sēr′) free from pretence or deceit; genuine in feeling; honest and straightforward: *a sincere expression of sympathy, a sincere person.* *adj.*, **sin·cer·er, sin·cer·est.** —**sin·cere′ly,** *adv.*

**sin·cer·i·ty** (sin ser′ə tē) freedom from pretence or deceit; honesty. *n., pl.* **sin·cer·i·ties.**

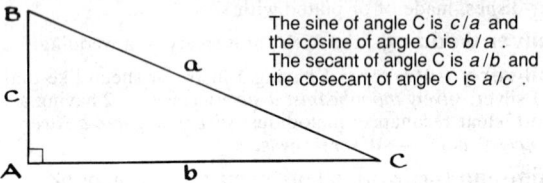

Triangle ABC is a right triangle of which A is the right angle and *a* is the hypotenuse.

The sine of angle C is *c/a* and the cosine of angle C is *b/a*. The secant of angle C is *a/b* and the cosecant of angle C is *a/c*.

**sine** (sīn) in a right triangle, the ratio of the length of the side opposite an acute angle to the length of the hypotenuse. *n.*
☛ *Hom.* SIGN.

**si·ne·cure** (sī′nə kyūr′ or sin′ə kyūr′) **1** an extremely easy job; a position requiring little or no work and usually paying well. **2** formerly, a position in the church that carried a salary but no parish duties. *n.*

**si·ne·cur·ist** (sī′nə kyū′rist or sin′ə kyū′rist) a person who has a SINECURE. *n.*

**sin·e di·e** (sin′ē dē′ā or sī′nē dī′ē) *Latin.* without a day fixed for future action (*literally*, 'without day'): *The committee adjourned* sine die.

**sin·e qua non** (sin′ē kwä′nōn′ or sī′nē kwä′non′) something essential; an indispensable condition or thing: *It was a* sine qua non *that all parties concerned should be included in the negotiations.*
☛ *Etym.* From late L *sine qua non* 'without which not'.

**sin·ew** (sin′yü) **1** a tough, strong band or cord that joins muscle to bone; tendon. **2** strength; energy: *moral sinew.* **3** strengthen by furnishing with sinews. **4** Usually, **sinews,** *pl.* a means of strength or power; mainstay: *Guns are the sinews of war.* 1, 2, 4 *n.*, 3 *v.*

**sin·ew·y** (sin′yü ē) **1** having strong sinews; strong; powerful: *The blacksmith had broad shoulders and sinewy arms.* **2** vigorous; forcible: *sinewy arguments, sinewy prose.* **3** of meat, having many or large sinews; tough; stringy. *adj.* —**sin′ew·i·ness.** *n.*

**sin·ful** (sin′fəl) characterized by sin or having a tendency to sin. *adj.* —**sin′ful·ly,** *adv.* —**sin′ful·ness,** *n.*

**sing** (sing) **1** make music with the voice: *She sings on television.* **2** utter musically: *He almost seemed to sing his lines from the play.* **3** chant; intone: *The priest sings Mass.* **4** make pleasant musical sounds: *Birds sing.* **5** cause something to happen with or by singing: *Sing the baby to sleep.* **6** tell in song or poetry: *Homer sang of Troy.* **7** tell of in song or poetry: *He sang the deeds of heroes.* **8** proclaim: *to sing a person's praises.* **9** make a ringing, whistling, humming, or buzzing sound: *The teakettle sang.* **10** have a sensation of a ringing, buzzing, or humming sound: *A bad cold made her ears sing.* **11** a singing, ringing, or whistling sound: *the sing of a bullet in flight.* **12** a singing, especially in a group. **13** admit of being sung: *This arrangement of the song sings more easily than that one.* 1–10, 13 *v.*, **sang, sung, sing·ing;** 11, 12 *n.* **sing out,** call loudly; shout.

**sing.** singular.

**singe** (sinj) **1** burn a little; scorch: *He got too close to the fire and singed his eyebrows.* **2** a slight burn. **3** expose the carcass of a chicken, etc. to flame for a very short while to burn off down, fuzz, etc. **4** burn the ends of hair after a haircut. 1, 3, 4 *v.*, **singed, singe·ing;** 2 *n.* **singe one's wings,** be slightly harmed, especially by some risky venture.

**sing·er** (sing′ər) **1** a person who sings, especially one who sings well or whose profession is singing: *He's an opera singer.* **2** a bird having a varied and musical call: *Our canary is a fine singer.* *n.*

**Sin·gha·lese** (sing′gə lēz′) SINHALESE. *n., adj.*

**sin·gle** (sing′gəl) **1** one and no more; only one: *Please give me a single piece of paper.* **2** for only one; individual: *The sisters share one room with two single beds in it.* **3** without others; alone: *He came to the party single.* **4** not married: *a single woman.* **5** having only one on each side: *The knights engaged in single combat.* **6** having only one set of petals: *Most cultivated roses have double flowers with many petals; wild roses have single flowers with five petals.* **7** not double; not multiple: *single houses.* **8** sincere; honest; genuine: *She showed single devotion to her religion.* **9** pick from among others: *The teacher singled Lois out for praise.* **10** a single thing or person. **11** in baseball, a hit that allows the batter to reach first base only. **12** make such a hit. **13** in cricket, a hit for which one run is scored. **14** a game for two people only. **15** in Canadian football, a single point scored by kicking into or beyond the end zone; a rouge. **16 singles,** *pl.* a game played with only one person on each side. 1–8 *adj.*, 10, 11, 13–16 *n.*, 9, 12 *v.*, **sin·gled, sin·gling.**

**single bed** a bed wide enough for one person: *The hotel room had two single beds.*

**sin·gle–breast·ed** (sing′gəl bres′tid) of a coat, jacket, etc., overlapping across the breast just enough to fasten with only one button or row of buttons. *adj.*

**single file** **1** a line of persons or things arranged one behind another. **2** in a line, one behind the other: *We walked single file along the narrow path.*

**sin·gle–foot** (sing′gəl fut′) **1** the gait of a horse in which one foot is put down at a time; rack. **2** go at a single-foot. 1 *n.*, 2 *v.*

**sin·gle–hand·ed** (sing′gəl han′did) **1** without help from others; working alone: *It was his single-handed effort that saved the ship.* **2** without help: *She built all the cupboards single-handed.* **3** using or requiring only one hand: *a single-handed sword.* 1, 3 *adj.*, 2 *adv.* —**sin′gle–hand′ed·ly,** *adv.*

**sin·gle–heart·ed** (sing′gəl här′tid) having or showing sincerity and devotion to one purpose or aim. *adj.* —**sin′gle–heart′ed·ly,** *adv.*

**sin·gle–mind·ed** (sing′gəl mīn′did) **1** having only one purpose in mind. **2** sincere; straightforward. *adj.* —**sin′gle–mind′ed·ly,** *adv.* —**sin′gle–mind′ed·ness,** *n.*

**sin·gle·ness** (sing′gəl nis) the state or quality of being single: *singleness of purpose. After years of singleness she decided to get married.* *n.*

**sin·gle–space** (sing′gəl spās′) type with no blank lines between lines of print: *Quotations set off within an essay should always be single-spaced.* *v.*

**sin·gle·stick** (sing′gəl stik′) **1** a stick held in one hand, used in FENCING (def. 1). **2** the act of FENCING (def. 1) with such a stick. *n.*

**sin·gle·ton** (sing′gəl tən) **1** something occurring singly or apart from others: especially, a child or animal born alone, without a twin. **2** a playing card that is the only one of a suit in a person's hand. *n.*

**sin·gle–track** (sing′gəl trak′) of a railway, etc., having only a single track. *adj.*

**sin·gle·tree** (sing′gəl trē′) the swinging bar of a carriage or wagon, to which the traces are fastened. *n.*

**sin·gly** (sing′glē) **1** as a single person or thing; separately: *Misfortunes never come singly.* **2** one by one; one at a time in sequence: *Let us consider each point singly.* **3** by one's own efforts; without help; single-handed. *adv.*

**sing·song** (sing′sông′) **1** a monotonous, up-and-down rhythm. **2** a monotonous tone or sound in speaking. **3** monotonous in rhythm: *a singsong recitation of the multiplication table.* **4** a monotonous or jingling verse. **5** a gathering for community singing. 1, 2, 4, 5 *n.*, 3 *adj.*

**sin·gu·lar** (sing′gyə lər) **1** extraordinary; unusual: *Lake Louise is a sight of singular beauty.* **2** strange; queer; peculiar: *The detectives were greatly puzzled by the singular nature of the crime.* **3** being the only one of its kind: *an event singular in history.* **4** in grammar, meaning or referring to one only: *Girl is singular; girls is plural.* **5** the form of a word used to show that only one is meant or referred to: *the singular of oxen is ox.* **6** a word in the singular. 1–4 *adj.*, 5, 6 *n.* —**sin′gu·lar·ly,** *adv.*

**sin·gu·lar·i·ty** (sing′gyə lar′ə tē or sing′gyə ler′ə tē) **1** a peculiarity; oddness; strangeness; unusualness: *The singularity of the stranger's appearance attracted much attention.* **2** something singular; peculiarity; oddity: *One of the giraffe's singularities is the length of its neck.* *n., pl.* **sin·gu·lar·i·ties.**

**Sin·ha·la** (sin′hə lä or sin′ə lä) the official language of Sri Lanka: *Sinhala is the language of the Sinhalese.* *n.*

**Sin·ha·lese** (sin′hə lēz′ *for noun,* sin′hə lēz′ *for adjective*) **1** a member of a people who make up the majority of the population of Sri Lanka. **2** the language

**sinister** 1108 **sire**

of these people; Sinhala. **3** of or having to do with these people or their language. **1, 2** *n.*, *pl.* **Sin·ha·lese; 3** *adj.*

**sin·is·ter** (sin′i stər) **1** showing or suggesting ill will or evil; wicked or malignant: *a sinister look, a sinister plan, a sinister motive.* **2** giving a warning of bad fortune or trouble; ominous: *a sinister sky, sinister rumblings of rebellion.* **3** extremely unfortunate; disastrous: *He met a sinister fate.* **4** of or on the left. **5** in heraldry, of or on the left-hand side of a shield, etc. from the point of view of the person bearing it; on the right of a person viewing it. *adj.*
☛ **Etym.** Through F *sinistre* from L *sinister* 'on or to the left'. In foretelling the future, the left side was considered by the Romans to be unlucky or ill-fated. Compare with note at DEXTERITY.

**sin·is·tral** (sin′i strəl) of or having to do with the left side; left; left-handed. *adj.*

**sink** (singk) **1** go down; fall slowly; go lower and lower: *The sun is sinking. She sank to the floor in a faint.* **2** make go down; make fall: *Lack of rain sank the water level of the lake.* **3** go under: *The ship is sinking.* **4** make go under: *The submarine sank two ships.* **5** become lower or weaker: *The wind has sunk down.* **6** make lower; reduce: *She sank her voice to a whisper.* **7** pass gradually into a state of sleep, silence, oblivion, etc. **8** go or cause to go deeply: *Let the lesson sink into your mind.* **9** make by digging or drilling: *to sink a well.* **10** set into a hole dug or drilled: *to sink a pipe.* **11** insert or fasten into a hollow space, etc.: *a stone sunk into the wall.* **12** become worse: *His spirits sank.* **13** invest money unprofitably: *We sank twenty dollars in a useless machine.* **14** keep quiet about; conceal: *to sink evidence.* **15** fall in; become hollow: *The sick man's cheeks have sunk.* **16** in basketball, score. **17** in golf, hit the ball into a hole; score thus with a stroke. **18** a shallow basin or tube with a drainpipe: *a kitchen sink.* **19** a drain; sewer. **20** a place where dirty water or any filth collects. **21** a place of vice or corruption. **22** a low-lying area in land where waters collect, or where they disappear by sinking downward or by evaporation. **1–17** *v.*, **sank** or **sunk, sunk, sink·ing; 18–22** *n.* —**sink′a·ble,** *adj.*
☛ **Hom.** SYNC.

**sink·er** (sing′kər) a person or thing that sinks, especially a lead weight for sinking a line or net for fishing. *n.*

**sink·hole** (singk′hōl′) **1** the hole in a sink, etc. for waste to pass through. **2** a hollow or cavity in limestone, etc. through which surface water drains into an underground passage or cavern. **3** a hollow place where water collects. **4** a place of vice and corruption. *n.*

**sinking fund** a fund set up by a government, corporation, etc. to offset a borrowing. Certain sums of money are regularly set aside to accumulate at interest so that when the debt, such as a debenture, matures, there will be enough money to pay it off.

**sin·less** (sin′lis) without sin; free from sin. *adj.* —**sin′less·ly,** *adv.* —**sin′less·ness,** *n.*

**sin·ner** (sin′ər) one who sins or does wrong. *n.*

**Sino-** (sī′nō) combining form. Chinese and ____: *Sino-Japanese* means Chinese and Japanese.

**Si·nol·o·gy** or **si·nol·o·gy** (sī nol′ə jē) the study of Chinese literature, art, culture, etc. *n.*

**sin·u·ate** (sin′yü āt′) especially in botany, having a wavy edge; having a margin with distinct inward and outward bends, as some leaves. See LEAF for picture. *adj.*

**sin·u·os·i·ty** (sin′yü os′ə tē) **1** a SINUOUS form or character; the quality or state of being sinuous. **2** something that is sinuous; a curve or bend. *n.*, *pl.* **sin·u·os·i·ties.**

**sin·u·ous** (sin′yü əs) **1** having many curves or turns; winding: *The motion of a snake is sinuous.* **2** indirect; devious. **3** morally devious. *adj.* —**sin′u·ous·ly,** *adv.*

**si·nus** (sī′nəs) **1** in anatomy: **a** a cavity or hollow in the body, especially one of the cavities in the bones of the skull that connect with the nose. **b** a large channel for venous blood. **2** in medicine, a long, narrow channel leading from an abscess and serving for the discharge of pus. **3** in botany, a curve or indentation between the lobes of a leaf. **4** any curved hollow or cavity. *n.*

**si·nus·i·tis** (sī′nə sī′tis) the inflammation of a SINUS (def. 1) of the skull. *n.*

**Siou·an** (sü′ən) **1** a stock or family of languages spoken by First Nations and Native American peoples of central and eastern North America. **2** a member of any of the peoples speaking one of these languages, including the Assiniboines and the Dakota. **3** of, having to do with, or referring to these peoples or their languages. **1, 2** *n.*, **3** *adj.*

**Sioux** (sü) **1** DAKOTA. **2** the Siouan language of this tribe. *n.*, *pl.* **Sioux** (sü *or* süz).
☛ **Hom.** SAULT, SUE.

**sip** (sip) **1** drink little by little: *She sipped her tea.* **2** a very small drink: *She took a sip.* **1** *v.*, **sipped, sip·ping; 2** *n.*

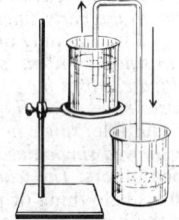

A siphon. The arrows show the direction of flow of the liquid.

**si·phon** (sī′fən) **1** a bent tube through which liquid can be drawn over the edge of one container into another at a lower level by air pressure. **2** draw off by means of a siphon or pass through a siphon: *She siphoned water from the rain barrel onto the garden.* **3** a bottle for soda water, having a tube through which the liquid is forced out by the pressure of the gas in the bottle. **4** a tube-shaped organ of some shellfish for drawing in and expelling water, etc. **1, 3, 4** *n.*, **2** *v.* Also, **syphon.**

**sir** (sėr; *unstressed,* sər) **1** a respectful or formal term of address used to a man (*used only alone, never with a name*): *Excuse me, sir.* **2 Sir,** the title used before the given name or full name of a knight or baronet: *Sir Wilfrid Laurier.* *n.*

**sire** (sīr) **1** the male parent of an animal, especially a domestic animal: *The sire of Danger, a great racehorse, was Lightning.* **2** be the father of; beget (*used especially for male domestic animals*): *Lightning sired Danger.* **3** a respectful form of address for a king or a great noble: *"I'm killed, Sire!" said the messenger to King Richard.* **1, 3** *n.*, **2** *v.*, **sired, sir·ing.**

**si·ren** (sī′rən)  1 a device that produces a loud, penetrating sound used as a warning of the approach of an ambulance, police vehicle, etc. or as a warning of an air raid.  2 in Greek mythology, one of a group of human or partly human female creatures who by their sweet, enchanting singing lured sailors to destruction upon the rocks where the sirens lived.  3 a dangerously seductive woman; temptress.  4 of a siren or like that of a siren; enchanting.  *n.*  —**sir′en·like′**, *adj.*

**Sir·i·us** (sir′ē əs)  the brightest fixed star in the sky; the Dog Star.  *n.*

**sir·loin** (sėr′loin)  a choice cut of beef or veal from the part of the loin in front of the rump.  See BEEF and VEAL for pictures.  *n.*

**si·roc·co** (sə rok′ō)  1 a hot, dry, dust-laden wind blowing from northern Africa across the Mediterranean and southern Europe.  2 a moist, warm, south or southeast wind in these same regions.  3 any hot, unpleasant wind.  *n., pl.* **si·roc·cos.**

**sir·up** (sėr′əp *or* sir′əp)  See SYRUP.  *n.*

**sir·up·y** (sėr′ə pē *or* sir′ə pē)  See SYRUPY.  *adj.*

**sis** (sis)  Informal.  sister.  *n.*

**sis·al** (sis′əl *or* sī′səl)  1 a strong white fibre used for making rope, twine, etc.  2 a West Indian plant of the amaryllis family from whose leaves this fibre is prepared.  *n.*

**sis·sy** (sis′ē)  Informal.  1 an effeminate boy or man.  2 a cowardly or very timid person: *Don't be such a sissy; there's nothing to be afraid of.*  3 sister.  *n., pl.* **sis·sies.**

**sis·ter** (sis′tər)  1 a woman or girl having the same parents as another person; a woman or girl thought of in her relationship to other children of her parents.  2 HALF SISTER.  3 SISTER-IN-LAW.  4 STEPSISTER.  5 a quality or thing thought of as female that resembles or is closely connected with another.  6 a woman closely associated with another, such as a fellow member of a club, church, etc.  7 a member of a religious order of women; nun: *Sisters of Charity.*  8 related as if by sisterhood: *sister ships.*  *n.*  —**sis′ter·less,** *adj.*

**sis·ter·hood** (sis′tər hùd′)  1 the state of being a sister.  2 a spiritual bond, like that between sisters; a sisterly relationship: *A feeling of sisterhood had developed between them over the years.*  3 an association or society of women with some common aim, characteristic, set of beliefs, etc.: *Nuns form a sisterhood.*  *n.*

**sis·ter-in-law** (sis′tə rin lo′)  1 the sister of one's husband or wife.  2 the wife of one's brother.  3 the wife of one's brother-in-law.  *n., pl.* **sis·ters-in-law.**

**sis·ter·ly** (sis′tər lē)  of, having to do with, or like a sister: *sisterly advice.*  *adj.*  —**sis′ter·li·ness,** *n.*

**sit** (sit)  1 rest on the lower part of the body, with the weight off the feet: *She sat in a chair.*  2 seat; cause to sit: *The woman sat the little boy down hard.*  3 bear oneself on; sit on: *He sat his horse well.*  4 be in a certain place or position: *The clock has sat on that shelf for years.*  5 have a seat in an assembly, etc.; be a member of a council: *to sit in Parliament.*  6 hold a session: *The court sits next month.*  7 place oneself as required for some purpose or activity; set oneself; pose: *to sit for a portrait.*  8 be in a state of rest; remain inactive.  9 press or weigh: *Care sat heavy on his brow.*  10 perch: *The birds were sitting on the fence rail.*  11 baby-sit.  12 cover eggs so that they will hatch; brood: *The hen will sit until the eggs are ready to hatch.*  13 fit: *Her coat sits well.*  *v.,* **sat, sit·ting.**

**sit down,**  take a seat; put oneself in a sitting position.
**sit in, a** take part in a game, conference, etc.  **b** take part in a SIT-IN.
**sit on** *or* **upon, a** sit in judgment or council on.  **b** have a seat on a jury, commission, etc.  **c** think about; consider over a period of time: *The committee sat on the request for several weeks.*  **d** *Informal.*  check, rebuke, or snub.
**sit out, a** remain seated during a dance.  **b** stay through; wait through: *to sit out a storm. They sat out the performance although the singing was poor.*  **c** stay later than another.
**sit up, a** raise the body to a sitting position.  **b** keep such a position.  **c** stay up instead of going to bed.  **d** *Informal.*  start up in surprise.
☛ *Usage.* See note at SET.

**si·tar** (si tär′)  a lutelike instrument having a very long neck and a varying number of strings: *The sitar was developed in India.*  *n.*

**sit·com** (sit′kom′)  *Informal.*  SITUATION COMEDY.  *n.*

**sit–down strike**  a strike in which employees stop working but stay in their place of employment until an agreement is reached.

**site** (sīt)  1 the ground on which a structure or group of structures is, was, or will be located: *the site of the new civic centre.*  2 the location or scene of something: *a company site. They visited the site of the Battle of Queenston Heights.*  3 choose a position for; locate; place: *They sited the new building on a hill.*  1, 2 *n.,* 3 *v.,* **sit·ed, sit·ing.**
☛ *Hom.*  CITE, SIGHT.

**sit-in** (sit′in′)  a form of protest in which a group of people occupy a public place and remain seated there for a long time: *The college students staged a sit-in to protest the increase in fees.*  *n.*

**sit·ka spruce** (sit′kə)  1 a very tall spruce tree found along the Pacific coast of North America, having stiff, very sharp yellowish-green needles and long, cylinder-shaped cones: *The sitka spruce is the largest of the spruces, usually between 38 and 50 metres high.*  2 the light, soft wood of this tree.

**si·tol·o·gy** (sī tol′ə jē)  the science of food or diet; dietetics.  *n.*

**sit·ter** (sit′ər)  1 a baby-sitter.  2 any person or thing that sits, especially a brooding hen.  *n.*

**sit·ting** (sit′ing)  1 the act of one that sits.  2 a single time of remaining seated; one uninterrupted occasion of sitting: *The portrait took five sittings. She read eight chapters at one sitting.*  3 a meeting or session of a legislature, court, etc.  4 the number of eggs on which a bird sits.  5 one of two or more consecutive fixed hours for serving a particular meal, when all cannot be served at once, as on a train, ship, etc.: *the second sitting for dinner.*  6 ppr. of SIT.  1–5 *n.,* 6 *v.*

**sitting duck**  an easy target or mark.

**sitting room**  a room furnished with comfortable chairs, chesterfields, etc.; parlour.

**sit·u·ate** (sich′ü āt′)  put in a certain place; locate:

They decided to situate the new city hall nearer the centre of town. *v.*, **sit·u·at·ed, sit·u·at·ing.**

**sit·u·at·ed** (sich′ü ā′tid) **1** having a location or site: *Montreal is well situated.* **2** having a certain financial or social position: *The doctor was quite well situated.* **3** pt. and pp. of SITUATE. 1, 2 *adj.*, 3 *v.*

**sit·u·a·tion** (sich′ü ā′shən) **1** circumstances; case; condition: *Act reasonably in all situations.* **2** site; location; place: *Our house has a beautiful situation on a hill.* **3** a place to work; job: *She is trying to find a situation.* **4** a critical state of affairs in a play, novel, etc. *n.*

**situation comedy** a radio or television comedy series consisting of unconnected, usually weekly episodes featuring the same cast of characters in each episode.

**sit-up** (sit′up′) a conditioning exercise that consists of raising the body from a lying to a sitting position without using the hands for support. *n.*

**Si·va** (sē′və *or* shē′və) one of the three great gods of classical Hinduism, a remote, austere god who remains in a state of constant meditation, worshipped as the highest god by many Hindus. *n.* Also, **Shiva.**

**six** (siks) **1** one more than five; 6: *He got seven points and I got six. They asked for six copies.* **2** the numeral 6: *Is that supposed to be a 6 or a 9?* **3** the sixth in a set or series; especially, a playing card or side of a die having six spots: *If you throw a six, you get another turn.* **4** being sixth in a set or series (*used mainly after the noun*): *I'm bogged down in Chapter Six.* **5** one of the sections into which a pack of Wolf Cubs or Brownies is divided: *Mario is in the Red six.* **6** any set or series of six persons or things: *He arranged the ten chips as a six and a four.* 1–3, 5, 6 *n.*, 1, 4 *adj.*
**at sixes and sevens,** in confusion or disagreement.
☞ *Etym.* From OE *siex*, related to German *sechs* and having the same Indo-European source as L *sex* and Gk. *hex*.

**six·er** (sik′sər) the leader of a six of Wolf Cubs or Brownies. *n.*

**six·fold** (sik′fōld′) **1** six times as much or as many. **2** having six parts. 1, 2 *adj.*, 1 *adv.*

**six-gun** (siks′gun′) SIX-SHOOTER. *n.*

**Six Nations** a federation of Iroquois tribes, called the FIVE NATIONS until the Tuscarora tribe joined in about 1722.

**six·pen·ny** (sik′spen′ē) referring to a kind of nail about 5 cm long, once costing six pennies per 100.

**six-shoot·er** (siks′shü′tər) a revolver that can fire six shots without being reloaded. *n.*

**six·teen** (sik′stēn′) **1** six more than ten; 16: *I got sixteen out of twenty. We had sixteen people for dinner yesterday.* **2** the numeral 16: *Is that a 91 or a 16?* **3** the sixteenth in a set or series. **4** being sixteenth in a set or series (*used after the noun*): *Section Sixteen.* **5** a set or series of sixteen persons or things. 1–3, 5 *n.*, 1, 4 *adj.*

**six·teenth** (sik′stēnth′) **1** next after the 15th; last in a series of 16; 16th. **2** one, or being one, of 16 equal parts. *adj.*, *n.*

**sixteenth note** in music, a note having one sixteenth of the time value of a whole note. See NOTE for picture.

**sixteenth rest** in music, a rest as long as a SIXTEENTH NOTE. See REST¹ for picture.

**sixth** (siksth) **1** next after the fifth; last in a series of six; 6th. **2** one, or being one, of six equal parts. *adj.*, *n.*

**sixth·ly** (siks′thlē) in the sixth place. *adv.*

**sixth sense** an unusual power of perception, beyond the common five senses; intuition.

**six·ti·eth** (sik′stē ith) **1** next after the 59th; last in a series of 60; 60th. **2** one, or being one, of 60 equal parts. *adj.*, *n.*

**six·ty** (sik′stē) **1** six times ten; 60. **2 sixties,** *pl.* the years from sixty through sixty-nine, especially of a century or of a person's life: *Rock music became popular in the sixties.* 1, 2 *n.*, *pl.* **six·ties;** 1 *adj.*

**six·ty·fold** (sik′stē fōld′) sixty times as much or as many. *adj.*, *adv.*

**sixty-fourth note** in music, a note having the time value of one sixty-fourth of a whole note. See NOTE for picture.

**siz·a·ble** (sī′zə bəl) fairly large: *He had a sizable income, but always seemed to be in debt.* *adj.*, Also, **sizeable.**

**siz·a·bly** (sī′zə blē) to a SIZABLE extent or degree. *adv.* Also, **sizeably.**

**size**¹ (sīz) **1** the amount of surface or space a thing takes up: *The two boys are of the same size. The library contains books of all sizes, big and little. We need a house of larger size.* **2** an extent; amount; magnitude: *the size of an industry.* **3** one of a series of measures: *His shoes are size 10. The size of card I want is 7 by 12 centimetres.* **4** *Informal.* the actual condition; true description: *That's the size of things.* **5** arrange according to size or in sizes: *Will you size these nails?* **6** make of certain size.
**7** SIZED (used only in compounds): *He cut the meat into bite-size pieces.* 1–4, 7 *n.*, 5, 6 *v.*, **sized, siz·ing.**
**of a size,** of the same size.
**size up,** *Informal.* **a** form an opinion of; estimate. **b** come up to some size or grade.

**size**² (sīz) **1** a sticky preparation made from materials like glue, starch, or resin and used as a glaze or filler for cloth, paper, plaster, leather, etc. **2** coat or treat with size. 1 *n.*, 2 *v.*, **sized, siz·ing.**

**size·a·ble** (sī′zə bəl) See SIZABLE. *adj.*

**size·a·bly** (sī′zə blē) See SIZABLY. *adv.*

**sized** (sīzd) **1** having a size of a particular kind (*used only in compounds*): *giant-sized.* **2** pt. and pp. of SIZE. 1 *adj.*, 2 *v.*

**siz·ing** (sī′zing) **1** SIZE². **2** ppr. of SIZE. 1 *n.*, 2 *v.*

**siz·zle** (siz′əl) **1** make a hissing sound, as fat does when it is frying or burning. **2** a hissing sound. **3** be very hot: *sizzle with anger.* 1, 3 *v.*, **siz·zled, siz·zling;** 2 *n.*

**SJAA** *or* **S.J.A.A.** St. John Ambulance Association.

**SJAB** *or* **S.J.A.B.** St. John Ambulance Brigade.

**SK** Saskatchewan.

**skald** (skold) in ancient times, a Scandinavian poet and singer. *n.*
☞ *Hom.* SCALD.

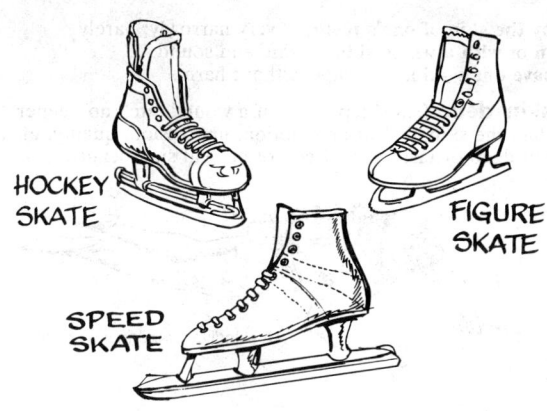

HOCKEY SKATE   FIGURE SKATE   SPEED SKATE

hat, āge, fär; let, ēqual, tėrm; it, īce
hot, ōpen, ôrder; oil, out; cup, pùt, rüle
ə above, takən, pencəl, lemən, circəs
ch, child; ng, long; sh, ship
th, thin; ᴛʜ, then; zh, measure

**skate**¹ (skāt)   1 a boot with a metal blade, or runner, attached to the sole, designed for gliding over ice.   2 the runner itself, together with its frame, especially when forming a separate part that is attached to a shoe or boot by means of clamps, straps, etc.   3 ROLLER SKATE.   4 glide or move along on skates.   1–3 *n.*, 4 *v.*, **skat·ed, skat·ing. —skat′er,** *n.*
☛ *Etym.*  Through Dutch *schaats* from OF *escache* 'stilt'. 17c.

**skate**² (skāt)   a kind of broad, flat fish.   *n., pl.* **skate** or **skates.**
☛ *Etym.*  From ON *skata*. 14c.

**skate·board** or **skate board** (skāt′bôrd′)   a small, narrow board of wood or plastic, usually about 45–50 cm long, shaped somewhat like a surfboard, but equipped with a pair of roller-skate wheels at each end and used for coasting along streets, sidewalks, etc.   *n.*

**skating rink**   1 a smooth sheet of ice for skating.   2 a smooth floor for roller skating.

**ske·dad·dle** (ski dad′əl) *Informal.*   run away; scatter in flight.   *v.*, **ske·dad·dled, ske·dad·dling.**

**skeet** (skēt)   in trapshooting, a type of target practice using clay plates that are released into the air so as to imitate the flight of birds.   *n.*

**skein** (skān)   1 a loosely coiled bundle of yarn or thread.   2 a confused tangle.   3 a flock of geese in flight.   *n.*

**skel·e·tal** (skel′ə təl)   of, having to do with, attached to, or forming a SKELETON.   *adj.*

**skel·e·ton** (skel′ə tən)   1 the framework of bones and cartilage of a vertebrate animal that supports the soft tissues and protects the internal organs.   2 a very thin person or animal: *He was just a skeleton after his long illness.*   3 the basic framework or structure of something: *The steel skeleton of an office tower, the skeleton of a story.*   4 of, like, or having the characteristics of a skeleton; basic or essential: *A skeleton crew remained on board while the ship was at the dock.*   *n.*
**skeleton in the closet,**   something shameful that is kept secret, as in a family.

**skeleton key**   a key made to open many locks.

**skep·tic** (skep′tik)   See SCEPTIC.   *n., adj.*

**skep·ti·cal** (skep′tə kəl)   See SCEPTICAL.   *adj.*
**—skep′ti·cal·ly,** *adv.*

**skep·ti·cism** (skep′tə siz′əm)   See SCEPTICISM.   *n.*

**sketch** (skech)   1 a rough, quickly done drawing, painting, or design.   2 make a sketch or sketches: *We spent the afternoon sketching.*   3 an outline; plan.   4 a short, light description, story, play, etc.: *Sunshine Sketches of a Little Town is a collection of short stories by Stephen Leacock.*   5 make a sketch of; draw or describe roughly.   1, 3, 4 *n.*, 2, 5 *v.* **—sketch′er,** *n.*

**sketch·book** (skech′bùk′)   a book of or for rough, quick drawings: *She takes her sketchbook along wherever she goes.*   *n.*

**sketch·y** (skech′ē)   1 like a sketch; having or giving only outlines or main features.   2 incomplete; slight; imperfect: *a sketchy meal.*   *adj.*, **sketch·i·er, sketch·i·est. —sketch′i·ly,** *adv.* **—sketch′i·ness,** *n.*

**skew** (skyü)   1 twisted to one side; slanting.   2 slant; twist.   3 having a part that deviates from a straight line, right angle, etc.   4 give a slanting form, position, or direction to.   5 turn aside; swerve.   6 represent unfairly; distort.   7 unsymmetrical.   1, 3, 7 *adj.*, 2 *n.*, 2, 4–6 *v.*

**skew·er** (skyü′ər)   1 a long pin of wood or metal stuck through meat to hold it together while it is cooking.   2 something shaped or used like a long pin.   3 fasten with a skewer or skewers.   4 pierce with or as if with a skewer: *Sarah skewered a hole in her hat.*   1, 2 *n.*, 3, 4 *v.*

**ski** (skē)   1 one of a pair of long pieces of wood, metal, or plastic, that can be fastened to boots to enable a person to glide over snow.   2 glide over the snow on skis.   3 a ski-like device fastened to the undercarriage of an aircraft and used in place of wheels for landing on snow, mud, sand, etc.   4 WATER SKI.   1, 3, 4 *n., pl.* **skis** or **ski;** 2 *v.*, **skied, ski·ing. —ski′er,** *n.*

**skid** (skid)   1 slip or slide sideways out of control, while moving: *The car skidded on the slippery road.*   2 a slip or slide sideways out of control: *His car went into a skid.*   3 a piece of wood or metal used to prevent a wheel from turning.   4 prevent from going round by means of a skid.   5 slide along without going round, as a wheel does when held by a skid.   6 a piece of timber or a runner on which something heavy may slide: *A stoneboat runs on skids.*   7 a frame on which heavy articles may be piled for moving to another position, often by lifting with a crane.   8 a runner on the bottom of an airplane to enable the airplane to skid along the ground when landing.   9 slide on a skid or skids.   1, 4, 5, 9 *v.*, **skid·ded, skid·ding;** 2, 3, 6–8 *n.*

**ski·doo** (ski dü′ or skē′dü) *Cdn.*   SNOWMOBILE (defs. 1 and 2).   *n., v.*
☛ *Etym.*  From *Ski-Doo,* a trademark.

**skid road**   1 *Cdn.*   in logging, a road of greased skids, over which logs were dragged by teams of mules, oxen, or horses.   2 SKID ROW.

**skid row**   a run-down district of cheap hotels and bars, used as a hangout by vagrants, petty criminals, etc.

**skies** (skīz)   *pl.* of SKY.   *n.*

**skiff** (skif)   1 a small, light rowboat with a rounded bottom and flat stern.   2 a small, light boat with a centreboard and a single sail.   *n.*

**ski jump**   1 a jump made by a person on skis.   2 a place for making such a jump.

**skil·ful** or **skill·ful** (skil′fəl) 1 having skill; expert: *a skilful surgeon.* 2 showing skill: *That operation was a skilful piece of work.* *adj.* —**skil′ful·ness** or **skill′ful·ness,** *n.*

**skil·ful·ly** or **skill·ful·ly** (skil′fə lē) with skill; expertly. *adv.*

**ski lift** a mechanism for transporting skiers to the top of a slope, usually by means of a chair running on a suspended cable.

**skill** (skil) 1 ability gained by practice or knowledge; expertness: *It takes skill to tune a piano.* 2 an ability or technique that can be learned: *One must master the basic language skills.* 3 an art or craft that is learned through training or experience: *the skill of carpentry.* *n.*

**skilled** (skild) 1 having skill; trained; experienced: *A carpenter is a skilled worker.* 2 showing skill; requiring skill: *Plastering is skilled labour.* *adj.*

**skil·let** (skil′it) a shallow pan with a long handle, used for frying; a frying pan: *He made the pancakes in a skillet.* *n.*

**skill·ful** (skil′fəl) See SKILFUL. *adj.*

**skill·ful·ly** (skil′fə lē) See SKILFULLY. *adv.*

**skim** (skim) 1 remove from the top: *The cook skims the cream from the milk.* 2 take something from the top of: *She skims the milk to get cream.* 3 that which is skimmed off. 4 move lightly over: *The pebble I threw skimmed the little waves. The skaters skimmed the ice.* 5 glide along: *The swallows were skimming by.* 6 send skimming: *You can skim a flat stone over the water.* 7 read rapidly or superficially; read with omissions, especially in order to get the general sense or purpose: *It took me an hour to skim the book.* 8 become covered with a thin layer of ice, scum, etc.: *The lake was skimmed with waste oil.* 9 cover with a thin layer of ice, scum, etc.: *Winter skimmed the stream with ice.* 10 the act of skimming. 1, 2, 4–9 *v.,* **skimmed, skim·ming;** 3, 10 *n.*

**skim·mer** (skim′ər) 1 a person or thing that skims; especially a long-handled, shallow ladle with small holes, used in skimming liquids. 2 a kind of sea bird that skims along the surface of water to get food. *n.*

**skim milk** milk from which the cream has been removed.

**skimp** (skimp) 1 supply in too small an amount: *Don't skimp the butter in making a cake.* 2 be very saving or economical: *She had to skimp to send her son to university.* 3 do imperfectly. *v.*

**skimp·y** (skim′pē) 1 scanty; not enough: *a skimpy meal.* 2 too saving or economical. *adj.,* **skimp·i·er, skimp·i·est.**

**skin** (skin) 1 the outer layer of tissue of the body in persons and animals, especially when soft and flexible: *Cows have thick skins.* 2 a hide; pelt: *The skin of a calf makes soft leather.* 3 any outer or surface layer, as the rind of a fruit, a sausage casing, etc. 4 take the skin off: *Jack skinned his knees when he fell. The hunter skinned the deer.* 5 shed skin. 6 be covered with skin. 7 cover with skin. 8 a container made of skin for holding liquids. 9 any outer covering: *the skin of a rocket.* 10 a planking or iron plating that covers the ribs of a ship. 1–3, 8–10 *n.,* 4–7 *v.,* **skinned, skin·ning.**

**by the skin of one's teeth,** very narrowly; barely.
**in** or **with a whole skin,** safe and sound.
**save one's skin,** escape without harm.

**skin–deep** (skin′dēp′) 1 of a wound, etc., no deeper than the skin. 2 of an emotion, impression, quality, etc., not deep or lasting in effect; of no real significance. *adj.*

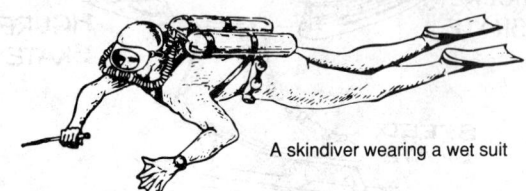

A skindiver wearing a wet suit

**skin·div·er** (skin′dī′vər) a person engaged in SKIN DIVING. *n.*

**skin diving** swimming under water, using a face mask and flippers, usually with a snorkel or scuba gear, and, in cold water, a rubber or rubberized suit to protect the body against the cold.

**skin·flint** (skin′flint′) a mean, stingy person. *n.*

**skin·ful** (skin′fùl) 1 as much as a skin container can hold. 2 *Informal.* as much as the stomach can hold; especially, as much wine, liquor, etc. as a person can take. *n., pl.* **skin·fuls.**

**skin graft** a piece of skin taken from another part of the body or another person to replace skin that has been burned or otherwise damaged or destroyed.

**skin grafting** the action or process of making a SKIN GRAFT; the surgical transplanting of skin.

**skin·less** (skin′lis) without a skin or casing: *skinless wieners.* *adj.*

**skin·ner** (skin′ər) 1 a person who prepares or deals in skins or furs. 2 a person who drives draft animals, especially mules. *n.*

**skin·ny** (skin′ē) 1 having too little flesh; too thin or lean: *She was always skinny as a child, but usually healthy.* 2 like skin. *adj.,* **skin·ni·er, skin·ni·est.** —**skin′ni·ness,** *n.*

**skin–tight** (skin′tīt′) of clothes, fitting closely to the skin. *adj.*

**skip¹** (skip) 1 leap lightly; spring; jump: *Lambs skipped in the fields.* 2 leap lightly over: *to skip rope.* 3 move along by stepping and hopping first with one foot, then with the other. 4 a moving in this way. 5 send bounding along a surface: *Children like to skip stones on the lake.* 6 go bounding along a surface. 7 pass over; fail to notice; omit: *She skips the hard words. Answer the questions in order without skipping.* 8 change quickly from one task, pleasure, subject, etc. to another. 9 a light spring, jump, or leap: *The child gave a skip of joy.* 10 a passing over; omission. 11 *Informal.* leave in a hurry: *He skipped town to avoid meeting his enemies.* 12 *Informal.* stay away from: *to skip classes.* 1–3, 5–8, 11, 12 *v.,* **skipped, skip·ping;** 4, 9, 10 *n.*

**skip²** (skip) the captain of a curling team or a lawn bowling team. *n.*

**ski pole** either of a pair of light poles used in skiing, having a leather strap and hand grip at one end and a pointed metal tip at the other with a disk slightly above the tip to keep the pole from sinking into the snow.

**skip·per**[1] (skip'ər)  **1** the captain of a ship, especially of a small trading or fishing boat.  **2** any captain or leader.  *n.*

**skip·per**[2] (skip'ər)  any of a large group of small insects belonging to the same order as butterflies and moths, having a heavy body and threadlike antennae with a hook at the end.  *n.*

**skipping rope**  a length of rope, often having a handle at each end, used to SKIP (def. 2) with.

**skirl** (skėrl)  **1** of bagpipes, sound loudly and shrilly.  **2** the sound of a bagpipe.  *1 v., 2 n.*

**skir·mish** (skėr'mish)  **1** a minor fight in war between small groups of soldiers, ships, aircraft, etc.  **2** a minor conflict, argument, contest, etc.  **3** take part in a skirmish.  *1, 2 n., 3 v.*

**skir·mish·er** (skėr'mi shər)  a person who engages in a SKIRMISH, especially one of a group of soldiers sent out in advance of an army to clear the way for the main attack or to prevent a surprise attack by the enemy, etc.  *n.*

**skirt** (skėrt)  **1** a women's and girls' garment for the lower body that hangs freely from the waist and may be wide or narrow, long or short: *She wore a skirt and blouse.*  **2** the free-hanging part of a dress, jumper, cassock, etc. that extends from the waist down.  **3** a cloth facing or hanging that resembles a skirt: *a dressing table with a skirt.*  **4** a border or edge.  **5** extend along or form a border or edge: *The road skirts the lake.*  **6** pass along the border or edge: *The boys skirted the forest because they did not want to go through it.*  **7** the rim or outer edge of an area.  **8** one of the flaps hanging from the sides of a saddle.  *1-4, 7, 8 n., 5, 6 v.*
☛ *Etym.*  See note at SHIRT.

**skirt·ing** (skėr'ting)  **1** cloth for making skirts.  **2** ppr. of SKIRT.  *1 n., 2 v.*

**skit** (skit)  a short dramatic sketch that contains humour or satire.  *n.*

**ski tow**  a motorized conveyor for towing skiers to the top of a slope on their skis, usually consisting of an endless moving rope or cable which the skiers hang onto.

**skit·ter** (skit'ər)  **1** move lightly or quickly; skim or skip along a surface.  **2** in fishing, draw a lure over the surface of the water with a skipping motion.  *v.*

**skit·tish** (skit'ish)  **1** apt to start, jump, or run; easily frightened: *a skittish horse.*  **2** fickle; changeable.  **3** coy.  *adj.*  —**skit'tish·ly**, *adv.*  —**skit'tish·ness**, *n.*

**skit·tle** (skit'əl)  **1** one of the pins used in the game of skittles.  **2 skittles**, *pl.*  a game in which the players try to knock down nine wooden pins by rolling or throwing wooden disks or balls at them.  *n.*
**beer and skittles**,  pure amusement; fun and games: *Life isn't all beer and skittles.*

**skoo·kum** (skü'kəm)  *Cdn.*  on the West Coast and in the Northwest, sturdy, husky, big, or brave: *a skookum bacon-and-egg breakfast.*  *adj.*
☛ *Etym.*  From Chinook Jargon.

**sku·a** (skyü'ə)  any of several large, brown sea birds that are related to the gulls; a jaeger.  *n.*

**skul·dug·ger·y** (skul dug'ə rē)  *Informal.*  trickery; dishonesty.  *n.*

**skulk** (skulk)  **1** move in a stealthy, furtive manner; slink: *The burglar skulked around the house, looking for an easy way in.*  **2** sneak away or keep out of sight to avoid danger, work, etc.: *He skulked at home to avoid facing the bully.*  **3** a person who skulks.  *1, 2 v., 3 n.*  —**skulk'er**, *n.*  —**skulk'ing·ly**, *adv.*

**skull** (skul)  **1** the bones of the head; the part of the skeleton of a vertebrate animal that encloses and protects the brain and organs of sight, hearing, and smell.  **2** the head, thought of as the seat of intelligence: *It's impossible to get anything into his thick skull.*  *n.*
☛ *Hom.* SCULL.

**skull and crossbones**  a picture of a human skull above two crossed bones, often used on pirates' flags as a symbol of death, and now often used on labels of poisonous drugs, etc.

**skull·cap** (skul'kap')  a close-fitting cap without a brim.  *n.*

A striped skunk—about 40 cm long excluding the tail

**skunk** (skungk)  **1** a black, bushy-tailed mammal, usually with white stripes along its back: *A skunk is about the size of a cat and gives off a very strong, unpleasant smell when frightened or attacked.*  **2** the fur of this animal, used on coats, etc.  **3** *Informal.*  a mean, contemptible person.  *n.*

**skunk cabbage**  a low, ill-smelling, broad-leaved plant, growing commonly in moist ground.

**sky** (skī)  **1** the space high above the earth, appearing as a great arch or dome covering the world; the region of the clouds or the upper air; the heavens: *a blue sky, a cloudy sky. A vapour trail stretched across the sky.*  **2** heaven.  **3** climate or weather.  **4** hit, throw, or raise high into the air.  *1-3 n., pl.* **skies**;  *4 v.,* **skied** *or* **skyed, sky·ing**.
**out of a clear (blue) sky**,  suddenly; unexpectedly.
**to the skies**,  very highly; extravagantly: *The review praised him to the skies.*
☛ *Hom.* SKYE.

**sky blue**  a clear, soft blue.

**sky·cap** (skī'kap')  a person whose work is carrying luggage at an airport.  *n.*

**sky·div·er** (skī'dī'vər)  a person who engages in SKY-DIVING.  *n.*

**sky·div·ing** (skī'dī'ving)  the sport of jumping from an airplane at a moderate height and making certain manoeuvres while falling free before opening one's parachute.  *n.*

**Skye terrier** or **Skye** (skī)  a breed of small terrier originally developed in Scotland, having short legs, a long body, and long, shaggy hair.  *n.*
☛ *Hom.* SKY.

**sky·ey** (skī'ē)  of or like the sky.  *adj.*

**sky–high** (skī'hī')  **1** to a great height; high up in the air: *to throw something sky-high.*  **2** to a high degree or level: *Prices have gone sky-high in the last month.* **3** to bits; completely apart: *The warehouse was blown sky-high.* **4** excessive: *sky-high prices.* 1–3 *adv.*, 4 *adj.*

**sky·jack** (skī′jak′) HIJACK (def. 3).

**sky·lark** (skī′lärk′) **1** an Old World lark having inconspicuous, brown-streaked plumage and famous for the beautiful song of the male, produced while the bird is soaring at great heights: *The skylark was introduced into southern British Columbia and has become established there.* **2** play pranks; frolic. 1 *n.*, 2 *v.*

**sky·light** (skī′līt′) a window in a roof. *n.*

**sky·line** (skī′līn′) **1** the line at which earth and sky seem to meet; horizon. **2** the outline of buildings, mountains, trees, etc. as seen against the sky, from a distance: *I took a picture of the Toronto skyline from Centre Island.* *n.*

**sky·rock·et** (skī′rok′it) **1** a firework that can be shot high into the air, where it bursts in a shower of sparks and stars; rocket. **2** rise or increase suddenly and quickly, like a skyrocket: *Prices were skyrocketing. The actor had skyrocketed to fame with his first movie.* 1 *n.*, 2 *v.*

**sky·sail** (skī′sāl′ *or* skī′səl) in a square-rigged ship, a light sail set at the top of the mast above the royal. *n.*

**sky·scrap·er** (skī′skrā′pər) a very tall building: *New York is famous for its skyscrapers.* *n.*

**sky·ward** (skī′wərd) toward the sky: *The rocket shot skyward (adv.). A quick skyward glance told him the storm was approaching fast (adj.).* *adv., adj.*

**sky·wards** (skī′wərdz) SKYWARD. *adv.*

**sky·way** (skī′wā′) **1** a route used by aircraft; air lane. **2** a stretch of elevated highway such as a bridge or overpass. **3** a covered walkway between upper storeys of two buildings or towers. *n.*

**sky·writ·ing** (skī′rī′ting) **1** the tracing of words, etc. against the sky from an airplane by means of smoke or some similar substance. **2** the letters, words, etc. so traced. *n.*

**slab** (slab) a broad, flat, thick piece of stone, wood, meat, etc.: *The hungry boy ate a slab of cheese as big as his hand.* *n.*

**slack**¹ (slak) **1** loose; not tight or firm: *The rope is too slack to hold anything.* **2** the part that hangs loose: *She pulled in the slack of the rope.* **3** careless: *He is a slack housekeeper.* **4** slow: *The horse was moving at a slack pace.* **5** not active; not brisk; dull: *Business is slack at this season.* **6** a dull season; quiet period. **7** make slack; let up on. **8** be or become slack; let up. **9** SLAKE (def. 4) lime. **10** in a slack manner. **11** a stopping of a strong flow of the tide or a current of water. **12 slacks,** *pl.* trousers for informal wear. **13** make slack; let up on. 1, 3–5 *adj.*, 2, 6, 11, 12 *n.*, 10 *adv.*, 7–9, 13 *v.*
**slack off,** **a** loosen. **b** lessen one's efforts.
**slack up,** slow down; go more slowly.

**slack**² (slak) dirt, coal dust, and small pieces of coal left after coal has been screened. *n.*

**slack·en** (slak′ən) **1** make or become slower; slow down: *Don't slacken now; we're almost finished. The work slackened as the temperature climbed.* **2** become less active, vigorous, brisk, etc.: *His business slackens in the winter.* **3** make or become looser: *Slacken the rope. The rope slackened as the boat neared the pier.* *v.*

**slack·er** (slak′ər) *Informal.* a person who shirks work or evades his or her duty. *n.*

**slag** (slag) **1** the rough, hard waste left after metal is separated from ore by smelting. **2** form slag; change into slag. **3** a light, spongy lava. 1, 3 *n.*, 2 *v.*, **slagged, slag·ging.**

**slain** (slān) pp. of SLAY: *The sheep were slain by the wolves.* *v.*

**slake** (slāk) **1** satisfy thirst, revenge, wrath, etc.: *We slaked our thirst at the spring.* **2** cause to be less active, intense, etc. **3** put out a fire. **4** change lime from calcium oxide to calcium hydroxide (**slaked lime**) by leaving it in the moist air or putting water on it: *Plaster contains slaked lime and sand.* **5** be changed thus. **6** *Rare.* become less active, vigorous, intense, etc. *v.*, **slaked, slak·ing.**

**slaked lime** lime combined with water; calcium hydroxide.

**sla·lom** (slä′ləm *or* slal′əm) **1** in skiing, a zigzag race downhill on a course set between a series of poles. **2** ski on such a course. 1 *n.*, 2 *v.*

**slam**¹ (slam) **1** shut with force and noise; close with a bang: *He slammed the window down. The door slammed.* **2** throw, push, hit, or move hard with force: *Joe slammed himself down on his bed. The car slammed into a truck.* **3** a violent and noisy closing, striking, etc.; bang: *John threw his books down with a slam.* **4** *Informal.* criticize harshly. **5** *Informal.* a harsh criticism. 1, 2, 4 *v.*, **slammed, slam·ming;** 3, 5 *n.*

**slam**² (slam) the winning of 12 (**little** or **small slam**) or all 13 (**grand slam**) tricks in the game of bridge. *n.*

**slan·der** (slan′dər) **1** in law, a false statement meant to do harm to the reputation of another: *Slander is spoken; libel is written or printed.* **2** talk falsely about. **3** the crime of speaking a slander. **4** speak or spread slander. **5** the spreading of false reports. 1, 3, 5 *n.*, 2, 4 *v.*
—**slan′der·er,** *n.*

**slan·der·ous** (slan′də rəs) using or containing SLANDER: *a slanderous remark.* *adj.*
—**slan′der·ous·ly,** *adv.*

**slang** (slang) **1** vocabulary and usage that differ from the standard, consisting mainly of new, usually colourful, humorous, or vigorous words or phrases, or such meanings for existing words or phrases: *Slang is often adopted by a particular group of people to set themselves apart from others; it often passes quickly out of use because it depends on novelty for much of its effect.* **2** jargon; shoptalk: *In the slang of the Canadian fur trade, stealing furs from a warehouse was called* indoor trapping. *n.*
☛ *Usage.* Slang is not usually considered acceptable in formal speech or writing, and should be avoided even in informal situations when one is communicating with people outside one's own group. See also notes at STANDARD and INFORMAL.

**slang·y** (slang′ē) using or containing much SLANG: *The writing is too slangy for an essay.* *adj.*, **slang·i·er, slang·i·est.**

**slant** (slant) **1** slope: *Most handwriting slants to the right.* **2** a slanting or oblique direction or position; a slope: *The greenhouse roof has a sharp slant.* **3** sloping: *a slant roof.* **4** a peculiar or personal attitude or viewpoint: *Her reminiscences provide us with an interesting slant on the political scene of the sixties.* **5** interpret or present from a particular angle to appeal to a particular group or interest: *a magazine slanted toward the teenage audience.* **6** distort on purpose to give a certain impression; falsify: *The* newspaper slanted the story by leaving out some of the facts. 1, 5, 6 *v.*, 2–4 *n.*

**slant·ing** (slan′ting)   **1** sloping.   **2** ppr. of SLANT. 1 *adj.*, 2 *v.*   —**slant′ing·ly**, *adv.*

**slant·ways** (slan′twāz′)   SLANTWISE (def. 1).   *adv.*

**slant·wise** (slan′twīz′)   **1** in a slanting manner; obliquely.   **2** slanting; oblique.   1 *adv.*, 2 *adj.*

**slap** (slap)   **1** a blow with the open hand or with something flat.   **2** strike with the open hand or with something flat: *He slapped at the fly with a newspaper.*   **3** put, dash, or cast with force: *She slapped the book down.*   **4** sharp words of blame; a direct insult or rebuff.   **5** *Informal.* straight; directly: *The thief ran slap into a police officer.*   **6** *Informal.* suddenly.   1, 4 *n.*, 2, 3 *v.*, **slapped, slap·ping;**   5, 6 *adv.*

**slap·dash** (slap′dash′) *Informal.*   **1** hastily and carelessly: *He always went at his work slapdash.*   **2** hasty and careless: *Slapdash people do slapdash work.*   **3** hasty, careless action, methods, or work.   1 *adv.*, 2 *adj.*, 3 *n.*

**slap·shot** (slap′shot′) *Cdn.*   in hockey, a fast, not always accurate shot on goal made with a powerful swinging stroke.   *n.*

**slap·stick** (slap′stik′)   **1** two long, narrow sticks fastened so as to slap together loudly when a clown, actor, etc. hits somebody with them.   **2** comedy full of broad humour and rough play.   **3** full of rough play: *In slapstick comedy, the actors knock each other around to make people laugh.*   1, 2 *n.*, 3 *adj.*

**slash** (slash)   **1** cut with a sweeping stroke of a sword, knife, etc.; gash: *He slashed his hand accidentally.*   **2** make a slashing stroke.   **3** a sweeping, slashing stroke: *the slash of a sword, the slash of the rain.*   **4** a cut or wound made by such a stroke; a gash.   **5** cut or slit to let a different cloth or colour show through.   **6** whip severely; lash.   **7** criticize sharply, severely, or unkindly.   **8** cut down severely; reduce a great deal: *Her salary was slashed when business became bad.*   **9** a sharp cutting down; great reduction: *a slash in prices.*   **10** cut out parts of a book, etc.; change greatly a book, etc.   **11** an open space in a forest, usually littered with chips, broken branches, etc.   **12** a litter of chips, broken branches, etc.   1, 2, 5–8, 10 *v.*, 3, 4, 9, 11, 12 *n.*   —**slash′er**, *n.*

**slat** (slat)   a long, thin, narrow piece of wood, metal, etc.: *The slats of the venetian blind need cleaning.*   *n.*

**slate** (slāt)   **1** a fine-grained, bluish-grey rock formed from the compression of layers of shale or clay that splits easily into thin, smooth layers: *Slate is used to cover roofs.*   **2** a thin piece of slate or material like slate, especially one used for writing on, or as a roofing tile: *Children used to do their schoolwork on slates they carried with them.*   **3** cover with slate.   **4** dark bluish-grey.   **5** a list of candidates, officers, etc. to be considered for appointment, nomination, etc.   **6** list as a candidate: *She is slated for the office of club president.*   1, 2, 4, 5 *n.*, 3, 6 *v.*, **slat·ed, slat·ing;**   4 *adj.* **a clean slate,** a record not marked by mistakes, dishonour, etc.: *She is entering public office with a clean slate.*

**slath·er** (slaᴛH′ər) *Informal.*   **1** spread thickly or lavishly.   **2 slathers,** *pl.* a great quantity: *slathers of bacon and eggs.*   1 *v.*, 2 *n.*

**slat·tern** (slat′ərn)   a woman who is dirty, careless, or untidy in her dress, her ways, her housekeeping, etc.   *n.*

**slat·tern·ly** (slat′ərn lē)   slovenly; untidy: *a slatternly woman, slatternly housekeeping.*   *adj.*

**slanting   1115   Slavey**

hat, āge, fär; let, ēqual, tėrm; it, īce hot, ōpen, ôrder; oil, out; cup, pút, rüle ə*b*ove, tak*e*n, penc*i*l, lem*o*n, circ*u*s ch, child; ng, long; sh, ship th, thin; ᴛH, then; zh, measure

**slat·y** (slā′tē)   **1** of or containing SLATE.   **2** SLATE-coloured.   *adj.*, **slat·i·er, slat·i·est.**

**slaugh·ter** (slot′ər)   **1** the killing of an animal or animals for food; butchering: *the slaughter of a steer, to fatten hogs for slaughter.*   **2** butcher: *Millions of beef cattle are slaughtered every year.*   **3** brutal killing; much or needless killing: *The battle resulted in a frightful slaughter.*   **4** kill brutally; massacre.   1, 3 *n.*, 2, 4 *v.*   —**slaugh′ter·er**, *n.*

**slaugh·ter·house** (slot′ər hous′)   a place where animals are killed for food; abattoir.   *n.*

**slaugh·ter·ous** (slot′ə rəs)   murderous; destructive.   *adj.*

**Slav** (slav *or* släv)   **1** a member of any of a group of eastern European peoples who speak Slavic languages: *Russians, Poles, Czechs, Serbs, Bulgarians, etc. are Slavs.*   **2** SLAVIC.   1 *n.*, 2 *adj.*

**slave** (slāv)   **1** a person who is the property of another: *Slaves were bought and sold like horses.*   **2** a person who is controlled or ruled by some desire, habit, or influence: *A drunkard is a slave of drink.*   **3** a person who works like a slave.   **4** work like a slave: *Some parents slave for their children.*   **5** of slaves; done by slaves: *slave labour.*   **6** an ant that is captured and forced to work for other ants.   1–3, 6 *n.*, 4 *v.*, **slaved, slav·ing;**   5 *adj.*   —**slave′like′**, *adj.*

**Slave** (slāv)   **1** a member of a First Nations people in the Northwest Territories between the Rockies and Great Slave Lake.   **2** the Athapascan language of these people.   **3** of or having to do with the Slaves or their language.   1, 2 *n.*, *pl.* **Slaves** or **Slave;**   3 *adj.*

**slave driver**   **1** a person who supervises slaves at work.   **2** an employer, supervisor, etc. who is excessively harsh or demanding.

**slave·hold·er** (slāv′hōl′dər)   an owner of slaves.   *n.*

**slave·hold·ing** (slāv′hōl′ding)   **1** owning slaves.   **2** the owning of slaves.   1 *adj.*, 2 *n.*

**slav·er**[1] (slā′vər)   **1** a dealer in slaves.   **2** a ship used in the slave trade.   *n.*

**slav·er**[2] (slav′ər)   **1** let saliva run from the mouth; drool.   **2** saliva running from the mouth.   1 *v.*, 2 *n.*

**slav·er·y** (slā′və rē)   **1** the condition of being a slave: *Many Africans were captured by Europeans and sold into slavery in America.*   **2** the custom of owning slaves: *They fought against slavery. Slavery was abolished in Upper Canada in 1793.*   **3** a condition like that of a slave: *slavery to the dictates of fashion.*   **4** hard work like that of a slave: *He said the job was pure slavery.*   *n.*

**slave trade**   traffic in slaves; the buying and selling of slaves for profit.

**slav·ey** (slā′vē) *Informal.*   a maid of all work.   *n.*, *pl.* **slav·eys.**

**Slav·ey** (slā′vē)   SLAVE.   *n.*, *adj.*

**Slav·ic** (slav′ik) **1** of or having to do with the SLAVS or their languages. **2** the group of languages spoken by the SLAVS. *1 adj., 2 n.*

**slav·ish** (slā′vish) **1** of or having to do with a slave or slaves. **2** like or characteristic of a slave; weakly submissive and servile: *a slavish personality, a slavish follower.* **3** lacking originality and independence: *a slavish translation of the original, slavish reliance on a pattern.* *adj.* —**slav′ish·ly,** *adv.* —**slav′ish·ness,** *n.*

**slaw** (slo) coleslaw, a salad of shredded raw cabbage. *n.*

**slay** (slā) kill with violence, especially in battle: *Many soldiers were slain on that hill.* *v.,* **slew, slain, slay·ing.** —**slay′er,** *n.*
☞ *Hom.* SLEIGH.

**slea·zy** (slē′zē) **1** flimsy and poor: *sleazy cloth.* **2** *Informal.* shoddy, squalid, or mean: *a sleazy, run-down hotel.* *adj.* **slea·zi·er, slea·zi·est.** —**slea′zi·ness,** *n.*

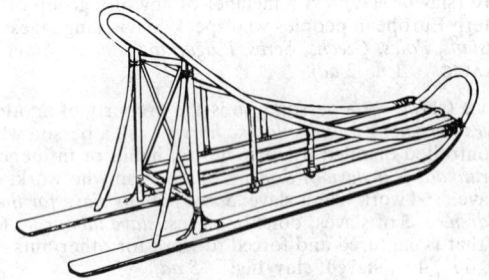

A sled designed to be pulled by a team of dogs

**sled** (sled) **1** a small, low vehicle having runners instead of wheels, used especially for carrying loads over ice and snow: *Before the snowmobile, the common means of winter transportation in the North was a sled pulled by a team of dogs.* **2** SLEIGH (def. 2). **3** ride or carry on a sled. *1, 2 n., 3 v.* **sled·ded, sled·ding.**

**sled·ding** (sled′ing) **1** riding or coasting on a sled. **2** the condition of the snow or ice as a surface for a sled: *The new snow made for good sledding.* **3** an advance toward a goal; progress: *Boris found it tough sledding at first because everything was strange to him.* **4** ppr. of SLED. *1–3 n., 4 v.*
**hard sledding,** unfavourable conditions.

**sled dog** a dog trained and used to draw a sled, especially in the Arctic.

**sledge¹** (slej) **1** a low, heavy vehicle mounted on runners, used for carrying loads and drawn over snow or ice or dragged over the ground by draft animals. **2** ride or carry on a sledge. *1 n., 2 v.,* **sledged, sledg·ing.**

**sledge²** (slej) SLEDGEHAMMER (def. 1). *n.*

**sledge·ham·mer** (slej′ham′ər) **1** a large, heavy hammer, usually swung with both hands. **2** powerful or crushing: *sledgehammer sarcasm.* **3** hit with, or as if with, a sledgehammer. *1, 2 n., 3 v.*

**sleek** (slēk) **1** smooth and glossy; looking highly polished: *sleek hair.* **2** having a well-groomed, well-fed appearance: *a sleek cat. He was looking very sleek and healthy after his holiday.* **3** too smooth in speech, manners, etc.; slick. **4** make glossy: *He sleeked his hair.* **5** trim and elegant: *a sleek ship.* *1–3, 5 adj., 4 v.* —**sleek′ly,** *adv.* —**sleek′ness,** *n.*

**sleep** (slēp) **1** rest the body and mind; be without ordinary consciousness: *She was very tired and slept for ten hours.* **2** a condition in which body and mind are very inactive, occurring naturally and regularly in animals: *I need more sleep than my sister does.* **3** be in a condition like sleep: *The seeds sleep in the ground all winter.* **4** a state or condition like sleep. **5** spend time in sleeping: *She slept the night in peace.* **6** provide space for sleeping: *This room sleeps two.* **7** mucus that is sometimes secreted by the eyes during sleep, and that collects and hardens especially in the inner corners of the eyes. *1, 3, 5, 6 v.,* **slept, sleep·ing;** *2, 4, 7 n.*
**last sleep,** death.
**put to sleep,** put an animal to death humanely, especially a pet: *We had to put our dog to sleep because she was old and sick.*
**sleep away,** pass or spend in sleeping: *Sarah slept away the whole morning.*
**sleep in, a** remain in bed later than usual: *We always sleep in on a Sunday morning.* **b** sleep late or oversleep: *He was late because he slept in.* **c** live at one's own place of work: *The maid slept in.*
**sleep like a log,** sleep soundly or heavily.
**sleep off,** get rid of by sleeping: *She was sleeping off a headache.*
**sleep on,** put off deciding on: *He said he would sleep on the idea.*

**sleep·er** (slē′pər) **1** a person or animal that sleeps: *They made their way silently past the sleepers. He's a sound sleeper.* **2** a railway SLEEPING CAR. **3** a horizontal beam, especially one on or near the ground, that supports a structure. **4** someone or something that is unexpectedly successful, especially a book, play, or motion picture that is an unexpected hit or winner: *Her first play was the sleeper of the season.* **5** a ring worn instead of an ordinary earring in a pierced ear: *She wore sleepers for three weeks after getting her ears pierced.* **6 sleepers,** *pl.* one-piece pyjamas for children, extending from the neck and covering the feet. *n.*

**sleeping bag** a zippered bag for sleeping in, usually waterproof and warmly lined, used especially when camping.

**sleeping car** a railway car with berths or small rooms for passengers to sleep in.

**sleeping partner** a partner who takes no active part in managing a business.

**sleeping pill** a pill or capsule containing a drug that causes sleep.

**sleeping sickness** a disease causing fever, inflammation of the brain, sleepiness, and usually death.

**sleep·less** (slē′plis) **1** not able to sleep: *He lay there sleepless for several hours.* **2** not providing or producing sleep: *sleepless nights.* **3** continually active or watchful: *a sleepless sentry, a sleepless memory.* *adj.* —**sleep′less·ly,** *adv.* —**sleep′less·ness,** *n.*

**sleep·walk** (slē′pwok′) walk about while asleep: *She used to sleepwalk when she was a child.* *v.*

**sleep·walk·er** (slē′pwok′ər) a person who walks about while asleep. *n.*

**sleep·walk·ing** (slē′pwok′ing) **1** the act or practice of walking while asleep. **2** ppr. of SLEEPWALK. *1 n., 2 v.*

**sleep·y** (slē'pē) **1** ready to go to sleep; inclined to sleep: *He never gets enough rest and is always sleepy.* **2** not active; quiet: *a sleepy day, a sleepy town.* *adj.*, **sleep·i·er, sleep·i·est.** —**sleep'i·ly**, *adv.* —**sleep'i·ness**, *n.*

**sleep·y·head** (slē'pē hed') a person who is sleepy or not paying attention: *Wake up, sleepyhead!* *n.*

**sleet** (slēt) **1** partly frozen rain; snow or hail mixed with rain. **2** come down in sleet: *It sleeted; then it snowed; then it rained.* **1** *n.*, **2** *v.*

**sleet·y** (slē'tē) of, like, or characterized by SLEET. *adj.*, **sleet·i·er, sleet·i·est.** —**sleet'i·ness**, *n.*

**sleeve** (slēv) **1** the tubelike part of a garment that extends from the shoulder and covers the arm or part of the arm. **2** a tube or tubelike machine part enclosing a rod or another tube. **3** a paper or plastic cover for a phonograph record. *n.*
**have up one's sleeve,** have in reserve, concealed but ready for use when needed: *She had one more trick up her sleeve.*

**sleeved** (slēvd) having sleeves of a particular kind (*used especially in compounds*): *a long-sleeved shirt.* *adj.*

**sleeve·less** (slēv'lis) without sleeves: *a sleeveless dress.* *adj.*

A sleigh (def. 2)

**sleigh** (slā) **1** a light carriage mounted on runners, used for carrying persons over snow or ice, and usually drawn by a horse or horses: *A cutter is a kind of sleigh.* See CUTTER for picture. **2** a small, low vehicle consisting of a platform of boards on narrow metal runners, used as a plaything for going over snow or ice and coasting down snow-covered hills. **3** travel or ride in a sleigh. **1, 2** *n.*, **3** *v.*
☞ Hom. SLAY.

**sleight** (slīt) **1** skill; dexterity. **2** a clever trick. *n.*
☞ Hom. SLIGHT.

**sleight of hand** **1** skill and quickness in moving the hands, as in juggling or conjuring tricks. **2** a display of skill and quickness with the hands; a trick or juggling act requiring such skill.

**slen·der** (slen'dər) **1** gracefully narrow and slight of frame; slim: *a tall, slender girl, a slender hand.* **2** long and thin; not wide or big around in proportion to length or height: *a slender sapling. A pencil is a slender piece of wood.* **3** scanty; meagre; not adequate: *a slender meal, a slender income, a slender hope.* *adj.* —**slen'der·ly**, *adv.* —**slen'der·ness**, *n.*

**slen·der·ize** (slen'də rīz') **1** make SLENDER. **2** cause to look SLENDER or less stout: *a slenderizing dress.* *v.*, **slen·der·ized, slen·der·iz·ing.**

**slept** (slept) pt. and pp. of SLEEP. *v.*

**sleuth** (slüth) **1** *Informal.* detective. **2** be or act like a detective. **1** *n.*, **2** *v.*

**sleuth·hound** (slüth'hound') **1** BLOODHOUND. **2** *Informal.* detective. *n.*

**slew¹** (slü) pt. of SLAY: *Jack slew the giant.* *v.*
☞ Hom. SLOUGH¹ (slü), SLUE.

**sleepy**     **1117**     **slide fastener**

hat, āge, fär; let, ēqual, tėrm; it, īce
hot, ōpen, ôrder; oil, out; cup, pút, rüle
ȧbove, tȧken, pencȧl, lemȧn, circȧs
ch, child; ng, long; sh, ship
th, thin; ᴛʜ, then; zh, measure

**slew²** (slü) **1** turn or swing on a pivot or as if on a pivot: *He slewed around in his seat to get a better look. We slewed the telescope around to the east.* **2** skid or turn sharply: *The car slewed around the curve. She slewed the car to the right to avoid the dog.* **3** a turn, twist, or skid. **1, 2** *v.*, **3** *n.* Also, **slue.**
☞ Hom. SLOUGH¹ (slü), SLUE.

**slew³** (slü) *Informal.* a lot; a large number or amount: *There was a whole slew of people waiting at the stage door.* *n.*
☞ Hom. SLOUGH¹ (slü), SLUE.
☞ Etym. From Irish Gaelic *sluagh* 'crowd, host'.

**slice** (slīs) **1** a thin, flat, broad piece cut from something, especially food: *a slice of bread, meat, or cake.* **2** cut into slices: *He sliced the loaf of bread.* **3** cut off as a slice: *I sliced a piece of the meatloaf for myself.* **4** cut or pass through like a knife: *A bullet sliced the air by his head. The plough sliced through the earth.* **5** a knife or spatula with a thin, broad blade. **6** a part; share: *She wanted a slice of the profits.* **7** in sports, hit a ball so that it curves away. Compare with HOOK (def. 19). **8** such a hit. **1, 5, 6, 8** *n.*, **2–4, 7** *v.*, **sliced, slic·ing.**

**slic·er** (slī'sər) a person or thing that slices, especially a mechanical device for slicing food: *a meat slicer.* *n.*

**slick** (slik) **1** sleek; smooth: *slick hair.* **2** make sleek or smooth. **3** slippery; greasy: *a road slick with ice or mud.* **4** a smooth place or spot: *Oil makes a slick on the surface of water.* **5** *Informal.* clever; ingenious. **6** smooth in speech, manners, etc., especially in a tricky or deceitful way. **7** *Informal.* a magazine printed on heavy, glossy paper. **1, 3, 5, 6** *adj.*, **2** *v.*, **4, 7** *n.*
—**slick'ly**, *adv.* —**slick'ness**, *n.*

**slick·er** (slik'ər) a long, loose waterproof coat. *n.*

**slid** (slid) pt. and pp. of SLIDE: *The minutes slid rapidly by. He has slid into bad habits.* *v.*

**slide** (slīd) **1** move smoothly over a surface: *The bureau drawers slide in and out.* **2** move easily or quietly or secretly: *The thief slid behind the curtains.* **3** pass without heeding or being heeded. **4** pass by degrees; slip: *He has slid into bad habits.* **5** pass or put quietly or secretly: *He slid a gun into his pocket.* **6** slip in an uncontrolled manner: *The car slid into the ditch.* **7** the act of sliding: *The children each take a slide in turn.* **8** a smooth surface for sliding on: *The frozen brook makes a good slide.* **9** a track, rail, etc. on which something slides. **10** something that works by sliding. **11** the U-shaped tube of a trombone that is pushed in or out to change the pitch of the tones. **12** a mass of earth, snow, etc. sliding down. **13** the sliding down of such a mass. **14** a small, thin sheet of glass on which objects are placed for microscopic examination. **15** a small transparent photograph made of glass or film: *Slides are put in a projector and shown on a screen.* **16** an inclined CHUTE (def. 1) on which children can play. **1–6** *v.*, **slid, slid·ing;** **7–16** *n.* —**slid'er,** *n.*
**let slide,** neglect; not bother about: *He has been letting his business slide lately.*

**slide fastener** ZIPPER.

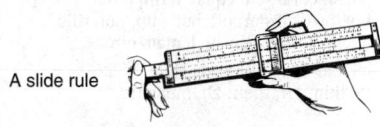
A slide rule

**slide rule** a ruler with a sliding piece, both marked with logarithmic scales, formerly used by engineers, physicists, etc. for making rapid calculations.

**slid·ing** (slī′ding) **1** moving or operating on a track or groove: *a sliding door.* **2** ppr. of SLIDE. *1 adj., 2 v.*

**sliding scale** a scale or standard, as for wages, tariffs, or fees, that is adjusted to fit certain conditions or situations: *Wages based on a sliding scale are adjusted according to the cost of living.*

**slight** (slīt) **1** not much; not important; small: *I have a slight headache.* **2** not big around; slender: *She is a slight girl.* **3** frail; flimsy: *a slight excuse.* **4** treat as of little value; pay too little attention to; neglect: *This maid slights her work. She felt slighted because she was not asked to the party.* **5** slighting treatment; an act showing neglect or lack of respect: *Cinderella suffered many slights from her sisters.* *1–3 adj., 4 v., 5 n.* —**slight′ness**, *n.*
☛ Hom. SLEIGHT.

**slight·ing** (slī′ting) **1** that detracts; contemptuous; disrespectful: *a slighting remark.* **2** ppr. of SLIGHT. *1 adj., 2 v.* —**slight′ing·ly**, *adv.*

**slight·ly** (slīt′lē) to a slight degree; somewhat; a little: *I knew him slightly.* *adv.*

**sli·ly** (slī′lē) See SLYLY. *adv.*

**slim** (slim) **1** slender; gracefully thin: *a slim girl, a slim waist.* **2** small or scanty; slight: *There is a slim chance that she will get the letter in time. His chances of escape were slim.* **3** make or become slender or more slender: *He is trying to slim down. Certain exercises are designed to slim the figure.* *1, 2 adj.,* **slim·mer, slim·mest**; *3 v.,* **slimmed, slim·ming.**

**slime** (slīm) **1** a soft, sticky mud or something like it: *His shoes were covered with slime from the swamp.* **2** a sticky substance given off by snails, snakes, fish, etc. **3** disgusting filth. *n.*

**slim·y** (slī′mē) **1** covered with SLIME: *The pond is too slimy to swim in.* **2** of SLIME; like slime. **3** disgusting; filthy. *adj.,* **slim·i·er, slim·i·est.**

**sling** (sling) **1** a strip of leather with a string fastened to each end, for throwing stones. **2** throw with a sling. **3** throw; cast; hurl; fling. **4** a throw; hurling. **5** a hanging loop of cloth fastened around the neck to support an injured arm or hand. **6** a loop of rope, band, chain, etc. by which heavy objects are lifted, carried, or held: *The men lowered the boxes into the cellar by a sling.* **7** raise, lower, etc. with a sling. **8** hang in a sling; hang so as to swing loosely: *The soldier's gun was slung over his shoulder.* *1, 4–6 n., 2, 3, 7, 8 v.,* **slung, sling·ing.**

**sling·shot** (sling′shot′) **1** a Y-shaped stick with a band of rubber between its prongs, used to shoot pebbles, etc.; a catapult. **2** SLING (def. 1). *n.*

**slink** (slingk) move in a sneaking, guilty manner; sneak: *After stealing the meat, the dog slunk away.* *v.,* **slunk, slink·ing.** —**slink′ing·ly**, *adv.*

**slink·y** (sling′kē) **1** furtive; sneaking. **2** of clothing, tight-fitting in an alluring, graceful way: *a slinky gown.* *adj.*

**slip¹** (slip) **1** go or move smoothly, quietly, easily, or quickly: *She slipped out of the room. Time slips by. The ship slips through the waves. The drawer slips into place.* **2** slide; move out of place: *The knife slipped and cut him.* **3** slide suddenly without wanting to: *He slipped on the icy sidewalk.* **4** the act or fact of slipping: *His broken leg was caused by a slip on a banana peel.* **5** cause to slip; put, pass, or draw smoothly, quietly, or secretly: *He slipped back the bolt. She slipped the ring from her finger. Slip the note into Maria's hand.* **6** put (*on*) or take (*off*) easily or quickly: *Slip on your coat. Slip off your shoes.* **7** PILLOWCASE. **8** a sleeveless garment worn under a dress or skirt. **9** pass without notice; pass through neglect; escape: *Don't let this opportunity slip.* **10** get loose from; get away from; escape from: *The dog has slipped his collar. Your name has slipped my mind.* **11** let go; release: *He slipped the hound. The ship has slipped anchor and is off.* **12** fall off; decline: *Sales are slipping.* **13** make a mistake or error. **14** a mistake; error: *He makes slips in grammar.* **15** a space for ships between wharves or in a dock. **16** an inclined platform alongside the water, on which ships are built or repaired. **17** a leash for a dog. **18** the position of a cricket player behind and to the side of the wicketkeeper. **19** the player in this position. *1–3, 5, 6, 9–13 v.,* **slipped, slip·ping;** *4, 7, 8, 14–19 n.*
**give someone the slip,** *Informal.* escape from or get away from someone: *She gave her creditors the slip.*
**let slip,** tell without meaning to: *He let the secret slip in a careless moment.*
**slip of the tongue,** a remark made by mistake.
**slip one over on,** *Informal.* get the advantage of, especially by trickery.
**slip up,** *Informal.* make a mistake or error.

**slip²** (slip) **1** a small stem or shoot cut from a plant, used to grow a new plant, either by rooting in water or earth or by grafting; cutting; scion. **2** a long, narrow strip of paper, wood, etc.: *a sales slip.* **3** a young, slender person: *She was just a slip of a girl.* **4** take a stem or shoot from a plant to grow a new plant. *1–3 n., 4 v.,* **slipped, slip·ping.**

**slip·cov·er** (slip′kuv′ər) a removable cloth cover for a chair, chesterfield, etc. *n.*

**slip·knot** (slip′not′) **1** a knot made to slip along the rope or cord around which it is made. **2** a knot that can be undone by a pull. See KNOT for picture. *n.*

**slip noose** a NOOSE made with a SLIP-KNOT.

**slip-on** (slip′on′) **1** that can be put on or taken off easily or quickly. **2** that must be put on or taken off over the head. **3** a slip-on glove, blouse, sweater, shoe, etc. *1, 2 adj., 3 n.*

**slip·per** (slip′ər) **1** a light, soft shoe that is easily slipped on and off the foot, especially one worn while resting indoors. **2** strike with a slipper, as in punishment. *1 n., 2 v.* —**slip′per·less**, *adj.*

**slip·pered** (slip′ərd) wearing slippers. *adj.*

**slip·per·y** (slip′ə rē) **1** causing or likely to cause sliding and slipping because of smoothness, greasiness, etc.: *Wet or icy streets are slippery. A waxed floor is slippery.* **2** slipping away easily; hard to hold firmly: *Wet soap is slippery.* **3** difficult to handle or pin down: *a slippery situation, a slippery concept.* **4** not to be depended on; tricky or deceitful: *a slippery character.* *adj.*
**slip·per·i·er, slip·per·i·est.** —**slip′per·i·ness**, *n.*

**slippery elm** **1** an elm tree of eastern North America

having an inner bark that becomes slimy or slippery when moistened. **2** the inner bark of this tree.

**slip·shod** (slip′shod′) **1** careless in dress, habits, speech, etc.; untidy, slovenly. **2** shuffling: *a slipshod gait.* **3** wearing shoes worn down at the heel. *adj.*

**slip·stitch** (slip′stich′) **1** an almost invisible kind of stitch used for sewing folded edges, such as hems, made by alternately taking a stitch inside the folded edge and a very tiny stitch in the body of the article being sewn. **2** a pattern stitch in knitting and crochet. *n.*

**slip·stream** (slip′strēm′) **1** a backward-moving stream of air created beside a rapidly moving object, such as an aircraft or a motor vehicle. **2** the area of decreased air pressure immediately behind such a moving object. *n.*

**slip–up** (slip′up′) *Informal.* a mistake; error: *There was a slip-up somewhere and the letter was never sent at all.* *n.*

**slit** (slit) **1** make a long, straight cut in; cut open: *The dentist had to slit the gum to take out the tooth. She used a paperknife to slit the envelope open.* **2** cut lengthwise into strips: *to slit leather into thongs.* **3** a straight, narrow cut or opening: *the slit in a letter box, a slit for a buttonhole. His eyes were just slits.* **1, 2** *v.*, **slit, slit·ting;** **3** *n.*
—**slit′ter,** *n.*

**slith·er** (sliᴛH′ər) **1** slide unsteadily down or along a gravelly surface: *We slithered down the embankment to the road.* **2** move or go with a gliding or sliding motion: *The snake slithered away into the grass.* **3** a slithering movement. **1, 2** *v.*, **3** *n.*

**sliv·er** (sliv′ər) **1** a long, thin piece that has been split off, broken off, or cut off; splinter: *a sliver of wood, a sliver of glass.* **2** split or break into slivers. **3** a loose fibre of wool, cotton, etc. **1, 3** *n.*, **2** *v.*

**slob** (slob) **1** an untidy or boorish person. **2** *Cdn.* SLOB ICE. *n.*

**slob·ber** (slob′ər) **1** let liquid run out from the mouth; drool: *The dog slobbered all over my skirt.* **2** saliva or other liquid running out from the mouth. **3** wet or smear with saliva, etc. **4** speak in a silly, sentimental way. **5** silly, sentimental talk or emotion. **1, 3, 4** *v.*, **2, 5** *n.*

**slob·ber·y** (slob′ə rē) **1** SLOBBERing. **2** disagreeably wet; sloppy. *adj.* —**slob′ber·i·ness,** *n.*

**slob ice** *Cdn.* a dense mass of small pieces of ice, especially sea ice: *The boat pushed its way through the slob ice.*

**sloe** (slō) **1** a dark-purple, plumlike fruit. **2** the thorny shrub that it grows on; blackthorn. *n.*
☛ *Hom.* SLOW.

**sloe–eyed** (slō′īd′) having very dark eyes. *adj.*

**sloe gin** a liqueur made from gin and flavoured with SLOES.

**slog** (slog) **1** plod heavily: *We slogged through the snow to the cabin. They had to slog their way through dense bush.* **2** work hard and steadily: *She slogged away at the hard assignment.* **3** a spell of hard, steady work. **4** hit hard. **5** a hard blow. **1, 2, 4** *v.*, **slogged, slog·ging;** **3, 5** *n.*

**slo·gan** (slō′gən) **1** a word or phrase used by a business, club, political party, etc. to advertise its purpose; motto: *"Service with a smile" was the store's slogan.* **2** formerly, a war cry. *n.*
☛ *Etym.* From Scots-Gaelic *sluagh-ghairm* 'war cry', made up of *sluagh* 'host, army' + *gairm* 'a cry, shout'.

**slipshod**     1119     **sloth**

hat, āge, fär; let, ēqual, tėrm; it, īce
hot, ōpen, ôrder; oil, out; cup, pu̇t, rüle
əbove, tākən, pencəl, lemən, circəs
ch, child; ng, long; sh, ship
th, thin; ᴛH, then; zh, measure

A sloop

**sloop** (slüp) a sailboat rigged fore-and-aft, having one mast, a mainsail, a jib, and sometimes other sails. *n.*

**sloop of war** a small warship having guns on the upper deck only.

**slop** (slop) **1** spill liquid upon; spill; splash. **2** liquid spilled or splashed about. **3** a thin liquid mud or slush. **4** splash through mud, slush, or water. **5** a weak liquid food, such as gruel. **6** Often, **slops**, *pl.* dirty water; liquid garbage. **1, 4** *v.*, **slopped, slop·ping;** **2, 3, 5, 6** *n.*

**slope** (slōp) **1** lie at an angle or slant; be inclined up or down: *a sloping roof. The land slopes toward the sea.* **2** cause to slant: *He sloped the ground so that rainwater would run away from the basement wall.* **3** any line, surface, land, etc. that goes up or down at an angle: *If you roll a ball up a slope, it will roll down again.* **4** the amount of slope: *The floor of the theatre has a slope of one metre from back to front.* **1, 2** *v.*, **sloped, slop·ing;** **3, 4** *n.*

**slop·py** (slop′ē) **1** very wet; slushy: *sloppy ground, sloppy weather.* **2** splashed or soiled with liquid: *a sloppy table.* **3** *Informal.* careless; slovenly: *to do sloppy work, to use sloppy English.* **4** *Informal.* weak; silly: *sloppy sentiment.* *adj.*, **slop·pi·er, slop·pi·est.**
—**slop′pi·ly,** *adv.* —**slop′pi·ness,** *n.*

**slops** (slops) **1** cheap ready-made clothing. **2** clothes, bedding, etc. supplied to sailors on a ship. *n.pl.*

**slosh** (slosh) **1** slush. **2** splash in slush, mud, or water. **3** *Informal.* a watery or weak drink. **4** go about idly. **1, 3** *n.*, **2, 4** *v.*

**slot¹** (slot) **1** a small, narrow opening or groove: *Vending machines have coin slots. We have a letter slot in our front door.* **2** make a slot or slots in. **3** a place or position in a series or scheme: *The new comedy series has a good time slot.* **4** place in a series or scheme: *The new show will be slotted after the six o'clock news.* **1, 3** *n.*, **2, 4** *v.*, **slot·ted, slot·ting.**

**slot²** (slot) a track or trail left by an animal: *They followed the deer's slot through the mud.* *n.*

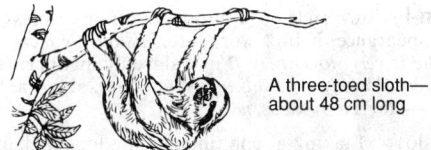
A three-toed sloth— about 48 cm long

**sloth** (slôth *or* sloth) **1** unwillingness to work or exert oneself; laziness; indolence: *His sloth keeps him from engaging in sports.* **2** a very slow-moving mammal of South and Central America that lives in trees: *Sloths hang upside down from tree branches.* *n.*

**sloth bear** a long-haired bear that lives in India.

**sloth·ful** (slôth′fəl *or* sloth′fəl) unwilling to work or exert oneself; lazy; idle. *adj.* —**sloth′ful·ly,** *adv.* —**sloth′ful·ness,** *n.*

**slot machine** a coin-operated machine, especially a gambling machine in which one pulls a handle to try to match up a series of symbols.

**slouch** (slouch) **1** stand, sit, walk, or move in an awkward, drooping manner: *The weary man slouched along.* **2** a bending forward of head and shoulders; an awkward, drooping way of standing, sitting, or walking. **3** droop or bend downward: *He slouched his shoulders.* **4** a drooping or bending downward of the brim of a hat, etc. **5** an awkward, slovenly, or inefficient person: *John is no slouch at cricket.* 1, 3 *v.*, 2, 4, 5 *n.*

**slouch·y** (slou′chē) not erect in posture or gait; slouching: *a slouchy walk.* *adj.*, **slouch·i·er, slouch·i·est.**

**slough**¹ (slü *for 1–4; usually,* slou *for 5*) **1** *Cdn.* in Western Canada, a body of fresh water formed by rain or melted snow: *Wild ducks nest on the prairie sloughs.* **2** a soft, deep, muddy place; mud hole. **3** a backwater or side channel of a stream; snye. **4** on the Pacific coast, a shallow or marshy inlet of the sea. **5** hopeless discouragement; degradation. *n.*
☞ *Hom.* SLEW, SLUE (for the first pronunciation of **slough**¹).

**slough**² (sluf) **1** the old skin shed, or cast off, by a snake. **2** drop off; throw off; shed: *The snake sloughed its skin.* **3** be shed or cast; drop or fall: *A scab sloughs off when new skin takes its place.* **4** a layer of dead skin or tissue that drops or falls off as a wound, sore, etc. heals. **5** cast off as undesirable, tiresome, bothersome, etc. (*usually used with* **off**): *to slough off a heavy backpack. Maureen sloughed off her depression and started anew.* **6** anything that has been shed or cast off: *the slough of outmoded ideas, the slough of grief.* **7** in card games, discard a losing card. 1, 4, 6 *n.*, 2, 3, 5, 7 *v.*

**slough of despond** (slou) hopeless dejection; deep despondency.

**Slo·vak** (slō′vak) **1** a member of a Slavic people living mainly in Slovakia, a country in eastern Europe. **2** the Slavic language of these people. **3** of or having to do with Slovakia, the Slovaks, or their language. 1, 2 *n.*, 3 *adj.*

**Slo·vak·i·an** (slō vak′ē ən) SLOVAK. *adj.*, *n.*

**slov·en** (sluv′ən) **1** a person who is untidy, dirty, or careless in dress, appearance, habits, work, etc. **2** SLOVENLY. **3** a cart used in the Maritimes. 1, 3 *n.*, 2 *adj.*

**slov·en·ly** (sluv′ən lē) **1** untidy, dirty, or careless in dress, appearance, habits, work, etc.: *a slovenly piece of work. She is very slovenly.* **2** in a slovenly manner: *He dresses very slovenly.* 1 *adj.*, **slov·en·li·er, slov·en·li·est;** 2 *adv.* —**slov′en·li·ness,** *n.*

**slow** (slō) **1** taking a long time; taking longer than usual; not fast or quick: *a slow journey.* **2** behind time; running less than proper speed: *a slow runner.* **3** indicating time earlier than the correct time: *a slow clock.* **4** causing a low or lower rate of speed: *slow ground, a slow track.* **5** burning or heating slowly or gently: *a slow flame.* **6** make slow or slower; reduce the speed of: *to slow down a car.* **7** become slow; go slower: *Slow up when you drive through a town.* **8** in a slow manner: *Drive slow.* **9** sluggish; naturally inactive: *a slow pupil.* **10** dull; not interesting: *a slow party.* 1–5, 9, 10 *adj.*, 6, 7 *v.*, 8 *adv.* —**slow′ly,** *adv.* —**slow′ness,** *n.*
☞ *Hom.* SLOE.
☞ *Usage.* **Slow** and **slowly** are both used as adverbs. In most written English **slowly** is preferred, except in certain set phrases (such as *go slow, drive slow*).

**slow·down** (slō′doun′) a slowing down: *There has been a slowdown in housing construction lately. The employees' protest took the form of a work slowdown.* *n.*

**slow match** a fuse that burns very slowly, used for setting fire to gunpowder, dynamite, etc.

**slow motion** **1** action at less than normal speed. **2** film or videotape showing action at less than its actual speed.

**slow–mo·tion** (slō′mō′shən) **1** moving at less than normal speed. **2** showing action at much less than its actual speed. *adj.*

**slow·poke** (slō′pōk′) *Informal.* a very slow person or thing. *n.*

**slow time** *Informal.* STANDARD TIME, as opposed to daylight-saving time, which is often called fast time: *We go back on slow time in the fall.*

**slow–wit·ted** (slō′wit′id) slow at thinking; dull; stupid. *adj.*

**sludge** (sluj) **1** soft mud; mire. **2** a soft, thick, muddy mixture, deposit, sediment, etc., such as that produced in sewage treatment processes. **3** small pieces of newly formed sea ice: *In winter there is sludge on the sea near the shore.* *n.*

**slue**¹ (slü) See SLEW². *v.*, **slued, slu·ing;** *n.*
☞ *Hom.* SLOUGH¹ (slü), SLEW.

**slue**² (slü) SLOUGH¹ (defs. 1, 3). *n.*
☞ *Hom.* SLOUGH¹ (slü), SLEW.

**slug**¹ (slug) **1** a slow-moving animal resembling a snail, without a shell or having only a partly developed shell. **2** a caterpillar or larva that resembles a slug. **3** bullet. **4** a roughly shaped, roundish lump of metal. **5** a small disk, such as one used illegally instead of a coin in a coin-operated machine. **6** in printing, a line of type cast in one piece by a linotype machine. *n.*

**slug**² (slug) *Informal.* **1** hit hard with the fist, a bat, or a blunt weapon. **2** a hard blow. 1 *v.*, **slugged, slug·ging;** 2 *n.* —**slug′ger,** *n.*

**slug·gard** (slug′ərd) **1** a person who is habitually lazy and idle. **2** lazy; idle. 1 *n.*, 2 *adj.*

**slug·gish** (slug′ish) **1** slow; lacking energy or vigour: *a sluggish mind.* **2** very slow in movement, growth or flow: *a sluggish river, sluggish blood circulation. The economy has been sluggish for the past few months.* **3** lazy or idle. *adj.* —**slug′gish·ly,** *adv.* —**slug′gish·ness,** *n.*

**sluice** (slüs) **1** a structure having a gate for holding back or controlling the water of a canal, river, or lake. **2** a gate that holds back or controls the flow of water: *When the water behind a dam gets too high, the sluices are opened.* **3** the water held back or controlled by such a gate. **4** something that controls the flow or passage of anything: *War opens the sluices of hatred and bloodshed.* **5** let out or draw off water by opening a sluice. **6** flow or pour in a stream; rush: *Water sluiced down the channel.*  **7** flush or cleanse with a rush of water; pour or throw water over.   **8** a long, sloping trough through which water flows, used to wash gold from sand, dirt, or gravel.   **9** wash gold from sand, dirt, or gravel in a sluice.   **10** a channel for carrying off overflow or surplus water.   **11** send logs, etc. along a channel of water.   1–4, 8, 10 *n.*, 5–7, 9, 11 *v.*, **sluiced, sluic·ing.**

**sluice gate**   a gate to control the flow of water in a SLUICE.

**slum** (slum)   **1** visit slums or other places considered inferior to one's usual surroundings, especially out of curiosity.   **2** Often, **slums,** *pl.*   a district or area in a city characterized by overpopulation, poor housing and sanitation, and social problems.   1 *v.*, **slummed, slum·ming;**   2 *n.*

**slum·ber** (slum′bər)   **1** sleep: *The baby slumbered peacefully through the uproar.*   **2** spend in sleep: *to slumber away the morning hours.*   **3** be inactive, dormant, or negligent: *The volcano had slumbered for years. The incident awakened his slumbering conscience.*   **4** an inactive, dormant, or negligent state or condition.   **5** Sometimes, **slumbers,** *pl.*   sleep: *Her slumbers were interrupted by the sound of a siren.*   1–3 *v.*, 4, 5 *n.*   —**slum′ber·er,** *n.*

**slum·ber·ous** (slum′bə rəs *or* slum′brəs)   **1** sleepy; heavy with drowsiness: *slumberous eyelids.*   **2** causing or inducing sleep.   **3** characterized by or suggestive of a state of sleep or inactivity: *the slumberous calm of a summer evening.* *adj.*   —**slum′ber·ous·ly,** *adv.*

**slum·brous** (slum′brəs)   SLUMBEROUS.   *adj.*   —**slum′brous·ly,** *adv.*

**slump** (slump)   **1** drop or fall suddenly: *He slumped to the floor in a dead faint.*   **2** have or assume a drooping posture: *The bored students slumped in their seats, waiting for the bell.*   **3** a great or sudden decline in prices, activity, etc.: *a slump in prices. The economy is in a slump.*   **4** go into a marked decline: *Business has slumped.*   **5** a long period during which a person is not working or performing as well as usual: *The team's pitcher is in a slump and they have lost several games in a row.*   1, 2, 4 *v.*, 3, 5 *n.*

**slung** (slung)   *pt.* and *pp.* of SLING: *They slung some stones and ran away. The boy had slung his books over his shoulders.*   *v.*

**slunk** (slungk)   *pt.* and *pp.* of SLINK: *The dog slunk away.*   *v.*

**slur** (slėr)   **1** pass lightly over; go through hurriedly or in a careless way.   **2** pronounce indistinctly: *Many persons slur "How do you do?"*   **3** speak or write sounds, letters, etc. so indistinctly that they run into each other.   **4** a slurred pronunciation, sound, etc.   **5** in music, sing or play two or more tones of different pitch without a break; run together in a smooth, connected manner.   **6** a slurring of tones.   **7** a curved mark ( ) ( ) indicating this.   **8** mark with a slur.   **9** a blot or stain upon one's reputation; an insulting or slighting remark: *a slur on a person's good name.*   **10** harm the reputation of; insult; slight.   1–3, 5, 8, 10 *v.*, **slurred, slur·ring,**   4, 6, 7, 9 *n.*

**slurp** (slėrp) *Informal.*   **1** eat or drink noisily or with a sucking sound.   **2** a slurping sound.   1 *v.*, 2 *n.*

**slush** (slush)   **1** partly melted snow; snow and water mixed.   **2** soft mud.   **3** *Informal.*   silly, sentimental talk, writing, etc.   **4** grease.   *n.*

**slush fund**   **1** money collected or set aside for dishonest purposes, such as bribery or improper political or business lobbying.   **2** money set aside for special projects.

**slush·y** (slush′ē)   **1** covered with slush; having much slush: *a slushy sidewalk.*   **2** made up of or like slush: *a slushy snow.*   *adj.,* **slush·i·er, slush·i·est.**   —**slush′i·ness,** *n.*

**slut** (slut)   **1** a slovenly, untidy woman; slattern.   **2** a woman of loose morals.   *n.*

**slut·tish** (slut′ish)   having to do with, like, or characteristic of a SLUT.   *adj.*   —**slut′tish·ly,** *adv.*   —**slut′tish·ness,** *n.*

**sly** (slī)   **1** clever in deceiving or tricking: *The sly cat stole the meat while the cook's back was turned.*   **2** not straightforward or open; cleverly underhanded; crafty: *Her sly questions were intended to get the men to reveal more than they realized. They had developed a sly scheme for taking over control of the organization.*   **3** playfully mischievous or knowing: *a sly wink.*   *adj.,* **sly·er** or **sli·er, sly·est** or **sli·est.**   —**sly′ness,** *n.*
**on the sly,**   in a way meant to avoid notice; secretly: *They got their information on the sly.*

**sly·ly** (slī′lē)   in a SLY manner.   *adv.*   Also, **slily.**

**Sm**   samarium.

**smack**[1] (smak)   **1** a slight taste or flavour: *The sauce had a smack of nutmeg.*   **2** a trace; suggestion: *The old sailor still had a smack of the sea about him.*   **3** have a smack: *The Irishman's speech smacked of the Old Country.*   1, 2 *n.,* 3 *v.*

**smack**[2] (smak)   **1** open the lips quickly so as to make a sharp sound.   **2** the sharp sound made in this way.   **3** kiss loudly.   **4** slap.   **5** crack a whip, etc.   **6** a loud kiss, slap, or crack.   **7** *Informal.*   directly; squarely: *He fell smack on his face.*   **8** *Informal.*   suddenly and sharply; with or as if with a smack.   1, 3–5 *v.,* 2, 6 *n.,* 7, 8 *adv.*

**smack**[3] (smak)   **1** a small sailboat with one mast.   **2** a similar fishing boat with a well for keeping fish alive.   *n.*

**smack·ing** (smak′ing)   **1** lively, brisk, or strong: *a smacking breeze.*   **2** making a quick, sharp sound: *a smacking kiss, a smacking blow.*   **3** ppr. of SMACK.   1, 2 *adj.,* 3 *v.*

**small** (smol)   **1** not large; little; not large as compared with other things of the same kind: *A cottage is a small house.*   **2** into small pieces.   **3** not great in amount, degree, extent, duration, value, strength, etc.: *a small dose, small hope of success. The cent is our smallest coin.*   **4** not important: *a small matter.*   **5** not prominent; of low social position; humble; poor: *People great and small mourned Laurier's death.*   **6** having little land, capital, etc.: *a small farmer, a small dealer.*   **7** gentle; soft; low: *a small voice, a small crumbling sound.*   **8** in low tones.   **9** mean: *A person with a small nature is not generous.*   **10** of letters, not capital.   **11** that which is small; a small, slender, or narrow part: *the small of the back.*   1, 3–7, 9, 10 *adj.,* 2, 8 *adv.,* 11 *n.*   —**small′ness,** *n.*
**feel small,**   be ashamed or humiliated.
**sing small,**   change to a humble tone or manner.

**small arms** weapons easily carried by a person, and held in the hand or hands while being fired: *Rifles and revolvers are classed as small arms.*

**small capital** a capital letter that is only about as high as a lower case letter: *In the sentence* Caesar conquered Britain in 54 B.C., BC *is printed in small capitals. Cross-references in this dictionary are printed in small capitals.*

**small change** 1 coins of small value, such as nickels, dimes, etc. 2 anything small and unimportant.

**small fry** 1 babies or children; small or young creatures. 2 small fish. 3 unimportant people or things.

**small hours** the early hours of the morning.

**small intestine** the long, narrow part of the INTESTINE where most of the absorption of digested food takes place, extending from the stomach to the large intestine: *In adults the small intestine is more than six metres long.* See ALIMENTARY CANAL for picture.

**small·ish** (smol′ish) somewhat small. *adj.*

**small letter** a lower-case letter, not a capital: *In this sentence, all the letters except the first one are small letters.*

**small–mind·ed** (smol′mīn′did) petty or mean. *adj.* —**small′-mind′ed·ness,** *n.*

**small of the back** the narrowest part of the back, at the waist.

**small potatoes** an unimportant person or thing or group of persons or things: *The last deal was just small potatoes, compared with what she's planning now.*

**small·pox** (smol′poks′) a contagious disease, now eradicated, characterized by fever and sores on the skin that often left permanent scars shaped like little pits. *n.*

**small–scale** (smol′skāl′) 1 small in operation or scope; limited: *She runs a small-scale import business.* 2 of a map, etc., drawn to a small scale, not permitting much detail. *adj.*

**small talk** light, informal conversation; chit-chat: *Laura makes people feel at ease because she's good at small talk.*

**small–town** (smol′toun′) 1 of or coming from a small town: *small-town friendliness, a small-town girl.* 2 narrow; provincial: *small-town bigotry.* *adj.*

**smart** (smärt) 1 feel sharp pain: *His eyes smarted.* 2 cause sharp pain: *The cut smarts.* 3 a sharp pain. 4 feel distress or irritation: *He smarted from the scolding.* 5 suffer: *He shall smart for this.* 6 sharp; severe: *She gave the horse a smart blow.* 7 keen; active; lively: *They walked at a smart pace.* 8 clever; bright: *a smart child.* 9 fresh and neat; in good order: *smart in his uniform.* 10 stylish; fashionable. 11 in a smart manner. 12 witty, humorous, or clever in an annoying way: *He thinks he is pretty smart.* 1, 2, 4, 5 *v.*, 3 *n.*, 6–10, 12 *adj.*, 11 *adv.* —**smart′ly,** *adv.* —**smart′ness,** *n.*

**smart al·eck** or **al·ec** (al′ik) a conceited, obnoxious person.

**smart·en** (smar′tən) 1 improve in appearance; brighten. 2 make or become brisker: *He smartened his walk when the sergeant approached.* *v.*
**smarten up,** *Informal.* move, behave, or work more briskly or efficiently: *The teacher told his idle class to smarten up.*

**smart·weed** (smär′twēd′) a weed growing in wet places, that causes a smarting sensation when brought into contact with the skin. *n.*

**smash** (smash) 1 break into pieces with violence and noise: *to smash a window.* 2 destroy; shatter; ruin: *to smash an argument.* 3 be broken to pieces: *The dishes smashed on the floor.* 4 become ruined. 5 rush violently; crash: *The car smashed into a tree.* 6 a violent breaking; shattering; crash: *the smash of two automobiles.* 7 the act or sound of a smash or crash: *the smash of broken glass.* 8 crush; defeat: *to smash an attack.* 9 a business failure; bankruptcy. 10 hit a tennis ball or baseball with a hard, fast overhand stroke. 11 a hard, fast overhand stroke in tennis. 12 *Informal.* hit a hard blow. 13 *Informal.* a hard blow. 1–5, 8, 10, 12 *v.*, 6, 7, 9, 11, 13 *n.*
**to smash, a** into broken pieces; into bits. **b** to ruin: *His business went to smash during the last depression.*

**smash hit** a very successful play, motion picture, recording, etc.

**smash–up** (smash′up′) 1 a bad collision of motor vehicles: *She was involved in a smash-up and is still in hospital.* 2 complete collapse or failure; ruin. *n.*

**smat·ter·ing** (smat′ə ring) a slight or superficial knowledge of a language or a subject: *Jeni has a smattering of Italian that she picked up on a visit to Italy last summer.* *n.*

**smear** (smēr) 1 cover or stain with anything sticky, greasy, or dirty: *She smeared her fingers with jam.* 2 rub or spread oil, grease, paint, etc. 3 blur or make a streak across a drawing, writing, etc.: *The corner of the painting was smeared a bit while it was still wet.* 4 a mark or stain left by smearing: *You have a smear of paint on your cheek.* 5 rub or wipe a brush, hand, cloth, etc. so as to make a mark or stain. 6 receive a mark or stain; be smeared: *Wet paint smears easily.* 7 a small amount of something such as blood, spread on a slide for examination with a microscope. 8 harm the reputation of: *She attempted to smear her opponent by suggesting that he had accepted bribes while in office.* 9 a charge or accusation, usually without any basis, against a person, group, etc.: *The smear was unsuccessful.* 1–3, 5, 6, 8 *v.*, 4, 7, 9 *n.*

**smear·y** (smē′rē) 1 smeared: *a small child's smeary drawing.* 2 tending to smear: *smeary lipstick.* *adj.*, **smear·i·er, smear·i·est.** —**smear′i·ness,** *n.*

**smell** (smel) 1 perceive with the nose. 2 an act of smelling; a sniff: *Have a smell at this rose.* 3 the sense of smelling: *Smell is keener in dogs than in people.* 4 detect or recognize smells. 5 the quality in a thing that affects the sense of smell; odour: *the smell of burning cloth.* 6 give out a smell. 7 give out a bad smell; have a bad smell. 8 find a trace or suggestion of: *We smelled trouble.* 9 have the smell of; have the trace of: *The plan smells of trickery.* 10 a trace; suggestion. 11 hunt or find by smelling or as if by smelling: *The dog will smell out the thief.* 12 sniff at: *She picked up a rose and smelled it.* 1, 4, 6–9, 11, 12 *v.*, **smelled** or **smelt, smell·ing;** 2, 3, 5, 10 *n.*
**smell up,** *Informal.* cause to have a bad smell.

**smell·er** (smel′ər) a person or thing that smells. *n.*

**smelling salts** a form of AMMONIA that, when inhaled, helps to relieve faintness, headaches, etc.

**smell·y** (smel′ē) giving off a strong, unpleasant odour: *The garbage can should be washed because it's getting smelly.* *adj.*, **smell·i·er, smell·i·est.**

**smelt**[1] (smelt) 1 melt ore in order to get the metal out of it. **2** obtain metal from ore by melting. **3** refine impure metal by melting. *v.*

**smelt²** (smelt) a small, edible fish having silvery scales. *n., pl.* **smelt** or **smelts.**

**smelt³** (smelt) a pt. and a pp. of SMELL. *v.*

**smelt·er** (smel′tər) **1** a person whose work or business is smelting ores or metals. **2** a place where ores or metals are smelted. *n.*

**smid·gen** (smij′ən) *Informal.* a tiny piece or amount; mite. *n.*

**smi·lax** (smī′laks) **1** a twining, trailing plant or vine, much used by florists in decoration. **2** any of a large group of woody vines having prickly stems, umbrella-shaped clusters of flowers, and blackish or red berries. *n.*

**smile** (smīl) **1** look pleased or amused; show pleasure, favour, kindness, amusement, etc. by an upward curve of the mouth. **2** look pleasant or agreeable; look with favour. **3** bring, put, drive, etc. by smiling: *Smile your tears away.* **4** give a smile: *She smiled a sunny smile.* **5** express by a smile: *She smiled consent.* **6** show scorn, disdain, etc. by a curve of the mouth: *She smiled bitterly.* **7** the act of smiling: *a friendly smile.* **8** a favouring look or regard; pleasant look or aspect. 1–6 *v.*, **smiled, smil·ing,** 7, 8 *n.* —**smil′ing·ly,** *adv.*

**smirch** (smėrch) **1** make dirty; soil or stain with soot, dirt, dust, etc. **2** bring dishonour or disgrace on; sully: *to smirch someone's reputation.* **3** a dirty mark; a smear or stain. **4** dishonour or disgrace. 1, 2 *v.*, 3, 4 *n.*

**smirk** (smėrk) **1** smile in a knowing, self-satisfied way. **2** a knowing or self-satisfied smile. 1 *v.*, 2 *n.*

**smit** (smit) a pp. of SMITE. *v.*

**smite** (smīt) have a sudden, strong effect on: *The thief's conscience smote him.* *v.*, **smote, smit·ten** or **smit, smit·ing.**

**smith** (smith) **1** a person who makes or shapes things out of metal (*used mainly in compounds*): *a goldsmith, a tinsmith.* **2** BLACKSMITH. *n.*

**smith·er·eens** (smiTH′ə rēnz′) *Informal.* small pieces; bits: *to smash a plate to smithereens.* *n.pl.*

**smith·y** (smith′ē or smiTH′ē) the workshop of a SMITH, especially a blacksmith. *n., pl.* **smith·ies.**

**smit·ten** (smit′ən) **1** hard hit; struck: *sudden sparks from smitten steel.* **2** suddenly and strongly affected: *smitten with terror.* **3** *Informal.* very much in love: *She's really smitten.* **4** a pp. of SMITE: *The giant had been smitten dead.* 1–3 *adj.*, 4 *v.*

**smock** (smok) **1** a loose, coatlike outer garment worn to protect clothing. **2** ornament with SMOCKING: *The little girl's dress was smocked from the neckline to the waist.* 1 *n.*, 2 *v.*

**smock·ing** (smok′ing) **1** decorative stitching used on clothing, made by gathering material closely with rows of stitches in a honeycomb pattern. **2** ppr. of SMOCK. 1 *n.*, 2 *v.*

**smog** (smog) a combination in the air of smoke or other chemical fumes and fog. *n.*
☛ *Etym.* A blend of *smoke* and *fog.*

**smoke** (smōk) **1** the visible mixture of gases and particles of carbon that rises when anything burns; a cloud from anything burning. **2** something resembling this. **3** something unsubstantial, quickly passing, or without result. **4** give off smoke or steam, etc.: *The fireplace smokes.* **5** draw the smoke from a pipe, cigar, or cigarette into the mouth and puff it out again. **6** that which is smoked; cigar, cigarette, pipe, etc. **7** the act or period of smoking tobacco. **8** preserve or flavour meat, fish, etc. by exposing to smoke: *People smoke fish to preserve them.* **9** drive out by smoke, or as if by smoke: *to smoke a groundhog from its hole.* **10** make, bring, pass, etc. by smoking. **11** colour, darken, or stain with smoke. 1–3, 6, 7 *n.*, 4, 5, 8–11 *v.*, **smoked, smok·ing.**
**smoke out, a** drive out with smoke. **b** find out and make known.

**smoke bomb** a kind of bomb containing chemicals that give out dense smoke when the bomb bursts.

**smoke·house** (smōk′hous′) a building where meat or fish is treated with smoke to preserve and flavour it. *n.*

**smoke·jump·er** (smōk′jump′ər) a person who is trained and equipped to fight forest fires and who is parachuted into an area where there is a fire. *n.*

**smoke·less** (smōk′lis) having or producing no smoke: *Anthracite coal burns with an almost smokeless flame.* *adj.*

**smok·er** (smō′kər) a person who smokes tobacco. *n.*

**smoke screen 1** a mass of thick smoke used to hide a ship, aircraft, etc. from the enemy. **2** anything that hides or obscures a plan, project, etc.: *a smoke screen of false information.*

**smoke·stack** (smōk′stak′) **1** a tall chimney. **2** a pipe that discharges smoke, etc.: *the smokestack of a boat.* *n.*

**smoke tree** a small tree or shrub having flower clusters that look somewhat like puffs of smoke.

**smok·y** (smō′kē) **1** giving off much smoke: *a smoky fire.* **2** full of smoke: *a smoky room.* **3** darkened or stained with smoke. **4** like smoke or suggesting smoke: *a smoky grey, a smoky taste.* *adj.*, **smok·i·er, smok·i·est.** —**smok′i·ly,** *adv.* —**smok′i·ness,** *n.*

**smol·der** (smōl′dər) See SMOULDER. *v., n.*

**smolt** (smōlt) a young salmon that has ceased to be a parr and is ready to descend, or has descended, to the sea for the first time. *n.*

**smooth** (smüTH) **1** having an even surface, like glass, silk, or still water; flat; level: *smooth stones.* **2** free from unevenness or roughness: *smooth sailing, a smooth voyage.* **3** without lumps: *smooth sauce.* **4** without hair: *a smooth face, smooth leaves.* **5** without trouble or difficulty; easy: *a smooth course of affairs.* **6** calm; serene: *a smooth temper.* **7** polished; pleasant; polite. **8** not harsh in sound or taste: *smooth verses, smooth wine.* **9** make smooth or smoother: *Smooth this dress with a hot iron. He smoothed out the ball of crushed paper and read it.* **10** make easy: *His tact smoothed the way to an agreement.* **11** in a smooth manner. **12** the act of smoothing. **13** a smooth part or place. 1–8 *adj.*, 9, 10 *v.*, 11 *adv.*, 12, 13 *n.* —**smooth′er,** *n.* —**smooth′ly,** *adv.* —**smooth′ness,** *n.*
**smooth away,** get rid of troubles, difficulties, etc.

**smooth down,** calm; soothe: *She smoothed down her father's temper.*
**smooth over,** make something seem less wrong, unpleasant, or noticeable: *The teacher tried to smooth over the argument between the two boys.*

**smooth·bore** (smüfH′bôr′) **1** of a gun, having no grooves on the inside of the barrel; not rifled. **2** a gun having a barrel with a smooth bore. 1 *adj.*, 2 *n.*

**smooth–faced** (smüfH′fāst′) **1** having a smooth face; beardless or clean-shaven: *a smooth-faced youth.* **2** having a smooth surface: *smooth-faced brick.* **3** having the appearance of being agreeable and sincere: *a smooth-faced hypocrite. adj.*

**smooth·ie** or **smooth·y** (smü′fHē) *Informal.* a smooth, persuasive, often insincere person. *n.*

**smooth–spok·en** (smüfH′spō′kən) speaking easily and pleasantly; polished in speech. *adj.*

**smooth–tongued** (smüfH′tungd′) speaking smoothly and agreeably; suave and plausible: *a smooth-tongued liar. adj.*

**smor·gas·bord** (smôr′gəs bôrd′) a buffet meal, featuring a large variety of meats, salads, etc. *n.*
☛ *Etym.* From Swedish *smörgåsbord* 'sandwich table'.

**smote** (smōt) pt. of SMITE. *v.*

**smoth·er** (smufH′ər) **1** make unable to get air; kill by depriving of air: *The murderer smothered his victim with a pillow.* **2** be unable to breathe freely; suffocate: *We are smothering in this stuffy room.* **3** cover thickly: *In the fall the grass is smothered with leaves.* **4** deaden or put out by covering thickly: *The fire is smothered by ashes.* **5** keep back; check; suppress: *She smothered a sharp reply.* **6** cook in a covered pot or baking dish: *smothered chicken.* **7** a cloud of dust, smoke, spray, etc. **8** anything that smothers. **9** the condition of being smothered. 1–6 *v.*, 7–9 *n.* —**smoth′er·er,** *n.*

**smoth·er·y** (smufH′ə rē) tending to SMOTHER; full of dust, smoke, spray, etc. *adj.*

**smoul·der** or **smol·der** (smōl′dər) **1** burn and smoke without flame: *The fire smouldered most of the night.* **2** a slow, smoky burning without flame; smouldering. **3** exist or continue in a suppressed condition: *The people's discontent smouldered for years before it broke out into open rebellion.* **4** show suppressed feeling: *The woman's eyes smouldered with anger.* 1, 3, 4 *v.*, 2 *n.*

**smudge** (smuj) **1** a dirty mark; smear. **2** mark with dirty streaks; smear: *The child's drawing was smudged.* **3** a smoky fire made to drive away insects or to protect plants from frost. **4** use a smudge or smudges, especially in an orchard. 1, 3 *n.*, 2, 4 *v.*, **smudged, smudg·ing.**

**smudg·y** (smuj′ē) smudged; marked with smudges. *adj.*, **smudg·i·er, smudg·i·est.**

**smug** (smug) **1** too pleased with one's own goodness, cleverness, respectability, etc.; self-satisfied; complacent: *Nothing disturbs the smug beliefs of some prim, narrow-minded people.* **2** sleek; neat; trim. *adj.*, **smug·ger, smug·gest.** —**smug′ly,** *adv.* —**smug′ness,** *n.*

**smug·gle** (smug′əl) **1** bring into or take out of a country secretly and against the law: *to smuggle drugs into Canada.* **2** bring, take, put, etc. secretly: *Rob tried to smuggle his puppy into the house.* *v.*, **smug·gled, smug·gling.** —**smug′gler,** *n.*

**smut** (smut) **1** soot, dirt, etc. **2** soil or be soiled with smut. **3** a place soiled with smut. **4** indecent or obscene talk, writing, or pictures. **5** a plant disease in which the ears of grain are changed to a black dust. **6** the fungus that causes this disease. **7** affect or become affected with this disease. 1, 3–6 *n.*, 2, 7 *v.*, **smut·ted, smut·ting.**

**smut·ty** (smut′ē) **1** soiled with smut, soot, etc.; dirty. **2** indecent or obscene. **3** having the plant disease called SMUT (def. 5). *adj.*, **smut·ti·er, smut·ti·est.** —**smut′ti·ness,** *n.*

**Sn** tin.

**snack** (snak) **1** a light meal: *She eats a snack before going to bed.* **2** eat a snack. 1 *n.*, 2 *v.*

**snack bar** a counter where light meals, coffee, etc. are served.

**snaf·fle** (snaf′əl) **1** a slender, jointed BIT[1] used on a bridle. See BRIDLE for picture. **2** control or manage by a snaffle. **3** *Informal.* pilfer; steal. 1 *n.*, 2, 3 *v.*, **snaf·fled, snaf·fling.**

**snag** (snag) **1** a tree or branch held fast in a river or lake: *Snags are dangerous to boats.* **2** any sharp or rough projecting point, such as the broken end of a branch. **3** the stump of a tooth; projecting tooth. **4** a hidden or unexpected obstacle: *Moira had to drop her plans because of a snag.* **5** hinder. **6** a pulled or broken thread in fabric. **7** run or catch on a snag. **8** clear of snags. 1–4, 6 *n.*, 5, 7, 8 *v.*, **snagged, snag·ging.**

**snag·gle–toothed** (snag′əl tütht′) having uneven, broken, or projecting teeth. *adj.*

**snag·gy** (snag′ē) **1** having SNAGS: *a snaggy tree, a snaggy river.* **2** projecting sharply or roughly. *adj.*, **snag·gi·er, snag·gi·est.**

A tree snail found in Florida— about 25 mm long

**snail** (snāl) **1** a small, soft-bodied MOLLUSC that crawls very slowly: *Most snails have spirally coiled shells into which they can withdraw for protection.* See WHORL for another picture. **2** a lazy, slow-moving person. *n.*

Snake: a prairie rattlesnake— about 120 cm long

**snake** (snāk) **1** any of a large group of reptiles having an elongated body, scaly skin, no legs, no eyelids or external ears, and moving by means of undulations of the body: *Snakes are found throughout most of the world and belong to the same order as lizards.* **2** a sly, treacherous person. **3** move, wind, or curve like a snake: *The road snaked through the hills.* **4** *Informal.* drag; haul. **5** a long, flexible metal rod used to clear drainpipes of obstructions. 1, 2, 5 *n.*, 3, 4 *v.*, **snaked, snak·ing.** —**snake′like′,** *adj.*

**snake·bite** (snāk′bīt′) **1** the bite of a snake, especially a poisonous one.  2 the condition resulting from the bite of a poisonous snake.  *n.*

**snake charmer**  a person who entertains an audience by demonstrating an apparent power to hypnotize, or charm, poisonous snakes.

**snake dance**  1 an informal single-file procession of people who join hands and dance in a weaving path through buildings, streets, etc., especially as part of an athletic victory celebration.  2 a ceremonial dance among certain peoples in which snakes are handled, invoked, etc.: *The Hopi Indian people of the southwestern United States have a traditional snake dance.*

**snake fence**  a fence made of horizontal tiers of wooden rails laid zigzag so that their ends overlap at an angle.

**snake in the grass**  a person who seems to be a friend but is actually faithless; a secret enemy.

**snake pit**  1 a pit filled with snakes.  2 a place of utter confusion and distress.

**snake·root** (snā′krüt′)  1 any of various plants whose roots have been regarded as a remedy for snakebites.  2 the root of such a plant.  *n.*

**snake·skin** (snāk′skin′)  1 the skin of a snake.  2 the leather made from it.  *n.*

**snak·y** (snā′kē)  1 of or like a snake or snakes.  2 curving, turning, or twisting, suggesting the movements of a snake: *a snaky path up the hillside.*  3 having many snakes.  4 sly; venomous; treacherous.  *adj.*, **snak·i·er, snak·i·est.**  —**snak′i·ly,** *adv.*  —**snak′i·ness,** *n.*

**snap** (snap)  1 make or cause to make a sudden, sharp sound: *This wood snaps as it burns. She snapped her fingers in time to the music.*  2 move, shut, catch, etc. with a snap: *He snapped the lid shut. The latch snapped into place.*  3 break suddenly with a sharp sound: *The violin string snapped.*  4 a sudden, sharp breaking of something hard or brittle: *the snap of a branch.*  5 the quick, sharp sound of a snap: *The box shut with a snap. The blade broke with a snap.*  6 become suddenly unable to endure a strain: *His nerves snapped.*  7 make a sudden, quick bite or snatch: *The dog snapped at the child's hand. The dog snapped up the meat.*  8 seize eagerly: *She snapped at the chance to go to Europe.*  9 a quick, sudden bite or snatch: *The dog made a snap at a fly.*  10 speak sharply or impatiently: *"Silence!" snapped the captain. Don't snap at him; he doesn't understand what you want.*  11 quick, sharp speech.  12 move quickly and sharply: *The soldiers snapped to attention. Her eyes snapped with anger.*  13 *Informal.* a quick, sharp way: *She moves with snap and energy.*  14 made or done quickly or unexpectedly: *A snap judgment is often wrong. The government called a snap election.*  15 DOME FASTENER: *The jacket closes with snaps.*  16 a thin, crisp cookie: *lemon snaps, gingersnaps.*  17 *Informal.* SNAPSHOT.  18 take a snapshot of.  19 *Informal.* a very easy job, piece of work, etc.: *The exam was a snap.*  20 *Informal.* very easy: *a snap assignment.*  21 in football, the act of passing the ball between the legs by the centre: *That was a bad snap.*  22 pass the ball between the legs in a football game.  23 in football, the player in the middle of the line of scrimmage; the centre.  1–3, 6–8, 10, 12, 18, 22 *v.*, **snapped, snap·ping;**  4, 5, 9, 11, 13–17, 19–21, 23 *n.*  **not a snap,** not at all.  **snap out of it,** *Informal.*  change one's attitude, habit, etc. suddenly.

**snap·drag·on** (snap′drag′ən)  1 a garden plant having spikes of showy flowers of crimson, purple, white, yellow,

etc.  2 an old game in which people try to snatch raisins from burning brandy.  *n.*

**snap fastener**  DOME FASTENER.

**snap·per** (snap′ər)  1 a person or thing that snaps.  2 a SNAPPING TURTLE.  3 a red fish of tropical seas, used for food.  *n.*

**snapping turtle**  a large, savage turtle of certain North American rivers, that has powerful jaws with which it snaps at its prey.

**snap·pish** (snap′ish)  1 quick and sharp in speech or manner; curt and irritable: *He's very snappish today.*  2 apt to bite or snap.  *adj.*

**snap·py** (snap′ē)  1 *Informal.*  brisk and vigorous: *We went at a snappy pace.*  2 *Informal.*  sharply chilly: *a snappy fall day.*  3 *Informal.*  smart; stylish: *a snappy sports jacket. She's a snappy dresser.*  4 SNAPPISH.  *adj.*, **snap·pi·er, snap·pi·est.**
**make it snappy,** *Informal.*  be quick about it; hurry: *We're waiting, so make it snappy with your phone call.*

**snap·shot** (snap′shot′)  an informal photograph, such as one taken by an amateur photographer with a hand-held camera, often without regard to artistic or creative effects: *We got some excellent snapshots at the picnic.*  *n.*

**snare**[1] (sner)  1 a noose for catching small animals and birds.  2 catch with a snare: *One day they snared a skunk.*  3 something that acts as a temptation and by which one is entangled; trap: *It is easy to be caught in the snare of quick profits.*  1, 3 *n.*, 2 *v.*, **snared, snar·ing.**

**snare**[2] (sner)  one of the twisted gut or rawhide strings or spiralled lengths of wire stretched across the bottom of a SNARE DRUM.  *n.*

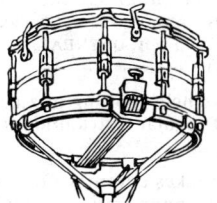

A snare drum, showing the snares on the bottom

**snare drum**  a small drum having lengths of wire, gut, or rawhide stretched across the bottom to make a rattling sound when the drum is struck.

**snarl**[1] (snärl)  1 of a dog, etc., growl while baring and snapping the teeth: *The dog snarled at the stranger.*  2 speak harshly in a sharp, menacing tone: *The kidnapper snarled at his prisoner.*  3 the act or sound of snarling.  4 say or express with a snarl: *The bully snarled a threat.*  1, 2, 4 *v.*, 3 *n.*  —**snarl′er,** *n.*  —**snarl′ing·ly,** *adv.*

**snarl**[2] (snärl)  1 a tangle, especially of hair, thread, yarn, etc.: *She combed the snarls out of her hair.*  2 confusion and disorder: *His legal affairs were in a snarl.*  3 tangle or become tangled: *The knitting yarn was badly snarled. Her hair snarls easily.*  4 complicate or confuse:

Traffic soon became snarled when the traffic lights broke down. 1, 2 n., 3, 4 v.

**snarl·y**¹ (snär′lē) inclined to snarl or growl; bad-tempered; cross. adj., **snarl·i·er, snarl·i·est.**

**snarl·y**² (snär′lē) tangled; full of snarls. adj., **snarl·i·er, snarl·i·est.**

**snatch** (snach) 1 seize suddenly; grasp hastily: *She snatched her jacket and ran.* 2 the act of snatching; a sudden grabbing movement: *The boy made a snatch at the ball.* 3 take suddenly: *He snatched off his hat and bowed.* 4 save or attain by quick action: *They snatched victory from defeat.* 5 a short time: *He had a snatch of sleep sitting in his chair.* 6 a small amount; bit; scrap: *to hear snatches of conversation.* 1, 3, 4 v., 2, 5, 6 n. —**snatch′er,** n.
**snatch at,** a try to seize or grasp: *Donna snatched at the railing to keep herself from falling.* b eagerly take advantage of: *He snatched at the chance to travel.*

**snatch·y** (snach′ē) done or occurring in snatches; disconnected; irregular: *She carried on a snatchy conversation with the man next to her in line.* adj. —**snatch′i·ly,** adv.

**sneak** (snēk) 1 move in a stealthy, sly way: *The man sneaked about the barn watching for a chance to steal the dog.* 2 the act of sneaking. 3 get, put, pass, etc. in a stealthy, sly way. 4 *Informal.* steal. 5 act in a mean, contemptible, cowardly way. 6 a person who sneaks; a sneaking, cowardly, contemptible person. 7 stealthy; underhand; sneaking: *a sneak thief, a sneak attack.* 8 someone who betrays his or her friends. 1, 3–5 v., **sneaked** or (*informal*) **snuck, sneak·ing;** 2, 6–8 n.
**sneak out of,** avoid by slyness.

**sneak·er** (snē′kər) 1 a light shoe with a cloth upper and pliable rubber sole, used for sports like tennis, badminton, etc. or for general casual wear: *She was dressed in a sweater, blue jeans, and sneakers.* 2 a person that sneaks; sneak. n.

**sneak·ing** (snē′king) 1 that one cannot justify or does not like to confess: *I have a sneaking suspicion that she doesn't know what she's talking about. He had a sneaking admiration for his adventuresome but irresponsible brother.* 2 mean and underhand; furtive and cowardly: *sneaking treachery, a sneaking manner.* 3 ppr. of SNEAK. 1, 2 adj., 3 v. —**sneak′ing·ly,** adv.

**sneak preview** a special single showing of a new motion picture in advance of regular distribution in order to test audience reaction.

**sneak thief** a person who takes advantage of open doors, windows, or other easy opportunities to steal.

**sneak·y** (snē′kē) sly, mean, or underhand. adj., **sneak·i·er, sneak·i·est.**

**sneer** (snēr) 1 smile, laugh, speak, etc. in such a way as to show contempt or scorn: *They sneered at his attempts to curry favour with the boss. She sneers at any expression of sentiment.* 2 a look or words expressing scorn or contempt: *There was a sneer on her face.* 3 say or express with scorn or contempt: *"Bah!" he sneered with a curl of his lip.* 1, 3 v., 2 n. —**sneer′er,** n. —**sneer′ing·ly,** adv.

**sneeze** (snēz) 1 expel air suddenly and violently through the nose and mouth by an involuntary spasm. 2 a sudden, violent expelling of air through the nose and mouth. 1 v., **sneezed, sneez·ing;** 2 n.
**not to be sneezed at,** *Informal.* not to be disregarded or despised; not to be made light of: *A saving of twenty dollars is not to be sneezed at.*

**snell** (snel) a short piece of gut, etc. by which a fish-hook is fastened to a longer line. n.

**snick**¹ (snik) 1 cut slightly; snip or nick. 2 a small cut; a nick. 3 in cricket, a light glancing blow given to the ball by the batsman, or the ball so hit. 4 give a cricket ball a light glancing blow. 1, 4 v., 2, 3 n.

**snick**² (snik) 1 make or cause to make a clicking sound. 2 a slight, sharp sound; click. 1 v., 2 n.

**snick·er** (snik′ər) 1 a half-suppressed and usually disrespectful laugh; sly or silly laugh; giggle. 2 laugh in this way. 1 n., 2 v.

**snide** (snīd) spitefully or slyly sarcastic: *When he did not get the part in the play, he started making snide remarks about the director.* adj.

**snies** (snīz) a pl. of SNYE. n.

**sniff** (snif) 1 draw air through the nose in short, quick breaths that can be heard. 2 smell with sniffs: *The dog sniffed suspiciously at the stranger.* 3 try the smell of. 4 draw in through the nose with the breath: *Louise sniffed the steam to clear her head.* 5 the act or sound of sniffing: *a loud sniff.* 6 a single breathing in of something; breath. 7 show contempt by sniffing: *to sniff at an inexpensive gift.* 8 suspect; detect: *The police sniffed a plot and broke up the meeting.* 1–4, 7, 8 v., 5, 6 n.

**snif·fle** (snif′əl) 1 sniff again and again: *Don't sniffle; blow your nose.* 2 the act or sound of sniffling. 3 **the sniffles,** *Informal.* a head cold marked by a runny nose and sniffling. 1 v., **snif·fled, snif·fling;** 2, 3 n. —**snif′fler,** n.

**sniff·y** (snif′ē) *Informal.* 1 inclined to sniff. 2 contemptuous; scornful; disdainful. adj., **sniff·i·er, sniff·i·est.**

**snif·ter** (snif′tər) 1 a pear-shaped glass having a short stem and used especially for brandy, the narrow top serving to retain the aroma of the liquor. 2 a small drink of liquor. n.

**snig·ger** (snig′ər) SNICKER. n., v.

**snip** (snip) 1 cut with a small, quick stroke or series of strokes with scissors: *She snipped the thread.* 2 the act of snipping: *With a few snips she cut out a paper doll.* 3 a small piece cut off: *Pick up the snips of cloth and thread from the floor.* 4 any small piece; bit; fragment. 5 *Informal.* a small or unimportant person. 6 **snips,** pl. hand shears for cutting metal. 1 v., **snipped, snip·ping;** 2–6 n.

**snipe** (snīp) 1 any of several related shore birds of the sandpiper family found in most parts of the world, having a long bill used in digging for worms in the mud, eyes set far back in the head, short legs with long toes, and a very short tail: *Only one species of snipe is found in North America. Snipe are important game birds in Europe.* 2 hunt snipe. 3 shoot as a SNIPER does. 1 n., pl. **snipe** or **snipes;** 2, 3 v., **sniped, snip·ing.**

**snip·er** (snī′pər) a person who shoots from a concealed place at one enemy or target at a time, as a hunter shoots at game. n.

**snip·pet** (snip′it) 1 a small piece snipped off; bit; scrap; fragment. 2 *Informal.* a small or unimportant person. n.

**snip·py** (snip′ē) 1 *Informal.* sharp; curt. 2 *Informal.* haughty; disdainful. 3 made up of scraps

**sniv·el** (sniv′əl) **1** cry with sniffling. **2** pretended grief or crying; whining. **3** put on a show of grief; whine. **4** run at the nose; sniffle. **5** a running from the nose; sniffling. 1, 3, 4 *v.*, **sniv·elled** or **sniv·eled**, **sniv·el·ling** or **sniv·el·ing**; 2, 5 *n.* —**sniv′el·ler** or **sniv′el·er**, *n.*

**snob** (snob) **1** a person who cares too much for rank, wealth, and position, being too anxious to please or imitate people above him or her and too ready to ignore those below him or her. **2** a person who is contemptuous of the popular taste in some field, and is attracted to esoteric or learned things for their own sake. *n.*

**snob·ber·y** (snob′ə rē) SNOBBISHness. *n., pl.* **snob·ber·ies**.

**snob·bish** (snob′ish) of or like a snob; looking down on those in a lower position. *adj.* —**snob′bish·ly**, *adv.* —**snob′bish·ness**, *n.*

**snood** (snüd) **1** a net or bag worn over a woman's hair: *A snood may be a part of a hat.* **2** a baglike hat. **3** in Scotland and northern England, a band or ribbon formerly worn around the hair by young unmarried women. **4** bind hair with a snood. 1–3 *n.*, 4 *v.*

**snook·er** (snúk′ər *or* snü′kər) a type of pool played with 15 red balls and six other balls of different colours. *n.*

**snoop** (snüp) *Informal.* **1** go about in a sneaking, prying way; prowl; pry: *The manager snooped into everybody's business.* **2** a person who snoops. 1 *v.*, 2 *n.* —**snoop′er**, *n.*

**snoot·y** (snü′tē) *Informal.* snobbish; conceited. *adj.* **snoot·i·er, snoot·i·est**.

**snooze** (snüz) *Informal.* **1** take a nap; sleep; doze. **2** a nap; doze. 1 *v.*, **snoozed, snooz·ing**; 2 *n.*

**snore** (snôr) **1** breathe during sleep with a harsh rough sound. **2** pass in snoring: *The lazy man snored away the afternoon.* **3** the sound made in snoring. 1, 2 *v.*, **snored, snor·ing**; 3 *n.*

**snor·kel** (snôr′kəl) **1** a shaft for taking in air and discharging gases that allows submarines to remain submerged for a long time. See SUBMARINE for picture. **2** a curved tube which enables swimmers to breathe under water while swimming near the surface. *n.*

**snort** (snôrt) **1** force the breath violently through the nose with a loud, harsh sound: *The horse snorted.* **2** make a sound like this: *The engine snorted.* **3** the act or sound of snorting. **4** show contempt, defiance, anger, etc. by snorting. **5** say or express with a snort: *"Indeed!" snorted my aunt.* 1, 2, 4, 5 *v.*, 3 *n.* —**snort′er**, *n.*

**snout** (snout) **1** the projecting part of an animal's head that contains the nose, mouth, and jaws: *Pigs, dogs, and crocodiles have snouts.* **2** anything like an animal's snout. **3** *Informal.* a person's nose, especially a large or ugly one. *n.*

**snout beetle** a small beetle whose head is prolonged to form a snout: *Snout beetles eat grain, nuts, and fruit.*

**snow** (snō) **1** water vapour frozen into crystals that fall to earth in soft, white flakes. **2** a fall of snow. **3** fall as snow: *to snow all day.* **4** let fall or scatter as snow: *Petals from the apple blossoms were snowing over the garden.* **5** cover, block up, etc. with snow or as if with snow. **6** something resembling or suggesting snow. **7** *Cdn.* SNOW APPLE. 1, 2, 6, 7 *n.*, 3–5 *v.*

---

## snivel 1127 snowflake

hat, āge, fär; let, ēqual, tėrm; it, īce
hot, ōpen, ôrder; oil, out; cup, pùt, rüle
above, takən, pencəl, lemən, circəs
ch, child; ng, long; sh, ship
th, thin; ᴛʜ, then; zh, measure

**snowed in**, shut in, covered, or blocked by snow: *The town was snowed in for a week.*
**snow under**, **a** cover with snow. **b** *Informal.* overwhelm: *He is snowed under with work.*

**snow apple** *Cdn.* a fine eating apple having crisp, white flesh and a deep-red skin.

**snow·ball** (snō′bol′) **1** a ball made of snow pressed together. **2** throw balls of snow at. **3** a shrub with white flowers in large clusters like balls. **4** increase rapidly by additions like a rolling snowball: *The number of signers of the petition for a swimming pool snowballed.* 1, 3 *n.*, 2, 4 *v.*

**snow·bank** (snō′bangk′) a large mass or drift of snow. *n.*

**snow·ber·ry** (snō′ber′ē) **1** a North American shrub that bears clusters of white berries in the fall. **2** the berry. *n., pl.* **snow·ber·ries**.

**snow·bird** (snō′bėrd′) *Cdn.* **1** SNOW BUNTING. **2** JUNCO. *n.*

**snow–blind** (snō′blīnd′) *Cdn.* suffering from SNOW BLINDNESS. *adj.*

**snow blindness** *Cdn.* a painful inflammation of the eyes caused by overexposure to the glare of sunlight on wide expanses of snow or ice, and resulting in temporary, partial, or complete blindness.

**snow·blow·er** (snō′blō′ər) *Cdn.* a machine that clears snow by drawing it in and blowing it out in another direction. *n.*

**snow·bound** (snō′bound′) shut in by snow; snowed in: *We were snowbound for two days after the blizzard and couldn't even get out for groceries.* *adj.*

**snow bunting** *Cdn.* a small songbird of the same family as grosbeaks, goldfinches, and sparrows that breeds in the Arctic and winters in northern temperate regions, having mostly white plumage with back and wings black in breeding season and mainly rusty brown in winter: *The snow bunting is a common sight in most of southern Canada in winter; in the Arctic, it is a harbinger of spring.*

**snow·capped** (snō′kapt′) having its top covered with snow. *adj.*

**snow·drift** (snō′drift′) **1** a mass or bank of snow piled up by the wind. **2** snow driven before the wind. *n.*

**snow·drop** (snō′drop′) a small plant having white flowers that blooms early in the spring. *n.*

**snow·fall** (snō′fol′) **1** a fall of snow. **2** the amount of snow falling within a certain time and area: *The snowfall in that one storm was 30 centimetres.* *n.*

**snow fence** *Cdn.* a lath-and-wire fence erected in winter alongside roads, etc. on the windward side to prevent snow from drifting.

**snow fencing** *Cdn.* **1** the material of which SNOW FENCES are made. **2** a SNOW FENCE.

**snow·flake** (snō′flāk′) a small, feathery piece of snow. *n.*

**snow goose** *Cdn.* a wild goose that breeds in the Arctic, the adult typically white with black wing tips and having a pinkish bill with a blackish patch on each side and reddish legs and feet: *Some snow geese are mainly bluish grey with a white head and are popularly called* **blue geese,** *but they belong to the same species.*

**snow·i·ness** (snō′ē nis) **1** being snowy. **2** whiteness. *n.*

**snow lily** *Cdn.* GLACIER LILY.

**snow line** a height on mountains, etc. above which there is snow all year round.

**snow·man** (snō′man′) a mass of snow made into a figure shaped somewhat like a person. *n., pl.* **snow·men** (-men′).

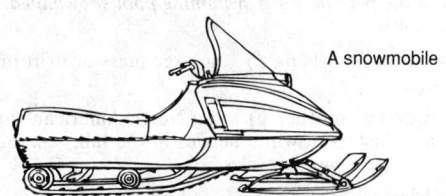
A snowmobile

**snow·mo·bile** (snō′mə bēl′) *Cdn.* **1** a small, open motor vehicle for travelling over snow and ice, equipped with skis at the front, by which it is steered, and a caterpillar track beneath the body: *Snowmobiles are used as a means of transportation, especially in the North, and also for sport.* **2** a large, closed-in vehicle similar to this, but having two tracks and designed to carry a number of persons, goods, etc.; Bombardier. See BOMBARDIER for picture. **3** travel by snowmobile. **1, 2** *n.,* **3** *v.,* **snow·mo·biled, snow·mo·bil·ing.**

**snow·plough** or **snow·plow** (snō′plou′) a machine for clearing away snow from streets, railway tracks, etc. by means of a large blade that pushes the snow aside as the machine moves forward. *n.*

**snow·shed** (snō′shed′) a long shed built over a railway track or a highway to protect it from snowslides. *n.*

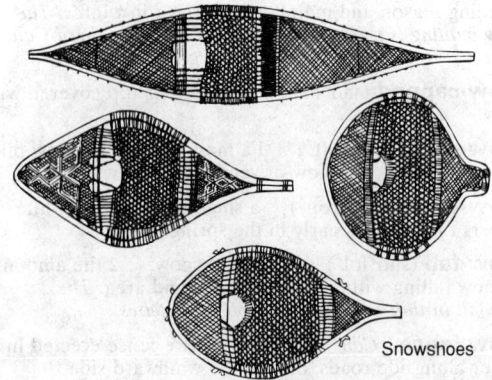
Snowshoes

**snow·shoe** (snō′shü′) **1** a light wooden frame with strips of leather stretched across it: *Trappers in the Far North wear snowshoes on their feet to keep from sinking in deep, soft snow.* **2** walk or travel on snowshoes. **1** *n.,* **2** *v.,* **snow·shoed, snow·shoe·ing.**

**snow shovel** a shovel having a square blade with a straight edge and slightly curved sides for clearing snow.

**snow·slide** (snō′slīd′) **1** the sliding down of a mass of snow on a steep slope. **2** the mass of snow that slides. *n.*

**snow snake 1** a North American Indian game in which a wooden stick is slid as far as possible along a smooth patch of ice or snow, or along a furrow in snow. **2** the stick used in this game.

**snow·storm** (snō′stôrm′) a storm with much snow. *n.*

**snow thrower** SNOWBLOWER.

**snow–white** (snō′wīt′ *or* snō′hwīt′) white as snow. *adj.*

**snow·y** (snō′ē) **1** having snow. **2** covered with snow: *Brush off your snowy clothing.* **3** like snow; white as snow: *Grandmother has snowy hair.* *adj.,* **snow·i·er, snow·i·est.**

**snowy owl** a large owl ranging the arctic tundras of the world, having mainly white plumage with some brown spots or bars (more in the female), yellow eyes, and feathered toes. The female is bigger than the male.

**snub** (snub) **1** treat coldly, scornfully, or with contempt: *The wealthy widow snubbed her poor cousin.* **2** cold, scornful, or disdainful treatment. **3** check or stop a boat, horse, etc. suddenly. **4** check or stop a rope or cable running out suddenly. **5** a sudden check or stop. **6** a sharp rebuke. **1, 3, 4** *v.,* **snubbed, snub·bing; 2, 5, 6** *n.*

**snub·by** (snub′ē) short and turned up at the tip. *adj.,* **snub·bi·er, snub·bi·est.**

**snub nose** a short, turned-up nose.

**snub–nosed** (snub′nōzd′) **1** having a short, turned-up nose. **2** of a handgun, having a short barrel. *adj.*

**snuff¹** (snuf) **1** draw in through the nose; draw up into the nose: *He snuffs up salt and water to cure a cold.* **2** sniff; smell: *The dog snuffed at the track of the fox.* **3** powdered tobacco that is snuffed into the nose. **4** take powdered tobacco into the nose by snuffing; use snuff. **1, 2, 4** *v.,* **3** *n.*
**up to snuff,** *Informal.* in perfect order or condition; as good as expected.

**snuff²** (snuf) **1** cut or pinch off the burned wick of a candle. **2** put out a candle; extinguish. **3** the burned part of a candlewick. **1, 2** *v.,* **3** *n.*
**snuff out, a** put out; extinguish. **b** put an end to suddenly and completely: *The new dictator snuffed out the people's hopes for freedom.*

**snuff·box** (snuf′boks′) a small box for holding SNUFF¹ (def. 3). *n.*

**snuff·ers** (snuf′ərz) small tongs for taking off burned wick or putting out the light of a candle. *n.pl.*

**snuf·fle** (snuf′əl) **1** breathe noisily through a partly clogged nose. **2** the act or sound of snuffling. **3** smell; sniff. **4** speak, sing, etc. through the nose or with a nasal tone. **5** the nasal tone of voice of a person who snuffles. **6 the snuffles, a** a fit of snuffling; a stuffed-up condition of the nose, caused by a cold, hay fever, etc. **b** a respiratory disease of animals. **1, 3, 4** *v.,* **snuf·fled, snuf·fling; 2, 5, 6** *n.*

**snug** (snug) **1** comfortable; warm; sheltered: *The cat has found a snug corner behind the stove.* **2** neat; trim; compact: *The cabins on the boat are snug.* **3** well-built;

**seaworthy:** *a snug ship.* **4** make snug. **5** fitting closely: *That coat is a little too snug.* **6** small but sufficient: *A snug income enables him to live in comfort.* **7** hidden; concealed: *He lay snug until the searchers passed by.* **8** in a snug manner. 1–3, 5–7 *adj.*, **snug·ger, snug·gest;** 4 *v.*, **snugged, snug·ging;** 8 *adv.* —**snug′ly,** *adv.* —**snug′ness,** *n.*

**snug·ger·y** (snug′ə rē) a snug place, position, room, etc. *n.*, *pl.* **snug·ger·ies.**

**snug·gle** (snug′əl) **1** lie or press closely for warmth or comfort or from affection; nestle; cuddle. **2** draw closely. *v.*, **snug·gled, snug·gling.**

**snye** or **sny** (snī) *Cdn.* a side channel of a stream: *There are many snyes in the Mackenzie River.* *n.*, *pl.* **snyes** or **snies.**
☞ *Etym.* From Cdn. F *chenail* 'channel' (especially a side channel that bypasses a falls or rapids), which came through OF *chanel* from L *canalem* 'pipe, channel'. OF *chanel* is also the source of CHANNEL.

**so**[1] (sō; unstressed before consonants, sə) **1** in this way; in that way; as shown: *Hold your pen so.* **2** in such a way as stated: *Is that really so?* **3** to this degree; to that degree: *Do not walk so fast.* **4** to such a degree; to the same degree: *He was not so cold as she was.* **5** very: *You are so kind.* **6** very much: *My head aches so.* **7** for this reason; for that reason; accordingly; therefore: *The dog was hungry; so we fed it.* **8** with the result that; in order that: *Go away so I can rest.* **9** with the purpose or intention that: *I did the work so she would not need to.* **10** on the condition that, if: *So it be done, I care not who does it.* **11** likewise; also: *She likes dogs; so does he.* **12** well! **13** let it be that way! all right! **14** is that true? **15** what now! so what? **16** more or less; approximately that: *a kilogram or so.* **17** the same: *He is unconscious and may remain so for some time.* **18** whatever has been or is going to be said; this; that: *She will say so.* 1–7, 11 *adv.*, 8–10 *conj.*, 12–15 *interj.*, 16–18 *pron.*
**and so,** **a** likewise; also: *Piet is here, and so is Josef.* **b** accordingly: *I said I would go, and so I shall.*
**or so,** more or less: *It came a day or so ago.*
**so as,** with the aim or purpose: *She goes to bed early so as to get enough sleep.*
**so that,** **a** with the result that. **b** with the purpose that. **c** provided that; if.
☞ *Hom.* SEW, SOW[1].

**so**[2] (sō) SOL. *n.*
☞ *Hom.* SEW, SOW[1].

**s.o.** or **so** in baseball: **1** struck out. **2** strike out.

**So.** **1** South. **2** Southern.

**soak** (sōk) **1** make very wet; wet through. **2** let remain in water or other liquid until wet through. **3** become very wet; remain until wet through. **4** make its way; enter; go: *Water will soak through the earth.* **5** suck: *The sponge soaked up the water.* **6** the act or process of soaking: *Give the clothes a long soak.* **7** the state of being soaked. **8** the liquid in which anything is soaked. 1–5 *v.*, 6–8 *n.*
**soak up,** **a** absorb or suck up: *soak up sunshine. The sponge soaked up the water.* **b** take into the mind: *soak up knowledge.*

**so-and-so** (sō′ənd sō′) **1** a person or thing not named. **2** *Informal.* an unpleasant or distasteful person. *n.*, *pl.* **so-and-sos.**

**soap** (sōp) **1** a substance used for washing, usually made of a fat and caustic soda or potash. **2** rub with soap: *Soap the dirty shirts well.* 1 *n.*, 2 *v.* —**soap′less,** *adj.*

# snuggery 1129 Soc.

hat, āge, fär; let, ēqual, tėrm; it, īce
hot, ōpen, ôrder; oil, out; cup, pùt, rüle
əbove, takən, pencəl, lemən, circəs
ch, child; ng, long; sh, ship
th, thin; ᴛʜ, then; zh, measure

**soap·ber·ry** (sōp′ber′ē) **1** any of a closely related group of mainly tropical woody plants or trees bearing fruit that is used as a soap substitute. **2** the fruit or nut of a soapberry. **3** *Cdn.* a low shrub closely related to the buffalo berry, found throughout Canada and the northern United States. *n.*, *pl.* **soap·ber·ries.**

**soap·box** (sōp′boks′) **1** a box, especially of wood, in which soap is packed. **2** an empty box used as a temporary platform by agitators or other speakers addressing gatherings in the open air. **3** address an audience in the open air. 1, 2 *n.*, 3 *v.*

**soap opera** a radio or television drama presented in serial form, often during the daytime, usually featuring emotional domestic situations.

**soap·stone** (sōp′stōn′) a heavy, soft stone that feels somewhat like soap: *Inuit carvings are often made of soapstone.* *n.*

**soap·suds** (sōp′sudz′) bubbles and foam made with soap and water. *n.pl.*

**soap·y** (sōp′ē) **1** covered with soap or soapsuds. **2** containing soap. **3** of or like soap; smooth; greasy. *adj.*, **soap·i·er, soap·i·est.**

**soar** (sôr) **1** fly at a great height; fly upward: *The eagle soared without flapping its wings.* **2** rise beyond what is common and ordinary; aspire: *Prices are soaring. Geza's hopes soared when he found there was a letter for him.* **3** reach in soaring. **4** fly or move through the air by means of rising air currents: *a hawk soaring in the sky. A glider can soar for a great distance.* *v.*
☞ *Hom.* SORE.

**sob** (sob) **1** cry or sigh with short, quick breaths. **2** a catching of short, quick breaths, because of grief, etc. **3** the sound of this. **4** put, send, etc. by sobbing: *Tuune sobbed herself to sleep.* **5** make a sound like a sob: *The wind sobbed.* **6** say or express with sobs: *Martina sobbed out her sad story.* 1, 4–6 *v.*, **sobbed, sob·bing;** 2, 3 *n.*

**so·ber** (sō′bər) **1** not drunk. **2** temperate; moderate: *The Puritans led sober, hard-working lives.* **3** quiet; serious; solemn: *a sober expression.* **4** calm; sensible: *The judge's sober opinion was not influenced by prejudice or strong feeling.* **5** free from exaggeration: *sober facts.* **6** make or become sober: *Seeing the car accident sobered us all.* **7** quiet in colour: *dressed in sober grey.* 1–5, 7 *adj.*, 6 *v.* —**so′ber·ly,** *adv.* —**so′ber·ness,** *n.*
**sober down,** become quiet, serious, or solemn.
**sober up** or **off,** recover from too much alcoholic drink.

**so·ber-mind·ed** (sō′bər mīn′did) having or showing a sober mind; self-controlled; sensible. *adj.*

**so·bri·e·ty** (sə brī′ə tē) **1** soberness. **2** temperance in the use of alcoholic liquors. **3** moderation. **4** quietness; seriousness. *n.*, *pl.* **so·bri·e·ties.**

**so·bri·quet** (sō′brə kā′) NICKNAME. *n.* Also, **soubriquet.**

**sob story** *Informal.* a story that is excessively pathetic or sentimental.

**Soc.** **1** Society. **2** Socialist.

**so-called** (sō′kold′) **1** called thus. **2** called thus improperly or incorrectly: *Nina's so-called friend dislikes her. adj.*

**soc·cer** (sok′ər) **1** a game played between two teams of eleven players each, using a round ball; association football: *In soccer, only the goalkeeper may touch the ball with hands and arms.* **2** of or having to do with soccer: *a soccer ball, a soccer team. n.*

**so·cia·bil·i·ty** (sō′shə bil′ə tē) one's social disposition or behaviour. *n., pl.* **so·cia·bil·i·ties.**

**so·cia·ble** (sō′shə bəl) **1** liking company; friendly: *The O'Hares are a sociable family and entertain a great deal.* **2** marked by conversation and companionship: *We had a sociable afternoon together.* **3** an informal social gathering. *1, 2 adj., 3 n.* —**so′cia·bly,** *adv.*

**so·cial** (sō′shəl) **1** of or dealing with human beings in their relations to each other; having to do with the life of human beings in a community: *social problems. History and geography are social sciences.* **2** living, or liking to live, with others: *Human beings are social creatures.* **3** for companionship or friendliness; having to do with companionship or friendliness: *a social club.* **4** liking company: *She has a social nature.* **5** connected with fashionable society: *a social leader.* **6** a social gathering or party: *Ice cream was served at the club social.* **7** of animals, living together in organized communities: *Ants and bees are social insects.* **8** SOCIALISTIC. *1–5, 7, 8 adj., 6 n.*

**Social Credit Party** a Canadian political party founded in Alberta in the 1930's.

**Social Credit Rally** a Canadian political party formed in 1962 from the Quebec wing of the SOCIAL CREDIT PARTY.

**social insurance** benefits, such as old-age pension, family allowance, unemployment insurance, etc., provided by a government.

**Social Insurance Number** *Cdn.* a nine-digit number by which the federal government identifies an individual for purposes of income tax, unemployment insurance, old-age pension, etc. *Abbrev.*: SIN

**so·cial·ism** (sō′shə liz′əm) a political and economic system in which the means of production and distribution are owned, managed, or controlled by a central, democratically elected authority. Compare with CAPITALISM and COMMUNISM. *n.*

**so·cial·ist** (sō′shə list) **1** a person who favours and supports SOCIALISM. **2** SOCIALISTIC. *1 n., 2 adj.*

**so·cial·is·tic** (sō′shə lis′tik) **1** of or having to do with SOCIALISM and socialists. **2** advocating or supporting SOCIALISM. *adj.* —**so′cial·is′ti·cal·ly,** *adv.*

**so·cial·ite** (sō′shə līt′) a person who is prominent in society. *n.*

**so·cial·ize** (sō′shə līz′) **1** make social; make fit for living with others. **2** establish or regulate in accordance with SOCIALISM. *v.,* **so·cial·ized, so·cial·iz·ing.**

**socialized medicine** the providing of medical care and hospital services for all classes of society, especially through government subsidization and administration.

**so·cial·ly** (sō′shə lē) **1** in a social way or manner; in relation to other people. **2** as a member of society or of a social group: *He is an able man, but socially he is a failure. adv.*

**social science** the study of people, their activities, and their customs in relationship to others: *History, sociology, economics, and civics are social sciences.*

**social security** *Esp. U.S.* SOCIAL INSURANCE.

**social service** SOCIAL WORK.

**social studies** school subjects, including history and geography, that deal with the development of peoples, their societies, and the parts of the world in which they live.

**social work** work directed toward the betterment of social conditions in a community: *Social work includes such services as medical clinics, counselling for families, and the organization of recreational activities.*

**social worker** a person who does SOCIAL WORK.

**so·ci·e·ty** (sə sī′ə tē) **1** a group of persons joined together for a common purpose or by a common interest: *A club, fraternity, lodge, or association may be called a society.* **2** all the people; the people of any particular time or place; their activities and customs: *Drug-control laws are passed for the good of society.* **3** those people thought of as a group because of common economic position, similar interests, etc.: *in cultivated society.* **4** company; companionship: *I enjoy his society.* **5** fashionable people; their doings: *She is a leader of society. n., pl.* **so·ci·e·ties.**

**so·ci·o–e·co·nom·ic** (sō′sē ō ē′kə nom′ik *or* sō′sē ō ek′ə nom′ik) of or having to do with social and economic matters: *a socio-economic study on poverty in big cities. adj.*

**so·ci·o·log·i·cal** (sō′sē ə loj′ə kəl) **1** of or having to do with human society or problems relating to it: *The care of the poor is a sociological problem.* **2** of SOCIOLOGY. *adj.*

**so·ci·o·log·i·cal·ly** (sō′sē ə loj′i klē) according to SOCIOLOGY. *adv.*

**so·ci·ol·o·gist** (sō′sē ol′ə jist) a student of human society and its problems; one skilled in SOCIOLOGY. *n.*

**so·ci·ol·o·gy** (sō′sē ol′ə jē) the study of the nature, origin, and development of human society and community life; science of society: *Sociology deals with social conditions, such as crime and poverty, and social institutions, such as marriage and religion.* *n.*

**sock** (sok) **1** a close-fitting, knitted covering for the foot and lower leg. **2** in ancient Greece and Rome, a light shoe worn by actors in comedy. *n.*

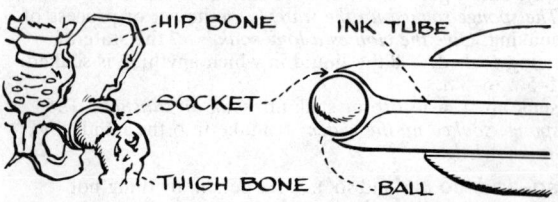

The hip joint, a ball-and-socket joint

The ball and socket forming the tip of a ball-point pen

**sock·et** (sok′it) **1** a hollow part or piece for receiving and holding something: *A candlestick has a socket in which to set a candle. A person's eyes are set in sockets. An electric* lamp has a socket into which a bulb is screwed. **2** a connecting place for electric wires and plugs. *n.*

**sock·eye** (sok′ī) *Cdn.* a species of small Pacific salmon found along the coasts of British Columbia and Alaska, greenish blue and metallic green in colour and having red, oily flesh highly valued for its flavour: *The sockeye changes colour to a bright red in spawning season.* *n., pl.* **sock·eye** or **sock·eyes.**

**So·crat·ic** (sō krat′ik) of or having to do with Socrates (469–399 B.C.), a famous Athenian philosopher, his philosophy, followers, etc. *adj.*

**So·cred** (sō′kred) *Cdn. Informal.* **1** Usually, **Socreds**, the SOCIAL CREDIT PARTY. **2** a member of this party. *n.*

**sod** (sod) **1** ground covered with grass. **2** a piece or layer of ground containing the grass and its roots. **3** cover with sods. 1, 2 *n.*, 3 *v.*, **sod·ded, sod·ding. under the sod,** buried.

**so·da** (sō′də) **1** any of several substances containing SODIUM, such as SODIUM CARBONATE, SODIUM BICARBONATE, CAUSTIC SODA, or sodium oxide: *Soda is used in the manufacture of soap and glass. Washing soda, or sal soda, is used in cleaning. Baking soda is used in cooking and as a medicine.* **2** SODA WATER. **3** SODA WATER flavoured with fruit juice or syrup, and often containing ice cream. *n.*

**soda ash** partly purified sodium carbonate.

**soda biscuit** a simple, light, thin biscuit made with little or no sugar or shortening.

**soda cracker** a SODA BISCUIT.

**soda fountain** **1** an apparatus for holding SODA WATER, syrups, ice, etc. and having taps for drawing off the liquids. **2** a counter with places for holding SODA WATER, flavoured syrups, ice cream, etc. **3** a store having such a counter.

**so·dal·i·ty** (sō dal′ə tē) **1** fellowship; friendship. **2** an association, society, or fraternity. **3** in the Roman Catholic Church, a society with religious or charitable purposes. *n., pl.* **so·dal·i·ties.**

**soda water** water charged with carbon dioxide to make it bubble and fizz, often served with the addition of syrup, ice cream, etc.

**sod·den** (sod′ən) **1** soaked through: *The girl's clothing was sodden with rain.* **2** heavy and moist: *This bread is sodden because it was not baked well.* **3** dull-looking; stupid. *adj.* —**sod′den·ness,** *n.*

**so·di·um** (sō′dē əm) a soft, silver-white metallic element which reacts violently with water and occurs in nature only in compounds: *Salt and soda contain sodium.* Symbol: Na *n.*

**sodium bicarbonate** a powdery white salt used in cooking, medicine, etc.; baking soda; bicarbonate of soda.

**sodium carbonate** a salt that occurs in a powdery white form and in a hydrated crystalline form; washing soda.

**sodium chloride** common salt.

**sodium cyanide** a very poisonous substance, composed of fine white crystals, used in the cyanide process for extracting gold and silver from ores, in fumigating, etc.

**sodium fluoride** a crystalline salt, poisonous in large quantities, used as an insecticide and disinfectant and as a preventive of tooth decay.

hat, āge, fär; let, ēqual, tėrm; it, īce
hot, ōpen, ôrder; oil, out; cup, pùt, rüle
əbove, takən, pencəl, lemən, circəs
ch, child; ng, long; sh, ship
th, thin; ᴛʜ, then; zh, measure

**sodium hydroxide** a white solid that is a strong, corrosive alkali; caustic soda.

**sodium nitrate** colourless crystals used in making fertilizers, explosives, etc.; Chile saltpetre.

**so·fa** (sō′fə) a long, upholstered seat or couch having a back and arms; chesterfield. *n.*

**soft** (soft) **1** not hard; yielding readily to touch or pressure: *a soft pillow.* **2** not hard compared with other things of the same kind: *Pine wood is softer than oak. Copper and lead are softer than steel.* **3** not hard or sharp; gentle and graceful: *soft shadows, soft outlines.* **4** fine in texture; not rough or coarse; smooth: *soft skin.* **5** not loud: *a soft voice.* **6** quietly pleasant; mild; not harsh: *soft air.* **7** not glaring or harsh: *soft light.* **8** gentle; kind; tender: *a soft heart.* **9** weak; unmanly: *The soldiers had become soft from idleness.* **10** silly. **11** softly; quietly; gently. **12** that which is soft; a soft part. **13** in pronunciation, having the sound of *c* and *g* as (s) (*city*) and (j) (*gem*), and not as stops as in *corn* and *go.* **14** *Informal.* easy; easy-going: *a soft job, a soft person.* **15** of wheat, containing little GLUTEN. 1–10, 13–15 *adj.*, 11 *adv.*, 12 *n.* —**soft′ly,** *adv.*

**soft·ball** (soft′bol) **1** a modified kind of baseball game that uses a larger and softer ball. **2** the ball used in that game. *n.*

**soft–boiled** (soft′boild′) of eggs, boiled only a little so that the yolk is still soft. *adj.*

**soft coal** BITUMINOUS COAL.

**soft copy** computer data that is not printed out but remains on the disk.

**soft drink** a refreshing cold drink that does not contain alcohol: *Ginger ale is a soft drink.*

**soft·en** (sof′ən) **1** make softer: *Hand lotion softens the skin.* **2** become softer: *Soap softens in water.* **3** (often used with **up**) lessen the ability of a country, region, etc. to resist invasion or attack through preliminary bombing, etc. *v.* —**soft′en·er,** *n.*

**soft–heart·ed** (soft′här′tid) gentle; kind; tender. *adj.* —**soft′-heart′ed·ness,** *n.*

**soft·ness** (soft′nis) the state of being soft; ease; comfort; mildness; gentleness; weakness. *n.*

**soft palate** the fleshy back part of the roof of the mouth.

**soft–ped·al** (soft′ped′əl) **1** use a pedal on a piano, organ, etc. to soften musical tones. **2** make quieter, less noticeable, or less strong. *v.*, **soft–ped·alled** or **soft–ped·aled, soft–ped·al·ling** or **soft–ped·al·ing.**

**soft return** a computer operation to start a new line, that is performed by the program and not by the user.

**soft sell** *Informal.* a sales approach that uses indirect, persuasive tactics rather than pushing, aggressive ones. Compare with HARD SELL.

**soft soap** 1 a liquid or partly liquid soap. 2 *Informal.* flattery.

**soft–soap** (soft′sōp′) *Informal.* flatter; cajole. *v.* —**soft′-soap′er**, *n.*

**soft–spo·ken** (soft′spō′kən) 1 speaking with a soft voice. 2 spoken softly. *adj.*

**soft spot** 1 a feeling of tenderness or affection: *She still had a soft spot in her heart for her first boyfriend.* 2 a vulnerable spot or point: *a soft spot in an otherwise strong argument.*

**soft touch** *Informal.* a person who lends or gives money easily.

**soft·ware** (sof′twer′) in computing science, the programs, programming languages, etc. that are necessary to the operation of computers. Compare with HARDWARE. *n.*

**soft water** water containing few or no minerals, in which soapsuds are easily formed and clothes, etc. are easily washed.

**soft·wood** (sof′twůd′) 1 wood that is easily cut. 2 a tree that has needles or does not have broad leaves: *Pines and firs are softwoods; oaks and maples are hardwoods.* 3 the wood of such a tree. *n.*

**soft·y** (sof′tē) *Informal.* 1 a soft, silly, or weak person. 2 one who is easily imposed upon. *n., pl.* **soft·ies.**

**sog·gy** (sog′ē) 1 thoroughly wet; soaked: *a soggy washcloth.* 2 damp and heavy: *soggy bread. adj.,* **sog·gi·er, sog·gi·est.** —**sog′gi·ness,** *n.*

**soil**[1] (soil) 1 ground; earth; dirt: *A farmer tills the soil.* 2 something thought of as a place for growth. 3 one's land; country: *my native soil. n.*

**soil**[2] (soil) 1 make dirty: *He soiled his clean clothes.* 2 become dirty: *White shirts soil easily.* 3 spot; stain: *Splashes of paint soiled the wall.* 4 disgrace; dishonour: *His actions have soiled the family name.* 5 corrupt morally. *v.*

**soi·ree** or **soi·rée** (swä rā′) an evening party or social gathering. *n.*

**so·journ** (sō jėrn′ *or* sō′jėrn *for verb,* sō′jėrn *for noun*) 1 stay for a time: *We sojourned for three weeks in Florida.* 2 a brief stay. 1 *v.,* 2 *n.* —**so·journ′er,** *n.*

**sol** (sōl) in music: 1 the fifth tone of an eight-tone major scale. 2 the tone G. See DO[2] for picture. *n.* Also, **so**[2].
☛ *Hom.* SOLE, SOUL.

**sol.** 1 solution. 2 soluble.

**sol·ace** (sol′is) 1 a comfort; relief: *She found solace from her troubles in music.* 2 comfort; relieve: *He solaced himself with a book.* 1 *n.,* 2 *v.,* **sol·aced, sol·ac·ing.**

**so·lar** (sō′lər) 1 of the sun: *a solar eclipse.* 2 having to do with the sun: *solar research.* 3 coming from the sun: *solar heat.* 4 See SOLAR SYSTEM. 5 measured or determined by the earth's motion in relation to the sun: *solar time.* 6 working by means of the sun's light or heat: *A solar battery traps sunlight and converts it into electrical energy.* 1–3, 5, 6 *adj.,* 4 *n.*

**solar cell** a small device for converting sunlight into electrical energy. It consists of thin wafers of a semiconductor such as silicon to which traces of certain other substances have been added. Sunlight striking the semiconductor produces charges which flow from the cell as an electric current.

**solar collector** a device, such as a glass-covered metal pan or plate that has been painted dull black, used to trap heat from sunlight: *Solar collectors are used together with a storage device and a distribution system to provide heating for buildings, etc.*

**solar day** the period of time from when the sun is at the meridian at any place on earth until the next time it reaches the same meridian.

**solar energy** energy derived from the sun's radiation as a source of electrical power.

**solar flare** a sudden discharge of gases on the sun, usually associated with sunspots.

**solar house** a house designed to obtain part or all of its space and water heating directly from the sun by means of solar collectors, large windows facing the winter sun, etc.

**so·lar·i·um** (sə ler′ē əm) a room, porch, etc. where people can lie or sit in the sun. *n., pl.* **so·lar·i·a** (-ler′ē ə).

**solar plex·us** (plek′səs) 1 the network of nerves situated at the upper part of the abdomen, behind the stomach and in front of the aorta. 2 *Informal.* the pit of the stomach.

**solar system** the sun and all the planets, satellites, comets, etc. that revolve around it.

**solar wind** a continuous flow of ionized gas particles from the sun into space.

**solar year** the period of time required for the earth to make one revolution around the sun, which equals about 365¼ days.

**sold** (sōld) pt. and pp. of SELL. *v.*

**sol·der** (sod′ər) 1 a metal or alloy that can be melted and used for joining or mending metal surfaces, parts, etc. 2 fasten, mend, or join with solder. 3 anything that unites firmly or joins closely. 4 unite firmly; join closely. 5 mend; repair; patch. 1, 3 *n.,* 2, 4, 5 *v.* —**sol′der·er,** *n.*

**sol·dier** (sōl′jər) 1 a person who serves in an army. 2 a private or non-commissioned officer. 3 a person having skill or experience in war. 4 a person who serves in any cause: *soldiers in the battle against drugs.* 5 in colonies of certain ants, a defending worker having a large head and powerful jaws. 6 in colonies of termites, a large-headed individual who fights in defence of the colony. 7 act or serve as a soldier. 1–6 *n.,* 7 *v.*

**sol·dier·ly** (sōl′jər lē) like a soldier; suitable for a soldier. *adj.*

**soldier of fortune** a man serving or ready to serve as a soldier under any government for money, adventure, or pleasure; military adventurer; mercenary.

**sol·dier·y** (sōl′jə rē) 1 soldiers collectively. 2 a body of soldiers. 3 military training or knowledge. *n., pl.* **sol·dier·ies.**

**sole**[1] (sōl) 1 one and only; single: *the sole heir.* 2 only: *the sole survivors.* 3 of or for only one person or group and not others; exclusive: *the sole right of use.* 4 alone: *a sole undertaking. adj.*
☛ *Hom.* SOL, SOUL.

**sole²** (sōl)  1 the bottom or under surface of the foot. 2 the bottom of a shoe, slipper, boot, etc.  3 a piece of leather, rubber, etc. cut in the shape of the bottom of a shoe, slipper, boot, etc.  4 put a sole on.  5 the under surface; under part; bottom.   1–3, 5 *n.*, 4 *v.*, **soled, sol·ing.**
☛ *Hom.* SOL, SOUL.

**sole³** (sōl)  a kind of flatfish: *European sole is valued highly as food.*  *n.*, *pl.* **sole** or **soles.**
☛ *Hom.* SOL, SOUL.

**sol·e·cism** (sol′ə siz′əm)  1 a violation of the grammatical or other accepted usages of a language; mistake in using words: *I done it is a solecism.*  2 a mistake in social behaviour; breach of good manners or etiquette.  *n.*

**sole·ly** (sōl′lē)  1 as the only one or ones; alone: *You will be solely responsible.*  2 only; purely; entirely: *She does it solely for convenience.*  *adv.*

**sol·emn** (sol′əm)  1 serious; grave; earnest: *a solemn face.*  2 causing serious or grave thoughts: *The organ played solemn music.*  3 done with form and ceremony: *a solemn procession.*  4 connected with religion; sacred.  *adj.*  —**sol′emn·ly,** *adv.*  —**sol′emn·ness,** *n.*

**so·lem·ni·ty** (sə lem′nə tē)  1 a solemn feeling; seriousness; impressiveness: *The solemnity of the funeral was felt even by the children.*  2 a solemn, formal ceremony: *The solemnities were concluded with the singing of the national anthem.*  *n.*, *pl.* **so·lem·ni·ties.**

**sol·em·nize** (sol′əm nīz′)  1 observe with ceremonies: *Remembrance Day is solemnized with special ceremonies.*  2 hold or perform a ceremony or service: *The marriage was solemnized before a large crowd.*  3 make serious or grave.  *v.*, **sol·em·nized, sol·em·niz·ing.**  —**sol′em·ni·za′tion,** *n.*

**so·le·noid** (sō′lə noid′)  a spiral or cylindrical coil of wire that acts like a magnet when an electric current passes through it.  *n.*

**so·lic·it** (sə lis′it)  1 ask earnestly; try to get: *The tailor sent around cards soliciting trade.*  2 make appeals or requests: *to solicit for contributions.*  3 influence to do wrong; tempt; entice: *To solicit a judge means to offer him or her bribes.*  *v.*

**so·lic·i·ta·tion** (sə lis′ə tā′shən)  1 an earnest request; entreaty.  2 an urging to do wrong; temptation; enticement.  *n.*

**so·lic·i·tor** (sə lis′ə tər)  1 a person who entreats or requests.  2 a person who seeks trade or business.  3 a lawyer, especially one who does not plead in court.  4 a lawyer for a town, city, etc.  *n.*

**so·lic·i·tor gen·er·al** (sə lis′ə tər jen′ə rəl or sə lis′ə tər jen′rəl)  1 in Canada, one of the two federal law officers of the Crown, the other being the ATTORNEY GENERAL.  2 a chief law officer, usually ranking next below an ATTORNEY GENERAL.  *n.*, *pl.* **so·lic·i·tors gen·er·al.**

**so·lic·it·ous** (sə lis′ə təs)  1 showing care or concern; anxious; concerned: *Parents are solicitous for their children's progress.*  2 desirous; eager: *solicitous to please.*  *adj.*  —**so·lic′it·ous·ly,** *adv.*  —**so·lic′it·ous·ness,** *n.*

**so·lic·i·tude** (sə lis′ə tyüd′ or sə lis′ə tüd′)  anxious care; anxiety; concern: *That woman shows great solicitude for her aging mother.*  *n.*

hat, āge, fär; let, ēqual, tėrm; it, īce
hot, ōpen, ôrder; oil, out; cup, pụt, rüle
əbove, takən, pencəl, lemən, circəs
ch, child; ng, long; sh, ship
th, thin; ᴛʜ, then; zh, measure

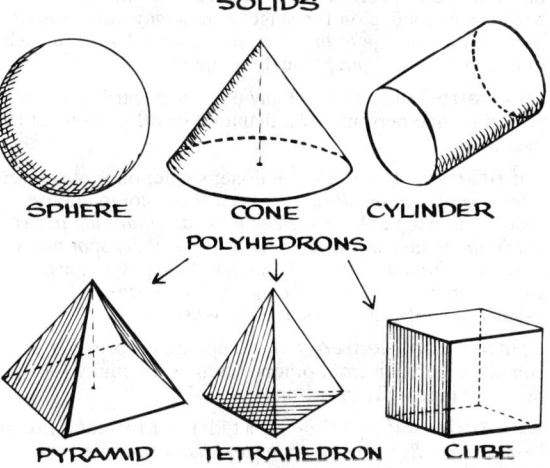

SOLIDS — SPHERE, CONE, CYLINDER
POLYHEDRONS — PYRAMID, TETRAHEDRON, CUBE

**sol·id** (sol′id)  1 not liquid or gas: *Water becomes solid when it freezes.*  2 a substance that is not a liquid or a gas.  3 not hollow: *A bar of iron is solid; a pipe is hollow.*  4 hard; firm: *They were glad to leave the boat and put their feet on solid ground.*  5 strongly made or put together: *This is not a very solid table.*  6 alike throughout: *The cloth is a solid blue.*  7 firmly united: *The country was solid for peace.*  8 serious; not superficial or trifling: *Chemistry and English are solid subjects.*  9 genuine; real: *solid comfort.*  10 that can be depended on: *She is a solid citizen.*  11 having good judgment; sound; sensible; intelligent: *a solid book by a solid thinker.*  12 financially sound or strong: *a solid business.*  13 whole; entire: *I waited three solid hours.*  14 undivided; continuous: *a solid row of houses.*  15 in printing, having the lines of type not separated by leads; having few open spaces.  16 written without a hyphen: *Earthworm is a solid compound.*  17 having length, breadth, and thickness.  18 a body that has length, breadth, and thickness: *A cube is a solid.*  2, 18 *n.*, 1, 3–17 *adj.*  —**sol′id·ly,** *adv.*  —**sol′id·ness,** *n.*

**sol·i·dar·i·ty** (sol′ə dar′ə tē or sol′ə der′ə tē)  unity or fellowship arising from common responsibilities and interests.  *n.*, *pl.* **sol·i·dar·i·ties.**

**solid geometry**  the branch of mathematics that deals with objects having the three dimensions of length, breadth, and thickness.

**sol·id·i·fy** (sə lid′ə fī′)  1 make or become solid; harden: *Extreme cold will solidify water.*  2 unite firmly.  *v.*, **so·lid·i·fied, so·lid·i·fy·ing.**  —**so·lid′i·fi·ca′tion,** *n.*

**so·lid·i·ty** (sə lid′ə tē)  being solid; firmness; hardness; density: *the solidity of marble or steel, the solidity of the statesman's character.*  *n.*, *pl.* **so·lid·i·ties.**

**sol·id–state** (sol′id stāt′)  1 of or having to do with the study of the properties of solid materials, especially of their molecular structure, the movement of their electrons, etc.: *The transistor was developed as a result of research in solid-state physics.*  2 proceeding from or produced by such study: *solid-state electronics, solid-state devices.*  *adj.*

**so·lil·o·quize** (sə lil′ə kwīz′)   1 talk to oneself. 2 speak a SOLILOQUY.   *v.*, **so·lil·o·quized, so·lil·o·quiz·ing.**

**so·lil·o·quy** (sə lil′ə kwē)   1 the act of talking to oneself.   2 a speech made by an actor to himself or herself when alone on the stage: *A soliloquy may be used to impart knowledge to the audience, to reveal a character's true motives, etc.*   *n., pl.* **so·lil·o·quies.**

**sol·i·taire** (sol′ə ter′)   1 any of various card games played by one person.   2 a diamond or other gem set by itself.   *n.*

**sol·i·tar·y** (sol′ə ter′ē)   1 alone; single; only: *A solitary rider was seen in the distance.*   2 without companions; away from people; lonely: *Irene leads a solitary life in her hut in the mountains. The house is in a solitary spot many kilometres from a town.*   3 a person living alone, away from people.   1, 2 *adj.*, 3 *n., pl.* **sol·i·tar·ies.** —**sol′i·tar′i·ly,** *adv.*  —**sol′i·tar′i·ness,** *n.*

**solitary confinement**   the keeping of a prisoner in complete isolation from others, often as a penalty for misbehaviour while in prison.

**sol·i·tude** (sol′ə tyüd *or* sol′ə tüd′)   1 the condition of being alone: *She likes company and hates solitude.*   2 a lonely place.   3 loneliness.   *n.*

**so·lo** (sō′lō)   1 a piece of music for one voice or instrument.   2 arranged for or performed by one voice or instrument: *a solo part.*   3 playing the solo part: *a solo violin.*   4 without a partner, companion, instructor, etc.; alone: *a solo flight, a solo dance.*   5 anything done without a partner, companion, instructor, etc.   6 make a solo flight in an airplane.   1, 5 *n., pl.* **so·los;** 2–4 *adj.*, 6 *v.*, **so·loed, so·lo·ing.**

**so·lo·ist** (sō′lō ist)   a person who performs a solo.   *n.*

**Solomon's seal**   a starlike figure formed of two triangles interlaced.   See STAR OF DAVID for picture.

**Sol·o·mon's–seal** (sol′ə mənz sēl′)   a kind of plant that has small flowers hanging from the bases of the leaves and a rootstock with seal-like scars.   *n.*

**so long**   *Informal.*   goodbye; farewell.

**sol·stice** (sol′stis)   either of the two times in the year when the sun is at its greatest distance from the celestial equator.   In the Northern Hemisphere, June 21 or 22, the **summer solstice,** is the longest day of the year and December 21 or 22, the **winter solstice,** is the shortest.   *n.*

**sol·sti·tial** (sol stish′əl)   having to do with a SOLSTICE.   *adj.*

**sol·u·bil·i·ty** (sol′yə bil′ə tē)   1 a quality that substances have of dissolving or being dissolved easily: *the solubility of sugar in water.*   2 a quality that problems, difficulties, questions, etc. have of being solved or explained.   *n., pl.* **sol·u·bil·i·ties.**

**sol·u·ble** (sol′yə bəl)   1 that can be dissolved: *Salt is soluble in water.*   2 that can be solved: *soluble puzzles.*   *adj.*

**sol·ute** (sol′yüt *or* sol′üt)   a solid, gas, etc. dissolved in a liquid to make a solution: *Salt is a solute in sea water.*   *n.*

**so·lu·tion** (sə lü′shən)   1 the solving of a problem: *The solution of the problem required many hours.*   2 an answer; explanation: *The police are seeking the solution to the crime.*   3 the process of dissolving; changing of a solid or gas to a liquid by treatment with a liquid.   4 a liquid or mixture formed by dissolving.   5 a separating into parts.   6 the condition of being dissolved: *Sugar and salt can be held in solution in water.*   *n.*

**solv·a·ble** (sol′və bəl)   1 capable of being solved. 2 capable of being dissolved.   *adj.*

**solve** (solv)   find the answer to; clear up; explain: *The mystery was never solved. She has solved all the problems in the lesson.*   *v.,* **solved, solv·ing.**

**sol·ven·cy** (sol′vən sē)   the ability to pay all one owes. *n., pl.* **sol·ven·cies.**

**sol·vent** (sol′vənt)   1 able to pay all that one owes: *A bankrupt firm is not solvent.*   2 able to dissolve: *Gasoline is a solvent liquid that removes grease spots.*   3 a substance, usually a liquid, that can dissolve other substances: *Water is a solvent of sugar and salt.*   4 a thing that solves.   1, 2 *adj.*, 3, 4 *n.*

**so·ma** (sō′mə)   all the tissues and organs of an animal or plant except the germ cells.   *n., pl.* **so·ma·ta** (sō′mə tə).

**So·ma·li** (sə mä′lē)   1 a member of a people of eastern Africa, apparently of mixed African and Mediterranean ancestry.   2 the language of these people.   *n., pl.* **So·ma·li** or **So·ma·lis.**

**so·mat·ic** (sō mat′ik)   1 of or having to do with the body.   2 having to do with the cavity of the body or its walls.   3 having to do with the SOMA.   *adj.*

**somatic cell**   any cell of an animal or plant, except a germ cell.

**som·bre** (som′bər)   1 dark; gloomy: *A cloudy winter day is sombre.*   2 melancholy; dismal: *Maura's losses made her very sombre.*   *adj.*   —**sombre′ly,** *adv.*   —**sombre′ness,** *n.* Also, **somber.**

**som·brer·o** (som brer′ō)   a broad-brimmed hat worn by men in Mexico, the southwestern United States, etc. See HAT for picture.   *n., pl.* **som·brer·os.**

**some** (sum; *unstressed,* səm)   1 certain, but not known or not named: *Some people sleep more than others.* 2 certain unnamed persons or things: *Some think so.*   3 a number of: *She left the city some years ago.*   4 a quantity of: *Drink some milk.*   5 a certain number or quantity: *Jacques ate some and threw the rest away.*   6 a; any: *Ask some girl to come here.*   7 about: *Some twenty people saw it.*   8 *Informal.*   to a great degree or extent: *That's going some!*   9 *Informal.*   big; good: *That was some storm!*   1, 3, 4, 6, 9 *adj.*, 2, 5 *pron.*, 7–8 *adv.* ☛ Hom. SUM.

**–some**[1]   an adjective-forming suffix meaning: 1 tending to, as in *frolicsome, meddlesome.*   2 causing, as in *awesome, troublesome.*   3 to a considerable degree, as in *lonesome.*

**–some**[2]   a suffix meaning a group of, as in *twosome, foursome.*

**some·bod·y** (sum′bud′ē *or* sum′bod′ē)   1 a person not known or named; some person; someone: *Somebody has taken my pen.*   2 a person of importance: *She acts as if she were somebody since she won the prize.*   1 *pron.*, 2 *n., pl.* **some·bod·ies.**

**some·day** (sum′dā′)   at some future time.   *adv.*

**some·how** (sum'hou') in a way not known or not stated; in one way or another: *I'll finish this work somehow.* *adv.*
**somehow or other,** in one way or another.

**some·one** (sum'wun' *or* sum'wən) some person; somebody. *pron.*

**some·place** (sum'plās') in or to some place; somewhere. *adv.*

A somersault

**som·er·sault** (sum'ər solt') **1** a complete roll of the body, forward or backward, bringing the feet over the head. **2** roll in this way. **1** *n.*, **2** *v.* Also, **summersault**.
**turn a somersault,** somersault.

**some·thing** (sum'thing') **1** some thing; a particular thing not named or not known: *I've got something important to tell you. He has something on his mind.* **2** a certain amount or quantity; part; little: *Something yet of doubt remains.* **3** somewhat; to some extent or degree: *He is something like his mother.* **4** a thing or person of some value or importance: *He thinks he's something.* **5** a thing or person that is to a certain extent an example of what is named: *to be something of a violinist.* **1, 2, 4, 5** *n.*, **3** *adv.*

**some·time** (sum'tīm') **1** at one time or another: *Come over sometime.* **2** at an indefinite point of time: *It happened sometime last March.* **3** former: *a sometime pupil of the school.* **1, 2** *adv.*, **3** *adj.*

**some·times** (sum'tīmz') now and then; at times: *She comes to visit sometimes.* *adv.*

**some·way** (sum'wā') in some way. *adv.*

**some·what** (sum'wut' *or* sum'hwut') **1** to some extent or degree; slightly: *somewhat round.* **2** some part; some amount: *Somewhat of the fun is lost when you hear a joke a second time.* **3** a little. **1** *adv.*, **2, 3** *n.*

**some·where** (sum'wer' *or* sum'hwer') **1** in or to some place; in or to one place or another: *She lives somewhere in the neighbourhood.* **2** at some time: *It happened somewhere in the last century.* *adv.*

**som·nam·bu·lism** (som nam'byə liz'əm) SLEEPWALKING. *n.*

**som·nam·bu·list** (som nam'byə list) SLEEPWALKER. *n.*

**som·nam·bu·lis·tic** (som nam'byə lis'tik) having to do with SLEEPWALKING or SLEEPWALKERS. *adj.*

**som·nif·er·ous** (som nif'ə rəs) **1** causing sleep. **2** sleepy. *adj.*

**som·no·lence** (som'nə ləns) sleepiness; drowsiness: *Many people have a feeling of somnolence after lunch.* *n.*

**som·no·lent** (som'nə lənt) sleepy; drowsy. *adj.* —**som'no·lent·ly**, *adv.*

**son** (sun) **1** a male child or person spoken of in relation to either or both of his parents. **2** a male descendant. **3** SON-IN-LAW. **4** a boy or man attached to a country, cause, etc. as a child is to its parents: *sons of liberty.* **5** anything thought of as a son in relation to its origin. **6** a term of address to a boy or from an older person, etc. *n.* —**son'less**, *adj.*
☞ *Hom.* SUN.

**so·nar** (sō'när) a device for detecting and locating objects under water by the reflection of sound waves. *n.*
☞ *Etym.* From the first letters of *sound navigation ranging.*

**so·na·ta** (sə nä'tə) a piece of music for one or two instruments, having three or four movements in contrasted rhythms but related keys. *n.*
☞ *Etym.* From Italian *sonata,* a feminine form of the past participle of *sonare* 'to sound'.

**song** (song) **1** something to sing; a short poem set to music. **2** poetry that has a musical sound. **3** a piece of music for, or as if for, a poem that is to be sung. **4** the act or practice of singing: *The canary burst into song.* **5** any sound like singing: *the cricket's song, the song of the teakettle, the song of the brook.* *n.*
**for a song,** very cheaply: *to buy things for a song.*
**song and dance,** fuss; disturbance; turmoil: *She made a great song and dance about having to do the job.*

**song·bird** (song'bėrd') **1** a bird that sings, especially a PASSERINE. **2** *Informal.* a woman singer. *n.*

**song·less** (song'lis) not able to sing. *adj.*

**song sparrow** a small North American sparrow having black, brown, and white plumage: *The song sparrow is noted for its pleasing song.*

**song·ster** (song'stər) **1** singer. **2** a writer of songs or poems. **3** SONGBIRD. *n.*

**song·stress** (song'stris) **1** a woman singer. **2** a woman writer of songs or poems. **3** a female SONGBIRD. *n.*

**song thrush** an Old World thrush having brown plumage above and white below, with a spotted breast; mavis: *The song thrush is noted for its singing.*

**son·ic** (son'ik) **1** of, having to do with, or using sound waves. **2** of or having to do with the speed of sound in the air (331 metres per second or about 1192 kilometres per hour at 0° Celsius). *adj.*

**sonic barrier** the sudden increase in aerodynamic resistance experienced by an aircraft when it approaches the speed of sound (331 m/s or about 1192 km/h at 0° C).

**sonic boom** the sound, like that of an explosion, of the shock wave formed in front of an aircraft travelling above the speed of sound.

**sonic mine** a container holding an explosive charge that is put under water and exploded by propeller vibrations; acoustic mine.

**so·nif·er·ous** (sō nif'ə rəs) carrying or producing sound. *adj.*

**son–in–law** (sun'in lo') the husband of one's daughter. *n., pl.* **sons-in-law.**

**son·net** (son'it) a poem having 14 lines, usually in iambic pentameter, and a certain arrangement of rhymes:

Elizabethan and Italian sonnets differ in the arrangement of the rhymes. *n.*

**son·net·eer** (son′ə tēr′) **1** a writer of sonnets. **2** write sonnets. 1 *n.*, 2 *v.*

**son·ny** (sun′ē) *Informal.* a word used in speaking to a young boy: *Say, sonny, can you tell me how to get to the city hall from here?* *n., pl.* **son·nies.**

**so·nom·e·ter** (sō nom′ə tər) **1** an instrument used in measuring the pitch of musical tones or for experimenting with vibrating strings. **2** an instrument used for testing a person's hearing. *n.*

**so·nor·i·ty** (sə nô′rə tē) a SONOROUS quality or condition. *n.*

**so·nor·ous** (sə nô′rəs *or* son′ə rəs) **1** giving out or having a deep, loud sound. **2** full and rich in sound. **3** having an impressive sound; high-sounding: *sonorous phrases, a sonorous style.* *adj.* —**so·no′rous·ly,** *adv.*

**son·ship** (sun′ship) the state of being a son. *n.*

**Sons of Freedom** *Cdn.* a sect of Doukhobors, located, for the most part, in British Columbia.

**soon** (sün) **1** in a short time; before long: *I will see you again soon.* **2** before the usual or expected time; early: *Why have you come so soon?* **3** promptly; quickly: *As soon as I hear, I will tell you.* **4** readily; willingly: *I would as soon die as yield.* *adv.*
**had sooner,** would more readily; prefer to.

**soot** (sùt) **1** a black substance in the smoke from burning coal, wood, oil, etc.: *Soot makes smoke dark and collects on the inside of chimneys.* **2** cover or blacken with soot. 1 *n.*, 2 *v.*

**soothe** (süᴛH) **1** quiet; calm; comfort: *The mother soothed the crying child.* **2** make less painful; relieve; ease: *Heat soothes some aches; cold soothes others.* *v.*, **soothed, sooth·ing.** —**sooth′er,** *n.* —**sooth′ing·ly,** *adv.*

**sooth·say·er** (süth′sā′ər) a person who claims to foretell the future; person who makes prophecies. *n.*

**sooth·say·ing** (süth′sā′ing) **1** the foretelling of future events. **2** a prediction or prophecy. *n.*

**soot·y** (sùt′ē) **1** covered or blackened with soot. **2** dark brown or black; dark-coloured. *adj.*, **soot·i·er, soot·i·est.** —**soot′i·ly,** *adv.* —**soot′i·ness,** *n.*

**sop** (sop) **1** a piece of food dipped or soaked in milk, broth, etc. **2** dip or soak: *She sopped the bread in milk.* **3** something given to soothe or quiet; bribe. **4** take up water, etc.; wipe; mop: *Please sop up that water with a cloth.* **5** be drenched. **6** soak thoroughly; drench. **7** a person or thing that is thoroughly soaked. **8** soak in or through. 1, 3, 7 *n.*, 2, 4–6, 8 *v.*, **sopped, sop·ping.**

**sop.** soprano.

**soph·ist** (sof′ist) **1** Usually, **Sophist,** one of a group of professional teachers of ancient Greece who gave instruction in rhetoric, grammar, science, the nature of virtue, the history of society, and other teachings designed especially to promote success in public life: *The Sophists were accused of not really seeking the truth, but being only interested in success in debate, even at the expense of honesty.* **2** a person who reasons cleverly but falsely. **3** in early use, a philosopher or sage. *n.*

**so·phis·ti·cate** (sə fis′tə kāt′ *for verb,* sə fis′tə kāt′ *or* sə fis′tə kət *for noun*) **1** make experienced in worldly ways. **2** a SOPHISTICATED person. **3** mislead. **4** use SOPHISTRY; quibble. **5** involve in SOPHISTRY. 1, 3–5 *v.*, **so·phis·ti·cat·ed, so·phis·ti·cat·ing;** 2 *n.*

**so·phis·ti·cat·ed** (sə fis′tə kā′tid) **1** experienced in worldly ways; informed; knowing; aware. **2** no longer having natural simplicity or frankness; artificial. **3** appealing to the tastes of sophisticated people. **4** of mechanical or electronic devices, complex and advanced in design: *sophisticated computers.* *adj.*

**so·phis·ti·ca·tion** (sə fis′tə kā′shən) **1** worldly experience or ideas. **2** a lessening or loss of naturalness, simplicity, or frankness; artificial ways. **3** SOPHISTRY.

**soph·ist·ry** (sof′i strē) **1** clever and plausible reasoning that is unsound or false. **2** a clever but misleading argument. *n., pl.* **soph·ist·ries.**

**soph·o·more** (sof′ə môr′) **1** a student in the second year of college. **2** of or having to do with second-year college students. 1 *n.*, 2 *adj.*

**soph·o·mor·ic** (sof′ə mô′rik) **1** of, having to do with, or like a SOPHOMORE or sophomores. **2** conceited and pretentious but crude and ignorant. *adj.*

**so·po·rif·ic** (sop′ə rif′ik *or* sō′pə rif′ik) **1** causing or tending to cause sleep. **2** sleepy; drowsy. **3** a drug that causes sleep. 1, 2 *adj.*, 3 *n.*

**sop·ping** (sop′ing) soaked; drenched. *adj.*
**sopping wet,** soaked; drenched.

**sop·py** (sop′ē) soaked; very wet: *soppy ground, soppy weather.* *adj.*, **sop·pi·er, sop·pi·est.**

**so·pran·o** (sə pran′ō) **1** the highest singing voice for women, girls, or boys. **2** a singer who has such a voice. **3** the part sung by a soprano: *Soprano is the highest part in standard four-part harmony for male and female voices.* **4** an instrument having the highest range in a family of musical instruments. **5** having to do with, having the range of, or designed for a soprano. 1–4 *n., pl.* **so·pran·os;** 5 *adj.*

**sor·cer·er** (sôr′sə rər) a man who supposedly practises magic with the aid of evil spirits; magician. *n.*

**sor·cer·ess** (sôr′sə ris) a woman who supposedly practises magic with the aid of evil spirits; witch. *n.*

**sor·cer·y** (sôr′sə rē) magic supposedly performed with the aid of evil spirits; witchcraft. *n., pl.* **sor·cer·ies.**

**sor·did** (sôr′did) **1** dirty; filthy: *The poor family lived in a sordid hut.* **2** mean; low; base; contemptible. **3** caring too much for money; meanly selfish; greedy. *adj.* —**sor′did·ly,** *adv.* —**sor′did·ness,** *n.*

**sore** (sôr) **1** painful; aching; tender; smarting: *a sore throat, a sore finger.* **2** a painful place on the body where the skin or flesh is broken or bruised. **3** sad; distressed: *The suffering of the poor makes her heart sore.* **4** *Informal.* offended; angered; vexed: *He is sore about missing the game.* **5** causing pain, misery, anger, or offence; vexing: *Their defeat is a sore subject with the members of the team.* **6** a cause of pain, sorrow, sadness, anger, offence, etc. **7** severe; distressing: *Your going away is a sore grief to us.* 1, 3–5, 7 *adj.*, **sor·er, sor·est;** 2, 6 *n.* —**sore′ly,** *adv.* —**sore′ness,** *n.*
☛ *Hom.* SOAR.

**sore·head** (sôr′hed′) *Informal.* a person who is angry or offended. *n.*

**sor·ghum** (sôr′gəm) **1** a tall cereal plant resembling corn: *One variety of sorghum has a sweet juice used for making molasses or syrup, others provide food for livestock* either by their grain or as hay, and still others furnish material for brushes or brooms. **2** molasses or syrup made from a sorghum plant. *n.*

**so·ri** (sô′rī *or* sô′rē) pl. of SORUS. *n.*

**so·ror·i·ty** (sə rô′rə tē) **1** sisterhood. **2** a club or society of women or girls. *n., pl.* **so·ror·i·ties.**

**sor·rel**[1] (sô′rəl) **1** reddish brown. **2** a reddish-brown horse. 1 *adj.*, 1, 2 *n.*

**sor·rel**[2] (sô′rəl) any of several plants having sour leaves and juice. *n.*

**sor·row** (sô′rō) **1** grief; sadness; regret: *Micaela felt sorrow at the news. She expressed sorrow at her mistake.* **2** a cause of grief, sadness, or regret; trouble; suffering; misfortune. *Her sorrows have aged her.* **3** feel or show grief, sadness, or regret. **4** be sad; feel sorry; grieve: *She sorrowed over the lost money.* 1, 2 *n.*, 3, 4 *v.*
—**sor′row·er,** *n.* —**sor′row·less,** *adj.*

**sor·row·ful** (sô′rə fəl) **1** full of sorrow; feeling sorrow; sad: *a sorrowful person.* **2** showing sorrow: *a sorrowful smile.* **3** causing sorrow: *a sorrowful event.* *adj.*
—**sor′row·ful·ly,** *adv.* —**sor′row·ful·ness,** *n.*

**sor·ry** (sô′rē) **1** feeling pity, regret, sympathy, etc.; sad: *I am sorry you are ill.* **2** wretched; poor; pitiful: *The blind beggar was a sorry sight.* *adj.*, **sor·ri·er, sor·ri·est.**
—**sor′ri·ly,** *adv.* —**sor′ri·ness,** *n.*
☛ *Hom.* SAURY (sô′rē).

**sort** (sôrt) **1** a kind; class: *What sort of work does she do?* **2** a character; quality; nature. **3** a person or thing of a certain kind or quality: *She is a good sort.* **4** arrange by kinds or classes; arrange in order: *Sort these cards according to their colours.* **5** in printing, a letter or piece in a font of type. **6** a way; fashion; manner. 1–3, 5, 6 *n.*, 4 *v.* —**sor′ter,** *n.*
**of sorts, a** of one kind or another. **b** of a poor or mediocre quality.
**out of sorts,** ill, cross, or uncomfortable.
**sort of,** *Informal.* somewhat; rather: *In spite of her faults I sort of like her. This bread is sort of dry.*
**sort out,** separate from others; put: *The farmer sorted out the best apples for eating.*

**sor·tie** (sôr′tē) **1** a sudden attack by troops from a defensive position. **2** a single round trip of an aircraft against the enemy. *n.*

**so·rus** (sô′rəs) a cluster of spore cases on the underside of a frond. *n., pl.* **so·ri** (-rī *or* rē).

**SOS** (es′ō′es′) **1** a signal of distress consisting of the letters *s o s* of the international Morse code (. . . — — — . . .), used in wireless telegraphy. **2** *Informal.* any urgent call for help.

**so-so** (sō′sō′) **1** neither very good nor very bad. **2** passably; indifferently; tolerably. 1 *adj.*, 2 *adv.*

**sos·te·nu·to** (sos′tə nü′tō) in music, sustained; prolonged. *adj., adv.*

**sot** (sot) a person made stupid and foolish by drinking too much alcoholic liquor; drunkard. *n.*
☛ *Hom.* SOUGHT.

**sot·tish** (sot′ish) **1** stupid and foolish from drinking too much alcoholic liquor; drunken. **2** of a SOT; like a sot. *adj.* —**sot′tish·ly,** *adv.* —**sot′tish·ness,** *n.*

**sot·to vo·ce** (sot′ō vō′chē; *Italian,* sôt′tō vō′chä) **1** in a low tone. **2** aside; privately.

**sou·brette** (sü bret′) an actress or singer acting the part of a pert young woman. *n.*

hat, āge, fär; let, ēqual, tėrm; it, īce
hot, ōpen, ôrder; oil, out; cup, pút, rüle
əbove, takən, pencəl, lemən, circəs
ch, child; ng, long; sh, ship
th, thin; ᴛʜ, then; zh, measure

**sou·bri·quet** (sü′brə kā′) SOBRIQUET. *n.*

**souf·flé** (sü flā′) *French.* **1** a frothy baked dish, usually made light by beaten eggs: *cheese soufflé.* **2** puffed up: *potatoes soufflé.* 1 *n.*, 2 *adj.*

**sough** (sou *or* suf) **1** make a rustling or murmuring sound: *The pines soughed when the wind blew.* **2** a rustling or murmuring sound. 1 *v.*, 2 *n.*
☛ *Hom.* SOW[2] (for the first pronunciation of **sough**).

**sought** (sot) pt. and pp. of **seek.** *v.*
☛ *Hom.* SOT.

**sought-after** (sot′af′tər) desirable; much in demand. *adj.*

**soul** (sōl) **1** the spiritual part of a person, regarded by some as the source of thought, feeling, and action, and considered as separate from the body: *Many religions believe that the soul and the body are separated in death and that the soul lives forever.* **2** energy of mind or feelings; spirit: *She puts her whole soul into her work.* **3** a cause of inspiration and energy: *Florence Nightingale was the soul of the movement to reform nursing.* **4** the essential part: *Brevity is the soul of wit.* **5** person: *Don't tell a soul.* **6** embodiment: *He is the soul of honour.* **7** the spirit of a dead person. *n.*
☛ *Hom.* SOL, SOLE.

**soul·ful** (sōl′fəl) **1** full of feeling; deeply emotional. **2** expressing or suggesting a deep feeling. *adj.*
—**soul′ful·ly,** *adv.* —**soul′ful·ness,** *n.*

**soul-less** (sōl′lis) having no soul; without spirit or noble feelings. *adj.* —**soul′-less·ly,** *adv.*

**soul-search·ing** (sōl′ sėr′ching) an examination of one's own motives, beliefs, etc. so as to evaluate one's conduct. *n.*

**sound**[1] (sound) **1** what is or can be heard; auditory sensation. **2** the vibrations causing this sensation: *Sound travels in waves.* **3** a noise, note, tone, etc. whose quality indicates its source or nature: *the sound of fighting.* **4** the distance within which a noise may be heard: *If you go outside, please stay within sound of the telephone.* **5** one of the simple elements composing speech: *a vowel sound.* **6** make a sound or noise: *The trumpet sounds for battle. The wind sounds like an animal howling.* **7** pronounce: *Sound each syllable.* **8** be pronounced: *Rough and ruff sound alike.* **9** be heard as a sound; issue or pass as sound; be mentioned. **10** be filled with sound. **11** cause to sound: *"Sound the trumpets; beat the drums."* **12** test by noting sounds: *to sound a person's lungs.* **13** order or direct by a sound: *to sound a retreat.* **14** make known; announce; utter: *The trumpets sounded the call to arms. Everyone sounded his praises.* **15** seem: *That excuse sounds ridiculous.* **16** the effect produced on the mind by what is heard: *a warning sound, a queer sound.* **17** mere noise without meaning. 1–5, 16, 17 *n.*, 6–15 *v.*

**sound**[2] (sound) **1** free from injury, decay, or defect: *a sound ship, sound fruit.* **2** free from disease; healthy: *a sound body and mind.* **3** strong; safe; secure: *a sound business firm.* **4** solid; deep. **5** correct; right; reasonable; reliable: *sound advice.* **6** without any legal defect: *a sound title.* **7** having orthodox or conventional ideas: *politically sound.* **8** thorough; hearty: *a sound whipping, a sound sleep.* **9** deeply; thoroughly: *She was sound asleep.* 1–8 *adj.*, 9 *adv.* —**sound'ly,** *adv.* —**sound'ness,** *n.*

**sound³** (sound) **1** measure the depth of water by letting down a weight fastened to the end of a line. **2** examine or test by a line arranged to bring up a sample. **3** inquire into the feelings, inclination, etc., of a person; examine; investigate: *We sounded Mother on the subject of a picnic.* **4** go toward the bottom; dive: *The whale sounded.* **5** a long, slender instrument used by doctors in examining body cavities. **6** examine with a sound. 1–4, 6 *v.*, 5 *n.*
**sound out,** inquire into a person's feelings, opinions, etc.; examine indirectly: *Johann sounded her out on the project, but she didn't seem interested.*

**sound⁴** (sound) **1** a narrow passage of water joining two larger bodies of water or separating an island and the mainland: *Queen Charlotte Sound.* **2** an arm of the sea: *Howe Sound.* **3** a sac in fish that contains air or gas and helps them float. *n.*

**sound barrier** SONIC BARRIER.

**sound·board** (sound'bôrd') a thin, resonant piece of wood forming part of a musical instrument, as in a violin or piano, to increase the fullness of its tone. *n.*

**sound effects** in the theatre, motion pictures, radio, and television, noises, as of rain, traffic, crowds, doorbells, etc., called for in the script and produced as required.

**sound·er¹** (soun'dər) **1** a person or thing that makes a sound. **2** a receiving instrument that converts a telegraph message into sound. *n.*

**sound·er²** (soun'dər) a person or thing that measures the depth of water. *n.*

**sound·ing¹** (soun'ding) **1** that sounds. **2** resounding. **3** ppr. of SOUND¹. 1, 2 *adj.*, 3 *v.*

**sound·ing²** (soun'ding) **1** the act of measuring the depth of water by letting down a weight fastened to the end of a line. **2** the depth of water found by measuring in this way. **3 soundings,** *pl.* **a** the depths of water found by a line and weight. **b** a place where the water is shallow enough for a SOUNDING LINE to touch bottom. **4** ppr. of SOUND³. 1–3 *n.*, 4 *v.*

**sounding board** **1** SOUNDBOARD. **2** a structure used to direct sound toward an audience. **3** a means of bringing opinions, etc. out into the open.

**sounding line** a line having a weight fastened to the end, used to measure the depth of water.

**sound·less¹** (soun'dlis) without sound; making no sound. *adj.*

**sound·less²** (soun'dlis) so deep that the bottom cannot be reached. *adj.*

**sound·proof** (sound'prüf') **1** not letting sound pass through. **2** make soundproof: *Father soundproofed his den.* 1 *adj.*, 2 *v.*

**sound track** a recording of the sounds of words, music, etc. made along one edge of a motion-picture film.

**sound waves** the progressive vibrations of which sounds consist: *People can hear sound waves in the range of 15 to 20 000 cycles per second.*

**soup** (süp) a liquid food made by boiling meat, vegetables, fish, etc. *n.*
**in the soup,** *Informal.* in difficulties; in trouble.

**soup·çon** (süp sôN') *French.* a slight trace or flavour. *n.*

**soup kitchen** a place that serves food free or at a very low charge to poor or unemployed people or to victims of a flood, fire, or other disaster.

**soup·y** (sü'pē) like soup. *adj.*, **soup·i·er, soup·i·est.**

**sour** (sour) **1** having a taste like vinegar or lemon juice; acidic; sharp and biting: *Most green fruit is sour.* **2** fermented; spoiled: *Sour milk is healthful, but most foods are not good to eat when they have become sour.* **3** having a sour or rank smell. **4** disagreeable; bad-tempered; peevish: *a sour face, a sour remark.* **5** unusually acid: *sour soil.* **6** cold and wet; damp: *sour weather.* **7** make or become sour; turn sour: *The milk soured in the heat.* **8** make or become peevish, bad-tempered, or disagreeable. **9** something sour. **10** in a sour manner. **11** fall below usual standards of excellence or interest: *Her liking for comic books has soured.* 1–6 *adj.*, 7, 8, 11 *v.*, 9 *n.*, 10 *adv.* —**sour'ly,** *adv.* —**sour'ness,** *n.*
**sour on,** take a dislike for; lose one's taste for: *He seems to have soured on dancing lately.*
**go sour,** fall below usual standards of excellence or interest; fall off.

**source** (sôrs) **1** a place from which anything comes or is obtained: *a source of iron, the source of a rumour.* **2** a person, book, statement, etc. that supplies information. **3** the beginning of a river or brook; fountain; spring. *n.*

**sour cream** a sour-tasting dairy product with a thick, smooth consistency, made from milk solids, bacterial culture, etc. It is used as a condiment and in cooking.

**sour·dough** (sour'dō) *Cdn.* **1** dough containing active yeast, saved from one baking for the next: *Prospectors and pioneers used sourdough for making bread to avoid the need for fresh yeast.* **2** a prospector or pioneer in northwestern Canada or Alaska. **3** any old resident, experienced hand, etc.; person who is not a tenderfoot. **4** a native or inhabitant of the Yukon. *n.*

**sour grapes** the attitude of pretending not to want or like something when actually it is impossible to have it: *When Elam wasn't allowed to go to the movies he said he didn't really want to go anyway, but that was just sour grapes.*

**souse** (sous) **1** plunge into liquid; drench; soak in a liquid. **2** a plunging into a liquid; drenching. **3** soak in vinegar, brine, etc.; pickle. **4** liquid used for pickling. **5** something soaked or kept in pickle, especially the head, ears, and feet of a pig. 1, 3 *v.*, **soused, sous·ing;** 2, 4–6 *n.*

**sou·tane** (sü tän') CASSOCK. *n.*

**south** (south) **1** the direction to the left as one faces the setting sun; the direction opposite to north. See COMPASS for picture. **2** lying toward or situated in the south. **3** originating in or coming from the south: *a south wind.* **4** toward the south: *Drive south.* **5** Also, **South,** that part of the world, country, or continent toward the south. **6 the South,** in the United States, the part of the country lying south of Pennsylvania, the Ohio River, Missouri, and Kansas. 1, 5, 6 *n.*, 2, 3 *adj.*, 4 *adv.*
**south of,** farther south than.

**South African** **1** of or having to do with South Africa, a country in southern Africa, or its people. **2** a native or inhabitant of South Africa. 1 *adj.*, 2 *n.*

**South American** **1** of or having to do with South America, a continent in the Western Hemisphere. **2** a native or inhabitant of South America. 1 *adj.*, 2 *n.*

**south–bound** (south′bound′) going toward the south. *adj.*

**south·east** (sou′thēst′) **1** the direction or compass point halfway between south and east. **2** a place that is in the southeast part or direction. **3** of, at, in, to, toward, or from the southeast: *a southeast wind.* (*adj.*) *She walked southeast.* (*adv.*) 1, 2 *n.*, 3 *adj.*, *adv.*

**south·east·er** (sou′thē′stər) a wind or storm from the southeast. *n.*

**south·east·er·ly** (sou′thē′stər lē) **1** toward the southeast. **2** from the southeast. *adj.*, *adv.*

**south·east·ern** (sou′thē′stərn) of, at, in, to, toward, or from the southeast. *adj.*

**south·east·ward** (sou′thē′stwərd) **1** toward the southeast. **2** SOUTHEAST. 1 *adv.*, *adj.*, 2 *n.*

**south·east·ward·ly** (sou′thē′stwər dlē) **1** toward the southeast. **2** of winds, from the southeast. *adj.*, *adv.*

**south·east·wards** (sou′thē′stwərdz) SOUTHEASTWARD. *adv.*

**south·er** (sou′ᴛʜər) a wind or storm from the south. *n.*

**south·er·ly** (suᴛʜ′ər lē) **1** toward the south: *The windows face southerly.* **2** from the south: *a southerly wind.* 1 *adv.*, 2 *adj.*

**south·ern** (suᴛʜ′ərn) **1** toward the south: *a southern view.* **2** from the south: *a southern breeze.* **3** of or in the south: *He has travelled in southern countries.* *adj.*

**Southern Cross** a group of four bright stars in the form of a cross, used in finding the direction south; it is visible mostly in the Southern Hemisphere.

**South·ern·er** (suᴛʜ′ər nər) a native or inhabitant of the South. *n.*

**Southern Hemisphere** the half of the earth that is south of the equator.

**south·ern·most** (suᴛʜ′ərn mōst′) farthest south: *Point Pelee, Ontario, is the southernmost part of Canada.* *adj.*

**south·ing** (sou′ᴛʜing) **1** a movement toward the south. **2** a distance due south. *n.*

**south·land** (sou′thlənd *or* sou′thland′) land in the south; southern part of a country. *n.*

**south·most** (sou′thmōst′) farthest south. *adj.*

**south·paw** (south′pô′) *Informal.* **1** a left-handed baseball pitcher or boxer. **2** any left-handed person. **3** left-handed. 1, 2 *n.*, 3 *adj.*

**South Pole** the southern end of the earth's axis.

**South Sea Islander** a native or inhabitant of the South Sea Islands in the southern Pacific Ocean.

**south–south·east** (south′sou′thēst′) **1** the direction or compass point midway between south and southeast. **2** in, toward, or from this direction. 1 *n.*, 2 *adj.*, *adv.*

**south–south·west** (south′sou′thwest′) **1** the direction or compass point midway between south and southwest. **2** in, toward, or from this direction. 1 *n.*, 2 *adj.*, *adv.*

**south·ward** (sou′thwərd) **1** toward the south; south: *He walked southward* (*adv.*). *The orchard is on the southward slope of the hill* (*adj.*). **2** a southward part, direction, or point. 1 *adv.*, *adj.*, 2 *n.*

**south·ward·ly** (sou′thwər dlē) **1** toward the south. **2** of winds, coming from the south. 1, 2 *adj.*, 1 *adv.*

**south·wards** (sou′thwərdz) SOUTHWARD. *adv.*

**south·west** (sou′thwest′) **1** the direction or compass point halfway between south and west. **2** a place that is in the southwest part or direction. **3** of, at, in, to, toward, or from the southwest: *a southwest wind* (*adj.*). *They walked southwest* (*adv.*). 1, 2 *n.*, 3 *adj.*, *adv.*

A southwester

**south·west·er** (sou′thwes′tər *or* sou′wes′tər) **1** a wind or storm from the southwest. **2** a waterproof hat having a broad brim at the back to protect the neck, worn especially by seamen. *n.*

**south·west·er·ly** (sou′thwes′tər lē) toward or from the southwest. *adj.*, *adv.*

**south·west·ern** (sou′thwes′tərn) of, at, in, to, toward, or from the southwest. *adj.*

**south·west·ward** (sou′thwes′twərd) **1** toward the southwest. **2** SOUTHWEST. 1 *adv.*, *adj.*, 2 *n.*

**south·west·ward·ly** (sou′thwes′twər dlē) **1** toward the southwest. **2** of winds, from the southwest. 1, 2 *adj.*, 1 *adv.*

**south·west·wards** (sou′thwes′twərdz) SOUTHWESTWARD. *adv.*

**sou·ve·nir** (sü′və nēr′ *or* sü′və nēr′) something to remind one of a place, person, or occasion; a keepsake. *n.*

**sou'west·er** (sou′wes′tər) SOUTHWESTER. *n.*

**sov·er·eign** (sov′rən) **1** a king or queen; supreme ruler; monarch. **2** having the rank or power of a sovereign. **3** greatest in rank or power: *a sovereign court.* **4** a person, group, or nation having supreme control or dominion; ruler; governor; lord; master: *sovereign of the seas.* **5** independent of the control of other governments: *a sovereign state.* **6** above all others; supreme; greatest: *Character is of sovereign importance.* **7** very excellent or powerful: *a sovereign cure for colds.* **8** a former British gold coin, worth one pound. 1, 4, 8 *n.*, 2, 3, 5–7 *adj.*

**sov·er·eign·ty** (sov′rən tē) **1** supreme power or authority. **2** freedom from outside control; independence in exercising power or authority: *Countries that are satellites lack full sovereignty.* **3** a state, territory, community, etc., that is independent or sovereign. **4** the rank, power, or jurisdiction of a sovereign. *n.*, *pl.* **sov·er·eign·ties.**

**sovereignty association** *Cdn.* a policy proposed in the late 1970's by the Quebec government, under which the province would become an independent state but would remain associated with Canada.

**so·vi·et** (sō′vē et′) **1** a council; assembly. **2** in the former Soviet Union, either of two elected local assemblies (**village soviets, town soviets**). **3** any of the higher elected assemblies in the former Soviet Union. The highest assembly of all was the **Supreme Soviet. 4** of or having to do with soviets. **5** any council like a Russian soviet. **6 Soviet,** of or having to do with the former Soviet Union. 1–3, 5 *n.*, 4, 6 *adj.*

**so·vi·et·ism** (sō′vē i tiz′əm) **1** a system of government by means of soviets. **2** COMMUNISM. *n.*

**so·vi·et·ize** (sō′vē i tīz′) bring under a soviet type of government; change to a soviet government. *v.*, **so·vi·et·ized, so·vi·et·iz·ing.**

**sow**[1] (sō) **1** scatter seed on the ground; plant seed: *He sows more wheat than oats.* **2** plant seed in: *The farmer sowed the field with oats.* **3** scatter seed. **4** scatter anything; spread about: *The enemy tried to sow discontent among our men.* *v.*, **sowed, sown** or **sowed, sow·ing.**
—**sow′er,** *n.*
☞ *Hom.* SEW, SO.

**sow**[2] (sou) a fully grown female pig. *n.*
☞ *Hom.* SOUGH (sou).

**sown** (sōn) a pp. of SOW[1]: *The field has been sown with oats.* *v.*
☞ *Hom.* SEWN.

**soy** (soi) **1** a sauce prepared from fermented soybeans, used especially in Chinese and Japanese dishes. **2** SOYBEAN. *n.*

**soy·bean** (soi′bēn′) **1** a bean widely grown in China, Japan, and North America: *Soybeans are used in making flour, oil, etc. and as a food.* **2** the plant that it grows on. *n.*

**sp. 1** special. **2** species. **3** spelling.

**spa** (spä) **1** a mineral spring. **2** a place where there is a mineral spring, especially a health resort at such a place. **3** any fashionable resort. *n.*

**space** (spās) **1** the unlimited room or expanse extending in all directions and in which all things exist: *The earth moves through space.* **2** a limited place or area: *a parking space.* **3** extent of area or volume: *We have plenty of space in this house.* **4** OUTER SPACE. **5** a distance; stretch: *The road is bad for a space of ten kilometres.* **6** a length of time: *He has not seen his brother for the space of ten years.* **7** a time in which to do something; opportunity. **8** a part of a surface; blank between words, etc.: *Fill in the spaces as directed.* **9** in printing, one of the blank types used to separate words, etc. **10** in music, one of the intervals between the lines of a staff. **11** accommodations on a train, etc. **12** fix the space or spaces of; divide into spaces. **13** separate by spaces: *Space your words evenly when you write.* 1–11 *n.*, 12, 13 *v.*, **spaced, spac·ing.**

**space age** the current period of history, thought of as being marked by the first efforts to explore and conquer OUTER SPACE.

**space·craft** (spās′skraft′) any manned or unmanned vehicle designed for flight into OUTER SPACE. *n., pl.* **space·craft.**

**space·man** (spās′smən) ASTRONAUT. *n., pl.* **space·men** (-smən).

**space ship** or **space·ship** (spās′ship′) SPACECRAFT. *n.*

**space shuttle** a spacecraft used more than once to go from earth to a space station.

**space station** a structure, usually a platform, sent into space to serve as an observation post or as a launching pad for other spacecraft.

**space suit** an airtight suit designed to protect astronauts from radiation, heat, lack of oxygen, etc., the conditions of the earth's atmosphere being maintained within the suit.

**spac·ing** (spā′sing) **1** the fixing or arranging of spaces. **2** the manner in which spaces are arranged: *even, close, or open spacing in printed matter.* **3** ppr. of SPACE. 1, 2 *n.*, 3 *v.*

**spa·cious** (spā′shəs) containing much space; with plenty of room; vast: *The rooms of the palace were spacious.* *adj.* —**spa′cious·ly,** *adv.* —**spa′cious·ness,** *n.*

A girl using a spade to dig a garden

**spade**[1] (spād) **1** a tool for digging, having a relatively flat blade which can be pressed into the ground with the foot, and a long handle with a grip or crosspiece at the top. **2** dig with a spade. 1 *n.*, 2 *v.*, **spad·ed, spad·ing. call a spade a spade,** call a thing by its real name; speak plainly and frankly.

**spade**[2] (spād) **1** a black figure (♠) used on playing cards. **2** a playing card bearing such figures. **3 spades,** *pl.* the suit of playing cards bearing such figures, usually the highest ranking suit in card games. *n.*

**spa·dix** (spā′diks) a spike composed of minute flowers on a fleshy stem: *A spadix is usually enclosed in a petal-like leaf called a spathe, as in the jack-in-the-pulpit and the calla lily.* See ARUM for picture. *n., pl.* **spa·dix·es** or **spa·di·ces** (spā dī′sēz).

**spa·ghet·ti** (spə get′ē) long, slender sticks of pasta, soft when cooked: *Spaghetti is thinner than macaroni.* *n.*

**span**[1] (span) **1** the distance between two supports: *The arch had a span of fifteen metres.* **2** the part between two supports: *The bridge crossed the river in three spans.* **3** a period of time: *"A life's but a span."* **4** the full extent: *the span of a bridge, the span of memory.* **5** extend over: *A bridge spanned the river.* **6** measure by the hand spread out: *This post can be spanned by one's two hands.* **7** a unit for measuring length based on the distance between the tip of the thumb and the tip of the little finger of a spread-out hand; about 23 cm. 1–4, 7 *n.*, 5, 6 *v.*, **spanned, span·ning.**

**span**[2] (span) a pair of horses or other animals harnessed and driven together. *n.*

**span·gle** (spang′gəl) **1** a small piece of glittering metal used for decoration: *The dress was covered with spangles.* **2** decorate with spangles. **3** any small, bright bit: *This* rock shows spangles of gold.   **4** sprinkle with, or as if with, small, bright bits: *The sky is spangled with stars.*   **5** glitter. 1, 3 *n.*, 2, 4, 5 *v.*, **span·gled, span·gling.**

**Span·iard** (span′yərd)   a native or inhabitant of Spain, a country in southwestern Europe.   *n.*

**span·iel** (span′yəl)   **1** any of various breeds of dog, usually of small or medium size, having long silky hair and drooping ears.   **2** a person who yields too easily to others.   *n.*

**Span·ish** (span′ish)   **1** of or having to do with Spain, a country in southwestern Europe, its people, or their language.   **2** the language of Spain and parts of Central and South America.   **3 the Spanish,** *pl.* the people of Spain.   1 *adj.*, 2, 3 *n.*

**Spanish American**   a native or inhabitant of a Spanish-American country, especially a person of Spanish descent.

**Span·ish–Amer·i·can** (span′ish ə mer′ə kən)   **1** of or having to do with Spain and America, or with Spain and the United States.   **2** of or having to do with the parts of America where Spanish is the standard language.   *adj.*

**Spanish Armada**   the great fleet sent by Philip II of Spain to attack England in 1588.

**Spanish Inquisition**   **1** the body of men appointed during the Renaissance by the Roman Catholic Church to suppress heresy in Spain.   **2** the activities of this body of men.

**Spanish Main**   **1** formerly, the mainland of America adjacent to the Caribbean Sea, especially between the mouth of the Orinoco River and the Isthmus of Panama.   **2** in later use, the Caribbean Sea.

**Spanish moss**   a plant growing on the branches of certain trees, from which it hangs in grey streamers: *Spanish moss is found in the rain forests of tropical America.*

**spank** (spangk)   **1** strike, usually on the buttocks, with the open hand, a slipper, etc., especially as a punishment.   **2** a blow with the open hand, a slipper, etc.; slap.   1 *v.*, 2 *n.*

**spank·er** (spang′kər)   **1** a fore-and-aft sail on the mast nearest the stern. See BRIG for picture.   **2** *Informal.* a fast horse.   **3** *Informal.* anything fine, large, unusual for its kind, etc.   *n.*

**spank·ing** (spang′king)   **1** brisk; lively; vigorous: *a spanking breeze, a spanking team of horses.*   **2** *Informal.* extremely, exceptionally: *a spanking good time.*   **3** the act of slapping with the open hand, a slipper, etc.: *The naughty boy was given a spanking.*   **4** ppr. of SPANK. 1 *adj.*, 2 *adv.*, 3 *n.*, 4 *v.*

**span·less** (span′lis)   that cannot be spanned.   *adj.*

**span·ner** (span′ər)   **1** one that spans: *the spanners of a bridge.*   **2** *Esp. Brit.* a tool for holding and turning a nut, bolt, etc.; wrench.   *n.*

**spar**[1] (spär)   **1** a stout pole used to support or extend the sails of a ship; mast, yard, boom, etc. of a ship. **2** provide a ship with spars.   **3** the main beam of an airplane wing.   **4** a large pole or boom used as part of a crane or derrick.   1, 3, 4 *n.*, 2 *v.*, **sparred, spar·ring.**

**spar**[2] (spär)   **1** make motions of attack and defence with the arms and fists; box.   **2** dispute.   **3** a dispute.   1, 2 *v.*, **sparred, spar·ring;**   3 *n.*

**spar**[3] (spär)   a shiny mineral that splits into flakes easily.   *n.*

# Spaniard 1141 sparrow

hat, āge, fär; let, ēqual, tėrm; it, īce
hot, ōpen, ôrder; oil, out; cup, pùt, rüle
əbove, takən, pencəl, lemən, circəs
ch, child; ng, long; sh, ship
th, thin; ᴛн, then; zh, measure

**spar deck**   the upper deck extending from one end of a ship to the other.

**spare** (sper)   **1** show mercy to; refrain from harming or destroying: *He spared his enemy.*   **2** show mercy; refrain from doing harm.   **3** show consideration for; save from labour, pain, etc.: *We walked uphill to spare the horse.* **4** get along without; do without: *Mother couldn't spare the car, so Michelle had to walk.*   **5** make a person, etc. free from something; relieve or exempt a person, etc. from something: *She did the work to spare you the trouble.* **6** use in small quantities or not at all; be saving of: *We spared no expense.*   **7** have free or available for use: *Can you spare the time? I have no money to spare.*   **8** be saving.   **9** free for other use: *spare time.*   **10** extra; in reserve: *a spare tire.*   **11** a spare thing, part, tire, etc. **12** thin; lean: *The minister was a tall, spare man.*   **13** small in quantity; meagre, scanty: *a spare diet.*   **14** the knocking down of all the pins with two rolls of a bowling ball.   1–8 *v.*, **spared, spar·ing,**   9, 10, 12, 13 *adj.*, **spar·er, spar·est;**   11, 14 *n.*   —**spare′ness,** *n.*

**spare·ly** (sper′lē)   sparingly; scantily; thinly.   *adv.*

**spare·rib** (sper′rib′)   a rib of meat, especially pork, having less meat than the ribs near the loins.   See PORK for picture.   *n.*

**spar·ing** (sper′ing)   **1** that spares.   **2** avoiding waste; economical; frugal: *a sparing use of sugar.*   **3** ppr. of SPARE.   1, 2 *adj.*, 3 *v.*   —**spar′ing·ly,** *adv.*

**spark** (spärk)   **1** a small bit of fire: *The burning wood threw off sparks.*   **2** a flash given off when electricity jumps across an open space: *An electric spark explodes the gas in the engine of an automobile.*   **3** flash; gleam: *a spark of light.*   **4** a small amount: *I haven't a spark of interest in the plan.*   **5** a trace of life or vitality.   **6** a glittering bit: *The moving sparks we saw were really fireflies.* **7** send out small bits of fire; produce sparks.   **8** stir to activity; stimulate: *to spark a revolt. She sparked the team to victory.*   1–6 *n.*, 7, 8 *v.*

**spark coil**   an induction coil for producing electric sparks.

**spar·kle** (spär′kəl)   **1** send out little sparks: *The fireworks sparkled.*   **2** a little spark.   **3** shine; glitter; flash; gleam: *The diamonds sparkled* (*v.*). *I like the sparkle of her eyes.* (*n.*).   **4** be brilliant; be lively: *His wit sparkles.* **5** brilliance; liveliness: *We admired the sparkle of his wit.* **6** bubble: *Her ginger ale sparkled.*   **7** cause to sparkle. 1, 3, 4, 6, 7 *v.*, **spar·kled, spar·kling;**   2, 3, 5 *n.*

**spar·kler** (spär′klər)   **1** a person or thing that sparkles. **2** a firework that sends out little sparks.   **3** *Informal.* a sparkling gem, especially a diamond.   *n.*

**spark plug**   **1** a device in the cylinder of a gasoline engine by which the mixture of gasoline and air is exploded by an electric spark.   See CYLINDER for picture. **2** *Informal.* a person who gives energy or enthusiasm to others.

**spar·row** (spar′ō *or* sper′ō)   any of many small finches, such as the song sparrow, the English sparrow, and the chipping sparrow.   *n.*

**sparrow hawk** a small hawk that feeds on sparrows and other small animals.

**sparse** (spärs) **1** thinly scattered; occurring here and there: *a sparse population, sparse hair.* **2** scanty; meagre. *adj.*, **spars·er, spars·est.** —**sparse′ly,** *adv.* —**sparse′ness,** *n.*

**spar·si·ty** (spär′sə tē) a sparse or scattered condition; sparseness. *n.*

**Spar·tan** (spär′tən) **1** of Sparta, a city in ancient Greece, or its people. **2** a native or inhabitant of Sparta: *The Spartans were noted for their simplicity of life, severity, courage, and brevity of speech.* **3** like the Spartans; simple, frugal, severe, sternly disciplined, brave, brief, or concise: *a Spartan diet.* **4** a person who is like the Spartans. 1, 3 *adj.*, 2, 4 *n.*

**spasm** (spaz′əm) **1** a sudden, involuntary contraction of a muscle or muscles. **2** any sudden, brief fit or spell of unusual energy or activity: *a spasm of temper, a spasm of industry.* *n.*

**spas·mod·ic** (spaz mod′ik) **1** having to do with spasms; resembling a spasm: *a spasmodic cough.* **2** sudden and violent, but brief; occurring very irregularly. **3** having or showing bursts of excitement. *adj.* —**spas·mod′i·cal·ly,** *adv.*

**spas·tic** (spas′tik) **1** caused by a spasm or spasms. **2** of, having to do with, or characterized by spasms. **3** a person suffering from cerebral palsy, a disorder involving continuous contraction of a muscle or muscles. 1, 2 *adj.*, 3 *n.*

**spat¹** (spat) **1** a slight quarrel. **2** *Informal.* have a slight quarrel. **3** a light blow; slap. **4** slap lightly. 1, 3 *n.*, 2, 4 *v.*, **spat·ted, spat·ting.**

**spat²** (spat) a pt. and a pp. of SPIT¹. *v.*

**spat³** (spat) Usually, **spats,** *pl.* a short gaiter covering the ankle. *n.*

**spat⁴** (spat) **1** the spawn of oysters; a young oyster. **2** of oysters, spawn. 1 *n.*, 2 *v.*, **spat·ted, spat·ting.**

**spate** (spāt) **1** a flood; downpour. **2** a sudden outburst: *a spate of words.* *n.*

**spathe** (spāTH) a large bract or pair of bracts that enclose a flower cluster: *The calla lily has a white spathe around a yellow flower cluster.* See ARUM for picture. *n.*

**spa·tial** (spā′shəl) **1** of or having to do with space. **2** existing in space. *adj.*

**spa·tial·ly** (spā′shə lē) in spatial respects; so far as space is concerned; in space. *adv.*

**spat·ter** (spat′ər) **1** scatter or dash in drops or particles: *to spatter mud.* **2** fall in drops or particles: *Rain spatters on the sidewalk.* **3** strike in a shower; strike in a number of places: *Bullets spattered the wall.* **4** a spattering: *a spatter of hail.* **5** the sound of spattering. **6** a splash or spot. **7** splash or spot with mud, paint, etc. **8** stain with slander, disgrace, etc. 1–3, 7, 8 *v.*, 4–6 *n.*

**spat·ter·dock** (spat′ər dok′) a yellow pond lily, especially a coarse, yellow-flowered plant common in stagnant waters. *n.*

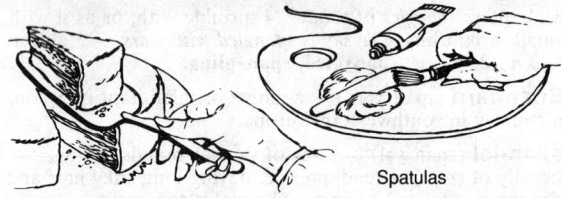
Spatulas

**spat·u·la** (spach′ə lə) a tool with a broad, flat, flexible blade, used for mixing drugs, in cooking and baking, for spreading paints, etc. *n.*

**spat·u·late** (spach′ə lit *or* spach′ə lāt′) shaped like a SPATULA; rounded somewhat like a spoon. *adj.*

**spav·in** (spav′ən) a disease of horses in which a bony swelling forms at the hock, causing lameness. *n.*

**spav·ined** (spav′ənd) having spavin; lame. *adj.*

**spawn** (spon) **1** the eggs of fish, frogs, shellfish, etc. **2** young fish, frogs, etc. when newly hatched from such eggs. **3** of fish, etc., produce eggs: *Salmon spawn in the rivers of British Columbia.* **4** give birth to; bring forth in great quantity: *The comedian spent ten minutes spawning poor jokes.* **5** offspring, especially a large number of offspring. **6** the product; result. **7** a mass of white, threadlike fibres from which mushrooms grow. 1, 2, 5–7 *n.*, 3, 4 *v.*

**spay** (spā) remove the ovaries of a female cat, dog, or other animal. *v.*

**SPCA** or **S.P.C.A.** Society for the Prevention of Cruelty to Animals.

**speak** (spēk) **1** say words; talk: *A cat cannot speak. Speak distinctly.* **2** make a speech: *Who is going to speak at the forum?* **3** tell; express; make known: *Speak the truth. Her eyes speak of suffering.* **4** use or know how to use in speaking: *I couldn't understand what they said because they were speaking Gaelic. Do you speak Swedish?* **5** express an idea, feeling, etc.; communicate: *Their eyes spoke.* **6** make a plea, request application, etc.; appeal: *to speak for seats ahead of time.* **7** speak to or with; address. **8** give forth sound: *The cannon spoke.* **9** of dogs, bark when told: *Speak for the biscuit, Fido.* *v.*, **spoke, spo·ken, speak·ing.**
**so to speak,** that is to say.
**speak for,** **a** speak in the interest of; represent: *She spoke for the group that wanted a picnic.* **b** ask or apply for.
**speak of,** mention; refer to: *She spoke of the matter to me. I have no complaints to speak of.*
**speak out** or **up,** **a** speak loudly and clearly. **b** speak freely and without restraint: *They were all too frightened to speak out. The children all spoke up in favour of the teacher's suggestion to have a party.*
**speak well for,** give a favourable idea of; be evidence in favour of.

**speak·er** (spē′kər) **1** a person who speaks, especially one who speaks before an audience: *Our next speaker is Professor Chapman.* **2** a device for amplifying the sound of a voice, music, etc. **3** a person who speaks on behalf of others; spokesman or spokeswoman. **4 Speaker,** a person who presides over an assembly: *the Speaker of the House of Commons.* *n.*

**Speaker of the House** the presiding officer of the House of Commons.

**speak·er·ship** (spē′kər ship′) the position of the presiding officer. *n.*

**speak·ing** (spē′king) **1** the act, utterance, or discourse of a person who speaks. **2** that speaks; giving information as if by speech: *a speaking example of a thing.* **3** used in, suited to, or involving speech: *within speaking distance, a speaking part in a play.* **4** permitting conversation: *a speaking acquaintance with a person.* **5** highly expressive: *speaking eyes.* **6** lifelike: *a speaking likeness.* **7** ppr. of SPEAK. 1 *n.*, 2–6 *adj.*, 7 *v.*

**spear**[1] (spēr) **1** a weapon having a long shaft and a sharp-pointed head. **2** pierce with a spear: *to spear a fish.* **3** pierce or stab with anything sharp: *to spear a wiener.* 1 *n.*, 2, 3 *v.*, —**spear′er**, *n.*

**spear**[2] (spēr) **1** a sprout or shoot of a plant: *a spear of grass.* **2** sprout or shoot into a long stem. 1 *n.*, 2 *v.*

**spear·head** (spēr′hed′) **1** the sharp-pointed striking end of a spear. **2** the part, person, or group that comes first in an attack, undertaking, etc.: *She was the spearhead of the project to make a park here.* **3** go first in an attack, undertaking, etc.: *Tanks spearhead the army's advance.* 1, 2 *n.*, 3 *v.*

**spear·man** (spēr′mən) a soldier armed with a spear. *n.*, *pl.* **spear·men** (-mən).

**spear·mint** (spēr′mint′) common mint, a fragrant herb much used for flavouring. *n.*

**spear side** the father's side of a family. Compare with DISTAFF SIDE.

**spec.** **1** special. **2** specification.

**spe·cial** (spesh′əl) **1** of a particular kind; distinct from others; not general: *This desk has a special lock.* **2** more than ordinary; unusual; exceptional: *Today's topic is of special interest.* **3** held in unusually high regard; valued in an exceptional way: *a special friend, a special favourite.* **4** for a particular person, thing, purpose, etc.: *The railway ran special trains on holidays. Send the letter by a special messenger.* **5** a special train, car, bus, etc. **6** any special person or thing. **7** a special edition of a newspaper. **8** in a store, restaurant, etc., a product which is specially featured; a bargain: *a weekend special.* **9** a specially produced television show, not one of the regular daily or weekly programs. 1–4 *adj.*, 5–9 *n.* —**spe′cial·ly**, *adv.*

**spe·cial·ist** (spesh′ə list) a person who devotes or restricts himself or herself to one particular branch of study, business, etc.: *Dr. Faber is a specialist in diseases of the ear, nose, and throat.* *n.*

**spe·ci·al·i·ty** (spesh′ē al′ə tē) *Esp. Brit* **1** a special or particular character. **2** a special quality or characteristic; the distinctive characteristic or feature of a thing. **3** a special point; particular; detail. **4** a special pursuit, branch, product, etc.; SPECIALTY. *n.*, *pl.* **spec·ial·i·ties**.

**spe·cial·ize** (spesh′ə līz′) **1** pursue some special branch of study, work, etc.: *Many students specialize in engineering.* **2** adapt to special conditions; give special form, use, duty, etc. to; limit: *Lungs and gills are specialized for breathing.* **3** develop in a special way; take on a special form, use, etc. **4** mention specially; SPECIFY. **5** go into particulars. *v.*, **spe·cial·ized**, **spe·cial·iz·ing**. —**spe′cial·i·za′tion**, *n.*

**spe·cial·ized** (spesh′ə līzd′) **1** designed for, fitted for, or devoted to a particular use, interest, or type of work: *An engineer needs much specialized knowledge.* **2** pt. and pp. of SPECIALIZE. 1 *adj.*, 2 *v.*

**spear**     1143     **specimen**

hat, āge, fär; let, ēqual, tėrm; it, īce
hot, ōpen, ôrder; oil, out; cup, pùt, rüle
əbove, takən, pencəl, lemən, circəs
ch, child; ng, long; sh, ship
th, thin; ŦH, then; zh, measure

**spe·cial·ty** (spesh′əl tē) **1** special study; special line of work, profession, trade, etc.: *Repairing watches is his specialty.* **2** a product, article, etc. to which special attention is given: *This store makes a specialty of children's clothes.* **3** a special character; special quality. **4** a special or particular characteristic; peculiarity. **5** a special point or item; particular; detail. *n.*, *pl.* **spe·cial·ties**.

**spe·cie** (spē′shē) money in the form of coins; metal money: *Silver dollars are specie.* *n.*

**spe·cies** (spē′sēz *or* spē′shēz) **1** in biology, the narrowest major category in the classification of plants and animals. See classification chart in the Appendix. **2** a kind; sort; distinct kind or sort: *There are many species of advertisements.* **3** an appearance; form; shape. **4 the species,** the human race. *n.*, *pl.* **spe·cies**.

**spe·cif·ic** (spə sif′ik) **1** definite; precise; particular: *There was no specific reason for the quarrel.* **2** characteristic of; peculiar to: *A scaly skin is a specific feature of snakes.* **3** any specific statement, quality, etc. **4** curing some particular disease. **5** a cure for some particular disease: *Quinine is a specific for malaria.* **6** produced by some special cause. **7** of or having to do with a SPECIES. 1, 2, 4, 6, 7 *adj.*, 3, 5 *n.* —**spe·cif′ic·ness**, *n.*

**spe·cif·i·cal·ly** (spə sif′i klē) in a specific manner; definitely; particularly: *The doctor told Kate specifically not to eat eggs.* *adv.*

**spec·i·fi·ca·tion** (spes′ə fə kā′shən) **1** the act of SPECIFYing; a definite mention; detailed statement of particulars: *Vezna made careful specification as to the kinds of cake and candy for her party.* **2** something specified; a particular item, article, etc. **3** Usually, **specifications,** *pl.* a detailed description of the dimensions, materials, etc. for a building, road, dam, boat, book, etc. *n.*

**specific gravity** RELATIVE DENSITY.

**specific heat** **1** a number that expresses the ratio of the quantity of heat needed to raise the temperature of a given substance one degree to that needed to raise the temperature of an equal mass of water one degree: *The specific heat of aluminum is about 0.2.* **2** SPECIFIC HEAT CAPACITY.

**specific heat capacity** the quantity of heat needed to raise the temperature of one unit of a substance one degree.

**spec·i·fy** (spes′ə fī′) **1** mention or name definitely; state or describe in detail: *Did you specify any particular time for us to call?* **2** include in the SPECIFICATIONS: *The contractor couldn't use shingles for the roof because slate was specified.* *v.*, **spec·i·fied**, **spec·i·fy·ing**.

**spec·i·men** (spes′ə mən) **1** one of a group or class taken to show what the others are like; a single part, thing, etc. regarded as an example of its kind: *a fine specimen of French art.* **2** taken or regarded as a specimen. **3** *Informal.* a human being; person: *The tramp was a pathetic old specimen.* **1, 3** *n.*, **2** *adj.*

**spe·cious** (spē'shəs) **1** seeming desirable, reasonable, or probable, but not really so; apparently good or right, but without real merit: *The teacher saw through Torvald's specious excuse.* **2** making a good outward appearance in order to deceive: *His dishonest actions showed him to be nothing but a specious hypocrite.* *adj.*
—**spe'cious·ly,** *adv.* —**spe'cious·ness,** *n.*

**speck** (spek) **1** a small spot; stain: *Can you clean the specks off this wallpaper?* **2** a tiny bit; particle: *I have a speck in my eye.* **3** mark with specks: *This fruit is badly specked.* **1, 2** *n.*, **3** *v.*

**speck·le** (spek'əl) **1** a small spot or mark: *This hen is grey with white speckles.* **2** mark with speckles. **1** *n.*, **2** *v.*

**speckled char** BROOK TROUT.

**specs** (speks) *Informal.* **1** SPECTACLES. **2** specifications. *n.pl.*

**spec·ta·cle** (spek'tə kəl) **1** something to look at; sight: *The children at play among the flowers made a charming spectacle.* **2** a public show or display: *The big parade was a fine spectacle.* **3 spectacles,** *pl.* a pair of glasses to help a person's sight or to protect the eyes. *n.*

**spec·ta·cled** (spek'tə kəld) **1** provided with or wearing spectacles. **2** having a marking resembling spectacles: *a spectacled snake.* *adj.*

**spec·tac·u·lar** (spek tak'yə lər) **1** making a great display: *The television program included a spectacular scene of a storm.* **2** having to do with a spectacle or show. **3** a spectacular display or show. **1, 2** *adj.*, **3** *n.*

**spec·tac·u·lar·ly** (spek tak'yə lər lē) **1** in a spectacular manner or degree. **2** as a spectacle. *adv.*

**spec·ta·tor** (spek'tā tər *or* spek tā'tər) a person who watches without taking part; onlooker: *Thousands of spectators lined the streets, waiting for the parade to come by.* *n.*

**spectator sport** a sport that attracts many spectators who do not practise the sport themselves: *Hockey and football are spectator sports.*

**spec·ter** (spek'tər) See SPECTRE. *n.*

**spec·tra** (spek'trə) pl. of SPECTRUM. *n.*

**spec·tral** (spek'trəl) **1** of or like a SPECTRE; ghostly: *She saw the spectral form of the headless horseman.* **2** of or produced by the SPECTRUM: *spectral colours.* *adj.*

**spec·tre** (spek'tər) **1** ghost. **2** something causing terror or dread. *n.* Also, **specter.**

**spec·trom·e·ter** (spek trom'ə tər) an instrument for measuring the rate of decay of radioactive elements in rocks. *n.*

**spec·tro·scope** (spek'trə skōp') an instrument for obtaining and examining the spectrum of radiation from any source by the passage of rays through a prism or a grating. *n.*

**spec·tros·co·py** (spek tros'kə pē) **1** a science having to do with the examination and analysis of spectra. **2** the use of the SPECTROSCOPE. *n.*

**spec·trum** (spek'trəm) **1** the band of colours formed when a beam of light is broken up by being passed through a prism or by some other means: *A rainbow has all the colours of the spectrum: red, orange, yellow, green, blue, indigo, and violet.* **2** the band of colours formed when any radiant energy is broken up: *The ends of such a spectrum are not visible to the eye but are studied by photography, heat effects, etc.* **3** in radio, the wavelength range between 30 000 metres and 3 centimetres. *n., pl.* **spec·tra** (-trə) or **spec·trums.**

**spec·u·late** (spek'yə lāt) **1** reflect; meditate; consider: *The philosopher speculated about time and space.* **2** guess; conjecture: *She refused to speculate about the possible winner.* **3** buy or sell when there is a large risk, with the hope of making a profit from future price changes. *v.*, **spec·u·lat·ed, spec·u·lat·ing.**

**spec·u·la·tion** (spek'yə lā'shən) **1** thought; reflection; conjecture: *Former speculations about electricity were often mere guesses.* **2** a guessing; conjecture: *His estimates of the cost were based on speculation.* **3** the act of buying or selling when there is a large risk, with the hope of making a profit from future price changes: *His speculations in stocks made him poor.* *n.*

**spec·u·la·tive** (spek'yə lə tiv *or* spek'yə lā'tiv) **1** thoughtful; reflective. **2** theoretical rather than practical. **3** risky. **4** of or involving speculation in land, stocks, etc. *adj.* —**spec'u·la'tive·ly,** *adv.* —**spec'u·la'tive·ness,** *n.*

**spec·u·la·tor** (spek'yə lā'tər) **1** a person who speculates, usually in business. **2** a person who buys tickets for shows, games, etc. in advance, hoping to sell them later at a higher price. *n.*

**sped** (sped) a pt. and a pp. of SPEED. *v.*

**speech** (spēch) **1** the act of speaking; talk. **2** the power of speaking: *Animals lack speech.* **3** a manner of speaking: *Her speech showed that she was a Newfoundlander.* **4** what is said; the words spoken: *We made the usual farewell speeches.* **5** a public talk: *after-dinner speeches.* **6** language: *His native speech was French.* *n.*

**Speech from the Throne** in Canada, a statement of government policy for the coming year read by the Governor General or, in a province, by the Lieutenant-Governor.

**speech·i·fy** (spē'chə fī') *Informal.* make a speech or speeches. *v.*, **speech·i·fied, speech·i·fy·ing.**
—**speech'i·fi'er,** *n.*

**speech·less** (spēch'lis) **1** not able to speak: *Teresa was speechless with anger.* **2** silent: *Her frown gave a speechless reply.* *adj.* —**speech'less·ness,** *n.*

**speech·less·ly** (spēch'li slē) **1** without speaking. **2** so as to be speechless. *adv.*

**speed** (spēd) **1** swift or rapid movement. **2** go quickly: *The boat sped over the water.* **3** make go quickly: *to speed a horse.* **4** send quickly. **5** a rate of movement; velocity: *a speed of 100 kilometres per hour. The horses ran at full speed.* **6** go faster than is safe or lawful: *The car was caught speeding near the school zone.* **7** an arrangement of gears to give a certain rate of movement: *An automobile usually has three speeds forward and one backward.* **8** help forward; promote: *to speed an undertaking.* **1, 5, 7** *n.*, **2-4, 6, 8** *v.*, **sped** or **speed·ed, speed·ing.**

**speed up,** go or cause to go more quickly; increase in speed.

**speed·boat** (spēd'bōt') a motorboat built to go quickly. *n.*

**speed·er** (spē′dər) 1 a person or thing that speeds, especially a person who drives an automobile at a higher speed than is legal or safe. 2 a small trolley powered by a gasoline engine, used on railway tracks by maintenance crews. *n.*

**speed·i·ly** (spē′də lē) quickly; with speed; soon. *adv.*

**speed limit** the top speed at which vehicles are allowed to travel on a particular road.

**speed·om·e·ter** (spē dom′ə tər *or* spi dom′ə tər) an instrument to indicate the speed of an automobile or other vehicle. *n.*

**speed skate** an ice skate made specially for SPEED SKATING.

**speed skating** the sport of competing with others to skate fastest on ice.

**speed trap** any place where police set up a means of catching motorists who are speeding.

**speed–up** (spē′dup′) an increase in speed. *n.*

**speed·way** (spē′dwā) a road or track for fast driving. *n.*

**speed·well** (spē′dwel) any of various low plants having blue, purple, pink, or white flowers; veronica. *n.*

**speed·y** (spē′dē) fast; rapid; quick; swift: *speedy workers, speedy progress, a speedy decision.* *adj.*, **speed·i·er, speed·i·est.** —**speed′i·ness,** *n.*

**spe·le·ol·o·gist** (spē′lē ol′ə jist) a person who knows much about SPELEOLOGY. *n.*

**spe·le·ol·o·gy** (spē′lē ol′ə jē) the branch of science dealing with caves. *n.*

**spell¹** (spel) 1 write or say the letters of in order: *Some words are easy to spell.* 2 write or say the letters of words in order: *Lisa can spell well.* 3 make up or form a word: *C-a-t spells cat.* 4 mean: *Delay spells danger.* 5 read with difficulty: *to spell out the meaning.* *v.*, **spelled** or **spelt, spel·ling.**

**spell²** (spel) 1 a word or set of words having magic power. 2 fascination; charm: *We were under the spell of the beautiful music.* *n.*
**cast a spell on,** put under the influence of a spell; fascinate.
**under a spell,** controlled by a spell; spellbound: *The explorer's story held the children under a spell.*

**spell³** (spel) 1 a period of work or duty: *The sailor's spell at the wheel was four hours.* 2 a period or time of anything: *a spell of coughing, a spell of hot weather.* 3 *Informal.* work in place of another for a while: *to spell another person at rowing a boat.* 4 give a time of rest to. 5 the relief of one person by another in doing something. 1, 2, 5 *n.*, 3, 4 *v.*, **spelled, spell·ing.**

**spell·bind** (spel′bīnd′) make SPELLBOUND; fascinate; enchant. *v.*, **spell·bound, spell·bind·ing.**

**spell·bind·er** (spel′bīn′dər) a speaker or writer who can hold his or her audience SPELLBOUND. *n.*

**spell·bound** (spel′bound′) too interested to move; fascinated; enchanted: *We were spellbound as we watched the great actor.* *adj.*

**spell check** a computer program for correcting misspellings.

**spell·er** (spel′ər) a book for teaching spelling. *n.*

**spell·ing** (spel′ing) 1 the writing or saying of the letters of a word in order. 2 the way in which a word is

---

**speeder**      1145      **sphere**

hat, āge, fär; let, ēqual, tėrm; it, īce
hot, ōpen, ôrder; oil, out; cup, pút, rüle
əbove, takən, pencəl, lemən, circəs
ch, child; ng, long; sh, ship
th, thin; ŦH, then; zh, measure

---

spelled: *Grey has two spellings,* grey *and* gray. 3 ppr. of SPELL. 1, 2 *n.*, 3 *v.*

**spelling bee** a spelling contest.

**spelt¹** (spelt) a pt. and a pp. of SPELL¹. *v.*

**spelt²** (spelt) a kind of wheat grown chiefly in Europe. *n.*

**spel·ter** (spel′tər) zinc, usually in the form of small bars. *n.*

**spe·lunk·er** (spi lung′kər) a person who studies and explores caves as a hobby. *n.*

**spend** (spend) 1 pay out: *She spent ten dollars today.* 2 pay out money: *Earn before you spend.* 3 use; use up: *Don't spend any more time on that job.* 4 pass time, etc.: *to spend a day at the beach.* 5 wear out: *The storm has spent its force.* *v.*, **spent, spend·ing.** —**spend′er,** *n.*

**spend·thrift** (spend′thrift′) 1 a person who wastes money. 2 extravagant with money; wasteful: *his spendthrift ways.* 1 *n.*, 2 *adj.*

**spent** (spent) 1 pt. and pp. of SPEND: *We spent Saturday at the beach. Have you spent all your money already?* 2 worn out; tired: *a spent swimmer, a spent horse.* 3 used up: *His energy was soon spent.* 1 *v.*, 2, 3 *adj.*

**sperm¹** (spėrm) 1 the mature male reproductive cell produced by almost all animals and plants that reproduce sexually; a male gamete: *The sperm of mammals are very tiny and consist of a head that contains the genes and a thin tail by which they propel themselves inside the female reproductive tract.* 2 SEMEN. *n.*, *pl.* **sperm** or **sperms.**

**sperm²** (spėrm) 1 SPERMACETI. 2 a SPERM WHALE. 3 SPERM OIL. *n.*

**sper·ma·cet·i** (spėr′mə set′ē *or* spėr′mə sē′tē) a whitish, waxy substance obtained from the oil in the head of the SPERM WHALE and used in making fine candles, ointments, cosmetics, etc. *n.*

**sper·ma·to·phyte** (spėr′mə tə fīt′) a plant that produces seeds: *The spermatophytes form the largest division of the plant kingdom and include the angiosperms and the gymnosperms.* *n.*

**sper·ma·to·zo·on** (spėr′mə tə zō′ən) a SPERM, especially of an animal. *n.*, *pl.* **sper·ma·to·zo·a** (-zō′ə).

**sperm oil** a light-yellow oil from the SPERM WHALE, used for lubricating.

**sperm whale** a large, square-headed, toothed whale that has a large cavity in its head filled with sperm oil and spermaceti. See WHALE¹ for picture.

**spew** (spyü) 1 vomit: *the dog spewed on the rug.* 2 cast forth; throw out: *The volcano was spewing lava. He spewed out a stream of insults.* *v.* —**spew′er,** *n.*

**sphag·num** (sfag′nəm) PEAT MOSS. *n.*

**sphere** (sfėr) 1 in geometry, a round solid figure bounded by a surface that is at all points equally distant from the centre. See SOLID for picture. 2 an object approximately like this in form; ball; globe. 3 the place or field in which a person or thing exists, acts, works, etc.:

**spherical** 1146 **spikelet**

*Her sphere is advertising.* **4** a range; extent; region: *England's sphere of influence.* **5** any of the stars or planets: *The earth, sun, and moon are spheres.* **6** a supposed hollow globe, with the earth at its centre, enclosing the stars, sun, and planets. **7** any one of a series of such globes, one inside another, in which the stars and planets were supposed to be set: *Movement of the spheres was believed to cause the stars and planets to revolve around the earth.* **8** the heavens; the sky. *n.*

**spher·i·cal** (sfer′ə kəl) **1** shaped like a sphere. **2** of or having to do with a sphere or spheres. *adj.*

**spher·i·cal·ly** (sfer′i klē) **1** in the form of a sphere, or of part of a sphere. **2** so as to be spherical. *adv.*

**sphe·ric·i·ty** (sfi ris′ə tē) spherical form; roundness. *n., pl.* **sphe·ric·i·ties.**

**sphe·roid** (sfē′roid) a body shaped somewhat like a sphere. *n.*

**sphe·roi·dal** (sfē roi′dəl) shaped somewhat like a sphere. *adj.*

**spher·ule** (sfer′ül) a small sphere or spherical body. *n.*

**sphinc·ter** (sfingk′tər) a ringlike muscle that surrounds an opening or passage of the body, and can contract to close it. *n.*

An Egyptian sphinx    The Sphinx of Greek mythology

**sphinx** (sfingks) **1** a statue of a lion's body with the head of a man, ram, or hawk: *There are many sphinxes in Egypt.* **2** a puzzling or mysterious person. *n., pl.* **sphinx·es.**

**Spi·ca** (spī′kə) a very bright star in the constellation Virgo. *n.*

**spice** (spīs) **1** any of various seasonings obtained from plants and used to flavour food: *Pepper, cinnamon, cloves, ginger, and nutmeg are common spices.* **2** a spicy, fragrant odour. **3** put spice in; season: *spiced peaches, spiced pickles.* **4** something that adds flavour or interest: *"Variety is the spice of life."* **5** a slight touch or trace: *a spice of wickedness.* **6** add flavour or interest to: *The principal spiced her speech with stories and jokes.* 1, 2, 4, 5 *n.*, 3, 6 *v.*, **spiced, spic·ing.**

**spice·bush** (spīs′bush′) a bush having yellow flowers and spicy-smelling bark. *n.*

**spic·er·y** (spī′sə rē) **1** spices. **2** a spicy flavour or fragrance. *n., pl.* **spic·er·ies.**

**spic·i·ness** (spī′sē nis) a spicy flavour or smell. *n.*

**spick–and–span** (spik′ənd span′) **1** neat and clean; spruce or smart: *a spick-and-span room, apron, or uniform.* **2** fresh; new. *adj.*

**spic·ule** (spik′yəl) **1** a small, slender, sharp-pointed piece, usually bony or crystalline. **2** such a piece in a sponge. **3** a small spike of a flower. *n.*

**spic·y** (spī′sē) **1** flavoured with spice: *The cookies were rich and spicy.* **2** having a taste or smell like that of spice: *spicy apples.* **3** lively; keen: *spicy conversation.* **4** somewhat improper: *a spicy joke.* **5** producing spices; abounding with spices. *adj.*, **spic·i·er, spic·i·est.** —**spic′i·ly,** *adv.*

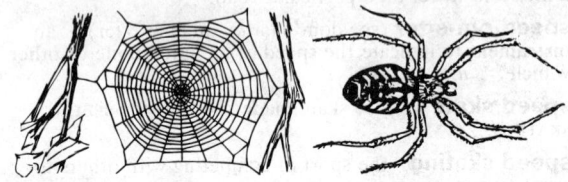

A house spider—
body about 6 mm long;
legs about 15 mm long

**spi·der** (spī′dər) **1** any of the eight-legged, wingless arachnids: *Many spiders spin webs to catch insects for food.* **2** something like or suggesting a spider. **3** a frame having three legs to support a pot or pan over a fire. *n.* —**spi′der·like′,** *adj.*
☛ *Etym.* Developed from OE *spīthra* 'spider', literally meaning 'spinner', related to modern German *Spinne* and Dutch *spin*, both meaning 'spider'. See also note at COBWEB.

**spider web** a web spun by a spider; COBWEB.

**spi·der·wort** (spī′dər wėrt′) **1** any of a closely related group of perennial plants having somewhat grasslike leaves and clusters of purple, blue, or white flowers: *The wandering jew is a spiderwort.* **2** referring to the family of mainly tropical plants that includes the spiderworts, all having jointed and often branching stems with parallel-veined leaves. *n.*

**spi·der·y** (spī′də rē) **1** long and thin like a spider's legs. **2** suggesting a spider web. **3** full of, or infested with, spiders. *adj.*

**spied** (spīd) pt. and pp. of SPY. *v.*

**spiel** or **′spiel** (spēl) *Cdn.* BONSPIEL. *n.*

**spiel·er** or **′spiel·er** (spē′lər) *Cdn.* a person who takes part in a BONSPIEL. *n.*

**spig·ot** (spig′ət) **1** a valve for controlling the flow of water or other liquid from a pipe, tank, barrel, etc. **2** a tap or faucet. **3** a peg or plug used to stop the small hole of a cask, barrel, etc.; bung. *n.*

**spike¹** (spīk) **1** a large, strong nail. **2** fasten with spikes: *The men spiked the rails to the ties when laying the track.* **3** a sharp-pointed piece or part: *Ballplayers wear shoes with spikes.* **4** provide or equip with spikes: *Runners wear spiked shoes to keep from slipping.* **5** pierce or injure with a spike. **6** make a cannon useless by driving a spike into the opening where the powder is set off. **7** put an end or stop to; make useless; block: *to spike an attempt.* 1, 3 *n.*, 2, 4–7 *v.*, **spiked, spik·ing.** —**spike′like′,** *adj.*

**spike²** (spīk) **1** an ear of grain. **2** a long, pointed flower cluster: *gladiolus spikes.* See INFLORESCENCE for picture. *n.*

**spike·let** (spī′klət) a small or secondary spike, especially one of the small spikes that make up a spike, or head, of grain or grass: *Each spikelet of wheat may produce one or more kernels.* *n.*

**spike·nard** (spīk′nərd *or* spīk′närd) **1** a sweet-smelling ointment used in ancient times. **2** a fragrant East Indian plant of the valerian family from which this ointment was probably obtained. *n.*

**spik·y** (spī′kē) **1** having spikes; set with sharp, projecting points. **2** having the shape of a spike. *adj.*

**spile** (spīl) **1** a peg or plug of wood used to stop the small hole of a cask or barrel. **2** a spout for drawing off sap from sugar maple trees. **3** stop up a hole with a peg or plug. **4** furnish with a spout. *1, 2 n., 3, 4 v.,* **spiled, spil·ing.**

**spill** (spil) **1** let liquid or any matter in loose pieces run or fall: *to spill milk or salt.* **2** fall or flow out: *Water spilled from the pail.* **3** scatter. **4** shed blood. **5** cause to fall from a horse, car, boat, etc.: *The boat upset and spilled the girls into the water.* **6** a spilling. **7** the quantity spilled. **8** *Informal.* a fall: *The horse gave Anita a bad spill.* **9** let wind out of a sail. *1–5, 9 v.,* **spilled** *or* **spilt, spill·ing;** *6–8 n.* —**spill′er,** *n.*

**spill·way** (spil′wā′) a channel or passage for the escape of surplus water from a dam, river, etc. *n.*

**spilt** (spilt) a pt. and a pp. of SPILL. *v.*

**spin** (spin) **1** turn or make turn rapidly: *The wheel spins round. The boy spins his top.* **2** feel as if one were whirling around; feel dizzy: *My head is spinning.* **3** draw out and twist cotton, flax, wool, etc. into thread. **4** make thread, yarn, etc. by drawing out and twisting cotton, wool, flax, etc. **5** make a thread, web, cocoon, etc. by giving out from the body sticky material that hardens into thread: *A spider spins a web.* **6** make glass, gold, etc. into thread. **7** a spinning. **8** a ride, run, or drive, especially a short one: *Get your bicycle and come for a spin with me.* **9** run, ride, drive, etc. rapidly. **10** produce; tell: *The old sailor used to spin yarns about adventures at sea.* **11** a rapid turning around of an airplane as it falls. *1–6, 9, 10 v.,* **spun, spin·ning;** *7, 8, 11 n.*
**spin out,** make long and slow; draw out; prolong: *Try not to spin out your story.*

**spin·ach** (spin′ich *or* spin′ij) **1** a plant whose green leaves are used as a vegetable. **2** the leaves of this plant. *n.*

**spi·nal** (spī′nəl) **1** of, having to do with, or located near the backbone. **2** of, having to do with, or affecting the SPINAL CORD. **3** an anesthetic for the lower part of the body. *1, 2 adj., 3 n.*

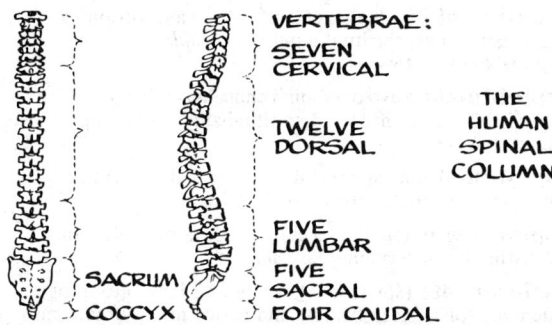

**spinal column** in human beings and other vertebrates, the series of small bones along the middle of the back that encloses and protects the spinal cord and provides support for the body: *The many bones of the spinal column, called vertebrae, are held together by muscles and tendons that*

hat, āge, fär; let, ēqual, tėrm; it, īce
hot, ōpen, ôrder; oil, out; cup, pu̇t, rüle
əbove, taken, pencəl, lemən, circəs
ch, child; ng, long; sh, ship
th, thin; ŦH, then; zh, measure

*allow movement in different directions.* See RIB for another picture.

**spinal cord** the thick whitish cord of nerve tissue that extends from the brain down through most of the backbone and from which nerves to various parts of the body branch off. See BRAIN for picture.

**spin·dle** (spin′dəl) **1** the rod or pin used in spinning to twist, wind, and hold thread. See SPINNING WHEEL for picture. **2** any rod or pin that turns around, or on which something turns: *Axles and shafts are spindles.* **3** grow tall and thin. *1, 2 n., 3 v.,* **spin·dled, spin·dling.**

**spin·dle–leg·ged** (spin′dəl leg′id *or* spin′dəl legd′) having long, thin legs. *adj.*

**spin·dle·legs** (spin′dəl legz′) **1** long, thin legs. **2** *Informal.* a person with long, thin legs. *n. pl.*

**spin·dle–shanked** (spin′dəl shangkt′) SPINDLE-LEGGED. *adj.*

**spin·dle·shanks** (spin′dəl shangks′) SPINDLELEGS. *n. pl.*

**spin·dling** (spin′dling) SPINDLY. *adj.*

**spin·dly** (spin′dlē) very long and slender; too tall and thin: *spindly legs, a spindly plant. adj.,* **spin·dli·er, spin·dli·est.**

**spin·drift** (spin′drift′) spray blown or dashed up from the waves. *n.* Also, **spoondrift.**

**spine** (spīn) **1** spinal column; backbone. **2** a stiff, sharp-pointed projection on an animal or plant body, such as on the tail of porcupines, in the fins of many kinds of fish, or on the stems of cactuses. **3** the back portion of a book where the pages are held together, or the part of the cover over this. **4** something that looks like a backbone or functions as a main support. *n.* —**spine′like′,** *adj.*

**spined** (spīnd) having a spine or spines. *adj.*

**spine·less** (spīn′lis) **1** without spines or sharp-pointed projections: *a spineless cactus.* **2** having no backbone: *All insects are spineless.* **3** having a weak spine; limp. **4** without moral force, resolution, or courage; weak-willed; feeble: *A spineless person will not stand up for his or her beliefs. adj.* —**spine′less·ly,** *adv.* —**spine′less·ness,** *n.*

**spin·et** (spin′it *or* spi net′) **1** an old-fashioned musical instrument like a small harpsichord. **2** a compact upright piano. *n.*

**spin·na·ker** (spin′ə kər) a large, triangular sail carried by yachts on the side opposite the mainsail when running before the wind. *n.*

**spin·ner** (spin′ər) a person, animal, or thing that spins. *n.*

**spin·ner·et** (spin′ə ret′) the organ by which spiders, silkworms, etc. spin their threads. *n.*

**spin·ney** (spin′ē) *Esp. Brit.* a thicket; small wood with undergrowth, especially one preserved for sheltering game birds; a small group of trees. *n., pl.* **spin·neys.**

**spin·ning** (spin′ing) **1** that spins. **2** the act of one that spins. **3** ppr. of SPIN. *1 adj., 2 n., 3 v.*

**spinning jenny** an early type of spinning machine having more than one spindle, whereby one person could spin a number of threads at the same time.

SPINDLE
A spinning wheel. The large wheel causes the smaller one to turn, and this revolves the horizontal spindle, twisting the thread and winding it up at the same time.

**spinning wheel** a large wheel with a spindle, arranged for spinning cotton, flax, wool, etc. into thread or yarn.

**spi·nose** (spī′nōs) full of spines; having spines; thorny; spinous. *adj.*

**spi·nous** (spī′nəs) 1 covered with spines; having spines; thorny. 2 spinelike; sharp. *adj.*

**spin·ster** (spin′stər) an unmarried woman. *n.*

**spin·ster·hood** (spin′stər hùd′) the state of being a SPINSTER. *n.*

**spin·y** (spī′nē) 1 covered with spines; having spines; thorny: *a spiny cactus, a spiny porcupine.* 2 spinelike. 3 difficult; troublesome. *adj.*, **spin·i·er, spin·i·est.**

**spi·ra·cle** (spī′rə kəl *or* spir′ə kəl) an opening for breathing: *Insects take in air through tiny spiracles. A whale breathes through a spiracle in the top of its head. n.*

**spi·rae·a** (spī rē′ə) any of various shrubs of the same family as the rose: *Spiraeas have clusters of small white, pink, or red flowers with five petals. n.*

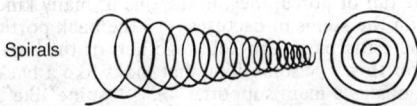

Spirals

**spi·ral** (spī′rəl) 1 a winding and gradually widening coil: *A watch spring is a spiral.* 2 coiled; coiling: *a spiral spring, the spiral stripes on a barber's pole.* 3 move in a spiral: *The flaming airplane spiralled to earth.* 4 form into a spiral. 5 a constant increasing or decreasing: *an inflationary spiral.* 1, 5 *n.*, 2 *adj.*, 3, 4 *v.*, **spi·ralled** *or* **spi·raled, spi·ral·ling** *or* **spi·ral·ing.** —**spi′ral·ly,** *adv.*

**spiral nebula** a cluster of stars in the form of a spiral.

**spire¹** (spīr) 1 the top part of a tower or steeple that narrows to a point. See STEEPLE for picture. 2 anything tapering and pointed: *The sunset shone on the rocky spires of the mountains.* 3 shoot up. 4 furnish with a spire. 1, 2 *n.* 3, 4 *v.*, **spired, spir·ing.** —**spire′like′,** *adj.*

**spire²** (spīr) 1 a coil; spiral. 2 a single twist of a coil or spiral. *n.*

**spi·re·a** (spī rē′ə) See SPIRAEA. *n.*

**spi·ril·lum** (spī ril′əm) any of a group of bacteria that have spirally twisted forms. See BACTERIA for picture. *n., pl.* **spi·ril·la** (-ril′ə).

**spir·it** (spir′it) 1 the soul; the immaterial part of a human being: *Many religions teach that at death the spirit leaves the body.* 2 a human being's moral, religious, or emotional nature. 3 a supernatural being: *Ghosts and fairies are spirits.* 4 conjure up. 5 a state of mind; disposition; temper: *He is low in spirit.* 6 a person; personality: *Montcalm was a noble spirit.* 7 an influence that stirs up and rouses: *A spirit of reform marked the 19th century.* 8 stir up; encourage; cheer. 9 courage; vigour; liveliness: *A racehorse must have spirit.* 10 enthusiasm and loyalty. 11 the real meaning or intent: *The spirit of a law is more important than its words.* 12 a solution in alcohol. 13 an alcoholic drink made by distilling the juice of certain fruits, grains, roots, etc.; liquor. 14 carry away or off secretly: *The child has been spirited away.* 15 **spirits,** *pl.* **a** a state of mind; disposition; mood: *She is in good spirits.* **b** vigour; liveliness; cheerfulness. 16 Often, **spirits,** *pl.* **a** a solution in alcohol: *spirits of camphor.* **b** distilled alcoholic liquor: *She drinks beer but no spirits.* 1–3, 5–7, 9–13, 15, 16 *n.,* 4, 8, 14 *v.*
**out of spirits,** sad; gloomy.

**spir·it·ed** (spir′ə tid) 1 full of energy and spirit; lively; dashing: *a spirited racehorse.* 2 pt. and pp. of SPIRIT. 1 *adj.,* 2 *v.* —**spir′it·ed·ly,** *adv.* —**spir′it·ed·ness,** *n.*

**spir·it·ism** (spir′ə tiz′əm) SPIRITUALISM. *n.*

**spir·it·less** (spir′i tlis) without spirit or courage; depressed. *adj.*

**spirit level** an instrument used to find out whether a surface is level: *When the bubble of air in the glass tube of a spirit level is exactly at the middle of the tube, the surface is level.* See LEVEL for picture.

**spir·i·tu·al** (spir′i chü əl) 1 of or having to do with the SPIRIT (defs. 1 and 2) as distinct from the body or material things: *a person's spiritual nature.* 2 sacred; religious: *spiritual songs.* 3 of religious, as opposed to secular, institutions: *lords spiritual, spiritual authority.* 4 a deeply emotional religious song or hymn with a jazz rhythm: *Spirituals developed from the folk music of the black people in the southern United States.* 5 of or having to do with spirits; supernatural. 6 of, having to do with, or involving SPIRITUALISM. 1–3, 5, 6 *adj.,* 4 *n.* —**spir′i·tu·al·ly,** *adv.*

**spir·i·tu·al·ism** (spir′i chü ə liz′əm) 1 the belief that spirits of the dead communicate with the living, especially through persons called mediums. 2 an insistence on the spiritual; doctrine that spirit alone is real. *n.*

**spir·i·tu·al·ist** (spir′i chü ə list) one who believes that the dead communicate with the living. *n.*

**spir·i·tu·al·is·tic** (spir′i chü ə lis′tik) of or having to do with SPIRITUALISM or SPIRITUALISTS. *adj.*

**spir·i·tu·al·i·ty** (spir′i chü əl′ə tē) a devotion to spiritual things; spiritual quality. *n., pl.* **spir·i·tu·al·i·ties.**

**spir·i·tu·al·i·za·tion** (spir′i chü ə lə zā′shən *or* spir′i chü ə lī zā′shən) 1 spiritualizing. 2 being SPIRITUALIZED. *n.*

**spir·i·tu·al·ize** (spir′i chü ə līz′) make spiritual. *v.,* **spir·i·tu·al·ized, spir·i·tu·al·iz·ing.**

**spir·i·tu·ous** (spir′i chü əs) 1 containing alcohol. 2 distilled, not fermented. *adj.*

**spi·ro·chete** (spī′rə kēt′) any of a large group of slender, spiral, very flexible and active micro-organisms that are usually classed as bacteria. *n.*

**spi·ro·gy·ra** (spī′rə jī′rə) any of several algae that grow in scumlike masses in freshwater ponds or tanks. *n.*

**spi·rom·e·ter** (spī rom′ə tər) an instrument for

measuring the capacity of the lungs, by the amount of air that can be breathed out after the lungs have been filled as full as possible. *n.*

**spirt** (spėrt) See SPURT. *v., n.*

**spir·y** (spī′rē) **1** having the form of a spire; tapering. **2** having many spires. *adj.*

**spit**[1] (spit) **1** eject saliva from the mouth. **2** eject from the mouth. **3** throw out: *The gun spits fire.* **4** the liquid produced in the mouth; saliva. **5** the noise or act of spitting. **6** make a spitting noise: *The cat spits when angry.* **7** a frothy or spitlike secretion given off by some insects. **8** rain or snow slightly. **9** a light rain or snow. 1–3, 6, 8 *v.,* **spat** or **spit, spit·ting;** 4, 5, 7, 9 *n.* —**spit′ter,** *n.*
**spit and image,** the exact likeness.
**the spit of,** *Informal.* just like.

**spit**[2] (spit) **1** a sharp-pointed, slender rod or bar on which meat is roasted: *The spit turns so that the meat is cooked evenly.* **2** run a spit through; put on a spit. **3** pierce; stab. **4** a narrow point of land running into the water. 1, 4 *n.,* 2, 3 *v.,* **spit·ted, spit·ting.**

**spit·ball** (spit′bol′) **1** a small ball of chewed-up paper, used as a missile. **2** in baseball, a curve pitched after moistening one side of the ball with saliva, now illegal. *n.*

**spite** (spīt) **1** ill will; a grudge: *She ruined his flowers out of spite.* **2** show ill will toward; annoy. 1 *n.,* 2 *v.,* **spit·ed, spit·ing.** —**spite′less,** *adj.*
**in spite of,** not prevented by; notwithstanding: *The children went to school in spite of the snowstorm.*

**spite·ful** (spīt′fəl) full of spite; eager to annoy; behaving with ill will and malice. *adj.* —**spite′ful·ly,** *adv.* —**spite′ful·ness,** *n.*

**spit·fire** (spit′fīr′) **1** a person, especially a woman or girl, who has a quick and fiery temper. **2** something that sends forth fire, such as a cannon or some kinds of fireworks. *n.*

**spit·tle** (spit′əl) SALIVA; SPIT. *n.*

**spitz** (spits) a kind of small dog with pointed muzzle and ears and long hair; a white variety of Pomeranian. *n.*

**splake** (splāk) *Cdn.* a game fish that is part speckled trout and part lake trout. *n., pl.* **splake** or **splakes.**

**splash** (splash) **1** cause water, mud, etc. to fly about. **2** dash liquid about: *The baby likes to splash in the tub.* **3** cause to scatter a liquid about: *He splashed the oars as he rowed.* **4** dash in scattered masses or drops: *The waves splashed on the beach.* **5** wet, spatter, or soil: *Our car is all splashed with mud.* **6** the act or sound of splashing; splashing: *The splash of the wave knocked her over. The boat upset with a loud splash.* **7** fall, move, or go with a splash or splashes: *She splashed across the brook.* **8** a spot of liquid splashed on something. **9** a spot; patch: *The dog is white with brown splashes.* **10** mark with spots or patches. 1–5, 7, 10 *v.,* 6, 8, 9 *n.*
**make a splash,** *Informal.* attract attention; cause excitement.

**splash·down** (splash′doun′) the landing of a capsule or other spacecraft in the ocean after re-entry. *n.*

**splash·er** (splash′ər) **1** one that splashes. **2** something that protects from splashes. *n.*

**splash·y** (splash′ē) **1** making a splash. **2** full of irregular spots or streaks. **3** *Informal.* attracting attention; causing excitement. *adj.,* **splash·i·er, splash·i·est.**

**splat·ter** (splat′ər) **1** splash; spatter. **2** a splash or spatter. 1 *v.,* 2 *n.*

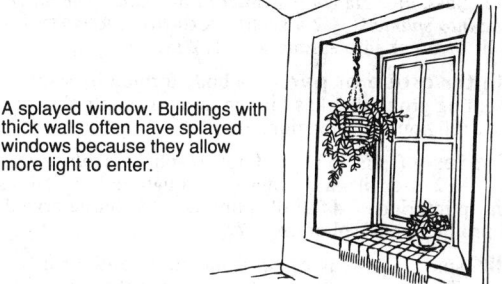

A splayed window. Buildings with thick walls often have splayed windows because they allow more light to enter.

**splay** (splā) **1** spread out. **2** spread; flare. **3** wide and flat. **4** awkward; clumsy. **5** a slanting surface; a surface that makes an oblique angle with another. **6** make slanting. 1, 2, 6 *v.,* 3, 4 *adj.,* 2, 5 *n.*

**splay·foot** (splā′fu̇t′) a broad, flat foot, especially one turned outward. *n., pl.* **splay·feet.**

**splay–foot·ed** (splā′fu̇t′id) **1** having splayfeet. **2** awkward; clumsy. *adj.*

**spleen** (splēn) **1** in human beings, a ductless gland at the left of the stomach; in other vertebrates, a similar gland near the stomach or intestine: *The spleen, which modifies the structure of the blood, was once believed to cause low spirits, bad temper, and spite.* **2** bad temper; spite; anger. **3** low spirits. *n.*

**splen·did** (splen′did) **1** brilliant; glorious; magnificent; grand: *a splendid sunset, a splendid palace, splendid jewels, a splendid victory.* **2** very good; fine; excellent: *a splendid chance. adj.* —**splen′did·ly,** *adv.* —**splen′did·ness,** *n.*

**splen·dif·er·ous** (splen dif′ə rəs) *Informal.* SPLENDID. *adj.*

**splen·dour** or **splen·dor** (splen′dər) **1** great brightness; brilliant light. **2** a magnificent show; pomp; glory. *n.*

**sple·net·ic** (spli net′ik) **1** having to do with the SPLEEN. **2** bad-tempered; irritable; peevish. *adj.* —**sple·net′i·cal·ly,** *adv.*

A spliced rope

**splice** (splīs) **1** join ropes, etc. by weaving together ends that have been untwisted. **2** join together two pieces of timber by overlapping. **3** join together film, tape, wire, etc. **4** a joining of ropes, timbers, tape, etc. by splicing. 1–3 *v.,* **spliced, splic·ing;** 4 *n.*
—**splic′er,** *n.*

**splint** (splint) **1** a rigid arrangement of wood, metal, plaster, etc. to hold a broken or dislocated bone in place until it heals. **2** a thin strip of wood, such as is used in making baskets. **3** a thin metal strip or plate: *Old armour often had overlapping splints to protect the elbow, knee, etc. and allow easy movement.* *n.*

**splint bone** in horses, mules, etc., one of the two smaller bones on either side of the large bone between the hock and the fetlock.

**splin·ter** (splin′tər) **1** a thin, sharp piece of wood, bone, glass, etc.: *He got a splinter in his hand. The mirror broke into splinters.* **2** a SPLINTER GROUP OR PARTY. **3** split or break into splinters. *1, 2 n., 3 v.*

**splinter group** or **party** a body formed by a small dissenting group that has broken away from a political party, religious organization, etc.

**splin·ter·y** (splin′tə rē) **1** apt to splinter: *splintery wood.* **2** of or like a splinter. **3** rough and jagged, as if from splintering. **4** full of splinters. **5** characterized by the production of splinters. *adj.*

**split** (split) **1** break or cut from end to end, or in layers: *The man is splitting wood. She split the cake and spread it with jelly.* **2** separate into parts; divide: *The huge tree split when it was struck by lightning. The two women split the cost of the dinner between them.* **3** divide into different groups, parties, etc. **4** a division in a group, etc.: *There was a split in the committee.* **5** a splitting; break; crack. **6** broken or cut from end to end; divided. **7** *Informal.* a bottle of a drink half the usual size. **8** a sweet dish made of sliced fruit, ice cream, etc. **9** divide a molecule into two or more smaller parts. **10** divide an atomic nucleus into two portions of approximately equal mass by forcing the absorption of a neutron. **11** Often, **splits**, *pl.* an exercise in which one lands on the floor with the legs stretched out in opposite directions. *1–3, 9, 10 v.,* **split, split·ting**; *4, 5, 7, 8, 11 n., 6 adj.* —**split′ter,** *n.*

**split hairs,** make distinctions that are too fussy: *It is splitting hairs to complain of having just 59 minutes instead of an hour in the pool.*

**split infinitive** an infinitive having an adverb between *to* and the verb. Example: *He wants to never work, but to always play.*

☛ *Usage.* Awkward split infinitives should be avoided. Awkward: *After a while I was able to, though not very accurately, distinguish the good customers from the sulky ones.* Improved: *After a while I was able to distinguish, though not very accurately, the good customers from the sulky ones.* Occasionally, a split infinitive is the least awkward construction, and is therefore acceptable: *I intended to partly cook the roast the night before.*

**split·ting** (split′ing) **1** that splits. **2** very painful; aching severely: *a splitting headache. My head is splitting.* **3** ppr. of SPLIT. *1, 2 adj., 3 v.*

**splotch** (sploch) **1** a large, irregular spot; splash. **2** make splotches on. *1 n., 2 v.*

**splotch·y** (sploch′ē) marked with splotches. *adj.*

**splurge** (splėrj) **1** a showing off. **2** show off. **3** spend money extravagantly. **4** a lavish or extravagant expenditure. *1, 4 n., 2, 3 v.,* **splurged, splurg·ing.**

**splut·ter** (splut′ər) **1** talk in a hasty, confused way: *People sometimes splutter when they are excited.* **2** make spitting or popping noises; sputter: *The baked apples are spluttering in the oven.* **3** a spluttering. *1, 2 v., 3 n.* —**splut′ter·er,** *n.*

**spoil** (spoil) **1** damage; injure; destroy: *to spoil a book by scribbling on it.* **2** be damaged; become bad or unfit for use: *Fruit spoils in the heat.* **3** injure the character or disposition of, especially by being too kind, generous, etc.: *The child is being spoiled by too much attention.* **4** an object of plundering; prey. **5** Often, **spoils**, *pl.* things taken by force; things won: *The soldiers carried off the spoils of war.* *1–3 v.,* **spoiled** or **spoilt, spoil·ing;** *4, 5 n.*

**be spoiling for,** *Informal.* be longing for a (fight, etc.); desire.

**spoil·er** (spoi′lər) **1** a person or thing that spoils. **2** a person who takes spoils.

**spoil·sport** (spoil′spôrt′) a person who spoils or prevents the fun of others. *n.*

**spoilt** (spoilt) a pt. and a pp. of SPOIL. *v.*

**spoke**[1] (spōk) pt. of SPEAK: *She spoke about that yesterday.* *v.*

**spoke**[2] (spōk) **1** one of the bars running from the centre of a wheel to the rim. See WHEEL for picture. **2** a rung of a ladder. *n.*

**put a spoke in someone's wheel,** stop or hinder someone.

**spo·ken** (spō′kən) **1** pp. of SPEAK: *They have often spoken about having a picnic.* **2** expressed with the mouth; uttered; told: *the spoken word.* **3** speaking in a certain way: *a soft-spoken man.* *1 v., 2, 3 adj.*

**spoke·shave** (spōk′shāv′) a cutting tool having a blade with a handle at each end, used for smoothing round surfaces. *n.*

**spokes·per·son** (spōk′spėr′sən) a person who speaks for another or others: *Ms. Moriyama was the spokesperson for the factory workers.* *n., pl.* **spokespersons.**

**spo·li·a·tion** (spō′lē ā′shən) **1** a plundering; robbery. **2** the plundering of neutrals at sea in time of war. *n.*

**sponge** (spunj) **1** a kind of sea animal that attaches itself to rocks and has a tough, fibrelike skeleton or framework. **2** the light, porous framework of any of these animals, used for soaking up water in bathing, cleaning, etc. **3** a similar article made artificially of rubber or plastic. **4** wipe or rub with a wet sponge; make clean or damp in this way: *Sponge the mud spots off the car. Sponge up the spilled water.* **5** absorb. **6** gather sponges. **7** something like a sponge, such as a pad of gauze used by doctors, a mop for cleaning the bore of a cannon, bread dough, or a kind of cake or pudding. **8** *Informal.* live or profit at the expense of another in a mean way: *The lazy man won't work; he just sponges on his family.* **9** *Informal.* a person who continually lives at the expense of others. *1–3, 7, 9 n., 4–6, 8 v.,* **sponged, spong·ing.** —**sponge′like′,** *adj.*

**sponge out,** blot out; remove all traces of.

**throw** or **toss in the sponge** or **throw up the sponge,** give up; admit defeat.

**sponge bath** a washing of the body with a wet sponge or cloth without getting into water.

**sponge cake** a light spongy cake made with eggs, sugar, flour, etc. but no butter.

**spong·er** (spun′jər) **1** a person who SPONGES (def. 8). **2** a machine for sponging cloth. **3** a person or vessel engaged in gathering sponges. **4** *Informal.* a person who gets on at the expense of others. *n.*

**spon·gy** (spun′jē) **1** like a sponge; soft, light, and full of holes: *spongy moss, spongy dough.* **2** full of holes: *a spongy rock. adj.*, **spon·gi·er, spon·gi·est.**
—**spon′gi·ness,** *n.*

**spon·son** (spon′sən) **1** a part projecting from the side of a ship or boat, used for support or protection. **2** an air-filled section on either side of an airplane, canoe, etc. to steady it. *n.*

**spon·sor** (spon′sər) **1** a person or group that supports or is responsible for a person or thing: *the sponsor of a law, the sponsor of a student applying for a scholarship. I will serve as her sponsor for admission to our club.* **2** a person who takes vows for an infant at baptism; godfather or godmother. **3** a company, store, or organization that, for purposes of advertising, public relations, etc., pays the costs of a radio or television program, concert, play, etc. **4** a person who pledges to donate money to an organization. **5** act as sponsor for.   1–4 *n.*, 5 *v.*

**spon·sor·ship** (spon′sər ship′)   the position, duties, etc. of a SPONSOR.   *n.*

**spon·ta·ne·i·ty** (spon′tə nē′ə tē *or* spon′tə nā′ə tē) **1** the state, quality, or fact of being SPONTANEOUS. **2** a SPONTANEOUS action, movement, etc. *n., pl.* **spon·ta·ne·i·ties.**

**spon·ta·ne·ous** (spon tā′nē əs)   **1** caused by natural impulse or desire; not forced or compelled; not planned beforehand: *Both sides burst into spontaneous cheers at the skilful play.* **2** happening without external cause or help; caused entirely by inner forces: *The eruption of a volcano is spontaneous.* **3** growing or produced naturally; not planted, cultivated, etc. *adj.* —**spon·ta′ne·ous·ly,** *adv.*
—**spon·ta′ne·ous·ness,** *n.*

**spontaneous abortion**   MISCARRIAGE (def. 3).

**spontaneous combustion**   the bursting into flame of a substance as a result of the heat produced by chemical action within the substance itself.

**spook¹** (spük) *Informal.*   a ghost; spectre.   *n.*

**spook²** (spük)   startle game or fish: *The noisy swimmers spooked all the trout.*   *v.*

**spook·y** (spü′kē) *Informal.*   like or suggesting SPOOKS¹; weird; scary.   *adj.*, **spook·i·er, spook·i·est.**

**spool** (spül)   **1** a cylinder of plastic, wood, or metal on which thread, wire, etc. is wound.   **2** something like a spool in shape or use.   **3** wind on a spool.   1, 2 *n.*, 3 *v.*

**spoon** (spün)   **1** a utensil consisting of a small, shallow bowl at the end of a handle: *Spoons are used to take up or stir food or drink.*   **2** take up in a spoon.   **3** something shaped like a spoon.   **4** a kind of golf club having a wooden head.   **5** a shiny, curved bait having hooks attached for catching fish.   1, 3–5 *n.*, 2 *v.*
—**spoon′like′,** *adj.*
**born with a silver spoon in one's mouth,**   born lucky or rich.

**spoon·bill** (spün′bil′)   **1** a long-legged wading bird that has a long, flat bill with a spoon-shaped tip.   **2** any of various birds that have a similar bill.   *n.*

**spoon·drift** (spün′drift′)   SPINDRIFT.   *n.*

**spoon·er·ism** (spü′nə riz′əm)   an unintentional, often humorous, transposing of the letters or sounds of successive words. Example: "kinkering kongs" for "conquering kings."
☞ *Etym.* After Rev. William. A. *Spooner* (1844–1930), of New College, Oxford, who was famous for such mistakes.

**spoon–feed** (spün′fēd′)   **1** feed with a spoon.   **2** spoil; coddle; overprotect: *Industry is being spoon-fed with government grants.*   *v.*, **spoon-fed, spoon-feed·ing.**

**spoon·ful** (spün′fùl′)   as much as a spoon can hold.   *n., pl.* **spoon·fuls.**

**spoor** (spür)   **1** the trail of a wild animal; track: *The hunters followed the spoor of the deer.*   **2** track by or follow a spoor.   1 *n.*, 2 *v.*

**spo·rad·ic** (spə rad′ik)   **1** appearing or happening at intervals in time: *sporadic outbreaks.*   **2** being or occurring apart from others; isolated.   **3** appearing in scattered instances: *sporadic cases of scarlet fever.*   *adj.*

**spo·rad·i·cal** (spə rad′ə kəl)   SPORADIC.   *adj.*

**spo·rad·i·cal·ly** (spə rad′i klē)   here and there; now and then; separately.   *adv.*

**spo·ran·gi·a** (spə ran′jē ə)   pl. of SPORANGIUM.   *n.*

**spo·ran·gi·um** (spə ran′jē əm)   a receptacle containing spores; spore case: *The little brown spots sometimes seen on the underside of ferns are sporangia.*   *n., pl.* **spo·ran·gi·a** (-jē ə).

**spore** (spôr)   **1** a single cell capable of growing into a new plant or animal: *Ferns produce spores.*   **2** a germ or seed.   *n.*

**spo·ro·phyll** or **spo·ro·phyl** (spô′rə fil′)   any leaf that bears spores or spore cases.   *n.*

**spo·ro·phyte** (spô′rə fīt′)   any plant or generation of a plant that produces asexual spores: *Sporophytes develop from the union of germ cells produced by gametophytes.*   *n.*

**spor·ran** (spô′rən)   in men's full Highland dress, a large purse, commonly of fur or leather, hanging from the belt in front. See KILT for picture.   *n.*

**sport** (spôrt)   **1** a game, contest, or other pastime requiring some skill and a certain amount of exercise: *Baseball and fishing are outdoor sports; bowling and basketball are indoor sports.*   **2** amusement; recreation.   **3** amuse oneself; play: *Lambs sport in the field.*   **4** of or suitable for sports.   **5** playful joking; fun: *That was great sport.*   **6** ridicule: *His clumsy dancing was a source of sport to his classmates.*   **7** the object of a joke; plaything: *Her hat blew off and became the sport of the wind.*   **8** JEST.   **9** SPORTSMAN.   **10** *Informal.*   a person who behaves in a SPORTSMANLIKE manner; good fellow: *to be a sport.*   **11** *Informal.*   gambler.   **12** *Informal.*   display: *to sport a new hat.*   **13** *Informal.*   a flashy or showy person.   **14** an animal or plant that varies suddenly or in a marked manner from the normal type: *A white blackbird would be a sport.*   **15** become or produce a sport.   1, 2, 4–7, 9–11, 13, 14 *n.*, 3, 8, 12, 15 *v.*
**for sport** or **in sport,**   in fun; as a joke: *to say a thing in sport.*
**make sport of,**   make fun of; laugh at; ridicule: *Don't make sport of my clumsiness.*

**sport·ing** (spôr′ting)   **1** of, interested in, or engaging in sports.   **2** playing fair: *Letting the little girl throw first was a sporting gesture.*   **3** willing to take a chance.   **4** *Informal.*   involving risk; uncertain: *a sporting chance.*   **5** ppr. of SPORT.   1–4 *adj.*, 5 *v.*   —**sport′ing·ly,** *adv.*

**spor·tive** (spôr′tiv) playful; merry: *The old dog seemed as sportive as the puppy.* *adj.*

**sports** (spôrts) of sports; suitable for sports: *a sports dress.* *adj.*

**sports car** 1 any low, fast, two-seater car, usually one having an open top. 2 any car appealing to driving enthusiasts and designed for high speeds and manoeuvrability.

**sports·cast** (spôrt′skast′) a radio or television broadcast of sports events, or of news or discussion of sports events. *n.* —**sports′cast′er,** *n.*

**sports·man** (spôrt′smən) 1 a person who takes part in sports, especially in hunting, fishing, or racing. 2 a person who plays fair. 3 a person who is willing to take a chance. *n., pl.* **sports·men** (-smən).

**sports·man·like** (spôrt′smən līk′) like or befitting a sportsman; fair and honourable. *adj.*

**sports·man·ship** (spôrt′smən ship′) 1 the qualities or conduct of a sportsman; fair play. 2 ability in sports. *n.*

**sports·wear** (spôrt′swer′) clothing designed for casual wear or recreation. *n.*

**sports·writ·er** (spôrts′rī′tər) a writer who reports sporting events. *n.*

**sport·y** (spôr′tē) *Informal.* 1 sportsmanlike; sporting. 2 gaudy or fast; flashy. 3 smart in dress, appearance, manners, etc. *adj.,* **sport·i·er, sport·i·est.** —**sport′i·ness,** *n.*

**spot** (spot) 1 a mark, stain, or speck: *a spot of ink.* 2 a stain or blemish on character or reputation; moral defect; fault; flaw: *Her character is without spot.* 3 a small part of a surface unlike the rest: *His tie is blue with white spots.* 4 make spots on: *to spot a dress.* 5 become spotted; have spots: *This silk will spot.* 6 stain; tarnish: *He spotted his reputation by lying.* 7 a place: *From this spot you can see the ocean.* 8 *Informal.* a position or place with reference to employment, radio or television scheduling, etc. 9 place in a certain spot; scatter in various spots: *Lookouts were spotted along the coast.* 10 on hand; ready: *a spot answer.* 11 *Informal.* pick out; find out; recognize: *The teacher spotted every mistake.* 12 *Informal.* a small amount; little bit: *a spot of lunch.* 13 a figure or dot on a playing card, domino, or die to show its kind and value. 1–3, 7, 8, 10, 12, 13 *n.,* 4–6, 9, 11 *v.,* **spot·ted, spot·ting.**
**hit the spot,** *Informal.* be just right; be satisfactory.
**in a spot,** in a difficult situation.
**on the spot, a** at the very place. **b** at once. **c** in trouble or difficulty: *She put me on the spot by asking a question I could not answer.*

**spot cash** money paid just as soon as goods are delivered or work is done.

**spot check** 1 a brief, rough sampling. 2 a checkup made without warning.

**spot·less** (spot′lis) without a spot or blemish. *adj.* —**spot′less·ly,** *adv.* —**spot′less·ness,** *n.*

**spot·light** (spot′līt′) 1 a strong light thrown upon a particular place or person. 2 a lamp that gives the light: *a spotlight in a theatre.* 3 light up with a spotlight or spotlights. 4 public notice; anything that focusses attention on a person or thing: *the spotlight of world events.* 5 call attention to; give public notice to. 1, 2, 4 *n.,* 3, 5 *v.*

**spot·ted** (spot′id) 1 stained with spots: *a spotted wall.* 2 marked with spots: *a spotted dog.* 3 sullied: *a spotted reputation.* *adj.*

**spotted fever** any of various fevers characterized by spots on the skin, especially cerebrospinal fever or typhus fever.

**spot·ter** (spot′ər) 1 a person who makes or removes spots. 2 a device for making or removing spots. 3 a civilian who watches for enemy aircraft over a city, town, etc. 4 a person employed to keep watch on employees for evidence of dishonesty or other misconduct. *n.*

**spot·ty** (spot′ē) 1 having spots; spotted. 2 not of uniform quality; irregular: *Her work was spotty.* *adj.,* **spot·ti·er, spot·ti·est.** —**spot′ti·ly,** *adv.* —**spot′ti·ness,** *n.*

**spouse** (spous) a husband or wife. *n.*

**spout** (spout) 1 throw out a liquid in a stream or spray: *A whale spouts water when it breathes.* 2 flow out with force: *Water spouted from a break in the pipe.* 3 a stream or jet. 4 a pipe for carrying off water: *Rain runs down a spout from our roof to the ground.* 5 a tube or lip by which liquid is poured: *A teakettle, a coffee pot, and a syrup jug have spouts.* 6 a column of spray thrown into the air by a whale in breathing. 7 *Informal.* speak in loud tones with affected emotion: *The old-fashioned actor spouted her lines.* 1, 2, 7 *v.,* 3–6 *n.* —**spout′er,** *n.*

**sprain** (sprān) 1 injure a joint or muscle by a sudden twist or wrench: *to sprain your ankle.* 2 an injury caused by a sudden twist or wrench. 1 *v.,* 2 *n.*

**sprang** (sprang) a pt. of SPRING. *v.*

**sprat** (sprat) 1 a small food fish related to the herring, found along the Atlantic coast of Europe. 2 any of various similar fishes. *n.*

**sprawl** (sprol) 1 lie or sit with limbs spread out, especially ungracefully: *The people sprawled on the beach in their bathing suits.* 2 toss or spread the limbs about. 3 spread out in an irregular or awkward manner: *She wrote in a large handwriting that sprawled across the page.* 4 the act or position of sprawling. 5 move awkwardly. 1–3, 5 *v.,* 4 *n.*

**spray**[1] (sprā) 1 liquid going through the air in small drops: *We were wet with the sea spray.* 2 something like this: *A spray of bullets hit the target.* 3 an instrument that sends a liquid out as spray. 4 any of a number of products that are dispensed from a container in a mist: *hair spray, spray paint.* 5 sprinkle; scatter a liquid in a mist or small drops: *Spray this paint on the far wall.* 6 scatter spray on or over: *We spray apple trees to keep the fruit free of disease.* 7 direct numerous small missiles, etc. upon: *The soldiers sprayed the enemy with bullets.* 1–4 *n.,* 5–7 *v.* —**spray′er,** *n.*

**spray**[2] (sprā) 1 a small branch or piece of some plant with its leaves, flowers, or fruit: *a spray of lilacs, a spray of ivy, a spray of berries.* 2 an ornament like this. *n.*

**spray gun** a device used to spray paint, insecticide, or other liquids.

**spread** (spred) 1 cover or cause to cover a large or larger area; stretch out; unfold; open: *to spread rugs on the floor, to spread one's arms, a fan that spreads when shaken.* 2 cause (a job or other activity) to be continued over a period of time: *Alicia spread her reading assignment over several days.* 3 move further apart: *The rails of the track have spread. She spread the end of the rivet with a hammer.*

**4** lie or cause to lie; extend: *Fields of corn spread out before us.* **5** make widely or generally prevalent; propagate: *to spread a religion.* **6** scatter; distribute: *She spread the news. The sickness spread rapidly.* **7** cover with a thin layer: *She spread each slice with butter.* **8** put as a thin layer: *He spread jam on his bread.* **9** be put as a thin layer: *This paint spreads evenly.* **10** the act of spreading: *Doctors fight the spread of disease.* **11** the width; extent; amount of or capacity for spreading: *the spread of a bird's wings, the spread of elastic.* **12** a stretch; expanse. **13** the difference between what something is bought for and what it is sold to another for. **14** the difference between any two prices, rates, etc. **15** stretched out; expanded; extended. **16** a cloth covering for a bed or table. **17** *Informal.* the food put on the table; feast. **18** something for spreading on bread, crackers, etc.: *Butter and jam are spreads.* **19** the area of land owned by a rancher: *She has a big spread near Calgary.* 1–9 *v.*, **spread, spread·ing;** 10–14, 16–19 *n.*, 15 *adj.* —**spread′er,** *n.*
**spread oneself,** *Informal.* **a** try hard to make a good impression. **b** display one's abilities fully. **c** brag.

**spread–ea·gle** (spred′ē′gəl) **1** having the form of an eagle with wings spread out. **2** stretch out flat and sprawling; tie with arms and legs outstretched. 1 *adj.*, 2 *v.*, **spread-ea·gled, spread-ea·gling.**

**spread·sheet** (spred′shēt′) a computer method of making calculations in rows and columns, allowing for manipulation, retrieval, and adjustment based on newly entered data. *n.*

**spree** (sprē) **1** a lively frolic; a jolly time. **2** a period during which a person drinks alcoholic liquor to excess; a bout of drinking. **3** a period of intense interest in an activity. *n.*

**sprig** (sprig) **1** a shoot, twig, or small branch: *a sprig of lilac.* **2** an ornament or design shaped like a sprig. **3** a young man. *n.*

**spright·ly** (sprīt′lē) lively and quick. *adj.*, **spright·li·er, spright·li·est.** —**spright′li·ness,** *n.*

**spring** (spring) **1** leap; jump; move or rise rapidly or suddenly: *The girl sprang to her feet.* **2** a leap or jump: *a spring over the fence.* **3** fly back or away as if by elastic force: *The door sprang to.* **4** cause to spring; cause to act by a spring: *to spring a trap.* **5** an elastic device that returns to its original shape after being pulled or held out of shape: *Beds have wire springs. The spring in a clock makes it go.* **6** elastic quality: *The old man's knees have lost their spring.* **7** be flexible, resilient, or elastic; be able to spring: *This branch springs enough to use as a snare.* **8** a flying back from a forced position. **9** having a spring or springs. **10** the season after winter when plants begin to grow again. **11** of, having to do with, characteristic of, or suitable for the season of spring: *spring hats, spring wheat.* **12** a small stream of water flowing naturally from the earth. **13** from a spring: *spring water.* **14** come from some source; arise; grow: *Plants spring from seeds.* **15** a source, origin; cause. **16** begin to move, act, grow, etc. suddenly; burst forth: *Towns spring up where oil is discovered.* **17** the first and freshest period: *the spring of life.* **18** bring out, produce, or make suddenly: *to spring a surprise on someone.* **19** to crack, split, warp, bend, strain, or break: *Frost had sprung the rock wall.* **20** a crack, bend, strain, or break. **21** rouse partridges, etc. 1, 3, 4, 7, 14, 16, 18, 19, 21 *v.*, **sprang** or **sprung, sprung, spring·ing;** 2, 5, 6, 8, 10–12, 15, 17, 20 *n.*, 9, 13 *adj.* —**spring′like′,** *adj.*

---

**spread-eagle  1153  sprint**

hat, āge, fär; let, ēqual, tėrm; it, īce
hot, ōpen, ôrder; oil, out; cup, pùt, rüle
əbove, takən, pencəl, lemən, circəs
ch, child; ng, long; sh, ship
th, thin; ᴛʜ, then; zh, measure

**spring a leak,** crack and begin to let water through.
**spring a mine,** cause the gunpowder or other explosive in a mine to explode.

**spring beauty** **1** a small, pink or white wildflower of early spring. **2** the plant it grows on, a member of the purslane family.

**spring·board** (spring′bôrd′) **1** a flexible board used to give added spring in diving, jumping, or vaulting. **2** anything that gives one a good start toward a goal or purpose: *Hard work was her springboard to success.* *n.*

**spring·bok** (spring′bok′) a gazelle or small antelope of South Africa. *n., pl.* **spring·boks** or (*esp. collectively*) **spring·bok.**

**spring·er** (spring′ər) **1** a person or thing that springs. **2** either of two breeds of large field spaniel, used to spring or flush game. *n.*

**spring fever** a listless, lazy feeling felt by some people, caused by the first sudden warm weather of spring.

**spring·halt** (spring′holt′) STRINGHALT. *n.*

**spring salmon** *Cdn.* the largest species of Pacific salmon, found from California to Alaska, including British Columbia, mainly dark greenish-blue and silver in colour and having red, white, or, sometimes, pink flesh: *Spring salmon are very highly valued as food fish.*

**spring·tail** (spring′tāl′) a small, wingless insect having a forked, tail-like appendage used in leaping. *n.*

**spring tide** **1** the high tide at its highest level. It comes at the time of the new moon or the full moon. **2** any great flood, swell, or rush.

**spring·tide** (spring′tīd′) SPRINGTIME. *n.*

**spring·time** (spring′tīm′) the season of spring. *n.*

**spring·y** (spring′ē) **1** yielding; flexible; elastic: *The wet lawn was springy to the feet.* **2** jaunty; happy; full of bounce: *a springy personality.* **3** having many springs of water. *adj.*, **spring·i·er, spring·i·est.** —**spring′i·ly,** *adv.* —**spring′i·ness,** *n.*

**sprin·kle** (spring′kəl) **1** scatter something in drops or tiny bits: *She sprinkled sand on the icy sidewalk.* **2** scatter in drops or tiny bits. **3** spray or cover with small drops: *to sprinkle flowers with water.* **4** dot or vary with something scattered here and there. **5** a sprinkling; small quantity. **6** rain a little. **7** a light rain. 1–4, 6 *v.*, **sprin·kled, sprin·kling;** 5, 7 *n.*

**sprin·kler** (spring′klər) **1** a device used to water lawns. **2** a device attached to the ceiling of a building from which water is sprayed in the event of a fire. *n.*

**sprin·kling** (spring′kling) **1** a small quantity or number scattered here and there. **2** ppr. of SPRINKLE. 1 *n.*, 2 *v.*

**sprint** (sprint) **1** run at top speed, especially for a short distance. **2** a short race or dash at full speed. 1 *v.*, 2 *n.* —**sprint′er,** *n.*

**sprit** (sprit)   a small pole that supports and stretches a sail.  *n.*

**sprite** (sprīt)   an elf; fairy; goblin.  *n.*

**sprit·sail** (sprit'sāl' *or* sprit'səl)   a sail supported and stretched by a SPRIT.  *n.*

A wheel with sprockets

**sprock·et** (sprok'it)   **1** one of a set of projections on the rim of a wheel, arranged so as to fit into the links of a chain: *The sprockets keep the chain from slipping.*   **2** Also, **sprocket wheel**, a wheel made with sprockets.

**sprout** (sprout)   **1** begin to grow; shoot forth: *Seeds sprout. Buds sprout in the spring.*   **2** cause to grow: *The rain has sprouted the corn.*   **3** a shoot or bud of a plant: *The gardener was setting out sprouts.*   **4** develop rapidly.   **5** *Informal.*   remove sprouts from: *He sprouted the potatoes twice every winter.*   **6** a small boy.   **7 sprouts**, *pl.* BRUSSELS SPROUTS.   1, 2, 4, 5 *v.*, 3, 6, 7 *n.*

A branch of spruce with cones

**spruce¹** (sprüs)   **1** any of a group of about 40 closely related species of evergreen tree of the pine family found throughout the northern areas of the world, having hanging cones and short, needle-like leaves growing singly along the stems: *There are five species of spruce native to Canada.*   **2** the wood of any of these trees.  *n.*

**spruce²** (sprüs)   **1** neat; trim: *Akbar looked very spruce in his new suit.*   **2** make or become spruce: *He spruced himself in front of the mirror. Spruce up before you go back to school.*   1 *adj.*, **spruc·er, spruc·est**;   2 *v.*, **spruced, spruc·ing.**   —**spruce'ly**, *adv.*   —**spruce'ness**, *n.*

**sprung** (sprung)   a pt. and pp. of SPRING: *The fox sprung the trap. The trap was sprung.*  *v.*

**spry** (sprī)   active; lively; nimble: *The spry old lady travelled everywhere.*   *adj.*, **spry·er** or **spri·er, spry·est** or **spri·est.**   —**spry'ly**, *adv.*   —**spry'ness**, *n.*

**spt.**   seaport.

**spud** (spud)   **1** a tool with a narrow blade, for digging up or cutting the roots of weeds.   **2** a tool resembling a chisel, for removing bark.   **3** dig up or remove with a spud.   **4** *Informal.*   potato.   **5** Often, **spud in**, make a hole for an oil well, as the first stage in drilling: *The new well was spudded in two weeks ago.*   1, 2, 4 *n.*, 3, 5 *v.*, **spud·ded, spud·ding.**

**spue** (spyü)   See SPEW.  *v.*, **spued, spu·ing.**

**spume** (spyüm)   foam; froth.  *n., v.*, **spumed, spum·ing.**

**spu·mo·ne** (spə mō'nē; *Italian*, spü mō'nā)   a type of Italian ice cream, usually containing fruit, nuts, etc.  *n.*

**spum·y** (spyü'mē)   covered with, consisting of, or resembling SPUME; foamy; frothy.  *adj.*, **spum·i·er, spum·i·est.**

**spun** (spun)   pt. and pp. of SPIN: *He spun the coin. Why have the spiders spun their webs here?*  *v.*

**spun glass**   glass made into threads.

**spunk** (spungk)   **1** *Informal.*   courage; pluck; spirit; mettle: *a little puppy full of spunk.*   **2** a spark.   **3** tinder or PUNK¹.   *n.*
**get one's spunk up**, *Informal.*   show courage, pluck, or spirit.

**spunk·y** (spung'kē) *Informal.*   courageous; plucky; spirited.   *adj.*, **spunk·i·er, spunk·i·est.**   —**spunk'i·ly**, *adv.*   —**spunk'i·ness**, *n.*

**spun rayon**   yarn made from rayon threads: *When woven, spun rayon resembles linen cloth.*

**spun silk**   silk waste spun into yarn.

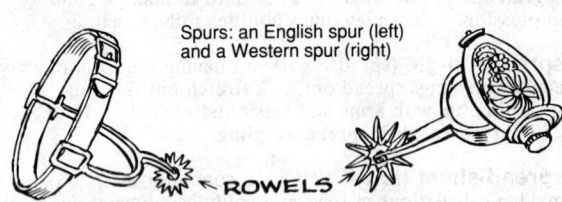
Spurs: an English spur (left) and a Western spur (right)

**spur** (spėr)   **1** a pricking instrument worn on a rider's heel for urging a horse on.   **2** prick with spurs: *The rider spurred her horse on.*   **3** something like a spur; a point sticking out: *A cock has spurs on his legs.*   **4** strike or wound with a spur or spurs.   **5** anything that urges on: *Ambition was the spur that made him work.*   **6** urge on: *Pride spurred the boy to fight.*   **7** provide with a spur or spurs.   **8** a ridge projecting from or subordinate to the main body of a mountain or mountain range.   **9** any short branch: *a spur of a railway.*   1, 3, 5, 8, 9 *n.*, 2, 4, 6, 7 *v.*, **spurred, spur·ring.**
**on the spur of the moment**,   on a sudden impulse; without previous planning or preparation.
**spur on**,   encourage.
**win one's spurs**,   make a reputation for oneself.

**spurge** (spėrj)   **1** any of a large, closely related group of plants having a bitter, milky juice and clusters of small flowers: *Some species and varieties of spurge are grown as garden flowers. The poinsettia is a spurge.*   **2** referring to a family of plants found in most temperate and tropical regions that includes spurge, croton, rubber, and cassava: *Most plants of the spurge family have milky juice.*  *n.*

**spu·ri·ous** (spyu'rē əs)   **1** not coming from the right source; not genuine; false; sham: *a spurious document.*   **2** illegitimate.  *adj.*   —**spu'ri·ous·ly**, *adv.*   —**spur'i·ous·ness**, *n.*

**spurn** (spėrn)   **1** refuse with scorn; scorn: *The judge spurned the bribe.*   **2** disdainful rejection; contemptuous treatment.   **3** oppose with scorn: *They spurned restraint.*   **4** strike with the foot; kick away.   **5** a kick.   1, 3, 4 *v.*, 2, 5 *n.*

**spurred** (spėrd)   **1** having spurs or a SPUR.   **2** pt. and pp. of SPUR.   1 *adj.*, 2 *v.*

**spurt** (spėrt)   **1** flow suddenly in a stream or jet; gush out; squirt: *Blood spurted from the cut.*   **2** cause to gush out.   **3** a sudden rushing forth; jet: *Spurts of flame broke through the roof.*   **4** a great increase of effort or activity for a short time: *to put on a spurt.*   **5** put forth great energy for a short time; show great activity for a short time: *The runners spurted near the end of the race.* 1, 2, 5 *v.*, 3, 4 *n.* Also, **spirt**.

**spur track** a branch railway track connected with the main track at one end only.

**sput·nik** (sput′nik *or* spùt′nik) any of a group of earth satellites put into orbit by the Soviet Union, especially those in 1957. *n.*
☛ *Etym.* From Russian *sputnik,* literally 'co-traveller'.

**sput·ter** (sput′ər) **1** make spitting or popping noises: *fat sputtering in the frying pan. The firecrackers sputtered.* **2** throw out drops of saliva, bits of food, etc. in excitement or in talking too fast. **3** say words or sounds in haste and confusion. **4** confused talk. **5** a sputtering; sputtering noise. 1–3 *v.*, 4, 5 *n.* —**sput′ter·er,** *n.*

**spu·tum** (spyü′təm) **1** SALIVA; spit. **2** what is coughed up from the lungs and spat out. *n., pl.* **spu·ta** (-tə).

**spy** (spī) **1** a person who keeps secret watch on the action of others. **2** a person paid by a government to get secret information about the government plans, military strength, etc. of another country. **3** find out or try to find out by careful observation; search. **4** keep secret watch: *Mr. Akiyama saw two men spying on him from behind a tree.* **5** act as a spy; be a spy: *The punishment for spying in wartime is death.* **6** catch sight of; see. 1, 2 *n., pl.* **spies;** 3–6 *v.*, **spied, spy·ing.**
**spy out, a** watch or examine secretly or carefully. **b** find out by watching secretly or carefully: *She spies out everything that goes on in the neighbourhood.*

**spy·glass** (spī′glas′) a small telescope: *Spyglasses were formerly very useful to naval officers.* *n.*

**sq.**[1] square.

**sq.**[2] the following.

**sq. ft.** square foot; square feet.

**sq. in.** square inch; square inches.

**sq. mi.** square mile; square miles.

**squab** (skwob) **1** a very young bird, especially a young pigeon. **2** newly hatched. **3** a short, stout person. **4** short and stout. **5** a thick, soft cushion. **6** a sofa; couch. 1, 3, 5, 6 *n.*, 2, 4 *adj.*

**squab·ble** (skwob′əl) **1** a petty, noisy quarrel: *Children's squabbles annoy their parents.* **2** take part in a petty, noisy quarrel: *I won't squabble over a dime.* 1 *n.*, 2 *v.*, **squab·bled, squab·bling.** —**squab′bler,** *n.*

**squad** (skwod) **1** a number of soldiers grouped for drill, inspection, or work: *A squad is the smallest tactical unit in an army.* **2** any small group of persons working together: *A squad of girls cleaned up the yard.* *n.*

**squad car** a police patrol car that keeps in communication with headquarters by special radio-telephone equipment.

**squad·ron** (skwod′rən) **1** a part of a naval fleet used for special service. **2** a body of cavalry. **3** a formation of airplanes, usually two or three flights, that fly or fight together. **4** a formation of armoured cars or tanks, smaller than a regiment and made up of several troops. *n.*

**squal·id** (skwol′id) filthy; degraded; wretched. *adj.* —**squal′id·ly,** *adv.* —**squal′id·ness,** *n.*

**squall**[1] (skwol) **1** a sudden, violent gust of wind, often with rain, snow, or sleet. **2** *Informal.* trouble. *n.*

**squall**[2] (skwol) **1** cry out loudly; scream violently: *The* 

---

**spur track**      **1155**      **square**

hat, āge, fär; let, ēqual, tėrm; it, īce
hot, ōpen, ôrder; oil, out; cup, pùt, rüle
əbove, tākən, pencəl, lemən, circəs
ch, child; ng, long; sh, ship
th, thin; ᴛʜ, then; zh, measure

*baby squalled.* **2** a loud, harsh cry: *the squall of a parrot.* 1 *v.*, 2 *n.* —**squall′er,** *n.*

**squall·y** (skwol′ē) **1** disturbed by sudden and violent gusts of wind: *squally weather.* **2** blowing in squalls. **3** *Informal.* threatening. *adj.*, **squall·i·er, squall·i·est.**

**squal·or** (skwol′ər) misery and dirt; wretchedness: *There is much squalor in a slum.* *n.*

**squan·der** (skwon′dər) spend foolishly; waste: *He squandered his time and money in gambling.* *v.*

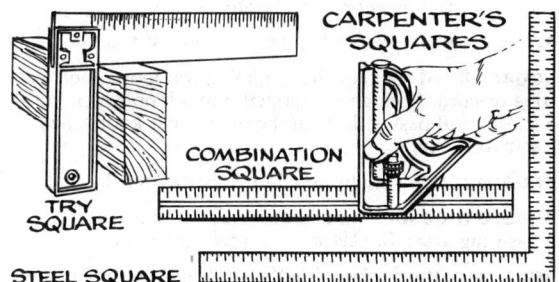

CARPENTER'S SQUARES
COMBINATION SQUARE
TRY SQUARE
STEEL SQUARE

**square** (skwer) **1** a plane figure with four equal sides and four interior right angles. See QUADRILATERAL for picture. **2** anything of or near this shape: *The troops were drawn up in a square.* **3** having this shape: *a square box. A block of stone is usually square.* **4** of a specified length on each side of a square: *a room five metres square.* **5** having breadth more nearly equal to length or height than is usual: *a square jaw.* **6** make square; make rectangular; make cubical. **7** mark out in squares: *The children squared off the sidewalk to play hopscotch.* **8** a space in a city or town bounded by streets on four sides: *This square is filled with stores.* **9** the distance along one side of such a space; block. **10** an open space in a city or town bounded by streets on four sides, often planted with grass, trees, etc. **11** any similar open space, such as at the meeting of streets. **12** the buildings surrounding such a place. **13** a parade ground. **14** forming a right angle: *a square corner.* **15** bring to the form of a right angle. **16** an instrument having two straight edges that meet to form a right angle, used in carpentry, etc. for drawing and testing right angles. **17** straight; level; even. **18** make straight, level, or even: *to square a picture on the wall.* **19** leaving no balance; even: *to make accounts square.* **20** adjust; settle: *Let us square accounts.* **21** agree; conform: *Denise's acts do not square with her promises.* **22** just; fair; honest: *a square deal.* **23** *Informal.* fairly or honestly. **24** straightforward; direct: *a square refusal.* **25** *Informal.* satisfying: *a square meal.* **26** regulate. **27** the product obtained when a number is multiplied by itself: *16 is the square of 4.* **28** in mathematics, find the equivalent in square measure: *Please square this circle.* **29** multiply a number by itself: *25 squared makes 625.* **30** squared: *a square centimetre.* **31** multiplied by itself. **32** so as to be square; in square or rectangular form; at right angles. **33** solid and strong. 1, 2, 8–13, 16, 27 *n.*, 3–5, 14, 17, 19, 22, 24, 25, 30, 31, 33

*adj.*, **squar·er, squar·est;** 6, 7, 15, 18, 20, 21, 26, 28, 29 *v.*, **squared, squar·ing;** 23, 32 *adv.* —**square′ly,** *adv.*
**on the square,** a at right angles. b *Informal.* justly; fairly; honestly.
**out of square,** not at right angles; out of order; incorrect or incorrectly.
**square away,** a set the sails of a ship so that it will stay before the wind. b prepare; put in order; get ready.
**square off,** *Informal.* put oneself in a position of defence or attack.
**square oneself,** *Informal.* a make up for something one has said or done. b get even.
**square the circle,** a find a square equal in area to a circle. b try to do something impossible.
**square up,** a adjust; settle: *to square up an account.* b take up a fighting stance; get ready to fight.

**square dance** a dance performed by a set of four couples arranged in some set form, usually a square: *The quadrille and Virginia reel are square dances.*

**square deal** *Informal.* fair and honest treatment.

**square knot** a knot firmly joining two loose ends of rope or cord. Each end is formed into a loop which both encloses and passes through the other; reef knot. See KNOT for picture.

**square meal** a substantial or satisfying meal.

**square measure** a unit or system of units for measuring area: *The hectare is a square measure.*

**square-rigged** (skwer′rigd′) having the principal sails set at right angles across the masts: *Brigs were square-rigged.* See BRIG for picture. *adj.*

**square-rig·ger** (skwer′rig′ər) a SQUARE-RIGGED ship. *n.*

**square root** a number that produces a given number when multiplied by itself: *If the given number is 16, the square root is 4.*

**square sail** a four-sided sail.

**square shooter** *Informal.* a fair and honest person.

**squash**[1] (skwosh) 1 press until soft or flat; crush: *The boy squashed the clay between his hands. Carry the cream puffs carefully for they squash easily.* 2 something squashed; a crushed mass. 3 a squashing; a squashing sound. 4 make a squashing sound; move with a squashing sound: *We heard her squash through the mud and slush.* 5 put an end to; stop by force: *The police quickly squashed the riot.* 6 *Informal.* silence with a crushing argument, reply, etc.: *The speaker neatly squashed her hecklers.* 7 crowd; squeeze. 8 a game resembling handball and tennis, played in a walled court with rackets and a rubber ball. See RACKET[2] for picture. 9 *Esp. Brit.* a drink containing crushed fruit: *lemon squash.* 1, 4–7 *v.*, 2, 3, 8, 9 *n.* —**squash′er,** *n.*
☛ *Etym.* From OF *esquasser* 'squeeze out', which developed from L *ex* 'out' + *quassare* 'press'.

**squash**[2] (skwosh) 1 the fruit of any of various vinelike plants: *Pumpkins and vegetable marrows are two kinds of squash.* 2 the plant it grows on. *n., pl.* **squash** or **squash·es.**
☛ *Etym.* A shortened form of an Algonquian name for this vegetable, probably *askootasquash*.

**squash·y** (skwosh′ē) 1 easily squashed: *squashy cream puffs.* 2 soft and wet: *squashy ground.* 3 having a crushed appearance. *adj.*, **squash·i·er, squash·i·est.** —**squash′i·ly,** *adv.* —**squash′i·ness,** *n.*

**squat** (skwot) 1 crouch on the heels. 2 sit on the ground or floor with the legs drawn up closely beneath or in front of the body. 3 seat oneself with the legs drawn up. 4 crouching: *We saw a squat figure in front of the fire.* 5 the act of squatting; squatting posture. 6 settle on another's land without title or right. 7 settle on public land to acquire ownership of it under government regulation. 8 short and thick; low and broad: *The burglar was a squat, dark man. I like that squat teapot.* 1–3, 6, 7 *v.*, **squat·ted** or **squat, squat·ting;** 4, 8 *adj.*, 5 *n.*

**squat·ter** (skwot′ər) 1 a person who settles on another's land or in another's house without right. 2 a person who settles on public land to acquire ownership of it. 3 a person, animal, etc. that crouches or squats. *n.*

**squat·ty** (skwot′ē) short and thick; low and broad. *adj.*, **squat·ti·er, squat·ti·est.**

**squawk** (skwok) 1 make a loud, harsh sound: *Chickens and ducks squawk when frightened.* 2 utter harshly and loudly. 3 a loud, harsh sound. 1, 2 *v.*, 3 *n.* —**squawk′er,** *n.*

**squeak** (skwēk) 1 make a short, sharp, shrill sound: *A mouse squeaks.* 2 such a sound: *We heard the squeak of the rocking chair.* 3 cause to squeak. 4 utter with a squeak. 5 *Informal.* get or pass (*by* or *through*) with difficulty. 6 *Informal.* a chance to get by or through; chance of escape: *a narrow squeak.* 1, 3–5 *v.*, 2, 6 *n.*

**squeak·y** (skwē′kē) SQUEAKing: *a squeaky door.* *adj.*, **squeak·i·er, squeak·i·est.** —**squeak′i·ly,** *adv.* —**squeak′i·ness,** *n.*

**squeal** (skwēl) 1 make a long, sharp, shrill cry: *A pig squeals when it is hurt.* 2 such a cry. 3 utter sharply and shrilly. 1, 3 *v.*, 2 *n.* —**squeal′er,** *n.*

**squeam·ish** (skwē′mish) 1 too proper, modest, etc.; easily shocked. 2 too particular; too scrupulous. 3 slightly sick at one's stomach; sickish. 4 easily turned sick. *adj.* —**squeam′ish·ly,** *adv.* —**squeam′ish·ness,** *n.*

**squeeze** (skwēz) 1 press hard: *Don't squeeze the kitten; you will hurt it.* 2 a squeezing; tight pressure: *a squeeze of the hand.* 3 hug: *She squeezed her child.* 4 force by pressing: *I can't squeeze another thing into my trunk.* 5 burden; oppress: *Heavy taxes squeezed the people.* 6 get by pressure, force, or effort: *The dictator squeezed money from the people.* 7 yield to pressure: *Sponges squeeze easily.* 8 force a way: *She squeezed through the crowd.* 9 a crush; crowd: *It's a tight squeeze to get five people in that little car.* 10 something made by pressing; a cast; impression. 11 *Informal.* a situation from which escape is difficult. 1, 3–8 *v.*, **squeezed, squeez·ing;** 2, 3, 9–11 *n.* —**squeez′er,** *n.*
**squeeze someone in,** *Informal.* accommodate someone.
**tight squeeze,** *Informal.* a difficult situation.

**squeeze play** 1 in baseball, a play executed when a runner on third base starts for home as soon as the pitcher begins to pitch. 2 *Informal.* an attempt to force somebody into a difficult situation or to make him or her act against his or her wishes.

**squelch** (skwelch) 1 cause to be silent; crush: *She squelched him with a look of contempt.* 2 a crushing retort. 3 strike or press on with crushing force. 4 walk in mud, water, wet shoes, etc. making a splashing sound. 5 make the sound of one doing so. 6 such a sound. 1, 3–5 *v.*, 2, 6 *n.* —**squelch′er,** *n.*

**squib** (skwib) 1 short witty attack in speech or writing; sharp sarcasm. 2 a brief item in a newspaper used mainly to fill space.   **3** a small firework that burns with a hissing noise and finally explodes.   **4** a broken firecracker.   *n.*

**squid** (skwid)   a sea MOLLUSC that is related to the octopus, having a long body, ten arms, and a pair of tail fins: *Small squid are used as bait in fishing for cod.*   *n., pl.* **squid** or **squids**.

**squill** (skwil)   a plant of the same family as the lily: *The onionlike bulb of the squill is used in medicine.*   *n.*

**squint** (skwint)   **1** look with the eyes partly closed.   **2** a looking with partly closed eyes.   **3** hold the eyes partly closed.   **4** a sidelong look; hasty look; look.   **5** look sideways.   **6** a tendency to look sideways.   **7** looking sideways; looking askance.   **8** cause to squint.   **9** incline; tend: *The general's remark squinted toward treason.*   **10** an inclination; tendency.   **11** a defect of the eyes that makes one look sideways or cross-eyed.   **12** look sideways or cross-eyed.   **13** cross-eyed.   **14** run or go obliquely.   1, 3, 5, 8, 9, 12, 14 *v.*, 2, 4, 6, 10, 11 *n.*, 7, 13 *adj.*   —**squint′er,** *n.*

**squire** (skwīr)   **1** in England, a country gentleman, especially the chief landowner in a district.   **2** a young man of noble family who attended a knight till he himself was made a knight; esquire.   **3** attendant.   **4** attend as squire.   **5** a woman's escort.   **6** escort a lady.   1–3, 5 *n.*, 4, 6 *v.*, **squired, squir·ing.**   —**squire′like′,** *adj.*

**squirm** (skwėrm)   **1** wriggle; writhe; twist: *The restless boy squirmed in his chair.*   **2** a wriggle; twist.   **3** show great embarrassment, annoyance, confusion, etc.   1, 3 *v.*, 2 *n.*

**squirm·y** (skwėr′mē)   squirming; wriggling.   *adj.*, **squirm·i·er, squirm·i·est.**

A grey squirrel—about 23 cm long excluding the tail

**squir·rel** (skwėr′əl *or* skwir′əl)   **1** a small, bushy-tailed rodent that usually lives in trees and eats nuts.   **2** its fur, usually black, grey, dark-brown, or reddish.   *n.*

**squirt** (skwėrt)   **1** force out liquid through a narrow opening: *to squirt water through a tube.*   **2** come out in a jet or stream: *Water squirted from the hose.*   **3** wet or soak by shooting liquid in a jet or stream: *The elephant squirted me with its trunk.*   **4** the act of squirting.   **5** a jet of liquid, etc.   **6** a small pump, syringe, or other device for squirting a liquid.   **7** *Informal.*   an insignificant person who is impudent or self-assertive.   **8** a young boy.   1–3 *v.*, 4–8 *n.*   —**squirt′er,** *n.*

**squirt gun**   WATER PISTOL.

**squish** (skwish)   **1** make a soft, splashing sound when walking in mud, water, etc.   **2** *Informal.*   squash; squeeze.   **3** a squishing sound.   1, 2 *v.*, 3 *n.*   —**squish′y,** *adj.*

**sq. yd.**   square yard; square yards.

**sq. yds.**   square yards.

**Sr**   strontium.

**Sr.**   **1** senior.   **2** Sir.   **3** Sister.

**squid**          1157          **stableboy**

hat, āge, fär; let, ēqual, tėrm; it, īce hot, ōpen, ôrder; oil, out; cup, pùt, rüle əbove, takən, pencəl, lemən, circəs ch, child; ng, long; sh, ship th, thin; ᴛʜ, then; zh, measure

**S.S.**   **1** steamship.   **2** Secretary of State.   **3** separate school.   **4** school section.   **5** staff sergeant.

**SSE** or **S.S.E.**   south-southeast.

**SSW** or **S.S.W.**   south-southwest.

**St.**   **1** Street.   **2** Saint.   **3** Strait.

**sta.**   **1** station.   **2** stationary.

**stab** (stab)   **1** pierce or wound with a pointed weapon.   **2** thrust with a pointed weapon; aim a blow.   **3** a thrust or blow made with a pointed weapon; any thrust.   **4** a wound made by stabbing.   **5** penetrate suddenly and sharply; pierce.   **6** wound sharply or deeply in the feelings: *The mother was stabbed to the heart by her son's thoughtlessness.*   **7** an injury to the feelings.   **8** *Informal.* an attempt.   1, 2, 5, 6 *v.*, **stabbed, stab·bing;**   3, 4, 7, 8 *n.*   —**stab′ber,** *n.*
**have** or **make a stab at,**   try; attempt.
**stab in the back,**   attempt to injure in a sly, treacherous manner; slander.

**sta·bil·i·ty** (stə bil′ə tē)   **1** the condition of being fixed in position; firmness: *A concrete wall has more stability than a light wooden fence.*   **2** permanence.   **3** steadfastness of character, purpose, etc.   **4** the ability of an object to return to its original position.   *n., pl.* **sta·bil·i·ties.**

**sta·bi·li·za·tion** (stā′bə lə zā′shən *or* stā′bə lī zā′shən)   a stabilizing; being STABILIZEd.   *n.*

**sta·bi·lize** (stā′bə līz′)   **1** make stable or firm.   **2** prevent changes in; hold steady: *to stabilize prices.*   **3** keep a ship, aircraft, spacecraft, etc. steady by special construction or automatic devices.   *v.*, **sta·bi·lized, sta·bi·liz·ing.**

**sta·bi·liz·er** (stā′bə lī′zər)   **1** a person or thing that makes something stable.   **2** a device for keeping a ship, aircraft, spacecraft, etc. steady. See AIRPLANE for picture.   *n.*

**sta·ble¹** (stā′bəl)   **1** a building fitted with stalls, rack and manger, etc. in which horses are kept.   **2** a barn, shed, or other building in which any domestic animals, such as cattle, goats, etc. are kept.   **3** a group of animals housed in such a building: *The black racehorse is one of Mr. Khan's stable.*   **4** the buildings and grounds where racehorses are quartered and trained.   **5** put or keep in a stable.   **6** lodge in a stable.   **7** a group of racehorses belonging to one owner.   **8** the persons caring for such a group.   **9** *Informal.*   a group of athletes, artists, writers, etc. who work under the same management.   1–4, 7–9 *n.*, 5, 6 *v.*, **sta·bled, sta·bling.**

**sta·ble²** (stā′bəl)   **1** not likely to move or change; firm; steady: *Concrete reinforced with steel is stable. The whole world needs a stable peace.*   **2** lasting without change; permanent.   **3** able to return to its original position.   **4** of a chemical compound, not easily decomposed.   **5** of people, mentally or emotionally steady.   *adj.*   —**sta′bly,** *adv.*

**sta·ble·boy** (stā′bəl boi′)   a boy who works in a stable.   *n.*

**sta·ble·girl** (stā′bəl gėrl′) a girl who works in a stable. *n.*

**stacc.** staccato.

**stac·ca·to** (stə kä′tō) **1** in music, short, sharp; with each note ended sharply: *staccato notes, a staccato passage.* **2** a staccato passage or composition; a piece to be sung or played staccato. **3** disconnected; abrupt. **4** in a staccato manner. *1, 3 adj., 2 n., 4 adv.*

**stack** (stak) **1** a large pile of hay, straw, etc.: *Haystacks, which are often round, are arranged so as to shed water.* **2** a pile of anything: *a stack of wood.* **3** a number of rifles arranged to form a cone or pyramid. **4** pile or arrange in a stack: *to stack hay, to stack firewood, to stack rifles, etc.* **5** arrange playing cards unfairly. **6** *Informal.* a large quantity. **7** a number of chimneys, flues, or pipes standing together in one group. **8** chimney. **9** *Brit.* a unit for measuring a quantity of firewood, equal to about 3.06 cubic metres. **10** a rack with shelves for books. **11 stacks,** *pl.* the part of a library in which the main collection of books is shelved. *1–3, 6–11 n., 4, 5 v.*
**have the cards stacked against one,** be at a great disadvantage.
**stack up,** *Informal.* measure up; compare against.

**Stad·a·co·na** (stad′ə kō′nə) the name of the Iroquois village on the site of the present city of Quebec when it was visited by Jacques Cartier in 1535. *n.*

**sta·di·a**[1] (stā′dē ə) an instrument for measuring distances or heights by means of angles: *A surveyor's transit is one kind of stadia.* *n.*

**sta·di·a**[2] (stā′dē ə) a pl. of STADIUM. *n.*

**sta·di·um** (stā′dē əm) **1** an oval or U-shaped structure with rows of seats around a large, open space for games, concerts, etc. **2** an ancient Greek running track for foot races, with rows of seats along each side and at one end: *The stadium of Athens was about 184 metres long.* *n., pl.* **sta·di·ums** or **sta·di·a.**

**staff** (staf) **1** a stick, pole, or rod used as a support, as an emblem of office, as a weapon, etc.: *The flag hangs on a staff.* **2** a group assisting a chief; a group of assistants working with their chief as a unit. **3** a group of service officers that assist a commanding officer in planning and supervisory operations. **4** provide with officers or employees. **5** in music, the five lines and four spaces between them on which the notes, rests, etc. are written. See DO[2] for picture. *1–3, 5 n., pl.* **staves** or **staffs,** (defs. 2, 3, and 5) **staffs;** *4 v.*
**staff of life,** something that sustains life.

**staff officer** a military officer who assists in planning and supervising operations.

**stag** (stag) **1** a full-grown male deer. **2** the male of various other animals. **3** a man who goes to a dance, party, etc. alone or with other men. **4** a dinner, party, etc. attended by men only. **5** attended by, or for, men only: *a stag party.* *1–4 n., 5 adj.*

**stage** (stāj) **1** one step or degree in a process; a period of development: *An insect passes through several stages before it is full-grown.* **2** the raised platform in a theatre on which the actors perform. **3** the theatre; the drama; an actor's profession: *Shakespeare wrote for the stage.* **4** the scene of action: *Queenston Heights was the stage of a famous battle.* **5** put on a stage; arrange: *The play was excellently staged.* **6** be suited to the theatre: *That scene will not stage well.* **7** arrange to have an effect: *The angry people staged a riot.* **8** a section of a rocket or missile having its own motor and fuel. **9** a stagecoach; bus. **10** travel by stagecoach. **11** a place of rest on a journey; regular stopping place. **12** the distance between two places of rest on a journey; distance between stops. **13** a platform; flooring. **14** a scaffold. *1–4, 8, 9, 11–14 n., 5–7, 10 v.,* **staged, stag·ing.** —**stage′like′,** *adj.*
**by** or **in easy stages,** a little at a time; slowly; often stopping: *We made the long journey in easy stages.*
**on the stage,** being an actor.

An early 19th century stagecoach

**stage·coach** (stāj′kōch′) a large, four-wheeled, horse-drawn coach formerly used for carrying passengers, mail, and parcels over a regular route. *n.*

**stage·craft** (stāj′kraft′) **1** skill in, or the art of, writing, adapting, or presenting plays. **2** skill in the techniques of staging plays. *n.*

**stage fright** nervous fear of appearing before an audience.

**stage·hand** (stāj′hand′) a person whose work is moving scenery, arranging lights, etc. in a theatre. *n.*

**stag·er** (stāj′ər) **1** a person of long experience. **2** a horse used for drawing a stagecoach. *n.*

**stage–struck** (stāj′struk′) extremely interested in acting; wanting very much to become an actor. *adj.*

**stage whisper 1** a loud whisper on a stage meant for the audience to hear. **2** a whisper meant to be heard by others than the person addressed.

**stag·ger** (stag′ər) **1** sway or reel, as from weakness, a heavy load, or drunkenness. **2** make sway or reel: *The blow staggered him for the moment.* **3** a swaying; reeling. **4** become unsteady; waver. **5** hesitate. **6** cause to hesitate or become confused: *The difficulty of the examination staggered her.* **7** confuse or astonish greatly: *We were staggered by the news of the air disaster.* **8** make helpless. **9** arrange in a zigzag or irregular order or way: *The rows of seats in the theatre were staggered so that each person could see past the one in front.* **10** arrange at intervals, often to prevent congestion or confusion: *The school was so crowded that classes had to be staggered. Vacations were staggered so that only one person was away at a time.* *1, 2, 4–10 v., 3 n.* —**stag′ger·er,** *n.* —**stag′ger·ing·ly,** *adv.*

**stag·gers** (stag′ərz) of horses, cattle, etc., a nervous disease that makes them stagger or fall suddenly. *n. pl.*

**stag·hound** (stag′hound′) one of a breed of hounds resembling the foxhound but larger, used for hunting deer. *n.*

**stag·ing** (stāj′ing) **1** a temporary platform or structure of posts and boards for support, as in building; scaffolding. **2** the act or process of putting a play on the stage. **3** a travelling by stages or by stagecoach. **4** the business of running stagecoaches. **5** ppr. of STAGE. *1–4 n., 5 v.*

**stag·nan·cy** (stag′nən sē) a stagnant condition. *n.*

**stag·nant** (stag′nənt) **1** not running or flowing: *stagnant air, stagnant water.* **2** foul from standing still: *a stagnant pool of water.* **3** not active; sluggish; dull: *a stagnant mind. During the summer, business is often stagnant.* *adj.* —**stag′nant·ly,** *adv.*

**stag·nate** (stag′nāt) **1** be stagnant; become stagnant. **2** make stagnant. *v.,* **stag·nat·ed, stag·nat·ing.**

**stag·na·tion** (stag nā′shən) a becoming or making stagnant; stagnant condition. *n.*

**stag·y** (stā′jē) **1** of or having to do with the stage. **2** suggestive of the stage; theatrical. **3** artificial; pompous; affected. *adj.,* **stag·i·er, stag·i·est.** —**stag′i·ly,** *adv.* —**stag′i·ness,** *n.*

**staid** (stād) having a settled, quiet character; sober; sedate. *adj.* —**staid′ly,** *adv.* —**staid′ness,** *n.*

**stain** (stān) **1** a discolouration; soil; spot: *He has ink stains on his shirt.* **2** discolour; spot: *The tablecloth is stained where food has been spilled.* **3** a cause of reproach, infamy, or disgrace; a moral blemish; stigma: *a stain on one's character or reputation.* **4** bring reproach or disgrace on a person's reputation, honour, etc.; blemish; soil. **5** a liquid dye used to colour or darken. **6** colour; dye: *She stained the chair a dark-green colour.* **1, 3, 5** *n.,* **2, 4, 6** *v.* —**stain′a·ble,** *adj.* —**stain′er,** *n.*

**stained glass 1** glass coloured by metallic oxides, used in church windows, etc. **2** a window or windows made of many pieces of stained glass, usually shaped to represent figures, scenes, etc. and joined together by grooved strips of lead.

**stain·less** (stān′lis) without stain; spotless: *a stainless reputation.* *adj.*

**stainless steel** steel containing chromium, nickel, or some other metal that makes it resistant to rust and corrosion.

**stair** (ster) **1** one of a series of steps for going from one level or floor to another. **2** Also, **stairs,** *pl.* a set of such steps; stairway: *the top of the stairs.* *n.* —**stair′less,** *adj.*
**below stairs, a** servants' quarters. **b** downstairs.
☛ *Hom.* STARE.

**stair·case** (ster′kās′) a flight of stairs with its framework; stairs. *n.*

**stair·way** (ster′wā′) a way up and down by stairs; a flight or flights of stairs. *n.*

**stake** (stāk) **1** a stick or post pointed at one end for driving into the ground. **2** fasten to a stake or with a stake. **3** mark with stakes; mark the boundaries of: *The miner staked his claim.* **4** risk money or something valuable on the result of a game or on any chance. **5** the money risked; what is staked: *The men played for high stakes.* **6** something to gain or lose; an interest; share in a property: *Each of us has a stake in the future of our country.* **7** Often, **stakes,** *pl.* the prize in a race or contest: *The stakes were divided up among the winners.* **8 the stake, a** a stake to which a person was tied and then burned to death. **b** death by being burned in this way. **1, 5-8** *n.,* **2-4** *v.,* **staked, stak·ing** —**stak′er,** *n.*
**at stake,** to be won or lost; risked: *Her honour is at stake.*
**pull up stakes,** *Informal.* move away: *After seven years of drought, they finally pulled up stakes and left the farm.*
☛ *Hom.* STEAK.

**stake·hold·er** (stāk′hōl′dər) the person who takes care of what is bet and pays it to the winner. *n.*

**stagnant**    **1159**    **stall**

hat, āge, fär; let, ēqual, tėrm; it, īce
hot, ōpen, ôrder; oil, out; cup, pút, rüle
əbove, takən, pencəl, lemən, circəs
ch, child; ng, long; sh, ship
th, thin; ᴛʜ, then; zh, measure

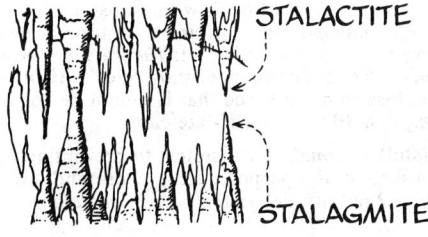

**sta·lac·tite** (stə lak′tīt *or* stal′ək tīt) **1** a formation of lime, shaped like an icicle, hanging from the roof of a cave: *Stalactites are formed by dripping water that contains lime.* **2** any similar formation. *n.*

**sta·lag·mite** (stə lag′mīt *or* stal′əg mīt) **1** a formation of lime, shaped like a cone, built up on the floor of a cave: *Stalagmites are formed by water dripping from stalactites.* See STALACTITE for picture. **2** any similar formation. *n.*

**stale** (stāl) **1** not fresh: *stale bread.* **2** no longer new or interesting: *a stale joke.* **3** out of condition: *The horse has gone stale from too much running.* **4** make stale. **5** become stale. **1–3** *adj.,* **stal·er, stal·est; 4, 5** *v.,* **staled, stal·ing.** —**stale′ly,** *adv.* —**stale′ness,** *n.*

**stale·mate** (stāl′māt′) **1** in chess, the position of the pieces when no move can be made without putting the king in check: *A stalemate makes the result a draw.* **2** any position in which no action can be taken; a complete standstill. **3** put in such a position; bring to a complete standstill. **1, 2** *n.,* **3** *v.,* **stale·mat·ed, stale·mat·ing.**

**stalk¹** (stok) **1** the stem or main axis of a plant. **2** any slender, supporting or connecting part of a plant: *A flower or leaf blade may have a stalk.* **3** any similar part of an animal: *The eyes of a crayfish are on stalks.* **4** a slender, upright support: *a wine glass with a tall stalk.* *n.*
☛ *Hom.* STOCK.

**stalk²** (stok) **1** approach or pursue without being seen or heard: *The lion stalked the antelope.* **2** spread silently and steadily: *Disease stalked through the land.* **3** walk proudly or haughtily. **4** a haughty gait. **5** an act of stalking. **1–3** *v.,* **4, 5** *n.*
☛ *Hom.* STOCK.

**stalk·ing-horse** (stok′ing hôrs′) **1** a horse or figure of a horse, behind which a hunter conceals himself or herself in stalking game. **2** anything used to hide plans or acts; pretext. *n.*

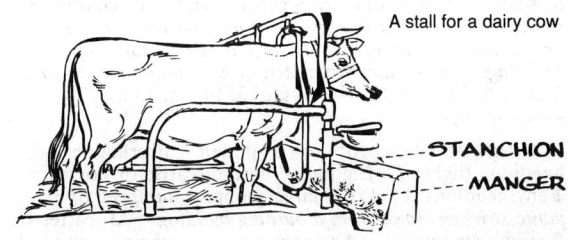

**stall¹** (stol) **1** a place in a stable for one animal.

**stall** **2** live in a stall, stable, kennel, etc. **3** a small place for selling things: *At the public market different things are sold at different stalls under one big roof.* **4** a seat in the choir of a church. **5** *Brit.* a seat in the front part of a theatre. **6** put or keep in a stall. **7** stop or bring to a standstill, usually against one's wish: *Roberta stalled the engine of her automobile.* **8** come to a stop because of too heavy a load or too little fuel: *The truck stalled on the steep hill.* **9** stick fast in mud, snow, etc. **10** of an airplane, lose so much speed that it cannot be controlled. 1, 3–5 *n.*, 2, 6–10 *v.* —**stall′-like′**, *adj.*

**stall²** (stol) *Informal.* **1** a pretext to prevent action, the accomplishment of a purpose, etc. **2** pretend; evade; deceive. **3** put off; delay: *You have been stalling long enough.* 1 *n.*, 2, 3 *v.*

**stal·lion** (stal′yən) an uncastrated male horse, especially one kept for breeding purposes. *n.*

**stal·wart** (stol′wərt) **1** strongly built. **2** strong and brave: *a stalwart knight.* **3** firm; steadfast: *a stalwart friend.* **4** a stalwart person. **5** a loyal supporter. 1–3 *adj.*, 4, 5 *n.* —**stal′wart·ly**, *adv.* —**stal′wart·ness**, *n.*

**sta·men** (stā′mən) the male reproductive organ of a flower, consisting of a threadlike stem called a filament and an anther: *The anther of the stamen produces pollen grains that become sperm.* See FLOWER for picture. *n.*

**stam·i·na** (stam′ə nə) strength; endurance: *A long-distance runner needs stamina.* *n.*

**stam·i·nate** (stam′ə nit *or* stam′ə nāt′) **1** having stamens but no pistils. **2** having a stamen or stamens; producing stamens. *adj.*

**stam·mer** (stam′ər) **1** repeat the same sound in an effort to speak; hesitate in speaking: *She stammers whenever she is nervous.* **2** utter in this manner: *to stammer an excuse.* **3** a stammering; stuttering: *Jacob has a nervous stammer.* 1, 2 *v.*, 3 *n.* —**stam′mer·er**, *n.* —**stam′mer·ing·ly**, *adv.*

**stamp** (stamp) **1** bring down one's foot with force: *to stamp on a spider, to stamp one's foot in anger.* **2** the act of stamping. **3** fix firmly or deeply: *Her words were stamped on my mind.* **4** a small piece of paper with a sticky back, put on letters, papers, parcels, etc. to show that a postal charge has been paid. **5** a similar piece of paper used for any of various purposes. **6** a mark printed by a machine to show that postage has been, or will be, paid. **7** put a stamp, or stamps, on. **8** pound; crush; trample; tread: *She stamped out the fire.* **9** a heavy metal piece used to crush or pound rock, etc. **10** a mill or machine that crushes rock, etc. **11** an instrument that cuts, shapes, or impresses a design on paper, wax, metal, etc.; a thing that puts a mark on. **12** mark with such an instrument: *She stamped the papers with the date.* **13** the mark made with such an instrument. **14** an official mark or seal. **15** show to be of a certain quality or character; indicate: *Her speech stamps her as an educated woman.* **16** the impression; marks: *Her face bore the stamp of suffering.* **17** a kind; type: *Men of his stamp are very rare.* 1, 3, 7, 8, 12, 15 *v.*, 2, 4–6, 9–11, 13, 14, 16, 17 *n.* —**stamp′er**, *n.*

**stam·pede** (stam pēd′) **1** a sudden scattering or headlong flight of a frightened herd of cattle or horses. **2** any headlong flight of a large group: *a stampede of a panic-stricken crowd from a burning building.* **3** scatter or flee in a stampede. **4** a general rush: *a stampede to newly discovered gold fields.* **5** make a general rush. **6** cause to stampede. **7** *Cdn.* a rodeo, often accompanied by other amusements usually found at a fair: *The Calgary Stampede began with a huge parade.* 1, 2, 4, 7 *n.*, 3, 5, 6 *v.*, **stam·ped·ed, stam·ped·ing.**

**stance** (stans) **1** in golf and other games, the position of the feet of a player when making a stroke. **2** the manner of standing; posture: *an erect stance.* *n.*

**stanch¹** (stonch) STAUNCH¹. *v.* —**stanch′er**, *n.*

**stanch²** (stonch) STAUNCH². *adj.* —**stanch′ly**, *adv.* —**stanch′ness**, *n.*

**stan·chion** (stan′shən) **1** an upright bar, post, or support in a window, in a stall for cattle, on a ship, etc. See STALL for picture. **2** fasten cattle by stanchions. **3** strengthen or support with stanchions. 1 *n.*, 2, 3 *v.*

**stand** (stand) **1** be upright on one's feet: *Don't stand if you are tired, but sit down.* **2** have specified height when upright: *He stands 180 centimetres in his socks.* **3** rise to one's feet: *He stood when she entered the room.* **4** be set upright; be placed; be located: *The box stands over there.* **5** set upright or in an indicated position, condition, etc.: *Stand the box here.* **6** be in a certain place, rank, scale, etc.: *Nina stood first in her class for service to the school.* **7** take or keep a certain position: *"Stand back!"* called the police officer to the crowd. **8** take a way of thinking or acting: *to stand for fair play, to stand on one's rights.* **9** be in a special condition: *She stands innocent of any wrong. The poor man stands in need of food and clothing.* **10** be unchanged; hold good; remain the same: *The rule against lateness will stand.* **11** stay in place; last: *The old house has stood for a hundred years.* **12** gather and stay: *Tears stood in her eyes.* **13** bear; endure: *Those plants cannot stand cold; they die in winter.* **14** withstand: *cloth that will stand wear.* **15** *Informal.* bear the expense of: *to stand treat.* **16** hold a specified course: *The ship stood out to sea.* **17** of a dog, point. **18** stop moving; halt; stop: *"Stand!"* cried the sentry. **19** a halt; stop. **20** a stop for defence, resistance, etc.: *We made a last stand against the enemy.* **21** a halt on a theatrical tour to give a performance: *a one-night stand.* **22** a place where a person stands; position: *The police officer took her stand at the street corner.* **23** a raised place where people can sit or stand. **24** something to put things on or in: *Leave your bicycle in the stand.* **25** a stall, booth, table, etc., for a small business: *a newspaper stand.* **26** an attitude; standpoint: *What is your stand on this topic?* **27** a group of growing trees or plants: *a stand of timber.* 1–18 *v.*, **stood, stand·ing;** 19–27 *n.*
**stand a chance,** have a chance.
**stand behind,** support; vouch for; guarantee.
**stand by, a** be near. **b** side with; help; support: *to stand by a friend.* **c** keep; maintain. **d** be or get ready for use, action, etc.: *The radio operator was ordered to stand by.*
**stand for, a** represent; mean: *N.S. stands for Nova Scotia.* **b** be on the side of; take the part of; uphold: *Our school stands for fair play.* **c** be a candidate for; run for; make oneself available for election: *to stand for parliament.* **d** *Informal.* put up with: *The teacher said she would not stand for talking during class.* **e** sail or steer toward.
**stand in,** *Informal.* serve as a substitute for somebody.
**stand off,** keep off; keep away.
**stand on, a** be based on; depend on. **b** demand; assert; claim.
**stand out, a** project: *His ears stood out.* **b** be noticeable or prominent: *Certain facts stand out.* **c** refuse to yield: *to stand out against popular opinion.*
**stand over,** be left for later consideration, treatment, or settlement.

**stand up,** a get to one's feet; rise: *She stood up and began to speak.* b endure; last.

**stand up for,** take the part of; defend; support: *to stand up for a friend.*

**stand up to,** meet or face boldly: *The young girl stood up to the bully.*

**stand·ard** (stan′dərd) 1 anything taken as a basis of comparison; model: *Your work is not up to standard.* 2 a rule, test, or requirement. 3 an authorized weight or measure. 4 of the accepted or normal size, amount, power, quality, etc.: *the standard rate of pay, a standard gauge.* 5 used as a standard; according to rule. 6 having recognized excellence or authority: *Jane Austen and Dickens are standard authors.* 7 a flag, emblem, or symbol: *The dragon was the standard of China.* 8 an upright support: *The floor lamp has a long standard.* 9 the largest of the four basic sizes of automobile. Compare with SUBCOMPACT, COMPACT, and INTERMEDIATE. 1–3, 7, 8, 9 *n.*, 4–6 *adj.*
➤ *Usage.* **Standard English** is the kind of English that educated people use in public and accept as appropriate for almost any situation. It includes **formal** and **informal** levels of language, but not **slang** or **non-standard** forms. See also notes at INFORMAL and SLANG.

**standard atmosphere** a unit for measuring pressure, equal to the normal atmospheric pressure at sea level: *One standard atmosphere is about* 101 kPa. *Symbol:* atm

**stand·ard·bear·er** (stan′dərd ber′ər) 1 an officer or soldier who carries a flag or standard. 2 a person who carries a banner in a procession. 3 a conspicuous leader of a movement, political party, etc. *n.*

**stand·ard·i·za·tion** (stan′dər də zā′shən or stan′dər dī zā′shən) a standardizing or being STANDARDIZEd. *n.*

**stand·ard·ize** (stan′dər dīz′) 1 make standard in size, shape, weight, quality, strength, etc.: *The parts of an automobile are standardized.* 2 regulate by a standard. 3 test by a standard. *v.*, **stand·ard·ized, stand·ard·iz·ing.**

**standard lamp** a household lamp on a tall pole.

**standard of living** the way of living that a person or community considers necessary to provide enough material things for comfort, happiness, etc.

**standard time** the time normally adopted for a region or country.

**stand–by** (stand′bī′) 1 a person or thing that can be relied upon; chief support; ready resource. 2 a ship kept in readiness for emergencies. 3 an order or signal for a boat to stand by. 4 a person or thing held in reserve, especially as a possible replacement or substitute. *n.*, *pl.* **stand-bys.**

**stand–in** (stan′din′) 1 a person whose work is to occupy the place of an actor while the lights, cameras, etc. are being arranged. 2 a person or thing that takes the place of another; substitute: *Will you be my stand-in at the next meeting? n.*

**stand·ing** (stan′ding) 1 position; reputation: *people of good standing.* 2 duration: *a feud of long standing between two families.* 3 straight up; erect: *standing timber.* 4 done from an erect position: *a standing jump.* 5 established; permanent: *a standing invitation, a standing army.* 6 that stands: *a standing lamp.* 7 not flowing; stagnant: *standing water.* 8 the act of standing; place of standing. 9 ppr. of STAND. 1, 2, 8 *n.*, 3–7 *adj.*, 9 *v.*

**standing room** 1 space to stand in. 2 space to stand in after all the seats are taken.

---

**standard** 1161 **stapler**

hat, āge, fär; let, ēqual, tėrm; it, īce
hot, ōpen, ôrder; oil, out; cup, pùt, rüle
əbove, takən, pencəl, lemən, circəs
ch, child; ng, long; sh, ship
th, thin; ŦH, then; zh, measure

**stand–off** (stan′dof′) 1 a standing off or apart; reserve; aloofness. 2 standing off or apart; reserved; aloof. 3 a tie or draw in a game. 1, 3 *n.*, 2 *adj.*

**stand–off·ish** (stan′dof′ish) reserved; aloof. *adj.*

**stand–out** (stan′dout′) *Informal.* a thing or person that is outstanding in appearance or performance. *n.*

**stand–pat** (stand′pat′) *Informal.* standing firm for things as they are; opposing any change. *adj.*

**stand–pat·ter** (stand′pat′ər) *Informal.* a person who stands firm for things as they are and opposes any change, especially in politics. *n.*

**stand·pipe** (stand′pīp′) a large vertical pipe or tower to hold water. *n.*

**stand·point** (stand′point′) the point at which one stands to view something; point of view; mental attitude. *n.*

**St. Andrew's cross** a diagonal cross. See CROSS for picture.

**stand·still** (stand′stil′) a complete stop; halt. *n.*

**stank** (stangk) a pt. of STINK: *The dead fish stank.* *v.*

**Stanley Cup** the cup presented annually to the winning team in a special end-of-season competition between National Hockey League clubs.

**stan·nic** (stan′ik) 1 of or having to do with tin. 2 containing tin with a valence of four. *adj.*

**stan·nous** (stan′əs) 1 of or having to do with tin. 2 containing tin with a valence of two. *adj.*

**stan·za** (stan′zə) a group of lines of poetry, commonly four or more, arranged according to a fixed plan; verse of a poem. *n.*

**sta·pes** (stā′pēz) the stirrup bone, the innermost of the three small bones in the middle ear. See EAR[1] for picture. *n.*

**sta·ple**[1] (stā′pəl) 1 a U-shaped piece of metal with pointed ends: *Staples are driven into doors, wood, etc. to hold hooks, pins, or bolts.* 2 a bent piece of wire used to hold together papers, parts of a book, etc. 3 fasten with a staple or staples. 1, 2 *n.*, 3 *v.*, **sta·pled, sta·pling.**

**sta·ple**[2] (stā′pəl) 1 the most important or principal article grown or manufactured in a place: *Wheat is the staple in Saskatchewan.* 2 any major article of trade. 3 the chief element or material. 4 most important; principal: *The weather is a staple subject of conversation.* 5 a raw material. 6 a fibre of cotton, wool, etc. 7 sort according to fibre: *to staple wool.* 8 established in commerce: *a staple trade.* 9 regularly produced in large quantities for the market. 1–3, 5, 6 *n.*, 4, 8, 9 *adj.*, 7 *v.*, **sta·pled, sta·pling.**

**sta·pler**[1] (stā′plər) a machine for driving wire staples into paper, cardboard, wood, or plaster. *n.*

**sta·pler²** (stā'plər) a person who sorts and grades fibres of wool, cotton, etc. *n.*

**star** (stär) **1** any of the heavenly bodies, especially one that is not the moon, a planet, a comet, or a meteor, appearing as a bright point in the sky at night. **2** a plane figure having five points, or sometimes six, like these: ★ ✶ **3** anything having or suggesting this shape. **4** mark or ornament with stars: *Nan's card was starred for perfect attendance.* **5** an asterisk (*). **6** mark with an asterisk. **7** in the United States, a representation of a star symbolizing one of the States in the Union. **8** a person of brilliant qualities: *an athletic star.* **9** a famous person in some art, profession, etc., especially one who plays the lead in a performance: *a young television star.* **10** chief; best; leading; excellent: *the star player on a football team.* **11** be prominent; be a leading performer; excel: *She has starred in many motion pictures.* **12** present as a star: *This play stars a rising young actress.* **13** fate; fortune: *under a lucky star.* 1–3, 5, 7–10, 13 *n.*, 4, 6, 11, 12 *v.*, **starred, star·ring.** —**star'like'**, *adj.* —**star'-shaped**, *adj.*
**see stars,** *Informal.* see flashes of light as a result of a hard blow on the head.
**thank one's (lucky) stars,** be thankful for one's good luck.

**star·board** (stär'bərd *or* stär'bôrd') **1** the right side of a ship or aircraft, when facing forward. See AFT for picture. **2** on the right side of a ship or aircraft. **3** turn the helm to the right side. 1 *n.*, 2 *adj., adv.*, 3 *v.*

**starch** (stärch) **1** a white, tasteless food substance: *Potatoes, wheat, rice, and corn contain much starch.* **2** a preparation of this substance used to stiffen clothes, fabric, etc. **3** stiffen clothes, fabric, etc. with starch. **4** a stiff formal manner; stiffness. **5** *Informal.* energy; vigour. **6 starches,** *pl.* foods containing much starch. 1, 2, 4–6 *n.*, 3 *v.*

**Star Chamber** *or* **star chamber 1** in England, a harsh court that used arbitrary, secret, and unfair methods of trial until it was abolished in 1641. **2** any similar court, committee, or group.

**starch·y** (stär'chē) **1** like starch; containing starch. **2** stiffened with starch. **3** stiff in manner; formal. *adj.*, **starch·i·er, starch·i·est.** —**starch'i·ness**, *n.*

**star·dom** (stär'dəm) **1** the condition or fact of being a star actor or performer. **2** star actors or performers as a group. *n.*

**star dust 1** masses of stars that look so small as to suggest particles of dust. **2** particles of matter falling from space to the earth. **3** *Informal.* glamour; happy enchantment.

**stare** (ster) **1** look long and directly with the eyes wide open: *A person stares in wonder, surprise, stupidity, curiosity, or from mere rudeness.* **2** a long and direct look with the eyes wide open: *The doll's eyes were set in an unwinking stare.* **3** bring to a named condition by staring: *to stare someone into confusion.* **4** gaze at. **5** be very striking or glaring: *Her eyes stared with anger.* 1, 3–5 *v.*, **stared, star·ing;** 2 *n.* —**star'er**, *n.*
**stare down** *or* **out of countenance,** confuse or embarrass by staring.
**stare one in the face,** **a** be very evident; force itself on the notice of: *Valerie's spelling mistake was staring her in the face.* **b** very likely or certain to happen soon.
☛ *Hom.* STAIR.

A common starfish of the Atlantic coasts of North America and Europe— about 9 cm across

**star·fish** (stär'fish') a star-shaped sea animal. *n., pl.* **star·fish** *or* **star·fishes.**

**star·gaze** (stär'gāz') **1** gaze at the stars. **2** be absent-minded; daydream. *v.*, **star·gazed, star·gaz·ing.**

**star·ing** (ster'ing) **1** very conspicuous; too bright; glaring. **2** gazing with a stare; wide-open. **3** ppr. of STARE. 1, 2 *adj.*, 3 *v.*

**stark** (stärk) **1** downright; complete: *That fool is talking stark nonsense.* **2** entirely; completely: *The boys went swimming stark naked.* **3** stiff: *The dog lay stark in death.* **4** bare; barren; desolate: *a stark landscape.* **5** harsh; stern. **6** in a stark manner. 1, 3–5 *adj.*, 2, 6 *adv.* —**stark'ly**, *adv.*

**star·less** (stär'lis) without stars; without starlight. *adj.*

**star·let** (stär'lit) **1** a young actress or singer who is being trained for leading roles in motion pictures or TV. **2** a little star. *n.*

**star·light** (stär'līt') **1** light from the stars. **2** lighted by the stars. 1 *n.*, 2 *adj.*

**star·like** (stär'līk') **1** shaped like a star. **2** shining like a star. *adj.*

**star·ling** (stär'ling) **1** a common European bird that nests about buildings. **2** a kind of North American blackbird. *n.*

**star·lit** (stär'lit') lighted by the stars: *a starlit night.* *adj.*

**star–of–Beth·le·hem** (stär'əv beth'lē əm) a plant of the same family as the lily, growing from a small bulb and having a tall cluster of white, star-shaped flowers. *n.*

Star of David

**Star of David** an ancient symbol comprising a six-pointed star made of two interlaced equilateral triangles, one upright and one inverted. It was adopted as a symbol of Judaism and appears on the flag of Israel.

**starred** (stärd) **1** decorated with stars. **2** marked with a star or stars. **3** presented as a star actor or performer. **4** influenced by the stars or by fate. **5** pt. and pp. of STAR. 1–4 *adj.*, 5 *v.*

**star·ry** (stä'rē) **1** lighted by stars; containing many stars: *a starry sky.* **2** shining like stars: *starry eyes.* **3** like a star in shape. **4** of or having to do with stars. *adj.*, **star·ri·er, star·ri·est.**

**Stars and Stripes** the flag of the United States.

**star·span·gled** (stär′spang′gəld) spangled with stars. *adj.*

**start** (stärt) **1** get in motion; set out; begin a journey: *The train started on time.* **2** begin: *to start a book.* **3** set moving, going, acting, etc.; cause to set out; cause to begin: *to start an automobile, to start a fire.* **4** the beginning of a movement, act, journey, race, etc. **5** a setting in motion; signal to start. **6** give a sudden involuntary jerk or twitch; move suddenly: *She started in surprise.* **7** come, rise, or spring out suddenly: *Tears started from her eyes.* **8** burst or stick out: *eyes seeming to start from their sockets.* **9** a sudden movement; jerk: *I awoke with a start. On seeing the snake, the man sprang up with a start.* **10** a surprise; fright: *The sudden appearance of the bear gave her quite a start.* **11** a beginning ahead of others; advantage: *He got the start of his rivals.* **12** a chance of starting a career, etc.: *His father gave him a start.* **13** a spurt of activity: *to work by fits and starts.* **14** the place, line, etc. where a race begins. **15** rouse: *to start a rabbit. to start a run in nylons.* 1–3, 6–8, 15 *v.*, 4, 5, 9–14 *n.*
**start in** or **start out,** begin to do something.

**start·er** (stär′tər) **1** a person or thing that starts. **2** a person who gives the signal for starting. **3** a SELF-STARTER. **4** a special kind of food for baby chicks and animals. *n.*

**starting point** a place of starting; beginning.

**star·tle** (stär′təl) **1** frighten suddenly; surprise. **2** a sudden shock of surprise or fright. **3** move suddenly in fear or surprise. **4** cause to make a sudden movement: *The hunters startled the deer.* 1, 3, 4 *v.*, **star·tled, star·tling;** 2 *n.*

**star·tling** (stär′tling) **1** surprising; frightening: *startling tales.* **2** ppr. of STARTLE. 1 *adj.*, 2 *v.*

**star·va·tion** (stär vā′shən) **1** a starving: *Starvation of prisoners is barbarous.* **2** the condition of suffering from extreme hunger; being starved: *Starvation caused her death.* *n.*

**starve** (stärv) **1** die because of hunger. **2** suffer severely because of hunger. **3** weaken or kill with hunger. **4** force or subdue by lack of food: *They starved the enemy into surrendering.* **5** *Informal.* feel hungry. **6** have a strong desire or craving. **7** weaken or destroy by lack of something needed. *v.*, **starved, starv·ing.**
**starve for,** suffer from lack of: *to starve for news. That child is starving for affection.*

**starve·ling** (stärv′ling) **1** starving; hungry. **2** a person or animal suffering from lack of food. 1 *adj.*, 2 *n.*

**stat·a·ble** (stā′tə bəl) that can be stated. *adj.*

**state** (stāt) **1** the condition of a person or thing: *She is in a state of poor health. Ice is water in a solid state.* **2** a particular condition of mind or feeling: *a state of uncertainty, a state of excitement.* **3** a person's position in life; rank: *humble state.* **4** nation. **5** the territory of a state. **6** civil government; the highest civil authority: *affairs of state.* **7** of or having to do with civil government or authority: *state control.* **8** tell in speech or writing; express; say: *to state one's views.* **9** settle; fix. **10** a high style of living; dignity; pomp: *Queens live in great state.* **11** used on or reserved for very formal and special occasions; ceremonious; formal: *state robes.* **12** Also, **State,** one of several organized political groups of people that together form a nation: *The State of Alaska is one of the United States.* 1–6, 10, 12 *n.*, 8, 9 *v.*, **stat·ed, stat·ing;** 7, 11 *adj.*
**in** or **into a state,** *Informal.* **a** in or into a bad or disordered condition. **b** in or into an agitated or excited condition of mind or feeling.
**lie in state,** of a corpse in its coffin and prepared for burial, be shown with dignity and ceremony so that the public may show their respect for the dead person.

**state·craft** (stāt′kraft′) **1** STATESMANSHIP. **2** crafty STATESMANSHIP. *n.*

**stat·ed** (stā′tid) **1** said; told: *done as stated.* **2** fixed; settled: *stated times, for a stated fee.* **3** pt. and pp. of STATE. 1, 2 *adj.*, 3 *v.*

**state·hood** (stāt′hud′) the condition of being a state. *n.*

**state·house** (stāt′hous′) *U.S.* the building in which the legislature of a state meets. *n.*

**state·less** (stāt′lis) **1** without nationality; without citizenship in any country. **2** without states or boundaries: *a stateless world.* *adj.*

**state·ly** (stāt′lē) dignified; imposing; grand; majestic: *Rideau Hall is a stately mansion.* *adj.*, **state·li·er, state·li·est.** —**state′li·ness,** *n.*

**state·ment** (stāt′mənt) **1** the act of stating; the manner of stating something. **2** something stated; report. **3** a summary of an account, showing the amount owed or due. *n.*

**state·room** (stāt′rüm′) a private room on a ship or railway train. *n.*

**states·man** (stāt′smən) a person skilled in the management of public or national affairs. *n., pl.* **states·men** (-smən).

**states·man·like** (stāt′smən līk′) having the qualities of a statesman. *adj.*

**states·man·ly** (stāt′smən lē) like, worthy of, or befitting a statesman. *adj.*

**states·man·ship** (stāt′smən ship′) the qualities of a statesman; skill in the management of public or national affairs. *n.*

**state socialism** a form of SOCIALISM in which government control, management, or ownership is used to improve social conditions.

**states of matter** the forms in which all substances can exist: solid, liquid, or gas.

**states·wom·an** (stāt′swum′ən) a woman skilled in the management of public or national affairs. *n., pl.* **states·wom·en** (-swim′ən).

**stat·ic** (stat'ik) **1** at rest; standing still: *Civilization does not remain static but changes constantly.* **2** having to do with bodies at rest or forces that balance each other. **3** acting by weight without producing motion: *static pressure.* **4** having to do with stationary electrical charges that balance each other: *Static electricity can be produced by rubbing a glass rod with a silk cloth.* **5** atmospheric electricity. **6** interference, especially with radio signals, due to such electricity. **7** of or having to do with such electricity. 1–4, 7 *adj.*, 5, 6 *n.*
—**stat'i·cal·ly,** *adv.*

**stat·ics** (stat'iks) the branch of mechanics that deals with the study of bodies at rest and the action of forces that balance each other to produce equilibrium. *n.*

**sta·tion** (stā'shən) **1** a place to stand in; place that a person is appointed to occupy in the performance of some duty; assigned post: *The police officer took her station at the corner.* **2** a building or place used for a definite purpose: *a police station.* **3** a regular stopping place: *a railway station.* **4** the place or equipment for sending out or receiving programs, messages, etc. by radio or television. **5** give a position or place to; place: *She stationed herself just outside the hotel.* **6** a military camp or establishment. **7** post or assign to such a camp or establishment. **8** social position; rank: *a humble station in life.* 1–4, 6, 8 *n.*, 5, 7 *v.*

**station agent** a person in charge of a railway station.

**sta·tion·ar·y** (stā'shə ner'ē) **1** having a fixed station or place; not movable: *A factory engine is stationary.* **2** standing still; not moving. **3** not changing in size, number, activity, etc.: *The population of this town has been stationary for years.* *adj.*
☞ *Hom.* STATIONERY.
☞ *Usage.* Do not confuse **stationary** and STATIONERY. **Stationary,** with an *a* in the second last syllable, is an *a*djective. **Stationery,** including 'writing material', is a noun.

**sta·tion·er** (stā'shə nər) a person who sells papers, pens, pencils, ink, etc. *n.*

**sta·tion·er·y** (stā'shə ner'ē) writing materials; paper, cards, and envelopes. *n.*
☞ *Hom.* STATIONARY.
☞ *Usage.* See note at STATIONARY.

**station house** a building used as a station, especially a police station.

**sta·tion·mas·ter** (stā'shən mas'tər) the person in charge of a railway station. *n.*

**station wagon** a closed automobile that can serve both as a passenger car and as a light truck: *The back end of our station wagon can be opened to permit loading.*

**stat·ism** (stā'tiz əm) a highly centralized governmental control of the economy, information media, etc. of a state or nation. *n.*

**stat·ist** (stā'tist) **1** STATISTICIAN. **2** one advocating STATISM. *n.*

**sta·tis·tic** (stə tis'tik) **1** STATISTICAL. **2** an item, element, etc. in a set of STATISTICS. 1 *adj.*, 2 *n.*

**sta·tis·ti·cal** (stə tis'tə kəl) of or having to do with STATISTICS; consisting of or based on statistics. *adj.*

**sta·tis·ti·cal·ly** (stə tis'ti klē) in a STATISTICAL manner; according to STATISTICS. *adv.*

**stat·is·ti·cian** (stat'i stish'ən) a person trained in the science of STATISTICS, especially one who makes it his or her work.

**sta·tis·tics** (stə tis'tiks) **1** numerical facts about people, the weather, business conditions, etc.: *Statistics are collected and classified systematically.* **2** the science of collecting and classifying such facts in order to show their significance. 1 *n. pl.*, 2 *n. sing.*

**stat·u·ar·y** (stach'ü er'ē) **1** statues collectively. **2** the art of making statues. **3** of or for statues: *statuary marble.* **4** SCULPTOR. 1, 2, 4 *n.*, *pl.* **stat·u·ar·ies;** 3 *adj.*

**stat·ue** (stach'ü) an image of a person or animal carved in stone, wood, etc., cast in bronze, or modelled. *n.*

**stat·u·esque** (stach'ü esk') like a statue in dignity, formal grace, or classic beauty. *adj.*

**stat·u·ette** (stach'ü et') a small statue. *n.*

**stat·ure** (stach'ər) **1** height: *A man 185 centimetres tall is above average stature.* **2** development; physical, mental, or moral growth. **3** reputation or distinction: *She is a woman of great stature in her line of business.* *n.*

**sta·tus** (stā'təs *or* stat'əs) **1** condition; state: *Diplomats are interested in the status of world affairs.* **2** one's social or professional standing; position; rank: *her status as a doctor.* **3** legal position. *n.*

**status quo** (kwō) the way things are; the existing state of affairs: *The club voted to maintain the status quo in election procedures.*

**stat·ute** (stach'üt') a law enacted by a legislative body: *The statutes for Canada are made by Parliament.* *n.*

**statute law** written law; expressed or stated by STATUTES.

**statute mile** a unit for measuring distance on land, equal to 5280 feet (about 1.61 km).

**statute of limitations** in law, any STATUTE that specifies a certain period of time after which legal action cannot be brought or offences punished.

**stat·u·to·ry** (stach'ü tô'rē) **1** having to do with a STATUTE. **2** fixed by STATUTE. **3** punishable by STATUTE. *adj.* —**stat'u·to'ri·ly,** *adv.*

**staunch**[1] (stonch) **1** stop a flow of blood, etc. **2** stop the flow of blood from a wound. **3** cease flowing. *v.* Also, **stanch.** —**staunch'er,** *n.*

**staunch**[2] (stonch) **1** firm; strong: *a staunch defence.* **2** loyal, steadfast: *a staunch friend.* **3** watertight: *a staunch boat.* *adj.* Also, **stanch.** —**staunch'ly,** *adv.* —**staunch'ness,** *n.*

**stave** (stāv) **1** one of the curved pieces of wood that form the sides of a barrel, tub, etc. **2** a stick or staff. **3** a rung of a ladder. **4** break a hole in a barrel, boat, etc. **5** become smashed or broken in. **6** a verse or stanza of a poem, song, etc. **7** in music, the STAFF (def. 6). **8** furnish with staves. 1–3, 6, 7 *n.*, 4, 5, 8 *v.*, **staved** or **stove, stav·ing.**

**stave off,** put off; keep back; delay or prevent: *The lost campers ate birds' eggs to stave off starvation.*

**staves** (stāvz) **1** a pl. of STAFF. **2** pl. of STAVE. *n.*

**stay**[1] (stā) **1** continue to be as indicated; remain: *to stay clean. Stay here till I call you.* **2** live for a while; dwell: *She is now staying with her aunt.* **3** a staying; a stop; time spent: *a pleasant stay in the country.* **4** stop; halt: *We have no time to stay.* **5** pause; wait: *"Time and tide stay for no man."* **6** wait for; await. **7** put an end to for a while; satisfy hunger, appetite, etc. **8** put off; hold back; delay; restrain; check: *The teacher stayed judgment till she could hear both sides.* **9** a check; restraint: *a stay on her activity.* **10** a delay in carrying out the order of a court: *The judge granted the condemned man a stay for an appeal.* **11** endure: *Our horse was unable to stay to the end of a race.* **12** *Informal.* staying power; endurance. 1, 2, 4–8, 11 *v.*, **stayed, stay·ing;** 3, 9, 10, 12 *n.* —**stay′er,** *n.*

**stay**[2] (stā) **1** a support; prop; brace: *The oldest daughter was the family's stay.* **2** support; prop; hold up. **3** strengthen mentally or spiritually; fix or rest in dependence or reliance. 1 *n.*, 2, 3 *v.*, **stayed, stay·ing.**

**stay**[3] (stā) **1** a strong rope, chain, or wire attached to something to steady it: *The mast of a ship is held in place by stays.* See SHROUD for picture. **2** support or secure with stays. **3** of a ship, change to the other tack. 1 *n.*, 2, 3 *v.*, **stayed, stay·ing.**
**in stays,** of a ship, in the act of changing from one tack to another.

**staying power** the ability to endure: *Sheena doesn't work very fast, but she has great staying power.*

**stay·sail** (stā′sāl′ *or* stā′səl) a sail fastened on a stay or rope. *n.*

**stbd.** starboard.

**stead** (sted) a place: *The sales manager could not come, but she sent her assistant in her stead.* *n.*
**stand in good stead,** be of advantage or service to.

**stead·fast** (sted′fast′) **1** loyal; unwavering: *The politician was a steadfast servant of his country.* **2** firmly fixed; not moving or changing. *adj.*
—**stead′fast′ly,** *adv.* —**stead′fast′ness,** *n.*

**stead·y** (sted′ē) **1** changing little; uniform; regular: *steady progress.* **2** firmly fixed; firm; not swaying or shaking: *to hold a ladder steady.* **3** not easily excited; calm: *steady nerves.* **4** resolute; steadfast: *steady friendship.* **5** having good habits; reliable: *a steady young woman.* **6** of a ship, keeping nearly upright in a heavy sea. **7** make steady; keep steady: *Steady the ladder while I climb to the roof.* **8** become steady: *The wind steadied.* **9** *Informal.* a regular girlfriend or boyfriend; a person who is being courted regularly by the same person. 1–6 *adj.*, **stead·i·er, stead·i·est;** 7, 8 *v.*, **stead·ied, stead·y·ing;** 9 *n., pl.* **stead·ies.** —**stead′i·ly,** *adv.* —**stead′i·ness,** *n.*
**go steady, a** *Informal.* date one person or each other only. **b** go carefully.

**steady–state** (sted′ē stāt′) maintaining the same basic condition; unchanging in quality, structure, behaviour, etc.: *a steady-state current.* *adj.*

**steady–state universe** the theory that in the universe, matter is continuously created to replace that which is naturally destroyed.

**steak** (stāk) **1** a thick slice of meat from a beef carcass, usually broiled or fried; beef steak: *One of the choice cuts of beef is a porterhouse steak.* **2** a similar slice of other meat or of fish for broiling or frying: *ham steak, salmon steak.* **3** ground meat shaped and cooked somewhat like a steak: *hamburger steak.* *n.*
☛ *Hom.* STAKE.

**steal** (stēl) **1** take something that does not belong to one; take dishonestly: *to steal money.* **2** take, get, or do secretly: *to steal a look at someone.* **3** take, get, or win by art, charm, or gradual means: *She steals all hearts.* **4** move secretly or quietly: *She stole out of the house.* **5** move slowly or gently: *The years steal by.* **6** *Informal.* the act of stealing. **7** *Informal.* the thing stolen. **8** *Informal.* something obtained very cheaply or very easily: *At that price the car is a steal.* **9** in baseball, run to a base without being helped by a hit or error. 1–5, 9 *v.*, **stole, sto·len, steal·ing;** 6–8 *n.*
☛ *Hom.* STEEL.

**stealth** (stelth) secret or sly action: *He took the letter by stealth while nobody was in the room.* *n.*

**stealth·y** (stel′thē) done in a secret manner; secret; sly: *The cat crept in a stealthy way toward the bird.* *adj.*, **stealth·i·er, stealth·i·est.** —**stealth′i·ly,** *adv.* —**stealth′i·ness,** *n.*

**steam** (stēm) **1** the invisible vapour or gas into which water is changed when it is heated to the boiling point. Compare with WATER VAPOUR. **2** the white cloud or mist formed when the invisible vapour from boiling water condenses as it cools. **3** give off steam: *The soup was steaming. Their mitts were steaming on the radiator.* **4** become covered with steam (*usually used with* **up**): *The windshield had steamed up inside the car.* **5** rise as vapour: *Mist was steaming off the lake.* **6** expose to the action of steam; prepare, treat, cook, etc. with steam: *to steam oneself for a cold, to steam vegetables, to steam a letter open.* **7** the vapour from boiling water, used to generate mechanical power and for heating and cooking: *Engines powered by steam were formerly used to run threshing machines, tractors, etc.* **8** move or travel by the power of steam: *The ship steamed away.* **9** *Informal.* power or energy. **10** *Informal.* be angry; fume: *She was steaming by the time he got there, half an hour late.* 1, 2, 7, 9 *n.*, 3–6, 8, 10 *v.* —**steam′like′,** *adj.*
**full steam ahead,** with all possible power or energy: *They went full steam ahead as soon as they got final approval.*
**let off steam,** *Informal.* **a** get rid of excess energy: *He took the kids to the playground so they could let off steam.* **b** relieve one's feelings of anger, frustration, etc.: *Wait till we get home before you let off steam.*
**steamed up,** *Informal.* **a** angry, fuming: *She gets all steamed up about nothing.* **b** full of energy and enthusiasm: *She's steamed up now about her science project.*

**steam bath** a kind of bath taken in a steam-filled room or chamber: *A steam bath is usually followed by massage.*

**steam·boat** (stēm′bōt′) a boat propelled by a STEAM ENGINE. *n.*

**steam chest** a chamber through which the steam of an engine passes from the boiler to the cylinder.

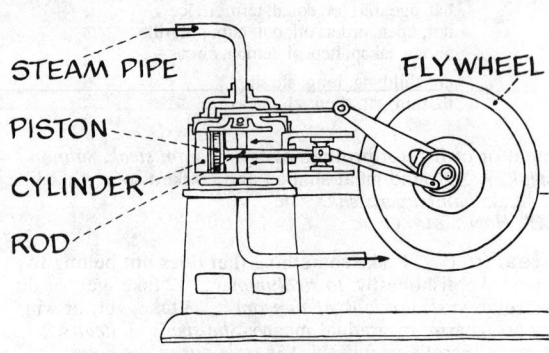

A steam engine. The pressure of the steam forced into the cylinder pushes the piston back and forth. This causes the rod to turn a shaft that passes on motion to wheels or other parts. The weight of the heavy flywheel attached to the shaft keeps the shaft turning evenly.

**steam engine** an engine operated by steam, typically one in which a sliding piston in a cylinder is moved by the expansive action of steam generated in a boiler.

**steam·er** (stē′mər) 1 a STEAMBOAT; STEAMSHIP. 2 an engine driven by steam. 3 a container in which something is steamed or kept warm. *n.*

**steamer rug** a blanket used to keep a person warm in a chair on the deck of a ship.

**steam fitter** a person who installs and repairs steam pipes, radiators, boilers, etc.

**steam iron** an electric iron in which water is heated to produce steam which is released through holes in its undersurface to dampen cloth while pressing it.

**steam roller** 1 a heavy roller formerly moved by steam, but now often by an INTERNAL-COMBUSTION ENGINE, used to crush and level materials in making roads. 2 *Informal.* a means of crushing opposition.

**steam–roll·er** (stēm′rō′lər) 1 *Informal.* override by crushing power or force; crush: *to steam-roller all opposition.* 2 *Informal.* force into or through by this means: *to steam-roller a convention into acceptance of a candidate.* 3 make level, smooth, etc. with a STEAM ROLLER. *v.*

**steam·ship** (stēm′ship′) a ship propelled by a STEAM ENGINE. *n.*

**steam shovel** a machine for digging, formerly always operated by steam, but now often by an INTERNAL-COMBUSTION ENGINE.

**steam·tight** (stēm′tīt′) so tight that no steam can get in or out: *a steamtight valve.* *adj.*

**steam·y** (stē′mē) 1 of steam; like steam. 2 full of steam; giving off steam; rising in steam. *adj.*, **steam·i·er, steam·i·est.** —**steam′i·ness,** *n.*

**ste·ap·sin** (stē ap′sən) a chemical, produced in the body, that aids digestion by changing fats into glycerol and fatty acids. It is an enzyme secreted in the pancreatic juice. *n.*

**ste·a·rate** (stē′ə rāt′) a salt of STEARIC ACID. *n.*

**ste·ar·ic** (stē ar′ik *or* stēr′ik) having to do with STEARIN, suet, or fat. *adj.*

**stearic acid** a solid white substance obtained from certain fats and used in making candles.

**ste·a·rin** (stē′ə rin *or* stē′rən) 1 a colourless, odourless substance that is the chief constituent of many animal and vegetable fats. 2 a mixture of fatty acids used for making candles, solid alcohol, etc. *n.*

**steed** (stēd) a horse, especially a high-spirited riding horse. *n.*

**steel** (stēl) 1 an alloy of iron and carbon that is very hard, strong, and tough: *Most tools are made from steel.* 2 something made from steel. 3 sword. 4 a piece of steel for making sparks. 5 a rod of steel for sharpening knives. 6 a narrow strip of steel in a corset. 7 made of steel. 8 point, edge, or cover with steel. 9 make hard or strong like steel: *He steeled his heart against our plea.* 10 steel-like hardness or strength: *nerves of steel.* 11 *Cdn.* a railway track: *Steel has been laid for 200 kilometres north.* 12 *Cdn.* the railway line: *They arranged to meet at steel.* 1–7, 10–12 *n.*, 8, 9 *v.* —**steel′-less,** *adj.* —**steel′-like′,** *adj.*
☛ *Hom.* STEAL.

**steel band** a group of musicians playing instruments made from oil drums, common in Trinidad and other parts of the West Indies.

**steel blue** lustrous dark-blue, like the colour of tempered steel.

**steel drum** a musical drum made from an oil drum, tuned and played in a STEEL BAND.

**steel·head** *or* **steel·head trout** (stēl′hed′) a trout of the Pacific coast from Alaska to California, including British Columbia, an important game and food fish that spends most of its life in the sea, but is born in fresh water and returns to fresh water to spawn: *Steelhead trout found in inland lakes and rivers are called rainbow trout because their colour changes in fresh water.* *n., pl.* **steel·head** *or* **steel·heads.**

**steel wool** fine steel threads or shavings in a pad, etc., used for cleaning or polishing.

**steel·work·er** (stēl′wėr′kər) one who works in a place where steel is made. *n.*

**steel·works** (stēl′wėrks′) a place where steel is made. *n.pl.* or *sing.*

**steel·y** (stē′lē) 1 made of steel. 2 like steel in colour, strength, or hardness. *adj.*, **steel·i·er, steel·i·est.** —**steel′i·ness,** *n.*
☛ *Hom.* STELE.

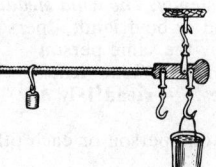

A steelyard. It is designed to be suspended from a hook or from the user's hand.

**steel·yard** (stēl′yärd′ *or* stil′yərd) a scale for weighing, having a horizontal bar on a pivot with a movable weight at the longer end and, at the shorter, a hook for holding the object to be weighed. *n.*

**steen·bok** (stēn′bok′ *or* stān′bok′) any of various small African antelopes frequenting rocky places. *n.*

**steep¹** (stēp) 1 having a sharp slope; almost straight up and down: *The hill is steep.* 2 a steep slope. 3 *Informal.* unreasonable: *a steep price.* 1, 3 *adj.*, 2 *n.* —**steep′ly,** *adv.* —**steep′ness,** *n.*

**steep²** (stēp) **1** soak: *Let the tea steep in boiling water for five minutes. His sword was steeped in blood.* **2** immerse; imbue: *ruins steeped in gloom.* **3** the process of soaking or being soaked. **4** the liquid or bath in which something is soaked. 1, 2 *v.*, 3, 4 *n.*
—**steep′er**, *n.*
**steeped in,** filled with; permeated by: *ruins steeped in gloom, a mind steeped in hatred.*

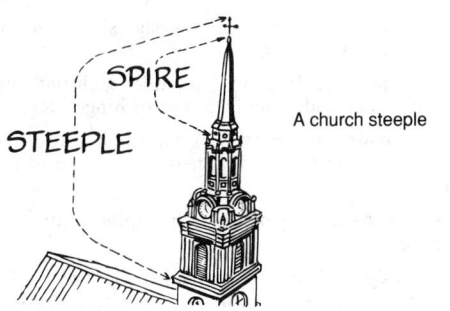
A church steeple

**stee·ple** (stē′pəl) a high tower on a church, usually with a spire. *n.*

**stee·ple·chase** (stē′pəl chās′) **1** a horse race over a course having ditches, hedges, and other obstacles. **2** a cross-country foot race. *n.*

**stee·ple·jack** (stē′pəl jak′) a person who climbs steeples, tall chimneys, etc. to paint them, make repairs, etc. *n.*

**steer¹** (stēr) **1** guide the course of: *to steer a ship, to steer a sled, to steer an automobile, to steer an airplane.* **2** set and follow: *She steered a course for home.* **3** be guided: *This car steers easily.* **4** guide a ship: *The pilot steered for the harbour.* **5** direct one's way or course: *Steer away from flattery.* *v.* —**steer′er**, *n.*
**steer clear of,** keep away from; avoid.

**steer²** (stēr) a full-grown, castrated male of cattle, less than three or four years old: *Steers are usually raised for their meat.* Compare with OX. *n.*

**steer·age** (stēr′ij) **1** formerly, the part of a passenger ship occupied by passengers travelling at the cheapest rate. **2** the act of steering. **3** the manner in which a ship is affected by the helm. *n.*

**steer·age·way** (stēr′ij wā′) the amount of forward motion a ship must have before it can be steered. *n.*

**steering gear** the apparatus for steering an automobile, ship, etc.

**steering wheel** the wheel that is turned to steer an automobile, ship, etc.

**steers·man** (stēr′zmən) a person who steers a ship. *n., pl.* **steers·men** (-zmən).

**steg·o·my·ia** (steg′ə mī′ə) a mosquito that transmits yellow fever. *n.*

**steg·o·sau·rus** (steg′ə sô′rəs) an extinct reptile of great size (sometimes nearly 13 metres long) with heavy, bony armour. *n., pl.* **steg·o·sau·ri** (-rī or -rē).

**stein** (stīn) a beer mug. *n.*

**ste·le** (stē′lē) an upright slab or pillar of stone bearing an inscription, sculptural design, or the like. *n., pl.* **ste·lae** (-lē or -lī) or **ste·les**.
☛ *Hom.* STEELY.

**stel·lar** (stel′ər) **1** of or having to do with the stars; of a star; like a star. **2** chief: *a stellar role.* *adj.*

---

**steep**     1167     **stenographic**

hat, āge, fär; let, ēqual, tėrm; it, īce
hot, ōpen, ôrder; oil, out; cup, pùt, rüle
above, takən, pencəl, lemən, circəs
ch, child; ng, long; sh, ship
th, thin; ᴛʜ, then; zh, measure

**St. El·mo's fire** (sān′tel′mōz) light due to a discharge of atmospheric electricity, often seen on masts, towers, etc.

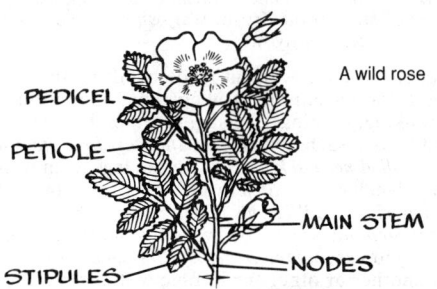
A wild rose

**stem¹** (stem) **1** the main part of a plant, usually above the ground: *The stem supports the branches, etc.* **2** the part of a flower, a fruit, or a leaf that joins it to the plant or tree. See FLOWER for picture. **3** remove the stem from a leaf, fruit, etc. **4** anything like or suggesting the stem of a plant: *the stem of a goblet, the stem of a pipe, etc.* **5** the line of descent of a family. **6** the part of a word to which endings are added and in which changes are made: *Run is the stem of running, runner, ran, etc.* **7** the bow or front end of a boat. 1, 2, 4–7 *n.*, 3 *v.*, **stemmed, stem·ming.** —**stem′like**, *adj.*
**from stem to stern,** from one end of the ship to the other.
**stem from,** come from; have as a source or cause: *The difficulty stems from his failure to plan properly.*

**stem²** (stem) **1** stop; check; dam up. **2** make progress against: *to stem the swift current.* *v.*, **stemmed, stem·ming.**

**stem·less** (stem′lis) having no stem; having no visible stem. *adj.*

**stemmed** (stemd) **1** having a stem. **2** having the stem removed. **3** pt. and pp. of STEM. 1, 2 *adj.*, 3 *v.*

**stem-wind·ing** (stem′wīn′ding) of a watch, winding by turning a knob on the stem. *adj.*

**stench** (stench) a very bad smell; stink: *the stench of a pigsty, the stench of gas.* *n.*

**sten·cil** (sten′səl) **1** a thin sheet of metal, paper, etc. having letters or designs cut through it: *When a stencil is laid on a surface and ink or colour is spread on, these letters or designs are made on the surface.* **2** the letters or designs so made. **3** mark, paint, or make with a stencil: *The curtains have a stencilled border.* 1, 2 *n.*, 3 *v.*, **sten·cilled** or **sten·ciled**, **sten·cil·ling** or **sten·cil·ing**.

**sten·o·graph** (sten′ə graf′) **1** a writing in shorthand. **2** any of various keyboard instruments, somewhat resembling a typewriter, used for writing in shorthand. **3** write in shorthand. 1, 2 *n.*, 3 *v.*

**ste·nog·ra·pher** (stə nog′rə fər) a person whose main work is STENOGRAPHY and keyboarding. *n.*

**sten·o·graph·ic** (sten′ə graf′ik) of or having to do

**with** STENOGRAPHY; written or produced by stenography. *adj.*

**sten·o·graph·i·cal·ly** (sten′ə graf′i klē) by means of STENOGRAPHY. *adv.*

**ste·nog·ra·phy** (stə nog′rə fē) SHORTHAND. *n.*

**sten·to·ri·an** (sten tô′rē ən) very loud or powerful in sound. *adj.*
☛ *Etym.* From the name of *Stentor*, in Greek legend, a Greek herald in the Trojan War, whose voice was as loud as the voices of fifty men.

**step** (step) **1** a movement made by lifting the foot and putting it down again in a new position; one motion of the leg in walking, running, dancing, etc. **2** the distance covered by one such movement: *She was three steps away when he called her back.* **3** move the legs as in walking, running, dancing, etc.: *Step lively!* **4** a short distance; little way: *The school is only a step away.* **5** walk a short distance: *Step this way.* **6** a way of walking, dancing, etc.: *a brisk step. Learn this new step.* **7** a pace uniform with that of another or others or in time with music: *keep step, be in step, be out of step.* **8** put the foot down: *to step on a worm.* **9** a place for the foot in going up or coming down: *A stair or a rung of a ladder is a step.* **10** make or arrange like a flight of steps. **11** the sound made by putting the foot down. **12** a footprint: *to see steps in the mud.* **13** an action: *The principal took steps to stop needless absence from school.* **14** a degree in a series; a grade in rank: *A colonel is three steps above a captain.* **15** in music, a degree of the staff or the scale consisting of a whole tone. **16** the interval of a whole tone between two successive degrees of the scale. **17** a part like a step; support, frame, etc. for holding the end of something upright: *the step of a mast.* **18** set a mast; fix or place in a support. **19** *Informal.* go fast. **20 steps,** *pl.* STEPLADDER. 1, 2, 4, 6, 7, 9, 11–17, 20 *n.*, 3, 5, 8, 10, 18, 19 *v.*, **stepped, step·ping.**
**in step,** **a** keeping one's pace uniform with that of another or others or in time with music. **b** making one's actions or ideas agree with those of another person or persons; in agreement.
**keep step,** move at the same pace as another person or persons or in time with music.
**out of step,** **a** not keeping pace with others or in time to music. **b** not in harmony or accord.
**step by step,** little by little; slowly.
**step down,** **a** come down. **b** surrender or resign from an office or position: *She stepped down from the presidency.* **c** decrease: *to step down the rate of flow in a pipeline.*
**step in,** come in; intervene; take part.
**step off,** measure by taking steps: *Step off the distance from the door to the window.*
**step on it,** *Informal.* go faster; hurry up.
**step out,** *Informal.* go out for entertainment.
**step up,** **a** go up. **b** make go higher, faster, etc.; increase: *to step up production, to step up the pressure in a boiler.*
**take steps,** adopt, put into effect, or carry out measures considered to be necessary, desirable, etc.: *Steps have already been taken to deal with the emergency.*
**watch one's step,** be careful.
☛ *Hom.* STEPPE.

**step·broth·er** (step′bruтH′ər) a stepfather's or stepmother's son by a former marriage. *n.*

**step·child** (step′chīld′) a child of one's husband or wife by a former marriage. *n., pl.* **step·chil·dren.**

**step·daugh·ter** (step′dot′ər) a daughter of one's husband or wife by a former marriage. *n.*

**step–down** (step′doun′) **1** serving or causing to decrease gradually. **2** in electricity, lowering the voltage of a current, especially by means of a transformer. *adj.*

**step·fa·ther** (step′foтH′ər) a man who has married one's mother after the death or divorce of one's father. *n.*

**step–in** (step′in′) of garments, shoes, etc., put on by being stepped into. *adj.*

**step·lad·der** (step′lad′ər) a ladder with flat steps instead of rungs and, usually, a pair of hinged legs. *n.*

**step·moth·er** (step′muтH′ər) a woman who has married one's father after the death or divorce of one's mother. *n.*

**step–par·ent** (step′per′ənt) a stepfather or stepmother. *n.*

**steppe** (step) **1** one of the vast, treeless plains in southeastern Europe and Asia. **2** a vast, treeless plain. *n.*
☛ *Hom.* STEP.

**step·per** (step′ər) a person or animal that steps, especially in a particular manner: *a high stepper.* *n.*

**step·ping–stone** (step′ing stōn′) **1** a stone or one of a line of stones in shallow water, a marshy place, etc., used in crossing. **2** a stone for use in mounting or ascending. **3** anything serving as a means of advancing or rising. *n.*

**step·sis·ter** (step′sis′tər) a stepfather's or stepmother's daughter by a former marriage. *n.*

**step·son** (step′sun′) a son of one's husband or wife by a former marriage. *n.*

**step–up** (step′up′) **1** serving or causing to increase gradually. **2** an increase. **3** in electricity, increasing the voltage of a current, especially by means of a transformer. 1, 3 *adj.*, 2 *n.*

**ste·ra·di·an** (stə rā′dē ən) an SI unit for measuring solid angles, equal to the angle from the centre of a sphere which cuts off an area on the surface of the sphere equal to the square of the radius: *The steradian is used mostly in mathematics; it is one of the two supplementary units in the SI.* Symbol: sr See RADIAN for picture. *n.*

**ster·e·o** (ster′ē ō′ *or* stē′rē ō′) *Informal.* **1** STEREOPHONIC. **2** produced for use with STEREOPHONIC equipment. **3** *Informal.* a radio, record player, or tape-recorder equipped with a STEREOPHONIC system. 1, 2 *adj.*, 3 *n.*

**ster·e·o·phon·ic** (ster′ē ə fon′ik *or* stē′rē ə fon′ik) in sound reproduction, of or produced by the use of two or more microphones, recording channels, loudspeakers, etc. in order to give a three-dimensional effect. *adj.*

A stereoscope

**ster·e·o·scope** (ster′ē ə skōp′ *or* stē′rē ə skōp′) an instrument through which two pictures of the same object or scene are viewed, one by each eye. The object or scene thus viewed appears to have three dimensions, as it would if really seen. *n.*

**ster·e·o·scop·ic** (ster′ē ə skop′ik *or* stē′rē ə skop′ik) having to do with STEREOSCOPES. *adj.*

**ster·e·o·type** (ster′ē ə tīp′ *or* stē′rē ə tīp′) **1** in printing, a one-piece plate of type metal cast from a mould made from a surface of composed type. **2** make a stereotype of. **3** something that has a fixed form, as if cast from a mould; especially, a kind of oversimplified mental picture shared by many people in a group: *He fits the stereotype of the insecure bully.* **4** a person or group that represents such a mental picture: *The novel's heroine is a stereotype of the ambitious young woman.* **5** have or show such a mental picture of. 1, 3, 4 *n.*, 2, 5 *v.*, **ster·e·o·typed, ster·e·o·typ·ing.** —**ster′e·o·typ′er,** *n.*

**ster·e·o·typed** (ster′ē ə tīpt′ *or* stē′rē ə tīpt′) **1** not original or individual; too conventional and rigid: *"It gives me great pleasure to be with you tonight" is a stereotyped opening for a speech.* **2** pt. and pp. of STEREOTYPE. 1 *adj.,* 2 *v.*

**ster·ile** (ster′il *or* ster′əl) **1** free from living germs: *The doctor kept her instruments sterile.* **2** barren; not fertile; not producing seed, offspring, crops, etc.: *a sterile cow. Sterile land does not produce good crops.* **3** not producing results: *sterile hopes. adj.* —**ster′ile·ly,** *adv.*

**ste·ril·i·ty** (stə ril′ə tē) barrenness; a sterile condition or character. *n., pl.* **ste·ril·i·ties.**

**ster·i·li·za·tion** (ster′ə lə zā′shən *or* ster′ə lī zā′shən) a sterilizing or being sterilized: *the sterilization of dishes by boiling them. n.*

**ster·i·lize** (ster′ə līz′) **1** make free from living germs: *The water had to be sterilized by boiling to make it fit to drink.* **2** deprive of fertility. *v.,* **ster·i·lized, ster·i·liz·ing.** —**ster′i·liz′er,** *n.*

**ster·ling** (ster′ling) **1** of standard quality for silver; containing 92.5 percent pure silver: *The candlesticks are sterling silver.* **2** sterling silver or things made of it. **3** made of sterling silver. **4** genuine; excellent; dependable: *a person of sterling character.* **5** British money, especially the pound as the standard British monetary unit in international trade: *pay in sterling.* **6** of British money; payable in British money. 1, 3, 4, 6 *adj.,* 2, 5 *n.*

**sterling silver** solid silver; silver 92.5 percent pure.

**stern**¹ (stėrn) **1** severe; strict; harsh: *a stern master, a stern frown.* **2** hard; not yielding; firm: *stern necessity.* **3** grim: *stern mountains. adj.* —**stern′ly,** *adv.* —**stern′ness,** *n.*

**stern**² (stėrn) the rear of a ship or boat. See AFT for picture. *n.*

**ster·nal** (ster′nəl) of or having to do with the breastbone or STERNUM. *adj.*

**stern·most** (stėrn′mōst′) **1** nearest the stern. **2** farthest in the rear. *adj.*

**stern sheets** the space at the stern of an open boat.

**ster·num** (stėr′nəm) BREASTBONE. *n., pl.* **ster·na** (-nə) *or* **ster·nums.**

**stern·ward** (stėrn′wərd) toward the stern; astern. *adj., adv.*

**stern·wards** (stėrn′wərdz) STERNWARD. *adv.*

### stereoscopic 1169 stick

hat, āge, fär; let, ēqual, tėrm; it, īce
hot, ōpen, ôrder; oil, out; cup, pùt, rüle
above, takən, pencəl, lemən, circəs
ch, child; ng, long; sh, ship
th, thin; ŦH, then; zh, measure

**stern·way** (stėrn′wā′) the backward movement of a ship. *n.*

**stern–wheel·er** (stėrn′wē′lər *or* stėrn′hwē′lər) a STEAMBOAT driven by a paddle wheel at the stern or rear. *n.*

**ster·to·rous** (ster′tə rəs) making a heavy snoring sound: *a stertorous breath. adj.* —**ster′to·rous·ness,** *n.*

**steth·o·scope** (steth′ə skōp′) an instrument used by doctors to hear sounds in the lungs, heart, etc. *n.*

**steth·o·scop·ic** (steth′ə skop′ik) **1** having to do with the STETHOSCOPE or its use. **2** made or obtained by the STETHOSCOPE. *adj.*

**ste·ve·dore** (stē′və dôr′) a man who loads and unloads ships. *n.*

**stew** (styü *or* stü) **1** cook by slow boiling or simmering: *to stew a chicken.* **2** a dish, usually consisting of meat, vegetables, etc., cooked by slow boiling or simmering. *beef stew.* **3** any food cooked in this way. **4** *Informal.* worry; fret. **5** *Informal.* a state of worry; fret: *She is in a stew over her lost diary.* 1, 4 *v.,* 2, 3, 5 *n.*

**stew in one's own juice,** suffer the consequence of one's own actions.

**stew·ard** (styü′ərd *or* stü′ərd) **1** a person who looks after the needs of persons in a club or on a ship, train, aircraft, etc., especially one in charge of food and table service. **2** a person who manages another's property: *Patrick is the steward of that great estate.* **3** a person appointed to manage a dinner, ball, show, etc. *n.*

**stew·ard·ship** (styü′ərd ship′ *or* stü′ərd ship′) **1** the position, duties, and responsibilities of a STEWARD. **2** management for others. *n.*

**stew·pan** (styü′pan′ *or* stü′pan′) a pan for stewing; saucepan. *n.*

**stib·i·um** (stib′ē əm) ANTIMONY. Symbol: Sb *n.*

**stick**¹ (stik) **1** a long, thin piece of wood. **2** such a piece of wood shaped for a special use: *a walking stick.* **3** something like a stick in shape: *a stick of candy.* **4** furnish with a stick or sticks to support or prop. **5** *Informal.* a stiff, awkward, or stupid person. **6** a lever used to work certain main controls of an airplane. **7** a mast; part of a mast; yard. **8** *Informal.* a portion of alcoholic liquor added to a drink. **9** a small metal tray in which type is set by hand. **10** the amount of type so set. **11 the sticks,** *pl. Informal.* the outlying districts; backwoods. 1–3, 5–11 *n.,* 4 *v.,* **sticked, stick·ing.**

**stick**² (stik) **1** pierce with a pointed instrument; thrust a point into; stab. **2** kill by stabbing or piercing. **3** fasten by thrusting the point or end into or through something: *He stuck a flower in his buttonhole.* **4** put in a place or position: *Don't stick your head out of the car window.* **5** be thrust; extend from, out, through, up, etc.: *His arms stick out of his coat sleeves.* **6** a thrust. **7** fasten; attach: *Stick a stamp on the letter.* **8** a sticky condition. **9** keep close: *The child stuck to her mother's heels.* **10** be or become fastened; become fixed; be at a

**standstill:** *Our car stuck in the mud.* **11** bring to a stop: *Our work was stuck by the breakdown of the machinery.* **12** a standstill; stop. **13** keep on; hold fast: *to stick to a task, to stick to one's friends when they are in trouble.* **14** *Informal.* puzzle. **15** be puzzled; hesitate. **16** *Informal.* stand or put up with; tolerate: *I won't stick his insults much longer.* 1–5, 7, 9–11, 13–16 *v.*, **stuck, sticking**; 6, 8, 12 *n.*
**stick around,** *Informal.* stay or wait nearby.
**stick at,** hesitate or stop for: *He sticks at nothing to get his own way.*
**stick by** or **to,** remain resolutely faithful or attached to; refuse to desert: *She sticks by her friends when they are in trouble.*
**stick it out,** *Informal.* put up with unpleasant conditions, circumstances, etc.; endure: *Try to stick it out for a few more days.*
**stick out, a** stand out; be plain. **b** *Informal.* put up with until the end.
**stick up,** *Informal.* hold up; rob.
**stick up for,** *Informal.* support; defend.

**stick·er** (stik′ər) **1** a person or thing that sticks. **2** a label or slip of paper for sticking to something. **3** a burr; thorn. **4** *Informal.* a puzzle. *n.*

**stick·han·dle** (stik′han′dəl) *Cdn.* in hockey, manoeuvre the puck by deft handling of the stick, especially to avoid opposing checkers. *v.*, **stick·han·dled, stick·han·dling.** —**stick′han′dler,** *n.*

**stick-in-the-mud** (stik′ in ᴛʜə mud′) *Informal.* **1** a person who prefers the old to the new; a conservative; fogey. **2** a person who lacks initiative or resourcefulness. *n.*

**stick·le** (stik′əl) **1** make objections about trifles; insist stubbornly. **2** feel difficulties about trifles; have objections; scruple. *v.*, **stick·led, stick·ling.**

**stick·le·back** (stik′əl bak′) a small scale-less fish with a row of sharp spines on the back. *n.*, *pl.* **stick·le·back** or **stick·le·backs.**

**stick·ler** (stik′lər) **1** a person who contends stubbornly or insists on trifles. **2** something that puzzles. *n.*

**stick·pin** (stik′pin′) a pin worn in a necktie for ornament. *n.*

**stick·tight** (stik′tīt′) a plant of the same family as the aster, having flat barbed seeds that stick to clothing. *n.*

**stick-up** (stik′up′) *Informal.* a holdup; robbery. *n.*

**stick·y** (stik′ē) **1** that sticks: *sticky glue.* **2** that makes things stick; covered with adhesive matter: *sticky tape.* **3** unpleasantly humid: *sticky weather.* **4** *Informal.* puzzling; difficult: *a sticky problem.* *adj.*, **stick·i·er, stick·i·est.** —**stick′i·ly,** *adv.* —**stick′i·ness,** *n.*

**sties** (stīz) *pl.* of STY. *n.*

**stiff** (stif) **1** not easily bent: *a stiff collar.* **2** hard to move: *stiff hinges.* **3** not able to move easily: *She was stiff and sore.* **4** drawn tight; tense: *a stiff cord.* **5** not fluid; firm: *stiff jelly.* **6** dense; compact: *stiff soil.* **7** not easy or natural in manner; formal: *a stiff bow, a stiff style of writing.* **8** strong and steady in motion: *a stiff breeze.* **9** hard to deal with; hard: *a stiff examination.* **10** harsh or severe: *a stiff penalty.* **11** strong: *a stiff drink.* **12** *Informal.* more than seems suitable: *a stiff price.* *adj.* —**stiff′ly,** *adv.* —**stiff′ness,** *n.*

**stiff·en** (stif′ən) **1** make stiff: *She stiffened the shirt with starch.* **2** become stiff: *The jelly will stiffen as it cools. Pat stiffened with anger. The wind was stiffening as the storm approached.* **3** become severe. *v.* —**stiff′en·er,** *n.*

**stiff·en·ing** (stif′ə ning) **1** a making or becoming stiff. **2** something used to stiffen a thing. **3** ppr. of STIFFEN. 1, 2 *n.*, 3 *v.*

**stiff-necked** (stif′nekt′) **1** having a stiff neck. **2** stubborn; obstinate. *adj.*

**sti·fle** (stī′fəl) **1** stop the breath of; smother: *The smoke stifled the firefighters.* **2** be unable to breathe freely: *to stifle in a close room.* **3** keep back; suppress; stop: *to stifle a cry, to stifle a yawn, to stifle business activity, to stifle revolt.* *v.*, **sti·fled, sti·fling.**

**stig·ma** (stig′mə) **1** a mark of disgrace; a stain or reproach on one's reputation. **2** a distinguishing mark or sign. **3** a small spot or mark; spot in the skin that bleeds or turns red. **4** the part of the pistil of a plant that receives the pollen. See COMPOSITE and FLOWER for pictures. *n.*, *pl.* **stig·mas** or **stig·ma·ta.**

**stig·ma·ta** (stig′mə tə *or* stig mä′tə) a pl. of STIGMA. *n.*

**stig·ma·tize** (stig′mə tīz′) **1** set some mark of disgrace upon; reproach. **2** brand. **3** produce stigmas on. *v.*, **stig·ma·tized, stig·ma·tiz·ing.** —**stig′ma·ti·za′tion,** *n.*

A stile

**stile** (stīl) **1** a step or steps for getting over a fence or wall. **2** TURNSTILE. **3** a vertical piece in a door, panelled wall, etc. *n.*
☞ *Hom.* STYLE.

**sti·let·to** (stə let′ō) **1** a dagger with a narrow blade. See DAGGER for picture. **2** a small, sharp-pointed instrument for making eyelet holes in embroidery. *n.*, *pl.* **sti·let·tos** or **sti·let·toes.**

**still¹** (stil) **1** remaining in the same position or at rest; motionless; stationary: *stand, sit, or lie still.* **2** quiet; tranquil; undisturbed: *The lake is still now.* **3** make calm or quiet: *to still a crying child.* **4** become calm or quiet. **5** calm; relieve. **6** silence: *the still of the night.* **7** soft; low; subdued: *a still, small voice.* **8** at this or that time: *He came yesterday and he is still here.* **9** up to this or that time: *The matter is still unsettled.* **10** in the future as in the past: *It will still be here.* **11** even; yet: *still more, still worse.* **12** yet; nevertheless: *Proof was given, but they still doubted* (*adv.*). *He is dull; still he tries hard* (*conj.*). **13** without moving; quietly. **14** not bubbling: *still wine.* **15** a photograph of a person or other subject at rest. **16** an individual picture or frame of a motion picture used in advertising. 1, 2, 7, 14 *adj.*; 3–5 *v.*; 6, 15, 16 *n.*; 8–13 *adv.*, 12 *conj.*

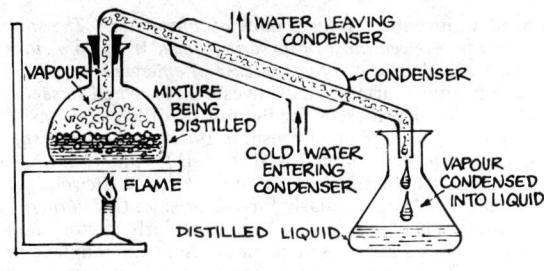

A still

**still²** (stil) **1** an apparatus for distilling liquids, especially alcoholic liquors. **2** a place where alcoholic liquors are distilled; distillery. *n.*

**still·born** (stil′bôrn′) dead when born. *adj.*

**still life** **1** fruit, flowers, furniture, pottery, dead animals, etc., shown in a picture. **2** a picture showing such things.

**still·ness** (stil′nis) **1** quiet; silence. **2** the absence of motion; calm. *n.*

**still·ly** (stil′lē) calmly; quietly. *adv.*

**stilt** (stilt) **1** one of a pair of poles to stand on and hold while walking, each with a support for the foot at some distance above the ground: *Stilts are used in walking through shallow water or for amusement.* **2** a long post or pole used to support a house, shed, etc. above the water. **3** a wading bird that lives in marshes and has a long bill and long, slender legs. *n.* —**stilt′like′**, *adj.*

**stilt·ed** (stil′tid) **1** stiffly dignified or formal: *stilted conversation.* **2** raised above the ordinary level. *adj.*

**Stil·ton cheese** (stil′tən) a rich, white cheese veined with mould when well ripened.

**stim·u·lant** (stim′yə lənt) **1** a food, drug, medicine, etc. that temporarily increases the activity of some part of the body: *Tea, coffee, and alcoholic drinks are stimulants.* **2** something that spurs one on or stirs one up; motive, influence, etc. that rouses one to action: *Hope is a stimulant.* **3** stimulating. **1, 2** *n.*, **3** *adj.*

**stim·u·late** (stim′yə lāt) **1** spur on; stir up; rouse to action: *Praise stimulated her to work hard.* **2** increase temporarily the functional activity of a part of the body, etc.: *Coffee stimulates the central nervous system.* **3** excite with alcoholic liquor; intoxicate. **4** act as a stimulant or a stimulus. *v.*, **stim·u·lat·ed, stim·u·lat·ing.** —**stim′u·lat′er, stim′u·la′tor,** *n.*

**stim·u·la·tion** (stim′yə lā′shən) a stimulating; being STIMULATED: *Lazy children need some stimulation to make them work.* *n.*

**stim·u·la·tive** (stim′yə lə tiv *or* stim′yə lā′tiv) **1** tending to STIMULATE; stimulating. **2** a stimulating thing; STIMULUS: *Brandy is sometimes used as a stimulative.* **1** *adj.*, **2** *n.*

**stim·u·li** (stim′yə lī′ *or* stim′yə lē′) pl. of STIMULUS. *n.*

**stim·u·lus** (stim′yə ləs) **1** something that stirs to action or effort: *Ambition is a great stimulus.* **2** something that excites some part of the body to activity: *The stimulus of a loud sound, carried by nerves to the brain, made the baby cry.* *n.*, *pl.* **stim·u·li** (-lī *or* -lē).

**sting** (sting) **1** prick with a sharp-pointed organ: *Bees, wasps, and hornets sting.* **2** the wound caused by stinging: *Put ointment on the sting to take away the pain.* **3** STINGER. **4** hurt sharply: *She was stung by the mockings*

of the other children. **5** a sharp pain: *The ball team felt the sting of defeat.* **6** something that causes a sharp pain. **7** cause a feeling like that of a sting: *Some antiseptics sting.* **8** drive or stir up as if by a sting: *Their ridicule stung him into making a sharp reply.* **9** something that drives or urges sharply. **1, 4, 7, 8** *v.,* **stung, sting·ing; 2, 3, 5, 6, 9** *n.* —**sting′ing·ly,** *adv.* —**sting′less,** *adj.*

**sting·er** (sting′ər) **1** the sharp part of an insect or animal that pricks or wounds and often poisons. **2** anything that stings. **3** *Informal.* a stinging blow, remark, etc. *n.*

**sting ray** a broad, flat-bodied fish that can inflict severe wounds with the sharp spines on its tail.

**stin·gy** (stin′jē) **1** mean about spending, lending, or giving money; not generous: *She tried to save money without being stingy.* **2** scanty; meagre. *adj.,* **stin·gi·er, stin·gi·est.** —**stin′gi·ly,** *adv.* —**stin′gi·ness,** *n.*

**stink** (stingk) **1** a bad smell. **2** have a bad smell: *Decaying fish stink.* **3** cause to have a very bad smell. **4** have a very bad reputation; be in great disfavour. **5** *Informal.* have poor quality or be unattractive in some way. **1** *n.,* **2–5** *v.,* **stank** or **stunk, stunk, stink·ing.** —**stink′ing·ly,** *adv.*

**raise a stink,** *Informal.* arouse much complaint, criticism, or disturbance.

**stink out,** drive out with stinking smoke or fumes.

**stink·er** (sting′kər) a person or thing that stinks. *n.*

**stint** (stint) **1** keep on short allowance; be saving or careful in using or spending; limit: *The parents stinted themselves of food to give it to their children.* **2** limit; limitation: *That generous man gives without stint.* **3** be saving; get along on very little. **4** an amount or share set aside. **5** a task assigned: *Washing the breakfast dishes was his daily stint.* **1, 3** *v.,* **2, 4, 5** *n.*

**stipe** (stīp) a stalk; stem: *the stipe of a mushroom, the stipe of a fern.* *n.*

**sti·pend** (stī′pend) **1** in some professions, fixed or regular pay; salary: *A magistrate receives a stipend.* **2** a regular allowance paid under the terms of a scholarship. *n.*

**stip·ple** (stip′əl) **1** paint, draw, or engrave by making dots. **2** this method of painting, drawing, or engraving. **3** the effect produced by this method. **4** produce this effect on. **5** stippled work. **1, 4** *v.,* **stip·pled, stip·pling; 2, 3, 5** *n.*

**stip·u·late** (stip′yə lāt′) arrange definitely; demand as a condition of agreement: *Olaf stipulated that he should receive a month's vacation every year if he took the job.* *v.,* **stip·u·lat·ed, stip·u·lat·ing.** —**stip′u·la′tor,** *n.*

**stip·u·la·tion** (stip′yə lā′shən) **1** a definite arrangement; agreement. **2** a condition in an agreement or bargain: *We rented the house with the stipulation that certain rooms should be papered.* *n.*

**stip·ule** (stip′yül) one of the pair of little leaflike parts at the base of a leaf stem. See STEM for picture. *n.*

**stir** (stėr) **1** move: *The wind stirred the leaves.* **2** move

**stirring** about: *No one was stirring in the house.* **3** mix by moving around with a spoon, fork, stick, etc.: *to stir sugar into one's coffee.* **4** be mixed with a spoon or the like: *This dough stirs hard.* **5** get going; affect strongly; excite: *Metin stirs the other children to mischief.* **6** become active, much affected, or excited: *The countryside was stirring with new life.* **7** a movement: *a stir in the bushes.* **8** a state of motion, activity, briskness, bustle, etc. **9** excitement: *The coming of the Queen caused a great stir.* **10** the act of stirring: *Joy gave the mixture a hard stir.* **11** a jog; thrust; poke. 1–6 *v.*, **stirred, stir·ring;** 7–11 *n.* —**stir′rer,** *n.*
**stir up,** **a** rouse to action, activity, or emotion; incite; stimulate. **b** excite; provoke; induce: *stir up a mutiny.*
**stir·ring** (stėr′ing) **1** moving; active; lively: *stirring times.* **2** rousing; exciting: *a stirring speech.* **3** ppr. of STIR. 1, 2 *adj.,* 3 *v.* —**stir′ring·ly,** *adv.*
**stir·rup** (stėr′əp *or* stir′əp) **1** one of a pair of foot supports that hang from a saddle: *The rider stood up in her stirrups.* See SADDLE for picture. **2** a piece resembling a stirrup used as a support or clamp. *n.*
**stirrup bone** the innermost of the three bones in the middle ear; the stapes. See EAR¹ for picture.
**stirrup cup** a cup of wine or other liquor offered to a rider mounted for departure; a drink at parting.
**stitch** (stich) **1** in sewing, embroidering, etc., a movement of a threaded needle through the cloth and back out again. **2** a particular method of making stitches: *buttonhole stitch. There are two basic stitches in knitting.* **3** the loop of thread, etc. made by a stitch: *The doctor will take the stitches out of the wound tomorrow.* **4** make stitches in; fasten with stitches: *She stitched his shirt. The doctor stitched the cut.* **5** sew. **6** a small piece of cloth or clothing: *His clothes were all burned, and he hadn't a stitch to wear.* **7** *Informal.* a small bit: *The lazy boy wouldn't do a stitch of work.* **8** a sudden, sharp pain: *a stitch in the side.* 1–3, 6–8 *n.,* 4, 5 *v.* —**stitch′er,** *n.*
**in stitches,** laughing uncontrollably.
**stitch·ing** (stich′ing) **1** the act or work of one who stitches. **2** stitches collectively. **3** ppr. of STITCH. 1, 2 *n.,* 3 *v.*
**St. John's Day** June 24; the anniversary holiday of Newfoundland, held then to commemorate the landing of John Cabot on the same day in 1497.
**St.–John's–wort** (sānt jonz′wėrt′) a shrub or plant that has many clusters of showy yellow flowers. *n.*
**stoat** (stōt) an ERMINE, especially in its brown summer coat. *n.*

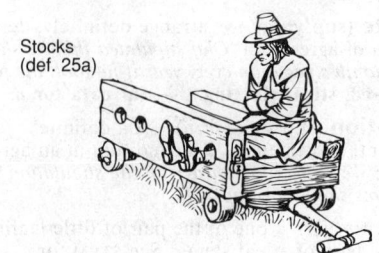
Stocks (def. 25a)

**stock** (stok) **1** a supply or store of goods, materials, equipment, etc. regularly kept on hand for sale or for use as needed; inventory: *a large stock of information. The store has already received most of its spring stock. We keep a stock of canned foods at the cottage in case of emergency.* **2** cattle or other farm animals; livestock: *purebred Jersey stock.* **3** for livestock or for the raising of livestock: *a stock farm.* **4** supply or furnish: *to stock a lake with fish, to stock a farm. Our camp is well stocked for the week.* **5** lay in a supply (used with **up**): *to stock up on firewood for the winter.* **6** keep regularly for use or sale: *Our corner store stocks school supplies.* **7** kept regularly in stock and available: *stock sizes.* **8** in common use; commonplace or trite: *a stock response. The weather is a stock topic of conversation.* **9** shares in the ownership of an incorporated business: *The holder of stock in a company owns a part of that company in proportion to the amount of stock he or she holds.* **10** of, having to do with, or dealing with stock or stocks: *a stock exchange, a stockbroker.* **11** a group having a common origin; family or race: *She is of Loyalist stock.* **12** an original ancestor of a family, tribe, or race. **13** a part used as a support or handle; a part or framework to which other parts are attached: *the wooden stock of a rifle, the stock of a whip.* See ANCHOR for picture. **14** fasten to or provide with a stock. **15** raw material used to manufacture something: *All the cabinetmaker's wood was kiln-dried stock.* **16** a particular kind of paper: *The advertisement was printed on heavy stock.* **17** liquid in which meat or fish has been cooked, used as a base for soups, sauces, etc.: *chicken stock.* **18** a stiff band of cloth worn around the neck by men especially in the 19th century: *A stock is still worn as part of a riding habit for both men and women.* **19** the repertoire of plays produced by a company at a single theatre. **20** the trunk or stump of a tree or the main stem of a plant. **21** an underground stem like a root. **22** a tree or plant that furnishes cuttings for grafting. **23** the stem into which a graft is inserted. **24** any of a closely related group of plants of the mustard family having flowers that are usually fragrant. **25 stocks,** *pl.* **a** a wooden frame having holes for the feet and, sometimes, for the hands, into which people were formerly locked in public as a punishment for minor offences. **b** a frame of timbers on which a ship rests during construction. 1–3, 7–13, 15–25 *n.,* 4–6, 14 *v.*
**in stock,** available for sale or use; on hand.
**out of stock,** sold out or used up; not immediately available for sale or use.
**take stock,** **a** find out how much stock there is on hand. **b** make an estimate or examination: *We decided to stop and take stock of our situation before continuing with the scheme.*
**take stock in,** **a** *Informal.* take an interest in; consider important; trust: *She takes no stock in his promises.* **b** take shares in a company.
☞ *Hom.* STALK.
**stock·ade** (sto kād′) **1** an enclosure for defence made of large, strong upright posts placed closely together in the ground: *A heavy stockade protected the trading post from attack.* **2** a fort, camp, etc. surrounded by a stockade. **3** protect, fortify, or surround with a stockade. **4** a pen or other enclosed space made with upright posts, stakes, etc. 1, 2, 4 *n.,* 3 *v.,* **stock·ad·ed, stock·ad·ing.**
**stock·bro·ker** (stok′brō′kər) a person who buys and sells stocks and bonds for others. *n.*
**stock car** **1** a railway freight car for livestock. **2** an automobile of a standard make that has been altered in various ways for use in racing.
**stock company** **1** a company whose capital is divided into shares. **2** a theatrical company employed more or less permanently under the same management, usually at one theatre, to perform many different plays.

**stock exchange** 1 a place where stocks and bonds are bought and sold. 2 an association of brokers and dealers in stocks and bonds.

**stock·hold·er** (stok′hōl′dər)   an owner of stocks or shares in a company.   *n.*

**stock·ing** (stok′ing)   1 a close-fitting, knitted covering of nylon, cotton, wool, etc. for the foot and leg.   2 sock. 3 something suggesting a stocking, especially a patch of different colour on the leg of an animal: *The horse was brown with a white mark on the forehead and white stockings.*   4 ppr. of STOCK.   1–3 *n.*, 4 *v.*
**in one's stocking feet,**   wearing socks or stockings but no shoes: *Don't run around in your stocking feet; the floor's too dirty. He's 188 cm tall in his stocking feet.*

**stocking cap**   TUQUE (def. 1).

**stock in trade**   1 the stock of a dealer or company; goods kept for sale.   2 tools or other materials needed to carry on a trade or business.   3 any resources, practices, etc. that are characteristic of a particular person, group, or business: *His stock in trade is a slightly rumpled look and a charming smile that audiences love.*

**stock–keep·er** (stok′kē′pər)   a person in charge of a stock of materials or goods in a warehouse, etc.: *The stock-keeper keeps an inventory of goods on hand, received, or shipped.*   *n.*

**stock·man** (stok′mən)   1 a person who owns or manages livestock.   2 STOCK-KEEPER.   *n.*, *pl.* **stock·men** (-mən).

**stock market**   1 a place where stocks and bonds are bought and sold; stock exchange.   2 the buying and selling in such a place.   3 the prices of stocks and bonds across a country: *The stock market is falling.*

**stock·pile** (stok′pīl′)   1 a supply of raw materials, manufactured items, etc. built up and held in reserve in case of a shortage or emergency: *a stockpile of weapons, a stockpile of canned goods.*   2 collect or bring together such a reserved supply: *to stockpile nuclear weapons.* 1 *n.*, 2 *v.*, **stock·piled, stock·pil·ing.**

**stock·pot** (stok′pot′)   a pot in which soup stock is prepared: *They keep all leftover bones for the stockpot.*   *n.*

**stock·room** (stok′rüm′)   a room where stock is kept.   *n.*

**stock–still** (stok′stil′)   motionless: *She stood stock-still and listened.*   *adj.*

**stock·tak·ing** (stok′tā′king)   the act of checking the supply of goods on hand: *The store will be closed two days for stocktaking.*   *n.*

**stock·y** (stok′ē)   having a solid, sturdy, somewhat thick form or build: *a stocky child, a stocky stem.*   *adj.*, **stock·i·er, stock·i·est.**   —**stock′i·ly,** *adv.* —**stock′i·ness,** *n.*

**stock·yard** (stok′yärd′)   a place with pens and sheds for cattle, sheep, hogs, and horses: *Livestock is kept in a stockyard before being slaughtered or sent to market.*   *n.*

**stodg·y** (stoj′ē)   1 dull or uninteresting; tediously commonplace: *a stodgy style of writing.*   2 very old-fashioned; out-of-date: *He's very stodgy and set in his ways.*   3 of food, heavy and indigestible.   4 heavily built and slow-moving: *A stodgy figure came lumbering through the fog.*   *adj.*, **stodg·i·er, stodg·i·est.**   —**stodg′i·ly,** *adv.* —**stodg′i·ness,** *n.*

**sto·gie** or **sto·gy** (stō′gē)   a long, slender, cheap cigar.   *n.*, *pl.* **sto·gies.**

hat, āge, fär; let, ēqual, tėrm; it, īce
hot, ōpen, ôrder; oil, out; cup, pút, rüle
əbove, takən, pencəl, lemən, circəs
ch, child; ng, long; sh, ship
th, thin; ŦH, then; zh, measure

**sto·ic** (stō′ik)   1 a person who remains calm, represses his or her feelings, and is indifferent to pleasure and pain. 2 STOICAL.   1 *n.*, 2 *adj.*

**sto·i·cal** (stō′ə kəl)   like a stoic; self-controlled; indifferent to pleasure and pain.   *adj.*
—**sto′i·cal·ly,** *adv.*

**sto·i·cism** (stō′ə siz′əm)   patient endurance; indifference to pleasure and pain.   *n.*

**stoke** (stōk)   1 stir up and feed fuel to: *to stoke a fire in a fireplace, to stoke a furnace.*   2 tend a boiler, furnace, etc.   *v.*, **stoked, stok·ing.**

**stoke·hold** (stōk′hōld′)   a place in a steamship where the furnaces, boilers, etc. are.   *n.*

**stoke·hole** (stōk′hōl′)   1 a hole through which fuel is put into a furnace.   2 the space in front of a boiler or furnace of a ship from which the fires are tended.   *n.*

**stok·er** (stō′kər)   1 a person who tends the fires of a furnace or boiler, especially in a steamship.   2 a mechanical device for tending and feeding a furnace.   *n.*

**STOL**   of an airplane, short takeoff and landing.

**stole**[1] (stōl)   pt. of STEAL: *He stole the money years ago.*   *v.*

**stole**[2] (stōl)   1 a long, narrow strip of silk or other material worn around the neck by a member of the clergy during certain church functions.   2 a woman's long, wide scarf or wrap worn around the shoulders with the ends usually hanging down in front: *a mink stole, a knitted stole.* 3 a long, loose robe worn by women in ancient Rome.   *n.*

**sto·len** (stō′lən)   pp. of STEAL: *The money was stolen by a thief.*   *n.*

**stol·id** (stol′id)   having or showing no emotion; hard to arouse; not excitable: *stolid opposition to new ideas. Her stolid presence was a comfort during the uproar.*   *adj.* —**stol′id·ly,** *adv.*

**sto·lid·i·ty** (stə lid′ə tē)   the quality or state of being STOLID.   *n.*, *pl.* **sto·lid·i·ties.**

STOLONS

**sto·lon** (stō′lon)   1 in botany, a slender horizontal branch growing from the base of a plant that takes root at the tip and produces a new plant; runner: *Strawberry plants have stolons.*   2 in zoology, a stemlike growth, as in certain polyps, that produces buds from which new individuals grow.   *n.*

**sto·ma** (stō′mə)   1 in botany, one of the very tiny openings in the surface of a leaf, etc., through which water vapour and gases pass in and out. 2 in zoology, a small, mouthlike opening in lower animals. *n., pl.* **sto·ma·ta.**

**stom·ach** (stum′ək) 1 a large internal organ, the part of the alimentary canal in which the first stage of digestion takes place: *Food passes into the stomach from the esophagus and from the stomach into the intestines.* See ALIMENTARY CANAL for picture. 2 a cavity in an invertebrate animal having a similar function. 3 the lower part of the front of the body; abdomen; belly: *My stomach aches. He was hit in the stomach.* 4 desire for food; appetite: *no stomach for dinner.* 5 eat or keep in one's stomach: *She can't stomach spinach.* 6 any desire or liking: *I had no stomach for a fight. He's got no stomach for that kind of behaviour.* 7 put up with; bear; endure: *She can't stomach arrogance.* 1–4, 6 *n.*, 5, 7 *v.*

**stom·ach·ache** (stum′ə kāk′) a steady pain in the abdomen. *n.*

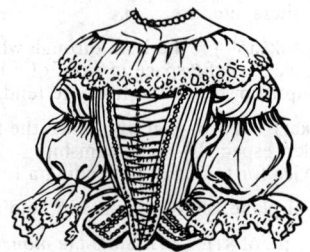

**stom·ach·er** (stum′ə kər) a stiff, often elaborately decorated panel located over the front of a tight-fitting bodice: *Stomachers were worn by men and women in the 16th century and by women also in the 17th and 18th centuries.* *n.*

**sto·ma·ta** (stō′mə tə *or* stom′ə tə) pl. of STOMA. *n.*

**stomp** (stomp) stamp with the foot. *v.*

**stone** (stōn) 1 hard mineral matter that is not metal; rock: *Stone is widely used in building.* 2 a small piece of rock. 3 a piece of rock of definite size, shape, etc. used for a particular purpose: *Her grave is marked by a fine stone.* 4 made of stone: *a stone wall, a stone house.* 5 having to do with stone. 6 put stone on; pave, build, line, etc. with stone. 7 rub with or on a stone. 8 a gem; jewel: *The queen's diamonds were very fine stones.* 9 something hard and rounded like a stone, which sometimes forms in the kidneys or gall bladder causing sickness and pain. 10 throw stones at; drive by throwing stones; kill by throwing stones: *The cruel children stoned the dog.* 11 the single seed, usually covered by a hard shell, found inside such fruits as peaches, plums, cherries, and avocados; pit. 12 take stones or seeds out of: *to stone cherries or plums.* 13 made of STONEWARE or coarse clay. 14 *Brit.* a unit of mass equal to about 6.34 kg: *He weighed more than fourteen stone.* 15 a curling stone. 1–3, 8, 9, 11, 14, 15 *n., pl.* **stones** or (for def. 14) **stone;** 4, 5, 13 *adj.*, 6, 7, 10, 12 *v.*, **stoned, ston·ing.** —**stone′like′,** *adj.*
**cast the first stone,** be the first to criticize.
**leave no stone unturned,** do everything that can be done.

**Stone Age** the earliest known period of any human culture, characterized by the use of tools and weapons made of stone.

**stone–blind** (stōn′blīnd′) totally blind. *adj.*
**stone·boat** (stōn′bōt′) a low kind of sledge often having runners made of logs, used for transporting stones taken from fields and for other heavy hauling. *n.*
**stone bruise** a bruise caused by a stone, especially one on the sole of the foot.
**stone–cold** (stōn′kōld′) cold as stone; completely cold: *By the time he got back, his soup was stone-cold.* *adj.*
**stone–crop** (stōn′krop′) 1 a low, creeping plant that has small, fleshy leaves and clusters of small yellow flowers. 2 any of various related plants. *n.*
**stone·cut·ter** (stōn′kut′ər) 1 a person who cuts or carves stone. 2 a machine for cutting or dressing stone. *n.*
**stoned** (stōnd) 1 having the stones, or pits, removed: *stoned peaches.* 2 pt. and pp. of STONE. 1 *adj.*, 2 *v.*
**stone–dead** (stōn′ded′) completely dead; lifeless. *adj.*
**stone–deaf** (stōn′def′) totally deaf. *adj.*
**stone fruit** any fruit that has a layer of pulp outside a hard shell containing a seed; any drupe: *Peaches, cherries, olives, etc. are stone fruits.*
**stone–ground** (stōn′ground′) of whole-grain flour, made by grinding the whole kernels of grain between millstones, instead of processing the grain to separate the bran from the pulp and then adding bran again after grinding. *adj.*
**stone·ma·son** (stōn′mā′sən) a person who cuts stone or builds walls, etc. of stone. *n.*
**stone's throw** a short distance.
**stone·ware** (stōn′wer′) a coarse, hard, glazed pottery. *n.*
**stone·work** (stōn′werk′) 1 work done in stone. 2 the part of a building made of stone. See MASONRY for picture. *n.*
**stone·work·er** (stōn′wer′kər) a person who shapes or cuts stone for use in buildings, sculpture, etc.; stonecutter. *n.*
**Ston·ey** (stō′nē) ASSINIBOINE. *n.*
**ston·y** (stō′nē) 1 having many stones: *The beach is stony.* 2 hard like stone: *The plate shattered on the stony floor.* 3 without expression or feeling: *a stony stare.* 4 cold and unfeeling: *a stony heart.* *adj.*, **ston·i·er, ston·i·est.** —**ston′i·ly,** *adv.* —**ston′i·ness,** *n.*
**ston·y·heart·ed** (stō′nē här′təd) pitiless and unfeeling; cold-hearted; cruel. *adj.*
**stood** (stud) pt. and pp. of STAND: *He stood at the corner for five minutes. This building has stood here for many years.* *v.*

Stooks of wheat

**stook** (stuk) 1 an upright arrangement of sheaves of grain intended to speed up drying in the field: *stooks of* golden wheat.   2 build such arrangements of sheaves: *He earned some money stooking on his uncle's farm.*   1 *n.*, 2 *v.*

**stool** (stül)   1 a seat for one person, without back or arms and supported on three or four legs or a central pedestal.   2 a low bench used to rest the feet on or to kneel on; footstool.   3 a seat to be used as a toilet.   4 waste matter from the bowels.   5 formerly, a pole to which a bird was fastened as a decoy.   6 decoy; STOOL PIGEON.   *n.* —**stool'-like'**, *adj.*

**stool pigeon**   1 a pigeon used to lead other pigeons into a trap.   2 *Informal.*   a spy for the police; informer.

**stoop**¹ (stüp)   1 bend forward: *to stoop over a desk.*   2 the act of bending forward.   3 carry the head and shoulders bent forward: *The old man stoops.*   4 a forward bend of the head and shoulders, especially when habitual: *She walks with a noticeable stoop.*   5 descend from a superior rank or position; condescend: *She would never stoop to speak to the workers.*   6 lower oneself morally; demean oneself: *He stooped to cheating his customers in trying to save his business.*   7 a lowering of oneself; condescension or a demeaning of oneself.   8 swoop down like a hawk attacking prey.   9 the descent of a hawk, etc. on its prey.   1, 3, 5, 6, 8 *v.*, 2, 4, 7, 9 *n.* —**stoop'er**, *n.*
☞ *Hom.* STOUP.

**stoop**² (stüp)   a porch or platform at the entrance of a house.   *n.*
☞ *Hom.* STOUP.

**stop** (stop)   1 keep from moving, acting, doing, being, etc.: *to stop a clock, to stop a speaker.*   2 cut off, withhold: *to stop supplies.*   3 put an end to; interrupt; check: *to stop a noise.*   4 stay; remain: *to stop at a hotel.*   5 leave off moving, acting, doing, being, etc.; cease: *All work stopped. We stopped and listened.*   6 close by filling; fill holes in; close: *to stop a hole, a leak, a wound.*   7 close a vessel with a cork, plug, or the like; shut up something in a closed vessel or place: *to stop a bottle.*   8 block; obstruct: *A fallen tree stopped traffic.*   9 check a blow, stroke, etc.; parry; ward off.   10 defeat by a knockout.   11 in games, defeat.   12 stopping; closing; blocking; checking: *We put a stop to his tricks.*   13 a stay or staying; a halt: *We made a stop for lunch.*   14 being stopped.   15 the place where a stop is made: *a bus stop.*   16 anything that stops; obstacle.   17 any piece or device that serves to check or control movement or action in a mechanism.   18 any of several punctuation marks: *A period is a full stop.*   19 punctuate.   20 something that controls the pitch of a musical instrument.   21 in organs, a graduated set of pipes of the same kind, or the knob or handle that controls them.   22 in music, close a finger hole, etc. in order to produce a particular note from a wind instrument.   23 press down a string of a violin, etc. in order to alter the pitch of tone produced.   24 in phonetics, a sudden, complete stopping of the breath stream, followed by its sudden release.   25 a consonant that involves such a stopping. *Examples:* p, t, k, b, d, *and* g (*as in* go).   1–11, 19, 22, 23 *v.*, **stopped, stop·ping;**   12–18, 20, 21, 24, 25 *n.*
**put a stop to,**   stop; end.
**stop off,** *Informal.*   stop for a short stay.
**stop over,**   **a** make a short stay.   **b** stop in the course of a trip.

**stop·cock** (stop'kok')   a cock or valve for regulating the flow of a gas or liquid in a pipe, etc.   *n.*

**stope** (stōp)   a steplike excavation formed in a mine as ore is extracted in successive layers.   *n.*

**stop·gap** (stop'gap')   1 anything that fills the place of something lacking; a temporary substitute.   2 serving as a stopgap: *stopgap legislation.*   *n.*

hat, āge, fär; let, ēqual, tėrm; it, īce
hot, ōpen, ôrder; oil, out; cup, put, rüle
əbove, takən, pencəl, lemən, circəs
ch, child; ng, long; sh, ship
th, thin; ᴛʜ, then; zh, measure

**stop·light** (stop'līt')   a traffic light or signal.   *n.*

**stop·o·ver** (stop'ō'vər)   1 a stopping over in the course of a journey, especially with the privilege of proceeding later on the ticket originally issued for the journey.   2 a place where such a stop is made: *Our first stopover was Regina.*   *n.*

**stop·page** (stop'ij)   1 a stopping: *The foreman called for a stoppage of operations to oil the machinery.*   2 being stopped: *During the work stoppage, many workers looked for other jobs.*   3 a block; obstruction.   *n.*

**stop·per** (stop'ər)   1 a plug or cork for closing a bottle, tube, etc.   2 close or fit with a stopper: *to stopper a flask.*   3 a person or thing that brings to a halt or causes to stop functioning; a check.   1, 3 *n.*, 2 *v.*

**stop street**   a side street from which vehicles may not enter a main street without first stopping.   Compare with THROUGH STREET.

**stop·watch** (stop'woch')   a watch having a hand that can be stopped or started at any instant: *A stopwatch indicates fractions of a second and is used for timing races and contests.*   *n.*

**stor·age** (stô'rij)   1 the act or fact of storing goods, data, etc.   2 the condition of being stored: *Cold storage is used to keep food from spoiling.*   3 a place or space for storing: *She put her furniture in storage. This house has very little storage.*   4 the cost of storing.   *n.*

**storage battery**   a device for producing electric current, consisting of a group of ELECTROCHEMICAL CELLS that can be recharged; BATTERY (def. 2).

**store** (stôr)   1 a place where goods are kept for sale: *a clothing store.*   2 a thing or things laid up for use; supply; stock: *She puts up stores of preserves and jellies every year.*   3 supply or stock.   4 put away for future use; lay up: *The squirrel stores away nuts. We stored our furs during the summer.*   5 a place where supplies are kept for future use; storehouse.   6 put in a warehouse or place used for preserving.   1, 2, 5 *n.*, 3, 4, 6 *v.*, **stored, stor·ing.** —**stor'er**, *n.*
**in store,**   on hand; in reserve; saved for the future.
**set store by,**   value; esteem: *She sets great store by her mother's opinion.*

**store·front** (stôr'frunt')   1 the front of a store or shop: *All the storefronts were newly painted.*   2 of a business office, social service, etc., situated at street level in a business district and providing direct access for the public: *a storefront legal office.*   3 operating a storefront business or service: *a storefront lawyer.*   *n.*

**store·house** (stôr'hous')   1 a place where things are stored; warehouse.   2 an abundant supply or source: *A library is a storehouse of information. She is a storehouse of knowledge.*   *n.*

**store·keep·er** (stôr'kē'pər)   a person who has charge of a store or stores: *My uncle was a country storekeeper.*   *n.*

**store·room** (stôr'rüm')   a room where things are stored.   *n.*

**sto·rey** (stô′rē) **1** a level or floor of a house or other building: *They are now building the second storey of our new house.* **2** the set of rooms or apartments on one level or floor: *The Bells occupy the second storey.* *n., pl.* **sto·reys.**

**sto·reyed** (stô′rēd) having a stated number of storeys or floors: *a two-storeyed house.* *adj.* ☛ Hom. STORIED.

**sto·ried** (stô′rēd) **1** celebrated in story or history: *"the storied Rhine."* **2** ornamented with designs representing happenings in history or legend: *storied tapestry.* *adj.* ☛ Hom. STOREYED.

White storks— about 105 cm long including the tail

**stork** (stôrk) a large, long-legged wading bird having a long neck and a long bill. *n.* —**stork′like′**, *adj.*

**storm** (stôrm) **1** a very strong wind, especially one with a velocity of about 100 to 120 km/h; windstorm. **2** a violent outbreak of rain with strong winds and, usually, thunder and lightning: *The clouds threatened an approaching storm.* **3** any heavy and especially sudden fall of snow, sleet, hail, etc. together with a strong wind. **4** be a storm: *It stormed for three days.* **5** anything like a storm: *a storm of arrows.* **6** a violent outburst or disturbance: *a storm of tears, a storm of angry words.* **7** be violent; rage: *She stormed at the guilty child.* **8** speak loudly and angrily. **9** rush violently: *to storm out of the room.* **10** attack violently: *The troops stormed the city.* **11** a violent attack: *The castle was taken by storm.* **12** a STORM WINDOW or STORM DOOR: *Our house has a complete set of storms and screens.* 1–3, 5, 6, 11, 12 *n.*, 4, 7–10 *v.*

**storm in a teacup**, *Esp. Brit.* great excitement or commotion over something unimportant. See TEMPEST.

**storm cellar** a cellar for shelter during cyclones, tornadoes, etc.

**storm centre** or **center** **1** the moving centre of a cyclone, where the pressure is lowest and the wind is comparatively calm. **2** any centre of trouble, tumult, etc.

**storm door** an extra door fixed outside a regular door as protection against cold, wind, etc.

**storm petrel** STORMY PETREL (def. 1).

**storm window** an extra window fixed on the outside of a regular window as protection against cold, wind, etc.

**storm·y** (stôr′mē) **1** having storms; likely to have storms; troubled by storms: *a stormy sea, stormy weather, a stormy night.* **2** rough and disturbed; violent: *They had stormy quarrels.* *adj.*, **storm·i·er, storm·i·est.** —**storm′i·ly**, *adv.* —**storm′i·ness**, *n.*

**stormy petrel** **1** any of several small, black-and-white petrels, sea birds whose presence is supposed to give warning of a storm; especially, a petrel of the northern Atlantic and Mediterranean. **2** anyone believed likely to cause trouble or to indicate trouble.

**sto·ry** (stô′rē) **1** an account of some happening or group of happenings: *Tell us the story of your life.* **2** such an account, either true or made-up, intended to interest the reader, or hearer; tale: *ghost stories, adventure stories.* **3** *Informal.* falsehood: *That boy is a liar; he tells stories.* **4** stories as a branch of literature: *a character famous in story.* **5** the plot of a play, novel, etc. **6** a newspaper article, or material for such an article. **7** a radio or television report. *n., pl.* **sto·ries.** —**sto′ry·less**, *adj.*

**sto·ry·book** (stô′rē bùk′) **1** a book containing one or more stories or tales, especially for children. **2** of or like that of a storybook; romantic: *a storybook hero, a storybook ending.* *n.*

**sto·ry·tell·er** (stô′rē tel′ər) **1** a person who tells stories. **2** *Informal.* a person who tells falsehoods; liar. *n.*

**sto·ry·tell·ing** (stô′rē tel′ing) **1** telling stories. **2** *Informal.* telling falsehoods; lying. *n., adj.*

**stoup** (stüp) **1** a drinking vessel of varying size for liquids, such as a cup, flagon, or tankard. **2** the amount it holds. **3** a basin for holy water at the entrance of a Christian church. *n.* ☛ Hom. STOOP.

**stout** (stout) **1** bulky; somewhat fat: *He's getting stout.* **2** strong or thick; solid; substantial: *a stout ship, a stout walking stick. The fort has stout walls.* **3** brave; bold: *He has a stout heart.* **4** not yielding; stubborn; determined: *stout resistance.* **5** a strong, dark-brown beer brewed with roasted malt. 1–4 *adj.*, 5 *n.* —**stout′ly**, *adv.* —**stout′ness**, *n.*

**stout-heart·ed** (stout′här′tid) brave; bold; courageous. *adj.* —**stout′-heart′ed·ly**, *adv.*

**stove**¹ (stōv) an apparatus for cooking and heating, using electricity or burning a fuel such as gas, oil, or wood. *n.*

**stove**² (stōv) a pt. and a pp. of STAVE: *The barrel was stove in when it dropped off the truck.* *v.*

**stove·pipe** (stōv′pīp′) a sheet-metal pipe of large diameter connected to a fuel-burning stove, used to carry smoke and gases from the stove to a chimney. *n.*

**stow** (stō) **1** pack: *The cargo was stowed in the ship's hold.* **2** pack things closely in; fill by packing: *The boys stowed the little cabin with supplies for the trip.* *v.* —**stow′er**, *n.*

**stow away**, hide on a ship, aircraft, etc. to avoid paying the fare or to escape.

**stow·age** (stō′ij) **1** stowing or being stowed: *The stowage of all their equipment took them two hours.* **2** a room or place for stowing: *The boat has stowage fore and aft.* **3** capacity for stowing: *Our boat has stowage for a three-day cruise.* **4** what is stowed. **5** the charge for stowing something. *n.*

**stow·a·way** (stō′ə wā′) a person who hides on a ship, aircraft, etc. to get a free passage or to escape. *n.*

**str.** **1** steamer. **2** strait.

**strad·dle** (strad′əl) **1** sit or stand with one's legs on either side of something: *He straddled the chair. She stood straddling the row of lettuce as she hoed.* **2** be or lie across something: *A footbridge straddled the brook. A pair of large glasses straddled her nose.* **3** be or be spread apart: *His legs straddled as he floundered through the snow.* **4** avoid committing oneself on an issue; favour or appear to favour both sides: *She is still straddling the question, but will soon have to decide one way or the other.* **5** the act or position of a person who straddles. 1–4 v., **strad·dled,** **strad·dling;** 5 n. —**strad′dler,** n.

**Strad·i·var·i·us** (strad′ə ver′ē əs) a violin, viola, or cello made by Antonio Stradivari, 1644–1737, a violin-maker of Cremona, Italy. These instruments are famous for their exquisite tone. n.

**strag·gle** (strag′əl) 1 wander in a scattered fashion: *Cows straggled along the lane.* 2 stray from the rest. 3 spread in an irregular, rambling manner: *Vines straggled over the old wall.* v., **strag·gled, strag·gling.** —**strag′gler,** n.

**strag·gly** (strag′lē) spread out in an irregular, rambling way; straggling. adj.

**straight** (strāt) 1 without a bend or curve; direct: *a straight line, a straight path.* 2 in a line; directly: *Walk straight. He went straight home.* 3 in an erect position; upright: *Stand up straight.* 4 frank; honest; upright: *straight conduct.* 5 frankly; honestly; uprightly: *Live straight.* 6 right; correct: *straight thinking.* 7 in proper order or condition: *Keep your accounts straight.* 8 continuous: *in straight succession.* 9 continuously: *Drive straight on.* 10 without delay. 11 unmodified; undiluted: *a straight comedy, straight whisky.* 12 thoroughgoing or unreserved: *a straight Tory.* 13 without qualification of any kind. 14 *Informal.* reliable: *a straight tip.* 15 the condition of being straight; straight form, position, or line. 16 a straight part, as of a race course. 17 in poker, a sequence of five cards. 18 made up of a sequence of five cards: *a straight flush.* 1, 4, 6–8, 11, 12, 14, 18 adj., 2, 3, 5, 9, 10, 13 adv., 15–17 n. —**straight′ly,** adv. —**straight′ness,** n.
**straight off,** at once.
☞ *Hom.* STRAIT.
☞ *Etym.* ME *streght, straght,* originally a past participle (meaning 'stretched at full length') of the verb *strecche,* which developed from OE *streccan* 'stretch'.

**straight angle** an angle of 180°.

**straight–arm** (strāt′ärm′) 1 prevent an opponent from making a tackle in football by holding one's arm straight in front. 2 the act of straight-arming. 1 v., 2 n.

**straight·a·way** (strāt′ə wā′) 1 a straight course; especially, the straight part of a closed racecourse or a straight stretch of highway: *They were now on a straightaway, making excellent time.* 2 in a straight course. 3 as quickly as possible; at once; immediately: *The captain read the letter and burned it straightaway.* 1, n., 2 adj., 3 adv.

**straight·edge** (strāt′ej′) a strip of wood or metal having one edge accurately straight, used in obtaining or testing straight lines and level surfaces. n.

**straight·en** (strāt′ən) 1 make or become straight: *Straighten your shoulders.* 2 put in the proper order or condition (usually used with **up** or **out**): *He straightened up his room. We have to straighten out our accounts to see how much we owe.* 3 *Informal.* make or become better in behaviour, etc.; reform (usually used with **out** or **up**): *His parents have tried to straighten him out but he still keeps getting in trouble.* v. —**straight′en·er,** n.
☞ *Hom.* STRAITEN.

**straight face** an expressionless face, especially one showing no trace of amusement: *She kept a straight face through the whole ridiculous story.*

**straight–faced** (strāt′fāst′) keeping a STRAIGHT FACE. adj.

**straight·for·ward** (strāt′fôr′wərd) 1 honest; frank: *a straightforward person, a straightforward answer.* 2 without complications; clear-cut and precise: *It was a straightforward plan.* 3 going straight ahead; direct. adj. —**straight′for′ward·ly,** adv. —**straight′for′ward·ness,** n.

**straight·for·wards** (strāt′fôr′wərdz) in a straightforward manner; openly or directly: *She always speaks straightforwards.* adv.

**straight–out** (strāt′tout′) *Informal.* out-and-out; complete; thorough. adj.

**strain**[1] (strān) 1 draw tight; stretch: *The weight strained the rope.* 2 pull hard: *The dog strained at its leash.* 3 a force or weight that stretches: *The strain on the rope made it break.* 4 stretch: *She strained the truth in telling the story.* 5 use to the utmost: *She strained her eyes to see.* 6 injure by too much effort or by stretching: *The runner strained his heart.* 7 be injured by too much effort. 8 too much muscular or physical effort. 9 an injury caused by too much effort or by stretching. 10 any severe, trying, or wearying pressure: *the strain of worry.* 11 the effect of such pressure on the body or mind. 12 make a very great effort. 13 press or pour through a material or device that allows only liquid to pass through it: *Consommé is a soup that has been strained.* 14 drip through. 15 press closely; squeeze; hug: *She strained her child to her breast.* 1, 2, 4–7, 12–15 v., 3, 8–11 n.

**strain**[2] (strān) 1 a line of descent; race; stock; breed: *The Irish strain in him makes him like jokes.* 2 a group of animals or plants that form a part of a breed, race, or variety. 3 an inherited quality: *There is a strain of musical talent in that family.* 4 a trace or streak: *That horse has a mean strain.* 5 a manner or style of doing or speaking: *She wrote in a playful strain.* 6 Often, **strains,** pl. a part of a piece of music; melody; song. n.

**strained** (strānd) 1 produced by efforts; forced; not natural: *a strained laugh. Their first meeting after the quarrel was strained.* 2 dangerously tense; near open conflict: *strained relations between the two nations.* 3 pt. and pp. of STRAIN. 1, 2 adj., 3 v.

**strain·er** (strā′nər) a utensil or device for straining, filtering, or sifting: *A filter, a sieve, and a colander are strainers.* n.

**strait** (strāt) 1 a narrow channel connecting two larger bodies of water. 2 **straits,** pl. difficulty; need; distress: *He was in desperate straits for money.* n.
—**strait′ly,** adv. —**strait′ness,** n.
☞ *Hom.* STRAIGHT.
☞ *Etym.* From OF *estreit* 'close, narrow, a narrow place', which came from L *strictus* 'drawn tight', past participle of *stringere* 'draw tight, bind tight'. STRICT came directly from L *strictus* in the 16c.

**strait·en** (strāt′ən) restrict or limit in range, scope, or amount: *a mind straitened by prejudice.* v.
**in straitened circumstances,** needing money badly.
☞ *Hom.* STRAIGHTEN.

**strait–jack·et** (strāt′jak′ət) 1 a strong, tight garment used to bind the arms in order to keep a violent person from harming himself or herself or others. 2 anything that hampers or confines: *a legal straight-jacket. She felt that the school system should break out of the straight-jacket*

**strait–laced** of tradition. **3** confine in or as if in a straight-jacket. 1, 2 *n.*, 3 *v.*

**strait–laced** (strā′tlāst′) very strict in matters of conduct; prudish. *adj.*

**stra·mo·ni·um** (strə mō′nē əm) **1** JIMSON WEED. **2** a drug made from its dried leaves. *n.*

**strand**[1] (strand) **1** leave in a helpless position: *He was stranded a thousand kilometres from home with no money.* **2** run aground; drive on the shore: *The ship was stranded on the rocks.* **3** a shore; land bordering a sea, lake, or river. 1, 2 *v.*, 3 *n.*

**strand**[2] (strand) **1** one of the threads, strings, or wires that are twisted together to make a rope or cable: *This is a rope of three strands.* **2** a fibre; hair, etc. **3** a string of beads, pearls, etc. *n.*

**strange** (strānj) **1** unusual; queer; peculiar: *It was a strange accident: he was unhurt, but the driver was killed. She had the strangest laugh. It's strange that you didn't get the book, because I left it right on your desk.* **2** not known, seen, or heard of before; unfamiliar: *strange faces, a strange language. The title of the book was strange to me. The procedure was entirely strange to her.* **3** unaccustomed; inexperienced (*used with* **to**): *She made the mistake because she is still strange to the job.* **4** foreign; alien: *travelling in strange lands. adj.*, **strang·er, strang·est.** —**strange′ly,** *adv.* —**strange′ness,** *n.*
**feel strange,** feel out of place; feel awkward: *He still feels strange in his brother-in-law's home.*
**make strange,** of a baby or small child, show fear or distress at the presence of someone unknown or not very well known: *She hardly ever makes strange.*

**stran·ger** (strān′jər) **1** a person not known, seen, or heard of before: *She is a stranger to me.* **2** a person new to a place; one who is not well acquainted with a place or its inhabitants, etc.; newcomer: *She is a stranger in this area.* **3** a person or thing that is unaccustomed to or not at home in something; one that has no experience of something (*used with* **to**): *He is no stranger to hard work.* **4** a person from another country; foreigner or alien. *n.*

**stran·gle** (strang′gəl) **1** kill by squeezing the throat to stop the breath: *Hercules strangled a snake with each hand.* **2** suffocate, choke: *His collar seemed to be strangling him. She almost strangled on a piece of meat that stuck in her throat.* **3** choke down; suppress; keep back: *Samuel strangled an impulse to laugh. v.*, **stran·gled, stran·gling.** —**stran′gler,** *n.*

**stran·gle·hold** (strang′gəl hōld′) **1** in wrestling, an illegal hold by which an opponent is choked. **2** a controlling or dominant position that chokes opposition, freedom of movement, etc.; an unshakable or deadly grip: *One company had a stranglehold on the market. n.*

**stran·gu·la·tion** (strang′gyə lā′shən) a strangling or being strangled. *n.*

**strap** (strap) **1** a narrow strip of leather, cloth, or other material that bends easily: *She wore a sun dress with narrow shoulder straps. The box was strengthened by straps of steel.* **2** fasten with a strap: *We strapped the trunk.* **3** punish by beating with a strap. **4** a narrow strip of leather to sharpen razors on; strop. **5** sharpen on a strap; strop. 1, 4 *n.*, 2, 3, 5 *v.*, **strapped, strap·ping.**

**strap·hang·er** (strap′hang′ər) *Informal.* a passenger in a streetcar, subway train, bus, etc. who cannot get a seat and stands holding on to a strap or bar. *n.*

**strap·less** (strap′lis′) having no shoulder straps; leaving the shoulders and arms completely bare: *a strapless evening gown. adj.*

**strapped** (strapt) *Informal.* **1** without money; having no ready cash: *I'm strapped, so I won't be able to go to the movie after all.* **2** pt. and pp. of STRAP. 1 *adj.*, 2 *v.*

**strap·per** (strap′ər) **1** a person or thing that straps. **2** *Informal.* a tall, robust person. *n.*

**strap·ping** (strap′ing) **1** tall, strong, and healthy: *a fine, strapping girl.* **2** a beating with a strap as punishment: *He got a strapping.* **3** ppr. of STRAP. 1 *adj.*, 2 *n.*, 3 *v.*

**stra·ta** (strā′tə *or* strat′ə) a pl. of STRATUM. *n.*

**strat·a·gem** (strat′ə jəm) **1** a scheme or trick for deceiving and outwitting the enemy in war: *The general's stratagem was successful.* **2** any clever scheme or trick designed to achieve a goal: *He got the position by an unusual stratagem.* **3** skill in using such schemes or tricks: *The plan requires stratagem to be effective. n.*

**stra·te·gic** (strə tē′jik) **1** of, having to do with, or based on STRATEGY: *a strategic retreat, a strategic move. The booth was in a strategic location, just inside the entrance to the fair grounds.* **2** important in or necessary to STRATEGY: *Each part of the armed forces is a strategic link in our national defence. He went over the strategic points again at the end of his talk.* **3** having to do with raw material necessary for warfare that must be obtained, at least partially, from an outside country. **4** especially trained or made for destroying enemy bases, industry, or communications behind the lines of battle: *a strategic bomber. adj.* —**stra·te′gi·cal·ly,** *adv.*

**stra·te·gics** (strə tē′jiks) STRATEGY. *n.*

**strat·e·gist** (strat′ə jist) a person trained or skilled in STRATEGY. *n.*

**strat·e·gy** (strat′ə jē) **1** the science and art of war; the overall planning and directing of the military operations of a nation or group of nations at war with another, including political and economic decisions affecting the nation or nations as a whole. **2** a plan based on this. **3** any skilful plan: *She needed a strategy to gain time until she was ready to move.* **4** the skilful planning and management of something: *Strategy is important in an election campaign. n.*

**strat·i·fi·ca·tion** (strat′ə fə kā′shən) an arrangement in layers or strata: *the stratification of rock, the stratification of society. n.*

**strat·i·fy** (strat′ə fī′) arrange, form, or deposit in layers or strata. *v.*, **strat·i·fied, strat·i·fy·ing.**

**stra·to–cu·mu·lus** (strā′tō kyü′myə ləs *or* strat′ō kyü′myə ləs) a cloud made up of large, dark, rounded heaps above a flat, horizontal base. *n.*

**strat·o·sphere** (strat′ə sfēr′) the upper region of the atmosphere, above the troposphere, which begins about eleven kilometres above the earth: *In the stratosphere, temperature varies little with changes in altitude, and the winds are chiefly horizontal. n.*

**strat·o·spher·ic** (strat′ə sfēr′ik) of or having to do with the STRATOSPHERE. *adj.*

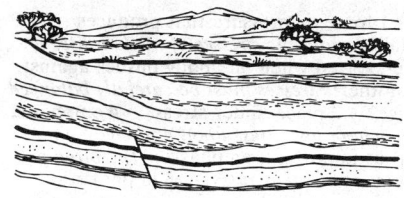
Strata of rock

**stra·tum** (strā′təm *or* strat′əm)   **1** a layer of material, especially one of several parallel layers placed one upon another: *In digging the well, the men struck first a stratum of sand, then several strata of rock.*   **2** a level of society; a group having about the same education, culture, development, etc.: *Professional people, such as doctors and lawyers, represent one stratum of society.*   *n., pl.* **stra·ta** *or* **stra·tums.**

**stra·tus** (strā′təs *or* strat′əs)   a low, horizontal layer of grey cloud that spreads over a large area.   *n., pl.* **stra·ti** (-tī *or* -tē).

**straw** (stro)   **1** the stalks or stems of grain after drying and threshing: *Straw is used for bedding horses and cows, for making hats, and for many other purposes.*   **2** a hollow stem or stalk.   **3** a slender tube made of waxed paper, plastic, etc., used for sucking up drinks.   **4** made of straw: *a straw hat.*   **5** a bit; trifle: *She doesn't care a straw.*   **6** of little value or consequence; worthless.   *n.*
**catch at a straw,**   try anything in desperation.
**the last straw,**   that which finally makes a situation intolerable.

**straw·ber·ry** (strob′er′ē)   **1** the small, juicy, edible red fruit of any of several closely related plants of the rose family: *A strawberry is not a fruit in the botanical sense; the juicy part is an enlarged flower receptacle and the actual fruits are the tiny, seedlike achenes on its surface.*   **2** a plant that produces strawberries: *There are many varieties of cultivated strawberry.*   *n., pl.* **straw·ber·ries.**

**strawberry blond**   reddish blond.

**strawberry blonde**   a woman or girl with reddish blond hair.

**strawberry mark**   a small, reddish birthmark.

**straw·board** (strob′ôrd′)   coarse cardboard made of straw pulp, used for boxes, packing, etc.   *n.*

**straw boss**   *Informal.*   an assistant foreman.

**straw man**   **1** a weak opposing argument or view put forward by a speaker or writer so that he or she may attack it and easily overcome it.   **2** a token candidate or opponent who is put in for appearances by one party or side, but who does not expect to win.

**straw vote**   an unofficial poll or vote taken to find out how a group of people feel about a particular candidate or issue.

**stray** (strā)   **1** lose one's way or get separated from a group: *The hen rounded up the chicks whenever they strayed. The two children had strayed off and got lost.*   **2** move or wander aimlessly or without conscious control: *Her gaze strayed around the room as she listened.*   **3** a person or thing that has strayed, such as a domestic animal wandering at large: *Our dog is a stray that we picked up a year ago.*   **4** wandering or lost: *A stray cat is crying at the door.*   **5** occurring here and there or now and then; scattered or isolated: *We could hear stray snatches of song from across the lake. There were a few stray fishermen's huts along the beach.*   **6** turn from the right course; go wrong.   **7** Usually, **strays,** *pl.*   electromagnetic waves that interfere with radio reception; static.   1, 2, 6 *v.,* 3, 7 *n.,* 4, 5 *adj.* —**stray′er,** *n.*

**streak** (strēk)   **1** a long, thin mark or line: *He has a streak of dirt on his face. We saw a streak of lightning.*   **2** layer: *Side bacon has streaks of fat and streaks of lean.*   **3** a vein; strain; element: *He has a streak of humour, though he looks very serious.*   **4** make streaks in or on: *hair streaked by the sun.*   **5** become streaked.   **6** *Informal.* a brief period; spell: *a streak of luck.*   **7** *Informal.* move very fast; go at full speed: *She streaked past the others and over the finish line.*   1–3, 6 *n.,* 4, 5, 7 *v.*
**like a streak,** *Informal.*   very fast; at full speed: *The dog went across the lawn like a streak to greet its mistress.*

**streak·y** (strē′kē)   **1** marked with streaks; streaked: *The wall is streaky where the paint did not cover properly.*   **2** occurring in streaks: *streaky clouds near the horizon. The colour is streaky and faded.*   **3** varying or uneven in quality, character, activity, etc.: *a streaky performance.* *adj.,* **streak·i·er, streak·i·est.**   —**streak′i·ly,** *adv.* —**streak′i·ness,** *n.*

**stream** (strēm)   **1** a body of flowing water in a channel or bed, especially a narrow river or a brook: *Many streams dried up that summer because of lack of rain.*   **2** any flow or current of water or other liquid: *A stream of water gushed from the run-off pipe.*   **3** a steady flow or current, like that of a liquid: *a stream of light, a stream of fresh air.*   **4** a continuous series or succession: *a stream of words, a stream of cars.*   **5** move in a stream: *The sunlight streamed in through the window. Tears streamed from his eyes. Soldiers streamed out of the fort.*   **6** give off or produce a stream: *Her eyes streamed with tears. The wound streamed blood.*   **7** be very wet; drip or run with water, etc.: *streaming windows, a streaming umbrella.*   **8** extend or float at full length: *The flag streamed in the wind. Her long hair streamed out behind her as she ran.*   1–4 *n.,* 5–8 *v.* —**stream′like′,** *adj.*

**stream·er** (strē′mər)   **1** any long, narrow, flowing thing: *Streamers of ribbon hung from her hat.*   **2** a long, narrow flag.   **3** a newspaper headline that runs all the way across the page.   *n.*

**stream·let** (strēm′lit)   a small stream.   *n.*

**stream·line** (strēm′līn′)   **1** the path of a fluid past a solid object.   **2** a shape, or contour, designed to offer as little resistance as possible for motion through air or water.   **3** give such a contour to; design or construct with a streamline: *They began to streamline cars in the 1930's.*   **4** bring up to date, modernize: *to streamline the curriculum.*   **5** organize to make simpler or more efficient: *to streamline a procedure.*   1, 2 *n.,* 3–5 *v.,* **stream·lined, stream·lin·ing.**

**stream·lined** (strēm′līnd′)   **1** having a contour designed to offer as little resistance as possible for motion through air or water: *The first streamlined car was the 1933 Chrysler.*   **2** organized and efficient: *a streamlined program.*   **3** without extra bulk, etc.: *a streamlined figure.*   **4** *pt.* and *pp.* of STREAMLINE.   1–3 *adj.,* 4 *v.*

**street** (strēt)   **1** a public road in a small or large community, usually having sidewalks and buildings along the sides: *They live on a fashionable street.*   **2** the part of

such a road for automobiles, trucks, etc.: *Don't play in the street.* **3** people who live in the buildings on a street: *The whole street was against the new bylaw.* **4** of, on, or near the street: *The camera department is on the street level of the store.* **5** of clothing, suitable for everyday wear in public: *She changed into her street clothes before leaving the hospital.* *n.* —**street′like,** *adj.*
**man in the street,** the typical person; average person.
**on** or **in the street,** homeless or without a job: *You'll be out in the street if you don't pay your rent soon. He was on the street for three months before he found another job.*

A streetcar

**street·car** (strēt′kär′) a large electrically powered vehicle that runs on rails on city streets and is used for public transportation. *n.*

**street·light** (strēt′līt′) a powerful light, usually mounted on a pole, that is one of a series used to provide illumination for the streets of a town or city. *n.*

**strength** (strength) **1** the capacity to exert or produce force; power or vigour: *Hercules was a man of great strength.* **2** the capacity to resist force or strain: *the strength of a rope, the strength of a wall. He doesn't have enough strength of mind to stick to a diet.* **3** the capacity to resist attack: *the strength of a fort, the strength of an argument.* **4** the number of effective soldiers, warships, team members, etc.; power measured in numbers: *Our team was not at full strength for the game.* **5** intensity: *the strength of a beverage, the strength of a sound.* **6** a person or thing that gives strength or firmness; support: *He said his children were his strength when his wife died.* *n.*
**on the strength of,** relying or depending on; with the support or help of: *We hired the woman on the strength of your recommendation.*

**strength·en** (streng′thən) make or become stronger: *The soldiers strengthened their defences. The reunion served to strengthen family ties.* *v.* —**strength′en·er,** *n.*

**stren·u·ous** (stren′yü əs) **1** requiring or marked by much energy or effort: *Squash is a strenuous game. We had a strenuous day moving into the new house.* **2** full of energy; persistently active and vigorous: *strenuous efforts. She was faced with strenuous opposition.* *adj.*
—**stren′u·ous·ly,** *adv.* —**stren′u·ous·ness,** *n.*

**strep** (strep) *Informal.* STREPTOCOCCUS. *n.*

**strep·to·coc·cal** (strep′tə kok′əl) of, having to do with, or caused by streptococci: *streptococcal organisms.* *adj.*

**strep·to·coc·cus** (strep′tə kok′əs) any of a group of spherical bacteria that multiply by dividing in only one direction, usually forming chains: *Many serious infections and diseases are caused by streptococci.* *n., pl.*
**strep·to·coc·ci** (-kok′sī *or* -kok′sē).

**strep·to·my·cin** (strep′tō mī′sən) a powerful substance similar to penicillin, effective against tuberculosis, typhoid fever, and certain other bacterial infections. *n.*

**stress** (stres) **1** force or pressure that produces physical or mental tension: *the stresses of modern life.* **2** a physical force exerted when one body pushes against, pulls, or twists another: *Stresses must be carefully balanced in building a bridge.* **3** place under stress. **4** emphasis; importance: *That school lays stress upon arithmetic and reading.* **5** treat as important; emphasize: *The principal stressed the importance of safety rules.* **6** in phonetics, a greater degree of force or loudness given to certain words or syllables in a word when speaking: *In* family, *the stress is on the first syllable; the second syllable has no stress. Many words have more than one degree of stress; for example,* swashbuckling *has the main, or primary, stress on the first syllable and a lesser, or secondary, stress on the second syllable.* **7** a mark written or printed to show that greater force or loudness is given to a word or syllable in speaking. A heavy mark (′) indicates primary stress; a light mark (′) indicates secondary stress. *Examples:* fam′i ly, swash′buck′ling, ac′a dem′ic. **8** pronounce with stress: *Accept* is stressed on the second syllable. 1, 2, 4, 6, 7 *n.,* 3, 5, 8 *v.*

**stretch** (strech) **1** draw out; extend to full length: *The blow stretched him out on the ground.* **2** continue over a distance; extend from one place to another; fill space; spread: *The forest stretches for many kilometres. We stretched a wire across the path.* **3** extend one's body or limbs. **4** straighten out. **5** reach out; hold out: *He stretched out his hand for the money.* **6** draw out to greater size: *Stretch the shoe a little.* **7** become longer or wider without breaking: *Rubber stretches.* **8** draw tight; strain: *She stretched the violin string until it broke.* **9** make great effort. **10** extend beyond proper limits: *He stretched the law to suit his own purpose.* **11** *Informal.* exaggerate: *to stretch the truth.* **12** an unbroken length; extent: *A stretch of sand hills lay between the road and the ocean.* **13** a continuous length of time. **14** one of the two straight sides of a racecourse, especially the part between the last turn and the finish line: *the home stretch.* **15** a stretching or being stretched. 1–11 *v.,* 12–15 *n.*

**stretch·er** (strech′ər) **1** a frame or other device for stretching something: *a glove stretcher.* **2** a frame having a canvas or similar covering and either wheels or carrying handles on which to move the sick, wounded, or dead. *n.*

**stretcher case** a person who has to be carried on a stretcher because of serious injury or illness: *Several bus passengers were hurt in the accident, but there were no stretcher cases.*

**strew** (strü) **1** scatter; sprinkle: *The pages were strewn all over the floor. He strewed shredded coconut on the cake.* **2** cover with something scattered or sprinkled: *The ground was strewn with leaves.* **3** be scattered over; be sprinkled over: *Litter strewed the sidewalk.* *v.,* **strewed, strewn** *or* **strewed, strew·ing.**

**strewn** (strün) a pp. of STREW. *v.*

**stri·a** (strī′ə) **1** a slight furrow or channel. **2** a narrow stripe or streak. *n., pl.* **stri·ae** (strī′ē *or* strī′ī).

**stri·at·ed** (strī′ā tid) striped, streaked, or furrowed: *the striated plumage of a bird, a striated muscle.* *adj.*

**stri·a·tion** (strī ā′shən) a striated condition or appearance. *n.*

**strick·en** (strik′ən) **1** affected or overwhelmed by disease, trouble, sorrow, etc.: *a stricken conscience. Help was rushed to the fire-stricken city.* **2** hit or wounded by or as if by a missile. **3** a pp. of STRIKE: *Their whole family has been stricken with measles.* 1, 2 *adj.,* 3 *v.*
**stricken in years,** old.

**strict** (strikt) **1** enforcing a rule or set of rules with great care: *The teacher was strict but not unfair.* **2** requiring complete obedience: *They were under strict orders not to leave the barracks.* **3** exact; precise: *a strict translation. She wasn't trespassing in the strict sense of the word.* **4** complete; absolute: *It was told to her in strict confidence. She lives in strict seclusion.* **5** very careful in following a standard or principle: *a strict Moslem.* *adj.* —**strict′ly**, *adv.* —**strict′ness**, *n.*
☛ *Etym.* See note at STRAIT.

**stric·ture** (strik′chər) **1** an unfavourable criticism; critical remark. **2** an abnormal narrowing of some duct or tube of the body. **3** something that binds or limits; restriction. *n.*

**strid·den** (strid′ən) pp. of STRIDE: *Gerard had stridden away angrily.* *v.*

**stride** (strīd) **1** walk with long steps: *She strode along the path.* **2** pass with one long step: *She strode over the brook.* **3** a long step: *With two strides he was at the door.* **4** a striding gait: *The child could not keep up with his father's stride.* **5** sit or stand with one leg on each side of: *to stride a fence.* **6** Usually, **strides**, *pl.* progress; advance: *Great strides have been made toward a settlement of the long-standing wage dispute.* 1, 2, 5 *v.*, **strode**, **strid·den**, **strid·ing**; 3, 4, 6 *n.* —**strid′er**, *n.*
**hit one's stride**, reach one's normal speed or level of efficiency: *By the second day of working together they had hit their stride and were making good progress.*
**take in (one's) stride**, do or handle without difficulty or hesitation; cope with easily: *He took the defeat in stride. The award came as a surprise, but she took it in her stride.*

**stri·dence** (strī′dəns) the state or quality of being STRIDENT. *n.*

**stri·dent** (strī′dənt) **1** making or having a harsh sound; grating or shrill: *a strident voice, the strident sound of a power saw.* **2** commanding attention in an unpleasant, irritating way: *strident colours. They agreed with his argument, but they didn't like the strident tone of the letter.* *adj.* —**stri′dent·ly**, *adv.*

**strid·u·late** (strij′ə lāt′) produce a shrill, grating sound, as a cricket or katydid does, by rubbing together certain parts of the body. *v.*, **strid·u·lat·ed**, **strid·u·lat·ing**.

**strid·u·la·tion** (strij′ə lā′shən) the action or sound of stridulating. *n.*

**strife** (strīf) **1** the act or fact of quarrelling or fighting; bitter or violent conflict: *The relationship between the brothers had always been full of strife.* **2** a struggle or contest between rivals. *n.*

**strike** (strīk) **1** hit; deal a blow to: *to strike a person in anger.* **2** deal; give: *to strike a blow in self-defence.* **3** make by stamping, printing, etc.: *to strike a medal.* **4** a number of coins made at one time. **5** set or be set on fire by hitting or rubbing: *to strike a match.* **6** appear to affect the mind or feeling of; impress: *The plan strikes me as silly.* **7** sound: *The clock strikes twelve times at noon.* **8** overcome by death, disease, suffering, fear, etc.: *They were struck with terror.* **9** attack; make an attack: *The enemy will strike at dawn.* **10** an attack. **11** occur to: *An amusing thought struck her.* **12** find or come upon ore, oil, water, etc. **13** the act or fact of finding rich ore in mining, in oil boring, etc.; sudden success. **14** stop work to get better pay, shorter hours, etc.: *The coal miners struck.* **15** a general quitting of work in order to force an employer or employers to agree to the workers' demands for higher wages, shorter hours, etc. **16** cross; rub: *Strike out the last word. Strike her name off the list.* **17** take

---

**strict**      **1181**      **string**

hat, āge, fär; let, ēqual, tėrm; it, īce
hot, ōpen, ôrder; oil, out; cup, pút, rüle
əbove, takən, pencəl, lemən, circəs
ch, child; ng, long; sh, ship
th, thin; ᴛʜ, then; zh, measure

away by a blow; take away: *Strike off his head.* **18** go: *We struck into a gallop. We walked along the road a kilometre, then struck out across the fields.* **19** assume: *He struck an attitude.* **20** enter or cause to enter; send or take root; fasten or be fastened: *The roots of oaks strike deep.* **21** get by figuring: *Strike an average.* **22** make; decide; enter upon: *The employer and the workers have struck an agreement.* **23** lower or take down a sail, flag, tent, stage set, etc.: *The ship struck its flag as a sign of surrender.* **24** make level; make level with the top edge of a measure. **25** an act of striking. **26** in baseball, failure of the batter to make a proper hit. **27** a pitched ball that passes above the plate at a height between the level of the batter's shoulders and that of his or her knees. **28** in bowling, an upsetting of all the pins with the first ball bowled. **29** the score so made. **30** take hold of the bait: *The fish are striking well today.* **31** a taking hold of the bait. **32** a metal piece in a doorjamb, into which the latch of a lock fits when the door closes. 1–3, 5–9, 11, 12, 14, 16–24, 30 *v.*, **struck**, **struck** or **strick·en**, **strik·ing**; 4, 10, 13, 15, 25–29, 31, 32 *n.*
**on strike**, stopping work to get more pay, shorter hours, etc.: *Most of the workers voted to go on strike.*
**strike it rich**, *Informal.* **a** find rich ore, oil, etc. **b** have a sudden or unexpected great success.
**strike off**, to take or remove by or as if by a stroke.
**strike out**, **a** cross out; rub out. **b** in baseball, fail to hit three times: *The batter struck out.* **c** in baseball, cause to fail to hit three times: *The pitcher struck out six men.* **d** use arms and legs to move forward.
**strike up**, begin: *The two girls struck up a friendship.*

**strike·bound** (strīk′bound′) immobilized by a labour strike. *adj.*

**strike·break·er** (strīk′brā′kər) a person actively involved in trying to break up a strike, especially one hired to replace a striking employee. *n.*

**strike·break·ing** (strīk′brā′king) action taken to halt a strike. *n.*

**strike·out** (strīk′kout) in baseball: **1** an out made by a pitcher throwing three strikes against the batter. **2** the act of striking out. *n.*

**strik·er** (strīk′kər) **1** a person or thing that strikes. **2** a worker who is on strike. *n.*

**strik·ing** (strī′king) **1** attracting attention because of some unusual quality; remarkable: *a striking use of colour, a striking dress.* **2** that strikes or is on strike: *The striking workers have rejected the latest offer.* **3** ppr. of STRIKE. 1, 2 *adj.*, 3 *v.*

**strik·ing·ly** (strī′king lē) in a way that attracts attention. *adv.*

**string** (string) **1** a thin strip or line of twisted fibre; fine cord. **2** a piece of this: *I need a string for the parcel.* **3** a series of objects threaded or hung on a string: *a string of pearls, a string of fish.* **4** thread or hang on a string: *to string beads.* **5** a length of wire or catgut for a musical instrument: *the strings of a violin.* **6 strings**, *pl.* in an orchestra, the violins, cellos, and other stringed instruments. **7** furnish with a string or strings: *to string a violin, to string a bow. Janice had her tennis racket strung.*

**8** anything used for tying: *apron strings.* **9** tie or hang with a string or rope: *We dry herbs by stringing them from the rafters in the barn.* **10** extend or stretch from one point to another: *to string a cable.* **11** tune the strings of a musical instrument. **12** make tense; key up: *The news had got them all strung up.* **13** a cordlike part of a plant, especially the tough fibre connecting the two halves of a string bean pod. **14** remove the strings from: *We sat there stringing beans.* **15** form into a string or strings. **16** a series or sequence of like things in a line or as if in a line: *a string of cars, a string of victories.* **17** move in a line or series. **18** arrange in a line or a row. **19** *Informal.* a condition; proviso: *an offer with a string attached to it.* 1–3, 5, 6, 8, 13, 16, 19 *n.*, 4, 7, 9–12, 14, 15, 17, 18 *v.*, **strung, string·ing.** —**string′less,** *adj.* —**string′like,** *adj.*
**have two strings to one's bow,** have more than one way of doing or getting something.
**no strings attached,** *Informal.* without conditions.
**pull strings,** use one's influence, especially secretly: *There were better qualified applicants, but he got the job because she pulled some strings for him.*
**pull the strings,** direct the actions of others, often secretly: *He is supposed to be retired, but he still pulls the strings on all the company's big deals.*
**string along,** *Informal.* **a** fool or deceive: *He's just stringing you along with that story of his adventures.* **b** go along; follow: *June asked if she could string along with them.*
**string out,** *Informal.* prolong; stretch; extend: *The program was strung out too long.*
**string up,** *Informal.* kill by hanging: *The horse thief was caught and strung up from the nearest tree.*

**string bean** a variety of kidney bean with stringlike fibres connecting the two halves of the pods.

**stringed instrument** a musical instrument having strings, played by striking, by plucking, or with a bow: *The violin, piano, harp, and guitar are stringed instruments.*

**strin·gen·cy** (strin′jən sē) the quality or state of being STRINGENT: *The public objected to the stringency of the regulations. n., pl.* **strin·gen·cies.**

**strin·gent** (strin′jənt) **1** strict; severe: *stringent laws.* **2** lacking ready money; tight: *a stringent market for loans.* **3** convincing; forcible: *stringent arguments. adj.* —**strin′gent·ly,** *adv.*

**string·er** (string′ər) **1** a person or thing that strings. **2** a long, horizontal timber in a building, bridge, or railway track. **3** a part-time or local correspondent for a newspaper or magazine. **4** a newspaper correspondent paid on the basis of linage. *n.*

**string·halt** (string′holt′) a lame condition of one or both hind legs of a horse, caused by spasms of the muscles that make the legs jerk when the horse walks. *n.* Also, **springhalt.**

**string·piece** (string′pēs′) a long horizontal beam used to strengthen or connect parts of a framework. *n.*

**string tie** a short, narrow necktie.

**string·y** (string′ē) **1** like, containing, or consisting of fibres or strings: *tough, stringy meat. Her hair was long and stringy.* **2** forming strings: *a stringy syrup.* **3** lean and sinewy; wiry: *a boy of about sixteen, tall and stringy. adj.*, **string·i·er, string·i·est.** —**string′i·ness,** *n.*

**strip**[1] (strip) **1** make bare or naked; undress a person, thing, etc. **2** undress. **3** take off the covering of: *The girl stripped the banana by taking off the skin.* **4** remove; pull off: *The boys stripped the fruit from the trees.* **5** rob: *Thieves stripped the house of everything valuable.* **6** take away the titles, rights, etc. of a person or thing. **7** tear off the teeth of a gear, etc. **8** break the thread of a bolt, nut, etc. **9** milk a cow thoroughly. *v.*, **stripped, strip·ping.** —**strip′per,** *n.*
**strip of,** **a** take away from; deprive of. **b** rob of money, possessions, etc.

**strip**[2] (strip) **1** a long, narrow, flat piece of material: *a strip of metal, a strip of paper. He tore the cloth into strips for a bandage. The bark came off in strips.* **2** a long, narrow tract of land, forest, etc. **3** AIRSTRIP. *n.*

**strip cropping** the planting of different crops in strips of equal width, running across the slopes instead of up and down.

**stripe**[1] (strīp) **1** a long, narrow band of different colour or texture: *A tiger has black stripes. The wallpaper is white with green stripes.* **2** fabric, wallpaper, etc. having a pattern of parallel stripes: *She used a stripe for the chair covers.* **3** mark with stripes. **4** a sort; type: *a man of quite a different stripe.* **5 stripes,** *pl.* a number or combination of stripes of braid on the sleeve of a uniform to show rank, length of service, etc.: *A corporal wears two stripes, a sergeant three.* 1, 2, 4, 5 *n.*, 3 *v.*, **striped, strip·ing.**

**stripe**[2] (strīp) a stroke or lash with a whip. *n.*

**striped** (strīpt) **1** having stripes; marked with stripes: *striped awnings, a striped design.* **2** pt. and pp. of STRIPE. 1 *adj.*, 2 *v.*

**strip·ling** (strip′ling) an adolescent boy; youth. *n.*

**strive** (strīv) **1** try hard; make a great effort: *to strive for self-control.* **2** fight or contend; vie: *The swimmer strove against the tide. The wrestlers strove with each other.* *v.*, **strove** or **strived, striv·en, striv·ing.**

**striv·en** (striv′ən) pp. of STRIVE: *She has striven hard to make the party a success.* *v.*

**strobe light** an apparatus for producing very brief, brilliant flashes of light, used in photography, theatre, etc.

**strob·o·scope** (strō′bə skōp′) an instrument for studying periodic motion by the illumination of a moving body in flashes or at intervals. *n.*

**strode** (strōd) pt. of STRIDE: *He strode over the ditch.* *v.*

**stro·ga·noff** (strō′gə nof) denoting a dish cooked with sour cream and, often, onions, mushrooms, and spices (*not used before a noun*): *beef stroganoff. adj.*

**stroke**[1] (strōk) **1** an act of striking; blow: *The house was hit by a stroke of lightning.* **2** a sound made by striking: *We arrived at the stroke of three.* **3** a piece of luck, fortune, etc.: *a stroke of bad luck.* **4** a single, complete movement to be made again and again: *She rowed with a strong stroke of the oars. He swims a fast stroke.* **5** in a game such as tennis and golf, the hitting of a ball. **6** a throb or pulsing, as of the heart. **7** a movement or mark made by a pen, pencil, brush, etc.: *She writes with a heavy down stroke.* **8** a vigorous attempt to attain some object: *a bold stroke for freedom.* **9** a feat or achievement: *a stroke of genius.* **10** an act, piece, or amount of work, etc.: *a stroke of work.* **11** a sudden inability to feel or move, with partial or complete loss of consciousness, caused by injury to the brain when a blood vessel breaks or becomes blocked by a clot. **12** a sudden attack of any of various illnesses (*used only in compounds*):

*heatstroke, sunstroke.* **13** a rower who sets the time for the other oarsmen. **14** act as the stroke of: *Who stroked the Vancouver crew?* **1–13** *n.*, **14** *v.*, **stroked, strok·ing.** —**strok′er,** *n.*
**keep stroke,** make strokes at the same time.

**stroke**² (strōk) **1** move the hand gently over: *She stroked the kitten.* **2** a stroking movement: *to brush away the crumbs with one stroke.* **1** *v.*, **stroked, strok·ing;** **2** *n.*

**stroke oar** **1** the oar nearest the stern of the boat. **2** the rower who pulls the oar nearest the stern of the boat, setting the time of the stroke for the other rowers; STROKE¹ (def. 13).

**stroll** (strōl) **1** take a quiet walk for pleasure; walk. **2** a leisurely walk. **3** go from place to place: *strolling musicians, strolling gypsies.* **4** stroll along or through: *Every evening they strolled the path by the river.* **1, 3, 4** *v.*, **2** *n.*

**stroll·er** (strō′lər) **1** a person who strolls: *The park was filled with strollers.* **2** a wanderer, especially an actor who goes from place to place in search of work. **3** a kind of light baby carriage in which a young child sits erect. *n.*

**strong** (strong) **1** having much force or power: *a strong wind, strong muscles, a strong nation.* **2** able to last, endure, resist, etc.: *a strong fort, a strong rope.* **3** not easily influenced, changed, etc.; firm: *a strong will.* **4** of great force or effectiveness: *strong arguments.* **5** having a certain number: *A group that is 100 strong has 100 in it.* **6** having a particular quality or property in high degree: *a strong acid, strong tea.* **7** containing much alcohol: *a strong drink.* **8** having much flavour or odour: *strong seasoning, strong perfume.* **9** having an unpleasant taste or smell: *strong butter.* **10** intense: *a strong light.* **11** vigorous; forceful: *a strong speech.* **12** hearty; zealous: *a strong dislike.* **13** with force; powerfully; vigorously; in a strong manner. **14** in grammar, inflecting by a vowel change within the stem of the word rather than by adding endings. *Examples: find, found; goose, geese.* **1–12, 14** *adj.*, **strong·er** (strong′gər), **strong·est** (strong′gist); **13** *adv.* —**strong′ly,** *adv.*

**strong-arm** (strong′ärm′) *Informal.* **1** having or using force or violence: *strong-arm tactics.* **2** use force or violence on. **1** *adj.*, **2** *v.*

**strong·box** (strong′boks′) a strongly made box for holding valuables. *n.*

**strong drink** drink containing alcohol; liquor.

**strong·hold** (strong′hōld′) **1** a fort or fortress. **2** a secure place or centre: *a stronghold of freedom. The city is the stronghold of the Conservative party in the province.* *n.*

**strong-mind·ed** (strong′mīn′did) having a strong mind; mentally vigorous. *adj.* —**strong-′mind′ed·ness,** *n.*

**stron·ti·um** (stron′tē əm *or* stron′shē əm) a soft, silver-white metallic element which occurs only in combination with other elements; *Strontium is used in making alloys and in fireworks and signal flares.* Symbol: Sr *n.*

**strontium 90** a radio-active isotope of strontium that occurs in the fall-out from nuclear explosions: *Strontium 90 is dangerous because it is absorbed by bones and tissues and may replace the calcium in the body.*

**strop** (strop) **1** a leather strap used for sharpening razors. **2** sharpen on a strop. **1** *n.*, **2** *v.*, **stropped, strop·ping.**

**stro·phe** (strō′fē) **1** the part of an ancient Greek ode

---

**stroke**     **1183**     **strychnine**

hat, āge, fär; let, ēqual, tėrm; it, īce
hot, ōpen, ôrder; oil, out; cup, pu̇t, rüle
əbove, takən, pencəl, lemən, circəs
ch, child; ng, long; sh, ship
th, thin; ᴛʜ, then; zh, measure

sung by the chorus when moving from right to left. Compare with ANTISTROPHE. **2** a group of lines of poetry; stanza. *n.*

**strove** (strōv) a pt. of STRIVE. *v.*

**struck** (struk) **1** pt. and a pp. of STRIKE: *Some idiot struck her. She was struck by a ball.* **2** closed or affected by a strike of workers. **1** *v.*, **2** *adj.*

**struc·tur·al** (struk′chə rəl) **1** used in building. *Structural steel is made into beams, girders, etc.* **2** of or having to do with structure or structures: *The geologist showed the structural difference in rocks of different ages.* *adj.*

**struc·tur·al·ly** (struk′chə rə lē) with regard to STRUCTURE: *The design is structurally sound, but it is not very attractive.* *adv.*

**struc·ture** (struk′chər) **1** a building; something built. **2** anything composed of parts arranged together: *The human body is a wonderful structure.* **3** the manner of building; the way parts are put together; construction: *The structure of the schoolhouse was excellent.* **4** the arrangement or interrelation of parts, elements, etc. forming something, especially as it determines its special character or nature: *the structure of a molecule, the structure of a sentence, a complex economic structure.* **5** make into a structure; build; fabricate. **6** organize; put together in a systematic way. **1–4** *n.*, **5, 6** *v.*, **struc·tured, struc·tur·ing.**

**stru·del** (strü′dəl; *German,* shtrü′dəl) a pastry, made of very thin dough rolled up around a filling and baked: *Apple strudel has an apple filling.* *n.*

**strug·gle** (strug′əl) **1** move one's arms and legs about violently in an effort to get free: *The child struggled to get down from her mother's lap.* **2** make strong efforts against difficulties; try hard: *For years she had to struggle to make a living. He struggled to control his anger.* **3** move or make one's way with great effort: *She struggled through the hedge. The old man struggled to his feet.* **4** great effort or hard work: *It was always a struggle for him to express himself.* **5** the act of fighting; conflict: *a struggle for control of the seas.* **1–3** *v.*, **strug·gled, strug·gling;** **4, 5** *n.* —**strug′gler,** *n.*

**strum** (strum) **1** play by brushing the fingers across the strings of: *to strum a guitar. We heard him strumming on his banjo.* **2** produce music in this way: *to strum a tune.* **3** the act or sound of strumming. **1, 2** *v.*, **strummed, strum·ming;** **3** *n.* —**strum′mer,** *n.*

**strum·pet** (strum′pit) PROSTITUTE. *n.*

**strung** (strung) pt. and pp. of STRING: *We strung along after the guide. The vines were strung on poles.* *v.*

**strut**¹ (strut) **1** walk in a stiff, erect manner, suggesting vanity or self-importance: *He strutted about the room in his new jacket.* **2** a strutting walk. **1** *v.*, **strut·ted, strut·ting;** **2** *n.* —**strut′ter,** *n.*

**strut**² (strut) a supporting bar fitted into a framework; brace. See TRUSS for picture. *n.*

**strych·nine** (strik′nin *or* strik′nēn) a bitter, poisonous compound consisting of colourless crystals obtained from nux vomica and related plants: *Strychnine is used in small doses as a stimulant for the central nervous system.* *n.*

**Stu·art** (styü′ərt *or* stü′ərt) **1** the royal family that ruled Scotland from 1371 to 1603, and Great Britain and Ireland from 1603 to 1649 and from 1660 to 1714. **2** a member of this family. *n.*

**stub** (stub) **1** a short piece that is left: *the stub of a pencil, a cigarette stub.* **2** something short and blunt; especially, something cut short or stunted in growth: *a stub of a tail.* **3** a pencil having a short, blunt point. **4** the stump of a tree, a broken tooth, etc. **5** strike one's toe against something. **6** clear land of tree stumps. **7** dig up by the roots. **8** put out a cigarette or cigar by crushing the burning end in an ashtray, etc. 1–4 *n.*, 5–8 *v.*, **stubbed, stub·bing.**

**stub·ble** (stub′əl) **1** the lower ends of stalks of grain that are left in the ground after the grain is cut. **2** any short, rough growth like this, especially a very short growth of beard. *n.*

**stub·bly** (stub′lē) **1** covered with stubble. **2** resembling stubble; bristly: *a stubbly mustache.* *adj.*

**stub·born** (stub′ərn) **1** too fixed or unyielding in purpose or opinion; pigheaded: *He's just too stubborn to admit he was wrong.* **2** determined; dogged; resolute: *a stubborn fight for freedom, stubborn courage.* **3** hard to deal with or manage: *a stubborn cough. Facts are stubborn things; they can't be changed.* *adj.* —**stub′born·ly,** *adv.* —**stub′born·ness,** *n.*
☞ *Syn.* See note at OBSTINATE.

**stub·by** (stub′ē) **1** short and thick or short and blunt like a stub: *stubby fingers, a stubby pencil.* **2** short, dense, and stiff: *a stubby beard.* **3** having many stubs or stumps. *adj.*, **stub·bi·er, stub·bi·est.** —**stub′bi·ness,** *n.*

**stuc·co** (stuk′ō) **1** a hard, rough, strong material usually made of cement, sand, and a small amount of lime, used as a covering for the outer walls of buildings. **2** a fine plaster used for moulding into architectural decorations. **3** STUCCOWORK. **4** cover or decorate with stucco. 1–3 *n.*, *pl.* **stuc·coes** *or* **stuc·cos;** 4 *v.*, **stuc·coed, stuc·co·ing.**

**stuc·co·work** (stuk′ō wėrk′) work done in STUCCO (defs. 1, 2). *n.*

**stuck** (stuk) pt. and pp. of STICK². *v.*

**stuck–up** (stuk′up′) *Informal.* too proud; conceited; haughty. *adj.*

**stud¹** (stud) **1** head of a nail, a knob, etc. sticking out from a surface: *The belt was ornamented with silver studs.* **2** set with studs or something like studs: *He plans to stud the sword hilt with jewels.* **3** be set or scattered over: *Little islands stud the harbour.* **4** set like studs; scatter at intervals: *Stooks of wheat were studded over the field.* **5** a kind of small button used to fasten the collar or front of a dress shirt. **6** one of a row of upright posts, usually wooden, which form part of the frame to which boards or laths are nailed in making a wall of a building. See FRAME for picture. **7** provide with studs. **8** a projecting pin on a machine. **9** a crosspiece put in each link of a chain cable to strengthen it. 1, 5, 6, 8, 9 *n.*, 2–4, 7 *v.*, **stud·ded, stud·ding.**

**stud²** (stud) **1** a male animal, especially a stallion, kept for breeding. **2** a group of horses or, sometimes, other animals, kept mainly for breeding. **3** a place where such animals are kept. **4** of, having to do with, or kept as a stud. *n.*

**at stud,** of a male animal, available for breeding.

**stud·ding** (stud′ing) **1** the studs forming the framework of a wall. **2** lumber for such studs. **3** ppr. of STUD. 1, 2 *n.*, 3 *v.*

**stu·dent** (styü′dənt *or* stü′dənt) **1** a person who is studying in a school, college, or university. **2** a person who studies; one who investigates or observes systematically: *a student of human nature.* *n.*

**student body** all the students at a school, etc., considered together.

**stud·horse** (stud′hôrs′) a stallion kept for breeding. *n.*

**stud·ied** (stud′ēd) **1** produced or marked by deliberate effort or design; intentional: *studied politeness. What she said to me was studied insult.* **2** prepared or planned carefully and thoughtfully: *a studied essay.* **3** pt. and pp. of STUDY. 1, 2 *adj.*, 3 *v.* —**stud′ied·ly,** *adv.* —**stud′ied·ness,** *n.*

**stu·dio** (styü′dē ō′ *or* stü′dē ō) **1** the workroom of a painter, sculptor, photographer, etc. **2** a place where music, dancing, etc. is taught. **3** a place where motion pictures are made. **4** a place from which a radio or television program is broadcast. *n.*, *pl.* **stu·di·os.**

**studio couch** a couch, usually without arms, that can be converted into a bed.

**stu·di·ous** (styü′dē əs *or* stü′dē əs) **1** fond of study: *She's very studious.* **2** thoughtful and painstaking; deliberate and careful: *Vito made a studious effort to please his customers.* **3** taking care; anxiously careful (*of*): *She was always studious of her mother's comfort.* *adj.* —**stu′di·ous·ly,** *adv.* —**stu′di·ous·ness,** *n.*

**stud·y** (stud′ē) **1** the effort to learn by reading or thinking. **2** try to learn: *Helen studied her spelling lesson for half an hour. Joseph is studying to be a doctor.* **3** a careful examination; investigation. **4** examine carefully: *We studied the map to find the shortest road home.* **5** a subject studied; branch of learning; something investigated or to be investigated. **6** a room for study, reading, writing, etc.: *The minister was reading in her study.* **7** a work of literature or art that deals in careful detail with one particular subject. **8** a sketch for a picture, story, etc. **9** a musical composition designed primarily for practice in a particular technical problem; a concert version of this, often of great difficulty and brilliance. **10** consider with care; think out; plan: *The prisoner studied ways to escape.* **11** give care and thought to; try hard: *The grocer studies to please his customers.* **12** an earnest effort, or the object of endeavour or effort: *Her constant study is to please her parents.* **13** deep thought; reverie: *The judge was absorbed in study about the case.* 1, 3, 5–9, 12, 13 *n.*, *pl.* **stud·ies;** 2, 4, 10, 11 *v.*, **stud·ied, stud·y·ing.**

**stuff** (stuf) **1** what a thing is made of; material: *She bought some white stuff for curtains.* **2** a woollen fabric. **3** a thing or things; substance: *The doctor rubbed some kind of stuff on the burn.* **4** goods; belongings: *He was told to move his stuff out of the room.* **5** silly words and thoughts; nonsense. **6** inward qualities; character: *That boy has good stuff in him.* **7** pack full; fill: *She stuffed the pillow with feathers.* **8** stop or block up: *My nose is stuffed up by a cold.* **9** fill the skin of a dead animal to make it look as it did when alive. **10** fill a chicken, turkey, etc. with seasoned bread crumbs, etc. **11** force; push; thrust: *He stuffed his clothes into the drawer.* **12** eat too much. 1–6 *n.*, 7–12 *v.*

**stuffed shirt** *Informal.* a pompous, conceited person, especially one who is old-fashioned or conservative.

**stuff·ing** (stuf′ing) **1** any soft material used to fill or stuff cushions, upholstered furniture, toys, etc. **2** seasoned bread crumbs, etc. for stuffing a chicken, turkey, etc. before cooking; dressing. **3** ppr. of STUFF. 1, 2 *n.*, 3 *v.*

**stuff·y** (stuf′ē) **1** lacking fresh air: *a stuffy room.* **2** lacking freshness or interest; dull: *a stuffy conversation.* **3** stopped up: *I've got a stuffy nose from hay fever.* **4** prim and proper; narrow-minded and stodgy: *Don't be so stuffy; it was only a harmless joke.* **5** angry or sulky. *adj.*, **stuff·i·er, stuff·i·est.** —**stuff′i·ly,** *adv.* —**stuff′i·ness,** *n.*

**stul·ti·fi·ca·tion** (stul′tə fə kā′shən) a STULTIFYing or being stultified. *n.*

**stul·ti·fy** (stul′tə fī) **1** cause to appear foolish or absurd; reduce to foolishness or absurdity. **2** make futile. **3** make passive or weak by requiring absolute obedience or conformity: *the stultifying atmosphere of a prison or dictatorship.* *v.*, **stul·ti·fied, stul·ti·fy·ing.**

**stum·ble** (stum′bəl) **1** trip by striking the foot against something: *She stumbled, but did not fall.* **2** walk unsteadily, stumbling often: *The tired hikers stumbled along.* **3** speak or act in a hesitating, faltering way: *The frightened boy stumbled through his recitation.* **4** make a mistake; do wrong. **5** come by accident or chance: *While in the country, she stumbled upon some fine antiques.* **6** the act or an instance of stumbling. 1–5 *v.*, **stum·bled, stum·bling.** 6 *n.* —**stum′bler,** *n.* —**stum′bling·ly,** *adv.*

**stum·bling-block** (stum′bling blok′) an obstacle or hindrance; something that causes difficulty or slows down progress. *n.*

**stump** (stump) **1** the lower end of a tree or plant, left after the main part is cut off. **2** remove stumps from land. **3** anything left after the main or important part is removed: *The dog wagged her stump of a tail.* **4** reduce to a stump; cut off. **5** a person with a short, thick build. **6** a place where a political speech is made. **7** go about or travel through an area, making speeches: *The four candidates for election will stump the riding.* **8** walk in a stiff, clumsy way: *The lame man stumped along.* **9** a heavy step. **10** the sound made by stiff walking or heavy steps. **11** a wooden leg. **12** *Informal.* leg. **13** *Informal.* make unable to answer, do, etc.: *The first question was easy but the second one stumped him.* **14** *Informal.* a dare; challenge. **15** a tight roll of paper, or other material, pointed at the ends and used to soften pencil marks in drawing. **16** one of the three upright sticks of a cricket wicket. 1, 3, 5, 6, 9–12, 14–16 *n.*, 2, 4, 7, 8, 13 *v.* —**stump′like′,** *adj.*

**up a stump,** *Informal.* unable to act, answer, etc.; impotent; baffled.

**stump·age** (stum′pij) *Cdn.* a price paid for the right to cut standing timber. *n.*

**stump·y** (stum′pē) **1** short and thick; stubby. **2** having many stumps. *adj.*, **stump·i·er, stump·i·est.** —**stump′i·ly,** *adv.* —**stump′i·ness,** *n.*

**stun** (stun) **1** make senseless; knock unconscious: *He was stunned by the fall.* **2** bewilder; shock; overwhelm: *She was stunned by the news of her friend's death.* *v.*, **stunned, stun·ning.**

**stung** (stung) pt. and pp. of STING: *A wasp stung Dave. He was stung on the neck.* *v.*

hat, āge, fär; let, ēqual, tėrm; it, īce
hot, ōpen, ôrder; oil, out; cup, pùt, rüle
above, takən, pencəl, lemən, circəs
ch, child; ng, long; sh, ship
th, thin; ᴛʜ, then; zh, measure

**stunk** (stungk) a pt. and pp. of STINK. *v.*

**stun·ner** (stun′ər) **1** a person, thing, or blow that stuns. **2** *Informal.* a very striking or attractive person or thing. *n.*

**stun·ning** (stun′ing) **1** that stuns: *a stunning blow.* **2** very attractive or good-looking; strikingly pretty: *a stunning girl, a stunning new hat.* **3** excellent or delightful; first-rate; splendid: *a stunning performance.* **4** ppr. of STUN. 1–3 *adj.*, 4 *v.* —**stun′ning·ly,** *adv.*

**stunt¹** (stunt) **1** check in growth or development: *Lack of proper food stunts a child.* **2** a check in growth or development. 1 *v.*, 2 *n.*

**stunt²** (stunt) *Informal.* **1** a feat or act intended to thrill an audience or to attract attention; an act showing boldness or skill: *Circus riders perform stunts on horseback.* **2** perform such feats. 1 *n.*, 2 *v.*

**stunt·man** (stunt′mən) a man who performs dangerous manoeuvres instead of the actor in a motion picture. *n.*, *pl.* **stunt·men** (-mən).

**stunt·wom·an** (stunt′wùm′ən) a woman who performs dangerous manoeuvres instead of the actress in a motion picture. *n.*, *pl.* **stunt·wom·en** (-wim′ən).

**stu·pe·fac·tion** (styü′pə fak′shən *or* stü′pə fak′shən) a STUPEFYing or being stupefied. *n.*

**stu·pe·fy** (styü′pə fī′ *or* stü′pə fī′) **1** make stupid, dull or senseless: *stupefied by a drug.* **2** overwhelm with shock or amazement; astound: *They were stupefied by the calamity.* *v.*, **stu·pe·fied, stu·pe·fy·ing.** —**stu′pe·fi′er,** *n.*

**stu·pen·dous** (styü pen′dəs *or* stü pen′dəs) **1** amazing; marvellous: *Niagara Falls is a stupendous sight.* **2** unusually large or great: *a stupendous meal, a stupendous structure.* *adj.* —**stu·pen′dous·ly,** *adv.* —**stu·pen′dous·ness,** *n.*

**stu·pid** (styü′pid *or* stü′pid) **1** not intelligent; dull: *a stupid person.* **2** not interesting: *a stupid book.* **3** showing lack of intelligence or good sense: *That was a stupid thing to do.* **4** dazed: *He was still stupid from the effect of the sedative.* **5** *Informal.* a stupid person. 1–4 *adj.*, 5 *n.* —**stu′pid·ly,** *adv.* —**stu′pid·ness,** *n.*

**stu·pid·i·ty** (styü pid′ə tē *or* stü pid′ə tē) **1** the quality or state of being stupid. **2** a stupid act, idea, etc. *n.*, *pl.* **stu·pid·i·ties.**

**stu·por** (styü′pər *or* stü′pər) **1** a loss or lessening of the power to feel: *The woman lay in a stupor, unable to tell what had happened to her.* **2** mental or moral numbness. *n.*

**stur·dy** (stėr′dē) **1** strong; stout: *sturdy legs.* **2** not yielding; firm: *sturdy resistance.* *adj.*, **stur·di·er, stur·di·est.** —**stur′di·ly,** *adv.* —**stur′di·ness,** *n.*

**stur·geon** (stėr′jən) a large food fish whose long body has a tough skin with rows of bony plates: *Caviar and isinglass are obtained from sturgeons.* *n.*, *pl.* **stur·geon** *or* **stur·geons.**

**stut·ter** (stut′ər) **1** repeat the same sound in an effort to speak. *Example: C-c-c-can't th-th-th-they c-c-c-come?*

**St. Vitus's dance   1186   subconsciousness**

---

**2** say, speak, or sound with a stutter: *to stutter a reply.* **3** the act or habit of stuttering.   1, 2 *v.*, 3 *n.*
—**stut′ter·er,** *n.*   —**stut′ter·ing·ly,** *adv.*

**St. Vi·tus's dance** (sānt′vī′təs siz)   a disorder of the nervous system with involuntary spasms of the muscles of the face and the arms and legs; chorea.

**sty**[1] (stī)   **1** a pen for pigs.   **2** any filthy place.   *n., pl.* **sties.**

**sty**[2] or **stye** (stī)   a small, inflamed swelling on the edge of the eyelid: *A sty is like a small boil.*   *n., pl.* **sties** or **styes.**

**Styg·i·an** (stij′ē ən)   **1** having to do with the river Styx, a river in the lower world in Greek mythology.   **2** having to do with the lower world.   **3** dark; gloomy.   *adj.*

**style** (stīl)   **1** fashion: *to dress in the latest styles.*   **2** a manner; method; way: *the Gothic style of architecture.* **3** a way of writing or speaking.   **4** a fashionable, elegant, or admirable way or manner: *She dressed in style. He lives in style.*   **5** literary or artistic excellence.   **6** give a distinctive design or manner to; design, fashion, or arrange: *dresses styled in Paris. She uses a blow dryer to style her hair.*   **7** name; call: *Joan of Arc was styled "the Maid of Orleans."*   **8** an official name; title: *Salute him with the style of King.*   **9** a pointed instrument for writing on wax. **10** something like this in shape or use.   **11** a pointer on a dial, chart, etc.   **12** the stemlike part of the pistil of a flower containing the stigma at its top. See FLOWER for picture.   1–5, 8–12 *n.*, 6, 7 *v.*, **styled, styl·ing.**
☛ *Hom.* STILE.

**style·book** (stīl′bůk′)   **1** a book containing rules of punctuation, capitalization, etc. used by printers.   **2** a book showing fashions in dress, etc.   *n.*

**styl·ish** (stī′lish)   fashionable; smart: *a stylish new coat. adj.*   —**styl′ish·ly,** *adv.*   —**styl′ish·ness,** *n.*

**styl·ist** (stī′list)   **1** a person, especially a writer, who has or aims at a good style or whose work is characterized by a particular style: *His editorials read well because he is a stylist.*   **2** a person who designs or advises concerning fashionable interior decoration, clothes, etc.   *n.*

**sty·lis·tic** (stī lis′tik)   of or having to do with artistic or literary style.   *adj.*

**sty·lis·ti·cal·ly** (stī lis′ti klē)   as regards style; in matters of style.   *adv.*

**styl·ize** (stī′līz)   make or design according to a particular or standard style or pattern rather than according to nature: *Our new bedroom wallpaper has tiny stylized tulips.*   *v.*, **styl·ized, styl·iz·ing.**

**sty·lus** (stī′ləs)   **1** a pointed instrument used in ancient times for writing on wax or clay tablets.   **2** a needle-like piece of steel, jewel, etc. used in playing phonograph records; needle.   **3** a similar device used for cutting the grooves on the original disk when recording music, etc.   *n.*

**sty·mie** (stī′mē)   **1** in golf, a situation on a putting green in which an opponent's ball is directly between the player's ball and the hole.   **2** hinder with a stymie. **3** block completely: *She was stymied by the last question on the exam and gave up on it.*   1 *n.*, 2, 3 *v.*, **sty·mied, sty·mie·ing.**

**styp·tic** (stip′tik)   **1** able to stop or check bleeding.

**2** a substance that stops or checks bleeding by contracting the tissue: *Alum is a common styptic.*   1 *adj.*, 2 *n.*

**styptic pencil**   a small stick of alum or other styptic substance, used on slight wounds to stop bleeding.

**sty·rene** (stī′rēn)   an aromatic liquid hydrocarbon used mainly in making synthetic rubber and plastics.   *n.*

**sty·ro·foam** (stī′rə fōm′)   a kind of lightweight, firm polystyrene plastic used for insulation, packaging, etc.   *n.*

**sua·sion** (swā′zhən)   PERSUASION: *Moral suasion is an appeal to one's sense of what is right.*   *n.*

**sua·sive** (swā′siv)   PERSUASIVE.   *adj.*

**suave** (swäv)   smoothly agreeable or polite: *He had a suave, well-bred manner.*   *adj.*   —**suave′ly,** *adv.* —**suave′ness,** *n.*

**sua·vi·ty** (swä′və tē)   smoothly agreeable quality of behaviour; smooth politeness.   *n., pl.* **sua·vi·ties.**

**sub** (sub) *Informal.*   **1** substitute.   **2** submarine. **3** subordinate.   **4** act as a substitute.   1–3 *n., adj.,* 4 *v.,* **subbed, sub·bing.**

**sub–**   a prefix meaning:   **1** under; below, as in *subway, submarine.*   **2** further or again, as in *subdivide, sublease.* **3** near; bordering upon, as in *subarctic.*   **4** nearly; almost, as in *subarid.*   **5** secondary, subordinate, or assistant, as in *substation, subhead.*   **6** resulting from further division; subordinate portion of, as in *subcommittee, subspecies.* **7** in a comparatively small degree or proportion; somewhat, as in *subacid.*   Also, (before *c*) **suc-,** (before *f*) **suf-,** (before *g*) **sug-,** (in some cases before *m*) **sum-,** (before *p*) **sup-,** (before *r*) **sur-,** (in some cases before *c, p, t*) **sus-.**

**sub.**   **1** substitute.   **2** subscription.   **3** suburban.

**sub·ac·id** (sub′as′id)   slightly acid: *Oranges are a subacid fruit.*   *adj.*

**sub·a·gent** (sub′ā′jənt)   a person employed as the agent of an agent; a subordinate or deputy agent.   *n.*

**sub·arc·tic** (sub′ärk′tik *or* sub′är′tik)   **1** of, having to do with, or like the region just south of the Arctic Circle. **2** the region just south of the Arctic Circle.   1 *adj.,* 2 *n.*

**sub·ar·id** (sub′ar′id *or* sub′er′id)   moderately arid. *adj.*

**sub·a·tom·ic** (sub′ə tom′ik)   of or having to do with the inside of the atom or with particles smaller than atoms.   *adj.*

**sub–base·ment** (sub′bā′smənt)   a storey below the main basement of a building.   *n.*

**sub·com·mit·tee** (sub′kə mit′ē)   a small committee chosen from a larger general committee for some special duty.   *n.*

**sub·com·pact** (sub′kom′pakt)   the smallest of the four basic sizes of automobile.   Compare with COMPACT, INTERMEDIATE, and STANDARD.   *n.*

**sub·con·scious** (sub′kon′shəs)   **1** existing in the mind and affecting thoughts, attitudes, or behaviour but not consciously felt: *a subconscious motive, subconscious inhibitions.*   **2** not completely conscious or aware: *In his subconscious state, he thought he heard a knocking.* **3** thoughts, feelings, etc. existing in the mind but not consciously recognized.   1, 2 *adj.,* 3 *n.*
—**sub′con′scious·ly,** *adv.*

**sub·con·scious·ness** (sub′kon′shəs nis)   **1** the quality or state of being not completely conscious.   **2** the SUBCONSCIOUS (def. 3).   *n.*

**sub·con·ti·nent** (sub′kon′tə nənt) 1 a very large land mass that is smaller than the land masses usually called continents: *Greenland is a subcontinent.* 2 a large section of a continent that has considerable geographical or political independence: *the Indian subcontinent.* *n.*

**sub·con·tract** (sub′kon′trakt *for noun,* sub′kon′trakt *or* sub′kən trakt′ *for verb*) 1 a contract under a previous contract; contract for carrying out a previous contract or part of it: *The contractor for the new school building gave my mother the subcontract to install the plumbing.* 2 make a subcontract: *The plumbing for the new school was subcontracted to my mother.* 1 *n.*, 2 *v.*

**sub·con·trac·tor** (sub′kon′trak tər, sub′kon′trak tər, *or* sub′kən trak′tər) a person or company that contracts to carry out part or all of a contract made by someone else. *n.*

**sub·cul·ture** (sub′kul′chər) 1 an element or cultural group within a larger culture, but distinguished from it by features of belief, custom, conduct, background, etc.: *the subculture of organized crime.* 2 a culture of bacteria, etc. derived from another culture. *n.*

**sub·di·vide** (sub′də vīd′) 1 divide again; divide into smaller parts. 2 divide land into lots for houses, etc.: *A developer bought the farm and subdivided it into building lots.* *v.*, **sub·di·vid·ed, sub·di·vid·ing.**

**sub·di·vi·sion** (sub′də vizh′ən) 1 a division into smaller parts. 2 a part of a part. 3 a tract of land divided into building lots. 4 the houses, community, etc. established on such a tract. *n.*

**sub·due** (səb dyü′ *or* səb dü′) 1 conquer: *The Spaniards subdued the Indian peoples of South America.* 2 keep down; hold back; suppress: *to subdue a desire to laugh.* 3 tone down; soften or reduce: *They pulled down the blinds to subdue the light.* 4 alleviate: *to subdue a fever.* *v.*, **sub·dued, sub·du·ing.** —**sub·du′a·ble,** *adj.* —**sub·du′er,** *n.*

**sub·dued** (səb dyüd′ *or* səb düd′) 1 lacking in intensity or strength: *The room was decorated in subdued colours.* 2 quietened down; less spirited or lively than usual: *He was quiet and subdued all afternoon.* 3 pt. and pp. of SUBDUE. 1, 2 *adj.*, 3 *v.*

**sub·en·try** (sub′en′trē) an entry listed under a main entry: *In this dictionary, idioms are included as subentries under the entry word.* *n.*

**sub·group** (sub′grüp′) a subordinate group; division of a group. *n.*

**sub·head** (sub′hed′) 1 the title, or heading, of a subdivision of an article, chapter, etc. 2 a subordinate title, headline, etc.: *Newspaper articles often have a subhead underneath the headline.* *n.*

**sub·head·ing** (sub′hed′ing) SUBHEAD. *n.*

**sub·hu·man** (sub′hyü′mən) 1 below the human race or type; less than human. 2 almost human: *subhuman primates.* *adj.*

**subj.** 1 subject. 2 subjective. 3 subjectively. 4 subjunctive.

**sub·ject** (sub′jikt *for noun and adjective,* səb jekt′ *for verb*) 1 something thought about, discussed, etc.: *She tried to change the subject. Juvenile delinquency is a broad subject.* 2 something learned or taught; a course of study, field of learning, etc.: *English, history, mathematics, and biology are required subjects in this school.* 3 a person under the power, control, or influence of another: *The people are the subjects of the queen.* 4 under some power or influence: *A colony is a subject nation.* 5 bring

**subcontinent** 1187 **sublease**

hat, āge, fär; let, ēqual, tėrm; it, īce
hot, ōpen, ôrder; oil, out; cup, pút, rüle
əbove, takən, pencəl, lemən, circəs
ch, child; ng, long; sh, ship
th, thin; ᴛʜ, then; zh, measure

under some power or influence: *Rome subjected all Italy to its rule.* 6 cause to undergo or experience something: *The savages subjected their captives to torture.* 7 a person or thing that undergoes or experiences something. 8 in grammar, the word or group of words in a sentence about which something is said in the predicate: *In the sentence* His little brother went to find him, His little brother *is the* subject; *in* Their travellers' cheques were stolen, Their travellers' cheques *is the subject.* 9 the theme of a book, poem, or other literary work. 10 the theme or melody on which a musical work or movement is based. 1–3, 7–10 *n.*, 4 *adj.*, 5, 6 *v.*

**subject to, a** under the power or influence of: *We are subject to our country's laws.* **b** likely to have: *Many children are subject to colds.* **c** depending on; on the condition of: *I bought the car subject to your approval.*

**sub·jec·tion** (səb jek′shən) 1 bringing under some power or influence: *The new dictator's first concern was the subjection of the rebel forces.* 2 being under some power or influence: *They lived in subjection to an old aunt.* *n.*

**sub·jec·tive** (səb jek′tiv) 1 existing in the mind; belonging to the person thinking rather than to the object thought of: *Ideas and opinions are subjective; facts are objective.* 2 about the thoughts and feelings of the speaker, writer, painter, etc.; personal: *a subjective poem.* 3 of, having to do with, or being the grammatical form of an English pronoun that shows that it is the subject of a sentence. There are six English pronouns with special subjective forms: *I, we, he, she, they,* and *who.* 4 the subjective form: *The English subjective corresponds roughly to the nominative case in German and Latin.* 5 a word in the subjective form: I *and* who *are subjectives.* 1–3 *adj.*, 4, 5 *n.* —**sub·jec′tive·ly,** *adv.* —**sub·jec′tive·ness,** *n.*

**sub·jec·tiv·i·ty** (sub′jek tiv′ə tē) the quality or condition of being SUBJECTIVE (def. 1): *The subjectivity of his account of the war makes it unreliable as a source of information.* *n.*

**subject matter** the thing or things discussed or considered in a book, speech, debate, etc.

**sub·join** (səb join′) add at the end; append: *Several appendixes were subjoined to the report.* *v.*

**sub·ju·gate** (sub′jə gāt′) subdue; conquer. *v.*, **sub·ju·gat·ed, sub·ju·gat·ing.** —**sub′ju·ga′tor,** *n.*

**sub·ju·ga·tion** (sub′jə gā′shən) conquest; subjection. *n.*

**sub·junc·tive** (səb jungk′tiv) 1 a set of verb forms used to express a state or act as possible, conditional, desirable, doubtful, etc. rather than as fact. 2 a verb form in the subjunctive: *In* Come what may, we will see it through, *and* If I were you I'd try again, *the verb forms* come *and* were *are subjunctives.* 3 of, having to do with, or referring to the subjunctive. 1, 2 *n.*, 3 *adj.*

**sub·king·dom** (sub′king′dəm) any primary division of the animal or plant kingdom, usually called a PHYLUM. *n.*

**sub·lease** (sub′lēs′ *for noun,* sub lēs′ *or* sub′lēs′ *for verb*) 1 a lease of all or part of some property by the person who rents the property himself or herself from the owner.

**2** grant or take a sublease of.  *1 n., 2 v.,* **sub·leased, sub·leas·ing.**

**sub·let** (sub let′)  **1** rent to another some property that has been rented to oneself: *She sublet her apartment while she was away last summer.*  **2** give part of a contract to another; subcontract: *The contractor for the whole building sublet the contract for the plumbing.*  *v.,* **sub·let, sub·let·ting.**

**sub·li·mate** (sub′lə māt′ *for verb,* sub′lə mit *or* sub′lə māt′ *for noun*)  **1** change the natural expression of an impulse or desire into one considered more socially or personally acceptable: *to sublimate one's aggressiveness.*  **2** SUBLIME (def. 3) a solid substance.  **3** a substance produced by the process of subliming: *Frost and snow are sublimates; they form directly from water vapour in the air.*  *1, 2 v.,* **sub·li·mat·ed, sub·li·mat·ing;**  *3 n.*

**sub·li·ma·tion** (sub′lə mā′shən)  **1** the act or process of sublimating or subliming.  **2** the resulting product or state.  *n.*

**sub·lime** (sə blīm′)  **1** lofty; noble; majestic; exalted: *We were awed by the sublime beauty of the Rocky Mountains.*  **2** perfect; supreme: *She carried on with sublime indifference to what people might say.*  **3** subject a solid substance to the action of heat to produce a vapour which is then condensed to a solid again: *Some substances can be purified by subliming them.*  **4** pass directly from a solid state to a vapour: *Some substances that will sublime are arsenic, camphor, and dry ice.*  **5 the sublime,** that which is lofty, noble, exalted, etc.  *1, 2 adj., 3, 4 v.,* **sub·limed, sub·lim·ing;**  *5 n.*

**sub·lim·i·nal** (sə blim′ə nəl)  existing or acting below the threshold of conscious awareness: *the subliminal self. The committee protested against the use of subliminal advertising on television.*  *adj.*

**sub·lim·i·ty** (sə blim′ə tē)  **1** the quality or state of being SUBLIME (def. 1); lofty excellence or grandeur.  **2** something SUBLIME (def. 1).  *n., pl.* **sub·lim·i·ties.**

**sub·ma·chine gun** (sub′mə shēn′)  a lightweight automatic or semi-automatic gun, designed to be fired from the shoulder or hip.

**sub·mar·gin·al** (sub mär′jə nəl)  **1** in biology, near the margin of an organ or part.  **2** below a required minimum standard: *submarginal living conditions.*  **3** of land, etc., not productive enough to be worth cultivating, developing, etc.  *adj.*

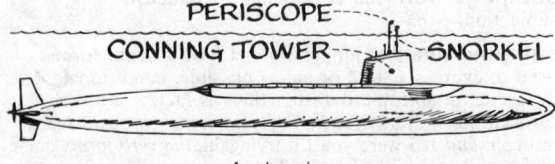

A submarine

**sub·ma·rine** (sub′mə rēn′ *for noun and verb,* sub′mə rēn′ *or* sub′mə rēn′ *for adjective*)  **1** a boat that can operate under water, used in warfare for discharging torpedoes, etc.  **2** attack or sink by a submarine.  **3** placed, growing, or used below the surface of the sea: *submarine plants.*  **4** a large sandwich consisting of a long roll that is split lengthwise and filled with a variety of cold meats, cheese, tomatoes, onions, coleslaw, etc.  *1, 4 n., 2 v.,* **sub·ma·rined, sub·ma·rin·ing;**  *3 adj.*
☛ *Etym.* See note at U-BOAT.

**sub·mar·i·ner** (sub mar′ə nər, sub mer′ə nər, *or* sub′mə rē′nər)  a member of the crew of a submarine.  *n.*

**sub·max·il·lar·y** (sub′mak′sə ler′ē)  **1** of, having to do with, or situated under the lower jaw.  **2** of or having to do with either of the salivary glands situated beneath the lower jaw, one on either side.  **3** a submaxillary part, especially the lower jawbone.  *1, 2 adj., 3 n., pl.* **sub·max·il·lar·ies.**

**sub·merge** (səb mėrj′)  **1** put under water; cover with water: *A big wave submerged us. At high tide this path is submerged.*  **2** cover; bury: *His talent was submerged by his shyness.*  **3** sink under water; go below the surface: *The submarine submerged.*  **4** sink out of sight.  *v.,* **sub·merged, sub·merg·ing.**

**sub·mer·gence** (səb mėr′jəns)  a submerging or being SUBMERGED.  *n.*

**sub·merse** (səb mėrs′)  SUBMERGE.  *v.,* **sub·mersed, sub·mers·ing.**

**sub·mers·i·ble** (səb mėr′sə bəl)  **1** that can be SUBMERGED.  **2** a ship or craft that can operate under water for research, exploration, etc.  *1 adj., 2 n.*

**sub·mer·sion** (səb mėr′zhən)  a submersing or being SUBMERSED.  *n.*

**sub·mis·sion** (səb mish′ən)  **1** submitting; yielding to the power, control, or authority of another: *The defeated general showed his submission by giving up his sword.*  **2** obedience or humbleness: *The servant bowed in submission to his master's order.*  **3** a referring or being referred to the consideration or judgment of another or others.  **4** a petition; a formal request: *The submission of the teachers was approved by the principal.*  **5** a report.  *n.*

**sub·mis·sive** (səb mis′iv)  yielding to the power, control, or authority of another; obedient; humble.  *adj.*
—**sub·mis′sive·ly,** *adv.*  —**sub·mis′sive·ness,** *n.*

**sub·mit** (səb mit′)  **1** yield to the power, control, or authority of another or others; surrender; yield: *The thief submitted to arrest by the police.*  **2** refer to the consideration or judgment of another or others: *The secretary submitted a report of the last meeting. She submitted a bid on the contract for the new shopping centre.*  **3** offer as an opinion; propose or affirm: *We submit that the proposed expansion of the airport is unnecessary.*  *v.,* **sub·mit·ted, sub·mit·ting.**

**sub–mul·ti·ple** (sub′mul′tə pəl)  a number or quantity contained exactly within another number or quantity: *The millimetre is a sub-multiple of the metre.*  *n.*

**sub·nor·mal** (sub′nôr′məl)  **1** lower or smaller than normal: *subnormal temperatures.*  **2** below normal, especially in mental ability.  *adj.*

**sub–or·bit·al** (sub′ôr′bi təl)  not in or going into a complete orbit: *The new space capsule was tested in a sub-orbital flight.*  *adj.*

**sub·or·der** (sub′ôr′dər)  in biology, a secondary category in the classification of plants and animals that is a grouping within an order and includes one or more families.  *n.*

**sub·or·di·nate** (sə bôr′də nit *for noun and adjective,* sə bôr′də nāt′ *for verb*)  **1** inferior in rank: *In the armed forces, lieutenants are subordinate to captains.*  **2** inferior in importance; secondary: *An errand boy has a subordinate* *position.* **3** under the control or influence of something else. **4** in grammar, of, having to do with, or referring to a clause that depends for its complete sense on a main clause: *A subordinate clause functions as an adjective, adverb, or noun in a complex sentence.* **5** a subordinate person or thing. **6** make subordinate: *A polite host subordinates his wishes to those of his guests.* 1–4 *adj.*, 5 *n.*, 6 *v.*, **sub·or·di·nat·ed, sub·or·di·nat·ing.**

**sub·or·di·na·tion** (sə bôr′də nā′shən) **1** the act of subordinating. **2** the quality or state of being subordinate. *n.*

**sub·orn** (sə bôrn′) **1** persuade by bribery or other means to do something illegal; especially, to give false testimony in court: *A friend of the accused was charged with suborning a witness.* **2** obtain by bribery or other means: *to suborn perjury.* *v.* —**sub·orn′er,** *n.*

**sub·or·na·tion** (sub′ôr nā′shən) the obtaining of an illegal act by a bribe or other means; especially, the crime of getting someone to commit perjury. *n.*

**subornation of perjury** the crime of persuading or causing a witness to give false testimony in court.

**sub·poe·na** (sə pē′nə) **1** in law, an official written order commanding a person to appear in court. **2** summon with a subpoena. 1 *n.*, 2 *v.*, **sub·poe·naed, sub·poe·na·ing.**

**sub ro·sa** (sub′ rō′zə) *Latin.* in strict confidence; privately.

**sub·scribe** (səb skrīb′) **1** promise to give or pay a sum of money: *She subscribed $50 to the hospital fund.* **2** arrange to receive a periodical or a service regularly for a given length of time (*used with* **to**): *He subscribes to several magazines.* **3** write one's name at the end of a document, etc.; sign one's name. **4** write one's name at the end of; show one's consent or approval by signing: *Thousands of citizens subscribed the petition.* **5** give one's consent or approval; agree: *He will not subscribe to anything unfair.* *v.*, **sub·scribed, sub·scrib·ing.** —**sub·scrib′er,** *n.*

**sub·script** (sub′skript) **1** a small number, letter, etc. written immediately below or below and to one side of another number, letter, etc. Example: *In* $H_2SO_4$ *the* $_2$ *and the* $_4$ *are subscripts.* **2** written underneath or low on the line. 1 *n.*, 2 *adj.*

**sub·scrip·tion** (səb skrip′shən) **1** a subscribing. **2** a sum of money subscribed: *Her subscription to the Fresh Air Fund was $50. We are raising a subscription for a new arena.* **3** the right obtained for the money: *His subscription to the newspaper expires next week.* **4** something written at the end of a thing; signature. *n.*

**sub·sec·tion** (sub′sek′shən) a part of a section. *n.*

**sub·se·quence** (sub′sə kwəns) **1** the quality or state of being SUBSEQUENT. **2** a SUBSEQUENT event or circumstance. *n.*

**sub·se·quent** (sub′sə kwənt) coming after; following; later: *Subsequent events proved him right. That problem is dealt with in a subsequent chapter. The package arrived on the day subsequent to her call.* *adj.* —**sub′se·quent·ly,** *adv.*

**sub·serve** (səb sėrv′) be of use or service in helping along a purpose, action, etc.; promote: *Chewing food well subserves digestion.* *v.*, **sub·served, sub·serv·ing.**

**sub·ser·vi·ence** (səb sėr′vē əns) **1** tame submission; slavish obedience; servility. **2** usefulness in a subordinate place or function. *n.*

---

**subordination**    **1189**    **substance**

hat, āge, fär; let, ēqual, tėrm; it, īce
hot, ōpen, ôrder; oil, out; cup, pùt, rüle
əbove, takən, pencəl, lemən, circəs
ch, child; ng, long; sh, ship
th, thin; ᴛʜ, then; zh, measure

**sub·ser·vi·ent** (səb sėr′vē ənt) **1** tamely submissive; slavishly obedient; servile. **2** useful as a means to help a purpose or end; serviceable. *adj.* —**sub·ser′vi·ent·ly,** *adv.*

**sub·set** (sub′set′) in mathematics and logic, a set whose members are also members of a larger set or series: *The set of dogs is a subset of the set of mammals.* *n.*

**sub·side** (səb sīd′) **1** sink to a lower level: *After the rain stopped, the flood waters subsided.* **2** grow less; die down; become less active; abate; ebb: *The storm finally subsided.* **3** fall to the bottom; settle. *v.*, **sub·sid·ed, sub·sid·ing.**

**sub·sid·ence** (səb sī′dəns *or* sub′sə dəns) the act or process of subsiding. *n.*

**sub·sid·i·ar·y** (səb sid′ē er′ē) **1** useful to assist or support; auxiliary; supplementary. **2** subordinate; secondary. **3** a thing or person that assists or supplements. **4** a company having over half of its stock owned or controlled by another company: *The bus line was a subsidiary of the railway.* **5** of, having to do with, or maintained by a SUBSIDY. 1, 2, 5 *adj.*, 3, 4 *n.*, *pl.* **sub·sid·i·ar·ies.**

**sub·si·dize** (sub′sə dīz′) **1** aid or assist with a grant of money: *The government subsidizes shipping services in coastal waters.* **2** buy the aid or assistance of with a grant of money. *v.*, **sub·si·dized, sub·si·diz·ing.** —**sub′si·diz′er,** *n.*

**sub·si·dy** (sub′sə dē) a grant or contribution of money, especially one made by a government. *n.*, *pl.* **sub·si·dies.**

**sub·sist** (səb sist′) **1** keep alive; live: *While the hikers were stranded they subsisted on berries.* **2** continue to be; exist: *Many superstitions still subsist.* *v.*

**sub·sist·ence** (səb sis′təns) **1** existence; continuance. **2** a means of keeping alive; livelihood: *The sea provides a subsistence for fishermen.* *n.*

**sub·soil** (sub′soil′) the layer of earth that lies just under the surface soil: *In our backyard we have clay subsoil under a thin layer of loam.* *n.*

**sub·son·ic** (sub son′ik) having to do with or designed for use at a speed less than that of sound. *adj.*

**sub·spe·cies** (sub′spē′sēz *or* sub′spē′shēz) a grouping within an animal or plant species based on inherited biological differences, often influenced by geography: *Subspecies often develop when groups of a particular species have been isolated from each other for many generations. The grizzly is a subspecies of brown bear.* *n.*, *pl.* **sub·spe·cies.**

**subst.** **1** substitute. **2** substantive.

**sub·stance** (sub′stəns) **1** what a thing consists of; matter; material: *Ice and water are the same substance in different forms.* **2** the real, main, or important part of anything: *The substance of an education is its effect on your life, not just the learning of lessons.* **3** the real meaning: *Give the substance of the speech in your own words.* **4** solid quality; body: *Pea soup has more substance than water.* **5** wealth; property. **6** a particular kind of

**substandard** 1190 **suburb**

matter: *The little pond is covered with a green substance.* *n.*
**in substance,** **a** essentially; mainly. **b** really; actually.

**sub·stand·ard** (sub stan′dərd) falling short of a minimum standard of quality: *The substandard sheets are being sold at very low prices.* *adj.*

**sub·stan·tial** (səb stan′shəl) 1 real; actual: *Dreams and ghosts are not substantial.* 2 large; important; ample: *Marta has made a substantial improvement in health.* 3 strong; firm; solid: *The house is substantial enough to last a hundred years.* 4 in the main; in essentials: *The stories told by the two girls were in substantial agreement.* 5 well-to-do; wealthy. *adj.* —**sub·stan′tial·ly,** *adv.*

**sub·stan·ti·al·i·ty** (səb stan′shē al′ə tē) the quality or state of being SUBSTANTIAL. *n., pl.* **sub·stan·ti·al·i·ties.**

**sub·stan·ti·ate** (səb stan′shē āt) 1 establish by evidence; prove: *to substantiate a rumour, a claim, a theory, etc.* 2 give concrete or substantial form to. *v.* **sub·stan·ti·at·ed, sub·stan·ti·at·ing.**

**sub·stan·ti·a·tion** (səb stan′shē ā′shən) a substantiating or being SUBSTANTIATED; embodiment or proof. *n.*

**sub·stan·ti·val** (sub′stən tī′vəl) of, having to do with, or being a SUBSTANTIVE. *adj.* —**sub′stan·ti′val·ly,** *adv.*

**sub·stan·tive** (sub′stən tiv) 1 a noun or pronoun; the name of a person or thing; an adjective, phrase, or clause used as a noun. 2 used as a noun. 3 showing or expressing existence: *The verb* to be *is the substantive verb.* 4 independent. 5 real; actual. 6 having a firm or solid basis. 1 *n.*, 2–6 *adj.* —**sub′stan·tive·ly,** *adv.*

**sub·sta·tion** (sub′stā′shən) a branch station; subordinate station. *n.*

**sub·sti·tute** (sub′stə tyüt *or* sub′stə tüt′) 1 a person or thing used instead, or taking the place, of another: *Margarine is a common substitute for butter. We were taught by a substitute today because our teacher was sick.* 2 put in the place of another: *We substituted brown sugar for molasses in these cookies.* 3 take the place of another: *She substituted for Ms. Divito who is ill.* 4 put in or taking the place of another: *a substitute teacher.* 1, 4 *n.*, 2, 3 *v.*, **sub·sti·tut·ed, sub·sti·tut·ing.**

**sub·sti·tu·tion** (sub′stə tyü′shən *or* sub′stə tü′shən) 1 the substituting of one person or thing for another. 2 something that functions as a SUBSTITUTE. *n.*

**sub·sti·tu·tion·al** (sub′stə tyü′shən əl *or* sub′stə tü′shən əl) 1 having to do with or characterized by SUBSTITUTION. 2 acting or serving as a SUBSTITUTE. *adj.* —**sub′sti·tu′tion·al·ly,** *adv.*

**sub·stra·ta** (sub strā′tə *or* sub strat′ə) a pl. of SUBSTRATUM. *n.*

**sub·stra·tum** (sub strā′təm *or* sub strat′əm) 1 a layer lying under another. 2 a layer of earth lying just under the surface soil; subsoil. 3 a basis; foundation: *The story has a substratum of truth.* *n., pl.* **sub·stra·ta** or **sub·stra·tums.**

**sub·struc·ture** (sub′struk′chər) a structure forming a foundation. *n.*

**sub·ten·an·cy** (sub ten′ən sē) the status, right, or holding of a SUBTENANT. *n., pl.* **sub·ten·an·cies.**

**sub·ten·ant** (sub ten′ənt *or* sub′ten′ənt) a tenant of a tenant; one who rents land, a house, or the like from a tenant. *n.*

**sub·tend** (səb tend′) in geometry: 1 define by marking off the endpoints of: *A chord subtends an arc of a circle.* 2 of a line, arc, etc., be opposite to an angle: *The hypotenuse subtends the right angle of a right-angled triangle. An arc of a circle subtends the central angle of the arc.* *v.*

**sub·ter·fuge** (sub′tər fyüj′) a trick, excuse, or expedient used to escape something unpleasant: *Her headache was a subterfuge to avoid work.* *n.*

**sub·ter·ra·ne·an** (sub′tə rā′nē ən) 1 underground: *A subterranean passage led from the castle to a cave.* 2 carried on secretly; hidden. *adj.*

**sub·ter·ra·ne·ous** (sub′tə rā′nē əs) SUBTERRANEAN. *adj.*

**sub·ti·tle** (sub′tī′təl) 1 an additional or subordinate title of a book, article, etc. 2 a piece of dialogue or description printed on the film and shown between the scenes of a silent motion picture or on the lower part of the scenes of a foreign-language motion picture. 3 give a subtitle to. 1, 2 *n.*, 3 *v.*, **sub·ti·tled, sub·ti·tling.**

**sub·tle** (sut′əl) 1 delicate; thin; fine: *a subtle odour of perfume.* 2 faint; mysterious: *a subtle smile.* 3 having a keen, quick mind; discerning; acute: *She is a subtle observer.* 4 sly; crafty; tricky: *a subtle scheme to get some money.* 5 skilful; clever; expert. *adj.* —**sub′tle·ness,** *n.* —**sub′tly,** *adv.*

**sub·tle·ty** (sut′əl tē) 1 the quality or state of being SUBTLE. 2 something SUBTLE, especially a fine distinction: *He did not understand all the subtleties of the author's argument.* *n., pl.* **sub·tle·ties.**

**sub·top·ic** (sub′top′ik) one of the secondary topics into which a main topic is divided. *n.*

**sub·to·tal** (sub′tō′təl) the total of a group of figures that form part of a series of figures to be added. *n.*

**sub·tract** (səb trakt′) 1 take away a number or quantity from a larger number or quantity: *Subtract 2 from 10 and you have 8.* 2 take away a part from a whole. *v.* —**sub·tract′er,** *n.*

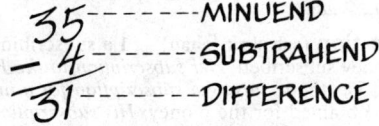

The parts of a subtraction calculation

**sub·trac·tion** (səb trak′shən) the act or process of subtracting one number or quantity from another; the process of finding the difference between two numbers or quantities: $10 - 2 = 8$ *is a simple subtraction.* *n.*

**sub·trac·tive** (səb trak′tiv) 1 tending to subtract; having power to subtract. 2 to be subtracted; having the minus sign (−). *adj.*

**sub·tra·hend** (sub′trə hend′) a number or quantity to be subtracted from another: *In* $10 - 2 = 8$, *the subtrahend is 2.* See SUBTRACTION for picture. *n.*

**sub·trop·i·cal** (sub trop′ə kəl) bordering on the tropics; nearly tropical. *adj.*

**sub·trop·ics** (sub trop′iks *or* sub′trop′iks) the region bordering on the tropics. *n.pl.*

**sub·urb** (sub′ėrb) 1 a district, town, or village just

outside or near a city or town.   **2 the suburbs,**   the residential section or sections on the outskirts of a city or town.   *n.*
☛ *Etym.*   From L *suburbium*, made up of *sub-* 'below' + *urbs, urbis* 'city'. 14c.

**sub·ur·ban** (sə bėr′bən)   **1** having to do with or in a suburb: *We have an excellent suburban train service.*   **2** characteristic of a suburb or its inhabitants.   *adj.*

**sub·ur·ban·ite** (sə bėr′bə nīt′)   a person who lives in a suburb.   *n.*

**sub·ur·bi·a** (sə bėr′bē ə)   **1** the suburbs of a city.   **2** the residents of the suburbs, thought of as a distinct social class.   **3** the values, attitudes, etc. thought to be characteristic of residents of the suburbs.   *n.*

**sub·ver·sion** (səb vėr′zhən)   a SUBVERTing or being subverted; overthrow; especially, an attempt to overthrow a government by working against it secretly from within the country.   *n.*

**sub·ver·sive** (səb vėr′siv)   **1** tending or designed to overthrow or destroy a government, institution, etc.: *a subversive scheme.*   **2** a person who seeks to overthrow or undermine a government, etc.   **1** *adj,* **2** *n.*

**sub·vert** (səb vėrt′)   **1** ruin; overthrow; destroy: *Dictators subvert democracy.*   **2** undermine the principles of; corrupt.   *v.*   —**sub·vert′er,** *n.*

**sub·way** (sub′wā′)   **1** an electric railway running for all or most of its length beneath the surface of the streets in a city.   **2** a road running under another road or under a railway track; an underpass: *The subway was flooded during the storm.*   **3** an underground passage for pipes, etc.   *n.*

**suc–**   a form of the prefix **sub-** occurring before *c,* as in *succeed.*

**suc·ceed** (sək sēd′)   **1** turn out well; have success: *Her plans succeeded.*   **2** accomplish what is attempted or intended: *The attack succeeded beyond all expectations.*   **3** come next after; follow; take the place of: *Diefenbaker succeeded St. Laurent as prime minister of Canada.*   **4** come into possession of an office, title, or property through right of birth, etc. (used with **to**): *The Prince of Wales succeeds to the throne of England.*   *v.*   —**suc·ceed′er,** *n.*

**suc·cess** (sək ses′)   **1** a favourable result; wished-for ending; good fortune.   **2** the gaining of wealth, position, etc.: *He has had little success in life.*   **3** a person or thing that succeeds: *The circus was a great success.*   **4** the result; outcome; fortune: *What success did they have in finding a gardener?*   *n.*

**suc·cess·ful** (sək ses′fəl)   **1** ending in success: *a successful plan.*   **2** having achieved success; prosperous: *a successful businessman.*   *adj.*   —**suc·cess′ful·ly,** *adv.*

**suc·ces·sion** (sək sesh′ən)   **1** a number of persons or things following one after the other; series: *a succession of capable leaders, a succession of misfortunes.*   **2** the act or process of following one after the other.   **3** the right of succeeding to an office, property, or rank: *There was a dispute about the rightful succession to the throne.*   **4** the order of persons having such a right: *The queen's oldest son is next in succession to the throne.*   **5** in biology, the process of replacing one community of organisms with another.   *n.*
**in succession,**   one after another: *We visited our sick friend several days in succession.*

**succession duty**   a tax payable on inherited money or property.

**suc·ces·sive** (sək ses′iv)   coming one after another;

# suburban 1191 suck

hat, āge, fär; let, ēqual, tėrm; it, īce
hot, ōpen, ôrder; oil, out; cup, pùt, rüle
əbove, takən, pencəl, lemən, circəs
ch, child; ng, long; sh, ship
th, thin; ᴛʜ, then; zh, measure

following in order; consecutive: *It rained for three successive days.*   *adj.*   —**suc·ces′sive·ly,** *adv.*

**suc·ces·sor** (sək ses′ər)   a person or thing that comes next after another in a series; especially a person who succeeds to an office, position, ownership of property, or title: *Elizabeth II was her father's successor to the throne.*   *n.*

**suc·cinct** (sək singkt′)   marked by clear, brief expression; concise: *She gave a succinct account of her meeting with the director.*   *adj.*   —**suc·cinct′ly,** *adv.*   —**suc·cinct′ness,** *n.*

**suc·co·tash** (suk′ə tash′)   a dish made of cooked sweet corn and lima beans or green beans, often with cream, butter, and green onions: *Succotash was originally an American Indian dish.*   *n.*

**suc·cour** or **suc·cor** (suk′ər)   **1** help; aid; relief: *to give succour in time of need.*   **2** a person or thing that gives help or aid.   **3** help or assist a person or animal in distress or need; relieve: *to succour the wounded.*   **1, 2** *n.,* **3** *v.*
☛ *Hom.*   SUCKER.

**suc·cu·lence** (suk′yə ləns)   juiciness.   *n.*

**suc·cu·lent** (suk′yə lənt)   **1** juicy: *a succulent fruit.*   **2** full of vigour and richness; not dull.   **3** any plant having thick, fleshy tissues adapted for storing water, either in the stem, as cactuses, or in the leaves, as agaves: *Most succulents are native to desert or semi-arid regions.*   **1, 2** *adj.,* **3** *n.*

**suc·cumb** (sə kum′)   **1** give way to superior force, etc. or to overwhelming desire; yield: *He succumbed to temptation and stole the money. After several days of fighting, the garrison succumbed.*   **2** die or die of: *She succumbed to her injuries two days after being admitted to hospital.*   *v.*

**such** (such)   **1** of that kind; of the same kind or degree: *I have never seen such a child.*   **2** of the kind that; of a particular kind: *She wore such thin clothes it is no wonder she caught cold.*   **3** of the kind already spoken of or suggested: *The ladies took only tea and coffee and such drinks.*   **4** so great, so bad, so good, etc.: *He is such a liar.*   **5** a certain one or ones not named or identified; some; certain: *The bank was robbed in such and such a town by such and such persons.*   **6** one or more persons or things of a certain kind: *The box contains blankets and towels and such.*   **1–5** *adj.,* **6** *pron.*
**as such,**   **a** as being what is indicated or implied: *A leader, as such, deserves respect.*   **b** in or by itself; intrinsically considered: *Mere good looks, as such, will not take you far.*
**such as,**   **a** the kind or degree that; of a particular kind: *Her behaviour was such as might be expected of a young child.*   **b** of a particular character or kind: *The food, such as it was, was plentiful.*   **c** for example: *members of the dog family, such as the wolf, fox, and jackal.*

**such·like** (such′līk′)   **1** of such kind; of a like kind.   **2** persons or things of the same kind: *deceptions, disguises, and suchlike.*   **1** *adj.,* **2** *pron.*

**suck** (suk)   **1** draw into the mouth: *Lemonade can be*

**sucker**     1192     **suffocate**

sucked through a straw.    **2** draw something from with the mouth: *to suck juice from oranges.*    **3** draw milk from the breast or a bottle.    **4** draw or be drawn by sucking: *He sucked at his pipe.*    **5** drink; take; absorb: *Plants suck up moisture from the earth. A sponge sucks in water.*    **6** draw in; swallow: *The whirlpool sucked down the boat.*    **7** draw air instead of water: *The pump sucked noisily.*    **8** hold in the mouth and lick: *The child sucked a lollipop.*    **9** the act of sucking: *The baby took one suck at the empty bottle and pushed it away.*    **10** a sucking force or sound.    *1–8 v., 9, 10 n.*

**suck·er** (suk′ər)    **1** an animal or thing that sucks.    **2** any of various freshwater fishes that suck in food or have mouths suggesting that they do so.    **3** in some animals, an organ for sucking or holding fast by a sucking force.    **4** a shoot growing from an underground stem or root.    **5** the piston of a suction pump.    **6** the valve of such a piston.    **7** take suckers from corn, tobacco, etc.    **8** form suckers.    **9** *Informal.* a person easily deceived.    **10** a lump of hard candy, usually on a stick: *Lollipops are suckers.*    *1–6, 9, 10 n., 7, 8 v.*
☛ *Hom.* SUCCOUR.

**suck·le** (suk′əl)    **1** feed with milk from the breast, udder, etc.: *The cat suckles her kittens.*    **2** suck at the breast.    **3** nourish; bring up.    *v.*, **suck·led, suck·ling.**

**suck·ling** (suk′ling)    a young animal or child that has not yet been weaned.    *n.*

**su·crase** (sü′krās)    a digestive enzyme in certain plants and in animal intestines which changes sucrose into dextrose and fructose.    *n.*

**su·crose** (sü′krōs)    ordinary sugar obtained from sugar cane, sugar beets, etc.    *n.*

**suc·tion** (suk′shən)    **1** the production of a vacuum by removing all or part of the air in a space with the result that atmospheric pressure forces fluid or gas into the vacant space or causes surfaces to stick together: *Lemonade is drawn through a straw by suction.*    **2** the force caused by sucking out or removing part of the air in a space.    **3** the act or process of sucking.    **4** causing a suction; working by suction: *a suction valve.*    *n.*

**suction cup**    a cuplike device of rubber, etc. designed to adhere to smooth surfaces by creating a vacuum when pressed against them and then let go: *Toy arrows are often tipped with suction cups.*

**Su·da·nese** (sü′də nēz′)    **1** of or having to do with Sudan, a country in northeastern Africa, or its inhabitants.    **2** of or having to do with the Sudan, a vast grassy region in Africa south of the Sahara desert, or its inhabitants.    **3** a native or inhabitant of Sudan or the Sudan.    *1, 2 adj., 3 n., pl.* **Su·da·nese.**

**sud·den** (sud′ən)    **1** not expected: *Our army made a sudden attack on the fort.*    **2** found or hit upon unexpectedly; abrupt: *a sudden turn in a road, a sudden shift in foreign policy.*    **3** quick; rapid: *The cat made a sudden jump at the mouse.*    *adj.* —**sud′den·ness**, *n.*
—**sud′den·ly**, *adv.*

**all of a sudden**,    in a sudden manner: *All of a sudden he stopped and listened.*

**sudden death**    **1** instant or unexpected death.    **2** in sports, an extra game played to break a tie, or an extra period of play for the same purpose, ending as soon as either side scores.

**su·dor·if·er·ous** (sü′də rif′ə rəs)    producing sweat: *sudoriferous glands.*    *adj.*

**su·dor·if·ic** (sü′də rif′ik)    causing sweat.    *adj.*

**suds** (sudz)    **1** soapy water.    **2** the bubbles and foam on soapy water.    **3** any froth or foam.    **4** *Informal.* beer.    **5** *Informal.* form suds: *This shampoo doesn't suds well.*    **6** *Informal.* wash in suds: *Just suds the stockings and hang them to dry.*    *1–4 n.pl., 5, 6 v.*

**sud·sy** (sud′zē)    full of suds; frothy: *sudsy dishwater.*    *adj.*

**sue** (sü)    **1** start a lawsuit against: *He sued the railway because his cow was killed by the engine.*    **2** take legal action: *He decided to sue for damages.*    **3** beg or ask for; plead: *Messengers came suing for peace.*    *v.*, **sued, su·ing.**
—**su′a·ble**, *adj.*

**sue out**,    apply for and get a writ, pardon, etc. from a law court.
☛ *Hom.* SAULT, SIOUX.

**suede** or **suède** (swād)    **1** a kind of soft leather that has a velvety nap on one or both sides.    **2** a kind of cloth with a short nap that looks and feels much like suede.    **3** made of suede.    *n.*

**su·et** (sü′it)    the hard fat about the kidneys and loins of cattle and sheep: *Suet is used in cooking and in making tallow.*    *n.*

**suf–**    a prefix meaning: under, from below, up, near, secondary, etc.; a form of **sub-** occurring before *f*, as in *suffer* and *suffice.*

**suf·fer** (suf′ər)    **1** have pain, grief, injury, etc.: *Sick people suffer.*    **2** have or feel pain, grief, etc.: *She suffered harm from being out in the storm.*    **3** experience harm, loss, etc.: *His business suffered greatly during the war.*    **4** allow; permit: *She suffers no criticism.*    **5** bear with patiently; endure: *I will not suffer insults.*    *v.*
—**suf′fer·er**, *n.*

**suf·fer·a·ble** (suf′ə rə bəl)    that can be endured or allowed.    *adj.*

**suf·fer·ance** (suf′ə rəns)    **1** permission or consent not actually given but only implied by a failure to object or prevent: *They managed to get their supplies through with the sufferance of the neutral country.*    **2** the power to bear or endure; patient endurance.    *n.*

**on sufferance,**    allowed or tolerated, but not really wanted: *Our cousin came with us to the party on sufferance.*

**suf·fer·ing** (suf′ə ring)    **1** pain, trouble, or distress.    **2** ppr. of SUFFER.    *1 n., 2 v.*

**suf·fice** (sə fīs′)    **1** be enough; be sufficient: *The money will suffice for one year.*    **2** satisfy; make content: *A small amount sufficed him.*    *v.*, **suf·ficed, suf·fic·ing.**
**suffice it to say,**    it is enough if I say only (that): *Suffice it to say that he was very upset.*

**suf·fi·cien·cy** (sə fish′ən sē)    **1** a sufficient amount; large enough supply: *The ship had a sufficiency of provisions for a voyage of two months.*    **2** the quality or state of being sufficient; adequacy: *They questioned the sufficiency of the preparations.*    *n., pl.* **suf·fi·cien·cies.**

**suf·fi·cient** (sə fish′ənt)    as much as is needed; enough: *sufficient proof.*    *adj.* —**suf·fi′cient·ly,** *adv.*

**suf·fix** (suf′iks *for noun,* sə fiks′ *for verb*)    **1** a syllable or syllables put at the end of a word to form another word of different meaning or function, as in *badly*, *goodness*, *spoonful*, *amazement*.    **2** add at the end; put after.    *1 n., 2 v.*

**suf·fo·cate** (suf′ə kāt′)    **1** kill by stopping the breath.

**2** have or cause to have difficulty in breathing: *the suffocating smell of sulphur. I was suffocating in that hot, smoky room.* **3** die for lack of air in the lungs: *The victims of the fire had not burned to death but had suffocated.* **4** be or cause to be unable to develop: *Celia longed to escape the suffocating environment of her home town.* *v.*, **suf·fo·cat·ed, suf·fo·cat·ing.** —**suf′fo·cat′ing·ly**, *adv.*

**suf·fo·ca·tion** (suf′ə kā′shən) a suffocating or being SUFFOCATED. *n.*

**suf·fo·ca·tive** (suf′ə kā′tiv) stifling. *adj.*

**suf·frage** (suf′rij) **1** the right to vote; franchise: *Alberta granted suffrage to women in 1916.* **2** a vote, especially a vote in support of a person or proposal. **3** a casting of votes. *n.*

**suf·fra·gette** (suf′rə jet′) a woman who advocates SUFFRAGE (def. 1) for women. *n.*

**suf·fra·gist** (suf′rə jist) a person who favours giving SUFFRAGE (def. 1) to more people, especially to women. *n.*

**suf·fuse** (sə fyüz′) overspread with colour, light, fluid, etc.: *At twilight the sky was suffused with colour. Her eyes were suffused with tears.* *v.*, **suf·fused, suf·fus·ing.**

**suf·fu·sion** (sə fyü′zhən) **1** a suffusing or being suffused. **2** that with which anything is overspread: *a suffusion of light or colour.* *n.*

**Su·fi** (sü′fē) **1** in Islam, any of the various sects which tend toward mysticism and asceticism. **2** a member of any of these sects. *n.*

**Suf·ism** (sü′fiz′əm) the system of mystical thought and ascetic practice of the Sufis. *n.*

**sug–** a form of the prefix **sub-** occurring before *g*, as in *suggest*.

**sug·ar** (shŭg′ər) **1** a sweet substance consisting entirely or mainly of sucrose and obtained especially from sugar cane or sugar beets: *Sugar is much used as a sweetener and preservative of foods and as a source of carbohydrate for the diet.* **2** any of the class of carbohydrates to which this substance belongs: *grape sugar, milk sugar.* **3** mix or sprinkle with sugar; put sugar in or on: *She sugared her tea. We sugared the buns before baking them.* **4** form crystals of sugar: *Honey sugars if kept too long.* **5** make maple sugar by boiling maple syrup until it is thick enough to crystallize (*usually used with* **off**). **6** make more pleasant or agreeable: *He sugared his criticism of the team with some praise for the individual players.* **7** *Informal.* sweetheart; darling. 1, 2, 7 *n.*, 3–6 *v.*

**sugar beet** a variety of beet having a white root with high sugar content, grown commercially for the sugar it yields.

**sugar bush** a grove of SUGAR MAPLES.

Sugar cane

**sugar cane** a very tall grass having a strong, jointed

---

**suffocation** 1193 **suicidal**

hat, āge, fär; let, ēqual, tėrm; it, īce
hot, ōpen, ôrder; oil, out; cup, pùt, rüle
ə*bove,* tak*ə*n, penc*ə*l, lem*ə*n, circ*ə*s
ch, child; ng, long; sh, ship
th, thin; ᴛʜ, then; zh, measure

stem and flat leaves, growing in warm regions: *Sugar cane and sugar beets are the main sources of sugar.*

**sug·ar–coat** (shŭg′ər kōt′) **1** cover with sugar. **2** cause to seem more pleasant or agreeable. *v.*

**sug·ar–coat·ing** (shŭg′ər kō′ting) **1** a covering with sugar. **2** anything that makes something seem more pleasant or agreeable. *n.*

**sugaring off** *Cdn.* **1** the converting of maple syrup into sugar by boiling it until it will crystallize. **2** a gathering of friends and neighbours to assist in this process and enjoy a party afterwards.

**sugar loaf 1** a cone-shaped mass of sugar. **2** something shaped like a sugar loaf, such as a hill or mountain.

**sugar maple** a large maple of eastern North America. It is a valuable timber tree having large, lobed leaves that turn bright crimson, scarlet, or yellow in fall, and yielding a sweet sap that is the main source of maple syrup and maple sugar: *The sugar maple is one of the largest Canadian maples, usually about 24 to 27 metres high, but sometimes reaching a height of 35 metres.*

**sugar of lead** a poisonous crystalline salt, lead acetate, used in making dyes, paints, and varnishes.

**sugar of milk** lactose, the sugar that occurs in milk.

**sug·ar·plum** (shŭg′ər plum′) a piece of candy; bonbon. *n.*

**sug·ar·y** (shŭg′ə rē) **1** consisting of, containing or like sugar. **2** too sweet, pleasant, or agreeable: *sugary compliments, a sugary voice.* *adj.* —**sug′ar·i·ness,** *n.*

**sug·gest** (sə jest′ *or* səg jest′) **1** bring to mind; call up the thought of: *An incident in his own life had suggested the plot of the story.* **2** propose: *Karen suggested a swim, and we all agreed.* **3** show in an indirect way; hint: *His yawns suggested that he would like to go to bed.* *v.*

**sug·gest·i·bil·i·ty** (sə jes′tə bil′ə tē *or* səg jest′tə bil′ə tē) the quality or condition of being SUGGESTIBLE. *n.*

**sug·gest·i·ble** (sə jes′tə bəl *or* səg jest′tə bəl) **1** easily influenced by SUGGESTION. **2** that can be SUGGESTED. *adj.*

**sug·ges·tion** (sə jes′chən *or* səg jes′chən) **1** a suggesting: *The trip was made at her suggestion.* **2** the thing suggested: *The picnic was an excellent suggestion.* **3** the calling up of one idea by another because they are connected or associated in some way. **4** a very small amount; slight trace: *She spoke English with just a suggestion of an accent.* *n.*

**sug·ges·tive** (sə jes′tiv *or* səg jes′tiv) **1** tending to suggest ideas, acts, or feelings: *a mild breeze suggestive of spring.* **2** tending to suggest something improper or indecent; risqué: *a suggestive remark.* *adj.* —**sug·ges′tive·ness,** *n.*

**su·i·cid·al** (sü′ə sī′dəl) **1** having to do with SUICIDE. **2** tending to consider committing SUICIDE: *He had been suicidal for some time.* **3** ruinous to one's own interests;

disastrous to oneself: *It would be suicidal for a store to sell many things below cost.* adj. —**su′i·cid′al·ly,** adv.

**su·i·cide** (sü′ə sīd′) **1** the killing of oneself on purpose. **2** a person who kills himself or herself on purpose. **3** the destruction of one's own interests or prospects. n.
**commit suicide,** kill oneself on purpose.

**suit** (süt) **1** a set of clothes to be worn together. **2** provide with clothes. **3** a case in a law court; application to a court for justice: *He started a suit to collect damages for his injuries.* **4** make suitable; make fit: *to suit the punishment to the crime.* **5** be suitable for; agree with: *The Canadian climate suits apples and wheat, but not oranges and tea.* **6** be agreeable or convenient to; please; satisfy: *Which date suits you best?* **7** be becoming to: *Her blue dress suits her fair skin.* **8** one of the four sets of cards in a deck: *Spades, hearts, diamonds, and clubs are the four suits.* **9** a request; asking; wooing. 1, 3, 8, 9 n., 2, 4–7 v.
**follow suit,** **a** play a card of the same suit as that first played. **b** follow the example of another.
**suit oneself,** do as one pleases.

**suit·a·bil·i·ty** (sü′tə bil′ə tē) the quality or state of being suitable. n.

**suit·a·ble** (sü′tə bəl) right for the occasion, purpose, condition, etc.; fitting; appropriate: *The park gives the children a suitable playground.* adj. —**suit′a·bly,** adv.

**suit·case** (süt′kās) a more or less rigid, flat, rectangular travelling bag. n.

**suit coat** or **suit-coat** (süt′kōt′) the long-sleeved upper part, or jacket, of a suit. n.

**suite** (swēt) **1** a set of connected rooms to be used as a unit by one person or group: *a suite in a hotel. She lives in a large suite above a store.* **2** a set of furniture that matches: *a bedroom suite.* **3** any set or series of like things. **4** in music, an instrumental composition consisting of a set of different movements: *A suite was originally an instrumental composition made up of a set of dances. The queen travelled with a large suite.* **5** a group of attendants: n.
☞ Hom. SWEET.

**suit·ing** (sü′ting) **1** cloth for making suits. **2** ppr. of SUIT. 1 n., 2 v.

**suit·or** (sü′tər) **1** a man who is courting a woman: *She had many suitors.* **2** a person bringing a suit in a law court. **3** anyone who sues or petitions. n.

**sul·fa** (sul′fə) See SULPHA. adj.

**sul·fa·di·a·zine** (sul′fə dī′ə zēn) See SULPHADIAZINE. n.

**sul·fa·nil·a·mide** (sul′fə nil′ə mīd′) See SULPHANILAMIDE. n.

**sul·fate** (sul′fāt) See SULPHATE. n.

**sul·fide** (sul′fīd) See SULPHIDE. n.

**sul·fite** (sul′fīt) See SULPHITE. n.

**sul·fur** (sul′fər) See SULPHUR. n.

**sul·fu·rate** (sul′fə rāt′ or sul′fyə rāt′) See SULPHURATE. v., sul·fu·rat·ed, sul·fu·rat·ing.

**sul·fu·ra·tion** (sul′fə rā′shən) See SULPHURATION. n.

**sulfur dioxide** See SULPHUR DIOXIDE.

**sul·fu·re·ous** (sul fyü′rē əs) See SULPHUREOUS. adj.

**sul·fu·ric** (sul fyü′rik) See SULPHURIC. adj.

**sulfuric acid** See SULPHURIC ACID.

**sul·fur·ous** (sul′fə rəs or sul fyü′rəs) See SULPHUROUS. adj.

**sulfurous acid** See SULPHUROUS ACID.

**sulk** (sulk) **1** hold aloof in a sullen manner; be sulky: *The child stood sulking in a corner.* **2** a fit of sulking; a sulky mood: *She was in a sulk because nothing was going her way.* **3** **the sulks,** pl. ill humour shown by sulking: *He has the sulks.* 1 v., 2, 3 n.

**sulk·y**[1] (sul′kē) silent and bad-humoured because of resentment; sullen: *He always became sulky as a child if he couldn't get his own way.* adj., **sulk·i·er, sulk·i·est.** —**sulk′i·ly,** adv. —**sulk′i·ness,** n.

A sulky for racing

**sulk·y**[2] (sul′kē) a very light two-wheeled carriage for one person. n., pl. **sulk·ies.**

**sul·len** (sul′ən) **1** silent because of bad humour or anger: *The sullen child refused to answer my question.* **2** showing bad humour or anger: *a sullen reply.* **3** gloomy; dismal: *The sullen skies threatened rain.* adj. —**sul′len·ly,** adv. —**sul′len·ness,** n.

**sul·ly** (sul′ē) soil; stain; tarnish: *to sully a person's reputation.* v., **sul·lied, sul·ly·ing.**

**sul·pha** or **sul·fa** (sul′fə) of or having to do with SULPHA DRUGS. adj.

**sul·pha·di·a·zine** or **sul·fa·di·a·zine** (sul′fə dī′ə zēn′) a SULPHA DRUG used mainly in treating meningitis, pneumonia, and infections of the intestines. n.

**sulpha drug** or **sulfa drug** any of a group of synthetic organic drugs, such as SULPHANILAMIDE, or a drug derived from it, that are used in treating various infections or diseases caused by bacteria.

**sul·pha·nil·a·mide** or **sul·fa·nil·a·mide** (sul′fə nil′ə mīd′) a white, crystalline, synthetic compound derived from coal tar, from which most SULPHA DRUGS are derived. n.

**sul·phate** or **sul·fate** (sul′fāt) a salt or ester of SULPHURIC ACID. n.

**sul·phide** or **sul·fide** (sul′fīd) a compound of SULPHUR with another element or radical. n.

**sul·phite** or **sul·fite** (sul′fīt) a salt or ester of SULPHUROUS ACID. n.

**sul·phur** or **sul·fur** (sul′fər) **1** a light-yellow, non-metallic chemical element that burns with a blue flame and a stifling odour: *Sulphur is used mainly in making gunpowder and matches, in vulcanizing rubber, and in treating skin diseases.* Symbol: S **2** light, somewhat greenish yellow. **3** any of several kinds of yellow butterfly. **4** treat with sulphur or a compound of sulphur. *1–3 n., 2 adj., 4 v.*

**sul·phu·rate** or **sul·fur·ate** (sul′fə rāt′ *or* sul′fyə rāt′) combine, treat, or impregnate with SULPHUR, the fumes of burning sulphur, etc. *v.*, **sul·phu·rat·ed**, **sul·phu·rat·ing**.

**sul·phur·a·tion** or **sul·fur·a·tion** (sul′fə rā′shən) **1** the act or process of treating with SULPHUR. **2** the state of being treated with SULPHUR. *n.*

**sulphur dioxide** or **sulfur dioxide** a heavy, colourless gas that has a sharp odour, used as a bleach, disinfectant, preservative, and refrigerant.

**sul·phu·re·ous** or **sul·fu·re·ous** (sul fyü′rē əs) **1** of, containing, or like SULPHUR. **2** SULPHUR-coloured; greenish yellow. *adj.*

**sul·phu·ric** or **sul·fu·ric** (sul fyü′rik) **1** of or having to do with SULPHUR. **2** containing SULPHUR, especially with a higher valence than SULPHUROUS compounds. *adj.*

**sulphuric acid** or **sulfuric acid** a heavy, colourless, oily, very strong acid; oil of vitriol: *Sulphuric acid is used in making explosives, in refining petroleum, etc.*

**sul·phur·ous** or **sul·fur·ous** (sul′fə rəs *or* sul fyü′rəs) **1** of or having to do with SULPHUR. **2** containing SULPHUR, especially with a lower valence than SULPHURIC compounds. **3** like SULPHUR, especially sulphur that is burning. **4** of or like the fires of hell; hellish. *adj.*

**sulphurous acid** or **sulfurous acid** a weak, unstable, colourless acid known only in solution or in the form of its salts, used as a bleach, reducing agent, etc.

**sul·tan** (sul′tən) the ruler of a Moslem country: *Turkey was ruled by a sultan until 1922. n.*

**sul·tan·a** (sul tan′ə) **1** the wife of a SULTAN. **2** the mother, sister, or daughter of a SULTAN. **3** a kind of small seedless raisin. *n.*

**sul·tan·ate** (sul′tə nāt′) **1** the position, authority, or period of rule of a SULTAN. **2** the territory ruled over by a SULTAN. *n.*

**sul·try** (sul′trē) **1** of weather or atmosphere, uncomfortably hot, humid, and close. **2** very hot; fiery: *the sultry sun.* **3** having or showing passion or sensuality: *a sultry glance. adj.*, **sul·tri·er**, **sul·tri·est**. —**sul′tri·ness**, *n.*

**sum** (sum) **1** an amount of money: *He paid a huge sum for that bicycle.* **2** the number or quantity obtained by adding two or more numbers or quantities together. See ADDITION for picture. **3** a problem in arithmetic: *She's very good at sums.* **4** the whole amount; total amount: *To win the prize seemed to her the sum of happiness.* **5** find the total of. *1–4 n., 5 v.*, **summed, sum·ming**.
**sum up**, **a** express or tell briefly; summarize: *to sum up the main points of a lesson.* **b** collect or add up into a whole. **c** review the chief points of evidence to a jury before it retires to consider a verdict. **d** form or express an idea of the qualities or character of; size up.
☛ *Hom.* SOME.

**sum–** a form of the prefix **sub–** occurring in some cases before *m*, as in *summon.*

**su·mac** (sü′mak *or* shü′mak) **1** any of a closely related group of trees, shrubs, and vines having compound leaves that turn a brilliant red in the fall: *Some species, such as the poison sumac, have leaves that are poisonous to the touch.* **2** a common species of sumac, also called **staghorn sumach**, having cone-shaped clusters of red fruit,

**sulphurate**    **1195**    **summerhouse**

hat, āge, fär; let, ēqual, tėrm; it, īce
hot, ōpen, ôrder, oil, out; cup, pùt, rüle
əbove, tāken, pencəl, lemən, circəs
ch, child; ng, long; sh, ship
th, thin; ᴛʜ, then; zh, measure

native to eastern Canada and often planted as an ornamental tree. **3** the dried, powdered leaves and flowers of various sumacs, used in tanning and dying. *n.*

**Su·ma·tran** (sü mä′trən *or* sü mat′rən) **1** of or having to do with the island of Sumatra in Indonesia or its inhabitants. **2** a native or inhabitant of Sumatra. *1 adj., 2 n.*

**Su·me·ri·an** (sü mēr′ē ən *or* sü mer′ē ən) **1** of or having to do with the earliest inhabitants of Sumer, an ancient region in the valley of the Euphrates River, or their language. **2** a native or inhabitant of Sumer. **3** their language. *1 adj., 2, 3 n.*

**sum·ma cum lau·de** (sùm′ə kùm′ lou′dā) *Latin.* with the highest honour.

**sum·ma·ri·ly** (sum′ə rə lē *or* sə mer′ə lē) in a SUMMARY (def. 3) manner; briefly or without delay. *adv.*

**sum·ma·ri·za·tion** (sum′ər ə zā′shən *or* sum′ə rī zā′shən) **1** the act of summarizing. **2** a SUMMARY. *n.*

**sum·ma·rize** (sum′ə rīz′) make or be a SUMMARY; express briefly: *The review summarized the plot of the novel. At the end of the speech, she took three minutes to summarize. v.*, **sum·ma·rized, sum·ma·riz·ing**.

**sum·ma·ry** (sum′ə rē) **1** a brief statement giving the main points: *The history book had a summary at the end of each chapter.* **2** concise and comprehensive; brief. **3** direct and prompt; without delay or formality: *a summary dismissal. We took summary measures to deal with the fire.* *1 n., pl.* **sum·ma·ries**; *2, 3 adj.*
☛ *Hom.* SUMMERY.

**summary offence** in law, a criminal offence that is less serious than an INDICTABLE OFFENCE. In Canada, a summary offence in most cases carries a maximum penalty of a $500 fine or six months' imprisonment, or both.

**sum·ma·tion** (su mā′shən) **1** the process of finding the sum or total; addition. **2** the total. **3** in law, the final charge of a judge to the jury before it considers the verdict. *n.*

**sum·mer** (sum′ər) **1** the warmest season of the year; season of the year between spring and autumn. **2** a year of age: *a girl of seventeen summers.* **3** a period or stage of maturity or fulfilment: *He was in the summer of his life.* **4** of or in summer: *the summer sun, summer holidays.* **5** fit for or used in summer: *summer clothes, a summer cottage.* **6** pass or spend the summer: *to summer at the seashore.* **7** keep or feed during the summer: *The cattle were summered on the mountain.* *1–5 n., 6, 7 v.*

**summer fallow** land ploughed and left unseeded for a season or more, in order to destroy weeds, improve the soil, etc.; FALLOW (def. 3).

**sum·mer-fal·low** (sum′ər fal′ō *or, esp. in the Prairie Provinces,* sum′ər fol′ō) prepare land as SUMMER FALLOW. *v.*

**sum·mer·house** (sum′ər hous′) a building in a park or garden in which to sit in warm weather: *Summerhouses often have no walls. n.*

**summer resort** a place in the mountains, on a lake, etc. where people go for summer holidays.

**sum·mer·sault** (sum′ər solt′) See SOMERSAULT. *n., v.*

**summer savory** a European herb of the mint family widely grown for its leaves, which are used as a flavouring in cooking meats and vegetables.

**summer solstice** the time in the Northern Hemisphere when the sun is farthest north from the equator, about June 21 or 22.

**summer squash** any of various squashes used as a vegetable in summer before they are fully ripe.

**sum·mer·time** (sum′ər tīm′) the summer season; summer. *n.*

**sum·mer·y** (sum′ə rē) of, like, or fit for summer: *a summery breeze. She wore a light, summery dress.* *adj.* ☞ *Hom.* SUMMARY.

**sum·mit** (sum′it) **1** the highest point; top; peak: *the summit of a mountain.* **2** the highest degree or state: *The summit of her ambition was to be a foreign correspondent.* **3** a conference at the highest level. *n.*

**sum·mon** (sum′ən) **1** call with authority or urgency; order to come; send for: *to summon firefighters to put out a fire. A telegram summoned Joselle home.* **2** call together: *to summon an assembly.* **3** order or notify formally to appear in court, especially to answer a charge. **4** call upon: *to summon a fort to surrender.* **5** stir to action; rouse: *Bela summoned his courage and entered the deserted house.* *v.* —**sum′mon·er,** *n.*

**sum·mons** (sum′ənz) **1** an urgent or authoritative call for the presence or attendance of a person. **2** in law, an order or notice to a person from an authority to appear before a court or judge on or before a certain date, especially to answer as a defendant to a charge made against him or her. **3** the written or printed notice by which such an order is made: *The police officer handed her a summons.* **4** summon to court. **5** something that summons; a message or signal to come or appear: *He heard the summons of his friend's car horn.* 1–3, 5 *n.,* pl. **sum·mons·es;** 4 *v.*

**sum·mum bo·num** (sùm′əm bō′nəm) *Latin.* the highest or chief good.

**sump** (sump) **1** a pit or reservoir for collecting water, oil, sewage, etc. **2** a pool at the bottom of a mine, where water collects and from which it is pumped. *n.*

**sump pump** a pump for removing collected water, sewage, etc. from a sump.

**sump·ter** (sump′tər) a pack animal. *n.*

**sump·tu·ar·y** (sump′chü er′ē) having to do with the regulating of expenses; especially, limiting personal expenditure on moral or religious grounds to prevent extravagance: *sumptuary laws.* *adj.*

**sump·tu·ous** (sump′chü əs) costly; magnificent; rich: *The emperor gave a sumptuous banquet.* *adj.* —**sump′tu·ous·ly,** *adv.* —**sump′tu·ous·ness,** *n.*

**sum total** **1** the total amount added up. **2** the total result; everything included.

**sun** (sun) **1** the brightest heavenly body in the sky; the star around which the earth and other planets revolve: *The sun lights and warms the earth.* **2** the light and warmth of the sun: *to sit in the sun.* **3** any heavenly body made up of burning gas and having satellites: *Many stars are suns and have their worlds that travel around them.* **4** something like the sun in brightness or splendour; something that is a source of light, honour, glory, or prosperity. **5** expose to the sun's rays: *The swimmers sunned themselves on the beach.* **6** warm or dry in the sunshine. 1–4 *n.,* 5, 6 *v.,* **sunned, sun·ning.**
**from sun to sun,** from sunrise to sunset.
**in the sun,** in a position easily seen.
**under the sun,** on earth; in the world.
☞ *Hom.* SON.

**Sun.** Sunday.

**sun·baked** (sun′bākt′) **1** baked by exposure to the sun: *sunbaked bricks.* **2** hardened, dried out, or cracked, etc. by too much sunlight: *sunbaked soil.* *adj.*

**sun·bath** or **sun bath** (sun′bath′) an exposure of the body to sunshine or a sunlamp. *n.*

**sun·bathe** (sun′bāᴛʜ′) take a SUNBATH; bask in the sun. *v.,* **sun·bathed, sun·bath·ing.** —**sun′bath·er,** *n.*

**sun·beam** (sun′bēm′) a ray of sunlight. *n.*

**sun·bon·net** (sun′bon′it) a large bonnet that shades the face and neck. *n.*

**sun·burn** (sun′bėrn′) **1** an inflammation of the skin caused by too much exposure to the rays of the sun: *A sunburn can be very painful.* **2** get a sunburn: *Her skin sunburns very quickly.* **3** cause to get a sunburn: *He is sunburned from a day at the beach.* 1 *n.,* 2, 3 *v.,* **sun·burned** or **sun·burnt, sun·burn·ing.**

**sun·burnt** (sun′bėrnt′) a pt. and a pp. of SUNBURN. *v.*

**sun·burst** (sun′bėrst′) **1** the sun shining suddenly through a break in clouds. **2** a brooch with jewels arranged to look like the sun with its rays. *n.*

**sun·dae** (sun′dā′ *or* sun′dē) a serving of ice cream with syrup, crushed fruits, nuts, etc. poured over it. *n.* ☞ *Hom.* SUNDAY.

**Sun·day** (sun′dā′ *or* sun′dē) **1** the first day of the week, observed in Canada and many other countries as the general day of rest and relaxation: *Most businesses are closed on Sundays. Sunday is the traditional day of rest and worship among most Christians.* **2** of, having to do with, or taking place on Sunday: *Sunday closing.* **3** associated with Sunday, especially as a special day or a day of leisure and recreation: *a Sunday painter, Sunday drivers, Sunday clothes.* *n.*
**a month of Sundays,** an indefinitely long time: *That wouldn't happen again in a month of Sundays.*
☞ *Hom.* SUNDAE.
☞ *Etym.* From OE *sunnandæg* 'day of the sun'.

**Sunday best** *Informal.* best clothes.

**Sunday school** **1** a school held by a Christian church on Sundays for teaching religion, especially to children. **2** its members.

**sun·der** (sun′dər) separate; part; sever; split. *v.*

**sun·dew** (sun′dyü *or* sun′dü) **1** any of a closely related group of insect-eating bog plants found throughout the world, having leaves covered with hairs with glands at the tips. The glands produce a sticky, glistening substance resembling dewdrops that attracts and captures insects. **2** referring to a small family of insect-eating plants which includes the sundews and three other groups of plants: *The Venus's-flytrap is a member of the sundew family.* *n.*

A sundial

**sun·di·al** (sun′dī′əl *or* sun′dīl′) an instrument for telling the time of day by the position of the shadow of a rod or pointer cast by the sun on a usually horizontal disk marked off in hours. *n.*

**sun·dog** (sun′dog′) a bright spot near the sun; parhelion. *n.*

**sun·down** (sun′doun′) SUNSET. *n.*

**sun–dried** (sun′drīd′) dried by exposure to the sun: *sun-dried apples. adj.*

**sun·dries** (sun′drēz) sundry things; items not named; odds and ends. *n.pl.*

**sun·dry** (sun′drē) **1** several; various: *From sundry hints, Hans guessed he was to be given a bicycle for his birthday.* **2** an indefinite number (now used only in the idiom **all and sundry**). 1 *adj.,* 2 *pron.*
**all and sundry,** everybody; one and all: *He sent out invitations to all and sundry to visit him in his new house.*

**sun·fast** (sun′fast′) made to resist fading by sunlight: *sunfast colours. adj.*

**sun·fish** (sun′fish′) **1** any of a family of freshwater food and game fishes of the temperate regions of North America, often very colourful and having fins with needle-sharp rays: *The most popular sunfishes in Canada are the smallmouth bass and the largemouth bass.* **2** referring to this family of fish: *The sunfish family is made up of about 25 species.* **3** any of a related group of large fish found in warm seas throughout the world, having a scale-less, silvery body that is about as deep as it is long, giving the fish a chopped-off look: *Sunfish often rest on the surface of the water in the sun.* *n., pl.* **sun·fish** *or* **sun·fish·es.**

**sun·flow·er** (sun′flou′ər) **1** a very tall annual plant of the same family as the aster and black-eyed Susan, having large leaves and a very large, flat flower head surrounded by rays of long yellow petals: *The sunflower is native to North and South America, but is widely cultivated throughout the world especially for its seeds and the oil they yield.* **2** any of a number of other annual and perennial plants closely related to the common sunflower, such as the prairie sunflower. *n.*

**sung** (sung) pp. of SING: *Many songs were sung at the concert. v.*

**sun·glass·es** (sun′glas′iz) eyeglasses with tinted lenses designed to protect the eyes from direct sunlight or glare. *n.pl.*

**sun–god** (sun′god′) a god who personifies the sun or is associated with it. *n.*

**sunk** (sungk) a pt. and pp. of SINK: *The ship had sunk to the bottom. v.*

**sunk·en** (sung′kən) **1** sunk: *a sunken ship.* **2** submerged: *a sunken rock.* **3** situated or constructed below the general level: *a sunken garden, a sunken living room.* **4** fallen in; hollow: *sunken eyes. adj.*

**sun·lamp** (sun′lamp′) an electric lamp that gives out ultraviolet rays, used for therapy or for producing an artificial suntan. *n.*

**sun·less** (sun′lis) without sunlight; dark: *a sunless day, sunless caverns. adj.*

**sun·light** (sun′līt′) the light of the sun; sunshine: *We moved the plants into the sunlight. This room doesn't get any sunlight. n.*

**sun·lit** (sun′lit′) lighted by the sun: *a sunlit meadow. adj.*

**Sun·ni** (sü′nē) **1** the larger of the two great divisions of Islam. **2** a member of this division. Compare with SHIAH. *n., pl.* **Sun·nis.**

**sun·ny** (sun′ē) **1** having much sunshine: *a sunny day.* **2** exposed to, lighted by, or warmed by the direct rays of the sun: *a sunny room.* **3** bright; cheerful; happy: *a sunny disposition. The baby gave a sunny smile. adj.,* **sun·ni·er, sun·ni·est.** —**sun′ni·ly,** *adv.* —**sun′ni·ness,** *n.*

**sun parlour** *or* **parlor** a room having many windows to let in sunlight.

**sun porch** a porch enclosed largely by glass or screen, designed to admit plenty of sunlight.

**sun·proof** (sun′prüf′) impervious to or unaffected by the rays of the sun: *These sunproof curtains will not fade. adj.*

**sun·rise** (sun′rīz′) **1** the rising of the sun; the first appearance of the sun in the morning: *There was a beautiful sunrise this morning.* **2** the time of day when the sun rises; the beginning of day: *We were packed and ready to go before sunrise. n.*

**sun·roof** (sun′rüf′) **1** an automobile roof having a panel that can be opened to admit air and sunlight. **2** the panel that opens. *n.*

**sun·room** (sun′rüm′) a room with many windows to let in sunlight. *n.*

**sun·screen** (sun′skrēn′) something that gives protection from the sun; especially, a substance put on the skin to block ultraviolet rays and prevent sunburn. *n.*

**sun·set** (sun′set′) **1** the setting of the sun; the last appearance of the sun in the evening. **2** the time of day when the sun sets; the close of a day: *They expect to be back by sunset.* **3** any decline or close: *Old age is often thought of as the sunset of life. n.*

**sun·shade** (sun′shād′) an umbrella, parasol, awning, etc. used to provide protection from the sun. *n.*

**sun·shine** (sun′shīn′) **1** the shining of the sun: *They had two days of sunshine during their holidays.* **2** light and heat from the rays of the sun: *Sunshine flooded the whole room. The sunshine made us drowsy.* **3** a place or surface on which the sun shines: *Kee was asleep in the sunshine.* **4** brightness; cheerfulness; happiness: *the sunshine of her smile. n.*

**sun·shin·y** (sun′shī′nē) **1** having much sunshine. **2** bright; cheerful; happy. *adj.,* **sun·shin·i·er, sun·shin·i·est.**

**sun·spot** (sun′spot′) one of the dark spots that appear at regular intervals on the surface of the sun: *Sunspots are usually visible only with a telescope. n.*

**sun·stroke** (sun′strōk′) a heatstroke caused by overexposure to direct sunlight: *Sunstroke is serious* because the body's sweating system has stopped functioning and can no longer cool the body. *n.*

**sun·tan** (sun′tan′) a bronzed colouring of a person's skin resulting from exposure to the sun. *n.*

**sun·tanned** (sun′tand′) having a suntan; browned by the sun: *suntanned vacationers.* *adj.*

**sun time** *Informal.* standard time.

**sun–up** (sun′up′) SUNRISE. *n.*

**sup**[1] (sup) eat the evening meal; take supper: *Chin supped alone on chicken and rice.* *v.*, **supped, sup·ping.**

**sup**[2] (sup) SIP. *v.*, **supped, sup·ping.**

**sup–** a form of the prefix **sub-** occurring before *p*, as in *suppress.*

**sup.** 1 superior. 2 superlative.

**su·per** (sü′pər) *Informal.* 1 a SUPERNUMERARY; extra person or thing: *Mobs on the stage are usually made up of supers.* 2 SUPERINTENDENT. 3 excellent; wonderful. *1, 2 n., 3 adj.*

**super–** a prefix meaning: 1 over; above, as in *superimpose, superstructure.* 2 besides; extra, as in *supertax.* 3 in high proportion; to excess; exceedingly, as in *superabundant, supersensitive.* 4 surpassing, as in *superman, supernatural.*

**su·per·a·ble** (sü′pə rə bəl) capable of being overcome; surmountable. *adj.* —**su′per·a·bly,** *adv.*

**su·per·a·bound** (sü′pə rə bound′) 1 be very abundant. 2 be too abundant. *v.*

**su·per·a·bun·dance** (sü′pə rə bun′dəns) a greater amount than is needed; surplus; excess: *a superabundance of rain.* *n.*

**su·per·a·bun·dant** (sü′pə rə bun′dənt) more than is needed; excessive. *adj.*

**su·per·an·nu·ate** (sü′pə ran′yü āt′) 1 retire on a pension because of age or infirmity. 2 make old-fashioned or out-of-date. *v.*, **su·per·an·nu·at·ed, su·per·an·nu·at·ing.**

**su·per·an·nu·at·ed** (sü′pə ran′yü ā′tid) 1 retired on a pension. 2 too old for work, service, etc. 3 old-fashioned; out-of-date. 4 pt. and pp. of SUPERANNUATE. *1–3 adj., 4 v.*

**su·per·an·nu·a·tion** (sü′pə ran′yü ā′shən) 1 a superannuating or being superannuated. 2 a pension or allowance granted to a superannuated person. *n.*

**su·perb** (sú pėrb′) 1 grand; stately; majestic; magnificent; splendid: *superb jewels, superb scenery.* 2 rich; elegant; sumptuous: *a superb dinner.* 3 very fine; first-rate; excellent: *The actor gave a superb performance.* *adj.* —**su·perb′ly,** *adv.*

**su·per·car·go** (sü′pər kär′gō) an officer on a merchant ship, who has charge of the cargo and the business affairs of the voyage. *n., pl.* **su·per·car·goes** or **su·per·car·gos.**

**su·per·charge** (sü′pər chärj′) 1 charge with excessive vigour, emotion, etc.: *The atmosphere at the trial was supercharged with tension.* 2 augment the power or efficiency of an engine, vehicle, etc. by fitting it with a SUPERCHARGER. *v.*, **su·per·charged, su·per·charg·ing.**

**su·per·charg·er** (sü′pər chär′jər) a blower, pump, etc. in an INTERNAL-COMBUSTION ENGINE for forcing more of the mixture of air and gasoline vapour into the cylinders than the action of the pistons would draw: *A supercharger is designed to increase the power or efficiency of an engine.* *n.*

**su·per·cil·i·ar·y** (sü′pər sil′ē er′ē) of or near the eyebrow; over the eye. *adj.*

**su·per·cil·i·ous** (sü′pər sil′ē əs) haughty, proud, and contemptuous; disdainful; showing scorn or indifference because of a feeling of superiority: *supercilious politeness, a supercilious desk clerk.* *adj.* —**su′per·cil′i·ous·ly,** *adv.*

**su·per·com·pu·ter** (sü′pər kəm pyü′tər) a very large and complex computer which can perform many operations at the same time. *n.*

**su·per·con·duc·tive** (sü′pər kən duk′tiv) showing SUPERCONDUCTIVITY. *adj.*

**su·per·con·duc·tiv·i·ty** (sü′pər kon′duk tiv′ə tē) the property of being able to conduct electricity without resistance, found in lead and tin and some other metals at temperatures near absolute zero (−273.16°C). *n.*

**su·per·con·duc·tor** (sü′pər kən duk′tər) a SUPERCONDUCTIVE metal. *n.*

**su·per·e·rog·a·to·ry** (sü′pə rə rog′ə tô′rē) 1 doing more than duty requires: *a supererogatory act of assistance.* 2 unnecessary; superfluous: *a supererogatory explanation of what everyone had seen quite clearly.* *adj.*

**su·per·fi·cial** (sü′pər fish′əl) 1 of, on, or affecting the surface: *superficial burns, superficial measurement.* 2 concerned with or understanding only what is on the surface; not thorough; shallow or casual: *a superficial reading.* 3 of or having to do with outward appearance only; general or external: *a superficial resemblance.* *adj.* —**su′per·fi′cial·ly,** *adv.*

**su·per·fi·ci·al·i·ty** (sü′pər fish′ē al′ə tē) 1 the quality or state of being SUPERFICIAL. 2 something SUPERFICIAL. *n., pl.* **su·per·fi·ci·al·i·ties.**

**su·per·fi·cial·ness** (sü′pər fish′əl nəs) the quality or state of being SUPERFICIAL. *n.*

**su·per·fine** (sü′pər fīn′) 1 very fine in texture or size; extra fine: *superfine cotton, superfine sugar.* 2 too refined or subtle: *superfine distinctions.* 3 of commercial goods, etc. very high in quality: *superfine craftsmanship, superfine china.* *adj.*

**su·per·flu·i·ty** (sü′pər flü′ə tē) 1 a greater amount than is needed; excess. 2 something not needed: *Luxuries are superfluities.* *n., pl.* **su·per·flu·i·ties.**

**su·per·flu·ous** (sú pėr′flü əs) 1 more than is sufficient or necessary: *In writing telegrams omit superfluous words.* 2 uncalled for; irrelevant: *a superfluous remark.* *adj.* —**su·per′flu·ous·ly,** *adv.*

**su·per·gi·ant** (sü′pər jī′ənt) a very large and brilliant star with a diameter greater than that of the sun, such as Betelgeuse. *n.*

**su·per·heat** (sü′pər hēt′) 1 heat a liquid above its boiling point without producing vaporization. 2 heat steam apart from water until it resembles a dry or perfect gas. 3 overheat. *v.*

**su·per·het·er·o·dyne** (sü′pər het′ər ə dīn′) 1 of or having to do with a kind of radio reception in which signals are received at a supersonic frequency and combined with locally produced oscillations of a lower supersonic frequency before being rectified and amplified. 2 a superheterodyne radio receiving set. *1 adj., 2 n.*

**su·per·high frequency** (sü′pər hī′) the range of radio frequencies between 3 and 30 gigahertz: *Superhigh frequency is the second highest range in the radio spectrum, above ultrahigh and below extremely high frequency.*

**su·per·high·way** (sü′pər hī′wā or sü′pər hī′wā′) a high-speed expressway or freeway divided by a median and having two or more traffic lanes in each direction. *n.*

**su·per·hu·man** (sü′pər hyü′mən) above or beyond ordinary human power, experience, etc.: *By superhuman effort, they survived the winter.* *adj.*
—**su′per·hu′man·ly,** *adv.*

**su·per·im·pose** (sü′pə rim pōz′) 1 put on top of something else. 2 put or join as an addition. *v.*, **su·per·im·posed, su·per·im·pos·ing.**

**su·per·im·po·si·tion** (sü′pə rim pə zish′ən) superimposing or being SUPERIMPOSEd. *n.*

**su·per·in·cum·bent** (sü′pə rin kum′bənt) lying or resting above and exerting pressure on something else: *a superincumbent stratum of rock.* *adj.*

**su·per·in·duce** (sü′pə rin dyüs′ or sü′pə rin düs′) bring in or develop as an addition. *v.*, **su·per·in·duced, su·per·in·duc·ing.**

**su·per·in·duc·tion** (sü′pə rin duk′shən) a superinducing or being SUPERINDUCEd. *n.*

**su·per·in·tend** (sü′pə rin tend′ or sü′prin tend′) oversee and direct work or workers; act as a SUPERINTENDENT of; supervise. *v.*

**su·per·in·ten·dence** (sü′pə rin ten′dəns or sü′prin ten′dəns) guidance and direction; SUPERVISION. *n.*

**su·per·in·ten·den·cy** (sü′pə rin ten′dən sē or sü′prin ten′dən sē) the position, authority, or work of a SUPERINTENDENT. *n., pl.* **su·per·in·tend·en·cies.**

**su·per·in·ten·dent** (sü′pə rin ten′dənt or sü′prin ten′dənt) 1 a person who oversees, directs, or manages; supervisor: *a superintendent of schools, a superintendent of a factory.* 2 a police officer of high rank. 3 a person in charge of the maintenance of an apartment building, office building, etc. *n.*

**su·pe·ri·or** (sə pē′rē ər) 1 very good; excellent: *superior work in school.* 2 higher in quality; better; greater: *The last brand of coffee we tried was superior to this.* 3 higher in position, rank, importance, etc.: *a superior officer.* 4 a person who is higher in rank or more accomplished than another: *A captain is a lieutenant's superior.* 5 showing a feeling of being above others; proud: *superior airs, superior manners.* 6 the head of a monastery or convent. 1–3, 5 *adj.,* 4, 6 *n.*
**superior to,** above yielding or giving in to: *superior to flattery.*

**su·pe·ri·or·i·ty** (sə pē′rē ô′rə tē) the quality or state of being SUPERIOR: *She was convinced of the superiority of the new data processing system over the old one.* *n.*

**superiority complex** a feeling of being superior to other people; an exaggerated feeling of self-importance.

**superl.** superlative.

**su·per·la·tive** (sü pėr′lə tiv, sü pėr′lə tiv, or sə pėr′lə tiv) 1 of the highest kind; above all others; supreme: *My grandmother had superlative wisdom.* 2 a person or thing above all others; supreme example. 3 in grammar, the third of three degrees of comparison, used when qualities are being compared: *Fairest* is the superlative of *fair.* *Most quickly* is the superlative of *quickly.* 4 expressing the highest degree of comparison of an adjective or adverb.

---

# superhigh frequency  1199  superscription

hat, āge, fär; let, ēqual, tėrm; it, īce
hot, ōpen, ôrder; oil, out; cup, pút, rüle
əbove, takən, pencəl, lemən, circəs
ch, child; ng, long; sh, ship
th, thin; ᴛʜ, then; zh, measure

---

*Fairest, best,* and *most slowly* are the superlative forms of *fair, good,* and *slowly.* 5 the form or combination of words that shows this degree. 1, 4 *adj.,* 2, 3, 5 *n.*
—**su·per′la·tive·ly,** *adv.* —**su·per′la·tive·ness,** *n.*
**talk in superlatives,** exaggerate.

**su·per·mar·ket** (sü′pər mär′kit) a large self-service store selling groceries and household articles. *n.*

**su·per·nal** (sù pėr′nəl) 1 heavenly; divine. 2 of, coming from, or in the sky. 3 lofty. *adj.*
—**su·per′nal·ly,** *adv.*

**su·per·nat·u·ral** (sü′pər nach′ə rəl or sü′pər nach′rəl) 1 of, having to do with, or caused by some agency or force outside the known laws of nature; especially, of, having to do with, or caused by God or a god or other spirit: *a supernatural event, supernatural powers.* 2 **the supernatural,** supernatural agencies, influences, or happenings. 1 *adj.,* 2 *n.* —**su′per·nat′u·ral·ly,** *adv.*

**su·per·nat·u·ral·ism** (sü′pər nach′ə ə liz′əm or sü′pər nach′rə liz′əm) 1 the quality or state of being SUPERNATURAL. 2 a belief in the SUPERNATURAL. *n.*

**su·per·no·va** (sü′pər nō′və) a star undergoing a massive explosion, which increases its brilliance by up to 20 times, leaving behind a large, expanding shell of gases and debris. *n.*

**su·per·nu·mer·ar·y** (sü′pər nyü′mə rer′ē or sü′pər nü′mə rer′ē) 1 more than the usual or necessary number; extra. 2 an extra person or thing. 3 a person who appears on the stage but has no lines to speak: *The drama group needs 20 supernumeraries for the mob scene.* 1 *adj.,* 2, 3 *n., pl.* **su·per·nu·mer·ar·ies.**

**su·per·pose** (sü′pər pōz′) place above or on something else. *v.*, **su·per·posed, su·per·pos·ing.**

**su·per·po·si·tion** (sü′pər pə zish′ən) superposing or being SUPERPOSEd. *n.*

**su·per·pow·er** (sü′pər pou′ər) 1 an extremely powerful nation; especially, one of a very small number of nations that dominate the world and compete with each other for economic or political control of blocs of less powerful nations. 2 extensive or extraordinary power. *n.*

**su·per·sat·u·rate** (sü′pər sach′ə rāt′) add to beyond the ordinary saturation point; saturate abnormally. A **supersaturated solution** is one in which more of a substance is dissolved than the solvent will hold under normal conditions. *v.,* **su·per·sat·u·rat·ed, su·per·sat·u·rat·ing.** —**su′per·sat′u·ra′tion,** *n.*

**su·per·scribe** (sü′pər skrīb′) 1 write words, letters, one's name, etc. at the top of, above, or on the outside of something: *Her name was superscribed on the document.* 2 write something at the top of or over: *to superscribe a document or a monument.* *v.,* **su·per·scribed, su·per·scrib·ing.**

**su·per·script** (sü′pər skript′) 1 written above. 2 a number, letter, etc. written directly above or above and to one side of another letter, number, etc. Example: *In* $a^3 = s^n$, *the* $^3$ *and the* $^n$ *are superscripts.* 1 *adj.,* 2 *n.*

**su·per·scrip·tion** (sü′pər skrip′shən) 1 a writing

above, on, or outside something. 2 something written above or on the outside. 3 the address on a letter or parcel. *n.*

**su·per·sede** (sü′pər sēd′) 1 cause to be set aside as obsolete or inferior; displace: *Electric lights had superseded gas lights in most homes by the 1920's.* 2 fill the place of; succeed: *Mrs. McKenzie has superseded Mr. Mossop as principal of the school.* *v.*, **su·per·sed·ed, su·per·sed·ing.** —**su′per·sed′er,** *n.*

**su·per·sen·si·tive** (sü′pər sen′sə tiv) extremely or morbidly sensitive. *adj.* —**su′per·sen′si·tive·ly,** *adv.* —**su′per·sen′si·tive·ness,** *n.*

**su·per·son·ic** (sü′pər son′ik) 1 having a frequency above the human ear's audibility limit of about 20 kilohertz. 2 of, having to do with, or produced by waves or vibrations of such frequency. 3 of, having to do with, or being a speed greater than the speed of sound in air (about 1200 kilometres per hour at sea level). 4 capable of moving at a speed greater than the speed of sound: *supersonic aircraft.* *adj.*

**su·per·sti·tion** (sü′pər stish′ən) 1 an unreasoning and abject fear of what is unknown or mysterious. 2 a belief or practice founded on ignorant fear or mistaken reverence: *It is a common superstition that breaking a mirror brings bad luck.* *n.*

**su·per·sti·tious** (sü′pər stish′əs) having to do with, caused by, or showing SUPERSTITION: *He was superstitious about the number 13.* *adj.* —**su′per·sti′tious·ly,** *adv.*

**su·per·struc·ture** (sü′pər struk′chər) 1 all of a building above the foundation. 2 the parts of a ship above the main deck. 3 a structure built on something else. 4 a concept, etc. based on a more general or fundamental one. *n.*

**su·per·tank·er** (sü′pər tang′kər) a very large TANKER. *n.*

**su·per·tax** (sü′pər taks′) a tax in addition to ordinary tax; surtax. *n.*

**su·per·vene** (sü′pər vēn′) come as something additional or interrupting. *v.*, **su·per·vened, su·per·ven·ing.**

**su·per·ven·tion** (sü′pər ven′shən) the act or fact of supervening. *n.*

**su·per·vise** (sü′pər vīz′) look after and direct work or workers, a process, etc.; oversee; superintend; manage: *Examinations are supervised by teachers.* *v.*, **su·per·vised, su·per·vis·ing.**

**su·per·vi·sion** (sü′pər vizh′ən) the act, process, or occupation of supervising: *Ken built the boat under his father's supervision.* *n.*

**su·per·vi·sor** (sü′pər vī′zər) a person who SUPERVISES: *The music supervisor has charge of the school choir and orchestra.* *n.*

**su·per·vi·so·ry** (sü′pər vī′zə rē) of or having to do with supervision or a SUPERVISOR: *supervisory duties. She was employed in a supervisory capacity.* *adj.*

**su·pine** (sü pīn′) 1 lying on the back with the face upwards: *The patient was placed in a supine position.* Compare with PRONE. 2 morally or mentally inactive or passive; sluggish: *supine indifference.* *adj.* —**su·pine′ly,** *adv.*

**supp.** or **suppl.** 1 supplement. 2 supplementary.

**sup·per** (sup′ər) 1 the evening meal; the third main meal of the day: *We usually have supper at 6 o'clock.* 2 the food served at this meal: *I enjoyed supper.* 3 an informal public social event that takes place in the evening, featuring a meal and often held to raise money: *a church supper.* *n.* —**sup′per·less,** *adj.*
☛ *Usage.* For some people, the evening meal is called *dinner*; for others, *dinner* is the name of the meal eaten at noon. *Supper* is never used for the noon meal.

**sup·plant** (sə plant′) 1 take the place of; displace or set aside: *Machinery has supplanted hand labour in the making of shoes.* 2 take the place of by unfair or treacherous means: *The prince plotted to supplant the king.* *v.*

**sup·ple** (sup′əl) 1 capable of being bent or folded without breaking or cracking: *a supple birch tree, supple leather.* 2 able to move and bend or twist easily and gracefully: *a supple dancer.* 3 readily adaptable to different ideas, circumstances, people, etc.; yielding: *a supple mind.* 4 make or become supple. 1–3 *adj.*, **sup·pler, sup·plest;** 4 *v.*, **sup·pled, sup·pling.** —**sup′ple·ly,** *adv.* —**sup′ple·ness,** *n.*

**sup·ple·ment** (sup′lə mənt *for noun,* sup′lə ment′ *for verb*) 1 something added to complete a thing, or to make it larger or better: *a diet supplement. The newspaper has a supplement every Saturday.* 2 supply what is lacking in; add to; complete: *Morag supplemented her income by taking an extra job on Saturdays.* 3 in geometry, an angle or arc that together with a given angle or arc equals 180°: *The supplement of a 60° angle is a 120° angle.* 1, 3 *n.*, 2 *v.*

**sup·ple·men·tal** (sup′lə men′təl) SUPPLEMENTARY. *adj.*

**sup·ple·men·ta·ry** (sup′lə men′tə rē) added to supply what is lacking; additional: *The new members of the class received supplementary instruction.* *adj.*

**supplementary angle** either of two angles or arcs which together equal 180° (*usually used in the plural*): *A 45° angle and a 135° angle are supplementary angles.*

**sup·pli·ance** (sup′lē əns) SUPPLICATION. *n.*

**sup·pli·ant** (sup′lē ənt) 1 asking humbly and earnestly; entreating: *a suppliant petitioner.* 2 expressing supplication: *suppliant gestures. They raised suppliant hands.* 3 a person who asks humbly and earnestly: *She knelt as a suppliant at the altar.* 1, 2 *adj.*, 3 *n.* —**sup′pli·ant·ly,** *adv.*

**sup·pli·cant** (sup′lə kənt) SUPPLIANT. *adj., n.*

**sup·pli·cate** (sup′lə kāt′) 1 beg humbly and earnestly: *The mother supplicated the judge to spare her son.* 2 beg humbly for (something); seek by entreaty: *to supplicate a blessing.* 3 pray humbly. *v.*, **sup·pli·cat·ed, sup·pli·cat·ing.** —**sup′pli·cat′ing·ly,** *adv.* —**sup′pli·ca′tor,** *n.*

**sup·pli·ca·tion** (sup′lə kā′shən) 1 the act of supplicating. 2 a humble and earnest request or prayer: *Their supplications were granted.* *n.*

**sup·pli·ca·to·ry** (sup′lə kə tô′rē) supplicating. *adj.*

**sup·ply**[1] (sə plī′) 1 furnish; provide: *The city supplies books for the children.* 2 a quantity ready for use; stock; store: *Our school gets its supply of paper from the city.* 3 the quantity of an article in the market ready for purchase: *a supply of coffee.* 4 make up for a loss, lack, absence, etc.: *to supply a deficiency.* 5 satisfy a want, need, etc.: *There was just enough to supply the demand.*

**6** fill a place, vacancy, etc. as a substitute. **7** one that supplies a vacancy: *a supply teacher.* **8** the act of supplying. **9 supplies,** *pl.* the food, equipment, etc. necessary for an army, expedition, or the like. 1, 4–6 *v.*, **sup·plied, sup·ply·ing;** 2, 3, 7–9 *n., pl.* **sup·plies.** —**sup·pli′er,** *n.*
**in supply,** available to a given extent: *Apples are in poor supply this year.*

**sup·ply**[2] (sup′lē) in a SUPPLE manner. *adv.*

**supply teacher** a teacher who is acting as a temporary substitute for a regular teacher.

**supply teaching** the act or occupation of substituting for regular teachers who are away temporarily because of sickness, etc.

**sup·port** (sə pôrt′) **1** keep from falling; hold up: *Walls support the roof.* **2** give strength or courage to; keep up; help: *Hope supports us in trouble.* **3** provide for: *She supported her nephew while he was at university.* **4** be in favour of; back; second: *She supports the Liberals.* **5** help prove; bear out: *The facts support his claim.* **6** put up with; bear; endure: *She couldn't support life without friends.* **7** the act of supporting; condition of being supported; help; aid: *He needs the support of a scholarship.* **8** maintenance: *the support of a family.* **9** a person or thing that supports; prop: *The neck is the support of the head.* **10** assist or protect another military unit in combat: *Artillery fire supported the infantry attack.* **11** in military use, assistance or protection given by one element or unit to another. **12** a unit which helps another unit in battle: *Aviation may be used as a support for infantry.* **13** act with a leading actor; assist; attend. 1–6, 10, 13 *v.*, 7–9, 11, 12 *n.* —**sup·port′er,** *n.*

**sup·port·a·ble** (sə pôr′tə bəl) capable of being supported; bearable or endurable. *adj.* —**sup·port′a·bly,** *adv.*

**sup·pose** (sə pōz′) **1** consider as a possibility; assume for the sake of argument: *Suppose it doesn't work; what will we do then?* **2** think probable; believe: *I suppose she will come as usual. I suppose I'll be left with the dishes again.* **3** involve as necessary; imply; presuppose: *An invention supposes an inventor.* *v.,* **sup·posed, sup·pos·ing.** —**sup·pos′a·ble,** *adj.*

**sup·posed** (sə pōzd′) **1** accepted as real or true, but mistakenly or without proof or evidence; believed or imagined: *a supposed insult. We need to take a closer look at the supposed improvements in the postal system.* **2** designed or intended: *What is that supposed to mean?* **3** obliged or expected (*to*): *I was supposed to bring the cake, but I forgot.* **4** permitted; allowed (*to*): *You are not supposed to jump on the bed.* **5** pt. and pp. of SUPPOSE. 1–4 *adj.*, 5 *v.*

**sup·pos·ed·ly** (sə pō′zi dlē) according to what is supposed or was supposed: *Winston was supposedly sleeping, but we discovered that he was out. adv.*

**sup·pos·ing** (sə pō′zing) **1** in the event that; assuming that: *Supposing it rains, shall we go?* **2** ppr. of SUPPOSE. 1 *conj.,* 2 *v.*

**sup·po·si·tion** (sup′ə zish′ən) **1** the act of supposing. **2** something supposed; assumption: *Ida entered the campaign on the supposition that her friends would support her.* *n.*

**sup·po·si·tion·al** (sup′ə zish′ə nəl) of or based on SUPPOSITION; hypothetical; supposed. *adj.*

**sup·pos·i·ti·tious** (sə poz′ə tish′əs) **1** put in place of another with intent to defraud; counterfeit: *supposititious writings, a supposititious heir.* **2** hypothetical; supposed. *adj.* —**sup·pos′i·ti′tious·ly,** *adv.*

**sup·pos·i·to·ry** (sə poz′ə tô′rē) medicine in the form of a cone or cylinder to be put into the rectum or other opening of the body. *n., pl.* **sup·pos·i·to·ries.**

**sup·press** (sə pres′) **1** put an end to; stop by force; put down: *The troops suppressed the rebellion.* **2** keep in; hold back; check: *She suppressed a yawn.* **3** hide; refuse to make known: *The government was accused of suppressing important facts.* **4** stop or prohibit the publication or circulation of: *The book was suppressed because it contained libellous statements.* **5** hinder or restrain the flow or growth of: *to suppress bleeding.* *v.* —**sup·press′er, sup·pres′sor,** *n.*

**sup·press·i·ble** (sə pres′ə bəl) that can be SUPPRESSed. *adj.*

**sup·pres·sion** (sə presh′ən) a SUPPRESSing or being suppressed: *the suppression of a revolt, the suppression of an impulse to cough, the suppression of facts.* *n.*

**sup·pres·sive** (sə pres′iv) tending to SUPPRESS; causing SUPPRESSION. *adj.*

**sup·pu·rate** (sup′yə rāt′) form or discharge PUS; fester. *v.,* **sup·pu·rat·ed, sup·pu·rat·ing.**

**sup·pu·ra·tion** (sup′yə rā′shən) **1** the formation or discharge of PUS. **2** PUS. *n.*

**su·pra·re·nal** (sü′prə rē′nəl) **1** situated above or on the kidney; adrenal: *The adrenal glands are sometimes called the suprarenal glands.* **2** a suprarenal part, especially an adrenal gland. 1 *adj.,* 2 *n.*

**su·prem·a·cy** (sə prem′ə sē) **1** the quality or state of being SUPREME. **2** SUPREME authority or power. *n.*

**su·preme** (sə prēm′) **1** highest in rank or authority: *a supreme ruler.* **2** highest in degree or quality; greatest; utmost: *supreme disgust, supreme courage.* *adj.* —**su·preme′ly,** *adv.*
**make the supreme sacrifice,** give one's life; die.

**Supreme Being** God.

**Supreme Court 1** in Canada: **a** the highest appeal court of Canada in civil and criminal matters. It consists of nine judges and hears appeals from the provincial courts of appeal and from the federal court dealing with matters of taxation, copyright, etc. **b** the highest appeal or trial court in some provinces. **2** a similar court in other countries.

**Supt.** or **supt.** Superintendent.

**sur–**[1] a prefix meaning: upon; above, as in *surcharge, surcoat, surtax.*

**sur–**[2] a form of the prefix **sub-** occurring before *r*, as in *surreptitious.*

**sur·charge** (sėr′chärj′ *for noun,* sər chärj′ *for verb*) **1** an extra charge: *The express company made a surcharge for delivering the trunk outside the city limits.* **2** charge extra. **3** overcharge. **4** an additional and usually excessive load, burden, or supply: *a surcharge of punishment.* **5** overload: *a heart surcharged with grief.*

**6** an additional mark printed on a postage stamp to change its value, date, etc. **7** print a surcharge on a postage stamp. *1, 4, 6 n., 2, 3, 5, 7 v.*, **sur·charged, sur·charg·ing.**

**sur·cin·gle** (sėr′sing gəl) a strap or belt around a horse's body to keep a saddle, blanket, or pack in place. *n.*

**sur·coat** (sėr′kōt) an outer coat or cloak, especially one once worn by knights over their armour. *n.*

**sure** (shùr) **1** free from doubt; certain; having ample reason for belief; confident; positive: *I am sure of his guilt.* **2** safe; reliable; to be trusted: *a sure messenger, sure ground.* **3** never missing, slipping, etc.; unfailing; unerring: *sure aim, a sure touch.* **4** certain to be or to happen: *The team faced sure defeat. She is sure to win the prize.* **5** *Informal.* surely; certainly: *Sure, we can go to the party.* *1–4 adj.*, **sur·er, sur·est;** *5 adv.* —**sure′ness,** *n.*
**for sure, a** surely; certainly: *He's coming for sure.* **b** sure; certain: *That's for sure.*
**make sure, a** act so as to make something certain. **b** get sure knowledge.
**to be sure,** surely; certainly.

**sure–fire** (shùr′fīr′) *Informal.* that will not fail; certain: *a sure-fire formula.* *adj.*

**sure–foot·ed** (shùr′fùt′id) not liable to stumble, slip, or fall. *adj.* —**sure′-foot′ed·ness,** *n.*

**sure·ly** (shùr′lē) **1** undoubtedly; certainly: *Half a loaf is surely better than none.* **2** really (*used to emphasize or intensify a statement*): *Surely you can't be serious!* **3** without mistake; without missing, slipping, etc.; firmly: *The goat leaped surely from rock to rock.* **4** without fail: slowly but surely. *adv.*

**sure·ty** (shü′rə tē) **1** security against loss, damage, or failure to do something: *An insurance company gives surety against loss by fire.* **2** a person who agrees to be legally responsible for another: *He was surety for his brother's appearance in court.* *n., pl.* **sur·e·ties.**

**surf** (sėrf) **1** the waves or swell of the sea breaking on the shore or upon shoals, reefs etc. **2** the deep pounding or thundering sound of this. **3** travel or ride on the crest of a wave, especially with a SURFBOARD. **4** *Informal.* search for material of interest on the INTERNET or WORLD WIDE WEB. *1, 2 n., 3, 4 v.* —**surf′er,** *n.*
☛ *Hom.* SERF.

**sur·face** (sėr′fis) **1** the outside of anything: *the surface of a golf ball, the surface of a mountain.* **2** the top of the ground or soil, or of a body of water or other liquid: *The stone sank below the surface.* **3** any face or side of a thing: *A cube has six surfaces.* **4** that which has length and breadth but no thickness: *a plane surface in geometry.* **5** the outward appearance: *He seems rough, but you will find him very kind below the surface.* **6** of the surface; on the surface; having to do with the surface: *a surface view, surface travel.* **7** put a surface on; make smooth: *to surface a road.* **8** bring or come to the surface: *to surface a submarine. The submarine surfaced.* *1–6 n., 7, 8 v.*, **sur·faced, sur·fac·ing.**

**surface mail** mail transported by land or sea, rather than by air.

**surface tension** the tension of the surface film of a liquid that makes it contract to a minimum area.

**surf·board** (sėrf′bôrd′) a more or less oblong board on which a person may stand or lie in order to ride on the crest of a wave as it comes in to the beach. *n.*

**surf·boat** (sėrf′bōt′) a strong boat specially made for use in heavy surf. *n.*

**sur·feit** (sėr′fit) **1** a grossly excessive amount of something; much; excess: *a surfeit of food, a surfeit of advice.* **2** disgust or nausea caused by this. **3** feed or cause to take too much, so as to cause nausea or disgust. **4** take too much of something; indulge too much. *1, 2 n., 3, 4 v.*

**surf·ing** (sėr′fing) **1** the sport of using a SURFBOARD to ride toward the shore on the crest of a wave. **2** ppr. of SURF. *1 n., 2 v.*

**surge** (sėrj) **1** rise and fall in waves or billows: *the surging sea.* **2** the swelling and rolling of the sea. **3** move as a wave; roll, swell, or sweep forward: *A great wave surged over us. Joy surged through him when he saw her. The crowd surged out of the arena.* **4** a swelling, rolling, or sweeping forward like a wave: *A surge of anger swept over her.* **5** a sudden increase: *a surge of power.* *1, 3 v.*, **surged, surg·ing;** *2, 4, 5 n.*

**sur·geon** (sėr′jən) a medical doctor who practises SURGERY. *n.*

**sur·ger·y** (sėr′jə rē) **1** the treatment of disease, injury, etc. by using the hands or instruments to mend or remove an organ, tissue, or part, or to remove foreign matter in the body: *The fracture was a serious one that required surgery.* **2** the branch of medicine that deals with such treatment. **3** an operating room. *n., pl.* **sur·ger·ies.**
☛ *Etym.* Through OF from L *chirurgia*, which came from Gk. *kheirourgos*, literally 'hand work', made up of *kheir* 'hand' + *erg* 'work'.

**sur·gi·cal** (sėr′jə kəl) **1** of or having to do with SURGEONS or SURGERY: *a surgical specialist.* **2** used in SURGERY: *surgical instruments.* **3** resulting from SURGERY: *a surgical scar.* *adj.* —**sur′gi·cal·ly,** *adv.*

**sur·ly** (sėr′lē) bad-tempered and unfriendly; rude; gruff: *They got a surly answer from the grouchy old man.* *adj.*, **sur·li·er, sur·li·est.** —**sur′li·ness,** *n.*

**sur·mise** (sər mīz′ *for verb,* sər mīz′ *or* sėr′mīz *for noun*) **1** guess: *We surmised that the delay was caused by some accident.* **2** the formation of an idea with little or no evidence; a guessing: *Her guilt was a matter of surmise; there was no proof.* *1 v.*, **sur·mised, sur·mis·ing;** *2 n.*

**sur·mount** (sər mount′) **1** overcome: *She surmounted many difficulties.* **2** be at or on the top of: *mountain peaks surmounted with snow.* **3** go up and across; get up and over: *to surmount a hill.* **4** place something on top of; cap. *v.* —**sur·mount′a·ble,** *adj.*

**sur·name** (sėr′nām′) **1** the name that members of a family have in common; family name; last name: *Kahn is the surname of Nathan Kahn.* **2** a name added to a person's real name: *William I of England had the surname "the Conqueror."* **3** give an added name to; call by a surname: *Simon was surnamed Peter.* *1, 2 n., 3 v.*, **sur·named, sur·nam·ing.**

**sur·pass** (sər pas′) **1** do or be better or greater than; be superior to: *The experience surpassed anything he had known before. She surpasses all the other team members in her ability to score.* **2** be too much or too great for; go beyond the range or capacity of: *The magnificence of the sight surpassed description.* *v.* —**sur·pass′a·ble,** *adj.* —**sur·pass′ing·ly,** *adv.*

**sur·plice** (sėr′plis) a loose, white, usually knee-length gown having very wide sleeves, worn over the clothing by the clergy and choir members during a service. *n.*

**sur·plus** (sėr′pləs *or* sėr′plus′) **1** an amount over and above what is needed; an extra quantity left over; excess: *We had a surplus of tomatoes this year, so we gave them away to the neighbours.* **2** an excess of assets over liabilities. **3** more than is needed; forming a surplus: *The store's surplus stock was put on sale at the end of the season.* 1, 2 *n.,* 3 *adj.*

**sur·pris·al** (sər prī′zəl *or* sə prī′zəl) a surprising or being surprised; SURPRISE. *n.*

**sur·prise** (sər prīz′ *or* sə prīz′) **1** a feeling caused by something unexpected. **2** cause to feel surprised; astonish: *The victory surprised us.* **3** something unexpected: *Mother always has a surprise for the children on holidays.* **4** that is not expected; surprising: *a surprise party, a surprise visit.* **5** catch unprepared; come upon suddenly; attack suddenly: *The enemy surprised the fort.* **6** a catching unprepared; coming upon suddenly; sudden attack. **7** lead or bring a person, etc. unawares: *The news surprised her into tears.* 1, 3, 4, 6 *n.,* 2, 5, 7 *v.,* **sur·prised, sur·pris·ing.**
**take by surprise, a** catch unprepared; come on suddenly and unexpectedly: *The fort was taken by surprise.* **b** astonish.

**sur·pris·ing** (sər prī′zing *or* sə prī′zing) **1** causing surprise: *a surprising recovery.* **2** ppr. of SURPRISE. 1 *adj.,* 2 *v.* —**sur·pris′ing·ly,** *adv.*

**sur·re·al·ism** (sə rē′ə liz′əm) in painting, sculpture, literature, etc., a 20th-century movement that tries to show what takes place in the subconscious mind: *In surrealism, the pictures, images, etc. have no conventional order or form.* *n.*

**sur·re·al·ist** (sə rē′ə list) **1** an artist or writer who uses SURREALISM. **2** of or having to do with SURREALISM or surrealists. 1 *n.,* 2 *adj.*

**sur·re·al·is·tic** (sə rē′ə lis′tik) **1** of or having to do with SURREALISM or surrealists. **2** having a strange and unreal quality, like a surrealist painting: *a surrealistic experience.* *adj.* —**sur·re·al·is′ti·cal·ly,** *adv.*

**sur·ren·der** (sə ren′dər) **1** give up control or possession of, especially under compulsion or demand from another: *to surrender a fort to an invader, to surrender an office. As the storm increased, the men on the raft surrendered all hope.* **2** give oneself up; stop resisting; give in to a demand for submission: *The captain had to surrender when the ammunition ran out.* **3** give in to an emotion, etc.: *to surrender to grief.* **4** cancel an insurance policy in return for a cash sum. **5** the act or an instance of surrendering. 1–4 *v.,* 5 *n.*

**surrender value** the value of an insurance policy in terms of the cash payable to the holder if the policy is cancelled or surrendered.

**sur·rep·ti·tious** (sėr′əp tish′əs) **1** done, made, or acquired secretly; secret and stealthy or unauthorized: *a surreptitious wink, a surreptitious gift.* **2** acting in a secret or stealthy way: *Sandra was very surreptitious in her movements.* *adj.* —**sur′rep·ti′tious·ly,** *adv.*

**sur·rey** (sėr′ē) a light, four-wheeled, horse-drawn carriage having two seats and, usually, a flat top. *n., pl.* **sur·reys.**

**sur·ro·gate** (sėr′ə gāt′ *or* sėr′ə git) **1** a person who acts for or takes the place of another; substitute or deputy. **2** having to do with the probate of wills, the administration of estates, etc.: *Some provinces have surrogate courts.* 1 *n.,* 2 *adj.*

| surplus | 1203 | surveyor's measure |

hat, āge, fär; let, ēqual, tėrm; it, īce
hot, ōpen, ôrder; oil, out; cup, put, rüle
əbove, takən, pencəl, lemən, circəs
ch, child; ng, long; sh, ship
th, thin; ᴛʜ, then; zh, measure

**sur·round** (sə round′) **1** come or be all around; shut in on all sides; enclose: *News reporters surrounded the minister as she emerged from the legislature. The little girl was surrounded by her toys. Police surrounded the house.* **2** extend around the outside or edge of: *A high fence surrounds the field. The inscription on the medal was surrounded by a design of flowers.* **3** be or form part of the environment of: *Love and goodwill surrounded her.* **4** cause to be surrounded by: *The invalid's family surrounded him with every comfort. The king surrounded himself with flatterers.* *v.*

**sur·round·ings** (sə roun′dingz) surrounding things, conditions, etc.: *rural surroundings. They lived in beautiful surroundings.* *n. pl.*

**sur·tax** (sėr′taks′) an additional or extra tax: *A surtax was temporarily levied by the government on incomes above $120 000.* *n.*

**sur·veil·lance** (sər vā′ləns) **1** a watch kept over a person: *She has been under police surveillance for several weeks.* **2** SUPERVISION. *n.*

**sur·vey** (sər vā′ *for verb,* sėr′vā *for noun*) **1** look over; take a general view of: *She surveyed the scene before her. They surveyed the wreckage.* **2** examine or inspect the condition, situation, etc. of: *He surveyed the alternatives open to him and decided he had to act at once.* **3** a general or comprehensive study or view of something: *Her book included a survey of twentieth century Canadian poetry.* **4** an inspection or investigation of the condition, situation, etc. of something: *Our first survey of the house showed us that it needed a lot of repairs. A recent survey shows that public opinion on the issue has changed.* **5** a written statement or description of the result of such an investigation or examination: *The government survey of food prices has just been published.* **6** determine the exact boundaries and contours of an area of land by measuring distances, angles, etc.: *The land is being surveyed for subdivision into building lots.* **7** survey land: *The crew is out surveying.* **8** the act or an instance of surveying land. **9** a map or plan of such a survey. **10** a tract of land divided into building lots; subdivision. **11** the houses or community built on such land. 1, 2, 6, 7 *v.,* 3–5, 8–11 *n., pl.* **sur·veys.**

**sur·vey·ing** (sər vā′ing) **1** the science or technique of measuring the boundaries and contours of particular areas on, above, or beneath the earth's surface by using the principles of geometry. **2** the act or business of making such measurements. **3** ppr. of SURVEY. 1, 2 *n.,* 3 *v.*

**sur·vey·or** (sər vā′ər) a person who surveys, especially one whose work is making land surveys. *n.*

**surveyor's measure** a system for measuring land area, formerly used by surveyors. The basic unit was the chain, a unit of length equal to 66 feet or about 20 metres, which was divided into 100 links, each equal to about 20 centimetres.

625 square links = 1 square pole
16 square poles = 1 square chain
10 square chains = 1 acre
640 acres = 1 section (or 1 square mile)
36 sections = 1 township

**sur·viv·al** (sər vī′vəl)   1 the act or fact of surviving; continuing to live, or exist: *Ethan had little chance of survival if his food ran out.*   2 a person, thing, custom, belief, etc. that has lasted from an earlier time: *Belief in the evil eye is a survival of ancient magic.*   3 of, having to do with, or assisting survival: *survival techniques, a survival kit.*   *n.*

**survival of the fittest**   the process or result of NATURAL SELECTION.

**sur·vive** (sər vīv′)   1 continue to live or exist; live on: *The family survived in spite of terrible hardship. Several of the original buildings still survive.*   2 live longer than; outlive: *He survived his wife by three years.*   3 continue to live or exist after: *Ten of the crew survived the shipwreck. The roses did not survive the winter.*   *v.*, **sur·vived, sur·viv·ing.**

**sur·vi·vor** (sər vī′vər)   a person or thing that SURVIVES.   *n.*

**sus–**   a form of the prefix **sub-** occurring in some cases before *c*, *p*, and *t*; for example, *susceptible, suspend, sustain.*

**sus·cep·ti·bil·i·ty** (sə sep′tə bil′ə tē)   1 the quality or state of being SUSCEPTIBLE: *susceptibility to disease.*   2 **susceptibilities,** *pl.* sensitive feelings.   *n., pl.* **sus·cep·ti·bil·i·ties.**

**sus·cep·ti·ble** (sə sep′tə bəl)   1 capable of receiving or undergoing a process or operation; allowing (*used with* **of**): *a statement not susceptible of proof. Oak is susceptible of high polish.*   2 open or liable to an influence, stimulus, etc.; readily affected (*used with* **to**): *He is susceptible to flattery. Children are susceptible to many diseases.*   3 sensitive and impressionable; easily influenced by feelings or emotions: *Tales of adventure appealed to her susceptible nature.*   *adj.* —**sus·cep′ti·bly,** *adv.*

**sus·pect** (sə spekt′ *for verb,* sus′pekt *for noun,* sus′pekt *or* sə spekt′ *for adjective*)   1 imagine to be so; have an impression of the presence or existence of: *The old fox suspected danger and did not touch the trap.*   2 tend to believe to be guilty, false, bad, etc. without proof: *The police officer suspected him.*   3 feel no confidence in; doubt: *The judge suspected the truth of the thief's excuse.*   4 be suspicious: *I'm sure she suspects.*   5 be inclined to think or believe that: *I suspect she was just trying to be funny.*   6 a person suspected: *The police have arrested two suspects in connection with the bank robbery.*   7 open to or viewed with suspicion; suspected or deserving to be suspected: *That version of the story is suspect.*   1–5 *v.*, 6 *n.*, 7 *adj.*

**sus·pend** (sə spend′)   1 hang from a support above so as to be free on all sides: *The lamp was suspended from the ceiling.*   2 hold, keep, or stay in place somewhere between the top and bottom: *We saw the smoke suspended in the still air.*   3 stop for a while: *to suspend work on the project, to suspend hostilities.*   4 remove or exclude for a while from some privilege or job: *to suspend a member of the team, to be suspended from school.*   5 keep undecided; put off: *to suspend judgment.*   *v.*

**suspended sentence**   in law, a sentence that remains unenforced subject to the convicted person's good behaviour for a certain length of time.

**sus·pend·ers** (sə spen′dərz)   1 straps worn over the shoulders to hold up the trousers; braces.   2 garters worn by men to hold up their socks.   *n.pl.*

**sus·pense** (sə spens′)   1 the condition of being uncertain about an outcome or decision: *The detective story kept me in suspense until the very end. They were kept in suspense while the doctors deliberated.*   2 a feeling of anxiety or excitement resulting from such uncertainty: *They had a long night of suspense before her fever broke. We all felt the suspense as we waited for the announcement of the winner.*   3 producing suspense, especially pleasant excitement: *a suspense novel.*   *n.*

**sus·pens·ion** (sə spen′shən)   1 the act of SUSPENDing or the state or period of being suspended.   2 a support on which something is SUSPENDed.   3 an arrangement of springs for supporting the body of an automobile, railway car, etc.   4 a mixture in which very small particles of a solid remain SUSPENDed (def. 2) without dissolving.   *n.*

**suspension bridge**   a bridge having its roadway hung on cables or chains between towers. See BRIDGE¹ for picture.

**sus·pen·so·ry** (sə spen′sə rē)   1 holding up; supporting.   2 a muscle, ligament, bandage, etc. that holds up or supports a part of the body.   1 *adj.*, 2 *n.*, *pl.* **sus·pen·so·ries.**

**sus·pi·cion** (sə spish′ən)   1 the act or an instance of SUSPECTing: *Her suspicion of the stranger turned out to be well founded.*   2 the feeling or state of mind of a person who SUSPECTS: *an atmosphere of suspicion. He had a suspicion that the document was forged.*   3 the condition of being SUSPECTed: *She tried to protect herself by diverting suspicion to someone else.*   4 a slight trace; suggestion: *She speaks with just a suspicion of an accent.*   *n.*
**above suspicion,**   so honourable as not to be suspected of wrong-doing: *They said their old servants were all above suspicion.*
**on suspicion,**   because of being SUSPECTed: *He was arrested on suspicion of robbery.*
**under suspicion,**   SUSPECTed; believed guilty but not proven to be so.

**sus·pi·cious** (sə spish′əs)   1 causing one to SUSPECT: *A man was seen loitering near the house in a suspicious manner. They left under suspicious circumstances.*   2 feeling SUSPICION; distrustful; suspecting: *It was the way she said it that made me suspicious.*   3 tending to SUSPECT; prone to distrust: *She has a very suspicious nature. Our dog is suspicious of strangers.*   4 showing SUSPICION: *The dog gave a suspicious sniff at my leg.*   *adj.*
—**sus·pi′cious·ly,** *adv.*   —**sus·pi′cious·ness,** *n.*

**sus·pi·ra·tion** (sus′pə rā′shən)   a SIGH.   *n.*

**sus·pire** (sə spīr′)   take a long, deep breath; especially, SIGH.   *v.*, **sus·pired, sus·pir·ing.**

**sus·tain** (sə stān′)   1 keep up; keep going: *Hope sustains him in his misery.*   2 supply with food, provisions, etc.: *to sustain an army.*   3 hold up; support: *Arches sustain the weight of the roof.*   4 bear; endure: *The sea wall sustains the shock of the waves.*   5 suffer; experience: *to sustain a great loss.*   6 allow; admit; favour: *The court sustained his suit.*   7 agree with; confirm: *The facts sustain her theory.*   *v.*   —**sus·tain′a·ble,** *adj.*

**sus·te·nance** (sus′tə nəns)   1 a means of SUSTAINing life; food or provisions: *He has gone for a week without sustenance.*   2 the means of living; support: *She gave money for their sustenance.*   3 sustaining or being SUSTAINed; especially, supplying or being supplied with food or provisions.   *n.*

**sut·ler** (sut′lər)   formerly, a person who followed an army to sell provisions, etc. to the soldiers.   *n.*

**sut·tee** (su tē′)   1 a Hindu widow who threw herself on

the burning funeral pyre of her husband and was burned with him.   **2** the former Hindu custom of a widow burning herself with the body of her husband, now illegal.   *n.*

**su·ture** (sü′chər)   **1** the act or process of joining together the edges of a cut or wound by stitching.   **2** a length of material, such as gut, thread, or wire, used in stitching wounds.   **3** one of the stitches closing a wound.   **4** join or unite by suture or as if by suture.   **5** the line where the edges of two bones form a rigid joint, as between the bones of the skull.   1–3, 5 *n.*, 4 *v.*, **su·tured, su·tur·ing.**

**su·ze·rain** (sü′zə rin *or* sü′zə rān′)   **1** a feudal lord.   **2** a state or government exercising political control over the foreign affairs of a dependent state.   *n.*

**su·ze·rain·ty** (sü′zə rin tē)   the position or authority of a SUZERAIN.   *n., pl.* **su·ze·rain·ties.**

**s.v.**   under the following word or heading (an abbreviation of Latin *sub verbo* 'under the word').

**svelte** (svelt)   slender and graceful; lithe: *a svelte figure.*   *adj.*

**SW, S.W.,** or **s.w.**   **1** southwest.   **2** southwestern.

**swab** (swob)   **1** a mop for cleaning decks, floors, etc.   **2** a bit of absorbent material usually attached to the end of a small stick, used for cleansing or removing material from some part of the body or for applying medicine to it.   **3** a specimen taken with a swab for examination for bacteria, etc.   **4** a sponge attached to a handle, used for cleaning the bore of a firearm.   **5** clean with or as if with a swab.   **6** apply medication to with a swab: *to swab a person's throat.*   1–4 *n.*, 5, 6 *v.*, **swabbed, swab·bing.**

**swab·ber** (swob′ər)   **1** a person who uses a SWAB.   **2** a SWAB.   *n.*

**swad·dle** (swod′əl)   **1** wrap a baby with SWADDLING CLOTHES.   **2** wrap tightly with bandages or thick layers of clothes; swathe.   **3** the cloth used for swaddling.   1, 2 *v.*, **swad·dled, swad·dling;**   3 *n.*

**swaddling clothes**   **1** long, narrow strips of cloth formerly used for wrapping a newborn infant.   **2** anything that restrains freedom of thought or action.

**swag** (swag)   an ornamental festoon of flowers, leaves, ribbons, etc.   *n.*

**swag·ger** (swag′ər)   **1** walk with a bold, defiant, or superior air; strut about or show off in a vain or insolent way: *The bully swaggered into the schoolyard.*   **2** boast or brag noisily.   **3** influence or force by bluster; bluff.   **4** a swaggering way of talking or acting: *The pirate captain moved among his prisoners with a swagger.*   1–3 *v.*, 4 *n.*   —**swag′ger·er,** *n.*   —**swag′ger·ing·ly,** *adv.*

**swagger stick**   a short, light stick or cane, sometimes carried by military officers.

**Swa·hi·li** (swä hē′lē)   **1** a member of a Bantu-speaking people of Zanzibar and the nearby African coast.   **2** a Bantu language spoken originally in Zanzibar and the nearby coast of Africa, characterized by a large proportion of words of Arabic origin: *Swahili is the common language of trade in Tanzania, Kenya, Zaire, and Uganda.*   *n., pl.* **Swa·hi·li** or **Swa·hi·lis.**
☛ *Etym.* From Arabic *sawahil*, plural of *sahil* 'coast'.

**swale** (swāl)   a low, wet piece of land.   *n.*

**swal·low**[1] (swol′ō)   **1** take into the stomach through the throat: *to swallow food.*   **2** perform the act of swallowing: *I cannot swallow.*   **3** take in; absorb: *The waves swallowed up the swimmer.*   **4** *Informal.*   believe too easily; accept without question or suspicion: *He will swallow any story.*   **5** put up with; take meekly: *He had to swallow the insult.*   **6** take back: *to swallow words said in anger.*   **7** keep back; keep from expressing: *She swallowed her displeasure and smiled.*   **8** the act of swallowing: *She took the medicine at one swallow.*   **9** an amount that is or can be swallowed at one time: *There are about four swallows of water left in the cup.*   **10** the throat; gullet.   1–7 *v.*, 8–10 *n.*   —**swal′low·er,** *n.*

**swal·low**[2] (swol′ō)   any of a family of small, swift-flying birds found in many parts of the world, having long, narrow, pointed wings, a long, more or less forked tail, and a short, broad bill that can open very wide to catch insects in flight.   See BARN SWALLOW for picture.   *n.*

**swal·low·tail** (swol′ō tāl′)   **1** a deeply forked tail, such as that of a swallow.   **2** something shaped like or suggesting a swallowtail.   **3** SWALLOW-TAILED COAT.   **4** any of a family of large, brightly coloured butterflies commonly having wings that end in a tail-like point.   *n.*

**swal·low–tailed** (swol′ō tāld′)   having a tail or end that is deeply forked or extends into long, tapering points.   *adj.*

A modern swallow-tailed coat, usually called a morning coat

**swallow–tailed coat**   a man's formal coat cut away in the front and extending at the back in two long tapering pieces; tailcoat.

**swam** (swam)   pt. of SWIM: *When the boat sank, we swam to shore.*   *v.*

**swa·mi** (swä′mē)   the title of a Hindu religious teacher.   *n., pl.* **swa·mis.**

**swamp** (swomp)   **1** an area of wet land sometimes partially covered with water, especially such an area having trees and shrubs as well as grasses and sedges.   **2** of, for use in, or found in swamps: *swamp grasses.*   **3** cover or fill with water; flood or soak: *A huge wave swamped the boat. All our provisions were swamped.*   **4** fill with water and sink: *Our boat swamped in the storm.*   **5** overwhelm as by a flood; make helpless with too much or too many of something: *swamped with work. The lottery winner was swamped with letters asking for money.*   1, 2 *n.*, 3–5 *v.*

**swamp·land** (swomp′land′)   a tract of land covered by SWAMPS.   *n.*

**swamp·y** (swom′pē)   **1** of, containing, or consisting of a SWAMP or swamps: *swampy meadowland.*   **2** like a

SWAMP; soft and wet: *The yard was swampy after the heavy rain.* *adj.*, **swamp·i·er, swamp·i·est.**

Trumpeter swans—about 150 cm long including the tail; wingspread about 275 cm

**swan** (swon) **1** any of about seven species of large water bird belonging to the same family as ducks and geese, having webbed feet, a long, slender neck that is curved back in swimming but stretched out straight in flight, and, in most species, pure white plumage: *Swans have a very long, convoluted windpipe that allows them to make a variety of far-reaching calls.* **2** a poet or singer: *Shakespeare is sometimes called the Swan of Avon.* *n.* —**swan′like′**, *adj.*

**swan dive** in swimming, a graceful dive in which the legs are held straight from the toes to the hips, the back is arched, and the arms are spread like the wings of a gliding bird. The diver brings his or her arms forward and together just before entering the water.

**swank** (swangk) *Informal.* **1** show off; swagger: *She was swanking around in her new outfit.* **2** a showing off; swaggering behaviour, speech, etc. **3** a person who behaves in this manner. **4** style and dash; smartness; elegance. **5** SWANKY: *Their apartment is very swank.* 1 *v.*, 2–4 *n.*, 5 *adj.*

**swank·y** (swang′kē) stylish and dashing; smart; elegant: *a swanky car.* *adj.*, **swank·i·er, swank·i·est.** —**swank′i·ly**, *adv.* —**swank′i·ness**, *n.*

**swans·down** (swonz′doun′) **1** the soft down of a swan, used for trimming, powder puffs, etc. **2** a fine, thick, soft cloth made of a mixture of cotton or silk with wool. **3** a very soft, absorbent cotton flannel. *n.*

**swan song** **1** the song that a swan is said to sing just before it dies. **2** a person's farewell performance or final statement, composition, painting, etc.

**swap** (swop) *Informal.* **1** exchange; barter; trade. **2** a trading; a trade. 1 *v.*, **swapped, swap·ping**; 2 *n.* Also, **swop.** —**swap′per**, *n.*

**swarm¹** (swôrm) **1** a large group of honeybees, led by a queen bee, leaving a hive to start a new colony elsewhere. **2** a colony of bees settled together in a hive. **3** of honeybees, fly off together to start a new colony. **4** a large number of insects, birds, people, etc. clustered together and usually moving about: *a swarm of children, swarms of migrating birds.* **5** fly or move about in great numbers; throng: *The mosquitoes swarmed about us.* **6** be crowded or overrun; teem: *The plaza was swarming with shoppers. Our camp swarmed with mosquitoes.* **7** a group of free-swimming, single-celled organisms. 1, 2, 4, 7 *n.*, 3, 5, 6 *v.*

**swarm²** (swôrm) climb with the hands and feet; shin: *The sailor swarmed up the rigging.* *v.*

**swarth·y** (swôr′ᴛʜē *or* swôr′ᴛʜē) having a dark skin. *adj.*, **swarth·i·er, swarth·i·est.** —**swarth′i·ly**, *adv.* —**swarth′i·ness**, *n.*

**swash** (swosh) **1** dash water, etc. about; splash. **2** move with a splashing, washing sound: *The water swashed against the boat.* **3** swagger. **4** the act of swaggering. **5** a narrow channel of water cutting through a sandbank or between a sandbank and the shore. 1–3 *v.*, 4, 5 *n.*

**swash·buck·ler** (swosh′buk′lər) a swaggering swordsman, bully, or boaster. *n.*

**swash·buck·ling** (swosh′buk′ling) swaggering; bullying; boasting. *n., adj.*

**swas·ti·ka** (swo stē′kə *or* swos′ti kə) an ancient symbol or ornament consisting of a cross with equal arms that are continued at the ends at right angles, all in the same direction: *The Nazis adopted the swastika with the arms bent in a clockwise direction.* *n.*

**swat** (swot) *Informal.* **1** hit with a smart or violent blow: *to swat a fly.* **2** a smart or violent blow. 1 *v.*, **swat·ted, swat·ting**; 2 *n.* —**swat′ter**, *n.*

**swatch** (swoch) a sample of cloth or other similar material. *n.*

**swath** (swoth) **1** the space covered by a single cut of a scythe or by one cut of a mowing machine. **2** a row of grass, grain, etc. cut by a scythe or mowing machine. **3** cut grain with a SWATHER. **4** a long, wide strip or belt. 1, 2, 4 *n.*, 3 *v.*
**cut a (wide) swath, a** make a destructive sweep: *The aggressive new company cut a swath through its competitors.* **b** make a forceful impression or effective display: *He cuts a wide swath in this town.*

**swathe** (swāᴛʜ *or* swoᴛʜ) **1** wrap up closely or completely: *swathed in a blanket.* **2** bind with bandages; bandage: *to swathe an injured arm.* **3** a wrapping; bandage. **4** envelop or surround like a wrapping: *The mountain top was swathed in cloud.* 1, 2, 4 *v.*, **swathed, swath·ing**; 3 *n.*

**swath·er** (swoᴛʜ′ər) a machine used for cutting grain that is not dry or is mixed with green weeds. *n.*

**sway** (swā) **1** swing slowly back and forth or from side to side from a base or pivot: *The tower of dominoes swayed and fell. The trees swayed in the wind.* **2** move or bend slowly down or to one side, as if from weight or pressure: *He suddenly felt dizzy and swayed against the wall.* **3** cause to sway: *The wind sways the grass.* **4** a swaying: *the sway of a branch in the wind.* **5** change in opinion, feeling, etc.: *Nothing could sway him after he had made up his mind.* **6** a controlling influence or power: *under the sway of a violent emotion. The rebel leader held sway over a large territory.* 1–3, 5 *v.*, 4, 6 *n.*

**sway·back** (swā′bak′) **1** in horses, etc., an abnormally hollow or sagging back, especially as a result of strain or overwork. **2** in human beings, an abnormal forward curve of the middle of the spine. *n.*

**sway·backed** (swā′bakt′) having a SWAYBACK. *adj.*

**swear** (swer) **1** make a solemn promise before a judge,

coroner, etc.: *A witness at a trial has to swear to tell the truth.*  **2** declare, calling God to witness; make a solemn oath; declare on oath.  **3** bind by an oath; require to promise: *Members of the club were sworn to secrecy.*  **4** admit to office or service by administering an oath to: *to swear a witness.*  **5** promise solemnly or on oath to observe or do something: *I swear to obey the rules of this club.*  **6** bring, set, take, etc. by swearing: *to swear a person's life away.*  **7** use profane language; curse.  *v.*, **swore, sworn, swear·ing.**  —**swear′er,** *n.*
**swear by,** a name as one's witness in taking an oath. **b** have great confidence in.
**swear in,** admit to office or service by giving an oath: *to swear in a jury.*
**swear off,** promise to give up: *to swear off smoking.*

**swear·word** (swer′werd′) a word or phrase used in cursing; a profane or obscene word or phrase. *n.*

**sweat** (swet)  **1** moisture coming through the pores of the skin; perspiration: *He wiped the sweat from his face.*  **2** give out moisture through the pores of the skin; perspire: *We sweated because it was very hot.*  **3** cause to sweat: *He sweated the horse by riding it too hard.*  **4** get rid of by sweating or as if by sweating: *sweat off excess weight.*  **5** cause to give off moisture; ferment: *to sweat hides or tobacco in preparing them for use.*  **6** come out in drops; ooze.  **7** send out in drops.  **8** a fit or condition of sweating: *He was in a cold sweat from fear.*  **9** *Informal.* a condition of anxiety, impatience, or anything that might make a person sweat: *We were all in a sweat over the big test we would get on Monday.*  **10** wet or stain with sweat.  **11** moisture given out by something or gathered on its surface: *The water pipes were covered with sweat.*  **12** give out moisture; collect or gather moisture on the surface: *A pitcher of ice water sweats on a hot day.*  **13** cause to work hard and under bad conditions: *That employer sweats her workers.*  **14** *Informal.* work very hard.  **15** heat solder till it melts; join metal parts by heating.  1, 8, 9, 11 *n.*, 2–7, 10, 12–15 *v.*, **sweat** or **sweat·ed, sweat·ing.**
**by the sweat of one's brow,** by one's own efforts and hard work.
**sweat it out,** *Informal.* wait anxiously or nervously for something to happen.

**sweat·band** (swet′band′)  **1** a band, usually of leather, lining the inside edge of a hat or cap to protect it from sweat.  **2** a cloth band tied around the head or wrist to absorb sweat.  *n.*

**sweat·er** (swet′ər) a knitted or crocheted outer garment for the upper body, made of wool, nylon, cotton, etc.; a pullover or cardigan.  *n.*

**sweat gland** a small gland, just under the skin, that secretes sweat. See EPIDERMIS for picture.

**sweat pants** loose trousers, usually gathered at the ankle, made of a warm, absorbent fabric such as fleece-lined cotton, worn for outdoor sports, warm-up exercises, etc.

**sweat shirt** a long-sleeved, collarless pullover, made of a warm, absorbent fabric such as fleece-lined cotton, worn for outdoor sports, warm-up exercises, etc.

**sweat·shop** (swet′shop′) a place where workers are employed at low pay for long hours under bad conditions.  *n.*

**sweat suit** a suit consisting of a sweat shirt and sweat pants, worn especially by athletes, etc. while exercising.

**sweat·y** (swet′ē)  **1** sweating; covered with sweat.  **2** causing sweat: *sweaty work, sweaty weather.*  **3** of or like sweat: *a sweaty odour.*  *adj.*, **sweat·i·er, sweat·i·est.**  —**sweat′i·ly,** *adv.*  —**sweat′i·ness,** *n.*

hat, āge, fär; let, ēqual, tėrm; it, īce
hot, ōpen, ôrder; oil, out; cup, put, rüle
əbove, takən, pencəl, lemən, circəs
ch, child; ng, long; sh, ship
th, thin; ŦH, then; zh, measure

**Swede** (swēd)  **1** a native or inhabitant of Sweden, a country in northern Europe.  **2** a person of Swedish descent.  *n.*

**Swed·ish** (swē′dish)  **1** of or having to do with Sweden, its people, or their language.  **2** the Germanic language of Sweden.  **3 the Swedish,** *pl.* the people of Sweden.  1 *adj.*, 2, 3 *n.*

**sweep** (swēp)  **1** clean or clear with a broom or brush; use a broom or something to remove dirt; brush: *Sweep the steps.*  **2** move, drive, or take away with or as with a broom, brush, etc.: *The wind sweeps the snow into drifts.*  **3** remove with a sweeping motion; carry along: *A flood swept away the bridge.*  **4** the act of sweeping; clearing away; removing: *Aino made a clean sweep of all her debts.*  **5** trail upon: *Her dress sweeps the ground.*  **6** pass over with a steady movement: *His fingers swept the strings of the harp. His eyes swept the sky, searching for signs of rain.*  **7** move swiftly; pass swiftly: *Pirates swept down on the town.*  **8** a steady, driving motion or swift onward course of something: *the sweep of the wind kept the trees from growing tall.*  **9** move with purpose and dignity: *The lady swept out of the room.*  **10** a smooth, flowing motion or line; dignified motion: *the sweep of verse.*  **11** move or extend in a long course or curve: *The shore sweeps to the south for some distance.*  **12** a curve; bend: *the sweep of a road.*  **13** a swinging or curving motion: *He cut the grass with strong sweeps of his scythe.*  **14** a continuous extent; stretch: *The house looked upon a wide sweep of farming country.*  **15** the reach; range; extent: *The mountain is beyond the sweep of your eye.*  **16** a winning of all the games in a series, match, contest, etc.; complete victory.  **17** a person who sweeps chimneys, streets, etc.  **18** a long oar.  **19** a long pole which pivots on a high post and is used to raise or lower a bucket in a well.  **20** a SWEEPSTAKES contest.  1–3, 5–7, 9, 11 *v.*, **swept, sweep·ing;**  4, 8, 10, 12–20 *n.*,  —**sweep·er,** *n.*

**sweep·ing** (swē′ping)  **1** passing or extending over a wide space: *a sweeping glance.*  **2** having wide range; extensive; thoroughgoing: *sweeping reforms.*  **3** not considering exceptions or limitations; indiscriminate: *a sweeping statement.*  **4** the act or work of a person or thing that sweeps: *The porch needs a good sweeping.*  **5** sweepings, *pl.* things that have been swept up; refuse: *Put the sweepings in that box.*  **6** ppr. of SWEEP.  1–3 *adj.*, 4, 5 *n.*, 6 *v.*  —**sweep′ing·ly,** *adv.*

**sweep·stake** (swēp′stāk′) SWEEPSTAKES.  *n.*

**sweep·stakes** (swēp′stāks′)  **1** a race or contest in which the prize or prizes come from the stakes of the participants, sometimes with additional contributions from the sponsor or sponsors.  **2** a form of lottery for gambling on horse races, etc., in which each participant pays a specified sum of money to draw a ticket bearing the name of one of the horses, etc. The sum of the stakes goes to the person or persons who draw the winning or placed horses, etc.  **3** a prize won in such a contest or race.  **4** the contest or race that determines the winner: *When is the sweepstakes?*  *n.sing.* or *pl.*

**sweet** (swēt)  **1** having a taste like sugar or honey.  **2** pleasing to the sense of smell; fragrant, like roses, perfume, etc.: *The air was sweet with the scent of lilacs.*

*Vanilla has a sweet smell.* **3** pleasing to the ear; harmonious: *sweet music.* **4** attractive, charming, kind, etc.: *She had a sweet smile. He's a sweet child. It's sweet of you to help.* **5** very pleasurable; gratifying or satisfying: *sweet praise, sweet dreams of success. Revenge is sweet.* **6** fresh; not sour, fermented, or spoiled: *sweet cider. Is the milk still sweet?* **7** not salty: *sweet butter.* **8** of soil, not too acid. **9** sweetheart; darling. **10** in a sweet manner; sweetly. **11 the sweet,** that which is sweet: *to take the bitter with the sweet.* **12 sweets,** *pl.* food, such as candy, cake, etc., containing a lot of sugar or other sweetening agent: *I like sweets.* 1–8 *adj.*, 9, 11, 12 *n.*, 10 *adv.* —**sweet′ly,** *adv.* —**sweet′ness,** *n.*
**be sweet on,** *Informal,* be in love with.
☞ *Hom.* SUITE.

**sweet alyssum** a common, low-growing garden plant of the mustard family native to Europe, having clusters of fragrant, small white or mauve flowers: *Sweet alyssum is popular for flower borders, window boxes, etc.*

**sweet-and-sour** (swē′tən sour′) of food, prepared with a sauce containing sugar together with vinegar or lemon juice: *sweet-and-sour pork.* *adj.*

**sweet basil** BASIL (def. 1): *Sweet basil is the only basil used in cooking.*

**sweet bay** **1** LAUREL (def. 1). **2** a small tree of the magnolia family native to the southeastern United States, having fragrant, creamy-white flowers.

**sweet·bread** (swēt′bred′) the pancreas or thymus of a calf, lamb, etc. used as meat. *n.*

**sweet·bri·er** (swēt′brī′ər) a wild rose native to Europe but now found in North America, having tall, branching stems with hooked prickles, fragrant leaves, and fragrant pink or white flowers; eglantine. *n.* Also, **sweetbriar.**

**sweet cider** unfermented cider.

**sweet clover** any of a closely related group of plants of the legume family, having small flowers and leaflets in groups of three: *Sweet clover is widely grown to improve the soil and for use as hay.*

**sweet corn** any of several varieties of corn having kernels rich in sugar, used as a vegetable when in the young, milky stage.

**sweet·en** (swē′tən) **1** make sweet. **2** become sweet. **3** make pleasant or agreeable. *v.*

**sweet·en·er** (swē′tə nər *or* swēt′nər) something that sweetens, especially an artificial substitute for sugar or honey, such as saccharin. *n.*

**sweet·en·ing** (swē′tə ning *or* swēt′ning) **1** something that sweetens. **2** ppr. of SWEETEN. 1 *n.*, 2 *v.*

**sweet flag** a tall, perennial marsh plant of the arum family, found in north temperate regions, having tiny flowers, long, sword-shaped leaves, and a thick, fragrant underground stem.

**sweet gale** a low-growing shrub of the wax myrtle family found along river banks and in marshy places in North America, Europe, and Asia: *The wood and leaves of the sweet gale are fragrant when crushed.*

**sweet gum** **1** a tall shade and timber tree of eastern North America having star-shaped leaves that turn scarlet or gold in the fall: *The bark of the sweet gum yields a fragrant, pleasant-tasting liquid balsam, or gum, used in* medicines and in making perfumes, etc. **2** the hard, fine-grained wood of this tree, highly valued for making fine furniture, mouldings, etc.

**sweet·heart** (swēt′härt′) **1** a loved one; lover. **2** darling. *n.*

**sweetheart neckline** a neckline for women's clothing that is low in front and scalloped in the shape of the top of a heart.

**sweet·ie** (swē′tē) *Informal.* SWEETHEART. *n.*

**sweetie pie** *Informal.* SWEETHEART.

**sweet·ing** (swē′ting) a sweet apple. *n.*

**sweet·ish** (swē′tish) somewhat sweet. *adj.*

**sweet marjoram** an herb of the mint family, having aromatic leaves commonly used as a seasoning in cookery.

**sweet·meat** (swēt′mēt′) food prepared with much sugar or honey; especially, candy or candied or crystallized fruit. *n.*

**sweet pea** **1** an annual climbing plant of the pea family, native to Italy but long cultivated in many parts of the world, having fragrant flowers of many different colours. **2** the flower of this plant.

**sweet pepper** **1** a large, mild-flavoured variety of capsicum fruit eaten raw in salads, etc. or cooked as a vegetable. **2** a pepper plant, or capsicum, bearing sweet peppers.

**sweet potato** **1** a perennial tropical vine of the morning glory family widely cultivated in tropical and warm temperate regions, having a large tuberous root that is used for food. **2** its sweet, starchy root, ranging in colour from white to orange inside and light brown to rose outside: *Sweet potatoes are usually served as a cooked vegetable.*

**sweet talk** FLATTERY.

**sweet-talk** (swēt′tok′) *Informal.* COAX *or* FLATTER: *Malik said he had let himself be sweet-talked into running for class president and now he was sorry.* *v.*

**sweet-tem·pered** (swēt′tem′pərd) having or showing a gentle or pleasant nature; amiable. *adj.*

**sweet tooth** a fondness or craving for sweet foods.

**sweet william** *or* **sweet William** a widely cultivated pink having flat clusters of small, fragrant, showy flowers often spotted or banded in different colours. See INFLORESCENCE for picture.

**swell** (swel) **1** grow or make larger in size, amount, degree, force, etc.: *Bread dough swells as it rises. The river is swollen by rain. His head is swollen where he bumped it. Savings may swell into a fortune. The sound swelled from a murmur to a roar.* **2** be larger or thicker in a particular place; stick out; cause to stick out: *A barrel swells in the middle.* **3** the act of swelling; increase in amount, degree, force, etc. **4** the condition of being swollen. **5** rise or cause to rise above the level: *Rounded hills swell gradually from the village plain.* **6** a part that swells out. **7** a piece of higher ground; rounded hill. **8** a long, unbroken wave or waves: *The boat rocked in the swell.* **9** a swelling tone or sound. **10** in music, a crescendo followed by a diminuendo. **11** the sign for this (< >). **12** a device in an organ to control the volume of sound. **13** *Informal.* become or make proud or conceited. **14** *Informal.* a fashionable person. **15** *Informal.* stylish; grand. **16** *Informal.* excellent; first-rate. 1, 2, 5, 13 *v.*, **swelled, swelled** *or* **swol·len, swell·ing;** 3, 4, 6–12, 14 *n.*, 15, 16 *adj.*

**swell·ing** (swel'ing) 1 a swollen part: *There is a swelling on her head where she bumped it.* 2 the condition of being swollen; an increase in size. 3 ppr. of SWELL. 1, 2 *n.*, 3 *v.*

**swel·ter** (swel'tər) 1 suffer from heat, as by sweating freely, feeling faint, etc. 2 a sweltering condition or atmosphere. 1 *v.*, 2 *n.* —**swel'ter·ing·ly**, *adv.*

**swept** (swept) a pt. and pp. of SWEEP: *He swept the room. Have the chimneys been swept?* *v.*

**swept–back** (swept'bak') of the wings of an aircraft, slanting backward from the base to the tip. *adj.*

**swerve** (swėrv) 1 turn aside sharply from a straight course or line: *The road swerves to the right here and goes around the lake. She swerved the car to avoid hitting the child.* 2 the act or instance of turning aside sharply: *The swerve of the ball made it hard to hit.* 1 *v.*, **swerved, swerv·ing;** 2 *n.*

**swift** (swift) 1 moving or able to move very fast: *a light, swift sailboat. She took the swiftest horse.* 2 coming or happening quickly: *a swift response.* 3 quick or prompt to act, etc.: *She is swift to repay a kindness.* 4 in a swift manner; swiftly: *a swift-flowing river.* 5 any of a family of small, mostly dull-coloured birds noted for their speed in flight, having long, narrow wings that when closed extend well past the tip of the tail: *Swifts resemble swallows when in flight, but are not related to them.* 1–4 *adj.*, 5 *n.* —**swift'ly**, *adv.* —**swift'ness**, *n.*

**swift–foot·ed** (swift'fùt'id) able to run swiftly: *Deer are nimble and swift-footed.* *adj.*

**swig** (swig) *Informal.* 1 a big or hearty drink or swallow, especially of liquor. 2 drink heartily or greedily. 1 *n.*, 2 *v.*, **swigged, swig·ging.** —**swig'ger**, *n.*

**swill** (swil) 1 kitchen scraps and other vegetable refuse, especially when partly liquid; garbage; slops: *Swill is sometimes fed to pigs.* 2 drink greedily or in great quantity; guzzle. 3 feed with swill: *to swill the pigs.* 4 a deep drink, especially of liquor; swig. 5 wash by flooding with water. 1, 4 *n.*, 2, 3, 5 *v.*

A woman swimming

**swim** (swim) 1 make oneself move in water by movements of the arms and legs, tail, or fins: *I'm learning to swim.* 2 cover or cross by swimming: *to swim a river. I swam four lengths of the pool.* 3 make swim: *Sif swam her horse across the stream.* 4 float on a liquid: *There were some bits of parsley swimming in the soup.* 5 be covered or flooded with a liquid: *a roast swimming in gravy, eyes swimming with tears. The floor was swimming with water.* 6 the act or a period of swimming: *We went for a swim.* 7 the distance covered or to be covered in swimming: *a four-kilometre swim.* 8 go smoothly; glide: *White clouds swam across the sky.* 9 have a feeling of floating or reeling; be dizzy: *The heat and noise made my head swim.* 10 of, having to do with, or involving swimming: *a swim meet.* 1–5, 8, 9 *v.*, **swam, swum, swim·ming;** 6, 7, 10 *n.* **in the swim,** in the main current of activity in fashion, business, politics, etc.: *She's socially very active and likes to be in the swim.*

**swim bladder** the air bladder of a fish.

**swim·mer** (swim'ər) a person or animal that swims. *n.*

**swim·mer·et** (swim'ə ret') in some crustaceans, a small appendage used in swimming and for carrying eggs. *n.*

**swim·ming** (swim'ing) 1 the practice or sport of swimming: *Sylvia is expert at both swimming and diving.* 2 the act of swimming: *Can you reach the island by swimming?* 3 of or for swimming or swimmers: *a swimming teacher, a swimming pool.* 4 faint; dizzy: *a swimming sensation.* 5 ppr. of SWIM. 1, 2 *n.*, 3, 4 *adj.*, 5 *v.*

**swim·ming·ly** (swim'ing lē) with great ease or success: *Our party went swimmingly.* *adv.*

**swimming pool** a large tank of concrete, plastic, etc., built into or on the ground for swimming or bathing in: *They have a swimming pool in their backyard.*

**swim–suit** (swim'süt') a close-fitting garment worn for swimming or bathing; bathing suit. *n.*

**swin·dle** (swin'dəl) 1 take money or property from by deceit or fraud; cheat: *They said he had swindled them. He swindled them out of their savings.* 2 get money or property by deceit or fraud: *She had swindled $200 from him.* 3 an act of swindling; cheating or defrauding: *The whole deal was a swindle.* 1, 2 *v.*, **swin·dled, swin·dling;** 3 *n.*

**swin·dler** (swin'dlər) a person who SWINDLES. *n.*

**swine** (swīn) 1 pig; hog. 2 a coarse or beastly person. *n.*, *pl.* **swine.**

**swine·herd** (swīn'hėrd') a person who tends SWINE. *n.*

**swing** (swing) 1 move freely to and fro in an arc or circle from an upper or overhead support that remains still: *A pendulum swings. His arms swung as he walked. Monkeys swing through the trees.* 2 move on or as if on hinges or a pivot: *The screen door was swinging in the wind. The gate swung slowly shut. She swung around and confronted them.* 3 cause to swing: *to swing a golf club. He swung his arms. She swung the car into the driveway.* 4 a swinging movement or stroke: *One swing of the axe split the log in two.* 5 the width or manner of a swing: *a wide swing. She has an excellent swing.* 6 carry or transport something that is suspended: *The crane swung the cargo into the hold.* 7 move or transport something with a sweeping motion: *I swung the suitcase up onto the rack.* 8 a seat hung from ropes or chains, on which one may swing for pleasure. 9 move or cause to move to and fro on a swing, in a hammock, etc.: *Several children were swinging in the playground. He was swinging his little sister.* 10 be suspended or hang freely: *The microphone swung from an overhead track.* 11 hang so as to swing; suspend: *We swung the hammock between two trees.* 12 *Informal.* manage successfully: *We didn't think she'd be able to swing the deal.* 13 move with a free, rhythmic motion: *The soldiers came swinging down the street.* 14 a swinging gait, movement, or rhythm: *She walked with a swing.* 15 the normal rhythm or sequence of activity: *to get into the swing of a new job.* 16 in music, a style of jazz that

evolved in the 1930's, characterized by a smooth but lively rhythm with more syncopation than in ragtime: *Swing was usually played by large bands.* **17** play or sing a melody in the style of swing. **18** of, having to do with, or playing music in this style: *a swing band.* **19** *Informal.* of a place, occasion, etc., be lively, exciting, and unrestrained: *The party was swinging by the time they got there. The town really swings these days.* **20** a trip around a country, region, etc.; tour: *a swing through the Maritimes.* **21** *Cdn.* in the North: **a** a train of sleighs or freight canoes, so called because they move, or swing, over a certain route in periodic trips. **b** a train of freight sleighs drawn by tractors; cat-train. 1–3, 6, 7, 9–13, 17, 19 *v.*, **swung, swing·ing,** 4, 5, 8, 14–16, 18, 20, 21 *n.*
**in full swing,** going on actively and completely; without restraint: *By eleven the party was in full swing.*

**swin·gle·tree** (swing'gəl trē') SINGLETREE. *n.*

**swin·ish** (swī'nish) of, characteristic of, or like swine; hoggish, beastly, or coarse: *swinish behaviour.* *adj.* —**swin'ish·ly,** *adv.* —**swin'ish·ness,** *n.*

**swipe** (swīp) **1** *Informal.* a sweeping stroke; hard blow: *She made two swipes at the golf ball without hitting it.* **2** *Informal.* strike with a sweeping blow. **3** *Informal.* steal. 1 *n.*, 2, 3 *v.*, **swiped, swip·ing.**
**take a swipe at,** *Informal.* try to hit; aim a blow at: *He took a swipe at me, but I ducked.*

**swirl** (swèrl) **1** move or drive along with a twisting motion; whirl: *dust swirling in the air, a stream swirling over rocks.* **2** a swirling movement or mass; eddy. **3** have a twisting shape or pattern. **4** something having a twisting shape or pattern: *a swirl of whipped cream.* 1, 3 *v.*, 2, 4 *n.*

**swish** (swish) **1** move, pass, or swing with a light hissing or brushing sound: *The whip swished through the air.* **2** make such a sound: *Her long skirt swished as she danced across the floor.* **3** cause to swish: *She swished the stick through the branches. The horse swished its tail.* **4** a swishing movement or sound: *the swish of little waves on the shore.* 1–3 *v.*, 4 *n.*

**Swiss** (swis) **1** of or having to do with Switzerland, a small country in west central Europe, or its people. **2** a native or inhabitant of Switzerland. **3** a person of Swiss descent. **4 the Swiss,** *pl.* the people of Switzerland. 1 *adj.*, 2–4 *n.*, *pl.* **Swiss.**

**Swiss chard** a variety of white beet whose leaves and stalks are eaten as a vegetable.

**Swiss cheese** a firm pale-yellow or whitish cheese having a mild, slightly nutty flavour and many large holes that form as the cheese ripens.

**Swiss steak** a cut of steak prepared by pounding it with flour and seasonings, browning it, and then cooking it slowly in a sauce with onions and, sometimes, tomatoes, sweet peppers, etc.

**switch** (swich) **1** a slender stick used in whipping. **2** whip; strike: *He switched the boys with a birch stick.* **3** a stroke; lash: *The dog broke a vase with a switch of its tail.* **4** move or swing like a switch: *The horse switched its tail to drive off the flies.* **5** a device for making or breaking a connection in an electric circuit. **6** pair of movable rails by which a train can shift from one track to another. **7** change, turn, or shift by using a switch: *switch off the light.* **8** move a train, railway car, etc. from one track to another by means of a switch: *to switch railroad cars from one track to another.* **9** turn aside; change course or direction: *He was driving on the outside lane but suddenly switched.* **10** turn; shift; divert something: *She quickly switched the subject.* **11** exchange: *The boys switched hats.* **12** a change or exchange. 1, 3, 5, 6, 12 *n.*, 2, 4, 7–11 *v.* —**switch'er,** *n.*

**switch·back** (swich'bak') **1** a railway or road climbing a steep grade in a zigzag course. **2** *Esp. Brit.* ROLLER COASTER. *n.*

**switch·blade** (swich'blād') a pocket knife whose blade springs open when a button or knob is pressed. *n.*

**switch·board** (swich'bôrd') a panel containing the necessary switches, meters, etc. for opening, closing, combining, or controlling electric circuits: *A telephone switchboard has plugs or buttons for connecting one line to another.* *n.*

**switch·man** (swich'mən) a person in charge of one or more railway switches. *n.*, *pl.* **switch·men** (-mən).

**swiv·el** (swiv'əl) **1** a fastening joining two parts so that one may turn without moving the other. **2** turn on a swivel or as if on a swivel: *She swivelled the chair around. He swivelled his eyes in our direction.* **3** fasten or support by a swivel. 1 *n.*, 2, 3 *v.*, **swiv·elled** or **swiv·eled, swiv·el·ling** or **swiv·el·ing.**

**swivel chair** a chair that turns on a SWIVEL in its base.

**swivel gun** a gun mounted on a SWIVEL so that it can be turned in any direction.

**swob** (swob) See SWAB. *n.*, *v.*, **swobbed, swob·bing.** —**swob'ber,** *n.*

**swol·len** (swō'lən) **1** swelled: *a swollen ankle.* **2** a pp. of SWELL. 1 *adj.*, 2 *v.*

**swoon** (swün) **1** faint: *He swooned at the sight of the blood.* **2** a loss of consciousness: *He fell in a swoon.* **3** of sound, fade or die away gradually. 1, 3 *v.*, 2 *n.*

**swoop** (swüp) **1** move with a rush; especially, make a sudden, swift attack (*usually used with* **down**): *The eagle swooped down on the mouse. The horsemen swooped down on the village and burned it.* **2** seize; snatch (*used with* **up**): *She swooped the puppy up in her arms.* **3** the act or an instance of swooping: *With one swoop, she had seized the pie and run off.* 1, 2 *v.*, 3 *n.* —**swoop'er,** *n.*

**swoosh** (swüsh) **1** move with or make a sound like a rush of liquid or air: *The car swooshed by.* **2** the act or an instance of swooshing: *We heard a swoosh as the water rushed into the tank.* 1 *v.*, 2 *n.*

**swop** (swop) See SWAP. *v.*, **swopped, swop·ping;** *n.* —**swop'per,** *n.*

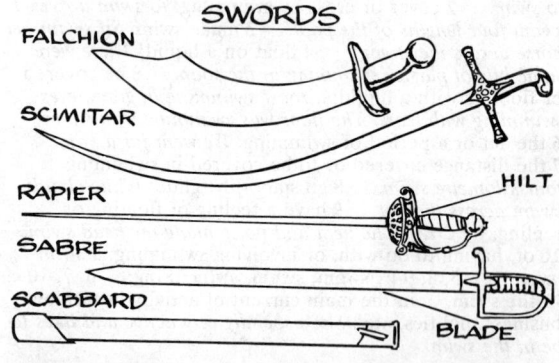

**sword** (sôrd) **1** a hand weapon, usually metal, with a

long, sharp blade fixed in a handle or hilt. 2 a symbol of honour or authority: *the sword of justice.* 3 **the sword,** war or military power: *The pen is mightier than the sword. The conqueror ruled by the sword.* *n.* —**sword'like',** *adj.*

**at swords' points,** very unfriendly; ready to fight or quarrel.

**cross swords,** fight or quarrel: *I wouldn't want to cross swords with him; he's mean.*

**put to the sword,** kill, especially in war: *He put his captives to the sword.*

A swordfish— usually about 215 cm long

**sword·fish** (sôrd'fish') a very large food and game fish found in tropical and temperate seas throughout the world, having a tall, scale-less back fin, a crescent-shaped fin and a very long, flat, swordlike upper jawbone with which it slashes and pierces its prey: *The swordfish makes up a separate family of fish but is distantly related to the marlins, sailfish, and tunas.* *n., pl.* **sword·fish** or **sword·fish·es.**

**sword·play** (sôrd'plā') the action, practice, or art of wielding a sword, especially in fencing. *n.*

**swords·man** (sôrdz'mən) 1 a person skilled in using a sword. 2 a person using a sword. *n., pl.* **swords·men** (-zmən).

**swords·man·ship** (sôrdz'mən ship') skill in using a sword. *n.*

**swore** (swôr) pt. of swear: *They swore to tell the truth. She swore to get even.* *v.*

**sworn** (swôrn) 1 pp. of swear: *A solemn oath of loyalty was sworn by all the knights.* 2 having taken an oath; bound by an oath. 3 declared, promised, etc. with an oath: *We have her sworn statement.* 1 *v.,* 2, 3 *adj.*

**swum** (swum) pp. of swim: *He had never swum before.* *v.*

**swung** (swung) pt. and pp. of swing. *v.*

**syb·a·rite** (sib'ə rīt') a person who cares very much for luxury and pleasure. *n.*

**syb·a·rit·ic** (sib'ə rit'ik) luxurious; voluptuous. *adj.*

**syc·a·more** (sik'ə môr') 1 any of a closely related group of trees that make up the plane tree family, native to North America, Europe, and Asia, especially a large hardwood tree of North America having broad, lobed leaves, spreading branches, and brownish outer bark that flakes off in large, irregular patches, revealing the whitish inner bark: *The common North American sycamore is also called the buttonball or buttonwood.* 2 a large species of maple native to Europe and Asia, having spreading branches and broad leaves: *The sycamore, also called the sycamore maple, is often planted as an ornamental tree in Canada.* 3 a species of fig tree of Egypt and Asia Minor. *n.*

**syc·o·phan·cy** (sik'ə fən sē) servile, self-seeking flattery. *n., pl.* **syc·o·phan·cies.**

**syc·o·phant** (sik'ə fənt) a servile, self-seeking flatterer; toady. *n.*

**syc·o·phan·tic** (sik'ə fan'tik) having to do with, characteristic of, or acting as a sycophant. *adj.*

hat, āge, fär; let, ēqual, tėrm; it, īce
hot, ōpen, ôrder; oil, out; cup, put, rüle
əbove, taken, pencəl, lemən, circəs
ch, child; ng, long; sh, ship
th, thin; ᴛʜ, then; zh, measure

**sy·e·nite** (sī'ə nīt') a grey crystalline rock composed of feldspar and hornblende. *n.*

**syl.** or **syll.** 1 syllable. 2 syllabus.

**syl·lab·ic** (sə lab'ik) 1 of, having to do with, or consisting of syllables. 2 forming a syllable or the nucleus of a syllable. *Example: The second* l *in* little *is syllabic because it forms a separate syllable.* 3 a syllabic speech sound. 4 a written sign or character representing a syllable. 5 pronounced syllable by syllable. 1, 2, 5 *adj.,* 3, 4 *n.*

**syl·lab·i·cal·ly** (sə lab'i klē) by or with regard to syllables. *adv.*

**syl·lab·i·cate** (sə lab'ə kāt') form or divide into syllables; syllabify. *v.,* **syl·lab·i·cat·ed, syl·lab·i·cat·ing.**

**syl·lab·i·ca·tion** (sə lab'ə kā'shən) the process of dividing into syllables; division into syllables. *n.*

**syl·lab·i·fi·ca·tion** (sə lab'ə fə kā'shən) syllabication. *n.*

**syl·lab·i·fy** (sə lab'ə fī') divide into syllables; syllabicate. *v.,* **syl·lab·i·fied, syl·lab·i·fy·ing.**

**syl·la·bize** (sil'ə bīz') 1 form or divide into syllables. 2 utter with careful distinction of syllables. *v.,* **syl·la·bized, syl·la·biz·ing.**

**syl·la·ble** (sil'ə bəl) 1 a word or part of a word spoken as a unit, usually consisting of a vowel sound alone or a vowel sound with one or more consonant sounds. *See* is a word of one syllable, consisting of a consonant sound (s) plus a vowel sound (ē). *Syllable* is a word of three syllables: (sil'ə bəl). 2 in writing or printing, a letter or group of letters corresponding roughly to a syllable of spoken language. The syllables of the entry word *syllable* in this dictionary are separated by dots: **syl·la·ble.** A word that has to be broken at the end of a line is usually hyphenated between two syllables. 3 the slightest bit or detail of something: *She promised not to breathe a syllable of the secret to anyone.* 4 pronounce or utter in or as if in syllables. 1–3 *n.,* 4 *v.,* **syl·la·bled, syl·la·bling.**

**syl·la·bus** (sil'ə bəs) a brief statement of the main points of a speech, a book, a course of study, etc. *n., pl.* **syl·la·bus·es** or **syl·la·bi** (-bī' or -bē').

**syl·lo·gism** (sil'ə jiz'əm) 1 a form of argument or reasoning consisting of two statements and a conclusion drawn from them. *Example: All trees have roots; an oak is a tree; therefore, an oak has roots.* 2 a reasoning in this form; deduction. *n.*

**syl·lo·gis·tic** (sil'ə jis'tik) of, having to do with or using syllogisms. *adj.*

**syl·lo·gize** (sil'ə jīz') 1 argue or reason by syllogisms. 2 deduce by syllogism. *v.,* **syl·lo·gized, syl·lo·giz·ing.**

**sylph** (silf) a slender, graceful girl or woman. *n.* —**sylph'like',** *adj.*

**syl·va** (sil'və) *See* silva. *n.*

**syl·van** (sil'vən) 1 of, having to do with, or

characteristic of the woods. 2 living or situated in the woods: *a sylvan retreat.* *adj.* Also, **silvan**.

**sym.** 1 symbol. 2 symmetrical. 3 symphony. 4 symptom.

**sym·bi·o·sis** (sim′bī ō′sis) the association or living together of two unlike organisms in a relationship that benefits each of them: *The lichen, which is composed of an alga and a fungus, is an example of symbiosis; the alga provides the food, and the fungus provides water and protection.* Compare with AMENSALISM, COMMENSALISM, MUTUALISM, and PARASITISM. *n.*

**sym·bi·ot·ic** (sim′bī ot′ik) having to do with or living in SYMBIOSIS. *adj.*

**sym·bol** (sim′bəl) 1 something that stands for or represents an idea, quality, condition, or other abstraction: *The lion is the symbol of courage; the lamb, of meekness; the olive branch, of peace.* 2 a letter, figure, or sign conventionally used in writing or printing, standing for a process, object, quantity, relation, etc.: *The marks +, −, ×, and ÷ are symbols for add, subtract, multiply, and divide.* 3 SYMBOLIZE. 1, 2 *n.*, 3 *v.*, **sym·bolled** or **sym·boled**, **sym·bol·ling** or **sym·bol·ing**.
☛ *Hom.* CYMBAL.

**sym·bol·ic** (sim bol′ik) 1 used as a SYMBOL: *The maple leaf is symbolic of Canada.* 2 of, expressed by, or using SYMBOLS: *Writing is a symbolic form of expression.* *adj.* —**sym·bol′i·cal·ly**, *adv.*

**sym·bol·i·cal** (sim bol′ə kəl) SYMBOLIC. *adj.*

**sym·bol·ism** (sim′bə liz′əm) 1 the use of conventional or traditional signs, etc. to represent things, especially things that are abstract or invisible; representation by symbols. 2 a system of symbols. *n.*

**sym·bol·ist** (sim′bə list) 1 a person who uses SYMBOLS or SYMBOLISM. 2 an artist or writer who makes much use of colours, sounds, etc. as SYMBOLS. 3 a person who is skilled in the study or interpretation of SYMBOLS. *n.*

**sym·bol·i·za·tion** (sim′bə lə zā′shən *or* sim′bə lī zā′shən) a symbolizing; representation by SYMBOLS. *n.*

**sym·bol·ize** (sim′bə līz′) 1 be a SYMBOL of; stand for; represent: *A dove symbolizes peace.* 2 represent or express by a SYMBOL or symbols: *We symbolize the chemical composition of water by the formula* $H_2O$. 3 use SYMBOLS. *v.*, **sym·bol·ized**, **sym·bol·iz·ing**.

**sym·met·ric** (si met′rik) SYMMETRICAL. *adj.*

**sym·met·ri·cal** (si met′rə kəl) having or showing SYMMETRY: *a symmetrical design, a symmetrical curve. The tree on our front lawn has an almost symmetrical crown.* See ASYMMETRIC for picture. *adj.*
—**sym·met′ri·cal·ly**, *adv.*

Symmetry. The figures in the top row show symmetry on opposite sides of a line; the figures in the bottom row show symmetry around a central point.

**sym·me·try** (sim′ə trē) 1 a regular, balanced arrangement on opposite sides of a line or plane, or around a centre or axis. 2 pleasing proportions between the parts of a whole; a well-balanced arrangement of parts; harmony: *A swollen cheek spoiled the symmetry of her face.* *n., pl.* **sym·me·tries**.

**sym·pa·thet·ic** (sim′pə thet′ik) 1 having or showing kind feelings toward others; sympathizing: *a sympathetic friend, a sympathetic gesture.* 2 inclined to agree or approve; favourably inclined: *They are sympathetic to our idea.* 3 enjoying the same things and getting along well together; congenial: *Rita enjoys the skating club because she finds most of the members sympathetic.* *adj.*

**sym·pa·thet·i·cal·ly** (sim′pə thet′i klē) in a sympathetic manner; with SYMPATHY. *adv.*

**sym·pa·thize** (sim′pə thīz′) 1 feel or show SYMPATHY: *to sympathize with a child who has hurt herself.* 2 share in or agree with a feeling or opinion: *My mother sympathizes with my plan to be a doctor.* *v.*, **sym·pa·thized**, **sym·pa·thiz·ing**. —**sym′pa·thiz′ing·ly**, *adv.*

**sym·pa·thiz·er** (sim′pə thī′zər) a person who SYMPATHIZES; especially, a person who is favourably inclined toward a particular belief or person. *n.*

**sym·pa·thy** (sim′pə thē) 1 a sharing of another's sorrow or trouble: *We feel sympathy for a person who is ill.* 2 an agreement in feeling; condition or fact of having the same feeling: *The sympathy between the twins was so great that they always smiled or cried at the same things.* 3 agreement; approval; favour: *He is in sympathy with my plan.* *n., pl.* **sym·pa·thies**.

**sym·phon·ic** (sim fon′ik) 1 of, having to do with, or having the character of a SYMPHONY (def. 1): *a symphonic composition.* 2 of or having to do with harmony of sounds; harmonious. *adj.*

**sym·pho·ny** (sim′fə nē) 1 a long and elaborate musical composition for a full orchestra and sometimes singers: *A symphony is usually in the form of a sonata, with three or four movements that are different in rhythm and speed but related in key.* 2 SYMPHONY ORCHESTRA. 3 *Informal.* a concert given by a symphony orchestra. 4 a harmony of sounds. 5 a harmony of colours: *In autumn the woods are a symphony in red, brown, and yellow.* *n., pl.* **sym·pho·nies**.

**symphony orchestra** a large orchestra for playing symphonies and similar works, made up of brass, woodwind, percussion, and stringed instruments.

**sym·po·si·um** (sim pō′zē əm) 1 a collection of the opinions of several persons on some subject: *This magazine contains a symposium on sports.* 2 a formal meeting at which several specialists give their views on a subject. *n., pl.* **sym·po·si·ums** or **sym·po·si·a** (-zē ə).

**symp·tom** (simp′təm) 1 something that indicates the existence of something else; sign: *symptoms of discontent.* 2 a noticeable change in the normal working of the body that indicates or accompanies disease or injury: *The doctor made his diagnosis after studying the patient's symptoms.* *n.*

**symp·to·mat·ic** (simp′tə mat′ik) 1 being a sign; indicative or characteristic: *Riots are symptomatic of political or social unrest.* 2 indicating or accompanying a disease, etc.: *a symptomatic fever.* 3 having to do with SYMPTOMS of disease, etc. *adj.*

**syn.** synonym; synonymous.

**syn·a·gogue** (sin′ə gog′) 1 a building used by a Jewish congregation as a house of worship and religious instruction. 2 a Jewish congregation or assembly. *n.*

**syn·apse** (si naps′ *or* sin′aps) a place where a nerve impulse passes from one nerve cell to another. *n.*

**sync** (singk) *Informal.* **1** SYNCHRONIZATION of sound and action or of speech and lip movement, as in television or motion pictures. **2** SYNCHRONIZE. 1 *n.*, 2 *v.*
**in sync,** synchronized.
**out of sync,** not synchronized.
☛ *Hom.* SINK.

**syn·chro·nal** (sing′krə nəl) SYNCHRONOUS. *adj.*

**syn·chro·nism** (sing′krə niz′əm) the quality or state of being SYNCHRONOUS. *n.*

**syn·chro·ni·za·tion** (sing′krə nə zā′shən *or* sing′krə nī zā′shən) a happening at the same time; coincidence. *n.*

**syn·chro·nize** (sing′krə nīz′) **1** happen at the same time; be simultaneous; coincide. **2** make occur or operate at the same time or speed: *to synchronize all the clocks in the building, to synchronize the flash with the camera shutter, to synchronize the sound with the action in a motion picture.* *v.*, **syn·chro·nized, syn·chro·niz·ing.** —**syn′chro·niz′er**, *n.*

**syn·chro·nous** (sing′krə nəs) **1** occurring or existing at exactly the same time; simultaneous. **2** moving or taking place at the same rate and exactly together. *adj.* —**syn′chro·nous·ly**, *adv.*

**syn·cli·nal** (sin klī′nəl *or* sing klī′nəl) **1** sloping downward from opposite directions so as to form a trough or inverted arch. **2** of, having to do with, or containing a SYNCLINE. *adj.*

Layers of sedimentary rock forming a syncline and anticline

**syn·cline** (sing′klīn) in geology, a downward fold, or trough, of stratified rock, in which the layers slope upward in opposite directions from the centre. Compare with ANTICLINE. *n.*

**syn·co·pate** (sing′kə pāt′) **1** in music: **a** change a regular rhythm by beginning a note on an unaccented beat and holding it into an accented one, or beginning it midway through a beat and continuing it midway into the next one. **b** introduce such shifted accents into a passage or piece of music. **2** shorten a word by SYNCOPE (def. 1). *v.*, **syn·co·pat·ed, syn·co·pat·ing.**

**syn·co·pa·tion** (sing′kə pā′shən). **1** the action or art of syncopating a musical rhythm or piece of music: *Syncopation is much used in jazz.* **2** a syncopated rhythm, piece of music, etc. **3** SYNCOPE (def. 1). *n.*

**syn·co·pe** (sing′kə pē′) **1** the contraction of a word by the loss or omission of a sound or sounds from the middle; as *batt'ry* for *battery.* **2** a temporary loss of consciousness due to an inadequate supply of blood to the brain; fainting: *Syncope can be caused by illness or by extreme pain or emotion.* *n.*

**syn·dic** (sin′dik) **1** a person who manages the business affairs of a university or other corporation. **2** a magistrate. *n.*

**syn·di·cal·ism** (sin′də kə liz′əm) a movement in industrial unions aimed at taking control of industry and government by direct means such as a general strike. *n.*

hat, āge, fär; let, ēqual, tėrm; it, īce
hot, ōpen, ôrder; oil, out; cup, put, rüle
əbove, takən, pencəl, lemən, circəs
ch, child; ng, long; sh, ship
th, thin; ᴛʜ, then; zh, measure

**syn·di·cal·ist** (sin′də kə list) a person who favours or supports SYNDICALISM. *n.*

**syn·di·cate** (sin′də kit *for noun,* sin′də kāt′ *for verb*) **1** a combination of persons or companies to carry out some undertaking, especially one requiring a large capital investment. **2** an agency that sells special articles, photographs, etc. to a large number of newspapers or magazines for publication at the same time. **3** a group of businesses, especially newspapers, under one management. **4** an association or combination of criminals controlling organized crime. **5** combine into a syndicate. **6** manage by a syndicate. **7** publish through a syndicate: *Her article was syndicated to over fifty newspapers.* 1–4 *n.*, 5–7 *v.*, **syn·di·cat·ed, syn·di·cat·ing.**

**syn·di·ca·tion** (sin′də kā′shən) a syndicating or being SYNDICATEd. *n.*

**syn·ec·do·che** (si nek′də kē′) a figure of speech by which a part is put for the whole, or the whole for a part, the special for the general, or the general for the special, etc. *Examples: a factory employing 500* hands (*persons*); *to eat of the* tree (*its fruit*); *a* marble (*a statue*) *on its pedestal.* *n.*

**syn·er·gism** (sin′ər jiz′əm) SYNERGY. *n.*

**syn·er·gy** (sin′ər jē) the combined or co-operative action of two or more agents, groups, or parts, etc. that together increase each other's effectiveness: *the synergy of the muscles of the body.* *n.*

**syn·od** (sin′əd) **1** an assembly called together under authority to discuss and decide church affairs; church council. **2** an assembly; convention; council. *n.*

**syn·od·al** (sin′ə dəl) of, having to do with, or made by a SYNOD: *a synodal assembly, a synodal decree.* *adj.*

**syn·od·i·cal** (si nod′ə kəl) **1** having to do with the conjunctions of the heavenly bodies: *The synodical period of the moon is the time between one new moon and the next.* **2** SYNODAL. *adj.*

**syn·o·nym** (sin′ə nim) **1** one of two or more words of a language having the same or nearly the same meaning: *St. Vitus's dance and chorea are synonyms. Sharp is a synonym for one meaning of keen; enthusiastic is a synonym for another meaning of keen.* Compare with ANTONYM. **2** a word or expression generally accepted as another name for something: *Churchill's name has become a synonym for patriotism.* *n.*

**syn·on·y·mous** (si non′ə məs) having the same or nearly the same meaning: *The words* velocity *and* speed *are synonymous.* *adj.* —**syn·on′y·mous·ly**, *adv.*

**syn·on·y·my** (si non′ə mē) **1** the quality or state of being SYNONYMOUS. **2** the study of SYNONYMS. **3** the use of SYNONYMS together in speaking or writing to add emphasis. *Example: in any shape or form.* **4** a set, list, or system of SYNONYMS. *n., pl.* **syn·on·y·mies.**

**syn·op·sis** (si nop′sis) a brief statement giving a general view of some subject, book, play, etc.; summary: *Write a synopsis of* Treasure Island *in 200 words or less.* *n., pl.* **syn·op·ses** (-sēz).

**syn·op·size** (si nop′sīz) make a SYNOPSIS of. *v.,* syn·op·sized, syn·op·siz·ing.

**syn·tac·tic** (sin tak′tik) of, having to do with, or according to the rules of SYNTAX. *adj.*

**syn·tac·ti·cal** (sin tak′tə kəl) SYNTACTIC. *adj.* —syn·tac′ti·cal·ly, *adv.*

**syn·tax** (sin′taks) 1 in grammar, the way in which words are arranged to form sentences, clauses, or phrases; sentence structure. 2 the patterns of such arrangement in a given language. 3 the use or function of a word, phrase, or clause in a sentence. 4 the part of grammar dealing with the construction of phrases, clauses, and sentences. *n.*

**syn·the·ses** (sin′thə sēz′) pl. of SYNTHESIS. *n.*

**syn·the·sis** (sin′thə sis) 1 a combination of parts or elements into a whole. Compare with ANALYSIS. 2 in chemistry, the formation of a compound or a complex substance by the chemical union of its elements, combination of simpler compounds, etc.: *Alcohol, ammonia, and rubber can be artificially produced by synthesis.* *n., pl.* syn·the·ses.

**syn·the·size** (sin′thə sīz′) 1 combine into a complex whole by SYNTHESIS. 2 make up or produce by combining parts or elements. *v.,* syn·the·sized, syn·the·siz·ing.

**syn·the·siz·er** (sin′thə sī′zər) 1 a person or thing that SYNTHESIZES. 2 an electronic device that simulates and blends conventional and ultrasonic sounds. *n.*

**syn·thet·ic** (sin thet′ik) 1 having to do with SYNTHESIS: *synthetic chemistry.* 2 made by chemical SYNTHESIS; artificial: *synthetic rubies.* 3 material, especially cloth or yarn, made by chemical SYNTHESIS: *Some people prefer synthetics for clothing because they are easy to care for.* 4 not real or genuine; artificial: *synthetic affection.* 5 **synthetics,** the branch of science or industry concerned with the production of synthetic articles. 1, 2, 4 *adj.,* 3, 5 *n.*

**syph·i·lis** (sif′ə lis) a contagious venereal disease which, if untreated, proceeds in three stages over many years, finally causing bones, muscles, and nerve tissue to degenerate: *Syphilis is usually transmitted through sexual intercourse. It is not hereditary but can be transmitted inside the womb from mother to child.* *n.*

**syph·i·lit·ic** (sif′ə lit′ik) 1 having to do with SYPHILIS. 2 affected with SYPHILIS. 3 a person affected with SYPHILIS. 1, 2 *adj.,* 3 *n.*

**sy·phon** (sī′fən) See SIPHON. *n., v.*

**Syr·i·an** (sir′ē ən) 1 of or having to do with ancient or modern Syria, situated in the Middle East, or its people. 2 a native or inhabitant of Syria. 1 *adj.,* 2 *n.*

**sy·rin·ga** (sə ring′gə) 1 mock orange. 2 lilac: *Syringa is the scientific name for the genus of shrubs and trees commonly called lilacs; unfortunately, botanists chose a name that was already in use as a common name for the unrelated mock orange, thus creating some confusion.* *n.*

**sy·ringe** (sə rinj′) 1 a device consisting of a narrow tube with a nozzle at one end and a compressible rubber bulb at the other, for drawing in a quantity of fluid and then forcing it out in a stream: *Syringes are used to clean wounds, inject fluids into body cavities, etc.* 2 a similar device consisting of a hollow needle attached to a hollow barrel with a plunger, used for injecting medicine under the skin, withdrawing body fluids, etc. See HYPODERMIC for picture. 3 clean, wash, inject, etc. by means of a syringe. 1, 2 *n.,* 3 *v.,* sy·ringed, sy·ring·ing.

**syr·inx** (sir′ingks) the vocal organ of birds, situated where the trachea divides into the right and left bronchi. *n., pl.* sy·rin·ges (sə rin′jēz) *or* syr·inx·es.

**syr·up** (sėr′əp *or* sir′əp) 1 a thick solution of sugar and water, usually combined with flavouring or medicine: *cough syrup.* 2 condensed juice of a plant or fruit; especially, sugar cane juice that remains uncrystallized in the refining of sugar, or the juice condensed from the sap of the sugar maple. *n.* —syr′up·like′, *adj.*

► *Etym.* **Syrup** and SHERBET can both be traced back to an Arabic word meaning 'to drink'. **Syrup** comes from OF *sirop* or Med. L *sirupus,* which came from colloquial Arabic *sharāb* 'a drink' from *shariba* 'to drink'. **Sherbet** comes from Turkish *sherbet* and Persian *sharbat* from Arabic *sharbah* 'a drink', also from *shariba.*

**syr·up·y** (sėr′ə pē *or* sir′ə pē) of, like, or suggesting SYRUP in consistency or sweetness. *adj.*

**sys·tem** (sis′təm) 1 a set of things or parts forming a whole: *a mountain system, a railway system, the digestive system, etc.* 2 an ordered group of facts, principles, beliefs, etc.: *a system of government.* 3 a plan; scheme; method: *a system for betting.* 4 an orderly way of getting things done. 5 the animal body as an organized whole: *to take food into the system.* 6 a group of heavenly bodies forming a whole that follows certain natural laws. 7 the world; universe. *n.* —sys′tem·less, *adj.*

**sys·tem·at·ic** (sis′tə mat′ik) 1 based on, involving, or forming a SYSTEM: *a systematic investigation, a systematic classification.* 2 orderly and methodical: *She is a systematic worker.* *adj.*

**sys·tem·at·i·cal** (sis′tə mat′ə kəl) SYSTEMATIC. *adj.*

**sys·tem·at·i·cal·ly** (sis′tə mat′i klē) in a SYSTEMATIC manner: *She checked all the desk drawers systematically, looking for a clue.* *adv.*

**sys·tem·a·tize** (sis′tə mə tīz′) arrange according to a SYSTEM; make into a system: *to systematize one's methods.* *v.,* sys·tem·a·tized, sys·tem·a·tiz·ing. —sys′tem·a·ti·za′tion, *n.* —sys′tem·a·tiz′er, *n.*

**sys·tem·ic** (sis tem′ik) 1 in physiology, of, having to do with, or affecting the body as a whole. 2 of or having to do with the general blood circulation, except for that supplied to the lungs through the pulmonary artery. 3 of an insecticide, fungicide, etc., entering the tissues of a plant and making the plant itself poisonous to pests. 4 a systemic pesticide. 1–3 *adj.,* 4 *n.*

**sys·tem·ize** (sis′tə mīz′) SYSTEMATIZE. *v.,* sys·tem·ized, sys·tem·iz·ing. —sys′tem·i·za′tion, *n.*

**systems analysis** a process or profession of using mathematical techniques to break down a complex activity into basic elements in order to discover ways for the goal or purpose of the activity to be accomplished most efficiently: *Systems analysis is used for business organizations, technical procedures, etc.*

**systems analyst** a person whose work is SYSTEMS ANALYSIS.

**sys·to·le** (sis′tə lē′) the normal rhythmical contraction of the heart. *n.*

**sys·tol·ic** (sis tol′ik) of or having to do with a contraction of the heart. Compare with DIASTOLIC. *adj.*

# T t  *T t*

hat, āge, fär; let, ēqual, tėrm; it, īce
hot, ōpen, ôrder; oil, out; cup, pu̇t, rüle
əbove, takən, pencəl, lemən, circəs
ch, child; ng, long; sh, ship
th, thin; ᴛн, then; zh, measure

**t or T** (tē) **1** the twentieth letter of the English alphabet. **2** any speech sound represented by this letter. **3** any person or thing identified as t, especially the twentieth in a series. **4** anything shaped like a T. *n.*, *pl.* **t's** or **T's**.
**to a T,** exactly; perfectly: *That suits me to a T.*

**t 1** temperature. **2** time. **3** tonne; tonnes.

**T 1** temperature (thermodynamic). **2** tritium.

**t. 1** teaspoon; teaspoons. **2** in grammar, tense. **3** transitive. **4** territory. **5** tenor. **6** in the time of (an abbreviation of Latin *tempore*). **7** town.

**T. 1** Territory. **2** Tuesday. **3** tablespoon; tablespoons.

**Ta** tantalum.

**tab** (tab) **1** a small flap, strap, loop, or piece: *He wore a fur cap with tabs over the ears.* **2** a small projection or attached piece on a card or folder used as a filing aid: *Tabs may be labelled, numbered, colour-coded, etc.* **3** put a tab on something: *to tab index cards.* **4** name or mark; identify: *He was very quickly tabbed as a show-off.* **5** *Informal.* a bill or check; a statement of costs: *to pay the tab.* 1, 2, 5 *n.*, 3, 4 *v.*, **tabbed, tab·bing.**
**keep tab, tabs,** or **a tab on,** keep track of; keep watch on: *He was asked to keep tab on his little sister.*

Tabards: on the left, a modern knitted tabard; on the right, a herald's tabard of the early 16th century.

**tab·ard** (tab′ərd) **1** a short, loose coat worn by a herald, emblazoned with his sovereign's coat of arms. **2** a short surcoat, or tunic, worn over armour by a knight, having short sleeves and open sides, and emblazoned with the knight's coat of arms. **3** a coarse, loose outer garment formerly worn out-of-doors by the lower classes and also by monks and foot soldiers. **4** a similar modern garment, sleeveless or short-sleeved and often open at the sides. *n.*

**tab·by** (tab′ē) **1** a domestic cat having a grey or brownish coat with dark stripes. **2** brown or grey with dark stripes. **3** any cat, especially a female. **4** a spiteful female gossip. 1, 3, 4 *n.*, *pl.* **tab·bies;** 2 *adj.*

**tab·er·nac·le** (tab′ər nak′əl) **1** a Jewish temple. **2** a building used as a place of worship for a large group of people. **3** the human body thought of as the temporary dwelling of the soul. **4** a tomb, shrine, etc. with a canopy. **5** in a church, a small chest or cupboard, often built into the altar, for keeping consecrated bread. **6 Tabernacle,** the covered wooden framework carried by the Israelites for use as a place of worship during their journey from Egypt to Palestine. *n.*

**ta·ble** (tā′bəl) **1** a piece of furniture having a smooth, flat top on legs. **2** the food put on a table to be eaten: *Mrs. Volo sets a good table.* **3** the persons seated at a table, especially at a dinner or for informal discussion: *a table of bridge. King Arthur and his Round Table* means *King Arthur and his knights.* **4** put on a table. **5** a flat surface; plateau. **6** very condensed tabulated information; a list: *a table of contents in the front of a book, the multiplication table.* **7** make a list or condensed statement. **8** a thin, flat piece of wood, stone, metal, etc.; tablet: *the twelve tables of Roman law.* **9** matter inscribed or written on tables. **10** present for consideration: *to table a motion in the House of Commons.* **11** *Esp. U.S.* put off a bill, motion, etc. **12 the tables,** certain laws cut or carved on thin, flat pieces of stone. 1–3, 5, 6, 8, 9, 12 *n.*, 4, 7, 10, 11 *v.*, **ta·bled, ta·bling.**
**on the table, a** of a bill, motion, etc.: **a** before a committee, legislative body, etc. for discussion. **b** *Esp. U.S.* put off or shelved.
**set** or **lay the table,** arrange cutlery, dishes, etc. on the table for a meal.
**turn the tables,** reverse conditions or circumstances completely: *The enemy troops had advanced, but our sudden attack turned the tables on them.*

**tab·leau** (tab′lō) **1** a striking scene; picture. **2** a representation of a picture, statue, scene, etc. by a person or group posing in appropriate costume: *Our school is going to present several tableaux from Canadian history.* *n.*, *pl.* **tab·leaux** (-lōz) or **tab·leaus.**

**ta·ble·cloth** (tā′bəl kloth′) a cloth for covering a table. *n.*

**ta·ble d'hôte** (tā′bəl dōt′) in hotels, etc., a meal served at a fixed time and price: *In meals table d'hôte, there is one price for the whole meal; but in meals à la carte, a person chooses what he or she wants and pays for each dish.* Compare with À LA CARTE.

**ta·ble·land** (tā′bəl land′) a plateau that rises sharply from a lowland area or the sea. *n.*

**table linen** tablecloths, napkins, etc.

**ta·ble·spoon** (tā′bəl spün′) **1** a spoon larger than a teaspoon or dessert spoon, used to serve vegetables, etc. **2** a standard unit of measurement in cookery, equal to three teaspoons, or about 15 mL. **3** TABLESPOONFUL: *The recipe calls for a tablespoon of sugar.* *n.*

**ta·ble·spoon·ful** (tā′bəl spün′fu̇l) as much as a tablespoon holds: *He added a tablespoonful of butter.* *n.*, *pl.* **ta·ble·spoon·fuls.**

**tab·let** (tab′lit) **1** a small, flat sheet of stone, wood, ivory, etc. used to write or draw on: *The ancient Romans used tablets as we use paper.* **2** a number of sheets of writing paper fastened together at one edge. **3** a small, flat surface with an inscription: *The names of the members of the first council are inscribed on a tablet in the city hall.* **4** a small, flat piece of medicine, candy, etc.: *vitamin tablets.* *n.*

**table talk** conversation at meals.

**table tennis** an indoor game resembling tennis, played on a table with small wooden paddles and a very light, hollow, plastic ball; ping-pong.

**ta·ble·top** (tā′bəl top′) **1** the top of a table: *The tabletop was scarred with cigarette burns.* **2** of a machine, instrument, or apparatus, designed to be used on a table; not having its own stand or support: *a tabletop loom.* *n.*

**ta·ble·ware** (tā′bəl wer′) the dishes, knives, forks, spoons, etc. used at meals. *n.*

**table wine** a red or white wine for drinking with meals, usually containing between 9 and 15 percent alcohol.

**tab·loid** (tab′loid) **1** a newspaper, usually having a page half the ordinary size, that presents the news through pictures and short articles. **2** condensed. *n.*

**ta·boo** (tə bü′) **1** forbidden by custom or tradition; banned: *Eating human flesh is taboo in all civilized countries.* **2** forbid; prohibit; ban. **3** a prohibition; ban. **4** set apart as sacred, unclean, or cursed, and forbidden to general use: *Among the Polynesians certain things, places, and persons are taboo.* **5** the system or act of setting things apart as sacred, unclean, or cursed. 1, 4 *adj.*, 2 *v.*, **ta·booed, ta·boo·ing;** 3, 5 *n., pl.* **ta·boos.** Also, **tabu.**

**ta·bor** (tā′bər) a small drum, used especially in the Middle Ages to accompany a pipe or fife played by the same person. *n.*

**ta·bu** (tə bü′) See TABOO. *adj., v.,* **ta·bued, ta·bu·ing;** *n., pl.* **ta·bus.**

**tab·u·lar** (tab′yə lər) **1** of, having to do with, or arranged in tables or lists; especially written or printed in columns and rows. Example:

| BOOK | AUTHOR | TYPE |
|---|---|---|
| *Ivanhoe* | Scott | Romantic novel |
| *Evangeline* | Longfellow | Narrative poem |
| *Tales* | Andersen | Fairy stories |

**2** flat like a table: *a tabular rock.* *adj.*

**tab·u·late** (tab′yə lāt′) arrange facts, figures, etc. in tables or lists. *v.,* **tab·u·lat·ed, tab·u·lat·ing.**

**tab·u·la·tion** (tab′yə lā′shən) an arrangement in tables or lists. *n.*

**tab·u·la·tor** (tab′yə lā′tər) **1** a person or machine that tabulates. **2** a device on a typewriter or computer for making even paragraph and column indentions. *n.*

**tac·a·ma·hac** (tak′ə mə hak′) **1** a strong-smelling gum resin used in incenses, ointments, etc. **2** any of several trees yielding this gum, such as the balsam poplar. *n.*

**ta·chom·e·ter** (tə kom′ə tər) an instrument for measuring speed of rotation, especially that of the crankshaft of a motor vehicle engine: *A tachometer measures engine rpm (revolutions per minute).* *n.*

**tac·it** (tas′it) **1** unspoken; silent: *a tacit prayer.* **2** implied or understood without being openly expressed: *Her eating the food was a tacit confession that she liked it.* *adj.* —**tac′it·ly,** *adv.*

**tac·i·turn** (tas′ə tėrn′) not fond of talking; usually saying very little. *adj.*

**tac·i·tur·ni·ty** (tas′ə tėr′nə tē) the habit of keeping silent; disinclination to talk much. *n.*

**tack** (tak) **1** any of various types of very short, sharp nail with a flat head, used for fastening upholstery, carpets, etc. in place, pinning paper to a drawing board, notices on a bulletin board, etc. **2** fasten with tacks: *She tacked mosquito netting over the windows.* **3** a stitch used as a temporary fastening. **4** sew with temporary stitches. **5** attach; add: *He tacked a postscript to the end of the letter.* **6** sail in a zigzag course against the wind: *The sloop was tacking, trying to make the harbour.* **7** a zigzag course against the wind. **8** the movement of a boat or ship in relation to the direction of the wind: *When on port tack, a ship has the wind on its left.* **9** change from one tack to another. **10** a zigzag movement; one of the movements in a zigzag course. **11** a course of action or conduct: *To demand what he wanted was the wrong tack to take with his mother.* **12** a rope to hold in place a corner of some sails. **13** the corner to which this is fastened. 1, 3, 7, 8, 10–13 *n.*, 2, 4–6, 9 *v.* —**tack′er,** *n.*

**tack·le** (tak′əl) **1** equipment; apparatus; gear: *Fishing tackle means the rod, line, hooks, etc.* **2** a set of ropes and pulleys for lifting, lowering, or moving heavy things: *The sails of a ship are raised and moved by tackle.* See BLOCK AND TACKLE for picture. **3** try to deal with: *Everyone has his or her own problems to tackle.* **4** lay hold of; seize: *John tackled the thief and held him till help arrived.* **5** in football, seize and stop an opponent having the ball by bringing him or her to the ground. **6** in soccer, obstruct an opponent in order to get the ball away from him or her. **7** the act of tackling. **8** in football, a player between the guard and the end on either side of the line. **9** fasten or attach by means of tackle. 1, 2, 7, 8 *n.*, 3–6, 9 *v.*, **tack·led, tack·ling.** —**tack′ler,** *n.*

**tack·y¹** (tak′ē) sticky: *The varnish is still tacky.* *adj.*

**tack·y²** (tak′ē) *Informal.* **1** of poor quality or appearance; shabby. **2** cheap and vulgar; in bad taste: *a tacky way to treat someone.* *adj.*, **tack·i·er, tack·i·est.**

**ta·co** (tä′kō) a Mexican food consisting of a tortilla folded around a filling of meat, cheese, beans, etc. *n., pl.* **tacos.**

**tac·o·nite** (tak′ə nīt′) a kind of rock consisting of about 30 percent iron ore. *n.*

**tact** (takt) a keen sense of the right or fitting thing to say or do so as to avoid hurting someone's feelings; sensitivity in dealing with people. *n.*

**tact·ful** (takt′fəl) **1** having TACT: *a tactful person.* **2** showing TACT: *A tactful reply does not hurt a person's feelings.* *adj.* —**tact′ful·ly,** *adv.* —**tact′ful·ness,** *n.*

**tac·tic** (tak′tik) a device or procedure for accomplishing a goal. *n.*

**tac·ti·cal** (tak′tə kəl) **1** of or having to do with TACTICS; especially, having to do with the disposal of naval, military, or air forces in action against an enemy. **2** having or showing cleverness and skill in planning or manoeuvring: *a tactical statesman.* *adj.* —**tac′ti·cal·ly,** *adv.*

**tac·ti·cian** (tak tish′ən) a person skilled or trained in TACTICS. *n.*

**tac·tics** (tak′tiks) **1** the science and art of managing naval, ground, or air forces in active combat (*used with a singular verb*). **2** the operations themselves: *The generals' tactics were successful.* **3** any procedures or devices to gain advantage or success: *Those are dangerous tactics to use. When his coaxing failed, the little boy changed his tactics and began to cry.* *n.pl.*

**tac·tile** (tak′tīl *or* tak′təl) **1** of, having to do with, or perceived by the sense of touch: *a tactile organ, a tactile impression.* **2** that can be felt by touch; tangible: *Heat and cold are tactile qualities.* *adj.*

**tac·til·i·ty** (tak til′ə tē) the capability of being felt by touch. *n.*

**tact·less** (takt′lis) **1** without TACT: *a tactless person.* **2** showing no TACT: *a tactless reply.* *adj.*

**tac·tu·al** (tak′chü əl) **1** of or having to do with the sense of touch; tactile. **2** arising from the sense of touch; giving sensations of touch. *adj.*

**tac·tu·al·ly** (tak′chü ə lē) by means of touch; as regards touch. *adv.*

**tad·pole** (tad′pōl′) the larva of a frog or toad that has a tail and gills and lives in the water. *n.*
☛ *Etym.* From ME *taddepol*, made up of *tadde* 'toad' + *poll* 'head', literally 'a toad that is only head'.

**taf·fe·ta** (taf′ə tə) a stiff cloth of silk, rayon, linen, etc. in a plain weave having a smooth, glossy surface on both sides. *n.*

**taff·rail** (taf′rāl′) **1** a rail around a ship's stern. **2** the upper part of the stern of a wooden ship. *n.*

**taf·fy** (taf′ē) **1** a kind of hard but chewy candy made of brown sugar or molasses boiled down, often with butter, and pulled to make it porous. **2** *Informal.* FLATTERY. *n.*

**tag¹** (tag) **1** a piece of card, paper, leather, etc. to be tied or fastened to something: *Each coat in the store has a tag with the price marked on it.* **2** a small hanging piece; a loosely attached piece; loose end: *Mother cut all the tags off the old frayed rug.* **3** a metal or plastic covering for the end of a shoelace. **4** a quotation, moral, etc. added for ornament or effect. **5** add for ornament or effect. **6** the last line or lines of a song, play, actor's speech, etc. **7** furnish with a tag or tags: *All Tema's suitcases are tagged with her name and address.* **8** *Informal.* follow closely: *The baby tagged after his sister.* **9** a piece of cardboard, etc., sometimes with a piece of string attached, sold by charitable organizations, etc. to raise money: *He bought a tag and tied it to his lapel.* **10** sell tags: *She tagged for the Cancer Society.* 1–4, 6, 9 *n.*, 5, 7, 8, 10 *v.*, **tagged**, **tag·ging**. —**tag′ger**, *n.*
**tag along**, *Informal.* go with someone or a group.

**tag²** (tag) **1** a children's game in which the player who is "it" chases the others until he or she touches one. The one touched is then "it" and must chase the others. **2** touch or tap with the hand. **3** in baseball, the act of touching a base runner with the ball, or a base with the foot while holding the ball. **4** put out a base runner with a touch of the ball. 1, 3 *n.*, 2, 4 *v.*, **tagged, tag·ging**.

**tag day** a day on which TAGS (def. 9) are sold by a charitable organization, etc.

**tag end** **1** a loosely hanging or attached bit or end. **2** the last part of something.

**Ta·hi·ti·an** (tə hē′shən) **1** of or having to do with Tahiti, an island country in the southern Pacific, its people, or their language. **2** a native or inhabitant of Tahiti. **3** the Polynesian language of the Tahitians. 1 *adj.*, 2, 3 *n.*

**tai·ga** (tī′gə) the moist evergreen forest of the subarctic regions, as in Siberia and northern Canada: *The taiga begins at the southern edge of the arctic tundra.* *n.*

**tail** (tāl) **1** a thin part that extends from the back of certain animals. **2** something like an animal's tail: *the tail of a kite.* **3** the after portion of an airplane. **4** the luminous train extending from the head of a comet. **5** the back part of anything; back; rear; conclusion: *the tail of a cart.* **6** a long braid or tress of hair. **7** furnish with a tail. **8** form a tail. **9** at the tail, back, or rear. **10** coming from behind: *a strong tail wind.* **11** follow close behind; form the tail of: *Some boys tailed after the parade.* **12** *Informal.* follow closely and secretly,

hat, āge, fär; let, ēqual, tėrm; it, īce
hot, ōpen, ôrder; oil, out; cup, pùt, rüle
əbove, takən, pencəl, lemən, circəs
ch, child; ng, long; sh, ship
th, thin; ᴛʜ, then; zh, measure

especially in order to watch or to prevent escaping. **13** join one thing to the end of another; fasten timber by an end. **14 tails**, *pl.* **a** the reverse side of a coin. **b** *Informal.* a coat with long tails, worn on formal occasions. See SWALLOW-TAILED COAT for picture. 1–6, 9, 10, 14 *n.*, 7, 8, 11–13 *v.* —**tail′-less**, *adj.*
**at the tail of,** following.
**turn tail,** run away from danger, trouble, etc.
**with one's tail between one's legs,** afraid; dejected; humiliated.
☛ *Hom.* TALE.

**tail·board** (tāl′bôrd′) a board at the back end of a vehicle such as a cart, wagon, or truck, that can be let down or removed when loading or unloading. *n.*

**tail·coat** (tāl′kōt′) a man's formal coat cut away at the front and extending at the back in two long, tapering pieces, or tails. See SWALLOW-TAILED COAT for picture. *n.*

**tail end** **1** the rear or bottom end: *the tail end of the parade.* **2** the concluding period: *the tail end of the school year.*

**tail·gate** (tāl′gāt′) **1** a TAILBOARD, especially on a truck or station wagon. **2** of a driver or a motor vehicle, follow another vehicle too closely. 1 *n.*, 2 *v.*, **tail·gated, tail·gat·ing.** —**tail′gat′er**, *n.*

**tail lamp** TAIL-LIGHT.

**tail–light** (tāl′līt′) a light, usually red, at the back end of an automobile, wagon, train, etc. *n.*

**tai·lor** (tā′lər) **1** a person whose business is making or repairing clothes, especially men's clothes. **2** make clothes, especially clothes that are cut and shaped to fit the body and that are finely finished. **3** make or adjust to suit a particular need: *The standard house design can be tailored to suit the individual buyer.* 1 *n.*, 2, 3 *v.*

**tai·lor·bird** (tā′lər bėrd′) any of a closely related group of small Asian and East Indian songbirds belonging to the same family as the kinglets, that stitch leaves together to hold and hide their nests. *n.*

**tai·lored** (tā′lərd) **1** having simple, shaped, and fitted lines; not loose, draped, frilly, etc.: *a tailored shirt or suit, a tailored bedspread.* **2** pt. and pp. of TAILOR. 1 *adj.*, 2 *v.*

**tai·lor·ing** (tā′lə ring) **1** the business or occupation of a tailor. **2** the workmanship or skill of a tailor: *expert tailoring.* **3** ppr. of TAILOR. 1, 2 *n.*, 3 *v.*

**tai·lor–made** (tā′lər mād′) **1** made by a tailor or as if by a tailor: *His suit was tailor-made.* **2** of women's clothes, simple, trim, and well-fitting; TAILORED. **3** made especially to suit a particular person, object, or purpose: *a tailor-made course of study.* *adj.*

**tailor's chalk** a usually thin, flat piece of hard chalk or soapstone, used in sewing for making temporary guide marks on cloth.

**tail·piece** (tāl′pēs′) a piece forming the end or added at the end. *n.*

**tail pipe** a pipe leading from the muffler to the rear of

**tail·race** (tāl′rās′) 1 the part of a MILLRACE below the wheel. 2 a channel for floating away refuse and residue from a mine. *n.*

**tail·spin** (tāl′spin′) 1 a downward spin of an aircraft with the nose pointed down. 2 a state of panic or confusion: *The news threw the whole household into a tailspin. n.*

**tail wind** a wind blowing in the direction of the course of an aircraft, ship, etc.; a wind coming from behind: *We made very good time because we had a tail wind all the way.*

**taint** (tānt) 1 a spot or trace of infection, decay, or corruption. 2 a moral blemish; a trace of discredit or dishonour: *a taint of vice. There was no taint of self-interest in her transactions.* 3 give a taint to; infect, spoil, or contaminate: *tainted meat. Her reputation had been tainted by a questionable business deal.* 4 become tainted; become infected or corrupted: *Meat taints quickly if not kept cold.* 1, 2 *n.*, 3, 4 *v.*

**take** (tāk) 1 lay hold of; grasp: *He took her by the hand.* 2 seize; catch; capture: *to take a wild animal in a trap.* 3 come upon suddenly: *take a person by surprise.* 4 have the proper effect; catch hold; lay hold: *The fire has taken.* 5 accept: *Take my advice. The woman won't take a cent less for the car.* 6 get; receive; assume the ownership or possession of: *She took the gifts and opened them.* 7 win: *He took first prize.* 8 absorb: *Wool takes a dye well.* 9 stick to a surface; stick; adhere: *This ink doesn't take on glossy paper.* 10 get; have: *to take a seat.* 11 use; make use of: *to take medicine.* 12 indulge in: *to take a rest, to take a vacation.* 13 submit to; put up with: *to take hard punishment.* 14 study: *to take physiology.* 15 teach: *I have a class to take.* 16 need; require: *It takes time and patience to learn how to drive an automobile.* 17 choose; select: *Take the shortest way home.* 18 remove: *Please take the waste basket away and empty it.* 19 remove by death: *Pneumonia took him.* 20 remove something; detract: *Her paleness takes from her beauty.* 21 subtract: *If you take 2 from 7, you have 5.* 22 lead: *Where will this road take me?* 23 go with; escort: *Take her home.* 24 carry: *Take your lunch along.* 25 do; make; obtain by some special method: *Please take my photograph.* 26 form and hold in mind; feel: *Marika takes pride in her schoolwork.* 27 find out: *The doctor took his temperature.* 28 of ice, to form; become thick enough to support people: *When the ice takes, cars are driven across the river.* 29 suppose: *I take it the train was late.* 30 regard; consider: *Let us take an example.* 31 assume: *She took charge of the household.* 32 engage; hire; lease: *to take a house.* 33 receive and pay for regularly: *to take a newspaper.* 34 become affected by: *to take a cold.* 35 in grammar, be used with: *A plural noun takes a plural verb.* 36 please; attract; charm: *The song took our fancy.* 37 win favour: *Do you think the new play will take?* 38 go: *The cat took to the woods.* 39 become: *He took sick.* 40 the amount or number taken: *a great take of fish.* 41 the act of taking. 42 that which is taken. 43 photograph: *to take a scene of a movie.* 44 in motion pictures, a scene or sequence photographed at one time. 45 the act or process of making a photograph or scene in a motion picture. 46 the act or process of making a recording for a record, tape, etc. 47 a record or tape of this. 1–39, 43 *v.,* **took, tak·en, tak·ing;** 40–42, 44–47 *n.* **—tak′er,** *n.*

**take aback,** surprise suddenly; startle.

**take after,** a be like; resemble: *Jeanne takes after her mother.* b chase in order to try to seize or capture: *The dog took after the rabbit.*

**take amiss,** a misinterpret. b be offended at.

**take back,** a withdraw; retract. b remind of the past: *The letter took her back ten years.*

**take down,** a write down. b lower the pride of.

**take for,** suppose to be.

**take in,** a receive; admit: *to take in boarders.* b of clothes, make smaller. c understand. d deceive; trick; cheat: *I was taken in by the strange girl's friendly manner; in fact, she wasn't friendly at all.* e include: *It's too late to take in Helen's party now.*

**take it out on,** *Informal.* relieve one's anger or annoyance by scolding or hurting.

**take lying down,** *Informal.* take without a protest.

**take off,** a leave the ground or water: *Three airplanes took off at the same time.* b *Informal.* give an amusing imitation of; mimic. c *Informal.* leave quickly; rush away: *He took off at the first sign of trouble.*

**take on,** a engage; hire. b undertake to deal with: *take on an opponent.* c *Informal.* show great excitement, grief, etc.

**take one's time,** not hurry.

**take out,** a remove; get rid of. b borrow a book, etc. from a library or similar collection. c apply for and obtain a licence, patent, etc. d escort.

**take over,** take the ownership or control of.

**take to,** a form a liking for; become fond of: *Good students take to books.* b go to: *The cat took to the woods and became wild.*

**take up,** a soak up; absorb: *A sponge takes up liquid.* b of clothes, make shorter. c begin; undertake: *She took up piano lessons in the summer.* d pay off. e lift. f establish a homestead; settle: *He took up land in Alberta.* g adopt an idea, purpose, etc.

**take up with,** *Informal.* begin to associate or be friendly with.

**tak·en** (tā′kən) *pp.* of TAKE: *Georg has taken his snowshoes with him. v.*

**take·off** (tā′kof′) 1 *Informal.* a mocking but generally good-humoured imitation: *The highlight of the evening was his clever takeoff on the prime minister.* 2 the act of leaving the ground or other surface, as in jumping or flying: *The plane was on the runway and ready for takeoff.* 3 the place or point at which a person or thing leaves the ground, etc. *n.*

**take·out** (tā′kout′) 1 of or referring to prepared food packaged in disposable containers and sold by a restaurant, etc. to be eaten away from the premises: *a takeout dinner.* 2 referring to a restaurant, etc. that sells such food. 3 in curling, a shot that hits an opposing stone so as to remove it from the house. 4 in bridge, a bid that releases a partner from a double or other bid. 5 any act of taking out. 1, 2 *adj.,* 3–5 *n.*

**take·o·ver** (tā′kō′vər) a taking over; seizure of ownership or control: *a takeover of a country by the army, the takeover of one business enterprise by a larger one.* *n.*

**take–up** (tā′kup′) 1 the action of taking up, as by absorbing, gathering, reeling in, etc. 2 a device for taking in or tightening. *n.*

**tak·ing** (tā′king) 1 attractive; pleasing; winning: *a taking smile.* 2 the act of a person or thing that takes. 3 something that is taken, such as a catch of fish. 4 **takings,** *pl.* money taken in; receipts. 5 *ppr.* of TAKE. 1 *adj.,* 2–4 *n.,* 5 *v.*

**talc** (talk) 1 a soft, smooth, white, grey, or greenish mineral with a soapy feel, used in making talcum or face

powder, lubricants, etc.: *Talc is magnesium silicate.*
**2** TALCUM POWDER.   *n.*

**tal·cum** (tal′kəm)   **1** TALCUM POWDER.   **2** TALC (def. 1).   *n.*

**talcum powder**   a powder made of purified white TALC (def. 1), often perfumed, for use on the face and body.

**tale** (tāl)   **1** a series of happenings or events related; recital or account: *They listened in shocked silence to his tale of the day's events.*   **2** a story of true, legendary, or fictitious events, especially when imaginatively treated: *tales of dragons. The old sea captain told the children tales of his adventures.*   **3** a malicious piece of gossip or scandal, either true or false: *She's always telling tales.*   *n.*
**tell tales**,   spread gossip or scandal; tattle.
☛ *Hom.* TAIL.

**tale·bear·er** (tāl′ber′ər)   a person who spreads gossip or scandal; TELLTALE.   *n.*

**tale·bear·ing** (tāl′ber′ing)   the spreading of gossip or scandal.   *n.*

**tal·ent** (tal′ənt)   **1** a special natural ability: *a talent for music.*   **2** general intelligence or ability: *a person of talent.*   **3** a person or persons having talent: *They were looking for local talent.*   **4** any of various units of mass or money used among the ancient Greeks, Romans, Assyrians, etc.   *n.*

**tal·ent·ed** (tal′ən tid)   having great natural ability; gifted: *a talented musician.*   *adj.*

**talent scout**   a person who looks for and recruits people having talent in a particular field of activity, especially in the public entertainment field.

**talent show**   a show made up of separate performances of singing, dancing, etc. by amateurs looking for recognition as performers.

**tales·man** (tāl′zmən *or* tā′lē zmən)   in law, a person chosen to fill a vacancy on a jury caused by the absence or disqualification of one of the original jury members.   *n.*, *pl.* **tales·men** (-zmən).

**tale·tell·er** (tāl′tel′ər)   TALEBEARER.   *n.*

**tal·is·man** (tal′i smən *or* tal′i zmən)   **1** a stone, ring, etc. engraved with figures or characters supposed to have magic power; charm.   **2** anything that acts as a charm.   *n.*, *pl.* **tal·is·mans.**

**tal·is·man·ic** (tal′i smən′ik *or* tal′i zmən′ik)   having to do with or serving as a TALISMAN.   *adj.*

**talk** (tok)   **1** use words; speak: *A child learns to talk.*   **2** exchange words; converse: *The two ministers talked for an hour.*   **3** use in speaking: *to talk sense, to talk French.*   **4** the use of words; spoken words; speech; conversation: *The old friends met for a good talk.*   **5** an informal speech: *The coach gave the team a talk about the need for more team spirit.*   **6** a way of talking: *baby talk.*   **7** bring, put, drive, influence, etc. by talk: *to talk a person to sleep.*   **8** discuss: *to talk politics, to talk business.*   **9** consult; confer: *to talk with one's doctor.*   **10** a conference; council.   **11** spread ideas by other means than speech: *to talk by signs.*   **12** make sounds that suggest speech: *The birds were talking loudly.*   **13** gossip; rumour: *She talked behind their backs.*   **14** gossip or rumour: *There is talk of a quarrel between them.*   **15** a subject for talk or gossip: *She is the talk of the town.*   **16** *Informal.* boastful or empty words: *His threat was just talk.*   1–3, 7–9, 11–13 *v.*, 4–6, 10, 14–16 *n.*
**talk back,** *Informal.*   answer rudely or disrespectfully.
**talk down,**   **a** make silent by talking louder or longer.   **b** speak condescendingly: *Adults should not talk down to*

**talcum**     **1219**     **tallyho**

hat, āge, fär; let, ēqual, tėrm; it, īce
hot, ōpen, ôrder; oil, out; cup, pùt, rüle
əbove, takən, pencəl, lemən, circəs
ch, child; ng, long; sh, ship
th, thin; ⟋H, then; zh, measure

*children.*   **c** belittle; disparage: *He talks down his competitor's products.*   **d** give a pilot radio instructions for landing because of instrument failure or poor visibility.
**talk off** or **out of the top of one's head,** *Informal.*   utter one's immediate thoughts or ideas without consideration.
**talk out,**   **a** discuss thoroughly.   **b** in Parliament, discuss a bill until the time for adjournment and so prevent its being put to a vote.
**talk over,**   **a** discuss; consider together.   **b** persuade or convince by arguing.
**talk up,**   talk earnestly in favour of; campaign for.

**talk·a·thon** (tok′ə thon′)   an extra-long public discussion or session of speech-making: *The city council's evening meeting turned into an all-night talkathon.*   *n.*
☛ *Etym.* A combination of *talk* + *-athon* from *Marathon.*

**talk·a·tive** (tok′ə tiv)   having the habit of talking a great deal; fond of talking: *She is a cheerful, talkative person who knows everyone in town.*   *adj.*
—**talk′a·tive·ly,** *adv.*   —**talk′a·tive·ness,** *n.*

**talk·er** (tok′ər)   **1** a person who talks.   **2** a talkative person.   *n.*

**talking point**   an important point in a discussion or argument; a point to be emphasized or that serves as a basis for discussion: *These facts may not prove our case but at least they are a talking point.*

**talk·ing–to** (tok′ing tü′) *Informal.*   SCOLDING.   *n., pl.* **talk·ing-tos.**

**talk show**   a radio or television show featuring interviews with well-known people or people who have some special interest or cause.

**tall** (tol)   **1** of considerable height; high: *Mountains are tall.*   **2** higher than the average or than surrounding things: *The trees in the valley were very tall. She is a tall woman.*   **3** of a particular height: *He is 185 centimetres tall.*   **4** *Informal.* high or large in amount or degree: *That's a tall order.*   **5** *Informal.* hard to believe; exaggerated: *a tall tale.*   *adj.*   —**tall′ness,** *n.*

**tall·ish** (tol′ish)   quite tall.   *adj.*

**tal·low** (tal′ō)   **1** the hard, white, rendered fat of cattle and sheep, used mainly for making candles, soap, lubricants, etc.: *Tallow is produced by melting suet.*   **2** smear or grease with tallow.   **1** *n.*, **2** *v.*

**tal·ly** (tal′ē)   **1** an account; reckoning; score: *a tally of a game.*   **2** anything on which a score or account is kept.   **3** a mark made for a certain number of objects in keeping account.   **4** a number or group used in tallying: *The dishes were counted in tallies of 20.*   **5** mark on a tally; count up: *to tally a score.*   **6** in sports, make scoring points; score: *The hockey team tallied seven goals in the last game.*   **7** a scoring point; a run, goal, etc.   **8** agree; correspond: *Your account tallies with mine.*   **9** cause to fit, suit, or correspond.   **10** anything corresponding to a certain other thing; duplicate; counterpart.   **11** correspondence; agreement.   **12** formerly, a stick of wood in which notches were cut to represent numbers: *The Roman captain kept count of the prisoners on a tally.*   1–4, 7, 10–12 *n., pl.* **tal·lies;**   5, 6, 8, 9 *v.*, **tal·lied, tal·ly·ing.**

**tal·ly·ho** (tal′ē hō′ *or* tal′ē hō′ for 1; tal′ē hō′ for 2)

**tally sheet** 1220 **tandem**

**1** a coach drawn by four horses: *We rode on a tallyho in Victoria.* **2** a hunter's cry on catching sight of the fox. 1, 2 *n.*, *pl.* **tal·ly·hos**; 2 *interj.*

**tally sheet**   a sheet on which a record or score is kept, especially a record of votes.

**tally stick**   TALLY (def. 12).

**Tal·mud** (tal′məd *or* täl′mùd)   the body of traditional Jewish civil and canonical law, made up of the Mishnah and the Gemara. *n.*

**tal·on** (tal′ən)   **1** a claw, especially of a bird of prey. **2** a human finger or hand resembling a claw in appearance or when thought of as grasping. *n.*

**ta·lus**[1] (tā′ləs)   in the foot, the highest tarsal bone, situated just below the bottom ends of the lower leg bones and joined to them: *The talus and the ends of the lower leg bones form the* ANKLE *(def. 3).* See LEG for picture. *n.*, *pl.* **ta·li** (-lī *or* -lē).

**ta·lus**[2] (tā′ləs)   **1** a slope. **2** a sloping side or face of a wall, rampart, parapet, or other fortification. **3** a sloping mass of rocky fragments lying at the base of a cliff or the like. *n.*

**tam** (tam)   TAM-O'-SHANTER. *n.*

**ta·ma·le** (tə mä′lē)   a Mexican food made of minced meat seasoned with red peppers, rolled in cornmeal, wrapped in cornhusks, and roasted or steamed. *n.*

**tam·a·rack** (tam′ə rak′)   **1** a small or medium-sized larch tree found mainly in muskeg and swamp areas throughout most of Canada: *Tannin, used in tanning leather, can be extracted from the bark of the tamarack.* **2** the wood of this tree. *n.*

**tam·a·rind** (tam′ə rind′)   **1** a tropical tree native to eastern Africa, having hard yellowish wood, yellow flowers with reddish veins, and fruit with an acid pulp. **2** the fruit, used in foods, drinks, and medicine. *n.*

**tam·a·risk** (tam′ə risk′)   any of a closely related group of shrubs or small trees found mainly in desert areas in warm or tropical climates, having long, slender branches and tiny, narrow leaves that give the trees a feathery appearance. *n.*

A tambourine

**tam·bou·rine** (tam′bə rēn′)   a small, shallow drum with one head and with jingling metal disks around the side, played by shaking, striking with the knuckles, or rubbing with the thumb. *n.*

**tame** (tām)   **1** of an animal, changed by people from a wild state to a state of being able to be handled or managed in order to serve as a beast of burden, source of food or clothing, pet, etc.   **2** gentle and easy to control; docile.   **3** make or become tame: *to tame a horse. Severe discipline had finally tamed him. White rats tame easily.*   **4** without spirit; dull and lifeless: *a tame story, a tame election campaign.* 1, 2, 4 *adj.*, **tam·er, tam·est;**   3 *v.*, **tamed, tam·ing.**   —**tame′a·ble, tam′a·ble,** *adj.* —**tame′ness,** *n.*   —**tame′ly,** *adv.*

**tam·er** (tā′mər)   a person who tames animals: *a lion tamer.* *n.*

A tam-o'-shanter

**tam-o'-shan·ter** (tam′ə shan′tər)   a type of peakless woollen cap originating in Scotland, having a tight headband, a flat, loose, round crown, and, often, a pompom. *n.* Also, **tam.**

**tamp** (tamp)   **1** pack down firmly by a series of taps or blows.   **2** in blasting, fill the hole containing explosive with dirt, etc. *v.*

**tam·per** (tam′pər)   interfere with or alter in an improper way, so as to damage or weaken (*used with* **with**): *The lock had been tampered with but not broken. It was obvious that someone had tampered with the evidence.* *v.* —**tam′per·er,** *n.*

**tam·pon** (tam′pon)   **1** a plug of cotton or other absorbent material inserted into a wound or body cavity to stop bleeding or to absorb blood, etc.   **2** plug with a tampon: *to tampon a wound.* 1 *n.*, 2 *v.*

**tan** (tan)   **1** make hide into leather by treating it with a solution containing TANNIN or a similar chemical agent to preserve it and keep it soft and flexible.   **2** medium, somewhat orange brown: *tan shoes.*   **3** the brown colour acquired by light skin from exposure to the sun or a sunlamp.   **4** make light skin brown by exposure to the sun or a sunlamp: *She was deeply tanned after a summer spent out-of-doors.*   **5** become tanned: *My sister tans more quickly than I do.*   **6** the liquid used in tanning hides, or the active ingredient in it, such as TANNIN.   **7** TANBARK.   **8** *Informal.*   spank or thrash in punishment. 1, 4, 5, 8 *v.*, **tanned, tan·ning;**   2 *adj.*, 2, 3, 6, 7 *n.*

**tan·a·ger** (tan′ə jər)   any of a family of small to medium-sized, mostly bright-coloured American songbirds found mainly in woodlands: *Most species of tanager are found only in the tropics, but three species, including the scarlet tanager, are regular summer visitors in Canada.* *n.*

**tan·bark** (tan′bärk′)   any bark rich in TANNIN, crushed or cut into small pieces and used in tanning hides. Used tanbark is often used to cover circus rings, race-tracks, etc. *n.*

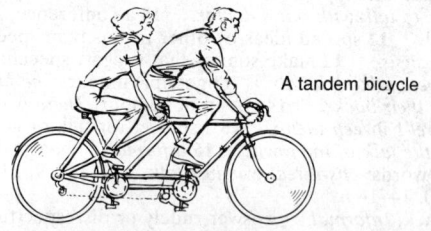
A tandem bicycle

**tan·dem** (tan′dəm)   **1** one behind the other: *to drive* *horses tandem.* **2** having animals, seats, parts, etc. arranged one behind the other. **3** a team of horses harnessed tandem. **4** a two-wheeled carriage drawn by horses harnessed tandem. **5** a bicycle with two seats and two sets of pedals, one behind the other. **6** a truck or other vehicle with two attached parts, such as a cab for pulling and a trailer to carry the load. 1 *adv.*, 2 *adj.*, 3–6 *n.*

**in tandem,** **a** one ahead of the other; in tandem formation: *mounted in tandem.* **b** closely together; in partnership or co-operation: *working in tandem.*

☛ *Etym.* From L *tandem* meaning 'at length' in reference to time, but here—humorously—interpreted as referring to a lengthened vehicle, or the arrangement of horses or riders one behind the other.

**tang**[1] (tang) **1** a strong, distinctive taste or flavour or smell: *the tang of blue cheese, the tang of sea air.* **2** a distinctive or characteristic quality or property: *We need a slogan with more tang.* **3** a slight touch or suggestion; trace. **4** a long, slender projecting point, shank, or prong forming the part of a chisel, file, sword, etc. that fits into the handle. *n.*

**tang**[2] (tang) **1** a sharp, ringing sound. **2** make a sharp, ringing sound. 1 *n.*, 2 *v.*

**tan·gent** (tan′jənt) **1** touching. **2** a tangent line, curve, or surface. **3** in geometry, touching at one point only and not intersecting. *These circles are tangent:* ∞. **4** in trigonometry, in a right triangle, the ratio of the length of the side opposite to an (acute) angle to the length of the side (not the hypotenuse) adjacent to the angle. **5** in geometry, the part of a line which intersects a curve at two coincident points. 1, 3 *adj.*, 2, 4, 5 *n.*

**fly off** or **go off at a tangent,** change suddenly from one course of action or thought to another.

**tan·ge·rine** (tan′jə rēn′ or tan′jə rēn′) **1** any of several varieties of mandarin orange having a reddish-orange skin and easily separated segments. **2** reddish-orange. 1, 2 *n.*, 2 *adj.*

**tan·gi·bil·i·ty** (tan′jə bil′ə tē) the quality or state of being TANGIBLE. *n.*

**tan·gi·ble** (tan′jə bəl) **1** capable of being touched or felt by touch: *A chair is a tangible object.* **2** real; actual; definite: *tangible evidence, a tangible advantage.* **3** whose value can be easily appraised: *Real estate is tangible property.* **4 tangibles,** *pl.* things whose value is easily appraised; material assets. 1–3 *adj.*, 4 *n.* —**tan′gi·bly,** *adv.*

**tan·gle** (tang′gəl) **1** twist and twine together in a confused mass: *The kitten got into the yarn and tangled it.* **2** a twisted or confused mass; a snarl or jumble: *The fighting children were a tangle of arms and legs. The detectives had to unsnarl a tangle of lies.* **3** become tangled: *Her hair tangles easily because it is fine and curly.* **4** involve in something that hampers or obstructs (often used with **up**): *He has tangled himself in a complicated business deal.* **5** get into a fight or argument (*with*): *Don't tangle with him.* **6** a complicated, confused, or bewildered state or condition: *Her business affairs are in a dreadful tangle. My mind was in such a tangle I didn't hear a word he said.* **7** a matted bit of hair: *It took 10 minutes to get all the tangles out of her hair.* 1, 3–5 *v.,* **tan·gled, tan·gling;** 2, 6, 7 *n.* —**tan′gle·ment,** *n.*

**tan·gled** (tang′gəld) **1** confused, disordered, or snarled: *a tangled pile of stockings, tangled hair.* **2** very involved or complicated: *a tangled web of lies, tangled relationships.* **3** pt. and pp. of TANGLE. 1, 2 *adj.*, 3 *v.*

**tan·gly** (tang′glē) full of tangles; TANGLED. *adj.*

**tang**    **1221**    **tantalize**

hat, āge, fär; let, ēqual, tėrm; it, īce
hot, ōpen, ôrder; oil, out; cup, put, rüle
əbove, takən, pencəl, lemən, circəs

ch, child; ng, long; sh, ship
th, thin; ᴛʜ, then; zh, measure

**tan·go** (tang′gō) **1** a Latin American ballroom dance of African origin, in 4/4 time and characterized by dips and slow glides. **2** the music for this dance. **3** dance the tango. 1, 2 *n., pl.* **tan·gos;** 3 *v.,* **tan·goed, tan·go·ing.**

**tang·y** (tang′ē) having a TANG[1] (def. 1): *a tangy sauce.* *adj.*

**tank** (tangk) **1** a large container for liquid or gas: *a tank for oil, a water tank, a gas tank.* **2** as much as a tank will hold; tankful: *They used up almost a tank of gas just driving around.* **3** put or store in a tank. **4** an armoured combat vehicle carrying machine guns and, usually, an artillery gun, and moving on tracks. 1, 2, 4 *n.*, 3 *v.*

**tank·age** (tang′kij) **1** the capacity of a tank or tanks. **2** storage in tanks. **3** the price charged for storage in tanks. **4** the waste matter left over from the rendering of fat in slaughterhouse tanks, dried and ground and used as fertilizer or feed. *n.*

**tank·ard** (tang′kərd) a large drinking mug with a handle and, often, a hinged cover. *n.*

**tank car** a railway car with a tank for carrying liquids or gases.

**tank·er** (tang′kər) a ship, aircraft, or truck with tanks for carrying oil, gasoline, or other liquid freight. *n.*

**tank farm** a tract of land containing many large tanks for storing oil.

**tank·ful** (tangk′ful′) as much as a tank will hold. *n.*

**tank top** a sleeveless, low-necked T-shirt.

**tank truck** a truck equipped with a large tank for carrying oil, gasoline, or other liquid freight.

**tan·ner** (tan′ər) a person whose work is tanning hides. *n.*

**tan·ner·y** (tan′ə rē) a place where hides are tanned. *n., pl.* **tan·ner·ies.**

**tan·nic** (tan′ik) of or obtained from TANBARK or TANNIN. *adj.*

**tannic acid** TANNIN.

**tan·nin** (tan′ən) an acid obtained from the bark or galls of oaks, etc. and from certain other plants, used in tanning, dyeing, making ink, and in medicine. *n.*

**tan·ning** (tan′ing) **1** the process or art of converting hide or skins into leather. **2** a making brown, as by exposure to sun. **3** *Informal.* a severe spanking or thrashing. **4** ppr. of TAN. 1–3 *n.*, 4 *v.*

**tan·sy** (tan′zē) **1** a coarse, strong-smelling, bitter-tasting perennial herb native to Europe, now common in North America, having large toothed leaves and small, yellow flowers: *Tansy was formerly much used as a food seasoning and medicine.* **2** any of a group of plants closely related to the common tansy. *n., pl.* **tan·sies.**

**tan·ta·lize** (tan′tə līz′) torment or tease by keeping something desired in sight but out of reach, or by holding

out hopes that are repeatedly disappointed. *v.*,
**tan·tal·ized, tan·ta·liz·ing. —tan'ta·li·za'tion,** *n.*
**—tan'ta·liz'er,** *n.* **—tan'ta·liz'ing·ly,** *adv.*
☛ *Etym.* From *Tantalus* + *-ize.* 16c. Tantalus was, in Greek mythology, a Greek king punished in the lower world by having to stand up to his chin in water, under branches laden with fruit. Whenever he tried to drink or eat, the water or fruit withdrew from his reach.

**tan·ta·lum** (tan'tə ləm) a rare, hard, greyish metallic element that is resistant to acids: *Tantalum is used in making surgical instruments.* Symbol: Ta *n.*

**tan·ta·mount** (tan'tə mount') having the same force, effect, etc.; equivalent (*to*): *His silence when questioned was tantamount to an admission of guilt.* *adj.*

**tan·tar·a** (tan tar'ə, tan ter'ə, *or* tan'tə rə) **1** a blast of a trumpet or horn. **2** any similar sound. *n.*

**tan·trum** (tan'trəm) a violent, childish outburst of bad temper: *He goes into a tantrum if anyone touches his rock collection.* *n.*

**Tan·za·ni·an** (tan zə nē'ən) **1** a native or inhabitant of Tanzania, a country in eastern Africa. **2** of or having to do with Tanzania or its people. 1 *n.*, 2 *adj.*

**Tao** (dou) **1** in TAOISM, "the way," the eternal, transcendent, and mystical entity that is the supreme creative force, the object of worship by Taoists. **2** the ultimate reality of the cosmos; the principle of harmony, orderliness, and integration. *n.*

**Tao·ism** (dou'iz əm) **1** a 2500-year-old Chinese philosophy that conceives of nature as being ordered by the balance between positive and negative forces produced by the universal creative spirit TAO. **2** a religion that was developed from this philosophy, with influence from CONFUCIANISM and BUDDHISM: *Taoism may involve magical, physical, alchemical, or meditative practices in order to achieve immortality and mystic union with the Tao.* *n.*

**Tao·ist** (dou'ist) **1** a believer in TAOISM. **2** of or having to do with TAOISM or Taoists. 1 *n.*, 2 *adj.*

**Tao Te Ching** (dou'də jing') an ancient text of philosophical speculation and mystical reflection, widely studied and revered in TAOISM. *n.*

**tap¹** (tap) **1** strike lightly: *to tap on a window.* **2** cause to strike lightly: *She tapped her foot on the floor.* **3** a light blow: *There was a tap at the door.* **4** the sound of a light blow. **5** make, put, etc. by light blows: *to tap a rhythm, to tap time, to tap the ashes out of a pipe.* **6** a piece of leather, etc. added to the sole or heel of a shoe to repair it. **7** repair with a tap. **8** a small steel plate on a shoe to reduce wear or to make a louder tap in tap-dancing. 1, 2, 5, 7 *v.*, **tapped, tap·ping;** 3, 4, 6, 8 *n.*

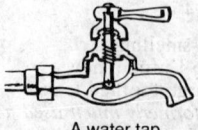
A water tap

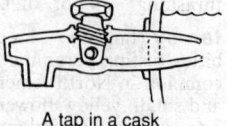
A tap in a cask

**tap²** (tap) **1** a device for turning on and off the flow of liquid in a pipe; a faucet: *Most sinks have taps for hot and cold water.* **2** a stopper or plug to close a hole in a cask containing liquid. **3** make a hole in to let out liquid:

*They tapped the sugar maples when the sap began to flow.* **4** draw the plug from: *to tap a cask.* **5** furnish with a tap. **6** let out liquid by piercing or by drawing a plug. **7** a certain kind or quality of liquor. **8** *Informal.* a room in which liquor is sold and drunk. **9** let out liquid from by surgery. **10** surgery to let out liquid: *spinal tap.* **11** make resources, reserves, etc. accessible; penetrate to; open up: *This highway taps a large district.* **12** on a coil, an electric connection somewhere other than at the end. **13** the place where an electric connection is or can be made. **14** make a connection with a telephone line in order to eavesdrop. 1, 2, 7, 8, 10, 12, 13 *n.*, 3–6, 9, 11, 14 *v.*, **tapped, tap·ping.**
**on tap,** **a** ready to be let out of a keg or barrel and served. **b** ready for use; on hand.

**tap dance** a dance in which the steps are accented by loud taps of the foot, toe, or heel, made using steel TAPS¹ (def. 8) on the sole of the shoe.

**tap–dance** (tap'dans') dance a TAP DANCE. *v.*, **tap–danced, tap–danc·ing. —tap'–danc'er,** *n.*

**tape** (tāp) **1** a long, narrow woven strip of cotton, linen, etc.: *Tape is used to make loops and bind seams.* **2** a long, narrow strip of other material: *Surveyors measure with a steel tape. Stock quotations are printed on paper tape.* **3** such a strip coated with a sticky substance to make it adhere to a surface: *Borje strengthened his hockey stick by wrapping tape around it.* **4** fasten with tape; wrap with tape. **5** a strip, string, etc. stretched across a race track at the finish line. **6** a thin, narrow strip of paper or plastic coated with magnetized iron oxide to record sound, as for a tape-recorder or videotape. **7** a recording made in this way. **8** record on tape. **9** VIDEOTAPE. 1–3, 5–7, 9 *n.*, 4, 8 *v.*, **taped, tap·ing. —tape'like',** *adj.*

**tape deck** an apparatus for making and playing tape recordings, especially a separate component of a stereo system.

**tape measure** a long, narrow strip of flexible steel or of cloth, paper, etc., marked off in millimetres, centimetres, etc. for measuring length or distance.

**ta·per** (tā'pər) **1** become gradually smaller toward one end: *The church spire tapers to a point.* **2** grow less gradually; diminish: *As people moved away, his business tapered to nothing.* **3** a gradual lessening in thickness, diameter, or width toward one end: *pant legs with a slight taper.* **4** a slender candle. **5** a long wick coated with wax, used to light candles, lamps, etc. 1, 2 *v.*, 3–5 *n.* **—ta'per·ing·ly,** *adv.*

**taper off,** gradually reduce, leave off or stop: *She thought she could taper off smoking rather than quit outright. He has been a heavy drinker but is trying to taper off. His voice tapered off and then stopped.*
☛ *Hom.* TAPIR.

**tape–re·cord** (tā'pri kôrd') record on magnetic tape. *v.*

**tape–re·cord·er** (tā'pri kôr'dər) a device for recording sound on magnetic tape and also playing back the recorded sound. In recording, the sound is converted into electric waves which activate the magnetic tape. When the recording is played back, the magnetic patterns on the tape create electric waves which are amplified and changed into sound. *n.*

**tape recording** **1** the recording of sound, etc. on magnetic tape. **2** a tape on which such a recording has been made.

**tap·es·tried** (tap'i strēd) covered or decorated with a TAPESTRY or tapestries: *tapestried walls.* *adj.*

**tap·es·try** (tap′i strē) **1** heavy, thick, handwoven fabric having designs or pictures woven into it, used to hang on walls, cover furniture, etc. **2** a machine-made fabric woven to resemble tapestry. *n., pl.* **tap·es·tries.**

**tape·worm** (tā′pwėrm) any of various flatworms that in the adult stage live as parasites in the intestines of human beings and other vertebrates. *n.*

**tap·i·o·ca** (tap′ē ō′kə) **1** a starchy food in the form of white grains prepared from the root of the cassava plant: *Tapioca is used for puddings and as a thickener for foods.* **2** pudding, etc. made from tapioca. *n.*

A Malay tapir — about 245 cm long excluding the tail

**ta·pir** (tā′pər) any of a closely related group of heavy, thick-skinned, woodland mammals having four toes on the front feet and three on the hind feet, and a long, tapered, flexible snout with the nostrils at the end: *Tapirs are distantly related to the rhinoceros but are much smaller and have no horns.* *n.*
☞ *Hom.* TAPER.

**tap·room** (tap′rüm′) a room where alcoholic liquor is sold; barroom. *n.*

**tap·root** (tap′rüt′) the main root of a plant, growing smaller straight downward and having smaller roots branching out from it: *A carrot is a taproot.* See ROOT¹ for picture. *n.*

**tap·ster** (tap′stər) a person who draws and serves liquor in a tavern or barroom. *n.*

**tar**¹ (tär) **1** a thick, brown or black, sticky substance obtained by the distillation of wood or coal. **2** a similar, condensible substance found in the smoke from burning tobacco. **3** cover or smear with tar: *a tarred roof.* **4** of, like, or covered with tar: *tar paper.* 1, 2, 4 *n.,* 3 *v.,* **tarred, tar·ring.**
**tar and feather,** smear heated tar on and then cover with feathers as a punishment.

**tar**² (tär) *Informal.* SAILOR. *n.*

**tar·an·tel·la** (tar′ən tel′ə *or* ter′ən tel′ə) **1** a rapid, whirling southern Italian dance in very quick rhythm, usually performed by couples. **2** the music for this dance. *n.*

Tarantula: a bird spider, one of the world's largest spiders — body about 8 cm long

**ta·ran·tu·la** (tə ran′chù lə) **1** a large, hairy, southern European wolf spider whose bite is painful, but not serious: *People used to think that the bite of the tarantula caused an uncontrollable desire to dance.* **2** any large, hairy spider thought of as poisonous; especially any of a family of spiders found in tropical America, Mexico, and the southern United States, some species reaching a body length of about 8 cm: *The bite of some South American tarantulas can be dangerous but all the species found in the United States are harmless to human beings.* *n., pl.* **ta·ran·tu·las** *or* **ta·ran·tu·lae** (-lē′ *or* -lī′).

**tar·boosh** (tär büsh′) a close-fitting, brimless cap like a fez, worn by Moslem men either alone or as the inner part of a turban. *n.*

**tar·di·ly** (tär′də lē) **1** late; delayed. **2** slowly or sluggishly. 1 *adj.,* 2 *adv.*

**tar·dy** (tär′dē) **1** after the proper or desired time; late: *a tardy attempt at reform. Tardy pupils were kept after school.* **2** slow or sluggish: *tardy growth, a tardy pace.* *adj.,* **tar·di·er, tar·di·est.** —**tar′di·ness,** *n.*

**tare**¹ (ter) **1** any of several species of vetch, especially the common vetch: *Tare is grown for fodder and for enriching the soil.* **2** the seed of a vetch. *n.*
☞ *Hom.* TEAR².

**tare**² (ter) a deduction made from the gross mass of something in a container, to allow for the mass of the wrapper, box, conveyance, etc. *n.*
☞ *Hom.* TEAR².

**tar·get** (tär′git) **1** a mark for shooting at: *We set up the target in a field.* See ARCHERY for picture. **2** something aimed at, as in a wartime operation: *The bomber's target was a bridge.* **3** a goal or objective: *The target for the fund-raising drive was $100 000.* **4** an object of scorn or abuse: *His absent-mindedness made him a target for their practical jokes.* **5** a shield, especially a small, round one; buckler. **6** make or put up as a target. **7** guide to a target. 1–5 *n.,* 6, 7 *v.,* **tar·get·ed, tar·get·ing.**
**on target,** to the purpose; to the point; appropriate or valid: *Her criticism of the book was right on target.*

**tar·iff** (tar′if *or* ter′if) **1** a list or schedule of duties or taxes imposed by a government on imports and, sometimes, exports. **2** any duty or tax in such a list or system: *There is a very high tariff on jewellery.* **3** a schedule of rates or prices of a business, etc.: *This hotel has the highest tariff in town.* **4** make subject to a tariff; set a tariff on. 1–3 *n.,* 4 *v.*

**tar·la·tan** (tär′lə tən) a thin, sheer, stiff, cotton cloth with a plain, open weave, used for costumes, dresses, trimming, etc. *n.*

**tar·mac** (tär′mak) an asphalt surface, especially a runway or other paved area of an airfield. *n.*

**tar·nish** (tär′nish) **1** dull the lustre or brightness of: *The salt tarnished the silver saltshaker.* **2** lose lustre or brightness, especially through exposure to the air or certain chemical substances: *Gold does not tarnish.* **3** the condition of being tarnished or the film or coating characteristic of this condition: *We took the tarnish off with silver polish.* **4** bring disgrace upon; sully: *His involvement in that business deal has tarnished his reputation.* 1, 2, 4 *v.,* 3 *n.*

**ta·ro** (tä′rō) **1** a tropical plant of the same family as the jack-in-the-pulpit, grown in the Pacific islands for its edible starchy roots. **2** the root of the taro. *n., pl.* **ta·ros.**

**tar paper** heavy paper coated with tar to make it waterproof, for use on roofs, outer walls, etc.

**tar·paul·in** (tär pol′ən) a sheet of waterproofed

canvas or other coarse strong cloth, used to protect goods against the weather. *n.*

**tar·pon** (tär′pon) a large, silver-coloured fish found in the warmer parts of the Atlantic Ocean. *n., pl.* **tar·pon** or **tar·pons.**

**tar·ry**¹ (tar′ē *or* ter′ē) **1** stay or lodge for a time: *He tarried at the inn till he felt well again.* **2** delay in going or coming, or in doing; be tardy: *Why do you tarry so long? v.,* **tar·ried, tar·ry·ing.**

**tar·ry**² (tä′rē) **1** of or like tar: *a tarry smell.* **2** covered with tar: *The dog's feet were tarry from the new pavement. adj.,* **tar·ri·er, tar·ri·est.**

**tar·sal** (tär′səl) **1** of or having to do with the TARSUS. **2** a tarsal bone or cartilage. 1 *adj.,* 2 *n.*

**tar sands** *Cdn.* a deposit of bitumen mixed with sand, clay, and various minerals, having the appearance and texture of asphalt paving, and found near the surface or hundreds of metres deep. The bitumen in the tar sands can be processed into a lighter, liquid form which is called synthetic crude oil to distinguish it from the traditional petroleum occurring naturally in a liquid state.

**tar·sus** (tär′səs) **1** the group of bones between the lower leg bones and the metatarsal bones, forming the ankle and the back half of the foot: *The tarsus contains seven bones, including the talus and the heel bone.* See LEG for picture. **2** the corresponding part in the hind leg of an animal, forming the backward-bending joint between the lower thigh and the shank; hock. **3** the small plate of connective tissue in the eyelid. *n., pl.* **tar·si** (-sī *or* -sē).

**tart**¹ (tärt) **1** having a pleasantly sharp, sour taste: *a tart apple.* **2** having a sharp, cutting quality: *a tart reply. adj.* —**tart′ly,** *adv.* —**tart′ness,** *n.*

**tart**² (tärt) **1** a piece of pastry filled with cooked fruit, jam, etc.: *In Canada and the United States, a tart is small and usually open at the top; in the British Isles, any fruit pie is a tart.* **2** *Informal.* dress or decorate in a cheap and gaudy way (*used with* **up**): *The resort was all tarted up for the tourist season.* 1 *n.,* 2 *v.*

**tar·tan** (tär′tən) **1** a plaid pattern for cloth originating in Scotland and designed with the stripes in varying widths and colours to distinguish the different families, or clans: *The main colour in the Douglas tartan is green.* **2** a similar pattern designed as an official symbol of a group, etc.: *The colours of Canada's Maple Leaf tartan represent the colours of maple leaves in different seasons.* **3** cloth woven with such a pattern, especially woollen cloth in a twill weave: *I bought a length of tartan.* **4** a garment made of such cloth: *He wore his tartan.* **5** made of tartan: *a tartan skirt.* **6** of or like tartan: *a tartan design. n.*

**tar·tar** (tär′tər) **1** an acid substance derived from grape juice that collects as a crustlike deposit on the inside of wine casks: *Purified tartar is called cream of tartar.* **2** a hard deposit on the teeth, consisting of proteins from saliva, calcium carbonate or other salts, and, usually, food particles; dental calculus. *n.*

**Tar·tar** (tär′tər) **1** a member of a Turkic people living mainly in the eastern European U.S.S.R. and the middle Volga region. **2** the Turkic language of the Tartars. **3** a member of any of various groups of Asian nomads of ancient and medieval times; especially, a Mongol people that formed part of the hordes of Genghis Khan. **4** of or having to do with the Tartars. **5 tartar,** a person with a bad temper: *That new supervisor is a tartar. n.*
**catch a tartar,** attack someone who is too strong; get the worst of it.

**tar·tar·ic** (tär tar′ik *or* tär ter′ik) of, having to do with, containing, or derived from TARTAR (def.1). *adj.*

**tartaric acid** a colourless crystalline acid found in many plants, especially grapes: *Tartaric acid is usually obtained commercially from tartar and is used in food and medicines, in photography, etc.*

**tartar sauce** a sauce made of mayonnaise with chopped pickles, olives, capers, etc.

**tar·trate** (tär′trāt) a salt or ester of TARTARIC ACID. *n.*

**tas·bih** (taz bē′) a ROSARY, or prayer beads, used by some Moslems as a memory aid during prayers. *n.*

**task** (task) **1** work to be done; a piece of work that has been assigned or undertaken: *One of her tasks was to take the garbage out.* **2** something hard or unpleasant that has to be done: *She was left with the task of breaking the news to her mother.* **3** put a strain on; burden: *The heavy work tasked him beyond his strength.* 1, 2 *n.,* 3 *v.*
**take to task,** reprove: *The teacher took him to task for not studying harder.*

**task force** a temporary group, specially organized under one leader for a particular task: *A naval task force was sent to turn away the spy ship. The mayor set up a task force to study the effects of the proposed expressway.*

**task·mas·ter** (task′mas′tər) a person who sets tasks for others to do; especially, one who is very demanding or severe. *n.*

**Tas·ma·ni·an** (taz mā′nē ən) **1** of or having to do with Tasmania, an island state of Australia just south of Victoria, or its people. **2** a native or inhabitant of Tasmania. 1 *adj.,* 2 *n.*

**TASS** (tas) the official news agency of the former Soviet Union. *n.*

**tas·sel** (tas′əl) **1** a hanging bunch of threads, small cords, beads, etc. of equal length fastened together at one end. **2** anything resembling a tassel: *The group of flower spikelets at the top of the main stem of a corn plant is called a tassel.* **3** put tassels on; ornament with tassels. **4** form or produce tassels, as corn does. 1, 2 *n.,* 3, 4 *v.,* **tas·selled** or **tas·seled, tas·sel·ling** or **tas·sel·ing.**

**taste** (tāst) **1** what is special about something to the sense organs of the mouth; flavour: *Sweet, sour, salt, and bitter are four important tastes.* **2** try the flavour of something by taking a little into the mouth. **3** the sense by which the flavour of things is perceived: *Her taste is unusually keen.* **4** get the flavour of by the sense of taste: *She tasted almond in the cake.* **5** have a particular flavour: *The soup tastes of onion.* **6** eat or drink a little bit of: *The children barely tasted their breakfast the day they went to the circus.* **7** eat or drink a little bit. **8** a little bit; sample: *to take a taste of a cake.* **9** experience; have: *to taste freedom.* **10** have experience: *to taste of pleasure.* **11** a liking: *Suit your own taste.* **12** the ability to perceive and enjoy what is beautiful and excellent: *Good books and pictures appeal to people of taste.* **13** a manner or style that shows such ability: *Her house is furnished in excellent taste.* **14** experience: *The snowstorm gave me a taste of northern winter.* 1, 3, 8, 11–14 *n.,* 2, 4–7, 9, 10 *v.,* **tast·ed, tast·ing.** —**tast′a·ble,** *adj.*
**to one's taste,** in harmony with one's preferences; to one's liking; pleasing: *That style of furniture is not to his taste.*

**to taste,** in the amount that suits one's palate: *Add salt and pepper to taste.*

**taste bud** any of certain small groups of cells, most of which are in the outer layer of the tongue, that are sense organs of taste.

**taste·ful** (tāst′fəl) **1** having or showing good taste: *tasteful furnishings.* **2** pleasing to the taste; tasty: *tasteful food.* *adj.* —**taste′ful·ly,** *adv.* —**taste′ful·ness,** *n.*

**taste·less** (tā′stlis) **1** not appealing to the sense of taste; without flavour; bland: *The meat was dry and tasteless.* **2** having or showing a lack of sensitivity to beauty and artistic worth: *a tasteless choice of accessories.* **3** showing a lack of sensitivity to what is appropriate or proper: *She made a tasteless remark about his having gained weight.* *adj.* —**taste′less·ly,** *adv.* —**taste′less·ness,** *n.*

**tast·er** (tā′stər) **1** a person who tastes; especially, one whose work is testing the quality of tea, wine, etc. by tasting it. **2** in former times, a person who ate a bit of food before it was touched by his master or employer as a precaution against poison. *n.*

**tast·y** (tā′stē) pleasing to the taste; appetizing; flavourful: *That cake is very tasty.* *adj.,* **tast·i·er, tast·i·est.** —**tast′i·ly,** *adv.* —**tast′i·ness,** *n.*

**tat** (tat) **1** do TATTING; work at tatting. **2** make by TATTING: *to tat a lace edging.* *v.,* **tat·ted, tat·ting.**

**tat·ter** (tat′ər) **1** a torn piece left hanging; shred: *After the storm the flag hung in tatters upon the mast.* **2** tear or wear to pieces; make or become ragged. **3 tatters,** *pl.* torn or ragged clothing. 1, 3 *n.,* 2 *v.*

**tat·ter·de·mal·ion** (tat′ər dē mā′lyən *or* tat′ər dē mal′yən) a person in tattered clothes; ragamuffin. *n.*

**tat·tered** (tat′ərd) **1** torn and ragged; in tatters: *a tattered dress.* **2** wearing torn or ragged clothes: *a tattered urchin.* **3** pt. and pp. of TATTER. 1, 2 *adj.,* 3 *v.*

**tat·ting** (tat′ing) **1** the act or process of making a delicate kind of lace by looping and knotting cotton or linen thread by hand, using a small shuttle. **2** the lace made in this way. **3** ppr. of TAT. 1, 2 *n.,* 3 *v.*

**tat·tle** (tat′əl) **1** reveal secrets; tell tales: *Don't tell her anything about it; she'll tattle.* **2** betray; give away (used with **on**): *He tattled on his sister and she was punished.* **3** talk idly or foolishly; gossip. **4** say or reveal by talking: *They tattled the story to the principal.* **5** idle talk or gossip. 1–4 *v.,* **tat·tled, tat·tling;** 5 *n.* —**tat′tler,** *n.*

**tat·tle·tale** (tat′əl tāl′) a person who tells secrets, especially to get other people into trouble. *n.*

**tat·too¹** (ta tü′) **1** a signal on a bugle or drum calling soldiers to their quarters at night. **2** a series of raps, taps, etc.: *The hail beat a loud tattoo on the roof.* **3** a military display, especially music and parading by show units. *n., pl.* **tat·toos.**
☞ *Etym.* From Dutch *taptoe,* made up of *tap* 'tap' (of a barrel) + *toe* 'shut', originally a signal for closing time (shutting off the taps) in a 'taproom' or bar. 17c.

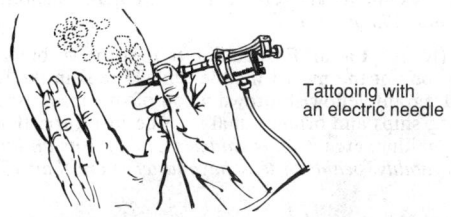
Tattooing with an electric needle

**tat·too²** (ta tü′) **1** mark the skin with designs or patterns by pricking it and putting in colours. **2** mark a design on the skin in this way: *The sailor had a ship tattooed on his arm.* **3** a mark or design made by tattooing. 1, 2 *v.,* **tat·tooed, tat·too·ing;** 3 *n., pl.* **tat·toos.** —**tat·too′er,** *n.*
☞ *Etym.* From Polynesian (probably Tahitian) *tatau.* 18c.

**taught** (tot) pt. and pp. of TEACH: *Miss Barbeau taught my mother. She has taught mathematics for many years.* *v.*
☞ *Hom.* TAUT, TOT.

**taunt** (tont) **1** tease or reproach in a scornful or insulting way; jeer at; mock: *At school she had been taunted with being poor. They taunted him with cowardice.* **2** a scornful or insulting remark. **3** get or drive by taunts: *They taunted him into taking the dare.* 1, 3 *v.,* 2 *n.*

**taupe** (tōp) medium brownish grey. *n., adj.*

**Tau·rus** (tô′rəs) **1** in astronomy, a northern constellation thought of as having the shape of a bull. **2** in astrology, the second sign of the zodiac. The sun enters Taurus about April 20. See ZODIAC for picture. **3** a person born under this sign. *n.*

**taut** (tot) **1** tightly drawn; having no slack: *a taut rope.* **2** strained; tense: *taut nerves, a taut smile.* **3** of a ship, etc., in neat condition; tidy. *adj.* —**taut′ly,** *adv.* —**taut′ness,** *n.*
☞ *Hom.* TAUGHT, TOT.

**tau·tog** (tot′og) a food and game fish of the wrasse family found mainly along the Atlantic coast of the United States; blackfish. *n.*

**tau·to·log·i·cal** (tot′ə loj′ə kəl) characterized by or using TAUTOLOGY; redundant. *adj.* —**tau′to·log′i·cal·ly,** *adv.*

**tau·tol·o·gy** (to tol′ə jē) **1** the saying of a thing over again in other words without making it clearer or more forceful; redundancy. Example: *the* modern *college student of today.* **2** an instance of tautology. *n., pl.* **tau·tol·o·gies.**

**tav·ern** (tav′ərn) **1** a place where alcoholic drinks are sold and drunk. **2** inn: *Hotels have taken the place of the old taverns.* *n.*

**taw** (to) **1** in the game of marbles, a large fancy marble used for shooting. **2** a game of marbles played with taws. **3** the line from which the players shoot their marbles. *n.*

**taw·dry** (tod′rē) showy and cheap; gaudy. *adj.,* **taw·dri·er, taw·dri·est.** —**taw′dri·ly,** *adv.* —**taw′dri·ness,** *n.*
☞ *Etym.* From Saint *Audrey*'s lace, sold at the fair of St. Audrey in Ely, England. 17c.

**taw·ny** (ton′ē) brownish yellow: *the tawny fur of a lion.* *n., adj.,* **taw·ni·er, taw·ni·est.** —**taw′ni·ness,** *n.*

**tax** (taks) **1** money paid by people for the support of the government, for public works, etc.: *Taxes are paid to the federal, provincial, and municipal governments.* **2** put a tax on: *People who own property are taxed to provide clean streets, protection against crime, free education, etc.* **3** a burden, duty, or demand that oppresses; strain: *Climbing stairs is a tax on a weak heart.* **4** lay a heavy burden on;

be hard for: *Reading in a poor light taxes the eyes.*
**5** accuse or charge (used with **with**): *The teacher taxed Rob with having neglected his work.* **1, 3** *n.*, **2, 4, 5** *v.*
—**tax′er**, *n.* —**tax′less**, *adj.*

**tax·a·bil·i·ty** (tak′sə bil′ə tē) being TAXABLE. *n.*

**tax·a·ble** (tak′sə bəl) liable to be taxed; subject to taxation: *Charities are not taxable.* *adj.*

**tax·a·tion** (tak sā′shən) **1** the act of taxing: *Taxation is necessary to provide roads, schools, and police protection.* **2** the amount people pay for the support of the government; taxes. *n.*

**tax-ex·empt** (tak′seg zempt′) free from taxes; not taxed. *adj.*

**tax·i** (tak′sē) **1** an automobile driven for hire, usually having a meter for recording the fare. **2** ride in a taxi. **3** move across the ground or water under its own power: *An airplane taxis down the runway before takeoff and taxis to the terminal building after landing.* **4** cause an aircraft to move in this way: *The pilot taxied the plane out onto the tarmac.* **1** *n.*, *pl.* **tax·is**; **2–4** *v.*, **tax·ied, tax·i·ing** or **tax·y·ing.**

**tax·i·cab** (tak′sē kab′) TAXI (def. 1). *n.*

**tax·i·der·mist** (tak′sə dėr′mist) a person trained in TAXIDERMY, especially one who makes it his or her work. *n.*

**tax·i·der·my** (tak′sə dėr′mē) the art of preparing the skins of animals and stuffing and mounting them in lifelike form. *n.*

**tax·i·me·ter** (tak′sē mē′tər) a device fitted to a hired vehicle for showing the fare as it accumulates. *n.*

**taxi stand** a place where taxis may park while waiting to be hired: *There is a taxi stand in front of the railway station.*

**tax·o·nom·ic** (tak′sə nom′ik) of or having to do with TAXONOMY. *adj.*

**tax·on·o·mist** (tak son′ə mist) an expert in TAXONOMY. *n.*

**tax·on·o·my** (tak son′ə mē) **1** the study of the principles of scientific classification. **2** in biology, the classification of animals and plants according to natural relationships based on structure, patterns of change and variation, etc. The basic categories, from the most general to the most specific are *kingdom, phylum* (or for plants, *division*), *class, order, family, genus*, and *species*. See classification chart in the Appendix. *n.*

**tax·pay·er** (tak′spā′ər) a person who pays a tax or is required by law to do so. *n.*

**tax rate** the rate of taxation on property, income, etc.

**Tb** terbium.

**T.B.** *Informal.* tuberculosis.

**T–bone** (tē′bōn′) a beefsteak taken from the middle part of the loin, containing a T-shaped bone and a bit of tenderloin. *n.*

**tbs.** or **tbsp.** tablespoon; tablespoons.

**Tc** technetium.

**TD** or **td** touchdown.

**Te** tellurium.

**tea** (tē) **1** a dark-brown or greenish drink made by pouring boiling water over the crushed, dried leaves of the tea plant. **2** the dried and prepared leaves from which this drink is made: *Most tea comes from China, Japan, and India.* **3** the plant itself: *Wild tea may grow to a height of nine metres.* **4** *Esp. Brit.* a meal in the late afternoon or early evening, at which tea is commonly served. **5** an afternoon reception at which tea is served: *Ms. Hsu gave a tea for her niece from Halifax.* **6** a hot drink made from herbs, meat broth, etc.: *mint tea, fruit tea, beef tea.* *n.*
**one's cup of tea,** *Informal.* just what one likes.
☞ *Hom.* TEE, TI.

**tea bag** a small paper or gauze bag containing enough tea leaves for one or two cups of tea.

**tea ball** a hollow metal or china ball with holes in it, which is filled with tea leaves and put in hot water to make tea.

**teach** (tēch) **1** show or explain how to do: *We taught our dog a new trick. His mother taught him to drive.* **2** make understand or know about: *She taught him honesty. That experience taught me not to believe everything I hear.* **3** give instruction to: *He taught my sister last year.* **4** give lessons in: *She teaches mathematics.* **5** give instruction; act as teacher: *He taught for 40 years.* *v.*, **taught, teach·ing.**

**teach·a·bil·i·ty** (tē′chə bil′ə tē) the fact or quality of being TEACHABLE. *n.*

**teach·a·ble** (tē′chə bəl) capable of being taught. *adj.* —**teach′a·ble·ness,** *n.*

**teach·er** (tē′chər) a person trained to teach, especially one who teaches in a school or college. *n.*

**teach·er·age** (tē′chə rij) formerly in rural areas and small towns, a house owned by a board of education for the use of the schoolteacher. *n.*

**teach·ing** (tē′ching) **1** the work or profession of a teacher. **2** the act of one who teaches. **3** what is taught; doctrine or precept: *the teachings of Islam.* **4** *ppr.* of TEACH. **1–3** *n.*, **4** *v.*

**teaching machine** a mechanical or electronic apparatus containing graded educational material and operated by a student so that he or she can learn at his or her own pace.

**tea cosy** a hatlike covering for putting over a teapot to keep the tea hot.

**tea·cup** (tē′kup′) **1** a cup used with a saucer for drinking tea, coffee, etc.: *A teacup is usually smaller than a mug or a measuring cup.* **2** as much as a teacup holds; teacupful. *n.*
**storm in a teacup,** great excitement or commotion over something unimportant. See TEMPEST.

**tea·cup·ful** (tē′kup fùl′) as much as a teacup holds. *n., pl.* **tea·cup·fuls.**

**tea·house** (tē′hous′) a place where tea and other light refreshments are served: *There are many teahouses in Japan and China.* *n.*

**teak** (tēk) **1** a tall East Indian tree of the verbena family, one of the most valuable timber trees in the world. **2** the fragrant yellowish-brown wood of this tree, used for building ships and bridges, making fine furniture, flooring and panelling, etc.: *Teak is valued mainly for its hardness and durability; beams of teak have lasted more than 1000 years.* *n.*

**tea·ket·tle** (tē′ket′əl) a covered kettle with a spout and handle, used for boiling water to make tea, etc. *n.*

**teak·wood** (tē′kwud′) the wood of the teak tree. *n.*

**teal** (tēl) **1** any of several varieties of small freshwater duck. **2** TEAL BLUE. *n., pl.* **teal** or **teals.**

**teal blue** a medium to dark greenish-blue.

**team** (tēm) **1** a group of people forming one of the sides in a game or competition: *a debating team, a football team.* **2** a group of people working or acting together; crew: *He was on the clean-up team.* **3** two or more horses or other animals harnessed together to work. **4** join together in a team (usually used with **up**): *We teamed up to clean the classroom after the party.* **5** drive a team. **6** work, carry, haul, etc. with a team. 1-3 *n.*, 4-6 *v.*
☛ *Hom.* TEEM.

**team–mate** (tēm′māt′) a fellow member of a team. *n.*

**team·ster** (tēm′stər) **1** a truck driver. **2** a person who drives a team of horses, especially as an occupation. *n.*

**team teaching** a system of teaching in which several teachers co-ordinate the instruction of a group of students: *Team teaching may involve bringing together different subject areas or different aspects of one subject.*

**team·work** (tē′mwėrk′) the acting together of a number of people to make the work of the group successful and effective: *Football requires teamwork even more than individual skill.* *n.*

**tea·pot** (tē′pot′) a container with a handle and a spout for making and serving tea. *n.*

**tear**[1] (tēr) **1** a drop of salty liquid secreted by a gland in the eyelid that serves to lubricate and wash the eye and that overflows the eyelids, especially in weeping: *There was a tear on the baby's cheek. He had tears in his eyes. We laughed till the tears came.* **2** something like or suggesting a tear. **3** fill with tears: *The bitter wind made her eyes tear.* **4** the act of weeping: *Tears will not help. She burst into tears.* 1, 2, 4 *n.*, 3 *v.*
**in tears,** shedding tears; crying: *The baby is in tears.*
☛ *Hom.* TIER[1].

**tear**[2] (ter) **1** pull apart by force: *to tear a box open.* **2** make by pulling apart: *She tore a hole in her dress.* **3** make a hole or a rent in by a pull: *The nail tore her coat.* **4** pull hard; pull violently: *He tore down the enemy's flag.* **5** cut badly; wound: *The jagged stone tore his skin.* **6** rend; divide: *The political party was torn by two factions.* **7** remove by effort: *He could not tear himself from that spot.* **8** make miserable; distress: *She was torn by grief.* **9** become torn: *Lace tears easily.* **10** a torn place: *She has a tear in her dress.* **11** the act or process of tearing. **12** *Informal.* move with great force or haste: *An automobile came tearing along.* **13** hurry; rush; dash. 1-9, 12, 13 *v.*, **tore, torn, tear·ing;** 10, 11, 13 *n.*
**tear down,** **a** pull down; raze; destroy: *The city tore down a whole block of houses.* **b** bring about the wreck of; discredit; ruin: *She tried to tear down his reputation.*
**tear into,** attack or criticize severely.
☛ *Hom.* TARE.

**tear·drop** (tēr′drop′) **1** a single tear. **2** something shaped like a tear, especially a gem. *n.*

**tear·ful** (tēr′fəl) **1** flowing with or accompanied by tears: *a tearful face, a tearful goodbye.* **2** causing tears; sad: *a tearful experience.* *adj.* —**tear′ful·ly,** *adv.*, —**tear′ful·ness,** *n.*

**tear gas** (tēr) a gas that irritates the eyes, causing tears and temporary blindness, used especially in breaking up riots.

**tear·jerk·er** (tēr′jėr′kər) *Informal.* a story, motion picture, etc. calculated to play on the emotions of the reader or audience. *n.*

**tear·less** (tēr′lis) without tears; not crying. *adj.*

**tea·room** (tē′rüm′) a room or shop where tea, coffee, and light meals are served. *n.*

**tear·y** (tēr′ē) TEARFUL. *adj.*

**tease** (tēz) **1** bother or annoy by means of jokes, questions, requests, etc.: *The other boys teased Jim about his curly hair.* **2** beg: *The child teases for every little thing that she sees.* **3** a person or thing that teases. **4** comb out or card wool, etc. **5** raise nap on cloth. **6** comb hair by holding it up and working the short hairs toward the scalp. **7** the act of teasing or the state of being teased. 1, 2, 4-6 *v.*, **teased, teas·ing;** 3, 7 *n.*
—**teas′ing·ly,** *adv.*

A flower head of the cultivated teasel, also called fuller's teasel

**tea·sel** (tē′zəl) **1** a plant with stiff, prickly flower heads. **2** one of these dried flower heads used for raising nap on cloth. **3** a mechanical device used for the same purpose. **4** raise a nap on cloth with teasels. 1-3 *n.*, 4 *v.*, **tea·selled** or **tea·seled, tea·sel·ling** or **tea·sel·ing.** Also, **teazel.**

**teas·er** (tē′zər) **1** a person or thing that teases. **2** *Informal.* annoying problem; puzzling task. *n.*

**tea service** a set of silver, china, etc. for serving tea, usually consisting of a teapot, hot water pitcher, cream jug, sugar bowl, and, sometimes, a coffee pot.

**tea set** **1** a set of china dishes for serving tea, etc., usually consisting of a teapot, sugar bowl, cream jug, teacups, saucers, and small plates. **2** TEA SERVICE.

**tea·spoon** (tē′spün′) **1** a spoon smaller than a dessert spoon and larger than a coffee spoon, commonly used to stir tea or coffee, eat desserts, etc. **2** a standard unit of measurement in cooking, equal to one third of a tablespoon, or about 5 mL. **3** TEASPOONFUL: *I put in a teaspoon of salt.* *n.*

**tea·spoon·ful** (tē′spün′fùl) as much as a teaspoon holds: *a teaspoonful of sugar.* *n., pl.* **tea·spoon·fuls.**

**teat** (tēt) the nipple of a breast or udder, from which the young suck milk. *n.*

**tea towel** a towel for drying dishes that have been washed.

**tea wagon** a small table on wheels, used in serving tea.

**tea·zel** (tē′zəl) See TEASEL. *n., v.*, **tea·zelled** or **tea·zeled, tea·zel·ling** or **tea·zel·ing.**

**techn.** 1 technical; technician. 2 technological; technology.

**tech·ne·ti·um** (tek nē′shē əm) a silver-grey metallic element produced artificially by irradiating molybdenum and in the fission of uranium: *All the isotopes of technetium are radio-active.* Symbol: Tc *n.*

**tech·nic** (tek′nik) 1 TECHNIQUE. 2 **technics**, TECHNOLOGY (*used with a singular or plural verb*). 3 **technics**, *pl.* technical details, points, terms, etc. *n.*

**tech·ni·cal** (tek′nə kəl) 1 of or having to do with a mechanical or industrial art or with applied science: *a technical school. Technical training is needed for many jobs in industry.* 2 of or having to do with the special facts or characteristics of a science or art; specialized: *Electrolysis, tarsus, and proteid are technical words.* 3 treating a subject technically; using technical terms: *The book gets very technical after the first chapter.* 4 strictly according to the rules or principles of a certain science, art, game, etc.: *a technical victory, a technical distinction.* 5 of or having to do with TECHNIQUE: *Her singing shows technical skill but her voice is weak.* *adj.* —**tech′ni·cal·ly,** *adv.* —**tech′ni·cal·ness,** *n.*

**tech·ni·cal·i·ty** (tek′nə kal′ə tē) 1 a technical matter, point, detail, term, etc.; especially one that only a specialist is likely to be aware of or to appreciate: *She was acquitted on a legal technicality.* 2 the quality or state of being technical: *The technicality of the article soon discouraged him.* *n., pl.* **tech·ni·cal·i·ties.**

**technical school** a school that provides training for work in industry, agriculture, etc.

**tech·ni·cian** (tek nish′ən) 1 a person trained or skilled in the technical details of a subject: *an electrical technician, a laboratory technician.* 2 a person skilled in the TECHNIQUE of an art: *a superb technician at the keyboard.* *n.*

**tech·nique** (tek nēk′) 1 a method or way of performing the technical details of an art; technical skill: *The pianist's technique was brilliant, but her interpretation of the piece lacked warmth.* 2 a special method or system used to accomplish something: *a new technique for removing tonsils.* *n.*

**tech·noc·ra·cy** (tek nok′rə sē) government or management of society by technical experts. *n.*

**tech·no·log·i·cal** (tek′nə loj′ə kəl) of, having to do with or used in TECHNOLOGY: *a technological age, technological advances.* *adj.* —**tech′no·log′i·cal·ly,** *adv.*

**tech·nol·o·gist** (tek nol′ə jist) a person skilled in a branch of TECHNOLOGY. *n.*

**tech·nol·o·gy** (tek nol′ə jē) 1 scientific knowledge applied to practical uses; applied science: *Engineering is a branch of technology.* 2 the system by which society is provided with the things needed to sustain life or desired for comfort. 3 technical language. *n.*

**tec·ton·ic** (tek ton′ik) 1 of or having to do with the architecture or construction of a building; structural. 2 in geology, of or having to do with structures that build up on the earth's crust: *tectonic plates.* *adj.*

**ted·der** (ted′ər) a machine that stirs and spreads out hay to speed up drying. *n.*

**ted·dy bear** (ted′ē) a stuffed toy made to look somewhat like a bear cub.

**te·di·ous** (tē′dē əs *or* tē′jəs) long and tiring: *A long talk that you cannot understand is tedious.* *adj.* —**te′di·ous·ly,** *adv.* —**te′di·ous·ness,** *n.*

**te·di·um** (tē′dē əm) the quality or state of being TEDIOUS; tiresomeness; tediousness. *n.*

**tee** (tē) 1 in quoits and other games, the mark aimed at. 2 in golf, a mark or place from which a player starts in playing each hole. 3 a little mound of sand or dirt or a short wooden or plastic peg on which a golf ball is placed when a player drives. 4 put a golf ball on a tee. 1–3 *n.,* 4 *v.,* **teed, tee·ing.**
**tee off,** drive a golf ball from a tee.
**tee up,** **a** in golf, put a ball on a tee. **b** prepare or get ready something to go into operation: *tee up a project.*
☛ Hom. TEA, TI.

**tee line** in curling, the line that runs through the centre of the house, parallel to the HOG LINE.

**teem¹** (tēm) be full of; abound; swarm: *The big swamp teemed with mosquitoes.* *v.*
☛ Hom. TEAM.

**teem²** (tēm) pour; come down in torrents: *It simply teemed all afternoon. A teeming rain spoiled the picnic.* *v.*
☛ Hom. TEAM.

**teen** (tēn) 1 *Informal.* TEENAGER: *a club for teens.* 2 *Informal.* TEENAGE. 3 **teens,** *pl.* of a century or a person's age, the years from thirteen to nineteen: *He was still in his teens when he got married. The songs in this book date from the teens and twenties.* 1, 3 *n.,* 2 *adj.*

**teen·age** (tē′nāj′) of, for, being, or having to do with teenagers: *a teenage club, teenage girls.* *adj.*

**teen·ag·er** (tē′nā′jər) a person in his or her teens: *She was still a teenager when she won her first Olympic gold medal.* *n.*

**tee·ny** (tē′nē) *Informal.* tiny; wee: *a teeny bit of sugar.* *adj.,* **tee·ni·er, tee·ni·est.**

**tee·pee** (tē′pē) a cone-shaped tent used mainly by the Plains Indians, consisting of a frame of poles spread out at the ground and joined at the top, covered with animal skins, canvas, etc.: *Teepees were originally covered with buffalo hide.* Compare with WIGWAM. *n.* Also, **tepee, tipi.**

**tee·ter** (tē′tər) 1 TEETER-TOTTER. 2 be badly balanced; move unsteadily; waver: *The tightrope walker teetered on the narrow wire.* 1 *n.,* 2 *v.*

**tee·ter–tot·ter** (tē′tər tot′ər) 1 a long plank balanced on a raised central support, used especially by children in a game in which they sit at opposite ends and move alternately up and down; seesaw. 2 play by moving up and down on a teeter-totter: *We watched the children teeter-tottering in the playground.* 3 the game of teeter-tottering. 1, 3 *n.,* 2 *v.*

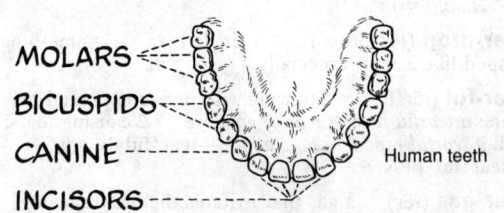

Human teeth

**teeth** (tēth) pl. of TOOTH. *n.*

**by the skin of one's teeth,** very narrowly, barely: *He escaped by the skin of his teeth.*

**grit** or **set one's teeth,** prepare to endure something without complaining.

**in the teeth of, a** straight against; in the face of: *He advanced in the teeth of the gale.* **b** in defiance of; in spite of.

**show one's teeth,** show anger; threaten.

**throw something in someone's teeth,** blame or reproach someone for something.

**to the teeth,** to the limit of what is possible; to the utmost: *She was armed to the teeth.*

**teethe** (tēᴛʜ) cut one's first teeth; grow primary teeth: *The baby is teething.* *v.*, **teethed, teeth·ing.**

**teeth·er** (tē′ᴛʜər) an object of hard rubber, plastic, etc. for babies to bite on when they are teething. *n.*

**teeth·ing ring** (tē′ᴛʜing) a ring of hard rubber, plastic, etc. for teething babies to bite on.

**tee·to·tal** (tē tō′təl) **1** of, having to do with, or practising total abstinence from alcoholic liquor. **2** *Informal.* absolute, complete, or entire. *adj.*

**tee·to·tal·ler** or **tee·to·tal·er** (tē tō′tə lər) a person who never drinks alcoholic liquor. *n.*

**tel.** **1** telephone. **2** telegram. **3** telegraph.

**tele–** or **tel–** a prefix meaning: **1** over, from, or to a long distance, as in *telegraph, telephone.* **2** of, in, or by television, as in *telecast.*
☛ *Etym.* From Gk. *tēle-*, combining form of *tēle* 'far, far off.'

**tel·e·cast** (tel′ə kast′) **1** broadcast by television: *The emergency session of the House of Commons was telecast.* **2** a television broadcast. **1** *v.*, **tel·e·cast** or **tel·e·cast·ed, tel·e·cast·ing;** **2** *n.* —**tel′e·cast′er,** *n.*

**tel·e·com·mu·ni·ca·tion** (tel′ə kə myü′nə kā′shən) **1** communication at a distance, as by cable, radio, telegraph, telephone, television, fax, etc. **2** Usually, **telecommunications,** the science that deals with such communication (used with a singular or plural verb). *n.*

**tel·e·com·mut·ing** (təl′ə kə myüt′ing) work at home that uses a computer link to one's place of employment. *n.* —**tel′e·com′mut·er,** *n.*

**tel·e·gram** (tel′ə gram′) a message sent by TELEGRAPH. *n.*

**tel·e·graph** (tel′ə graf′) **1** an apparatus, system, or process for sending or receiving coded messages or pictures by electricity, especially over a wire. **2** send by telegraph: *They telegraphed the news of the escape.* **3** send a telegram to: *She telegraphed us yesterday.* **4** send by means of an order made by telegraph: *to telegraph flowers.* **1** *n.*, **2–4** *v.*

**te·leg·ra·pher** (tə leg′rə fər) a person whose work is sending and receiving messages by TELEGRAPH. *n.*

**tel·e·graph·ic** (tel′ə graf′ik) of, having to do with, or transmitted by TELEGRAPH: *a telegraphic message.* *adj.* —**tel′e·graph′i·cal·ly,** *adv.*

**te·leg·ra·phy** (tə leg′rə fē) the making or operating of TELEGRAPHS. *n.*

**te·lem·e·ter** (tə lem′ə tər *for noun*, tel′ə mē′tər *for verb*) **1** a device for measuring heat, radiation, speed, etc. and transmitting the information, especially by radio, to a distant station where it is recorded: *Telemeters are used in rockets, etc.* **2** measure and transmit by this means. **3** range finder. **1, 3** *n.*, **2** *v.*

## teethe 1229 telephoto lens

hat, āge, fär; let, ēqual, tėrm; it, īce
hot, ōpen, ôrder; oil, out; cup, put, rüle
əbove, takən, pencəl, lemən, circəs
ch, child; ng, long; sh, ship
th, thin; ᴛʜ, then; zh, measure

**tel·e·met·ric** (tel′ə met′rik) of or having to do with TELEMETERS or TELEMETRY. *adj.*

**te·lem·e·try** (tə lem′ə trē) **1** the use of TELEMETERS for measuring and transmitting information. **2** the equipment used in this process: *The ground telemetry indicated that the rocket was on course.* *n.*

**tel·e·path·ic** (tel′ə path′ik) **1** of or having to do with TELEPATHY. **2** by TELEPATHY. *adj.*

**tel·e·path·i·cal·ly** (tel′ə path′i klē) by TELEPATHY. *adv.*

**te·lep·a·thist** (tə lep′ə thist) **1** a student of or believer in TELEPATHY. **2** a person who has TELEPATHIC power. *n.*

**te·lep·a·thy** (tə lep′ə thē) the communication of one mind with another without using speech, hearing, sight, or any other sense used normally to communicate. *n.*

**tel·e·phone** (tel′ə fōn′) **1** an apparatus, system, or process for transmitting sound or speech over distances by converting it into electrical impluses that are sent through a wire. **2** talk through a telephone; communicate by telephone: *Wait till she's finished telephoning.* **3** make a telephone call to: *Did you telephone her?* **4** send by telephone: *to telephone a message.* **1** *n.*, **2–4** *v.*, **tel·e·phoned, tel·e·phon·ing.** —**tel′e·phon′er,** *n.*

**telephone book** TELEPHONE DIRECTORY.

**telephone booth** a small enclosure in a public place containing a telephone that is usually coin-operated.

**telephone directory** a book containing an alphabetical or classified list of names of telephone subscribers, together with their addresses and telephone numbers.

**tel·e·phon·ic** (tel′ə fon′ik) of, having to do with, or sent by telephone. *adj.*

**te·leph·o·ny** (tə lef′ə nē) the making or operating of telephones. *n.*

**tel·e·pho·to** (tel′ə fō′tō) **1** of or referring to a system of lenses for a camera designed to produce a large image of a distant object. **2** a TELEPHOTO LENS. **3** a photograph taken with a camera having a TELEPHOTO LENS. **1** *adj.*, **2, 3** *n.*

**tel·e·pho·to·graph** (tel′ə fō′tə graf′) **1** a picture taken with a camera having a TELEPHOTO LENS. **2** take a picture in this way. **3** a picture sent by TELEGRAPHY. **4** send such a picture. **1, 3** *n.*, **2, 4** *v.*

**tel·e·pho·to·graph·ic** (tel′ə fō′tə graf′ik) of, having to do with, or referring to the process of TELEPHOTOGRAPHY. *adj.*

**tel·e·pho·tog·ra·phy** (tel′ə fə tog′rə fē) **1** the method or process of photographing distant objects by using a camera with a TELEPHOTO LENS. **2** the method or process of sending and reproducing pictures by TELEGRAPH. *n.*

**tel·e·pho·to lens** (tel′ə fō′tō) a lens for a camera that produces a large image of a distant object.

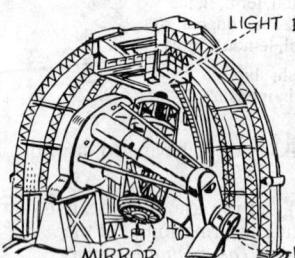

A large reflecting telescope in an observatory. A large concave mirror at the bottom reflects light from the object being studied to one or more flat mirrors and then to a magnifying lens called the eyepiece.

**tel·e·scope** (tel′ə skōp′) **1** an instrument for directly viewing distant objects, using lenses or mirrors or both to make the object viewed appear nearer and larger. **2** RADIO TELESCOPE. **3** slide one within the other like the sections of a hand telescope: *Built-in radio aerials are made so that they can be telescoped.* **4** force or be forced one into the other as in a collision: *When the two trains collided, the force of the crash telescoped the first few cars.* **5** shorten; condense. 1, 2 *n.*, 3–5 *v.*, **tel·e·scoped, tel·e·scop·ing.**

**tel·e·scop·ic** (tel′ə skop′ik) **1** of or having to do with a telescope. **2** obtained or seen by means of a telescope: *a telescopic view of the moon.* **3** visible only through a telescope: *telescopic stars.* **4** far-seeing: *telescopic vision.* **5** consisting of parts that slide inside one another like the tubes of some telescopes: *a telescopic antenna.* *adj.*

**tel·e·scop·i·cal·ly** (tel′ə skop′i klē) **1** in a TELESCOPIC manner. **2** by a telescope. *adv.*

**tel·e·text** (tel′ə tekst′) **1** a method of superimposing printed words on a television picture. **2** the words so shown. *n.*

**tel·e·type** (tel′ə tīp′) **1** a telecommunication system that transmits messages, typed on an electronic typewriter, by cable or telephone to be received and typed by a compatible machine. **2** the message or messages so transmitted and received. **3** use such a system. 1, 2 *n.*, 3 *v.*, **tel·e·typed, tel·e·typ·ing.**

**tel·e·type·writ·er** (tel′ə tī′prī′tər) a machine resembling a typewriter, used in teletyping. *n.*

**tel·e·view** (tel′ə vyü′) watch by means of television. *v.* —**tel′e·view′er,** *n.*

**tel·e·vise** (tel′ə vīz′) pick up and transmit by television: *All the games are being televised.* *v.*, **tel·e·vised, tel·e·vis·ing.**

**tel·e·vi·sion** (tel′ə vizh′ən) **1** the process of transmitting the image of an object, scene, or event by radio or wire so that a person in some other place can see it at once: *In television, waves of light from an object are changed into electric waves that are transmitted by radio or wire, and then changed back into waves of light that produce an image of the object on a screen.* **2** the apparatus on which these pictures may be seen. **3** the business of television broadcasting; the television industry. *n.*

**tell** (tel) **1** put in words; say: *Tell the truth.* **2** tell to; inform: *Tell us about it.* **3** make known: *Don't tell where the money is.* **4** tell something: *He was always telling, never doing.* **5** act as talebearer; reveal something secret or private: *Promise not to tell.* **6** recognize; know; distinguish: *She couldn't tell which house it was.* **7** say to; order; command: *Tell him to stop!* **8** say to with force: *I don't like it, I tell you.* **9** count; count one by one: *The nun tells her beads.* **10** have effect or force: *Every blow told.* *v.*, **told, tell·ing.**
**all told,** counting everyone or everything; altogether: *We'll be 15 people all told.*
**tell apart,** distinguish one from the other or others: *Nobody could tell the twin sisters apart.*
**tell off,** **a** count off; count off and detach for some special duty. **b** *Informal.* rebuke strongly; castigate: *His father told him off for staying out late.*
**tell on,** **a** inform on; tell tales about: *Please don't tell on us.* **b** have a harmful effect on; break down: *The strain was telling on the man's health.*
**tell time,** know what time it is by the clock.

**tell·a·ble** (tel′ə bəl) capable or worthy of being told. *adj.*

**tell·er** (tel′ər) **1** a person who tells a story. **2** a cashier in a bank: *A teller in a bank takes in, gives out, and counts money.* **3** a person appointed to count votes. *n.*

**tell·ing** (tel′ing) **1** having a marked effect or great force; impressive or effective: *a telling blow.* **2** ppr. of TELL. 1 *adj.*, 2 *v.* —**tell′ing·ly,** *adv.*

**tell·tale** (tel′tāl′) **1** a person who tells tales on others; tattletale; talebearer. **2** revealing thoughts, actions, etc. that are supposed to be secret: *telltale fingerprints, a telltale blush.* **3** any of various devices that indicate or record something: *A time clock is sometimes called a telltale.* *n.*

**tel·lu·ri·um** (te lü′rē əm) a rare, silver-white chemical element resembling sulphur in its chemical properties, and usually occurring in nature combined with gold, silver, or other metals. Symbol: Te *n.*

**tel·ly** (tel′ē) *Brit. Informal.* **1** television. **2 tellies,** *pl.* television programs. *n.*

**te·mer·i·ty** (tə mer′ə tē) reckless boldness; rashness. *n.*

**temp.** **1** temperature. **2** temporary.

**tem·per** (tem′pər) **1** a state of mind; disposition; condition: *She was in a good temper.* **2** an angry state of mind: *In her temper she broke a vase.* **3** a calm or controlled state of mind: *He became angry and lost his temper.* **4** moderate; soften: *Temper justice with mercy.* **5** bring to a proper or desired condition of hardness, toughness, etc. by mixing or preparing: *A painter tempers his or her colours by mixing them with oil. Steel is tempered by heating it and working it till it has the proper degree of hardness and toughness.* **6** the degree of hardness, toughness, etc. of a substance: *The temper of the clay was right for shaping.* **7** a substance added to something to modify its properties or qualities. **8** tune or adjust the pitch of an instrument, a voice, etc. 1–3, 6, 7 *n.*, 4, 5, 8 *v.*

**tem·per·a** (tem′pə rə) a method of painting in which colours are mixed with egg, especially the yolk, or SIZE² or CASEIN instead of oil, to produce a dull finish. *n.*

**tem·per·a·ment** (tem′pə rə mənt *or* tem′prə mənt) **1** an individual's usual way of thinking, feeling, and acting; natural disposition: *a person of shy temperament, the artistic temperament.* **2** great or extreme sensitivity, especially when characterized by irritability or an unwillingness to submit to ordinary rules and restraints: *Temperament is often attributed to actors and artists.* *n.*

**tem·per·a·men·tal** (tem′pə rə men′təl *or* tem′prə men′təl) **1** of, having to do with, or due to TEMPERAMENT (def. 1); constitutional: *Cats have a temperamental dislike for water.* **2** extremely sensitive and excitable or unpredictable in behaviour: *a temperamental* actress. When he gets temperamental like that, it's impossible to reason with him. *adj.* —**tem′per·a·men′tal·ly,** *adv.*

**tem·per·ance** (tem′pə rəns *or* tem′prəns)
**1** moderation in action, speech, habits, etc.
**2** moderation in the use of alcoholic drinks.   **3** the principle and practice of not using alcoholic drinks at all.   *n.*

**tem·per·ate** (tem′pə rit *or* tem′prit)   **1** not very hot and not very cold: *a temperate climate, the temperate regions of the world.*   **2** having to do with or found in regions with a moderate climate: *temperate plants.*
**3** self-restrained; moderate: *She spoke in a calm, temperate manner.*   **4** moderate in using alcoholic drinks.   *adj.*
—**tem′per·ate·ly,** *adv.*   —**tem′per·ate·ness,** *n.*

**tem·per·a·ture** (tem′pə rə chər *or* tem′prə chər)   **1** the degree of heat or cold measured on a scale: *The temperature of freezing water is zero degrees Celsius.*   **2** the degree of heat contained in a living body: *The normal temperature of the human body is about 37 degrees Celsius.*
**3** a level of body heat that is above normal; fever: *Does he have a temperature? The baby was running a temperature yesterday.*   *n.*

**tem·pered** (tem′pərd)   **1** softened; moderated: *justice tempered with mercy.*   **2** having a particular disposition (*used in compounds*): *an even-tempered person.*   **3** treated by tempering; brought to a desired condition of hardness and toughness: *a sword of tempered steel.*   **4** pt. and pp. of TEMPER.   1–3 *adj.,* 4 *v.*

**tem·pest** (tem′pist)   **1** a violent windstorm, usually accompanied by rain, hail or snow: *The tempest drove the ship onto the rocks.*   **2** a violent disturbance; uproar; tumult: *a tempest of cheers.*   *n.*
**tempest in a teapot** *or* **tea cup,**   great excitement or commotion over something unimportant.   See STORM.

**tem·pes·tu·ous** (tem pes′chü əs)   **1** stormy: *a tempestuous night.*   **2** violent: *a tempestuous argument.*
*adj.*   —**tem·pes′tu·ous·ly,** *adv.*
—**tem·pes′tu·ous·ness,** *n.*

**tem·plate** (tem′plit)   a thin piece of wood, metal, plastic, or cardboard used as a pattern in cutting an object or shape out of wood, metal, cloth, etc.   *n.*

**tem·ple**[1] (tem′pəl)   **1** a building used for religious services or worship.   **2** SYNAGOGUE.   **3** a place in which God is thought of as residing.   **4** Often, **Temple,** any of three religious buildings built in succession by the Jews in ancient Jerusalem.   *n.*

**tem·ple**[2] (tem′pəl)   **1** the flattened part on either side of the forehead.   **2** either of the side supports of a pair of eyeglasses passing above and behind the ears.   *n.*

**tem·po** (tem′pō)   **1** in music, the time or rate of speed of a composition or passage: *The tempo of this piece is very fast. He didn't play it at the correct tempo.*
**2** characteristic rate of activity or motion; pace: *the fast tempo of modern life.*   *n., pl.* **tem·pos** *or* **tem·pi** (-pē).

**tem·po·ral**[1] (tem′pə rəl *or* tem′prəl)   **1** of, having to do with, or referring to time or earthly life, as opposed to eternity.   **2** of or having to do with secular things; worldly: *temporal concerns.*   *adj.*   —**tem′po·ral·ly,** *adv.*

**tem·po·ral**[2] (tem′pə rəl *or* tem′prəl)   of or having to do with the temples of the head: *the temporal artery.*   *adj.*

**tem·po·ral·i·ty** (tem′pə ral′ə tē)   **1** the quality or state of being TEMPORAL[1].   **2** Usually, **temporalities,** *pl.* secular possessions of a church, especially revenues or properties.   *n., pl.* **tem·po·ral·i·ties.**

**tem·po·rar·i·ly** (tem′pə rer′ə lē *or* tem′pə rer′ə lē)

**temperance**     **1231**     **tenacious**

hat, āge, fär; let, ēqual, tėrm; it, īce
hot, ōpen, ôrder; oil, out; cup, pùt, rüle
əbove, takən, pencəl, lemən, circəs
ch, child; ng, long; sh, ship
th, thin; ᴛʜ, then; zh, measure

for a short time; for the present: *Classes for the new course are temporarily being held in the auditorium.*   *adv.*

**tem·po·rar·y** (tem′pə rer′ē)   **1** lasting or used for a short time only; not permanent: *a temporary shelter, a temporary inconvenience.*   **2** a person employed for a short time: *They hired several temporaries last summer.*
1 *adj.,* 2 *n.*   —**tem′po·rar′i·ness,** *n.*

**tem·po·ri·za·tion** (tem′pə rə zā′shən *or* tem′pə rī za′shən)   the act or practice of temporizing; a compromise.   *n.*

**tem·po·rize** (tem′pə rīz′)   **1** evade immediate action or decision in order to gain time, avoid trouble, etc.: *He temporized until we promised to help.*   **2** fit one's acts to the time or occasion.   **3** make or discuss terms; negotiate.   *v.,* **tem·po·rized, tem·po·riz·ing.**
—**tem′po·riz′er,** *n.*

**tempt** (tempt)   **1** make, or try to make a person do something wrong by promising pleasure or some advantage: *He was tempted to steal.*   **2** appeal to strongly; be very attractive to: *sweets that tempt one's appetite.*
**3** cause to feel strongly inclined (*usually used after the verb* **to be**): *After three failures he was tempted to quit.*
**4** provoke or defy: *It would be tempting fate to take that old car on the road.*   *v.*   —**tempt′a·ble,** *adj.*

**temp·ta·tion** (temp tā′shən)   **1** the act of tempting or the state of being tempted: *No temptation could make her false to her friend.*   **2** something that tempts: *The money lying on the counter was a temptation to him.*   *n.*

**tempt·er** (temp′tər)   a person who tempts.   *n.*

**tempt·ing** (temp′ting)   **1** that tempts; alluring; inviting: *A party is a tempting idea.*   **2** ppr. of TEMPT.   1 *adj.,* 2 *v.*
—**tempt′ing·ly,** *adv.*

**tempt·ress** (temp′tris)   a woman who tempts.   *n.*

**ten** (ten)   **1** one more than nine; 10: *Six and four make ten. I still have ten dollars.*   **2** the numeral 10: *That's a 10, not a 16.*   **3** the tenth in a set or series; especially, a playing card having ten spots: *She played a ten of clubs.*
**4** a 10-dollar bill: *I changed the twenty for two tens.*
**5** being tenth in a set or series (*used mainly after the noun*): *Chapter Ten will be discussed tomorrow.*   **6** a set or series of ten persons or things: *I got my ten right.*   1–4, 6 *n.,* 1, 5 *adj.*
☞ *Etym.* From OE *tēne, tīene,* related to German *zehn* and having the same Indo-European source as L *decem* and Gk. *deka.*

**ten.**   tenor.

**ten·a·bil·i·ty** (ten′ə bil′ə tē)   the fact or quality of being TENABLE.   *n.*

**ten·a·ble** (ten′ə bəl)   capable of being held or defended: *a tenable position, a tenable theory.*   *adj.*
—**ten′a·bly,** *adv.*

**te·na·cious** (ti nā′shəs)   **1** holding fast; not readily letting go: *a tenacious grip, the tenacious jaws of a bulldog. He is tenacious of his rights and will fight to the end.*
**2** stubborn or persistent; not readily giving up: *a tenacious salesman, tenacious courage.*   **3** especially good at remembering: *a tenacious memory.*   **4** tending to stick or

**tenaciousness**    **tenpins**

cling: *tenacious burrs.*   **5** holding fast together; not easily pulled apart; tough: *a tenacious metal.* *adj.* —**te·na′cious·ly**, *adv.*

**te·na·cious·ness** (ti nā′shə snəs)    the quality or state of being TENACIOUS; tenacity. *n.*

**te·nac·i·ty** (ti nas′ə tē)    the quality or state of being TENACIOUS. *n.*

**ten·an·cy** (ten′ən sē)    **1** the state of being a tenant; the occupying of and paying rent for land or buildings.   **2** the length of time a tenant occupies a property. *n., pl.* **ten·an·cies**.

**ten·ant** (ten′ənt)    **1** a person paying rent for the temporary use of the land or buildings of another person: *They have tenants on the second floor of their house.*   **2** a person or thing that occupies: *Birds are tenants of the trees.*   **3** hold or occupy as a tenant; inhabit.   *1, 2 n., 3 v.* —**ten′ant·less**, *adj.*

**ten·ant·ry** (ten′ən trē)    **1** all the tenants on an estate.   **2** TENANCY. *n., pl.* **ten·ant·ries**.

**tend¹** (tend)    **1** have an inclination or TENDENCY: *She tends to use large canvases for her paintings. He tends to dress conservatively.*   **2** move or extend; be directed: *The coastline tends to the south here.* *v.*

**tend²** (tend)    **1** take care of; look after; attend to: *He tends shop for his father. A shepherd tends his flock.*   **2** serve; wait upon.   **3** *Informal.* pay attention (*to*): *Just tend to your work and never mind what everyone else is doing.* *v.*

**tend·en·cy** (ten′dən sē)    **1** an inclination or leaning toward a particular kind of action, behaviour, etc.: *a tendency to favour pastel colours, a tendency to reject new ideas without considering them.*   **2** a natural disposition to move, proceed, or act in some direction or toward some point, end, or result: *Wood has a tendency to swell if it gets wet.* *n., pl.* **tend·en·cies**.

**ten·den·tious** (ten den′shəs)    having or promoting a particular aim or point of view; biassed: *tendentious writings.* *adj.*

**ten·der¹** (ten′dər)    **1** not hard or tough; soft: *tender meat.*   **2** not strong and hard; delicate: *tender young grass.*   **3** kind; affectionate; loving; *She spoke tender words to the child.*   **4** not rough or crude; gentle: *He patted the dog with tender hands.*   **5** young; immature: *Two years is a tender age.*   **6** sensitive; painful; sore: *a tender wound, a tender subject.*   **7** feeling pain or grief easily: *She has a tender heart and would never hurt anyone.*   **8** considerate; careful: *He handles people in a tender manner.*   **9** requiring careful or tactful handling: *a tender situation.* *adj.* —**ten′der·ly**, *adv.* —**ten′der·ness**, *n.*

**ten·der²** (ten′dər)    **1** offer formally: *He tendered his thanks.*   **2** a formal offer: *She refused his tender of marriage. The contract was put out to tender.*   **3** the thing offered: *Money that may be offered as payment for a debt is called legal tender.*   *1 v., 2, 3 n.* —**ten′der·er**, *n.*

**tend·er³** (ten′dər)    **1** a person or thing that tends another: *a bartender.*   **2** a small boat carried or towed by a big one and used for landing passengers.   **3** a small ship used for carrying supplies and passengers to and from larger ships.   **4** the car attached behind a steam locomotive: *The tender carries coal and water for the locomotive.* *n.*

**ten·der·foot** (ten′dər fùt′) *Informal.*    **1** a newcomer to the pioneer life of the West.   **2** a person not used to rough living and hardships.   **3** an inexperienced person; beginner.   **4** a beginning BOY SCOUT or GIRL GUIDE.   *n., pl.* **ten·der·foots** or **ten·der·feet**.

**ten·der–heart·ed** (ten′dər här′tid)    kindly; sympathetic. *adj.*

**ten·der·ize** (ten′də rīz′)    make meat tender; soften. *v.*, **ten·der·ized**, **ten·der·iz·ing**.

**ten·der·loin** (ten′dər loin′)    a tender part of the loin of beef or pork. *n.*

**ten·di·nous** (ten′də nəs)    **1** of or like a TENDON.   **2** consisting of TENDONS. *adj.*

**ten·don** (ten′dən)    a tough, strong band or cord of tissue that joins a muscle to a bone or some other part; sinew. *n.*

**tendon of A·chil·les** (ə kil′ēz)    the tendon that connects the muscles of the calf of the leg with the bone of the heel.

**ten·dril** (ten′drəl)    **1** a threadlike part of a climbing plant that attaches itself to something and helps support the plant.   **2** something resembling such a part of a plant: *tendrils of hair curling about a child's face.* *n.*

**ten·e·ment** (ten′ə mənt)    **1** any house or building to live in; dwelling house.   **2** a part of a house or building occupied by a tenant as a separate dwelling.   **3** a building, especially in a poor section of a city, divided into sets of rooms for separate families.   **4** an abode; habitation. *n.*

**ten·et** (ten′it)    a doctrine, principle, belief, or opinion held as true. *n.*

**ten·fold** (ten′fōld′)    ten times as much or as many. *adj., adv.*

**ten·nis** (ten′is)    a game played on a special court by two or four players who knock a ball back and forth over a net with a racket (**tennis racket**). See RACKET² for picture.

**ten·on** (ten′ən)    **1** the end of a piece of wood cut so as to fit into a hole, the mortise, in another piece and so form a joint. See JOINT for picture.   **2** cut so as to form a tenon.   **3** fit together with tenon and mortise.   *1 n., 2, 3 v.*

**ten·or** (ten′ər)    **1** a general tendency or direction; a settled course: *The calm tenor of her life has never been disturbed by excitement or trouble.*   **2** the general meaning or drift: *I understand French well enough to get the tenor of his speech.*   **3** the highest ordinary, or natural, adult male singing voice. Compare with COUNTERTENOR.   **4** a singer who has such a voice.   **5** the part sung by a tenor: *Tenor is the second lowest part, above bass, in standard four-part harmony for men's and women's voices.*   **6** an instrument having a range next above that of the bass in a family of musical instruments.   **7** having to do with, having the range of, or designed for a tenor.   **8** a high-pitched male speaking voice.   *1–6, 8 n., 7 adj.*
☞ *Etym.* Through Old French from L *tenor* 'course, general substance or meaning' (originally 'a holding on'), which came from L *tenere* 'to hold'. The musical senses came from the tenor part being the one that held the melody.

**ten·pen·ny** (ten′pen′ē)    **1** worth or costing ten pennies.   **2** designating a kind of large-sized nail, once costing ten pennies per hundred. *adj.*

**ten·pins** (ten′pinz′)    **1** a bowling game in which a ball is bowled at 10 wooden pins to knock them down.   **2** the pins used in this game.   *1 n. sing., 2 n. pl.*

**tense¹** (tens) 1 stretched tight; strained to stiffness: *a tense rope, a face tense with pain.* 2 stretch tight; stiffen: *He tensed his muscles.* 3 strained; keyed up: *a tense moment.* 1, 3 *adj.*, **tens·er, tens·est**; 2 *v.*, **tensed, tens·ing.** —**tense′ly,** *adv.* —**tense′ness,** *n.*

**tense²** (tens) 1 a set of verb forms to show the time, duration, etc. of the action or state expressed by the verb: *The simple past tense in English is used to express an action or state that is completed or ended.* 2 a form of a verb indicating a particular time, etc. of an action or state: *The simple past tense of* go *is* went. *n.*

**ten·sile** (ten′sīl *or* ten′səl) 1 of or having to do with tension: *Steel has great tensile strength.* 2 capable of being stretched; ductile. *adj.*

**ten·sil·i·ty** (ten sil′ə tē) a TENSILE quality; ductility. *n.*

**ten·sion** (ten′shən) 1 stretching. 2 a stretched condition: *The tension of the spring is caused by the weight.* 3 mental strain: *A mother feels tension when her baby is sick.* 4 a strained condition: *political tension.* 5 a stress caused by the action of a pulling force: *An elevator exerts tension on the cables supporting it.* 6 a device or method to control the pull or strain on something: *The tension in a sewing machine may be adjusted to hold the thread tight or loose. In knitting and crocheting, you must keep the tension even.* 7 voltage: *high-tension wires.* 8 the pressure of a gas. *n.*

**ten·si·ty** (ten′sə tē) a TENSE quality or state. *n.*

**ten·sor** (ten′sər) a muscle that stretches or tightens some part of the body. *n.*

**ten–strike** (ten′strīk′) 1 in the game of tenpins, the stroke that knocks down all the pins. 2 *Informal.* any completely successful stroke or act. *n.*

**tent** (tent) 1 a movable shelter, usually made of canvas and often supported by one or more poles and ropes or wires. 2 camp out or live in a tent: *They plan on spending their holidays tenting in the Maritimes.* 3 cover with a tent. 1 *n.*, 2, 3 *v.* —**tent′like′,** *adj.*

**ten·ta·cle** (ten′tə kəl) 1 a long, slender, flexible growth on the head or around the mouth of an animal, used to touch, hold, or move; feeler: *An octopus has tentacles.* See OCTOPUS for picture. 2 a sensitive, hairlike growth on a plant. *n.*

**ten·ta·tive** (ten′tə tiv) done as a trial or experiment; experimental: *a tentative plan.* *adj.* —**ten′ta·tive·ly,** *adv.* —**ten′ta·tive·ness,** *n.*

**ten·ter** (ten′tər) 1 a framework on which cloth is stretched so that it may set or dry evenly without shrinking. 2 stretch cloth on a tenter. 1 *n.*, 2 *v.*

**ten·ter·hook** (ten′tər hůk′) one of the hooks or bent nails that hold the cloth stretched on a TENTER. *n.*
**on tenterhooks,** in painful suspense; anxious.

**tenth** (tenth) 1 next after the 9th; last in a series of ten; 10th. 2 one, or being one, of 10 equal parts. *adj., n.*

**tenth·ly** (ten′thlē) in the tenth place. *adv.*

**ten·u·i·ty** (ti nyü′ə tē *or* ti nü′ə tē) a rarefied condition; thinness; slightness. *n.*

**ten·u·ous** (ten′yü əs) 1 thin; slender: *a tenuous thread.* 2 not dense; tenuous air. 3 having slight importance; not substantial: *a tenuous claim.* *adj.* —**ten′u·ous·ly,** *adv.* —**ten′u·ous·ness,** *n.*

**ten·ure** (ten′yər) 1 a holding or possessing. 2 the length of time of holding or possessing: *The tenure of office of the president of our club is one year.* 3 a manner of holding land, buildings, etc. from a feudal lord or superior. 4 the conditions, terms, etc. on which anything is held or occupied. 5 security of position for a university teacher. *n.*

**te·pee** (tē′pē) See TEEPEE. *n.*

**tep·id** (tep′id) slightly warm; lukewarm. *adj.* —**tep′id·ness,** *n.*

**te·pid·i·ty** (ti pid′ə tē) lukewarmness; TEPID condition. *n.*

**ter·bi·um** (tėr′bē əm) a rare metallic element of the yttrium group. Symbol: Tb *n.*

**ter·cel** (tėr′səl) a male falcon or goshawk, especially the male of the peregrine falcon. *n.*

**ter·cen·ten·ar·y** (tėr′sən ten′ə rē *or* tėr′sən tē′nə rē) 1 having to do with a period of 300 years. 2 a period of 300 years. 3 a 300th anniversary. 1 *adj.*, 2, 3 *n., pl.* **ter·cen·te·nar·ies.**

**te·re·do** (tə rē′dō) a small wormlike MOLLUSC that bores into and destroys the wood of ships, etc. *n., pl.* **te·re·dos.**

**term** (tėrm) 1 a word or phrase used in a recognized and definite sense in some particular subject, science, art, business, etc.: *medical terms, terms about radio.* 2 name; call; describe as: *He might be termed handsome.* 3 a set period of time; length of time that a thing lasts: *a president's term of office.* 4 one of the long periods into which the school year may be divided: *the fall term.* 5 one of the periods of time when certain law courts are in session. 6 one of the members in a proportion or ratio. 7 in mathematics, one or more numerals or symbols that make a product. Terms in an algebraic expression are always separated by + and −. $x$ and $xy$ are expressions consisting of one term; $xy + ab$ is an expression consisting of two terms. 8 having a definite end or limit: *a term deposit, term insurance.* 9 **terms,** *pl.* **a** conditions: *the terms of a treaty.* **b** a way of speaking: *flattering terms.* **c** personal relations: *on good terms, on speaking terms.* 1, 3–7, 9 *n.*, 2 *v.*, 8 *adj.*
**bring to terms,** compel to agree, assent, or submit.
**come to terms,** reach an agreement.
**terms of reference,** the matters referred to a person, committee, etc. for study; instructions indicating the scope of an inquiry.

**ter·ma·gant** (tėr′mə gənt) 1 a violent, quarrelling, scolding woman. 2 violent; quarrelling; scolding. 1 *n.*, 2 *adj.*

**ter·mi·na·bil·i·ty** (tėr′mə nə bil′ə tē) the fact or quality of being TERMINABLE. *n.*

**ter·mi·na·ble** (tėr′mə nə bəl) 1 that can be ended: *The contract was terminable by either party.* 2 coming to an end after a certain time: *a loan terminable in 10 years.* *adj.* —**ter′mi·na·ble·ness,** *n.* —**ter′mi·na·bly,** *adv.*

**ter·mi·nal** (tėr′mə nəl) 1 at the end; forming the end part: *A terminal flower or bud is one growing at the end of a stem, branch, etc.* 2 the end; end part. 3 coming at the end: *a terminal examination.* **4** leading to death: *a terminal illness.* **5** having to do with a term. **6** either end of a railway line, airline, shipping route, etc. where sheds, hangars, garages, offices, etc., and stations to handle freight and passengers are located; terminus. **7** at the end of a railway line: *a terminal station.* **8** having to do with the handling of freight at a terminal. **9** marking a boundary, limit, or end. **10** a device for making an electrical connection: *the terminals of a battery.* See GENERATOR for picture. **11** an apparatus, such as a visual display unit, by which a user can give information to or receive information from a computer, communications system, etc. *1, 3–5, 7–9 adj., 2, 6, 10, 11 n.*

**ter·mi·nal·ly** (tėr′mə nə lē) **1** at the end. **2** with respect to a TERMINATION. *adv.*

**ter·mi·nate** (tėr′mə nāt) **1** bring to an end; put an end to: *to terminate a partnership.* **2** come to an end: *Her contract terminates soon.* **3** occur at or form the end of; bound; limit. *v.,* **ter·mi·nat·ed, ter·mi·nat·ing.**

**ter·mi·na·tion** (tėr′mə nā′shən) **1** an ending; end: *the termination of a war.* **2** an end part. **3** the ending of a word. *Example: In* gladly, *the adverbial termination is* -ly. *n.*

**ter·mi·nol·o·gy** (tėr′mə nol′ə jē) the special words or terms used in a science, art, business, etc.: *medical terminology. n., pl.* **ter·mi·nol·o·gies.**

**term insurance** life insurance that expires at the end of a specified period of time.

**ter·mi·nus** (tėr′mə nəs) **1** either end of a railway line, bus line, etc. **2** a city or station at the end of a railway line, bus line, etc. **3** an ending place; final point; goal; end. **4** a stone, post, etc. marking a boundary or limit. *n., pl.* **ter·mi·nus·es** or **ter·mi·ni** (-nī′ *or* -nē′).

**ter·mite** (tėr′mīt) any of various insects that have a soft, pale body and live in colonies: *Termites, which are sometimes called white ants, are destructive to buildings, furniture, provisions, etc. n.*

**tern** (tėrn) a sea bird resembling a gull but having a more slender body and bill and a long, forked tail. *n.* ☞ *Hom.* TURN.

**terp·si·cho·re·an** (tėrp′sə kə rē′ən) having to do with dancing: *the terpsichorean art. adj.*

A series of terraces on a mountainside in Peru

**ter·race** (ter′is) **1** a flat level of land like a large step, especially one of a series of such levels on a slope. **2** form into a terrace or terraces; furnish with terraces. **3** a street along the side or top of a slope. **4** a row of houses on such a street. **5** a paved outdoor space adjoining a house, used for lounging, dining, etc. **6** the flat roof of a house, especially of an Oriental or Spanish house. *1, 3–6 n., 2 v.,* **ter·raced, ter·rac·ing.**

**ter·ra cot·ta** (ter′ə kot′ə) **1** a kind of hard, brownish-red earthenware, used for vases, statuettes, decorations on buildings, etc. **2** dull, brownish red.

**ter·ra fir·ma** (ter′ə fėr′mə) *Latin.* solid earth; dry land.

**ter·rain** (te rān′) land; a tract of land, especially considered as to its extent and natural features in relation to its use in warfare. *n.*

**ter·ra·pin** (ter′ə pin) a North American turtle used for food. *n.*

**ter·rar·i·um** (tə rer′ē əm) a glass enclosure in which plants or small land animals are kept. *n., pl.* **ter·rar·i·ums** or **ter·rar·i·a** (-ē ə).

**ter·res·tri·al** (tə res′trē əl) **1** of the earth; having to do with the earth. **2** of land, not water or air: *Islands and continents make up the terrestrial parts of the earth.* **3** living on the ground, not in the air, in water, or in trees: *terrestrial animals.* **4** growing on land; growing in the ground: *terrestrial plants.* **5** worldly; earthly. **6** an inhabitant of earth. *1–5 adj., 6 n.*

**ter·ri·ble** (ter′ə bəl) **1** causing great fear; dreadful; awful: *a terrible leopard.* **2** distressing; severe: *the terrible suffering caused by war.* **3** *Informal.* extremely bad, unpleasant, etc.: *She has a terrible temper. adj.* —**ter′ri·ble·ness,** *n.*

**ter·ri·bly** (ter′ə blē) **1** in a terrible manner: *The lightning flashed terribly.* **2** *Informal.* extremely: *I am terribly sorry I stepped on your toe. adv.*

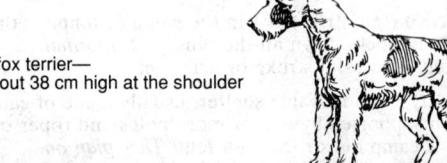

A fox terrier—
about 38 cm high at the shoulder

**ter·ri·er** (ter′ē ər) any of several breeds of dog, such as the fox terrier, Airedale, or Scottish terrier, having either a short-haired, smooth coat or a long-haired, rough coat. Terriers were formerly used to pursue burrowing animals. *n.*

**ter·rif·ic** (tə rif′ik) **1** causing great fear; terrifying. **2** *Informal.* very unusual; remarkable; extraordinary: *A terrific hot spell ruined many of the crops. adj.*

**ter·rif·i·cal·ly** (tə rif′i klē) in a terrific manner or to a terrific degree. *adv.*

**ter·ri·fied** (ter′ə fīd) **1** filled with great fear; frightened. **2** pt. and pp. of TERRIFY. *1 adj., 2 v.*

**ter·ri·fy** (ter′ə fī) fill with great fear; frighten very much. *v.,* **ter·ri·fied, ter·ri·fy·ing.**

**ter·ri·to·ri·al** (ter′ə tô′rē əl) **1** of or having to do with territory: *Many wars have been fought for territorial gain.* **2** of a particular territory or region; restricted to a particular region. *adj.*

**ter·ri·to·ri·al·ly** (ter′ə tô′rē ə lē) in respect to territory; as to territory. *adv.*

**ter·ri·to·ry** (ter′ə tô′rē) **1** land: *Much territory in the northern part of Africa is desert.* **2** a region; an area of land: *The company leased a large territory for oil explorations.* **3** land under the rule or control of a distant government: *The British Empire included many territories.* **4** a region assigned to a salesperson or agent.

**5** the facts investigated by some branch of science or learning: *the territory of biochemistry.* **6 Territory,** in Canada, a region having its own elected council and administered by a commissioner appointed by the federal government: *the Northwest Territories, Yukon Territory.* *n., pl.* **ter‧ri‧to‧ries.**

**ter‧ror** (ter′ər) **1** great fear: *The child has a terror of thunder.* **2** a cause of great fear: *Pirates were once the terror of the sea.* **3** *Informal.* a person or thing that causes much trouble and unpleasantness. *n.*

**ter‧ror‧ism** (ter′ə riz′əm) **1** the act of terrorizing; use of terror. **2** the condition of fear and submission produced by frightening people. **3** a method of opposing a government internally through the use of terror. **4** the use of violence, taking of hostages, etc., to gain specific demands. *n.*

**ter‧ror‧ist** (ter′ə rist) a person who uses or favours TERRORISM (defs. 3, 4). *n.*

**ter‧ror‧is‧tic** (ter′ə ris′tik) using or favouring methods that inspire terror. *adj.*

**ter‧ror‧i‧za‧tion** (ter′ə rə zā′shən *or* ter′ə rī zā′shən) a terrorizing or being terrorized; rule by terror. *n.*

**ter‧ror‧ize** (ter′ə rīz′) **1** fill with terror: *The sight of the growling dog terrorized the little child.* **2** rule or subdue by causing terror: *The village was terrorized by bandits during the revolution.* *v.,* **ter‧ror‧ized, ter‧ror‧iz‧ing.**

**ter‧ror–strick‧en** (ter′ər strik′ən) terrified. *adj.*

**ter‧ry** (ter′ē) a rough cloth made of uncut looped yarn. *n., pl.* **ter‧ries.**

**terry cloth** TERRY.

**terse** (tėrs) of writers, writing, speakers, or speaking, brief and to the point. *adj.,* **ters‧er, ters‧est.** —**terse′ly,** *adv.* —**terse′ness,** *n.*

**ter‧tian** (tėr′shən) **1** a fever or ague with a bad spell recurring every other day. **2** recurring every other day. 1 *n.,* 2 *adj.*

**ter‧ti‧ar‧y** (tėr′shē er′ē) of the third order, rank, formation, etc.; third. *adj.*

**tes‧sel‧late** (tes′ə lāt′ *for verb,* tes′ə lit *or* tes′ə lāt′ *for adjective*) **1** make of small squares or blocks, or in a checkered pattern. **2** made in small squares or blocks or in a checkered pattern. 1 *v.,* **tes‧sel‧lat‧ed, tes‧sel‧lat‧ing;** 2 *adj.*

**tes‧ser‧a** (tes′ə rə) **1** a small piece of marble, glass, etc. used in mosaic work. **2** a small square of bone, wood, etc. used in ancient times as a token, tally, ticket, die, etc. *n., pl.* **tes‧ser‧ae** (-ē′ *or* -ī′).

**test** (test) **1** an examination; trial: *People who want to drive an automobile must pass a test. The teacher gave the class a test in arithmetic.* **2** a means of trial: *Trouble is a test of character.* **3** an examination of a substance to see what it is or what it contains: *A test showed that the water from our well was pure.* **4** a process or substance used in such an examination. **5** put to a test; try out: *She tested the boy's honesty by leaving the money on the table.* 1–4 *n.,* 5 *v.* —**test′a‧ble,** *adj.* —**test′er,** *n.*

**tes‧ta** (tes′tə) **1** a shell; hard covering of certain animals. **2** the hard outside coat of a seed. *n., pl.* **tes‧tae** (-tē *or* -tī).

**terror**     **1235**     **test pilot**

hat, āge, fär; let, ēqual, tėrm; it, īce
hot, ōpen, ôrder; oil, out; cup, pùt, rüle
əbove, takən, pencəl, lemən, circəs
ch, child; ng, long; sh, ship
th, thin; ᴛʜ, then; zh, measure

**tes‧ta‧cy** (tes′tə sē) the leaving of a will at death. *n.*

**tes‧ta‧ment** (tes′tə mənt) **1** written instructions telling what to do with a person's property after his or her death; a will. **2 Testament,** the Old Testament or the New Testament of the Bible. *n.*

**tes‧ta‧men‧ta‧ry** (tes′tə men′tə rē) **1** of or having to do with a testament or will. **2** given, done, or appointed by a testament or will. **3** in a testament or will. *adj.*

**tes‧tate** (tes′tāt) having made and left a valid will. Compare with INTESTATE. *adj.*

**tes‧ta‧tor** (tes tā′tər *or* tes′tā tər) **1** a person who makes a will. **2** a person who has died leaving a valid will. *n.*

**tes‧ta‧trix** (tes tā′triks) **1** a woman who makes a will. **2** a woman who has died leaving a valid will. *n., pl.* **tes‧ta‧tri‧ces** (-trə sēz′).

**tes‧tes** (tes′tēz) pl. of TESTIS. *n.*

**tes‧ti‧cle** (tes′tə kəl) the male reproductive organ of most animals, which produces sperm: *In most mammals, the testicles are contained in an external pouch called the scrotum.* *n.*

**tes‧ti‧fy** (tes′tə fī′) **1** give evidence; bear witness: *The excellence of Shakespeare's plays testifies to his genius.* **2** give evidence of; bear witness to: *The firm testified their appreciation of her work by raising her pay.* **3** declare solemnly; affirm. **4** declare or give evidence under oath before a judge, coroner, etc.: *The police testified that the speeding car had crashed into the truck. The witness was unwilling to testify.* *v.,* **tes‧ti‧fied, tes‧ti‧fy‧ing.** —**tes′ti‧fi′er,** *n.*

**tes‧ti‧mo‧ni‧al** (tes′tə mō′nē əl) **1** a certificate of character, conduct, qualifications, value, etc.; recommendation: *The girl looking for a job has testimonials from her teachers and former employer. Advertisements of patent medicines often contain testimonials from people who have used them.* **2** something given or done to show esteem, admiration, gratitude, etc.: *The members of the club collected money for a testimonial to their retiring president.* **3** given or done as a testimonial. 1, 2 *n.,* 3 *adj.*

**tes‧ti‧mo‧ny** (tes′tə mō′nē *or* tes′tə mə nē) **1** a statement used for evidence or proof: *A witness gave a testimony that Mr. Tymchuk was at home at 9 p.m.* **2** evidence: *The pupils presented their teacher with a watch in testimony of their respect and affection.* **3** an open declaration or profession of one's faith. *n., pl.* **tes‧ti‧mo‧nies.**

**tes‧tis** (tes′tis) TESTICLE. *n., pl.* **tes‧tes** (-tēz).

**tes‧tos‧ter‧one** (tes tos′tər ōn′) a hormone, which can be made synthetically. Formula: $C_{19}H_{28}O_2$. *n.*

**test pilot** a pilot employed to test new or experimental airplanes by subjecting them to greater than normal stress.

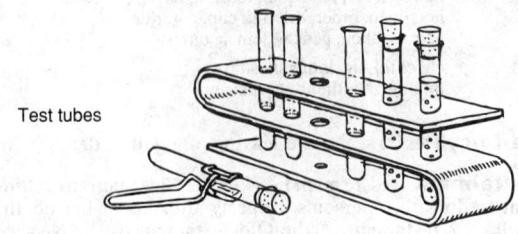
Test tubes

**test tube** a thin glass tube closed at one end, used in making chemical tests.

**tes·ty** (tes′tē) easily irritated; impatient. *adj.*, **tes·ti·er, tes·ti·est.** —**tes′ti·ly,** *adv.* —**tes′ti·ness,** *n.*

**tet·a·nus** (tet′ə nəs) a disease caused by certain bacilli usually entering the body through wounds, characterized by violent spasms, stiffness of many muscles, and even death: *Tetanus of the lower jaw is called lockjaw.* *n.*

**tetch·y** (tech′ē) irritable; touchy. *adj.*, **tetch·i·er, tetch·i·est.**

**tête-à-tête** (tā′tə tāt′) **1** two together in private: *They dined tête-à-tête.* **2** of or for two people in private: *tête-à-tête conversation.* **3** a private conversation between two people. **4** an S-shaped seat built so that two people can sit facing one another. 1 *adv.*, 2 *adj.*, 3, 4 *n.*

**teth·er** (teᴛH′ər) **1** a rope or chain for fastening an animal so that it can graze only within certain limits: *The cow had broken her tether and was in the cornfield.* **2** fasten with a tether: *The horse is tethered to a stake.* 1 *n.*, 2 *v.*
**at the end of one's tether,** *Informal.* at the end of one's resources or endurance: *After the class had gone wild for an hour, the teacher was at the end of her tether.*

**tetra–** combining form. four: *tetrahedron.*

**tet·ra·he·dron** (tet′rə hē′drən) a solid bounded by four plane sides: *The most common tetrahedron is a pyramid whose base and three sides are equilateral triangles.* See SOLID for picture. *n., pl.* **tet·ra·he·drons** or **tet·ra·he·dra** (-drə).

**tet·rar·chy** (tet′rär kē) **1** government by four persons. **2** a set of four rulers. **3** a country divided into four governments. *n., pl.* **tet·rar·chies.**

**te·trox·ide** (ti trok′sīd) any oxide having four atoms of oxygen in each molecule. *n.*

**Teu·ton** (tyü′tən *or* tü′tən) **1** a member of an ancient Germanic people of northern Europe. **2** a member of any of the northern European people speaking a Germanic language, especially a German. *n.*

**Teu·ton·ic** (tyü ton′ik *or* tü ton′ik) **1** of or having to do with the ancient Teutons. **2** of, having to do with, or referring to the Germanic languages or the peoples who speak them. **3** German. *adj.*

**text** (tekst) **1** the main body of reading matter in a book: *This history contains 300 pages of text and about 50 pages of notes, explanations, and questions for study.* **2** the original words of a writer: *Always quote the exact words of a text.* **3** any one of the various wordings of a poem, play, etc. **4** a topic; subject: *Town improvement was the speaker's text.* **5** TEXTBOOK. *n.*

**text·book** (tekst′bùk′) a book used as a basis of instruction or as a standard reference in a particular course of study. *n.*

**tex·tile** (tek′stīl *or* tek′stəl) **1** woven: *Linen is a textile material.* **2** a woven or knit fabric. **3** suitable for weaving: *Cotton, silk, and wool are common textile fibres.* **4** material suitable for weaving. **5** of or having to do with weaving: *the textile art.* **6** of or having something to do with the making, selling, etc. of textiles: *Her father is in the textile business.* 1, 3, 5, 6 *adj.*, 2, 4 *n.*

**tex·tu·al** (teks′chü əl) of a TEXT; having to do with the text: *A misprint is a textual error.* *adj.*

**tex·tu·al·ly** (teks′chü ə lē) in regard to the TEXT. *adv.*

**tex·tur·al** (teks′chə rəl) of TEXTURE; having to do with texture. *adj.*

**tex·ture** (teks′chər) **1** the arrangement of threads in a woven fabric: *Burlap has a much coarser texture than a linen handkerchief.* **2** the arrangement of the parts of anything; structure; constitution; make-up; feel: *Sandstone and granite have very different textures.* **3** give a texture to. 1, 2 *n.*, 3 *v.*, **tex·tured, tex·tur·ing.**

**tex·tured** (teks′chərd) **1** having a certain TEXTURE. **2** bulky; looped: *textured wool.* *adj.*

**Th** thorium.

**Thai** (tī) **1** of or having to do with Thailand, a country in southern Asia, its people, or their language. **2** a native or inhabitant of Thailand. **3** the language of Thailand. 1 *adj.*, 2, 3 *n.*

**thal·a·mus** (thal′ə məs) a part of the brain where a nerve emerges or appears to emerge. The **optic thalami** are two large, oblong masses of grey matter forming a part of the midbrain. *n., pl.* **thal·a·mi** (-mī′ *or* -mē′).

**tha·ler** (tä′lər) a former German silver coin. *n., pl.* **tha·ler.**

**thal·li·um** (thal′ē əm) a malleable, rare metallic element. Symbol: Tl *n.*

**thal·lo·phyte** (thal′ə fīt′) any plant belonging to the subkingdom **Thallophyta** of the plant kingdom, having no leaves, stems, or roots: *Bacteria, algae, fungi, and lichens are thallophytes.* *n.*

**thal·lus** (thal′əs) a plant not divided into leaves, stems, and roots: *Mushrooms, toadstools, and lichens are thalli.* *n., pl.* **thal·li** (-lī *or* -lē) or **thal·lus·es.**

**than** (ᴛHan; *unstressed*, ᴛHən) **1** in comparison with; compared to that which: *This train runs faster than that one does.* **2** except; besides: *How else can we come than on foot?* 1 *conj.*, 2 *prep.*
**than whom,** compared with whom.

**thane** (thān) **1** in early England, a man who ranked between an earl and an ordinary freeman: *Thanes held lands of the king or lord and gave military service in return.* **2** a Scottish baron or lord. *n.*

**thank** (thangk) **1** say that one is pleased and grateful for something given or done; express gratitude to: *She thanked them for their hospitality.* **2 thanks,** *pl.* **a** the act of thanking; an expression of gratitude: *to give thanks for a favour, to give thanks before a meal.* **b** a feeling of kindliness and gratitude: *You have our heartful thanks.*

**3 thanks,** *Informal.* thank you: *Many thanks for your help.* 1 *v.,* 2 *n.,* 3 *interj.*
**have oneself to thank,** be to blame: *You have yourself to thank if you eat too much.*
**thanks to,** owing to; because of: *Thanks to her efforts, we won the game.*
**thank you,** the standard courteous expression of appreciation: *"It's a lovely present. Thank you."*

**thank·ful** (thangk′fəl) feeling or expressing thanks; grateful. *adj.*

**thank·ful·ly** (thangk′fə lē) with thanks; gratefully. *adv.*

**thank·ful·ness** (thangk′fəl nis) a thankful feeling; gratitude. *n.*

**thank·less** (thang′klis) **1** not likely to be rewarded with thanks; not appreciated: *Giving advice is usually a thankless act.* **2** not feeling or expressing thanks; without a desire to do a favour in return; ungrateful: *The thankless woman did nothing for the neighbour who had helped her. adj.* —**thank′less·ly,** *adv.* —**thank′less·ness,** *n.*

**thanks·giv·ing** (thangks′giv′ing) **1** a giving of thanks. **2** an expression of thanks: *They offered thanksgiving for the bountiful harvest.* **3 Thanksgiving,** THANKSGIVING DAY. *n.*

**Thanksgiving Day** in Canada, the second Monday in October, a day set apart every year to give thanks for the harvest. *n.*

**that** (ᴛHat; *unstressed,* ᴛHət) a word used: **1** to point out, indicate, or emphasize some person, thing, idea, etc. already mentioned or understood, especially one some distance away in place or time. When used with *this, that* refers to something far or farther away and *this* refers to something near. Examples: *Do you know that girl over there? What was that? That is a shorter way than this. I will not allow that piano to be misused. After that they went home.* **2** to introduce a noun clause and connect it with the preceding verb: *I know that 6 and 4 are 10.* **3** to show purpose: *Juanita ran fast so that she might not be late.* **4** to show result: *She ran so fast that she was five minutes early.* **5** to show cause: *I wonder what happened, not that I care.* **6** to express a wish: *Oh, that she were here!* **7** to show anger, surprise, etc.: *That one so fair should be so false!* **That** also means: **8** which, who, or whom: *Is he the man that trains dogs? Bring the box that's in the kitchen.* **9** when; at or in which: *The year that we went to England, they had a terrible drought.* **10** to such an extent or degree; so: *The baby cannot stay up that late.* 1 *adj.,* 1, 8, 9 *pron., pl.* (for *def.* 1) **those;** 2–7 *conj.,* 10 *adv.*
**at that,** *Informal.* **a** with no more talk, work, etc. **b** considering everything.
**in that,** because: *I prefer her plan to yours, in that I think it is more practical.*
**that's that,** *Informal.* that is finished, settled, or decided.
☞ *Usage.* **That** may be used to refer to people, animals, or things: *The man that talked to you is the new teacher. What happened to the car that was used by the bank robbers?* **Who** and **whom** are used for people and sometimes for animals (especially when thought of as pets): *The man who talked to you is the new teacher. It was Rex, our collie, who got lost in the woods.* **Which** is used only for things and animals: *The dog, which had looked tame enough, began to bark wildly.*
☞ *Usage.* **That** may be used for people only in defining clauses, without comma (as illustrated above). See wHO, wHICH.

**thankful** 1237 **theatrical**

hat, āge, fär; let, ēqual, tėrm; it, īce
hot, ōpen, ôrder; oil, out; cup, pu̇t, rüle
əbove, takən, pencəl, lemən, circəs
ch, child; ng, long; sh, ship
th, thin; ᴛH, then; zh, measure

An English house with a roof of thatch

**thatch** (thach) **1** straw, rushes, palm leaves, etc. used as a roof or covering. **2** a roof or covering of thatch. **3** roof or cover with thatch. **4** *Informal.* the hair covering the head. 1, 2, 4 *n.,* 3 *v.*

**that's** (ᴛHats) **1** that is. **2** that has: *That's never stopped him.*

**thaw** (tho) **1** melt ice, snow, or anything frozen; free from frost: *Salt was put on the sidewalk to thaw the ice.* **2** become warm enough to melt ice, snow, etc.: *If the sun stays out, it will probably thaw today.* **3** a thawing; weather above the freezing point (0°C); time of melting. **4** become free of frost, ice, etc.: *The ground has begun to thaw. The pond thaws in April.* **5** make or become less stiff and formal in manner; soften: *His shyness thawed under her kindness.* **6** a becoming less stiff and formal in manner; softening. 1, 2, 4, 5 *v.,* 3, 6 *n.*

**the** (*unstressed before a consonant,* ᴛHə; *before a vowel and stressed,* ᴛHē) The word **the** shows that a certain one or ones is meant. Various special uses are: **1** to mark a noun as indicating something well-known or unique: *the* (ᴛHē) *Alps.* **2** denoting the time in question or under consideration, now or then present: *the hour of victory. Was that the moment to act?* **3** with or as part of a title: *the Duke of Wellington.* **4** to mark a noun as indicating the best-known or most important of its kind: *the* (ᴛHē) *place to dine.* **5** to mark a noun as being used generically: *The dog is a quadruped.* **6** to indicate a part of the body or a personal belonging: *to hang the head in shame.* **7** before adjectives used as nouns: *to visit the sick.* **8** distributively, to denote any one separately: *grapes at four dollars the kilo.* **9** to modify an adjective or adverb in the comparative degree; signifying "in or by that," "on that account," "in some or any degree": *If you start now, you will be back the sooner.* **10** used correlatively, in one instance with relative force and in the other with demonstrative force, and signifying "by how much...by so much," "in what degree...in that degree": *the more the merrier, the sooner the better.* *definite article.*

**the·a·tre** (thē′ə tər) **1** a place where plays and other stage performances are acted or where motion pictures are shown. **2** a place that looks like a theatre in its arrangement of seats: *The surgeon performed an operation before the medical students in the operating theatre.* **3** a place of action: *Belgium and France were the theatre of the First World War.* **4** plays; the writing and producing of plays; the drama. **5** a play, situation, dialogue, etc. considered as to its effectiveness on the stage: *This scene is bad theatre. n.* Sometimes, **theater.**

**the·at·ric** (thē at′rik) THEATRICAL. *adj.*

**the·at·ri·cal** (thē at′rə kəl) **1** of or having to do with

the theatre or actors: *theatrical performances, a theatrical company.* **2** suggesting a theatre or acting; for display or effect; artificial. **3 theatricals,** *pl.* **a** dramatic performances, especially as given by amateurs. **b** matters having to do with the stage and acting. **c** actions of a theatrical or artificial character. 1, 2 *adj.*, 3 *n.*
—**theat′ri·cal·ly,** *adv.*

**the·at·ri·cal·i·ty** (thē at′rə kal′ə tē) the quality of being THEATRICAL. *n.*

**theft** (theft) **1** the act of stealing: *The man was put in prison for theft.* **2** an instance of stealing: *The theft of the jewels caused much excitement.* *n.*

**the·in** (thē′ən) THEINE. *n.*

**the·ine** (thē′ēn *or* thē′ən) CAFFEINE. *n.*

**their** (ᴛHer; *unstressed,* ᴛHər) a possessive form of THEY: of, belonging to, or made or done by them or themselves: *They did their best. They all raised their hands. That's their house.* *adj.*
☞ Hom. THERE, THEY'RE.
☞ Usage. **Their** and THEIRS are possessive forms of THEY. **Their** is a determiner and is always followed by a noun: *This is their farm.* **Theirs** is a pronoun and stands alone: *This farm is theirs.*

**theirs** (ᴛHerz) a possessive form of THEY: that which belongs to them: *The painting isn't theirs, it's just rented.* *pron.*
☞ Hom. THERE'S.
☞ Usage. See note at THEIR.

**the·ism** (thē′iz əm) **1** a belief in one God, the creator and ruler of the universe. **2** belief in any god or gods. *n.*

**the·ist** (thē′ist) a believer in THEISM. *n.*

**the·is·tic** (thē is′tik) of THEISM or THEISTS. *adj.*

**them** (ᴛHem; *unstressed,* ᴛHəm) the objective form of THEY: *The books were a gift, but I don't really like them.* *pron.*

**the·mat·ic** (thē mat′ik) of a THEME; having to do with themes. *adj.*

**theme** (thēm) **1** a topic; subject: *Protecting the whales was the speaker's theme.* **2** a short written composition. **3** the principal melody in a piece of music. **4** a short melody repeated in different forms in an elaborate musical composition. **5** a melody used to identify a particular radio or television program. *n.*

**them·selves** (ᴛHem selvz′ *or* ᴛHəm selvz′) **1** a reflexive pronoun, the object of a reflexive verb with **they** as subject: *They injured themselves.* **2** an intensive pronoun, used to emphasize the noun or pronoun it follows: *The teachers themselves said that the test was too hard.* **3** their usual selves: *They were ill and were not themselves.* *pron.*

**then** (ᴛHen) **1** at that time: *Prices were lower then.* **2** that time: *By then we shall know the result.* **3** being at that time in the past; existing then: *the then premier.* **4** soon afterwards: *The noise stopped, and then began again.* **5** next in time or place: *First comes spring, then summer.* **6** at another time: *Now one girl does best and then another.* **7** also; besides: *The dress seems too good to throw away, and then it is very attractive.* **8** in that case; therefore: *If Harry broke the window, then he should pay for it.* 1, 4–8 *adv.*, 2 *n.*, 3 *adj.*
**but then,** but at the same time; but on the other hand.

**then and there,** at that time and place; at once and on the spot.

**thence** (ᴛHens *or* thens) **1** from that place; from there: *A few kilometres thence is a river.* **2** for that reason; therefore: *You didn't work, thence no pay.* **3** from that time; from then: *a year thence.* *adv.*

**thence·forth** (ᴛHens′fôrth′ *or* thens′fôrth′) from then on; from that time forward: *Women were given the same rights as men; thenceforth they could vote.* *adv.*

**thence·for·ward** (ᴛHens′fôr′wərd *or* thens′fôr′wərd) THENCEFORTH. *adv.*

**the·oc·ra·cy** (thē ok′rə sē) **1** a system of government in which God is recognized as the supreme civil ruler and His laws are taken as the laws of the state. **2** a system of government by priests. **3** a country governed by a theocracy. *n.*, *pl.* **the·oc·ra·cies.**

**the·o·crat** (thē′ə krat′) **1** a ruler, or member of a governing body, in a THEOCRACY. **2** a person who favours THEOCRACY. *n.*

**the·o·crat·ic** (thē′ə krat′ik) **1** of or having to do with THEOCRACY. **2** having a THEOCRACY. *adj.*

**the·od·o·lite** (thē od′ə līt′) a surveying instrument for measuring horizontal and vertical angles. *n.*

**the·o·lo·gian** (thē′ə lō′jən) a person skilled or trained in THEOLOGY. *n.*

**the·o·log·i·cal** (thē′ə loj′ə kəl) **1** of THEOLOGY; having to do with theology: *A theological school trains young men and women for the ministry.* **2** referring to the nature and will of God. *adj.* —**the′o·log′i·cal·ly,** *adv.*

**the·ol·o·gy** (thē ol′ə jē) **1** the study of the nature of God and His relations to people and the universe. **2** the study of religion and religious beliefs. **3** a system of religious beliefs. *n.*, *pl.* **the·ol·o·gies.**

**the·o·rem** (thē′ə rəm) **1** in mathematics, a statement to be proved. **2** a statement of mathematical relations that can be expressed by an equation or formula. **3** any statement or rule that can be proved to be true. *n.*

**the·o·ret·ic** (thē′ə ret′ik) THEORETICAL. *adj.*

**the·o·ret·i·cal** (thē′ə ret′ə kəl) **1** planned or worked out in the mind, not from experience; based on THEORY, not on fact; limited to theory. **2** dealing with THEORY only; not practical: *Books provide only a theoretical knowledge of farming.* *adj.*

**the·o·ret·i·cal·ly** (thē′ə ret′i klē) in THEORY; according to theory; in a theoretical manner. *adv.*

**the·o·re·ti·cian** (thē′ə rə tish′ən) one who knows much about the THEORY of an art, science, etc. *n.*

**the·o·rist** (thē′ə rist) one who forms theories. *n.*

**the·o·rize** (thē′ə rīz′) form a THEORY or theories; speculate. *v.,* **the·o·rized, the·o·riz·ing.**
—**the′o·riz′er,** *n.*

**the·o·ry** (thē′ə rē) **1** an explanation based on thought or speculation. **2** an explanation based on observation and reasoning: *the theory of evolution, Einstein's theory of relativity.* **3** the principles or methods of a science or art rather than its practice: *the theory of music.* **4** an idea or opinion about something. **5** thought or fancy as opposed to fact or practice. *n.*, *pl.* **the·o·ries.**
☞ Syn. Both **theory** and HYPOTHESIS are explanations. The difference between them is this: A theory is an explanation that has been proved to be correct, but a hypothesis is simply a possible explanation that has not been tested.

**the·o·soph·ic** (thē′ə sof′ik) of or having to do with THEOSOPHY. *adj.*

**the·os·o·phist** (thē os′ə fist) a person who believes in THEOSOPHY. *n.*

**the·os·o·phy** (thē os′ə fē) a philosophy or religion that claims to have a special insight into the divine nature through spiritual self-development: *Modern theosophy includes many of the teachings of Buddhism and Brahmanism.* *n.*

**ther·a·peu·tic** (ther′ə pyü′tik) having to do with the treatment or curing of disease; curative. *adj.*

**ther·a·peu·tics** (ther′ə pyü′tiks) a branch of medicine that deals with the treating or curing of disease; therapy. *n.*

**ther·a·peu·tist** (ther′ə pyü′tist) a person who specializes in THERAPEUTICS. *n.*

**ther·a·pist** (ther′ə pist) THERAPEUTIST. *n.*

**ther·a·py** (ther′ə pē) the treatment of diseases or disorders. *n., pl.* **ther·a·pies.**

**Ther·a·va·da** (ter′ə vä′də) one of the major branches of Buddhism, the "Southern School." It emphasizes the humanity of Buddha. *n.*

**Ther·a·va·din** (ter′ə vä′din) a follower of THERAVADA Buddhism. *n.*

**there** (THer; *unstressed,* THər) **1** in or at that place: *Sit there.* **2** to or into that place: *Go there at once.* **3** that place: *From there go on to Hamilton.* **4** at that point in an action, speech, etc.: *You have done enough, you may stop there.* **5** in that matter, particular, or respect: *You are mistaken there.* **6 There** is used at the beginning of sentences to replace the subject, which then follows its verb: *There are three new houses on our street. Is there a drugstore near here?* **7 There** is used to call attention to some person or thing: *There goes the bell.* **8 There** is also used to express satisfaction, triumph, dismay, encouragement, comfort, etc.: *There, there! Don't cry.* 1, 2, 4–7 *adv.,* 3 *n.,* 8 *interj.*
**all there,** *Informal.* **a** wide-awake; alert. **b** not crazy; sane.
☞ *Hom.* THEIR, THEY'RE.

**there·a·bout** (THer′ə bout′) THEREABOUTS. *adv.*

**there·a·bouts** (THer′ə bouts′) **1** near that place: *She lives downtown, on Main Street or thereabouts.* **2** near that time: *She went home in the late afternoon, at 5 o'clock or thereabouts.* **3** near that number or amount: *The book cost me twenty dollars or thereabouts.* *adv.*

**there·af·ter** (THer af′tər) **1** after that; afterward: *He was very ill as a child and was considered delicate thereafter.* **2** accordingly. *adv.*

**there·at** (THer at′) **1** when that happened; at that time. **2** because of that; because of it. **3** at that place; there. *adv.*

**there·by** (THer bī′ or THer′bī′) **1** by means of that; in that way: *She wished to travel and thereby study the customs of other countries.* **2** in connection with that: *George won the game, and thereby hangs a tale.* **3** near there: *A farm lay thereby.* *adv.*

**there·for** (THer fôr′) for that; for this; for it: *She promised to give a building for a hospital and as much land as should be necessary therefor.* *adv.*

**there·fore** (THer′fôr′) for that reason; as a result of that; consequently: *Helen went to a party and therefore did not study her lessons.* *adv.*

**theosophic**     1239 **thermodynamics**

hat, āge, fär; let, ēqual, tèrm; it, īce
hot, ōpen, ôrder; oil, out; cup, pùt, rüle
əbove, takən, pencəl, lemən, circəs
ch, child; ng, long; sh, ship
th, thin; TH, then; zh, measure

**there·from** (THer from′ *or* THer frum′) from that; from this; from it: *Lee opened her bag and took therefrom an apple.* *adv.*

**there·in** (THer in′) **1** in that place; in it. **2** in that matter; in that way; in that respect: *The captain thought all danger was past; therein he made a mistake.* *adv.*

**there·in·to** (THer in′tü *or* THer′in tü′) **1** into that place; into it. **2** into that matter. *adv.*

**there'll** (THerl) **1** there will. **2** there shall.

**there·of** (THer ov′ *or* THer uv′) **1** of that; of it. **2** from it; from that source. *adv.*

**there·on** (THer on′) **1** on that; on it: *Before the window was a table and a huge book lay thereon.* **2** immediately after that: *The witch cast a spell; thereon the prince was changed into a frog.* *adv.*

**there's** (THerz) **1** there is. **2** there has: *There's been an accident.*
☞ *Hom.* THEIRS.

**there·to** (THer tü′) **1** to that; to it: *The castle stands on a hill, and the road thereto is steep and rough.* **2** in addition to that; also: *The queen gave her servant rich garments and added thereto a bag of gold.* *adv.*

**there·to·fore** (THer′tə fôr′) before that time; until then. *adv.*

**there·un·der** (THer un′dər) **1** under that; under it. **2** under the authority of that; according to that. *adv.*

**there·un·to** (THer un′tü *or* THer′un tü′) to that; to it. *adv.*

**there·up·on** (THer′ə pon′) **1** immediately after that: *The Queen appeared, and thereupon the people clapped.* **2** because of that; therefore: *The stolen jewels were found in his room; thereupon he was put in jail.* **3** on that; on it: *The knight carried a shield with a bear painted thereupon.* *adv.*

**there·with** (THer wiTH′ *or* THer with′) **1** with that; with it: *The lady gave him a rose and a smile therewith.* **2** immediately after that; then: *"Avenge me!" said the ghost and therewith disappeared.* *adv.*

**there·with·al** (THer′wiTH ol′) **1** with that; with this; with it. **2** in addition to that; also. *adv.*

**ther·mal** (thėr′məl) **1** of or having to do with heat. **2** warm; hot. *adj.*

**thermal barrier** the point of speed beyond which a VEHICLE (def. 2) is subjected to dangerously high temperatures as a result of friction with the atmosphere.

**ther·mo·cline** (thėr′mō klīn′) a layer of water that gets colder by 1°C for each metre of increasing depth. *n.*

**ther·mo·dy·nam·ic** (thėr′mō dī nam′ik) **1** of or having to do with THERMODYNAMICS. **2** using force due to heat or to the conversion of heat into mechanical energy. *adj.*

**ther·mo·dy·nam·ics** (thėr′mō dī nam′iks) the

**thermo-electric** branch of physics that deals with the relations between heat and mechanical energy or work. *n.*

**ther·mo·e·lec·tric** (thėr′mō i lek′trik) of or having to do with THERMO-ELECTRICITY. *adj.*

**ther·mo·e·lec·tric·i·ty** (thėr′mō i lek′tris′ə tē) electricity produced directly by heat. *n.*

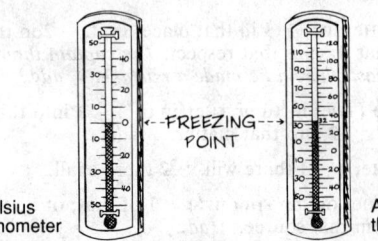

A Celsius thermometer — FREEZING POINT — A Fahrenheit thermometer

**ther·mom·e·ter** (thər mom′ə tər) an instrument for measuring temperature, usually by means of the expansion and contraction of mercury or alcohol in a capillary tube and bulb. *n.*

**ther·mo·nu·cle·ar** (thėr′mō nyü′klē ər *or* thėr′mō nü′klē ər) of or designating the heat generated by nuclear fusion: *a thermonuclear reactor. adj.*

**ther·mo·plas·tic** (thėr′mō plas′tik) 1 becoming soft and capable of being moulded when heated. 2 a thermoplastic material, especially one of certain synthetic resins. 1 *adj.*, 2 *n.*

**ther·mos** (thėr′məs) 1 a double-walled bottle or flask made with a vacuum between its inner and outer walls, used to keep a beverage, soup, etc. hot or cold for a long time; vacuum bottle. See VACUUM BOTTLE for picture. 2 of or using such a vacuum: *a thermos bottle or flask.* 1 *n.*, 2 *adj.*
☛ *Etym.* From *Thermos*, a trademark for such a bottle or flask.

**ther·mo·set·ting** (thėr′mō set′ing) becoming hard and permanently set after being heated: *thermosetting plastics. adj.*

**ther·mo·sphere** (thėr′mō sfēr′) the ionosphere; part of the earth's atmosphere beginning at an altitude of about 80–100 km: *Air is very thin in the thermosphere, where it is very hot.*

**ther·mo·stat** (thėr′mə stat′) an automatic device for regulating temperature. In most thermostats, the expansion and contraction of a metal, liquid, or gas opens and closes an electric circuit by which an appliance or device, such as an air conditioner or furnace, is made to work or to stop working. *n.*

**ther·mo·stat·ic** (thėr′mə stat′ik) of, having to do with, or like a THERMOSTAT. *adj.*

**ther·mo·stat·i·cal·ly** (thėr′mə stat′i klē) by means of a THERMOSTAT. *adv.*

**the·sau·rus** (thi sô′rəs) 1 a treasury; storehouse. 2 a dictionary, etc., especially a classified dictionary that groups together words with related meanings. 3 a computer program serving a similar purpose. *n., pl.* **the·sau·ri** (-rī *or* -rē) *or* **the·sau·rus·es**.
☛ *Etym.* Through Latin from Gk. *thēsauros* 'treasure, treasure house'.

**these** (ᴛʜēz) 1 pl. of the adjective THIS: *These two problems are hard.* 2 pl. of the pronoun THIS: *These are my books.* 1 *adj.*, 2 *pron.*

**the·sis** (thē′sis) 1 a proposition or statement to be proved or to be maintained against objections. 2 an essay; an essay presented by a candidate for a diploma or degree. *n., pl.* **the·ses** (-sēz).

**Thes·pi·an** (thes′pē ən) 1 having to do with Thespis, a tragic poet in ancient Greece. 2 of or having to do with the drama or tragedy; dramatic; tragic. 3 an actor or actress. 1, 2 *adj.*, 3 *n.*

**thews** (thüz *or* thyüz) 1 muscles. 2 sinews. *n.pl.*

**they** (ᴛʜā) 1 nom. pl. of HE, SHE, or IT: *Where are they? They are on the kitchen table.* 2 *Informal.* some people; any people; persons: *They say we should have a new school. pron., pl. nom.; poss.,* **their, theirs;** *obj.,* **them.**
☛ *Usage.* In informal speech **they** is often used as an indefinite pronoun, to mean 'people unnamed': *They will raise income taxes again.* This usage should be avoided in writing: *The government will raise income taxes again* or *Income taxes will be raised again.*

**they'd** (ᴛʜād) 1 they had. 2 they would.

**they'll** (ᴛʜāl) 1 they will. 2 they shall.

**they're** (ᴛʜer; *unstressed,* ᴛʜər) they are.
☛ *Hom.* THERE, THEIR.

**they've** (ᴛʜāv) they have.

**thi·a·min** (thī′ə min) a complex organic compound found in cereals, yeast, etc., or prepared synthetically; vitamin B1. *n.* Also, **thi·a·mine**.

**thi·a·mine** (thī′ə min *or* thī′ə mēn′) THIAMIN. *n.*

**thick** (thik) 1 filling much space from one surface to the other; not thin: *The castle has thick stone walls.* 2 measuring between two opposite surfaces: *three centimetres thick.* 3 set close together; dense: *thick hair.* 4 many and close together; abundant: *The butterflies were thick on the ground.* 5 filled; covered: *thick with flies.* 6 like glue or syrup, not like water; rather dense of its kind: *Thick liquids pour much more slowly than thin liquids.* 7 not clear; foggy: *The weather was thick and the airports were shut down.* 8 not clear in sound; hoarse: *She had a thick voice because of a cold.* 9 stupid; dull: *He has a thick head.* 10 thickly: *The field was planted so thick with corn that you could hide among the stalks.* 11 the part that is thickest, most crowded, most active, etc.: *in the thick of the fight.* 12 *Informal.* very friendly; intimate: *as thick as thieves.* 13 *Informal.* too much to be endured: *That's a bit thick.* 1–9, 12, 13 *adj.,* 10 *adv.,* 11 *n.*
**lay it on thick,** *Informal.* praise or blame too much.
**thick skin,** the ability to take criticism, etc. without being affected by it.
**through thick and thin,** in good times and bad: *A true friend stays loyal through thick and thin.*

**thick·en** (thik′ən) 1 make or become thick or thicker. 2 of the plot of a play, novel, etc., become more complex or intricate. *v.* —**thick′en·er,** *n.*

**thick·en·ing** (thik′ə ning) 1 a material or ingredient used to thicken something. 2 a thickened part. 3 ppr. of THICKEN. 1, 2 *n.,* 3 *v.*

**thick·et** (thik′it) shrubs, bushes, or small trees growing close together. *n.*

**thick-head·ed** (thik′hed′id) stupid; dull. *adj.* —**thick′-head′ed·ness,** *n.*

**thick·ly** (thik′lē) 1 in a thick manner; closely; densely:

*a thickly settled region.* **2** in great numbers; in abundance. **3** frequently. **4** with thick consistency. **5** hoarsely. *adv.*

**thick·ness** (thik′nis) **1** the quality or state of being thick. **2** the distance between opposite surfaces; the third measurement of a solid, not length nor breadth: *The length of the board is three metres, the width fourteen centimetres, the thickness five centimetres.* **3** the thick part. **4** layer: *The pad was made up of three thicknesses of cloth.* *n.*

**thick–set** (thik′set′) **1** closely placed, planted, etc.: *a thick-set hedge.* **2** thick in form or build: *a thick-set man.* **3** THICKET. **4** a thick hedge. 1, 2 *adj.*, 3, 4 *n.*

**thick–skinned** (thik′skind′) **1** having a thick skin. **2** not sensitive to criticism, reproach, rebuff, or the like. *adj.*

**thick–wit·ted** (thik′wit′id) stupid; dull. *adj.*

**thief** (thēf) a person who steals, especially one who steals secretly and without using force: *A thief stole the little girl's bicycle from the yard.* *n.*, *pl.* **thieves.**

**thieve** (thēv) STEAL. *v.*, **thieved, thiev·ing.**

**thiev·er·y** (thē′və rē) the act of stealing; theft. *n.*, *pl.* **thiev·er·ies.**

**thieves** (thēvz) *pl.* of THIEF. *n.*

**thiev·ish** (thē′vish) **1** having the habit of stealing; likely to steal. **2** like a thief; stealthy; sly: *That cat has a thievish look.* *adj.* —**thiev′ish·ly,** *adv.* —**thiev′ish·ness,** *n.*

**thigh** (thī) the part of the leg between the hip and the knee. See LEG for picture. *n.*

**thigh·bone** (thī′bōn′) the bone of the leg between the hip and knee; femur. See LEG, PELVIS and SOCKET for pictures. *n.*

**thig·mo·tro·pism** (thig mot′rə piz′əm) the growth of a plant in response to touch, such as when a vine tendril coils around a support. *n.*

**thill** (thil) either of the shafts between which a single animal drawing a vehicle is placed. *n.*

**thim·ble** (thim′bəl) **1** a small cap of metal, bone, plastic, etc. worn on the finger to protect it when pushing the needle in sewing. **2** a short metal tube. **3** a metal ring fitted in a rope, to save wear on the rope. **4** a type of printing mechanism in a computer printer. It is like a daisy wheel in which the spokes are bent up so as to look like a thimble. *n.*

**thim·ble·ber·ry** (thim′bəl ber′ē) any of several plants closely related to and resembling the raspberry, especially a tall, thornless shrub of central and western North America, having large, very broad, lobed leaves, white flowers, and red, thimble-shaped fruit. *n.*, *pl.* **thim·ble·ber·ries.**

**thim·ble·ful** (thim′bəl fül′) as much as a THIMBLE (def. 1) will hold; a very small quantity. *n.*, *pl.* **thim·ble·fuls.**

**thin** (thin) **1** filling little space from one surface to the other; not thick: *thin paper, thin wire.* **2** having little flesh or fat; slender or lean: *a long, thin face. She is dieting to get thin again. She is still thin after her illness.* **3** not set close together; scanty: *He has thin hair.* **4** not dense: *The air on the top of those high mountains is thin.* **5** few and far apart; not abundant: *The actors played to a thin audience.* **6** not like glue or syrup; like water; of less substance than usual: *thin milk.* **7** not deep or strong: *a shrill, thin voice.* **8** having little depth, fullness, or

**thickness**     1241     **thin-skinned**

hat, āge, fär; let, ēqual, tėrm; it, īce
hot, ōpen, ôrder; oil, out; cup, pùt, rüle
əbove, takən, pencəl, lemən, circəs
ch, child; ng, long; sh, ship
th, thin; ᴛH, then; zh, measure

intensity: *a thin colour.* **9** easily seen through; flimsy: *a thin excuse.* **10** in a thin manner. **11** make or become thin: *to thin paint.* **12** make less crowded or close by removing individuals: *to thin a row of beets.* **13** of a place, become less full or crowded. **14** of a crowd, become less numerous. 1–9 *adj.*, **thin·ner, thin·nest;** 10 *adv.*, 11–14 *v.*, **thinned, thin·ning.** —**thin′ly,** *adv.* —**thin′ner,** *n.* —**thin′ness,** *n.*

**thin skin,** the condition of being easily affected by criticism, etc.

**thing** (thing) **1** any object or substance: *All the things in the house were burned. Put these things away.* **2** whatever is spoken or thought of; any act, deed, fact, event, happening, idea, or opinion: *A strange thing happened. It was a good thing to do. How are things going?* **3** a person or creature: *a silly old thing, a dear little thing. I feel sorry for the poor thing.* **4 the thing,** anything considered desirable, suitable, appropriate, etc.: *the latest thing in swimsuits, the thing to do.* **5 things,** *pl.* **a** belongings; possessions. **b** clothes. *n.*

**know a thing** or **two,** *Informal.* be experienced or wise.
**make a good thing of,** *Informal.* profit from.
**see** or **hear things,** have hallucinations.

**thing·a·ma·bob** (thing′ə mə bob′) *Informal.* THINGUMBOB. *n.*

**thing·a·ma·jig** (thing′ə mə jig′) *Informal.* THINGUMBOB. *n.*

**thing·um·bob** (thing′əm bob′) *Informal.* something whose name one forgets or does not bother to mention. *n.*

**think** (thingk) **1** have ideas; use the mind: *You must learn to think clearly.* **2** have in the mind: *Helena thought that she would go.* **3** have one's thoughts full of: *He thinks of nothing but sports.* **4** have an idea: *He had thought of her as still a child.* **5** have an opinion; believe: *Do what you think fit. They think their teacher an angel.* **6** reflect; consider: *I must think before answering.* **7** imagine: *You can't think how surprised I was.* **8** remember: *I can't think of her name.* **9** intend: *He thinks to escape punishment.* **10** expect: *I did not think to find you here.* *v.*, **thought, think·ing.** —**think′er,** *n.*

**think aloud,** say what one is thinking.
**think out, a** plan or discover by thinking. **b** solve or understand by thinking: *Bill thought out the reasons for his mom's anger.* **c** think through to the end.
**think out loud,** say what one is thinking.
**think over,** consider carefully: *Think over our plan before you go.*
**think through,** think about until one reaches an understanding or conclusion.
**think twice,** think again before acting; hesitate.
**think up,** plan or discover by thinking: *We will think up a way to get the candy.*

**think·a·ble** (thing′kə bəl) capable of being thought; conceivable. *adj.*

**think·ing** (thing′king) **1** that thinks; reasoning. **2** thoughtful or reflective. **3** thought. **4** ppr. of THINK. 1, 2 *adj.*, 3 *n.*, 4 *v.*

**thin–skinned** (thin′skind′) **1** having a thin skin.

**2** sensitive to criticism, reproach, rebuff, or the like; touchy. *adj.*

**third** (thėrd) **1** next after the 2nd; last in a series of three; 3rd. **2** one, or being one, of three equal parts: *Mother divided the pizza into thirds.* **3** in music, a tone three degrees from another tone. **4** the interval between such tones. **5** the combination of such tones. **6** in automobiles and similar machines, the forward gear or speed next above second; high gear in a three-gear system. 1 *adj.*, 1–6 *n.*

**third–class** (thėrd′klas′) of or belonging to a class after the second. *adj.*

**third estate** persons not in the nobility or clergy; ordinary people.

**third·ly** (thėr′dlē) in the third place. *adv.*

**third person** the form of a pronoun or verb used to refer to a thing or things, person or persons spoken about. *He, she, it* and *they* are pronouns of the third person.

**third rail** a rail parallelling the ordinary rails of a railway: *The third rail carries a powerful electric current and is used instead of an overhead wire.*

**third–rate** (thėrd′drāt′) **1** of the third class. **2** distinctly inferior. *adj.*

**Third World** the developing countries of the world, especially those in Africa, Asia, and Latin America where the standard of living is relatively low.

**thirst** (thėrst) **1** a dry, uncomfortable feeling in the mouth or throat caused by having had nothing to drink; desire or need for something to drink: *The traveller in the desert died of thirst. Bella satisifed her thirst at the spring.* **2** feel thirst; be thirsty. **3** a strong desire: *a thirst for adventure.* **4** have a strong desire. 1, 3 *n.*, 2, 4 *v.*

**thirst·y** (thėr′stē) **1** feeling thirst; having thirst. **2** without water or moisture; dry. **3** having a strong desire; eager. *adj.*, **thirst·i·er, thirst·i·est.** —**thirst′i·ly,** *adv.* —**thirst′i·ness,** *n.*

**thir·teen** (thėr′tēn′) **1** three more than ten; 13: *She counted fourteen people, but I counted thirteen. She has thirteen pairs of earrings.* **2** the numeral 13: *The 13 is very faint.* **3** the thirteenth in a set or series. **4** being thirteenth in a set or series (*used after the noun*): *Section Thirteen.* **5** a set or series of thirteen persons or things. 1–3, 5 *n.*, 1, 4 *adj.*

**thir·teenth** (thėr′tēnth′) **1** next after the 12th; last in a series of thirteen; 13th. **2** one, or being one, of 13 equal parts. *adj., n.*

**thir·ti·eth** (thėr′tē ith) **1** next after the 29th; last in a series of thirty; 30th. **2** one, or being one, of 30 equal parts. *adj., n.*

**thir·ty** (thėr′tē) **1** three times ten; 30. **2 thirties,** *pl.* the years from twenty through twenty-nine, especially of a century or of a person's life: *Her grandmother still vividly remembered the drought of the thirties.* 1 *adj.*, 1, 2 *n., pl.* **thir·ties.**

**thirty–second note** in music, a note one thirty-second of a whole note (♪). See NOTE for picture.

**this** (ᴛʜis) **1** a word used to point out, indicate, or emphasize some person, thing, idea, etc. already mentioned or understood, especially one present or near in place or time. When used with *that, this* refers to something near and *that* refers to something far or farther away. *Example:* What's this? she asked, holding up my torn sweater. I liked this book a lot. This dress is nicer than that one. After this, we'd better go home. **2** to such an extent or degree; so: *You can have this much.* 1 *adj., pron., pl.* **these;** 2 *adv.*

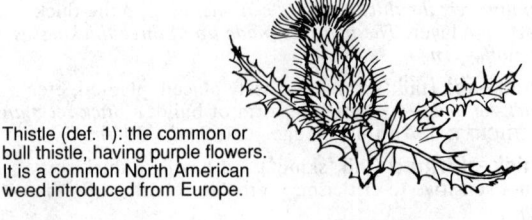

Thistle (def. 1): the common or bull thistle, having purple flowers. It is a common North American weed introduced from Europe.

**this·tle** (this′əl) **1** any of various plants of the composite family having prickly leaves and stem and showy heads of purple, pink, or yellow flowers: *Some thistles are common weeds.* **2** any of various other prickly plants. *n.*

**this·tle·down** (this′əl doun′) the down or fluff of a THISTLE. *n.*

**this·tly** (this′lē) **1** like THISTLES; prickly. **2** having many THISTLES. *adj.*

**thith·er** (thiᴛʜ′ər) **1** to or toward that place; there. **2** on that side; farther. 1 *adv.*, 2 *adj.*

**thith·er·ward** (thiᴛʜ′ər wərd) toward that place; THITHER (def. 1). *adv.*

**tho′** (ᴛʜō) THOUGH. *conj., adv.*

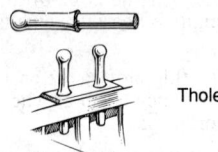

Tholes

**thole** (thōl) a peg on the side of a boat to hold an oar in rowing. *n.*

**thole·pin** (thōl′pin′) THOLE. *n.*

**thong** (thong) **1** a narrow strip of leather, etc., especially one used as a fastening: *The ancient Greeks laced their sandals on with thongs.* **2** the lash of a whip. **3** a kind of sandal held on the foot by a narrow piece of leather, plastic, etc. that passes between the toes. *n.*

**tho·rac·ic** (thô ras′ik) of or having to do with the thorax: *The thoracic cavity contains the heart and lungs.* See SPINAL COLUMN for picture. *adj.*

**tho·rax** (thô′raks) **1** the part of the body between the neck and the abdomen: *A human being's chest is the thorax.* **2** the second division of an insect's body, between the head and the abdomen. See INSECT for picture. *n., pl.* **tho·rax·es** or **tho·ra·ces** (-rə sēz′).

**tho·rite** (thô′rīt) a mineral consisting essentially of a silicate of THORIUM. *n.*

**tho·ri·um** (thô′rē əm) a radio-active metallic element present in thorite and monozite. Symbol: Th *n.*

**thorn** (thôrn) **1** a sharp-pointed growth on a stem or branch of a tree or plant: *Roses have thorns.* **2** a tree or plant that has thorns on it: *Thorns sprang up and choked the wheat.* *n.*

**thorn in the flesh** or **side,** a cause of trouble or annoyance.

**thorn apple** 1 the fruit of the HAWTHORN; haw. 2 HAWTHORN. 3 JIMSON WEED.

**thorn·y** (thôr′nē) 1 full of thorns. 2 troublesome; annoying: *The girls argued over the thorny points in the lesson.* *adj.,* **thorn·i·er, thorn·i·est.**

**tho·ron** (thô′ron) an isotope of radon, given off by thorium: *Thoron is a radio-active gas.* Symbol: Tn *n.*

**thor·ough** (thėr′ō or thėr′ə) 1 being all that is needed; complete: *a thorough search.* 2 doing all that should be done and neglecting nothing: *The doctor was very thorough in her examination of the patient.* 1, 2 *adj.* Also, **thoro.** —**thor′ough·ly,** *adv.* —**thor′ough·ness,** *n.*

**thor·ough·bred** (thėr′ə bred′) 1 of pure breed or stock. 2 a thoroughbred horse or other animal. 3 of persons, well-bred; thoroughly trained. 4 a well-bred or thoroughly trained person. 1, 3 *adj.*, 2, 4 *n.*

**thor·ough·fare** (thėr′ə fer′) 1 a passage, road, or street open at both ends. 2 a main road; highway: *The Queen Elizabeth Way is a well-known thoroughfare between Toronto and Niagara Falls.* *n.*

**thor·ough·go·ing** (thėr′ə gō′ing) thorough; complete. *adj.*

**those** (ᴛнōz) 1 pl. of the adjective THAT: *She owns that dog; the boys own those dogs.* 2 pl. of the pronoun THAT: *These are her books; those are my books.* 1 *adj.*, 2 *pron.*

**though** (ᴛнō) 1 in spite of the fact that; notwithstanding the fact that: *Though it was pouring, the girls went to school.* 2 yet; still; nevertheless: *He is better, though not yet cured.* 3 even if; granting or supposing that: *Though I fail, I shall try again.* 4 however: *I am sorry about our quarrel; you began it, though.* 1–3 *conj.,* 4 *adv.*

**as though,** as if; as it would be if: *You look as though you are tired.*

**thought** (thot) 1 what one thinks; an idea; notion: *Her thought was to have a picnic.* 2 the power or process of thinking; mental activity: *Thought helps us solve problems.* 3 reasoning: *He applied thought to the problem.* 4 the way of thinking characteristic of the thinkers of a specified group, time, or place: *in modern scientific thought, 16th-century thought.* 5 consideration; attention; care; regard: *Show some thought for others who are less fortunate.* 6 intention: *His thought was to avoid controversy.* 7 a little bit; trifle: *Be a thought more polite.* 8 pt. and pp. of THINK: *We thought it would snow yesterday.* 1–7 *n.,* 8 *v.*

**thought control** the strict limiting or regimentation of ideas, reasoning, etc. to make them conform to those of a particular group, government, etc.

**thought·ful** (thot′fəl) 1 deep in thought; thinking: *She was thoughtful for a while and then replied, "No."* 2 careful; showing careful thought: *a thoughtful plan.* 3 careful of others; considerate: *She is always thoughtful of her mother.* *adj.* —**thought′ful·ly,** *adv.* —**thought′ful·ness,** *n.*

**thought·less** (thot′lis) 1 without thought; doing things without thinking; careless. 2 showing little or no care or regard for others; not considerate. *adj.* —**thought′less·ly,** *adv.* —**thought′less·ness,** *n.*

**thou·sand** (thou′zənd) ten hundred; 1000. *n., adj.*

**thou·sand·fold** (thou′zənd fōld′) a thousand times as much or as many. *adj., adv., n.*

**thou·sandth** (thou′zəndth) 1 last in a series of a thousand. 2 one, or being one, of a thousand equal parts. *adj., n.*

**thral·dom** (throl′dəm) See THRALLDOM. *n.*

**thrall** (throl) 1 a person in bondage; slave. 2 THRALLDOM; bondage; slavery. *n.*

**thrall·dom** or **thral·dom** (throl′dəm) bondage; slavery: *A sorcerer held the knight in thralldom.* *n.*

**thrash** (thrash) 1 beat: *The man thrashed the boy for stealing the apples.* 2 move violently; toss: *Unable to sleep, the patient thrashed about in her bed.* 3 THRESH.

**thrash out,** settle by thorough discussion: *Let's stay until we thrash out the problem.*

**thrash over,** go over again and again.

**thrash·er** (thrash′ər) 1 any of several North American songbirds belonging to the same family as the mocking bird, having a long tail and long bill: *Thrashers are noted for their song.* 2 a person or thing that thrashes. *n.*

**thread** (thred) 1 cotton, silk, flax, etc. spun out into a fine cord: *Thread is used for sewing.* 2 pass a thread through: *She threaded her needle. Maaike threaded a hundred beads.* 3 something long and slender like a thread: *Threads of gold could be seen in the ore.* 4 form into a thread: *Cook the syrup until it will thread.* 5 something that connects the parts of a story, speech, etc.: *He lost the thread of their conversation when he heard the phone ring.* 6 pass like a thread through; pervade. 7 make one's way through; make one's way carefully; go on a winding course: *He threaded his way through the crowd. The path threads through the forest.* 8 the sloping ridge that winds around a bolt, screw, pipe joint, etc.: *The thread of a nut interlocks with the thread of a bolt.* 9 cut threads into a bolt, screw, pipe joint, etc.: *The plumber threaded the pipe.* 10 **threads,** *Informal.* clothes. 1, 3, 5, 8, 10 *n.,* 2, 4, 6, 7, 9 *v.* —**thread′like′,** *adv.*

**thread·bare** (thred′ber′) 1 having the nap worn off; worn so much that the threads show: *a threadbare coat.* 2 wearing clothes worn to the threads; shabby: *a threadbare beggar.* 3 old and worn; stale: *Saying "I forgot" is a threadbare excuse.* *adj.*

**thread·y** (thred′ē) 1 consisting of or resembling a thread. 2 fibrous; stringy or viscid. 3 of the pulse, thin and feeble. 4 of the voice, etc., lacking in fullness. *adj.* —**thread′i·ness,** *n.*

**threat** (thret) 1 a statement of what will be done to hurt or punish someone. 2 a sign or cause of possible harm or unpleasantness: *Those black clouds are a threat of rain.* *n.*

**threat·en** (thret′ən) 1 make a threat against; say what will be done to hurt or punish: *to threaten a person with imprisonment.* 2 be a sign of possible evil or harm, etc.: *Black clouds threaten rain.* 3 be a threat. 4 utter threats: *Do you mean to threaten?* 5 be a cause of possible evil or harm to: *A flood threatened the city.* *v.* —**threat′en·er,** *n.* —**threat′en·ing·ly,** *adv.*

**three** (thrē) 1 one more than two; 3: *I bought two T-shirts and she bought three. She ate three pieces of cake.* 2 the numeral 3: *There's a 3 at the bottom of the page.*

**3** the third in a set or series; especially, a playing card or side of a die having three spots: *the three of hearts.*
**4** being third in a set or series (*used mainly after the noun*): *Have you read Chapter Three?* **5** a set or series of three persons or things: *The soldiers marched past in threes.* 1–3, 5 *n.*, 1, 4 *adj.*
☛ *Etym.* From OE *thrēo*, related to German *drei* and having the same Indo-European source as L *tres* and Gk. *treis.*

**three–D** or **3–D** (thrē′dē′)   a THREE-DIMENSIONAL motion picture. *n.*

**three–di·men·sion·al** (thrē′di men′shə nəl)   **1** having the three dimensions of height, width, and depth: *A cube is a three-dimensional object.*   **2** appearing to have depth as well as height and width, especially of flat images which have the illusion of depth.   *adj.*

**three–fold** (thrē′fōld′)   **1** three times as much or as many.   **2** having three parts: *Clover has a three-fold leaf.* 1, 2 *adj.*, 1 *adv.*, *n.*

**three–ply** (thrē′plī′)   having three thicknesses, layers, folds, or strands: *My socks are knitted of three-ply yarn.* *adj.*

**three R's**   reading, writing, and arithmetic.

**three·score** (thrē′skôr′)   three times twenty; 60. *n.*, *adj.*

**three·some** (thrē′səm)   **1** a group of three people.   **2** any game played by three people.   **3** the players in such a game.   *n.*

**thren·o·dy** (thren′ə dē)   a song of lamentation, especially at a person's death.   *n.*, *pl.* **thren·o·dies.**

**thresh** (thresh)   **1** separate the grain or seeds from wheat, etc.: *Nowadays most farmers use a machine to thresh their wheat.*   **2** toss about; thrash.   *v.*   Also, **thrash.**
**thresh out,**   settle by thorough discussion.
**thresh over,**   go over again and again.

**thresh·er** (thresh′ər)   **1** a person who threshes.   **2** a machine used for separating the grain or seeds from the stalks and other parts of wheat, oats, etc.   **3** a large shark having a long tail.   *n.*

**thresh·old** (thresh′ōld or thresh′hōld)   **1** a piece of wood or stone under a door.   **2** doorway.   **3** the point of entering; beginning point: *The scientist was on the threshold of an important discovery.*   *n.*

**threw** (thrü)   pt. of THROW: *He threw a stone and ran away.*   *v.*
☛ *Hom.* THROUGH, THRO'.

**thrift** (thrift)   the absence of waste; economical management; the habit of saving: *By thrift she managed to get along on her small salary.*   *n.*

**thrift·less** (thrift′lis)   without thrift; wasteful.   *adj.*

**thrift·y** (thrif′tē)   **1** careful in spending; economical; saving.   **2** thriving; flourishing: *a thrifty business.* **3** prosperous; well-to-do; successful: *The countryside has many fine, thrifty farms.*   *adj.*, **thrift·i·er, thrift·i·est.** —**thrift′i·ly,** *adv.*   —**thrift′i·ness,** *n.*

**thrill** (thril)   **1** a shivering, exciting feeling.   **2** give a shivering, exciting feeling to: *Stories of adventure thrilled him.*   **3** have a shivering, exciting feeling: *The children thrilled with joy at the sight of the ponies.*   **4** quiver; tremble: *Her voice thrilled with terror.*   1 *n.*, 2–4 *v.*
—**thrill′ing·ly,** *adv.*

**thrill·er** (thril′ər)   **1** a person or thing that thrills.   **2** *Informal.*   a sensational play or story, especially one involving a murder.   *n.*

**thrill·ing** (thril′ing)   **1** exciting.   **2** ppr. of THRILL. 1 *adj.*, 2 *v.*

**thrips** (thrips)   a small, destructive insect having long, narrow wings fringed with hairs.   *n.*

**thrive** (thrīv)   **1** grow strong; grow vigorously: *Flowers will not thrive without sunshine.*   **2** be successful; grow rich: *Her business is thriving.*   *v.*, **throve** or **thrived, thrived** or **thriv·en, thriv·ing.**   —**thriv′ing·ly,** *adv.*

**thriv·en** (thriv′ən)   a pp. of THRIVE.   *v.*

**thro'** (thrü)   THROUGH.   *prep.*, *adv.*, *adj.*
☛ *Hom.* THREW.

**throat** (thrōt)   **1** the front of the neck.   **2** the passage from the mouth to the stomach or the lungs.   **3** any narrowed opening or passage: *the throat of a mine.*   *n.*
**lump in the throat, a** a feeling of inability to swallow.
**b** a feeling of sadness: *The beggar's story brought a lump in my throat.*
**stick in one's throat,**   be hard or unpleasant to say.

**throat·ed** (thrō′tid)   having a certain kind of throat: *white-throated.*   *adj.*

**throat·y** (thrō′tē)   **1** produced or uttered from far back in the throat; low-pitched and resonant: *a throaty voice.* **2** deep and resonant as if produced far back in the throat. *adj.*, **throat·i·er, throat·i·est.**   —**throat′i·ness,** *n.*

**throb** (throb)   **1** beat more rapidly or strongly than normally: *Our hearts were still throbbing from the long climb up the hill.*   **2** an abnormally rapid or strong beat: *the throb of our hearts.*   **3** beat or vibrate steadily.   **4** a steady beat or vibration: *She felt the throb of the little plane's engine.*   **5** quiver; tremble: *They were throbbing with excitement.*   1, 3, 5 *v.*, **throbbed, throb·bing;**   2, 4, 5 *n.*   —**throb′bing·ly,** *adv.*

**throe** (thrō)   Usually, **throes,** *pl.*   **1** a violent pang or pangs; great pain: *the throes of death, the throes of childbirth.*   **2** a hard or agonizing struggle: *a poet in the throes of creation, the throes of revolution.*   *n.*

**throm·bo·sis** (throm bō′sis)   the formation of a blood clot in a blood vessel or the heart.   *n.*

**throne** (thrōn)   **1** the chair on which a king, queen, bishop, or other person of high rank sits during ceremonies.   **2** the power or authority of king, queen, etc.: *The throne commands respect but no longer commands armies.*   **3** ENTHRONE.   1, 2 *n.*, 3 *v.*, **throned, thron·ing.**
☛ *Hom.* THROWN.

**throng** (throng)   **1** a crowd; multitude.   **2** crowd; fill with a crowd: *People thronged the theatre to see the famous actress.*   **3** come together in a crowd; go or press in large numbers: *The people thronged to see the Queen.*   1 *n.*, 2, 3 *v.*

**throt·tle** (throt′əl)   **1** a valve regulating the flow of steam, gasoline vapour, etc. to an engine; especially, the valve controlling the gasoline vapour entering the cylinders of an internal-combustion engine.   **2** a lever or pedal working such a valve: *The throttle of a car is called an accelerator.*   **3** lessen the speed of an engine by closing a throttle (*often used with* **down** *or* **back**): *to throttle down a steam engine.*   **4** stop the breath of by pressure on the throat; choke; strangle: *The thief throttled the dog to keep it from barking.*   **5** stop or check the expression or action of; suppress: *Increased tariffs soon throttled trade between the two countries.*   **6** throat or windpipe.   1, 2, 6 *n.*, 3–5 *v.*, **throt·tled, throt·tling.**

**through** (thrü) **1** from end to end of; from side to side of; between the parts of; from beginning to end of: *The soldiers marched through the town. The men cut a tunnel through a mountain.* **2** from end to end; from side to side; between the parts: *The bullet hit the wall and went through.* **3** here and there in; over; around: *We travelled through Quebec, visiting many old towns.* **4** because of; by reason of: *The woman refused help through pride.* **5** by means of: *She became rich through hard work and ability.* **6** completely; thoroughly: *He walked home in the rain and was wet through.* **7** going all the way without change: *a through train from Montreal to Vancouver.* **8** having reached the end of; finished with: *We are through school at three o'clock.* **9** from beginning to end: *She read the book through.* **10** along the whole distance; all the way: *The train goes through to Vancouver.* **11** having reached the end; finished: *I am almost through.* 1, 3–5, 8 *prep.*, 2, 6, 9, 10 *adv.*, 7, 11 *adj.*
**through and through,** completely; thoroughly.
☞ Hom. THREW, THRO'.

**through·out** (thrü out′) **1** all the way through; through all; in every part or during the whole course of: *Canada Day is celebrated throughout Canada. She skied almost every weekend throughout the winter.* **2** in or to every part or from beginning to end: *The house is well built throughout. He remained stubborn throughout.* 1 *prep.*, 2 *adv.*

**through street** a street on which traffic is given the right of way at intersections. Compare with STOP STREET.

**throve** (thrōv) a pt. of THRIVE. *v.*

**throw** (thrō) **1** cast; toss; hurl: *to throw a ball. The fire hose threw water on the fire.* **2** a cast, toss, etc. **3** the distance a thing is or may be thrown. **4** bring to the ground: *His horse threw him.* **5** put carelessly or in haste: *She threw a cloak over her shoulders.* **6** put into a certain condition: *to throw a person into confusion.* **7** turn, direct, or move, especially quickly: *She threw a glance at each car that passed us.* **8** move a lever, etc. that connects or disconnects parts of a switch, clutch, or other mechanism. **9** connect or disconnect thus. **10** shed: *A snake throws its skin.* **11** of some animals, bring forth young. **12** *Informal.* let an opponent win a race, game, etc., often for money. **13** a scarf; light covering. **14** make a specified cast with dice. **15** a cast at dice; venture. **16** twist silk into threads. 1, 4–12, 14, 16 *v.*, **threw, thrown, throw·ing;** 2, 3, 13, 15 *n.* —**throw′er,** *n.*
**throw away,** **a** get rid of; discard. **b** waste: *to throw away an opportunity.*
**throw back,** revert to an ancestral type.
**throw cold water on,** discourage.
**throw in,** add as a gift: *Our grocer often throws in an extra apple.*
**throw off,** **a** get rid of. **b** *Informal.* produce a poem, etc., in an offhand manner.
**throw oneself at,** try very hard to get the love, friendship, or favour of.
**throw open,** **a** open suddenly or widely. **b** remove all obstacles or restrictions from.
**throw out,** **a** get rid of; discard. **b** reject.
**throw over,** give up; discard; abandon.
**throw up,** **a** *Informal.* vomit. **b** give up; abandon: *Stan threw up his plan to go to Europe.* **c** build rapidly.

**throw·a·way** (thrō′ə wā′) **1** a free handbill or leaflet carrying advertising or other information; handout. **2** meant to be discarded or thrown away after use; disposable: *throwaway bottles.* 1 *n.*, 2 *adj.*

**throw·back** (thrō′bak′) **1** a reversion to an ancestral type or character. **2** an instance of such a reversion: *The boy seemed to be a throwback to his great-grandfather.* *n.*

---

**through 1245 thumb**

hat, āge, fär; let, ēqual, tėrm; it, īce
hot, ōpen, ôrder; oil, out; cup, pút, rüle
əbove, takən, pencəl, lemən, circəs
ch, child; ng, long; sh, ship
th, thin; ᴛʜ, then; zh, measure

**thrown** (thrōn) pp. of THROW. *v.*
☞ Hom. THRONE.

**thrum¹** (thrum) **1** play on a stringed instrument by plucking the string, especially in an idle way; strum: *to thrum a guitar.* **2** of a guitar, etc. or its strings, sound when thrummed on. **3** drum or tap idly with the fingers: *to thrum on a table.* **4** the sound made by thrumming. **5** recite or tell in a monotonous way. 1–3, 5 *v.*, **thrummed, thrum·ming;** 4 *n.*

**thrum²** (thrum) **1** an end of the warp thread left unwoven on the loom after the web is cut off. **2** loose thread or yarn. **3** a tuft or fringe. *n.*

**thrush¹** (thrush) any of a large group of migratory songbirds that includes the robin, the bluebird, the wood thrush, etc. *n.*

**thrush²** (thrush) a contagious disease, especially of very young babies, in which white blisters form in the mouth and throat and on the lips: *Thrush is caused by a fungus.* *n.*

**thrust** (thrust) **1** push with force: *He thrust his hands into his pockets. She thrust her brother aside and grabbed the plate of cookies.* **2** drive into or cause to pierce by pushing; stab: *He thrust his fork into the potato.* **3** a sudden or forceful push: *With a quick thrust, she hid the book behind the pillow.* **4** a push or lunge with a pointed weapon: *A thrust with the pin broke the balloon.* **5** a military attack. **6** in mechanics, the continuous sideways force of one part of a structure against another, such as the pressure of an arch against a pillar. **7** the endwise push exerted by the rotation of a propeller, producing forward motion. **8** the force exerted by a high-speed jet of gas, etc. ejected to the rear, as in a jet engine, producing forward motion. **9** main purpose or direction: *the thrust of an argument.* 1, 2 *v.*, **thrust, thrust·ing;** 3–9 *n.*

**thud** (thud) **1** a dull sound caused by a blow or fall: *The book hit the floor with a thud.* **2** a blow or thump. **3** hit, move, or strike with a thud: *The heavy box fell and thudded on the floor.* 1, 2 *n.*, 3 *v.*, **thud·ded, thud·ding.**

**thug** (thug) **1** a ruffian; cutthroat; gangster. **2** a member of a former religious organization of robbers and murderers in India. *n.*

**thu·li·um** (thü′lē əm *or* thyü′lē əm) a metallic element of the rare-earth group. Symbol: Tm *n.*

**thumb** (thum) **1** the short finger of the human hand that is nearest the wrist and can be opposed to the other fingers. See ARM for picture. **2** the part of a glove, mitten, etc. that covers the thumb. **3** leaf through or turn the pages of a book, magazine, etc. rapidly. **4** soil or wear by repeated thumbing or as if by thumbing: *The table in the waiting room was covered with badly thumbed magazines.* **5** *Informal.* ask for or get a free ride by signalling with the thumb to passing motorists: *He thumbed a ride into town when his car broke down.* **6** travel by thumbing rides; hitchhike: *She thumbed her way from Calgary to Winnipeg.* 1, 2 *n.*, 3–6 *v.*
—**thumb′like′,** *adj.*

**all thumbs,** very clumsy, awkward, etc.: *I'm all thumbs when it comes to tying bows.*

**thumb one's nose,** express scorn or defiance by or as if by placing one's thumb on the end of one's nose and extending the fingers: *The rude little girl thumbed her nose at a passer-by. He thumbed his nose at the promise of success and went his own way.*

**thumbs down,** **a** a sign of disapproval, rejection, or disappointment, made by closing the hand and pointing the thumb downward: *She just gave us a thumbs down when we asked how she liked the slogan.* **b** an expression of disapproval, rejection, or disappointment: *The principal turned thumbs down on the proposal for another field trip.*

**thumbs up,** **a** a sign of acceptance or satisfaction, made by closing the hand and pointing the thumb up: *He smiled and signalled thumbs up as he came out of the employment office.* **b** an expression of satisfaction: *"Thumbs up!" he called as he came out of the examination room.*

**under someone's thumb,** under someone's control or influence: *He's got them all under his thumb and they'll do anything he tells them.*

**thumb·nail** (thum′nāl) the nail of the thumb. *n.*

**thumbnail sketch** 1 a small or quickly drawn picture: *a thumbnail sketch of the children at play.* 2 a short description.

**thumb·screw** (thum′skrü) 1 a screw made so that its head can be easily turned with the thumb and a finger. 2 an old instrument of torture that squeezed the thumbs. *n.*

**thumb·tack** (thum′tak) a tack having a broad, flat head for pressing into a surface with the thumb. *n.*

**thump** (thump) 1 strike with something thick and heavy: *He thumped the table with his fist.* 2 strike against something heavily and noisily: *The shutters thumped the wall in the wind.* 3 a blow with something thick and heavy; heavy knock: *The thief hit him a thump on the head.* 4 the dull sound made by a blow, knock, or fall: *We heard the thump as he fell.* 5 make a dull sound; pound: *The hammer thumped against the wood.* 6 beat violently or heavily: *His heart thumped as he walked past the cemetery at night.* 7 defeat, beat, or thrash severely. 1, 2, 5–7 *v.*, 3, 4 *n.* —**thump′er,** *n.*

**thump·ing** (thum′ping) 1 *Informal.* great; huge; whopping: *a thumping victory.* 2 ppr. of THUMP. 1 *adj.*, 2 *v.*

**thun·der** (thun′dər) 1 the loud noise that often follows a flash of lightning: *Thunder is caused by a disturbance of the air resulting from the discharge of electricity.* 2 give forth thunder: *We heard it thunder in the distance.* 3 any noise like thunder: *the thunder of Niagara Falls, a thunder of applause.* 4 make a noise like thunder: *The cannon thundered.* 5 utter very loudly; roar: *to thunder a reply.* 6 utter a threat or denunciation loudly, violently, or impressively: *The newspaper article thundered against the injustices of the political system.* 7 a threat or denunciation. 1, 3, 7 *n.*, 2, 4–6 *v.* —**thun′der·er,** *n.*

**steal someone's thunder,** make someone's idea, method, etc. less effective by using it first or doing something better or more startling: *The Liberals stole the Tories' thunder by announcing their election plans first.*

**thun·der·bird** (thun′dər bėrd′) in the culture of certain North American Indians, a huge bird believed to cause thunder and lightning. It is often carved at the top of totem poles and used in other west coast Indian designs. *n.*

**thun·der·bolt** (thun′dər bōlt′) 1 a flash of lightning and the thunder that follows it. 2 something sudden, startling, and terrible: *The news of her death came as a thunderbolt.* *n.*

**thun·der·clap** (thun′dər klap′) 1 a loud crash of thunder. 2 something sudden or startling. *n.*

**thun·der·cloud** (thun′dər kloud′) a dark, electrically charged cloud that brings thunder and lightning. *n.*

**thun·der·head** (thun′dər hed′) one of the round, swelling masses of cumulus clouds often appearing before thunderstorms and frequently developing into thunderclouds. *n.*

**thun·der·ous** (thun′də rəs) 1 producing thunder. 2 making a noise like thunder: *thunderous applause.* *adj.*

**thun·der·show·er** (thun′dər shou′ər) a shower accompanied by thunder and lightning. *n.*

**thun·der·squall** (thun′dər skwol′) a squall accompanied by thunder and lightning. *n.*

**thun·der·storm** (thun′dər stôrm′) a storm accompanied by thunder and lightning and, usually, by heavy rain. *n.*

**thun·der·struck** (thun′dər struk′) overcome, as if hit by a thunderbolt; astonished; amazed. *adj.*

**Thurs.** or **Thur.** Thursday.

**Thurs·day** (thėrz′dā′ *or* thėrz′dē) the fifth day of the week, following Wednesday. *n.*
☛ *Etym.* From OE *thuresdæg* 'day of thunder' or 'day of Thor (the Germanic god of thunder)', equivalent to L *Jovis dies* 'day of Jove or Jupiter'.

**thus** (ᴛʜus) 1 in this way; in the way just indicated or about to be indicated: *She spoke thus.* 2 accordingly; consequently; therefore: *Thus we decided that he was wrong.* 3 to this extent or degree; so: *thus far.* *adv.*

**thwack** (thwak) 1 strike vigorously with a stick or something flat. 2 a sharp blow with a stick or something flat. 1 *v.*, 2 *n.*

**thwart** (thwôrt) 1 hinder, defeat, or frustrate; keep from doing something: *The boy's lack of money thwarted his plans for a trip. The enemy's attack was thwarted.* 2 a seat across a boat, on which a rower sits. 3 a brace in a canoe. See CANOE for picture. 4 lying or situated across something else; transverse or oblique. 5 across; ATHWART. 1 *v.*, 2, 3 *n.*, 4 *adj.*, 5 *adv.*

**thyme** (tīm) a small plant that has a mintlike fragrance. The leaves of the common **garden thyme** are used for seasoning. The common **wild thyme** is a creeping evergreen. *n.*
☛ *Hom.* TIME.

**thy·mus** (thī′məs) a ductless glandlike body situated near the base of the neck, present in the young of most vertebrates but becoming very small or disappearing altogether in adults: *The thymus is thought to function in the development of the body's immune system.* *n.*

**thy·roid** (thī′roid) 1 THYROID GLAND. 2 a medicine made from the thyroid glands of animals, used in the treatment of goitre, obesity, etc. 3 THYROID CARTILAGE. 4 of or having to do with the THYROID GLAND or THYROID CARTILAGE. *n.*

**thyroid cartilage** the principal cartilage of the larynx, which in men forms the Adam's apple.

**thyroid gland** an important ductless gland in the neck

of vertebrates producing a hormone that regulates growth and metabolism.

**thy·rox·in** (thī rok′sin)  THYROXINE.  *n.*

**thy·rox·ine** (thī rok′sēn *or* thī rok′sin)  an amino acid that is the active hormone produced by the THYROID GLAND: *Thyroxine is also prepared synthetically or obtained from the thyroid glands of animals and is used in the treatment of thyroid disorders.*  *n.*

**ti** (tē)  in music:  **1** the seventh tone of an eight-tone major scale.  **2** the tone B. See DO² for picture.  *n.*
☞ *Hom.* TEA, TEE.

**Ti**  titanium.

**ti·ar·a** (tē ä′rə *or* tī er′ə)  **1** a band of gold, jewels, flowers, etc., worn around the head by women as an ornament.  **2** the triple crown of the Pope.  **3** an ancient Persian headdress for men.  *n.*

**Ti·bet·an** (ti bet′ən)  **1** of or having to do with Tibet, its people, or their language.  **2** a member of an Asiatic people who are the original inhabitants of Tibet.  **3** a native or inhabitant of Tibet.  **4** the language of Tibet, related to Burmese and Chinese.  1 *adj.*, 2–4 *n.*

**tib·i·a** (tib′ē ə)  the inner and thicker of the two bones of the leg from the knee to the ankle; shinbone. See LEG for picture.  *n.*, *pl.* **tib·i·ae** (-ē ē′ *or* -ē ī′) *or* **tib·i·as**.

**tic** (tik)  a habitual, involuntary twitching of the muscles, especially those of the face.  *n.*
☞ *Hom.* TICK.

**tick¹** (tik)  **1** a sound made by a clock or watch.  **2** make a tick.  **3** a sound like it.  **4** mark off: *The clock ticked away the minutes.*  **5** *Informal.*  a moment; instant.  **6** a small mark used in checking (✓).  **7** mark an item in a list, etc. with a tick; check (*usually used with* **off**): *He ticked off the groceries he had already bought.*  **8** *Informal.*  function, work, or go: *What makes that gadget tick?*  1, 3, 5, 6 *n.*, 2, 4, 7, 8 *v.*
**ticked off,** *Informal.*  fed up.
**tick off,** *Informal.*  scold; tell off: *She got ticked off for being late again.*
**what makes a person tick,**  what motivates a person to act or behave in a certain way: *He's very quiet; I wonder what makes him tick.*
☞ *Hom.* TIC.

**tick²** (tik)  **1** any of a large group of small bloodsucking animals belonging to the same class as spiders, scorpions, and mites, that feed on the blood of dogs, cattle, human beings, etc.: *Some ticks carry infectious diseases.*  **2** any of various species of usually wingless insect that live as parasites on cattle, sheep, birds, etc.  *n.*
☞ *Hom.* TIC.

**tick³** (tik)  **1** the cloth covering of a mattress or pillow.  **2** *Informal.*  TICKING.  *n.*
☞ *Hom.* TIC.

**tick·er** (tik′ər)  **1** something that ticks, especially a clock or watch.  **2** a telegraphic instrument that records stock market reports or news on a paper tape.  *n.*

**ticker tape**  the paper tape on which a TICKER (def. 2) records its information.

**tick·et** (tik′it)  **1** a card or other piece of paper showing that a fee or fare has been paid: *a theatre ticket, an airline ticket, a lottery ticket.*  **2** an official notification that a person is charged with a traffic violation: *a parking ticket, a ticket for speeding.*  **3** a label or tag attached to an article for sale, showing its size, price, etc.  **4** put a ticket on; mark with a ticket: *All articles in the store are ticketed with the price.*  **5** give or attach a ticket to, indicating a traffic violation: *She was ticketed for speeding.*  1–3 *n.*, 4, 5 *v.*
**that's the ticket,** *Informal.*  that's the correct or desirable thing.

**tick·ing** (tik′ing)  **1** a strong cotton or linen cloth, used to cover mattresses and pillows and to make tents and awnings.  **2** ppr. of TICK¹.  1 *n.*, 2 *v.*

**tick·le¹** (tik′əl)  **1** touch lightly causing little thrills, shivers, or wriggles.  **2** have a feeling like this; cause to have such a feeling: *My nose tickles.*  **3** a tingling or itching feeling.  **4** excite pleasantly; amuse: *The story tickled her. The child was tickled with his new toys.*  **5** play, stir, get, etc. with light touches or strokes.  **6** the act of tickling.  1, 2, 4, 5 *v.*, **tick·led, tick·ling;**  3, 6 *n.*

**tick·le²** (tik′əl) *Cdn.*  esp. in Newfoundland:  **1** a narrow channel between an island and the mainland, or sometimes, between islands.  **2** a narrow entrance to a harbour.  *n.*

**tick·ler** (tik′lər)  **1** a person or device that tickles, especially a small feather brush used to tickle the faces of others at a carnival, etc.  **2** *Informal.*  a memorandum book, card index, or other device kept as a reminder.  **3** *Informal.*  a difficult or puzzling problem.  *n.*

**tick·lish** (tik′lish)  **1** sensitive to tickling.  **2** requiring careful handling; delicate; risky: *Mending the radio was a ticklish job.*  **3** easily upset; unstable: *A canoe is a ticklish craft.*  **4** easily annoyed or offended: *a proud and ticklish fellow.*  *adj.*  —**tick′lish·ly,** *adv.*  —**tick′lish·ness,** *n.*

**tick–tack–toe** (tik′tak tō′)  a game in which two players alternately put circles or crosses in a figure of nine squares, each player trying to be the first to fill three spaces in a row with his or her mark.  *n.*

**tick–tock** (tik′tok′)  the sound made by some clocks or watches.  *n.*

**tick·y–tack·y** (tik′ē tak′ē) *Informal.*  **1** rubbish; worthless material.  **2** worthless; in poor taste.  1 *n.*, 2 *adj.*

**tid·al** (tī′dəl)  **1** of, having to do with, caused by, or having tides: *tidal waters, a tidal breeze.*  **2** dependent on the state of the tide as to time of arrival and departure: *a tidal steamer.*  *adj.*

**tidal energy**  the kinetic energy of large bodies of water, manifested in waves: *Tidal energy can be harnessed to make electricity.*

**tidal wave**  **1** a large wave or sudden increase in the level of water along a shore, caused by unusually strong winds.  **2** a destructive ocean wave which is caused by an underwater earthquake.  **3** any great movement or manifestation of feeling, opinion, or the like: *a tidal wave of popular indignation.*

**tid·bit** (tid′bit′)  a very pleasing bit of food, news, etc.  *n.*  Also, **titbit.**

**tid·dly·winks** (tid′lē wingks′)  a game in which the players try to make small coloured disks jump into a cup by pressing on their edges with a larger disk (*used with a singular verb*).  *n.*

**tide** (tīd) **1** the rise and fall of the ocean, usually taking place about every twelve hours, caused by the attraction of the moon and the sun. **2** anything that rises and falls like the tide: *the tide of popular opinion*. **3** drift with the tide; especially, get a ship into or out of a harbour, etc. with the help of the tide. **4** a stream; current; flood. **5** a season; time (*usually used in compounds*): *Eastertide*. 1, 2, 4, 5 *n.*, 3 *v.*, **tid·ed, tid·ing.** —**tide′less,** *adj.*
**tide over,** help to overcome a difficulty, etc.: *He said twenty dollars would tide him over until payday.*
**turn the tide,** change from one condition to the opposite.

**tide·mark** (tīd′märk′) a mark left by the tide at its highest point, or sometimes, at its lowest point. *n.*

**tide·wa·ter** (tīd′dwot′ər) **1** water having tides. **2** water brought by tides; water flooding land at high tide. **3** a low-lying seacoast. *n.*

**tide·way** (tīd′dwā′) **1** a channel through which a tide runs. **2** the current or ebb and flow in such a channel. **3** the tidal part of a river. *n.*

**ti·dings** (tī′dingz) news; information: *The letter brought tidings from their daughter and her family.* *n.pl.*

**ti·dy** (tī′dē) **1** neat and in order: *a tidy room.* **2** put in order; make tidy (*often used with* **up**): *She quickly tidied the room. We tidied up before we left.* **3** inclined to keep things neat and in order: *a tidy person.* **4** *Informal.* fairly large; considerable; substantial: *He already has a tidy sum saved up toward a stereo.* **5** *Informal.* fairly good; acceptable; satisfactory: *They've worked out a tidy solution.* **6** a small decorative cover used to protect the back or arms of a chair, chesterfield, etc. 1, 3–5 *adj.*, **ti·di·er, ti·di·est;** 2 *v.*, **ti·died, ti·dy·ing;** 6 *n.*, *pl.* **ti·dies.** —**ti′di·ly,** *adv.* —**ti′di·ness,** *n.*

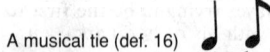
A musical tie (def. 16)

**tie** (tī) **1** fasten, attach, or close with cord, ribbon, rope, or the like: *Tie the package securely and tie a label on it. She tied the dog to the fence. Tie your shoes. He tied down the tarpaulin to keep it from flapping.* **2** arrange to form a bow or knot: *to tie a scarf.* **3** make by tying: *to tie a knot, to tie a fishing fly.* **4** be capable of being tied: *This paper ribbon doesn't tie very well.* **5** close or join by means of cord, ribbon, etc.: *The apron ties at the back.* **6** a cord, ribbon, etc. used for fastening parts together, especially one already attached: *An apron has ties. I don't like shoes with ties.* **7** a shaped, folded length of cloth worn under a shirt collar and knotted in front, either to form a bow or, more often, so that the two ends hang straight down: *He always wears a shirt and tie to work.* **8** anything that unites or binds; a bond or obligation: *family ties.* **9** restrain or limit: *He did not want to be tied to a steady job.* **10** connect or join in any way: *When the river was low, a narrow strip of sand tied the island to the shore.* **11** one of the parallel wooden beams placed crosswise at intervals on a railway bed to form a foundation and support for the rails. See RAIL¹ for picture. **12** a connecting beam or rod, as in a framework supporting a roof, etc. **13** equality in points, votes, etc.: *The game ended in a tie, 3–3.* **14** make the same score; be equal in points: *The two teams tied.* **15** make the same score as: *Halifax tied Charlottetown in the last game of the series.* **16** in music, a curved line joining two notes of the same pitch to show that they are to be played or sung without a break between them. **17** connect notes by a tie. 1–5, 9, 10, 14, 15, 17 *v.*, **tied, ty·ing;** 6–8, 11–13, 16 *n.*

**tie down,** confine or restrict: *She's tied down with a full-time job and night school.*

**tie in,** **a** connect: *Where does this line tie in with the main circuit?* **b** co-ordinate or relate: *The illustrations tie in very well with the story.*

**tie into,** *Informal.* start in on vigorously: *She forgot everything else and tied into her food.*

**tie up,** **a** confine in bonds; bind with cord, etc.: *The thieves tied him up and left him.* **b** hinder or stop the progress of: *The stalled truck tied up traffic for half an hour.* **c** invest or place money or property in such a way as to make it unavailable for other uses: *Since her money was tied up in real estate, she was unable to buy the bonds.* **d** have one's program full; be very busy: *He's tied up and can't make it to the dinner.* **e** take for oneself so as to make unavailable for others: *Don't tie up the phone too long.* **f** complete a sale; bring to completion; conclude: *They've nearly got the details tied up.*

**tie-and-dye** (tī′ən dī′) TIE-DYE. *n.*

**tie·back** (tī′bak′) **1** a cord, ribbon, strip of cloth, etc., usually decorative, used to drape a curtain to the side of a window instead of allowing it to hang straight down. **2 tiebacks,** *pl.* curtains having tiebacks. *n.*

**tie breaker** a contest or game held to determine a winner from among contestants with equal scores.

**tie clip** a long clip, usually having an ornamental face, used to clip a necktie to the front of a shirt.

**tie-dye** (tī′dī′) **1** a method of dyeing cloth in patterns by tying parts of the cloth with string so that they will not absorb the dye. **2** a design made in this way. **3** cloth decorated with such a design. **4** dye cloth or a garment in this way: *to tie-dye a scarf.* 1–3 *n.*, 4 *v.*, **tie-dyed, tie-dye·ing.**

**tie-in** (tī′in′) a link; association; connection: *There was no tie-in between the murder and the robbery.* *n.*

**tie·pin** (tī′pin′) a pin, usually having an ornamental head and a protective sheath for the point, used to hold a necktie or cravat in place. *n.*

**tier¹** (tēr) **1** one of a series of rows arranged one above another: *tiers of seats in a football stadium.* **2** arrange in tiers. 1 *n.*, 2 *v.*
☛ *Hom.* TEAR¹.

**ti·er²** (tī′ər) a person or thing that ties. *n.*

**tierce** (tērs) **1** a cask, of varying sizes, for provisions. **2** a sequence of three playing cards of the same suit. **3** in fencing, the third position. **4** in music, a third. *n.*

**tie tack** a kind of pin to hold a necktie in place, having an ornamental head with a short stud behind it that is passed through the tie and shirt and held in place with a small clasp on the inside.

**tie-up** (tī′up′) **1** a stopping of work or action on account of a strike, storm, accident, etc. **2** *Informal.* a connection; relation. *n.*

**tiff** (tif) **1** a slight quarrel. **2** a slight fit of ill humour or peevishness; a pet. **3** have or be in a tiff. 1, 2 *n.*, 3 *v.*

A tiger— about 2 m long excluding the tail

hat, āge, fär; let, ēqual, tėrm; it, īce
hot, ōpen, ôrder; oil, out; cup, pùt, rüle
əbove, takən, pencəl, lemən, circəs
ch, child; ng, long; sh, ship
th, thin; ᴛн, then; zh, measure

**ti·ger** (tī′gər) 1 a large, fierce, Asiatic mammal of the cat family that has dull-yellow fur striped with black. 2 a fierce and wild person: *He becomes a tiger if you criticize his work.* 3 a vigorous or energetic person: *a tiger for work.* 4 *Informal.* an extra yell at the end of a cheer. *n.* —**ti′ger·like′**, *adj.*
**have a tiger by the tail**, be in a situation more difficult than was expected.

**tiger beetle** a beetle whose larvae live in burrows in sandy soil and catch insects that come near.

**tiger cat** 1 any of various medium-sized wild members of the cat family resembling the tiger, such as the ocelot or serval. 2 a striped domestic cat.

**ti·ger·ish** (tī′gə rish) like a tiger; wild and fierce. *adj.*

**tiger lily** a lily that has dull-orange flowers spotted with black.

**tiger moth** any of a group of moths having conspicuously spotted or striped wings.

**ti·ger's-eye** (tī′gər zī′) a golden-brown semi-precious stone with a changeable lustre, composed chiefly of quartz, coloured with iron oxide. *n.*

**tiger swallowtail** a large butterfly, a species of swallowtail found in eastern North America, having yellow wings with black stripes and margins.

**tight** (tīt) 1 firm; held firmly; packed or put together firmly: *a tight knot.* 2 closely; securely; firmly: *The rope was tied too tight.* 3 drawn; stretched: *a tight canvas.* 4 fitting closely; close: *Since she gained weight, her skirt has a tight fit.* 5 well-built; trim; neat: *a tight craft.* 6 not letting water, air, or gas in or out: *The caulking of the boat is tight.* 7 hard to deal with or manage; difficult: *His lies got him in a tight place.* 8 *Informal.* almost even; close: *It was a tight race.* 9 hard to get; scarce: *Money is tight just now.* 10 characterized by scarcity or eager demand: *a tight money market.* 11 *Informal.* stingy: *A miser is tight with his money.* 12 *Informal.* drunk. 1, 3–12 *adj.*, 2 *adv.* —**tight′ly**, *adv.* —**tight′ness**, *n.*
**sit tight,** *Informal.* keep the same position, opinion, etc.

**tight·en** (tī′tən) 1 make tight or tighter: *Carla tightened her belt.* 2 become tight or tighter: *The rope tightened as I pulled it.* *v.*

**tight-fist·ed** (tīt′fis′tid) STINGY. *adj.*

**tight-lipped** (tī′tlipt′) 1 keeping the lips firmly together, as in determination or when controlling strong emotion: *She stood there in tight-lipped fury.* 2 saying little or nothing; reluctant to speak: *He's very tight-lipped; you won't get any information out of him.* *adj.*

**tight·rope** (tī′trōp′) 1 a rope or wire stretched tight some distance above the ground, for acrobats to perform on. 2 a dangerous or extremely delicate situation: *She was on a tightrope now; one wrong word and she would lose their confidence.* *n.*

**tights** (tīts) a close-fitting, usually knitted, garment covering the lower body and each leg and foot separately, worn by acrobats, dancers, etc. or as stockings in cold weather. *n.pl.*

**tight·wad** (tīt′twod′) *Informal.* a stingy person. *n.*

**ti·gress** (tī′gris) 1 an adult female tiger. 2 a woman thought of as being like a tiger in fierceness or wildness. *n.*

**ti·ki·na·gan** (tik′ə nä′gən) *Cdn.* CRADLE-BOARD. *n.*

**til·de** (til′də; *Spanish,* tēl′dā) 1 a diacritical mark (~) used over *n* in Spanish when it is pronounced *ny,* as in *cañon* (kä nyōn′). 2 the same mark, used over certain vowels in Portuguese to indicate that they are nasalized as in *São* (souɴ). The Portuguese name for this mark is **til.** *n.*

**tile** (tīl) 1 a thin piece of baked clay, stone, etc.: *Tiles are used for covering roofs and floors, and for ornamenting.* 2 a thin square of plastic, rubber, etc., used for surfacing floors, walls, or ceilings: *It took sixty tiles to cover the bathroom floor.* 3 a pipe for draining land. 4 tiles collectively: *We have tile on the ceiling of our classroom.* 5 put tiles on or in; cover with tile: *to tile a bathroom floor.* 6 covered with tile; made of tile; tiled: *There is a tile floor in the bathroom.* 7 *Informal.* a stiff hat; a high silk hat. 1–4, 6, 7 *n.,* 5 *v.,* **tiled, til·ing.**

**til·ing** (tī′ling) 1 tiles collectively. 2 the work of a person who tiles. 3 a surface or structure consisting of tiles. 4 *ppr.* of TILE. 1–3 *n.,* 4 *v.*

**till**¹ (til) 1 up to the time of; until: *The child played till eight.* 2 up to the time when; until: *Walk till you come to a white house.* 1 *prep.,* 2 *conj.*

**till**² (til) cultivate; plough, harrow, etc.: *Farmers till the land.* *v.* —**till′a·ble,** *adj.*

**till**³ (til) 1 a small drawer for money: *The till is under the counter.* 2 a cash register. 3 formerly, a drawer or tray for keeping valuables. *n.*

**till**⁴ (til) glacial drift composed of clay, stones, gravel, boulders, etc. mixed together. *n.*

**till·age** (til′ij) 1 the cultivation of land. 2 tilled land. *n.*

**till·er**¹ (til′ər) a bar or handle used to turn the rudder in steering a boat. See RUDDER for picture. *n.*

**till·er**² (til′ər) 1 a person who tills the land. 2 a machine for tilling; cultivator. *n.*

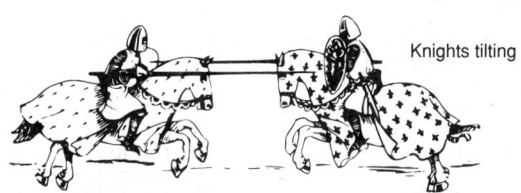

Knights tilting

**tilt** (tilt) 1 tip or cause to tip; slope; slant; lean: *You tilt your head forward when you bow. This table tilts.* 2 a slope; slant: *This table is on a tilt.* 3 rush, charge, or fight with lances: *Knights used to tilt on horseback.* 4 a fight on horseback with lances. 5 point or thrust a lance. 6 any dispute or quarrel. 7 a heavy, pivoted hammer. 8 forge or hammer with a heavy, pivoted hammer. 9 in

the Maritimes, a TEETER-TOTTER.   **10** in Newfoundland, a tent, shanty, or lean-to, especially one used as a temporary shelter.   *1, 3, 5, 8 v., 2, 4, 6, 7, 9, 10 n.*
**full tilt,**   at full speed; with full force: *Her car ran full tilt against the tree.*
**tilt at,**   attack; fight; protest against.
**tilt at windmills,**   attack imaginary enemies.

**tilth** (tilth)   **1** the cultivation of land.   **2** tilled land.   **3** the condition of tilled soil: *a garden in bad tilth.*   *n.*

**tim·bale** (tim′bəl)   **1** minced meat, fish, vegetables, etc. prepared with a sauce and cooked in a mould.   **2** a mould made of pastry.   *n.*

**tim·ber** (tim′bər)   **1** wood suitable for building and making things.   **2** a large squared piece of wood ready to use in building or forming part of a structure: *Beams and rafters are timbers.*   **3** a curved piece forming a rib of a ship.   **4** trees that are growing and suitable for cutting: *Half of their land is covered with timber.*   **5** cover, support, or furnish with timber.   *1–4 n., 5 v.*

**tim·bered** (tim′bərd)   **1** made or furnished with timber.   **2** covered with growing trees.   **3** pt. and pp. of TIMBER.   *1, 2 adj., 3 v.*

**timber hitch**   a knot used to fasten a rope around a spar, post, etc.   See KNOT for picture.

**tim·ber·ing** (tim′bə ring)   **1** building material of wood.   **2** timbers collectively.   **3** an arrangement or structure of timbers.   **4** ppr. of TIMBER.   *1–3 n., 4 v.*

**tim·ber·land** (tim′bər land′)   land with trees that are, or will be, useful for timber.   *n.*

**timber limit**   *Cdn.*   **1** TIMBERLINE.   **2** in logging, a tract of land in which a person or company has the right to fell trees and remove timber; concession.

**tim·ber·line** (tim′bər līn′)   a limit on mountains and in high latitudes beyond which trees will not grow because of climatic conditions such as extreme cold and strong winds: *In Canada, the country north of the timberline is called the Barrens.*   *n.*

**timber wolf**   *Cdn.*   a large, grey North American wolf, especially a subspecies found in the northern forests of Canada.   See WOLF for picture.

**tim·bre** (tim′bər *or* tam′bər; *French,* taNbR)   the quality in sounds that distinguishes a certain voice, instrument, etc. from other voices, instruments, etc.: *Notes of the same pitch and loudness may differ in timbre.*   *n.*

**tim·brel** (tim′brəl)   TAMBOURINE.   *n.*

**time** (tīm)   **1** all the days there have been or ever will be; the past, present, and future: *We measure time in years, months, days, hours, minutes, seconds, etc.*   **2** a part of time: *A minute is a short time.*   **3** a period of time; epoch: *the time of the Stuarts in England.*   **4** a long time: *What a time it took you!*   **5** some point in time; a particular point in time: *What time is it?*   **6** the right part or point of time: *It is time to eat.*   **7** an occasion: *This time we will succeed.*   **8** a way of reckoning time: *daylight-saving time.*   **9** amount of time: *I have some time for rest.*   **10** an experience during a certain time: *She had a good time at the party.*   **11** in music or poetry, a rate of movement; rhythm: *march time, waltz time, to beat time, to keep time.*   **12** in music, the length of a note or rest.   **13** the grouping of such notes into rhythmic beats, divided into bars or measures of equal length.   **14** the amount of time that one has worked or should work.   **15** the pay for this.   **16** leisure: *to have time to read.*   **17** measure the time of: *to time a race.*   **18** fix, set, or regulate the length of in time: *time an exposure correctly.*   **19** do in rhythm with; set the time of: *The dancers timed their steps to the music.*   **20** choose the moment or occasion for: *The demonstrators timed their march through the business section so that most shoppers would see them.*   **21** of or having to do with time.   **22** provided with a clocklike mechanism so that it will explode or ignite at a given moment: *a time bomb.*   **23** having to do with purchases to be paid for at a future date.   **24 times,** *pl.*   conditions of life: *War brings hard times.*   **25 times,** *pl.*   multiplied by: *Four times three is twelve.*   **26** multiplied instances: *five times as much.*   *1–16, 24, 26 n., 17–20 v.,* **timed, tim·ing;**   *21–23 adj., 25 prep.*

**against time,**   trying to finish before a certain time.
**at the same time,**   however; nevertheless.
**at times,**   now and then; once in a while.
**behind the times,**   old-fashioned; out-of-date.
**do** or **serve time,** *Informal.*   be imprisoned as a criminal: *a man doing time for bank robbery.*
**for the time being,**   for the present; for now.
**from time to time,**   now and then; once in a while: *From time to time we visited Uncle Jim's fruit farm.*
**in good time,**   **a** at the right time: *We reached the theatre in good time for the first act.*   **b** soon; quickly.
**in no time,**   shortly; before long.
**in time,**   **a** after a while.   **b** soon enough: *Will the groceries arrive in time to cook for supper?*   **c** in music, dancing, marching, etc. in the right rate of movement.
**keep time,**   **a** of a watch or clock, go correctly.   **b** sound or move at the right rate: *The marchers kept time to the martial music.*
**make time,**   go with speed.
**on time,**   **a** at the right time; not late.   **b** with time in which to pay; on credit: *She bought a car on time.*
**tell time,**   read the clock; tell what time it is by the clock.
**time after time** or **time and again,**   again and again.
**time out of mind,**   beyond memory or record.
☛ *Hom.* THYME.

**time bomb**   **1** a bomb equipped with a timing device, so that it can be set to explode at a certain moment.   **2** *Informal.*   a condition or situation leading to inevitable disaster, unless action can be taken to avert it.

**time capsule**   a container with documents and other items representative of the current civilization, that is buried or sealed into the cornerstone of a building, etc., to be discovered in a future age.

**time·card** (tīm′kärd′)   a card for recording the amount of time that a person works.   *n.*

**time clock**   a clock with a device to stamp an employee's time card with the time he or she arrives or leaves.

**time–con·sum·ing** (tīm′kən sü′ming *or* tīm′kən syü′ming)   taking up or requiring a great deal of time: *The calculations weren't hard, but they were time-consuming.*   *adj.*

**time exposure**   **1** the exposure of a photographic film for a certain time, usually longer than half a second.   **2** a photograph taken in this way.

**time fuse**   a fuse that will burn for a certain time.

**time–hon·oured** or **time–hon·ored** (tī′mon′ərd)   honoured because old and established: *a time-honoured custom.*   *adj.*

**time·keep·er** (tīm′kē′pər)   a measurer of time; a person or thing that keeps time: *The factory timekeeper* keeps account of the hours of work done. *My watch is an excellent timekeeper.* *n.*

**time–lapse photography** motion photography in which separate pictures are taken at intervals of a slow-moving object, such as a flower unfolding, and then projected at normal speed to give the illusion of speeded-up action.

**time·less** (tīm′lis) **1** never ending; eternal: *the timeless beauty of the Taj Mahal.* **2** referring to no special time. *adj.*

**time line** a usually long line marked with dates and events at approximate intervals, for use in teaching history.

**time·ly** (tīm′lē) at the right time: *The timely arrival of the police stopped the riot.* *adj.*, **time·li·er, time·li·est.** —**time′li·ness,** *n.*

**time·piece** (tīm′pēs′) a clock or watch. *n.*

**tim·er** (tī′mər) **1** a person or thing that times; TIMEKEEPER. **2** a device for indicating or recording intervals of time, such as a stop watch. **3** a clockwork device for indicating when a certain period of time has elapsed: *Many stoves have timers for baking.* **4** in an INTERNAL-COMBUSTION ENGINE, an automatic device that causes the spark for igniting the charge to occur just at the time required. *n.*

**time·sav·er** (tīm′sā′vər) a person or thing that saves time: *A pocket calculator can be a timesaver for mathematical problems.* *n.*

**time·sav·ing** (tīm′sā′ving) that saves time: *timesaving household appliances.* *adj.*

**time·serv·er** (tīm′sėr′vər) a person who for selfish purposes shapes his or her conduct to conform with the opinions of the time or of the person in power. *n.*

**time·serv·ing** (tīm′sėrv′ing) **1** the practice or behaviour of a TIMESERVER. **2** having or showing a lack of integrity or independent thinking: *a timeserving little wretch.* **1** *n.*, **2** *adj.*

**time·ta·ble** (tīm′tā′bəl) **1** a schedule showing the times when trains, buses, airplanes, or boats arrive and depart. **2** any list or schedule showing a planned sequence; especially, a list showing the times of different classes for students. *n.*

**time–test·ed** (tīm′tes′təd) having a value or effectiveness that has been proven over a long period of time: *a time-tested recipe for bread.* *adj.*

**time warp** a theoretical change in the nature of time, according to certain conditions in the universe.

**time·worn** (tīm′wôrn′) **1** worn by long existence or use: *They walked up the timeworn steps of the old house.* **2** worn out by use; trite: *a timeworn excuse.* *adj.*

The Canadian time zones

TIME ZONES: 1 PACIFIC STANDARD 2 MOUNTAIN STANDARD 3 CENTRAL STANDARD 4 EASTERN STANDARD 5 ATLANTIC STANDARD 5½ NEWFOUNDLAND STANDARD

**time zone** a geographical region within which the same standard of time is used. The world is divided into 24 time zones beginning and ending at the INTERNATIONAL DATE LINE.

**tim·id** (tim′id) **1** lacking courage or self-confidence; easily frightened: *He's a very timid person.* **2** showing lack of self-confidence or determination: *a timid voice, a timid excuse.* *adj.* —**tim′id·ly,** *adv.* —**tim′id·ness,** *n.*

**ti·mid·i·ty** (tə mid′ə tē) the quality of being timid: *Her timidity prevents her from asking questions.* *n.*

**tim·ing** (tī′ming) **1** the choice or regulation of the speed or the moment of occurrence of something so as to produce the best possible effect: *Her timing couldn't have been worse—she asked for the car just after her mother had discovered the mess in the living room. Timing is very important in a golf swing.* **2** the measurement and recording of time taken by an action or process: *Timing is often done with a stopwatch.* **3** ppr. of TIME. **1, 2** *n.*, **3** *v.*

**tim·or·ous** (tim′ə rəs) **1** easily frightened; timid: *a timorous child.* **2** marked or caused by fear or lack of self-confidence: *The puppy's timorous advances were ignored.* *adj.* —**tim′or·ous·ly,** *adv.* —**tim′or·ous·ness,** *n.*

**tim·o·thy** (tim′ə thē) a kind of coarse grass with long, cylindrical spikes, often grown for fodder. *n.*

**tim·pa·ni** (tim′pə nē′) a set of kettledrums played by one person in an orchestra or band. *n., pl.* of **tim·pa·no** (tim′pə nō′).

**tim·pa·nist** (tim′pə nist) a person who plays the kettledrums in an orchestra or band. *n.*

**tin** (tin) **1** a soft, silver-white metallic element used as a coating on other metals and in making alloys. *Symbol:* Sn **2** thin sheets of iron or steel coated with tin. **3** made of tin: *tin cans, a tin box.* **4** cover or plate with tin or a tin alloy. **5** any box, can, pan, or other container made of tin or tin plate: *Sardines are packed in tins.* **6** such a container together with its contents: *a tin of peas.* **7** any of various kinds of metal containers, especially pans used for baking: *a cake tin, a muffin tin.* **8** *Esp. Brit.* put up in tin cans or tin boxes; can. **1–3, 5–7** *n.*, **4, 8** *v.*, **tinned, tin·ning.**

**tinc·ture** (tingk′chər) **1** a solution of medicine in alcohol: *tincture of iodine.* **2** a trace or tinge of something. **3** give a trace or tinge to; affect slightly with a certain quality (*used with* **with**): *Everything he says is tinctured with conceit.* **4** a slight colour or flavour. **5** colour or flavour slightly. **1, 2, 4** *n.*, **3, 5** *v.*, **tinc·tured, tinc·tur·ing.**

**tin·der** (tin′dər) **1** anything that catches fire easily. **2** material used to catch fire from a spark: *Before matches were invented, people carried a box holding tinder, flint, and steel.* *n.*

**tin·der·box** (tin′dər boks′) **1** a box formerly used for holding tinder, flint, and steel for making a fire. **2** an object, structure, etc. that is highly flammable. **3** a situation or place likely to burst into conflict or violence of some kind. *n.*

**tine** (tīn) a sharp, projecting point or prong: *the tines of a fork.* *n.*

**tin foil** 1 very thin sheet of tin, aluminum, or an alloy of tin and lead, used for wrapping food products, for insulation, etc. 2 SILVER PAPER.

**ting** (ting) 1 a light, clear ringing sound, as that made by crystal goblets striking each other lightly. 2 make or cause to make such a sound: *The glass tinged when I touched it with the spoon.* 1 *n.*, 2 *v.*

**tinge** (tinj) 1 colour slightly: *A drop of ink will tinge a glass of water.* 2 a slight colouring or tint: *There is a tinge of red in her cheeks.* 3 add a trace of some quality to; change slightly: *Sad memories tinged their present joy.* 4 a very small amount; trace: *She likes just a tinge of lemon in her tea. There was a tinge of envy in his voice.* 1, 3 *v.*, **tinged, tinge·ing** or **ting·ing**; 2, 4 *n.*

**tin·gle** (ting′gəl) 1 have a pricking or stinging feeling, especially from excitement: *He tingled with delight on his first train trip.* 2 a pricking, stinging feeling: *The cold caused a tingle in my fingers.* 3 cause this feeling in: *Shame tingled his cheeks.* 4 be thrilling: *The newspaper story tingled with excitement.* 5 tinkle; jingle. 1, 3–5 *v.*, **tin·gled, tin·gling**; 2, 5 *n.*

**tink·er** (ting′kər) 1 a person who mends pots, pans, etc., usually one who travels from place to place to practise his or her trade. 2 work as a tinker. 3 work with, adjust, or repair in an unskilled or experimental way: *Someone has been tinkering with my bicycle. She likes to tinker with old radios and TV sets.* 4 work at or keep busy with in an irregular or purposeless way: *to tinker with a new idea.* 5 a clumsy or unskilful worker. 1, 5 *n.*, 2–4 *v.*

**tin·kle** (ting′kəl) 1 make short, light, ringing sounds: *Little bells tinkle.* 2 cause to tinkle: *The baby tinkled the little bell.* 3 a series of short, light, ringing sounds: *the tinkle of sleigh bells.* 4 indicate, make known, etc. by tinkling: *The little clock tinkled out the hours.* 1, 2, 4 *v.*, **tin·kled, tin·kling**; 3 *n.*

**tin·man** (tin′mən) TINSMITH. *n.*, *pl.* **tin·men** (-mən).

**tin·ner** (tin′ər) 1 a person who works in a tin mine; a tin miner. 2 TINSMITH. *n.*

**tin·ny** (tin′ē) 1 of or containing tin. 2 shrill or thin in sound: *a tinny voice, the tinny music of an old juke box.* 3 thin and cheap; of poor quality: *tinny cutlery, tinny jewellery.* 4 tasting of tin: *The salmon tastes tinny.* *adj.*, **tin·ni·er, tin·ni·est. —tin′ni·ness,** *n.*

**tin–pan alley** 1 a district or area of a city serving as a centre for composers and publishers of popular music. 2 the people concerned with writing and publishing popular music.

**tin plate** thin sheets of iron or steel coated with tin: *Ordinary tin cans are made of tin plate.*

**tin·sel** (tin′səl) 1 thin sheets, strips, or threads of a metallic substance, used to add glitter to cloth, yarn, or decorations. 2 something like tinsel; something showy and attractive, but not worth much. 3 decorate or trim with or as if with tinsel. 4 cloth woven with threads of gold, silver, or copper. 5 made of or decorated with tinsel. 6 showy but cheap; gaudy. 1, 2, 4–6 *n.*, 3 *v.*, **tin·selled** or **tin·seled, tin·sel·ling** or **tin·sel·ing. —tin′sel·like′,** *adj.*

**tin·smith** (tin′smith′) a person who works with tin or other light metal; maker of TINWARE. *n.*

**tint** (tint) 1 a variety of a colour, especially one mixed with white. 2 a suggestion of or tendency toward a different colour: *white with a bluish tint.* 3 a delicate or pale colour. 4 a preparation for colouring hair; dye. 5 put a tint on; colour: *to tint a black-and-white photograph, to tint one's hair.* 1–4 *n.*, 5 *v.*

**tin·type** (tin′tīp′) photograph taken on a sheet of enamelled tin or iron. *n.*

**tin·ware** (tin′wer′) articles made of or lined with tin. *n.*

**ti·ny** (tī′nē) very small; wee. *adj.*, **ti·ni·er, ti·ni·est.**

**–tion** a suffix meaning: 1 the act or process of _____ing: *Addition means the act or process of adding.* 2 the condition of being _____ed: *Exhaustion means the condition of being exhausted.* 3 the result of _____ing: *Reflection means the result of reflecting.*

**tip¹** (tip) 1 the end part; end; point: *the tips of the fingers.* 2 a small piece put on the end of something: *Buy rubber tips to put on the legs of the stool.* 3 put a tip on; furnish with a tip: *spears tipped with steel.* 4 cover or adorn at the tip: *mountains tipped with snow. Sunlight tips the steeple.* 1, 2 *n.*, 3, 4 *v.*, **tipped, tip·ping.**

**tip²** (tip) 1 slope; slant: *She tipped the table toward her.* 2 upset; overturn: *He tipped over the milk jug. We fell in the water when the canoe tipped.* 3 take off a hat in greeting: *Men used to tip their hats when meeting a lady.* 4 empty out; dump: *She tipped the contents of her purse out onto the table.* 5 a slope or slant: *There is such a tip to that table that everything slides off.* 1–4 *v.*, **tipped, tip·ping;** 5 *n.*

**tip³** (tip) 1 a small present of money in return for service: *He gave the waiter a tip.* 2 give a small present of money to: *She tipped the porter.* 3 give a tip: *He always tips too much.* 4 a piece of secret information: *Fred had a tip that the black horse would win the race.* 5 give secret information to. 6 a useful hint, suggestion, etc.: *a book of tips on caring for your pet.* 1, 4, 6 *n.*, 2, 3, 5 *v.*, **tipped, tip·ping.**
**tip off,** *Informal.* **a** give secret information to: *They tipped me off about a good bargain.* **b** warn: *Someone tipped off the criminal and he escaped before the police arrived.*

**tip⁴** (tip) 1 a light, sharp blow; tap. 2 hit lightly and sharply; tap. 1 *n.*, 2 *v.*, **tipped, tip·ping.**

**ti·pi** (tē′pē) See TEEPEE. *n.*

**tip–off** (tip′of′) *Informal.* 1 a piece of secret information. 2 warning. *n.*

Tippet (def. 2): a dress of the 12th century with tippets on the sleeves

**tip·pet** (tip′it) 1 a scarf for the neck and shoulders with ends hanging down in front. 2 a long, narrow, hanging part of a hood, sleeve, or scarf. *n.*

**tip·ple** (tip′əl) 1 drink alcoholic liquor often. 2 an alcoholic liquor. 1 *v.*, **tip·pled, tip·pling;** 2 *n.*

**tip·pler** (tip′lər) a habitual drinker of alcoholic liquor. *n.*

**tip·ster** (tip′stər) *Informal.* a person who makes a business of furnishing private or secret information for use in betting, speculation, etc. *n.*

**tip·sy** (tip′sē) 1 tipping easily; unsteady; tilted. 2 somewhat intoxicated but not thoroughly drunk. *adj.* **tip·si·er, tip·si·est.** —**tip′si·ly,** *adv.* —**tip′si·ness,** *n.*

**tip·toe** (tip′tō′) 1 the tips of the toes. 2 walk on one's toes, without using the heels: *She tiptoed quietly up the stairs.* 1 *n.*, 2 *v.*, **tip·toed, tip·toe·ing.** **on tiptoe,** **a** walking on one's toes. **b** eager: *The children were on tiptoe for vacation to begin.* **c** in a silent or stealthy manner: *He crossed the room on tiptoe to avoid waking her.*

**tip·top** (tip′top′) 1 the very top; highest point. 2 at the very top or highest point. 3 *Informal.* first-rate; excellent: *The car is in tiptop shape.* 1 *n.*, 2, 3 *adj.*

**ti·rade** (tī′rād *or* tə rād′) a long, vehement, usually scolding, speech. *n.*

**tire**[1] (tīr) 1 lower or use up the strength of; make weary: *The hard work tired him.* 2 become weary: *He tires easily.* 3 wear down the patience, interest, or appreciation of: *Dull filing jobs tired the office boy.* *v.*, **tired, tir·ing.**
**tire out,** make very weary.

**tire**[2] (tīr) 1 a circular tube made of cord and rubber or similar synthetic material and filled with air for placing around the wheel of a car, plane, bicycle, etc.: *Some tires have inner tubes; others are tubeless.* See WHEEL for picture. 2 a band of rubber or metal around a wheel: *We had a bumpy ride on a wagon with steel tires.* 3 furnish with a tire. 1, 2 *n.*, 3 *v.*, **tired, tir·ing.**

**tired**[1] (tīrd) 1 weary; wearied; exhausted: *I am tired, but I must get back to work.* 2 pt. and pp. of TIRE. 1 *adj.*, 2 *v.* —**tired′ly,** *adv.* —**tired′ness,** *n.*
**tired of,** no longer interested in; bored with: *I'm tired of hearing about their holidays.*

**tired**[2] (tīrd) having tires: *a rubber-tired vehicle.* *adj.*

**tire·less**[1] (tīr′lis) 1 never becoming tired; requiring little rest: *a tireless worker.* 2 never stopping: *tireless efforts.* *adj.* —**tire′less·ly,** *adv.* —**tire′less·ness,** *n.*

**tire·less**[2] (tīr′lis) having no tire or tires. *adj.*

**tire·some** (tīr′səm) tiring, because boring: *a tiresome speech.* *adj.* —**tire′some·ly,** *adv.* —**tire′some·ness,** *n.*

**ti·ro** (tī′rō) See TYRO. *n., pl.* **ti·ros.**

**Ti·ro·le·an** (tə rō′lē ən *or* tir′ə lē′ən) See TYROLEAN. *adj., n.*

**Ti·ro·lese** (tir′ə lēz′) See TYROLESE. *adj., n.*

**Tir·than·ka·ra** (tir tung′kə rə) any of the twenty-four venerated prophets and teachers in Jain belief. *n.*

**'tis** (tiz) it is.

**tis·sue** (tish′ü) 1 a mass of similar cells that together form some part of an animal or a plant: *muscle tissue, skin tissue.* 2 a thin, light cloth. 3 a web; network: *Her whole story was a tissue of lies.* 4 TISSUE PAPER. 5 a thin, soft paper that absorbs moisture easily: *toilet tissue,*

hat, āge, fär; let, ēqual, tėrm; it, īce
hot, ōpen, ôrder; oil, out; cup, pùt, rüle
above, takən, pencəl, lemən, circəs
ch, child; ng, long; sh, ship
th, thin; ᴛʜ, then; zh, measure

*cleansing tissue.* 6 a piece or a sheet of this paper: *There are 450 tissues in each box.* *n.*

**tissue paper** a very thin, soft paper used mainly for wrapping.

**tit**[1] (tit) any of various small birds, especially a titmouse. *n.*

**tit**[2] (tit) a nipple; teat. *n.*

**ti·tan** (tī′tən) 1 a person or thing of great size, power, or strength. 2 having great size, strength, or power; titanic. *n.*

**ti·tan·ic** (tī tan′ik) having or showing great size, strength, or power; colossal: *titanic energy.* *adj.*

**ti·ta·ni·um** (tī tā′nē əm) a light, silvery or grey metallic element occurring in various minerals. Symbol: Ti *n.*

**tit·bit** (tit′bit′) TIDBIT. *n.*

**tit for tat** blow for blow; like for like.

**tithe** (tīᴛʜ) 1 one tenth. 2 a tax or a donation of one tenth of the yearly produce of land, animals, and personal work, given for the support of the church and the clergy. 3 put a tax, or levy, of a tenth on. 4 pay a tithe on. 5 give one tenth of one's income to the church or to charity. 6 a very small part. 7 any small tax, levy, etc. 1, 2, 6, 7 *n.*, 3–5 *v.*, **tithed, tith·ing.**

**ti·tian** (tish′ən) auburn; golden red. *n., adj.*

**tit·il·late** (tit′ə lāt′) 1 excite pleasantly; stimulate agreeably. 2 TICKLE. *v.*, **tit·il·lat·ed, tit·il·lat·ing.**

**tit·il·la·tion** (tit′ə lā′shən) 1 pleasant excitement; agreeable stimulation. 2 a tickling. *n.*

**tit·i·vate** *or* **tit·ti·vate** (tit′ə vāt′) *Informal.* dress up; make smart; spruce up. *v.*, **tit·i·vat·ed** *or* **tit·ti·vat·ed, tit·i·vat·ing** *or* **tit·ti·vat·ing.** —**tit′i·va′tion** *or* **tit′ti·va′tion,** *n.*

**tit·lark** (tit′lärk′) PIPIT. *n.*

**ti·tle** (tī′təl) 1 the name of a book, poem, picture, song, etc. 2 a person's name showing rank, occupation, or condition in life. *Examples:* King, Duke, Lord, Countess, Captain, Doctor, Professor, Madame, and Miss. 3 call by a title; name. 4 a first-class position; championship: *the tennis title.* 5 a book; volume: *There are 5000 titles in our library.* 6 the legal right to the possession of property: *When a house is sold, the seller gives title to the buyer.* 7 the evidence showing such a right. 8 a recognized right; claim. 1, 2, 4–8 *n.*, 3 *v.*, **ti·tled, ti·tling.**

**ti·tled** (tī′təld) 1 having a title, such as that of a Duke, Countess, Lord, Dame, etc.: *She married a titled diplomat.* 2 pt. and pp. of TITLE. 1 *adj.*, 2 *v.*

**title page** the page at the beginning of a book that contains the title, the author's name, etc.

**tit·mouse** (tit′mous′) any of certain small birds having short bills and dull-coloured feathers: *A chickadee is one kind of titmouse.* *n., pl.* **tit·mice.**

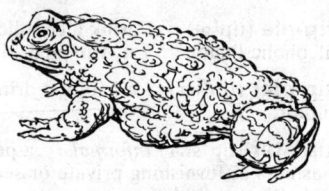
A common toad—
usually about 9 cm long

**ti·trate** (tī′trāt)  **1** find the strength of an acid or base solution by TITRATION.  **2** be subjected to TITRATION. *v.*, **ti·trat·ed, ti·trat·ing.**

**ti·tra·tion** (tī trā′shən)  the process of determining the amount of some substance present in a solution by measuring the amount of a different substance that must be added to cause a chemical change.  *n.*

**tit·ter** (tit′ər)  **1** laugh or giggle in a partly checked way: *Some people in the audience tittered nervously when the actor forgot his lines.*  **2** such a laugh or giggle: *A titter ran through the classroom.*  **3** say with such a laugh or giggle: *"He's got his sweater on inside out," she tittered.*  1, 3 *v.*, 2 *n.* —**tit′ter·er,** *n.*

**tit·tle** (tit′əl)  **1** a very little bit; particle; whit.  **2** in writing or printing, a small stroke or mark over a letter. The dot over an *i* is a tittle.  *n.*

**tit·tle-tat·tle** (tit′əl tat′əl)  GOSSIP.  *n., v.*, **tit·tle-tat·tled, tit·tle-tat·tling.**

**tit·u·lar** (tich′ə lər)  **1** in title or name only: *He is a titular prince without any power.*  **2** having a title; titled.  **3** having to do with a title.  *adj.* —**tit′u·lar·ly,** *adv.*

**TKO, T.K.O.,** or **t.k.o.**  technical knockout.

**Tl**  thallium.

**Tlin·git** (tling′git)  **1** a member of a group of First Nations peoples of the northern Pacific coast.  **2** the group of Athapascan languages spoken by these peoples.  **3** of or having to do with the Tlingit or their languages.  1, 2 *n.*, *pl.* (*for def. 1*) **Tlin·git** or **Tlin·gits;**  3 *adj.*

**Tm**  thulium.

**tn.**  ton; tons.

**Tn**  thoron.

**T.N.T.** or **TNT**  a colourless solid used as an explosive; trinitrotoluene.

**to** (tü; *unstressed,* tu̇ *or* tə)  **1** in the direction of: *Go to the right.*  **2** as far as; until: *rotten to the core, faithful to the end.*  **3** for; for the purpose of: *She came to the rescue.*  **4** toward or into the position, condition, or state of: *He went to sleep.*  **5** so as to produce, cause, or result in: *To her horror, the beast approached.*  **6** into: *She tore the letter to pieces.*  **7** along with; with: *We danced to the music.*  **8** compared with: *Those dogs are as different as black is to white. The score was 9 to 5.*  **9** in agreement or accordance with: *It is not to my liking.*  **10** belonging with; of: *the key to my room.*  **11** in honour of: *Drink to the king.*  **12** on; against: *Fasten it to the wall.*  **13** about; concerning: *What did she say to that?*  **14** included, contained, or involved in: *seven apples to the kilogram.*  **15 To** is used to show action toward: *Give the book to me. Speak to her.*  **16 To** is used with some infinitive forms of verbs: *He likes to read. The birds began to sing. "To err is human; to forgive, divine."*  **17** forward: *He wore his cap wrong side to.*  **18** together; touching; closed: *The door slammed to.*  **19** to action or work: *We turned to gladly.*  **20** to consciousness: *She came to.*  1–16 *prep.*, 17–20 *adv.*
**to and fro,**  first one way and then back again; back and forth.
☞ *Hom.* TOO, TWO.

**toad** (tōd)  **1** any of numerous small amphibians resembling frogs, but living mostly on land and having a more squat body, weaker hind legs, and rough, dry, often warty skin: *Toads return to water to breed.*  **2** a contemptible or disgusting person.  *n.*
☞ *Hom.* TOED.

**toad·fish** (tōd′fish′)  any of various related saltwater fishes having a thick head, a wide mouth, and slimy skin without scales.  *n.*

**toad·flax** (tōd′flaks′)  any of several closely related plants of the same family as the snapdragon: *The common toadflax has yellow-and-orange flowers.*  *n.*

**toad·stool** (tōd′stül′)  a mushroom, especially a poisonous mushroom.  *n.*

**toad·y** (tō′dē)  **1** a fawning flatterer.  **2** act like a toady; fawn upon; flatter.  1 *n.*, *pl.* **toad·ies;**  2 *v.*, **toad·ied, toad·y·ing.**

**toad·y·ism** (tō′dē iz′əm)  the action or behaviour of a TOADY; interested flattery; mean servility.  *n.*

**toast**[1] (tōst)  **1** a slice or slices of bread browned by heat.  **2** brown by heat.  **3** heat thoroughly: *He toasted his feet by the fire.*  1 *n.*, 2, 3 *v.* —**toast′er,** *n.*
☞ *Etym.* Through OF *toster* from L *tostus*, past participle of *torrere* 'parch'.

**toast**[2] (tōst)  **1** take a drink and wish good fortune to; drink to the health of: *The men toasted the general.*  **2** a person or thing whose health is proposed and drunk: *"The Queen" was the first toast drunk by the officers.*  **3** a person having many admirers: *She was the toast of the town.*  **4** the act of drinking to the health of a person or thing.  1 *v.*, 2–4 *n.* —**toast′er,** *n.*
☞ *Etym.* Applied in the early 17c. to a lady whose health was drunk. Saying her name was supposed to add to the drink as much flavour as did the spiced toast that was often added to hot wine.

**toast·er** (tō′stər)  an appliance for toasting bread.  *n.*

**toast·mas·ter** (tōst′mas′tər)  **1** a person who presides at a dinner and introduces the speakers.  **2** a person who proposes toasts.  *n.*

**to·bac·co** (tə bak′ō)  **1** the prepared leaves of a cultivated plant of the nightshade family, used for smoking or chewing or as snuff.  **2** the products from such leaves: *Does this store sell tobacco?*  **3** the practice of using tobacco for smoking, etc.: *She has sworn off tobacco.*  **4** any of a closely related group of plants including the plant cultivated for its leaves and several other species grown for their sweet-smelling flowers.  *n., pl.* **to·bac·cos** or **to·bac·coes.**

**to·bac·co·nist** (tə bak′ə nist)  a dealer in TOBACCO.  *n.*

**To·ba·go·ni·an** (tob′ā go′nē ən)  **1** a native or inhabitant of Tobago, an island in the West Indies.  **2** of or having to do with Tobago.  1 *n.*, 2 *adj.*

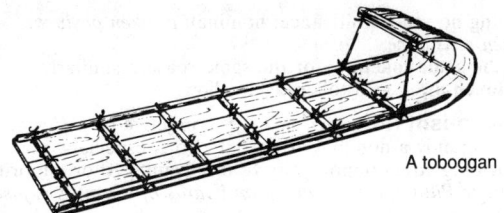

A toboggan

**to·bog·gan** (tə bog′ən) *Cdn.* **1** a long, light, narrow sleigh with a flat bottom and no runners, and having the front end curved up and back. **2** ride or carry on a toboggan: *We went tobogganing yesterday. The supplies were tobogganed to camp.* **3** decline sharply and rapidly in value: *House prices tobogganed.* **1** *n.,* **2, 3** *v.*
☛ *Etym.* Through Cdn. F *tabagane* from an Algonquian word, such as Micmac *tobakun* 'handsled'. 19c.

**to·by** or **To·by** (tō′bē) a small jug or mug in the form of a fat man wearing a long coat and a three-cornered hat. *n., pl.* **to·bies** or **To·bies**.

**toc·sin** (tok′sən) **1** an alarm sounded on a bell; a warning signal. **2** a bell used to sound an alarm. *n.*

**to·day** (tə dā′) **1** on or during this day: *I have to go to the dentist today.* **2** the present day, time, or period: *The photographer of today has many types of camera to choose from.* **3** at the present time or period; these days: *Most Canadian homes today have a refrigerator.* **1, 3** *adv.,* **2** *n.*

**tod·dle** (tod′əl) **1** walk with short, unsteady steps, as a baby does. **2** a toddling way of walking. **1** *v.,* **tod·dled, tod·dling;** **2** *n.*

**tod·dler** (tod′lər) a young child, especially one between the ages of one and two or three. *n.*

**tod·dy** (tod′ē) **1** the fresh or fermented sap of various palm trees, especially of the East Indies. **2** a usually hot drink made of an alcoholic liquor such as whisky or brandy mixed with water, sugar, and spices. *n., pl.* **tod·dies**.

**to-do** (tə dü′) *Informal.* a fuss; flurry; excitement: *There was a great to-do when the new puppy arrived.* *n., pl.* **to-dos**.

**toe** (tō) **1** one of the five end parts of the foot. **2** the part of a stocking, shoe, etc. that covers the toes. **3** the forepart of a foot or hoof. **4** anything like a toe: *the toe and heel of a golf club.* **5** touch or reach with the toes: *to toe a line.* **6** turn the toes in walking, standing, etc.: *to toe in, to toe out.* **7** furnish with a toe or toes. **8** drive a nail slantwise. **9** fasten by nails driven slantwise. **1–4** *n.,* **5–9** *v.,* **toed, toe·ing.** —**toe′less,** *adj.*
**on one's toes,** ready for action, alert.
**toe in,** adjust the front wheels of an automobile, etc. so that they point forward and slightly inward.
**toe the line, a** have one's toes on the starting line of a race. **b** obey rules, conform to a doctrine, etc. strictly.
☛ *Hom.* TOW.

**toed** (tōd) **1** having a certain number or kind of toes (used only in compounds): *square-toed shoes. The camel is a two-toed animal.* **2** of a nail, driven slantwise. **3** fastened by nails driven slantwise. *adj.*
☛ *Hom.* TOAD.

**toe·hold** (tō′hōld′) **1** a small place of support for the toes when climbing: *The climber cut toeholds in the glacier as she went.* **2** any means of support in progressing, especially at the start of a venture, etc.: *She opened a small neighbourhood store to get a toehold in the business.* **3** in wrestling, a hold in which an opponent's foot is bent back or twisted. *n.*

hat, āge, fär; let, ēqual, tėrm; it, īce hot, ōpen, ôrder; oil, out; cup, put, rüle
əbove, takən, pencəl, lemən, circəs
ch, child; ng, long; sh, ship
th, thin; ᴛʜ, then; zh, measure

**toe·nail** (tō′nāl′) **1** the nail growing on a toe. **2** in carpentry, a nail driven slantwise. *n.*

**toe rubber** a very low rubber overshoe worn by men, covering only the toe, heel, and the sole of the shoe.

**tof·fee** (tof′ē) a hard, chewy candy; taffy. *n., pl.* **tof·fees**.

**tog** (tog) **1** a garment. **2** clothe; dress. **3** **togs,** *pl. Informal.* clothes. **1, 3** *n.,* **2** *v.,* **togged, tog·ging.**

A Roman toga of the first century A.D.

**to·ga** (tō′gə) **1** in ancient Rome, the loose flowing outer garment worn by citizens: *A toga was made of a single piece of cloth with no sleeves or armholes, covering the whole body except for the right arm.* **2** a robe of office. *n., pl.* **to·gas** or **to·gae** (-jē).

**to·geth·er** (tə geᴛʜ′ər) **1** in company or association; with each other: *They walked down the road together. I like navy and red together. They worked together for many years.* **2** in or into one unit, mass, piece, etc.: *She mixed the two colours together.* **3** considered as a whole: *All the dimes and nickels together don't even make up three dollars. All together, there were 25 people at the party.* **4** into one gathering, company, or collection: *They get together every Friday to play bridge.* **5** at the same time: *Day and night cannot occur together.* **6** without a stop or break; continuously: *He worked for days together.* *adv.*
**together with,** along with.
☛ *Usage.* **Together with.** In formal writing a singular subject followed by 'together with———' still takes a singular verb: *My aunt, together with my two cousins, was there to meet me.* Compare this with: *My aunt and my two cousins were there to meet me.*

**to·geth·er·ness** (tə geᴛʜ′ər nis) the condition of being closely associated or united, especially in family or social activities. *n.*

**tog·ger·y** (tog′ə rē) *Informal.* **1** garments; clothes. **2** a clothing store. *n.*

**tog·gle** (tog′əl) **1** a pin, bolt, or rod put through the eye of a rope or the link of a chain to keep it in place, to hold two ropes together, to serve as a hold for the fingers, etc. **2** an oblong piece that is attached crosswise by its centre and is passed through a loop or hole to act as a fastening for a coat, etc. **3** a toggle joint, or a device furnished with one. **4** fasten or furnish with a toggle or toggles. **1–3** *n.,* **4** *v.,* **tog·gled, tog·gling.**

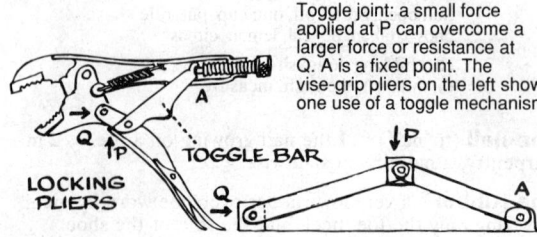

Toggle joint: a small force applied at P can overcome a larger force or resistance at Q. A is a fixed point. The vise-grip pliers on the left show one use of a toggle mechanism.

**toggle joint** a knee-like joint that transmits pressure at right angles.

**toggle switch** an electric switch having a projecting lever that is pushed through a small arc to open or close the circuit.

**toil¹** (toil) **1** hard work; labour: *to succeed finally after years of toil.* **2** work hard: *to toil with one's hands for a living.* **3** move with difficulty, pain, or weariness: *They toiled up the hill.* 1 *n.*, 2, 3 *v.* —**toil′er**, *n.*

**toil²** (toil) a net for trapping game. *Archaic except in* **toils,** *pl.* anything that holds one fast; a snare or trap: *caught in the toils of the law. n.*

**toi·let** (toi′lit) **1** a fixture, usually a porcelain bowl flushed by water, into which to pass waste matter from the body. **2** a room containing a toilet. **3** for a toilet: *a toilet brush.* **4** the act or process of washing, dressing, and grooming oneself: *She took an hour to complete her toilet.* **5** of or for use in the process of dressing and grooming: *Combs and brushes are toilet articles. n.*
**go to the toilet,** *Informal.* urinate or defecate: *The child said he had to go to the toilet.*

**toilet paper** thin, soft, absorbent paper for use in a toilet, especially after passing waste matter.

**toi·let·ry** (toi′li trē) Usually, **toiletries,** *pl.* soap, face powder, perfume or cologne, shaving cream, etc. used in washing and grooming oneself. *n.*

**toilet soap** mild soap that is usually perfumed and coloured.

**toi·lette** (toi let′; *French,* twä let′) **1** the process of washing, dressing, and grooming oneself. **2** fashionable attire or costume. *n.*

**toilet tissue** TOILET PAPER.

**toi·let–train·ing** (toi′lət trā′ning) the process of training a child to control bladder and bowel movements and to use a toilet. *n.* —**toi′let-train′**, *v.*

**toilet water** a fragrant liquid not so strong as perfume.

**toil·some** (toil′səm) requiring hard work; laborious; wearisome. *adj.*

**toil·worn** (toil′wôrn′) worn by toil; showing the effects of toil: *toilworn hands. adj.*

**to·ken** (tō′kən) **1** a mark or sign: *Black is a token of mourning in most Western societies.* **2** a sign of friendship; keepsake: *She received many birthday tokens.* **3** a piece of metal, plastic, etc. stamped for a higher value than that of the material: *Tokens are used on some buses and trains instead of money.* **4** a piece of metal, plastic, etc. indicating a right or privilege: *This token will admit you to the swimming pool.* **5** something that is a sign of genuineness or authority. **6** serving only as a symbol; having no real significance; nominal: *a token payment, token resistance. n.*
**by the same token,** for the same reason; similarly.
**in token of,** as a token of; to show.

**to·ken·ism** (tō′kə niz′əm) the practice or policy of making only a nominal or partial effort, especially in providing equal opportunity to disadvantaged or minority groups: *Putting a few women on boards of directors is just tokenism. n.*

**told** (tōld) pt. and pp. of TELL: *You told me that last week. We were told to wait. v.*
**all told,** including all.

**tol·er·a·ble** (tol′ər ə bəl) **1** that can be endured: *The pain has not disappeared, but it has become tolerable.* **2** fairly good: *She is in tolerable health. adj.*
—**tol′er·a·ble·ness,** *n.* —**tol′er·a·bly,** *adv.*

**tol·er·ance** (tol′ə rəns) **1** a willingness to be tolerant and patient toward people whose opinions or ways differ from one's own. **2** the power of enduring or resisting the action of a drug, poison, etc. **3** the action of tolerating: *His tolerance of their bad behaviour surprised us.* **4** an allowed amount of variation from a standard, as in the mass of coins or the dimensions of a machine or part. *n.*

**tol·er·ant** (tol′ə rənt) **1** willing to let other people do as they think best; willing to allow beliefs and actions of which one does not approve: *A more tolerant person would not have walked out in the middle of the meeting.* **2** easy-going; not readily saying no: *The teacher was tolerant toward the high-spirited children.* **3** able to endure or resist the action of a drug, poison, etc. *adj.*
—**tol′er·ant·ly,** *adv.*

**tol·er·ate** (tol′ə rāt′) **1** allow; permit: *He was an informal teacher, but would never tolerate insolence.* **2** bear; endure; put up with: *They tolerated the grouchy old man only because he was their employer.* **3** endure or resist the action of a drug, poison, etc. *v.,* **tol·er·at·ed, tol·er·at·ing.**

**tol·er·a·tion** (tol′ə rā′shən) **1** the act or practice of tolerating. **2** the recognition of a person's right to worship as he or she thinks best without loss of civil rights or social privileges; freedom of worship. *n.*

**toll¹** (tōl) **1** sound a church bell, etc. with single strokes slowly and regularly repeated: *Bells were tolled all over the country at the king's death.* **2** of a bell, sound with slow, single strokes: *The bell tolled.* **3** the stroke or sound of a bell being tolled. **4** the act or fact of tolling. **5** call, announce, etc. by tolling: *The bells tolled the death of the king.* 1, 2, 5 *v.,* 3, 4 *n.*

**toll²** (tōl) **1** a tax or fee paid for some right or privilege: *We pay a toll when we use the bridge.* **2** a charge for a certain service: *There is a toll on long-distance telephone calls.* **3** something paid, lost, suffered, etc.: *Automobile accidents take a heavy toll of human lives. n.*

**toll bar** a barrier, especially a gate, across a road or bridge where toll is taken.

**toll bridge** a bridge at which a toll is charged.

**toll call** a long-distance telephone call.

**toll·gate** (tōl′gāt′) a gate where toll is collected. *n.*

**toll·keep·er** (tōl′kē′pər) a person who collects the toll at a tollgate. *n.*

**toll road** a road on which tolls are charged; turnpike.

**tol·u·ene** (tol′yü ēn′) a colourless liquid hydrocarbon resembling benzene and obtained from coal tar and coal gas: *Toluene is used as a solvent and for making explosives and dyes.* *n.*

**tol·u·ol** (tol′yü ōl′) a commercial grade of TOLUENE. *n.*

**tom** (tom) the male of some animals; male: *a tom turkey. This cat is a tom.* *n.*

**tom·a·hawk** (tom′ə hok′) **1** a light axe used by many First Nations and Native American peoples, as a weapon and as a tool. **2** strike or kill with a tomahawk. **1** *n.*, **2** *v.*
**bury the tomahawk,** stop fighting; make peace.

**to·ma·to** (tə mā′tō, tə mä′tō, *or* tə mat′ō) **1** a juicy, pulpy, red or yellow fruit commonly eaten as a vegetable, either raw or cooked. **2** the widely cultivated annual plant this fruit grows on, having hairy leaves and stems and small, yellow flowers. *n., pl.* **to·ma·toes.**

**tomb** (tüm) **1** a vault or chamber for the dead, often built partly or completely above ground. **2** a grave. **3** a monument or tombstone to commemorate the dead. **4 the tomb,** death. *n.*

**tom·boy** (tom′boi′) a girl who is more active and enjoys rougher games than most girls. *n.*

**tomb·stone** (tüm′stōn′) a stone that marks a tomb or grave. *n.*

**tom·cat** (tom′kat′) a male cat. *n.*

**tom·cod** (tom′kod′) *Cdn.* any of several small, closely related saltwater fishes resembling and related to the cod. Also, **tommy cod.** *n.*

**tome** (tōm) a book, especially a large and scholarly book. *n.*

**tom·fool** (tom′fül′) **1** a silly fool; stupid person. **2** very stupid or foolish: *That was a tomfool thing to do.* **1** *n.*, **2** *adj.*

**tom·fool·er·y** (tom′fü′lə rē) silly behaviour; nonsense. *n., pl.* **tom·fool·er·ies.**

**Tom·my** *or* **tom·my** (tom′ē) a nickname for a British soldier. *n., pl.* **Tom·mies** *or* **tom·mies.**

**tommy cod** *Cdn.* TOMCOD.

**to·mor·row** (tə mô′rō) **1** the day after today: *You'll have to wait until tomorrow.* **2** on the day after today: *We're going fishing tomorrow.* **3** the indefinite future: *the world of tomorrow.* **1, 3** *n.*, **2** *adv.*

**Tom Thumb** **1** in the children's story, a dwarf no bigger than his father's thumb. **2** any very small thing or person.

**tom·tit** (tom′tit′) *Esp. Brit.* any of various small birds, especially a TITMOUSE. *n.*

**tom–tom** (tom′tom′) a usually long, narrow drum beaten with the hands; especially, any of various such drums of India or Africa. *n.*
☛ *Etym.* From Hindi *tam-tam*; the drum was probably named for its sound.

**ton** (tun) **1** either of two formerly standard units for measuring mass: the **short ton,** used in Canada, the United States, etc., equal to 2000 pounds (about 907 kg) and the **long ton,** used in the United Kingdom, equal to 2240 pounds (about 1016 kg). **2** a unit for measuring the internal capacity of a ship, equal to 100 cubic feet (about 2.8 m³); in full, **register ton.** **3** a unit for measuring the cargo or carrying capacity of a ship, equal to 40 cubic feet (about 1.1 m³); in full, **freight ton** or **measurement ton.** **4** a unit for measuring the amount of water a ship will displace, equal to 35 cubic feet (about 1 m³), which is

---

toluol    **1257**    tongue

hat, āge, fär; let, ēqual, tėrm; it, īce
hot, ōpen, ôrder; oil, out; cup, pùt, rüle
əbove, takən, pencəl, lemən, circəs
ch, child; ng, long; sh, ship
th, thin; ᴛʜ, then; zh, measure

approximately equal to a long ton mass of sea water; in full, **displacement ton.** **5** *Informal.* a very large number or amount: *These books weigh a ton. She's got tons of records.* *n.*
☛ *Hom.* TONNE, TUN.

**ton·al** (tō′nəl) **1** of or having to do with tones or tone. **2** characterized by TONALITY: *tonal music.* *adj.*

**to·nal·i·ty** (tō nal′ə tē) **1** in music: **a** the relations existing between the tones that make up a scale or musical system. **b** a particular arrangement of tones in a scale or musical system; key. **2** in painting, etc., the overall tone or colour scheme of a picture: *The colours in the painting are sombre, but the tonality is good.* *n., pl.* **to·nal·i·ties.**

**ton·al·ly** (tō′nə lē) with respect to tone. *adv.*

**tone** (tōn) **1** any sound considered with reference to its quality, pitch, strength, source, etc.: *sweet, shrill, or loud tones.* **2** the quality of sound: *a voice silvery in tone.* **3** in music: **a** a sound of definite pitch and character. **b** the difference in pitch between two notes: *C and D are one tone apart.* **4** a manner of speaking or writing: *We disliked the haughty tone of her letter.* **5** spirit; character; style: *a tone of elegance.* **6** a normal, healthy condition; vigour. **7** the effect of colour and of light and shade in a picture: *I like the soft green tone of that painting.* **8** a shade of colour: *tones of brown.* **9** harmonize: *This rug tones in well with the wallpaper.* **10** give a tone to. **11** change the tone of. **1–8** *n.*, **9–11** *v.*, **toned, ton·ing.**
**tone down,** soften: *Tone down your voice. Tone down the colours in that painting.*
**tone up,** give more sound, colour, or vigour to; strengthen: *Bright curtains would tone up this dull room.*

**tone arm** the part of a record player that carries the pickup and needle: *The tone arm moves on a pivot.*

**tone block** one of a set of tuned percussion instruments, consisting of shaped wooden pieces struck with a mallet.

**tone–deaf** (tōn′def′) not able to distinguish differences in musical pitch accurately. *adj.*

**tone·less** (tōn′ləs) lacking in expression or variation of tone: *She spoke in a toneless voice.* *adj.*
—**tone′less·ly,** *adv.* —**tone′less·ness,** *n.*

**to·nette** (tō net′) a simple flutelike instrument having easy finger guides and a range slightly more than an octave, used for basic education in music. *n.*

**tong** (tong) **1** in China, an association or club. **2** a secret organization or club in North American Chinese communities. *n.*

**tongs** (tongz) a tool for seizing, holding, or lifting, usually consisting of two long arms joined like a pair of scissors, or by a spring piece: *Fire tongs are used for placing logs in a fireplace.* *n.pl.*

**tongue** (tung) **1** the movable fleshy organ in the mouth of human beings and most vertebrates: *The tongue*

is used in tasting and, by people, for talking. See WINDPIPE for picture. **2** an animal's tongue used as food. **3** the power of speech: *Have you lost your tongue?* **4** a way of speaking; speech; talk: *a flattering tongue.* **5** the language of a people: *the English tongue.* **6** something shaped or used like a tongue. **7** the strip of material under the laces of a shoe. **8** a narrow strip of land running out into water. **9** a tapering jet of flame: *Tongues of flame leaped from the fire.* **10** the pin of a buckle, brooch, etc. **11** the pole by which a team of horses draws a wagon. **12** a projecting strip along the edge of a board for fitting into a groove of another board. **13** the pointer of a dial, balance, etc. **14** in a bell, the movable piece that strikes and rings the outer part. **15** a vibrating reed or the like in a musical instrument. **16** the short movable rail of a railway switch. **17** modify tones of a flute, cornet, etc. with the tongue. **18** use the tongue. *1–16 n., 17, 18 v.,* **tongued, tongu·ing.**
**give tongue,** of hounds, etc., bark or bay.
**hold one's tongue,** keep silent.
**on the tip of one's tongue, a** on the verge of being remembered. **b** ready to be spoken.

**tongue–and–groove joint** (tung′ən grüv′) in carpentry, a joint made by fitting a projecting strip, or tongue, along one edge of a board into a groove in another board. See JOINT for picture.

**tongue–in–cheek** (tung′in chēk′) meant to be ironic or joking: *a tongue-in-cheek criticism. adj.*

**tongue–lash·ing** (tung′lash′ing) a severe scolding: *Her mother gave her a tongue-lashing for letting her ice cream drip all over the carpet. n.* —**tongue-′lash,** *v.*

**tongue–tied** (tung′tīd′) **1** unable to speak because of shyness or embarrassment. **2** having the motion of the tongue hindered or limited because the membrane that connects its lower side to the bottom of the mouth is abnormally short. *adj.*

**tongue twister** a phrase or sentence having a sequence of similar consonants or consonant groups that is difficult to say quickly without getting the sounds mixed up. *Example: She sells sea shells on the seashore.*

**ton·ic** (ton′ik) **1** anything that gives strength; a medicine to give strength: *Cod-liver oil is a tonic.* **2** restoring to health and vigour; giving strength; bracing: *The mountain air is tonic.* **3** characterized by continuous contraction of the muscles: *a tonic convulsion.* **4** in music, the first note of a scale; keynote. **5** in music, having to do with a tone or tones. **6** of or based on a keynote. **7** having to do with tone or accent in speaking. **8** TONIC WATER: *gin and tonic.* *1, 4, 8 n., 2, 3, 5–7 adj.*

**to·nic·i·ty** (tō nis′ə tē) **1** a tonic quality or condition. **2** the property of possessing bodily tone; the normal elastic tension of muscles, arteries, etc. *n.*

**tonic water** a type of flavoured carbonated water.

**to·night** (tə nīt′) **1** on or during the present or the coming night or evening: *I want to get to bed early tonight. She is coming tonight at eight o'clock.* **2** the present or the coming night or evening: *I wish tonight would come. 1 adv., 2 n.*

**ton·nage** (tun′ij) **1** the internal capacity of a ship expressed in tons of 100 cubic feet, or register tons (about 2.8 m³): *A ship with a tonnage of 500 has an internal capacity of 50 000 cubic feet.* **2** ships in terms of their total carrying capacity or the total amount carried: *the tonnage of Canada's navy.* **3** a duty or tax on ships at so much a ton. **4** total mass in tons shipped or carried. *n.*

**tonne** (tun) a unit used with the SI for measuring mass, equal to one thousand kilograms: *A very small car has a mass of about one tonne.* Symbol: t *n.*
☛ *Hom.* TON, TUN.

**ton·neau** (tun ō′ *or* tə nō′) the part of an automobile that contains the back seats. *n., pl.* **ton·neaus** or **ton·neaux** (-ōz′).

**ton·sil** (ton′səl) either of the two oval masses of tissue on the inner sides of the throat, just at the back of the mouth. See ADENOIDS for picture. *n.*

**ton·sil·lec·to·my** (ton′sə lek′tə mē) the removal of the TONSILS by surgery. *n., pl.* **ton·sil·lec·to·mies.**

**ton·sil·li·tis** (ton′sə lī′tis) inflammation of the TONSILS. *n.*

**ton·so·ri·al** (ton sô′rē əl) of or having to do with a barber or his or her work. *adj.*

**ton·sure** (ton′shər) **1** the act or the rite of clipping the hair or of shaving a part or the whole of the head of a person entering the priesthood or an order of monks. **2** the shaved part of the head of a priest or monk. **3** shave the head of. *1, 2 n., 3 v.,* **ton·sured, ton·sur·ing.**

**ton·tine** (ton′tēn *or* ton tēn′) a system of annuity or insurance in which subscribers share a fund: *The shares of survivors increase as members of a tontine die, until the last gets all that is left. n.*

**too** (tü) **1** also; besides: *The dog is hungry, and thirsty too.* **2** beyond what is desirable, proper, or right; more than enough: *My dress is too long for you. He ate too much. The summer passed too quickly.* **3** very; exceedingly: *I am only too glad to help you. I didn't do too well on the exam.* **4** indeed; most definitely (used to contradict a negative statement): *I didn't take it. You did too! adv.*
☛ *Hom.* TO, TWO.

**took** (tůk) pt. of TAKE: *She took the car an hour ago. v.*

**tool** (tül) **1** a knife, hammer, saw, shovel, or any instrument used in doing work: *Plumbers, mechanics, carpenters, and shoemakers need tools.* **2** anything used to achieve some purpose: *Books are a student's tools.* **3** a person used by another like a tool: *He is a tool of the departmental boss.* **4** a part of a machine that cuts, bores, smooths, etc. **5** the whole of such a machine. **6** use a tool on; work or shape with a tool: *She tooled beautiful designs in the leather with a knife.* **7** ornament with a tool. *1–5 n., 6, 7 v.*
**tool up,** prepare for a certain task; get ready for some job: *The factory is tooling up for the production of the new cars.*

**tool·ing** (tü′ling) **1** ornamentation made with a hand tool; especially, lettering or designs made on leather. **2** any work done with a tool. **3** ppr. of TOOL. *1, 2 n., 3 v.*

**toonie** or **toony** (tü′nē) the Canadian two-dollar coin. Also, **twoonie.** *n., pl.* **-ies.**

**toot** (tüt) **1** the sound of a horn, whistle, etc. **2** give forth a short blast: *He heard the train toot three times.* **3** sound a horn, whistle, etc. in short blasts: *She tooted as she drove past the house.* *1 n., 2, 3 v.* —**toot′er,** *n.*

**tooth** (tüth) **1** one of the hard, bonelike parts in the

mouth, used for biting and chewing. **2** something like a tooth: *Each one of the projecting parts of a comb, rake, or saw is a tooth.* **3** furnish with teeth; put teeth on. **4** cut teeth on the edge of; indent. **5** a taste, liking: *to have no tooth for fruit, a sweet tooth.* 1, 2, 5 *n.*, *pl.* **teeth;** 3, 4 *v.*
**fight tooth and nail,** fight fiercely, with all one's force.

**tooth·ache** (tü′thāk′) a pain in a tooth or the teeth. *n.*

**tooth·brush** (tüth′brush′) a small brush for cleaning the teeth. *n.*

**toothed** (tütht *or* tüTHd) **1** having teeth, especially of a certain kind or number (*often used in compounds*): *yellow-toothed.* **2** notched or indented: *a toothed blade.* **3** pt. and pp. of TOOTH. 1, 2 *adj.*, 3 *v.*

**tooth·less** (tü′thlis) without teeth. *adj.*

**tooth·paste** (tüth′pāst′) a paste for use in cleaning the teeth. *n.*

**tooth·pick** (tüth′pik′) a small, pointed piece of wood, plastic, quill, etc., for removing bits of food from between the teeth. *n.*

**tooth powder** a powder for cleaning the teeth.

**tooth·some** (tüth′səm) pleasing to the taste; tasting good. *adj.*

**top**¹ (top) **1** the highest point or part: *the top of a mountain.* **2** the upper end or surface: *the top of a table.* **3** the highest or leading place, rank, etc.: *He is at the top of his class.* **4** one that occupies the highest or leading position: *He is top in his profession.* **5** the highest point, pitch, or degree: *The girl was yelling at the top of her voice.* **6** the best or most important part: *the top of the morning.* **7** the part of a plant that grows above ground: *carrot tops.* **8** head. **9** the cover of an automobile, carriage, can, etc. **10** the upper part of a shoe or boot. **11** a piece of clothing for the upper part of the body: *She wore white shorts and a pink top.* **12** having to do, situated at, or forming the top: *the top shelf.* **13** highest in degree; greatest: *at top speed.* **14** chief; foremost: *top honours.* **15** put a top on: *to top a box.* **16** be on top of; be the top of: *A windmill tops the hill.* **17** reach the top of: *They topped the mountain.* **18** rise high; rise above: *The sun topped the horizon.* **19** be higher than; be greater than. **20** do better than; outdo; excel: *Her story topped all the rest.* **21** in golf, hit a ball above centre. **22** remove the top of a plant, etc.: *to top a tree.* **23** a platform around the top of a lower mast on a ship. See MAST for picture. 1–14, 23 *n.*, 15–22 *v.*, **topped, top·ping.**
**from top to toe,** **a** from head to foot. **b** completely.
**on top,** with success; with victory: *to come out on top.*
**over the top,** **a** over the front of a trench to attack. **b** over a target or limit: *We aimed for 50 subscriptions to our magazine, but we went over the top and collected 73.*
**top off,** complete; finish; end.

**top**² (top) a rounded or cone-shaped toy having a point at one end on which it is made to spin. *n.*
**sleep like a top,** sleep soundly.

**to·paz** (tō′paz) **1** a mineral that is a silicate of aluminum, occurring usually in transparent or translucent crystals in various colours: *Transparent yellow or brownish topaz is used as a gem.* **2** any of various yellow gemstones, such as a yellow sapphire. *n.*

**top boot** a high boot usually having the upper part of the top in a different colour or material and made to look as if turned down.

**top·coat** (top′kōt′) an overcoat, especially a light-weight one. *n.*

hat, āge, fär; let, ēqual, tėrm; it, īce
hot, ōpen, ôrder; oil, out; cup, pùt, rüle
əbove, tāken, pencəl, lemən, circəs
ch, child; ng, long; sh, ship
th, thin; ᴛʜ, then; zh, measure

**top dog** *Informal.* the best, most successful or most important individual or group.

**top drawer** *Informal.* the highest level of excellence, importance, good breeding, etc.: *a family in the top drawer of society.*

**tope** (tōp) drink excessively or habitually; tipple. *v.*, **toped, top·ing.**

**top·er** (tō′pər) a person who drinks a great deal of alcoholic liquor. *n.*

**top–flight** (top′flīt′) superior; of the highest excellence. *adj.*

**top·gal·lant** (top′gal′ənt *or* tə gal′ənt) **1** the mast or sail above the topmast; the third section of a mast above the deck. **2** next above the topmast. 1 *n.*, 2 *adj.*

**top hat** a tall, black silk hat worn by men in formal clothes. See HAT for picture.

**top–heav·y** (top′hev′ē) too heavy at the top: *The load was top-heavy and soon fell off.* *adj.*

**top·ic** (top′ik) **1** a subject that people think, write, or talk about: *The main topics at the dinner party were the weather and the election.* **2** a short phrase or sentence used in an outline to give the main point of a part of a speech, writing, etc. *n.*

**top·i·cal** (top′ə kəl) **1** having to do with topics of the day; of current or local interest. **2** of or using topics; having to do with the topics of a speech, writing, etc.: *Some books have topical outlines.* **3** of or designed for a particular part of the body; local: *a topical medicine.* *adj.*

**top·knot** (top′not′) a knot of hair or a tuft of feathers on the top of the head. *n.*

**top·less** (top′ləs) **1** having no top: *a topless table.* **2** wearing no clothes on the upper part of the body: *a topless waitress.* **3** *Informal.* of a restaurant, etc., featuring topless waitresses, dancers, etc. **4** so high or tall that the top cannot be seen: *topless mountains.* *adj.*

**top–lev·el** (top′lev′əl) *Informal.* of the highest importance, authority, etc.: *top-level decisions.* *adj.*

**top·mast** (top′mast′ *or* top′məst) the second section of a mast above the deck. See MAST for picture. *n.*

**top·most** (top′mōst′) highest. *adj.*

**top–notch** (top′noch′) *Informal.* first-rate; best possible. *adj.*

**to·pog·ra·pher** (tə pog′rə fər) a person trained in TOPOGRAPHY, especially one who makes it his or her work. *n.*

**top·o·graph·ic** (top′ə graf′ik) TOPOGRAPHICAL. *adj.*

**top·o·graph·i·cal** (top′ə graf′ə kəl) of or having to do with TOPOGRAPHY: *A topographical map shows mountains, rivers, etc.* *adj.* —**top′o·graph′i·cal·ly,** *adv.*

**to·pog·ra·phy** (tə pog′rə fē) **1** the art or practice of detailed description or mapping of the natural and artificial features of a region or place. **2** a detailed description of the surface features of a place or region. **3** the surface features of a place or region. The topography of a region includes hills, valleys, streams, lakes, bridges, tunnels, roads, etc.   *n., pl.* **to‧pog‧ra‧phies.**

**top‧ping** (top′ing)   **1** something that forms a top, such as a garnish placed on food to add flavour or for decoration: *pudding with a topping of whipped cream, a cake with a crumb topping.*   **2** ppr. of TOP.   1 *n.*, 2 *v.*

**top‧ple** (top′əl)   **1** fall forward; tumble down: *The chimney toppled over on the roof.*   **2** throw over or down; overturn: *The wrestler toppled his opponent.*   **3** hang over in an unsteady way: *beneath toppling crags.*   *v.*, **top‧pled, top‧pling.**

**tops** (tops) *Informal.*   **1** of the highest degree in quality, excellence, popularity, etc. (never used before a noun): *She's tops in her field.*   **2 the tops,**   an excellent person or thing of its kind.   1 *adj.*, 2 *n.*

**top‧sail** (top′sāl *or* top′səl)   the second sail above the deck on a mast.   *n.*

**top–se‧cret** (top′sē′krit)   of utmost secrecy; extremely confidential: *top-secret information. The file was labelled top-secret.*   *adj.*

**top‧side** (top′sīd′)   **1** to or on the bridge or an upper deck; on deck.   **2** Often, **topsides,** *pl.*   the upper part of a ship's side, especially the part above the waterline.   1 *adv.*, 2 *n.*

**top‧soil** (top′soil′)   surface soil suitable for growing plants in: *People buy topsoil for gardens and lawns.*   *n.*

**top‧stitch** (top′stich′)   decorate or finish with TOPSTITCHING.   *v.*

**top‧stitch‧ing** (top′stich′ing)   a decorative line of stitching on the outside of a garment near an edge or seam: *The jacket has topstitching around the collar and down the front.*   *n.*

**top‧sy–tur‧vy** (top′sē tėr′vē)   **1** upside down.   **2** in confusion or disorder: *Her room was always topsy-turvy because she never put anything away.*   **3** confusion; disorder.   1, 2 *adv., adj.*, 3 *n., pl.* **top‧sy‧tur‧vies.**

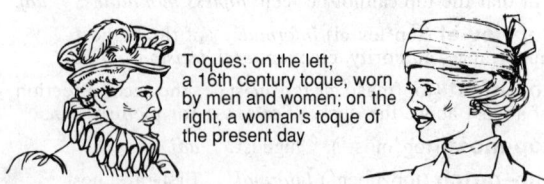

Toques: on the left, a 16th century toque, worn by men and women; on the right, a woman's toque of the present day

**toque** (tōk)   **1** a hat with no brim or with very little brim.   **2** TUQUE.   *n.*
☞ *Etym.* From F *toque,* which came through Spanish from Basque *tauka,* a certain kind of cap. 16c.

**to‧rah** or **to‧ra** (tô′rə)   **1** in Jewish usage, a doctrine, teaching, or law.   **2 the Torah,**   the law of Moses; Pentateuch.   *n.*

**torch** (tôrch)   **1** a light to be carried around or stuck in a holder on a wall: *A piece of pine wood or anything that burns easily makes a good torch.*   **2** a device for producing a very hot flame, used especially to burn off paint or to solder or melt metal.   **3** *Brit.*   FLASHLIGHT.   **4** something thought of as a source of enlightenment: *the torch of civilization.*   *n.*   —**torch′like′,** *adj.*
**carry a torch** or **carry the torch,** *Informal.*   crusade for; support a cause.

**torch‧bear‧er** (tôrch′ber′ər)   **1** one who carries a torch.   **2** *Informal.*   one who is prominent in support of a crusade, a cause, or an individual.   *n.*

**torch‧light** (tôrch′līt′)   the light of a torch or torches.   *n.*

**tore** (tôr)   pt. of TEAR². *Yesterday she tore her dress on a nail.*   *v.*

**tor‧e‧a‧dor** (tô′rē ə dôr′)   BULLFIGHTER.   *n.*

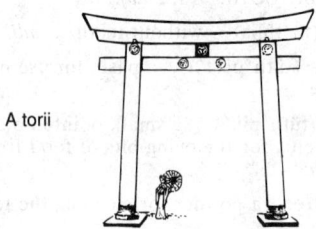

A torii

**to‧ri‧i** (tô′rē ē′)   a gateway at the entrance to a Japanese Shinto temple, built of two uprights and two crosspieces: *The torii marks off the sacred Shinto shrine from the ordinary world.*   *n., pl.* **to‧ri‧i.**

**tor‧ment** (tôr ment′ *for verb,* tôr′ment *for noun*)   **1** cause very great pain to: *Headaches tormented him.*   **2** a cause of very great pain: *Instruments of torture were torments.*   **3** very great pain: *He suffered torments from his aching teeth.*   **4** a cause of very much worry or annoyance.   **5** worry or annoy very much: *He torments everyone with silly questions.*   1, 5 *v.*, 2–4 *n.*

**tor‧men‧tor** or **tor‧ment‧er** (tôr men′tər)   a person or thing that torments.   *n.*

**torn** (tôrn)   pp. of TEAR². *She has torn up the plant by the roots. His coat was old and torn.*   *v.*

**tor‧na‧do** (tôr nā′dō)   **1** a violent, destructive kind of cyclone from a few hundred metres to a few kilometres wide, seen as a slender, funnel-shaped, whirling cloud that moves across the land.   **2** any whirlwind or hurricane.   **3** a violent outburst.   *n., pl.* **tor‧na‧does** or **tor‧na‧dos.**

A torpedo. When it is launched from a ship, aircraft, etc. it travels much like a small ship. It contains a motor and devices for controlling its course and depth.

**tor‧pe‧do** (tôr pē′dō)   **1** a large, cigar-shaped metal tube that contains explosives and travels by its own power: *Torpedoes are sent under water to blow up enemy ships.*   **2** a submarine mine, shell, etc. that explodes when hit.   **3** attack or destroy with a torpedo.   **4** an explosive put on a railway track that makes a loud noise for a signal when a wheel of the engine runs over it.   **5** a kind of firework that explodes when it is thrown against something hard.   **6** any of a closely related group of fishes of the Mediterranean and subtropical Atlantic, having a flat, disk-shaped body, a short tail, and a pair of electric organs which can produce a current of 2000 volts to stun their prey.   **7** bring to an end; destroy: *He torpedoed my plan.*   1, 2, 4–6 *n., pl.* **tor‧pe‧does;**   3, 7 *v.*, **tor‧pe‧doed, tor‧pe‧do‧ing.**

**tor·pe·do boat** a small, fast warship designed for firing torpedoes.

**tor·pid** (tôr′pid) **1** lacking in vigour; dull or sluggish: *a torpid mind.* **2** dormant, as a hibernating animal. **3** numb. *adj.* —**tor′pid·ly,** *adv.* —**tor′pid·ness,** *n.*

**tor·pid·i·ty** (tôr pid′ə tē) the quality or state of being TORPID. *n.*

**tor·por** (tôr′pər) **1** a state of being dormant or inactive. **2** sluggishness or dullness. *n.*

**torque** (tôrk) **1** a force that produces rotation: *The engine of a motor vehicle transmits torque to the axle.* **2** a necklace of twisted metal, especially such necklaces worn by the ancient Celts. *n.*

**tor·rent** (tô′rənt) **1** a violent, rushing stream of liquid, especially water or lava. **2** any violent, rushing stream or flood: *a torrent of abuse.* *n.*

**tor·ren·tial** (tô ren′shəl) of, caused by, or like a TORRENT: *torrential rains, a torrential flow of words.* *adj.* —**tor·ren′tial·ly,** *adv.*

**tor·rid** (tô′rid) **1** very hot: *a torrid climate.* **2** passionate; intense: *torrid love letters.* *adj.*

**tor·rid·i·ty** (tô rid′ə tē) extreme heat. *n.*

**tor·sion** (tôr′shən) **1** the act or process of twisting or wrenching by turning one end of something while the other end is held fast or twisted in the opposite direction. **2** the state of being twisted. **3** the TORQUE exerted by a body being twisted. *n.*

**tor·sion·al** (tôr′shə nəl) of, having to do with, or resulting from TORSION. *adj.*

**tor·so** (tôr′sō) **1** the trunk or body of a statue without any head, arms, or legs. **2** the trunk of the human body. *n., pl.* **tor·sos.**

**tort** (tôrt) any civil, not criminal, wrong for which the law requires damages (except a breach of contract): *If a person's car breaks a fence, he or she has committed a tort against the owner.* *n.*

**tor·til·la** (tôr tē′yə) Spanish American. a thin, flat, round corn or wheat cake. *n.*

**tor·toise** (tôr′təs) a turtle, especially a land turtle. *n., pl.* **tor·tois·es** or **tor·toise.**

**tortoise beetle** a small beetle shaped rather like a tortoise.

**tor·toise–shell** (tôr′təs shel′ *or* tôr′tə shel′) **1** the mottled yellow-and-brown shell of some species of turtle, used for ornaments, combs, etc. **2** made of or resembling tortoise-shell. **3** a butterfly, cat, etc. with mottled colours like those of tortoise-shell: *Tortoise-shell cats are usually female.* Compare with CALICO. *n.*

**tor·tu·ous** (tôr′chü əs) **1** full of twists, turns, or bends; twisting; winding; crooked: *a tortuous path.* **2** mentally or morally crooked; not straightforward; devious or indirect: *tortuous reasoning.* *adj.* —**tor′tu·ous·ly,** *adv.* —**tor′tu·ous·ness,** *n.*

☛ *Usage.* Do not confuse **tortuous** and TORTUROUS. **Tortuous** simply suggests the idea of twisting and turning or devious, whereas **torturous** describes a situation which always involves torture.

**tor·ture** (tôr′chər) **1** the act or fact of inflicting extreme pain: *Torture used to be widely used to make people give evidence about crimes, or to make them confess.* **2** extreme pain: *She suffered torture from rheumatism.* **3** cause extreme pain to: *That cruel boy tortures animals.* **4** something that causes extreme pain. **5** twist the

---

**torpedo boat    1261    totalitarianism**

hat, āge, fär; let, ēqual, tèrm; it, īce
hot, ōpen, ôrder; oil, out; cup, pùt, rüle
əbove, takən, pencəl, lemən, circəs
ch, child; ng, long; sh, ship
th, thin; ᴛʜ, then; zh, measure

---

meaning of. **6** twist or force out of its natural form: *Winds tortured the trees.* **1, 2, 4** *n.,* **3, 5, 6** *v.,* **tor·tured, tor·tur·ing.** —**tor′tur·er,** *n.*

**tor·tur·ous** (tôr′chə rəs) full of, involving, or causing TORTURE. *adj.*
☛ *Usage.* See note at TORTUOUS.

**To·ry** (tô′rē) **1** in Canada, a member or supporter of the PROGRESSIVE CONSERVATIVE PARTY: *His mother is a Tory.* **2** in the United Kingdom, originally, a member of the political party that favoured royal power and the established church and that opposed change: *Strictly speaking, there is no Tory party in Britain nowadays, although members of the Conservative Party are often called Tories.* **3** *U.S.* during the American Revolution, a person who supported continued allegiance to Britain; Loyalist. **4** of or having to do with the Tories or their policies: *a strong Tory opposition.* **1–3** *n., pl.* **Tor·ies; 4** *adj.*

**To·ry·ism** (tô′rē iz′əm) **1** the principles and practices of the Tories. **2** the fact or state of being a TORY. *n.*

**toss** (tos) **1** throw lightly with the palm upward; cast; fling: *to toss a ball.* **2** throw about; roll or pitch about: *The ship was tossed by the heavy waves.* **3** lift quickly; throw upward: *She tossed her head. He was tossed by the bull.* **4** mix the ingredients of lightly: *to toss a salad.* **5** throw a coin to decide something by the side that falls upward. **6** the distance to which something is or can be tossed. **7** throw oneself about in bed; roll restlessly. **8** a throw; tossing: *A toss of a coin decided who should play first.* **1–5, 7** *v.,* **6, 8** *n.*

**toss off, a** do or make quickly and easily. **b** drink all at once.

**toss–up** (tos′up′) **1** a tossing of a coin to decide something. **2** an even chance: *It was a toss-up whether he or his brother would get the nomination.* *n.*

**tot** (tot) **1** a little child. **2** a small portion of alcoholic liquor. *n.*
☛ *Hom.* TAUGHT, TAUT.

**to·tal** (tō′təl) **1** whole; entire: *The total cost of the house and land will be $455 000.* **2** the whole amount; sum: *Her expenses reached a total of $200.* **3** find the sum of; add: *Total that column of figures.* **4** reach an amount of; amount to: *The money spent yearly on chewing gum totals millions of dollars.* **5** complete; absolute: *The lights went out and we were in total darkness.* **6** *Informal.* wreck completely: *Her car was totalled in the accident.* **1, 5** *adj.,* **2** *n.,* **3, 4, 6** *v.* **to·talled** or **to·taled, to·tal·ling** or **to·tal·ing.**

**to·tal·i·tar·i·an** (tō tal′ə ter′ē ən) **1** of, having to do with, or referring to a form of government in which a centralized state authority permits no competing political group and exercises strict control over economic, social, and cultural aspects of life. **2** supporting or favouring such a form of government. **3** a person who supports or practises TOTALITARIANISM. **1, 2** *adj.,* **3** *n.*

**to·tal·i·tar·i·an·ism** (tō tal′ə ter′ē ə niz′əm) **1** a TOTALITARIAN system of government. **2** the political principle that the individual citizen should be under the complete control of a government or ruler. *n.*

**to·tal·i·ty** (tō tal′ə tē) **1** a total number or amount; whole; sum. **2** the quality or state of being total; entirety. **3** the total eclipse of the sun or moon or the period during which this takes place. *n., pl.* **to·tal·i·ties.**

**to·tal·ly** (tō′tə lē) wholly; entirely; completely: *He was totally exhausted. The experiment was totally successful.* *adv.*

**total recall** the ability to remember clearly every detail about an experience or situation in the past.

**total war** war in which all the resources of a nation are used, and in which attack is made not only on the armed forces of the opponent, but also (subject to certain limitations) on all its people and property.

**tote** (tōt) *Informal.* carry; haul: *I had to tote all the stuff home by myself.* *v.*, **tot·ed, tot·ing.**

**tote bag** a large handbag of canvas, straw, vinyl, etc., usually open at the top, used for carrying small packages, clothing, etc.: *She carried her swimsuit and towel in a tote bag.*

**to·tem** (tō′təm) **1** among Amerindian peoples of the northern Pacific coast, an animal or plant taken as the emblem of a tribe, clan, or family. **2** among many peoples throughout the world, a creature or object that is associated with their ancestral traditions and is looked on with awe and reverence by a tribe, clan, etc.: *Many peoples never kill the animals that are their totems.* **3** a representation of a totem, usually carved or painted. **4** anything that is used as an emblem or symbol. *n.*

**to·tem·ic** (tō tem′ik) of or having to do with a TOTEM or TOTEMISM. *adj.*

**to·tem·ism** (tō′tə miz′əm) **1** belief in a mystical relationship or kinship between human beings and animals and plants, usually taking the form of a special reverence felt by a people or a person for particular creatures or objects. **2** the use of totems to distinguish tribes, clans, or families. *n.*

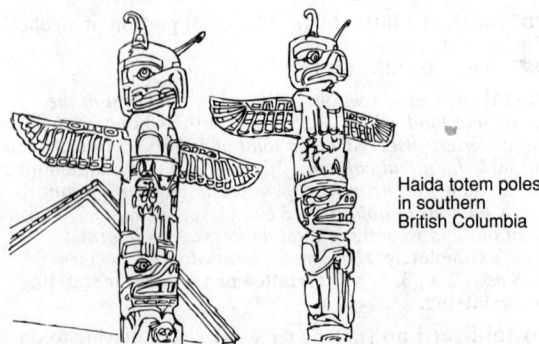

Haida totem poles in southern British Columbia

**totem pole** a large upright log carved and painted with representations of totems, traditionally erected by many of the Amerindian peoples of the northern Pacific coast: *Totem poles served as a record of the ancestry of a family and sometimes also of historical or mythological happenings.*

**tot·ter** (tot′ər) **1** walk with shaky, unsteady steps: *The baby tottered three steps all by herself.* **2** tremble or rock as if about to fall: *The old wall tottered in the storm and fell.* **3** become unstable; be about to fail or collapse: *The old regime was already tottering before the revolution broke out.* **4** an unsteady way of walking. 1–3 *v.*, 4 *n.*
—**tot′ter·er,** *n.*

**tot·ter·y** (tot′ə rē) tottering; shaky. *adj.*

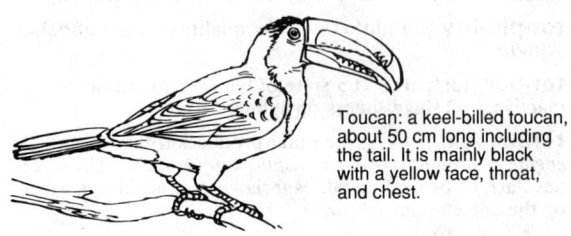

Toucan: a keel-billed toucan, about 50 cm long including the tail. It is mainly black with a yellow face, throat, and chest.

**tou·can** (tü′kan) any of a family of bright-coloured birds of tropical America, having an enormous beak. *n.*

**touch** (tuch) **1** put the hand or some other part of the body on or against: *She touched the pan to see whether it was still hot.* **2** put against; make contact with: *He touched the post with his umbrella.* **3** be against; come against: *Your sleeve is touching the butter.* **4** be in contact: *Our hands touched.* **5** a touching or being touched: *A bubble bursts at a touch.* **6** the sense by which a person perceives things by feeling, handling, or coming against them: *The blind have a keen touch.* **7** a coming or being in contact: *the touch of their hands.* **8** communication or connection: *A newspaper keeps one in touch with the world. He has been out of touch with his mother since he left home.* **9** a slight amount; little bit: *We had a touch of frost.* **10** a stroke with a brush, pencil, pen, etc.: *The artist finished my picture with a few touches.* **11** a detail in any artistic work: *a story with charming poetic touches.* **12** strike lightly or gently: *She touched the strings of the harp.* **13** injure slightly: *The flowers were touched by the frost.* **14** affect with some feeling: *The sad story touched us.* **15** make slightly crazy. **16** have to do with; concern: *The matter touches your interest.* **17** speak of; deal with; refer to; treat lightly: *Our conversation touched many subjects.* **18** handle; use: *He won't touch liquor or tobacco.* **19** reach; come up to: *His head almost touches the top of the doorway. Nobody in our class can touch her in music.* **20** stop at; visit in passing: *The ship touched port.* **21** make a brief stop: *Most ships touch at that port.* **22** the act or manner of playing a musical instrument: *a pianist with an excellent touch.* **23** the way the keys of a musical instrument work. **24** a distinctive manner or quality: *The work showed an expert's touch.* **25** a slight attack: *a touch of fever.* 1–4, 12–21, *v.*, 5–11, 22–25 *n.*
—**touch′a·ble,** *adj.* —**touch′er,** *n.*

**touch down, a** land an aircraft. **b** in football, score a TOUCHDOWN (def. 1).

**touch off, a** represent exactly or cleverly. **b** cause to go off; fire: *The new tax touched off a rebellion.*

**touch on** or **upon, a** speak of; treat lightly: *Our conversation touched on many subjects.* **b** come close to.

**touch up, a** change a little; improve: *She touched up a photograph.* **b** rouse.

**touch and go** an uncertain or risky situation: *So far it's been touch and go, but we're still hoping for the best.*

**touch–and–go** (tuch′ən gō′) uncertain; risky. *adj.*

**touch·down** (tuch′doun′) **1** in football, the act of scoring by being in possession of the ball on or behind the opponents' goal line. **2** the score made in this way. **3** the landing or moment of landing of an aircraft: *The pilot had to make an unexpected touchdown because of engine trouble.* *n.*

**touched** (tucht) **1** stirred emotionally, especially by gratitude or sympathy; moved: *He was touched by their offer to help.* **2** *Informal.* slightly unbalanced mentally. **3** pt. and pp. of TOUCH. 1, 2 *adj.*, 3 *v.*

**touch football** a variety of football, usually played informally and without protective equipment, in which the person carrying the ball is touched rather than tackled.

**touch·hole** (tuch′hōl′) the small opening in early cannon or firearms through which the gunpowder inside was set on fire. *n.*

**touch·ing** (tuch′ing) **1** arousing tender feeling: *The Old Curiosity Shop is a touching story.* **2** concerning; about: *She asked many questions touching my home life.* **3** ppr. of TOUCH. 1 *adj.*, 2 *prep.*, 3 *v.* —**touch′ing·ly**, *adv.*

**touch–me–not** (tuch′mē not′) any of several wild species of IMPATIENS found in wet places and woods in North America and Europe. *n.*

**touch·stone** (tuch′stōn′) **1** a black stone formerly used to test the purity of gold or silver by the colour of the streak on the stone after it was rubbed with the metal. **2** any test or standard for determining the genuineness or value of something: *His work has for many years been the touchstone of excellence in architecture.* *n.*

**touch–ty·ping** (tuch′tī′ping) a method of keyboarding without looking at the keyboard by always using a particular finger to strike a particular key. *n.* —**touch′-type**, *v.*

**touch·wood** (tuch′wùd) **1** wood decayed by fungi so that it catches fire easily, used as tinder. **2** a fungus found on old tree trunks, used as tinder. *n.*

**touch·y** (tuch′ē) **1** apt to take offence at trifles; too sensitive: *He is tired and very touchy this afternoon.* **2** requiring skill in handling; ticklish; precarious: *It was a touchy situation; he didn't know whether to stay or leave.* **3** of a part of the body, very sensitive to touch: *The skin around the wound is very touchy.* *adj.*, **touch·i·er**, **touch·i·est.** —**touch′i·ly**, *adv.* —**touch′i·ness**, *n.*

**tough** (tuf) **1** bending without breaking: *Leather is tough.* **2** hard to cut, tear, or chew: *The steak was so tough he couldn't eat it.* **3** stiff; sticky: *tough clay.* **4** strong; hardy: *a tough plant. Donkeys are tough little animals and can carry big loads.* **5** hard; difficult: *tough work.* **6** hard to bear; bad; unpleasant: *A spell of tough luck discouraged him.* **7** hard to influence; stubborn: *a tough customer.* **8** rough; disorderly: *We lived in a tough neighbourhood.* **9** a rough person; rowdy. 1–8 *adj.*, 9 *n.* —**tough′ly**, *adv.* —**tough′ness**, *n.*

**tough·en** (tuf′ən) **1** make tough or tougher: *She decided to toughen her muscles by doing regular exercises.* **2** become tough or tougher: *His muscles gradually toughened.* *v.*

**tou·pee** (tü pā′) a wig or patch of false hair worn to cover a bald spot. *n.*

**tour** (tür) **1** travel from place to place: *He's touring next winter with the Canadian Opera Company.* **2** a long journey through a country or countries, in which one returns to the starting point: *a European tour.* **3** travel through: *Last year they toured Europe.* **4** a regular spell or turn of work or duty, or the length of time such a spell lasts: *Her last tour of duty was in France.* **5** a short trip or walk around, as for inspection: *a tour of the boat.* **6** walk around in: *The children will tour the museum.* 1, 3, 6 *v.*, 2, 4, 5 *n.*

**on tour**, touring: *A show on tour travels around the country giving performances in various places.*

**tour de force** (tür′də fôrs′; *French*, türdəfôrs′) **1** a notable feat of strength, skill, or ingenuity. **2** something done that is merely clever or ingenious: *His later work showed that his first novel was little more than a tour de force.*

**tour·ism** (tür′iz′əm) **1** a touring or travelling as a pastime or recreation. **2** the business of providing services for tourists. *n.*

**tour·ist** (tür′ist *or* tùr′ist) **1** a person travelling for pleasure. **2** TOURIST CLASS. **3** of or for tourists. *n.*

**tourist class** the cheapest class of accommodation for passengers on a ship, train, etc.; economy class.

**tourist trap** a place or business establishment that exploits tourists.

**tour·ma·line** (tür′mə lin *or* tür′mə lēn′) a complex mineral occurring in various colours: *The transparent varieties of tourmaline are used for gems.* See CRYSTAL for picture. *n.*

**tour·na·ment** (tèr′nə mənt *or* tür′nə mənt) **1** a series of contests testing the skill of many persons: *a golf tournament. Her uncle won the chess tournament.* **2** in the Middle Ages, a contest between two groups of knights on horseback who fought for a prize. **3** a series of knightly jousts, sports, etc. occurring at one time at a particular place. *n.*

**tour·ney** (tèr′nē *or* tür′nē) **1** TOURNAMENT. **2** take part in a TOURNAMENT. 1 *n.*, *pl.* **tour·neys;** 2 *v.*, **tour·neyed, tour·ney·ing.**

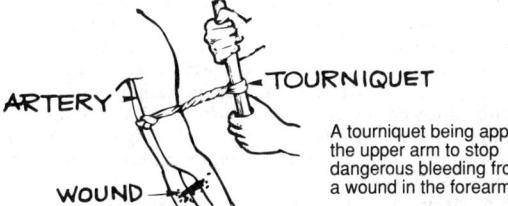

A tourniquet being applied on the upper arm to stop dangerous bleeding from a wound in the forearm

**tour·ni·quet** (tür′nə ket′ *or* tür′nə kā′) a device for stopping bleeding by compressing a blood vessel, such as a bandage tightened by twisting with a stick, or a pad pressed down by a screw. *n.*

**tour·ti·ere** (tür tyer′) *Cdn.* a pie made with ground pork, often mixed with some veal or chicken, associated especially with French Canada. *n.*

**tou·sle** (tou′zəl) **1** put into disorder; make untidy; muss: *She tousled her brother's hair to tease him.* **2** a disordered or tangled mass of hair, etc. 1 *v.*, **tou·sled, tou·sling;** 2 *n.*

**tout** (tout) *Informal.* **1** try to get customers, jobs, votes, etc. **2** *Esp. Brit.* spy out information about racehorses for use in betting. **3** give special information about racehorses. **4** praise highly and insistently. **5** a person who touts. 1–4 *v.*, 5 *n.* —**tout′er**, *n.*

**tout à fait** (tü tà fe′) *French.* entirely; completely.

**tow¹** (tō) **1** pull by a rope, chain, etc.: *The tug is towing three barges.* **2** the act or an instance of towing: *He charges twenty dollars for a tow.* **3** the fact or condition of being towed. **4** that which is towed: *Each tug had a tow of three barges.* **5** something that tows: *a ski tow.* **6** the rope, chain, etc. used for towing. **1** *v.*, **2–6** *n.*
**in tow, a** in the state of being towed: *The launch had a sailboat in tow.* **b** under protection or guidance: *He was taken in tow by his aunt as soon as he arrived.* **c** under one's influence; in the position of follower or dependent: *The movie producer arrived at the reception with several admirers in tow.*
☞ *Hom.* TOE.

**tow²** (tō) **1** the coarse, broken fibres of flax, hemp, etc., prepared for spinning: *This string is made of tow.* **2** made from tow. *n.*
☞ *Hom.* TOE.

**tow·age** (tō′ij) **1** towing or being towed. **2** a charge for towing. *n.*

**to·ward** (tôrd *or* tə wôrd′ *for preposition,* tôrd *for adjective*) **1** in the direction of: *She walked toward the north.* **2** with respect to; regarding; about; concerning: *What is your attitude toward war?* **3** near: *It must be toward four o'clock.* **4** as a help to; for: *Will you give something toward our new hospital?* **5** about to happen; impending. **1–4** *prep.*, **5** *adj.*

**tow·boat** (tō′bōt′) TUGBOAT. *n.*

**tow·el** (tou′əl) **1** an absorbent piece of cloth or paper for wiping and drying something wet. **2** dry with a towel. **1** *n.*, **2** *v.*, **tow·elled** *or* **tow·eled, tow·el·ling** *or* **tow·el·ing.**
**throw** *or* **toss in the towel,** *Informal.* admit defeat.

**tow·el·ling** *or* **tow·el·ing** (tou′ə ling) **1** the looped cotton cloth from which towels are made. **2** ppr. of TOWEL. **1** *n.*, **2** *v.*

**tow·er** (tou′ər) **1** a high structure that may be completely walled in or may consist only of a framework of metal or wood, and that may stand alone or form part of a church, castle, etc.: *a lookout tower, a bell tower, a water tower.* **2** a fortress or prison consisting of or including a tower: *the Tower of London.* **3** a very tall building; highrise: *an office tower.* **4** rise high up: *The girl towered over her baby brother. A mountain towered over the village.* **1–3** *n.*, **4** *v.*
**tower of strength,** a person or thing that acts as a defence, protection, or support: *She proved to be a tower of strength during the emergency.*

**tow·er·ing** (tou′ə ring) **1** very high: *a towering peak.* **2** very tall: *a towering basketball player.* **3** very great: *Making electricity from atomic power is a towering achievement.* **4** very violent: *a towering rage.* **5** ppr. of TOWER. **1–4** *adj.*, **5** *v.*

**Tower of London** an ancient palace-fortress in London. It has been used as a palace, prison, mint, and arsenal.

**tow·head** (tō′hed′) a person having light, pale-yellow hair. *n.*

**tow·head·ed** (tō′hed′id) having light, pale-yellow hair. *adj.*

**tow·hee** (tou′hē *or* tō′hē) any of several long-tailed North American finches, especially a common bird of central and eastern North America having rusty-coloured flanks and a black head, back, and tail with white patches; chewink. *n.*

**tow·line** (tō′līn′) a rope, chain, etc. for towing. *n.*

**town** (toun) **1** a large group of houses, stores, schools, churches, etc. that together with the people living there forms a community with fixed boundaries and its own local government: *A town is usually smaller than a city but larger than a village.* **2** any large place with many people living in it: *Toronto is an exciting town.* **3** the people of a town: *The whole town was having a holiday.* **4** the part of a town or city where the stores and office buildings are: *Let's go to town.* **5** TOWNSHIP (def. 1). *n.*
**go to town,** *Informal.* **a** achieve success. **b** do or go through thoroughly: *The hungry girls really went to town on that pie.*
**in town,** in a specified town or city: *She is not in town today.*
**on the town,** out for entertainment and pleasure as available in a city or town.

**town clerk** an official who keeps the records of a town.

**town crier** a public crier in a city or town.

**town hall** the headquarters of a town's government.

**town house** a house in town, belonging to a person who also has a house in the country.

**town·house** (toun′hous′) a house that is one of a row of attached houses two or more storeys high, each having a small yard and its own entrance from the street. *n.*

**town meeting** a general meeting of the inhabitants of a town.

**towns–folk** (tounz′fōk′) the people of a town. *n.pl.*

**town·ship** (toun′ship) **1** in Canada and the United States, a part of a county having certain powers of government; municipality. **2** a land-survey area on which later subdivisions may be based: *In the Prairie Provinces, a township is an area of 36 square miles (about 93 km²), divided into 36 sections.* *Abbrev.:* Tp., tp., *or* twp. *n.*

**town·site** (toun′sīt′) **1** the site of a town. **2** a piece of land being developed or to be developed as a town. *n.*

**towns·man** (toun′zmən) **1** a native or resident of a city or town. **2** a person who lives in one's own town. *n., pl.* **towns·men** (-zmən).

**towns·peo·ple** (tounz′pē′pəl) the people of a town. *n.pl.*

**towns·wom·an** (toun′zwum′ən) **1** a woman who is a native or inhabitant of a city or town. **2** a woman who lives in one's own town. *n., pl.* **towns·wom·en** (-zwim′ən).

**tow·path** (tō′path′) a path along the bank of a canal or river for use in towing boats. *n.*

**tow·rope** (tō′rōp′) a rope used for towing. *n.*

**tow truck** a truck equipped for towing away disabled or illegally parked vehicles.

**tox·e·mi·a** (tok sē′mē ə) a form of blood poisoning, especially one in which the toxins produced by certain micro-organisms enter the blood. *n.* Also, **toxaemia.**

**tox·e·mic** (tok sē′mik) **1** of or having to do with TOXEMIA. **2** suffering from TOXEMIA. *adj.* Also, **toxaemic.**

**tox·ic** (tok′sik) **1** of, having to do with, or caused by a poison or TOXIN: *a toxic reaction.* **2** poisonous: *Automobile exhaust fumes are toxic.* *adj.*

**tox·ic·i·ty** (tok sis′ə tē) the quality or state of being TOXIC or poisonous. *n., pl.* **tox·ic·i·ties.**

**tox·i·co·log·i·cal** (tok′sə kə loj′ə kəl) of or having to do with the science of poisons. *adj.*

**tox·i·col·o·gist** (tok′sə kol′ə jist) a person trained in TOXICOLOGY, especially one who makes it his or her work. *n.*

**tox·i·col·o·gy** (tok′sə kol′ə jē) the science that deals with poisons, their effects, antidotes, detection, etc. *n.*

**tox·in** (tok′sən) any poisonous product of animal or vegetable metabolism, especially one of those produced by bacteria: *The symptoms of a disease caused by bacteria, such as diphtheria, are due to toxins.* *n.*

**toy** (toi) **1** something for a child to play with; plaything: *His toys are all over the living room again.* **2** made for use as a toy; especially, being a small model of a real thing: *a toy truck, a toy soldier.* **3** something that resembles a child's toy in being small or having little real value, usefulness, or importance, etc.: *That little calculator is nothing but a toy.* **4** referring to a small variety of certain breeds of dog: *Pekinese, pugs, and chihuahuas are toys.* **6** handle or deal with in a light, careless, or trifling way (used with **with**): *She toyed with her beads as she talked. She has been toying with the idea of writing a book but so far has not done anything about it.* 1–5 *n.,* 6 *v.* —**toy′-like**′, *adj.*

**to·yon** (tō′yən) a shrub of the Pacific coast of North America, whose evergreen leaves and scarlet berries look much like holly: *The toyon belongs to the rose family.* *n.*

**Tp.** or **tp.** **1** township. **2** troop.

**tr.** **1** transitive. **2** transpose. **3** translation. **4** translator. **5** train.

**trace**[1] (trās) **1** a sign or evidence of the existence, presence, or action of something in the past; vestige: *The explorer found traces of an ancient city.* **2** a footprint or other mark left; track; trail: *We saw traces of rabbits on the snow.* **3** follow by means of marks, tracks, or signs: *to trace deer.* **4** follow the course of; follow a trail of evidence to: *She traced the river to its source. He traced his family back through eight generations.* **5** find signs of; observe. **6** a very small amount; little bit: *There wasn't a trace of grey in her hair.* **7** mark out; draw: *The spy traced a plan of the fort.* **8** something marked out or drawn. **9** copy by following the lines of: *He put thin paper over the map and traced it.* 1, 2, 6, 8 *n.,* 3–5, 7, 9 *v.,* **traced, trac·ing.**

**trace**[2] (trās) either of the two straps, ropes, or chains by which an animal pulls a wagon, carriage, etc. See HARNESS for picture. *n.*
**kick over the traces,** throw off control; become unruly.

**trace·a·bil·i·ty** (trā′sə bil′ə tē) the quality or condition of being TRACEABLE. *n.*

**trace·a·ble** (trā′sə bəl) capable of being traced: *Find out if the letter is traceable.* *adj.* —**trace′a·bly,** *adv.*

**trac·er** (trā′sər) **1** a person whose work is tracing missing persons or property. **2** an inquiry sent from place to place to trace a missing person, letter, parcel, etc. **3** a person whose work is tracing patterns, designs, markings, etc. **4** a device or machine for making tracings of drawings, plans, etc. **5** a bullet or shell containing a substance that marks its course with a trail of smoke or fire. **6** an element (**tracer element**) or atom (**tracer atom**), usually radio-active, used in a chemical or biological process to permit the course of the process to be traced. *n.*

Tracery ornamenting a church window

**trac·er·y** (trā′sə rē) **1** ornamental openwork in stone, consisting of branching or interlacing lines, especially such ornament at the top of a window in Gothic architecture. **2** any decorative pattern or natural outline suggesting this: *the tracery in a butterfly's wing. Tracery is sometimes used in embroidery.* *n., pl.* **trac·er·ies.**

**tra·che·a** (trā′kē ə *or* trə kē′ə) the windpipe. See LUNG and WINDPIPE for pictures. *n., pl.* **tra·che·ae** (-ē′ *or* -ī′).

**tra·che·al** (trā′kē əl *or* trə kē′əl) of or having to do with the TRACHEA. *adj.*

**tra·cho·ma** (trə kō′mə) a contagious disease of the eye caused by a micro-organism and characterized by inflamed granulations on the inner surface of the eyelids. *n.*

**trac·ing** (trā′sing) **1** a copy of a map, drawing, etc. made by following its lines on a transparent sheet that has been placed over it. **2** a line made by a recording instrument that registers movement: *An electrocardiograph makes tracings of the contractions of the heart, which are used to diagnose heart disease.* **3** made for the purpose of tracing: *tracing paper.* **4** ppr. of TRACE. 1–3 *n.,* 4 *v.*

**track** (trak) **1** a line of metal rails for cars to run on: *A railway has tracks.* **2** a mark left: *The dirty road showed many automobile tracks.* **3** a footprint: *We saw a wild animal's tracks near the camp.* **4** follow by means of footprints, marks, smell, etc.: *The hunter tracked the bear and killed it.* **5** trace in any way: *to track down a criminal.* **6** make footprints or other marks on a floor, etc.: *Don't track the floor.* **7** bring snow or mud into a place on one's feet: *to track mud into the house.* **8** a path or trail: *A track runs through the woods to the farmhouse.* **9** a way of doing or acting: *to go on in the same track year after year.* **10** a course for running or racing: *a race track, a cinder track.* **11** the sport made up of contests in running. See TRACK AND FIELD. **12** of or for use in such sport: *track shoes.* **13** an endless belt of linked steel treads by which a tank, bulldozer, etc. is driven forward. 1–3, 8–13 *n.,* 4–7 *v.* —**track′er,** *n.* —**track′less,** *adj.*
**in one's tracks,** *Informal.* right where one is.
**keep track of,** keep within one's sight, knowledge, or attention: *The noise of the crowd made it difficult to keep track of what was going on.*
**lose track of,** fail to keep track of.
**make tracks,** *Informal.* go very fast; run away.

# track and field 1266 traditional

**off the track,** off the subject; wrong.
**on the track,** on the subject; right.

**track and field** the group of competitive athletic events performed on a running track and the field next to it, including running, jumping, pole-vaulting, and throwing: *John doesn't play hockey but he's good at track and field.*
—**track'-and-field'**, *adj.*: *Joan entered several track-and-field events.*

**track meet** a series or group of contests in track-and-field events.

**tract¹** (trakt) 1 a stretch of land, water, etc.; extent; area: *A tract of desert land has little value to farmers.* 2 a system of related parts or organs in the body: *The stomach and intestines are part of the digestive tract.* *n.*

**tract²** (trakt) a pamphlet on a religious or political subject intended to support or speak out against a particular cause or point of view. *n.*

**trac·ta·bil·i·ty** (trak'tə bil'ə tē) the quality or condition of being TRACTABLE. *n.*

**trac·ta·ble** (trak'tə bəl) 1 easily managed or controlled; easy to deal with; docile: *Dogs are more tractable than mules.* 2 easily worked: *Copper and gold are tractable.* *adj.* —**trac'ta·ble·ness**, *n.*
—**trac'ta·bly**, *adv.*

**trac·tion** (trak'shən) 1 the friction between a body and the surface on which it moves, enabling the body to move without slipping: *Wheels slip on ice because there is too little traction.* 2 the kind of power used by a locomotive, streetcar, etc.: *Some railways use electric traction.* 3 the act or process of pulling a load or vehicle over a surface or the state of being pulled. 4 the pulling of muscles of an arm, leg, etc. by means of a special device to relieve pressure, bring a fractured bone into place, etc. or the state of tension produced by such a device: *He spent several months in traction as a result of the accident.* *n.*

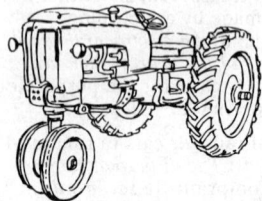 

A tractor (def. 1)   A tractor (def. 2) with trailer

**trac·tor** (trak'tər) 1 a vehicle with a powerful gasoline or diesel engine, having four wheels or running on continuous tracks, used for pulling farm implements, wagons, etc. 2 a powerful truck having a cab for the driver, a short chassis, and no body, used to pull one or more large trailers along the highway. *n.*

**trac·tor–trail·er** (trak'tər trā'lər) a very large truck, consisting of a TRACTOR (def. 2) together with a trailer or semitrailer, used for hauling freight. *n.*

**trade** (trād) 1 the process of buying and selling; exchange of goods; commerce: *Canada has much trade with foreign countries.* 2 buy and sell; exchange goods; be in commerce: *Some Canadian companies trade all over the world.* 3 make an exchange: *to trade seats. If you don't like your book, I'll trade with you. He traded a package of gum for a ride on her bicycle.* 4 an exchange: *an even trade.* 5 bargain; deal: *She made a good trade.* 6 a kind of work; business, especially one requiring skilled mechanical work: *She is learning the carpenter's trade.* 7 people in the same kind of work or business: *the building trade.* 8 *Informal.* customers: *That store has a lot of trade.* 9 **the trades**, *pl.* the TRADE WINDS. 1, 4–9 *n.*, 2, 3, 5 *v.*, **trad·ed, trad·ing.**

**trade in,** give an automobile, radio, etc. as part payment for something else: *She traded her old car in for a new one.*

**trade off,** get rid of by trading.

**trade on,** take advantage of: *She traded on her father's good name.*

**trade–in** (trād'in') 1 something, such as a used appliance or car, given or accepted as part payment for a new thing of the same kind. 2 the value or price allowed by the seller on a trade-in: *The dealer gave her $600 trade-in on her old car.* 3 of or as a trade-in: *My car has a trade-in value close to zero.* *n.*

**trade·mark** (trād'märk') 1 a mark, picture, symbol, or name that identifies a product or service as being produced or sold by a particular company, and that is protected by law: *A trademark may legally be applied only to goods or services produced or sold by the company that owns it.* 2 distinguish by means of a trademark. 3 register the trademark of. 1 *n.*, 2, 3 *v.*

**trade name** a distinctive name that identifies a product or service as being produced or sold by a particular company; brand name.

**trad·er** (trā'dər) 1 a person who trades; merchant. 2 a ship used in trading: *a coastal trader.* 3 a person who buys and sells stocks and securities for himself or herself rather than for customers. *n.*

**trade school** a school where trades are taught.

**trades·man** (trādz'mən) 1 a storekeeper; shopkeeper. 2 one who practises a trade, as, a carpenter, baker, etc. *n., pl.* **trades·men** (-zmən).

**trades·peo·ple** (trādz'pē'pəl) 1 storekeepers; shopkeepers. 2 people who practise a trade, as, welding. *n.pl.*

**trades union** *Esp. Brit.* a TRADE UNION.

**trade union** an association of workers in any trade or craft or group of allied trades to protect and promote their interests; labour union.

**trade unionism** 1 the system of having trade unions. 2 the methods or practices of trade unions.

**trade unionist** 1 a member of a trade union. 2 a person who favours TRADE UNIONISM.

**trade wind** a tropical wind blowing steadily toward the equator: *North of the equator, the trade wind blows from the northeast; south of the equator, it blows from the southeast.*

**trading post** a store or station of a trader, especially in a remote place: *The Hudson's Bay Company operates trading posts in the North.*

**tra·di·tion** (trə dish'ən) 1 the handing down of beliefs, opinions, customs, stories, etc. from one generation to another. 2 what is handed down in this way: *Many traditions of the past are still kept today.* 3 among the Jews, the unwritten laws and doctrines received from Moses. 4 in the Christian Church, the unwritten precepts and doctrines received from Christ and his apostles. 5 a way of behaving or doing things based on long practice: *The navy has many old traditions.* *n.*

**tra·di·tion·al** (trə dish'ə nəl) of, based on, or handed down by TRADITION: *The coronation is a traditional* ceremony. *They prefer traditional furniture to modern furniture.* *adj.* —**tra·di′tion·al·ly,** *adv.*

**tra·duce** (trə dyüs′ *or* trə düs′) speak evil of a person falsely; slander. *v.*, **tra·duced, tra·duc·ing.** —**traduc′er,** *n.*

**traf·fic** (traf′ik) **1** the people, automobiles, wagons, ships, etc. coming and going along a way of travel. **2** buying and selling; commerce; trade. **3** carry on trade; buy; sell; exchange: *The men trafficked with the natives for pearls.* **4** the business done by a railway line, a steamship line, etc. **5** the number of passengers or the amount of freight carried. **6** intercourse; dealings. **7** have social dealings with; have to do with: *He refuses to traffic with strangers.* 1, 2, 4–6 *n.*, 3, 7 *v.*, **traf·ficked, traf·fick·ing.**

**traffic island** a usually raised area in a road or street designed to direct the flow of traffic into particular lanes, protect pedestrians, etc.

**traf·fick·er** (traf′i kər) a person who buys and sells, especially one who deals illicitly in drugs or other goods. *n.*

**traffic light** an electrically operated device for controlling traffic at intersections, consisting of a standard series of coloured lights. A green light means go ahead, an amber light means caution, and a red one means stop.

**trag·a·canth** (trag′ə kanth′) **1** a gum obtained from certain Asian or eastern European shrubs of the pea family used for stiffening cloth, thickening medicines, etc. **2** a plant yielding this gum. *n.*

**tra·ge·di·an** (trə jē′dē ən) **1** a writer of tragedies. **2** an actor who specializes in tragic roles. *n.*

**tra·ge·di·enne** (trə jē′dē en′) an actress who specializes in tragic roles. *n.*

**trag·e·dy** (traj′ə dē) **1** a serious play having an unhappy ending. In many tragedies the hero or heroine experiences great mental suffering and, finally, meets his or her death: *Hamlet is a tragedy.* **2** the branch of drama that includes such plays. **3** the writing of such plays. **4** a novel, long poem, etc. similar to a tragic play. **5** a very sad or terrible happening: *The father's death was a tragedy to his family.* *n., pl.* **trag·e·dies.**

**trag·ic** (traj′ik) **1** of tragedy; having to do with tragedy: *a tragic actor, a tragic poet.* **2** very sad; dreadful: *a tragic event.* *adj.* —**trag′i·cal·ly,** *adv.*

**trag·i·cal** (traj′ə kəl) TRAGIC. *adj.*

**tragic flaw** a flaw in the character of a tragic hero or heroine that brings about his or her downfall.

**trag·i·com·e·dy** (traj′i kom′ə dē) **1** a play having both tragic and comic elements: *The Merchant of Venice is a tragicomedy.* **2** an incident or situation in which serious and comic elements are blended. *n., pl.* **trag·i·com·e·dies.**

**trag·i·com·ic** (traj′i kom′ik) having both tragic and comic elements. *adj.*

**trail** (trāl) **1** a path across a wild or unsettled region: *The men had followed mountain trails for days.* **2** track or smell: *The dogs found the trail of the rabbit.* **3** hunt by track or smell: *The dogs trailed the rabbit.* **4** anything that follows along behind: *The car left a trail of dust behind it.* **5** follow along behind; follow: *The dog trailed its mistress constantly.* **6** pull or be pulled along behind: *The child trailed a toy horse after her. Her dress trails on the ground.* **7** follow the trail or track of; track: *to trail a bear or thief.* **8** follow in a long, uneven line: *The ten campers trailed their leader down the mountainside.*

**traduce** 1267 **trainee**

hat, āge, fär; let, ēqual, tėrm; it, īce
hot, ōpen, ôrder; oil, out; cup, pùt, rüle
əbove, takən, pencəl, lemən, circəs
ch, child; ng, long; sh, ship
th, thin; ᴛʜ, then; zh, measure

**9** grow along: *Poison ivy trailed by the road.* **10** go along slowly: *The children trailed to school.* **11** tread down grass to make a path. **12** the lower end of a gun carriage. **13** pass little by little: *Her voice trailed off into silence.* 1, 2, 4, 12 *n.*, 3, 5–11, 13 *v.*

**trail·bla·zer** (trāl′blā′zər) **1** a person who blazes a trail. **2** a person who pioneers or prepares the way to something new. *n.*

**trail·er** (trā′lər) **1** a small or large vehicle having one or more pairs of wheels, designed to be pulled along by a truck, tractor, automobile, etc., and used for transporting goods, animals, a boat or snowmobile, etc. **2** a closed-in vehicle having one or more pairs of wheels, designed to be pulled by an automobile or truck and equipped for use as a dwelling or place of business: *We have a trailer that we take to the lake every summer. Large trailers are often called mobile homes.* **3** a short film made up of selected scenes from a motion picture, shown to advertise the motion picture. **4** a trailing plant. **5** a person or animal that follows a trail. *n.*

**trailer camp** or **park** an area equipped to accommodate TRAILERS (def. 2): *Many trailer camps have electricity and running water.*

**trailing arbutus** a trailing plant of the heath family found in the woodlands of eastern North America, having evergreen leaves and clusters of fragrant, pink or white flowers very early in spring; mayflower: *The trailing arbutus is the provincial flower of Nova Scotia.*

**train** (trān) **1** a connected line of railway cars pulled by an engine. **2** a line of people, animals, wagons, trucks, etc. moving along together: *A train of snowmobiles sped across the ice.* **3** a collection of vehicles, animals, and men accompanying an army to carry supplies, baggage, ammunition, or any equipment or materials. **4** a part of a cloak or gown that trails behind the wearer: *Two attendants carried the bride's train.* **5** something that is drawn along behind; a trailing part. **6** a TRAIL (def. 4): *the train of a peacock, the train of a comet.* **7** a group of followers: *the rodeo star and his train.* **8** a series; succession: *a long train of misfortunes.* **9** a continuous course: *a train of ideas.* **10** a succession of results or conditions following some event: *The flood brought starvation and disease in its train.* **11** bring up; rear; teach: *to train a child.* **12** make skilful by teaching and practice: *Saint Bernard dogs were trained to hunt for travellers lost in the snow.* **13** become skilful: *She is training as a nurse.* **14** make fit by exercise and diet: *The runners trained for races.* **15** make oneself fit. **16** point; aim: *to train cannon upon a fort.* **17** bring into a particular position: *We trained the vine around the post.* **18** a line of gunpowder that acts as a fuse. **19** in machinery, a series of connected parts, such as wheels and pinions, through which motion is transmitted. 1–10, 18, 19 *n.*, 11–17 *v.*

**train of thought,** a succession of thoughts passing through one's mind at a particular time: *From the way the speaker paused, it was obvious that he had lost his train of thought.*

**train·ee** (trā nē′) one who is receiving training. *n.*

**train·er** (trā′nər) **1** a person who trains individual athletes or sports teams. **2** a person who trains racehorses, circus beasts, or other animals. **3** a device, machine, etc. used in training: *The pilot was flying a single-engined trainer.* *n.*

**train·ing** (trā′ning) **1** practical education in some art, profession, etc.: *training for teachers.* **2** the development of strength and endurance. **3** a good condition maintained by exercise, diet, etc.: *to keep in training.* **4** ppr. of TRAIN. 1–3 *n.*, 4 *v.*

**training camp** in sports, a session of intensive training undertaken by a team or an athlete at a place away from home base in preparation for a regular season or for a special contest or event.

**training school** in Canada, an institution for the custody and education of juvenile offenders, operated by a provincial government or by a private organization under a provincial charter.

**training wheels** small wheels attached on either side of the rear wheel of a bicycle to steady the vehicle for a child learning to ride.

**train·load** (trān′lōd′) as much as a train can hold or carry. *n.*

**train·man** (trān′mən) a man who works on a railway train, especially a brakeman. *n., pl.* **train·men** (-mən).

**train oil** oil obtained from a sea animal, especially a whale.

**traipse** (trāps) *Informal.* **1** trudge or tramp, especially wearily or aimlessly: *He traipsed all over town looking for a job. Don't traipse through here with your muddy boots on.* **2** the act of traipsing. 1 *v.*, **traipsed, traips·ing**; 2 *n.*

**trait** (trāt *or* trā) a quality of mind, character, etc.; a distinguishing feature; characteristic: *Courage, love of justice, and common sense are desirable traits.* *n.*
☛ *Hom.* TRAY (for the second pronunciation of **trait**).

**trai·tor** (trā′tər) **1** a person who betrays his or her country or ruler; one who commits TREASON. **2** a person who betrays a trust, duty, friend, etc. *n.*

**trai·tor·ous** (trā′tə rəs) like a TRAITOR; treacherous; faithless. *adj.* —**trai′tor·ous·ly,** *adv.*

**trai·tress** (trā′tris) a female TRAITOR. *n.*

**tra·jec·to·ry** (trə jek′tə rē) the curved path of something moving through space, such as a bullet from a gun or a planet in its orbit. *n., pl.* **tra·jec·to·ries.**

**tram** (tram) **1** *Esp.Brit.* STREETCAR. **2** TRAMWAY. **3** a truck or car on which loads are carried in coal mines. *n.*

**tram·mel** (tram′əl) **1** anything that hinders or restrains: *A large bequest freed the artist from the trammels of poverty.* **2** hinder; restrain. **3** a fine net to catch fish, birds, etc. **4** entangle. **5** a hook in a fireplace to hold pots, kettles, etc. over the fire. **6** a shackle for controlling the motions of a horse and making it amble. 1, 3, 5, 6 *n.*, 2, 4 *v.*, **tram·melled** *or* **tram·meled, tram·mel·ling** *or* **tram·mel·ing**.

**tramp** (tramp) **1** walk heavily: *He tramped across the room in his heavy boots.* **2** step heavily on: *He tramped on the flowers.* **3** the sound of heavy footsteps: *Hear the tramp of the parade.* **4** go on foot; walk: *We tramped through the streets.* **5** travel through on foot: *to tramp the streets.* **6** a long, steady walk; hike: *The girls took a tramp together over the hills.* **7** walk steadily; march: *We tramped all day.* **8** a person who goes about on foot, living by begging, doing odd jobs, etc.; a hobo. **9** go or wander as a tramp. **10** a freight ship that takes a cargo when and where it can. 1, 2, 4, 5, 7, 9 *v.*, 3, 6, 8, 10 *n.* —**tramp′er,** *n.*

**tram·ple** (tram′pəl) **1** crush, destroy, violate, etc. by or as if by treading on heavily: *The cattle broke through the fence and trampled the farmer's crops.* **2** the act or sound of trampling: *We heard the trample of many feet.* 1 *v.*, **tram·pled, tram·pling;** 2 *n.* —**tram′pler,** *n.*
**trample under foot, trample on** *or* **upon,** treat with scorn or cruelty: *The dictator trampled on the rights of the people.*

A trampoline

**tram·po·line** (tram′pə lēn′) an apparatus for tumbling, acrobatics, etc. consisting of a taut piece of canvas or other sturdy fabric attached by springs to a metal frame: *The children liked to bounce around on the trampoline.* *n.*

**tram·way** (tram′wā) **1** *Esp.Brit.* a track for streetcars. **2** in mining: **a** a track or roadway for carrying ore from mines. **b** a cable or system of cables on which suspended cars carry ore, etc. *n.*

**trance** (trans) **1** a state of unconsciousness resembling sleep: *A person may be in a trance from illness, from the influence of some other person, or from his or her own will.* **2** a dreamy, absorbed condition that is like a trance: *The old man sat before the fire in a trance, thinking of his past life.* **3** a high emotion; rapture. **4** hold in a trance; enchant. 1–3 *n.*, 4 *v.*, **tranced, tranc·ing**. —**trance′like′,** *adj.*

**tran·quil** (trang′kwəl) calm; peaceful; quiet: *a tranquil mood, the tranquil evening air.* *adj.* —**tran′quil·ly,** *adv.*

**tran·quil·ize** (trang′kwə līz′) See TRANQUILLIZE. *v.*, **tran·quil·ized, tran·quil·iz·ing**.

**tran·quil·iz·er** (trang′kwə lī′zər) See TRANQUILLIZER. *n.*

**tran·quil·li·ty** *or* **tran·quil·i·ty** (trang kwil′ə tē) calmness; peacefulness; quiet. *n.*

**tran·quil·lize** *or* **tran·quil·ize** (trang′kwə līz′) **1** make tranquil; especially, reduce mental tension and anxiety by the use of drugs. **2** become tranquil. *v.*, **tran·quil·lized** *or* **tran·quil·ized, tran·quil·liz·ing** *or* **tran·quil·iz·ing**.

**tran·quil·liz·er** *or* **tran·quil·iz·er** (trang′kwə lī′zər) a person or thing that tranquillizes; especially, any of several drugs used to reduce mental tension and anxiety, control certain psychoses, etc. *n.*

**trans–** a prefix meaning: **1** across, over, or through, as in *transcontinental, transmit.* **2** beyond; on the other side of, as in *Transjordan, transcend.* **3** across, etc.; and also beyond, on the other side of, as in *transmarine, transoceanic,* and many other geographical terms, such as

*trans-African.* **4** into a different place, condition, etc., as in *transform, transmute.*
☞ *Etym.* From L *trans* 'across, over'.

**trans.** **1** transitive. **2** transportation. **3** translation. **4** transferred.

**trans·act** (tran zakt′) attend to; manage; do; carry on business: *She transacts business with stores all over the country.* *v.*

**trans·ac·tion** (tran zak′shən) **1** the carrying on of business: *Dawn attends to the transaction of important matters herself.* **2** a piece of business: *A record is kept of all the firm's transactions.* **3 transactions,** *pl.* a record of what was done at the meetings of a society, club, etc. *n.*

**trans·al·pine** (tran zal′pīn) across or beyond the Alps, especially as viewed from Italy. *adj.*

**trans·at·lan·tic** (tran′sə tlan′tik) **1** crossing or extending across the Atlantic Ocean. **2** having to do with crossing the Atlantic Ocean: *transatlantic air fares.* **3** on the other side of the Atlantic Ocean. *adj.*

**trans–Can·a·da** (tran′skan′ə də) **1** extending right across Canada, from the Atlantic to the Pacific oceans: *the trans-Canada microwave system.* **2 the Trans-Canada,** the Trans-Canada Highway, a series of paved roads extending across Canada through each province and conforming to agreed standards of construction. *adj.*

**trans·cei·ver** (tran sē′vər) a combined transmitter and receiver, as, for radio signals. *n.*

**tran·scend** (tran send′) **1** go beyond the limits or powers of; exceed: *The grandeur of Niagara Falls transcends description.* **2** be higher or greater than; surpass; excel: *The speed of jet planes transcends that of any previous form of transportation.* **3** be superior or extraordinary to. *v.*

**tran·scend·ent** (tran sen′dənt) **1** surpassing ordinary limits; excelling; superior; extraordinary. **2** existing apart from the universe. *adj.* —**tran·scend′ent·ly,** *adv.*

**tran·scen·den·tal** (tran′sen den′təl) **1** TRANSCENDENT. **2** SUPERNATURAL. **3** obscure; incomprehensible; fantastic. **4** explaining matter and objective things as products of the mind that is thinking about them; idealistic. **5** implied in and necessary to human experience. *adj.* —**tran′scen·den′tal·ly,** *adv.*

**trans·con·ti·nen·tal** (tran′skon tə nen′təl) **1** crossing or extending across a continent: *a transcontinental railway.* **2** a train that crosses a continent: *We went from Halifax to Vancouver on the transcontinental.* **3** on the other side of a continent. **1, 3** *adj.,* **2** *n.*

**tran·scribe** (tran skrīb′) **1** copy in writing or in typewriting: *The account of the trial was transcribed from the stenographer's shorthand notes.* **2** set down in writing or print: *Her entire speech was transcribed in the newspapers, word for word.* **3** arrange a piece of music for a different instrument or voice. **4** in radio and television, make a recording of a program, commercial, etc., especially for broadcasting at a later time. **5** broadcast a program, commercial, etc. that has been previously recorded. *v.,* **tran·scribed, tran·scrib·ing.** —**tran·scrib′er,** *n.*

**tran·script** (tran′skript) **1** a written or typewritten copy: *They were waiting for a transcript of the tapes.* **2** any copy or reproduction: *The university requires a transcript of your high-school grades.* *n.*

**tran·scrip·tion** (tran skrip′shən) **1** the act or process of transcribing. **2** a transcript; copy. **3** an arrangement of a piece of music for a different instrument or voice.

**trans.** 1269 **transformer**

hat, āge, fär; let, ēqual, tėrm; it, īce
hot, ōpen, ôrder; oil, out; cup, put, rüle
əbove, takən, pencəl, lemən, circəs
ch, child; ng, long; sh, ship
th, thin; ᴛʜ, then; zh, measure

**4** a recording of a program, commercial, etc. made for broadcasting on radio or television. **5** the act or practice of broadcasting such a recording. *n.*

**trans·du·cer** (trans dyü′sər *or* trans dü′sər) an electrical device which converts one form of energy into another: *Microphones and loudspeakers are transducers.* *n.*

**tran·sept** (tran′sept) **1** the part of a cross-shaped church at right angles to the long main part. **2** either projecting end of this part. *n.*

**trans·fer** (tran sfėr′ *for verb,* tran′sfėr *for noun*) **1** convey or remove from one person or place to another; hand over: *This farm has been transferred from father to son for generations. My trunks were transferred by express.* **2** convey a drawing, design, pattern from one surface to another: *You transfer the embroidery design from the paper to cloth by pressing it with a warm iron.* **3** a transferring or being transferred. **4** a drawing, pattern, etc. printed or to be printed from one surface onto another. **5** change from one streetcar, bus, train, etc. to another without having to pay another fare. **6** a ticket allowing a passenger to continue his or her journey on another streetcar, bus, train, etc. **7** a point or place for transferring. **1, 2, 5** *v.,* **trans·ferred, trans·fer·ring; 3, 4, 6, 7** *n.*

**trans·fer·a·bil·i·ty** (tran sfėr′ə bil′ə tē) the quality of being TRANSFERABLE. *n.*

**trans·fer·a·ble** (tran sfėr′ə bəl) capable of being TRANSFERred. *adj.*

**trans·fer·ence** (tran sfėr′əns *or* tran′sfə rəns) TRANSFERring or being transferred. *n.*

**trans·fig·u·ra·tion** (tran sfig′ə rā′shən *or* tran sfig′yə rā′shən) a change in form or appearance; transformation. *n.*

**trans·fig·ure** (tran sfig′ər *or* tran sfig′yər) **1** change in form or appearance, usually for the better: *New paint had transfigured the old house.* **2** change so as to glorify; exalt. *v.,* **trans·fig·ured, trans·fig·ur·ing.**

**trans·fix** (tran sfiks′) **1** pierce through: *The hunter transfixed the lion with a spear.* **2** fasten by piercing through with something pointed. **3** make motionless with amazement, terror, etc. *v.*

**trans·form** (tran sfôrm′) **1** change in form or appearance: *The blizzard transformed the bushes into glittering mounds of snow.* **2** change in condition, nature, or character: *The witch transformed men into pigs. A generator transforms mechanical energy into electricity.* **3** change an electric current to a different voltage or type. *v.*

**trans·for·ma·tion** (tran′sfər mā′shən) a transforming or being transformed: *The witch's transformation of the men into pigs was terrifying. We were amazed at the transformation of a thief into an honest man.* *n.*

**trans·form·er** (tran sfôr′mər) a device for changing the voltage of an electric current: *North American electrical appliances cannot be used in Europe without a transformer*

# transfuse 1270 transmission

because the voltage there is much higher than in North America. *n.*

**trans·fuse** (tran sfyüz′) **1** pour from one container into another. **2** transfer blood from one person or animal to another. **3** inject a solution into a blood vessel. **4** infuse; instil: *The speaker transfused her enthusiasm into the audience.* *v.*, **trans·fused, trans·fus·ing.**

**trans·fu·sion** (tran sfyü′zhən) **1** the act or process of transfusing; especially, the process of transfusing blood or blood plasma into a blood vessel of a person or animal. **2** an instance of transfusing blood: *The wounded soldier was given three transfusions in a week.* *n.*

**trans·gress** (trans gres′ *or* tranz gres′) **1** break a law, command, etc.; sin: *He knew he had transgressed.* **2** go contrary to; sin against: *to transgress the divine law.* **3** go beyond a boundary or limit: *The interviewer's questions transgressed the bounds of good taste.* *v.*

**trans·gres·sion** (trans gresh′ən *or* tranz gresh′ən) the act of transgressing; breaking a law, command, etc. *n.*

**trans·gres·sor** (trans gres′ər *or* tranz gres′ər) a person who transgresses; sinner. *n.*

**tran·ship** (tran ship′) See TRANSSHIP. *v.*, **tran·shipped, tran·ship·ping. —tran·ship′ment,** *n.*

**tran·sience** (tran′zē əns) the quality or state of being TRANSIENT. *n.*

**tran·sient** (tran′zē ənt) **1** passing soon; fleeting; not lasting; transitory: *Joy and sorrow are often transient.* **2** passing through and not staying long: *a transient guest in a hotel.* **3** a visitor or boarder who stays for a short time. **4** a tramp or hobo. 1, 2 *adj.*, 3, 4 *n.* **—tran′sient·ly,** *adv.*

**tran·sis·tor** (tran zis′tər) **1** a small electronic device similar to an electron tube in use, that amplifies electricity by controlling the flow of electrons: *Transistors are used in computers, radios, television sets, etc.* **2** a portable radio that has transistors instead of tubes: *She carries her transistor wherever she goes.* *n.*

**tran·sis·tor·ize** (tran zis′tə rīz′) equip with transistors. *v.*, **tran·sis·tor·ized, tran·sis·tor·iz·ing.**

Transit (def. 6). The instrument includes a telescope and levels and scales for measuring angles both vertically and horizontally.

**trans·it** (tran′sit *or* tran′zit) **1** the act or process or an instance of passing across or through. **2** the process of carrying or being carried across or through: *The goods were damaged in transit.* **3** transportation by trains, buses, etc.: *All systems of transit are crowded during the rush hour.* **4** a transition or change. **5** pass; pass across; pass through. **6** an instrument used in surveying to measure angles. **7** the apparent passage of a heavenly body across the meridian of a place. **8** the passage of a small heavenly body across the disk of a larger one. 1–4, 6–8 *n.*, 5 *v.*, **trans·it·ed, trans·it·ing.**

**tran·si·tion** (tran zish′ən) **1** a change or passing from one condition, place, form, stage, etc. to another: *a transition from poverty to wealth and power. The time between two distinct periods of history, art, etc. is called a period of transition. Abrupt transitions in a book confuse the reader.* **2** in music: **a** a change of key. **b** a passage linking one section, subject, etc. of a composition with another. *n.*

**tran·si·tion·al** (tran zi′shə nəl) of, having to do with, or involving TRANSITION: *a transitional stage in his life.* *adj.* **—tran·si′tion·al·ly,** *adv.*

**tran·si·tive** (tran′sə tiv *or* tran′zə tiv) **1** of verbs, taking a direct object. *Bring* and *raise* are transitive verbs. Compare with INTRANSITIVE. **2** a transitive verb. **3** TRANSITIONAL. 1, 3 *adj.*, 2 *n.* **—tran′si·tive·ly,** *adv.* **—tran′si·tive·ness,** *n.*

**tran·si·to·ry** (tran′sə tô′rē *or* tran′zə tô′rē) passing soon or quickly; lasting only a short time. *adj.* **—tran′si·to′ri·ly,** *adv.* **—tran′si·to′ri·ness,** *n.*

**trans·late** (tran slāt′, tran zlāt′ *or* tran′zlāt′) **1** change from one language into another: *to translate a book from French into English.* **2** explain the meaning of: *He translated his idea into language we could understand.* **3** change from one place, position, state, or form to another; transform or transfer: *to translate one's ideas into practice.* *v.*, **trans·lat·ed, trans·lat·ing.** **—trans·lat′a·ble,** *adj.*

**trans·la·tion** (tran slā′shən *or* tran zlā′shən) **1** translating or being translated: *Her translation of the German novel was very successful. The translation of a promise into a deed is not always easy.* **2** the result of translating; version: *a translation of a French poem.* *n.*

**trans·la·tor** (tran slā′tər *or* tran zlā′tər) a person who TRANSLATES (def. 1). *n.*

**trans·lu·cence** (tran slü′səns *or* tran zlü′səns) the quality or state of being TRANSLUCENT. *n.*

**trans·lu·cen·cy** (tran slü′sən sē *or* tran zlü′sən sē) **1** TRANSLUCENCE. **2** something that is TRANSLUCENT. *n.*

**trans·lu·cent** (tran slü′sənt *or* tran zlü′sənt) letting light through without being TRANSPARENT: *Frosted glass is translucent.* *adj.* **—trans·lu′cent·ly,** *adv.*

**trans·ma·rine** (tran′smə rēn′ *or* tran′zmə rēn′) across or beyond the sea. *adj.*

**trans·mi·grate** (tran smī′grāt *or* tran zmī′grāt) **1** of the soul, pass at death into another body. **2** move from one place or country to another; migrate. *v.*, **trans·mi·grat·ed, trans·mi·grat·ing.**

**trans·mi·gra·tion** (tran′smī grā′shən *or* tran′zmī grā′shən) **1** in certain religions, the passing of the soul at death into another body: *Belief in the transmigration of souls is an important part of Hinduism.* **2** going from one place or country to another; migration. *n.*

**trans·mis·si·ble** (tran smis′ə bəl *or* tran zmis′ə bəl) capable of being transmitted: *Scarlet fever is a transmissible disease.* *adj.*

**trans·mis·sion** (tran smish′ən *or* tran zmish′ən) **1** a sending over; passing on or along; letting through: *Mosquitoes are the only means of transmission of malaria.* **2** something transmitted. **3** the part of a motor vehicle that transmits power from the engine to the driving axle. **4** the passage through space of radio waves from the transmitting station to the receiving station: *When* *transmission is good, distant radio stations can be heard.* *n.*

**trans·mit** (tran smit′ *or* tran zmit′) **1** send over; pass on; pass along; let through: *I will transmit the money by special messenger. Rats transmit disease.* **2** cause light, heat, sound, etc. to pass through a medium. **3** of a medium, allow light, heat, etc. to pass through: *Glass transmits light.* **4** send out signals, voice, music, etc. by electromagnetic waves or by wire: *Some broadcasting stations transmit every hour of the day.* *v.*, **trans·mit·ted, trans·mit·ting.**

**trans·mit·tal** (tran smit′əl *or* tran zmit′əl) a TRANSMITting. *n.*

**trans·mit·ter** (tran smit′ər *or* tran zmit′ər) **1** the part of a telephone into which one speaks and which contains a device that converts the sound waves of speech into corresponding electric waves. **2** the part of a telegraph by which a message is sent. **3** in radio and television broadcasting, the apparatus that generates and modulates radio-frequency waves and sends them to the station's antenna. **4** any person or thing that transmits. *n.*

**trans·mu·ta·tion** (tran′smyə tā′shən *or* tran′zmyə tā′shən) **1** a change into another nature, substance, or form. **2** in physics and chemistry, the conversion of atoms of one element into atoms of a different element or a different isotope, either naturally, as by radio-active disintegration, or artificially, as by bombardment with neutrons, etc. **3** in alchemy, the attempted conversion of a base metal into gold or silver. *n.*

**trans·mute** (tran smyüt′ *or* tran zmyüt′) change from one nature, substance, or form into another: *We can transmute water power into electrical power.* *v.*, **trans·mut·ed, trans·mut·ing.** —**trans·mut′er,** *n.*

**trans·o·ce·an·ic** (tran′sō shē an′ik *or* tran′zō shē an′ik) **1** crossing or extending across the ocean: *a transoceanic airline.* **2** on the other side of the ocean. *adj.*

**tran·som** (tran′səm) **1** a window over a door or other window, usually hinged at the top or bottom for opening. **2** a horizontal crossbar in a window, over a door, or between a door and a window above it. *n.*

**tran·son·ic** (tran son′ik) of, having to do with, or designed for operation at speeds close to the speed of sound in air, which is about 1190 km/h at sea level. *adj.*

**trans·pa·cif·ic** (tran′spə sif′ik) **1** crossing or extending across the Pacific Ocean. **2** having to do with crossing the Pacific Ocean: *transpacific air fares.* **3** on the other side of the Pacific Ocean. *adj.*

**trans·par·ence** (tran sper′əns *or* tran spar′əns) TRANSPARENCY. *n.*

**trans·par·en·cy** (tran sper′ən sē *or* tran spar′ən sē) **1** the quality or state of being TRANSPARENT. **2** something TRANSPARENT; especially, a photograph, picture, or design on glass or clear plastic made visible by light shining through from below or behind. *n., pl.* **trans·par·en·cies.**

**trans·par·ent** (tran sper′ənt *or* tran spar′ənt) **1** transmitting light so that something behind or beyond can be distinctly seen: *Window glass is transparent.* **2** of fabrics, etc., so fine, or open in weave that something on the other side can be seen quite clearly; sheer. **3** easily seen through or detected; obvious: *The excuse he gave was transparent.* **4** free from deceit or guile; frank: *She had led a simple and transparent life.* *adj.*
—**trans·par′ent·ly,** *adv.*

## transmit 1271 transposition

hat, āge, fär; let, ēqual, tėrm; it, īce
hot, ōpen, ôrder; oil, out; cup, pùt, rüle
əbove, takən, pencəl, lemən, circəs
ch, child; ng, long; sh, ship
th, thin; ᴛH, then; zh, measure

**tran·spi·ra·tion** (tran′spə rā′shən) the act or process or an instance of transpiring; especially, the passage of moisture through the pores of the skin or the surface of plant leaves. *n.*

**tran·spire** (tran spīr′) **1** take place; happen. **2** leak out; become known. **3** pass off or send off in the form of vapour through a wall or surface, as from the human body or from leaves. *v.*, **tran·spired, tran·spir·ing.**

**trans·plant** (tran splant′ *for verb,* tran′splant *for noun*) **1** plant again in a different place: *We start the flowers indoors and then transplant them to the garden.* **2** remove from one place to another: *The colony was transplanted to a more healthful location.* **3** transfer skin, an organ, etc. from one person or animal to another, or from one part of the body to another: *to transplant a kidney.* **4** the transfer of an organ, etc. from one person or animal to another, or from one part of the body to another: *a heart transplant.* **5** bear transplanting: *Poppies do not transplant well and should be planted where they are to grow.* 1–3, 5 *v.*, 4 *n.* —**trans·plant′a·ble,** *adj.*
—**trans·plant′er,** *n.*

**trans·plan·ta·tion** (tran′splan tā′shən) **1** TRANSPLANTing or being transplanted. **2** something that has been TRANSPLANTED. *n.*

**trans·port** (tran spôrt′ *for verb,* tran′spôrt *for noun*) **1** carry from one place to another: *Wheat is transported from the farms to the mills.* **2** a carrying from one place to another: *Trucks are much used for transport.* **3** a large truck used to carry freight long distances by road. **4** a ship used to carry troops and supplies. **5** an airplane that transports passengers, mail, freight, etc. **6** carry away by strong feeling: *She was transported with joy by the good news.* **7** a strong feeling: *a transport of rage.* **8** send away to another country as a punishment. **9** a transported convict. 1, 6, 8 *v.*, 2–5, 7, 9 *n.*
—**trans·port′er,** *n.*

**trans·port·a·ble** (tran spôr′tə bəl) **1** capable of being transported. **2** involving, or liable to, punishment by TRANSPORTATION (def. 4): *a transportable offence.* *adj.*

**trans·por·ta·tion** (tran′spər tā′shən) **1** a transporting or being transported: *The railway allows free transportation for a certain amount of a passenger's baggage.* **2** a means of transport: *A small bus serves as transportation to the airport.* **3** the cost of transport; a ticket for transport: *The transportation for our summer trip came to $800.* **4** sending or being sent away to another country as a punishment. *n.*

**trans·pos·al** (tran spō′zəl) TRANSPOSITION (def. 1). *n.*

**trans·pose** (tran spōz′) **1** change the position or order of; interchange. **2** change the usual order of letters, words, or numbers. *Example:* Up came the wind, and off went her hat. **3** in music, change the key of. **4** transfer a term to the other side of an algebraic equation, changing plus to minus or minus to plus. *v.*, **trans·posed, trans·pos·ing.** —**trans·pos′er,** *n.*

**trans·po·si·tion** (tran′spə zish′ən) **1** transposing or being transposed. 2 something transposed, such as a piece of music transposed into a different key. *n.*

**trans·pro·vin·cial** (tran′sprə vin′shəl)  crossing a province from one end to the other: *a transprovincial bus service. adj.*

**trans·ship** (trans ship′ *or* tran ship′)  transfer from one ship, train, car, etc., to another. *v.*, **trans·shipped, trans·ship·ping.** Also, **tranship.** —**trans·ship′ment,** *n.*

**trans·son·ic** (tran son′ik)  See TRANSONIC. *adj.*

**tran·sub·stan·ti·a·tion** (tran′səb stan′shē ā′shən)  1 a changing of one substance into another. 2 in the Roman Catholic and the Eastern Orthodox church, the miraculous changing of the substance of the bread and wine of the Eucharist into the substance of the body and blood of Christ, only the appearance of the bread and wine remaining. *n.*

**trans·ver·sal** (tran svėr′səl *or* tran zvėr′səl)  1 TRANSVERSE (def. 1).  2 a line intersecting two or more other lines.  1 *adj.*, 2 *n.*

**trans·verse** (tran svėrs′ *or* tran zvėrs′)  1 lying or placed across or crosswise: *The transverse beams in the barn were walnut.*  2 a transverse part or piece.  1 *adj.*, 2 *n.* —**trans·verse′ly,** *adv.*

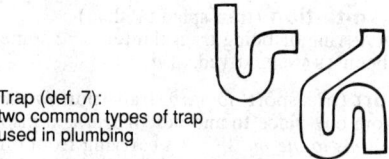

Trap (def. 7): two common types of trap used in plumbing

**trap** (trap)  1 a device for catching animals, lobsters, birds, etc.  2 a trick or other means for catching someone off guard: *She knew that the question was a trap.*  3 catch in a trap: *The wily old bear was trapped.*  4 set traps for animals: *He makes his living by trapping animals for their fur.*  5 make a business of catching animals in traps for their furs.  6 TRAPDOOR.  7 a bend in a pipe for holding a small amount of water to prevent the escape of air, gas, etc.  8 provide with a trap.  9 stop with a trap.  10 a light two-wheeled carriage.  11 a device to throw clay pigeons, etc. into the air to be shot at.  12 **traps,** *pl.*  drums, cymbals, bells, gongs, etc.  1, 2, 6, 7, 10–12 *n.*, 3–5, 8, 9 *v.*, **trapped, trap·ping.**

**trap·door** (trap′dôr′)  a door in a floor, ceiling, or roof.  *n.*

**tra·peze** (trə pēz′)  a short, horizontal bar hung by ropes like a swing, used in gymnastics and acrobatics.  *n.*

**tra·pe·zi·um** (trə pē′zē əm)  1 a four-sided plane figure having no sides parallel.  See QUADRILATERAL for picture.  2 *Brit.*  a four-sided plane figure having two parallel and two non-parallel sides; TRAPEZOID.  *n., pl.* **tra·pe·zi·ums** or **tra·pe·zi·a** (-zē ə).

**trap·e·zoid** (trap′ə zoid′)  1 a four-sided plane figure having two sides parallel and two sides not parallel.  See QUADRILATERAL for picture.  2 *Brit.*  a four-sided plane figure having no sides parallel; TRAPEZIUM.  *n.*

**trap·line** (trap′līn′)  in trapping, the way or route along which traps are set for beaver and other small animals.  *n.*

**trap·per** (trap′ər)  a person who traps wild animals for food or for their fur.  *n.*

**trap·pings** (trap′ingz)  1 ornamental coverings for a horse.  2 things worn; ornamental dress: *the trappings of a king and his court.*  3 outward appearances: *He had all the trappings of a cowboy, but he couldn't even ride a horse.* *n.pl.*

**Trap·pist** (trap′ist)  1 a monk belonging to an extremely austere branch of the Cistercian order established in 1664.  2 of or having to do with the Trappists.  1 *n.*, 2 *adj.*

**trap·shoot·er** (trap′shü′tər)  a person who takes part in TRAPSHOOTING.  *n.*

**trap·shoot·ing** (trap′shü′ting)  the sport or act of shooting at clay pigeons, etc. thrown into the air.  *n.*

**trash** (trash)  1 discarded or worthless stuff; rubbish: *There was a lot of trash in the yard of the vacant house.*  2 worthless or inferior writing: *That novel is trash; I can't imagine how it ever got published.*  3 a person of worthless character or such persons as a group; riffraff.  4 destroy: *Last winter our summer cottage was broken into and trashed by vandals.*  1–3 *n.*, 4 *v.*

**trash·y** (trash′ē)  like or containing trash; of inferior quality: *a trashy magazine.*  *adj.*, **trash·i·er, trash·i·est.** —**trash′i·ness,** *n.*

**trau·ma** (trom′ə *or* trou′mə)  1 a physical or psychic wound; injury.  2 the condition produced by such a wound.  3 an emotional shock that has lasting effects for the victim.  *n., pl.* **trau·ma·ta** (-mə tə) or **trau·mas.**

**trau·mat·ic** (tro mat′ik *or* trou mat′ik)  1 of, having to do with, or produced by a TRAUMA.  2 *Informal.* shocking or unpleasant: *It was a traumatic experience to run into his old enemy after all those years.*  *adj.* —**trau·mat′i·cal·ly,** *adv.*

**trav·ail** (trav′āl)  1 hard work; toil.  2 trouble or pain.  3 the pains of childbirth; labour pains.  4 suffer the pains of childbirth.  5 work hard.  1–3 *n.*, 4, 5 *v.*

**trav·el** (trav′əl)  1 go from one place to another; journey: *to travel across the country.*  2 going in airplanes, trains, ships, cars, etc. from one place to another; journeying.  3 go from place to place on business: *She travels for a large firm.*  4 move; proceed; pass: *Light and sound travel in waves.*  5 walk or run: *A deer travels a considerable distance in a day.*  6 pass through or over: *to travel a road.*  7 movement in general.  8 the length of stroke, speed, way of working, etc. of a part of a machine.  9 **travels,** *pl.*  **a** journeys.  **b** a book about one's experiences, visits, etc. while travelling.  1, 3–6 *v.*, 2, 7–9 *n.*  **trav·elled** or **trav·eled, trav·el·ling** or **trav·el·ing;**

**trav·elled** or **trav·eled** (trav′əld)  1 that has done much travelling: *a travelled man.*  2 much used by travellers: *It was a well-travelled road.*  3 pt. and pp. of TRAVEL.  1, 2 *adj.*, 3 *v.*

**trav·el·ler** or **trav·el·er** (trav′ə lər)  1 a person who travels: *The town had little accommodation for travellers.*  2 a travelling sales representative; TRAVELLING SALESMAN: *He's a traveller for a drug company.* *n.*

**travelling** or **traveling salesman**  a person whose work is going from place to place, usually in an assigned area, selling things for a company.

**trav·e·logue** (trav′ə log′)  1 a lecture describing travel, usually accompanied by pictures.  2 a motion picture depicting travel.  *n.*  Also, **travelog.**

☛ **Etym.** A blend of *travel* + *-logue*, as in *dialogue* and *monologue*.

**tra·verse** (trav′ərs *or* trə vėrs′) **1** pass across, over, or through: *The caravan traversed the desert.* **2** the act of crossing. **3** lying across; being across. **4** something put or lying across: *A traverse was laid across the trench to protect it from the gunfire from the side.* **5** an earth wall protecting a trench or an exposed place in a fortification. **6** a gallery from side to side in a church. **7** across; crosswise. **8** walk or move in a crosswise direction; move back and forth: *That horse traverses.* **9** go to and fro over or along a place, etc. **10** a distance across. **11** move sideways; turn from side to side. **12** turn big guns to right or left. **13** turn on a pivot, or as if on a pivot. **14** a sideways motion of a ship, part in a machine, mountain climbers, etc. **15** the zigzag line taken by a ship because of contrary winds or currents. **16** a line that crosses other lines. **17** oppose; hinder; thwart. **18** opposition; an obstacle; hindrance. **19** examine carefully. 1, 8, 9, 11–13, 17, 19 *v.*, **trav·ersed**, **trav·ers·ing**; 2, 4–6, 10, 14–16, 18 *n.*, 3 *adj.*, 7 *adv.* —**trav′ers·a·ble**, *adj.* —**trav′ers·er**, *n.*

**trav·es·ty** (trav′i stē) **1** an imitation of a serious literary work in such a way as to make it seem ridiculous. **2** any treatment or imitation that makes a serious thing seem ridiculous: *The trial was a travesty of justice.* **3** make a serious subject or matter ridiculous; imitate in an absurd or grotesque way. 1, 2 *n.*, *pl.* **trav·es·ties**; 3 *v.*, **trav·es·tied**, **trav·es·ty·ing**.

Two kinds of travois

**tra·vois** (trə voi′ *or* trav′wo; *French*, trȧ vwä′) *Cdn.* **1** a simple wheel-less vehicle used by Indians of the plains and made of two shafts, or poles, to which was attached a platform or net for holding a load: *Travois were pulled by horses or dogs.* **2** a sled used for transporting logs. *n.*, *pl.* **tra·vois**.
☛ **Etym.** From a Canadian French variant of F *travail*, one of the shafts by which a wheeled vehicle is drawn.

**trawl** (trol) **1** a strong net dragged along the bottom of the sea. **2** fish with such a net. **3** a line supported by buoys and having attached to it many short lines with baited hooks. **4** fish with such a line. **5** catch with a trawl: *to trawl fish.* 1, 3 *n.*, 2, 4, 5 *v.*

**trawl·er** (trol′ər) **1** a boat used in trawling. **2** a person who fishes by trawling. *n.*

**tray** (trā) a flat, open holder or container with a low rim around it: *We carried the dishes into the dining room on a tray. The sewing basket has an accessory tray that can be lifted out.* *n.*
☛ **Hom.** TRAIT (trā).

**treach·er·ous** (trech′əs) **1** not to be trusted; not faithful; disloyal: *The treacherous soldier carried reports to* the enemy. **2** having a false appearance of strength, security, etc.; not reliable; deceiving: *Thin ice is treacherous.* *adj.* —**treach′er·ous·ly**, *adv.* —**treach′er·ous·ness**, *n.*

**treach·er·y** (trech′ə rē) **1** a breaking of faith; treacherous behaviour; deceit. **2** TREASON. *n.*, *pl.* **treach·er·ies**.

**trea·cle** (trē′kəl) *Esp. Brit.* MOLASSES. *n.*

**tread** (tred) **1** walk; step; set the foot down: *Don't tread on the flower beds.* **2** set the feet on; walk on or through; step on: *to tread the streets.* **3** press under the feet; trample; trample on; crush: *to tread grapes.* **4** make, form, or do by walking: *Cattle had trodden a path to the pond.* **5** the act or sound of treading: *the tread of marching feet.* **6** a way of walking: *He walks with a heavy tread.* **7** the part of stairs or a ladder that a person steps on: *The stair treads were covered with rubber.* **8** the part of something, such as a wheel or shoe, that touches the ground. **9** the raised pattern on the surface of a tire: *The tread on the back tires is almost gone.* **10** the part of a rail or rails that the wheels touch. **11** the sole of the foot or of a shoe. 1–4 *v.*, **trod**, **trod·den** or **trod**, **tread·ing**; 5–11 *n.* —**tread′er**, *n.*
**tread on air**, feel happy.
**tread on one's toes**, offend or annoy one.
**tread the boards**, be an actor or actress; play a part in a play.
**tread water**, keep afloat in water, with the body upright and the head above the surface, by slowly moving the legs as if bicycling.

**trea·dle** (tred′əl) **1** a lever or pedal worked by the foot to make a machine move: *My grandmother's sewing machine was worked by a treadle.* See GRINDSTONE for picture. **2** work a treadle. 1 *n.*, 2 *v.*, **trea·dled**, **trea·dling**.

**tread·mill** (tred′mil) **1** an apparatus for producing motion by having a person or animal walk on the moving steps of a wheel or of a sloping, endless belt. **2** any wearisome or monotonous round of work or life that seems to go nowhere. *n.*

**treas.** **1** treasurer. **2** treasury.

**trea·son** (trē′zən) the act or fact of betraying one's country or ruler: *Helping the enemies of one's country is treason.* *n.*

**trea·son·a·ble** (trē′zə nə bəl) having to do with, consisting of, or involving TREASON. *adj.* —**trea′son·a·ble·ness**, *n.* —**trea′son·a·bly**, *adv.*

**trea·son·ous** (trē′zə nəs) TREASONABLE. *adj.*

**trea·sure** (trezh′ər) **1** wealth or riches stored up; valuable things. **2** any thing or person that is much loved or valued: *The silver teapot was the old lady's chief treasure. My cleaning woman is a treasure.* **3** value highly: *She treasures that doll more than all her other toys.* **4** put away for future use; store up. 1, 2 *n.*, 3, 4 *v.*, **treas·ured**, **treas·ur·ing**.

**treas·ur·er** (trezh′ə rər) a person in charge of the finances of a club, society, corporation, government body, etc. *n.*

**treas·ur·y** (trezh′ə rē) **1** a place where money is kept; especially one where public revenues are deposited and kept: *The national treasury is in Ottawa.* **2** money owned; funds: *We paid for the party out of the club treasury.* **3** a government department that has charge of the collection, management and expenditure of public revenues. **4** a place where treasure or anything valuable is kept. **5** a book, person, etc. thought of as a valued source: *a treasury of adventure stories. She is a treasury of information on rocks.* *n., pl.* **treas·ur·ies.**

**treat** (trēt) **1** act toward; handle: *He treats his dog gently. My mother treats our new car with care.* **2** think of; consider; regard: *He treated his mistake as a joke.* **3** deal with to relieve or cure: *The dentist is treating my toothache.* **4** deal with to bring about some special result: *to treat a metal plate with acid in engraving.* **5** deal with; discuss: *Her talk treated of recent political developments in Europe. This magazine treats the progress of medicine.* **6** express in literature or art: *to treat a theme realistically.* **7** deal with a subject. **8** discuss terms; arrange terms: *Messengers came to treat for peace.* **9** entertain by giving food, drink, or amusement: *Fatima treated her friends to ice cream.* **10** pay the cost of entertainment: *I'll treat today.* **11** a gift of food, drink, or amusement: *"This is my treat," she said, as she paid for the tickets.* **12** anything that gives pleasure: *Being in the country is a treat to her.* 1–10 *v.*, 11, 12 *n.* —**treat′er,** *n.*

**treat·a·ble** (trē′tə bəl) capable of being treated; that will respond to treatment: *Cancer is treatable.* *adj.*

**trea·tise** (trē′tis) a book or writing dealing formally and systematically with some subject. *n.*

**treat·ment** (trēt′mənt) **1** the act or process of treating: *My cold won't respond to treatment.* **2** a way of treating: *This cat has suffered from bad treatment.* **3** something done or used to treat something else, such as a disease: *We read about old treatments for colds.* *n.*

**trea·ty** (trē′tē) **1** an agreement, especially one between nations, signed and approved by each nation. **2** *Cdn.* one of a number of official agreements between the federal government and certain Indian bands whereby the Indians give up their land rights except for reserves and accept treaty money and other kinds of government assistance. **3** TREATY MONEY. *n., pl.* **trea·ties.**

**treaty Indian** *Cdn.* a member of a First Nations band or people living on a reserve and receiving TREATY MONEY and other TREATY RIGHTS.

**treaty money** *Cdn.* annual payments made to TREATY INDIANS.

**treaty rights** *Cdn.* the rights guaranteed to Indians in their treaties with the federal government.

**tre·ble** (treb′əl) **1** three times; threefold; triple. **2** make or become three times as much: *She trebled her income when she changed to a career in advertising.* **3** the highest voice part in choral music, especially for a boys' choir; soprano. **4** a singer who sings such a part. **5** the upper half of the whole musical range for a voice or instrument. Compare with BASS¹ (def. 6). **6** an instrument having the highest range in a family of musical instruments. **7** having to do with, having the range of, or designed for the treble. **8** of a voice or sound, shrill and high-pitched. **9** a shrill, high-pitched voice or sound. 1, 7, 8 *adj.,* 2 *v.,* **tre·bled, tre·bling;** 3–6, 9 *n.*

**treble clef** in music, the symbol indicating that the pitch of the notes on a staff is above middle C. See CLEF for picture.

**tre·bly** (treb′lē) three times. *adv.*

**tree** (trē) **1** a large perennial plant having a woody trunk, branches, and leaves. **2** less accurately, any of certain other plants that resemble trees in form or size. **3** a piece or structure of wood, etc. for some special purpose: *a clothes tree, a shoe tree.* **4** stretch a shoe on a tree. **5** anything suggesting a tree and its branches. **6** See FAMILY TREE. **7** assume a tree-like or branching form. **8** chase up a tree: *The cat was treed by a dog.* **9** take refuge in a tree. **10** *Informal.* put into a difficult position. 1–3, 5, 6 *n.,* 4, 7–10 *v.,* **treed, tree·ing. up a tree, a** chased up a tree. **b** *Informal.* in a difficult position.

**treed** (trēd) **1** planted or covered with trees: *treed lands.* **2** pt. and pp. of TREE. 1 *adj.,* 2 *v.*

**tree fern** any of various tropical ferns that grow to the size of a tree, with a trunklike stem and large fronds at the top.

**tree frog** **1** any of a large family of frogs found mainly in the western hemisphere, most of which live in trees: *Tree frogs have suckerlike, sticky disks on the tips of their toes which help them in climbing.* **2** any of various other frogs and toads that live in trees.

**tree house** a structure, such as a playhouse, built in the branches of a tree.

**tree line** a limit on mountains and in high latitudes beyond which trees will not grow because of the cold, etc.; timberline.

**tree of heaven** an Asian species of AILANTHUS that is widely grown as an ornamental and shade tree.

**tree surgeon** one whose work is TREE SURGERY.

**tree surgery** the cutting and other treatment of diseased trees, and moving of trees for preservation.

**tree toad** TREE FROG.

**tree·top** (trē′top′) the top of a tree: *From our place in the treetop, we could see for a very long way.* *n.*

**tre·foil** (trē′foil′) **1** any of several herbs having leaves made up of three leaflets, especially clover. **2** a leaf made up of three leaflets. **3** an ornamental figure shaped like such a leaf. See CINQUEFOIL for picture. *n.*

**trek** (trek) **1** travel, especially slowly and for a long distance or under difficult conditions; migrate. **2** a journey, especially a slow or difficult one: *It was a long trek over the mountains.* **3** *Informal.* go; proceed: *I had to trek all the way back to the car because I had forgotten my swimsuit.* **4** especially in South Africa, travel by ox wagon. **5** a journey by ox wagon. **6** a stage of such a journey, from one stopping place to the next. 1, 3, 4 *v.,* **trekked, trek·king;** 2, 5, 6 *n.*

A trellis

**trel·lis** (trel′is) **1** a frame of light strips of wood or metal crossing one another with open spaces in between; lattice, especially one supporting growing vines. See LATTICE for another picture. **2** furnish with a trellis. **3** support on a trellis. **4** cross or interlace like a trellis; interweave. *1 n., 2–4 v.*

**trel·lis·work** (trel′is wėrk′) trellises; latticework. *n.*

**trem·a·tode** (trem′ə tōd′) any of a class of flatworms that live as parasites in or on other animals; fluke. *n.*

**trem·ble** (trem′bəl) **1** shake because of fear, excitement, weakness, cold, etc.: *The old woman's hand trembled. His voice trembled with fear.* **2** feel fear, anxiety, etc.: *She trembled for their safety. He trembled at the thought of having to ask for the money.* **3** move gently: *The leaves trembled in the breeze.* **4** a trembling or quivering: *There was a tremble in her voice as she began to recite.* *1–3 v.,* **trem·bled, trem·bling;** *4 n.*
—**trem′bling·ly**, *adv.*

**trem·bly** (trem′blē) trembling; tremulous: *His voice was trembly with fear.* *adj.*

**tre·men·dous** (tri men′dəs) **1** dreadful; awful: *The team suffered a tremendous defeat.* **2** *Informal.* very great; enormous: *That is a tremendous house for a family of three.* **3** *Informal.* especially good: *We saw a tremendous movie yesterday.* *adj.*
—**tre·men′dous·ly**, *adv.*

**trem·o·lo** (trem′ə lō′) **1** in music, a trembling or vibrating quality: *The tremolo is used to express emotion.* **2** a device in an organ used to produce this quality. *n., pl.* **trem·o·los.**

**trem·or** (trem′ər) **1** an involuntary shaking or trembling as from physical weakness, emotional upset, or disease: *a nervous tremor in the voice.* **2** a thrill of emotion or excitement. **3** a shaking movement: *An earthquake is called an earth tremor.* *n.*

**trem·u·lous** (trem′yə ləs) **1** trembling; quivering: *The child's voice was tremulous with sobs.* **2** timid; fearful: *He was shy and tremulous in the presence of strangers.* *adj.*
—**trem′u·lous·ly**, *adv.* —**trem′u·lous·ness**, *n.*

**trench** (trench) **1** a long, narrow cut in the ground; especially one having the excavated earth thrown up in front, used as a defence for soldiers in battle. **2** surround or fortify with a trench or trenches. **3** a long, narrow, deep area in the ocean floor. **4** dig a trench in. **5** dig ditches. **6** make a cut in. *1, 3 n., 2, 4–6 v.* **trench on** or **upon**, **a** trespass upon. **b** come close to; border on: *The demagogue's speech trenched closely on treason.*

**trench·an·cy** (tren′chən sē) the quality or state of being TRENCHANT. *n.*

**trench·ant** (tren′chənt) **1** sharp; keen; cutting: *trenchant wit.* **2** vigorous; effective: *a trenchant policy.* **3** clear-cut; distinct: *in trenchant outline against the sky.* *adj.* —**trench′ant·ly**, *adv.*

**trench coat** a loose-fitting raincoat worn with a belt, often double-breasted and usually having wide lapels and epaulets: *A classic trench coat is a beige or camel colour.*

**trench·er** (tren′chər) a wooden platter formerly used for serving food, especially meat. *n.*

**trench·er·man** (tren′chər mən) a heavy eater; person who has a hearty appetite. *n., pl.* **trench·er·men** (-mən).

**trench mouth** a contagious disease of the gums and, sometimes, the inside of the lips and cheeks, etc., caused by bacteria and characterized by foul-smelling breath.

**trend** (trend) **1** the general direction; a course or

**trelliswork**     **1275**     **trial**

hat, āge, fär; let, ēqual, tėrm; it, īce
hot, ōpen, ôrder; oil, out; cup, pu̇t, rüle
ə above, taken, pencəl, lemən, circəs
ch, child; ng, long; sh, ship
th, thin; ᴛʜ, then; zh, measure

tendency: *a western trend, the trend of modern living.* **2** a current style in fashion, etc. **3** have a general direction; tend; run: *The road trends to the north.* *1, 2 n., 3 v.*

**trend·y** (tren′dē) following the very latest fashions or trends: *a trendy boutique, trendy styles.* *adj.*

**trep·i·da·tion** (trep′ə dā′shən) **1** nervous dread; apprehension; fear. **2** a trembling. *n.*

**tres·pass** (tres′pəs *or* tres′pas) **1** go on somebody's property without any right: *The farmer put up "No Trespassing" signs to keep people off her farm.* **2** go beyond the limits of what is right, proper, or polite: *I won't trespass on your time any longer.* **3** the act or fact of trespassing. **4** do wrong; sin. **5** a wrong; sin. **6** an unlawful act done by force against the person, property, or rights of another. **7** in law, an action to recover damages for such an injury. *1, 2, 4 v., 3, 5–7 n.*
—**tres′pass·er**, *n.*

**tress** (tres) **1** a lock, curl, or braid of hair. **2 tresses,** *pl.* a woman's or girl's hair, especially when long: *She had thick dark brown tresses.* *n.*

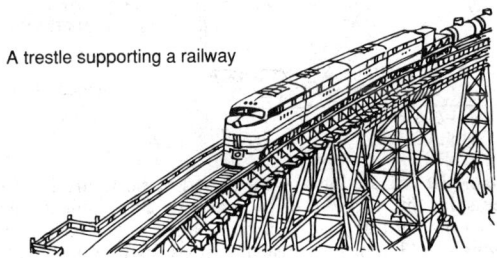

A trestle supporting a railway

**tres·tle** (tres′əl) **1** a structure, such as a sawhorse, used to support a tabletop, platform, etc. See SAWHORSE for picture. **2** a framework used as a bridge to support a road, railway tracks, etc. *n.*

**tres·tle·work** (tres′əl wėrk′) a system of connected trestles supporting a bridge, etc. *n.*

**trews** (trüz) *Scottish.* tight-fitting tartan trousers. *n.*

**trey** (trā) a card, die, domino, etc. having three spots. *n.*

**tri–** a prefix meaning: **1** three; having three; having three parts, as in *triangle, tripod, triplane.* **2** three times; into three parts, as in *trisect.* **3** containing three atoms, etc. of the substance specified, as in *trioxide.* **4** once in three; every third, as in *trimonthly.*
☞ *Etym.* From a combining form of L *tres* and Gk. *treis* 'three'. Some words beginning with *tri-* have come or been formed from Latin, while others come directly from Greek.

**tri·ad** (trī′ad) **1** a group of three, especially of three closely related persons or things. **2** in music, a chord of three tones; especially, a root tone with its third and its fifth. *n.*

**tri·al** (trī′əl) **1** the process of examining and deciding a case in court: *The suspected thief was arrested and brought to trial.* **2** the process of trying or testing: *He gave the* machine another trial to see if it would work. **3** for a try or test: *a trial run, a trial model.* **4** the condition of being tried or tested: *She is employed on trial.* **5** a trouble; hardship: *Her life has been full of trials—sickness, poverty, and loss of loved ones.* **6** a cause of trouble or hardship: *She is a trial to her big sister.* **7** an attempt; effort. *n.*

**trial and error** the process of arriving at a solution of a problem by trying several ways and learning from the mistakes so made.

**trial jury** a group of persons, usually twelve in number, chosen to decide a case in court.

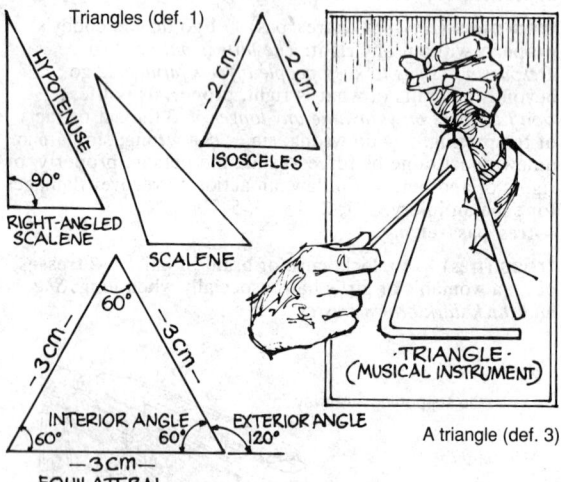

Triangles (def. 1)

A triangle (def. 3)

**tri·an·gle** (trī′ang′gəl) **1** a closed plane figure having three sides and three interior angles. **2** any object, part, or area having three sides or three angles: *Our backyard is a triangle.* **3** a musical instrument consisting of a steel rod bent in a triangle with one corner open, that produces a light ringing sound when struck with a small steel rod. **4** an instrument for drafting, consisting of a flat right-angled triangle of wood, plastic, etc. **5** a group of three. *n.*

**tri·an·gu·lar** (trī ang′gyə lər) **1** of, having to do with, or shaped like a TRIANGLE: *a triangular piece of cloth.* **2** concerned with three persons, groups, etc. *adj.*

**tri·an·gu·late** (trī ang′gyə lāt′ *for verb;* trī ang′gyə lit *or* trī ang′gyə lāt′ *for adj.*) **1** divide into triangles. **2** survey or map out (a region) by dividing (it) into triangles and measuring their angles. **3** find by trigonometry: *to triangulate the height of a mountain.* **4** make triangular. **5** composed of or marked with triangles. **6** triangular. 1–4 *v.,* **tri·an·gu·lat·ed, tri·an·gu·lat·ing,** 5, 6 *adj.*

**tri·ath·lete** (trī ath′lēt) one who competes in the TRIATHLON. *n.*

**tri·ath·lon** (trī ath′lon) an Olympic sport in which athletes compete in swimming, bicycling, and running. *n.*

**trib·al** (trī′bəl) of, having to do with, or characteristic of a TRIBE: *tribal customs, tribal lore.* adj.

**trib·al·ly** (trī′bə lē) according to tribe; by tribe or tribes: *a tribally organized society.* adv.

**tribe** (trīb) **1** a group of families, clans, etc. united by race, custom, etc. under one leader or ruling group. **2** a group of people having a common interest, profession, etc.: *the tribe of artists, the whole tribe of gossips.* **3** a minor category in the classification of animals and plants, ranking below a subfamily. *n.*

**tribes·man** (trībz′mən) a member of a TRIBE. *n., pl.* **tribes·men** (-zmən).

**trib·u·la·tion** (trib′yə lā′shən) great trouble or affliction, especially as a result of persecution or oppression: *the tribulations of the early settlers.* *n.*

**tri·bu·nal** (tri byü′nəl *or* trī byü′nəl) **1** a court of justice; place of judgment: *He was brought before the tribunal for trial.* **2** a place where judges sit in a law court. **3** something by or in which judgment is rendered; judicial or deciding authority: *the tribunal of the polls, the tribunal of the press.* *n.*

**trib·une**[1] (trib′yün) **1** in ancient Rome, an official chosen by the plebeians to protect their rights and interests. **2** a defender of the people. *n.*

**trib·une**[2] (trib′yün) a raised platform or dais. *n.*

**trib·une·ship** (trib′yün ship′) the position, duties, or term of a TRIBUNE[1]. *n.*

**trib·u·tar·y** (trib′yə ter′ē) **1** a stream that flows into a larger stream: *The Ottawa River is a tributary of the St. Lawrence River.* **2** flowing into a larger stream or body of water. **3** paying or required to pay TRIBUTE (defs. 1, 2). **4** paid as TRIBUTE (defs. 1, 2); of the nature of tribute. **5** one that pays TRIBUTE (defs. 1, 2). **6** contributing; helping. 1, 5 *n., pl.* **trib·u·tar·ies;** 2–4, 6 *adj.*

**trib·ute** (trib′yüt) **1** money paid by one nation to another for peace or protection or because of some agreement. **2** any forced payment: *The pirates demanded tribute from passing ships.* **3** an acknowledgment of thanks or respect; compliment: *Remembrance Day is a tribute to our dead soldiers.* *n.*

**trice** (trīs) haul up and fasten with a rope: *to trice up a sail.* *v.,* **triced, tric·ing.**

**tri·ceps** (trī′seps) the large muscle at the back of the upper arm. It extends, or straightens, the arm. *n.*

**tri·chi·na** (tri kī′nə) a small, slender worm that lives in the intestines and muscles of humans and some animals: *Trichinae usually get into the human body from pork that is infected with the larvae and is not cooked long enough to destroy them.* *n., pl.* **tri·chi·nae** (-nē *or* -nī).

**trich·i·no·sis** (trik′ə nō′sis) a disease due to the presence of TRICHINAE in the intestines and muscular tissues. *n.*

**trich·i·nous** (trik′ə nəs) **1** having TRICHINOSIS; infected with trichinae. **2** of, having to do with, or involving trichinae or TRICHINOSIS: *a trichinous infection.* *adj.*

**trick** (trik) **1** something done to deceive or cheat: *The false message was a trick to get him to leave the house.* **2** deceive; cheat: *We were tricked into buying a poor car.* **3** something pretended or unreal; illusion: *Those two lines are really the same length, but a trick of the eyesight makes one of them look longer.* **4** a clever act; feat of skill: *We enjoyed the tricks of the trained animals.* **5** the best way of doing or dealing with something: *the trick of making pies.* **6** a piece of mischief; prank: *Stealing the girl's lunch was a mean trick.* **7** play pranks. **8** a peculiar habit or way of acting: *He has a trick of pulling at his collar.* **9** single round of certain card games. **10** a turn or

period of duty at a job, especially at steering a ship. **11** a turn at any job. **12** dress or adorn, especially in an ornate or fanciful way (used with **out** or **up**): *She was tricked out in her mother's clothes.* 1, 3–6, 8–11 *n.*, 2, 7, 12 *v.*
**do** or **turn the trick,** do what one wants done.

**trick·er·y** (trik′ər ē) the act or practice of deceiving or cheating; fraud. *n., pl.* **trick·er·ies.**

**trick·le** (trik′əl) **1** flow or fall in drops or in a small stream: *Tears trickled down her cheeks. The brook trickled through the valley.* **2** a small flow or stream. **3** cause to flow in drops or in a small stream: *He trickled the water into the container.* **4** come, go, pass, etc. slowly and unevenly: *An hour before the show began, people started to trickle into the theatre.* **5** a trickling. 1, 3, 4 *v.*, **trick·led, trick·ling;** 2, 5 *n.*

**trick·ster** (trik′stər) a cheat; deceiver. *n.*

**trick·y** (trik′ē) **1** full of tricks; deceiving. **2** not reliable; difficult to handle: *Our back door has a tricky lock.* *adj.,* **trick·i·er, trick·i·est.** —**trick′i·ly,** *adv.* —**trick′i·ness,** *n.*

**tri·col·our** or **tri·col·or** (trī′kul′ər) **1** having three colours. **2** a flag having three colours: *The tricolour of France has three equal vertical stripes of blue, white, and red. The tricolour of Italy is green, white, and red.* 1 *adj.,* 2 *n.*

**tri·cot** (trē′kō) **1** a knitted fabric made by hand or machine. **2** a kind of woollen cloth. *n.*

**tri·cus·pid** (trī kus′pid) **1** having three points. **2** having three flaps: *the tricuspid valve of the heart.* **3** a tricuspid tooth. 1, 2 *adj.,* 3 *n.*

**tri·cy·cle** (trī′sə kəl) a three-wheeled vehicle usually worked by pedals attached to the large single wheel in front: *Children often ride tricycles before they are old enough to ride bicycles.* *n.*

**tri·dent** (trī′dənt) **1** a three-pronged spear. **2** three-pronged. 1 *n.*, 2 *adj.*

**tried** (trīd) **1** tested; proved: *a worker of tried abilities.* **2** pt. and pp. of TRY: *I tried to call him last night. I haven't tried this morning.* 1 *adj.,* 2 *v.*

**tri·en·ni·al** (trī en′ē əl) **1** lasting three years. **2** occurring every three years. **3** an event that occurs every three years. **4** the third anniversary of an event. 1, 2 *adj.,* 3, 4 *n.* —**tri·en·ni·al·ly,** *adv.*

**tri·er** (trī′ər) a person or thing that tries. *n.*

**tri·fle** (trī′fəl) **1** something having little value or importance. **2** a small amount; a little bit. **3** a small amount of money. **4** talk or act lightly, not seriously: *Don't trifle with serious matters.* **5** play or toy (*with*): *Eden trifled with his pen while he was talking to me.* **6** spend time, effort, money, etc. on things having little value: *She had trifled away the whole morning.* **7** a rich dessert made of sponge cake, whipped cream, custard, fruit, jelly, etc. 1–3, 7 *n.*, 4–6 *v.*, **tri·fled, tri·fling.**

**tri·fler** (trī′flər) a frivolous or shallow person. *n.*

**tri·fling** (trī′fling) **1** having little value; not important; small: *The friends treated their quarrel as only a trifling matter.* **2** frivolous; shallow. **3** ppr. of TRIFLE. 1, 2 *adj.,* 3 *v.* —**tri′fling·ly,** *adv.*

**trig** (trig) neat; trim; smart-looking. *adj.*

**trig.** **1** trigonometry. **2** trigonometric.

**trig·ger** (trig′ər) **1** the small lever pulled back by the finger in firing a gun. See PISTOL for picture. **2** any

**trickery**     127

hat, āge, fär; let, ēqual, tėrm; it, īce;
hot, ōpen, ôrder; oil, out; cup, pùt, rüle;
above, taken, pencil, lemon, circus
ch, child; ng, long; sh, ship
th, thin; ᴛʜ, then; zh, measure

lever that releases a spring, catch, etc. when pulled pressed. **3** set off: *The explosion was triggered by a s*. **4** cause to start; begin: *The fiery speech triggered an outburst of violence.* 1, 2 *n.*, 3, 4 *v.*
**quick on the trigger,** **a** quick to shoot. **b** *Informal.* quick to act; mentally alert.

**trigger–happy** (trig′ər hap′ē) *Informal.* **1** too readily inclined to shoot a gun. **2** too readily inclined to overreact, especially with violent action or adverse criticism. *adj.*

**trig·o·no·met·ric** (trig′ə nə met′rik) of or having to do with TRIGONOMETRY. *adj.*

**trig·o·no·met·ri·cal·ly** (trig′ə nə met′ri klē) by or according to TRIGONOMETRY. *adv.*

**trig·o·nom·e·try** (trig′ə nom′ə trē) the branch of mathematics that deals with the relations between the sides and angles of triangles and the calculations based on these: *The principles of trigonometry are used in surveying, navigation, and engineering.* *n.*

**tri·graph** (trī′graf) three letters used to spell a single sound. *Example: the* eau *in* beau. *n.*

**trike** (trīk) *Informal.* TRICYCLE. *n.*

**tri·lin·gual** (trī ling′gwəl *or* trī ling′gyə wəl) **1** able to speak three languages: *a trilingual person.* **2** using or involving three languages. *adj.*

**trill** (tril) **1** sing, play, sound, or speak with a quivering, vibrating sound. **2** the act or sound of trilling. **3** in music, a quick alternating of two notes a tone or a half tone apart. **4** sing or play with a trill: *Some birds trill.* 1, 4 *v.*, 2, 3 *n.*

**tril·lion** (tril′yən) **1** in Canada and the United States, a thousand billion; 1 followed by 12 zeros; 1 000 000 000 000. **2** in the British Isles, France, Germany, etc., 1 followed by 18 zeros. *n., adj.*

White trilliums

**tril·li·um** (tril′ē əm) any of a closely related group of small plants of the lily family having a short stem with a whorl of three leaves and a single flower with three narrow green sepals and three white, pink, or reddish petals: *The white trillium is the provincial flower of Ontario.* *n.*

**tri·lo·bate** (trī lō′bāt) having three lobes: *a trilobate leaf.* *adj.*

**tri·lo·bite** (trī′lə bīt′) an extinct arthropod having three divisions of the body and jointed limbs: *Fossil trilobites are widely found in various rocks.* *n.*

**tril·o·gy** (tril′ə jē) three plays, operas, novels, etc. that fit together to make a related series: *Any section of a trilogy is itself a complete work.* *n., pl.* **tril·o·gies.**

**trim** (trim) ...d order; make neat by cutting ...as to be trimmed for the carpenter. ... the hedge. **2** remove parts that are away ...med dead leaves off the plants. The gard...ondition or order: *She keeps her desk trim.* not ne...on or order: *Is our team in trim for the* **3** ...neat condition; order: *That ship is in poor trim for a* **4** go **6** trimming: *the trim on a dress.* **7** decorate: ga...ldren trimmed the Christmas tree.* **8** equipment; ...t. **9** balance a boat, airplane, etc. by arranging the ...ad carried. **10** the position of a ship or aircraft when properly balanced. **11** be or keep in balance. **12** arrange the sails to fit wind and direction. **13** change opinions, views, etc. to suit circumstances. **14** the visible woodwork inside a building. **15** the upholstery, handles, and accessories inside an automobile. **16** woodwork used as a finish or ornament on the outside of a building. **17** *Informal.* defeat heavily; beat: *We trimmed that team twice last year.* **18** *Informal.* scold. 1, 2, 7, 9, 11–13, 17, 18 *v.*, **trimmed, trim·ming;** 3 *adj.*, **trim·mer, trim·mest;** 4–6, 8, 10, 14–16 *n.* —**trim′ly,** *adv.* —**trim′ness,** *n.*

**tri·ma·ran** (trī′mə ran′) a boat with three hulls side by side. Compare with CATAMARAN. *n.*

**tri·mes·ter** (trī mes′tər) **1** a third part of a school year. **2** a three-month period; a quarter of a year. *n.*

**trim·mer** (trim′ər) **1** a person or thing that trims: *a hat trimmer, a window trimmer.* **2** a person who changes his or her opinions, actions, etc. to suit the circumstances: *a political trimmer.* *n.*

**trim·ming** (trim′ing) **1** something added as a decoration or accessory: *I'm putting red and blue trimming on my costume.* **2** *Informal.* a decisive defeat. **3** *Informal.* a scolding or thrashing. **4** act of a person or thing that trims. **5** ppr. of TRIM. **6 trimmings,** *pl.* **a** parts cut away in trimming. **b** *Informal.* additions to food: *We ate turkey with all the trimmings.* 1–4, 6 *n.*, 5 *v.*

**tri·month·ly** (trī mun′thlē) occurring every three months. *adj.*

**Trin·i·dad·i·an** (trin′i dad′ē ən *or* trin′i dā′dē ən) **1** of or having to do with Trinidad, an island in the West Indies, or its people. **2** a native or inhabitant of Trinidad. 1 *adj.*, 2 *n.*

**tri·ni·tro·tol·u·ene** (trī nī′trō tol′yü ēn′) a powerful explosive, known as T.N.T. *n.*

**Trin·i·ty** (trin′ə tē) in Christianity, the union of Father, Son, and Holy Ghost in one divine nature. *n.*

**trin·i·ty** (trin′ə tē) **1** a group of three. **2** being three. *n.*

**trin·ket** (tring′kit) **1** any small fancy article, bit of jewellery, etc. **2** a TRIFLE (def. 1). *n.*

**tri·no·mi·al** (trī nō′mē əl) **1** in mathematics, an expression consisting of three terms connected by plus or minus signs. Example: $a + bx^2 - 2$ is a trinomial. **2** the name of an animal or plant consisting of three words. **3** consisting of three terms. 1, 2 *n.*, 3 *adj.*

**tri·o** (trē′ō) **1** a piece of music for three voices or instruments. **2** a group of three singers or players performing together. **3** any group of three persons or things. *n.*, *pl.* **tri·os.**

**tri·ode** (trī′ōd) a vacuum tube that has an anode, a cathode, and a controlling grid. *n.*

**tripper**

**tri·ox·ide** (trī ok′sīd) any oxide having three atoms of oxygen in each molecule. *n.*

**trip** (trip) **1** a journey; voyage: *We took a trip to Europe.* **2** stumble: *to trip on the stairs.* **3** a stumble; slip. **4** cause to stumble and fall: *The loose board tripped him.* **5** the act of catching a person's foot to throw him or her down. **6** make a mistake; do something wrong: *He tripped on that difficult question.* **7** cause to make a mistake or blunder: *The difficult question tripped him.* **8** detect in an inconsistency or inaccuracy: *The examining board tripped her up several times.* **9** take light, quick steps: *She tripped across the floor.* **10** a light, quick tread; stepping lightly. **11** tip; tilt. **12** release or operate a catch, clutch, etc. suddenly; operate, start, or set free a mechanism, weight, etc. **13** a projecting part, catch, etc. for starting or checking some movement. 1, 3, 5, 10, 11, 13 *n.*, 2, 4, 6–9, 11, 12 *v.*, **tripped, trip·ping.**

**tri·par·tite** (trī pär′tīt) **1** divided into or composed of three parts. **2** having three corresponding parts or copies. **3** made or shared by three parties: *a tripartite treaty between Britain, the United States, and France.* *adj.*

**tripe** (trīp) the walls of the first and second stomachs of an ox, etc. used as food: *tripe and onions.* *n.*

**trip·ham·mer** (trip′ham′ər) a heavy power-driven hammer, operated by a tripping device by which it is raised and allowed to fall repeatedly. *n.*

**Tri·pi·ta·ka** (tri pit′ə kə) the corpus of sacred texts containing the teachings of Buddha, originally written in the Pali language and collected between the 6th and the 1st centuries B.C. *n.*

**tri·plane** (trī′plān′) an airplane having three sets of wings, one above another. See ECHELON for picture. *n.*

**tri·ple** (trip′əl) **1** including three; having three parts: *the triple petals of the trillium.* **2** three times as much or as many: *She has triple the foreign stamps I have.* **3** a number, amount, etc. that is three times as much or as many: *Nine is the triple of three.* **4** make or become three times as much or as many: *My older brother has tripled his wages in five years.* **5** in baseball, a three-base hit. **6** make such a hit: *He tripled in the eighth inning.* 1, 2 *adj.*, 3, 5 *n.*, 4, 6 *v.*, **tri·pled, tri·pling.**

**triple crown** in horse racing, a championship won by a horse that in a single season wins the three classic races for its category.

**triple play** in baseball, a play that puts three men out.

**trip·let** (trip′lit) **1** one of three children born at the same time from the same mother. **2** a group of three similar or equal things. *n.*

**triple time** in music, time or rhythm having three beats to the measure.

**trip·li·cate** (trip′lə kāt′ *for verb,* trip′lə kit *for adjective and noun*) **1** make threefold; triple. **2** triple; threefold. **3** one of three things exactly alike. 1 *v.*, **trip·li·cat·ed, trip·li·cat·ing;** 2 *adj.*, 3 *n.* **in triplicate,** in three copies exactly alike.

**tri·ply** (trip′lē) in a triple manner; three times. *adv.*

**tri·pod** (trī′pod) **1** a support or stand having three legs, as for a camera, telescope, etc. **2** a stool or other article having three legs. *n.*

**trip·per** (trip′ər) **1** a person or thing that trips; especially, a device in a machine that releases a catch, etc. or one that operates a railway signal. **2** *Esp. Brit.* a person who takes a trip or short excursion. *n.*

**trip·ping** (trip′ing) **1** light and quick: *That poem has a tripping rhythm.* **2** ppr. of TRIP. 1 *adj.*, 2 *v.*

**trip·tych** (trip′tik) **1** a set of three panels side by side, having pictures, carvings, etc. on them; especially, an altarpiece consisting of a central panel and two smaller, hinged side panels that fold over it. **2** a hinged three-leaved writing tablet used in ancient Rome. *n.*

**tri·rat·na** (trē rut′nə) in Jainism, the "three jewels" of belief and practice by which to attain liberation from the world and rebirth, namely: right faith, right knowledge, and right conduct. *n.*

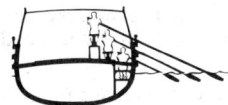
A sectional diagram of a trireme, showing the positions of the rowers

**tri·reme** (trī′rēm) an ancient Greek or Roman warship having three rows of oars, one above the other, on each side. *n.*

**tri·sect** (trī sekt′) **1** divide into three parts. **2** divide into three equal parts. *v.* —**tri·sec′tion**, *n.*

**tri·ser·vice** or **tri–ser·vice** (trī sėr′vis) *Cdn.* of or for all three commands (land, sea, and air) of the armed forces: *Royal Military College is a triservice college.* *adj.*

**tri·syl·lab·ic** (trī′sə lab′ik or tris′ə lab′ik) having three syllables: *Fantasy is a trisyllabic word.* *adj.*

**tri·syl·lab·i·cal·ly** (trī′sə lab′i klē or tris′ə lab′i klē) as or in three syllables. *adv.*

**tri·syl·la·ble** (trī sil′ə bəl or tri sil′ə bəl) a word of three syllables: *Educate is a trisyllable.* *n.*

**trite** (trīt) ordinary; commonplace; no longer interesting: *The movie turned out to be very trite, so we left early.* *adj.*, **trit·er**, **trit·est.** —**trite′ly**, *adv.* —**trite′ness**, *n.*

**trit·i·um** (trit′ē əm) a radio-active isotope of hydrogen that occurs in minute amounts in natural water, having a mass three times that of ordinary hydrogen: *Tritium is the explosive used in a hydrogen bomb.* Symbol: T or H³ *n.*

**tri·ton¹** (trī′tən) any of various large sea snails having a heavy, cone-shaped shell. *n.*

**tri·ton²** (trī′tən) the nucleus of a TRITIUM atom. *n.*

**trit·u·rate** (trich′ə rāt′) **1** rub, crush, or grind into a very fine powder. **2** any substance that is ground into a very fine powder. 1 *v.*, **trit·u·rat·ed, trit·u·rat·ing;** 2 *n.*

**trit·u·ra·tion** (trich′ə rā′shən) **1** the act or process of triturating or the state of being TRITURATED. **2** a TRITURATEd powder, especially one consisting of a powdered medicinal substance mixed with lactose. *n.*

**tri·umph** (trī′umf) **1** the state of being victorious or successful: *a final triumph over the enemy. They returned home in triumph.* **2** a great success or achievement: *a triumph of modern science.* **3** gain victory; win success: *Our team triumphed over theirs.* **4** joy because of victory or success: *There was triumph in her eyes as she accepted the medal.* **5** exult or rejoice because of victory or success: *They triumphed in their success.* **6** in ancient Rome, a procession in honour of a victorious general. 1, 2, 4, 6 *n.*, 3, 5 *v.*

**tri·um·phal** (trī um′fəl) of or for a TRIUMPH; celebrating a victory: *a triumphal march.* *adj.*

**tri·um·phant** (trī um′fənt) **1** victorious; successful: *a triumphant army.* **2** rejoicing because of victory or success: *The winner of the election spoke in triumphant tones to her supporters.* *adj.* —**tri·um′phant·ly**, *adv.*

**tri·um·vir** (trī um′vər) **1** in ancient Rome, one of three men who shared the same public office. **2** one of any three persons sharing power or authority. *n., pl.* **tri·um′virs** or **tri·um·vi·ri** (-və rī′ or -və rē′).

**tri·um·vi·rate** (trī um′və rit) **1** the position or term of office of a TRIUMVIR. **2** government by three persons together. **3** any association of three in office or authority. **4** any group of three. *n.*

**triv·et** (triv′it) a stand or support usually having three legs or feet: *Trivets are used over or beside fires and under hot platters, etc.* *n.*

**triv·i·a** (triv′ē ə) trifles; unimportant matters (*sometimes used with a singular verb*). *n.pl.*

**triv·i·al** (triv′ē əl) minor; not important; trifling; insignificant: *The essay had only a few trivial mistakes.* *adj.* —**triv′i·al·ly**, *adv.*

**triv·i·al·i·ty** (triv′ē al′ə tē) **1** the quality or state of being TRIVIAL. **2** something TRIVIAL; trifle. *n., pl.* **triv·i·al·i·ties.**

**tri·week·ly** (trī wē′klē) **1** once every three weeks. **2** three times a week. **3** a newspaper or magazine published triweekly. **4** occurring or appearing triweekly. 1, 2 *adv.*, 3 *n., pl.* **tri·week·lies;** 4 *adj.*

**tro·che** (trō′kē) a small medicinal tablet or lozenge. *n.* ☞ *Hom.* TROCHEE.

**tro·chee** (trō′kē) in poetry, a foot or measure consisting of two syllables, the first accented and the second unaccented, or the first long and the second short. Example:

Sing a/ song of/ sixpence. *n.*

☞ *Hom.* TROCHE.

**trod** (trod) pt. and a pp. of TREAD: *He trod on a tack. You have trod on my foot again.* *v.*

**trod·den** (trod′ən) a pp. of TREAD: *The cattle have trodden down the corn.* *v.*

**trog·lo·dyte** (trog′lə dīt′) **1** a member of a prehistoric people who lived in caves. **2** a person living in seclusion; hermit. **3** an anthropoid ape, such as a gorilla. *n.*

**troi·ka** (troi′kə) **1** in Russia, a sleigh, wagon, or other vehicle pulled by three horses abreast. **2** a group of three rulers sharing power; triumvirate. *n.*

**Tro·jan** (trō′jən) **1** of or having to do with Troy or its people. **2** a native or inhabitant of Troy. **3** a person who shows courage or energy: *They all worked like Trojans.* 1 *adj.*, 2, 3 *n.*

**troll¹** (trōl) **1** sing in a full, rolling voice. **2** sing as a round is sung, each person or group starting one after the other. **3** a song whose parts are sung in succession, as a round: *"Three Blind Mice" is a well-known troll.* **4** fish with a moving line, usually by trailing the line behind the boat near the surface: *He trolled for bass.* **5** the reel of a fishing rod. **6** a fishing lure or bait, especially one used

**troll** for trolling.   **7** make revolve; roll.   **8** the act of trolling.   1, 2, 4, 7 v., 3, 5, 6, 8 n.   —**troll′er,** n.

**troll²** (trōl)   in Scandinavian folklore, any of a race of supernatural beings, thought of as giants or, more recently, as dwarfs.   n.

**trol·ley** (trol′ē)   **1** a pulley moving against a wire to carry electricity to a streetcar, electric engine, etc. See STREETCAR for picture.   **2** a streetcar or TROLLEY BUS.   **3** a basket, carriage, etc., suspended from a pulley running on an overhead track.   **4** Brit.   a truck pushed by hand; handcart.   n., pl. **trol·leys.**

**trolley bus**   an electrically powered bus having two overhead trolleys and running on tires like a motor bus.

**trolley car**   STREETCAR.

**trol·lop** (trol′əp)   **1** an untidy or slovenly woman.   **2** prostitute.   n.

A trombone

**trom·bone** (trom′bōn or trom bōn′)   a musical brass wind instrument resembling a trumpet and having either a sliding piece or, less often, valves for varying the pitch.   n.

**trom·bon·ist** (trom′bō nist or trom bō′nist)   a person who plays the trombone, especially a skilled player.   n.

**troop** (trüp)   **1** a group or collection of people or animals: a troop of deer. A troop of children burst into the kitchen.   **2** a formation of armoured or cavalry forces smaller than a squadron; a similar group in other army units.   **3** a group of BOY SCOUTS or GIRL GUIDES, made up of several patrols: She belongs to the 4th Kingston troop.   **4** gather or move in a troop or band: We all trooped into the living room to sing happy birthday.   **5** walk; go: The young girls trooped off after the older ones.   **6 troops,** pl. armed forces; soldiers.   1–3, 6 n., 4, 5 v.
☛ Hom. TROUPE.

**troop·er** (trü′pər)   **1** a soldier in a cavalry regiment or an armoured regiment.   **2** a cavalry horse.   **3** TROOPSHIP.   **4 a** a mounted police officer.   **b** U.S.   a state police officer.   n.

**troop·ship** (trüp′ship′)   a ship used to carry soldiers; transport.   n.

**trope** (trōp)   **1** the use of a word or phrase in a sense different from its ordinary meaning; figurative use of a word or phrase.   **2** a word or phrase so used; figure of speech. Example:
All in a hot and copper sky,
The bloody sun at noon.   n.

**tro·phy** (trō′fē)   **1** something taken or won in war, etc., especially if displayed as a memorial or souvenir: The helmet was a trophy of the last war.   **2** a prize, often in the form of a silver cup, awarded in sports or other competitions: Francine kept her tennis trophy on the mantelpiece.   **3** in ancient Greece and Rome, captured arms, flags, etc. of a defeated enemy set up on the field of battle or in a public place as a memorial of victory.   **4** a representation of such a memorial on a medal or in the form of a monument.   **5** anything serving as a remembrance.   n., pl. **tro·phies.**

**trop·ic** (trop′ik)   **1** either of two parallels of latitude, one 23°27′ north and the other 23°27′ south of the equator. The northern parallel is the tropic of Cancer and the southern parallel is the tropic of Capricorn.   **2 the tropics** or **Tropics,** pl.   the region between these parallels: The equator runs through the middle of the tropics, which include the hottest parts of the earth.   **3** of or belonging to the tropics.   **4** either of two corresponding circles in the celestial sphere, the limits reached by the sun in its apparent journey north and south.   n.

**trop·i·cal** (trop′ə kəl)   **1** of, characteristic of, or found in the tropics: tropical fruits, tropical diseases, a tropical climate.   **2** suitable for or used in the tropics: tropical suiting.   **3** very hot; burning or fervent.   adj.
—**trop′i·cal·ly,** adv.

**tropic of Cancer**   the parallel of latitude that is 23°27′ north of the equator; the northern boundary of the Torrid Zone.

**tropic of Capricorn**   the parallel of latitude that is 23°27′ south of the equator; the southern boundary of the Torrid Zone.

**tro·pism** (trō′piz əm)   the tendency of an animal or plant to turn or move in response to a stimulus.   n.

**tro·pis·tic** (trō pis′tik)   of or having to do with TROPISM.   adj.

**trop·o·sphere** (trop′ə sfēr′)   the lowest layer of the atmosphere, extending about 10 to 16 kilometres from the earth upward to the stratosphere: The troposphere is characterized by winds, cloud formation, and a rapid decrease in temperature with increase in altitude.   n.

**trot** (trot)   **1** of horses, etc., go at a gait between a walk and a run by lifting the right forefoot and the left hind foot at about the same time and then the other two feet in the same way: Some horses gallop more smoothly than they trot.   **2** of a person, run at a moderate pace: The child trotted along after her mother.   **3** the gait of a trotting animal or person: We started off at a trot.   **4** the action or exercise of trotting: to go for a trot.   **5** cause to trot: to trot a horse.   **6** ride a horse at a trot: She trotted up to the stables.   **7** a brisk, steady movement.   1, 2, 5, 6 v., **trot·ted, trot·ting;** 3, 4, 7 n.
**trot out,** Informal.   bring out for others to see.

**troth** (troth or trōth)   **1** faithfulness; loyalty.   **2** a promise, especially a promise or engagement to marry.   **3** pledge; betroth.   1, 2 n., 3 v.
**by my troth** or **in troth,**   truly; upon my word: By my troth, I'll see him revenged.
**plight one's troth,**   pledge one's word, especially in an engagement to marry.

**trot·ter** (trot′ər)   **1** an animal that trots, especially a horse bred and trained for harness racing.   **2** the foot of a sheep or a pig used for food: pig's trotters.   n.

**trou·ba·dour** (trü′bə dôr′ or trü′bə dür′)   one of a class of medieval lyric poets of southern France, northern Spain, and northern Italy who wrote poems of chivalry and courtly love: The troubadours had great social influence and were often of knightly rank.   n.

**trou·ble** (trub′əl)   **1** distress; worry or difficulty: That dog has caused them a lot of trouble. We're still having trouble with the furnace.   **2** a distressing or annoying fact,

event, or experience: *Her life was full of troubles.* **3** cause distress or worry to: *The lack of business troubled him.* **4** public disturbance or unrest: *There was some trouble on the picket line.* **5** extra work; bother; effort: *She took the trouble to make extra copies.* **6** require extra work or effort of: *May I trouble you to do something for me?* **7** cause oneself inconvenience or effort: *Don't trouble to come to the door; I can let myself out.* **8** illness or disease: *She has stomach trouble.* **9** cause pain or discomfort to; afflict: *His arthritis is troubling him again. The baby has been troubled with colds.* **10** faulty operation; malfunction: *They were delayed because of engine trouble.* **11 the trouble,** the cause of annoyance, worry, etc.: *The trouble is that he never bothers to let us know. She's just too easy going; that's the trouble.* 1, 2, 4, 5, 8, 10, 11 *n.*, 3, 6, 7, 9 *v.*, **trou·bled, trou·bling.**
**in** or **into trouble,** **a** in or into a situation in which one is caught in wrongdoing and is liable to be blamed, punished, etc.: *They're very mischievous and are always getting into trouble. Her boyfriend is in trouble with the police.* **b** *Informal.* pregnant without being married.
**make trouble,** cause problems or unpleasantness: *Mind your own business and don't make trouble.*

**trou·ble·mak·er** (trub′əl māˊkər) a person who causes trouble, especially one who deliberately causes disagreement between people. *n.*

**trou·ble·shoot** (trubˊəl shüt′) work as a TROUBLESHOOTER: *She troubleshoots for a large construction firm.* *v.*, **trou·ble·shot, trou·ble·shoot·ing.**

**trou·ble·shoot·er** (trubˊəl shü′tər) **1** a person employed to discover and eliminate causes of trouble in equipment, machinery, etc. **2** a person who is skilled in mediating diplomatic or political disputes. *n.*

**trou·ble·some** (trubˊəl səm) causing trouble; annoying: *a troublesome zipper. Bullies are troublesome people.* *adj.* —**trouˊble·some·ly,** *adv.* —**trouˊble·some·ness,** *n.*

**trough** (trof) **1** a long, narrow container for holding food or water for animals: *a watering trough.* **2** a container shaped like this: *The baker uses a trough for kneading dough.* **3** a channel for carrying water; gutter. **4** a long hollow between two ridges, etc.: *the trough between two waves.* **5** in meteorology, a long, narrow area of relatively low barometric pressure. *n.* —**troughˊlike,** *adj.*

**trounce** (trouns) **1** beat; thrash. **2** *Informal.* defeat severely in a contest, game, etc.: *The home team was trounced by the visitors.* *v.*, **trounced, trounc·ing.**

**troupe** (trüp) **1** a troop, band, or company, especially a group of actors, singers, or acrobats. **2** tour or travel with a troupe. 1 *n.*, 2 *v.*, **trouped, troup·ing.**
☛ Hom. TROOP.

**troup·er** (trüˊpər) **1** a member of a theatrical troupe. **2** an old, experienced actor. *n.*

**trou·sers** (trouˊzərz) **1** a two-legged outer garment reaching from the waist to the ankles or, sometimes, to the knees: *These old trousers are too short.* **2 trouser,** of, having to do with, or designed for trousers: *trouser cuffs.* *n.pl.*

**trous·seau** (trüˊsō *or* trü sōˊ) a bride's outfit of clothes, linen, etc. *n., pl.* **trous·seaux** (trüˊsōz *or* trü sōzˊ) or **trous·seaus.**

**trout** (trout) **1** any of a closely related group of food and game fish belonging to the salmon family and trout family, found mainly in northern lakes and rivers: *Trout belonging to this group, such as the rainbow trout, are often called true trout to distinguish them from char.* See FISH for picture. **2** any of several species of char, also belonging to the salmon and trout family: *lake trout, brook trout.* *n., pl.* **trout** or **trouts.**

Trowels

**trow·el** (trouˊəl) **1** a hand tool with a thin, flat blade, used for smoothing or spreading plaster, mortar, etc. **2** a garden hand tool similar to a scoop, used for taking up plants, loosening dirt, etc. *n.*

**troy** (troi) expressed in TROY WEIGHT; *a troy ounce.* *adj.*

**troy weight** a system of units for measuring mass, traditionally used for weighing gems and precious metals: *One pound troy weight is equal to about 0.373 kilograms.*
24 grains = 1 pennyweight
20 pennyweight = 1 ounce
12 ounces = 1 pound

**trs.** transpose.

**tru·an·cy** (trüˊən sē) the act or habit of staying away from school without permission; TRUANT behaviour. *n., pl.* **tru·an·cies.**

**tru·ant** (trüˊənt) **1** a person who neglects work, especially a student who stays away from school without permission. **2** being a truant; especially, staying away from school without permission. **3** of, like, or characteristic of a truant: *truant habits.* 1, 2 *n.*, 3 *adj.*
**play truant,** neglect one's work or duty; especially, stay away from school without permission.

**truce** (trüs) **1** a stop in fighting by agreement between opposing armed forces; peace for a time: *A truce was declared between the two armies.* **2** a rest from quarrelling, turmoil, trouble, etc.: *After this argument there was a family truce for several days.* *n.*

**truck¹** (truk) **1** a motor vehicle designed primarily for carrying heavy things or animals rather than people. **2** carry on a truck: *The fruit was trucked to market.* **3** drive a truck. **4** a small vehicle, sometimes with a motor, for carrying trunks, boxes, etc.: *Giulia uses a truck in the warehouse. The porter is coming with a truck.* **5** a swivelling frame with two or more pairs of wheels supporting each end of a railway car, locomotive, etc. **6** a low, flat car. **7** on a ship or boat, a wooden disk at the top of a flagstaff or mast with holes for the ropes. **8** of, for, or used on a truck. 1, 4–8 *n.*, 2, 3 *v.*

**truck²** (truk) **1** vegetables raised for market. **2** small articles of little value; odds and ends. **3** *Informal.* rubbish. **4** *Informal.* dealings: *She has no truck with peddlers.* **5** exchange; barter. **6** the payment of wages

**trucker** 1282 **truncheon**

in goods, etc. rather than in money. **7** make an exchange; swap. *1–6 n., 7 v.*

**truck·er** (truk′ər) **1** a person who drives a truck. **2** a person whose business is carrying goods, etc. by trucks. *n.*

**truck farm** a farm where vegetables are raised for market. —**truck farmer,** *n.*

**truck·le** (truk′əl) give up or submit tamely; be servile: *That man got his position by truckling to his superiors.* *v.,* **truck·led, truck·ling.** —**truck′ler,** *n.*

**truck·man** (truk′mən) TRUCKER. *n., pl.* **truck·men** (-mən).

**truc·u·lence** (truk′yə ləns) the quality or state of being TRUCULENT. *n.*

**truc·u·lent** (truk′yə lənt) **1** showing a readiness to fight or quarrel; arrogant and hostile: *a truculent attitude.* **2** fierce and cruel: *at the mercy of a truculent ruffian.* **3** of speech or writing, ruthless and scathing; harsh: *truculent satire.* *adj.* —**truc′u·lent·ly,** *adv.*

**trudge** (truj) **1** walk, especially wearily or with effort: *The tired hikers trudged home.* **2** a hard or weary walk: *It was a long trudge up the hill.* **1** *v.,* **trudged, trudg·ing;** **2** *n.* —**trudg′er,** *n.*

**trudg·en stroke** (truj′ən) a swimming stroke using a double overarm stroke together with a scissors movement of the legs.

**true** (trü) **1** agreeing with fact; not false: *It is true that 6 and 4 are 10.* **2** real; genuine: *true gold, true kindness.* **3** faithful; loyal: *a true friend.* **4** agreeing with a standard; right; proper; correct; exact; accurate: *a true copy, a true voice, true to type.* **5** representative of the class named: *A sweet potato is not a true potato.* **6** rightful; lawful: *the true heir to the property.* **7** reliable; sure: *a true sign.* **8** accurately formed, fitted, or placed: *a true angle.* **9** exact or accurate formation, position, or adjustment: *A slanting door is out of true.* **10** make true; shape, place, or make in the exact position, form, etc. required. **11** steady in direction, force, etc.; unchanging: *The arrow made a true course through the air.* **12** that which is true. **13** honest. **14** in a true manner; truly; exactly: *Her words ring true.* **15** in agreement with the ancestral type: *to breed true.* *1–8, 11, 13 adj.,* **tru·er, tru·est;** *9, 12 n., 10 v.,* **trued, tru·ing;** *14, 15 adv.* **come true,** happen as expected; become real.

**true bill** *Esp. U.S.* a bill of indictment found by a grand jury to be supported by enough evidence to justify the case being brought to trial.

**true–blue** (trü′blü′) staunch and unchanging; very loyal: *She's a true-blue conservative.* *adj.*

**true–heart·ed** (trü′här′tid) faithful; loyal: *a true-hearted lover.* *adj.*

**truf·fle** (truf′əl) **1** any of several species of European underground fungus valued as food. **2** a soft chocolate candy. *n.*

**tru·ism** (trü′iz əm) a statement that is obviously true, especially one that is too obvious to mention, such as "You're only young once." *n.*

**tru·ly** (trü′lē) **1** in a true manner; exactly; rightly; faithfully: *Tell me truly what you think.* **2** in fact, really: *It was truly a beautiful sight.* *adv.*

**trump** (trump) **1** any playing card of a suit that for a time ranks higher than the other suits. **2** the suit itself. **3** take a trick, card, etc. with a trump: *He trumped my king.* **4** play a trump when another suit was led: *We didn't expect him to trump.* **5** any resource or advantage held back until needed. **6** *Informal.* a fine, dependable person. *1, 2, 5, 6 n., 3, 4 v.*

**trump up,** think up or invent falsely: *He trumped up an excuse for being late.*

**trump card** **1** any playing card of a suit that for a particular hand ranks higher than the other suits. **2** a decisive fact, argument, etc., especially one that is held in reserve until needed; clincher.

**trumped–up** (trump′tup′) invented in order to deceive; fraudulent: *trumped-up charges.* *adj.*

**trump·er·y** (trump′ə rē) **1** something showy but without value; worthless ornaments; useless stuff; rubbish; nonsense. **2** showy but without value; trifling; worthless; useless; nonsensical. *1 n., pl.* **trump·er·ies;** *2 adj.*

A trumpet

**trum·pet** (trum′pit) **1** a musical brass wind instrument having a looped tube that is bell-shaped at one end and usually has three valves to vary the pitch: *The trumpet has a sharp, clear tone and can produce great volume.* **2** anything shaped like a trumpet: *Some people used ear trumpets before small hearing aids were invented.* **3** blow a trumpet. **4** a sound like that of a trumpet. **5** make a sound like a trumpet: *The elephant trumpeted in fright.* **6** proclaim loudly or widely: *They'll trumpet that story all over town.* *1, 2, 4 n., 3, 5, 6 v.* —**trum′pet·like′,** *adj.*

**blow one's own trumpet,** talk boastfully; praise oneself.

**trumpet creeper** a climbing woody vine native to the warm regions of the Western Hemisphere, having clusters of large, red, trumpet-shaped flowers.

**trum·pet·er** (trum′pə tər) **1** a person who plays a trumpet, especially a skilled player. **2** any of three closely related species making up a family of large birds living mainly on the ground in the tropical rain forests of South America, having a long neck and legs, short tail and wings, and mainly black plumage: *Trumpeters have a loud, deep call.* **3** TRUMPETER SWAN. *n.*

**trumpeter swan** the largest species of swan, found in western Canada and the northwestern United States, weighing up to 18 kg and with a wingspread of often more than 2.5 m, having a deep, very far-carrying, trumpetlike call. See SWAN for picture.

**trumpet vine** TRUMPET CREEPER.

**trun·cate** (trung′kāt) **1** shorten by cutting off the top or end of. **2** in biology, having a blunt or square end: *the truncate leaf of the tulip tree.* See LEAF for picture. **3** truncated. *1 v.,* **trun·cat·ed, trun·cat·ing;** *2, 3 adj.* —**trun·ca′tion,** *n.*

**trun·cat·ed** (trung′kā tid) **1** especially in geometry, having the top or apex cut off: *a truncated cone.* **2** cut short: *a truncated version of a speech.* **3** pt. and pp. of TRUNCATE. *1, 2 adj., 3 v.*

**trun·cheon** (trun′chən) **1** *Esp. Brit.* a short stick or club; billy: *a police officer's truncheon.*   2 a staff of office or authority; baton: *a herald's truncheon.*   *n.*

**trun·dle** (trun′dəl)   1 roll or push along: *The worker trundled a wheelbarrow full of cement.*   2 the motion or sound of rolling.   3 roll or revolve.   4 a small wheel; caster.   5 TRUNDLE BED.   6 a low cart or wagon on small wheels or casters.   1, 3 *v.*, **trun·dled, trun·dling;** 2, 4–6 *n.*

**trundle bed**   a low bed on small wheels or casters that can be rolled under a higher bed when not in use.

**trunk** (trungk)   1 the main stem of a tree, as distinct from the branches and the roots.   2 the main part of anything: *The marble trunk of the column rested on a granite base.*   3 an enclosed compartment in an automobile for storing luggage, tools, etc.   4 a large, heavy box with a hinged lid, used for transporting or storing clothes and other personal property.   5 the body apart from the head, arms, and legs; torso.   6 the long, muscular, flexible snout of an elephant.   7 a main channel or passage.   8 TRUNK LINE.   9 **trunks,** *pl.* very short pants worn by male athletes, swimmers, acrobats, etc.   *n.*

Trunk hose of the late Tudor period, about 1565

**trunk hose**   short, full, baggy breeches reaching about halfway down the thigh, worn by men, especially in the 16th and 17th centuries.

**trunk line**   1 the main line of a railway, canal, etc.   2 a line between telephone exchanges.

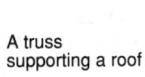
A truss supporting a roof
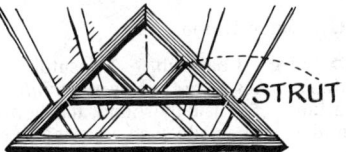

**truss** (trus)   1 tie; fasten; bind (*often used with* **up**): *We trussed the burglar up and called the police.*   2 fasten the wings or legs of a fowl in preparation for cooking.   3 a framework of beams or other braces for supporting a roof, bridge, etc.   4 support or strengthen with a truss or trusses.   5 a pad or other device worn as a support for a hernia.   6 a bundle or pack.   7 on a ship or boat, an iron fitting by which a lower yard is fastened to the mast.   1, 2, 4 *v.*, 3, 5–7 *n.*

**trust** (trust)   1 a firm belief in the honesty, truthfulness, justice, or power of a person or thing; faith: *A child puts trust in his mother.*   2 have faith; rely; be confident: *Trust in God.*   3 believe firmly in the honesty, truth, justice, or power of; have faith in: *She is a woman to be trusted.*   4 rely on; depend on: *A forgetful man should not trust his memory.*   5 a person or thing trusted: *God is our trust.*   6 a confident expectation or hope: *Our trust is that she will soon be well.*   7 hope; believe: *I trust you will soon feel better.*   8 a group of people or companies that controls much of a certain kind of business: *a steel trust.*   9 a group of business people or firms having a central committee that controls stock of the constituent companies, thus simplifying management and defeating competition.   10 something managed for the benefit of another; something of value committed to one's care.   11 the obligation or responsibility imposed on a person in whom confidence or authority is placed: *Mr. Chung will be faithful to his trust.*   12 the condition of one in whom trust has been placed; being relied on: *A guardian is in a position of trust.*   13 keeping; care: *The will was left in my trust.*   14 in law, a confidence reposed in a person by making him or her nominal owner of property, which he or she is to hold, use, or dispose of for the benefit of another: *Mr. Chung does not own the house; it is a trust that he holds for his dead sister's children.*   15 an estate, etc. committed to a trustee or trustees.   16 the right of a person to enjoy the use or profits of property held in trust for him or her.   17 managing for an owner: *a trust company.*   18 of or having to do with trust or trusts; held in trust: *a trust fund.*   19 commit to the care of; leave without fear: *Can I trust the keys to her?*   20 confidence in the ability or intention of a person to pay at some future time for goods, etc.; business credit.   21 give business credit to: *The butcher will trust us for the meat.*   1, 5, 6, 8–18, 20 *n.*, 2–4, 7, 19, 21 *v.*   —**trust′er,** *n.*
**in trust,**   as a thing taken charge of for another.
**on trust,**   **a** on business credit; with payment later. **b** without investigation.
**trust to,**   rely on; depend on: *Don't trust to luck.*

**trust company**   a business concern formed primarily to act as a TRUSTEE (def. 1) but also often engaging in other financial activities normally performed by banks.

**trus·tee** (trus tē′)   1 a person responsible for the property or affairs of another person, of a company, or of an institution: *A trustee will manage the children's property until they grow up.*   2 a person elected to a board or committee that is responsible for the schools in a district; school trustee.   3 a country made responsible for a trust territory.   *n.*

**trus·tee·ship** (trus tē′ship)   the position of TRUSTEE.   *n.*

**trust·ful** (trust′fəl)   ready to confide; ready to have faith; believing.   *adj.*   —**trust′ful·ly,** *adv.*   —**trust′ful·ness,** *n.*

**trust fund**   money, property, or other valuables held in trust by one person for the benefit of another.

**trust·ing** (trus′ting)   1 that trusts; trustful: *She has a trusting nature.*   2 ppr. of TRUST.   1 *adj.*, 2 *v.*   —**trust′ing·ly,** *adv.*

**trust territory**   a territory placed under the administrative control of a particular country by the United Nations.

**trust·wor·thy** (trust′wėr′ᴛʜē)   that can be depended on; reliable: *The class chose a trustworthy girl for treasurer.*   *adj.*   —**trust′wor′thi·ness,** *n.*

**trust·y** (trus′tē)   1 that can be depended on; reliable: *a trusty servant.*   2 a convict who is given special privileges because of his or her good behaviour: *The trusties were allowed to work on the gardens outside the prison walls.* 1 *adj.*, **trust·i·er, trust·i·est;** 2 *n., pl.* **trust·ies.** —**trust′i·ly,** *adv.* —**trust′i·ness,** *n.*

**truth** (trüth) 1 the quality or property of being in accord with fact or reality: *She doubted the truth of the story.* 2 something that is in accord with fact or reality: *to tell the whole truth. The truth is that I haven't seen him for over a year.* 3 a fixed or established principle, law, etc.; an accepted or proven doctrine or fact: *a basic scientific truth. n., pl.* **truths** (trüᴛʜz *or* trüths).
**in truth,** truly; really; in fact.

**truth·ful** (trüth′fəl) 1 telling the truth: *a truthful child.* 2 conforming to truth: *a truthful report. adj.* —**truth′ful·ly,** *adv.* —**truth′ful·ness,** *n.*

**truth serum** *Informal.* any drug thought to make a person speak freely and openly when questioned.

**try** (trī) 1 make an attempt or effort: *He tried to open the window, but it was stuck. You'll never know till you try. She's going to try for her lifesaving certificate next week.* 2 attempt to do or accomplish: *It seems easy until you try it.* 3 find out the quality or qualities of by experimenting or sampling: *Try your skill at trap-shooting. He tried the candy but didn't like it.* 4 find out the effectiveness or usefulness of an action, process, or thing: *Try opening the window to get the smoke out. Did you try the hardware store to see if they had any?* 5 attempt to open a door, window, etc.: *Try the doors to see if they are locked.* 6 an attempt or effort: *We each had three tries at the high jump. She made a good try for the ball but missed it.* 7 examine the evidence against in a court of law; determine the guilt or innocence of with respect to a particular accusation: *The woman was tried and found guilty.* 8 put to a severe test; strain: *Don't try your eyes by reading in a poor light. His constant complaining tried her patience.* 9 subject to trials; afflict: *Mother was greatly tried by the children's squabbles.* 10 melt down or extract by melting (*often used with* **out**): *to try lard, to try out oil from blubber.* 1–5, 7–10 *v.,* **tried, try·ing;** 6 *n., pl.* **tries.**
**try on,** put on to test the fit, looks, etc.: *I tried on four blouses but didn't like any of them.*
**try out, a** test thoroughly by using: *She took the car onto the highway to try it out.* **b** take a test to show fitness for a particular role or place: *to try out for the hockey team, to try out for a part in a play. Are you going to try out?*
☛ *Usage.* **Try and** is commonly used in informal speech and writing: *They will try and make me stay home.* In more careful English, especially in formal situations, **try to** is preferred: *We will try to do better.*

**trying** (trī′ing) 1 hard to endure; annoying: *It's been a trying day.* 2 ppr. of TRY. 1 *adj.,* 2 *v.*

**try–on** (trī′on′) *Informal.* the act or process of trying on an unfinished garment to check the fit, etc.; a fitting: *I have to go to the dressmaker's tomorrow for a try-on. n.*

**try–out** (trī′out′) a test made to determine fitness for a particular role or place: *The tryouts are tomorrow. n.*

**tryp·sin** (trip′sən) an enzyme in the digestive juice secreted by the pancreas: *Trypsin changes proteins into peptones. n.*

**try·sail** (trī′sāl′ *or* trī′səl) a small fore-and-aft sail used in stormy weather on the foremast or mainmast. *n.*

**try square** an instrument for drawing right angles and testing the squareness of anything. See SQUARE for picture.

**tryst** (trist) 1 an agreement or appointment to meet at a certain time and place, especially an agreement by lovers for a secret meeting. 2 a meeting held by appointment. 3 a place of meeting. *n.*

**trysting place** an appointed meeting place.

**tsar** (zär) See CZAR. *n.*

**tsa·ri·na** (zä rē′nə) See CZARINA. *n.*

**tset·se** (tset′sē) TSETSE FLY. *n.*

**tsetse fly** any of a closely related group of African bloodsucking, two-winged flies, many species of which carry disease: *At least one species of tsetse fly transmits African sleeping sickness.*

**T–shirt** (tē′shėrt′) a light, knitted sport shirt or undershirt having no collar and, usually, short sleeves. It is frequently made of cotton. *n.*

**tsp.** teaspoonful; teaspoonfuls.

A T-square

**T–square** (tē′skwer′) a T-shaped ruler used for making parallel lines, etc.: *The shorter arm of a T-square slides along the edge of the drawing board, which serves as a guide. n.*

**T–strap** (tē′strap′) 1 a T-shaped strap on a shoe, consisting of a strap along the instep joined to a strap around the ankle. 2 a shoe having such a strap. *n.*

**tsu·na·mi** (tsu nam′ē) a gigantic sea wave caused by an earthquake on the ocean floor, occurring especially in the Pacific Ocean and often causing great destruction in coastal regions. *n.*

**Tu.** Tuesday.

**T.U.** Trade Union.

**tub** (tub) 1 bathtub. 2 washtub. 3 *Informal.* a bath: *He takes a cold tub every morning.* 4 wash or bathe in a tub. 5 a usually round, flat-bottomed, open container, especially such a container made of wooden staves bound by hoops, used for holding butter, lard, etc. 6 as much as a tub can hold: *a tub of butter.* 7 *Informal.* a clumsy, slow-moving boat or ship. 1–3, 5–7 *n.,* 4 *v.,* **tubbed, tub·bing.**

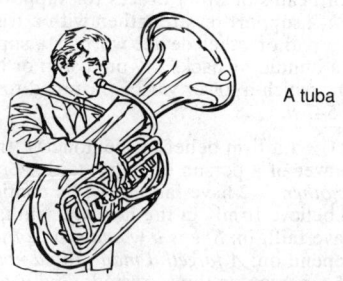

A tuba

**tu·ba** (tyü′bə *or* tü′bə) a large musical brass wind instrument resembling a trumpet, having valves to vary the pitch. It has the lowest range of the brasses. *n.*

**tub·bing** (tub′ing) 1 a bath. 2 ppr. of TUB. 1 *n.*, 2 *v.*

**tub·by** (tub′ē) 1 like a tub in shape. 2 short and fat or pudgy. 3 of a violin, etc., having a dull, wooden sound; not having proper resonance. *adj.*, **tub·bi·er**, **tub·bi·est**. —**tub′bi·ness**, *n.*

**tube** (tyüb *or* tüb) 1 a long, hollow cylinder, especially one used to hold or carry liquids or gases: *The mercury or alcohol of a thermometer is held in a glass tube. A plastic tube runs from the pump to the filter of our fish tank.* 2 a small cylinder of thin, flexible metal or plastic with a cap that screws onto the open end, used for holding paste substances, such as toothpaste or paint, ready for use. 3 a channel in an animal or plant body: *the bronchial tubes.* 4 a separate, inflatable casing of rubber that fits inside the outer casing of a tire; inner tube. 5 a pipe or tunnel through which something travels: *The subway runs under the city in a tube.* 6 *Informal.* SUBWAY. 7 ELECTRON TUBE. 8 the picture tube of a television set. *n.* —**tube′like′**, *adj.*

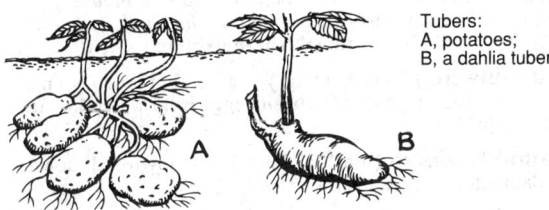

Tubers: A, potatoes; B, a dahlia tuber

**tu·ber** (tyü′bər *or* tü′bər) the thick part of an underground stem: *A potato is a tuber.* *n.*

**tu·ber·cle** (tyü′bər kəl *or* tü′bər kəl) 1 a small, rounded swelling or knob on an animal or plant: *The roots of some plants have tubercles. There is a tubercle near the end of each rib where it connects with the backbone.* 2 a small, hard lump in an organ or the skin, especially such a lump in the lungs that is characteristic of TUBERCULOSIS. *n.*

**tubercle bacillus** the bacterium that causes TUBERCULOSIS.

**tu·ber·cu·lar** (tyü bėr′kyə lər *or* tü bėr′kyə lər) 1 TUBERCULOUS. 2 of, having to do with, or having TUBERCLES. 3 a person having TUBERCULOSIS. 1, 2 *adj.*, 3 *n.*

**tu·ber·cu·lin** (tyü bėr′kyə lin *or* tü bėr′kyə lin) a sterile liquid prepared from a culture of the bacteria that cause TUBERCULOSIS, used in the diagnosis of the disease. *n.*

**tu·ber·cu·lo·sis** (tyü bėr′kyə lō′sis *or* tü bėr′kyə lō′sis) an infectious disease caused by the TUBERCLE BACILLUS, affecting human beings and some other mammals, and characterized by the formation of TUBERCLES in various tissues of the body: *Tuberculosis in human beings usually affects the lungs.* *n.*

**tu·ber·cu·lous** (tyü bėr′kyə ləs *or* tü bėr′kyə ləs) 1 of, having to do with, or affected with TUBERCULOSIS: *a tuberculous patient.* 2 caused by the TUBERCLE BACILLUS: *tuberculous ulcers in the lungs, a tuberculous infection.* *adj.*

**tube·rose** (tyü′brōz′ *or* tü′brōz′) a tropical plant of the amaryllis family, having sword-shaped leaves and spikes of very fragrant, white, funnel-shaped flowers: *The tuberose grows from a bulb.* *n.*

**tu·ber·os·i·ty** (tyü′bə ros′ə tē *or* tü′bə ros′ə tē) 1 the quality or condition of being TUBEROUS. 2 a rounded knob or swelling, especially on a bone where muscles or ligaments are attached. *n.*, *pl.* **tu·ber·os·i·ties.**

**tu·ber·ous** (tyü′bə rəs *or* tü′bə rəs) 1 of, like, or having a TUBER or tubers. 2 covered with rounded knobs or swellings. *adj.*

**tub·ing** (tyü′bing *or* tü′bing) 1 material in the form of a tube: *rubber tubing.* 2 a piece of tube. 3 a system of tubes. *n.*

**tu·bu·lar** (tyü′byə lər *or* tü′byə lər) 1 shaped like a tube; round and hollow. 2 made of or provided with tube-shaped pieces: *tubular furniture.* *adj.*

**tu·bule** (tyü′byül *or* tü′byül) a very small tube, especially a narrow channel in an animal or plant. *n.*

**tuck** (tuk) 1 put into a narrow place or space where it is held tightly or concealed: *She tucked the newspaper under her arm. He tucked the letter away in an inside pocket.* 2 push the loose edge or end of tightly into place: *Tuck your shirt in. He tucked a serviette under his chin.* 3 cover snugly by tucking in the bedclothes (*used with* **in**): *He always came up to tuck the children in.* 4 draw close together into a fold or folds; make shorter by gathering or folding together (*used with* **up**): *She tucked up her long skirt and waded into the lake.* 5 a narrow, straight fold sewn into a garment, etc. for decoration or to shorten or control fullness. 6 make a tuck or tucks in: *to tuck the bodice of a dress. The pillowcases have tucked edges.* 7 fold the legs back or up when sitting or lying: *She sat with her legs tucked under her.* 8 in diving, etc., a position in which the knees are drawn up to the body. 9 eat heartily (*used with* **away** *or* **in**): *He tucked away a big meal.* 10 pull in or back: *to tuck in one's stomach.* 11 sew tucks. 1–4, 6, 7, 9–11 *v.*, 5, 8 *n.*

**tuck·er**[1] (tuk′ər) 1 a piece of lace, embroidered fabric, etc. worn by women in the 17th and 18th centuries as a yoke above a low-cut bodice. 2 a person or thing that makes tucks, especially an attachment or device on a sewing machine for making tucks. *n.*

**tuck·er**[2] (tuk′ər) *Informal.* tire; weary; exhaust (*usually used with* **out**): *We were all tuckered out after four hours of wandering around the zoo.* *v.*

**Tu·dor** (tyü′dər *or* tü′dər) 1 of or having to do with the royal family that ruled England from 1485 to 1603. 2 a member of the Tudor family: *Elizabeth I was the last Tudor.* 3 referring to, having to do with, or characteristic of the time of the Tudors, especially of the style of architecture that was common then: *Tudor architecture was characterized by shallow, pointed or slightly rounded arches, half-timbered construction, etc.* 1, 3 *adj.*, 2 *n.*

**Tues.** Tuesday.

**Tues·day** (tyüz′dā *or* tüz′dā, tyüz′dē *or* tüz′dē′) the third day of the week, following Monday. *n.*
☛ *Etym.* From OE *Tīwesdæg* 'day of Tiw (the Germanic god of war)'.

**tu·fa** (tyü′fə *or* tü′fə) 1 a soft porous form of limestone produced as a deposit from a spring or stream rich in lime. 2 TUFF. *n.*

**tuff** (tuf) a soft, porous rock formed from volcanic ash

or dust thrown out by an erupting volcano: *Tuff can vary greatly in texture and composition.* *n.*

**tuft** (tuft) **1** a bunch of feathers, hair, grass, etc. growing close together: *A goat has a tuft of hair on its chin.* **2** a clump of bushes, trees, etc. **3** a bunch of short, fluffy, often decorative threads or lengths of yarn held together at one end, especially the ends of thread or yarn sewn through a comforter, mattress, cushion, etc. to keep the padding in place. **4** provide or decorate with a tuft or tufts. **5** secure the padding of a comforter, etc. by sewing through it at intervals. **6** grow in or form into tufts. 1–3 *n.*, 4–6 *v.*

**tuft·ed** (tuf′tid) **1** having or furnished with a tuft or tufts. **2** formed into a tuft or tufts. **3** pt. and pp. of TUFT. 1, 2 *adj.*, 3 *v.*

**tug** (tug) **1** pull with force or effort; pull hard: *I tugged the rope and it came loose. The child tugged at his mother's hand.* **2** move by pulling hard: *We tugged the boat up onto the sand.* **3** a hard pull: *The baby gave a tug at Mary's hair.* **4** a hard strain, struggle, effort, or contest. **5** TUGBOAT. **6** tow by a tugboat. **7** a rope, chain, or strap used for pulling, especially the harness trace. See HARNESS for picture. 1, 2, 6 *v.*, **tugged, tug·ging;** 3, 4, 5, 7 *n.*

**tug·boat** (tug′bōt′) a small, powerful boat used to tow or push ships or boats. *n.*

**tug–of–war** (tug′ə vwôr′) **1** a contest between two teams pulling at the ends of a rope, each trying to drag the other over a line marked between them. **2** any hard struggle for power. *n.*

**tu·i·tion** (tyü ish′ən *or* tü ish′ən) **1** the price of or money paid for instruction: *Her yearly tuition is $1300.* **2** teaching; instruction: *The child made excellent progress under his capable tuition.* *n.*

**tu·la·re·mi·a** (tü′lə rē′mē ə) an infectious disease of rabbits and other rodents, sometimes transmitted to human beings through insect bites or contact with diseased animals. *n.*

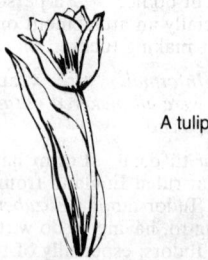
A tulip

**tu·lip** (tyü′lip *or* tü′lip) **1** any of a closely related group of plants belonging to the lily family, that grow from bulbs and have long, pointed leaves and large, cup-shaped, usually single flowers: *There are many varieties of cultivated tulips.* **2** the flower or bulb of a tulip. *n.*
☛ Etym. Through modern Latin *tulipa* and F *tulipe* from Turkish *tuliband* (now *tülbend*), which came from Persian *dulband* 'turban', which the flower was thought to resemble.

**tulip tree** a large North American hardwood tree of the magnolia family having broad, lobed leaves and large, cup-shaped, greenish-yellow flowers that appear after the leaves.

**tulle** (tül) a fine, stiff, machine-made net, usually of silk, used especially for veils and ballet costumes: *Tulle was used for evening gowns in the 1950's.* *n.*

**tul·li·bee** (tul′ə bē′) *Cdn.* a species of whitefish found throughout most Canadian lakes from Quebec westward, particularly valued as a food fish: *The tullibee is also often called a cisco.* *n.*, *pl.* **tul·li·bee** *or* **tul·li·bees.**

**tum·ble** (tum′bəl) **1** fall, especially helplessly, headlong, or end over end: *The child tumbled down the stairs.* **2** a fall: *The tumble hurt him badly. He took a tumble on the ice.* **3** throw over or down; cause to fall: *The earthquake tumbled several buildings.* **4** roll or toss about: *The sick child tumbled restlessly in her bed.* **5** move or go in a headlong or awkward way: *He tumbled out of bed to answer the phone. The excited children tumbled through the door.* **6** perform leaps, springs, somersaults, etc. **7** turn over and over; whirl: *to tumble clothes in a dryer.* **8** decline rapidly in amount, etc.: *The stock market tumbled.* **9** *Informal.* understand; catch on (used with *to*): *She tumbled to the trick right away.* **10** a state of confusion or disorder: *Her room was all in a tumble.* **11** a confused or disordered heap: *a tumble of clothes on the floor.* 1, 3–9 *v.*, **tum·bled, tum·bling;** 2, 10, 11 *n.*

**tum·ble·bug** (tum′bəl bug′) a beetle that rolls up a ball of dung in which it deposits eggs from which larvae develop. *n.*

**tum·ble–down** (tum′bəl doun′) ready to fall down; dilapidated: *a tumble-down shack.* *adj.*

**tum·bler** (tum′blər) **1** a person who performs leaps, springs, etc.; acrobat. **2** a glass for drinking out of, made without a handle or a foot or stem, and having a heavy, flat bottom: *Tumblers originally had rounded or pointed bottoms so that they could not be set down until empty.* **3** the amount a glass will hold: *to drink a tumbler of water.* **4** the part in the lock that must be moved from a certain position in order to release the bolt. **5** the part of a gunlock that forces the hammer forward when the trigger is pulled. **6** a kind of domestic pigeon that does backward somersaults while flying. **7** a toy figure with a rounded, weighted bottom that will rock when touched but will always right itself. **8** a revolving device that tumbles things for a particular purpose: *The drum in a clothes dryer is often called a tumbler.* *n.*

**tum·ble·weed** (tum′bəl wēd′) any of various plants that after drying up in the fall break off from their roots and are blown about by the wind. *n.*

**tum·bling** (tum′bling) **1** the sport or practice of performing leaps, somersaults, and other gymnastic feats without the use of any apparatus. **2** ppr. of TUMBLE. 1 *n.*, 2 *v.*

**tum·brel** *or* **tum·bril** (tum′brəl) **1** a farmer's cart that can be tipped for emptying. **2** an open cart used in the French Revolution to carry prisoners to the guillotine. **3** formerly, a two-wheeled covered cart for carrying ammunition and military tools. *n.*

**tu·me·fac·tion** (tyü′mə fak′shən *or* tü′mə fak′shən) **1** swelling or being swollen. **2** a swollen part. *n.*

**tu·me·fy** (tyü′mə fī′ *or* tü′mə fī′) SWELL. *v.* **tu·me·fied, tu·me·fy·ing.**

**tu·mes·cence** (tyü mes′əns *or* tü mes′əns) the quality or state of being swollen. *n.*

**tu·mes·cent** (tyü mes′ənt *or* tü mes′ənt) **1** becoming swollen; beginning to swell. **2** somewhat swollen. *adj.*

**tu·mid** (tyü′mid *or* tü′mid) **1** SWOLLEN. **2** swollen with big words; bombastic: *a tumid style of writing.* *adj.* —**tu′mid·ly,** *adv.* —**tu′mid·ness,** *n.*

**tum·my** (tum′ē) *Informal.* stomach. *n., pl.* **tum·mies.**

**tu·mor·ous** (tyü′mə rəs *or* tü′mə rəs) **1** of or having to do with a TUMOUR or tumours. **2** having a TUMOUR or tumours. *adj.*

**tu·mour** *or* **tu·mor** (tyü′mər *or* tü′mər) an abnormal, separate mass of tissue in any part of the body, that develops from existing tissue, but has no physiological function: *Tumours can be either benign (doing little or no harm) or malignant (cancerous).* *n.*

**tump** (tump) TUMPLINE. *n.*

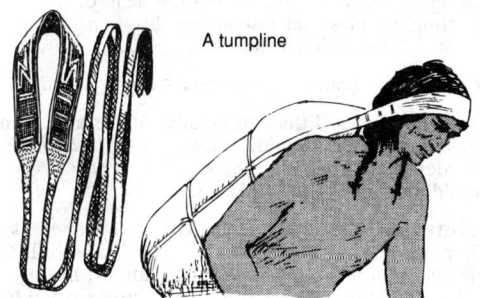

A tumpline

**tump·line** (tum′plīn′) a kind of harness for carrying or pulling heavy loads, consisting of a long strap with a broad middle part that is placed around the forehead or chest, the two ends being attached to the pack or load. *n.*

**tu·mult** (tyü′mult *or* tü′mult) **1** a violent disturbance or disorder; uproar: *We heard the tumult of the storm. The shout of "Fire!" caused a tumult in the theatre.* **2** a great disturbance of mind or feeling; confusion and excitement: *I was in a state of tumult after the policeman's questions.* *n.*

**tu·mul·tu·ous** (tyü mul′chü əs *or* tü mul′chü əs) **1** very noisy or disorderly; violent: *a tumultuous celebration.* **2** greatly disturbed: *tumultuous emotion.* **3** rough; stormy: *Tumultuous waves beat upon the rocks.* *adj.* —**tu·mul′tu·ous·ly,** *adv.* —**tu·mul′tu·ous·ness,** *n.*

**tu·mu·lus** (tyü′myə ləs *or* tü′myə ləs) a mound of earth, especially an ancient burial mound. *n., pl.* **tu·mu·lus·es** *or* **tu·mu·li** (-lī′ *or* -lē′).

**tun** (tun) **1** a large cask for holding liquids, especially wine, beer or ale. **2** a unit formerly used for measuring the volume of liquids, equal to 252 gallons (about 954 L). *n.* ☞ *Hom.* TON, TONNE.

**tu·na** (tü′nə *or* tyü′nə) **1** any of a group of important food and game fish of the same family as the mackerels, found in warm seas throughout the world, having a rounded, tapering body and a crescent-shaped tail: *The largest and commercially most important tuna is the* **bluefin tuna,** *which may weigh as much as 500 kilograms.* **2** the flesh of a tuna, especially when canned for use as food. *n., pl.* **tu·na** *or* **tu·nas.**

**tun·a·ble** *or* **tune·a·ble** (tyü′nə bəl *or* tü′nə bəl) capable of being tuned. *adj.*

**tuna fish** the flesh of a TUNA, especially when canned for use as food: *a tuna-fish casserole.*

**tun·dra** (tun′drə) a vast, level, treeless plain in the arctic regions: *The subsoil of the tundra remains frozen all year round.* *n.*

**tune** (tyün *or* tün) **1** a succession of musical tones in a particular rhythm, forming a unit; melody: *He was humming a tune to himself as he worked.* **2** the proper pitch: *She can't sing in tune. The piano is out of tune.* **3** a mood or manner; attitude: *He was very cocky at first, but soon changed his tune.* **4** agreement; harmonious relation: *He's happier now that he's in tune with his surroundings again. She won't be elected because she's out of tune with the times.* **5** adjust to the proper pitch; put in tune: *to tune a piano or a violin.* **6** of an orchestra, adjust instruments to the proper pitch (*used with* **up**): *The orchestra was already tuning up when we arrived.* **7** adjust a motor, etc. for precise performance (*often used with* **up**): *She took her car in to have the engine tuned.* **8** adjust a radio or television set to receive a particular frequency of signals (*often used with* **in**): *He tuned his radio to the news from London. Tune in tomorrow for another episode. We tuned in the new FM station.* 1–4 *n.,* 5–8 *v.,* **tuned, tun·ing.**

**call the tune,** have control; be in a position to dictate what will be done: *He talks big to the press, but it is his partner who calls the tune.*

**sing a different tune,** talk or behave differently: *She's singing a different tune since she lost her job.*

**to the tune of,** *Informal.* to the amount or sum of, especially when it is considered excessive: *He received a bill to the tune of $800 for car repairs.*

**tune out, a** adjust a radio or television set to cut out interference or static. **b** *Informal.* turn one's mind away from; ignore: *Our boss tunes out complaints he doesn't want to hear.*

**tune·ful** (tyün′fəl *or* tün′fəl) musical; melodious: *a tuneful song.* *adj.* —**tune′ful·ly,** *adv.* —**tune′ful·ness,** *n.*

**tune·less** (tyün′lis *or* tün′lis) not tuneful; not having a pleasing or recognizable tune: *His absent-minded tuneless humming began to get on their nerves.* *adj.*

**tun·er** (tyü′nər *or* tü′nər) **1** a person whose work is tuning musical instruments, especially pianos. **2** any person or thing that tunes. *n.*

**tune–up** (tyü′nup′ *or* tü′nup′) adjustment of a motor, etc. to the proper running condition: *He took his car in for an engine tune-up.* *n.*

**tung oil** (tung) an oil obtained from the seeds of the TUNG TREE, widely used as a drying oil in paints and varnishes, as a waterproofing agent, etc.

**tung·sten** (tung′stən) a hard, heavy, steel-grey metallic element with a very high melting point, used especially for the filaments of electric light bulbs and in making steel alloys; wolfram. *Symbol:* W *n.*

**tung tree** (tung) a tree native to China but now cultivated in other warm regions of the world, belonging to the same family as the poinsettia, having large, heart-shaped leaves and white flowers: *The seeds of the tung tree yield tung oil.*

**tu·nic** (tyü′nik *or* tü′nik) **1** a loose garment with or without sleeves, usually reaching to the knees, worn by the ancient Greeks and Romans. **2** a woman's garment somewhat like a dress but shorter, worn over a skirt or long pants: *Sleeveless tunics, sometimes open at the sides, are often worn over blouses and skirts, etc.* **3** a hip-length overblouse. **4** a short, close-fitting coat or jacket worn as part of the uniform by soldiers, police officers, etc. *n.*

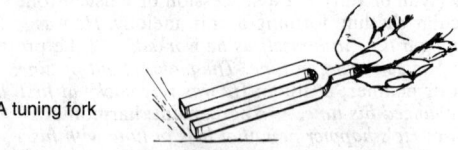
A tuning fork

**tuning fork** a small, two-pronged steel instrument that sounds a fixed tone when struck, used to determine a standard pitch for singing or for tuning a musical instrument.

**Tu·ni·sian** (tü nē′zhən, tü nē′zē ən, or tü nē′shən) **1** a native or inhabitant of Tunisia, a country in northern Africa, or its capital city, Tunis. **2** of or having to do with Tunisia, Tunis, or the Tunisians. 1 *n.*, 2 *adj.*

**tun·nel** (tun′əl) **1** an artificial underground passage under a river, road, building, etc. or through a hill or mountain, for a railway, road, or walkway: *The railway passes through several tunnels on its way through the Rockies. There is a tunnel connecting the university residences with the food-services building.* **2** a horizontal passage in a mine. **3** an animal's burrow. **4** make a tunnel: *The mole tunnelled in the ground. The workers are tunnelling under the river.* **5** make a tunnel through or under: *to tunnel a hill or river.* **6** make one's way or a passage by tunnelling: *She tunnelled a narrow passage through the snowdrift. They tunnelled their way under the prison wall.* 1–3 *n.*, 4–6 *v.*, **tun·nelled** or **tun·neled**, **tun·nel·ling** or **tun·nel·ing**. —**tun′nel·ler** or **tun′nel·er**, *n.*

**tunnel vision** **1** a very narrow field of vision; a field of vision that is restricted at the sides.
**2** narrow-mindedness: *His tunnel vision makes him too intolerant to be a good politician.*

**tun·ny** (tun′ē) TUNA. *n.*, *pl.* **tun·nies** or **tun·ny**.

**tu·pik** (tü′pək) *Cdn.* a compact, portable tent of skins, traditionally used by Inuit as a summer dwelling. *n.* Also, **tupek**.

Two styles of tuque

**tuque** (tük *or* tyük) *Cdn.* **1** a knitted cap resembling a long stocking, usually knotted at the end: *Tuques are popular at the winter carnival.* **2** a tight-fitting, short knitted cap, often having a round tassel on top. *n.*
☛ *Etym.* From a Canadian French variant of *toque* 'cap'. See also the note at TOQUE.

A turban

**tur·ban** (tėr′bən) **1** a headdress for men worn especially by Muslims and Sikhs, consisting of a scarf wound around the head, sometimes over a cap. **2** any similar headdress, especially one worn by women, consisting of a scarf wound around the head or a close-fitting, brimless hat resembling this. *n.*
☛ *Hom.* TURBINE (tėr′bən).

**tur·baned** (tėr′bənd) wearing a TURBAN. *adj.*

**tur·bid** (tėr′bid) **1** thick or cloudy with or as if with churned up sediment; muddy: *a turbid river.* **2** confused or disordered: *a turbid and restless mind.* *adj.*
—**tur′bid·ly**, *adv.* —**tur′bid·ness**, *n.*

**tur·bi·nate** (tėr′bə nit *or* tėr′bə nāt′) **1** shaped like an upside-down cone. **2** shaped like a spiral or scroll: *Many molluscs have turbinate shells.* **3** in anatomy, having to do with or referring to certain spongy, scroll-shaped bones in the nasal passages. **4** a turbinate shell or bone. 1–3 *adj.*, 4 *n.*

**tur·bine** (tėr′bīn *or* tėr′bən) a rotary engine or motor driven by a current of water, steam, or air that pushes against the blades of a wheel or system of wheels attached to a drive shaft, causing the wheel and drive shaft to turn: *Turbines are used to turn generators that produce electric power.* See JET ENGINE for picture. *n.*
☛ *Hom.* TURBAN (for the second pronunciation of **turbine**).

**turbo–** *combining form.* consisting of or driven by a TURBINE, as in *turbojet.*

**tur·bo·gen·er·a·tor** (tėr′bō jen′ə rā tər) a generator attached to a TURBINE, by which it is driven. *n.*

**tur·bo·jet** (tėr′bō jet′) **1** TURBOJET ENGINE. **2** an aircraft powered by a TURBOJET ENGINE or engines. *n.*

**turbojet engine** a jet engine using a TURBINE to drive an air compressor which supplies compressed air to the combustion chamber: *A turbojet engine is started with an auxiliary power source that spins the turbine. Most military aircraft are powered by turbojet engines.*

**tur·bo·prop** (tėr′bō prop′) **1** TURBOPROP ENGINE. **2** an aircraft powered by a TURBOPROP ENGINE or engines. *n.*

**turboprop engine** a jet engine using a propeller and a TURBOJET ENGINE with two TURBINES. The turbojet engine is used mainly to turn the propeller, which supplies most of the power for the aircraft: *The jet exhaust of a turboprop engine adds only a little to the power provided by the propeller.*

**tur·bot** (tėr′bət) **1** a large European flatfish, valued as food. **2** any of various similar fishes, such as certain flounders. *n.*, *pl.* **tur·bot** or **tur·bots**.

**tur·bu·lence** (tėr′byələns) **1** the quality or state of being TURBULENT; disturbance or commotion: *He was glad to retire from the turbulence of public life. The weather* *forecast was for some turbulence later in the day.* **2 a** disturbance in the air: *The captain is expecting some turbulence and suggests that you fasten your seat belts.* *n.*

**tur·bu·lent** (tėr′byə lənt) **1** greatly disturbed or agitated; characterized by trouble or commotion: *the turbulent sea, a turbulent state of mind.* **2** causing disturbance; unruly; boisterous: *a turbulent mob.* *adj.*

**tu·reen** (tu̇ rēn′) a deep, covered dish for serving soup, etc. *n.*

**turf** (tėrf) **1** grass with its roots and the soil it is growing in, forming a thick layer like a mat. **2** a piece of turf; sod: *We cut turfs from the back lawn to fill in bare spots in the front.* **3** an artificial surface for a playing field, etc., made to resemble grass. **4** cover with turf. **5** *Informal.* a particular territory or area: *He could relax now that he was back on his own turf.* **6** PEAT, especially a block of peat used for fuel. **7** Usually, **the turf, a** a track for horse racing. **b** the sport or business of horse racing. 1–3, 5, 6, 7 *n., pl.* **turfs;** 4 *v.*

**turf·y** (tėr′fē) **1** covered with turf; grassy. **2** like turf. **3** full of peat; like peat. **4** of or having to do with horse racing. *adj.*, **turf·i·er, turf·i·est.** —**turf′i·ness,** *n.*

**tur·ges·cence** (tėr jes′əns) the process of swelling or the condition of being swollen. *n.*

**tur·ges·cent** (tėr jes′ənt) becoming TURGID; swelling. *adj.*

**tur·gid** (tėr′jid) **1** swollen; bloated. **2** using big words and elaborate comparisons; bombastic; inflated; pompous. *adj.* —**tur′gid·ly,** *adv.*

**tur·gid·i·ty** (tėr jid′ə tē) the quality or state of being TURGID. *n.*

**tur·gor pressure** the pressure of water in the cytoplasm against the cell wall of a plant.

**Turk** (tėrk) **1** a native or inhabitant of Turkey, a country in Asia Minor and southeastern Europe. **2** a native or inhabitant of the Ottoman Empire. **3** a member of any of the peoples traditionally speaking Turkic languages and inhabiting the region from the Adriatic Sea to eastern Siberia. *n.*

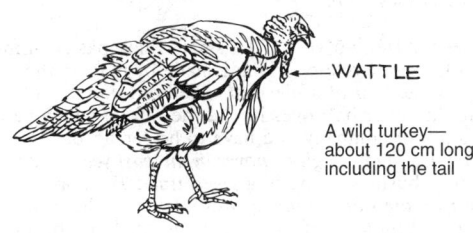

A wild turkey—about 120 cm long including the tail

**tur·key** (tėr′kē) **1** a large domestic fowl having metallic green, copper, and bronze plumage, with black-tipped body feathers and white-tipped tail feathers and having no feathers on the head and neck. **2** the flesh of a turkey, used for food: *Turkey is associated especially with Christmas and Thanksgiving.* **3** either of two species of large forest bird of the Western Hemisphere, distantly related to the pheasants and grouse: *The domestic turkey is derived from the wild turkey of Mexico.* **4** *Cdn.* especially in the Prairie Provinces, SANDHILL CRANE. *n., pl.* **tur·keys.**

**cold turkey,** *Informal.* instantly; not gradually: *He decided to stop smoking, cold turkey.*

hat, āge, fär; let, ēqual, tėrm; it, īce
hot, ōpen, ôrder; oil, out; cup, pu̇t, rüle
ə above, takən, pencəl, lemən, circəs
ch, child; ng, long; sh, ship
th, thin; ᴛʜ, then; zh, measure

**talk turkey,** *Informal.* talk frankly and bluntly: *They decided it was time to get together and talk turkey.*
☛ Etym. A shortened form of *turkey-cock* and *turkey-hen*, names that were originally applied to the guinea fowl, which was imported into England through Turkey. The names were later applied to the North American turkey because it was at first confused with the guinea fowl. See also note at GUINEA FOWL.

**turkey buzzard** TURKEY VULTURE.

**turkey·cock** (tėr′kē kok′) **1** a male turkey. **2** a strutting, conceited person. *n.*

**turkey vulture** a vulture found in the Western Hemisphere as far north as southern Canada, having dark plumage and a red upper neck and head that are bare of feathers: *The turkey vulture looks somewhat like a turkey.*

**Tur·kic** (tėr′kik) **1** of, having to do with or referring to a group of languages including Turkish, Turkoman, and Tartar. **2** the Turkic languages. **3** of or having to do with the peoples speaking Turkic languages. 1, 3 *adj.*, 2 *n.*

**Turk·ish** (tėr′kish) **1** of, having to do with, or characteristic of Turkey, its inhabitants, or their language. **2** the Turkic language of Turkey. 1 *adj.*, 2 *n.*

**Turkish bath 1** a kind of bath in which the bather stays in a hot, usually steam-filled room until he or she sweats freely and then is washed and massaged. **2** Often, **Turkish baths,** *pl.* a place used for such baths. *n.*

**Turkish delight** a fruit-flavoured candy made of sugar and gelatin cut into cubes and dusted with powdered sugar.

**turkish towel** a thick towel made of cotton terry.

**Tur·ko·man** (tėr′kə mən) **1** a member of any of several Turkic peoples living near the Aral Sea and in parts of Iran and Afghanistan. **2** the Turkic language of these people. **3** of or having to do with the Turkomans or their language. 1, 2 *n., pl.* **Tur·ko·mans;** 3 *adj.*

**tur·mer·ic** (tėr′mə rik) **1** a yellow powder prepared from the underground stem of an East Indian perennial herb, used as a seasoning, as a yellow dye, and in medicine. **2** the plant itself. **3** the underground stem of this plant. *n.*

**tur·moil** (tėr′moil) a commotion; disturbance; tumult: *Six robberies in one night put our village in a turmoil.* *n.*

**turn** (tėrn) **1** move round as a wheel does; rotate: *The merry-go-round turned.* **2** cause to move round as a wheel does: *I turned the crank three times.* **3** a motion like that of a wheel: *At each turn, the screw goes in further.* **4** move part way around; change from one side to the other: *Turn over on your back.* **5** cause to move around in order to open, close, raise, lower, or tighten: *She turned the key in the lock.* **6** take a new direction: *The road turns to the north here.* **7** give a new direction to: *Hanna turned her steps to the north.* **8** a change of direction: *a turn to the left.* **9** a place where there is a change in direction: *a turn in the road.* **10** change in direction or position; invert; reverse: *to turn a page.* **11** change so as

to become: *She turned pale.* **12** change for or to a worse condition; sour; spoil: *Warm weather turns milk. The milk has turned.* **13** a change in affairs, conditions, or circumstances: *The sick man has taken a turn for the better.* **14** give form to; make: *He can turn pretty compliments.* **15** change from one language into another: *Turn this sentence into Latin.* **16** a form; style: *A scholar often has a serious turn of mind.* **17** put out of order; unsettle: *Too much praise turns his head.* **18** cause to go, send, etc.: *to turn a person from one's door.* **19** drive back; stop: *to turn a punch.* **20** direct one's thoughts or attention: *He turned his thoughts toward home.* **12** direct thought, eyes, etc.: *He turned to his father for help.* **22** put to use: *to turn money to good use.* **23** move to the other side of; go round; get beyond: *to turn the corner.* **24** a twist; bend: *Give that rope a few more turns around the tree.* **25** a time or chance to do something: *My turn comes after yours.* **26** a time or spell of action: *to have a turn at a thing.* **27** a deed; act: *One good turn deserves another.* **28** performance. **29** an inclination; bent: *She has a turn for mathematics.* **30** a walk, drive, or ride: *a turn in the park.* **31** shape on a lathe. **32** make sick; become sick: *The sight of blood turns my stomach.* **33** become dizzy. **34** a spell of dizziness or fainting. **35** *Informal.* a nervous shock. **36** in music, a grace consisting of a principal tone with those above and below it. **37** of leaves, change colour. 1, 2, 4–7, 10–12, 14, 15, 17–23, 31–33, 37 *v.*, 3, 8, 9, 13, 16, 24–30, 34–36 *n.*
**by turns,** one after another,
**in turn,** in proper order.
**out of turn, a** not in proper order. **b** at an inappropriate time, stage, etc.: *She was tactless to speak out of turn.*
**take turns,** play, act, etc. one after another in proper order.
**to a turn,** to just the right degree: *meat done to a turn.*
**turn about** or **turn and turn about,** one after another in proper order.
**turn down, a** fold down. **b** bend downward. **c** place with face downward. **d** refuse: *to turn down a plan.* **e** lower by turning something.
**turn in, a** turn and go in. **b** point toes inward. **c** *Informal.* go to bed: *I think I'll turn in now.* **d** give back. **e** exchange: *to turn an old bike in for a new one.*
**turn off, a** shut off: *Is the tap turned off?* **b** put out: *Turn off the lights.* **c** turn aside. **d** discharge.
**turn on, a** start the flow of; put on. **b** attack; oppose. **c** be about; have to do with. **d** depend on: *The success of the picnic turns on the weather.*
**turn out, a** put out; shut off. **b** let go out. **c** drive out. **d** come or go out: *We all turned out for hockey.* **e** go out on strike. **f** make; produce. **g** result. **h** become. **i** be found or known. **j** equip; fit out. **k** *Informal.* get out of bed.
**turn over, a** give; hand over; transfer: *He turned the job over to his assistant.* **b** think carefully about; consider in different ways: *I will turn the idea over in my mind.* **c** buy and then sell; use in business. **d** invest and get back capital. **e** change in position, especially change from lying on one side to the other. **f** convert to different use. **g** do business to the amount of.
**turn to, a** refer to. **b** go to for help. **c** get busy; set to work.
**turn up, a** fold up or over, especially so as to shorten; give an upward turn to; bring underside up. **b** make a lamp, etc. burn stronger. **c** make a radio, etc. louder. **d** turn and go up. **e** be directed upwards. **f** appear.
☞ *Hom.* TERN.

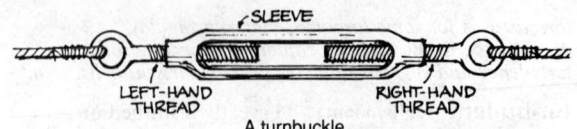
A turnbuckle

**turn·buck·le** (tėrn′buk′əl) a device for connecting and tightening metal rods, sections of wire, etc., consisting of a hollow metal link with an inside screw thread at either end or a swivel at one end and a screw thread at the other. *n.*

**turn·coat** (tėrn′kōt′) a person who changes his or her political party or principles; person who goes over to the opposing side. *n.*

**turn·down** (tėrn′doun′) that is or can be turned down; folded or doubled down: *a turndown collar.* *adj.*

**turn·er** (tėr′nər) **1** a device or tool that is used for turning: *A lathe is one kind of turner.* **2** a person who forms or shapes things with a lathe. *n.*

**turning point** a point in time at which a significant change takes place: *That experience was the turning point of her life.*

**tur·nip** (tėr′nip) **1** a biennial plant of the mustard family, having hairy leaves and a thick round, whitish root. **2** the rutabaga, closely related to this plant. **3** the root of either of these plants, used as a vegetable. *n.*

**turn·key** (tėrn′kē′) formerly, a person in charge of the keys of a prison; keeper of a prison. *n., pl.* **turn·keys.**

**turn·off** (tėr′nof′) **1** the act of turning off. **2** a place where one can leave a highway, especially an exit ramp leading off an expressway: *It's two kilometres to the next turnoff.* *n.*

**turn·out** (tėr′nout′) **1** a gathering of people for a special purpose or event: *There was a good turnout at the dance.* **2** output: *What was your turnout last month?* **3** the way in which a person or thing is equipped or dressed: *an elegant turnout.* **4** a carriage together with its horse or horses. *n.*

**turn·o·ver** (tėr′nō′vər) **1** a small, filled pastry in the shape of a semicircle or triangle made by placing the filling on one half of a piece of rolled-out dough and folding the other half over it. **2** the rate at which people leave a job or company and have to be replaced: *The company has had a high turnover in the past year.* **3** the amount of business done in a given time: *There was a large turnover on the stock exchange this week.* **4** the paying out and getting back of the money involved in a business transaction: *The store reduced prices to make a quick turnover.* **5** in football, the act or an instance of losing possession of the ball to the opposing team through a fumble, pass interception, etc.: *Two touchdowns were scored as a result of turnovers.* **6** the act or an instance of turning over; upset or reversal. *n.*

**turn·pike** (tėrn′pīk′) **1** *Esp. U.S.* a road on which toll is or used to be charged. **2** TOLLGATE. *n.*

**turn·spit** (tėrn′spit′) formerly, a person or animal, especially a dog in a treadmill, that worked a device for turning meat on a spit. *n.*

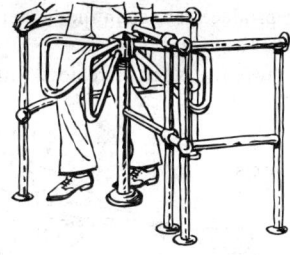

A turnstile

hat, āge, fär; let, ēqual, tėrm; it, īce
hot, ōpen, ôrder; oil, out; cup, put, rüle
əbove, taken, pencəl, lemən, circəs
ch, child; ng, long; sh, ship
th, thin; ŦH, then; zh, measure

**turn·stile** (tėrn′stīl′) an entrance barrier consisting of bars set into a revolving central post, allowing people to pass through only on foot, one at a time, and only in one direction. *n.*

**turn·ta·ble** (tėrn′tā′bəl) **1** on a record player, the revolving disk on which a record is placed to be played. **2** any similar disk or platform that revolves, such as a platform with track, used for turning a locomotive around. *n.*

**tur·pen·tine** (tėr′pən tīn′) **1** a thick, sticky fluid consisting of oil and resin, obtained from pines and various other coniferous trees. **2** a volatile oil distilled from this fluid, used especially as a solvent and thinner for paints, varnishes, etc. **3** apply turpentine to. **1, 2** *n.*, **3** *v.*

**tur·pi·tude** (tėr′pə tyüd′ *or* tėr′pə tüd′) shameful wickedness; baseness. *n.*

**tur·quoise** (tėr′kwoiz *or* tėr′koiz) **1** a sky-blue or greenish-blue mineral which is used as a gem. **2** light greenish blue. **1, 2** *n.*, **2** *adj.*

**tur·ret** (tėr′it) **1** a small tower, often on the corner of a building. **2** any of various low, rotating armoured structures, in which guns are mounted. **3** a cockpit in a military aircraft, usually enclosed by a strong, transparent plastic material and sometimes containing movable machine guns. **4** a kind of tower on wheels, formerly used in attacking walled castles, forts, or towns. *n.*

**tur·ret·ed** (tėr′ə tid) **1** having a TURRET or turrets. **2** of a shell, having whorls forming a long spiral. *adj.*

A green sea turtle—
upper shell about 1 m long

**tur·tle** (tėr′təl) **1** any of an order of four-legged, toothless, generally slow-moving reptiles found throughout the world, having the body encased in a protective bony shell with an outside layer of horny plates, or, in some species, tough skin. Most species of turtle can withdraw the head, legs, and tail into the shell for protection: *Land turtles are often called tortoises.* **2** a special cursor that moves about on a computer screen under program control: *The turtle is used to draw lines on a cathode-ray tube.* *n.* **turn turtle,** turn bottom side up.

**tur·tle·dove** (tėr′təl duv′) any of a closely related group of wild doves, especially a small, grey or brownish European wild dove found in woods and around farms, noted for its sad-sounding cooing note and the affection that it appears to have for its mate. *n.*

**tur·tle·neck** (tėr′təl nek′) **1** a high, snugly fitting, usually turned-over collar, especially on a sweater. **2** a sweater, etc., having a turtleneck. *n.*

**Tus·can** (tus′kən) **1** of or having to do with Tuscany, a district in central Italy, or its people. **2** a native or inhabitant of Tuscany. **3** the language of Tuscany, regarded as the classical form of Italian and forming the basis of modern standard Italian. **4** of or referring to one of the five classical styles of architecture, characterized by plain, round columns and no decoration. See ORDER for picture. **1, 4** *adj.*, **2, 3** *n.*

**Tus·ca·ro·ra** (tus′kə rô′rə) **1** a member of a First Nations and Native American people of Iroquois stock who occupied what is now North Carolina at the time of their first contact with Europeans, but later migrated to New York and Ontario: *The Tuscarora were the sixth nation to join the Iroquois Confederacy.* **2** the language of these people. *n., pl.* **Tus·ca·ro·ra.**

**tush**[1] (tush) an exclamation expressing impatience, contempt, etc. *interj., n.*

**tush**[2] (tush) **1** a canine tooth of a horse. **2** TUSK. *n.*

**tusk** (tusk) **1** a very long, large, pointed tooth, usually one of a pair projecting from the sides of the closed mouth in animals like the elephant, walrus, and wild boar: *Animals with tusks use them for digging, as weapons, etc.* **2** any tooth or other object like a tusk. **3** gore, dig up, or tear with the tusks. **1, 2** *n.*, **3** *v.*

**tusk·er** (tus′kər) an animal with well-developed tusks, such as a mature elephant, walrus, or wild boar. *n.*

**tus·sah** (tus′ə) **1** a coarse, strong silk from a wild or semi-domesticated silkworm of India or China: *Undyed tussah is a brownish colour.* **2** the silkworm that produces this silk: *The tussah feeds on oak or castor bean leaves and makes a larger cocoon than the domestic silkworm.* *n.*

**tus·sle** (tus′əl) **1** a scuffle or struggle: *There was a short tussle as everyone tried to get through the door first.* **2** struggle or wrestle: *The two sisters liked to tussle with one another.* **1** *n.*, **2** *v.*, **tus·sled, tus·sling.**

**tus·sock** (tus′ək) a tuft or clump of growing grass or the like. *n.*

**tussock moth** any of numerous species of dull-coloured moth whose larvae have thick tufts of hair.

**tut** (tut) **1** an exclamation of impatience, contempt, or rebuke. **2** exclaim in this way; utter a tut or tuts. **1** *interj., n.,* **2** *v.,* **tut·ted, tut·ting.**

**tu·te·lage** (tyü′tə lij *or* tü′tə lij) **1** instruction: *They learned very quickly under her expert tutelage.* **2** guardianship; protection. **3** the condition of being in the care of a guardian. *n.*

**tu·te·lar** (tyü′tə lər *or* tü′tə lər) tutelary. *adj.*

**tu·te·lar·y** (tyü′tə ler′ē *or* tü′tə ler′ē) **1** protecting; guardian: *a tutelary saint.* **2** a tutelary saint, spirit, divinity, etc. **3** of or having to do with a guardian. **1, 3** *adj.*, **2** *n., pl.* **tu·te·lar·ies.**

**tu·tor** (tyü′tər *or* tü′tər) **1** a private teacher. **2** in some colleges and universities, a teacher, especially an

**tutorial** 1292 **twilight**

assistant teacher who gives extra instruction to students individually or in small groups. **3** teach; instruct, especially individually or privately. **4** in certain universities of the British Isles, a college official appointed to advise students, direct their work, etc. **5** act as tutor. *1, 2, 4 n., 3, 5 v.*

**tu·to·ri·al** (tyü tô′rē əl *or* tü tô′rē əl) **1** of or having to do with a tutor: *tutorial authority.* **2** using tutors: *the tutorial system.* **3** in some colleges and universities, a class given by a tutor to an individual or a small group of students. *1, 2 adj., 3 n.*

**tu·tor·ship** (tyü′tər ship′ *or* tü′tər ship′) the position, rank, or duties of a tutor. *n.*

**tut·ti–frut·ti** (tü′tē frü′tē) **1** a preserve of mixed fruits. **2** ice cream containing a variety of fruits or fruit flavourings. **3** flavoured by mixed fruits. *n.*

**tu·tu** (tü′tü; *French*, TY TY′) a female ballet dancer's very short, frilly skirt. *n.*

**tux** (tuks) *Informal.* TUXEDO. *n.*

**tux·e·do** (tuk sē′dō) **1** a man's semiformal jacket for evening wear, usually black and with satin lapels, and made without tails; dinner jacket. **2** a man's evening clothes including such a jacket. *n., pl.* **tux·e·dos** *or* **tux·e·does.**

**TV** *or* **T.V.** **1** television. **2** a television set.

**TV dinner** a frozen, precooked, packaged dinner that is ready to serve after simply being heated in its aluminum container.

**twad·dle** (twod′əl) **1** silly, feeble, tiresome talk or writing; nonsense; drivel. **2** talk or write in a silly, feeble, tiresome way. *1 n., 2 v.,* **twad·dled, twad·dling.** —**twad′dler,** *n.*

**twang** (twang) **1** a sharp, ringing sound like that made by a bowstring or rubber band when plucked: *We could hear the twang of her bow as she shot the arrow.* **2** make or cause to make a sharp, ringing sound: *The banjos twanged.* **3** play, pluck, shoot, etc. with a twang: *to twang a guitar. He twanged an arrow into the target.* **4** a sharp, nasal tone: *Some Nova Scotians speak with a twang.* **5** speak with a sharp, nasal tone. *1, 4 n., 2, 3, 5 v.*

**'twas** (twoz *or* twuz; *unstressed*, twəz) it was.

**tweak** (twēk) **1** pull sharply and twist with the fingers: *She tweaked her little brother's ear and made him cry.* **2** a sharp pull and twist: *His mother told him to give his sister's ear a tweak in return.* *1 v., 2 n.*

**tweed** (twēd) **1** a woollen cloth with a rough surface, usually woven in a twill weave with yarns of two or more colours, used especially for suits and coats. **2** any cloth resembling tweed, made of other fibres. **3 tweeds,** *pl.* clothes made of tweed, especially a suit: *He was wearing tweeds.* *n.*

**twee·dle·dum and twee·dle·dee** (twē′dəl dum′ən twē′dəl dē′) **1** two persons or things that are practically identical. **2 Tweedledum and Tweedledee,** identical twin brothers in Lewis Carroll's *Through the Looking Glass.*

**tweet** (twēt) **1** the note of a young bird. **2** utter a tweet or tweets. *1 n., interj., 2 v.*

**tweet·er** (twē′tər) a small high-fidelity loudspeaker used to reproduce sounds in the higher frequency range. *n.*

**tweeze** (twēz) pluck or remove with or as if with TWEEZERS. *v.*

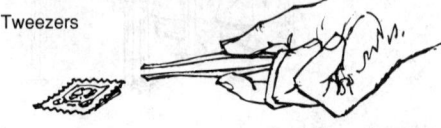
Tweezers

**tweez·ers** (twē′zərz) small pincers or tongs for pulling out hairs or slivers, picking up small objects, etc. *n.pl.*

**twelfth** (twelfth) **1** next after the 11th; last in a series of twelve; 12th. **2** one, or being one, of 12 equal parts. *adj., n.*

**twelve** (twelv) **1** two more than ten; 12: *That makes twelve you ate. I sold twelve tickets.* **2** the numeral 12: *The 12 is too small.* **3** the twelfth in a set or series. **4** being twelfth in a set or series (*used mainly after the noun*): *Section Twelve.* **5** a set or series of twelve persons or things. *1–3, 5 n., 1, 4 adj.*

**twelve·fold** (twelv′fōld′) **1** twelve times as much or as many. **2** having 12 parts. *1, 2 adj., 1 adv.*

**twelve·month** (twelv′munth′) a period of twelve months; a year. *n.*

**twen·ti·eth** (twen′tē ith) **1** next after the 19th; last in a series of twenty; 20th. **2** one, or being one, of 20 equal parts. *adj., n.*

**twen·ty** (twen′tē) **1** two times ten; 20. **2** the numeral 20. **3** the twentieth in a set or series. **4** a 20-dollar bill. **5** being twentieth in a set or series (*used mainly after the noun*): *Lesson Twenty.* **6 twenties,** *pl.* the years from twenty through twenty-nine, especially of a century or of a person's age: *He was in his twenties when his mother died.* **7** a set or series of twenty persons or things. *1–4, 6, 7 n., pl.* **twen·ties;** *1, 5 adj.*

**twen·ty·fold** (twen′tē fōld′) **1** twenty times as much or as many. **2** having 20 parts. *1, 2 adj., 1 adv.*

**twice** (twīs) **1** two times: *twice a day. Twice two is four.* **2** doubly: *twice as much.* *adv.*

**twice–told** (twīs′tōld′) told many times before; trite or very familiar: *twice-told tales.* *adj.*

**twid·dle** (twid′əl) **1** twirl: *to twiddle one's pencil.* **2** play with idly. **3** a twirl. *1, 2 v.,* **twid·dled, twid·dling; 3** *n.* **twiddle one's thumbs, a** keep turning one's thumbs idly about each other. **b** do nothing; be idle.

**twig¹** (twig) a slender shoot of a tree or other plant; a very small branch. *n.*

**twig²** (twig) *Informal.* **1** get the meaning; catch on (*often used with* **to**): *I didn't twig that he wanted a lift. They soon twigged to our plan.* **2** observe; notice: *The boys were sure the security guard would twig them.* *v.* **twigged, twig·ging.**

**twi·light** (twī′līt′) **1** the faint light reflected from the sky before the sun rises and after it sets. **2** the period during which this light lasts, especially after sunset. **3** any faint light. **4** a period of gradual decline in fame, vigour, achievement, etc.: *the twilight of a golden age in history, twilight of one's life.* **5** any undefined or intermediate state or condition: *She lived in an uneasy* twilight between sickness and health.   **6** of, like, or produced by twilight: *the twilight hour, a twilight glow.*   *n.*

**twill** (twil)   **1** a textile weave in which the crosswise threads pass alternately over one and then under two or more lengthwise threads, producing raised diagonal lines. See WEAVE for picture.   **2** fabric woven in this way: *Denim is a twill.*   *n.*

**twilled** (twild)   woven in raised diagonal lines.   *adj.*

**twin** (twin)   **1** one of two children or animals born at the same time from the same mother: *Twins sometimes look just alike.*   **2** being two or either one of two born at the same time from the same mother: *twin girls. That's his twin sister.*   **3** one of two persons or things very much or exactly alike in structure, appearance, etc.: *This table is the twin of one we have at home.*   **4** being two persons or things very much or exactly alike; paired or matching: *twin houses, twin dresses.*   **5** having or consisting of two identical parts or units; double: *a twin-engined aircraft.*   **6** of bed linen, designed to fit a TWIN BED.   **7** give birth to twins.   **8** join closely; pair.   1, 3 *n.*, 2, 4–6 *adj.*, 7, 8 *v.*, **twinned, twin·ning.**

**twin bed**   a single bed about one metre wide: *Twin beds are still often sold in matching pairs.*

**twine** (twīn)   **1** a strong thread or string made of two or more strands twisted together.   **2** twist together: *She twined holly into wreaths.*   **3** make or form by twisting: *to twine a wreath of flowers.*   **4** wind or wrap around; cause to encircle or be encircled: *We are training the vine to twine around the post. He twined the string around his finger. They twined their arms around each other.*   **5** the act of twisting together, encircling or embracing.   **6** something that is twisted together or interlaced.   1, 5, 6 *n.*, 2–4 *v.*, **twined, twin·ing.**

**twin–en·gine** (twin′en′jən)   TWIN-ENGINED.   *adj.*

**twin–en·gined** (twin′en′jənd)   of an aircraft, powered by two engines.   *adj.*

**twinge** (twinj)   **1** a sudden sharp, pinching pain that lasts only a moment: *He felt a twinge of rheumatism in his leg as he stooped to pick up the paper.*   **2** a sudden, brief mental pain; pang: *a twinge of remorse, a twinge of fear.*   **3** feel or cause to feel a twinge: *The theft occasionally twinged his conscience.*   1, 2 *n.*, 3 *v.*, **twinged, twing·ing.**

**twin·kle** (twing′kəl)   **1** shine with quick little gleams; sparkle: *The stars twinkled.*   **2** of a person's eyes, light up or shine with amusement or fun: *Tony's eyes twinkled when he laughed.*   **3** a twinkling; sparkle; gleam: *She didn't say anything, but there was a twinkle in her eyes.*   **4** of the feet, move quickly: *The dancer's feet twinkled.*   **5** a quick motion, especially of the feet in dancing.   **6** a quick motion of the eyelid; wink; blink.   **7** the time required for a wink; twinkling: *He was gone in a twinkle.*   **8** wink or blink one's eyes.   **9** cause to twinkle.   1, 2, 4, 8, 9 *v.*, **twin·kled, twin·kling;**   3, 5–7 *n.*

**twin·kling** (twing′kling)   **1** a little, quick gleam.   **2** a very short period of time; instant: *When I called my dog, he was there in a twinkling.*   **3** that twinkles: *twinkling stars.*   **4** ppr. of TWINKLE.   1, 2 *n.*, 3 *adj.*, 4 *v.*

**twin–screw** (twin′skrü′)   **1** of a steamship, having two screw propellers that revolve in opposite directions.   **2** a steamship powered by such propellers.   1 *adj.*, 2 *n.*

**twirl** (twėrl)   **1** revolve rapidly; spin; whirl: *to twirl a top. The skaters twirled over the ice.*   **2** turn or twist round and round idly with the fingers: *He twirled the ends of his mustache.*   **3** the act of twirling; spin; whirl: *a twirl in a dance.*   **4** a twist, curl, or flourish, as made in writing,

etc.   **5** throw a baseball; pitch.   1, 2, 5 *v.*, 3, 4 *n.* —**twirl′er,** *n.*

**twist** (twist)   **1** wind together; twine: *to twist flowers into a wreath.*   **2** make by winding together: *to twist a wreath of flowers.*   **3** wind a cord, ribbon, wire, etc. around something: *She twisted the wire around the post.*   **4** give a spiral form to by turning one end while the other remains stationary or is turned in the opposite direction: *to twist a rubber band. The belt is twisted at the back.*   **5** move part way around: *He twisted around in his seat to see who had come in. She twisted the steering wheel sharply to the left.*   **6** spin or twirl: *She twisted the ring on her finger.*   **7** pull off or break by turning one end (*used with* **off**): *to twist off the stem of an apple.*   **8** pull or force out of the natural shape or position: *I twisted my ankle when I fell. His face was twisted with pain. Your skirt is twisted.*   **9** a wrench or sprain.   **10** give a wrong meaning to: *Don't twist my words; I didn't mean that at all.*   **11** a twisting or being twisted: *There's a twist in the rope.*   **12** something made by twisting, such as a roll or a loaf of bread made of twisted pieces of dough.   **13** a strong, heavy kind of sewing thread usually made of silk or polyester: *buttonhole twist.*   **14** have a winding shape; follow a winding course; have many curves or bends: *The path twists in and out among the rocks.*   **15** a curve or bend: *a path full of twists and turns.*   **16** an unexpected change or variation: *an old story with a new twist. The plot had several twists that kept us in suspense right to the end.*   **17** a peculiar bias or inclination; quirk: *an action prompted by some mental twist.*   **18** give an abnormal bias or inclination to: *Years of bitterness had twisted his mind.*   **19** a dance in which the hips are vigorously turned back and forth while the dancer stands in one place.   **20** dance the twist.   1–8, 10, 14, 18, 20 *v.*, 9, 11–13, 15–17, 19 *n.* —**twist′a·ble,** *adj.*

**twist·er** (twis′tər)   **1** a tornado, whirlwind, etc.   **2** any person or thing that twists.   *n.*

**twist–tie** (twist′tī′)   a short length of thin wire between two narrow strips of paper or embedded in a narrow strip of soft plastic, used for closing plastic bags, tying up plants, etc.   *n.*

**twit** (twit)   **1** taunt lightly; make fun of; tease: *His friends twitted him about his schemes to make money.*   **2** the act of twitting.   **3** *Informal.*   an annoyingly silly or stupid person; fool; nitwit.   1 *v.*, **twit·ted, twit·ting,** 2, 3 *n.*

**twitch** (twich)   **1** move with slight, quick jerks: *The child's mouth twitched as if she were about to cry.*   **2** a quick, jerky movement of some part of the body.   **3** pull or move with a sudden tug; jerk: *He twitched the curtain aside.*   **4** a short, sudden pull or jerk.   1, 3 *v.*, 2, 4 *n.*

**twitch grass**   COUCH GRASS.

**twit·ter** (twit′ər)   **1** make a series of light, trembling sounds; chirp: *Birds began to twitter just before sunrise.*   **2** a series of light, trembling sounds; chirping: *the twitter of birds in the garden.*   **3** talk or laugh in a rapid, excited or nervous way; chatter or titter.   **4** utter by twittering: *a sparrow twittering its morning song. She nervously twittered a greeting.*   **5** an excited condition: *My nerves are in a twitter* when I have to sing in public. **6** tremble with excitement. 1, 3, 4, 6 *v.*, 2, 5 *n.*

**two** (tü) **1** one more than one; 2: *She said there were three mistakes in the sentence, but I see only two. I have two arms and two legs.* **2** the numeral 2: *I can't see it very well, but I think it's a 2.* **3** the second in a set or series; especially, a playing card or side of a die having two spots: *the two of clubs.* **4** a two-dollar bill: *Do you have any twos?* **5** being second in a set or series (used mainly after the noun): *Chapter Two tells about his childhood.* **6** a set or series of two persons or things: *The audience came in in twos and threes.* 1–4, 6 *n.*, 1, 5 *adj.*
**in two,** in two parts or pieces: *She broke the cookie in two.*
**put two and two together,** form an obvious conclusion from the facts.
☞ *Hom.* TO, TOO.
☞ *Etym.* From OE *twā*, related to German *zwei* and having the same Indo-European source as L *duo* and Gk. *duo*.

**two-bag·ger** (tü′bag′ər) a TWO-BASE HIT. *n.*

**two-base hit** in baseball, a hit where the ball goes far enough for the batter to reach second base.

**two bits** *Informal.* twenty-five cents; a quarter.

**two-by-four** (tü′bī fôr′) **1** especially of lumber, measuring about two inches by four inches (about 5 by 10 cm): *They used two-by-four studs for the inside walls.* **2** a piece of lumber about two inches thick and four inches wide, untrimmed: *Two-by-fours are much used in building.* **3** *Informal.* small; narrow or limited: *a two-by-four apartment.* 1, 3 *adj.*, 2 *n.*

**two-edged** (tü′ejd′) **1** of a sword, etc., having two cutting edges; cutting both ways. **2** of a comment, etc., able to be taken in two ways; ambiguous: *a two-edged compliment.* **3** able to be used or to be effective in two ways: *a two-edged policy. adj.*

**two-faced** (tü′fāst′) **1** having two faces. **2** deceitful; hypocritical. *adj.*

**two-fist·ed** (tü′fis′tid) *Informal.* vigorous and aggressive: *a two-fisted bully. adj.*

**two·fold** (tü′fōld′) **1** two times as much or as many; double. **2** made up of two parts or elements: *Her meaning was twofold; part joking and part serious.* 1, 2 *adj.*, 1 *adv.*

**two-four** (tü′fôr′) in music, of or referring to a rhythm with two quarter notes to a bar. *adj.*

**two-hand·ed** (tü′han′did) **1** having two hands. **2** using both hands equally well. **3** involving the use of both hands; requiring both hands to wield or manage: *a two-handed sword.* **4** requiring two persons to operate: *a two-handed saw.* **5** engaged in by two persons. *adj.*

**two-part time** in music, a time or rhythm with two beats to the measure, or multiples of two beats to the measure.

**two-par·ty system** (tü′pär′tē) a political system in which two political parties predominate over any others, one of the two generally having a majority in the legislature.

**two-piece** (tü′pēs′) **1** of a dress, swimsuit, etc., consisting of separate, matching top and bottom parts. **2** a two-piece dress, swimsuit, etc. 1 *adj.*, 2 *n.*

**two-ply** (tü′plī′) having two thicknesses, folds, layers, or strands. *adj.*

**two·some** (tü′səm) **1** a group of two people. **2** a game played by two people. **3** the players in such a game. *n.*

**two-step** (tü′step′) **1** a dance in march time. **2** the music for such a dance. *n.*

**two-time** (tü′tīm′) *Informal.* **1** be unfaithful to in love. **2** betray; double-cross. *v.*, **two-timed, two-tim·ing.** —**two-tim′er,** *n.*

**two-tone** (tü′tōn′) having two colours or two shades of one colour: *two-tone shoes. Her car is two-tone blue. adj.*

**two-way** (tü′wā′) **1** of a street, bridge, etc., allowing traffic to move in either direction. **2** of traffic, moving in both directions on the same street, etc. **3** designed for both sending and receiving messages: *a two-way radio. adj.*

**two-wheel·er** (tü′wē′lər *or* tü′hwē′lər) a vehicle having two wheels, especially a bicycle or motorcycle: *She got her first two-wheeler when she was seven. n.*

**twp.** township.

**-ty**[1] a suffix meaning: tens, as in *sixty, seventy, eighty.*

**-ty**[2] a noun-forming suffix meaning: the fact, quality, state, condition, etc. of being _____, as in *safety, sovereignty, surety.* See also **-ity.**

**Ty.** Territory.

**ty·coon** (tī kün′) *Informal.* a person who holds a very important position in business, industry, etc.; magnate. *n.*

**ty·ee** (tī′ē) *Cdn.* **1** a spring salmon, especially one weighing more than about 13 kg. **2** especially in British Columbia, the chief of an Indian tribe or band. *n., pl.* **ty·ees** or (for def. 2) **ty·ee.**
☞ *Etym.* From a Chinook jargon word meaning 'chief' or 'champion'.

**tyee salmon** TYEE (def. 1).

**ty·ing** (tī′ing) ppr. of TIE: *He is tying a knot. v.*

**tyke** (tīk) **1** *Informal.* a small child. **2** a dog, especially an inferior or worthless one. *n.*

**tym·pa·ni** (tim′pə nē′) See TIMPANI. *n., pl.* of **tym·pa·no.**

**tym·pan·ic** (tim pan′ik) **1** of, having to do with, or being the eardrum or the middle ear. **2** like a drum. *adj.*

**tympanic membrane** EARDRUM.

**tym·pa·nist** (tim′pə nist) See TIMPANIST. *n.*

**tym·pa·num** (tim′pə nəm) **1** EARDRUM. **2** the middle ear. *n., pl.* **tym·pa·nums** or **tym·pa·na** (-nə).

**type** (tīp) **1** a class or group having qualities or characteristics in common: *type O blood, a new type of engine. He doesn't like that type of work.* **2** a person or thing having the qualities or characteristics of a particular class or group; model, representative, or symbol: *She is a fine type of student.* **3** the general form, style, or character that distinguishes some class or group: *They weren't surprised when he got angry, because he was behaving true to type.* **4** *Informal.* an unusual or eccentric person: *He's a real type.* **5** classify according to type: *to type a blood sample. The new boy was immediately typed as a bully.* **6** TYPECAST: *He's been typed as the boy next door ever since his first film.* **7** in printing, a block, usually of metal, having a raised letter, numeral, or sign in reverse on its upper surface, from which an inked impression can be made.   **8** a collection of such pieces: *a box of type*.   **9** a collection of letters, numerals, or signs that are reproduced photographically for printing.   **10** a particular kind or size of letters, numerals, or signs used in printing: *The poem was set in italic type*.   **11** printed or typewritten letters, numerals, or signs: *The page looks crowded with so much type on it*.   **12** write with a typewriter: *He usually types his letters. She can type at a rate of 75 words per minute*.   **13** the figure, writing, or design on either side of a coin or medal.   1–4, 7–11, 13 *n*., 5, 6, 12 *v*., **typed, typ·ing**.

**type·script** (tīp′skript′)   a typewritten manuscript.   *n*.

**type·set·ter** (tīp′set′ər)   a person, company, or machine that sets type for printing.   *n*.

**type·set·ting** (tīp′set′ing)   **1** the act or process of setting type for printing.   **2** of, having to do with, or used for setting type: *typesetting machines, typesetting methods*. 1 *n*., 2 *adj*.

**type·write** (tīp′rīt′)   write with a typewriter; type. *v*., **type·wrote, type·writ·ten, type·writ·ing**.

**type·writ·er** (tīp′rī′tər)   a machine for producing letters, numerals, and signs similar to those produced by printer's type, operated by means of a keyboard. When a key is struck, the corresponding type hits an inked ribbon, transferring the imprint of the letter, etc. onto paper behind the ribbon.   *n*.

**type·writ·ing** (tīp′rī′ting)   **1** the act or art of using a typewriter.   **2** work done on a typewriter.   **3** ppr. of TYPEWRITE.   1, 2 *n*., 3 *v*.

**type·writ·ten** (tīp′rit′ən)   **1** written with a typewriter: *a typewritten letter*.   **2** pp. of TYPEWRITE: *Her manuscripts have all been typewritten*.   1 *adj*., 2 *v*.

**ty·phoid** (tī′foid)   **1** of or having to do with TYPHOID FEVER.   **2** TYPHOID FEVER.   **3** like TYPHUS.   1, 3 *adj*., 2 *n*.

**typhoid fever**   a severe infectious disease caused by a bacterium that enters the body in contaminated food or drink, most often from a polluted public water supply: *Typhoid fever is characterized by fever, a rash of small red spots and, often, inflammation of the intestines*.

**ty·phoon** (tī fün′)   a violent tropical cyclone that forms over the Pacific Ocean.   *n*.

**ty·phus** (tī′fəs)   a very serious infectious disease caused by micro-organisms called rickettsias which are carried especially by lice or fleas: *Typhus is characterized by chills and fever, dark-red spots on the skin, and extreme weakness; it used to occur in epidemics in which many people died*.   *n*.

**typ·i·cal** (tip′ə kəl)   **1** very much like others of the same type or kind; serving as an example; representative: *a typical Canadian. The typical Thanksgiving dinner has roast turkey as its main course*.   **2** of, having to do with, or serving to distinguish a type; characteristic: *the hospitality typical of the pioneer. It was typical of her to sign it without reading it first*.   *adj*.

**typ·i·cal·ly** (tip′i klē)   in a typical manner or to a typical degree: *typically high-handed behaviour*.   *adv*.

**typ·i·fy** (tip′ə fī)   **1** be a symbol of; signify or represent: *The dove typifies peace*.   **2** have the common characteristics of; be an example of: *Alexander Mackenzie typifies the adventurous explorer*.   *v*., **typ·i·fied, typ·i·fy·ing**.   —**typ′i·fi·ca′tion**, *n*.

## typescript 1295 tzarina

hat, āge, fär; let, ēqual, tėrm; it, īce
hot, ōpen, ôrder; oil, out; cup, pùt, rüle
əbove, takən, pencəl, lemən, circəs
ch, child; ng, long; sh, ship
th, thin; ᴛʜ, then; zh, measure

**typ·ist** (tī′pist)   a person who operates a typewriter, especially one who makes a living by typewriting.   *n*.

**ty·po** (tī′pō) *Informal*.   a typographical error; a small mistake made in typing or in setting type.   *n*.

**ty·pog·ra·pher** (tī pog′rə fər)   PRINTER.   *n*.

**ty·po·graph·ic** (tī′pə graf′ik)   of or having to do with printing: *Catt and hoRse contain typographic errors*.   *adj*.

**ty·po·graph·i·cal** (tī′pə graf′ə kəl)   TYPOGRAPHIC. *adj*.   —**ty′po·graph′i·cal·ly**, *adv*.

**ty·pog·ra·phy** (tī pog′rə fē)   **1** the art or process of printing with type; the work of setting and arranging type and of printing from it.   **2** the arrangement, appearance, or style of printed matter.   *n*.

**ty·ran·nic** (tə ran′ik)   TYRANNICAL.   *adj*.

**ty·ran·ni·cal** (tə ran′ə kəl)   of or like a TYRANT; arbitrary, cruel, or unjust: *a tyrannical king*.   *adj*. —**ty·ran′ni·cal·ly**, *adv*.

**tyr·an·nize** (tir′ə nīz′)   **1** use power cruelly or unjustly (used with **over**): *Those who are strong should not tyrannize over those who are weaker*.   **2** rule cruelly; oppress.   *v*., **tyr·an·nized, tyr·an·niz·ing**.

**ty·ran·no·sau·rus** (ti ran′ə sô′rəs)   a huge carnivorous dinosaur of the late Cretaceous period of North America, noted for its ability to walk upright on its two hind legs.   *n*.

**tyr·an·nous** (tir′ə nəs)   tyrannical; despotic.   *adj*. —**tyr′an·nous·ly**, *adv*.

**tyr·an·ny** (tir′ə nē)   **1** cruel or unjust use of power: *The boy ran away to sea to escape his father's tyranny*. **2** severe or demanding condition: *the tyranny of public opinion, living all one's life under the tyranny of the clock*. **3** a tyrannical act: *She had suffered many tyrannies*. **4** government by an absolute ruler.   *n., pl.* **tyr·an·nies**.

**ty·rant** (tī′rənt)   **1** a person who uses his or her power cruelly or unjustly.   **2** a cruel or unjust ruler.   **3** a ruler with absolute power: *Some tyrants in ancient Greece were kind and just rulers*.   *n*.

**Tyr·i·an** (tir′ē ən)   **1** of or having to do with Tyre, a seaport in ancient Phoenicia.   **2** a native of Tyre. 1 *adj*., 2 *n*.

**Tyrian purple**   **1** a crimson or purple dye used by the ancient Greeks and Romans.   **2** bluish red.

**ty·ro** (tī′rō)   a beginner in learning anything; novice; greenhorn: *Much practice changed the tyro into an expert. n., pl.* **ty·ros**. Also, **tiro**.

**Ty·ro·le·an** (tə rō′lē ən *or* tir′ə lē′ən)   **1** of or having to do with Tyrol, a region in the Alps, partly in Austria and partly in Italy, or its inhabitants.   **2** a native or inhabitant of the Tyrol.   1 *adj*., 2 *n*., Also, **Tirolean**.

**Ty·ro·lese** (tir′ə lēz′)   TYROLEAN.   *adj., n*. Also, **Tirolese**.

**tzar** (zär)   See CZAR.   *n*.

**tza·ri·na** (zä rē′nə)   See CZARINA.   *n*.

# U u  U u

**u** or **U** (yü) **1** the twenty-first letter of the English alphabet. **2** any speech sound represented by this letter. **3** a person or thing identified as u, especially the twenty-first of a series. **4** anything shaped like a U. *n., pl.* **u's** or **U's.**

**U** uranium.

**U.** University.

**u·biq·ui·tous** (yü bik′wə təs) being or seeming to be everywhere at the same time; found or turning up everywhere: *He wanted a quiet place to read, but found it impossible to escape from his ubiquitous little sister.* *adj.* —**u·biq′ui·tous·ly,** *adv.*

**u·biq·ui·ty** (yü bik′wə tē) the fact or condition of being or seeming to be everywhere at the same time. *n.*

**U-boat** (yü′bōt′) a German submarine: *U-boats were first used during World War I.* *n.*
☞ *Etym.* An abbreviation of German *Unterseeboot* 'under-sea boat'. The English term *submarine* also means 'under-sea' but was made up from L *sub* 'under' + *marinus* 'of the sea'. See also note at **marine.**

**u.c.** upper case; one or more capital letters.

**U.C.** Upper Canada.

**ud·der** (ud′ər) in a cow, female sheep, goat, etc., a large baglike organ containing two or more milk-producing glands, each gland provided with one teat. *n.*

**U.E.L.** United Empire Loyalist.

**UFO** (yü′ef ō′) an UNIDENTIFIED FLYING OBJECT, especially a flying saucer or other object regarded as possibly being a spacecraft from another planet. *n., pl.* **UFOs** or **UFO's.**

**u·fol·o·gist** (yü fol′ə jist) a person who studies UFOs, especially one who believes them to be from outer space. *n.*

**u·fol·o·gy** (yü fol′ə jē) the study of UFOs. *n.*

**U·gan·dan** (yü gan′dən) **1** of or having to do with Uganda, a country in East Africa, or its people. **2** a native or inhabitant of Uganda. 1 *adj.*, 2 *n.*

**ugh** (u̇H *or* u) an exclamation expressing disgust or horror. *interj.*

**ug·li·ness** (ug′lē nis) the quality or state of being UGLY. *n.*

**ug·ly** (ug′lē) **1** very unpleasant to look at or listen to: *an ugly house, an ugly sound.* **2** morally bad; objectionable; vile: *ugly rumours, an ugly deed.* **3** threatening; dangerous: *an ugly wound, ugly clouds.* **4** *Informal.* ill-natured or bad-tempered; quarrelsome: *an ugly dog. He gets ugly when he's drunk.* *adj.*, **ug·li·er, ug·li·est.** *n.*

**UHF** or **U.H.F.** ultrahigh frequency.

**UI** or **U.I.** unemployment insurance.

**UIC** or **U.I.C.** Unemployment Insurance Commission.

**U.K.** United Kingdom.

**U·krain·i·an** (yü krā′nē ən) **1** of or having to do with Ukraine, its people, or their language. **2** a native or inhabitant of Ukraine. **3** the language of Ukraine, closely related to Russian. **4** a person of Ukrainian descent: *There are many Ukrainians in Canada, especially in the West.* 1 *adj.*, 2–4 *n.*

A ukulele

**u·ku·le·le** (yü′kə lā′lē) a small guitar-shaped instrument having four strings. *n.*
☞ *Etym.* From Hawaiian *uku* 'flea' + *lele* 'jumping'. With the meaning 'a small, quick person', it was the nickname given in Hawaii to a British army officer, Edward Purvis, who made this instrument popular there in the 1880's.

**u·la·ma** (ü′lə mä′) in Islam, a collective term for religious scholars and leaders. *n.*

**ul·cer** (ul′sər) **1** an open sore on the skin or a mucous membrane such as the lining of the stomach or the inside of the mouth. **2** a moral sore spot; corrupting influence. *n.*

**ul·cer·ate** (ul′sə rāt′) affect or be affected with an ULCER: *An ulcerated tooth may be very painful.* *v.*, **ul·cer·at·ed, ul·cer·at·ing.**

**ul·cer·a·tion** (ul′sə rā′shən) **1** ulcerating or being ulcerated. **2** ULCER. *n.*

**ul·cer·ous** (ul′sə rəs) **1** having an ulcer or ulcers. **2** of or having to do with ulcers. *adj.*

**ul·na** (ul′nə) **1** the bone of the forearm on the side opposite the thumb. See ARM¹ for picture. **2** a corresponding bone in the foreleg of an animal. *n., pl.* **ul·nae** (-nē *or* -nī) or **ul·nas.**

**ul·nar** (ul′nər) **1** of or having to do with the ULNA. **2** in or supplying the part of the forearm near the ULNA. *adj.*

**ul·ster** (ul′stər) a long, loose, heavy overcoat, often belted at the waist. *n.*

**ul·te·ri·or** (ul tē′rē ər) **1** beyond what is seen or expressed; hidden, especially for a bad purpose: *He had an ulterior motive in inviting my sister: he wanted to make another girl jealous.* **2** more distant or on the farther side. **3** further; later. *adj.* —**ul·te′ri·or·ly,** *adv.*

**ul·ti·ma** (ul′tə mə) the last syllable of a word. *n.*

**ul·ti·mate** (ul′tə mit) **1** coming at the end; last possible; final: *He never stopped to consider the ultimate result of his actions.* **2** beyond which nothing further may be discovered by investigation or analysis; primary; basic: *the ultimate principal, the ultimate source.* **3** greatest possible. **4** an ultimate point, result, fact, etc. 1–3 *adj.*, 4 *n.*

**ul·ti·mate·ly** (ul′tə mit lē) finally; in the end. *adv.*

**ul·ti·ma·tum** (ul′tə mā′təm) a final proposal, statement of conditions, or demand, especially one whose rejection may result in a breaking off of relations between negotiating parties or, sometimes, in international negotiations, a declaration of war. *n., pl.* **ul·ti·ma·tums** or **ul·ti·ma·ta** (-tə).

**ul·tra** (ul′trə) **1** beyond what is usual; very; excessive; extreme: *an ultra conservative.* **2** a person who holds extreme views or urges extreme measures. **1** *adj.,* **2** *n.*

**ultra–** a prefix meaning: **1** beyond, as in *ultraviolet.* **2** very; extremely; unusually, as in *ultra-ambitious, ultramodest, ultraradical.*

**ul·tra·high frequency** (ul′trə hī′) the range of radio frequencies between 300 and 3000 megahertz: *Ultrahigh frequency is the range next above very high frequency.*

**ul·tra·light** (ul′trə līt′) MICROLIGHT. *n.*

**ul·tra·ma·rine** (ul′trə mə rēn′) **1** deep blue. **2** a blue pigment made from powdered LAPIS LAZULI. **3** a chemically similar pigment made from other substances: *Artificial ultramarine is much cheaper than the natural pigment and also occurs in reddish and greenish hues.* **4** beyond the sea. **1–3** *n.,* **1, 4** *adj.*

**ul·tra·son·ic** (ul′trə son′ik) of or referring to sound waves having a pitch above the upper limit of human hearing, that is, a frequency above 20 000 cycles per second. *adj.*

**ul·tra·vi·o·let** (ul′trə vī′ə lit) of, having to do with, or referring to the invisible rays, or waves, just beyond the violet end of the colour spectrum: *Ultraviolet rays are present in sunlight.* *adj.*

**ultraviolet light** ULTRAVIOLET rays.

An ulu

**u·lu** (ü′lü) *Cdn.* a crescent-shaped, bone-handled knife used by Inuit women. *n.* Also, **ooloo**.
☞ *Etym.* From Inuktitut *ulu*. 19c.

**ul·u·lant** (yü′lyə lənt *or* ul′yə lənt) howling or wailing. *adj.*

**ul·u·late** (yü′lyə lāt′ *or* ul′yə lāt′) **1** of a dog, wolf, etc., howl. **2** lament loudly. *v.,* **ul·u·lat·ed, ul·u·lat·ing.** —**ul′u·la′tion,** *n.*

**um·bel** (um′bəl) a type of flower cluster in which stalks nearly equal in length spring from a common centre and form a flat or slightly curved surface, as in parsley. See INFLORESCENCE for picture. *n.*

**um·ber** (um′bər) **1** an earth used in its natural state (**raw umber**) as a brown pigment, or after heating (**burnt umber**) as a reddish-brown pigment. **2** brown or reddish brown. **1, 2** *n.,* **2** *adj.*

**um·bil·i·cal cord** (um bil′ə kəl *or* um′bi li′kəl) **1** in mammals, a cordlike structure through which a fetus in the womb receives food and discharges waste. The cord runs from the navel of the fetus to the placenta. **2** an

hat, āge, fär; let, ēqual, tėrm; it, īce
hot, ōpen, ôrder; oil, out; cup, pút, rüle
əbove, takən, pencəl, lemən, circəs
ch, child; ng, long; sh, ship
th, thin; ŦH, then; zh, measure

electric cable, fuel line, or the like, connected to a rocket or spacecraft on its launching site and disconnected just before takeoff.

**um·bra** (um′brə) **1** a shadow of the earth or moon that completely hides the sun. See ECLIPSE for picture. **2** the dark central part of a sunspot. **3** shade; shadow. *n., pl.* **um·brae** (-brē *or* -brī).

**um·brage** (um′brij) a feeling that one has been slighted or insulted; resentment (*now used mainly in the phrases* **take umbrage** *and* **give umbrage**): *He took umbrage at the slightest criticism. She didn't say anything for fear of giving umbrage to her host.* *n.*

An umbrella

**um·brel·la** (um brel′ə) **1** a collapsible device used for protection against rain or sun, especially a small, light one meant to be carried in the hand and consisting of a circular, convex screen of cloth or plastic stretched over a framework of hinged ribs radiating from a central pole. **2** anything that protects or provides shelter. **3** a sphere of interest or control: *chartered banks under the umbrella of the Bank of Canada.* **4** an organization covering a broad range of activities, a wide sphere of interest, etc.: *an umbrella organization. The Community Chest is an umbrella for many local charities.* *n.*
☞ *Etym.* From Italian *ombrella,* diminutive of *ombra* 'shade', which came from L *umbra* 'shade, shadow'.

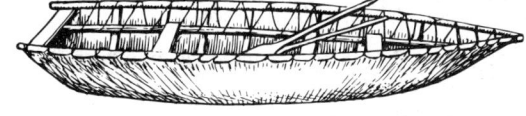

An umiak

**u·mi·ak** (ü′mē ak′) *Cdn.* a large, flat-bottomed boat made of skins stretched over a wooden frame and propelled by paddles: *Umiaks are used by Inuit for carrying freight and are usually worked by women.* *n.* Also, **oomiak**.
☞ *Etym.* From Inuktitut *umiaq*. 18c.

**um·ma** (um′ə) in Islam, the world-wide community of believers, including Sunnis, Shiites, and other Moslem sects. *n.*

**um·pire** (um′pīr) **1** a person who rules on the plays in certain games: *The umpire called the ball a foul.* **2** a person chosen to settle a dispute. **3** act as umpire. **4** act as umpire in. **1, 2** *n.,* **3, 4** *v.,* **um·pired, um·pir·ing.**

**ump·teen** (ump′tēn′) *Informal.* a great many: *I've heard umpteen different suggestions, but not one of them is practical.* *adj.*

**ump·teenth** (ump′tēnth′) *Informal.* the last in an extremely long series: *I've just dialled her number for the umpteenth time, but there's still no answer.* *adj.*

**un–**[1] an adjective-forming prefix meaning: not or the opposite of, as in *unfair, unjust, unequal.*

**un–**[2] a verb-forming prefix meaning: do the opposite of or do what will reverse the act, as in *undress, unlock, untie.*

**UN** or **U.N.** United Nations.

**un·a·bashed** (un′ə basht′) not embarrassed, ashamed, or awed: *They looked at him accusingly, but he remained unabashed.* *adj.* —**un′a·bash′ed·ly**, *adv.*

**un·a·bridged** (un′ə brijd′) 1 complete; not shortened: *an unabridged book.* 2 of or referring to any large dictionary more comprehensive than an ordinary desk dictionary, especially the largest one of a series. *adj.*

**un·ac·com·pa·nied** (un′ə kum′pə nēd or un′ə kump′nēd) 1 not accompanied: *She was unaccompanied on her journey.* 2 in music, without an accompaniment: *She sang unaccompanied.* 1 *adj.*, 2 *adv.*

**un·ac·count·a·ble** (un′ə koun′tə bəl) 1 that cannot be accounted for or explained; strange or puzzling: *He suddenly flew into one of his unaccountable rages.* 2 not obliged or bound to account for; not responsible: *The accused was judged insane and therefore unaccountable for his actions.* *adj.*

**un·ac·count·a·bly** (un′ə koun′tə blē) in a way that cannot be explained; strangely: *unaccountably sad.* *adv.*

**un·ac·cus·tomed** (un′ə kus′təmd) 1 not used to; not accustomed: *John did not like his new job at first because he was unaccustomed to the routines.* 2 not familiar; unusual; strange: *The unaccustomed heat made us all very tired.* *adj.*

**un·ad·vised** (un′əd vīzd′) 1 not prudent or discreet; rash. 2 not advised; without advice. *adj.*

**un·ad·vis·ed·ly** (un′əd vī′zi dlē) in an indiscreet manner; rashly. *adv.*

**un·af·fect·ed** (un′ə fek′tid) 1 not affected; not influenced: *He was completely unaffected by their criticism.* 2 simple and natural; sincere: *an unaffected style of writing. Her manner was straightforward and unaffected.* *adj.* —**un′af·fect′ed·ly**, *adv.* —**un′af·fect′ed·ness**, *n.*

**u·na·nim·i·ty** (yü′nə nim′ə tē) the quality or state of being UNANIMOUS; complete accord or agreement. *n.*

**u·nan·i·mous** (yü nan′ə məs) 1 in complete accord or agreement; agreed: *The delegates were unanimous that the issue needed to be discussed further.* 2 formed by or showing complete accord; having the consent of everyone: *unanimous consent. The vote was unanimous.* *adj.* —**u·nan′i·mous·ness**, *n.* —**u·nan′i·mous·ly**, *adv.*

**un·an·swer·a·ble** (un an′sə rə bəl) 1 that cannot be answered or has no answer: *unanswerable questions about life and death.* 2 that cannot be disproved: *an unanswerable argument.* *adj.* —**un·an′swer·a·bly**, *adv.*

**un·ap·proach·a·ble** (un′ə prō′chə bəl) 1 very hard to approach; aloof; distant. 2 unrivalled; without an equal: *unapproachable excellence.* *adj.*
—**un′ap·proach′a·ble·ness**, *n.*
—**un′ap·proach′a·bly**, *adv.*

**un·arm** (un ärm′) 1 take weapons or armour from; disarm. 2 lay down one's weapons. 3 take off armour. *v.*

**un·armed** (un ärmd′) 1 without weapons or armour: *The intruder turned out to be unarmed.* 2 of plants and animals, without horns, teeth, prickles, spines, thorns, etc. 3 pt. and pp. of UNARM. 1, 2 *adj.*, 3 *v.*

**un·as·sum·ing** (un′ə sü′ming or un′ə syü′ming) modest; not putting on airs: *The people were delighted by the duchess's unassuming manner.* *adj.*
—**un′as·sum′ing·ly**, *adv.* —**un′as·sum′ing·ness**, *n.*

**un·at·tached** (un′ə tacht′) 1 not attached. 2 not connected or associated with a particular body, group, organization, or the like; independent. 3 not engaged or married. *adj.*

**un·at·tend·ed** (un′ə ten′did) 1 without attendants; alone. 2 not accompanied. 3 not taken care of; not attended to: *The switchboard was left unattended while the receptionist took a coffee break.* *adj.*

**un·a·vail·ing** (un′ə vā′ling) not successful; useless: *His attempt to climb the fence was unavailing.* *adj.*
—**un′a·vail′ing·ly**, *adv.*

**un·a·ware** (un′ə wer′) 1 not aware; ignorant: *They were unaware of her change in plans. He had gone out in the boat, unaware that there was a storm warning.* 2 UNAWARES. 1 *adj.*, 2 *adv.*

---

*In each of the words below* **un–** *means not; the pronunciation of the main part of each word is not changed.*

| | | | | |
|---|---|---|---|---|
| un′a·bat′ed | un′ac·cred′it·ed | un′al·pha·bet′ized′ | un′ap·peased′ | un′as·signed′ |
| un′ab·bre′vi·at·ed | un′ac·knowl′edged | un′al·ter·a·ble | un′ap·pe′tiz′ing | un′as·sist′ed |
| un′a·bet′ted | un′a·dapt′a·ble | un′al·ter·ing | un′ap·pre′ci·at·ed | un′at·tain′a·ble |
| un·a′ble | un′ad·just′a·ble | un′am·big′u·ous | un′ap·pre′ci·a·tive | un′at·tempt′ed |
| un′ab·solved′ | un′ad·just′ed | un′am·bi′tious | un′ap·proached′ | un′at·tract′ive |
| un′ab·sorbed′ | un′a·dorned′ | un′a·mi·a·ble | un′ap·pro·pri′at·ed | un′au·then′tic |
| un′ac·a·dem′ic | un′a·dul′ter·at·ed | un′am·pli·fied′ | un′ap·proved′ | un′au·then·ti·cat′ed |
| un′ac·cent′ed | un′ad·ver·tised′ | un′a·mused′ | un·apt′ | un′au′thor·ized |
| un′ac·cept′a·ble | un′ad·vis′a·ble | un′a·mus′ing | un·ar′moured | un′a·vail′a·ble |
| un′ac·cept′ed | un′a·fraid′ | un′an·i·mat′ed | un·ar·rest′ed | un′a·venged′ |
| un′ac·cli′mat·ed | un·ai′ded | un′an·nounced′ | un·ar′tis′tic | un′a·void′a·ble |
| un′ac·cli′ma·tized | un′a·like′ | un′an·tic′i·pat·ed | un′a·shamed′ | un′a·vowed′ |
| un′ac·com·mo·dat′ing | un′al·lied′ | un′a·pol′o·get′ic | un·asked′ | un′a·wak′ened |
| un′ac·com′plished | un′al·low′a·ble | un′ap·peal′ing | un′as·sail′a·ble | |
| un′ac·count′ed-for | un′al·loyed′ | un′ap·peas′a·ble | un′as·sign′a·ble | |

**un·a·wares** (un′ə werz′) **1** without being expected; by surprise: *The police caught the burglar unawares.* **2** without knowing or being aware: *We made the error unawares.* *adv.*

**un·bal·ance** (un bal′əns) **1** a lack of balance; unbalanced condition; imbalance. **2** throw out of balance; disorder or derange. **1** *n.*, **2** *v.*, **un·bal·anced, un·bal·anc·ing.**

**un·bal·anced** (un bal′ənst) **1** not balanced. **2** mentally disordered; unstable or deranged. **3** pt. and pp. of UNBALANCE. **1, 2** *adj.*, **3** *v.*

**un·bar** (un bär′) remove the bars from; unbolt. *v.*, **un·barred, un·bar·ring.**

**un·beat·en** (un bē′tən) **1** not defeated or surpassed. **2** not trodden; not travelled: *unbeaten paths.* **3** not beaten or pounded: *unbeaten by the storm.* **4** not mixed by stirring: *Add two unbeaten eggs.* *adj.*

**un·be·com·ing** (un′bi kum′ing) **1** not attractive; not suited to the wearer: *an unbecoming dress.* **2** not fitting or proper: *unbecoming behaviour.* *adj.*
—**un′be·com′ing·ly,** *adv.* —**un′be·com′ing·ness,** *n.*

**un·be·known** (un′bi nōn′) not known: *He arrived unbeknown to anyone.* *adj.*

**un·be·knownst** (un′bi nōnst′) UNBEKNOWN; not known. *adj.*

**un·be·lief** (un′bi lēf′) a lack of belief, especially in God or in a particular religion or doctrine. *n.*

**un·be·liev·er** (un′bi lē′vər) **1** one who does not believe. **2** one who does not believe in a particular religion. *n.*

**un·bend** (un bend′) **1** straighten: *to unbend the fingers.* **2** release from strain: *to unbend a bow.* **3** relax: *The judge unbent and behaved like a boy.* **4** unfasten a sail, rope, etc. *v.*, **un·bent, un·bend·ing.**

**un·bend·ing** (un ben′ding) **1** not bending or curving; rigid: *the unbending boughs of an old oak.* **2** not yielding; firm or inflexible: *an unbending attitude.* **3** a relaxing or freeing from constraint: *In a rare moment of unbending, he told us about his boyhood.* **4** ppr. of UNBEND. **1, 2** *adj.*, **3** *n.*, **4** *v.* —**un·bend′ing·ly,** *adv.*
—**un·bend′ing·ness,** *n.*

**un·bid·den** (un bid′ən) not bidden; not invited or commanded. *adj.*

**un·bind** (un bīnd′) release from bonds or restraint; untie; unfasten; let loose. *v.*, **un·bound, un·bind·ing.**

**un·blessed** or **un·blest** (un blest′) **1** not blessed. **2** wicked, evil, or malignant: *a soul unblessed.* **3** unhappy; miserable; wretched. *adj.*

**un·blush·ing** (un blush′ing) **1** not blushing. **2** shameless or unabashed: *unblushing impudence.* *adj.*
—**un·blush′ing·ly,** *adv.*

unawares     1299     unbutton

hat, āge, fär; let, ēqual, tėrm; it, īce
hot, ōpen, ôrder; oil, out; cup, pùt, rüle
əbove, takən, pencəl, lemən, circəs
ch, child; ng, long; sh, ship
th, thin; ᴛʜ, then; zh, measure

**un·bolt** (un bōlt′) open or unlock a door, etc. by drawing back the bolt or bolts. *v.*

**un·bolt·ed**¹ (un bōl′tid) **1** not bolted or fastened: *an unbolted door.* **2** pt. and pp. of UNBOLT. **1** *adj.*, **2** *v.*

**un·bolt·ed**² (un bōl′tid) not sifted: *unbolted flour.* *adj.*

**un·born** (un bôrn′) **1** within the mother's womb; not yet born: *an unborn child.* **2** not brought into being: *That joke should have stayed unborn.* **3** still to come; future: *unborn generations.* *adj.*

**un·bos·om** (un bùz′əm *or* un bü′zəm) reveal; disclose. *v.*
**unbosom oneself,** tell or reveal one's thoughts, feelings, secrets, etc.

**un·bound** (un bound′) **1** not fastened or bound together; loose: *unbound sheets of music.* **2** having no binding: *an unbound book.* **3** pt. and pp. of UNBIND. **1, 2** *adj.*, **3** *v.*

**un·bound·ed** (un boun′did) not bounded; without bounds or limits; very great: *Her unbounded good spirits cheered all of us up.* *adj.*

**un·braid** (un brād′) separate the strands of. *v.*

**un·bri·dle** (un brī′dəl) remove a bridle or restraint from: *to unbridle a horse.* *v.*, **un·bri·dled, un·bri·dling.**

**un·bri·dled** (un brī′dəld) **1** not having a bridle on. **2** not controlled; not restrained: *unbridled anger.* **3** pt. and pp. of UNBRIDLE. **1, 2** *adj.*, **3** *v.*

**un·bro·ken** (un brō′kən) **1** not broken; whole: *There was only one unbroken cup left in the whole set.* **2** not interrupted; continuous: *She had eight hours of unbroken sleep.* **3** not tamed: *an unbroken colt.* *adj.*

**un·buck·le** (un buk′əl) open the buckle or buckles of: *She unbuckled her belt and took it off.* *v.*, **un·buck·led, un·buck·ling.**

**un·bur·den** (un bėr′dən) **1** free from a burden. **2** relieve oneself or one's conscience or mind by confessing or revealing: *He decided to unburden himself of the problem. She unburdened her mind to her friend.* *v.*

**un·busi·ness·like** (un biz′ni slīk′) without system and method; not efficient. *adj.*

**un·but·ton** (un but′ən) unfasten the button or buttons of. *v.*

---

*In each of the words below* **un-** *means* not; *the pronunciation of the main part of each word is not changed.*

| | | | | |
|---|---|---|---|---|
| un·awed′ | un·be·hold′en | un·blam′a·ble | un·both′ered | un·broth′er·ly |
| un·backed′ | un·be·liev′a·ble | un·blamed′ | un·bought′ | un·bruised′ |
| un·baked′ | un·be·liev′ing | un·bleached′ | un·bowed′ | un·brushed′ |
| un·band′aged | un·belt′ed | un·blem′ished | un·braced′ | un·burnt′ |
| un·barbed′ | un·be·seem′ing | un·blink′ing | un·branched′ | |
| un·bear′a·ble | un·be·trothed′ | un·blocked′ | un·brand′ed | |
| un·beat′a·ble | un·be·wailed′ | un·blurred′ | un·break′a·ble | |
| un·be·fit′ting | un·bi′assed | un·bod′ied | un·brib′a·ble | |

**un·but·toned** (un but′ənd)   **1** not buttoned: *His coat was unbuttoned.*   **2** unrestricted in expression or action; casual; informal: *He was in an unbuttoned mood, talking freely of his past.*   **3** pt. and pp. of UNBUTTON.   *1, 2 adj., 3 v.*

**un·called–for** (un kold′fôr′)   unnecessary and unjustified; impertinent or rude: *an uncalled-for remark.*   *adj.*

**un·can·ny** (un kan′ē)   **1** strange and mysterious; eerie: *The trees had uncanny shapes in the dim light.*   **2** seeming to have or show powers beyond what is natural or normal: *an uncanny sense of timing, an uncanny knack for solving puzzles.*   *adj.*   —**un·can′ni·ly,** *adv.*   —**un·can′ni·ness,** *n.*

**un·cap** (un kap′)   remove a cap or cover from: *to uncap a bottle.*   *v.,* **un·capped, un·cap·ping.**

**un·cer·e·mo·ni·ous** (un′ser ə mō′nē əs)   **1** not ceremonious; informal.   **2** not as courteous as would be expected; abrupt or rude: *an unceremonious dismissal.*   *adj.*   —**un′cer·e·mo′ni·ous·ly,** *adv.*   —**un′cer·e·mo′ni·ous·ness,** *n.*

**un·cer·tain** (un sėr′tən)   **1** not known with certainty; not finally established; indefinite: *The election results are still uncertain. Her arrival time is uncertain.*   **2** not sure; problematical: *an uncertain future.*   **3** likely to change; unreliable: *a dog of uncertain temper. The weather remains uncertain.*   **4** dubious or doubtful; hesitating: *an uncertain smile. He was uncertain about the reception he would get.*   **5** not definite or defined; vague: *an uncertain shape in the mist.*   **6** not constant; varying: *an uncertain flicker of light.*   *adj.*   —**un·cer′tain·ly,** *adv.*

**un·cer·tain·ness** (un sėr′tən nəs)   the quality or state of being UNCERTAIN.   *n.*

**un·cer·tain·ty** (un sėr′tən tē)   **1** the quality or state of being UNCERTAIN; doubt.   **2** something UNCERTAIN: *Our trip is still an uncertainty.*   *n., pl.* **un·cer·tain·ties.**

**un·chain** (un chān′)   free from chains or as if from chains; set free.   *v.*

**un·char·i·ta·ble** (un char′ə tə bəl *or* un cher′ə tə bəl)   not generous; not charitable; severe; harsh.   *adj.*   —**un·char′i·ta·ble·ness,** *n.*   —**un·char′i·ta·bly,** *adv.*

**un·chart·ed** (un chär′tid)   not yet mapped; not recorded on a chart: *sailing uncharted seas.*   *adj.*

**un·chris·tian** (un kris′chən)   **1** not Christian.   **2** unworthy of Christians.   **3** *Informal.* such as any civilized person would object to; barbarous; outrageous: *routed out of bed at a most unchristian hour.*   *adj.*

**un·church** (un chėrch′)   **1** expel from a church; excommunicate.   **2** deprive of status and rights as a church.   *v.*

**un·ci·al** (un′shē əl)   **1** a kind of letter or writing having heavy, rounded strokes, used especially in Greek and Latin manuscripts from the 4th to the 8th century.   **2** a manuscript written in uncial.   **3** having to do with or written in this style or such letters.   *1, 2 n., 3 adj.*

**un·cir·cum·cised** (un sėr′kəm sīzd′)   **1** not circumcised.   **2** heathen.   *adj.*

**un·civ·il** (un siv′əl)   **1** not civil; rude; impolite: *an uncivil retort.*   **2** not civilized.   *adj.*   —**un·civ′il·ly,** *adv.*

**un·clad** (un klad′)   **1** not dressed; not clothed; naked.   **2** a pt. and a pp. of UNCLOTHE.   *1 adj., 2 v.*

**un·clasp** (un klasp′)   **1** unfasten.   **2** release or be released from a clasp or grasp.   *v.*

**un·clas·si·fied** (un klas′i fīd′)   **1** not placed in a category or class.   **2** not classified as secret or restricted: *Employees without security clearance have access only to unclassified information.*   *adj.*

**un·cle** (ung′kəl)   **1** the brother of one's father or mother.   **2** the husband of one's aunt.   *n.*
**say** or **cry uncle,** *Informal.*   give in; surrender: *She wouldn't let him up until he said uncle.*

**un·clean** (un klēn′)   **1** not clean; dirty; filthy.   **2** not pure morally; evil.   **3** ceremonially impure.   *adj.*   —**un·clean′ness,** *n.*

**un·clean·ly**[1] (un klen′lē)   not cleanly; unclean.   *adj.*   —**un·clean′li·ness,** *n.*

**un·clean·ly**[2] (un klēn′lē)   in an unclean manner.   *adv.*

**un·clench** (un klench′)   open or become opened from a clenched state: *to unclench one's fists.*   *v.*

**Uncle Sam**   *Informal.*   the government or people of the United States.
☞ *Etym.* From the initials of the United States. First used scornfully in the War of 1812, it became a popular nickname for the U.S. government. In 1961, the name and character of Uncle Sam became an official symbol of the United States.

**un·cloak** (un klōk′)   **1** remove the coat from.   **2** reveal; expose: *to uncloak an impostor.*   **3** take off the cloak or outer garment.   *v.*

**un·clog** (un klog′)   free from an obstruction: *to unclog a drain.*   *v.,* **un·clogged, un·clog·ging.**

**un·close** (un klōz′)   open: *Favia unclosed her eyes and looked around her.*   *v.,* **un·closed, un·clos·ing.**

**un·clothe** (un klōᴛH′)   **1** strip clothes; undress.   **2** lay bare; uncover.   *v.,* **un·clothed** or **un·clad, un·cloth·ing.**

**un·coil** (un koil′)   unwind: *to uncoil a rope.*   *v.*

---

*In each of the words below* **un-** *means not; the pronunciation of the main part of each word is not changed.*

| | | | | |
|---|---|---|---|---|
| un·can′celled | un·cer′ti·fied′ | un·chas′tened | un·clas′si·fi′a·ble | un·cocked′ |
| un′ca·non′i·cal | un·chained′ | un′chas·tised′ | un·cleaned′ | un′co·erced′ |
| un·cared′-for′ | un·chal′lenged | un·checked′ | un·clear′ | un·col·lect′a·ble |
| un·car′ing | un·change′a·ble | un·chewed′ | un·cleared′ | un·col·lect′ed |
| un·cat′a·logued′ | un·changed′ | un·chiv′al·rous′ | un·closed′ | un·col·lect′i·ble |
| un·caught′ | un·chap′er·oned′ | un·chris′tened | un·clothed′ | un·col′oured |
| un·ceas′ing | un·char·ac·ter·is′tic | un·civ′i·lized | un·cloud′ed | un·combed′ |
| un·cen′sored | un·charged′ | un·claimed′ | un·clut′tered | un·com′bined′ |
| un·cen′sured | un·chaste′ | un·clar′i·fied | un·coat′ed | un·come′ly |

**un·com·fort·a·ble** (un kum′fər tə bəl)   **1** not comfortable: *I am uncomfortable in this chair.* **2** uneasy: *I feel uncomfortable at formal dinners.* **3** disagreeable; causing discomfort: *This is an uncomfortable chair.* *adj.*
—**un·com′fort·a·ble·ness,** *n.*   —**un·com′fort·a·bly,** *adv.*

**un·com·mit·ted** (un′kə mit′id)   **1** not bound or pledged to a certain viewpoint, course, program, etc.: *an uncommitted candidate.* **2** not committed to prison or other institution. *adj.*

**un·com·mon** (un kom′ən)   **1** not commonly encountered; rare; unusual: *The tulip tree is uncommon in Canada.* **2** remarkable: *uncommon strength, an uncommon grasp of the subject.* *adj.*
—**un·com′mon·ly,** *adv.*   —**un·com′mon·ness,** *n.*

**un·com·mu·ni·ca·tive** (un′kə myü′nə kə tiv or un′kə myü′nə kā′tiv)   not giving out any information, opinions, etc.; silent and reserved; taciturn. *adj.*
—**un′com·mu′ni·ca·tive·ness,** *n.*

**un·com·pro·mis·ing** (un kom′prə mī′zing) unyielding; firm; unwilling to compromise: *His uncompromising attitude makes him very hard to deal with.* *adj.*   —**un·com′pro·mis′ing·ly,** *adv.*

**un·con·cern** (un′kən sėrn′)   lack of care, interest, or anxiety; indifference: *The children looked with complete unconcern at their strange surroundings.* *n.*

**un·con·cerned** (un′kən sėrnd′)   **1** free from care, interest or anxiety; indifferent or nonchalant: *unconcerned about the results of the exam.* **2** not involved: *She was unconcerned with that aspect of the inquiry. They need an unconcerned person to settle the dispute.* *adj.*

**un·con·cern·ed·ly** (un′kən sėr′ni dlē)   in an unconcerned manner. *adv.*

**un·con·di·tion·al** (un′kən dish′ə nəl or un′kən dish′nəl) without conditions; absolute; unqualified; unrestricted: *The victorious general demanded unconditional surrender of the enemy.* *adj.*   —**un·con·di′tion·al·ly,** *adv.*

**un·con·di·tioned** (un′kən dish′ənd)   **1** without conditions; UNCONDITIONAL. **2** not learned; not dependent on conditioning; natural or instinctive: *Withdrawing one's hand on contact with fire is an unconditioned reflex.* *adj.*

**un·con·form·i·ty** (un′kən fôr′mə tē)   a lack of agreement; nonconformity. *n., pl.* **un·con·form·i·ties.**

**un·con·nect·ed** (un′kə nek′tid)   **1** separated; disconnected. **2** not connected; separate or unrelated: *What she had written was not a paragraph; it was just a series of unconnected sentences.* *adj.*

**un·con·scion·a·ble** (un kon′shə nə bəl)   **1** not influenced or guided by conscience; unscrupulous: *unconscionable business practices, an unconscionable liar.* **2** unreasonable; excessive: *to wait an unconscionable time for someone.* *adj.*   —**un·con′scion·a·bly,** *adv.*

hat, āge, fär; let, ēqual, tėrm; it, īce
hot, ōpen, ôrder; oil, out; cup, pùt, rüle
əbove, takən, pencəl, leməl, circəs
ch, child; ng, long; sh, ship
th, thin; ᴛʜ, then; zh, measure

**un·con·scious** (un kon′shəs)   **1** not conscious; not able to feel or think: *He was knocked unconscious when the car struck him.* **2** not aware: *The general was unconscious of being followed by a spy.* **3** not meant; not intended: *unconscious neglect.* **4 the unconscious,** the part of a person's mind of which the person is not normally aware, but which can affect behaviour; a person's unconscious thoughts, desires, fears, etc. 1–3 *adj.,* 4 *n.*
—**un·con′scious·ly,** *adv.*   —**un·con′scious·ness,** *n.*

**un·con·sti·tu·tion·al·i·ty** (un′kon stə tyü′shə nal′ə tē or un′kon stə tü′shə nal′ə tē)   the fact, state, or condition of being contrary to the constitution. *n.*

**un·con·ven·tion·al** (un′kən ven′shə nəl)   not bound by or conforming to convention, rule, or precedent; being out of the ordinary: *an unconventional way of dressing. She is an unconventional person.* *adj.*
—**un′con·ven′tion·al·ly,** *adv.*

**un·con·ven·tion·al·i·ty** (un′kən ven′shə nal′ə tē)   the quality or state of being unconventional: *His unconventionality amused his friends.* *n.*

**un·cork** (un kôrk′)   pull the cork from: *to uncork a bottle of wine.* *v.*

**un·count·ed** (un koun′tid)   **1** not counted; not reckoned. **2** very many; innumerable. *adj.*

**un·cou·ple** (un kup′əl)   disconnect; unfasten: *to uncouple a freight car.* *v.,* **un·cou·pled, un·cou·pling.**

**un·couth** (un küth′)   awkward or crude in appearance, conduct, etc.: *uncouth manners, an uncouth young man.* *adj.*   —**un·couth′ness,** *n.*

**un·cov·er** (un kuv′ər)   **1** remove the cover from. **2** make known; reveal; expose: *The plot was uncovered when the letter was found.* **3** remove one's hat or cap in respect: *The men uncovered as the flag passed by.* *v.*

**un·cov·ered** (un kuv′ərd)   **1** having no cover or covering: *Don't leave the milk uncovered.* **2** not protected by insurance, etc. **3** not wearing a hat or cap. **4** pt. and pp. of UNCOVER. 1–3 *adj.,* 4 *v.*

**un·cross** (un kros′)   change from a crossed position: *She uncrossed her legs and stretched them out.* *v.*

**un·crown** (un kroun′)   take the crown from; depose. *v.*

---

*In each of the words below* **un-** *means* not; *the pronunciation of the main part of each word is not changed.*

| | | | | |
|---|---|---|---|---|
| un′com·fort·ed | un′con·cealed′ | un′con·sid′ered | un′con·trolled′ | un′cor·rob′o·rat′ed |
| un′com·pan′ion·a·ble | un′con·cert′ed | un′con·soled′ | un′con·vert′ed | un′cor·rupt′ed |
| un′com·plain′ing | un′con·fined′ | un′con·sti·tu′tion·al | un′con·vinced′ | un′count′a·ble |
| un′com·plai′sant | un′con·firmed′ | un′con·strained′ | un′con·vin′cing | un′cour′te·ous |
| un′com·plet′ed | un′con·gealed′ | un′con·sumed′ | un′cooked′ | un′court′ly |
| un com′pli·ca·ted | un′con·gen′i·al | un′con·tam′i·nat′ed | un·cooled′ | un′cre·at′ed |
| un′com·pli′men·tary | un′con·gest′ed | un′con·test′ed | un′co-op′e·ra·tive | un·cred′it·ed |
| un′com·pound′ed | un′con·quer·a·ble | un′con·tra·dict′a·ble | un′co-or′di·nat·ed | un·crit′i·cal |
| un′com·pre·hend′ing | un′con·quered | un′con·tra·dict′ed | un·cor′dial | un·cropped′ |
| un·com′pro·mised′ | un′con·se·crat′ed | un′con·trol′la·ble | un′cor·rect′ed | un·crowd′ed |

**un·crowned** (un kround′) **1** not crowned; not having yet assumed the crown. **2** having royal power without being king, queen, etc. **3** pt. and pp. of UNCROWN. 1, 2 *adj.*, 3 *v.*

**unc·tion** (ungk′shən) **1** the act of anointing with oil, ointment, etc. for medical purposes or as a religious rite: *The priest gave the dying woman extreme unction.* **2** the oil, ointment, etc. used for anointing. **3** something soothing or comforting: *the unction of flattery.* **4** a fervent or earnest quality in behaviour or expression. **5** affected fervour or earnestness; unctuousness. *n.*

**unc·tu·ous** (ungk′chü əs) **1** like an oil or ointment; oily or greasy. **2** of a person or a person's manner, very smooth, fervent, or earnest, especially in a false or affected way when trying to please or persuade: *The stranger's unctuous manner made us suspicious.* *adj.* —**unc′tu·ous·ly,** *adv.* —**unc′tu·ous·ness,** *n.*

**un·curl** (un kėrl′) straighten out. *v.*

**un·cut** (un kut′) **1** not cut into or cut down: *The cake was on the table, still uncut.* **2** of a gem, not shaped: *uncut diamonds.* **3** of a book, having the folded edges of the leaves not cut open, or having untrimmed margins. **4** of a book, film, etc., not shortened; unabridged or unexpurgated: *They saw the uncut version of the film.* *adj.*

**un·de·ceive** (un′di sēv′) free from error, illusion, or deception. *v.*, **un·de·ceived, un·de·ceiv·ing.**

**un·de·cid·ed** (un′di sī′did) **1** not decided or settled: *The matter was still undecided when the meeting was adjourned.* **2** not having one's mind made up: *She is undecided about her future.* *adj.* —**un′de·cid′ed·ly,** *adv.* —**un′de·cid′ed·ness,** *n.*

**un·de·ni·a·ble** (un′di nī′ə bəl) **1** that cannot be denied; certain; indisputable: *the undeniable rudeness of his answer, undeniable excellence.* **2** unquestionably genuine or excellent: *Her references were undeniable.* *adj.* —**un′de·ni′a·bly,** *adv.*

**un·der** (un′dər) **1** in, at, or to a place or position directly below: *The marble rolled under the table. Write your name under mine.* **2** under and through to the other side of: *The road goes under that bridge.* **3** below the surface of: *under the ground, swimming under water.* **4** on the inside of; covered or hidden by: *She was wearing a heavy sweater under her parka. He has a soft heart under his gruff exterior.* **5** in or to a place or position below something: *We saw the swimmer go under.* **6** lower than the required or standard degree, amount, etc.: *under par. You cannot sign a contract if you are underage.* **7** facing or projecting downward: *The under surface was rough.* **8** less than: *It will cost under twenty dollars.* **9** less than some quantity or limit: *ten dollars or under.* **10** subject to the authority, control, influence, or guidance of: *She studied under a famous pianist. The soldiers acted under orders.* **11** during the time of the rule of: *England under Queen Elizabeth I.* **12** in the position or state of being affected by: *under the new rules. He doesn't work well under pressure. Under these conditions we must cancel the picnic.* **13** within a particular group or category: *Books on gymnastics are classed under sports.* **14** represented by: *under a new name.* 1–4, 6, 8, 10–14 *prep.*, 5, 9 *adv.*, 7 *adj.*

**under–** a prefix meaning: **1** in, on, or to a lower place or side; below or beneath, as in *underground, underline, underarm, underlip.* **2** on or for the inside; covered or concealed, as in *underwear.* **3** lower in rank; subordinate, as in *undersecretary.* **4** not enough; insufficiently, as in *underfed, underripe.* **5** below normal, as in *undersized.*

**un·der·age** (un′də rāj′ *for adjective,* un′də rāj′ *for adverb*) **1** of less than full age. **2** being less than the legal age for voting, marrying, drinking liquor in public bars, etc.: *You can't drink underage.* 1 *adj.*, 2 *adv.*

**un·der·arm** (un′də rärm′) **1** on or under the inside of the arm where it joins the shoulder; on or under the armpit: *an underarm scar, the underarm seam in a shirt.* **2** ARMPIT. **3** of, having to do with, or for the armpit: *underarm deodorant.* **4** UNDERHAND (def. 3): *an underarm throw (adj.). He threw the ball underarm (adv.).* 1, 3, 4 *adj.*, 2 *n.*, 4 *adv.*

**un·der·bid** (un′dər bid′) **1** make a lower bid than, as in seeking a contract for work, at an auction, etc. **2** bid less than the full point value of: *to underbid a hand in bridge.* *v.*, **un·der·bid, un·der·bid·ding.** —**un′der·bid′der,** *n.*

**un·der·bred** (un′dər bred′) **1** marked by lack of good breeding; ill-mannered or vulgar. **2** of a horse, dog, etc., not of pure breed. *adj.*

**un·der·brush** (un′dər brush′) bushes and small trees growing under large trees in a forest or wood; undergrowth. *n.*

**un·der·car·riage** (un′dər kar′ij *or* un′dər ker′ij) **1** the supporting framework of an automobile, carriage, etc. **2** the under part of an aircraft that receives the impact on landing and supports the aircraft on the ground or water; landing gear. *n.*

**un·der·charge** (un′dər chärj′ *for verb,* un′dər chärj′ *for noun*) **1** put an insufficient charge or load into. **2** an insufficient charge or load. **3** charge less than the proper or fair price: *I think the clerk undercharged me. He undercharged me one dollar.* **4** a charge or price less than is proper or fair. 1, 3 *v.*, **un·der·charged, un·der·charg·ing;** 2, 4 *n.*

**un·der·clothes** (un′dər klōz′ *or* un′dər klōᴛHz′) UNDERWEAR. *n.pl.*

**un·der·cloth·ing** (un′der klō′ᴛHing) underwear. *n.*

---

*In each of the words below* **un–** *means* not; *the pronunciation of the main part of each word is not changed.*

| | | | | |
|---|---|---|---|---|
| un·crys′tal·lized′ | un·cur′tained | un′de·cayed′ | un′de·feat′a·ble | un′de·mand′ing |
| un·cul′ti·va·ble | un·dam′aged | un′de·ceiv′a·ble | un′de·feat′ed | un′dem·o·crat′ic |
| un·cul′tured | un·damped′ | un′de·ceived′ | un′de·fend′ed | un′de·mon′stra·ble |
| un·curbed′ | un·dat′ed | un′de·ci′pher·a·ble | un′de·filed′ | un′de·mon′stra·tive |
| un·cured′ | un·daugh′ter·ly | un′de·clared′ | un′de·fin′a·ble | un′de·nied′ |
| un·cur′i·ous | un·daun′ted | un′de·clin′a·ble | un′de·layed′ | un′de·pend′a·ble |
| un·curled′ | un·daz′zled | un′de·clined′ | un′de·liv′er·a·ble | un′de·pre′ci·at′ed |
| un·cur′rent | un′de·bat′a·ble | un′dec·o·rat′ed | un′de·liv′ered | |

**un·der·coat** (un′dər kōt′) **1** a coat or layer of paint, etc. applied before the finishing coat. **2** apply undercoating or an undercoat to: *to undercoat a car.* **3** the soft, thick fur of certain mammals that is hidden by the longer, coarser hair of the outer coat. 1, 3 *n.*, 2 *v.*

**un·der·coat·ing** (un′dər kō′ting) **1** a heavy, tarry coating sprayed on the underside of a motor vehicle to protect it against rust, etc.: *Every new car should have undercoating.* **2** ppr. of UNDERCOAT. 1 *n.*, 2 *v.*

**un·der·cov·er** (un′dər kuv′ər) **1** working in secret: *The jeweller was an undercover man for the police.* **2** done in secret: *an undercover attack.* *adj.*

**un·der·cur·rent** (un′dər kėr′ənt) **1** a current flowing below the upper currents or the surface of a body of water, air, etc. **2** an underlying tendency that is often contrary to what is expressed or shown: *There was an undercurrent of sadness beneath her joking manner.* *n.*

**un·der·cut** (un′dər kut′ *for verb,* un′dər kut′ *for adjective and noun*) **1** cut under or beneath; cut away material from so as to leave a portion overhanging. **2** that is cut away underneath: *an undercut rim on a vase.* **3** the act or result of cutting away underneath. **4** sell or work for less than a competitor. **5** a notch cut in a tree below the main cut and on the side toward which the tree is to fall: *An undercut prevents the tree from splitting when it falls.* **6** cut such a notch in. **7** in golf, tennis, etc., hit a ball with a downward slant to give it a backward spin. **8** the act or an instance of hitting a ball in this way. 1, 4, 6, 7 *v.*, **un·der·cut, un·der·cut·ting;** 2 *adj.*, 3, 5, 8 *n.*

**un·der·de·vel·oped** (un′dər di vel′əpt) **1** not developed in a normal way: *an underdeveloped limb.* **2** of a region, country, etc., poorly or inadequately developed in industry and commerce and having a relatively low standard of living. *adj.*

**un·der·dog** (un′dər dog′) **1** a person or group that is expected to lose or is losing a struggle or contest: *We've been the underdogs in the league so far, but this year we're going to win.* **2** a person or group that is a victim of persecution or injustice. **3** a dog having the worst of a fight. *n.*

**un·der·done** (un′dər dun′) not cooked enough; cooked very little. *adj.*

**un·der·es·ti·mate** (un′də res′tə māt′ *for verb,* un′də res′tə mit *or* un′də res′tə māt′ *for noun*) **1** estimate at too low a value, amount, rate, etc.: *He lost the match because he underestimated his opponent's strength.* **2** an estimate that is too low. 1 *v.*, **un·der·es·ti·mat·ed, un·der·es·ti·mat·ing;** 2 *n.*

**un·der·ex·pose** (un′də rek spōz′) in photography, expose to light for too short a time. *v.*, **un·der·ex·posed, un·der·ex·pos·ing.**

**un·der·ex·po·sure** (un′də rek spō′zhər) an exposure to the light for too short a time: *Underexposure makes a photograph look dim.* *n.*

**un·der·feed** (un′dər fēd′) feed too little. *v.*, **un·der·fed, un·der·feed·ing.**

**un·der·foot** (un′dər fut′) **1** under one's foot or feet; down on or against the ground: *He walked straight through the flower bed, crushing several plants underfoot.* **2** at, before, or underneath one's feet: *enjoying the soft grass underfoot.* **3** in the way: *That dog is always underfoot.* *adv.*

**un·der·fur** (un′dər fėr′) the soft, thick fur of certain

hat, āge, fär; let, ēqual, tėrm; it, īce
hot, ōpen, ôrder; oil, out; cup, pùt, rüle
əbove, takən, pencəl, lemən, circəs
ch, child; ng, long; sh, ship
th, thin; ᴛʜ, then; zh, measure

mammals that is hidden by the longer, coarser hair of the outer coat. *n.*

**un·der·gar·ment** (un′dər gär′mənt) any garment worn under outer clothing, especially an article of underwear. *n.*

**un·der·glaze** (un′dər glāz′) in ceramics, a design, decoration, or colour applied to an article before the glaze is put on. *n.*

**un·der·go** (un′dər gō′) **1** go through; be subjected to; experience: *The town has undergone many changes in the past few years.* **2** endure; suffer: *They underwent a great deal of hardship on the long trek.* *v.*, **un·der·went, un·der·gone, un·der·go·ing.**

**un·der·gone** (un′dər gon′) pp. of UNDERGO: *Tina has undergone much pain during her illness.* *v.*

**un·der·grad·u·ate** (un′dər graj′ü it) **1** a student at a college or university who has not yet received the first degree for a course of study; a student without a bachelor's degree. **2** for, having to do with, or referring to undergraduates: *undergraduate activities.* **3** characteristic of undergraduates. 1 *n.*, 2, 3 *adj.*

**un·der·ground** (un′dər ground′ *for adverb,* un′dər ground′ *for adjective and noun*) **1** beneath the surface of the ground. **2** being, working, or used beneath the surface of the ground: *underground telephone cables.* **3** *Esp. Brit.* an underground railway system in a city; subway. **4** a place or space beneath the surface of the ground. **5** in or into concealment or secret operation: *The thieves went underground after the robbery.* **6** done or operating secretly: *The revolution began as an underground movement in the cities.* **7** a secret organization of citizens or a grouping of such organizations, working to free a country from foreign domination or an autocratic regime: *The French underground was active during World War II.* **8** of, having to do with, or produced by a group or groups outside the establishment, especially avant-garde or radical groups: *an underground newspaper. Her first plays were produced by an underground theatre.* 1, 5 *adv.*, 2, 6, 8 *adj.*, 3, 4, 7 *n.*

**Underground Railroad** a secret system set up by opponents of slavery in Canada and the United States before the Civil War to help slaves escape to freedom in the northern states and Canada.

**un·der·growth** (un′dər grōth′) **1** UNDERBRUSH. **2** short, fine hair under longer outer hair. *n.*

**un·der·hand** (un′dər hand′) **1** not open or honest; secret and sly; underhanded. **2** secretly and slyly; underhandedly. **3** with an upward movement of the hand from below shoulder level: *an underhand pitch* (*adj.*), *throw a ball underhand* (*adv.*). 1, 3 *adj.*, 2, 3 *adv.*

**un·der·hand·ed** (un′dər han′did) not open or honest; secret and sly: *an underhanded trick.* *adj.*
—**un′der·hand′ed·ly,** *adv.* —**un′der·hand′ed·ness,** *n.*

**un·der·hung** (un′dər hung′) **1** of the lower jaw, projecting beyond the upper jaw: *A bulldog has an underhung jaw.* **2** having a projecting lower jaw. **3** resting on a track beneath, instead of being hung from above: *underhung sliding doors.* **4** UNDERSLUNG. *adj.*

**un·der·laid** (un′dər lād′)  pp. of UNDERLAY.  v.

**un·der·lain** (un′dər lān′)  pp. of UNDERLIE.  v.

**un·der·lay** (un′dər lā′ for verb, un′dər lā′ for noun)  **1** lay something under; raise, support, cushion, etc. with something laid underneath.  **2** something laid beneath to raise, support, cushion, etc.: *The carpet has a foam rubber underlay.*  **3** pt. of UNDERLIE.  1 v., **un·der·laid**, **un·der·lay·ing**;  3 v., 2 n.

**un·der·lie** (un′dər lī′)  **1** lie under; beneath: *A layer of limestone underlies the gravel you see here.*  **2** form the basis of; be a reason or cause for: *Strong resentment underlay his outburst.*  v., **un·der·lay**, **un·der·lain**, **un·der·ly·ing**.

**un·der·line** (un′dər līn′ or un′dər līn′)  **1** draw a line or lines under: *In writing, we underline titles of books.*  **2** emphasize; make emphatic or more emphatic: *Her speech underlined the importance of co-operation.*  **3** a line drawn underneath something: *The underline is too faint.*  1, 2 v., **un·der·lined, un·der·lin·ing**;  3 n.

**un·der·ling** (un′dər ling)  a person of lower rank or position; inferior.  n.

**un·der·lip** (un′dər lip′)  the lower lip.  n.

**un·der·ly·ing** (un′dər lī′ing)  **1** lying under or beneath.  **2** fundamental; basic; essential: *the underlying cause.*  **3** not clearly evident or expressed; implicit: *His complimentary remarks had an underlying tone of sarcasm.*  **4** ppr. of UNDERLIE.  1–3 adj., 4 v.

**un·der·manned** (un′dər mand′)  having not enough crew, staff, etc.; understaffed: *The ship was undermanned, but still carried out its mission.*  adj.

**un·der·mine** (un′dər mīn′)  **1** wear away the base or foundations of: *The wave had undermined the cliff.*  **2** injure or damage by secret or unfair means: *The editorial was obviously intended to undermine her influence in the community.*  **3** weaken, wear out, or destroy gradually: *Several months of stress and insufficient sleep had undermined her health.*  **4** make a passage or hole under; dig under: *to undermine a wall.*  v., **un·der·mined, un·der·min·ing**.  —**un′der·min′er,** n.

**un·der·most** (un′dər mōst′)  lowest.  adj., adv.

**un·der·neath** (un′dər nēth′)  **1** directly below; beneath; under: *a cellar underneath a house. Write the date underneath your name.*  **2** on the inside of; covered or hidden by; under: *He wore a T-shirt underneath his shirt.*  **3** on the inside of or below something: *He crawled underneath. She was wearing her swimsuit underneath.*  **4** on or at the lower part or surface: *The box is wet underneath.*  **5** lower: *the underneath side.*  **6** the lower part or surface: *Let me see the underneath.*  1, 2 prep., 3, 4 adv., 5 adj., 6 n.

**un·der·nour·ished** (un′dər nėr′isht)  not sufficiently nourished.  adj.

**un·der·nour·ish·ment** (un′dər nėr′ishmənt)  not having enough food; lack of nourishment.  n.

**un·der·pants** (un′dər pants′)  long or short pants worn as an undergarment.  n.pl.

**un·der·pass** (un′dər pas′)  a way underneath; a road under railway tracks or under another road; subway.  n.

**un·der·pay** (un′dər pā′)  pay too little.  v., **un·der·paid, un·der·pay·ing**.

**un·der·pin** (un′dər pin′)  support or strengthen with props, stones, masonry, etc.  v., **un·der·pinned, un·der·pin·ning**.

**un·der·pin·ning** (un′dər pin′ing)  **1** the material or structure used to support a building or wall from below.  **2** Often, **underpinnings,** pl.  anything used as a foundation or support: *The new evidence provided good underpinnings for the detective's theory.*  n.

**un·der·priv·i·leged** (un′dər priv′ə lijd)  **1** having fewer advantages than most people have, especially because of poor economic or social status.  **2** the **underprivileged,** pl.  all persons who are underprivileged.  1 adj., 2 n. pl.

**un·der·pro·duc·tion** (un′dər prə duk′shən)  production that is less than normal or less than there is demand for.  n.

**un·der·rate** (un′dər rāt′)  rate or estimate too low; put too low a value on: *One should take care not to underrate the ability of one's rivals.*  v., **un·der·rat·ed, un·der·rat·ing**.

**un·der·ripe** (un′dər rīp′)  not completely ripe or not ripe enough: *The tomatoes were somewhat underripe, but edible.*  adj.

**un·der·score** (un′dər skôr′ for verb, un′dər skôr′ for noun)  **1** UNDERLINE.  **2** an UNDERLINE.  **3** EMPHASIZE.  1, 3 v., **un·der·scored, un·der·scor·ing**;  2 n.

**un·der·sea** (un′dər sē′ for adjective, un′dər sē′ for adverb)  **1** being, carried on, or used beneath the surface of the sea: *an undersea cable, undersea explorations, undersea oil deposits.*  **2 underseas,**  beneath the surface of the seas: *exploring underseas.*  1 adj., 2 adv.

**un·der·seas** (un′dər sēz′)  beneath the surface of the sea: *Submarines go underseas.*  adv.

**un·der·sec·re·tar·y** (un′dər sek′rə ter′ē)  an assistant secretary, especially of a government department.  n., pl. **un·der·sec·re·tar·ies**.

**un·der·sell** (un′dər sel′)  sell things at a lower price than: *This store can undersell other stores because it sells in bulk.*  v., **un·der·sold, un·der·sell·ing**.

**un·der·shirt** (un′dər shėrt′)  a collarless, often sleeveless, knitted undergarment for the upper part of the body.  n.

**un·der·shoot** (un′dər shüt′)  **1** of an aircraft, come down short of the runway or landing field.  **2** shoot short of or below a target, mark, etc.  v., **un·der·shot, un·der·shoot·ing**.

**un·der·shorts** (un′dər shôrts′)  short underpants worn by men and boys.  n.pl.

An undershot water wheel. The force of the water pushing against the blades makes the wheel turn. Its axle is connected to machinery.

**un·der·shot** (un′dər shot′)  **1** of a water wheel, driven by water passing beneath.  **2** of the lower jaw, projecting beyond the upper; UNDERHUNG.  **3** pt. and pp. of UNDERSHOOT.  1, 2 adj., 3 v.

**un·der·side** (un′dər sīd′) the surface lying underneath; the bottom side: *The underside of the stone was crawling with ants.* *n.*

**un·der·signed** (un′dər sīnd′) **1** signed or having signed at the end of a letter or document: *the undersigned witnesses.* **2 the undersigned,** the person or persons signing a letter or document: *The undersigned accepts the agreement. We, the undersigned, testify that we have read the document.* 1 *adj.*, 2 *n.*, *pl.* **un·der·signed.**

**un·der·sized** (un′dər sīzd′) smaller than the usual, desired, or required size: *undersized trout.* *adj.*

**un·der·skirt** (un′dər skėrt′) a skirt worn under another skirt: *a lace skirt with a satin underskirt.* *n.*

**un·der·slung** (un′dər slung′) **1** of a vehicle frame, suspended below the axles. **2** having an underslung frame. *adj.*

**un·der·staffed** (un′dər staft′) having too small a staff; having not enough personnel. *adj.*

**un·der·stand** (un′dər stand′) **1** get the meaning of; comprehend: *Now I understand the teacher's words.* **2** get the meaning: *People listen but often do not understand.* **3** know how to deal with; know well; know: *A good teacher should understand children.* **4** be informed; learn: *I understand that he is leaving town.* **5** take as a fact; believe: *It is understood that you will come.* **6** take as meaning; take as meant: *What are we to understand from his words?* *v.*, **un·der·stood, un·der·stand·ing.**

**un·der·stand·a·ble** (un′dər stan′də bəl) able to be understood. *adj.* —**un′der·stand′a·bly,** *adv.*

**un·der·stand·ing** (un′dər stan′ding) **1** the mental process or state of one that understands; comprehension; knowledge: *a clear understanding of the problem.* **2** the ability to learn and know; intelligence: *The doctor was a person of understanding.* **3** intelligent and sympathetic: *an understanding reply.* **4** a knowledge of each other's meaning and wishes: *True friendship is based on understanding.* **5** an agreement: *You and I must come to an understanding.* 1, 2, 4, 5 *n.*, 3 *adj.*
—**un′der·stand′ing·ly,** *adv.*

**un·der·state** (un′dər stāt′) **1** state restrainedly. **2** say less than the full truth about. *v.*, **un·der·stat·ed, un·der·stat·ing.**

**un·der·state·ment** (un′dər stāt′mənt) **1** a statement that expresses a fact with restraint. **2** a statement that says less than could be said truly. *n.*

**un·der·stood** (un′dər stud′) pt. and pp. of UNDERSTAND: *Have all of you understood today's lesson?* *v.*

**un·der·stud·y** (un′dər stud′ē *for noun,* un′dər stud′ē *for verb*) **1** a person who is ready to substitute in an emergency for an actor or any other regular performer. **2** learn a part in order to replace the regular performer when necessary. **3** act as an understudy to. 1 *n.*, *pl.* **un·der·stud·ies;** 2, 3 *v.*, **un·der·stud·ied, un·der·stud·y·ing.**

**un·der·take** (un′dər tāk′) **1** set about; try; attempt. **2** agree to do; take upon oneself: *Kate undertook the feeding of my dogs.* **3** promise; guarantee. *v.*, **un·der·took, un·der·tak·en, un·der·tak·ing.**

**un·der·tak·er** (un′dər tā′kər *for 1,* un′dər tā′kər *for 2*) **1** a person whose business is preparing the dead for burial and taking charge of funerals: *An undertaker is a funeral director.* **2** a person who undertakes something. *n.*

**un·der·tak·ing** (un′dər tā′king *for 1, 2 and 4,* un′dər tā′king *for 3*) **1** something undertaken; task; enterprise. **2** a promise; guarantee. **3** the business of preparing the dead for burial and taking charge of funerals. **4** ppr. of UNDERTAKE. 1–3 *n.*, 4 *v.*

**un·der·tone** (un′dər tōn′) **1** a low or very quiet tone: *to talk in undertones.* **2** a subdued colour; a colour seen through other colours: *There was an undertone of brown beneath all the gold and crimson of autumn.* **3** a quality or feeling that is beneath the surface: *an undertone of sadness in her gaiety.* *n.*

**un·der·took** (un′dər tuk′) pt. of UNDERTAKE: *Gabriella undertook more than she could do.* *v.*

**un·der·tow** (un′dər tō′) **1** any strong current below the surface, moving in a direction different from that of the surface current. **2** the backward flow from waves breaking on a beach. *n.*

**un·der·val·u·a·tion** (un′dər val′yü ā′shən) too low a valuation. *n.*

**un·der·val·ue** (un′dər val′yü) put too low a value on. *v.*, **un·der·val·ued, un·der·val·u·ing.**

**un·der·wa·ter** (un′dər wot′ər *for adjective,* un′dər wot′ər *for adverb*) **1** growing, done, or used below the surface of the water: *underwater plants. A submarine is an underwater ship.* **2** below the surface of the water: *She stayed underwater for two minutes.* 1 *adj.*, 2 *adv.*

**un·der·wear** (un′dər wer′) clothing worn under outer clothing and not meant to be visible when one is fully dressed. *n.*

**un·der·weight** (un′dər wāt′) **1** of a person or animal, having a mass that is too small in proportion to height and build: *You are a little underweight, but it is nothing to worry about.* **2** having less mass than is needed, desired, or specified: *He claimed that the roast was underweight.* *adj.*

**un·der·went** (un′dər went′) pt. of UNDERGO: *Transportation underwent a great change with the development of the automobile.* *v.*

**un·der·world** (un′dər wėrld′) **1** the criminal part of society. **2** in Roman myths, the world of the dead; Hades. **3** antipodes. *n.*

**un·der·write** (un′dər rīt′ *or* un′dər rīt′) **1** insure property against loss. **2** sign an insurance policy, thereby accepting the risk of insuring something against loss. **3** write under other written matter; sign one's name to a document, etc. **4** agree to buy all the stocks or bonds of a certain issue that are not bought by the public: *The bankers underwrote the steel company's bonds.* **5** agree to meet the expense of. *v.*, **un·der·wrote, un·der·writ·ten, un·der·writ·ing.**

**un·der·writ·er** (un′dər rī′tər) **1** a person who underwrites an insurance policy or carries on an insurance business; insurer. **2** an official of an insurance company who determines the risks to be accepted, the premiums to be paid, etc. **3** a person who underwrites (usually with others) issues of bonds, stocks, etc. *n.*

**un·der·writ·ten** (un′dər rit′ən *or* un′dər rit′ən) pp. of UNDERWRITE. *v.*

---

hat, āge, fär; let, ēqual, tėrm; it, īce
hot, ōpen, ôrder; oil, out; cup, pùt, rüle
above, taken, pencəl, lemən, circəs

ch, child; ng, long; sh, ship
th, thin; ∓H, then; zh, measure

**un·der·wrote** (un′dər rōt′ *or* un′dər rōt′) pt. of UNDERWRITE.

**un·de·sir·a·ble** (un′di zīr′ə bəl) 1 objectionable; disagreeable: *That drug was taken off the market because it was found to have undesirable effects.* 2 a person that is not wanted. 1 *adj.*, 2 *n.*

**un·de·vel·oped** (un′di vel′əpt) 1 not fully grown. 2 not put to full use. *adj.*

**un·did** (un did′) pt. of UNDO: *He undid his shoes. The fire in the artist's studio undid years of work.* *v.*

**un·dis·guised** (un′dis gīzd′) 1 not disguised. 2 unconcealed; open; plain; frank. *adj.*

**un·do** (un dü′) 1 unfasten; untie: *Please undo the package. I undid the string.* 2 do away with; cancel or reverse: *We mended the roof, but a heavy storm undid our work.* 3 bring to ruin; spoil; destroy. 4 explain; solve: *to undo a puzzle.* *v.*, **un·did, un·done, un·do·ing.** —**un·do′er,** *n.*
☛ Hom. UNDUE (un dü′).

**un·do·ing** (un dü′ing) a cause of destruction or ruin: *Drink was his undoing.* *n.*

**un·done** (un dun′) 1 not done; not finished: *I left all my homework undone and went to a movie.* 2 pp. of UNDO. 1 *adj.*, 2 *v.*

**un·doubt·ed·ly** (un dou′ti dlē) beyond doubt; certainly. *adv.*

**un·dress** (un dres′ for verb, un′dres′ or un dres′ for noun, un′dres′ for adjective) 1 take the clothes off; strip. 2 loose, informal dress. 3 ordinary clothes. 4 of or having to do with informal or ordinary clothes. 5 strip of ornament. 6 take dressing from a wound. 7 take off one's clothes. 8 lack of clothing; nakedness. 1, 5–7 *v.*, 2, 3, 8 *n.*, 4 *adj.*

**un·due** (un dyü′ *or* un dü′) 1 not fitting; not right; improper: *He made undue remarks about those around him.* 2 too great; too much: *A miser gives undue importance to money.* *adj.*
☛ Hom. UNDO (for the second pronunciation of **undue**).

**un·du·lant** (un′jə lənt) waving; wavy. *adj.*

**un·du·late** (un′jə lāt′ *or* un′dyə lāt′) 1 move in waves: *undulating water.* 2 have a wavy form or surface: *undulating hair.* 3 cause to move in waves. 4 give a wavy form or surface to. 5 wavy. 1–4 *v.*, **un·du·lat·ed, un·du·lat·ing;** 5 *adj.*

**un·du·la·tion** (un′jə lā′shən) 1 a waving motion. 2 a wavy form. 3 one of a series of wavelike bends, curves, swellings, etc. 4 a sound wave. 5 VIBRATION. *n.*

**un·du·la·to·ry** (un′jə lə tô′rē) undulating; wavy. *adj.*

**un·du·ly** (un dyü′lē *or* un dü′lē) 1 improperly: *He was punished unduly.* 2 excessively; too much: *unduly harsh, unduly optimistic.* *adj.*

**un·dy·ing** (un dī′ing) deathless; immortal; eternal: *undying beauty.* *adj.* —**un·dy′ing·ly,** *adv.*

**un·earned** (un ėrnd′) 1 not earned; not gained by labour or service. 2 not deserved. *adj.*

**un·earth** (un ėrth′) 1 dig up: *to unearth a buried city.* 2 find out; discover: *to unearth a plot.* *v.*

**un·earth·ly** (un er′thlē) 1 not of this world; supernatural. 2 strange; weird; ghostly. 3 *Informal.* unnatural; extraordinary; preposterous. *adj.*
—**un·earth′li·ness,** *n.*

**un·eas·y** (un ē′zē) 1 restless; disturbed; anxious. 2 not comfortable. 3 not easy in manner; awkward. *adj.*, **un·eas·i·er, un·eas·i·est.** —**un·eas′i·ly,** *adv.*
—**un·eas′i·ness,** *n.*

**UNEF** (yü′nef) United Nations Emergency Force.

**un·em·ployed** (un′em ploid′) 1 not employed; not in use: *an unemployed skill.* 2 not having a job; having no work: *an unemployed person.* 3 **the unemployed,** people out of work: *Some of the unemployed receive aid from the government.* 1, 2 *adj.*, 3 *n. pl.*

**un·em·ploy·ment** (un′em ploi′mənt) 1 a lack of employment; being out of work. 2 the number or percentage of persons unemployed at a particular time: *a period of high unemployment.* 3 UNEMPLOYMENT INSURANCE (def. 2). *n.*

**unemployment insurance** 1 a program providing regular payments of money for a fixed period to persons in the regular labour force who are temporarily unemployed due to layoffs, illness, maternity, etc.: *Unemployment insurance benefits in Canada are paid for through the contributions of employees, employers, and the federal government.* 2 benefits paid through such a

---

*In each of the words below* **un-** *means* not; *the pronunciation of the main part of each word is not changed.*

| | | | | |
|---|---|---|---|---|
| un′de·served′ | un′dig′ni·fied′ | un′dis·heart′ened | un′do·mes′tic | un·eat′a·ble |
| un′de·serv′ing | un′di·lut′ed | un′dis·mayed′ | un′do·mes′ti·cat′ed | un·eat′en |
| un′des′ig·nat′ed | un′di·min′ished | un′dis·put′ed | un·dou′bled | un′e·clipsed′ |
| un′de·sign′ing | un′di·min′ish·ing | un′dis·so′ci·at′ed | un·doubt′ed | un′e·co·nom′ic |
| un′de·sired′ | un·dimmed′ | un′dis·solved′ | un·doubt′ing | un′eco·nom′i·cal |
| un′des·pair′ing | un′dip·lo·mat′ic | un′dis·tilled′ | un·drained′ | un′ed′i·fy′ing |
| un′de·stroyed′ | un′di·rect′ed | un′dis·tin′guish·a·ble | un′dra·mat′ic | un′ed′u·ca·ble |
| un′de·tach′a·ble | un′dis·cern′i·ble | un′dis·tin′guished | un·draped′ | un′ed′u·cat′ed |
| un′de·tect′a·ble | un′dis·cern′ing | un′dis·tin′guish·ing | un·dreamed′ | un′ef·faced′ |
| un′de·tect′ed | un′dis·charged′ | un′dis·tort′ed | un·dreamt′ | un′e·lim′i·nat′ed |
| un′de·ter′min·a·ble | un′dis·ci′plined | un′dis·tract′ed | un·dressed′ | un′em·bar′rassed |
| un′de·ter′mined | un′dis·closed′ | un′dis·trib′ut·ed | un·dried′ | un′em·bel′lished |
| un′de·terred′ | un′dis·cour′aged | un′dis·turbed′ | un·drilled′ | un′e·mo′tion·al |
| un′de·vi′at·ing | un′dis·cov′er·a·ble | un′di·ver′si·fied′ | un·drink′a·ble | un′em·phat′ic |
| un′dif·fer·en′ti·at′ed | un′dis·cov′ered | un′di·vid′ed | un·dut′i·ful | |
| un′di·gest′ed | un′dis·crim′i·nat′ing | un′di·vulged′ | un·dyed′ | |

program: *She collected unemployment insurance for two months.*

**un·e·qual** (un ē′kwəl) **1** not the same in amount, size, number, value, merit, rank, etc.: *unequal sums of money.* **2** not balanced; not well matched. **3** not fair; one-sided: *an unequal contest.* **4** not enough; not adequate: *His strength was unequal to the task.* **5** not regular; not even; variable. *adj.* —**un·e′qual·ly,** *adv.* —**un·e′qual·ness,** *n.*

**un·e·quiv·o·cal** (un′i kwiv′ə kəl) clear; plain. *adj.* —**un′e·quiv′o·cal·ly,** *adv.* —**un′e·quiv′o·cal·ness,** *n.*

**UNESCO** (yü nes′kō) the United Nations Educational, Scientific, and Cultural Organization, an independent organization related to and recognized by the United Nations as one of its specialized agencies. *n.*

**un·es·sen·tial** (un′ə sen′shəl) **1** not essential; not of prime importance. **2** something not essential. 1 *adj.*, 2 *n.*

**un·e·ven** (un ē′vən) **1** not level: *uneven ground.* **2** not equal; one-sided: *an uneven contest.* **3** of a number, leaving a remainder of 1 when divided by 2; odd: *The numbers 27 and 9 are uneven.* *adj.* —**un·e′ven·ly,** *adv.* —**un·e′ven·ness,** *n.*

**un·e·vent·ful** (un′i vent′fəl) without important or striking occurrences: *an uneventful day.* *adj.* —**un′e·vent′ful·ly,** *adv.*

**un·ex·am·pled** (un′eg zam′pəld) having no equal or like; without precedent or parallel; without anything like it. *adj.*

**un·ex·cep·tion·a·ble** (un′ek sep′shə nə bəl) beyond criticism; wholly admirable. *adj.*

**un·ex·cep·tion·al** (un′ek sep′shə nəl) **1** ordinary. **2** admitting of no exception. *adj.*

**un·fail·ing** (un fā′ling) **1** never failing; tireless; loyal. **2** never running short; endless. **3** sure; certain. *adj.*

**un·fail·ing·ly** (un fā′ling lē) always; without fail. *adv.*

**un·faith·ful** (un fāth′fəl) **1** not faithful; not true to duty or one's promises; faithless. **2** not accurate; not true to the original: *an unfaithful translation.* *adj.* —**un·faith′ful·ly,** *adv.* —**un·faith′ful·ness,** *n.*

**un·fal·ter·ing** (un fol′tə ring) firm; steadfast; not hesitating. *adj.*

**un·fa·mil·iar** (un′fə mil′yər) **1** not well-known; unusual; strange: *That face is unfamiliar to me.* **2** not acquainted: *She is unfamiliar with the Greek language.* *adj.*

**un·fa·mil·i·ar·i·ty** (un′fə mil yar′ə tē or un′fə mil yer′ə tē, un′fə mil′ē ar′ə tē or un′fə mil′ē er′ə tē) lack of familiarity. *n.*

**un·fas·ten** (un fas′ən) undo; loose; open. *v.*

**un·fath·om·a·ble** (un faᴛʜ′ə mə bəl) **1** so deep that the bottom cannot be reached. **2** too mysterious to be understood. *adj.*

**un·fath·omed** (un faᴛʜ′əmd) **1** not measured. **2** not understood. *adj.*

**un·fa·vour·a·ble** or **un·fa·vor·a·ble** (un fā′və rə bəl) **1** opposed or adverse: *Most of the reviews were unfavourable.* **2** not propitious or advantageous: *an unfavourable aspect.* *adj.* —**un·fa′vour·a·ble·ness** or **un·fa′vor·a·ble·ness,** *n.* —**un·fa′vour·a·bly** or **un·fa′vor·a·bly,** *adv.*

**un·feel·ing** (un fē′ling) **1** hard-hearted; cruel: *a cold, unfeeling person.* **2** not able to feel: *numb, unfeeling hands.* *adj.* —**un·feel′ing·ly,** *adv.* —**un·feel′ing·ness,** *n.*

**un·feigned** (un fānd′) sincere; real; unaffected; genuine. *adj.*

**un·feign·ed·ly** (un fā′ni dlē) really; sincerely. *adv.*

**un·fet·ter** (un fet′ər) remove fetters from; unchain. *v.*

**un·fin·ished** (un fin′isht) **1** not finished; not complete: *unfinished homework.* **2** without some special finish; not polished; rough; not painted: *unfinished furniture.* *adj.*

**un·fit** (un fit′) **1** not fit; not suitable. **2** not good enough; unqualified. **3** not adapted. **4** make unfit; spoil. 1–3 *adj.*, 4 *v.*, **un·fit·ted, un·fit·ting.** —**un·fit′ness,** *n.*

**un·fix** (un fiks′) loosen; detach; unfasten. *v.*

---

*In each of the words below* **un-** *means* not; *the pronunciation of the main part of each word is not changed.*

| | | | | |
|---|---|---|---|---|
| un′en·closed′ | un′en·ter·pris′ing | un′ex·cit′ing | un′ex·pur·gat′ed | un′fenced′ |
| un′en·cour′aged | un′en·ter·tain′ing | un′ex·cused′ | un′ex·tend′ed | un′fer·ment′ed |
| un′en·cum′bered | un′en·thu′si·as′tic | un′ex·e·cut′ed | un′ex·tin′guished | un′fer′ti·lized′ |
| un′en·dan′gered | un′en·vi′a·ble | un′ex·haust′ed | un·fa′ded | un′fet′tered |
| un·end′ing | un·en′vied | un′ex·pand′ed | un·fa′ding | un·filed′ |
| un′en·dorsed′ | un·en′vi·ous | un′ex·pect′ed | un·fair′ | un·fil′i·al |
| un′en·dur′a·ble | un′e·qualled | un′ex·pend′ed | un·fash′ion·a·ble | un·filled′ |
| un·en·dur′ing | un′e·quipped′ | un′ex·pired′ | un·fas′tened | un·fil′tered |
| un′en·force′a·ble | un·er′ring | un′ex·plain′a·ble | un·fa′vour·a·ble | un·fired′ |
| un′en·forced′ | un′es·ti·mat′ed | un′ex·plained′ | un·fazed′ | un·fit′ting |
| un′en·gaged′ | un·eth′i·cal | un′ex·plod′ed | un·fea′si·ble | un·fixed′ |
| un′en·joy′a·ble | un′ex·ag′ger·at′ed | un′ex·ploit′ed | un·feath′ered | un·flag′ging |
| un′en·larged′ | un′ex·am′ined | un′ex·plored′ | un·fed′ | un·flat′ter·ing |
| un′en·light′ened | un′ex·celled′ | un′ex·posed′ | un·fed′er·at′ed | un·fla′voured |
| un′en·riched′ | un′ex·change′a·ble | un′ex·pressed′ | un·felt′ | |
| un′en·rolled′ | un′ex·cit′ed | un′ex·pres′sive | un·fem′i·nine | |

**un·fledged** (un flejd′) 1 of a bird, too young to fly; not having full-grown feathers. 2 undeveloped; immature. *adj.*

**un·flinch·ing** (un flin′ching) not drawing back from difficulty, danger, or pain; firm; resolute: *unflinching courage. adj.* —**un·flinch′ing·ly**, *adv.*

**un·fold** (un fōld′) 1 open the folds of; spread out: *to unfold a serviette, to unfold your arms.* 2 reveal; show; explain: *The story unfolded.* 3 open; develop: *Buds unfold into flowers. v.*

**un·forced** (un fôrst′) 1 not forced; not compelled; willing. 2 natural; spontaneous. *adj.*

**un·fore·seen** (un′fôr sēn′) not known beforehand; unexpected: *They had to change their plans because of an unforeseen crisis. adj.*

**un·formed** (un fôrmd′) 1 shapeless. 2 undeveloped. *adj.*

**un·for·tu·nate** (un fôr′chə nit) 1 not lucky; having bad luck. 2 not suitable; not fitting: *The child's outburst of temper was an unfortunate thing for the guest to see.* 3 an unfortunate person. *1, 2 adj., 3 n.* —**un·for′tu·nate·ly**, *adv.* —**un·for′tu·nate·ness**, *n.*

**un·found·ed** (un foun′did) without foundation; baseless: *an unfounded complaint. adj.*

**un·fre·quent·ed** (un′fri kwen′tid) not frequented; seldom visited; rarely used. *adj.*

**un·friend·ly** (un fren′dlē) 1 not friendly; hostile: *an unfriendly dog.* 2 not favourable: *unfriendly weather. adj.* —**un·friend′li·ness**, *n.*

**un·frock** (un frok′) 1 take away a frock from. 2 deprive a priest or minister of his or her rank, position, and privileges. *v.*

**un·fruit·ful** (un früt′fəl) not fruitful; barren; not productive. *adj.*

**un·furl** (un fėrl′) spread out; shake out; unfold: *to unfurl a sail. The flag unfurled. v.*

**un·gain·ly** (un gān′lē) awkward; clumsy: *The boy's long arms and large hands give him an ungainly appearance. adj.* —**un·gain′li·ness**, *n.*

**un·god·li·ness** (un god′lē nis) a lack of godliness; wickedness; sinfulness. *n.*

**un·god·ly** (un god′lē) 1 not religious. 2 wicked; sinful. 3 *Informal.* very annoying; shocking: *an ungodly noise, pay an ungodly price. adj.*

**un·gov·ern·a·ble** (un guv′ər nə bəl) impossible to control; very hard to control or rule; unruly: *an ungovernable temper. adj.* —**un·gov′ern·a·ble·ness**, *n.* —**un·gov′ern·a·bly**, *adv.*

**un·gra·cious** (un grā′shəs) 1 not polite; rude. 2 unpleasant; disagreeable: *With his tousled hair and dirty face, the man had an ungracious appearance. adj.* —**un·gra′cious·ly**, *adv.* —**un·gra′cious·ness**, *n.*

**un·grate·ful** (un grāt′fəl) 1 not grateful; not thankful. 2 unpleasant; disagreeable. *adj.* —**un·grate′ful·ly**, *adv.* —**un·grate′ful·ness**, *n.*

**un·ground·ed** (un groun′did) without foundation; without reasons. *adj.*

**un·grudg·ing** (un gruj′ing) willing; hearty; liberal. *adj.* —**un·grudg′ing·ly**, *adv.*

**un·gual** (ung′gwəl) of, having to do with, bearing, or shaped like a nail, claw, or hoof. *adj.*

**un·guard·ed** (un gär′did) 1 not protected: *an unguarded camp.* 2 careless: *In an unguarded moment, she gave away the secret. adj.* —**un·guard′ed·ly**, *adv.* —**un·guard′ed·ness**, *n.*

**un·guent** (ung′gwənt) an ointment for sores, burns, etc.; salve. *n.*

**un·gu·late** (ung′gyə lit *or* ung′gyə lāt) 1 having hoofs; belonging to the group of animals having hoofs. 2 an animal that has hoofs: *Horses, cows, sheep, and deer are ungulates.* 1 *adj.*, 2 *n.*

**un·hal·lowed** (un hal′ōd) 1 not made holy; not sacred. 2 wicked. *adj.*

**un·hand** (un hand′) let go of; take the hands from. *v.*

**un·hand·y** (un han′dē) 1 not easy to handle. 2 not skilful. *adj.* —**un·hand′i·ly**, *adv.* —**un·hand′i·ness**, *n.*

**un·hap·py** (un hap′ē) 1 sad; sorrowful. 2 unlucky. 3 not suitable. *adj.*, **un·hap·pi·er**, **un·hap·pi·est**. —**un·hap′pi·ly**, *adv.* —**un·hap′pi·ness**, *n.*

**un·har·ness** (un här′nis) 1 remove the harness from; free from harness or gear: *to unharness a horse.* 2 remove harness or gear. 3 divest of armour: *The knight unharnessed. v.*

**un·health·i·ness** (un hel′thē nis) 1 a lack of health; sickness. 2 a condition causing disease or harmful to health. *n.*

**un·health·y** (un hel′thē) 1 not possessing good health; not well: *an unhealthy child.* 2 characteristic of or resulting from poor health: *an unhealthy paleness.* 3 harmful to health; unwholesome: *an unhealthy climate.* 4 morally harmful. *adj.*

**un·heard** (un hėrd′) 1 not perceived by the ear: *unheard melodies.* 2 not given a hearing: *to condemn a person unheard. adj.*

---

In each of the words below **un-** means *not*; the pronunciation of the main part of each word is not changed.

| | | | | |
|---|---|---|---|---|
| un′fore·see′a·ble | un·free′ | un·gen′er·ous | un·grad′ed | un·har′assed |
| un·for′est·ed | un·fre′quent | un′gen·teel′ | un·gram·mat′i·cal | un·hard′ened |
| un·for·get′ta·ble | un·friend′ed | un·gen′tle | un·grat′i·fied | un·harmed′ |
| un·for·get′ting | un·froz′en | un·gen′tle·man·ly | un·guar·an·teed′ | un·har·mo′ni·ous |
| un′for·giv′a·ble | un·ful·filled′ | un·gift′ed | un·hack′neyed | un·har′nessed |
| un·for·giv′en | un·fur′nished | un·glam′or·ous | un·ham′pered | un·hatched′ |
| un·for·giv′ing | un·gained′ | un·glazed′ | un·hand′i·capped′ | un·healed′ |
| un·for′mu·lat′ed | un·gal′lant | un·gloved′ | un·hand′led | |
| un·for′ti·fied′ | un·gar′nished | un·gov′erned | un·hand′some | |
| un·framed′ | un·gath′ered | un·grace′ful | un·hanged′ | |

**un·heard–of** (un hėr′duv′ *or* un hėr′dov′) **1** never heard of; unknown: *Electric light was unheard-of 200 years ago.* **2** not known before; unprecedented: *A price of $7 a dozen for eggs is unheard-of.* *adj.*

**un·heed·ed** (un hē′did) not heeded; disregarded; unnoticed: *Her advice went unheeded.* *adj.*

**un·hes·i·tat·ing** (un hez′ə tā′ting) ready; prompt; immediate: *His unhesitating acceptance of the job surprised us all, for the work looked difficult.* *adj.* —**un·hes′i·tat′ing·ly**, *adv.*

**un·hinge** (un hinj′) **1** take a door, etc. off its hinges. **2** remove the hinges from. **3** separate from something; detach. **4** unsettle; disorganize; upset: *Trouble has unhinged this poor woman's mind.* *v.*, **un·hinged**, **un·hing·ing**.

**un·hitch** (un hich′) free from being hitched; unfasten: *Unhitch the team.* *v.*

**un·ho·ly** (un hō′lē) **1** not holy; wicked; sinful. **2** *Informal.* outrageous or dreadful: *They were raising an unholy row.* *adj.*, **un·ho·li·er**, **un·ho·li·est**. —**un·ho′li·ness**, *n.*

**un·hook** (un huk′) **1** loosen from a hook. **2** undo by loosening a hook or hooks. **3** become loosed from hooks; become undone. *v.*

**un·horse** (un hôrs′) **1** pull or knock from a horse's back; cause to fall from a horse: *The knight was unhorsed by the sharp thrust of his opponent's lance.* **2** dislodge; overthrow. *v.*, **un·horsed**, **un·hors·ing**.

**un·hy·gien·ic** (un′hī jē′nik *or* un′hī jen′ik) not healthful; unsanitary. *adj.*

**uni–** combining form. one: *unilateral, unicellular.*

**u·ni·cam·er·al** (yü′nə kam′ə rəl) having only one house in a lawmaking body: *All Canadian provinces have unicameral legislatures.* *adj.*

**UNICEF** (yü′ni sef′) United Nations Children's Fund (originally, United Nations International Children's Emergency Fund). *n.*

**u·ni·cel·lu·lar** (yü′nə sel′yə lər) having one cell only: *The amoeba is a unicellular animal.* *adj.*

An ancient Roman idea of a unicorn. It was thought to have the body of a horse, the head of a stag, the feet of an elephant, and the tail of a boar.

**u·ni·corn** (yü′nə kôrn′) a legendary animal like a horse, but having a single long horn in the middle of its forehead. *n.*

☛ *Etym.* Through OF *unicorne* from L *unicornus* 'one-horned', made up of *unus* 'one' + *cornu* 'horn'.

**u·ni·cy·cle** (yü′nə sī′kəl) a vehicle with a single wheel and a saddle, propelled by pedals: *Unicycles are ridden mostly by acrobats and entertainers.* *n.*

**un·i·den·ti·fied flying object** (un′ī den′tə fīd′) an object in the sky that cannot be identified as a known aircraft from earth or explained as any natural phenomenon. *Abbrev.:* UFO

**u·ni·fi·ca·tion** (yü′nə fə kā′shən) **1** a formation into one unit; union: *the unification of many states into one nation.* **2** making or being made more alike: *The traffic laws of the different provinces need unification.* *n.*

**u·ni·flo·rous** (yü′nə flô′rəs) having or bearing one flower only. *adj.*

**u·ni·form** (yü′nə fôrm′) **1** always the same; not changing: *The earth rotates at a uniform rate.* **2** all alike; not varying: *All the bricks have a uniform size.* **3** regular; even: *a uniform pace.* **4** the distinctive clothes worn by the members of a group, by which they may be recognized as belonging to that group: *Soldiers, police officers, and nurses wear uniforms.* **5** clothe or furnish with a uniform. 1–3 *adj.*, 4 *n.*, 5 *v.* —**u′ni·form′ness**, *n.*

**u·ni·form·i·ty** (yü′nə fôr′mə tē) a uniform condition or character; sameness throughout. *n., pl.* **u·ni·form·i·ties.**

**u·ni·form·ly** (yü′nə fôrm′lē) always; regularly; without variation. *adv.*

**u·ni·fy** (yü′nə fī′) make or form into one; unite. *v.*, **u·ni·fied**, **u·ni·fy·ing**. —**u′ni·fi′er**, *n.*

**u·ni·lat·er·al** (yü′nə lat′ə rəl) **1** of, on, or affecting one side only. **2** having all the parts arranged on one side of an axis; turned to one side; one-sided. **3** concerned with or considering only one side of a matter. **4** of a contract, etc., affecting one party or person only; done by one side only; putting obligation on one party only: *unilateral disarmament.* *adj.* —**un′i·lat′er·al·ly**, *adv.*

**un·i·mag·i·na·tive** (un′i maj′ə nə tiv) **1** showing little or no imagination. **2** not able to imagine well. *adj.*

**un·im·por·tance** (un′im pôr′təns) an unimportant nature or quality. *n.*

---

*In each of the words below* **un-** *means* not; *the pronunciation of the main part of each word is not changed.*

| | | | | |
|---|---|---|---|---|
| un·heed′ful | un·hoped′-for′ | un′il·lu′mi·nat′ed | un′im·pressed′ | un′in·flect′ed |
| un·heed′ing | un·housed′ | un′i·mag′i·na·ble | un′im·press′i·ble | un′in·flu′enced |
| un·help′ful | un·hur′ried | un′im·paired′ | un′im·press′ion·a·ble | un′in·form′a·tive |
| un·her′ald·ed | un·hur′ry·ing | un′im·pas′sioned | un′im·press′ive | un′in·formed′ |
| un·her·o′ic | un·hurt′ | un′im·peach′a·ble | un′im·proved′ | |
| un·hes′i·tant | un·hurt′ful | un′im·ped′ed | un′in·cor′po·rat′ed | |
| un·hin′dered | un·i·den′ti·fied′ | un′im·port′ant | un′in·cum′bered | |
| un·hon′oured | un·id′i·o·mat′ic | un′im·pos′ing | un′in·fect′ed | |

**un·in·hab·it·ed** (un′in hab′ə tid) not lived in; without inhabitants: *an uninhabited wilderness. adj.*

**un·in·spired** (un in spīrd′) 1 not inspired. 2 dull; tiresome. *adj.*

**un·in·ter·est·ed** (un in′tri stəd *or* un in′tə res′tid) not interested; showing no interest. *adj.*
☛ *Usage.* See note at INTERESTED.

**un·ion** (yü′nyən) 1 a uniting or being united: *The United States was formed by the union of thirteen former colonies of the United Kingdom.* 2 something formed by combining two or more members or parts: *The ten provinces of Canada form a union.* 3 a group of workers joined together to protect and promote their interests; LABOUR UNION; trade union. 4 marriage. 5 any of various devices for connecting parts of machinery or apparatus, especially a piece to join pipes or tubes together. *n.*

**un·ion·ism** (yü′nyə niz′əm) 1 the principle of union. 2 an attachment to a union. 3 the system, principles, or methods of LABOUR UNIONS. *n.*

**un·ion·ist** (yü′nyə nist) 1 one who promotes or advocates union. 2 a member of a LABOUR UNION. 3 Unionist, **a** a person who was in favour of union among the provinces of British North America, especially of Upper and Lower Canada. **b** a supporter of the federal government of the United States during the Civil War. **c** up to 1922, a person who opposed the political separation of Ireland from Great Britain. **d** since 1920, a member or supporter of the Unionist Party in Northern Ireland which opposes the political separation of Northern Ireland from Great Britain. *n.*

**un·ion·i·za·tion** (yü′nyə nə zā′shən *or* yü′nyə nī zā′shən) unionizing or being unionized. *n.*

**un·ion·ize** (yü′nyə nīz′) 1 form into a LABOUR UNION. 2 organize under a LABOUR UNION. 3 join in a LABOUR UNION. *v.,* **un·ion·ized, un·ion·iz·ing.**

The Union Jack

**Union Jack** the red, white, and blue flag of the United Kingdom, formed by combining the crosses of St. George, St. Andrew, and St. Patrick, for England, Scotland, and Ireland.

**union shop** a factory or business firm that by agreement hires only employees who are, or will become, members of a labour union.

**union station** a station used jointly by two or more railways.

**u·nique** (yü nēk′) 1 having no like or equal; being the only one of its kind: *She discovered a unique specimen of rock in the cave.* 2 *Informal.* rare; unusual: *His style of singing is rather unique. adj.* —**u·nique′ly,** *adv.* —**u·nique′ness,** *n.*
☛ *Usage.* In formal English **unique** means 'being one of a kind', and so it cannot be compared or qualified; something is either unique or not. In informal English **unique** is sometimes used with **more** or **most** and more often with a qualifier like **quite, rather,** or **really**: *Her clothes are rather unique.* This usage should be avoided in careful speech and writing.

**u·ni·son** (yü′nə sən) 1 a doing together as one, at the same time, etc.: *The feet of marching soldiers move in unison.* 2 an agreement in pitch of two or more tones. 3 performing together by voices, instruments, etc. of the same melody, etc. at the same pitch or an octave apart. 4 agreement: *There was unison among the club members on the question of increasing fees. n.*

**u·nit** (yü′nit) 1 a single thing or person. 2 any group of things or persons considered as one. 3 one of the individuals or groups of which a whole is composed: *The body consists of units called cells.* 4 a standard quantity or amount, used as a basis for measuring: *A metre is a unit of length; a minute is a unit of time.* 5 the smallest whole number; 1. 6 regiment: *My father and my uncle served in the same unit.* 7 in schools, a section of a course usually on one theme or topic: *Our reader is divided into eight units. n.*

**u·ni·tar·y** (yü′nə ter′ē) 1 of or having to do with a unit or units. 2 having to do with unity. 3 like that of a unit; used as a unit. *adj.*

**u·nite** (yü nīt′) 1 join together; make one; combine: *Bricks united by mortar make a strong wall.* 2 bring together; amalgamate or consolidate into one body; join in action, interest, opinion, feeling, etc.: *Several firms united to form one company.* 3 become one; join in action, etc. *v.,* **u·nit·ed, un·it·ing.** —**u·nit′er,** *n.*

**u·nit·ed** (yü nī′tid) 1 joined together to make one. 2 joined together. 3 pt. and pp. of UNITE. 1, 2 *adj.,* 3 *v.*

**United Church of Canada** *Cdn.* a Christian church formed by the union of former Methodist, Presbyterian, and other churches.

**United Empire Loyalist** one of the persons who came to Canada during and after the American Revolution of 1776: *The United Empire Loyalists left the United States because they preferred to remain British subjects.*

**United Kingdom** GREAT BRITAIN and Northern Ireland.

**United Nations** 1 a world-wide organization devoted to establishing world peace and promoting economic and social welfare: *The United Nations charter was put into effect on October 24, 1945.* See OLIVE BRANCH for

---

*In each of the words below* **un-** *means* not; *the pronunciation of the main part of each word is not changed.*

| un′in·ha′bit·a·ble | un′in·spect′ed | un′in·sured′ | un′in·ter·est′ing | un′in·vest′ed |
| un′in·hab′i·ted | un′in·spir′ing | un′in·te·grat′ed | un′in·ter·mit′tent | un′in·vit′ed |
| un′in·hib′i·ted | un′in·struct′ed | un′in·tel′i·gent | un′in·ter·rupt′ed | un′in·volved′ |
| un·in′i·ti·at′ed | un′in·struct′ive | un′in·tend′ed | un′in·tim′i·dat′ed | un·is′sued |
| un′in·quir′ing | un′in·su·lat′ed | un′in·ten′tion·al | un′in·ven′tive | |

picture. **2** the nations that belong to this organization: *Canada is one of the United Nations.*

**unit fraction** a common fraction in which the numerator is 1. *Examples:* ⅛, ¹⁄₁₀₀.

**u·ni·ty** (yü′nə tē) **1** oneness; being united: *A circle has more unity than a row of dots.* **2** a union of parts forming a complex whole. **3** harmony: *Brothers and sisters should live together in unity.* **4** the number one (1). **5** an arrangement and choice of material to give a single effect, main idea, etc.: *A pleasing picture has unity; so has a well-written composition.* **6 the unities,** *pl.* In Greek drama, the rules of action, time, and place that used to require a play to have one plot occurring on one day in one place. *n., pl.* **u·ni·ties.**

**univ.** or **Univ.** university.

**u·ni·valve** (yü′nə valv′) **1** an animal having a shell made of one piece: *Snails are univalves; clams are bivalves.* **2** its shell. **3** having a shell made of one piece. 1, 2 *n.*, 3 *adj.*

**u·ni·ver·sal** (yü′nə vėr′səl) **1** of all; belonging to all; concerning all; done by all: *Food, fire, and shelter are universal needs.* **2** existing everywhere: *The law of gravity is universal.* **3** covering a whole group of persons, things, cases, etc.; general. **4** a proposition that asserts or denies something of every member of a class. *Example: All men are mortal.* **5** adaptable to different sizes, angles, kinds of work, etc.: *a universal joint.* 1–3, 5 *adj.*, 4 *n.* —**u·ni·ver′sal·ly,** *adv.*

**u·ni·ver·sal·i·ty** (yü′nə vėr sal′ə tē) the fact or condition of being UNIVERSAL. *n., pl.* **u·ni·ver·sal·i·ties.**

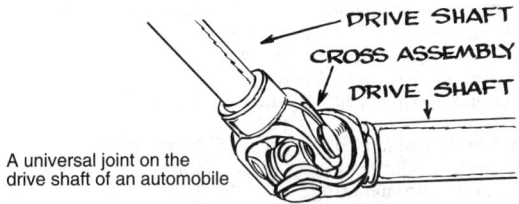

A universal joint on the drive shaft of an automobile

**universal joint** **1** a joint that moves in any direction. **2** a coupling for transmitting power from one shaft to another when they are not in line.

**Universal Product Code** a bar code printed on consumer products, indicating product classification, price, etc., that be read by an electronic scanner.

**u·ni·verse** (yü′nə vėrs′) all things; everything there is: *Our world is but a small part of the universe.* *n.*

**u·ni·ver·si·ty** (yü′nə vėr′sə tē) **1** an educational institution attended after secondary school for studies leading to a degree: *Universities offer advanced courses in general subjects such as literature, history, and science, and also often have schools of law, medicine, business, etc.* **2** a

**unit fraction**     **1311**     **unlikeness**

hat, āge, fär; let, ēqual, tėrm; it, īce
hot, ōpen, ôrder; oil, out; cup, pùt, rüle
əbove, takən, pencəl, lemən, circəs
ch, child; ng, long; sh, ship
th, thin; ᴛʜ, then; zh, measure

building or buildings used by a university. *n., pl.* **u·ni·ver·si·ties.**

**un·just** (un just′) not just; not fair: *It is unjust to punish lawbreakers who are insane.* *adj.* —**un·just′ly,** *adv.* —**un·just′ness,** *n.*

**un·kempt** (un kempt′) **1** not combed. **2** neglected; untidy. *adj.*

**un·kind·ly** (un kīn′dlē) **1** harsh; unfavourable. **2** in an unkind way; harshly. 1 *adj.*, 2 *adv.*

**un·known** (un nōn′) **1** not known; not familiar; strange; unexplored: *an unknown country, an unknown number.* **2** a person or thing that is unknown: *The diver descended into the unknown. The main actor in this movie is an unknown.* 1 *adj.*, 2 *n.*

**un·lace** (un lās′) undo the laces of. *v.*, **un·laced, un·lac·ing.**

**un·latch** (un lach′) unfasten or open by lifting a latch. *v.*

**un·law·ful** (un lof′əl) **1** contrary to the law; against the law; forbidden; illegal. **2** ILLEGITIMATE. *adj.* —**un·law′ful·ly,** *adv.* —**un·law′ful·ness,** *n.*

**un·learn** (un lėrn′) get rid of ideas, habits, or tendencies; forget. *v.*

**un·learn·ed** (un lėr′nid for 1, 3, un lėrnd′ for 2, 4) **1** not educated; ignorant: *The man was unlearned and could not write his name.* **2** not learned; known without being learned: *A baby's ability to suck is unlearned.* **3** not showing education. **4** pt. and pp. of UNLEARN. 1–3 *adj.*, 4 *v.*

**un·leash** (un lēsh′) **1** release from a leash: *to unleash a dog.* **2** let loose: *to unleash one's temper.* *v.*

**un·less** (un les′) if it were not that; if not: *We shall go unless it rains.* *conj.*

**un·let·tered** (un let′ərd) **1** not educated. **2** not able to read or write. *adj.*

**un·like** (un līk′) **1** not like; different: *The two problems are quite unlike.* **2** different from: *to act unlike others.* 1 *adj.*, 2 *prep.*

**un·like·li·hood** (un lī′klē hùd′) improbability. *n.*

**un·like·ly** (un lī′klē) **1** not likely; not probable: *She is unlikely to win the race.* **2** not likely to succeed: *an unlikely undertaking.* *adj.* —**un·like′li·ness,** *n.*

**un·like·ness** (un līk′nis) being unlike; difference. *n.*

*In each of the words below* **un-** *means not; the pronunciation of the main part of each word is not changed.*

| un·just′i·fi·a·ble | un·know′a·ble | un·lad′en | un·la·ment′ed | un·li′censed |
| un·kept′ | un·know′ing | un·la·dy-like | un·laun′dered | un·light′ed |
| un·kind′ | un·la′belled | un·laid′ | un·leav′ened | un·lik′a·ble |
| un·knight′ly | | | | |

**un·lim·ber**[1] (un lim′bər) make or become supple: *The pianist unlimbered her fingers.* *v.*

**un·lim·ber**[2] (un lim′bər) 1 detach the limber or forepart of the carriage from an artillery piece. 2 prepare for action. *v.*

**un·lim·it·ed** (un lim′ə tid) 1 without limits; boundless: *The girl seems to have unlimited energy.* 2 not restrained; not restricted: *a government of unlimited power.* *adj.* —un·lim′it·ed·ness, *n.*

**un·load** (un lōd′) 1 remove a load: *We unloaded as soon as we got home.* 2 take the load from: *Please help us unload the car.* 3 get rid of: *She began to unload her troubles onto her mother.* 4 remove powder, shot, bullets, or shells from a gun. 5 discharge a cargo: *The ship is unloading.* *v.* —un·load′er, *n.*

**un·lock** (un lok′) 1 open the lock of; open anything firmly closed. 2 disclose; reveal. 3 become unlocked. *v.*

**un·looked–for** (un lukt′fôr′) unexpected; unforeseen. *adj.*

**un·loose** (un lüs′) let loose; set free; release. *v.*, un·loosed, un·loos·ing.

**un·loos·en** (un lü′sən) unloose; loosen. *v.*

**un·luck·y** (un luk′ē) 1 not lucky; unfortunate. 2 bringing or thought to bring bad luck: *The number 13 is considered unlucky by some people.* *adj.* —un·luck′i·ly, *adv.* —un·luck′i·ness, *n.*

**un·make** (un māk′) undo; destroy; ruin. *v.*, un·made, un·mak·ing.

**un·man** (un man′) 1 deprive of the qualities of a man. 2 weaken or break down the spirit of. 3 deprive of men: *to unman a ship.* *v.*, un·manned, un·man·ning.

**un·man·ner·ly** (un man′ər lē) 1 having bad manners; discourteous. 2 with bad manners; rudely. 1 *adj.*, 2 *adv.* —un·man′ner·li·ness, *n.*

**un·mar·ried** (un mar′ēd *or* un mer′ēd) not married; single. *adj.*

**un·mask** (un mask′) 1 remove a mask or disguise: *The guests unmasked at midnight.* 2 take off a mask or disguise from: *The police caught the burglar and unmasked him.* 3 expose the true character of: *to unmask a hypocrite.* 4 reveal the presence of guns, etc. by firing: *to unmask a battery.* *v.*

**un·mean·ing** (un mē′ning) 1 without meaning. 2 without sense; without expression: *an unmeaning stare.* *adj.* —un·mean′ing·ly, *adv.*

**un·meas·ured** (un mezh′ərd) 1 not measured; unlimited; measureless. 2 unrestrained; intemperate. *adj.*

**un·meet** (un mēt′) not fit; not proper; unsuitable. *adj.*

**un·mer·ci·ful** (un mėr′si fəl) 1 having or showing no mercy; cruel. 2 excessive: *He kept us waiting an unmerciful length of time.* *adj.* —un·mer′ci·ful·ly, *adv.* —un·mer′ci·ful·ness, *n.*

**un·mind·ful** (un mīnd′fəl) regardless; heedless; careless: *She went ahead despite our warning and unmindful of the results.* *adj.* —un·mind′ful·ly, *adv.*

**un·mit·i·gat·ed** (un mit′ə gā′tid) 1 not softened or lessened: *unmitigated harshness.* 2 unqualified or absolute: *an unmitigated fraud.* *adj.*

**un·mor·al** (un mô′rəl) neither moral nor immoral; not perceiving or involving right and wrong. *adj.* —un·mor′al·ly, *adv.*

**un·moved** (un müvd′) 1 not moved; firm. 2 not disturbed; indifferent: *He was unmoved by the scenes of horror.* *adj.*

**un·muz·zle** (un muz′əl) 1 take off a muzzle from a dog, etc. 2 free from restraint; allow to speak or write freely. *v.*, un·muz·zled, un·muz·zling.

**un·nat·u·ral** (un nach′ə rəl *or* un nach′rəl) 1 not natural; artificial. 2 not normal; strange: *Unnatural cruelty is frequent in horror movies.* 3 artificial or affected: *an unnatural laugh.* *adj.* —un·nat′u·ral·ly, *adv.* —un·nat′u·ral·ness, *n.*

**un·nerve** (un nėrv′) deprive of firmness or self-control: *The sight of so much blood unnerved him.* *v.*, un·nerved, un·nerv·ing.

**un·no·ticed** (un nō′tist) 1 not observed. 2 not receiving any attention. *adj.*

**un·num·bered** (un num′bərd) 1 not numbered; not counted: *The pages of this composition have been left unnumbered.* 2 too many to count: *There are unnumbered fish in the ocean.* *adj.*

---

*In each of the words below* **un-** *means* not; *the pronunciation of the main part of each word is not changed.*

| | | | | |
|---|---|---|---|---|
| un·lined′ | un·man′age·a·ble | un·meant′ | un′mis·tak′en | un·nam′a·ble |
| un·liq′ue·fied′ | un·man′ly | un·meas′ur·a·ble | un′mixed′ | un·named′ |
| un·liq′ui·dat′ed | un·man′nered | un′me·chan′i·cal | un′mod′i·fied′ | un·nat′u·ral·ized′ |
| un·lit′ | un′man·u·fac′tured | un′me·lo′di·ous | un′mod′u·lat′ed | un·nav′i·ga·ble |
| un·lit′tered | un·mapped′ | un·melt′ed | un′mo·lest′ed | un·nec′es·sar′y |
| un·lov′a·ble | un·marked′ | un·men′tion·a·ble | un·mo′ti·vat′ed | un·need′ed |
| un·loved′ | un·mar′ket·a·ble | un·men′tioned | un·mount′ed | un·need′ful |
| un·love′ly | un·marred′ | un·mer′it·ed | un·mourned′ | un·ne·go′ti·a·ble |
| un·lov′ing | un·mar′riage·a·ble | un′meth·od′i·cal | un·mov′a·ble | un·neigh′bour·ly |
| un·mag′ni·fied′ | un·mas′tered | un·mil′i·tar′y | un·mov′ing | un·neigh′bor·ly |
| un·maid′en·ly | un·match′a·ble | un·milled′ | un·mown′ | un·not′ed |
| un·mailed′ | un·matched′ | un·min′gled | un·mu′si·cal | un·note′wor′thy |
| un·mal′le·a·ble | un·mat′ed | un·mirth′ful | un·muz′zled | un·no′tice·a·ble |

**UNO** or **U.N.O.** United Nations Organization.

**un·ob·tru·sive** (un′əb trü′siv)   modest; inconspicuous. *adj.*

**un·oc·cu·pied** (un ok′yə pīd′)   **1** not occupied; vacant: *The driver pulled her car into the one unoccupied parking space.* **2** not in action or use; idle: *an unoccupied mind.* *adj.*

**un·of·fend·ing** (un′ə fen′ding)   inoffensive; harmless; innocent. *adj.*

**un·or·gan·ized** (un ôr′gə nīzd′)   **1** not formed into an organized or systematized whole. **2** not organized into LABOUR UNIONS. **3** not being a living organism: *An enzyme is an unorganized ferment.* *adj.*

**un·pack** (un pak′)   **1** take out things packed in a box, trunk, etc. **2** take things out of. **3** take out things packed. *v.*

**un·pal·at·a·ble** (un pal′ə tə bəl)   not agreeable to the taste; distasteful; unpleasant: *unpalatable food, unpalatable remarks.* *adj.* —**un·pal′at·a·ble·ness**, *n.*

**un·par·al·leled** (un par′ə leld′ *or* un per′ə leld′)   having no parallel; unequalled; matchless. *adj.*

**un·peo·ple** (un pē′pəl)   deprive of people. *v.*, **un·peo·pled, un·peo·pling.**

**un·pin** (un pin′)   take out a pin or pins from; unfasten. *v.*, **un·pinned, un·pin·ning.**

**un·pleas·ant·ness** (un plez′ənt nis)   **1** an unpleasant quality. **2** something unpleasant. **3** a quarrel. *n.*

**un·plumbed** (un plumd′)   **1** not fathomed; not measured; of unknown depth. **2** having no plumbing. *adj.*

**un·pop·u·lar·i·ty** (un′pop yə lar′ə tē *or* un′pop yə ler′ə tē)   a lack of popularity; the state of being unpopular. *n.*

**un·prac·tised** or **un·prac·ticed** (un prak′tist)   **1** not skilled; not expert. **2** not put into practice; not used. *adj.*

**UNO**  **1313**  **unqualified**

hat, āge, fär; let, ēqual, tėrm; it, īce
hot, ōpen, ôrder; oil, out; cup, pút, rüle
above, takən, pencəl, lemən, circəs
ch, child; ng, long; sh, ship
th, thin; ᵺ, then; zh, measure

**un·prec·e·dent·ed** (un pres′ə den′tid *or* un prē′sə den′tid)   having no precedent; never done before; never known before: *An unprecedented event took place in 1961, when a human being travelled in outer space.* *adj.*

**un·prej·u·diced** (un prej′ə dist)   **1** without prejudice; impartial. **2** not weakened. *adj.*

**un·pre·pared** (un′pri perd′)   **1** not made ready; not worked out ahead: *an unprepared speech.* **2** not ready: *a person unprepared to answer.* *adj.*

**un·pre·par·ed·ness** (un′pri per′id nis *or* un′pri perd′nis)   **1** being unprepared. **2** a lack of preparation. *n.*

**un·pre·tend·ing** (un′pri ten′ding)   unassuming; modest. *adj.* —**un′pre·tend′ing·ly**, *adv.*

**un·pre·ten·tious** (un′pri ten′shəs)   MODEST. *adj.* —**un′pre·ten′tious·ly**, *adv.* —**un′pre·ten′tious·ness**, *n.*

**un·prin·ci·pled** (un prin′sə pəld)   lacking good moral principles; bad. *adj.*

**un·print·a·ble** (un prin′tə bəl)   not fit to be printed. *adj.*

**un·pro·fes·sion·al** (un′prə fesh′ə nəl)   **1** contrary to professional etiquette; unbecoming in members of a profession. **2** not having to do with or connected with a profession. **3** not belonging to a profession. *adj.* —**un′pro·fes′sion·al·ly**, *adv.*

**un·qual·i·fied** (un kwol′ə fīd′)   **1** not qualified; not fitted. **2** not modified, limited, or restricted in any way: *unqualified praise.* **3** complete; absolute: *an unqualified failure.* *adj.*

---

*In each of the words below* **un-** *means* not; *the pronunciation of the main part of each word is not changed.*

| | | | | |
|---|---|---|---|---|
| un′o·beyed′ | un·par′doned | un·planned′ | un·prac′ti·cal | un′pro·nounce′a·ble |
| un′ob·jec′tion·a·ble | un′par·lia·men′ta·ry | un·plant′ed | un·praised′ | un′pro·nounced′ |
| un′o·blig′ing | un·par·ti′tioned | un·play′a·ble | un′pre·dict′a·ble | un′pro·pi′tious |
| un′ob·scured′ | un′pas·teur·ized′ | un·played′ | un′pre·med′i·tat′ed | un′pro·por′tioned |
| un′ob·serv′a·ble | un′pa·tri·ot′ic | un·pleas′ant | un′pre·pos·sess′ing | un·pros′per·ous |
| un′ob·serv′ing | un·paved′ | un·pleased′ | un′pre·scribed′ | un′pro·tect′ed |
| un′ob·struct′ed | un·peace′a·ble | un·pleas′ing | un′pre·sent′a·ble | un′pro·test′ed |
| un′ob·tain′a·ble | un′per·ceived′ | un·pledged′ | un·pressed′ | un′pro·test′ing |
| un′oc·ca′sioned | un′per·ceiv′ing | un·ploughed′ | un·pret′ty | un·prov′en |
| un′of·fend′ing | un′per·cep′tive | un·plowed′ | un′pre·vail′ing | un′pro·vid′ed |
| un·of′fered | un′per·formed′ | un·po′et·ic | un′pre·vent′a·ble | un′pro·voked′ |
| un·of·fi′cial | un′per·plexed′ | un′po·et′i·cal | un·print′ed | un′pro·vok′ing |
| un·oiled′ | un′per·suad′ed | un·point′ed | un·priv′i·leged | un·pruned′ |
| un·o′pened | un′per·sua′sive | un·poised′ | un·prized′ | un′pub·li·cized′ |
| un′or·dained′ | un′per·used′ | un′po·lar·ized′ | un′pro·cessed′ | un·punc′tu·al |
| un·or′dered | un·phil′o·soph′ic | un′po·liced′ | un′pro·cur′a·ble | un·pun′ished |
| un′o·rig′in·al | un′phil·o·soph′i·cal | un·pol′ished | un′pro·duc′tive | un·pur′chas·a·ble |
| un′or·tho·dox′ | un·pho·net′ic | un·po·lit′i·cal | un′pro·faned′ | un·pur′posed |
| un′os·ten·ta′tious | un·picked′ | un·polled′ | un·prof′it·a·ble | un·pur′su·ing |
| un·owned′ | un·pierced′ | un·pol·lut′ed | un′pro·gres′sive | un·quail′ing |
| un·paid′ | un·pit′ied | un·pop′u·lar | un′pro·hib′ited | un·qual′i·fy·ing |
| un·paint′ed | un·pit′y·ing | un·pop′u·lat′ed | un′pro·ject′ed | |
| un·paired′ | un·placed′ | un·posed′ | un·prom′is·ing | |
| un·par′don·a·ble | un·plagued′ | un·post′ed | un·prompt′ed | |

**un·quench·a·ble** (un kwench′ə bəl) that cannot be extinguished. *adj.*

**un·ques·tion·a·ble** (un kwes′chə nə bəl) beyond dispute or doubt; certain: *It is an unquestionable advantage to know several languages. adj.*
—**un·ques′tion·a·bly,** *adv.*

**un·quote** (un kwōt′) end a quotation. Used only in the expression "Quote (i.e. begin a quotation), unquote (i.e. end the quotation)." *v.*

**un·rav·el** (un rav′əl) **1** separate the threads of: *The kitten unravelled my knitting.* **2** come apart; ravel: *My knitted gloves are unravelling at the wrist.* **3** bring or come out of a tangled state; clear up: *to unravel a mystery. v.,* **un·rav·elled** or **un·rav·eled, un·rav·el·ling** or **un·rav·el·ing.**

**un·read** (un red′) **1** not read: *an unread book.* **2** not having read much: *an unread person. adj.*

**un·read·y** (un red′ē) **1** not ready; not prepared. **2** not prompt or quick. *adj.* —**un·read′i·ly,** *adv.* —**un·read′i·ness,** *n.*

**un·re·al** (un rē′əl) imaginary; not real; not substantial; fanciful. *adj.* —**un·re′al·ly,** *adv.*

**un·re·al·i·ty** (un′rē al′ə tē) **1** a lack of reality; imaginary or fanciful quality. **2** something unreal: *Unrealities, such as elves and goblins, are fun to imagine. n., pl.* **un·re·al·i·ties.**

**un·rea·son·a·ble** (un rē′zə nə bəl) **1** not reasonable; not sensible: *The little boy was very timid and had an unreasonable fear of the dark.* **2** not moderate; excessive: *$200 is an unreasonable price for that pair of shoes. adj.* —**un·rea′son·a·ble·ness,** *n.*

**un·rea·son·a·bly** (un rē′zə nə blē) **1** in a way that is not reasonable; contrary to reason; foolishly. **2** extremely; immoderately: *unreasonably angry. adv.*

**un·rea·son·ing** (un rē′zə ning) not reasoning; not using reason; reasonless. *adj.*
—**un·rea′son·ing·ly,** *adv.*

**un·re·flect·ing** (un′ri flek′ting) unthinking; thoughtless. *adj.* —**un′re·flect′ing·ly,** *adv.*

**un·re·gard·ed** (un′ri gär′did) disregarded; not heeded. *adj.*

**un·re·gen·er·ate** (un′ri jen′ə rit) **1** not born again spiritually; not turned to the love of God. **2** wicked; bad. *adj.* —**un′re·gen′er·ate·ness,** *n.*

**un·re·lent·ing** (un′ri len′ting) **1** not yielding to feelings of kindness or compassion; merciless. **2** not slackening or relaxing in severity or determination. *adj.* —**un′re·lent′ing·ly,** *adv.* —**un′re·lent′ing·ness,** *n.*

**un·re·li·a·bil·i·ty** (un′ri lī′ə bil′ə tē) a lack of reliability. *n.*

**un·re·mit·ting** (un′ri mit′ing) never stopping; not slackening; maintained steadily: *unremitting vigilance. adj.* —**un′re·mit′ting·ly,** *adv.*

**un·re·served** (un′ri zėrvd′) **1** frank; open. **2** not restricted; without reservation. *adj.*

**un·re·serv·ed·ly** (un′ri zėr′vi dlē) **1** frankly; openly. **2** without reservation or restriction. *adv.*

**un·rest** (un rest′) **1** a lack of ease and quiet; restlessness. **2** an agitation or disturbance amounting almost to rebellion. *n.*

**un·re·strained** (un′ri strānd′) not held back; not checked: *unrestrained laughter, unrestrained freedom. adj.*

**un·re·straint** (un′ri strānt′) a lack of restraint. *n.*

**un·right·eous** (un rī′chəs) wicked; sinful; unjust. *adj.* —**un·right′eous·ly,** *adv.* —**un·right′eous·ness,** *n.*

**un·ri·valled** or **un·ri·valed** (un rī′vəld) having no rival; without an equal. *adj.*

**un·roll** (un rōl′) **1** open or spread out something rolled. **2** become opened or spread out. **3** reveal; display: *She soon unrolled the story of the burglary.* **4** become revealed or displayed: *As the story unrolled, everyone became interested. v.*

**un·ruf·fled** (un ruf′əld) **1** not ruffled; smooth. **2** not disturbed; calm. *adj.*

**un·ruled** (un rüld′) **1** not kept under control; not governed. **2** not marked with lines: *unruled paper. adj.*

**un·ru·ly** (un rü′lē) hard to rule or control: *an unruly horse, a disobedient and unruly child, an unruly section of the country. adj.* —**un·ru′li·ness,** *n.*

---

*In each of the words below* **un-** *means* not; *the pronunciation of the main part of each word is not changed.*

| | | | | |
|---|---|---|---|---|
| un·quenched′ | un′re·claimed′ | un′re·mem′bered | un′rep·re·sent′ed | un′re·turn′a·ble |
| un·ques′tioned | un′rec·og·niz′a·ble | un′re·mit′ted | un′re·pressed′ | un′re·turned′ |
| un·ques′tion·ing | un′rec·og·nized′ | un′re·mov′a·ble | un′re·proached′ | un′re·vealed′ |
| un·qui′et | un′rec·om·pensed′ | un′re·moved′ | un′re·proved′ | un′re·venged′ |
| un·quot′able | un′rec·on·cil′a·ble | un′re·mu′ner·at′ed | un′re·quit′ed | un′re·voked′ |
| un·raised′ | un′rec·on·ciled′ | un′re·mu′ner·a·tive | un′re·signed′ | un′re·ward′ing |
| un·ran′somed | un′re·cord′ed | un′re·nowned′ | un′re·sist′ant | un·rhymed′ |
| un·rat′ed | un′reg′is·tered | un′re·rent′ed | un′re·sist′ed | un·rhyth′mi·cal |
| un·rat′i·fied′ | un′reg′u·lat′ed | un′re·paid′ | un′re·sist′ing | un·ri′fled |
| un·read′a·ble | un′re·laxed′ | un′re·paired′ | un′re·solved′ | un·right′ful |
| un·re′al·is′tic | un′re·lax′ing | un′re·pealed′ | un′re·spon′sive | un·rimed′ |
| un·re′al·ized′ | un′re·li′a·ble | un′re·pent′ant | un′re·strict′ed | un·ripe′ |
| un·rea′soned | un′re·lieved′ | un′re·pent′ing | un′re·ten′tive | un·rip′ened |
| un′re·buked′ | un′re·mark′a·ble | un′re·port′ed | un′re·tract′ed | un·ro·man′tic |
| un′re·ceived′ | un′re·rem′e·died | un′rep·re·sent′a·tive | un′re·trieved′ | |

**un·sad·dle** (un sad′əl) **1** take the saddle off a horse. **2** cause to fall from a horse. *v.*, **un·sad·dled, un·sad·dling.**

**un·san·i·tar·y** (un san′ə ter′ē) unhealthful. *adj.* —**un·san′i·tar′i·ness,** *n.*

**un·sa·vour·y** or **un·sa·vor·y** (un sā′və rē) **1** tasteless. **2** unpleasant in taste or smell. **3** morally unpleasant; offensive: *That man has an unsavoury reputation. adj.* —**un·sa′vour·i·ly** or **un·sa′vor·i·ly,** *adv.* —**un·sa′vour·i·ness** or **un·sa′vor·i·ness,** *n.*

**un·say** (un sā′) take back or cancel something said: *What is said cannot be unsaid. v.*, **unsaid, un·say·ing.**

**un·scathed** (un skāᴛʜd′) not harmed; uninjured. *adj.*

**un·schooled** (un sküld′) not schooled; not taught; not disciplined. *adj.*

**un·sci·en·tif·ic** (un′sī ən tif′ik) **1** not in accordance with the facts or principles of science: *an unscientific notion.* **2** not acting in accordance with such facts or principles: *an unscientific farmer. adj.* —**un′sci·en·tif′i·cal·ly,** *adv.*

**un·scram·ble** (un skram′bəl) reduce from confusion to order; bring out of a scrambled condition. *v.*, **un·scram·bled, un·scram·bling.**

**un·screw** (un skrü′) **1** take out the screw or screws from. **2** loosen or take off by turning; untwist: *to unscrew an electric light bulb. v.*

**un·scru·pu·lous** (un skrü′pyə ləs) not careful about right or wrong; without principles or conscience: *The unscrupulous girls cheated on the test. adj.* —**un·scru′pu·lous·ly,** *adv.* —**un·scru′pu·lous·ness,** *n.*

**un·seal** (un sēl′) **1** break or remove the seal of: *to unseal a letter.* **2** open: *The threat unsealed her lips. v.*

**un·search·a·ble** (un sėr′chə bəl) not to be searched into; that cannot be understood by searching; mysterious. *adj.*

**un·sea·son·a·ble** (un sē′zə nə bəl) **1** not suitable to the season. **2** coming at the wrong time. *adj.* —**un·sea′son·a·bly,** *adv.* —**un·sea′son·a·ble·ness,** *n.*

**un·seat** (un sēt′) **1** displace from a seat: *The bronco unseated everyone who tried to ride it.* **2** remove from office: *Our previous MP was unseated in the last election. v.*

**unsaddle**     **1315**     **unsnarl**

hat, āge, fär; let, ēqual, tėrm; it, īce
hot, ōpen, ôrder; oil, out; cup, pùt, rüle
əbove, takən, pencəl, lemən, circəs
ch, child; ng, long; sh, ship
th, thin; ᴛʜ, then; zh, measure

**un·seem·ly** (un sēm′lē) **1** not suitable; improper: *His unseemly laughter annoyed the rest of the audience.* **2** improperly; unsuitably. **1** *adj.*, **2** *adv.* —**un·seem′li·ness,** *n.*

**un·seen** (un sēn′) **1** not seen: *an unseen error.* **2** not visible: *an unseen spirit. adj.*

**un·set·tle** (un set′əl) make or become unstable; disturb; shake; weaken: *The shock unsettled her mind. v.*, **un·set·tled, un·set·tling.**

**un·set·tled** (un set′əld) **1** disordered; not in proper condition or order: *Our house is still unsettled after our move.* **2** not fixed or stable. **3** liable to change; uncertain: *The weather is unsettled.* **4** not adjusted or disposed of: *an unsettled estate, an unsettled bill.* **5** not determined or decided: *an unsettled question.* **6** not inhabited: *Large parts of Canada are still unsettled. adj.*

**un·sex** (un seks′) deprive of the attributes of one's sex, especially to deprive of womanly character. *v.*

**un·shack·le** (un shak′əl) remove shackles from; set free. *v.*, **un·shack·led, un·shack·ling.**

**un·shak·en** (un shā′kən) not shaken; firm: *Virginia still had an unshaken belief in Santa Claus. adj.*

**un·sheathe** (un shēᴛʜ′) draw a sword, knife, etc. from a sheath. *v.*, **un·sheathed, un·sheath·ing.**

**un·sight·ly** (un sīt′lē) ugly or unpleasant to look at: *Her cluttered room was an unsightly mess. adj.* —**un·sight′li·ness,** *n.*

**un·skil·ful** or **un·skill·ful** (un skil′fəl) awkward; clumsy. *adj.* —**un·skil′ful·ly** or **un·skill′ful·ly,** *adv.* —**un·skil′ful·ness** or **un·skill′ful·ness,** *n.*

**un·skilled** (un skild′) **1** not skilled; not trained: *Unskilled workers usually earn less than skilled workers.* **2** not requiring special skills or training: *unskilled labour. adj.*

**un·snap** (un snap′) unfasten the snap or snaps of. *v.*, **un·snapped, un·snap·ping.**

**un·snarl** (un snärl′) remove the snarls from; untangle. *v.*

---

*In each of the words below* **un-** *means* not; *the pronunciation of the main part of each word is not changed.*

| | | | | |
|---|---|---|---|---|
| un·safe′ | un·scaled′ | un·sea′wor′thy | un·served′ | un·shield′ed |
| un·said′ | un·scared′ | un·sec′ond·ed | un·serv′ice·a·ble | un·shod′ |
| un·saint′ly | un·scarred′ | un·se′cured′ | un·set′ | un·shorn′ |
| un·sal′a·ble | un·scent′ed | un·seed′ed | un·shad′ed | un·shrink′a·ble |
| un·sal′a·ried | un·sched′uled | un·see′ing | un·shad′owed | un·shrink′ing |
| un·sale′a·ble | un·schol′ar·ly | un·seg′ment·ed | un·shak′a·ble | un·sift′ed |
| un·salt′ed | un·scorched′ | un·seg′re·gat′ed | un·shaped′ | un·sight′ed |
| un·sanc′ti·fied′ | un·scoured′ | un·seized′ | un·shape′ly | un·signed′ |
| un·sanc′tioned | un·scraped′ | un·se·lect′ed | un·shared′ | un·sing′a·ble |
| un·sat′ed | un·scratched′ | un·se·lect′ive | un·sharp′ened | un·sink′a·ble |
| un·sa′ti·at·ed | un·screened′ | un·self-con′scious | un·shaved′ | un·sis′ter·ly |
| un·sat′is·fac·to·ry | un·scrip′tur·al | un·self′ish | un·shav′en | un·sized′ |
| un·sat′is·fied′ | un·sculp′tured | un·sen′si·tive | un·shed′ | un·slacked′ |
| un·sat′is·fy′ing | un·sealed′ | un·sen·ti·ment′al | un·shelled′ | un·slaked′ |
| un·sat′u·rat·ed | un·sea′soned | un·sep′a·rat·ed | un·shel′tered | un·sliced′ |

**un·so·cia·bil·i·ty** (un′sō shə bil′ə tē)   an unsociable nature or behaviour; lack of friendliness. *n.*

**un·sought** (un sot′)   not sought; not looked for; not asked for. *adj.*

**un·sound** (un sound′)   **1** not in good condition; not sound: *A diseased mind or body is unsound. Unsound walls are not firm. An unsound business is not reliable.*   **2** not based on truth or fact: *an unsound doctrine, theory, etc.*   **3** not restful; disturbed: *an unsound sleep.*   *adj.*   —**un·sound′ly**, *adv.*   —**un·sound′ness**, *n.*

**un·spar·ing** (un sper′ing)   **1** very generous; liberal.   **2** not merciful; severe. *adj.*   —**un·spar′ing·ly**, *adv.*   —**un·spar′ing·ness**, *n.*

**un·speak·a·ble** (un spē′kə bəl)   **1** that cannot be expressed in words: *unspeakable joy, an unspeakable loss.*   **2** extremely bad; so bad that it can hardly be spoken of: *That was an unspeakable thing to do!* *adj.*   —**un·speak′a·bly**, *adv.*

**un·spot·ted** (un spot′id)   without spot or stain; pure. *adj.*

**un·sta·ble** (un stā′bəl)   **1** not firmly fixed; easily moved, shaken, or overthrown.   **2** not constant; variable.   **3** in chemistry, easily decomposed; readily changing into other compounds.   **4** not normal: *emotionally unstable.* *adj.*   —**un·sta′ble·ness**, *n.*   —**un·sta′bly**, *adv.*

**unstable element**   a radio-active element that eventually changes into a radio-active isotope.

**un·stained** (un stānd′)   without stain or spot. *adj.*

**un·stead·y** (un sted′ē)   **1** not steady; shaky: *an unsteady voice, an unsteady flame.*   **2** likely to change; not reliable: *unsteady winds.*   **3** not regular in habits. *adj.*   —**un·stead′i·ly**, *adv.*   —**un·stead′i·ness**, *n.*

**un·strap** (un strap′)   loosen the strap of a trunk, box, etc. *v.*, **un·strapped, un·strap·ping.**

**un·string** (un string′)   **1** take off or loosen the string or strings of.   **2** take from a string.   **3** weaken the nerves of; make nervous. *v.*, **unstrung, un·string·ing.**

**un·strung** (un strung′)   **1** upset; emotionally disturbed.   **2** pt. and pp. of UNSTRING.   **1** *adj.*, **2** *v.*

**un·stud·ied** (un stud′ēd)   not studied; not planned ahead; natural. *adj.*

**un·sub·stan·tial** (un′səb stan′shəl)   not substantial; flimsy; slight; unreal. *adj.*   —**un′sub·stan′tial·ly**, *adv.*

**un·suit·a·bil·i·ty** (un sü′tə bil′ə tē)   the fact or state of being unsuitable. *n.*

**un·sul·lied** (un sul′ēd)   without spot or stain; pure: *an unsullied reputation.* *adj.*

**un·sung** (un sung′)   **1** not sung.   **2** not honoured in song or poetry; unpraised. *adj.*

**un·sus·pect·ed** (un′sə spek′tid)   **1** not suspected: *He had already committed several burglaries but was still unsuspected.*   **2** not thought of: *an unsuspected danger.* *adj.*

**un·tan·gle** (un tang′gəl)   **1** take the tangles out of; disentangle.   **2** straighten out or clear up anything confused or perplexing. *v.*, **un·tan·gled, un·tan·gling.**

**un·taught** (un tot′)   **1** not taught; not educated.   **2** known without being taught; learned naturally. *adj.*

**un·thank·ful** (un thangk′fəl)   **1** ungrateful.   **2** not appreciated; thankless. *adj.*   —**un·thank′ful·ly**, *adv.*   —**un·thank′ful·ness**, *n.*

**un·think·a·ble** (un thing′kə bəl)   that can hardly be imagined: *It is unthinkable that she could be a thief.* *adj.*

**un·think·ing** (un thing′king)   thoughtless; heedless; careless: *An unthinking comment can sometimes cause a lot of trouble.* *adj.*   —**un·think′ing·ly**, *adv.*

---

*In each of the words below* **un-** *means* not; *the pronunciation of the main part of each word is not changed.*

| | | | | |
|---|---|---|---|---|
| un·so′cia·ble | un·spent′ | un·strat′i·fied′ | un·swayed′ | un·tar′nished |
| un·so′cial | un·spiced′ | un·stressed′ | un·sweet′ened | un·tast′ed |
| un·soil′ed | un·spir′i·tu·al | un·sub·dued′ | un·swept′ | un·tax′a·ble |
| un·sold′ | un·split′ | un′sub·mis′sive | un·swerv′ing | un·teach′a·ble |
| un·sol′dier·ly | un·spoiled′ | un·sub·stan′ti·at·ed | un·sworn′ | un·tech′ni·cal |
| un·so·lic′i·ted | un·spoilt′ | un·sub′tle | un·sym·met′ri·cal | un·tem′pered |
| un·so·lic′i·tous | un·spok′en | un·suc·cess′ful | un·sym·pa·thet′ic | un·ten′a·ble |
| un·sol′id | un·sports′man·like′ | un·suf′fer·a·ble | un·sym′pa·thiz′ing | un·ten′ant·ed |
| un·solv′able | un·stain′a·ble | un·suit′a·ble | un·sys′tem·at′ic | un·tend′ed |
| un·solved′ | un·stamped′ | un·suit′ed | un·sys′tem·a·tized′ | un·ter′ri·fied |
| un·so·phis′ti·cat·ed | un·stand′ard·ized′ | un·sup·port′a·ble | un·tab′u·lat·ed | un·test′ed |
| un·sort′ed | un·stat′ed | un·sup·port′ed | un·tact′ful | un·thanked′ |
| un·sound′ed | un·states′man·like′ | un·sup·pressed′ | un·taint′ed | un·thatched′ |
| un·soured′ | un·ster′i·lized′ | un·sure′ | un·ta′ken | un·thawed′ |
| un·sowed′ | un·stig′ma·tized′ | un·sur·mount′a·ble | un·tal′ent·ed | un·the·at′ri·cal |
| un·sown′ | un·stint′ed | un·sur·passed′ | un·tam′a·ble | un·thought′ |
| un·spec′ial·ized′ | un·stint′ing | un·sus·pect′ing | un·tamed′ | un·thought′ful |
| un·spe·cif′ic | un·stitched′ | un·sus·pi′cious | un·tanned′ | |
| un·spec′i·fied | un·stopped′ | un·sus·tained′ | un·tapped′ | |
| un·spec·tac′u·lar | un·strained′ | | | |

**un·thought–of** (un thot′uv′ or un thot′ov′) not imagined or considered. *adj.*

**un·thread** (un thred′) **1** take the thread out of. **2** unravel. **3** find one's way through. *v.*

**un·tie** (un tī′) **1** loosen; unfasten; undo: *to untie a knot.* **2** make free; release: *She untied her horse.* **3** make clear. *v.*, **un·tied, un·ty·ing.**

**un·til** (un til′) **1** up to the time of: *It was cold from January until April.* **2** up to the time when: *She waited until the sun had set.* **3** before: *She did not leave until morning* (prep.). *He did not come until the meeting was half over* (conj.). **4** to the point or stage that: *Elam worked until he was too tired to do more.* 1, 3 prep., 2–4 conj.

**un·time·ly** (un tīm′lē) **1** at a wrong time or season: *Snow in May is untimely.* **2** too early; too soon: *his untimely death.* 1, 2 adj., adv. —**un·time′li·ness,** *n.*

**un·tir·ing** (un tī′ring) tireless; unwearying: *an untiring runner. adj.* —**un·tir′ing·ly,** *adv.*

**un·told** (un tōld′) **1** not told; not revealed: *an untold secret.* **2** too many to be counted; countless: *There are untold stars in the sky.* **3** not counted; immense: *untold wealth. adj.*

**un·touch·a·ble** (un tuch′ə bəl) **1** that cannot be touched; out of reach. **2** that must not be touched. **3** in India, formerly a person of the lowest CASTE, whose touch supposedly defiled members of higher castes. 1, 2 *adj.,* 3 *n.*

**un·touched** (un tucht′) **1** not touched: *The cat left the milk untouched.* **2** not emotionally moved: *The miser was untouched by the poor man's story. adj.*

**un·to·ward** (un′tə wôrd′ or un tôrd′) **1** unfavourable; unfortunate: *an untoward wind, an untoward accident.* **2** perverse; stubborn; willful. *adj.* —**un·toward′ly,** *adv.* —**un·toward′ness,** *n.*

**un·tram·melled** or **un·tram·meled** (un tram′əld) not hindered; not restrained; free. *adj.*

**un·true** (un trü′) **1** false; incorrect. **2** not faithful. **3** not true to a standard or rule. *adj.*

**un·truth** (un trüth′) **1** a lack of truth; falsity. **2** a lie; falsehood. *n.*

**un·tu·tored** (un tyü′tərd *or* un tü′tərd) untaught. *adj.*

**un·twist** (un twist′) **1** undo or loosen something twisted; unravel. **2** become untwisted. *v.*

**un·used** (un yüzd′) **1** not in use; not being used: *an unused room.* **2** never having been used: *We'll keep the unused paper cups for our next picnic. adj.*

**un·used to** (un yüst′tü *or* un yüzd′tü) not accustomed to: *The actor's hands were unused to manual labour.*

**un·ut·ter·a·ble** (un ut′ə rə bəl) that cannot be expressed; unspeakable. *adj.* —**un·ut′ter·a·bly,** *adv.*

**un·var·nished** (un vär′nisht) **1** not varnished. **2** plain; unadorned: *the unvarnished truth. adj.*

**un·var·y·ing** (un ver′ē ing) steady; constant; not changing. *adj.*

**un·veil** (un vāl′) **1** remove a veil from; disclose; reveal: *The statue was unveiled the day the graduating class presented it to the school.* **2** take off one's veil; reveal onself: *The princess unveiled. v.*

**un·war·rant·a·ble** (un wôr′ən tə bəl) not justifiable; illegal; improper. *adj.* —**un·war′rant·a·bly,** *adv.*

**un·war·y** (un wer′ē) not cautious; not careful; unguarded. *adj.* —**un·war′i·ly,** *adv.* —**un·war′i·ness,** *n.*

**un·wea·ried** (un wē′rēd) **1** not weary; not tired. **2** never growing weary. *adj.*

**un·wept** (un wept′) **1** not wept for; not mourned. **2** not shed: *unwept tears. adj.*

**un·wield·y** (un wēl′dē) not easily handled or managed, because of size, shape, or weight; bulky and clumsy: *the unwieldy armour of knights, an unwieldy bundle. adj.* —**un·wield′i·ness,** *n.*

**un·will·ing** (un wil′ing) not willing; not consenting. *adj.* —**un·will′ing·ly,** *adv.* —**un·will′ing·ness,** *n.*

**un·wind** (un wīnd′) **1** wind off; take from a spool, ball, etc. **2** become unwound. **3** disentangle. **4** *Informal.* relax: *I need an hour to unwind when I come home from a meeting. v.,* **un·wound, un·wind·ing.**

**un·wise** (un wīz′) not wise; not showing good judgment; foolish: *It is unwise to delay going to the doctor if you are sick. adj.* —**un·wise′ly,** *adv.*

---

In each of the words below **un-** means *not; the pronunciation of the main part of each word is not changed.*

| | | | | |
|---|---|---|---|---|
| un·thrift′y | un·trav′eled | un·twist′ed | un·wak′ened | un·wed′ded |
| un·ti′dy | un·trav′ers·a·ble | un·typ′i·cal | un·walled′ | un·weed′ed |
| un·tilled′ | un·trav′ersed | un·us′a·ble | un·want′ed | un·wel′come |
| un·tired′ | un·treat′ed | un·vac′ci·nat·ed | un·war′like′ | un·well′ |
| un·torn′ | un·tried′ | un·val′ued | un·war′rant·ed | un·wel′ded |
| un·trace′a·ble | un·trimmed′ | un·van′quished | un·washed′ | un·whole′some |
| un·traced′ | un·trod′ | un·var′ied | un·wast′ed | un·wife′like′ |
| un·tracked′ | un·trod′den | un·veiled′ | un·watched′ | un·wife′ly |
| un·tract′a·ble | un·trou′bled | un·ven′ti·lat·ed | un·wa′tered | un·willed′ |
| un·trained′ | un·trust′wor·thy | un·ver′i·fi′a·ble | un·wa′ver·ing | un·wink′ing |
| un′trans·fer′a·ble | un·truth′ful | un·ver′i·fied′ | un·weaned′ | un·wished′ |
| un′trans·lat′a·ble | un·tuft′ed | un·versed′ | un·wear′a·ble | un·wit′nessed |
| un′trans·lat′ed | un·tun′a·ble | un·vexed′ | un·wea′ry·ing | |
| un′trans·mit′ted | un·tuned′ | un·vis′it·ed | un·weath′ered | |
| un·trav′elled | un·turned′ | un·voiced′ | un·wed′ | |

**un·wit·ting** (un wit′ing) not knowing; unaware; unconscious; unintentional. *adj.* —**un·wit′ting·ly,** *adv.*

**un·wont·ed** (un wōn′tid) **1** not customary; not usual. **2** not accustomed; not used. *adj.* —**un·wont′ed·ly,** *adv.* —**un·wont′ed·ness,** *n.*

**un·world·ly** (un wėrl′dlē) not caring much for the things of this world, such as money, pleasure, and power. *adj.* —**un·world′li·ness,** *n.*

**un·wor·thi·ly** (un wėr′ᴛHə lē) **1** in a way that is not worthy or honourable; shamefully. **2** not according to one's merits. *adv.*

**un·wor·thy** (un wėr′ᴛHē) **1** not worthy; not deserving: *Such a silly story is unworthy of belief.* **2** base; shameful: *unworthy conduct.* *adj.* —**un·wor′thi·ness,** *n.*

**un·wound** (un wound′) pt. and pp. of UNWIND. *v.*

**un·wrap** (un rap′) **1** remove a wrapping from; open. **2** become opened. *v.,* **un·wrapped, un·wrap·ping.**

**un·writ·ten** (un rit′ən) **1** not written. **2** understood or customary, but not actually expressed in writing. **3** not written on; blank. *adj.*

**unwritten law** law that is based on custom or on decisions of previous judges, rather than on a written command, decree, statute, etc.; common law.

**un·yoke** (un yōk′) **1** free from a yoke; separate; disconnect. **2** remove a yoke. *v.,* **un·yoked, un·yok·ing.**

**up** (up) **1** from a lower to a higher place or condition; to, toward, or near the top: *The bird flew up.* **2** in a higher place or condition; on or at a higher level: *She stayed up in the mountains several days.* **3** to or at a higher place on or in something: *The cat ran up the tree.* **4** to, toward, or near the top of: *They climbed up the hill.* **5** from a smaller to a larger amount: *Prices have gone up.* **6** along; through: *She walked up the street.* **7** toward or in the inner or upper part of: *We sailed up the river.* **8** to or at any point, place, or condition that is considered higher: *He lives up north.* **9** moving upward; directed upward: *an up trend.* **10** *Informal.* a period of good luck, prosperity or happiness: *Her life is full of ups and downs.* **11** above the horizon: *The sun is up.* **12** in or into an erect position: *Stand up.* **13** above the ground: *The wheat is up.* **14** out of bed: *Please get up or you will be late* (*adv.*). *The children were up at dawn* (*adj.*). **15** thoroughly; completely; entirely: *The paper burned up in a few minutes. My eraser is almost used up.* **16** at an end; over: *Your time is up now.* **17** in or into being or action: *Don't stir up trouble.* **18** together: *Add these numbers up.* **19** to or in an even position; not behind: *to catch up in a race. Keep up with the times.* **20** in or into view, notice, or consideration: *to bring up a new topic.* **21** in or into a state of tightness, etc.: *Shut him up in his cage.* **22** into safekeeping, storage, etc.; aside; by: *to store up supplies. Squirrels lay up nuts for the winter.* **23** at bat in baseball. **24** ahead of an opponent by a certain number: *We are three games up.* **25** in tennis, etc., apiece; for each one. **26** *Informal.* put, lift, or get up. **27** *Informal.* increase: *They upped the price of eggs.* 1, 2, 5, 8, 11–23, 25 *adv.,* 3, 4, 6, 7 *prep.,* 9, 11, 13, 14, 23, 24 *adj.,* 10 *n.,* 26, 27 *v.,* **upped, up·ping.**

**up against,** facing as a thing to be dealt with.
**up against it,** *Informal.* in difficulties.
**up and about,** active; occupied as usual, especially after an illness.
**up and doing,** busy; active.
**up on,** *Informal.* well informed about: *The engineer is up on the newest methods.*
**up to, a** doing; about to do: *She is up to some mischief.* **b** equal to; capable of doing: *Do you feel up to going out so soon after being sick?* **c** plotting; scheming: *What are you up to?* **d** *Informal.* before a person as a duty or task to be done: *It's up to the judge to decide.*

**up–and–down** (up′ən doun′) variable: *an up-and-down existence.* *adj.*

**up·braid** (up brād′) find fault with; blame; reprove: *The captain upbraided his men for falling asleep.* *v.*

**up·braid·ing** (up brā′ding) **1** a severe reproof; scolding. **2** ppr. of UPBRAID. 1 *n.,* 2 *v.*

**up·bring·ing** (up′bring′ing) the care and training given to a child while growing up; especially, a particular way of training or educating a child: *a very casual upbringing, a Buddhist upbringing.* *n.*

**UPC** UNIVERSAL PRODUCT CODE

**up·com·ing** (up′kum′ing) forthcoming; approaching: *the upcoming school year.* *adj.*

**up·date** (up′dāt′) bring up to date: *to update one's wardrobe. The files are updated once a month.* *v.,* **up·dat·ed, up·dat·ing.**

**up·draft** (up′draft′) an upward movement of gas, air, etc. *n.* Also, **updraught.**

**up·end** (up end′) set on end; stand on end: *If you upend the box, it will take up less space.* *v.*

**up·grade** (up′grād′ for noun, adjective, and adverb; up′grād′ or up′grād′ for verb) **1** an upward slope or incline. **2** uphill. **3** improve the grade, quality, or rank of: *to upgrade livestock by selective breeding.* **4** promote to a higher position with a higher salary: *The company has set up a training program to upgrade its secretaries.* 1 *n.,* 2 *adv., adj.,* 3, 4 *v.,* **up·grad·ed, up·grad·ing.**
**on the upgrade,** rising; improving.

**up·heav·al** (up hē′vəl) **1** the action or an instance of heaving up, especially of part of the earth's crust: *Geologists say that the Rocky Mountains were formed by an upheaval of the earth's crust.* **2** a sudden or violent agitation in affairs; social turmoil: *The sale of the family business caused a great upheaval.* *n.*

**up·heave** (up hēv′) **1** heave up; lift up. **2** rise. *v.,* **up·heaved** or **up·hove, up·heav·ing.**

**up·held** (up held′) pt. and pp. of UPHOLD. *v.*

**up·hill** (up′hil′ for adjective, up′hil′ for adverb) **1** up the slope of a hill; upward: *It is an uphill road all the way.* **2** upward: *We walked a kilometre uphill.* **3** difficult: *an uphill fight.* 1, 3 *adj.,* 2 *adv.*

**up·hold** (up hōld′) **1** give moral support to: *Their beliefs upheld them in difficulties.* **2** hold up; keep from

---

*In each of the words below* **un-** *means* not; *the pronunciation of the main part of each word is not changed.*

| un·wom′an·ly | un·work′a·ble | un·worn′ | un·wo′ven | un·wrought′ |
| un·won′ | un·worked′ | un·wor′ried | un·wrin′kled | un·yield′ing |
| un·wood′ed | un·work′man-like′ | un·wound′ed | | |

falling; not let down: *We uphold the good name of our school.*
**3** sustain; approve; confirm: *The higher court upheld the lower court's decision.* *v.*, **up·held, up·hold·ing.**
—**up·hold′er,** *n.*

**up·hol·ster** (up hōl′stər) provide furniture with cushions, springs, padding, etc. and a covering of cloth, leather, vinyl, etc. *v.*

**up·hol·ster·er** (up hōl′stə rər) a person whose business is upholstering furniture. *n.*

**up·hol·ster·y** (up hōl′stə rē *or* up hōl′strē) **1** the materials and fittings used in upholstering. **2** the business of upholstering. *n., pl.* **up·hol·ster·ies.**

**up·hove** (up hōv′) a pp. of UPHEAVE. *v.*

**up·keep** (up′kēp′) **1** maintaining or being maintained in good condition: *The upkeep of that big house and yard takes up a lot of their time.* **2** the cost of maintaining in good condition: *What's the upkeep on your car?* *n.*

**up·land** (up′lənd *or* up′land′) **1** high land. **2** of or found in high land: *an upland meadow, upland flowers.* **1** *n.*, **2** *adj.*

**upland plover** a North American sandpiper found in open, grassy uplands, having streaked, buff-coloured plumage, a long neck, and a small head with a straight, somewhat short bill.

**up·lift** (up lift′ *for verb*, up′lift′ *for noun*) **1** lift up; raise; elevate; especially, cause a part of the earth's crust to be raised. **2** the act, process, or result of lifting up: *A good bra can provide needed uplift.* **3** improve mentally, socially, or morally: *Hsiu had been greatly uplifted by her friends' cheerful optimism.* **4** mental, social, or moral improvement or a movement toward it: *Good music gives her an uplift when she is discouraged.* **1, 3** *v.*, **2, 4** *n.*
—**up·lift′er,** *n.*

**up·link** (up′lingk′) **1** the sending of communication from an earth station to a space station. **2** the earth station used to send such communication. *n.*

**up·most** (up′mōst′) UPPERMOST. *adj.*

**up·on** (ə pon′) on. *prep.*

**up·per** (up′ər) **1** higher: *the upper lip, the upper floor, the upper range of a singer's voice.* **2** higher in rank, office, etc.; superior: *the upper house of a parliament.* **3** of a river, farther from the sea or nearer the source: *He explored the upper reaches of the great Orinoco River.* **4** the part of a shoe or boot above the sole. **5** upper berth or bunk: *I had the upper, and my sister had the lower.* **6** an upper tooth or denture: *Her new uppers are much more comfortable than the old ones were.* **7 Upper,** in geology and archaeology, of or having to do with a recent or late division or part of a specified period, epoch, system, or formation: *Upper Cambrian.* **1–3, 7** *adj.*, **4–6** *n.*

**on one's uppers,** in financial difficulty; having very little or no money left: *He was obviously on his uppers but refused to accept charity.*

**Upper Canada** *Cdn.* **1** especially in the Maritimes, the province of Ontario. **2** the name of the present province of Ontario before 1841, when Upper and Lower Canada were united in the Province of Canada: *Upper Canada was further up the St. Lawrence than Lower Canada.*

**Upper Canadian** *Cdn.* especially in the Maritimes, Ontarian.

**upper case** capital letters. Compare with LOWER CASE.

hat, āge, fär; let, ēqual, tėrm; it, īce
hot, ōpen, ôrder; oil, out; cup, pùt, rüle
əbove, takən, pencəl, lemən, circəs
ch, child; ng, long; sh, ship
th, thin; ᴛʜ, then; zh, measure

☛ *Etym.* From the printers' practice of keeping the individual characters of sets of metal type in two trays or cases, the lower one for small letters and the upper one for capitals.

**up·per–case** (up′ər kās′) capital; in capital letters. *adj.*

**Upper Chamber** or **upper chamber** UPPER HOUSE.

**upper class** the social class that has the greatest prestige or power in a society, usually due to wealth, birth, or education.

**up·per–class** (up′ər klas′) **1** of, having to do with, or suitable for the upper class of society: *upper-class tastes.* **2** in universities, schools, etc., of or having to do with the senior classes. *adj.*

**up·per·class·man** (up′ər klas′mən) a senior student. *n., pl.* **up·per·class·men** (-mən).

**upper crust** *Informal.* the upper classes.

**up·per·cut** (up′ər kut′) **1** in boxing, a swinging blow directed upwards from beneath. **2** strike with an uppercut. **1** *n.*, **2** *v.*, **up·per·cut, up·per·cut·ting.**

**upper hand** a position of control; mastery or advantage: *During the first two periods, the visiting team had the upper hand.*

**Upper House** or **upper house** in a legislature having two branches, the branch that has the smaller number of members and is less representative. In some countries, the members of the Upper House are elected, as in the United States; in others they are appointed: *The Senate is the Upper House of the Canadian Parliament.*

**Upper Lakes** the most northerly of the Great Lakes; Lakes Superior and Huron and, sometimes, Lake Michigan.

**up·per·most** (up′ər mōst′) **1** highest; topmost: *The uppermost branches of the tree had the most fruit.* **2** having the most force or influence; most prominent. **3** in or into the highest place: *The watch lay with the back turned uppermost.* **4** in or into the first or most prominent position. **1, 2** *adj.*, **3, 4** *adv.*

**up·pi·ty** (up′ə tē) *Informal.* inclined to put on airs; arrogant or conceited. *adj.*

**up·raise** (up rāz′) raise or lift up. *v.*, **up·raised, up·rais·ing.**

**up·rate** (up rāt′) raise to a higher level of rank, speed, etc.; upgrade. *v.*, **up·rat·ed, up·rat·ing.**

**up·rear** (up rēr′) lift up; raise. *v.*

**up·right** (up′rīt′) **1** standing up straight; erect. **2** straight up; in a vertical position: *Hold yourself upright.* **3** vertical or upright position. **4** something standing erect; a vertical part or piece: *The boards for the fence were nailed across the uprights.* **5** UPRIGHT PIANO. **6** good; honest; righteous: *an upright citizen.* **1, 6** *adj.*, **2** *adv.*, **3–5** *n.* —**up′right′ly,** *adv.* —**up′right′ness,** *n.*

**upright piano** a piano with a vertical frame and strings. Compare with GRAND PIANO.

**up·rise** (up rīz′ *for verb,* up′rīz′ *for noun*) 1 rise up. 2 an upward rise. 3 slope upward. 4 increase in volume, amount, etc. 1, 3, 4 *v.,* **up·rose, up·ris·en, up·ris·ing;** 2 *n.*

**up·ris·en** (up riz′ən) pp. of UPRISE. *v.*

**up·ris·ing** (up′rī′zing) 1 a revolt; rebellion: *The revolution began with small uprisings in several towns.* 2 ppr. of UPRISE. 1 *n.*, 2 *v.*

**up·riv·er** (up′riv′ər) of, at, or to the upper part of a river. *adj., adv.*

**up·roar** (up′rôr′) 1 a noisy or violent disturbance; tumult; commotion: *We heard an uproar in the hall and went to see what it was. There was a great uproar when the theft was discovered.* 2 a loud or confused noise. *n.*

**up·roar·i·ous** (up rô′rē əs) 1 marked by UPROAR; noisy and confused: *an uproarious disturbance.* 2 loud and boisterous: *uproarious laughter, in uproarious good spirits.* 3 very funny: *an uproarious comedy, an uproarious scene. adj.* —**up·roar′i·ous·ly,** *adv.* —**up·roar′i·ous·ness,** *n.*

**up·root** (up rüt′) 1 tear up by the roots: *The storm uprooted two trees.* 2 force away from: *Famine uprooted many families from their homes in Ireland during the 1840's. v.*

**up·rose** (up rōz′) pt. of UPRISE. *v.*

**up·set** (up set′ *for verb,* up′set′ *for noun,* up′set′ *or* up set′ *for adjective*) 1 tip over; overturn: *to upset a boat.* 2 a tipping over; overturn. 3 tipped over; overturned. 4 disturb greatly; disorder: *Rain upset our plans for a picnic. The shock upset his nerves.* 5 a great disturbance; disorder. 6 greatly disturbed; disordered: *an upset stomach.* 7 overthrow; defeat: *to upset a will, to upset an argument. The young candidate upset the mayor in the election.* 8 a defeat: *The hockey team suffered an upset.* 1, 4, 7 *v.,* **up·set, up·set·ting;** 2, 5, 8 *n.,* 3, 6 *adj.* **upset price,** the lowest price at which a thing offered for sale will be sold.

**up·shot** (up′shot′) the end result; outcome: *The upshot of all the delays will probably be that we'll have to cancel the program. n.*

**up·side** (up′sīd′) the upper side. *n.*

**upside down** 1 having at the bottom what should be on top: *The slice of bread and butter fell upside down on the floor.* 2 in or into complete disorder: *The room was upside down. The children turned the house upside down.*

**up·side–down cake** (up′sīd doun′) a cake baked with a layer of fruit on the bottom and served upside down with the fruit on top.

**up·stage** (up′stāj′ *or* up′stāj′ *for adjective,* up′stāj′ *for adverb and verb*) 1 in a theatre, toward or at the back of the stage. 2 having to do with the back part of the stage. 3 in the theatre, force (another actor) to turn away from the audience by moving or staying upstage of him or her. 4 make oneself the centre of attention at the expense of; steal the show from: *She upstaged the hostess by welcoming everyone herself.* 5 haughty; snobbish: *I didn't like his upstage manner.* 1 *adv.,* 1, 2, 5 *adj.,* 3, 4 *v.*

**up·stairs** (up′sterz′ *for adverb,* up′sterz′ *for adjective and noun*) 1 up the stairs: *The girl ran upstairs.* 2 on or of an upper floor: *She lives upstairs* (*adv.*). *He is waiting in an upstairs hall* (*adj.*). 3 the upper storey or storeys

(used with a singular verb): *The upstairs of the house is very small.* 1, 2 *adv.,* 2 *adj.,* 3 *n.*
**kick a person upstairs,** get rid of a person by promoting him or her to a higher but ineffectual position.

**up·stand·ing** (up stan′ding) 1 having integrity; honourable: *a fine, upstanding young man.* 2 standing up; erect: *He had very short, upstanding hair. adj.*

**up·start** (up′stärt′) 1 a person who has suddenly risen from a humble position to wealth, power, or importance. 2 suddenly risen from a humble position to wealth, power, or importance. 3 an unpleasant, conceited, and self-assertive person. 4 conceited; self-assertive. 1, 3 *n.,* 2, 4 *adj.*

**up·stream** (up′strēm′ *for adverb,* up′strēm′ *for adjective*) in the direction opposite to the current of a stream: *It is hard to swim upstream. They stopped at an upstream camping site. adv., adj.*

**up·stroke** (up′strōk′) a stroke or movement in an upward direction: *the upstroke of a choir leader's baton. n.*

**up·surge** (up′sėrj′ *for noun,* up′sėrj′ *for verb*) 1 a sudden or rapid rise; a surge of growth, development, emotion, etc.: *an upsurge in prices, an upsurge of feeling.* 2 surge up; rise. 1 *n.,* 2 *v.,* **up·surged, up·surg·ing.**

**up·swing** (up′swing′) 1 a swing or movement upward. 2 a marked improvement; strong advance: *an upswing in business. n.*

**up·take** (up′tāk′) 1 the act or process of taking or drawing up. 2 a flue or ventilating shaft. *n.*
**quick (or slow) on the uptake,** quick (or slow) to understand: *He's a very nice fellow, but a little slow on the uptake.*

**up·thrust** (up′thrust′) 1 an upward push. 2 a movement upward of part of the earth's crust. *n.*

**up·tight** (up′tīt′ *for 1, 2,* up′tīt′ *for 3*) *Informal.* 1 angry and defensive: *Don't get uptight; she didn't mean anything by it.* 2 tense, worried, or anxious: *His mother gets uptight if he's late getting home.* 3 rigid and conformist in attitude; straitlaced: *an uptight approach to new ideas. adj.* —**up′tight′ness,** *n.*

**up–to–date** (up′tə dāt′ *or* up′tə dāt′) 1 extending to the present time; including the latest information: *an up-to-date record of sales, an up-to-date map of the city.* 2 keeping up with the times in style, ideas, or methods; modern: *an up-to-date dress shop. Ina is very up-to-date in her selling methods. adj.*

**up·town** (up′toun′ *for adverb,* up′toun′ *for adjective*) to or in a main part of a town or city that is higher, further north, or further from a lake, river, harbour, etc. than other parts: *to go uptown, an uptown store. adv., adj.*

**up·turn** (up tėrn′ *for verb,* up′tėrn′ *for noun*) 1 turn up or over. 2 any upward turn: *The airplane made a sudden upturn to avoid the mountain.* 3 an improvement: *As business improved, his income took an upturn.* 1 *v.,* 2, 3 *n.*

**up·turned** (up′tėrnd′) 1 turned upside down; overturned: *She set the upturned chair on its feet.* 2 turned upward: *a mustache with upturned ends. She kissed the child's upturned face.* 3 pt. and pp. of UPTURN. 1, 2 *adj.,* 3 *v.*

**up·ward** (up′wərd) 1 toward a higher place. 2 directed or moving toward or situated in a higher place: *an upward glance.* 3 toward a higher or greater rank, amount, age, etc.: *From public school upward she studied French.* 4 above; more: *Children of five years and upward*

must pay carfare.   **5** to or toward the source: *We traced the brook upward.*   1, 3–5 *adv.*, 2 *adj.*
**upwards of** or **upward of,**   more than: *Repairs to the car will cost upwards of $800.*

**up·ward·ly** (up′wər dlē)   in an upward manner or direction; upward.   *adv.*

**up·wards** (up′wərdz)   UPWARD (defs. 1, 3–5).   *adv.*

**up·well·ing** (up′wel′ing)   a current of warm water which rises from the depths of the sea to the surface: *An upwelling is rich in nutrients that attract fish.*   *n.*

**u·ra·ni·um** (yü rā′nē əm)   a heavy, white, radio-active metallic element: *Uranium is a source of atomic energy.* Symbol: U   *n.*

**U·ra·nus** (yü rā′nəs *or* yü′rə nəs)   one of the larger planets, seventh in order from the sun.   *n.*
☞ *Etym.* From *Uranus,* in early Greek mythology, the first god of the heavens, the father of the Titans and the Cyclopes.

**ur·ban** (ėr′bən)   **1** of, having to do with, or in cities or towns: *an urban district, urban planning, the urban population.*   **2** characteristic of cities or towns: *urban problems.*   *adj.*

**ur·bane** (ėr bān′)   courteous and refined; smoothly polite; polished.   *adj.*   —**ur·bane′ly,** *adv.* —**ur·bane′ness,** *n.*

**ur·ban·i·ty** (ėr ban′ə tē)   **1** the quality or state of being URBANE.   **2 urbanities,** *pl.*   URBANE acts; courteous, polite conduct.   *n., pl.* **ur·ban·i·ties.**

**ur·ban·i·za·tion** (ėr′bə nə zā′shən *or* ėr′be nī zā′shən) the quality or state of rendering or being rendered urban.   *n.*

**urban renewal**   a program, policy, or the process of rehabilitating or replacing rundown or substandard buildings in a city, especially in the downtown core.

**urban sprawl**   the uncontrolled spreading of urban development, in the form of new subdivisions, shopping centres, etc., into rural areas.

**ur·chin** (ėr′chin)   **1** a small child, especially a mischievous one.   **2** SEA URCHIN.   *n.*

**Ur·du** (ùr′dü *or* ėr′dü)   an Indo-European language closely related to Hindi: *Urdu is an official language of Pakistan and is widely used in India.*   *n.*

**–ure**   a noun-forming suffix meaning:   **1** the act or fact of _____ing, as in *failure.*   **2** the state of being _____ing, as in *pleasure.*   **3** the result of _____ing, as in *enclosure.*   **4** the thing that _____s, as in *legislature.*   **5** the thing that is _____ed, as in *disclosure.*   **6** other special meanings, as in *procedure, sculpture, denture.*

**u·re·a** (yü rē′ə)   a soluble crystalline compound present especially in the urine of mammals: *Urea is manufactured synthetically for use in making fertilizers, adhesives, and plastics.*   *n.*

**u·re·mi·a** (yü rē′mē ə)   a poisoned condition resulting from the accumulation in the blood of waste products that should normally be eliminated in the urine.   *n.*

**u·re·mic** (yü rē′mik)   **1** of or having to do with UREMIA.   **2** suffering from UREMIA.   *adj.*

**u·re·ter** (yü rē′tər *or* yü′rə tər)   in anatomy and zoology, a duct that carries urine from a kidney to the bladder or the cloaca.   See KIDNEY for picture.   *n.*

---

hat, āge, fär; let, ēqual, tėrm; it, īce
hot, ōpen, ôrder; oil, out; cup, pùt, rüle
əbove, takən, pencəl, lemən, circəs
ch, child; ng, long; sh, ship
th, thin; ᴛʜ, then; zh, measure

**u·re·thane** (yü′rə thān′ *or* yü reth′ān)   **1** a white, crystalline compound used especially in the plastics industry to manufacture polyurethane and in medicine to treat certain forms of leukemia, etc.   **2** POLYURETHANE.   *n.*

**u·re·thra** (yü rē′thrə)   in most mammals, the duct by which urine is discharged from the bladder and, in males, through which semen is discharged.   *n., pl.* **u·re·thrae** (-thrē *or* -thrī) *or* **u·re·thras.**

**urge** (ėrj)   **1** push, force, or drive: *The rider urged on her horse with whip and spurs.*   **2** a driving force or impulse: *The urge of hunger led him to beg.*   **3** try to persuade with arguments; ask earnestly: *They urged her to stay.*   **4** plead or argue earnestly for; recommend strongly: *Motorists urged better roads.*   **5** press upon the attention; refer to often and with emphasis: *to urge a claim, to urge an argument.*   **6** the act of urging.   1, 3–5 *v.,* **urged, urg·ing,**   2, 6 *n.*

**ur·gen·cy** (ėr′jən sē)   the quality or state of being URGENT: *They said it was a matter of great urgency. His captors were moved by the urgency of his plea. There was a note of urgency in her voice.*   *n., pl.* **ur·gen·cies.**

**ur·gent** (ėr′jənt)   **1** demanding immediate action or attention; pressing; important: *an urgent duty. She said the matter was urgent.*   **2** insistent: *an urgent appeal for funds.* *adj.*   —**ur′gent·ly,** *adv.*

**u·ric** (yü′rik)   of, having to do with, or found in urine. *adj.*

**uric acid**   a white, odourless, tasteless, crystalline compound only slightly soluble in water, that is found in small quantities in the urine of mammals and in large quantities in the urine of birds and reptiles.

**u·ri·nal** (yü′rə nəl *or* yü rī′nəl)   **1** an upright plumbing fixture into which to urinate, for use by men and boys.   **2** a room or structure containing such fixtures.   **3** a container for urine.   *n.*

**u·ri·nal·y·sis** (yü′rə nal′ə sis)   an analysis of a sample of urine.   *n., pl.* **u·ri·nal·y·ses** (-sēz′).

**u·ri·nar·y** (yü′rə ner′ē)   **1** of or having to do with urine.   **2** of or having to do with the organs that secrete and discharge urine.   *adj.*

**u·ri·nate** (yü′rə nāt′)   discharge urine from the body. *v.,* **u·ri·nat·ed, u·ri·nat·ing.**

**u·ri·na·tion** (yü′rə nā′shən)   the act or process of urinating.   *n.*

**u·rine** (yü′rən)   waste material that is produced by the kidneys of vertebrates and that forms a clear, usually slightly acid fluid in mammals but is semi-solid in birds and reptiles.   *n.*

An urn (def. 1)

An urn (def. 2)

**urn** (ėrn) **1** a vase or similar vessel having a base or pedestal: *Urns were used in Greece and Rome to hold ashes of the dead.* **2** a large coffee pot or teapot with a tap. *n.*
☛ *Hom.* EARN.

**Ur·sa Ma·jor** (ėr′sə mā′jər) the most conspicuous northern constellation, situated near the north pole of the heavens and including the stars that form the Big Dipper; the Great Bear.

**Ur·sa Mi·nor** (ėr′sə mī′nər) the northern constellation that includes the north pole of the heavens and the stars that form the Little Dipper; the Little Bear.

**ur·sine** (ėr′sīn) of, having to do with, or resembling a bear or the bear family; bearlike. *adj.*

**U·ru·guay·an** (yü′rə gwä′ən *or* yü′rə gwī′ən) **1** of or having to do with Uruguay, a country in the southeastern part of South America, or its people. **2** a native or inhabitant of Uruguay. 1 *adj.*, 2 *n.*

**u·rus** (yü′rəs) AUROCHS (def. 1). *n.*

**us** (us; *unstressed*, əs) the objective form of **we**: *Mother went with us.* *pron.*

**U.S.** United States.

**U.S.A.** or **USA** United States of America.

**us·a·bil·i·ty** (yü′zə bil′ə tē) the quality or state of being USABLE. *n.*

**us·a·ble** (yü′zə bəl) that can be used; fit for use. *adj.* Also, **useable.** —**us′a·ble·ness,** *n.*

**us·age** (yü′sij *or* yü′zij) **1** a way or manner of using; treatment: *The car has had rough usage.* **2** a long-continued practice; customary use; habit; custom: *Travellers should learn many of the usages of the countries they visit.* **3** the customary way of using words: *It is best to follow standard usage in writing.* *n.*

**use** (yüz *for verb*, yüs *for noun*) **1** put into action or service; avail oneself of for a particular purpose: *We use our legs in walking. He used a knife to cut the meat. May I use your telephone?* **2** act toward; treat: *She used us well.* **3** consume or expend by using: *We have used most of the money.* **4** using: *the use of tools.* **5** being used: *methods long out of use. Our telephone is in constant use.* **6** usefulness: *a thing of no practical use.* **7** the purpose that a thing is used for: *to find a new use for something.* **8** a way of using: *a poor use of materials.* **9** a need; occasion: *She had no further use for it.* **10** the power, right, or privilege of using: *to have the use of a boat for the summer.* **11** a custom; habit; usage: *It was his use to rise early.* 1–3 *v.,* **used, us·ing.**; 4–11 *n.* —**us′er,** *n.*
**have no use for,** a not need or want. b *Informal.* dislike.
**make use of,** use; employ.
**out-of-use,** no longer being used.
**put to use,** use.

**used** (yüst *or* yüs) **to,** a accustomed to: *used to hardships.* b formerly did: *She used to come every day.*
**use up,** a consume or expend entirely. b *Informal.* tire out; weary; exhaust.

**use·a·ble** (yü′zə bəl) See USABLE. *adj.*

**used** (yüzd) **1** not new; that has belonged to another or others: *We bought a used car.* **2** pt. and pp. of USE. 1 *adj.,* 2 *v.*

**use·ful** (yüs′fəl) of use; giving service; helpful: *a useful gadget. She learned a useful lesson from that experience.* *adj.* —**use′ful·ly,** *adv.* —**use′ful·ness,** *n.*

**use·less** (yü′slis) having no use or being of no use: *She is completely useless in the kitchen. That walkie-talkie is useless for any distance over a kilometre. It was useless to complain.* *adj.* —**use′less·ly,** *adv.* —**use′less·ness,** *n.*

**u·ser–friend·ly** (yü′zər fren′dlē) of a computer or computer program, easy to understand and use; not confusing. *adj.*

**U–shaped** (yü′shāpt′) having the shape of the letter U: *a U-shaped kitchen counter.* *adj.*

**ush·er** (ush′ər) **1** a person who shows people to their seats in a church, theatre, etc. **2** a person who has charge of the door of a court, hall, or chamber. **3** act as usher to; conduct; escort: *The patrons were ushered to their seats.* **4** go or come before; introduce or inaugurate (*used with* **in**): *to usher in a new age. Winter was ushered in by a week of cold rains.* 1, 2 *n.*, 3, 4 *v.*

**ush·er·ette** (ush′ə ret′) a girl or woman acting as USHER (def. 1) in a theatre. *n.*

**U.S.S.R.** or **USSR** Union of Soviet Socialist Republics, the name of the former country which consisted of a union of fifteen eastern European and northern Asian republics, including Russia.

**u·su·al** (yü′zhü əl) **1** commonly done, used, occurring, etc.; ordinary or customary: *He didn't take his usual route home last night. It's the usual thing to tip a waiter in a restaurant.* **2 the usual,** something that is customarily done, used, etc.: *She sat down at our table and ordered the usual.* 1 *adj.,* 2 *n.* —**u′su·al·ly,** *adv.* —**u′su·al·ness,** *n.*
**as usual,** in the usual manner, at the usual time, or in the usual way.

**u·su·rer** (yü′zhə rər) a person who lends money at an extremely high or unlawful rate of interest. *n.*

**u·su·ri·ous** (yü zhú′rē əs) **1** taking extremely high or unlawful interest for the use of money; practising USURY. **2** of, having to do with, or involving USURY: *Fifty percent is a usurious rate of interest.* *adj.*

**u·surp** (yü zėrp′ *or* yü sėrp′) seize and hold power, position, authority, etc., by force or without right: *The prince usurped the throne.* *v.* —**u·surp′er,** *n.*

**u·sur·pa·tion** (yü′zər pā′shən *or* yü′sər pā′shən) the act of usurping: *the usurpation of the throne by a pretender.* *n.*

**u·su·ry** (yü′zhə rē) **1** the lending of money at an extremely high or unlawful rate of interest. **2** an extremely high or unlawful rate of interest. *n., pl.* **u·su·ries.**

**u·ten·sil** (yü ten′səl) **1** a container or implement used for practical household purposes, especially in the kitchen: *Pots, pans, kettles, and mops are utensils.* **2** an instrument or tool used for some special purpose: *Pens and pencils are writing utensils.* *n.*

**u·ter·us** (yü′tə rəs)   in female mammals, an organ of the body that holds and nourishes the young till birth; womb.   *n., pl.* **u·ter·i** (-tər ī′ *or* -tər ē′).

**u·til·i·dor** (yü til′ə dôr′) *Cdn.*   in the North, a large, insulated tube mounted on short posts above ground and housing water, steam, and sewage pipes that supply services to buildings in a town or settlement built on permafrost.   *n.*

**u·til·i·tar·i·an** (yü til′ə ter′ē ən)   **1** of, having to do with, or aimed at utility: *a utilitarian furniture design.*   **2** of, having to do with, or referring to UTILITARIANISM: *utilitarian philosophy.*   **3** a person who believes in UTILITARIANISM.   1, 2 *adj.*, 3 *n.*

**u·til·i·tar·i·an·ism** (yü til′ə ter′ē ə niz′əm)   **1** the doctrine or belief that the greatest good of the greatest number should be the purpose of human conduct.   **2** the doctrine or belief that actions are good if they are useful.   **3** a utilitarian quality or character.   *n.*

**u·til·i·ty** (yü til′ə tē)   **1** the power to satisfy needs; usefulness: *The cottage was obviously designed more for utility than beauty.*   **2** something that is useful.   **3** designed or serving strictly for usefulness rather than appearance or luxury: *utility furnishings.*   **4** the supplying of gas, water, electricity, etc. to the public: *They pay a lot more for utilities than we do.*   **5** of, having to do with, or referring to the supplying of electricity, etc. to the public or the equipment used for this: *The car struck a utility pole.*   **6** PUBLIC UTILITY.   **7** referring to the lowest and cheapest government grade of meat: *A utility grade turkey may be an A or B grade that has had the skin broken, or has a wing missing, etc.*   *n., pl.* **u·til·i·ties.**

**u·ti·li·za·tion** (yü′tə lə zā′shən *or* yü′tə lī zā′shən)   utilizing or being UTILIZED.   *n.*

**u·ti·lize** (yü′tə līz′)   make use of; put to some practical use: *to utilize leftovers in cooking.*   *v.,* **u·ti·lized, u·ti·liz·ing.**  —**u′ti·liz′a·ble,** *adj.*  —**u′ti·liz′er,** *n.*

**ut·most** (ut′mōst′)   **1** of the greatest or highest degree, amount, or quantity: *Sunshine is of the utmost importance to health.*   **2** farthest or most distant; extreme: *the utmost ends of the earth.*   **3** the most that is possible; extreme limit: *a car of the utmost serviceability.*   **4** all that one can do; the greatest or highest of one's powers or abilities: *She did her utmost to help him find a good job. She strained her resources to the utmost.*   1–3 *adj.*, 4 *n.*

**u·to·pi·a** (yü tō′pē ə)   **1 Utopia,** an ideal commonwealth where perfect justice and social harmony exist, described in *Utopia,* by Sir Thomas More.   **2** any ideal place or state with perfect laws.   **3** a visionary, impractical system of political or social perfection.   *n.*

**u·to·pi·an** (yü tō′pē ən)   **1** Usually, **Utopian,** of, having to do with, or characteristic of Utopia.   **2** of, having to do with, or like a UTOPIA.   **3** visionary; impractical.   **4** an ardent but impractical reformer; idealist.   1–3 *adj.*, 4 *n.*

**u·to·pi·an·ism** (yü tō′pē ə niz′əm)   **1** the ideas, beliefs, and aims of Utopians.   **2** ideal schemes for the improvement of life, social conditions, etc.   *n.*

**ut·ter**[1] (ut′ər)   complete; total; absolute: *utter surprise, utter darkness, an utter failure.*   *adj.*

**ut·ter**[2] (ut′ər)   **1** speak; make known; express: *the last words he uttered, to utter one's thoughts.*   **2** give out as sound: *She uttered a cry of pain.*   *v.*  —**ut′ter·a·ble,** *adj.*  —**ut′ter·er,** *n.*

**ut·ter·ance** (ut′ə rəns)   **1** an uttering; expression in words or sounds: *The child gave utterance to his grief.*   **2** the power or a way of speaking: *defective utterance.*   **3** something uttered; a spoken word or words: *Some of his famous political utterances are included in the book.*   *n.*

**ut·ter·ly** (ut′ər lē)   completely; totally; absolutely: *She was utterly flabbergasted.*   *adv.*

**ut·ter·most** (ut′ər mōst′)   UTMOST: *the uttermost parts of the earth.*   *adj., n.*

**U–turn** (yü′tėrn′)   a complete reversal of direction on a road, as, from the northbound to the southbound lane: *U-turns are illegal on some roads.*   *n.*

**UV**   ultraviolet.

**u·vu·la** (yü′vyə lə)   the small lobe of flesh hanging down from the soft palate in the back of the mouth.   *n., pl.* **u·vu·las** or **u·vu·lae** (-lē′ *or* -lī′).

**ux·o·ri·ous** (uk sô′rē əs)   excessively or foolishly fond of one's wife.   *adj.*  —**ux·o′ri·ous·ness,** *n.*

# V v  V v

**v** or **V** (vē) **1** the twenty-second letter of the English alphabet. **2** any speech sound represented by this letter. **3** a person or thing identified as v, especially the twenty-second of a series. **4** V, the Roman numeral for 5. **5** anything shaped like a V. *n., pl.* **v's** or **V's**.

**V** **1** vanadium. **2** volt. **3** victory. **4** vector.

**v.** **1** verb. **2** verse. **3** versus. **4** see (for Latin *vide*). **5** voice. **6** vice-. **7** volume. **8** violin. **9** velocity.

**va·can·cy** (vā′kən sē) **1** the state of being unoccupied or empty. **2** an unfilled post, office, or position: *The company has a vacancy for a sales representative.* **3** a space, room, apartment, etc. that is unoccupied and available: *There were no vacancies in the parking lot. The hotel had one vacancy.* **4** empty space; void: *Robin stared into the vacancy of the night.* **5** emptiness of mind; a lack of thought or intelligence. *n., pl.* **va·can·cies**.

**va·cant** (vā′kənt) **1** empty; not occupied or filled: *a vacant house, a vacant chair, a vacant space.* **2** without thought or intelligence: *a vacant smile.* **3** having no expression: *a vacant face.* **4** free from work, business, etc.: *vacant time.* *adj.* —**va′cant·ly,** *adv.*

**va·cate** (və kāt′ *or* vā′kāt) **1** go away from and leave empty or unoccupied; make VACANT: *They will vacate the house next month.* **2** leave: *We are waiting for them to vacate so that we can move in.* **3** in law, make void; annul; cancel. *v.,* **va·cat·ed, va·cat·ing.**

**va·ca·tion** (və kā′shən *or* vā kā′shən) **1** a scheduled time of rest and freedom from work or activity, especially in schools and courts of law: *The school has a vacation in the spring.* **2** a period of time spent away from work; holidays: *Is he taking a vacation this year? She spent her vacation at the cottage.* **3** take or spend a vacation: *They are vacationing in the North.* **4** the act or an instance of vacating. **1, 2, 4** *n.,* **3** *v.* —**va·ca′tion·less,** *adj.*

**va·ca·tion·er** (və kā′shə nər *or* vā kā′shə nər) a person who is taking a vacation, especially away from home; vacationist: *The resort town was crowded with vacationers.* *n.*

**va·ca·tion·ist** (və kā′shə nist *or* vā kā′shə nist) VACATIONER. *n.*

**vac·ci·nate** (vak′sə nāt′) inoculate with VACCINE as a protection against polio or other diseases. *v.,* **vac·ci·nat·ed, vac·ci·nat·ing.**

**vac·ci·na·tion** (vak′sə nā′shən) **1** the act or process of vaccinating: *Vaccination has made smallpox extinct.* **2** the sore or the scar left by vaccinating. *n.*

**vac·cine** (vak′sēn *or* vak sēn′) **1** a preparation, often made of weakened viruses of a disease, used to inoculate people in order to protect them from that disease: *Salk vaccine is used against polio.* **2** a program whose purpose is to protect a computer from viruses. *n.*
☞ *Etym.* From L *vaccinus* 'having to do with cows' (from *vacca* 'cow'), used in the modern Latin phrase *virus vaccinus* 'virus of cowpox'. This virus became the first vaccine when it was found to protect people against smallpox.

**vac·il·late** (vas′ə lāt′) **1** move first one way and then another; waver. **2** waver in mind or opinion: *Ali vacillated so long about which car to buy that when he went back they were both gone.* *v.,* **vac·il·lat·ed, vac·il·lat·ing.**

**vac·il·la·tion** (vas′ə lā′shən) **1** the act or an instance of vacillating. **2** the inability to make up one's mind or take a stand. *n.*

**va·cu·i·ty** (va kyü′ə tē) **1** the quality or state of being empty or without thought or intelligence. **2** an empty space; vacuum. **3** something, such as an idea, that is foolish or stupid. *n., pl.* **va·cu·i·ties.**

**vac·u·ole** (vak′yü ōl′) **1** a tiny cavity in a living cell, containing fluid. See CELL for picture. **2** formerly, any very small cavity in organic tissue. *n.*

**vac·u·ous** (vak′yü əs) **1** showing no thought or intelligence; foolish; stupid: *a vacuous remark, a vacuous mind.* **2** empty. *adj.* —**vac′u·ous·ly,** *adv.*

**vac·u·um** (vak′yü əm *or* vak′yəm) **1** an empty space utterly devoid of matter, even air. **2** an enclosed space from which almost all air, gas, etc. has been removed. **3** a decrease of air pressure below normal atmospheric pressure. **4** of, containing, using, or producing a vacuum: *vacuum brakes, a vacuum pump.* **5** an empty space; void: *His wife's death left a vacuum in his life.* **6** VACUUM CLEANER. **7** clean with a VACUUM CLEANER: *to vacuum a carpet. I still have to vacuum before I can go.* **1–6** *n., pl.* **vac·u·ums** or (defs. 1–3, 5) **vac·u·a** (vak′yü ə); **7** *v.*

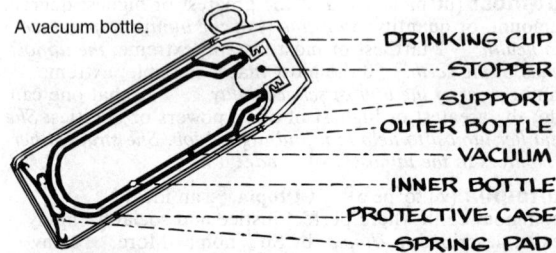
A vacuum bottle. — DRINKING CUP, STOPPER, SUPPORT, OUTER BOTTLE, VACUUM, INNER BOTTLE, PROTECTIVE CASE, SPRING PAD

**vacuum bottle** a bottle or flask made with a vacuum between its inner and outer walls so that its contents will stay hot or cold for a long time. Compare with THERMOS.

**vacuum cleaner** an electrical appliance for cleaning carpets, curtains, floors, etc. by suction.

**vacuum flask** VACUUM BOTTLE.

**vac·u·um-packed** (vak′yü əm pakt′ *or* vak′yəm pakt′) **1** of a container, having most of the air removed before being sealed: *Coffee, nuts, etc. are often sold in vacuum-packed cans.* **2** packed in airtight containers from which most of the air has been removed: *vacuum-packed tennis balls.* *adj.*

**vacuum pump** **1** a pump or device by which a partial vacuum can be produced. **2** a pump in which a partial vacuum is used to raise water.

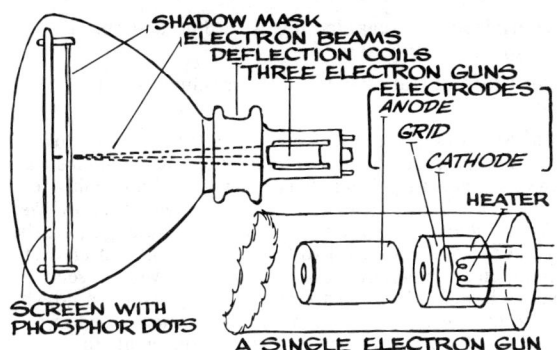

Vacuum tube: a colour television picture tube

**vacuum tube** an electron tube from which almost all the air has been removed, leaving an almost perfect vacuum through which an electric current can pass freely.

**vag·a·bond** (vag′ə bond′) 1 a wanderer, especially a tramp. 2 wandering: *Gypsies are traditionally a vagabond people.* 3 of, having to do with, or characteristic of a wanderer: *a vagabond life.* 4 an idle, shiftless person; rascal. 5 shiftless and irresponsible. 1, 4 *n.*, 2, 3, 5 *adj.*

**vag·a·bond·age** (vag′ə bon′dij) the fact or state of being a VAGABOND; idle wandering. *n.*

**va·gar·y** (və ger′ē or vā′gə rē) 1 an odd fancy; extravagant notion: *the vagaries of a dream.* 2 an odd action; caprice: *the vagaries of fashion.* *n., pl.* **va·gar·ies.**

**va·gi·na** (və jī′nə) 1 in female mammals, the passage from the uterus to the vulva or external opening. 2 in botany, a sheathlike part in certain plants formed around the stem by the base of the leaf. *n., pl.* **va·gi·nas** or **va·gi·nae** (-nē or -nī).

**vag·i·nal** (vaj′ə nəl or və jī′nəl) 1 of or having to do with the VAGINA of a female mammal. 2 of or resembling a sheath. *adj.*

**vag·i·ni·tis** (vaj′ə nī′tis) inflammation of the VAGINA. *n.*

**va·gran·cy** (vā′grən sē) 1 a wandering idly from place to place without proper means or ability to earn a living. 2 in law, the criminal offence of being a VAGRANT (def. 2): *The tramp was charged with vagrancy.* *n., pl.* **va·gran·cies.**

**va·grant** (vā′grənt) 1 an idle wanderer; a person who goes from place to place without a regular residence, often living by begging, etc. 2 in law, a beggar, prostitute, drunkard, etc. living without lawful or visible means of support. 3 moving in no definite direction or course; wandering. 4 of, having to do with, or being a vagrant. 1, 2 *n.*, 3, 4 *adj.* —**va′grant·ly,** *adv.*

**vague** (vāg) 1 not clearly expressed or defined: *a vague statement, a vague notion, a vague longing.* 2 having no definite meaning or character: "Nice" is a vague term. 3 not thinking or expressing oneself clearly: *Jo was very vague about his plans.* 4 having no definite outline: *a vague shape in the mist.* *adj.,* **va·guer, va·guest.** —**vague′ly,** *adv.* —**vague′ness,** *n.*

**va·gus** (vā′gəs) either of the tenth pair of nerves extending from the brain to the heart, larynx, lungs, stomach, and most of the abdominal organs. *n., pl.* **va·gi** (vā′jī or vā′jē).

**vain** (vān) 1 having too much pride in one's looks, ability, etc.: *She is vain about her beauty.* 2 of no use;

without effect or success; producing no good result: *a vain hope. Kin made several vain attempts to pull himself out of the icy water.* 3 of no value or importance; worthless; empty: *a vain boast.* *adj.* —**vain·ly,** *adv.* —**vain′ness,** *n.*

**in vain,** without effect or success: *My shout for help was in vain, for no one was near enough to hear me.*
☞ Hom. VANE, VEIN.

**vain·glo·ri·ous** (vān′glô′rē əs) excessively proud or boastful; extremely vain. *adj.* —**vain′glo′ri·ous·ly,** *adv.*

**vain·glo·ry** (vān′glô′rē) 1 an extreme pride in oneself; boastful vanity. 2 worthless pomp or show. *n.*

**vain·ly** (vān′lē) 1 in vain. 2 with conceit. *adv.*

**val·ance** (val′əns) 1 a short drapery or a decorative wooden or metal frame around the top of a window, used to hide curtain fixtures, etc. 2 a short curtain hanging around the edge of a bed, dressing table, etc. *n.*

**vale** (vāl) *Poetic.* valley. *n.*
☞ Hom. VEIL.

**val·e·dic·tion** (val′ə dik′shən) the act of bidding farewell. *n.*

**val·e·dic·to·ri·an** (val′ə dik tô′rē ən) a student who gives the farewell address at the graduation of his or her class. *n.*

**val·e·dic·to·ry** (val′ə dik′tə rē) 1 a farewell address, especially at the graduating exercises of a school or college. 2 bidding farewell. 1 *n., pl.* **val·e·dic·to·ries;** 2 *adj.*

**va·lence** (vā′ləns) in chemistry, the quality of an atom or radical that determines the number of other atoms or radicals with which it can combine, indicated by the number of hydrogen atoms with which it can combine or which it can displace. Elements whose atoms lose electrons, such as hydrogen and the metals, have a positive valence. Elements whose atoms add electrons, such as oxygen and other non-metals, have a negative valence: *Oxygen has a negative valence of two; hydrogen has a positive valence of one; one atom of oxygen combines with two of hydrogen to form a molecule of water.* *n.*

**va·len·cy** (vā lən sē) VALENCE. *n., pl.* **va·len·cies.**

**val·en·tine** (val′ən tīn′) 1 a greeting card or small gift sent or given on Saint Valentine's Day, February 14. 2 a sweetheart chosen on this day. *n.*

**va·le·ri·an** (və lē′rē ən) 1 any of a closely related group of perennial herbs, especially the common valerian, a tall garden plant having clusters of small, very fragrant white or reddish flowers and a strong-smelling root. 2 a drug made from the dried roots of the common valerian, formerly used in medicine. 3 referring to a family of perennial or annual herbs or shrubs found mainly in the Northern Hemisphere: *The valerian family includes the valerian and spikenard.* *n.*

**val·et** (val′it or val′ā) 1 a male servant who takes care of a man's clothes, helps him dress, etc. 2 an employee in a hotel, etc. who cleans or presses clothes. 3 serve as a valet. 1, 2 *n.*, 3 *v.*, **val·et·ed, val·et·ing.**

**val·e·tu·di·nar·i·an** (val′ə tyü′də ner′ē ən or val′ə tü′də ner′ē ən)   **1** a weak or sickly person, especially one who thinks too much about being sick.   **2** of, having to do with, or characteristic of a valetudinarian.   *1 n., 2 adj.*

**val·iant** (val′yənt)   brave; courageous: *a valiant soldier, a valiant effort.*   *adj.*   —**val′iant·ly**, *adv.*   —**val′iant·ness**, *n.*

**val·id** (val′id)   **1** supported by facts or authority; sound; true: *a valid argument.*   **2** having legal force; legally binding: *a valid passport. A contract made by a person who is a minor is not valid.*   **3** appropriate in a particular situation or for a particular goal or end; effective: *a valid approach to a problem, a valid excuse.*   *adj.*   —**val′id·ly**, *adv.*

**val·i·date** (val′ə dāt)   **1** make or declare legally binding; give legal force to: *to validate election results.*   **2** support by facts or authority; confirm: *The results of the experiments validated her hypothesis.*   *v.*, **val·i·dat·ed**, **val·i·dat·ing**.

**va·lid·i·ty** (və lid′ə tē)   the quality, fact, or condition of being VALID: *He questioned the validity of the contract.*   *n., pl.* **va·lid·i·ties**.

**va·lise** (və lēs′)   a travelling bag to hold clothes, etc.   *n.*

**val·ley** (val′ē)   **1** low land between hills or mountains, usually having a stream or river flowing through it.   **2** a wide region drained by a great river system: *the Ottawa Valley.*   **3** any hollow or structure like a valley.   **4** in architecture, a trough formed where two slopes of a roof meet or where a roof meets a wall.   *n., pl.* **val·leys**.

**val·or·ous** (val′ə rəs)   valiant; brave; courageous.   *adj.*   —**val′or·ous·ly**, *adv.*   —**val′or·ous·ness**, *n.*

**val·our** or **val·or** (val′ər)   bravery; courage.   *n.*

**val·u·a·ble** (val′yü ə bəl or val′yə bəl)   **1** having value; being worth something: *valuable information, a valuable friend.*   **2** that can have its value measured.   **3** Usually, **valuables**, *pl.* articles of value: *She keeps her jewellery and other valuables in a safe.*   *1, 2 adj., 3 n.*   —**val′u·a·ble·ness**, *n.*   —**val′u·a·bly**, *adv.*

**val·u·a·tion** (val′yü ā′shən)   **1** the value estimated or determined: *The jeweller's valuation of the necklace was $10 000.*   **2** an estimating or determining of the value of something.   *n.*

**val·ue** (val′yü)   **1** worth; excellence; usefulness; importance: *the value of education.*   **2** the real worth; the proper price: *She bought the house for less than its value.*   **3** the power to buy: *The value of the dollar has varied greatly.*   **4** rate at a certain value or price; estimate the value of: *The land is valued at $80 000.*   **5** an estimated worth: *Rajiv placed a value on his furniture.*   **6** think highly of; regard highly: *to value one's judgment.*   **7** the meaning; effect; force: *the value of a symbol.*   **8** a number or amount represented by a symbol: *The value of XIV is fourteen.*   **9** in music, the relative length of a tone indicated by a note.   **10** in speech, a special quality of sound.   **11** the degree of lightness or darkness in a painting, etc.   **12** the relative importance or effect of an object, part, spot of colour, etc. in a painting.   **13 values**, *pl.* the established ideals of life.   *1–3, 5, 7–13 n., 4, 6 v.*, **val·ued**, **val·u·ing**.   —**val′u·er**, *n.*

**val·ued** (val′yüd)   **1** having its value estimated or determined.   **2** regarded highly.   *3 pt. and pp. of* VALUE.   *1, 2 adj., 3 v.*

**val·ue·less** (val′yü lis)   without value; worthless.   *adj.*

**valve** (valv)   **1** a movable part that controls the flow of a liquid, gas, etc. through a pipe by opening and closing the passage: *A tap is one kind of valve.*   **2** a membrane that works like a valve: *The valves of the heart control the flow of blood.*   **3** control the flow of a liquid, gas, etc. by a valve.   **4** one of the two halves of the shell of an oyster, clam, etc.   **5** one of the sections formed when a seed vessel bursts open.   **6** a section that opens like a lid when an anther opens.   **7** a vacuum tube formerly used in a radio.   **8** a device in musical wind instruments for changing the pitch of the tone by changing the direction and length of the column of air: *Cornets, trumpets, and French horns have valves; they are pressed separately or in combination to alter the pitch.*   *1, 2, 4–8 n., 3 v.*, **valved**, **valv·ing**.   —**valve′less**, *adj.*   —**valve′like′**, *adj.*

**val·vu·lar** (val′vyə lər)   **1** of or having to do with a VALVE, especially of the heart: *a valvular disorder.*   **2** having the form of a VALVE.   **3** furnished with or working by VALVES.   *adj.*

**vamp¹** (vamp)   **1** the upper front part of a shoe or boot covering the instep and, sometimes, the toes.   **2** furnish with a new vamp.   **3** a piece or patch added to an old thing to make it look new.   **4** patch up; make an old thing look new (*usually used with* **up**).   **5** invent, especially in order to deceive (*often used with* **up**): *He vamped up a big story about needing the money to help out a friend.*   **6** in music, improvise an accompaniment, introduction, etc.   **7** an improvised musical accompaniment, introduction, etc.   *1, 3, 7 n., 2, 4–6 v.*   —**vamp′er**, *n.*

**vamp²** (vamp) *Informal.*   **1** a woman who seduces and exploits men; unscrupulous flirt.   **2** act as a vamp; use wiles and charm on: *to vamp an unsuspecting man.*   *1 n., 2 v.*

**vam·pire** (vam′pīr)   **1** an imaginary creature believed to be a corpse that comes back to life at night and sucks the blood of people while they sleep.   **2** a person who ruthlessly takes advantage of others.   **3** a woman who seduces and ruins men.   **4** any of various tropical American bats that live by sucking the blood of vertebrates and that can be dangerous to human beings and animals because they transmit diseases such as rabies.   **5** any of various other species of bat that are believed to feed on blood but do not actually do so.   *n.*

**vam·pir·ism** (vam′pī riz′əm)   belief in the existence of VAMPIRES (def. 1).   *n.*

**van¹** (van)   the front part of an army, fleet, or other advancing group; VANGUARD: *The magazine tries to be in the van of current fashion.*   *n.*
☛ *Etym.* From the first syllable of VANGUARD.

**van²** (van)   **1** a large, enclosed motor truck or trailer used for moving furniture, etc.   **2** a small, light motor truck with a completely enclosed body, used as a camper, for delivering goods to customers, etc.   **3** *Brit.* a railway car for luggage or freight.   *n.*
☛ *Etym.* From the last syllable of CARAVAN.

**va·na·di·um** (və nā′dē əm)   a rare metallic element used in making certain kinds of steel.   *Symbol:* V   *n.*

**vanadium steel**   a steel alloy containing VANADIUM to make it tougher and harder.

**Van Al·len belt** (van′al′ən)   a broad zone or belt of high-intensity radiation above the earth's atmosphere, produced by a high concentration of charged particles trapped in the magnetic field of the earth.

**van·dal** (van′dəl)  **1 Vandal,** a member of a Germanic people originally living in the area south of the Baltic between the Vistula and the Oder, who ravaged Gaul, Spain, and North Africa and in A.D. 455 sacked Rome. Many books and works of art were destroyed by them. **2 Vandal,** of or having to do with the Vandals. **3** a person who willfully destroys or damages things, especially beautiful or valuable ones. **4** of or like a vandal; willfully or senselessly destructive. *1, 3 n., 2, 4 adj.*
☛ *Etym.* From L *Vandali* 'Vandals'. 16c. VANDALISM came in the 18c. through F *vandalisme* from the same original source.

**van·dal·ism** (van′də liz′əm)  willful destruction or defacement of things, especially works of art or other valuable things or property. *n.*
☛ *Etym.* See note at VANDAL.

**van·dal·ize** (van′də līz′)  destroy or damage willfully; subject to VANDALISM: *The school was vandalized during the holidays. v.,* **van·dal·ized, van·dal·iz·ing.**
☛ *Etym.* See note at VANDAL.

**vane** (vān)  **1** a movable device attached to a spire, roof, or other high point to show which way the wind is blowing.  **2** a blade, wing, or similar part attached to an axis, wheel, etc., so as to be turned by a current of air or liquid or to produce a current when turned: *The vanes of a windmill are turned by the wind; the vanes of an electric fan produce air currents as they turn.*  **3** the flat, soft part of a feather. *n.*
☛ *Hom.* VAIN, VEIN.

**van·guard** (van′gärd′)  **1** a body of soldiers marching ahead of the main part of an army to clear the way and guard against surprise.  **2** the foremost or leading position.  **3** the leaders of a movement. *n.*

**va·nil·la** (və nil′ə)  **1** a food flavouring made from the beanlike pods of a tropical American climbing orchid.  **2** VANILLA BEAN.  **3** the plant producing the pods. *n.*

**vanilla bean** the long, beanlike fruit of a tropical American plant from which the food flavouring VANILLA is extracted.

**van·ish** (van′ish)  **1** pass suddenly out of sight; disappear: *The fairy godmother vanished.*  **2** pass away; cease to be: *Dinosaurs have vanished from the earth. v.*
—**van′ish·er,** *n.*

**van·i·ty** (van′ə tē)  **1** too much pride in one's looks, ability, etc.: *The man's vanity made him look in the mirror often.*  **2** a lack of real value; worthlessness: *the vanity of wealth.*  **3** a useless or worthless thing.  **4** worthless pleasure or display.  **5** lack of effect or success.  **6** VANITY CASE.  **7** a low dresser with a mirror, usually with a matching chair or stool: *She always puts on her make-up at her vanity.*  **8** a bathroom counter or cabinet with a built-in sink and storage space. *n., pl.* **van·i·ties.**

**vanity case** a small travelling case used by some women, containing a mirror and fitted for carrying cosmetics, etc.

**van·quish** (vang′kwish)  conquer; defeat; overcome. *v.* —**van′quish·a·ble,** *adj.*
—**van′quish·er,** *n.*

**vantage ground** a favourable position.

**vantage point**  **1** a superior position from which a person can see to advantage.  **2** a favourable condition that gives a person an advantage.

hat, āge, fär; let, ēqual, tėrm; it, īce
hot, ōpen, ôrder; oil, out; cup, pủt, rüle
əbove, takən, pencəl, lemən, circəs
ch, child; ng, long; sh, ship
th, thin; ᴛʜ, then; zh, measure

**vap·id** (vap′id)  without much life or flavour; flat; dull. *adj.* —**vap′id·ly,** *adv.* —**vap′id·ness,** *n.*

**va·pid·i·ty** (va pid′ə tē)  insipidity; flatness of flavour. *n.*

**va·por** (vā′pər)  See VAPOUR. *n., v.*

**va·por·ish** (vā′pə rish)  **1** like vapour.  **2** abounding in vapour. *adj.*

**va·por·ize** (vā′pə rīz′)  change from a solid or liquid to a vapour: *To distil water, we first have to vaporize it. v.,* **va·por·ized, va·por·iz·ing.** —**va′por·iz′a·ble,** *adj.*
—**va′por·i·za′tion,** *n.*

**va·por·ous** (vā′pə rəs)  **1** full of vapour; misty.  **2** like vapour.  **3** soon passing; worthless. *adj.*

**va·por·y** (vā′pə rē)  VAPOROUS. *adj.*

**va·pour** or **va·por** (vā′pər)  **1** moisture in the air that can be seen; fog; mist.  **2** steam from boiling water.  **3** a gas formed from a substance that is usually a liquid or a solid: *We could smell the gasoline vapour as the gas tank of the car was being filled.*  **4** pass off as vapour.  **5** send out in vapour.  **6** give out vapour.  **7** something without substance; empty fancy. *1–3, 7 n., 4–6 v.*

**vapour trail** or **vapor trail** a white trail of water droplets or ice crystals that is sometimes seen in the wake of an aircraft flying at high altitudes: *A vapour trail is caused by the condensation of moisture in the atmosphere or of exhaust gases from the aircraft.*

**var.**  **1** variant.  **2** variation.  **3** variable.

**va·re·ny·ky** (və ren′ə kē)  PEROGY. *n.pl.*

**var·i·a·bil·i·ty** (ver′ē ə bil′ə tē *or* var′ē ə bil′ə tē)  **1** the fact or quality of being VARIABLE.  **2** a tendency to VARY. *n.*

**var·i·a·ble** (ver′ē ə bəl *or* var′ē ə bəl)  **1** apt to change; changeable; uncertain: *variable winds.*  **2** that can be varied: *This curtain rod is of variable length.*  **3** a thing, quality, or quantity that varies: *Temperature and rainfall are variables.*  **4** a shifting wind.  **5** deviating from the normal biological species, type, etc.  **6** in computer science, a change in the value assigned to data stored in memory.  **7 the variables,** the region between the northeast and the southeast trade winds. *1, 2, 5 adj., 3, 4, 6, 7 n.* —**var′i·a·ble·ness,** *n.* —**var′i·a·bly,** *adv.*

**variable star** any of several stars whose brightness varies as a result of forces outside the atmosphere of the earth.

**var·i·ance** (ver′ē əns *or* var′ē əns)  **1** disagreement; dispute; difference of opinion: *She had had a slight variance with her brother over the matter.*  **2** a varying or a tendency to vary; variation. *n.*
**at variance,** differing; disagreeing; in disagreement: *His actions are at variance with his promises.*

**var·i·ant** (ver′ē ənt *or* var′ē ənt)  **1** showing difference, disagreement, or variety: *variant readings of a poem, a variant pronunciation of a word.*  **2** something that is somewhat different from a standard or norm: *She showed us two variants of the original design.*  **3** one of two or more slightly different things, especially forms,

**variation** | 1328 | **vault**

pronunciations, or spellings of one word: *The spellings* colour *and* color *are almost equally common variants in Canada.* 1 *adj.*, 2, 3 *n.*

**var·i·a·tion** (ver′ē ā′shən *or* var′ē ā′shən) 1 a varying in condition, degree, etc.; change. 2 the amount of change. 3 a varied or changed form. 4 in music, a changing or ornamenting of a tune or theme. 5 a deviation of an animal or plant from type. 6 the deviation of a heavenly body from its average orbit or motion. *n.*

**var·i·col·oured** *or* **var·i·col·ored** (ver′ē kul′ərd *or* var′ē kul′ərd) having various colours. *adj.*

**var·i·cose** (var′ə kōs′ *or* ver′ə kōs′) 1 swollen or enlarged: *William has varicose veins on his legs.* 2 of, having to do with, or affected with varicose veins. *adj.*

**var·ied** (ver′ēd *or* var′ēd) 1 of different kinds; having variety: *a varied assortment of candies.* 2 changed; altered. 3 pt. and pp. of VARY. 1, 2 *adj.*, 3 *v.*

**var·i·e·gate** (ver′ē ə gāt′ *or* var′ē ə gāt′) 1 vary in appearance; mark, spot, or streak with different colours. 2 give variety to. *v.*, **var·i·e·gat·ed, var·i·e·gat·ing.**

**var·i·e·gat·ed** (ver′ē ə gā′tid *or* var′ē ə gā′tid) 1 varied in appearance; marked with different colours: *variegated pansies.* 2 having variety. 3 pt. and pp. of VARIEGATE. 1, 2 *adj.*, 3 *v.*

**var·i·e·ga·tion** (ver′ē ə gā′shən *or* var′ē ə gā′shən) variegating or being variegated; especially, variety of colour. *n.*

**va·ri·e·ty** (və rī′ə tē) 1 a lack of sameness; difference; variation: *Variety is the spice of life.* 2 a number of different kinds: *The store has a great variety of toys.* 3 a kind; sort: *Which variety of cake do you prefer?* 4 a grouping within an animal or plant species, based on inherited biological differences; subspecies. 5 VARIETY SHOW. *n., pl.* **va·ri·e·ties.**

**variety show** an entertainment in a theatre or night club, on television, etc., made up of different kinds of acts such as songs, dances, and comic skits.

**variety store** a store selling a large variety of different things, especially small, inexpensive items such as sewing supplies, small toys, magazines, greeting cards, candy, and tobacco.

**var·i·form** (ver′ə fôrm′ *or* var′ə fôrm′) varied in form; having various forms. *adj.*

**var·i·ous** (ver′ē əs *or* var′ē əs) 1 differing from one another; different: *various opinions.* 2 several; many: *We have looked at various houses, but have decided to buy this one.* 3 varied; many-sided: *lives made various by learning.* 4 varying; changeable. *adj.*

**var·i·ous·ly** (ver′ē ə slē *or* var′ē ə slē) 1 in various ways or at various times: *She has been variously involved in editing, proofreading, and research.* 2 by various names or classifications: *He was known variously as Harry the Hooligan, Deadeye, and Jaws McGee.* *adv.*

**var·nish** (vär′nish) 1 a liquid that gives a smooth, glossy appearance to wood, metal, etc., made of resinous substances dissolved in oil or turpentine. 2 the smooth, hard surface made by this liquid when dry: *The varnish on the car has been scratched.* 3 put varnish on. 4 a glossy appearance. 5 a false or deceiving appearance; pretence: *She covers her selfishness with a varnish of good manners.* 6 give a false or deceiving appearance to: *to varnish over the truth with a lie.* 1, 2, 4, 5 *n.*, 3, 6 *v.* —**var′nish·er,** *n.*

**var·si·ty** (vär′sə tē) *Informal.* UNIVERSITY. *n., pl.* **var·si·ties.**

**var·y** (ver′ē *or* var′ē) 1 make or become different; change: *The driver can vary the speed of an automobile. The weather varies.* 2 in music, change or ornament a basic tune or theme. 3 be different; differ: *The stars vary in brightness.* 4 alternate. 5 in mathematics or physics, undergo or be subject to a change in value according to some law: *Pressure varies inversely as volume.* 6 in biology, exhibit or be subject to variation, as by natural or artificial selection. *v.*, **var·ied, var·y·ing.** —**var′y·ing·ly,** *adv.*
☛ *Hom.* VERY (for the first pronunciation of **vary**).

**vas·cu·lar** (vas′kyə lər) having to do with, made of, or provided with vessels that carry blood, sap, etc. *adj.*

**vascular bundle** in botany, a unit of the system of specialized, tubelike cells by which food and water are carried through a plant.

**vase** (vāz, väz, *or* vōz) an open holder or container, usually taller than it is wide, used for ornament or for holding flowers. *n.* —**vase′like′,** *adj.*

**vas·ec·to·my** (va sek′tə mē) the surgical removal of part or all of the **vas deferens,** a duct that conveys semen from the testicles to the penis, especially as a means of sterilization. *n.*

**vas·sal** (vas′əl) 1 in feudal times, a person who held land from a lord or superior, to whom in return he gave help in war or some other service: *A great noble could be a vassal of the king and have many other men as his vassals.* 2 of or like a vassal. 3 a person in a subordinate position; a servant, slave, etc. *n.*

**vas·sal·age** (vas′ə lij) 1 the state of being a vassal. 2 the homage or service due from a vassal to his lord or superior. 3 dependence; servitude. 4 the land held by a vassal. *n.*

**vast** (vast) extremely great; immense: *a vast desert, a vast amount of money.* *adj.* —**vast′ly,** *adv.* —**vast′ness,** *n.*

**vat** (vat) a large container for liquids; tank. *n.*

**Vat·i·can** (vat′ə kən) 1 in Vatican City, the buildings of the Roman Catholic Church and the palace of the Pope. 2 the government, office, or authority of the Pope. *n.*

**vau·de·ville** (vod′ə vil′ *or* vod′vil) theatrical entertainment consisting of a variety of acts, such as singing, dancing, juggling, short plays, and animal acts. *n.*

 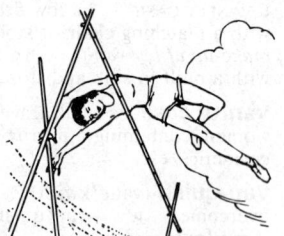

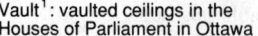

Vault[1]: vaulted ceilings in the Houses of Parliament in Ottawa     Vault[2]: a woman pole-vaulting

**vault**[1] (volt) 1 an arched roof or ceiling; a series of arches. 2 an arched space or passage. 3 something like an arched roof. The **vault of heaven** means the sky. **4** make in the form of a vault: *The roof was vaulted.* **5** cover with a vault. **6** an underground cellar or storehouse. **7** a place for storing valuable things and keeping them safe: *Vaults are often made of steel.* **8** a place for burial. *1–3, 6–8 n., 4, 5 v.* —**vault′like′**, *adj.*

**vault²** (volt) **1** jump or leap over by using a pole or the hands: *She easily vaulted the fence.* **2** the act of vaulting. **3** jump or leap: *He vaulted over the wall.* *1, 3 v., 2 n.*

**vault·ed** (vol′tid) **1** in the form of a vault; arched. **2** built or covered with a vault. **3** pt. and pp. of VAULT. *1, 2 adj., 3 v.*

**vault·ing¹** (vol′ting) **1** a vaulted structure. **2** vaults collectively. **3** ppr. of VAULT. *1, 2 n., 3 v.*

**vault·ing²** (vol′ting) **1** reaching or leaping over. **2** too confident; overreaching: *vaulting ambition.* **3** for use in vaulting or gymnastics: *a vaulting-horse.* **4** ppr. of VAULT². *1–3 adj., 4 v.*

**vaunt** (vont) boast. *v., n.* —**vaunt′ing·ly**, *adv.*

**vb.** **1** verb. **2** verbal.

**V.C.** **1** the Victoria Cross. **2** a person who has won a Victoria Cross: *There were several V.C.'s at the reunion.* **3** Vice-Chairman. **4** Vice-Chancellor. **5** Vice-Consul.

**VCR** video cassette recorder.

**V.D.** or **VD** venereal disease.

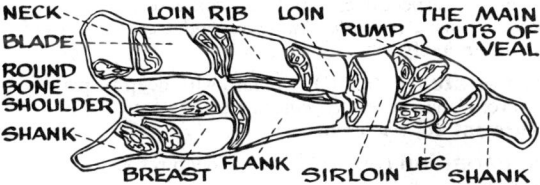
THE MAIN CUTS OF VEAL

**veal** (vēl) the flesh of a calf, used for food. *n.*

**vec·tor** (vek′tər) **1** a quantity involving direction as well as magnitude. **2** a line representing both the direction and the magnitude of some force, etc. *n.*

**Ve·da** (vā′də *or* vē′də) any or all of the four collections of Hindu sacred writings. *n.*

**Ve·dan·ta** (vi dän′tə *or* vi dan′tə) one of the leading schools of Hindu religious philosophy based on the Vedas, dealing with the relations of people and the universe with the Divine spirit. *n.*

**veer** (vēr) **1** change in direction; shift; turn: *The wind veered to the south. The talk veered to ghosts.* **2** change the direction of: *We veered our boat.* **3** a change in direction: *a veer to the left.* *1, 2 v., 3 n.*

**Ve·ga** (vē′gə) a bluish-white star of the first magnitude, in the constellation Lyra. *n.*

**veg·e·ta·ble** (vej′ə bəl *or* vej′tə bəl) **1** a part of a plant, such as leaves, seeds, roots, stem, or fruit, used for food and usually eaten with the main part of the meal: *Some common vegetables are potatoes, beans, peas, carrots, cabbage, tomatoes, sweet peppers, and spinach.* **2** a usually non-woody plant grown for such parts. **3** any plant. **4** of, having to do with, or like plants: *the vegetable kingdom, vegetable life.* **5** consisting of or made from vegetables: *vegetable soup.* **6** a person apparently lacking in thought or feeling, or one who has lost the use of his or her mind or, sometimes, limbs, etc. *n.*

**vault**     1329     **vein**

hat, āge, fär; let, ēqual, tėrm; it, īce
hot, ōpen, ôrder; oil, out; cup, pùt, rüle
əbove, takən, pencəl, lemən, circəs
ch, child; ng, long; sh, ship
th, thin; ŦH, then; zh, measure

**vegetable marrow** any of various oblong summer squashes having a smooth, light-yellow skin when ripe.

**vegetable oil** any fatty oil extracted from the seeds or fruit of plants, used in cooking.

**veg·e·tar·i·an** (vej′ə ter′ē ən) **1** a person who eats no meat and, sometimes, no animal products such as eggs, milk, or cheese. **2** of or having to do with vegetarians or VEGETARIANISM. **3** containing no meat: *a vegetarian diet.* *1 n., 2, 3 adj.*

**veg·e·tar·i·an·ism** (vej′ə ter′ē ə niz′əm) the practice or principle of eating vegetables, fruits, grains, and nuts, but no meat and, sometimes, no animal products. *n.*

**veg·e·tate** (vej′ə tāt′) **1** grow as plants do. **2** live with very little mental or physical activity; lead a dull, passive existence. *v.,* **veg·e·tat·ed, veg·e·tat·ing.**

**veg·e·ta·tion** (vej′ə tā′shən) **1** plant life; growing plants: *There is not much vegetation in deserts.* **2** vegetating; the growth of plants. **3** an existence similar to that of a vegetable; dull, empty, or stagnant life. *n.*

**veg·e·ta·tive** (vej′ə tā′tiv) **1** growing as plants do. **2** of plants or plant life. **3** having very little action, thought, or feeling. *adj.* —**veg′e·ta′tive·ly**, *adv.* —**veg′e·ta′tive·ness**, *n.*

**ve·he·mence** (vē′ə məns) the quality or state of being VEHEMENT: *The vehemence of her retort surprised us.* *n.*

**ve·he·ment** (vē′ə mənt) **1** having, showing, or caused by strong feeling; intense or passionate: *a vehement denial, vehement patriotism. She was vehement about not wanting to go.* **2** forceful; violent: *a vehement wind.* *adj.* —**ve′he·ment·ly**, *adv.*

**ve·hi·cle** (vē′ə kəl) **1** a carriage, cart, wagon, automobile, sled, or any other conveyance used on land. **2** any form of conveyance or transportation: *a space vehicle.* **3** a means by which something is communicated, shown, done, etc.: *Language is the vehicle of thought.* **4** a painting medium, such as linseed oil, in which the pigment is suspended: *Linseed oil is a vehicle for paint.* *n.*

**ve·hic·u·lar** (vē hik′yə lər) of or having to do with VEHICLES. *adj.*

**veil** (vāl) **1** a length of cloth worn by women so as to fall over the head and shoulders and, sometimes, the face or part of the face. **2** a piece of very thin cloth or netting worn by women over the head or face as a protection or as an ornament: *A veil is sometimes attached to a hat.* **3** cover with a veil: *In some places, Moslem women still veil their faces before going out in public.* **4** anything that covers or hides: *A veil of clouds hid the sun.* **5** cover; screen, or hide: *Fog veiled the shore. The spy veiled his plans in secrecy.* *1, 2, 4 n., 3, 5 v.,* —**veil′-like′**, *adj.*
☞ Hom. VALE.

**veil·ing** (vā′ling) **1** a VEIL. **2** material for veils. **3** ppr. of VEIL. *1, 2 n., 3 v.*

**vein** (vān) **1** one of the blood vessels or tubes that carry blood to the heart from all parts of the body. See HEART for picture. **2** a rib of an insect's wing. **3** one of the bundles of tubes and fibres that carry food and

**veined** 1330 **vengeance**

water through a leaf and form its main framework.  **4** a crack or seam in rock filled with a different mineral: *a vein of copper.*  **5** any streak or marking of a different shade or colour in wood, marble, etc.  **6** a strain or streak of some quality in character, conduct, writing, etc.: *There is a vein of fun in these poems. He has a vein of cruelty.*  **7** cover with veins; mark with veins.  *1–6 n., 7 v.* —**vein′less**, *adj.* —**vein′like′**, *adj.*
☛ *Hom.* VAIN, VANE.

**veined** (vānd)  **1** having veins or veinlike markings: *veined marble.*  **2** pt. and pp. of VEIN.  *1 adj., 2 v.*

**vein·ing** (vā′ning)  **1** an arrangement or pattern of veins.  **2** ppr. of VEIN.  *1 n., 2 v.*

**veld** or **veldt** (velt *or* felt)  in South Africa, open country having grass or bushes but few trees.  *n.*
☛ *Etym.* Through Afrikaans from Dutch *veld* 'field', which has the same Germanic source as FIELD.

**vel·lum** (vel′əm)  **1** the finest kind of parchment, originally made from calfskin, used especially for writing on or for binding books.  **2** a manuscript written on vellum.  **3** strong writing paper made to imitate vellum.  **4** of, resembling, or bound in vellum: *a vellum finish.*  *n.*

**ve·loc·i·pede** (və los′ə pēd′)  **1** a child's tricycle.  **2** an early kind of bicycle or tricycle.  *n.*

**ve·loc·i·ty** (və los′ə tē)  **1** speed; swiftness; quickness of motion: *to fly with the velocity of a bird.*  **2** the rate of motion: *The velocity of light is about 300 000 kilometres per second.*  *n., pl.* **ve·loc·i·ties.**

**ve·lo·drome** (vē′lə drōm′)  a building having a track for bicycle racing and, usually, seats and other facilities for spectators.  *n.*

**ve·lour** or **ve·lours** (və lür′)  any of various fabrics with a nap or pile like velvet, used for upholstery, draperies, clothing, etc.  *n.*

**ve·lum** (vē′ləm)  a veil-like membrane or membranous part, especially the soft palate.  *n., pl.* **ve·la** (-lə).

**vel·vet** (vel′vit)  **1** cloth, usually of cotton, rayon, or nylon, having a thick, short, cut pile that makes it smooth and soft to the touch: *Velvet is made by weaving two layers of fabric together and then shearing the faces apart.*  **2** made of or covered with velvet: *a velvet chesterfield.*  **3** like velvet; soft, smooth, rich, etc.: *the velvet paws of a kitten, a velvet voice.*  **4** something like velvet or suggesting velvet, especially in softness or smoothness.  **5** the soft, furry skin that covers and nourishes the growing antlers of a deer.  *n.*

**vel·vet·een** (vel′və tēn′)  **1** cotton or rayon cloth having a soft, cut pile similar to velvet, but which is woven singly instead of face to face like velvet.  **2** made of or covered with velveteen.  *n.*

**vel·vet·y** (vel′və tē)  smooth and soft like velvet.  *adj.*

**ve·na ca·va** (vē′nə kā′və)  either of the two large veins that in air-breathing vertebrates return blood to the right atrium of the heart.  See HEART and KIDNEY for pictures.  *n., pl.* **ve·nae ca·vae** (vē′nē kā′vē).

**ve·nal** (vē′nəl)  **1** willing to sell one's services or influence basely; open to bribes; corrupt: *a venal person.*  **2** influenced or obtained by bribery: *venal conduct.*  *adj.* —**ve′nal·ly**, *adv.*

**ve·nal·i·ty** (vē nal′ə tē)  the quality of being VENAL.  *n.*

**ve·na·tion** (vē nā′shən)  the arrangement of veins in a leaf or in an insect's wing.  *n.*

**vend** (vend)  sell, especially by peddling or hawking.  *v.*

**vend·er** (ven′dər)  See VENDOR.  *n.*

**ven·det·ta** (ven det′ə)  a feud in which the relatives of a person who has been wronged or murdered try to take vengeance on the wrongdoer or killer or his or her relatives.  *n.*

**vend·i·ble** (ven′də bəl)  **1** salable.  **2** a salable thing.  *1 adj., 2 n.*

**vending machine**  a coin-operated machine from which one may obtain coffee, candies, cigarettes, stamps, etc.

**ven·dor** or **ven·der** (ven′dər)  **1** a person who sells, especially by peddling or hawking.  **2** a person who is selling a house, etc.  **3** vending machine.  *n.*

**ve·neer** (və nēr′)  **1** a thin layer of fine wood or other material covering a cheaper grade of wood, fibreboard, etc.: *a desk made of pine with a walnut veneer, a wall with a veneer of brick.*  **2** cover with a veneer.  **3** cover anything with a layer of something else to give an appearance of superior quality.  **4** surface appearance or show: *a veneer of honesty.*  *1, 4 n., 2, 3 v.*

**ven·er·a·bil·i·ty** (ven′ə rə bil′ə tē)  the fact or quality of being VENERABLE.  *n.*

**ven·er·a·ble** (ven′ə rə bəl)  worthy of reverence; deserving respect because of age, character, or associations: *a venerable leader, venerable customs.*  *adj.* —**ven′er·a·bly**, *adv.*

**ven·er·ate** (ven′ə rāt′)  regard with deep respect; revere: *He venerates his father's memory.*  *v.*, **ven·er·at·ed, ven·er·at·ing.**

**ven·er·a·tion** (ven′ə rā′shən)  deep respect or reverence.  *n.*

**ve·ne·re·al** (və nē′rē əl)  **1** of or having to do with sexual intercourse.  **2** caused by sexual intercourse.  **3** having to do with diseases transmitted by sexual intercourse.  **4** infected with syphilis, gonorrhea, or some other VENEREAL DISEASE.  *adj.*

**venereal disease**  a contagious disease that is transmitted only or mainly by sexual intercourse, such as gonorrhea or syphilis.

**Ve·ne·tian** (və nē′shən)  **1** of Venice, a city on the northeastern coast of Italy, or its people.  **2** a native or inhabitant of Venice.  **3** a dialect of Italian spoken in parts of the province of Veneto.  *1 adj., 2, 3 n.*

**Venetian blind**  a window blind consisting of horizontal plastic, metal, or wooden slats that can be set at different angles to vary the amount of light that is let in.

**Ven·e·zue·lan** (ven′ə zwā′lən *or* ven′ə zwē′lən)  **1** of or having to do with Venezuela, a country in northern South America, or its people.  **2** a native or inhabitant of Venezuela.  *1 adj., 2 n.*

**venge·ance** (ven′jəns)  **1** the inflicting of injury as a punishment for a wrong or injury; revenge: *to swear vengeance for a wrong, to take vengeance on an enemy.*  **2** the desire to punish in this way: *There was vengeance in his heart.*  *n.*
**with a vengeance**, **a** with great force or intensity: *By six o'clock it was raining with a vengeance. She started in on the job with a vengeance.*  **b** to an unusual degree; extremely:

Leo was getting his own back with a vengeance. That escapade was adventure with a vengeance.

**venge·ful** (venj′fəl)   feeling or showing a strong desire for VENGEANCE.   adj.   —**venge′ful·ly**, adv.

**ve·ni·al** (vē′nē əl)   that can be forgiven; not very wrong; pardonable: *a venial sin, venial faults.*   adj.

**ven·i·son** (ven′ə sən)   the flesh of a deer, used for food; deer meat.   n.

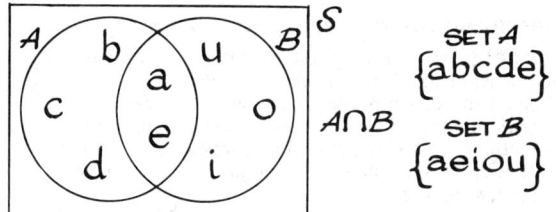

A Venn diagram showing the intersection of two sets having common elements. S is the set of all the letters of the alphabet, A is the set of the first five letters, and B is the set of vowels.

**Venn diagram** (ven)   a diagram using circles, rectangles, or ellipses to show the relationships between sets, propositions, etc.

**ven·om** (ven′əm)   **1** the poison produced by some snakes, spiders, etc. and introduced into the body of prey or an enemy mainly by a bite or sting.   **2** spite; malice: *There was venom in her voice.*   n.   —**ven′om·less**, adj.

**ven·om·ous** (ven′ə məs)   **1** poisonous: *Rattlesnakes are venomous.*   **2** spiteful; malicious.   adj.   —**ven′om·ous·ly**, adv.   —**ven′om·ous·ness**, n.

**ve·nous** (vē′nəs)   **1** of, in, or having to do with veins: *venous blood.*   **2** having veins: *the venous wings of insects.*   adj.

**vent**¹ (vent)   **1** a hole; opening, especially one serving as an outlet: *She used a pencil to make air vents in the box top so the frog could breathe.*   **2** an outlet; way out: *His great energy found vent in hard work.*   **3** expression: *She gave vent to her grief in tears.*   **4** let out; express freely: *He vented his anger on the dog.*   **5** the end of the intestine, especially in birds and reptiles.   **6** the small opening in the barrel of certain old guns through which the powder was fired; touchhole.   **7** in an automobile, etc., a small window that can be opened for indirect ventilation.   **8** make a vent in.   1–3, 5–7 n., 4, 8 v.

**vent**² (vent)   a slit or opening in a garment: *His new leather jacket has side vents.*   n.

**ven·ti·late** (ven′tə lāt′)   **1** change the air in: *We ventilate a room by opening windows.*   **2** purify by fresh air: *The lungs ventilate the blood.*   **3** make known publicly; discuss openly: *to ventilate one's opinions.*   **4** furnish with a vent or opening for the escape of air, gas, etc.   v., **ven·ti·lat·ed**, **ven·ti·lat·ing**.

**ven·ti·la·tion** (ven′tə lā′shən)   **1** the act or process of ventilating.   **2** a means of supplying fresh air: *That small window is the only ventilation in the warehouse.*   **3** circulation of air: *The room has good ventilation.*   **4** the circulation and exchange of gases in the lungs in the process of breathing.   n.

**ven·ti·la·tor** (ven′tə lā′tər)   any apparatus or means for changing or improving the air in an enclosed space.   n.

**ven·tral** (ven′trəl)   **1** of or having to do with the belly; abdominal.   **2** of, having to do with, or located on or

hat, āge, fär; let, ēqual, tėrm; it, īce
hot, ōpen, ôrder; oil, out; cup, put, rüle
ə*bove,* ə*taken,* ə*pencil,* ə*lemon,* ə*circus*
ch, child; ng, long; sh, ship
th, thin; ŦH, then; zh, measure

near the part or surface opposite the back: *a ventral fin.*   adj.   —**ven′tral·ly**, adv.

**ven·tri·cle** (ven′trə kəl)   **1** either of the two lower chambers of the heart that receive blood and force it into the arteries. See HEART for picture.   **2** any of a series of connecting cavities in the brain. See BRAIN for picture.   **3** any hollow organ of the body.   n.

**ven·tric·u·lar** (ven trik′yə lər)   of, having to do with, or being a VENTRICLE.   adj.

**ven·tril·o·quism** (ven tril′ə kwiz′əm)   the art or practice of speaking or uttering sounds without moving the lips so that the voice may seem to come from some source other than the speaker.   n.
☞ *Etym.* See note at VENTRILOQUY.

**ven·tril·o·quist** (ven tril′ə kwist)   a person who is skilled in VENTRILOQUISM, especially one who uses it to entertain an audience by appearing to carry on a conversation with a puppet manipulated by hand.   n.
☞ *Etym.* See note at VENTRILOQUY.

**ven·tril·o·quy** (ven tril′ə kwē)   VENTRILOQUISM.   n.
☞ *Etym.* From modern L *ventriloquium*, made up from *venter*, *ventri-* 'belly' (as in F *ventre*) + *loqui* 'speak', literally 'speaking in the belly'. 16c. VENTRILOQUIST and VENTRILOQUISM were formed from **ventriloquy** in the 17c. and 18c. respectively.

**ven·ture** (ven′chər)   **1** a risky or daring undertaking: *Her courage was equal to any venture.*   **2** a speculation to make money: *A lucky venture in oil stock made his fortune.*   **3** expose to risk or danger: *People venture their lives in war.*   **4** run a risk.   **5** the thing risked; stake.   **6** dare: *No one ventured to interrupt the speaker.*   **7** dare to come, go, or proceed: *She ventured out on the thin ice and fell through.*   **8** dare to say or make: *He ventured an objection.*   1, 2, 5 n., 3, 4, 6–8 v., **ven·tured**, **ven·tur·ing**.
**at a venture**, at random; by chance: *She went to the shelf and, without looking, took out a book at a venture.*

**ven·ture·some** (ven′chər səm)   **1** inclined to take risks; rash; daring: *a venturesome explorer.*   **2** hazardous; risky: *A trip to the moon is a venturesome journey.*   adj.

**ven·tu·ri** (ven chü′rē or ven tü′rē)   a short, narrow piece of tubing between wider sections in a pump or pipeline, used to measure or regulate the rate of flow of a liquid or gas.   n.

**venturi tube**   VENTURI.

**ven·tur·ous** (ven′chə rəs)   VENTURESOME.   adj.

**ven·ue** (ven′yü)   **1** the place or neighbourhood of a crime or other cause of legal action.   **2** the place where the jury is gathered and the case tried: *A change of venue is allowed when strong local feeling may prevent a defendant from getting a fair trial.*   **3** the location of a conference, an important sporting event, etc.   n.

**Ve·nus** (vē′nəs)   the most brilliant planet, second in distance from the sun and coming closest to the earth.   n.
☞ *Etym.* From *Venus*, in Roman mythology, th love and beauty, corresponding to the Greek Aphrodite.

**Ve·nus's–fly·trap** (vē′nə səz flī′trap′) an insect-eating bog plant of the sundew family native to the eastern United States, having hairy leaves with two lobes at the end that snap together to trap insects. *n.*

**ver.** 1 verse. 2 version.

**ve·ra·cious** (və rā′shəs) 1 truthful. 2 true. *adj.* —**ve·ra′cious·ly**, *adv.* —**ve·ra′cious·ness**, *n.*
☛ *Hom.* VORACIOUS (və rā′shəs).

**ve·rac·i·ty** (və ras′ə tē) 1 truthfulness: *Her veracity was not questioned.* 2 correctness; accuracy: *to check the veracity of a statement.* 3 something that is true. *n., pl.* **ve·rac·i·ties**.
☛ *Hom.* VORACITY (və ras′ə tē).

**ve·ran·da** (və ran′də) a large, covered porch along one or more sides of a house. *n.*

**verb** (vėrb) a part of speech that expresses the tense (past, present, future), voice (active or passive) and duration (complete or progressive) of an action or state: *The verb is the main part of the predicate of a sentence.* Do, see, impose, introduce, eat, *and* translate *are verbs.* *n.*

**ver·bal** (vėr′bəl) 1 in or of words: *A description is a verbal picture.* 2 expressed in spoken words; oral: *a verbal promise, a verbal message.* 3 word for word; literal: *a verbal translation from the French.* 4 of, having to do with, or derived from a verb: *a verbal noun.* 5 a verb form that functions as a noun, adjective, or adverb: *Participles, gerunds, and infinitives are verbals.* 1–4 *adj.*, 5 *n.* —**ver′bal·ly**, *adv.*

**ver·bal·ism** (vėr′bə liz′əm) 1 a verbal expression; word, phrase, etc. 2 too much attention to mere words. 3 a stock phrase or formula in words with little meaning. *n.*

**ver·bal·i·za·tion** (vėr′bə lə zā′shən *or* vėr′bə lī zā′shən) 1 expression in words. 2 the use of too many words. *n.*

**ver·bal·ize** (vėr′bə līz′) 1 express in words. 2 use too many words; be wordy. *v.*, **ver·bal·ized**, **ver·bal·iz·ing**.

**ver·ba·tim** (vėr bā′tim) word for word; in exactly the same words: *Her speech was printed verbatim in the newspaper.* *adv., adj.*

**ver·be·na** (vər bē′nə) 1 any of a closely related group of plants, most of which are native to the Western Hemisphere, having flowers of various colours growing in clusters or spikes: *Some verbenas have long been cultivated as garden plants.* 2 referring to a family of mainly tropical herbs, shrubs, and trees: *The verbena family includes the verbenas and also some trees important for timber, such as teak.* *n.*

**ver·bi·age** (vėr′bē ij) the use of too many words; abundance of useless words. *n.*

**ver·bose** (vėr bōs′) containing or using too many words; wordy. *adj.* —**ver·bose′ly**, *adv.* —**ver·bose′ness**, *n.*

**ver·bos·i·ty** (vėr bos′ə tē) the use of too many words; wordiness. *n.*

**ver·dan·cy** (vėr′dən sē) the quality or state of being VERDANT; greenness. *n.*

**ver·dant** (vėr′dənt) 1 green in colour: *fields covered with verdant grass.* 2 covered with growing green plants: *verdant fields.* *adj.* —**ver′dant·ly**, *adv.*

**ver·dict** (vėr′dikt) 1 the decision of a jury: *The jury returned a verdict of not guilty.* 2 any decision or judgment: *the public's verdict, the verdict of history.* *n.*

**ver·di·gris** (vėr′də grēs *or* vėr′də gris) 1 a green or bluish coating that forms on brass, copper, or bronze when exposed to the air for long periods of time. 2 a green or bluish-green poisonous compound used as a pigment for paints. *n.*

**ver·dure** (vėr′jər) 1 fresh greenness. 2 a fresh growth of green grass, plants, or leaves. *n.*

**ver·dur·ous** (vėr′jə rəs) green and fresh. *adj.*

**verge**¹ (vėrj) 1 the point at which something begins or happens; brink: *Their business is on the verge of ruin.* 2 be on the verge; border (used with **on**): *Her silly talk verged on nonsense.* 3 a limiting belt, strip, or border of something. 4 a rod, staff, etc. carried as an emblem of authority. 5 the shaft of a column. 1, 3–5 *n.*, 2 *v.*, **verged**, **verg·ing**.

**verge**² (vėrj) tend; incline: *She was plump, verging on fatness.* *v.*, **verged**, **verg·ing**.

**ver·ger** (vėr′jər) 1 in some churches, an attendant who shows people to their seats, passes the collection plate, etc. 2 an officer or attendant who carries the staff or wand before a bishop, dean, etc. *n.*

**ver·i·est** (ver′ē ist) utmost: *the veriest nonsense.* *adj.*

**ver·i·fi·a·ble** (ver′ə fī′ə bəl) capable of being verified; that can be checked for truth or correctness. *adj.*

**ver·i·fi·ca·tion** (ver′ə fə kā′shən) verifying or being verified; proof by evidence or testimony; confirmation. *n.*

**ver·i·fy** (ver′ə fī′) 1 prove something to be true; confirm: *The driver's report of the accident was verified by eyewitnesses.* 2 test the correctness of; check for accuracy: *Verify the spelling of a word by looking in a dictionary.* *v.*, **ver·i·fied**, **ver·i·fy·ing**. —**ver′i·fi′er**, *n.*

**ver·i·si·mil·i·tude** (ver′ə sə mil′ə tyüd′ *or* ver′ə sə mil′ə tüd′) 1 appearance of truth or reality; probability: *A story must have verisimilitude to interest most people.* 2 something having merely the appearance of truth. *n.*

**ver·i·ta·ble** (ver′ə tə bəl) true; real; actual: *a veritable flood of letters.* *adj.* —**ver′i·ta·ble·ness**, *n.* —**ver′i·ta·bly**, *adv.*

**ver·i·ty** (ver′ə tē) 1 the quality or state of being true or real. 2 something that is true or real, especially a basic principle or belief: *the eternal verities.* *n., pl.* **ver·i·ties**.

**ver·meil** (vėr′məl) silver or bronze coated with gilt. *n.*

**ver·mi·cel·li** (vėr′mə sel′ē; *Italian*, vėr′mē chel′lē) a kind of pasta similar to spaghetti, but thinner. *n.*

**ver·mi·cide** (vėr′mə sīd′) any agent that kills worms, especially a drug used to kill parasitic intestinal worms. *n.*

**ver·mic·u·lite** (vėr mik′yə līt′) any of various silicate minerals in the form of small, lightweight granules or flakes that readily absorb water: *Vermiculite is used as a medium for growing seedlings, for insulation, etc.* *n.*

**ver·mi·form** (vėr′mə fôrm′) shaped like a worm. *adj.*

**vermiform appendix** a slender tube, closed at one end, growing out of the large intestine in the lower right-hand part of the abdomen: *Appendicitis is inflammation of the vermiform appendix.*

**ver·mi·fuge** (vėr′mə fyüj′) a medicine to expel worms from the intestines. *n.*

**ver·mil·ion** (vər mil′yən) **1** bright, somewhat orangy red. **2** a pigment having this colour, especially one consisting of mercuric sulphide. *1, 2 n., 1 adj.*

**ver·min** (vėr′mən) **1** small animals that are troublesome or destructive: *Fleas, lice, bedbugs, rats, and mice are vermin.* **2** *Esp. Brit.* animals or birds that destroy game, poultry, etc. **3** a vile, worthless person or persons. *n.pl. or sing.*

**ver·min·ous** (vėr′mə nəs) **1** infested with VERMIN. **2** caused by VERMIN. **3** like VERMIN; vile; worthless. *adj.*

**ver·mouth** (vər müth′) a dry or sweet white wine flavoured with wormwood or other herbs and used as a liqueur or in cocktails. *n.*

**ver·nac·u·lar** (vər nak′yə lər) **1** a native language; a language used by the people of a certain country or place. **2** used by the people of a certain country, place, etc.; native: *French is their vernacular tongue.* **3** of or in the native or everyday language, rather than a literary or learned language. **4** everyday language; informal speech. **5** the language of a profession, trade, etc.: *the vernacular of lawyers.* *1, 4, 5 n., 2, 3 adj.*

**ver·nal** (vėr′nəl) **1** of, having to do with, or occurring in spring: *vernal green, vernal flowers, vernal months, the vernal equinox.* **2** like spring; fresh or new. **3** youthful: *Everyone admired the young girl's vernal freshness.* *adj.* —**ver′nal·ly,** *adv.*

**vernal equinox** the equinox that occurs about March 21.

**ver·ni·er** (vėr′nē ər) a small, movable scale for measuring a fractional part of one of the divisions of a fixed scale. *n.*

**ve·ron·i·ca** (və ron′ə kə) SPEEDWELL. *n.*

**ver·sa·tile** (vėr′sə tīl′ *or* vėr′sə təl) **1** able to do many things well: *He is very versatile: he is an actor, a poet, a singer, and a language teacher.* **2** having many uses: *a versatile dress that is suitable for different occasions. A pocketknife is a versatile tool.* **3** capable of turning forward or backward: *the versatile toe of an owl.* **4** moving freely up and down and from side to side: *versatile antennae.* **5** in botany, attached at or near the middle so as to swing or turn freely: *a versatile anther.* **6** fickle; inconstant. *adj.* —**ver′sa·tile·ly,** *adv.*

**ver·sa·til·i·ty** (vėr′sə til′ə tē) the quality or state of being VERSATILE. *n., pl.* **ver·sa·til·i·ties.**

**verse** (vėrs) **1** lines of words usually having a regularly repeated stress pattern and often with rhyme; poetry. **2** a single line of verse. **3** a group of such lines: *Sing the first verse of "O Canada."* **4** a type of verse; METRE (def. 2): *blank verse, iambic verse.* **5** in the Bible, a short division of a chapter. *n.*

**versed** (vėrst) experienced; practised; skilled: *A doctor should be well versed in medical theory.* *adj.*

**ver·si·fi·ca·tion** (vėr′sə fə kā′shən) **1** the making of verses. **2** the form or style of poetry; metrical structure. **3** a version in verse of a prose writing. *n.*

**ver·si·fi·er** (vėr′sə fī′ər) a person who makes verses. *n.*

**ver·si·fy** (vėr′sə fī) **1** write verses. **2** tell in verse. **3** turn prose into poetry. *v.,* **ver·si·fied, ver·si·fy·ing.**

**ver·sion** (vėr′zhən) **1** a translation from one language

**vermifuge**     **1333**     **very high frequency**

hat, āge, fär; let, ēqual, tėrm; it, īce
hot, ōpen, ôrder; oil, out; cup, put, rüle
əbove, takən, pencəl, lemən, circəs
ch, child; ng, long; sh, ship
th, thin; ᴛʜ, then; zh, measure

to another. **2** a statement or description from a particular point of view: *Each of the three boys gave his own version of the quarrel.* **3** a special form or variant of something: *The tent trailer is a modern version of the travois.* *n.*

**ver·sus** (vėr′səs) **1** against: *It was our team versus a much older one.* **2** in contrast to: *the new versus the old, strength versus agility.* *prep.*
☛ *Etym.* From Med. L *versus* 'toward, against', formed from the verb *vertere* 'to turn'.

**ver·te·bra** (vėr′tə brə) one of the bones of the spinal column. See SPINAL COLUMN for picture. *n., pl.* **ver·te·brae** (-brā′ *or* -brē′) *or* **ver·te·bras.**

**ver·te·bral** (vėr′tə brəl) **1** of or having to do with a VERTEBRA or the vertebrae. **2** composed of VERTEBRAe. *adj.*

**ver·te·brate** (vėr′tə brit *or* vėr′tə brāt′) **1** any animal that has a segmented spinal column, or backbone: *Fish, amphibians, reptiles, birds, and mammals are all vertebrates.* **2** having a backbone. *1 n., 2 adj.*

**ver·tex** (vėr′teks′) **1** the highest point; top; summit. **2** the point opposite to and farthest away from the base of a triangle, pyramid, etc. **3** the point of meeting of lines that form an angle. **4** a point in the heavens directly overhead; zenith. **5** any point of a triangle or polygon. *n., pl.* **ver·tex·es** *or* **ver·ti·ces.**

**ver·ti·cal** (vėr′tə kəl) **1** straight up and down; PERPENDICULAR to a level surface: *A person standing up straight is in a vertical position.* See HORIZONTAL for picture. **2** a vertical line, plane, circle, position, part, etc. **3** of or at the highest point; of the VERTEX. **4** directly overhead; at the zenith. **5** so organized as to include many or all stages in the production of some manufactured product: *a vertical union, vertical trusts.* *1, 3–5 adj., 2 n.* —**ver′ti·cal·ly,** *adv.*

**ver·ti·ces** (vėr′tə sēz′) a pl. of VERTEX. *n.*

**ver·ti·go** (vėr′tə gō′) a sensation of dizziness or of giddiness. *n., pl.* **ver·ti·goes** *or* **ver·tig·i·nes** (vėr tij′ə nēz′).

**ver·vain** (vėr′vān) verbena; especially, any of several wild North American herbs or a European species formerly used in medicine. *n.*

**verve** (vėrv) enthusiasm; energy; vigour; spirit; liveliness. *n.*

**ver·y** (vėr′ē) **1** much; greatly; extremely: *The sunshine is very hot in July.* **2** absolutely; exactly: *She stood in the very same place for an hour.* **3** same; identical: *The very people who used to love her hate her now.* **4** even; mere; sheer: *The very thought of blood makes her sick. She wept from very joy.* **5** real; true; genuine: *She seemed a very queen.* **6** actual: *He was caught in the very act of stealing.* *1, 2 adv., 3–6 adj.*
☛ *Hom.* VARY (vėr′ē).

**very high frequency** the band of radio frequencies between 30 and 300 megahertz: *Very high frequency is the range next above high frequency.* *Abbrev.:* VHF, V.H.F., vhf

**very low frequency** the band of radio frequencies between 3 and 30 kilohertz: *Very low frequency is the range next above voice frequency.* *Abbrev.:* VLF, V.L.F., vlf

**ves·i·cate** (ves′ə kāt′) cause blisters on; blister. *v.*, **ves·i·cat·ed, ves·i·cat·ing.**

**ves·i·cle** (ves′ə kəl) **1** in biology, a small bladder, pouch, sac, or cyst. **2** a small, abnormal, raised part in the outer layer of skin, containing a watery fluid; blister. **3** in geology, a small cavity in a rock or mineral. *n.*

**ve·sic·u·lar** (və sik′yə lər) **1** of, having to do with, or having VESICLES. **2** like a VESICLE; having the form or structure of a vesicle. *adj.*

**ves·sel** (ves′əl) **1** a large boat; ship. **2** an airship. **3** a hollow holder or container: *Cups, bowls, pitchers, bottles, barrels, tubs, etc., are vessels.* **4** a tube carrying blood or other fluid: *Veins and arteries are blood vessels.* *n.*

A man's vest

**vest** (vest) **1** a short, sleeveless garment worn by men and boys under a suit coat. **2** a similar garment worn by women. **3** UNDERSHIRT. **4** clothe; robe; dress in vestments: *The vested priest stood before the altar.* **5** furnish with powers, authority, rights, etc.: *Parliament is vested with the power to declare war.* **6** put in the possession or control of a person or persons: *The management of the hospital is vested in a board of trustees.* 1–3 *n.*, 4–6 *v.* —**vest′less,** *adj.*

**ves·tal** (ves′təl) **1** of or having to do with the Roman goddess Vesta, the goddess of the hearth. **2** chaste. *adj.*

**vestal virgin** a virgin consecrated to the service of the Roman goddess Vesta: *Six vestal virgins tended an undying fire in honour of Vesta at her temple in Rome.*

**vest·ed** (ves′tid) **1** in law, placed in the permanent possession or control of a person or persons; fixed; absolute: *vested rights.* **2** pt. and pp. of VEST. 1 *adj.*, 2 *v.*

A vestibule

**ves·ti·bule** (ves′tə byül′) **1** a passage or hall between the outer door and the inside of a building. **2** the enclosed space at the end of a railway passenger car. **3** a cavity of the body that leads to another cavity: *The vestibule of the ear is the central cavity of the inner ear.* See EAR¹ for picture. *n.*

**ves·tige** (ves′tij) a slight remnant; trace: *Ghost stories are vestiges of a former widespread belief in ghosts.* *n.*

**ves·tig·i·al** (ves tij′ē əl) remaining as a VESTIGE of something that has disappeared. *adj.*

**vest·ment** (vest′mənt) **1** an outer garment, especially for ceremonial or official wear. **2** any of the official garments worn by members of the Christian clergy and assistants during church services. **3 vestments,** *pl.* clothing. *n.*

**vest–pock·et** (vest′pok′it) **1** able to fit into a vest pocket. **2** very small. *adj.*

**ves·try** (ves′trē) **1** a room in a Christian church, where vestments, etc. are kept; sacristy. **2** a room in a church or an attached building, used for Sunday school, prayer meetings, etc. **3** in Anglican churches, a committee that helps manage church business. **4** in Anglican churches, a meeting of parishioners on church business. *n., pl.* **ves·tries.**

**ves·try·man** (ves′trē mən) a member of a committee that helps manage church business. *n., pl.* **ves·try·men** (-mən).

**ves·ture** (ves′chər) **1** clothing; garments. **2** a covering: *In the spring the meadows have a vesture of grass.* *n.*

**vet¹** (vet) *Informal.* **1** VETERINARIAN. **2** examine and care for as a VETERINARIAN or, sometimes, a doctor. **3** examine carefully; check: *to vet a report, to vet a candidate.* **4** be a veterinarian. 1 *n.*, 2–4 *v.*, **vet·ted, vet·ting.**

**vet²** (vet) *Informal.* VETERAN. *n.*

**vetch** (vech) any of a closely related group of trailing or climbing plants of the pea family, including several species that are valuable fodder and soil-enriching plants. *n.*

**vet·er·an** (vet′ə rən *or* vet′rən) **1** a person who has served in the armed forces, especially during wartime. **2** a person who has had much experience in war; an old soldier, sailor, or airman, etc. **3** having had much experience in war: *Veteran troops fought side by side with new recruits.* **4** a person who has had much experience in some position, occupation, etc. **5** grown old in service; having had much experience: *a veteran farmer.* *n.*

**Veterans Affairs Canada** a branch of the federal government dealing with the needs and rights of former servicemen and servicewomen.

**vet·er·i·nar·i·an** (vet′ə rə ner′ē ən) a person who is qualified to treat diseases and injuries of animals and who makes this his or her work. *n.*

**vet·er·i·nar·y** (vet′ə rə ner′ē) **1** of, having to do with, or being the art or science of the prevention or treatment of diseases and injuries of animals. **2** VETERINARIAN. 1 *adj.*, 2 *n., pl.* **vet·er·i·nar·ies.**

**veterinary surgeon** VETERINARIAN.

**ve·to** (vē′tō) **1** the right or power to forbid or reject: *The Senate has the power of veto over most bills passed in the House of Commons.* **2** having to do with a veto: *veto power.* **3** the use of this right; a refusal of consent: *The Senate's veto kept the bill from becoming a law.* **4** a statement of the reasons for disapproval of a bill passed by a legislature. **5** reject by a veto. **6** refuse to consent to: *His parents vetoed his plan to buy a motorcycle.* *1, 3, 4 n., pl.* **ve·toes;** *2 adj.,* 5, 6 *v.,* **ve·toed, ve·to·ing.** —**ve′to·er,** *n.*

**vex** (veks) **1** anger by trifles; annoy; provoke: *It is vexing to have to wait for anyone.* **2** disturb; trouble: *Cape Sable is much vexed by storms.* *v.*

**vex·a·tion** (vek sā′shən) **1** the quality or state of being vexed: *Her vexation at the delay was obvious.* **2** the act of vexing. **3** something that vexes: *Rain on Saturday was a vexation to the children.* *n.*

**vex·a·tious** (vek sā′shəs) vexing; annoying. *adj.* —**vex·a′tious·ly,** *adv.*

**vex·ed·ly** (vek′si dlē) with vexation; with a sense of annoyance or vexation: *"What can be keeping them?" he asked vexedly.* *adv.*

**VHF, V.H.F.,** or **vhf** very high frequency.

**v.i.** intransitive verb (an abbreviation of Latin *verbum intransitivum*).

**V.I.** **1** Vancouver Island. **2** Virgin Islands.

**vi·a** (vī′ə *or* vē′ə) **1** by way of; by a route that passes through or along: *They travelled from Winnipeg to Saskatoon via Regina.* **2** by means or through the medium of: *We sent the package via airmail.* *prep.* ☞ *Etym.* From L *via* 'by way of', a form of *via* 'road, way'.

**vi·a·bil·i·ty** (vī′ə bil′ə tē) the quality or state of being VIABLE: *the viability of a plan.* *n.*

**vi·a·ble** (vī′ə bəl) **1** able to stay alive: *a viable animal or plant.* **2** able to keep operating or functioning: *a viable economy.* *adj.*

**vi·a·duct** (vī′ə dukt′) a bridge, especially one consisting of a series of arches or short spans resting on high piers or towers, for carrying a road or railway over a valley, a part of a city, etc. *n.*

**vi·al** (vī′əl) a small bottle, especially a glass bottle, for holding medicines, perfumes, etc. *n.* ☞ *Hom.* VIOL.

**vi·and** (vī′ənd *or* vē′ənd) Usually, **viands,** *pl.* articles of food, especially choice food. *n.*

**vibes** (vībz) *Informal.* **1** VIBRAPHONE: *She plays the vibes.* **2** a distinctive emotional atmosphere; vibrations: *He left the party early because he said the vibes were bad.* *n.pl.*

**vi·brant** (vī′brənt) **1** vibrating. **2** throbbing with vitality, enthusiasm, etc.; full of life and vigour: *a vibrant personality.* **3** resounding or resonant: *a vibrant voice.* *adj.* —**vi′brant·ly,** *adv.*

**vi·bra·phone** (vī′brə fōn′) a musical instrument similar to a xylophone but having motor-driven resonators and metal tubes that produce a VIBRATO. *n.*

**vi·brate** (vī′brāt) **1** move rapidly to and fro: *A piano string vibrates and makes a sound when a key is struck.* **2** cause to swing to and fro; set in motion. **3** measure by moving to and fro: *A pendulum vibrates seconds.* **4** respond with feeling; thrill: *Their hearts vibrated to the appeal.* **5** resound: *The clanging vibrated in his ears.* *v.,* **vi·brat·ed, vi·brat·ing.**

**vi·bra·tion** (vī brā′shən) **1** a rapid movement to and fro; quivering motion; vibrating: *The heavy trucks shake the house so much that we feel the vibration.* **2** a rapid or slow movement to and fro. **3** motion back and forth across the position of rest. *n.* —**vi·bra′tion·less,** *adj.*

hat, āge, fär; let, ēqual, tėrm; it, īce
hot, ōpen, ôrder; oil, out; cup, pu̇t, rüle
əbove, takən, pencəl, lemən, circəs
ch, child; ng, long; sh, ship
th, thin; ᴛʜ, then; zh, measure

**vi·bra·to** (vē brä′tō) in music, a vibrating or tremulous effect produced by slight variations of pitch. *n., pl.* **vi·bra·tos.**

**vi·bra·tor** (vī′brā tər) **1** an electrical appliance or device that vibrates, used in massage. **2** a vibrating device in an electric bell or buzzer. *n.*

**vi·bra·to·ry** (vī′brə tô′rē) **1** vibrating or capable of vibration. **2** having to do with or causing vibration: *a vibratory force.* **3** consisting of vibration: *a vibratory movement.* *adj.*

**vi·bur·num** (vī bėr′nəm) any of a closely related group of shrubs and small trees of the honeysuckle family: *The snowball is a viburnum.* *n.*

**vic·ar** (vik′ər) **1** in the Anglican church, a member of the clergy who carries out the duties of a parish but is not officially the rector: *A rector may be responsible for several parishes, with a different vicar representing him in each one.* **2** in the Roman Catholic church, a deputy or representative of another official: *The cardinal vicar of Rome is appointed to represent the pope.* **3** any person who takes the place of another; a substitute or representative. *n.*

**vic·ar·age** (vik′ə rij) **1** the residence of a vicar. **2** the position or duties of a vicar. *n.*

**vi·car·i·ous** (vī ker′ē əs *or* vi ker′ē əs) **1** felt or realized by sharing in one's imagination the actual experience of another person: *She obtains a vicarious delight in foreign countries from reading travel books.* **2** done or suffered for others: *vicarious work, a vicarious sacrifice.* **3** taking the place of or doing the work of another: *As a ghost writer, he is a vicarious autobiographer.* *adj.* —**vi·car′i·ous·ly,** *adv.* —**vi·car′i·ous·ness,** *n.*

**vice**[1] (vīs) **1** moral corruption; evil; wickedness. **2** an evil or immoral habit: *the vice of gluttony.* **3** a fault; a bad habit: *He said that his horse had no vices.* **4** prostitution. *n.* ☞ *Hom.* VISE.

**vice**[2] (vīs) See VISE. *n.* ☞ *Hom.* VISE.

**vi·ce**[3] (vī′sē) instead of; in the place of. *prep.*

**vice–** a prefix meaning: a substitute; deputy; subordinate, as in *vice-president, vice-admiral.*

**vice–chan·cel·lor** (vīs′chan′sə lər) a person who substitutes for the regular chancellor or acts as his or her assistant. *n.*

**vice–con·sul** (vīs′kon′səl) a person next in rank below a consul. *n.*

**vice–ge·ren·cy** (vīs′jē′rən sē) the position of VICEGERENT. *n., pl.* **vice·ge·ren·cies.**

**vice–ge·rent** (vīs′jē′rənt) **1** a person exercising the powers or authority of another; a deputy, especially of a ruler. **2** acting as vicegerent. **1** *n.,* **2** *adj.*

**vi·cen·ni·al** (vī sen′ē əl) **1** of or for twenty years. **2** occurring once every twenty years. *adj.*

An English victoria of the late 19th century

**vice‑pres‧i‧den‧cy** (vīs′prez′ə dən sē) the position of vice-president. *n.*

**vice‑pres‧i‧dent** (vīs′prez′ə dənt) the officer next in rank to the president, who takes the president's place when necessary. *n.*

**vice‑pres‧i‧den‧tial** (vīs′prez ə den′shəl) of or having to do with a vice-president. *adj.*

**vice‑re‧gal** (vīs′rē′gəl) of or having to do with a VICEROY. *adj.*

**vice‑re‧gent** (vīs′rē′jənt) a deputy of a regent. *n.*

**vice‧roy** (vīs′roi) a person governing a province or colony as the representative of the sovereign. *n.*

**vice‧roy‧al‧ty** (vīs′roi′əl tē) the position or district of a VICEROY. *n.*

**vi‧ce ver‧sa** (vī′sə vėr′sə *or* vīs′ vėr′sə) the other way round; conversely: *John blamed Harry, and vice versa (Harry blamed John).*

**vi‧cin‧i‧ty** (və sin′ə tē) **1** a region near or about a place; neighbourhood; surrounding district: *She knew many people in Toronto and its vicinity.* **2** a nearness in place; closeness: *The vicinity of the school to the house was an advantage on rainy days.* *n., pl.* **vi‧cin‧i‧ties.**

**vi‧cious** (vish′əs) **1** depraved or wicked: *He had led a vicious life.* **2** dangerously aggressive or unruly: *a vicious dog, a vicious horse.* **3** fierce or violent: *a vicious brawl.* **4** spiteful; malicious: *a vicious rumour, a vicious retort.* **5** *Informal.* unpleasantly severe: *a vicious headache.* *adj.* —**vi′cious‧ly,** *adv.* —**vi′cious‧ness,** *n.*

**vicious circle** **1** two or more undesirable things each of which keeps causing the other: *It's a vicious circle: the more you scratch a mosquito bite, the more it itches.* **2** false reasoning that uses one statement to prove a second statement when the first statement really depends upon the second for proof.

**vi‧cis‧si‧tude** (və sis′ə tyüd′ *or* və sis′ə tüd′) **1** a change in circumstances, fortune, etc. that occurs by chance: *The vicissitudes of life may suddenly make a rich man poor or a poor man rich.* **2** constant change or variation; mutability. **3** a regular alternation or succession: *the vicissitude of day and night.* *n.*

**vi‧comte** (vē kôNt′) *French.* VISCOUNT. *n.*

**vic‧tim** (vik′təm) **1** a person or animal injured, destroyed, sacrificed, or mistreated: *victims of war, a victim of heart disease, victims of an unjust economic system. She has been the victim of several harsh attacks in the press.* **2** a person tricked by another; dupe: *the victim of a swindler.* **3** a person or animal sacrificed as part of a religious rite. *n.*

**vic‧tim‧i‧za‧tion** (vik′tə mə zā′shən *or* vik′tə mī zā′shən) victimizing or being VICTIMIZED. *n.*

**vic‧tim‧ize** (vik′tə mīz′) **1** make a VICTIM of; cause to suffer. **2** cheat; swindle. *v.,* **vic‧tim‧ized, vic‧tim‧iz‧ing.**

**vic‧tor** (vik′tər) **1** a winner; conqueror. **2** victorious: *the victor army.* *n.*

**vic‧to‧ri‧a** (vik tô′rē ə) **1** a low, four-wheeled carriage with a folding top and a seat for two passengers: *A victoria is a type of phaeton.* **2** any of a closely related group of South American water lilies having huge rose-white flowers and very large leaves. *n.*

**Victoria Cross** a medal in the shape of a cross awarded to members of the armed forces for remarkable valour in the presence of the enemy: *The Victoria Cross is the highest award given for bravery in the armed forces of the Commonwealth.* See MEDAL for picture.

**Victoria Day** in Canada, a national holiday falling on the Monday before or on the 24th of May, the birthday of Queen Victoria.

**Vic‧to‧ri‧an** (vik tô′rē ən) **1** of or having to do with the time of Queen Victoria: *Victorian furniture, Victorian drama.* **2** a person who lived during the reign of Queen Victoria, especially an author, artist, statesman, etc. considered representative of the time. **3** possessing characteristics considered typical of the Victorians, especially prudishness, smugness, bigotry, etc. **4** a native or inhabitant of any place called Victoria, such as Victoria, B.C. or the state of Victoria, Australia. 1, 3 *adj.,* 2, 4 *n.*

**Victorian age** the period during the reign of Queen Victoria, from 1837 to 1901.

**Vic‧to‧ri‧an‧ism** (vik tô′rē ə niz′əm) **1** the quality or state of being Victorian, especially in attitudes or tastes. **2** an idea, belief, etc. common during the Victorian age. *n.*

**vic‧to‧ri‧ous** (vik tô′rē əs) having won a victory; conquering: *a victorious army.* *adj.* —**vic‧to‧ri‧ous‧ly,** *adv.*

**vic‧to‧ry** (vik′tə rē) a defeat of an enemy or opponent; success in a contest. *n., pl.* **vic‧to‧ries.**

**vic‧tro‧la** (vik trō′lə) a former term for phonograph. *n.*

**vic‧tual** (vit′əl) **1** supply with food or provisions: *The captain victualled his ship for the voyage.* **2** take on a supply of food: *The ship will victual before sailing.* **3** **victuals,** *pl.* food, especially when prepared for use. 1, 2 *v.,* **vict‧ualled** *or* **vict‧ualed, vict‧ual‧ling** *or* **vict‧ual‧ing;** 3 *n.*

**vict‧ual‧ler** *or* **vict‧ual‧er** (vit′ə lər) **1** a person who supplies food or provisions to a ship, an army, etc. **2** *Esp. Brit.* the keeper of an inn, tavern, saloon, etc. *n.*

**vi‧cu‧ña** (vi kü′nyə *or* vi kyü′nə) **1** a wild animal of South America closely related to the llama and alpaca, highly valued for its soft, fine wool. **2** the wool of a vicuña. **3** cloth made from this wool. *n.*

**vid‧e‧o** (vid′ē ō′) **1** of or used in the transmission or reception of images in television. **2** TELEVISION. **3** the visual part, as opposed to the sound, of a film or television program. **4** a VIDEOTAPE, especially a recording of a motion picture or other entertainment. **5** VIDEO CASSETTE. **6** using a computer screen. 1, 6 *adj.,* 2–5 *n.*

**video cassette** a videotape mounted in a CASSETTE, for recording and playing back video programs.

**video cassette recorder** a device for recording and playing back video cassettes. *Abbrev.*: VCR.

**vid·e·o·disk** (vid′ē ō disk′) a disk containing data and instructions for playback on a television screen, computer screen, or video game.

**video game** an electronic game in which the player manipulates the action on a screen.

**video recorder** VIDEO CASSETTE RECORDER.

**vid·e·o·tape** (vid′ē ō tāp′) **1** a magnetic tape for recording video and audio signals. **2** a recording made on such a tape. **3** record on videotape. 1, 2 *n.*, 3 *v.*, **vid·e·o·taped, vid·e·o·tap·ing.**

**vie** (vī) strive for superiority; contend in rivalry; compete: *The children vied with each other to be first in line. v.*, **vied, vy·ing.**

**Vi·en·nese** (vē′ə nēz′) **1** of or having to do with Vienna, the capital of Austria, or its people. **2** a native or inhabitant of Vienna. 1 *adj.*, 2 *n.*, *pl.* **Vi·en·nese.**

**Vi·et·nam·ese** (vē′ət nə mēz′) **1** of or having to do with Vietnam, a country in southeast Asia, or its people. **2** a native or inhabitant of Vietnam. **3** the official language of Vietnam. 1 *adj.*, 2, 3 *n.*, *pl.* (for def. 2) **Vi·et·nam·ese.**

**view** (vyü) **1** an act of seeing; sight: *It was our first view of the ocean.* **2** the power of seeing; range of the eye: *A ship came into view.* **3** see; look at: *They viewed the scene with pleasure.* **4** something seen; a scene: *The view from our house is beautiful.* **5** a picture of some scene: *Various views of the mountains hung on the walls.* **6** a mental picture; idea: *This book will give you a general view of the way the pioneers lived.* **7** a way of looking at or considering a matter; opinion: *A child's view of school is different from a teacher's.* **8** consider; regard: *The plan for having classes on Saturdays was not viewed with favour by the students.* **9** an aim; purpose: *It is my view to leave tomorrow.* **10** a prospect; expectation: *with no view of success.* 1, 2, 4–7, 9, 10 *n.*, 3, 8 *v.*
**in view,** **a** in sight: *As the noise grew louder, the airplane came in view.* **b** under consideration: *Keep the teacher's advice in view as you try to improve your work.* **c** as a purpose or intention: *She works hard and has a definite aim in view.* **d** as a hope; as an expectation.
**in view of,** considering; because of.
**on view,** to be seen; open for people to see: *The exhibit is on view from 9 a.m. to 5 p.m.*
**take a dim view of,** *Informal.* look upon or regard with disapproval, doubt, pessimism, etc.
**with a view to,** **a** with the purpose or intention of: *She worked hard after school with a view to earning money for a new bicycle.* **b** with a hope of; expecting to.

**view·er** (vyü′ər) **1** a person who views: *a television viewer.* **2** a device for viewing, especially a small instrument for viewing photographic transparencies. *n.*

**view·less** (vyü′lis) **1** without views or opinions. **2** without a view: *a viewless room. adj.*

**view·point** (vyü′point′) **1** the place from which one looks at something. **2** an attitude of mind; a point of view: *A heavy rain is good from the viewpoint of farmers. n.*

**vig·il** (vij′əl) **1** staying awake for some purpose; a watching; watch: *All night the mother kept vigil over the sick child.* **2** a night spent in prayer. **3** the day and night before a religious festival. **4** **vigils,** *pl.* devotions, prayers, services, etc. on the night before a religious festival. *n.*

**vig·i·lance** (vij′ə ləns) the quality or state of being VIGILANT; watchfulness or alertness. *n.*

**vigilance committee** a self-appointed committee of citizens organized for protection or to maintain order and punish criminals in places or situations where official law enforcement appears inadequate.

**vig·i·lant** (vij′ə lənt) watchful; alert: *The watchdog was vigilant. adj.* —**vig′i·lant·ly,** *adv.*

**vig·i·lan·te** (vij′ə lan′tē) a member of a VIGILANCE COMMITTEE. *n.*

**vi·gnette** (vi nyet′) **1** a decorative design on a page of a book, especially on the title page. **2** a literary sketch; a short verbal description. **3** a short incident or scene, as in a movie or play. **4** an engraving, drawing, photograph, or the like, that shades off gradually at the edge. **5** finish a photograph in the manner of a vignette. 1–4 *n.*, 5 *v.*

**vig·or** (vig′ər) See VIGOUR. *n.*

**vig·or·ous** (vig′ə rəs) **1** full of vigour; strong and active: *The old man is still vigorous and lively.* **2** requiring or carried out with vigour; done energetically: *vigorous denial, vigorous exercises, a vigorous election campaign. adj.* —**vig′or·ous·ly,** *adv.*

**vig·our** or **vig·or** (vig′ər) **1** active physical strength or force; flourishing physical condition: *A man's vigour lessens as he grows old.* **2** mental energy, activity, or power; moral strength or force. **3** strong or energetic action; intensity of action. *n.*

**Vi·king** or **vi·king** (vī′king) one of the daring Norse adventurers and pirates who raided the coasts of Europe during the 8th, 9th, and 10th centuries A.D. *n.*

**vile** (vīl) **1** despicable or evil: *a vile attempt to defraud an old woman of her savings.* **2** physically repulsive: *the vile smell of rotting garbage.* **3** very bad or unpleasant: *vile language. The weather has turned really vile. She has a vile temper.* **4** degrading; mean and low: *He was reduced to the vile task of cleaning out the stables. adj.*, **vil·er, vil·est.** —**vile′ly,** *adv.* —**vile′ness,** *n.*

**vil·i·fi·ca·tion** (vil′ə fə kā′shən) a VILIFYing or being vilified. *n.*

**vil·i·fy** (vil′ə fī) speak evil of; revile; slander. *v.*, **vil·i·fied, vil·i·fy·ing.** —**vil′i·fi′er,** *n.*

**vil·la** (vil′ə) a house in the country or suburbs, sometimes at the seashore: *A villa is usually a large or elegant residence. n.*

**vil·lage** (vil′ij) **1** a group of houses, stores, schools, churches, etc. that together with the people living there forms a community with fixed boundaries and some local powers of government: *In Canada, a village is the smallest community that can have its own local government.* **2** the people of a village: *The whole village was out to see the fire. n.*

**vil·lag·er** (vil′i jər) a person who lives in a VILLAGE (def. 1). *n.*

**vil·lain** (vil′ən) **1** a scoundrel; a wicked person: *The villain stole the money and cast the blame on his friend.* **2** a character in a play, novel, etc. whose evil motives or actions form an important element in the plot. **3** a person or thing blamed for a particular problem: *City health experts studying the epidemic decided the chief villain was overcrowding.* *n.*

**vil·lain·ous** (vil′ə nəs) **1** very wicked. **2** extremely bad; vile: *a villainous temper.* *adj.*
—**vil′lain·ous·ly,** *adv.*

**vil·lain·y** (vil′ə nē) **1** great wickedness. **2** a wicked act; crime. *n., pl.* **vil′lain·ies.**

**vil·li** (vil′ī *or* vil′ē) *n., pl.* of VILLUS.

**vil·lus** (vil′əs) **1** any of the tiny hairlike parts growing out of the mucous membrane of the small intestine: *The villi absorb certain substances.* **2** any of the soft hairs covering the fruit, flowers, etc. of certain plants. *n., pl.* **vil·li.**

**vin·di·cate** (vin′də kāt′) **1** clear from suspicion, dishonour, or charge of wrongdoing, etc.: *The verdict of "Not guilty" vindicated her.* **2** defend successfully against opposition: *He vindicated his claim to his uncle's fortune.* **3** confirm or justify: *Their faith in him has been vindicated.* *v.,* **vin·di·cat·ed, vin·di·cat·ing.** —**vin′di·ca′tor,** *n.*

**vin·di·ca·tion** (vin′də kā′shən) **1** the act or process of clearing from any charge of wrongdoing. **2** JUSTIFICATION: *The success of her invention was a vindication of her new idea.* *n.*

**vin·di·ca·tive** (vin dik′ə tiv *or* vin′də kā′tiv) tending to VINDICATE; justifying. *adj.*

**vin·dic·tive** (vin dik′tiv) **1** feeling a strong tendency toward revenge; bearing a grudge: *He is so vindictive that he never forgives anybody.* **2** intended for revenge; involving revenge: *vindictive punishment.* **3** spiteful; malicious: *He has a vindictive nature. She wrote a vindictive column in the local paper.* *adj.* —**vin·dic′tive·ly,** *adv.* —**vin·dic′tive·ness,** *n.*

**vine** (vīn) **1** any plant having a long, slender stem that does not stand up by itself, but creeps along the ground or climbs on a support by twining or by putting out tendrils: *Melons and pumpkins grow on vines. Ivy is a vine.* **2** any of the group of woody-stemmed climbing or creeping plants whose fruit is the grape; GRAPEVINE (def. 1): *the fruit of the vine.* *n.* —**vine′like′,** *adj.*

**vin·e·gar** (vin′ə gər) a sour liquid produced by the fermentation of cider, wine, etc., consisting largely of dilute, impure ACETIC ACID. *n.*
☞ *Etym.* From OF *vyn egre* (modern F *vinaigre*) 'wine (that is) sour'.

**vin·e·gar·y** (vin′ə gə rē *or* vin′ə grē) of or like VINEGAR; sour. *adj.*

**vine·yard** (vin′yərd) a place planted with GRAPEVINES (def. 1). *n.*

**vi·nous** (vī′nəs) **1** of, like, or having to do with wine. **2** caused by drinking wine. *adj.*

**vin·tage** (vin′tij) **1** the wine or grapes of one season from a particular vineyard: *The finest vintages cost much more than others.* **2** the year's harvest from which a particular wine was produced: *The vintage of this wine is 1978.* **3** of a good vintage; of superior quality: *a cellar full of vintage wines.* **4** a particular period or year of origin: *songs of prewar vintage.* **5** being or representing the best example or model; classic: *Sunshine Sketches of a Little Town is vintage Stephen Leacock.* **6** of or belonging to an earlier time; old or old-fashioned: *shelves full of vintage comic books. She rattled around town in her vintage Ford.* **1, 2, 4** *n.,* **3, 5, 6** *adj.*

**vintage year** **1** a year in which a vintage wine is produced: *The year 1972 was a vintage year.* **2** an outstandingly successful year: *a vintage year in the history of sports.*

**vi·nyl** (vī′nil *or* vin′il) **1** a polymer of any of several organic chemical compounds that are derived from ethylene: *Vinyls are used to make floor and furniture coverings, toys, phonograph records, etc.* **2** made of vinyl: *The car has a vinyl roof.* *n.*

**vi·ol** (vī′əl) one of a family of usually six-stringed musical instruments similar to the violin family, used mainly in the 16th and 17th centuries: *Viols are played with a curved bow and have a softer, less rich and varied tone than the violin.* *n.*
☞ *Hom.* VIAL.

**vi·o·la**¹ (vē ō′lə *or* vī ō′lə) a musical instrument of the violin family that is slightly larger and tuned a fifth lower than the violin. *n.*

**vi·o·la**² (vī ō′lə *or* vī′ə lə) any of a closely related group of plants including the violets and pansies; especially, any of numerous garden varieties that are hybrids, having yellow, purple, or white flowers somewhat smaller than pansies. *n.*

**vi·o·late** (vī′ə lāt′) **1** break a law, rule, agreement, promise, etc.; act contrary to: *Speeding violates the traffic regulations.* **2** treat with disrespect or contempt: *The soldiers violated the church by using it as a stable.* **3** break in upon; disturb: *The sound of the explosion violated the usual calm of Sunday morning.* **4** trespass on; infringe on: *to violate the right of free speech.* **5** commit rape on. *v.,* **vi·o·lat·ed, vi·o·lat·ing.** —**vi′o·la′tor,** *n.*

**vi·o·la·tion** (vī′ə lā′shən) **1** violating or being VIOLATED; infringement of a law, rule, agreement, promise, etc. **2** an interruption or disturbance. **3** the treatment of a holy thing with disrespect or contempt. **4** RAPE. *n.*

**vi·o·lence** (vī′ə ləns) **1** rough force in action: *He slammed the door with violence.* **2** rough or harmful action or treatment: *The police had to use violence in arresting the gunman.* **3** harm; injury: *It would do violence to her principles to work on Sunday.* **4** the illegal or unjust use of physical force to injure or damage persons or property. **5** strength of feeling: *We were shocked by the violence of her hate.* *n.*

**vi·o·lent** (vī′ə lənt) **1** acting or done with strong, rough force: *a violent blow.* **2** caused by strong, rough force: *a violent death.* **3** showing or caused by very strong feeling, action, etc.: *violent language.* **4** severe; extreme; very great: *a violent pain, violent heat.* *adj.*
—**vi′o·lent·ly,** *adv.*

**vi·o·let** (vī′ə lit) **1** any of numerous closely related plants having small, solid-coloured, usually yellow, white, or purple flowers: *The purple violet is the provincial flower of New Brunswick.* **2** any plant belonging to the closely related group of mainly temperate plants that includes the violas and pansies as well as the violets. **3** the flower of a violet. **4** referring to a worldwide family of herbs, shrubs, and small trees to which the violets belong: *The violet family is made up of 800 species.* **5** any of various unrelated plants having violetlike flowers: *dogtooth violet, African violet.* **6** medium bluish purple. *1–6 n., 6 adj.*

**vi·o·lin** (vī′ə lin′) **1** a musical instrument with four strings tuned at intervals of a fifth, played by drawing a bow across the strings: *The violin can produce tones of great variety and richness.* **2** referring to a family of stringed musical instruments of which the violin is the smallest: *The other members of the violin family are the viola, cello, and double bass.* *n.*

**vi·o·lin·ist** (vī′ə lin′ist) a person who plays the violin, especially a skilled player. *n.*

**vi·ol·ist** (vē ō′list) a person who plays the VIOLA or VIOL, especially a skilled player. *n.*

**vi·os·ter·ol** (vī os′tə rōl′) an oil containing a form of vitamin D, used as a medicine to prevent or cure rickets. *n.*

**VIP** *Informal.* very important person.

**vi·per** (vī′pər) **1** a thick-bodied poisonous snake having a pair of large, perforated fangs. **2** a spiteful, treacherous person. *n.*

**vi·per·ine** (vī′pə rīn′) of, having to do with, or resembling a VIPER. *adj.*

**vi·per·ous** (vī′pə rəs) like a VIPER; treacherous and malicious. *adj.*

**vi·ra·go** (və rā′gō *or* və rä′gō) a violent, bad-tempered, or scolding woman. *n., pl.* **vi·ra·goes** or **vi·ra·gos.**

**vi·ral** (vī′rəl) of, having to do with, or caused by a VIRUS: *viral pneumonia.* *adj.*

**vir·e·o** (vir′ē ō′) a small, insect-eating North American songbird. *n., pl.* **vir·e·os.**

**vir·gin** (vėr′jən) **1** a person, especially a woman, who has never had sexual intercourse. **2** an unmarried girl or young woman. **3** a member of any religious order of women who have vowed to remain virgins. **4** having to do with or suitable for a virgin: *virgin modesty.* **5** being a virgin. **6** pure or spotless: *virgin snow.* **7** not yet used or altered by human beings: *virgin forest.* **8** of wool, spun or woven only once or not yet spun at all. **9** initial; first: *a virgin effort.* **10 the Virgin,** VIRGIN MARY. *1–3, 10 n., 4–9 adj.*

**vir·gin·al**[1] (vėr′jə nəl) **1** of or suitable for a VIRGIN; maidenly. **2** fresh; pure; unsullied; untouched. *adj.*

**vir·gin·al**[2] (vėr′jə nəl) a musical instrument like a small piano, but set in a box without legs. It was much used in the 16th and 17th centuries. *n.*

**Virginia creeper** a climbing plant having leaves with five leaflets and bluish-black berries; woodbine; North American ivy.

**Virginia reel** **1** a North American country dance in which the partners form two lines facing each other and perform a number of dance steps. **2** the music for such a dance.

**vir·gin·i·ty** (vər jin′ə tē) the quality or state of being a VIRGIN; maidenhood. *n.*

**Virgin Mary** the mother of Jesus.

**Vir·go** (vėr′gō) **1** in astronomy, a constellation on the celestial equator thought of as having the form of a woman. **2** in astrology, the sixth sign of the zodiac. The sun enters Virgo about August 22. See ZODIAC for picture. **3** a person born under this sign. *n.*

**vir·ile** (vir′īl *or* vir′əl) **1** belonging to or characteristic of a man; masculine; manly. **2** having masculine vigour or forcefulness: *a virile writing style.* **3** of a male, capable of copulation; sexually potent. *adj.*

**vi·ril·i·ty** (və ril′ə tē) the quality or state of being VIRILE. *n., pl.* **vi·ril·i·ties.**

**vir·tu·al** (vėr′chü əl) being something in effect, though not so in name or according to strict definition: *a virtual promise. The battle was won with so great a loss of soldiers that it was a virtual defeat. He is the virtual president, though his title is secretary.* *adj.*

**vir·tu·al·ly** (vėr′chü ə lē) almost entirely or for all practical purposes: *The house was virtually destroyed in the fire. The two houses are virtually identical.* *adv.*

**virtual reality** a realistic set of effects in which the user or viewer of a specially programmed computer system can see, hear, or feel the physical sensations associated with scenes, events, or an environment, and can interact with them as though they were real.

**vir·tue** (vėr′chü) **1** moral excellence; goodness: *Her virtue is shown in her many good deeds.* **2** a particular kind of goodness: *Justice and kindness are virtues.* **3** a good quality; merit or value: *There is virtue in making a detailed plan. He praised the virtues of his car.* **4** chastity, especially in a woman. **5** the power to produce effects: *There is little virtue in that medicine.* *n.*
**by** or **in virtue of,** relying on; because of; on account of: *By virtue of getting to the theatre early, they got the best seats. He was able to get a copy of the letter by virtue of his position in the company.*
**make a virtue of necessity,** do willingly what must be done anyway.

**vir·tu·os·i·ty** (vėr′chü os′ə tē) the character or skill of a VIRTUOSO. *n., pl.* **vir·tu·os·i·ties.**

**vir·tu·o·so** (vėr′chü ō′sō) **1** a person highly skilled in the methods of an art, especially in playing a musical instrument. **2** a person who has a cultivated appreciation of artistic excellence. **3** a student or collector of objects of art, curios, antiquities, etc. *n., pl.* **vir·tu·o·sos** or **vir·tu·o·si** (-sē).

**vir·tu·ous** (vėr′chü əs) **1** good; moral; righteous: *a virtuous conduct, a virtuous life, a virtuous person.* **2** CHASTE. *adj.* —**vir′tu·ous·ly,** *adv.* —**vir′tu·ous·ness,** *n.*

**vir·u·lence** (vir′yə ləns) **1** the quality of being very poisonous or harmful; deadliness: *the virulence of a disease, the virulence of a rattlesnake's bite.* **2** intense bitterness or spite; violent hostility. *n.*

**vir·u·len·cy** (vir′yə lən sē) VIRULENCE. *n.*

**vir·u·lent** (vir′yə lənt) **1** very poisonous or harmful; deadly: *a virulent form of a disease.* **2** intensely bitter or spiteful; violently hostile. *adj.* —**vir′u·lent·ly,** *adv.*

**vi·rus** (vī′rəs) 1 any of a group of disease-producing agents smaller than any known bacteria and dependent upon the living tissue of hosts for their reproduction and growth. 2 a disease produced by a virus. 3 anything that poisons the mind or morals; a corrupting influence: *the virus of racism.* 4 *Informal.* a piece of code inserted in a computer program to destroy or corrupt the system and data stored on it. A virus may then be passed accidentally between systems. *n.*

**vi·sa** (vē′zə) 1 an official document or endorsement on a passport allowing the person or persons identified in the passport to visit a particular country or region: *Some countries will not allow a foreign traveller to enter without a visa.* 2 give a visa to. 1 *n.*, 2 *v.*, **vi·saed, vi·sa·ing.**
☛ *Etym.* Through French from a modern use of L *visa* 'things seen', a form of the past participle of *videre* 'to see'. See also note at VISIBLE.

**vis·age** (viz′ij) 1 the face, especially with reference to its form or expression: *a grim visage, a visage of despair.* 2 appearance; aspect: *the sad visage of the late autumn.* *n.*
☛ *Etym.* Through OF *visage* from *vis* 'face', which came from L *visus* 'sight, appearance', a noun use of the past participle of *videre* 'to see'. VISOR came from Norman French *viser*, which also developed from OF *vis*. See also note at VISIBLE.

**vis·cer·a** (vis′ə rə) the internal organs of the body, especially those in the cavity of the trunk, such as the stomach, intestines, kidneys, and liver. *n.*, *pl.* of **vis·cus** (vis′kəs).

**vis·cer·al** (vis′ə rəl) 1 of, having to do with, or affecting the VISCERA. 2 of or springing from instinct or emotion, rather than reason: *a visceral reaction.* *adj.*

**vis·cid** (vis′id) thick and sticky like heavy syrup or glue. *adj.*

**vis·cose** (vis′kōs) 1 a viscous solution made from cellulose and used especially in making rayon. 2 rayon fibres, yarn, or fabric. 3 of, having to do with, or made of viscose. *n.*

**vis·cos·i·ty** (vis kos′ə tē) 1 the quality or state of being VISCOUS. 2 the property of a liquid that tends to prevent it from flowing; the frictional resistance of a fluid to the motion of its molecules. *n.*, *pl.* **vis·cos·i·ties.**

**vis·count** (vī′kount) a nobleman ranking next below an earl or count and next above a baron. *n.*

**vis·count·ess** (vī′koun tis) 1 the wife or widow of a viscount. 2 a woman who holds in her own right a rank equivalent to that of a viscount. *n.*

**vis·cous** (vis′kəs) 1 of a liquid, sticky; thick like syrup or glue; viscid. 2 having the property of VISCOSITY (def. 2). *adj.*

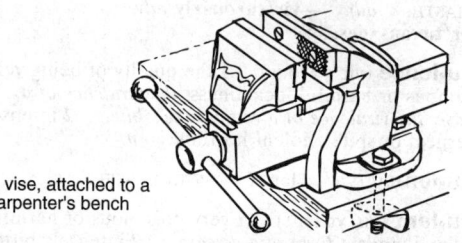

A vise, attached to a carpenter's bench

**vise** or **vice** (vīs) a tool having two jaws moved by a screw, lever, etc., used to hold an object firmly while work is being done on it. *n.*
☛ *Hom.* VICE.

**vise–grip pliers** pliers with a grip like that of a vise.

**Vish·nu** (vish′nü) one of the three great gods of classical Hinduism, widely regarded as the highest god, and usually worshipped in one of his human forms, especially Krishna or Rama. *n.*

**vis·i·bil·i·ty** (viz′ə bil′ə tē) 1 the quality or state of being VISIBLE. 2 the condition of light, atmosphere, etc. with reference to the distance at which things can be clearly seen: *Poor visibility was the main reason for the accident.* 3 the distance at which things are clearly visible: *Fog and rain decreased visibility to about 50 metres.* *n.*

**vis·i·ble** (viz′ə bəl) 1 that can be seen: *The shore was barely visible through the fog. Bacteria are visible only with the aid of a microscope.* 2 that can be observed; apparent; obvious: *There was no visible improvement in the patient's condition. The tramp had no visible means of support.* *adj.* —**vis′i·bly,** *adv.*
☛ *Etym.* **Visible,** VISION, VISUAL, and words derived from them come either directly or through French from Latin words that developed from *visus,* the past participle of *videre* 'to see'. See also the note at VISIT. Other words derived from *videre* include VIDEO, VISA, VISAGE, VISOR, and VISTA.

**Vis·i·goth** (viz′ə goth′) a member of the western division of the Goths: *The Visigoths plundered Rome in* A.D. 410, *and formed a monarchy in France and northern Spain about* A.D. 418. *n.*

**vi·sion** (vizh′ən) 1 the power of seeing; sense of sight: *She wears glasses because of poor vision.* 2 the act or fact of seeing; sight. 3 the power of perceiving by the imagination or by clear thinking: *a prophet of great vision.* 4 something seen in the imagination, in a dream, in one's thoughts, etc.: *The beggar had visions of great wealth.* 5 phantom. 6 imagine or envision. 7 a very beautiful person, scene, etc. 1–5, 7 *n.*, 6 *v.*
☛ *Etym.* See note at VISIBLE.

**vi·sion·ar·y** (vizh′ə ner′ē) 1 having a tendency to indulge in advanced schemes or theories: *a visionary thinker.* 2 a person whose ideas are far more advanced than those of the current time. 3 based on ideas far more advanced than the accepted ones: *a visionary scheme for a just society.* 4 sometimes, a person who is not practical; a dreamer. 5 of, having to do with, or seen in a vision: *The visionary scene faded and she awoke.* 6 a person who sees visions. 7 able or likely to see visions. 1, 3, 5, 7 *adj.*, 2, 4, 6 *n.*, *pl.* **vi·sion·ar·ies.**

**vis·it** (viz′it) 1 make a call on or stay with for social reasons: *I'm going to visit my aunt tomorrow. They're visiting friends in Europe this month.* 2 go or come to see or stay at a place, especially for sightseeing, etc.: *Last year we visited Newfoundland.* 3 go or come to see officially in order to inspect or examine: *The inspector visits the factory once a month.* 4 make a call or stay as a guest: *They are visiting in the country.* 5 a call or stay as a guest or for the purpose of inspection, etc.: *They had to cut their visit short because he got sick.* 6 *Informal.* a friendly talk or chat: *We had a nice visit while we were waiting.* 7 come upon; afflict: *The poor old man was visited by many troubles.* 8 send upon; inflict: *He visited his anger upon them.* 9 punish or avenge a person or sin: *to visit the sins of the fathers upon the children.* 1–4, 7–9 *v.*, 5, 6 *n.*
**visit with,** *Informal.* talk with.
☛ *Etym.* **Visit,** VISITANT, VISITATION, and VISITOR all developed from words derived from OF *visiter* or L

*visitare* 'go to see', a form of *visare* 'view, see', which was formed from *visus*, past participle of *videre* 'to see'. See also note at VISIBLE.

**vis·it·ant** (viz′ə tənt)  1 a visitor, especially one thought to be supernatural.  2 in biology, a migrating bird in any of the places it stays temporarily.  *n.*
☞ *Etym.*  See note at VISIT.

**vis·it·a·tion** (viz′ə tā′shən)  1 the act or an instance of visiting; especially, a visit for the purpose of making an inspection or examination: *the visitation of a foreign ship.*  2 a punishment or reward sent by God.  *n.*
☞ *Etym.*  See note at VISIT.

**vis·i·tor** (viz′ə tər)  a person who visits or is visiting; guest: *Our visitors from the East arrived last night. I don't live here; I'm just a visitor.*  *n.*
☞ *Etym.*  See note at VISIT.

**vi·sor** (vī′zər)  1 the movable front part of a helmet, covering the face. See ARMOUR for picture.  2 a projecting part, such as the peak of a cap, intended to protect the eyes from the sun or other strong light. See CAP for picture.  3 a mask or disguise.  4 a small movable shade attached inside an automobile at the top of the windshield.  *n.*  Also, **vizor.**
☞ *Etym.*  See note at VISAGE.

**vi·sored** (vī′zərd)  furnished or equipped with a VISOR.  *adj.*

**vis·ta** (vis′tə)  1 the view seen through a narrow opening or passage: *The opening between the rows of elms afforded a vista of the lake.*  2 such an opening or passage itself: *a shady vista of elms.*  3 a mental view over a period of time or series of events in the past or future: *The book had opened up a new vista for her future.*  *n.*
☞ *Etym.*  From Italian *vista*, past participle of *vedere* 'to see', which comes from L *videre*. 17c. See also note at VISIBLE.

**vis·u·al** (vizh′ü əl)  1 of, having to do with, or used in sight or vision: *Near-sightedness is a visual defect.*  2 that can be seen; visible: *the visual arts.*  3 done by sight only: *visual navigation.*  4 of the nature of a mental vision; produced or occurring as a picture in the mind: *She tried to form a visual conception of the author's description.*  *adj.*  —**vis·u·al·ly,** *adv.*
☞ *Etym.*  See note at VISIBLE.

**visual aid**  a device or means such as a chart, diagram, motion picture, etc. for aiding the learning process through the sense of sight.

**vis·u·al·i·za·tion** (vizh′ü ə lə zā′shən *or* vizh′ü ə lī zā′shən)  1 the act or process of visualizing.  2 the thing visualized.  *n.*

**vis·u·al·ize** (vizh′ü ə līz′)  1 form a mental picture of: *I can visualize his reaction when he hears the news.*  2 make visible; especially, make an internal organ visible by surgical means or X ray.  3 form mental pictures.  *v.*, **vis·u·al·ized, vis·u·al·iz·ing.**

**vis·u·al·ly** (vizh′ü ə lē)  in a visual manner or respect; by sight.  *adv.*

**vi·tal** (vī′təl)  1 of, having to do with, or necessary to life: *vital forces. Eating is a vital function. The heart is one of the vital organs of the body.*  2 of the greatest importance; essential: *vital national interests. Perfect timing was vital to the success of their plan.*  3 causing death, failure, or ruin: *a vital wound, a vital blow to an industry.*  4 full of life and spirit; lively.  5 **vitals,** *pl.*  **a** the vital organs, such as the heart, brain, lungs, etc.  **b** the essential parts or elements of anything.  1–4 *adj.*, 5 *n.* —**vi′tal·ly,** *adv.*
☞ *Etym.*  VITAL and related words developed from L *vitalis*

hat, āge, fär; let, ēqual, tėrm; it, īce
hot, ōpen, ôrder; oil, out; cup, pu̇t, rüle
əbove, takən, pencəl, lemən, circəs
ch, child; ng, long; sh, ship
th, thin; ŦH, then; zh, measure

'of life', formed from *vita* 'life', which was related to L *vivus* 'living', and *vivere* 'to live'. See also note at VIVA.

**vi·tal·ism** (vī′tə liz′əm)  a doctrine that the behaviour of a living organism is, at least in part, due to a vital principle that cannot possibly be explained by physics and chemistry.  *n.*
☞ *Etym.*  See note at VITAL.

**vi·tal·i·ty** (vī tal′ə tē)  1 mental or physical vigour; liveliness: *She has great vitality.*  2 the power to endure or remain active: *the vitality of a tradition.*  3 vital force; the power to live; that which distinguishes the living from the non-living.  *n.*, *pl.* **vi·tal·i·ties.**
☞ *Etym.*  See note at VITAL.

**vi·tal·ize** (vī′tə līz′)  1 make more energetic, lively, or enterprising.  2 give life to.  *v.*, **vi·tal·ized, vi·tal·iz·ing.** —**vi′tal·i·za′tion,** *n.*
☞ *Etym.*  See note at VITAL.

**vital statistics**  facts or data about births, deaths, marriages, etc.

**vi·ta·min** (vī′tə min)  1 any of certain substances required for the normal growth and nourishment of the body, found especially in milk, butter, raw fruit and vegetables, brewers' yeast, wheat, and cod-liver oil: *Lack of vitamins in food causes such diseases as rickets and scurvy as well as general poor health.*  2 of, having to do with, or containing vitamins: *Richard protected himself against vitamin deficiency by taking vitamin tablets.*  *n.*
☞ *Etym.*  From German *vitamine*, made up of L *vita* 'life' + *amine*, because vitamins were mistakenly thought to contain amino acids. See also note at VITAL.

**vitamin A**  the fat-soluble vitamin occurring in two known forms, $A_1$ and $A_2$, and found especially in animal products such as milk, butter, cod-liver oil, egg yolk and liver, carrots, and leafy green vegetables: *Vitamin A helps the body resist infection and prevents night blindness.*

**vitamin $B_1$**  THIAMINE.

**vitamin $B_2$**  RIBOFLAVIN.  Also, **vitamin G.**

**vitamin $B_6$**  PYRIDOXINE.

**vitamin $B_{12}$**  a complex crystalline compound found especially in liver, that is necessary for blood formation and is used particularly in treating pernicious anemia.

**vitamin B complex**  a group of different water-soluble vitamins found especially in yeast, liver, eggs, and seed germs. They include vitamin $B_1$, $B_2$, $B_6$, $B_{12}$, biotin, choline, nicotinic acid, and pantothenic acid.

**vitamin C**  a water-soluble compound found especially in citrus fruits and also made synthetically; ascorbic acid. It is used in the prevention and treatment of scurvy.

**vitamin D**  any of several fat-soluble compounds that are necessary for normal growth of bones and teeth and found especially in fish-liver oils, egg yolk, and milk. The most abundant form of this vitamin is $D_3$, which is found in fish-liver oils and is also formed in the skin by the action of sunlight.

**vitamin E**  any of several fat-soluble vitamins found especially in leaves and seed germ oils. Lack of vitamin E

**vitamin G** vitamin B₂; RIBOFLAVIN.

**vitamin H** BIOTIN.

**vi·ta·min·ize** (vī′tə mi nīz′) provide with VITAMINS. *v.*, **vi·ta·min·ized, vi·ta·min·iz·ing.**

**vitamin K** either of two fat-soluble compounds necessary to the normal clotting of blood, found especially in leafy vegetables, alfalfa, etc. and formed in the intestines of mammals by the action of bacteria. The two forms of vitamin K that occur naturally are K₁ and K₂. There are also several compounds produced synthetically that are closely related to K₁ and K₂ and have the same function.

**vitamin P** a vitamin that promotes capillary resistance to hemorrhaging, obtained from citrus fruits and paprika.

**vi·ti·ate** (vish′ē āt′) **1** impair the quality of; spoil: *His illness vitiated his chances of success.* **2** destroy the legal force or authority of: *The contract was vitiated because one person signed under compulsion.* *v.*, **vi·ti·at·ed, vi·ti·at·ing.** —**vi′ti·a′tion,** *n.*

**vit·re·ous** (vit′rē əs) **1** of, having to do with, derived from or consisting of glass. **2** like glass in texture, brittleness, etc.; glassy: *vitreous rocks.* **3** of or having to do with the VITREOUS HUMOUR. *adj.*

**vitreous humour** or **humor** the transparent, jelly-like substance that fills that part of the eyeball behind the lens. See EYE for picture.

**vit·ri·fi·ca·tion** (vit′rə fə kā′shən) **1** the process of making or becoming glass or a glasslike substance. **2** something vitrified. *n.*

**vit·ri·form** (vit′rə fôrm′) having the structure or appearance of glass. *adj.*

**vit·ri·fy** (vit′rə fī′) change into glass or a glasslike substance by heat and fusion. *v.*, **vit·ri·fied, vit·ri·fy·ing.**

**vit·ri·ol** (vit′rē əl) **1** any of certain sulphates, as of copper (**blue vitriol**), iron (**green vitriol**), zinc (**white vitriol**). **2** SULPHURIC ACID: *Vitriol burns deeply.* **3** very sharp speech or severe criticism. *n.*

**vit·ri·ol·ic** (vit′rē ol′ik) **1** of or containing vitriol. **2** like vitriol. **3** bitterly severe; sharp: *vitriolic criticism. adj.*

**vi·tu·per·ate** (vi tyü′pə rāt′ *or* vi tü′pə rāt′, vī tyü′pə rāt′ *or* vī tü′pə rāt′) scold very severely; find fault with in abusive words; revile. *v.*, **vi·tu·per·at·ed, vi·tu·per·at·ing.**

**vi·tu·per·a·tion** (vi tyü′pə rā′shən *or* vi tü′pə rā′shən, vī tyü′pə rā′shən *or* vī tü′pə rā′shən) bitter abuse in words; very severe scolding. *n.*

**vi·tu·per·a·tive** (vi tyü′pə rə tiv *or* vi tü′pə rə tiv, vī tyü′pə rə tiv *or* vī tü′pə rə tiv) abusive; reviling. *adj.* —**vi·tu′per·a·tive·ly,** *adv.*

**vi·va** (vē′və) **1** an exclamation used as a salute or expression of approval. **2** a shout of approval or good will: *The crowd greeted her with a loud viva.* **1** *interj.*, **2** *n.*
☞ *Etym.* Words beginning in **viv-** can all be traced back to L *vivus* 'alive' or *vivere* 'to live'. **Viva** itself comes directly from an Italian subjunctive-imperative form of the verb, meaning 'may (he/she) live'. See also note at VITAL.

**vi·va·cious** (vi vā′shəs *or* vī vā′shəs) lively; sprightly; animated: *a vivacious personality, a vivacious smile. adj.* —**vi·va′cious·ly,** *adv.* —**vi·va′cious·ness,** *n.*
☞ *Etym.* See note at VIVA.

**vi·vac·i·ty** (vi vas′ə tē *or* vī vas′ə tē) liveliness; sprightliness; animation; gaiety. *n., pl.* **vi·vac·i·ties.**
☞ *Etym.* See note at VIVA.

**vi·var·i·um** (vī ver′ē əm) an enclosed place for keeping animals in an environment as close as possible to their natural one. *n., pl.* **vi·var·i·ums, vi·var·i·a** (-ē ə).
☞ *Etym.* See note at VIVA.

**vi·va vo·ce** (vī′və vō′sē *or* vē′və vō′chā) **1** spoken; oral: *a viva voce examination.* **2** orally: *We voted viva voce instead of by ballot.*
☞ *Etym.* From Med. L *viva voce* 'with the living voice'. The second English pronunciation developed through the influence of modern Italian.

**viv·id** (viv′id) **1** brilliant; strikingly bright: *Dandelions are a vivid yellow.* **2** full of life; lively: *a vivid description.* **3** clearly and strikingly perceived or felt: *a vivid impression, a vivid sensation.* **4** very strong and active: *a vivid imagination. adj.* —**viv′id·ly,** *adv.* —**viv′id·ness,** *n.*
☞ *Etym.* See note at VIVA.

**viv·i·fy** (viv′ə fī′) **1** give life or vigour to. **2** enliven; make vivid. *v.*, **viv·i·fied, viv·i·fy·ing.** —**viv′i·fi·ca′tion,** *n.*
☞ *Etym.* See note at VIVA.

**vi·vip·a·rous** (vi vip′ə rəs *or* vī vip′ə rəs) bringing forth living young, rather than eggs: *Dogs, cats, cows, and human beings are viviparous.* Compare with OVIPAROUS. *adj.*
☞ *Etym.* From L *viviparus,* made up from *vivus* 'alive' + *parere* 'produce, bring forth' (as in PARENT). See also note at VIVA. 17c.

**viv·i·sect** (viv′ə sekt′) **1** perform VIVISECTION on: *to vivisect an animal.* **2** practise VIVISECTION. *v.*

**viv·i·sec·tion** (viv′ə sek′shən) the act or practice of cutting into or experimenting on living animals for scientific study. *n.*
☞ *Etym.* From L *vivus* 'alive' + English *section.* See also the note at VIVA. 18c.

**viv·i·sec·tion·ist** (viv′ə sek′shə nist) **1** a person who practises VIVISECTION. **2** a person who favours or defends VIVISECTION. *n.*

**vix·en** (vik′sən) **1** a female fox. **2** a bad-tempered or quarrelsome woman. *n.*

**vix·en·ish** (vik′sə nish) ill-tempered; scolding. *adj.*

**viz.** that is to say; namely (an abbreviation of L *videlicet,* which came from *videre licet* 'it is permitted to see'): *Two members have been asked to attend the conference, viz., Ms. Sanchez and Mr. Faber.*
☞ *Usage.* **Viz.** is a written form only and is usually spoken or read as 'namely'.

**vi·zier** or **vi·zir** (vi zēr′) in Moslem countries, especially in the former Turkish Empire, a high official or minister of state. *n.*

**vi·zor** (vī′zər) See VISOR. *n.*

**VLF, V.L.F.,** or **vlf** very low frequency.

**vocab.** vocabulary.

**vo·cab·u·lar·y** (və kab′yə ler′ē *or* vō kab′yə ler′ē) **1** the stock of words used by a person, class of people, profession, etc.: *Reading will increase your vocabulary.* **2** a collection or list of words, usually in alphabetical order, with their translations or meanings: *There is a* *vocabulary in the back of our French book.* **3** all the words of a language. *n., pl.* **vo‧cab‧u‧lar‧ies.**

**vocabulary entry** **1** a word, term, or item entered in a vocabulary. **2** in dictionaries, any word or phrase in alphabetical order and defined, or any related word listed for identification under the word from which it is derived.

**vo‧cal** (vō′kəl) **1** of, by, for, with, or having to do with the voice: *vocal organs, vocal power, a vocal message, vocal music.* **2** having a voice; giving forth sound: *We are vocal beings. The gorge was vocal with the roar of the cataract.* **3** aroused to speech; inclined to talk freely: *She became vocal with indignation.* **4** of a vowel. **5** a VOICED (def. 2) speech sound: *All vowels are vocals.* **6** a musical composition for the voice. **7** the part of a musical composition that is to be sung. 1–4 *adj.*, 5–7 *n.* —**vo′cal‧ly,** *adv.*
☛ *Etym.* See note at VOICE.

**vocal cords** either of two pairs of folds of mucous membrane in the larynx. Voice is produced when the edges of the lower pair of folds vibrate as air from the lungs passes between them. See WINDPIPE for picture.

**vo‧cal‧ic** (vō kal′ik) **1** of, having to do with, or consisting of a vowel or vowels: *a vocalic sound. I is a vocalic word.* **2** being or functioning as a vowel: *In* bit, *only* /i/ *is vocalic.* *adj.*

**vo‧cal‧ist** (vō′kə list) SINGER. *n.*

**vo‧cal‧ize** (vō′kə līz′) **1** speak, sing, shout, etc. **2** make vocal; utter: *The dog vocalized its pain in a series of long howls.* **3** in phonetics, change into a vowel; use as a vowel. *v.,* **vo‧cal‧ized, vo‧cal‧iz‧ing.** —**vo′cal‧i‧za′tion,** *n.*

**vo‧ca‧tion** (vō kā′shən) **1** an occupation, business, profession, or trade: *He chose teaching as his vocation.* **2** an inclination or summons to a particular activity, especially to religious work: *Since childhood she had felt a vocation for nursing.* *n.*

**vo‧ca‧tion‧al** (vō kā′shə nəl) of or having to do with some occupation, trade, etc.: *Trades such as carpentry and printing are taught in vocational schools.* *adj.* —**vo‧ca′tion‧al‧ly,** *adv.*

**voc‧a‧tive** (vok′ə tiv) **1** of, having to do with, or being the grammatical case which in some languages shows that a noun, pronoun, or adjective refers to a person or thing being addressed or invoked: *Latin has a vocative case.* **2** the vocative case. **3** a word or group of words in the vocative case. 1 *adj.*, 2, 3 *n.*

**vo‧cif‧er‧ate** (və sif′ə rāt *or* vō sif′ə rāt′) cry out loudly or noisily; shout: *The speaker vociferated against fluoridation.* *v.,* **vo‧cif‧er‧at‧ed, vo‧cif‧er‧at‧ing.**

**vo‧cif‧er‧a‧tion** (və sif′ə rā′shən *or* vō sif′ə rā′shən) a vociferating; noisy oratory or clamour. *n.*

**vo‧cif‧er‧ous** (və sif′ə rəs *or* vō sif′ə rəs) loud and noisy; shouting; clamouring: *a vociferous person, vociferous cheers.* *adj.* —**vo‧cif′er‧ous‧ly,** *adv.* —**vo‧cif′er‧ous‧ness,** *n.*

**vod‧ka** (vod′kə) a colourless alcoholic liquor distilled from a mash of rye, wheat, etc. *n.*
☛ *Etym.* From Russian *vodka,* which developed from *voda* 'water'.

**vogue** (vōg) **1** something that is in fashion at a particular time: *Hoopskirts were the vogue many years ago.* **2** general favour; popularity: *That song had a great vogue at one time.* *n.*

**voice** (vois) **1** the sound produced by specific organs in the throat and uttered through the mouth and nose,

## vocabulary entry 1343 voice-over

hat, āge, fär; let, ēqual, tėrm; it, īce
hot, ōpen, ôrder; oil, out; cup, pu̇t, rüle
əbove, takən, pencəl, lemən, circəs
ch, child; ng, long; sh, ship
th, thin; ᴛʜ, then; zh, measure

especially the sounds human beings make in speaking, singing, shouting, etc.: *The voices of the children could be heard coming from the playground.* **2** such sound regarded as having a particular quality that distinguishes one person from another, expresses emotion, etc.: *to recognize someone's voice, a low voice, a gentle voice, an angry voice.* **3** the power to make such sounds: *He lost his voice because of a sore throat.* **4** anything thought of as being like speech or song: *the voice of the wind, the voice of one's conscience.* **5** ability as a singer: *He has a very good voice.* **6** singer: *The chorus consists of 70 voices.* **7** a part of a composition for one kind of singer or instrument. **8** express; utter: *They voiced their approval of the plan.* **9** expression: *They gave voice to their joy.* **10** an expressed opinion, choice, wish, etc.: *Her voice was for compromise.* **11** a means or instrument of expression: *That newspaper claims to be the voice of the people.* **12** the right to express an opinion or choice: *We had no voice in the matter.* **13** in grammar, a form of a verb showing the relation of the subject of the verb to the action expressed by the verb: *The active voice, as* sees *in* he sees, *shows that the subject is performing the action. The passive voice, as* is seen *in* he is seen, *shows that the subject is receiving the action.* **14** in phonetics, utter with a sound made by vibration of the vocal cords, not with breath alone: *The consonants* z, v, *and* d *are voiced;* s, f, *and* t *are not.* **15** the proper use of the voice, as in acting or singing: *She is studying voice.* 1–7, 9–13, 15 *n.,* 8, 14 *v.,* **voiced, voic‧ing.**
**in voice,** in condition to sing or speak well.
**lift up one's voice,** **a** shout; yell. **b** protest; complain.
**with one voice,** unanimously.
☛ *Etym.* VOCAL, **voice,** and words derived from them can be traced back to L *vox, vocis* 'voice'. **Voice** came through OF *vois* (modern F *voix*), while **vocal** came in the 14c. directly from L *vocalis* 'with the sound of the voice'.

**voice box** LARYNX.

**voiced** (voist) **1** having a voice, especially of a particular kind (*usually used in compounds*): *deep-voiced.* **2** in phonetics, produced or uttered by means of vibration of the vocal cords: *All vowel sounds are voiced; many consonants, such as* b, d, *and* g *have voice added to their basic articulation.* Compare with VOICELESS (def. 2). **3** *pt.* and *pp.* of VOICE. 1, 2 *adj.,* 3 *v.*

**voice frequency** the range of radio frequencies between 300 and 3000 hertz: *Voice frequency is the second lowest range in the radio spectrum, above extremely low frequency.*

**voice mail** **1** an answering machine or automated electronic system that records and stores telephone messages, which can later be listened to by the person for whom they were intended. **2** a message or messages recorded on such a machine or system.

**voice‧less** (vois′lis) **1** having no voice; mute. **2** in phonetics, produced or uttered without vibration of the vocal cords; not voiced: *The consonants* p, t, *and* k *are voiceless.* Compare with VOICED (def. 2). *adj.*

**voice–o‧ver** (vois′ō′vər) **1** the voice of an unseen narrator or commentator in a motion picture or on television. **2** made with an unseen narrator: *He does voice-over commercials for television.* *n.*

**void** (void) **1** without legal force or effect; not binding in law: *A contract made by a person under legal age is void.* **2** make of no force or effect in law. **3** an empty space: *The death of his dog left an aching void in Bob's heart.* **4** empty; vacant: *a void space.* **5** empty out. **6** without effect; useless. 1, 4, 6 *adj.*, 2, 5 *v.*, 3 *n.* —**void′er,** *n.*
**void of,** devoid of; without; lacking: *void of sense.*

**void·a·ble** (voi′də bəl) capable of being voided or given up: *The contract was voidable by either party after twelve months.* *adj.*

**voile** (voil) a thin, sheer, somewhat crisp cloth in a plain weave, used for blouses, light dresses, curtains, etc.: *Voile is usually made of cotton or a cotton blend.* *n.*

**vol.** **1** volume. **2** volunteer. **3** volcano.

**vol·a·tile** (vol′ə til *or* vol′ə təl) **1** evaporating rapidly; changing into a vapour easily at a relatively low temperature: *Gasoline is volatile.* **2** changing rapidly from one mood or interest to another; fickle; frivolous: *He has a volatile disposition; he changes very quickly from being happy to being sad.* *adj.* —**vol′a·tile·ness,** *n.*

**vol·a·til·i·ty** (vol′ə til′ə tē) the quality or state of being VOLATILE. *n.*

**vol·a·til·ize** (vol′ə tə līz′) change into vapour; evaporate. *v.*, **vol·a·til·ized, vol·a·til·iz·ing.**

**vol·can·ic** (vol kan′ik) **1** of, having to do with, or caused by a volcano: *a volcanic eruption.* **2** characterized by the presence of volcanoes: *volcanic country.* **3** made of materials from volcanoes: *volcanic rock.* **4** like a volcano in being likely to break forth violently: *a volcanic temper.* *adj.*

**vol·can·ism** (vol′kə niz′əm) volcanic activity. *n.*

**vol·ca·no** (vol kā′nō) **1** an opening in the earth's crust through which steam, ashes, and lava are expelled. **2** a hill or mountain around this opening, built up of the material that has been forced out. *n., pl.* **vol·ca·noes** or **vol·ca·nos.**

**vole** (vōl) any of numerous rodents belonging to the same family as rats and mice, usually of heavier build and having short limbs and tail. *n.*

**vo·li·tion** (vō lish′ən *or* və lish′ən) **1** the act or an instance of using one's will to make a choice or decision: *He gave himself up to the police of his own volition.* **2** the power of making a choice or decision; will: *By a tremendous exercise of volition, she made one last effort.* *n.*

**vo·li·tion·al** (vō lish′ə nəl *or* və lish′ə nəl) of or having to do with VOLITION. *adj.*
—**vo·li′tion·al·ly,** *adv.*

**vol·ley** (vol′ē) **1** a shower of stones, bullets, arrows, etc.: *A volley of arrows rained down from the walls upon the attacking troops.* **2** the discharge of a number of guns at once. **3** a burst or outpouring of words, oaths, shouts, cheers, etc.: *A volley of questions met the prime minister as he stepped from the car.* **4** discharge or be discharged in a volley: *Cannons volleyed on all sides.* **5** in tennis, etc., the hitting or return of the ball before it touches the ground. **6** hit or return the ball before it touches the ground. 1–3, 5 *n., pl.* **vol·leys;** 4, 6 *v.*, **vol·ley·ed, vol·ley·ing.**

**vol·ley·ball** (vol′ē bol′) **1** a game played with a large ball and a high net: *In volleyball, two teams of players try to hit the ball with their hands back and forth across the net without letting it touch the ground and losing a point.* **2** the ball used in this game. *n.*

**vol·plane** (vol′plān′) **1** glide toward the earth in an airplane without using motor power. **2** the act of gliding in this way. 1 *v.*, **vol·planed, vol·plan·ing;** 2 *n.*

**vols.** volumes.

**volt** (vōlt) an SI unit for measuring the pressure, or push, of an electric current: *One volt of pressure is needed to drive a current of one ampere through a conductor with a resistance of one ohm.* Symbol: V *n.*
☛ *Etym.* Named after an Italian physicist, Count Alessandro *Volta* (1745–1827), who invented the electric battery.

**volt·age** (vōl′tij) the strength of electric pressure measured in VOLTS: *A current of high voltage is used in transmitting electric power over long distances.* *n.*

**vol·ta·ic** (vol tā′ik) of, having to do with, or producing direct electric current by chemical action; galvanic: *a voltaic cell.* *adj.*

**voltaic battery** **1** a battery composed of VOLTAIC CELLS. **2** VOLTAIC CELL.

**voltaic cell** an ELECTROCHEMICAL CELL.

**volt·am·e·ter** (vol tam′ə tər) a device for measuring the quantity of electricity passing through a conductor by the amount of ELECTROLYSIS it produces. *n.*

**volt·me·ter** (vōlt′mē′tər) an instrument for measuring the number of VOLTS of an electric circuit. *n.*

**vol·u·bil·i·ty** (vol′yə bil′ə tē) **1** readiness to talk much; the habit of talking much. **2** a great flow of words. *n.*

**vol·u·ble** (vol′yə bəl) **1** ready to talk much; talkative. **2** characterized by a rapid or ready flow of words: *a voluble protest. Leah was voluble in her account of the accident.* *adj.* —**vol′u·bly,** *adv.*

**vol·ume** (vol′yüm *or* vol′yəm) **1** a collection of printed or written sheets bound together to form a book; book: *We own a library of five hundred volumes.* **2** a book forming part of a set or series: *Her memoirs were published in three volumes.* **3** a series of a periodical, usually all the issues published in one year. **4** space occupied, measured in cubic units: *The storeroom has a volume of 20 cubic metres.* **5** an amount or quantity, especially a large quantity: *Volumes of smoke poured from the chimneys of the factory.* **6** a degree of loudness and fullness of tone: *A pipe organ gives much more volume than a violin or flute.* **7** a roll of parchment, papyrus, etc. containing written matter (the ancient form of a book); scroll. *n.*
**speak volumes,** express much; be full of meaning: *His loving glance spoke volumes.*

**vol·u·met·ric** (vol′yə met′rik) of or having to do with measurement by VOLUME (def. 4). *adj.*

**vo·lu·mi·nous** (və lü′mə nəs) **1** of great size or volume; very bulky or full: *A voluminous cloak covered him from head to foot.* **2** forming or filling a large book or several books: *a voluminous report.* **3** writing or speaking much: *a voluminous author.* *adj.*
—**vo·lu′mi·nous·ly,** *adv.*

**vol·un·tar·i·ly** (vol′ən ter′ə lē) of one's own free will; without force or compulsion: *He went to the police voluntarily to give himself up.* *adv.*

**vol·un·tar·y** (vol′ən ter′ē) **1** done, made, given, etc. of one's own free will; not forced or compelled: *The state is supported by taxes, charities by voluntary contributions.* **2** supported entirely by voluntary gifts: *She works for several voluntary organizations.* **3** acting of one's own free will or choice and usually without pay: *Voluntary workers built a road to the boys' camp.* **4** able to act of one's own free will: *a voluntary agent.* **5** in law, deliberately intended; done on purpose: *voluntary manslaughter.* **6** controlled by the will: *Talking is voluntary; breathing is only partly so.* *adj.*

**vol·un·teer** (vol′ən tēr′) **1** a person who enters military or other service of his or her own free will. **2** offer one's services: *As soon as war was declared, many volunteered.* **3** a person who serves without pay: *In some towns, the firefighters are volunteers.* **4** offer of one's own free will: *She volunteered to do the job.* **5** made up of volunteers: *Our village has a volunteer fire department.* **6** serving as a volunteer: *That man is a volunteer firefighter in this town.* **7** tell or say voluntarily: *She volunteered the information.* **8** VOLUNTARY (def. 1). **9** a plant that grows from seeds dropped by other plants: *We have lots of volunteers in our garden this year.* 1, 3, 9 *n.*, 2, 4, 7 *v.*, 5, 6, 8 *adj.*

**vo·lup·tu·ar·y** (və lup′chü er′ē) **1** a person who cares much for luxury and sensual pleasures. **2** caring much for luxury and sensual pleasures. 1 *n., pl.* **vo·lup·tu·ar·ies;** 2 *adj.*

**vo·lup·tu·ous** (və lup′chü əs) **1** full of or giving pleasure to the senses: *voluptuous music, a voluptuous dance.* **2** occupied with or directed toward luxury and the pleasures of the senses. *adj.* —**vo·lup′tu·ous·ly,** *adv.* —**vo·lup′tu·ous·ness,** *n.*

**vo·lute** (və lüt′) **1** a spiral or scroll-shaped thing or form. **2** in architecture, a spiral or scroll-like ornament, especially on an Ionic or Corinthian capital. See ORDER for picture. **3** any of numerous sea snails having a short spiral shell. **4** the shell of such a snail or one of the whorls of the shell. **5** rolled up or spiral. 1–4 *n.*, 5 *adj.*

**vom·it** (vom′it) **1** expel the contents of the stomach through the mouth; throw up what has been eaten. **2** the substance thrown up from the stomach. **3** the act or an instance of vomiting. **4** throw up; throw out with force: *The chimneys vomited forth smoke.* **5** come out with force or violence. 1, 4, 5 *v.*, 2, 3 *n.*

**voo·doo** (vü′dü) **1** a religion that originated in Africa and is still practised among some black peoples, especially in Haiti: *Voodoo involves belief in the magical powers of charms and spells.* **2** a person who practises this religion. **3** of or having to do with voodoo. 1, 2 *n., pl.* **voo·doos;** 3 *adj.*

**voo·doo·ism** (vü′dü iz′əm) VOODOO rites or practices. *n.*

**voo·doo·ist** (vü′dü ist) a believer in VOODOO. *n.*

**voo·doo·is·tic** (vü′dü is′tik) of or having to do with VOODOOISM. *adj.*

**vo·ra·cious** (vô rā′shəs *or* və rā′shəs) **1** eating much; having an enormous appetite; ravenous: *voracious sharks.* **2** very eager; unable to be satisfied: *She is a voracious reader.* *adj.* —**vo·ra′cious·ly,** *adv.*
☛ Hom. VERACIOUS (for the second pronunciation of **voracious**).

**vo·ra·cious·ness** (vô rā′shəs nəs *or* və rā′shəs nəs) the quality or state of being voracious; VORACITY. *n.*

**vo·rac·i·ty** (vô ras′ə tē *or* və ras′ə tē) the quality or state of being VORACIOUS. *n.*

**volunteer**     1345     **voucher**

hat, āge, fär; let, ēqual, tėrm; it, īce
hot, ōpen, ôrder; oil, out; cup, put, rüle
əbove, takən, pencəl, lemən, circəs

ch, child; ng, long; sh, ship
th, thin; ᴛʜ, then; zh, measure

☛ Hom. VERACITY (for the second pronunciation of **voracity**).

**vor·tex** (vôr′teks) **1** a whirling mass of water, air, etc. that sucks everything near it into its centre: *A whirlpool is a kind of vortex.* **2** a whirl of activity or other situation from which it is hard to escape: *The two nations were unwillingly drawn into the vortex of war.* *n., pl.* **vor·tex·es** *or* **vor·ti·ces.**

**vor·ti·ces** (vôr′tə sēz′) a pl. of VORTEX. *n.*

**vot·a·ble** (vō′tə bəl) capable of being submitted to a vote; that can be voted on. *adj.*

**vo·ta·ress** (vō′tə ris) a female VOTARY. *n.*

**vo·ta·rist** (vō′tə rist) VOTARY. *n.*

**vo·ta·ry** (vō′tə rē) **1** a person devoted to something; devotee: *She was a votary of golf.* **2** a person, such as a monk or nun, bound by vows to a religious life. *n., pl.* **vo·ta·ries.**

**vote** (vōt) **1** a formal expression of a person's opinion or decision in response to a specific question, a choice between candidates, etc.: *My vote is for peace. She won the election by twenty votes.* **2** the formal decision or expression of opinion by a group resulting from the majority of the individual choices of its members: *The vote may go against the government.* **3** the right to contribute to such a formal decision: *We don't have the vote until we are 18 years old. In our club, only those who have paid their fees have a vote.* **4** the written or printed slip, token, etc. used to indicate one's decision; ballot: *The votes were placed in a sealed box.* **5** what is expressed or decided by a majority of voters: *a vote of confidence, a vote of $500 000 for a new gymnasium.* **6** the total number of votes cast; votes collectively: *The vote was higher than in the last election.* **7** a particular group of voters or their votes: *the labour vote, the under-25 vote.* **8** give or cast a vote: *He voted for the Liberals. She has gone to vote.* **9** the act or process of voting: *They decided to take a vote on the matter.* **10** support by one's vote: *to vote Conservative.* **11** pass, determine, or grant by a vote: *The committee voted $60 000 for renovating the building.* **12** declare by general consent: *The trip was voted a success.* **13** *Informal.* suggest: *I vote we quit.* 1–7, 9 *n.*, 8, 10–13 *v.*, **vot·ed, vot·ing.**
**vote down,** defeat by voting against.
**vote in,** elect.

**vot·er** (vō′tər) **1** a person who votes. **2** a person who has the right to vote. *n.*

**voters' list** at an election, a list giving the names, addresses, and occupations of all those entitled to vote.

**voting machine** a mechanical device for registering and counting votes.

**vo·tive** (vō′tiv) done, given, etc. to fulfill a vow: *a votive offering.* *adj.*

**vouch** (vouch) **1** be responsible; give a guarantee (*for*): *I can vouch for the truth of the story. The principal vouched for Mata's honesty.* **2** answer for; confirm; guarantee. *v.*

**vouch·er** (vou′chər) **1** a person or thing that vouches

**voucher** for something. **2** a written evidence of payment; receipt: *Cancelled cheques returned from one's bank are vouchers.* *n.*

**vous·soir** (vü swär′) any of the wedge-shaped pieces forming an arch or vault. See ARCH for picture. *n.*

**vow** (vou) **1** a solemn promise: *a vow of secrecy, marriage vows.* **2** a promise made to God: *a nun's vows.* **3** make a vow: *She vowed not to tell the secret.* **4** make a vow to do, give, get, etc.: *to vow revenge.* **5** declare earnestly or emphatically: *She vowed she would never shop there again.* 1, 2 *n.*, 3–5 *v.*
**take vows,** become a member of a religious order.

**vow·el** (vou′əl) **1** a speech sound in which the vocal cords are vibrating and the breath is not blocked at any point in the mouth by the tongue, teeth, or lips: *When you say awe, you are uttering a vowel. The vowel is the most prominent sound in any syllable.* **2** a letter representing such a sound: *There are five vowels used in writing:* a, e, i, o, *and* u. **3** of or having to do with a vowel: *Voluntary has four vowel sounds; strength has only one.* *n.*

**voy·age** (voi′ij) **1** a journey by water, especially a long journey: *a voyage to Japan.* **2** a journey through the air or through space: *an airplane voyage, the earth's voyage around the sun.* **3** make or take a voyage; travel by water or air: *Columbus voyaged on unknown seas.* **4** a written account of a voyage, especially by sea. 1, 2, 4 *n.*, 3 *v.*, **voy·aged, voy·ag·ing.** —**voy′ag·er,** *n.*

**voy·a·geur** (voi′ə zhèr′; *French,* vwä yä zhœR′) *Cdn.* **1** a canoeman or boatman, especially a French Canadian, in the service of the early fur-trading companies. **2** a person who travels the northern wilderness, especially by canoe. *n., pl.* **vo·ya·geurs** (-zhèrz′; *French,* -zhœR′).

**V.P.** or **V. Pres.** Vice-President.

**vs.** **1** versus. **2** verse.

**V-shaped** (vē′shăpt′) shaped like the letter V: *There is a V-shaped burn on the table.* *adj.*

**v.t.** transitive verb (an abbreviation of Latin *verbum transitivum*).

**VTOL** vertical takeoff and landing.

**vul·can·ite** (vul′kə nīt′) a hard black rubber made by treating crude rubber with sulphur and heating it to high temperatures; ebonite. *n.*

**vul·can·ize** (vul′kə nīz′) treat crude rubber or a similar synthetic material chemically, especially with sulphur and intense heat, to make it stronger and more elastic. *v.,* **vul·can·ized, vul·can·iz·ing.**
—**vul′can·i·za′tion,** *n.* —**vul′can·iz′er,** *n.*

**vulg.** vulgar.

**vul·gar** (vul′gər) **1** lacking good manners, taste, sensitivity, etc.; coarse; boorish: *vulgar language, vulgar ambition.* **2** in common use; ordinary. **3** of the people: *Modern French, Italian, Portuguese, Spanish, and Romanian developed from vulgar varieties of Latin.* *adj.*
—**vul′gar·ly,** *adv.* —**vul′gar·ness,** *n.*
☞ *Etym.* From L *vulgaris* 'of the people, ordinary', which was formed from *vulgus* 'a crowd, the people or public'. 14c.

**vul·gar·ian** (vul ger′ē ən) a vulgar person, especially a rich person who lacks good manners, taste, etc. *n.*

**vul·gar·ism** (vul′gə riz′əm) **1** a word, phrase, or expression that is regarded as nonstandard, coarse, or obscene. **2** VULGARITY. *n.*

**vul·gar·i·ty** (vul gar′ə tē *or* vul ger′ə tē) **1** the quality or state of being vulgar. **2** an action, habit, word, etc. that is vulgar. *n., pl.* **vul·gar·i·ties.**

**vul·gar·ize** (vul′gə rīz′) **1** make vulgar; make cheap or coarse. **2** make widely known; popularize. *v.,* **vul·gar·ized, vul·gar·iz·ing.**

**Vulgar Latin** the popular, spoken form of Latin, the main source of French, Spanish, Italian, Portuguese, and Romanian.

**Vulgate** (vul′gāt) **1** the Latin translation of the Bible used by the Roman Catholic church: *The Vulgate was made by St. Jerome in the fourth century* A.D. **2 vulgate,** the traditionally accepted text or reading of any author. *n.*

**vul·ner·a·bil·i·ty** (vul′nə rə bil′ə tē) the quality or state of being VULNERABLE; being open to attack or injury. *n.*

**vul·ner·a·ble** (vul′nə rə bəl) **1** capable of being wounded or injured; open to attack: *The head is a vulnerable part of the body. The fort was vulnerable while the walls were being repaired.* **2** in the game of contract bridge, in the position where penalties and premiums are increased. *adj.* —**vul′ner·a·bly,** *adv.*
**vulnerable to,** sensitive to or affected by certain influences: *Most people are vulnerable to ridicule.*

**vul·pine** (vul′pīn) of, having to do with, or like a fox. *adj.*

**vul·ture** (vul′chər) **1** any of various large birds of prey belonging to two different but related families, having a more or less naked head and neck, weaker feet and claws than the distantly related hawk, eagles, and falcons, and feeding mainly on the flesh of dead animals: *The condors and the turkey vulture are Western Hemisphere vultures.* **2** a greedy, ruthless person who preys on others. *n.*

**vul·va** (vul′və) the external genitals of the human female. *n., pl.* **vul·vae** (-vē *or* -vī) or **vul·vas.**

**vv** **1** versus. **2** violins.

**v.v.** vice versa.

**vy·ing** (vī′ing) ppr. of VIE. *v.*

# W w *W w*

hat, āge, fär; let, ēqual, tėrm; it, īce
hot, ōpen, ôrder; oil, out; cup, put, rüle
əbove, takən, pencəl, lemən, circəs
ch, child; ng, long; sh, ship
th, thin; ŦH, then; zh, measure

**w or W** (dub′əl yü′) **1** the twenty-third letter of the English alphabet. **2** any speech sound represented by this letter. **3** a person or thing identified as w, especially the twenty-third of a series. **4** anything shaped like a W. *n., pl.* **w's** or **W's.**

**w. 1** week; weeks. **2** wide; width. **3** west; western. **4** weight. **5** wife. **6** with.

**W 1** watt. **2** west; western. **3** tungsten; wolfram. **4** in physics, work; energy or force.

**W. 1** Wednesday. **2** west; western. **3** Wales; Welsh.

**wab·ble** (wob′əl) See WOBBLE. *v.* **wab·bled, wab·bling;** *n.*

**wab·bly** (wob′lē) See WOBBLY. *adj.*

**wad** (wod) **1** a small, soft or loose mass of material, such as cotton batting or crumpled paper: *He plugged his ears with wads of cotton to keep out the noise. She stuck a wad of paper into the crack to keep the window from rattling.* **2** crush, press, or roll into a wad: *She wadded up the paper and threw it into the wastebasket.* **3** a small compact lump of something: *a wad of chewing gum.* **4** *Informal.* a roll of paper money: *Jan took a wad out of his pocket and counted off five tens.* **5** a round plug of felt, cardboard, etc. used to hold the powder and shot in place in a gun or cartridge. **6** stuff with a wad: *to wad a gun.* **7** hold in place by a wad: *to wad a charge in a gun.* **8** pad or line with wadding. 1, 3–5 *n.,* 2, 6–8 *v.,* **wad·ded, wad·ding.**

**wad·ding** (wod′ing) **1** a soft material for padding, stuffing, packing, etc., especially carded cotton in sheets. **2** material for making wads for guns or cartridges. **3** a wad or wads. **4** ppr. of WAD. 1–3 *n.,* 4 *v.*

**wad·dle** (wod′əl) **1** walk with short steps and an awkward swaying motion, as a duck does: *The duck waddled across the road.* **2** an awkward, swaying gait: *It made us laugh to see its waddle.* 1 *v.,* **wad·dled, wad·dling;** 2 *n.* —**wad′dler,** *n.*

**wade** (wād) **1** walk through water, snow, sand, mud, or anything that hinders free motion: *We had to wade through deep snowdrifts to get to the door.* **2** walk about in shallow water for amusement: *We loved to go wading in the spring.* **3** make one's way with difficulty (*used with* **through**): *to wade through an uninteresting book.* **4** *Informal.* attack or go to work on vigorously (*used with* **in**): *He waded right in and got the job done in half an hour.* **5** cross or pass through by wading: *to wade a creek.* **6** the act of wading. 1–5 *v.,* **wad·ed, wad·ing;** 6 *n.*

**wad·er** (wā′dər) **1** wading bird. **2** any person or thing that wades. **3** Usually, **waders,** *pl.* high waterproof boots or combination boots and trousers used for wading, especially by fishermen, etc. *n.*

**wa·di** (wä′dē) **1** in parts of the Arabian peninsula, northern Africa, etc., a valley or ravine through which a stream flows during the rainy season. **2** a stream or torrent running through such a ravine. *n., pl.* **wa·dis.**

**wading bird** any long-legged bird that wades in water to look for food: *Herons, cranes, sandpipers, and flamingos are wading birds.*

**wa·fer** (wā′fər) **1** a very thin, crisp biscuit or cookie: *an ice cream wafer.* **2** a very thin piece of candy: *a chocolate wafer.* **3** in some Christian churches, a thin, round piece of unleavened bread used in the Communion service. **4** a small disk of paper or sealing wax used as a seal on letters, documents, etc. *n.* —**wa′fer·like′,** *adj.*

**waf·fle¹** (wof′əl) a light, crisp, moulded cake made from a batter and baked in a waffle iron. See WAFFLE IRON for picture. *n.*

**waf·fle²** (wof′əl) **1** avoid making a decision or commitment by speaking ambiguously or evasively: *The ratepayers' association accused their MP of waffling on the airport issue.* **2** talk nonsense; talk on and on; prattle. **3** nonsense; foolish talk. 1, 2 *v.,* **waf·fled, waf·fling;** 3 *n.*

A waffle iron and waffles

**waffle iron** a device for cooking waffles, consisting of two hinged metal plates with a gridlike pattern of surface projections, which close together and cook the waffles between them.

**waft** (waft *or* woft) **1** carry over water or through air: *The waves wafted the boat to shore. The night wind wafted the sound of singing across the lake.* **2** float: *A single feather wafted down to the ground.* **3** a breath or puff of air, wind, etc.: *A waft of fresh air came through the open window.* **4** a waving movement: *a waft of the hand.* 1, 2 *v.,* 3, 4 *n.*

**wag¹** (wag) **1** move from side to side or up and down, especially rapidly and repeatedly: *He wagged his finger at me in disapproval. The dog's tail started wagging even before the car turned into the driveway.* **2** of a person's tongue, move in speaking, especially to chatter or gossip: *Tongues began to wag almost immediately after the police left.* **3** move the tongue in chatter or gossip: *They don't really know anything about it; they're just wagging their tongues.* **4** the act of wagging: *Donna refused with a wag of her head.* 1–3 *v.,* **wagged, wag·ging;** 4 *n.*

**wag²** (wag) a person who is fond of making jokes. *n.*

**wage** (wāj) **1** carry on: *to wage war, to wage a campaign.* **2** an amount paid for work, especially on an hourly or daily basis: *He earns a decent wage. That company pays good wages.* **3** **wages,** a result: *The wages of hard work are often success.* 1 *v.,* **waged, wag·ing;** 2, 3 *n.* —**wage′less,** *adj.*
☛ *Syn.* See note at SALARY.

**wage earner** a person who works for a wage or a salary.

**wa·ger** (wā′jər) **1** an agreement between two persons that the one who is proved wrong about the outcome of an event will give a particular thing or sum of money to the person who is proved right; bet: *They made a wager on the result of the election.* **2** the thing or sum risked in a wager; stake: *What's your wager? She paid the wager promptly.* **3** make a wager; bet; gamble: *He wagered $5 on the first race.* 1, 2 *n.*, 3 *v.* —**wa′ger•er**, *n.*

**wag•ger•y** (wag′ə rē) **1** joking or merriment. **2** a joke, especially a practical joke. *n.*, *pl.* **wag•ger•ies.**

**wag•gish** (wag′ish) **1** fond of making jokes. **2** done or made in fun; playful or funny: *a waggish look.* *adj.* —**wag′gish•ly**, *adv.* —**wag′gish•ness**, *n.*

**wag•gle** (wag′əl) **1** move quickly and repeatedly from side to side; wag. **2** a wagging motion. 1 *v.*, **wag•gled, wag•gling;** 2 *n.*

**wag•gon** (wag′ən) *Esp. Brit.* See WAGON. *n.*

**wag•gon•er** (wag′ə nər) *Esp. Brit.* See WAGONER. *n.*

**wag•on** (wag′ən) **1** a four-wheeled vehicle, especially one for carrying loads: *a milk wagon.* **2** a child's four-wheeled cart. **3** *Informal.* STATION WAGON. *n.* Also, **waggon.**
**hitch one's wagon to a star,** have high hopes and ambitions; aim high.

**wag•on•er** (wag′ə nər) a person who drives a WAGON. *n.* Also, **waggoner.**

**wag•on•load** (wag′ən lōd′) the load that a WAGON can carry. *n.*

**wagon train** a group of WAGONs moving along in a line one after another, especially such a group carrying a company of settlers travelling together for protection: *Many wagon trains crossed the plains during the settlement of the American West.*

**waif** (wāf) **1** a person without home or friends, especially a homeless or neglected child. **2** anything without an owner; a stray thing, animal, etc. *n.*

**wail** (wāl) **1** cry loud and long because of grief or pain: *The baby wailed.* **2** a long cry of grief or pain. **3** a sound like such a cry: *the wail of a hungry coyote.* **4** make a mournful sound: *The wind wailed around the old house.* **5** lament; mourn. 1, 4, 5 *v.*, 2, 3 *n.* —**wail′er**, *n.*
☞ *Hom.* WALE, WHALE (wāl).

**wain** (wān) WAGON (def. 1). *Archaic* except in WAINWRIGHT. *n.*

**wain•scot** (wān′skət *or* wān′skot′) **1** a lining of wood, usually in panels, on the walls of a room. **2** line with wood: *a room wainscotted in oak.* **3** the lower part of the wall of a room when it is decorated differently from the upper part. 1, 3 *n.*, 2 *v.* **wain•scot•ted** *or* **wain•scot•ed, wain•scot•ting** *or* **wain•scot•ing.**

**wain•scot•ting** *or* **wain•scot•ing** (wān′skot′ing *or* wān′skə ting) **1** a WAINSCOT. **2** material used for WAINSCOTs. *n.*

**wain•wright** (wān′rīt′) a person who makes and repairs WAGONs (def. 1). *n.*
☞ *Etym.* See note at WRIGHT.

**waist** (wāst) **1** the part of the human body between the ribs and the hips. **2** the WAISTLINE. **3** a garment or part of a garment covering the body from the neck or shoulders to the waistline; bodice or blouse. **4** a narrow middle part: *the waist of a violin.* **5** the part of a ship amidships, as that between the forecastle and the quarterdeck of a sailing vessel, or between the forward and stern superstructure of an oil tanker. **6** the middle section of the fuselage of an aircraft, especially that of a bomber. *n.*
☞ *Hom.* WASTE.

**waist•band** (wāst′band′) a band of cloth attached to the top of a skirt or trousers to fit around the waist: *a wide waistband. The waistband on these slacks is too loose.* *n.*

**waist•coat** (wāst′kōt′ *or* wes′kət) *Esp. Brit.* a man's vest: *The modern waistcoat is basically the same garment as that worn by British and European men in the 16th century.* See VEST for picture. *n.*

**waist•line** (wāst′līn′) **1** the smallest part of the waist. **2** the measurement around the body at this part: *Her waistline is 84 centimetres.* **3** the part of a garment that fits around the waist: *The dress has an elasticized waistline.* **4** the line where the bodice and skirt of a dress join: *a loose-fitting dress without a waistline.* *n.*

**wait** (wāt) **1** stay or be inactive until someone comes or something happens: *Let's wait in the shade. We waited for him for two hours.* **2** *Informal.* put off serving a meal: *Can you wait dinner for her?* **3** the act or time of waiting: *I had a long wait at the doctor's office.* **4** look forward expectantly: *waiting impatiently for the holidays.* **5** await: *to wait one's chance. Wait your turn.* **6** be ready and available: *The car was waiting for us when we got there.* **7** be left undone; be put off: *That matter can wait till tomorrow.* 1, 2, 4–7 *v.*, 3 *n.*
**lie in wait,** stay hidden ready to surprise or attack: *Two assassins were lying in wait for the dictator.*
**wait on,** supply the wants of, as a clerk in a store, a waiter in a restaurant, etc.; serve: *A polite, elderly man waited on us.*
**wait on** *or* **upon,** **a** be a servant to: *He waits on the prince.* **b** pay a respectful visit to a superior: *Tomorrow the prime minister will wait on the Queen.*
**wait out,** do nothing until something has passed or is finished: *There was nothing to do but wait out the storm.*
**wait up, a** delay going to bed until someone comes or something happens: *I'll probably be late, so don't wait up for me.* **b** *Informal.* stop and wait for someone to catch up: *Wait up! She's fallen behind again.*
☞ *Hom.* WEIGHT.

**wait•er** (wā′tər) a person who waits, especially a man who waits on table in a hotel, restaurant, etc. *n.*

**wait•ing** (wā′ting) **1** the act of a person who waits. **2** that waits: *a waiting crowd.* **3** used to wait in: *a waiting room.* **4** ppr. of WAIT. 1 *n.*, 2, 3 *adj.*, 4 *v.*
**in waiting,** in attendance on royalty: *a lady-in-waiting to the queen.*

**waiting list** a list of people who have applied for something that may become available in the future: *There is already a long waiting list so you probably won't get on that flight.*

**waiting room** a room at a railway station, doctor's office, etc. for people to wait in.

**waiting woman** formerly, a female servant or attendant.

**wait–list** (wā′tlist) enter on a list of persons waiting, especially for a seat on an airliner: *Leon is booked to fly tomorrow morning, but he is wait-listed for tonight's flight.* *v.*

**wait•ress** (wā′tris) a woman who waits on table in a hotel, restaurant, etc. *n.*

**waive** (wāv) **1** refrain from claiming or pressing; give

up or forgo: *The defendant's lawyer waived her right to cross-examine the witness.* **2** put off; postpone; delay. *v.*, **waived, waiv·ing.**
☞ *Hom.* WAVE.

**waiv·er** (wā′vər) **1** a giving up of a right, claim, etc. **2** a written statement of this: *For $10 000 the man signed a waiver of all claims against the railway. n.*
☞ *Hom.* WAVER.

**wake¹** (wāk) **1** stop sleeping (*often used with* **up**): *to wake up early in the morning.* **2** cause to stop sleeping (*often used with* **up**): *The noise will wake the baby. Wake me up early.* **3** be or stay awake: *Waking or sleeping, he could not seem to get the accusation out of his mind.* **4** become alive or active: *Her conscience woke. The flowers wake in the spring.* **5** make alive or active; rouse to action, alertness, or liveliness (*often used with* **up**): *Mario needs some interest to wake him up.* **6** a watch held by the body of a dead person before burial, sometimes accompanied by festivities. 1–5 *v.*, **woke** or **waked, woken** or **waked, wak·ing;** 6 *n.*
**wake (up) to,** become conscious or aware of: *Niki finally woke up to the fact that his money was almost gone.*

**wake²** (wāk) **1** the track left behind a moving ship. **2** the track left by anything. *n.*
**in the wake of,** close behind; very soon after: *Floods came in the wake of the hurricane.*

**wake·ful** (wāk′fəl) **1** not able to sleep: *Even after reading till midnight, she was still wakeful.* **2** without sleep; sleepless: *They spent a wakeful night.* **3** watchful; alert. *adj.* —**wake′ful·ness,** *n.*

**wak·en** (wā′kən) WAKE (def. 2): *The sudden noise wakened him. v.* —**wak′en·er,** *n.*

**wale** (wāl) **1** a streak or ridge made on the skin by a stick or whip; welt. **2** mark with welts; raise welts on. **3** a long, narrow, raised surface, especially one of a series of parallel ribs or ridges in cloth such as corduroy. **4** weave with ridges. **5** Usually, **wales,** *pl.* a continuous line of thick, outside planking on the sides of a wooden ship. 1, 3, 5 *n.*, 2, 4 *v.*, **waled, wal·ing.**
☞ *Hom.* WAIL, WHALE (wāl).

**walk** (wok) **1** go on foot: *Walk down to the post office with me.* **2** appear after death: *The ghost will walk tonight.* **3** go over, on, or through on foot: *The captain walked the deck.* **4** make, put, drive, etc. by walking: *to walk off a headache.* **5** go step by step: *Walk, do not run.* **6** cause to walk: *The rider walked her horse.* **7** the act of walking, especially walking for pleasure or exercise: *a walk in the country.* **8** a distance to walk: *It is a long walk from here.* **9** a manner or way of walking; gait: *We knew the man was a sailor from his rolling walk.* **10** a route, sidewalk, or path for walking: *We always preferred the walk down by the river. I shovelled the snow off the walk.* **11** occupation or social position: *A street cleaner and a letter carrier are in different walks of life.* **12** conduct oneself in a particular manner; follow a particular course in life: *walk in fear.* **13** go to first base after the pitcher has thrown four balls. **14** a chance to do this. **15** of a pitcher, give such a chance. **16** an enclosed place; tract: *a poultry walk.* 1–6, 12, 13, 15 *v.*, 7–11, 14, 16 *n.*
**walk away from,** progress much faster than.
**walk off with, a** take; get; win. **b** steal.
**walk out, a** *Informal.* go on strike. **b** leave suddenly.
**walk out on,** *Informal.* desert.
**walk over,** defeat easily and by a wide margin.
☞ *Hom.* WOK.

**walk·a·way** (wok′ə wā′) *Informal.* an easy victory. *n.*

hat, āge, fär; let, ēqual, tėrm; it, īce
hot, ōpen, ôrder; oil, out; cup, pút, rüle
əbove, takən, pencəl, lemən, circəs
ch, child; ng, long; sh, ship
th, thin; ŦH, then; zh, measure

**walk·er** (wok′ər) **1** a person who walks, especially one who walks in a particular way: *She's a fast walker.* **2** a framework on wheels designed to support a child learning to walk. **3** a framework designed to help a lame or handicapped person walk. *n.*

**walk·ie-talk·ie** (wok′ē tok′ē) a small, portable two-way radio set. *n.*

**walk–in** (wok′in′) **1** large enough to be walked into: *a walk-in closet.* **2** a sure or easy victory. 1 *adj.*, 2 *n.*

**walk·ing** (wok′ing) **1** the action of a person or thing that walks: *Walking is good exercise.* **2** for use in walking: *Bring your walking shoes.* **3** including or consisting of the action of walking: *We went on a walking tour of the city centre.* **4** in human form; personified: *She's a walking encyclopedia.* **5** the quality or condition of a road, etc. for walking: *The walking was treacherous after the ice-storm.* **6** ppr. of WALK. 1, 5 *n.*, 2–4 *adj.*, 6 *v.*

**walking papers** *Informal.* dismissal from a position, etc.

**walking stick** **1** a stick used for support in walking; cane. **2** any of various insects having a body like a stick or twig.

**walk–on** (wok′on′) **1** a small part in a dramatic production in which an actor appears on stage but usually has no lines to speak. **2** an actor having such a part. *n.*

**walk·out** (wok′out′) **1** a work stoppage; strike. **2** the departure of a group of people from a meeting, etc. as a protest. *n.*

**walk·o·ver** (wok′ō′vər) *Informal.* an easy victory. *n.*

**walk–up** (wok′up′) **1** an apartment house or office building of more than two storeys having no elevator. **2** a room, apartment, or office above the ground floor in such a building. **3** located above the ground floor in such a building: *a walk-up apartment.* **4** having several storeys and no elevator: *There is a walk-up annex.* 1, 2 *n.*, 3, 4 *adj.*

**wall** (wol) **1** the side of a building or room joining the floor or foundation and the ceiling or roof. **2** a solid structure of stone, brick, or other material built up to enclose, divide, support, or protect: *Cities used to be surrounded by high walls to keep out enemies. There was a low wall around the garden.* **3** something like a wall in looks or use: *The flood came in a wall of water four metres high. The soldiers kept their ranks a solid wall.* **4** the side of any hollow thing: *the wall of a cylinder, the wall of the heart.* **5** enclose, divide, protect, or fill with a wall or as if with a wall: *The garden is walled. Workers walled up the doorway.* 1–4 *n.*, 5 *v.* —**wall′-less,** *adj.* —**wall′-like′,** *adj.*

**come, be,** etc. **up against a blank wall,** be completely unsuccessful, as when seeking information; be stymied: *She tried several angles, but always came up against a blank wall.*

**drive** or **push to the wall,** make desperate or helpless: *driven to the wall by debts.*

**drive, send,** etc. **up the wall,** *Informal.* make frantic with

frustration or anger: *His constant whining drives me up the wall!*
**go to the wall, a** give way; be defeated. **b** fail in business.
**off the wall,** *Informal.* eccentric; bizarre; crazy.
**with one's back to** or **against the wall,** in an extreme or desperate situation.

**wal·la·by** (wol'ə bē) any of various small kangaroos, some of which are no bigger than a rabbit. *n., pl.* **wal·la·bies** or (*esp. collectively*) **wal·la·by.**

**wal·la·roo** (wol'ə rü') a species of large kangaroo having thick, coarse, dark-grey or reddish-brown fur. *n.*

**wall·board** (wol'bôrd') a building material made in large sheets, used in place of plaster or wooden panelling to finish interior walls and ceilings. It is made of a variety of materials, such as gypsum covered with heavy paper, pressed wood chips, or plastic. *n.*

**walled** (wold) **1** having walls: *a walled garden.* **2** pt. and pp. of WALL. *1 adj., 2 v.*

**wal·let** (wol'it) a small, flat, folding case, usually made of leather or vinyl, having compartments for carrying money, credit cards, etc. in one's pocket or purse. *n.*

**wall·eye** (wol'ī') **1** especially in a horse, an eye with an almost colourless iris. **2** an eye having an opaque, white cornea. **3** the condition of having such an eye or such eyes. **4** an eye that turns outward. **5** a condition of the eyes in which one or both eyes are turned outward because of an imbalance of the muscles. **6** a large, staring eye, as in some fish. **7** a common North American freshwater game fish of the perch family occurring in two forms, or subspecies: the **yellow walleye** marked with gold or yellow spots and weighing an average of about 1.5 kg, and the much smaller **blue walleye,** having a bluish colouring. *n.*

**wall·eyed** (wol'īd') having WALLEYES. *adj.*

**walleyed pike** or **walleye pike** YELLOW WALLEYE.

**wall·flow·er** (wol'flou'ər) **1** *Informal.* a person, especially a girl or woman, who remains alone at a dance, either from shyness or because of not being asked to dance. **2** any of numerous perennial plants of the mustard family that often grow from chinks in walls: *Several wallflowers having fragrant yellow, orange, or red flowers are widely cultivated.* *n.*

**wall hanging** a large woven, knotted, appliquéd, etc. decoration hung on a wall: *I made a macramé wall hanging for our front hall.*

**wal·lop** (wol'əp) *Informal.* **1** beat soundly; thrash. **2** hit very hard; strike with a vigorous blow. **3** a very hard blow: *The wallop knocked him down.* **4** the power to hit very hard blows: *He's got a real wallop! My arm still hurts.* **5** defeat thoroughly, as in a game. *1, 2, 5 v., 3, 4 n.*

**wal·lop·ing** (wol'ə ping) *Informal.* **1** a sound beating or thrashing. **2** a thorough defeat. **3** very big or impressive; whopping: *a walloping big baby.* **4** ppr. of WALLOP. *1, 2 n., 3 adj., 4 v.*

**wal·low** (wol'ō) **1** roll about lazily or pleasurably, as animals in dust or mud: *The pigs wallowed in the cool mud.* **2** roll about clumsily or out of control: *The boat wallowed helplessly in the stormy sea.* **3** indulge oneself excessively in some pleasure, state of mind, way of living, etc.: *to wallow in luxury, to wallow in self-pity.* **4** the act of wallowing. **5** a place where an animal wallows: *There used to be many buffalo wallows on the prairies.* *1–3 v., 4, 5 n.*

**wall·pa·per** (wol'pā'pər) **1** paper, commonly with printed decorative patterns in colour, for pasting on and covering the walls and, often, the ceiling of a room. **2** put wallpaper on. *1 n., 2 v.*

**wal·nut** (wol'nut' *or* wol'nət) **1** any of a closely related group of hardwood trees found in many parts of the world, having compound leaves with 5 to 23 toothed leaflets and fruit that is a large woody nut enclosed in a thick husk: *Two species of walnut, the butternut and the black walnut, are native to eastern Canada.* **2** the roundish, edible nut of any of these trees. **3** the hard, dark wood of any of these trees, valued for making furniture, etc. **4** referring to a family of trees, including the walnuts and hickories. **5** medium reddish brown. *1–5 n., 5 adj.*
☛ *Etym.* From OE *wealhhnutu,* made up of *wealh* 'foreign' and *hnutu* 'nut'.

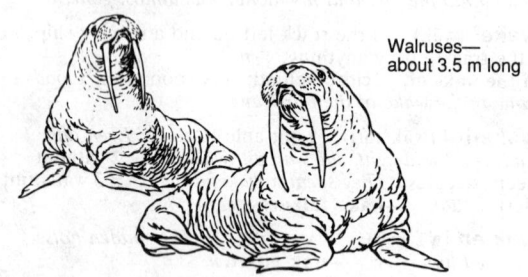

Walruses— about 3.5 m long

**wal·rus** (wol'rəs) a large sea mammal of the arctic regions, resembling a seal but larger and having long tusks: *Walruses have long been hunted, especially for their thick hide, their ivory tusks, and the oil obtained from their blubber.* *n., pl.* **wal·rus** or **wal·rus·es.**
☛ *Etym.* From Dutch *walrus, walros* (literally 'whale horse'), made up of *wal* 'whale' + *ros* 'horse'.

**waltz** (wolts) **1** a smooth, even, gliding ballroom dance in three-four time. **2** the music for the waltz. **3** dance a waltz. **4** move nimbly, quickly, or showily: *She waltzed through the room, cheerfully greeting all the guests.* **5** *Informal.* advance or proceed easily and successfully (*used with* **through**): *She waltzed through the exam in half the time it took me.* **6** *Informal.* approach boldly or abruptly; accost (*used with* **up**): *He just waltzed up to the foreman and said he was quitting.* **7** *Informal.* make a person advance by or as if by taking him or her by the arm and leading him or her; march: *His mother waltzed him into the living room to apologize to his sister.* *1, 2 n., 3–7 v.* —**waltz'er,** *n.*

Wampum. The circular piece is the wampum record of the founding of the Iroquois League of Five Nations. It consists of an outer ring of shells with 50 separate strings representing the 50 chiefs of the League. The other piece is a standard Iroquois wampum sash.

**wam·pum** (wom'pəm) beads made from polished shells strung in belts and sashes, formerly used by eastern

North American Indian peoples as money, as a reminder of a treaty, and as ornament. *n.*

**wan** (won) **1** pale and sickly; lacking natural colour: *Her face looked wan after her long illness.* **2** looking worn or tired; faint or weak: *The sick boy gave the doctor a wan smile.* *adj.*, **wan·ner, wan·nest.** —**wan′ly,** *n.* —**wan′ness,** *n.*

**wand** (wond) a slender stick or rod: *The magician waved her wand and a rabbit popped out of the hat.* *n.* —**wand′like′,** *adj.*

**wan·der** (won′dər) **1** move about without any special purpose: *I was too early for my appointment, so I wandered through the stores for a while.* **2** go aimlessly over or through: *to wander the earth.* **3** go from the right way; stray: *The dog wandered off and got lost.* **4** talk or think in a rambling or incoherent way; drift away in thought or be delirious: *The fever made his mind wander. As she talked, she kept wandering away from her subject and glancing at the door.* **5** of a river, path, etc., follow a winding, irregular course. *v.* —**wan′der·er,** *n.*

**wandering Jew 1** any of a number of plants of the spiderwort family, especially any of several trailing or creeping plants having showy leaves that are striped with white or cream on the upper side and are reddish purple beneath: *Wandering Jews are commonly grown as house plants.* **2 Wandering Jew,** in medieval legend, a Jew who insulted Christ on the way to the Crucifixion and was condemned to wander on earth till Christ's Second Coming.

**wan·der·lust** (won′dər lust′) a strong desire to wander: *Otto's wanderlust led him all over the world.* *n.*

**wane** (wān) **1** of the moon, go through the regular decrease in the size of its visible portion: *The moon wanes after it has become full.* See MOON for picture. **2** become less brilliant or intense: *The light of day wanes in the evening.* **3** lose strength, power, or importance: *Her influence in the club has waned.* **4** of a period of time, draw to a close: *Summer wanes as autumn nears.* **5** the process of waning. 1–4 *v.*, **waned, wan·ing;** 5 *n.* **on the wane,** growing less; waning: *His popularity was on the wane.*

**wan·gle** (wang′gəl) *Informal.* manage to get by schemes, tricks, persuasion, etc: *She wangled an invitation to the party.* *v.*, **wan·gled, wan·gling.** **wangle out of,** escape from by trickery: *He wangled out of the unpleasant job.*

**wan·i·gan** (won′ə gən) *Cdn.* **1** a logger's chest or trunk. **2** a large sled equipped as living quarters and pulled by tracked vehicles as part of a train for carrying troops and supplies in the North. **3** a kind of boat used by loggers for carrying supplies, tools, etc. and as a houseboat. *n.*
☛ *Etym.* From Algonquian *wanigan* 'a trap' or 'a place for stray objects'.

**want** (wont) **1** wish for; desire: *Aled wants to become a singer. She wants a new car.* **2** something wanted; a desire or need: *The new park supplied a long-felt want. Paul is a man of few wants.* **3** be without what is desired or needed; lack: *a reply that wants courtesy. The building fund still wants several thousand dollars.* **4** the quality or state of lacking something desired or needed; shortage or lack: *The plant died for want of water.* **5** need; require: *Plants want water. You want more exercise.* **6** suffer from a lack, especially of the necessities of life: *In spite of the new aid program, many people are still wanting. "Waste not, want not."* **7** extreme poverty: *Many families were in want this past winter.* **8** wish to see, speak to, or use the help of a

---

**wan**     **1351**     **war bonnet**

hat, āge, fär; let, ēqual, tėrm; it, īce
hot, ōpen, ôrder; oil, out; cup, pùt, rüle
əbove, takən, pencəl, lemən, circəs
ch, child; ng, long; sh, ship
th, thin; ᴛʜ, then; zh, measure

---

person: *Call me if you want me. You're wanted on the phone.* **9** seek or go after in order to question or arrest: *The police want him for questioning. She is wanted for theft.* **10** have or feel a shortage (*used with* **for**): *They are wealthy and want for nothing. She has never wanted for friends.* **11** *Informal.* ought: *You want to eat a balanced diet.* **12** *Informal.* of animals, wish to enter or leave (*used with* **in** *or* **out**): *The dog wants in. Our cat wants out.* **13** be short or lacking: *It wants an hour until train time.* 1, 3, 5, 6, 8–13 *v.*, 2, 4, 7 *n.*

**want ad** *Informal.* a notice in a newspaper that an employee, an apartment, an article of some kind, etc. is wanted, or is for sale or rent.

**want·ing** (won′ting) **1** not coming up to a standard or need; not satisfactory: *The stranger was wanting in courtesy.* **2** lacking or missing: *One volume of the set is wanting.* **3** ppr. of WANT. 1, 2 *adj.*, 3 *v.*

**wan·ton** (won′tən) **1** without excuse or reason; senseless, reckless, or heartless: *a wanton attack, a wanton disregard of others' rights. His mistreatment of animals is wanton cruelty.* **2** sexually immoral; not chaste: *a wanton woman.* **3** an immoral or unchaste person. 1, 2 *adj.*, 3 *n.* —**wan′ton·ly,** *adv.* —**wan′ton·ness,** *n.*

**wap·i·ti** (wop′i tē) *Cdn.* the North American ELK. *n.*, *pl.* **wap·i·ti** or **wap·i·tis.**
☛ *Etym.* From the Algonquian name *wapitā* 'white', referring to the animal's white rump and tail.

**war** (wôr) **1** open fighting carried on by armed forces between nations or parts of a nation. **2** any active struggle, strife, or conflict: *the war against disease, a gang war.* **3** the art or science of fighting against an opposing armed force; military science: *Soldiers are trained in war.* **4** fight; make war: *to war against poverty. Germany warred against France.* **5** of, having to do with, or used in war: *war materials, war crimes.* 1–3, 5 *n.*, 4 *v.*, **warred, war·ring.** —**war′less,** *adj.*
**at war,** taking part in a war.
**go to war,** **a** start a war. **b** go as a soldier.
☛ *Hom.* WORE.

**war·ble** (wôr′bəl) **1** sing in a lilting, melodious way, with trills, quavers, etc.: *Birds warbled in the trees.* **2** make a sound like that of a bird warbling: *The brook warbled over its rocky bed.* **3** express by warbling: *to warble a greeting.* **4** the act of warbling. **5** a bird's song or a sound like it. 1–3 *v.*, **war·bled, war·bling;** 4, 5 *n.*

**war·bler** (wôr′blər) **1** any of numerous related birds of the Eastern Hemisphere distantly related to the thrushes: *Many warblers are noted for their song.* **2** any of various small, brightly coloured songbirds of the Western Hemisphere: *wood warbler.* **3** any person or thing that warbles. *n.*

**war bonnet** a ceremonial headdress traditionally worn as a mark of honour among Amerindian peoples of the North American plains, consisting of a row or rows of feathers attached to a headband and trailing down the back.

**war club** a heavy club used as a weapon.

**war cry** 1 a word or phrase shouted in fighting; battle cry. 2 a party cry in any contest.

**ward** (wôrd) 1 a division of a hospital, especially a section for a particular class or group of patients, consisting of one large room or a group of rooms: *a maternity ward, the children's ward.* 2 a division of a prison, such as a block of cells. 3 a district of a city or town, especially one represented by an alderman. 4 a person under the care of a guardian or of a court: *a ward of the Children's Aid Society.* 5 guard: *The soldiers kept ward over the castle.* 6 being kept under guard; custody; prison. *n.*
**ward off,** turn aside or keep away; avert: *He warded off the blow with his arm. She raised her collar to ward off the icy wind.*
☛ *Etym.* From OE *weard* (*n.*), *weardian* (*v.*), coming together with Norman French *warde, warder,* which had been separately borrowed from Germanic. WARDEN also came from Norman French. GUARD and GUARDIAN came in the 15c. from later (central French) forms of the same words.

**-ward** a suffix meaning: in or to a particular direction or point in time, as *afterward, backward, seaward, upward.*
☛ *Usage.* Words ending in **-ward** may be used as adjectives (*the seaward side of the house*), adverbs (*She glanced upward*), prepositions (*He came toward me*), or, in some cases, nouns (*to the southward*). See also -WARDS.

**ward·en** (wôr′dən) 1 an official who enforces certain laws or rules: *a fire warden.* 2 a person in charge of the operation of a prison. 3 in certain colleges, churches, or other institutions, an official with administrative, academic, or supervisory duties. 4 *Cdn.* in provinces having county governments, the head of the county council, generally chosen by the members from among themselves. *n.*
☛ *Etym.* See note at WARD.

**ward·er** (wôr′dər) 1 a guard or watchman. 2 jailer. *n.*

**ward·robe** (wôr′drōb′) 1 a stock of clothes: *She is shopping for her spring wardrobe.* 2 a closet or piece of furniture for holding clothes. 3 a room in which clothes are kept. 4 all the costumes of a theatrical show or film. *n.*

**wardrobe mistress** the woman in charge of the costumes in a theatrical show or film.

**-wards** suffix meaning: in or to a particular direction or point in time, as *afterwards, backwards, towards.*
☛ *Usage.* Words ending in **-wards** are used most often as adverbs (*She fell over backwards*) but are also used as prepositions (*He came towards me*) and as adjectives (*He left her without a backwards glance*). With adjectives the usual suffix is **-ward** (*He left her without a backward glance*). See also -WARD.

**ward·ship** (wôrd′ship) 1 guardianship; custody; especially of a minor or other ward. 2 the condition of being a WARD (def. 4), or of being under a legal or feudal guardian. *n.*

**ware** (wer) 1 articles or goods of a particular kind or used for a particular purpose (now used mainly in compounds): *tinware, hardware, kitchenware. The silverware needs polishing.* 2 articles of fired clay; pottery: *blue-and-white ware from Delft. Biscuit ware is unglazed porcelain.* 3 Usually, **wares,** *pl.* manufactured articles or goods for sale (as by merchants, peddlers, etc.); merchandise: *She peddled her wares from door to door.* *n.*
☛ *Hom.* WEAR, WHERE (wer).

**warehouse** (wer′hous′) 1 a building or large room where goods are stored. 2 store or keep in a warehouse. 1 *n.*, 2 *v.*

**ware·house·man** (wer′hou′smən) a person who owns or works in a warehouse. *n., pl.* **ware·house·men** (-smən).

**war·fare** (wôr′fer′) war; fighting. *n.*

**war·head** (wôr′hed′) the forward part of a rocket, missile, torpedo, etc.: *The warhead contains the explosive charge.* *n.*

**war horse** *Informal.* a person, especially a veteran soldier or a person in public life, who has survived many battles or struggles.

**war·i·ly** (wer′ə lē) cautiously; carefully. *adv.*

**war·i·ness** (wer′ē nis) caution; care. *n.*

**war·like** (wôr′līk′) 1 fond of and ready for war: *a warlike nature, warlike peoples.* 2 threatening war; belligerent: *a warlike speech.* 3 of, for, or having to do with war: *warlike preparations.* *adj.*

**war·lock** (wôr′lok) a man who practises black magic; sorcerer. Compare with WITCH[1] (def. 1). *n.*

**warm** (wôrm) 1 more hot than cold; having or giving forth some heat: *a warm fire. She sat in the warm sunshine.* 2 having a feeling of heat: *to be warm from running.* 3 that makes or keeps warm: *a warm coat.* 4 having or showing affection, enthusiasm, etc.: *a warm welcome, a warm friend, a warm heart.* 5 quick to show irritation or anger: *a warm temper.* 6 showing irritation or anger: *a warm dispute.* 7 fresh and strong: *a warm scent.* 8 *Informal.* in games, treasure hunts, etc., near what one is searching for. 9 suggesting heat: *Red, orange, and yellow are called warm colours.* 10 uncomfortable; unpleasant: *to make things warm for a person.* 11 make or become warm: *to warm a room.* 12 make or become cheered, interested, friendly, or sympathetic: *The speaker warmed to his subject. Her happiness warms my heart.* 1–10 *adj.,* 11, 12 *v.* —**warm′er,** *n.* —**warm′ly,** *adv.* —**warm′ness,** *n.*
**warm up,** **a** heat or cook again. **b** make or become more interested, friendly, etc. **c** practise or exercise for a few minutes before entering a game, contest, etc. **d** of an engine, radio, etc., run or operate in order to reach a proper working temperature: *It takes the car a long time to warm up on cold mornings.* **e** run or operate an engine, radio, etc. until it reaches a proper working temperature.

**warm–blood·ed** (wôrm′blud′id) 1 having warm blood that stays about the same temperature regardless of the surrounding air or water: *Warm-blooded animals have body temperatures between 36 and 44 degrees Celsius.* 2 having or showing a passionate or ardent spirit. *adj.*

**warmed–o·ver** (wôrm′dō′vər) 1 of food, warmed again; reheated: *warmed-over chili.* 2 of ideas, etc., not new or fresh or interesting; stale and trite. *adj.*

**warm front** in meteorology, the front edge of a warm air mass advancing into and replacing a colder one.

**warm–heart·ed** (wôrm′här′tid) having or showing a kind, sympathetic, affectionate, or friendly nature: *a warm-hearted person, a warm-hearted response.* *adj.*

A warming pan being placed in a bed

**warming pan** 1353 **wary**

hat, āge, fär; let, ēqual, tėrm; it, īce
hot, ōpen, ôrder; oil, out; cup, pùt, rüle
əbove, takən, pencəl, lemən, circəs
ch, child; ng, long; sh, ship
th, thin; ŦH, then; zh, measure

**warming pan** a covered pan having a long handle and designed to hold hot coals, formerly used to warm beds.

**warm·ish** (wôr′mish) somewhat warm. *adj.*

**war·mon·ger** (wôr′mung′gər) a person who is in favour of war or attempts to bring about war. *n.*

**warmth** (wôrmth) 1 the quality or state of being more hot than cold; being warm: *the warmth of an open fire.* 2 the quality or state of being lively, excited, fervent, etc.: *She spoke with warmth of the natural beauty of the countryside.* 3 a friendly, affectionate, or kind feeling or nature: *the warmth of family life.* 4 in painting, interior decorating, etc., a glowing effect produced by the use of reds and yellows. *n.*

**warm–up** (wôr′mup′) exercise or practice taken for a few minutes before entering a game, contest, etc. *n.*

**warn** (wôrn) 1 give notice to in advance about a possible or approaching unpleasantness or danger; put on guard: *The clouds warned us that a storm was coming. They had been warned against using the old bridge. She warned us to keep away from the dog.* 2 give notice of something that requires attention or action; inform: *His mother warned us that we would have to leave by eight.* 3 give notice to stay away, go away, keep out, etc. (*used with* **off** or **away**): *There was a sign warning off trespassers.* 4 caution or admonish about certain actions, conduct, etc.: *They warned us not to smoke in the auditorium.* *v.* —**warn′er**, *n.*
☞ *Hom.* WORN.

**warn·ing** (wôr′ning) 1 something that warns; notice given in advance. 2 that warns: *The police fired a warning shot over the heads of the mob.* 3 ppr. of WARN. 1 *n.*, 2 *adj.*, 3 *v.* —**warn′ing·ly**, *adv.*

**War of 1812** a war between the United States and the United Kingdom, 1812–1815, fought on the Atlantic Ocean and in North America. This war confirmed Canada's independence of the United States.

**War of Independence** *U.S.* the REVOLUTIONARY WAR.

**war of nerves** a conflict or struggle characterized by the use of propaganda, bluffing, threats, etc. in order to break the morale of an opponent or enemy.

**warp** (wôrp) 1 bend or twist out of shape: *The heat from the radiator has warped the table. If you use green wood to build something, it is liable to warp.* 2 make or become perverted or distorted: *Prejudice warps our judgment. He has a warped sense of humour.* 3 a bend or twist in something that should be straight, especially wood: *The board has a warp.* 4 a distortion of the mind, judgment, etc.; a bias or quirk. 5 move a ship, etc. by pulling on a rope fastened at one end to a fixed object. 6 a rope used for warping a ship or boat. 7 the threads stretched lengthwise in a loom, through which the crosswise threads are woven. See WEAVE for picture. 8 the basis or foundation of something: *the warp of our society.* 1, 2, 5 *v.*, 3, 4, 6–8 *n.*
☞ *Etym.* See note at WEB.

**war paint** 1 paint put on the face or body by certain peoples, as formerly some Amerindian peoples, before going to war. 2 *Informal.* make-up; cosmetics for the face. 3 *Informal.* ceremonial costume; full dress.

**war·path** (wôr′path′) formerly, the way or route taken by a fighting expedition of North American Indians. *n.*
**on the warpath, a** on a warlike expedition or at war. **b** looking for a fight; very angry.

**war·plane** (wôr′plān′) an aircraft used in war. *n.*

**war·rant** (wô′rənt) 1 a written order giving legal authority for something, especially one authorizing a search, arrest etc.: *The police have a warrant for his arrest.* 2 something that gives a right; authorization or sanction: *Their vote of confidence was her warrant to continue her investigation.* 3 a good and sufficient reason for an action, belief, etc.; justification or grounds: *She had no warrant for her suspicions.* 4 justify: *It was a crisis that warranted immediate action.* 5 a promise; guarantee. 6 guarantee the quality, condition, etc. of: *to warrant the genuineness of goods purchased.* 7 *Informal.* declare positively or confidently: *I warrant I'll get there before you.* 8 a document certifying something, especially to a purchaser. 9 formerly, the official certificate of appointment of a warrant officer: *In the armed services a warrant officer ranked below a commissioned officer.* 1–3, 5, 8, 9 *n.*, 4, 6, 7 *v.*

**war·rant·a·ble** (wô′rən tə bəl) capable of being warranted; justifiable. *adj.* —**war′rant·a·ble·ness**, *n.* —**war′rant·a·bly**, *adv.*

**war·ran·tee** (wô′rən tē′) a person to whom a WARRANTY is made. *n.*

**war·ran·tor** (wô′rən tər) a person who makes a WARRANTY; GUARANTOR. *n.* Also, **warranter.**

**war·ran·ty** (wô′rən tē) 1 a promise or pledge, usually written, that a product is what it is claimed to be and that the manufacturer will take the responsibility for repairing or replacing it if it proves to be defective. 2 authority or justification; warrant. *n., pl.* **war·ran·ties.**

**war·ren** (wô′rən) 1 a piece of ground having many burrows, where rabbits live or where they are raised. 2 the rabbits living in a warren. 3 a crowded district or building. *n.*

**war·ri·or** (wô′rē ər) a fighting man; an experienced soldier. *n.* —**war′ri·or·like′**, *adj.*

**war·ship** (wôr′ship′) a ship used in war. *n.*

**wart** (wôrt) 1 a small, usually hard growth on the skin, caused by a virus. 2 anything resembling a wart, such as a hard lump on a plant. *n.*

**wart hog** a wild pig of Africa, that has two large tusks and two large wartlike growths on each side of its face.

**war·time** (wôr′tīm′) time of war. *n.*

**wart·y** (wôr′tē) 1 having WARTS or lumps that are like warts. 2 of or like a WART. *adj.*, **wart·i·er, wart·i·est.**

**war whoop** a war cry.

**war·y** (wer′ē) 1 on one's guard against danger,

**was** (wuz or woz; unstressed, wəz) the 1st and 3rd person singular, past tense, of **be**: *I was late. Was he late too?* *v.*

**wash** (wosh) **1** clean with water or other liquid: *to wash clothes, to wash one's face, to wash dishes.* **2** make clean. **3** remove dirt, stains, paint, etc. by or as if by the action of water: *to wash a spot out.* **4** wash oneself: *She washed before eating dinner.* **5** wash clothes: *They wash for a living.* **6** a washing or being washed. **7** a quantity of clothes washed or to be washed: *They hung the wash on the line.* **8** undergo washing without damage: *That cloth washes well.* **9** that can be washed without damage: *a wash dress.* **10** carry or be carried along or away by water or other liquid: *The road washed out during the storm. Wood is often washed ashore by the waves.* **11** the material carried along by moving water and then deposited as sediment: *A delta is formed by the wash of a river.* **12** wear by water or other liquid: *The cliffs are being washed away by waves.* **13** flow or beat with a lapping sound: *The waves washed upon the rocks.* **14** the motion, rush, or sound of water: *We listened to the wash of the waves against the boat.* **15** make wet: *The flowers are washed with dew.* **16** a tract of land sometimes overflowed with water and sometimes left dry; a tract of shallow water; fen, marsh, or bog. **17** a liquid for a special use: *a hair wash, a mouthwash.* **18** waste liquid matter; liquid garbage. **19** washy or weak liquid food. **20** a thin coating of colour or metal: *He began his watercolour with a wash of blue for the sky.* **21** cover with a thin coating of colour or of metal: *walls washed with blue, silver washed with gold.* **22** sift earth, ore, etc. by action of water to separate. **23** earth, etc. from which gold or the like can be washed. **24** the rough or broken water left behind a moving ship; wake. **25** a disturbance in air made by a moving aircraft. **26** *Informal.* stand being put to the proof: *patriotism that won't wash.* 1–5, 8, 10, 12, 13, 15, 21, 22, 26 *v.*, 6, 7, 9, 11, 14, 16–20, 23–25 *n.*

**wash down, a** wash from top to bottom or from end to end. **b** swallow liquid along with or after solid food to help in swallowing or digestion.

**wash out, a** wash the dirt from: *He washed out his socks.* **b** fail or cause to fail an examination. **c** carry or be carried away by water: *The rain washed out part of the pavement.* **d** *Informal.* cancel: *The whole program was washed out.*

**wash up, a** wash the hands and face, as before meals. **b** wash the dishes after meals: *We washed up right after supper.*

**wash·a·ble** (wosh′ə bəl) **1** that can be washed without damage: *washable silk.* **2** that can be removed by washing: *washable paint or ink.* *adj.*

**wash–and–wear** (wosh′ən wer′) of a fabric or garment, easily washed and dried and needing little or no ironing. *adj.*

**wash·ba·sin** (wosh′bā′sən) a basin for holding water to wash one's face and hands, do laundry by hand, etc., especially a porcelain, metal, or plastic fixture in a bathroom, with attached water taps and a drain. *n.*

**wash·board** (wosh′bôrd′) **1** a rectangular sheet of heavy glass, metal, etc. with a surface of rounded crosswise ridges, set in a wooden frame and used for rubbing the dirt out of clothes, etc. **2** a road having a surface with many crosswise ridges. *n.*

**wash·bowl** (wosh′bōl′) a bowl for holding water to wash one's hands and face. *n.*

**wash·cloth** (wosh′kloth′) **1** a small cloth for washing oneself; facecloth. **2** DISHCLOTH. *n.*

**wash·day** (wosh′dā′) a day when clothes and household linens are washed: *Monday used to be the traditional washday.* *n.*

**washed–out** (wosh′tout′) **1** lacking colour; pale or faded, as from much washing: *an old washed-out shirt.* **2** *Informal.* lacking vigour or spirit; exhausted: *She was feeling washed-out after a day of meetings.* *adj.*

**washed–up** (wosh′tup′) *Informal.* **1** no longer able to function; failed; finished: *After three unsuccessful films, he is probably washed-up as a director.* **2** fatigued; washed-out. *adj.*

A washer for a bolt

**wash·er** (wosh′ər) **1** a person or thing that washes, especially an automatic washing machine: *Many homes have a washer and dryer for the laundry.* **2** a flat ring of metal, rubber, leather, etc. used to protect surfaces held by bolts or nuts, to seal joints, to reduce friction, etc. *n.*

**wash·er·wom·an** (wosh′ər wum′ən) a woman whose work is washing clothes and linens; laundress. *n., pl.* **wash·er·wom·en** (-wim′ən).

**wash·ing** (wosh′ing) **1** clothes or linens that have been washed or are to be washed; laundry; WASH (def. 7). **2** material obtained in washing something: *washings of gold obtained from earth.* **3** the act of cleaning with water or other liquid. **4** ppr. of WASH. 1–3 *n.*, 4 *v.*

**washing machine** a machine for washing clothes, etc.

**washing soda** a crystalline form of sodium carbonate, used dissolved in water for washing clothes, etc.

**wash·out** (wosh′out′) **1** a washing away of earth, a road, etc. by heavy rainfall, a flood, or other sudden rush of water. **2** the hole or break made by such action. *n.*

**wash·room** (wosh′rüm′) **1** a room equipped with a toilet and sink, especially such a room in a public building: *Most restaurants and gas stations have washrooms for their customers.* **2** a room for washing. *n.*

**wash·stand** (wosh′stand′) **1** a bowl with pipes and taps for running water to wash one's hands and face. **2** a stand for holding a basin, pitcher, etc. for washing. *n.*

**wash·tub** (wosh′tub′) a tub used to wash or soak laundry in. *n.*

**wash·y** (wosh′ē) **1** too watery or thin: *washy tea.* **2** too weak; not having enough colour, substance, or force; insipid: *washy colours, washy poetry.* *adj.*, **wash·i·er, wash·i·est.**

**was·n't** (wuz′ənt or woz′ənt) was not.

**wasp** (wosp) any of numerous winged insects belonging to the same order as bees, ants, and sawflies, having biting mouth parts, a slender body with the abdomen attached to the thorax by a thin stalk, and, in the females and workers, a powerful sting: *Some species of wasps live in colonies, but most do not.* *n.*

**WASP** (wosp) *Informal.* White Anglo-Saxon Protestant.

**wasp·ish** (wos′pish) 1 of or like a WASP. 2 irritable or snappish: *a waspish temper.* *adj.* —**wasp′ish·ly,** *adv.* —**wasp′ish·ness,** *n.*

**wasp waist** a very slender waist.

**wasp–waist·ed** (wosp′wā′stid) having a very slender waist. *adj.*

**was·sail** (wos′əl) 1 a drinking party; revel with drinking of healths. 2 take part in a wassail; revel. 3 spiced ale or other liquor drunk at a wassail. 4 an old English toast meaning "Be healthy!" 5 drink to the health of. 1, 3, 4 *n.,* 2, 5 *v.,* 4 *interj.*

**was·sail·er** (wos′ə lər) 1 reveller. 2 a drinker of healths. *n.*

**wast·age** (wā′stij) 1 loss by use, wear, decay, leakage, etc., especially preventable loss of something useful or valuable; waste. 2 the amount wasted. *n.*

**waste** (wāst) 1 make poor use of; spend uselessly; fail to get value from: *Don't waste time or money. We try not to waste food.* 2 poor use; useless spending; failure to get the most out of something. 3 thrown away as useless or worthless. 4 useless or worthless material; stuff to be thrown away: *Garbage or sewage is waste.* 5 left over; not used: *waste food.* 6 bare or wild land; desert; wilderness: *We travelled through treeless wastes. Before us stretched a waste of snow and ice.* 7 not cultivated; that is a desert or wilderness; bare; wild. 8 wear down little by little; destroy or lose gradually: *The sick man was wasted by disease.* 9 wearing down little by little; gradual destruction or loss: *Both waste and repair are constantly going on in our bodies.* 10 destruction or devastation caused by war, floods, fire, etc. 11 damage greatly; destroy: *The soldiers wasted the enemy's fields.* 12 in a state of desolation or ruin. 13 material left over or rejected during the manufacture of textiles, used to wipe off oil, dirt, etc. 1, 8, 11 *v.,* **wast·ed, wast·ing;** 2, 4, 6, 9, 10, 13 *n.,* 3, 5, 7, 12 *adj.*
**go to waste,** be wasted.
**lay waste,** damage greatly; destroy; ravage: *The invading army laid waste the countryside.*
☞ Hom. WAIST.

**waste·bas·ket** (wāst′bas′kit) a basket or other open container for wastepaper, etc. *n.*

**waste·ful** (wāst′fəl) using or spending too much. *adj.* —**waste′ful·ly,** *adv.* —**waste′ful·ness,** *n.*

**waste·land** (wā′stland′) 1 barren, uncultivated land: *desert wastelands.* 2 a devastated, ruined region: *The advancing troops left a wasteland behind them.* 3 anything that has been improperly managed or is unproductive or barren: *This factory is a technological wasteland.* *n.*

**waste·pa·per** (wāst′pā′pər) paper thrown away or to be thrown away as useless or worthless. *n.*

**wastepaper basket** WASTEBASKET.

**waste pipe** a pipe for carrying off waste water, etc.

**wast·er** (wā′stər) a person or thing that wastes, especially a person who is a spendthrift. *n.*

**wast·ing** (wā′sting) 1 gradually destructive to the body: *Tuberculosis is a wasting disease.* 2 laying waste; devastating. 3 ppr. of WASTE. 1, 2 *adj.,* 3 *v.*

# WASP 1355 water

hat, āge, fär; let, ēqual, tėrm; it, īce
hot, ōpen, ôrder; oil, out; cup, pu̇t, rüle
əbove, takən, pencəl, lemən, circəs
ch, child; ng, long; sh, ship
th, thin; ᴛʜ, then; zh, measure

**wast·rel** (wā′strəl) 1 WASTER. 2 a good-for-nothing. *n.*

**watch** (woch) 1 look attentively or carefully; observe closely: *The medical students watched while the doctor performed the operation.* 2 look at; observe; view: *to watch a play.* 3 look or wait with care and attention; be very careful: *The girl watched for a chance to cross the busy street.* 4 look at or wait for with care and attention: *The police watched the prisoners.* 5 a careful looking; attitude of attention: *Be on the watch for cars when you cross the street.* 6 keep guard: *He watched throughout the night.* 7 keep guard over; guard: *The dog watched the house.* 8 a protecting; guarding: *A man keeps watch over the bank at night.* 9 a person or persons kept to guard: *The man's cry aroused the town watch, who came running to his aid.* 10 a period of time for guarding: *a watch in the night.* 11 stay awake for some purpose: *The nurse watched with her patient.* 12 a staying awake for some purpose. 13 a spring-driven or electronic device for indicating time, small enough to be carried in a pocket or worn on the wrist. 14 the time of duty of one part of a ship's crew: *A watch usually lasts four hours.* 15 the part of a crew on duty at one time. 1–4, 6, 7, 11 *v.,* 5, 8–10, 12–15 *n.* —**watch′er,** *n.*
**watch and ward,** the act of guarding: *to keep watch and ward over the captive.*
**watch out,** be careful; be on guard: *Watch out for cars.*
**watch over,** guard or supervise; protect or preserve from danger, harm, error, etc.

**watch·band** (woch′band′) a band or strap of leather, metal, etc. for holding a wristwatch on the wrist. *n.*

**watch·case** (woch′kās′) the outer covering for the works of a watch. *n.*

**watch·dog** (woch′dog′) 1 a dog kept to guard property. 2 a watchful guardian. *n.*

**watch fire** a fire kept burning at night in camps, etc.

**watch·ful** (woch′fəl) watching carefully; on the lookout; alert and vigilant: *They knew they could not get by the watchful guard. Lee is watchful of her health.* *adj.* —**watch′ful·ly,** *adv.* —**watch′ful·ness,** *n.*

**watch·mak·er** (woch′mā′kər) a person who makes and repairs watches and clocks. *n.*

**watch·man** (woch′mən) a person who keeps watch; guard: *A watchman guards the grounds at night.* *n., pl.* **watch·men** (-mən).

**watch·tow·er** (woch′tou′ər) a tower from which watch is kept for enemies, fires, ships, etc. *n.*

**watch·word** (woch′wėrd′) 1 a secret word that allows a person to pass a guard; password: *She gave the watchword, and the sentinel let her pass.* 2 a motto or slogan: *"Forward" is our watchword.* *n.*

**wa·ter** (wot′ər) 1 the liquid that falls as rain and makes up the seas, lakes, and rivers and that is also the main constituent of all living matter: *Pure water is a transparent, colourless, odourless, tasteless compound of hydrogen and oxygen ($H_2O$) that can be converted into steam by heating it to 100°C and into ice by cooling it to 0°C.*

**water beetle**     1356     **waterless**

**2** a body of water; a sea, river, lake, etc.: *She lived across the water from them.*    **3** found or living in or near water: *water rodents, water lilies, waterfowl.*    **4** the water of a river, etc. with reference to the tide: *high or low water.*    **5** a liquid containing and resembling water: *rose water, soda water. When you cry, water runs from your eyes.*    **6** sprinkle or wet with water: *to water the grass.*    **7** provide with water to drink: *to water the horses.*    **8** supply water to a region, etc.: *British Columbia is well watered by rivers and brooks.*    **9** fill with or discharge water: *Her mouth watered when she saw the cake. Strong sunlight can make your eyes water.*    **10** weaken by adding water; adulterate with water: *It is against the law to sell watered milk.*    **11** get or take in a supply of water: *A ship waters before sailing.*    **12** of animals, drink water: *The cattle usually watered at the creek.*    **13** the degree of clearness and brilliance of a precious stone, especially a diamond: *A diamond of the first water is a very clear and brilliant one.*    **14** an irregular wavy, lustrous pattern on silk, metal, etc.    **15** make a wavy pattern on: *Watered silk is often called moiré.*    **16 waters,** *pl.*   **a** a particular part of the ocean, a lake, etc.: *fishing in Canadian waters, the upper waters of the St. Lawrence, warm Pacific waters.*   **b** mineral or spring water, as at a spa: *to take the waters.* 1–5, 13, 14, 16 *n.,* 6–12, 15 *v.*   —**wa′ter·er,** *n.*

**back water, a** make a boat go backward. **b** reverse one's course; withdraw from a position, claim, etc.
**by water,** by means of a ship or boat: *He would rather travel by water than by air.*
**hold water,** stand the test; be shown to be consistent, logical, effective, etc.: *That argument won't hold water.*
**keep one's head above water,** keep out of trouble or difficulty, especially financial difficulty: *Business is so bad that he is finding it hard to keep his head above water.*
**like water,** very freely or recklessly: *to spend money like water. Blood flowed like water.*
**make one's mouth water,** arouse one's appetite or desire: *a sports car to make your mouth water.*
**make** or **pass water,** urinate.
**of the first water,** of the highest quality or most extreme degree: *a musical composition of the first water. He is a bungler of the first water.*
**throw** or **pour cold water on,** actively discourage or belittle: *She didn't tell her friends her scheme because she knew they'd throw cold water on it.*
**water down, a** reduce in strength by diluting with water: *We watered down the punch because it was too strong.* **b** reduce the effectiveness or force of by altering; weaken: *The original bill had been watered down before being presented to Parliament.*

**water beetle** any of numerous beetles belonging to several different families, all having broad, fringed hind legs well adapted for swimming: *Water beetles are found in freshwater streams and lakes.*

**water bird** a bird that swims or wades in water.

**water biscuit** an unsweetened cracker made of flour and water and, sometimes, oil or shortening.

**water boatman** any of a number of related species of bug that live in water and have paddle-like legs used in swimming.

**wa·ter–borne** (wot′ər bôrn′) **1** supported by water; floating. **2** conveyed by a boat or the like. *adj.*

**water bottle** a bottle, bag, etc. for holding water.

**wa·ter·buck** (wot′ər buk′) any of various African antelopes that frequent rivers, marshes, etc. *n.*

**water buffalo** the common buffalo of southern Asia and the Philippines, having large, spreading horns: *The water buffalo is used as a draft animal.* See BUFFALO for picture.

**water bug 1** CROTON BUG. **2** WATER BOATMAN.

**water clock** an instrument for measuring time by the flow of water.

**water closet 1** a room or compartment having a toilet with a bowl that can be flushed with water. **2** the toilet itself.

**water colour** or **color 1** paint mixed with water instead of oil. **2** the art or skill of painting with water colours: *She is good at water colour.* **3** a picture painted with water colours: *A lovely water colour hung in her room.*

**water cooler** a device for cooling drinking water.

**wa·ter·course** (wot′ər kôrs′) **1** a stream of water; river or brook. **2** a natural or artificial channel for water; a stream bed, canal, etc. *n.*

**wa·ter·craft** (wot′ər kraft′) **1** skill in handling boats or in water sports. **2** a ship or boat. *n., pl.* (def. 2) **wa·ter·craft.**

**wa·ter·cress** (wot′ər kres′) a perennial plant of the mustard family that grows in running water and has crisp leaves often used in salads. *n.*

**water cure** the treatment of disease by the use of water; HYDROPATHY.

**wa·ter·fall** (wot′ər fol′) a stream or river falling over a cliff or down a very steep hill; cataract. *n.*

**wa·ter·fowl** (wot′ər foul′) **1** a water bird, especially one that swims. **2 waterfowl,** *pl.* swimming game birds as a group, as opposed to shore birds, etc. *n., pl.* (def. 1) **wa·ter·fowl** or **wa·ter·fowls.**

**wa·ter·front** (wot′ər frunt′) **1** the part of a city, town, etc. by a river, lake, or harbour. **2** land at the water's edge. **3** of, having to do with, or on the waterfront: *a waterfront hotel.* *n.*

**water gap** a gap in a mountain ridge through which a stream flows.

**water gas** a poisonous gas used for lighting or fuel: *Water gas is largely carbon monoxide and hydrogen, made by passing steam over very hot coal or coke.*

**water gate 1** a gate that controls the flow of water; floodgate. **2** a gate giving access to a river, etc., as from a building.

**water glass 1** a glass to hold water; tumbler. **2** sodium or potassium silicate, a substance used especially to coat eggs in order to preserve them.

**water hole** a hole in the ground where water collects; a small pond or pool.

**water ice** a confection or dessert consisting of a frozen mixture of water, sugar, and flavouring.

**watering place 1** a place where water may be obtained, especially a pool, a part of a stream, etc. where animals go to drink. **2** *Esp. Brit.* a resort with springs containing mineral water; spa.

**water jacket** a casing with water or other liquid in it, surrounding something to keep it at a certain temperature; especially, in an INTERNAL-COMBUSTION ENGINE, the part of the cylinder block that contains the coolant.

**wa·ter·less** (wot′ər lis) **1** not having water; dry. **2** not needing or using water: *waterless cooking.* *adj.*

**water level** 1 the surface level of a body of water. 2 WATER TABLE.

*Water lilies*

**water lily** any of a family of water plants found in temperate and tropical parts of the world, having floating leaves and showy, fragrant flowers: *The stems of a water lily grow from thick, creeping underground stems buried in the mud at the bottom of a pond, etc.*

**wa·ter·line** (wot′ər līn′) 1 the line where the surface of the water touches the side of a ship or boat. 2 any of several lines marked on a ship's hull to show the depth to which it sinks when unloaded, partly loaded, or fully loaded. 3 a line showing how high water has risen or may rise; WATERMARK (def. 1). *n.*

**wa·ter-logged** (wot′ər logd′) 1 of a boat, etc., so full of water that it will barely float. 2 completely soaked with water. *adj.*

**Wa·ter·loo** (wot′ər lü′) 1 the battle in which Napoleon was finally defeated in 1815. 2 any decisive or crushing defeat: *She has met her Waterloo and will not run for election again. His first international tennis competition turned out to be his Waterloo.* *n.*

**water main** a main pipe in a system of water pipes.

**wa·ter·man** (wot′ər mən) 1 a boatman, especially one who rents out boats. 2 OARSMAN. *n., pl.* **wa·ter·men** (-mən).

**wa·ter·mark** (wot′ər märk′) 1 a mark showing how high water has risen or may rise. 2 a faint mark produced on some paper by pressure of a projecting design during manufacture, indicating the maker, etc.: *The watermark may be seen by holding the paper up to the light.* 3 put a watermark on: *Fine writing paper is often watermarked.* 1, 2 *n.,* 3 *v.*

**wa·ter·mel·on** (wot′ər mel′ən) 1 a large, oblong or roundish edible fruit having sweet, juicy red, pink, or yellowish pulp with seeds scattered through it and a hard, thick green rind. 2 the trailing vine it grows on: *The watermelon, which is native to Africa, is a member of the gourd family.* *n.*

**water meter** a device that registers the quantity of water supplied to a house, etc. through a water supply system.

**water moccasin** 1 a poisonous snake of the southern United States, that lives in swamps and along streams. 2 any of various similar but harmless snakes.

**water of crystallization** water that is a constituent of certain crystalline substances and that usually is necessary to maintain a particular crystalline structure: *When water of crystallization is removed by heating, the crystals usually break up into a powder.*

**water ouzel** any of various wading birds, related to the thrushes, that dive in deep water for food.

**water pipe** 1 a pipe for conveying water. 2 HOOKAH.

**water pistol** a toy pistol designed to shoot a jet of water.

**water polo** a game played in a swimming pool by two teams of seven players who try to throw or push a round inflated ball into the opponents' goal.

**water power** 1 the power from flowing or falling water, used to drive machinery and make electricity. 2 a fall in a stream that can supply power.

**wa·ter·proof** (wot′ər prüf′) 1 that will not let water through; sealed, or treated or coated with something so as to keep water out: *a waterproof tarpaulin, a waterproof watch.* 2 a waterproof material. 3 *Esp. Brit.* raincoat. 4 make waterproof. 1 *adj.,* 2, 3 *n.,* 4 *v.*

**water rat** 1 a large European field mouse that lives in the banks of streams or lakes. 2 *Cdn.* MUSKRAT.

**wa·ter-re·pel·lent** (wot′ər ri pel′ənt) resistant to water; that repels water, but is not waterproof: *Most raincoats are water-repellent but those treated or coated with rubber or plastic are waterproof.* *adj.*

**wa·ter-re·sis·tant** (wot′ər ri zis′tənt) water-repellent: *a water-resistant watch.* *adj.*

**wa·ter·shed** (wot′ər shed′) 1 a high ridge that divides two areas drained by different river systems; a divide: *On one side of a watershed, rivers and streams flow in one direction; on the other side, they flow in a different direction.* 2 the region drained by one river system. *n.*

**wa·ter·side** (wot′ər sīd′) 1 land along the sea, a lake, a river, etc. 2 of, at, or on the waterside: *a waterside park.* *n.*

**water ski** a broad ski, usually one of a pair, for skimming over the water while being towed by a boat.

**wa·ter-ski** (wot′ər skē′) skim over the water on water skis. *v.,* **wa·ter-skied, wa·ter-ski·ing.** —**wa′ter-ski′er,** *n.*

**wa·ter-ski·ing** (wot′ər skē′ing) 1 the practice or sport of skimming over the water on water skis. 2 ppr. of WATER-SKI. 1 *n.,* 2 *v.*

**water snake** any of various snakes that live in or near water, especially any of a closely related group of non-poisonous freshwater snakes that feed mainly on fish and other water creatures.

**water softener** 1 a chemical added to HARD (def. 16) water to soften it by dissolving and removing minerals. 2 a device using such a chemical and attached to a water supply.

**water spaniel** either of two breeds of spaniel, the Irish water spaniel and the American water spaniel, both having thick, curly, reddish-brown hair and often trained to retrieve game birds from water.

**wa·ter·spout** (wot′ər spout′) 1 a pipe which takes away or spouts water. 2 a rotating funnel-shaped or tube-shaped column of spray and water between a cloud and the surface of the ocean or a large lake, produced by the action of a whirlwind. *n.*

**water table** the level below which the ground is saturated with water.

**wa·ter·tight** (wot′ər tīt′) 1 so tight that no water can get in or out: *Large ships are often divided into watertight* compartments by watertight partitions. **2** leaving no opening for misunderstanding, criticism, etc.; perfect: *a watertight argument.* *adj.*

**water tower** **1** an elevated tank or reservoir for storing water and maintaining a steady pressure in a water supply system. **2** any of several types of firefighting equipment designed to deliver water under pressure to a nozzle at a great height for fighting fires in the upper parts of tall buildings: *The original water tower was a large, vertical, telescoping steel pipe with a nozzle at the top.*

**water vapour** or **vapor** water in a gaseous state, especially when below the boiling point and fairly diffused, as in the atmosphere. Compare with STEAM.

**wa·ter·way** (wot′ər wā′) **1** a river, canal, or other body of water that ships can go on. **2** a channel for water. *n.*

**water wheel** a wheel turned by running or falling water, used to supply power: *The grindstones of grain mills used to be powered by water wheels.* See MILL and OVERSHOT for pictures.

**water wings** a device consisting of two air-filled floats joined together, designed to give support to a swimmer or a person learning to swim: *Water wings are worn under the arms, extending out behind the shoulders.*

**wa·ter·works** (wot′ər wėrks′) **1** a system of pipes, reservoirs, water towers, pumps, etc. for supplying a city or town with water. **2** a building containing engines and pumps for pumping water; pumping station. *n. pl.*

**wa·ter·worn** (wot′ər wôrn′) worn or smoothed by the action of water: *waterworn rocks.* *adj.*

**wa·ter·y** (wot′ə rē) **1** too wet; soaked; sodden: *watery soil. The potatoes were overcooked and watery.* **2** of eyes, full of tears; tending to water: *The old man's eyes were watery.* **3** of a liquid, too thin; containing too much water: *watery soup, watery tea.* **4** like water in consistency or appearance: *A blister is filled with a watery fluid.* **5** weak or pale: *a watery blue, watery winter sunlight.* **6** indicating rain: *a watery sky.* **7** consisting of water: *a watery grave.* *adj.*

**watt** (wot) an SI unit for measuring electric power, or energy available per second: *One watt is equal to one joule of energy per second.* Symbol: W *n.*
☞ *Hom.* WHAT (wot).
☞ *Etym.* Named after James *Watt* (1736–1819), a Scottish engineer and inventor.

**watt·age** (wot′ij) electric power expressed in WATTS: *Our new heater has a higher wattage than our old one.* *n.*

**watt hour** a unit of electric energy, equal to the power of one watt maintained for one hour: *A watt hour is equal to 3.6 kJ.*

**wat·tle** (wot′əl) **1** sticks interwoven with slender branches, twigs, or reeds to form a wall, fence, etc.: *a hut built of wattle.* **2** poles used to support a roof of thatch. **3** build or form of wattle: *to wattle a fence.* **4** twist or weave together into wattle: *to wattle twigs and branches.* **5** the fleshy, wrinkled skin hanging down from the throat of certain birds: *The wattle of a turkey is bright red.* See TURKEY for picture. 1, 2, 5 *n.*, 3, 4 *v.*, **wat·tled, wat·tling.**

**wat·tled** (wot′əld) **1** having WATTLES. **2** formed by interwoven twigs; interlaced. **3** pt. and pp. of WATTLE. 1, 2 *adj.,* 3 *v.*

**wave** (wāv) **1** move back and forth or up and down from a fixed base, with a slow, sweeping or undulating motion, as in a current of air or water: *tall grasses waving. A flag waved in the breeze.* **2** make a signal or greeting with an up-and-down or back-and-forth movement of the hand or arm: *We waved until the train was out of sight.* **3** make a signal or greeting by such a movement of something held in the hand: *She waved her handkerchief.* **4** signal or direct by waving: *He waved us away. She waved goodbye.* **5** the action of waving, especially as a signal or greeting: *a wave of the hand.* **6** a moving ridge or swell of water, as on the sea: *The boat rose and fell on the waves.* **7** a group or one of a series of groups advancing in a surging or swelling movement, like ocean waves: *A wave of new settlers followed the completion of the railway.* **8** an emotion, activity, etc. passing from one person to the next in a group: *A wave of hysteria passed through the crowd.* **9** a swell or sudden temporary increase of emotion, influence, activity, etc.; upsurge or rush: *We're having a heat wave. A wave of fear swept over him.* **10** shake in the air; brandish: *She waved the stick at them.* **11** a curve or series of curves: *hair set in waves.* **12** have a wavelike form or follow a curving line: *Her hair waves naturally.* **13** give a wavelike form or pattern to: *to wave hair.* **14** in physics, a disturbance consisting of an oscillating movement of particles of liquid or gas by which energy is transferred from one to the next continuously in one direction without the liquid or gas itself being moved any great distance: *Sound and light travel in waves.* **15** Often, **waves,** *pl.* a body of water, especially the sea. 1–4, 10, 12, 13 *v.,* **waved, wav·ing;** 5–9, 11, 14, 15 *n.* —**wave′like′,** *adj.* —**wav′er,** *n.*
☞ *Hom.* WAIVE.

**wave·length** (wāv′length′) **1** in physics, the distance between any point in a wave and the next point that is in the same phase, as from one peak to the next: *Radio wavelengths are measured in metres.* **2** *Informal.* a person's line of thought: *He and I were just never on the same wavelength.* *n.*

**wave·less** (wāv′lis) having no waves; still. *adj.*

**wave·let** (wāv′lit) a little wave. *n.*

**wa·ver** (wā′vər) **1** move unsteadily to and fro; flutter or totter: *Her hand wavered as she reached for the phone.* **2** vary in intensity; flicker: *a wavering light.* **3** hesitate between choices; be undecided in opinion, direction, etc.: *He wavered, not knowing which road to take.* **4** become unsteady; be about to give way; falter: *The battle line wavered and then broke.* **5** the act of wavering. 1–4 *v.,* 5 *n.* —**wa′ver·er,** *n.* —**wa′ver·ing·ly,** *adv.*
☞ *Hom.* WAIVER.

**wa·vey** (wā′vē) *Cdn.* a wild goose, especially the snow goose. *n.*
☞ *Hom.* WAVY.
☞ *Etym.* From an Algonquian word for 'goose', such as Ojibwa *wewe.* **Wavey** may have come from a Canadian French version or from a related Algonquian word.

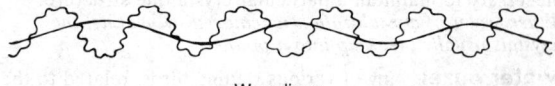

Wavy lines

**wav·y** (wā′vē) **1** having waves; curving back and forth: *wavy hair, a wavy line.* **2** moving to and fro or up and down with a wavelike motion: *wavy grass.* *adj.,* **wav·i·er, wav·i·est.** —**wav′i·ness,** *n.*
☞ *Hom.* WAVEY.

**wa·wa** (wä′wə *or* wä′wä) *Cdn.* WAVEY. *n.*
☛ *Etym.* See note at WAVEY.

**wax¹** (waks) **1** a yellowish, somewhat greasy, pleasant-smelling substance secreted by bees for constructing their honeycomb cells; beeswax: *Wax is hard when cold, but can be easily shaped when warm; it is used for candles, modelling, etc.* **2** any of various substances resembling this: *Paraffin, commonly used for candles, etc., is often called wax. Sealing wax is a mixture of resin and turpentine. Scale insects secrete a kind of wax.* **3** rub or treat with wax or something like wax to polish, stiffen, condition, etc.: *We wax that floor once a month.* **4** made of wax: *a wax model for a sculpture.* 1, 2, 4 *n.*, 3 *v.* —**wax′like′**, *adj.*
**wax in one's hands,** a person easy to influence and manage.

**wax²** (waks) **1** of the moon, go through the regular increase in the size of its visible portion: *The moon waxes till it becomes full and then it wanes.* See MOON for picture. **2** grow bigger or greater; increase in size, strength, prosperity, numbers, etc.: *During this period his wealth waxed steadily.* **3** become: *to wax indignant. The party waxed merry.* *v.*

**wax·en** (wak′sən) like wax, being smooth, pale, and lustrous: *a waxen skin.* *adj.*

**wax myrtle** *or* **wax–myr·tle** (wak′mėr′təl) **1** BAYBERRY (def. 1). **2** referring to a small family of aromatic trees and shrubs found in many parts of the world: *The wax-myrtle family includes the bayberry and sweet gale.* *n.*

**wax paper** *or* **waxed paper** paper coated with a waxy substance such as paraffin, used mostly for wrapping food.

**wax·wing** (wak′swing′) any of three closely related species of small perching bird having silky greyish or brownish plumage and a large crest, and often having red, waxlike tips on the secondary wing feathers. Two species are found in Canada: the **cedar waxwing**, common in all provinces, and the **Bohemian waxwing**, found in western and northern Canada. *n.*

**wax·work** (wak′swėrk′) **1** a figure or figures made of wax. **2 waxworks,** *pl.* an exhibition of such figures, especially one showing figures of famous or notorious people. *n.*

**wax·y** (wak′sē) **1** made of, containing, or covered with wax: *Bayberries are waxy.* **2** like wax; smooth, glossy, pale, etc.: *waxy skin.* *adj.*, **wax·i·er, wax·i·est.** —**wax′i·ness,** *n.*

**way** (wā) **1** a manner or style: *a queer way of talking.* **2** a method or means: *Doctors are using new ways of preventing disease.* **3** a point or feature; respect; detail: *This plan is bad in several ways.* **4** a direction: *Look this way.* **5** movement or progress along a course: *The guide led the way.* **6** distance: *The sun is a long way off.* **7** *Informal.* at or to a great distance; far: *The cloud of smoke stretched way out to the pier.* **8** a road; path; street; course: *a way through the forest.* **9** a space for passing or going ahead: *Cars must make way for the fire engine.* **10** a habit or custom: *Don't mind her teasing; it's just her way.* **11** one's wish or will: *Spoiled children want their own way all the time.* **12** *Informal.* a condition or state: *That sick man is in a bad way.* **13** movement; forward motion: *The ship slowly gathered way as it slid through the water.* **14** the range of experience or notice: *The best idea that ever came my way.* **15** a course of life, action, or experience: *a way of life.* **16** *Informal.* district; area; region: *She lives out our way.* **17 ways,** *pl.*

hat, āge, fär; let, ēqual, tėrm; it, īce
hot, ōpen, ôrder; oil, out; cup, put, rüle
əbove, takən, pencəl, lemən, circəs
ch, child; ng, long; sh, ship
th, thin; ᴛʜ, then; zh, measure

the timbers on which a ship is built and launched. 1–6, 8–17 *n.*, 7 *adv.*
**by the way,** **a** while coming or going. **b** in that connection; incidentally.
**by way of,** **a** by the route of; through. **b** as; for: *By way of an answer he just nodded.*
**come one's way,** happen to one.
**give way,** **a** make way; retreat; yield: **b** break down or fall: *Several people were hurt when the platform gave way.* **c** abandon oneself to emotion: *to give way to tears.*
**go out of the way,** make a special effort.
**have a way with one,** be persuasive.
**in a way,** to some extent.
**in the way,** being an obstacle, hindrance, etc.
**in the way of,** **a** in a favourable position for doing or getting: *She put me in the way of a good investment.* **b** in the matter or business of; as regards: *We have a small stock in the way of shoes.*
**make one's way,** **a** go: *They made their way through the bushes to the road.* **b** get ahead; succeed: *He's sure to make his way in the world.*
**make way,** **a** give space for passing or going ahead; make room. **b** move forward.
**once in a way,** occasionally.
**out of the way,** **a** so as not to be an obstacle, hindrance, etc. **b** far from where most people live or go; awkward to reach. **c** unusual; strange: *Her clothes seemed out of the way to us.* **d** finished; taken care of: *I'd like to get this job out of the way first.* **e** going or being off the right path; improper; wrong.
**put out of the way,** put to death; kill or murder.
**see one's way,** be willing or able.
**take one's way,** go.
**under way,** going on; in motion; in progress: *The program is under way.*
☛ *Hom.* WEIGH, WHEY (wā).

**way·bill** (wā′bil′) a paper listing the goods in a shipment and stating where the goods are to be shipped, by what route, and the cost involved: *The waybill is sent with the shipment.* *n.*

**way·far·er** (wā′fer′ər) a traveller, especially one who travels on foot. *n.*

**way·far·ing** (wā′fer′ing) travelling, especially on foot. *adj.*

**way·laid** (wā′lād′ *or* wā′lād′) pt. and pp. of WAYLAY. *v.*

**way·lay** (wā′lā′ *or* wā′lā′) **1** lie in wait for and attack; ambush: *Robin Hood waylaid rich travellers and robbed them.* **2** stop a person on his or her way: *Newspaper reporters waylaid the famous woman as she left her hotel and asked her a number of questions.* *v.*, **way·laid, way·lay·ing.** —**way′lay′er,** *n.*

**–ways** a suffix meaning: in a particular direction, position, or manner, as in *edgeways, sideways.*

**ways and means** the resources, methods, etc. available to accomplish a particular purpose: *The plan seemed attractive but the committee still had to consider ways and means.*

**way·side** (wā′sīd′) **1** the edge of a road or path: *We* ate lunch on the wayside. **2** along the edge of a road or path: *We slept in a wayside inn.* 1 *n.*, 2 *adj.*

**way station** **1** a station between main stations on a railway. **2** any stopping place along a route.

**way·ward** (wā′wərd) **1** tending to go against the advice, wishes, or orders of others; wrong-headed; willful: *In a wayward mood, the boy ran away from home.* **2** irregular; unpredictable. *adj.* —**way′ward·ly,** *adv.* —**way′ward·ness,** *n.*

**W.C.** or **w.c.** *Brit. Informal.* water closet.

**we** (wē) **1** the speaker or writer plus the person or persons spoken or written to or about: *We are going to a movie; would you like to come? Bring your swimsuit so we can go to the pool.* **2** the speaker or writer, thinking of himself or herself as in a formal or official role: *An author, a sovereign, a judge, or a newspaper editor sometimes uses* we *when others would say* I. **3** people in general, including the speaker; ONE (def. 7); YOU (def. 2): *We need some starch in our diet.* *pron.* 1st person plural, **us, our, ours.**
☞ *Hom.* WEE.

**weak** (wēk) **1** lacking physical strength or health: *She is still weak from her illness. He realized he was too weak to move the rock.* **2** resulting from or showing lack of normal strength or health: *weak eyes. He spoke in a weak voice. She gave the door a weak push.* **3** that can too easily be broken, crushed, torn, overcome, etc.: *weak defences, a weak link in a chain. The building collapsed because the foundation was weak.* **4** lacking authority, force, or power: *a weak government, a weak argument.* **5** lacking mental power: *a weak mind.* **6** lacking moral strength or firmness; not able to resist persuasion or temptation: *a weak character.* **7** containing less of the active ingredient or ingredients than is usual or desired: *a weak solution of boric acid. The tea is too weak.* **8** less strong or potent than is usual or normal: *a weak strain of a virus.* **9** lacking skill or aptitude: *The weaker students were given extra help in the subject.* **10** showing lack of skill or aptitude: *I am weak in English.* **11** lacking or poor in a particular thing: *The composition was weak in spelling, but otherwise quite good.* *adj.*
☞ *Hom.* WEEK.

**weak·en** (wē′kən) **1** make weak or weaker: *You can weaken tea by adding water. The new evidence weakened the case against him.* **2** become weak or weaker: *The patient was gradually weakening.* **3** take a less firm attitude; begin to give way: *He weakened when the child began to cry.* *v.*

**weak·fish** (wēk′fish′) a spiny-finned saltwater food fish that has a tender mouth. *n., pl.* **weak·fish** or **weak·fish·es.**

**weak–kneed** (wēk′nēd′) lacking determination or resolution; giving in easily to opposition, intimidation, etc. *adj.*

**weak·ling** (wē′kling) a weak person or animal. *n.*

**weak·ly** (wē′klē) **1** in a weak manner: *She smiled weakly.* **2** weak; feeble; sickly. 1 *adv.*, 2 *adj.*, **weak·li·er, weak·li·est.** —**weak′li·ness,** *n.*
☞ *Hom.* WEEKLY.

**weak–mind·ed** (wēk′mīn′did) **1** having or showing little intelligence; feeble-minded. **2** lacking firmness of mind: *Because she was so shy, she appeared weak-minded and unsure of herself.* *adj.*

**weak·ness** (wēk′nis) **1** the condition of being weak; lack of power, force, or vigour: *Weakness kept him in bed.* **2** a weak point; fault: *Putting things off is her weakness.* **3** fondness: *She has a weakness for candy.* *n.*

**weal** (wēl) a streak or ridge on the skin made by a stick or whip; welt. *n.*
☞ *Hom.* WE'LL, WHEAL (wēl), WHEEL (wēl).

**wealth** (welth) **1** much money or property; riches: *a man of wealth, the wealth of a city.* **2** in economics, all things that have money value or that add to the capacity for production. **3** a large quantity; abundance: *a wealth of hair, a wealth of words.* *n.*

**wealth·y** (wel′thē) having much money or property; rich. *adj.*, **wealth·i·er, wealth·i·est.** —**wealth′i·ness,** *n.*

**wean** (wēn) **1** accustom a child or young animal to food other than its mother's milk. **2** accustom a person to do without something; cause to turn away: *Tom was sent to a different school to wean him from bad companions.* *v.*

**weap·on** (wep′ən) **1** any instrument or device designed or used to injure or kill, such as a sword, gun, bomb, club, or knife: *weapons of war. The murder weapon was a rock.* **2** an organ or part of an animal or plant used for fighting or protection, such as claws, teeth, thorns, or stings. **3** a procedure or means used to get the better of an opponent: *Drugs are used as weapons against disease.* *n.* —**weap′on·less,** *adj.*

**wear** (wer) **1** have or carry on the body as clothing, adornment, etc.: *He always wears a suit to work. She was wearing pearls. He wore a sword.* **2** the act of wearing or the state of being worn: *clothing for summer wear.* **3** things worn or to be worn; clothing: *children's wear. Casual wear is sold on the second floor.* **4** have habitually as part of one's person: *He wears a beard. I used to wear my hair long.* **5** carry on the body to assist or replace a natural part or organ: *He wears a hearing aid. She wore a brace on her leg.* **6** show as part of one's appearance: *wearing a grin. The old house wore an air of sadness.* **7** change, make less, or damage by constant handling, using, rubbing, etc.: *These shoes are badly worn. Water had worn the stones smooth. The mountains were worn down by glacial action.* **8** suffer damage or deterioration from constant handling, using, rubbing, etc. (*often used with* **away** *or* **down**): *The cuffs of the shirt are starting to wear at the edges.* **9** damage or deterioration due to use: *The rug showed signs of wear.* **10** produce gradually by rubbing, scraping, washing away, etc.: *I wore a hole in my shoe.* **11** tire; exhaust (*often used with* **out**): *The job was extremely wearing. A visit with him always wears me out.* **12** endure being used; last under use: *This coat has worn well. The shoes are beautiful but they won't wear.* **13** capacity for resisting deterioration and damage through use; lasting quality: *The shoes still have a lot of wear in them.* **14** stand the test of experience, familiarity, criticism, etc.: *The friendship did not wear.* **15** of time, pass or go gradually: *It grew hotter as the day wore on.* **16** pass time gradually (*used with* **away** *or* **out**): *to wear one's life away in regrets.* **17** hold the rank or office symbolized by an ornament or article of dress: *"Uneasy lies the head that wears a crown".* **18** of a ship, turn or be turned so that the bow is pointing away from the wind. 1, 4–8, 10–12, 14–18 *v.,* **wore, worn, wear·ing;** 2, 3, 9, 13 *n.*
—**wear′a·ble,** *adj.,* —**wear′er,** *n.*

**wear down,** overcome by persistent effort: *He tried to wear his parents down by asking again and again why they wouldn't let him go.*

**wear off,** become less: *As the freezing wore off, my tooth started to ache.*

**wear out,** a wear until no longer fit for use; make useless by long or hard wear: *She wore the shoes out in six months.* b become useless from long or hard wear: *I don't think this coat will ever wear out.*

**wear thin,** a become weak from being used too much: *My patience was wearing thin.* b become tiresome and unconvincing because of repetition: *That excuse of hers is wearing thin.*
☛ *Hom.* WARE, WHERE (wer).

**wear and tear** damage or deterioration as a result of ordinary use over a period of time.

**wear·i·ness** (wē′rē nis) the quality or state of being WEARY. *n.*

**wea·ri·some** (wē′rē səm) wearying; tiring; tiresome: *a long and wearisome tale.* *adj.* —**wea′ri·some·ly,** *adv.* —**wea′ri·some·ness,** *n.*

**wea·ry** (wē′rē) 1 tired: *weary feet. We were all weary after the long ride.* 2 causing tiredness; tiring: *a weary wait.* 3 having one's patience, liking, or tolerance exhausted (*used with* **of**): *She was weary of his stupid jokes.* 4 showing weariness: *a weary smile.* 5 make weary; tire: *Walking up the hill wearied Grandfather.* 6 become weary. 1–4 *adj.,* **wea·ri·er, wea·ri·est;** 5, 6 *v.,* **wea·ried, wea·ry·ing.** —**wea′ri·ly,** *adv.*

A long-tailed weasel—about 30 cm long excluding the tail

**wea·sel** (wē′zəl) 1 any of several closely related species of small meat-eating mammal having a long, slender body, a long, flexible neck, short legs, and short, thick fur that is mainly reddish brown above and creamy below: *Northern weasels turn white in winter.* 2 referring to the family of meat-eating mammals that includes the weasels, minks, and otters: *The weasel family is found throughout the world.* 3 *Informal.* a sly and sneaky person. 4 *Informal.* use misleading or ambiguous words to avoid committing oneself or making a direct statement: *Stop weaselling and give me a straight answer.* 5 *Informal.* escape from or evade in a crafty way; get out of a situation or obligation (*used with* **out**): *She had promised to help but weaselled out at the last minute.* 1–3 *n.,* 4, 5 *v.,* **wea·selled** or **wea·seled, wea·sel·ling** or **wea·sel·ing.**

**weasel word** Often, **weasel words,** *pl.* A word intended to soften what one says, making the message vague or confusing.

**weath·er** (weTH′ər) 1 the condition of the atmosphere at a particular time and place with respect to temperature, moisture, cloudiness, or windiness: *windy weather. The weather was beautiful for the entire trip.* 2 disagreeable conditions of the atmosphere, such as wind, rain, storm, or cold; bad weather: *a shelter for protection against the weather.* 3 expose to the weather; subject to the action of sun, rain, frost, etc.: *Wood turns grey if weathered for a long time.* 4 become discoloured or worn by air, rain, sun, frost, etc.: *The house had weathered to a silvery grey.* 5 pass safely through bad weather or a difficult time: *The ship weathered the storm.* 6 sail to the windward of: *The ship weathered the cape.* 7 of or referring to the side of a ship toward the wind; windward. 8 make boards, tiles, etc. overlap and slope downward so as to shed water. 9 resist the effects of the weather: *This paint weathers well.* 1, 2, 7 *n.,* 3–6, 8, 9 *v.*

**under the weather,** *Informal.* a somewhat sick; ailing: *She's been feeling under the weather for several days.* b slightly drunk.
☛ *Hom.* WETHER, WHETHER (weTH′ər).

**weather beam** the side of a ship toward the wind.

**weath·er-beat·en** (weTH′ər bē′tən) worn or hardened by the wind, rain, and other forces of the weather: *an old farmer's weather-beaten face, a weather-beaten ship.* *adj.*

**weath·er·board** (weTH′ər bôrd′) 1 clapboard; siding. 2 cover with weatherboards. 3 the side of a ship toward the wind; weather beam. 1, 3 *n.,* 2 *v.*

**weath·er-bound** (weTH′ər bound′) delayed by bad weather: *a weather-bound ship.* *adj.*

**weath·er·cock** (weTH′ər kok′) a WEATHER VANE, especially one in the shape of a rooster. *n.*

**weather eye** 1 an eye alert to signs of change in the weather. 2 a close watch for expected change of any kind: *The news media were keeping a weather eye on the labour situation.* *n.*

**keep a weather eye open,** be on the lookout for possible danger or trouble.

**weather forecast** a prediction of future weather, based on scientific observation of current weather patterns and developments.

**weath·er·glass** (weTH′ər glas′) an instrument to show the weather: *A barometer is a weatherglass.* *n.*

**weath·er·ing** (weTH′ə ring) 1 the destructive or discolouring action of air, water, frost, etc., especially on rocks. 2 ppr. of WEATHER. 1 *n.,* 2 *v.*

**weath·er·man** (weTH′ər man′) *Informal.* a person who forecasts the weather or one who presents weather forecasts, as on television. *n., pl.* **weath·er·men** (-men′).

**weath·er·proof** (weTH′ər prüf′) 1 protected against rain, snow, or wind; able to stand exposure to all kinds of weather: *They built a small weatherproof cabin and lived there all winter.* 2 make weatherproof: *I'm looking for something that will weatherproof my boots.* 1 *adj.,* 2 *v.*

**weather strip** a narrow strip to fill or cover the space between a door or window and the casing, so as to keep out rain, snow, and wind.

**weather vane** a VANE (def. 1).

**weath·er-wise** (weTH′ər wīz′) skilful in forecasting the changes of the weather. *adj.*

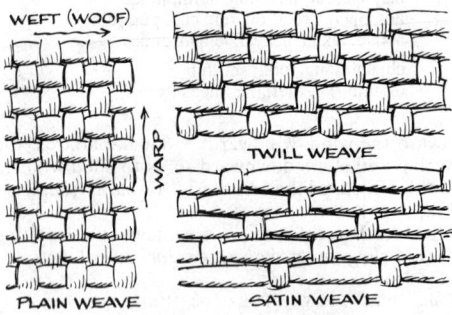

The three basic weaves for cloth

**weave** (wēv)  1 form threads or strips into a texture or fabric; interlace: *People weave threads into cloth, straw into hats, and reeds into baskets.*  2 make out of thread, etc.: *She is weaving a rug.*  3 work with a loom.  4 a method or pattern of weaving: *Homespun is a cloth of coarse weave.*  5 combine into a whole: *The author wove three plots together into one story.*  6 make by combining parts: *The author wove a story from three plots.*  7 make with care and skill.  8 go by twisting and turning: *We weaved around beds and boxes to the back door.*  1–3, 5–8 *v.*, **wove** or (for def. 8) **weaved, wo‧ven** or **wove, weav‧ing;**  4 *n.*
**weave one's way,**  make one's way by twisting and turning.
☞ *Hom.*  WE'VE (wēv).
☞ *Etym.*  See note at WEB.
☞ *Usage.*  **Woven** is the regular past participle. **Wove** is now used chiefly as an adjective in certain technical phrases, such as *wire-wove* and *wove paper*.

**weav‧er** (wē′vər)  1 one who weaves.  2 one whose work is weaving.  3 WEAVERBIRD.  *n.*

**weav‧er‧bird** (wē′vər bėrd′)  in Asia, Africa, and Australia, a bird that builds an elaborately woven nest.  *n.*

**web** (web)  1 a woven length of fabric, especially while on the loom or as it comes off the loom.  2 a COBWEB or something similar produced by any of various insects.  3 any complicated network, especially one that entangles like a cobweb: *a web of lies.*  4 the skin joining the toes of swimming birds and animals.  5 the vane of a feather.  6 a thin metal sheet or plate.  7 connective tissue.  8 a large roll of paper, especially newsprint, for use in a rotary printing press.  9 **the Web,** *Informal.*  WORLD WIDE WEB.  *n.* —**web′like′,** *adv.*
☞ *Etym.*  OE *webb* 'woven fabric'. It later came to mean the "fabric" woven by a spider, and also 'tissue, membrane'. Related words that survive in modern English are WEAVE (OE *wefan* 'weave'), and also WEFT (OE *wefta*) and WOOF (OE *ōwef*), both meaning the threads that extend from side to side of a web. Another related word is the surname *Webster,* which developed from OE *webbestre* 'female weaver'. WARP, however, meaning the lengthwise threads on a loom, developed from OE *weorpan* 'to cast, throw'. The modern meaning of **warp** 'twist, bend' also developed from a form of the OE verb.

**webbed** (webd)  1 formed like a web or with a web.  2 having the toes joined by a web: *Ducks have webbed feet.*  See DUCK for picture.  *adj.*

**web‧bing** (web′ing)  1 cloth woven into strong strips, used in upholstery and for belts.  2 the plain foundation fabric left for protection at the edge of some rugs, etc.  3 skin joining the toes, as in a duck's feet.  *n.*

**web‧foot** (web′fut)  1 a foot in which the toes are joined by a web.  2 a bird or animal having webfeet.  *n., pl.* **web‧feet.**

**web–foot‧ed** (web′fut′id)  having the toes joined by a web.  *adj.*

**web‧site** (web′sīt)  A site on the WORLD WIDE WEB. Each website contains a home page, which is the first file a user sees, and may contain more files. Each website is owned and managed by individual companies or organizations.

**web–toed** (web′tōd′)  WEB-FOOTED.  *adj.*

**wed** (wed)  1 marry.  2 unite.  *v.*, **wed‧ded, wed‧ded** or **wed, wed‧ding.**

**we'd** (wēd; *unstressed,* wid)  1 we had.  2 we should; we would.
☞ *Hom.*  WEED.

**Wed.**  Wednesday.

**wed‧ded** (wed′id)  1 married.  2 united.  3 devoted.  4 pt. and a pp. of WED.  1–3 *adj.*, 4 *v.*

**wed‧ding** (wed′ing)  1 the marriage ceremony.  2 an anniversary of this ceremony: *A golden wedding is the fiftieth anniversary of a marriage.*  3 joining or uniting: *Her writing shows a remarkable wedding of thought and language.*  4 ppr. of WED.  1–3 *n.*, 4 *v.*

Wedges being used to raise a support post

**wedge** (wej)  1 a piece of wood or metal with a tapering thin edge, used in splitting, separating, etc.  2 something shaped like a wedge: *He cut the big pie into eight wedges.*  3 something used like a wedge to make an opening or opportunity: *Her grand party was a wedge for her entry into society.*  4 anything that divides in some way: *Their disagreement about politics drove a wedge between the friends.*  5 thrust or pack in tightly; squeeze: *He wedged himself into the narrow space.*  6 split or separate with a wedge.  7 fasten or tighten with a wedge.  8 force a way.  9 a particular kind of golf club having a metal head.  1–4, 9 *n.*, 5–8 *v.*, **wedged, wedg‧ing.**

**wed‧lock** (wed′lok)  married life; marriage.  *n.*

**Wednes‧day** (wenz′dā *or* wenz′dē′)  the fourth day of the week, following Tuesday.  *n.*
☞ *Etym.*  From OE *Wōdnesdæg* 'Woden's day'. Woden, or Odin, was the chief Germanic god.

**wee** (wē)  very small; tiny.  *adj.*, **we‧er, we‧est.**
☞ *Hom.*  WE.

**weed** (wēd)  1 a wild plant growing where it is not wanted, as in grainfields, gardens, lawns, pastures, etc., especially one that grows fast and is hard to get rid of: *Russian thistle, milkweed, ragweed, and wild mustard are common weeds.*  2 take weeds out of: *to weed a garden.*  3 take out weeds: *I spent all morning weeding.*  1 *n.*, 2, 3 *v.* —**weed′like′,** *adj.*
**weed out,**  remove or discard as not wanted: *The weak players were weeded out before the regular season began.*
☞ *Hom.*  WE'D.

**weed·er** (wē′dər) 1 a person who weeds. 2 a tool or machine for digging up weeds. *n.*

**weed·y** (wē′dē) 1 full of weeds: *a weedy garden.* 2 of or like a weed or weeds, especially in fast and vigorous growth. 3 thin and lanky: *a tall and weedy youth. adj.,* **weed·i·er, weed·i·est.** —**weed′i·ness,** *n.*

**week** (wēk) 1 seven days, one after another. 2 the time from Sunday through Saturday: *This is the last week of holidays.* 3 the working days of a seven-day period: *A school week is five days. Some people work a six-day week. n.*
**Monday week,** the Monday one week from this Monday.
**this day week,** one week from today.
**week in, week out,** week after week.
☞ *Hom.* WEAK.

**week·day** (wēk′dā′) 1 any day except Sunday. 2 any day except Saturday or Sunday. 3 of or on a weekday. *n.*

**week·end** (wē′kend′) 1 Saturday and Sunday as a time for recreation, visiting, etc.; the time between the end of one week of work or school and the beginning of the next: *a weekend in the country, Thanksgiving weekend.* 2 of or on a weekend. 3 spend a weekend: *They are weekending at their cottage.* 1, 2 *n.,* 3 *v.*

**week·ly** (wē′klē) 1 of a week; for a week; lasting a week: *His weekly wage is $1400.* 2 done or happening once a week: *She writes a weekly letter to her grandmother.* 3 once each week; every week: *The clerks in the store are paid weekly.* 4 a newspaper or magazine published once a week. 1, 2, *adj.,* 3 *adv.,* 4 *n., pl.* **week·lies.**
☞ *Hom.* WEAKLY.

**weep** (wēp) 1 shed tears; cry: *She wept for joy when she won the award.* 2 shed tears for; mourn. 3 spend in crying: *to weep one's life away.* 4 let fall in drops; shed: *They wept bitter tears.* 5 give off moisture in drops; ooze or drip: *The basement wall sometimes weeps. v.,* **wept, weep·ing.**

**weep·er** (wē′pər) a person who weeps. *n.*

**weep·ing** (wē′ping) 1 that weeps. 2 having thin, drooping branches: *a weeping willow.* 3 ppr. of WEEP. 1, 2 *adj.,* 3 *v.*

**weeping willow** a large willow tree native to eastern Asia, having long, feathery, drooping branches: *Weeping willows are often planted as ornamental trees.*

**wee·vil** (wē′vəl) 1 a small beetle whose larvae destroy grain, nuts, cotton, fruit, etc. 2 any of various small insects that destroy stored grain. *n.*

**wee·vil·ly** or **wee·vil·y** (wē′və lē) infested with WEEVILS. *adj.*

**weft** (weft) the threads running from side to side across a fabric; the woof. See WEAVE for picture. *n.*
☞ *Etym.* See note at WEB.

**weigh** (wā) 1 find the mass of: *I weighed myself this morning.* 2 have a measure of mass: *I weigh 45 kilograms.* 3 measure a quantity of something by mass: *The grocer weighed out two kilograms of potatoes.* 4 find how heavy a thing is at a certain altitude. 5 have as a measure by WEIGHT (def. 3): *Things weigh much less on the moon than on earth.* 6 bend by weight; burden: *The boughs of the apple tree are weighed down with fruit. She is weighed down with many troubles.* 7 balance in the mind; consider carefully: *He weighed his words before speaking.* 8 have importance or influence: *The amount of his salary does not weigh with Mr. Black at all, because he is very rich.* 9 bear down: *The mistake weighed heavily upon her mind.*

hat, āge, fär; let, ēqual, tėrm; it, īce
hot, ōpen, ôrder; oil, out; cup, pu̇t, rüle
əbove, takən, pencəl, lemən, circəs
ch, child; ng, long; sh, ship
th, thin; ᴛʜ, then; zh, measure

10 lift up an anchor: *The ship weighed anchor and sailed away.* 11 lift anchor. *v.* —**weigh′er,** *n.*
**weigh in,** find out one's weight before a contest.
**weigh on,** be a burden to.
☞ *Hom.* WAY, WHEY (wā).

**weight** (wāt) 1 MASS (def. 7): *The dog's weight is 20 kilograms.* 2 a piece of metal having a particular mass, used to weigh (def. 1) something on a balance: *a fifty-gram weight.* 3 how heavy a thing is; the quality of anything that makes it tend toward the centre of the earth: *Gas has hardly any weight at all. Your weight is a little less on a mountain than at sea level.* 4 a system of units for expressing mass: *avoirdupois weight, troy weight.* 5 a unit of such a system. 6 a quantity that has a certain weight: *Five tonnes is a heavy weight.* 7 a heavy thing or mass: *A weight keeps the papers in place.* 8 a load; burden: *The pillars support the weight of the roof.* 9 load down; burden: *The manager was weighted with troubles.* 10 add weight to; put weight on: *The elevator is weighted too heavily.* 11 influence; importance; value: *What he says carries weight with me.* 12 attach importance or value to. 13 load cloth or thread with mineral to make it seem of better quality: *weighted silk.* 1–8, 11 *n.,* 9, 10, 12, 13 *v.*
**by weight,** measured by weighing.
**pull one's weight,** do one's part or share: *We will finish the job quickly if we all pull our weight.*
☞ *Hom.* WAIT.

**weight–arm** (wā′tärm′) the distance from the weight to the fulcrum in a lever. *n.*

**weight·less** (wā′tlis) 1 appearing to have no weight: *The snow felt weightless on my shoulders.* 2 being free from the pull of gravity: *In outer space, all things are weightless. adj.*

**weight·less·ness** (wā′tlis nis) in astronautics, the state or condition of being free from the pull of gravity. *n.*

**weight·y** (wā′tē) 1 heavy. 2 too heavy; burdensome: *weighty cares of state.* 3 important; influential: *a weighty speaker.* 4 convincing: *weighty arguments. adj.,* **weight·i·er, weight·i·est.** —**weight′i·ly,** *adv.* —**weight′i·ness,** *n.*

**weir** (wēr) 1 a dam built in a river to raise the level of the water or to divert its flow. 2 a fence of stakes or broken branches put in a stream or channel to catch fish. 3 an obstruction erected across a channel or stream to divert the water through a special opening in order to measure the rate of flow. *n.*
☞ *Hom.* WE'RE.

**weird** (wērd) 1 unearthly; mysterious: *We were awakened by a weird shriek.* 2 odd; fantastic; queer: *The shadows made weird figures on the wall. adj.*
—**weird′ly,** *adv.* —**weird′ness,** *n.*

**wel·come** (wel′kəm) 1 greet kindly: *We always welcome guests at our house.* 2 a kind reception: *You will always have a welcome here.* 3 receive gladly: *We welcome new ideas and suggestions.* 4 gladly received; pleasing: *a welcome visitor, a welcome letter, a welcome rest.* 5 gladly or freely permitted: *You are welcome to pick the flowers.* 6 as a reply to thanks, free to have or do

something, to enjoy some favour, etc.: *You are quite welcome.* **7** an exclamation of friendly greeting: *Welcome!* **1, 3** *v.,* **wel·comed, wel·com·ing;** **2** *n.,* **4–6** *adj.,* **7** *interj.* —**wel′com·er,** *n.*
**wear out one's welcome,** visit a person too often or too long.

**weld** (weld) **1** join together metal, plastic, etc. by hammering or pressing while hot and soft. **2** a welded joint. **3** welding. **4** unite closely: *Working together welded them into a strong team.* **5** become welded or be capable of being welded: *Some metals weld better than others.* **1, 4, 5** *v.,* **2, 3** *n.* —**weld′er,** *n.*

**wel·fare** (wel′fer′) health, happiness, and prosperity; a condition of being or doing well: *Uncle Charles asked about the welfare of everyone in our family.* *n.*
**on welfare,** receiving benefits from the government or from some organization to provide a basic standard of living: *There was no harvest and many families were on welfare.*

**welfare state** a state whose government provides for the welfare of its citizens through social security, unemployment insurance, medical treatment, etc.

**welfare work** work done to improve lives and living conditions of people who need help because of poverty, sickness, family problems, etc.: *Welfare work is carried on by governments, private organizations, and sometimes individuals.*

**welfare worker** a person who does WELFARE WORK.

**well¹** (wel) **1** in a satisfactory, favourable, or advantageous manner; all right: *The job was well done. Is everything going well at school?* **2** satisfactory; good; right: *It is well you came along.* **3** thoroughly: *Shake well before using.* **4** to a considerable degree; much: *The fair brought in well over a hundred dollars.* **5** in detail; intimately: *She knows the subject well.* **6** easily or reasonably: *I can't very well refuse. You might well ask what he was doing there. They could well be here before dark.* **7** in good health: *I am very well.* **8** an expression used to show mild surprise, agreement, etc., or merely to fill in: *Well! Well! Here's Nina. Well, I'm not sure.* **1, 3–6** *adv.,* **bet·ter, best;** **2, 7** *adj.,* **8** *interj.*
**as well,** **a** also; besides. **b** equally.
**as well as,** **a** in additon to; besides: *I have skates as well as skis.* **b** as an equal with: *I can ride as well as you can.*

**well²** (wel) **1** a hole dug or bored in the ground to get water, oil, gas, etc. **2** fountain or source: *Our class president is a well of ideas.* **3** something like a well in shape or use: *the well of a fountain pen.* **4** a shaft for light, or for stairs or an elevator, extending vertically through the floors of a building. **5** a compartment around a ship's pumps. **6** spring; rise; gush: *Tears welled up in her eyes.* **1–5** *n.,* **6** *v.*

**we'll** (wēl; *unstressed,* wil) we shall; we will.
☛ Hom. WEAL, WHEAL (wēl), WHEEL (wēl).

**well–ap·point·ed** (wel′ə poin′tid) having good furnishings or equipment. *adj.*

**well–bal·anced** (wel′bal′ənst) **1** rightly balanced, adjusted, or regulated. **2** sensible; sane. *adj.*

**well–be·haved** (wel′bi hāvd′) showing good manners or conduct. *adj.*

**well–be·ing** (wel′bē′ing) health and happiness; welfare. *n.*

**well–born** (wel′bôrn′) belonging to a good family. *adj.*

**well–bred** (wel′bred′) well brought up; having or showing good manners. *adj.*

**well–con·tent** (wel′kən tent′) highly pleased or satisfied. *adj.*

**well–de·fined** (wel′di fīnd′) clearly defined or indicated; distinct. *adj.*

**well–dis·posed** (wel′di spōzd′) **1** rightly or properly disposed. **2** well-meaning. **3** favourably or kindly disposed. *adj.*

**well–do·ing** (wel′dü′ing) the act of doing right; good conduct. *n.*

**well–fa·voured** or **well–fa·vored** (wel′fā′vərd) good-looking. *adj.*

**well–fed** (wel′fed′) showing the result of good feeding; fat; plump. *adj.*

**well–fixed** (wel′fikst′) *Informal.* well-to-do. *adj.*

**well–found** (wel′found′) well supplied or equipped. *adj.*

**well–found·ed** (wel′foun′did) rightly or justly founded: *a well-founded faith in democracy.* *adj.*

**well–groomed** (wel′grümd′) well cared for; neat and trim. *adj.*

**well–ground·ed** (wel′groun′did) **1** based on good reasons. **2** thoroughly instructed in the fundamental principles of a subject. *adj.*

**well·head** (wel′hed′) **1** a spring of water. **2** source. *n.*

**well–in·formed** (wel′in fôrmd′) **1** having reliable or full information on a subject. **2** having information on a wide variety of subjects. *adj.*

**well–kept** (wel′kept′) well cared for; carefully tended. *adj.*

**well–knit** (wel′nit′) **1** firmly constructed or joined together; closely connected or linked. **2** of strong, supple build; well-built. *adj.*

**well–known** (wel′nōn′) generally or widely known. *adj.*

**well–man·nered** (wel′man′ərd) polite; courteous. *adj.*

**well–marked** (wel′märkt′) clearly marked or distinguished; distinct. *adj.*

**well–mean·ing** (wel′mē′ning) **1** having good intentions. **2** proceeding from good intentions. *adj.*

**well–nigh** (wel′nī′) very nearly; almost. *adv.*

**well–off** (wel′of′) **1** in a good condition or position: *Your whole family is healthy, so you should consider yourself well-off.* **2** fairly rich; prosperous: *Her family is well-off but not wealthy.* *adj.*

**well–or·dered** (wel′ôr′dərd) ordered or arranged well; regulated well. *adj.*

**well–pre·served** (wel′pri zėrvd′) showing few signs of age. *adj.*

**well–pro·por·tioned** (wel′prə pôr′shənd) having good or correct proportions. *adj.*

**well–read** (wel′red′) having read much; knowing a great deal about books and literature. *adj.*

**well-spo·ken** (wel′spō′kən) 1 speaking well, fittingly, or pleasingly; polite in speech. 2 spoken well. *adj.*

**well·spring** (wel′spring′) 1 FOUNTAINHEAD. 2 a source, especially of a supply that never fails. *n.*

**well-suit·ed** (wel′sü′tid) suitable; convenient. *adj.*

**well sweep** a device used to draw water from a well, consisting of a pole attached to a pivot and having a bucket at one end.

**well-timed** (wel′tīmd′) timely: *His well-timed intervention settled the dispute. adj.*

**well-to-do** (wel′tə dü′) having enough money to live well; prosperous. *adj.*

**well-wish·er** (wel′wish′ər) a person who wishes well to a person, cause, etc. *n.*

**well-worn** (wel′wôrn′) 1 much worn by use. 2 used too much; trite; stale. *adj.*

**Welsh** (welsh) 1 of or having to do with Wales, a division of Great Britain, its people, or their Celtic language. 2 the Celtic language of Wales. 3 **the Welsh**, *pl.* the people of Wales. 1 *adj.*, 2, 3 *n.*
☛ *Etym.* From OE *Wēlisc*, which developed from *wealh* 'stranger, foreigner', a Germanic term that came originally from a Celtic tribal name and was applied especially to Celts.

**Welsh·man** (welsh′mən) 1 a native or inhabitant of Wales. 2 a person of Welsh descent. *n., pl.* **Welsh·men** (-mən).

**Welsh rabbit** a thick sauce containing cheese, cooked and served on toast.

**Welsh rarebit** WELSH RABBIT.

**Welsh·wom·an** (welsh′wum′ən) 1 a woman who is a native or inhabitant of Wales. 2 a woman of Welsh descent. *n., pl.* **Welsh·wom·en** (-wim′ən).

**welt** (welt) 1 a strip of leather between the upper part and the sole of a shoe. 2 the narrow border, trimming, etc. on the edge of a garment or upholstery. 3 put a welt on. 4 a streak or ridge made on the skin by a blow, especially from a stick or whip. 5 a heavy blow. 6 *Informal.* beat severely. 1, 2, 4, 5 *n.*, 3, 6 *v.*

**wel·ter** (wel′tər) 1 roll or toss about; wallow. 2 a surging or confused mass: *All we saw was a welter of arms, legs, and bodies.* 3 confusion; commotion. 4 lie soaked; be drenched. 1, 4 *v.*, 2, 3 *n.*

**wel·ter·weight** (wel′tər wāt′) a boxer or wrestler weighing between 63.5 and 67 kg. *n.*

**wen** (wen) a harmless tumour of the skin. *n.*
☛ *Hom.* WHEN (wen).

**wend** (wend) 1 direct one's way: *We wended our way home.* 2 go. *v.*, **wend·ed** or (*archaic*) **went, wend·ing.**

**wen·di·go** (wen′di gō′) 1 among Algonquian Indians, an evil spirit. 2 *Cdn.* a kind of trout; splake. *n., pl.* (def. 1) **wen·di·gos,** (def. 2) **wen·di·go** or **wen·di·gos.**

**went** (went) originally the pt. of WEND and now the pt. of GO: *I went home. v.*

**wept** (wept) pt. and pp. of WEEP: *She wept for hours. She has often wept. v.*

**were** (wėr; *unstressed,* wər) 1 plural and 2nd person singular, past tense, of BE: *The officers were obeyed by the soldiers.* 2 past subjunctive of BE: *If I were rich, I would travel. v.*
**as it were,** as if it were; so to speak; in some way.
☛ *Hom.* WHIR (wėr).

---

hat, āge, fär; let, ēqual, tėrm; it, īce
hot, ōpen, ôrder; oil, out; cup, put, rüle
əbove, tākən, pencəl, lemən, circəs
ch, child; ng, long; sh, ship
th, thin; ŦH, then; zh, measure

**we're** (wēr) we are.
☛ *Hom.* WEIR.

**weren't** (wėrnt *or* wərnt) were not.

**were·wolf** (wēr′wulf′ *or* wer′wulf′) in folklore, a man who has been changed into a wolf, or who can change himself into a wolf, while keeping his human intelligence. *n., pl.* **were·wolves** (-wulvz′). Also, **werwolf.**
☛ *Etym.* From Germanic through OE *werewulf*, made up of *wer* 'man' + *wulf* 'wolf'.

**wer·wolf** (wėr′wulf′ *or* wer′wulf′) See WEREWOLF. *n., pl.* **wer·wolves.**

**We·sak** (wes′ak) in Buddhism, the New Year festival celebrated at the full moon in the month of May, and commemorating the birth, enlightenment, and death of Buddha. *n.*

**west** (west) 1 the direction of the sunset; the point of the compass to the left as one faces north. See COMPASS for picture. 2 toward the west; farther toward the west: *Walk west three blocks.* 3 from the west: *a warm west wind.* 4 in the west; living in the west: *the west wing of a house.* 5 Also, **West,** the part of the world, country, or continent toward the west. 6 **the West,** **a** in Canada, the western part of Canada or the United States. **b** the countries in Europe and America as distinguished from those in Asia. **c** the United States, the United Kingdom, and their allies as distinguished from the U.S.S.R. and its allies. 1, 5, 6 *n.*, 2 *adv.*, 3, 4 *adj.*
**out West,** in Canada: **a** any point to the west of Winnipeg. **b** in or toward any place west of Winnipeg.
**west of,** farther west than: *Alberta is west of Saskatchewan.*

**west·bound** (west′bound′) going toward the west. *adj.*

**west·er·ly** (wes′tər lē) 1 toward the west: *The wind blew westerly.* 2 from the west: *a westerly wind.* 3 a wind that blows from the west. 1 *adv.*, 2 *adj.*, 3 *n.*

**west·ern** (wes′tərn) 1 toward the west. 2 from the west. 3 of or in the west; of or in the western part of the world, country, or continent: *Vancouver is a western port.* 4 of, in, or having to do with the West. 5 *Informal.* a story or motion picture dealing with life in the western part of North America, especially cowboy life in the United States. 1–4 *adj.*, 5 *n.*

**Western civilization** European and American civilization as contrasted with oriental civilization.

**West·ern·er** (wes′tər nər) a native or inhabitant of the West. *n.*

**western flowering dogwood** a tree of the DOGWOOD family, having blossoms with white, petal-like bracts, red berries, and hard wood: *The blossom of the western flowering dogwood is the floral emblem of British Columbia.*

**Western Hemisphere** the half of the world that includes North and South America.

**western hemlock** 1 a tall hemlock found in the forest regions of British Columbia and the northwestern United States, an important timber-producing tree having flat needles and small, egg-shaped cones. **2** the moderately light, hard, and strong wood of this tree.

**west·ern·ize** (wes′tər nīz′) introduce or adopt western ideas, customs, culture, etc. *v.*, **west·ern·ized, west·ern·iz·ing.** —**west′ern·i′zer,** *n.*

**western juniper** ROCKY MOUNTAIN JUNIPER.

**western larch** a very tall larch tree found mainly in the forests of southern British Columbia, often growing to heights of 30 to 50 metres, having oval cones and heavy, hard, strong wood: *The western larch is one of the most important timber-producing trees in western Canada.*

**west·ern·most** (wes′tərn mōst′) farthest west. *adj.*

**western red cedar** a very large evergreen tree, a species of arborvitae found along the Pacific coast and in interior British Columbia, a very long-lived tree often reaching a height of 45 to 60 metres and a diameter of 2.5 metres or more: *The western red cedar was used by the Indians of the Pacific northwest for carving totem poles and building canoes and lodges.*

**western yew** a species of yew occurring as a small tree or shrub in the forests of British Columbia: *The hard, strong wood of the western yew is valued for archery bows, canoe paddles, and carving.*

**West Indian** **1** of or having to do with the West Indies, a large group of islands between Florida and South America, or the people of these islands. **2** a native or inhabitant of the West Indies. **3** a person whose recent ancestors came from the West Indies.

**West·min·ster Abbey** (west′min′stər) in London, an ABBEY (def. 3) in which many British monarchs and famous men are buried.

**west–north·west** (west′nôr′thwest′) **1** a direction or compass point midway between west and northwest. **2** in, toward, or from this direction. 1 *n.*, 2 *adj., adv.*

**west–south·west** (west′sou′thwest′) **1** a direction or compass point midway between west and southwest. **2** in, toward, or from this direction. 1 *n.*, 2 *adj., adv.*

**west·ward** (wes′twərd) **1** toward the west; west: *He walked westward* (adv.). *We live on the westward slope of the hill* (adj.). **2** a westward part, direction, or point. 1 *adj., adv.*, 2 *n.*

**west·ward·ly** (wes′twər dlē) **1** toward the west. **2** of winds, from the west. *adj., adv.*

**west·wards** (wes′twərdz) WESTWARD. *adv.*

**wet** (wet) **1** covered or soaked with water or other liquid: *wet hands.* **2** not yet dry: *Don't touch wet paint.* **3** watery; liquid: *Her eyes were wet with tears.* **4** make or become wet: *Wet the cloth before you wipe off the window.* **5** water or other liquid: *I dropped my scarf in the wet.* **6** rainy: *wet weather.* **7** wetness; rain: *Come in out of the wet.* **8** *Informal.* having or favouring laws that permit the making and selling of alcoholic drinks. **9** *Informal.* one who favours laws that permit the making and selling of alcoholic drinks. 1–3, 6, 8 *adj.*, **wet·ter, wet·test;** 4 *v.*, **wet** or **wet·ted, wet·ting;** 5, 7, 9 *n.* —**wet′ness,** *n.*
**wet behind the ears,** too young to know very much; green; inexperienced.
☞ *Hom.* WHET (wet).

**wet blanket** *Informal.* a person who has a discouraging or depressing effect: *He's really a wet blanket; when we were planning our picnic he said it would probably be cold, and besides, we'd get bugs in our food.*

**wet cell** an ELECTROCHEMICAL CELL having a liquid electrolyte.

**weth·er** (weᴛн′ər) a castrated male sheep. *n.*
☞ *Hom.* WEATHER, WHETHER (weᴛн′ər).

**wet nurse** a woman employed to suckle the infant of another.

**wet suit** a skin-tight suit of sponge rubber or a similar material that is not watertight but that will retain body heat, worn especially by skindivers in cold water. See SKINDIVER for picture.

**wet·tish** (wet′ish) somewhat wet. *adj.*

**we've** (wēv; *unstressed,* wiv) we have.
☞ *Hom.* WEAVE (for the first pronunciation of **we've**).

**whack** (wak *or* hwak) **1** a sharp, resounding blow or the sound of such a blow. **2** strike with a sharp, resounding blow: *The batter whacked the ball out of the park.* 1 *n.*, 2 *v.*
**out of whack,** *Informal.* not in proper condition; out of order: *The timing of the engine is out of whack.*

**whack·ing** (wak′ing *or* hwak′ing) *Informal.* **1** large or tremendous: *a whacking success.* **2** ppr. of WHACK. 1 *adj.*, 2 *v.*

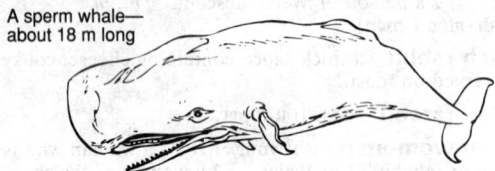
A sperm whale—about 18 m long

**whale**[1] (wāl *or* hwāl) **1** any member of the order Cetacea, a group of water mammals that are shaped like fish; especially, any of the larger members of this order (which are the largest known animals) as distinguished from the porpoises and dolphins: *Whales breathe air and bear live young.* **2** hunt and catch whales. **3** *Informal.* something very big, great, impressive, etc. 1, 3 *n., pl.* **whales** *or* **whale;** 2 *v.*, **whaled, whal·ing.**
**a whale of,** *Informal.* a big or impressive example or type of: *a whale of a car, a whale of a good time.*
☞ *Hom.* WAIL, WALE (for the first pronunciation of **whale**).

**whale**[2] (wāl *or* hwāl) *Informal.* **1** beat; whip severely. **2** hit hard. *v.*, **whaled, whal·ing.**
☞ *Hom.* See note at WHALE[1].

**whale·back** (wāl′bak′ *or* hwāl′bak′) a freight steamer having a rounded upper deck shaped like a whale's back. *n.*

**whale·boat** (wāl′bōt′ *or* hwāl′bōt′) a long, narrow rowboat, sharp at both ends, formerly much used in WHALING. *n.*

**whale·bone** (wāl′bōn′ *or* hwāl′bōn′) an elastic, horny substance growing in place of teeth in the upper jaw of certain whales and forming a series of thin, parallel plates. *n.*

**whal·er** (wā′lər *or* hwā′lər) **1** a person who hunts whales. **2** a ship used for hunting whales. *n.*

**whal·ing** (wā′ling *or* hwā′ling) **1** the hunting and killing of whales. **2** ppr. of WHALE. 1 *n.*, 2 *v.*

**whang** (wang *or* hwang) *Informal.* **1** a resounding blow or bang. **2** strike a blow or bang. 1 *n.*, 2 *v.*

**wharf** (wôrf *or* hwôrf) a platform built on the shore or out from the shore, beside which ships can load and unload. *n., pl.* **wharves** *or* **wharfs**.

**wharves** (wôrvz *or* hwôrvz) a pl. of WHARF. *n.*

**what** (wut *or* wot, hwut *or* hwot) **1** a word used in asking questions about persons or things: *What is your name?* (pron.). *What time is it?* (adj.). **2** that which: *I know what you mean* (pron.). *Give me what paper you don't use* (adj.). **3** whatever; anything that; any that: *Do what you please* (pron.). *Take what supplies you will need* (adj.). **4** how much; how: *What does it matter?* **5** having regard to; taking into account: *What with the wind and the rain, our picnic was spoiled.* **6** a word used to show surprise, liking, anger, or to add emphasis: *What! Are you late again?* (interj.) *What a pity!* (adj.). *What a good time we had* (adv.). *1–3 pron., 1–3, 6 adj., 4–6 adv., 6 interj.*
**and what not,** and all kinds of other things.
**but what,** but that.
**give one what for,** *Informal.* give one something to cry, suffer, or be miserable for; punish; castigate.
**what for,** why.
**what have you,** *Informal.* anything else like this; and so on.
**what if,** what would happen if: *What if it rains on the day of the game?*
**what's what,** *Informal.* the true state of affairs: *That girl knows what's what.*
**what with,** because of; considering: *We were very tired, what with our long walk and the lateness of the hour.*
☞ *Hom.* WATT (for the second pronunciation of WHAT).

**what·ev·er** (wə tev′ər *or* wot ev′ər, hwə tev′ər *or* hwot ev′ər) **1** anything that: *Do whatever you like.* **2** any that: *Ask whatever girls you like to the party.* **3** at all: *Any person whatever can tell you the way.* **4** no matter what: *Whatever happens, he is safe* (pron.). *Whatever excuse he makes will not be believed* (adj.). **5** *Informal.* a word used for emphasis instead of *what: Whatever do you mean?* *1, 4, 5 pron., 2–4 adj.*

**what·not** (wot′not′ *or* hwot′not′) a stand with several shelves for books, ornaments, etc. *n.*

**what's** (wuts *or* wots, hwuts *or* hwots) **1** what is: *What's the latest news?* **2** what has: *What's been going on here lately?*

**what·so·ev·er** (wut′sō ev′ər *or* wot′sō ev′ər, hwut′sō ev′ər *or* hwot′sō ev′ər) WHATEVER. *pron., adj.*

**wheal** (wēl *or* hwēl) a small burning or itching swelling on the skin. *n.*
☞ *Hom.* WEAL and WE'LL (for the first pronunciation of **wheal**); WHEEL.

Wheat

**wheat** (wēt *or* hwēt) **1** any of numerous closely related cereal grasses bearing grain in dense spikes: *There are thirty thousand varieties of wheat cultivated throughout the world.* **2** the grain yielded by any of these plants, one of the world's most important sources of flour for bread, pasta, etc. *n.*

**wheat·en** (wē′tən *or* hwē′tən) made of wheat. *adj.*

**wheat germ** the tiny golden embryo of the wheat kernel, used as a cereal and as a vitamin supplement.

**whee·dle** (wē′dəl *or* hwē′dəl) **1** persuade by flattery, smooth words, caresses, etc.; coax: *The children wheedled their mother into letting them go out.* **2** get by wheedling: *They finally wheedled the secret out of him.* *v.,* **whee·dled, whee·dling.** —**whee′dler,** *n.* —**whee′dling·ly,** *adv.*

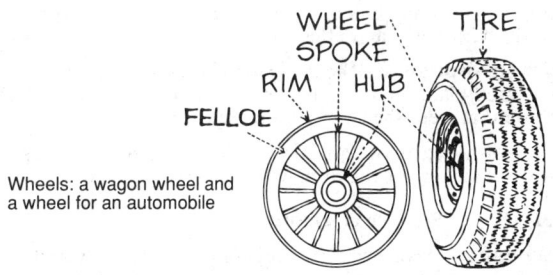

Wheels: a wagon wheel and a wheel for an automobile

**wheel** (wēl *or* hwēl) **1** a round frame or disk that can turn on a pin or shaft in its centre. **2** any instrument, machine, apparatus, etc. shaped or moving like a wheel: *A ship's wheel is used in steering. Clay is shaped into dishes, etc. on a potter's wheel.* **3** *Informal.* bicycle. **4** *Informal.* ride a bicycle. **5** any force thought of as moving or propelling: *the wheels of government.* **6** turn: *He wheeled around suddenly.* **7** cause to turn: *The rider wheeled her horse about.* **8** move or perform in a curved or circular direction. **9** move on wheels: *The workman was wheeling a load of bricks on a wheelbarrow.* **10** travel along smoothly. **11** provide with wheels. **12 wheels,** *pl. Informal.* a car, cars, or other means of transportation. *1–3, 5, 12 n., 4, 6–11 v.*
**at the wheel,** **a** at the steering wheel. **b** in control: *The variety night is bound to be a success with Maria at the wheel.*
**big wheel,** *Informal.* an important person.
**wheels within wheels,** complicated circumstances, motives, influences, etc.
☞ *Hom.* WEAL and WE'LL (for the first pronunciation of **wheel**); WHEAL.

A wheelbarrow

**wheel·bar·row** (wēl′bar′ō *or* wēl′ber′ō, hwēl′bar′ō

or hwĕl′bėr′ō) a small vehicle for carrying loads, having one wheel at the front and two handles at the back. *n.*

**wheel·base** (wēl′bās′ *or* hwēl′bās′) in motor vehicles, the distance from the centre of the front axle to the centre of the rear axle. *n.*

**wheel chair** a chair mounted on wheels so that it can be pushed from behind or moved by the person sitting in it: *Wheel chairs are used by invalids, amputees, and people who are paralysed.*

**wheeled** (wēld *or* hwēld) 1 having a wheel or wheels. 2 pt. and pp. of WHEEL. 1 *adj.*, 2 *v.*
☛ *Hom.* WIELD (for the first pronunciation of **wheeled**).

**wheel·er** (wē′lėr *or* hwē′lėr) 1 a person or thing that wheels. 2 a thing that has a wheel or wheels. 3 WHEEL HORSE. *n.*

**wheel horse** 1 the horse nearest to the front wheels of the vehicle being pulled. 2 *Informal.* a person who works hard, long, and effectively.

**wheel–house** (wēl′hous′ *or* hwēl′hous′) a small, enclosed place on a ship to shelter the steering wheel and those that steer the ship; pilothouse. *n.*

**wheel–wright** (wēl′rīt′ *or* hwēl′rīt′) a person whose work is making or repairing wheels, carriages, and wagons. *n.*
☛ *Etym.* See note at WRIGHT.

**wheeze** (wēz *or* hwēz) 1 breathe with difficulty and with a whistling sound. 2 a whistling sound caused by difficult breathing. 3 make a sound like this: *The old engine wheezed, but it didn't stop.* 4 say with a wheeze. 1, 3, 4 *v.*, **wheezed, wheez·ing;** 2 *n.*

**wheez·y** (wē′zē *or* hwē′zē) wheezing: *The old dog was fat and wheezy.* *adj.*, **wheez·i·er, wheez·i·est.**
—**wheez′i·ly,** *adv.* —**wheez′i·ness,** *n.*

The shell of a whelk— about 7 cm long

**whelk** (welk *or* hwelk) a MOLLUSC with a spiral shell, used for food in Europe. *n.*

**whelm** (welm *or* hwelm) 1 OVERWHELM. 2 SUBMERGE. *v.*

**whelp** (welp *or* hwelp) 1 a puppy or cub; a young dog, wolf, bear, lion, tiger, etc. 2 give birth to whelps. 3 a good-for-nothing boy or young man. 1, 3 *n.*, 2 *v.*

**when** (wen *or* hwen; *unstressed,* wən *or* hwən) 1 at what time: *When does school close?* 2 at the time that: *Rise when your name is called.* 3 at any time that: *He is impatient when he is kept waiting.* 4 at which time; and then: *The dog growled till his master spoke, when he gave a joyful bark.* 5 although: *We have only three books when we need five.* 6 considering that; inasmuch as; since: *How can I help you when I don't know how to do the problem myself?* 7 what time; which time: *Since when have they had a car?* 8 the time or occasion: *the when and where of an act.* 1 *adv.*, 2–6 *conj.*, 7 *pron.*, 8 *n.*
☛ *Hom.* WEN (for the first pronunciation of **when**).

**when·ev·er** (we nev′ėr *or* hwe nev′ėr) at whatever time; when; at any time. *conj., adv.*

**where** (wer *or* hwer) 1 in what place; at what place: *Where is she?* 2 to what place: *Where are you going?* 3 from what place: *Where did you get that story?* 4 what place: *Where does he come from?* 5 in which; at which: *the house where he was born.* 6 to which: *the place where he is going.* 7 in or at which place: *I don't know where he is.* 8 to the place to which: *I will go where you go.* 9 in the place in which; at the place at which: *The book is where you left it.* 10 in any place in which; at any place at which: *Use the salve where the pain is felt.* 11 in or at which place: *They came to the town, where they stayed for the night.* 12 the place or scene: *the when and the where of it.* 13 in the case, circumstances, respect, etc., in which: *Some people worry where it does no good.* 1–3, 5–7 *adv.*, 4, 12 *n.*, 8–11, 13 *conj.*
☛ *Hom.* WARE, WEAR (for the first pronunciation of **where**).

**where·a·bout** (wer′ə bout′ *or* hwer′ə bout′) WHEREABOUTS. *adv., conj., n.*

**where·a·bouts** (wer′ə bouts′ *or* hwer′ə bouts′) 1 where; near what place: *Whereabouts can I find a doctor?* (*adv.*) *We did not know whereabouts we were.* (*conj.*) 2 the place where a person or thing is: *Do you know the whereabouts of the cottage?* 1 *adv., conj.*, 2 *n.*

**where·as** (wer az′ *or* hwer az′) 1 on the contrary; but; while: *Some children like school, whereas others do not.* 2 considering that; since: *Whereas all people are human, so all people should show humanity.* *conj.*

**where·by** (wer bī′ *or* hwer bī′) by what; by which: *There is no other way whereby it can be saved.* *adv.*

**where·in** (wer in′ *or* hwer in′) in what; in which; how. *adv., conj.*

**where·in·to** (wer in′tü *or* hwer in′tü) into what; into which. *adv., conj.*

**where·of** (wer uv′ *or* wer ov′, hwer uv′ *or* hwer ov′) of what; of which; of whom: *Solomon knew whereof he spoke.* *adv., conj.*

**where·on** (wer on′ *or* hwer on′) on which; on what: *Summer cottages occupy the land whereon the old farmhouse used to stand.* *adv., conj.*

**where·to** (wer tü′ *or* hwer tü′) 1 to what; to which; where: *He went to that place whereto he had been sent.* 2 for what purpose; why: *Whereto do you lay up riches?* *adv., conj.*

**where·up·on** (wer′ə pon′ *or* hwer′ə pon′) 1 upon what; upon which. 2 at which; after which: *The prince kissed the princess, whereupon she awoke.* *adv., conj.*

**wher·ev·er** (wer ev′ėr *or* hwer ev′ėr) where; to whatever place, in whatever place: *Wherever are you going? Sit wherever you like. She will be happy wherever she lives.* *conj., adv.*

**where·with** (wer wiŦH′ *or* wer with′, hwer wiŦH′ *or* hwer with′) with what; with which: *Wherewith shall we be fed?* *adv., conj.*

**where·with·al** (wer′wiŦH ol′ *or* hwer′ wiŦH ol′) means, supplies, or money needed: *Has she the wherewithal to pay for the trip?* *n.*

**wher·ry** (wer′ē *or* hwer′ē) 1 a light, shallow rowboat for carrying passengers and goods on rivers. 2 a light rowboat for one person, used for racing. 3 *Esp. Brit.* a broad sailboat, used chiefly on rivers. *n., pl.* **wher·ries.**

**whet** (wet *or* hwet) 1 sharpen by rubbing: *to whet a knife.* 2 stir up; awaken: *The smell of food whetted my appetite. An exciting story whets your interest.* 3 the act of

whetting.   **4** something that whets.   **5** an appetizer. **1, 2** *v.*, **whet·ted, whet·ting;**   **3–5** *n.*
☞ *Hom.* WET (for the first pronunciation of **whet**).

**wheth·er** (we<small>TH</small>′ər *or* hwe<small>TH</small>′ər)   **1** *Whether* is a conjunction expressing a choice or an alternative: *It matters little whether we go or stay. She does not know whether to work or play.*   **2** either: *Whether sick or well, she is always cheerful.*   **3** if: *He asked whether he should finish the work.*   *conj.*
**whether or no,**   in any case; no matter what happens.
☞ *Hom.* WEATHER and WETHER (for the first pronunciation of **whether**).

**whet·stone** (wet′stōn′ *or* hwet′stōn′)   a stone for sharpening knives or tools.   *n.*

**whew** (hwyü)   .  an exclamation of surprise, relief, dismay, etc.: *Whew! It's hot!*   *interj.*, *n.*

**whey** (wā *or* hwā)   the watery part of milk that separates from the curd when milk sours and becomes coagulated or when cheese is made.   *n.*
☞ *Hom.* WAY, WEIGH (for the first pronunciation of **whey**).

**which** (wich *or* hwich)   a word used:   **1** in asking questions about one or more persons or things from a group: *Which girl won the prize? (adj.) Which books are yours? (adj.) Which seems the best plan? (pron.)*   **2** in connecting a group of words with some other word in the sentence: *Take the book which is on the desk (pron.). The house was very expensive, for which reason they did not buy it (adj.).*   **3** in making statements about one or more persons or things from a group: *I don't know which dress to wear (adj.). Tell me which is best (pron.).*   **4** to mean a thing or fact that: *And, which was worse, he was late.* **1–4** *pron.*, **1–3** *adj.*
**which is which,**   which is one and which is the other.
☞ *Hom.* WITCH (for the first pronunciation of **which**).
☞ *Usage.* See note at THAT.

**which·ev·er** (wi chev′ər *or* hwi chev′ər)   **1** any one that; any that: *Take whichever you want (pron.). Buy whichever coat you like (adj.).*   **2** no matter which: *Whichever side wins, I shall be satisfied.*   *pron.*, *adj.*

**which·so·ev·er** (wich′sō ev′ər *or* hwich′sō ev′ər)   WHICHEVER.   *pron.*, *adj.*

**whiff** (wif *or* hwif)   **1** a slight gust; puff; breath: *A whiff of fresh air cleared her head.*   **2** breathe in or out gently.   **3** a slight smell; a puff of air having an odour: *We thought we detected a whiff of perfume in the empty room.*   **4** a puff of tobacco smoke.   **5** puff tobacco smoke from a pipe, etc.; smoke.   **6** a slight outburst.   **1, 3, 4, 6** *n.*, **2, 5** *v.*

**whif·fle** (wif′əl *or* hwif′əl)   **1** blow in puffs or gusts. **2** veer; shift.   **3** blow lightly; scatter.   *v.*, **whif·fled, whif·fling.**

**whif·fle·tree** (wif′əl trē′ *or* hwif′əl trē′) WHIPPLETREE.   *n.*

**Whig** (wig *or* hwig)   **1** a member or supporter of a British political party of the 18th and 19th centuries that favoured sweeping social and political reforms: *The Whig Party became the Liberal Party.*   **2** composed of, having to do with, or characteristic of Whigs.   *n.*
☞ *Hom.* WIG (for the first pronunciation of **Whig**).

**while** (wīl *or* hwīl)   **1** a time; period of time: *He kept us waiting a long while. The postman came a while ago.* **2** during the time that; in the time that; in the same time that: *While I was speaking he said nothing. Summer is pleasant while it lasts.*   **3** in contrast with the fact that; although: *While I like the colour of the coat, I do not like its shape.*   **4** pass or spend in an easy, pleasant manner

---

**whether**   1369   **whip**

hat, āge, fär; let, ēqual, tėrm; it, īce
hot, ōpen, ôrder; oil, out; cup, pút, rüle
əbove, takən, pencəl, lemən, circəs
ch, child; ng, long; sh, ship
th, thin; <small>TH</small>, then; zh, measure

(usually used with **away**): *We whiled away the day playing at the beach.*   **1** *n.*, **2, 3** *conj.*, **4** *v.* **whiled, whil·ing.**
**between whiles,**   at times; at intervals.
**the while,**   during the time.
**worth while,**   worth time, attention, or effort: *The visit to New York was certainly worth while.*
☞ *Hom.* WILE (for the first pronunciation of **while**).

**whilst** (wīlst *or* hwīlst)   WHILE (defs. 2, 3).   *conj.*

**whim** (wim *or* hwim)   **1** a sudden fancy or notion; freakish or capricious idea or desire: *She has a whim for gardening, but it won't last.*   **2** in mining, a kind of capstan used in hoisting.   *n.*
**on a whim,**   suddenly; without planning: *She went to Alberta on a whim.*

**whim·per** (wim′pər *or* hwim′pər)   **1** cry with soft broken sounds: *The sick child whimpered.*   **2** a whimpering cry or sound.   **3** say with a whimper. **4** complain in a weak way; whine.   **1, 3, 4** *v.*, **2** *n.*
—**whim′per·er,** *n.*   —**whim′per·ing·ly,** *adv.*

**whim·sey** (wim′zē *or* hwim′zē)   See WHIMSY.   *n.*, *pl.* **whim·seys.**

**whim·si·cal** (wim′zə kəl *or* hwim′zə kəl)   **1** having many odd notions or fancies; fanciful; odd.   **2** full of whims.   *adj.*   —**whim′si·cal·ly,** *adv.*

**whim·si·cal·i·ty** (wim′zə kal′ə tē *or* hwim′zə kal′ə tē)   **1** a WHIMSICAL character or quality.   **2** a WHIMSICAL notion, speech, act, etc.   *n.*, *pl.* **whim·si·cal·i·ties.**

**whim·sy** (wim′zē *or* hwim′zē)   **1** an odd or fanciful idea; whim: *It was just one of her whimsies; don't take it seriously.*   **2** odd or fanciful humour; quaintness: *Alice in Wonderland is full of whimsy.*   **3** an object or creation showing whimsy.   *n.*, *pl.* **whim·sies.**   Also, **whimsey.**

**whin** (win *or* hwin)   FURZE, GORSE.   *n.*
☞ *Hom.* WIN (for the first pronunciation of **whin**).

**whine** (wīn *or* hwīn)   **1** make a soft, drawn-out complaining cry or sound: *The dog whined to go out with us.*   **2** a soft, drawn-out complaining cry or sound. **3** complain in a peevish, childish way: *Some people are always whining about trifles.*   **4** say with a whine.   **5** a peevish, childish complaint.   **1, 3, 4** *v.*, **whined, whin·ing;** **2, 5** *n.*   —**whin′er,** *n.*   —**whin′ing·ly,** *adv.*
☞ *Hom.* WINE (for the first pronunciation of **whine**).

**whin·ny** (win′ē *or* hwin′ē)   **1** the sound that a horse makes.   **2** make such a sound: *The horse whinnied as we approached the stable.*   **3** express with such a sound. **1** *n.*, *pl.* **whin·nies;**   **2, 3** *v.*, **whin·nied, whin·ny·ing.**

**whin·stone** (win′stōn′ *or* hwin′stōn′)   BASALT or some similar hard rock.   *n.*

**whip** (wip *or* hwip)   **1** a thing to strike or beat with, usually a stick with a cord at the end.   **2** strike or beat with or as with a whip; lash: *He whipped the horse to make it go faster.*   **3** move, put, or pull quickly and suddenly: *He whipped off his coat and whipped out his knife. The thief whipped behind a tree and escaped.*   **4** a whipping motion: *a whip of the wrist.*   **5** *Informal.*   defeat: *The mayor whipped her opponent in the election.*   **6** beat cream, eggs, etc. to a froth.   **7** a dessert made by beating cream, eggs,

etc., into a froth: *Prune whip is my favourite dessert.*   **8** rouse; incite: *He whipped the crowd into a state of frenzy.*   **9** sew with stitches passing over and over an edge.   **10** wind a rope, stick, etc. closely with thread or string; wind cord, twine, or thread around something.   **11** a member of a political party who oversees the attendance of other members in a lawmaking body.   **12** a person who manages the hounds of a hunting pack.   **13** coachman.   **14** a rope and pulley.   **15** cast a fish line with a motion like that of using a whip.   **16** fish in: *to whip a stream.*   1, 4, 7, 11–14 *n.*, 2, 3, 5, 6, 8–10, 15, 16 *v.*, **whipped** or **whipt, whip·ping.**   —**whip′like′,** *adj.*   —**whip′per,** *n.*
**whip up, a** prepare or make quickly: *She whipped up some masks for us to wear on Halloween.*   **b** stir up: *We are trying to whip up some interest in speed skating.*

**whip·cord** (wip′kôrd′ *or* hwip′kôrd′)   **1** a strong, twisted cord, sometimes used for the lashes of whips.   **2** a strong worsted cloth with diagonal ridges on it.   *n.*

**whip hand**   **1** the hand that holds the whip while driving.   **2** a position of control; advantage: *A clever person often gets the whip hand over others.*

**whip·lash** (wip′lash′ *or* hwip′lash′)   **1** a lash of a whip.   **2** an injury to the neck resulting from a sudden jolt that snaps the head backward and then forward: *A person in a vehicle that is struck from behind by another vehicle can suffer whiplash.*   *n.*

**whip·per–snap·per** (wip′ər snap′ər *or* hwip′ər snap′ər) an insignificant person who thinks he or she is clever or important.   *n.*

**whip·pet** (wip′it *or* hwip′it)   a breed of swift, lean racing and hunting dog that looks like a small greyhound: *The whippet was developed from a cross between the greyhound and a terrier.*   *n.*

**whip·ping** (wip′ing *or* hwip′ing)   **1** a beating; flogging.   **2** an arrangement of cord, twine, or the like, wound about a thing: *We fastened the broken rod with a whipping of wire.*   **3** ppr. of WHIP.   1, 2 *n.*, 3 *v.*

**whipping boy**   **1** formerly, a boy who was educated with a young prince and made to take punishment due to the prince.   **2** any person who takes the blame for the wrongdoings of others; a scapegoat.

**whip·ple·tree** (wip′əl trē′ *or* hwip′əl trē′)   the swinging bar of a carriage or wagon, to which the traces of a harness are fastened.   *n.*   Also, **whiffletree.**

**whip–poor–will** (wip′ər wil′ *or* wip′ər wil′, hwip′ər wil′ *or* hwip′ər wil′)   a North American bird whose call sounds somewhat like its name: *The whip-poor-will is active at night or in the twilight.*   *n.*

**whip·saw** (wip′sô *or* hwip′sô)   **1** a long, narrow saw with its ends held in a frame.   **2** cut with a whipsaw.   **3** *Informal.*   get the better of a person no matter what he or she does.   1 *n.*, 2, 3 *v.*

**whip·stock** (wip′stok′ *or* hwip′stok′)   the handle of a whip.   *n.*

**whir** or **whirr** (wėr *or* hwėr)   **1** a buzzing noise as of something turning at high speed: *the whir of a small machine.*   **2** operate or move with such a noise: *The motor whirs.*   1 *n.*, 2 *v.*, **whirred, whir·ring.**
☛ *Hom.* WERE (for the first pronunciation of **whir**).

**whirl** (wėrl *or* hwėrl)   **1** turn or swing round and round; spin: *The leaves whirled in the wind.*   **2** move round and round: *We whirled about the room. He whirled the club.* **3** move or carry quickly: *We were whirled away in an airplane.*   **4** a whirling movement: *whirls of smoke.*   **5** something that whirls.   **6** feel dizzy or confused.   **7** a dizzy or confused condition: *Her thoughts are in a whirl.*   **8** great activity; a rapid round of happenings, parties, etc.: *We had a rest after the whirl of Christmas holidays.*   1–3, 6 *v.*, 4, 5, 7, 8 *n.*   —**whirl′er,** *n.*
☛ *Hom.* WHORL (wėrl, hwėrl).

**whirl·i·gig** (wėr′lē gig′ *or* hwėr′lē gig′)   **1** a toy that whirls.   **2** MERRY-GO-ROUND.   **3** something that whirls round and round.   **4** a beetle that circles about on the surface of water.   *n.*

**whirl·pool** (wėrl′pül′ *or* hwėrl′pül′)   **1** water whirling round and round rapidly and violently.   **2** anything like a whirlpool.   *n.*

**whirl·wind** (wėrl′wind′ *or* hwėrl′wind′)   **1** a current of air whirling violently round and round; whirling windstorm.   **2** anything like a whirlwind.   *n.*

**whirr** (wėr′ *or* hwėr)   See WHIR.   *n., v.*

**whish** (wish *or* hwish)   **1** a soft rushing sound; whiz; swish.   **2** make a soft rushing sound.   1 *n.*, 2 *v.*
☛ *Hom.* WISH (for the first pronunciation of **whish**).

**whisk** (wisk *or* hwisk)   **1** remove, wipe, brush, etc. with a quick sweeping motion: *He whisked the crumbs from the table. She whisked the letter out of sight. The waitress whisked my plate away.*   **2** move or carry quickly or nimbly: *They whisked the children off to bed. The mouse whisked into its hole. The prime minister was whisked away in his limousine.*   **3** a quick sweeping or whipping movement: *with a whisk of the broom, a whisk of the horse's tail.*   **4** WHISK BROOM.   **5** a small wire kitchen utensil for beating eggs, cream, etc. by hand.   **6** beat or whip eggs, etc. to a froth.   1, 2, 6 *v.*, 3–5 *n.*

**whisk broom**   a small, short-handled broom for brushing clothes, etc.

**whisk·er** (wis′kər *or* hwis′kər)   **1** one of the hairs growing on a man's face.   **2** a long, stiff hair growing near the mouth of a cat, rat, etc.   **3** Usually, **whiskers,** *pl.* the hair growing on a man's face, especially that on his cheeks and chin.   *n.*

**whisk·ered** (wis′kərd *or* hwis′kərd)   having WHISKERS.   *adj.*

**whisk·er·y** (wis′kə rē *or* hwis′kə rē)   **1** WHISKERED.   **2** resembling WHISKERS.   *adj.*

**whis·key** (wis′kē *or* hwis′kē)   See WHISKY.   *n., pl.* **whis·keys.**

**whis·ky** (wis′kē *or* hwis′kē)   a strong alcoholic drink made from grain: *Whisky is about half alcohol.*   *n., pl.* **whis·kies.**   Also, **whiskey.**
☛ *Etym.* A shortened form of *whiskybae,* originally *usquebaugh,* from Gaelic *uisge beatha* 'water of life'.

**whisky–jack** (wis′kē jak′ *or* hwis′kē jak′) *Cdn.* CANADA JAY.   *n.*   Also, **whiskey-jack.**
☛ *Etym.* A variation of older *whisky-john,* from an Algonquian word, such as Cree *weskuchanis* (literally, 'little blacksmith', from the bird's sooty colour), which would have sounded like *whisky-john* to English ears.

**whis·per** (wis′pər *or* hwis′pər)   **1** speak very softly, with little or no vibration of the vocal cords: *We could hear them whispering behind us. She whispered the news in my ear.*   **2** the act or an instance of whispering: *She spoke in a whisper. They were speaking in whispers.*   **3** tell secretly or privately: *It is whispered that his health is failing.*   **4** something told secretly or privately: *No whisper about having a new teacher has come to our ears.*   **5** make a soft, rustling sound: *The wind whispered in the pines.* **6** a soft, rustling sound. 1, 3, 5 *v.*, 2, 4, 6 *n.* —**whis′per•er,** *n.*

**whist** (wist *or* hwist) a card game, resembling bridge, for two pairs of players: *Contract bridge developed from whist.* *n.*

**whis•tle** (wis′əl *or* hwis′əl) **1** make a clear, shrill sound by forcing breath through one's teeth or lips: *The boy whistled and his dog ran to him quickly.* **2** the sound made by whistling. **3** an instrument for making whistling sounds. **4** blow a whistle: *The police officer whistled for the automobile to stop.* **5** produce or utter by whistling: *to whistle a tune.* **6** call, signal, or direct by a whistle. **7** move with a shrill sound: *The wind whistled around the house.* 1, 4–7 *v.*, **whis•tled, whis•tling;** 2, 3 *n.*
**wet one's whistle,** *Informal.* take a drink.
**whistle for,** *Informal.* go without; fail to get.
**whistle in the dark,** try to be courageous or hopeful in a fearful or trying situation.

**whis•tler** (wis′lər *or* hwis′lər) **1** a person or thing that whistles. **2** any of several whistling birds. **3** *Cdn.* an animal related to the groundhog and gopher, found in the mountainous parts of western Canada; hoary marmot. *n.*

**whis•tle-stop** (wis′əl stop′ *or* hwis′əl stop′) *Informal.* **1** a small, little-known town along a railway line at which a train stops only when signalled. **2** a stop at such a town or station for a brief appearance or speech, as in a political campaign tour. **3** of or having to do with a whistle-stop. **4** make a series of electioneering appearances or speeches at stations along a railway line. 1, 2 *n.*, 3 *adj.*, 4 *v.*, **whis•tle-stopped, whis•tle-stop•ping.**

**whit** (wit *or* hwit) a very small bit: *The sick woman is not a whit better.* *n.*
☞ *Hom.* WIT (for the first pronunciation of **whit**).

**white** (wīt *or* hwīt) **1** the colour of snow or salt. **2** having this colour or one approaching it: *white hair.* **3** white colouring matter. **4** white clothing. **5** wearing white clothing. **6** something white; a white or colourless part: *Take the whites of four eggs.* **7** the central part of a butt in archery (formerly painted white). **8** a blank space in printing. **9** pale: *She turned white with fear.* **10** light-coloured: *white wines, white meat.* **11** having a light-coloured skin; noting or pertaining to the Caucasoid race. **12** a member of a light-skinned race. **13** silvery; grey. **14** snowy. **15** blank. **16** spotless; pure; innocent. **17** *Informal.* honourable, trustworthy; fair. **18** ultra-conservative; reactionary; royalist. **19** good; beneficent: *white magic.* 1, 3, 4, 6–8, 12 *n.*, 2, 5, 9–11, 13–19 *adj.*, **whit•er, whit•est.** —**white′ness,** *n.*
**bleed white,** use up or take away all of someone's money, strength, etc.: *His good-for-nothing son has bled the old man white.*

**white ant** a pale-white insect; termite: *White ants eat wood and are very destructive to buildings.*

**white•bait** (wīt′bāt *or* hwīt′bāt) **1** a young herring or sprat about 3 to 5 cm long. **2** any of various very small fish used for food. *n., pl.* **white•bait.**

**white blood cell** any of the white or colourless blood cells found in the blood and lymph of vertebrates; leucocyte: *White blood cells help the body to fight infection.*

**white•cap** (wīt′kap *or* hwīt′kap) a wave with a foaming white crest: *Whitecaps are seen on windy days.* *n.*

**white cedar** **1** an arborvitae of eastern North America, found in Canada from Nova Scotia to Manitoba. **2** the wood of this tree.

hat, āge, fär; let, ēqual, tėrm; it, īce
hot, ōpen, ôrder; oil, out; cup, put, rüle
above, taken, pencil, lemon, circus
ch, child; ng, long; sh, ship
th, thin; ᴛʜ, then; zh, measure

**white clover** a kind of clover with white flowers, common in fields and lawns.

**white coal** water used as a source of power.

**white–col•lar** (wīt′kol′ər *or* hwīt′kol′ər) of or having to do with clerical, professional, or business work or workers. Compare with BLUE-COLLAR. *adj.*

**white corpuscle** WHITE BLOOD CELL.

**white dwarf** a small star of little brightness. Compare with RED GIANT.

**white elephant** anything that is expensive and troublesome to keep and take care of.

**white feather** a symbol of cowardice.
**show the white feather,** act like a coward.

**white•fish** (wīt′fish *or* hwīt′fish′) a food fish having white or silvery sides, found in lakes and streams. *n., pl.* **white•fish** or **white•fish•es.**

**white flag** a plain white flag used as a sign of truce or surrender.

**white gold** an alloy of gold that looks much like platinum and is used for jewellery, commonly containing gold, nickel, copper, and zinc.

**White•hall** (wīt′hol′ *or* hwīt′hol) **1** in London: **a** a former palace. **b** a street where many government offices are located. **2** the British government or its policies. *n.*

**white heat** **1** extremely great heat at which things give off a dazzling, white light. **2** a state of extremely great activity, excitement, or feeling.

**white–hot** (wīt′hot′ *or* hwīt′hot′) **1** white with heat; extremely hot. **2** very enthusiastic; excited; violent. *adj.*

**White House** (wīt′hous′ *or* hwīt′hous′) **1** in Washington, D.C., the official residence of the President of the United States. **2** *Informal.* the office, authority, opinion, etc. of the President of the United States.

**white lead** a compound of lead used in making paint; basic carbonate of lead.

**white lie** a lie about some small matter, especially one told to avoid being rude or hurting someone's feelings: *I was very tempted to tell a white lie and say that I liked her ugly dress.*

**white magic** good magic. Compare with BLACK MAGIC.

**white matter** tissue of the brain, spinal cord, etc. that consists chiefly of nerve fibres.

**whit•en** (wī′tən *or* hwī′tən) make or become white: *She used bleach to whiten the sheets. He whitened when he heard the bad news.* *v.*

**white noise** the sound produced by using the whole range of audible frequencies at once.

**white oak** **1** an oak tree of eastern North America having light grey or whitish bark and hard, durable wood.

See OAK for picture.    2 any similar species of oak.   3 the wood of any of these trees.

**white·out** (wī′tout′ *or* hwī′tout′) *Cdn.*    1 an arctic weather condition in which the snow-covered ground, the cloudy sky, and the horizon become a continuous, shadowless mass of dazzling white.   2 a temporary blindness resulting from this condition.   3 a winter weather condition in which blowing snow completely fills the range of vision: *Many highway traffic accidents are caused by whiteouts. n.*

**white paper**   a minor type of government report.

**white pepper**   a hot-tasting seasoning made by grinding the dried, husked berries of the black pepper vine.

**white pine**   1 any of several species of pine having soft, light wood, especially the **eastern white pine** of the Great Lakes and St. Lawrence forest regions, and the **western white pine** of southern British Columbia.   2 the wood of any of these trees, much used for building.

**white plague**   TUBERCULOSIS.

**white potato**   a very common variety of potato with a whitish inside; an Irish potato.

**White Russian**   1 a Russian living in Belarus, north of the Ukraine.   2 a Russian who fought on the czarist side during the Russian Revolution.

**white sauce**   a sauce made of milk, butter, and flour cooked together.

**white sound**   WHITE NOISE.

**white spruce**   a common spruce tree of the northern forest, also found throughout the rest of Canada, larger and taller than the black spruce, having long, slender cones, and bluish-green needles often covered with a whitish, powdery coating called a bloom.

**white–tail** (wīt′tāl′ *or* hwīt′tāl′)   WHITE-TAILED DEER. *n.*

**white–tailed deer** (wīt′tāld′ *or* hwīt′tāld′)   a North American deer closely resembling the mule deer, but having a broad, relatively long tail with a wide white fringe and underside, and antlers that arch forward.

**white·thorn** (wīt′thôrn′ *or* hwīt′thôrn′)   the common HAWTHORN. *n.*

**white·wash** (wī′twosh *or* hwī′twosh)   1 a liquid for whitening walls, woodwork, etc., usually made of lime and water.   2 whiten with whitewash.   3 cover up the faults or mistakes of.   4 a covering up of faults or mistakes.   5 anything that covers up faults or mistakes.   6 *Informal.* defeat in a game without a score for the loser: *We whitewashed our opponents 7-0.*   7 *Informal.*   a defeat of this kind.    1, 4, 5, 7 *n.*, 2, 3, 6 *v.*

**white water**   RAPIDS (def. 3).

**white·wood** (wī′twùd′ *or* hwī′twùd′)   1 a tree with light-coloured wood, such as a tulip tree, linden, etc.   2 the wood. *n.*

**whith·er** (wiᴛH′ər *or* hwiᴛH′ər)   to what place; to which place; where: *He did not know whither she had gone. adv., conj.*
☛ *Hom.* WITHER (for the first pronunciation of **whither**).

**whit·ing**[1] (wī′ting *or* hwī′ting)   1 a European fish like the cod.   2 the silver hake.   3 any of several other food fishes of the cod family.   *n.*, *pl.* **whit·ing** *or* **whit·ings**.

**whit·ing**[2] (wī′ting *or* hwī′ting)   a powdered white chalk, used in making putty, whitewash, and silver polish.  *n.*

**whit·ish** (wī′tish *or* hwī′tish)    almost white: *a whitish dress. adj.*

**whit·low** (wit′lō *or* hwit′lō)   a usually pus-filled inflammation of a finger or toe, especially near the nail; felon. *n.*

**Whit·sun** (wit′sən *or* hwit′sən)   of or having to do with Whitsunday or Whitsuntide. *adj.*

**Whit·sun·day** (wit′sən dā′ *or* hwit′sən dā′, wit′sən′dē *or* hwit′sun′dē)   the seventh Sunday after Easter; Pentecost. *n.*

**Whit·sun·tide** (wit′sən tīd′ *or* hwit′sən tīd′)   the week beginning with Whitsunday, especially the first three days. *n.*

**whit·tle** (wit′əl *or* hwit′əl)   1 cut shavings or chips from wood, etc. with a knife.   2 shape wood with a knife; carve: *The old sailor whittled a boat for Jim. v.,*
**whit·tled, whit·tling.  —whit′tler,** *n.*
**whittle down** *or* **away,**   cut down little by little: *We tried to whittle down our expenses.*

**whiz** *or* **whizz** (wiz *or* hwiz)   1 a humming or hissing sound.   2 make a humming or hissing sound; move or rush with such a sound: *An arrow whizzed past his head.*   3 *Informal.*   a very clever person; an expert.    1, 3 *n.*, 2 *v.*, **whizzed, whiz·zing.**

**who** (hü)   a word used:   1 in asking about the identity of a person or persons: *Who is your friend? Who told you?*   2 in connecting a group of words with some previous word in the sentence: *The girl who spoke is my best friend. We saw men who were working in the fields.*   3 in making statements about the identity of a person or persons: *I don't know who will be there.    pron., poss.* **whose,** *obj.* **whom.**
**who's who,**   **a** which is one person and which is the other.   **b** which people are important.
☛ *Usage.*  **Who** is used mainly as a subject in a sentence: *Who gave you the book? The woman who spoke at the meeting is a friend of my parents.* However, it is also often used in informal English as an object: *Who were you talking to?* In formal and most written English, the standard object form of this pronoun is **whom:** *The woman whom you heard at the meeting is a friend of my parents.* When a preposition comes first, **whom** is always used, in informal and formal English: *To whom were you talking?* See also usage notes at WHOSE and THAT.

**WHO**   World Health Organization.

**whoa** (wō *or* hwō)   stop! (*used especially to horses*). *interj.*

**who'd** (hüd)   1 who would: *Who'd like to go along?*   2 who had: *He didn't know who'd committed the crime.*

**who·dun·it** (hü dun′it) *Informal.*   a story or motion picture dealing with crime, especially murder, and its detection. *n.*

**who·ev·er** (hü ev′ər)   1 who; any person that: *Whoever wants the book may have it.*   2 no matter who: *Whoever else goes hungry, she won't. pron.*

**whole** (hōl)   1 having all its parts or elements; complete: *a whole set of dishes.*   2 comprising the full quantity, amount, extent, number, etc.; entire: *a whole melon, a whole day.*   3 all of a thing; the total: *Four quarters make a whole.*   4 anything complete in itself; a

system. **5** not injured, broken or defective: *to escape with a whole skin.* **6** in one piece; undivided: *to swallow a piece of meat whole.* **7** not fractional; integral: *a whole number.* **8** well; healthy. **9** having the same father and mother: *They are whole brothers.* 1, 2, 5–9 *adj.*, 3, 4 *n.*
**as a whole,** as one complete thing; altogether.
**made out of whole cloth,** *Informal.* entirely false or imaginary.
**on the whole, a** considering everything. **b** for the most part.
☞ *Hom.* HOLE.

**whole–heart·ed** (hōl′här′tid) earnest; sincere; hearty; cordial: *The returning athletes were given a whole-hearted welcome.* *adj.* —**whole′-heart′ed·ly,** *adv.* —**whole′-heart′ed·ness,** *n.*

**whole note** in music, a note having the longest time value in standard notation, used as the basis for determining the time value of all other notes. It is equal to two half notes, four quarter notes, etc. See NOTE for picture.

**whole number** a number denoting zero or one or more whole things or units; a number that does not contain a fraction; integer. 1, 2, –15, 106, etc., are whole numbers; ½, ¾, and ⅞ are fractions; 1⅜, 2½, and 12⅔ are mixed numbers.

**whole rest** in music, a rest as long as a WHOLE NOTE. See REST for picture.

**whole·sale** (hōl′sāl′) **1** the sale of goods in large quantities at a time, usually to retailers rather than to consumers directly: *She buys at wholesale and sells at retail.* **2** in large lots or quantities: *The wholesale price of this coat is $100; the retail price is $130 (adj.). He bought the team sweaters wholesale (adv.).* **3** selling in large quantities: *a wholesale fruit business.* **4** sell or be sold in large quantities: *They wholesale these jackets at $40 each. Such jackets usually wholesale for much less.* **5** broad and general; extensive and indiscriminate: *Avoid wholesale condemnation.* 1 *n.*, 2, 3, 5 *adj.*, 2 *adv.*, 4 *v.*, **whole·saled, whole·sal·ing.**

**whole·sal·er** (hōl′sā′lər) a merchant who sells goods wholesale. *n.*

**whole·some** (hōl′səm) **1** good for the health; healthful: *Milk is a wholesome food.* **2** healthy-looking; suggesting health: *a wholesome face.* **3** good for the mind or morals; beneficial: *She reads only wholesome books.* *adj.* —**whole′some·ly,** *adv.* —**whole′some·ness,** *n.*

**whole step** in music, an interval equal to one sixth of an octave, such as D to E, or E to F♯.

**whole tone** WHOLE STEP.

**whole–wheat** (hōl′wēt′ or hōl′hwēt′) made of the entire wheat kernel. *adj.*

**who'll** (hül) who will; who shall.

**whol·ly** (hōl′lē or hō′lē) to the whole amount or extent; completely; entirely: *The boy was wholly cured.* *adv.*
☞ *Hom.* HOLEY, HOLY, HOLI, (for the second pronunciation of **wholly**).

**whom** (hüm) the object form of **who**: *Whom do you like best? He does not know whom to believe. The girl to whom I spoke is my cousin.* *pron.*
☞ *Usage.* See notes at WHO and THAT.

**whom·ev·er** (hü′mev′ər) **1** whom; any person whom. **2** no matter whom. *pron.*

# whole-hearted 1373 whorl

hat, āge, fär; let, ēqual, tėrm; it, īce
hot, ōpen, ôrder; oil, out; cup, pút, rüle
əbove, takən, pencəl, lemən, circəs
ch, child; ng, long; sh, ship
th, thin; ᴛʜ, then; zh, measure

**whom·so·ev·er** (hüm′sō ev′ər) any person whom. *pron.*

**whoop** (hüp, wüp, or hwüp) **1** a loud cry or shout: *When land was sighted, the sailor let out a whoop of joy.* **2** shout loudly. **3** call, urge, drive, etc. with shouts: *to whoop dogs on.* **4** the cry of an owl, crane, etc.; a hoot. **5** hoot. **6** the loud, gasping noise a person with whooping cough makes after a fit of coughing. **7** make this noise. 1, 4, 6 *n.*, 2, 3, 5, 7 *v.*
**whoop it up,** *Informal.* make a noisy disturbance.
☞ *Hom.* HOOP (for the first pronunciation of **whoop**).

**whoop·ing cough** (hü′ping) an infectious disease of children, characterized by fits of coughing that end with a loud, gasping sound.

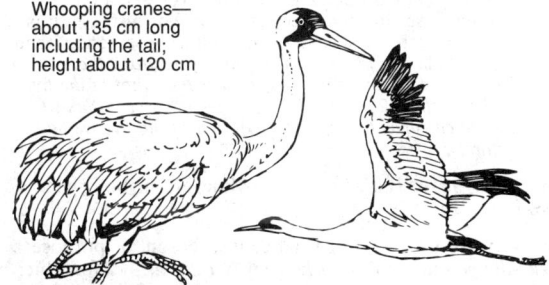
Whooping cranes—about 135 cm long including the tail; height about 120 cm

**whooping crane** a very large white bird having a long neck and legs, with black wing tips and a red patch on the face: *The whooping crane is the tallest of Canadian birds.*

**whop·per** (wop′ər or hwop′ər) *Informal.* **1** something very large. **2** a big lie. *n.*

**whop·ping** (wop′ing or hwop′ing) *Informal.* very large of its kind; huge: *a whopping great steak, a whopping defeat.* *adj., adv.*

**whore** (hôr) **1** prostitute. **2** an unchaste woman. **3** have sexual intercourse with whores. 1, 2 *n.*, 3 *v.*, **whored, whor·ing.**
☞ *Hom.* HOAR.

A fingerprint with a whorl  The whorled shell of a snail  The whorled leaves of the starflower, a North American wildflower

**whorl** (wėrl or hwėrl, wôrl or hwôrl) **1** a circle of leaves or flowers round a stem of a plant. **2** one of the turns of a spiral shell. **3** any coil or curl, especially of something

that is whirling or that suggests a whirling movement. **4** a type of fingerprint in which the ridges in the centre turn through at least one complete circle. *n.*
☞ *Hom.* WHIRL (for the first two pronunciations of **whorl**).

**whorled** (wėrld *or* hwėrld, wôrld *or* hwôrld) **1** having a WHORL or whorls. **2** arranged in a WHORL. *adj.*
☞ *Hom.* WORLD (for the first pronunciation of **whorled**).

**whor·tle·ber·ry** (wėr′təl ber′ē *or* hwėr′təl ber′ē) **1** a small, blackish berry much like the huckleberry. **2** the shrub that it grows on. *n., pl.* **whor·tle·ber·ries.**

**who's** (hüz) **1** who is: *Who's that man?* **2** who has: *Who's been eating my porridge?*
☞ *Hom.* **whose.**

**whose** (hüz) the possessive form of **who** and of **which**; of or relating to whom or which: *The girl whose work got the prize is the youngest in her class. Whose book is this? pron.*
☞ *Hom.* WHO'S.
☞ *Usage.* **Whose** is usually used to refer to people, but it can also be used for things, in order to make a long written or spoken sentence smoother. For instance, it is easier to read the second of the following sentences than the first: 1) *The plant has three new generators, the combined capacity of which is greater than that of the five we had before.* 2) *The plant has three new generators whose combined capacity is greater than that of the five we had before.*

**who·so·ev·er** (hü′sō ev′ər) whoever; anybody who. *pron.*

**why** (wī *or* hwī) **1** for what cause, reason, or purpose: *Why did you do it? I don't know why I did it.* **2** for which; because of which: *That is the reason why he failed.* **3** the reason for which: *That is why he raised the question.* **4** the cause; reason: *I can't understand the whys and wherefores of her behaviour.* **5** an expression used to show surprise, doubt, etc., or just to fill in: *Why! The cage is empty. Why, yes, I will if you wish.* 1–3 *adv.,* 4 *n., pl.* **whys;** 5 *interj.*

**W.I. 1** West Indies. **2** West Indian.

**Wic·ca** (wic′ə) the belief in the power of witchcraft, whose followers are organized in covens. *n.*

**Wic·can** (wik′ən) **1** a devotee of WICCA: *Wiccans hold regular meetings in groups called* COVENS. **2** of or having to do with WICCA. 1 *n.,* 2 *adj.*

**wick** (wik) the part of an oil lamp or candle that is lighted, usually a loosely-twisted cord through which oil or melted wax is drawn up and burned. *n.*

**wick·ed** (wik′id) **1** bad; evil; sinful: *a wicked person, wicked deeds.* **2** mischievous; playfully sly: *a wicked smile.* **3** *Informal.* unpleasant; severe: *a wicked task, a wicked storm. adj.* —**wick′ed·ly,** *adv.*

**wick·ed·ness** (wik′id nis) **1** sin; the state of being wicked. **2** a wicked thing or act; something evil. *n.*

**wick·er** (wik′ər) **1** slender, easily bent branches or twigs that can be woven together: *Wicker is used in making baskets and furniture.* **2** made of wicker. **3** covered with wicker. *n.*

**wick·er·work** (wik′ər wėrk′) **1** twigs or branches woven together; wicker. **2** anything made of wicker. **3** the art or business of making things of wicker. *n.*

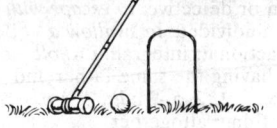
A croquet wicket

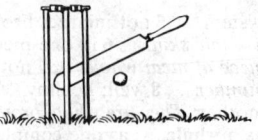
A cricket wicket—
71 cm high and 23 cm wide

**wick·et** (wik′it) **1** a small door or gate: *The big door has a wicket in it.* **2** a small window or opening, often protected by a screen or grating: *to buy tickets at a wicket.* **3** in croquet, a wire arch stuck in the ground to knock the ball through. **4** in cricket, either of the two sets of sticks that the batsman protects by hitting the ball. **5** the level space between these. **6** one batsman's turn. *n.*

**wick·et-keep·er** (wik′it kē′pər) in cricket, the player who stands behind the wicket. *n.*

**wick·ing** (wik′ing) material for wicks. *n.*

**wick·i·up** (wik′ē up′) a rude shelter, such as a lean-to; originally, a brush or mat-covered shelter among certain Algonquian Indians. *n.*

**wide** (wīd) **1** filling space from side to side; not narrow; broad: *a wide street, the wide ocean.* **2** extending a certain distance from side to side, measured at right angles to length: *The door is 90 centimetres wide.* **3** to a great or relatively great extent from side to side: *wide apart.* **4** over an extensive space or region: *They travel far and wide.* **5** a wide space or expanse. **6** full; ample; roomy: *wide shoes.* **7** of great range: *wide reading.* **8** far or fully open; distended: *to stare with wide eyes.* **9** to the full extent; fully: *Open your mouth wide.* **10** far from a named point, object, target, etc. **11** aside; astray. **12** uttered with a relatively relaxed tongue. 1, 2, 6–8, 10, 12 *adj.,* **wid·er, wid·est;** 3, 4, 9–11 *adv.,* 5 *n.*
—**wide′ness,** *n.*

**wide of,** far from: *Her guess was wide of the truth. The shot was wide of the mark.*

**wide-a·wake** (wī′də wāk′) **1** with the eyes wide open; fully awake. **2** alert; keen; knowing: *A watchdog must be a wide-awake guard against danger. adj.*

**wide-eyed** (wī′dīd′) **1** with the eyes wide open. **2** greatly surprised; astonished: *The little girl was wide-eyed with surprise. adj.*

**wide·ly** (wī′dlē) **1** to a wide extent: *a widely distributed plant, a man who is widely known, to be widely read, widely opened eyes.* **2** very; extremely: *The boys gave two widely different accounts of the quarrel. adv.*

**wid·en** (wī′dən) make or become wide or wider: *He widened the path through the forest. The river widens as it flows. v.*

**wide-o·pen** (wī′dō′pən) **1** opened as much as possible. **2** lax in the enforcement of laws, especially those having to do with the sale of liquor, with gambling, and with prostitution. *adj.*

**wide·spread** (wīd′spred′) **1** spread widely or fully: *widespread wings.* **2** spread over a wide space: *a widespread flood.* **3** occurring in many places or among many persons far apart: *a widespread belief. adj.*

**widg·eon** (wij′ən) any of several closely related freshwater ducks, especially the European widgeon, having a rusty head and neck with a buff forehead and crown, and the American widgeon, or baldpate, having a white forehead and crown and a green patch on either side of the head. *n., pl.* **widg·eons** or (*esp. collectively*) **widg·eon.**

**wid·ow** (wid′ō)  1 a woman whose husband is dead and who has not married again.  2 make a widow or widower of: *She was widowed when she was only thirty years old.*  3 in typesetting or word processing, a word left alone on a line.   1, 3 *n.*, 2 *v.*

**wid·ow·er** (wid′ō ər)   a man whose wife is dead and who has not married again.   *n.*

**wid·ow·hood** (wid′ō hu̇d′)   the condition or time of being a widow.   *n.*

**widow's mite**   a small amount of money given cheerfully by a poor person.

**width** (width)   1 how wide a thing is; distance across; breadth: *The width of the room is four metres.*  2 a piece of a certain width: *curtains taking two widths of cloth.*   *n.*

**wield** (wēld)   hold and use; manage; control: *to wield a sword, to wield power.*   *v.*  —**wield′er,** *n.*
☛ *Hom.* WHEELED (wēld).

**wie·ner** (wē′nər)   a bland reddish sausage, usually made of beef and pork; frankfurter.   *n.*

**wiener roast**   an outdoor social function at which wieners are roasted or boiled over an open fire.

**wie·ner·wurst** (wē′nər wėrst′)   wiener; frankfurter.   *n.*

**wife** (wīf)   a married woman: *Ella is Tom's wife.*   *n.*, *pl.* **wives.**  —**wife′less,** *adj.*
**take to wife,**   marry.

**wife·hood** (wīf′hu̇d′)   the condition of being a wife.   *n.*

**wife·ly** (wīf′lē)   of a wife; like a wife; suitable for a wife.   *adj.*, **wife·li·er, wife·li·est.**

**wig** (wig)   an artificial covering of hair for the head: *The bald man wore a wig. British judges wear wigs in court.*   *n.*
☛ *Hom.* WHIG (wig).

**wig·gle** (wig′əl)   1 move with short, quick movements from side to side; wriggle: *Worms wiggle.*  2 a wiggling movement.   1 *v.*, **wig·gled, wig·gling;**   2 *n.*

**wig·gler** (wig′lər)   1 a person or thing that wiggles.  2 the larva of a mosquito.   *n.*

**wig·gly** (wig′lē)   1 wiggling: *a wiggly little caterpillar.*  2 wavy: *He drew a wiggly line under the heading.*   *adj.*, **wig·gli·er, wig·gli·est.**

**wig·wag** (wig′wag′)   1 move to and fro.  2 signal by movements of arms, flags, lights, etc., according to a code.  3 such signalling.  4 the message signalled.   1, 2 *v.*, **wig·wagged, wig·wag·ging;**   3, 4 *n.*  —**wig′wag′ger,** *n.*

An Algonquian wigwam

**wig·wam** (wig′wom)   1 a kind of dwelling traditionally used by Amerindian peoples from Manitoba to the Atlantic Provinces, consisting of an arched or cone-shaped framework of poles covered with hide, bark, mats made from rushes, etc. Compare with TEEPEE.  2 TEEPEE.   *n.*

**widow**   1375   **wild oats**

hat, āge, fär; let, ēqual, tėrm; it, īce
hot, ōpen, ôrder; oil, out; cup, pu̇t, rüle
əbove, takən, pencəl, lemən, circəs

ch, child; ng, long; sh, ship
th, thin; ᴛʜ, then; zh, measure

**wild** (wīld)   1 living or growing in the forests or fields; not tamed or cultivated: *The tiger is a wild animal.*  2 with no people living in it: *wild land.*  3 not civilized; savage: *He is reading about the wild tribes of ancient times in Europe.*  4 not checked; not restrained: *a wild rush for the ball.*  5 not in proper control or order: *wild hair.*  6 boisterous: *wild boys.*  7 violently excited; frantic: *wild with rage, wild with joy.*  8 violent: *a wild storm.*  9 rash; crazy: *a wild scheme.*  10 *Informal.* very eager.  11 unconventional, barbaric, or fanciful: *a wild tune or song.*  12 far from the mark.  13 of a playing card, able to be used to represent any number or suit: *The jokers are used as wild cards in some games.*  14 in a wild manner or to a wild degree.  15 **wilds,** *pl.* wild country.   1–13 *adj.*, 12, 14 *adv.*, 15 *n.*  —**wild′ly,** *adv.*  —**wild′ness,** *n.*
**run wild,**   live or grow without restraint.
**wild and woolly,**   rough and uncivilized like the Canadian West during frontier times; rough-and-tumble.

**wild boar**   a wild pig of Europe, southern Asia, and northern Africa.

**wild·cat** (wīld′kat′)   1 any of several kinds of wild animal related to the common cat, but larger: *The cougar and the lynx are two kinds of wildcat.* See COUGAR and LYNX for pictures.  2 BOBCAT.  3 a fierce fighter.  4 a well drilled for oil or gas in a region where none has been found before; a test well.  5 drill wells in regions not known to contain oil.  6 not authorized by proper union officials; precipitated by small groups or local unions: *a wildcat strike.*  1–4, 6 *n.*, 5 *v.*, **wild·cat·ted, wild·cat·ting.**  —**wild′cat′ter,** *n.*

**wil·de·beest** (wil′də bēst′)   the GNU, an African antelope.   *n.*

**wil·der·ness** (wil′dər nis)   1 a wild or desolate region with few or no people living in it.  2 a bewildering mass or collection: *a wilderness of streets.*   *n.*

**wild–eyed** (wīld′īd′)   staring wildly or angrily.   *adj.*

**wild·fire** (wīld′fīr′)   1 a substance that burns fiercely and is hard to put out, formerly used in warfare; GREEK FIRE.  2 WILL-O'-THE-WISP.   *n.*
**like wildfire,**   very rapidly: *The news spread like wildfire.*

**wild·flow·er** (wīld′flou′ər)   1 any flowering plant that grows in the woods, fields, etc.; an uncultivated plant.  2 a flower of such a plant.   *n.* Also, **wild flower.**

**wild·fowl** (wīld′foul′)   birds ordinarily hunted, such as wild ducks or geese, partridges, quail, and pheasants.   *n.*

**wild–goose chase** (wīld′güs′chās′)   a useless search or pursuit.

**wild·life** (wīl′dlīf′)   wild animals and birds as a group, especially those native to a particular area: *the northern wildlife.*   *n.*

**wild mustard**   one of the commonest Canadian weeds, an annual plant growing up to one metre high, having somewhat hairy leaves and clusters of small, bright-yellow flowers: *Wild mustard was introduced to North America from Europe and Asia.*

**wild oats**   1 oatlike grass growing as a weed in meadows, etc.  2 youthful dissipation.

**sow one's wild oats,** indulge in youthful dissipation before settling down in life.

**wild pansy** a common European wildflower, a species of violet having small, usually purple flowers: *The pansy commonly found in gardens is derived mainly from the wild pansy.*

**wild rice** *Cdn.* **1** a tall North American grass that grows in wet places, as along the edges of lakes. **2** its edible grain, which resembles rice.

**wild rose** *Cdn.* any uncultivated rose, especially the prickly rose: *The wild rose is the floral emblem of Alberta.*

**wild West** or **Wild West** western Canada during pioneer days.

**wile** (wīl) **1** a trick to deceive; cunning way: *The princess was turned to stone by the witch's wiles.* **2** subtle trickery; slyness; craftiness. **3** coax; lure; entice: *The sunshine wiled me outside.* 1, 2 *n.*, 3 *v.*, **wiled, wil·ing.**
☛ *Hom.* WHILE (wīl).

**wil·ful** (wil'fəl) See WILLFUL. *adj.*

**wil·ful·ly** (wil'fə lē) See WILLFULLY. *adv.*

**wil·i·ness** (wī'lē nis) a wily quality; craftiness; slyness. *n.*

**will**[1] (wil; *unstressed*, wəl) a word used: **1** to express a promise: *"I will come at 4 o'clock" means that the speaker has made a definite appointment. The doctor will see you now.* **2** to refer to future happenings: *The train will be late. If they leave now, they will arrive in time for dinner.* **3** to introduce a polite request: *Will you please hand me that book?* **4** to express a capacity or power that something has: *This pail will hold eight litres.* **5** to refer to something done again and again: *She will read for hours at a time.* **6** with "you" to mean that a person has to do something: *Don't argue with me; you will do it at once!* *v.*, **would.**
☛ *Usage.* See note at SHALL.

**will**[2] (wil) **1** the power of the mind to decide and do; deliberate control over thought and action: *A good leader must have a strong will.* **2** decide by using this power; use the will: *She willed to keep awake.* **3** influence or try to influence by deliberate control over thought and action: *She willed the person in front of her to turn around.* **4** determine: *Fate has willed it otherwise.* **5** purpose; determination: *the will to live.* **6** wish; desire: *The servants had to do their master's will.* **7** a legal statement of a person's wishes about what shall be done with his or her property after he or she is dead. **8** a document containing such a statement. **9** give by a will: *to will a house to someone.* **10** a feeling toward another: *good will, ill will.* 1, 5–8, 10 *n.*, 2–4, 9 *v.*, **willed, will·ing.**
**at will,** whenever one wishes.
**with a will,** with energy and determination.

**wil·let** (wil'it) a North American wading bird related to the snipes and sandpipers. *n.*

**will·ful** or **wil·ful** (wil'fəl) **1** wanting or taking one's own way; stubborn: *The willful child would not eat his supper.* **2** done on purpose; intended: *willful waste.* *adj.* —**will'ful·ness** or **wil'ful·ness,** *n.*

**will·ful·ly** or **wil·ful·ly** (wil'fə lē) **1** by choice; voluntarily. **2** by design; intentionally. **3** selfishly; perversely; obstinately; stubbornly. *adv.*

**wil·lies** (wil'ēz) *Informal.* a feeling of nervousness and uneasiness: *That movie gave me the willies—I won't go to that kind of show again.* *n. pl.*

**will·ing** (wil'ing) **1** ready; consenting: *He is willing to wait.* **2** cheerfully ready: *willing obedience.* **3** ppr. of WILL. 1, 2 *adj.*, 3 *v.* —**will'ing·ly,** *adv.* —**will'ing·ness,** *n.*

**will-o'-the-wisp** (wil'ə ᴛʜə wisp') **1** a moving light appearing at night over marshy places, caused by combustion of marsh gas. **2** something that deceives or misleads by luring on: *Any scheme to get rich quickly is likely to be a will-o'-the-wisp.* *n.*

**wil·low** (wil'ō) **1** any of a closely related group of trees and shrubs found mainly in the Northern Hemisphere, usually having long, narrow, pointed leaves arranged alternately on the twigs, and flowers that appear in early spring before or at the same time as the leaves: *Many willows have tough, slender branches that bend easily.* **2** the wood of any of these trees or shrubs: *Willow is the best wood for cricket bats.* **3** made of willow. **4** referring to a family of trees and shrubs that consists of the willows and poplars. *n.*

**wil·low·y** (wil'ō ē *or* wil'ə wē) **1** like a willow; slender; supple; graceful: *a tall, willowy girl.* **2** having many willows: *the willowy bank of a river.* *adj.*

**will·pow·er** (wil'pou'ər) power exercised by the will; self-control or determination: *He hasn't got enough willpower to keep to a diet.* *n.*

**wil·ly-nil·ly** (wil'ē nil'ē) **1** willingly or not; whether one wishes it or not: *He found himself involved willy-nilly in the promotion campaign.* **2** that is or happens whether one wishes it or not: *a willy-nilly candidate.* 1 *adv.*, 2 *adj.*

**wilt** (wilt) **1** become limp and drooping; wither: *Flowers wilt when they do not get enough water.* **2** lose strength, vigour, assurance, etc. **3** cause to wilt: *The early frost wilted the plant's leaves.* **4** any of various plant diseases that cause leaves to wilt. 1–3 *v.*, 4 *n.*

**Wil·ton** (wil'tən) a kind of velvety carpet. *n.*

**wil·y** (wī'lē) using subtle tricks to deceive; crafty; cunning; sly. *adj.*, **wil·i·er, wil·i·est.** —**wil'i·ly,** *adv.*

A wimple, as worn in the early 14th century in England

**wim·ple** (wim'pəl) **1** a cloth for the head arranged in folds about the head, cheeks, chin, and neck, worn by nuns and formerly by other women. **2** cover or muffle with a wimple. **3** ripple or cause to ripple. 1 *n.*, 2, 3 *v.*, **wim·pled, wim·pling.**

**win** (win) **1** get victory or success: *The tortoise won in the end. I will win.* **2** get victory or success in: *He won the race.* **3** the act or fact of winning; success; victory: *We had five wins and no defeats.* **4** get by effort, ability, or skill; gain: *to win fame, to win a prize.* **5** gain the favour of; persuade: *The speaker soon won his audience. Lisa won her mother over to her side.* **6** attract; get the love of: *His ready smile won him many friends.* **7** persuade to marry. **8** get to; reach, often by effort: *to*

win the summit of a mountain. 1, 2, 4-8 v., **won**, **win·ning;** 3 n.
**win out,** *Informal.* get victory or success.
☞ *Hom.* WHIN (win).

**wince** (wins) 1 draw back suddenly; flinch slightly: *The boy winced at the sight of the dentist's drill.* 2 the act of wincing. 1 v., **winced, winc·ing;** 2 n.

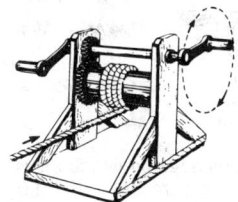

A winch, or windlass. When the crank on the right is turned clockwise, the rope is wound onto the spool.

**winch** (winch) 1 a machine for lifting or pulling, having a roller around which a rope or cable is wound: *The crank of a winch is turned by hand or by an engine.* 2 move by a winch. 1 n., 2 v.

**wind**[1] (wind) 1 air in motion: *The wind bends the branches. The wind varies in force from a slight breeze to a strong gale.* 2 a current of air filled with some smell: *The deer caught wind of the hunter and ran off.* 3 smell; follow by scent: *The dogs winded the rabbit and ran off after it.* 4 expose to wind or air. 5 gas in the stomach or bowels. 6 follow a scent; smell. 7 the power of breathing; breath: *A runner needs good wind.* 8 put out of breath; cause difficulty in breathing: *The fat man was winded by walking up the steep hill.* 9 let recover breath: *They stopped in order to wind their horses.* 10 empty, useless talk. 11 in music: **a** a wind instrument. **b winds,** *pl.* wind instruments. 1, 2, 5, 7, 10, 11 n., 3, 4, 6, 8, 9 v., **wind·ed, wind·ing.**
**before the wind,** in the direction toward which the wind is blowing.
**between wind and water, a** near the water line of a ship. **b** in a dangerous place.
**down (the) wind,** in the direction that the wind is blowing.
**get wind of, a** find out about; get a hint of: *Don't let him get wind of our plans.* **b** smell: *The deer soon got wind of the hunter.*
**in the teeth of the wind,** directly against the wind.
**in the wind,** happening; about to happen; impending: *There's an election in the wind.*
**into the wind,** pointing toward the direction from which the wind is blowing.
**off the wind,** with the wind blowing from behind.
**on the wind,** as nearly as possible in the direction from which the wind is blowing.
**take the wind out of one's sails,** take away one's advantage, argument, etc. suddenly or unexpectedly.

**wind**[2] (wīnd) 1 move this way and that; move in a crooked way; change direction; turn: *A brook winds through the woods. We wound our way through the narrow streets.* 2 proceed in a roundabout or indirect manner: *His speech wound slowly toward its conclusion.* 3 fold, wrap, or place about something: *The mother wound her arms about the child.* 4 cover with something put, wrapped, or folded around: *The man's arm is wound with bandages.* 5 roll into a ball or on a spool: *Machines were winding yarn. Thread comes wound on spools.* 6 a bend; turn; twist. 7 twist or turn around something: *The vine winds round a pole.* 8 be warped or twisted: *That board will wind.* 9 make some machine go by turning some part of it: *to wind a clock.* 10 be wound: *This clock winds easily.* 11 haul or hoist by means of a winch,

windlass, or the like. 1-5, 7-11 v., **wound** or (*rare*) **wind·ed, wind·ing;** 6 n. —**wind'er,** n.
**wind off,** unwind.
**wind up, a** end; settle; conclude: *We expect to wind up the project tomorrow.* **b** in baseball, make swinging and twisting movements of the arm and body just before pitching the ball. **c** roll or coil; wind completely. **d** put into a state of tension, great strain, intensity of feeling, etc.; excite.

**wind·age** (win'dij) 1 the power of the wind to turn a missile from its course. 2 the distance that a missile is turned from its course by the wind. n.

**wind–blown** (wind'blōn') 1 blown by the wind. 2 with the hair cut short and brushed forward. adj.

**wind–borne** (wind'bôrn') of pollen, seed, etc., carried by the wind. adj.

**wind–break** (wind'brāk') *Cdn.* 1 a row or clump of trees planted to provide protection from the wind and, often, to prevent soil erosion. 2 any temporary shelter from the wind. n.

**wind·break·er** (wind'brā'kər) *Cdn.* a short outdoor jacket of wool, leather, nylon, etc. that closes to the neck and has close-fitting cuffs and waist. n.

**wind–bro·ken** (wind'brō'kən) of horses, etc., having the power of breathing injured; having the HEAVES (def. 11). adj.

**wind–charg·er** (wind'chär'jər) *Cdn.* 1 a windmill used to drive a generator: *Wind-chargers were formerly much used on the Prairies to supply electricity for individual homes.* 2 the generator of a wind-charger. n.

**wind chill** *Cdn.* the rate at which exposed human skin cools under given conditions of temperature and wind speed. When the wind chill count is 2400, exposed flesh begins to freeze immediately. See Appendix for table.

**wind chill factor** a measure of the combined chilling effect of wind and low temperature on living things or inanimate objects, expressed in watts per square metre. See Appendix for chart.

**wind·ed** (win'did) 1 out of breath. 2 having wind or breath of a certain kind (*used only in compounds*): *short-winded.* 3 pt. and pp. of WIND[1]. 1, 2 adj., 3 v.

**wind·fall** (wind'fol') 1 fruit blown down by the wind. 2 a tree blown down by the wind. 3 an unexpected piece of good luck. n.

**wind·flow·er** (wind'flou'ər) *Cdn.* in the West, any of several anemones, especially the PRAIRIE CROCUS. n.

**win·di·go** (win'di gō') WENDIGO (def. 1). n., pl. **win·di·gos.**

**wind·ing** (wīn'ding) 1 the act of one that winds. 2 a bend; turn. 3 bending; turning. 4 something that is wound or coiled. 5 in electricity, a continuous coil of wire forming a conductor in a generator, motor, etc. 6 the manner in which the wire is coiled: *a series winding.* 7 ppr. of WIND[2]. 1, 2, 4-6 n., 3 adj., 7 v.
—**wind'ing·ly,** adv.

**winding sheet** the cloth in which a dead person is wrapped for burial.

**wind instrument** a musical instrument sounded by blowing air into it: *Horns, flutes, and trombones are wind instruments.*

**wind·jam·mer** (wind′jam′ər) *Informal.* **1** a sailing ship. **2** a member of its crew. *n.*

**wind·lass** (wind′ləs) a machine for pulling or lifting things; winch. See WINCH for picture. *n.*

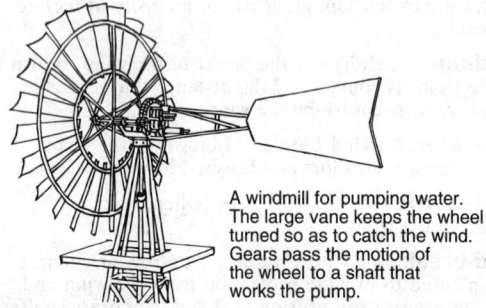
A windmill for pumping water. The large vane keeps the wheel turned so as to catch the wind. Gears pass the motion of the wheel to a shaft that works the pump.

**wind·mill** (wind′mil′) a mill or machine operated by the action of the wind upon a wheel of vanes or sails mounted on a tower: *Windmills are often used to pump water.* *n.*
**tilt at** or **fight windmills,** expend one's energy in futile attacks on what cannot be overcome (in allusion to the story of Don Quixote tilting at windmills under the illusion that they were giants).

**win·dow** (win′dō) **1** an opening in the wall or roof of a building, boat, car, etc. to let in light or air. **2** such an opening with the frame, panes of glass, etc. that fill it. **3** an opening like a window in shape or function, such as the transparent part of some envelopes through which the address is seen. **4** furnish with windows. **5** a method of interrupting a computer program with a boxlike screen compartment that enables the user to perform some other function without disturbing the existing file. **6** a period of time favourable for launching a spacecraft. 1–3, 5, 6 *n.,* 4 *v.* —**win′dow·less,** *adj.*
☛ *Etym.* From ON *vindauga* (literally, 'wind eye'), made up of *vindr* 'wind' + *auga* 'eye'.

**window box** a long, narrow box placed outside a window, or inside on a window sill, and used for growing plants and flowers.

**window dressing** **1** the art of attractively displaying merchandise in shop windows. **2** any display or statement made, often misleadingly, to create a favourable impression: *Much of the president's report was window dressing.*

**win·dow·pane** (win′dō pān′) a piece of glass in a window. *n.*

**win·dow–shop** (win′dō shop′) examine or gaze at articles in store windows without going in to buy anything. *v.,* **win·dow–shopped, win·dow–shop·ping.** —**win′dow–shop′per,** *n.*

**window sill** a piece of wood or stone across the bottom of a window. See LINTEL for picture.

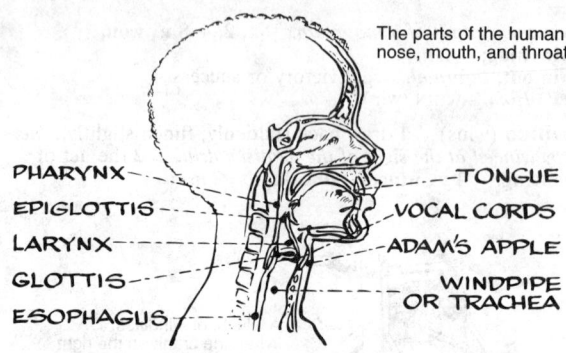
The parts of the human nose, mouth, and throat

**wind·pipe** (wind′pīp′) the passage by which air is carried from the throat to the lungs; trachea. See LUNG for another picture. *n.*

**wind·row** (win′drō′) **1** a row of hay raked together to dry before being made into cocks or heaps. **2** any similar row, as of sheaves of grain, made for the purpose of drying; a row of dry leaves, dust, etc. swept together by wind or the like. **3** arrange in a windrow or windrows. 1, 2 *n.,* 3 *v.*

**wind shear** a sudden, violent change in the direction or speed of the wind: *Wind shear can cause aircraft to crash.*

**wind·shield** (wind′shēld′) the front window of an automobile, etc. *n.*

**wind sleeve** or **wind sock** a cone-shaped sleeve mounted on a pole or the like, showing the direction of the wind.

**Wind·sor chair** (win′zər) a kind of comfortable wooden chair, having a spindle back and slanting legs.

**Windsor tie** a wide necktie of soft silk, tied in a loose bow.

**wind·storm** (wind′stôrm′) a storm with much wind but little or no rain. *n.*

**wind·surf·ing** (wind′sėr′fing) the sport of gliding over water on a board that resembles a surfboard but is equipped with a sail. *n.*

**wind tunnel** a structure in which the effect of air pressures on aircraft, missiles, etc. can be calculated by means of artificially made winds.

**wind–up** (wīn′dup′) **1** a winding up; ending; close; conclusion. **2** in baseball, a series of movements made by a pitcher just before throwing the ball. *n.*

**wind·ward** (wind′wərd *or* win′dərd) **1** on the side toward the wind. **2** in the direction from which the wind is blowing. **3** the direction from which the wind is blowing: *They saw a ship to windward.* 1, 2 *adv., adj.,* 3 *n.*

**wind·y** (win′dē) **1** having much wind: *a windy street, windy weather.* **2** made of wind; empty: *windy talk.* **3** talking a great deal; voluble: *Those two are windy and we won't have a chance to say much.* **4** causing or having gas in the stomach or intestines. *adj.,* **wind′i·er, wind′i·est.** —**wind′i·ly,** *adv.* —**wind′i·ness,** *n.*

**wine** (wīn) **1** the juice of grapes, when it is fermented and contains alcohol. **2** the fermented juice of other fruits or plants: *currant wine, dandelion wine.* **3** entertain with wine: *We wined and dined our guests.* **4** the colour of red wine. **5** dark purplish-red. 1, 2, 4 *n.,* 3 *v.,* **wined, win·ing;** 5 *adj.*

**new wine in old bottles,** something new presented in an old form or style, or without a necessary change of form. ☞ *Hom.* WHINE (wīn).

**wine cellar** 1 a cellar where wine is stored. 2 the wine stored there.

**wine-col·oured** or **wine-col·ored** (wīn′kul′ərd) dark purplish-red. *adj.*

**wine gallon** an old English gallon equal to 231 cubic inches (about 3.8 L), now the standard United States gallon.

**wine press** 1 a machine for pressing the juice from grapes. 2 a vat in which grapes are trodden in the process of making wine.

**win·er·y** (wī′nə rē) a place where wine is made. *n., pl.* **win·er·ies.**

**wing** (wing) 1 the part of a bird, insect, or bat used in flying, or a corresponding part in a bird or insect that does not fly. 2 anything like a wing in shape or use, such as one of the major lifting and supporting surfaces of an airplane, the vanes of a windmill, and the feather of an arrow. See AIRPLANE for picture. 3 a part that sticks out from the main part or body, such as an extension at the side of a building, etc. 4 either of the side portions of an army or fleet ready for battle. 5 any of the pieces of side scenery on the stage. 6 a part of an organization; faction: *The left wing of the party opposed the new policy.* 7 fly or fly through: *The birds are winging south.* 8 supply with wings. 9 make able to fly; give speed to: *Terror winged his steps as the bear drew nearer.* 10 wound in the wing or arm: *The bullet winged the bird but did not kill it.* 11 in certain games, a player whose position is on either side of the centre. 12 in the air force, an administrative and tactical unit made up of several squadrons. 13 **wings,** *pl.* a in a theatre, the area at either side of the stage, out of sight of the audience. b the insignia, or badge, of a pilot. 1–6, 11–13 *n.,* 7–10 *v.* —**wing′less,** *adj.* —**wing′like′,** *adj.*

**in the wings,** *Informal.* about to happen.

**on the wing,** a flying. b moving; active; busy. c going away.

**take wing,** fly away.

**under the wing of,** under the protection or sponsorship of.

**wing one's way,** fly: *The bird wings its way south.*

**wing case** either of the hardened front wings of certain insects.

**winged** (wingd; *esp. poetic,* wing′id) 1 having wings: *winged insects.* 2 swift; rapid: *a winged messenger.* 3 pt. and pp. of WING. 1, 2 *adj.,* 3 *v.*

**wing·er** (wing′ər) in certain games, a player whose position is on either side of the centre. *n.*

**wing·span** (wing′span′) the distance between the tips of the wings of an airplane, bird, or insect; wingspread. *n.*

**wing·spread** (wing′spred′) the distance between the tips of the wings when they are spread out. *n.*

**wing tip** 1 the outer end of the wing of a bird or airplane. 2 a special decoration on the toe of a shoe. 3 a shoe with such a decorated toe.

**wink** (wingk) 1 close the eyes and open them again quickly: *The bright light made her wink.* 2 close and open quickly. 3 close one eye and open it again as a hint or signal: *Father winked at Jag as a sign for him to keep still.* 4 a winking. 5 a hint or signal given by winking. 6 move by winking: *to wink back tears.* 7 twinkle: *The stars winked.* 8 give a signal or express a message by a winking of the eye, a flashlight, etc. 9 a very short time: *I didn't sleep a wink.* 10 **forty winks,** *pl.* a short sleep; nap. 1–3, 6–8 *v.,* 4, 5, 9, 10 *n.*

**wink at,** pretend not to see.

**wink·er** (wing′kər) 1 a person or thing that winks. 2 *Informal.* an eyelash. 3 a blinder or blinker for a horse's eye. *n.*

**win·kle** (wing′kəl) a sea snail used for food. *n.*

**win·ner** (win′ər) a person or thing that wins. *n.*

**win·ning** (win′ing) 1 that wins: *a winning team.* 2 charming; attractive: *a winning smile.* 3 **winnings,** *pl.* what is won; money won: *He pocketed his winnings.* 4 ppr. of WIN. 1, 2 *adj.,* 3 *n.,* 4 *v.* —**win′ning·ly,** *adv.*

**Win·ni·peg couch** (win′ə peg′) *Cdn.* a kind of couch having no arms or back and opening out into a double bed.

**Winnipeg goldeye** *Cdn.* GOLDEYE.

**win·now** (win′ō) 1 blow off the chaff from grain; drive or blow away chaff. 2 blow chaff from grain. 3 sort out; separate; sift: *to winnow truth from falsehood.* 4 fan with wings; flap wings. *v.*

**win·now·er** (win′ō ər) 1 a person who winnows. 2 a machine for winnowing grain, etc. *n.*

**win·some** (win′səm) charming; attractive; pleasing: *a winsome girl.* *adj.* —**win′some·ly,** *adv.* —**win′some·ness,** *n.*

**win·ter** (win′tər) 1 the coldest of the four seasons; time of the year between fall and spring. 2 a year as denoted by this season: *a woman of eighty winters.* 3 of, having to do with, or characteristic of winter: *winter clothes, winter weather.* 4 of the kind that may be kept for use during the winter: *winter apples.* 5 pass the winter: *Robins winter in the south.* 6 keep, feed, or manage during winter: *We wintered our cattle in the warm valley.* 7 the last period of life. 8 a period of decline, dreariness, or adversity. 1–4, 7, 8 *n.,* 5, 6 *v.*

**win·ter·green** (win′tər grēn′) 1 a small evergreen plant of North America having bright red berries and aromatic leaves. An oil made from its leaves (**oil of wintergreen** or **wintergreen oil**) is used in medicine and as a flavouring. 2 the oil of this plant. 3 its flavour. *n.*

**win·ter·ize** (win′tə rīz′) 1 make an automobile, etc. ready for operation or use during the winter. 2 prepare a building, such as a cottage, for use in the winter. 3 safeguard an unoccupied building against damage in winter by draining taps, boarding windows, etc.: *We winterized our summer cottage in October.* *v.* **win·ter·ized, win·ter·iz·ing.**

**win·ter·kill** (win′tər kil′) 1 kill by or die from exposure to cold weather: *The rosebushes were winterkilled.* 2 an instance of this: *The trees died from winterkill.* 1 *v.,* 2 *n.*

**winter solstice** for the Northern Hemisphere, the time when the sun is farthest south from the equator, December 21 or 22.

**win·ter·time** (win′tər tīm′) the season of winter. *n.*

**winter wheat** wheat planted in the fall to ripen in the following spring or summer.

**win·ter·y** (win′tə rē) WINTRY. *adj.*, **win·ter·i·er, win·ter·i·est.**

**win·tri·ness** (win′trē nis) a WINTRY quality. *n.*

**win·try** (win′trē) **1** of or having to do with winter; like winter: *a wintry sky.* **2** devoid of fervour or affection; cold; chilling: *a wintry smile.* **3** destitute of warmth or brightness; dismal; dreary; cheerless: *a wintry gathering.* *adj.*, **win·tri·er, win·tri·est.**

**wipe** (wīp) **1** rub with paper, cloth, etc. in order to clean or dry: *to wipe the table.* **2** take away, off, or out by rubbing: *Wipe away your tears. She wiped off the dust.* **3** remove: *The rain wiped away all the footprints.* **4** rub or draw something over a surface. **5** the act of wiping: *He gave his face a hasty wipe.* **6** form a joint in lead pipe by spreading solder with a leather pad. 1–4, 6 *v.*, **wiped, wip·ing;** 5 *n.*

**wipe out, a** destroy completely: *The pollution in the river has wiped out all the fish.* **b** cancel: *Tema generously wiped out all the debts owed her.*

**wip·er** (wī′pər) **1** a person who wipes. **2** anything used for wiping: *a windshield wiper. n.*

**wire** (wīr) **1** metal drawn out into a thin, flexible rod or thread: *telephone wire.* **2** such metal as a material. **3** made of or consisting of wire: *a wire fence.* **4** wire netting. **5** a piece of such metal: *Use wire to connect these two batteries.* **6** furnish with wire: *to wire a house for electricity.* **7** fasten with wire: *She wired the two pieces together.* **8** catch by a wire or wires. **9** telegraph: *to wire a birthday greeting (v.). He sent a message by wire (n.).* **10** *Informal.* telegram: *The news of her arrival came in a wire.* 1–5, 9, 10 *n.*, 6–9 *v.*, **wired, wir·ing.** —**wire′like′,** *adj.* —**wir′er,** *n.*

**get (in) under the wire,** arrive or finish just before it is too late.

**pull wires,** *Informal.* **a** direct the actions of others secretly. **b** use secret influence to accomplish one's purposes.

**wire gauge** a device, usually a disk with different-sized notches in it, for measuring the diameter of wire, the thickness of metal sheets, etc.

**wire–haired** (wīr′herd′) having coarse, stiff hair: *a wire-haired fox terrier. adj.*

**wire·less** (wīr′lis) **1** using no wires; transmitting by radio waves instead of by electric wires: *wireless telegraphy.* **2** *Esp. Brit.* formerly, radio. **3** *Esp. Brit.* a message sent by radio. **4** *Esp. Brit.* send or transmit by radio. 1, 2 *adj.*, 2, 3 *n.*, 4 *v.*

**wire·pho·to** (wīr′fō′tō) **1** a method of transmitting photographs by reproducing a facsimile through electric signals. **2** a photograph transmitted in this fashion. *n.*

**wire puller** *Informal.* a person who uses secret influence to accomplish his or her purposes.

**wire pulling** *Informal.* the use of secret influence to accomplish a purpose.

**wire·tap** (wīr′tap′) **1** WIRETAPPING. **2** the information obtained by WIRETAPPING. **3** make a wiretap, legally or illegally. **4** record by WIRETAPPING. 1, 2 *n.*, 3, 4 *v.*, **wire·tapped, wire·tap·ping.** Also, **wire tap.**

**wire·tap·per** (wīr′tap′ər) a person who taps telephone wires secretly. *n.*

**wire·tap·ping** (wīr′tap′ing) the act or practice of making a secret connection with telephone or telegraph wires to find out the messages sent over them. *n.* Compare with BUG (defs. 7, 8).

**wire·worm** (wīr′wėrm′) the slender, hard-bodied larva of a beetle: *Wireworms feed on the roots of plants and do much damage to crops. n.*

**wire–wove** (wīr′wōv′) a grade of paper, very smooth, made in a frame of fine wire. *n.*

**wir·ing** (wī′ring) a system of wires to carry an electric current. *n.*

**wir·y** (wī′rē) **1** made of wire. **2** like wire. **3** lean, strong, and tough: *The athlete had a wiry body. adj.*, **wir·i·er, wir·i·est.** —**wir′i·ly,** *adv.* —**wir′i·ness,** *n.*

**wis·dom** (wiz′dəm) **1** knowledge and good judgment based on experience; being wise. **2** wise conduct; wise words: *Her wisdom guided us.* **3** scholarly knowledge. *n.*

**wisdom tooth** the back tooth on either side of the upper and lower jaw, ordinarily appearing between the ages of 17 and 25.

**wise**[1] (wīz) **1** having knowledge and good judgment: *a wise judge.* **2** showing wisdom: *wise advice.* **3** having knowledge or information: *We are none the wiser for his explanations.* **4** learned; erudite. *adj.*, **wis·er, wis·est.** —**wise′ly,** *adv.* —**wise′ness,** *n.*

**wise**[2] (wīz) way; manner: *Tito is in no wise a student; he prefers sports and machinery. n.*

**–wise** an adverb-forming suffix meaning: **1** in _____ manner: *Likewise means in like manner.* **2** in a _____ ing manner: *Slantwise means in a slanting manner.* **3** in the characteristic way of a _____: *Clockwise means in the characteristic way of a clock, with hands turning from left to right. Turn the screw clockwise.* **4** in the _____ respect or case: *Otherwise means in the other case.* **5** in the direction of _____: *Lengthwise means in the direction of length.* **6** with regard to _____: *Businesswise means with regard to business.* **7** special meanings, as in *sidewise.*

☞ Usage. In Old and Middle English, -wise was freely added to nouns to form adverbs, as in def. 6. This usage has recently been revived and is popularly used to form words as needed: *He is doing well salarywise.* However, many people regard the usage as a fad appropriate only to informal speech. It should, therefore, be avoided in writing.

**wise·a·cre** (wī′zā′kər) a person who thinks that he or she knows everything. *n.*

**wise·crack** (wīz′krak′) **1** a smart remark; a quick, witty reply. **2** make wisecracks. 1 *n.*, 2 *v.* —**wise′crack′er,** *n.*

**wi·sent** (vē′zent) the European bison, somewhat smaller than the North American bison, or buffalo, and having a much smaller hump over the shoulder: *The wisent is now nearly extinct as a wild animal, but survives in parks. n.*

**wish** (wish) **1** have a need or longing for; desire; want: *Do you wish to go home?* **2** have a desire or express a hope: *She wished for a new house. I wish that I had enough money to buy that model boat.* **3** a wishing; desire: *What is your wish? He had no wish to be king.* **4** the expression

of a wish: *She sends you best wishes for a Happy New Year.*
**5** desire something for someone; desire that someone shall be or have; have a hope for; express a hope for: *We wish peace for all people. I wish you a Happy New Year.*   **6** the thing wished for: *She got her wish.*   1, 2, 5 *v.*, 3, 4, 6 *n.*
—**wish′er,** *n.*
**wish on,** *Informal.*   pass on to; foist on: *They wished the hardest job on him.*
☛ *Hom.* WHISH (wish).

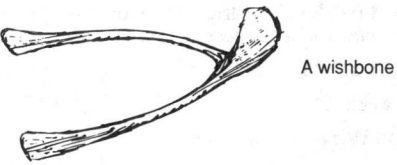
A wishbone

**wish·bone** (wish′bōn′)   in poultry and other birds, the forked bone in the front of the breast.   *n.*

**wish·ful think·ing** (wish′fəl)   belief that reality is as one would wish, not as it is: *Her boast about winning the race was only wishful thinking.*

**wish·y–wash·y** (wish′ē wosh′ē)   **1** thin and weak; watery: *wishy-washy soup with no flavour.*   **2** lacking in substantial qualities; feeble; inferior: *a wishy-washy story.*   *adj.*

**wisp** (wisp)   **1** a small bundle; small bunch: *a wisp of hay.*   **2** a small portion of anything; a little bit: *a wisp of hair, a wisp of smoke.*   **3** a little thing: *a wisp of a child.*   *n.*

**wisp·y** (wis′pē)   like a WISP; thin; slight.   *adj.*
wisp·i·er, wisp·i·est.

**wis·tar·i·a** (wis ter′ē ə *or* wis tar′ē ə)   a climbing shrub having large clusters of purple or white flowers.   *n.*
Also, **wisteria.**

**wist·ful** (wist′fəl)   **1** longing; yearning: *A child stood looking with wistful eyes at the toys in the window.*
**2** pensive; melancholy.   *adj.*   —**wist′ful·ly,** *adv.*
—**wist′ful·ness,** *n.*

**wit**[1] (wit)   **1** the power to perceive quickly and express cleverly ideas that are unusual, striking, and amusing: *Her wit made even trouble seem amusing.*   **2** a person with such power: *Stephen Leacock was a wit.*   **3** the power of understanding; mind; sense: *People with quick wits learn easily. The child was out of his wits with fright. That poor man hasn't wit enough to earn a living.*   *n.*
**at one's wit's end,**   not knowing what to do or say.
**have** or **keep one's wits about one,**   be alert.
**live by one's wits,**   survive without regular work.
☛ *Hom.* WHIT (wit).

**wit**[2] (wit) *Archaic*   except in
**to wit,**   that is to say; namely: *To my son I leave all I own—to wit: my house, what is in it, and the land on which it stands.*   *v.*

**witch**[1] (wich)   **1** a woman supposed to be under the influence of evil spirits and to have magic power. Compare with WARLOCK.   **2** an ugly old woman.   **3** use the power of a witch on.   **4** *Informal.*   a fascinating girl or woman.   **5** charm; fascinate; bewitch.   1, 2, 4 *n., pl.*
**witch·es;**   3, 5 *v.*
☛ *Hom.* WHICH (wich).

**witch**[2] (wich)   **1** a WICCAN priest or priestess.   **2** a devotee of WICCA.   *n., pl.* **witch·es.**

**witch·craft** (wich′kraft′)   what a witch does or can do; magic power or influence.   *n.*

**wishbone**   **1381**   **withdrew**

hat, āge, fär; let, ēqual, tėrm; it, īce
hot, ōpen, ôrder; oil, out; cup, pùt, rüle
əbove, takən, pencəl, lemən, circəs
ch, child; ng, long; sh, ship
th, thin; ᴛʜ, then; zh, measure

**witch doctor**   especially among African tribes, a MEDICINE MAN.

**witch·er·y** (wich′ə rē)   **1** witchcraft; magic.   **2** charm; fascination: *There was witchery in the moonlit scene.*   *n., pl.* **witch·er·ies.**

**witch hazel**   **1** a shrub of North America that has yellow flowers in the fall or winter after the leaves have fallen.   **2** a lotion for cooling and soothing the skin, made from the bark and leaves of this shrub.

**witch hunt**   *Informal.*   the persecuting or defaming of a person to gain an advantage, especially a political advantage.

**witch·ing** (wich′ing)   **1** bewitching; magical; enchanting.   **2** ppr. of WITCH.[1]   1 *adj.*, 2 *v.*
—**witch′ing·ly,** *adv.*

**with** (with *or* wiᴛʜ)   **1** in the company of: *Come with me.*   **2** among: *They will mix with the crowd.*   **3** having, wearing, carrying, etc.: *a student with brains, a telegram with bad news.*   **4** by means of; by using: *Cut meat with a knife.*   **5** using; showing: *Work with care.*   **6** as an addition to; added to: *Do you want sugar with your tea?*
**7** including; and: *tea with sugar and lemon.*   **8** in relation to: *They are friendly with us.*   **9** in regard to: *We are pleased with the house.*   **10** in proportion to: *An army's power increases with its size.*   **11** because of: *to shake with cold.*   **12** in the keeping or service of: *Leave the dog with me.*   **13** in the region, sphere, experience, opinion, or view of: *It is day with us while it is night with the Chinese. High taxes are unpopular with many people.*   **14** at the same time as: *With this event the field day ended.*   **15** in the same direction as: *The boat floated along with the current.*   **16** on the side of; for: *They are with us in our plan.*   **17** from: *I hate to part with my favourite things.*
**18** against: *We fought with that gang.*   **19** receiving; having; being allowed: *I went with her permission.*   **20** in spite of: *With all his weight he was not a strong man.*
*prep.*
☛ *Hom.* WITHE (with).

**with·draw** (wiᴛʜ drô′ *or* with drô′)   **1** draw back; draw away: *The guilty child quickly withdrew his hand from the cookie jar.*   **2** take back; remove: *Worn-out paper money is withdrawn from use by the government.*   **3** go away: *She withdrew from the room.*   *v.*, **with·drew, with·drawn, with·draw·ing.**

**with·draw·al** (wiᴛʜ drô′əl *or* with drô′əl)   **1** a drawing back or taking back; taking away or going away: *The chairman noticed her withdrawal from the meeting.*   **2** a mental condition during which a person ceases to communicate with others and draws back into himself or herself.   *n.*

**with·drawn** (wiᴛʜ drôn′ *or* with drôn′)   **1** pp. of WITHDRAW.   **2** unsociable or unresponsive; introverted: *He was always shy and withdrawn.*   1 *v.*, 2 *adj.*

**with·drew** (wiᴛʜ drü′ *or* with drü′)   pt. of WITHDRAW.   *v.*

**withe** (wiTH *or* with) **1** a willow twig. **2** any tough easily bent twig suitable for binding things together. *n.*
☛ *Hom.* WITH (with).

**with·er** (wiTH′ər) **1** lose or cause to lose freshness, vigour, etc.; dry up; fade: *a face withered with age. Flowers wither after they are cut.* **2** cause to feel ashamed or confused: *She blushed under her aunt's withering look.* *v.*
☛ *Hom.* WHITHER (wiTH′ər).

**with·ers** (wiTH′ərz) the highest part of a horse's or other animal's back, behind the neck. See HORSE for picture. *n. pl.*

**with·held** (with held′) pt. and pp. of WITHHOLD. *v.*

**with·hold** (with hōld′) **1** refrain from giving or granting: *to withhold one's consent.* **2** hold back; keep back: *The captain withheld his men from attack.* *v.*, **with·held, with·hold·ing.**

**with·in** (with in′ *or* wiTH in′) **1** inside the limits of; not beyond: *The task was within the man's powers. She guessed my weight within two kilograms.* **2** in or into the inner part of; inside of: *By the use of X rays doctors can see within the body.* **3** in or into the inner part; inside: *The house has been painted within and without. The curtains were white without and green within.* 1, 2 *prep.*, 3 *adv.*

**with·out** (with out′ *or* wiTH out′) **1** with no; not having; free from; lacking: *A cat walks without noise. He drinks tea without sugar.* **2** so as to omit, avoid, or neglect: *She walked past without noticing us.* **3** outside of; beyond: *Soldiers are camped within and without the city walls.* **4** on the outside; outside: *The house is painted without and within.* 1–3 *prep.*, 4 *adv.*
**do** *or* **go without,** remain in want of something; manage in spite of not having a certain thing: *Either cook your own supper or go without.*

**with·stand** (with stand′) stand against; hold out against; oppose, especially successfully: *Explorers have to withstand hardships. These shoes will withstand hard wear.* *v.*, **with·stood, with·stand·ing.**

**with·stood** (with stůd′) pt. and pp. of WITHSTAND. *v.*

**wit·less** (wit′lis) lacking intelligence; stupid; foolish: *Walking into the street without looking is a witless thing to do.* *adj.* —**wit′less·ly,** *adv.* —**wit′less·ness,** *n.*

**wit·ness** (wit′nis) **1** a person who saw something happen; spectator: *He started the fight in the presence of several witnesses.* **2** see; perceive: *They witnessed the accident.* **3** a person who gives evidence or testifies under oath before a judge, coroner, etc. **4** evidence; testimony: *This document is witness to my honesty.* **5** testify to; give evidence of: *Her whole manner witnessed her surprise.* **6** give evidence; testify. **7** a person who signs a document to show that another person's signature on it is genuine. **8** sign a document as witness: *to witness a will.* 1, 3, 4, 7 *n.*, 2, 5, 6, 8 *v.*
**bear witness,** be evidence; give evidence; testify: *The thief's fingerprints bore witness to his guilt.*

**witness box** the place where a WITNESS stands or sits to give evidence in a law court.

**wit·ti·cism** (wit′ə siz′əm) a WITTY remark. *n.*

**wit·ti·ly** (wit′ə lē) in a WITTY manner; with wit. *adv.*

**wit·ting·ly** (wit′ing lē) knowingly; intentionally. *adv.*

**wit·ty** (wit′ē) full of WIT; clever and amusing: *A witty person makes witty remarks.* *adj.*, **wit·ti·er, wit·ti·est.** —**wit′ti·ness,** *n.*

**wives** (wīvz) pl. of WIFE. *n.*

**wiz·ard** (wiz′ərd) **1** a man supposed to have magic power. **2** *Informal.* a very clever person; expert: *Edison was a wizard at invention.* *n.*

**wiz·ard·ry** (wiz′ər drē) magic; magic skill. *n.*

**wiz·ened** (wiz′ənd) dried up; withered; shrivelled: *a wizened apple, a wizened face.* *adj.*

**wk.** **1** week. **2** work.

**wkly.** weekly.

**WNW** *or* **W.N.W.** west-northwest.

**woad** (wōd) **1** a European plant from whose leaves a blue dye is made. **2** the dye. *n.*

**wob·ble** (wob′əl) **1** move unsteadily from side to side; shake; tremble: *A baby wobbles when it begins to walk alone.* **2** be uncertain, unsteady, or inconstant; waver. **3** a wobbling motion. 1, 2 *v.*, **wob·bled, wob·bling;** 3 *n.* Also, **wabble.** —**wob′bler,** *n.*

**wob·bly** (wob′lē) unsteady; shaky; wavering. *adj.* Also, **wabbly.**

**wo·be·gone** (wō′bi gon′) See WOEBEGONE. *adj.*

**woe** (wō) great grief, trouble, or distress: *Sickness and poverty are common woes.* *n.*

**woe·be·gone** *or* **wo·be·gone** (wō′bi gon′) looking sad, sorrowful, or wretched. *adj.*

**woe·ful** (wō′fəl) **1** full of WOE; sad; sorrowful; wretched: *a woeful expression.* **2** pitiful: *a woeful sight.* **3** of wretched quality. *adj.* Also, **woful.** —**woe′ful·ly,** *adv.* —**woe′ful·ness,** *n.*

**wok** (wok) a wide, somewhat shallow metal cooking utensil having sides that curve in to a small, flat bottom, used especially in Chinese cooking. *n.*
☛ *Hom.* WALK.

**woke** (wōk) a pt. of WAKE¹. *v.*

**wo·ken** (wō′kən) a pp. of WAKE¹: *I was woken by my alarm clock.* *v.*

A timber wolf—about 70 cm high at the shoulder

**wolf** (wůlf) **1** either of two closely related wild members of the dog family found in the northern parts of the Northern Hemisphere, having long legs, a wide head, erect ears, and a long, bushy tail: *Wolves may vary in colour from almost white to black or reddish brown, but most wolves are mainly grey.* **2** a cruel, greedy person. **3** eat greedily: *The starving men wolfed down the food.* 1, 2 *n., pl.* **wolves;** 3 *v.* —**wolf′like′,** *adj.*
**cry wolf,** give a false alarm.
**keep the wolf from the door,** keep safe from hunger or poverty.
**wolf in sheep's clothing,** a person who pretends to be friendly or harmless, but intends to do harm.

**Wolf Cub** a member of the junior branch of the BOY SCOUTS.

**wolf·hound** (wulf′hound′) any of several breeds of very large dog, such as the Russian BORZOI or the IRISH WOLFHOUND, formerly used in hunting wolves. *n.*

**wolf·ish** (wul′fish) 1 of or having to do with wolves. 2 resembling a wolf: *a wolfish-looking dog.* 3 characteristic of wolves; fierce, greedy, etc.: *He ate with wolfish impatience.* *adj.* —**wolf′ish·ly,** *adv.* —**wolf′ish·ness,** *n.*

**wol·fram** (wul′frəm) 1 a metallic element used in making steel and for electric lamp filaments; also called tungsten. It has stable and radio-active isotopes. Symbol: W 2 WOLFRAMITE. *n.*

**wolf·ram·ite** (wul′frə mīt′) an ore consisting of compounds of WOLFRAM (def. 1) with iron and manganese. *n.*

**wolf's–bane** or **wolfs·bane** (wulfs′bān′) ACONITE, especially a poisonous species having dull-yellow flowers, found in the mountainous regions of Europe. *n.*

**wolf spider** any of a family of ground spiders ranging in size from a body length of about 6 mm to about 45 mm, that do not spin webs but leap on their prey: *Some wolf spiders, such as the European tarantula, live in silk-lined burrows in the ground; others live in the open.*

**wolf–wil·low** (wulf′wil′ō) *Cdn.* especially in the Prairie Provinces, a common shrub of western North America having silvery foliage and small, yellow, fragrant flowers. *n.*

A wolverine— about 17 cm long including the tail

**wol·ver·ine** or **wol·ver·ene** (wul′və rēn′ *or* wul′və rēn′) a very powerful, heavily built, meat-eating animal related to the badger and the skunk; carcajou: *The wolverine is found in the forests of Canada and the northern United States.* *n.*

**wolves** (wulvz) pl. of WOLF. *n.*

**wom·an** (wum′ən) 1 an adult female human being: *In most provinces a girl is considered a woman after the age of eighteen.* 2 women as a group; the average woman: *a magazine designed for the modern woman.* 3 a female servant: *The princess always travelled with her woman.* *n.*, *pl.* **wom·en** (wim′ən). —**wom′an·less,** *adj.*
☛ *Usage.* See note at LADY.

**wom·an·hood** (wum′ən hud′) 1 the condition or time of being a woman. 2 the character or qualities of a woman. 3 women as a group: *Marie Curie was an honour to womanhood.* *n.*

**wom·an·ish** (wum′ə nish) 1 characteristic of or suited for a woman or women; womanly. 2 effeminate: *He had a womanish way about him.* *adj.*

**wom·an·kind** (wum′ən kīnd′) women as a group. *n.*

**wom·an·like** (wum′ən līk′) 1 like a woman; womanly. 2 suitable for a woman. *adj.*

hat, āge, fär; let, ēqual, tėrm; it, īce hot, ōpen, ôrder; oil, out; cup, put, rüle əbove, takən, pencəl, lemən, circəs
ch, child; ng, long; sh, ship th, thin; ᴛʜ, then; zh, measure

**wom·an·ly** (wum′ən lē) 1 having or showing the best qualities of a woman: *a womanly nature. She is very womanly.* 2 proper or suitable for a woman: *I'd prefer some more womanly clothes. To enter politics is a womanly thing.* *adj.* —**wom′an·li·ness,** *n.*

**woman of the world** a woman who has wide experience of different kinds of people and customs; a sophisticated and worldly-wise or practical woman.

**woman suffrage** 1 the political right of women to vote: *In 1918 leaders of woman suffragist movements gained for all Canadian women over 21 the right to vote federally.* 2 women's votes.

**wom·an–suf·fra·gist** (wum′ən suf′rə jist) a person who favours the right of women to vote: *Mrs. Nellie McClung was a famous woman suffragist.* *n.*

**womb** (wüm) 1 the organ of the female body that holds and provides food for the young until birth; uterus. 2 a place where something is conceived and developed: *the womb of Western civilization.* *n.*

**wom·bat** (wom′bat) a burrowing Australian mammal that resembles a small bear: *A female wombat has a pouch for carrying her young.* *n.*

**wom·en** (wim′ən) pl. of WOMAN. *n.*

**wom·en·folk** (wim′ən fōk′) women. *n. pl.*

**women's rights** social, political, and legal rights for women, equal to those of men.

**won** (wun) pt. and pp. of WIN. *v.*
☛ *Hom.* ONE.

**won·der** (wun′dər) 1 a strange and surprising thing or event: *He saw the wonders of the city. It is a wonder he turned down the offer.* 2 the feeling caused by what is strange and surprising: *The baby looked with wonder at the new snow.* 3 feel wonder: *We wonder at the splendour of the stars.* 4 be surprised or astonished: *I shouldn't wonder if he wins the prize.* 5 be curious; be curious about; think about; wish to know: *I wonder what happened.* 1, 2 *n.*, 3–5 *v.* —**won′der·ing·ly,** *adv.*
**do wonders,** do wonderful things; achieve or produce extraordinary results.
**for a wonder,** as a strange and surprising thing.
**no wonder, a** no marvel or prodigy: *The lecturer is no wonder.* **b** nothing surprising; not surprising: *No wonder he resigned.*

**won·der·ful** (wun′dər fəl) 1 causing wonder; marvellous; remarkable: *The explorer had wonderful adventures.* 2 excellent; splendid; fine: *We had a wonderful time at the party.* *adj.* —**won′der·ful·ly,** *adv.* —**won′der·ful·ness,** *n.*

**won·der·land** (wun′dər land′) a land full of wonders. *n.*

**won·der·ment** (wun′dər mənt) wonder; surprise: *He stared at the northern lights in wonderment.* *n.*

**won·drous** (wun′drəs) 1 wonderful. 2 wonderfully. 1 *adj.*, 2 *adv.* —**won′drous·ly,** *adv.*

**wont** (wōnt) **1** accustomed: *He was wont to read the paper at breakfast.* **2** a custom or habit: *He rose early, as was his wont.* 1 *adj.*, 2 *n.*
☞ *Hom.* WON'T.

**won't** (wōnt) will not.
☞ *Hom.* WONT.

**wont·ed** (wōn'tid) accustomed; customary; usual: *The cat was in its wonted place by the stove.* *adj.*

**woo** (wü) **1** seek to marry; court. **2** seek to win; try to get: *Some people woo fame; some woo riches.* **3** try to persuade; urge. *v.*

**wood** (wùd) **1** the hard substance beneath the bark of trees and shrubs. **2** trees cut up for use: *Put some wood on the fire. The carpenter brought wood to build a garage.* **3** made of wood; wooden: *a wood house.* **4** something made of wood. **5** a cask; barrel; keg: *wine drawn from the wood.* **6** used for or on wood: *We have a wood basket for the fireplace.* **7** in printing, woodcuts collectively or a woodcut. **8** dwelling or growing in woods: *wood moss.* **9** supply with wood; get wood for. **10** get supplies of wood. **11** plant with trees. **12** a golf club with a wooden head. **13** Often, **woods**, *pl.* a large number of growing trees; forest: *looking for wildflowers in the woods. There is a large wood north of the village.* 1–8, 12, 13 *n.*, 9–11 *v.*
**out of the woods,** out of danger or difficulty.
**saw wood,** *Informal.* **a** work steadily at one's task, without attention to anything else. **b** sleep heavily.
☞ *Hom.* WOULD.

**wood alcohol** a poisonous, inflammable liquid often made by distilling wood, used as a solvent, fuel, etc.; methyl alcohol.

**wood·bine** (wùd'bīn') **1** HONEYSUCKLE. **2** the VIRGINIA CREEPER, a climbing vine that has leaves with five leaflets and bluish-black berries. *n.*

**wood·chuck** (wùd'chuk') a MARMOT found in Eastern Canada and the northeastern United States, having a thickset body, a flat head on a very short neck, and short, rounded ears; groundhog. *n.*
☞ *Etym.* Earlier **woodshock**, from an Algonquian word such as Cree *ochāk* 'fisher' and originally applied in English to the fisher.

**wood·cock** (wùd'kok') a small game bird having a long bill and short legs. *n.*, *pl.* **wood·cocks** or (*esp. collectively*) **wood·cock**.

**wood·craft** (wùd'kraft') **1** knowledge about how to get food and shelter in the woods; skill in hunting, trapping, finding one's way, etc. **2** skill in making things of wood. *n.*

**wood·cut** (wùd'kut') **1** an engraved block of wood to print from. **2** a print from such a block. *n.*

**wood·cut·ter** (wùd'kut'ər) a person who cuts down trees or chops wood. *n.*

**wood·ed** (wùd'id) **1** covered with trees: *The park is well wooded.* **2** pt. and pp. of WOOD. 1 *adj.*, 2 *v.*

**wood·en** (wùd'ən) **1** made of wood. **2** stiff; awkward: *The boy gave a wooden bow and left the stage.* **3** dull; stupid. *adj.* —**wood'en·ly**, *adv.* —**wood'en·ness,** *n.*

**wood·land** (wùd'lənd) **1** land covered with trees: *sounds of the woodland.* **2** of or in the woods; having to do with woods: *woodland animals.* *n.*

**wood·lark** (wùd'lärk') a European lark closely related to the skylark. *n.*

**wood lice** *pl.* of WOOD LOUSE.

**wood lily** PRAIRIE LILY.

**wood·lot** (wùd'lot') a piece of land on which trees are grown and cut; a bush lot. *n.*

**wood louse** **1** any of several small crustaceans that have flat, oval bodies and live in decaying wood, damp soil, etc. **2** any of certain small insects that live in the woodwork of houses.

**wood·man** (wùd'mən) **1** a person who cuts down trees. **2** a person who lives in the woods. **3** a person who takes care of forests. *n.*, *pl.* **wood·men** (-mən).

**wood nymph** **1** a nymph supposed to live in the woods. **2** a moth that destroys grapevines.

A downy woodpecker—about 17 cm long including the tail

**wood·peck·er** (wùd'pek'ər) a bird having a hard, pointed bill for pecking holes in trees to get insects. *n.*

**wood·pile** (wùd'pīl') a pile of wood, especially wood for fuel. *n.*

**wood rat** any of a closely related group of rats of western North America having large ears, a furry tail, and thick grey fur.

**wood·ruff** (wùd'ruf') a fragrant plant having small flowers and pointed leaves. *n.*

**wood·shed** (wùd'shed') a shed for storing wood. *n.*

**woods·man** (wùdz'mən) **1** a person used to life in the woods and skilled in hunting, fishing, trapping, etc. **2** a person whose work is cutting down trees; logger. *n.*, *pl.* **woods·men** (-mən).

**wood sorrel** a plant with sour juice and with leaves composed of three heartshaped leaflets; oxalis.

**wood thrush** a thrush common in the thickets and woods of eastern North America.

**wood warbler** **1** any of numerous small, brightly coloured songbirds of the Western Hemisphere: *Most wood warblers do not have a very musical song.* **2** any of a family of small, mostly brightly coloured birds of the Western Hemisphere: *Forty-two species of wood warbler are found in Canada.*

**wood·wind** (wùd'wind') **1 woodwinds**, *pl.* the wind instruments of an orchestra, including clarinets, oboes, etc. **2** any of this group of instruments: *Woodwinds were formerly made of wood, but many are now made of metal.* *n.*

**wood–wind** (wùd'wind') of or having to do with wooden wind instruments. *adj.*

**wood·work** (wùd'werk') **1** things made of wood, especially the doors, stairs, mouldings, etc. inside a house. **2** carpentry, especially as a school subject. *n.*

**wood·work·er** (wùd'wer'kər) a person who makes things of wood. *n.*

**wood·work·ing** (wüd′wėr′king)   making or shaping things of wood.   *n., adj.*

**wood·worm** (wüd′wėrm′)   a worm or larva that is bred in wood or bores in wood.   *n.*

**wood·y** (wüd′ē)   **1** having many trees; covered with trees: *a woody hillside.*   **2** of a plant, having stems containing xylem, the tissue that is the main element of wood: *Trees, shrubs, and some vines are woody plants.*   **3** consisting of wood: *the woody parts of a shrub.*   **4** like wood: *Turnips become woody when they are left in the ground too long.*   *adj.*, **wood·i·er, wood·i·est.** —**wood′i·ness,** *n.*

**woo·er** (wü′ər)   one that woos; suitor.   *n.*

**woof** (wüf)   **1** the threads running from side to side across a woven fabric: *The woof crosses the warp.* See WEAVE for picture.   **2** woven fabric or its texture.   *n.*
☛ *Etym.* See note at WEB.

**wool** (wùl)   **1** the soft, curly hair or fur of sheep and some other animals.   **2** short, thick, curly hair.   **3** something like wool: *Glass wool for insulation is made from fibres of glass.*   **4** yarn, cloth, or garments made of wool: *We wear wool in winter.*   **5** made of wool.   *n.*
**pull the wool over someone's eyes,** *Informal.*   deceive or trick someone.

**wool·en** (wùl′ən)   See WOOLLEN.   *adj., n.*

**wool·gath·er·ing** (wùl′gaTH′ə ring)   **1** absorption in thinking or daydreaming; absent-mindedness.   **2** inattentive; absent-minded; dreamy.   **1** *n.,* **2** *adj.*

**wool·grow·er** (wùl′grō′ər)   a person who raises sheep for their wool.   *n.*

**wool·len** or **wool·en** (wùl′ən)   **1** made of wool: *a woollen suit.*   **2** of or having to do with wool or cloth made of wool: *a woollen mill.*   **3 woollens** or **woolens,** *pl.* cloth or clothing made of wool.   **1, 2** *adj.,* **3** *n.*

**wool·ly** (wùl′ē)   **1** consisting of wool: *the woolly coat of a sheep.*   **2** like wool.   **3** covered with wool or something like it.   **4** *Informal.*   an article of clothing made from wool.   **5** not definite; confused; muddled: *woolly thinking.*   **1–3, 5** *adj.,* **wool·li·er, wool·li·est; 4** *n., pl.* **wool·lies.** Also, **wooly.** —**wool′li·ness,** *n.*

**wool·pack** (wùl′pak′)   **1** a large cloth bag for packing wool.   **2** formerly, a bundle or bale of wool weighing 240 pounds.   **3** a round, fleecy cloud.   *n.*

**wool·sack** (wùl′sak′)   **1** a bag of wool.   **2** the cushion on which the Lord Chancellor sits in the British House of Lords.   **3** the office of Lord Chancellor.   *n.*

**wool·y** (wùl′ē)   See WOOLLY.   *adj.,* **wool·i·er, wool·i·est.** —**wool′i·ness,** *n.*

**wooz·y** (wü′zē or wùz′ē)   *Informal.*   **1** somewhat dizzy or weak: *He was just over an illness and still a little woozy.*   **2** muddled; confused.   *adj.*

**Worces·ter·shire** (wùs′tər shər)   a highly seasoned sauce.   *n.*

**word** (wėrd)   **1** a sound or a group of sounds that has meaning and is an independent unit of speech: *She answered in one word, "No."*   **2** the writing or printing that stands for a word. *Bat, bet, bit,* and *but* are words: *This page is filled with words.*   **3** a short talk: *May I have a word with you?*   **4** speech: *honest in word and deed.*   **5** a brief expression or comment: *The teacher gave us a word of advice.*   **6** a command: *We have to wait till she gives the word.*   **7** a signal: *The word for tonight is "the King."*   **8** a promise: *The boy kept his word.*   **9** news: *No word has come from the battle front.*   **10** put into words:

*He worded his message clearly.*   **11** a string of bits, characters, or bytes treated as a single unit by a computer.   **12 words,** *pl.*   **a** angry talk; a quarrel or dispute: *They had words about whose fault it was.*   **b** the text of a song as distinguished from the notes.   **1–9, 11, 12** *n.,* **10** *v.*
**be as good as one's word,**   keep one's promise.
**by word of mouth,**   by spoken words; orally.
**eat one's words,**   take back what one has said; retract.
**have the last word,**   in an argument, have the final, decisive say.
**in a word,**   briefly.
**in so many words,**   exactly; precisely.
**man of his word,**   a man who keeps his promise.
**mince words,**   avoid coming to the point, telling the truth, or taking a stand by using ambiguous or evasive words.
**My word!**   an expression of surprise.
**take a person at his or her word,**   take a person's words seriously and act accordingly.
**take the words out of one's mouth,**   say exactly what one was just going to say oneself.
**the last word,**   **a** the last or latest thing or example in a class or field.   **b** the final thing or example, beyond which no advance or improvement is possible.
**upon my word,**   **a** I promise.   **b** an expression of surprise.
**woman of her word,**   a woman who keeps her promise.
**word for word,**   in the exact words.

**word·book** (wėrd′bùk′)   a list of words, usually with explanation, etc.; dictionary; vocabulary.   *n.*

**word element**   combining form.

**word·ing** (wėr′ding)   **1** the way of saying a thing; the choice and use of words: *Careful wording helps you make clear to others what you really mean.*   **2** ppr. of WORD.   **1** *n.,* **2** *v.*

**word·less** (wėr′dlis)   **1** without words; speechless.   **2** not put into words; unexpressed.   *adj.*

**word of honour** or **honor**   a solemn promise.

**word order**   the arrangement of words in a sentence, phrase, etc. In English the usual word order for statements is subject + predicate, as in *Johann hit the ball. The ball hit Johann.* Some other patterns of word order (*Away ran Johann. Sweet are the uses of adversity*) are chiefly rhetorical and poetic. In English, with its relative absence of inflections, word order is the chief grammatical device for indicating the function of words and their relation to each other.

**word processing**   the production of printed material, such as letters and reports, using a computer system for the input, editing, and organizing of information.

**word processor**   **1** a computer or computer program for use in word processing. It usually includes a keyboard, printer, storage, memory, and a display screen.   **2** a person who operates a word processor.

**word·y** (wėr′dē)   using too many words.   *adj.* **word·i·er, word·i·est.** —**word′i·ly,** *adv.* —**word′i·ness,** *n.*

**wore** (wôr) pt. of WEAR. *v.*
☛ Hom. WAR.

**work** (wėrk) **1** the effort of doing or making something: *Moving the piano was hard work.* **2** something to do; occupation; employment: *Many people are out of work.* **3** something made or done, especially something creative; the result of work: *The artist considers that picture to be his greatest work.* **4** that on which effort is put: *The dressmaker took her work out on the porch.* **5** do work; labour: *Most people must work for a living.* **6** work for pay; be employed: *He works in a bank.* **7** carry on operations in districts, etc. *The salesman worked the Toronto area.* **8** put one's effort or labour into; perform a required or expected activity on or in: *They worked their farm with success.* **9** act; operate, especially effectively: *This pump will not work. The plan worked well.* **10** put into operation; use; manage: *to work a scheme.* **11** cause to do work: *He worked his employees long hours.* **12** treat or handle in making; knead; mix: *Dough is worked to mix it thoroughly.* **13** make, get, do, or bring about by effort: *The injured man worked his way across the room on his hands and knees. He worked his way through college.* **14** move as if with effort: *His face worked as he tried to keep back the tears.* **15** bring about; cause; do: *The plan worked harm.* **16** go, do, manipulate, etc. slowly or with effort: *The ship worked to windward. Work the cork loose.* **17** gradually become: *The window catch has worked loose.* **18** form; shape: *He worked a silver dollar into a bracelet.* **19** influence; persuade: *to work people to one's will.* **20** move; stir; excite: *Don't work yourself into a temper.* **21** solve: *Work all the problems on the page.* **22** a fortification. **23** the transference of energy from one body or system to another. **24** that which is accomplished by a force when it acts through a distance. **25** an engineering structure. **26** *Informal.* use tricks on to get something: *to work a friend for a loan.* **27** ferment: *Yeast makes the brew work.* **28 works,** *pl.* **a** a factory or other place for doing some kind of work: *His first job was in the boiler works.* **b** the moving parts of a machine or device: *the works of a watch.* **c** buildings, bridges, docks, etc. **d** actions; deeds: *good works.* **29 the works,** *Informal.* everything involved; the complete set, collection, or treatment: *He invested $50 000 and lost the works.* 1–4, 22–25, 28, 29 *n.*, 5–21, 26, 27 *v.*, **worked** or **wrought, work·ing.**
**at work,** working.
**in the works,** *Informal.* in the planning stage; upcoming.
**make short work of,** do or get rid of quickly.
**out of work,** having no job; unemployed.
**work in,** put in with effort.
**work off,** get rid of by means of effort.
**work on** or **upon,** try to persuade or influence.
**work out, a** plan; develop. **b** solve; find out. **c** use up. **d** give exercise to; practise. **e** accomplish. **f** result.
**work up, a** plan; develop. **b** excite; stir up.

**work·a·ble** (wėr′kə bəl) that can be worked. *adj.*

**work·a·day** (wėr′kə dā′) of working days; practical; commonplace; ordinary. *adj.*

**work·bench** (wėrk′bench′) a table at which a mechanic, artisan, etc. works. *n.*

**work·book** (wėrk′bůk′) **1** a book containing outlines for the study of some subject, questions to be answered, etc.; a book in which a student does parts of the written work. **2** a book containing rules for doing certain work. **3** a book for notes of work planned or work done. *n.*

**work·day** (wėrk′dā′) **1** a day for work; a day that is not Sunday or a holiday. **2** the part of a day during which work is done. **3** WORKADAY. 1, 2 *n.*, 3 *adj.*

**work·er** (wėr′kər) **1** a labourer who works with hands or machines; a workman; a workingman or workingwoman. **2** a person who works for a living. **3** a bee, ant, wasp, or other insect that works for its community. *n.*
☛ Usage. See note at WORKINGMAN.

**work·horse** (wėrk′hôrs′) **1** a horse used mostly for work, not for racing, hunting, or showing. **2** a person who is an exceptionally hard worker. **3** a machine that is especially powerful, productive, etc. *n.* Also, **work horse.**

**work·house** (wėrk′hous′) *Esp. Brit.* formerly, a house where very poor people were lodged and were expected to perform some work in return. *n.*

**work·ing** (wėr′king) **1** the action, method, or performance of one that works. **2** that works. **3** used in working: *working hours, working clothes.* **4** used to operate with or by: *a working majority.* **5** performing its function; that goes: *a working model of a train.* **6** providing a basis for further work: *a working hypothesis.* **7** Often, **workings,** *pl.* operations; action: *the workings of a machine.* **8 workings,** *pl.* the parts of a mine, quarry, tunnel, etc. where work is being done. **9** ppr. of WORK. 1, 7, 8 *n.*, 2–6 *adj.*, 9 *v.*

**work·ing·man** (wėr′king man′) a man who works for wages, especially one who works with his hands or with machines. *n., pl.* **work·ing·men** (-men′).
☛ Usage. Although any person who makes a living by working can be described as a *workingman* or *workingwoman,* these names, along with WORKER (def. 2), are usually restricted to people who do not work at one of the PROFESSIONS (def. 2) such as law, medicine, or teaching.

**work·ing·wom·an** (wėr′king wům′ən) a woman who works for wages, especially one who works with her hands or with machines. *n., pl.* **work·ing·wom·en** (-wim′ən).
☛ Usage. See note at WORKINGMAN.

**work·load** (wėr′klōd′) the amount of work assigned to a person, position, department, etc. *n.*

**work·man** (wėrk′mən) **1** WORKINGMAN. **2** a person skilled in a trade or craft; craftsman. *n., pl.* **work·men** (-mən).

**work·man·like** (wėrk′mən līk′) worthy of a good worker; skilful: *The job was done quickly and in a workmanlike manner. adj.*

**work·man·ship** (wėrk′mən ship′) **1** the art or skill of a worker; craftsmanship: *His workmanship is not always good.* **2** the quality of something that has been made: *jewellery of fine workmanship.* **3** the work done. *n.*

**work·out** (wėr′kout′) **1** an exercise; practice: *The team had a good workout before the game.* **2** a trial or test: *He gave the car a thorough workout before buying it. n.*

**work·room** (wėr′krům′) a room set aside for working in: *We have a workroom in the basement. n.*

**work·shop** (wėrk′shop′) **1** a room or building where work, especially manual work, is done. **2** a meeting of people for discussion, study, etc. of a particular subject: *The social studies teachers held a workshop in September. n.*

**work station** a desk and other equipment where a computer system is set up for work by one person.

**work·ta·ble** (wėrk′tā′bəl) a table to work at. *n.*

**world** (wėrld)  **1** the earth: *Ships can sail around the world.*  **2** all of certain parts, people, or things of the earth: *the insect world, a woman's world. The New World is North America and South America. The Old World is Europe, Asia, and Africa.*  **3** a sphere of interest, activity, thought, etc.: *the world of music.*  **4** human affairs; the activities and circumstances of social, business, and public life: *a man of the world. The young graduate was ready to go out into the world.*  **5** all people; the human race; the public: *The whole world knows it.*  **6** the things of this life and the people devoted to them: *Monks and nuns live apart from the world.*  **7** a star or planet, especially when considered inhabited.  **8** any time, condition, or place of life: *Heaven is in the world to come.*  **9** all things; everything; the universe.  **10** a great deal; very much; a large amount: *The rest did her a world of good.*  *n.*
**for all the world,**  **a** for any reason, no matter how great.  **b** in every respect; exactly.
**in the world,**  **a** anywhere.  **b** at all; ever.
**on top of the world,**  in high spirits: *I was on top of the world when I found out I had won.*
**out of this world,** *Informal.*  great; wonderful; distinctive: *Our plans for the decorations are out of this world.*
**world without end,**  forever.
☞ *Hom.* WHORLED (wėrld).

**World Bank**  the International Bank for Reconstruction and Development, an agency of the United Nations.

**World Court**  an informal name for the Permanent Court of International Justice, a court made up of representatives of various nations and having the power to settle certain disputes between nations: *The World Court is located in The Hague.*

**world·li·ness** (wėrl′dlē nis)  worldly ideas, ways, or conduct.  *n.*

**world·ly** (wėrl′dlē)  **1** of this world; not of heaven: *worldly wealth.*  **2** caring much for the interests and pleasures of this world.  **3** WORLDLY-WISE.  *adj.*, **world·li·er, world·li·est.**

**world·ly–wise** (wėrl′dlē wīz′)  wise about the ways and affairs of this world.  *adj.*

**world series**  in baseball, the series of games played each fall between the winners of the two major league championships, to decide the professional championship of the United States.

**World War I**  the war in Europe, Asia, Africa, and at sea, from July 28, 1914 to Nov. 11, 1918. France, Russia, Italy, Canada, the United Kingdom, the United States (1917-18), and their allies were on one side; Germany, Austria-Hungary, and their allies were on the other side.

**World War II**  the war in Europe, Asia, Africa, and at sea, from September 1, 1939 to August 14, 1945, beginning as a war between the United Kingdom, France, Poland, and their allies on one side and Germany on the other, ultimately involving most of the world's nations, notably the United States, the Soviet Union and Japan.

**world–wea·ry** (wėrl′dwē′rē)  tired of living.  *adj.*

**world–wide** (wėrl′dwīd′)  spread throughout the world: *Gasoline now has world-wide use.*  *adj.*

**World Wide Web**  a branch of the Internet that consists of stored, interlinked data in the form of documents. By using specialized software, the user of the World Wide Web can create or link such data in any order. Also called **the Web.** *Abbrev.:* WWW

**worm** (wėrm)  **1** any of many small, slender, elongated, often segmented animals, usually soft-bodied and without legs, including the earthworm and parasites such as tapeworms or roundworms, etc.  **2** something like a worm in shape or movement, such as the thread of a screw.  **3** a short, continuously threaded shaft or screw, the thread of which gears with the teeth of a toothed wheel.  **4** something that slowly eats away; the pain or destruction it causes.  **5** move like a worm; crawl or creep like a worm: *We wormed under the high fence.*  **6** work or get by persistent and secret means: *He tried to worm the secret out of me. He wormed himself into our confidence.*  **7** a person who deserves contempt or pity.  **8 worms,** *pl.*  a disease caused by worms in the body.  **9** remove worms from.  1–4, 7, 8 *n.*, 5, 6, 9 *v.*
—**worm′like**′, *adj.*

**worm–eat·en** (wėrm′ē′tən)  **1** eaten into by worms: *worm-eaten timbers.*  **2** worn-out; worthless; out-of-date.  *adj.*

**worm gear**  **1** a WORM WHEEL.  **2** a WORM WHEEL and an endless screw together: *By a worm gear the rotary motion of one shaft can be transmitted to another shaft at right angles to it.*

**worm·hole** (wėrm′hōl′)  a hole made by a worm.  *n.*

**worm wheel**  a wheel with teeth that fit into a revolving screw.

**worm·wood** (wėrm′wud′)  **1** a bitter plant used in medicine, absinthe, etc.  **2** something bitter or extremely unpleasant.  *n.*

**worm·y** (wėr′mē)  **1** having worms; containing many worms: *a wormy apple.*  **2** damaged by worms: *wormy wood.*  *adj.*, **worm·i·er, worm·i·est.**  —**worm′i·ness,** *n.*

**worn** (wôrn)  **1** pp. of WEAR: *He has worn that suit for two years.*  **2** damaged by use: *worn rugs.*  **3** tired; wearied: *a worn face.*  1 *v.*, 2, 3 *adj.*
☞ *Hom.* WARN.

**worn–out** (wôr′nout′)  **1** used until no longer fit for use: *You should throw those worn-out shoes away.*  **2** fatigued; very tired; exhausted: *I'm worn-out after all that running.*  *adj.*

**wor·ri·ment** (wėr′ē mənt) *Informal.*  **1** a worrying.  **2** worry; anxiety.  *n.*

**wor·ri·some** (wėr′ē səm)  **1** causing worry.  **2** inclined to worry.  *adj.*

**wor·ry** (wėr′ē)  **1** feel anxious or uneasy: *She will worry if we are late.*  **2** cause to feel anxious or troubled: *The problem worried him.*  **3** anxiety; uneasiness; trouble; care: *Worry kept her awake.*  **4** a cause of trouble or care: *A mother of sick children has many worries.*  **5** annoy; bother: *Don't worry me with so many questions.*  **6** seize and shake with the teeth; bite at; snap at: *A cat will worry a mouse.*  1, 2, 5, 6 *v.*, **wor·ried, wor·ry·ing;**  3, 4 *n.*, *pl.* **wor·ries.**  —**wor′ri·er,** *n.*
**worry along,**  manage somehow.

**worse** (wėrs)  **1** more ill: *The patient is worse.*  **2** more bad; more evil: *He is dishonest enough, but his brother is*

**worsen**     much worse.    **3** in a more severe or worse manner or degree: *It is raining worse than ever.*    **4** that which is worse: *He thought the loss of his property bad enough, but worse followed.*    1, 2 *adj.*, comparative of BAD; 3 *adv.*, 4 *n.*
**for the worse,**    to a worse state: *The change was for the worse.*
**none the worse for,**    not suffering because of: *Pearl was rescued from the water, and was none the worse for her adventure.*
**worse off,**    **a** in a worse condition.    **b** having less money.

**wors·en** (wėr′sən)    make or become worse: *You will only worsen the situation if you talk about it. She was taken to hospital, but her condition worsened through the night.*    *v.*

**wor·ship** (wėr′ship)    **1** great honour and respect paid to someone or something regarded as sacred: *the worship of God, idol worship.*    **2** pay great honour and respect to: *Moslems worship Allah.*    **3** religious ceremonies or services in which one pays such respect: *Prayers and hymns are part of worship.*    **4** take part in a religious service.    **5** great love and admiration: *hero worship.*    **6** consider extremely precious; hold very dear; adore: *A miser worships money. She worships her mother.*    **7** a title used in addressing or referring to a mayor or certain magistrates: *"Yes, Your Worship," he said to the judge.*    1, 3, 5, 7 *n.*, 2, 4, 6 *v.*, **wor·shipped** or **wor·shiped**, **wor·ship·ping** or **wor·ship·ing.** —**wor′ship·per** or **wor′ship·er,** *n.*

**wor·ship·ful** (wėr′ship fəl)    **1** having or showing reverence: *worshipful silence.*    **2** Often, **Worshipful,** *Esp. Brit.* a title of respect for mayors and certain other people of distinguished rank.    *adj.*

**worst** (wėrst)    **1** most ill: *This is the worst cold I ever had.*    **2** most bad; most evil: *He is the worst boy in school.*    **3** in the worst manner or degree: *He acts worst when he's tired.*    **4** that which is worst: *Yesterday was bad, but the worst is yet to come.*    **5** beat; defeat: *The hero worsted his enemies.*    1, 2 *adj.*, superlative of BAD; 3 *adv.*, 4 *n.*, 5 *v.*
**at worst,**    under the least favourable circumstances.
**give one the worst of it,**    defeat one.
**if worst comes to worst,**    if the very worst thing happens.

**wor·sted** (wėr′stid *or* wus′tid)    **1** smooth, firm yarn or thread made from long wool fibres that have been combed: *Worsted is used especially for firm, smooth-finished fabrics, carpets, and in knitting.*    **2** fabric made from worsted.    **3** made of worsted.    *n.*
☛ *Etym.* From the name of a parish in Norfolk, England, now *Worstead,* where this kind of cloth was first made.

**worth** (wėrth)    **1** good or important enough for; deserving of: *Vancouver is a city worth visiting.*    **2** merit; usefulness; importance: *We should read books of real worth.*    **3** value in money: *She needed money and had to sell her car for less than its worth.*    **4** a quantity of something of specified value: *ten dollars' worth of gasoline.*    **5** equal in value to: *That book is worth fifteen dollars.*    **6** having property that amounts to: *That man is worth millions.*    1, 5, 6 *adj.*, 2–4 *n.*

**worth·less** (wėrth′lis)    without worth; good-for-nothing; useless.    *adj.*    —**worth′less·ly,** *adv.* —**worth′less·ness,** *n.*

**worth·while** (wėr′thwīl′ *or* wėrth′hwīl′)    worth time, attention, or effort; having real merit: *Pauline ought to spend her time on some worthwhile reading.*    *adj.*

**wor·thy** (wėr′ŦHē)    **1** having worth or merit.    **2** deserving; meriting: *Her courage was worthy of high praise.*    **3** a person of great merit; admirable person: *Sir Winston Churchill stands high among English worthies.*    1, 2 *adj.*, **wor·thi·er, wor·thi·est;**    3 *n.*, *pl.* **wor·thies.** —**wor′thi·ly,** *adv.* —**wor′thi·ness,** *n.*
**worthy of,**    **a** deserving: *Bad acts are worthy of punishment.*    **b** having enough worth for.

**would** (wud; *unstressed,* wəd)    a word used:    **1** to introduce a request or command in a polite manner: *Would you please close the window?*    **2** to soften a statement or express uncertainty: *I wouldn't like to ask him.*    **3** to express an unlikely or an impossible condition: *If he would say no, I would be surprised. If she would take her work seriously, she could graduate this year.*    **4** to express repeated, or habitual, action in the past: *When we were small, we would spend hours playing in the sand.*    **5** pt. of WILL¹.    *v.*
☛ *Hom.* WOOD.
☛ *Usage.* **Would** as the past tense of **will** is used most often in reported speech. Compare *She said, "I will come"* with *She said that she would come.*

**would–be** (wud′bē′)    **1** wishing or pretending to be.    **2** intended to be.    *adj.*

**would·n't** (wud′ənt)    would not.

**wound¹** (wünd)    **1** a hurt or injury caused by cutting, stabbing, shooting, etc.    **2** injure by cutting, stabbing, shooting, etc.; hurt.    **3** any hurt or injury to feelings, reputation, etc.: *The loss of his job was a wound to his pride.*    **4** injure in feelings, reputation, etc.: *His unkind words wounded her.*    1, 3 *n.*, 2, 4 *v.*

**wound²** (wound)    a pt. and a pp. of WIND².    *v.*

**wove** (wōv)    a pt. and a pp. of WEAVE: *wove paper.*    *v.*

**wo·ven** (wō′vən)    a pp. of WEAVE.    *v.*

**wrack** (rak)    **1** wreckage.    **2** ruin; destruction.    **3** seaweed cast ashore.    *n.*
☛ *Hom.* RACK.

**wraith** (rāth)    **1** the ghost of a person seen before or soon after his or her death.    **2** a ghost; spectre.    *n.*

**wran·gle** (rang′gəl)    **1** argue or dispute in a noisy or angry way; quarrel: *The children wrangled about who should sit in front.*    **2** a noisy dispute; angry quarrel.    **3** in the western parts of Canada and the United States, herd or tend livestock, especially horses, on the range.    1, 3 *v.*, **wrang·led, wran·gling;**    2 *n.*

**wran·gler** (rang′glər)    **1** a person who wrangles.    **2** in the western parts of Canada and the United States, a cowboy, especially one who looks after saddle horses.    *n.*

**wrap** (rap)    **1** cover by winding or folding something around: *She wrapped herself in a shawl.*    **2** wind or fold as a covering: *Wrap a shawl around you.*    **3** cover with paper and tie up or fasten.    **4** cover; envelop; hide: *The mountain peak is wrapped in clouds. She sat wrapped in thought.*    **5** an outer covering: *Shawls, scarfs, coats, and furs are wraps.*    1–4 *v.*, **wrapped** or **wrapt, wrap·ping;**    5 *n.*
**wrapped up in,**    **a** devoted to; thinking mainly of: *She is wrapped up in her children.*    **b** involved in; associated with.
**wrap up,**    put on warm outer clothes.
☛ *Hom.* RAP.

**wrap·per** (rap′ər)  1 anything in which something is wrapped; a covering; cover: *Magazines are mailed in paper wrappers.*  2 a person or thing that wraps.  3 a woman's long, loose-fitting garment for wearing in the house. *n.*

**wrap·ping** (rap′ing)  1 the paper or other material in which something is wrapped.  2 ppr. of WRAP.  1 *n.*, 2 *v.*

**wrapt** (rapt)  a pt. and a pp. of WRAP. *v.*
☞ Hom. RAPT.

**wrasse** (ras)  any of a number of related and usually brightly coloured sea fishes having thick, fleshy lips, powerful teeth, and spiny fins. *n.*

**wrath** (rath *or* roth)  very great anger; rage. *n.*

**wrath·ful** (rath′fəl *or* roth′fəl)  feeling or showing wrath; very angry: *a wrathful mood, a group of wrathful citizens. adj.* —**wrath′ful·ly,** *adv.* —**wrath′ful·ness,** *n.*

**wrath·y** (rath′ē *or* roth′ē)  WRATHFUL. *adj.*, **wrath·i·er, wrath·i·est.**

**wreak** (rēk)  1 give expression to; work off feelings, desires, etc.: *The cruel boy wreaked his bad temper on his dog.*  2 inflict: *The hurricane wreaked havoc on the city. v.*
☞ Hom. REEK.

**wreath** (rēth)  1 a ring of flowers or leaves twisted together.  2 something suggesting a wreath: *a wreath of smoke. n., pl.* **wreaths** (rēTHz).

**wreathe** (rēTH)  1 make into a wreath; twist: *The children wreathed flowers to put on their grandmother's grave.*  2 decorate or adorn with wreaths: *The hall was wreathed with Christmas greens.*  3 make a ring around; encircle: *Mist wreathed the hills.*  4 envelop: *wreathed in smiles.*  5 move in rings: *The smoke wreathed upward. v.,* **wreathed, wreath·ing.**

**wreck** (rek)  1 the destruction of a ship, building, train, automobile, or aircraft: *The hurricane caused many wrecks. I heard there was a bad train wreck in the Maritimes.*  2 any destruction or serious injury: *Heavy rains caused the wreck of many crops.*  3 what is left of anything that has been destroyed or much injured: *The wreck of a ship was cast upon the shore.*  4 cause the wreck of; destroy; ruin.  5 be wrecked; suffer serious injury.  6 a person or animal that has lost physical or mental health: *He's been a wreck ever since his bout with pneumonia.*  7 goods cast up by the sea, especially after a shipwreck.  8 act as WRECKER. 1–3, 6, 7 *n.*, 4, 5, 8 *v.*

**wreck·age** (rek′ij)  1 what is left by wreck or wrecks: *The shore was covered with the wreckage of ships.*  2 a wrecking or being wrecked: *She wept at the wreckage of her hopes. n.*

**wreck·er** (rek′ər)  1 a person or machine that tears down buildings: *Pat operates the wrecker that is demolishing the vacant building.*  2 a person, car, train, or machine that removes wrecks.  3 a person or ship that recovers wrecked or disabled ships or their cargoes.  4 a person who causes shipwrecks by false lights on shore so as to plunder the wrecks. *n.*

**wren** (ren)  a small brown or grey songbird having a slender bill and a short tail, often held erect: *Wrens often build their nests near houses. n.*

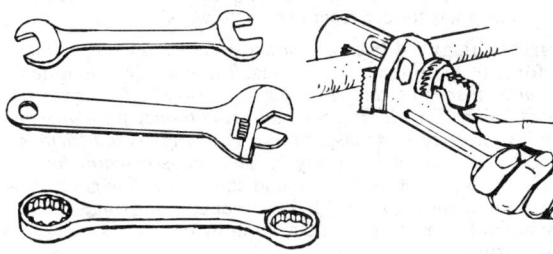

hat, āge, fär; let, ēqual, tėrm; it, īce
hot, ōpen, ôrder; oil, out; cup, pút, rüle
əbove, takən, pencəl, lemən, circəs
ch, child; ng, long; sh, ship
th, thin; ᴛH, then; zh, measure

Three kinds of wrench

A pipe wrench. The jaws have ridged surfaces for gripping. They can be moved together or apart by means of a screw.

**wrench** (rench)  1 a violent twist or twisting pull: *He broke the branch off the tree with a sudden wrench. He gave his ankle a wrench when he jumped off the bus.*  2 twist or pull violently: *The policewoman wrenched the gun out of the man's hand.*  3 injure by twisting: *He wrenched his back in wrestling.*  4 an injury caused by twisting: *She was suffering from a wrench in the back.*  5 grief; pain: *It was a wrench to leave our old home.*  6 twist the meaning of.  7 a tool for holding and turning nuts, bolts, etc.  1, 4, 5, 7 *n.*, 2, 3, 6 *v.*

**wrest** (rest)  1 twist, pull, or tear away with force; wrench away: *He bravely wrested the knife from the insane man.*  2 take by force: *to wrest power from someone.*  3 twist or turn from the proper meaning, use, etc.: *to wrest words from their meanings.*  4 the act of wresting; forcible twist.  1–3 *v.*, 4 *n.* —**wrest′er,** *n.*
☞ Hom. REST.

**wres·tle** (res′əl)  1 try to throw or force an opponent to the ground.  2 a wrestling match.  3 contend with in wrestling, or as if in wrestling.  4 struggle: *We wrestle with problems, temptations, and difficulties.*  1, 3, 4 *v.*, **wres·tled, wres·tling;**  2, 4 *n.* —**wres′tler,** *n.*

**wres·tling** (res′ling)  1 a sport or contest in which each of usually two opponents tries to throw or force the other to the ground: *The rules for wrestling do not allow using the fists or certain holds on the body.*  2 ppr. of WRESTLE.  1 *n.*, 2 *v.*

**wretch** (rech)  1 a very unfortunate or unhappy person.  2 scoundrel. *n.*
☞ Hom. RETCH.

**wretch·ed** (rech′id)  1 very unfortunate or unhappy.  2 very unsatisfactory; miserable: *a wretched hut.*  3 vicious; wicked; degenerate: *a wretched traitor. adj.* —**wretch′ed·ly,** *adv.* —**wretch′ed·ness,** *n.*

**wrig·gle** (rig′əl)  1 twist and turn: *Children wriggle when they are restless.*  2 move by twisting and turning: *A snake wriggled across the road.*  3 make one's way by tricks, excuses, etc.: *to wriggle out of a difficulty.*  4 the act of wriggling: *With one wriggle, he was under the bed.*  1–3 *v.*, **wrig·gled, wrig·gling;**  4 *n.*

**wrig·gler** (rig′lər)  1 a person who wriggles.  2 the larva of a mosquito. *n.*

**wrig·gly** (rig′lē)  twisting and turning. *adj.*

**wright** (rīt) a maker or author of something (*used usually in compounds*): *A wheelwright makes wheels. A playwright writes plays for the theatre.* *n.*
☛ *Hom.* RIGHT, RITE, WRITE.
☛ *Etym.* From OE *wryhta*, a variant of *wyrhta* 'maker', which was formed from *wyrcan* 'to work'.

**wring** (ring) **1** twist and squeeze hard: *to wring clothes.* **2** force by twisting and squeezing: *The hikers wrung water from their soaking clothes.* **3** get by force, effort, or persuasion: *The old beggar could wring money from anyone by his sad story.* **4** clasp; press: *He wrung his old friend's hand.* **5** cause pain or pity in: *Their poverty wrung her heart.* **6** the act of twisting and squeezing: *She gave her swimsuit a good wring.* 1–5 *v.*, **wrung, wring·ing**; 6 *n.*
**wring out,** force water, etc. from by twisting or squeezing.
☛ *Hom.* RING.

**wring·er** (ring'ər) a person or thing that wrings, especially a device or machine for squeezing water from clothes. *n.*
☛ *Hom.* RINGER.

**wrin·kle**[1] (ring'kəl) **1** an irregular ridge or fold; crease: *The old woman's face has wrinkles. I must press out the wrinkles in this dress.* **2** make a wrinkle or wrinkles in: *He wrinkled his forehead.* **3** have wrinkles; acquire wrinkles: *This shirt will not wrinkle.* 1 *n.*, 2, 3 *v.*, **wrin·kled, wrin·kling.**

**wrin·kle**[2] (ring'kəl) *Informal.* a useful hint or idea; clever trick: *She will give you some wrinkles for using empty cartons to make toys.* *n.*

**wrin·kly** (ring'klē) WRINKLEd. *adj.*, **wrin·kli·er, wrin·kli·est.**

**wrist** (rist) **1** the part of the human arm between the palm of the hand and the forearm: *Her wrists are thicker than mine.* See ARM for picture. **2** the joint formed by the end of the larger bone of the forearm and the carpus, connecting the arm with the hand: *flexible wrists.* **3** one or more of the bones of this joint: *Urho broke his wrist when he fell.* **4** the part of a sleeve, glove, or mitten covering the wrist. *n.*

**wrist·band** (rist'band') the band of a sleeve or glove fitting around the wrist. *n.*

**wrist·watch** (ris'twoch) a small watch worn on a strap around the wrist. *n., pl.* **wrist·watches.**

**writ** (rit) **1** something written; a piece of writing. Archaic except in **Holy Writ. 2** a formal order directing a person to do or not to do something: *A writ from the judge ordered the man's release from jail.* *n.*

**write** (rīt) **1** make letters or words with pen, pencil, chalk, etc.: *She learned to write.* **2** mark with letters or words: *She had to write a cheque.* **3** put down the letters or words of: *Write your name and address.* **4** give in writing; record: *She writes all that happens.* **5** make up books, stories, articles, poems, letters, etc.; compose: *He writes for the magazines.* **6** be a writer: *Her ambition was to write.* **7** write a letter: *She writes to her mother every week.* **8** write a letter to: *Mary wrote her friends to come.* **9** show plainly: *Honesty is written on his face.* *v.*, **wrote, writ·ten, writ·ing.**
**write down,** **a** put into writing: *Many early folk songs were never written down.* **b** put a lower value on.
**write off,** cancel as by entering in accounts as a loss: *My father agreed to write off my debt to him.*
**write out,** **a** put into writing. **b** write in full: *She made quick notes during the interview and wrote out her report later.*
**write up,** **a** write a description or account of. **b** write in detail. **c** bring up to date in writing. **d** put a higher value on.
☛ *Hom.* RIGHT, RITE, WRIGHT.

**writ·er** (rī'tər) a person who writes, especially one whose profession or business is writing, such as an author or journalist. *n.*

**write–off** (rī'tof') **1** something cancelled or recognized as a loss: *We treated the money we had lent him as a write-off.* **2** a total wreck, such as might be written off as a loss: *They weren't hurt badly in the accident, but their car was a write-off.* *n.*

**write–up** (rī'tup') *Informal.* a written description or account. *n.*

**writhe** (rīᴛʜ) **1** twist and turn; twist: *The snake writhed along the branch. The wounded man writhed with pain.* **2** suffer mentally; be very uncomfortable: *We writhed when we heard the angry man insult our friend.* *v.*, **writhed, writh·ing.**

**writ·ing** (rī'ting) **1** written form: *Put your ideas in writing.* **2** handwriting: *Her writing is hard to read.* **3** something written; a letter, paper, document, etc. **4** a literary work; a book or other literary production: *the writings of Stephen Leacock.* **5** the profession or business of a person who writes. **6** used in writing: *writing paper.* **7** ppr. of WRITE. 1–6 *n.*, 7 *v.*

**writ·ten** (rit'ən) pp. of WRITE: *She has written a letter.* *v.*

**wrong** (rong) **1** not right; bad; unjust; unlawful: *It is wrong to tell lies.* **2** incorrect: *He gave the wrong answer.* **3** unsuitable; improper: *the wrong clothes for the occasion.* **4** in a bad state or condition; out of order; amiss: *Something is wrong with the car.* **5** in a wrong manner; in the wrong direction; badly: *Everything went wrong today.* **6** what is wrong; wrong thing or things: *Two wrongs do not make a right.* **7** an injustice; injury: *You do an honest man a wrong if you call him a liar or a thief.* **8** do wrong to; treat unjustly; injure: *Una forgave those who had wronged her.* **9** not meant to be seen or shown: *the wrong side of cloth.* 1–4, 9 *adj.*, 5 *adv.*, 6, 7 *n.*, 8 *v.*
—**wrong'ly,** *adv.* —**wrong'ness,** *n.*
**go wrong,** **a** turn out badly. **b** stop being good and become bad.
**in the wrong,** at fault; guilty.

**wrong·do·er** (rong'dü'ər) a person who does wrong. *n.*

**wrong·do·ing** (rong'dü'ing) the doing of wrong; bad acts: *The thief was guilty of wrongdoing.* *n.*

**wrong·ful** (rong'fəl) **1** wrong; unjust. **2** unlawful. *adj.* —**wrong'ful·ly,** *adv.*

**wrong–head·ed** (rong'hed'id) **1** wrong in judgment or opinion. **2** stubborn even when wrong. *adj.*
—**wrong'-head'ed·ness,** *n.*

**wrote** (rōt) pt. of WRITE. *v.*
☛ *Hom.* ROTE.

**wroth** (roth) angry. *adj.*

**wrought** (rot) **1** a pt. and a pp. of WORK. **2** shaped or formed with skill and care; fashioned: *elegantly wrought vases.* **3** of metals, shaped by hammering, etc.: *a plate of wrought silver.* 1 *v.*, 2, 3 *adj.*
☛ *Hom.* ROT.
☛ *Etym.* From ME *wrohte*, a variant of *worhte*, past participle of WORK.

**wrought iron** a tough, durable form of iron that is soft enough to be easily forged and welded, but that will not break as easily as cast iron: *Wrought iron is often used for decorative furniture, gates, or railings.*

**wrought–up** (rot′up′) stirred up; excited: *After all the work of planning, she was too wrought-up to enjoy the party.* *adj.*

**wrung** (rung) pt. and pp. of WRING. *v.*
☛ *Hom.* RUNG.

**wry** (rī) **1** made by distorting the mouth or other features to show disgust, bitterness, doubt, or irony: *a wry face, a wry grin.* **2** marked by grim or bitter irony: *wry humour, wry remarks.* **3** turned to one side in an abnormal way: *a wry nose.* **4** perversely wrong or inappropriate: *wry behaviour.* *adj.*, **wri·er, wri·est.** —**wry′ly,** *adv.*
☛ *Hom.* RYE.

**wry·neck** (rī′nek′) **1** a twisted neck caused by unequal contraction of the muscles. **2** any of several birds related to the woodpecker, able to twist its neck. *n.*

**WSW** or **W.S.W.** west-southwest.

**wt.** weight.

hat, āge, fär; let, ēqual, tėrm; it, īce
hot, ōpen, ôrder; oil, out; cup, pút, rüle
əbove, takən, pencəl, lemən, circəs

ch, child; ng, long; sh, ship
th, thin; ᴛʜ, then; zh, measure

**x or X** (eks) **1** the twenty-fourth letter of the English alphabet. **2** any speech sound or sounds represented by this letter. **3** a person or thing identified as x, especially the twenty-fourth of a series or the first of a series consisting of x, y, and sometimes z. **4** an unknown quantity. **5** X, the Roman numeral for 10. **6** anything shaped like an X. **7** x is also used: **a** to indicate a certain place on a map, etc.: *X marks the spot.* **b** to symbolize a kiss. **c** to represent the signature of a person who cannot write. *n., pl.* **x's** or **X's.**

**x** (eks) **1** mark with an x. **2** cancel or cross out with an x or a series of x's (*often used with* **out**): *to x out a mistake. v.,* **x-ed** or **x'd, x-ing** or **x'ing.**

**X chromosome** one of the chromosomes that determine sex: *An embryo containing two X chromosomes, one from each parent, develops into a female.*

**Xe** xenon.

**xe·bec** (zē′bek) a small three-masted vessel of the Mediterranean. *n.*

**xe·non** (zē′non *or* zen′on) a heavy, colourless gas that is chemically inactive. It is a rare element that occurs in the air in very small quantities. *Symbol:* Xe *n.*

**xen·o·pho·bi·a** (zen′ə fō′bē ə) a hatred or fear of foreigners. *n.*

**xe·rog·ra·phy** (zē rog′rə fē) a process for making copies of written or printed material, pictures, etc., by the action of magnetic attraction rather than ink and pressure. Tiny, negatively-charged particles are spread on positively-charged paper in an arrangement that exactly copies the printing, etc. on the original paper. *n.*

**xe·ro·phyte** (zē′rə fīt′) a plant that needs very little water and can grow in deserts or very dry ground: *Cactuses, sagebrush, etc. are xerophytes. n.*

**Xer·ox** (zē′roks) **1** a copy made by Xerox. **2** make such copies. 1 *n., pl.* **Xer·ox·es;** 2 *v.,* **xer·oxed, xer·ox·ing.**
☛ *Usage.* The spelling **xerox** is sometimes seen, but both the noun and the verb **xerox** are derived from the trademark for the photocopying machine, Xerox, and the xerographic process used.

**Xmas** (kris′məs) *Informal.* Christmas. *n.*

**Xn.** Christian.

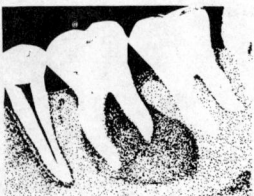

An X ray of an abscessed tooth. The abscess is shown by the dark area around the roots of the tooth.

**X ray** or **X–ray** (eks′rā′) **1** radiation of the same type as visible radiation (i.e. light) but having an extremely short wavelength. It can go through substances that ordinary light rays cannot penetrate, but will act in the same way as light does on a photographic film or plate to produce a picture: *X rays are used to locate breaks in bones, a bullet lodged in the body, etc., and in treating certain diseases.* **2** a picture obtained by means of X rays. *n.*

**X–ray** or **x–ray** (eks′rā′) **1** examine, photograph, or treat with X rays. **2** of, by, or having to do with X rays: *an X-ray examination of one's teeth.* 1 *v.,* 2 *adj.*

**Xtian.** Christian.

**Xty.** Christianity.

**xy·lem** (zī′lem) in botany, the woody tissue in the vascular system of plants and trees that conducts water and mineral salts and supports the softer tissue. Compare with PHLOEM. *n.*

A xylophone

**xy·lo·phone** (zī′lə fōn′) a tuned percussion instrument consisting of two rows of wooden bars of varying lengths, which are sounded by striking them with small wooden hammers. *n.*

# Yy Yy

hat, āge, fär; let, ēqual, tėrm; it, īce
hot, ōpen, ôrder; oil, out; cup, pút, rüle
əbove, takən, pencəl, lemən, circəs
ch, child; ng, long; sh, ship
th, thin; ŦH, then; zh, measure

**y** or **Y** (wī)  **1** the twenty-fifth letter of the English alphabet.  **2** any speech sound represented by this letter.  **3** a person or thing identified as y, especially the twenty-fifth of a series or the second of a series consisting of x, y, and sometimes z.  **4** anything shaped like a Y. *n., pl.* **y's** or **Y's.**

**y.**  **1** yard; yards.  **2** year; years.

**Y¹**  yttrium.

**Y²** (wī) *Informal.*  YMCA, YWCA, YMHA, or YWHA: *We spent the afternoon at the Y.*

**-y¹**  a suffix meaning:  **1** full of, composed of, containing, having, or characterized by, as in *airy, cloudy, dewy, icy, juicy, watery.*  **2** somewhat, as in *chilly, salty.*  **3** inclined to, as in *chatty, fidgety.*  **4** resembling; suggesting, as in *sugary, willowy.*  **5** in certain words, usually archaic or poetic, such as *stilly, vasty,* the presence of the *-y* does not change the meaning.

**-y²**  a suffix used to indicate that someone or something is considered as small and attractive, thought of with affection, etc.: *doggy, dolly, mummy.*

**-y³**  a suffix meaning:  **1** a state or quality, as in *jealousy, victory.*  **2** an activity, as in *delivery, entreaty.*

**yacht** (yot)  **1** a boat for pleasure trips or racing.  **2** sail or race on a yacht.  **1** *n.,* **2** *v.*

**yacht·ing** (yot′ing)  **1** the art of sailing a yacht.  **2** the pastime of sailing on a yacht.  **3** ppr. of YACHT.  **1, 2** *n.,* **3** *v.*

**yachts·man** (yot′smən)  a person who owns or sails a yacht. *n., pl.* **yachts·men** (-smən).

**yachts·man·ship** (yot′smən ship′)  skill or ability in handling a yacht. *n.*

**yah** (yä)  a noise made to express derision, disgust, or impatience. *interj.*

**yak** (yak)  a large, long-haired animal of central Asia, related to the North American buffalo and to cattle: *Yaks are often domesticated and used for food and as beasts of burden. n.*

**yam** (yam)  **1** a kind of sweet potato.  **2** the starchy root of a vine grown for food in warm countries.  **3** the vine itself. *n.*

**yang** (yang)  in Taoism, the positive force in the cosmos. It refers to the "bright side" of reality. Compare with YIN. *n.*

**yank** (yangk)  **1** *Informal.*  pull with a sudden motion; jerk: *You almost yanked my arm off!*  **2** a sudden pull; jerk: *He gave the door a yank.*  **1** *v.,* **2** *n.*

**yank out,** *Informal.*  take out with a jerk.

**Yan·kee** (yang′kē) *Informal.*  **1** a native of one of the six New England states of the northeastern part of the United States.  **2** a native of any of the northern states of the United States.  **3** a person born in or living in the United States; an American.  **4** of or having to do with Yankees. *n.*

**Yankee Doo·dle** (dü′dəl)  an American song, probably of English origin and taken over by the Revolutionary soldiers in the American Revolution.

**yap** (yap)  **1** a snappish bark; yelp.  **2** bark snappishly; yelp.  **1** *n.,* **2** *v.,* **yapped, yap·ping.**

**yard¹** (yärd)  **1** a piece of ground near or around a house, barn, school, etc.  **2** a piece of enclosed ground for some special purpose or business: *a chicken yard, a junk yard.*  **3** a space with tracks where railway cars are stored, shifted around, etc.: *My brother works at the CN yards.*  **4** a clearing where animals feed.  **5** put into or enclose in a yard.  **1–4** *n.,* **5** *v.*

**yard²** (yärd)  **1** a unit for measuring length, equal to 3 feet or 36 inches (about 91.4 cm).  **2** a long, slender beam, or spar, with tapered ends, fastened across a mast and used to support a sail.  See BRIG for picture. *n.*

**yard·age** (yär′dij)  **1** length in yards.  **2** an amount measured in yards. *n.*

**yard·arm** (yärd′ärm′)  either end of a YARD (def. 2) supporting a sail on a square-rigged ship. *n.*

**yard goods**  cloth, etc. sold by the yard.

**yard·mas·ter** (yärd′mas′tər)  a person in charge of a railway yard. *n.*

**yard·stick** (yärd′stik′)  **1** a stick one yard long, used for measuring.  **2** any standard of judgment or comparison: *She is the yardstick for success. n.*

**yar·mul·ke** (yär′məl kə)  a skullcap worn by Jewish men and boys, especially for prayer and on ceremonial occasions. *n.*

**yarn** (yärn)  **1** any spun thread, especially that prepared for weaving or knitting.  See SHUTTLE for picture.  **2** a tale; story: *An old sailor told me that yarn.*  **3** tell stories.  **1, 2** *n.,* **3** *v.*

**spin a yarn,** *Informal.*  tell a story.

**yar·row** (yar′ō *or* yer′ō)  a common plant having finely divided leaves and flat clusters of white or pink flowers. *n.*

**yaw** (yo)  **1** turn from a straight course; go unsteadily.  **2** of an aircraft, turn from a straight course by a motion about its vertical axis.  **3** a movement away from a straight course.  **1, 2** *v.,* **3** *n.*

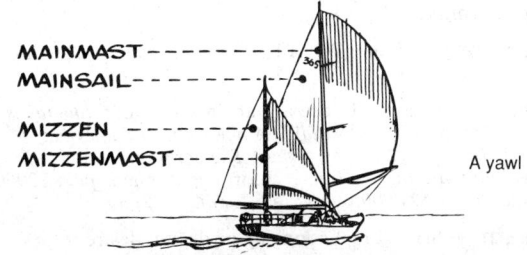

A yawl

**yawl** (yol)  **1** a boat like a sloop having a large mast near the bow and a short mast near the stern: *A yawl has its sails rigged fore-and-aft.*  **2** a ship's boat rowed by four or six oars. *n.*

**yawn** (yon) **1** open the mouth wide and inhale deeply involuntarily because one is sleepy, tired, or bored. **2** utter with a yawn; cause by yawning. **3** open wide; gape: *A wide gorge yawned beneath our feet.* **4** an act or instance of yawning. 1–3 *v.*, 4 *n.*

**yaws** (yoz) a contagious disease of the tropics, characterized by sores on the skin. *n. pl.*

**Yb** ytterbium.

**Y chromosome** one of the two chromosomes that determine sex: *An embryo containing one Y chromosome develops into a male.*

**yd.** yard; yards.

**yds.** yards.

**ye** (yē) an early form of YOU. *pron.*

**yea** (yā) **1** yes (used in affirmation or assent). **2** indeed; truly (used to introduce a sentence or clause). **3** an affirmative vote or voter. 1, 2 *adv.*, 3 *n.*

**yean** (yēn) give birth to a lamb or kid. *v.*

**yean·ling** (yēn′ling) a lamb or kid; the young of a sheep or goat. *n.*

**year** (yēr) **1** 12 months or 365 days; January 1 to December 31. Leap year has 366 days. **2** 12 months reckoned from any point. A **fiscal year** is a period of 12 months at the end of which the accounts of a government, business, etc. are balanced: *We moved here five years ago this week. They came with their six-year-old daughter.* **3** the part of a year spent in a certain activity: *The school year goes from September to June.* **4** the exact period of the earth's revolution around the sun. The **solar** or **astronomical year** is 365 days, 5 hours, 48 minutes, 46 seconds. **5** the time required (365 days, 6 hours, 9 minutes of mean solar time) for the earth to orbit the sun relative to a fixed star. The **sidereal year** is 20 minutes, 23 seconds longer than the solar year. **6** the time in which any planet completes its revolution around the sun. **7 years**, *pl.* **a** age: *a child of tender years.* **b** a very long time: *They hadn't seen each other for years.* *n.*
**year by year,** with each succeeding year; as years go by.
**year in, year out,** always; continuously: *She has always worked hard, year in, year out.*

**year·book** (yēr′bůk′) **1** a book or report published every year. **2** a school annual containing pictures and information of school activities. *n.*

**year·ling** (yēr′ling *or* yėr′ling) **1** an animal one year old: *The rancher decided to sell her yearlings.* **2** one year old: *a yearling colt.* *n.*

**year·long** (yēr′long′) **1** lasting for a year. **2** lasting for years. *adj.*

**year·ly** (yēr′lē) **1** once a year; in every year: *She takes a yearly trip to Toronto (adj.). A new volume comes out yearly (adv.).* **2** lasting a year: *The earth makes a yearly revolution around the sun.* **3** for a year: *She is paid $2000 a month, or $24 000 yearly.* 1, 2 *adj.*, 1, 3 *adv.*

**yearn** (yėrn) **1** feel a longing or desire; desire earnestly: *He yearns for home.* **2** feel pity; have tender feelings: *Her heart yearned for the homeless children.* *v.*

**yearn·ing** (yėr′ning) an earnest or strong desire; longing. *n.*

**year–round** (yēr′round′) throughout the year: *Our town has many summer visitors but few year-round residents.* *adj.*

**yeast** (yēst) **1** a yellowish, frothy substance consisting of very small fungi, which occurs especially on the surface of liquids containing sugar and produces fermentation: *Yeast is used to make bread rise, in the making of beer and other alcoholic liquors, etc.* **2** a product containing yeast, often in the form of a small pressed block or cake. **3** any of a family of fungi that produce yeast. **4** something that acts like yeast, in causing activity or ferment: *the yeast of rebellion.* **5** foam; froth. *n.*

**yeast·y** (yē′stē) **1** of, containing, or resembling yeast. **2** frothy or foamy: *yeasty waves.* **3** light or trifling; frivolous. *adj.*

**yell** (yel) **1** cry out with a strong, loud sound: *He yelled with pain.* **2** a strong, loud cry. **3** say with a yell: *We yelled our goodbyes as the bus left.* **4** a special shout or cheer, especially one used by a school or college to encourage its sports teams. 1, 3 *v.*, 2, 4 *n.*

**yel·low** (yel′ō) **1** the colour of gold, butter, or ripe lemons. **2** having a yellow colour. **3** turn yellow: *Paper yellows with age.* **4** make yellow: *Buttercups yellowed the field.* **5** a yellow pigment or dye. **6** something yellow, especially the yolk of an egg: *We used the whites of six eggs for cake and the yellows for custards.* **7** having a yellowish-brown skin. **8** jealous; envious. **9** *Informal.* cowardly. **10** sensational in an offensive way: *yellow journalism.* 1, 5, 6 *n.*, 2, 7–10 *adj.*, 3, 4 *v.*
—**yel·low·ness**, *n.*

**yel·low·bird** (yel′ō bėrd′) **1** the goldfinch of North America. **2** the yellow warbler of North America. **3** any of various other yellow birds, such as an oriole of Europe. *n.*

**yellow cypress** or **cedar** a medium large evergreen tree of the cypress family found along the Pacific coast of North America, usually about 25 metres tall, having small, sharply pointed, scale-like leaves and small, round, reddish-brown cones: *The hard wood of the yellow cypress is much used for boat building.*

**yellow fever** a dangerous, infectious disease of warm climates, caused by a virus transmitted by the bite of a mosquito.

**yel·low·ham·mer** (yel′ō ham′ər) **1** a European bird having a yellow head, neck, and breast. **2** the flicker or golden-winged woodpecker of eastern North America. *n.*

**yel·low·ish** (yel′ō ish) somewhat yellow. *adj.*

**yellow jacket** a wasp or hornet marked with bright yellow.

**yel·low·legs** (yel′ō legz′) a shore bird having yellow legs, a brownish back streaked with white, and a white breast with brown markings. *n.*

**yellow pages** a telephone directory, or part of one, that lists and advertises firms classified by the nature of their business. It is printed on yellow paper.

**yellow pickerel** YELLOW WALLEYE.

**yellow pine 1** any of several species of pine having relatively hard wood, especially the ponderosa pine. **2** the wood of any of these pines.

**yellow walleye** a common game fish of the perch family found in rivers and lakes from New Brunswick to

British Columbia, having an olive-brown back and yellow sides and mottled all over with gold or yellow spots.

**yellow warbler** a small North American warbler. The male has yellow plumage streaked with brown.

**yelp** (yelp) **1** a quick, sharp bark or cry: *The yelps of the small puppy didn't bother the Newfoundland dog.* **2** make such a bark or cry: *I yelped when the rock fell on my toe.* **3** utter with a yelp. *1 n., 2, 3 v.*

**yen** (yen) **1** a fanciful desire or longing: *a yen to see the world. You're free to do whatever you have a yen for.* **2** a desire: *a yen for Chinese food.* **3** desire. *1, 2 n., 3 v.*, **yenned, yen·ning.**
☛ *Etym.* From Chinese *yen* 'craving, addiction'. The word came into English in the 19c., probably with reference to addiction to opium.

**yeo·man** (yō′mən) **1** a petty officer in the navy, especially the chief signalman on a ship. **2** especially in England, a person who owns land, but not a large amount. *n., pl.* **yeo·men** (-mən).
**yeoman service** or **yeoman's service**, extremely valuable service or assistance.

**yeo·man·ly** (yō′mən lē) **1** sturdy; honest. **2** bravely. *1 adj., 2 adv.*

**yeoman of the guard** in England, a member of a force once forming the sovereign's bodyguard, now having ceremonial duties and providing warders for the Tower of London.

**yeo·man·ry** (yō′mən rē) yeomen as a group. *n.*

**yes** (yes) **1** a word used to indicate that one can or will, or that something is so; a word used to affirm, accept, or agree: *"Yes, five and two are seven," said Barbara. Will you go? Yes.* **2** agreement; acceptance; consent: *You have my yes to that.* **3** say yes. **4** and what is more; in addition to that: *The soldier found that he could endure hardships; yes, even enjoy them.* *1, 4 adv., 2 n., pl.* **yes·es**; *3 v.*, **yessed, yes·sing.**

**Ye·shi·va** (yə shē′və) **1** a Jewish school for higher studies. **2** a Jewish day school. *n., pl.* **Ye·shi·vas** or **Ye·shi·voth** (yə shē′vōt′).

**yes man** *Informal.* a person who always agrees with his or her employer, superior officer, party, etc., especially one who does so obsequiously and in order to curry favour.

**yes·ter·day** (yes′tər dā′ *or* yes′tər dē) **1** the day before today. **2** on the day before today. **3** the recent past: *We are often amused by the fashions of yesterday.* **4** recently. *1, 3 n., 2, 4 adv.*

**yet** (yet) **1** up to the present time; thus far: *The work is not yet finished.* **2** now; at this time: *Don't go yet.* **3** then; at that time: *It was not yet dark.* **4** still; even now: *She is talking yet.* **5** sometime: *The thief will be caught yet.* **6** also; again: *Yet once more I forbid you to go.* **7** even: *She spoke yet more loudly when asked to be quiet.* **8** nevertheless: *The story was strange, yet true.* **9** however; but: *The work is good, yet it could be better.* *1-8 adv., 9 conj.*
**as yet,** up to now.

**ye·ti** (yet′ē) ABOMINABLE SNOWMAN. *n.*

**yew** (yū) **1** any of a closely related group of evergreen trees and shrubs found in many parts of the northern hemisphere, having broad, flat needles that are dark green above and light green below and small, red cones that look like berries: *The two species of yew native to Canada are the ground hemlock, or Canada yew, and the western yew.* **2** the wood of the yew, especially the hard, fine-grained wood of the English yew, used in cabinetmaking and for archery bows. **3** referring to a family of evergreen trees and shrubs including the yews and several other groups of trees. *n.*
☛ *Hom.* EWE, YOU.

hat, āge, fär; let, ēqual, tėrm; it, īce
hot, ōpen, ôrder; oil, out; cup, pút, rüle
әbove, takәn, pencәl, lemәn, circәs

ch, child; ng, long; sh, ship
th, thin; ŦH, then; zh, measure

**Yid·dish** (yid′ish) **1** a language that developed from medieval German, containing many Hebrew and Slavic words, and written in Hebrew characters: *Yiddish is spoken mainly by Jews in eastern and central Europe.* **2** having to do with the Yiddish language. *1 n., 2 adj.*

**yield** (yēld) **1** produce; bear: *This land yields good crops. Mines yield ore.* **2** the amount yielded; product: *This year's yield from the silver mine was very large.* **3** give; grant: *Her mother yielded her consent to the plan.* **4** give up; submit; surrender: *The enemy yielded to our soldiers. I yielded to temptation and ate all the candy.* **5** give way: *The door yielded to her touch.* **6** give place: *We yield to nobody in love of freedom.* *1, 3-6 v., 2 n.*

**yield·ing** (yēl′ding) **1** not resisting; submissive: *Nita loses most arguments because of her yielding nature.* **2** soft; giving way under weight or force: *We lay back in the yielding grass.* **3** ppr. of YIELD. *1, 2 adj., 3 v.*

**yin** (yin) in Taoism, the negative cosmic force; the counterpart to the YANG. *n.*

**yip** (yip) *Informal.* **1** especially of dogs, bark or yelp briskly. **2** a sharp, barking sound. *1 v.,* **yipped, yip·ping**; *2 n.*

**YMCA** or **Y.M.C.A.** Young Men's Christian Association.

**YMHA** or **Y.M.H.A.** Young Men's Hebrew Association.

**yo·del** (yō′dəl) **1** sing or call with frequent, sudden changes from the ordinary voice pitch to a much higher pitch: *The Swiss mountaineer was yodelling as we came up the valley.* **2** the act or sound of yodelling. *1 v.,* **yo·delled** or **yo·deled, yo·del·ling** or **yo·del·ing**; *2 n.* —**yo′del·ler** or **yo′del·er,** *n.*

**yo·ga** or **Yo·ga** (yō′gə) a system to improve the condition of the body under the control of the mind and spirit through the practice of slow, rhythmic body movements, controlled breathing exercises, and complete relaxation of the body and the mind. Yoga originated in India about 6000 years ago as one of the six systems of Hindu philosophy. *n.*

**yo·gi** (yō′gē) a person who practises or follows YOGA. *n., pl.* **yo·gis.**

**yo·gurt** (yō′gėrt) a semisolid food made from milk fermented by a bacterial culture and often sweetened and flavoured with honey, fruit, etc. *n.* Also, **yoghurt, yoghourt.**

Yoke (def. 6): a nightgown with a yoke

Yoke (def. 1): a double yoke for oxen

**yoke** (yōk) **1** a wooden frame which fits around the neck of two work animals to fasten them together for pulling a plough or vehicle. **2** a pair fastened together by a yoke: *The plough was drawn by a yoke of oxen.* **3** any frame connecting two other parts: *The woman carried two buckets on a yoke, one at each end.* **4** put a yoke on; fasten with a yoke. **5** harness or fasten a work animal or animals to: *The farmer yoked his plough.* **6** a part of a garment fitted closely to the shoulders. **7** the top piece to a skirt, fitting the hips. **8** something that binds together: *the yoke of marriage.* **9** something that holds people in slavery or submission: *the yoke of ignorance.* **10** rule; dominion: *Slaves are under the yoke of their masters.* 1–3, 6–10 *n.*, 4, 5 *v.*, **yoked, yok·ing.**
☞ *Hom.* YOLK.

**yo·kel** (yō′kəl) a person from the country, especially one who is unused to city ways: *Some city people look down on country folk and call them yokels.* *n.*

**yolk**[1] (yōk) the yellow and principal substance of an egg, as distinguished from the white. *n.*
☞ *Hom.* YOKE.

**yolk**[2] (yōk) the fat or grease in sheep's wool. *n.*
☞ *Hom.* YOKE.

**Yom Kip·pur** (yom′kip′ər) the Day of Atonement, an annual Jewish day of fasting and atoning for sin, observed on the tenth day of the first month of the Jewish year.

**yon·der** (yon′dər) **1** over there; within sight, but not near: *Look yonder.* **2** situated over there; being within sight, but not near: *She lives in yonder cottage.* **3** farther; more distant: *Look at the snow on yonder mountains.* 1 *adv.*, 2, 3 *adj.*

**yore** (yôr) *n.*
**of yore,** of long ago; formerly; in the past: *in days of yore, tales of yore.* *n.*

A York boat

**York boat** *Cdn.* formerly, a type of heavy freight canoe developed by the Hudson's Bay Company at York Factory on Hudson Bay.

**York·shire pudding** (yôrk′shər) a batter that is baked and often served with roast beef.

**Yorkshire terrier** one of a breed of small dogs having long, silky steel-blue hair.

**you** (yü; *unstressed,* yù *or* yə) **1** the person or persons spoken to: *Are you ready? Then you may go. She will bring you the book tomorrow.* **2** one; anybody: *You can push this button to get a light. You never can tell. His speeches put you to sleep.* *pron. pl.* and *sing.*
☞ *Hom.* EWE, YEW.
☞ *Usage.* The use of **you** and **your** to refer to people in general is common in speech: *The pay is good if you can stand the long hours.* In formal writing, however, most people prefer **one** or some other impersonal construction: *This work develops one's powers of concentration.* The important thing is to be consistent; avoid using **you** and **one** for the same purpose in the same piece of writing.

**you'd** (yüd; *unstressed,* yùd *or* yəd) **1** you had: *You'd better go quickly.* **2** you would: *You'd like this story.*

**you'll** (yül; *unstressed,* yùl *or* yəl) you will: *You'll be surprised when I tell you.*
☞ *Hom.* YULE.

**young** (yung) **1** in the early part of life or growth; not old: *A puppy is a young dog.* **2** young offspring: *An animal will fight to protect its young.* **3** having the looks or qualities of youth or a young person; youthful; lively: *She looks young for her age.* **4** of youth; early: *one's young days.* **5** not so old as another: *Young Mr. Lee worked for his father.* **6** in an early stage; not far advanced: *The night was still young when they left the party.* **7** without much experience or practice: *She was too young in the business.* **8 the young,** young people. 1, 3–7 *adj.*, **young·er** (yung′gər), **young·est** (yung′gist); 2, 8 *n. pl.*
**with young,** pregnant.

**young blood** **1** young people. **2** youthful vigour, energy, enthusiasm, etc.

**young·ish** (yung′ish) rather young. *adj.*

**young·ling** (yung′ling) **1** a young person, animal, or plant. **2** young; youthful. **3** a novice; beginner. 1, 3 *n.*, 2 *adj.*

**young·ster** (yung′stər) **1** child: *She is a lively youngster.* **2** a young person: *The old farmer was as spry as a youngster.* *n.*

**your** (yür; *unstressed,* yər) **1** a possessive form of YOU; of, belonging to, or made or done by you or yourself: *Give me your hand. Is this your pen? We enjoyed your visit.* **2** of, having to do with, or belonging to you or oneself: *The government guarantees your basic freedoms.* **3** *Informal.* that you know or speak of: *your real lover of music, your modern girl.* **4** a word used as part of a formal title: *Your Highness, Your Ladyship, Your Worship.* *pron.*
☞ *Hom.* YOU'RE.
☞ *Usage.* **Your** and YOURS are possessive forms of **you**. **Your** is always followed by a noun: *This is your ball.* **Yours** stands alone: *This ball is yours.*

**you're** (yür; *unstressed,* yər) you are.
☞ *Hom.* YOUR.

**yours** (yürz) **1** a possessive form of **you**: that which belongs to you: *I think this scarf is yours. I don't like our set as well as yours.* **2** at your service: *yours sincerely. I am yours to command.* *pron. sing.* and *pl.*
**of yours,** belonging to or having to do with you: *Is he a friend of yours?*
**yours truly,** *Informal.* I, me, or myself: *Yours truly is going home.*
☞ *Usage.* See note at YOUR.

**your·self** (yür self′; *unstressed,* yər self′) **1** a reflexive pronoun, the object of a reflexive verb with **you** as subject: *You will hurt yourself if you aren't careful.* **2** an intensive pronoun, used to emphasize the noun or pronoun it follows: *You yourself know the story is not true.* **3** your usual self: *Come see us when you feel better and are yourself again.* *pron., pl.* **your·selves.**

**your·selves** (yür selvz′; *unstressed,* yər selvz′)   pl. of YOURSELF.   *pron.*

**youth** (yüth)   **1** the fact or quality of being young: *He has the vigour of youth.*   **2** the appearance, freshness, vigour or other quality characteristic of the young: *She keeps her youth well.*   **3** the time between childhood and manhood or womanhood.   **4** a young man.   **5** young people: *the pleasures common to youth.*   **6** the first or early stage of anything; early period of growth or development: *during the youth of this country.*   *n., pl.* **youths** (yüths *or* yüTHz) *or* (*collectively*) **youth.**

**youth·ful** (yüth′fəl)   **1** young.   **2** of youth; suitable for young people: *Everyone admired his youthful enthusiasm.*   **3** having the looks or qualities of youth; fresh and lively: *The old man had a very happy and youthful spirit.*   *adj.* —**youth′ful·ly,** *adv.*   —**youth′ful·ness,** *n.*

**youth hostel**   a supervised, inexpensive lodging place for young people travelling, usually one of a system of such places: *Many European countries have excellent youth hostels.*

**you've** (yüv; *unstressed,* yùv *or* yəv)   you have: *You've gone too far.*

**yowl** (youl)   **1** a long, distressful, or dismal cry; a howl.   **2** howl.   **1** *n.,* **2** *v.*

**yo–yo** (yō′yō)   a small wheel-shaped toy made up of two disks, usually wooden, joined by a central peg to which is attached a long string. The string is held by one hand, and the toy is spun out and reeled in on the string.   *n., pl.* **yo-yos.**

**yr.**   **1** year; years.   **2** your; yours.

**yrs.**   years.

**Yt**   yttrium.

**YT** *or* **Y.T.**   Yukon Territory.

**yt·ter·bi·um** (i tėr′bē əm)   a rare metallic element belonging to the yttrium group.   *Symbol*: Yb   *n.*

**yt·tri·um** (it′rē əm)   a rare metallic element: *Compounds of yttrium are used for incandescent gas mantles.*   *Symbol*: Y *or* Yt   *n.*

**yuc·ca** (yuk′ə)   any of a closely related group of plants of the lily family having long, stiff, sword-shaped leaves and a single erect cluster of large, white, lily-like flowers.   *n.*

**Yu·go·slav** (yü′gō slav′ *or* yü′gō släv′)   **1** a native or inhabitant of the Federal Republic of Yugoslavia, made up of Serbia and Mntenegro.   **2** any member of a southern Slav people living in southeastern Europe.   **3** of or having to do with the Federal Republic of Yugoslavia.   **4** of or having to do with any southern Slav people.   **1, 2** *n.,* **3, 4** *adj.*

**Yu·go·slav·i·an** (yü′gō slav′ē ən *or* yü′gō slä′vē ən)   YUGOSLAV.   *adj., n.*

**Yu·kon·er** (yü′kon ər)   a native or long-term resident of Yukon Territory.   *n.*

**Yukon Legislative Council** (yü′kon)   a legislative body responsible for government in the Yukon, consisting of sixteen members elected by political party, the party with a majority of elected representatives forming the government. It has powers similar to a provincial legislature, although control of oil and gas resources at present remain with the federal government.

hat, āge, fär; let, ēqual, tėrm; it, īce
hot, ōpen, ôrder; oil, out; cup, pùt, rüle
əbove, takən, pencəl, lemən, circəs
ch, child; ng, long; sh, ship
th, thin; ᴛʜ, then; zh, measure

**Yule** *or* **yule** (yül)   **1** Christmas.   **2** Yuletide.   *n.*
☞ **Hom.** YOU'LL.

**Yule log**   a large log burned at Christmas.

**Yule·tide** *or* **yule·tide** (yül′tīd′)   Christmas time; the Christmas season.   *n.*

**Yup·pie** *or* **yup·pie** (yup′ē)   young urban professional.   *n.*

**yurt** (yùrt)   a portable, domed tent made of felt stretched over a framework of branches, used by the Mongolian nomads of Siberia.   *n.*

**YWCA** *or* **Y.W.C.A.**   Young Women's Christian Association.

**YWHA** *or* **Y.W.H.A.**   Young Women's Hebrew Association.

# Z z  Z z

A zebu

**z or Z** (zed) **1** the twenty-sixth and last letter of the English alphabet. **2** any speech sound represented by this letter. **3** a person or thing identified as z, especially the twenty-sixth of a series or the last in a series consisting of x, y, and z. **4** anything shaped like a Z. *n., pl.* **z's** or **Z's.**

**z.** or **Z.** zone.

**Z** atomic number.

**za·ny** (zā′nē) **1** foolish; ludicrous: *His zany stories make everyone laugh.* **2** fool. **3** clown. *1 adj., 2, 3 n., pl.* **za·nies.**

**zap** (zap) *Informal.* **1** a word used to express or indicate a sudden, swift happening: *I was just standing there when—zap—something hit me on the head.* **2** the sound of a sudden slap, blow, blast, etc. **3** hit with a hard blow. **4** kill. **5** beat; defeat. **6** move very fast; zip; zoom. **7** delete commercials while videotaping a television program. *1 interj., 2 n., 3–7 v.,* **zapped, zap·ping.**

**zeal** (zēl) earnest enthusiasm; passionate eagerness in favour of a person or cause: *A good citizen works with zeal for his or her country's interests. n.*

**zeal·ot** (zel′ət) a person who shows too much zeal; fanatic. *n.*

**zeal·ot·ry** (zel′ə trē) too great zeal; fanaticism. *n.*

**zeal·ous** (zel′əs) full of zeal; eager; earnest; enthusiastic: *The children made zealous efforts to clean up for the party. That salesman seems zealous to please. adj.* —**zeal′ous·ly,** *adv.* —**zeal′ous·ness,** *n.*

A zebra— about 125 cm high at the shoulder

**ze·bra** (zē′brə *or* zeb′rə) a wild animal of Africa, related to the horse and donkey, but striped with dark bands on white. *n.*

**ze·bu** (zē′byü) any of several breeds of cattle first developed in India having a high, fatty hump over the shoulders, large, drooping ears, and loose folds of skin hanging from the throat and chest; BRAHMAN (def. 3): *Zebus are usually light grey or tan. n.*

**Zen Buddhism** a Japanese form of Buddhism that emphasizes contemplation to achieve self-discipline and intuitive truth.

**ze·nith** (zen′ith *or* zē′nith) **1** the point in the heavens directly overhead. See NADIR for picture. **2** the highest or greatest point: *At the zenith of its power Rome ruled the whole of civilized Europe. n.*

**zeph·yr** (zef′ər) **1** the west wind. **2** any soft, gentle wind; mild breeze. **3** a fine, soft yarn or worsted. *n.*

**Zep·pe·lin** or **zep·pe·lin** (zep′ə lən) an early type of airship shaped like a cigar with pointed ends, having compartments for gas, engines, passengers, etc. See DIRIGIBLE for picture. *n.*
☛ *Etym.* Named after Count Ferdinand von *Zeppelin* (1838–1917), a German pioneer in the design of such aircraft.

**ze·ro** (zē′rō) **1** nought; the figure 0: *There are three zeros in 40 006.* **2** the point marked as 0 on the scale of a thermometer, etc.: *A thermometer reads up and down from zero.* **3** the temperature that corresponds to zero on the scale of a thermometer: *The forecast is zero. Water freezes at zero degrees Celsius.* **4** of or at zero: *a zero score.* **5** the complete absence of quantity; nothing: *The other team's score was zero.* **6** not any; none at all: *The weather station at the airport announced zero visibility.* **7** the lowest point: *The team's spirit sank to zero after its third defeat.* *1–3, 5, 7 n., pl.* **ze·ros** *or* **ze·roes;** *4, 6 adj.*
**zero in, a** adjust the sights of a rifle for a given range so a bullet will strike the centre of the target. **b** with a telephoto lens, focus on and enlarge part of a scene being photographed or filmed.
**zero in on, a** get the range of by adjusting the sights of a firearm, etc. **b** direct with precision toward a target, etc. **c** locate as a target; find the range of.
☛ *Etym.* From F or Italian *zero*, which in turn came through Old Spanish from Arabic *çifr* 'zero'. 17c. See also note at CIPHER.

**ze·ro–g** (zē′rō jē′) in physics ZERO GRAVITY, the point at which weightlessness is reached. *n.*

**zero gravity** in physics, a condition in which gravity does not operate; weightlessness.

**zero hour** **1** the time set for beginning an attack, etc. **2** any point in time viewed as similar to this; crucial moment.

**zest** (zest) **1** keen enjoyment; relish: *The hungry girls ate with zest.* **2** a pleasant or exciting quality, flavour, etc.: *Wit gives zest to conversation.* **3** give a zest to. *1, 2 n., 3 v.*

**zest·ful** (zest′fəl)   characterized by ZEST.   *adj.*
—**zest′ful·ly,** *adv.*   —**zest′ful·ness,** *n.*

**zig·gu·rat** (zig′ú rat′)   an ancient Assyrian or Babylonian temple in the form of a pyramid of terraced towers.   *n.*

A zigzag design

**zig·zag** (zig′zag′)   **1** with short, sharp turns from one side to the other: *The path ran zigzag up the hill.*   **2** turning sharply from one side to the other: *go in a zigzag direction.*   **3** move in a zigzag way: *Lightning zigzagged across the sky.*   **4** a zigzag line or course.   **5** one of the short, sharp turns of a zigzag.   1 *adv.*, 2 *adj.*, 3 *v.*, **zig·zagged, zig·zag·ging;**   4, 5 *n.*

**zinc** (zingk)   **1** a bluish-white metal, a chemical element, very little affected by air and moisture at ordinary temperatures: *Zinc is used as a roofing material, in electric batteries, in paint, in medicine, and for coating some metals.* Symbol: Zn   **2** coat or cover with zinc.   1 *n.*, 2 *v.*, **zincked** or **zinced** (zingkt), **zinck·ing** or **zinc·ing** (zing′king).

**zinc ointment**   a salve containing ZINC OXIDE, used especially in treating skin disorders.

**zinc oxide**   an insoluble white powder used in making paint, rubber, glass, cosmetics, ointments, etc.

**zing** (zing)   **1** a sharp humming sound.   **2** *Informal.* spirit; vitality; liveliness; zest: *Put more zing in your story; it's too dull.*   **3** make a sharp humming sound, especially in going fast: *A fly zinged past my ear.*   1, 2 *n.*, 3 *v.*

**zin·ni·a** (zin′ē ə)   a garden plant grown for its showy flowers of many colours.   *n.*
☛ *Etym.*   Named after Johann Zinn (1727–1759), a German botanist.

**Zi·on** (zī′ən)   **1** a hill in Jerusalem on which, in ancient times, the royal palace and the temple were built.   **2** Israel; the people of Israel.   **3** heaven; the heavenly city.   **4** the church of God.   *n.*   Also, **Sion.**
☛ *Etym.*   Through OE from L *Sion* and Gk. *Seiōn*, which came from Hebrew *tsīyōn* 'hill'.

**Zi·on·ism** (zī′ə niz′əm)   a movement, begun in the late 19th century, to make modern Palestine (now Israel) a Jewish national state.   *n.*

**Zi·on·ist** (zī′ə nist)   a supporter of ZIONISM.   *n.*

**zip** (zip)   **1** a sudden, brief hissing sound, as of a flying bullet.   **2** make such a sound.   **3** *Informal.* energy.   **4** *Informal.* proceed with energy.   **5** fasten or close with a zipper: *Etta zipped up her jacket.*   1, 3 *n.*, 2, 4, 5 *v.*, **zipped, zip·ping.**

**zip code**   in the United States:   **1** a system for addressing and sorting mail, in which an identifying number is assigned to each delivery area; POSTAL CODE.   **2** an identifying number of this system.

**zip·gun** (zip′gun′)   a homemade pistol or gun consisting of a piece of tubing, a wooden handle, and a rubber band or spring to fire the bullet.   *n.*

**zip·per** (zip′ər)   **1** a metal or plastic sliding fastener for clothing, shoes, etc.   **2** fasten or close with a zipper: *Zipper up your coat before you go out in the cold.*   1 *n.*, 2 *v.*
☛ *Etym.*   From *Zipper*, a trademark for such a device.

**zestful**     **1399**     **zone**

hat, āge, fär; let, ēqual, tėrm; it, īce
hot, ōpen, ôrder; oil, out; cup, pút, rüle
əbove, takən, pencəl, lemən, circəs
ch, child; ng, long; sh, ship
th, thin; ŦH, then; zh, measure

**zip·py** (zip′ē)   *Informal.*   full of energy; lively; gay.   *adj.*, **zip·pi·er, zip·pi·est.**

**zir·con** (zėr′kon)   a mineral that occurs in crystals of many forms and colours; a silicate of zirconium: *Transparent zircon is used as a gem.*   *n.*

**zir·co·ni·um** (zėr kō′nē əm)   a rare metallic element used in alloys for wires, filaments, etc.   Symbol: Zr   *n.*

**zith·er** (ziŦH′ər)   a musical instrument having 30 to 40 strings, played with the fingers and a pick.   *n.*
☛ *Etym.*   See note at GUITAR.

**Zn**   zinc.

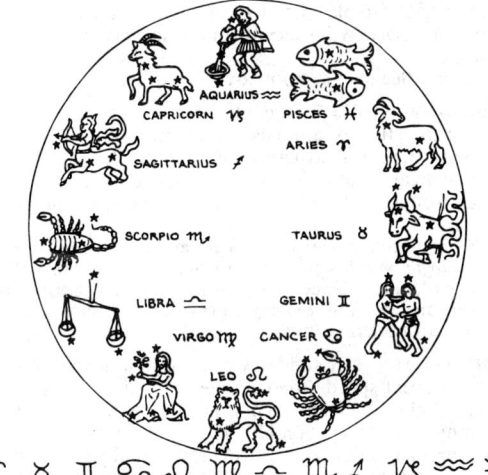

The zodiac

**zo·di·ac** (zō′dē ak′)   **1** an imaginary belt of the heavens extending on both sides of the apparent yearly path of the sun: *The zodiac is divided into 12 equal parts, called signs, named after 12 groups of stars.*   **2** a diagram representing the zodiac, used in astrology.   *n.*

**zo·di·a·cal** (zō dī′ə kəl)   **1** of or having to do with the zodiac.   **2** situated in the zodiac.   *adj.*

**zom·bi** (zom′bē)   ZOMBIE.   *n., pl.* **zom·bis.**

**zom·bie** (zom′bē)   **1** a corpse supposedly brought back to life by a supernatural power in West Africa.   **2** a drink of several kinds of rum, fruit juice, sugar, and brandy.   *n., pl.* **zom·bies.**

**zon·al** (zō′nəl)   **1** of a zone; having to do with zones.   **2** divided into zones.   *adj.*

**zone** (zōn)   **1** an area, region, district, etc. set off as distinct from surrounding or neighbouring areas, etc.: *a hospital zone, an industrial zone in a city. A combat zone is a region where fighting is going on. Alberta, British Columbia, and the Yukon are in the same postal-rate zone.*   **2** a region or area having a particular environment or climate and characterized by certain forms of plant and animal life.   **3** set an area or areas apart for a special purpose, especially in a city or town: *This area is zoned for apartment buildings.*   1, 2 *n.*, 3 *v.*, **zoned, zon·ing.**

**zoned** (zōnd)   **1** marked with or having zones.   **2** divided into zones.   **3** pt. and pp. of ZONE.   1, 2 *adj.*, 3 *v.*

**zon·ing** (zō'ning)   **1** building restrictions in an area of a city or town.   **2** ppr. of ZONE.   1 *n.*, 2 *v.*

**zoo** (zü)   a place where animals are kept and shown; zoological garden.   *n.*
☛ *Etym.* See note at ZOOLOGY.

**zool.**   **1** zoology.   **2** zoologist.   **3** zoological.

**zo·o·log·i·cal** (zō'ə loj'ə kəl *or* zü'ə loj'ə kəl)   **1** of animals and animal life.   **2** having to do with ZOOLOGY: *zoological science.*   *adj.*   —**zo'o·log'i·cal·ly**, *adv.*
☛ *Etym.* See note at ZOOLOGY.

**zoological garden**   ZOO.

**zo·ol·o·gist** (zō ol'ə jist *or* zü ol'ə jist)   a person trained in ZOOLOGY, especially one who makes it his or her work.   *n.*
☛ *Etym.* See note at ZOOLOGY.

**zo·ol·o·gy** (zō ol'ə jē *or* zü ol'ə jē)   the science of animals; the study of animals and animal life. Zoology deals with the form, structure, physiology, development, and classification of animals. It also includes the study of special groups, such as birds, insects, snakes, mammals, etc.   *n.*
☛ *Etym.* From modern L *zoologia* and modern Gk. *zōiologia*, which were formed from Gk. *zōion* 'animal' + *-logia* 'study, science'. 17c. ZOOLOGICAL and ZOOLOGIST were formed from **zoology**. ZOO was a 19c. shortening of ZOOLOGICAL GARDEN.

**zoom** (züm)   **1** fly suddenly upward in a nearly vertical ascent at great speed: *The airplane zoomed.*   **2** a sudden upward flight.   **3** make a continuous, low-pitched humming or buzzing sound.   **4** travel or move with a humming or buzzing sound.   **5** move rapidly from one focus to another, as with a ZOOM LENS.   **6** move or travel rapidly.   **7** a humming or buzzing sound.   1, 3, 4–6 *v.*, 2, 7 *n.*

**zoom in on,**   photograph by means of a ZOOM LENS.

**zoom lens**   especially in television or movie cameras, a type of lens that can be adjusted from telephoto close-ups to wide-angle shots without loss of focus.

**zo·o·phyte** (zō'ə fīt')   any of various invertebrate animals that resemble plants in form, such as corals, sponges, or sea anemones.   *n.*

**Zo·ro·as·ter** (zô'rō as'tər)   the prophet and founder of Zoroastrianism, born in Persia about 600 B.C. His birthday is celebrated each year by Zoroastrians on the 26th of March.   *n.*

**Zo·ro·as·tri·an** (zô'rō as'trē ən)   **1** of or having to do with Zoroastrianism or Zoroaster.   **2** a follower of Zoroaster or believer in Zoroastrianism: *Zoroastrians in North America have their centre in Toronto.*   1 *adj.*, 2 *n.*

**Zo·ro·as·tri·an·ism** (zô'rō as'trē ə niz'əm)   a religion founded by the Persian prophet Zoroaster in the 6th century B.C. It is expounded in the Zend-Avesta and teaches that the supreme god Ormazd (or Ahura Mazda) is struggling continuously with Ahriman, the spirit of evil, and needs the good deeds of people to help him ultimately to overcome evil.   *n.*

**Zr**   zirconium.

**zuc·chi·ni** (zü kē'nē)   **1** any of various summer squash, small and cylindrical in shape, having smooth, flecked, dark-green skin and tender white flesh.   **2** the plant this fruit grows on.   *n., pl.* **zuc·chi·ni** *or* **zuc·chi·nis.**

**Zu·lu** (zü'lü)   **1** a member of a Bantu-speaking people of Natal in South Africa.   **2** a Bantu language spoken by these people: *Zulu is an important literary language of southern Africa.*   **3** of or having to do with the Zulus or their language.   1, 2 *n.*, 3 *adj.*

**zwie·back** (zwē'bäk'; *German,* tsvē'bäk')   a kind of bread cut into slices and toasted dry in an oven.   *n.*
☛ *Etym.* From German *Zwieback*, formed from a translation of Italian *biscotto*, which (like F *biscuit*) developed from L *bis coctus* 'twice cooked'. See also note at BISCUIT.

**zy·gote** (zī'gōt *or* zig'ōt)   any cell formed by the union of two gametes. A fertilized egg is a zygote.   *n.*

**zy·mase** (zī'mās)   an enzyme in yeast that changes sugar into alcohol and carbon dioxide.   *n.*

# Appendix 1: General Information

## GEOLOGICAL TIME CHART

| Eras | Periods, Epochs, and Their Beginnings (years ago) | | Changes and Characteristics |
|---|---|---|---|
| CENOZOIC ERA | Quaternary Period | Recent or Holocene Epoch (11 thousand) | Glaciers melt and Great Lakes are formed. Climate warm. Humans live in most parts of the earth, develop agriculture, use metals, domesticate animals. |
| | | Pleistocene Epoch (2 million) | Great ice sheets cover northern hemisphere. Climate cool. Mountains continue to rise in western North America. Early humans reach Europe and North America. Massive extinctions of plants and animals. |
| | Tertiary Period | Pliocene Epoch (11 million) | Climate cooling. Grasslands replace forests. Many volcanoes. Birds and mammals spread around the world. Humans appear near end of epoch. |
| | | Miocene Epoch (24 million) | Climate mild. Sierra Nevadas forming. Flowering plants and trees resemble modern kinds. Apes first appear. |
| | | Oligocene Epoch (37 million) | Climate mild. Hawaiian Islands start to form. Red Sea opens up. |
| | | Eocene Epoch (57 million) | Climate mild. Seas flood shores of continents. Primitive apes, early horses, and elephants appear. |
| | | Paleocene Epoch (66 million) | Dinosaurs are extinct. First placental mammals appear. |
| MESOZOIC ERA | Cretaceous Period (144 million) | | Seas spread over the land. Flowering plants appear. Dinosaurs die out. Rockies, Himalayas, Alps, and Andes begin to form. |
| | Jurassic Period (208 million) | | Shallow seas invade continents. Dinosaurs reach their largest size. First birds and simple mammals appear. |
| | Triassic Period (245 million) | | Dinosaurs first appear. Continents rise and deserts form. |
| PALEOZOIC ERA | Permian Period (280 million) | | Ural Mountains are formed. Major glaciation occurs. Major extinction of plants and animals. |
| | Carboniferous Period (360 million) | | Warm, moist climate produces great forests that later become coal beds. Large insects and reptiles appear. Appalachian and central European mountains are formed. |
| | Devonian Period (405 million) | | Many kinds of fish in seas and fresh water. Immense trees. Climate warm and humid. |
| | Ordovician Period (505 million) | | Coral reefs are formed. First amphibians and forests of fernlike trees appear. Land starts to emerge from sea and dry out. |
| | Cambrian Period (570 million) | | Seas spread across North America. First fishes appear. Greatest development of invertebrates. |
| | PRECAMBRIAN TIME (4.5 billion?) | | Cooling and melting of the earth's crust. Evidence of bacteria, the first known living things, about 3.5 billion years ago. |

# PERIODIC TABLE OF THE ELEMENTS

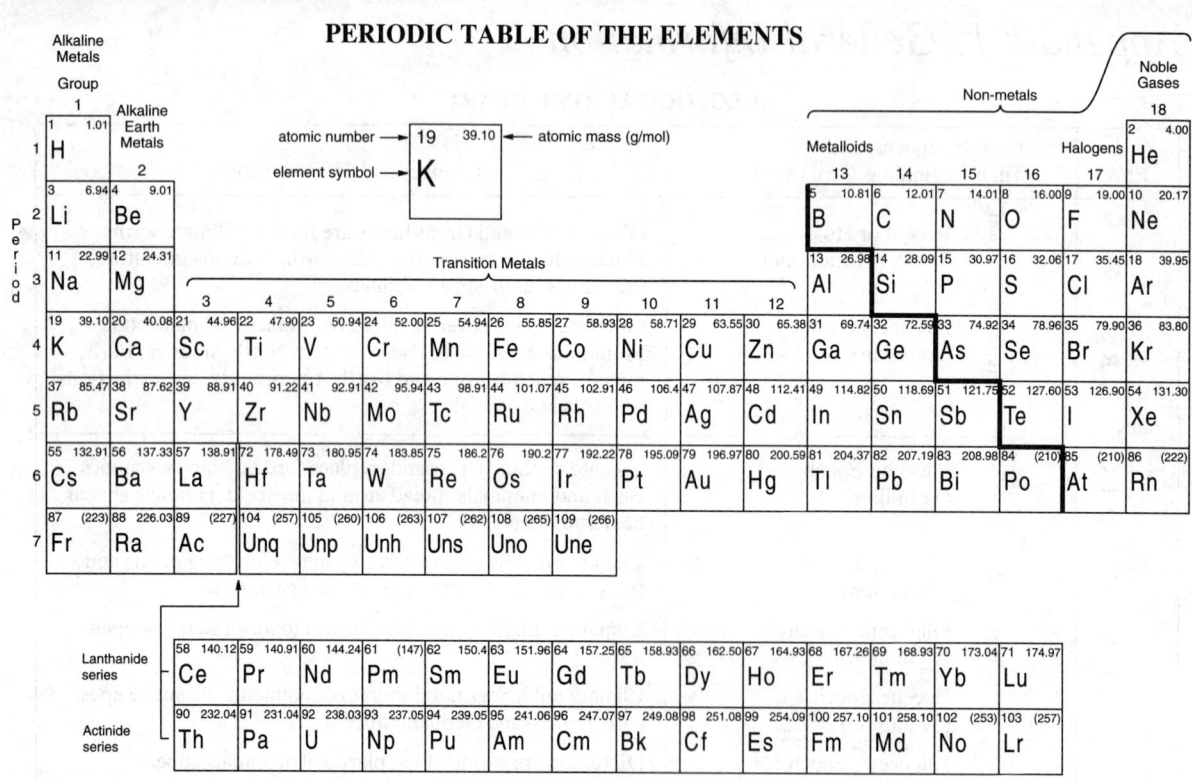

## ALPHABETICAL LIST OF THE ELEMENTS, WITH THEIR SYMBOLS AND ATOMIC NUMBERS

| Symbol | Name | Atomic Number | Symbol | Name | Atomic Number | Symbol | Name | Atomic Number | Symbol | Name | Atomic Number |
|---|---|---|---|---|---|---|---|---|---|---|---|
| Ac | actinium | 89 | Fm | fermium | 100 | Np | neptunium | 93 | Sr | strontium | 38 |
| Al | aluminum | 13 | F | fluorine | 9 | Ni | nickel | 28 | S | sulphur | 16 |
| Am | americium | 95 | Fr | francium | 87 | Nb | niobium | 41 | Ta | tantalum | 73 |
| Sb | antimony | 51 | Gd | gadolinium | 64 | N | nitrogen | 7 | Tc | technetium | 43 |
| Ar | argon | 18 | Ga | gallium | 31 | No | nobelium | 102 | Te | tellurium | 52 |
| As | arsenic | 33 | Ge | germanium | 32 | Os | osmium | 76 | Tb | terbium | 65 |
| At | astatine | 85 | Au | gold | 79 | O | oxygen | 8 | Tl | thallium | 81 |
| Ba | barium | 56 | Hf | hafnium | 72 | Pd | palladium | 46 | Th | thorium | 90 |
| Bk | berkelium | 97 | He | helium | 2 | P | phosphorus | 15 | Tm | thulium | 69 |
| Be | beryllium | 4 | Ho | holmium | 67 | Pt | platinum | 78 | Sn | tin | 50 |
| Bi | bismuth | 83 | H | hydrogen | 1 | Pu | plutonium | 94 | Ti | titanium | 22 |
| B | boron | 5 | In | indium | 49 | Po | polonium | 84 | Unh | unnilhexium | 106 |
| Br | bromine | 35 | I | iodine | 53 | K | potassium | 19 | Une | unnilennium | 109 |
| Cd | cadmium | 48 | Ir | iridium | 77 | Pr | praseodymium | 59 | Uno | unniloctium | 108 |
| Ca | calcium | 20 | Fe | iron | 26 | Pm | promethium | 61 | Unp | unnilpentium | 105 |
| Cf | californium | 98 | Kr | krypton | 36 | Pa | protactinium | 91 | Uns | unnilseptium | 107 |
| C | carbon | 6 | La | lanthanum | 57 | Ra | radium | 88 | Unq | unnilquadium | 104 |
| Ce | cerium | 58 | Lr | lawrencium | 103 | Rn | radon | 86 | U | uranium | 92 |
| Cs | cesium | 55 | Pb | lead | 82 | Re | rhenium | 75 | V | vanadium | 23 |
| Cl | chlorine | 17 | Li | lithium | 3 | Rh | rhodium | 45 | W | tungsten | 74 |
| Cr | chromium | 24 | Lu | lutetium | 71 | Rb | rubidium | 37 | Xe | xenon | 54 |
| Co | cobalt | 27 | Mg | magnesium | 12 | Ru | ruthenium | 44 | Yb | ytterbium | 70 |
| Cu | copper | 29 | Mn | manganese | 25 | Sm | samarium | 62 | Y | yttrium | 39 |
| Cm | curium | 96 | Md | mendelevium | 101 | Sc | scandium | 21 | Zn | zinc | 30 |
| Dy | dysprosium | 66 | Hg | mercury | 80 | Se | selenium | 34 | Zr | zirconium | 40 |
| Es | einsteinium | 99 | Mo | molybdenum | 42 | Si | silicon | 14 | | | |
| Er | erbium | 68 | Nd | neodymium | 60 | Ag | silver | 47 | | | |
| Eu | europium | 63 | Ne | neon | 10 | Na | sodium | 11 | | | |

## TABLE OF MEASURES

### The International System (SI) as Used in Canada

**SI base units**

| name | symbol | quantity |
|---|---|---|
| metre | m | length |
| kilogram | kg | mass |
| second | s | time |
| ampere | A | electric current |
| kelvin | K | thermodynamic temperature |
| mole | mol | amount of substance |
| candela | cd | luminous intensity |

**SI prefixes**

| name | symbol | multiplying factor* |
|---|---|---|
| exa- | E | $\times 10^{18}$ |
| peta- | P | $\times 10^{15}$ |
| tera- | T | $\times 10^{12}$ |
| giga- | G | $\times 10^{9}$ |
| mega- | M | $\times 10^{6}$ |
| kilo- | k | $\times 10^{3}$ |
| hecto- | h | $\times 10^{2}$ |
| deca- | da | $\times 10$ |
| deci- | d | $\times 10^{-1}$ |
| centi- | c | $\times 10^{-2}$ |
| milli- | m | $\times 10^{-3}$ |
| micro- | μ | $\times 10^{-6}$ |
| nano- | n | $\times 10^{-9}$ |
| pico- | p | $\times 10^{-12}$ |
| femto- | f | $\times 10^{-15}$ |
| atto- | a | $\times 10^{-18}$ |

*$10^2 = 100$; $10^3 = 1000$
$10^{-1} = 0.1$; $10^{-2} = 0.01$
Thus, 2 km = $2 \times 1000$ = 2000 m
3 cm = $3 \times 0.01$ = 0.03 m

**Common SI derived units with special names**

| name | symbol | quantity |
|---|---|---|
| hertz | Hz | frequency |
| pascal | Pa | pressure, stress |
| watt | W | power, radiant flux |
| volt | V | electric potential, electromotive force |
| newton | N | force |
| joule | J | energy, work |
| coulomb | C | electric charge |
| ohm | Ω | electric resistance |
| farad | F | electric capacitance |

**Common units used with the SI**

| name | symbol | quantity |
|---|---|---|
| litre | L | volume or capacity (= 1 dm³) |
| degree Celsius | °C | temperature (= 1 K; 0°C = 273.2 K) |
| hectare | ha | area (= 10 000 m²) |
| tonne | t | mass (= 1000 kg) |
| electronvolt | eV | energy (= 0.160 aJ) |
| nautical mile | M | distance (navigation)(= 1852 m) |
| knot | kn | speed (navigation)(= 1 M/h) |

**SI supplementary units**

| name | symbol | quantity |
|---|---|---|
| radian | rad | plane angle |
| steradian | sr | solid angle |

### Common Conversion Factors

| | | |
|---|---|---|
| 1 centimetre | = | 0.39 in. |
| 1 metre | = | 39.4 in. |
| 1 kilometre | = | 0.62 mi. |
| 1 gram | = | 0.04 oz. |
| 1 kilogram | = | 2.20 lb. |
| 1 tonne | = | 1.10 short tons |
| 1 square centimetre | = | 0.16 sq.in. |
| 1 square metre | = | 1.20 sq.yd. |
| 1 litre | = | 0.88 qt. |
| 1 cubic centimetre | = | 0.06 cu.in. |
| 1 cubic metre | = | 1.31 cu.yd. |

**Conversion factors for common U.S. liquid measures**

| U.S. | Cdn. | metric |
|---|---|---|
| 1 fl.oz. | = 1.041 fl.oz. | (29.57 cm³) |
| 1 pt. | = 0.833 pt. | (0.473 dm³) |
| 1 qt. | = 0.833 qt. | (0.946 dm³) |
| 1 gal. | = 0.833 gal. | (3.785 dm³) |

### Traditional Canadian Measures

| name | abbrev. or symbol | equivalent in related units | metric equivalent |
|---|---|---|---|
| **LENGTH** | | | |
| inch | in. or " | — | 2.54 cm |
| foot | ft. or ' | 12 in. | 30.48 cm |
| yard | yd. | 3 ft.; 36 in. | 0.91 m |
| mile | mi. | 1760 yd.; 5280 ft. | 1.609 km |
| **MASS (WEIGHT)** | | | |
| grain | gr. | — | 0.06 g |
| dram | dr. | 27.343 gr. | 1.77 g |
| ounce | oz. | 16 dr. | 28.35 g |
| pound | lb. | 16 oz. | 0.453 kg |
| hundredweight | | | |
| (short) | cwt. | 100 lb. | 45.36 kg |
| (long) | cwt. | 112 lb. | 50.80 kg |
| ton (short) | — | 2000 lb. | 0.907 t |
| ton (long) | — | 2240 lb. | 1.016 t |
| **VOLUME AND CAPACITY** | | | |
| fluid dram | fl.dr. | 0.22 cu.in. | 3.55 cm³ |
| fluid ounce | fl.oz. | 8 fl.dr.; 1.7 cu.in. | 28.41 cm³ |
| pint | pt. | 20 fl.oz.; 34.7 cu.in. | 568.3 cm³ |
| quart | qt. | 2 pt.; 69.4 cu.in. | 1.14 dm³ |
| gallon | gal. | 4 qt.; 277 cu.in. | 4.55 dm³ |
| peck | pk. | 2 gal.; 555 cu.in. | 9.09 dm³ |
| bushel | bu. | 4 pk.; 2219 cu.in. | 36.37 dm³ |
| barrel (oil) | — | 35 gal. | 159 dm³ |
| **AREA** | | | |
| acre | — | 4840 sq.yd. | 4047 m² |
| square mile | sq.mi. | 640 acres | 2.590 km² |

# MONEY: MAJOR CURRENCIES OF THE WORLD

| Country | Currency Unit | Lesser Unit | Country | Currency Unit | Lesser Unit |
|---|---|---|---|---|---|
| Afghanistan | afghani | 100 puls | Iran | rial | 100 dinars |
| Albania | lek | 100 qindarka | Iraq | dinar | 1000 fils |
| Algeria | dinar | 100 centimes | Ireland | pound | 100 pence |
| Angola | kwanza | 100 lwei | Israel | shequel | 100 agorot |
| Argentina | peso | 100 centavos | Italy | lira | 100 centesimi |
| Armenia | dram | 100 lumma | Ivory Coast | franc CFA | 100 centimes |
| Australia | dollar | 100 cents | Jamaica | dollar | 100 cents |
| Austria | schilling | 100 groschen | Japan | yen | 100 sen |
| Azerbaijan | manat | 100 qepiq | Jordan | dinar | 1000 fils |
| Bahamas | dollar | 100 cents | Kampuchea | riel | 100 su |
| Bahrain | dinar | 1000 fils | Kazakhstan | tenge | 100 cents |
| Bangladesh | taka | 100 poisha | Kenya | shilling | 100 cents |
| Barbados | dollar | 100 cents | Kirghizia | som | 100 tyyn |
| Belarus | ruble | 100 kapeik | Korea | won | 100 chon |
| Belgium | franc | 100 centimes | Kuwait | dinar | 1000 fils |
| Belize | dollar | 100 cents | Laos | kip | 100 att |
| Benin | franc CFA | 100 centimes | Latvia | lat | 100 santimi |
| Bermuda | dollar | 100 cents | Lebanon | livre | 100 piastres |
| Bhutan | ngultrum | 100 chetrums | Lesotho | loti | 100 lisente |
| Bolivia | Boliviano | 100 centavos | Liberia | dollar | 100 cents |
| Bosnia-Hercegovina | new dinar | | Libya | dinar | 1000 dirhams |
| Botswana | pula | 100 thebe | Liechtenstein | Swiss franc | 100 centimes |
| Brazil | real | 100 centavos | Lithuania | lita | 100 centas |
| Brunei | ringgit | 100 cents | Luxembourg | franc | 100 centimes |
| Bulgaria | lev | 100 stotinki | Macao | pataca | 100 avos |
| Burkina Faso | franc CFA | 100 centimes | Macedonia | denar | 100 deni |
| Burundi | franc | 100 centimes | Madagascar | franc | 100 centimes |
| Cameroon | franc CFA | 100 centimes | Malawi | kwacha | 100 tambala |
| Canada | dollar | 100 cents | Malaysia | ringgit | 100 sen |
| Cape Verde | escudo | 100 centavos | Maldives | rufiyaa | 100 lari |
| Cayman Islands | dollar | 100 cents | Mali | franc CFA | 100 centimes |
| Central African Republic | franc CFA | 100 centimes | Malta | lira | 100 cents |
| Chad | franc CFA | 100 centimes | Mauritania | ougiya | 5 khoum |
| Chile | peso | 100 centavos | Mauritius | rupee | 100 cents |
| People's Republic of China | yuan | 100 fen | Mexico | peso | 100 centavos |
| | | | Moldova | leu | 100 bani |
| Colombia | peso | 100 centavos | Monaco | French franc | 100 centimes |
| Congo | franc CFA | 100 centimes | Mongolia | tugrik | 100 mongo |
| Costa Rica | colon | 100 centimos | Morocco | dirham | 100 centimes |
| Croatia | kuna | 100 lipa | Mozambique | metical | 100 centavos |
| Cuba | peso | 100 centavos | Myanmar | kyat | 100 pyas |
| Cyprus | pound | 100 cents | Namibia | dollar | 100 cents |
| Czech Republic | koruna | 100 haléru | Nepal | rupee | 100 paisa |
| Denmark | krone | 100 öre | The Netherlands | gulden | 100 cents |
| Djibouti | franc | 100 centimes | New Zealand | dollar | 100 cents |
| Dominican Republic | peso oro | 100 centavos | Nicaragua | córdoba | 100 centavos |
| Ecuador | sucre | 100 centavos | Niger | franc CFA | 100 centimes |
| Egypt | pound | 100 piastres | Nigeria | naira | 100 kobo |
| El Salvador | colón | 100 centavos | Norway | krone | 100 öre |
| Equatorial Guinea | franc CFA | 100 centimes | Oman | rial | 1000 baisa |
| Eritrea | birr | 100 cents | Pakistan | rupee | 100 paisas |
| Estonia | kroon | 100 senti | Panama | balboa | 100 centésimos |
| Ethiopia | birr | 100 cents | Papua New Guinea | kina | 100 toea |
| Fiji Islands | dollar | 100 cents | Paraguay | guaraní | 100 céntimos |
| Finland | markka | 100 pennia | Peru | nuevo sol | 100 centimos |
| France | franc | 100 centimes | Philippines | piso | 100 sentimos |
| Gabon | franc CFA | 100 centimes | Poland | zloty | 100 groszy |
| Gambia | dalasi | 100 bututs | Portugal | escudo | 100 centavos |
| Georgia | kupon | | Qatar | riyal | 100 dirhems |
| Germany | Deutsche mark | 100 pfennige | Romania | leu | 100 bani |
| Ghana | cedi | 100 pesewas | Russia | ruble | 100 kopeks |
| Greece | drachma | 100 lepta | Rwanda | franc | 100 centimes |
| Grenada | dollar EC | 100 cents | São Tomé e Principe | dobra | 100 centimos |
| Guatemala | quetzal | 100 centavos | Saudi Arabia | riyal | 100 halalas |
| Guinea | franc | 100 centimes | Senegal | franc CFA | 100 centimes |
| Guinea-Bissau | peso | 100 centavos | Serbia | dinar | 100 paras |
| Guyana | dollar | 100 cents | Seychelles | rupee | 100 cents |
| Haïti | gourde | 100 centimes | Sierra Leone | leone | 100 cents |
| Honduras | lempira | 100 centavos | Singapore | dollar | 100 cents |
| Hong Kong | dollar | 100 cents | Slovak Republic | koruna | 100 halier |
| Hungary | forint | 100 fillér | Slovenia | tolar | |
| Iceland | króna | 100 aurar | Solomon Islands | dollar | 100 cents |
| India | rupee | 100 paise | Somalia | shilin | 100 senti |
| Indonesia | rupiah | 100 sen | South Africa | rand | 100 cents |
| | | | Spain | peseta | 100 céntimos |

| Country | Currency Unit | Lesser Unit | Country | Currency Unit | Lesser Unit |
|---|---|---|---|---|---|
| Sri Lanka | rupee | 100 cents | Turkmenistan | manat | 100 tenesi |
| Sudan | dinar | 10 pounds | Uganda | shilling | 100 cents |
| Surinam | gulden | 100 cents | Ukraine | karbovanets | |
| Swaziland | lilangeni | 100 cents | United Arab Emirates | dirham | 100 fils |
| Sweden | krona | 100 öre | United Kingdom | pound sterling | 100 pence |
| Switzerland | franc | 100 centimes | United States | dollar | 100 cents |
| Syria | pound | 100 piastres | Uruguay | peso Uruguayo | 100 centésimos |
| Tajikistan | ruble | | Uzbekistan | som | 100 tyyn |
| Taiwan | yuan | 100 cents | Vanuatu | vatu | |
| Tanzania | shilingi | 100 senti | Venezuela | bolívar | 100 céntimos |
| Thailand | baht | 100 satang | Vietnam | dong | 10 hao |
| Togo | franc CFA | 100 centimes | Western Samoa | tala | 100 sene |
| Tonga | pa'anga | 100 seniti | Yemen | rial | 100 fils |
| Trinidad and Tobago | dollar | 100 cents | Zaïre | nouveau zaïre | 100 makuta |
| Tunisia | dinar | 1000 millim | Zambia | kwacha | 100 ngwee |
| Turkey | lira | 100 kurus | Zimbabwe | dollar | 100 cents |

## PRIME MINISTERS OF CANADA

| | | |
|---|---|---|
| Sir John A. Macdonald | Conservative | July 1, 1867–Nov. 5, 1873 |
| | | Oct. 9, 1878–June 6, 1891 |
| Alexander Mackenzie | Liberal | Nov. 5, 1873–Oct. 9, 1878 |
| Sir John Abbot | Conservative | June 15, 1891–Nov. 24, 1892 |
| Sir John Thompson | Conservative | Nov. 25, 1892–Dec. 12, 1894 |
| Sir Mackenzie Bowell | Conservative | Dec. 13, 1894–Apr. 27, 1896 |
| Sir Charles Tupper | Conservative | Apr. 27, 1896–July 8, 1896 |
| Sir Wilfrid Laurier | Liberal | July 11, 1896–Oct. 6, 1911 |
| Sir Robert Borden | Conservative/Unionist | Oct. 10, 1911–Oct. 12, 1917 |
| | | Oct. 12, 1917–July 10, 1920 |
| Arthur Meighen | Unionist/Conservative | July 10, 1920–Dec. 29, 1921 |
| | | June 29, 1926–Sept. 25, 1926 |
| Mackenzie King | Liberal | Dec. 29, 1921–June 28, 1926 |
| | | Sept. 25, 1926–Aug. 6, 1930 |
| | | Oct. 23, 1935–Nov. 15, 1948 |
| Richard B. Bennett | Conservative | Aug. 7, 1930–Oct. 23, 1935 |
| Louis St. Laurent | Liberal | Nov. 15, 1948–June 21, 1957 |
| John Diefenbaker | Progressive Conservative | June 21, 1957–Apr. 22, 1963 |
| Lester Pearson | Liberal | Apr. 22, 1963–Apr. 20, 1968 |
| Pierre Trudeau | Liberal | Apr. 20, 1968–June 4, 1979 |
| | | Mar. 3, 1980–June 30, 1984 |
| Joe Clark | Progressive Conservative | June 4, 1979–Mar. 3, 1980 |
| John Turner | Liberal | June 30, 1984–Sept. 17, 1984 |
| Brian Mulroney | Progressive Conservative | Sept. 17, 1984–June 25, 1993 |
| Kim Campbell | Progressive Conservative | June 25, 1993–Nov. 4, 1993 |
| Jean Chrétien | Liberal | Nov. 4, 1993– |

## EXAMPLES OF WIND CHILL FACTOR

| Wind Chill Factor | Description |
|---|---|
| 700 | Conditions considered comfortable when dressed for skiing. |
| 1200 | Conditions no longer pleasant for outdoor activities on overcast days. |
| 1400 | Conditions no longer pleasant for outdoor activities on sunny days. |
| 1600 | Freezing of exposed skin begins for most people, depending on the degree of activity and the amount of sunshine. |
| 2300 | Conditions for outdoor travel such as walking become dangerous. Exposed areas of the face freeze in less than 1 minute for the average person. |
| 2700 | Exposed flesh will freeze within half a minute for the average person. |

Atmospheric Environmental Service. Government of Canada

## BEAUFORT SCALE OF WIND SPEEDS

| Beaufort Number | International Description | Wind Speed km/h |
|---|---|---|
| 0 | Calm | 0-1 |
| 1 | Light air | 1-5 |
| 2 | Light breeze | 6-11 |
| 3 | Gentle breeze | 12-19 |
| 4 | Moderate breeze | 20-28 |
| 5 | Fresh breeze | 29-38 |
| 6 | Strong breeze | 39-49 |
| 7 | Moderate gale | 50-61 |
| 8 | Fresh gale | 62-74 |
| 9 | Strong gale | 75-88 |
| 10 | Whole gale | 89-102 |
| 11 | Storm | 103-117 |
| 12-17 | Hurricane | above 117 |

# Appendix II: Grammar and Usage

**Abbreviation** An abbreviation is a shortened form of a word or phrase. There is a trend away from using periods in many abbreviations, especially names of companies or organizations. While abbreviations are useful in lists, tables, footnotes, and technical documents, most are inappropriate in formal writing. A few exceptions are:
- titles, such as Mrs., Mr., Ms., and Dr.
- St. for Saint in place names
- degrees and professional titles, such as Ph.D., B.A., C.A., when placed after a person's name
- indications of time, when used with figures, such as 7:00 p.m., A.D. 500

**Active and Passive Voice** A verb is in the active voice if its subject is the doer of the action. A verb is in the passive voice (*be* + past participle) when the subject of the verb receives the action:

Active: *The firefighters extinguished the fire.*
Passive: *The fire was extinguished.*

The passive voice allows the doer of the action to be omitted. Thus the doer may be unknown, unimportant, or obvious. Writers of scientific papers usually prefer the passive voice: *the experiment was conducted.*

**Adjective** An adjective is a word that describes a noun or a pronoun: *We heard a loud noise. His icy blue eyes stared at nothing. She looked pale.*

**Adverb** An adverb can describe a verb, an adjective, another adverb, or a whole clause or sentence. Adverbs usually tell how, when, where, or in what manner. Adverbs such as *who, when, where, what,* and *how* are also used to indicate a question: *That singer sings beautifully. I have an extremely tight schedule today. I work too hard! Strangely, the door was unlocked. Where are you going?*

**Agreement** SEE Pronoun; Subject/Verb Agreement

**Apostrophe** ['] Use an apostrophe
- to show possession: *Jane's boat*
- to indicate a contraction: *don't, can't*
- to replace missing letters in speech: *"How 'bout you?"*
- to replace missing numbers in a date: *class of '99*
- to show the plural of letters or symbols: *There are three a's in Saskatchewan and two 9's in 1998.*

**Bias** SEE Racist Language; Sexist Language

**Bibliography** A bibliography is a list of all the works used in an essay or paper. Place it on a separate page at the end of the paper. Although there are variations in style, all bibliographies include the same basic information: the name of the author(s), the title of the work, and the name, date, and place of publication. (NOTE: If the author is unknown, start with the title of the work.) Indent all lines except the first line of each entry. Arrange the sources alphabetically, by author's name. Below are some examples.

- book with one author:
Smucker, Barbara Claasen. *Days of Terror.* Toronto: Clarke, Irwin, 1979.
- book with more than one author:
Nida, Patricia Cooney, and Wendy M. Heller. *The Teenager's Survival Guide to Moving.* New York: Macmillan, 1985.
- work in an anthology:
London, Jack. "The Hunger Cry." *Great Canadian Animal Stories.* Ed. Muriel Whitaker. Edmonton: Hurtig, 1978.
- magazine or newspaper article:
Place the volume number after the title of the magazine. Place the page numbers, preceded by a colon, at the end of the citation.
Jarzen, David. "Pollen Power." *Owl* 22 (Mar. 1997): 12-14.
- video or film
*Perspectives in Science.* Dir. Julie Stanfel. National Film Board, 1989.
- CD-ROM
*Canadian Encyclopedia Plus.* CD-ROM, videodisc. Toronto: McClelland & Stewart Inc., 1996.
- Internet document
[Author]. [Year]. [*Title of document*]. Available: [address] [date accessed]
- interview
Singh, T. Jai. Personal interview. 10 March 1997.

SEE ALSO Citation and Footnote

**Capitalization** Capitalize the following.
- the first word in a sentence or a quotation: *The novelist Farley Mowat once said, "Truth I have no trouble with."*
- the name of a particular person, place, or nation: *My English penpal, Sterling Sawyer, will be visiting Canada this fall.*
- the main words in a title: *Roughing It in the Bush, Mathematics 201, Romeo and Juliet, O Canada*
- titles and family relationships, when used as part of a person's name: *I saw Dad go downstairs.*
(BUT *I saw my dad go downstairs.*)
*Doctor Namis* (BUT *the doctor*)
*Prime Minister Macdonald* (BUT *the prime minister*)
- days of the week, months, and holidays: *Tuesday; September; Ramadan*
- organizations, political parties, religions: *the United Nations; the Liberal Party; Judaism*
- historical events, eras, and documents: *the Seven Years War; the Great Depression; the BNA Act*

**Citation and Footnote** In essays and papers, use citations or footnotes to acknowledge the sources of quotations, charts, tables, diagrams, and all ideas other than your own. Below are some general guidelines for writing **citations**.

- Place the author's name and the page numbers (if appropriate) in parentheses, as close to the relevant material as possible. If the citation is at the end of a sentence, the period follows the citation: *Inventors are enchanted by ideas, beguiled into following a trail of investigation to its very end (Carpenter 8).*
- If you have already mentioned the author, you do not need to repeat the name in the citation: *According to Thomas Carpenter, "Inventors are enchanted by ideas, beguiled into following a trail of investigation to its very end." (8).*
- If you have referred to more than one work by the same author in your paper, include a shortened version of the title in the citations. For example, if you mentioned two of Alice Munroe's short stories in a paper, perhaps "Miles City, Montana" and "Jesse and Meribeth," you could refer to *("Miles" 119)* or *("Jesse" 249)* in your citations.

For **footnotes**, instead of placing information in parentheses within the text, put a small raised number at the end of the relevant material, and add a corresponding footnote at the bottom of the page, separated from the text by a short line (about ten spaces). Indent the first line of the footnote. Here is an example: *"Inventors are enchanted by ideas, beguiled into following a trail of investigation to its very end."*[1]

[1]*Thomas Carpenter, Inventors: Profiles in Canadian Genius (Camden East, Ont.: Camden House, 1990), p. 8.*

The first time you cite a source, give a full reference. Then cite only the author's last name and the page number: [2]*Carpenter, p. 23.*

Here are some other sample footnote references:
- book with more than one author:
  [3]Patricia Cooney Nida and Wendy M. Heller, *The Teenager's Survival Guide to Moving* (New York: Macmillan, 1985), p. 34.
- work in an anthology:
  [4]Jack London, "The Hunger Cry," in *Great Canadian Animal Stories*, ed. Muriel Whitaker. (Edmonton: Hurtig, 1978), p. 37.
- magazine or newspaper article
  [5]David Jarzen, "Pollen Power," *Owl*, Mar. 1997, p. 12.
- video or film
  [6]*Perspectives in Science*, dir. Julie Stanfel. National Film Board, 1989.
- CD-ROM
  [7]"Film Animation," *Canadian Encyclopedia* (Edmonton: Hurtig, 1996). CD-ROM.
- Internet document
  [8][Author]. [Year]. [*Title of document*]. Available: [address] [date accessed]
- interview
  [9]Singh, T. Jai. Personal interview. 10 March 1997.

**Clause**  A clause is a group of words that has a subject and a verb. Main clauses (also known as independent or principal clauses) can stand on their own as full sentences, while subordinate clauses (also known as dependent clauses) need a main clause to complete them.

A sentence may have more than one clause within it. In the following examples, main clauses are underlined, and subordinate clauses are in italics.
<u>This is the secret place</u> *that I like to visit*. <u>Marta</u>, *who sometimes looks after our dog*, <u>is going to veterinary college</u>. *When Riswan smiles* <u>the whole room lights up</u>.
SEE ALSO Sentence

**Cliché**  Clichés are overworked expressions that no longer have much impact. They are best avoided. Here are some examples: *free as a bird; sick as a dog; stay the course; between a rock and a hard place; last but not least; in the home stretch; under the weather*

**Colon [:]**  A colon warns you that something is to follow. Use colons in the following situations.
- to introduce a list: *Colours have different meanings in western culture: red for danger, black for mourning, and white for purity.*
- to introduce a quotation in formal writing: *Back in 1957, Professor Kenneth Boulding said: "Canada has no cultural unity, no linguistic unity, no religious unity, no economic unity, no geographic unity. All it has is unity."*
- to express time: *8:45; 20:00*
- to separate the volume and page numbers of a magazine: *Food Lovers Digest, 4:17-19*
- after the salutation of a business letter: *Dear Ms. Rosen:*

**Comma [,]**  A comma indicates a slight pause in a sentence. The common practice, especially in informal writing, is to use as few commas as possible without obscuring the meaning. Use commas as follows.
- between compound sentences: *Rula thought hard, but no solutions came to mind.*
- with nouns of address: *David, take the garbage out.*
- with words, phrases, or clauses that interrupt a sentence: *We will<u>, nevertheless,</u> do our best to win. Mother was delighted when<u>, for the first time,</u> the baby smiled. Marcus<u>, who has thick hair,</u> can never get his bathing cap on.*
- with introductory words, phrases, or clauses: <u>*Naturally,*</u> *George was pleased.* <u>*In the end,*</u> *I stayed home and read.* <u>*When we had finished eating,*</u> *we took the boat out for a spin.*
- between items in a series: *They took a <u>long, slow, boring</u> flight to Calgary. <u>Jim, Walter, and Aviva</u> work together at the factory.* NOTE: some people omit the comma just before the *and* in a series. This is acceptable, as long as the use is consistent and it does not make the sentence unclear.
- to set off *which* clauses: *The house<u>, which I own,</u> is on a hill.* (*which I own* is not essential to the main idea) BUT *The house that I own is on a hill.* (*that I own* identifies which house is being discussed, so it is considered part of the main idea).
SEE ALSO That and Which
- in some forms of dates: *January 14, 1997* BUT *14 January 1997*

- in addresses: *Please send an information kit to Serge Laflamme, 334 Grosvenor Avenue, Montréal, Québec H3H 3C7.* BUT
  *Serge Laflamme
  334 Grosvenor Avenue
  Montréal, Québec H3H 3C7*
  NOTE: there is no comma before the postal code.
- between a city and a country: *Ottawa, Canada*
- in salutations of personal letters: *Dear Sam,*
- to set off degrees and titles: *Peter Mishinski, Ph.D; Lorraine Markotic, M.P.*

SEE ALSO Quotation and Quotation Marks

**Comma Splice** SEE Run-on Sentence

**Conjunction** A conjunction is a word that connects other words, phrases, clauses, or sentences. There are three types of conjunction, as follows.
- co-ordinating conjunctions (*and, or, nor, for, but, so, yet*): *Mico and I are best friends.*
- subordinating conjunctions (*whenever, after, if, since, because, before, unless*): *I break out in hives whenever I eat pickles.*
- correlative conjunctions (*both...and, either...or, neither...nor, not only...but also*): *My watch is neither on my wrist nor by my bed.*

**Dangling Modifier** SEE Misplaced or Dangling Modifier

**Dash (—)** A dash marks a strong break in a sentence: *It wasn't until Friday—or it may have been Saturday—that I discovered my wallet was missing. Did you ever see the film—but no, it was made before you were born. Three students—Ruby, Amina, and Michael—were named as finalists. Jack works hard—when he has to.*

Dashes are useful for emphasis. However, using many dashes can make your writing disjointed and difficult to read. Consider using other punctuation instead.

**Double Negative** Using two negative words (such as *not* and *never*) in the same sentence creates a double negative. Avoid confusion by removing or replacing one of the two words. Double negatives are often created in sentences where the word not is hidden in a contraction, such as *can't, won't,* or *don't.*

Confusing: *I can't barely see!*
Better: *I can barely see!* OR *I can't see!*

Confusing: *There isn't scarcely enough to go around.*
Better: *There is scarcely enough to go around.* OR *There isn't enough to go around.*

**Euphemism** A euphemism is a word or expression that is meant to blunt the impact of harsh or unpleasant words or phrases. Some common euphemisms are: *pass away; senior citizen; rest room; special needs.* As the military use of terms like *collateral damage* instead of *deaths* shows, there can be a fine line between using a euphemism and obscuring the truth. As a general rule, the direct way to say something is usually best.

**Exclamation Mark [!]** An exclamation mark gives emphasis, and expresses surprise, delight, or alarm: *Hey! How sweet! Watch out!* Most writers trust their words to express whatever mood or emotion they wish to convey. When used sparingly, exclamation marks can be helpful, but too many may weaken their effect.

Weak: *The room was a mess! Tables were overturned! The drawers had been pulled out! I understood immediately! The house had been robbed!!!!*
Better: *The room was a mess. Tables were overturned. The drawers had been pulled out. I understood immediately—the house had been robbed!*

SEE ALSO Quotation and Quotation Marks

**Footnote** SEE Citation and Footnote

**Homonym** Homonyms are words that are pronounced the same but have different meanings, such as *see* and *sea*. The following homonyms are often confused: *complement/compliment; hear/here; its/it's; passed/past; piece/peace; principal/principle; their/they're/there; to/too/two; through/threw; who's/whose; your/you're.* If you are unsure of the correct spelling, check your dictionary.

**Homograph** Homographs are words that are written the same, but have different meanings, such as *bank* (edge of a river) and *bank* (place that lends money).

**Hyphen [-]** Use hyphens in the following ways.
- in compound numbers between 21 and 99: *twenty-one*
- in time: *the five-fifteen bus*
- in fractions: *one-half of the pie*
- in some numerical expressions: *a ten-year-old boy; a twenty-dollar bill*
- to divide a word between syllables at the end of a line: *dis-satisfied; dissat-isfied; dissatis-fied*
  NOTE: Never break proper nouns or words of only one syllable.
- in many expressions formed with prefixes: *all-round; co-operate; de-ice; ex-boyfriend; half-baked; post-mortem; pre-test; pro-Canadian; re-elect; self-centred*
  Note: As there are many exceptions to these rules, it is safest to check your dictionary for guidance.
- when a compound modifier precedes a noun, unless the first word ends in *-ly*: *rosy-fingered dawn; black-eyed Susan* BUT *carefully woven cloth*
- in some compound words: since compound words are often written as one word (*checklist*), or as two words with or without a hyphen (*check-out; check mark*), it is best to consult your dictionary for the proper form.

**Italics and Underlining** Use italics in print (or underline when writing by hand) to identify a whole work, such as the title of a play, piece of music, movie, book, newspaper, or magazine: *I read a great article about Margaret Atwood's book, <u>Alias Grace</u>, in <u>Saturday Night</u> the other day.*

Italics and underlining can also be used to indicate emphasis (*To avoid charges of bias, the committee listened to arguments both for and against the proposal.*); to indicate a word that is being referred to (*My dictionary defines fatuous as "stupid but self-satisfied."*); or to indicate a foreign phrase: (*ad hoc*).

SEE ALSO Title

**Metaphor and Simile** Metaphors and similes are both forms of comparison. A simile compares two things or ideas using *like* or *as*. A metaphor makes the comparison implicitly, without using like or as.

simile: *The icicles looked like bony fingers, pointing down at him accusingly.*
metaphor: *Bony fingers of ice pointed down at him accusingly.*

SEE ALSO Cliché

**Misplaced or Dangling Modifier** When a modifier (a word or phrase that limits or describes other words) is too far from what it modifies, the result can be a misplaced modifier. In the following examples, the modifiers are in italics, and the word being modified is underlined.

Misplaced: *Growling*, my hat was being eaten by the dog.
Better: *Growling*, the dog was eating my hat.
Better: My hat was being eaten by a *growling* dog.
Misplaced: She watched the moon rise *from her chair*.
Better: *From her chair*, she watched the moon rise.

A dangling modifier occurs when the word being modified is implied but does not appear in the sentence.

Dangling: *While on holiday*, a thief broke into our house.
Better: *While we were on holiday*, a thief broke into our house.

**Noun** A noun is a word that refers to people, places, qualities, things, actions, or ideas: *When Joe was at the library in Guelph, curiosity enticed him to read an article that claimed fear could be cured by meditation.*

SEE ALSO Subject/Verb Agreement

**Number** The number of a noun, pronoun, or verb indicates whether it is singular or plural.

SEE Pronoun; Subject/Verb Agreement

**Object** English has three types of objects. In the following examples, the direct object is in italics, and the indirect object is underlined.
- A direct object is a noun or pronoun that answers the question *what?* or *who?* about the verb: He bought a *kite*.
- An indirect object answers the question *to what?*, *to whom?*, *for what?*, or *for whom?* about the verb: He bought me a *kite*.
- The object of a preposition is a noun or pronoun that comes at the end of a phrase that begins with a preposition: He bought a *kite* for me.

**Paragraph** A paragraph is a group of sentences that develop one aspect of a topic, or one phase of a narrative. The sentences in a paragraph should be clearly related to each other. Sometimes, especially in essays, the aspect or point being developed is expressed in a topic sentence, and the other sentences in the paragraph expand on this statement.

**Parallel Structure** In a sentence, two or more elements that are of equal importance, expressed in similar grammatical terms to emphasize their relationship, are called parallel. Sentences without parallel structure can sound both confusing and awkward. Parallel structure is especially important in lists; with expressions like *both...and*, *not only...but also*, *whether...or*, and *either...or*; and in words, phrases, or clauses joined by *and*.

Not Parallel: *Campers are taught hiking, swimming, and how to paddle a canoe.*
Parallel: *Campers are taught to hike, swim, and canoe.* OR
*Campers are taught hiking, swimming, and canoeing.*
Not Parallel: *Raoul can't decide whether to work as a lifeguard or if he would prefer to renovate houses.*
Parallel: *Raoul can't decide whether to work as a lifeguard or to renovate houses.* OR
*Raoul can't decide whether to work as a lifeguard or as a renovator.*

**Parentheses** [()] Use parentheses to set off comments or asides in a sentence: They lived happily ever after (and so did the dog). When necessary, you can use punctuation marks within the parentheses, even if the parenthetical comment is in the middle of a sentence: *All of us except Peter (Peter is always optimistic!) were sure it was going to rain on our picnic.*

You can place whole sentences in parentheses. If the sentence stands alone and is not grammatically related to the ones before and after it, punctuate the sentence within the parentheses as you would a regular sentence: *The French colony of Upper Volta, now called Burkina Faso, gained its independence in 1960. (Burkina Faso means land of honest men.)*

**Participle** The present participle is the form of the verb that ends in *-ing* (*wanting, eating, burning, hearing, growing*). The past participle usually ends in *-ed, -en, -t, -d,* or *-n* (*wanted, eaten, burnt, heard, grown*). Participles have three main uses.
- as part of certain verb tenses: *I am thinking about what I will eat for lunch. I had been there too long.* NOTE: a participle cannot act as a verb on its own. It must be accompanied by a helping verb, such as *is, have, were*.
- to modify a noun or pronoun, either alone or as part of a phrase: *a broken doll; a spoiled child; The man standing at the back is my father; Exhausted by our long hike, we arrived back at the campsite.*

- to modify a whole sentence, either alone or as part of a phrase: *Talking of food, here comes the lunch truck! All things considered, we did quite well.*

**Part of Speech** Parts of speech are nouns, adjectives, verbs, adverbs, conjunctions, pronouns, interjections, and prepositions.

**Period [.]** Use a period
- to mark the end of a sentence: *The sky is blue.*
- after abbreviations and initials: *J.J. Cale; Mr.; St.*

SEE ALSO: Quotation and Quotation Marks

**Phrase** A phrase is a group of words, used together in a sentence, that does not have a subject and a verb:
Marcel spoke *for the first time*.   (prepositional phrase)
*Thinking fast*, I covered my face. (participial phrase)
Catrina wants *to be a scientist*.   (infinitive phrase)

COMPARE: Clause

**Plagiarism** Plagiarism is the presenting of the ideas of others as if they were your own. This is a very serious offence. To avoid unintentional plagiarism, be sure to include a citation or footnote whenever you borrow ideas or quote directly from another source.

SEE Citation and Footnote.

**Possessive** Use possessive forms of nouns and pronouns to show ownership.
- To form the possessive of most singular nouns, add *'s*: *Jim's idea; the cat's paw; Toronto's night life*
- To form the possessive of plurals that end in *-s*, add only an apostrophe: *the students' project; the Livakos' pet; the cars' lights*
- Plurals that do not end in *-s* form the possessive in the same way as singular nouns: *children's games; people's pets; geese's flying patterns*
- Proper nouns of two or more syllables that end in *-s* sometimes sound awkward when an *'s* is added to form the possessive. In such cases, some writers omit the final *-s*: *Jesus' words; Laertes' death*

**Prefix** A prefix is a word or syllable added on to the beginning of a word to make a new word. For example, *dis-* added to *appear* makes *disappear*. Often, knowing what a prefix means can help you to figure out the meaning of a new word. Here is a list of some common prefixes and their meanings:

*a-* (not)
*ante-* (before)
*anti-* (against)
*multi-* (many)
*bi-* (two)
*circum-* (around)
*co-* (together)
*dis-* (not)
*extra-* (beyond)
*fore-* (before)
*hyper-* (excessively)
*in-* (not)
*inter-* (between; among)
*mal-* (bad)
*mis-* (wrong)
*mono-* (one)
*non-* (not)
*post-* (after)
*pseudo-* (false)
*re-* (again)
*retro-* (back)
*semi-* (half)
*super-* (over)
*trans-* (across)
*tri-* (three)
*un-* (not)
*uni-* (one)

**Preposition** A preposition is a word that shows a relationship between a noun (called the object of the preposition; SEE Object) and some other word in the sentence. Some words that sometimes function as prepositions are: above, at, before, behind, by, down, for, from, in, of, on, past, since, to, under, until, with. In this example, the prepositions are underlined, and the objects of the prepositions are in italics: The house in *the valley* was swept away by *the flood*.

**Pronoun** A pronoun is a word that replaces a noun or another pronoun. There are many different types of pronouns, and most of them cause no problems. However, there are a few pitfalls.
- Antecedent: It should be clear what word the pronoun replaces (its antecedent). Here are some examples of sentences with unclear antecedents.

Unclear: *Linda loves looking after Sandra, because she is so good.*
Clear: *Linda loves looking after Sandra, because Sandra is so good.*
Unclear: *I completed the report, which pleased my boss.*
Clear: *My boss was pleased with the report that I completed.* OR
*My boss was pleased that I completed the report.*

- Case: Personal pronouns have three forms, or cases:
the subject form (*I, you, he, she, we, they*)
the object form (*me, you, him, her, us, them*)
the possessive form (*mine, yours, his, hers, ours, theirs*).
Usually you will have no trouble choosing the right form. However, pay attention when the pronoun is joined to another noun or pronoun by and, or, or nor. Use the form of the pronoun that you would use if the other noun or pronoun were not there:

Incorrect: *Neither John nor me had done the work.*
  (*me had done* is wrong)
Correct: *Neither John nor I had done the work.*
  (*I had done* is correct)
Incorrect: *Ms. Singh read the book to Saritsa and I.*
  (*read the book to I* is wrong)
Correct: *Ms. Singh read the book to Saritsa and me.*
  (*read the book to me* is correct)

When we use a personal pronoun immediately after a form of the verb *be* (*am, is, are, was, were, had been, will be*, etc.), most of us use the object form when we are talking: *It is me.* However, in formal language, it is more correct to use the subject form: *It is I who did all the work.*

SEE ALSO Who/Whom

- Agreement: Personal pronouns (*I, me, you, they, us,* etc.) should agree in number and gender with the noun or pronoun they replace:

Incorrect: *A clown always looks happy, even if they are crying inside.*
Better: *Clowns always look happy, even if they are crying inside.*

Indefinite pronouns (*any, every, some, each, all*, etc.) do not refer to a specific person or thing. When an indefinite pronoun is the subject of a verb, the verb should agree in number with the pronoun. Some are considered singular (*no one, each, another, either, neither*, and words with *any-, every-, no-,* or *some-*, such as *anybody, everything*); some are treated as plural (*many, few, and several*); some can be singular or plural, depending on the context (*all, any, enough, more, most, none, one(s), other(s), plenty, some*):

Singular: *Most of the pie is gone.*
Plural:   *Most of the people are gone.*

Singular: *Some of the money is lost.*
Plural:   *Some of the tickets are lost.*

A pronoun that refers to an indefinite pronoun should also agree with the indefinite pronoun in number and gender: *Everyone who is going on the trip should bring his or her own lunch.* (*everyone* is singular, so the pronouns *his or her* must be singular)

SEE ALSO Sexist Language

- We and you before a noun: sometimes the pronouns *we* and *us* are used just before a noun. In sentences like the following examples, check that you are using the right form of the pronoun by reading the sentence without the following noun, to see if it is correct:

Incorrect: *Us dog lovers love to talk about our pets.*
           (*Us...love* is wrong)
Correct:   *We dog lovers love to talk about our pets.*
           (*We...love* is correct)

Incorrect: *The actors gave we students a preview.*
           (*The cast gave we* is wrong)
Correct:   *The actors gave us students a preview.*
           (*The cast gave us* is correct)

SEE ALSO Who/Whom; That/Which

**Proofreading Symbols** The following symbols may be used to mark changes on your writing.

| Symbol | Name | Example |
|---|---|---|
| ∧ | INSERT | The house on fire. (*is*) |
| ℯ | DELETE | Rattlesnakes are very very dangerous. |
| ∼ | TRANSPOSE (SWITCH) | Raisa, Louise, and Karin are 12, 14, and 16 years old, respectively. |
| ≡ | CAPITAL | Planet earth may be in danger. |
| / | LOWER CASE | We Compost all our food scraps. |
| ¶ | NEW PARAGRAPH | So that day ended badly. The next day... |
| ⊙ | ADD PERIOD | Liu wondered which way to go |
| ∧ | ADD COMMA | Bring your tent, a sleeping bag, and a flashlight. |
| ∨ | APOSTROPHE | "It's Hans!" he cried. |
| # | ADD SPACE | Daniel and I are leaving tomorrow. |
| ⌒ | CLOSE SPACE | Chickens can't fly, but ducks can. |
| .... | LEAVE AS IS (NO CHANGE) | The pictures are not ready. |

**Proofreading Tips** Proofreading is the final stage in the writing process, before you present your work to your audience. Before you reach this stage, you will have already edited your writing to the point where you are satisfied with the content, style, and words used. When proofreading written work, do the following.
- Read slowly, focussing on each word.
- Check for errors in spelling (especially those items that have been troublesome to you in the past), capitalization, and punctuation.
- Check that all place names and proper names are spelled correctly.
- Check that each paragraph is indented, and that each sentence begins with a capital letter.
- Spend extra time checking lists, charts, and tables.
- Ensure that you have acknowledged all your sources correctly and completely. (SEE Citation and Footnote)
- Make sure you have used quotation marks correctly (SEE Quotation and Quotation Marks).

**Question Mark [?]** A question mark indicates a direct question: *Where is the remote?* BUT *Sasha asked where the remote was.*

SEE ALSO Quotation and Quotation Marks

**Quotation and Quotation Marks [" "]** Indicate a direct quotation by enclosing it in quotation marks. NOTE: Very long quotations (over 100 words, or over 3 lines of your writing) must be indented from the body of the text, and begun on a separate line. When you use this method, do not use quotation marks.
- Separate the words that introduce the quotation (*Camila asked*) from the quotation itself by commas: *Camila asked, "Where is the notebook that you borrowed from me?"*
- Indicate deleted words within a sentence by three dots (...). If the missing words come after the end of a sentence, add a fourth dot (....) . Any added words or explanations that are not part of the original should be placed in square brackets:
Original quotation:
*Our concepts of what is attractive or worthwhile are learned, so we can modify our ideas of style and esthetics to include durability and quality. Instead of stressing something as arbitrary and temporary as fashion, we can take pride in clothing that will last for years.*
Shortened version:
*In 1989, David Suzuki wrote, "...we can modify our ideas [of what is attractive]...to include durability and quality...[and] take pride in clothing that will last for years."*
- A question mark or exclamation mark goes inside the quotation marks if it relates to the quoted material, and outside if it applies to the whole sentence: *Theo called out, "Where are you going?" I'm sick of hearing you say, "I'll clean it up tomorrow"!*
- A period or comma at the end of a quotation goes inside the quotation marks: *"The trouble is,"* he muttered, *"I can't get the machine to work."*

- A semicolon at the end of a quotation goes outside the quotation marks: *Kathy announced, "I don't want any more cookies, thank you"; then she sank back down in the bed and stayed asleep until morning.*
- A quotation within a quotation should be marked by single quotation marks: *Camila wailed, "Did I hear you say, 'I lost them both'?"*
- You can use quotation marks in place of italics or underlining to indicate a word that is being defined or explained: *The term "downsizing" is a euphemism that usually means firing a lot of employees.*

**Racist Language** Racist language is any language that refers to a particular cultural or ethnic group in insulting terms. But racism also exists in more subtle forms. Be sensitive to the issues.
- Mention a person's race only if that is relevant to the context:
  Relevant: *Mr. Wilkes, who is black, says he faced a lot of racism growing up in rural Alberta.*
  Unnecessary: *A Chinese man has been charged after four stores were set on fire deliberately in the downtown area yesterday.*
  Better: *A man has been charged after four stores were set on fire deliberately in the downtown area yesterday.*
- If a person's race or ethnic origin is relevant, be as specific as possible:
  Vague: *Ying Yee emigrated from Asia in 1963.*
  Better: *Ying Yee emigrated from Beijing, China, in 1963.*
- Avoid making generalizations about any racial or cultural group:
  Stereotyped *The Welsh are great singers.*
  Better: *The Welsh have a long tradition of singing.*
- The word "ethnic" should only be used as an adjective, never as a noun:
  Inappropriate: *Many ethnics live in this area.*
  Better: *Many ethnic groups live in this area.*

**Redundancy** Redundancy is the use of unnecessary words in a sentence:
Redundant: *I woke up at 7:30 a.m. in the morning.*
Better: *I woke up at 7:30 a.m.*
Redundant: *The reason I stayed home is because I was sick.*
Better: *I stayed home because I was sick.*
Redundant: *That area is restricted and not everyone is allowed in there.*
Better: *That area is restricted.*

**Run-on Sentence** A run-on sentence is formed when two sentences are run into one. To fix a run-on sentence, add the proper punctuation, or change the wording to make it a single sentence:

Run-on: *The sky is clear it is spring at last.*
Better: *The sky is clear; it is spring at last.* OR
*The sky is clear, and it is spring at last.* OR
*The sky is clear because it is spring at last.*

Two sentences separated only by a comma is called a comma splice. Fix a comma splice the same way you would fix a run-on sentence:
Comma Splice: *The doctor said I need rest, I am taking the week off.*
Better: *The doctor said I need rest; I am taking the week off.* OR
*The doctor said I need rest, so I am taking the week off.* OR
*Because the doctor said I need rest, I am taking the week off.*

**Semicolon [;]** Use a semicolon to separate two related sentences: *I love watching television after school; it relaxes me.* A semicolon may also be used along with a co-ordinating conjunction (*and, or, nor, for, but, so, yet*) to join main clauses, if one or more of the clauses already contains a comma: *I threw on my coat, picked up my jacket, and raced to the bus stop; but the bus had already left.* Finally, semicolons are used to separate items in a list, when one or more of the items contains a comma: *Walter has lived in Tokyo, Japan; London, England; and Esteban, Saskatchewan.*

SEE ALSO Quotation and Quotation Marks

**Sexist Language** Sexist language is language that degrades either women or men. As with racist language, it is best to avoid generalizing about men or women unless you are basing your claims on scientific fact.

Also, whenever possible, replace words such as *fireman, policeman,* and *man-made* with non-sexist alternatives such as *firefighter, police officer,* and *fabricated.*

Finally, avoid using the masculine pronouns *he, him, his* (or the feminine pronouns, *she, her, hers*) to refer to both men and women. Instead, try one or more of the following methods.
- Use the plural.
  Sexist: *A good teacher can always command the respect of his students.*
  Better: *Good teachers can always command the respect of their students.*
- Replace the pronoun with *the, a,* or *an.*
  Sexist: *Whoever holds the winning ticket has not claimed his prize.*
  Better: *Whoever holds the winning ticket has not claimed the prize.*
- Substitute *one* or *you.* Use *one* in more formal writing, and *you* in informal contexts.
  Sexist: *A man never knows when his time will come.*
  Better: *One never knows when one's time will come.*
  *You never know when your time will come.*
- Use *her or his, her or him, she or he.*
  Sexist: *Each child will be given his own seat.*
  Better: *Each child will be given her or his own seat.*

  Choose this method only when necessary, as some people object to it.

- Sometimes, the best way to avoid sexism is to change the wording of the sentence.
  Sexist: *I have never met a nurse who was not rushed off her feet.*
  Better: *I have never met a nurse who was not in a great hurry.*

**Sentence** A sentence is a group of words that expresses a complete thought. Every sentence needs a subject and an action.

A **simple sentence** has one subject and one verb:
*Yukio's house has six bedrooms.*

A **compound sentence** has two or more main clauses (that is, smaller sentences that can stand alone). The sentences are usually joined together either by a semicolon, or by a comma or semicolon followed by *and, or, nor, for, but, so,* or *yet*:
*Yukio's house has six bedrooms, and the yard is huge.*

A **complex sentence** has a main clause that can stand alone as a sentence, and one or more subordinate clauses that cannot stand on their own as sentences. In the following example of a complex sentence, the main clause is underlined, and the subordinate clause is in italics:
<u>Yukio's house</u>, *which he built himself*, <u>has six bedrooms</u>.
SEE ALSO Clause

**Sentence Fragment** A sentence fragment is a group of words that is set off like a sentence, but that lacks either a verb or a subject. Sentence fragments are acceptable in informal writing, dialogue, and spoken English, but are not appropriate in formal writing:
Fragment: *We went to the game on Saturday. Josh and I.*
  (lacks a verb)
Revised: *Josh and I went to the game on Saturday.*
Fragment: *Never did understand those engines.*
  (lacks a subject)
Revised: *I never did understand those engines.*

**Split Infinitive** A split infinitive occurs when an adverb is placed between *to* and a verb. Try to avoid this construction, unless doing so will make the sentence sound awkward.
Split: *I want to really try hard in math this year.*
Better: *I want to try really hard in math this year.*
Split: *He is going to fully recover from the accident.*
Better: *He is going to recover fully from the accident.*
Split: *The girl pretended to almost drop the card.*
Confusing: *The girl pretended almost to drop the card.*
In this last example, the split infinitive is preferable.

**Subject/Verb Agreement** A verb should always agree in number with its subject. Singular subjects take singular verbs, and a plural subject takes a plural verb. When you are looking for the subject of a verb, remember the following tips.

- Prepositional phrases like *at school, under my desk, through the woods, with great sadness* never contain the subject of a sentence:
  Wrong:     *One of the cars were stolen.*
      (*cars* is not the subject)
  Corrected: *One of the cars was stolen.*
      (the subject *one* needs a singular verb)
- *There* and *here* are not usually the subject of the verb: *There are many reasons why I like you.*
  (subject is *reasons*)
  *Here are my workbooks.*
  (subject is *workbooks*)
- If a subject has two parts, joined by *or, not, either...or,* or *neither...nor,* make the verb agree with the part of the subject nearest to it: *Neither my brother nor <u>my parents were</u> at my recital. Neither my brother nor <u>my sister was</u> at my recital*
- Some subjects look like they are plural, but they are really singular: <u>*The Diviners is*</u> *a remarkable book.* <u>*The news is*</u> *about to come on.* <u>*Five dollars is*</u> *not enough to go to a movie.*

SEE ALSO Pronoun (agreement of indefinite pronouns)

**Subordinate Clause** SEE Clause

**Suffix** A suffix is a syllable or letters added to the end of a word to make a new word. Knowing the meaning of some common suffixes can help you to figure out the meaning of new words.

*-able* (able to/inclined to/causing):
  *agreeable; capable, comfortable*
*-en* (become/made of):
  *strengthen; wooden*
*-er* (more/one who does):
  *longer; writer*
*-ful* (characterized by):
  *delightful*
*-ish* (belonging to/having the qualities of/somewhat):
  *English; boyish; blueish*
*-ize* (cause to become/become/affect):
  *caramelize; crystallize; paralyze*
*-less* (without/not able to):
  *loveless; countless*
*-ly* (in a certain manner):
  *kindly*
*-ment* (state, condition, or result of):
  *abandonment*
*-ness* (state, condition, or result of):
  *awareness*

**Synonym** Synonyms are words that mean the same thing, although they differ in the way they are used or the shade of meaning they imply. For example, *discuss, talk,* and *chat* can all be said to mean more or less the same thing, but each has a different use, or connotation: *The council discussed the proposal at length. We need to talk to you about your report card. Eli chatted to me on the phone.* When choosing the right word for a particular context, check in your dictionary or thesaurus.

**Tense** A tense of a verb is the form of the verb that indicates whether the action took place in the past, present, or future.

| Tense | Example | Use |
|---|---|---|
| Present | *She knows* | action that takes place in the present, to express general truths |
| Simple Past | *She knew* | action completed in the past |
| Present Perfect | *She has known* | action begun in the past extending to the present |
| Past Perfect | *She had known* | action completed in the past, before some action in the past |
| Future | *She will know* | action that will occur in the future |
| Future Perfect | *She will have known* | action that will be completed by a specific time in the future. |

The present tense can be used to describe events in the past. However, it is important not to switch tenses in the middle of a piece of writing. If you have chosen to write in the present tense, remember to keep that perspective:

Confusing: *Pedro walks up to the door. He had been waiting for this moment for the last two years. He reaches for the knocker and lets it fall. The door opens slowly, and there stood the biggest giant he ever saw.*

Better: *Pedro walked up to the door. He had been waiting for this moment for the last two years. He reached for the knocker and let it fall. The door opened slowly, and there stood the biggest giant he had ever seen.*

OR *Pedro walks up to the door. He has been waiting for this moment for the last two years. He reaches for the knocker and lets it fall. The door opens slowly, and there stands the biggest giant he has ever seen.*

**That/Which** Use *that* when the information that follows is a necessary part of the main idea in the sentence; use *which* (preceded by a comma) when the information is not necessary to the sentence. Consider the change in meaning in the following two sentences:
*The coat that Mary bought is blue.*
(*that Mary bought* tells us which specific coat we are talking about, so it is necessary to the main idea)
*The coat, which Mary bought, is blue.*
(*which Mary bought* tells us something else about the coat, but it is not part of the main idea, which is that the coat is blue)

**Title** Use italics or underlining for titles of whole works:

| | |
|---|---|
| Books | *The Wars* |
| Films | *The Empire Strikes Back* |
| Newspapers | *The Vancouver Sun* |
| Magazines | *Sports Illustrated* |
| Plays | *Romeo and Juliet* |
| Long Poems | *Four Quartets* |
| Works of Art | *Mona Lisa* |
| TV Programs or Series | *Hockey Night in Canada* |
| Musicals | *Phantom of the Opera* |
| Ballets | *The Nutcracker* |

Quotation marks are generally used for the titles of works within a larger work, as well as for songs:

| | |
|---|---|
| Short Stories: | "Survival Ship" |
| Magazine Articles: | "Canada's Comedians" |
| News articles: | "Election Called for June 2" |
| Short Poems: | "The Bull Calf" |
| Songs: | "Suzanne" |

**Transitive/Intransitive Verb** A transitive verb is one that has a direct object to complete its meaning. An intransitive verb does not need a direct object. Many verbs can be transitive or intransitive:

Transitive: *I breathed air into his lungs to revive him.*
Intransitive: *The child beside me was breathing in my face.*

**Verb** A verb is a word that expresses an action or a state of being. Verbs that express a state of being are sometimes called linking verbs, because they link the subject to another word that describes the subject.

Action verbs: *Sunil ran to school.*
 *Dana thought about retiring.*
Linking verb: *Mariko seemed tired.*

The verb *be* is the most common linking verb, but verbs like *seem, appear, feel, smell,* and *look* can act as linking verbs. To find out if a verb is a linking verb, try replacing it with a form of the verb *be*. If the meaning of the sentence remains the same, the verb is a linking verb:
*John felt bad about what he had done.*
(*John was bad* does not have the same meaning, so *felt* is not a linking verb here)
*The blankets felt soft.*
(*The blankets were soft* does have the same meaning, so *felt* is a linking verb here)

SEE ALSO Transitive/Intransitive Verbs; Tense; Subject/Verb Agreement

**Who/Whom** *Who* is the subject form and *whom* is the object form (SEE Pronoun). If you are unsure which form to use, try rewording the sentence by replacing the pronoun with *he* or *him*. If *he* works, use *who*, but if *him* sounds right, use *whom*:
*The boy who starred in the play won an award.*
(*he starred* is correct, so use *who*)
*The boy whom I saw in the play won an award.*
(*I saw him* is correct, so use *whom*)

# Abbreviations

## Parts of speech

| | | | |
|---|---|---|---|
| *n.* | noun | *pron.* | pronoun |
| *v.* | verb | *prep.* | preposition |
| *adj.* | adjective | *conj.* | conjunction |
| *adv.* | adverb | *interj.* | interjection |

## Languages

| | |
|---|---|
| OE | Old English (before A.D. 1100) |
| ME | Middle English (about 1100 - 1500) |
| OF | Old French (before 1400) |
| F | French (modern) |
| Cdn. F | Canadian French |
| ON | Old Norse (before 1300) |
| L | Latin (classical: about 200 B.C. to A.D. 300) |
| Med. L | Medieval Latin (about 700 - 1500) |
| Gk. | Greek (classical: about 900 B.C. to A.D. 200) |

| | | | |
|---|---|---|---|
| c. | century | pt. | past tense |
| *pl.* | plural | ppr. | present participle |
| *Abbrev.* | abbreviation | | |

## Fistnotes

| | |
|---|---|
| *Hom.* | homonym |
| *Syn.* | synonym |
| *Pron.* | pronunciation |
| *Etym.* | etymology |